Acronyms, Initialisms & Abbreviations Dictionary

ISSN 0270-4404

Acronyms, Initialisms & Abbreviations Dictionary

*A Guide to Acronyms, Initialisms, Abbreviations,
Contractions, Alphabetic Symbols, and Similar Condensed Appellations*

Covering: Aerospace, Associations, Banking, Biochemistry, Business, Data
Processing, Domestic and International Affairs, Economics, Education, Electronics, Genetics,
Government, Information Technology, Investment, Labor, Law, Medicine, Military Affairs,
Periodicals, Pharmacy, Physiology, Politics, Religion, Science, Societies, Sports, Technical
Drawings and Specifications, Telecommunications, Trade, Transportation, and Other Fields

Eighteenth Edition
1994

Volume 1

Part 3
P-Z

Jennifer Mossman,
Editor

Pamela Dear
Jacqueline L. Longe
Allison K. McNeill
Kelle S. Sisung
Rita H. Skirpan
Associate Editors

Gale Research Inc. • *DETROIT* • *WASHINGTON, D.C.* • *LONDON*

Senior Editor:	Donna Wood
Editor:	Jennifer Mossman
Associate Editors:	Pamela Dear, Jacqueline L. Longe, Allison K. McNeill, Kelle S. Sisung, Rita H. Skirpan
Assistant Editors:	Erin E. Holmberg, Matt Merta, Lou Ann Shelton, Gerda Sherk, Bradford J. Wood
Contributing Editors:	Leland G. Alkire, Jr., Mildred Hunt, Miriam M. Steinert
Data Entry Supervisor:	Benita L. Spight
Data Entry Group Leader:	Gwen Tucker
Data Entry Associate:	Nancy Jakubiak
Production Manager:	Mary Beth Trimper
Production Assistant:	Catherine Kemp
Art Director:	Cynthia Baldwin
Keyliners:	C.J. Jonik, Yolanda Y. Latham
Supervisor of Systems and Programming:	Theresa A. Rocklin
Programmer:	Charles Beaumont

Library of Congress Catalog Card Number 84-643188
ISBN 0-8103-8203-2 (Volume 1 Complete)
ISBN 0-8103-8204-0 (Part 1: A-F only)
ISBN 0-8103-8205-9 (Part 2: G-O only)
ISBN 0-8103-8206-7 (Part 3: P-Z only)
ISSN 0270-4404

Printed in the United States of America

Published simultaneously in the United Kingdom
by Gale Research International Limited
(An affiliated company of Gale Research Inc.)

The trademark **ITP** is used under license.

Contents

Gale's publications in the acronyms and abbreviations field include:

Acronyms, Initialisms & Abbreviations Dictionary series:

Acronyms, Initialisms & Abbreviations Dictionary (Volume 1). A guide to acronyms, initialisms, abbreviations, and similar contractions, arranged alphabetically by abbreviation.

New Acronyms, Initialisms & Abbreviations (Volume 2). An interedition supplement in which terms are arranged alphabetically both by abbreviation and by meaning.

Reverse Acronyms, Initialisms & Abbreviations Dictionary (Volume 3). A companion to Volume 1 in which terms are arranged alphabetically by meaning of the acronym, initialism, or abbreviation.

Acronyms, Initialisms & Abbreviations Dictionary Subject Guide series:

Computer & Telecommunications Acronyms (Volume 1). A guide to acronyms, initialisms, abbreviations, and similar contractions used in the field of computers and telecommunications in which terms are arranged alphabetically both by abbreviation and by meaning.

Business Acronyms (Volume 2). A guide to business-oriented acronyms, initialisms, abbreviations, and similar contractions in which terms are arranged alphabetically both by abbreviation and by meaning.

International Acronyms, Initialisms & Abbreviations Dictionary series:

International Acronyms, Initialisms & Abbreviations Dictionary (Volume 1). A guide to foreign and international acronyms, initialisms, abbreviations, and similar contractions, arranged alphabetically by abbreviation.

New International Acronyms, Initialisms & Abbreviations (Volume 2). An interedition supplement in which terms are arranged alphabetically both by abbreviation and by meaning.

Reverse International Acronyms, Initialisms & Abbreviations Dictionary (Volume 3). A companion to Volume 1 in which terms are arranged alphabetically by meaning of the acronym, initialism, or abbreviation.

Periodical Title Abbreviations series:

Periodical Title Abbreviations: By Abbreviation (Volume 1). A guide to abbreviations commonly used for periodical titles, arranged alphabetically by abbreviation.

Periodical Title Abbreviations: By Title (Volume 2). A guide to abbreviations commonly used for periodical titles, arranged alphabetically by title.

New Periodical Title Abbreviations (Volume 3). An interedition supplement in which terms are arranged alphabetically both by abbreviation and by title.

User's Guide

The following examples illustrate possible elements of entries in AIAD:

---

    1   **2**   **3**   **4** **5**

FATAC....Force Aerienne Tactique [*Tactical Air Force*] [*French*] (NATG)

                                 6   **7**

MMT...Multiple-Mirror Telescope [*Mount Hopkins, AZ*] [*Jointly operated by Smithsonian Institution and the University of Arizona*] [Astronomy]

                                           8

---

1 Acronym, Initialism, or Abbreviation

2 Meaning or Phrase

3 English translation

4 Language (for non-English entries)

5 Source code (Allows you to verify entries or find additional information. Decoded in the List of Selected Sources)

6 Location or Country of origin (Provides geographic identifiers for airports, colleges and universities, libraries, military bases, political parties, radio and television stations, and others)

7 Sponsoring organization

8 Subject category (Clarifies entries by providing appropriate context)

The completeness of a listing is dependent upon both the nature of the term and the amount of information provided by the source. If additional information becomes available during future research, an entry is revised.

Arrangement of Entries

Acronyms, initialisms, and abbreviations are arranged alphabetically in letter-by-letter sequence. Spacing, punctuation, and capitalization are not considered. If the same term has more than one meaning, the various meanings are subarranged in word-by-word sequence.

Should you wish to eliminate the guesswork from acronym formation and usage, a companion volume could help. *Reverse Acronyms, Initialisms and Abbreviations Dictionary* contains essentially the same entries as *AIAD*, but arranges them alphabetically by meaning, rather than by acronym or initialism.

List of Selected Sources

Each of the print sources included in the following list contributed at least 50 terms. It would be impossible to cite a source for every entry because the majority of terms are sent by outside contributors, are uncovered through independent research by the editorial staff, or surface as miscellaneous broadcast or print media references.

For sources used on an ongoing basis, only the latest edition is listed. For most of the remaining sources, the edition that was used is cited. The editors will provide further information about these sources upon request.

Unless further described in an annotation, the publications listed here contain no additional information about the acronym, initialism, or abbreviation cited.

(AABC) *Catalog of Abbreviations and Brevity Codes.* Washington, DC:U.S. Department of the Army, 1981. [Use of source began in 1969]

(AAG) *Aerospace Abbreviations Glossary.* Report Number AG60-0014. Prepared by General Dynamics/Astronautics. San Diego: 1962.

(AAMN) *Abbreviations and Acronyms in Medicine and Nursing.* By Solomon Garb, Eleanor Krakauer, and Carson Justice. New York: Springer Publishing Co., 1976.

(ADA) *The Australian Dictionary of Acronyms and Abbreviations.* 2nd ed. Compiled by David J. Jones. Leura, NSW, Australia: Second Back Row Press Pty. Ltd., 1981.

(AEBS) *Acronyms in Education and the Behavioral Sciences.* By Toyo S. Kawakami. Chicago: American Library Association, 1971.

(AF) *Reference Aid: Abbreviations in the African Press.* Arlington, VA: Joint Publications Research Service, 1979.

(AFIT) *Compendium of Authenticated Systems and Logistics.* Washington, DC:Air Force Institute of Technology. [Use of source began in 1984]

(AFM) *Air Force Manual of Abbreviations.* Washington, DC: U.S. Department of the Air Force, 1975. [Use of source began in 1969]

(AIA) *Aviation Insurance Abbreviations,* Organisations and Institutions. By M.J. Spurway. London: Witherby & Co. Ltd., 1983.

(APAG) *Associated Press Abbreviations Guide.* New York: Associated Press. [Online database]

(APTA) *Australian Periodical Title Abbreviations.* Compiled by David J. Jones. Leura, NSW, Australia: Second Back Row Press Pty. Ltd., 1985.

(ARC) *Agricultural Research Centres: A World Directory of Organizations and Programmes.* 2 vols. Edited by Nigel Harvey. Harlow, Essex, England: Longman Group, 1983; distributed in the U.S. by Gale Research Inc., Detroit.
> A world guide to official, educational, industrial, and independent research centers which support research in the fields of agriculture, veterinary medicine, horticulture, aquaculture, food science, forestry, zoology, and botany.

(ASF)   *Guide to Names and Acronyms of Organizations, Activities, and Projects.* Food and Agriculture Organization of the United Nations. Fishery Information, Data, and Statistics Service and U.S. National Oceanic and Atmospheric Administration. Aquatic Sciences and Fisheries Information System Reference Series, Number 10, 1982. n.p.

(BIB)   *Bibliotech.* Ottawa, Canada: National Library of Canada, 1988-89.

(BJA)   *Biblical and Judaic Acronyms.* By Lawrence Marwick. New York: Ktav Publishing House, Inc., 1979.

(BUR)   *Computer Acronyms and Abbreviations Handbook.* Tokyo: Burroughs Co. Ltd., 1978.

(BYTE)   *Byte: The Small Systems Journal.* Peterborough, NH: McGraw-Hill Information Systems, Inc., 1987-89.

(CAAL)   *CAAL COMOPTEVFOR Acronym and Abbreviation List.* Norfolk, VA: (CAAL-U) Operational Test and Evaluation Force, 1981.

(CB)   *Centres & Bureaux: A Directory of Concentrations of Effort, Information and Expertise.* Edited by Lindsay Sellar. Beckenham, Kent, England: CBD Research Ltd., 1987.
           A guide to British organizations which include the words "centre" or "bureau" in their names. Entries include name and address; telephone and telex numbers; chief official; and a description of the purposes, activities, and services of the organization.

(CDAI)   *Concise Dictionary of Acronyms and Initialisms.* By Stuart W. Miller. New York: Facts on File Publications, 1988.

(CED)   *Current European Directories.* 2nd ed. Edited by G.P. Henderson, Beckenham, Kent, England: CBD Research, 1981; distributed in U.S. by Gale Research Inc., Detroit.

(CET)   *Communications-Electronics Terminology.* AFM 11-1. Vol. 3 U.S. Department of the Air Force, 1973.

(CINC)   *A CINCPAC Glossary of Commonly Used Abbreviations and Short Titles.* By Ltc. J.R. Johnson. Washington, DC: 1968.

(CMD)   *Complete Multilingual Dictionary of Computer Terminology.* Compiled by Georges Nania. Chicago: National Textbook Co., 1984.
           Computer-related terms in Spanish, French, Italian, Portuguese, and English. Indexes in French, Italian, Spanish, and Portuguese are also provided.

(CNC)   *American National Standard Codes for the Representation of Names of Countries, Dependencies, and Areas of Special Sovereignty for Information Interchange.* U.S. National Bureau of Standards. Washington, DC: Government Printing Office, 1986. [Use of source began in 1977]
           These standard codes, approved by the International Organization for Standardization and the American National Standards Institute, are used in the international interchange of data in many fields.

(CRD)   *Computer-Readable Databases: A Directory and Data Sourcebook.* 6th ed. Edited by Kathleen Young Marcaccio. Detroit: Gale Research Inc., 1990.
           A guide to online databases, offline files available in various magnetic formats, and CD-ROM files. Entries include producer name, address, telephone number, description of coverage, vendors, and contact person.

(CSR)   *Computer Science Resources: A Guide to Professional Literature.* Edited by Darlene Myers. White Plains, NY: Knowledge Industry Publications, Inc., 1981.
           Covers several types of computer-related literature including journals, technical reports, directories, dictionaries, handbooks, and university computer center newsletters. Five appendices cover career and salary trends in the computer industry, user group acronyms, university computer libraries, and trade fairs and shows.

(CTT)   *Corporate TrendTrac.* Edited by A. Dale Timpe. Detroit: Gale Research Inc., 1988-89.
            Covers mergers and acquisitions, stock exchange listings and suspen-
            sions, company name changes, bankruptcies, liquidations, and reorgani-
            zations.

(DAS)   *Dictionary of Abbreviations and Symbols.* By Edward Frank Allen. London: Cassell and
            Co. Ltd.

(DBQ)   *A Dictionary of British Qualifications.* London: Kogan Page Ltd., 1985.

(DCTA)   *Dictionary of Commercial Terms and Abbreviations.* By Alan E. Branch. London: Witherby
            & Co. Ltd., 1984.

(DEN)   *Dictionary of Electronics and Nucleonics.* By L.E.C. Hughes, R.W.B. Stephens, and L.D.
            Brown. New York: Barnes & Noble, 1969.

(DHSM)   *Dictionary of Health Services Management.* 2nd ed. By Thomas C. Timmreck. Owings
            Mills, MD: Rynd Communications, 1987.

(DI)   *The Dictionary of Initials-What They Mean.* Compiled and edited by Harriette Lewis.
            Kingswood, Surrey, England: Paper fronts Elliot Right Way Books, 1983.

(DIT)   *Dictionary of Informatics Terms in Russian and English.* By G.S. Zhdanov, E.S. Kolobrodov,
            V.A. Polushkin, and A.I. Cherny. Moscow: Nauka, 1971.

(DLA)   *Bieber's Dictionary of Legal Abbreviations.* 3rd ed. By Mary Miles Prince. Buffalo, NY:
            William S. Hein & Co., 1988.

(DMA)   *Dictionary of Military Abbreviations: British, Empire, Commonwealth.* By. B.K.C. Scott.
            Hastings, East Sussex, England: Tamarisk Books, 1982.

(DNAB)   *Dictionary of Naval Abbreviations.* 3rd ed. Compiled and edited by Bill Wedertz. Annapolis,
            MD: Naval Institute Press, 1984.

(DS)   *Dictionary of Shipping International Trade Terms and Abbreviations.* 3rd ed. By Alan E.
            Branch. London: Witherby & Co. Ltd., 1986.

(DSA)   *Dictionary of Sigla and Abbreviations to and in Law Books before 1607.* By William
            Hamilton Bryson. Charlottesville, VA: University Press of Virginia, 1975.

(DSUE)   *A Dictionary of Slang and Unconventional English.* 8th ed. By Eric Partridge. New York:
            Macmillan Publishing Co., 1984.

(DUND)   *Directory of United Nations Databases and Information Services.* 4th ed. Compiled by the
            Advisory Committee for the Coordination of Information Systems. New York: United
            Nations, 1990.
            A guide to computerized databases and information systems/services.
            Entries include sponsoringorganization, year established, type, scope,
            coverage, timespan, and contact information.

(DWSG)   *Defense Weapon Systems Glossary.* By David Trotz. Piscataway, NJ: Target Marketing,
            1992.

(EA)   *Encyclopedia of Associations.* 26th ed. Vol. 1, National Organizations of the U.S. Edited
            by Deborah M. Burek. Detroit: Gale Research Inc., 1991. (and supplement, 1992) [Use of
            source began in 1960]
            A guide to trade, professional, and other nonprofit associations that are
            national and international in scope and membership and that are headquar-
            tered in the United States. Entries include name and address; telephone
            and telex number; chief official; and a description of the purpose, activities,
            and structure of the organization.

(EAAP)   *Encyclopedia of Associations: Association Periodicals.* 3 vols. Edited by Denise M. Allard and Robert C. Thomas. Detroit: Gale Research Inc., 1987.
> A directory of publications issued by all types of national nonprofit organizations in the United States. Entries include title and organization name, address, telephone number; description of periodical, frequency of publication, and price.

(EAIO)   *Encyclopedia of Associations: International Organizations.* 27th ed. Edited by Linda Irvin. Detroit: Gale Research Inc., 1993. [Use of source began in 1985]
> A guide to trade, professional, and other nonprofit associations that are national or international in scope and membership and that are headquartered outside the United States. Entries include name and address; principal foreign language name; telephone and telex number; chief official; and a description of the purpose, activities, and structure of the organization.

(ECED)   *The European Communities Encyclopedia and Directory 1992.* London: Europa Publications Ltd., 1991; distributed in U.S. by Gale Research Inc., Detroit.
> A comprehensive guide to the European Communities. Entries explain widley-used acronyms and include address, telephone, telex, fax numbers and chief officers for EC-level organizations.

(ECON)   *The Economist.* London: The Economist Newspaper Ltd., 1993. [Use of source began in 1988]

(EE)   *Eastern Europe and the Commonwealth of Independent States 1992.* London: Europa Publications Ltd., 1992; distributed in U.S. by Gale Research Inc., Detroit.

(EG)   *Environmental Glossary.* 4th ed. Edited by G. William Frick and Thomas F.P. Sullivan. Rockville, MD: Government Institutes, Inc., 1986.

(EGAO)   *Encyclopedia of Government Advisory Organizations.* 6th ed. Edited by Denise M. Allard and Donna Batten. Detroit: Gale Research Inc., 1988 [Use of source began in 1975]
> A reference guide to permanent, continuing, and ad hoc U.S. presidential advisory committees, interagency committees, and other government-related boards, panels, task forces, commissions, conferences, and other similar bodies serving in a consultative, coordinating, advisory, research, or investigative capacity. Entries include name and address, telephone number, designated federal employee, history, recommendation and findings of the committee, staff size, publications, and subsidiaries. Also includes indexes to personnel, reports, federal agencies, presidential administration, and an alphabetical and keyword index.

(EPA)   *Glossary of EPA Acronyms.* Washington, DC: Environmental Protection Agency, 1987.

(EY)   *The Europa World Year Book 1992.* London: Europa Publications Ltd., 1992. distributed in U.S. by Gale Research Inc., Detroit.
> An annual survey containing detailed information about the political, economic, statistical, and commercial situation of the regions and countries covered.

(FAAC)   *Contractions Handbook. Changes.* U.S. Department of Transportation. Federal Aviation Administration, 1985. [Use of source began in 1969]

(FAAL)   *Location Identifiers.* U.S. Department of Transportation. Federal Aviation Administration. Air Traffic Service, 1982.

(FEA)   *The Far East and Australasia 1987.* 18th ed. London: Europa Publications Ltd., 1986; distributed in U.S. by Gale Research Inc., Detroit.
> An annual survey containing detailed information about the political, economic, statistical, and commercial situation of the regions and countries covered.

(GEA)   *Government Economic Agencies of the World: An International Directory of Governmental Organisations Concerned with Economic Development and Planning.* A Keesing's Reference Publication. Edited by Alan J. Day. Harlow, Essex, England: Longman Group Ltd., 1985; distributed in U.S. by Gale Research Inc., Detroit.

        Covers over 170 countries and territories. Two introductory sections for each area cover economic data and prevailing economic and political conditions. Individual entries provide title, address, and names of chief officials of each agency. Current activities and financial structure of each agency are also detailed. An index of agency officials is provided.

(GFGA)   *Guide to Federal Government Acronyms.* Edited by William R. Evinger. Phoenix: The Oryx Press, 1989.

(GPO)   *Style Manual.* Washington, DC: Government Printing Office, 1984.

        Terms are included in Chapter 24, Foreign Languages.

(GRD)   *Government Research Directory.* 5th ed. Edited by Kay Gill and Susan E. Tufts. Detroit: Gale Research Inc., 1989. (and supplement, 1989)

        A descriptive guide to U.S. government research and development centers, institutes, laboratories, bureaus, test facilities, experiment stations, data collection and analysis centers, and grants management and research coordinating offices in agriculture, business, education, energy, engineering, environment, the humanities, medicine, military science, and basic applied sciences.

(HGAA)   *The Handy Guide to Abbreviations and Acronyms for the Automated Office.* By Mark W. Greenia. Seattle: Self-Counsel Press Inc., 1986.

(IAA)   *Index of Acronyms and Abbreviations in Electrical and Electronic Engineering.* Compiled by Buro Scientia. New York: VCH Publishers, 1989.

(IBMDP) *IBM Data Processing Glossary.* 6th ed. White Plains, NY: IBM Corp., 1977.

(ICAO)   *Aircraft Type Designators.* 13th ed. International Civil Aviation Organization, August, 1981.

(ICDA)   *Designators for Aircraft Operating Agencies, Aeronautical Authorities and Services.* 49th ed. International Civil Aviation Organization, June 1982.

        Document also includes telephony designators and postal and telegraphic addresses of government civil aviation authorities.

(ICLI)   *Location Indicators.* 51st ed. International Civil Aviation Organization, February 1987.

        Document also contains addresses of flight information centers.

(IEEE)   *IEEE Standard Dictionary of Electrical and Electronics Terms.* Edited by Frank Jay. New York: The Institute of Electrical and Electronics Engineers, Inc., 1977, 1984.

        Includes definitions for thousands of electrical and electronics terms. Each entry includes a numeric source code.

(IIA)   *Index of Initials and Acronyms.* Compiled by Richard Kleiner. New York: Auerbach Publishers, 1971.

(IID)   *Information Industry Directory.* 11th ed. Edited by Bradley J. Morgan. Detroit: Gale Research Inc., 1991 (and supplement, 1991).

        An international guide to computer-readable databases, database producers, and publishers, online vendors and time-sharing companies, telecommunications networks, and many other information systems and services. Entries include name and address, telephone number, chief official, and a detailed description of the purpose and function of the system or service.

(ILCA)   *Index to Legal Citations and Abbreviations.* By Donald Raistrick. Abingdon, Oxfordshire, England: Professional Books Ltd., 1981.

(IMH) *International Marketing Handbook.* 2nd ed. Edited by Frank Bair. Detroit: Gale Research Inc., 1985.

> An in-depth guide to commercial and trade data on 142 countries of the world. Features include a list of European trade fairs and a report on growth markets in Western Europe.

(INF) *Infantry.* Fort Benning, GA: U.S. Army Infantry Training School, 1993. [Use of source began in 1983]

(IRC) *International Research Centers Directory 1992-93.* 6th ed. Edited by Annette Piccirelli. Detroit: Gale Research Inc., 1991.

> A world guide to government, university, independent, nonprofit, and commercial research and development centers, institutes, laboratories, bureaus, test facilities, experiment stations, and data collection and analysis centers, as well as foundations, councils, and other organizations which support research.

(IRUK) *Industrial Research in the United Kingdom.* 12th ed. Harlow, Essex, England: Longman Group UK Ltd., 1987.

> A guide to all groups conducting or funding research relevant to British industrial development. Entries include name, address, telephone and telex numbers; chief officials; and scope of activities.

(IT) *Information Today: The Newspaper for Users and Producers of Electronic Information Services.* Medford, NJ: Learned Information Inc., 1988-89.

(ITD) *International Tradeshow Directory.* 5th ed. Frankfurt am Main: M + A Publishers for Fairs, Exhibitions and Conventions Ltd., 1989.

> A guide to trade fairs and exhibitions throughout the world. Entries include event name, dates, frequency, location, description of purpose, profile of exhibitors and attendees.

(IYR) *The 1989-92 International Yacht Racing Rules.* London: International Yacht Racing Union, 1989.

(KSC) *A Selective List of Acronyms and Abbreviations.* Compiled by the Documents Department, Kennedy Space Center Library, 1971, 1973.

(LCCP) *MARC Formats for Bibliographic Data.* Appendix II. Washington, DC: Library of Congress, 1982.

(LCLS) *Symbols of American Libraries.* 13th ed. Washington, DC: Catalog Management and Publication Division, Library of Congress, 1985. [Use of source began in 1980]

(MAE) *Medical Abbreviations and Eponyms.* By Sheila B. Sloane. Philadelphia: W.B. Saunders Co., 1985.

(MCD) *Acronyms, Abbreviations, and Initialisms.* Compiled by Carl Lauer. St. Louis: McDonnell Douglas Corp., 1989 [Use of source began in 1969]

(MDG) *Microcomputer Dictionary and Guide.* By Charles J. Sippl. Champaign, IL: Matrix Publishers, Inc., 1975.

> A listing of definitions for over 5,000 microelectronics terms. Seven appendices.

(MENA) *The Middle East and North Africa 1987.* 33rd ed. London: Europa Publications Ltd., 1986; distributed in U.S. by Gale Research Inc., Detroit.

> An annual survey containing detailed information about the political, economic, statistical, and commercial situation of the regions and countries covered.

(MSA) *Military Standard Abbreviations for Use on Drawings, and in Specifications, Standards, and Technical Documents.* MIL-STD-12D. U.S. Department of Defense, 1981. [Use of source began in 1975]

(MSC) *Annotated Acronyms and Abbreviations of Marine Science Related Activities.* 3rd ed. Revised by Charlotte M. Ashby and Alan R. Flesh. Washington, DC: U.S. Department of Commerce. National Oceanographic and Atmospheric Administration. Environmental Data Service. National Oceanographic Data Center, 1976, 1981.

(MUGU) *The Mugu Book of Acronyms and Abbreviations.* Management Engineering Office, Pacific Missile Range, California, 1963, 1964.

(NASA) *Space Transportation System and Associated Payloads: Glossary, Acronyms, and Abbreviations.* Washington, DC: U.S. National Aeronautics and Space Administration, 1985.

(NATG) *Glossary of Abbreviations Used in NATO Documents.* AAP 15(B), n.p., 1979. [Use of source began in 1976]

(NCC) *NCC The National Centre for Information Technology. Guide to Computer Aided Engineering, Manufacturing and Construction Software.* Manchester, England: NCC Publications. The National Computing Centre Ltd., 1985.
   Includes software classifications and descriptions, names and addresses of suppliers, processor manufacturers, and operating systems.

(NG) *NAVAIR Glossary of Unclassified Common-Use Abbreviated Titles and Phrases.* NAVAIRNOTE 5216 AIR-6031, n.p., July 1969.

(NLC) *Symbols of Canadian Libraries.* 12th ed. National Library of Canada. Minister of Supply and Services Canada, 1987.

(NOAA) *NOAA Directives Manual.* 66-13 Acronyms. 1977.

(NQ) *NASDAQ Company Directory. New York: National Association of Securities Dealers Inc., 1990.* [Use of source began in 1983]
   Entries include company name, SIC code, contact person's name, title, address, and telephone number.

(NRCH) *A Handbook of Acronyms and Initialisms.* Washington, DC: U.S. Nuclear Regulatory Commission. Division of Technical Information and Document Control, 1985.

(NVT) *Naval Terminology.* NWP3. Rev. B. U.S. Department of the Navy. Office of the Chief of Naval Operations, 1980. [Use of source began in 1974]
   Includes a section on definitions of naval terminology.

(OA) *Ocran's Acronyms: A Dictionary of Abbreviations and Acronyms Used in Scientific and Technical Writing.* By Emanuel Benjamin Ocran. London: Routledge & Kegan Paul Ltd., 1978.

(OAG) *Official Airline Guide Worldwide Edition.* Oak Brook, IL: Official Airlines Guide, Inc., 1984. [Use of source began in 1975]

(OCD) *Oxford Classical Dictionary.* 2nd ed. Edited by N.G. Hammond and H.H. Scullard. London: Oxford University Press, 1970.

(OCLC) *OCLC Participating Institutions Arranged by OCLC Symbol.* Dublin, OH: OCLC, 1981.

(OICC) *Abbreviations and Acronyms.* Des Moines, IA: Iowa State Occupational Information Coordinating Committee, 1986.

(OLDSS) *Online Database Search Services Directory.* 2nd ed. Edited by Doris Morris Maxfield. Detroit: Gale Research Inc., 1988.
   Provides detailed descriptions of the online information retrieval services offered by libraries, private information firms, and other organizations in the United States and Canada. Entries include name and address, telephone number, and key contact, as well as online systems accessed, frequently searched databases, and access hardware.

(PCM)   *PC Magazine*. New York: Ziff-Davis Publishing Co., 1993. [Use of source began in 1987]

(PD)   *Political Dissent: An International Guide to Dissident, Extra-Parliamentary, Guerrilla and Illegal Political Movements*. A Keesing's Reference Publication. Compiled by Henry W. Degenhardt. Edited by Alan J. Day. Harlow, Essex, England: Longman Group, 1983; distributed in U.S. by Gale Research Inc., Detroit.
> Includes the history and aims of approximately 1,000 organizations, with details of their leaderships.

(PDAA) *Pugh's Dictionary of Acronyms and Abbreviations: Abbreviations in Management, Technology and Information Science*. 5th ed. Eric Pugh. Chicago: American Library Association, 1987.

(PPE)   *Political Parties of Europe*. 2 vols. Edited by Vincent E. McHale. The Greenwood Historical Encyclopedia of the World's Political Parties. Westport, CT: Greenwood Press, 1983.
> One of a series of reference guides to the world's significant political parties. Each guide provides concise histories of the political parties of a region and attempts to detail the evolution of ideology, changes in organization, membership, leadership, and each party's impact upon society.

(PPW)   *Political Parties of the World*. 2nd ed. A Keesing's Reference Publication. Compiled and edited by Alan J. Day and Henry W. Degenhardt. Harlow, Essex, England: Longman Group, 1980, 1984; distributed in U.S. by Gale Research Inc., Detroit.
> Covers historical development, structure, leadership, membership, policy, publications, and international affiliations. For each country, an overview of the current political situation and constitutional structure is provided.

(PS)   *Popular Science*. New York: Times-Mirror Magazines, Inc., 1993. [Use of source began in 1992]

(RCD)   *Research Centers Directory*. 14th ed. Edited by Peter D. Dresser and Karen Hill. Detroit: Gale Research Inc., 1989 (and supplement, 1990). [Use of source began in 1986]
> A guide to university-related and other nonprofit research organizations carrying on research in agriculture, astronomy and space sciences, behavioral and social sciences, computers and mathematics, engineering and technology, physical and earth sciences and regional and area studies.

(RDA)   *Army RD and A Magazine*. Alexandria, VA: Development, Engineering, and Acquisition Directorate, Army Materiel Command, 1993. [Use of source began in 1979]

(ROG)   *Dictionary of Abbreviations*. By Walter T. Rogers. London: George Allen & Co. Ltd., 1913; reprinted by Gale Research Inc., 1969.

(SAA)   *Space-Age Acronyms, Abbreviations and Designations*. 2nd ed. By Reta C. Moser. New York: IFI/Plenum, 1969.

(SDI)   *Report to the Congress on the Strategic Defense Initiative*. U.S. Department of Defense. Strategic Defense Initiative Organization, April 1987.

(SEIS) *Seismograph Station Codes and Characteristics*. Geological Survey. Circular 791. By Barbara B. Poppe, Debbi A. Naab, and John S. Derr. Washington, DC: U.S. Department of the Interior, 1978.

(SLS)   *World Guide to Scientific Associations and Learned Societies/Internationales Verzeichnis Wissenschaftlicher Verbande und Gesellschaften*. 4th ed. Edited by Barbara Verrel. New York: K.G. Saur, 1984.
> A directory of more than 22,000 societies and associations in all fields of science, culture, and technology. International, national, and regional organizations from 150 countries are also included.

(SPSG) *Security Owner's Stock Guide*. New York: Standard & Poor's Corp., 1992. [Use of source began in 1988]

(SSD)   *Space Station Directory and Program Guide.* Edited and compiled by Melinda Gipson, Jane Glass, and Mary Linden. Arlington, VA: Pasha Publications Inc., 1988.

(TEL)   *Telephony's Dictionary.* 2nd ed. By Graham Langley. Chicago: Telephony Publishing Corp., 1986.
> Includes definitions for U.S. and international telecommunications terms.
> Ten appendices.

(TSPED) *Trade Shows and Professional Exhibits Directory.* 2nd ed. Edited by Robert J. Elster. Detroit: Gale Research Inc., 1987. [Use of source began in 1986]
> A guide to scheduled events providing commercial display facilities including conferences, conventions, meetings, fairs and festivals, etc. Entries include name of trade show; sponsor name, address, and telephone number; attendance figures; principal exhibits; special features; publications; and date and location of shows.

(TSSD)   *Telecommunications Systems and Services Directory.* 4th ed. (and supplement) Edited by John Krol. Detroit: Gale Research Inc., 1989. [Use of source began in 1985]
> An international descriptive guide to telecommunications organizations, systems, and services. Entries include name and address, telephone number, chief official, and a description of the purposes, technical structure, and background of the service or system.

(WDMC)   *Webster's New World Dictionary of Media and Communications.* By Richard Weiner. New York: Webster's New World, 1990.

(WGA)   *Webster's Guide to Abbreviations.* Springfield, MA: Merriam-Webster Inc., 1985.

Acronyms, Initialisms
& Abbreviations
Dictionary *was named
an "Outstanding
Reference Source,"
the highest honor given
by the American
Library Association
Reference and Adult
Services Division.*

Acronyms, Initialisms & Abbreviations Dictionary

P-Z

P

P .... Aircraft [*Wind triangle problems*]
P .... All India Reporter, Patna [*A publication*]   (DLA)
P .... Armour Pharmaceutical Co. [*Research code symbol*]
P .... Assistant in Private Practice [*Chiropody*] [*British*]
P .... Asta Werke AG [*Germany*] [*Research code symbol*]
P .... Bristol Laboratories [*Research code symbol*]
P .... cis-Platinum [*Cisplatin*] [*Also, cis-DDP, CDDP, CPDD, CPT, DDP*] [*Antineoplastic drug*]
P .... Dainippon Pharmaceutical Co. [*Japan*] [*Research code symbol*]
p .... Density [*Heat transmission symbol*]
P .... Departure
p .... Difficulty [*Of a test item*] [*Psychology*]
P .... Farbenfabriken Bayer [*Germany*] [*Research code symbol*]
P .... Farmitalia [*Italy*] [*Research code symbol*]
P .... Faulty Punctuation [*Used in correcting manuscripts, etc.*]
P .... Force of Concentrated Load
P .... Games [*or Matches*] Played [*Sports statistics*]
P .... Hole P-Type Semiconductor Material
P .... Indian Law Reports, Patna Series [*A publication*]   (DLA)
P .... Law Reports, Probate, Divorce, and Admiralty [*Since 1890*] [*England*] [*A publication*]   (DLA)
P .... Lepetit [*Italy*] [*Research code symbol*]
p .... Momentum [*Symbol*] [*IUPAC*]
P .... Office of Personnel [*Coast Guard*]
p .... On Probation [*Navy*] [*British*]
P .... Orbital Period [*of a comet*] [*In years*]
p .... P-Doped Semiconductor [*Photovoltaic energy systems*]
P .... P-Register [*Data processing*]
P .... Pacer
P .... Pacht [*A publication*]
P .... Pacific Coast Stock Exchange [*Later, PSE*]
p------ .... Pacific Ocean [*MARC geographic area code*] [*Library of Congress*]   (LCCP)
P .... Pacific Reporter [*A publication*]   (DLA)
P .... Pacific Standard Time   (FAAC)
P .... Pack [*JETDS*]
P .... Packed Lunches [*School meals*] [*British*]
P .... Pad   (SAA)
P .... Paddington Railway Station   (ROG)
P .... Paddle   (DS)
P .... Page
P .... Paid This Year [*In stock listings of newspapers*]
P .... Pain [*Medicine*]
P .... Paired [*for or against*] [*Votes in Congress*]
P .... Paise [*Monetary unit*] [*India*]
P .... Palace   (ROG)
P .... Palacio [*A publication*]
P .... Palaestra [*A publication*]
P .... Pale   (ADA)
P .... Palimpsest [*A publication*]
P .... Pallet [*Spacelab*] [*NASA*]   (NASA)
P .... Pamphlet
P .... Pancuronium [*A muscle relaxant*]
P .... Pandects [*A publication*] [*Authority cited in pre-1607 legal work*]   (DSA)
P .... Papa [*Pope*] [*Latin*]
P .... Papa [*Phonetic alphabet*] [*International*]   (DSUE)
P .... Paper
P .... Paperback   (WGA)
P .... Papilla [*Optic*] [*Medicine*]
P .... Papillate [*A type of seed*] [*Botany*]
p .... Para [*Chemistry*]
P .... Para [*Monetary unit*] [*Former Yugoslavia*]
P .... Parachutist [*Army skill qualification identifier*]   (INF)
P .... Paragraph   (ADA)
P .... Paralegal Program [*Association of Independent Colleges and Schools specialization code*]
P .... Parallax
P .... Parallel
P .... Paramecin [*A protozoan toxin*]
P .... Parashah   (BJA)

P .... Pardon   (ADA)
P .... Parenchyma [*Botany*]
P .... Parental
P .... Parish   (ROG)
P .... Parity [*Atomic physics*]
P .... Park
P .... Parking Place [*Traffic sign*] [*British*]
P .... Parlophone [*Record label*] [*Great Britain, Italy, Australia, etc.*]
P .... Parson
P .... Part
P .... Parthian [*Language, etc.*]
P .... Partial [*Astronomy*]
P .... Partial Pressure   (MAE)
P .... Participle [*Grammar*]
P .... Partim [*In Part*]
P .... Partnership
P .... Party
P .... Parve [*or Pareve*] [*In food labeling, indicates food is kosher and can be used with either meat or dairy products*]
P .... Passed [*Examination*]
P .... Passing Showers [*Meteorology*]
P .... Past
P .... Paste
P .... Pasteurella [*Genus of bacteria*]
P .... Pastor
P .... Patchy [*Decelerometer readings*] [*Aviation*]   (FAAC)
P .... Patent
P .... Pater [*Father*] [*Latin*]
P .... Patient
P .... Patrol [*Designation for all US military aircraft*]
P .... Patrol Service Gunnery Instructor [*Officer's rating*] [*British Royal Navy*]
P .... Patron
P .... Pattern
P .... Paulus de Liazaris [*Deceased, 1356*] [*Authority cited in pre-1607 legal work*]   (DSA)
P .... Paused Program [*Data processing*]
P .... Pavilion   (ROG)
P .... Pawn [*Chess*]
P .... Pax [*Peace*] [*Latin*]
P .... Pay
P .... Payee
P .... Paymaster [*Military*]   (ROG)
P .... Pazmaveb [*A publication*]
P .... Peak
P .... Peat   (ROG)
P .... Pebbles [*Quality of the bottom*] [*Nautical charts*]
P .... Pectoral [*Anatomy*]   (ROG)
P .... Peculiar [*Astronomy*]
p .... Pelagius [*Deceased, 1232*] [*Authority cited in pre-1607 legal work*]   (DSA)
P .... Pen [*Sports*]
p .... Pence [*Monetary unit*] [*British*]
P .... Pencil Tube   (MDG)
P .... Pengo [*Monetary unit in Hungary until 1946*]
P .... Penicillin
p .... Penni(a) [*Penny or Pence*] [*Monetary unit*] [*Finland*]   (GPO)
P .... Pennsylvania   (DLA)
P .... Pennsylvania State Library, Harrisburg, PA [*Library symbol*] [*Library of Congress*]   (LCLS)
P .... Penny
P .... Pensamiento [*A publication*]
P .... Pentachlorophenol [*Also, PCP*] [*Wood preservative*] [*Organic chemistry*]   (TEL)
P .... Pentode [*Electronics*]   (OA)
P .... Peony [*Horticulture*]
P .... People
P .... Per
P .... Percentile
P .... Perceptual
P .... Perceptual Speed [*A factor ability*] [*Psychology*]

P................ Perch
P................ Perchloroethylene [*Also, TCE*] [*Dry cleaning*]
P................ Percussion
P................ Pere [*Father*] [*French*]
P................ Perforation
P................ Performance [*Army*]   (INF)
P................ Performer
P................ Perianth
P................ Pericardium [*Medicine*]
P................ Perimeter
P................ Period
P................ Perishable
P................ Permanent Stay [*in hospital*] [*British*]
P................ Perpetuus [*Uninterrupted*] [*Latin*]
p................ Perseverate [*Psychology*]
P................ Persian   (DLA)
P................ Persimmon
P................ Persistence [*Medicine*]
P................ Person
P................ Person to Person [*Telecommunications*]   (TEL)
P................ Personality Organization and Stability [*Eysenck*] [*Psychology*]
P................ Personnel
P................ Perspectives [*A publication*]
P................ Perstetur [*Continue*] [*Pharmacy*]   (ROG)
P................ Persuasion [*Novel by Jane Austen*]
P................ Peseta [*Monetary unit*] [*Spain and Latin America*]
P................ Pesewa [*Monetary unit*] [*Ghana*]
P................ Pesher   (BJA)
P................ Peshitta   (BJA)
P................ Peso [*Monetary unit*] [*Spain and Latin America*]
P................ Peta [*A prefix meaning multiplied by 10^{15}*] [*SI symbol*]
P................ Peter [*New Testament book*]
P................ Peter [*Phonetic alphabet*] [*World War II*]   (DSUE)
P................ Peters' United States Supreme Court Reports [*26-41 United States*] [*A publication*]   (DLA)
P................ Petiole [*Botany*]
P................ Petite   (WGA)
P................ Petrol [*British Waterways Board sign*]
P................ Petrus Hispanus [*Authority cited in pre-1607 legal work*]   (DSA)
P................ Peyote
P................ Pfizer, Inc. [*Research code symbol*]
P................ Pharmacopoeia
P................ Phencyclidine [*An anesthetic*]
P................ Phenolphthalein [*Chemical indicator*]
P................ Philadelphia [*Pennsylvania*] [*Mint mark, when appearing on US coins*]
P................ Phillips Petroleum Co. [*NYSE symbol*]   (SPSG)
P................ Philosophy [*A publication*]
P................ Phoenician   (BJA)
P................ Phon [*Unit of loudness level*]
p................ Phosphate [*One-letter symbol*] [*Biochemistry*]
p................ Phosphoric Residue [*As substituent on nucleoside*] [*Biochemistry*]
P................ Phosphorus [*Chemical element*]
P................ Photographic Reconnaissance Capability [*When suffix to Navy aircraft designation*]
P................ Phototropism [*Botany*]
P................ Phrase Structure Rule [*Linguistics*]
P................ Physics [*Secondary school course*] [*British*]
P................ Physiology [*Medical Officer designation*] [*British*]
P................ Phytophthora [*A fungus*]
P................ Piaggio Rinaldo [*Industria Aeronautiche & Meccaniche SpA*] [*Italy*] [*ICAO aircraft manufacturer identifier*]   (ICAO)
P................ Pianissimo [*Very Softly*] [*Music*]
P................ Piano [*Softly*] [*Music*]
P................ Piano [*Musical instrument*]
P................ Piaster [*Monetary unit*] [*Spain, Republic of Vietnam, and some Middle Eastern countries*]
P................ Pica [*Typography*]   (ADA)
P................ Pickering's Massachusetts Reports [*18-41 Massachusetts*] [*A publication*]   (DLA)
p................ Pico [*A prefix meaning divided by one trillion*] [*SI symbol*]
P................ Picot [*Crochet*]   (ROG)
P................ Pie
P................ Pied [*Foot*] [*French*]
P................ Pierced [*Quilting*]
P................ Pigs   (ROG)
P................ Pilaster [*Technical drawings*]
P................ Pillar [*Buoy*]
P................ Pilot
P................ [*Marc*] Pincherle [*When used in identifying Vivaldi's compositions, refers to cataloging of his works by musicologist Pincherle*]
P................ Pink
P................ Pinnule
P................ Pint
P................ Pip [*Phonetic alphabet*] [*Pre-World War II*]   (DSUE)
P................ Pipe
P................ Pipe Rolls [*British*]
P................ Pique; Inclusions [*Diamond clarity grade*]

P................ Pitch [*or Pitcher*] [*Baseball*]
P................ Pitch [*Technical drawings*]
P................ Pith [*Botany*]
P................ Pitman Examination Institute [*British*]
P................ Pitman-Moore Co. [*Research code symbol*]
P................ Pius [*Dutiful*] [*Latin*]
P................ Placebo [*Medicine*]
P................ Placentinus [*Deceased, 1192*] [*Authority cited in pre-1607 legal work*]   (DSA)
P................ Placitum [*or Placita*] [*Agreeable, Agreed Upon*] [*Latin*] [*Legal term*]   (DLA)
P................ Planed
P................ Planning
P................ Plasma
P................ Plasmodium [*Biology*]   (MAE)
P................ Plastid [*Botany*]
P................ Plate [*Electron tube*] [*Technical drawings*]
P................ Platform   (DCTA)
P................ Players League [*Major league in baseball, 1890*]
P................ Pleasant
P................ Pleinsbachian [*Geology*]
P................ Plotter [*British military*]   (DMA)
P................ Plug
P................ Plus [*More*]
P................ Poco [*Somewhat*] [*Music*]
P................ Poetry [*A publication*]
P................ Point [*Lacrosse position*]
P................ Point
P................ Point-to-Point Radio [*FAA designator*]   (CET)
P................ Poise [*Unit of dynamic viscosity*]
P................ Poison
P................ Polar [*Air mass*]   (FAAC)
P................ Polar Distance [*Navigation*]
P................ Polarization
P................ Pole
P................ Political Division [*Geography*]
P................ Polka [*Music*]
P................ Pollen [*Botany*]
P................ Polonystyka [*A publication*]
P................ Polymorphic [*Biology*]
P................ Polyneuropathy [*Medicine*]
P................ Polyphagous [*Biology*]
P................ Pond [*Maps and charts*]
P................ Pondere [*By Weight*] [*Latin*]
p................ Pondus [*Weight*] [*Latin*]   (MAE)
P................ Ponendum [*To Be Placed*] [*Latin*]
P................ Ponte [*A publication*]
P................ Pontifex [*Bishop*] [*Latin*]
P................ Pool
P................ Poop [*Portion of a ship*]
P................ Poor Skiing Conditions
P................ Poorly Organized, Unstable Personality [*Eysenck*] [*Psychology*]
P................ Pope
P................ Popular Response [*Rorschach*] [*Psychology*]
P................ Population
P................ Populus [*People*] [*Latin*]
P................ Porcelain
P................ Port [*Maps and charts*]
P................ Portable [*JETDS nomenclature*]
P................ Portable   (MDG)
P................ Portion
P................ Portugal [*IYRU nationality code*]
P................ Position
p................ Positive [*Crystal*]
P................ Post
P................ Post [*After*] [*Latin*]
P................ Postage
P................ Posten [*Sentry*] [*German military*]
P................ Posterior
P................ Postpartum [*Medicine*]
P................ Pouce [*Inch*] [*French*]
P................ Pounds [*As measurement of total stress*] [*Aerospace*]   (AAG)
P................ Pour [*For*] [*French*]
P................ Power [*Symbol*] [*IUPAC*]
P................ Poynting Vector [*Electromagnetism*]   (DEN)
P................ Practical
P................ Practical Intelligence
P................ Pre-1920 [*Deltiology*]
P................ Preceding
P................ Precipitation Ceiling [*Aviation weather reports*]   (FAAC)
P................ Precipitation Static
P................ Predators Present [*Ecology*]
P................ Predicate
P................ Predictor [*British military*]   (DMA)
P................ Prednisolone [*Endocrinology*]
P................ Prednisone [*Also, PDN, Pr, Pred, Pro*] [*Antineoplastic drug*] [*Endocrinology*]
P................ Preferred
P................ Prefix [*Indicating a private radiotelegram*]
P................ Preliminary
P................ Premolar [*Dentistry*]

P..............	Presbyopia [*Ophthalmology*]
P..............	Presbyterian
P..............	Prescribing
P..............	Present
P..............	Present BIT [*Binary Digit*] [*Data processing*]
P..............	Preset
P..............	President
P..............	Press [*Publishing*]
P..............	Pressure [*or p*] [*Symbol*] [*IUPAC*]
P..............	Pressurized Tank [*Liquid gas carriers*]
P..............	Preview
P..............	Prey [*Zoology*]
P..............	Price [*Economics*]
P..............	Pridie [*The Day Before*] [*Latin*]
P..............	Priest
P..............	Priestly Source [*Biblical scholarship*]
P..............	Prilled
P..............	Primary
P..............	Primary [*or Push*] Wave [*Earthquakes*]
P..............	Primipara [*Woman bearing first child*] [*Medicine*] (MAE)
P..............	Primitive
P..............	Primus [*First*] [*Latin*]
P..............	Prince
P..............	Princeps [*First Edition*] [*French*]
P..............	Princess (ROG)
P..............	Principal
P..............	Print
P..............	Priority [*Telecommunications*] (TEL)
P..............	Priory
P..............	Prisoner [*Military*]
P..............	Private
P..............	Private Trust [*Includes testamentary, investment, life insurance, holding title, etc.*] [*Legal term*] (DLA)
P..............	Private Venture
P..............	Privy (ROG)
P..............	Pro [*For*] [*Latin*]
P..............	Probability [*or Probability Ratio*] [*Statistics*]
P..............	Probate
P..............	Probe (MSA)
P..............	Probucol [*Anticholesteremic*]
P..............	Procarbazine [*Also, PC, PCB, Pr*] [*Antineoplastic drug*]
P..............	Procedure
P..............	Processor [*Data processing*]
P..............	Proconsul
P..............	Producer [*Films, television, etc.*]
P..............	Product
P..............	Production [*of Energy*]
P..............	Profession
P..............	Professional [*Civil Service employees designation*]
P..............	Proficiency
P..............	Profit
P..............	Progesterone [*A hormone*]
P..............	Program (KSC)
P..............	Programmable
P..............	Progressive
P..............	Prohibited Area [*Followed by identification*]
P..............	Proliferation [*Biology*]
P..............	Proline [*One-letter symbol; see Pro*]
P..............	Promoter [*Genetics*]
P..............	Prompt [*i.e., the right side*] [*A stage direction*]
P..............	Proof [*Philately*]
P..............	Prop (DS)
P..............	Propagation Distribution [*Broadcasting*]
P..............	Proportion in a Specific Class
P..............	Proposed Departure [*Aviation*] (FAAC)
P..............	Propulsion (AAG)
P..............	Protein
P..............	Proteinuria [*Clinical chemistry*]
P..............	Protestant
P..............	Protet [*Protest*] [*French*]
P..............	Proteus [*Genus of bacteria*] (MAE)
P..............	Proto [*Linguistics*]
p..............	Proton [*A nuclear particle*]
P..............	Protoplasmic [*Freeze etching in microscopy*]
P..............	Prototroch
P..............	Prototype (AAG)
P..............	Provisional
p..............	Proximum [*Near*] [*Latin*] (MAE)
P..............	Psychiatry
P..............	Psychometrist [*Psychology*]
P..............	Public Houses [*Public-performance tariff class*] [*British*]
P..............	Publications
P..............	Pudding [*Phonetic alphabet*] [*Royal Navy*] [*World War I*] (DSUE)
P..............	Pugillus [*A Handful*] [*Pharmacy*] (ROG)
P..............	Pulled Up [*Horse racing*]
P..............	Pulse
P..............	Pump (AAG)
P..............	Punch
P..............	Punic (BJA)
P..............	Punkt [*Point*] [*German military*]

P..............	Punter [*Football*]
P..............	Pupil
P..............	Purchased (AAG)
P..............	Purified [*Animal breeding*]
P..............	Purinethol [*Mercaptopurine*] [*Also, M, MP*] [*Antineoplastic drug*]
P..............	Purkinje Cell [*Neuroanatomy*]
P..............	Purl [*Knitting*]
P..............	Purple
P..............	Purpure [*Purple*] [*Heraldry*]
P..............	Pursuit [*Airplane designation*]
P..............	Put [*In options listings of newspapers*]
P..............	Pya [*Monetary unit*] [*Myanmar*]
p..............	Pyranose [*One-letter symbol*] [*Biochemistry*]
P..............	Pyroxene Subgroup [*Acmite, sodium metasilicate, potassium metasilicate, diopside, wollastonite, hypersthene*] [*CIPW classification*] [*Geology*]
P..............	RADAR [*JETDS nomenclature*]
P..............	Reproducing [*JETDS nomenclature*]
P..............	Single Paper [*Wire insulation*] (AAG)
P..............	Soft Pad [*Missile launch environment symbol*]
P..............	Warner-Lambert Pharmaceutical Co. [*Research code symbol*]
P$_1$.............	Parental Generation (MAE)
P1.............	Pershing 1 [*Missile*] (GFGA)
P-2.............	Propaganda Due [*Secret Italian Masonic organization, allegedly tied to the Roman Catholic church*]
P$_2$.............	Pulmonic Second Sound [*Medicine*]
P2.............	Second Pilot [*Aviation*] (AIA)
P3.............	Industry Composites and Polymer Processing Program [*Massachusetts Institute of Technology*] [*Research center*] (RCD)
P3.............	Phillips Post Processor
P3.............	Portable Plotting Package [*Nuclear energy*] (NRCH)
3P.............	Three-Pole [*or Triple Pole*] [*Switch*]
4P.............	Four-Pole [*Switch*]
P 14...........	Pattern 14 Rifle [*Made in the US for Great Britain, beginning in 1914*]
P$_{50}$.............	Partial pressure of oxygen at 50% hemoglobin saturation [*Medicine*]
5P's...........	Poet, Printer, Publisher, Publican, and Player [*Nickname given to William Oxberry (fl. 1784-1824)*]
P (Card)	Personal Card [*Containing person's name, address, age, description, job, habits, haunts, movements*] [*Used in Belfast, Northern Ireland*]
P (Day)......	Production Day [*Army*] (AABC)
PA	B. F. Jones Memorial Library, Aliquippa, PA [*Library symbol*] [*Library of Congress*] (LCLS)
PA	[*The*] Item Requested Is a Controlled Item That May Be Released Only By Written Authority of the Proponent. Please See DA Pamphlet 310-1 for Identification of and Address of Proponent [*Supply action error code*] [*Army*]
PA	Office of Public Affairs [*DoD*]
PA	Onze Pius-Almanak [*A publication*]
PA	Pacific Affairs [*A publication*]
PA	Pad Abort [*NASA*] (KSC)
P & A.........	Page and Adams' Code [*1912*] [*A publication*] (DLA)
PA	Paging and Area Warning (MCD)
Pa	Paideia [*A publication*]
Pa	Paine's United States Circuit Court Reports [*A publication*] (DLA)
PA	Paired Associates [*Psychometrics*]
PA	Pakistan Army
PA	Paleopathology Association
PA	Palestine Affairs [*New York*] [*A publication*] (BJA)
PA	Palladium [*Chemical element*] (ROG)
PA	Pamatky Archeologicke [*A publication*]
PA	Pan American World Airways, Inc. [*See also PAA, PAN-AM, PN*] [*ICAO designator*] (MCD)
PA	Panama [*ANSI two-letter standard code*] (CNC)
PA	Panatlas Energy, Inc. [*Toronto Stock Exchange symbol*]
PA	Paper (WGA)
PA	Paper Advance (BUR)
PA	Par Amitie [*By Favor*] [*French*]
PA	Par Autorite [*By Authority*] [*French*]
PA	Para-Amps (EA)
Pa	Parachutist [*British military*] (DMA)
P in A	Parallax in Altitude [*Navigation*]
PA	Paralysis Agitans
PA	Parametric Amplifier
Pa	Paranoia [*Psychology*]
PA	Parapsychological Association (EA)
PA	Parents Anonymous (EA)
PA	Parents' Association
PA	Parish
Pa	Parkett [*A publication*]
PA	Parliamentary Affairs [*A publication*]
PA	Parti de l'Action [*Party of Action*] [*Morocco*] [*Political party*] (PPW)
PA	Parti Affectae [*To the Affected Part*] [*Pharmacy*]
PA	Partial Application [*Military*] (AFIT)
Pa	Partial Pressure in Arterial Blood (MAE)

PA .... Participating Activity [*Responsible for standardization efforts*] [*DoD*]
PA .... Participial Adjective [*Grammar*]
PA .... Particular Average
PA .... Partido Andalucista [*Spain*] [*Political party*]　(ECED)
PA .... Partido Arnulfista [*Panama*] [*Political party*]　(EY)
PA .... Partners of the Americas　(EA)
Pa .... Paru [*A publication*]
Pa .... Pascal [*Symbol*] [*SI unit of pressure*]
PA .... Passenger Agent
PA .... Passenger Ship
PA .... Pastoral Music [*A publication*]
PA .... Pathfinder Association　(EAIO)
PA .... Pathology　(AAMN)
PA .... Patient
PA .... Patrol Aircraft　(NATG)
PA .... Pattern Analysis [*Test*]
P & A .... Pay and Allowances
PA .... Paying Agent [*Legal term*]　(DLA)
P/A .... Payment Authority [*Business term*]
PA .... Pending Availability
PA .... Pendulous Axis [*Accelerometer*]　(IEEE)
PA .... Pennsylvania [*Postal code*]
P & A .... Pennsylvania & Atlantic Railroad Co.　(IIA)
Pa .... Pennsylvania State Reports [*A publication*]
PA .... Pennsylvania Supreme Court Reports [*1845-date*] [*A publication*]　(DLA)
PA .... People's Alliance [*Althydubandalag*] [*Iceland*] [*Political party*]　(PPW)
PA .... Peptide Absorption
PA .... Per Abdomen
PA .... Per Adresse [*Care Of*] [*German*]
PA .... Per Annum [*By the Year*] [*Latin*]
PA .... Per Auguri [*Used on visiting cards to express congratulations, birthday wishes, etc.*] [*Italian*]
P & A .... Percussion and Auscultation [*Medicine*]
PA .... Performance Alertness　(AEBS)
PA .... Performance Analysis
PA .... Performance Appraisal Required [*Civil Service*]
PA .... Performing Arts [*US Copyright Office class*]
PA .... Periodic Acid [*Inorganic chemistry*]
pA .... Periplanone A [*Biochemistry*]
PA .... Permanent Abeyance [*FDA*]
PA .... Permanent Address　(ROG)
PA .... Permanent Appointment
PA .... Permanently Associated [*Telecommunications*]　(TEL)
PA .... Pernicious Anemia [*Hematology*]
PA .... Personal Accident [*Insurance*]　(AIA)
PA .... Personal Affairs　(AFM)
PA .... Personal Appearance
PA .... Personal Assistant [*British*]
PA .... Personal Audit [*Psychological testing*]
P & A .... Personnel and Administration [*Army*]　(AABC)
PA .... Personnel Administrator [*American Society for Personnel Administration*] [*A publication*] [*Information service or system*]
PA .... Personnel Area　(NRCH)
PA .... Petroleum Abstracts [*Also, an information service or system*] [*A publication*]
PA .... Pfizer, Inc. [*Research code symbol*]
PA .... Phakic-Aphakic [*Ophthalmology*]　(MAE)
PA .... Pharmacology, Clinical [*Medical specialty*]　(DHSM)
PA .... Phentolamine [*Antiadrenergic*]
PA .... Philippine Army
PA .... Philippine Association　(EA)
PA .... Philosophische Abhandlungen [*A publication*]
PA .... Phonocardiogram Amplifier [*Cardiology*]
PA .... Phosphatidic Acid [*Biochemistry*]
PA .... Phosphoarginine [*Biochemistry*]
PA .... Photoallergenic [*Response*] [*Medicine*]
PA .... Photodiode Amplifier
PA .... Phthalic Anhydride [*Organic chemistry*]
PA .... Physical Activity　(MCD)
PA .... Physician's Assistant
PA .... Physics Abstracts [*Institution of Electrical Engineers*] [*Information service or system*] [*A publication*]　(CRD)
PA .... Phytoalexin [*Plant pathology*]
PA .... Piaster [*Monetary unit*] [*Spain, Republic of Vietnam, and some Middle Eastern countries*]
PA .... Picatinny Arsenal [*New Jersey*] [*Later, Armament Development Center*] [*Army*]
pA .... Picoampere [*One trillionth of an ampere*]
PA .... Pierre Allain [*Lightweight rock-climbing boot named after its designer*]
PA .... Pierre Arpels [*Jewelry designer*]
PA .... Pills Anonymous [*Later, DA*] [*An association*]　(EA)
P/A .... Pilotless Aircraft
P & A .... Pioneer and Ammunition
PA .... Piper Aircraft Corp. [*ICAO aircraft manufacturer identifier*]　(ICAO)
PA .... Pirke Avot　(BJA)

PA .... [*Pension*] Plan Administrator
P/A .... Planetary Atmosphere　(SAA)
PA .... Planning Assistance　(EA)
P & A .... Plans and Analysis
PA .... Plasma Aldosterone [*Endocrinology*]
PA .... Plasminogen Activator [*Biochemistry*]
PA .... Platelet Adhesiveness [*Hematology*]
PA .... Platform Assembly　(MCD)
PA .... Point of Aim [*Military*]
PA .... Points Against [*Football*]
P/A .... Polar to Analog　(KSC)
PA .... Polar Atlantic [*American air mass*]
PA .... Polarization Approximation [*Physical chemistry*]
PA .... Polarographic Analyzer
PA .... Police Academy
PA .... Pollution Abstracts [*A publication*]
Pa .... Polonystyka [*A publication*]
PA .... Polyacetal [*Organic chemistry*]
PA .... Polyacrylic [*Organic chemistry*]
PA .... Polyamide [*Organic chemistry*]
PA .... Polyanhydride [*Organic chemistry*]
PA .... Polyarteritis [*Medicine*]
PA .... Polymer Adhesive
PA .... Port Agency [*Army*]
PA .... Position Angle [*Astronomy*]
PA .... Position Approximate [*Nautical charts*]
PA .... Positive Addiction [*Self-improvement method developed by William Glasser, MD*]
PA .... Positive Attitude
PA .... Post Adjutant
PA .... Post Amplifier
PA .... Postal Assistant　(DCTA)
PA .... Posterior Anterior [*Medicine*]
PA .... Posterior Aorta
PA .... Postmortem Aging [*of meat*]
PA .... Potato Agar [*Microbiology*]
PA .... Potsmokers Anonymous　(EA)
PA .... Power Amplifier
PA .... Power Approach [*Aerospace*]
PA .... Power of Attorney
P/A .... Power of Authority
PA .... Practice Amendment　(AAG)
PA .... Prealbumin [*Biochemistry*]
PA .... Preamplifier
PA .... Preapproved
PA .... Prearm
PA .... Preavailability
PA .... Precision Approach　(FAAC)
PA .... Precision Architecture [*Hewlett-Packard Co.*] [*Data processing*]
PA .... Precomputed Altitude
P & A .... Prediction and Allocation
PA .... Predictive Analyzer [*Data processing*]　(DIT)
PA .... Prefect-Apostolic [*Roman Catholic*]
PA .... Pregnancy-Associated [*Gynecology*]　(MAE)
PA .... Preliminary Acceptance　(KSC)
PA .... Preparing Activity [*Responsible for Federal document and study projects*]
P/A .... Presence or Absence
PA .... Presence Africaine [*A publication*]
PA .... Present Again　(ADA)
PA .... Preservation Action　(EA)
PA .... Presidents Association [*New York, NY*]　(EA)
PA .... Press Agent
PA .... Press Association Ltd.　(IID)
PA .... Pressure Actuated [*Switch*]
PA .... Pressure Alarm [*Nuclear energy*]　(NRCH)
PA .... Pressure Altitude [*Aviation*]
PA .... Pressure Angle　(MSA)
PA .... Pressure Area [*Medicine*]
PA .... Price Analyst
P & A .... Price and Availability
PA .... Primary Aerospace Vehicle [*or Aircraft*]
PA .... Primary Amenorrhea [*Gynecology*]　(MAE)
PA .... Primary Anemia [*Medicine*]
PA .... Primerica Corp. [*NYSE symbol*]　(SPSG)
PA .... Prince Albert Coat [*Slang*]
PA .... Principal Assistant　(NOAA)
PA .... Principal Axes
PA .... Principle of Adding [*New math*]
PA .... Prior to Admission [*Medicine*]
P & A .... Priorities and Allocations　(MUGU)
PA .... Priority A　(MCD)
PA .... Priority Aggregate
PA .... Privacy Act
PA .... Private Account [*Banking*]
PA .... Private Architect [*British*]
PA .... Pro Anno [*For the Year*] [*Latin*]
PA .... Pro Applicatione [*To Be Applied*] [*Pharmacy*]　(ROG)
PA .... Pro Arte [*A publication*]
PA .... Proactivator [*Medicine*]
PA .... Proanthocyanidin (Assay) [*Analytical chemistry*]

PA .... Probability of Acceptance (KSC)
PA .... Probability of Acquisition [Military]
P/A .... Problem Analysis (NASA)
PA .... Probleme der Agyptologie [A publication] (BJA)
PA .... Procainamide [Cardiac depressant]
P & A .... Procedures and Analysis
PA .... Process Allocator [Telecommunications] (TEL)
PA .... Process Automation (CMD)
PA .... Procurement Agency (MCD)
PA .... Procurement Appropriations [Army] (AABC)
PA .... Procurement, Army
P & A .... Procurement and Assignment
PA .... Procurement Authorization
PA .... Procuring Activity [Military]
PA .... Product Acceptance [Automotive engineering]
PA .... Product Analysis (IEEE)
PA .... Product Assurance (NASA)
PA .... Production Adjustment
PA .... Production Assistant
PA .... Professional Administration [A publication]
P & A .... Professional and Administrative (AAG)
PA .... Professional Administrator [Australia] [A publication]
PA .... Professional Agent [Professional Insurance Agents] [A publication]
PA .... Professional Association [Telecommunications]
PA .... Profile Analysis [Medicine]
PA .... Profile Angle (MSA)
PA .... Program Access
PA .... Program Account (NG)
PA .... Program Address
PA .... Program Administrator (MCD)
PA .... Program Agent (OICC)
PA .... Program for the Aging (OICC)
PA .... Program Aid [A publication]
PA .... Program Analysis [Data processing]
PA .... Program Application Instructions [Telecommunications] (TEL)
PA .... Program Assessment (MCD)
PA .... Program Attention Key [Data processing]
PA .... Program Authorization (AFM)
PA .... Programmable Automation
PA .... Progressive Alliance [Defunct] (EA)
PA .... Project Administration (MCD)
PA .... Project Authorization
PA .... Proliferating Angioendotheliomatosis
PA .... Prolonged-Action [Pharmacy]
PA .... Prolotherapy Association (EA)
PA .... Property Administrator [DoD]
PA .... Prophylactic Antibiotic
PA .... Proponent Agency [Army]
PA .... Proportional Action (AAG)
PA .... Proposal Authorization
PA .... [The] Proprietary Association [Later, NDMA] (EA)
PA .... Propulsion Assistance (DS)
PA .... Prosecuting Attorney
PA .... Prostitutes Anonymous (EA)
Pa .... Protactinium [or Protoactinium] [Chemical element]
PA .... Protected Area [Nuclear energy] (NRCH)
P & A .... Protection and Advocacy [System] [To protect the rights of developmentally disabled persons]
PA .... Protective Antigen
PA .... Prothonotary Apostolic
PA .... Proton Affinity [Surface ionization]
PA .... Provisional Allowance
PA .... Pseudo-Astronomy
PA .... Pseudoaneurysm [Medicine]
PA .... Pseudomonas aeruginosa [Bacterium]
PA .... Psychoanalyst
PA .... Psychogenic Aspermia [Medicine]
PA .... Psychological Abstracts [A publication]
PA .... Psychological Age
PA .... Public Accountant
PA .... Public Act
PA .... Public Address [Amplification equipment] [Communications]
PA .... Public Administration [A publication] (APTA)
PA .... Public Administration
PA .... Public Advocate (EA)
PA .... Public Affairs
PA .... Public Archives [of Canada]
PA .... Public Assistance
PA .... Publication Announcement
PA .... Publishers' Alliance (EA)
PA .... Publishers' Association [London, England] (DIT)
PA .... Pull and Adjust [Brace] [Medicine]
PA .... Pulmonary Angiography [Medicine]
PA .... Pulmonary Artery [Medicine]
PA .... Pulmonary Atresia [Medicine]
PA .... Pulpoaxial [Dentistry]
PA .... Pulse Amplifier
PA .... Puppeteers of America (EA)
PA .... Purchasing Agent

PA .... Purge Alarm [Nuclear energy] (NRCH)
PA .... Puromycin Aminonucleoside [Biochemistry] (OA)
PA .... Put Away [Papers] [British]
PA .... Puumala [Vole virus]
PA .... Pyro Ammonia (ROG)
PA .... Pyrrolizidine Alkaloid [Toxicology]
PA .... Pythium aphanidermatum [A fungus]
P1a .... Pershing 1a [Missile] (GFGA)
PA0$_2$ .... Arterial Oxygen Pressure (MAE)
PAA .... Pa-An [Myanmar] [Airport symbol] (OAG)
PAA .... Pacific Arts Association (EA)
PAA .... Pan American Minerals Corp. [Toronto Stock Exchange symbol] [Vancouver Stock Exchange symbol]
PAA .... Pan American World Airways, Inc. [See also PA, PAN-AM, PN]
PAA .... Pancretan Association of America (EA)
PAA .... Pancyprian Association of America [Defunct] (EA)
PAA .... Panguna [Solomon Islands] [Seismograph station code, US Geological Survey] (SEIS)
paa .... Papuan-Australian [MARC language code] [Library of Congress] (LCCP)
PAA .... Para-Azoxyanisole [Organic chemistry]
PAA .... Parke, Davis & Co. [Research code symbol]
PAA .... Parti Affectae Applicandus [Apply to the Affected Part] [Pharmacy]
PAA .... Pay Adjustment Authorization
PAA .... Peracetic Acid [Organic chemistry]
PAA .... Peruvian American Association (EA)
PAA .... Petroleum Administration Act [Canada]
PAA .... Phased Array Antenna
PAA .... Phenanthrene Amino Alcohol [Organic chemistry]
PAA .... Phenanthrylacetamide [Organic chemistry]
PAA .... Phenylacetic Acid [Organic chemistry]
PAA .... Phosphonoacetic Acid [Antiviral compound]
PAA .... Photographers Association of America [Later, Professional Photographers of America]
PAA .... Photon Activation Analysis
PAA .... Pi Alpha Alpha (EA)
PAA .... Planar Array Antenna
PAA .... Plasminogen Activator Activity [Biochemistry]
PAA .... Platelet Associated Activity [Pharmacology]
PAA .... Polish Association of America [Later, NFLI] (EA)
PAA .... Polyacrylamide [Also, PAAM, PAM] [Organic chemistry]
PAA .... Polyacrylic Acid [Organic chemistry]
PAA .... Polyaspartic Acid [Biochemistry]
PAA .... Polycyclic Aromatic Amine [Organic chemistry]
PAA .... Population Association of America (EA)
PAA .... Port Autonome d'Abidjan [The Ivory Coast] (EY)
PAA .... Post Award Action
PAA .... Potato Association of America (EA)
PAA .... Power Amplifier Assembly
PAA .... Pragmateiai tes Akademias Athenon [A publication]
PAA .... Praktika tes Akademias Athenon [A publication]
PAA .... Pre-Apprenticeship Allowance
PAA .... Primary Aircraft Authorized [Air Force]
PAA .... Primary Auxiliary Area [Nuclear energy] (NRCH)
PAA .... Print Advertising Association [Defunct] (EA)
PAA .... Procurement of Ammunition, Army (AABC)
PAA .... Procurement Appropriation, Army (MCD)
PAA .... Professional Archers Association (EA)
PAA .... Programme d'Aide aux Athletes [Athlete Assistance Program] [Canada]
PAA .... Pyridineacetic Acid [Organic chemistry]
P/AA3 .... Probationary Aircraft Artificer 3rd Class [British military] (DMA)
PAAA .... Asian Affairs. An Americaan Review [A publication]
PAAA .... Premium Advertising Association of America [Later, PMAA] (EA)
P/AAA2 ..... Probationary Aircraft Artificer, Acting, 2nd Class [British military] (DMA)
PAAAS ...... Proceedings. American Academy of Arts and Sciences [A publication]
PAAAS ...... Publication. American Association for the Advancement of Science [A publication]
PAAB .... PERSCOM [Personnel Command] Acquisition Accession Board [Army] (INF)
PAABA ...... Para-Acetamidobenzoic Acid [Biochemistry]
PAABS ...... PanAmerican Association of Biochemical Societies (EA)
PAABS Symp ... PAABS [Pan-American Association of Biochemical Societies] Symposium [A publication]
PAAC .... Journal of Aesthetics and Art Criticism [A publication]
PAAC .... Pacific and Asian Affairs Council
PAAC .... Program Analysis Adaptable Control [Data processing]
PA Acad Sci Proc ... Pennsylvania Academy of Science. Proceedings [A publication]
PAACE ...... Precision Aircraft Armament Control Experiment (RDA)
PAACS ...... Prior Active Army Commissioned Service
PAACT ...... Patient Advocates for Advanced Cancer Treatments
PAADAR... Passive Airborne Detection and Ranging (MSA)
PAADC ...... Principal Air Aide-de-Camp [RAF] [British]
PA Admin Bull ... Pennsylvania Bulletin [A publication] (DLA)
PA Admin Code ... Pennsylvania Administrative Code [A publication] (DLA)

PAAECI .... Pan American Association of Educational Credit Institutions [*See also APICE*] (EAIO)
PAAES ...... Prior Active Army Enlisted Service
PAAES ...... Publications. American Archaeological Expedition to Syria [*A publication*] (BJA)
PAAF .... African Affairs [*A publication*]
PAAFB ...... Patrick Auxiliary Air Force Base [*Florida*] (SAA)
PAAFCS .... Prior Active Air Force Commissioned Service
PAAFES .... Prior Active Air Force Enlisted Service
PAAG .... Annals. Association of American Geographers [*A publication*]
PAAGE ...... Panel on Alternate Approaches to Graduate Education (EA)
PA Ag Exp ... Pennsylvania. Agricultural Experiment Station. Publications [*A publication*]
PA Agric Exp Stn Bull ... Pennsylvania. Agricultural Experiment Station. Bulletin [*A publication*]
PA Agric Exp Stn Prog Rep ... Pennsylvania. Agricultural Experiment Station. Progress Report [*A publication*]
PAAH .... Polyacrylamide-Hydrazide [*Organic chemistry*]
PAAH .... Praktika tes en Athenais Archaiologikes Hetaireias [*A publication*]
PAAHA ..... Para-Acetamidohippuric Acid [*Biochemistry*]
PAAJR ...... Proceedings. American Academy for Jewish Research [*A publication*]
PAAM ...... Physicians Association for Anthroposophical Medicine (EA)
PAAM ...... Polyacrylamide [*Also, PAA, PAM*] [*Organic chemistry*]
PAAM ...... Projective Assessment of Aging Method [*Personality development test*] [*Psychology*]
P/AAMHRC ... Pacific/Asian American Mental Health Research Center [*University of Illinois at Chicago*] [*Research center*] (RCD)
PAAN .... Product Assurance Alert Notice (MCD)
PAANA ..... Proceedings. Australian Society of Animal Production [*A publication*]
PAANS ...... Pan African Association of Neurological Sciences (EAIO)
PAAO .... Pan-American Association of Ophthalmology (EA)
PAAOD8 ... Proceedings. American Association for Cancer Research and American Society of Clinical Oncology [*A publication*]
PAAORLBE ... Pan-American Association of Oto-Rhino-Laryngology and Broncho-Esophagology [*Mexico City, Mexico*] (EAIO)
PAAP .... Panjabi Adabi Academy. Publication [*A publication*]
PAAP .... Peaceful Alternatives to the Atlantic Pact
PAAP .... Provisional Algal Assay Procedure [*Test measuring impact of chemicals on algal growth*]
PAAQ .... Palmer [*Alaska*] [*ICAO location identifier*] (ICLI)
PAAR .... African Arts [*A publication*]
PAAR .... American Academy in Rome. Papers and Monographs [*A publication*]
PA Arch ..... Pennsylvania Archaeologist [*A publication*]
PA Archaeol ... Pennsylvania Archaeologist [*A publication*]
PAAS .... Pan American Allergy Society (EA)
PAAS .... Performance Assessment and Appraisal System
PAAS .... Phased Array Analysis System
PAAS .... Phased Array Antenna System
PAAS .... Proceedings. American Antiquarian Society [*A publication*]
PAAT .... Parent as a Teacher Inventory [*Psychology*]
PAAT .... Personnel and Administrative Assistance Team [*Navy*] (NVT)
PAAT .... Personnel Assistance and Audit Team [*Military*]
PAAT .... Programmer Analyst Aptitude Test
PAAT .... Public Affairs Assist Team [*Hazardous substance emergency response*]
PAATA ...... Praktika tes Akademias Athenon [*A publication*]
PAATI .... Phased Array Antenna Technology Investigation
PAATLANT ... Personnel and Administration Assistance Team, Atlantic [*Navy*] (DNAB)
PAATPAC ... Personnel and Administration Assistance Team, Pacific [*Navy*] (DNAB)
PAAWWW ... Pacific Asian American Women Writers West (EA)
PAAXOP ... Pan-Dodecanesian Association of America "Xanthos O Philikos" (EA)
PAAZA ...... Progressive Agriculture in Arizona [*A publication*]
PAb .... Abington Free Library, Abington, PA [*Library symbol*] [*Library of Congress*] (LCLS)
PAB .... Cabrini College, Library, Radnor, PA [*OCLC symbol*] (OCLC)
PAB .... Panair do Brasil, SA
PAB .... Para-Aminobenzoic Acid [*Also, PABA*] [*Biochemistry*]
PAB .... Paramaribo [*Suriname*] [*Geomagnetic observatory code*]
PAB .... Parti des Paysans, Artisans, et Bourgeois [*Farmers', Artisans', and Burghers' Party*] [*Switzerland*] [*Political party*] (PPE)
PAB .... Patent Abstracts Bibliography [*NASA*]
PAB .... Patrick Air Force Base [*Florida*]
PAB .... Peanut Advisory Board (EA)
PAB .... Pension Appeals Board [*Canada*]
PAB .... Petroleum Administrative Board [*Terminated, 1936*]
PAB .... Plastic Assault Boat [*Navy*]
PAB .... Police Administration Building
PAB .... Policies Allotment Board [*Navy*] (DNAB)
PAB .... Polyclonal Antibody [*Immunochemistry*]
P/AB .... Port Side Abreast (DNAB)
PAB .... Power-Assisted Brakes
PAB .... Prealbumin [*Biochemistry*]
PAB .... Precision Aneroid Barometer (DNAB)

PAB .... Preliminary As-Built [*Nuclear energy*] (NRCH)
PAB .... Premature Atrial Beat [*Cardiology*] (AAMN)
PAB .... Price Adjustment Board
PAB .... Price Agreement Bulletin
PAB .... Primary Auxiliary Building [*Nuclear energy*] (NRCH)
PAB .... Priorities Allotment Board
PAB .... Priority Assignment Base (MCD)
PAB .... Product Application Bulletins [*A publication*] (EAAP)
PAB .... Program Advisory Board (MCD)
PAB .... Psychiatric Attitudes Battery [*Psychology*]
PAB .... Psychology of Addictive Behaviors [*An association*] (EA)
PAB .... Pulmonary Artery Banding [*Cardiology*]
PAB .... Pulsed Adsorption Bed [*Process*]
PAB .... Purple Agar Base [*Media*] [*Microbiology*]
PABA .... Barter Island [*Alaska*] [*ICAO location identifier*] (ICLI)
PABA .... Para-Aminobenzoic Acid [*Also, PAB*] [*Biochemistry*]
PA BA .... Pennsylvania Bar Association. Reports [*A publication*] (DLA)
PABA .... Progressive Angus Breeders Association
PABAQ .... Pennsylvania Bar Association. Quarterly [*A publication*]
PA Bar Asso Q ... Pennsylvania Bar Association. Quarterly [*A publication*]
PA B Ass'n Q ... Pennsylvania Bar Association. Quarterly [*A publication*]
PA B Brief ... Pennsylvania Bar Brief [*A publication*] (DLA)
PABC .... Pacific Bancorporation [*NASDAQ symbol*] (NQ)
PABC .... Pan American Basketball Confederation [*See also CPB*] (EAIO)
PABCA8 .... Annual Biology Colloquium [*A publication*]
PABD .... Precise Access Block Diagram
PABE .... Bethel [*Alaska*] [*ICAO location identifier*] (ICLI)
PABE .... Program and Budget Estimate (MCD)
P Aberd ...... Catalogue of Greek and Latin Papyri and Ostraca in the Possession of the University of Aberdeen [*A publication*]
PABF .... Precision Air-Bearing Floor (SSD)
PABFSA .... Pediatric Association of Black French-Speaking Africa (EAIO)
PABG .... Big Delta [*Alaska*] [*ICAO location identifier*] (ICLI)
P Abh .... Philosophische Abhandlungen [*A publication*]
PABI .... Delta Junction/Allen Army Air Field [*Alaska*] [*ICAO location identifier*] (ICLI)
PABIA ...... Pathologie et Biologie [*A publication*]
PA Bk Cas ... Pennsylvania Bank Cases [*A publication*] (DLA)
PABLA ...... Problem Analysis by Logical Approach
PABLE ...... Payable (ROG)
PABLI .... Pages Bleues Informatisees [*Commission of the European Communities*] [*Information service or system*] (CRD)
PABM .... Big Mountain Air Force Station [*Alaska*] [*ICAO location identifier*] (ICLI)
PABMI .... Performing Arts Biography Master Index [*A publication*]
PABP .... Poly(A)-Binding Protein
PABR .... Barrow [*Alaska*] [*ICAO location identifier*] (ICLI)
PABR .... Planning Appeals Board. Reports [*A publication*]
P Abr .... Pulton's Abridgment of the Statutes [*A publication*] (DLA)
PA Browne (PA) ... Browne's Reports (Pennsylvania) [*A publication*] (DLA)
PA Browne R ... Browne's Reports [*Pennsylvania*] [*A publication*] (DLA)
PABS .... Pan-American Biodeterioration Society (EA)
PABS .... Para-Aminobenzensulfonamide [*Antibiotic*]
PA Bsns Survey ... Pennsylvania Business Survey [*A publication*]
PABST ...... Primary Adhesively Bonded Structural Technology [*Aviation*]
PABT .... American Biology Teacher [*A publication*]
PABT .... Bettles [*Alaska*] [*ICAO location identifier*] (ICLI)
PABT .... Pabst Brewing Co. [*NASDAQ symbol*] (NQ)
Pa Bull ...... Pennsylvania Bulletin [*A publication*]
PA Bur Topogr Geol Surv Miner Resour Rep ... Pennsylvania. Bureau of Topographic and Geologic Survey. Mineral Resource Report [*A publication*]
PABV .... Pyroactuated Ball Valve
PABVA ...... Pesquisa Agropecuaria Brasileira. Serie Veterinaria [*A publication*]
P(A)BX ...... Private (Automatic) Branch Exchange [*Telecommunications*] (DEN)
PAC .... Canada. Fisheries and Marine Service. Northern Operations Branch. Pacific Region. Data Report Series [*A publication*]
PAC .... cis-Platinum [*Cisplatin*], Adriamycin, Cyclophosphamide [*Antineoplastic drug regimen*]
PAC .... Pacific (AFM)
Pac .... Pacific [*Record label*] [*France*]
PAC .... Pacific Air Command [*Air Force*]
PAC .... Pacific Command [*Military*] (GFGA)
PAC .... Pacific Ocean
Pac .... Pacific Reporter [*A publication*] (DLA)
PAC .... Pacific Telesis Group [*NYSE symbol*] (SPSG)
Pac .... Pacifica: Australian Theological Studies [*A publication*] (APTA)
PAC .... Package Attitude Control [*NASA*]
PAC .... Packaged Assembly Circuit
Pac .... Packaging [*A publication*]
PAC .... Packard Automobile Classics (EA)
PAC .... Pacto de Alianza de Centro [*Chile*] [*Political party*] (EY)
PAC .... Pak-Man Resources, Inc. [*Vancouver Stock Exchange symbol*]
PAC .... Palo Alto - Branner [*California*] [*Seismograph station code, US Geological Survey*] [*Closed*] (SEIS)
PAC .... Pan-Africanist Congress [*South Africa*]
PAC .... Pan American College [*Texas*]
PAC .... Pan-American Congress

PAC .... Panama City [*Panama*] Paitilla Airport [*Airport symbol*] (OAG)
PAC .... Papular Acrodermatitis of Childhood
PAC .... Para-Aminoclonidine [*Biochemistry*]
PAC .... Para-Aminosalicylic Acid Calcium Salt [*Pharmacology*]
PAC .... Parachute and Cable Defence [*British military*]
PAC .... Parametric Amplifier Converter
P-A-C .... Parent-Adult-Child [*Transactional analysis*]
PAC .... Parker Aircraft Corp. (MCD)
PAC .... Partido Autentico Constitucional [*Authentic Constitutional Party*] [*El Salvador*] [*Political party*]
PAC .... Parts Allocation Chart (MCD)
PAC .... Pascagoula, MS [*Location identifier*] [*FAA*] (FAAL)
PAC .... Passed the Final Examination of the Advanced Class [*Military College of Science*] [*British*]
PAC .... Passive Acoustic Classification (NVT)
PAC .... Patents Advisory Committee [*British*]
PAC .... Patient Airlift Center [*Aeromedical evacuation*]
PAC .... Payment after Closing [*Insurance*]
PAC .... Peace Action Center [*Defunct*] (EA)
PAC .... Pearson Aircraft, Inc. [*Port Angeles, WA*] [*FAA designator*] (FAAC)
PAC .... Pedagogic Automatic Computer (IEEE)
PAC .... Pediatric AIDS [*Acquired Immune Deficiency Syndrome*] Coalition (EA)
PAC .... Penetration Aids Deployment Concept (SAA)
PA C.......... Pennsylvania Commonwealth Court Reports [*A publication*] (DLA)
Pa C .... Pennsylvania County Reports [*A publication*]
PAC .... People's Army Congress
PAC .... Peptide Acid [*Organic chemistry*]
PAC .... Performance Analysis and Control
PAC .... Performance Assured Certification
PAC .... Person in Addition to Crew [*Sailing*]
PAC .... Personal Analog Computer
PAC .... Personnel Action Center [*Army*] (INF)
PAC .... Personnel Action Code
PAC .... Personnel and Administration Center [*Army*] (AABC)
PAC .... Perturbed Angular Correlation
PAC .... Petroleum Advisory Committee [*of Organization for Economic Cooperation and Development*] [*Terminated, 1976*] (EGAO)
PAC .... Pharmaceutical Advertising Council [*New York, NY*] (EA)
PAC .... Phenacetin [*Acetophenetidin*], Aspirin, Caffeine [*Pharmacology*]
PAC .... Photo Aperture Card (SAA)
PAC .... Photoacoustic [*Spectroscopy*]
PA-C .... Physician's Assistant-Certified (WGA)
PAC .... Piper Aircraft Corp.
PAC .... Place Complement of Address in Index Register (SAA)
PAC .... Planned-Amortization-Class Bond [*Investment term*]
PAC .... Planning Advisory Committee (OICC)
PAC .... Plasma Arc Chamber
PAC .... Plasma Arc Cutting [*Welding*]
PAC .... Platinol [*Cisplatin*], Adriamycin, Cyclophosphamide [*Antineoplastic drug regimen*]
PAC .... Plowshare Advisory Committee [*AEC*]
PAC .... Pneumatic Analog Computer
PAC .... Pneumatic Auxiliary Console (AAG)
PAC .... Pod Air Conditioner (AAG)
PAC .... Policy Advisory Center
PAC .... Policy Advisory Committee [*National Cancer Institute*] [*Department of Health and Human Services*] (GFGA)
PAC .... Policy Advisory Committee [*Office of Economic Opportunity*]
PAC .... Polish American Congress (EA)
PAC .... Political Action Caucus [*Superseded by LPAC*] (EA)
PAC .... Political Action Committee [*Generic term*]
PAC .... Polled Access Circuit
PAC .... Pollution Abatement and Control
PAC .... Polyanionic Cellulose [*Organic chemistry*]
PAC .... Polycyclic Aromatic Compound [*Organic chemistry*]
PAC .... Population Action Council (EA)
PAC .... Porterfield Airplane Club (EA)
PAC .... Post-Adoption Centre [*British*] (CB)
PAC .... Post Award Conference (MCD)
PAC .... Post Award Contract
PAC .... Powdered Activated Carbon [*Adsorbent*]
PAC .... Pre-Action Calibration [*Gunnery*] (NVT)
PAC .... Preauthorized Check Plan [*Insurance*]
PAC .... Premature Atrial Contraction [*Medicine*]
PAC .... Premature Auricular Contraction [*Cardiology*] (AAMN)
PAC .... Pressure Alpha Center (MCD)
PAC .... Primary Address Code (AFM)
PAC .... Prime [*or Principal*] Associate Contractor (MCD)
PAC .... Principal Associate Contractor (MCD)
PAC .... Printing Accountants Club (EA)
PAC .... Privacy Act Coordinator [*Navy*] (DNAB)
PAC .... Probe Aerodynamic Center [*NASA*]
PAC .... Problem Action Center [*NASA*] (NASA)
PAC .... Process Analytical Chemistry
PAC .... Production Acceleration Capacity [*Manufacturing*]

PAC .... Professional Activities Survey [*Medicine*]
PAC .... Program Acquisition Cost (MCD)
PAC .... Program Adjustment Committee
PAC .... Program Advisory Committee
PAC .... Program Allocation Checker
PAC .... Program Application Code (DNAB)
PAC .... Program Authorized Credentials [*Data processing*]
PAC .... Programmable Automatic Comparator
PAC .... Programme Activity Center [*Advisory Committee on Pollution of the Sea*]
PAC .... Progress Assessment Chart [*Psychology*]
PAC .... Project Advisory Committee (EGAO)
PAC .... Promoting Achievement through Communications [*Education*]
PAC .... Protect America's Children [*An association*] (EA)
PAC .... Protection Auxiliary Cabinet [*Nuclear energy*] (NRCH)
PAC .... Public Access Catalogue (ADA)
PAC .... Public Access Control
PAC .... Public Accounts Committee [*British government*]
PAC .... Public Affairs Committee [*Defunct*] (EA)
PAC .... Public Affairs Coordinator [*Nuclear energy*] (NRCH)
PAC .... Public Affairs Council (EA)
PAC .... Public Archives of Canada
PAC .... Publishers' Ad Club [*New York, NY*] (EA)
PAC .... Pulmonary Artery Catheter [*Medicine*]
PAC .... Pure and Applied Chemistry [*IUPAC*]
PAC .... Pursuant to Authority Contained In [*Army*]
PAC .... Put and Call [*Stock exchange term*]
PAC-10 ...... Pacific 10 Conference (EA)
Pac A......... Pacific Affairs [*A publication*]
PACA........ Perishable Agricultural Commodities Act, 1930
PACA........ Picture Agency Council of America (EA)
PACA........ Principal Assistant County Architect [*British*]
PACA........ Proceedings. African Classical Association [*A publication*]
PACA........ Propulsion and Control Assembly
PACA....... Proyecto Ambiental para Centro America [*Environmental Project for Central America*] [*Spanish*] (ECON)
PACAB..... Pacific Affairs. Current Awareness Bulletin [*A publication*] (APTA)
PACADIV ... Pacific Fleet Advance Headquarters Division (DNAB)
PACADV... Pacific Fleet Advance Headquarters [*Guam*]
PACAF...... Pacific Air Forces
PACAFBASECOM ... Pacific Air Forces Base Command
Pac Aff ...... Pacific Affairs [*A publication*]
Pac Affairs ... Pacific Affairs [*A publication*]
PACAF-OA ... Pacific Air Forces Operations Analysis
PACAF-OA ... Pacific Air Forces Operations Analysis Office [*Hickam Air Force Base, HI*]
PACAH ..... Pitch Attitude Command/Attitude Hold [*Aviation*] (MCD)
Pac Arts Newsl ... Pacific Arts Newsletter [*A publication*]
PacAS .... Pacific American Income Shares, Inc. [*Associated Press abbreviation*] (APAG)
PACAS ..... Patient Care System [*Army*] (AABC)
PA Cas....... Pennsylvania Supreme Court Cases (Sadler) [*A publication*] (DLA)
PACAS ...... Personnel Access Control Accountability System [*NASA*] (MCD)
PACAS ...... Psychological Abstracts Current Awareness Service (IID)
PACB........ Pan-American Coffee Bureau [*Defunct*] (EA)
PACBAR... Pacific Barrier RADAR (MCD)
Pac Bird Obs ... Pacific Bird Observer [*A publication*]
Pac Builder Eng ... Pacific Builder and Engineer [*A publication*]
PA CC........ Pennsylvania County Court Reports [*A publication*] (DLA)
PACC........ Portable Arm Control Console (KSC)
P(ACC)...... Probability of Acceptance
PACC........ Problem Action Control Center [*NASA*] (NASA)
PACC........ Products Administration Contract Control
PACC........ Professional Association of Custom Clothiers (EA)
PACC........ Propulsion and Auxiliary Control Console [*NASA*] (DNAB)
PACC........ Protected Air-Cooled Condenser [*Nuclear energy*] (NRCH)
PACCA...... Policy Alternatives for the Caribbean and Central America (EA)
PACCALL ... Pacific Fleet Calls [*Radio call signs*]
PACCAR ... Pacific Car and Foundry
Pac Chem Eng Cong Proc ... Pacific Chemical Engineering Congress. Proceedings [*United States*] [*A publication*]
Pac Chem Eng Congr ... Pacific Chemical Engineering Congress [*A publication*]
Pac Chem Metall Ind ... Pacific Chemical and Metallurgical Industries [*A publication*]
PACCIOS ... Pan American Council of International Committee of Scientific Management
PACCO...... Cisplatin, Adriamycin, Cyclophosphamide, CCNU [*Lomustine*], Oncovin [*Vincristine*] [*Antineoplastic drug regimen*]
Pac Coast Gas Assoc Proc ... Pacific Coast Gas Association. Proceedings [*A publication*]
Pac Coast Int ... Pacific Coast International [*A publication*] (ILCA)
Pac Coast LJ ... Pacific Coast Law Journal [*A publication*] (DLA)
Pac Coast Med ... Pacific Coast Medicine [*A publication*]
PACCOM ... Pacific Command [*Military*]
Pac Com..... Pacific Community [*Tokyo*] [*A publication*]

PACCOM ... Pacific Fleet Communications Instructions
Pac Commun ... Pacific Community [*A publication*]
PACCOMOPCONCEN ... Pacific Fleet Command Operational Control Center (DNAB)
PA CCR ..... Pennsylvania County Court Reports [*A publication*] (DLA)
PA CC Reps ... Pennsylvania County Court Reports [*A publication*] (DLA)
PACCS ...... Pan American Cancer Cytology Society [*Defunct*] (EA)
PACCS ...... Post-Attack Command and Control System [*Military*]
PACCS/ADA ... Post-Attack Command and Control System/Airborne Data Automation [*Military*]
PACCSq .... Post-Attack Command Control Squadron [*Air Force*]
PACCT ...... PERT [*Program Evaluation and Review Technique*] and Cost Correlation Technique
PACD .... Cold Bay [*Alaska*] [*ICAO location identifier*] (ICLI)
PACD .... Pacific Division [*Military*]
PACD .... Parachute and Cable Defence [*British military*] (DMA)
Pac 2d .... Pacific Reporter, Second Series [*A publication*] (DLA)
PACDA...... Personnel and Administration, Combat Development Activity [*Army*] (AABC)
PA C Dec WCC ... Pennsylvania Courts, Decisions in Workmen's Compensation Cases [*A publication*] (DLA)
Pac Discov ... Pacific Discovery [*A publication*]
Pac Discovery ... Pacific Discovery [*A publication*]
PACDIV .... Pacific Division [*Military*]
Pac D Rep .. Pacific Defence Reporter [*A publication*]
PACE......... PACE. Pacing and Clinical Electrophysiology [*A publication*]
PACE......... PACE. Process and Chemical Engineering [*A publication*] (APTA)
PACE......... Pacesetter Homes, Inc. [*NASDAQ symbol*] (NQ)
PACE......... Pacific Agricultural Cooperative for Export [*Corte Madera, CA*] (EA)
PACE........ Pacific Alternate Command Element (CINC)
PACE........ Pacific Atoll Cratering Experiment [*Military*] (DNAB)
PACE......... Packaged CRAM [*Card Random-Access Memory*] Executive [*NCR Corp.*] [*Data processing*]
PACE......... Packet of Accelerated Christian Education [*Educational material marketed by fundamentalist company, Accelerated Christian Education*]
PACE........ Passive Attitude Control Experimental [*Satellite*]
PACE........ Patrol Airship Concept Evaluation
PACE........ Performance Advantage with Cummins Electronics [*Automotive engineering*]
PACE........ Performance and Cost Evaluation
PACE........ Performing Arts, Culture, and Entertainment [*Proposed cable television system*]
PACE........ Peripheral Automatic Channel Emulator [*Data processing*]
PACE........ Personalized Aerobics for Cardiovascular Enhancement
PACE........ Petroleum Association for Conservation of the Canadian Environment
PACE........ Phased Array Control Electronics
PACE........ Physics and Chemistry Experiment
PACE........ Plan for Action by Citizens in Education
PACE........ Planetary Association for Clean Energy (EA)
PACE........ Planned Action with Constant Evaluation [*Data processing*]
PACE........ Plant Acquisition and Construction Equipment [*Nuclear energy*] (NRCH)
PACE........ Plant and Capital Equipment (MCD)
PACE........ Plasma-Assisted Chemical Etching [*Metallurgy*]
PACE........ Police and Criminal Evidence Act [*1964*] [*British*]
PACE........ Policy Analysis for California Education [*Research center*] (RCD)
PACE........ Portable Acoustic Collection Equipment (MCD)
PACE........ Precision Analog Computing Equipment
PACE........ Preflight Acceptance Checkout Equipment
PACE........ Prelaunch Automatic Checkout Equipment [*NASA*]
PACE........ Priority Activities in Cancer Education
PACE........ Prisoners Accelerated Creative Exposure [*An association*]
PACE........ Procedural Approach to the Composition of Essays [*In book title*]
PACE........ Professional Activities for Continuing Education [*AEC*]
PACE........ Professional and Administrative Career Examination [*Formerly, FSEE*] [*Civil Service*]
PACE........ Professional Association of Consulting Engineers
PACE........ Program for Afloat College Education [*Navy*] (NVT)
PACE........ Programmable Autonomously-Controlled Electrode [*Instrumentation*]
PACE........ Programmed Automatic Communications Equipment
PACE........ Programming Analysis Consulting Education (IEEE)
PACE........ Progressive Aerobic Circuit Exercise [*Fitness training*]
PACIA........ Project for the Advancement of Church Education
PACE........ Projects to Advance Creativity in Education [*HEW*]
PACE........ Providing Avenues for Continuing Encouragement [*Scholarship awarded by Fraternity of Recording Executives*]
PACE........ Provisioning Action Control Evaluation [*Military*] (AFIT)
PACE........ Pulse-Synthesized Advanced Conversion Equipment
P/ACEA2 .. Probationary Control Electrical Artificer, Acting, 2nd Class [*British military*] (DMA)
PACED........ Program for Advanced Concepts in Electronic Design
PACEE...... Propulsion and Auxiliary Control Electronic Enclosure (DNAB)
Pace LR...... Pace Law Review [*A publication*]

Pace L Rev ... Pace Law Review [*A publication*]
PACE/LV ... Preflight Acceptance Checkout Equipment-Launch Vehicle
PACEMAKER ... Public Agency Career Employment Maker [*OEO project*]
PACEN...... Public Affairs Center [*Navy*] (DNAB)
PACENLANT ... Public Affairs Center, Atlantic [*Navy*] (DNAB)
PACENPAC ... Public Affairs Center, Pacific [*Navy*] (DNAB)
PACENS ... Patient Census
PacEnt .... Pacific Enterprises [*Associated Press abbreviation*] (APAG)
PACEO...... Professional Application Creation Environment (HGAA)
PACE Process Chem Eng ... PACE. Process and Chemical Engineering [*A publication*]
PACER...... Part and Component Evaluation Report [*NASA*]
PACER...... Planning Automation and Control for Evaluating Requirements
PACER...... Portable Aircraft Condition Evaluator Recorder
PACER...... Postadoption Center for Education and Research
PACER...... Postoperational Analysis Critique and Exercise Report [*Military*] (CAAL)
PACER...... Prescriptive Analysis for Curriculum Evaluation [*Vocational guidance*]
PACER...... Priority for Allocation/Application of COMSEC Equipment Resources (MCD)
PACER...... Process Assembly Case Evaluator Routine [*Data processing*]
PACER...... Program of Active Cooling Effects and Requirements
PACER...... Program-Assisted Console Evaluation and Review [*Air Force*]
PACER...... Programmed Automatic Circuit Evaluator and Recorder
PACERS.... Pacing and Cardiac Electrophysiology Retrieval System [*Intermedics, Inc.*] [*Information service or system*] (IID)
PACES ..... Political Action Committee for Engineers and Scientists
PACE-S/C ... Preflight Acceptance Checkout Equipment for Spacecraft
PAC-EX..... Canadian National Packaging Exposition [*Packaging Association of Canada*] (TSPED)
PACEX...... Pacific Exchange [*System*] [*Military*] (AFM)
PACF........ Pacific
Pacf........... PacifiCorp [*Associated Press abbreviation*] (APAG)
PACF......... Partial Autocorrelation Function [*Statistics*]
PACFAST ... Pacific Forward Area Support Team (DNAB)
PACFASTDET ... Pacific Forward Area Support Team Detachment (DNAB)
PACFASTREP ... Pacific Forward Area Support Team Representative (DNAB)
PACFDP ... Proceedings. Annual Conference on Restoration of Coastal Vegetation in Florida [*A publication*]
PacFIN ...... Pacific Fishery Information Network [*Database*] [*National Marine Fisheries Service*]
Pac Fisherman ... Pacific Fisherman [*A publication*]
PACFLAP ... Pacific Fleet Augmentation Plan [*Navy*] (NVT)
PACFLT.... Pacific Fleet
PACFLTCOM ... Pacific Fleet Command
PACFLTMOPHOTOU ... Pacific Fleet Mobile Photographic Unit (MUGU)
PACFLTPROPEXAMBD ... Pacific Fleet Propulsion Examining Board (DNAB)
PACFORNET ... Pacific Coast Forest Research Information Network [*Later, WESTFORNET*] [*Forest Service*] (IID)
PACFW ..... President's Advisory Committee for Women [*Terminated, 1980*] (EGAO)
PacGate ..... Pacific Gateway Properties [*Associated Press abbreviation*] (APAG)
PACGCS ... Prior Active Coast Guard Commissioned Service
PacGE........ Pacific Gas & Electric Co. [*Associated Press abbreviation*] (APAG)
PACGEEIA ... Pacific Area Ground Environment Electronic Installation Agency (CINC)
Pac Geol..... Pacific Geology [*A publication*]
PACGES ... Prior Active Coast Guard Enlisted Service
PACGO ..... President's Advisory Committee on Government Organization [*Abolished, 1961*]
PACGSR ... Pan American Center for Geographical Studies and Research [*See also CEPEIGE*] (EAIO)
PacH .... Pacific Historian [*A publication*]
PACH .... Performing Arts Center for Health [*New York University/ Bellevue Hospital, New York, NY*] [*Superseded by Center for Dance Medicine -CDM*]
PACH .... Public Administration Clearing House [*1931-1956*]
PACHACH ... Partizanim-Chayalim-Chalutzim (BJA)
PACHEDPEARL ... Pacific Headquarters, Pearl Harbor, Hawaii [*Navy*]
Pac Hist R ... Pacific Historical Review [*A publication*]
Pac Hist Rev ... Pacific Historical Review [*A publication*]
Pac Hist Rev ... Pacific History Review [*A publication*] (APTA)
Pac Hortic ... Pacific Horticulture [*A publication*]
PacHR .... Pacific Historical Review [*A publication*]
PACIA .... Particle Counting Immunoassay
PACIF .... Pacific
Pacif........... PacifiCorp [*Associated Press abbreviation*] (APAG)
Pacif Aff..... Pacific Affairs [*A publication*]
Pacif Bs N ... Pacific Business News [*A publication*]
Pacif Coa J Nurs ... Pacific Coast Journal of Nursing [*A publication*]
PacifCp...... PacifiCorp [*Associated Press abbreviation*] (APAG)
Pacif Defence Reporter ... Pacific Defence Reporter [*A publication*]
Pacif Hist R ... Pacific Historical Review [*A publication*]
Pacific Bus ... Pacific Business [*A publication*]
Pacific CLJ ... Pacific Coast Law Journal [*San Francisco*] [*A publication*] (DLA)

Pacific His R ... Pacific Historical Review [*A publication*]
Pacific Islands Com J ... Pacific Islands Communication Journal [*A publication*]
Pacific Islands M ... Pacific Islands Monthly [*A publication*] (APTA)
Pacific Islands Yrbk ... Pacific Islands Year Book [*A publication*] (APTA)
Pacific J Math ... Pacific Journal of Mathematics [*A publication*]
Pacific Law Mag ... Pacific Law Magazine [*A publication*] (DLA)
Pacific L J ... Pacific Law Journal [*A publication*]
Pacific Med Surg ... Pacific Medicine and Surgery [*A publication*]
Pacific Northw Q ... Pacific Northwest Quarterly [*A publication*]
Pacific Perspect ... Pacific Perspective [*A publication*]
Pacific Rep ... Pacific Reporter [*A publication*] (DLA)
Pacific Sci .. Pacific Science [*A publication*]
Pacific Sociol R ... Pacific Sociological Review [*A publication*]
Pacif Imp ... Pacific Imperialism Notebook [*A publication*]
Pacif Insects ... Pacific Insects [*A publication*]
Pacif Is Mon ... Pacific Islands Monthly [*A publication*]
Pacif J Math ... Pacific Journal of Mathematics [*A publication*]
Pacif Rep .... Pacific Reporter [*A publication*] (DLA)
Pacif Sci ..... Pacific Science [*A publication*]
Pacif Soc Rev ... Pacific Sociological Review [*A publication*]
PACIFY ..... Parents and Alumni Committee Involved for Youth [*Brown University*]
PACIMS .... Passive Chemical Ionization Mass Spectrometry
Pac Insects ... Pacific Insects [*A publication*]
Pac Insects Mongr ... Pacific Insects Monograph [*A publication*]
Pac Insects Monogr ... Pacific Insects Monograph [*A publication*]
PACINTCEN ... Pacific Intelligence Center (DNAB)
PACIR ...... Practical Approach to Chemical Information Retrieval
PACIT ...... Passive and Active Interface Test [*Electronic warfare*]
Pac J Math ... Pacific Journal of Mathematics [*A publication*]
Pack .... Packaging [*A publication*]
PACK .... Packing and Allocation for a COMPOOL [*Communications Pool*] Kaleidoscope (SAA)
PACK .... Pontoon Air Cushion Kit [*Army*] (RDA)
Packag Abstr ... Packaging Abstracts [*A publication*]
PACKAGE ... Planned Aids for Cross-Culture Knowledge, Action and Growth in Effectiveness
Package Dev ... Package Development [*A publication*]
Package Dev Syst ... Package Development and Systems [*A publication*]
Package Eng ... Package Engineering [*A publication*]
Package Engng ... Package Engineering [*A publication*]
Packag (India) ... Packaging (India) [*A publication*]
Packag Inst Spec Rep ... Packaging Institute. Special Report [*A publication*]
Packag Plast ... Packaging with Plastics [*A publication*]
Packag Rev ... Packaging Review [*A publication*]
Packag Rev (S Afr) ... Packaging Review (South Africa) [*A publication*]
Packa Rev .. Packaging Review [*A publication*]
Pack Encyc ... Packaging Encyclopedia [*A publication*]
Packer Process ... Packer, Processor [*A publication*]
Pack Print and Dyecutting ... Package Printing and Dyecutting [*A publication*]
PACL .... Clear [*Alaska*] [*ICAO location identifier*] (ICLI)
Pac Law Mag ... Pacific Law Magazine [*A publication*] (DLA)
Pac Law Reptr ... Pacific Law Reporter [*San Francisco*] [*A publication*] (DLA)
Pac Leg N .. Pacific Legal News [*A publication*] (DLA)
Pac LJ .... Pacific Law Journal [*A publication*]
PACM .... Passive Countermeasures (MSA)
PACM .... Pulse Amplitude Code Modulation [*Electronics*]
Pac Mar Fish Comm Annu Rep ... Pacific Marine Fisheries Commission. Annual Report [*A publication*]
Pac Mar Fish Comm Bull ... Pacific Marine Fisheries Commission. Bulletin [*A publication*]
Pac Mar Sci Rep ... Pacific Marine Science Report [*A publication*]
PACMD .... Philadelphia Contract Management District (SAA)
Pac Med Surg ... Pacific Medicine and Surgery [*A publication*]
PACMETNET ... Pacific Meteorological Network (AAG)
PACMI ...... President's Advisory Committee on Management Improvement [*Terminated, 1973*]
Pac Miner Rev ... Pacific Minerals Review [*A publication*]
PACMISCEN ... Pacific Missile Center [*Marine science*] (DNAB)
PACMISRAN ... Pacific Missile Range [*Later, WTR*] (MUGU)
PACMISRANFAC ... Pacific Missile Range Facility [*Obsolete*]
PACMISRANFACDET ... Pacific Missile Range Facility Detachment [*Obsolete*] (DNAB)
PACMISRANFACREP ... Pacific Missile Range Facility Representative [*Obsolete*] (DNAB)
PACMISTESTCEN ... Pacific Missile Test Center [*Navy*]
PACMISTESTCEN LO ... Pacific Missile Test Center Liaison Office [*Navy*] (DNAB)
Pac Mo .... Pacific Monthly [*Portland, Oregon*] [*A publication*]
PA Cmwlth ... Pennsylvania Commonwealth Court Reports [*A publication*] (DLA)
PACN .... Pacific Area Communicatios Network (SAA)
PACN .... Pacific Nuclear Systems, Inc. [*Federal Way, WA*] [*NASDAQ symbol*] (NQ)
P Ac Nat S ... Proceedings. Academy of Natural Sciences of Philadelphia [*A publication*]
PACNAVCONSTFOR ... Pacific Naval Construction Force (DNAB)
PACNAVFACENGCOM ... Pacific Division Naval Facilities Engineering Command

PACNCF ... Pacific Naval Construction Force (DNAB)
PACNCO .. Personnel Assistance Center Noncommissioned Officer (INF)
PACNDF ... AAZPA [*American Association of Zoological Parks and Aquariums*] Annual Proceedings [*A publication*]
Pac Neighbours ... Pacific Neighbours [*A publication*] (APTA)
PACNET ... OCLC Pacific Network [*Claremont, CA*] [*Information service or system*] (IID)
PACNET ... Plymouth Audioconferencing Network [*Plymouth Polytechnic*] [*Plymouth, England*] [*Telecommunications*] (TSSD)
PACNET ... POCC [*Payload Operations Control Center*] Automated Computer Network
Pac Northw ... Pacific Northwest Quarterly [*A publication*]
Pac Northwest ... Pacific Northwesterner [*A publication*]
Pac Northwesterner ... Pacific Northwesterner [*A publication*]
Pac Northwest For Range Exp Stn Res Note PNW ... Pacific Northwest Forest and Range Experiment Station. Research Note PNW [*A publication*]
Pac Northwest For Range Exp Stn Res Pap PNW ... Pacific Northwest Forest and Range Experiment Station. Research Paper PNW [*A publication*]
Pac Northwest Q ... Pacific Northwest Quarterly [*A publication*]
Pac Northwest Sea ... Pacific Northwest Sea [*A publication*]
PacNQ .... Pacific Northwest Quarterly [*A publication*]
Pac NWQ .. Pacific Northwest Quarterly [*A publication*]
PACNY ...... Pawnbrokers' Association of the City of New York (EA)
PacO .... Pacific Ocean
PACO .... Pivot Ambulating Crutchless Orthosis [*Medicine*]
PACO .... Polaris Accelerated Change Operation [*Missiles*]
PACO .... Primary Administrative Contracting Officer [*Military*] (AFIT)
Paco$_2$ .... Arterial Carbon Dioxide Pressure, Tension [*Medicine*] (MAE)
PACOB ..... Propulsion Auxiliary Control Box (AAG)
PA Co Ct .... Pennsylvania County Court Reports [*A publication*] (DLA)
PA Co Ct R ... Pennsylvania County Court Reports [*A publication*] (DLA)
Pa Code ...... Pennsylvania Code [*A publication*]
PACOM ...... Pacific Command [*Military*]
PACOM ..... Pacific Communications Group
PACOMBPO ... Pacific Command Blood Program Office [*Military*] (DNAB)
PACOMDET ... Pacific Command Detachment [*Military*] (DNAB)
PACOMEP ... Pacific Command Emergency Procedures (CINC)
PACOMEW ... Pacific Command Electronic Warfare (CINC)
PACOMINTS ... Pacific Command Intelligence School (CINC)
PACOMJRO ... Pacific Command Joint Medical Regulating Office (DNAB)
PA Commw ... Pennsylvania Commonwealth Court Reports [*A publication*] (DLA)
PA Commw Ct ... Pennsylvania Commonwealth Court Reports [*A publication*] (DLA)
PA Com Pl ... Pennsylvania Common Pleas Reporter [*A publication*] (DLA)
PA Cons Stat ... Pennsylvania Consolidated Statutes [*A publication*] (DLA)
PA Cons Stat Ann ... Pennsylvania Consolidated Statutes, Annotated [*A publication*] (DLA)
PA Cons Stat Ann (Purdon) ... Pennsylvania Consolidated Statutes, Annotated (Purdon) [*A publication*] (DLA)
PACOPS ... Pacific Air Combat Operations Staff
PACOPS ... Pacific Air Force Operations (MCD)
PACOR ...... Passive Correlation and Ranging
PACORE ... Parabolic Corner Reflector
PACORNALOG ... Pacific Coast Coordinator of Naval Logistics
PA Corp ...... Pennsylvania Corp. Reporter [*A publication*] (DLA)
PA Corp R ... Pennsylvania Corp. Reporter [*A publication*] (DLA)
PA Corp Rep ... Pennsylvania Corp. Reporter [*A publication*] (DLA)
PA County Ct ... Pennsylvania County Court Reports [*A publication*] (DLA)
PA CP .... Pennsylvania Common Pleas Reporter [*A publication*] (DLA)
PACP .... Photo Aperture Card Program (SAA)
PACP .... Propulsion Auxiliary Control Panel [*NASA*] (KSC)
PACP .... Pulmonary Artery Counter-Pulsation [*Cardiology*] (MAE)
Pac Pack Rep ... Pacific Packers Report [*A publication*]
PACPhA .... Proceedings. American Catholic Philosophical Association [*A publication*]
Pac Pharm ... Pacific Pharmacist [*A publication*]
Pac Philos Q ... Pacific Philosophical Quarterly [*A publication*]
Pac Phil Q ... Pacific Philosophical Quarterly [*A publication*]
Pac Phil Quart ... Pacific Philosophical Quarterly [*A publication*]
PACPIP ..... Public Advocate - Coalition of Public Interest Professionals (EA)
Pac Plast .... Pacific Plastics [*A publication*]
P Ac Poli S ... Proceedings. Academy of Political Science [*A publication*]
Pac Pulp Pap Ind ... Pacific Pulp and Paper Industry [*A publication*]
PACQ .... Atlantic Community Quarterly [*A publication*]
Pac Q .... Pacific Quarterly [*A publication*]
PACQI .... Probability of Acquisition [*Military*]
PACR .... Pacer Corp. [*Bothell, WA*] [*NASDAQ symbol*] (NQ)
Pac R .... Pacific Reporter [*Commonly cited as P*] [*A publication*] (DLA)
PA CR .... Pennsylvania County Court Reports [*A publication*] (DLA)
PACR .... Performance and Compatibility Requirements
PACR .... Perimeter Acquisition RADAR (MSA)
PACRAO ... Pacific Association of Collegiate Registrars and Admission Officers
PACRED ... Pacific Area Cooperative Renewable Energy Development [*University of Hawaii*]
Pac Rep ...... Pacific Reporter [*Commonly cited as P*] [*A publication*] (DLA)
PACREP .... Port Activities Report [*Navy*]

PACREPCOMNAVSURFRES ... Pacific Representative for Commander Naval Surface Reserve Force (DNAB)
PACREPNAVRES ... Pacific Representative of the Chief of Naval Reserve (DNAB)
Pac Repr .... Pacific Reporter [*A publication*] (DLA)
Pac Res ...... Pacific Research [*Formerly, Pacific Research and World Empire Telegram*] [*A publication*]
PACRESFLT ... Pacific Reserve Fleet
Pac Rockets ... Pacific Rockets [*A publication*]
Pac Rocket Soc Bull ... Pacific Rocket Society. Bulletin [*A publication*]
PACS .... Cape Sarichef Air Force Station [*Alaska*] [*ICAO location identifier*] (ICLI)
PACS .... Pacific Area Communications System (MCD)
PACS .... Particle Analysis Cameras for the Shuttle [*NASA*]
PACS .... Patient Accounting, Census, and Statistics
PACS .... Peace and Common Security (EA)
PACS .... Photo Aperture Card System (SAA)
PACS .... Physics and Astronomy Classification Scheme
PACS .... Picture Archival and Communication System
PACS .... Plant Automation Communication System [*IBM Corp.*]
PACS .... Pointing and Attitude Control System [*Aerospace*] (NASA)
PACS .... Post-Attack Communication System
PACS .... Principal Appreciation Conversion Security [*Finance*]
PACS .... Process Automation & Computer Systems
PACS .... Program Authorization Control System (MCD)
Pa CSA ...... Pennsylvania Consolidated Statutes, Annotated [*A publication*] (DLA)
PACSAT ... Passive Communications Satellite
PA/CSC ..... Payload Accommodation/Carrier Support Center [*NASA*] (SSD)
PACSCAT ... Pacific Ionospheric Scatter (CINC)
Pac Sci .... Pacific Science [*A publication*]
PacSci .... Pacific Scientific Co. [*Associated Press abbreviation*] (APAG)
Pac Sci Congr Proc ... Pacific Science Congress. Proceedings [*A publication*]
Pac Sci Congr Rec Proc ... Pacific Science Congress. Record of Proceedings [*A publication*]
Pac Search ... Pacific Search [*United States*] [*A publication*]
Pac Sociol R ... Pacific Sociological Review [*A publication*]
Pac Soc R ... Pacific Sociological Review [*A publication*]
Pac Soc Rev ... Pacific Sociological Review [*A publication*]
PacSp .... Pacific Spectator [*A publication*]
PACSUBDSEC ... Pacific Submarine Direct Support Element Coordinator (DNAB)
PACT .... Pan American Commission of Tampa (EA)
PACT .... Participating and Assertive Consumer Training [*Health education*]
PACT .... Paved Concrete Track [*Railways*]
PACT .... Pay Actual Computer Time
PACT .... Performing Arts for Crisis Training [*In association name, PACT Training*] (EA)
PACT .... Perturbed-Anisotropic-Chain Theory [*Chemistry*]
PACT .... Philco Automatic Circuit Tester
PACT .... Plan of Action for Challenging Times (EA)
PACT .... Portable Aircraft Calibration Tracker [*NASA*]
PACT .... Poseidon Automatic Cable Tester [*Missiles*] (DNAB)
PACT .... Powdered Activated Carbon Treatment [*For wastewater*] [*E. I. Du Pont De Nemours & Co., Inc.*]
PACT .... Precision Aircraft Control Technology (MCD)
PACT .... Prevention des Accidents, Controles Techniques, Hygiene, et Maladies Professionnelles [*A publication*]
PACT .... Print Active Computer Tables (SAA)
PACT .... Private Agencies Collaborating Together (EA)
PACT .... Processing and Communications Terminal (MCD)
PACT .... Production Action Control Technique (SAA)
PACT .... Production Analysis Control Technique [*Navy*]
PACT .... Professional Association of Canadian Theatres
PACT .... Program for Automatic Coding Techniques [*Data processing*]
PACT .... Programmable Asynchronous Clustered Teleprocessing
PACT .... Programmed Analysis Computer Transfer (KSC)
PACT .... Programmed Automatic Circuit Tester
PACT .... Project for the Advancement of Coding Techniques
PACT .... Provide Addict Care Today [*Later, NADAP*]
PACT .... Public Action Coalition on Toys [*Opposes sexist toys*]
PACTA ...... Packed Tape Assembly
PACTEL .... PA Computers & Telecommunications [*Information service or system*] (IID)
PacTel .... Pacific Telesis Group [*San Francisco, CA*] (TSSD)
PacTel .... Pacific Telesis Group [*Associated Press abbreviation*] (APAG)
PACTEX ... Pacific-Texas [*Pipeline*]
PACTIV .... Principos Activos [*Ministerio de Sanidad y Consumo*] [*Spain*] [*Information service or system*] (CRD)
PACTOA ... Pacific Technical Operations Area [*Military*]
PACTS ...... Parents, Administrators, Community, Teachers, and Students [*School-community groups*]
PACTS ...... Programmer Aptitude Competence Test System
PACUSA ... Pacific Air Command, United States Army
PACV .... Cordova [*Alaska*] [*ICAO location identifier*] (ICLI)
PACV .... Patrol Air-Cushion Vehicle [*Also called Hovercraft*] [*Navy*]
PACV .... Personnel Air-Cushion Vehicle
PACV .... Post-Accident Containment Venting [*Nuclear energy*] (NRCH)

PACVD ...... Plasma-Assisted Chemical Vapor Deposition [*Coating technology*]
Pac View .... Pacific Viewpoint [*New Zealand*] [*A publication*]
Pac Viewp .. Pacific Viewpoint [*A publication*]
Pac Wine Spirit Rev ... Pacific Wine Spirit Review [*A publication*]
PACWST .. Pacific Western Bancshares [*Associated Press abbreviation*] (APAG)
PACX .... Private Automatic Computer Exchange
PACZ .... Cape Romanzof Air Force Station [*Alaska*] [*ICAO location identifier*] (ICLI)
PAD .... Anthropology of Development Programme [*McGill University*] [*Canada*] [*Research center*] (RCD)
PAD .... Packet Assembler/Disassembler [*Switching technique*] [*Data processing*]
PAD .... Padder [*Capacitor*] [*Electronics*]
PAD .... Paderborn [*Germany*] [*Airport symbol*] (OAG)
PAD .... Padova [*Italy*] [*Seismograph station code, US Geological Survey*] (SEIS)
PAD .... Padstow [*Town in England*]
PAD .... Palestine Arab Delegation (EA)
PAD .... Partido de Accion Democrata [*Democratic Action Party*] [*Spain*] [*Political party*] (PPW)
PAD .... Partido Accion Democratica [*Democratic Action Party*] [*El Salvador*] [*Political party*] (PPW)
PAD .... Passive Acoustic Detection [*Military*] (CAAL)
PAD .... Passive Air Defense [*British*]
PAD .... Patriot Arm Decoy [*Weaponry*] (DWSG)
PAD .... Payable after Death [*Insurance*] (ADA)
PAD .... Pedagogischer Austauschdienst [*Pedagogical Exchange Service*] [*German*]
PAD .... Penetration Aids Deployment [*Weaponry*] (DWSG)
Pa D .... Pennsylvania District Reports [*A publication*]
PAD .... Performance Analysis and Design [*Nuclear energy*] (NRCH)
PAD .... Performing Arts Directory [*A publication*]
PAD .... Peripheral Arterial Disease [*Medicine*]
PAD .... Permissible Accumulated Dose
PAD .... Personal Articulation Device [*Facetious term for pre-word-processing equipment*]
PAD .... Personnel Administrator [*A publication*]
PAD .... Peters' United States District Court Reports, Admiralty Decisions [*A publication*] (DLA)
PAD .... Petroleum Administration for Defense [*Abolished, 1954*]
PAD .... Phenacetin [*Acetophenetidin*], Aspirin, Deoxyephedrine [*Pharmacology*]
PAD .... Pilotless Aircraft Division [*Navy*]
PAD .... Pitch Axis Definition
PAD .... Pitless Adapter Division of Water Systems Council (EA)
PAD .... Planning Action Directive [*Military*] (AFIT)
PAD .... Planning and Analysis Division [*Environmental Protection Agency*] (GFGA)
PAD .... Player Assessment Device
PAD .... Polar and Auroral Dynamics [*Meteorology*]
PAD .... Polyaperture Device [*NASA*] (KSC)
PAD .... Pontoon Assembly Depot (NVT)
PAD .... Pontoon Assembly Detachment
PAD .... Poor Acquisition Data (AAG)
PAD .... Port of Aerial Debarkation [*Air Force*]
PAD .... Positioning Arm Disk
PAD .... Post-Activation Diffusion (IEEE)
PAD .... Potential Area of Danger [*Navigation*]
PAD .... Power Amplifier Device [*or Driver*]
PAD .... Preadvisory Data (KSC)
PAD .... Precise Access Diagram
PAD .... Preferred Arrival Date (AFM)
PAD .... Preliminary Advisory Data (MCD)
PAD .... Presence and Amplitude Detector
PAD .... Preventive Aggressive Device [*Restraint*] [*Medicine*]
PAD .... Primary Aeronautical Designation (DNAB)
PAD .... Primary Afferent Depolarization [*Electrophysiology*]
PAD .... Procurement Acquisition Directive
PAD .... Product Assurance Directorate [*Armament, Munitions, and Chemical Command*] [*Army*]
PAD .... Professional Administrative Development [*Medicine*]
PAD .... Program Action Directive (AFM)
PAD .... Program Analysis for Documentation [*Data processing*]
PAD .... Program Approval Document [*NASA*] (KSC)
PAD .... Project Approval Document [*NASA*]
PAD .... Propellant Acquisition Device (NASA)
PAD .... Propellant-Actuated Device
PAD .... Provisional Acceptance Date (NATG)
PAD .... Public Affairs Division [*Military*] (AABC)
PAD .... Public Assistance Director [*Federal disaster planning*]
PAD .... Pueblo Army Depot [*Colorado*]
PAD .... Pulmonary Artery Diastolic [*Pressure*] [*Cardiology*]
PAD .... Pulsatile Assist Device [*Cardiology*]
PAD .... Pulse Averaging Discriminator
PAD .... Pulsed Activation Doppler (MCD)
PAD .... Pulsed Amperometric Detection [*Electroanalytical chemistry*]
PADA .... Payroll Automation for Department of Agriculture
PADA .... Pharmacists Against Drug Abuse (EA)
PADA .... Poly(adipicanhydride) [*Organic chemistry*]

PADA .... Prespin Automatic Dynamic Alignment
PADA .... Public Address Assembly [*Ground Communications Facility, NASA*]
PADA .... (Pyridylazo)dimethylaniline [*Organic chemistry*]
PADAC...... Professional Art Dealers Association of Canada
PADAF..... Pacific Command Air Defense Analysis Facility (CINC)
PADAL...... Pattern for Analysis, Decision, Action, and Learning
PADAR...... Passive Airborne Detection and Ranging
PADAR...... Program Approval Disposal and Redistribution [*Army*] (AABC)
PADAT...... Psychological Abstracts Direct Access Terminal
PADC .... Pennsylvania Avenue Development Corp. [*Washington, DC*] [*Federal corporatio n*]
PA D & C... Pennsylvania District and County Reports [*A publication*] (DLA)
PADC .... Piccole Apostole della Carita [*Ponte Lambro, Italy*] (EAIO)
PA D & C 2d ... Pennsylvania District and County Reports, Second Series [*A publication*] (DLA)
PA D & C 3d ... Pennsylvania District and County Reports, Third Series [*A publication*] (DLA)
PADCP...... Paul Andrew Dawkins Children's Project (EA)
PA D & C Rep ... Pennsylvania District and County Reports [*A publication*] (DLA)
PADD .... Passive Antidrown Device (DWSG)
PADD .... Petroleum Administration for Defense District [*Department of Energy*]
PADD .... Planned Active Duty Date [*Military*]
PADD .... Portable Acoustic Doppler Detector
PADDS...... Procurement Automated Data Document System [*Military*] (RDA)
PADEL...... Pattern Description Language
PA Dent J .. Pennsylvania Dental Journal [*A publication*]
PA Dep Environ Resour Water Resour Bull ... Pennsylvania. Department of Environmental Resources. Water Resources Bulletin [*A publication*]
PA Dep For Waters Water Resour Bull ... Pennsylvania. Department of Forests and Waters. Water Resources Bulletin [*A publication*]
PA Dep L & I Dec ... Pennsylvania Department of Labor and Industry Decisions [*A publication*] (DLA)
PA Dep Rep ... Pennsylvania Department Reports [*A publication*] (DLA)
PA Dept Int Affairs Monthly Bull ... Pennsylvania. Department of Internal Affairs. Monthly Bulletin [*A publication*]
PADF......... Driftwood Bay Air Force Station [*Alaska*] [*ICAO location identifier*] (ICLI)
PADF......... Pan American Development Foundation (EA)
PADGEM ... Platelet Activation-Dependent Granulocyte External Membrane Protein [*Biochemistry*]
PADGERC ... PACOM [*Pacific Command*] Air Defense Ground Environment Requirements Committee (CINC)
PADGT...... Past Assistant Deputy Grand Treasurer [*Freemasonry*]
PADI.......... Parti pour l'Avancement de la Democratie en Ituri [*Party for Democratic Advancement in Ituri*] [*Political party*]
PADI.......... Professional Association of Diving Instructors (EA)
Padiatr Pad ... Paediatrie und Paedologie [*A publication*]
PADIE....... Prevention and Detection of Illegal Entry [*Military*] (DNAB)
Padin.......... Partido de Integracion Nacional [*National Integration Party*] [*Peru*] [*Political party*] (PPW)
PADIS .... Pan-African Documentation and Information System [*Economic Commission for Africa*] [*United Nations*] (IID)
PA Dist ...... Pennsylvania District Reporter [*A publication*] (DLA)
PA Dist & Co R ... Pennsylvania District and County Reports [*A publication*] (DLA)
PA Dist & Co Repts ... Pennsylvania District and County Reports [*A publication*] (DLA)
PA Dist & C Rep ... Pennsylvania District and County Reports [*A publication*] (DLA)
PA Dist R... Pennsylvania District Reporter [*A publication*] (DLA)
PA Dist Rep ... Pennsylvania District Reports [*A publication*] (DLA)
PADK .... Adak/Davis [*Alaska*] [*ICAO location identifier*] (ICLI)
PADL......... Dillingham [*Alaska*] [*ICAO location identifier*] (ICLI)
PADL......... Part and Assembly Description Language [*Data processing*]
PADL......... Pilotless Aircraft Development Laboratory [*Navy*]
PADLA...... Programmable Asynchronous Dual Line Adapter
PADLOC... Passive Active Detection and Location (IEEE)
PADLOC... Passive Detection and Location of Countermeasures [*Air Force*]
PADMIS... Patient Administration Information System [*Army*] (AABC)
PADO .... Proposed Advanced Development Objective [*Army*] (AABC)
PADOC..... Pay Adjustment Document [*Army*]
PADP......... Physicians Against the Death Penalty (EA)
PADP......... Proposal for Advanced Development Program
PADP......... Pulmonary Artery Diastolic Pressure [*Cardiology*] (AAMN)
PA Dp Agr An Rp ... Pennsylvania. Department of Agriculture. Annual Report [*A publication*]
PADQ .... Kodiak [*Alaska*] [*ICAO location identifier*] (ICLI)
PADR .... Parts and Data Record System
PA DR....... Pennsylvania District Reports [*A publication*] (DLA)
PADR .... Preferential Arrival/Departure Route [*Aviation*] (FAAC)
PADR .... Production Administration Deficiency Report [*DoD*]
PADRA...... Pass to Air Defense RADAR (FAAC)

PADRE...... Particle Analysis and Data Reduction [*Environmental Protection Agency*] (GFGA)
PADRE...... Particulate Data Reduction (EPA)
PADRE...... Patient Automatic Data Recording Equipment (IEEE)
PADRE...... Portable Automatic Data Recording Equipment
PADS........ Passive-Active Data Simulation
PADS........ Passive Advanced Sonobuoy
PADS........ Pen Application Development System [*Computer software*] [*Slate Corp.*] (PCM)
PADS........ Performance Analysis and Design Synthesis [*Computer program*] [*NASA*]
PADS........ Peroxylaminedisulfonate [*Organic chemistry*]
PADS........ Personnel Automated Data System [*TIMMS*] [*Navy*]
PADS........ Plant Alarm and Display System [*Nuclear energy*] (NRCH)
PADS........ Position and Azimuth Determining System [*Aviation*]
PADS........ Precision Aerial Delivery System
PADS........ Precision Aerial Display System
PADS........ Professional Application Development System [*Slate*] [*Data processing*]
PADS........ Programmer Advanced Debugging System [*Data processing*]
PADS........ Publications. American Dialect Society [*A publication*]
PADS........ Sports Marketing, Inc. [*Minneapolis, MN*] [*NASDAQ symbol*] (NQ)
PADSD...... Proceedings. Analytical Division. Chemical Society [*A publication*]
PADT .... Postalloy Diffusion Transistor
PADU .... Dutch Harbour [*Alaska*] [*ICAO location identifier*] (ICLI)
PADUD ...... Program of Advanced Professional Development, University of Denver College of Law (DLA)
PAE .... Everett, WA [*Location identifier*] [*FAA*] (FAAL)
PAE .... Executive Air Charter [*San Jose, CA*] [*FAA designator*] (FAAC)
PAE .... Paea [*Society Islands*] [*Seismograph station code, US Geological Survey*] (SEIS)
Pae .... Paedagogik [*A publication*]
P AE........... Partes Aequales [*Equal Parts*] [*Pharmacy*]
PAE .... Passed Assistant Engineer [*British*]
PAE .... Payload Accomodations Equipment [*NASA*] (SSD)
PAE .... Payload Attach Equipment [*NASA*] (SSD)
PAE .... Peoria & Eastern Railway [*Absorbed into Consolidated Rail Corp.*] [*AAR code*]
PAE .... Phase Angle Error
PAE .... Phthalic Acid Esters [*Organic chemistry*]
PAE .... Physical Aptitude Examination (AFM)
PAE .... Pioneer Systems, Inc. [*AMEX symbol*] (SPSG)
PAE .... Polyarylether [*Organic chemistry*]
PAE .... Port of Aerial Embarkation [*Air Force*]
PAE .... Post-Accident Environment [*Nuclear energy*] (IEEE)
PAE .... Preliminary Airworthiness Evaluations
PAE .... Preliminary Army Evaluation (MCD)
PAE .... Preventive Action Engineer (NASA)
PAE .... Problem Assessment Engineering (NASA)
PA & E .... Program Analysis and Evaluation
PAE .... Projets pour une Agriculture Ecologique [*Ecological Agriculture Projects - EAP*] [*Sainte Anne De Bellevue, PQ*] (EAIO)
PAE .... Public Affairs Event (NVT)
PAEAC...... Parliamentary Association for Euro-Arab Cooperation (EA)
PAEC........ Pakistan Army Education Corps [*British military*] (DMA)
PAECI .... Pan American Association of Educational Credit Institutions [*Bogota, Colombia*] (EAIO)
PAECT ...... Pollution Abatement and Environmental Control Technology [*Army*] (AABC)
PAED .... Anchorage/Elmendorf Air Force Base [*Alaska*] [*ICAO location identifier*] (ICLI)
PAED .... Paediatric [*or Paediatrics*]
PAED .... Plans, Analysis, and Evaluation Division [*Army*] (MCD)
Paedag Hist ... Paedagogica Historica [*A publication*]
Paedagog Hist ... Paedagogica Historica [*A publication*]
Paedagogica Hist ... Paedagogica Historica [*A publication*]
Paedagog Run ... Paedagogische Rundschau [*A publication*]
Paediatr Fortbildungskurse Prax ... Paediatrische Fortbildungskurse fuer die Praxis [*A publication*]
Paediatr Grenzgeb ... Paediatrie und Grenzgebiete [*A publication*]
Paediatr Indones ... Paediatrica Indonesiana [*A publication*]
Paediatr Paedol ... Paediatrie und Paedologie [*A publication*]
Paediatr Paedol (Suppl) ... Paediatrie und Paedologie (Supplementum) [*A publication*]
Paediatr Univ Tokyo ... Paediatria Universitatis Tokyo [*A publication*]
PAEDP...... Pulmonary Artery End-Diastolic Pressure [*Cardiology*]
PAEH .... Cape Newenham Air Force Station [*Alaska*] [*ICAO location identifier*] (ICLI)
PAEI......... Fairbanks/Eielson Air Force Base [*Alaska*] [*ICAO location identifier*] (ICLI)
PAEI......... Periscope Azimuth Error Indicator
PAEI......... Purchasing Agents of the Electronic Industry [*Rosedale, NY*] (EA)
PAEK........ Polyaryletherketone [*Organic chemistry*]
PAEL........ Preliminary Allowance Equipage List [*Military*] (CAAL)
PA Elec Ass Eng Sect Transm Distrib ... Pennsylvania Electric Association. Engineering Section. Transmission and Distribution Committee. Minutes [*A publication*]

PA Electr Assoc Annu Rep ... Pennsylvania Electric Association. Annual Report [*A publication*]
PA Electr Assoc Eng Sect Minutes Meet ... Pennsylvania Electric Association. Engineering Section. Minutes of the Meeting [*A publication*]
PAEM........ Program Analysis and Evaluation Model (IEEE)
PAEN .... Kenai [*Alaska*] [*ICAO location identifier*] (ICLI)
PA Energy Ext Serv News ... Pennsylvania Energy Extension Service. News [*A publication*]
PAEP........ Preliminary Annual Engineering Plan [*Military*] (AFIT)
P AEQ........ Partes Aequales [*Equal Parts*] [*Pharmacy*]
PAES........ Phenyl(aminoethyl)sulfide [*Biochemistry*]
PAES........ Publications. Princeton University Archaeological Expeditions to Syria [*A publication*]
PAET........ American Ethnologist [*A publication*]
PAET........ Planetary Atmosphere Experimental [*or Experiments*] Test [*NASA*]
PAEWCC.. Peace Activists East and West Coordinating Committee (EA)
PAF........... Pacific Affairs [*A publication*]
PAF........... Pacific Air Forces
PAF........... Pacific American Airlines, Inc. [*Burbank, CA*] [*FAA designator*] (FAAC)
PAF........... Pacific Aqua Foods Ltd. [*Toronto Stock Exchange symbol*]
PAF........... Page Address Field
PAF........... Pan American Foundation [*Defunct*] (EA)
PAF........... Paroxysmal Atrial [*or Auricular*] Fibrillation [*Medicine*] (MAE)
PAF........... Payload Attachment Fitting [*NASA*]
PAF........... Peak Annual Funding (NASA)
PA F........... Pennsylvania Folklife [*A publication*]
PA & F........ Percussion, Auscultation, and Fremitus [*Medicine*]
PAF........... Performing Arts Foundation (EA)
PAF........... Peripheral Address Field
PAF........... Peroxisome Assembly Factor [*Biochemistry*]
PAF........... Personal Ancestry File [*Data processing*] (PCM)
PAF........... Personal Article Floater [*Air baggage insurance*]
PAF........... Philippine Air Force
PAF........... Platelet-Activating Factor [*Hematology*]
PAF........... Platelet Aggregation Factor [*Hematology*]
PAF........... Polaris Accelerated Flight [*Chamber*] [*Missiles*]
PAF........... Port-Aux-Francais [*Kerguelen Islands*] [*Seismograph station code, US Geological Survey*] [*Closed*] (SEIS)
PAF........... Portable Arc Furnace
PAF........... Portuguese Air Force
PAF........... Posterior Auditory Field
PAF........... Preadmission Assessment Form [*Health Care Financing Administration*]
PAF........... Prearranged Fire
PAF........... Preatomized Fuel [*Trademark*] [*Petroferm product*]
PAF........... Premature Anti-Fascist [*World War II designation used by Army Counterintelligence Department*]
PAF........... Price Analysis File (AFIT)
PAF........... Printed and Fired Circuit
PAF........... Pro-American Forum (EA)
PAF........... Production Assembly Facility [*Manufacturing*]
PAF........... Pseudo-Archaic Forgery
PAF........... Pseudoamniotic Fluid [*Gynecology*]
PAF........... Psychoanalytic Assistance Fund (EA)
PAF........... Public Agenda Foundation (EA)
PAF........... Public Art Fund (EA)
PAF........... Publication Authority Form (AAG)
PAF........... Pulmonary Arteriovenous Fistula [*Medicine*]
PAF........... Pulse-Air Feeder [*Automotive engineering*]
PAFA........ Fairbanks/International [*Alaska*] [*ICAO location identifier*] (ICLI)
PAFA........ Pan-American Festival Association (EA)
PAFA........ Pennsylvania Academy of the Fine Arts
PAFA........ Presidential Academic Fitness Award [*Department of Education*] (GFGA)
PAFAM..... Performance and Failure Assessment Monitor (MCD)
PAFAMS... Pan American Federation of Associations of Medical Schools [*See also FEPAFEM*] [*Caracas, Venezuela*] (EAIO)
PA Farm Econ ... Pennsylvania Farm Economics [*A publication*]
PAFATU ... Pan-African Federation of Agricultural Trade Unions (EA)
PAFB........ Fairbanks/Wainwright Army Air Field [*Alaska*] [*ICAO location identifier*] (ICLI)
PAFB........ Patrick Air Force Base [*Florida*]
PAFC........ Paul Anka Fan Club (EA)
PAFC........ Phase-Locked Automatic Frequency Control [*Telecommunications*]
PAFC........ Phosphoric Acid Fuel Cell [*Energy source*]
PAFCOMNET ... Pacific Air Forces Communications Network (SAA)
PAFCS...... Prior Active Foreign Commissioned Service
PAFDEFNET ... Pacific Air Forces Defense Network (SAA)
PAFE........ Place Accepted for Enlistment
PAFEA..... Patologicheskaya Fiziologiya i Eksperimental'naya Terapiya [*A publication*]
PAFES...... Prior Active Foreign Enlisted Service (DNAB)
PAFIB........ Paroxysmal Atrial [*or Auricular*] Fibrillation [*Medicine*] (MAE)
PA Fid........ Pennsylvania Fiduciary Reporter [*A publication*] (DLA)

PA Fiduc... Pennsylvania Fiduciary Reporter [*A publication*] (DLA)
PAFMECSA ... Pan African Freedom Movement for East, Central, and Southern Africa [*Superseded in 1963 by the liberation committee of the Organization of African Unity*] (PD)
PA Folklife ... Pennsylvania Folklife [*A publication*]
PA For ...... Pennsylvania Forests [*A publication*]
PAFP......... Photochemical Aerosol-Forming Potential of Polluted Air [*Environmental chemistry*]
PAFR......... Fort Richardson/Bryant Army Air Field [*Alaska*] [*ICAO location identifier*] (ICLI)
PA Fruit News ... Pennsylvania Fruit News [*A publication*]
PAFS .... Asian Folklore Studies [*A publication*]
PAFS .... Primary Air Force Specialty
PAFS .... Publications. American Folklore Society [*A publication*]
PAFSC...... Primary Air Force Specialty Code
PAFT........ Polish American Folk Theatre
PAFT .... Programme for Alternative Fluorocarbon Toxicity Testing [*British*]
PAFTT ...... Program for Alternative Fluorocarbon Toxicity Testing [*Environmental science*]
PAFU........ Patriot Arm Fire Unit [*Weaponry*] (MCD)
PAFVA ..... Polish Air Force Veterans Association (EA)
PAFW........ Farewell [*Alaska*] [*ICAO location identifier*] (ICLI)
PAFZDW .. Fundacao Zoobotanica do Rio Grande Do Sul. Publicacoes Avulsas [*A publication*]
PAG .... I Pagliacci [*Opera*] (DSUE)
PAG .... Packaging [*A publication*]
PAG .... Pagadian [*Philippines*] [*Airport symbol*] (OAG)
Pag .... Page's Three Early Assize Rolls, County of Northumberland [*Surtees Society Publications, Vol. 88*] [*A publication*] (ILCA)
PAG .... Paget Resources Ltd. [*Vancouver Stock Exchange symbol*]
Pag .... Pagoda
PAG .... Panagjuriste [*Bulgaria*] [*Geomagnetic observatory code*]
PAG .... Parts Acquisition Group
PAG .... Party for the Autonomy of Gibraltar [*Political party*] (PPW)
PAG .... Pentaacetylglucose [*Laundry bleach activator*]
PAG .... Periaqueductal Gray Matter [*Brain anatomy*]
PAG .... Polyacrylamide Gel [*Analytical chemistry*]
PAG .... Polyalkylene Glycol [*Organic chemistry*]
PAg .... Poultry-Related Antigens [*Immunology*]
PAG .... Poverty Advisory Group
PAG .... Prealbumin Globulin [*Biochemistry*] (OA)
PAG .... Precision Alignment Gyrocompass
PAG .... Precursor Active Galaxies
PAG .... Pregnancy-Associated alpha-Glycoprotein [*Gynecology*]
PAG .... Preliminary Analysis Group (NATG)
PAG .... Prince Albert's Guard [*British military*] (DMA)
PAG .... Professional Activities Group
PAG .... Professional Auto Group, Inc.
PAG .... Program Assessment Guide [*Department of Labor*] (OICC)
PAG .... Progress Analysis Group [*Navy*] (MCD)
PAG .... Project Advisory Group [*Army*]
PAG .... Property Advisory Group [*British*] (DCTA)
PAG .... Protective Action Guide [*Nuclear energy*]
PAG .... Protein Advisory Group [*United Nations*]
PAG .... Spring Garden College, Philadelphia, PA [*OCLC symbol*] (OCLC)
PAGA .... Galena [*Alaska*] [*ICAO location identifier*] (ICLI)
PAGA .... Pan American Grace Airways, Inc. [*Also, PANAGRA*]
PaGa .... Printing and Graphic Arts [*A publication*]
PAGAA ..... Pesquisa Agropecuaria Brasileira. Serie Agronomia [*A publication*]
PAGAN .... Pattern Generation Language [*Data processing*]
PAGDC ..... Past Assistant Grand Director of Ceremonies [*Freemasonry*] (ROG)
Page .... Page's Three Early Assize Rolls, County of Northumberland [*Surtees Society Publications, Vol. 88*] [*A publication*] (DLA)
PAGE........ Paging Network [*NASDAQ symbol*] (SPSG)
PAGE........ PERT [*Program Evaluation and Review Technique*] Automated Graphical Extension (KSC)
PAGE........ Philatelic Association of Government Employees
PAGE........ Piston Arrestment Gas Entrapment System [*SPRINT launch cell*] [*Army*] (AABC)
PAGE........ Polyacrylamide Gel Electrophoresis [*Analytical chemistry*]
PAGE........ Preliminary Automated Ground Environment
PAGEAM ... Page America Group, Inc. [*Associated Press abbreviation*] (APAG)
Page Contr ... Page on Contracts [*A publication*] (DLA)
Page Div..... Page on Divorce [*A publication*] (DLA)
PAGEL...... Priced Aerospace Ground Equipment List
PA Gen As ... Pennsylvania General Assembly [*A publication*]
PA Geol..... Pennsylvania Geology [*A publication*]
PA Geol Surv Atlas ... Pennsylvania. Geological Survey. Atlas [*A publication*]
PA Geol Surv Gen Geol Rep ... Pennsylvania. Geological Survey. General Geology Report [*A publication*]
PA Geol Surv Inf Circ ... Pennsylvania. Geological Survey. Information Circular [*A publication*]
PA Geol Surv Miner Resour Rep ... Pennsylvania. Geological Survey. Mineral Resource Report [*A publication*]

PA Geol Surv Prog Rep ... Pennsylvania. Geological Survey. Progress Report [*A publication*]
PA Geol Surv Water Resour Rep ... Pennsylvania. Geological Survey. Water Resource Report [*A publication*]
PAGEOS... Passive Geodetic Earth-Orbiting Satellite [*NASA*]
PA-Ger...... Pennsylvania-German [*A publication*]
PA Ger Folk Soc Yr Bk ... Pennsylvania German Folklore Society. Year Book [*A publication*]
PAGES...... Program Affinity Grouping and Evaluation System
PAGH....... Agricultural History [*A publication*]
PAGH....... Pacific Agricultural Holdings, Inc. [*NASDAQ symbol*] (NQ)
PAGICEP ... Petroleum and Gas Industry Communications Emergency Plan [*FCC*]
Pag Jud Puz ... Paget's Judicial Puzzles [*A publication*] (DLA)
PAGK .... Gulkana [*Alaska*] [*ICAO location identifier*] (ICLI)
PAGL......... Pulsed Argon Gas LASER
PAGMK .... Primary African Green Monkey Kidney [*Cells*]
PAGN....... Pagnall [*England*]
PAGO .... Pacific Gold Corp. [*NASDAQ symbol*] (NQ)
PAGR .... Professional Agricultural Management, Inc. [*Firebaugh, CA*] [*NASDAQ symbol*] (NQ)
PAGS........ Parti de l'Avant-Garde Socialiste [*Socialist Vanguard Party*] [*Algeria*] [*Political party*] (PD)
PA G S....... Pennsylvania. Geological Survey [*A publication*]
PAGS........ Polish-American Guardian Society (EA)
PAGS........ Proceedings. Australian Goethe Society [*A publication*]
PAGTU ..... Pan-American Ground Training Unit
PAGVA...... Progres Agricole et Viticole [*A publication*]
PAGYB....... Pennsylvania Geology [*A publication*]
PAGYDY... Pediatric and Adolescent Gynecology [*A publication*]
PAH.......... Paducah [*Kentucky*] [*Airport symbol*] (OAG)
PAH.......... Pahoa [*Hawaii*] [*Seismograph station code, US Geological Survey*] [*Closed*] (SEIS)
PAH.......... Panorama Air Tour, Inc. [*Honolulu, HI*] [*FAA designator*] (FAAC)
PAH.......... Para-Aminohippuric [*Biochemistry*]
PAH.......... Parts Application Handbook
PAH.......... Pathtechnics Ltd. [*Vancouver Stock Exchange symbol*]
PAH.......... Payload Accommodations Handbook [*NASA*] (NASA)
PAH.......... Phase Adjusting Hub
PAH.......... Phenylalanine Hydroxylase [*An enzyme*]
PAH.......... Pitch Attitude Hold [*Aviation*] (MCD)
PAH.......... Polycyclic [*or Polynuclear*] Aromatic Hydrocarbon [*Organic chemistry*]
PAH.......... Pulmonary Artery Hypertension [*Medicine*]
PAH.......... Push and Hold [*Push button*]
PAHA....... Para-Aminohippuric Acid
PAHA....... Polish American Historical Association (EA)
Pahasapa Q ... Pahasapa Quarterly [*A publication*]
PAHBAH.. Para-Hydroxybenzoic Acid Hydrazide [*Organic chemistry*]
PAHC........ Pan American Highway Congresses (EA)
PAHC........ Pioneer American Holding Corp. [*Carbondale, PA*] [*NASDAQ symbol*] (NQ)
PAHC........ Pontifical Association of the Holy Childhood (EA)
PAHEA ..... Pharmaceutica Acta Helvetiae [*A publication*]
PAHEF...... Pan American Health and Education Foundation (EA)
PAHEL...... Pay Records and Health Records
PAHEO..... Particle Accelerators in High Earth Orbit [*Proposed*]
PAHF .... Pan American Hockey Federation [*Winnipeg, MB*] (EAIO)
PA His ...... Pennsylvania History [*A publication*]
PA Hist...... Pennsylvania History [*A publication*]
PAHL......... Pressure Alarm, High-Limit [*Nuclear energy*] (NRCH)
Pahlavi Med J ... Pahlavi Medical Journal [*A publication*]
PAHO........ Homer [*Alaska*] [*ICAO location identifier*] (ICLI)
PAHO........ Pan American Health Organization (EA)
PAHO........ Paraho Development Corp. [*NASDAQ symbol*] (NQ)
PAHO/B .... Bulletin. Pan American Health Organization [*A publication*]
PAHR....... Post-Accident Heat Removal [*Nuclear energy*]
PAHS .... Passive Annual Heat Storage [*Housing technology*]
PAI............ Pacific Aerospace Index (DIT)
PAI............ Pacific American Income Shares, Inc. [*NYSE symbol*] (SPSG)
PAI............ Pacific American Institute (EA)
PAI............ Pacoima, CA [*Location identifier*] [*FAA*] (FAAL)
Pai............ Paige's New York Chancery Reports [*A publication*] (DLA)
Pai............ Paine's United States Circuit Court Reports [*A publication*] (DLA)
PAI............ Pair Attraction Inventory [*Premarital, marital, and family counseling test*] [*Psychology*]
PAI............ Parti Africain de l'Independance [*African Independence Party*] [*Senegal*] [*Political party*] (PPW)
PAI............ Partido Aragones Independiente [*Spain*] [*Political party*] (EY)
PAI............ Parts Application Information [*Manufacturing*]
PAI............ Passive-Aggressive Index [*Psychology*]
PAI............ Percent Adherence Index
PAI............ Performance Audit Inspection [*Environmental Protection Agency*] (GFGA)
PAI............ Personal Accident Insurance
PAI............ Personal Adjustment Inventory [*Psychology*]
PAI............ Personnel Accreditation Institute (EA)
PAI............ Phosphate Adsorption Index [*Analytical chemistry*]
PAI............ Photographic Administrators, Inc. (EA)

PAI............ Piedmont Aviation, Inc. [*Air carrier designation symbol*]
PAI............ Pirchei Agudath Israel (EA)
PA & I........ Planning, Analysis, and Integration
PAI............ Plasminogen-Activator Inhibitor [*Biochemistry*]
PAI............ Plunger Actuated Indexer
PAI............ Poale Agudath Israel of America (EA)
PAI............ Polish Assistance, Inc. (EA)
PAI............ Polyamide-Imide [*Organic chemistry*]
PAI............ Prearrival Inspection
PAI............ Precise Angle Indicator
PAI............ Primary Aerospace Vehicle [*or Aircraft*] Inventory
PAI............ Process Analytical Instrument
PAI............ Processed Apples Institute (EA)
PAI............ Production Adjustment Index [*Word processing*]
PAI............ Professional Athletes International [*Later, NFLPA*] (EA)
PAI............ Programmer Appraisal Instrument [*Data processing*] (IEEE)
PAI............ Project Assignment Instruction (MCD)
PAI............ Property Agents International
PAI............ Public Affairs Information, Inc. [*Sacramento, CA*] [*Database producer*] [*Information service or system*]
PAI............ Public Affairs Institute [*Defunct*] (EA)
PAI............ Public Assistance Information [*A publication*]
PAIA......... Pan American Implant Association (EA)
PAIAA....... Proceedings. National Academy of Sciences (India). Section A [*A publication*]
PAIB......... Polish-American Information Bureau [*Later, PATIB*] (EA)
PAIC......... Persia and Iraq Command [*World War II*]
PAIC......... Public Address Intercom System (NRCH)
PAICC .... Professional Association of the Interstate Commerce Commission
Pai Ch .... Paige's New York Chancery Reports [*A publication*] (DLA)
PAID......... Pan African Institute for Development (EAIO)
PAID......... Personnel and Accounting Integrated Data [*System*] [*Veterans Administration*]
PAID......... Price and Item Display [*British*]
Paid Dues... Paid My Dues [*A publication*]
Paideia Studies in Nature of Modern Math ... Paideia Studies in the Nature of Modern Mathematics [*A publication*]
PAIDOL..... Paidologist [*A publication*]
PAIDS....... Pediatric Acquired Immune Deficiency Syndrome [*Medicine*]
PAIF .... Persia and Iraq Force [*World War II*]
PAIFORCE ... Persia and Iraq Force [*World War II*] (DMA)
PAIg.......... Platelet-Associated Immunoglobulin [*Hematology*]
PAIGC....... Partido Africano da Independencia da Guine e do Cabo Verde [*African Party for the Independence of Guinea and Cape Verde*] [*Political party*] (PPW)
Paige .... Paige's New York Chancery Reports [*A publication*] (DLA)
Paige Ch..... Paige's New York Chancery Reports [*1828-45*] [*A publication*] (DLA)
Paige Ch Rep ... Paige's New York Chancery Reports [*A publication*] (DLA)
Paige's Ch ... Paige's New York Chancery Reports [*A publication*] (DLA)
PAIgG........ Platelet-Associated Immunoglobulin G [*Hematology*]
PAIGH ...... Pan American Institute of Geography and History [*Research center*] [*Mexico*] (IRC)
PAIGS........ Performing Arts Information Guide Series [*A publication*]
PAIL.......... Iliamna [*Alaska*] [*ICAO location identifier*] (ICLI)
PAIL.......... Post-Attack Intercontinental Link
PAILS........ Projectile Airburst and Impact Location System
PAILS........ Publication Automated Information Locator System [*Army*]
PAIM........ Indian Mountain Air Force Station [*Alaska*] [*ICAO location identifier*] (ICLI)
PAIM........ Parti Africain pour l'Independance des Masses [*African Party for the Independence of the Masses*] [*Senegal*] [*Political party*] (PPW)
PAIM........ Primary Air Inlet Muffler (MCD)
PAIMEG ... Pan American Institute of Mining, Engineering, and Geology [*Defunct*]
PAIN .... Pain Suppression Labs, Inc. [*Elmwood Park, NJ*] [*NASDAQ symbol*] (NQ)
Paine .... Paine's United States Circuit Court Reports [*A publication*] (DLA)
Paine CC.... Paine's United States Circuit Court Reports [*A publication*] (DLA)
Paine CCR ... Paine's United States Circuit Court Reports [*A publication*] (DLA)
Paine Cir Ct R ... Paine's United States Circuit Court Reports [*A publication*] (DLA)
Paine & D Pr ... Paine and Duer's Practice [*A publication*] (DLA)
Paine Elect ... Paine on Elections [*A publication*] (DLA)
Paine Webb ... Paine, Webber, Jackson & Curtis, Inc. Research Notes [*A publication*]
Pain Fr .... Pain Francais [*A publication*]
Pain Suppl ... Pain. Supplement [*A publication*]
Paint.......... Paintbrush [*A publication*]
PAINT .... Painting (ROG)
PAINT....... Post-Attack Intelligence
Paint Colour J Master Painter Aust ... Paint Colour; Journal of the Master Painter of Australia [*A publication*]
Paint Colour Rec ... Paint and Colour Record [*A publication*]
Paint Dec J ... Painting and Decorating Journal [*A publication*]
Paint Decor ... Painting and Decorating [*A publication*]

Painters J... Painters and Allied Trades Journal [*A publication*]
Paint Ind .... Paint Industry [*A publication*]
Paint Ind Mag ... Paint Industry Magazine [*A publication*]
Painting Technol (Tokyo) ... Painting Technology (Tokyo) [*A publication*]
Paint J........ Paint Journal [*A publication*]
Paint J........ Paint Journal of Australia and New Zealand [*A publication*] (APTA)
Paint J Aust NZ ... Paint Journal of Australia and New Zealand [*A publication*]
Paint Manuf ... Paint Manufacture [*England*] [*A publication*]
Paint Manuf Assoc US Tech Circ Educ Bur Sci Sect ... Paint Manufacturers Association. United States. Technical Circulars. Educational Bureau. Scientific Section [*A publication*]
Paint Oil Chem Rev ... Paint Oil and Chemical Review [*A publication*]
Paint Oil Colour J ... Paint Oil and Colour Journal [*A publication*]
Paint Res.... Paint and Resin [*A publication*]
Paints Pak ... Paints in Pakistan [*A publication*]
Paint Technol ... Paint Technology [*A publication*]
Paint Varn Prod ... Paint and Varnish Production [*A publication*]
Paint Varn Prod Manager ... Paint and Varnish Production Manager [*A publication*]
PainW........ PaineWebber Group, Inc. [*Associated Press abbreviation*] (APAG)
PainWb...... PaineWebber Group, Inc. [*Associated Press abbreviation*] (APAG)
PainWP ..... Paine Webber Premier Tax Free Income [*Associated Press abbreviation*] (APAG)
PAIP......... Preverbal Assessment-Intervention Profile [*Test*]
PAIP......... Production Acceleration Insurance Program
PAIP......... Public Affairs and Information Program [*Atomic Industrial Forum*] (NRCH)
PAIR......... Performance Assessment in Reading [*Educational test*]
PAIR......... Performance and Improved Reliability
PAIR......... Performance and Integration Retrofit
PAIR......... Precision Approach Interferometer RADAR (MCD)
PAIR......... Preliminary Assessment Information Rule [*Environmental Protection Agency*]
PAIR......... Presidential Airways, Inc. [*Herndon, VA*] [*NASDAQ symbol*] (NQ)
PAIR......... Procurement Automated Integrated Requirements (MCD)
PAIR......... Psychological Audit for Interpersonal Relations [*Psychology*]
PAIR......... Pulse-Air Injection Reactor [*Automotive engineering*]
PAIRC....... Polish American Immigration and Relief Committee (EA)
PAIRS .... Product Assurance Information Retrieval System [*Boeing*]
PAIRS .... Program for the Analysis of Infrared Spectra [*Computer program*] [*Analytical chemistry*]
PAIS .... Padre Island National Seashore [*National Park Service designation*]
PAIS .... Partido Amplio de Izquierda Socialista [*Chile*] [*Political party*] (EY)
PAIS .... Partido Autentico Institucional Salvadoreno [*Salvadoran Authentic Institutional Party*] [*Political party*] (PPW)
PAIS .... Personnel Authentication Identification System (MCD)
PAIS .... Petroleum Abstracts Information Services [*University of Tulsa*] [*Oklahoma*] [*Information service or system*] (IID)
PAIS .... Project Analysis Information System [*Agency for International Development*]
PAIS .... Prototype Advanced Indicator System (MCD)
PAIS .... Psychological Abstracts Information Services [*American Psychological Association*]
PAIS .... Psychosocial Adjustment to Illness Scale [*Personality development test*] [*Psychology*]
PAIS .... Public Affairs Information Service [*Bibliographic database*] [*A publication*]
PAISA .... Partido Autentico Institucional Salvadoreno [*Salvadoran Authentic Institutional Party*] [*Political party*] (EY)
PAIS Bull .. PAIS [*Public Affairs Information Service*] Bulletin [*A publication*]
PAISER..... Proceedings. Annual Conference and International Symposium of the North American Lake Management Society [*A publication*]
PAIS Foreign Lang Index ... PAIS [*Public Affairs Information Service*] Foreign Language Index [*A publication*]
PAIT......... Program for Advancement of Industrial Technology [*Canada*]
PAIX......... Pacific Alaska Airlines [*Air carrier designation symbol*]
PA J.......... American Academy of Physicians' Assistants. Journal [*A publication*]
PAJ.......... Kansas City, MO [*Location identifier*] [*FAA*] (FAAL)
PA J.......... PA Journal [*Formerly, Physician's Associate*] [*A publication*]
PAJ.......... Pan-African Journal [*A publication*]
PAJ.......... Performing Arts Journal [*A publication*]
PAJA........ American Journal of Archaeology [*A publication*]
PAJA........ Parachute Jumping Activity (FAAC)
PAJAR....... Parti Rakyat Jati Sarawak [*Sarawak Native People's Party*] [*Malaysia*] [*Political party*] (PPW)
PAJF......... American Journal of Family Therapy [*A publication*]
PAJH......... American Jewish History [*A publication*]
PAJHS....... Publication. American Jewish Historical Society [*A publication*]
PAJM....... Journal. American Musicological Society [*A publication*]
PAJN........ Juneau [*Alaska*] [*ICAO location identifier*] (ICLI)
PAJO........ American Journal of Psychoanalysis [*A publication*]

PAJP .... American Journal of Philology [*A publication*]
PAK .... Hanapepe, HI [*Location identifier*] [*FAA*] (FAAL)
PAK .... Pacific Alaska Airlines [*Fairbanks, AK*] [*FAA designator*] (FAAC)
PAK .... Pakistan [*ANSI three-letter standard code*] (CNC)
PAK .... Panzer Abwehr Kanone [*Cannon Against Armor*] [*German antitank gun*]
PAK .... Performance Advantage Kit [*Personal computers*]
PAK .... Polycyclic Aromatic Ketone [*Organic chemistry*]
PAK .... Power Amplifier Klystron
PAK .... Program Attention Key [*Data processing*] (BUR)
Pak Acad Sci Proc ... Pakistan Academy of Sciences. Proceedings [*A publication*]
Pak Agric... Pakistan Agriculture [*A publication*]
Pak Assoc Adv Sci Annu Rep ... Pakistan Association for the Advancement of Science. Annual Report [*A publication*]
PAKBA...... Promyshlennost Armenii [*A publication*]
Pak Bar J... Pakistan Bar Journal [*A publication*] (DLA)
Pak Cottons ... Pakistan Cottons [*A publication*]
Pak Crim LJ ... Pakistan Criminal Law Journal [*A publication*] (DLA)
Pak CSIR Bull Monogr ... Pakistan Council of Scientific and Industrial Research. Bulletin. Monograph [*A publication*]
Pak Dent Rev ... Pakistan Dental Review [*A publication*]
Pak Dev R ... Pakistan Development Review [*A publication*]
Pak Dev Rev ... Pakistan Development Review [*A publication*]
Pak DR...... Pakistan Development Review [*A publication*]
Pak Eng ..... Pakistan Engineer [*A publication*]
PAKEX...... International Packaging Exhibition [*British*] (ITD)
Pak Geogr R ... Pakistan Geographical Review [*A publication*]
Pak Geogr Rev ... Pakistan Geographical Review [*A publication*]
Pak Geol Surv Inf Release ... Pakistan Geological Survey. Information Release [*A publication*]
Pak Geol Surv Rec ... Pakistan Geological Survey. Records [*A publication*]
PAKISTAN ... Nation in Asia, the name of which is said to be coined from Punjab (P), Afghan border states (A), Kashmir (K), Sind (S), and Baluchistan (TAN). Name also means "land of the pure" in Hindustani.
Pakistan Develop R ... Pakistan Development Review [*A publication*]
Pakistan Econ and Social R ... Pakistan Economic and Social Review [*A publication*]
Pakistan Eng ... Pakistan Engineer [*A publication*]
Pakistan J Biol Agr Sci ... Pakistan Journal of Biological and Agricultural Sciences [*A publication*]
Pakistan J For ... Pakistan Journal of Forestry [*A publication*]
Pakistan J Med Res ... Pakistan Journal of Medical Research [*A publication*]
Pakistan J Sci ... Pakistan Journal of Science [*A publication*]
Pakistan J Sci Ind Res ... Pakistan Journal of Scientific and Industrial Research [*A publication*]
Pakistan J Sci Res ... Pakistan Journal of Scientific Research [*A publication*]
Pakistan J Soil Sci ... Pakistan Journal of Soil Sciences [*A publication*]
Pakistan Lib Bull ... Pakistan Library Bulletin [*A publication*]
Pakistan Lib R ... Pakistan Library Review [*A publication*]
Pakistan Phil J ... Pakistan Philosophical Journal [*A publication*]
Pakist J Agric Sci ... Pakistan Journal of Agricultural Sciences [*A publication*]
Pakist J Bot ... Pakistan Journal of Botany [*A publication*]
Pakist J Scient Res ... Pakistan Journal of Scientific Research [*A publication*]
Pakist J Zool ... Pakistan Journal of Zoology [*A publication*]
Pakistn Pl .. Sixth Five-Year Plan, 1983-88 (Pakistan) [*A publication*]
Pak J Agric Sci ... Pakistan Journal of Agricultural Sciences [*A publication*]
Pak J Agri Res ... Pakistan Journal of Agricultural Research [*A publication*]
Pak J Biochem ... Pakistan Journal of Biochemistry [*A publication*]
Pak J Biol Agric Sci ... Pakistan Journal of Biological and Agricultural Sciences [*A publication*]
Pak J Bot ... Pakistan Journal of Botany [*A publication*]
Pak J Fam Plann ... Pakistan Journal of Family Planning [*A publication*]
Pak J For ... Pakistan Journal of Forestry [*A publication*]
Pak J Geriatr ... Pakistan Journal of Geriatrics [*A publication*]
Pak J Health ... Pakistan Journal of Health [*A publication*]
Pak J Med Res ... Pakistan Journal of Medical Research [*A publication*]
Pak J Nematol ... Pakistan Journal of Nematology [*A publication*]
Pak J Pharm ... Pakistan Journal of Pharmacy [*A publication*]
Pak J Pharmacol ... Pakistan Journal of Pharmacology [*A publication*]
Pak J Pharm Sci ... Pakistan Journal of Pharmaceutical Sciences [*A publication*]
Pak J Sci.... Pakistan Journal of Science [*A publication*]
Pak J Sci Ind Res ... Pakistan Journal of Scientific and Industrial Research [*A publication*]
Pak J Sci Res ... Pakistan Journal of Scientific Research [*A publication*]
Pak J Surg Gynaecol Obstet ... Pakistan Journal of Surgery, Gynaecology, and Obstetrics [*A publication*]
Pak J Surg Gyn Obst ... Pakistan Journal of Surgery, Gynaecology, and Obstetrics [*A publication*]
Pak J Zool ... Pakistan Journal of Zoology [*A publication*]
Pak Libr Ass Q J ... Pakistan Library Association. Quarterly Journal [*A publication*]
Pak Libr Rev ... Pakistan Library Review [*A publication*]
Pak LR....... Pakistan Law Reports [*India*] [*A publication*] (DLA)
Pak L Rev .. Pakistan Law Review [*A publication*] (DLA)
Pak Med For ... Pakistan Medical Forum [*A publication*]
Pak Med Forum ... Pakistan Medical Forum [*A publication*]
Pak Med J ... Pakistan Medical Journal [*A publication*]

Pak Med Rev ... Pakistan Medical Review [*A publication*]
PAKN .... King Salmon [*Alaska*] [*ICAO location identifier*]   (ICLI)
Pak Nurs Health Rev ... Pakistan Nursing and Health Review [*A publication*]
Pak Philos Congr Proc ... Pakistan Philosophical Congress. Proceedings [*A publication*]
PakQ .... Pakistan Quarterly [*A publication*]
PakR .... Pakistan Review [*A publication*]
Pak Rev Agric ... Pakistan Review of Agriculture [*A publication*]
PAKS .... Packaging Systems Corp. [*NASDAQ symbol*]   (NQ)
Pak Sci Conf Proc ... Pakistan Science Conference. Proceedings [*A publication*]
Pak Sup Ct Q ... Pakistan Supreme Court Law Quarterly [*Lahore, Pakistan*] [*A publication*]   (DLA)
PAKT .... Ketchikan [*Alaska*] [*ICAO location identifier*]   (ICLI)
PAKT .... Petroleum Acreage Corp. of Texas [*NASDAQ symbol*]   (NQ)
Pak Text J ... Pakistan Textile Journal [*A publication*]
Pak Vet J ... Pakistan Veterinary Journal [*A publication*]
PAL .... Allegheny County Law Library, Pittsburgh, PA [*OCLC symbol*]   (OCLC)
PAL .... Pacific Aeronautical Library
PAL .... Pacific Air Lines
pal .... Pahlavi [*MARC language code*] [*Library of Congress*]   (LCCP)
PAL .... Paired-Associates Learning [*Task*] [*Psychology*]
PAL .... Palace
Pal .... Palamedes [*of Gorgias*] [*Classical studies*]   (OCD)
PAL .... Palatine [*or Palatinate*] [*Genealogy*]
PAL .... Paleography   (ROG)
PAL .... Paleontology
PAL .... Paleozoic [*Period, era, or system*] [*Geology*]
PAL .... Palestine
PAL .... Palisades [*New York*] [*Seismograph station code, US Geological Survey*]   (SEIS)
PAL .... Pallor   (KSC)
Pal .... Palmer's Assizes at Cambridge [*England*] [*A publication*]   (DLA)
Pal .... Palmer's English King's Bench Reports [*1619-29*] [*A publication*]   (DLA)
Pal .... Palmer's Reports [*53-60 Vermont*] [*A publication*]   (DLA)
PAL .... Paloma Petroleum Ltd. [*Toronto Stock Exchange symbol*]
PAL .... Paradox Application Language [*ANSA*] [*Data processing*]
PAL .... Parcel Air Lift [*US Postal Service*]
PAL .... Parents Anonymous Lifeline [*British*]   (DI)
PAL .... Parser Assembly Language [*Data processing*]
PAL .... Parts and Assemblies Locator [*ADP/CES*]
PAL .... Parts Authorization List   (KSC)
PAL .... Patent Associated Literature
PAL .... Pathology Laboratory [*Test*]
PAL .... Pectin Acid Lyase [*An enzyme*]
PAL .... Pedagogic Algorithmic Language [*Data processing*]
PAL .... People Against Chlordane   (EA)
PAL .... People-Animals-Love   (EA)
PAL .... Perceptual Alternatives Laboratory [*University of Louisville*] [*Research center*]   (RCD)
PAL .... Performance Assessment Logic
PAL .... Peripheral Access Lattices
PAL .... Permanent Artificial Lighting   (IEEE)
PAL .... Permissive Action Link [*Army*]
PAL .... Permissive Arming Line [*or Link*]
PAL .... Peroxide Assisted Leach [*Ore processing*]
PAL .... Personal Assets Line
PAL .... Personnel Accounting Level [*Air Force*]   (AFM)
PAL .... Personnel Address Listing   (SAA)
PAL .... Personnel Airlock [*Nuclear energy*]   (NRCH)
PAL .... Personnel Augmentation List [*Military*]
PAL .... Phase Alternation Line [*West German color television system*]
PAL .... Phenylalanine Ammonia-Lyase [*An enzyme*]
PAL .... Philippine Air Lines
PAL .... Pipe Analysis Log [*Gas well*]
PAL .... Point, Area, and Line Source Air Quality Model [*Environmental Protection Agency*]   (GFGA)
PAL .... Police Athletic League
PAL .... Poly-DL-alanine Poly-L-lysine [*Biochemical analysis*]
PAL .... Positive Arming Link [*Military*]   (DNAB)
PAL .... Posterior Axillary Line [*Medicine*]
PAL .... Power Assist Lathe
PAL .... Pre-Academic Learning Inventory [*Child development test*]
PAL .... Preapproved Loan [*Business term*]
PAL .... Precision Artwork Language [*Data processing*]
PAL .... Preliminary Allowance List [*Military*]   (DNAB)
PAL .... Prescribed Action Link [*DoD*]
PAL .... Present Atmospheric Level
PAL .... Price and Availability List   (CINC)
PAL .... Princeton Accelerator Laboratory
PAL .... Princeton Air Link
PAL .... Prisoner-at-Large
PAL .... Privileged Architecture Library Code
PAL .... Pro Alesia [*A publication*]
PAL .... Problem Action Log   (AAG)
PAL .... Process Assembler Language
PAL .... Process Audit List   (MCD)
PAL .... Production and Application of Light   (MCD)

PAL .... Profile Automobile League   (EA)
PAL .... Programmable Algorithm Machine Assembly Language [*Data processing*]
PAL .... Programmable Array Logic [*Data processing*]   (IEEE)
PAL .... Programmed Application Library [*IBM Corp.*]
PAL .... Programmed Audit Library
PAL .... Programmer Assistance and Liaison [*Data processing*]   (NRCH)
PAL .... Progressive Alliance of Liberia [*Political party*]   (PPW)
PAL .... Prototype Application Loop [*Nuclear energy*]   (NRCH)
PAL .... Psycho-Acoustic Laboratory [*Harvard University*]   (MCD)
PAL .... Public Archives of Canada Library [*UTLAS symbol*]
PAL .... Publications Allowance List [*Military*]   (CAAL)
PAL .... Pulsed Argon LASER
PAL .... Push and Latch [*Push button*]
PA L .... University of Pennsylvania. Law Review [*A publication*]
PALA .... N-(Phosphoacetyl)-L-aspartate [*Biochemistry*]
Pala .... Partido Laborista [*Labor Party*] [*Panama*] [*Political party*]   (PPW)
PALA .... Partition Affinity Ligand Assay [*Analytical microbiology*]
PALA .... Passenger Acceptance and Load Accumulation [*Aviation*]
PALA .... Phosphonoacetyl-L-Aspartate [*Biochemistry*]
PALA .... Polish American Librarians Association   (EA)
PALA .... Prison Atheist League of America   (EA)
Palabra Hom ... Palabra y el Hombre [*A publication*]
PALAEOB ... Palaeobotany
Palaeoecol Afr Surround Isl ... Palaeoecology of Africa and the Surrounding Islands [*A publication*]
PALAEOG ... Palaeography
Palaeogeogr Palaeoclimatol Palaeoecol ... Palaeogeography, Palaeoclimatology, Palaeoecology [*A publication*]
Palaeogeo P ... Palaeogeography, Palaeoclimatology, Palaeoecology [*A publication*]
Palaeont ..... Palaeontographica [*A publication*]
PALAEONT ... Palaeontology
Palaeont Abh (Dames u Kayser) ... Palaeontologische Abhandlungen (Dames und Kayser) [*A publication*]
Palaeontogr Abt A ... Palaeontographica. Abteilung A. Palaeozoologie-Stratigraphie [*A publication*]
Palaeontogr Abt A Palaeozool-Stratigr ... Palaeontographica. Abteilung A. Palaeozoologie-Stratigraphie [*A publication*]
Palaeontogr Abt B ... Palaeontographica. Abteilung B. Palaeophytologie [*A publication*]
Palaeontogr Abt B Palaeophytol ... Palaeontographica. Abteilung B. Palaeophytologie [*A publication*]
Palaeontogr Am ... Palaeontographica Americana [*A publication*]
Palaeontogr Can ... Palaeontographica Canadiana [*A publication*]
Palaeontogr Ital ... Palaeontographica Italia [*A publication*]
Palaeontogr Soc Monogr ... Palaeontographical Society. Monographs [*A publication*]
Palaeontogr Soc Monogr (Lond) ... Palaeontographical Society. Monographs (London) [*A publication*]
Palaeontol Afr ... Palaeontologia Africana [*A publication*]
Palaeontol Jugosl ... Palaeontologia Jugoslavica [*A publication*]
Palaeontol Jugoslav ... Palaeontologia Jugoslavica [*A publication*]
Palaeontol Mex Inst Geol (Mex) ... Palaeontologia Mexicana. Instituto de Geologia (Mexico) [*A publication*]
Palaeontol Pap Publ Geol Surv Queensl ... Palaeontology Papers. Geological Survey of Queensland [*A publication*]   (APTA)
Palaeontol Pol ... Palaeontologia Polonica [*A publication*]
Palaeontol Sin Ser B ... Palaeontologia Sinica. Series B [*A publication*]
Palaeontol Sin Ser C ... Palaeontologia Sinica. Series C [*A publication*]
Palaeontol Sin Ser D ... Palaeontologia Sinica. Series D [*A publication*]
Palaeontol Soc Japan Trans Proc NS ... Palaeontological Society of Japan. Transactions and Proceedings. New Series [*A publication*]
Palaeontol Soc Jpn Spec Pap ... Palaeontological Society of Japan. Special Papers [*A publication*]
Palaeontol Stratigr Lithol ... Palaeontology, Stratigraphy, and Lithology [*A publication*]
Palaeont Soc Japan Trans and Proc ... Palaeontological Society of Japan. Transactions and Proceedings [*A publication*]
Palaeont Soc Mon ... Palaeontographical Society. Monographs [*A publication*]
Palaeovertebrata. Mem Extraordinaire ... Palaeovertebrata. Memoire Extraordinaire [*A publication*]
Palaeovertebr (Montp) ... Palaeovertebrata (Montpellier) [*A publication*]
Pal Ag .... Paley on Principal and Agent [*3rd ed.*] [*1833*] [*A publication*]   (DLA)
Pa Lang & Lit ... Papers on Language and Literature [*A publication*]
PALASM .. Programmable Array Logic Assembler [*Data processing*]   (IEEE)
Pa Law Finder ... Pennsylvania Law Finder [*A publication*]
PA Law J ... Pennsylvania Law Journal [*A publication*]   (DLA)
PA Law Jour ... Pennsylvania Law Journal [*Philadelphia*] [*A publication*]   (DLA)
PA Laws ..... Laws of the General Assembly of the Commonwealth of Pennsylvania [*A publication*]   (DLA)
Pa Laws ..... Laws of Pennsylvania [*A publication*]
PA Law Ser ... Pennsylvania Law Series [*A publication*]   (DLA)
PALAY .... Palabora Mining Cl A ADR [*NASDAQ symbol*]   (NQ)
PALB .... Animal Learning and Behavior [*A publication*]
Pal B .... Paleontological Bulletins [*A publication*]
PALC .... Passenger Acceptance and Load Control [*Aviation*]

PALC......... Point Arguello Launch Complex
PALC......... Precastable Autoclaved Lightweight Concrete [*Residential construction*]
PAL-C........ Profile of Adaptation to Life - Clinical [*Personality development test*] [*Psychology*]
PALCDR ... Annual Lightwood Research Conference. Proceedings [*A publication*]
PalCl......... Palestra del Clero [*Rovigo, Italy*] [*A publication*]
PALCO...... Pan American Liaison Committee of Women's Organizations   (EA)
PALCON... Pallet-Size Container   (MCD)
Pal Conv..... Paley on Summary Convictions [*10th ed.*] [*1953*] [*A publication*]   (DLA)
PALCOR ... Palestine Correspondence [*A publication*]
PALCR...... Propulsion Auxiliaries Local Control Rack   (DNAB)
PALCRU ... Pay and Allowances Accrue From [*Air Force*]
PALCS........ Permissive Action Link Cypher System   (MCD)
PAL-D .... Phase Alternation Line Delay   (IEEE)
PALDS ...... Point, Area, and Line Source with Deposition and Settling of Pollutants [*Air quality model*] [*Environmental Protection Agency*]   (GFGA)
PALE......... Pelvis and Legs Elevating [*Pilot seat*]
PA Leg Gaz ... Legal Gazette (Pennsylvania) [*A publication*]   (DLA)
PA Leg Gaz ... Legal Gazette Reports (Campbell) [*Pennsylvania*] [*A publication*]   (DLA)
PA Legis Serv ... Pennsylvania Legislative Service (Purdon) [*A publication*]   (DLA)
Pa Legis Serv (Purdon) ... Pennsylvania Legislative Service (Purdon) [*A publication*]
Paleobiol Cont ... Paleobiologie Continentale [*A publication*]
PALEOECOL ... Paleoecologic
paleog......... Paleography
PALEOGEOG ... Paleogeographic
Paleolimnol Lake Biwa Jpn Pleistocene ... Paleolimnology of Lake Biwa and the Japanese Pleistocene [*A publication*]
paleon........ Paleontology
PALEONT ... Paleontologic
Paleontol Evol-Barc Inst Prov Paleontol ... Paleontologia y Evolucion-Barcelona. Instituto Provincial de Paleontologia [*A publication*]
Paleontol J ... Paleontological Journal [*A publication*]
Paleontol J (Engl Transl Paleontol Zh) ... Paleontological Journal (English Translation of Paleontologicheskii Zhurnal) [*A publication*]
Paleontol Mex ... Paleontologia Mexicana [*A publication*]
Paleontol Soc Mem ... Paleontological Society. Memoir [*A publication*]
Paleontol Stratigr Litol ... Paleontologiya Stratigrafiya i Litologiya [*A publication*]
Paleont Pap Publs Geol Suv QD ... Paleontology Papers. Publications. Geological Survey of Queensland [*A publication*]   (APTA)
Paleont Research Lab Special Inv Rept ... Paleontological Research Laboratories. Special Investigation. Report [*A publication*]
Paleopathol Newsl ... Paleopathological Newsletter [*A publication*]
PalEQ .... Palestine Exploration Quarterly [*A publication*]
Palest Board Sci Ind Res Rep ... Palestine Board for Scientific and Industrial Research. Reports [*A publication*]
Palest Citrogr ... Palestine Citrograph [*A publication*]
Palest Econ ... Palestine Economist [*A publication*]
Palestine Explor Q ... Palestine Exploration Quarterly [*A publication*]
Palestine Explor Quart ... Palestine Exploration Quarterly [*A publication*]
Palest J Bot Hortic Sci ... Palestine Journal of Botany and Horticultural Science [*A publication*]
Palest J Bot Jerusalem Ser ... Palestine Journal of Botany. Jerusalem Series [*A publication*]
Palest J Bot Jerus Ser ... Palestine Journal of Botany. Jerusalem Series [*A publication*]
Palest J Bot Rehovot Ser ... Palestine Journal of Botany. Rehovot Series [*A publication*]
Palest Trib ... Palestine Tribune [*A publication*]
PALEX ...... Pacific Armies Look Exercise
Pal Expl Qu ... Palestine Exploration Quarterly [*London*] [*A publication*]
Pal Ex Q .... Palestine Exploration Quarterly [*A publication*]
Paley Ag..... Paley on Principal and Agent [*A publication*]   (DLA)
Paley Mor Ph ... [*William*] Paley's Moral Philosophy [*England*] [*A publication*]   (DLA)
Paley Princ & Ag ... Paley on Principal and Agent [*3rd ed.*] [*1833*] [*A publication*]   (DLA)
PA LG........ Legal Gazette (Pennsylvania) [*A publication*]   (DLA)
PA LG........ Legal Gazette Reports (Campbell) [*Pennsylvania*] [*A publication*]   (DLA)
Palg Ch ...... Palgrave's Proceedings in Chancery [*A publication*]   (DLA)
Palgrave..... Palgrave's Proceedings in Chancery [*A publication*]   (DLA)
Palgrave..... Palgrave's Rise and Progress of the English Commonwealth [*A publication*]   (DLA)
Palg Rise Etc ... Palgrave's Rise and Progress of the English Commonwealth [*A publication*]   (DLA)
Palg Rise & Prog ... Palgrave's Rise and Progress of the English Commonwealth [*1832*] [*A publication*]   (DLA)
PAL-H .... Profile of Adaptation to Life - Holistic [*Personality development test*] [*Psychology*]
PALI......... Pacific and Asian Linguistics Institute [*University of Hawaii*]
Pali........... Partido Liberal [*Nicaragua*] [*Political party*]   (EY)

PALI......... Prince Albert's Light Infantry [*Military unit*] [*British*]
PA Lib Assn Bull ... Pennsylvania Library Association. Bulletin [*A publication*]
PALIKA .... Parti de Liberation Kanak [*New Caledonia*] [*Political party*]   (EY)
PALINET ... Pennsylvania Area Library Network
PALINET/ULC ... PALINET and Union Library Catalogue of Pennsylvania [*Philadelphia, PA*] [*Library network*]
PALIS........ Property and Liability Information System
PalJ.......... Palaestina-Jahrbuch [*A publication*]
PA LJ........ Pennsylvania Law Journal [*A publication*]   (DLA)
PA LJ........ Pennsylvania Law Journal Reports [*1842-52*] [*A publication*]   (DLA)
PalJb.......... Palaestina-Jahrbuch [*A publication*]
PA LJR...... Clark's Pennsylvania Law Journal Reports [*A publication*]   (DLA)
PA LJ Rep ... Pennsylvania Law Journal-Reporter [*A publication*]
PALL........ Pallet [*Freight*]
Pall Mall M ... Pall Mall Magazine [*A publication*]
PALM........ PALFED, Inc. [*NASDAQ symbol*]   (NQ)
Palm.......... Palmer's Assizes at Cambridge [*England*] [*A publication*]
Palm.......... Palmer's English King's Bench Reports [*1619-29*] [*A publication*]   (DLA)
Palm.......... Palmer's Reports [*53-60 Vermont*] [*A publication*]   (DLA)
PALM........ Palmistry   (ADA)
Palm.......... Palmyrene   (BJA)
PALM........ Precision Altitude and Landing Monitor [*Aircraft location*]
Palm Comp L ... Palmer's Company Law [*22nd ed.*] [*1976*] [*A publication*]   (DLA)
Palm Comp Prec ... Palmer's Company Precedents [*17th ed.*] [*1956-60*] [*A publication*]   (DLA)
Palmer........ Palmer's Assizes at Cambridge [*England*] [*A publication*]   (DLA)
Palmer........ Palmer's English King's Bench Reports [*A publication*]   (DLA)
Palmer........ Palmer's Reports [*53-60 Vermont*] [*A publication*]   (DLA)
Palmer Co Prec ... Palmer's Company Precedents [*16 eds.*] [*1877-1952*] [*A publication*]   (DLA)
Palmer Pr Comp ... Palmer's Private Companies [*41st ed.*] [*1950*] [*A publication*]   (DLA)
Palm Pr Lords ... Palmer's Practice in the House of Lords [*1830*] [*A publication*]   (DLA)
PALMS ..... Provisioning Automated Logistics Material System   (MCD)
Palm Sh ..... Palmer's Shareholders [*34th ed.*] [*1936*] [*A publication*]   (DLA)
Palm Wr..... Palmer's Law of Wreck [*1843*] [*A publication*]   (DLA)
PALO .... Phosphonoacetyl-L-Ornithine [*Biochemistry*]
PALO .... Port Amenities Liaison Officer [*British*]   (DSUE)
PALOS ...... Pacific Logistic Operations - Streamline [*Army*]
PALP........ Palpable [*Medicine*]
PALP........ Pyridoxal Phosphate [*Also, PLP*] [*Biochemistry*]
PALPI........ Palpitation [*Medicine*]
palpit......... Palpitation [*Medicine*]
PALR........ Permissive Action Link Report [*Army*]   (AABC)
PA L Rec ... Pennsylvania Law Record [*A publication*]   (DLA)
PA L Rev.... University of Pennsylvania. Law Review [*A publication*]
PALS .... [*Child's*] Parental Authority-Love Statement   (AEBS)
PALS .... Patient Advocacy Legal Service [*An association*] [*Defunct*]   (EA)
PA LS .... Pennsylvania Law Series [*A publication*]   (DLA)
PALS .... People Against Loneliness [*British*]   (DI)
PALS .... Periarteriolar Lymphocyte Sheath   (AAMN)
PALS .... Permissive Action Link System [*Army*]
PALS .... Phase Alternation Line Simple [*TV decoding system*]
PALS .... Photo Area and Location System   (NASA)
PALS .... Point Arguello Launch Site   (AAG)
PALS .... Precision Approach and Landing System   (NASA)
PALS .... Prestaged Ammunition Loading System [*Army*]   (RDA)
PALS .... Principle of the Alphabet Literacy System [*Software*] [*IBM Corp.*]
PALS .... Protection Against Limited Strikes [*Military defence system*]
PALSD ...... Program: Automated Library and Information Systems [*A publication*]
PA L Ser .... Pennsylvania Law Series [*A publication*]   (DLA)
PALS-G..... Passive Artillery Locating System - Ground Based   (MCD)
PALSG ...... Personnel and Logistics Systems Group [*Army*]   (AABC)
PALSGR.... Palsgrave Dictionary [*A publication*]
PA-LS-ID.. Pernicious Anemia-Like Syndrome and Immunoglobulin Deficiency [*Hematology*]   (AAMN)
PALST....... Picture Articulation and Screening Test
PAlt........... Altoona Area Public Library, Altoona, PA [*Library symbol*] [*Library of Congress*]   (LCLS)
PALT........ Present Altitude [*Aviation*]   (FAAC)
PALT........ Procurement Administrative Lead Time
PALTREU .. Palaestina Treuhandstelle zur Beratung Deutscher Juden [*A publication*]
PALU........ Cape Lisburne Air Force Station [*Alaska*] [*ICAO location identifier*]   (ICLI)
PALU........ Progressive Arbeiders- en Landbouwersunie [*Progressive Workers' and Farm Laborers' Union*] [*Surinam*] [*Political party*]   (PPW)

Palud......... Paludonus [*Pierre de la Palu*] [*Deceased, 1342*] [*Authority cited in pre-1607 legal work*] (DSA)
PALV......... Passiflora Latent Virus [*Plant pathology*]
Palyaval Tanacs ... Palyavalasztasi Tanacsadas [*A publication*]
Palynol Bull ... Palynological Bulletin [*A publication*]
PAM......... Palermo [*California*] [*Seismograph station code, US Geological Survey*] (SEIS)
PAM......... Pamida Holdings Corp. [*AMEX symbol*] (SPSG)
PAM......... Pamour, Inc. [*Toronto Stock Exchange symbol*]
Pam........... Pampa [*Record label*] [*Brazil*]
PAM......... Pamphlet (AFM)
PAM......... Panama City, FL [*Location identifier*] [*FAA*] (FAAL)
PAM......... Panoramic
PAM......... Parameter Adjusting Mechanism
PAM......... Parametric Amplifier (NATG)
PAM......... Parents Against Molesters (EA)
PAM......... Partial Mobilization Expansion Plan [*Army*] (GFGA)
PAM......... Partitioned Access Method [*Data processing*]
PAM......... Payload Assist Module [*NASA*] (MCD)
PAM......... Penetration Augmented Munition
PAM......... Penicillin Aluminum Monostearate [*Antibiotic*]
PA M........ Pennsylvania Magazine of History and Biography [*A publication*]
PAM......... People's Action Movement [*Nevis*] [*Political party*] (PPW)
PAM......... People's Anti-War Mobilization (EA)
PAM......... Performance Analysis Model (MCD)
PAM......... Performance Assessment Monitoring (MCD)
PAM......... Performing Arts Medicine
PAM......... Peripheral Adapter Module
PAM......... Personal Accounting Management
PAM......... Personal Applications Manager [*Hewlett-Packard Co.*]
PAM......... Personnel Action Memorandum [*Military*]
PAM......... Phase-Amplitude Modulation
PAM......... Phased Array Module
PAM......... Phenylalanine Mustard (AAMN)
PAM......... Philosophies, Ancient and Modern [*A publication*]
PAM......... Phoenix Airborne Missile
PAM......... Pittsburgh, Allegheny & McKees Rocks Railroad Co. [*AAR code*]
PAM......... Planning, Activation, Modification [*Army reorganization*]
PAM......... Plasma-Arc Machining [*Manufacturing term*]
PAM......... Pledged Account Mortgage
PAM......... Pole Amplitude Modulation (IEEE)
PAM......... Polyacrylamide [*Also, PAA, PAAM*] [*Organic chemistry*]
PAM......... Portable Alpha Monitor
PAM......... Portable Automated Mesonet [*Meteorology*]
PAM......... Position and Altitude Monitor (MCD)
PAM......... Post-Accident Monitoring [*Nuclear energy*] (NRCH)
PAM......... Postacceptance Modification
PAM......... Potential Acuity Meter [*Instrumentation*]
PAM......... Power Assist Module [*NASA*]
PAM......... Pozzolan Aggregate Mixture (OA)
PAM......... Pralidoxime Methiodide [*Biochemistry*]
PAM......... Presbyterian Association of Musicians (EA)
PAM......... Pressure-Acoustic-Magnetic [*Minesweeping system*] (DNAB)
PAM......... Primary Access Method [*Sperry UNIVAC*]
PAM......... Primary Acquired Melanosis [*Oncology*]
PAM......... Primary Amoebic Meningitis [*or Meningoencephalitis*] [*Medicine*]
PAM......... Primary Auxiliary Memory [*Unit*] [*Data processing*] (MCD)
PAM......... Priorities and Allocations Manual [*Army*] (AABC)
PAM......... Process Automation Monitor [*Texas Instruments, Inc.*]
PAM......... Processor and Memory [*Data processing*]
PAM......... Procurement Aids Man [*Marine Corps*]
PAM......... Procurement of Aircraft and Missiles
PAM......... Program Analysis Memorandum (MCD)
PA-M........ Program Authorization - Map [*Military*] (AFIT)
PAM......... Program Automated Method [*Data processing*]
PAM......... Programmable Algorithm Machine [*Data processing*]
PAM......... Propulsion Assistance Module (MCD)
PAM......... Pulmonary Alveolar Macrophage [*Attacks inhaled particles*]
PAM......... Pulmonary Alveolar Microlithiasis [*Medicine*] (MAE)
PAM......... Pulse-Address MODEM
PAM......... Pulse Amplitude Modulation [*Electronics*]
PAM......... Pyridine Aldoxime Methiodide [*Biochemistry*]
PAM......... Pyridine Aldoxime Methyl [*Pharmacology*]
PAM......... University of Pennsylvania, School of Medicine, Philadelphia, PA [*OCLC symbol*] (OCLC)
PAm........... Wissahickon Valley Public Library, Ambler, PA [*Library symbol*] [*Library of Congress*] (LCLS)
PAMA....... American Antiquity [*A publication*]
PAM-A...... PAM [*Payload Assist Module*] Atlas-Centaur Class Spacecraft (NASA)
Pam A........ Pamatky Archeologicke [*A publication*]
PAMA....... Pan American Medical Association [*Also known as Association Medica Pan Americana*] (EA)
PAMA....... Para-Dimethylaminophenylazopyridine [*An indicator*] [*Chemistry*]
PAM-A...... Payload Assist Module - Atlas Class Spacecraft (MCD)
PAMA....... Polish Alma Mater of America (EA)
PAMA....... Professional Aviation Maintenance Association (EA)

PAMA ...... Pulse-Address Multiple Access [*Satellite communications*]
PAMAC.... Parts and Materials Accountability Control
P Am Ac Ins ... Proceedings. American Academy and Institute of Arts and Letters [*A publication*]
PAMAD .... Parents Against Middle-Aged Discrimination [*British*] (DI)
PA Mag Hist ... Pennsylvania Magazine of History and Biography [*A publication*]
PA Mag Hist Biogr ... Pennsylvania Magazine of History and Biography [*A publication*]
PAMAI...... Program of Action for Mediation, Arbitration, and Inquiry [*American Library Association*]
PAMAM ... Polyamidoamine [*Organic chemistry*]
P Am Antiq ... Proceedings. American Antiquarian Society [*A publication*]
P Am Ass Ca ... Proceedings. American Association for Cancer Research [*A publication*]
Pamatky Prir ... Pamatky a Priroda [*A publication*]
PAMB....... American Behavioral Scientist [*A publication*]
PAMB....... Pressure Ambient (NASA)
PAMC ...... McGrath [*Alaska*] [*ICAO location identifier*] (ICLI)
PAMC ...... Pakistan Army Medical Corps
PAMC ...... Provident American Corp. [*Norristown, PA*] [*NASDAQ symbol*] (NQ)
PAMC ...... Provisional Acceptable Means of Compliance (MCD)
PAmC .... Temple University, Ambler Campus, Ambler, PA [*Library symbol*] [*Library of Congress*] (LCLS)
P Am Cath P ... Proceedings. American Catholic Philosophical Association [*A publication*]
PAMCCS .. Prior Active Marine Corps Commissioned Service
PAMCES .. Prior Active Marine Corps Enlisted Service
PAMCI...... Pyridinealdoxime Methochloride [*Organic chemistry*]
PAMCS ..... Phoenix Airborne Missile Control System
PAM-D...... PAM [*Payload Assist Module*] Delta Class Spacecraft (NASA)
PAM-D...... Payload Assist Module - Delta Class Spacecraft (MCD)
PAMD ...... Periodic Acid Mixed Diamine (OA)
PAMD ...... Price and Management Data
PAMD ...... Process Automation Monitor/Disk Version [*Texas Instruments, Inc.*]
PAMDA .... Progress in Atomic Medicine [*A publication*]
Pam Div Wood Technol For Comm NSW ... Pamphlet. Division of Wood Technology. Forestry Commission. New South Wales [*A publication*] (APTA)
PAMDS..... Price and Management Data Section [*of a stock list*] [*Navy*]
PAME....... Pandemokratiki Agrotikon Metapon Ellados [*Pan-Democratic Agrarian Front of Greece*] [*Political party*] (PPE)
PAME....... Primary Amoebic Meningoencephalitis [*Medicine*]
P/AMEA2 ... Probationary Marine Engineering Artificer, Acting, 2nd Class [*British military*] (DMA)
PA Med..... Pennsylvania Medicine [*A publication*]
PA Med J .. Pennsylvania Medical Journal [*A publication*]
PAMETON ... Paracetamol and Methionine [*Pain-relief drug*]
PAMF....... American Forests [*A publication*]
PAMF....... Portable Arc Melting Furnace
PAM-FM .. Pulse Amplitude Modulation - Frequency Modulation [*Electronics*]
PAmh........ Amherst Papyri [*A publication*] (OCD)
PAMHLD ... Pamida Holdings Corp. [*Associated Press abbreviation*] (APAG)
PAMI........ Personnel Accounting Machine Installation
PAMI........ Prairie Agricultural Machinery Institute [*Canada*]
PAMI........ Professional Arts Management Institute (EA)
Pamiet Konf Nauk Otolaryngol Dzieciecej Zakopane ... Pamietnik Konferencji Naukowej Otolaryngologii Dzieciecej Zakopane [*A publication*]
Pamietnik L ... Pamietnik Literacki [*A publication*]
Pamiet Pulawski ... Pamietnik Pulawski [*A publication*]
Pamiet Zjazdu Otolaryngol Pol Katowicach ... Pamietnik Zjazdu Otolaryngologow Polskich w Katowicach [*A publication*]
PAMII....... Protection and Advocacy for Mentally Ill Individuals Act [*1986*]
Pam Iowa State Univ Sci Tech Coop Ext Serv ... Pamphlet. Iowa State University of Science and Technology. Cooperative Extension Service [*A publication*]
PAMIS ...... Processing and Manufacturing in Space [*European Space Agency*]
PAMIS ...... Psychological Operations Automated Management Information System (MCD)
PA Misc..... Pennsylvania Miscellaneous Reports [*A publication*] (DLA)
PamL .... Pamietnik Literacki [*A publication*]
PAMLPU .. Pianoforte Action Makers' Labour Protection Union [*British*]
P Am Math S ... Proceedings. American Mathematical Society [*A publication*]
PAMN .... American Midland Naturalist [*A publication*]
PAMN .... Procurement Aircraft and Missiles, Navy [*An appropriation*]
PAMO ...... Pacific Air Management Office [*Military*]
PAMO ...... Port Air Materiel Office
PAMP....... Pampero [*River Plate gale*] [*Nautical term*] (DSUE)
PAMPA..... Pacific Area Movement Priority Agency [*Military*]
PamPAC.... Pamela's Political Action Committee [*Nickname of "Democrats for the '80's," a committee founded by Pamela Harriman*]
PAMPER .. Practical Application of Mid-Points for Exponential Regression
PAMPH .... Pamphlet [*Freight*]
Pamph........ Pamphleteer [*A publication*]

Pamph Amat Ent Soc ... Pamphlet. Amateur Entomologists' Society [*A publication*]
Pamph Dep Agric (Qd) ... Pamphlet. Department of Agriculture (Queensland) [*A publication*]
Pamph Dep Agric (Tanganyika) ... Pamphlet. Department of Agriculture (Tanganyika Territory) [*A publication*]
Pamph Dep Agric Un S Afr ... Pamphlet. Department of Agriculture. Union of South Africa [*A publication*]
Pamph Div Sci Publs Volcani Cent Agric Res Orgn ... Pamphlet. Division of Scientific Publications. Volcani Center. Agricultural Research Organisation [*A publication*]
Pamph Div Wood Technol For Comm NSW ... Pamphlet. Division of Wood Technology. Forestry Commission. New South Wales [*A publication*]   (APTA)
Pamph Idaho Bur Mines Geol ... Pamphlet. Idaho Bureau of Mines and Geology [*A publication*]
P Am Phil S ... Proceedings. American Philosophical Society [*A publication*]
Pamph Laws ... Pamphlet Laws, Acts [*A publication*]   (DLA)
Pamphlet Archre ... Pamphlet Architecture [*A publication*]
Pamphl For Res Educ Proj For Dep (Sudan) ... Pamphlet. Forestry Research and Education Project. Forests Department (Khartoum, Sudan) [*A publication*]
Pamphl Laws ... Pamphlet Laws, Acts [*A publication*]   (DLA)
Pamph Volcani Inst Agric Res ... Pamphlet. Volcani Institute of Agricultural Research [*A publication*]
PAMPS ..... Poly(Acrylamidomethyl Propane) Sulphonic Acid [*Organic chemistry*]
Pam Pulaw ... Pamietnik Pulawski [*A publication*]
Pam Pulawski ... Pamietnik Pulawski [*A publication*]
PAMPUS .. Photons for Atomic and Molecular Processes and Universal Studies [*Physics*]
PAMR .... Anchorage/Merrill Field [*Alaska*] [*ICAO location identifier*]   (ICLI)
PAMREA ... Proceedings. American Association for Cancer Research. Annual Meeting [*A publication*]
PAMRF ..... Palo Alto Medical Research Foundation [*Research center*]   (RCD)
PAMRS ..... Parameter Adaptive Model Reference System
PAMS .... North-Holland Series in Probability and Applied Mathematics [*Elsevier Book Series*] [*A publication*]
PAMS .... Pacific Armies Management Seminar
PAMS .... Pad Abort Measuring System [*NASA*]   (KSC)
PAMS .... Papers. American Musicological Society [*A publication*]
PAMS .... Portable Acoustic Monitoring System
PAMS .... Post-Accident Monitoring System [*Nuclear energy*]   (NRCH)
PAMS .... Predictive Aircraft Maintenance System
PAMS .... Preselected Alternate Master-Slave [*Telecommunications*]   (TEL)
PAMS .... Proceedings. American Mathematical Society [*A publication*]
PAMS .... Procurement Action Management System   (MCD)
PAMS .... Public Access Message System
PAMSB ..... Pharos of Alpha Omega Alpha Honor Medical Society [*A publication*]
P Am S Info ... Proceedings. American Society for Information Science [*A publication*]
PamSL .... Pamietnik Slowianski Czasopismo Naukowe Posiecone Slowianoznawstwu [*A publication*]
PAMTGG ... Pan Am Makes the Going Great [*Title of ballet choreographed by George Balanchine, taken from Pan American World Airways' slogan*] [*Pronounced "pam-ti-guh-guh"*]
PAMUSA ... Post-Attack Mobilization of the United States Army
PAMV .... Petunia Asteroid Mosaic Virus [*Plant pathology*]
PAMWA ... Pan American Medical Women's Alliance   (EA)
PAMWS .... Proceedings. Annual Meeting. Western Society for French History [*A publication*]
PAMX .... Pancho's Mexican Buffet, Inc. [*NASDAQ symbol*]   (NQ)
PAMYA ..... Proceedings. American Mathematical Society [*A publication*]
PAN .... National Action Party [*Mexico*] [*Political party*]   (PD)
PAN .... Packaging News [*A publication*]
PAN .... Pagans Against Nukes [*British*]   (DI)
PAN .... Paladin Fuel Technology [*Vancouver Stock Exchange symbol*]
Pan .... Panache [*A publication*]
PAN .... Panama [*ANSI three-letter standard code*]   (CNC)
PAN .... Panchromatic   (DEN)
Pan .... Panegyricus [*of Pliny the Younger*] [*Classical studies*]   (OCD)
PAN .... Paneled   (WGA)
PAN .... Panimavida [*Chile*] [*Seismograph station code, US Geological Survey*] [*Closed*]   (SEIS)
PAN .... Panis [*Bread*] [*Pharmacy*]   (ROG)
pan .... Panjabi [*MARC language code*] [*Library of Congress*]   (LCCP)
Pan .... Panorama [*A publication*]
PAN .... Panoramic   (MSA)
Pan .... Panormitanus [*Nicholas de Tudeschis*] [*Deceased, 1445*] [*Authority cited in pre-1607 legal work*]   (DSA)
Pan .... Pantheon [*Record label*] [*France, etc.*]
PAN .... Pantry   (MSA)
PAN .... Partido de Accion Nacional [*Nicaragua*] [*Political party*]   (EY)
PAN .... Pastoral Music Notebook [*A publication*]
PAN .... Pattani [*Thailand*] [*Airport symbol*]   (OAG)
PAN .... Peace Action Network   (EA)

PAN .... Pennsylvania Animal Network [*Coalition operated by Trans-Species Unlimited*]
PAN .... Pennsylvania Association of Notaries   (EA)
PAN .... Performing Artists Network [*Electronic network*]
PAN .... Periarteritis Nodosa [*Also, PN*] [*Medicine*]
PAN .... Periodic Alternating Nystagmus [*Ophthalmology*]
PAN .... Peroxyacetyl Nitrate [*Lacrimator*]
PAN .... Pesticides Action Network   (EA)
PAN .... Polled Access Network
PAN .... Polska Akademia Nauk [*Polish Academy of Sciences*] [*Also, an information service or system*]   (IID)
PAN .... Polyacrylonitrile [*Organic chemistry*]
PAN .... Polyarteritis Nodosa [*Medicine*]
PAN .... Positional Alcohol Nystagmus [*Physiology*]
PAN .... Primary Account Number [*Business term*]
PAN .... Project Authorization Notice   (MCD)
PAN .... Propodial Anlage [*Zoology*]
PAN .... Publications Account Number [*DoD*]
PAN .... Pyridylazonaphthol [*An indicator*] [*Chemistry*]
PAN .... Switchboard Panel [*Telecommunications*]   (TEL)
PanA .... Pan-Africanist [*A publication*]
PanA .... Pan American Corp. [*Associated Press abbreviation*]   (APAG)
PANA .... Pan-Asia News Agency Ltd. [*Also, PANASIA*] [*Hong Kong*]
PANA .... PanAfrican News Agency   (EAIO)
PANA .... Polish-American Numismatic Association   (EA)
PANABANK ... Banco Panamericano [*Panama*]   (EY)
PANAGRA ... Pan American Grace Airways, Inc. [*Also, PAGA*]
PANAIR .... Panama Air Lines
PANAL ...... Papuan National Alliance [*Political party*]   (PPW)
PANALU ... Parti National Lumumba [*Lumumba National Party*] [*Political party*]
PAN-AM ... Pan American World Airways, Inc. [*See also PA, PAA, PN*]
Panama Admin Recursos Minerales Mapa ... Republica de Panama. Administracion de Recursos Minerales. Mapa [*A publication*]
PANAMAC ... Pan American World Airways Communications System
Panama Univ Dept Geografia Pub ... Panama Universidad. Departamento de Geografia. Publicacion [*A publication*]
Pan Am Fisherman ... Pan American Fisherman [*A publication*]
Pan Am Health Organ Off Doc ... Pan American Health Organization. Official Document [*A publication*]
Pan Am Health Organ Res Prog ... Pan American Health Organization. Research in Progress [*A publication*]
Pan Am Health Organ Sci Publ ... Pan American Health Organization. Scientific Publication [*A publication*]
Pan-Am Inst Geography and History Pub ... Pan-American Institute of Geography and History. Publication [*A publication*]
Pan Am Inst Min Eng Geol US Sect Tech Pap ... Pan American Institute of Mining Engineering and Geology. United States Section. Technical Paper [*A publication*]
Pan Am M ... Pan American Magazine [*A publication*]
PanAmSat ... Pan American Satellite [*Greenwich, CT*] [*Telecommunications service*]   (TSSD)
Pan-Am TS ... Pan-American Treaty Series [*A publication*]   (DLA)
Pan Am Union Bol Ciencia y Tecnologia ... Pan American Union. Boletin de Ciencia y Tecnologia [*A publication*]
Pan Am Union Bul ... Pan American Union. Bulletin [*A publication*]
Pan Am Womans J ... Pan American Woman's Journal [*A publication*]
PanAR .... Pan American Review [*A publication*]
PANAR ..... Panoramic RADAR
PANASIA ... Organization of Pan Asian American Women   (EA)
PANASIA ... Pan-Asia News Agency Ltd. [*Also, PANA*] [*Hong Kong*]
PANB .... Panic Bolt
PANC .... Anchorage/International [*Alaska*] [*ICAO location identifier*]   (ICLI)
PANC .... Pasta & Cheese, Inc. [*Long Island City, NY*] [*NASDAQ symbol*]   (NQ)
PANC .... Power Amplifier Neutralizing Capacitor   (DEN)
PANCAN .. [*The*] Panama Canal
PANCANCO ... Panama Canal Co. [*Superseded by Panama Canal Commission*]
PANCAP ... Practical Annual Capacity [*FAA*]
P de Ancha ... Petrus de Ancharano [*Deceased, 1416*] [*Authority cited in pre-1607 legal work*]   (DSA)
Pancir .... [*Guido*] Pancirolus [*Deceased, 1599*] [*Authority cited in pre-1607 legal work*]   (DSA)
Pancirol ...... [*Guido*] Pancirolus [*Deceased, 1599*] [*Authority cited in pre-1607 legal work*]   (DSA)
PANCO ..... Procurement Aids Noncommissioned Officer [*Marine Corps*]
Pand .... [*The*] Pandects [*A publication*]   (DLA)
PAND .... Pandering [*FBI standardized term*]
PAND .... Passive Air Navigation Device
PAND .... Performing Artists for Nuclear Disarmament   (EA)
PANDA ..... Portable Array for Numerical Data Acquisition [*Instrumentation*]
PANDA ..... Prestel Advanced Network Design Architecture
Pand B .... Pandectes Belges [*A publication*]
Pandect Flor ... Pandectae Florentinae [*A publication*]   (DSA)
PANDEX ... Name of an all-inclusive index covering fields of science, technology and medicine; composed of Greek prefix Pan meaning all and -Dex from word index

Pand Flo..... Pandectae Florentinae [*A publication*]   (DSA)
PANDLCHAR ... Pay and Allowances Chargeable
PANDORA ... Passive and Active Signal Digital Correlator Analyzer   (MCD)
PANDS..... Pay and Supply [*Coast Guard*]
PANDS..... Print and Search Processor [*Data processing*]
PANE .... Park News [*A publication*]
PANE .... Performance Analysis of Networks, Electrical
PanEC........ Panhandle Eastern Corp. [*Associated Press abbreviation*]   (APAG)
Paneg .... Panegyricus [*of Isocrates*] [*Classical studies*]   (OCD)
panendo..... Panendoscopy [*Medicine*]
PAN/ES .... Estudios Latinoamericanos. Polska Akademia Nauk [*A publication*]
PANES ..... Prior Active Navy Enlisted Service
PANES ...... Program for Analysis of Nonlinear Equilibrium and Stability [*NASA*]
PANF........ Plan Account Number File [*IRS*]
PANFI....... Precision Automatic Noise Figure Indicator
PANGCS... Prior Active National Guard Commissioned Service
PANGES... Prior Active National Guard Enlisted Service
PANGIS .... Pan-African Network for a Geological Information System [*UNESCO*]   (DUND)
PANH....... Panhandling [*FBI standardized term*]
PANH........ Picolinaldehyde Nicotinoylhydrazone [*Reagent*]
Panhandle Geol Soc Strat Cross Sec ... Panhandle Geological Society. Stratigraphic Cross Section [*A publication*]
PANHONLIB ... Panama, Honduras, and Liberia [*Acronym used to refer to merchant ships operating under "flags of convenience"*]
PANI .... Patriarch Athenagoras National Institute   (EA)
PANIC....... Planned Attack on Nine Inner Cities [*to build education parks*]
Pan Indian Ocean Sci Congr Proc Sect D Agr Sci ... Pan Indian Ocean Science Congress. Proceedings. Section D. Agricultural Sciences [*A publication*]
Panjab Univ (Chandigarh) Cent Adv Stu Geol Publ ... Panjab University (Chandigarh). Centre of Advanced Study in Geology. Publication [*A publication*]
Panj C .... Panjab Code [*India*] [*A publication*]   (DLA)
Pank Jur .... Pankhurst's Jurisprudence [*A publication*]   (DLA)
PAnL.......... Lebanon Valley College, Annville, PA [*Library symbol*] [*Library of Congress*]   (LCLS)
PANL .... PanelGraphic Corp. [*NASDAQ symbol*]   (CTT)
PANLAR... PanAmerican League Against Rheumatism [*Canada*]   (EAIO)
PANLIBHON ... Panama, Liberia, and Honduras [*Acronym used to refer to merchant ships operating under "flags of convenience"*]
PANLIBHONCO ... Panama-Liberia-Honduras-Costa Rica
Panminerva Med ... Panminerva Medica [*A publication*]
PANMV .... Panicum Mosaic Virus [*Plant pathology*]
PANNAP... Panavia New Aircraft Project   (MCD)
PANNDA.. Precedent Analysis by Nearest Neighbor Discriminant Analysis
PANNR ..... Previous Applicants Need Not Reapply [*Civil Service*]
Panor.......... Panormitanus [*Nicholas de Tudeschis*] [*Deceased, 1445*] [*Authority cited in pre-1607 legal work*]   (DSA)
Panorama Democr Chr ... Panorama Democrate Chretien [*A publication*]
Panorama Econ (Chile) 2a Epoca ... Panorama Economico (Chile). Segunda Epoca [*A publication*]
Panorama Econ (Mexico) ... Panorama Economico (Mexico) [*A publication*]
Panorama M Instruments ... Panorama de la Musique et des Instruments [*A publication*]
PA NP........ Brightly's Pennsylvania Nisi Prius Reports [*A publication*]   (DLA)
PANP .... Pan Petroleum Master LP [*NASDAQ symbol*]   (NQ)
PANPA...... Pacific Area Newspaper Publishers Association   (EAIO)
Pan-Pac Ent ... Pan-Pacific Entomologist [*A publication*]
Pan-Pac Entomol ... Pan-Pacific Entomologist [*A publication*]
Pan-Pacif Ent ... Pan-Pacific Entomologist [*A publication*]
Pan Pipes ... Pan Pipes of Sigma Alpha Iota [*A publication*]
PANPRA... Parti Nationaliste Progressiste Revolutionnaire [*Haiti*] [*Political party*]   (EY)
Pan i Prawo ... Panstwo i Prawo [*A publication*]
PANPUB... Panel Publishers   (DLA)
PANR .... Antioch Review [*A publication*]
P An Rel M ... Proceedings. Annual Reliability and Maintainability Symposium [*A publication*]
PANS........ Ageing and Society [*A publication*]
PANS........ Pest Articles News Summaries [*Commonwealth Mycological Institute*] [*Kew, England*] [*A publication*]
PANS........ Positioning and Navigation System
PANS........ Procedures for Air Navigation Services [*ICAO*]
PANS........ Programmable Augmented Noise Source [*Military*]   (CAAL)
PANS........ Puromycin Aminonucleoside [*Biochemistry*]
PANSDOC ... Pakistan National Scientific and Documentation Center [*Later, PASTIC*]
PANSEAFRON ... Panama Sea Frontier
PANSMET ... Procedures for Air Navigation Services - Meteorology   (IEEE)
PANS Pest Artic News Summ ... PANS. Pest Articles and News Summaries [*A publication*]
Panstw Sluzba Geol Panstw Inst Geol Biul ... Panstwowa Sluzba Geologiczna. Pantswowy Instytut. Geologiczny Biuletyn [*A publication*]
PANT .... Annette Island [*Alaska*] [*ICAO location identifier*]   (ICLI)
PANT .... Pantera's Corp. [*NASDAQ symbol*]   (NQ)
PANT .... Pantograph   (KSC)

pant .... Pantomine
Panta J Med ... Panta Journal of Medicine [*A publication*]
PANTDK... Progress in Anatomy [*A publication*]
PANTIES ... Passive Automatic Nighttime Tracking Investigation and Evaluation Studies [*DoD*]
PAntin........ [*The*] Antinoe Papyrus of Theocritus [*Classical studies*]   (OCD)
PAntinoop ... Antinoopolis Papyri [*A publication*]   (OCD)
PantiP .... Peroxidase-Antiperoxidase [*Immunochemistry*]
Pantnagar J Res ... Pantnagar Journal of Research [*A publication*]
PANTO ..... Pantomime
pantrop...... Pantropical [*Botany*]
PANTS...... Pantaloons   (DSUE)
PA Nurse ... Pennsylvania Nurse [*A publication*]
PANW....... Pan-Western Corp. [*NASDAQ symbol*]   (NQ)
PANX .... Panex Industries [*NASDAQ symbol*]   (NQ)
PANY .... Platinumsmiths Association of New York   (EA)
PANY .... Port Authority of New York [*Later, PANYNJ*]
PANYNJ... Port Authority of New York and New Jersey [*Formerly, PANY*]
Panz Ann ... Panzer Annales [*A publication*]
PAO.......... Palo Alto, CA [*Location identifier*] [*FAA*]   (FAAL)
PAO.......... Paotow [*Republic of China*] [*Seismograph station code, US Geological Survey*]   (SEIS)
PAO.......... Paramount Resources, Inc. [*Vancouver Stock Exchange symbol*]
PaO.......... Paranoia Obvious [*Psychology*]
PAO.......... Peacetime Acquisition Objective [*DoD*]   (AFIT)
PAO.......... Peak Acid Output [*Physiology*]
PAO.......... Penalty Appeals Officer [*IRS*]
PA/O........ Performing Arts/Omaha [*Nebraska*]
PAO.......... Phenylarsine Oxide
PAO.......... Pinellas Area Office [*Energy Research and Development Administration*]
PAO.......... Polyalkyleneoxide [*Organic chemistry*]
PAO.......... Polyalphaolefin [*Organic chemistry*]
PAO.......... Primary Action Office [*or Officer*] [*Army*]
PAO.......... Prince Albert's Own [*Military unit*] [*British*]
PAO.......... Principal Administrative Officer
PAO.......... Pro Athletes Outreach   (EA)
PAO.......... Product Activity/Operational Code   (MCD)
PAO.......... Product Assurance Operations [*Army*]
PAO.......... Program Action Officer [*Navy*]   (CAAL)
PAO.......... Project Action Officer [*Air Force*]   (AFIT)
PAO.......... Project Administration Officer [*Military*]   (AFIT)
PAO.......... Property Action Order
PAO.......... Public Affairs Office [*NASA*]
PAO.......... Public Affairs Officer [*Embassies*]
PAO.......... Pulsed Avalanche Diode Oscillator [*Telecommunications*]   (IEEE)
PAOA .... Pan American Odontological Association   (EA)
PAOC .... Pakistan Army Ordnance Corps [*British military*]   (DMA)
PAOC .... Pan-African Ornithological Congress
PAOC .... Pentacostal Assemblies of Canada
PAOC .... Pollution Abatement Operations Center   (MCD)
PAOC .... Principal Administrative Officers Committee [*Chiefs of Staff*] [*World War II*]
PAOD .... Peripheral Arteriosclerotic Occlusive Disease [*Medicine*]   (MAE)
P/AOEA2 ... Probationary Ordnance Electrical Artificer, Acting, 2nd Class [*British military*]   (DMA)
PAOL .... Poly-alpha-olefin [*Organic chemistry*]
PAOM .... Nome [*Alaska*] [*ICAO location identifier*]   (ICLI)
PAOP .... Pulmonary Artery Occlusion Pressure [*Cardiology*]
PAOR .... Northway [*Alaska*] [*ICAO location identifier*]   (ICLI)
PAORB...... Problemes Actuels d'Oto-Rhino-Laryngologie [*A publication*]
PAOS........ Proceedings. American Oriental Society [*A publication*]
PAOT .... Kotzebue [*Alaska*] [*ICAO location identifier*]   (ICLI)
PAOT .... Persons at One Time
PAOTA ...... Problemes Actuels d'Ophtalmologie [*A publication*]
P/AP......... Painter/Apprentice Painter   (AAG)
PAP........... Papain [*An enzyme*]
PAP........... Papanicolaou [*Diagnosis, smear, stain, or test*] [*Medicine*]
PAP........... Paper   (DSUE)
PAP........... Paper Bound [*Books*]   (ROG)
pap .... Papilla [*Medicine*]
Pap .... [*Aemilius*] Papinianus [*Deceased, 212*] [*Authority cited in pre-1607 legal work*]   (DSA)
PAP........... Papyrologica [*A publication*]
Pap .... Papyrus   (BJA)
PAP........... Para-Aminophenol [*Organic chemistry*]
PAP........... Parallel Applications Programme [*British*]
PAP........... Parti d'Action Paysanne [*Farmers Actions Party*] [*Burkina Faso*] [*Political party*]
PAP........... Participatory Anthropic Principle [*Term coined by authors John Barrow and Frank Tipler in their book, "The Anthropic Cosmological Principle"*]
PAP........... Partido Accion Popular [*Popular Action Party*] [*Ecuador*] [*Political party*]
PAP........... Partido Accion Popular [*Popular Action Party*] [*Peru*] [*Political party*]
PaP........... Past and Present [*A publication*]
PAP........... Patrol Amphibian Plane

PaP............ Patterns of Prejudice [*A publication*]
PAP........... Paulin [*H.*] & Co. Ltd. [*Toronto Stock Exchange symbol*]
PAP........... Payload Activity Planner [*NASA*]
PAP........... Peak Airway Pressure [*Physiology*]
PAP.......... Pension Administration Plan [*Insurance*]
PAP........... People's Action Party [*Papua New Guinea*] [*Political party*] (EY)
PAP........... People's Action Party [*Singapore*] [*Political party*] (PPW)
PAP........... People's Action Party [*Malaya*] [*Political party*]
PAP........... People's Alliance Party [*Solomon Islands*] [*Political party*] (PPW)
PAP........... Peroxidase-Antiperoxidase [*Immunochemistry*]
PAP........... Personal Auto Policy [*Insurance*]
PAP........... Personnel Allocation Plan [*Navy*]
PAP........... Personnel Assistance Point [*Army*] (AABC)
PAP........... Phase Advance Pulse
PAP........... Phenolphthalein in Paraffin [*Emulsion*]
PAP........... Phenyl Acid Phosphate [*Organic chemistry*]
PAP........... Philippine Aid Plan
PAP........... Phosphoadenosine Phosphate [*Biochemistry*]
PAP........... Photodiode Array Processing (MCD)
PAP........... Photonic Array Processor [*Device for manipulating light beams in an optical computer*]
PAP........... Physics and Astronomy Programs [*NASA*]
PAP........... Pierced Aluminum Plank [*Technical drawings*]
PAP........... Pilotless Aircraft Program (NG)
PAP........... Platelet Aggregation Profiler [*Hematology*]
PAP........... Platelet Alkaline Phosphatase [*An enzyme*]
PAP........... Pokeweed Antiviral Protein [*Immunochemistry*]
PAP........... Political Asylum Project (EA)
PAP........... Politiki Aneksartitos Parataksis [*Independent Political Front*] [*Greek*] [*Political party*] (PPE)
PAP........... Polska Agencja Prasowa [*Polish Press Agency*]
PAP........... Poly-a-polymerase [*An enzyme*]
PAP........... Poly(acryloylpyrrolidine) [*Organic chemistry*]
PAP........... Port-Au-Prince [*Haiti*] [*Airport symbol*] (OAG)
PAP........... Positive Airway Pressure (MAE)
PAP........... Prearranged Payments [*Business term*]
PAP........... Primary Atypical Pneumonia [*Medicine*]
PAP........... Printer Access Protocol (BYTE)
PAP........... Prison-Ashram Project (EA)
PAP........... Procurement and Production (AFIT)
PAP........... Product Assurance Plan [*Army*] (AABC)
PAP........... Production Allocation Program
PAP........... Project Aerospace Plane (AAG)
PAP........... Projected Average Progress (NG)
PAP........... Prostatic Acid Phosphatase [*An enzyme*]
PAP........... Proton Attenuation Procedure
PAP........... Psychobiology and Psychopathology [*Elsevier Book Series*] [*A publication*]
PAP........... Public Affairs Program [*of the American Friends Service Committee*] (EA)
PAP........... Public Assistance Program
PAP........... Pulmonary Alveolar Proteinosis [*Medicine*]
PAP........... Pulmonary Arterial [*or Artery*] Pressure [*Medicine*]
PAPA......... Philippines Alien Property Administration
PAPA......... Probabilistic Automatic Pattern Analyzer [*Data processing*]
PAPA......... Proceedings. American Philological Association [*A publication*]
PAPA......... Programmer and Probability Analyzer [*Data processing*] (IEEE)
PAPA......... Publications. Arkansas Philological Association [*A publication*]
PAPAA4.... American Psychopathological Association. Proceedings [*A publication*]
Pap Am Chem Soc Div Paint Plast Print Ink ... Papers. American Chemical Society. Division of Paint, Plastics, and Printing Ink [*A publication*]
Pap Amer Soc Agr Eng ... Paper. American Society of Agricultural Engineers [*A publication*]
Pap Am Sch Ath ... Papers. American School of Classical Studies at Athens [*A publication*]
Pap Am Soc Ch Hist ... Papers. American Society of Church History [*A publication*]
Pap Annu Conv West Can Water Sewage Conf ... Papers Presented at the Annual Convention. Western Canada Water and Sewage Conference [*A publication*]
Pap Anthro ... Papers in Anthropology [*Oklahoma*] [*A publication*]
Pap Archit Sci Unit Univ Queensl ... Paper. Architectural Science Unit. University of Queensland [*A publication*] (APTA)
PAPAS ...... Pin and Pellet Assay System [*Nuclear energy*] (NRCH)
Pap ASAE ... Paper. American Society of Agricultural Engineers [*A publication*]
PAPAV...... Papaver Poppy [*Botany*] (ROG)
Pap Avulsos Dep Zool (Sao Paulo) ... Papeis Avulsos. Departamento de Zoologia (Sao Paulo) [*A publication*]
Pap Avulsos Dep Zool Secr Agric Ind Comer (Sao Paulo) ... Papeis Avulsos. Departamento de Zoologia. Secretaria de Agricultura Industria e Comercio (Sao Paulo) [*A publication*]
Pap Avul Zool ... Papeis Avulsos de Zoologia [*A publication*]
PAPB........ Point Barrow [*Alaska*] [*ICAO location identifier*] (ICLI)
Pap Bibliog ... Papers. Bibliographical Society of America [*A publication*]

Pap Bibliogr Soc Am ... Papers. Bibliographical Society of America [*A publication*]
Pap Bibliog Soc Am ... Papers. Bibliographical Society of America [*A publication*]
Pap Bibl Soc Am ... Papers. Bibliographical Society of America [*A publication*]
Pap Board Abstr ... Paper and Board Abstracts [*A publication*]
Papbrd Pkg ... Paperboard Packaging [*A publication*]
Pap Brit Sch Rome ... Papers. British School at Rome [*A publication*]
PAPC........ Philological Association of the Pacific Coast [*A publication*]
PAPCA ...... Pan-American Progressive Consumers Alliance [*Later, NPCA*] (EA)
Pap Carton Cellul ... Papier. Carton et Cellulose [*A publication*]
Pap Celul ... Papir a Celuloza [*A publication*]
PAPCNY ... Portuguese American Progressive Club of New York (EA)
Pap Coal Util Symp Focus SO₂ Emiss Control ... Papers. Coal Utilization Symposium. Focus on SO_2 Emission Control [*A publication*]
Pap Commonw For Conf ... Paper. Commonwealth Forestry Conference [*A publication*]
Pap Congr Aust NZ Assoc Adv Sci ... Australian and New Zealand Association for the Advancement of Science. Congress. Papers [*A publication*] (APTA)
Pap Congr Fed Int Precontrainte ... Papers. Congress of the Federation Internationale de la Precontrainte [*A publication*]
Pap Conv Am Nurs Assoc ... Papers from the Convention. American Nurses' Association [*A publication*]
Pap Converting ... Paper Converting [*A publication*]
Pap Czech Soil Sci Conf ... Papers. Czechoslovak Soil Science Conference [*A publication*]
Pap Dep Agric QD Univ ... Papers. Department of Agriculture. University of Queensland [*A publication*] (APTA)
Pap Dep Geol QD Univ ... Papers. Department of Geology. University of Queensland [*A publication*] (APTA)
Pap Dep Geol Queensl Univ ... Papers. Department of Geology. University of Queensland [*A publication*] (APTA)
Pap Dep Geol Univ QD ... Papers. Department of Geology. University of Queensland [*A publication*] (APTA)
Pap Dep Zool QD Univ ... Papers. Department of Zoology. University of Queensland [*A publication*] (APTA)
Pap & Disc Vic Inst Eng ... Papers and Discussions. Victorian Institute of Engineers [*Australia*] [*A publication*]
PAPE........ Aperature [*A publication*]
PAPE........ Parkside Petroleum, Inc. [*NASDAQ symbol*] (NQ)
PAPE........ Photoactive Pigment Electrophotography (IEEE)
PAPEDJ.... Pesquisa Agropecuaria Pernambucana [*A publication*]
Pap Egypt Geol Surv ... Paper. Egyptian Geological Survey [*A publication*]
PAPER ...... Prairie Association of Publishers Education Representatives [*Canada*]
Paper & Board Abs ... Paper and Board Abstracts [*A publication*]
Paperboard Packag ... Paperboard Packaging [*A publication*]
Paperboard Pkg ... Paperboard Packaging [*A publication*]
Paper Bul ... Paper and Packaging Bulletin [*A publication*]
PAPERCHEM ... Paper Chemistry [*Institute of Paper Chemistry*] [*Appleton, WI*] [*Bibliographic database*]
Paper Film Foil Conv ... Paper, Film, and Foil Converter [*A publication*]
Paper Jour ... Paper Trade Journal [*A publication*]
Paper Makers Merch Dir ... Paper Makers and Merchants. Directory of All Nations [*A publication*]
PAPERMAN ... Payroll and Accounting, Personnel Management, Manpower Utilization [*Air Force*]
Paper Mkr ... Paper Maker [*A publication*]
Paper Pulp Mill Catalogue ... Paper and Pulp Mill Catalogue/Engineering Handbook [*A publication*]
Papers Biblio Soc Am ... Papers. Bibliographical Society of America [*A publication*]
Papers Brit School Rome ... Papers. British School at Rome [*A publication*]
Papers in Ed (Anstey Coll) ... Papers in Education (Anstey College of Physical Education) [*A publication*]
Papers Far East Hist ... Papers on Far Eastern History [*A publication*]
Papers & Proc Roy Soc Tas ... Papers and Proceedings. Royal Society of Tasmania [*A publication*] (APTA)
Papers Proc Roy Soc Tasmania ... Papers and Proceedings. Royal Society of Tasmania [*A publication*]
Papers & Proc Tas Hist Res Assn ... Papers and Proceedings. Tasmanian Historical Research Association [*A publication*] (APTA)
Paper Technol ... Paper Technology [*A publication*]
Paper Technol Ind ... Paper Technology and Industry [*A publication*]
Paper Tr J ... Paper Trade Journal [*A publication*]
Paper Twine J ... Paper and Twine Journal [*A publication*]
Paper Yrb ... Paper Year Book [*A publication*]
Papeterie Numero Spec ... Papeterie. Numero Special [*A publication*]
Pap FAO/IUFRO World Consult For Tree Breed ... Paper. FAO [*Food and Agriculture Organization of the United Nations*]/IUFRO [*International Union of Forestry Research Organization*] World Consultation on Forest Tree Breeding [*A publication*]
Pap Far Eas ... Papers on Far Eastern History [*A publication*]
Pap Far East Hist ... Papers on Far Eastern History [*Australia*] [*A publication*]
Pap Film Foil Converter ... Paper, Film, and Foil Converter [*A publication*]

Pap Geol Surv Can ... Papers. Geological Survey of Canada [*A publication*]
Pap Gifu Univ Sch Med ... Papers. Gifu University. School of Medicine [*Japan*] [*A publication*]
Pap Grt Barrier Reef Comm ... Papers. Great Barrier Reef Committee [*A publication*] (APTA)
PAPH .... (Pyridinealdehyde)pyridylhydrazone [*Organic chemistry*]
PAPhilosS ... Proceedings. American Philosophical Society [*A publication*]
PAPhS .... Proceedings. American Philosophical Society [*A publication*]
Papi .... Papi [*Aemilius*] Papinianus [*Deceased, 212*] [*Authority cited in pre-1607 legal work*] (DSA)
Papi .... Papirius Justus [*Flourished, 2nd century*] [*Authority cited in pre-1607 legal work*] (DSA)
PAPI .... Precision Approach Path Indicator [*Aviation*] (FAAC)
PAPI .... Professional Association of Pet Industries (EA)
Pap IAALD World Congr ... Papers. International Association of Agricultural Librarians and Documentalists. World Congress [*A publication*]
Papier (Darmstadt) Beil ... Papier (Darmstadt). Beilage [*A publication*]
Papierfabr Wochenbl Papierfabr ... Papierfabrikant - Wochenblatt fuer Papierfabrikation [*A publication*]
Papiergesch ... Papier Geschichte [*A publication*]
Papierverarb ... Papier- und Kunststoffverarbeiter [*A publication*]
Pap Ind ...... Paper Industry [*A publication*]
Pap Ind Pap World ... Paper Industry and Paper World [*A publication*]
Pap Inst Def Anal ... Paper. Institute for Defense Analyses [*A publication*]
Pap Inst Post Off Electr Eng ... Printed Papers. Institution of Post Office Electrical Engineers [*A publication*]
Pap Inst Therm Spring Res Okayama Univ ... Papers. Institute for Thermal Spring Research. Okayama University [*A publication*]
Pap Int Conf Fluid Sealing ... Paper. International Conference on Fluid Sealing [*A publication*]
Papirip Magy Grafika ... Papiripar es Magyar Grafika [*A publication*]
Pap Is Afr .. Papers in International Studies. Africa Series. Ohio University [*A publication*]
Pap Is Se A ... Papers in International Studies. Southeast Asia Series. Ohio University [*A publication*]
Pap J .... Papir-Journalen [*A publication*]
Pap Karanis ... Papyri from Karanis [*A publication*]
PaPL .... Pennsylvania Power & Light Co. [*Associated Press abbreviation*] (APAG)
PAPL .... Preliminary Allowance Parts List [*Military*] (CAAL)
Pap Lab Tree-Ring Res Univ Ariz ... Papers. Laboratory of Tree-Ring Research. University of Arizona [*A publication*]
Pap Lanc Co Hist Soc ... Historical Papers. Lancaster County Historical Society [*Pennsylvania*] [*A publication*]
Pap Lang L ... Papers on Language and Literature [*A publication*]
Pap Lang Lit ... Papers on Language and Literature [*A publication*]
Pap Ling .... Papers in Linguistics [*A publication*]
PAPM .... Passed Assistant Paymaster [*British*]
PAPM .... Port Moller Air Force Station [*Alaska*] [*ICAO location identifier*] (ICLI)
Pap Maker Br Pap Trade J ... Paper Maker and British Paper Trade Journal [*A publication*]
Pap Maker (London) ... Paper Maker and British Paper Trade Journal (London) [*A publication*]
Pap Makers Assoc (GB Irel) Proc Tech Sect ... Paper Makers' Association (Great Britain and Ireland). Proceedings of the Technical Section [*A publication*]
Pap Makers Mon J ... Paper Makers' Monthly Journal [*A publication*]
Pap Maker (Wilmington Del) ... Paper Maker (Wilmington, Delaware) [*A publication*]
Pap Meteorol Geophys (Tokyo) ... Papers in Meteorology and Geophysics (Tokyo) [*A publication*]
Pap Met Geo ... Papers in Meteorology and Geophysics [*A publication*]
Pap Mich Acad ... Papers. Michigan Academy of Science, Arts, and Letters [*A publication*]
Pap Mich Acad Sci ... Papers. Michigan Academy of Science, Arts, and Letters [*A publication*]
Pap Mich Acad Sci Arts Lett ... Papers. Michigan Academy of Science, Arts, and Letters [*A publication*]
Pap Mill News ... Paper Mill News [*A publication*]
Pap Mill Wood Pulp News ... Paper Mill and Wood Pulp News [*A publication*]
Pap Miner Explor Res Inst McGill Univ ... Paper. Mineral Exploration Research Institute. McGill University [*A publication*]
Pap Minist Energy Mines Pet Resour (Br Columbia) ... Paper. Ministry of Energy, Mines, and Petroleum Resources (Province of British Columbia) [*A publication*]
PAPMOP ... Product Assurance Program Management Operations Plan (MCD)
PAPMV ..... Papaya Mosaic Virus [*Plant pathology*]
Pap Natl Conf Prof Nurses Physicians ... Papers. National Conference for Professional Nurses and Physicians [*US*] [*A publication*]
Pap N Haven Col Hist Soc ... Papers. New Haven Colony Historical Society [*A publication*]
Pap Norw State Game Res Inst ... Papers. Norwegian State Game Research Institute [*A publication*]
Pap Nova Scotia Dep Mines ... Paper. Nova Scotia Department of Mines [*A publication*]
Pap Nyomdatech ... Papir es Nyomdatechnika [*A publication*]

Papo .... Partido de Accion Popular [*Popular Action Party*] [*Panama*] [*Political party*] (PPW)
PAPOC ...... Parents' Alliance to Protect Our Children (EA)
PAPOILA ... Pacis Amico, Persecutionis Osore, Joanne Lockio Anglo [*Pseudonym used by John Locke*]
Pap Oreg State Univ For Res Lab ... Paper. Oregon State University. Forest Research Laboratory [*A publication*]
PAPOVA ... Papilloma Virus, Polyoma Virus, Vacuolating Virus
PapOxy ...... Oxyrhynchus Papyri [*A publication*]
PAPP .... Para-Aminopropiophenone [*Pharmacology*]
PAPP .... Parametric Aircraft Performance Program (MCD)
PAPP .... Pregnancy-Associated Plasma Protein
PAPPA ...... Pulp and Paper Prepackaging Association [*Later, SSI*] (EA)
Pap Peabody Mus Archaeol Ethnol Harv Univ ... Papers. Peabody Museum of Archaeology and Ethnology. Harvard University [*A publication*]
PAPPGM .. Preliminary Army Planning and Program Guidance Memorandum (MCD)
Pap Phil Ling ... Papers in Philippine Linguistics. Pacific Linguistics. Series A [*Canberra*] [*A publication*]
Pap Presentations Proc Digital Equip Comput Users Soc ... Papers and Presentations-Proceedings. Digital Equipment Computer Users Society [*A publication*]
Pap Primer ... Papyrological Primer [*A publication*]
Pap Print Dig ... Paper and Printing Digest [*A publication*]
Pap & Proc Roy Soc Tas ... Papers and Proceedings. Royal Society of Tasmania [*A publication*]
Pap Proc R Soc Tas ... Papers and Proceedings. Royal Society of Tasmania [*A publication*] (APTA)
Pap Proc R Soc Tasm ... Papers and Proceedings. Royal Society of Tasmania [*A publication*] (APTA)
Pap Proc R Soc Tasmania ... Papers and Proceedings. Royal Society of Tasmania [*A publication*]
Pap Proc Tas Hist Res Assoc ... Tasmanian Historical Research Association. Papers and Proceedings [*A publication*] (APTA)
Pap ja Puu ... Paperi ja Puu [*A publication*]
Pap Puu ...... Paperi ja Puu - Papper och Tra [*A publication*]
Pap Puu B Painos ... Paperi ja Puu. B Painos [*A publication*]
Pap Puu Painos ... Paperi ja Puu. A Painos [*A publication*]
PAPQ .... American Philosophical Quarterly [*A publication*]
PAPR .... American Poetry Review [*A publication*]
PAPR .... Paper Corp. of America [*Valley Forge, PA*] [*NASDAQ symbol*] (NQ)
PA Prac ...... Standard Pennsylvania Practice [*A publication*] (DLA)
Pap Res Appl Technol Symp Mined Land Reclam ... Papers. Research and Applied Technology Symposium on Mined-Land Reclamation [*A publication*]
PAPRICAN ... Pulp and Paper Research Institute of Canada [*McGill University*] [*Research center*] (RCD)
Pap Roy Soc Tasm ... Royal Society of Tasmania. Papers and Proceedings [*A publication*] (APTA)
PAPS .... Periodic Acid-Schiff with Phenylhydrazine Interposition [*A stain*]
PAPS .... Periodic Armaments Planning System (MCD)
PAPS .... Permissive Arming and Protection System [*AEC*]
PAPS .... Phosphoadenosine Phosphosulfate [*Also, APPS*] [*Biochemistry*]
PAPS .... Phosphoadenylyl Sulfate [*Biochemistry*]
PAPS .... Proceedings. American Philosophical Society [*A publication*]
PAPS .... Procurement and Production Status System
PAPS .... Public Assistance Processing System
PA PSC ...... Pennsylvania Public Service Commission Annual Report [*A publication*] (DLA)
PA PSC Dec ... Pennsylvania Public Service Commission Decisions [*A publication*] (DLA)
Pap Sci Ser ... Papers in Science Series [*A publication*]
Pap SE As Ling ... Papers in South East Asian Linguistics. Pacific Linguistics. Series A [*Canberra*] [*A publication*]
Pap SESA ... Paper. SESA [*Society for Experimental Stress Analysis*] [*A publication*]
Pap Ship Res Inst (Tokyo) ... Papers. Ship Research Institute (Tokyo) [*A publication*]
PAPSI .... Pregnancy-Associated Prostaglandin Synthetase Inhibitor [*Endocrinology*]
Pap S Shields Archaeol Hist Soc ... Papers. South Shields Archaeological and Historical Society [*A publication*]
P Ap St Dalho ... Applied Statistics. Proceedings of Conference at Dalhousie University [*A publication*]
Pap Sthn Afr ... Paper Southern Africa [*A publication*]
PA Psychiatr Q ... Pennsylvania Psychiatric Quarterly [*A publication*]
Pap Symp Coal Manage Tech ... Papers Presented before the Symposium on Coal Management Techniques [*A publication*]
Pap Symp Coal Mine Drainage Res ... Papers Presented before the Symposium on Coal Mine Drainage Research [*A publication*]
Pap Symp Coal Prep Util ... Papers Presented before the Symposium on Coal Preparation and Utilization [*A publication*]
Pap Symp Coal Prep (Washington DC) ... Papers Presented before the Symposium on Coal Preparation (Washington, DC) [*A publication*]

Pap Symp Coal Util ... Papers Presented before the Symposium on Coal Utilization [*A publication*]
Pap Symp Manage ... Papers Presented before the Symposium on Management [*A publication*]
Pap Symp Surf Min Reclam ... Papers Presented before the Symposium on Surface Mining and Reclamation [*A publication*]
Pap Symp Underground Min ... Papers Presented before the Symposium on Underground Mining [*A publication*]
Pap Synth Conf Proc ... Paper Synthetics Conference. Proceedings [*United States*] [*A publication*]
PAPTC ...... Pakistan Army Physical Training Corps [*British military*]   (DMA)
PAPTC ...... Practical Approach to Patents, Trademarks, and Copyrights [*A publication*]
PAPTE ...... President's Advisory Panel on Timber and the Environment
Pap Tech Mtg Int Union Conserv Nature ... Paper. Technical Meeting. International Union for the Conservation of Nature and Natural Resources [*A publication*]
Pap Technol ... Paper Technology [*England*] [*A publication*]
Pap Technol ... Paper Technology and Industry [*A publication*]
Pap Technol Ind ... Paper Technology and Industry [*A publication*]
Pap Trade J ... Paper Trade Journal [*A publication*]
Papua New Guin Agric J ... Papua and New Guinea Agricultural Journal [*A publication*]
Papua New Guinea Agric J ... Papua and New Guinea Agricultural Journal [*A publication*]
Papua New Guinea Agr J ... Papua and New Guinea Agricultural Journal [*A publication*]
Papua New Guinea Dep Agric Stock Fish Annu Rep ... Papua New Guinea. Department of Agriculture, Stock, and Fisheries. Annual Report [*A publication*]
Papua New Guinea Dep Agric Stock Fish Res Bull ... Papua New Guinea. Department of Agriculture, Stock, and Fisheries. Research Bulletin [*A publication*]
Papua New Guinea Geol Surv Mem ... Papua New Guinea. Geological Survey. Memoir [*A publication*]
Papua New Guinea Inst Med Res Monogr Ser ... Papua New Guinea. Institute of Medical Research. Monograph Series [*A publication*]
Papua New Guinea J Agric For Fish ... Papua New Guinea Journal of Agriculture, Forestry, and Fisheries [*A publication*]
Papua New Guinea Med J ... Papua New Guinea Medical Journal [*A publication*]
Papua & NG ... Papua and New Guinea Law Reports [*A publication*]
PAPUFA ... Physiologically Active Polyunsaturated Fatty Acid [*Nutrition*]
Pap Univ Maine Technol Exp Stn ... Paper. University of Maine. Technology Experiment Station [*A publication*]
Pap Univ MO-Columbia Dep Agric Econ ... Paper. University of Missouri-Columbia. Department of Agricultural Economics [*A publication*]
Pap Univ Queensland Dep Geol ... Papers. University of Queensland. Department of Geology [*A publication*]
Pap US Geol Surv Wat Supply ... Paper. United States Geological Survey. Water Supply [*A publication*]
PAPVC ...... Partial Anomalous Pulmonary Venous Connection   (MAE)
PAPVR ...... Partial Anomalous Pulmonary Venous Return
PAPW .... Papworth [*England*]
Papy ... Papy's Reports [*5-8 Florida*] [*A publication*]   (DLA)
Pap Zenon ... Selected Papyri from the Archives of Zenon [*A publication*]
Pap Ztg ...... Papier-Zeitung [*A publication*]
PAQ .... Palmer, AK [*Location identifier*] [*FAA*]   (FAAL)
PAQ .... Partially Allocated Quotas [*Ocean fishery management*]
PAQ .... Personal Attributes Questionnaire
PAQ .... Position Analysis Questionnaire
PAQ .... Preliminary Allowance Quantity [*Military*]   (CAAL)
PAQ .... Process Average Quality
PAQ .... Public Administration Quarterly [*A publication*]
PAQR .... Polyacenequinone Radical [*Organic chemistry*]
PAQT .... American Quarterly [*A publication*]
Par .... Guiraudus Pargues [*Authority cited in pre-1607 legal work*]   (DSA)
PAR .... Kosmetiek [*A publication*]
PAR .... Page Address Register
PAR .... Parabolic Aluminized Reflector [*Lamp*]
PAR .... Paracel Islands [*ANSI three-letter standard code*]   (CNC)
PAR .... Parachute
PAR .... Paragon Resources Ltd. [*Vancouver Stock Exchange symbol*]
Par .... Paragone [*A publication*]
PAR .... Paragraph   (AAG)
Par .... Paraguay
Par .... Parah   (BJA)
PAR .... Paralipomenon [*Old Testament book*] [*Douay version*]
PAR .... Parallax
PAR .... Parallel   (KSC)
PAR .... Parallelogram [*Geometry*]   (ADA)
PAR .... Parameter
PAR .... Parametric Amplifier
PAR .... Paraphrase   (ADA)
PAR .... Parcel
PAR .... Parenthesis
Par .... Parents' Magazine and Better Family Living [*Later, Parents' Magazine*] [*A publication*]

PAR .... Paris [*France*] [*Airport symbol*]   (OAG)
PAR .... Paris - Parc St. Maur [*France*] [*Seismograph station code, US Geological Survey*]   (SEIS)
PAR .... Parish
PAR .... Parity   (ADA)
Par .... Parker's English Exchequer Reports [*A publication*]   (DLA)
Par .... Parker's New York Criminal Reports [*A publication*]   (DLA)
PAR .... Parochial
Par .... Parsons' Reports [*65-66 New Hampshire*] [*A publication*]   (DLA)
PAR .... Partheite [*A zeolite*]
PAR .... Partido Aragones Regionalista [*Aragonese Regional Party*] [*Spain*] [*Political party*]   (PPW)
PAR .... Partito Anti-Reformista [*Anti-Reform Party*] [*Malta*] [*Political party*]   (PPE)
PAR .... Parts Approval Request   (MCD)
PAR .... Payload Adapter Ring
PAR .... [*The*] Payment Analysis Report [*Dun & Bradstreet Credit Services*] [*Information service or system*]   (CRD)
PAR .... Peacetime Airborne Reconnaissance   (AFM)
PAR .... Peak Accelerometer Recorder   (IEEE)
PAR .... Peak-to-Average Ratio [*Telecommunications*]
PAR .... Pennsylvania Advanced Reactor
PAR .... People Against Racism [*Civil rights organization*]
PAR .... People Against Rape   (EA)
PAR .... Perennial Allergic Rhinitis [*Medicine*]
PAR .... Performance Analysis and Review
PAR .... Performance Analysis Routine [*Data processing*]
PAR .... Performance Appraisal Report [*Nuclear energy*]   (NRCH)
PAR .... Performance Assessment Report [*Small Cities Community Development Block Grant*] [*Department of Housing and Urban Development*]   (GFGA)
PAR .... Performance Augmentation Ring   (MCD)
PAR .... Performing Arts Resources [*A publication*]
PAR .... Performing Arts Review [*A publication*]
PAR .... Perimeter Acquisition RADAR [*Army*]
PAR .... Perimeter Array RADAR   (MCD)
PAR .... Personnel Activity Report [*Office of Management and Budget*]
PAR .... Personnel Activity Request
PAR .... Personnel Advancement Requirement [*Navy*]   (NVT)
PAR .... PERT [*Program Evaluation and Review Technique*] Analysis Report   (KSC)
PAR .... Phased Array RADAR
PAR .... Phosphoric Acid-Resistant
PAR .... Photosynthetically Active Radiation
PAR .... Physiological Aging Rate
PAR .... Planning Action Request [*NASA*]   (MCD)
PAR .... Planning Activity Report
PAR .... Platelet Aggregate Ratio [*Hematology*]
PAR .... Pollen Accumulation Rate [*Botany*]
PAR .... Polyarylate [*Resin*]
PAR .... Positive Attitudinal Reinforcement [*In George Lee Walker novel "The Chronicles of Doodah"*]
PAR .... Post Adjudicative Review [*Social Security Administration*]   (OICC)
PAR .... Post Attach Requirements   (AAG)
PAR .... Postanesthesia [*or Postanesthetic*] Room [*Medicine*]
PAR .... Postanesthetic Recovery [*Medicine*]
PAR .... Potassium-Adsorption-Ratio
PAR .... Power Analysis Report [*Automobile testing*]
PAR .... Precedent, Action, and Result
PAR .... Precision Aerotech, Inc. [*AMEX symbol*]   (SPSG)
PAR .... Precision Aircraft Reference
PAR .... Precision Approach RADAR [*Aviation*]
PAR .... Prime Assets Ratio
PAR .... Princeton Applied Research Corp. [*Princeton University*]
PAR .... Priority Action Report   (AAG)
PAR .... Priority Action Request   (AAG)
PAR .... Probabilistic Analysis of Risk   (KSC)
PAR .... Problem Accountability Record   (NASA)
PAR .... Problem Action Record   (KSC)
PAR .... Problem Action Request   (NASA)
PAR .... Problem Analysis Report   (MCD)
PAR .... Problem Analysis and Resolution
PAR .... Process Action Request
PAR .... Product Acceptance & Research [*Commercial firm*]   (WDMC)
PAR .... Product Acceptance Review   (NASA)
PAR .... Product of Antigenic Recognition [*Immunochemistry*]
PAR .... Production Acceptance Review
PAR .... Production Action Request   (MCD)
PAR .... Production Analysis Report
PAR .... Production, Augmentation, and Reliability   (NG)
PAR .... Production Automated Riveting
PAR .... Professional Abstracts Registries [*Database Innovations, Inc.*]
PAR .... Profile of Average Reflectivity
PAR .... Program Action Request   (SSD)
PAR .... Program Address Register
PAR .... Program Adjustment Request [*Navy*]
PAR .... Program Administrator's [*Progress*] Report [*DoD*]
PAR .... Program-Aid Routine [*Data processing*]
PAR .... Program for Alcohol Recovery

PAR .... Program Allocation and Reimbursements (AFIT)
PAR .... Program Analysis and Review
PAR .... Program Appraisal Report
PAR .... Program Appraisal and Review (IEEE)
PAR .... Program Assessment Report [*or Review*] (MCD)
PAR .... Program Audience Rating
PAR .... Progressive Aircraft Repair [*or Rework*]
PAR .... Project Audit Report
PAR .... Projected Automation Requirement
PAR .... Promotion Appraisal Report (FAAC)
PAR .... Propulsion and Aeroballistics Research (SAA)
PAR .... Pseudoautosomal Region [*Genetics*]
PAR .... Public Administration Review [*A publication*]
PAR .... Public Affairs Research Council [*Research center*] (RCD)
PAR .... Publication Analysis Report (SAA)
PAR .... Pulmonary Arteriolar Resistance [*Medicine*] (MAE)
PAR .... Pulse Acquisition RADAR [*Military*] (NG)
PAR .... Purchasing Approval Request (NRCH)
PAR .... Push and Release [*Push button*]
PAR .... (Pyridylazo)resorcinol [*Organic chemistry*]
para .... Paracentesis [*Medicine*] (MAE)
PARA........ Parachute
PARA........ Paragon Resources Ltd. [*NASDAQ symbol*] (NQ)
PARA........ Paragraph (AFM)
PARA........ Paraguay
para .... Paraplegic
PARA........ Particle Aiding Replication of Adenovirus [*Virology*]
PARA........ Policy Analysis and Resource Allocation [*Department of State*]
PARA........ Polyarylamid [*Organic chemistry*]
PARA........ Professional Audiovideo Retailers Association (EA)
P-88/ARA ... Project '88: Americans for the Reagan Agenda (EA)
PARABAT ... Parachute Battalion [*Army*]
paracent ..... Paracentesis [*Medicine*]
PARACOMPT ... Parameter Analysis of Respiration Agents Considering Operations Motivation Protection and Time Model (MCD)
PARACS ... Perimeter Acquisition RADAR Attack Characterization System (MCD)
PARADE... Passive-Active Range Determination
Par Adm..... Parsons on the Law of Shipping and Admiralty [*A publication*] (DLA)
PARADROP ... Airdrop by Parachute
PAR AFF... Pars Affecta [*The Part Affected*] [*Pharmacy*]
PARAFRAG ... Parachute Fragmentation Bomb [*Air Force*]
ParagT .... Paragon Trade Brands [*Associated Press abbreviation*] (APAG)
PARAKU... Pasokan Rakyat Kalimantan Utara [*North Kalimantan People's Forces*] [*Malaya*]
PARAM..... Parameter (KSC)
Paramagn Rezon ... Paramagnitnyj Rezonans [*A publication*]
Paramaribo-Suriname Agric Exp Stn Bull ... Paramaribo-Suriname. Agricultural Experiment Station. Bulletin [*A publication*]
Para-Med... Para-Medico [*A publication*]
PARAMEDIC ... [*A*] Medical Service Person Qualified to Participate in Parachute Activities [*Air Force*] [*In a nonmilitary context, may refer to one who serves as a physician's assistant*]
Paramed Int ... Paramedics International [*A publication*]
PARAMI... Parsons Active Ring-Around Miss Indicator
PARAMIS ... Parsons Passive Miss Distance Indicating System (SAA)
Par Am Law ... Parsons' Commentaries on American Law [*A publication*] (DLA)
Par Am Law Comm ... Parsons' Commentaries on American Law [*A publication*] (DLA)
PARAMP.. Parametric Amplifier
Par Ant ...... Parochial Antiquities [*A publication*] (DLA)
PARAPSYCH ... Parapsychology
PARARESCUE ... Rescue by Individuals Parachuted to Distressed Persons [*Air Force*]
Par Arter.... Paroi Arterielle-Arterial Wall [*A publication*]
PARASEV ... Paraglider Research Vehicle [*NASA*]
Parasit........ Parasitica [*A publication*]
Parasite Immunol ... Parasite Immunology [*A publication*]
Parasite Immunol (Oxf) ... Parasite Immunology (Oxford) [*A publication*]
Parasit Hung ... Parasitologia Hungarica [*A publication*]
PARASITOL ... Parasitology
Parasitol..... Parasitology [*A publication*]
Parasitol Hung ... Parasitologia Hungarica [*A publication*]
Parasitol Res ... Parasitology Research [*A publication*]
Parasitol Schriftenr ... Parasitologische Schriftenreihe [*A publication*]
Parasitol Today ... Parasitology Today [*A publication*]
Parasit Res ... Parasitology Research [*A publication*]
PARASYN ... Parametric Synthesis [*Data processing*]
PARATHORMONE ... Parathyroid Hormone [*Endocrinology*]
PARATROOPS ... Parachute Infantry [*Military*]
Parazity Zhivotn Rast ... Parazity Zhivotnykh i Rastenii [*A publication*]
PARB........ Perimeter Acquisition RADAR Building [*Army*] (AABC)
Parbhani Agric Coll Mag ... Parbhani Agricultural College. Magazine [*A publication*]
PARBICA ... Pacific Regional Branch of the International Council on Archives (EAIO)
Par Bills & N ... Parsons on Bills and Notes [*A publication*] (DLA)
PARC......... Pacific Air Rescue Center [*or Command*] (CINC)

PARC........ Pacific-Asia Resources Center [*Japan*] (EAIO)
PARC........ Palo Alto Research Center [*Xerox Corp.*]
PARC........ Pan-African Resource Center (EA)
PARC........ Pan-African Rinderpest Campaign [*Organization of African Unity*]
PARC........ Park Communications, Inc. [*NASDAQ symbol*] (NQ)
PARC........ Periodic Aircraft Reconditioning Cycle (DNAB)
PARC........ Plains Aquatic Research Conference. Proceedings [*A publication*]
PARC........ Predator and Rodent Control [*US Fish and Wildlife Service*] (IIA)
PARC........ President's Appalachian Regional Commission
PARC........ Princeton Applied Research Corp.
PARC........ Principal Assistant Responsible for Contracting [*Army*]
PARC........ Progressive Aircraft Reconditioning [*or Repair*] Cycle
PARCA...... Pan American Railway Congress Association
PARCH ..... Parchment (ADA)
PARCHM ... Parchment (ROG)
PARCHT ... Parchment
PaRCL .... Parsec Research Control Language [*Pronounced "parkul"*] [*Parsec Reseach*] [*Robotics*]
ParCom...... Paramount Communications, Inc. [*Associated Press abbreviation*] (APAG)
PARCOM ... Paris Commission [*See also CP*] (EAIO)
Par Cont..... Parsons on Contracts [*A publication*] (DLA)
Par Costs .... Parsons on Costs [*A publication*] (DLA)
PARCP ...... PEMARS [*Procurement of Equipment and Missiles, Army Management and Accounting Reporting System*] Accounting and Reporting Control Point [*Army*]
PARCS ...... Perimeter Acquisition RADAR Attack Characterization System [*Army*]
PARD .... Parts Application Reliability Data (IEEE)
PARD .... Periodic and Random Deviation
PARD .... Personnel Actions and Records Directorate [*Military Personnel Center*] (AABC)
PARD .... Pilot Airborne Recovery Device [*A balloon-parachute*]
PARD .... Pilotless Aircraft Research Division [*Later, Applied Materials and Physics Division*] [*Langley Research Center*]
PARD .... Post-Accident Radioactivity Depletion [*Nuclear energy*] (NRCH)
PARD .... Precision Annotated Retrieval Display [*System*] [*Data processing*]
PARDAC.... Parallel Digital-to-Analog Converter
Par Dec ..... Parsons' Decisions [*2-7 Massachusetts*] [*A publication*] (DLA)
PARDENTL ... Paradental
Pard Lois Mar ... Pardessus' Lois Maritimes [*A publication*] (DLA)
PARDON .. Pastors' Anonymous Recovery-Directed Order for Newness [*Rehabilitation program for troubled clergymen*] [*Defunct*]
PARDOP... Passive Ranging Doppler
PARDP...... Perimeter Acquisition RADAR Data Processor [*Army*] (AABC)
Pard Serv ... Pardessus' Traites des Servitudes [*A publication*] (DLA)
PARE........ People Against Racism in Education
PAREA...... Pharmacological Reviews [*A publication*]
P/AREA .... Probationary Acting Radio Electrical Artificer [*British military*] (DMA)
PAREC...... Pay Record
PA Rec....... Pennsylvania Record [*A publication*] (DLA)
PAREN...... Parenthesis [*or Parentheses*] (AFM)
PAREN...... Progressive Aircraft Engine Repair
PARENT ... Parenteral
Parent Aust ... Parent Australia [*A publication*] (APTA)
Parent & Cit ... Parent and Citizen [*A publication*] (APTA)
Parents....... Parents' Magazine [*A publication*]
PARENTS ... People of America Responding to Educational Needs of Today's Society (EA)
Parents Cit Guide ... Parents and Citizens Guide [*A publication*]
Parents' Mag ... Parents' Magazine and Better Family Living [*Later, Parents' Magazine*] [*A publication*]
PARENTSQ ... Parent Squadron Base [*Military*] (NVT)
PA Rep....... Pennsylvania Reports [*A publication*] (DLA)
Par Eq Cas ... Parsons' Select Equity Cases [*1842-51*] [*Pennsylvania*] [*A publication*] (DLA)
Par Eq Cases ... Parsons' Select Equity Cases [*Pennsylvania*] [*A publication*] (DLA)
PARESEV ... Paraglider Research Vehicle [*NASA*] (MCD)
Par Ess....... Parsons' Essays on Legal Topics [*A publication*] (DLA)
PARET ...... Parallel Architecture Research and Evaluation Tool [*Data processing*]
PAREX...... Programmed Accounts Receivable Extra Service [*Data processing*]
PARF........ Paradise Fruit Co., Inc. [*NASDAQ symbol*] (NQ)
PARF........ Practical Allergy Research Foundation (EA)
PARFAS.... Passive Radio Frequency Acquisition System
Par & Fonb Med Jur ... Paris and Fonblanque's Medical Jurisprudence [*A publication*] (DLA)
PARFOX.... [*Front*] Parapet Foxhole (MCD)
PARFR ...... Program for Applied Research on Fertility Regulation [*Northwestern University*] [*Research center*]

Parfuem Kosmet ... Parfuemerie und Kosmetik [*West Germany*] [*A publication*]
Parfum Cosmet Savons ... Parfums, Cosmetiques, Savons [*A publication*]
Parfum Mod ... Parfumerie Moderne [*A publication*]
Parfums Cos ... Parfums, Cosmetiques, Aromes [*A publication*]
Parfums Cosmet Savons ... Parfums, Cosmetiques, Savons [*A publication*]
Parfums Cosmet Savons Fr ... Parfums, Cosmetiques, Savons de France [*A publication*]
Parfums Fr ... Parfums de France [*A publication*]
Pargs .... Guiraudus Pargues [*Authority cited in pre-1607 legal work*] (DSA)
PARGS ...... Parks and Recreation Girls Service
PARH .... Art History [*A publication*]
PARI .... Ariel, A Review of International English Literature [*A publication*]
PARI .... Parent Attitude Research Instrument [*A questionnaire*]
PARIS ...... Pictorial and Artifact Retrieval and Information System [*Canadian Heritage Information Network*] [*Information service or system*]
PARIS ...... Planning Aid for Retail Information System [*IBM Corp.*]
PARIS ...... Pour l'Amenagement et le Renouveau Institutionel et Social [*France*] [*Political party*]
PARIS ...... Pulse Analysis-Recording Information System
Parisi .... [*Petrus Paulus*] Parisius [*Flourished, 16th century*] [*Authority cited in pre-1607 legal work*] (DSA)
Paris Med .. Paris Medical [*A publication*]
ParisR .... Paris Review [*A publication*]
Paris Rev .... Paris Review [*A publication*]
PARK .... Parkerized [*Metallurgy*] [*Tradename*]
Park .... Parker's English Exchequer Reports [*1743-67*] [*A publication*] (DLA)
Park .... Parker's New Hampshire Reports [*A publication*] (DLA)
Park .... Parker's New York Criminal Cases [*1823-68*] [*A publication*] (DLA)
PARK .... Parks. International Journal for Managers of National Parks, Historic Sites, and Other Protected Areas [*A publication*]
PARKA ...... Pacific Acoustic Research Kaneohe-Alaska [*Navy*]
Park Adm ... Park Administration [*A publication*]
Park Arb .... Parker on Arbitration [*1820*] [*A publication*] (DLA)
Park Ch ...... Parker's Practice in Chancery [*A publication*] (DLA)
Park CR ...... Parker's New York Criminal Reports [*A publication*] (DLA)
Park Cr Cas ... Parker's New York Criminal Cases [*A publication*] (DLA)
Park Crim L ... Parker's New York Criminal Reports [*A publication*] (DLA)
Park Crim (NY) ... Parker's New York Criminal Cases [*A publication*] (DLA)
Park Crim R ... Parker's New York Criminal Reports [*A publication*] (DLA)
Park Crim Rep ... Parker's New York Criminal Reports [*A publication*] (DLA)
Park Cr Rep ... Parker's New York Criminal Reports [*A publication*] (DLA)
Park Dig .... Parker's California Digest [*A publication*] (DLA)
Park Dow ... Park. Dower [*1819*] [*A publication*] (DLA)
ParkDrl ...... Parker Drilling Co. [*Associated Press abbreviation*] (APAG)
ParkEl .... Park Electrochemical Corp. [*Associated Press abbreviation*] (APAG)
Parker .... Parker on the Laws of Shipping and Insurance [*England*] [*A publication*] (DLA)
Parker .... Parker's English Exchequer Reports [*A publication*] (DLA)
Parker .... Parker's New Hampshire Reports [*A publication*] (DLA)
Parker .... Parker's New York Criminal Reports [*6 vols.*] [*A publication*] (DLA)
Parker Cr Cas ... Parker's New York Criminal Reports [*A publication*] (ILCA)
Parker Cr Cas (NY) ... Parker's New York Criminal Reports [*A publication*] (ILCA)
Parker Cr R ... Parker's New York Criminal Reports [*A publication*] (ILCA)
Parker Cr R (NY) ... Parker's New York Criminal Reports [*A publication*] (ILCA)
Parker's Crim R ... Parker's New York Criminal Reports [*A publication*] (DLA)
Parker's Crim Rep (NY) ... Parker's New York Criminal Reports [*A publication*] (DLA)
Parker's Cr R ... Parker's New York Criminal Reports [*A publication*] (DLA)
Park Exch ... Parker's English Exchequer Reports [*1743-67*] [*A publication*] (DLA)
Park Hist Ch ... Parkes' History of Court of Chancery [*1828*] [*A publication*] (DLA)
ParkHn ...... Parker-Hannifin Corp. [*Associated Press abbreviation*] (APAG)
Park Ins ..... Parker's Insurance [*8 eds.*] [*1787-1842*] [*England*] [*A publication*] (DLA)
Park NH .... Parker's New Hampshire Reports [*A publication*] (DLA)
ParkPar ..... Parker & Parsley Petroleum [*Associated Press abbreviation*] (APAG)
Park Pract Grist ... Park Practice Grist [*A publication*]
Park Pract Prog ... Park Practice Program. Design, Grist, Trends. Index [*A publication*]
Park Pr Ch ... Parker's Practice in Chancery [*A publication*] (DLA)
Park Rev Cas ... Parker's English Exchequer Reports (Revenue Cases) [*A publication*] (DLA)
Parks and R ... Parks and Recreation [*A publication*]
Parks & Rec ... Parks and Recreation [*A publication*]
Parks & Wild ... Parks and Wildlife [*A publication*]

Parks Wildl ... Parks and Wildlife [*A publication*] (APTA)
PARL .... Parallel
Parl .... Parlament [*A publication*]
PARL .... Parliament
Parl .... Parliamentarian [*British*] [*A publication*]
PARL .... Parlux Fragrances, Inc. [*NASDAQ symbol*] (NQ)
Par L .... Parsons' Law by Hughes [*A publication*] (DLA)
PARL .... Prince Albert RADAR Laboratory
Parl Aff ...... Parliamentary Affairs [*A publication*]
Parlam Beil Polit Zeitgesch ... Parlament Beilage aus Politik und Zeitgeschichte [*A publication*]
PARLARS ... Particulars
Par Laws Bus ... Parsons' Laws of Business [*A publication*] (DLA)
PARLB ...... Parliamentary Borough
Parl Cas ..... Parliamentary Cases [*House of Lords Reports*] [*A publication*] (DLA)
Parl Deb ..... Parliamentary Debates [*A publication*] (APTA)
Parl Deb HC ... Parliamentary Debates. House of Commons [*United Kingdom*] [*A publication*]
Parl Deb HL ... Parliamentary Debates. House of Lords [*United Kingdom*] [*A publication*]
PAR Legis Bul ... PAR [*Public Affairs Research*] Legislative Bulletin [*A publication*]
Parl Hist Eng ... Parliamentary History of England [*Pre-1803*] [*A publication*] (DLA)
Parliam Aff ... Parliamentary Affairs [*A publication*]
Parliamentary Aff ... Parliamentary Affairs [*A publication*]
Parliament Pap (Commonw Aust) ... Parliamentary Paper (Commonwealth of Australia) [*A publication*]
Parliam Liaison Group Altern Energy Strategies Bull ... Parliamentary Liaison Group for Alternative Energy Strategies. Bulletin [*A publication*]
PARLIKDER ... Partiya Litsom k Derevne [*The Party Face to Face with the Countryside*] [*Given name popular in Russia after the Bolshevik Revolution*]
Parlim Aff ... Parliamentary Affairs [*A publication*]
PARLO ...... Parlando [*Music*] (ROG)
Parl Reg ..... Parliamentary Register [*England*] [*A publication*] (DLA)
PARLT ...... Parliament
PARLTY .. Parliamentary
PARLV ...... Parsley Latent Virus [*Plant pathology*]
PARLY ...... Parliamentary
PARM .... Arts Magazine [*A publication*]
PARM .... Parallelogram [*Geometry*] (ROG)
PARM .... Parameter [*Data processing*]
Par M .... Parents' Magazine [*A publication*]
PARM .... Participating Manager
PARM .... Partido Autentico de la Revolucion Mexicana [*Authentic Party of the Mexican Revolution*] [*Political party*] (PPW)
PARM ...... Persistent Antiradiation Missile (MCD)
PARM ...... Post-Attack Resource Management System (MCD)
PARM ...... Program Analysis for Resource Management
PARMA ..... Program for Analysis, Reporting, and Maintenance [*Data processing*]
PARMA ..... Public Agency Risk Managers Association [*San Jose, CA*] (EA)
Par Mar Ins ... Parsons on Marine Insurance and General Average [*A publication*] (DLA)
Par Mar L ... Parsons on Maritime Law [*A publication*] (DLA)
Par Med ..... Paris Medical [*A publication*]
PARMEDL ... Paramedical
Par Merc Law ... Parsons on Mercantile Law [*A publication*] (DLA)
PARMV ..... Parsnip Mosaic Virus [*Plant pathology*]
Par N & B .. Parsons' Notes and Bills [*A publication*] (DLA)
Par Nucl ..... Particles and Nuclei [*A publication*]
PARO .... Partners Oil Co. [*NASDAQ symbol*] (NQ)
PAROCH .. Parochial (ROG)
Paroch Ant ... Kennett's Parochial Antiquities [*A publication*] (DLA)
Parod Epic Gr Rel ... Parodorum Epicorum Graecorum Reliquiae [*A publication*] (OCD)
Parodontol Stomatol Nuova ... Parodontologia e Stomatologia Nuova [*A publication*]
Par Or .... Parole de l'Orient [*A publication*]
PAROS ...... Passive Ranging on Submarines [*Navy*]
PAROSS ... Passive/Active Reporting Ocean Surveillance System [*Navy*] (NVT)
PAROX ..... Paroxysmal [*Medicine*]
PARP .... Partially Acidulated Rock Phosphate (OA)
PARP .... Procyclic Acidic Repetitive Protein [*Biochemistry*]
PARP .... Production Assistance Report to Pricing [*DoD*]
Parpal .... [*Thomas*] Parpalea [*Flourished, 16th century*] [*Authority cited in pre-1607 legal work*] (DSA)
Par Part ..... Parsons on Partnership [*1889*] [*A publication*] (DLA)
Par Pass ..... Parola del Passato [*A publication*]
ParPf .... Partners Preferred Yield [*Associated Press abbreviation*] (APAG)
PARPFD ... Partners Preferred Yield [*Associated Press abbreviation*] (APAG)
PARPRO ... Peacetime Aerial Reconnaissance Program [*Military*] (NVT)
PAR Pseudo-Allerg React ... PAR. Pseudo-Allergic Reactions [*A publication*]

PAR Pseudo-Allerg React Involvement Drugs Chem ... PAR. Pseudo-Allergic Reactions. Involvement of Drugs and Chemicals [*A publication*]
PARQ .... Parental Acceptance-Rejection Questionnaire [*Psychology*]
Parques Jard ... Parques y Jardines [*A publication*]
PARR .... Pakistan Atomic Research Reactor
ParR .... Paris Review [*A publication*]
Par R .... Parsons' Select Equity Cases [*Pennsylvania*] [*A publication*] (DLA)
ParR .... Partisan Review [*A publication*]
PARR .... Performance Analysis Reliability Reporting (DNAB)
PARR .... Post-Accident Radioactivity Removal [*Nuclear energy*] (NRCH)
PARR .... Procurement Authorization and Receiving Report [*NASA*] (KSC)
PARR .... Program Analysis and Resources Review
PARR .... Program Assessment Review Report [*Military*] (GFGA)
PARRC .... Pacific Aerospace Rescue and Recovery Center [*Air Force*]
Par Rights Cit ... Parsons on the Rights of a Citizen of the United States [*A publication*] (DLA)
PARRS ...... Postal Analysis Response and Reporting System [*Computer system designed to track mail through the US Postal Service*] [*R. R. Donnelley & Sons Co.*]
PARRS ...... Psychological Abstracts Reference Retrieval System [*Syracuse University*]
PARS .... Parachute Altitude Recognition System (MCD)
Pars .... Parsons' Select Equity Cases [*1842-51*] [*Pennsylvania*] [*A publication*] (DLA)
PARS .... Passenger Airlines Reservation System
PARS .... Patrol Analysis Recording System [*British*]
PARS .... Pedestrians Association for Road Safety [*British*] (DI)
PARS .... Perimeter Acquisition RADAR [*Characterization*] System (MCD)
PARS .... Photoacoustic Raman Spectroscopy
PARS .... Pilotless Aircraft Research Station [*NASA*]
PARS .... Precision and Accuracy Reporting System [*Environmental Protection Agency*] (GFGA)
PARS .... Procurement Accounting and Reporting System [*Navy*] (NVT)
PARS .... Programmed Airline Reservation System
PARS .... Property Accountability Record System (NASA)
PARS .... Provincial Archives and Records Service [*Canada*]
PARSA ...... Parasitological Society of Southern Africa (EAIO)
Pars Ans .... Parsons' Answer to the Fifth Part of Coke's Reports [*A publication*] (DLA)
Pars Bills & N ... Parsons on Bills and Notes [*A publication*] (DLA)
Pars Cont ... Parsons on Contracts [*A publication*] (DLA)
Pars Dec ..... Parsons' Decisions [*2-7 Massachusetts*] [*A publication*] (DLA)
PARSEC ..... Parallax Second [*Unit of interstellar-space measure*]
PARSEC .... Parser and Extensible Compiler [*Programming language*] (CSR)
PARSECS ... Program for Astronomical Research and Scientific Experiments Concerning Space
Pars Eq Cas ... Parsons' Select Equity Cases [*1842-51*] [*Pennsylvania*] [*A publication*] (DLA)
PARSET .... Precision Askania Range System of Electronic Timing (MUGU)
PARSEV .... Paraglider Research Vehicle [*NASA*] (KSC)
Par Sh & Adm ... Parsons on the Law of Shipping and Admiralty [*A publication*] (DLA)
PARSIM ... Perimeter Acquisition RADAR Simulation [*Missile system evaluation*] (RDA)
PARSIP ..... Point Arguello Range Safety Impact Predictor (MUGU)
Pars Mar Ins ... Parsons on Marine Insurance [*A publication*] (DLA)
Pars Mar Law ... Parsons on Maritime Law [*A publication*] (DLA)
Pars Merc Law ... Parsons on Mercantile Law [*A publication*] (DLA)
Parsons' ..... Parsons' Select Equity Cases [*Pennsylvania*] [*A publication*] (DLA)
Parsons J ... Parsons Journal [*A publication*]
PARSQ ..... Pararescue
Pars Sel Eq Cas (PA) ... Parsons' Select Equity Cases [*Pennsylvania*] [*A publication*] (DLA)
Pars S Eq Cas ... Parsons' Select Equity Cases [*Pennsylvania*] [*A publication*] (DLA)
Pars Shipp & Adm ... Parsons on Shipping and Admiralty [*A publication*] (DLA)
PARSYM .. Partial Symmetry
PARSYN ... Parametric Synthesis [*Data processing*]
PART .... Pan American Round Tables in the USA [*Defunct*] (EA)
PART .... Partial (MSA)
PART .... Participate (AABC)
PART .... Participle [*Grammar*]
PART .... Particular
PART .... Partis [*A Part*] [*Pharmacy*]
PART .... Partition [*Ballistics*]
PART .... Partner (ADA)
PART .... Parts Allocation Requirements Technique
PART .... People Against Racist Terror (EA)
PART .... Performing Arts Repertory Theater
PARTAC ... Precision Askania Range Target Acquisition and Control (MUGU)
Part Accel .. Particle Accelerators [*A publication*]

PART AEQ ... Partes Aequales [*Equal Parts*] [*Pharmacy*]
PART AEQUAL ... Partes Aequales [*Equal Parts*] [*Pharmacy*] (ROG)
Part An ...... De Partibus Animalium [*of Aristotle*] [*Classical studies*] (OCD)
ParTch .... PAR Technology Corp. [*Associated Press abbreviation*] (APAG)
Part Charact ... Particle Characterization [*A publication*]
PART DOLENT ... Partes Dolentes [*Painful Parts*] [*Pharmacy*]
Parth .... Parthenius [*First century BC*] [*Classical studies*] (OCD)
Partic .... Participating [*or Participation*] (DLA)
PARTIC .... Participial [*Grammar*]
PARTIC .... Particle
PARTIC .... Particular
Particle B ... Particleboard and Medium Density Fibreboard. Annual Publication and Shipments [*A publication*]
Particleboard/Compos Mater Ser ... Particleboard/Composite Materials Series [*A publication*]
PARTICO ... Parti d'Interets Congolais [*Party for Congolese Interests*] [*Political party*]
Partidas ...... Moreau-Lislet and Carleton's Laws of Las Siete Partidas in Force in Louisiana [*A publication*] (DLA)
Partisan R ... Partisan Review [*A publication*]
Partisan Rev ... Partisan Review [*A publication*]
PARTN .... Partnership (ADA)
PARTNER ... Proof of Analog Results through a Numerical Equivalent Routine [*Data processing*]
Part Nucl ... Particles and Nuclei [*A publication*]
Part Or .... Partitiones Oratoriae [*of Cicero*] [*Classical studies*] (OCD)
PARTR .... Particular (ROG)
Part R .... Partisan Review [*A publication*]
PARTS ...... Precision Approach RADAR Training System (MCD)
PARTS ...... Price Analysis and Review Technique for Spares
Part Sci Technol ... Particulate Science and Technology [*A publication*]
PART VIC ... Partitis Vicibus [*In Divided Parts*] [*Pharmacy*]
Party .... Party Newspapers [*A publication*]
Part Z .... Partiinaya Zhizn [*A publication*]
PARU .... Personnel Applied Research Unit [*Canadian military*]
PARU .... Photographic and Reproduction Unit
PARU .... Police Aerial Reinforcement [*or Resupply*] Unit [*Thailand*] (CINC)
PARU .... Postanesthetic Recovery Unit [*Medicine*]
PARV .... Paravane [*Anti-moored-mine device*] (KSC)
PARV .... Parvus [*Small*] [*Pharmacy*]
PARV3 .... Parsnip Virus 3 [*Plant pathology*]
ParVec .... Purdue Center for Parallel and Vector Computing [*Purdue University*] [*Research center*] (RCD)
PARVSTRCRA ... Paravane and Stores Crane [*Engineering*]
PARWAC ... Archivum Veterinarium Polonicum [*A publication*]
Par WC ...... Parish Will Case [*A publication*] (DLA)
Par Wills .... Parsons on Wills [*1854*] [*A publication*] (DLA)
PARZEP .... Pochvoznanie Agrokhimiya i Rastitelna Zashtita [*A publication*]
PAS .... National Postsecondary Agriculture Student Organization (EA)
PAS .... Palestine Aid Society of America (EA)
PaS .... Pamietnik Slowianski [*A publication*]
PAS .... Papers. American School of Classical Studies [*Athens*] [*A publication*]
PAS .... Para-Aminosalicylic [*Acid*] [*Organic chemistry*]
PAS .... Parametric Amplifier System
PaS .... Paranoia Subtle [*Psychology*]
PAS .... Parent Attitude Scale
PAS .... Paros [*Greece*] [*Airport symbol*] (OAG)
PAS .... Parti Islam se Malaysia [*Islamic Party of Malaysia*] [*Political party*] (PPW)
PAS .... Partido de Accion Socialista [*Socialist Action Party*] [*Costa Rica*] [*Political party*] (PPW)
PAS .... Partito de Azione di Sardegna [*Sardinian Action Party*] [*Italy*] [*Political party*] (PPW)
PAS .... Pasadena [*California*] [*Seismograph station code, US Geological Survey*] (SEIS)
PA S .... Pascal Second
PAS .... Pascal Source File [*Data processing*]
PAS .... Passage (AABC)
PAS .... Passed to the Adjacent Sector
Pas .... Passipoverus [*Flourished, 13th century*] [*Authority cited in pre-1607 legal work*] (DSA)
PAS .... Patient Administration System [*British*]
PAS .... Patients' Aid Society
PAS .... Payload Accommodations Studies [*NASA*] (NASA)
PA S .... Pennsylvania Superior Court Reports [*A publication*] (DLA)
PAS .... Percussive Arts Society (EA)
PAS .... Perigee-Apogee Satellite [*Aerospace*]
PAS .... Perigee-Apogee Stage [*Aerospace*]
PAS .... Perigee-Apogee System [*Aerospace*]
PA/S .... Periodic Acid/Schiff [*A stain*]
PAS .... Peripheral Anterior Synechia [*Ophthalmology*]
PAS .... Personal Acquaintance Service
PAS .... Personnel Accounting Symbol [*Air Force*] (AFM)
PAS .... Personnel Accounting System [*Marine Corps*]
PAS .... Personnel Activity Sequence (AAG)

PAS........... Personnel Administration Section [*Library Administration Division of ALA*]
PAS........... Personnel Assignment Survey   (MCD)
PAS........... Phase Address System
PAS........... Phase Array System
PAS........... Philanthropic Advisory Service
PAS........... Phosphoric Acid-Sensitive
PAS........... Photoacoustic Spectrometry [*Also, OAS*]
PAS........... Physicians for Automotive Safety [*Defunct*]   (EA)
PAS........... Pierce-Arrow Society   (EA)
PAS........... Pilots Advisory Service
PAS........... Pilot's Attack Sight [*British*]
PAS........... Pioneer America Society   (EA)
PAS........... Plasma Arc System
PAS........... Pneumatic Air Saw
PAS........... Policy Analysis Staff [*Environmental Protection Agency*]   (GFGA)
PAS........... Polish Academy of Sciences
PAS........... Polish Astronautical Society [*See also PTA*]
PAS........... Poly(alkyl Sulfone) [*Organic chemistry*]
PAS........... Polyaminosiloxane [*Organic chemistry*]
PAS........... Polyarylsulfone [*Organic chemistry*]
PAS........... Positron Annihilation Spectroscopy   (MCD)
PAS........... Post Abortion Syndrome
PAS........... Postacoustic Spectroscopy
PAS........... Posterior Area of [*Loose*] Skin
PAS........... Postponed Accounting System [*Banking*]
PAS........... Power Apparatus and Systems   (MCD)
PAS........... Power-Assisted Steering [*Automotive feature*]
PAS........... Preaward Survey [*To determine a contractor's capability*] [*DoD*]
PAS........... Precise Acquisition System
PAS........... Pregnancy Advisory Service [*British*]
PAS........... Presidential Appointee Subject
PAS........... President's Advisor for Science
PAS........... Pressure-Assisted Sintering [*Forging*] [*Automotive engineering*]
PAS........... Pressurized Air Subsystem
PAS........... Price Analysis Sheet
PAS........... Primary Alerting System
PAS........... Primary Ascent System [*Aerospace*]   (NASA)
PAS........... Principal Assistant Secretary
PAS........... Privacy Act Statement   (NRCH)
PAS........... Problem Appraisal Scales [*Personality development test*] [*Psychology*]
PAS........... Proceedings. Aristotelian Society [*A publication*]
PAS........... Processed Array Signal
PAS........... Procurement Action System   (MCD)
PAS........... Procurement Appropriation, Secondary   (MCD)
PAS........... Product Acceptance Standard [*Automotive engineering*]
PAS........... Product Assurance Survey
PAS........... Product Availability Search   (MCD)
PAS........... Professional Activity Study [*Later, CPHA*]
PAS........... Professor of Aerospace Studies [*Air Force*]   (AFIT)
PAS........... Professor of Air Science [*Air Force*]
PAS........... Program Activity Structure
PAS........... Program Address Storage   (IEEE)
PAS........... Program of Advanced Studies
PAS........... Program Allowance Schedule
PAS........... Progressive Accumulated Stress [*Psychiatry*]
PAS........... Propulsion and Auxiliary Systems Department [*David W. Taylor Naval Ship Research and Development Center*]
PAS........... Public Address System
PAS........... Public Administration Service   (EA)
PAS........... Pulmonary Artery Stenosis [*Medicine*]
PAS........... Pulsating Air System [*Automotive engineering*]
PAS........... Pump Actuator Set
PAS........... Pyrotechnics Arming Switch
Pas .... Terminus Paschae [*Easter Term*] [*Latin*] [*Legal term*]   (DLA)
PASA .... Pacific American Steamship Association [*Later, AIMS*]
PASA .... Papers. American School of Classical Studies at Athens [*A publication*]
PASA......... Para-Aminosalicylic Acid [*Organic chemistry*]
PASA......... Personnel Administrative Services Agency [*Army*]
PASA......... Primary Acquired Sideroblastic Anemia [*Medicine*]
PASAR ...... Psychological Abstracts Search and Retrieval
PASARR ... Preadmission Screening and Annual Resident Review [*Medicare*]
PASAT ...... Poppleton-Allen Sales Aptitude Test
PASB .... Archives of Sexual Behavior [*A publication*]
PASb.......... Predneaziatskii Sbornik Voprosy Khattologii i Khurritologii [*A publication*]   (BJA)
PASBI........ Palo Alto Social Background Inventory [*Psychology*]
PASC .... Deadhorse [*Alaska*] [*ICAO location identifier*]   (ICLI)
PASC .... Pacific Area Standards Congress [*American National Standards Institute*]
PASC .... Palestine Armed Struggle Command   (PD)
PASC .... Pan American Sanitary Conference
PASC .... Pan American Standards Commission [*See also COPANT*]   (EAIO)
PAS-C........ Para-Aminosalicylic Acid Crystallized with Ascorbic Acid [*Organic chemistry*]   (MAE)

PASC........ Parkscan. Parks Canada [*A publication*]
Pasc........... Paschal [*Easter Term*] [*Legal term*]   (DLA)
Pasc........... Paschal's Reports [*25, 28-31 Texas*] [*A publication*]   (DLA)
PASC .... Precision Adaptive Sub-Band Coding [*Electronics*]
PASC .... Primitive Art Society of Chicago   (EA)
PASCA ...... Positron Annihilation Spectroscopy for Chemical Analysis
PASCAL.... [*A*] programming language [*1968*] [*Named after French mathematician Blaise Pascal, 1623-62*]
PASCAL.... Philips Automatic Sequence Calculator
PASCAL.... Program Applique a la Selection et a la Compilation Automatique de la Litterature [*Centre National de la Recherche Scientifique-Informascience*] [*Bibliographic database*]
PASCALS ... Projected Antisubmarine Classification and Location System   (DNAB)
PASCH...... Pascha [*Easter*] [*Church calendars*]   (ROG)
Pasch......... Paschal [*Easter Term*] [*Legal term*]   (DLA)
Paschal ...... Paschal's Reports [*28-31 Texas*] [*Supplement to Vol. 25*] [*A publication*]   (DLA)
Paschal's Ann Const ... Paschal's United States Constitution, Annotated [*A publication*]   (DLA)
Pasch Dig... Paschal's Texas Digest of Decisions [*A publication*]   (DLA)
PA Sch J .... Pennsylvania School Journal [*A publication*]
PAS Cl St... Papers. American School of Classical Studies at Athens [*A publication*]
PASCOSS ... Passive and Active Control of Space Structures
PASCT ...... Pan American Society for Chemotherapy of Tuberculosis [*See also SAQT*] [*Buenos Aires, Argentina*]   (EAIO)
PASE .... Post-Apollo Space Electrophoresis [*European Space Agency*]
PASE .... Power-Assisted Storage Equipment   (IEEE)
PASED ...... Proceedings. Annual Symposium. Society of Flight Test Engineers [*A publication*]
PASEP...... Passed Separately [*Military*]
PASES...... Performance Assessment of Syntax: Elicited and Spontaneous [*Educational test*]
PASF .... Asian Affairs [*A publication*]
PASF .... Photographic Art and Science Foundation   (EA)
PASG........ Patent Abstracts Section, Official Gazette [*Federal government*] [*A publication*]
PASG........ Pneumatic Antishock Garment [*Roentgenology*]
PASG........ Pulse Amplifier/Symbol Generator
PASG........ Pulse Analyzer Signal Generator
PASGT...... Personnel Armor System for Ground Troops   (RDA)
PASI .... American Studies International [*A publication*]
PASI .... Pacific Silver Corp. [*NASDAQ symbol*]   (NQ)
PASI .... Pikunas Adult Stress Inventory [*Psychology*]
PASI .... Professional Associate, Chartered Surveyors' Institution [*Later, ARICS*]
PASI .... Sitka [*Alaska*] [*ICAO location identifier*]   (ICLI)
PASIC .... Percussive Arts Society International Convention [*Percussive Arts Society*]
PASITAM ... Program of Advanced Studies of Institution Building and Technical Assistance Methodologies [*MUCIA*]
PASJD...... Passive Solar Journal [*A publication*]
Pas L......... Pasicrisie Luxembourgeoise [*A publication*]
PASL .... Polish Americans for the Statue of Liberty   (EA)
PASLA ...... Programmable Asynchronous Line Adapter
Pa Slow ..... Pamietnik Slowianski [*A publication*]
Pas Lux...... Pasicrisie Luxembourgeoise [*Luxembourg Law Reports*] [*A publication*]   (ILCA)
PASM....... Partitionable SIMD/MIMD [*Single Instruction, Multiple Data/Multiple Instruction, Multiple Data*]   (MCD)
PASM....... Periodic Acid - Silver Methenamine [*Biological stain*]
PASM....... Preaward Survey Monitor [*DoD*]
PASMB ..... Proceedings. Australian Society for Medical Research [*A publication*]
Pas Mus..... Pastoral Music [*A publication*]
PASN........ Parisian, Inc. [*NASDAQ symbol*]   (NQ)
PASN........ St. Paul Island [*Alaska*] [*ICAO location identifier*]   (ICLI)
PASO........ Pan American Sanitary Organization
PASO........ Pan American Sports Organization [*See also ODEPA*] [*Mexico City, Mexico*]   (EAIO)
PA/SO........ Port Antisubmarine Officer [*Navy*]
PASO........ Principal Armament Supply Officer [*British military*]   (DMA)
PASOC...... Partido de Accion Socialista [*Party of Socialist Action*] [*Spain*] [*Political party*]   (PPW)
PASOCO... Parti Socialiste des Comores [*Socialist Party of Comoros*] [*Political party*]   (EY)
PASOH ..... Partido de Accion Socialista de Honduras [*Political party*]   (EY)
PASOH ..... Partido Socialista de Honduras [*Honduran Socialist Party*] [*Political party*]
PASOK...... Panellinion Sosialistikon Kinema [*Pan-Hellenic Socialist Movement*] [*Greek*] [*Political party*]   (PPE)
PASOLS.... Pacific Area Senior Officer Logistics Seminar   (MCD)
PASP .... American Speech [*A publication*]
PASP .... Port Autonome de San Pedro [*The Ivory Coast*]   (EY)
PA/SP....... Positioner Antenna and Solar Panel [*NASA*]
PAS(PR).... Principal Assistant Secretary (Priority)
PASQ........ Pasquale Food Co., Inc. [*NASDAQ symbol*]   (NQ)
PASR .... African Studies Review [*A publication*]

PASRB	Preaward Survey Review Board [*DoD*]
PASS	Panic Attack Sufferers' Support Groups (EA)
PASS	Parents Against Subliminal Seduction (EA)
PASS	Parts Analysis Summary Sheet
PASS	Passage [*Maps and charts*] (KSC)
PASS	Passenger (KSC)
PASS	Passenger Automated Selection System (ADA)
PASS	Passim [*Everywhere*] [*Latin*]
PASS	Passive
PASS	Passive-Active Surveillance System (MCD)
PASS	Patrol Advanced Surveillance System (MCD)
PASS	Pay/Personnel Administrative Support System (NVT)
PASS	Penetration Aids/Strike System (NG)
PASS	Performance Analysis Subsystem [*Military*] (CAAL)
PASS	Personalized Automotive Security System [*In product name, PASS-Key*] [*Delco Electronics*] [*Automotive engineering*]
PASS	Petroleum Abstracts Search Service [*Online information service*]
PASS	Phased Array Sector Scanner [*Instrument for measuring ultrasound*] [*Trademark of General Electric Co.*]
PASS	Phoenix Ability Survey System [*Test*]
PASS	Pilot Aerial Survival System (SAA)
PASS	Planning and Scheduling Session
PASS	Planning and Scheduling System (NASA)
PASS	Policyowner Attitude Survey Service [*LIMRA*]
PASS	Polymeric Aluminum Silicate Sulfate [*Inorganic chemistry*]
PASS	Positioning and Surveying System (MCD)
PASS	Post-Accident Sampling Systems [*Nuclear energy*]
PASS	Precision Autocollimating Solar Sensor
PASS	Pressurized Air Starter System (MCD)
PASS	Primary Academic Sentiment Scale [*Child development test*]
PASS	Primary Avionics Software System (NASA)
PASS	Private Alarm Signalling System
PASS	Private Automatic Switching System [*Telecommunications*]
PASS	Procurement Aging and Staging System [*Army*] (AABC)
PASS	Procurement Automated Source System [*Small Business Administration*] [*Washington, DC*] [*Information service or system*] (IID)
PASS	Production Automated Scheduling System (IEEE)
PASS	Professional Airways Systems Specialists (EA)
PASS	Professional Amateur Sports Systems [*Cable-television network*]
PASS	Professional Association of Secretarial Services [*Later, NASS*] (EA)
PASS	Program Aid Software Systems [*Data processing*] (IEEE)
PASS	Program Alternative Simulation System (KSC)
PASS	Program Analysis of Service Systems [*Procedure to evaluate human service programs*]
PASS	Programmed Access/Security System [*Card Key Systems*]
PASSA	Pacific American Steamship Association [*Later, AIMS*] (EA)
Passenger Transp ...	Passenger Transport [*A publication*]
Passeng Transp J ...	Passenger Transport Journal [*England*] [*A publication*]
PASSIM	President's Advisory Staff on Scientific Information Management
PASS-IN-REVIEW ...	Priority Aircraft Subsystem Suitability Intensive Review (MCD)
PASSION ...	Program for Algebraic Sequences Specifically of Input-Output Nature [*Data processing*]
PASSMAN ...	Pay/Personnel Administrative Support System Manual (DNAB)
PASSR	Passenger (DCTA)
PASSWD ..	Password [*Data processing*]
PAST	Pasteurella [*Genus of bacteria*]
PAST	Pastillus [*A Lozenge, Troch, Pastil*] [*Pharmacy*] (ROG)
Past	Pastoral Epistles (BJA)
PAST	Pastorate
PA St	Pennsylvania State Reports [*A publication*] (DLA)
PAST	Portable Arming System Trainer (MCD)
PAST	Process Accessible Segment Table
PAST	Professor of Air Science and Tactics
PAST	Propulsion and Associated Systems Test (MCD)
PA Stat Ann ...	Pennsylvania Statutes, Annotated [*A publication*] (DLA)
Pa Stat Ann ...	Purdon's Pennsylvania Statutes Annotated [*A publication*]
PA Stat Ann (Purdon) ...	Pennsylvania Statutes, Annotated (Purdon) [*A publication*] (DLA)
PA State	Pennsylvania State Reports [*A publication*] (DLA)
PA State Coll Miner Ind Exp Stn Bull ...	Pennsylvania State College. Mineral Industries Experiment Station. Bulletin [*A publication*]
PA State Coll Miner Ind Exp Stn Circ ...	Pennsylvania State College. Mineral Industries Experiment Station. Circular [*A publication*]
PA State Coll Stud ...	Pennsylvania State College. Studies [*A publication*]
PA State R ...	Pennsylvania State Reports [*A publication*] (DLA)
PA State Univ Coll Agric Agric Exp Stn Prog Rep ...	Pennsylvania State University. College of Agriculture. Agricultural Experiment Station. Progress Report [*A publication*]
PA State Univ Coll Agric Ext Serv Spec Circ ...	Pennsylvania State University. College of Agriculture. Agricultural Extension Service. Special Circular [*A publication*]
PA State Univ Coll Earth Miner Sci Exp Stn Circ ...	Pennsylvania State University. College of Earth and Mineral Sciences. Experiment Station. Circular [*A publication*]

PA State Univ Coll Earth Miner Sci Spec Publ ...	Pennsylvania State University. College of Earth and Mineral Sciences. Special Publication [*A publication*]
PA State Univ Coll Eng Eng Proc ...	Pennsylvania State University. College of Engineering. Engineering Proceedings [*A publication*]
PA State Univ Coll Eng Eng Res Bull ...	Pennsylvania State University. College of Engineering. Engineering Research Bulletin [*A publication*]
PA State Univ Earth Miner Sci Exp Stn Circ ...	Pennsylvania State University. Earth and Mineral Sciences Experiment Station. Circular [*A publication*]
PA State Univ Miner Ind Exp Stn Bull ...	Pennsylvania State University. Mineral Industries Experiment Station. Bulletin [*A publication*]
PA State Univ Miner Ind Exp Stn Circ ...	Pennsylvania State University. Mineral Industries Experiment Station. Circular [*A publication*]
PA State Univ Sch For Resour Res Briefs ...	Pennsylvania State University. School of Forest Resources. Research Briefs [*A publication*]
PA State Univ Stud ...	Pennsylvania State University. Studies [*A publication*]
PastBl	Pastoralblaetter [*Stuttgart*] [*A publication*]
Pastbl	Pastoralblatt [*A publication*]
Past Care & Couns Abstr ...	Pastoral Care and Counseling Abstracts [*A publication*]
PA St Coll An Rp ...	Pennsylvania State College. Annual Report [*A publication*]
Pasteur Inst South India (Coonoor) Annu Rep Dir Sci Rep ...	Pasteur Institute of Southern India (Coonoor). Annual Report of the Director and Scientific Report [*A publication*]
Past Forum ...	Pastorales Forum fuer die Seelsorger im Erzbistum Muenchen-Freising [*A publication*]
PASTIC	Pakistan Scientific and Technological Information Center [*Formerly, PANSDOC*] [*Quaid-I-Azan University Campus*] [*Islamabad, Pakistan*]
Past Mus....	Pastoral Music [*A publication*]
PAstO	Our Lady of Angels College, Aston, PA [*Library symbol*] [*Library of Congress*] (LCLS)
Pastoralist ...	Pastoralist and Grazier [*A publication*] (APTA)
Pastoral Rev ...	Pastoral Review [*A publication*]
Pastoral Rev Graz Rec ...	Pastoral Review and Graziers' Record [*A publication*] (APTA)
Pastor Care Couns Abstr ...	Pastoral Care and Counseling Abstracts [*A publication*]
Pastor Care Educ ...	Pastoral Care in Education [*A publication*]
Past & Pres ...	Past and Present [*A publication*]
Past Pres....	Past and Present. Studies in the History of Civilization [*A publication*]
Past Presen ...	Past and Present [*A publication*]
Past Psych ...	Pastoral Psychology [*A publication*]
Past R.........	Pastoral Review and Graziers' Record [*A publication*] (APTA)
PA St R	Pennsylvania State Reports [*A publication*] (DLA)
PASTRAM ...	Passenger Traffic Management System [*Army*]
Past Rev......	Pastoral Review and Graziers' Record [*A publication*] (APTA)
PA St Tr.....	Pennsylvania State Trials (Hogan) [*A publication*] (DLA)
PASU	American Studies [*A publication*]
PASU	Pan-African Socialist Union [*Southern Rhodesia*]
PASU	Patrol Aircraft Service Unit
PASU	Performing Arts Study Unit (EA)
PASU	Polyarylsulfone [*Organic chemistry*]
PASU	Preliminary Approval for Service Use [*Military*]
PASU	Provisional Approval for Service Use [*Navy*] (NVT)
PA Summary ...	Summary of Pennsylvania Jurisprudence [*A publication*] (DLA)
PA Super....	Pennsylvania Superior Court Reports [*A publication*] (DLA)
PA Super Ct ...	Pennsylvania Superior Court Reports [*A publication*] (DLA)
PA Superior Ct ...	Pennsylvania Superior Court Reports [*A publication*] (DLA)
PASUS	Pan American Society of the United States (EA)
PASV	Pangola Stunt Virus [*Plant pathology*]
PASV	Sparrevohn Air Force Station [*Alaska*] [*ICAO location identifier*] (ICLI)
PASWEPS ...	Passive Antisubmarine Warfare Environmental Protection System [*Navy*] (NATG)
PASY	Shemya Air Force Base [*Alaska*] [*ICAO location identifier*] (ICLI)
PASYD	Policy Analysis and Information Systems [*A publication*]
Pat.............	All India Reporter, Patna Series [*A publication*] (ILCA)
PAt............	Allentown Public Library, Allentown, PA [*Library symbol*] [*Library of Congress*] (LCLS)
PAT	Athenaeum of Philadelphia (EA)
PAT	Athenaeum of Philadelphia, Philadelphia, PA [*OCLC symbol*] (OCLC)
Pat.............	Indian Law Reports, Patna Series [*A publication*] (DLA)
Pat.............	Indian Rulings, Patna Series [*A publication*] (DLA)
PAT	International Brotherhood of Painters and Allied Trades
PAT	National Patents Appeal Tribunal [*England*] (DLA)
PAT	Paper Trade Journal [*A publication*]
PAT	Parametric Artificial Talker
PAT	Paroxysmal Atrial [*or Auricular*] Tachycardia [*Medicine*]
PAT	Parts Accountability Technique (MCD)
PAT	Passive Acoustic Target [*Military*]

PAT .... Passive Acoustic Torpedo [*Military*]
PAT .... Passive Angle Track   (NVT)
PAT .... Patent   (KSC)
PAT .... Patent Rolls [*British*]
Pat............. Paterson's Scotch Appeals, House of Lords [*A publication*]   (DLA)
Pat............. Pathe [*Record label*] [*France*]
PAT .... Patient
PAT .... Patna [*India*] [*Airport symbol*]   (OAG)
Pat............ Paton's Scotch Appeal Cases, House of Lords [*A publication*]   (DLA)
PAT .... Patras [*Greece*] [*Seismograph station code, US Geological Survey*]   (SEIS)
PAT .... Patriarch [*Greek Church*]   (ROG)
PAT .... Patrick Air Force Base [*Florida*]   (KSC)
PAT .... Patrol
PAT .... Patten Corp. [*NYSE symbol*]   (SPSG)
PAT .... Pattern
PAT .... Pattern Analysis Test [*Army*]
PAT .... Peninsula Air Transport Co. [*Michigan*]   (FAAC)
PAT .... People's Action Team [*South Vietnam*]
PAT .... Performance Acceptance Test   (SAA)
PAT .... Performance Appraisal Team [*Nuclear energy*]   (NRCH)
PAT .... Peripheral Assignment Table   (CMD)
PAT .... Permit Assistance Team [*Environmental Protection Agency*]   (GFGA)
PAT .... Personalized Array Translator   (IEEE)
PAT .... Personnel Assistance Team [*Military*]
PAT .... Personnel Authorization Table [*Air Force*]
PAT .... Petroleum Air Transport, Inc. [*Lafayette, IN*] [*FAA designator*]   (FAAC)
PAT .... Phenylaminotetrazole [*Psychology*]
PAT .... Phosphinothricin Acetyl Transferase [*An enzyme*]
PAT .... Photo Articulation Test
PAT .... Physics Achievement Test
PAT .... Picric Acid Turbidity Test
PAT .... Picture Arrangement Test
PAT .... Plasma Arc Tunnel
PAT .... Plastic Apply Template   (MCD)
PAT .... Platoon Anti-Tank   (SAA)
PAT .... Plenum Air Tread [*Army amphibian vehicle*]
PAT .... Plutonium Air Transportable [*Nuclear energy*]   (NRCH)
PAT .... Point after Touchdown [*Football*]
PAT .... Polar Adjectives Test   (AEBS)
PAT .... Polar Auxin Transport [*Botany*]
PAT .... Polaris Acceleration Test [*Military*]   (SAA)
PAT .... Political Action Teams
PAT .... Polyaminotriazole [*Organic chemistry*]
PAT .... Polyarlterephthalate [*Organic chemistry*]
PAT .... Position Adjusting Type
PAT .... Postavailability Trials
PAT .... Power Ascension Testing   (IEEE)
PAT .... Preadmission Testing
PAT .... Prearranged Transfers
PAT .... Precision Aim Technique [*for helicopters*] [*Army*]   (RDA)
PAT .... Prediction Analysis Techniques
PAT .... Pregnancy at Term [*Gynecology*]
PAT .... Preliminary Acceptance Trials [*Navy*]
PAT .... Prescription Athletic Turf [*Trademark for an artificial turf*]
PAT .... Pressure Assembled Thyristor
PAT .... Printer Action Table [*Data processing*]   (HGAA)
PAT .... Priority Air Travel [*Army*]
PAT .... Prism Adaptation Test [*Ophthalmology*]
PAT .... Problem Action Team [*NASA*]   (NASA)
PAT .... Procedures Authorized Task   (MCD)
PAT .... Process-Activation Table [*Data processing*]
PAT .... Process Analysis Team
PA & T ...... Product Assurance and Test
PAT .... Production Acceptance Test [*NASA*]   (KSC)
PAT .... Production Assessment Test
PAT .... Professional, Administrative, and Technical   (OICC)
PAT .... Professional Association of Teachers [*British*]
PAT .... Proficiency Analytical Testing [*National Institute on Occupational Safety and Health*]
PAT .... Program Analysis Team   (KSC)
PAT .... Program Attitude Test   (IEEE)
PAT .... Programmable Actuator-Transducer [*Automotive engineering*]
PAT .... Programmed Activity Transmission   (MCD)
PAT .... Programmer Aptitude Test
PAT .... Property and Accounting Technician [*Navy*]
PAT .... Pseudoadder Tree [*Data processing*]
PAT .... Psychoacoustic Testing
PAT .... PSYOP [*Psychological Operation*] Automated Terminal   (RDA)
PAT .... Public Administration and Development [*A publication*]
PAT .... Public Administration Times [*A publication*]   (EAAP)
PAT .... Pulsed Amplifier Tube
PaT .... Purge-and-Trap [*Technique*] [*Environmental Protection Agency*]
PAtA .... Air Products & Chemicals, Inc., Allentown, PA [*Library symbol*] [*Library of Congress*]   (LCLS)

PATA......... Pacific American Tankship Association [*Defunct*]   (EA)
PATA......... Pacific Area Travel Association [*San Francisco, CA*]
PATA......... Pacific Asia Travel Association   (EA)
PATA......... Patagonia [*Region of South America*]   (ROG)
PATA......... Plenum Air Tread, Amphibious [*Army vehicle*]
PATA......... Pneumatic All-Terrain Amphibian   (IEEE)
PATA......... Professional Aeromedical Transport Association   (EA)
PATA......... Tanana [*Alaska*] [*ICAO location identifier*]   (ICLI)
Pat Abr....... Paterson's Abridgment of Poor Law Cases [*1857-63*] [*A publication*]   (DLA)
Pat App...... Craigie, Stewart, and Paton's House of Lords Appeals from Scotland [*1726-1857*] [*A publication*]   (DLA)
Pat App Cas ... Paterson's Scotch Appeal Cases [*A publication*]   (DLA)
Pat App Cas ... Paton's Scotch Appeal Cases [*Craigie, Stewart, and Paton*] [*A publication*]   (DLA)
PATAS ...... Portable Air-Launched Missile Telemetry Acquisition System   (MCD)
PATASWDEVGRU ... Patrol Antisubmarine Warfare Development Group
PATB........ Patriot Bancorp [*NASDAQ symbol*]   (NQ)
Pat Bl .... Patentblatt [*A publication*]
PATBOMRON ... Patrol-Bombing Squadron
PAtC .... Cedar Crest College, Allentown, PA [*Library symbol*] [*Library of Congress*]   (LCLS)
PATC........ Paroxysmal Atrial [*or Auricular*] Tachycardia [*Medicine*]
PATC........ PATCLASS [*Pergamon ORBIT InfoLine, Inc.*] [*Information service or system*] [*No longer available online*]   (CRD)
PATC........ Pioneer Automobile Touring Club   (EA)
PAT-C .... Position, Attitude, Trajectory-Control [*Aerospace*]   (AAG)
PATC........ Potomac Appalachian Trail Club   (EA)
PATC........ Professional, Administrative, Technical, and Clerical [*Bureau of Labor Statistics survey*]
PATC........ Tin City Air Force Station [*Alaska*] [*ICAO location identifier*]   (ICLI)
PATCA...... Panama Air Traffic Control Area
PATCA...... Phase Lock Automatic Tuned Circuit Adjustment [*Telecommunications*]
PATCA...... Professional and Technical Consultants Association   (EA)
Pat Cas...... Reports of Patent, Design, and Trade Mark Cases [*England, Scotland, Ireland*] [*A publication*]   (DLA)
PATCENT ... Patching Central [*Army*]   (AABC)
PA-TCH-SP ... Periodic Acid-Thiocarbohydrazide-Silver Proteinate [*Test*] [*Cytology*]
PATCO...... Prednisone, ara-C [*Cytarabine*], Thioguanine, Cyclophosphamide, Oncovin [*Vincristine*] [*Antineoplastic drug regimen*]
PATCO...... Professional, Administrative, Technical, Clerical, and Other [*Bureau of Labor Statistics survey*]   (DNAB)
PATCO...... Professional Air Traffic Controllers Organization [*Defunct*]   (EA)
PATCOM ... Patriot Communications Model   (MCD)
Pat Comp ... Paterson's Compendium of English and Scotch Law [*A publication*]   (DLA)
PATD .... Patented
Pat Dec....... Decisions of the Commissioner of Patents [*A publication*]   (DLA)
Pat Des & TM Rev ... Patent, Design, and Trade Mark Review [*India*] [*A publication*]   (DLA)
Pat Dig....... Pattison's Missouri Digest [*A publication*]   (DLA)
PATDPA ... Deutsche Patent Datenbank [*German Patent Database*] [*German Patent Office*] [*Information service or system*]   (IID)
PAT & E .... Product Acceptance Testing and Evaluation [*Marketing*]   (MCD)
PATE........ Programmed Automatic Telemetry Evaluator
PATE........ Programmed Automatic Test Equipment
PATE........ Psychodynamics and Therapeutic Education
PATEFA News ... Printing and Allied Trades Employers' Federation. News [*A publication*]
PATELL.... Psychological Abstracts Tape Edition Lease or Licensing
Patentbl...... Patentblatt [*A publication*]
Patentbl Ausg A ... Patentblatt. Ausgabe A [*A publication*]
Patentbl Ausg B ... Patentblatt. Ausgabe B [*A publication*]
Patentjoernaal (S Afr) ... Patentjoernaal (South Africa) [*A publication*]
Patent Off Soc Jour ... Patent Office Society. Journal [*A publication*]
Pater.......... Paterson's New South Wales Reports [*A publication*]   (DLA)
Pater.......... Paterson's Scotch Appeal Cases [*A publication*]   (DLA)
Pater Ap Cas ... Paterson's Scotch Appeal Cases [*A publication*]   (DLA)
Pater App... Paterson's Scotch Appeal Cases [*A publication*]   (DLA)
Paters App ... Paterson's Appeal Cases [*A publication*]   (ILCA)
Paters Comp ... Paterson's Compendium of English and Scotch Law [*A publication*]   (DLA)
Paterson..... Paterson on the Game Laws [*A publication*]   (DLA)
Paterson..... Paterson on the Liberty of the Subject [*A publication*]   (DLA)
Paterson..... Paterson's Compendium of English and Scotch Law [*A publication*]   (DLA)
Paterson..... Paterson's Law and Usages of the Stock Exchange [*A publication*]   (DLA)
Paterson..... Paterson's Scotch Appeal Cases [*A publication*]   (DLA)
Paterson Sc App Cas ... Paterson's Scotch Appeal Cases [*A publication*]   (DLA)
PATF......... Pathfinder Petroleum [*NASDAQ symbol*]   (NQ)

PATF .... Program Activation Task Force [*Military*] (AFIT)
PATF .... Property Accountability Task Force [*Army*] (MCD)
Pat Fiz Eksp Ter ... Patologiceskaya Fiziologiya i Eksperimental'naya Terapija [*A publication*]
PATFOR ... Patrol Force
Pat Game L ... Paterson on the Game Laws [*1861*] [*A publication*] (DLA)
PATGC ...... Purge-and-Trap Gas Chromatography [*Environmental Protection Agency*]
PatGlb .... Patriot Global Dividend Fund [*Associated Press abbreviation*] (APAG)
PATH .... Pathology (AABC)
Pat & H ...... Patton, Jr., and Heath's Reports [*Virginia Special Court of Appeals*] [*A publication*] (DLA)
PATH .... Performance Analysis and Test Histories (KSC)
PATH .... Pituitary Adrenotrophic Hormone [*Endocrinology*]
PATH .... Port Authority Trans-Hudson [*New York*]
PATH .... Preserve American Patriotic Holidays Committee (EA)
PATH .... Program on Advanced Technology for the Highway
PATH .... Program for Appropriate Technology in Health (EA)
PATH .... Prospectors and Treasure Hunters Guild (EA)
PATHAT... Precision Aim-Technique Heliborne Antitank [*Gun system concept*] [*Ballistic Research Laboratory*] (RDA)
Path Biol.... Pathologie et Biologie [*Paris*] [*A publication*]
Path Europ ... Pathologia Europaea [*A publication*]
Pat HL Sc .. Paterson's Scotch Appeal Cases [*A publication*] (DLA)
Pat HL Sc .. Paton's Scotch Appeal Cases [*A publication*] (DLA)
Path Microb ... Pathologia et Microbiologia [*A publication*]
Pathobiol Annu ... Pathobiology Annual [*A publication*]
PATHOL... Pathological (MSA)
Pathol........ Pathology [*A publication*] (APTA)
Pathol Annu ... Pathology Annual [*A publication*]
Pathol Biol ... Pathologie et Biologie [*Paris*] [*A publication*]
Pathol Biol (Paris) ... Pathologie et Biologie (Paris) [*A publication*]
Pathol Biol Sem Hop ... Pathologie et Biologie. La Semaine des Hopitaux [*A publication*]
Pathol Clin Med (Tokyo) ... Pathology and Clinical Medicine (Tokyo) [*A publication*]
Pathol Eur ... Pathologia Europaea [*A publication*]
Pathol Eur Suppl ... Pathologia Europaea. Supplement [*A publication*]
Pathol Gen ... Pathologie Generale [*A publication*]
Pathol Immunopathol Res ... Pathology and Immunopathology Research [*A publication*]
Pathol Microbiol ... Pathologia et Microbiologia [*A publication*]
Pathol Microbiol Suppl ... Pathologia et Microbiologia. Supplementum [*Switzerland*] [*A publication*]
Pathol Res Pract ... Pathology. Research and Practice [*A publication*]
Pathol Vet ... Pathologia Veterinaria [*A publication*]
Path Res Pract ... Pathology. Research and Practice [*A publication*]
PATHS ...... Peer Attitudes Toward the Handicapped Scale [*Educational testing*]
PATHS ...... Precursor above the Horizon Sensor [*Strategic Defense Initiative*]
PATI .... Passive Airborne Time-Difference Intercept [*Navy*]
PATI .... Phoenix Advanced Technology, Inc. [*NASDAQ symbol*] (NQ)
PATIA ...... Pacific Area Trading and Investment Area
Patiala........ Indian Law Reports, Patiala Series [*A publication*] (DLA)
PATIB .... Polish-American Travel Information Bureau (EA)
Patient Acc ... Patient Accounts [*A publication*]
Patient Couns Health Educ ... Patient Counselling and Health Education [*A publication*]
Patient Educ Couns ... Patient Education and Counseling [*A publication*]
Patient Educ Newsl ... Patient Education Newsletter [*A publication*]
PATINA.... Potomac Antique Tools and Industries Association (EA)
Pat Ins........ Paton on Insurance [*1962*] [*A publication*] (DLA)
Pat J........... Patent Journal, Including Trademarks and Models [*South Africa*] [*A publication*] (DLA)
Pat J Incl Trade Marks Des ... Patent Journal, Including Trade Marks and Designs [*A publication*]
Pat J Incl Trade Marks Des Copyright Cinematogr Films ... Patent Journal, Including Trade Marks, Designs, and Copyright in Cinematograph Films [*A publication*]
PATK........ Patrick Industries, Inc. [*NASDAQ symbol*] (NQ)
PATK........ Talkeetna [*Alaska*] [*ICAO location identifier*] (ICLI)
PAtL......... Lehigh County Historical Society, Allentown, PA [*Library symbol*] [*Library of Congress*] (LCLS)
PATL......... Pan Atlantic, Inc. [*NASDAQ symbol*] (NQ)
PATL........ Tatalina Air Force Station [*Alaska*] [*ICAO location identifier*] (ICLI)
Pat L Ann... Patent Law Annual [*A publication*]
Pat Law Rev ... Patent Law Review [*A publication*] (DLA)
Pat Licens .. Paterson's Licensing Acts Annual [*A publication*] (DLA)
Pat LJ .... Patna Law Journal [*India*] [*A publication*] (DLA)
Pat LR........ Patent Law Review [*A publication*] (DLA)
Pat LR........ Patna Law Reports [*India*] [*A publication*] (DLA)
Pat L Reptr ... Patna Law Reporter [*India*] [*A publication*] (DLA)
Pat L Rev ... Patent Law Review [*A publication*] (DLA)
Pat LT........ Patna Law Times [*India*] [*A publication*] (DLA)
Pat LW ...... Patna Law Weekly [*A publication*] (DLA)
PAtM........ Muhlenberg College, Allentown, PA [*Library symbol*] [*Library of Congress*] (LCLS)
PATMI...... Powder Actuated Tool Manufacturers' Institute (EA)

PATMKG ... Patternmaking (WGA)
Pat Mort .... Patch on Mortgages [*1821*] [*A publication*] (DLA)
Pat & Mr.... Paterson and Murray's Reports [*1870-71*] [*New South Wales*] [*A publication*] (DLA)
PATMRG ... PACOM [*Pacific Command*] Air Target Materials Review Group (CINC)
PATN .... Pattern (MDG)
Patna J Med ... Patna Journal of Medicine [*A publication*]
PATO .... Partial Acceptance and Takeover Date [*Telecommunications*] (TEL)
PATO .... Pattetico [*Pathetically*] [*Music*] (ROG)
PATO .... Principal Ammunition Technical Officer [*British military*] (DMA)
Pat Off .... Patent Office (DLA)
Pat Off Gaz ... Official Gazette. United States Patent Office [*A publication*]
Pat Off J .... Patent Office Journal [*India*] [*A publication*] (DLA)
Pat Off Rep ... Patent Office Reports [*A publication*] (DLA)
Pat Off Soc J ... Patent Office Society. Journal [*A publication*]
Patog Ter Dermatozov ... Patogenez i Terapiya Dermatozov [*A publication*]
Patol Clin Ostet Ginecol ... Patologia e Clinica Ostetrica e Ginecologica [*A publication*]
Patol Fiziol Eksp Ter ... Patologicheskaya Fiziologiya i Eksperimental'naya Terapiya [*A publication*]
PATOLIS ... Patent Online Information System [*Database*] [*Japan*]
Patol-Mex ... Patologia-Mexico City [*A publication*]
Patol Pol .... Patologia Polska [*A publication*]
Patol Sper .. Patologia Sperimentale [*A publication*]
Paton......... Craigie, Stewart, and Paton's Scotch Appeal Cases [*1726-1821*] [*A publication*] (DLA)
Paton App Cas ... Paton's Scotch Appeal Cases [*A publication*] (DLA)
Paton Sc App Cas ... Paton's Scotch Appeal Cases [*A publication*] (DLA)
PATOOMB ... Phage and the Origins of Molecular Biology
PA Top G S Com ... Pennsylvania Topographic and Geologic Survey Commission [*A publication*]
PA Topogr Geol Surv Bull A ... Pennsylvania Topographic and Geologic Survey. Bulletin A. Atlas Series [*A publication*]
PA Topogr Geol Surv Bull C ... Pennsylvania. Bureau of Topographic and Geologic Survey. Bulletin C [*County Report*] [*A publication*]
PA Topogr Geol Surv Bull G ... Pennsylvania. Bureau of Topographic and Geologic Survey. Bulletin G [*General Geology Report*] [*A publication*]
PA Topogr Geol Surv Bull M ... Pennsylvania Topographic and Geologic Survey. Bulletin M [*A publication*]
PA Topogr Geol Surv Bull W ... Pennsylvania Topographic and Geologic Survey. Bulletin W [*A publication*]
PA Topogr Geol Surv Geol Atlas PA ... Pennsylvania. Bureau of Topographic and Geologic Survey. Geologic Atlas of Pennsylvania [*A publication*]
Pa Topogr Geol Surv Ground Water Rep ... Pennsylvania. Topographic and Geologic Survey. Ground Water Report [*A publication*]
PA Topogr Geol Surv Inform Circ ... Pennsylvania. Bureau of Topographic and Geologic Survey. Information Circular [*A publication*]
PA Topogr Geol Surv Miner Resour Rep ... Pennsylvania Topographic and Geologic Survey. Mineral Resources Report [*A publication*]
PA Topogr Geol Surv Progr Rep ... Pennsylvania. Bureau of Topographic and Geologic Survey. Progress Report [*A publication*]
PA Topogr Geol Surv Spec Bull ... Pennsylvania. Bureau of Topographic and Geologic Survey. Special Bulletin [*A publication*]
PATOS ...... Patent-Online-System [*Bertelsmann Datenbankdienste GmbH*] [*Database*]
PATP .... Preliminary Authority to Proceed (NASA)
PATP .... Production Acceptance Test Procedure (MCD)
PATP .... (Pyridylcarbonylamino)tetrahydropyridine [*Biochemistry*]
PATPEND ... Patent Pending
Pat Pol .... Patologia Polska [*A publication*]
PatPtr .... Patrick Petroleum Co. [*Associated Press abbreviation*] (APAG)
PAT-PTR .. US Patent Data Base - Patent Technology Reports [*Patent and Trademark Office*] [*Database*]
PATQ .... ATQ. The American Transcendental Quarterly [*A publication*]
PATR........ Patriarch
PATR........ Patriotic (ROG)
PATR........ Patron
PATR........ Production Acceptance Test Requirement (MCD)
PATRA...... Printing, Packaging, and Allied Trades Research Association
PATRA...... Professional and Technical Role Analyses [*Occupational therapy*]
Pa Trade J ... Paper Trade Journal [*A publication*]
PATRDL... Pan American Tung Research and Development League [*Defunct*] (EA)
Patr Elect Cas ... Patrick's Election Cases [*1824-49*] [*Upper Canada*] [*A publication*] (DLA)
PATREU... Palaestina Treuhandstelle zur Beratung Deutscher Juden [*A publication*]
PATRIC .... Pattern Recognition and Information Correlations [*Police crime-detection computer*]
PATRIC .... Pattern Recognition Interpretation and Correlation (CET)
PATRIC .... Position and Time-Resolved Ion Counting [*Detector*]
PATRICIA ... Practical Algorithm to Receive Information Coded in Alphanumeric [*Information retrieval*]

Patrick El Cas ... Patrick's Election Cases [*Canada*] [*A publication*] (DLA)
PATRIOT ... Phased Array Tracking to Intercept of Target [*Air defense system unit*] [*Army*] (RDA)
Patrist Sorb ... Patristica Sorbonensia [*A publication*]
Pa Tr J .... Paper Trade Journal [*A publication*]
PATROL ... Program for Administrative Traffic Reports On-Line [*Computer program*] [*Bell System*]
PatrolGr ..... Patrologia Graeca (BJA)
PatrolLat .... Patrologia Latina (BJA)
PATRON .. Patrol Squadron
Patronato Invest Cient Tec "Juan De La Cierva" Mem ... Patronato de Investigacion Cientifica y Tecnica "Juan De La Cierva." Memoria [*A publication*]
Patronato Invest Cient Tec "Juan De La Cierva" Publ Tec ... Patronato de Investigacion Cientifica y Tecnica "Juan De La Cierva." Publicaciones Tecnicas [*A publication*]
PatrPr .... Patriot Premium Dividend Fund, Inc. [*Associated Press abbreviation*] (APAG)
PATS .... Payload Avionics Test Station [*NASA*] (SSD)
PATS .... Payment and Telecommunication Services Corp. [*New York, NY*] [*Telecommunications*] [*Defunct*] (TSSD)
PATS .... People Against Tobacco Smoke (EA)
PATS .... Personnel Assistance Teams [*Military*]
PATS .... Personnel in an Awaiting Training Status [*Air Force*] (AFM)
PATS .... Portable Acoustic Tracking System for Divers (MCD)
PATS .... Preacademic Training Student [*Military*]
PATS .... Preauthorized Automatic Transfer Scheme [*Banking*]
PATS .... Precision Altimeter Techniques Study
PATS .... Predicasts Abstract Terminal System [*Data processing*]
PATS .... Primary Aircraft Training System (MCD)
PATS .... Program for Analysis of Time Series (NASA)
PATS .... Programmatic and Technical Support [*Army*]
PATS .... Propulsion Analysis Trajectory Simulation [*Computer program*] [*NASA*]
PATSEARCH ... Patent Search [*Data processing*]
PatSel .... Patroit Select Dividend Trust [*Associated Press abbreviation*] (APAG)
Pat Ser .... Indian Law Reports, Patna Series [*A publication*] (DLA)
Pat Specif (Aust) ... Patent Specification (Australia) [*A publication*]
Pat St Tr .... Paton on Stoppage in Transitu [*1859*] [*A publication*] (DLA)
PATSU .... Patrol Aircraft Service Unit
PATSY ...... Parametric Test Synthesis [*Data processing*]
PATSY ...... Picture Animal Top Star of the Year [*or Performing Animal Television Star of the Year*] [*American Humane Association award*]
PATSY ...... Programmer's Automatic Testing System
PATT .... Partial Automatic Translation Technique
PATT .... Patent (ROG)
PATT .... Pattern (AAG)
PATT .... Patton Oil Co. [*NASDAQ symbol*] (NQ)
PATT .... Project for the Analysis of Technology Transfer [*NASA*]
Patten .... Patten Corp. [*Associated Press abbreviation*] (APAG)
PATTERN ... Planning Assistance Through Technical Evaluation of Relevance Numbers [*RAND Corp.*]
Pattern Recogn ... Pattern Recognition [*A publication*]
Pattern Recognition ... Journal. Pattern Recognition Society [*A publication*]
Pattern Recognition Lett ... Pattern Recognition Letters [*A publication*]
Patt & H ..... Patton, Jr., and Heath's Reports [*Virginia*] [*A publication*] (DLA)
PATTH ...... People Against Telephone Terrorism and Harassment (EA)
Patt & Heath R ... Patton, Jr., and Heath's Reports [*Virginia*] [*A publication*] (DLA)
Patt & H (VA) ... Patton, Jr., and Heath's Reports [*Virginia*] [*A publication*] (DLA)
PATTI .... Prompt Action to Telephone Inquiries (SAA)
Pat TM & Copy J ... Patent, Trademark, and Copyright Journal [*A publication*]
Pat TM & Copyr J of R & Educ ... Patent, Trademark, and Copyright Journal of Research and Education [*A publication*] (DLA)
Pat and TM Rev ... Patent and Trade Mark Review [*A publication*]
Patton & H ... Patton, Jr., and Heath's Reports [*Virginia Special Court of Appeals*] [*A publication*] (DLA)
Patton & Heath ... Patton, Jr., and Heath's Reports [*Virginia*] [*A publication*] (DLA)
Patton & H (VA) ... Patton, Jr., and Heath's Reports [*Virginia Special Court of Appeals*] [*A publication*] (DLA)
Pat Trademark & Copyright J (BNA) ... Patent, Trademark, and Copyright Journal (Bureau of National Affairs) [*A publication*] (DLA)
Pat Trademark & Copyright J BNA ... Patents, Trademark, and Copyright Journal. Bureau of National Affairs [*A publication*]
Patt Recog ... Pattern Recognition [*A publication*]
Pat & Tr Mk Rev ... Patent and Trade Mark Review [*A publication*]
PATU .... Pan American Taekwondo Union (EA)
PATU .... PanAfrican Telecommunications Union (EAIO)
PATUA ...... Proceedings. Research Institute of Atmospherics. Nagoya University [*A publication*]
PATWAS .. Pilots Automatic Telephone Weather Answering Service
PATWING ... Patrol Wing [*Later, Fleet Air Wing*]
PATWINGDET ... Patrol Wing [*Later, Fleet Air Wing*] Detachment (DNAB)
PATWINGLANTFLT ... Patrol Wing [*later, Fleet Air Wing*] Atlantic Fleet

PATWINGSCOFOR ... Patrol Wing [*later, Fleet Air Wing*] Scouting Force
PAU .... Pacific Command Frequency Allocation and Uses (CINC)
PAU .... Pamietnik Akademii Umiejetnosci Krakowie [*A publication*]
PAU .... Pan American Union [*Central organ and permanent secretariat of the OAS*]
PAU .... Pattern Articulation Unit [*Data processing*]
PAU .... Pauk [*Myanmar*] [*Airport symbol*] (OAG)
PAU .... Paulingite [*A zeolite*]
Pau .... [*Julius*] Paulus [*Flourished, 3rd century*] [*Authority cited in pre-1607 legal work*] (DSA)
Pau .... Paulus de Liazaris [*Deceased, 1356*] [*Authority cited in pre-1607 legal work*] (DSA)
PAU .... Pauzhetka [*Former USSR*] [*Seismograph station code, US Geological Survey*] (SEIS)
pau .... Pennsylvania [*MARC country of publication code*] [*Library of Congress*] (LCCP)
PAU .... Pilotless Aircraft Unit
PAU .... Polska Akademia Umiejetnosci [*A publication*]
PAU .... Portable Annotation Unit [*Military*] (CAAL)
PAU .... Position Analog Unit [*Manufacturing term*]
PAU .... Precision Approach - UNICOM [*Aviation*]
PAU .... Present Address Unknown
PAU .... Probe Aerodynamic Upper [*NASA*] (MCD)
PAU .... Production Assurance Unit (MCD)
PAU .... Programmes Analysis Unit [*British*] (MCD)
PAU .... University of Pennsylvania, Philadelphia, PA [*OCLC symbol*] (OCLC)
PAU-AN ... Polska Akademia Umiejetnosci. Archivum Neophilologicum [*A publication*]
PAUBM .... Pan American Union of Baptist Men [*Defunct*] (EA)
PAUCA ..... Proceedings. Royal Australian Chemical Institute [*A publication*]
PAUCA ..... Providence Association of Ukrainian Catholics in America (EA)
Pau de Cast ... Paulus de Castro [*Deceased, 1441*] [*Authority cited in pre-1607 legal work*] (DSA)
PAUDGET ... Photometer, Automated Universal Distribution Gonielectric Type
Pau Hunga ... Paulus Hungarus [*Deceased, 1242*] [*Authority cited in pre-1607 legal work*] (DSA)
Pau Hungar ... Paulus Hungarus [*Deceased, 1242*] [*Authority cited in pre-1607 legal work*] (DSA)
PAUKO ..... Pan-American Union of Karatedo Organizations [*Later, PUKO*] (EA)
PAUL .... Paullum [*A Little*] [*Pharmacy*]
Pau de La ... Paulus de Liazaris [*Deceased, 1356*] [*Authority cited in pre-1607 legal work*] (DSA)
Paul de Cast ... Paulus de Castro [*Deceased, 1441*] [*Authority cited in pre-1607 legal work*] (DSA)
Paul de Castr ... Paulus de Castro [*Deceased, 1441*] [*Authority cited in pre-1607 legal work*] (DSA)
Pau Leon .... Paulus Leonius [*Flourished, 16th century*] [*Authority cited in pre-1607 legal work*] (DSA)
Paul Liaz .... Paulus de Liazaris [*Deceased, 1356*] [*Authority cited in pre-1607 legal work*] (DSA)
PAULS ..... Pennsylvania Union List of Serials
Paulus .... Julius Paulus. Sententiae Receptae [*A publication*] (DLA)
Pau de Montep ... Paulus Ruinus de Montepico [*Flourished, 15th century*] [*Authority cited in pre-1607 legal work*] (DSA)
PAUMV .... Potato Aucuba Mosaic Virus [*Plant pathology*]
PAUN .... Unalakleet [*Alaska*] [*ICAO location identifier*] (ICLI)
PA Univ Lab Contr ... Pennsylvania University. Laboratory Contributions [*A publication*]
PA Univ Mus Bul ... Pennsylvania University. University Museum. Bulletin [*A publication*]
PA Univ Schoolmen's Week Proc ... Pennsylvania University. Schoolmen's Week. Proceedings [*A publication*]
PAUP .... Phylogenic Analysis Using Parsimony [*Biology*]
Paus .... Pausanias [*Second century AD*] [*Classical studies*] (OCD)
PAUS .... Piedmontese Association of the United States (EA)
PAus .... Poetry Australia [*A publication*]
PAUSE .... People Against Unconstitutional Sex Education
PAusL .... Papers in Australian Linguistics [*A publication*]
P Aust Bioc ... Proceedings. Australian Biochemical Society [*A publication*]
PAUT .... Pennsylvania & Atlantic Railroad Co. [*Absorbed into Consolidated Rail Corp.*] [*AAR code*]
PAUTDL ... Proceedings. Australian Society of Sugar Cane Technologists [*A publication*]
P Automtn ... Process Automation [*A publication*]
PAUX .... Pauxillum [*A Little*] [*Pharmacy*]
PAV .... Packaging Review [*A publication*]
P/AV .... Particular Average
PaV .... Pathe-Vox [*Record label*] [*France*]
PAV .... Paulo Afonso [*Brazil*] [*Airport symbol*] (OAG)
PAV .... Pavia [*Italy*] [*Seismograph station code, US Geological Survey*] (SEIS)
PAV .... Pavilion
Pav .... Pavo [*Constellation*]
PAV .... Pay Adjustment Voucher [*Military*]
PAV .... Personnel Allotment Voucher [*Army*]
PAV .... Phase Angle Voltmeter

PAV .... Position and Velocity
PAV .... Poste-Avion [*Airmail*] [*French*]
PAV .... Potential Acquisition Valuation Method [*Management*]
PAV .... Pressure-Actuated Valve (NASA)
PAV .... Pressure Altitude Variation [*Aviation*]
PAV .... Propellant-Actuated Valve
PAV .... Public Access Videotex
PAV .... Public Against Violence [*Former Czechoslovakia*] [*Political party*]
PAV .... Puella Americana Vallensis [*Valley Girl*] [*Teenaged girl who follows the fads, fashions, and slang originated among teenagers in California's San Fernando Valley*]
PAVA .... Polish Army Veterans Association of America (EA)
PAVAS ..... Performing and Visual Arts Society (EA)
PAVD .... Valdez [*Alaska*] [*ICAO location identifier*] (ICLI)
PAVE........ Position and Velocity Extraction
PAVE........ Primary Auditory Visual Experience [*National Visitor Center*]
PAVE........ Principles and Applications of Value Engineering
PAVe.......... Procarbazine, Alanine Nitrogen Mustard [*L-Phenylanine mustard, L-PAM*], Velban [*Vinblastine*] [*Antineoplastic drug regimen*]
PAVE........ Professional Audiovisual Education Study
PAVE........ Programmed Analysis for Value Engineers
PAVE PAWS ... Precision Acquisition of Vehicle Entry Phased Array Warning System
PAVF........ Pulmonary Arteriovenous Fistula [*Medicine*]
PAVFC ..... Princeton Azimuthally-Varying-Field Cyclotron
PAVG .... Prince Albert's Volunteer Guards [*British military*] (DMA)
Pavia Univ Ist Geol Atti ... Pavia Universita. Istituto Geologico. Atti [*A publication*]
Pav J Biol... Pavlovian Journal of Biological Science [*A publication*]
PAVLA ...... Papal Volunteers for Latin America [*Defunct*]
Pavlovian J Biol Sci ... Pavlovian Journal of Biological Science [*A publication*]
Pavlov J Biol Sci ... Pavlovian Journal of Biological Science [*A publication*]
Pavlov J Higher Nerv Act ... Pavlov Journal of Higher Nervous Activity [*A publication*]
PAVM .... Patrons of the Arts in the Vatican Museum (EA)
PAVM .... Phase Angle Voltmeter
PAVMT..... Pavement
PAVN .... People's Army of Vietnam
PAVO .... Prince Albert Victor's Own [*British military*] (DMA)
PAVOC ..... Prince Albert Victor's Own Cavalry [*British military*] (DMA)
PA/VR....... Public Assistance/Vocational Rehabilitation
PAVS........ Pulmonary Arterial Vasconstrictor Substance [*Medicine*]
PAVT........ Position and Velocity Tracking
P & AW..... Paging and Area Warning
PAW .... Pambwa [*Papua New Guinea*] [*Airport symbol*] (OAG)
PAW .... Panel of American Women (EA)
PA of W .... Pentecostal Assemblies of the World (EA)
PAW .... People for the American Way (EA)
PAW .... Percussive Arc Welder
PAW .... Performance Analysis Workstation [*Data processing*]
PAW .... Petroleum Administration for War [*World War II*]
PAW .... Plasma Arc Welding
PAW .... Port Angeles Western Railroad (IIA)
PAW .... Powered All the Way
PAW .... Public Administered Whipping [*Slang*]
PAW .... Pulmonary Artery Wedge Pressure [*Cardiology*]
PAWA .... Pan American Women's Association (EA)
PAWA .... PanAmerican Women's Association (EAIO)
PAWAF..... Polish American Workmen's Aid Fund (EA)
PAWC .... Pan-American Weightlifting Confederation (EA)
PA WC Bd Dec ... Pennsylvania Workmen's Compensation Board Decisions [*A publication*] (DLA)
PA WC Bd Dec Dig ... Digest of Decisions, Pennsylvania Workmen's Compensation Board [*A publication*] (DLA)
PA WC Bd (Dep Rep Sup) ... Workmen's Compensation Supplement to Department Reports of Pennsylvania [*A publication*] (DLA)
PAWD .... Kodiak/Municipal [*Alaska*] [*ICAO location identifier*] (ICLI)
PAWE........ Program for Analysis of the World Ecosystem
PAWI........ Parks and Wilderness [*A publication*]
PAWLC..... Pan-American Weightlifting Confederation (EA)
PAWN .... Poole, Aberley, Worthington, and Nolen [*Four early residents of Pawn, Oregon. The city derives its name from the initial letters of their surnames*]
PAWOS..... Portable Automatic Weather Observing Station (MCD)
PAWP........ Pulmonary Artery Wedge Pressure [*Medicine*]
PAWS........ Parachute Altitude Wind Sensor
PAWS........ Pet Animal Welfare Scheme [*British*] (DI)
PAWS........ Pets Are Worth Safeguarding [*An association*]
PAWS........ Phased Array Warning System
PAWS........ Polar Automatic Weather Station (NG)
PAWS........ Portable Automatic Weather Station (MUGU)
PAWS........ Programmed Automatic Welding System
PAWT........ Wainwright [*Alaska*] [*ICAO location identifier*] (ICLI)
PAWW ...... Wildwood [*Alaska*] [*ICAO location identifier*] (ICLI)
PAX .... OPTEVFOR [*Operational Test and Evaluation Force*] Detachment, Patuxent River, MD [*Navy*] (CAAL)

PAX .... Pan Central Explorations Ltd. [*Toronto Stock Exchange symbol*]
PAX .... Parallel Architecture Extended [*Data processing*]
PAX .... Passenger (AFM)
PAX .... Patuxent River [*Maryland*] (MCD)
PAX .... Paxson [*Alaska*] [*Seismograph station code, US Geological Survey*] (SEIS)
Pax .... Paxton [*Record label*] [*Great Britain*]
PAX .... Person-to-Person Accelerated Xerography [*Office technology*] [*British*]
PAX .... Physical Address Extension
PAX .... Place Address in Index Register (SAA)
PAX .... Private Automatic Exchange [*Telecommunications*]
PAXAR...... Paxar Corp. [*Associated Press abbreviation*] (APAG)
PAXCON .. Passenger Airlift Contract [*Military*]
PAXT........ Paxton [*Frank*] Co. [*NASDAQ symbol*] (NQ)
PAY .... Pamol [*Malaysia*] [*Airport symbol*] (OAG)
PAYA .... Yakutat [*Alaska*] [*ICAO location identifier*] (ICLI)
PAYC........ Payco American Corp. [*NASDAQ symbol*] (NQ)
PAYCOM ... Payload Command [*NASA*] (MCD)
PAYDAT... Payload Data [*NASA*] (MCD)
PAYE........ Pay As You Earn
PAYE........ Pay As You Enter
PAYE........ Pitch and Yaw Engine (MCD)
PAYERS... Program Accomplishment Year to Date Evaluation Reviews
PAYES ...... Program for Assessing Youth Employment Skills [*Vocational guidance test*]
PAYFON... Pay-Fone Systems, Inc. [*Associated Press abbreviation*] (APAG)
Pay & Iv Carr ... Payne and Ivamy's Carriage by Sea [*10th ed.*] [*1976*] [*A publication*] (DLA)
PAYLD...... Payload
PAYM .... Paymaster [*Military*] [*British*] (ROG)
PAYMARCORPS ... Paymaster, Marine Corps
PAYMR..... Paymaster
PAYMT..... Payment
PAYMTR.. Paymaster [*Military*] [*British*] (ROG)
PAYN .... Pay'n Save, Inc. [*NASDAQ symbol*] (NQ)
PAYR........ Paymaster (WGA)
PAYS........ Patriotic American Youth Society
Pays .... Paysans [*A publication*]
PAYSOP ... Payroll/Stock Ownership Plan
PAYSU ..... P'Eylim-American Yeshiva Student Union (EA)
PAYT........ Payment
PAYX........ Paychex, Inc. [*NASDAQ symbol*] (NQ)
PAZ .... Palaeozoic Axial Zone [*Geophysics*]
PAZ .... Paper and Packaging Bulletin [*A publication*]
PAZ .... Poza Rica [*Mexico*] [*Airport symbol*] (OAG)
PAZA........ Anchorage [*Alaska*] [*ICAO location identifier*] (ICLI)
PAZA........ Pan American Zebu Association [*Later, IZBA*] (EA)
PAZF........ Fairbanks [*Alaska*] [*ICAO location identifier*] (ICLI)
PAZO .... American Zoologist [*A publication*]
PAZT........ Aztlan [*A publication*]
PB .... Air Burundi [*ICAO designator*] (FAAC)
PB .... Bethlehem Public Library, Bethlehem, PA [*Library symbol*] [*Library of Congress*] (LCLS)
PB .... Dr. Karl Thomae GmbH [*Germany*] [*Research code symbol*]
PB .... Document PB. National Technical Information Service [*A publication*]
P/B............. Pad and Boom [*Refueling*] [*Aerospace*] (MSA)
PB .... Paedagogische Blaetter [*A publication*]
PB .... Painted Base (AAG)
PB .... Panama Basin
PB .... Panic Bar [*Technical drawings*]
PB .... Pantheon Babylonicum: Nomina Deorum [*A publication*]
PB .... Paper Base (MSA)
PB .... Paperback (CDAI)
PB .... Paperboard Industries Corp. [*Toronto Stock Exchange symbol*]
PB .... Papua Besena [*Political party*] [*Papua New Guinea*] (FEA)
PB .... Paraffin Bath [*Medicine*]
PB .... Paris Bourse [*The French stock exchange*]
PB .... Parke-Bernet [*Later, SPB*] [*Manhattan art auction house*]
PB .... Parliamentary Bill [*British*] (ROG)
PB .... Particle-Beam Weapon
PB .... Parts Breakdown
PB .... Passbook [*Banking*]
PB .... Passed Ball
PB .... Pastor Bonus [*A publication*]
PB .... Patrol Boat [*Navy symbol*]
PB .... Patrol Bomber
PB .... Paul-Bunnell [*Test*] [*Immunology*] (AAMN)
PB .... Pawnbroker
PB .... Pay Board
PB .... Peaceful Beginnings (EA)
PB .... Peanut Butter [*Brand name of the Red Wing Co.*]
PB .... Pennsylvania Ballet
PB .... Pentaborane [*Rocket fuel*]
PB .... Pentobarbital [*Organic chemistry*]
PB .... Peribrachialis [*Anatomy*]
PB .... Peripheral Blood [*Medicine*] (AAMN)
PB .... Peripheral Buffer

PB .... Permanent Ballast (DS)
PB .... Permanent Bunkers
PB .... Permanently Blind
P de B .... Petrus de Bellapertica [*Deceased, 1308*] [*Authority cited in pre-1607 legal work*] (DSA)
PB .... Petrus Brito [*Flourished, 13th century*] [*Authority cited in pre-1607 legal work*] (DSA)
PB .... Phalangeal Bracket [*i.e., cup handle*] [*Slang*]
PB .... Pharmacopoeia Britannica [*British Pharmacopoeia*]
PB .... Phenobarbital [*A drug*]
P & B .... Phenobarbital and Belladonna [*A drug regimen*]
PB .... Philosophiae Baccalaureus [*Bachelor of Philosophy*]
PB .... Phonetically Balanced [*With reference to word lists*]
PB .... Phosphate Buffer
PB .... Phosphoribosyl
PB .... Photon Barrier [*Astrophysics*]
PB .... Physics Briefs [*Physikalische Berichte*] [*American Institute of Physics*] [*Database*] [*Information service or system*] (IID)
PB .... Picket Boat [*Navy*]
PB .... Piebald
PB .... Pilotless Bomber [*Air Force*]
PB .... Pinchbeck [*Jewelry*] (ROG)
PB .... Pine Bark
PB .... Pink Bollworm [*Cotton pest*]
PB .... Pipe Break [*Nuclear energy*] (NRCH)
PB .... Piperonyl Butoxide [*Organic chemistry*]
PB .... Pit Border [*Paleobotany*]
PB .... Pitney-Bowes, Inc.
PB .... Planen und Bauen [*A publication*]
PB .... Planning Board
P & B .... Planning and Budgeting [*Military*] (AFIT)
PB .... Plasminogen Binding [*Hematology*]
PB .... Plate Block [*Philately*]
PB .... Playback (KSC)
Pb .... Playboy [*A publication*]
PB .... Plot Board (KSC)
PB .... Plugboard
Pb .... Plumbum [*Lead*] [*Chemical element*]
PB .... Plymouth Brethren (ROG)
PB .... Pocket Book
PB .... Poetry Bag [*A publication*]
PB .... Police Burgh
PB .... Policy Board (OICC)
PB .... Pollen Body [*Botany*]
PB .... Polybenzene [*Organic chemistry*]
PB .... Polybutylene [*Organic chemistry*]
PB .... Polymyxin B [*An antibiotic*]
PB .... Pony Baseball (EA)
PB .... Poop and Bridge [*of a ship*] (DS)
PB .... Population Biology
PB .... Ports and Beaches (NATG)
PB .... Power Boiler
PB .... Power Brakes [*Automotive engineering*]
PB .... Prabuddha Bharata [*Calcutta*] [*A publication*]
P and B ...... Pragmatics and Beyond [*A publication*]
PB .... Praktische Betriebswirt [*A publication*]
PB .... Pravoslav'nija Bukovyna [*A publication*]
PB .... Prayer Book
PB de B .... Preburner [*NASA*] (NASA)
PB .... Preliminary Breakdown
Pb .... Presbyopia [*Ophthalmology*]
PB .... Presentation Brothers [*See also FPM*] (EAIO)
PB .... Presiding Bishop [*Episcopal Church*]
PB .... Pressure Breathing
P & B .... Price and Budgeting (MCD)
PB .... Primary Buffer [*Chemistry*]
PB .... Primary Bus [*Data processing*] (CAAL)
PB .... Primitive Baptist
P & B .... Printing and Binding [*Publishing*]
PB .... Prisoners' Barracks (ADA)
PB .... Private Business [*Slang*] [*British*]
PB .... Privately Bonded
Pb .... Probability (PCM)
PB .... Process Bulletin
PB .... Production Base (MCD)
PB .... Professional Books Ltd. (ILCA)
PB .... Profile Block (MCD)
PB .... Program Breakdown
P-as-B .... Program as Broadcast [*Radio*] (DEN)
PB .... Program Budgeting (ADA)
PB .... Property Book [*Army*] (AABC)
PB .... Proportional Band
PB .... Protein-Binding (MAE)
PB .... Provisional Battalion [*Military*] [*A publication*] (ROG)
PB .... Przeglad Biblioteczny [*A publication*]
PB .... Pseudoterminal Bud [*Botany*]
PB .... Psychological Bulletin [*A publication*]
PB .... Ptychodiscus brevis [*An alga, the cause of the red tide*]
PB .... Public (DSUE)

Pb .... Publicatieblad van de Europese Gemeenschappen [*A publication*]
PB .... Publications Board [*Later, CFSTI, NTIS*]
PB .... Publications Bulletin
PB .... Publisher's Name [*Online database field identifier*]
P & B .... Pugsley and Burbridge's New Brunswick Reports [*A publication*] (DLA)
PB .... Pull Box (AAG)
PB .... Pulse Beacon (KSC)
PB .... Purplish Blue
PB .... Push from the Bush [*A publication*] (APTA)
PB .... Push Button
PB4 .... Plate Block of Four [*Philately*]
PBA .... Academy of the New Church, Bryn Athyn, PA [*OCLC symbol*] (OCLC)
PBa .... Academy of the New Church, Bryn Athyn, PA [*Library symbol*] [*Library of Congress*] (LCLS)
Pba .... Brachial Arterial Pressure [*Medicine*] (MAE)
PBA .... Pacific Broadcasting Association (EAIO)
PBA .... Paid by Agent [*Business term*] (DCTA)
PBA .... Partido Barrientista Autentico [*Bolivia*] [*Political party*] (PPW)
PBA .... Patrol Boat, Air Cushion (MCD)
PBA .... Patrolmen's Benevolent Association
PBA .... Pencil Beam Antenna
PBA .... Permanent Budget Account
PBA .... Phenylboronic Acid [*Organic chemistry*]
PBA .... Phenylbutyric Acid [*Organic chemistry*]
PBA .... Physical Blowing Agent [*Plastics technology*]
PBA .... Pill Box Antenna
PBA .... Pine Bluff Arsenal [*Army*] (AABC)
PBA .... Plant Breeding Abstracts [*A publication*]
PbA .... Plasmodium Berghei Anka [*Bacteriology*]
PBA .... Plastic Bag Association (EA)
PBA .... Polar Bear Association (EA)
PBA .... Polish Beneficial Association (EA)
PBA .... Polska Bibliografia Analityczna [*A publication*]
PBA .... Polybenzamide [*Organic chemistry*]
PBA .... Polyclonal B Cell Activator [*Hematology*]
PBA .... Port Blair [*Andaman Islands*] [*Seismograph station code, US Geological Survey*] (SEIS)
PBA .... Port of Bristol Authority [*British*]
PBA .... Poultry Breeders of America (EA)
PBA .... Prescott Builders Association (EA)
PBA .... President of the British Academy
PBA .... Pressure Breathing Assistor [*Medicine*]
PBA .... Principal Business Activity (GFGA)
PBA .... Printing Brokerage Association (EA)
PBA .... Proceedings. British Academy [*A publication*]
PBA .... Production Base Analysis (MCD)
PBA .... Professional Bookmen of America [*Later, Pi Beta Alpha*] (EA)
PBA .... Professional Bowlers Association of America (EA)
PBA .... Provincetown-Boston Airlines, Inc.
PBA .... Public Buildings Administration [*Functions transferred to PBS, 1949*]
PBA .... Pulpobuccoaxial [*Dentistry*]
PBA .... Pyrenebutyric Acid [*Organic chemistry*]
PBA .... Schoenvisie. Maandblad voor de Schoenhandel en Schoenindustrie [*A publication*]
PBAA .... Periodical and Book Association of America (EA)
PBAA .... Poly(butadiene-acrylic Acid) [*Organic chemistry*]
PBAC .... Pacific Bantam Austin Club (EA)
PBAC .... ProBac International Corp. [*NASDAQ symbol*] (NQ)
PBAC .... Program Budget Advisory Committee [*Army*]
PBAE .... Publications. Bureau of American Ethnology [*A publication*]
PB-AESRS ... Property Book - Army Equipment Status Reporting System (AABC)
PBAL .... Black American Literature Forum [*A publication*]
PBAL .... Provincetown-Boston Airlines, Inc. [*NASDAQ symbol*] (NQ)
PBAN .... Pheromone Biosynthesis-Activating Neuropeptide [*Biochemistry*]
PBAN .... Poly(butadiene-acrylonitrile) [*Organic chemistry*]
PBAN .... Popular Bancshares Corp. [*NASDAQ symbol*] (NQ)
PBANB .... Pathobiology Annual [*A publication*]
PBAPRS .... Program/Budget Accounting and Progress Reporting System [*Proposed*] [*Navy*]
PBAPS ...... Peach Bottom Atomic Power Station (NRCH)
PBAPS ...... Pipe Break Air Piping System (IEEE)
PBAPS ...... Pipe Break Automatic Protective System (IEEE)
PBAR .... Baker Island Army Air Field [*Baker Island*] [*ICAO location identifier*] (ICLI)
PBAS .... Program Budget Accounting System [*Military*] (GFGA)
PBASA ...... Proceedings. Bihar Academy of Agricultural Sciences [*A publication*]
PBAT .... Pyro Battery (KSC)
P Bat Conf ... Proceedings. Battle Conference on Anglo-Norman Studies [*A publication*]
PBB .... Bloomsburg State College, Bloomsburg, PA [*OCLC symbol*] (OCLC)
PBB .... Parallel by Bit
PBB .... Paranaiba [*Brazil*] [*Airport symbol*] (OAG)

PBB............ Parti Pesaka Bumiputera Bersatu Sarawak [*United Bumiputra Party*] [*Political party*] [*Malaysia*]   (FEA)
PBB............ Polybrominated Biphenyl [*Flame retardant, toxic chemical*]
PBB............ Posterior Basal Body [*Botany*]
PBB............ Private Boxes and Bags
PBB............ Project Blue Book [*An association*]   (EA)
PBBCAS.... Program-Based Budget Classification and Analysis System [*Pronounced "pib-kaz"*] [*Office of Management and Budget*]
PBBCD...... Promoclim B. Bulletin du Genie Climatique [*A publication*]
PBbCHi ..... Columbia County Historical Society, Bloomsburg, PA [*Library symbol*] [*Library of Congress*]   (LCLS)
PBBFI........ Pearl S. Buck Birthplace Foundation, Inc.   (EA)
PBBH .... Peter Bent Brigham Hospital [*Boston*]
PBBHA...... Pharmacology, Biochemistry, and Behavior [*A publication*]
PBbS.......... Bloomsburg State College, Bloomsburg, PA [*Library symbol*] [*Library of Congress*]   (LCLS)
PBBS .... Pertubuhan Bumiputera Bersatu Sarawak [*United Sarawak National Association*] [*Political party*] [*Malaysia*]   (FEA)
PBC............ Columbia/Mt. Pleasant, TN [*Location identifier*] [*FAA*]   (FAAL)
PBC............ Pacific Bible College [*California*]
PBC............ Packed by Carrier
PBC............ Pakistan Broadcasting Corp.   (IMH)
PBC............ Panamerican Badminton Confederation   (EAIO)
PBC............ Parallel by Character
PBC............ Pedal Branch of Columellar [*Muscle*]
PBC............ Pen and Brush Club   (EA)
PBC............ People's Bank of China   (ECON)
PBC............ People's Bicentennial [*later, Business*] Commission
PBC............ Peripheral Blood Cells [*Medicine*]
PBC............ Peripheral Bus Computer [*Bell System*]
PBC............ Personnel/Burden Carrier Manufacturers Association   (EA)
PBC............ Plain Bond Copier [*Pitney Bowes*]
PBC............ Planning and the Black Community   (EA)
PBC............ Point of Basal Convergence
PBC............ Practice Bomb Contained   (NG)
PBC............ Prebed Care [*Medicine*]   (MAE)
PBC............ Presbyterians for Biblical Concerns   (EA)
PBC............ Primary Biliary Cirrhosis [*Medicine*]
PBC............ Program Booking Center [*Telecommunications*]   (TEL)
PBC............ Program Budget Committee [*Military*]
PBC............ Psychometric Behavior Checklist [*Psychology*]
PBC............ Public Buildings Commission [*Functions transferred to PBA, 1939*]
PBCA........ Pacific Bible College of Azusa [*California*]
PBCA........ Paperboard Butter Chip Association
PBCB........ Pierce-Blank Die (Class B)   (MCD)
PBCC........ Pitney Bowes Credit Corp.
PBCCH...... Pentabromochlorocyclohexane [*Flame retardant*] [*Organic chemistry*]
PBCE .... Boston College Environmental Affairs Law Review [*A publication*]
PBCE .... Pine Bluff Cotton Exchange   (EA)
PBCF .... Prudential-Bache Capital Funding
PBCI .... Pamrapo Bancorp, Inc. [*NASDAQ symbol*]   (NQ)
PBCMO..... Poly(bis(chloromethyl)oxetane) [*Organic chemistry*]
PBCO .... Praseodymium Barium Copper Oxide [*Inorganic chemistry*]
PB/COC.... Plymouth Barracuda/Cuda Owners Club   (EA)
PBCS .... Persian Bicolor and Calico Society   (EA)
PBCS .... Post Boost Control System [*Aerospace*]
PBCT........ People's Bank [*NASDAQ symbol*]   (NQ)
PBCT........ Proposed Boundary Crossing Time [*Aviation*]
PBC-USA.. Polar Bear Club - USA   (EA)
PBC-WS.... Polar Bear Club - Winter Swimmers [*Later, PBC-USA*]   (EA)
PBD .... Pacific Basin Development Corp. [*Vancouver Stock Exchange symbol*]
PBD .... Paperboard   (MSA)
PBD .... Parallel Blade Damper   (OA)
PBD .... Particle Board [*Technical drawings*]
PBD .... Paul-Bunnell-Davidsohn [*Test*] [*Immunology*]
PBD .... Payload Bay Door [*NASA*]   (NASA)
PBD .... Phenylbiphenylyloxadiazole [*Analytical biochemistry*]
PBD .... Pierce-Blank Die   (MCD)
PBD .... Plasterboard
PBD .... Plenum Bleed Duct [*Hovercraft*]
PBD .... Polybutadiene [*Organic chemistry*]
PBD .... Porbandar [*India*] [*Airport symbol*]   (OAG)
PBD .... Power Building   (NATG)
PBD .... Precise Block Diagram
PBD .... Pressboard   (MSA)
PBD .... Program Budget Decision [*DoD*]
PBD .... Program Budget Directive   (MCD)
PBD .... Program Budget Document   (MCD)
PBD .... Proliferative Breast Disease [*Medicine*]
Pbd Abstr.. Paper and Board Abstracts [*A publication*]
PBDC........ Pacific Basin Development Council   (EA)
PBDF........ Payload Bay Door Forward [*NASA*]   (MCD)
PBDG .... Push-Button Data Generator   (IEEE)
PBDI........ Position Bearing and Distance Indicator   (MCD)
PBDM .... Payload Bay Door Mechanism [*NASA*]   (NASA)

PBDMA.... Poly(butadiene-malic Acid) [*A polymer*]
Pbd Pkg .... Paperboard Packaging [*A publication*]
PBDS........ Parti Bansa Dayak Sarawak [*Political party*] [*Malaysia*]   (FEA)
PBDU .... Pancreaticobiliary Ductal Union [*Anatomy*]
PBe............ Beaver Memorial Library, Beaver, PA [*Library symbol*] [*Library of Congress*]   (LCLS)
PBE............ Paint, Body, and Equipment [*Automotive engineering*]
PBE............ Paschen-Back Effect [*Spectroscopy*]
PBE............ Pemberton Exploration [*Vancouver Stock Exchange symbol*]
PBE............ Perlsucht Bacillary Emulsion [*Medicine*]
PBE............ Piggyback Experiment
PBE............ Present-Barrel-Equivalent
PBE............ Problemes Economiques. Selection de Textes Francais et Etrangers [*A publication*]
PBE............ Prompt Burst Experiments [*Nuclear energy*]   (NRCH)
PBE............ Prompt-by-Example [*Data processing*]
PBE............ Proton Balance Equation
PBE............ Proton Binding Energy
PBE............ Puerto Berrio [*Colombia*] [*Airport symbol*]   (OAG)
PBE............ Pulsed Bridge Element [*Telecommunications*]   (OA)
PBEA........ Paint, Body, and Equipment Association   (EA)
PBEA Newsletter ... Pennsylvania Business Education Association. Newsletter [*A publication*]
PBEB .... Pentabromoethylbenzene [*Flame retardant*] [*Organic chemistry*]
PBeC.......... Beaver County Court House, Beaver, PA [*Library symbol*] [*Library of Congress*]   (LCLS)
PBEC .... Pacific Basin Economic Council   (FEA)
PBEC .... Public Broadcasting Environment Center [*Corporation for Public Broadcasting*]
P Bef G....... Personenbefoerderungsgesetz [*A publication*]
PBEIST ..... Planning Board European Inland Surface Transport [*Army*]   (AABC)
PBel .... Centre County Library, Bellefonte, PA [*Library symbol*] [*Library of Congress*]   (LCLS)
PBELB...... Promyshlennost Belorussii [*A publication*]
PBelC......... Centre County Court House, Bellefonte, PA [*Library symbol*] [*Library of Congress*]   (LCLS)
PBEN........ Puritan-Bennett Corp. [*NASDAQ symbol*]   (NQ)
PBER .... Program Budget Execution Review [*Army*]
PBerol .... Berlin Papyri [*A publication*]   (OCD)
PBf............ Carnegie Free Library, Beaver Falls, PA [*Library symbol*] [*Library of Congress*]   (LCLS)
PBF .... Fast Patrol Boat [*Ship symbol*] [*NATO*]   (NATG)
PBF .... Patriotic Burmese Forces [*World War II*]
PBF .... Patrol Boat, Fast [*British military*]   (DMA)
PBF .... Peribronchial Fibrosis [*Medicine*]
PBF .... Pine Bluff [*Arkansas*] [*Airport symbol*] [*Obsolete*]   (OAG)
PBF .... Plastic Bottle Feeder
PBF .... Plates for Beam Forming   (DEN)
PBF .... Poop, Bridge, and Forecastle [*of a ship*]   (DS)
PBF .... Portal Blood Flow [*Physiology*]
PBF .... Potential Benefit Factor   (OA)
PBF .... Power Burst Facility [*Nuclear energy*]
PBF .... Praehistorische Bronzefunde [*A publication*]
PBF .... Public Budgeting and Finance [*A publication*]
PBF .... Pulmonary Blood Flow [*Medicine*]
PBFA .... Particle Beam Fusion Accelerator
PBFA .... Provincial Booksellers' Fairs Association [*British*]   (DI)
PBFC .... Peter Breck Fan Club   (EA)
PBFC .... Pierce Brosnan Fan Club   (EA)
PBFD........ Pierce Bland and Form Die   (MSA)
PB-Fe........ Protein-Bound Iron   (MAE)
PBfG .... Geneva College, Beaver Falls, PA [*Library symbol*] [*Library of Congress*]   (LCLS)
PBFG .... Guided Missile Fast Patrol Boat [*Ship symbol*]   (NATG)
PBFG .... Patrol Boat, Fast, Guided Weapon [*British military*]   (DMA)
PBFI .... Paris Business Forms, Inc. [*Burlington, NJ*] [*NASDAQ symbol*]   (NQ)
PBFL .... Planning for Better Family Living [*UN Food and Agriculture Organization*]
PBFP .... Provisioning Budget Forecast Procedure   (MCD)
PBFPA...... Protides of the Biological Fluids. Proceedings of the Colloquium [*A publication*]
PBF/WR.... Presiding Bishop's Fund for World Relief   (EA)
PBG .... Phenylbiguanide [*Biochemistry*]
PBG .... Plattsburgh, NY [*Location identifier*] [*FAA*]   (FAAL)
PBG .... Porphobilinogen [*Clinical chemistry*]
PBG .... Program and Budget Guidance [*Army*]
PBGC........ Pension Benefit Guaranty Corp. [*Government agency*]
PBGC Manual of Opinion Letters ... Pension Benefit Guaranty Corporation. Manual of Opinion Letters [*A publication*]
PBGI......... Piedmont BankGroup, Inc. [*NASDAQ symbol*]   (NQ)
PBH .... Partial Bulkhead   (DS)
PBH .... Patrol Boat, Hydrofoil   (MCD)
PBH .... Phillips, WI [*Location identifier*] [*FAA*]   (FAAL)
PBH .... Post Biblical Hebrew [*Language, etc.*]   (BJA)
PBH .... Primordial Black Hole [*Astrophysics*]
PBHF........ President Benjamin Harrison Foundation   (EA)
PBHP......... Pounds per Brake Horsepower
PB-HTGR ... Peach Bottom High-Temperature Gas-Cooled Reactor

PBI............ Paper Bag Institute   (EA)
PBI............ Parental Bonding Instrument
PBI............ Partial Background Investigation [*Army*]
PBI............ Paving Brick Institute
PBI............ Peace Brigades International   (EA)
PBI............ Pen and Brush, Inc.   (EA)
PBI............ Philadelphia Bible Institute [*Pennsylvania*]
PBI............ Pitch Boundary Indicator   (MCD)
PBI............ Pitney-Bowes, Inc. [*NYSE symbol*]   (SPSG)
PBI............ Plant Biological Institute [*University of Saskatchewan*] [*Canada*]
PBI............ Plant Biotechnology Institute [*National Research Council of Canada*] [*Research center*]   (RCD)
PBI............ Plant Breeding Institute [*British*]
PBI............ Plastic Bottle Institute   (EA)
PBI............ Plumbing Brass Institute [*Later, PMI*]   (EA)
PBI............ Polybenzimidazole [*Organic chemistry*]   (NATG)
PBI............ Poly(phenylenebibenzimidazole) [*Organic chemistry*]
PBI............ Poor Bloody Infantry [*British military slang*]
PBI............ Process Branch Indicator
PBI............ Programme Biologique Internationale [*International Biological Program - IBP*]   (MSC)
PBI............ Projected Books, Inc. [*Defunct*]   (EA)
PBI............ Prophylactic Brain Irradiation [*Oncology*]
PBI............ Protein-Bound Iodine [*Clinical chemistry*]
PBI............ Public Interest [*A publication*]
PBI............ Pupil Behavior Inventory [*Psychology*]
PBI............ Push-Button Indicator
PBI............ Puzzle Buffs International   (EA)
PBI............ West Palm Beach [*Florida*] [*Airport symbol*]
PBIB.......... Biological Bulletin [*A publication*]
PBIBA........ Pochvy Bashkirii i Puti Ratsional'nogo Ikh Ispol'zovaniya [*A publication*]
PBIC.......... Poly(butyl Isocyanate) [*Organic chemistry*]
PBIC.......... Programmable Buffer Interface Card [*Data processing*]   (NASA)
PBICSGH ... Permanent Bureau of International Congresses for the Sciences of Genealogy and Heraldry   (EA)
PBIF.......... Pacific Bible Institute of Fresno [*California*]
PBIL.......... Polybenzimidazolone [*Organic chemistry*]
PBIM.......... Programmable Buffer Interface Module   (MCD)
PBIOEM.... Plant Biology [*New York*] [*A publication*]
PBIP.......... Paperbound Books in Print [*A publication*]
PBIP.......... Pulse Beacon Impact Predictor   (AAG)
PBIR.......... Biological Reviews. Cambridge Philosophical Society [*A publication*]
PBIS.......... Prospezioni. Bollettino di Informazioni Scientifiche [*A publication*]
PBISTP ..... Peter Burwash International Special Tennis Programs   (EA)
PBIT.......... Parity BIT [*Binary Digit*] [*Data communications*]
PB/IWT..... Ports and Beaches and Inland Waterways Transports [*Military*]   (NATG)
PB and J .... Peanut Butter and Jelly
PBJ........... Presa Benito Juarez [*Mexico*] [*Seismograph station code, US Geological Survey*]   (SEIS)
PBJA......... British Journal of Aesthetics [*A publication*]
PBJC......... British Journal of Criminology [*A publication*]
PBJC......... Palm Beach Junior College [*Lakeworth, FL*]
PBJH......... British Journal for the History of Science [*A publication*]
PBJO......... British Journal of Sociology [*A publication*]
PBJOD...... Plant Biochemical Journal [*A publication*]
PBJP......... British Journal for the Philosophy of Science [*A publication*]
PBJS......... British Journal of Political Science [*A publication*]
PBK........... Pamietnik Biblioteki Kornickiej [*A publication*]
PBK........... Paperback
PBK........... Payload Bay Kit [*NASA*]   (NASA)
PBK........... Peoples Bancorporation [*AMEX symbol*]   (SPSG)
PBK........... Phi Beta Kappa [*Honorary society*]
PBK........... Phosphorylase B Kinase [*An enzyme*]   (MAE)
PBKB........ People's Savings Bank of Brockton [*Brockton, MA*] [*NASDAQ symbol*]   (NQ)
PBKC........ Premier Bankshares Corp. [*NASDAQ symbol*]   (NQ)
PBKL........ Booklist [*A publication*]
PBKS........ Provident Bankshares Corp. [*NASDAQ symbol*]   (NQ)
PBL........... Bethlehem Public Library, Bethlehem, PA [*OCLC symbol*]   (OCLC)
PBl............ Blairsville Public Library, Blairsville, PA [*Library symbol*] [*Library of Congress*]   (LCLS)
PBL........... Lehigh University, Bethlehem, PA [*Library symbol*] [*Library of Congress*]   (LCLS)
PBL........... Papers in Borneo Linguistics [*A publication*]
PBL........... Pastoralblaetter [*A publication*]
P Bl........... Patentblatt [*A publication*]
PBL........... Payload Bay Liner [*NASA*]   (MCD)
PBL........... Peripheral Blood Leukocyte [*or Lymphocyte*] [*Hematology*]
PBL........... [*The*] Philadelphia Belt Line Railroad Co. [*AAR code*]
PBL........... Photo Butt Line   (MSA)
PBL........... Planetary Boundary Layer [*Aerospace*]
PBL........... Potential Binding Level [*Of natural waters for metal ions*]
PBL........... Probable   (FAAC)
PBL........... Product Baseline   (MCD)
PBL........... Prune Brownline [*Plant pathology*]

PBL........... Public Broadcast Laboratory
Pbl............ Publicatieblad van de Europese Gemeenschappen [*A publication*]
pbl .... Publisher [*MARC relator code*] [*Library of Congress*]   (LCCP)
PBL........... Puerto Cabello [*Venezuela*] [*Airport symbol*]   (OAG)
PBlbM....... Montgomery County Community College, Blue Bell, PA [*Library symbol*] [*Library of Congress*]   (LCLS)
PBLD........ Progressive Base Line Dimensioning   (SAA)
PBLG........ Polybenzyl-L-glutamate [*Biochemistry*]
PBLS........ Production Baseline Set   (MCD)
PBLSA....... Publius [*A publication*]
PBm .... Bryn Mawr College, Bryn Mawr, PA [*Library symbol*] [*Library of Congress*]   (LCLS)
PBM .... Paramaribo [*Surinam*] [*Airport symbol*]   (OAG)
PBM .... Patrol Search Plane [*Navy designation for Mariner aircraft*]
PBM .... Peripheral Blood Mononuclear [*Cells*] [*Hematology*]
PBM .... Permanent Bench Mark
PBM .... PIXEL Block Mode [*Data processing*]   (BYTE)
PBM .... Poetry Book Magazine [*A publication*]
PBM .... Pressure Bias Modulation   (MCD)
PBM .... Principal Beach Master [*RAF*] [*British*]
PBM .... Probability Based-Matched [*Database search techniques*]
PBM .... Production Base Modernization   (MCD)
PBM .... Program Budget Manager   (MCD)
PBM .... Program Business Management   (NASA)
PBM .... Public Management [*A publication*]
PBmA .... American College of Life Underwriters, Bryn Mawr, PA [*Library symbol*] [*Library of Congress*]   (LCLS)
PBMA....... Peanut Butter Manufacturers Association [*Later, PBNPA*]   (EA)
PBMA....... Plastic Bath Manufacturers Association [*British*]   (DI)
PBMAA.... Publications. Research Institute for Mathematical Sciences. Series A [*Japan*] [*A publication*]
PBMC....... Moravian College and Theological Seminary, Bethlehem, PA [*Library symbol*] [*Library of Congress*]   (LCLS)
PBMC....... Peripheral Blood Mononuclear Cells [*Hematology*]
PBMCA..... Archives of the Moravian Church, Bethlehem, PA [*Library symbol*] [*Library of Congress*]   (LCLS)
PBMEA.... Perspectives in Biology and Medicine [*A publication*]
PBmL........ Ludington Public Library, Bryn Mawr, PA [*Library symbol*] [*Library of Congress*]   (LCLS)
PBML....... Prague Bulletin of Mathematical Linguistics [*A publication*]
PBMOE8... Progress in Behavior Modification [*A publication*]
PBMR....... International Bulletin of Missionary Research [*A publication*]
PBMR....... Pennsylvania Bureau of Municipal Research   (MCD)
PBMR....... Provisional Basic Military Requirements   (NATG)
PBM/STIRS ... Probability Based Matching and Self-Trained Interpretive and Retrieval Systems [*Database*] [*John Wiley & Sons, Inc.*] [*Information service or system*]   (CRD)
PBMW ...... Moravian College, Bethlehem, PA [*Library symbol*] [*Library of Congress*]   (LCLS)
PBN .... Northampton County Area Community College, Bethlehem, PA [*Library symbol*] [*Library of Congress*]   (LCLS)
PBN .... Paralytic Brachial Neuritis [*Medicine*]   (MAE)
PBN .... PE Ben Oilfield Services Ltd. [*Toronto Stock Exchange symbol*]
PBN .... Peribrachialis Nuclei [*Neurology*]
PBN .... Phenyl(butyl)nitrone [*Organic chemistry*]
PBN .... Physical Block Number
PBN .... Polymixin-B Sulfate/Bacitracin/Neomycin [*Antibacterial regime*]
PBN .... Porto Amboin [*Angola*] [*Airport symbol*]   (OAG)
PBN .... Primary Block Number [*Data processing*]
PBN .... Pyrolytic Boron Nitride [*Inorganic chemistry*]
PBNA .... Partial Body Neutron Activation [*Radiology*]
PBNA .... Phenyl-beta-naphthylamine [*Organic chemistry*]
PBNB........ People's Savings Financial Corp. [*Formerly, People's Savings Bank New Britain*] [*NASDAQ symbol*]   (NQ)
PBNC........ Peoples Bancorporation [*NASDAQ symbol*]   (NQ)
PBNE........ Philadelphia, Bethlehem & New England Railroad Co. [*AAR code*]
PBNM ...... Parallel Bar Noise Maker [*Antiacoustic torpedo device*]
PBNP........ Phipps Bend Nuclear Plant   (NRCH)
PBNP........ Point Beach Nuclear Plant   (NRCH)
PBNP........ Porcine Brain Natriuretic Peptide [*Biochemistry*]
PBNPA...... Peanut Butter and Nut Processors Association   (EA)
PBNS........ Prospects Business News Survey [*A publication*]
PBO .... Packed by Owner
PBO .... Paleobioclimatic Operator
PBO .... Paraburdoo [*Australia*] [*Airport symbol*]   (OAG)
PBO .... Pauling Bond Order [*Physical chemistry*]
P Bo........... Petrus Boaterius [*Flourished, 1285-1321*] [*Authority cited in pre-1607 legal work*]   (DSA)
pbo .... Placebo [*Medicine*]
PBO .... Plotting Board Operator   (MUGU)
PBO .... Polski Biuletyn Orientalistyczny [*A publication*]
PBO .... Poor Bloody Observer [*British World War I military slang*]   (DSUE)
PBO .... Print Business Opportunities [*A publication*]   (EAAP)
PBO .... Property Book Officer [*Army*]   (AABC)
PBO .... Push-Button Operation
PBoC.......... People's Bank of China

PBOD .... Phytoplankton Biochemical Oxygen Demand [*Oceanography*]
PBOG .... Botanical Gazette [*A publication*]
PBOI .... Public Board of Inquiry
PBOIP .... Preliminary Basis of Issue Plan [*Military*]   (MCD)
PBOR .... Botanical Review [*A publication*]
PBOS......... Planning Board for Ocean Shipping [*Army*] [*NATO*]
PBP .... [*The*] Paper Bag Players   (EA)
PBP........... Paperbound Books in Print [*A publication*]
PBP........... Para-(Benzyloxy)phenol [*Organic chemistry*]
PB/P .... Particleboard/Plywood
PBP........... Pay-Back Period [*Finance*]
PBP........... Pay by Phone [*Business term*]
PBP........... Pellin-Broca Prism [*Physics*]
PBP........... Penicillin-Binding Protein [*Biochemistry*]
P de Bp....... Petrus de Bellapertica [*Deceased, 1308*] [*Authority cited in pre-1607 legal work*]   (DSA)
PBP........... Phosphate-Binding Protein [*Biochemistry*]
PBP........... Pinkas Bractwa Pogrzebowego [*A publication*]
PBP........... Play-by-Play   (WDMC)
PBP........... Plotting Board Plot   (MUGU)
PBP........... Point by Point
PBP........... Porphyrin Biosynthetic Pathway [*Biochemistry*]   (AAMN)
PBP........... Power Bias Panel
PBP........... Pregnenolone Binding Protein [*Endocrinology*]
PBP........... Private Brand Proneness [*Marketing*]
PBP........... Production Base Plan   (MCD)
PBP........... Program Board Panel
PBP........... Program and Budget Planning
PBP........... Provider Based Physician
PBP........... Push-Button Panel
PBPB .... Para-bromophenacyl Bromide [*Organic chemistry*]
PBPB .... Pyridinium Bromide Perbromide [*Inorganic chemistry*]
PBPC .... Passenger and Baggage Processing Committee [*IATA*]   (DS)
PBPE .... Population Biology/Physiological Ecology [*Program*] [*National Science Foundation*]
PBPITMT ... Production Base Productivity Improvement through Manufacturing Technology   (MCD)
PBPK .... Physiologically Based Pharmacokinetics [*Biochemistry*]
PBPM........ Black Perspective in Music [*A publication*]
PBPM........ Poultry Byproduct Meal
PBPS .... Painting Brushmakers' Provident Society [*A union*] [*British*]
PBPS .... Paulist Bible Pamphlet Series [*Glen Rock, NJ*] [*A publication*]   (BJA)
PBPS .... Post-Boost Propulsion System [*Aerospace*]
PBPTC ...... Palm Beach Psychotherapy Training Center   (EA)
PBQ .... Poste De La Baleine [*Quebec*] [*Seismograph station code, US Geological Survey*]   (SEIS)
PBQ .... Preschool Behavior Questionnaire
PBr............ Carnegie Public Library, Bradford, PA [*Library symbol*] [*Library of Congress*]   (LCLS)
PBR .... Pabst Blue Ribbon [*Beer*]
PBR .... Packed Bed Reactor
PBR .... Particle Bed Reactor [*Department of Energy*]
PBR .... Patapsco & Back Rivers Railroad Co. [*AAR code*]
P and BR .... Patristic and Byzantine Review [*A publication*]
PBR .... Patrol Boat, River [*Navy symbol*]
PBR .... Payment by Results [*Payment system*]
PBR .... Pebble-Bed Reactor [*Nuclear energy*]
PBR .... Pembroke, NH [*Location identifier*] [*FAA*]   (FAAL)
PBR .... Pencil Beam RADAR
PBR .... Permit by Rule [*Pollution control*]
PBR .... Pigment-Binder Ratio [*Weight*]
PBR .... Plant Breeders' Rights
PBR .... Plum Brook Reactor [*Nuclear energy*]
PBR .... Pole Broken [*Telecommunications*]   (TEL)
PBR .... Power Breeder Reactor   (AAG)
PBR .... Precision Bombing Range [*Army*]
PBR .... Pressurized Ballistic Range [*NASA*]
PBR .... Progress in Brain Research [*Elsevier Book Series*] [*A publication*]
PBR .... Pyridine-Butadiene Rubber
PBra .... Carnegie Free Library, Braddock, PA [*Library symbol*] [*Library of Congress*]   (LCLS)
PBRA........ Polska Bibliografja Biblijna Adnotowana [*A publication*]
PBRA........ Practical Bomb Rack Adapter   (NG)
PBRA........ Professional Bicycle Racers Association [*Defunct*]   (EA)
PBracAL.... Allegheny International, Inc., Brackenridge, PA [*Library symbol*] [*Library of Congress*]   (LCLS)
PBRCA...... Proceedings. British Ceramic Society [*A publication*]
PBRE......... Pebble-Bed Reactor Experiment [*Nuclear energy*]
PBREE3 ..... Plant Breeding Reviews [*A publication*]
PBRERP.... Permanent Board for Review of the Enlisted Retention Program
PBRERS.... Permanent Board for Review of the Enlisted Rating Structure
PBRESD.... Polar Branch, Research Environmental Science Division [*Army*]
PBRF .... Plant Breeding Research Forum   (EA)
PBRF .... Plum Brook Reactor Facility [*Lewis Research Center*]
PBriR........ Rohm & Haas Co., Bristol, PA [*Library symbol*] [*Library of Congress*]   (LCLS)
P/BRK .... Power Brake [*Automotive engineering*]

PBroGS...... Church of Jesus Christ of Latter-Day Saints, Genealogical Society Library, Philadelphia Branch, Broomall, PA [*Library symbol*] [*Library of Congress*]   (LCLS)
PBRS .... Pupil Behavior Rating Scale [*Psychology*]
PBRS .... Push-Button Rotary Switch
PBRT .... Behaviour Research and Therapy [*A publication*]
PBRV .... Potato Black Ringspot Virus [*Plant pathology*]
PBS........... Bethlehem Steel Corp., Charles H. Herty, Jr., Memorial Library, Bethlehem, PA [*Library symbol*] [*Library of Congress*]   (LCLS)
PBS........... Pacific Biological Station [*Department of Fisheries and Oceans*] [*Canada*] [*Research center*]   (RCD)
PBS........... Palestine Broadcasting Service   (BJA)
PBS........... Parenchymatous Bundle Sheath [*Botany*]
PBS........... Parimutuel Betting System
PBS........... Particulate Biogenic Silica [*Environmental science*]
PBS........... Parts Breakdown Structure
PBS........... Peninsular Base Section [*Military*]
PBS........... Periscope Bombsight Stabilizer
PBS........... Personal Bibliographic Software, Inc. [*Information service or system*]   (IID)
PBS........... Peterborough Board of Education [*UTLAS symbol*]
PBS........... Phosphate-Buffered Saline
PBS........... Phosphate-Buffered Sodium   (MAE)
PBS........... Pigeon Bay [*South Carolina*] [*Seismograph station code, US Geological Survey*]   (SEIS)
PBS........... Pilgrim Regional Bank Shares, Inc. [*NYSE symbol*]   (SPSG)
PBS........... Podiatry Bibliographical Society [*Defunct*]   (EA)
PBS........... Polarization Beam Splitter
PBS........... Poly(butenesulfone) [*Organic chemistry*]
PBS........... Polysteel Building Systems Ltd. [*Toronto Stock Exchange symbol*]
PBS........... Potere Battericida del Sangue [*Bactericidal Property of the Blood*] [*Medicine*]
PBS........... Poverty Budget Share [*Bureau of the Census*]   (GFGA)
PBS........... Power Breakfast Syndrome [*Suffered by late-risers forced to attend breakfast meetings*]
PBS........... Prefabricated Bituminous Surfacing
PBS........... Pressedienst fuer das Bauspar [*A publication*]
PBS........... Pressure Boundary Subsystem [*Nuclear energy*]   (NRCH)
PBS........... Primer Binding Site [*Genetics*]
PBS........... Production Base Support [*Army*]   (AABC)
PBS........... Professional Bibliographic System [*Database manager package*] [*Personal Bibliographic Software, Inc.*] [*Ann Arbor, MI*]
PBS........... Professional Bowhunters Society   (EA)
PBS........... Program Board Stowage
PBS........... Program Breakdown Structure [*Nuclear energy*]
PBS........... Program and Budgeting System   (OICC)
PBS........... Project Breakdown Structure [*Nuclear energy*]   (NRCH)
PBS........... Protestant Big Sisters
PBS........... Public Brand Software   (PCM)
PBS........... Public Broadcasting Service   (EA)
PBS........... Public Buildings Service [*of General Services Administration*]
PBS........... Publications. Babylonian Section. University Museum. University of Pennsylvania [*Philadelphia*] [*A publication*]
PBS........... Push-Button Switch
PBSA......... Papers. Bibliographical Society of America [*A publication*]
PBSA......... Phosphate-Buffered Saline Azide [*Culture medium*]
PBSA......... Publications. Bibliographical Society of America [*A publication*]
PBSB......... Prudential Bancorporation [*NASDAQ symbol*]   (NQ)
PBSC........ Behavioral Science [*A publication*]
PBSC........ Panelized Building Systems Council   (EA)
PBSC........ Papers. Bibliographical Society of Canada [*A publication*]
PBSCMA .. Peanut Butter Sandwich and Cookie Manufacturers Association [*Later, PBNPA*]   (EA)
PBSE .... Philadelphia-Baltimore Stock Exchange [*Later, Philadelphia-Baltimore-Washington Stock Exchange*]
PBSED ...... Proceedings. Bioenergy R and D Seminar [*A publication*]
PBSF......... Pacific Bank NA [*NASDAQ symbol*]   (SPSG)
PBSM .... Plastic Bonded Starter Mix
PBSP .... Prognostically Bad Sign During Pregnancy [*Obstetrics*]   (MAE)
PBSR .... Papers. British School at Rome [*A publication*]
PBST .... Public Storage Properties [*Associated Press abbreviation*]   (APAG)
PBSteel ...... Bethlehem Steel Corp., Charles M. Schwab Memorial Library, Bethlehem, PA [*Library symbol*] [*Library of Congress*]   (LCLS)
PBSU......... Portable Beacon and Scoring Unit   (MCD)
PBSUV ...... Papers. Bibliographical Society. University of Virginia [*A publication*]
PBSW .... Push-Button Switch
PBSWA .... Proceedings. Biological Society of Washington [*A publication*]
PBSY .... British Journal of Psychology [*A publication*]
PBT........... Pacific Ballet Theatre
PBT........... Para-Bandit Target
PBT........... Parity BIT [*Binary Digit*] Test
PBT........... Passband Tuning
PBT........... Peoria Board of Trade   (EA)
PBT........... Permian Basin Royalty Trust [*NYSE symbol*]   (SPSG)
PBT........... Philippine Ballet Theater   (ECON)

PBT............ Pierce-Blank Tool (MCD)
PBT............ Piggyback Tape [*or Twistor*] [*Data processing*]
PBT............ Pittsburgh Ballet Theatre
PBT............ Polybay Tier
PBT............ Polybenzothiazole [*Organic chemistry*]
PBT............ Polybutylene Terephthalate [*Organic chemistry*]
PBT............ Preferred Body Temperature [*Physiology*]
PBT............ Preliminary-Breath-Test [*Device used by police to determine whether or not a driver is legally intoxicated*]
PBT............ Push-Button Telephone
PBT............ Red Bluff, CA [*Location identifier*] [*FAA*] (FAAL)
PBTC........ Postal Business Training Centre [*British*]
PBTE........ Performance-Based Teacher Evaluation (OICC)
PBTF........ Pump Bearing Test Facility [*Nuclear energy*]
P/BTN....... Push Button [*Automotive engineering*]
PBTO........ Boundary 2 [*A publication*]
PBTP........ Polybutylene Terephthalate [*Organic chemistry*]
PBTS .... Proton Beam Transport System
PBTX........ Ptychodiscus brevis Toxin [*Florida red-tide toxin*]
PBU .... Bucknell University, Lewisburg, PA [*OCLC symbol*] (OCLC)
PBU .... Palm Beach County Utility Corp. [*Toronto Stock Exchange symbol*]
PBU .... Perry Basin [*Utah*] [*Seismograph station code, US Geological Survey*] (SEIS)
PBU .... Premature Baby Unit [*National Health Service*] [*British*] (DI)
PBU .... Putao [*Myanmar*] [*Airport symbol*] (OAG)
PBUP........ Perforated Backup Plate
PBut........ Butler Public Library, Butler, PA [*Library symbol*] [*Library of Congress*] (LCLS)
PButV .... United States Veterans Administration Hospital, Butler, PA [*Library symbol*] [*Library of Congress*] (LCLS)
PBUZ........ Buzzworm. The Environmental Journal [*A publication*]
PBV........... English Prayer Book Version (BJA)
PBV........... Pedal Blood Vessel
PBV........... Platinol [*Cisplatin*], Bleomycin, Vinblastine [*Antineoplastic drug regimen*]
PBV........... Post Boost Vehicle [*Missiles*] (AFM)
PBV........... Predicted Blood Volume [*Medicine*]
PBV........... Pulmonary Blood Volume [*Medicine*]
PBVM........ Presentation of the Blessed Virgin Mary [*Roman Catholic women's religious order*]
PBVP........ Post Boost Vehicle Propulsion [*Missiles*] (MCD)
PBVR........ [*The*] Port Bienville Railroad [*AAR code*]
PBvu.......... Andrew Bayne Memorial Library, Bellevue, PA [*Library symbol*] [*Library of Congress*] (LCLS)
PBW .... Particle-Beam Weapon
PBW .... Parts by Weight (IEEE)
PBW .... Percussive Butt Welder
PBW .... Pink Bollworm [*Cotton pest*]
PBW .... Posterior Bite Wing [*Dentistry*]
PBW .... Power by Wire [*Flight control*]
PBW .... Proportional Bandwidth (MCD)
PBW .... Pulse Burst Wave
PBWA........ Plasma Beta-Wave Accelerator [*Plasma physics*]
PBWAA.... Professional Basketball Writers' Association of America (EA)
PBWEE ..... Pilot Boll Weevil Eradication Experiment [*Department of Agriculture*]
PBWF........ Pulse Burst Waveform
PBWSE ..... Philadelphia-Baltimore-Washington Stock Exchange [*Later, Philadelphia Stock Exchange*]
PBX........... PBX Resources [*Vancouver Stock Exchange symbol*]
PBX........... Plastic Bonded Explosive
PBX........... Private Branch Exchange [*Telecommunications*]
PBY........... Kayenta, AZ [*Location identifier*] [*FAA*] (FAAL)
PBY........... Patrol Bomber [*Navy designation for Catalina aircraft*]
PBY........... Pep Boys - Manny, Moe & Jack [*NYSE symbol*] (SPSG)
PBZ........... Phenoxybenzamine [*Also, POB*] [*Adrenergic blocking agent*]
PBZ........... Phenylbutazone [*Anti-inflammatory compound*]
PBZ........... Plettenberg [*South Africa*] [*Airport symbol*] (OAG)
PBZ........... Pyribenzamine [*Antihistamine*] [*Trademark*]
PBzN........ Peroxybenzoyl Nitrate [*Lacrimator*]
PBZT........ Poly-P-Phenylene Benzobesthiazole
PC .... All India Reporter, Privy Council [*1914-50*] [*A publication*] (DLA)
PC .... British and Colonial Prize Cases [*A publication*] (DLA)
PC .... Civilian Personnel Division [*Coast Guard*]
PC .... Coastal Escort [*Ship symbol*] (NATG)
PC .... Communist Party [*Peru*] [*Political party*] (PD)
PC .... Indian Rulings, Privy Council [*1929-47*] [*A publication*] (DLA)
PC .... J. Lewis Crozer [*Chester Public*] Library, Chester, PA [*Library symbol*] [*Library of Congress*] (LCLS)
PC .... Judicial Committee of the Privy Council (DLA)
PC .... Pacific Coast Railroad [*AAR code*] [*Terminated*]
PC .... Package Control [*or Controller*]
PC .... Packed Cell [*Hematology*] (MAE)
PC .... Pad Coordinator [*NASA*]
PC .... Palmitoyl Carnitine [*Biochemistry*]
PC .... Pan Malaysian Air Transport [*Malaysia*] [*ICAO designator*] (FAAC)
PC .... [*The*] Panama Canal

Pc .... Pancuronium [*A muscle relaxant*]
PC .... Panoramic Camera
PC .... Paper Chromatography
PC .... Paper or Cloth [*Freight*]
PC .... Paper Copy
PC .... Paracortical Hyperplasia [*Oncology*]
PC .... Parametric Cubic [*Data processing*] (OA)
PC .... Paraula Cristiana [*A publication*]
PC .... Parent Care (EA)
PC .... Parent Cells
PC .... Parental Control [*Channel lockout*] [*Video technology*]
P & C......... Parge and Core [*Construction*]
PC .... Parish Church [*British*] (ROG)
PC .... Parish Council
PC .... Parliamentary Cases [*A publication*] (DLA)
PC .... PARSEC [*Parallax Second*] [*See PARSEC*]
PC .... Parti Communiste [*Communist Party*] [*Luxembourg*] [*Political party*] (PPW)
PC .... Participation Certificate
PC .... Partido Colorado [*Colorado Party*] [*Uruguay*] [*Political party*] (PPW)
PC .... Partido Conservador [*Conservative Party*] [*Nicaragua*] [*Political party*] (EY)
PC .... Partido Conservador [*Conservative Party*] [*Ecuador*] [*Political party*] (PPW)
PC .... Parts Catalog (KSC)
PC .... Passenger Certificate [*Shipping*] (DS)
PC .... Past Commander
PC .... Patent Cases [*A publication*] (DLA)
PC .... Patent Committee (MCD)
PC .... Path Control [*Data processing*] (IBMDP)
PC .... Patres Conscripti [*Senators*] [*Latin*]
PC .... Patrol Car [*British military*] (DMA)
PC .... Patrol Craft
PC .... Patrol Vessel, Submarine Chaser [*Navy symbol*]
PC .... Pay Clerk
PC .... Paymaster-Captain [*Navy*] [*British*]
PC .... Paymaster-Commander [*Navy*] [*British*]
PC .... Peace Commissioner [*Ireland*]
PC .... Peace Corps (EA)
PC .... Peak Capacity
PC .... Peake's Commentary on the Bible [*A publication*]
PC .... Peg Count [*Telecommunications*] (TEL)
PC .... Penal Code [*A publication*] (DLA)
PC .... Penetrating Cell
PC .... [*The*] Penn Central Corp. [*NYSE symbol*] (SPSG)
PC .... Penn Central Transportation Co. [*Subsidiary of Penn Central Corp.*] [*Absorbed into Consolidated Rail Corp.*] [*AAR code*]
PC .... Penny Cyclopaedia [*British*] [*A publication*] (ROG)
PC .... Pensiero Critico [*A publication*]
PC .... Penske Car [*Racing model*]
PC .... Pentose Cycle [*Biochemistry*] (MAE)
PC .... People for a Change [*An association*] (EA)
PC .... People's China [*A publication*]
PC .... People's Conference [*India*] [*Political party*] (PPW)
PC .... Per Centum [*By the Hundred*] [*Latin*]
PC .... Per Condoglianza [*Used on visiting cards to express condolence*] [*Italian*]
PC .... Perciconia circinata [*A toxin-producing fungus*]
PC .... Perfins Club (EA)
PC .... Performance Code
PC .... Performance Contract (OICC)
P & C......... Performance and Control (SSD)
PC .... Pericarditis [*Avian pathology*]
PC .... Pericentral
PC .... Pericynthion [*Perilune, or low point, in lunar orbit*]
PC .... Period Contract
PC .... Peripheral Cell
PC .... Peripheral Control (BUR)
PC .... Perpetual Curate
PC .... Personal Call (OA)
PC .... Personal Computer
PC .... Personal Copier [*In product name, PC-10*] [*Canon Inc.*]
PC .... Personal Correction
PC .... Personnel Carrier [*A vehicle*]
PC .... Petro-Canada
PC .... Petty Cash
PC .... Pharmacy Corps [*Army*]
PC .... Phase Coherent (CET)
PC .... Phenol Coefficient (IIA)
PC .... Pheochromocytoma [*Oncology*]
PC .... Philosophical Classics [*A publication*]
PC .... Phobia Clinic (EA)
PC .... Phosphate Cycle [*Chemistry*] (MAE)
PC .... Phosphatidylcholine [*Lecithin*] [*Biochemistry*]
PC .... Phosphocholine [*Biochemistry*]
PC .... Phosphocreatine [*Also, PCr*] [*Creatine phosphate; see CP*] [*Biochemistry*]
PC .... Phosphorylcholine [*Biochemistry*]
PC .... Photocell

PC	Photoconductor
PC	Photocounting
Pc	Phthalocyanine [Organic chemistry]
P & C	Physical and Chemical (AAG)
PC	Physocyanin [Biochemistry]
PC	Phytophthora Cinnamoni [A fungus]
PC	Pica [Typography] (WDMC)
PC	Pick Up Cargo (AFM)
pC	Picocoulomb [One trillionth of a coulomb]
pC	Picocurie [Also, pCi] [One trillionth of a curie]
PC	Picture (MDG)
PC	Piece (AAG)
pc	Pied Carre [Square Foot] [French]
pc	Pied Cube [Cubic Foot] [French]
PC	Pierre Cardin [Fashion designer]
PC	Pilotage Charts [Air Force]
PC	Pioneer Clubs (EA)
PC	Pioneer Corps [British military] (DMA)
pc	Pitcairn [MARC country of publication code] [Library of Congress] (LCCP)
PC	Pitch Channel
PC	Pitch Circle [Technical drawings]
PC	Pitch Control (KSC)
PC	Pitch Cycle (DNAB)
PC	Pittsburgh Commerce Institute
PC	Plaid Cymru [Welsh national liberation party] [Political party]
P/C	Plane Captain (MUGU)
PC	Plane Change (MCD)
PC	Plane Commander
PC	Planetary Citizens (EA)
PC	Planning Card (AAG)
PC	Planning Concept (MCD)
PC	Plant Computer (NRCH)
PC	Planting Council (EA)
PC	Plasma Cell [Oncology]
PC	Plasma Chromatography
PC	Plasmacytoma [Medicine]
PC	Plastic Core
Pc	Plastocyanin
PC	Plate Circuit (DEN)
PC	Platelet Concentrate [Hematology]
PC	Platelet Count [Hematology]
PC	Platform/Crane (DCTA)
PC	Pleas of the Crown [A publication] (DLA)
P/C	Pledges/Cost (WDMC)
PC	Plenum Chamber
PC	Plug Cock (AAG)
PC	Plug Compatible [Data processing] (BUR)
PC	Pneumotoxic Center (AAMN)
PC	Pocket Computer
PC	Poesia e Critica [A publication]
P & C	Poet and Critic [A publication]
PC	Poetry Criticism [A publication]
PC	Point of Curve [Technical drawings]
P-C	Polar to Cartesian
PC	Polar Continental [American air mass]
PC	Polar Crane [Nuclear energy] (NRCH)
PC	Pole Cell [Insect embryology]
P/C	Police Car
PC	Police Commissioner (WGA)
PC	Police-Constable [Scotland Yard]
PC	Police Court [British] (ROG)
PC	Policy Control (ADA)
PC	Political Code [A publication] (ILCA)
PC	Political Correctness
PC	Politically Correct
P/C	Polizza di Carico [Bill of Lading] [Italian] [Shipping]
PC	Polycarbonate [Organic chemistry]
PC	Polycarbosilane [Organic chemistry]
PC	Polymer-Concrete (KSC)
PC	Pondus Civile [Civil (Avoirdupois) Weight] [Pharmacy] (ROG)
PC	Poni Curavit [Caused to Be Placed] [Latin]
PC	Poor Clares [Roman Catholic women's religious order]
PC	Poor Classes [British] (DSUE)
pc	Pop Corn [Crochet]
PC	Popular Cult
PC	Population Census
PC	Population Communication (EA)
PC	Population Council (EA)
PC	Port Call [Army]
PC	Port Committee (NATG)
PC	Port Control [Telecommunications] (TEL)
PC	Portable Computer
PC	Portacaval [Medicine]
PC	Portion Control [Food service]
PC	Portland Cement
PC	Position Classification (GFGA)
PC	Positive Control
Pc	Positive Wave in Children [Neurophysiology]
PC	Post Card (ROG)
PC	Post Cibum [After Meals] [Pharmacy]
PC	Post Commander [Military]
PC	Post Consulatum [After the Consulate] [Latin]
PC	Postal Clerk [Navy rating]
PC	Postcard
PC	Postcode (ADA)
PC	Postcoital [Medicine]
PC	Posterior Chamber [Ophthalmology]
PC	Posterior Commissure [Neuroanatomy]
PC	Postinflammatory Corticoid [Medicine]
pc	Pottery Cache (BJA)
PC	Pour Condoler [To Offer Sympathy] [French]
PC	Power Contactor
PC	Power Control [System] (NG)
P-C	Power Conversion (CET)
PC	Practice Cases [A publication] (DLA)
PC	Pre-Chamber [Automotive engineering]
PC	Pre-Emphasis Circuit (OA)
PC	Precarrier
PC	Precast
PC	Precaution Category [For clinical laboratories]
PC	Precedents in Chancery [A publication] (DLA)
PC	Precision Control [Computer programming] (BYTE)
PC	Precordia [Anatomy]
PC	Preliminary Commitment (IMH)
PC	Preparatory Commission
PC	Preparatory Committee
PC	Presence Chretienne [A publication]
PC	Present Complaint [Medicine]
PC	Presidents Club [Commercial firm] (EA)
PC	Press Council [British]
PC	Pressure Chamber
PC	Pressure Controller [Nuclear energy]
PC	Price Commission [Cost of Living Council]
PC	Price Control Cases [A publication] (DLA)
PC	Price per Copy [of books]
P/C	Price/Cost
PC	Prices Current
P & C	Prideaux and Cole's English Reports [4 New Sessions Cases] [A publication] (DLA)
P-in-C	Priest-in-Charge [Church of England]
PC	Priest Confessor
PC	Primary Center
PC	Primary Circuit (MCD)
PC	Primary Code
PC	Primary Contributor
PC	Primary Control (MCD)
PC	Prime Contractor
PC	Prime Cost
PC	Prince Consort (IIA)
PC	Prince Edward Island Provincial Library, Charlottetown, Prince Edward Island [Library symbol] [National Library of Canada] (NLC)
PC	Principal Chaplain (ADA)
PC	Principal Component
PC	Print Club (EA)
PC	Printed Circuit
PC	Printer Control
P & C	Prism and Cover (Test) [Ophthalmology]
PC	Prisoner of Conscience (BJA)
PC	Private Concerns [An association] [Defunct] (EA)
PC	Private Contract [Tea trade] (ROG)
PC	Private Corporation
PC	Privatization Council [New York, NY] (EA)
PC	Privilege Car [on a train] [Theatre slang]
PC	Privileged Character [A favored student] [Teen slang]
PC	Privy Council [or Councillor] [British]
PC	Prize Court (DLA)
PC	Probable Cause [Legal term]
PC	Probate Court [British] (ROG)
PC	Problems of Communism [A publication]
PC	Procaer SpA [Italy] [ICAO aircraft manufacturer identifier] (ICAO)
PC	Procarbazine [Also, P, PCB, Pr] [Antineoplastic drug]
PC	Procerebral Lobe [Neuroanatomy]
PC	Process Chemistry
PC	Process Computer (NRCH)
PC	Process Control (DEN)
PC	Processing Center [Telecommunications] (TEL)
PC	Processor Controller [Data processing] (MDG)
PC	Procurement Command [Army]
PC	Procurement Communication [Military]
P & C	Procurement and Contracting (AFM)
PC	Producers' Council [Later, CPMC] (EA)
PC	Production Certificate (MCD)
PC	Production Company [Films, television, etc.]
PC	Production Control (MCD)
PC	Production Costs
PC	Professional Communication (MCD)
PC	Professional Corporation
PC	Professors of Curriculum (EA)

PC .... Program Change
PC .... Program Committee [*UN Food and Agriculture Organization*]
PC .... Program Communications [*Military*]   (AFIT)
PC .... Program Control
PC .... Program Coordination   (IEEE)
PC .... Program Counter
PC .... Programmable Computer
PC .... Programmed Check   (AAG)
PC .... Progressive Conservative [*Canada*] [*Political party*]
PC .... Project Censored   (EA)
PC .... Project Children   (EA)
PC .... Project Control   (NASA)
PC .... Project Coordinator   (NG)
PC .... Projector Charge
PC .... Proof Coins [*Numismatics*]
P/C............. Property/Casualty [*Insurance*]
PC .... Proportional Counter [*Instrumentation*]
PC .... Proposed Change
PC .... Propositional Calculus [*Logic*]
PC .... Propulsive Coefficient
PC .... Propylene Carbonate [*Organic chemistry*]
PC .... Prospectors Club [*Later, PCI*]
PC .... Prosthetics Center [*Veterans Administration*]
PC .... Protective Climate [*Solar heating*]
PC .... Protective Cover   (MCD)
PC .... Proto-Canaanite   (BJA)
PC .... Protocol Converter   (MCD)
PC .... Provincial Commissioner [*British government*]
PC .... Provisional Costs
PC .... Provocative Concentration [*Immunology*]
PC .... Pseudocode   (AAG)
PC .... Pseudoconditioning Control [*Neurophysiology*]
PC .... Public Citizen   (EA)
PC .... Public Contract
PC .... Publications in Climatology   (MCD)
PC .... [*The*] Publishers' Circular [*A publication*]   (ROG)
PC .... Pubococcygeus [*Muscle*] [*Anatomy*]
PC .... Pulmonary Capillary [*Medicine*]
PC .... Pulmonic Closure [*Medicine*]   (MAE)
PC .... Pulsating Current
PC .... Pulse Cleaned [*Dust filtration*]
PC .... Pulse Comparator   (AAG)
PC .... Pulse Compression
PC .... Pulse Controller
PC .... Pulse Counter [*Data processing*]   (MDG)
PC .... Pulverized Coal [*Fuel technology*]
PC .... Punched Card [*Data processing*]
PC .... Punjab Cavalry [*British military*]   (DMA)
PC .... Puns Corps   (EA)
PC .... Purchase Card
PC .... Purchasing and Contracting [*Army*]
P & C......... Purchasing and Contracting
PC .... Pure Clairvoyance [*Psychical research*]
PC .... Purified Concentrate
PC .... Purkinje Cell [*Neuroanatomy*]
P & C......... Put and Call [*Stock exchange term*]
PC .... Pyrrolinecarboxylic Acid [*Biochemistry*]
PC .... Pyruvate Carboxylase [*An enzyme*]   (MAE)
PC .... Single Paper Single Cotton [*Wire insulation*]   (AAG)
PC .... Submarine Chaser [*173 foot*] [*Navy symbol*] [*Obsolete*]
PC .... Sumitomo Chemical Co. [*Japan*] [*Research code symbol*]
PC .... Veterans of the US Posse Comitatus   (EA)
PC1 .... Postal Clerk, First Class [*Navy rating*]
PC1 .... Power Control One [*Hydraulic*]   (MCD)
PC2 .... Postal Clerk, Second Class [*Navy rating*]
PC2 .... Power Control Two [*Hydraulic*]   (MCD)
PC3 .... Postal Clerk, Third Class [*Navy rating*]
PCA .... Acts of the Privy Council [*England*] [*A publication*]   (DLA)
PCA .... Calgon Corp., Pittsburgh, PA [*OCLC symbol*]   (OCLC)
PCA .... Pacific Communications Area [*Air Force*]   (MCD)
PCA .... Panama Canal Authority
PCA .... Paper Converters Association [*Defunct*]   (EA)
PCA .... Paperweight Collectors' Association   (EA)
PCA .... Papillon Club of America   (EA)
PCA .... Para-Chloroaniline [*Organic chemistry*]
PCA .... Para-Coumaric Acid [*Organic chemistry*]
PCA .... Parachute Club of America [*Later, USPA*]   (EA)
PCA .... Parietal Cell Antibodies [*Immunology*]
PCA .... Parliamentary Commissioner for Administration [*British*]
PCA .... Parti Communiste Algerien [*Algerian Communist Party*] [*Political party*]
PCA .... Partido Comunista de Argentina [*Communist Party of Argentina*] [*Political party*]   (PD)
PCA .... Parts Control Area [*NASA*]   (KSC)
PCA .... Party of the Civic Alliance [*Romania*] [*Political party*]   (EY)
PCA .... Passive Cutaneous Anaphylaxis [*Immunochemistry*]
PCA .... Patient-Controlled Analgesia
PCA .... Patriotic Catholic Association [*Name given to nationalized Catholic Church in China*]
P & CA....... Paying and Collecting Area   (AFM)
PCA .... Peak Clipping Amplifier

PCA .... Pekingese Club of America   (EA)
PCA .... Pennsylvania Commuter Airlines [*New Cumberland, PA*] [*FAA designator*]   (FAAC)
PCA .... Pentachloraniline [*Organic chemistry*]
PCA .... Pentachloroanisole [*Organic chemistry*]
PCA .... Percent Cortical Area [*Neurology*]
PCA .... Perchloric Acid [*Inorganic chemistry*]
PCA .... Percutaneous Carotid Arteriogram [*Medicine*]   (MAE)
PCA .... Pericruciate Association [*Cortex, of cat*]
PCA .... Period Contract Acceptance
PCA .... Peripheral Circulatory Assist [*Medicine*]
PCA .... Peritoneal Carcinomatosis [*Oncology*]
PCA .... Permanent Change of Assignment [*Army*]
PCA .... Permanent Court of Arbitration [*See also CPA*] [*Hague, Netherlands*]   (EAIO)
PCA .... Personal Care Aide [*or Assistant or Attendant*]
PCA .... Personal Cash Allowance
PCA .... Photon Counting Array [*Instrumentation*]
PCA .... Physical Configuration Audit [*Military, NASA*]
PCA .... Pinnacle [*Alaska*] [*Seismograph station code, US Geological Survey*]   (SEIS)
PCA .... Pitcairn Cierva Autogiro [*Aeronautics*]
PCA .... Pitch Control Assembly   (MCD)
PCA .... Plane Circular Aperture
PCA .... Plasma Catecholamine [*Biochemistry*]
PCA .... Plasma-Covered Antenna
PCA .... Plate Count Agar [*Microbiology*]
PCA .... Pneumatic Control Assembly   (NASA)
PCA .... Point of Closest Approach
PCA .... Polar Cap Absorption
PCA .... Police Complaint Authority [*British*]
PCA .... Polycrystalline Alumina
PCA .... Poodle Club of America   (EA)
PCA .... Pool Critical Assembly [*Nuclear reactor*]
PCA .... Popular Culture Association   (EA)
PCA .... Porous-Coated Anatomical [*Prosthesis*]
PCA .... Porsche Club of America   (EA)
PCA .... Port Communications Area [*Telecommunications*]   (TEL)
PCA .... Portacaval Anastomosis [*Animal model of chronic liver disease*]
PCA .... Portage Creek [*Alaska*] [*Airport symbol*]   (OAG)
PCA .... Portland Cement Association   (EA)
PCA .... Ports Canada
PCA .... Positive Control Area
PCA .... Positive Controlled Airspace
PCA .... Postconstruction Availability   (NVT)
PCA .... Posterior Cerebral Artery [*Brain anatomy*]
PCA .... Posterior Communicating Artery [*Anatomy*]
PCA .... Posterior Cricoarytenoid [*A muscle of the larynx*]
PCA .... Potash Co. of America, Inc. [*Toronto Stock Exchange symbol*]
PCA .... Potentially Contaminated Area   (DNAB)
PCA .... Poultrymen's Cooperative Association   (EA)
PCA .... Power Conditioning Assembly
PCA .... Power Control Assembly   (NASA)
PCA .... Precision Clearing Agent   (DNAB)
PCA .... Precontractual Authorization
PCA .... Prescribed Concentration of Alcohol   (ADA)
PCA .... President's Council on Aging [*Inactive*]
PCA .... Primary Carbon Assimilation [*Botany*]
PCA .... Primary Control Assembly [*Nuclear energy*]   (NRCH)
PCA .... Primary Coolant Activity [*Nuclear energy*]   (NRCH)
PCA .... Prime Candidate Alloy   (MCD)
PCA .... Prime Condition Aircraft
PCA .... Principal Component Analysis
PCA .... Principal Control Authority   (NATG)
PCA .... Prindle Class Association   (EA)
PCA .... Print Council of America   (EA)
PCA .... Printed Circuit Assembly [*Telecommunications*]   (TEL)
PCA .... Printer Communications Adapter
PCA .... Printing Corp. of America
PCA .... Private Communications Association [*Later, NCA*]
PCA .... Proceedings. Classical Association [*A publication*]
PCA .... Process Control Analyzer
PCA .... Procoagulant Activity
PCA .... Procrastinators' Club of America   (EA)
PCA .... Producers Commission Association   (EA)
PCA .... Professional Chess Association   (EA)
PCA .... Professional Comedians' Association   (EA)
PCA .... Program Change Analysis [*DoD*]
PCA .... Program Coupler Assembly   (KSC)
PCA .... Programmable Communications Adapter [*Data processing*]
PCA .... Progress Change Authority
PCA .... Progressive Citizens of America
PC & A .... Project Control and Administration [*NASA*]
PCA .... Protective Clothing Arrangement [*Telecommunications*]   (TEL)
PCA .... Protective Connecting Arrangement [*Telecommunications*]   (TEL)
PCA .... Public Archives, Charlottetown, Prince Edward Island [*Library symbol*] [*National Library of Canada*]   (NLC)
PCA .... Puli Club of America   (EA)

PCA .... Pulp Chemicals Association (EA)
PCA .... Pulse Counter Adapter
PCA .... Putnam California Investment Grade Municipal [*AMEX symbol*] (SPSG)
PCA .... Pyrotechnic Control Assembly [*NASA*]
PCA .... Pyrrolidonecarboxylic Acid [*Organic chemistry*]
PCAA........ Pancretan Association of America (EA)
PCaab .... Parietal Cell Autoantibody [*Immunology*]
PCAABC ... Centre for Agricultural Publications and Documentation [*Wageningen*]. Annual Report [*A publication*]
PCAAS ...... Proceedings. Connecticut Academy of Arts and Sciences [*A publication*]
PCAC........ Partially Conserved Axial-Vector Current
PCAC........ Private College Admissions Center [*Later, NAAPHE*]
PC Act....... Probate Court Act [*A publication*] (DLA)
PCAD .... Package Computer-Aided Design [*Data processing*]
PCADS....... Panoramic Control and Display System (MCD)
PCAE........ Polar Cap Absorption Event
PC-AEO .... Personal Computer - Annual Energy Outlook Forecasting Model [*Department of Energy*] (GFGA)
PCAG .... Pentobarbital-Chlorpromazine-Alcohol Group [*Medicine*]
PCAG .... Research Station, Agriculture Canada [*Station de Recherches, Agriculture Canada*] Charlottetown, Prince Edward Island [*Library symbol*] [*National Library of Canada*] (NLC)
PCAI......... PCA International, Inc. [*NASDAQ symbol*] (NQ)
P Cal .... Petrus Calvelli [*Flourished, 14th century*] [*Authority cited in pre-1607 legal work*] (DSA)
PCalS........ California State College, California, PA [*Library symbol*] [*Library of Congress*] (LCLS)
PCAM .... Partitioned Content Addressable Memory
PCAM .... Punched Card Accounting Machine [*Data processing*]
PCamA ...... Alliance College, Cambridge Springs, PA [*Library symbol*] [*Library of Congress*] (LCLS)
P Camb Ph S ... Proceedings. Cambridge Philological Society [*A publication*]
PCAMIC ... People Concerned about MIC [*Methyl Isocyanate*] (EA)
PCAMP..... Protective Coatings and Metalizing Process (DNAB)
PCAN .... Program Change Action Notice (DNAB)
PCAO .... President's Commission on Americans Outdoors
PCAP........ Physical Correlation Analysis Program [*Military*]
P-CAP....... Physically-Challenged Assistance Program [*Chrysler Motors Corp.*] [*Detroit, MI*] [*Information service or system*] (IID)
PCAP........ Post Commercial Action Plan [*International Trade Administration*]
PCAP........ Programmer Capacity
PC App ...... Law Reports, Privy Council, Appeal Cases [*England*] [*A publication*] (DLA)
PCAPS....... Production Control and Planning System (MCD)
PCAR........ PACCAR, Inc. [*NASDAQ symbol*] (NQ)
PCarl......... Bosler Free Library, Carlisle, PA [*Library symbol*] [*Library of Congress*] (LCLS)
PCarlA....... United States Army War College, Carlisle Barracks, PA [*Library symbol*] [*Library of Congress*] (LCLS)
PCarlD....... Dickinson College, Carlisle, PA [*Library symbol*] [*Library of Congress*] (LCLS)
PCarlD-L... Dickinson School of Law, Sheeley-Lee Law Library, Carlisle, PA [*Library symbol*] [*Library of Congress*] (LCLS)
PCarlH ...... Cumberland County Historical Society and Hamilton Library Association, Carlisle, PA [*Library symbol*] [*Library of Congress*] (LCLS)
PCarlMH .. United States Army, Military History Research Collection, Carlisle Barracks, PA [*Library symbol*] [*Library of Congress*] (LCLS)
PCarlPL..... United States Army, Carlisle Barracks Post Library, Carlisle Barracks, PA [*Library symbol*] [*Library of Congress*] (LCLS)
PCARS ...... Point Credit Accounting and Reporting System (AFM)
PCAS........ Persistent Chemical Agent Stimulant
PCAS........ Possible Carotid Artery System [*Medicine*]
PCAS........ Primary Central Alarm Station [*Nuclear energy*] (NRCH)
P Cas......... Prize Cases [*1914-22*] [*England*] [*A publication*] (DLA)
P Cas......... Prize Cases (Trehearn and Grant) [*England*] [*A publication*] (DLA)
PCAS........ Proceedings. Cambridge Antiquarian Society [*A publication*]
PCAS........ Proceedings. Classical Association of Scotland [*A publication*]
PCAS........ Punch Card Accounting System [*Data processing*]
PCAS/CADS ... Persistent Chemical Agent Stimulant/Chemical Agent Disclosure Solution [*Army*]
PCASP....... Passive-Cavity Aerosol Spectrometer Probe [*Meteorology*]
PCASS....... Parts Control Automated Support System [*Database*]
PCAST ...... President's Council of Advisers on Science and Technology [*1989*]
PCAT........ Pharmacy College Admission Test
pCAT .... Plasmid Chloramphenicol Acetyltransferase [*An enzyme*]
PCAT........ Procedures for the Control of Air Traffic (SAA)
P Cath .... Pensee Catholique [*A publication*]
PCAU .... Parachute Course Administrative Unit [*Military*] [*British*] (INF)
PCAU .... Philippine Civil Affairs Unit [*Army unit which supplied emergency subsistence after end of Japanese dominance*] [*World War II*]

PCAV........ Principal Component Analysis with Varimax Rotation
PCB........... Central Pennsylvania District Library Center, Bellefonte, PA [*OCLC symbol*] (OCLC)
PcB........... Near Point of Convergence [*Ophthalmology*]
PCB........... Page Control Block [*Data processing*] (IBMDP)
PCB........... Paracervical Block [*Anesthesiology*]
PCB........... Parti Communiste de Belgique [*Communist Party of Belgium*] [*See also KPB*] [*Political party*] (PPE)
PCB........... Partido Comunista de Bolivia [*Communist Party of Bolivia*] [*Political party*] (PPW)
PCB........... Partido Comunista do Brasil [*Communist Party of Brazil*] [*Pro-Albanian*] [*Political party*] (PPW)
PCB........... Parts Control Board
PCB........... Patent Compensation Board [*Energy Research and Development Administration*]
PC & B .... Personnel Compensation and Benefits (GFGA)
PCB........... Petty Cash Book [*Business term*]
PCB........... Planning Change Board (AAG)
PCB........... Plenum Chamber Burning
PCB........... Poetry Chapbook [*A publication*]
PCB........... Pollution. Environmental News Bulletin [*A publication*]
PCB........... Polychlorinated Biphenyl [*Organic chemistry*]
PCB........... Polychlorobenzene
PCB........... Port Check BIT [*Binary Digit*] [*Telecommunications*] (TEL)
PCB........... Power Circuit Breaker (MSA)
PCB........... Power Control Box (NASA)
PCB........... Precambrian Shield Resources Ltd. [*Toronto Stock Exchange symbol*]
PCB........... Premier Commercial Bank Ltd. [*Nigeria*]
PCB........... Primary Carpet Backing
PCB........... Printed Circuit Board (MCD)
PCB........... Prix de Cession de Base [*Basic Wholesale Price*] [*French*]
PCB........... Procarbazine [*Also, P, PC, Pr*] [*Antineoplastic drug*]
PCB........... Process Control Block
PCB........... Product Configuration Baseline (NASA)
PCB........... Program Communication Block
PCB........... Program Control Block [*Data processing*] (BUR)
PCB........... Project Change Board (AAG)
PCB........... Project Control Branch [*Social Security Administration*]
PCB........... Projected Control Board
PCB........... Property Control Branch [*of Allied Military Government*] [*Post-World War II*]
PCB........... Proprietor of Copyright on a Work by a Corporate Body
PCB........... Propulsion [*Ground*] Control Box (AAG)
PCB........... Public Coin Box [*Telecommunications*] (TEL)
PCB........... Publisher's Central Bureau
PCBA........ Para-Chlorobenzoic Acid [*Organic chemistry*]
PCBA........ Pepsi-Cola Bottlers Association (EA)
PCBA........ Polyclonal B Cell Activation [*Hematology*]
PCBA........ Printed Circuit Board Assembly (MCD)
PCBB........ Power Conditioning Brass Board (MCD)
PCBB........ Primary Commercial Blanket Bond [*Insurance*]
PCBC........ Para-Chlorobenzyl Chloride [*Organic chemistry*]
PCBC........ Partially Conserved Baryon Current (IEEE)
PCBC........ Polk County Biomedical Consortium [*Library network*]
PCBC........ Progressive Conservative Broadcasting Corp. [*Fictional version of the Cana dian Broadcasting Corp.*]
PCBCL ...... Printed Circuit Board Configuration List (MCD)
PCBD........ Polychlorinated Benzodioxin [*Organic chemistry*]
PCBDA...... Put and Call Brokers and Dealers Association [*Inactive*] (EA)
PCBG........ Primary Care Block Grant
PCBMEM ... Progress in Clinical Biochemistry and Medicine [*A publication*]
PCB-ML.... Partido Comunista Marxista-Leninista de Bolivia [*Marxist-Leninist Communist Party of Bolivia*] [*Political party*] (PPW)
PCBN........ Para-Chlorobenzonitrile [*Organic chemistry*]
PCBN........ Polycrystalline Cubic Boron Nitride
PCBPA...... Personal Computer Board Panel Assembly (DWSG)
PCBPB ..... Pesticide Biochemistry and Physiology [*A publication*]
PCBQ........ Catholic Biblical Quarterly [*A publication*]
PCBR........ Printed Circuit Board Repair (MCD)
PCBR........ Progress in Clinical and Biological Research [*Elsevier Book Series*] [*A publication*]
PC/BRD .... Printed Circuit Board [*Automotive engineering*]
PCBRD...... Progress in Clinical and Biological Research [*A publication*]
PCBS .... Plastic Connector Backing Shell
PCBS .... Positive Control Bombardment System [*Air Force*]
PCBS .... Printed Circuit Board Socket
PCBS .... Pupil Classroom Behavior Scale
PCBSA2 .... Canadian Federation of Biological Societies. Proceedings [*A publication*]
PCBTF....... Para-Chlorobenzotrifluoride [*Organic chemistry*]
PCBTS....... Portable Cesium Beam Time Standard
PCC........... Acts of the Privy Council, Colonial Series [*A publication*] (DLA)
PCC........... Chief Postal Clerk [*Navy rating*]
PCC........... Pacific Cal Air [*Oakland, CA*] [*FAA designator*] (FAAC)
PCC........... Pacific Cruise Conference [*Formerly, TPPC*] [*Defunct*] (EA)
PCC........... Package Carrier Committee (EA)
PCC........... Pad Control Center [*NASA*] (NASA)
PCC........... Paid Circulation Council [*Later, ASCMP*]

PCC............ Palestinian Ceramic Chronology [*200BC-70AD*] [*A publication*]   (BJA)
PCC............ Panama Canal Commission [*Independent government agency*]
PCC............ Panama Canal Co. [*Superseded by Panama Canal Commission*]
PCC............ Panamerican Cultural Circle   (EA)
PCC............ Parent and Child Center [*Project Head Start*]
PCC............ Parklawn Health Library Computer Center [*Department of Health and Human Services*]   (GFGA)
PCC............ Parochial Church Council [*Church of England*]
PCC............ Partial Crystal Control   (IEEE)
PCC............ Partido Comunista Chileno [*Communist Party of Chile*] [*Political party*]   (PD)
PCC............ Partido Comunista Cubano [*Communist Party of Cuba*] [*Political party*]   (PPW)
PCC............ Partido Conservador Colombiano [*Conservative Party of Colombia*] [*Political party*]   (PPW)
PCC............ Party of Catalan Communists [*Political party*]   (PPW)
PCC............ Pasadena City College [*California*]
PCC............ Pathe Communications Corp. [*NYSE symbol*]   (SPSG)
PCC............ Patient Care Coordinator [*Medicine*]
PCC............ Payload Control and Checkout [*NASA*]   (NASA)
PCC............ Peak Cathode Current
PCC............ People's Caretakers' Council [*Rhodesian*]
PCC............ People's Christian Coalition [*Later, Sojourners*]   (EA)
PCC............ Pepper Community [*Later, IPC*]
PCC............ Per-Command Course   (MCD)
PCC............ Per Copia Conforme [*True Copy*] [*Italian*]
PCC............ Performance Certification Component [*SQT*]   (MCD)
PCC............ Performance Criteria Categories   (MCD)
PCC............ Peripheral Control Computer
PCc............ Periscopic Concave [*Ophthalmology*]
PCC............ Personal Computer Coprocessor
PCC(C)........ Personnel Control Center [*Air Force*]   (AFM)
PCC............ Personnel Coordination Center [*Army*]
PCC............ Peters' United States Circuit Court Reports [*A publication*]   (DLA)
PCC............ Phenylchlorocarbene [*Organic chemistry*]
PCC............ Pheochromocytoma [*Oncology*]
PCC............ Philippine Christian College   (AEBS)
PCC............ Phosphate Carrier Compound
PCC............ Physical Coal Cleaning [*Fuel technology*]
PCC............ Pilarcitos Creek [*California*] [*Seismograph station code, US Geological Survey*]   (SEIS)
PCC............ Pilot Control Console
PCC............ Piperidinocyclohexanecarbonitrile [*Organic chemistry*]
PCC............ Planning Coordination Conference [*NATO*]   (NATG)
PCC............ Plastics in Construction Council [*Later, CCS*]
PCC............ Platform Control Center [*NASA*]   (SSD)
PCC............ Platoon Command Center [*Army*]
PCC............ Plug Compatible Computer   (ADA)
PCC............ Plutonium Concentrator Concentrate [*Nuclear energy*]   (NRCH)
PCC............ Point of Compound Curve   (KSC)
PCC............ Pointe Claire Public Library [*UTLAS symbol*]
PCC............ Poison Control Center
PCC............ Polarity Coincidence Correlator
PCC............ Political Consultative Committee [*Warsaw Pact*]
PCC............ Political Consultative Council   (CINC)
PCC............ Polycore Composite Construction [*Automotive engineering*]
PCC............ Polymer-Cement Concrete   (KSC)
PCC............ Polynesian Cultural Center   (EA)
PCC............ Pontifical Council for Culture [*Vatican City*]   (EAIO)
PCC............ Poor Clares of St. Colette [*Roman Catholic women's religious order*]
PCC............ Population Crisis Committee   (EA)
PCC............ Portable Cable Checker
PCC............ Portland Cement Concrete
PCC............ Positive Control Communication
PCC............ Postal Concentration Center [*Army*]
PCC............ Postal and Courier Communications [*British*]
PCC............ Pour Copie Conforme [*Certified True Copy*] [*French*]
PCC............ Power Control Console [*Diving apparatus*]
PCC............ Pre-Command Course [*Military*]
PCC............ Precast Concrete [*Technical drawings*]
PCC............ Precipitated Calcium Carbonate [*Inorganic chemistry*]
PCC............ Precompressor Cooling   (MCD)
PCC............ Premature Chromosome Condensation [*Genetics*]
PCC............ Prerogative Court of Canterbury [*English court previously having jurisdiction over wills*]
PCC............ Presbyterian Charismatic Communion [*Later, PRR*] [*An association*]   (EA)
PCC............ President of the Canteen Committee [*Military*] [*British*]
PCC............ President's Conference Committee
PCC............ Press Complaints Commission   (ECON)
PCC............ Printed Circuit Card
PCC............ Printed Circuit Conference
PCC............ Private Carrier Conference [*of ATA*]   (EA)
PCC............ Privy Council Cases [*British*]
PC(C)........ Privy Councillor (Canada)
PCC............ Problem Control and Contact Unit [*IRS*]
PCC............ Process Chemistry Cell   (NRCH)

PCC............ Process Control Computer
PCC............ Processor Control Console [*Telecommunications*]   (TEL)
PCC............ Product Control Center [*DoD*]
PCC............ Production Compression Capability
PCC............ Productivity Communication Center   (EA)
PCC............ Program Control Counter
PCC............ Program-Controlled Computer   (DIT)
PCC............ Program Coordination Committee   (SSD)
PCC............ Progress Control Clerk [*DoD*]
PCC............ Project Control Center
PCC............ Project Coordination Centre [*Defence Research Board*] [*Canada*]
PCC............ Propionyl CoA Carboxylase [*An enzyme*]
PCC............ Prothrombin Complex Concentrates [*Hematology*]
PCC............ Provincial Congress Committee
PCC............ Provisioning Control Code [*Military*]   (AFIT)
PCC............ Psychometric Colorimeter Chamber   (MCD)
PCC............ Pulse Counter Chain
PCC............ Pulverized Coal Combustion [*or Combustor*]
PCC............ Pure Car Carrier [*Shipping*]   (DS)
PCC............ Pyridinium Chlorochromate [*Organic chemistry*]
PCC............ Pyroconvective Cooling
PC(C)........ Submarine Chaser (Control) [*173 foot*] [*Navy symbol*] [*Obsolete*]
PCCA........ Confederation Art Gallery and Museum, Charlottetown, Prince Edward Island [*Library symbol*] [*National Library of Canada*]   (NLC)
PCCA........ Pacific Class Catamaran Association   (EA)
PCCA........ Pattern-Contingent Chromatic Aftereffects
PCCA........ Pewter Collectors Club of America   (EA)
PCCA........ Pipe Collectors Club of America   (EA)
PCCA........ Playing Card Collectors' Association   (EA)
PCCA........ Police Car Collectors Association   (EA)
PCCA........ Postcard Collector's Club of America [*Defunct*]   (EA)
PCCA........ Power and Communication Contractors Association   (EA)
PCCADS ... Panoramic Cockpit Control and Display System   (MCD)
PCCAF ...... Procedure Change Control Action Form   (AAG)
PCCAF ...... Procedure Committee Change Authorization Form   (AAG)
PCCB........ Payload Configuration Control Board [*NASA*]   (MCD)
PCCB........ Program Configuration Control Board [*NASA*]   (NASA)
PCCB........ Project Configuration Control Board [*Army*]   (AABC)
PCCC........ Participating College Correspondence Course   (MUGU)
PCCCD...... Proceedings. Annual Allerton Conference on Communication, Control, and Computing [*A publication*]
PCCD........ Peristaltic Charge-Coupled Device   (IEEE)
PCCDS ...... Patrol Craft Combat Direction System [*Navy*]   (SAA)
PCCE........ Pacific Coast Coin Exchange
PCCE........ Payload Common Communication Equipment [*NASA*]   (NASA)
PCCEI .... Permanent Charities Committee of the Entertainment Industries   (EA)
PCCEMRSP ... Permanent Commission for the Conservation and Exploitation of the Maritime Resources of the South Pacific
PCCES....... Planning and Coordinating Committee for Environmental Studies [*National Research Council*]
PCCF .... Plan Case Control File [*IRS*]
PCCG .... Protestant Cinema Critics Guild [*Later, PCG*]   (EA)
PCCh .... Partido Comunista de Chile [*Chilean Communist Party*] [*Political party*]   (EY)
PCCH .... Pentachlorocyclohexene [*Organic chemistry*]
PCCI .... Paper Cup and Container Institute [*Later, SSI*]   (EA)
PCCI .... President's Committee on Consumer Interests [*Terminated, 1971*]
PCCL........ People's Community Civic League   (EA)
PCCL........ Precontract Cost Letter [*Navy*]   (NG)
PCCLAS/P ... Proceedings. Pacific Coast Council on Latin American Studies [*A publication*]
PCCM....... Master Chief Postal Clerk [*Navy rating*]
PCCM....... Private Circuit Control Module [*Telecommunications*]   (TEL)
PCCM....... Program Change Control Management   (NASA)
PCCM....... Program Control Contract Manager   (MCD)
PCC (M-L) ... Parti Communiste Canadien (Marxiste-Leniniste) [*Marxist-Leninist Communist Party of Canada*] [*Political party*]
PCCN .... Part Card Change Notice   (KSC)
PCCN .... Port Call Control Number [*Army*]   (AABC)
PCCN .... Preliminary Configuration Control Number   (AAG)
PCCN .... Provisioning Contract Control Number   (NASA)
PCCNL...... Pacific Coast Coordinator of Naval Logistics
PCCO .... Plant Clearance Contracting Officer [*DoD*]
PCCOA...... Coles Associates Ltd., Charlottetown, Prince Edward Island [*Library symbol*] [*National Library of Canada*]   (NLC)
PCCOA...... Professional Contributions. Colorado School of Mines [*A publication*]
PCCP........ Canadian Pension Commission [*Commission Canadienne des Pensions*], Charlottetown, Prince Edward Island [*Library symbol*] [*National Library of Canada*]   (BIB)
PCCP........ Preliminary Contract Change Proposal [*NASA*]   (KSC)
PCCPS....... Pacific Coast Canned Pear Service   (EA)
PCCR........ Publishing Center for Cultural Resources   (EA)
PCCRD7.... Proceedings. Serono Clinical Colloquia on Reproduction [*A publication*]

PCCS	Parti Conservateur Chretien-Social [*Conservative Christian-Social Party*] [*Switzerland*] [*Political party*] (PPE)
PCCS	Photographic Camera Control System (KSC)
PCCS	Ported Coax Cable Sensor [*Military*] (DWSG)
PCCS	Positive Control Communications System
PCCS	Processor Common Communications System
PCCS	Program Change Control System (NG)
PCCS	Program and Cost Control System [*Army*] (RDA)
PCCS	Project Cost Control System
PCCS	Publications Contract Coverage Schedule (MCD)
PCCS	Senior Chief Postal Clerk [*Navy rating*]
PCCSD	Proceedings. International Conference on Cybernetics and Society [*A publication*]
PCCT	Percept and Concept Cognition Test [*Psychology*]
P-CCU	Post Coronary Care Unit
PCCU	President's Commission on Campus Unrest (EA)
PCCU	Punched Card Control Unit [*Data processing*] (AABC)
PCD	Democratic Conservative Party [*Nicaragua*] [*Political party*] (PD)
PCD	Pacific Car Demurrage Bureau, San Francisco CA [*STAC*]
PCD	Pacific Communications Division [*Military*]
PCD	Panama Canal Department
PCD	Parti Communiste du Dahomey [*Communist Party of Dahomey*] [*Political party*] [*Benin*]
PCD	Partido Comunista Dominicano [*Dominican Communist Party*] [*Dominican Republic*] [*Political party*] (PPW)
PCD	Patriotic Coalition for Democracy [*Political group*] [*Guyana*]
PCD	Phenylchlorodiazirine [*Organic chemistry*]
PCD	Phosphate-Citrate-Dextrose Polycystic Disease (MAE)
PCD	Photoconductive Decay [*Semiconductor material*]
PCD	Pine Channel Gold [*Vancouver Stock Exchange symbol*]
PCD	Planned Completion Date (TEL)
PCD	Plasma Cell Dyscrasia [*Medicine*]
PCD	Plasma-Coupled Device
PCD	Plutonium Concentrator Distillate [*Nuclear energy*] (NRCH)
PCD	Pneumatic Control Distributors (KSC)
PCD	Polar Cap Disturbance (DNAB)
PCD	Polycrystalline Diamond (ECON)
PCD	Polycystic Disease [*of kidneys*] [*Medicine*]
PCD	Port Control Diagnostic [*Telecommunications*] (TEL)
PCD	Positive Control Document (MCD)
PCd	Post Card [*Philately*]
Pcd	Postcard (BJA)
PCD	Posterior Corneal Deposit [*Ophthalmology*] (MAE)
PCD	Pounds per Capita per Day (AAG)
PCD	Power Control Device [*Nuclear energy*] (NRCH)
PCD	Power Control and Distribution
PCD	Power Conversion Distributor
PCD	Precision Course Direction [*Aerospace*] (MCD)
PCD	Pressure Control Distributor (KSC)
PC & D	Priest, Confessor, and Doctor (ROG)
PCD	Primary Ciliary Dyskinesia [*Medicine*]
PCD	Primary Current Distribution [*Electroplating*]
PCD	Problem Control and Display
PCD	Procedural Change Directive (KSC)
PCD	Procurement and Contracts Division [*NASA*]
PCD	Procurement Control Document [*NASA*] (MCD)
PCD	Production Common Digitizer
PCD	Program Change Decision [*Army*]
PCD	Program Control Display System [*NATO Air Defense Ground Environment*] (NATG)
PCD	Program Control Document (KSC)
PCD	Project Control Drawing (AAG)
PCD	Protocatechuatedioxygenase [*An enzyme*]
PCD	Pulmonary Clearance Delay [*Medicine*]
PCDA	Post Card Distributors Association
PCDA	Professional Currency Dealers Association (EA)
PCDB	Poison Control Data Base [*Database*]
PCDC	Diagnostic Chemicals Ltd., Charlottetown, Prince Edward Island [*Library symbol*] [*National Library of Canada*] (NLC)
PCDC	Plutonium Canister Decontamination Cell [*Nuclear energy*] (NRCH)
PCDD	Pentachlorodioxin [*Organic chemistry*]
PCDD	Polychlorinated Dibenzodioxin [*Organic chemistry*]
PCDDS	Private Circuit Digital Data Service [*Telecommunications*] (TEL)
PCDESIG ...	Plane Captain Designated [*or Designation*] (DNAB)
PCDF	Polychlorinated Dibenzofuran [*Organic chemistry*]
PCDHi	Delaware County Historical Society, Chester, PA [*Library symbol*] [*Library of Congress*] (LCLS)
PCDI	Per Capita Disposable Income [*Economics*]
PCDI	Pierce Die
PCDJ	Pakistan Committee for Democracy and Justice (EA)
PCDL	Pro-Choice Defense League (EA)
PCdoB	Partido Comunista do Brasil [*Communist Party of Brazil*] [*Political party*] (PPW)
PC-DOS	Personal Computer Disk Operating System [*IBM's version of Microsoft program*]
PCDP	Contemporary Drug Problems [*A publication*]
PCDP	Parti Comorien pour la Democratie et le Progres [*Political party*] (EY)
PCDP	Pilot Control and Display Panel
PCDP	Punched Card Data Processing
PCD-PRP ..	Pueblo, Cambio, y Democracia - Partido Roldosista Popular [*People, Change, and Democracy - Popular Roldosista Party*] [*Ecuador*] [*Political party*] (PPW)
PCDR	Comparative Drama [*A publication*]
PCDR	Procedure (AAG)
PCDRR	PC Digest Ratings Report [*A publication*]
PCDS	Payload Command Decoder Subunit [*NASA*] (KSC)
PCDS	Power Conversion and Distribution System
PCDS	Procurement Congressional Descriptive Summary [*Army*] (RDA)
PCDS	Project Control Drawing System (AAG)
PCDU	Payload Command Decoder Unit [*NASA*] (NASA)
PCDUS	Plasma Cell Dyscrasias of Unknown Significance [*Medicine*]
PCE	Pacific East Air, Inc. [*Los Angeles, CA*] [*FAA designator*] (FAAC)
PCE	Page Communications Engineers, Inc. [*Canada*] (MCD)
PCE	Painter Creek, AK [*Location identifier*] [*FAA*] (FAAL)
PCE	Partido Comunista Ecuatoriano [*Communist Party of Ecuador*] [*Political party*] (PPW)
PCE	Partido Comunista de Espana [*Communist Party of Spain*] [*Political party*] (PPE)
PCE	Patrol Escort [*Patrol Craft Escort*] [*Navy symbol*]
PCE	Pedco Energy Ltd. [*Vancouver Stock Exchange symbol*]
PCE	Perchloroethylene [*Organic chemistry*]
PCE	Peripheral Control Element
PCE	Personal Consumption Expenditure
PCE	Petrozavodsk Commodity Exchange [*Russian Federation*] (EY)
PCE	Physical Capacities Evaluation [*Test of hand skills*]
PCE	Piece [*Numismatics*]
PCE	Plasma Chamber Evacuation Subsystem (MCD)
PCE	Plug Compatible Ethernet
PCE	Pollution Control Equipment (GFGA)
PCE	Polyarthrite Chronique Evolutive [*Chronic Evolutive Polyarthritis*] [*Medicine*] [*French*]
PCE	Positive Continuous Engagement [*Automotive engineering*]
PCE	Power Conditioning Equipment
PCE	Power Conversion Equipment (DNAB)
PC of E	Presbyterian Church of England
PCE	Pressure to Clutch Engage [*Aerospace*] (AAG)
PCE	Prince Edward Island Department of Education, Charlottetown, Prince Edward Island [*Library symbol*] [*National Library of Canada*] (NLC)
PCE	Privy Councillor, England (ROG)
PCE	Production Check Equipment (MCD)
PCE	Professional Care, Inc. [*AMEX symbol*] (SPSG)
PCE	Program Cost Estimate (AFM)
PCE	Prohormone-Converting Endopeptidase
PCE	Pseudocholinesterase [*Same as ACAH*] [*An enzyme*]
PCE	Pulmocutaneous Exchange
PCE	Punch Card Equipment [*Data processing*] (AFM)
PCE	Pyrometric Cone Equivalent [*Refractory industry*]
PCE	Submarine Chaser Escort
PCEA	Pacific Coast Electrical Association
PCEA	Phosphate Chemicals Export Association (EA)
P/CEA3	Probationary Control Electrical Artificer 3rd Class [*British military*] (DMA)
PCEAA	Professional Construction Estimators Association of America (EA)
PCEA Bol Trimest Exp Agropecu ...	PCEA [*Programa Cooperativo de Experimentacion Agropecuaria*] Boletin Trimestral de Experimentacion Agropecuaria [*A publication*]
PCE(C)	Patrol Vessel, Escort (Control) [*180 feet*] [*Navy symbol*] [*Obsolete*]
PCEDURE ...	Procedure (ROG)
PCEEDGS ...	Proceedings (ROG)
PCEEO	President's Committee on Equal Employment Opportunity [*Later, OFCCP*] [*Department of Labor*]
PCEH	President's Committee on Employment of the Handicapped [*Washington, DC*]
PCEI	Prime Contract End Item (MCD)
PCEM	Parliamentary Council of the European Movement
PCEM	Process Chain Evaluation Model (IEEE)
PCEM	Program Committee on Education for Mission (EA)
PCEM	Propulsion Contamination Effects Module (NASA)
PcEn	Pacific Enterprises [*Associated Press abbreviation*] (APAG)
PCEP	Perception Technology Corp. [*Canton, MA*] [*NASDAQ symbol*] (NQ)
PCE-R	Partido Comunista de Espana - Reconstituido [*Reconstituted Spanish Communist Party*] [*Political party*] (PD)
PCER	Patrol Rescue Escort [*Patrol Craft Escort Rescue*] [*Navy symbol*]
P Cert Ed ...	Professional Certificate in Education
PCES	President's Committee on Economic Security [*New Deal*]
PCET	Personal Computer Extended Technology [*Computer bus*]
PCETF	Power Conversion Equipment Test Facility [*Nuclear energy*]

PCEU......... Partido Comunista de Espana Unificado [*Unified Communist Party of Spain*] [*Political party*] (PPW)
PCEU......... Pulse Compression/Expansion Unit
PCEZ......... PC Etcetera, Inc. [*NASDAQ symbol*] (NQ)
PCF........... Pacific Air Express [*Honolulu, HI*] [*FAA designator*] (FAAC)
PCF........... Pacific Ridge Resources [*Vancouver Stock Exchange symbol*]
PCF........... Pacificulture Foundation (EA)
PCF........... Parents' Choice Foundation (EA)
PCF........... Parti Communiste Francais [*French Communist Party*] [*Political party*] (PPW)
PCF........... Patrol Craft (Fast) [*Navy symbol*]
PCF........... Payload Control Facility [*NASA*] (MCD)
PCF........... Peace Centers Foundation [*Later, UDC*] (EA)
PCF........... Pentagon Counterintelligence Force
PCF........... Personal Card File
PCF........... Personnel Control Facility [*Army*] (AABC)
PCF........... Pharyngoconjunctival Fever [*Medicine*]
PCF........... Plan Characteristics File [*IRS*]
PCF........... Polycationized Ferritin [*Biochemistry*]
PCF........... Postcard Club Federation (EA)
PCF........... Posterior Carotid Foramen [*Anatomy*]
PCF........... Posterior Cranial Fossa [*Anatomy*] (MAE)
PCF........... Potential Conflict Forecasts [*Army*]
PCF........... Potentially Critical Failures
PCF........... Pounds per Cubic Foot
PCF........... Power Cathode Follower
PCF........... Power per Cubic Foot
PCF........... Prairie Chicken Foundation (EA)
PCF........... Primary Checkpoint File
PCF........... Probability of Consequence Factor
PCF........... Processed Citation File
PCF........... Program Change Factor
PCF........... Program Characteristics File [*Medicaid*] (GFGA)
PCF........... Program Checkout Facility
PCF........... Program Control Facility
PCF........... Programmed Cryptographic Facility [*Data processing*]
PCF........... Prothrombin Conversion Factor [*Hematology*]
PCF........... Public Concern Foundation (EA)
PCF........... Pulse Compression Filter
PCF........... Pulse-to-Cycle Fraction
PCF........... Pulverized Coal-Fired Plant
PCF........... Putnam High Income Convertible & Bond Fund [*NYSE symbol*] (SPSG)
PCFA......... Pin, Clip, and Fastener Association [*Later, PCFS*] (EA)
PCFC......... Phil Collins Fan Club (EA)
PCFC......... Polytechnics and Colleges Funding Council [*British*]
PCFE......... Polytrifluoroethylene [*Organic chemistry*]
PCFE......... Prime Contractor Furnished Equipment (MCD)
PCFFA...... Pacific Coast Federation of Fishermen's Associations (EA)
PC/FGD .... Pulverized Coal / Flue Gas Desulfurization [*Energy technology*]
PCFIA .... Particle Concentration Fluorescence Immunoassay
PCFO........ Position Classification Field Office
PCFP .... Predicted Comparative Failure Probability
PCFR........ Programmatic Center for Fire Research [*National Institute of Standards and Technology*]
PCFS .... Journal of Comparative Family Studies [*A publication*]
PCFS .... Pin, Clip, and Fastener Services (EA)
PCFT .... Information Centre, Prince Edward Island Food Technology Centre, Charlottetown [*Library symbol*] [*National Library of Canada*] (BIB)
PCG .... Guided Missile Coastal Escort [*Ship symbol*] (NATG)
PCG .... Pacific Gas & Electric Co. [*NYSE symbol*] (SPSG)
PCG .... Package Engineering [*A publication*]
PCG .... Paracervical Ganglion [*Anatomy*]
PCG .... Parti Communiste de Guadeloupe [*Communist Party of Guadeloupe*] [*Political party*] (PPW)
PCG .... PezCorona Gold Corp. [*Vancouver Stock Exchange symbol*]
PCG .... Phonocardiogram [*Cardiology*]
PCG .... Plain Clothes Gratuity [*British military*] (DMA)
PCG .... Plains Cotton Growers (EA)
PCG .... Planning Career Goals [*Vocational guidance test*]
PCG .... Planning and Control Guide
PCG .... Power Conditioning Group (MCD)
PCG .... Printed Circuit Generator
PCG .... Programmable Character Generator
PCG .... Protestant Cinema Guild [*Formerly, PCCG*] [*Defunct*]
PCG .... Pulsed Coaxial Gun
PCGD........ Pollution Control Guidance Document
PCGE........ Canadian Geographer [*A publication*]
PCGF........ Protein Crystal Growth Facility (SSD)
PCGLA...... Physics and Chemistry of Glasses [*A publication*]
PCGM...... Pacific Coast Garment Manufacturers [*Later, AAMA*] (EA)
PCGN .... Permanent Committee of Geographical Names [*Later, BGN*]
PCGO........ Canadian Geographic [*A publication*]
PCGOV .... Port Charges Paid by Foreign Government (DNAB)
PCGS........ Protein Crystal Growth System
PCGU........ Protein Crystal Growth Unit (SSD)
PCGVB...... Pairwise Correlated Generalized Valence Bond [*Physics*]
PCH.......... Cheyney State College, Cheyney, PA [*OCLC symbol*] (OCLC)
PCH.......... Packing, Crating, and Handling [*Shipping*]
PC & H ...... Packing, Crating, and Handling [*Shipping*] (AFM)

PCH........... Parent Compound Handbook [*Later, Ring Systems Handbook*] [*American Chemical Society*]
PCH........... Paroxysmal Cold Hemoglobinuria [*Medicine*]
PCH........... Partido Comunista de Honduras [*Communist Party of Honduras*] [*Political party*] (PD)
PCH........... Patrol Craft (Hydrofoil) [*Navy symbol*]
PCH........... PCH Post Career [*Vancouver Stock Exchange symbol*]
PCh........... Phosphocholine [*Biochemistry*]
PCH........... Physicochemical Hydrodynamics [*A publication*]
PCH........... Pitch
P Ch.......... Planovoe Chozjajstvo [*A publication*]
PCH........... Porch (WGA)
PCH........... Potlatch Corp. [*Formerly, PFI*] [*NYSE symbol*] (SPSG)
PCH........... Prepare Chassis
Pch........... Principal Chaplain [*Navy*] [*British*]
PCH........... Punch (KSC)
PCH........... Purchase (DCTA)
PCHA........ Chaucer Review [*A publication*]
PCHAR ..... Printing Character [*Data processing*]
PCHBD...... Patchboard (MSA)
PCHC .... Holland College, Charlottetown, Prince Edward Island [*Library symbol*] [*National Library of Canada*] (NLC)
PCHC .... People's Center for Housing Change (EA)
PChCo .... Conococheague District Library, Chambersburg, PA [*Library symbol*] [*Library of Congress*] (LCLS)
PCHCY...... Parents Campaign for Handicapped Children and Youth (EA)
PCHD........ Purchased (ROG)
PCHE .... Poor Clare Nuns of the Holy Eucharist [*Roman Catholic religious order*]
PCHE .... Purchase (ROG)
PCHEA ..... Petro/Chem Engineer [*A publication*]
Pchela Sof ... Pchela Sofiya [*A publication*]
Pchel Mir... Pchelovodnyi Mir [*A publication*]
Pchel Zhizn ... Pchelovodnaya Zhizn' [*A publication*]
PCheS........ Cheyney State College, Cheyney, PA [*Library symbol*] [*Library of Congress*] (LCLS)
PCHG .... Punching
PCHH....... Church History [*A publication*]
PCHI .... Chicago Review [*A publication*]
PCHK .... Parity Check [*Data communications*] (TEL)
PCHL .... Pacific Coast Hockey League [*Later, Western Hockey League*] (EA)
PCHLT..... Pressurized Cabin Hydraulic Leakage Tester (DWSG)
PCHM...... PharmChem Laboratories [*NASDAQ symbol*] (SPSG)
PCHN....... Peerless Chain [*NASDAQ symbol*] (NQ)
PCHN....... Programmed Course, Home Nursing [*Red Cross*]
PCHO....... Choice [*A publication*]
PCH PhysicoChem Hydrodyn ... PCH: PhysicoChemical Hydrodynamics [*Later, Physicochemical Hydrodynamics*] [*England*] [*A publication*]
PCHR .... Canadian Historical Review [*A publication*]
PCHR .... Panamanian Committee for Human Rights (EA)
PCHR .... Paraguay Committee for Human Rights [*British*]
PCHR .... Pentecostal Coalition for Human Rights (EA)
PCHR .... Purchaser (ROG)
PCHRG ..... Public Citizen Health Research Group (EA)
P Ch S........ Proceedings. Chemical Society [*A publication*]
PCHS......... Purchase (WGA)
PCHSR....... Purchaser
PCHT .... Packaging, Crating, Handling, and Transportation [*Shipping*] (AABC)
PCH & T.... Packaging, Crating, Handling, and Transportation [*Shipping*] (CINC)
PCHT .... Parchment (MSA)
PChW .... Wilson College, Chambersburg, PA [*Library symbol*] [*Library of Congress*] (LCLS)
PCI............. Pacific Viewpoint [*A publication*]
PCI............. Packet Communications, Inc.
PCI............. Panel Call Indicator
PCI............. Pantone Color Institute (EA)
PCI............. Paramount Communications, Inc. [*NYSE symbol*] (SPSG)
PCI............. Parti Communiste Internationaliste [*Internationalist Communist Party*] [*France*] [*Political party*] (PPE)
PCI............. Partito Comunista Italiano [*Italian Communist Party*] [*Political party*]
PCI............. Paterson Candy International [*British*]
PCI............. Pattern of Cockpit Indication
PCI............. Pattern Correspondence Index
PCI............. Pax Christi International (EAIO)
PCI............. PCL Industries Ltd. [*Toronto Stock Exchange symbol*]
PCI............. Pellet Clad Interaction [*Nuclear energy*] (NRCH)
PCI............. Per Column Inch [*Publishing*]
PCI............. Periodic Conformance Inspection (MCD)
PCI............. Peripheral Command Indicator
PCI............. Peripheral Component Interconnect [*Intel Corp.*] (PCM)
PCI............. Peripheral Controller Interface
PCI............. Personal Computer Interface [*Varitronics Systems, Inc.*]
PCI............. Photographic Credit Institute (EA)
PCI............. Physical Configuration Inspection (AFIT)
PCI............. Physical Configuration Item [*Military*]
Pci............. Phytophthora Citricola [*A fungus*]

pCi............ Picocurie [*Also, pC*] [*One trillionth of a curie*]
PCI............ Pilot Club International   (EA)
PCI............ Pilot Controller Integration   (IEEE)
PCI............ Pilots for Christ International   (EA)
PCI............ Pipe Collectors International [*Later, PCCA*]   (EA)
PCI............ Planning Card Index   (AAG)
PCI............ Plant Control Interface
PCI............ Pneumatic Circuit Indicator
PCI............ Pneumatosis Cystoides Intestinorum [*Medicine*]   (AAMN)
PCI............ Political Campaign Institute [*Commercial firm*]   (EA)
PCI............ Population Communications International [*An association*]   (EA)
PCI............ Portable Cesium Irradiator
PCI............ Portable Compass Indicator
PCI............ Possible Criminal Informant
PCI............ Potato Chip Institute, International [*Later, PC/SFA*]   (EA)
PCI............ Powder Coating Institute   (EA)
PCI............ Pre-Combat Inspection   (INF)
PCI............ Pre-Counseling Inventory [*Psychology*]
PCI............ Precision Components, Inc. [*Addison, IL*] [*Telecommunications service*]   (TSSD)
PCI............ Prestressed Concrete Institute   (EA)
PCI............ Prime Ceiling Incentive
PCI............ Private Citizen, Inc. [*An association*]   (EA)
PCI............ Privy Council Decisions [*India*] [*A publication*]   (DLA)
PCI............ Privy Councillor, Ireland   (ROG)
PCI............ Proceedings. Canadian Institute [*A publication*]
PCI............ Process Control Interface
PCI............ Product Configuration Identification   (KSC)
PCI............ Product Cost Index
PCI............ Production Control Information [*Software supplier*] [*Sheffield, England*]   (NCC)
PCI............ Program Check Interruption [*Data processing*]   (MDG)
PCI............ Program Control Input   (NASA)
PCI............ Program-Controlled Interruption [*Data processing*]   (IBMDP)
PCI............ Program in Correctional Institutions   (OICC)
PCI............ Programmable Communications Interface
PCI............ Project Concern International   (EA)
PCI............ Prophylactic Cranial Irradiation [*Oncology*]
PCI............ Proportional Change Index [*Occupational therapy*]
PCI............ Prospectors Club International   (EA)
PCI............ Protein C Inhibitor [*Organic chemistry*]
PCIAC....... Petro-Canada International Assistance Corp.
PCIAOH ... Permanent Commission and International Association on Occupational Health   (EAIO)
PCIC......... Poison Control Information Center
PC & IC ..... Polaris Control and Information Center [*Missiles*]
PCICP....... Primary Control Inventory Control Point [*Navy*]
PCICS....... Permanent Council of the International Convention of Stresa on Cheeses   (EAIO)
PCIE......... President's Council on Integrity and Efficiency in Government   (EPA)
PCIEC .... Permanent Committee for International Eucharistic Congresses   (EA)
PCIFC....... Patsy Cline International Fan Club   (EA)
PCIFC........ Permanent Commission of the International Fisheries Convention
PCII .... Protocol Computers [*NASDAQ symbol*]   (NQ)
PCIJ.......... Permanent Court of International Justice Cases [*A publication*]   (DLA)
PCIJ Ann R ... Permanent Court of International Justice Annual Reports [*A publication*]   (DLA)
pCi/L .... Picocuries per Liter [*Measure of radioactivity*]
PCIL .... Pilot-Controlled Instrument Landing [*Aviation*]   (NASA)
PCILO .... Perturbative Configuration Interaction [*Based on*] Localized Orbitals [*Quantum mechanics*]
PCIM........ Packet Channel Interface Module [*Telecommunications*]
PCIM........ Parti du Congres de l'Independance de Madagascar [*Party of the Congress for Malagasy Independence*]
PCIMP ...... President's Commission on Income Maintenance Programs   (EA)
PCIMR...... Centre for Information and Technical Assistance, Institute of Man and Resources, Charlottetown, Prince Edward Island [*Library symbol*] [*National Library of Canada*]   (NLC)
PCIN......... Program Change Identification Number   (NASA)
PCIN......... Program Change Integration   (NASA)
PCI/O .... Program-Controlled Input-Output
PC-IOC...... Posterior Chamber - Intraocular Lens [*Ophthalmology*]
PCIOMR... Preconditioning Interim Operating Management Recommendation [*Nuclear energy*]   (NRCH)
PCIOS .... Processor Common Input/Output System [*Data processing*]
PCIP .... Personal Computer, Instrument Product
PCIP .... Poseidon [*Missile*] Communication Improvement Program [*Navy*]
PCIPI........ Permanent Committee on Industrial Property [*World Intellectual Property Organization*] [*Switzerland*] [*Information service or system*]   (IID)
PCIRO....... Preparatory Commission for International Refugee Organization
PCIS .... Canton Island [*Phoenix Islands*] [*ICAO location identifier*]   (ICLI)

PCIS .... Patient Care Information System   (IID)
PCIS .... Primary Containment Isolation System [*Nuclear energy*]   (NRCH)
PCIS .... Processed Commodities Inventory System [*Department of Agriculture*]   (GFGA)
PCIS .... Production Control Information System   (NVT)
PCIS .... Professional Career Information Service [*Department of Labor*]
PCIU........ Programmable Communications Interface Unit
PCIV......... Civil War History [*A publication*]
PC/IX .... Personal Computer / Interactive Executive   (HGAA)
PCIYA .... Progress in Clinical Immunology [*A publication*]
PCIYRA .... Pacific Coast Intercollegiate Yacht Racing Association
PCJ .... Bangladesh Development Studies [*A publication*]
PCJ .... Peoples Jewellers Ltd. [*Toronto Stock Exchange symbol*]
PCJ .... Pontifical College Josephinum [*Worthington, OH*]
PCJ .... Pontifical College Josephinum, Worthington, OH [*OCLC symbol*]   (OCLC)
PCJ .... Sisters of the Poor Child Jesus [*Roman Catholic religious order*]
PCJC .... Canadian Journal of Criminology [*A publication*]
PCJH........ Canadian Journal of History [*A publication*]
PCJILMCC ... Philip C. Jessup International Law Moot Court Competition   (EAIO)
PCJOAU ... Pharmaceutical Chemistry Journal [*A publication*]
PCJP......... Canadian Journal of Philosophy [*A publication*]
PC Judg .... Privy Council Judgments [*India*] [*A publication*]   (DLA)
pck............ Peacock [*Philately*]
PCK .... Phase Control Keyboard
PCK .... Pilot Check   (FAAC)
PCK .... Porcupine Creek, AK [*Location identifier*] [*FAA*]   (FAAL)
PCK .... Premarital Counseling Kit [*Psychology*]
PCK .... Primary Chicken Kidney [*Cell line*]
PCK .... Printed Circuit Keyboard
PCK .... Processor Controlled Keying [*Data processing*]   (DCTA)
PCKB........ Printed Circuit Keyboard
PCKD .... Polycystic Kidney Disease [*Medicine*]
Pckg Eng En ... Package Engineering Encyclopedia, Including Modern Packaging Encyclopedia [*A publication*]
Pckgng Eng ... Packaging Engineering [*A publication*]
Pckgng Rev ... Packaging Review [*A publication*]
Pckgng Wek ... Packaging Week [*A publication*]
PCL........... Alberta Attorney General, Provincial Court Libraries [*UTLAS symbol*]
PCI .... Clarion Free Library, Clarion, PA [*Library symbol*] [*Library of Congress*]   (LCLS)
PCL........... Confederation Centre Library, Charlottetown, Prince Edward Island [*Library symbol*] [*National Library of Canada*]   (NLC)
PCL........... Pachaco Lake [*California*] [*Seismograph station code, US Geological Survey*]   (SEIS)
PCL........... Pacific Coast League [*Baseball*]
PCL........... Pallet Coolant Loop   (NASA)
PCL........... Parallel Communications Link
PCL........... Parcel
PCL........... Parti Communiste Libanais [*Lebanese Communist Party*] [*Political party*]   (PPW)
PCL........... Parti Communiste de Luxembourg [*Communist Party of Luxembourg*] [*Political party*]   (PPE)
PCL........... Pencil   (MSA)
PCL........... Permissible Contamination Limits [*Nuclear energy*]   (NRCH)
PCL........... Persistent Corpus Luteum [*Medicine*]
PCL........... Personnel Security Clearance
PCL........... Perspectives on Contemporary Literature [*A publication*]
P Cl .... Petrus Calvelli [*Flourished, 14th century*] [*Authority cited in pre-1607 legal work*]   (DSA)
PCL........... Phillips Cables Ltd. [*Toronto Stock Exchange symbol*]
PCL........... Pilot-Controlled Lighting [*Aviation*]   (FAAC)
PCL........... Planning Configuration List
PCL........... Planning and Conservation League   (EA)
PCL........... Plasma Cell Leukemia [*Oncology*]
PCL........... Playboy Club of London
PCL........... Plum Creek Timber Co., Inc. [*NYSE symbol*]   (SPSG)
PCL........... Pocket Checklist   (MCD)
PCL........... Polycaprolactone [*Organic chemistry*]
PCL........... [*The*] Polytechnic of Central London
PCL........... Positive Control Line
PCL........... Post Conference List
PCL........... Posterior Cruciate Ligament [*Anatomy*]
PCL........... PostScript and LASERJet-Type [*LASER printer*]
PCL........... Power Control Lever   (DNAB)
PCL........... Power Control List   (MCD)
PCL........... Preliminary Change Letter [*Navy*]   (NG)
PCL........... Premier Cruise Lines
PCL........... Primary Coolant Line   (NASA)
PCL........... Primary Coolant Loop   (NASA)
PCL........... Printed Circuit Lamp
PCL........... Printer Control Language
PCL........... Procedural Control Language [*1971*] [*Data processing*]   (CSR)
PCL........... Process Capability Laboratory
PCL........... Programming Checklist   (MCD)
PCL........... Programming Control Language [*Data processing*]   (PCM)
PCL........... Project Control Ledgers [*Navy*]   (NG)

PCL............ Pseudocleistogamous [*Botany*]
PCL............ Pucallpa [*Peru*] [*Airport symbol*] (OAG)
PCL............ Pulse Compression Loop
PCLA......... Polish Canadian Librarians Association
PCLA........ Power Control Linkage Assembly
P Cl A........ Proceedings. Classical Association [*A publication*]
PCLA........ Process Control Language [*Texas Instruments, Inc.*]
PCLA........ Project Coordination and Liaison Administration (OICC)
PCLAC...... Proceedings. California Linguistics Association Conference [*A publication*]
PCLB........ [*The*] Price Co. [*NASDAQ symbol*] (NQ)
PCLC........ Journal of Criminal Law and Criminology [*A publication*]
PCLD........ Dependent Political Entity [*Board on Geographic Names*]
PCLDI....... Prototype Closed-Loop Development Installation [*Nuclear energy*] (NRCH)
PCLG........ Public Citizen Litigation Group (EA)
PCLI......... Canadian Literature [*A publication*]
PCLI......... Independent Political Entity [*Board on Geographic Names*]
PCLI......... Parti de la Convergence pour les Libertes et l'Integration [*Burkina Faso*] [*Political party*] (EY)
P Clin North America ... Pediatric Clinics of North America [*A publication*]
PCLJ........ Pacific Coast Law Journal [*A publication*] (DLA)
PCLK........ Pay Clerk
PCLLG...... Ollennu's Principles of Customary Land Law in Ghana [*A publication*] (DLA)
PCLMP..... President's Advisory Committee on Labor-Management Policy [*Abolished, 1973*]
PCLN........ Personalcomputer Literaturnachweis [*Datendienst Weiss*] [*Database*]
PC-LNIM ... Personal Computer Local Network Interface Module (TSSD)
PCLO........ Passenger Control Liaison Office [*or Officer*] [*Army*] (AABC)
PCLP........ Classical Philology [*A publication*]
PCLQ........ Classical Quarterly [*A publication*]
PCLQA...... Physics and Chemistry of Liquids [*A publication*]
P Cl R....... Parker's New York Criminal Reports [*A publication*] (DLA)
PCLR........ PR [*Public Relations*] Committee for Licensing and Registration (EA)
P Cl R....... Privy Council Reports [*A publication*] (DLA)
PCIS.......... Clarion State College, Clarion, PA [*Library symbol*] [*Library of Congress*] (LCLS)
PCLS .... Classical Antiquity [*A publication*]
PCLS .... Law Society of Prince Edward Island, Charlottetown, Prince Edward Island [*Library symbol*] [*National Library of Canada*] (NLC)
PCLS .... People's Committee for Libyan Students (EA)
PCLS .... Proceedings. Comparative Literature Symposium [*A publication*]
PCLS .... Prototype Closed-Loop System [*Nuclear energy*] (NRCH)
PCLT .... Children's Literature. An International Journal [*A publication*]
PCLT .... Portable Coded LASER Target
PCLT .... Prototype Closed-Loop Test [*Nuclear energy*] (NRCH)
PCLU .... Pioneer Civil Labour Unit [*British*]
PClvU .... Ursinus College, Collegeville, PA [*Library symbol*] [*Library of Congress*] (LCLS)
PCLX .... Section of Independent Political Entity [*Board on Geographic Names*]
PCM .... Coastal Escort Medium [*200-500 tons*] [*Ship symbol*] (NATG)
PCM .... Pacific Comox Resources [*Vancouver Stock Exchange symbol*]
PCM .... Parabolic Collimator Mirror
PCM .... Parallel Cutter Mechanism
PCM .... Parity Check Matrix (MCD)
PCM .... Parti des Classes Moyennes [*Middle Class Party*] [*Luxembourg*] [*Political party*] (PPE)
PCM .... Parti Communiste Marocain [*Moroccan Communist Party*] [*Political party*]
PCM .... Parti Communiste Martiniquais [*Communist Party of Martinique*] [*Political party*] (PPW)
PCM .... Partido Comunista Mexicano [*Mexican Communist Party*] [*Political party*] (PPW)
PCM .... Passive Countermeasure
PCM .... Penalty Cost Model
PCM .... Pending Contractual Matters (NRCH)
PCM .... Per Calendar Month [*Business term*] (ADA)
PCM .... Percent Milli (NRCH)
PCM .... Phase Change Materials [*Solar energy*]
PCM .... Phase Conjugate Mirror
PCM .... Phase Contrast Microscopy
PCM .... Philippine Campaign Medal
PCM .... Photochemical Machining [*Desktop manufacturing*]
PCM .... Photoformed Ceramic Modules [*Du Pont process for making microconductors*]
PCM .... PIPES Buffer with Calcium and Magnesium
PCM .... Pitch Control Motor
PCM .... Planning and Control Memorandum [*Army*]
PCM .... Plug Compatible Mainframe [*Data processing*]
PCM .... Plug Compatible Manufacturer [*Data processing*]
PCM .... Plug Compatible Memory
PCM .... Plutonium Contaminated Material
PCM .... Police Court Mission [*British*] (ROG)
PCM .... Polyimide Composite Material
PCM .... Port Command Area [*Telecommunications*] (TEL)

PCM .... Post Column Method [*Chromatography*]
PCM .... Postmammillary Caudal Magnocellular Nuclei [*Neuroanatomy*]
PCM .... Power Control Mission (NASA)
PCM .... Power-Cooling Mismatch [*Nuclear energy*]
PCM .... Powertrain Control Module [*Automotive engineering*]
PCM .... Precision Condenser Microphone
PCM .... President's Certificate of Merit [*Military decoration*] (AFM)
PCM .... Process Control Module [*Telecommunications*] (TEL)
PCM .... Productive Cost Management (ADA)
PCM .... Profiling Current Meter [*Oceanography*] (MSC)
PCM .... Program Configuration Manager
PCM .... Program Continuity Memorandum [*Military*]
PCM .... Program Cost Management (MCD)
PCM .... Project Cost Model [*Project Software Ltd.*] [*Software package*] (NCC)
PCM .... Protein-Calorie Malnutrition [*Medicine*]
PCM .... Pulse Code Modulation [*Telecommunications*]
PCM .... Pulse-Count Modulation [*Data processing*]
PCM .... Punch Card Machine [*Data processing*]
PCM .... Pyrotechnic Countermeasure [*Military*] (SDI)
PCMA .... Pennsylvania Coal Mining Association (EA)
PCMA .... Personal Computer Management Association [*Commercial firm*] [*Orange, CA*] [*Information service or system*] (EA)
PCMA .... Phenylcyclopropanemethylamine [*Organic chemistry*]
PCMA .... Post Card Manufacturers Association [*Inactive*] (EA)
PCMA ...... Prince Edward Island Department of Municipal Affairs, Charlottetown, Prince Edward Island [*Library symbol*] [*National Library of Canada*] (NLC)
PCMA .... Professional Convention Management Association [*Birmingham, AL*] (EA)
PCMA .... Provincial Carters' and Motormen's Association [*A union*] [*British*]
PCMB....... Para-Chloromercuribenzoate [*Organic chemistry*]
PCMC....... Para-Chloro-meta-cresol [*Organic chemistry*]
PCMC....... Provided Chief of Mission Concurs [*Army*]
PCMC....... Psychemedics Corp. [*NASDAQ symbol*] (NQ)
PCMCIA ... Personal Computer Memory Card International Association (PCM)
PCMD ...... Particle Count Monitoring Device (KSC)
PCMD ...... Passive Count Monitoring Device (KSC)
PCMD .... Procurement and Contracts Management Division [*Environmental Protection Agency*] (GFGA)
PCMD ...... Pulse Code Modulation, Digital
PCMDI...... Program for Climate Model Diagnosis and Intercomparison [*Department of Energy*]
PCME........ Pulse Code Modulation Event
PCMF....... Phi Chi Medical Fraternity (EA)
PCM-FM... Pulse Code Modulation - Frequency Modulation
PCM/FSK/AM ... Pulse Code Modulation/Frequency Shift Keying/ Amplitude Modulation (SAA)
PCMGS ..... Pulse Code Modulated Ground Station
PCMH ...... Community Mental Health Journal [*A publication*]
PCMH ...... Postgraduate Center for Mental Health (EA)
PCMI........ Photo-Chemical Machining Institute (EA)
PCMI........ Photochromic Microimage [*Microfiche*]
PCMI........ Plastic Container Manufacturers Institute (EA)
PCMI........ President's Council on Management Improvement [*Executive Office of the President*] (GFGA)
PCMIA ..... Pittsburgh Coal Mining Institute of America (EA)
PCMIP ...... Pontifical Commission for Migrants and Itinerant Peoples [*See also PCMT*] [*Vatican City, Vatican City State*] (EAIO)
PCMJ .... College Mathematics Journal [*A publication*]
PCMK....... Piece Mark
PC-ML ...... Marxist-Leninist Communist Party [*Bolivia*] [*Political party*] (PPW)
PCML....... Parti Communiste Marxiste-Leniniste [*Marxist-Leninist Communist Party*] [*France*] [*Political party*] (PPW)
PCML....... Partito Comunista Marxista-Leninista [*Marxist-Leninist Communist Party*] [*San Marino*] [*Political party*] (PPE)
PCML....... President's Committee on Migratory Labor [*Terminated, 1964*]
PCMLF ..... Parti Communiste Marxiste-Leniniste Francais [*French Marxist-Leninist Communist Party*] [*Dissolved, 1978*] [*Political party*] (PPW)
PC(ML)I.... Partito Comunista (Marxista-Leninista) de Italia [*Communist Party of Italy (Marxist-Leninist)*] [*Political party*] (PPE)
PCMMU ... PCM [*Punch Card Machine*] Master Unit [*Data processing*] (GFGA)
PCMMU ... Pulse Code Modulation Master Unit [*Electronics*] (NASA)
PCM/NRZ ... Pulse Code Modulation/Nonreturn to Zero (KSC)
PCMO ...... Principal Clinical Medical Officer [*British*]
PCMO ...... Principal Colonial Medical Officer [*British*]
PCMOD .... Personal Computer Modification Program
PCMP....... (Phenylcyclohexyl)methylpiperidine [*Organic chemistry*]
PCMP....... Preliminary Configuration Management Plan (MCD)
PCMPS ..... Para-Chloromercuriphenylsulfonic Acid [*Organic chemistry*]
PCM-PS.... Pulse Code Modulation - Phase-Shift
P Cmp Sc St ... Proceedings. Computer Science and Statistics [*A publication*]
PCMQ....... Communication Quarterly [*A publication*]
PCMR....... Communication Research [*A publication*]
PCMR....... Patient Computer Medical Record
PCMR....... Photochromic Microreproduction (DIT)

PCMR........ President's Committee on Mental Retardation [*Washington, DC*]
PCMS........ Current Musicology [*A publication*]
PCMS........ Para-Chloromercuriphenyl Sulfonate [*or Sulfonic Acid*] [*Organic chemistry*]
PCMS........ Photographic Cabinet Makers' Society [*A union*] [*British*]
PCMS........ Plasma Chromatography Mass Spectroscopy
PCMS........ Production Control Monitoring System   (NVT)
PCMS........ Pulse Code Modulation Shared   (MCD)
PCMS........ Punch Card Machine System [*Data processing*]
PCMT........ Pontificia Commissione Migrazioni e Turismo [*Pontifical Commission for Migrants and Itinerant Peoples - PCMIP*] [*Vatican City, Vatican City State*]   (EAIO)
PCMTE..... Pulse Code Modulation and Timing Equipment   (KSC)
PCMTEA .. Pulse Code Modulation and Timing Electronics Assembly
PCMTS ..... Pulse Code Modulation Telemetry System   (AAG)
PCMU .... Physico-Chemical Measurements Unit [*British*]
PCMU .... Propellant Calibration Measuring Unit '(KSC)
PCMV....... Porcine Cerebral Microvascular [*Cell line*]
PCMX....... Para-Chloro-meta-xylenol [*Organic chemistry*]
PCN .... Package Control Number
PCN .... Page Change Notice   (MCD)
PCN .... PanCana Minerals [*Toronto Stock Exchange symbol*]
PCN .... Part Control Number   (AAG)
PCN .... Partido Comunista de Nicaragua [*Communist Party of Nicaragua*] [*Political party*]   (PD)
PCN .... Partido de Conciliacion Nacional [*National Reconciliation Party*] [*El Salvador*] [*Political party*]   (PPW)
PCN .... Partido Conservador Nicaraguense [*Nicaraguan Conservative Party*] [*Political party*]   (PPW)
PCN .... Parts Change Notice   (MCD)
PCN .... Penicillin [*Antibiotic*]
PCN .... Permanent Control Number   (MCD)
PCN .... Personal Communications Network [*British*]
PCN .... Personal Computer Network [*Telecommunications*]
PCN .... Piacenza [*Italy*] [*Seismograph station code, US Geological Survey*] [*Closed*]   (SEIS)
PCN .... Pitcairn Islands [*ANSI three-letter standard code*]   (CNC)
PCN .... Planning Change Notice
PCN .... Players Chess News [*A publication*]
PCN .... Point Comfort & Northern Railway Co. [*AAR code*]
PCN .... Polychlorinated Naphthalene [*Organic chemistry*]
PCN .... Position Control Number   (AFM)
PCN .... Post Christum Natum [*After the Birth of Christ*] [*Latin*]   (ROG)
PCN .... Potato Cyst Nematode [*Plant pathology*]
PCN .... Primary Care Network [*Medical insurance*]
PCN .... Primary Care Nursing
PCN .... Princeton Aviation Corp. [*Princeton, NJ*] [*FAA designator*]   (FAAC)
PCN .... Print Collector's Newsletter [*A publication*]
PCN .... Procedure Change Notice
PCN .... Processing Control Number
PCN .... Procurement Control Number   (AFM)
PCN .... Product Control Number   (AFM)
PCN .... Production Change Number   (KSC)
PCN .... Program Change Notice   (MCD)
PCN .... Program Composition Notation [*Data processing*]
PCN .... Program Control Number   (AFM)
PCN .... Project Control Number   (AAG)
PCN .... Proposal Control Number   (AAG)
PCN .... Public Convenience and Necessity [*Department of Transportation*]
PCN .... Publication Change Notice   (MCD)
PCN .... Pulse Compression Network
PCNA .... Palestine Congress of North America [*Defunct*]   (EA)
PCNA .... Porsche Cars North America, Inc.
PCNA .... Proliferating Cell Nuclear Antigen [*Cytology, immunology*]
PCNAC...... Professionals Coalition for Nuclear Arms Control   (EA)
PCNB........ Pentachloronitrobenzene [*Agricultural fungicide*]
PCNB........ Permanent Control Narcotics Board
PCNC .... Capital and Class [*A publication*]
PCNCDH .. Publications. Centre National pour l'Exploitation des Oceans. Actes de Colloques [*A publication*]
PCNDP...... Publication. Centre National de Documentation Pedagogique [*A publication*]
PCNF........ Pacific Central NOTAM [*Notice to Airmen*] Facility [*Military*]
PCNFDQ... Publications. Centre National pour l'Exploitation des Oceans. Rapports Scientifiques et Techniques [*A publication*]
PCNH........ Computers and the Humanities [*A publication*]
PCNI......... Physician Computer Network [*NASDAQ symbol*]   (SPSG)
PCNMDD ... Publications. Centre National pour l'Exploitation des Oceans. Resultats des Campagnes a la Mer [*A publication*]
PCNP........ Personal Computer Network Program   (HGAA)
PCNR .... Part Control Number Request   (AAG)
PCNR .... Planning Change Notice Request
PCNS........ Polar Coordinates Navigation System
PCNT........ Conde Nast Traveler [*A publication*]
PCNY .... Proofreaders Club of New York   (EA)
PCO .... Conococheague District Library, Chambersburg, PA [*OCLC symbol*]   (OCLC)

PCO .... Parcel Concentration Office [*British*]
PCO .... Passport Control Officer [*British*]
PCO .... Patient Complains Of [*Medicine*]
PCO .... Pest Control Operator
PCO .... Philadelphia College of Osteopathy [*Pennsylvania*]
PCO .... Phoenix Canada Oil Co. Ltd. [*Toronto Stock Exchange symbol*]
PCO .... Photosynthetic Carbon Oxidation [*Plant metabolism*]
PCO .... [*The*] Pittston Co. [*NYSE symbol*]   (SPSG)
PCO .... Placement Contracting Officer [*Army*]   (AABC)
P & CO...... Plans and Combat Operations
PCO .... Plant Clearance Officer [*DoD*]
PCO .... Plant Clearance Order
PCO .... Police Commissioner's Office
PCO .... Polycystic Ovary [*Gynecology*]
PCO .... Ponca City [*Oklahoma*] [*Seismograph station code, US Geological Survey*]   (SEIS)
PCO .... Post Checkout
PCO .... Postcheckout   (NASA)
PCO .... Postcheckout Operations
PCO .... Potassium Channel Opener [*Vasodilator*]
PCO .... Primary Contracting Officer   (MCD)
PCO .... Prime Contracting Officer   (SAA)
PCO .... Prince Consort's Own [*Military unit*] [*British*]
PCO .... Principal Coast Officer [*Customs*] [*British*]   (ROG)
PCO .... Principal Contracting Officer [*Air Force*]
PCO .... Printer Control Option   (SAA)
PCO .... Printing Control Officer [*Air Force*]   (AFM)
PCO .... Privy Council Office [*British*]
PCO .... Proceedings. Congress of Orientalists [*A publication*]
PCO .... Procurement Change Order   (MCD)
PCO .... Procuring Contracting Office [*or Officer*] [*Military*]
PCO .... Procuring Contrast Offer
PCO .... Professional Conference Organizer
PCO .... Program Comparator
PCO .... Program-Controlled Output   (NASA)
PCO .... Program Coordination Office   (AAG)
PCO .... Project Control Office   (MCD)
PCO .... Property Control Office [*of Allied Military Government*] [*Post-World War II*]
PCO .... Proposed Change Order   (AFIT)
PCO .... Prospective Commanding Officer [*Navy*]
PCO .... Provisioning Contracting Officer [*Military*]   (AFIT)
PCO .... Public Call Office   (DAS)
PCO .... Public Communications Office
PCO .... Publications Control Officer [*DoD*]
PCO .... Purchase Change Order   (MCD)
pCO$_2$ .... Partial Pressure of Carbon Dioxide   (AAMN)
pCO$_2$ .... Pressure of Carbon Dioxide   (HGAA)
PCOA .... Pharmacy Corp. of America [*NASDAQ symbol*]   (NQ)
PCoA........ Principal Co-Ordinates Analysis
PCOAD...... Powder Coatings [*A publication*]
P Coast LJ ... Pacific Coast Law Journal [*A publication*]   (DLA)
PCOB(UN) ... Permanent Central Opium Board (United Nations)
PCOC .... Partit Comunista Obrero de Catalunya [*Communist Workers' Party of Catalonia*] [*Political party*]   (PPW)
PCOD....... Permanent Change of Duty [*Navy*]   (DNAB)
PCOD....... Polycystic Ovarian Disease [*Medicine*]
PCOE .... Partido Comunista Obrero de Espana [*Communist Workers' Party of Spain*] [*Political party*]   (PPW)
PCOF........ Probable Cause of Failure   (MCD)
PCOG....... Press Clippings of Greenland [*A publication*]
PCOGA ..... Pacific Coast Oyster Growers Association   (EA)
PCOI........ Purcell Co., Inc. [*NASDAQ symbol*]   (NQ)
PCOL........ College Literature [*A publication*]
PCOM ...... Philadelphia College of Osteopathic Medicine
PCOM ...... Photocomm, Inc. [*NASDAQ symbol*]   (NQ)
PCOMB..... Physics of Condensed Matter [*A publication*]
P Comp Lit ... Proceedings. Comparative Literature Symposium [*A publication*]
PCON....... Para-Chloro-ortho-nitroaniline [*Also, PCONA*] [*Organic chemistry*]
PCON....... Personnel Continuity
PCONA ..... Para-Chloro-ortho-nitroaniline [*Also, PCON*] [*Organic chemistry*]
PCONA ..... Pest Control [*A publication*]
PCOP........ Port Charges Operator   (DNAB)
PCOP........ Port Charges Paid by Commercial Operator   (DNAB)
PCOPF...... President's Council on Physical Fitness [*Later, PCPFS*]   (KSC)
PCOR .... Corrections Today [*A publication*]
PC & OR... Procurement, Commitment, and Obligation Record [*Navy*]
PCOR .... Profit Commission on Renewal [*Insurance*]   (AIA)
PCOR .... PSICOR, Inc. [*NASDAQ symbol*]   (NQ)
PCoR......... Robert Morris College, Coraopolis, PA [*Library symbol*] [*Library of Congress*]   (LCLS)
PCORN ..... Perpetual Convertible or Redeemable Note [*Economics*]
P Cornell.... Greek Papyri in the Library of Cornell University [*A publication*]
PCOS........ Comparative Literature Studies [*A publication*]
PCOS........ Polycystic Ovarian Syndrome [*Also, POS*] [*Gynecology*]
PCOS........ Primary Communications-Oriented System   (IEEE)
PCOS......... Process Control Operating System

PCOS........	Project Concern's Options Service (EA)
PCOSD2.....	Psychoanalysis and Contemporary Science [*A publication*]
P-COSWA ...	Pugwash Conferences on Science and World Affairs
PCOT	Payload Center Operations Team [*NASA*] (MCD)
PCOTES ...	Prototype Carrier Operational Test and Evaluation Site [*Military*] (CAAL)
PCOU	Counseling Psychologist [*A publication*]
PCOUNT ..	Parameter Count [*Data processing*]
PCOV	Precombustor Oxidizer Valve (KSC)
P(COV)......	Probability of No Covariate Effect [*Statistics*]
PCOYO	President's Council on Youth Opportunity [*Defunct*] (EA)
PCP...........	Centre for Personal Construct Psychology [*British*] (CB)
PCP...........	Pacific Coast Philology [*A publication*]
PCP...........	Paired Cone Pigments [*Vision physiology*]
PCP...........	Palestinian Communist Party [*Political party*] (PD)
PCP...........	PanCanadian Petroleum Ltd. [*Toronto Stock Exchange symbol*] [*Vancouver Stock Exchange symbol*]
PCP...........	Para-Chlorophenol [*Organic chemistry*]
PCP...........	Paraguayan Communist Party
PCP...........	Parallel Cascade Processor (IEEE)
PCP...........	Parallel Circular Plate (IEEE)
PCP...........	Partido Comunista Paraguayano [*Paraguayan Communist Party*] [*Political party*] (PD)
PCP...........	Partido Comunista Peruano [*Peruvian Communist Party*] [*Political party*] (PPW)
PCP...........	Partido Comunista Portugues [*Portuguese Communist Party*] [*Political party*] (PPE)
PCP...........	Partido Comunista Puertorriqueno [*Puerto Rican Communist Party*] [*Political party*] (PPW)
PCP...........	Passenger Control Point [*Army*] (AABC)
PCP...........	Past Chief Patriarch [*Freemasonry*]
PCP...........	Patient Care Publications
PCP...........	Payload Control Processor [*NASA*]
PCP...........	Peace Corps Physician
PCP...........	Pentachlorophenol [*Wood preservative*] [*Organic chemistry*]
PCP...........	Peripheral Control Program
PCP...........	Peripheral Control Pulse [*Data processing*]
PCP...........	Peripheral Coronary Pressure [*Cardiology*] (AAMN)
PCP...........	Personal Communications Programme [*British*]
PCP...........	Peter Collins Publishing [*British*]
PCP...........	(Phenylcyclohexyl)piperidine [*or Phencyclidine*] [*Anesthetic*] [*A street drug*]
PCP...........	Philadelphia College of Pharmacy and Science, Philadelphia, PA [*OCLC symbol*] (OCLC)
PCP...........	Phosphor Coated Paper
PCP...........	Photon-Coupled Pair (IEEE)
PCP...........	Pilot Control Panel
PCP...........	Planar Combat Problem
PCP...........	Plastic Clad Plastic [*Materials science*]
PCP...........	Platoon Command Post [*Military*] (RDA)
PCP...........	Pneumatics Control Panel (AAG)
PCP...........	Pneumocystis Carinii Pneumonia [*Microbiology*]
PCP...........	Polaroid Color Pack Camera
PCP...........	Polychloroprene [*Organic chemistry*]
PCP...........	Poorly Characterized Phase [*Mineralogy*]
PCP...........	Portable Code Processor
PCP...........	Portuguese Communist Party
PCP...........	Post-Construction Permit [*Nuclear energy*] (NRCH)
PCP...........	Posted County Price [*Agriculture*]
PCP...........	Postgraduate Center for Psychotherapy [*Later, Postgraduate Center for Mental Health*] (EA)
PCP...........	Potential Contractor Program (MCD)
PCP...........	Power Control Panel [*Aerospace*] (AAG)
PCP...........	Preassembled Cable in Pipe
PCP...........	Precision Castparts Corp. [*NYSE symbol*] (SPSG)
PCP...........	Preliminary Cost Proposal (MCD)
PCP...........	Pressurization Control Panel [*NASA*] (KSC)
PCP...........	Primary Care Physician
PCP...........	Primary Command Point [*Military*] (CAAL)
PCP...........	Primary Control Program [*Data processing*]
PCP...........	Primary Coolant Pump [*Nuclear energy*] (NRCH)
PCP...........	Printed Circuit Patchboard
PCP...........	Process Control Processor (IEEE)
PCP...........	Process Control Program [*Nuclear energy*] (NRCH)
PCP...........	Processor Control Program
PCP...........	Product Change Proposal (MCD)
PCP...........	Production Change Point
PCP...........	Program Change Procedure
PCP...........	Program [*or Project*] Change Proposal
PCP...........	Program Control Plan (AAG)
PCP...........	Program Control Procedure [*Nuclear energy*] (NRCH)
PCP...........	Programmable Communication Processor
PCP...........	Progressive Conservative Party [*Canada*] [*Political party*] (PPW)
PCP...........	Progressive Conservative Party [*Australia*] [*Political party*]
PCP...........	Progressive Constitutionalist Party [*Malta*] [*Political party*] (PPE)
PCP...........	Project Control Plan (IEEE)
PCP...........	Project Cost Plan (NASA)
PCP...........	Prototype Communications Processor
PCP...........	Pulse Comparator
PCP...........	Pulse Cytophotometry [*Hematology*]
PCP...........	Punched Card Punch [*Data processing*] (IEEE)
PcP...........	Reflected P Wave [*Earthquakes*]
PCPA........	Pacific Conservatory of the Performing Arts
PCPA........	Panel of Consultants for the Performing Arts [*of CFC*]
PCPA........	Para-Chlorophenoxyacetic Acid [*Organic chemistry*]
PCPA........	Para-Chlorophenylacetic Acid [*Organic chemistry*]
PCPA........	Para-Chlorophenylalanine [*Biochemistry*]
PCPA........	Poor Clares of Perpetual Adoration [*Roman Catholic women's religious order*]
PCPA........	Protestant Church-Owned Publishers Association (EA)
PCPAC......	Parker-Coltrane Political Action Committee (EA)
PCPBMA ..	Pacific Coast Paper Box Manufacturers' Association (EA)
PCPC........	Power Conversion Products Council [*Later, PCPCI*] (EA)
PCPCA......	Pairpoint Cup Plate Collectors of America (EA)
PCPCI	Power Conversion Products Council International (EA)
PCPCN......	Part Card Procurement Change Notice (KSC)
PCPE........	Partido Comunista de los Pueblos de Espana [*Communist Party of the Peoples of Spain*] [*Political party*] (EY)
PCPF	President's Council on Physical Fitness [*Later, PCPFS*]
PCPFS	President's Council on Physical Fitness and Sports (EGAO)
PCPG........	Primary Clock Pulse Generator
PCPHA......	Plant and Cell Physiology [*A publication*]
PCPhS	Proceedings. Cambridge Philological Society [*A publication*]
PCPI	Parent Cooperative Pre-Schools International (EA)
PCPI	Permanent Committee on Patent Information [*World Intellectual Property Organization*] [*Information service or system*] (IID)
PCPI	Personal Computer Products, Inc. [*San Diego, CA*] [*NASDAQ symbol*] (NQ)
PCPI	President's Commission on Personnel Interchange [*Later, President's Commission on Executive Exchange*]
PCPJ.........	Peoples Coalition for Peace and Justice [*Defunct*]
PCPL........	Government Services Library, Charlottetown, Prince Edward Island [*Library symbol*] [*National Library of Canada*] (NLC)
PCPL........	Planning Library, Charlottetown, Prince Edward Island [*Library symbol*] [*National Library of Canada*] (NLC)
PCPL........	Production Control Priority List (MCD)
PCPL........	Proposed Change Point Line [*NASA*] (KSC)
PCPM.......	PERT [*Program Evaluation and Review Technique*] Cost Performance Measurement
PCPMDN ...	Annual Research Reviews. Proteins of Animal Cell Plasma Membranes [*A publication*]
PCP M-L...	Partido Comunista de Portugal, Marxista-Leninista [*Marxist-Leninista Communist Party of Portugal*] [*Political party*] (PPE)
PCPN........	Precipitation (FAAC)
PCPO........	Comparative Politics [*A publication*]
PCPP	(Para-Chlorophenoxy)propionic Acid [*Organic chemistry*]
PCPP	Peace Corps Partnership Program (EA)
PCPP	Plasma Chemistry and Plasma Processing [*A publication*]
PCPPD	Plasma Chemistry and Plasma Processing [*A publication*]
PCPS	Canadian Journal of Political Science [*A publication*]
PCPS	Philadelphia College of Pharmacy and Science [*Pennsylvania*]
PCPS	Pool Cooling and Purification System [*Nuclear energy*] (NRCH)
PCPS	Proceedings of the Cambridge Philological Society [*A publication*] (OCD)
PCPS	Pulse-Coded Processing System
PCPSA......	Proceedings. Cambridge Philosophical Society [*England*] [*A publication*]
PCPSD	Progress in Colloid and Polymer Science [*A publication*]
PCPT	Para-Chlorophenylthio [*Organic chemistry*]
PCPT	Perception
PCPT	Perception. Canadian Magazine of Social Comment [*A publication*]
PCPT	Physical Combat Proficiency Test [*Army*]
PCPT	Post Conference Provisioning Tape (MCD)
PCPU........	Comparative Political Studies [*A publication*]
PCPV	Partido Comunista del Pais Valenciano [*Spain*] [*Political party*] (EY)
PCPV	Prestressed Concrete Pressure Vessel
PCQ	Production Control Quantometer
PCQ	Productivity Criteria Quotient
PCQ	Professional Capabilities Questionnaire [*Jet Propulsion Laboratory, NASA*]
PCQ	Yuma, AZ [*Location identifier*] [*FAA*] (FAAL)
PCQEH	Queen Elizabeth Hospital, Charlottetown, Prince Edward Island [*Library symbol*] [*National Library of Canada*] (NLC)
PCQT........	Personal Computer Query Tool [*Military software package*] (INF)
PC Quote ...	PC Quote, Inc. [*Associated Press abbreviation*] (APAG)
PCR...........	Island Pacific Air [*Maui, HI*] [*FAA designator*] (FAAC)
PCR...........	Page Control Register
PCR...........	Parker's Criminal Reports [*New York*] [*A publication*] (DLA)
PCR...........	Parti Communiste Reunionnais [*Communist Party of Reunion*] [*Political party*] (PPW)
PCR...........	Partido Comunista Revolucionario [*Revolutionary Communist Party*] [*Peru*] [*Political party*] (PPW)

PCR........... Partidul Comunist Roman [*Romanian Communist Party*] [*Political party*]   (PPE)
PCR........... Pass Card Reader [*Telecommunications*]   (TEL)
PCR........... Patient Charge Ratio
PCR........... Payload Certification Review   (SSD)
PCR........... Payload Changeout Room [*NASA*]   (NASA)
PCR........... Payload Checkout Room [*NASA*]   (NASA)
P Cr........... Paymaster-Commander [*Navy*] [*British*]   (DMA)
PCR........... PC Resource [*A publication*]
PCR........... Peninsular Chemresearch [*Calgon Corp.*]
PCR........... Pennsylvania Corp. Reporter [*A publication*]   (DLA)
PCR........... Pennsylvania County Court Reports [*A publication*]   (DLA)
P & CR...... Performance and Compatibility Requirements
PCR........... Perini Corp. [*AMEX symbol*]   (SPSG)
PCR........... Period Contract Request
PCR........... Periodic Current Reversal [*Electrochemistry*]
PCR........... Peripheral Control Routine   (CMD)
PCR........... Personal Communications Report [*FutureComm Publications, Inc.*] [*Information service or system*] [*Defunct*]   (CRD)
PCr........... Phosphocreatine [*Also, CP, PC*] [*Biochemistry*]
PCR........... Photoconductive Relay   (IEEE)
PCR........... Photoconductive Resonance [*Physics*]
PCR........... Photosynthetic Carbon Reduction [*Plant metabolism*]
PCR........... Pine Creek Railroad [*An association*]   (EA)
PCR........... Planned Component Replacement [*Predictive maintenance schedule*]
PCR........... Planning Change [*or Check*] Request   (AAG)
P & CR...... Planning and Compensation Reports [*British*]
PCR........... Pneumatic Checkout Rack   (KSC)
PCR........... Pneumatic Control Regulator   (KSC)
PCR........... Pollution Control Report [*Navy*]
PCR........... Polychromatic Color Removal [*Printing technology*]
PCR........... Polymerase Chain Reaction [*Genetics*]
PCR........... Population Census Report   (OICC)
PCR........... Positive Control Route [*Aviation*]   (OA)
PCR........... Post-Consumer Recycle [*or Reclaim*] [*Plastics industry*]
PCR........... Powell Cycle Registry   (EA)
PCR........... Power Change Request [*NASA*]   (NASA)
PCR........... Power Conversion Room
PCR........... Pressure Check Range
PCR........... Prestressed Ceramic RADOME
PCR........... Preventative Cyclic Retransmission [*Telecommunications*]   (TEL)
PCR........... Primary Chemotherapy-Radiotherapy [*Oncology*]
PCR........... Primary Cosmic Radiation
PCR........... Principal Components Regression
PCR........... Print Command Register
PCR........... Procedure Change Request [*NASA*]
PCR........... Procurement Center Representative [*Small Business Administration*]
PCR........... Production Capability Review [*Army*]
PCR........... Production Change Request   (MCD)
PCR........... Production Control Record [*NASA*]   (KSC)
PCR........... Professional Casting Report [*A publication*]
PCR........... Program Change Request [*DoD*]
PCR........... Program to Combat Racism [*British*]   (DI)
PCR........... Program Control Register
PCR........... Program Control Report
PCR........... Progress Curve Report
PCR........... Project Control Room [*NASA*]   (NASA)
PCR........... Project on Corporate Responsibility   (EA)
PCR........... Project Cost Record [*or Report*] [*NASA*]   (KSC)
P & CR...... Property and Compensation Reports [*A publication*]   (DLA)
PCR........... Proven Commercial Registration [*Advertising*]   (WDMC)
PCR........... Publication Change Request   (MCD)
PCR........... Publication Contract Requirements
PCR........... Puerto Carreno [*Colombia*] [*Airport symbol*]   (OAG)
PCR........... Pulse Compression RADAR
PCR........... Punched Card Reader [*Data processing*]   (BUR)
PCR........... Punched Card Requisition [*Data processing*]   (MCD)
PCRA........ Phantom Class Racing Association   (EA)
PCR & A.... Picked Cold, Rolled, and Annealed [*Metallurgy*]   (ROG)
PCRA........ Poland China Record Association   (EA)
PCRAP...... Personal Computer Response Analysis Program
PCRB........ Parks Canada. Research Bulletin [*A publication*]
PCRB........ Personnel and Control Room Building [*Nuclear energy*]   (NRCH)
PCRB........ Pollution Control Revenue Bond [*Environmental Protection Agency*]
PCRB........ Program Change Review Board [*NASA*]
PCRC........ Pacific Concerns Resource Center   (EA)
PCRC........ Paraffined Carton Research Council [*Later, Paperboard Packaging Council*]
PCRC........ Perinatal Clinical Research Center [*Case Western Reserve University*] [*Research center*]   (RCD)
PCRC........ Primary Communications Research Centre [*University of Leicester*] [*Canada*]
PCRCA...... Pickled, Cold-Rolled, and Close-Annealed [*Metal*]
PCRD........ Primary Control Rod Driveline [*Nuclear energy*]   (NRCH)
PCRDM..... Primary Control Rod Drive Mechanism [*Nuclear energy*]   (NRCH)

PCRE......... Catholic Historical Review [*A publication*]
PCRE......... ProCare Industries, Inc. [*Englewood, CO*] [*NASDAQ symbol*]   (NQ)
PC Rep....... English Privy Council Reports [*A publication*]   (DLA)
PCRF......... Paralysis Cure Research Foundation   (EA)
PCRF......... Parker Chiropractic Resource Foundation   (EA)
PCRI......... Papanicolaou Cancer Research Institute [*University of Miami*] [*Research center*]
PCRJ......... Criminal Justice Ethics [*A publication*]
PCRM....... Physicians Committee for Responsible Medicine   (EA)
PCRM....... Primary Certified Reference Material [*Nuclear energy*]   (NRCH)
PCRMGPS ... Poor Clerks Regular of the Mother of God of the Pious Schools [*Rome, Italy*]   (EAIO)
PCRML..... Parti Communiste Revolutionnaire - Marxiste-Leniniste [*Revolutionary Marxist-Leninist Communist Party*] [*France*] [*Political party*]   (PPW)
PCRPD8.... Plant Cell Reports [*A publication*]
Pcr/Pi........ Phosphocreatine to Inorganic Phosphate Ratio
PCRPS...... Program for Collaborative Research in the Pharmaceutical Sciences [*University of Illinois at Chicago*] [*Information service or system*]   (IID)
PCRQ .... Critical Quarterly [*A publication*]
PCRR........ Pennsylvania Central Railroad   (ROG)
PCRS........ Canadian Review of Sociology and Anthropology [*A publication*]
PCRS........ Poor Clergy Relief Society [*British*]
PCRS........ Precision Chiropractic Research Society [*Also known as Spinal Stress Research Society*]   (EA)
PCRS........ Primary Control Rod System [*Nuclear energy*]   (NRCH)
PCRS........ Primary CRITICOMM [*Critical Intelligence Communications System*] Relay Station   (CET)
PCRSAE.... Colston Research Society. Proceedings of the Symposium [*A publication*]
PCRSB...... Proceedings. Canadian Rock Mechanics Symposium [*A publication*]
PCRV........ Poinsettia Cryptic Virus [*Plant pathology*]
PCRV........ Pressurized Concrete Reactor Vessel [*Nuclear energy*]
PCRV........ Prestressed Concrete Reactor Vessel [*Nuclear energy*]
PCRY........ Criminology [*A publication*]
PCS........... IEEE Professional Communication Society   (EA)
PCS........... Pace Car Society   (EA)
PCS........... Pacific Command Ship
PCS........... Palliative Care Service
PCS........... Paracas [*Peru*] [*Seismograph station code, US Geological Survey*] [*Closed*]   (SEIS)
PCS........... Parents' Confidential Statement [*Education*]
PCS........... Parti Chretien-Social [*Christian Social Party*] [*Luxembourg*] [*Political party*]   (PPW)
PCS........... Parti Communiste Suisse [*Communist Party of Switzerland*] [*Political party*]   (PPE)
PCS........... Particle Counting System
PCS........... Particulates, Condensables, and Solubles [*In gases*]
PCS........... Partido Comunista Salvadoreno [*Salvadoran Communist Party*] [*Political party*]   (PPW)
PCS........... Partito Comunista Sammarinese [*Communist Party of San Marino*] [*Political party*]   (PPE)
PCS........... Parts, Components, Subassemblies
PCS........... Parts Control System [*DoD*]
PCS........... Passive Containment System [*Nuclear energy*]   (NRCH)
PCS........... Patient Care System
PCS........... Patrol Vessel, Submarine Chaser (Control) [*136 feet*] [*Navy symbol*] [*Obsolete*]
PCS........... Patterns of Care Study [*Roentgenography*]
PCS........... Paul Claudel Society   (EA)
PCS........... Payload Checkout System [*NASA*]   (NASA)
PCS........... Payload Control Supervisor [*NASA*]   (MCD)
PCS........... Pergamon Compact Solution [*CD-ROM publisher*]   (IT)
PCS........... Periodical Control System [*Libraries*]
PCS........... Permanent Change of Station [*Army*]
PCS........... Permanent Cruiser Service [*British military*]   (DMA)
PCS........... Permit Compliance System [*Environmental Protection Agency*]   (GFGA)
PCS........... Personal Communications Service [*Provided by Personal Communications Network*]
PCS........... Personal Computing System
PCS........... Personnel Capabilities System [*Jet Propulsion Laboratory, NASA*]
PCS........... Personnel Change of Station
PCS........... Personnel Consultancy Services Ltd. [*British*]
PCS........... Pharmaceutical Card System   (MCD)
PCS........... Phase Combining System [*Trademark*] [*A solubilizer in scintillation counting*]
PCS........... Phase Compensator System
PCS........... Philippine Collectors Society   (EA)
PCS........... PhonoCardioScan [*Cardiology*]
PCS........... Photoformed Ceramic Substrates [*Du Pont process for making microconductors*]
PCS........... Photon Correlation Spectroscopy
PCS........... Physical-Chemical System   (SAA)
PCS........... Physical Control System

PCS........... Physically Controlled Space [*Military*] (GFGA)
PCS........... Pictorial Cancellation Society (EA)
PCS........... Pieces
PCS........... Pilot Control System (MCD)
PCS........... Pitch Control System (MCD)
PCS........... Planning Control Sheet
PCS........... Plant Computer System (NRCH)
PCS........... Plant Control System [*Nuclear energy*] (NRCH)
PCS........... Plastic-Clad Silica [*Optics*]
PCS........... Plastic Connector Shell
PCS........... Platoon Combat Skills [*Army*] (INF)
PCS........... Plausible Conflict Situations [*Army*]
PCS........... Pneumatic Control System [*Gas chromatography*]
PCS........... Pointing-Control System [*Aerospace*]
PCS........... Polymer-Clad Silica [*Chemistry*]
PCS........... Port Command Store [*Telecommunications*] (TEL)
PCS........... Port Control Store [*Telecommunications*] (TEL)
PCS........... Port Control System [*Telecommunications*] (TEL)
PCS........... Portable Communications System
PCS........... Portacaval Shunt [*Medicine*]
PCS........... Position Classification Standard [*Civil Service*]
PCS........... Position Control System
PCS........... Position, Course, and Speed
PCS........... Positive Concatenation Structures [*Mathematics*]
PCS........... Postal Church Service
PCS........... Postal Commemorative Society (EA)
PCS........... Postcardiotomy Syndrome [*Medicine*]
PCS........... Postcaval [*or Portacaval*] Shunt [*Medicine*]
PCS........... Posterior Concave Side
PC & S....... Posts, Camps, and Stations [*Military*]
PCS........... Posts, Camps, and Stations [*Military*]
PCS........... Potash Corp. of Saskatchewan [*Canada*]
PCS........... Power Conditioning System
PCS........... Power Conversion System
PCS........... Powered Causeway Section [*Military*] (CAAL)
PCS........... Precision Casting Standard (MCD)
PCS........... Preconscious
PCS........... Preferred Capital Stock [*Investment term*]
PC & S....... Preliminary Command and Sequencing [*Viking lander mission*] [*NASA*]
PCS........... Preliminary Component Specification
PCS........... Pressure Control System
PCS........... Pressure Cycling Switch [*Automotive engineering*]
PCS........... Primary Calibration System
PCS........... Primary Cancer Site [*Oncology*]
PCS........... Primary Conditioning Solution
PCS........... Primary Control Ship [*Navy*]
PCS........... Primary Coolant System (MSA)
PCS........... Principal Clerk of Session
PCS........... Principal Coordinating Scientist [*NASA*] (KSC)
PCS........... Print Contrast Scale (IEEE)
PCS........... Print Contrast Signal [*Data processing*]
PCS........... Print Contrast System (BUR)
PCS........... Probability of Command Shutdown (MCD)
PCS........... Probability of Correct Selection [*Statistics*]
PCS........... Probability of Crew Survival (AAG)
PCS........... Procedure Completion Sheet [*NASA*] (MCD)
PCS........... Process Computer System (NRCH)
PCS........... Process Control Sheet [*Nuclear energy*] (NRCH)
PCS........... Process Control System
PCS........... Production Control Section
PCS........... Production Control System (BUR)
PCS........... Professional Car Society (EA)
PCS........... Professional Careers Sourcebook [*A publication*]
PCS........... Program Coordination Staff [*Environmental Protection Agency*] (GFGA)
PCS........... Program Cost Status [*Report*] (MCD)
PCS........... Program Counter Store
PCS........... Programmable Communications Subsystem
PCS........... Project Control Sheet [*Data processing*]
PCS........... Project Control System [*Data processing*]
PCS........... Project Coordination Staff [*NASA*] (KSC)
PCS........... Property Control System
PCS........... Proprietary Computer Systems, Inc. [*Information service or system*] (IID)
PCS........... Provision Coordinate Schedule (MCD)
PCS........... Public Choice Society (EA)
PCS........... Publication Control Sheet (MCD)
PCS........... Pump Control Sensor
PCS........... Punched Card System [*Data processing*]
PCS........... Pyrotechnics Circuit Simulator
PCS........... Sabah Chinese Party [*Political party*] [*Malaysia*] (FEA)
PCS........... Submarine Chaser
PCS........... Sun Shipbuilding & Dry Dock Co., Chester, PA [*Library symbol*] [*Library of Congress*] (LCLS)
PCSA........ Patrol Craft Sailors Association (EA)
PCSA........ Personal Computing Systems Architecture
PCSA........ Power Crane and Shovel Association (EA)
PCSA........ Seaman Apprentice, Postal Clerk, Striker [*Navy rating*]
PCS(A)...... Submarine Chaser (Air Cushion) (MCD)

PCsB........ Baptist Bible College of Pennsylvania, Clarks Summit, PA [*Library symbol*] [*Library of Congress*] (LCLS)
PCSC........ Control Submarine Chaser [*136 feet*] [*Navy symbol*] [*Obsolete*]
PCSC........ Plant Cell Suspension Cultures [*Biotechnology*]
PCSC........ Power Conditioning, Switching, and Control
PCSC........ Principal Commonwealth Supply Committee [*World War II*]
PCS-CSS... Parents' Confidential Statement of the College Scholarship Service [*Education*] (IIA)
PCSD........ Partido Cristao Social Democratico [*Christian Social Democratic Party*] [*Portugal*] [*Political party*] (PPE)
PCSD........ Polychloro(chloromethylsulfonamido)diphenyl Ether [*Insectproofing agent for wool*]
PCSE........ Pacific Coast Stock Exchange [*Later, PSE*] (EA)
PCSE........ President's Committee on Scientists and Engineers [*Expired, 1958*]
PCSE........ Printed Circuit Soldering Equipment
PC/SFA..... Potato Chip/Snack Food Association [*Formerly, NPCI, PCI*] [*Later, SFA*]
PCSFSK ... Phase Comparison Sinusoidal Frequency Shift Keying
PCSG....... Public Cryptography Study Group [*Defunct*] (EA)
PCSH....... Pierce Shell
PCS(H)...... Submarine Chaser (Hydrofoil) (MCD)
PCSI........ PCS, Inc. [*NASDAQ symbol*] (NQ)
PCSIB....... Protection Civile et Securite Industrielle [*A publication*]
PCSIG ...... Personal Computer-Software Interest Group (EA)
PCSJ......... All-Party Parliamentary Committee for the Release of Soviet Jewry (EAIO)
PCSM....... Criticism [*A publication*]
PCSM....... Percutaneous Stone Manipulation [*Medicine*]
PCSN....... PC Satellite Network
PCSN....... Precision Standard, Inc. [*NASDAQ symbol*] (NQ)
PCSN....... Seaman, Postal Clerk, Striker [*Navy rating*]
PCSNA...... Processing [*England*] [*A publication*]
PCSO........ Current Sociology [*A publication*]
PCSP .... Programmed Communications Support Program [*Air Force*] (AFM)
PCSPS....... Principal Civil Service Pension Scheme [*British*]
PCSS......... Comparative Studies in Society and History [*A publication*]
PCSS......... Platform Check Subsystem
PCSS......... Princess (ROG)
PCST .... President's Committee on Science and Technology
PCSW....... Clinical Social Work Journal [*A publication*]
PCSW....... Police Chiefs Spouses - Worldwide [*An association*] (EA)
PCSW....... President's Commission on the Status of Women
PCSY....... Canadian Journal of Psychology [*A publication*]
PCT........... Pacific Coast Tariff Bureau, San Francisco CA [*STAC*]
PCT........... Pacific Crest Trail
PCT........... Paper Crepe Tape
PCT........... Para-Chlorotoluene [*Organic chemistry*]
PCT........... Parti Communiste Tunisien [*Tunisian Communist Party*] [*Political party*] (PD)
PCT........... Parti Congolais du Travail [*Congolese Labor Party*] [*Political party*] (PPW)
PCT........... Partido Conservador Tradicional [*Traditionalist Conservative Party*] [*Nicaragua*] [*Political party*]
PCT........... Patent Cooperation Treaty [*1978*]
PCT........... Peak Centerline Temperature [*Nuclear energy*] (NRCH)
PCT........... Peak Cladding Temperature [*Nuclear energy*] (NRCH)
PCT........... Percent [*or Percentage*]
PCT........... Percentage [*Used instead of "average"*] [*Baseball*]
PCT........... Performance Correlation Technique
PCT........... Periodic Confidence Test
PCT........... Peripheral Control Terminal
PC/T......... Personal Computer/Technology (HGAA)
PCT........... Personality Completion Test [*Psychology*]
PCT........... Pharmacy and Chemistry Technician [*Navy*]
PCT........... Philadelphia College of Textiles and Science, Philadelphia, PA [*OCLC symbol*] (OCLC)
PCT........... Photoinduced Charge Transfer [*Electrochemistry*]
PCT........... Photon-Coupled Transistor (IEEE)
PCT........... Physical Correlate Theory [*Psychophysics*]
PCT........... Picture
PCT........... Pitch Centering Torquer (SAA)
PCT........... Planning and Control Techniques
PCT........... Plasmacrit Test [*Medicine*]
PCT........... Plasmacytoma [*Medicine*]
PCT........... Platelet Count [*Hematology*]
PCT........... Polychemotherapy [*Oncology*]
PCT........... Polychlorinated Terphenyl [*Pesticide*]
PCT........... Polychloroterphenyl [*Organic chemistry*]
PCT........... Porcine Calcitonin [*Biochemistry*] (AAMN)
PCT........... Porphyria Cutanea Tarda [*Disease*] [*Medicine*]
PCT........... Portable Camera-Transmitter
PCT........... Portable Conference Telephone [*Bell Laboratories*]
PCT........... Portacaval Transposition [*Medicine*] (MAE)
PCT........... Positron Computed Tomography
PCT........... Potato Curly Top Disease [*Plant pathology*]
PCT........... Potential Current Transformer
PCT........... Precinct
PCT........... Preliminary Change Transmittal (AAG)
PCT........... Pressure Concentration Temperature

PCT........... Prime Contract Termination   (AAG)
PCT........... Princeton [*New Jersey*] [*Airport symbol*] [*Obsolete*]   (OAG)
P Ct........... Probate Court   (DLA)
PCT........... Production Confirmatory Test   (MCD)
PCT........... Program Control Table [*Data processing*]
PCT........... Programa de Cooperacion Tecnica [*Program of Technical Cooperation - PTC*] [*Organization of American States*] [*Washington, DC*]
PCT........... Project Control Tool   (BUR)
PCT........... Property Capital Trust [*AMEX symbol*]   (SPSG)
PCT........... Proximal Convoluted Tubule [*of a nephron*]
PCT........... Puangchon Chao Thai [*Thai Mass Party*] [*Thailand*] [*Political party*]
PCT........... Pulse Compression Tube
PCT........... Pulse Count [*Telecommunications*]   (TEL)
PCT........... Wesman Personnel Classification Test
PCTA........ Pentachlorothioanisole [*Organic chemistry*]
PCTB........ Pacific Coast Tariff Bureau
PCTC......... Penn Central Transportation Co.
PCTC........ Pure Car Truck Carrier [*Shipping*]   (DS)
PCTC........ Pyrotechnic Circuit Test Console   (KSC)
PCTCA ...... Protection [*London*] [*A publication*]
PCTDS ...... Problem and Change Tracking Directory System
PCTE........ Portable Commercial Test Equipment   (NASA)
PCTE........ Portable Common Test Environment [*British*]
PCTEB ...... Pennsylvania Council of Teachers of English. Bulletin [*A publication*]
PCTE Bull ... Pennsylvania Council of Teachers of English. Bulletin [*A publication*]
PCTE Bulletin ... Pennsylvania Council of Teachers of English. Bulletin [*A publication*]
PCTF .... Plant Component Test Facility [*Nuclear energy*]
PCTF .... Power Conversion Test Facility   (SAA)
PCTFE....... Polychlorotrifluoroethylene [*Organic chemistry*]
PCT-GF..... Plasmacytoma Growth Factor [*Oncology*]
PCTHDS... Psychoanalysis and Contemporary Thought [*A publication*]
PCTL......... PictureTel Corp. [*NASDAQ symbol*]   (NQ)
PCTM........ PC Telemart, Inc. [*NASDAQ symbol*]   (NQ)
PC/TM...... Performance Criteria and Test Methods Task
PCTM....... Pulse-Count Modulation   (MSA)
PCTNB...... Perception [*A publication*]
PCTO .... Payload Cost Tradeoff Optimization [*NASA*]   (NASA)
PCTP........ Partido Comunista dos Trabalhadores Portugueses [*Portuguese Workers' Communist Party*] [*Political party*]   (PPW)
PCTP........ Pierce Template
PCTQ........ Critique. Studies in Contemporary Fiction [*A publication*]
PCTR........ Physical Constant Test Reactor [*Nuclear energy*]
PCTR........ Program Counter
PCTR........ Property Control Transaction Report
PCTR........ Pulsed Column Test Rig [*Chemical engineering*]
PCTS .... Pentagon Consolidated Telecommunications System   (MCD)
PCTS .... Portable Cesium Time Standard
PCTS .... President's Committee for Traffic Safety   (EA)
PCTT .... Precommit Track Time [*DoD*]
PCTUULAW ... Permanent Congress of Trade Union Unity of Latin American Workers [*See also CPUSTAL*] [*Mexico City, Mexico*]   (EAIO)
PCTV........ Private Channel Television
PCtvL........ Lukens Steel Co., Coatesville, PA [*Library symbol*] [*Library of Congress*] [*Obsolete*]   (LCLS)
PCtvVA...... United States Veterans Administration Hospital, Medical Library, Coatesville, PA [*Library symbol*] [*Library of Congress*]   (LCLS)
PCU .... Packet Communications Unit
PCU .... Paging Control Unit [*Telecommunications*]   (TEL)
PCU .... Pain Control Unit
PCU .... Partido Conservador Unido [*Chilean Catholic political party*]
PCU .... Passenger Control Unit   (MCD)
PCU .... Payload Checkout Unit [*NASA*]   (MCD)
PCU .... Peripheral Control Unit   (CMD)
PCU .... Picayune, MS [*Location identifier*] [*FAA*]   (FAAL)
PCU .... Pneumatic Checkout Unit   (AAG)
PCU .... Pod Cooling Unit   (AAG)
PCU .... Portable Checkout Unit
PCU .... Portable Computer Unit
PCU .... Portuguese Continental Union of the United States of America   (EA)
PCU .... Pound Centigrade Unit
PCU .... Power Conditioning Unit
PCU .... Power Control Unit
PCU .... Power Conversion Unit   (IEEE)
PCU .... Pressure Control Unit   (MCD)
PCU .... Price [*Utah*] [*Seismograph station code, US Geological Survey*]   (SEIS)
PCU .... Print Control Unit   (SAA)
PCU .... Printed Control Unit [*Military*]   (GFGA)
PCU .... Processor Control Unit
PCU .... Product Co-Ordination Unit [*British Overseas Trade Board*]   (DS)
PCU .... Program Control Unit [*Data processing*]
PCU .... Progress Control Unit   (KSC)

PCU .... Progressive Care Unit [*Medicine*]
PCU .... Propellant Control Unit   (SAA)
PCU .... Protective Care Unit [*Medicine*]
PCU .... Protein-Calorie Undernutrition [*Medicine*]
PCU .... Punched Card Utility [*Data processing*]
PCU .... University of Prince Edward Island, Charlottetown, Prince Edward Island [*Library symbol*] [*National Library of Canada*]   (NLC)
PCUA .... Power Controller Unit Assembly   (IEEE)
PCUA .... Pressure Control Unit, Atlas   (MCD)
PCUA .... PROFIT Control Users Association   (EA)
PCUC .... Positive Continuous Ullage Control
PCU/HDR ... Primary Control Unit, Hydraulics   (AAG)
PCUI......... Partito Comunista Unificado de Italia [*Unified Communist Party of Italy*] [*Political party*]   (PPE)
PCUR .... Cross Currents [*A publication*]
PCUR .... Pulsating Current
PCUS......... Port Charges Paid by United States Army, Navy, or Air Force   (DNAB)
PCUS........ Propeller Club of the United States   (EA)
PC-USA..... Pax Christi - USA   (EA)
PCUSAW .. Pen Center USA West   (EA)
PCUSEQ ... Pressure Control Unit Sequencer   (AAG)
pcut .... Percutaneous [*Medicine*]   (AAMN)
PCUUS...... Polish Council of Unity in the United States   (EA)
PCV .... Pacific Concord Resources Corp. [*Vancouver Stock Exchange symbol*]
PCV .... Packed Cell Volume [*Hematocrit value*]
PCV .... Parietal Cell Vagotomy [*Medicine*]   (AAMN)
PCV .... Partido Comunista Venezolana [*Venezuelan Communist Party*] [*Political party*]   (PPW)
PCV .... Passenger Carrying Vehicle [*Military*]   (GFGA)
PCV .... Peace Corps Volunteer
PCV .... Peanut Clump Virus [*Plant pathology*]
PCV .... Petty Cash Voucher   (MCD)
PCV .... Phenetic Coefficient of Variation
PCV .... Pneumatic Control Valve
PCV .... Pollution Control Valve   (IEEE)
PCV .... Polycythemia Vera [*Also, PV*] [*Hematology*]
PCV .... Porcine Cirovirus
PCV .... Positive Crankcase Ventilation [*For automotive antipollution systems*]
PCV .... Precheck Verification [*NASA*]   (NASA)
PCV .... Pressure [*or Pressurizer*] Control Valve   (AAG)
PCV .... Primary Control Vessel   (DNAB)
PCV .... Primate Calicivirus
PCV .... Purge Control Valve   (NASA)
PCV .... Pyrocatechol Violet [*Also, PV*] [*An indicator*] [*Chemistry*]
PCV .... Veterans Affairs, Canada [*Affaires des Anciens Combattants Canada*] Charlottetown, Prince Edward Island [*Library symbol*] [*National Library of Canada*]   (NLC)
PCvA.......... Allentown College of Saint Francis De Sales, Center Valley, PA [*Library symbol*] [*Library of Congress*]   (LCLS)
PCVB........ Pyro Continuity Verification Box [*NASA*]   (NASA)
PCVC........ Public Citizens Visitors Center [*An association*] [*Defunct*]   (EA)
PCVD .... Plasma Chemical Vapor Deposition
PCVDA...... Progress in Cardiovascular Diseases [*A publication*]
PCVL......... Pilot-Controlled Visual Landing [*Aviation*]   (NASA)
PCV-M ...... Myeloid Metaplasia with Polycythemia Vera [*Hematology*]   (MAE)
PCW .... Personal Computer World Show [*Montbuild Ltd.*]   (TSPED)
PCW .... Plate Control Wedge [*Printing technology*]
PCW .... Port Clinton, OH [*Location identifier*] [*FAA*]   (FAAL)
PCW .... Post Consumer Waste   (EG)
PCW .... Previously Complied With
PCW .... Primary Cooling Water [*Reactor*]
PCW .... Princess Charlotte of Wales [*Military unit*] [*British*]
PCW .... Principal Conductor of the Works [*Freemasonry*]
PCW .... Program Control Word
PCW .... Proprietor of Copyright on a Composite Work
PCW .... Pulmonary Capillary Wedge [*Medicine*]
PCW .... Pulsed Continuous Wave   (IEEE)
PCW .... Widener College, Chester, PA [*Library symbol*] [*Library of Congress*]   (LCLS)
PCWBS ..... Preliminary Contract Work Breakdown Structure   (MCD)
PCWCA..... Poured Concrete Wall Contractors Association   (EA)
PC-WNIM ... Personal Computer Wide Area Network Interface Module   (TSSD)
PCWO .... Production Control Work Order   (MCD)
PCWP....... Pulmonary Capillary Wedge Pressure [*Medicine*]
PCWU ...... Port Commissioners Workers' Union [*India*]
PCX.......... Pacific Express [*Chico, CA*] [*FAA designator*]   (FAAC)
PCx.......... Periscopic Convex [*Ophthalmology*]
PCX.......... Plasma Confinement Experiment [*Physics*]
PCY........... Pacific Cypress Minerals Ltd. [*Vancouver Stock Exchange symbol*]
PCY........... Pittsburgh, Chartiers & Youghiogheny Railway Co. [*AAR code*]
PCY........... Plastocyanin
PCY........... Prerogative Court of York [*English court previously having jurisdiction over wills*]

PCYF .... President's Council on Youth Fitness (EA)
PCYF .... Progressive Conservative Youth Federation of Canada
PCYL .... Contemporary Literature [*A publication*]
PCYMF ..... Pacific Cypress Minerals Ltd. [*NASDAQ symbol*] (NQ)
PCZ .... Canal Zone [*ANSI three-letter standard code*] [*Obsolete*] (CNC)
PCZ .... Paracomp Technology, Inc. [*Vancouver Stock Exchange symbol*]
PCZ .... Physical Control Zone (NASA)
PCZ .... Positive Control Zone (DNAB)
PCZ .... Prochlorperazine [*Antiemetic*]
PCZ .... Waupaca, WI [*Location identifier*] [*FAA*] (FAAL)
PD .... Democratic Party [*Ecuador*] [*Political party*] (PD)
PD .... Doctor of Pedagogy
PD .... Doctor of Pharmacy
Pd .... Dorsal Pressure Neuron [*of a leech*]
PD .... Dublin Pharmacopoeia
PD .... Interpupillary Distance
PD .... Ipec Aviation Pty. Ltd. [*Australia*] [*ICAO designator*] (FAAC)
P & D .... Law Reports, Probate and Divorce [*England*] [*A publication*] (DLA)
PD .... Law Reports, Probate, Divorce, and Admiralty Division [*1875-90*] [*England*] [*A publication*] (DLA)
p/d .... Packs per Day [*Cigarettes*] [*Medicine*]
PD .... Pad (MCD)
PD .... Paget's Disease [*Medicine*]
PD .... Paid
PD .... Paix et Droit [*Paris*] [*A publication*]
PD .... Palisade Diabase [*Geology*]
Pd .... Palladium [*Chemical element*]
PD .... Pancreatic Divisum [*Medicine*]
PD .... Pancreatic Duct [*Anatomy*]
PD .... Pants Down [*At a disadvantage*] [*Slang*] (DSUE)
PD .... Papier und Druck [*A publication*]
pd .... Papilla Diameter [*Medicine*]
PD .... Papillary Distance
PD .... Parental Ditype [*Genetics*]
PD .... Parkinsonism Dementia [*Medicine*]
PD .... Parkinson's Disease [*Medicine*]
PD .... Parliamentary Debates [*A publication*]
PD .... Pars Distalis [*Medicine*]
PD .... Part Damaged (ROG)
PD .... Parti Democratique [*Democratic Party*] [*Luxembourg*] [*Political party*] (EAIO)
PD .... Partial Discharge [*High-voltage testing*] (IEEE)
PD .... Particle-Density [*Forensic science*]
PD .... Partido Democrata [*Democratic Party*] [*Chile*] [*Political party*]
PD .... Partido Democrata [*Democratic Party*] [*Costa Rica*] [*Political party*] (PPW)
PD .... Partner Air Services A/S [*Norway*] [*ICAO designator*] (FAAC)
PD .... Passed
PD .... Passive Detection [*Electronics*]
PD .... Past Due
PD .... Paste-Down [*Album*] [*Photography*] (ROG)
PD .... Patent Ductus [*Cardiology*] (MAE)
PD .... Pay Department [*Army*] [*British*] (ROG)
PD .... Pay Dirt
PD .... Payload Diameter
PD .... Peak Detector
PD .... Pediatric [*or Pediatrics*]
PD .... Pennsylvania Dutchman [*A publication*]
PD .... People's Democracy [*Ireland*] [*Political party*]
PD .... Pepper Dust [*An adulterating element*]
PD .... Per Diem [*By the Day*] [*Latin*]
PD .... Per Diliquium [*By Deliquescence*] [*Pharmacy*] (ROG)
PD .... Perfect Diffuser [*Optics*]
PD .... Performance Demonstration (MCD)
PD .... Periderm [*Botany*]
PD .... Period (AABC)
PD .... Peripheral Device (BUR)
PD .... Peritoneal Dialysis [*Medicine*]
PD .... Permanent Deactivation
PD .... Permits Division [*Environmental Protection Agency*] (GFGA)
P & D .... Perry and Davison's English Queen's Bench Reports [*1834-44*] [*A publication*] (DLA)
PD .... Personnel Department
PD .... Personnel Distribution [*Army*]
PD .... Pharmacy Dispenser [*British military*] (DMA)
PD .... Phase Discriminator
PD .... Phelps Dodge Corp. [*NYSE symbol*] (SPSG)
PD .... Phenyldichlorarsine [*A war gas*]
PD .... Philosophiae Doctor [*Doctor of Philosophy*]
PD .... Phosphate Dehydrogenase
PD .... Phosphodiester [*Organic chemistry*]
PD .... Photodiode
PD .... Phyllis Dorothy James White [*In name P. D. James*] [*Author*]
PD .... Physical Damage [*Insurance*]
PD .... Physical Disabilities
PD .... Physical Distribution (ADA)
PD .... Physics Department
P & D .... Pick Up and Delivery [*Business term*]

PD .... Picknick Dam [*TVA*]
P/D .... Pickup and Deposit
PD .... Pictorial Display (MCD)
PD .... Pierce's Disease [*Plant pathology*]
PD .... Pilot Dogs (EA)
P & D .... Pioneer and Demolition Section [*Army*]
PD .... Piskei Din Shel Bet ha-Mishpat ha-'Elyon le-Yisrael (BJA)
PD .... Pitch Diameter
PD .... Pitch Down (MCD)
PD .... Pivoted Door (AAG)
PD .... Plane Disagreement [*Telecommunications*] (TEL)
PD .... Planned Derating [*Electronics*] (IEEE)
PD .... Planning Directive (NG)
PD .... Planning Document
PD .... Plans Division [*Military*]
PD .... Plasma Defect [*Medicine*] (MAE)
PD .... Plasma Desorption [*of ions for analysis*]
PD .... Plasma Display
PD .... Plate Dissipation
PD .... Platelet Deaggregation [*Hematology*]
PD .... Plausible Deniability
PD .... Poetic Drama [*A publication*]
PD .... Point Defense
PD .... Point Delay Fuze [*Army*]
PD .... Point Detonating [*Projectile*]
PD .... Polar Distance [*Navigation*]
PD .... Police Department
pd .... Pond [*Pound*] [*Monetary unit*] [*Afrikaans*]
PD .... Pontoon Dock
PD .... Pool Density [*Pisciculture*]
PD .... Poorly Differentiated [*Medicine*]
PD .... Population Density (NRCH)
PD .... Population Distribution (NRCH)
PD .... Population Doubling
PD .... Pore Diameter
PD .... Porphobilinogen Deaminase [*Clinical chemistry*] (MAE)
PD .... Port of Debarkation [*Navy*]
PD .... Port Director
PD .... Port Du [*Carriage Forward*] [*French*]
PD .... Port Dues
PD .... Position Description
PD .... Position Document
PD .... Position Doubtful [*Nautical charts*]
PD .... Positive Displacement
PD .... Post Diluvium [*After the Flood*] [*Latin*] (ROG)
PD .... Postage Due
PD .... Postal District
PD .... Postdated
PD .... Postdoctorate
PD .... Posterior Deltoid [*Myology*]
PD .... Posterior Digestive [*Gland*]
PD .... Postnasal Drainage [*Medicine*]
PD .... Postural Drainage [*Medicine*] (MAE)
PD .... Potential Difference [*Electricity*]
PD .... Pound (ROG)
PD .... Power Distribution
PD .... Precision Device [*British military*] (DMA)
PD .... Precision Drilling (1987) Ltd. [*Toronto Stock Exchange symbol*]
PD .... Predeployment
P/D .... Predicted [*NASA*] (KSC)
PD .... Predilute
PD .... Preference for Duty
PD .... Pregnanediol [*Biochemistry*]
PD .... Preliminary Design
PD .... Prescription Drug
PD .... Presidential Determination
PD .... Presidential Directive
PD .... Presidential Documents [*A publication*]
PD .... Press Division [*Environmental Protection Agency*] (GFGA)
P & D .... Pressing and Distribution (WDMC)
PD .... Pressor Dose [*Medicine*]
Pd .... Pressure, Diastolic [*Cardiology*]
PD .... Pressure Drop (KSC)
PD .... Presumptive Disability [*Title XVI*] [*Social Security Administration*] (OICC)
PD .... Prevention Detention [*Scotland Yard*]
PD .... Prime Driver
PD .... Principal Distance [*Graphic arts*] (OA)
PD .... Printer Driver
PD .... Printer's Devil (ROG)
PD .... Priority Designator [*Army*]
PD .... Priority Directive
PD .... Prism Diopter
PD .... Prisoner's Dilemma [*Psychology*]
PD .... Privatdozent [*Tutor*] [*German*]
PD .... Private Detective
pd .... Pro Defendente [*On Behalf of Defendant*] [*Latin*] [*Legal term*] (DLA)
PD .... Probability of Damage (MCD)
PD .... Probability of Death [*Biology*]
PD .... Probability of Detection

P & D	Probate and Divorce [*Legal*] [*British*]
PD	Problem Definition [*Army*]
PD	Probleme der Dichtung [*A publication*]
PD	Process Diagnostic [*Interpersonal skills and attitudes test*]
PD	Procurement Data
PD	Procurement Directive [*Army*]
P & D	Procurement and Distribution [*Military*]
PD	Procurement District [*Air Force*] (AFIT)
PD	Procurement Division
PD	Procurement Document (NASA)
PD	Procurement Drawing
PD	Product Design [*Phase*]
P/D	Product Development
PD	Production Department
PD	Production and Deployment Phase [*Military*] (MCD)
PD	Professional Development (ADA)
PD	Program Deceleration (KSC)
PD	Program Decoder
PD	Program Directive (NG)
PD	Program Director [*Television*]
PD	Programa Democratico [*Democratic Program*] [*Spain*] [*Political party*] (PPE)
PD	Progression of Disease [*Medicine*]
PD	Progressive Democrats [*Ireland*] [*Political party*]
PD	Project Directive (NASA)
PD	Project Document
PD	Projected Decision Date (NRCH)
PD	Projected Display
P & D	Promote and Develop Fishery Products Pertaining to American Fisheries Account [*National Oceanic and Atmospheric Administration*] (GFGA)
PD	Promotion Director
PD	Propellant Dispersion (KSC)
PD	Property Damage
PD	Proposal Development (AAG)
PD	Protective Device (BUR)
PD	Prototype Demonstration
PD	Provisioning Document
PD	Proximity Detector
PD	Prussian Dollar [*Monetary unit*] (ROG)
PD	Przemysl Drzewny [*A publication*]
PD	Pseudohomogeneous Axial Dispersion Model [*Fluid dynamics*]
PD	Psychodynamic
Pd	Psychopathic Deviate [*Psychology*]
PD	Psychotic Depression [*Medicine*]
PD	Public Domain
PD	Publication Date [*Online database field identifier*]
PD	Publisher's Directory [*Formerly, BPD*] [*A publication*]
PD	Pulmonary Disease [*Medicine*]
PD	Pulpodistal [*Dentistry*]
PD	Pulse Detector [*Spectroscopy*]
PD	Pulse Doppler
PD	Pulse Driver
PD	Pulse Duration
P-D	Punch-Die (MSA)
PD	Punch Driver
pd	Pupillary Distance [*Medicine*]
PD	Purchase Description
PD	Pyloric Dilator [*Neuron*]
PD	Pyramidal Decussation [*Neuroanatomy*]
PD1	Portable Dictionary 1 [*English/Japanese electronic dictionary*] [*Sanyo Electric*]
P 2d	Pacific Reporter. Second [*A publication*]
P 2d	Pacific Reporter, Second Series [*A publication*] (DLA)
PDA	Pacific Dance Association (EA)
PDA	Pacific Dermatologic Association (EA)
PDA	Parallel Data Adapter
PDA	Parametric Design Analysis (RDA)
PDA	Parenteral Drug Association (EA)
PdA	Partei der Arbeit [*Labor Party*] [*Switzerland*] [*Political party*] (PPE)
PDA	Parti Democratico da Angola [*Democratic Party of Angola*] [*Political party*]
PDA	Parti Dolonti Applicandum [*Apply to Painful Part*] [*Pharmacy*] (ROG)
PDA	Partido Democratico Arubano [*Democratic Party of Aruba*] [*Political party*] (EY)
PDA	Partit Democrata d'Andorra [*Andorran Democratic Party*] [*Political party*] (PPW)
Pd'A	Partito d'Azione [*Action Party*] [*Italy*] [*Political party*] (PPE)
PDA	Parts Disposal Area
PDA	Party of Democratic Action [*Bosnia-Herzegovina*] [*Political party*] (EY)
PDA	Pasadena Energy [*Vancouver Stock Exchange symbol*]
PDA	Patent Ductus Arteriosus [*Cardiology*]
PDA	Patient Data Automation
PDA	Payroll Deduction Authorization (MCD)
PDA	Peak Distribution Analyzer
PDA	Pediatric Allergy
PDA	Pentadecanoic Acid [*Organic chemistry*]
PDA	Permanent Duty Assignment [*Air Force*] (AFM)

PDA	Personal Deposit Account [*Banking*]
PDA	Personal Digital Assistant (ECON)
PDA	Petrol Dealers' Association [*British*]
PDA	Phenylenediamine [*Chemistry*]
PDA	Philadelphia Dance Alliance
PDA	Phorbol Diacetate [*Organic chemistry*]
PDA	Photodiode Array [*Instrumentation*]
PDA	Photon Detector Assembly (MCD)
PDA	Physical Device Address [*Data processing*] (IBMDP)
PDA	Piperidinedicarboxylic Acid [*Organic chemistry*]
PDA	Pisatin Demethylase [*An enzyme*]
PDA	Planning and Development in the Netherlands (Assen) [*A publication*]
PDA	Point Density Analysis [*Mathematics*]
PDA	Point Director Array
PDA	Pointing Device Adapter [*Data processing*]
PDA	Poise Distribution Amplifier (AFM)
PDA	Polarization Diversity Array
PDA	Polydiacetylene [*Organic chemistry*]
PDA	Poly(dimethylacrylamide) [*Organic chemistry*]
PDA	Ponta Delgada [*Azores*] [*Seismograph station code, US Geological Survey*] (SEIS)
PDA	Population Drainage Area [*Civil Defense*]
PDA	Portable Diagnostic Analyzer (SSD)
PDA	Post-Deflection Accelerator (DEN)
PDA	Post-Delivery Availability [*Military*] (NVT)
PDA	Post-Design Analysis
PDA	Potato Dextrose Agar [*Culture media*]
PDA	Pour Dire Adieu [*To Say Farewell*] [*On visiting cards*] [*French*]
PDA	Power Distribution Assembly (KSC)
PDA	Precision Drive Axis (KSC)
PDA	Predelivery Acceptance Test [*NASA*]
PDA	Predialyzed Human Albumin [*Medicine*] (MAE)
PDA	Predicted Drift Angle [*Navigation*]
PDA	Predocketed Application (NRCH)
PDA	Preliminary Design Acceptance (NRCH)
PDA	Preliminary Design Approval [*or Authorization*] (NRCH)
PDA	Preliminary Design Assessment [*Nuclear energy*] (NRCH)
PDA	Present Duty Assignment Option [*Military*]
PDA	Princeton Diagnostic Laboratories of America, Inc. [*AMEX symbol*] (SPSG)
PDA	Principal Development Activity [*Navy*]
PDA	Principal Development Authority (MCD)
PDA	Private Doctors of America (EA)
PDA	Probabilistic Decision Algorithm [*Artificial intelligence job performance aid*] [*Army*]
PDA	Probability Discrete Automata (IEEE)
PDA	Probability Distribution Analyzer [*Statistics*]
PDA	Probate, Divorce, and Admiralty [*British*] [*Legal term*] (DLA)
PDA	Processor and Distribution Assembly [*Viking lander analysis equipment*] [*NASA*]
PDA	Procurement Defense Agencies [*DoD*]
PDA	Product Departure Authorization
PDA	Professional Drivers Association
PDA	Program Developing Agency [*Military*] (CAAL)
PDA	Prolonged Depolarizing Afterpotential [*Neurophysiology*]
PDA	Propanediamine [*Organic chemistry*]
PDA	Propellant Drain Area (NASA)
PDA	Property Disposal Account [*Military*] (NG)
PDA	Property Disposal Agent [*Military*] (NG)
PDA	Property Disposition Authorization
PDA	Proposed Development Approach [*Navy*]
PDA	Propylenediamine [*Organic chemistry*]
PDA	Prospectors' and Developers' Association [*Canada*]
PDA	Prototype Development Associate
PDA	Public Display of Affection [*Slang*]
PDA	Puerto Inirida [*Colombia*] [*Airport symbol*] (OAG)
PDA	Pulse Demodulation Analysis
PDA	Pulse Distribution Amplifier
PDA	Pump Drive Assembly
PDA	Pushdown Automation [*Data processing*] (HGAA)
PDAAP	Plume Data Analysis of Advanced Propellants (MCD)
PDAB	Para-(Dimethylamino)benzaldehyde [*Organic chemistry*]
PDAB	Physical Disability Appeals Board [*Military*] (AFM)
PDAC	Professional Development Advisory Committee [*American Occupational Therapy Association*]
PDAD	Photodiode Array Detector [*Spectrophotometry*]
PDAD	Probate, Divorce, and Admiralty Division [*Legal*] [*British*] (ROG)
PDAFSC....	Projected Duty Air Force Specialty Code (AFM)
PDAGA	Pediatriia, Akusherstvo, i Ginekologiia [*A publication*]
PDAID......	Problem Determination Aid [*Data processing*] (MDG)
PDA-KM ...	Party of Democratic Action of Kosovo-Metohija [*Serbia*] [*Political party*] (EY)
PDAL........	Dalhousie Review [*A publication*]
PDalCM	College Misericordia, Dallas, PA [*Library symbol*] [*Library of Congress*] (LCLS)
PDAM	Periodontal Disease-Associated Microbiotae [*Dentistry*]
PDANB	Pediatric Annals [*A publication*]
PDANHS ..	Proceedings. Dorset Natural History and Archaeological Society [*A publication*]

PDanMHi ... Montour County Historical Society, Danville, PA [*Library symbol*] [*Library of Congress*] (LCLS)
PDanSH .... Danville State Hospital, Danville, PA [*Library symbol*] [*Library of Congress*] (LCLS)
PDAP........ Programmable Digital Autopilot (MCD)
PDAP........ Provincial Development Assistance Program [*Agency for International Development*]
PDAR .... Parts Drawing Approval Request (MCD)
PDAR .... Producibility Design Analysis Report (AAG)
PDAR .... Program Description and Requirements [*NASA*] (NASA)
PDARR...... Production Drawing and Assembly Release Record (AAG)
PDA-S .... Party of Democratic Action of the Sandjak [*Serbia*] [*Political party*] (EY)
PDAS........ PDA Engineering [*NASDAQ symbol*] (NQ)
PDAS........ Photo Data Analysis System [*Navy*]
PDAS........ Plant Data Acquisition System (NRCH)
PDAS........ [*A*] Popular Dictionary of Australian Slang [*A publication*]
PDAS........ Portable Data Acquisition System (MCD)
PDASD...... Principal Deputy Assistant Secretary of Defense
PDate........ Pay Date
PDATE....... Production Date [*Data processing*]
Pd B .... Bachelor of Pedagogy
PDB .... Packard Data Bank (EA)
PDB .... Pakistan Development Review [*A publication*]
PDB .... Para-Dichlorobenzene [*Insecticide for moths, etc.*]
PDB .... Partei der Deutschsprachigen Belgier [*Party of German-Speaking Belgians*] [*Political party*] (PPW)
PDB .... Pedro Bay [*Alaska*] [*Airport symbol*] (OAG)
PDB .... Pee Dee Belemnite [*An isotopic standard for oxygen and carbon*]
PDB .... Pentadecylbenzene [*Organic chemistry*]
PDB .... Performance Data Book (NASA)
PDB .... Periodical Directories and Bibliographies [*A publication*]
PDB .... Personality Data Base
PDB .... Phorbol Dibutyrate [*Also, PDBu*] [*Organic chemistry*]
PDB .... Phosphorus-Dissolving Bacteria [*Microbiology*]
PDB .... Pierce's Disease Bacterium [*Plant pathology*]
PDB .... Plasma Diagnostic Base
PDB .... Positive Displacement Blower
PDB .... Potato Dextrose Broth [*Microbiology*]
PDB .... Power Distribution Box (NASA)
PDB .... President's Daily Brief
PDB .... Price Decontrol Board [*Post-World War II*]
PDB .... Primary Data Bus [*Data processing*]
PDB .... Process Descriptor Base [*Telecommunications*] (TEL)
PDB .... Project Development Brochure [*Military*]
PDB .... Protein Data Bank [*Brookhaven National Laboratory*] [*Information service or system*] (CRD)
PDB .... Psychic Detective Bureau (EA)
PDBA .... Personnel Database Application (MCD)
PDBA/SIPM ... Personnel Database Application / Student Instructor Performance Module (DNAB)
PDBH........ Production Broach (AAG)
PDBIA .... Periodicum Biologorum [*A publication*]
PDBM .... Pulse Delay Binary Modulation (MCD)
PDBMI...... Periodical Directories and Bibliographies Master Index [*A publication*]
PDBP........ Powered Disposal Bomb Pod (AAG)
PDBR........ Page-Directory Base Register [*Data processing*] (BYTE)
PDBU .... Pesticides Documentation Bulletin
PDBu .... Phorbol Dibutyrate [*Also, PDB*] [*Organic chemistry*]
PDBz .... Phorbol Dibenzoate [*Organic chemistry*]
PDC .... Community College of Philadelphia, Philadelphia, PA [*OCLC symbol*] (OCLC)
PDC .... Mueo [*New Caledonia*] [*Airport symbol*] (OAG)
PDC .... Pacific Defense College (CINC)
PDC .... Package Design Council [*New York, NY*] (EA)
PDC .... Pacte Democratica per Catalunya [*Democratic Pact for Catalonia*] [*Spain*] [*Political party*] (PPE)
PDC .... Paper Distribution Centers
PDC .... Paper Distribution Council (EA)
PDC .... Parallel Data Communicator (AAG)
PDC .... Parallel Data Controller
PDC .... Parametric Defense Coverage
PDC .... Parti Democrate Chretien [*Christian Democratic Party*] [*Burundi*] [*Political party*]
PDC .... Parti Democrate-Chretien Suisse [*Christian Democratic Party of Switzerland*] [*Political party*] (PPE)
PDC .... Parti des Democrates Camerounais [*Political party*] (EY)
PDC .... Partido da Democracia Cristao [*Christian Democratic Party*] [*Portugal*] [*Political party*] (PPW)
PDC .... Partido Democracia Cristiana [*Christian Democratic Party*] [*Guatemala*] [*Political party*] (PPW)
PDC .... Partido Democrata de Confianza Nacional [*Nicaragua*] [*Political party*] (EY)
PDC .... Partido Democrata Cristiano [*Christian Democratic Party*] [*Paraguay*] [*Political party*] (PPW)
PDC .... Partido Democrata Cristiano [*Christian Democratic Party*] [*Peru*] [*Political party*] (PPW)
PDC .... Partido Democrata Cristiano [*Christian Democratic Party*] [*Costa Rica*] [*Political party*] (PPW)

PDC .... Partido Democrata Cristiano [*Christian Democratic Party*] [*Honduras*] [*Political party*] (PPW)
PDC .... Partido Democrata Cristiano [*Christian Democratic Party*] [*El Salvador*] [*Political party*]
PDC .... Partido Democrata Cristiano [*Christian Democratic Party*] [*Bolivia*] [*Political party*] (PPW)
PDC .... Partido Democrata Cristiano [*Christian Democratic Party*] [*Panama*] [*Political party*] (PPW)
PDC .... Partido Democratico Cristao [*Christian Democratic Party*] [*Brazil*] [*Political party*]
PDC .... Partido Democratico Cristiano [*Christian Democratic Party*] [*Chile*] [*Political party*] (PPW)
PDC .... Partido Democratico Cristiano [*Christian Democratic Party*] [*Argentina*] [*Political party*] (PPW)
PDC .... Partito della Democrazia Cristiana [*Christian Democratic Party*] [*Italy*] [*Political party*]
PDC .... Pediatric Cardiology [*Medical specialty*] (DHSM)
PDC .... Pentadecylcatechol [*An allergen*]
PDC .... Per Diem, Travel and Transportation Allowance Committee for Departments of the Army, Navy, and Air Force
PDC .... Performance Data Computer
PDC .... Personnel Data Card
PDC .... Personnel Distribution Command
PDC .... Philosophy Documentation Center (EA)
PDC .... Photo-Data Card [*Trademark*] [*Data processing*]
PDC .... Photonuclear Data Center [*National Institute of Standards and Technology*]
PDC .... Pieve Di Cadore [*Italy*] [*Seismograph station code, US Geological Survey*] [*Closed*] (SEIS)
PDC .... Piston-Driven Compaction (MCD)
PDC .... Plastic Dielectric Capacitor
PDC .... Polaris Documentation Control [*Missiles*]
PDC .... Policy Determination Committee (AAG)
PDC .... Polycrystalline Diamond Compact Drill Bit
PDC .... Polystyrene Dielectric Capacitor
PDC .... Population Documentation Center [*Food and Agriculture Organization*] [*United Nations*] [*Information service or system*] (IID)
PDC .... Portable Data Carrier
PDC .... Portable Data Communications [*British*]
PDC .... Position Depth Charge
PDC .... Power Distribution and Control
PDC .... Power Distribution Cubiale (NATG)
PDC .... Practice Depth Charge
PDC .... Prairie Du Chien, WI [*Location identifier*] [*FAA*] (FAAL)
PDC .... Predefined Command (MCD)
PDC .... Predeparture Check [*Aviation*] (AIA)
PDC .... Predocketed Construction (NRCH)
PDC .... Preliminary Diagnostic Clinic
PDC .... Premission Documentation Change [*NASA*] (KSC)
PDC .... Premium and Dispersion Credits [*Insurance*]
PDC .... Prescott Development Corp. [*Vancouver Stock Exchange symbol*]
PDC .... Presley Co. [*NYSE symbol*] (SPSG)
PDC .... Pressure Die Casting [*Commercial firm*] [*British*]
PDC .... Prevention of Deterioration Center [*Defunct*] (EA)
PDC .... Price Decontrol Board [*Post-World War II*] [*A publication*] (DLA)
PDC .... Private Diagnostic Clinic
PDC .... Probability of Detection and Conversion [*Military*]
PDC .... Procurement Document Change (NASA)
PDC .... Production Decision Criteria
PDC .... Production Drawing Control
PDC .... Proficiency Data Card [*Army*]
PDC .... Program Data Cards (OICC)
PDC .... Program Data Coordinator (MCD)
PDC .... Programmes Directorate Committee [*British*]
PDC .... Project Data Card
PDC .... Project Data Control (MCD)
PDC .... Prosthetic Distribution Center [*Veterans Administration*]
PDC .... Public Documents Commission [*Government agency*]
PDC .... Publications Distribution Center [*Military*] (AFM)
PDC .... Publishers' Data Center, Inc.
PDC .... Pulse-Duration Commutator
PDC .... Pyridinium Dichromate [*Organic chemistry*]
PDC .... Pyrotechnic Devices Checker
PDC .... Pyruvate Dehydrogenase Complex [*Also, PDHC*] [*Biochemistry*]
PDC .... Single Paper Double Cotton [*Wire insulation*] (AAG)
PDCA .... Painting and Decorating Contractors of America (EA)
PDCA .... Pioneer Dairymen's Club of America (EA)
PDCA .... Pug Dog Club of America (EA)
PDCA .... Purebred Dairy Cattle Association (EA)
PDCA .... United States Professional Diving Coaches Association (EA)
PDCAU ..... Pete Duel - Clube da Amizade do Universo [*Pete Duel Universal Friendship Club - PDUFC*] (EAIO)
PDCG .... Partido Democracia Cristiana Guatemalteca [*Guatemalan Christian Democratic Party*] [*Political party*] (PPW)
PDCH........ Dance Chronicle [*A publication*]
PDCH........ Parti Democratique Chretien d'Haiti [*Political party*] (EY)

PDCI.......... Parti Democratique de la Cote-D'Ivoire [*Democratic Party of the Ivory Coast*] [*Political party*]   (PPW)
Pdck .... Probability of Detection Conversion and Kill [*for an interceptor system*] [*Military*]
PDCL......... Provisioning Data Check List [*NASA*]   (KSC)
PDCN .... Partido Democratico de Cooperacion Nacional [*Democratic Party of National Cooperation*] [*Guatemala*] [*Political party*]
PDCN .... Public Data Communications Network [*Library science*]
PDCO .... Perennial Development Corp. [*NASDAQ symbol*]   (NQ)
PDCO .... Property Disposal Contracting Officer [*Military*]
PDCP........ Pilot's Display Control Panel
PDCP........ Private Development Corp. of the Philippines
PDCPD...... Polydicyclopentadiene [*Organic chemistry*]
PDCR........ Project Data Compliance Report   (MCD)
PDCR........ Proprietary Data Control Record   (NASA)
PDCRC...... Periodontal Disease Clinical Research Center [*State University of New York at Buffalo*] [*Research center*]   (RCD)
PDCS........ Parallel Digital Computing System
PDCS......... Partito Democratico Cristiano Sammarinese [*Christian Democratic Party of San Marino*] [*Political party*]   (PPE)
PDCS........ Performance Data Computer System   (MCD)
PDCS......... Power Distribution and Control System [*or Subsystem*] [*NASA*]   (NASA)
PDCS....... Processing Distribution and Control System
PDCS....... Programmable Data Collection System [*Military*]   (CAAL)
PDCS........ Prototype Die Casting Service
PDCU .... Plotting Display Control Unit
PDCU .... Power Distribution and Control Unit
Pd D .... Doctor of Pedagogy
PDD .... Pancreatic Dorsal Duct [*Anatomy*]
PDD .... Participacion Democratica de Tzquierda [*Chile*] [*Political party*]   (EY)
PDD .... Past Due Date
PDD .... Pervasive Developmental Disorder [*Medicine*]
PDD .... Phenyldodecane [*Organic chemistry*]
PDD .... Phorbol Didecanoate [*Organic chemistry*]
PDD .... Physical Damage Division [*Navy*]
PDD .... Physical Defense Division [*Army*]
PDD .... Plotting Data Distributor   (MCD)
P & DD ...... Plumbing and Deck Drain   (MSA)
PDD .... Post Dialing Delay [*Telecommunications*]   (TEL)
PDD .... Precision Depth Digitizer [*Oceanography*]
PDD .... Preferred Delivery Date   (AFM)
PDD .... Preliminary Design and Development   (MCD)
PDD .... Premodulation Processor - Deep Space - Data
PDD .... Primary Degenerative Dementia [*Medicine*]
PDD .... Principal Distribution Depot [*DoD*]
PDD .... Priority Delivery Date   (AFM)
PDD .... Probability Density Distribution [*Statistics*]
PdD .... Probleme der Dichtung [*A publication*]
PDD .... Procurement Description Data [*DoD*]
PD & D ...... Product Design & Development [*Radnor, PA*] [*A publication*]
PDD .... Professional Development Division [*American Occupational Therapy Association*]
PDD .... Program Description Document [*Military*]   (CAAL)
PDD .... Program Design Data
PDD .... Program Dimension Drawing   (MCD)
PDD .... Program Directive Document   (RDA)
PDD .... Projected Data Display
PDD .... Projected Decision Date   (NRCH)
PDD .... Prospective Decision Date   (NRCH)
PDD .... Provisioning Description Data
PDD .... Public Documents Department [*Government Printing Office*]
PDD .... Pulse Delay Device
PDD .... Puy-De-Dome [*France*] [*Seismograph station code, US Geological Survey*] [*Closed*]   (SEIS)
PDD .... Pyridoxine-Deficient Diet   (MAE)
PDDA .... Power Driver Decontamination Apparatus   (NATG)
PDDAIO ... Parts for Direct Discrete Analog Input/Output   (MCD)
PDDB .... Phenododecinium [*or Phenoxyethyldimethyl-dodecylammonium*] Bromide [*Antiseptic*]
PDDB .... Product Definition Database   (MCD)
PDDD........ Program Demonstration and Development Division [*ACTION*]
PDDF........ Propargyl(dideaza)folic Acid [*Biochemistry*]
PDDGM.... Past District Deputy Grand Master [*Freemasonry*]
PDDI .... Product Definition Data Interface   (MCD)
PD Div'l Ct ... Probate, Divorce, and Admiralty Divisional Court [*England*]   (DLA)
PDDLS ..... Post D-Day Logistic Support [*Army*]   (AABC)
PDDM....... Disciples of the Divine Master [*Roman Catholic women's religious order*]
PDD/RDD ... Priority Delivery Date/Required Delivery Date   (AFM)
PDDS........ Parasitic Disease Drug Service   (MAE)
PDDS........ Program Definition Data Sheet
PDE .... Page-Directory Entry [*Data processing*]   (BYTE)
PDE .... Pandie Pandie [*Australia*] [*Airport symbol*] [*Obsolete*]   (OAG)
PDE .... Parade
Pde .... Parade [*Record label*]
PDE .... Paroxysmal Dyspnea on Exertion [*Medicine*]

PDE .... Partei fuer Deutschland und Europa [*Party for Germany and Europe*] [*Germany*] [*Political party*]   (PPW)
PDE .... Partial Differential Equation
PDE .... Pediatric Endocrinology [*Medical specialty*]   (DHSM)
PDE .... Pee Dee Air Express, Inc. [*Florence, SC*] [*FAA designator*]   (FAAC)
PDE .... Personnel Development and Education   (MCD)
PDE .... Phosphatidyl(dimethyl)ethanolamine [*Biochemistry*]
PDE .... Phosphodiesterase [*An enzyme*]
PDE .... Pilot's Discrete Encoder
PDE .... Position-Determining Equipment
PDE .... Preliminary Determination of Epicenters [*A publication*] [*National Oceanic and Atmospheric Administration*]
PDE .... Pride Resources Ltd. [*Vancouver Stock Exchange symbol*]
PDE .... Principal DOD [*Department of Defense*] Executive
PDE .... Producers' Durable Equipment   (GFGA)
PDE .... Production Design Engineers
PDE .... Projectile Development Establishment [*British*]
PDE .... Propellant Disposition Effects
PDE .... Prospective Data Element [*Army*]   (AABC)
PD & E....... Provisioning Documentation and Effort [*Military*]   (AFIT)
PDEA .... Phenyldiethanolamine [*Organic chemistry*]
PDECS ..... Portable Detector and Cueing System
PDED .... Partial Double Error Detection
PDED .... Program Development and Evaluation Division [*Environmental Protection Agency*]   (GFGA)
PDEI......... Phosphodiesterase Inhibitor [*Biochemistry*]
PDEL........ Partial Differential Equation Language [*Data processing*]
PDELAN... Partial Differential Equation Language [*Data processing*]   (CSR)
PDEM .... Demography [*A publication*]
PDENA ..... Production Engineer [*London*] [*A publication*]
PDEP........ Preliminary Draft Equipment Publication   (MCD)
PDEQ .... Profile of DARCOM Environmental Quality   (MCD)
PDES........ Preliminary Draft Environmental Statement   (NRCH)
PDES........ Product Definition Exchange Specification [*Army*]
P Det .... Port Detachment [*British military*]   (DMA)
PDET........ Post-Diapause Eclosion Time [*Entomology*]
PDET........ Probability of Detection, Evaluation, and Transfer   (MCD)
PDEX........ Pro-Dex, Inc. [*NASDAQ symbol*]   (NQ)
PDF........... Packaging Technology [*A publication*]
PDF........... Paget's Disease Foundation   (EA)
PDF........... Pair Distribution Function [*Physical chemistry*]
PDF........... Pakistan Democratic Front
PDF........... Panama Defense Forces [*Later, Public Forces*]
PDF........... Parkinson's Disease Foundation   (EA)
PDF........... Parti Democrate Francais [*French Democratic Party*] [*Political party*]   (PPW)
PDF........... Particle Distribution Function
PDF........... Passive Direction Finding
PDF........... Pavement Depth Factor   (ADA)
PDF........... Peace Development Fund   (EA)
PDF........... Pele Defense Fund   (EA)
PDF........... People's Democratic Force [*The Bahamas*] [*Political party*]   (EY)
PDF........... Planar Deformation Feature [*Geology*]
PDF........... Planet Drum Foundation   (EA)
PDF........... Plant Design Factor [*Nuclear energy*]   (NRCH)
PDF........... Plant Design Flood [*Nuclear energy*]   (GFGA)
PDF........... Point Detonating Fuze [*Army*]
PDF........... Popular Democratic Front [*Jordan*] [*Political party*]
PDF........... Porsche Dual-Function Transmission [*Automotive engineering*]
PDF........... Post Defense Force
PDF........... Post Detection Filter [*Telecommunications*]   (TEL)
PDF........... Primordial Density Fluctuation [*Cosmology*]
PDF........... Principal Direction of Fire [*Military*]
PDF........... Probability Density Function [*Statistics*]
PDF........... Probability Distribution Function [*Statistics*]
PDF........... Processor Defined Function
PDF........... Production and Distribution of Foodstuffs [*British*]
PDF........... Program Data File
PDF........... Program Data Form [*Army*]
PDF........... Project Design Flood   (NRCH)
PDF........... Protected Difference Fat   (OA)
PDFCS ..... Pennsylvania Dutch Folk Culture Society   (EA)
PDFD........ Predemonstration Fusion Device
PDFD........ Pulsed Doppler Frequency Diversity   (NG)
PDFLP....... Popular Democratic Front for the Liberation of Palestine
PDFM....... Phillips and Drew Fund Management [*England*] [*British*]
PDFRR...... Program Directors Flight Readiness Review [*NASA*]   (KSC)
PDFWPR .. Physical Disabilities Fieldwork Performance Report [*Occupational therapy*]
PDG .... Padang [*Indonesia*] [*Airport symbol*]   (OAG)
PDG .... Parachute Drop Glider
PDG .... Paradigm   (WGA)
PDG .... Parti Democratique Gabonais [*Gabonese Democratic Party*] [*Political party*]   (PPW)
PDG .... Parti Democratique de Guinee [*Democratic Party of Guinea*] [*Political party*]   (PPW)
PDG .... Passive Defense Group   (MUGU)
PDG .... Patent Documentation Group   (DIT)

PDG .... Personalistic Discussion Group - Eastern Division (EA)
PDG .... Placer Dome, Inc. [*NYSE symbol*] [*Toronto Stock Exchange symbol*] [*Vancouver Stock Exchange symbol*] (SPSG)
PDG .... Precision Drop Glider [*Army*]
PDG .... Pregnanediol Glucuronide [*Endocrinology*]
PDG .... President Directeur General [*President Director General*] [*French*]
PDG .... Pretty Damn Good
PDG .... Professional Dyers Guild [*Defunct*]
PDG .... Programs Development Group (MUGU)
PDG .... Proposal Development Group [*Aerospace*] (AAG)
PDGA .... Pteroyldiglutamic Acid [*Pharmacology*]
PDGDL ..... Plasma Dynamics and Gaseous Discharge Laboratory [*MIT*] (MCD)
PDGE .... Partido Democratico de Guinea Ecuatorial [*Democratic Party of Equatorial Guinea*][*Political party*] (EY)
PDGF .... Platelet-Derived Growth Factor [*Genetics*]
PDGFR ...... Platelet-Derived Growth Factor Receptor [*Genetics*]
PDGMS .... Peabody Developmental Gross Motor Scale
PDGS .... Precision Delivery Glider System
P-DGs .... Presidents-Directeurs Generaux
PDGS .... Probe Drill Guidance System
PDGS .... Product Design Graphics System [*Prime Computer Ltd.*] [*Software package*] (NCC)
PDGW .... Principle Directorate of Guided Weapons [*British*] (SAA)
PDGY .... Prodigy Systems, Inc. [*NASDAQ symbol*] (NQ)
PDH.......... Packaged Disaster Hospital [*Public Health Service*]
PDH.......... Passive Defense Handbook [*Navy*] (MCD)
PDH.......... Past Dental History
PDH.......... Phosphate Dehydrogenase (MAE)
PDH.......... Planned Derated Hours [*Electronics*] (IEEE)
PDH.......... Pocket Dosimeter-High (MCD)
PDH.......... Pyruvate Dehydrogenase [*An enzyme*]
PDHC .... Pyruvate Dehydrogenase Complex [*Biochemistry*]
PDH & DS ... Plant Data Handling and Display System [*Nuclear energy*] (NRCH)
PDHF .... Postdilution Hemofiltration [*Medicine*]
PDHMUA ... Publication. Department of History. Muslim University (Aligarh) [*A publication*]
PDHV-RDA ... Parti Democratique de la Haute Volta-Rassemblement Democratique Africain [*Democratic Party of Upper Volta-African Democratic Rally*]
PDI .... Palmer Drought Index
PDI .... Partai Demokrasi Indonesia [*Indonesian Democratic Party*] [*Political party*] (PPW)
PDI .... Parti Democratique de l'Independance [*Democratic Independence Party*] [*Morocco*] [*Political party*]
PDI .... Partial Delivery Injection [*Materials science*]
PDI .... Partito Democratica Italiana [*Italian Democratic Party*] [*Political party*] (PPE)
PDI .... Payload Data Interleaver [*NASA*] (NASA)
PDI .... Perfect Digital Invariant (OA)
PDI .... Personal Disposable Income [*Economics*]
PDI .... Pictorial Deviation Indicator (AAG)
PDI .... Picture Description Instruction [*Telecommunications*]
PDI .... Pilot Direction Indicator [*Electronic communications*]
PDI .... Planned Innovation [*A publication*]
PDI .... Plumbing and Drainage Institute (EA)
PDI .... Porto D'Ischia [*Italy*] [*Seismograph station code, US Geological Survey*] [*Closed*] (SEIS)
PDI .... Post Detection Integration (MCD)
PDI .... Potential Determining Ions
PDI .... Powered Descent Initiation [*Aerospace*]
PDI .... Pre-Delivery Inspection (DCTA)
PDI .... Predeployment Inspection [*Navy*] (NVT)
PDI .... Premdor, Inc. [*Toronto Stock Exchange symbol*]
PDI .... Professional Development Institute [*Canada*]
PDI .... Program Design, Inc. [*Commercial firm*]
PDI .... Program with Developing Institutions (EA)
PDI .... Project Data Index [*Jet Propulsion Laboratory, NASA*]
PDI .... Protein Dispersibility Index [*Analytical chemistry*]
PDI .... Protein Disulfide-Isomerase [*An enzyme*]
PDI .... Psychiatric Diagnostic Interview [*Personality development test*] [*Psychology*]
PDI .... Psychological Distress Inventory [*Student personality test*]
PDI .... Psychomotor Development Index [*Bayley Scales of Infant Development*]
PDI .... Public Debt Interest (ADA)
PDI .... Public Demographics, Inc. (IID)
PDI .... Putnam Dividend Income [*NYSE symbol*] (SPSG)
Pdi............. Transdiaphragmatic [*Pressure*]
PDial.......... Poetry Dial [*A publication*]
PDIC.......... Periodic (AFM)
PDIC.......... Professional Driver Improvement Course
PDIF .... Putnam Dividend Income Fund [*Associated Press abbreviation*] (APAG)
PDII .... Pusat Dokumentasi dan Informasi Ilmiah [*Indonesian Center for Scientific Documentation and Information*] [*Information service or system*] (IID)
PDIIS .... Priority Defense Items Information System
PDIL.......... Power-Dependent Insertion Limit [*Nuclear energy*] (NRCH)

PDIO .... Diogenes [*English edition*] [*A publication*]
PDIO .... Parallel Digital Input/Output
PDIO .... Photodiode
P-DIOL ..... Pregnanediol [*Biochemistry*]
PDIP .... Diplomatic History [*A publication*]
PDIP.......... Preflight Data Insertion Program (NVT)
PDIP.......... Program Development Increment Package [*Military*]
PDIQ .... Protein Databases, Inc. [*NASDAQ symbol*] (NQ)
PDIR.......... Priority Disassembly and Inspection Report
PDIR.......... Program Directive
PDIS.......... Parts Dissection Information System
PDIS.......... Payload Data Interleaver System [*NASA*] (MCD)
PDIS.......... Proceedings. National Symposia [*A publication*]
PDIS.......... Product Description Information Standards [*or System*]
PDISCH ..... Pump Discharge
PDISPL..... Positive Displacement [*Engineering*]
PDIT .... Provision for Deferred Income Tax
PDIUM ..... Partito Democratico Italiano di Unita Monarchica [*Italian Democratic Party of Monarchical Unity*] [*Political party*] (PPE)
P Div .... Law Reports, Probate Division [*England*] [*A publication*] (DLA)
PDJ .... Plaine Des Jarres [*South Vietnam*]
PDJ .... Precision Drill Jig
PDJB .... Precision Drill Jig Bushing
PD/JV .... Project Definition/Joint Validation (MCD)
PDK .... Atlanta [*Georgia*] De Kalb/Peachtree Airport [*Airport symbol*] [*Obsolete*] (OAG)
PDK .... Phase-Delay Keying [*Data processing*]
PDK .... Phi Delta Kappa [*Fraternity*]
PDK .... Phileleftheron Demokratikon Kendron [*Liberal Democratic Union*] [*Greek*] (PPE)
PDK .... Phileleftheron Demokratikon Komma [*Liberal Democratic Party*] [*Greek*] [*Political party*] (PPE)
PDK .... Poop Deck [*Naval engineering*]
PDK .... Promenade Deck [*of a ship*] (DS)
PDL .... Page Description Language [*Computer graphics*]
PDL .... Partido Democrata Liberal [*Liberal Democratic Party*] [*Spain*] [*Political party*] (EY)
PDL .... Parts Deletion List (MSA)
PDL .... Parts Difference List (MCD)
PDL .... Parts Documentation List (MCD)
PDL .... Pass Down the Line [*Book*] [*Navy*] (MUGU)
PDL .... Patent Depository Library [*Designated by the Patent and Trademark Office*]
PDL .... Periodontal Ligament [*Dentistry*]
PDL .... Permanent Duty Location
PDL .... Photodissociation Dye LASER
PDL .... Placer Development Ltd. [*Toronto Stock Exchange symbol*] [*Vancouver Stock Exchange symbol*]
PDL .... Pocket Dosimeter-Low (MCD)
PDL .... Ponta Delgada [*Portugal*] [*Airport symbol*] (OAG)
PDL .... Poorly Differentiated Lymphocytic [*Oncology*]
PDL .... Population Doubling Level [*Cytology*]
PDL .... Portable Data Loader [*Aviation*]
pdl .... Poundal [*Unit of force*]
PDL .... Poverty Datum Line
PDL .... Precision Delay Line
PDL .... Presidential Realty Corp. [*AMEX symbol*] (SPSG)
PDL .... Procedure Definition Language [*Data processing*] (BUR)
PDL .... Procedure Distribution List (MCD)
PDL .... Procurement Data List
PDL .... Product Disaster Loans [*Small Business Administration*]
PDL .... Professional Development League (EA)
PDL .... Program Description Language (MCD)
PDL .... Program Design Language (NASA)
PDL .... Programmed Digital Logic
PDL .... Project Document List
PdL .... Provincia di Lucca [*A publication*]
PDL .... Publishers' Databases Ltd. [*Publishing consortium*] [*British*]
pdl .... Pudendal [*Anatomy*] (MAE)
PDL .... Pulsed Dye LASER
PDL .... Pumped Dye LASER
PDLC........ Partido Liberal de Cataluna [*Liberal Democratic Party of Catalonia*] [*Political party*] (PPW)
PDLC........ Polymer Dispersed Liquid Crystal [*Physical chemistry*]
PDL/FT² .... Poundals per Square Foot
PDLL........ Poorly Differentiated Lymphatic [*or Lymphocytic*] Lymphoma [*Oncology*]
PDLM ...... Periodic Depot Level Maintenance
PDLM ...... Planned Depot Level Maintenance (MCD)
PDLM ...... Programmed Depot Level Maintenance [*Air Force*]
PDLP........ Pacific Dunlop Ltd. [*NASDAQ symbol*] (NQ)
PDLS........ Party of the Democratic Left of Slovakia [*Former Czechoslovakia*] [*Political party*] (EY)
PDL S/FT² ... Poundal Seconds per Square Foot
PDLT........ P-Channel Depletion-Load Triode Inverter
Pd M .... Master of Pedagogy
PDM......... Parti Democratique Malgache [*Malagasy Democratic Party*]
PDM......... Partial Descriptive Method

PDM .... Partido de los Democratas Melillenses [*Political party*] [*Spanish North Africa*] (MENA)
PDM .... Patient Data Management
PDM .... Pendant Drop Method
PDM .... People's Democratic Movement [*Turks and Caicos Islands*] [*Political party*] (PPW)
PDM .... People's Democratic Movement [*Papua New Guinea*] [*Political party*] (FEA)
PDM .... People's Democratic Movement [*Guyana*] [*Political party*] (EY)
PDM .... Percent Deviation from the Median
PDM .... Physical Distribution Management
PDM .... Physicians Drug Manual [*A publication*]
PDM .... Physiological Data Monitor
PDM .... Pinch Design Method [*Heat exchange design*]
PDM .... Pittsburgh - Des Moines, Inc. [*AMEX symbol*] (SPSG)
PDM .... Poetry and Drama Magazine [*A publication*]
PDM .... Portable Differential Magnetometer
PDM .... Power Density Meter
PDM .... Practical Data Manager [*Hitachi Ltd.*] [*Japan*]
PDM .... Precedence Diagraming Method (MCD)
PDM .... Predictive Maintenance
PDM .... Preliminary Development Model
PDM .... Preliminary Draft Manuscript
PDM .... Presidential Decision Memorandum [*Jimmy Carter Administration*]
PDM .... Print Down Module
PDM .... Processor Data Monitor (NASA)
PDM .... Production Decision Criteria Matrix
PDM .... Program Data Manager (MCD)
PDM .... Program Decision Memorandum [*Military*]
PDM .... Programmed Depot Maintenance (MCD)
PDM .... Progres et Democratie Moderne [*Progress and Modern Democracy*] [*France*] [*Political party*] (PPE)
PDM .... Project Design Memo
PDM .... Protected Difference Milk (OA)
PDM .... Publications Distribution Manager [*Military*] (AFM)
PDM .... Pulse Delay Mechanism [*British military*] (DMA)
PDM .... Pulse Delta Modulation (IEEE)
PDM .... Pulse-Duration Modulation [*Data transmission*]
PDM .... Pursuit Deterrent Munition
PDM .... Push Down Memory [*Data processing*]
PDMA ...... Peninsula Drafting Management Association
PDMA ...... Prescription Drug Marketing Act [*1987*]
PDMA ...... Product Development and Management Association [*Indianapolis, IN*] (EA)
PDMAC .... Prescription Drug Maximum Allowable Cost
PDMAMS ... Product Design Minuteman Airborne Mechanical System (SAA)
PDME ...... Pendant-Drop Melt Extraction [*Metal fiber technology*]
PDME ...... Precision Distance Measuring Equipment (MCD)
PDM-FM .. Pulse-Duration Modulation - Frequency Modulation (CET)
PDMLA .... PDM. Physicians' Drug Manual [*A publication*]
PDMLR.... Post-Development Maintainability Logistics Review (MCD)
PDMM ...... Push Down Memory MODEM [*Data processing*]
PDMO ...... Production Mold (AAG)
PDMP .... Positive Displacement Mechanical [*or Metering*] Pump
PDMR ...... Provisioning Data Master Record (MCD)
PDMS....... Particle Desorption Mass Spectrometry
PDMS....... Pesticide Document Management System [*Environmental Protection Agency*] (GFGA)
PDMS....... Physiological Data Monitoring System
PDMS....... Plant Design and Management System [*Computer Aided Design Centre*] [*Software package*] (NCC)
PDMS....... Plasma Desorption Mass Spectroscopy
PDMS....... Point Defense Missile System [*NATO*] (NATG)
PDMS....... Polydimethylsiloxane [*Organic chemistry*]
PDMS....... Power-Plant and Process Design Management System [*Data processing*]
PDMS....... Program Definition and Management System (MCD)
PDMT ...... Predominate (FAAC)
PDMU ...... Passive Data Memory Unit
PDMU ...... Production Mock-Up (AAG)
PDN.......... Partido Democratico Nacional [*National Democratic Party*] [*Venezuela*] [*Political party*]
PDN.......... Partido Democratico Nacional [*National Democratic Party*] [*Chile*] [*Political party*]
PDN.......... Partito Democratico Nazionalista [*Democratic Nationalist Party (1921-1926)*] [*Malta*] [*Political party*] (PPE)
PDN.......... Partnerships Data Net (EA)
PDN.......... Petition Denied
PDN.......... Port Heiden, AK [*Location identifier*] [*FAA*] (FAAL)
PDN.......... Prednisone [*Also, P, Pr, Pred, Pro*] [*Antineoplastic drug*] [*Endocrinology*]
PDN.......... Problem Documentation Number (AAG)
PDN.......... Production (AFM)
PDN.......... Properly Driven Net
PDN.......... Public Data Network [*Packet-switching network*] [*British Telecommunications Ltd.*] [*London*]
PDN.......... Putnam Diversified Premium [*NYSE symbol*] (SPSG)
PDNC........ Presidents' Day National Committee (EA)

PDNPD ..... Physica D. Nonlinear Phenomena [*A publication*]
PD/NSC .... Presidential Directives/National Security Council
PDO.......... Philips & Du Pont Optical Co. [*Wilmington, DE*]
PDO.......... Postman's Delivery Office (DCTA)
PDO.......... Printer Direction Optimizer (BUR)
PD-O......... Program Directive - Operations (KSC)
PDO.......... Property Disposal Officer [*Army*]
PdO........... Psychopathic Deviate Obvious [*Psychology*]
PDO.......... Publications Distribution Officer [*Military*]
PDoB .... Bucks County Free Library, Doylestown, PA [*Library symbol*] [*Library of Congress*] (LCLS)
PDoBHi .... Bucks County Historical Society, Doylestown, PA [*Library symbol*] [*Library of Congress*] (LCLS)
PDOC .... Particulate and/or Dissolved Organic Carbon [*Chemistry*]
PDOC .... Proceed on Course by Course [*Aviation*] (FAAC)
PDOD .... Phytoplankton Dissolved Oxygen Deficit [*Oceanography*]
PDOF .... Principal Direction of Force [*Mechanical engineering*]
PDOIS...... People's Democratic Organisation for Independence and Socialism [*Senegambia*] [*Political party*]
PDOL .... Publishers Discount Option List
PDoN .... Delaware Valley College of Science and Agriculture, Doylestown, PA [*Library symbol*] [*Library of Congress*] (LCLS)
PDOP .... Position Dilution of Precision
PDOP .... Prospective Designated Overhaul Point (MCD)
PDOS .... Parent Diabetes Opinion Survey [*Test*]
PDowN ...... Newcomen Society in North America, Downingtown, PA [*Library symbol*] [*Library of Congress*] (LCLS)
PDP .... Packaging Development Plan
PDP .... Pakistan Democratic Party [*Political party*] (PD)
PDP .... Parallel Detection Polychromator [*Instrumentation*]
PDP .... Parallel Distributed Processing [*A simulation of mental processes*]
PDP .... Parker & Parsley Development Ltd. [*AMEX symbol*] [*NYSE symbol*] (SPSG)
PDP .... Parliamentary Democratic Party [*Myanmar*] [*Political party*]
PdP .... Parola del Popolo [*A publication*]
PDP .... Parti Democrate Populaire [*Popular Democratic Party*] [*France*] [*Political party*] (PPE)
PDP .... Partido Democrata Popular [*Popular Democratic Party*] [*Dominican Republic*] [*Political party*] (PPW)
PDP .... Partido Democrata Popular [*Popular Democratic Party*] [*Spain*] [*Political party*] (PPW)
PDP .... Partido Democratico para o Progresso [*Democratic Progressive Party*] [*Guinea-Bissau*] [*Political party*] (EY)
PDP .... Partido da Direita Portuguesa [*Party of the Portuguese Right*] [*Political party*] (PPE)
PDP .... Partito Democratico Populare [*Popular Democratic Party*] [*San Marino*] [*Political party*] (PPE)
PDP .... Party for Democratic Prosperity [*Macedonia*] [*Political party*]
PDP .... Payload Distribution Panel [*NASA*] (MCD)
PDP .... Payload Distribution Plan
PDP .... Pentadecylphenol [*Organic chemistry*]
PDP .... People's Democratic [*Saint Christopher and Nevis*] [*Political party*] (EY)
PDP .... People's Democratic Party [*Sudan*] [*Political party*]
PDP .... People's Democratic Party [*Sierra Leone*] [*Political party*] (EY)
PDP .... People's Democratic Party [*South Korea*] [*Political party*] (EY)
PDP .... People's Democratic Party [*Netherlands Antilles*] [*Political party*] (EY)
PDP .... Personal Development Program (MCD)
PDP .... Philadelphia, PA [*Location identifier*] [*FAA*] (FAAL)
PDP .... Philippine Democratic Party [*Pilipino Lakas Ng Bayan*] [*Political party*] (PPW)
PDP .... Pilot District Project [*Office of Economic Opportunity*] [*Defunct*] (EA)
PDP .... Piperidino-Pyrimidine [*Biochemistry*] (MAE)
PDP .... Pitch-Depitch (AAG)
PDP .... Planning Development Program (OICC)
PDP .... Plasma Diagnostics Package [*NASA*]
PDP .... Plasma Display Panel [*Data processing*]
PDP .... Plasma Display Processor [*Data processing*]
PDP .... Popular Democratic Party [*Puerto Rico*] [*Political party*]
PDP .... Positive Displacement Pump
PDP .... Post Detection Processor [*Military*] (CAAL)
PDP .... Post-Drug Potentiation
PDP .... Post-Insertion Deorbit Preparation [*NASA*] (MCD)
PDP .... Power Distribution Panel
PDP .... Preliminary Definition Plan (NASA)
PDP .... Preliminary Design Phase
PDP .... Preliminary Design Proposal (MCD)
PDP .... Preprototype Demonstration
PDP .... Present-Day Primers [*A publication*]
PDP .... Pressure Distribution Panel (AAG)
PDP .... Principal Display Panel [*Packaging*]
PDP .... Procedure Definition Processor [*Data processing*]
PDP .... Process Development Pile NE
PDP .... Procurement Data Package [*Military*] (AABC)
PDP .... Production Data Package (MCD)

PDP .... Professional Development Program [*Military*]
PDP .... Program Decision Package [*Military*]
PDP .... Program Definition Phase [*Army*]
PDP .... Program Development Paper   (MCD)
PDP .... Program Development Plan [*NASA*]
PDP .... Programmed Data Processor
PDP .... Programmed Digital Processor
PDP .... Progressive Democratic Party [*St. Vincent*] [*Political party*]   (PPW)
PDP .... Progressive Democratic Party [*Montserrat*] [*Political party*]   (PPW)
PDP .... Project Definition Phase   (NRCH)
PDP .... Project Development Plan
PDP .... Punta Del Este [*Uruguay*] [*Airport symbol*]   (OAG)
PDPA......... People's Democratic Party of Afghanistan [*Political party*]   (PPW)
PDPA......... Production Pattern   (AAG)
PDPC........ Position Display Parallax Corrected
PDPC........ Post Detection Pulse Compression [*Military*]   (CAAL)
PDPF........ Packet Data Processing Facility   (MCD)
PDPGM..... Past Deputy Provincial Grand Master [*Freemasonry*]
PDPL........ Property Damage, Personal Liability [*Insurance*]
PD & PL .... Property Damage and Public Liability [*Insurance*]   (IIA)
PDPM .... Preliminary Draft Presidential Memo
PDPOA ..... Proposal Directive Plan of Action   (MCD)
PDPR........ Pandick Press [*NASDAQ symbol*]   (NQ)
PDPR........ Present-Day Preachers [*A publication*]
PDPRA...... Plastics Design and Processing [*A publication*]
PDPS .... Parts Data Processing System [*Bell Telephone*]
PDPS........ Program Data Processing Section   (AAG)
PDPS........ Program Definition Phase Studies [*Navy*]
PDPS........ Project Data Processing System   (MCD)
PDPT........ Parti Democratique des Populations Togolaises [*Togolese Democratic People's Party*] [*Political party*]
PDPUB...... Pedicel Pubescence [*Botany*]
PDPVF ...... Presidential and Democratic Party Victory Fund   (EA)
PDQ.......... Packages Delivered Quick [*Allegheny Airlines service*]
PDQ.......... Parental Diagnostic Questionnaire [*Speech evaluation test*]
PDQ.......... Parodies Done Quirkily [*Humorous translation of Peter Schickele's PDQ Bach*]
PDQ.......... PDQ Air Charter, Inc. [*Pontiac, MI*] [*FAA designator*]   (FAAC)
PDQ.......... Permanent Durable Quality [*Paper*]
PDQ.......... Personal Description Questionnaire
PDQ.......... Pertinent Data Quest   (MCD)
PDQ.......... Pesikta de-Rav Kahana
PDQ.......... Photo Data Quantizer
PDQ.......... Physician's Data Query [*NIH*]
PDQ.......... Please Draw Quickly [*Initialism used as title of TV series*]
PDQ.......... Point, Digital, Qualifier [*In automobile name Opel PDQ*]
PDQ.......... Prescreening Developmental Questionnaire [*Child development test*]
PDQ.......... Pretty Damn Quick
PDQ.......... Price and Delivery Quotations
PDQ.......... Prime Hospitality [*NYSE symbol*]   (SPSG)
PDQ.......... Prime Motor Inns [*NYSE symbol*]   (SPSG)
PDQ ..... Programmed Data Quantizer
PDQ.......... Protocol Data Query [*Database*] [*National Institutes of Health*]
PDQC........ Physicians Data Query: Cancer Information File [*Database*]
PDQD........ Physicians Data Query: Directory File [*Database*]
PDQP........ Physicians Data Query: Protocol File [*Database*]
PDR .... Page Data Register
PDR .... Pakistan Development Review [*A publication*]
PDR .... Parti Democratique Progressif [*Algeria*] [*Political party*]   (EY)
PDR .... Particulate Data Reduction   (EPA)
PDR .... Party of Democratic Reform [*Slovenia*] [*Political party*]   (EY)
PDR .... Peak Dose Rate [*Radiation*]   (AAG)
PDR .... Pediatric Radiology [*Medical specialty*]   (DHSM)
PDR .... Periscope Depth Range [*SONAR*]
PDR .... Periscope Detection RADAR   (NG)
PDR .... Peter De Ridder Press Publications [*A publication*]
PDR .... Pharma-Dokumentationsring [*Pharma Documentation Ring*] [*Information service or system*]   (IID)
PDR .... Phase Data Recorder   (KSC)
PDR .... Phase Delay Rectifier
PDR .... Philippine Defense Ribbon [*Military decoration*]
PDR .... Physicians' Desk Reference [*Also, an information service or system*] [*A publication*]
PDR .... Pilot's Display Recorder
PDR .... Piskei Din Shel Batei ha-Din ha-Rabaniyim be-Yisrael   (BJA)
PDR .... Plant Disease Reporter [*A publication*]
PDR .... Plasma-Developed Resist Processing [*Lithography*]
PD & R...... Policy Development and Research
PDR .... Position Distribution Report [*DoD*]
PDR .... Pounder   (MSA)
PDR .... Powder
PDR .... Power Directional Relay
PDR .... Precision Depth Recorder
PDR .... Predetection Recording
PDR .... Predetermined Demand Rate
PDR .... Preferential Departure Route [*Aviation*]   (FAAC)
PDR .... Preliminary Data Report
PDR .... Preliminary Data Requirements   (NASA)

PDR .... Preliminary Design Report   (NRCH)
PDR .... Preliminary Design Review   (NASA)
PDR .... Pressurized Deuterium Reactor [*Nuclear energy*]
P & DR....... Price and Delivery Request
PDR .... Price Description Record [*Data processing*]   (IBMDP)
PDR .... Priority Data Reduction
PDR .... Process Dynamics Recorder
PDR .... Processed Data Recorder
PDR .... Processing Data Rate   (IEEE)
PDR .... Procurement Data Reference
PDR .... Product Design Review [*Army*]
PDR .... Program Design Review   (MCD)
PDR .... Program Director's Review [*NASA*]   (NASA)
PDR .... Program Discrepancy Report   (IEEE)
PDR .... Program Document Requirement   (BUR)
PDR .... Program Drum Recording
PDR .... Proliferative Diabetic Retinopathy [*Ophthalmology*]
PDR .... Public Document Room   (NRCH)
PDR .... Publications Data Request
PDR .... Pulse Doppler RADAR
PDR .... Pulse Duty Ratio
PDRA........ Professional Drag Racing Association   (EA)
PDRC........ Clinical Research Center for Periodontal Disease [*University of Florida*] [*Research center*]   (RCD)
PDRC........ Personnel Despatch and Reception Centre [*British military*]   (DMA)
PDRC........ Peter Duel Remembrance Club   (EA)
PDRC........ Poultry Disease Research Center [*University of Georgia*] [*Research center*]   (RCD)
PDRC........ Preliminary Design Review Commercial   (MCD)
PDRC........ Pressure Difference Recording Controller
PDRC........ Professional Development and Recruitment Career Program [*Military*]
PDRC........ Program Development Review Committee [*Navy*]   (CAAL)
PDRD .... Procurement Data Requirements Document   (NASA)
PDRD .... Program Definition and Requirements Document   (SSD)
PDRE........ People's Democratic Republic of Ethiopia
PDRF........ Passive Defense Recovery Force   (MUGU)
PDRF........ Presbyterians for Democracy and Religious Freedom   (EA)
PDRH........ Partido Democratico Revolucionario Hondureno [*Revolutionary Democratic Party of Honduras*] [*Political party*]
PDRI......... Publications. Diaspora Research Institute [*A publication*]
PDRJ .... Dance Research Journal [*A publication*]
PdRK .... Pesikta de-Rav Kahana   (BJA)
PDRL........ Permanent Disability Retired List
PDRL........ Procurement Data Requirements List   (NASA)
PDRM .... Payload Deployment and Retrieval Mechanism [*NASA*]
PDRM .... Post-Depositional Remanent Magnetization [*Geophysics*]
PDRM .... Postdetrital Remanent Magnetization [*Geophysics*]
PDRMA .... Portable Drilling Rig Manufacturers Association [*Defunct*]   (EA)
PDRP........ Program Data Requirement Plan [*Nuclear Regulatory Commission*]   (NRCH)
PD & RS .... Payload Deployment and Retrieval Subsystem [*NASA*]   (NASA)
PDRS......... Payload Deployment and Retrieval System [*NASA*]   (GFGA)
PDRSS ...... Payload Deployment and Retrieval System Simulation [*NASA*]   (SSD)
PDRSTA ... Payload Deployment and Retrieval System Test Article [*NASA*]   (NASA)
PDRY .... People's Democratic Republic of Yemen [*Political party*]
PDS........... Auburn/Lewiston, ME [*Location identifier*] [*FAA*]   (FAAL)
PDS........... Package Data System   (NASA)
PDS........... Packet Data Satellites [*Telecommunications*]   (TSSD)
PDS........... Paid-during-Service [*Billing*]
PDS........... Pain Dysfunction Syndrome [*Medicine*]   (AAMN)
PDS........... Parkinson's Disease Society [*British*]
PDS........... Paroxysmal Depolarizing Shift [*Physiology*]
PDS........... Partei des Demokratischen Sozialismus [*Party of Democratic Socialism*] [*Germany*] [*Political party*]   (EAIO)
PDS........... Parti Democratique Senegalais [*Senegalese Democratic Party*] [*Political party*]   (PPW)
PDS........... Partido Democrata Socialista [*Socialist Democratic Party*] [*Panama*] [*Political party*]   (PPW)
PDS........... Partitioned Data Set [*or System*] [*Data processing*]   (NASA)
PDS........... Partito Democratico della Sinistra [*Democratic Party of the Left*] [*Formerly, Italian Communist Party*] [*Political party*]   (EY)
PDS........... Partito di Democrazia Socialista [*Socialist Democracy Party*] [*San Marino*] [*Political party*]   (PPW)
PDS........... Party of Democratic Socialism [*Germany*] [*Political party*]
PDS........... Passive Detection System   (NVT)
PDS........... Pediatric Surgery [*Medical specialty*]   (DHSM)
PDS........... Penultimate Digit Storage [*Telecommunications*]   (TEL)
PDS........... Performer Design Sheet
PDS........... Perimeter Defense System   (MCD)
PDS........... Permanent Duty Station [*Air Force*]   (AFM)
PDS........... Perry Drug Stores, Inc. [*NYSE symbol*]   (SPSG)
PDS........... Personal Decision Series   (HGAA)
PDS........... Personal Development Study [*Psychology*]

PDS............	Personnel Daily Summary [*Army*] (AABC)
PDS............	Personnel Data Summary (FAAC)
PDS............	Personnel Data System [*Air Force*]
PDS............	Personnel Decontamination Station (MCD)
PDS............	Personnel Delivery System
PDS............	Petroleum Data System [*University of Oklahoma*] [*Databank*] (IID)
PDS............	Petroleum Data System [*Petroleum Information Corp.*] [*Information service or system*] (IID)
PDS............	Pharma-Dokumentations-Service [*Pharma Documentation Service*] [*Information service or system*] (IID)
PDS............	Phased Development Shuttle [*NASA*] (KSC)
PDS............	Photo-Digital Store
PDS............	Photodischarge Spectroscopy (MCD)
PDS............	Photothermal Deflection Spectroscopy (MCD)
PDS............	Planning Data Sheet
PDS............	Planning Data Systems [*Information service or system*] (IID)
PDS............	Plant Data System [*Nuclear energy*] (NRCH)
PDS............	Plasma-Derived Serum
PDS............	Plasma Display (MCD)
PDS............	Plotter Display System (DNAB)
PDS............	Pneumatic Distribution System
PDS............	Polydimethylsiloxane [*Organic chemistry*]
PDS............	Polydioxanone [*Organic chemistry*]
PDS............	Portable Data System (MCD)
PDS............	Portable Duress Sensor (MCD)
PDS............	Position-Determining System
PDS............	Post Design Services [*British*] (RDA)
PDS............	Power Density Spectra (IEEE)
PDS............	Power Distribution System [*or Subsystem*]
PDS............	Power Drive System
PDS............	Preadsorb-Dilute-Shake [*Phage growth method*]
PDS............	Predialyzed Human Serum [*Medicine*] (MAE)
PDS............	Predocketed Special Project (NRCH)
PDS............	Premises Distribution System [*AT & T Corp.*]
PDS............	Priority Distribution System [*Military*] (AFM)
PDS............	Prisoner Detention System
PDS............	Probability Distribution Subprogram [*Data processing*] (BUR)
PDS............	Problem Data System (MCD)
PD/S..........	Problem Definition/Solution
PDS............	Problem Descriptor System
PDS............	Procedures Development Simulator (KSC)
PDS............	Processor Direct Slot [*Data processing*]
PDS............	Procurement Data Sheet
PDS............	Product Design Standard
PDS............	Production Data Sheet (MCD)
PDS............	Professional Development School
PDS............	Professional Development Seminar (HGAA)
PDS............	Professional Development System [*PC software*] [*Microsoft, Inc.*] (PCM)
PDS............	Program Data Sheets [*Army*] (AABC)
PDS............	Program Data Source (BUR)
PDS............	Program Design Specification (CAAL)
PDS............	Program Development Specialist
PDS............	Program Development System [*Data processing*]
PDS............	Program Distribution System
PDS............	Programmable Data Station [*or System*]
PDS............	Propellant Delivery System
PDS............	Propellant Dispersion System (MCD)
PDS............	Protected Distribution System [*Military*] (GFGA)
PdS............	Psychopathic Deviate Subtle [*Psychology*]
PDS............	Pulse Doppler Seeker
PDS............	Punch Driver Selectric
PDS............	Purchasing Department Specification (MSA)
PDS............	Pyrotechnic Devices Simulator (SAA)
PDSA.........	People's Dispensary for Sick Animals [*British*]
PDS-A	Personnel Data System - Airmen [*Air Force*]
PDSA.........	Predesign and Systems Analysis [*NASA*] (KSC)
PDS-A(I) ...	Personnel Data System - Airmen (Interim) [*Air Force*] (AFM)
PDSC.........	PACOM [*Pacific Command*] Data Systems Center (MCD)
PDSC.........	Parti Democrate et Social Chretien [*Zaire*] [*Political party*] (EY)
PDS-C.......	Personnel Data System - Civilian [*Air Force*] (AFM)
PDSC.........	Pressure Differential Scanning Calorimetry [*Analytical technique*]
PDSC.........	Publishers Data Service Corp. [*Monterey, CA*]
PDSD........	Point Detonating Self-Destroying [*Projectile*]
PDSD........	US Department of State Dispatch [*A publication*]
PDSDD.......	Plotting Display Subchannel Data Distributor (MCD)
PDSE........	Production Sample (AAG)
P & DSEC ...	Pioneer and Demolition Section [*Army*]
PDSI..........	Palmer Drought Severity Index [*Meteorology*]
PDSI..........	Performance Data Services, Inc. [*Falls Church, VA*] [*Software manufacture r*]
PDSI..........	Portable Digital Strain Indicator
PDSK........	Petroleum Distribution System - Korea [*Army*] (MCD)
PDSM........	Powder Diffraction Search-Match System [*International Data Center*]
PDS/MAGEN ...	Problem Descriptor System/Matrix Generation [*Programming language*] [*1965*] (CSR)
PDSMS	Point Defense Surface Missile System

PDS-O	Personnel Data System - Officers [*Air Force*] (AFM)
PDSOF	Public Domain Software on File [*Facts on File, Inc.*] [*Information service or system*] (IID)
PDSP.........	Personnel Data System - Planning [*Air Force*] (AFM)
PDSPI.......	Polyurethane Division, Society of the Plastics Industry (EA)
PDSQ........	Point Detonating Super-Quick Fuze (NATG)
PDS-R.......	Parti Democratique Senegalais - Renovation [*Senegalese Democratic Party - Reform*] [*Political party*]
PDSS	Physical Disabilities Special Interest Section [*American Occupational Therapy Association*]
PDSS	Post-Deployment Software System (MCD)
PDST........	Death Studies [*A publication*]
PDST........	Pacific Daylight Saving Time (KSC)
PDSTT	Pulse Doppler Single Target Track [*Military*] (CAAL)
PDT	Pacific Daylight Time
PDT	Panoramic Design Technique
PDT	Parallel Data Transmission
PdT	Parti du Travail [*Labor Party*] [*Switzerland*] [*Political party*] (PPE)
PDT	Patriot Premium Dividend, Inc. II [*NYSE symbol*] (SPSG)
Pd T	Pedagogisk Tidskrift [*A publication*]
PDT	Pendleton [*Oregon*] [*Airport symbol*] (OAG)
PDT	Performance Demonstration Test
PDT	Personal Data Transmitter [*From the movie "Aliens"*]
PDT	Phenyldimethyltriazine [*Organic chemistry*] (AAMN)
PDT	Photodynamic Therapy [*Oncology*]
PDT	Planned Data to Transportation [*DoD*]
PDT	Plasma Display Terminal [*Data processing*]
PDT	Pollable Data Terminal [*Bell System*]
PDT	Population Doubling Time [*Cytology*]
PDT	Posting Data Transfer [*Air Force*] (AFM)
PDT	Power Distribution Trailer (NATG)
PDT	Predelivery Test (MCD)
PDT	Predictor Display Technique
PDT	President Mines [*Vancouver Stock Exchange symbol*]
PDT	Proceedings. European Society of Drug Toxicity [*Elsevier Book Series*] [*A publication*]
PDT	Processed Directional Transmission [*Military*] (NVT)
PDT	Programmable Data Terminal [*Digital Equipment Corp.*] (IEEE)
PDT	Published Data Tape [*A. C. Nielsen Co.*] [*A publication*] (WDMC)
PDT	Pulse Delay Time
PDT	(Pyridyl)diphenyltriazine [*Analytical chemistry*]
PDT-1	Picatinny Arsenal Detonation Trap Number 1 [*Army*] (AABC)
3PDT	Triple-Pole, Double-Throw [*Switch*] (MUGU)
4PDT	Four-Pole, Double-Throw [*Switch*]
PDTA	Production Tape (AAG)
PDTA	Professional Dance Teachers Association (EA)
PDTA	Propylenediaminetetraacetic Acid [*Organic chemistry*]
PDTC	Philadelphia Depository Trust Co.
PDTF........	Program Development and Test Facility [*Social Security Administration*]
PDTMR....	Phalloidin Tetramethylrhodamine [*Biochemistry*]
PDTNBH ..	Paediatrician [*A publication*]
PDTP........	Plasma Display Touch Panel [*Data processing*]
PDTRDV..	Pediatria [*Buenos Aires*] [*A publication*]
PDTS........	Procurement Document Tracking System (MCD)
PDTS........	Program Development Tracking System [*Data processing*]
PDTS........	Programmable Data Terminal Set [*Military*] (CAAL)
PDT & T ..	Post-Delivery Test and Trials [*Military*] (CAAL)
PDTTT	Post-Delivery Test and Trial Team (MCD)
PDU..........	Pacific Democrat Union (EAIO)
PDU..........	Parti Dahomeen de l'Unite [*Dahomean Unity Party*] [*Benin*] [*Political party*]
PDU..........	Parti Democrate Unifie [*Unified Democratic Party*] [*Name replaced by Section Voltaique de Rassemblement*] [*Burkina Faso*] [*Political party*]
PDU..........	Paysandu [*Uruguay*] [*Airport symbol*] (OAG)
PDU..........	Phase Demodulation Unit
PDU..........	Photomultiplier Detector Unit (KSC)
PDU..........	Pilot's Display Unit (MCD)
PDU..........	Power Distribution Unit (AAG)
PDU..........	Power Drive Unit (MCD)
PDU..........	Pressure Distribution Unit
PDU..........	Process Demonstration Unit [*Chemical engineering*]
PDU..........	Process Development Unit [*Chemical engineering*]
PDU..........	Production Distribution Unit (AAG)
PDU..........	Programmable Delay Unit
PDU..........	Programmable Diagnostic Unit [*TACOM*] [*Army*] (RDA)
PDU..........	Project Development Unit [*Chemical engineering*]
PDU..........	Projection Display Unit
PDU..........	Protocol Data Unit
PDU..........	Pulse Detection Unit (NASA)
PDUFC.....	Pete Duel Universal Friendship Club (EAIO)
PdUP	Partito di Unita Proletaria per il Comunismo [*Democratic Party of Proletarian Unity for Communism*] [*Italy*] [*Political party*] (PPE)
PDur	Papyri Durani (BJA)
PDUR	Predischarge Utilization Review [*Medicine*]
PDV	Parcel Delivery Van

PDV .... Phocine Distemper Virus
PDV .... Polyhedra Derived Virus
PDV .... Ponderosa Ventures, Inc. [*Vancouver Stock Exchange symbol*]
PDV .... Premodulation Processor - Deep Space - Voice
PDV .... Pressure Disconnect Valve   (MCD)
PDV .... Probability of Detection and Verification [*Military*]   (CAAL)
PDV .... Prune Dwarf Virus
PDVN .... Power-Driven
PDW .... Evansville, IN [*Location identifier*] [*FAA*]   (FAAL)
PDW .... Partially Delactosed Whey   (OA)
PDW .... Personal Defense Weapon [*Army*]   (INF)
PDW .... Platelet Distribution Width [*Hematology*]
PDW .... Priority Delayed Weather [*Aviation*]   (FAAC)
PDWHF .... Platelet-Derived Wound-Healing Factor [*Biochemistry*]
PDWP....... Partially Delactosed Whey Powder   (OA)
PDX .... Passive Dosimeter Experiment   (KSC)
PDX .... Place Decrement in Index
PDX .... Poloidal Divertor Experiment [*Princeton University*]
PDX .... Portland [*Oregon*] [*Airport symbol*]   (OAG)
PDX .... Prado Explorations Ltd. [*Toronto Stock Exchange symbol*]
PDX .... Private Digital Exchange
PDY .... Piccadilly Resources Ltd. [*Vancouver Stock Exchange symbol*]
PDY .... Principal Duty [*Military*]
PDZ .... Ontario, CA [*Location identifier*] [*FAA*]   (FAAL)
PDZ .... Pedernales [*Venezuela*] [*Airport symbol*]   (OAG)
PdZ .... Perspektiven der Zukunft [*A publication*]
PDZBDD... Publicaciones. Departamento de Zoologia [*Barcelona*] [*A publication*]
PDZI.......... Przeglad Zachodni [*A publication*]
PE .... British Aircraft Corp. Ltd. [*ICAO aircraft manufacturer identifier*]   (ICAO)
PE .... Easton Area Public Library, Easton, PA [*Library symbol*] [*Library of Congress*]   (LCLS)
PE .... Ice Pellets [*Meteorology*]
PE .... Pacific Electric Railway [*AAR code*]
PE .... Packaging Engineering [*A publication*]
PE .... Page-End Character [*Data processing*]
PE .... Paper Electrophoresis [*Medicine*]   (MAE)
PE .... Parabolic Equation
PE .... Parity Error
PE .... Partes Aequales [*Equal Parts*] [*Pharmacy*]
PE .... Patrol Vessel, Eagle [*Eagle boat*] [*Navy symbol*] [*Obsolete*]
PE .... Peacetime Establishment [*Military*]   (NATG)
Pe .... Peclet Number [*IUPAC*]
PE .... Pectinesterase [*Also, PME*] [*An enzyme*]
Pe .... Pelagius [*Deceased, 1232*] [*Authority cited in pre-1607 legal work*]   (DSA)
PE .... Pennsylvania English [*A publication*]
Pe .... Pentyl [*Biochemistry*]
PE .... Percussionist [*A publication*]
PE .... Period Ending
PE .... Periodic   (AAG)
PE .... Peripheral Equipment   (AAG)
PE .... Periscope
PE .... Peritoneal Exudate [*Medicine*]
PE .... Perkin Elmer Corp.
PE .... Permanent Echo [*RADAR*]
PE .... Permissible Error   (ADA)
PE .... Perry Ellis [*Fashion designer, 1940-86*]
PE .... Persistent Estrus [*Endocrinology*]
PE .... Personal Effects
PE .... Personal Equipment
PE .... Personnel, Enlisted [*or Enlisted Personnel Division*] [*Coast Guard*]
PE .... Personnel Equipment [*Air Force*]   (AFM)
PE .... Personnel Equivalent [*DoD*]
PE .... Personnel Executive [*A publication*]
pe............... Peru [*MARC country of publication code*] [*Library of Congress*]   (LCCP)
PE .... Peru [*ANSI two-letter standard code*]   (CNC)
Pe .... Perylene [*Organic chemistry*]   (AAMN)
PE .... Petroleum Economist [*London*] [*A publication*]   (BJA)
PE .... Petroleum Engineer
Pe .... Petrus de Bellapertica [*Deceased, 1308*] [*Authority cited in pre-1607 legal work*]   (DSA)
Pe .... Petrus Hispanus [*Authority cited in pre-1607 legal work*]   (DSA)
PE .... Pharmacopaeia Edinensis [*Edinburgh Pharmacopoeia*] [*A publication*]   (ROG)
PE .... Pharyngoesophageal [*Medicine*]
PE .... Phase Encoding [*Magnetic tape recording*] [*Data processing*]   (MDG)
PE .... Phenylephrine
PE .... Philadelphia Electric Co. [*NYSE symbol*]   (SPSG)
PE .... Philadelphia Stock Exchange   (CDAI)
PE .... Philippine Educator [*A publication*]
PE .... Phoenix Air Service GmbH, Munchen [*West Germany*] [*ICAO designator*]   (FAAC)
PE .... Phosphatidylethanolamine [*Biochemistry*]
PE .... Photoelectric
PE .... Photoemission [*Physics*]

PE .... Photographic Effect   (MAE)
PE .... Photon Echo [*Spectroscopy*]
PE .... Phycoerythrin [*Biochemistry*]
PE .... Physical Education
PE .... Physical Evaluation [*Medicine*]   (MAE)
PE .... Physical Examination
PE .... Physiological Ecology
PE .... Pictorial Eleven [*Later, PES*] [*An association*]   (EA)
PE .... Pigment Epithelium [*of the retina*]
P & E .... Pike and Eel [*A pub at Cambridge University*] [*British*]   (DSUE)
PE .... Pilot Error
PE .... Pinion End
PE .... Pistol Expert
PE .... Planetary Explorer [*NASA*]
PE .... Planification de l'Emploi [*Canadian Jobs Strategy - CJS*]
P/E .... Planning Economics Group, Boston [*Information service or system*]   (IID)
PE .... Planning Estimate
P & E .... Planning and Estimating   (AAG)
PE .... Plant Engineering   (AAG)
PE .... Plant Equipment   (MCD)
PE .... Plant Extrusion   (OA)
PE .... Plasma Emission [*Spectrophotometry*]
PE .... Plasma Exchange [*Medicine*]
PE .... Plastic Explosive   (NATG)
PE .... Pleural Effusion [*Medicine*]
PE .... Poesia Espanola [*A publication*]
PE .... Politique Etrangere [*A publication*]
PE .... Pollen Equivalent [*Immunology*]
PE .... Polyelectrolyte [*Organic chemistry*]
PE .... Polyethylene [*Organic chemistry*]
PE .... Porcelain Enamel [*Technical drawings*]
PE .... Port of Embarkation [*Military*]
P of E .... Port of Embarkation [*Military*]
PE .... Port Engineer   (DNAB)
PE .... Portable Executable File [*Data processing*]
P of E .... Portal of Entry [*Bacteriology*]
PE .... Position Effect [*Parapsychology*]
PE .... Position Error
PE .... Positive Expulsion   (SAA)
PE .... Post Engineer [*Army*]   (AABC)
PE .... Post Exchange [*Marine Corps*]
PE .... Postexposure [*Medicine*]
PE .... Potato Eaters   (EA)
PE .... Potential Energy
PE .... Potential Excess [*of stock*] [*DoD*]
PE .... Powdered Extract [*Pharmacy*]
PE .... Practical Exercise
PE .... Pre-Eclampsia [*Medicine*]
PE .... Pre-Emption [*Telecommunications*]   (TEL)
P-E .... Precipitation-Evaporation
PE .... Preliminary Evaluation
PE .... Preliminary Exploitation   (MCD)
PE .... Presiding Elder
PE .... Pressure Enclosure   (MCD)
Pe .... Pressure on Expiration [*Medicine*]
P/E............ Price [*or Profit*]/Earnings Ratio [*Relation between price of a company's stock and its annual net income*]
PE .... Priced Exhibit   (MCD)
PE .... Primary Electricity
PE .... Prime Equipment
PE .... Primitive Endoderm [*Cytology*]
PE .... Primitive Equation
PE .... Prince Edward Island [*Canadian province*] [*Postal code*]
PE .... Principal Engineer   (AAG)
PE .... Printer's Error
P & E .... Privileges and Elections Subcommittee [*US Senate*]
PE .... Probable Error [*Statistics*]
PE .... Problems of Economics [*A publication*]
PE .... Procedures Evaluation [*DoD*]
PE .... Processing Element [*of central processing unit*]
PE .... Procurement Executive [*British*]
P & E .... Procurement and Expedition
PE .... Production Engineering
PE .... Production Engineering Division [*Frankford Arsenal*] [*Philadelphia, PA*]
PE .... Production Executive [*British*]
PE .... Professional Education   (AFM)
PE .... Professional Engineer
P/E .... Professional and Executive [*Employment register*] [*British*]
PE .... Program Element   (AFM)
PE .... Program Evaluation   (OICC)
PE .... Programmed Exciter
PE .... Project Engineer
PE .... Project Equality   (EA)
PE .... Prometheus-Europe [*Paris, France*]   (EAIO)
P & E .... Propellants and Explosives [*Military*]   (AABC)
PE .... Proponent Evaluation   (MCD)
PE .... Protect Enable [*Data processing*]   (PCM)
PE .... Protected Environment

PE .... Protestant Episcopal
PE .... Proteus Engine [Hovercraft]
PE .... Proton Event
PE .... Pseudomonas Exotoxin [Bacterial toxin]
PE .... Pulley End
PE .... Pulmonary Edema [Medicine]
PE .... Pulmonary Effusion [Medicine]
PE .... Pulmonary Embolism [Medicine]
PE .... Pulse Echo [Materials research]
PE .... Pulse Encoding [Data processing]
PE .... Punta Europa [A publication]
PE .... Purchased Equipment
PE .... Pyroelectric
P & E........ Pyrotechnical and Explosive [NASA]   (KSC)
Pe .... Warner-Lambert Pharmaceutical Co. [Research code symbol]
2PE .... Two-Pulse Photon Echo [Spectroscopy]
PEA .... Papillary Eccrine Adenoma [Oncology]
PEA .... Parking Enforcement Aide   (ECON)
PEA .... Pattern Error Analysis
PEA .... Patterson Experimental Array   (MCD)
PEA .... Payload Enclosure Assembly   (MCD)
Pea .... Peake's English Nisi Prius Reports [1790-1812] [A
                 publication]   (DLA)
PEA .... Pella, IA [Location identifier] [FAA]   (FAAL)
PEA .... Penneshaw [Australia] [Airport symbol]   (OAG)
PEA .... Phenethyl Alcohol [Organic chemistry]
PEA .... Phenylethanolamine [Organic chemistry]
PEA .... Phenylethylamine [Biochemistry]
PEA .... Phosphoethanolamine [Organic chemistry]
PE(A)........ Physical Education (Association) [British]
PEA .... Pilot's Employment Agency
PEA .... Pitch Error Amplifier
PEA .... Plant Engineering Agency
PEA .... Plastics Engineers Association [Defunct]   (EA)
PEA .... Platform Electronics Assembly   (KSC)
PEA .... Poly(ethyl Acrylate) [Organic chemistry]
PEA .... Portuguese East Africa [Mozambique]
PEA .... Potash Export Association   (EA)
PEA .... Preliminary Environmental Assessment   (MCD)
PEA .... Primary Expense Account
PEA .... Private Employment Agency   (OICC)
PEA .... Process Environmental Analysis
PEA .... Process Equipment Accessory   (MCD)
PEA .... Program Element Administrator [Navy]   (NG)
PEA .... Progressive Education Association [Defunct]
PEA .... Public Education Association
PEA .... Push-Effective Address [Data processing]   (IEEE)
PEA .... Pyridylethylamine [Organic chemistry]
Pea (2)....... Peake's Additional Cases Nisi Prius [170 English Reprint]
                 [1795-1812] [A publication]   (DLA)
PEAA........ Program Elements Activity Accounts   (MCD)
P/EA(A)3 .. Probationary Electrical Artificer (Air) 3rd Class [British
                 military]   (DMA)
Pea Add Cas ... Peake's English Nisi Prius Reports [Vol. 2] [A
                 publication]   (DLA)
PEABA...... Petroleum Abstracts [A publication]
Peab L Rev ... Peabody Law Review [A publication]   (DLA)
Peabody J E ... Peabody Journal of Education [A publication]
Peabody J Ed ... Peabody Journal of Education [A publication]
Peabody J Educ ... Peabody Journal of Education [A publication]
Peabody Mus Nat Hist Yale Univ Bull ... Peabody Museum of Natural
                 History. Yale University. Bulletin [A publication]
PEAC........ Photoelectric Auto Collimator
PEAC........ Photoelectroanalytical Chemistry
PEACA...... Progress in Nuclear Energy. Series 9 [A publication]
Peace........ Peace Newsletter [A publication]
Peace.......... Peace/Non-Violence [A publication]
PEACE...... People Emerging Against Corrupt Establishments
                 [Underground military newspaper]
PEACE...... Project Evaluation and Assistance, Civil Engineering [Air
                 Force]
Peaceful Nucl Explos ... Peaceful Nuclear Explosions. Proceedings of a
                 Technical Committee [A publication]
Peacemak... Peacemaker [A publication]
Peace Nws ... Peace News [A publication]
PeaceResAb ... Peace Research Abstracts [A publication]
Peace Res Abstr J ... Peace Research Abstracts Journal [A publication]
Peace Res Ja ... Peace Research in Japan [A publication]
Peace Res Rev ... Peace Research Reviews [A publication]
PEACESAT ... Pan-Pacific Education and Communication Experiments by
                 Satellites [University of Hawaii] [NASA]
Peace and Sci ... Peace and the Sciences [A publication]
Peace Science Soc Internat Pas ... Peace Science Society. International Papers
                 [A publication]
PEACU...... Plastic Energy Absorption in Compression Unit   (IEEE)
PEAD........ Presidential Emergency Action Document
PEADS ...... Presidential Emergency Action Direction System   (MCD)
Peake .... Peake's Cases [1790-1812] [A publication]   (DLA)
Peake Add Cas ... Peake's Additional Cases Nisi Prius [1795-1812] [A
                 publication]   (DLA)
Peake Ev ... Peake on the Law of Evidence [A publication]   (DLA)

Peake NP... Peake's English Nisi Prius Cases [170 English Reprint] [A
                 publication]   (DLA)
Peake NP Add Cas ... Peake's Additional Cases Nisi Prius [170 English
                 Reprint] [England] [A publication]   (DLA)
Peake NP Add Cas (Eng) ... Peake's Additional Cases Nisi Prius [170 English
                 Reprint] [England] [A publication]   (DLA)
Peake NP Cas ... Peake's English Nisi Prius Cases [170 English Reprint]
                 [1790-1812] [A publication]   (DLA)
Peake NP Cas (Eng) ... Peake's English Nisi Prius Cases [170 English Reprint]
                 [A publication]   (DLA)
PEAL........ Early American Literature [A publication]
PEAL........ Petro-Global, Inc. [NASDAQ symbol]   (NQ)
PEAL........ Publishing, Entertainment, Advertising, and Allied Fields Law
                 Quarterly [A publication]
PEALQ...... Publishing, Entertainment, Advertising, and Allied Fields Law
                 Quarterly [A publication]
PEAM....... Personal Electronic Aid for Maintenance [Military]
Pea MS ...... Peachey on Marriage Settlements [1860] [A
                 publication]   (DLA)
PEAMUSE ... Peabody Museum of Archaeology and Ethnology [Harvard
                 University] [Research center]   (RCD)
PEANA...... Proceedings. Easter School in Agricultural Science. University
                 of Nottingham [A publication]
Pe de Ancar ... Petrus de Ancharano [Deceased, 1416] [Authority cited in pre-
                 1607 legal work]   (DSA)
Pe de Anch ... Petrus de Ancharano [Deceased, 1416] [Authority cited in pre-
                 1607 legal work]   (DSA)
Pe de Ancha ... Petrus de Ancharano [Deceased, 1416] [Authority cited in pre-
                 1607 legal work]   (DSA)
Peanut J Nut World ... Peanut Journal and Nut World [A publication]
Peanut Sci ... Peanut Science [A publication]
PEAP......... Pad Emergency Air Pack [NASA]   (KSC)
PEAP........ Pesticide Education and Action Project   (EA)
PEAP........ Principal Error Axis for Position
PEAP........ Program Evaluation Analysis Plan   (MCD)
PeAR......... Die Provinzeinteilung des Assyrischen Reiches [A
                 publication]   (BJA)
Pearce CC .. Pearce's Reports in Dearsley's English Crown Cases [A
                 publication]   (DLA)
Pearce-Sellards Ser Tex Mem Mus ... Pearce-Sellards Series. Texas Memorial
                 Museum [A publication]
PEARL ...... Committee for Public Education and Religious Liberty   (EA)
PEARL ...... Performance Evaluation of Amplifiers from a Remote Location
PEARL ...... Periodicals Automation, Rand Library
PEARL ...... Personal Equipment and Rescue/Survivable Lowdown   (MCD)
PEARL ...... Process and Experiment Automation Real-Time Language
                 [Data processing]
PEARL ...... Program for EPS [Electrical Power System] Analysis and Rapid
                 Look-Ahead [NASA computer program]
PEARL ...... Programmed Editor and Automated Resources for Learning
PEARLA ... Pupils Equal and React to Light and Accomodation [Medicine]
Pears .... Pearson's Reports [1850-80] [Pennsylvania] [A
                 publication]   (DLA)
Pearson ...... Pearson's Common Pleas [Pennsylvania] [A
                 publication]   (DLA)
Pears (PA) ... Pearson's Reports [1850-80] [Pennsylvania] [A
                 publication]   (DLA)
PEART ...... Passive Electronic Advanced Receiver   (MCD)
PEAS .... Physical Estimation and Attraction Scales
PEAS .... Policy and External Affairs Staff [Environmental Protection
                 Agency]   (GFGA)
PEAS .... Presbyterian Educational Association of the South
                 [Defunct]   (EA)
Peasant Stud Newsl ... Peasant Studies Newsletter [A publication]
PEAT........ Phenylethanolaminotetralin [Organic chemistry]
PEAT........ Pricing Evaluation for Audit Technique [Finance]
PEAT........ Programme Elargi d'Assistance Technique [Expanded Program
                 of Technical Assistance] [United Nations]
PEAT........ Programmer Exercised Autopilot Test   (AAG)
Peat Abstr ... Peat Abstracts [A publication]
Peat Plant Yearb ... Peat and Plant Yearbook [A publication]
PEAV........ Principal Error Axis for Velocity
PE B.......... Bachelor of Pedagogy   (ROG)
Pe B........... Bachelor of Pediatrics
PEB........... Parametric Empirical Bayes [Statistics]
Peb .... Pebble [A publication]
PEB........... Pebble [Jewelry]   (ROG)
PEB........... Pebble Gold Resources [Vancouver Stock Exchange symbol]
PEB........... Pensioners' Employment Bureau [British]
PEB........... Performance Evaluation Board [NASA]   (MCD)
PEB........... Philippine Economy Bulletin [A publication]
PEB........... Phycoerythrobilin [Biochemistry]
PEB........... Physical Evaluation Board [Military]
PEB........... Population-Environment Balance   (EA)
PEB........... Porcelain Enamel Bath [Classified advertising]   (ADA)
PEB........... Positive Expulsion Bladder
PEB........... Pre-Expanded Bin   (DNAB)
PEB........... Production Efficiency Board [British] [World War II]
PEB........... Propulsion Examining Board [Navy]   (NVT)
PEB........... Prototype Environmental Buoy [Marine science]   (MSC)
PEB........... Psycho-Educational Battery [Educational test]

PEB............ Pulmonary Ectopic Beat [Cardiology]
PEB............ Pulsed Electron Beam   (IEEE)
PEBA......... Polyether Block Amide [Plastics technology]
PEBA......... Pulsed Electron Beam Annealer [Photovoltaic energy systems]
PEBA......... Purified Extract of Brucella abortus
PEBAB....... Para-(Ethoxybenzylidene)aminobenzonitrile [Also, EBCA]
            [Organic chemistry]
PEB & B .... Porcelain Enamel Bath and Basin [Classified
            advertising]   (ADA)
PEBB......... Public Employees Blanket Bond
PEBCO...... Program Evaluation and Budget Committee [American Library
            Association]
PEBD......... Pay Entry Base Date
Pe de Bel .... Petrus de Bellapertica [Deceased, 1308] [Authority cited in pre-
            1607 legal work]   (DSA)
Pe de Belper ... Petrus de Bellapertica [Deceased, 1308] [Authority cited in
            pre-1607 legal work]   (DSA)
Pe de Bepe ... Petrus de Bellapertica [Deceased, 1308] [Authority cited in pre-
            1607 legal work]   (DSA)
PEBES....... Personal Earning and Benefit Estimate Statement [Social
            Security Administration]
PEBG......... Phenethylbiguanide [Same as PEDG] [Antidiabetic compound]
PEBH......... Physical Evaluation Board Hospital [Military]
PEBIDN .... Perspectives in Biometrics [A publication]
PEBK......... Peoples Bank [Newton, NC] [NASDAQ symbol]   (NQ)
PEBL......... Port Everglades Belt Line Railway [AAR code] [Obsolete]
PEBLO....... Physical Evaluation Board Liaison Officer [Air Force]   (AFM)
Pe de Blpti ... Petrus de Bellapertica [Deceased, 1308] [Authority cited in pre-
            1607 legal work]   (DSA)
PEBS .... Pulsed Electron Beam Source   (MCD)
PEBV......... Pea Early-Browning Virus [Plant pathology]
PEBW....... People's Bancorp of Worcester, Inc. [NASDAQ symbol]   (NQ)
PEC............ Aero Sport [Vancouver, WA] [FAA designator]   (FAAC)
PEC............ American Irish Political Education Committee   (EA)
PEc............ Ellwood City Area Public Library, Ellwood City, PA [Library
            symbol] [Library of Congress]   (LCLS)
PEC............ IEEE Power Electronics Council   (EA)
PEC............ Pacific Command Electronic Intelligence Center   (MCD)
PEC............ Pacific Economic Community   (FEA)
PEC............ Palestine Economic Commission
PEC............ Panasonic Energy Corp. [Vancouver Stock Exchange symbol]
PEC............ Passive Equipment Cabinet [Military]   (CAAL)
PEC............ Peak Electrode Current
PEC............ Pectoral [Lungs and Chest] [Medicine]   (ROG)
PEC............ Pedal Excretory Cell
PEC............ Pelican [Alaska] [Airport symbol]   (OAG)
PEC............ Pennsylvania Engineering Corp. [AMEX symbol]   (SPSG)
PEC............ Perfil de Evaluacion del Comportamiento [Standardized test of
            elementary through high school students' behavior at
            school, at home, and with peers]
PEC............ Peritoneal Exudate Cells [Hematology]
PEC............ Perkin-Elmer Corp.   (MCD)
PEC............ Perris [California] [Seismograph station code, US Geological
            Survey]   (SEIS)
PEC............ Persistent Early Curvature
PEC............ Personal Education Counseling   (DNAB)
PEC............ Personal Effects Coverage [Insurance]
PEC............ Petro-Canada
PEC............ Phenylene Ether Copolymer [Organic chemistry]
PECUS........ Photoelectric Cell
PEC............ Photoelectrochemical Cell [Energy conversion device]
PEC............ Physics, Engineering, and Chemistry   (AAG)
PEC............ Pigmented Emulsified Creosote
PEC............ Planetary Entry Capsule [Aerospace]
PEC............ Plant Equipment Codes [DoD]
PEC............ Platform Electron Card [Electronics]   (OA)
PeC............ Poesia e Critica [A publication]
PEC............ Polish Economic News [A publication]
PEC............ Positive Engagement Clutch
PEC............ Potasse et Engrais Chimiques
PEC............ Potential Enviromental Concentration [Pollution technology]
PEC............ Predicted Environmental Concentration   (DCTA)
PEC............ Presbyterian Evangelical Coalition   (EA)
PEC............ Previous Element Coding
PEC............ Production Equipment Code [Military]
PEC............ Production Executive Committee
PEC............ Program Element Code   (AFM)
PEC............ Program Environment Control
PEC............ Program Evaluation Center [Navy]   (AFIT)
PEC............ Propulsion Environmental Chamber
PEC............ Prova Elementi Combustibili [An Italian fast reactor]
PEC............ Pugwash Etudiant du Canada
PEC............ Pyridylethylcysteine [Biochemistry]
PEC............ Pyrogenic Exotoxin C [Medicine]
PECA......... Petroleum Equipment Contractors Association   (EA)
Peca........... Petrus de Bellapertica [Deceased, 1308] [Authority cited in pre-
            1607 legal work]   (DSA)
PECAD4.... Pediatric Cardiology [A publication]
PECAM...... Platelet-Endothelial Cell Adhesion Molecule [Cytology]
PECAN...... Pulse Envelop Correlation Air Navigation
Pecan Q...... Pecan Quarterly [A publication]

PE CARD .. Production Estimate Card   (MSA)
PECBI....... Professional Engineers Conference Board for Industry   (EA)
PECC........ Journal of Ecclesiastical History [A publication]
PECC........ Panel of Experts on Climatic Change [WMO]   (MSC)
PECC......... Precanceled Envelope Collectors Club   (EA)
PECC......... Product Engineering Control Center
            [Telecommunications]   (TEL)
PECDS...... Professional Engineering Career Development Series [Book
            series]
PECE......... Proposed Engineering Change Estimate
PECF .... Pseudoextracellular Fluid [for biocompatibility testing]
PECFA ...... Presidential Election Campaign Fund Act of 1966
PECG......... Economic Geography [A publication]
PECH .... Economic History Review [A publication]
PECHA ..... Petroleum Chemistry USSR [English Translation] [A
            publication]
Peche Mar ... Peche Maritime [A publication]
Peche Marit ... Peche Maritime [A publication]
Pecho .... Prostatic Echogram [Medicine]   (AAMN)
PECI .... Preliminary Equipment Component Index [or Inventory]
PECI .... Productivity Enhancing Capital Investment [DoD]
PECIP....... Productivity Enhancing Capital Investment Program   (MCD)
Peck .... Peck's Reports [24-30 Illinois] [A publication]   (DLA)
Peck .... Peck's Reports [7 Tennessee] [1921-24] [A publication]   (DLA)
Peck .... Peckwell's English Election Cases [1802-06] [A
            publication]   (DLA)
Peck El Cas ... Peckwell's English Election Cases [A publication]   (DLA)
Peck Elec Cas ... Peckwell's English Election Cases [1802-06] [A
            publication]   (DLA)
Peck (Ill).... Peck's Reports, Illinois Supreme Court Reports [11-22, 24-30]
            [A publication]   (DLA)
Peck (Tenn) ... Peck's Reports [7 Tennessee] [A publication]   (DLA)
Peck Tr ...... Peck's Trial (Impeachment) [A publication]   (DLA)
Peckw....... Peckwell's English Election Cases [A publication]   (DLA)
PECL........ Preliminary Engineering Configuration List
PECM........ Journal of Ecumenical Studies [A publication]
PECM....... Passive Electronics Countermeasures [Military]   (NG)
PECM....... Preliminary Engineering Change Memorandum [Air
            Force]   (CET)
PECN........ Publishers Equipment Corp. [NASDAQ symbol]   (NQ)
PECO .... Pays d'Europe Centrale et Orientale   (ECON)
PECO .... Peace Country [Grande Prairie, Alberta] [A publication]
PECO .... Pecos National Monument
PECO .... Premier Energy Corp. [NASDAQ symbol]   (NQ)
PECOS ...... Pentagon Computer Operations Support   (MCD)
PECOS ...... Program Environment Checkout System
PECOS ..... Project Evaluation and Control System   (MCD)
PECP .... Preliminary Engineering Change Proposal
PECR........ Program Error Correction Report
Pe Cri .... Petrus Crispanus [Authority cited in pre-1607 legal
            work]   (DSA)
PECS .... Plant Engineering Check Sheet   (AAG)
PECS .... Portable Environmental Control System [NASA]
PECS .... Princeton Encyclopedia of Classical Sites [A publication]
Pecsi Muesz Sz ... Pecsi Mueszaki Szemle [Hungary] [A publication]
PECT........ Pectori [To the Chest] [Pharmacy]
PECTFE..... Polyethylene-Chlorotrifluoroethylene [Organic chemistry]
PECU...... Ecumenical Review [A publication]
PECUL...... Peculiar   (ROG)
PECUS ...... Personal Engineering Computer User's Society   (EA)
PECUY...... Pecuniary   (ROG)
PECVD...... Plasma-Enhanced Chemical Vapor Deposition [Coating
            technology]
PECWBS... Proposed Extended Contract Work Breakdown Structure
            [Military]
PECWG..... Piaster Expenditure Control Working Group [Military]
Ped .... Pedagogia [A publication]
PED .... Pedagogue
PED .... Pedal
PED .... Peddler [or Peddling] [FBI standardized term]
PED .... Pedestal   (AAG)
PED .... Pedestrian
PED .... Pediatrics   (AABC)
PED .... Pedlary   (ROG)
PED .... Pedro Aguirre Cerda [Antarctica] [Seismograph station code,
            US Geological Survey] [Closed]   (SEIS)
PED .... Period End Date   (MCD)
PED .... Personnel Equipment Data [Army]
PED .... Photoemission Diode
PEd .... Physical Education
PED .... Positive Expulsion Device
PED .... Production Eligibility Date   (MUGU)
PED .... Production Engineering Division [University of Wisconsin -
            Madison] [Research center]   (RCD)
PED .... Program Element Description
PED .... Program Element Directive
PED .... Program Evaluation Division [Environmental Protection
            Agency]   (GFGA)
PED .... Program Execution Directive   (AAG)
PED .... Promotion Eligibility Date [Military]
PED .... Proton-Enhanced Diffusion

PED .... Public Employee Department (of AFL-CIO)   (EA)
PEd .... Pulmonary Edema [*Medicine*]
PED .... Pulse Edge Discrimination   (OA)
PED .... Pure Edge Dislocation
PED .... Pyramid Element Designator
PED .... Springfield, TN [*Location identifier*] [*FAA*]   (FAAL)
PEDA .... Pedal Artery
PEDA .... Personnel Equipment Data Analysis
Pedag Meddel ... Pedagogiska Meddelanden fran Skoloeverstyrelsen [*A publication*]
Pedagog Fak Plzni Sb Ser Chem ... Pedagogicka Fakulta v Plzni. Sbornik. Serie Chemie [*A publication*]
Pedagog Sem ... Pedagogical Seminary [*A publication*]
Pedag i Psihol ... Pedagogika i Psihologija [*A publication*]
Pedag Szle ... Pedagogiai Szemle [*A publication*]
Pedag Tidskr ... Pedagogisk Tidskrift [*A publication*]
Ped Akus Ginek ... Pediatriia, Akusherstvo, i Ginekologiia [*A publication*]
Ped B .... Bachelor of Pedagogy
PEDB .... Payload Engineering Data Base [*NASA*]   (SSD)
PEDB .... Process Engineering Database
PEDBA9 .... Pediatria [*Bucharest*] [*A publication*]
PEDC .... Personal Effects Distribution Center
Ped Cal ...... Pediatria in Calabria [*A publication*]
Ped Clin NA ... Pediatric Clinics of North America [*A publication*]
PEDCUG... Planning Engineers Desktop Computer Users Group   (EA)
Ped D .... Doctor of Pedagogy
PEDD .... Program Element Descriptive Data   (CAAL)
PEddyB...... Baldwin Locomotive Works, Eddystone, PA [*Library symbol*] [*Library of Congress*] [*Obsolete*]   (LCLS)
PEDET ...... Pedetemptim [*Gradually*] [*Pharmacy*]
PEDF .... Potential-Energy Distribution Function [*Physical chemistry*]
PEDG .... Phenethyldiguanide [*Same as PEBG*] [*Antidiabetic compound*]
PEDI .... Pediatrics [*Medicine*]   (DHSM)
Pedia .... Pediatrics [*A publication*]
Pediat Akush Ginek ... Pediatriia, Akusherstvo, i Ginekologiia [*A publication*]
Pediat Clins N Am ... Pediatric Clinics of North America [*A publication*]
Pediat Inf ... Pediatric Infectious Disease [*A publication*]
Pediat Nurs ... Pediatric Nursing [*A publication*]
Pediatr Adolesc Endocrinol ... Pediatric and Adolescent Endocrinology [*A publication*]
Pediatr Adolesc Gynecol ... Pediatric and Adolescent Gynecology [*A publication*]
Pediatr Akush Ginekol ... Pediatriia, Akusherstvo, i Ginekologiia [*A publication*]
Pediatr Ann ... Pediatric Annals [*A publication*]
Pediatr Cardiol ... Pediatric Cardiology [*A publication*]
Pediatr Clin N Am ... Pediatric Clinics of North America [*A publication*]
Pediatr Clin North Am ... Pediatric Clinics of North America [*A publication*]
Pediatr Contin Educ Courses Pract ... Pediatric Continuing Education Courses for the Practitioner [*A publication*]
Pediatr Dent ... Pediatric Dentistry [*A publication*]
Pediatr Dermatol ... Pediatric Dermatology [*A publication*]
Pediatr Emerg Care ... Pediatric Emergency Care [*A publication*]
Pediat Res ... Pediatric Research [*A publication*]
Pediatr Esp ... Pediatria Espanola [*A publication*]
Pediatria Arch ... Pediatria. Archivio di Patologia e Clinica Pediatrica [*A publication*]
Pediatrics Suppl ... Pediatrics Supplement [*A publication*]
Pediatr Infect Dis ... Pediatric Infectious Disease [*A publication*]
Pediatr Int ... Pediatria Internazionale [*A publication*]
Pediatr Listy ... Pediatricke Listy [*A publication*]
Pediatr Med Chir ... Pediatria Medica e Chirurgica [*A publication*]
Pediatr Mod ... Pediatria Moderna [*A publication*]
Pediatr Nephrol ... Pediatric Nephrology [*A publication*]
Pediatr Neurosci ... Pediatric Neuroscience [*A publication*]
Pediatr News ... Pediatric News [*A publication*]
Pediatr Nurs ... Pediatric Nursing [*A publication*]
Pediatr Nurse Pract ... Pediatric Nurse Practitioner [*A publication*]
Pediatr Pathol ... Pediatric Pathology [*A publication*]
Pediatr Pharmacol ... Pediatric Pharmacology [*A publication*]
Pediatr Pol ... Pediatria Polska [*A publication*]
Pediatr Prat ... Pediatria Pratica [*A publication*]
Pediatr Pulmonol ... Pediatric Pulmonology [*A publication*]
Pediatr Radiol ... Pediatric Radiology [*A publication*]
Pediatr Res ... Pediatric Research [*A publication*]
Pediatr Update ... Pediatrics Update [*A publication*]
PEDIEY .... Pedoatrocoam [*A publication*]
PEDIN....... Peapod Dinghy
P Edin Math ... Proceedings. Edinburgh Mathematical Society [*A publication*]
Ped Int .... Pediatria Internazionale [*A publication*]
PE Dir....... Physical Education Director
PEdiS......... Edinboro State College, Edinboro, PA [*Library symbol*] [*Library of Congress*]   (LCLS)
PEDL......... Pedicel Length [*Botany*]
Ped M .... Master of Pedagogy
PEDMAN ... PACFLT [*Pacific Fleet*] Enlisted Personnel Distribution Manual   (CINC)
PEDN .... Planned Event Discrepancy Notification [*NASA*]   (KSC)
Pedobiolog ... Pedobiologia [*A publication*]
Pedod Fr .... Pedodontie Francaise [*A publication*]
PEDOL...... Pedology

Pedology (Leningr) ... Pedology (Leningrad) [*A publication*]
PEDP........ Pacific Energy Development Program [*Fiji*] [*United Nations*]
Ped Panam ... Pediatria Panamericana [*A publication*]
PEDRO ..... Pneumatic Energy Detector with Remote Optics
PEDRO ..... Pride, Efficiency, Dedication, Reliability, and Order   (DNAB)
PEDRTC ... Pediatric
PEDS......... Packaging Engineering Data System   (AFM)
PEDS........ Pediatrics
PEDS........ Peltier Effect Diffusion Separation [*Physical chemistry*]
PEDS........ Pilgrim Edward Doty Society   (EA)
PEDS........ Program Element Descriptive Summary   (CAAL)
PEDS........ Protective Equipment Decontamination Section [*Nuclear energy*]   (NRCH)
Ped Sem ..... Pedagogical Seminary [*A publication*]
PEDSTL.... Pedestal [*Freight*]
PEDT........ Pendant [*Jewelry*]   (ROG)
PEDT........ Peridot [*Jewelry*]   (ROG)
PEDTAT ... Pediatriya [*Moscow*] [*A publication*]
PEDUC.... Professeurs d'Economie Domestique des Universites Canadiennes [*Canadian University Teachers of Home Economics - CUTHE*]
P Educator ... Physical Educator [*A publication*]
PEE............ Photoelectron Emission [*Also, OSEE*]
PEE............ Photoemission Effect
PEE............ Pressure Environmental Equipment   (NVT)
PEE............ Program Estimating Equation
PEE............ Proof and Experimental Establishment [*British*]
P & EE ...... Proof and Experimental Establishments   (RDA)
PEE............ Talkeetna, AK [*Location identifier*] [*FAA*]   (FAAL)
PEEA........ (Phenyl)(ethyl)ethanolamine [*Organic chemistry*]
PEEAD...... Promoclim E. Etudes Thermiques et Aerauliques [*A publication*]
PEEC .... Personnel Emergency Estimator Capability
PEEC .... Programmable Electronic Engine Control [*Automotive engineering*]
PEEC .... Project for an Energy-Enriched Curriculum [*Department of Energy*]
PEECD...... Petroleum Economist [*A publication*]
PEEH .... Journal of European Economic History [*A publication*]
PEEIC .... Programme des Economies d'Energie dans l'Industrie Canadienne
PEEID ...... Petroleum Engineer International [*A publication*]
PEEK........ Peek 'n' Peak Recreation, Inc. [*Clymer, NY*] [*NASDAQ symbol*]   (NQ)
PEEK........ People for the Enjoyment of Eyeballing Knees [*Group opposing below-the-knee fashions introduced in 1970*]
PEEK........ Periodically Elevated Electronic Kibitzer
PEEK......... Polyetherketone [*Organic chemistry*]
Peel Valley Hist Soc J ... Peel Valley Historical Society. Journal [*A publication*]   (APTA)
PEEM....... Photoemission Electron Microscope
PEEM....... Photoemission Electron Microscopy   (MCD)
PEEP .... Panel of Experts on Environmental Pollution [*WMO*]   (MSC)
PEEP .... Pilot's Electronic Eyelevel Presentation [*British*]
PEEP .... Porous Electrode Electrostatic Precipitation
PEEP .... Positive End Expiratory Pressure [*Medicine*]
PEEP .... Production Electronic Equipment Procurement Status Report
Peeples & Stevens ... Peeples and Stevens' Reports [*80-97 Georgia*] [*A publication*]   (DLA)
PEEQ........ East European Quarterly [*A publication*]
PEER .... Pediatric Examination of Educational Readiness [*Child development test*]
Peer........... Peerless [*Record label*] [*USA, Mexico*]
PEER .... Planned Experience for Effective Relating
PEER .... Price Escalation Estimated Rates
PEER .... Program of Equal Employment Opportunity Evaluation Reports
PEER .... Project Engineer Evaluation Report   (HGAA)
PEER .... Project on Equal Education Rights   (EA)
PEERAMID ... Pediatric Examination of Educational Readiness at Middle Childhood [*Child development test*] [*Psychology*]
PEERC ...... Production Engineering Education and Research Center
Peere Wms ... Peere-Williams' English Chancery and King's Bench Cases [*1695-1736*] [*A publication*]   (DLA)
PEERTU ... Peerless Tube Co. [*Associated Press abbreviation*]   (APAG)
PEET .... Environmental Ethics [*A publication*]
PEET .... Printing Equipment Education Trust [*British*]
PEEX........ Pediatric Early Elementary Examination [*Child development test*] [*Psychology*]
PEF........... Pacific-European Growth Fund [*AMEX symbol*]   (SPSG)
PEF........... Packaging Education Foundation   (EA)
PEF........... Palestine Endowment Funds [*Later, PEF Israel Endowment Funds*]   (EA)
PEF........... Palestine Exploration Fund
PEF........... Peak Expiratory Flow [*Pulmonary function*]
PEF........... Performance Efficiency Factor   (AFIT)
PEF........... Personal Effects Floater [*Insurance*]
PEF........... Personality Evaluation Form [*Psychology*]
PEF........... Phil Esposito Foundation   (EA)
PEF........... Physical Electronics Facility   (MCD)
PEF........... Plastics Education Foundation   (EA)

PEF........... Polyethylene Foam
PEF........... Potential-Energy Function [*Physical chemistry*]
PEF........... Prediction Error Filter [*Wave frequency and phase modifier*]
PEF........... Presbyterian Evangelistic Fellowship (EA)
PEF........... Pro Ecclesia Foundation (EA)
PEF........... Program Estimating Factor (AFM)
PEF........... Proposal Evaluation Form (AAG)
PEF........... Psychiatric Evaluation Form [*Psychology*]
PEFA......... Palestine Exploration Fund. Annual [*A publication*]
PEFC........ Private Export Funding Corp. (IMH)
PEFCO ..... Private Export Funding Corp.
Pe Fi......... Petrus Filipi [*Authority cited in pre-1607 legal work*] (DSA)
Pe Fili....... Petrus Filipi [*Authority cited in pre-1607 legal work*] (DSA)
PEFM....... Palestine Exploration Fund. Memoirs [*A publication*]
PEF/NET ... Public Education Fund Network (EA)
PEFO........ Payload Effects Follow-On Study [*NASA*] (NASA)
PEFO........ Petrified Forest National Park
PEFOS ..... Program Evaluation and Field Operations Staff [*Environmental Protection Agency*] (GFGA)
PEFQ........ Palestine Exploration Fund. Quarterly Statement [*A publication*]
PEFQS ..... Palestine Exploration Fund. Quarterly Statement [*London*] [*A publication*] (BJA)
PEFQST.... Palestine Exploration Fund. Quarterly Statement [*London*] [*A publication*] (BJA)
PEFR........ Peak Expiratory Flow Rate
PEFSR....... Partial Expiratory Flow-Static Recoil Curve [*Physiology*] (MAE)
PEFT .... Peripheral Equipment Functional Test (CAAL)
PEFT .... Preschool Embedded Figures Test [*Child development test*]
PEFTOK ... Philippine Expeditionary Force to Korea [*United Nations*]
PEFU .... Panel of Experts on Fish Utilization [*FAO*] (ASF)
PEFV .... Partial Expiratory Flow-Volume [*Physiology*]
PEG .... General Analine & Film Co., General Research Laboratory, Easton, PA [*Library symbol*] [*Library of Congress*] [*Obsolete*] (LCLS)
PEG .... Pac Engo Materials [*Vancouver Stock Exchange symbol*]
PEG .... Pacific Environmental Group [*Marine science*] (MSC)
Peg .... Pegaso [*A publication*]
Peg .... Pegasus [*Constellation*]
PEG .... Performance Evaluation Group (CINC)
PEG .... Petrochemical Energy Group (EA)
PEG .... Photo Exploitation Group
PEG .... Pneumatic Explosion Generator
PEG .... Pneumoencephalogram [*Medicine*]
PEG .... Polyethylene Glycol [*Organic chemistry*]
PEG .... Previous Endorsement(s) Guaranteed [*Banking*]
PEG .... Principle of the Equivalent Generator
PEG .... Prior Endorsement Guaranteed (HGAA)
PEG .... Priorities for ELINT Guidance (MCD)
PEG .... Priorities Exploitation Group
PEG .... Process Evaluation Guide [*Graphic Communications Association*]
PEG .... Production Engineering [*A publication*]
PEG .... Production Entitlement Guarantee [*International Agricultural Trade Research Consortium*] (ECON)
PEG .... Program Evaluation Group [*Air Force*]
PEG .... Project Engineering Guide (MCD)
PEG .... Protected Employee Group [*Program*]
PEG .... Protection Engineers Group [*United States Telephone Association*] [*Telecommunications*]
PEG .... Public Service Electric & Gas Co. (CDAI)
PEG .... Public Service Enterprise Group, Inc. [*NYSE symbol*] (SPSG)
PEG .... Pyrotechnic Electron Generator (MCD)
PEGA........ Polyethylene Glycol Adipate [*Organic chemistry*]
PEG-ADA ... Polyethylene Glycol-Adenosine Deaminase [*A modified enzyme*]
PEGDE...... Pentaethylene Glycol Dodecyl Ether [*Organic chemistry*]
PEGE........ Program for Evaluation of Ground Environment
PEGEA...... Petroleum Geology [*English Translation*] [*A publication*]
PEGGLD... Pegasus Gold, Inc. [*Associated Press abbreviation*] (APAG)
PEGLN...... Petiole Gland Pairs, Number Of [*Botany*]
Pegmatitovye Redkomet Mestorozhd ... Pegmatitovye Redkometal'nye Mestorozhdeniya [*A publication*]
PEGR........ Ethnic Groups [*A publication*]
PEGR........ Press Extracts on Greenland [*A publication*]
PEGR........ Proportional Exhaust Gas Recirculation [*Engines*]
PEGS........ Ecologist [*A publication*]
Pegs........... Pegasus [*Constellation*]
PEGS........ Polyethylene Glycol Succinate [*Organic chemistry*]
PEGS........ Project Engineering Graphics System [*Computer Aided Design Centre*] [*Software package*] (NCC)
PEGS........ Publications. English Goethe Society [*A publication*]
PEGY....... Ethnology [*A publication*]
PEH .... Pehpei [*Republic of China*] [*Seismograph station code, US Geological Survey*] (SEIS)
PEH .... Pehuajo [*Argentina*] [*Airport symbol*] (OAG)
PEH .... Periods of European History [*A publication*]
PEH .... Planning Estimate Handbook (SAA)
PEH .... Plus Each Hour [*Aviation*] (FAAC)
PEHA .... Pentaethylenehexamine [*Organic chemistry*]

PEHA .... Pony Express Historical Association (EA)
PEHD .... Polyethylene-High Density [*Organic chemistry*]
PEHI .... Journal of Economic History [*A publication*]
PEHi......... Northampton County Historical and Genealogical Society, Mary Illick Memorial Library, Easton, PA [*Library symbol*] [*Library of Congress*] (LCLS)
Pe His .... Petrus Hispanus [*Authority cited in pre-1607 legal work*] (DSA)
PEHPA..... Progress in Nuclear Energy. Series 12 [*A publication*]
PEHQ....... European History Quarterly [*A publication*]
PEHR .... English Historical Review [*A publication*]
PEHYA ..... Petroleum and Hydrocarbons [*A publication*]
PEI............ Haszard and Warburton's Reports. Prince Edward Island [*Canada*] [*A publication*]
PeI............ Parole e le Idee [*A publication*]
PEI............ Patriotic Education, Inc. (EA)
PEI............ Peine [*Chile*] [*Seismograph station code, US Geological Survey*] [*Closed*] (SEIS)
PEI............ Pennsylvania Real Estate Investment Trust [*AMEX symbol*] (SPSG)
PEI............ Pereira [*Colombia*] [*Airport symbol*] (OAG)
PEI............ Petrocel Industries, Inc. [*Vancouver Stock Exchange symbol*]
PEI............ Petroleum Equipment Institute (EA)
PEI............ Physical Education Index [*A publication*]
PEI............ Planning Executives Institute [*Later, PF*]
PEI............ Plant Engineering Inspection (AAG)
PEI............ Playboy Enterprises, Inc.
PEI............ Polyethylenimine [*Organic chemistry*]
PEI............ Porcelain Enamel Institute (EA)
PEI............ Postejaculatory Interval [*Physiology*]
PEI............ Precipitation-Efficiency Index
PEI............ Preliminary Engineering Inspection [*NASA*] (KSC)
PEI............ Prince Edward Island [*Canadian province*]
PEI............ Prince Edward Island Provincial Library [*UTLAS symbol*]
PEI............ Prince Edward Island Reports (Haviland's) [*A publication*] (DLA)
PEI............ Professional Engineers in Industry
PEIA .... Poultry and Egg Institute of America (EA)
PEI Acts .... Acts of Prince Edward Island [*Canada*] [*A publication*]
PEIC .... Essays in Criticism [*A publication*]
PEIC .... Periodic Error Integrating Controller
PEID......... Program Element Identifier [*Military*] (AFIT)
PEIDD9..... Personality and Individual Differences [*A publication*]
PEIF .... Productivity Enhancing Incentive Fund (DNAB)
PEIG......... Eighteenth-Century Studies [*A publication*]
PEIL .... Essays in Literature [*A publication*]
PEILS....... PACOM [*Pacific Command*] Executive Intelligence Summary (MCD)
PEIN......... PEI, Inc. [*NASDAQ symbol*] (NQ)
Peine Salzgitter Ber ... Peine und Salzgitter Berichte [*A publication*]
Peint Pigm Vernis ... Peintures, Pigments, Vernis [*A publication*]
PEIP .... Presidential Executive Interchange Program [*Federal government*]
PEIR .... Problem Equipment Indicator Reports (MCD)
PEIR .... Project Equipment Inspection Record [*NASA*] (KSC)
PEI Rep ..... Prince Edward Island Reports (Haviland's) [*1850-1914*] [*A publication*] (DLA)
PEI Rev Regs ... Revised Regulations of Prince Edward Island [*Canada*] [*A publication*]
PEI Rev Stat ... Prince Edward Island Revised Statutes [*Canada*] [*A publication*] (DLA)
PEIS .... Programmatic Environmental Impact Statement (NRCH)
PEI Stat..... Prince Edward Island Statutes [*Canada*] [*A publication*] (DLA)
PEITA .... Professional Equestrian Instructors and Trainers Association (EA)
PEITV .... Preliminary Encapsulated Inert Test Vehicle (MCD)
PEJ .... Pakistan Economic Journal [*A publication*]
PEJ .... Personnel Journal [*A publication*]
PEJ .... Premolded Expansion Joint [*Technical drawings*]
Pe Ja .... Petrus Jacobi [*Flourished, 14th century*] [*Authority cited in pre-1607 legal work*] (DSA)
PEJO .... Plant Engineering Job Order (AAG)
PEJOA ...... Personnel Journal [*A publication*]
PEK.......... Beijing [*China*] [*Airport symbol*] (OAG)
PEK.......... Jacksonville, FL [*Location identifier*] [*FAA*] (FAAL)
PEK.......... Peking [*Republic of China*] [*Geomagnetic observatory code*]
PEK.......... Peking [*Chiufeng*] [*Republic of China*] [*Seismograph station code, US Geological Survey*] (SEIS)
PEK.......... Pekoe [*Tea trade*] (ROG)
PEK.......... Perkiomen Airways Ltd. [*Reading, PA*] [*FAA designator*] (FAAC)
PEK.......... Phase-Exchange Keying [*Data processing*] (IEEE)
PEK.......... Phi Epsilon Kappa [*Fraternity*]
PEK.......... Polyetherketone [*Organic chemistry*]
Peking Nat Hist Bull ... Peking Natural History Bulletin [*A publication*]
Peking R .... Peking Review [*A publication*]
PEL........... Lafayette College, Easton, PA [*Library symbol*] [*Library of Congress*] (LCLS)
PEL........... Panhandle Eastern Pipe Line Co. [*NYSE symbol*] (SPSG)
Pel .... Pelagius [*Deceased, 1232*] [*Authority cited in pre-1607 legal work*] (DSA)

PEL............ Pelaneng [*Lesotho*] [*Airport symbol*] (OAG)
PEL............ Peldehue [*Chile*] [*Seismograph station code, US Geological Survey*] (SEIS)
Pel.............. Pelopidas [*of Plutarch*] [*Classical studies*] (OCD)
PEL............ Penguin English Library [*A publication*]
PEL............ Peritoneal Exudate Lymphocytes [*Hematology*]
PEL............ Permissible Exposure Level
PEL............ Permissible Exposure Limit [*OSHA*]
PEL............ Personal Exposure Level [*or Limit*]
PEL............ Personnel Licensing and Training [*ICAO*] (AIA)
PEL............ Philatelic Esperanto League [*See also ELF*] [*Solna, Sweden*] (EAIO)
PEL.......... Photoelectron Layer
PEL............ Picture Element [*Single element of resolution in image processing*] (IBMDP)
PEL............ Precision Elastic Limit
PEL............ Priests Eucharistic League (EA)
PEL............ Professional Education Libraries [*UTLAS symbol*]
PEL............ Proportional Elastic Limit
PEL.......... Public Exposure Limit (MCD)
PELAA...... Progress in Nuclear Energy. Series 10 [*A publication*]
PElC .... Elizabethtown College, Elizabethtown, PA [*Library symbol*] [*Library of Congress*] (LCLS)
PELC......... Professional Engineers' Legislative Committee
PELEC ...... Photoelectric (MSA)
PEleph....... Elephantine Papyri [*A publication*] (OCD)
PELG......... Poly(ethyl L-Glutamate) [*Organic chemistry*]
PELL .... Papers on English Language and Literature [*A publication*]
PELN......... English Language Notes [*A publication*]
PELR......... Peeler
PELR........ Pelsart Resources NL [*NASDAQ symbol*] (NQ)
PELRV ...... Pea Leafroll Virus [*Plant pathology*]
PELS .... Precision Emitter Location System [*Air Force*] (MCD)
PELS .... Propionyl Erythromycin Lauryl Sulfate [*Antimicrobial agent*]
PELSS...... Precision Emitter Location Strike System [*Air Force*]
Pelt............ Peltier's Decisions. Court of Appeal. Parish of Orleans [*A publication*]
Pelt............ Peltier's Orleans Appeals [*1917-23*] [*A publication*] (DLA)
PELT .... Princeton Electronic Products, Inc. [*NASDAQ symbol*] (NQ)
PELV......... Pepino Latent Virus [*Plant pathology*]
PEM .... Parametric Earth Model [*Geodynamics*]
PEM .... Parasitic Encephalitis Meningitis [*Medicine*]
PeM .... Parole e Metodi [*A publication*]
PEM .... Particle Environmental Monitor (MCD)
PEM .... Partido Ecologista Mexicano [*Political party*] (EY)
PEM .... Payload Ejection Mechanism
PEM .... Pem Air Ltd. [*Pembroke, ON*] [*FAA designator*] (FAAC)
PEM .... Pembrokeshire [*County in Wales*] (ROG)
PEM .... Performance Evaluation Model
PEM .... Peritoneal Exudate Macrophage [*Hematology*]
PEM .... Perrot Memorial Library, Old Greenwich, CT [*OCLC symbol*] (OCLC)
PEM .... Personal Exposure Monitor [*Environmental chemistry*]
PEM .... Perspectivas de la Economia Mundial [*A publication*]
PEM .... Perspectives de l'Economie Mondiale [*A publication*]
PEM .... Petite Ensemble Model (MCD)
PEM .... Petrox Energy & Mineral Corp. [*Toronto Stock Exchange symbol*]
PEM .... Phased Equipment Modernization [*Army*] (AABC)
PEM .... Philco Electronic Module
PEM .... Photoelastic Modulator [*Instrumentation*]
PEM .... Photoelectromagnetic
PEM .... Photoelectron Microscopy
PEM .... Photoemission Microscope
PEM .... Photographic Equipment and Materials (NATG)
PEM .... Plant Engineer Mechanical (AAG)
PE & M...... Plant Engineering and Maintenance (MCD)
PEM .... Plant Engineering and Maintenance (NASA)
PEM .... Plastic-Encapsulated Microcircuit [*Telecommunications*]
PEM .... Polaris Evaluation Missile
PEM .... Polymer Electrolyte Membrane [*Fuel technology*]
PEM .... Position Encoding Module (CAAL)
PEM .... Prescription-Event Monitoring
PEM .... Primary Enrichment Medium [*Microbiology*]
PEM .... Probable Error of Measurement
PEM .... Processing Element Memory [*Data processing*]
PEM .... Product Effectiveness Manual
PEM .... Production Engineering Measure [*Army*] (MCD)
PEM .... Production Evaluation Missile [*Military*] (CAAL)
PEM .... Program Element Manager (MCD)
PEM .... Program Element Monitor (AFM)
PEM .... Project Engineering Memorandum
PEM .... Proposal Evaluation Manager
PEM .... Protein Energy Malnutrition [*Medicine*]
PEM .... Puerto Maldonado [*Peru*] [*Airport symbol*] (OAG)
PEMA....... Process Equipment Manufacturers Association (EA)
PEMA....... Procurement Equipment Maintenance, Army (MCD)
PEMA....... Procurement, Equipment, Missiles, Army
PEMA....... Procurement of Equipment and Munition Appropriations [*Military*] (AABC)
PEMA....... Production-Equipment-Missile Agency [*Army*]

PEMAP..... President's Environmental Merit Award Program [*Environmental Protection Agency*]
PEMARS .. Procurement of Equipment and Missiles, Army Management and Accounting Reporting System (AABC)
PEMB....... Pembroke College [*Oxford and Cambridge Universities*] (ROG)
PEMB....... Pembrokeshire [*County in Wales*]
Pemb Eq..... Pemberton's Practice in Equity by Way of Revivor and Supplement [*1867*] [*A publication*] (ILCA)
Pemb Judg ... Pemberton's Judgments and Orders [*A publication*] (DLA)
Pembroke Mag ... Pembroke Magazine [*A publication*]
PEMBS ..... Pembrokeshire [*County in Wales*]
PEMC....... Pele Medical Corp. [*NASDAQ symbol*] (NQ)
PEMCONS ... Photographic Equipment Management Control System
PEMD .... Program Evaluation and Methodology Division [*General Accounting Office*] [*Federal government*] (GFGA)
PEMD .... Program for Export Market Development [*Canada*]
PEMF....... Pulsating Electromagnetic Field
PEMFC .... Proton Exchange Membrane Fuel Cell [*Energy source*]
PEMJ .... Pemmican Journal [*A publication*]
PEMJA ..... Pesticides Monitoring Journal [*A publication*]
P & EML ... Personnel and Equipment Modification List [*Air Force*]
PEMO ...... Ecological Monographs [*A publication*]
Pe Mo........ Petrus Morini [*Authority cited in pre-1607 legal work*] (DSA)
PEMO ...... Plant Engineering Maintenance Order
PEMO ...... Production Engineering and Manufacturing Organization (AAG)
PE-MOCVD ... Plasma-Enhanced Metalorganic Chemical Vapor Deposition [*Coating technology*]
Pe Mori...... Petrus Morini [*Authority cited in pre-1607 legal work*] (DSA)
PEMOV .... Peanut Mottle Virus [*Plant pathology*]
PEM Process Eng Mag ... PEM Process Engineering Magazine [*A publication*]
PEMS........ Physical, Emotional, Mental, Safety [*Model for charting procedure*] [*Medicine*]
PEMS........ Portable Environmental Measuring System
PEMS........ Professional Education of the Media Specialist
PEMS........ Propulsion Energy Management Study (MCD)
PEMT........ Phosphatidylethanolamine Methyltransferase [*An enzyme*]
PEMU ...... Early Music [*A publication*]
PEMV........ Pea Enation Mosaic Virus [*Plant pathology*]
PeMV .... Pepper Mottle Virus
Pem Yeo..... Pembroke Yeomanry [*British military*] (DMA)
PEN .... Astoria, OR [*Location identifier*] [*FAA*] (FAAL)
PEN .... International PEN [*Official name; PEN, never spelled out in use, is said to stand for poets, playwrights, editors, essayists, novelists*] (EAIO)
PEN .... Peace Education Network (EA)
PEN .... PEN American Center (EA)
PEN .... Penang [*Malaysia*] [*Airport symbol*] (OAG)
PEN .... Pendeli [*Greece*] [*Geomagnetic observatory code*]
PEN .... Penetration (AFM)
PEN .... Penicillin [*Antibiotic*]
PEN .... Peninsula [*Maps and charts*]
PEN .... Penitent
Pen .... Pennewill's Delaware Reports [*A publication*] (DLA)
Pen .... Pennington's New Jersey Reports [*2, 3 New Jersey*] [*A publication*] (DLA)
PEN .... Pensacola [*Florida*] [*Seismograph station code, US Geological Survey*] [*Closed*] (SEIS)
Pen .... Pensamiento [*Madrid*] [*A publication*]
PEN .... Pentazocine [*An analgesic*]
PEN .... Pentobarbital [*Sedative*]
PEN .... Pentode (DEN)
PEN .... Pentron Industries, Inc. [*Later, KOA*] [*AMEX symbol*] (SPSG)
PEN .... Permanent Entry Number [*Data processing*]
PEN .... Petroleum News. Asia's Energy Journal [*A publication*]
PEN .... Pharmacology Equivalent Name
PEN .... Physicians Enrichment Network (EA)
PEN .... Polyethylene Naphthalate [*Organic chemistry*]
PEN .... Professional Enrichment News [*Portuguese*] (BJA)
PEN .... Program Element Number [*Data processing*] (KSC)
PEN .... Program Error Note [*Data processing*]
PEN .... Purchasing Electronic Notebook (HGAA)
PENA .... Primary Emission Neuron Activation (IEEE)
PENAID.... Penetration Aid [*Weaponry*]
PENB........ Environment and Behavior [*A publication*]
PENB........ Poultry and Egg National Board [*Later, AEB*] (EA)
PENBASE ... Peninsular Base Section [*Military*]
Pen C......... Penal Code [*A publication*] (DLA)
PENCIL .... Pictorial Encoding Language [*Data processing*] (IEEE)
PENCIL .... Portable Encoder/Illustrator [*Facetious term for pre-word-processing equipment*]
PenCn .... [*The*] Penn Central Corp. [*Associated Press abbreviation*] (APAG)
PencpF .... Penncorp Financial Group [*Associated Press abbreviation*] (APAG)
PENCPR ... PEN [*Poets, Playwrights, Essayists, Editors, and Novelists*] Club of Puerto Rico (EA)
PEND .... Endeavour [*A publication*]
Pend .... Pendant (ROG)

PEND .... Pendens [*Weighing*] [*Pharmacy*]
PEND .... Pending
PENDA ..... Polish Endocrinology [*A publication*]
Pen Dec...... Pension Decisions [*Department of the Interior*] [*A publication*] (DLA)
PENDORF ... Penetrate Dorfman [*FBI investigation of Teamster leader Allen Dorfman*]
PENEE4.... Pediatric Neuroscience [*A publication*]
Penelitian Indones ... Penelitian Laut di Indonesia [*Marine Research in Indonesia*] [*A publication*]
Penelitian Laut Indones (Mar Res Indones) ... Penelitian Laut di Indonesia (Marine Research in Indonesia) [*A publication*]
PENEM..... Penn Engineering & Manufacturing Corp. [*Associated Press abbreviation*] (APAG)
P/E NEWS ... Petroleum/Energy Business News Index [*American Petroleum Institute*] [*New York, NY*] [*Bibliographic database*]
PenG .... Penicillin G [*Antibacterial agent*]
PEng.......... Pennsylvania English [*A publication*]
PENG .... Photo-Electro-Nystagmography [*Medicine*]
PENG .... Prima Energy Corp. [*NASDAQ symbol*] (NQ)
PEng .... Professional Engineer
PENGEM ... Penetrate Gray Electronics Markets [*FBI "sting" operation, 1982, in which employees of Japanese computer firms were caught attempting to obtain proprietary information illegally from IBM Corp.*]
Pengum Lemb Penelit Kehutanan ... Pengumuman. Lembaga Penelitian Kehutanan [*A publication*]
PENIC....... Penicillin [*Antibiotic*]
Penic Cam ... Penicillum Camelinum [*A Camel's-Hair Brush*] [*Pharmacy*]
penin .... Peninsula
PENIT....... Penitentiary
Penjelidikan Indones ... Penjelidikan Laut di Indonesia [*A publication*]
PENJERDEL ... Pennsylvania, New Jersey, Delaware
Penn .... Pennewill's Delaware Reports [*A publication*] (DLA)
Penn .... Pennington's New Jersey Reports [*A publication*] (DLA)
PENN .... Pennsylvania
Penn .... Pennsylvania State Reports [*A publication*] (DLA)
PENN .... Pennsylvanian [*Period, era, or system*] [*Geology*]
Penn .... Pennypacker's Unreported Pennsylvania Cases [*A publication*] (DLA)
PENNA ..... Pennsylvania
Penna Law Journal ... Pennsylvania Law Journal [*A publication*] (DLA)
Penna LJ.... Pennsylvania Law Journal [*A publication*] (DLA)
Penna R...... Pennsylvania State Reports [*A publication*] (DLA)
Penna SR ... Pennsylvania State Reports [*A publication*] (DLA)
Penna St..... Pennsylvania State Reports [*A publication*] (DLA)
Penna State Rep ... Pennsylvania State Reports [*A publication*] (DLA)
Penn Ba Q ... Pennsylvania Bar Association. Quarterly [*A publication*]
Penn BAR ... Pennsylvania Bar Association. Report [*A publication*]
Penn Bar Assc Q ... Pennsylvania Bar Association. Quarterly [*A publication*]
Penn Beekpr ... Pennsylvania Beekeeper [*A publication*]
Penn Co Ct Rep ... Pennsylvania County Court Reports [*A publication*] (DLA)
Penn Corp Rep ... Pennsylvania Corporation Reporter [*A publication*] (DLA)
Penn Del .... Pennewill's Delaware Reports [*A publication*] (DLA)
Penn Dent J ... Penn Dental Journal [*A publication*]
Penn Dist & Co Rep ... Pennsylvania District and County Reports [*A publication*] (DLA)
Penn Dist Rep ... Pennsylvania District Reports [*A publication*] (DLA)
Penne .... Pennewill's Delaware Reports [*17-23 Delaware*] [*1897-1909*] [*A publication*] (DLA)
Pennew....... Pennewill's Delaware Reports [*A publication*] (DLA)
Pennewill ... Pennewill's Delaware Supreme Court Reports [*1897-1909*] [*A publication*] (DLA)
Penney .... Penney [*J.C.*] Co., Inc. [*Associated Press abbreviation*] (APAG)
Penn Geol Surv Atlas ... Pennsylvania. Geological Survey. Atlas [*A publication*]
Penn Geol Surv Bull ... Pennsylvania. Geological Survey. Bulletin [*A publication*]
Penn Geol Surv Gen Geol Rep ... Pennsylvania. Geological Survey. General Geology Report [*A publication*]
Penn Geol Surv Ground Water Rep ... Pennsylvania. Geological Survey. Ground Water Report [*A publication*]
Penn Geol Surv Inform Circ ... Pennsylvania. Geological Survey. Information Circular [*A publication*]
Penn Geol Surv Progr Rep ... Pennsylvania. Geological Survey. Progress Report [*A publication*]
Penn German Soc Proc ... Pennsylvania German Society. Proceedings [*A publication*]
Penn Hist... Pennsylvania History [*A publication*]
Penn Hosp Rep ... Pennsylvania Hospital Reports [*A publication*]
Penning...... Pennington's New Jersey Reports [*2, 3 New Jersey*] [*A publication*] (DLA)
Pen NJ .... Pennington's New Jersey Reports [*2, 3 New Jersey*] [*A publication*] (DLA)
Penn Law .... Pennsylvania Lawyer [*A publication*]
Penn Law Jour ... Pennsylvania Law Journal [*A publication*] (DLA)
Penn LG..... Pennsylvania Legal Gazette [*A publication*] (DLA)
Penn LG..... Pennsylvania Legal Gazette Reports (Campbell) [*A publication*] (DLA)

Penn Lib Assn Bull ... Pennsylvania Library Association. Bulletin [*A publication*]
Penn LJ...... Pennsylvania Law Journal [*A publication*] (DLA)
Penn LJR... Pennsylvania Law Journal Reports, Edited by Clark [*1842-52*] [*A publication*] (DLA)
Penn L Rec ... Pennsylvania Law Record [*Philadelphia*] [*A publication*] (DLA)
Penn L Rev ... Pennsylvania Law Review [*A publication*] (DLA)
Penn Mag H ... Pennsylvania Magazine of History and Biography [*A publication*]
Penn Mag Hist Biog ... Pennsylvania Magazine of History and Biography [*A publication*]
Penn Mo .... Penn Monthly [*A publication*]
Penn Nurse ... Pennsylvania Nurse [*A publication*]
PENNORTH ... Pennyworth [*British*] (ROG)
Penn R .... Pennsylvania State Reports [*A publication*] (DLA)
Penn Rep.... Pennsylvania State Reports [*A publication*] (DLA)
Penn Rep... Penrose and Watts' Pennsylvania Reports [*A publication*] (DLA)
PennsF....... Pennsylvania Folklife [*A publication*]
Penn St...... Pennsylvania State Reports [*A publication*] (DLA)
PENNSTAC ... Penn State University Automatic Digital Computer
Penn Stat ... Pennsylvania State Reports [*A publication*] (DLA)
Penn State F ... Penn State Farmer [*A publication*]
Penn State Rep ... Pennsylvania State Reports [*A publication*] (DLA)
Penn State Univ Exp Sta Bull ... Pennsylvania State University. Experiment Station. Bulletin [*A publication*]
Penn State Univ Exp Sta Circ ... Pennsylvania State University. Experiment Station. Circular [*A publication*]
Penn St M Q ... Penn State Mining Quarterly [*A publication*]
Penn Stock & F ... Pennsylvania Stockman and Farmer [*A publication*]
Penn St R ... Pennsylvania State Reports [*A publication*] (ILCA)
Penn St Rep ... Pennsylvania State Reports [*A publication*] (DLA)
Penn Super ... Pennsylvania Superior Court Reports [*A publication*] (DLA)
Pennsyl M ... Pennsylvania Magazine of History and Biography [*A publication*]
Pennsylvania Acad Sci Newsletter ... Pennsylvania Academy of Science. Newsletter [*A publication*]
Pennsylvania Acad Sci Proc ... Pennsylvania Academy of Science. Proceedings [*A publication*]
Pennsylvania Bus Survey ... Pennsylvania Business Survey [*A publication*]
Pennsylvania Geol ... Pennsylvania Geology [*A publication*]
Pennsylvania Geol Survey Bull ... Pennsylvania. Geological Survey. Bulletin [*A publication*]
Pennsylvania Geol Survey Inf Circ ... Pennsylvania. Geological Survey. Information Circular [*A publication*]
Pennsylvania Geol Survey Prog Rept ... Pennsylvania. Geological Survey. Progress Report [*A publication*]
PENNTAP ... Pennsylvania Technical Assistance Program [*Pennsylvania State University*] [*University Park, PA*]
PENNTR... Penn Traffic Co. [*Associated Press abbreviation*] (APAG)
Penn Univ Mus Bul ... Pennsylvania University. University Museum. Bulletin [*A publication*]
Penny .... Pennypacker's Pennsylvania Colonial Cases [*A publication*] (DLA)
Penny .... Pennypacker's Unreported Pennsylvania Cases [*A publication*] (DLA)
Penny Col Cas ... Pennypacker's Pennsyulvania Colonial Cases [*A publication*] (DLA)
Penny M .... Penny Magazine [*A publication*]
Penny Mech Chem ... Penny Mechanic and the Chemist [*A publication*]
Pennyp........ Pennypacker's Unreported Pennsylvania Cases [*A publication*] (DLA)
Pennyp Col Cas ... Pennypacker's Pennsylvania Colonial Cases [*A publication*] (DLA)
Pennyp (PA) ... Pennypacker's Unreported Pennsylvania Cases [*A publication*] (DLA)
Pennzol ...... Pennzoil Co. [*Associated Press abbreviation*] (APAG)
PENOB ...... Penobscot Shoe Co. [*Associated Press abbreviation*] (APAG)
PENOL...... Penology
Pen P......... Penault's Prerosti de Quebec [*A publication*] (DLA)
Pen Pow .... Penny Power [*A publication*]
PENR .... Ethnic and Racial Studies [*A publication*]
PENR .... Pennant Resources Ltd. [*NASDAQ symbol*] (NQ)
PENR .... Penryn [*England*]
PENRAD... Penetration RADAR
Penr Anal... Penruddocke's Short Analysis of Criminal Law [*2nd ed.*] [*1842*] [*A publication*] (DLA)
PENRB...... Professional Engineer [*Washington, DC*] [*A publication*]
PENRE...... Pennsylvania Real Estate Investment Trust [*Associated Press abbreviation*] (APAG)
Pen Ref....... Penal Reformer [*1934-39*] [*A publication*] (DLA)
Pen Ref League M Rec ... Penal Reform League Monthly Record [*1909-12*] [*A publication*] (DLA)
Pen Ref League Q Rec ... Penal Reform League Quarterly Record [*1912-20*] [*A publication*] (DLA)
PENREP ... Penetration Report [*National Security Agency*]
Penrose Ann ... Penrose Annual [*A publication*]
Penr & W ... Penrose and Watts' Pennsylvania Reports [*1829-32*] [*A publication*] (DLA)
PENS........ Magic Marker Industries [*NASDAQ symbol*] (NQ)

PENS......... Partido Espanol Nacional Sindicalista [*Political party*] [*Spain*]
PENS......... Polymer Ejection for Noise Suppression
PENSAM .. Penetration Survivability Assessment Model   (MCD)
Pensamiento Econ ... Pensamiento Economico [*A publication*]
Pensamiento Polit ... Pensamiento Politico [*A publication*]
PensCr .... Pensamiento Cristiano. Tribuna de Exposicion del Pensamiento
                Evangelico [*Cordoba, Argentina*] [*A publication*]   (BJA)
Pensee Nat ... Pensee Nationale [*A publication*]
Pensez Plast ... Pensez Plastiques [*A publication*]
Pensiero Med ... Pensiero Medico [*A publication*]
Pensiero Polit ... Pensiero Politico [*A publication*]
Pension FA ... Pension Fund Sponsors Ranked by Assets [*A publication*]
Pension Fc ... Pension Facts [*A publication*]
Pension Rep ... Pension Reporter [*Bureau of National Affairs*] [*A
                publication*]   (DLA)
Pensions..... Pensions and Investments [*Later, Pension & Investment Age*]
                [*A publication*]
Pensions Investm Age ... Pensions and Investment Age [*A publication*]
Pension Wld ... Pension World [*A publication*]
Pens Plan Guide CCH ... Pension Plan Guide. Commerce Clearing House [*A
                publication*]
Pens & Profit Sharing (P-H) ... Pension and Profit Sharing (Prentice-Hall,
                Inc.) [*A publication*]   (DLA)
Pens Rep (BNA) ... Pension Reporter (Bureau of National Affairs) [*A
                publication*]   (DLA)
PenST .... Penicillin Skin Test [*Immunology*]
Pen St R ... Pennsylvania State Reports [*A publication*]   (DLA)
PENT........ Penetrate   (AABC)
PENT........ Penna Enterprises [*NASDAQ symbol*]   (SPSG)
PENT........ Pennsylvania Enterprises, Inc. [*NASDAQ symbol*]   (NQ)
PENT........ Pentagon
PENT........ Pentameter
Pent........... Pentateuch   (BJA)
PENT........ Pentecost
PENT........ Pentode   (AAG)
Pent........... Pentothal [*Anesthetic*]   (AAMN)
PENTAC... Penetration for Tactical Aircraft [*Air Force*]
Pentax Photogr ... Pentax Photography [*A publication*]
PENTENG ... Pentagon English [*Pseudotechnical language*]
P Ent S Ont ... Proceedings. Entomological Society of Ontario [*A publication*]
P Ent S Was ... Proceedings. Entomological Society of Washington [*A
                publication*]
PENV .... Journal of Environmental Health [*A publication*]
PENVAL... Penetration Evaluation [*Military*]   (NVT)
PENVDK... Population and Environment [*A publication*]
PENW ...... Penetrating Wound
Pen & W..... Penrose and Watts' Pennsylvania Reports [*1829-32*] [*A
                publication*]   (DLA)
PENW ...... PENWEST Ltd. [*Bellevue, WA*] [*NASDAQ symbol*]   (NQ)
PENW ...... Penwith [*England*]
Pen Wld ..... Pension World [*A publication*]
PENZ........ Penzance [*City in England*]   (ROG)
Penzuegyi Szemle ... Penzuegyi Szemle [*A publication*]
Penzugyi Szle ... Penzugyi Szemle [*A publication*]
PEO .... Pankypria Ergatiki Omospondia [*Pancyprian Federation of
                Labour*] [*The "Old Trade Unions"*] [*Cyprus*]
PEO .... Patrol Emergency Officer [*Nuclear energy*]   (NRCH)
PEO .... People
peo.............. Persian, Old [*MARC language code*] [*Library of
                Congress*]   (LCCP)
PEO .... Petroleum & Resources Corp. [*NYSE symbol*]   (SPSG)
PEO .... Petrolia Oil & Gas [*Vancouver Stock Exchange symbol*]
PEO .... Philanthropic and Educational Organization [*Facetious
                translation "Pop Eats Out"*]
PEO .... Planners for Equal Opportunity [*Defunct*]   (EA)
PEO .... Plant Engineering Order
PEO .... Plant Equipment Operator [*Nuclear energy*]   (NRCH)
PEO .... Poly(ethylene oxide) [*Acronym is trade name owned by Seitetsu
                Kagaku Co.*]
PEO .... Principal Executive Officer [*Civil Service*] [*British*]
PEO .... Process Engineering Order
PEO .... Product Engineering Office
PEO .... Production Engineering Order
PEO .... Program Evaluation Office [*Army*]
PEO .... Program Executive Office [*or Officer*]
PEO .... Progressive External Ophthalmoplegia
PEO .... Propulsion Engineering Officer   (MCD)
PEO .... Prospective Engineer Officer
PEO .... Public Employment Office [*State Employee Security
                Agency*]   (OICC)
PEOC .... Essays on Canadian Writing [*A publication*]
PEOC .... Publishing Employees Organizing Committee [*AFL-CIO*]
PEOED...... Proceedings. European Offshore Petroleum Conference and
                Exhibition [*A publication*]
PEO-GPALS ... Program Executive Officer, Global Protection Against
                Limited Strikes [*Army*]   (RDA)
Peo L Adv .. People's Legal Advisor [*Utica, NY*] [*A publication*]   (DLA)
PEOPD7.... Perspectives in Ophthalmology [*A publication*]
PeopEn....... Peoples Energy Corp. [*Associated Press abbreviation*]   (APAG)
Peop J .... People's Journal [*A publication*]
People .... People Weekly [*A publication*]

People and Plann ... People and Planning [*A publication*]
Peoples....... Peoples' Reports [*77-97 Georgia*] [*A publication*]   (DLA)
People Wkly ... People Weekly [*A publication*]
Peopl Tax... People and Taxes [*A publication*]
Peoria Med Month ... Peoria Medical Monthly [*A publication*]
PEOS......... Propulsion and Electrical Operating System   (IEEE)
PEOUD ..... Petroleum Outlook [*A publication*]
Peo World ... People's World [*A publication*]
PEOX .... Polyethyleneoxide [*Organic chemistry*]
PEP........... All India Reporter, Patiala and East Punjab States Union Series
                [*A publication*]   (ILCA)
PEP............ Charlotte, NC [*Location identifier*] [*FAA*]   (FAAL)
PEP............ Packetized Ensemble Protocol [*Data processing*]
PEP............ Paperless Electronic Payment [*Business term*]
PEP............ Paperless Entry Processing User Group [*Defunct*]   (CSR)
PEP............ Parenting, Education, and Political Involvement [*Jack and Jill
                of America*]
PEP............ Parti Ecologiste pour le Progres [*Burkina Faso*] [*Political
                party*]   (EY)
PEP............ Parti Evangelique Populaire [*Popular Protestant Party*]
                [*Switzerland*] [*Political party*]   (PPE)
PEP............ Partitioned Emulation Program [*Data processing*]   (BUR)
PEP............ Pauli Exclusion Principle [*Physics*]
PEP............ Peak Effective Power
PEP............ Peak Energy Product
PEP............ Peak Envelope Power [*Telecommunications*]
PEP............ Peer Evaluation Program [*College of American Pathologists*]
PEP............ People for Energy Progress   (EA)
PEP............ Pepitilla [*Race of maize*]
PEP............ Peppermint   (DSUE)
PEP............ PepsiCo Inc. [*NYSE symbol*]   (SPSG)
PEP............ Peptide [*Biochemistry*]
PEP............ Performance Effectiveness [*or Evaluation*] Program [*Navy*]
PEP............ Performance Evaluation Procedure [*Joint Commission on
                Accreditation of Hospitals*]   (DHSM)
PEP............ Peripheral Event Processor [*Data processing*]
PEP............ Perkin-Elmer Processor [*Computer*]
PEP............ Personal Employee Profiling [*Information service or
                system*]   (IID)
PEP............ Personal Equity Plan [*Finance*]
PEP............ Personal Exemption Phase-Out [*Income tax*]
PEP............ Personal Exercise Programmer
PEP............ Personality-Profile Exam
PEP............ Personnel Exchange Program [*Military*]   (NVT)
PEP............ Pfizer, Inc., Research Center Library, Easton, PA [*Library
                symbol*] [*Library of Congress*]   (LCLS)
PEP............ Phenethyl Propionate [*Insect attractant*] [*Organic chemistry*]
PEP............ Phosphoenolpyruvate [*Biochemistry*]
PEP............ Photoelectric Potential
PEP............ Photoelectrophoresis
PEP............ Photographic Exploitation Products   (MCD)
PEP............ Physical Education Program
PEP............ Physiological Evaluation of Primates
PEP............ Pictorial End-Papers [*Publishing*]
PEP............ Pipeline Expanding Polymer
PEP............ Piping Efficiency Program
PEP............ Planar Epitaxial Passivated
PEP............ Planetary Ephemeris Program   (IEEE)
PEP............ Planetary Exploration Plan [*NASA*]
PEP............ Plant Equipment Package [*DoD*]
PEP............ Platform Electronic Package
PEP............ Platform Evaluation Program
PEP............ Plessey Electronic Payroll   (DEN)
PEP............ Plume Exposure Pathway [*Nuclear emergency planning*]
PEP............ Political and Economic Planning [*A British organization*]
                [*Later, Policy Studies Institute*]
PEP............ Polyestradiol Phosphate [*Endocrinology*]
PEP............ Polyethylene Powder
PEP............ Polynominal Error Protection   (MCD)
PEP............ Porsche Experimental Prototype [*Automotive engineering*]
PEP............ Portable Energy Provision   (SSD)
PEP............ Positive Energy [*Vancouver Stock Exchange symbol*]
PEP............ Positron-Electron Project [*High-energy accelerator*]
PEP............ Positron Electron Proton [*Physics*]
PEP............ Postal Efficiency Plan   (SAA)
PEP............ Power Evaluation Program
PEP............ Power Extension Package   (MCD)
PEP............ Power Extension Plant   (MCD)
PEP............ Practical Engineering Paperwork
PEP............ Pratt & Whitney Engine Program [*Aviation*]   (NG)
PEP............ Pre-Ejection Period [*Cardiology*]
PEP............ Pre-Employment Program
PEP............ Preamplifier Extension Plug
PEP............ Preferred Equipment Package [*Automotive retailing*]
PEP............ President's Economy Program
PEP............ Preventive Enforcement Patrol [*New York City police*]
PEP............ Primary Education Program [*Child development test*]
PEP............ Primate Equilibrium Platform
PEP............ Princeton Experiment Package [*NASA*]
PeP............ Principal of Pedagogy [*Academic degree*]
PEP........... Printer-Emulation Package [*Software*]

PEP............ Priority Energy Policy [*Environmental Protection Agency*]
PEP............ Processing Enhancing Protein [*Biochemistry*]
PEP............ Procurement Evaluation Panel [*Air Force*] (MCD)
PEP............ Procytox [*Cyclophosphamide*], Epipodophyllotoxin Derivative [*VM-26*], Prednisolone [*Antineoplastic drug regimen*]
PEP............ Producibility Engineering and Planning [*Army*] (AABC)
PEP............ Product Engineering and Production (MCD)
PEP............ Production EAGLE [*Elevation Angle Guidance Landing Equipment*] Package
PEP............ Production Engineering Planning
PEP............ [*The*] Production Engineering and Productivity Exhibition and Conference [*British*] (ITD)
PEP............ Production Equipment Package
PEP............ [*The*] Productivity Effectiveness Program [*Title of a pamphlet by Robert Gedaliah that describes sedentary exercises for desk-bound workers*]
PEP............ Professional Enhancement Project [*American Occupational Therapy Association*]
PEP............ Proficiency Examination Program (MCD)
PEP............ Program Element Plan (AFIT)
PEP............ Program Evaluation Procedure [*Air Force*]
PEP............ Progressive Exercise Program
PEP............ Projects and Exports Policy [*Board of Trade*] [*British*]
PEP............ Promoting Enduring Peace (EA)
PEP............ Promotion Evaluation Pattern
PEP............ Proposal Equipment Packages (MCD)
PEP............ Proposal Evaluation Panel (MCD)
PEP............ Proposal Evaluation Plan [*or Program*] (MCD)
PEP............ Proposal Exploitation Product
PEP............ Propulsion Evaluation Plan
PEP............ Protection in Evaluation Procedures
PEP............ Proton-Electron-Proton [*Nuclear physics*]
PEP............ Psychiatric Evaluation Profile [*Psychology*] (MAE)
PEP............ Psychoeducational Profile [*Test for autistic children*]
PEP............ Psychoepistemological Profile [*Student personality test*]
PEP............ Pulse Echo Pattern
PEPA........ Peptidase A [*An enzyme*]
PEPA........ Petroleum Electric Power Association [*Later, EUIPA*] (EA)
PEPA........ Protected Environment plus Prophylactic Antibiotics [*Oncology*]
PEPA........ Pulse Echo Pattern Analyzer
PEPAG...... Physical Electronics and Physical Acoustics Group [*MIT*] (MCD)
Pe de Pal .... Pierre de la Palu [*Deceased, 1342*] [*Authority cited in pre-1607 legal work*] (DSA)
PEPAOP ... (Phenylethyl)phenylacetoxypiperidine [*Organic chemistry*]
PEPAS....... WHO [*World Health Organization*] Western Pacific Regional Centre for the Promotion of Environmental Planning and Applied Studies (EAIO)
PepBoy...... Pep Boys-Manny, Moe & Jack [*Associated Press abbreviation*] (APAG)
PEPC........ Peptidase C [*An enzyme*]
PEPC........ Phosphoenolpyruvate Carboxylase [*An enzyme*]
PEPC........ Polynomial Error Protection Code [*Data processing*]
PEPC........ Potomac Electric Power Co.
PEPCK .... Phosphoenolopyruvate Carboxykinase [*An enzyme*]
PEPCK .... Phosphoenolpyruvate Carboxykinase [*An enzyme*]
PEPCO .... Potomac Electric Power Co.
PEPD........ Peptidase D [*An enzyme*]
PEPE .... Parallel Element Processing Ensemble [*Burroughs Corp.*] (BUR)
PEPE .... Prolonged Elevated-Pollution Episode [*Environmental Protection Agency*]
PEPG........ Piezoelectric Power Generation
PEPG........ Port Emergency Planning Group [*NATO*] (NATG)
PEPI .... Physical Education Public Information [*Film*]
PEPI .... Piezo Electric Products, Inc. [*NASDAQ symbol*] (NQ)
PEPI .... Pre-Ejection Period Index [*Cardiology*]
PEPIA ...... Physics of the Earth and Planetary Interiors [*A publication*]
Pepinier Hortic Maraichers ... Pepinieristes, Horticulteurs, Maraichers [*France*] [*A publication*]
PEPL .... Peoples Restaurants [*NASDAQ symbol*] (NQ)
PEPL .... Preliminary Engineering Parts List
PEPLAN ... Polaris Executive Plan [*British*]
PEPMC ..... Printing Estimators and Production Men's Club [*New York, NY*] (EA)
PEPMIS.... Plant Equipment Packages Management Information System (MCD)
PEPMOV ... Pepper Mottle Virus [*Plant pathology*]
PEPMV ..... Pepino Mosaic Virus [*Plant pathology*]
PEPP .... Planetary Entry Parachute Program [*NASA*]
PEPP .... Positive Expiratory Pressure Plateau [*Medicine*] (MAE)
PEPP .... Professional Engineers in Private Practice
PEPPA ...... Preparedness for Emergency Plant Pest Action [*In Animal and Plant Health Inspection Service publication PEPPA Pot*]
PEPPARD ... Propellant, Explosive, Pyrotechnic Pollution Abatement Research and Development (DNAB)
Pepperdine LR ... Pepperdine Law Review [*A publication*]
Pepperdine L Rev ... Pepperdine Law Review [*A publication*]
Pepper & L Dig ... Pepper and Lewis' Digest of Laws [*Pennsylvania*] [*A publication*] (DLA)

Pepper & L Dig Laws ... Pepper and Lewis' Digest of Laws [*Pennsylvania*] [*A publication*] (DLA)
Pepp LR..... Pepperdine Law Review [*A publication*]
PEPR .... Precision Encoding and Pattern Recognition Device [*Data processing*]
PEPS .... National Committee on Public Employee Pension Systems (EA)
PEPS .... Peperomia and Exotic Plant Society (EA)
PEPS .... Peptidase S [*An enzyme*]
PEPS .... Pesticide Enforcement Policy Statement [*Environmental Protection Agency*]
PEPS .... Primary Environmental Prediction System
PEPS .... Primary Environmental Processing Systems [*Navy*] (GFGA)
PEPS .... Production Engineering Productivity System [*Camtek Ltd.*] [*Software package*]
PEPS .... Productivity Environmental Preference Survey [*Test*]
PEPS .... Program Element Plan Supplement
PEPSB....... Perception and Psychophysics [*A publication*]
PEP-SEP ... Peptide Separation [*Biochemistry*]
PEPSI .... Plasma Electron Profiles, Symmetric Integrals (MCD)
PepsiC...... Pepsico, Inc. [*Associated Press abbreviation*] (APAG)
PEPSS .... Preschool and Early Primary Skills Survey [*Child development test*]
PEPSS ...... Programmable Equipment for Personnel Subsystem Simulation
PEPSU ...... All India Reporter, Patiala and East Punjab States Union [*1950-57*] [*A publication*] (DLA)
PEPSU ...... Patiala and East Punjab States Union
PEPSY ...... Precision Earth-Pointing System (MCD)
PEPTDO ... Peptides [*New York*] [*A publication*]
Pept Protein Rev ... Peptide and Protein Reviews [*A publication*]
Pept Res..... Peptide Research [*A publication*]
PEP/USA ... Parkinson's Educational Program - USA (EA)
PEPUSL.... Pepperdine University School of Law (DLA)
PEpW .... Westinghouse Electric Corp., East Pittsburgh, PA [*Library symbol*] [*Library of Congress*] (LCLS)
PEQ .... Palestine Exploration Quarterly [*A publication*]
PEQ .... Pecos City, TX [*Location identifier*] [*FAA*] (FAAL)
PEQ .... Personal Experience Questionnaire [*Psychology*]
PEQ .... Petroquin Resources Ltd. [*Vancouver Stock Exchange symbol*]
PEQL......... Palestine Exploration Quarterly (London) [*A publication*]
PEQUA ..... Production Equipment Agency [*Army*]
PEQUOD .. Pacific Equatorial Ocean Dynamics
PEr........... Erie Public Library, Erie, PA [*Library symbol*] [*Library of Congress*] (LCLS)
PER........... Par Exchange Rate [*Business term*]
PER........... Parity Error Rate
PER........... Partido Estadista Republicano [*Puerto Rico*] [*Political party*]
PER........... Path Extension Ratio (MCD)
PER........... Peak Ejection Rate [*Cardiology*]
PER........... Peak Expiration Rate [*Medicine*]
Pe R........... Pennewill's Delaware Reports [*A publication*] (DLA)
Per con ...... Per Contra [*On the Other Side*] [*Latin*]
per .... Perennial [*Botany*]
Per............ Perera's Select Decisions [*Ceylon*] [*A publication*] (DLA)
PER........... Performance Evaluation Report [*DoD*]
PER........... Perhaps (ROG)
Per............ Pericles [*Shakespearean work*]
Per............ Pericles [*of Plutarch*] [*Classical studies*] (OCD)
PER........... Perigee (KSC)
per .... Perineal [*Gynecology*] (MAE)
Per............ Periochae [*of Livy*] [*Classical studies*] (OCD)
PER........... Period
Per............ Period [*Record label*]
per .... Periodic (AAMN)
PER........... Periodical (ROG)
PER........... Permian Airways, Inc. [*Midland, TX*] [*FAA designator*] (FAAC)
PER........... Permission (AABC)
Per............ Perseus [*Constellation*]
PER........... Persia [*Obsolete*]
per .... Persian, Modern [*MARC language code*] [*Library of Congress*] (LCCP)
PER........... Person
PER........... Personnel [*A publication*]
PER........... Personnel (KSC)
Per............ Perspective [*A publication*]
Per............ Perspectives [*A publication*]
PER........... PERT [*Program Evaluation and Review Technique*] Event Report
PER........... Perth [*Australia*] [*Seismograph station code, US Geological Survey*] [*Closed*] (SEIS)
PER........... Perth [*Australia*] [*Airport symbol*] (OAG)
PER........... Peru [*ANSI three-letter standard code*] (CNC)
PER........... Phase Engineering Report
PER........... Physical Examination Rate [*Military*] (AFM)
PER........... Planning, Evaluation, and Reporting [*Education-improvement system*]
PER........... Pominex Ltd. [*Toronto Stock Exchange symbol*]
PER........... Ponca City, OK [*Location identifier*] [*FAA*] (FAAL)
PER........... Pope, Evans & Robbins, Inc. [*AMEX symbol*] (SPSG)
PER........... Port Everglades Railway [*AAR code*]

PER........... Post Engineer Request
PER........... Postelectrophoresis Relaxation
PER........... Potential Excess Report
PER........... Preedited Region [*Genetics*]
PER........... Preliminary Engineering Report   (KSC)
PER........... PressNet Environmental Reports [*Information service or system*]   (IID)
PER........... Price Earnings Ratio [*Relation between price of a company's stock and its annual net income*]
PER........... Product Engineering Recommendation [*Automotive engineering*]
PER........... Production Engine Remanufacturers Program [*Automotive engineering*]
PER........... Professional and Executive Recruitment Service [*British*]
PER........... Proficiency Evaluation Review
PER........... Program Event Recording [*Data processing*]   (MDG)
PER........... Program Execution Request
PER........... Proposal Evaluation Report   (MCD)
PER........... Protein Efficiency Ratio [*Nutrition*]
PER..... Public Employees Roundtable   (EA)
PER........... Pyrotechnical Evaluation Range [*Army*]   (RDA)
PERA........ Planning and Engineering for Repair and Alteration [*Navy*]
PERA........ Production Engine Remanufacturers Association   (EA)
PERA........ Production Engineering Research Association [*Research center*] [*British*]   (IRC)
Per AJ....... Performing Arts Journal [*A publication*]
PERAM...... Personnel Action Memorandum [*Military*]
PER AN..... Per Annum [*By the Year*] [*Latin*]
PER ANN ... Per Annum [*By the Year*] [*Latin*]
Per A R ...... Performing Arts Review [*A publication*]
Pe Rave...... Petrus Ravennas [*Flourished, 1468-1508*] [*Authority cited in pre-1607 legal work*]   (DSA)
Per Biol...... Periodicum Biologorum [*A publication*]
PERC........ Peace on Earth Research Center
PERC........ Perceptronics, Inc. [*NASDAQ symbol*]   (NQ)
PERC........ Percolator   (DSUE)
PERC........ Percussion   (AAG)
PERC........ Pittsburgh Energy Research Center [*Later, PETC*] [*Energy Research and Development Administration*]
PERC........ Political Economy Research Center [*Research center*]   (RCD)
PERC........ Processor Emergency Recovery Circuit [*Bell System*]
PERC........ Professional Engineering and Research Consultants
PERC........ Psoriasis Education and Research Centre [*University of Toronto*] [*Canada*] [*Research center*]   (RCD)
PERCAM.. Performance and Cost Analysis Model   (MCD)
Per Cap ..... Per Capita [*By the Individual*] [*Latin*]
PERCAP..... Persian Gulf Requirements and Capabilities [*Military*]
PERCASREPT ... Personnel Casualty Report [*Military*]   (NVT)
PERCENT ... Per Centum [*By the Hundred*] [*Latin*]
Percept Cogn Dev ... Perceptual Cognitive Development [*A publication*]
Percept Cognit Devel ... Perceptual Cognitive Development [*A publication*]
Percept & Motor Skills ... Perceptual and Motor Skills [*A publication*]
Percept and Mot Sk ... Perceptual and Motor Skills [*A publication*]
Percept Mot Skills ... Perceptual and Motor Skills [*A publication*]
Percept Psychophys ... Perception and Psychophysics [*A publication*]
PERCHLOR ... Perchloride [*Chemistry*]   (ROG)
PERCI .... Personnel Contamination Instrumentation
Perc Mot Sk ... Perceptual and Motor Skills [*A publication*]
Perc Notes ... Percussive Notes [*A publication*]
Perc Notes Res Ed ... Percussive Notes. Research Edition [*A publication*]
PERCOM ... Peripheral Communications   (FAAC)
PERCOM ... Personnel Command [*Army*]   (MCD)
PERCOMPASIA ... South East Asian Personal Computer Hardware and Software Show
Per Comp T ... Personal Computers Today [*A publication*]
PERCOS ... Performance Coding System
Perc Psych ... Perception and Psychophysics [*A publication*]
Per CS........ Perrault's Conseil Superieur [*Canada*] [*A publication*]   (DLA)
PERCS....... Preference Equity Redemption Cumulative Stock   (ECON)
PERCUSS & AUSC ... Percussion and Ausculation [*Medicine*]   (DHSM)
PERD........ Perdendo [*or Perdendosi*] [*Softer and Slower*] [*Music*]
PERD........ Periodic   (MSA)
PERD........ Perused   (ROG)
PERDA...... Per Diem [*By the Day*] [*Latin*]   (NOAA)
Per & Dav .. Perry and Davison's English King's Bench Reports [*1838-41*] [*A publication*]   (DLA)
PERDDiMS ... Personnel Deployment and Distribution Management System [*Military*]   (AABC)
PERDEN.... Perdendo [*or Perdendosi*] [*Softer and Slower*] [*Music*]
PERDEX.... Permuted Formula Index [*Molecular formula indexing*]
Peredovoi Opyt Stroit Ekspl Shakht ... Peredovoi Opyt v Stroitel'stve i Ekspluatatsii Shakht [*A publication*]
Peredovoi Opyt Stroit Eksp Shakht ... Peredovoi Opyt v Stroitel'stve i Ekspluatatsii Shakht [*Former USSR*] [*A publication*]
PEREF....... Personal Effects
PEREF....... Propellant Engine Research Environmental Facility
Pereg.......... Peregrinus Fabius [*Authority cited in pre-1607 legal work*]   (DSA)
Pererab Gaza Gazov Kondens Nauchno-Tekh Obz ... Pererabotka Gaza i Gazovogo Kondensata. Nauchno-Tekhnicheskii Obzor [*A publication*]

Pererab Tverd Topl ... Pererabotka Tverdogo Topliva [*Former USSR*] [*A publication*]
PE Rev .... Physical Education Review [*A publication*]
PERF .... Perfect
PERF .... PerfectData Corp. [*NASDAQ symbol*]   (NQ)
PERF .... Perforate   (KSC)
PERF .... Perforation   (DSUE)
PERF .... Performance   (KSC)
PERF .... Police Executive Research Forum   (EA)
Perf Art C .. Performing Arts in Canada [*A publication*]
Perf Art J ... Performing Arts Journal [*A publication*]
Perf Art R .. Performing Arts Review [*A publication*]
Perf Arts .... Performing Arts in Canada [*A publication*]
Perf Arts Can ... Performing Arts in Canada [*A publication*]
Perf Arts R ... Performing Arts Review [*A publication*]
PERFCE.... Performance
PERFD ...... Performed   (ROG)
Perf Eval .... Performance Evaluation [*A publication*]
Perf Eval Rev ... Performance Evaluation Review [*A publication*]
PERFINS.. Perforated Insignia [*Philately*]
PERFM ..... Perform   (ROG)
Performance Eval ... Performance Evaluation [*A publication*]
Performance Eval Rev ... Performance Evaluation Review [*A publication*]
Performing Arts Rev ... Performing Arts Review [*A publication*]
Perform Instr J ... Performance and Instruction Journal [*A publication*]
Perf Right .. Performing Right [*A publication*]
Perfumer .... Perfumer and Flavorist [*A publication*]
Perfum Essent Oil Rec ... Perfumery and Essential Oil Record [*A publication*]
Perfum Flavorist ... Perfumer and Flavorist [*A publication*]
Perfum Flavorist Int ... Perfumer and Flavorist International [*A publication*]
Perfum Flavour ... Perfumery and Flavouring [*Japan*] [*A publication*]
Perfum J ..... Perfumers' Journal [*A publication*]
Perfum Kosmet ... Perfumerie und Kosmetik [*A publication*]
PERFW ..... Perforating Wound
PErG .... Gannon University, Erie, PA [*Library symbol*] [*Library of Congress*]   (LCLS)
PERG........ Pergola [*Classified advertising*]   (ADA)
PERG........ Production Emergency Redistribution Group
PERG........ Production Equipment Redistribution Group [*Army*]
Pergamon Gen Psychol Ser ... Pergamon General Psychology Series [*A publication*]
Pergamon Ser Environ Sci ... Pergamon Series on Environmental Science [*A publication*]
Pergamon Ser Monogr Lab Tech ... Pergamon Series of Monographs in Laboratory Techniques [*A publication*]
Pergamon Texts Inorg Chem ... Pergamon Texts in Inorganic Chemistry [*A publication*]
Perg I S Da ... Pergamon International Series on Dance and Related Disciplines [*A publication*]
PERGO ..... Project Evaluation and Review with Graphic Output   (IEEE)
PERGRA ... Permission Granted [*Military*]
PERH .... Perhaps
PerHi .... Erie County Historical Society, Erie, PA [*Library symbol*] [*Library of Congress*]   (LCLS)
PERI .... Pacific Energy Resources, Inc. [*NASDAQ symbol*]   (NQ)
PERI .... Pea Ridge National Military Park
PERI .... Perigee
PERI .... Perimeter   (AABC)
PERI .... Periscope
PERI .... Platemakers Educational and Research Institute [*Later, IAP*]
PERI .... Production Equipment Redistribution Inventory [*Army*]
PERI .... Production Equipment Reserve Inventory [*Navy*]   (NG)
PERI .... Protein Engineering Research Institute [*Japanese governmental and industrial consortium*]
PERI .... Psychiatric Epidemiology Research Interview
PERIAP..... Periapical [*Dentistry*]
PERIF........ Peripheral
Pe Rigal...... Petrus Rigaldi [*Flourished, 14th century*] [*Authority cited in pre-1607 legal work*]   (DSA)
PERIM ...... Perimeter   (KSC)
Perinat Med ... Perinatal Medicine [*A publication*]
Perinat Neonat ... Perinatology/Neonatology [*A publication*]
PERINIC... Perini Corp. [*Associated Press abbreviation*]   (APAG)
PERINTREP ... Periodic Intelligence Report   (NATG)
PERINTREPT ... Periodic Intelligence Report
PERINTSUM ... Periodic Intelligence Summary [*Army*]   (AABC)
Period Anim Prod ... Periodical on Animal Production [*A publication*]
Period Biol ... Periodicum Biologorum [*A publication*]
Period Bull Int Sugar Confect Manuf Assoc Int Off Cocoa Choc ... Periodic Bulletin. International Sugar Confectionery Manufacturers' Association and International Office of Cocoa and Chocolate [*A publication*]
Period Guide Comput ... Periodical Guide for Computerists [*A publication*]
Period Mat ... Periodico di Matematiche [*A publication*]
Period Mat 5 ... Periodico di Matematiche. Serie V [*A publication*]
Period Math Hung ... Periodica Mathematica Hungarica [*A publication*]
Period Math Hungar ... Periodica Mathematica Hungarica [*A publication*]
Period Mineral ... Periodico di Mineralogia [*Italy*] [*A publication*]
Periodont Abstr ... Periodontal Abstracts. Journal of the Western Society of Periodontology [*A publication*]
Periodont Case Rep ... Periodontal Case Reports [*A publication*]

Period Polytech ... Periodica Polytechnica [*A publication*]
Period Polytech Chem Eng ... Periodica Polytechnica. Chemical Engineering [*A publication*]
Period Polytech Civ Eng ... Periodica Polytechnica. Civil Engineering [*Hungary*] [*A publication*]
Period Polytech Civ Engng ... Periodica Polytechnica. Civil Engineering [*A publication*]
Period Polytech Electr Eng ... Periodica Polytechnica. Electrical Engineering [*A publication*]
Period Polytech Eng ... Periodica Polytechnica. Engineering [*A publication*]
Period Polytech Mech Eng ... Periodica Polytechnica. Mechanical Engineering [*Hungary*] [*A publication*]
Period Polytech Mech Engng ... Periodica Polytechnica. Mechanical Engineering [*A publication*]
Period Polytech Trans Engng ... Periodica Polytechnica. Transportation Engineering [*A publication*]
Period Speaking ... Periodically Speaking [*A publication*]
Periopr Nurs Q ... Perioperative Nursing Quarterly [*A publication*]
PERIPH .... Periphery (KSC)
Peripl M Eux ... Periplus Maris Euxini [*of Arrian*] [*Classical studies*] (OCD)
PERIS........... Periscope (KSC)
Periton Dia ... Peritoneal Dialysis Bulletin [*A publication*]
PERJ .... Perjury [*FBI standardized term*]
PERJY......... Perjury (ROG)
PERK........... Payroll Earnings Record Keeping
Perk............ Perkins on Conveyancing [*A publication*] (DLA)
Perk............ Perkins Journal [*A publication*]
Perk............ Perkins on Pleading [*A publication*] (DLA)
Perk............ Perkins' Profitable Book (Conveyancing) [*A publication*] (DLA)
PERK........ Perquisite
PERK........ Prospective Evaluation of Radial Keratotomy [*for eye surgery*]
PERKARA ... Parti Perpaduan Kebangsaan Ra'ayat Brunei [*Brunei People's National United Party*] [*Political party*] (EY)
PerkEl........ Perkin-Elmer Corp. [*Associated Press abbreviation*] (APAG)
PerkF........ Perkins Family Restaurants Ltd. [*Associated Press abbreviation*] (APAG)
Perkin-Elmer Tech News ... Perkin-Elmer Technical News [*A publication*]
Perkins J.... Perkins School of Theology. Journal [*A publication*]
Perkins Obs Contrib Ser 2 ... Perkins Observatory. Contributions. Series 2 [*A publication*]
Per & Kn .... Perry and Knapp's English Election Reports [*1838*] [*A publication*] (DLA)
Perk Pr Bk ... Perkins' Profitable Book (Conveyancing) [*A publication*] (DLA)
PERL......... Pathologically Eclectic Rubbish Lister
PERL......... Perkin-Elmer Robot Language
PERL......... Perle Systems Ltd. [*Scarborough, ON*] [*NASDAQ symbol*] (NQ)
PERL......... Perusal (ROG)
PERL......... Pictorial Engineering and Research Laboratory
PERL......... Prepositioned Equipment Requirements List [*Navy*] (MCD)
PERL......... Public Employee Relations Library [*of International Personnel Management Association*]
PERLA ...... Pupils Equal, React to Light and Accommodation [*Medicine*]
PERLS....... Principal Exchange-Rate-Linked Securities [*Investment term*]
PERM........ Permanent
PERM........ Permanent Employee (DSUE)
PERM........ Permeability
PERM........ Permian [*Period, era, or system*] [*Geology*]
PERM........ Permission (MSA)
PERM........ Permutation (DSUE)
PERM........ Program Evaluation for Repetitive Manufacture (IEEE)
PERMACAP ... Personnel Management and Accounting Card Processor [*Military*]
PERMACAPS ... Personnel Management and Accounting Card Processing System (MCD)
PERMAFROST ... Permanent Frost
PerManAb ... Personal Management Abstracts [*A publication*]
PERMAS .. Persatuan Rakyat Malaysian Sarawak [*Political party*] (EY)
PERMAS .. Personnel Management Assistance System [*Military*] (AABC)
PERMB..... Permeability
Permbledhje Stud ... Permbledhje Studimesh [*A publication*]
Permbledhje Stud Inst Kerkimeve Gjeol Miner ... Permbledhje Studimesh. Instituti i Kerkimeve Gjeologijke dhe Minerale [*A publication*]
Permbledhje Stud Inst Stud Kerkimeve Ind Miner ... Permbledhje Studimesh. Instituti i Studimeve dhe Kerkimeve Industirale e Minerale [*A publication*]
PErMC...... Mercyhurst College, Erie, PA [*Library symbol*] [*Library of Congress*] (LCLS)
PERME..... Propellants, Explosives, and Rocket Motors Establishment [*British Ministry of Defense*] [*Research center*] (RDA)
Perm Found Med Bull ... Permanente Foundation Medical Bulletin [*A publication*]
PERMIC ... Personnel Management Information Center [*Navy*] (NVT)
PERMINVAR ... Permeability Invariant
PERMIXT ... Permixtus [*Mixed*] [*Pharmacy*] (ROG)
PERMLY .. Permanently
PERMR..... Permanent Residence

PERMREP ... Permanent Representation to North Atlantic Council [*NATO*] (NATG)
PERMS ..... Personnel Electronic Record Management System [*Army*] (RDA)
PERMS ..... Process and Effluent Radiological Monitoring System [*Nuclear energy*] (NRCH)
PERMSS... Process and Effluent Radiological Monitoring and Sampling System [*Nuclear energy*] (NRCH)
PERMT.... Permanent (ROG)
PERMU..... Permanent Magnet Users Association [*Defunct*] (EA)
Perm Way ... Permanent Way [*A publication*]
Pernamb Odont ... Pernambuco Odontologica [*A publication*]
PernC........ Perini Corp. [*Associated Press abbreviation*] (APAG)
PERNOGRA ... Permission Not Granted [*Military*]
PER OP EMET ... Peracta Operatione Emetici [*When the Operation of the Emetic is Finished*] [*Pharmacy*] (ROG)
Per Or Cas ... Perry's Oriental Cases [*Bombay*] [*A publication*] (DLA)
PEROX...... Peroxide
PERP........ Pan-Ethnic Republican Party of Australia [*Political party*]
PERP........ Perpendicular (AAG)
PERP........ Perpetual (ADA)
Per P .... Perrault's Prevoste de Quebec [*A publication*] (DLA)
PERP........ Personnel Processing (MUGU)
perpad...... Perineal Pad [*Gynecology*] (MAE)
Perpet........ Perpetual (DLA)
Per Poly CE ... Periodica Polytechnica. Chemical Engineering [*A publication*]
Per Poly EE ... Periodica Polytechnica. Electrical Engineering [*A publication*]
Per Poly ME ... Periodica Polytechnica. Mechanical Engineering [*A publication*]
Per Pract B ... Personnel Practice Bulletin [*A publication*] (APTA)
PER PROC ... Per Procurationem [*By Proxy, By the Action Of*] [*Legal term*] [*Latin*]
Per Psy....... Personnel Psychology [*A publication*]
PERR........ Premature Engine Removal Rate (AAG)
Perrault...... Perrault's Conseil Superieur [*Canada*] [*A publication*] (DLA)
Perrault...... Perrault's Prevoste de Quebec [*A publication*] (DLA)
Perrault...... Perrault's Quebec Reports [*A publication*] (DLA)
Per Rel St.... Perspectives in Religious Studies [*A publication*]
PERRLA ... Pupils Equal, Round, React to Light and Accommodation [*Medicine*]
Perry .... Perry's Oriental Cases [*Bombay*] [*A publication*] (DLA)
Perry .... [*Sir Erskine*] Perry's Reports in Morley's East Indian Digest [*A publication*] (DLA)
Perry & D... Perry and Davison's English King's Bench Reports [*A publication*] (DLA)
Perry & D (Eng) ... Perry and Davison's English King's Bench Reports [*A publication*] (DLA)
Perry Ins .... Perry's English Insolvency Cases [*1831*] [*A publication*] (DLA)
Perry & K... Perry and Knapp's English Election Cases [*A publication*] (DLA)
Perry & Kn ... Perry and Knapp's English Election Cases [*A publication*] (DLA)
Perry OC.... Perry's Oriental Cases [*Bombay*] [*A publication*] (DLA)
PERS .... Performance Evaluation Reporting System [*DoD*]
PERS .... Periodical Source Index [*A publication*]
Pers .... Persae [*of Aeschylus*] [*Classical studies*] (OCD)
Pers .... Perseus [*Constellation*]
PERS .... Persia [*Obsolete*]
Pers .... Persius [*34-62AD*] [*Classical studies*] (OCD)
PERS .... Person
PERS .... Personal
PERS .... Personal Diagnostics, Inc. [*NASDAQ symbol*] (NQ)
PERS .... Personal Emergency Response System [*Telecommunications*]
Pers .... Personalist [*A publication*]
Pers .... Personnel [*A publication*]
PERS .... Personnel (AFM)
PERS .... Personnel Squadron
Pers .... Perspektiv [*A publication*]
PERS .... Preliminary Engineering Reports (MUGU)
PERSACLIT ... Peritus in Sacred Liturgy [*Roman Catholic*]
PERSACS ... Personnel Structure and Accounting System [*Army*]
PERSACS ... Personnel Structure and Composition System [*Military*]
Pers Adm ... Personnel Administration [*A publication*]
Pers Adm ... Personnel Administrator [*A publication*]
Pers Admin ... Personnel Administrator [*A publication*]
Pers Am Hist ... Perspectives in American History [*A publication*]
PERSC....... Public Education Religion Studies Center (EA)
PERSCEN ... Personnel Center
PERSCO ... Personnel Support of Contingency Operations [*Military*]
PersCom ... Personnel Command [*Army*] (INF)
Pers Commun ... Personal Communications [*A publication*]
Pers Comput World ... Personal Computer World [*A publication*]
PERSCON ... Personnel Control [*Military*]
PERSD ...... Personnel Department [*Marine Corps*]
PERSDEP ... Personnel Deployment Report [*Military*]
PERSEP.... Pershing Survivability Evaluation Program [*Military*] (MCD)
PERSEPCOMD ... Personnel and Separation Command (DNAB)
PERSEREC ... [*Defense*] Personnel Security Research and Education Center
PERSERVDEPSERVS ... Personal Services and Dependents' Services Support System [*Navy*] (DNAB)
PERSET.... Personnel Standardization and Evaluation Team [*Military*]

PERSEVCE ... Perseverance (ROG)
PERSEXP ... Personal Expense Money [*Army*]
Pers Finance LQ ... Personal Finance Law Quarterly Report [*A publication*]
Pers Finance LQ Rep ... Personal Finance Law Quarterly Report [*A publication*]
Pers Guid J ... Personnel and Guidance Journal [*A publication*]
PERSH ... Perishable (WGA)
Pershad ...... Privy Council Judgments [*1829-69*] [*India*] [*A publication*] (DLA)
PERSIL ..... Peroxide Silicate [*Detergent and bleach*]
Pers Indiv ... Personality and Individual Differences [*A publication*]
Pers Individ Differ ... Personality and Individual Differences [*A publication*]
Pers Inj Ann ... Personal Injury Annual [*A publication*]
Pers Inj Comment'r ... Personal Injury Commentator [*A publication*] (DLA)
Pers Inj Deskbook ... Personal Injury Deskbook [*A publication*]
Pers Inj LJ ... Personal Injury Law Journal [*A publication*] (DLA)
PERSINS .. Personnel Information System [*Army*]
PERSINSCOM ... Personnel Information Systems Command [*Army*] (AABC)
PERSINSD ... Personnel Information Systems Directorate [*Military Personnel Center*] (AABC)
PERSIR ..... Personnel Inventory Report [*Army*] (AABC)
Pers J .... Personnel Journal [*A publication*]
Pers Jrl ...... Personnel Journal [*A publication*]
PERSL .... Personal
Pers Lit ...... Personnel Literature [*A publication*]
Pers Man ... Personnel Management [*A publication*]
Pers Manage ... Personnel Management [*A publication*]
Pers Manage Abstr ... Personnel Management Abstracts [*A publication*]
PERSMAR ... Personnel Manning Assistance Report (DNAB)
Pers Mgmt Abstr ... Personnel Management Abstracts [*A publication*]
Pers Mgt .... Personnel Management [*A publication*]
PERSNET ... Personnel Network [*Army*]
Pers New Mus ... Perspectives of New Music [*A publication*]
PERSO ...... Personnel Officer [*Air Force*]
PERSOF .... Personnel Officer [*Navy*]
Person .... Personalist [*A publication*]
PERSON .. Personnel Simulation On-Line [*Department of State*] [*Computer program*]
Personal & Soc Psychol Bull ... Personality and Social Psychology Bulletin [*A publication*]
Person Manage Abstr ... Personnel Management Abstracts [*A publication*]
Personnel Exec ... Personnel Executive [*A publication*]
Personnel Guidance J ... Personnel and Guidance Journal [*A publication*]
Personnel & Guid J ... Personnel and Guidance Journal [*A publication*]
Personnel J ... Personnel Journal [*A publication*]
Personnel Manag (London) ... Personnel Management (London) [*A publication*]
Personnel Mgmt ... Personnel Management [*A publication*]
Personnel Mgmt P-H ... Personnel Management. Prentice-Hall [*A publication*]
Personnel Mgt Abstracts ... Personnel Management Abstracts [*A publication*]
Personnel Practice B ... Personnel Practice Bulletin [*A publication*]
Personnel Practice Bul ... Personnel Practice Bulletin [*A publication*] (APTA)
Personnel Psych ... Personnel Psychology [*A publication*]
Personnel Psychol ... Personnel Psychology [*A publication*]
Personn Pract Bull ... Personnel Practice Bulletin [*A publication*] (APTA)
PERSP .... Perspective (MSA)
Persp .... Perspective [*Record label*]
Persp .... Perspectives [*A publication*]
PERSPAY ... Personnel and Pay [*Project*] [*Navy*]
Persp Biol .. Perspectives in Biology and Medicine [*A publication*]
Perspec....... Perspective (MSA)
Perspec....... Perspective [*A publication*]
Perspec Biol & Med ... Perspectives in Biology and Medicine [*A publication*]
Perspec Ed ... Perspectives on Education [*A publication*]
Perspect Accredit ... Perspectives on Accreditation [*A publication*]
Perspect Am Hist ... Perspectives in American History [*A publication*]
Perspect Biol Med ... Perspectives in Biology and Medicine [*A publication*]
Perspect Biom ... Perspectives in Biometrics [*A publication*]
Perspect Brain Sci ... Perspectives in the Brain Sciences [*A publication*]
Perspect Cardiovasc Res ... Perspectives in Cardiovascular Research [*A publication*]
Perspect Clin Pharmacol ... Perspectives in Clinical Pharmacology [*A publication*]
Perspect Comput ... Perspectives in Computing [*A publication*]
Perspect in Educ ... Perspectives in Education [*A publication*]
Perspect Hum Reprod ... Perspectives in Human Reproduction [*A publication*]
Perspect Ind Psychol ... Perspectives in Industrial Psychology [*A publication*]
Perspect Int ... Perspectives Internationales [*A publication*]
Perspective K ... Perspective (Karachi) [*A publication*]
Perspectives Biol Med ... Perspectives in Biology and Medicine [*A publication*]
Perspectives Civ Rights Q ... Perspectives. The Civil Rights Quarterly [*A publication*]
Perspectives Euro-Afr ... Perspectives Euro-Africaines [*A publication*]
Perspectives Latino-Am ... Perspectives Latino-Americaines [*A publication*]
Perspectives New M ... Perspectives of New Music [*A publication*]
Perspect Med ... Perspectives in Medicine [*A publication*]
Perspect Medicaid Manage ... Perspectives on Medicaid Management [*A publication*]

Perspect Medicaid Medicare Manage ... Perspectives on Medicaid and Medicare Management [*A publication*]
Perspect Nephrol Hypertens ... Perspectives in Nephrology and Hypertension [*A publication*]
Perspect Ophthalmol ... Perspectives in Ophthalmology [*A publication*]
Perspect Pediatr Pathol ... Perspectives in Pediatric Pathology [*A publication*]
Perspect Polon ... Perspectives Polonaises [*A publication*]
Perspect Powder Metall ... Perspectives in Powder Metallurgy [*A publication*]
Perspect Psychiatr ... Perspectives Psychiatriques [*A publication*]
Perspect Psychiatr Care ... Perspectives in Psychiatric Care [*A publication*]
Perspect Vertebr Sci ... Perspectives in Vertebrate Science [*A publication*]
Perspect Virol ... Perspectives in Virology [*A publication*]
Perspekt Phil ... Perspektiven der Philosophie [*A publication*]
Persp N Mus ... Perspectives of New Music [*A publication*]
Persp Pol.... Perspectives Polonaises [*A publication*]
Pers Prac B ... Personnel Practice Bulletin [*A publication*]
Pers Prac Bul ... Personnel Practice Bulletin [*A publication*] (APTA)
Pers Pract Bull ... Personnel Practice Bulletin [*A publication*] (APTA)
Pers Pract Newsl ... Personnel Practices Newsletter [*A publication*]
PERSPROC ... Personnel Processing [*Army*]
Persp Soc ... Perspectives Socialistes [*A publication*]
Pers Psych ... Personnel Psychology [*A publication*]
Pers Psych C ... Perspectives in Psychiatric Care [*A publication*]
Pers Psychol ... Personnel Psychology [*A publication*]
Persp Teol ... Perspectiva Teologica [*A publication*]
Pers Rep Exec ... Personal Report for the Executive [*A publication*]
PERSRSCHSYSTM ... Personnel Management and Training Research Statistical Data System [*Navy*] (DNAB)
PERSRU ... Personnel Reporting Unit
PERSSEPCENT ... Personnel Separation Center
PERSSO.... Personnel System Staff Officer
PERSTAT ... Personnel Status Report [*Military*]
PERSTATREP ... Personnel Status Report [*Military*]
PERS & TRACOMD ... Personnel and Training Command
PERSTRAN ... Personal Transportation [*Navy*]
Pers V .... Personalvertretung [*A publication*]
PERT .... Patients Experience of the Relationship with the Therapist Method
PERT .... Performance Evaluation Review Technique
PERT .... Pertain (AABC)
PERT .... Pertussis [*Whooping cough*]
PERT .... Phenol Enhanced Reassociation Technique [*Clinical chemistry*]
PERT .... Program Evaluation Research Task (IEEE)
PERT .... Program Evaluation and Review Technique [*Data processing*] [*Computer performance management*]
PERTCO ... Program Evaluation and Review Technique with Cost
PERT-CS... Program Evaluation and Review Technique - Cost System (DNAB)
PERTHS ... Perthshire [*County in Scotland*]
Perti .... [*Petrus de*] Bellapertica [*Deceased, 1308*] [*Authority cited in pre-1607 legal work*] (DSA)
Pertica .... [*Petrus de*] Bellapertica [*Deceased, 1308*] [*Authority cited in pre-1607 legal work*] (DSA)
PERT-NAP ... Program Evaluation and Review Technique - Network Automatic Plotting (SAA)
PERTO ...... Pertaining To (NVT)
Per Tr........ Perry on Trusts [*A publication*] (DLA)
PERTRAN ... Perturbation Transport [*NASA*]
PERTSIM ... Program Evaluation and Review Technique Simulation [*Game*]
PERT-TAM ... Program Evaluation and Review Technique Task, Action, and Milestone Items
PERT/TIME ... Program Evaluation and Review Technique/Time Analyzer [*Sperry UNIVAC*]
PERU........ Production Equipment Records Unit (IEEE)
Peru Dir Gen Mineria Bol ... Peru. Ministerio de Fomento y Obras Publicas. Direccion General de Mineria. Boletin [*A publication*]
PERUG...... Perusing (ROG)
Peru Indig.. Peru Indigena [*A publication*]
Peru Minist Agric Dir Gen Invest Agropecu Bol Tec ... Peru. Ministerio de Agricultura. Direccion General de Investigaciones Agropecuarias. Boletin Tecnico [*A publication*]
Peru Minist Agric Serv Invest Promoc Agrar Bol Tec ... Peru. Ministerio de Agricultura. Servicio de Investigacion y Promocion Agraria. Boletin Tecnico [*A publication*]
PERUSA ... Perspectives - United States of America [*History course*]
Peru Serv Geol Min Bol ... Peru. Servicio de Geologia y Mineria. Boletin [*A publication*]
Peru Serv Geol Min Estud Espec ... Peru. Servicio de Geologia y Mineria. Estudios Especiales [*A publication*]
Peru Serv Geol Min Geodinamica Ing Geol ... Peru. Servicio de Geologia y Mineria. Geodinamica e Ingenieria Geologica [*A publication*]
PERUV...... Peruvian
PERV......... Pervert [*or Perverted*] [*FBI standardized term*]
PErV .... United States Veterans Administration Hospital, Erie, PA [*Library symbol*] [*Library of Congress*] (LCLS)
PErVM ...... Villa Maria College, Erie, PA [*Library symbol*] [*Library of Congress*] (LCLS)
PERY........ Ethnohistory [*A publication*]
PeryDr .... Perry Drugs Stores, Inc. [*Associated Press abbreviation*] (APAG)

PERYLENE ... Peri-Dinaphthalene [*A fluorophore*] [*Organic chemistry*]
PES............ IEEE Power Engineering Society   (EA)
PES............ Paid Educational Services [*British*]
PES............ Pan European Survey [*A publication*]
PES............ Paraendocrine Syndrome [*Endocrinology*]
PES............ Parent Egg Seed
PES............ Partial Energy Service [*Electric power*]
PES............ Partido Ecuatoriano Socialista [*Ecuadorean Socialist Party*]
                    [*Political party*]
PES............ Parts Engineering Support
PES............ Patent Examining System
PES............ Pecos Resources [*Vancouver Stock Exchange symbol*]
Pes............ Pesahim   (BJA)
PES............ Peshawar [*Pakistan*] [*Seismograph station code, US Geological
                    Survey*] [*Closed*]   (SEIS)
PES............ Philosophy of Education Society   (EA)
PES............ Photoelectric Scanner
PES............ Photoelectron Spectroscopy
PES............ Photoemission Spectroscopy
PES............ Photojet Edge Sensor
PES............ Physicians Equity Services
PES............ Pictorial Eleven Society [*Formerly, PE*] [*Absorbed by
                    PCS*]   (EA)
PES............ Pointing Error Sensor   (MCD)
PES............ Polish Economic Survey [*A publication*]
PES............ Polyethersulfone [*Organic chemistry*]
PES............ Polyethylene Sodium Sulfonate [*Anticoagulant*]
PES............ Post-Enumeration Survey [*Bureau of the Census*]
PES............ Postextrasystolic Potentiation [*Cardiology*]
PES............ Potential Energy Source [*Physiology*]
PES............ Potential-Energy Surface [*Chemical kinetics*]
PES............ Poultry and Egg Situation
PES............ Power Engineering Society
PES............ Power Engineering Specification
PES............ Preexcitation Syndrome [*Cardiology*]
Pes............ Pressure, End-Systole [*Cardiology*]
P(ES) .... Probability of Equal Regressive Slopes [*Statistics*]
PES............ Problem-Etiology-Signs [*or Symptoms*] [*Nursing*]
PES............ Processor Enhancement Socket [*Data processing*]   (PCM)
PES............ Production Engineering Service
PES............ Production Engineering Specification   (NG)
PES............ Professional Examination Service
PES............ Program Element Summary
PES............ Program Emphasis Statement [*US Employment Service*]
                    [*Department of Labor*]
PES............ Program Execution System
PES............ Programmed Electrical Stimulation [*Neurophysiology*]
PES............ Projected Engagement Scheduler [*Military*]   (CAAL)
PES............ Public Expenditure Survey [*British*]
PESA .... Petroleum Electric Supply Association [*Defunct*]   (EA)
PESA .... Petroleum Equipment Suppliers Association   (EA)
PESA .... Propellant Expulsion and Storage Assembly
PESA .... Proton Elastic-Scattering Analysis
PESABC.... Permanent Executive Secretariat of the Andres Bello
                    Convention [*See also SECAB*]   (EAIO)
Pe de Sal .... Petrus de Salinis [*Flourished, 13th century*] [*Authority cited in
                    pre-1607 legal work*]   (DSA)
Pe de Samp ... Petrus de Sampsone [*Flourished, 1246-58*] [*Authority cited in
                    pre-1607 legal work*]   (DSA)
Pesca Mar ... Pesca y Marina [*A publication*]
Pesca Pesqui ... Pesca y Pesquisa [*A publication*]
PESC Rec IEEE Power Electron Spec Conf ... PESC Record. IEEE [*Institute
                    of Electrical and Electronics Engineers*] Power Electronics
                    Specialists Conference [*A publication*]
PESD........ Pacific Electronic Security Division [*Military*]
PESD........ Postsecondary Education Statistics Division [*Department of
                    Education*]   (GFGA)
PESD........ Program Element Summary Data [*DoD*]
PESD........ Program Execution Subdirective   (AABC)
PESDC ...... Properties of Electrolyte Solutions Data Center [*National
                    Institute of Standards and Technology*]
PESDS....... Program Element Summary Data Sheet [*DoD*]
PESGB ...... Petroleum Exploration Society of Great Britain
Pesh .... Peshitta [*Syriac translation of the Bible*]   (BJA)
Peshawar ... All India Reporter, Peshawar [*1933-50*] [*A publication*]   (DLA)
Peshawar ... Indian Rulings, Peshawar Series [*1933-47*] [*A
                    publication*]   (DLA)
Peshawar Univ Dep Geol Geol Bull ... Peshawar. University. Department of
                    Geology. Geological Bulletin [*A publication*]
PESI .... Physical Education/Sports Index [*A publication*]
P & ESI...... Physical and Engineering Sciences Division [*Army Research
                    Office*]
PESIA........ Postal Employees Salary Increase Act of 1960
PESIC........ Parti du Progres Economique et Social des Independants
                    Congolais Luluabourg [*Party for Economic and Social
                    Progress of the Congolese Independents in Luluabourg*]
                    [*Political party*]
Pesik .... Pesikta de-Rav Kahana   (BJA)
Pesikt........ Pesikta de-Rav Kahana   (BJA)
PesiktR ...... Pesikta Rabbati   (BJA)
PESM........ Photoelectron Spectromicroscope

PeSMoT .... Penn State Microoxidation Test [*Analytical chemistry*]
PESO........ Participation Enriches Science, Music, and Art Organizations
                    [*Orlando, Florida*]
PESO........ Performance Evaluation Support Office
PESO........ Plant Engineering Shop Order   (AAG)
PESO........ Product Engineering Services Office [*DoD*]
PESOD...... Proceedings. Electrochemical Society [*A publication*]
PESOS ...... Perkin-Elmer Solvent Optimization System [*Chemistry*]
PESOS ...... Prepare, Explain, Show, Observe, Supervise [*Formula*]
                    [*LIMRA*]
PESPD ...... Periodically Speaking [*A publication*]
Pesqu......... Pesquisas [*A publication*]
Pesqui Agropecuar Brasil Ser Agron ... Pesquisa Agropecuaria Brasileira. Serie
                    Agronomia [*A publication*]
Pesqui Agropecuar Brasil Ser Vet ... Pesquisa Agropecuaria Brasileira. Serie
                    Veterinaria [*A publication*]
Pesqui Agropecu Bras ... Pesquisa Agropecuaria Brasileira [*A publication*]
Pesqui Agropecu Bras Ser Agron ... Pesquisa Agropecuaria Brasileira. Serie
                    Agronomia [*A publication*]
Pesqui Agropecu Bras Ser Vet ... Pesquisa Agropecuaria Brasileira. Serie
                    Veterinaria [*A publication*]
Pesqui Agropecu Bras Ser Zootec ... Pesquisa Agropecuaria Brasileira. Serie
                    Zootecnia [*A publication*]
Pesqui Agropecu Nordeste Recife ... Pesquisas Agropecuarias do Nordeste
                    Recife [*A publication*]
Pesqui Agropecu Pernambucana ... Pesquisa Agropecuaria Pernambucana [*A
                    publication*]
Pesqui Bot (Porto Alegre) ... Pesquisas Botanica (Porto Alegre) [*A publication*]
Pesqui Commun (Porto Alegre) ... Pesquisas Communications (Porto Alegre)
                    [*A publication*]
Pesqui Med ... Pesquisa Medica [*A publication*]
Pesquisa e Planejamento Econ ... Pesquisa e Planejamento Economico [*A
                    publication*]
Pesquisas Antropol ... Pesquisas Antropologia [*A publication*]
Pesqui Secc B Cienc Nat (Porto Alegre) ... Pesquisas. Seccao B. Ciencias
                    Naturais (Porto Alegre) [*A publication*]
Pesqui Zool (Porto Alegre) ... Pesquisas Zoologia (Porto Alegre) [*A
                    publication*]
PESR .... Earth-Science Reviews [*A publication*]
PesR........... Pesikta Rabbati   (BJA)
PESR .... Planning Element System Report   (NATG)
PESR .... Precision Echo Sounder Recorder
PESR .... Pseudoequivalent Service Rounds [*Military*]   (NVT)
PEsS .... East Stroudsburg State College, East Stroudsburg, PA [*Library
                    symbol*] [*Library of Congress*]   (LCLS)
PESS......... Pessus [*Pessary*] [*Pharmacy*]
PESSO .... Personnel System Staff Officer
PEST .... Parameter Entity Symbol Translator [*Elstree Computing Ltd.*]
                    [*Software package*]   (NCC)
PEST .... Parameter Estimation by Sequential Testing [*Computer*]
PEST .... Patterned Elicitation Syntax Test [*Educational test*]
PEST .... Pesticide Evaluation Summary Tabulation
PEST .... Pressure for Economic and Social Toryism [*Tory Reform
                    Group*] [*British*]   (DI)
PEST .... Production Evaluation Surveillance Test
PEST .... Reuter Laboratories, Inc. [*Detroit, MI*] [*NASDAQ
                    symbol*]   (NQ)
Pest Bioch ... Pesticide Biochemistry and Physiology [*A publication*]
Pest Contr ... Pest Control [*A publication*]
Pest Contro ... Pest Control [*A publication*]
Pest Control Circ ... Pest Control Circular [*A publication*]
PESTD ...... Proceedings. European Society of Toxicology [*A publication*]
PESTDOC ... Pest Control Literature Documentation [*Derwent Publications
                    Ltd.*] [*Bibliographic database*] [*Information service or
                    system*]   (IID)
PESTF .... Proton Event Start Forecast [*Solar weather information*]
PESTIC ..... Pesticide
Pestic Abstr ... Pesticides Abstracts and News Summary [*A publication*]
Pestic Abstr News Sum Sect C Herbic ... Pesticides Abstracts and News
                    Summary. Section C. Herbicides [*A publication*]
Pestic Biochem Physiol ... Pesticide Biochemistry and Physiology [*A
                    publication*]
Pestic CIPAC Methods Proc Ser ... Pesticides. CIPAC [*Collaborative
                    International Pesticides Analytical Council*] Methods and
                    Proceedings Series [*A publication*]
Pestic Doc Bull ... Pesticides Documentation Bulletin [*A publication*]
Pesticide A ... Pesticides Annual [*A publication*]
Pestic Monit J ... Pesticides Monitoring Journal [*A publication*]
Pestic Progr ... Pesticide Progress [*A publication*]
Pestic Res Rep Agric Can ... Pesticide Research Report. Agriculture Canada
                    [*A publication*]
Pestic Sci.... Pesticide Science [*A publication*]
Pestic Tech ... Pesticide and Technique [*A publication*]
Pestic Toxic Subst Mon Rep ... Pesticides and Toxic Substances Monitoring
                    Report [*A publication*]
Pest Infest Control Lab Rep (Lond) ... Pest Infestation Control. Laboratory
                    Report (London) [*A publication*]
Pest Infest Control (Lond) ... Pest Infestation Control. Laboratory Report
                    (London) [*A publication*]

Pest Infest Res Rep Pest Infest Lab Agric Res Counc ... Pest Infestation Research Report. Pest Infestation Laboratory. Agricultural Research Council [*A publication*]

Pest Leafl Pac For Res Cent ... Pest Leaflet. Pacific Forest Research Centre [*A publication*]

Pest Mon J ... Pesticides Monitoring Journal [*A publication*]

Pest Sci ...... Pesticide Science [*A publication*]

PESU .... Polyethersulfone [*Organic chemistry*]

PESV .... Pea Streak Virus [*Plant pathology*]

PESY .... People Say. Bimonthly Newsletter [*Canada*] [*A publication*]

PET .... Pacific Enterprises [*NYSE symbol*]   (SPSG)

PET .... Panel on Education and Training [*COSATI*]

PET .... Panel on Educational Terminology [*Office of Education*]

PET .... Parent Effectiveness Training [*A course of study*]

PET .... Particle Electrostatic Thruster

PET .... Patterned Epitaxial Technology   (IEEE)

PET .... Pelotas [*Brazil*] [*Airport symbol*]   (OAG)

PET .... Pentaerythritol [*Organic chemistry*]

PET .... Pentaerythritol Tetranitrate [*Also, PETN*] [*Explosive, vasodilator*]

PET .... Penthouse Entertainment Network [*Cable television system*]

PET .... Performance Efficiency Test [*Employee screening and placement test*]

PET .... Performance Evaluation Team [*Nuclear energy*]   (NRCH)

PET .... Performance Evaluation Test

PET .... Periodic Environmental Test

PET .... Periodic Evaluation Test

PET .... Peripheral Equipment Tester [*Data processing*]   (BUR)

PET .... Personal Effectiveness Training   (MCD)

PET .... Personal Electronic Transactor [*Computer*] [*Commodore Business Machines*]

PET .... Personal Employee Time   (DHSM)

Pet .... Pet, Inc. [*Associated Press abbreviation*]   (APAG)

PET .... Pet, Inc., Corporate Information Center, St. Louis, MO [*OCLC symbol*]   (OCLC)

Pet .... Peter [*New Testament book*]

Pet .... Peters Notes [*A publication*]

Pet .... Peters' Prince Edward Island Reports [*1850-72*] [*Canada*] [*A publication*]   (DLA)

Pet .... Peters' United States Circuit Court Reports [*A publication*]   (DLA)

Pet .... Peters' United States District Court Reports, Admiralty Decisions [*A publication*]   (DLA)

Pet .... Peters' United States Supreme Court Reports [*26-41 United States*] [*A publication*]   (DLA)

Pet .... Petihta   (BJA)

PET .... Petition

PET .... Petrine [*Of, or relating to, Peter the Apostle or Peter the Great*]

PET .... Petrolatum   (WGA)

PET .... Petroleum

PET .... Petropavlovsk [*Former USSR*] [*Geomagnetic observatory code*]

PET .... Petropavlovsk [*Former USSR*] [*Seismograph station code, US Geological Survey*]   (SEIS)

PET .... Petrotech, Inc. [*Toronto Stock Exchange symbol*]

Pet .... Petrus [*Authority cited in pre-1607 legal work*]   (DSA)

Pet .... Petrus de Bellapertica [*Deceased, 1308*] [*Authority cited in pre-1607 legal work*]   (DSA)

PET .... Phase Elapsed Time   (NASA)

PET .... Photoemission Tube

PET .... Photoinduced Electron Transfer

PET .... Phototropic Energy Transfer

PET .... Physical Equipment Table

PET .... Pierre Elliott Trudeau [*Canadian prime minister*] [*Acronymic designation considered derogatory*]

PET .... Point of Equal Time [*Aviation*]

PET .... Polyester

PET .... Poly(ethylene Terephthalate) [*Organic chemistry*]

PET .... Portable Earth Terminal [*NASA*]

PET .... Portable Electronic Telephone

PET .... Position-Event-Time

PET .... Positron-Emission Tomography

PET .... Potential Evapotranspiration

PET .... Pre-Eclamptic Toxemia [*Medicine*]

PET .... Pre-Employment Training   (OICC)

PET .... Preliminary Evaluation Team

PET .... Preliminary Examination Team [*NASA*]

PET .... Preprimary Evaluation and Training

PET .... Pressurization Events Trainer

PET .... Probe Ephemeris Tape

PET .... Process Evaluation Tester

PET .... Production Environmental Tests

PET .... Production Evaluation Test

PET .... Production Experimental Test   (SAA)

PET .... Program Evaluator and Tester [*Data processing*]

PET .... Property Enterprise Trust [*Investment term*] [*British*]   (ECON)

PET .... Propulsion Experimental Test   (SAA)

PET .... Prototype Evaluation Test

PET .... Psychiatric Emergency Team

PET .... Pulsed Electrothermal   (MCD)

PET .... Pupil Evaluation Team [*Education*]

PETA .... Pentaerythritol Triacrylate [*Organic chemistry*]

PETA .... People for the Ethical Treatment of Animals   (EA)

PETA .... Performance Evaluation and Trend Analysis   (NASA)

PETA .... Plutonium Equipment Transfer Area [*Nuclear energy*]   (NRCH)

PETA .... Portable Electronic Traffic Analyzer [*British*]

Pet Ab .... Petersdorff's Abridgment [*A publication*]   (DLA)

Pet Abr ...... Petersdorff's Abridgment [*1660-1823*] [*A publication*]   (DLA)

Pet Abstr .... Petroleum Abstracts [*A publication*]

Pet Abstracts ... Petroleum Abstracts [*A publication*]

Pet Ad .... Peters' United States District Court Reports, Admiralty Decisions [*A publication*]   (DLA)

Pet Ad Dec ... Peters' United States District Court Reports, Admiralty Decisions [*A publication*]   (DLA)

Pet Adm ..... Peters' United States District Court Reports, Admiralty Decisions [*A publication*]   (DLA)

Pet Adm App ... Peters' United States District Court Reports, Admiralty Decisions (Appendix) [*A publication*]   (DLA)

Pet Ad R ..... Peters' United States District Court Reports, Admiralty Decisions [*A publication*]   (DLA)

Pet Age .... Petroleum Age [*A publication*]

Pet de Anch ... Petrus de Ancharano [*Deceased, 1416*] [*Authority cited in pre-1607 legal work*]   (DSA)

Pet Aret ...... Petrus Aretinus [*Flourished, 1088-91*] [*Authority cited in pre-1607 legal work*]   (DSA)

PETAT ...... Periodic Inspection Turn-Around Time [*Military*]   (AFIT)

Pet Bail ...... Petersdorff on Bail [*1824*] [*A publication*]   (DLA)

Pet de Bel ... Petrus de Bellapertica [*Deceased, 1308*] [*Authority cited in pre-1607 legal work*]   (DSA)

Pet de Bellap ... Petrus de Bellapertica [*Deceased, 1308*] [*Authority cited in pre-1607 legal work*]   (DSA)

Pet de Belper ... Petrus de Bellapertica [*Deceased, 1308*] [*Authority cited in pre-1607 legal work*]   (DSA)

Pet Br .... Bellewe's Cases Tempore Henry VIII [*Brooke's New Cases*] [*England*] [*A publication*]   (DLA)

Pet Br .... Brooke's New Cases (Petit Brooke) [*1515-58*] [*A publication*]   (DLA)

PETC .... Et Cetera [*A publication*]

PETC .... Pittsburgh Energy Technology Center [*Formerly, PERC*] [*Department of Energy*] [*Pittsburgh, PA*]   (GRD)

PETC .... Portable Equipment Test Chamber   (MCD)

Pet CC .... Peters' United States Circuit Court Reports [*A publication*]   (DLA)

Pet Chem Ind Conf Rec Conf Pap ... Petroleum and Chemical Industry Conference. Record of Conference Papers [*United States*] [*A publication*]

Pet Chem Ind Dev ... Petroleum and Chemical Industry Developments [*India*] [*A publication*]

Pet Chem USSR ... Petroleum Chemistry USSR [*A publication*]

Pet Cir CR ... Peters' Condensed United States Circuit Court Reports [*A publication*]   (DLA)

Pet Cond .... Peters' Condensed Reports, United States Supreme Court [*A publication*]   (DLA)

Pet Cond Rep ... Peters' Condensed United States Circuit Court Reports [*A publication*]   (DLA)

PETD .... Petroleum Development Corp. [*NASDAQ symbol*]   (NQ)

Pet Dig ...... Peters' United States Digest [*A publication*]   (DLA)

Pet Dig ...... Peticolas' Texas Digest [*A publication*]   (DLA)

PETE .... Petersburg National Battlefield

PETE .... Pneumatic End to End

PETE .... Portable Electronics Test Equipment   (DNAB)

PETE .... Portable Emergency Thermal Environment

PETE .... Product Engineering Tribute to Excellence

PETE .... Proof and Experimental Test Establishment [*Canada*]   (MCD)

Pet Econ ..... Petroleum Economist [*A publication*]

Pet Energy Bus News Index ... Petroleum/Energy Business News Index [*A publication*]

Pet Eng ...... Petroleum Engineer [*A publication*]

Pet Eng Int ... Petroleum Engineer International [*A publication*]

Pet Equip ... Petroleum Equipment [*A publication*]

Pet Equip Serv ... Petroleum Equipment and Services [*A publication*]

Peter .... Analysis and Digest of the Decisions of Sir George Jessel, by A. P. Peter [*England*] [*A publication*]   (DLA)

Petermanns Geog Mitt ... Petermanns Geographische Mitteilungen [*A publication*]

Petermanns Geogr Mitt ... Petermanns Geographische Mitteilungen [*A publication*]

Petermanns Mitt ... Petermanns. A. Mitteilungen aus J. Perthes Geographischer Anstalt [*A publication*]

Petermanns Mitt Erg ... Petermanns Mitteilungen. Ergaenzungsheft [*Gotha*] [*A publication*]

Peterm Geog ... Petermanns Geographische Mitteilungen [*A publication*]

Peter Phot Mag ... Petersen's Photographic Magazine [*A publication*]

Peters .... Haviland's Prince Edward Island Chancery Reports, by Peters [*1850-72*] [*Canada*] [*A publication*]   (DLA)

PETERS .... Peters [*J. M.*] Co. [*Associated Press abbreviation*]   (APAG)

Peters .... Peters' United States Supreme Court Reports [*26-41 United States*] [*A publication*]   (DLA)

Peters' Ad .. Peters' United States District Court Reports, Admiralty Decisions [*A publication*]   (DLA)

Peters Adm ... Peters' United States District Courts Reports, Admiralty Decisions [*A publication*]   (DLA)

Peters' Adm Dec ... Peters' United States District Court Reports, Admiralty Decisions [*A publication*]   (DLA)

Peters' Admiralty Dec ... Peters' United States District Court Reports, Admiralty Decisions [*A publication*]   (DLA)

Peters' Adm R ... Peters' United States District Court Reports, Admiralty Decisions [*A publication*]   (DLA)

Peters Adm Rep ... Peters' United States District Court Reports, Admiralty Decisions [*A publication*]   (DLA)

Peters CC... Peters' United States Circuit Court Reports [*A publication*]   (DLA)

Petersd Ab ... Petersdorff's Abridgment [*A publication*]   (DLA)

Pet Explor Dev ... Petroleum Exploration and Development [*A publication*]

PETFE...... Polyethylenetetrafluoroethylene [*Organic chemistry*]

PETFEM... Postsecondary Education Task Force on Energy Management [*Canada*]

PETG........ Phenylethyl(thiogalactoside) [*Organic chemistry*]

Pet Gas Process ... Petroleum and Gas Processing [*A publication*]

Pet Gaz...... Petroleum Gazette [*A publication*]   (APTA)

Pet & Gaze ... Petrol si Gaze [*Romania*] [*A publication*]

Pet Gaze Supl ... Petrol si Gaze. Supliment [*Romania*] [*A publication*]

Pet Geogr Mitt ... Petermanns Geographische Mitteilungen [*A publication*]

Pet Geol ..... Petroleum Geology [*A publication*]

Pet Geol Taiwan ... Petroleum Geology of Taiwan [*A publication*]

Petg Pr & Ag ... Petgrave's Principal and Agent [*1857*] [*A publication*]   (DLA)

Pet Greg..... Petrus Gregorius [*Deceased, 1617*] [*Authority cited in pre-1607 legal work*]   (DSA)

PETH .... Ethics [*A publication*]

Peth Dis ..... Petheram's Discovery by Interrogations [*1864*] [*A publication*]   (DLA)

Pet Hydrocarbons ... Petroleum and Hydrocarbons [*India*] [*A publication*]

PETI .... Percent of Travel Involved   (FAAC)

PETI .... Portable Electronic Typewriter Interface [*Applied Creative Technology, Inc.*]

PETIA .... Particle-Enhanced Turbidometric Immunoassay [*Clinical chemistry*]

Pet Indep.... Petroleum Independent [*A publication*]

Pet Inf .... Petrole Informations [*A publication*]

Pet Int .... Petroleo Internacional [*A publication*]

Pet Interam ... Petroleo Interamericano [*A publication*]

Pet Interamericano ... Petroleo Interamericano [*A publication*]

Pet Int (London) ... Petroleum International (London) [*A publication*]

Petit Br....... Petit Brooke, or Brooke's New Cases, English King's Bench [*1515-58*] [*A publication*]   (DLA)

Petit J Brass ... Petit Journal du Brasseur [*A publication*]

PETITN ..... Petition

Pet Land J ... Petroleum Land Journal [*A publication*]

Pet L Nat ... Petersdorff's Law of Nations [*A publication*]   (DLA)

Pet Manage ... Petroleum Management [*A publication*]

Pet Mitt...... Petermanns Mitteilungen [*A publication*]

Pet de Mont ... Petrus Piccoli de Monteforte [*Flourished, 14th century*] [*Authority cited in pre-1607 legal work*]   (DSA)

Pet M & S.. Petersdorff's Master and Servant [*1876*] [*A publication*]   (DLA)

PETN........ Pentaerythritol Tetranitrate [*Also, PET*] [*Explosive, vasodilator*]

PETN........ Petition

Pet News.... Petroleum News [*Taiwan*] [*A publication*]

Pet Newsl... Petroleum Newsletter [*A publication*]

PETNR...... Petitioner

PETOA....... Petrotecnica [*A publication*]

Pet Outlook ... Petroleum Outlook [*A publication*]

PETP .... (Phenylethyl)phenyltetrahydropyridine [*Organic chemistry*]

PETP .... Poly(ethylene Terephthalate) [*Organic chemistry*]

PETP .... Preliminary Engineering Technical Proposal

Pet Peck Zir ... Petrus Peckius (Ziricaeus) [*Deceased, 1589*] [*Authority cited in pre-1607 legal work*]   (DSA)

Pet Petrochem ... Petroleum and Petrochemicals [*Japan*] [*A publication*]

Pet Petrochem Int ... Petroleum and Petrochemical International [*England*] [*A publication*]

Pet Petrochem (Tokyo) ... Petroleum and Petrochemicals (Tokyo) [*Japan*] [*A publication*]

Pet P M...... Petersen's Photographic Magazine [*A publication*]

Pet Press Serv ... Petroleum Press Service [*England*] [*A publication*]

Pet Press Service ... Petroleum Press Service [*A publication*]

PetPRO...... Pet Professional Retailers Organization   (EA)

Pet Process ... Petroleum Processing [*A publication*]

Pet Process Eng ... Petroleum Process Engineering [*A publication*]

PETQ........ Petro Quest, Inc. [*NASDAQ symbol*]   (NQ)

PETR......... Petitioner

PETR......... Petra Resources, Inc. [*NASDAQ symbol*]   (NQ)

PETRA ...... Positron-Electron Tandem Ring Accelerator [*Nuclear*]

PETRA ...... Program for the Vocational Training of Young People and their Preparation for Adult and Working Life [*EC*]   (ECED)

PETRASAFE ... Petroleum Transport Scheme for Assistance in Freight Emergencies [*A publication*]   (APTA)

PETRB ...... Petroleum Review [*A publication*]

Petr Bellug ... Petrus Belluga [*Flourished, 1446-68*] [*Authority cited in pre-1607 legal work*]   (DSA)

Petr de Benint ... Petrus de Benintendis [*Flourished, 16th century*] [*Authority cited in pre-1607 legal work*]   (DSA)

Petr de Bezut ... [*Johannes*] Petrus de Bezutio [*Deceased circa 1582*] [*Authority cited in pre-1607 legal work*]   (DSA)

PETRD...... Petrologie [*A publication*]

Pet Refiner ... Petroleum Refiner [*A publication*]

Pet Refin Petrochem Lit Abstr ... Petroleum Refining and Petrochemicals Literature Abstracts [*A publication*]

PETRES.... Petroleum Reserves [*Navy*]

PETRESO ... Petroleum Reserves Office [*or Officer*]

Pet Rev...... Petrocorp Review [*A publication*]

Pet Rev...... Petroleum Review [*A publication*]

Petr Greg ... Petrus Gregorius [*Deceased, 1617*] [*Authority cited in pre-1607 legal work*]   (DSA)

PETRIBURG ... Petriburgensis [*Signature of the Bishops of Peterborough*] [*Latin*]   (ROG)

Petrie......... Petrie Stores Corp. [*Associated Press abbreviation*]   (APAG)

Petr Inde .... Petroleum Independent [*A publication*]

PETRL ...... Petroleum   (AABC)

Petr Nuni ... Petrus Nunius de Avendano [*Flourished, 16th century*] [*Authority cited in pre-1607 legal work*]   (DSA)

PETRO...... Petroleum

PETROCH ... Rock Chemical Database [*Ontario Geological Survey*] [*Canada*] [*Information service or system*]   (CRD)

Petro/Chem Eng ... Petro/Chem Engineer [*A publication*]

PETRODEG ... Petroleum Degrading [*Agent*]

PETROG..... Petrographic

PETROGAL ... Petroleos de Portugal, EP [*Portuguese Petroleum Co.*]

PETROGR ... Petrography

PETROL ... Petroleum

PETROL ... Petrology

Petrol Abstr ... Petroleum Abstracts [*A publication*]

Petrol Eng ... Petroleum Engineer [*A publication*]

Petrol Eng Int ... Petroleum Engineer International [*A publication*]

Petroleo...... Petroleo Internacional [*A publication*]

Petroleos Mexicanos Servicio Inf ... Petroleos Mexicanos Servicio de Informacion [*A publication*]

Petroleum... Petroleum Economist [*A publication*]

Petroleum Gaz ... Petroleum Gazette [*A publication*]   (APTA)

Petrol Gaz ... Petroleum Gazette [*A publication*]   (APTA)

Petrol Geol ... Petroleum Geology [*A publication*]

Petrolieri Int ... Petrolieri International [*A publication*]

Petrol Independ ... Petroleum Independent [*A publication*]

Petrol Inform ... Petrole Informations [*A publication*]

Petrol Int.... Petroleo Internacional [*A publication*]

Petrol News ... Petroleum News [*A publication*]

Petrol Ref... Petroleum Refiner [*A publication*]

Petrol Rev ... Petroleum Review [*A publication*]

Petrol Tech ... Petrole et Techniques [*A publication*]

Petrol Technol ... Petroleum Technology [*A publication*]

Petrol Tecnol ... Petroleo y Tecnologia [*A publication*]

PETROMIN ... General Petroleum & Mineral Organization [*Saudi Arabia state-owned oil company*]

Petron .... Petronius [*First century AD*] [*Classical studies*]   (OCD)

PETRONET ... Petroleum Network [*Distribution and interdiction model*]   (MCD)

Petron Satyric ... Petronius' [*Titus*] Arbiter, Satyricon, Etc. [*A publication*]   (DLA)

PETROPHIL ... Petroleum Philatelic Society International   (EAIO)

PETROPOL ... Petropolis [*St. Petersburg*] [*Imprint*] [*Latin*]   (ROG)

Petr Prog.... Petrole-Progres [*A publication*]

Petr Rave ... Petrus Ravennas [*Flourished, 1468-1508*] [*Authority cited in pre-1607 legal work*]   (DSA)

PetRs.......... Petroleum & Resources Corp. [*Associated Press abbreviation*]   (APAG)

Petr Sit....... Petroleum Situation [*A publication*]

Petr Techn ... Petroleum Technology [*A publication*]

Petr Times ... Petroleum Times [*A publication*]

Petr Tm R .. Petroleum Times Price Report [*A publication*]

PETS .... P/L Experiment Test System [*NASA*]   (GFGA)

PETS .... Pacific Electronics Trade Show

PETS .... Payload Environmental Transportation System [*NASA*]   (NASA)

PET & S.... Performance Evaluation, Test, and Simulation [*Air Force*]

PETS .... Peripheral Equipment Test Set

PETS .... POCC [*Payload Operations Control Center*] Experiments Timeline System [*Ground Data Systems Division and Spacelab*] [*NASA*]   (NASA)

PETS .... Polaris Engineering Technical Service [*Missiles*]

PETS .... Portable Engine Test Stand   (MCD)

PETS .... Positions Equipment Task Summary   (AAG)

PETS .... Prior to Expiration of Term of Service [*Reenlistments*] [*Military*]

PETS .... Programmed Extended Time Sharing [*Data processing*]

PETS .... Proximity Effect Tunneling Spectroscopy   (MCD)

Pet de Sam ... Petrus de Sampsone [*Flourished, 1246-58*] [*Authority cited in pre-1607 legal work*]   (DSA)

Pet de Samp ... Petrus de Sampsone [*Flourished, 1246-58*] [*Authority cited in pre-1607 legal work*]   (DSA)

Pet SC .... Peters' United States Supreme Court Reports [*26-41 United States*] [*A publication*]   (DLA)

PETSEC.... Petroleum Section [*Allied Force Headquarters*]

Pet Substitutes ... Petroleum Substitutes [*A publication*]

Pet Suppl ... Supplement to Petersdorff's Abridgment [*A publication*]   (DLA)

PETT .... Pettibone Corp. [*NASDAQ symbol*]   (NQ)
PETT .... Phototropic Energy Transfer Technique
PETT .... Positron Emission Transaxial [*or Transverse*] Tomography [*Roentgenography*]
PETTA ...... Petroleum Times [*A publication*]
Pet Tech..... Petrole et Techniques [*A publication*]
Pet Technol ... Petroleum Technology [*A publication*]
Pet Tech Rev ... Petroleum Technical Review [*A publication*]
Pet Times... Petroleum Times [*A publication*]
Pet Today... Petroleum Today [*A publication*]
Petty SR..... Petty Sessions Review [*A publication*]   (APTA)
PETU......... Ethnomusicology [*A publication*]
PETV......... Planar Epitaxial Tuning Varactor
PETV......... Process Evaluation Test Vehicle
Pet W .... Petroleum Week [*A publication*]
Pet Week.... Petroleum Week [*A publication*]
Pet World... Petroleum World [*London*] [*A publication*]
Pet World (London) ... Petroleum World (London) [*A publication*]
Pet World (Los Angeles) ... Petroleum World (Los Angeles) [*A publication*]
Pet World Oil ... Petroleum World and Oil [*A publication*]
Pet World Oil Age ... Petroleum World and Oil Age [*A publication*]
PETX......... PETX Petroleum [*NASDAQ symbol*]   (NQ)
PEU .... Paneuropa-Union [*Paneuropean Union*]   (EAIO)
PEU .... Port Expander Unit
PEU .... Protected Environment Unit [*Medicine*]
PEUA .... Pelvic Exam under Anesthesia [*Medicine*]
PEUBA...... Publikacije Elektrotehnickog Fakulteta Univerziteta u Beogradu. Serija Matematika i Fizika [*A publication*]
PEUS........ Journal of European Studies [*A publication*]
PEUU .... Polyether Polyurethane Urea [*Organic chemistry*]
peV............ Peak Electron Volts
PEV........... Peak Envelope Voltage [*Telecommunications*]   (TEL)
PEV........... Pleasant Valley [*California*] [*Seismograph station code, US Geological Survey*]   (SEIS)
P Evang...... Pentecostal Evangel [*A publication*]
PEVCV...... Petunia Vein Clearing Virus [*Plant pathology*]
PEVE .... Prensa Venezolana [*Press agency*] [*Venezuela*]
PEVI .... Perry's Victory and International Peace Memorial National Monument
PEVL........ Polyethylene Expanded Video Longitudinal Cable   (MCD)
PEVM....... Personal'naia Elektronnaia Vychislitel'naia Mashina [*Personal Computer*] [*Russian*]
PEVM....... Professional'naia Elektronnaia Vychislitel'naia Mashina [*Professional Computer*] [*Russian*]
PEVO .... Evolution [*A publication*]
PEVR........ Power-Enrichment Vacuum Regulator [*Automotive engineering*]
PEW .... Passive Electronics Warfare   (NG)
PEW .... Percussion Welding
PEW .... Peshawar [*Pakistan*] [*Airport symbol*]   (OAG)
PEW .... Philosophy East and West [*A publication*]
PEW .... Politiek Economisch Weekblad [*A publication*]
PEWO .... Plant Engineering Work Order   (MCD)
PEWR........ Plant Engineering Work Release   (AAG)
PEWS........ Platoon Early Warning System   (RDA)
PEWS........ Plutonium Equipment Warm Shop [*Nuclear energy*]   (NRCH)
PEWV....... Pulmonary Extravascular Water Volume [*Physiology*]
PEX........... People Express [*Newark, NJ*] [*FAA designator*]   (FAAC)
PEX........... Per Example
PEX........... Phenazine Ethosulfate [*Biochemistry*]
PEx .... Physical Examination   (MAE)
PEX........... Pronto Explorations Ltd. [*Vancouver Stock Exchange symbol*]
PEXP .... People Express Airlines, Inc. [*NASDAQ symbol*]   (NQ)
PEXRAD... Programmed Electronic X-Ray Automatic Diffractometer
PEY.......... Pengelly Mines Ltd. [*Vancouver Stock Exchange symbol*]
PEY.......... Photoelectric Yield
PEYS .... Photoelectron Yield Spectroscopy   (MCD)
PEZ........... Pezgold Resource Corp. [*Vancouver Stock Exchange symbol*]
PEZ........... Pleasanton, TX [*Location identifier*] [*FAA*]   (FAAL)
PEZAF ...... Pezamerica Resources Corp. [*NASDAQ symbol*]   (NQ)
PF.............. American First Preparation Fund 2 LP [*AMEX symbol*]   (SPSG)
PF.............. Frankford Public Library, Frankford, PA [*Library symbol*] [*Library of Congress*]   (LCLS)
PF.............. French Polynesia [*ANSI two-letter standard code*]   (CNC)
PF.............. Pacifica Foundation   (EA)
PF.............. Package Freighter [*Shipping*]
PF.............. Paderewski Foundation [*Defunct*]   (EA)
PF.............. Paedagogische Forschungen [*A publication*]
PF.............. Page Footing   (BUR)
PF.............. Page Formatter   (MDG)
PF.............. Paling Fence
PF.............. Panchromatic Film   (ADA)
PF.............. Paper and Foil [*Capacitor*]   (DEN)
pf.............. Paracel Islands [*MARC country of publication code*] [*Library of Congress*]   (LCCP)
PF.............. Parachute Facility   (NASA)
PF.............. Parachute Flare   (NVT)
PF.............. Parafascicular Nucleus [*Neuroanatomy*]
PF.............. Parallel Fiber [*Neuroanatomy*]
PF.............. Parallel Fold

PF.............. Paramount Funding Corp. [*Toronto Stock Exchange symbol*]
PF.............. Parapsychology Foundation   (EA)
PF.............. Partition Factor   (NRCH)
P/F............ Pass-Fail [*System*]   (MAE)
PF.............. Passage Free   (ROG)
PF.............. Path Finder [*British military*]   (DMA)
PF.............. Pathfinder Fund   (EA)
PF.............. Patriotic Front [*Zimbabwe*] [*Political party*]   (PPW)
PF.............. Patrol Vessel, Frigate [*Navy symbol*]
P/F............ Pattern Flight [*Also, P/FLT*]   (MUGU)
PF.............. Payload Forward [*NASA*]   (MCD)
PF.............. Payload Function [*NASA*]   (MCD)
PF.............. Peace and Freedom Party [*Political party*]   (DLA)
PF.............. Peak Flow [*Medicine*]
PF.............. Peak Frequency
PF.............. Peanut Flour
PF.............. Pedal Furrow
PF.............. Pen Friends   (EA)
PF.............. Pennsylvania Folklife [*A publication*]
PF.............. Pensee Francaise [*A publication*]
PF.............. Pension Fund
PF.............. Peregrine Fund   (EA)
PF.............. Perfect
PF.............. Performance Factor
PF.............. Perfusion Fixation [*Histology*]
PF.............. Peritoneal Fluid [*Medicine*]   (MAE)
PF.............. Permanent Fireman
PF.............. Permanent Force [*Canadian Militia before 1940*]
PF.............. Permeability Factor
pf.............. Perofskite [*CIPW classification*] [*Geology*]
PF.............. Personal Fouls [*Basketball*]
PF.............. Personal Security File Number [*British Secret Service*]
PF.............. Personality Factor
P & F......... Petroleum and Fuel
Pf.............. Pfeifferella [*Genus of bacteria*]
PF.............. Pfennig [*Penny*] [*Monetary unit*] [*German*]
PF.............. Pfleuger Flug-Betriehs GmbH [*Germany*] [*ICAO designator*]   (FAAC)
PF.............. Phenol-Formaldehyde [*Organic chemistry*]
PF.............. Philatelic Foundation   (EA)
PF.............. Philosophische Forschungen [*A publication*]
PF.............. Philosophy Forum [*A publication*]
PF.............. Photogrammetric Facility [*Army*]
P & F......... Photography and Focus [*A publication*]
PF.............. Physicians Forum   (EA)
PF.............. Pianoforte [*Soft, then Loud*] [*Music*]
pF.............. Picofarad
PF.............. Picture Frustration [*Study*]   (MAE)
P & F......... Pike and Fischer's Administrative Law [*A publication*]   (DLA)
P & F......... Pike and Fischer's Federal Rules Service [*A publication*]   (DLA)
P & F......... Pike and Fischer's OPA Price Service [*A publication*]   (DLA)
PF.............. Pilgrim Fellowship   (EA)
PF.............. Pininfarina [*Automotive coachworks*]
PF.............. [*The*] Pioneer & Fayette Railroad Co. [*AAR code*]
PF.............. Piu Forte [*A Little Louder*] [*Music*]
PF.............. Plain Face [*Construction*]
PF.............. Plane Frame [*Camutek*] [*Software package*]   (NCC)
P & F......... Planning and Forecasting   (MCD)
PF.............. Planning Forum   (EA)
P & F......... Plant and Facilities
PF.............. Plantar Fasciaitis [*Medicine*]
PF.............. Plantar Flexion [*Medicine*]
PF.............. Platelet Factor [*Hematology*]
PF.............. Platform   (SSD)
PF.............. Plentiful Foods [*A publication*] [*Department of Agriculture*]
PF.............. Plot Function [*Data processing*]
PF.............. Pneumatic Float
PF.............. Poco Forte [*Rather Loud*] [*Music*]
PF.............. Poe Foundation   (EA)
PF.............. Poesie Francaise [*A publication*]
PF.............. Point Foundation   (EA)
PF.............. Point of Frog [*Electronics*]   (MSA)
PF.............. Points For [*Football*]
PF.............. Pole Fittings [*JETDS nomenclature*] [*Military*]   (CET)
PF.............. Police Forces [*British*]
PF.............. Police Foundation   (EA)
PF.............. POLISARIO [*Frente Popular para la Liberacion de Saguia El Hamra y Rio De Oro*] [*Popular Front for the Liberation of Saguia El Hamra and Rio De Oro*] [*Morocco*]   (PD)
PF.............. Polish Folklore [*A publication*]
PF.............. Poloidal Field   (MCD)
PF.............. Polyurethane Foam
PF.............. Pool Frequency [*Pisciculture*]
PF.............. Poop and Forecastle [*of a ship*]   (DS)
PF.............. Popular Foodservice [*A publication*]
PF.............. Popular Forces [*ARVN*]
PF.............. Por Favor [*Please*] [*Portuguese*]
PF.............. Portal Fibrosis [*Medicine*]
PF.............. Portfolio [*A publication*]
PF.............. Position Failure

PF............... Position Finder [*British military*]   (DMA)
P/F............. Post Flight   (AFIT)
PF............. Postage Free   (ROG)
PF............. Postman's Federation [*A union*] [*British*]
PF............. Posture Foundation [*Initialism is used in brand of sneaker shoe, PF Flyers*]
PF............. Power Factor [*Radio*]
PF............. Power Frame [*Telecommunications*]   (TEL)
PF............. Powered Flight   (NASA)
P/F............. Practical Factors
PF............. Preference
PF............. Preferred
PF............. Preflight
PF............. Pressure Fan   (AAG)
PF............. Prime Function   (NASA)
PF............. Prison Fellowship Ministries   (EA)
pf............. Pro Forma [*As a Matter of Form*] [*Latin*]   (WGA)
PF............. Probability of Failure   (NASA)
PF............. Procurator Fiscal
PF............. Profile   (KSC)
PF............. Program Function [*Data processing*]   (IBMDP)
PF............. Programmable Format [*Perforating keyboard*]
PF............. Progressive Foundation   (EA)
PF............. Project Friend   (EA)
PF............. Projectile Fragment
PF............. Proof
PF............. Prop Forward
PF............. Proposed Finding [*Nuclear energy*]   (NRCH)
PF............. Protection Factor
PF............. Protein-Free
PF............. Protoplasmic Fracture [*Freeze etching in microscopy*]
PF............. Proximity Fuze [*Bomb, rocket, or shell*]
PF............. PsychoHistory Forum   (EA)
PF............. Psychologische Forschung [*A publication*]
PF............. Psynetics Foundation   (EA)
P/F............. Pteropod/Foramifera [*Ratio in coastal waters*]
PF............. Public Finance [*A publication*]
PF............. Pulmonary Factor [*Medicine*]
PF............. Pulse Frequency
PF............. Pulverized Fuel
P F............. Pump-Out Facilities [*Nautical charts*]
PF............. Punch Off [*Data processing*]   (BUR)
PF............. Purge Fan [*Nuclear energy*]   (NRCH)
PF............. Purple Finch [*Ornithology*]
PF............. Pygmy Fund   (EA)
PFA............. Korte Berichten over Buitenlandse Projecten [*A publication*]
PFA............. Palmdale Final Assembly [*NASA*]   (NASA)
PFA............. Panarcadian Federation of America   (EA)
PFA............. Papermakers Felt Association   (EA)
PFA............. Para-Fluorophenylalanine [*Biochemistry*]
PFA............. Parti de la Federation Africaine [*African Federation Party*] [*Political party*]
PFA............. Participating Field Activity [*DoD*]
PFA............. Pension Fund Association [*Japan*]   (ECON)
PFA............. Perfluoroalkoxy [*Organic chemistry*]
PFA............. Petroflame International [*Vancouver Stock Exchange symbol*]
Pf A............. Pfluegers Archiv fuer die Gesamte Physiologie des Menschen und der Tiere [*A publication*]
PFA............. Phosphonoformic Acid [*Antiviral compound*]
PFA............. Pianists Foundation of America   (EA)
PFA............. Pierce Ferry [*Arizona*] [*Seismograph station code, US Geological Survey*] [*Closed*]   (SEIS)
PFA............. Pierre Fauchard Academy   (EA)
PFA............. Pioneer Fraternal Association   (EA)
PFA............. Pitch Follow-Up Amplifier
PFA............. Plan for Action   (MCD)
PFA............. Polish Falcons of America   (EA)
PFA............. Polyfurfuryl Alcohol [*Organic chemistry*]
PFA............. Polyurethane Foam Association   (EA)
PFA............. Popular Flying Association [*British*]
PFA............. Post Flight Analysis
PFA............. Prescription Footwear Association   (EA)
PFA............. Prison Families Anonymous   (EA)
PFA............. Professional Farmers of America   (EA)
PFA............. Professional Fraternity Association   (EA)
PFA............. Program and File Analysis
PFA............. Proportional Fluid Amplifier
PFA............. Public Finance and Accountancy [*A publication*]
PFA............. Pulverized Fuel Ash   (IEEE)
PFA............. Pure Fluid Amplification
PFAA............. Prairie Farm Assistance Act
8PFAB............. Eight-Parallel-Form Anxiety Battery [*Psychology*]
PFAC............. Panepirotic Federation of America and Canada [*Later, PFACA*]   (EA)
PFAC............. People for a Change   (EA)
PFACA............. Panepirotic Federation of America, Canada, and Australia   (EA)
P/FACCTL ... Pad Facility Controls [*Aerospace*]   (AAG)
PFAD............. Palm Fatty Acid Distillate [*Organic chemistry*]
PFAE............. Perfluoroalkyl Ether [*Organic chemistry*]
Pfaelzer H ... Pfaelzer Heimat [*A publication*]

Pfaelz Heimat ... Pfaelzer Heimat [*A publication*]
PFAM............. Programmed Frequency Amplitude Modulation
PFAP............. Poly(fluoroalkoxyphosphazene) [*Organic chemistry*]
PFAR............. Popular Front for Armed Resistance [*Pakistan*]
PFAR............. Power Fail Automatic Restart [*Data processing*]
PFAR............. Preliminary Failure Analysis Report [*NASA*]   (KSC)
PFAS............. Performic Acid-Schiff Reaction [*Medicine*]   (MAE)
PFAS............. President of the Faculty of Architects and Surveyors [*British*]   (DBQ)
PFAT............. Pre-First Article Test
PFAT............. Preliminary Flight Appraisal Test   (MCD)
PFAVC............. Pacific Fleet Audio-Visual Command   (DNAB)
PFAW............. People for the American Way   (EA)
PFAX............. Primefax, Inc. [*NASDAQ symbol*]   (NQ)
PFB............. Partei Freier Buerger [*Free Citizens' Party*] [*Germany*] [*Political party*]   (PPW)
PFB............. Passo Fundo [*Brazil*] [*Airport symbol*]   (OAG)
PFB............. Payload Feedback [*NASA*]   (MCD)
PFB............. Payload Forward Bus [*NASA*]   (MCD)
PFB............. Pentafluorobenzyl [*Organic radical*]
PFB............. Pentafluorobenzyl Bromide [*Organic chemistry*]
PFB............. Photo Flash Battery
PFB............. Plasti-Fab Ltd. [*Toronto Stock Exchange symbol*]
PFB............. Pneumatic Float Bridge
PFB............. Position Feedback   (MCD)
PFB............. Prefabricated [*Technical drawings*]
PFB............. Preformed Beams [*SONAR*]
PFB............. Pressure Fed Booster   (NASA)
PFB............. Pressurized Fluid-Bed [*Chemical engineering*]
PFB............. Provisional Frequency Board [*ITU*]
PFB............. Pseudofollicutitis Barbae [*Medicine*]
PFBA............. Poly(perfluorobutyl Acrylate) [*Organic chemistry*]
PFBC............. Pressurized Fluidized-Bed Combustion
PFBFA............. Power Farming and Better Farming Digest (Australia) [*A publication*]
PFBHA............. Pentafluorobenzylhydroxylamine Hydrochloride [*Analytical biochemistry*]
PFBI............. FBI Law Enforcement Bulletin [*A publication*]
PFBK............. Pioneer Federal Savings Bank [*NASDAQ symbol*]   (NQ)
PFBRG............. Pneumatic Float Bridge
PFBS............. Ponce Federal Bank FSB [*Ponce, PR*] [*NASDAQ symbol*]   (NQ)
PFBV............. Pelargonium Flower Break Virus [*Plant pathology*]
PFC............. Pacific City, OR [*Location identifier*] [*FAA*]   (FAAL)
PFC............. Parti Feministe du Canada
PFC............. Passed Flying College [*British*]
PFC............. Passenger Facility Charge [*Airports*]
PFC............. Pathfinder Industries Ltd. [*Formerly, Pathfinder Financial Corporation*] [*Toronto Stock Exchange symbol*]
PFC............. Peak Follower Circuit
PFC............. Peculiar Facility Change   (AAG)
PFC............. Pen Fancier's Club   (EA)
PFC............. Pennsylvania Public Library Film Center, University Park, PA [*OCLC symbol*]   (OCLC)
PFC............. Perfluorocarbon [*Organic chemistry*]
PFC............. Perfluorochemical [*Organic chemistry*]
PFC............. Performance Flight Certification [*NASA*]   (NASA)
PFC............. Permanent Families for Children [*Defunct*]   (EA)
PFC............. Persistent Fetal Circulation [*Medicine*]
PFC............. Physicians for Choice   (EA)
PFC............. Plan Filing Cabinet
PFC............. Plaque-Forming Cell [*Immunochemistry*]
PFC............. Pneumatic Function Controller
PFC............. Point Focusing and Centering [*Optics*]
PFC............. Police Forces [*British*]
PFC............. Positive Feedback Circuit
PFC............. Postflight Checklist   (MCD)
PFC............. Power Factor Corrector   (MCD)
PFC............. Prairie Fiction Collection, Alberta Culture [*UTLAS symbol*]
PFC............. Praying for Corporal [*Private First Class desirous of promotion, or female in wartime desirous of a boyfriend*]
PFC............. Preflight Console   (MCD)
PFC............. Prefrontal Cortex [*Anatomy*]
PFC............. Preliminary Flight Certification [*NASA*]
PFC............. Presley-ites Fan Club   (EA)
PFC............. Pressure Function Controller
PFC............. Primary Flight Control
PFC............. Priority Foreign Country [*International trade*]   (ECON)
PFC............. Private, First Class [*Army*]
PFC............. Programmed Fuel Computer [*Automotive engineering*]
PFC............. Progreso y Futuro de Ceuta [*Political party*]   (EY)
PFC............. Progressive Fish-Culturist [*A publication*]
PFC............. Pulse-Flow Coulometry
PFC............. Pulsed Flame Combustor
PFCA............. Performance Ford Club of America   (EA)
PFCA............. Plastic Food Container Association [*Defunct*]
PFCCG............. Pacific Fleet Combat Camera Group   (DNAB)
PFCD............. Primary Flight Control Display
PFCE............. Performance   (WGA)
PFCE............. Preface   (ROG)
PFCE............. Preference   (AAG)

PFCF .... Payload Flight Control Facility [*NASA*] (MCD)
PFCF .... Producer Fixed Capital Formation (MCD)
PFCH......... Prefilled Clutch Hydraulic Actuation [*Automotive Products, Inc.*] [*Automotive engineering*]
PFCM....... Pittsburgh Festival of Contemporary Music [*Record label*]
PFCO......... Position Field Classification Officer
PFCO......... Preferred Financial [*NASDAQ symbol*] (NQ)
PFCP .... Perpetual Financial Corp. [*NASDAQ symbol*] (NQ)
PFCR .... Plaque-Forming Cell Response [*Immunochemistry*] (OA)
PFCRA ...... Program Fraud Civil Remedies Act
PFCRN ...... Partido del Frente Cardenista de Reconstruccion Nacional [*Mexico*] [*Political party*] (EY)
PFCS .... Primary Flight Control System [*NASA*] (MCD)
PFCS .... Primary Flow Control System [*Nuclear energy*] (NRCH)
PFCS .... Program and Funds Control System (MCD)
PFCT .... Pre-Flight Certification Test
PFCUA ...... Progressive Fish-Culturist [*A publication*]
PFD........... Particle [*or Proton*] Flux Density
PFD........... Perfluorodecalin [*Organic chemistry*]
PFD........... Personal, Fatigue, and Delay [*Work measurement factors*]
PFD........... Personal Flotation Device [*Life jacket*]
PFD........... Planning Factors Development (MCD)
PFD........... Position Fixing Device (ADA)
PFD........... Power Flux Density [*Telecommunications*] (TEL)
PFD........... Preferred (AAG)
PFD........... Preferred Income Fund [*NYSE symbol*] (SPSG)
PFD........... Preliminary Functional Description (CINC)
PFD........... Present for Duty
PFD........... Primary Flash Distillate [*Chemical technology*]
PFD........... Primary Flight Display
PFD........... Process Flow Diagram (NRCH)
PFD........... Puffed [*Freight*]
PFD........... Pulse-Frequency Diversity [*Electronics*] (NG)
PFDA........ Perfluorodecanoic Acid [*Organic chemistry*]
PFDA........ Post Flight Data Analysis
PFDA........ Precision Frequency Distribution Amplifier
PFDA........ Pulse-Frequency Distortion Analyzer
PFDBAD ... Pathfinder Badge [*Military decoration*] (GFGA)
PFDC......... Peoples Federal Savings Bank of DeKalb City [*NASDAQ symbol*] (NQ)
PFDCCA ... Prodema: Friends of the Democratic Center in the Americas (EA)
PFDF .... Pacific Fisheries Development Foundation (EA)
PFDHLTH ... Preferred Health Care Ltd. [*Associated Press abbreviation*] (APAG)
PfdInco ...... Preferred Income Fund [*Associated Press abbreviation*] (APAG)
PFDM....... Preliminary Final Draft Manuscript
PFDR........ Pathfinder [*Aircraft*]
PFDR........ Preferred Risk Life Insurance Co. [*NASDAQ symbol*] (NQ)
PfdrBad..... Pathfinder Badge [*Military decoration*] (AABC)
PFDS .... Pergamon Financial Data Services [*Pergamon Orbit Infoline Ltd.*] [*British*] [*Information service or system*] (IID)
PFDTM ..... Preliminary Flightweight Demonstration Test Motor (MCD)
PFE........... Pacific Fruit Express Co. [*AAR code*]
PFE........... Paper, Film, and Foil Converter [*A publication*]
PFE........... Partido Feminista de Espana [*Feminist Party of Spain*] [*Political party*] (PPW)
PFE........... Performance Fitness Examination [*Military*] (DNAB)
PFE........... Pfizer, Inc. [*NYSE symbol*] (SPSG)
PFE........... Photoferroelectric Effect [*Physics*]
PFE........... Physics of Failure in Electronics [*A publication*] (MCD)
PFE........... Plenum Fill Experiment [*Nuclear energy*] (NRCH)
PFE........... Popular Front of Estonia [*Political party*]
PFE........... Post Fire Evaluation [*Military*] (CAAL)
PFE........... Post Flight Evaluation
PFE........... Pressure Feedback Exhaust [*Automotive engineering*]
PFE........... Priests for Equality (EA)
PFE........... Process Fuel Equivalent (MCD)
PFE........... Pulsed Field Electrophoresis [*Analytical biochemistry*]
PFE........... Purchaser Furnished Equipment (NATG)
PFEC........ Philatelic Friends Exchange Circuit (EA)
PFEFES..... Pacific and Far East Federation of Engineering Societies
PFEL........ Pacific Far East Line
PFEM....... Feminist Review [*A publication*]
PFEP .... Programmable Front-End Processor [*Data processing*]
PFES......... Pan American Federation of Engineering Societies
PFES......... Proposed Final Environmental Statement [*Department of Energy*]
PFES......... Pure Fluid Encoder System
PFF........... Pathfinder Force [*British RADAR designation which became overall synonym for RADAR*] [*Military*]
PFF........... Permanent Family File [*Navy*] (NG)
PFF........... Phenolfurfural [*Organic chemistry*]
PFF........... Planning Factors File (MCD)
PFF........... Police Field Force (CINC)
PFF........... Porcine Follicular Fluid [*Endocrinology*]
PFF........... Primary Focus Feed [*Satellite communications*]
PFF........... Proposed Fabric Flammability Standard [*Consumer Product Safety Commission*]
PFF........... Protein Fat-Free [*Food technology*]

PFF........... Punjab Frontier Force [*British military*] (DMA)
PFFC .... Parallel-Flow Film Cooling
PFFC .... Philadelphia Flyers Fan Club (EA)
PFF Convrt ... Paper, Film, and Foil Converter [*A publication*]
PFF Convt ... Paper, Film, and Foil Converter [*A publication*]
PFF Inc...... Police-FBI Fencing, Incognito [*Phony fencing ring operated by Washington, DC, law enforcement agents during 1976 to identify and arrest area thieves*]
PFFS......... Pacific First Financial Corp. [*Formerly, Pacific First Federal Savings Bank*] [*NASDAQ symbol*] (NQ)
PFFX .... Profiling Fixture
PFG........... Pacific Rim Mining Corp. [*Vancouver Stock Exchange symbol*]
PFG........... Paeoniflorigenone [*Biochemistry*]
PFG........... Paper Flow Group [*Nuclear Regulatory Commission*] (GFGA)
PFG........... Peak Flow Gauge [*Medicine*] (AAMN)
PFG........... PennCorp Financial Group [*NYSE symbol*] (SPSG)
PFG........... Pfennig [*Penny*] [*Monetary unit*] [*German*]
PFG........... Piping and Filter Gallery [*Nuclear energy*] (NRCH)
PFG........... Primary Frequency Generator
PFG........... Pulsed Field Gradient [*Electroanalytical chemistry*]
PFG........... Purple Flower Gang (EA)
PFGC........ Parameters from Group Contribution [*Equation of state*]
PFGE........ Pulsed Field Gel Electrophoresis
PFGE........ Pulsed Field Gradient Gel Electrophoresis
PFGGA ...... Professional Geographer [*A publication*]
PFGM....... Guided Missile Patrol Escort [*Ship symbol*] (NATG)
PFGX........ Pacific Fruit Growers Express
PFH .... Hudson, NY [*Location identifier*] [*FAA*] (FAAL)
PFH .... Pafco Financial Holdings Ltd. [*Toronto Stock Exchange symbol*]
PfH .... Pfaelzische Heimatblaetter [*A publication*]
PFH .... Pressurized Fluidized-Bed Hydroretorting [*Chemical engineering*]
PFHA .... Paso Fino Horse Association (EA)
PFHEDE.... Pfaelzer Heimat [*A publication*]
PFHM....... Protein-Free Hybridoma Medium
PFHS........ French Historical Studies [*A publication*]
PFHS......... Precipitation from Homogeneous Solution [*Catalyst preparation process*]
PFI .... Pacific Forest Industries (EA)
PFI .... People First International (EA)
PFI .... Pet Food Institute (EA)
PFI .... Photo Finishing Institute [*Defunct*] (EA)
PFI .... Physical Fitness Index
PFI .... Picture and Frame Institute [*Defunct*] (EA)
PFI .... Pie Filling Institute [*Defunct*] (EA)
PFI .... Pipe Fabrication Institute (EA)
PFI .... Port Fuel Injector [*Automotive engines*]
PFI .... Position Finding Instrument (DS)
PFI .... Power Failure Indicator [*NASA*] (KSC)
PFI .... Prison Fellowship International (EA)
PFI .... Profile Index. Micromedia Ltd. [*A publication*]
PFIA .... Police and Firemen's Insurance Association (EA)
PFIA .... Prevention of Fraud Investments Act [*British*]
PFIAB....... President's Foreign Intelligence Advisory Board (AFM)
PFIB .... Pentafluoroiodosylbenzene [*Organic chemistry*]
PFIB .... Perfluoroisobutene [*Organic chemistry*]
PFIB .... Perfluoroisobutylene [*Organic chemistry*] (MAE)
PFIC .... Passive Foreign Investment Company [*IRS*]
PFIEP....... Perfluorinated Ion-Exchange Polymer [*Organic chemistry*]
PFil .... Przeglad Filozoficzny [*A publication*]
PFIM......... Pure Fluid Impact Modulator
PFIN......... P & F Industries, Inc. [*NASDAQ symbol*] (NQ)
PfIOF......... Preferred Income Opportunity Fund [*Associated Press abbreviation*] (APAG)
PFI & R ..... Part Fill In and Ram [*Construction*]
Pfitzner .... Hans Pfitzner-Gesellschaft. Mitteilungen [*A publication*]
PFIU......... Plot File Import Utility [*IBM Corp.*]
Pfizer....... Pfizer, Inc. [*Associated Press abbreviation*] (APAG)
Pfizer Med Monogr ... Pfizer Medical Monographs [*A publication*]
PFJ .... Patreksfjordur [*Iceland*] [*Airport symbol*] (OAG)
PFJ .... Polar Front Jet Stream (ADA)
PFJR......... Patellofemoral Joint Reaction [*Physiology*]
PFK........... Payload Function Key [*NASA*] (MCD)
PFK........... Perfluorokerosene [*Heat transfer agent*]
PFK........... Phosphofructokinase [*An enzyme*]
PFK........... Programmed Function Keyboard [*Data processing*]
PFL .... Fort Sill, OK [*Location identifier*] [*FAA*] (FAAL)
PFL .... Pacific Cassiar Ltd. [*Toronto Stock Exchange symbol*]
PFL .... Pennsylvania Folklife [*A publication*]
PFL .... People for Life (EA)
PFL .... Pharmacists for Life (EA)
PFL .... Pounds per Lineal Foot [*Technical drawings*]
PFL .... Primary Freon Loop (NASA)
PFL .... Propulsion Field Laboratory
PFL .... Public Facility Loans
PFLA .... Popular Front for the Liberation of Ahvaz [*Iran*]
PFLAB....... Pfluegers Archiv. European Journal of Physiology [*A publication*]
P-FLAG..... Federation of Parents and Friends of Lesbians and Gays (EA)
Pflanzenschutzber ... Pflanzenschutzberichte [*A publication*]

Pflanzenschutz-Nachr ... Pflanzenschutz-Nachrichten [*A publication*]
Pflanzenschutz-Nachr (Am Ed) ... Pflanzenschutz-Nachrichten (American Edition) [*A publication*]
Pflanzenschutz Nachr Bayer ... Pflanzenschutz-Nachrichten Bayer [*A publication*]
Pflanz-Nach Bayer ... Pflanzenschutz-Nachrichten Bayer [*A publication*]
PflBau PflSchutz PflZucht ... Pflanzenbau, Pflanzenschutz, Pflanzenzucht [*A publication*]
PFLDA ...... Physics of Fluids [*A publication*]
PFLF .... People, Food and Land Foundation (EA)
PFLFT .... Pubblicazioni. Facolta di Lettere e Filosofia. Universita di Torino [*A publication*]
P Flo .... Pandectae Florentinae [*A publication*] (DSA)
PFLO .... Popular Front for the Liberation of Oman [*Political party*] (PD)
PFLOAG ... Popular Front for the Liberation of Oman and the Arabian Gulf [*Political party*] (PD)
PFLOLS .... Portable Fresnel-Lens Optical-Landing System (NG)
P Florent .... Pandectae Florentinae [*A publication*] (DSA)
PFLP .... Popular Front for the Liberation of Palestine [*Political party*] (PD)
PFLP-GC ... Popular Front for the Liberation of Palestine - General Command [*Political party*] (PD)
PFLSA .... Physics of Fluids. Supplement [*A publication*]
PFLSH ...... Publications. Faculte des Lettres et Sciences Humaines de Paris [*A publication*]
P/FLT .... Pattern Flight [*Also, P/F*] (MUGU)
PFLT .... People's Front of the Liberation Tigers [*Sri Lanka*] [*Political party*] (EY)
PFLTS ...... Parquet Floor Layers' Trade Society [*A union*] [*British*]
Pflueg Arch ... Pfluegers Archiv. European Journal of Physiology [*A publication*]
Pfluegers Arch Eur J Physiol ... Pfluegers Archiv. European Journal of Physiology [*A publication*]
Pfluegers Arch Ges Physiol ... Pfluegers Archiv fuer die Gesamte Physiologie [*A publication*]
Pfluegers Archiv Gesamte Physiol Menschen Tiere ... Pfluegers Archiv fuer die Gesamte Physiologie des Menschen und der Tiere [*A publication*]
PFLUS .... Publications. Faculte des Lettres. Universite de Strasbourg [*A publication*]
PFLV .... Pressure Fed Launch Vehicle [*NASA*] (KSC)
PFLY .... Polifily Finance Corp. [*NASDAQ symbol*] (NQ)
PFM .... Little Franciscan Sisters of Mary [*Roman Catholic religious order*]
PFM .... Pacific Minesearch Ltd. [*Vancouver Stock Exchange symbol*]
PFM .... Patriots of Fort McHenry (EA)
PFM .... Peak Flow Meter [*Medicine*] (AAMN)
PFM .... Physiological Flow Model [*For simulating medical conditions*]
PFM .... Pitch Follow-Up Motor
PFM .... Plan for Maintenance [*Navy*]
PFM .... Planning Factors Management (MCD)
PFM .... Platform (NASA)
PFM .... Political Freedom Movement [*British*]
PFM .... Porcelain Fused to Metal [*Dentistry*]
PFM .... Potato Futures Market [*Finance*]
PFM .... Poultry Feather Meal [*Fisheries*]
PFM .... Power Factor Meter
PFM .... Precision Frequency Multivider (KSC)
PFM .... Predictor Frame Memory
PFM .... Preliminary Flight Motor (MCD)
PFM .... Pressure Flow Meter
PFM .... Prison Fellowship Ministries (EA)
P & FM ...... Programs and Financial Management [*Navy*]
PFM .... Pulse-Forming Machine
PFM .... Pulse-Frequency Modulation [*RADAR*]
P/FM .... Pylon/Fin Movement
PFM .... University of Pittsburgh, Falk Library - Health Professions, Pittsburgh, PA [*OCLC symbol*] (OCLC)
PFMA .... Pipe Fittings Manufacturers Association [*Later, APFA*] (EA)
PFMA .... Plumbing Fixture Manufacturers Association [*Defunct*] (EA)
PFMC .... Pacific Fishery Management Council (EA)
PFMO .... Planning Factors Management Office
PFMPG ...... Pacific Fleet Mobile Photographic Group (DNAB)
PFMR ...... Pasadena Foundation for Medical Research [*California*]
PFMR ...... Plug-Flow Membrane Reactor [*Chemical engineering*]
PFMR ...... Project Funds Management Record (MCD)
PFN .... Panama City [*Florida*] [*Airport symbol*] (OAG)
PFN .... Pantyffynnon [*British depot code*]
PFN .... Parti des Forces Nouvelles [*New Forces Party*] [*France*] [*Political party*] (PPW)
PFN .... Passamaquoddy Ferry & Navigation Co. [*AAR code*]
PFN .... Permanent File Name
PFN .... Plasma Fibronectin [*Biochemistry*]
PFN .... PMC Corp. [*Toronto Stock Exchange symbol*]
PFN .... Prefinished [*Technical drawings*]
PFN .... Pulse-Forming Network
PFNA .... Pentecostal Fellowship of North America (EA)
PFNA .... Pulsed Fast Neutron Analysis [*for detection of explosives*] (PS)
PFNC .... Progress Financial Corp. [*Plymouth Meeting, PA*] [*NASDAQ symbol*] (NQ)

PFNP .... Partido Federalista Nacionalista Popular [*Panama*] [*Political party*] (EY)
PFNS .... Position Fixing Navigation System (AABC)
PFNTU ...... Pathfinder Navigation Training Unit [*Military*]
PFO .... Paphos [*Cyprus*] [*Airport symbol*] (OAG)
PFO .... Partly Filled Out [*Questionnaire*]
PFO .... Patent Foramen Ovale [*Cardiology*]
PFO .... Physical Fitness Officer [*British military*] (DMA)
PFO .... Pitch Follow-Up Operation
PFO .... Pomona Public Library, Pomona, CA [*OCLC symbol*] (OCLC)
PFO .... Postal Finance Officer [*Army*]
PFO .... Procurement Field Office
PFO .... Pyrolysis Fuel Oil [*Petroleum refining*]
PFO .... Spofford, TX [*Location identifier*] [*FAA*] (FAAL)
PFOBA ...... Paso Fino Owners and Breeders Association [*Later, PFHA*] (EA)
PFOD .... Presumed Finding of Death [*DoD*]
PFol .... Ridley Township Public Library, Folsom, PA [*Library symbol*] [*Library of Congress*] (LCLS)
PFouad ...... Les Papyrus Fouad I [*A publication*] (OCD)
PFP .... Partnership for Productivity International (EA)
PFP .... Peace and Freedom Party (EA)
PFP .... Pensions for Professionals, Inc.
PFP .... Pentafluoropropionate [*or Pentafluoropropionyl*] [*Organic chemistry*]
PFP .... Personal Financial Planning (ADA)
PFP .... Pet-Facilitated Psychotherapy [*Psychiatry*]
PFP .... Platelet-Free Plasma [*Hematology*]
PFP .... Pleiades Foundation for Peace [*Later, PFPSE*] (EA)
PFP .... Policy-Framework Paper (ECON)
PFP .... Popular Front Party [*Ghana*] [*Political party*] (PPW)
PFP .... Pore Forming Protein [*Biochemistry*]
PFP .... Post Flight Processor
PFP .... Postage Forward Parcels [*Shipping*]
PFP .... Primary Failed Part (DNAB)
PFP .... Prime Financial Partnership [*AMEX symbol*] (SPSG)
PFP .... Probability of Failure, Performance [*NASA*] (SAA)
PFP .... Products for Power [*Automotive components manufacturer*]
PFP .... Program File Processor
PFP .... Program Financial Plan (NASA)
PFP .... Program Forecast Period [*Military*] (AFIT)
PFP .... Programmable Function Panel (NASA)
PFP .... Progressiewe Federale Party [*Progressive Federal Party*] [*South Africa*] [*Political party*] (PPW)
PFP .... Proving for Production (MCD)
PFP .... Publishers for Peace [*An association*]
PFPA .... Pentafluoropropionic Anhydride [*Organic chemistry*]
PFPA .... Pro-Family Press Association (EA)
PFPC .... Passenger Form and Procedures Committee [*IATA*] (DS)
PFPE .... Perfluorinated Polyether [*Organic chemistry*]
PFPI .... Partnership for Productivity International (EA)
PFPI .... Pentafluoropropionyl Imidazole [*Organic chemistry*]
PFPM .... Production Flight Procedures Manual (MCD)
PFPR .... Federal Probation [*A publication*]
PFPS .... Potential for Foster Parenthood Scale [*Psychology*]
PFPS .... Progressive French Polishers' Society [*A union*] [*British*]
PFPSE ...... Pleiades Foundation for Peace and Space Education (EA)
PFPUT ...... Pension Fund Property Unit Trust [*British*]
PFPXA6 .... Pediatric Continuing Education Courses for the Practitioner [*A publication*]
PFQ .... Personality Factor Questionnaire (MAE)
PFQ .... Preflight Qualification
PFQ .... Public Finance Quarterly [*A publication*]
PFr .... Franklin Public Library, Franklin, PA [*Library symbol*] [*Library of Congress*] (LCLS)
PFR .... Part Failure Rate
PFR .... Peak Flow Rate [*or Reading*] [*Medicine*]
PFR .... Perforator (DEN)
PFR .... Perkins Family Restaurants LP [*NYSE symbol*] (SPSG)
PFR .... Permanent Factory Repairable (MCD)
PFR .... Persistent Fat Retention [*Syndrome*]
PFR .... Personal Financial Record [*Army*] (AABC)
PFR .... Pfarrer [*Pastor*] [*German*] (EY)
PFR .... Photoflash Relay
PFR .... Pike Fry Rhabdovirus
PFR .... Plug-Flow Reactor [*Engineering*]
PFR .... Polarized Frequency Relay
PFR .... Portable Foot Restraint (NASA)
PFR .... Post-Fielding Review [*DoD*]
PFR .... Power Fail Recovery System [*Data processing*] (MDG)
PFR .... Power Fail/Restart
PFR .... Power Failure Release
PFR .... Precision Fathometer Recorder [*Raytheon Co.*]
PFR .... Preferred Resources, Inc. [*Vancouver Stock Exchange symbol*]
PFR .... Preflight Review [*NASA*] (KSC)
PFR .... Preheating, Falling-Film, Rising-Film [*Sections of a concentrator*] [*Chemical engineering*]
PFR .... Preliminary Flight Rating [*Air Force*]
PFr .... Presence Francophone [*A publication*]
PFR .... Problem/Failure Report
PFR .... Programmed Film Reader [*System*]

pfr.............. Proofreader [*MARC relator code*] [*Library of Congress*] (LCCP)
PFR............ Prototype Fast Reactor
PFR............ Pulmonary Blood Flow Redistribution [*Medicine*]
PFR............ Pulse Frequency (MDG)
PFR............ Punch Feed Read (CMD)
PFRA........ Percent of Females Reproductively Active [*Ecology*]
PFRA........ Prairie Farm Rehabilitation Administration [*Canada*]
PFRA........ Problem-Focused Research Applications [*of ASRA*] [*National Science Foundation*]
PFRA........ Professional Football Referees Association (EA)
PFRA........ Professional Football Researchers Association (EA)
P & F Radio Reg ... Pike and Fischer's Radio Regulation Reporter [*A publication*] (DLA)
PFRC........ Pacific Forest Research Centre [*Canada*] (ARC)
PFRD........ Preferred Homecare of America, Inc. [*NASDAQ symbol*] (NQ)
PFRD........ Preferred Stock [*Investment term*]
PFredY...... Joseph A. Yablonski Memorial Clinic, Fredericktown, PA [*Library symbol*] [*Library of Congress*] (LCLS)
PFRMG..... Performing (ROG)
PFRS .... French Studies [*A publication*]
PFRS .... Portable Field Recording System [*NASA*] (KSC)
PFRT .... Preliminary Flight Rating Test
PFRT .... Preliminary Flight Readiness Test [*NASA*] (KSC)
PFS .... Parallel Filter System
P & FS....... Particles and Fields Subsatellite [*NASA*] (KSC)
PFS .... Particles and Fields Subsatellite [*NASA*]
PFS .... Percent Full Scale (KSC)
PFS .... Performance Funding System [*Department of Housing and Urban Development*] (GFGA)
PFS .... Peripheral Fixed Shim [*Nuclear energy*] (NRCH)
PFS .... Personal and Family Survival [*Civil Defense*]
PFS .... Personal Filing System [*Data-base program*] [*Software Publishing Corp.*]
PFS .... Photofragment Spectroscopy
PFS .... Pioneer Financial Services, Inc. [*NYSE symbol*] (SPSG)
PFS .... Pitch Follow-Up System
PFS .... Pittsburgh, PA [*Location identifier*] [*FAA*] (FAAL)
PFS .... Plasterers' Friendly Society [*A union*] [*British*]
PFS .... Porous Friction Surface [*Airfield pavement*]
PFS .... Positive Fuel Stop
PFS .... Precision Frequency Source
PFS .... Preflight School [*Military*]
PFS .... Press Fit Socket
PFS .... Primary Flight System (NASA)
PFS .... Primary Frequency Supply [*Telecommunications*] (TEL)
PFS .... Probability of Failure, Stress [*NASA*] (SAA)
PFS .... Programmable Frequency Standard
PFS .... Progress in Filtration and Separation [*Elsevier Book Series*] [*A publication*]
PFS .... Propellant Feed System
PFS .... Propellant Field System
PFS .... Pulmonary Function Score [*Physiology*]
PFS .... Pure Fluid System
PFS .... [*P. F.*] Smith's Pennsylvania State Reports [*51-81 1/2 Pennsylvania*] [*A publication*] (DLA)
PFSB......... Piedmont Federal Corp. [*NASDAQ symbol*] (NQ)
P Fsch .... Philosophische Forschungen [*A publication*]
PFSCL....... Papers on French Seventeenth Century Literature [*A publication*]
PFSh .... Partia Fashimit e Shqiperise [*Fascist Party of Albania*] [*Political party*] (PPE)
PFSH......... Porcine Follicle Stimulating Hormone [*Endocrinology*]
PFSL......... Prudential Financial Services Corp. [*NASDAQ symbol*] (NQ)
PFSM .... Physical Fitness/Sports Medicine [*A publication*]
P F Smith... [*P. F.*] Smith's Pennsylvania State Reports [*51-81 1/2 Pennsylvania*] [*A publication*] (DLA)
PFSN .... Food Sciences and Nutrition [*A publication*]
PFSO........ Postal Finance and Supply Office (AFM)
PFSP......... Polyfactorial Study of Personality [*Psychology*] (AEBS)
PFS/PRS... Patent Family Service/Patent Register Service [*Database*] [*International Patent Documentation Center*] [*Information service or system*] (CRD)
PFSR .... Journal of Feminist Studies in Religion [*A publication*]
PFSR .... Program Financial Status Report (AAG)
PFSS........ Particles and Fields Subsatellite [*Telecommunications*] (OA)
PFSS........ Patellofemoral Stress Syndrome [*Medicine*]
PFSV .... Pilot-to-Forecaster Service (FAAC)
PFT........... Pacific Asia Tech [*Vancouver Stock Exchange symbol*]
PFT........... Pacific Fisheries Technologists [*An association*]
PFT........... Page Frame Table (BUR)
PFT........... Pancreatic Function Test [*Medicine*]
PFT........... Paper, Flat Tape
PFT........... Parafascicular Thalamotomy [*Medicine*]
PFT........... Parallel Fourier Transform (MCD)
PFT........... Permanent Full-Time (GFGA)
PFT........... Pet-Facilitated Therapy [*Psychiatry*]
PFT........... Phenylalanine mustard [*Melphalan*], Fluorouracil, Tamoxifen [*Antineoplastic drug regimen*]
PFT........... Physical Fitness Test
PFT........... Pittsburgh, Fort Wayne & Chicago Railway Co. (IIA)

PFT............ Plastic Fuel Tank
PFT............ Portable Flame Thrower [*Army*]
PFT............ Positive Flight Termination (MUGU)
PFT............ Posterior Fossa Tumor [*Anatomy*] (MAE)
PFT............ Preflight Team [*Air Force*] (AFM)
PFT............ Preflight Tool (MCD)
PFT............ Professional Football Trainers (EA)
PFT............ Program Flying Training [*Air Force*] (AFM)
PFT............ Projective Field Theory
PFT............ Pulmonary Function Test [*Medicine*]
PFT............ Pulse Fourier Transform
PFTA .... Payload Flight Test Article [*NASA*] (MCD)
PFTA .... Post-Fielding Training Analysis
PFTB .... Preflight Test Bus (MCD)
PFTC .... Pestalozzi-Froebel Teachers College [*Illinois*]
PFTE .... Permanent Full-Time Equivalent (GFGA)
PFTE .... Pianoforte [*Soft, then Loud*] [*Music*]
PFTE .... Portable Field Trainer/Evaluator (MCD)
PFTEA ..... Post-Fielding Training Effectiveness Analysis
PFTM .... Preliminary Flight Test Memo
PFTR .... Preliminary Flight Test Report
PFTS .... Permanent Field Training Site
PFTS.......... Profit Systems, Inc. [*NASDAQ symbol*] (NQ)
PFU .... Passive Filtration Unit
PFU .... Physical Fitness Uniform [*Army*] (INF)
PFU .... Plan for Use (DNAB)
PFU .... Plaque-Forming Unit [*Immunochemistry*]
PFU .... Please Follow Up
PFU .... Pock-Forming Unit
PFU .... Preparation for Use
PFUA........ Pitch Follow-Up Amplifier
PFUEI ...... Prime Focus Universal Extragalactic Instrument [*Astronomy*]
PFUM....... Pitch Follow-Up Motor
PFUO .... Pitch Follow-Up Operation
PFUS .... Pitch Follow-Up System
PFV .... Peak Flow Velocity [*Cardiology*]
PFV .... Pestalozzi-Froebel-Verband [*Pestalozzi-Froebel Association*]
PFV............ Philippine Forces, Vietnam
PFV............ Physiological Full Value
PFV............ Probability of Failure, Vehicle [*NASA*] (SAA)
PFVEA ...... Professional Film and Video Equipment Association (EA)
PFW.......... Power, Fulcrum, Weight
PFW.......... Predicted Fire Weapon
PFW.......... Progressive Free Wave
PFWA....... Professional Football Writers of America (EA)
PFwB .... Budd Co., Fort Washington, PA [*Library symbol*] [*Library of Congress*] (LCLS)
PFWOAD ... Place from Which Ordered to Active Duty [*Military*]
PFwR .... William H. Rorer, Inc., Fort Washington, PA [*Library symbol*] [*Library of Congress*] (LCLS)
PFX........... Prefix (ROG)
PFX........... Proflex Ltd. [*Vancouver Stock Exchange symbol*]
PFY........... Prior Fiscal Year (AFIT)
PFYA........ Predicted First-Year Average [*Law school*]
PFZ........... Polar Front Zone [*Marine science*] (MSC)
PFZ........... Potassium Hexafluorozirconate [*Inorganic chemistry*]
PFZ........... Precipitate-Free Zone (MCD)
PF-ZAPU .. Patriotic Front - Zimbabwe African People's Union [*Political party*] (PD)
PG .... Air Gabon Cargo [*ICAO designator*] (FAAC)
PG .... Page [*or Pagination*] [*Online database field identifier*]
PG .... Palestine Gazette [*A publication*]
PG .... Papua New Guinea [*ANSI two-letter standard code*] (CNC)
PG .... Paralysie Generale [*General Paralysis*] [*Medicine*] [*French*]
PG .... Paregoric [*Slang*]
PG .... Parental Guidance Suggested [*Formerly, GP*] [*Some material may not be suitable for preteenagers*] [*Movie rating*]
PG .... Paris Granite
PG .... Paris Group [*See also GP*] [*France*] (EAIO)
PG .... Partial Gum [*Philately*]
PG .... Past Grand [*Freemasonry*]
PG .... Paste Grain [*Bookbinding*]
PG .... Patrol Combatant [*Gunboat*] [*Navy symbol*]
PG .... Patrologia Graeca [*A publication*]
PG .... Patrologiae Cursus. Series Graeca [*A publication*] (OCD)
PG .... Pay Grade
PG .... Pay Group
PG .... Paying Guest
PG .... PEACE [*Program for Emergency Assistance, Cooperation, and Education*] for Guatemala (EA)
PG .... Pedal Ganglion
PG .... Pedal Groove
PG .... Pelham Grenville Wodehouse [*British humorist, 1881-1975*]
Pg.............. Pentagram [*One billion metric tons*]
PG .... Peptidoglycan [*Biochemistry*]
PG .... Permanent Glow [*Telecommunications*] (TEL)
PG .... Permanent Grade
PG .... Persian Gulf (MCD)
PG .... Pharmacopoeia Germanica [*German Pharmacopoeia*]
PG .... Phosphatidylglycerol
PG .... Phosphogluconate [*Biochemistry*]

PG .... Phosphogypsum [*Inorganic chemistry*]
PG .... Photogrammetry
pg .... Picogram [*One trillionth of a gram*]
PG .... Pine Grosbeak [*Ornithology*]
PG .... Pipers Guild   (EA)
PG .... Pituitary Gonadotropin [*Endocrinology*]   (MAE)
PG .... Placebo Group [*Medicine*]
PG .... Planning Group [*DoD*]
PG .... Planning Guide [*HUD*]
PG .... Plasma Gastrin [*Endocrinology*]   (AAMN)
PG .... Plasma Glucose [*Hematology*]
PG .... Plate Glass
PG .... Plate-Glazed [*Paper*]
PG .... Pointer Game   (AEBS)
PG .... Politie-Gids [*A publication*]
PG .... Pollen Grain [*Botany*]
PG .... Polyethylene Glycol [*Organic chemistry*]
PG .... Polygalacturonase [*An enzyme*]
PG .... Polyglycine [*Biochemistry*]
PG .... Pontius Guillelmi [*Authority cited in pre-1607 legal work*]   (DSA)
PG .... Port Group [*Telecommunications*]   (TEL)
PG .... Portugal
PG .... Portuguese [*Language, etc.*]
pg .... Portuguese Guinea [*Guinea-Bissau*] [*MARC country of publication code*] [*Library of Congress*]   (LCCP)
PG .... Position Guide   (MCD)
P/G .... Postagram [*British military*]   (DMA)
PG .... Postgraduate [*Refers to courses or students*] [*Slang*]
PG .... Power Gain
PG .... Power Gate [*Electronics*]   (OA)
PG .... Power Generation   (MCD)
PG .... Preacher General
PG .... Predicted Grade [*IRS*]
PG .... Pregnanediol Glucuronide [*Endocrinology*]
PG .... Pregnant
PG .... Pregnant Guppy [*Reference to Boeing 377 aircraft*]   (SAA)
PG .... Press Gallery [*US Senate*]
PG .... Pressure Gauge   (KSC)
PG .... Priority Group
PG .... Prisonnier de Guerre [*Prisoner of War - POW*] [*French*]
PG .... Pro-German [*Prisoner of war term*] [*World War I*]   (DSUE)
PG .... Procter & Gamble Co. [*NYSE symbol*]   (SPSG)
P & G .... Procter & Gamble Co.
PG .... Procureur Generaal [*Public Attorney*] [*Dutch*]   (ILCA)
PG .... Producers Group   (EA)
PG .... Professional Group   (MCD)
PG .... Program [*Telecommunications*]
PG .... Program Generic [*Data processing*]   (TEL)
PG .... Program Guidance
PG .... Programmer   (AAG)
PG .... Project Group
PG .... Proof Gallon [*Wines and spirits*]
PG .... Propyl Gallate [*Antioxidant*] [*Organic chemistry*]
PG .... Propylene Glycol
PG .... Prostaglandin [*Also, Pg*] [*Biochemistry*]
PG .... Protein Granule
PG .... Proteoglycan [*Biochemistry*]
PG .... Prothoracic Gland [*Insect anatomy*]
PG .... Province Guard [*Cambodia*]   (CINC)
PG .... Proving Ground [*Army*]
PG .... Przeglad Geograficzny [*A publication*]
PG .... Public Gaol [*British*]
PG .... Pulse Gate
PG .... Pulse Generator
PG .... Pure Gum [*of envelopes*]
PG .... Pyoderma Gangrenosum [*Medicine*]
PG .... Pyrolytic Graphite   (MCD)
PG .... Pyrotechnic Gyro   (AAG)
PG-13........ Parental Guidance Suggested [*Now: Parents Strongly Cautioned. Some material may be inappropriate for children under 13*] [*Movie rating*]
PGA .... Page [*Arizona*] [*Airport symbol*]   (OAG)
PGA .... Paragould [*Arkansas*] [*Seismograph station code, US Geological Survey*]   (SEIS)
PGA .... Pega Capital Resources Ltd. [*Toronto Stock Exchange symbol*]
PGA .... Pendulous Gyro Accelerometer
PGA .... PGI, Inc. [*AMEX symbol*]   (SPSG)
PGA .... Phosphoglyceric Acid [*Biochemistry*]
PGA .... Pin-Grid-Array [*Motorola, Inc.*]
PGA .... Polyglycolic Acid [*Organic chemistry*]   (RDA)
PGA .... Poly(L-glutamic Acid) [*Organic chemistry*]
PGA .... Power Gain Antenna
PGA .... Power Generating Assembly   (KSC)
PGA .... Pressure Garment Assembly
PGA .... Printing and Graphic Arts [*A publication*]
PGA .... Producers Guild of America   (EA)
PGA .... Professional Golfers' Association of America   (EA)
PGA .... Professional Graphics Adapter [*IBM Corp.*]
PGA .... Professional Group Audio
PGA .... Programmable Gain Amplifier   (MCD)

PGA .... Programmable Gate Array
PGA .... Prostaglandin A [*Biochemistry*]
PGA .... Prostaglandin Analog [*Biochemistry*]
PGA .... Pteroylmonoglutamic Acid [*Folic acid*] [*Also, FA, PteGlu*] [*Biochemistry*]
PGA .... Purchased Gas Adjustment
PGA .... Pure Grain Alcohol
PGA .... Pyrolysis Gas Analysis
PGA .... Upjohn Co. [*Research code symbol*]
PGAA .... Professional Guides Association of America   (EA)
PGAA .... Prompt Gamma-Ray Activation Analysis
P-GABA .... Phenyl-gamma-aminobutyric Acid [*Tranquilizer*]
PGAC .... Guam/Taguac [*Mariana Islands*] [*ICAO location identifier*]   (ICLI)
PG-AC .... Phenylglycine Acid Chloride [*Biochemistry*]   (AAMN)
PGAC .... Professional Group - Automatic Control
PGAEA ...... Proceedings. Geologists' Association (England) [*A publication*]
PGAH........ Pineapple Growers Association of Hawaii   (EA)
PGAI......... Pension Insurance Group of America, Inc. [*Valley Forge, PA*] [*NASDAQ symbol*]   (NQ)
PGAM .... Pacific Gamble Robinson Co. [*NASDAQ symbol*]   (NQ)
PGAM .... Phosphoglyceromutase [*An enzyme*]
PGANE ..... Professional Group on Aeronautical and Navigational Electronics
PGA-NOC ... Permanent General Assembly of National Olympic Committees
PGAP........ Professional Group - Antennas and Propagation
PGAPL...... Preliminary Group Assembly Parts List
PGAR .... Georgia Review [*A publication*]
PGAR .... Provisional Government of the Algerian Republic
PGase........ Polygalacturonase [*An enzyme*]
PGAZA ..... Petrol si Gaze [*A publication*]
Pg B............ Bachelor of Pedagogy
PGB .... Patrol Gunboat [*Navy symbol*]   (NATG)
PGB .... Phoenix Global [*Vancouver Stock Exchange symbol*]
PGB .... Prostaglandin B [*Biochemistry*]
PGB .... Protestant Guild for the Blind   (EA)
PGB .... Pyrographalloy Boron
PGBA........ Piece Goods Buyers Association [*Defunct*]   (EA)
PGBA........ Possum Growers and Breeders Association   (EA)
PGBD....... Pegboard [*Freight*]
PGBM .... Pulse Gate Binary Modulation   (MCD)
PGbSH ...... Seton Hill College, Greensburg, PA [*Library symbol*] [*Library of Congress*]   (LCLS)
PGBTR ..... Professional Group - Broadcast and Television Receivers
PGBTS ..... Professional Group - Broadcast Transmission Systems
PGbU .... University of Pittsburgh at Greensburg, Greensburg, PA [*Library symbol*] [*Library of Congress*]   (LCLS)
PGC .... Geneva College, Beaver Falls, PA [*OCLC symbol*]   (OCLC)
PGC .... Gettysburg College, Gettysburg, PA [*Library symbol*] [*Library of Congress*]   (LCLS)
PGC .... Pacific Geoscience Centre [*Research center*]   (RCD)
PGC .... Pagurian Corp. [*Toronto Stock Exchange symbol*]
PGC .... Past Grand Commander [*Freemasonry*]   (ROG)
PGC .... Pelican Gospel Commentaries [*Harmondsworth*] [*A publication*]
PGC .... Per Gyro Compass [*Navigation*]
PGC .... Persian Gulf Command [*World War II*]
PGC .... Phillips Gas [*NYSE symbol*]   (SPSG)
PGC .... Pontine Gaze Center [*Eye anatomy*]
PGC .... Poorly Graphitized Carbon [*Physical chemistry*]
PGC .... Port Group Control [*Telecommunications*]   (TEL)
PGC .... Potassium Gold Cyanide [*Inorganic chemistry*]
PGC .... Potential Gas Committee
PGC .... Primordial Germ Cell
PGC .... Process Gas Chromatography
PGC .... Process Gas Consumers Group   (EA)
PGC .... Professional Graphics Controller [*IBM Corp.*]
PGC .... Program Generation Center [*Military*]   (CAAL)
PGC .... Programmed Gain Control
PGC .... Proving Ground Command [*Air Force*]
PGC .... Pulsed Gas Crymotography
PGC .... Pyrolysis Gas Chromatography
PGcC........ Grove City College, Grove City, PA [*Library symbol*] [*Library of Congress*]   (LCLS)
PGCC........ Power Generation Control Complex [*Nuclear energy*]   (NRCH)
PGCE........ Post Graduate Certificate of Education
PGCh .... Past Grand Chaplain [*Freemasonry*]
PGCOA ..... Pennsylvania Grade Crude Oil Association   (EA)
PGCP........ Professional Group - Component Parts
PGCRA ..... Professional Golf Club Repairmen's Association   (EA)
PGCS........ Professional Group - Communications Systems
PGCT........ Professional Group - Circuit Theory
PGCU .... International Printing and Graphic Communications Union
PGD .... Pango Gold Mines Ltd. [*Toronto Stock Exchange symbol*]
PGD .... Past Grand Deacon [*Freemasonry*]
PGD .... Patriot Global Dividend Fund [*NYSE symbol*]   (SPSG)
PGD .... Personnel and Guidance Journal [*A publication*]
PGD .... Phosphogluconate Dehydrogenase [*Also, PGDH*] [*An enzyme*]
PGD .... Phosphoglyceraldehyde Dehydrogenase [*An enzyme*]   (MAE)
PGD .... Pikwitonei Granulite Domain [*Geology*]
PGD .... Pinion Gear Drive

PGD .... Planar Gas Discharge (MCD)
PGD .... Policy and Grants Division [*Environmental Protection Agency*] (GFGA)
PGD .... Prostaglandin D [*Biochemistry*]
PGD .... Pulse Generator Display
PGD .... Punta Gorda [*Florida*] [*Airport symbol*] (OAG)
PGDB .... Propylene Glycol Dibenzoate [*Organic chemistry*]
PGDC .... Provincial Grand Director of Ceremonies [*Freemasonry*]
PGDCS ...... Power Generation, Distribution, and Control Subsystem (MCD)
PGDF .... Pilot Guide Dog Foundation (EA)
PGDH .... 15-Hydroxyprostaglandin Dehydrogenase [*An enzyme*]
PGDH .... Phosphogluconate Dehydrogenase [*Also, PGD*] [*An enzyme*]
PGDN .... Propylene Glycol Dinitrate [*Organic chemistry*]
PGDR .... Plasma-Glucose Disappearance Rate [*Hematology*] (MAE)
PGDS .... Pioneer Ground Data System
PGDS .... Pulse Generator Display System
PG & E ...... Pacific Gas and Electric [*Rock music group*]
PG & E ...... Pacific Gas & Electric Co.
PGE .... Pacific Great Eastern Railway Co. [*Nicknames: Prince George Eventually, Please Go Easy*] [*Later, British Columbia Railway*] [*AAR code*]
PGE .... Page Petroleum Ltd. [*Toronto Stock Exchange symbol*] (SPSG)
PGE .... Phenyl Glycidyl Ether [*Organic chemistry*]
PGE .... Platelet Granule Extract [*Hematology*] (MAE)
PGE .... Platinum Group Element [*Chemistry*]
PGE .... Population Growth Estimation
PGE .... Pore Gradient Electrophoresis
PGE .... Portland General Electric Co., Library, Portland, OR [*OCLC symbol*] (OCLC)
PGE .... Portland Grain Exchange (EA)
PGE .... Precision Gimbal Experiment
PGE .... Prime Group Engineer (AAG)
PGE .... Professional Group - Education
PGE .... Prostaglandin E [*Biochemistry*]
PGE .... Purge (NASA)
PGEC .... Professional Group on Electronic Computers [*IEEE*]
PGED .... Professional Group - Electronic Devices
PGEM .... Professional Group - Engineering Management
PGEN .... Plant Genetics, Inc. [*NASDAQ symbol*] (NQ)
PGEO .... Geography [*A publication*]
PGEPF ...... Pacific Gas & Electric Co. [*Associated Press abbreviation*] (APAG)
PGER .... Geographical Review [*A publication*]
PGEWS ..... Professional Group on Engineering Writing and Speech [*Institute of Radio Engineers; now IEEE*]
PGF .... Pacific Gamefish Foundation (EA)
PGF .... Pengrowth Gas Income Fund Trust Units [*Toronto Stock Exchange symbol*]
PGF .... Peptide Growth Factor [*Biochemistry*]
PGF .... Perpignan [*France*] [*Airport symbol*] (OAG)
PGF .... Plerocercoid Growth Factor [*Endocrinology*]
PGF .... Portugal Fund [*NYSE symbol*] (SPSG)
PGF .... Presentation Graphic Feature [*Data processing*]
PGF .... Prostaglandin F [*Biochemistry*]
PGFC .... Periodical Guide for Computerists [*Applegate Computer Enterprises*] [*Information service or system*] [*Defunct*] (IID)
PGFEL ...... Preliminary Government-Furnished Equipment List (MCD)
PGFS .... Pennsylvania German Folklore Society. Bulletin [*A publication*]
PGFW .... Guam [*Mariana Islands*] [*ICAO location identifier*] (ICLI)
PGG .... Page America Group, Inc. [*AMEX symbol*] (SPSG)
PGG .... Petrogold Financial Corp. [*Vancouver Stock Exchange symbol*]
PGG .... Pneumatic Ground Group
PGG .... Power Generation Group [*Nuclear Regulatory Commission*] (NRCH)
PGG .... Prostaglandin G [*A prostaglandin endoperoxide*] [*Biochemistry*]
PGGJ-A ..... Philippine Geographical Journal [*A publication*]
PGGUDU ... Annual Research Reviews. Prostaglandins and the Gut [*A publication*]
PGH .... Patrol Gunboat (Hydrofoil) [*Navy symbol*]
PGH .... Phosphoglycolohydroxamate [*Biochemistry*]
PGH .... Pituitary Growth Hormone [*Endocrinology*]
PGH .... Plasma Growth Hormone [*Hematology*] (MAE)
PGH .... Porcine Growth Hormone [*Biochemistry*]
PGH .... Port Group Highway [*Telecommunications*] (TEL)
PGH .... Prostaglandin H [*A prostaglandin endoperoxide*] [*Biochemistry*]
PGHA .... Park Gallatin Hereford Association (EA)
PGHFE ...... Professional Group - Human Factors in Electronics
Pgh Leg Journal ... Pittsburgh Legal Journal [*Pennsylvania*] [*A publication*] (DLA)
PGHM .... Payload Ground Handling Mechanism [*NASA*] (MCD)
PGHS .... Public-General Hospital Section [*American Hospital Association*] (EA)
PGHTA ..... Progress in Hemostasis and Thrombosis [*A publication*]
PGHTS ...... Port Group Highway Timeslot [*Telecommunications*] (TEL)
PGI .... Chitato [*Angola*] [*Airport symbol*] [*Obsolete*] (OAG)

PGI .... General Information Programme [*Acronym is based on foreign phrase*] [*UNESCO*]
PGi .... Paragigantocellularis [*Neuroanatomy*]
PGI .... Paris Gestion Informatique [*Paris Informatics Administration*] [*France*] [*Information service or system*] (IID)
PGI .... Peripheral Graphics, Inc.
PGI .... Phosphoglucoisomerase [*An enzyme*]
PGI .... Ply-Gem Industries, Inc. [*AMEX symbol*] (SPSG)
PGI .... Port Group Interface [*Telecommunications*] (TEL)
PGI .... Potassium, Glucose, and Insulin (MAE)
PGI .... Professional Group - Instrumentation
PGI .... Project Group, Inc. [*Advertising agency*] [*Acronym now used as official name of agency*]
PGI .... Prostaglandin I [*Biochemistry*]
PGI .... Provigo, Inc. [*Toronto Stock Exchange symbol*]
PGI .... Pyrotechnics Guild International (EA)
PGIE .... Professional Group - Industrial Electronics
PGiess .... Griechische Papyri im Museum des Oberhessischen Geschichtsvereins zu Giessen [*A publication*] (OCD)
PGIM .... Professional Group on Instrumentation and Measurement [*National Bureau of Standards*]
PGIS .... Project Grant Information System
PGIT .... Professional Group - Information Theory
PGJ .... Personnel and Guidance Journal [*A publication*]
PGJ .... Pipeline Girth Joint
PGJD .... Past Grand Junior Deacon [*Freemasonry*]
PGJN .... Pomegranate Guild of Judaic Needlework (EA)
P & G Jour ... Pipeline and Gas Journal [*A publication*]
P & G Jour BG ... Pipeline and Gas Journal Buyer's Guide Issue Handbook [*A publication*]
PGJW .... Past Grand Junior Warden [*Freemasonry*] (ROG)
PGK .... Pangkalpinang [*Indonesia*] [*Airport symbol*] (OAG)
PGK .... Phosphoglycerate Kinase [*An enzyme*]
PGK .... Preussischer Gesamtkatalog [*A publication*]
PGl .... Glenside Free Library, Glenside, PA [*Library symbol*] [*Library of Congress*] (LCLS)
PGL .... Lutheran Theological Seminary, Gettysburg, PA [*Library symbol*] [*Library of Congress*] (LCLS)
PGL .... Paraglossa of Labium [*Entomology*]
PGL .... Pascagoula, MS [*Location identifier*] [*FAA*] (FAAL)
PGL .... Peoples Energy Corp. [*NYSE symbol*] (SPSG)
PGL .... Persistent Generalized Lymphadenopathy [*Medicine*]
PGL .... Phosphoglycolipid
PGL .... Polyglutaraldehyde [*Organic chemistry*]
PGL .... Portable Gas LASER
PGL .... Professional Graphics Language [*Software*] [*IBM Corp.*] (BYTE)
PGL .... Provincial Grand Lodge [*Freemasonry*]
PGL .... Pulsed Gas LASER
PGladM ..... Mary J. Drexel Home, Gladwyne, PA [*Library symbol*] [*Library of Congress*] [*Obsolete*] (LCLS)
PGlB .... Beaver College, Glenside, PA [*Library symbol*] [*Library of Congress*] (LCLS)
PGLC .... Pyrolysis Gas Liquid Chromatography
PGL-Hi ...... Lutheran Historical Society, Gettysburg, PA [*Library symbol*] [*Library of Congress*] (LCLS)
PGLO .... NV Philips Gloeilampenfabrieken [*NASDAQ symbol*] (NQ)
PGM .... Messiah College Learning Center, Grantham, PA [*OCLC symbol*] (OCLC)
PGM .... Papyri Graecae Magicae [*A publication*] (OCD)
PGM .... Past Grand Master [*Freemasonry*]
PGM .... Patrol Vessel, Motor Gunboat [*Navy symbol*] [*Obsolete*]
PGM .... Perron Gold Mines [*Vancouver Stock Exchange symbol*]
PGM .... Persatuan Geologi Malaysia [*Geological Society of Malaysia*] (EAIO)
PGM .... Petermanns Geographische Mitteilungen [*A publication*]
PGM .... Phosphoglucomutase [*An enzyme*]
PGM .... Planetary Gearhead Motor [*Aerospace*]
PGM .... Platinum Group Metal [*In meteorites*]
PGM .... Port Graham, AK [*Location identifier*] [*FAA*] (FAAL)
PGM .... Postgraduate Medicine [*A publication*]
PGM .... Precision Guided Missile
PGM .... Precision-Guided Munition (MCD)
PGM .... Program
PGM .... Program Guidance Memorandum
PGM .... Program Manager [*A publication*]
PGM .... Putnam Investment Grade Municipal Trust [*NYSE symbol*] (SPSG)
PGMA .... Poly(glyceryl Methacrylate) [*Organic chemistry*]
PGMA .... Pulsed Gas Metal Arc (KSC)
PGME .... Professional Group - Medical Electronics
PGM-FI .... Programmed Fuel Injection [*Automotive engineering*]
PGMIL ...... Professional Group - Military Electronics (MUGU)
PGMILE ... Professional Group - Military Electronics (AAG)
PGMS .... Professional Grounds Management Society (EA)
PGMSJ .... Professional Group of Mathematical Symbol Jugglers (MUGU)
PGMT .... Pigment (MSA)
PGMTT .... Professional Group - Microwave Theory and Techniques
PGMV .... Pea Green Mottle Virus [*Plant pathology*]
PGN .... Paragon Petroleum Ltd. [*Toronto Stock Exchange symbol*]
PGN .... Perigeniculate Nucleus [*Anatomy*]

PGN.......... Phi Gamma Nu [*Fraternity*]
PGN.......... Pigeon   (ADA)
PGN.......... Platinum Group Nugget [*In meteorites*]
PGN.......... Portland General Corp. [*NYSE symbol*]   (SPSG)
PGN.......... Proliferative Glomerulonephritis [*Medicine*]
PGN.......... Pulse Generator
PGNAA ..... Prompt Gamma Neutron Activation Analysis [*Analytical chemistry*]
PGNCS...... Primary Guidance, Navigation, and Control System [*or Subsystem*] [*Apollo*] [*NASA*]   (MCD)
PGND....... Propaganda   (AABC)
P & G News ... Plants and Gardens News [*A publication*]
PGNMA .... Progress in Nuclear Medicine [*A publication*]
PGNO........ Government and Opposition [*A publication*]
PGNR........ Greece and Rome [*A publication*]
PGNS........ Polar Gas News [*A publication*]
PGNS........ Primary Guidance and Navigation System [*Apollo*] [*NASA*]
PGNS........ Professional Group - Nuclear Science
PGNT .... Sabanettan, Tinian Island [*Mariana Islands*] [*ICAO location identifier*]   (ICLI)
PGNW .... Ritidian Point, Guam Island [*Mariana Islands*] [*ICAO location identifier*]   (ICLI)
PGNY .... Journals of Gerontology [*A publication*]
PGO.......... Page, OK [*Location identifier*] [*FAA*]   (FAAL)
PGO.......... Pagecorp, Inc. [*Toronto Stock Exchange symbol*]
PGO.......... Past Grand Orient [*Freemasonry*]   (ROG)
PGO.......... Peroxidase-Glucose Oxidase [*Also, GOD-POD*] [*Enzyme mixture*]
PGO.......... Ponto-Geniculate-Occipital [*Electroencephalography*]
PGO.......... Positive Grid Oscillator
PGO.......... Progressive Grocer [*A publication*]
PGOC........ Payload Ground Operations Contractor [*NASA*]   (SSD)
P Goodsp Cair ... Greek Papyri from the Cairo Museum. Together with Papyri of Roman Egypt from American Collections. Goodspeed [*A publication*]
PGOR .... Payload Ground Operation Requirements [*NASA*]   (NASA)
PGORS...... Payload Ground Operation Requirements Study [*NASA*]   (MCD)
PGP .... Pacific Gateway Properties [*Formerly, Perini Investment Properties, Inc.*] [*AMEX symbol*]   (SPSG)
PGP .... Parti Gabonais du Progres [*Political party*]   (EY)
PGP .... Peace Garden Project [*Later, NPG*]   (EA)
PGP .... Phosphoglycolate Phosphatase [*An enzyme*]
PGP .... Pico Glass Pellet
PGP .... Planning Grant Program
PGP .... Postgamma Proteinuria [*Medicine*]   (MAE)
PGP .... Precision Gas Products [*Commercial firm*]
PGP .... Prepaid Group Practice [*Insurance*]
PGP .... Programmable Graphics Processor
PGP .... Project on Government Procurement   (EA)
PGP .... Prostaglandin Production
PGP .... Puerta Galera [*Philippines*] [*Seismograph station code, US Geological Survey*]   (SEIS)
PGP .... University of Southern Maine at Portland, Portland, ME [*OCLC symbol*]   (OCLC)
PGPEP ..... Professional Group - Product Engineering and Production
PGPI......... Protein Grain Products International   (EA)
PGPR........ Plant-Growth-Promoting Rhizobacteria
PGPS........ Packaged Gas Pressure System
PGPSDZ ... Pergamon General Psychology Series [*A publication*]
PGPT .... Professional Group - Production Techniques
PGR .... Pakistan Geographical Review [*A publication*]
PGR .... Paragould, AR [*Location identifier*] [*FAA*]   (FAAL)
PGR .... Parental Guidance Recommended [*Movie rating*] [*Australia*]
P Gr.......... Patrologia Graeca [*A publication*]
PGR .... Peregrine Petroleum [*Vancouver Stock Exchange symbol*]
PGR .... Petition Granted   (DNAB)
PGR .... PGR. Press Gallery Report [*A publication*]   (ADA)
PGR .... [*Spacelab*] Planning and Ground Rule [*NASA*]   (NASA)
PGR .... Plant Growth Regulation [*A publication*]
PGR .... Polymerized Grass Extract [*Immunology*]
PGR .... Population Growth Rate
PGR .... Precision Graphic Recorder
PgR .... Progesterone Receptor [*Endocrinology*]
PGR .... Progressive Corp. [*NYSE symbol*]   (SPSG)
Pgr........... Progressive Grocer [*A publication*]
PGR .... Psychogalvanic Reflex [*or Response*] [*Psychology*]
PGR .... Pyrogallol Red [*Also, PR*] [*An indicator*] [*Chemistry*]
PGRAA...... Progressive Architecture [*A publication*]
PGraM...... Messiah College, Grantham, PA [*Library symbol*] [*Library of Congress*]   (LCLS)
PGRB........ Greek, Roman, and Byzantine Studies [*A publication*]
PGRC........ Plant Gene Resources of Canada [*See also RPC*]
PGRC........ Program Guidance and Review Committee [*Army*]   (AABC)
PGrev........ Greenville Area Public Library, Greenville, PA [*Library symbol*] [*Library of Congress*]   (LCLS)
PGrevT ...... Thiel College, Greenville, PA [*Library symbol*] [*Library of Congress*]   (LCLS)
PGRF........ Pacific Gamefish Research Foundation [*Later, PORF*]   (EA)
PGRF........ Pulse Group Repetition Frequency
PGRFI .... Professional Group - Radio Frequency Interference

PGRM .... Parti Gerakan Rakyat Malaysia [*People's Action Party of Malaysia*] [*Political party*]   (PPW)
PGRO .... Processors and Growers Research Organisation [*British*]   (IRUK)
PGRO .... Rota/International [*Mariana Islands*] [*ICAO location identifier*]   (ICLI)
PGRQC ..... Professional Group - Reliability and Quality Control
PGRS........ Pergerakan Guerilja Rakyat Sarawak [*Sarawak People's Guerrilla Forces*] [*Malaya*]
PGRSA....... Plant Growth Regulator Society of America   (EA)
PGRT........ Petroleum Gas and Revenue Tax [*Canada*]
PGRV .... Precision Guided Reentry Vehicle
PGRVT..... Precisely Guided Reentry Test Vehicle   (SAA)
PGRWG ..... Payload Ground Requirements Working Group [*NASA*]   (NASA)
PGS........... Naval Postgraduate School
PGS........... Pagosa Springs [*Colorado*] [*Seismograph station code, US Geological Survey*] [*Closed*]   (SEIS)
PGS........... Papergram System [*Military*]   (CAAL)
PGS........... Parallel Gap Soldering
PGS........... Passive Geodetic Satellite [*NASA*]
PGS........... Passive Gravity Stabilization
PGS........... Peach Springs, AZ [*Location identifier*] [*FAA*]   (FAAL)
PGS........... Pegasus Club [*St. Louis, MO*] [*FAA designator*]   (FAAC)
PGS........... Pennsylvania German Society [*Later, TPGS*]   (EA)
PGS........... Pennsylvania German Society. Proceedings and Addresses [*A publication*]
PGS........... Pikunas Graphoscopic Scale [*Personality development test*] [*Psychology*]
PGS........... Plane Grating Spectrograph
PGS........... Plant Growth Substance
PGS........... Plasma Generator System
PGS........... Polish Genealogical Society   (EA)
PGS........... Polymer Glass Sealant
PGS........... Portable Ground Station
PGS........... Power Generation Satellite   (HGAA)
PGS........... Power Generation System [*or Subsystem*]
PGS........... Power Generator Section   (KSC)
PGS........... Precision Gunnery System [*Army training device*]   (INF)
PGS........... Predicted Ground Speed [*Navigation*]
PGS........... President of the Geographical Society [*British*]   (ROG)
PGS........... President of the Geological Society [*British*]
PGS........... Pressure-Gradient Single-Ended [*Microphone*]   (DEN)
PGS........... Pretty Good Stuff [*Liquor*]
PGS........... Primary Guidance Subsystem   (MCD)
PGS........... Professional Guidance Systems, Inc. [*Information service or system*]   (IID)
PGS........... Progenitor Genealogical Society   (EA)
PGS........... Program Generation System [*Data processing*]   (MDG)
PGS........... Propellant Gauging System
PGS........... Prostaglandin Synthase [*An enzyme*]
PGS........... Provincial Grand Secretary [*Freemasonry*]
PGSB .... Past Grand Sword Bearer [*Freemasonry*]   (ROG)
PGSB .... Provincial Grand Sword-Bearer [*Freemasonry*]
PGSC........ Payload and General Support Computer [*NASA*]
PGSC........ Persian Gulf Service Command
PGSCOL ... Naval Postgraduate School
PGSD........ Past Grand Senior Deacon [*Freemasonry*]
PGSE .... Payload Ground Support Equipment [*NASA*]   (MCD)
PGSE .... Peculiar Ground Support Equipment [*DoD*]
PGSE .... Pulsed Field Gradient Spin-Echo
PGSE .... Pulsed Gradient Spin Echo [*Physics*]
PGSEL ...... Priced Ground Support Equipment List   (AAG)
PGSET ...... Professional Group on Space Electronics and Telemetry   (AAG)
PGSN........ Saipan Island (Obyan)/International [*Mariana Islands*] [*ICAO location identifier*]   (ICLI)
PGSP .... Pennsylvania German Society. Proceedings and Addresses [*A publication*]
PGSR........ Psychogalvanic Skin Resistance [*Otolaryngology*]
PGST .... Grand Street [*A publication*]
PGSTAP.... Pressure, Gas, Start, Turbine, Auxiliary Pump-Drive Assembly [*Pronounced "pigstap"*]
PGSU........ Propellant [*or Propulsion*] Gas Supply Unit
PGSW .... Journal of Gerontological Social Work [*A publication*]
PGSW .... Past Grand Senior Warden [*Freemasonry*]
PGT .... Page Table [*Data processing*]   (IBMDP)
PGT .... Partido Guatemalteco del Trabajo [*Guatemalan Labor Party*] [*Political party*]   (PD)
PGT .... Past Grand Treasurer [*Freemasonry*]
PGT .... Per Gross Ton [*Shipping*]
PGT .... Photo Glow Tube
PGT .... Pigtail   (MSA)
PGT .... Pollen Grain Trajectory [*Botany*]
PGT .... Potato Extract-Glucose-Thiamine Hydrochloride [*Growth medium*]
PGT .... Power Grid Tube
PGT .... Putnam Intermediate Government Income [*NYSE symbol*]   (SPSG)
PGTAA...... Prager Tieraerztliches Archiv [*A publication*]
PGTO .... Portuguese Government Trade Office   (EA)
PGTR........ Plasma-Glucose Tolerance Rate [*Hematology*]   (MAE)

PGTS......... Precision Gunnery Training System [*Army*]   (INF)
PGTSND... Puget Sound [*FAA*]   (FAAC)
PGTTT...... Precision Gear Train Tools and Test
PGTW....... Guam [*Mariana Islands*] [*ICAO location identifier*]   (ICLI)
PGTWA..... Petroleum Geology of Taiwan [*A publication*]
PGU.......... Gannon University, Nash Library, Erie, PA [*OCLC symbol*]   (OCLC)
PGU.......... Pegasus Gold, Inc. [*AMEX symbol*] [*Toronto Stock Exchange symbol*]
PGU.......... Plant Growth Unit [*NASA*]   (MCD)
PGU.......... Postgonococcal Urethritis [*Medicine*]
PGU.......... Pressure Gas Umbilical   (KSC)
PGU.......... Propulsion Gas Umbilical
PGUA........ Andersen Air Force Base, Guam Island [*Mariana Islands*] [*ICAO location identifier*]   (ICLI)
PGUE........ Professional Group - Ultrasonic Engineering
PGUL........ Pegasus Gold, Inc. [*NASDAQ symbol*]   (NQ)
PGUM....... Agana Naval Air Station, Guam Island [*Mariana Islands*] [*ICAO location identifier*]   (ICLI)
PGUT........ Phosphogalactose Uridyltransferase [*An enzyme*] [*Known as Galactose-1-phosphate Uridylyltransferase*]
PGV.......... Greenville [*North Carolina*] [*Airport symbol*]   (OAG)
PGV.......... Proximal Gastric Vagotomy [*Medicine*]
PGVC........ Professional Group - Vehicular Communications
PGW......... Parallel Gap Welding
PGW......... Past Grand Warden [*Freemasonry*]
PGW......... Practice Guided Weapon   (MCD)
PGW......... Pressure Gas Welding
PGW......... Pressurized Stone Groundwood [*Pulp and paper technology*]
PGW......... United Plant Guard Workers of America
PGWG...... Parliamentary Group for World Government
PGWG...... Particles and Gases Working Group [*NASA*]   (NASA)
PGWS....... P. G. Wodehouse Society   (EA)
PGWT....... Peipeinimaru, Tinian Island [*Mariana Islands*] [*ICAO location identifier*]   (ICLI)
PGwvG...... Gwynedd-Mercy College, Gwynedd, PA [*Library symbol*] [*Library of Congress*]   (LCLS)
PGX.......... Prostaglandin X [*or Prostacyclin*] [*Biochemistry*]
PGY.......... Global Yield Fund, Inc. [*NYSE symbol*]   (SPSG)
PGY.......... Postgraduate Year
PGY.......... San Diego, CA [*Location identifier*] [*FAA*]   (FAAL)
PGZ.......... Ponta Grossa [*Brazil*] [*Airport symbol*]   (OAG)
PH............. Czechoslovakia [*License plate code assigned to foreign diplomats in the US*]
pH............. Hydrogen Ion Concentration   (MAE)
PH............. Netherlands [*Aircraft nationality and registration mark*]   (FAAC)
Ph............. [*The*] New Testament in Modern English [*1958*] [*J. B. Phillips*] [*A publication*]   (BJA)
PH............. Paedigogica Historica [*A publication*]
PH............. Page Heading   (BUR)
PH............. Pakistan Horizon [*A publication*]
PH............. Parker-Hannifin Corp. [*NYSE symbol*]   (SPSG)
PH............. Past History [*Medicine*]
P of H........ Patron of Husbandry
P & H........ Patton, Jr., and Heath's Reports [*Virginia Special Court of Appeals*] [*A publication*]   (DLA)
PH............. Pearl Harbor, Hawaii
PH............. Pennsylvania History [*A publication*]
pH............. Percent Hydrogen   (SSD)
PH............. Performance History
PH............. Persistent Hepatitis [*Medicine*]
PH............. Personal History [*Medicine*]   (AAMN)
PH............. Personal Hygiene   (MCD)
Ph............. Phallacidin [*Biochemistry*]
Ph............. Phantom Circuit [*Telecommunications*]   (TEL)
Ph............. Pharmacia AB [*Sweden*] [*Research code symbol*]
Ph............. Pharmacopoeia
Ph............. Phase   (KSC)
Ph............. Phenanthrene [*Organic chemistry*]   (AAMN)
Ph............. Phenyl [*Organic chemistry*]
PH............. Phiala [*Bottle*] [*Pharmacy*]
Ph'............. Philadelphia [*Chromosome*]
Ph............. Philippians [*New Testament book*]   (BJA)
ph............. Philippines [*IYRU nationality code*] [*MARC country of publication code*] [*Library of Congress*]   (LCCP)
PH............. Philippines [*ANSI two-letter standard code*]   (CNC)
Ph............. Philippus [*Flourished, 13th century*] [*Authority cited in pre-1607 legal work*]   (DSA)
Ph............. Phillimore's English Ecclesiastical Reports [*A publication*]   (DLA)
Ph............. Phillips' English Chancery Reports [*1841-49*] [*A publication*]   (DLA)
Ph............. Phillips' English Election Cases [*1780-81*] [*A publication*]   (DLA)
Ph............. Philosophisches Jahrbuch [*A publication*]
Ph............. Philosophy [*A publication*]
Ph............. Phoenix [*A publication*]
PH............. Phone   (MDG)
Ph............. Phosphate
PH............. Phot [*Electronics*]   (DEN)

PH............. Photographer's Mate [*Navy rating*]
PH............. Photography Program [*Association of Independent Colleges and Schools specialization code*]
Ph............. Photoreceptor
Ph............. Photostat   (BJA)
PH............. Phrase   (ADA)
Ph............. Physica [*of Aristotle*] [*Classical studies*]   (OCD)
Ph............. Physically Handicapped   (OICC)
Ph............. Phytane [*Organic chemistry*]
PH............. Piano Type Hinge
PH............. Picohenry [*One trillionth of a henry*]
P/H............. Pier to House [*Classified advertising*]   (ADA)
Ph............. Pilot-Helicopter [*Navy*] [*British*]
PH............. Pilot House
PH............. Pinch Hitter [*Baseball*]
PH............. Plane Handler [*Navy*]
PH............. Plant Height [*Botany*]
PH............. Polynesian Airlines Ltd. [*ICAO designator*]   (FAAC)
PH............. Porta Hepatis [*Anatomy*]
PH............. Porter House [*Initials often used as a pattern on clothing designed by this firm*]
P/H............. Postage and Handling [*Shipping*]
pH............. Pouvoir Hydrogene [*Hydrogen Power*] [*Negative logarithm of effective H ion concentration*] [*Chemistry*]
PH............. Powerhouse
PH............. Practical Homeowner [*A publication*]
PH............. Practitioner's Handbooks [*A publication*]
PH............. Precipitation Hardening
P-H............. Prentice-Hall, Inc. [*Publishers*]
PH............. Presidential Medal of Honour [*Botswana*]
PH............. Previous History [*Medicine*]
PH............. Primary Hyperparathyroidism
PH............. Private Hotel
PH............. Probability of Hit [*Military*]   (MCD)
PH............. Project Handclasp   (EA)
PH............. Prospect Hill [*Vole virus*]
PH............. Prostatic Hypertrophy [*Medicine*]   (MAE)
PH............. Provence Historique [*A publication*]
PH............. Przeglad Historyczny [*A publication*]
PH............. Public Health
PH............. Public House [*A drinking establishment*] [*British*]
PH............. Pulmonary Hypertension [*Medicine*]   (MAE)
PH............. Purple Heart [*Given to personnel wounded in military service*] [*Military decoration*]
Ph¹............. Philadelphia Chromosome   (MAE)
PH1........... Photographer's Mate, First Class [*Navy rating*]
1PH........... Single-Phase
PH2........... Photographer's Mate, Second Class [*Navy rating*]
2PH........... Two-Phase
PH3........... Photographer's Mate, Third Class [*Navy rating*]
3PH........... Three-Phase
PHA.......... Chicago, IL [*Location identifier*] [*FAA*]   (FAAL)
PHa........... Hazelton Public Library, Hazelton, PA [*Library symbol*] [*Library of Congress*]   (LCLS)
PHA.......... Pachena Industries Ltd. [*Vancouver Stock Exchange symbol*]
PHA.......... Palomino Horse Association   (EA)
PHA.......... Parts per Hundred of Asphalt [*Chemical technology*]
PHA.......... Passive Hemagglutination [*Immunology*]
PHA.......... Peripheral Hyperalimentation (Solution) [*Medicine*]
PHA.......... Peruvian Heart Association   (EA)
PHA.......... Pharmaceutisch Weekblad [*A publication*]
Pha........... Philologica [*A publication*]
PHA.......... Philosophia Antiqua [*A publication*]
PHA.......... Phytohemagglutinin [*Immunology*]
PHA.......... Polyhydroxyalkanoate [*Organic chemistry*]
PHA.......... Poly(hydroxystearic Acid) [*Organic chemistry*]
PHA.......... Port Heiden [*Alaska*] [*Seismograph station code, US Geological Survey*] [*Closed*]   (SEIS)
PHA.......... Poultry Husbandry Adviser [*Ministry of Agriculture, Fisheries, and Food*] [*British*]
PHA.......... Preferred Hotels Association [*Also known as Preferred Hotel Worldwide*]   (EA)
PHA.......... Prelaunch Hazard Area   (MUGU)
PHA.......... Preliminary Hazard Analyses   (NASA)
PHA.......... Professional Handlers Association   (EA)
PHA.......... Professional Horsemen's Association of America   (EA)
PHA.......... Public Health Act   (DAS)
PHA.......... Public Housing Administration [*or HHFA; disbanded 1965*]
PHA.......... Public Housing Agency [*Department of Housing and Urban Development*]   (GFGA)
PHA.......... Pulse Height Analysis [*Spectroscopy*]
PHA.......... State Library of Pennsylvania, Harrisburg, PA [*OCLC symbol*]   (OCLC)
PHAA........ Airman Apprentice, Photographer's Mate, Striker [*Navy rating*]
PHAA........ Percheron Horse Association of America   (EA)
PHAA........ Photographer's Airman Apprentice [*Navy*]
PHAA........ Positive High-Angle of Attack
PHAA........ Professional Horsemen's Association of America [*Later, PHA*]   (EA)
PHAABO.. Purebred Hanoverian Association of American Breeders and Owners   (EA)

PHAB .... Pharmacia AB [*NASDAQ symbol*]   (NQ)
PhAb .... Photographic Abstracts [*A publication*]
PHAB .... Physically Handicapped and Able Bodied [*Charitable organization*] [*British*]
PHACCK ... PHAC. Pathologie Humaine et Animale Comparee [*A publication*]
PHADA ..... Public Housing Authorities Directors Association   (EA)
PHADS ..... Phoenix Air Defense Sector   (SAA)
PHAGA ..... Philippine Agriculturist [*A publication*]
PHAH .... Hispanic American Historical Review [*A publication*]
PHAID ...... Positive Hostile Aircraft Identification
Phal CC ..... Phalen's Criminal Cases [*A publication*]   (DLA)
PHALCM ... Phytohemagglutinin Stimulated Leukocyte Conditioned Medium
PHALSE ... Phreakers, Hackers, and Laundry Service Employees [*East Coast group of computer trespassers raided by the FBI*]
PHA-M ...... Phytohemagglutinin M [*Immunology*]   (MAE)
P-H Am Lab Arb Awards ... American Labor Arbitration Awards (Prentice-Hall, Inc.) [*A publication*]   (DLA)
P-H Am Lab Cas ... American Labor Cases (Prentice-Hall, Inc.) [*A publication*]   (DLA)
PHAMOS ... Premote Hemodynamics and Metabolism in an Orbiting Satellite   (KSC)
PHAN .... Airman, Photographer's Mate, Striker [*Navy rating*]
Phanerogamarum Monogr ... Phanerogamarum Monographiae [*A publication*]
PHANT ..... Phantom-Glass [*Theater term*]   (DSUE)
PHAOMU ... Pianoforte, Harmonium, and American Organ Makers' Union [*British*]
PHAP .... Palmitoyl Hydrolyzed Animal Protein [*Organic chemistry*]
PHAP .... Provincial Health Assistance Program [*Vietnam*]
PHAR .... Pharmacology
PHAR .... PharmaControl Corp. [*NASDAQ symbol*]   (NQ)
PHAR .... Pharmacopoeia   (ROG)
PHAR .... Pharmacy [*or Pharmacist*]   (MSA)
PHarA .... AMP, Inc., Harrisburg, PA [*Library symbol*] [*Library of Congress*]   (LCLS)
PHARA ..... Pharmazie [*A publication*]
Phar B .... Pharmaciae Baccalaureus [*Bachelor of Pharmacy*]
PHarC .... Harrisburg Area Community College, Harrisburg, PA [*Library symbol*] [*Library of Congress*]   (LCLS)
PharC .... Pharmaceutical Chemist [*British*]
PHarD .... Dauphin County Library System, Harrisburg, PA [*Library symbol*] [*Library of Congress*]   (LCLS)
Phar D .... Pharmaciae Doctor [*Doctor of Pharmacy*]
PHARE ..... Poland and Hungary Assistance for Economic Restructuring [*EC*]   (ECED)
Phar G .... Graduate in Pharmacy   (AAMN)
PHarH .... Pennsylvania Historical and Museum Commission, Harrisburg, PA [*Library symbol*] [*Library of Congress*]   (LCLS)
PHARM .... Pharmaceutical
Phar M .... Pharmaciae Magister [*Master of Pharmacy*]
PHARM .... Pharmacist [*or Pharmacy*]
PHARM .... Pharmacology
Pharm Abstr ... Pharmaceutical Abstracts [*A publication*]
PHARMAC ... Pharmacology
Pharmaceutical J ... Pharmaceutical Journal and Transactions [*A publication*]
Pharmacochem Libr ... Pharmacochemistry Library [*A publication*]
Pharmacog Tit ... Pharmacognosy Titles [*A publication*]
PHARMACOL ... Pharmacological   (MSA)
Pharmacol ... Pharmacology [*A publication*]
Pharmacol Biochem Behav ... Pharmacology, Biochemistry, and Behavior [*A publication*]
Pharmacol Clin ... Pharmacologia Clinica [*A publication*]
Pharmacol Cond Learn Retention Proc Int Pharmacol Meet ... Pharmacology of Conditioning, Learning, and Retention. Proceedings. International Pharmacological Meeting [*A publication*]
Pharmacol Eating Disord ... Pharmacology of Eating Disorders (Monograph). Theoretical and Clinical Developments [*A publication*]
Pharmacol Eff Lipids ... Pharmacological Effect of Lipids [*A publication*]
Pharmacol Med ... Pharmacology in Medicine [*A publication*]
Pharmacolog ... Pharmacologist [*A publication*]
Pharmacol Physicians ... Pharmacology for Physicians [*A publication*]
Pharmacol R ... Pharmacological Research Communications [*A publication*]
Pharmacol Res ... Pharmacological Research [*A publication*]
Pharmacol Res Commun ... Pharmacological Research Communications [*A publication*]
Pharmacol Rev ... Pharmacological Reviews [*A publication*]
Pharmacol Sleep ... Pharmacology of Sleep [*A publication*]
Pharmacol Ther ... Pharmacology and Therapeutics [*A publication*]
Pharmacol Ther (B) ... Pharmacology and Therapeutics. Part B. General and Systematic Pharmacology [*A publication*]
Pharmacol Ther Dent ... Pharmacology and Therapeutics in Dentistry [*A publication*]
Pharmacol Ther Part A Chemother Toxicol Metab Inhibitors ... Pharmacology and Therapeutics. Part A. Chemotherapy, Toxicology, and Metabolic Inhibitors [*A publication*]
Pharmacol Ther Part B Gen Syst Pharmacol ... Pharmacology and Therapeutics. Part B. General and Systematic Pharmacology [*A publication*]

Pharmacol Ther Part C ... Pharmacology and Therapeutics. Part C. Clinical Pharmacology and Therapeutics [*A publication*]
Pharmacol Toxicol (Amsterdam) ... Pharmacology and Toxicology (Amsterdam) [*A publication*]
Pharmacol Toxicol (Copenhagen) ... Pharmacology and Toxicology (Copenhagen) [*A publication*]
Pharmacol Toxicol (Engl Transl) ... Pharmacology and Toxicology (English Translation of Farmakologiya Toksikologiya) [*Moscow*] [*A publication*]
Pharmacol Toxicol (USSR) ... Pharmacology and Toxicology (USSR) [*A publication*]
Pharmac Res ... Pharmacological Research [*A publication*]
Pharm Acta Helv ... Pharmaceutica Acta Helvetiae [*A publication*]
Pharm Act H ... Pharmaceutica Acta Helvetiae [*A publication*]
Pharma Int ... Pharma International [*A publication*]
Pharma Int Engl Ed ... Pharma International (English Edition) [*A publication*]
Pharma Jpn ... Pharma Japan [*A publication*]
Pharmakeutickon Delt Epistem Ekodosis ... Pharmakeutikon Deltion. Epistemonike Ekodosis [*A publication*]
Pharmakopsy ... Pharmakopsychiatrie Neuro-Psychopharmakologie [*A publication*]
Pharmakopsychiatr Neuro-Psychopharmakol ... Pharmakopsychiatrie Neuro-Psychopharmakologie [*A publication*]
Pharm Aquitaine ... Pharmacien d'Aquitaine [*A publication*]
Pharm Arch ... Pharmaceutical Archives [*A publication*]
Pharmazie Beih ... Pharmazie. Beihefte [*A publication*]
Pharm Bio B ... Pharmacology, Biochemistry, and Behavior [*A publication*]
Pharm Biol ... Pharmacien Biologiste [*A publication*]
Pharm Bull ... Pharmaceutical Bulletin [*A publication*]
Pharm Bull Fukuoka Univ ... Pharmaceutical Bulletin. Fukuoka University [*A publication*]
Pharm Bull Nihon Univ ... Pharmaceutical Bulletin. Nihon University [*A publication*]
Pharm Chem J ... Pharmaceutical Chemistry Journal [*A publication*]
Pharm Chem J (Engl Transl Khim Farm Zh) ... Pharmaceutical Chemistry Journal (English Translation of Khimiko-Farmatsevticheskii Zhurnal) [*A publication*]
Pharm Chem J (USSR) ... Pharmaceutical Chemistry Journal (USSR) [*A publication*]
PharmChem Newsl (Menlo Park Calif) ... PharmChem Newsletter (Menlo Park, California) [*A publication*]
PHARMCL ... Pharmaceutical
Pharm Cosmet ... Pharmaceuticals and Cosmetics [*A publication*]
Pharm Cosmet Rev ... Pharmaceutical and Cosmetics Review [*South Africa*] [*A publication*]
Pharm D .... Doctor of Pharmacy
Pharm Delt Epistem Ekdosis ... Pharmkeutikon Deltion Epistemonike Ekdosis [*A publication*]
Pharm Era ... Pharmaceutical Era [*A publication*]
Pharm Fr ... Pharmacien de France [*A publication*]
Pharm Heute ... Pharmazie Heute [*A publication*]
Pharm Hist ... Pharmacy in History [*A publication*]
Pharm Hosp Fr ... Pharmacie Hospitaliere Francaise [*A publication*]
Pharm Ind ... Pharmazeutische Industrie [*A publication*]
Pharm Ind (Shanghai) ... Pharmaceutical Industry (Shanghai) [*A publication*]
Pharm Ind Yugosl ... Pharmaceutical Industry of Yugoslavia [*A publication*]
Pharm Int ... Pharmacy International [*Netherlands*] [*A publication*]
Pharm J ..... Pharmaceutical Journal [*A publication*]
Pharm J (Dunedin NZ) ... Pharmaceutical Journal (Dunedin, New Zealand) [*A publication*]
Pharm J NZ ... Pharmaceutical Journal of New Zealand [*A publication*]
Pharm J Pharm ... Pharmaceutical Journal and Pharmacist [*A publication*]
Pharm Libr Bull ... Pharmaceutical Library Bulletin [*A publication*]
Pharm M ... Master of Pharmacy
Pharm Manage ... Pharmacy Management [*A publication*]
Pharm Manage Comb Am J Pharm ... Pharmacy Management Combined with the American Journal of Pharmacy [*A publication*]
Pharm Manuf Assoc Yearb ... Pharmaceutical Manufacturers Association. Yearbook [*A publication*]
Pharm Med ... Pharmaceutical Medicine [*A publication*]
Pharm Med Future Int Meet Pharm Physicians ... Pharmaceutical Medicine - the Future. International Meeting of Pharmaceutical Physicians [*A publication*]
Pharm Med (Hamps) ... Pharmaceutical Medicine (Hampshire) [*A publication*]
Pharm Mon ... Pharmaceuticals Monthly [*A publication*]
Pharm Monatsbl ... Pharmazeutische Monatsblaetter [*A publication*]
Pharm Monatsh ... Pharmazeutische Monatshefte [*A publication*]
Pharm Monogr ... Pharmaceutical Monographs [*A publication*]
Pharm News Index ... Pharmaceutical News Index [*A publication*]
Pharm Pak ... Pharmacy Pakistan [*A publication*]
Pharm Post ... Pharmazeutische Post [*A publication*]
Pharm Prax ... Pharmazeutische Praxis [*A publication*]
Pharm Presse ... Pharmazeutische Presse [*A publication*]
Pharm Presse Wiss Prakt Hefte ... Pharmazeutische Presse. Wissenschaftlich-Praktische Hefte [*A publication*]
Pharm Prod Pharm ... Pharmacie-Produits Pharmaceutiques [*A publication*]
Pharm Rep (Beijing) ... Pharmacy Reports (Beijing) [*A publication*]
Pharm Res ... Pharmaceutical Research [*A publication*]
Pharm Rev ... Pharmaceutical Review [*A publication*]
Pharm Rev ... Pharmacological Reviews [*A publication*]

Pharm Rev (Tokyo) ... Pharmaceutical Review (Tokyo) [*A publication*]
Pharm Rundsch ... Pharmazeutische Rundschau [*A publication*]
Pharm Rural ... Pharmacien Rural [*A publication*]
Pharm Soc Jpn J ... Pharmaceutical Society of Japan. Journal [*A publication*]
Pharm Soc (Pilani) J ... Pharmaceutical Society (Pilani). Journal [*A publication*]
Pharm Tech Jpn ... Pharm Tech Japan [*A publication*]
Pharm Technol ... Pharmaceutical Technology [*A publication*]
Pharm Times ... Pharmacy Times [*A publication*]
Pharm Tox ... Pharmacology and Toxicology [*A publication*]
Pharm Unserer Zeit ... Pharmazie in Unserer Zeit [*A publication*]
Pharm Weekbl ... Pharmaceutisch Weekblad [*A publication*]
Pharm Weekbl Ned ... Pharmeceutisch Weekblad voor Nederland [*A publication*]
Pharm Weekbl Sci ... Pharmaceutisch Weekblad. Scientific Edition [*A publication*]
Pharm Zentralhalle ... Pharmazeutische Zentralhalle [*A publication*]
Pharm Zentralhalle Dtl ... Pharmazeutische Zentralhalle fuer Deutschland [*A publication*]
Pharm Zentralhalle Dtschl ... Pharmazeutische Zentralhalle fuer Deutschland [*A publication*]
Pharm Ztg ... Pharmazeutische Zeitung [*A publication*]
Pharm Ztg (Berl) ... Pharmazeutische Zeitung (Berlin) [*A publication*]
Pharm Ztg Nachr ... Pharmazeutische Zeitung Nachrichten [*A publication*]
Pharm Ztg Ver Apotheker-Ztg ... Pharmazeutische Zeitung. Vereinigt mit Apotheker-Zeitung [*West Germany*] [*A publication*]
Pharos .... Pharos of Alpha Omega Alpha Honor Medical Society [*A publication*]
PHAROS... Phased Array RADAR Operational Simulation [*Army*]　(AABC)
PHarP .... Harrisburg Polyclinic Hospital, Harrisburg, PA [*Library symbol*] [*Library of Congress*]　(LCLS)
P Harr .... Rendel Harris Papyri of Woodbrooke College. Birmingham [*A publication*]
PHAS .... Harvard Journal of Asiatic Studies [*A publication*]
PHAS .... Phaser Systems, Inc. [*NASDAQ symbol*]　(NQ)
PHAS .... Pollution Hazard Assessment System [*Environmental science*]
PHAS .... Pulse Height Analyzer System
Phase Transitions Proc Conf Chem ... Phase Transitions. Proceedings. Conference on Chemistry [*A publication*]
PHASR ...... Personnel Hazards Associated with Space Radiation [*Satellite*]
PHatfB .... Biblical School of Theology, Hatfield, PA [*Library symbol*] [*Library of Congress*]　(LCLS)
PHatU .... Union Library Co., Hatboro, PA [*Library symbol*] [*Library of Congress*] [*Obsolete*]　(LCLS)
PHav .... Haverford Township Free Library, Havertown, PA [*Library symbol*] [*Library of Congress*]　(LCLS)
P Hawaii En ... Proceedings. Hawaiian Entomological Society [*A publication*]
Ph B .... Bachelor of Pharmacy
Ph B .... Bachelor of Physical Culture
PHB .... Para-Hexadecylaminobenzoate [*Clinical chemistry*]
PHB .... Para-Hydroxybenzoate [*Organic chemistry*]
PHB .... Parliament House Book [*Scotland*] [*A publication*]　(DLA)
PHB .... Parnaiba [*Brazil*] [*Airport symbol*]　(OAG)
PhB .... Philobiblon [*A publication*]
Ph B .... Philosophiae Baccalaureus [*Bachelor of Philosophy*]
PhB .... Philosophische Bibliothek [*Meiner*] [*A publication*]
PHB .... Photochemical Hole Burning [*Spectrometry*]
PHB .... Photographic Bulletin　(MCD)
PHB .... Poly(hydroxybenzoate) [*Organic chemistry*]
PHB .... Polyhydroxybutyrate [*Organic chemistry*]
PHB .... Pre-Homeobox [*Genetics*]
PHB .... Public Health Bibliography
PHB .... Public Health Service Building
PHBA .... Palomino Horse Breeders of America　(EA)
PHBA .... Para-Hydroxybenzoic Acid [*Organic chemistry*]
Ph B in Arch ... Bachelor of Philosophy in Architecture
PHBB .... Propylhydroxybenzyl Benzimidazole [*Organic chemistry*]　(MAE)
PHBCD ..... Physica B + C [*A publication*]
Ph B in Com ... Bachelor of Philosophy in Commerce
Ph BD .... Doctor of Bible Philosophy
Ph B in Ed ... Bachelor of Philosophy in Education
PHBHA ..... Physiology and Behavior [*A publication*]
PHBI .... Human Biology [*A publication*]
PHBIA .... Pharmacien Biologiste [*A publication*]
PHBK .... Barking Sands, Kauai Island [*Hawaii*] [*ICAO location identifier*]　(ICLI)
PHBK .... People's Heritage Financial Group, Inc. [*NASDAQ symbol*]　(NQ)
PHBLA ...... Physikalische Blaetter [*A publication*]
PHBOA ..... Physiologia Bohemoslovenica [*Later, Physiologia Bohemoslovaca*] [*A publication*]
PHBRZ ...... Phosphor Bronze
PHBV .... Hydroxy Butyric Valeric Acid [*Polymer*]
PHC .... Chief Photographer's Mate [*Navy rating*]
PHC .... Children's Hospital of Pittsburgh, Pittsburgh, PA [*OCLC symbol*]　(OCLC)
PHC .... Haverford College, Haverford, PA [*Library symbol*] [*Library of Congress*]　(LCLS)
PHC .... Pacific Hurricane Centers [*National Weather Service*]

PHC .... Palmitoyl Homocysteine [*Biochemistry*]
PHC .... Pathonic Network, Inc. [*Toronto Stock Exchange symbol*]
PHC .... Personal Holding Company [*Generic term*]
PHC .... Perturbed-Hardness Chain [*Molecular thermodynamics*]
Ph C .... Pharmaceutical Chemist
Ph C .... Philosopher of Chiropractic
PHC .... Photographic Change　(MCD)
PHC .... Population Housing Census　(OICC)
PHC .... Port Harcourt [*Nigeria*] [*Airport symbol*]　(OAG)
PHC .... Port Hardy [*British Columbia*] [*Seismograph station code, US Geological Survey*]　(SEIS)
PHC .... Posthospital Care [*Medicine*]
PHC .... [*A*] Prairie Home Companion [*National Public Radio program*]
PHC .... Pratt Hotel Corp. [*AMEX symbol*]　(SPSG)
PHC .... Primary Health Care
PHC .... Primary Health Centre [*British*]
PHC .... Primary Hepatic Carcinoma [*Medicine*]
PH'c .... Proliferative Helper Cells [*Immunology*]
Ph'c .... Philadelphia Chromosome
PHCA .... Philippine Heart Center for Asia　(PDAA)
PHCA .... Pig Health Control Association [*British*]
PHCA .... Pleasure Horse Club of America　(EA)
PHCAA .... Physics in Canada [*A publication*]
PHCAA .... Public Health Cancer Association of America [*Defunct*]　(EA)
P-H Cas ..... American Federal Tax Reports (Prentice-Hall, Inc.) [*A publication*]　(DLA)
PHCBA .... Photochemistry and Photobiology [*A publication*]
P-HCC .... Piston-Hand Control Clutch　(DNAB)
PHCC .... Punjab High Court Cases [*India*] [*A publication*]　(DLA)
PHCCA .... Progress in Histochemistry and Cytochemistry [*A publication*]
Ph Ch .... Phillips' English Chancery Reports [*1841-49*] [*A publication*]　(DLA)
PHCI .... Peak Health Care, Inc. [*NASDAQ symbol*]　(NQ)
PHCIB .... Plumbing-Heating-Cooling Information Bureau　(EA)
PhCL .... Pharmacochemistry Library [*Elsevier Book Series*] [*A publication*]
PHCLIS .... Protected Home Circle Life Insurance Society　(EA)
PHCM .... Master Chief Photographer's Mate [*Navy rating*]
P-H Corp ... Corporation [*Prentice-Hall, Inc.*] [*A publication*]　(DLA)
PHCP .... [*International Trade Show for*] Plumbing, Heating, Cooling, and Piping　(ITD)
PHCS .... Senior Chief Photographer's Mate [*Navy rating*]
PHCSC .... Piers-Harris Children's Self-Concept Scale [*Child development test*] [*Psychology*]
PHCT .... Perturbed Hard Chain Theory [*Equation of state*]
PHCTB ...... Photophysiology [*A publication*]
PHCV-SD ... Phase Conversion and Step-Down　(MSA)
PHCYAQ .. Specialist Periodical Reports. Photochemistry [*A publication*]
PHD .... Dixmont State Hospital, Sewickley, PA [*OCLC symbol*]　(OCLC)
Ph D .... Doctor of Pharmacy
PH D .... Doctor of Philosophy
PHD .... Doctor of Public Health [*British*]　(DAS)
PHD .... Duncan Aviation, Inc. [*Lincoln, NE*] [*FAA designator*]　(FAAC)
PHD .... New Philadelphia, OH [*Location identifier*] [*FAA*]　(FAAL)
PHD .... Parallel Head Disk
PhD .... Perfect Hard Disk [*Century Data Systems*] [*Data processing*]
Phd .... Phaedo [*of Plato*] [*Classical studies*]　(OCD)
PHD .... Phase-Shift Driver　(CET)
Ph D .... Philosophiae Doctor [*Doctor of Philosophy*] [*Facetious translation: Piled Higher and Deeper*]
PHD .... Photoelectron Diffraction [*Spectroscopy*]
PHD .... Photohydrodynamic [*Astrophysics*]
PHD .... Pilot's Horizontal Display [*Aviation*]　(CAAL)
PHD .... Poly Harnstoff Dispersion [*Organic chemistry*]
PHD .... Port Huron & Detroit Railroad Co. [*AAR code*]
PHD .... Positioning-Head Drum　(DNAB)
PH D .... Pre-Pearl Harbor Dad [*A humorous wartime degree*]
PHD .... Precision High Dose
PHD .... Pride, Hustle, and Drive
PHD .... Public Health Department
PHD .... Public Health Director
PHD .... Public Housing Development [*Department of Housing and Urban Development*]　(GFGA)
PHD .... Pulse Height Discrimination
PHD .... Pulsed Holograpy Development [*Department of Energy*]
PHDAN ..... Physically Dangerous　(DNAB)
PHDDS ..... PSRO [*Professional Standards Review Organization*] Hospital Discharge Data Set
PHDEA ..... Public Housing Drug Elimination Act [*1988*]
PhDEd ..... Doctor of Philosophy in Education [*British*]　(ADA)
PHDH .... Dillingham Air Force Base, Oahu Island [*Hawaii*] [*ICAO location identifier*]　(ICLI)
PHDK .... Phi Delta Kappan [*A publication*]
PHDLAQ .. Farmakeftikon Deltion. Edition Scientifique [*A publication*]
PhD(Med) ... Doctor of Philosophy (Medicine)　(ADA)
PhDMH ..... Doctor of Philosophy in Mechanics and Hydraulics
PHDr .... Doctor of Philosophy
Phdr .... Phaedrus [*of Plato*] [*Classical studies*]　(OCD)
PHDR .... Preliminary Hardware Design Review

PhD(RCA) ... Doctor of Philosophy (Royal College of Art) [*British*] (DBQ)
PHDS .... Post-Harvest Documentation Service [*Kansas State University*] (IID)
PHE .... Aviation POL [*Petroleum, Oil, and Lubrication*] Handling Equipment (NATG)
PHE .... Eastern State School and Hospital, Trevose, PA [*OCLC symbol*] (OCLC)
PHE .... Periodic Health Examination
PHE .... Petroleum Handling Equipment (MCD)
Phe .... Phenylalanine [*Also, F*] [*An amino acid*]
PHE .... Pheophytin [*Biochemistry*]
PhE .... Philadelphia Electric Co. [*Associated Press abbreviation*] (APAG)
Phe .... Phoenix [*Constellation*]
PHE .... Photo Engravers & Electrotypers Ltd. [*Toronto Stock Exchange symbol*]
PHE .... Plate Heat Exchanger [*Chemical engineering*]
PHE .... Port Hedland [*Australia*] [*Airport symbol*] (OAG)
PHE .... Post-Heparin Esterase [*Medicine*] (MAE)
PHE .... Preflight Heat Exchanger [*NASA*] (KSC)
PHEA .... Public Health Engineering Abstracts [*A publication*]
Phear Wat ... Phear's Rights of Water [*1859*] [*A publication*] (DLA)
PHEC .... Human Ecology [*A publication*]
PHEDA ..... Physics Education [*A publication*]
PHEF .... Human Ecology Forum [*A publication*]
PhEI .... Penetrator, High-Explosive, Incendiary (MCD)
PhEJ .... Philippine Economic Journal [*A publication*]
PHEL .... Petroleum Helicopters, Inc. [*NASDAQ symbol*] (NQ)
P Helm Soc ... Proceedings. Helminthological Society of Washington [*A publication*]
PhelpD ...... Phelps Dodge Corp. [*Associated Press abbreviation*] (APAG)
PHEM .... Hemingway Review [*A publication*]
PHeM .... Hershey Medical Center, Hershey, PA [*Library symbol*] [*Library of Congress*] (LCLS)
PHEMA .... Poly(hydroxyethyl Methacrylate) [*Organic chemistry*]
phen .... o-Phenanthroline [*Organic chemistry*]
PHEN .... Phenolic (AAG)
Pheney Rep ... Pheney's New Term Reports [*England*] [*A publication*] (DLA)
PH Eng ...... Public Health Engineer
PHENO ..... Phenobarbital [*A drug*]
pheno .... Phenotype
PHENO ..... Precise Hybrid Elements for Nonlinear Operation (IEEE)
Phenom Ioniz Gases Contrib Pap Int Conf ... Phenomena in Ionized Gases. Contributed Papers. International Conference [*A publication*]
Phen & Ped ... Phenomenology and Pedagogy [*A publication*]
PHEO .... Pheochromocytoma [*Oncology*]
PHER .... Journal of Heredity [*A publication*]
PHER .... Photographic Mechanical Equipment Repair [*Course*] (DNAB)
PHER .... Plate Heat Exchanger [*Chemical Engineering*] (DNAB)
PHERMEX ... Pulsed High-Energy Radiographic Machine Emitting X-Rays
PHESA ...... Proceedings. Hawaiian Entomological Society [*A publication*]
P-H Est Plan ... Estate Planning (Prentice-Hall, Inc.) [*A publication*]
Ph Ev .... Phillips on Evidence [*A publication*] (DLA)
Ph E W ...... Philosophy East and West [*A publication*]
PHEWA .... Presbyterian Health, Education, and Welfare Association (EA)
PHF .... Fairview State Hospital, Waymart, PA [*OCLC symbol*] (OCLC)
PHF .... Newport News [*Virginia*] [*Airport symbol*] (OAG)
PHF .... Paired Helical Filaments [*Neuroanatomy*] [*Term coined by Dr. Robert Terry to describe the components of neurofibrillary tangles in the brains of Alzheimer's Disease patients*]
PHF .... Patrick Henry Foundation [*Liberty, NY*] (EA)
PHF .... Patrol Hydrofoil [*Missile*] (HGAA)
PHF .... Peak Hour Factor [*Transportation*]
PHF .... Peanut Hull Flour
PHF .... Pergamon Holding Foundation [*Liechtenstein*]
PHF .... Personal Hygiene Facility [*NASA*] (NASA)
PHF .... Phoenix House Foundation (EA)
PHF .... Plug Handling Fixture (NRCH)
PHF .... Process Holding Fixture (MCD)
PHF .... Procurement History File [*DoD*]
PHF .... Public Health Foundation [*Information service or system*] (IID)
PHF .... USF & G Pacholder Fund, Inc. [*AMEX symbol*] (CTT)
PHFA .... Potomac Horse Fever Agent
PHFC .... Phoenix Financial Corp. [*Medford, NJ*] [*NASDAQ symbol*] (NQ)
PHFEA ...... Physica Fennica [*A publication*]
P-H Fed Taxes ... Federal Taxes (Prentice-Hall, Inc.) [*A publication*] (DLA)
PHFF .... Oahu [*Hawaii*] [*ICAO location identifier*] (ICLI)
PHFG .... Primary Human Fetal Glial [*Cytology*]
PHFTX ...... Prentice-Hall Federal Taxes [*Database*] (IT)
Ph G .... Graduate in Pharmacy
PhG .... Pharmacopoeia Germanica [*German Pharmacopeia*] (MAE)
PHG .... Phenate-Hexamine Goggle [*British World War I anti-poison-gas helmet*]
PHG .... Philips NV [*NYSE symbol*] (SPSG)
PHG .... Phillipsburg, KS [*Location identifier*] [*FAA*] (FAAL)
Phg .... Phytophthora Megasperma Glycinea [*A fungus*]
PHG .... Postman, Higher Grade [*British*] (DI)

PHG .... Prototype Hydrofoil Gunboat
PHG .... Scranton State General Hospital, Scranton, PA [*OCLC symbol*] (OCLC)
PHGA .... Pteroylhexaglutamylglutamic [*or Pteroylheptaglutamic*] Acid [*Biochemistry*]
PhGABA ... Phenyl-gamma-aminobutyric Acid [*Tranquilizer*]
PHGLTF ... Physiological Training Flight [*Air Force*]
Phgly .... Phenylglycine [*An amino acid*]
PHGM .... Patrol Hydrofoil Guided Missile [*Navy*] (DNAB)
Phgn .... Physiognomonica [*of Aristotle*] [*Classical studies*] (OCD)
P HGT ...... Package Height [*Freight*]
PHH .... Andrews, SC [*Location identifier*] [*FAA*] (FAAL)
PHH .... Haverford State Hospital, Haverford, PA [*OCLC symbol*] (OCLC)
PHH .... PHH Corp. [*NYSE symbol*] [*Toronto Stock Exchange symbol*] (SPSG)
PHH .... PHH Corp. [*Associated Press abbreviation*] (APAG)
PHH .... Phillips Head [*Screw*]
PHH .... Puu Huluhulu [*Hawaii*] [*Seismograph station code, US Geological Survey*] [*Closed*] (SEIS)
PHHA .... Pearl Harbor History Associates (EA)
PHHC .... Programmable Hand-Held Calculator (RDA)
PHHI .... Wheeler Air Force Base, Oahu Island [*Hawaii*] [*ICAO location identifier*] (ICLI)
PHHN ...... Hana, Maui Island [*Hawaii*] [*ICAO location identifier*] (ICLI)
PHHSA .... Protestant Health and Human Services Assembly (EA)
PHi .... Historical Society of Pennsylvania, Philadelphia, PA [*Library symbol*] [*Library of Congress*] (LCLS)
PhI .... International Pharmacopoeia
PHI .... Permanent Health Insurance [*British*]
PHI .... Petroleum Helicopters, Inc. (MCD)
PHI .... Philadelphia [*Pennsylvania*] [*Seismograph station code, US Geological Survey*] [*Closed*] (SEIS)
PHI .... Philippine Long Distance Telephone Co. [*AMEX symbol*] (SPSG)
Phi .... Philippus [*Flourished, 13th century*] [*Authority cited in pre-1607 legal work*] (DSA)
Phi .... Philips [*Holland & International*] [*Record label*]
PHI .... Philipsburg State General Hospital, Philipsburg, PA [*OCLC symbol*] [*Inactive*] (OCLC)
PHI .... Phillipsite [*A zeolite*]
PHI .... Philosophie Informationsdienst [*Philosophy Information Service*] [*University of Dusseldorf*] [*Information service or system*] (IID)
Phi .... Philosophy [*A publication*]
PHI .... Philosophy (WGA)
PHI .... Phosphohexose Isomerase [*An enzyme*]
Phi .... Physeptone [*A narcotic substitute*]
PHI .... Physiological Hyaluronidase Inhibitor [*Biochemistry*]
PHI .... Polarity Health Institute (EA)
PHI .... Position and Homing Indicator
PHI .... Prentice-Hall International [*Publisher*]
PHI .... Programme Hydrologique International [*International Hydrological Program - IHP*] [*UNESCO*] (MSC)
PHI .... Public Health Inspector [*British*]
PHIA .... Phenylalanine (MAE)
PHIAL .... Phiala [*Bottle*] [*Pharmacy*]
PHIB .... Amphibious
PHib .... Hibeh Papyri [*A publication*] (OCD)
PHIBB .... Project for Historical Biobibliography [*A publication*]
PHIBCB .... Amphibious Construction Battalion [*Also, ACB*] (NVT)
PHIBCORPAC ... Amphibious Corps, Pacific Fleet [*Marine Corps*]
PHIBCORPS ... Amphibious Corps [*Marine Corps*]
PHIBDET ... Amphibious Detachment
PHIBDETIND ... Amphibious Detachment, India
PHIBEU .... Amphibious Forces, Europe
PHIBEX .... Amphibious Exercise [*NATO*]
PHIBFOR ... Amphibious Forces
PHIBGROUP ... Amphibious Group
PHIBGRU ... Amphibious Group
PHIBLANT ... Amphibious Forces, Atlantic Fleet
PHIBLEX ... Amphibious Landing Exercise [*Navy*] (NVT)
PHIBNAW ... Amphibious Forces, Northwest African Waters
PHIBOPS ... Amphibious Operations [*Navy*] (NVT)
PHIBPAC ... Amphibious Forces, Pacific Fleet
PHIBRAIDEX ... Amphibious Raid Exercise [*Navy*] (NVT)
PHIBRECONEX ... Amphibious Reconnaissance Exercise [*Navy*] (NVT)
PHIBREFTRA ... Amphibious Refresher Training [*Navy*] (CAAL)
PHIBRFT ... Amphibious Refresher Training [*Navy*] (NVT)
PHIBRON ... Amphibious Squadron [*Army*]
PHIBSEU ... Amphibious Forces, Europe
PHIBSFORPAC ... Amphibious Forces, Pacific Fleet
PHIBSKDN ... Amphibious Ship Shakedown Cruise [*Navy*] (NVT)
PHIBSLANT ... Amphibious Forces, Atlantic Fleet
PHIBSPAC ... Amphibious Forces, Pacific Fleet
PHIBSS ...... Amphibious Schoolship [*Navy*] (NVT)
PHIBSTRAPAC ... Training Command Amphibious Forces, US Pacific Fleet
PHIBSUKAY ... Amphibious Bases, United Kingdom
PHIBTF .... Amphibious Task Force [*Navy*] (NVT)
PHIBTRA ... Training Command Amphibious Forces
PHIBTRABASE ... Amphibious Training Base [*Navy*]

PHIBTRAEX ... Amphibious Training Exercise [*Navy*] (NVT)
PHIBTRAINLANT ... Training Command Amphibious Forces, US Atlantic Fleet
PHIBTRAINPAC ... Training Command Amphibious Forces, US Pacific Fleet
PHIBTRALANT ... Training Command Amphibious Forces, US Atlantic Fleet
PHIBTRANS ... Amphibious Transport [*Navy*]
PHIBTRAPAC ... Training Command Amphibious Forces, US Pacific Fleet
PHIBTRBASE ... Amphibious Training Base [*Navy*]
PHIBWARTRACEN ... Amphibious Warfare Training Center [*Navy*]
PHIC .... Poly(hexyl Isocyanate) [*Organic chemistry*]
PHICB .... Putnam High Income Convertible & Bond Fund [*Associated Press abbreviation*] (APAG)
Phi D .... Doctor of Philanthropy
PHID .... Positive Hostile Identification Device [*Air Force*]
Phi Del Kap ... Phi Delta Kappan [*A publication*]
Phi D K ...... Phi Delta Kappan [*A publication*]
PHIGS .... Programmers Hierarchical Interactive Graphics System [*IBM Corp.*]
PHIJ .... Historical Journal [*A publication*]
PHIK .... Honolulu/Hickam Air Force Base, Oahu Island [*Hawaii*] [*ICAO location identifier*] (ICLI)
Phil............ Orationes Philippicae [*of Cicero*] [*Classical studies*] (OCD)
PHIL......... Philadelphia [*Pennsylvania*]
Phil............ Philadelphia Reports [*A publication*] (DLA)
Phil............ Philemon [*New Testament book*]
Phil............ Philharmonia [*Record label*]
PHIL......... Philharmonic
Phil............ Philippians [*New Testament book*]
Phil............ Philippine Island Reports [*A publication*] (DLA)
PHIL......... Philippines (AFM)
Phil............ Phillimore's English Ecclesiastical Reports [*A publication*] (DLA)
Phil............ Phillips' English Chancery Reports [*1841-49*] [*A publication*] (DLA)
Phil............ Phillips' English Election Cases [*1780-81*] [*A publication*] (DLA)
Phil............ Phillips' Illinois Reports [*152-245 Illinois*] [*A publication*] (DLA)
Phil............ Phillips' North Carolina Law Reports [*A publication*] (DLA)
Phil............ Phillips' Treatise on Insurance [*A publication*] (DLA)
Phil............ Philoctetes [*of Sophocles*] [*Classical studies*] (OCD)
PHIL......... Philology
Phil............ Philopoemen [*of Plutarch*] [*Classical studies*] (OCD)
PHIL......... Philosophy
PHIL......... Programmable Algorithm Machine High-Level Language [*Data processing*]
PHILA....... Philadelphia [*Pennsylvania*]
Phila........... Philadelphia Reports [*Pennsylvania*] [*A publication*] (DLA)
Phila Bs J .. Philadelphia Business Journal [*A publication*]
Philad........ Philadelphia Reports [*Pennsylvania*] [*A publication*] (DLA)
PHILADA ... Philadelphia (ROG)
Philada R ... Philadelphia Reports [*Pennsylvania*] [*A publication*] (DLA)
Philada Rep ... Philadelphia Reports [*Pennsylvania*] [*A publication*] (DLA)
PHILADEL ... Philadelphia (ROG)
Philadelphia Leg Int ... Philadelphia Legal Intelligencer [*Pennsylvania*] [*A publication*] (DLA)
Philadelphia Med ... Philadelphia Medicine [*A publication*]
Philadelphia Rep ... Philadelphia Reports [*Pennsylvania*] [*A publication*] (DLA)
PhilaEl....... Philadelphia Electric Co. [*Associated Press abbreviation*] (APAG)
Phil Ag....... Philippine Agriculturist [*A publication*]
Phila Geog Soc Bull ... Philadelphia Geographical Society. Bulletin [*A publication*]
Phil Ag R ... Philippine Agricultural Review [*A publication*]
PHILAGRP ... Philadelphia Group (DNAB)
Phila Inqr... Philadelphia Inquirer [*A publication*]
Phila Leg Int ... Philadelphia Legal Intelligencer [*Pennsylvania*] [*A publication*] (DLA)
Phila LJ ..... Philadelphia Law Journal [*A publication*] (DLA)
Phila Med ... Philadelphia Medicine [*A publication*]
Phila Med J ... Philadelphia Medical Journal [*A publication*]
Phila Med Phys J ... Philadelphia Medical and Physical Journal [*A publication*]
Phila Mus Bull ... Philadelphia Museum of Art. Bulletin [*A publication*]
philan......... Philanthropical (BJA)
PHILANTHR ... Philanthropic (ROG)
Philanthrop ... Philanthropist [*A publication*]
Phila Orch ... Philadelphia Orchestra. Program Notes [*A publication*]
Phila (PA) ... Philadelphia Reports [*Pennsylvania*] [*A publication*] (DLA)
Phila Phot ... Philadelphia Photographer [*A publication*]
Phila Reports ... Philadelphia Reports [*Pennsylvania*] [*A publication*] (DLA)
philat......... Philately
Philat Aust ... Philately from Australia [*A publication*] (APTA)
Philat Bul... Philatelic Bulletin [*A publication*] (APTA)
Philately from Aust ... Philately from Australia [*A publication*] (APTA)
Philat Pregl ... Philatelen Pregled [*A publication*]
Phil Books ... Philosophical Books [*A publication*]
Philbro....... Philipp Brothers Ltd. [*Commercial firm*]

Phil Bull..... Philatelic Bulletin [*A publication*] (APTA)
(Phil) Busn ... Business Journal (Philadelphia) [*A publication*]
Phil Bus R ... Philippine Business Review [*A publication*]
Phil C......... Philosophy in Chiropractic
Phil Civ & Can Law ... Phillimore's Civil and Canon Law [*A publication*] (DLA)
PHILCOM ... Philippine Global Communications, Inc. [*Manila*] [*Telecommunications*]
PHILCON ... Philippine Contingent [*Military*]
Phil Context ... Philosophy in Context [*A publication*]
Phil Cop..... Phillips' Law of Copyright Designs [*A publication*] (DLA)
Phil D......... Philosophiae Doctor [*Doctor of Philosophy*] [*See also Ph D*] [*Latin*]
PHILDANCO ... Philadelphia Dance Company
Phil Dec..... Philippus Decius [*Deceased circa 1537*] [*Authority cited in pre-1607 legal work*] (DSA)
Phil Dev..... Philippine Development [*A publication*]
Phil Dom.... Phillimore's Law of Domicil [*A publication*] (DLA)
Phil East West ... Philosophy East and West [*A publication*]
Phil Ecc..... Phillimore's Ecclesiastical Judgments [*A publication*] (DLA)
Phil Ecc...... Phillimore's English Ecclesiastical Law [*2 eds.*] [*1873, 1895*] [*A publication*] (DLA)
Phil Ecc...... Phillimore's English Ecclesiastical Reports [*1809-21*] [*A publication*] (DLA)
Phil Ecc Judg ... Phillimore's Ecclesiastical Judgments [*1867-75*] [*A publication*] (DLA)
Phil Ecc Law ... Phillimore's English Ecclesiastical Law [*2 eds.*] [*1873, 1895*] [*A publication*] (DLA)
Phil Ecc R .. Phillimore's English Ecclesiastical Reports [*1809-21*] [*A publication*] (DLA)
Phil Educ Proc ... Proceedings. Far Western Philosophy of Education Society [*A publication*]
Phil El Cas ... Phillips' English Election Cases [*1780-81*] [*A publication*] (DLA)
Philem........ Philemon [*New Testament book*]
Phil Eq....... Phillips' North Carolina Equity Reports [*A publication*] (DLA)
Phil Ev ...... Phillips on Evidence [*A publication*] (DLA)
Phil Ev Cow & H & Edw Notes ... Phillips on Evidence, Notes by Cowen, Hill, and Edwards [*A publication*] (DLA)
PHILEX .... Philadelphia Stock Exchange
Phil Exch ... Philosophic Exchange [*A publication*]
Phil Fam Cas ... Phillipps' Famous Cases in Circumstantial Evidence [*A publication*] (DLA)
Phil Forum (Boston) ... Philosophical Forum (Boston) [*A publication*]
Phil Forum (De Kalb) ... Philosophy Forum (De Kalb) [*A publication*]
Phil Geog J ... Philippine Geographical Journal [*A publication*]
PhilGl .... Philips NV [*Associated Press abbreviation*] (APAG)
Phil Grand ... Phillips' Grandeur of the Law [*A publication*] (DLA)
Philhar....... Philharmonic [*A publication*]
Phili Fran... Philippus Francus [*Deceased, 1471*] [*Authority cited in pre-1607 legal work*] (DSA)
Phil ILJ ..... Philippine International Law Journal [*A publication*] (DLA)
Phil Ind...... Philosopher's Index [*A publication*]
Phil Inq...... Philosophical Inquiry [*A publication*]
Phil Ins ...... Phillips on Insurance [*A publication*] (DLA)
Phil Insan .. Phillips on Lunatics [*1858*] [*A publication*] (DLA)
Phil Int Law ... Phillimore's International Law [*A publication*] (DLA)
Phil Int LJ ... Philippine International Law Journal [*A publication*] (DLA)
Phil Int Rom Law ... Phillimore's Introduction to the Roman Law [*A publication*] (DLA)
Phil Invest ... Philosophical Investigators [*A publication*]
Philip .... Philippines
Philip Abstr ... Philippine Abstracts [*A publication*]
Philip Fran ... Philippus Franchus [*Deceased, 1471*] [*Authority cited in pre-1607 legal work*] (DSA)
Philip Morris Sci Symp Proc ... Philip Morris Science Symposium. Proceedings [*A publication*]
Philipp AEC ... Philippine Atomic Energy Commission. Publications [*A publication*]
Philipp AEC Annu Rep ... Philippine Atomic Energy Commission. Annual Report [*A publication*]
Philipp AEC Rep ... Philippine Atomic Energy Commission. Reports [*A publication*]
Philipp Agric ... Philippine Agriculturist [*A publication*]
Philipp Agric Eng J ... Philippine Agricultural Engineering Journal [*A publication*]
Philipp Agric Rev ... Philippine Agricultural Review [*A publication*]
Philipp At Bull ... Philippine Atomic Bulletin [*A publication*]
Philipp Biochem Soc Bull ... Philippine Biochemical Society. Bulletin [*A publication*]
Philipp Bur Mines Geo Sci Rep Invest ... Philippines. Bureau of Mines and Geo-Sciences. Report of Investigation [*A publication*]
Philipp Bur Mines Inf Circ ... Philippines. Bureau of Mines. Information Circular [*A publication*]
Philipp Bur Mines Rep Invest ... Philippines. Bureau of Mines. Report of Investigations [*A publication*]
Philipp Bur Mines Spec Proj Ser Publ ... Philippines. Bureau of Mines. Special Projects Series. Publication [*A publication*]
Philipp Dep Agric Nat Resour Bur Mines Inf Circ ... Philippines. Department of Agriculture and Natural Resources. Bureau of Mines. Information Circular [*A publication*]

Philipp Dep Agric Nat Resour Bur Mines Rep Invest ... Philippines. Department of Agriculture and Natural Resources. Bureau of Mines. Report of Investigation [*A publication*]
Philipp Dep Agric Nat Resour Bur Mines Spec Proj Ser Publ ... Philippines. Department of Agriculture and Natural Resources. Bureau of Mines. Special Projects Series Publication [*A publication*]
Philipp Dep Nat Resour Bur Mines Rep Invest ... Philippines. Department of Natural Resources. Bureau of Mines. Report of Investigation [*A publication*]
Philipp Ent ... Philippine Entomologist [*A publication*]
Philipp Entomol ... Philippine Entomologist [*A publication*]
Philipp For ... Philippine Forests [*A publication*]
Philipp For Prod Res Ind Dev Comm FORPRIDE Dig ... Philippines. Forest Products Research and Industries Development Commission. FORPRIDE Digest [*A publication*]
Philipp Geogr J ... Philippine Geographical Journal [*A publication*]
Philipp Geol ... Philippine Geologist [*A publication*]
Philippine .. Philippine Reports [*A publication*]   (DLA)
Philippine Ag R ... Philippine Agricultural Review [*A publication*]
Philippine Agr ... Philippine Agriculturist [*A publication*]
Philippine Agr Situation ... Philippine Agricultural Situation [*A publication*]
Philippine Co ... Philippine Code [*A publication*]   (DLA)
Philippine Econ J ... Philippine Economic Journal [*A publication*]
Philippine Economy and Ind J ... Philippine Economy and Industrial Journal [*A publication*]
Philippine Farm Gard ... Philippine Farms and Gardens [*A publication*]
Philippine Internat LJ ... Philippine International Law Journal [*Manila, Philippines*] [*A publication*]   (DLA)
Philippine Int'l LJ ... Philippine International Law Journal [*A publication*]   (DLA)
Philippine J Nutr ... Philippine Journal of Nutrition [*A publication*]
Philippine J Plant Ind ... Philippine Journal of Plant Industry [*A publication*]
Philippine J Pub Adm ... Philippine Journal of Public Administration [*A publication*]
Philippine J Pub Admin ... Philippine Journal of Public Administration [*A publication*]
Philippine J Public Admin ... Philippine Journal of Public Administration [*A publication*]
Philippine J Sci ... Philippine Journal of Science [*A publication*]
Philippine LJ ... Philippine Law Journal [*A publication*]   (DLA)
Philippine L Rev ... Philippine Law Review [*A publication*]   (DLA)
Philippine Planning J ... Philippine Planning Journal [*A publication*]
Philippine Rice Corn Progr ... Philippines Rice and Corn Progress [*A publication*]
Philippines Bur Mines Geo-Sci Rep Invest ... Philippines. Bureau of Mines and Geo-Sciences. Report of Investigation [*A publication*]
Philippine Sociol R ... Philippine Sociological Review [*A publication*]
Philippine Stud ... Philippine Studies [*A publication*]
Philipp J Agric ... Philippine Journal of Agriculture [*A publication*]
Philipp J Anesthesiol ... Philippine Journal of Anesthesiology [*A publication*]
Philipp J Anim Ind ... Philippine Journal of Animal Industry [*A publication*]
Philipp J Cancer ... Philippine Journal of Cancer [*A publication*]
Philipp J Cardiol ... Philippine Journal of Cardiology [*A publication*]
Philipp J Coconut Stud ... Philippine Journal of Coconut Studies [*A publication*]
Philipp J Crop Sci ... Philippine Journal of Crop Science [*A publication*]
Philipp J Fish ... Philippine Journal of Fisheries [*A publication*]
Philipp J Food Sci Technol ... Philippine Journal of Food Science and Technology [*A publication*]
Philipp J For ... Philippine Journal of Forestry [*A publication*]
Philipp J Intern Med ... Philippine Journal of Internal Medicine [*A publication*]
Philipp J Nurs ... Philippine Journal of Nursing [*A publication*]
Philipp J Nutr ... Philippine Journal of Nutrition [*A publication*]
Philipp J Ophthal ... Philippine Journal of Ophthalmology [*A publication*]
Philipp J Ophthalmol ... Philippine Journal of Ophthalmology [*A publication*]
Philipp J Pediat ... Philippine Journal of Pediatrics [*A publication*]
Philipp J Pediatr ... Philippine Journal of Pediatrics [*A publication*]
Philipp J Plant Ind ... Philippine Journal of Plant Industry [*A publication*]
Philipp J Pub Admin ... Philippine Journal of Public Administration [*A publication*]
Philipp J Sci ... Philippine Journal of Science [*A publication*]
Philipp J Sci Sect A ... Philippine Journal of Science. Section A. Chemical Sciences [*A publication*]
Philipp J Sci Sect B ... Philippine Journal of Science. Section B. Medical Sciences [*A publication*]
Philipp J Sci Sect C ... Philippine Journal of Science. Section C. Botany [*A publication*]
Philipp J Surg ... Philippine Journal of Surgery [*A publication*]
Philipp J Surg Obstet Gynecol ... Philippine Journal of Surgery, Obstetrics, and Gynecology [*A publication*]
Philipp J Surg Surg Spec ... Philippine Journal of Surgery and Surgical Specialties [*A publication*]
Philipp J Trop Med ... Philippine Journal of Tropical Medicine [*A publication*]
Philipp J Vet Anim Sci ... Philippine Journal of Veterinary and Animal Sciences [*A publication*]
Philipp J Vet Med ... Philippine Journal of Veterinary Medicine [*A publication*]

Philipp Lumberm ... Philippine Lumberman [*A publication*]
Philipp Med Dent J ... Philippine Medical-Dental Journal [*A publication*]
Philipp Med World ... Philippine Medical World [*A publication*]
Philipp Med World (1946-1951) ... Philippine Medical World (1946-1951) [*A publication*]
Philipp Med World (1952-1962) ... Philippine Medical World (1952-1962) [*A publication*]
Philipp Met ... Philippine Metals [*A publication*]
Philipp Min J ... Philippine Mining Journal [*A publication*]
Philipp Nucl J ... Philippines Nuclear Journal [*A publication*]
Philip Popul J ... Philippine Population Journal [*A publication*]
Philipp Phytopathol ... Philippine Phytopathology [*A publication*]
Philipp Popul J ... Philippine Population Journal [*A publication*]
Philipp Q Cult Soc ... Philippine Quarterly of Culture and Society [*A publication*]
Philipp Quart Cult Soc ... Philippine Quarterly of Culture and Society [*A publication*]
Philipp Sci ... Philippine Scientist [*A publication*]
Philipp Sci Index ... Philippine Science Index [*A publication*]
Philipp Sugar Inst Q ... Philippine Sugar Institute. Quarterly [*A publication*]
Philipp Text Inf Dig ... Philippine Textile Information Digest [*A publication*]
Philipp Weed Sci Bull ... Philippine Weed Science Bulletin [*A publication*]
Philips........ Philips Music Herald [*A publication*]
PhilipSa..... Philippiana Sacra [*Manila*] [*A publication*]
Philips Ind Eng Bul ... Philips Industrial Engineering Bulletin [*A publication*]   (APTA)
Philips J Res ... Philips Journal of Research [*A publication*]
Philips Res Rep ... Philips Research Reports [*A publication*]
Philips Res Rep Suppl ... Philips Research Reports. Supplements [*A publication*]
Philips Serv Sci Ind ... Philips Serving Science and Industry [*A publication*]
PhilipSt...... Philippine Studies [*Manila*] [*A publication*]
Philips Tech Rev ... Philips Technical Review [*A publication*]
Philips Tech Rundsch ... Philips Technische Rundschau [*A publication*]
Philips Tech Rundschau ... Philips Technische Rundschau [*Netherlands*] [*A publication*]
Philips Telecommun Rev ... Philips Telecommunication Review [*A publication*]
Philips Weld Rep ... Philips Welding Reporter [*A publication*]
Phili S Rev ... Philippine Sociological Review [*A publication*]
Phil J Ag ... Philippine Journal of Agriculture [*A publication*]
Phil Jahr ... Philosophisches Jahrbuch [*A publication*]
Phil J Ling ... Philippine Journal of Linguistics [*A publication*]
Phil J Pub Admin ... Philippine Journal of Public Administration [*A publication*]
Phil Jrl....... Business Journal (Philippines) [*A publication*]
Phil J Sci ... Philippine Journal of Science [*A publication*]
Phil Jud ..... Phillimore's Ecclesiastical Judgments [*1867-75*] [*England*] [*A publication*]   (DLA)
Phil Judg... Phillimore's Ecclesiastical Judgments [*1867-75*] [*A publication*]   (DLA)
Phill .... Phillips' English Chancery Reports [*1841-49*] [*A publication*]   (DLA)
Phill .... Phillips' English Election Cases [*1780-81*] [*A publication*]   (DLA)
Phill .... Phillips' Illinois Reports [*152-245 Illinois*] [*A publication*]   (DLA)
Phill .... Phillips' North Carolina Equity Reports [*A publication*]   (DLA)
Phill .... Phillips' North Carolina Law Reports [*A publication*]   (DLA)
Phil Lab R ... Philippine Labor Review [*A publication*]
Phil Lab Rel J ... Philippine Labour Relations Journal [*A publication*]   (DLA)
Phil Law..... Phillips' North Carolina Law Reports [*A publication*]   (DLA)
Phill Ch...... Phillips' English Chancery Reports [*1841-49*] [*A publication*]   (DLA)
Phill Ch (Eng) ... Phillips' English Chancery Reports [*1841-49*] [*A publication*]   (DLA)
Phil LD ...... Doctor of Lithuanian Philology
Phill Ecc Judg ... Phillimore's Ecclesiastical Judgments [*1867-75*] [*A publication*]   (DLA)
Phill Ecc R ... Phillimore's English Ecclesiastical Reports [*1809-21*] [*A publication*]   (DLA)
Phill Eq (NC) ... Phillips' North Carolina Equity Reports [*A publication*]   (DLA)
Phil Lic ...... Licentiate of Philosophy [*British*]
Phillim .... Phillimore's English Ecclesiastical Reports [*1809-21*] [*A publication*]   (DLA)
Phillim Dom ... Phillimore's Law of Domicil [*A publication*]   (DLA)
Phillim Eccl ... Phillimore's Ecclesiastical Judgments [*1867-75*] [*A publication*]   (DLA)
Phillim Eccl ... Phillimore's English Ecclesiastical Reports [*1809-21*] [*A publication*]   (DLA)
Phillim Ecc Law ... Phillimore's English Ecclesiastical Law [*A publication*]   (DLA)
Phillim Eccl (Eng) ... [*J.*] Phillimore's English Ecclesiastical Reports [*1809-21*] [*A publication*]   (DLA)
Phillim Int Law ... Phillimore's International Law [*A publication*]   (DLA)
Phil Ling.... Philosophical Linguistics [*A publication*]
Phill Ins ..... Phillips on Insurance [*A publication*]   (DLA)
Phillip J Sci ... Philippine Journal of Science [*A publication*]
Phillips....... Phillips' English Chancery Reports [*1841-49*] [*A publication*]   (DLA)

Phillips....... Phillips' English Election Cases [*1780-81*] [*A publication*] (DLA)
Phillips....... Phillips' Illinois Reports [*152-245 Illinois*] [*A publication*] (DLA)
Phillips....... Phillips' North Carolina Equity Reports [*A publication*] (DLA)
Phillips....... Phillips' North Carolina Law Reports [*A publication*] (DLA)
Phillips Dir ... Phillips' Paper Trade Directory of the World [*A publication*]
Phil Lit....... Philosophy and Literature [*A publication*]
Phil LJ....... Philippine Law Journal [*Manila*] [*A publication*] (DLA)
Phill L (NC) ... Phillips' North Carolina Law Reports [*A publication*] (DLA)
Phil Log ..... Philosophie et Logique [*A publication*]
Phil L Rev ... Philippine Law Review [*A publication*] (DLA)
Phil Lun ..... Phillips on Lunatics [*1858*] [*A publication*] (DLA)
Philly .... Philadelphia
Phil Mag.... Philosophical Magazine [*A publication*]
Phil Math .. Philosophia Mathematica [*A publication*]
Phil Mech Liens ... Phillips on Mechanics' Liens [*A publication*] (DLA)
PhilMr....... Philip Morris Companies, Inc. [*Associated Press abbreviation*] (APAG)
Phil Mus .... Philological Museum [*A publication*]
philn........... Philanthropy
Phil Natur ... Philosophia Naturalis [*A publication*]
Phil NC...... Phillips' North Carolina Law Reports [*A publication*] (DLA)
Philo........... Philo Judaeus [*First century AD*] [*Classical studies*] (OCD)
Philol .... Philologus [*A publication*] (OCD)
PHILOL.... Philology
Philol Q..... Philological Quarterly [*A publication*]
Philol Suppl ... Philologus. Supplement [*A publication*] (OCD)
PHILOM .. Philomathes [*Lover of Learning*] (ROG)
PHILOMATH ... Philomathematicus [*Lover of Mathematics*] (ROG)
Philos .... Philosophy [*A publication*]
PHILOS .... Philosophy (EY)
Philos Abhandlungen ... Philosophische Abhandlungen [*A publication*]
Philos Bibliothek ... Philosophische Bibliothek [*Hamburg*] [*A publication*]
Philos Book ... Philosophical Books [*A publication*]
Philos Collect R Soc London ... Philosophical Collections. Royal Society of London [*A publication*]
Philos Curr ... Philosophical Currents [*A publication*]
Philos East & West ... Philosophy East and West [*A publication*]
Philos EW ... Philosophy East and West [*A publication*]
Philos Foru ... Philosophy Forum [*A publication*]
Philos Forum ... Philosophical Forum [*A publication*]
Philos Forum ... Philosophy Forum [*A publication*]
Philos Forum Quart ... Philosophical Forum. A Quarterly [*A publication*]
Philos His.. Philosophy and History [*A publication*]
Philos Hist ... Philosophy and History. German Studies Section I [*A publication*]
PhilosI .... Philosopher's Index [*A publication*]
Philos Index ... Philosopher's Index [*A publication*]
Philos J ...... Philosophical Journal [*A publication*]
Philos Jahr ... Philosophisches Jahrbuch [*A publication*]
Philos Lit ... Philosophy and Literature [*A publication*]
Philos M .... Philosophical Magazine [*A publication*]
Philos Mag ... Philosophical Magazine [*A publication*]
Philos Mag A ... Philosophical Magazine A. Physics of Condensed Matter, Defects, and Mechanical Properties [*A publication*]
Philos Mag B ... Philosophical Magazine B. Physics of Condensed Matter, Electronic, Optical, and Magnetic Properties [*A publication*]
Philos Mag Lett ... Philosophical Magazine Letters [*A publication*]
Philos Mag Suppl ... Philosophical Magazine. Supplement [*A publication*]
Philos Math ... Philosophia Mathematica [*A publication*]
Philos Med ... Philosophy and Medicine [*A publication*]
Philos Nat ... Philosophia Naturalis [*A publication*]
Philos Natur ... Philosophia Naturalis [*A publication*]
Philosophy of Ed Soc Proc ... Philosophy of Education Society of Great Britain. Proceedings [*A publication*]
Philos Pap ... Philosophical Papers [*A publication*]
Philos Phen ... Philosophy and Phenomenological Research [*A publication*]
Philos Phenomenol Res ... Philosophy and Phenomenological Research [*A publication*]
Philos & Phenom Res ... Philosophy and Phenomenological Research [*A publication*]
Philos Pub ... Philosophy and Public Affairs [*A publication*]
Philos & Pub Affairs ... Philosophy and Public Affairs [*A publication*]
Philos Publ Aff ... Philosophy and Public Affairs [*A publication*]
PhilosQ...... Philosophical Quarterly [*A publication*]
Philos Quart ... Philosophical Quarterly [*A publication*]
Philos R ..... Philosophical Review [*A publication*]
Philos Rd ... Philosophische Rundschau [*A publication*]
PhilosRdschau ... Philosophische Rundschau [*A publication*]
Philos Rev ... Philosophical Review [*A publication*]
Philos Rhet ... Philosophy and Rhetoric [*A publication*]
Philos Rund ... Philosophische Rundschau [*A publication*]
Philos Sci ... Philosophy of Science [*A publication*]
Philos Soc Sci ... Philosophy of the Social Sciences [*A publication*]
Philos S Sc ... Philosophy of the Social Sciences [*A publication*]
Philos Stud ... Philosophical Studies [*A publication*]
Philos Studies ... Philosophical Studies [*Dordrecht*] [*A publication*]
Philos Stud Ser Philos ... Philosophical Studies Series in Philosophy [*A publication*]

Philo Stds .. Philosophical Studies [*A publication*]
Philos Tod ... Philosophy Today [*A publication*]
Philos Top ... Philosophical Topics [*A publication*]
Philostr ...... Philostratus [*Second century AD*] [*Classical studies*] (OCD)
Philos Trans Roy Soc London Ser A ... Philosophical Transactions. Royal Society of London. Series A. Mathematical and Physical Sciences [*A publication*]
Philos Trans R Soc A ... Philosophical Transactions. Royal Society of London. Series A. Mathematical and Physical Sciences [*A publication*]
Philos Trans R Soc Lond A Math Phys Sci ... Philosophical Transactions. Royal Society of London. Series A. Mathematical and Physical Sciences [*A publication*]
Philos Trans R Soc Lond Biol ... Philosophical Transactions. Royal Society of London. Series B. Biological Sciences [*A publication*]
Philos Trans R Soc London ... Philosophical Transactions. Royal Society of London [*A publication*]
Philos Trans R Soc London A ... Philosophical Transactions. Royal Society of London. Series A. Mathematical and Physical Sciences [*A publication*]
Philos Trans R Soc London Ser A ... Philosophical Transactions. Royal Society of London. Series A. Mathematical and Physical Sciences [*A publication*]
Philos Trans R Soc London Ser B ... Philosophical Transactions. Royal Society of London. Series B. Biological Sciences [*A publication*]
Phil (PA).... Philadelphia Reports [*Pennsylvania*] [*A publication*] (DLA)
Phil Papers ... Philosophical Papers [*A publication*]
Phil Pat...... Phillips on Patents [*A publication*] (DLA)
Phil Perspekt ... Philosophische Perspektiven [*A publication*]
PhilPet....... Phillips Petroleum Co. [*Associated Press abbreviation*] (APAG)
Phil Phenomenol Res ... Philosophy and Phenomenological Research [*A publication*]
Phil Plan J ... Philippine Planning Journal [*A publication*]
Phil Pln 87 ... Five-Year Philippine Development Plan, 1983-1987 [*A publication*]
Phil Pol Sci J ... Philippine Political Science Journal [*A publication*]
Phil Post .... Philharmonic Post [*A publication*]
Phil Pub Affairs ... Philosophy and Public Affairs [*A publication*]
PHILPUC ... Philippine Presidential Unit Citation Badge [*Military decoration*]
Phil Q........ Philippines Quarterly [*A publication*]
Phil Q........ Philosophical Quarterly [*A publication*]
Phil Q Cult Soc ... Philippine Quarterly of Culture and Society [*A publication*]
Phil Qy....... Philological Quarterly [*A publication*]
Phil R........ Philadelphia Reports [*Pennsylvania*] [*A publication*] (DLA)
Phil R........ Philosophical Review [*A publication*]
PhilR.......... Philosophy and Rhetoric [*A publication*]
Phil R Bus Econ ... Philippine Review of Business and Economics [*A publication*]
Phil Reform ... Philosophia Reformata [*A publication*]
Phil Rep ..... Philadelphia Reports [*Pennsylvania*] [*A publication*] (DLA)
Phil Res Arch ... Philosophy Research Archives [*A publication*]
Phil Res R ... Philips Research Reports [*A publication*]
Phil Rev ..... Philosophical Review [*A publication*]
Phil Rev (Taiwan) ... Philosophical Review (Taiwan) [*A publication*]
Phil Rhet.... Philosophy and Rhetoric [*A publication*]
Phil Rom Law ... Phillimore's Private Law among the Romans [*A publication*] (DLA)
Phil Rundsch ... Philosophische Rundschau [*A publication*]
PhilS .... Philosophical Studies [*A publication*]
Phil Sacra .. Philippine Sacra [*A publication*]
Phil Sci...... Philosophy of Science [*A publication*]
PHILSEAFRON ... Philippine Sea Frontier
Phil Soc...... Philological Society. Transactions [*A publication*]
Phil Soc Act ... Philosophy and Social Action [*A publication*]
Phil Soc Cr ... Philosophy and Social Criticism [*A publication*]
Phil Soc Crit ... Philosophy and Social Criticism [*A publication*]
Phil Sociol R ... Philippine Sociological Review [*A publication*]
Phil Soc Sci ... Philosophy of the Social Sciences [*A publication*]
Phil Soc Sci Hum R ... Philippine Social Sciences and Humanities Review [*A publication*]
PHILSOM ... Periodical Holdings in the Library of the School of Medicine [*Washington University School of Medicine*] [*Library network*]
Phil St........ Philologische Studien [*A publication*]
Phil St Leg R ... Phillips' Studii Legalis Ratio [*A publication*] (DLA)
Phil St Tr... Phillipps' State Trials [*Prior to 1688*] [*A publication*] (DLA)
Phil Stud ... Philippine Studies [*A publication*]
Phil Stud.... Philosophical Studies [*A publication*]
Phil Stud Educ ... Philosophical Studies in Education [*A publication*]
Phil Stud (Ireland) ... Philosophical Studies (Ireland) [*A publication*]
PhilSub ...... Philadelphia Suburban Corp. [*Associated Press abbreviation*] (APAG)
PhilT .... Philosophy Today [*A publication*]
Phil Techn Rd ... Philips Technische Rundschau [*A publication*]
Phil Techn Rev ... Philips Technical Review [*A publication*]
Phil Tech R ... Philips Technical Review [*A publication*]
Phil Today ... Philosophy Today [*A publication*]
Phil Topics ... Philosophical Topics [*A publication*]

Phil Trans ... Philosophical Transactions [*A publication*]
Phil Trans Royal Soc London Ser A ... Philosophical Transactions. Royal Society of London. Series A. Mathematical and Physical Sciences [*A publication*]
Phil Trans Roy Soc Lond ... Philosophical Transactions. Royal Society of London [*A publication*]
Phil Trans Roy Soc Lond B ... Philosophical Transactions. Royal Society of London. Series B. Biological Sciences [*A publication*]
Phil Trans Roy Soc Lond Ser A Math Phys Sci ... Philosophical Transactions. Royal Society of London. Series A. Mathematical and Physical Sciences [*A publication*]
Phil Trans R Soc ... Philosophical Transactions. Royal Society of London [*A publication*]
Phil Unters ... Philologische Untersuchungen [*A publication*]   (OCD)
Phil US Pr ... Phillips' United States Practice [*A publication*]   (DLA)
Phil Woch ... Philologische Wochenschrift [*A publication*]
Phil Wochenschr ... Philologische Wochenschrift [*A publication*]   (OCD)
Phil Yb Int'l L ... Philippine Yearbook of International Law [*Manila, Philippines*] [*A publication*]   (DLA)
PHIN .... Position and Homing Inertial Navigator
PHINA ...... Pharmazeutische Industrie [*A publication*]
PHIND ...... Pharmaceutical and Healthcare Industries News Database [*PJB Group Publications Ltd.*] [*Information service or system*]   (IID)
PHIND ...... Pharmacy International [*A publication*]
P-H Ind Rel Lab Arb ... Industrial Relations, American Labor Arbitration (Prentice-Hall, Inc.) [*A publication*]   (DLA)
P-H Ind Rel Union Conts ... Industrial Relations, Union Contracts, and Collective Bargaining (Prentice-Hall, Inc.) [*A publication*]   (DLA)
PHINet ...... Prentice-Hall Information Network [*Prentice-Hall Information Services*] [*Information service or system*]   (IID)
Phip .... Phipson's Digest, Natal Reports [*South Africa*] [*A publication*]   (DLA)
Phip .... Phipson's Reports, Natal Supreme Court [*South Africa*] [*A publication*]   (DLA)
Phip Ev ...... Phipson on Evidence [*12th ed.*] [*1976*] [*A publication*]   (DLA)
PHIPS .... Professional Hi-Resolution Image Processing System [*TerraVision, Inc.*]   (PCM)
Phipson ...... Reports of Cases in the Supreme Court of Natal [*A publication*]   (DLA)
PHIS .... History. The Journal of the Historical Association [*A publication*]
PHIS .... Program Hardware Interface Specification   (CAAL)
PHITAP .... Predesigned [*or Priority*] High-Interest Tactical Air [*Acoustic forecast*] Prediction   (MCD)
PHITAR .... Predesignated High-Interest Tactical Area [*Navy*]   (NVT)
Phi T Roy A ... Philosophical Transactions. Royal Society of London. Series A. Mathematical and Physical Sciences [*A publication*]
Phi T Roy B ... Philosophical Transactions. Royal Society of London. Series B. Biological Sciences [*A publication*]
PHIX .... [*The*] Phoenix Group International, Inc. [*NASDAQ symbol*]   (NQ)
PHJ .... Danville State Hospital, Danville, PA [*OCLC symbol*]   (OCLC)
Ph J .... Philosophical Journal [*A publication*]
PhJ .... Philosophisches Jahrbuch [*A publication*]
Ph J .... Philosophisches Jahrbuch der Goerres-Gesellschaft [*A publication*]
Ph Jb .... Philosophisches Jahrbuch [*A publication*]
Ph Jb .... Philosophisches Jahrbuch der Goerres-Gesellschaft [*A publication*]
PHJC .... Penn Hall Junior College [*Pennsylvania*] [*Closed, 1973*]
PHJC .... Poor Handmaids of Jesus Christ [*Ancilla Domini Sisters*] [*Roman Catholic religious order*]
PHJC .... Port Huron Junior College [*Michigan*]
PHJH .... Historian. A Journal of History [*A publication*]
PH/JO .... Photojournalist   (DNAB)
PHJRD ...... Philips Journal of Research [*A publication*]
PHK .... Pahokee, FL [*Location identifier*] [*FAA*]   (FAAL)
PHK .... Personal Hygiene Kit   (MCD)
PhK .... Phosphorylase Kinase [*An enzyme*]
PHK .... Platelet Phosphohexokinase   (MAE)
PHK .... Pootaardappelwereld [*A publication*]
PHK .... Porter [*H. K.*] Co., Inc. [*NYSE symbol*]   (SPSG)
PHK .... Postmortem Human Kidney [*Cells*]
PHKO .... Kona/Ke-Ahole, Hawaii Island [*Hawaii*] [*ICAO location identifier*]   (ICLI)
PHKOA ..... Photographische Korrespondenz (Austria) [*A publication*]
PHKP .... Kaanapali, Maui Island [*Hawaii*] [*ICAO location identifier*]   (ICLI)
PHKU .... Kunia [*Hawaii*] [*ICAO location identifier*]   (ICLI)
PHL .... Allentown State Hospital, Allentown, PA [*OCLC symbol*]   (OCLC)
Ph L .... Licentiate of Pharmacy
Ph L .... Licentiate in Philosophy
PHL .... Periodical Holdings List [*Libraries*]
PHL .... Philadelphia [*Pennsylvania*] [*Airport symbol*]
PHL .... Philippines [*ANSI three-letter standard code*]   (CNC)
PHL .... Philips Industries, Inc. [*NYSE symbol*]   (SPSG)
PHL .... Phillips Michigan City Flying Service [*Michigan City, IN*] [*FAA designator*]   (FAAC)

PHL .... Pressure to Horizontal Locks [*Missiles*]   (AAG)
PHL .... Public Health Law
Ph La .... Philosophischer Literaturanzeiger [*A publication*]
PHLA .... Plasma Postheparin Lipolytic Activity [*Clinical chemistry*]
PHLAG ..... Phillips Petroleum Load and Go [*System*]
PHLAGS ... Phillips Petroleum Load and Go System   (DNAB)
Phlb .... Philebus [*of Plato*] [*Classical studies*]   (OCD)
PHLBA ...... Phlebologie [*A publication*]
Phld .... Philodemus [*First century BC*] [*Classical studies*]   (OCD)
Phl Freep ... Philadelphia Free Press [*A publication*]
PHLH .... Phillips Head [*Screw*]
PHLI .... Lihue, Kauai Island [*Hawaii*] [*ICAO location identifier*]   (ICLI)
Ph Lit .... Philosophischer Literaturanzeiger [*A publication*]
PHLLD ...... Philippine Long Distance Telephone Co. [*Associated Press abbreviation*]   (APAG)
Phlm .... Philemon [*New Testament book*]
PHLO .... Phloretin [*Biochemistry*]
PHLODOT ... Phase Lock Doppler Tracking [*System*]   (MUGU)
PhlpGs .... Phillips Gas [*Associated Press abbreviation*]   (APAG)
PHLS .... Public Health Laboratory Service [*British*]
PHLSB ...... Public Health Laboratory Service Board [*British*]
PHLTA ...... Physics Letters [*A publication*]
PhlVH .... Phillips-Van Heusen Corp. [*Associated Press abbreviation*]   (APAG)
PHLX .... Philadelphia Stock Exchange
Ph M .... Master in Pharmacy
Ph M .... Master of Philosophy
PHM .... Mayview State Hospital, Bridgeville, PA [*OCLC symbol*]   (OCLC)
PHM .... Patrol Hydrofoil Missile [*Navy symbol*]
PHM .... Patterson-Harker Method [*Physics*]
PHM .... Per Hundred Million   (NASA)
PHM .... Petroleum Helicopters, Inc. [*Lafayette, LA*] [*FAA designator*]   (FAAC)
PHM .... Phantom   (MSA)
PHM .... Pharmacist's Mate [*Navy rating*]
PHM .... Phase Meter
PHM .... Phase Modulation [*Radio data transmission*]   (DEN)
Phm .... Philemon [*New Testament book*]   (BJA)
PhM .... Philips Minigroove [*Record label*]
PHM .... PHM Corp. [*Formerly, Pulte Home Corp.*] [*NYSE symbol*]   (SPSG)
PHM .... PHM Corp. [*Formerly, Pulte Home Corp.*] [*Associated Press abbreviation*]   (APAG)
PHM .... Post-Holiday Movie
PHM .... Posterior Hyaloid Membrane [*Eye anatomy*]
PHM .... Power Hybrid Microcircuit
PHMA ...... Plastic Houseware Manufacturers Association
PHMAA .... Philosophical Magazine [*A publication*]
Ph Mag ...... Philosophical Magazine [*A publication*]
Phm B .... Bachelor of Pharmacy
PHMB .... Para-Hydroxymercuribenzoate [*Biochemistry*]
PHMBA .... Physics in Medicine and Biology [*A publication*]
PHMC .... Probe Heater Motor Controller [*NASA*]   (MCD)
PHMDEH ... Pharmaceutical Medicine [*Hampshire*] [*A publication*]
PHMDP .... Pharmacist's Mate, Dental Prosthetic Technician [*Navy rating*]
Phm G .... Graduate in Pharmacy
PHMGB ..... Pharmacology [*A publication*]
PHMK .... Molokai, Molokai Island [*Hawaii*] [*ICAO location identifier*]   (ICLI)
PHMMA ... Physics of Metals and Metallography [*English Translation*] [*A publication*]
PHMO .... Partially Hydrogenated Menhaden Oil [*Food science*]
PHMODF ... Phanerogamarum Monographiae [*A publication*]
PHMOV ..... Phleum Mottle Virus [*Plant pathology*]
PhmRes ...... Pharmaceutical Resources, Inc. [*Associated Press abbreviation*]   (APAG)
PHMS .... Para-Hydroxymercuriphenylsulfonate [*Organic chemistry*]
PHMS .... Patrol Hydrofoil Missile Ship [*Navy/NATO*]
PHMS .... Polish Historical Military Society   (EA)
PHMT .... PhoneMate, Inc. [*NASDAQ symbol*]   (NQ)
PHMTD .... Previews of Heat and Mass Transfer [*A publication*]
PHMU .... Waimea-Kohala, Kamuela, Hawaii Island [*Hawaii*] [*ICAO location identifier*]   (ICLI)
PhMV .... Phleum Mottle Virus
PHMV .... Physalis Mosaic Virus [*Plant pathology*]
PHMWO ... Prospect Hill Millimeter Wave Observatory [*Waltham, MA*] [*Air Force*]
PHN .... Norristown State Hospital, Norristown, PA [*OCLC symbol*]   (OCLC)
PHN .... Phone   (KSC)
PHN .... Port Huron, MI [*Location identifier*] [*FAA*]   (FAAL)
PHN .... Public Health Network [*Information service or system*]   (IID)
PHN .... Public Health Nurse
PHNA .... Barbers Point Naval Air Station, Oahu Island [*Hawaii*] [*ICAO location identifier*]   (ICLI)
Ph Nat .... Philosophia Naturalis [*A publication*]
PHNC .... Pearl Harbor, Oahu Island [*Hawaii*] [*ICAO location identifier*]   (ICLI)
PHNG .... Kaneohe Bay Marine Corps Air Station, Oahu Island [*Hawaii*] [*ICAO location identifier*]   (ICLI)

PHNL........ Honolulu/International, Oahu Island [*Hawaii*] [*ICAO location identifier*] (ICLI)
PHNOA..... Physica Norvegica [*A publication*]
PHNT........ History and Theory [*A publication*]
PHNTA...... Phonetica [*A publication*]
PHNX........ Phoenix Medical Technology, Inc. [*Andrews, SC*] [*NASDAQ symbol*] (NQ)
PhnxLs ...... Phoenix Laser Systems, Inc. [*Associated Press abbreviation*] (APAG)
PhnxRs ...... Phoenix Resource Companies, Inc. [*Associated Press abbreviation*] (APAG)
PHNY........ Lanai City, Lanai Island [*Hawaii*] [*ICAO location identifier*] (ICLI)
PHNY........ Pearl Harbor Navy Yard [*Later, Pearl Harbor Naval Shipyard*]
P-H NYETR ... Prentice-Hall New York Estate Tax Reports [*A publication*] (DLA)
PHO.......... Pediatric Hematology-Oncology [*Medical specialty*] (DHSM)
PHO.......... Phenolic Heavy Oil
PHO.......... Philco Houston Operations (SAA)
PhO.......... Philologia Orientalis [*A publication*]
Pho........... Photographer [*British military*] (DMA)
PHO.......... Point Hope [*Alaska*] [*Airport symbol*] (OAG)
PHO.......... Polk State School and Hospital, Polk, PA [*OCLC symbol*] (OCLC)
PHO.......... Port Health Officer
PHO.......... Puu Honuaula [*Hawaii*] [*Seismograph station code, US Geological Survey*] (SEIS)
PHOAC..... Photographer's Mate, Combat Aircrewman [*Navy rating*] [*Obsolete*]
Phob.......... Previous Highroller, on a Budget [*Lifestyle classification*]
PHOBOS ... Photometric Instrument for Biological Optical Sections
PHOC........ Photo Control Corp. [*NASDAQ symbol*] (NQ)
PHOC........ Photocopy (MSA)
PHOD........ Philadelphia Ordnance Depot [*Military*] (AAG)
PHODEC .. Photometric Determination of Equilibrium Constants [*Data processing*]
Phoe .... Phoenix [*Constellation*]
Phoen .... Phoenician (BJA)
Phoen .... Phoenissae [*of Euripides*] [*Classical studies*] (OCD)
PHOENIX .. Plasma Heating Obtained by Energetic Neutral Injection Experiment (IEEE)
Phoenix BJ ... Phoenix Business Journal [*A publication*]
PhoenixC ... Phoenix: The Classical Association of Canada [*A publication*]
Phoenix Ex Or Lux ... Phoenix. Bulletin Uitgegeven door het Vooraziatisch-Egyptisch Genootschap Ex Oriente Lux [*A publication*]
PhoenixK ... Phoenix (Korea) [*A publication*]
Phoenix Q ... Phoenix Quarterly [*A publication*]
Phoe Sh...... Phoenix Shocker [*A publication*]
PHOFEX... Photofragment Excitation [*Spectroscopy*]
PHOFL...... Photoflash (AAG)
PHOG........ Kahului, Maui Island [*Hawaii*] [*ICAO location identifier*] (ICLI)
PHOM....... Photographer's Mate [*Navy rating*] [*Obsolete*]
PHON .... Phoenician
Phon........... Phonetica [*A publication*]
PHON .... Phonetics
PHON .... Phonogram (ROG)
PHON .... Phonograph (AAG)
PHON .... Photon Technology International, Inc. [*NASDAQ symbol*] (NQ)
PHONCON ... Telephone Conversation [*or Conference*]
PHONET.. Phonetics (ROG)
P HONG.... Ponchong [*Tea trade*] (ROG)
PHONO .... Phonograph (MSA)
PHONOG ... Phonography
PHONOL ... Phonology
Phonon Scattering Condens Matter Proc Int Conf ... Phonon Scattering in Condensed Matter. Proceedings. International Conference [*A publication*]
Phonons Proc Int Conf ... Phonons. Proceedings. International Conference [*A publication*]
PhonPr...... Phonetica Pragensia [*A publication*]
PHOPD..... Photobiochemistry and Photobiophysics [*A publication*]
PHOPT..... Pseudohypoparathyroidism [*Endocrinology*]
Phorm .... Phormio [*of Terence*] [*Classical studies*] (OCD)
PHOS........ Phosphate (KSC)
PHOS........ Phosphorescent (KSC)
PHOS........ Phosphorus [*Chemical symbol is P*]
PhosBro ..... Phosphor Bronze
PHOSCHEM ... Phosphate Chemicals Export Association (EA)
PHOSI....... Preliminary Handbook of Operations and Service Instructions
PHOSIAC ... Photographically Stored Information Analog Comparator
PHosp .... Post Hospital [*Army*]
Phospho Potas ... Phosphorus and Potassium [*A publication*]
Phosphore Agric ... Phosphore et Agriculture [*France*] [*A publication*]
Phosphor Sulfur Relat Elem ... Phosphorus and Sulfur and the Related Elements [*A publication*]
Phosphorus ... Phosphorus and Potassium [*A publication*]
Phosphorus Agric ... Phosphorus in Agriculture [*A publication*]
Phosphorus Relat Group V Elem ... Phosphorus and the Related Group V Elements [*A publication*]

Phosphorus Sulfur Silicon Relat Elem ... Phosphorus, Sulfur, and Silicon and the Related Elements [*A publication*]
Phot........... Photius [*Ninth century AD*] [*Classical studies*] (OCD)
PHOT........ Photograph
PHOT........ Photograph [*Navy rating*] [*British*]
Phot........... Photon [*A publication*]
PHOT........ Photronics Corp. [*NASDAQ symbol*] (NQ)
PHOTABS ... Photographic Abstracts [*Pergamon*] [*Database*]
Phot Abstr ... Photographic Abstracts [*A publication*]
PHOTAC .. Phototypesetting and Composing [*AT & T*]
Phot Appln Sci ... Photographic Applications in Science, Technology, and Medicine [*A publication*]
Phot Appl Sci Tech Med ... Photographic Applications in Science, Technology, and Medicine [*A publication*]
Phot Arch... Photographisches Archiv [*A publication*]
PHOTEX... [*Day*] Photographic Exercise [*Military*] (NVT)
Phot Industrie ... Photographische Industrie [*A publication*]
PHOTINT ... Photographic Intelligence [*Military*]
Phot J........ Photographic Journal [*A publication*]
Phot J Amer ... Photographic Journal of America [*A publication*]
Phot Ko ...... Photographische Korrespondenz [*A publication*]
Phot Korr ... Photographische Korrespondenz [*A publication*]
PHOTO..... Photograph (AAG)
Photo.......... Photogravure [*Philately*]
Photo Abstr ... Photographic Abstracts [*A publication*]
Photo Art Mon ... Photo Art Monthly [*A publication*]
Photobiochem Photobiophys ... Photobiochemistry and Photobiophysics [*A publication*]
Photobiol Bull ... Photobiology Bulletin [*A publication*]
Photobl....... Photoblaetter [*A publication*]
Photo Can .. Photo Canada [*A publication*]
Photochem Convers Storage Sol Energy Int Conf ... Photochemical Conversion and Storage of Solar Energy. International Conference on Photochemical Conversion and Storage of Solar Energy [*A publication*]
Photo Chem Mach Photo Chem Etching ... Photo Chemical Machining - Photo Chemical Etching [*A publication*]
Photochem P ... Photochemistry and Photobiology [*A publication*]
Photochem Photobiol ... Photochemistry and Photobiology [*A publication*]
Photochem Photobiol Rev ... Photochemical and Photobiological Reviews [*A publication*]
Photo Cine Rev ... Photo-Cine-Review [*A publication*]
Photodermatol ... Photo-Dermatology [*A publication*]
Photoelastic J ... Photoelastic Journal [*A publication*]
Photoelastic Soil Mech J ... Photoelastic and Soil Mechanics Journal [*A publication*]
Photoelectr Spectrom Group Bull ... Photoelectric Spectrometry Group Bulletin [*A publication*]
Photo Engravers Bull ... Photo-Engravers' Bulletin [*A publication*]
Photo Era Mag ... Photo-Era Magazine [*A publication*]
PHOTOG ... Photographic
Photog Abstr ... Photographic Abstracts [*A publication*]
PHOTOGR ... Photography
Photogr Abstr ... Photographic Abstracts [*A publication*]
Photogr Alle ... Photographie fuer Alle [*A publication*]
Photogram Eng Remote Sensing ... Photogrammetric Engineering and Remote Sensing [*A publication*]
Photogramma ... Photogrammetria [*A publication*]
Photogramm Eng ... Photogrammetric Engineering [*Later, Photogrammetric Engineering and Remote Sensing*] [*A publication*]
Photogramm Eng Remote Sensing ... Photogrammetric Engineering and Remote Sensing [*A publication*]
Photogrammetric Eng ... Photogrammetric Engineering [*Later, Photogrammetric Engineering and Remote Sensing*] [*A publication*]
Photogramm Rec ... Photogrammetric Record [*A publication*]
Photographie Forsch ... Photographie und Forschung [*A publication*]
Photogr Appl Sci Technol Med ... Photographic Applications in Science, Technology, and Medicine [*A publication*]
Photogr Canadiana ... Photographic Canadiana [*A publication*]
Photogr Chron ... Photographische Chronik [*A publication*]
Photogr Chron Allg Photogr Ztg ... Photographische Chronik und Allgemeine Photographische Zeitung [*A publication*]
Photogr Collector ... Photographic Collector [*A publication*]
Photogr Eng ... Photographic Engineering [*A publication*]
Photogr E R ... Photogrammetric Engineering and Remote Sensing [*A publication*]
Photogr Focus ... Photography and Focus [*A publication*]
Photogr Forsch ... Photographie und Forschung [*A publication*]
Photogr Ind ... Photographische Industrie [*A publication*]
Photogr Index ... Photography Index [*A publication*]
Photogr Ind Tokyo ... Photographic Industries (Tokyo) [*A publication*]
Photogr J ... Photographic Journal [*A publication*]
Photogr J Sect A ... Photographic Journal. Section A. Pictorial and General Photography [*A publication*]
Photogr J Sect B ... Photographic Journal. Section B. Scientific and Technical Photography [*A publication*]
Photogr Korresp ... Photographische Korrespondenz [*A publication*]
Photogr Mag ... Photography Magazine [*A publication*]
Photogr Sci Eng ... Photographic Science and Engineering [*A publication*]

Photogr Sci Photochem ... Photographic Science and Photochemistry [*A publication*]
Photogr Sci Symp ... Photographic Science. Symposium [*A publication*]
Photogr Sci Tech ... Photographic Science and Technique [*A publication*]
Photogr Sensitivity ... Photographic Sensitivity [*A publication*]
Photogr Soc Am J ... Photographic Society of America. Journal [*A publication*]
Photogr Soc Am J Sect B ... Photographic Society of America. Journal. Section B. Photographic Science and Technique [*A publication*]
Photogr Soc Am J Suppl ... Photographic Society of America. Journal. Supplement [*A publication*]
Photogr Tech Sci Res ... Photographic Techniques in Scientific Research [*A publication*]
Photogr Welt ... Photographische Welt [*A publication*]
Photogr Wiss ... Photographie und Wissenschaft [*A publication*]
Photo Ind ... Photo-Industrie und -Handel [*A publication*]
Photo Ind ... Photographische Industrie [*A publication*]
Photo Ind ... Wolfman Report on the Photographic Industry in the United States [*A publication*]
Photo Kino Chem Ind ... Photo-Kino-Chemical Industry [*A publication*]
Photo Lab Manag ... Photo Lab Management [*A publication*]
Photo Lit .... Photographic Literature [*A publication*]
PHOTOLITH ... Photolithographic
Photo-M .... Photo-Miniature [*A publication*]
PHOTOM ... Photometry
Photo-Mag ... Photo-Magazin [*A publication*]
Photomethd ... Photomethods [*A publication*]
Photo Methods Ind ... Photo Methods for Industry [*A publication*]
Photo Min ... Photo-Miniature [*A publication*]
Photo Mkt ... Photo Marketing [*A publication*]
Photon Correl Tech Fluid Mech Proc Int Conf ... Photon Correlation Techniques in Fluid Mechanics. Proceedings. International Conference [*A publication*]
Photon Detect Proc Int Symp Tech Comm ... Photon-Detectors. Proceedings. International Symposium. Technical Committee [*A publication*]
Photonic Meas Photon Detect Proc Int Symp Tech Comm ... Photonic Measurements Photon-Detectors. Proceedings. International Symposium. Technical Committee [*A publication*]
Photonics Appl Nucl Phys ... Photonics Applied to Nuclear Physics [*A publication*]
Photon Photon Collisions Proc Int Workshop ... Photon Photon Collisions. Proceedings. International Workshop on Photon Photon Collisions [*A publication*]
Photophysiol Curr Top ... Photophysiology. Current Topics [*A publication*]
Photoplay... Photoplay, Movies, and Video [*A publication*]
Photosel Chem ... Photoselective Chemistry [*A publication*]
Photo Spec ... Photonics Spectra [*A publication*]
Photosynthe ... Photosynthetica [*A publication*]
Photosynth Proc Int Congr ... Photosynthesis. Proceedings. International Congress on Photosynthesis [*A publication*]
Photosynth Res ... Photosynthesis Research [*A publication*]
Photosynth Sol Energy Convers ... Photosynthetic Solar Energy Conversion [*A publication*]
Photo Tech ... Photo Technique [*A publication*]
PHOTOTRIGULANT ... Photographic Triangulation Group, Atlantic [*Military*] (DNAB)
PHOTOTRIGUPAC ... Photographic Triangulation Group, Pacific [*Military*] (DNAB)
Photovoltaic Gener Space Proc Eur Symp ... Photovoltaic Generators in Space. Proceedings. European Symposium [*A publication*]
Photovoltaic Sol Energy Conf Proc Int Conf ... Photovoltaic Solar Energy Conference. Proceedings. International Conference [*A publication*]
PHOTRIPART ... Photo Triangulation Party [*Military*]
PHOTRON ... Photographic Squadron [*Navy*]
Phot Sci En ... Photographic Science and Engineering [*A publication*]
Phot Sci Eng ... Photographic Science and Engineering [*A publication*]
Phot Sci Tech ... Photographic Society of America. Journal. Section B. Photographic Science and Technique [*A publication*]
Phot Tech... Photo Technique [*A publication*]
Phot Tech Wirt ... Photo-Technik und -Wirtschaft [*A publication*]
PHOTUB .. Phototube (KSC)
PHO/TY ... Photo Type [*Deltiology*]
PHP .... Pacific Hawaiian Products Co. [*Later, PHP Co.*]
PHP .... Packing-House Products [*Food industry*]
PHP .... Parents Helping Parents [*An association*] (EA)
PHP .... Parts, Hybrids, and Packaging (MCD)
PHP .... Passive Hyperpolarizing Potential [*Neurochemistry*]
PHP .... Payload Handling Panel [*NASA*] (MCD)
PHP .... Peace, Happiness, Prosperity for All [*A publication*]
PH and P ... Peace, Health, and Prosperity
PHP .... Pennhurst State School and Hospital, Spring City, PA [*OCLC symbol*] (OCLC)
PHP .... Petroleum Heat & Power Co. [*AMEX symbol*] (SPSG)
PHP .... Philip, SD [*Location identifier*] [*FAA*] (FAAL)
PHP .... Phillip Resources, Inc. [*Vancouver Stock Exchange symbol*]
PhP .... Philologica Pragensia [*A publication*]
PhP .... Philologike Protochronia [*A publication*]
PHP .... Philosophia Patrum [*A publication*] (BJA)

PHP .... PHP Healthcare Corp. [*Associated Press abbreviation*] (APAG)
PHP .... Physician's Health Plan
PHP .... Pinane Hydroperoxide [*Organic chemistry*]
PHP .... Planetary Horizon Platform [*Aerospace*]
PHP .... Post-Heparin Phospholipase [*Medicine*] (MAE)
PHP .... Post-Hostilities Planning Subcommittee of the Chiefs of Staff Committee [*World War II*]
PHP .... Pounds per Horsepower
PHP .... Prentice Hall Press [*Publisher*]
PHP .... Prepaid Health Plan [*Insurance*]
PHP .... Presbyterian Hunger Program (EA)
PHP .... Primary Hyperparathyroidism (MAE)
PHP .... Propeller Horsepower
PHP .... Pseudohypoparathyroidism [*Endocrinology*]
PHP .... Pump Horsepower
PHPA .... Pacific Herring Packers Association (EA)
PHPC .... Post-Hostilities Planning Committee [*Navy*] [*World War II*]
PHPE .... History of Political Economy [*A publication*]
PHPG .... Poly(hydroxypropylglutamine) [*Organic chemistry*]
PHPHB .... P-heptyl-p-hydroxy Benzoate [*A preservative used in the making of American and British beer*]
Ph & Phen R ... Philosophy and Phenomenological Research [*A publication*]
PHPL .... Parallel Hardware Processing Language [*1977*] [*Data processing*] (CSR)
PHPLA ...... Physiologia Plantarum [*A publication*]
PHPO .... Private Health Plan Option [*Medicare*] (GFGA)
Ph Prag ..... Philologica Pragensia [*A publication*]
PHPS .... Post-Hostilities Planning Staff [*World War II*]
PHPT .... Portable High-Potential Tester
PHPT .... Primary Hyperparathyroidism
PHPV .... Persistent Hyperplastic Primary Vitreous [*Ophthalmology*]
PHPXA ...... Pharmazeutische Praxis [*A publication*]
PHQ .... Phenylhydroquinone [*Organic chemistry*]
PhQ .... Philosophical Quarterly [*A publication*]
PHQ .... Postal Headquarters [*British*]
PHR .... Pacific Harbour [*Fiji*] [*Airport symbol*] (OAG)
PHR .... Pacific Historical Review [*A publication*]
PHR .... Parts per Hundred of Rubber [*Chemical technology*]
PHR .... Payload Hazardous Report (NASA)
PHR .... Peak Heart Rate [*Cardiology*]
PHR .... Peak Height Ratio
PHR .... Pharmazeutische Industrie [*A publication*]
PHR .... Philippine Historical Review [*A publication*]
PhR .... Philosophical Review [*A publication*]
Ph R .... Philosophische Rundschau [*A publication*]
PHR .... Phorbol [*Organic chemistry*]
PHR .... Photographic Reconnaissance
PHR .... Phrase
Phr .... Phrenomena: an Annual Review [*A publication*] (APTA)
PHR .... Physical Record [*Data processing*]
PHR .... Physicians for Human Rights (EA)
PHR .... Pound-Force per Hour (MCD)
PHR .... Pounds per Hour (AAG)
PHR .... Preheater (KSC)
PHR .... Process Heat Reactor Program [*Nuclear Regulatory Commission*]
PHR .... Public Health Reports [*A publication*]
PHR .... Pulse-Height Resolution [*By photomultiplier tubes*]
PHR .... Retreat State Hospital, Hunlock Creek, PA [*OCLC symbol*] (OCLC)
PHRA .... Poverty and Human Resources Abstracts [*A publication*]
PHRC .... Palestine Human Rights Campaign (EA)
Ph Rdschau ... Philosophische Rundschau [*A publication*]
PHRE .... Public Health Reports [*A publication*]
PHREA ...... Physiological Reviews [*A publication*]
PHRED ...... Public Health Risk Evaluation Data [*Environmental Safety*]
PHREN ..... Phrenology
Ph Rep ...... Philadelphia Reports [*Pennsylvania*] [*A publication*] (DLA)
Ph Res .... Philosophy and Phenomenological Research [*A publication*]
Ph Rev .... Philosophical Phenomenological Review [*A publication*]
Ph Rev .... Philosophical Review [*A publication*]
PHRF .... Performance Handicap Racing Formula [*Sailing*]
PHRG .... Parliamentary Human Rights Group (EAIO)
Ph & Rh ..... Philosophy and Rhetoric [*A publication*]
PHRHD ..... Pump, Hydraulic Ram, Hand-Driven (MSA)
PHRI .... Human Rights [*A publication*]
PHRI .... Public Health Research Institute of the City of New York, Inc. [*Research center*] (RCD)
PHRIC .... Palestine Human Rights Information Center (EA)
PHRK .... Power and Heat Rejection Kit [*NASA*]
PHRM .... Pharmetics, Inc. [*NASDAQ symbol*] (NQ)
PHRQ .... Human Rights Quarterly [*A publication*]
PHRR .... Parenchymal Hepatic Resection Rate [*Medicine*]
PHRS .... Paul Harris Stores, Inc. [*NASDAQ symbol*] (NQ)
PHRS .... Portable Heat Rejection System
Ph Ru .... Philosophische Rundschau [*A publication*]
PHRV .... Public Health Reviews [*A publication*]
PHRVA ..... Physical Review [*A publication*]
PHS .... Packaging, Handling, and Storage (MCD)
PHS .... Pallottine House of Studies
PHS .... Paternal Half Sister (OA)

PHS .... Pathological Human Serum [*Serology*]
PHS .... Payload Handling Station [*NASA*]　(MCD)
PHS .... Personal Health Survey [*Psychology*]
PHS .... Personal Hygiene Subsystem [*NASA*]　(KSC)
PhS .... Philologische Studien [*A publication*]
PhS .... Philosophical Studies [*A publication*]
PHS .... Phitsanuloke [*Thailand*] [*Airport symbol*]　(OAG)
PHS .... Photographic Historical Society　(EA)
PHS .... Postal History Society　(EA)
PHS .... Postcard History Society　(EA)
PHS .... Posthypnotic Suggestion [*Psychology*]
PHS .... Prepared Hessian Surfacing [*Air Force*]
PHS .... Presbyterian Historical Society　(EA)
PHS .... Price History System　(MCD)
PHS .... Printing Historical Society [*British*]
PHS .... Probability of Having a Space
PHS .... Progressive Hongkong Society [*Political party*]
PHS .... Public Health Service [*Department of Health and Human Services*]
PHS .... Public Health Service. Publications [*A publication*]
PHS .... Pumped Hydro Storage [*Power source*]
PHS .... Schippersweekblad [*A publication*]
PHS .... Somerset State Hospital, Somerset, PA [*OCLC symbol*]　(OCLC)
PHSA .... Pearl Harbor Survivors Association　(EA)
PHSA .... Polyhydroxystearic Acid [*Organic chemistry*]
PHSA .... Polymerized Human Serum Albumin [*Biochemistry*]
PHS of A.... Postal History Society of the Americas　(EA)
PHSA .... Public Health Service Act　(GFGA)
PHSAR...... Public Health Service Acquisition Regulations [*Department of Health and Human Services*]　(GFGA)
PHSB........ Journal of Health and Social Behavior [*A publication*]
PHSBB .... Physics Bulletin [*A publication*]
PHSC........ Pluripotent Hematopoietic Stem Cells [*Cytology*]
PHSC........ Postal History Society of Canada　(EA)
PHSC........ Private Hospital Supplementary Charges　(ADA)
PHSCA...... Philippine Journal of Science [*A publication*]
PHSE........ Phase [*Data processing*]
PHSE........ Piedmont Health Survey of the Elderly [*Department of Health and Human Services*]　(GFGA)
PHSF........ Bradshaw Field, Hawaii Island [*Hawaii*] [*ICAO location identifier*]　(ICLI)
PHSG .... Postal History Study Group　(EA)
PHSI......... Pearle Health Service [*NASDAQ symbol*]　(NQ)
PHSI......... Plant Health and Seeds Inspectorate [*Ministry of Agriculture, Fisheries, and Food*] [*British*]
PHSIA...... Physiotherapy [*A publication*]
PHSIG...... Pan Hellenic Society Inventors of Greece in USA　(EA)
PHSNA ..... Philosophia Naturalis [*A publication*]
PHSNB..... Physics of Sintering [*A publication*]
PHSNZ..... Postal History Society of New Zealand [*Auckland*]　(EA)
PHSO .... Partially Hydrogenated Soybean Oil [*Cooking fat*]
PHSO .... Postal History Society of Ontario [*Later, PHSC*]　(EA)
Ph Soc...... Philosophy/Social Theory/Sociology [*A publication*]
PHSOC ..... Photographical Historical Society of Canada
Ph Soc Glasgow Pr ... Philosophical Society of Glasgow. Proceedings [*A publication*]
P-H Soc Sec Taxes ... Social Security Taxes (Prentice-Hall, Inc.) [*A publication*]　·(DLA)
Ph Soc Wash B ... Philosophical Society of Washington. Bulletin [*A publication*]
PHSP........ Phase-Splitter　(MSA)
PHSP........ Public Health Service Publications
PHSPS ...... Preservation, Handling, Storage, Packaging, and Shipping　(NRCH)
PhSR........ Philippine Sociological Review [*A publication*]
PHSSA...... Physica Status Solidi [*A publication*]
PHS & T.... Packaging, Handling, Storage, and Transportation [*Shipping*]
PHST........ Packaging, Handling, Storage, and Transportation [*Shipping*]
PhSt........ Philosophical Studies [*A publication*]
PHSTB..... Physica Scripta [*A publication*]
Ph St Tr.... Phillipps' State Trials [*A publication*]　(DLA)
PHSW ...... Health and Social Work [*A publication*]
PHSWA..... Proceedings. Helminthological Society of Washington [*A publication*]
PHSY........ PacifiCare Health Systems, Inc. [*Cypress, CA*] [*NASDAQ symbol*]　(NQ)
PHSYB...... Photosynthetica [*A publication*]
PHT .... Paris, TN [*Location identifier*] [*FAA*]　(FAAL)
PHT .... Passive Hemagglutination Technique [*Immunology*]
PHT .... Personhistorisk Tidskrift [*A publication*]
PhT .... [*The*] Phoenix and the Turtle [*Shakespearean work*]
pht............ Photographer [*MARC relator code*] [*Library of Congress*]　(LCCP)
PHT .... Phototube
Pht............ Phthaloyl [*Also, Phth*] [*Organic chemistry*]
PHT .... Physical Therapy Technician [*Navy*]
PHT .... Pitch, Hit, and Throw [*Youth competition sponsored by professional baseball*]
PHT .... Portal Hypertension [*Medicine*]
PHT .... Preheat

PHT .... Putting Hubby Through [*College "degree" earned by some wives*]
PHT .... Pyridohomotropane [*Organic chemistry*]
PHT .... Torrance State Hospital, Torrance, PA [*OCLC symbol*]　(OCLC)
PHTab ...... President's Hundred Tab [*Military decoration*]　(AABC)
PHTAT..... Para-Hydroxytriamterene [*Biochemistry*]
PHTATS ... Para-Hydroxytriamterene Sulfate [*Biochemistry*]
P-H Tax...... Federal Taxes (Prentice-Hall, Inc.) [*A publication*]　(DLA)
P-H Tax Ct Mem ... Tax Court Memorandum Decisions (Prentice-Hall, Inc.) [*A publication*]　(DLA)
P-H Tax Ct Rep & Mem Dec ... Tax Court Reported and Memorandum Decisions (Prentice-Hall, Inc.) [*A publication*]　(DLA)
PHTC .... Pharmatec, Inc. [*NASDAQ symbol*]　(NQ)
PHTC .... Pneumatic Hydraulic Test Console　(KSC)
PHTC .... Pulse Height to Time Converter　(OA)
PhTD .... Physical Therapy Doctor
PHTEA..... Physics Teacher [*A publication*]
PHTED .... Physiology Teacher [*A publication*]
PHTF....... Pearl Harbor Training Facility [*Navy*]
Ph TF .... Philologiae Turcicae Fundamenta [*A publication*]
Phth .... Phthaloyl [*Also, Pht*] [*Organic chemistry*]
PHTN....... Photon Sources, Inc. [*NASDAQ symbol*]　(NQ)
PHTO........ Hilo/General Lyman Field, Hawaii Island [*Hawaii*] [*ICAO location identifier*]　(ICLI)
PHTOA..... Physics Today [*A publication*]
PHTR .... Harvard Theological Review [*A publication*]
PHTS........ Primary Heat Transport System [*Nuclear energy*]　(NRCH)
PHU......... Pressure, Hydraulic Unit
PHUD....... Hudson Review [*A publication*]
PHuJ .... Juniata College, Huntingdon, PA [*Library symbol*] [*Library of Congress*]　(LCLS)
PHum........ Przeglad Humanistyczny [*A publication*]
PHUN ...... Huntington Library Quarterly [*A publication*]
P-H Unrep Tr Cas ... Prentice-Hall Unreported Trust Cases [*A publication*]　(DLA)
Phus Plu..... Philippus Puldericus [*Authority cited in pre-1607 legal work*]　(DSA)
PHUZA ..... Physik in Unserer Zeit [*A publication*]
PHV......... Paramount Home Video
PHV .... Phase Velocity
PHV......... Pro Haec Vice [*For This Turn*] [*Latin*]　(ROG)
PHV......... Wernersville State Hospital, Wernersville, PA [*OCLC symbol*]　(OCLC)
PHVA .... Plasma Homovanillic Acid [*Biochemistry*]
PHVPS...... Primary High-Voltage Power Supply
PHW .... Pemberton Houston Willoughby Investment Corp. [*Toronto Stock Exchange symbol*] [*Vancouver Stock Exchange symbol*]
PHW......... Phalaborwa [*Airport symbol*] [*South Africa*]　(OAG)
PHW......... Philatelic Hobbies for the Wounded　(EA)
PhW......... Philologische Wochenschrift [*A publication*]
PHW......... Warren State Hospital, Warren, PA [*OCLC symbol*]　(OCLC)
PHWA ...... Professional Hockey Writers' Association　(EA)
PHWA ...... Protestant Health and Welfare Assembly [*Later, PHHSA*]　(EA)
PHWC...... Polish Helsinki Watch Committee　(EAIO)
PHWEA .... Pharmaceutisch Weekblad [*A publication*]
PHWFJD.. Partners in Harmony, World Family of John Denver　(EA)
PHWR ...... Hickam United States Air Force Automatic Weather Switch, Oahu Island [*Hawaii*] [*ICAO location identifier*]　(ICLI)
PHWR ...... Pressurized Heavy Water Reactor [*Nuclear energy*]
PHX......... Partial Hepectomy [*Medicine*]
PHx........... Past History [*Medicine*]　(MAE)
PHX........... PHL Corp. [*NYSE symbol*]　(SPSG)
PHX......... Phoenix [*Arizona*] [*Airport symbol*]　(OAG)
PHX......... Woodville State Hospital, Carnegie, PA [*OCLC symbol*]　(OCLC)
PHXA .... Phoenix American, Inc. [*NASDAQ symbol*]　(NQ)
PHXN ...... Phoenix Network, Inc. [*NASDAQ symbol*]　(NQ)
PHXQA .... Phoenix Quarterly [*A publication*]
PHY .... C. Howard Marcy State Hospital, Pittsburgh, PA [*OCLC symbol*]　(OCLC)
PHY .... Norman, OK [*Location identifier*] [*FAA*]　(FAAL)
PHY .... Pharyngitis
Phy............ Phylon [*A publication*]
Phy............ Physalaemin [*Biochemistry*]
PHY .... Physical
PHY .... Physician
PHY .... Physics
PHY .... Phytohemagglutinin [*Immunology*]　(AAMN)
PHY .... Prospect Street High Income Portfolio, Inc. [*NYSE symbol*]　(SPSG)
PHYBA .... Phyton (Buenos Aires) [*A publication*]
PHYC .... PhyCor, Inc. [*NASDAQ symbol*]　(SPSG)
PHYCA .... Physics [*A publication*]
PHYCOM ... Physicians Communications Service [*Fisher-Stevens, Inc.*] [*Merged into BRS/COLLEAGUE*]
PHY ED .... Physical Education　(WGA)
Phyl........... Phylon [*A publication*]
PHYL .... Physiological
PHYLIP .... Phylogeny Inference Package [*Botany*]

PHYM .... Putnam High Yield Municipal Trust [*Associated Press abbreviation*] (APAG)
PHYMA .... Phytomorphology [*A publication*]
PHYP .... Physicians' Pharmaceutical Services, Inc. [*NASDAQ symbol*] (NQ)
PHYS. .... Physical (AFM)
PHYS. .... Physician
PHYS. .... Physicist [*or Physics*] (ADA)
PHYS. .... Physiology
Phys .... Physis [*A publication*]
Phys A .... Physica A. Europhysics Journal [*A publication*]
PHYSA ...... Physica (Amsterdam) [*A publication*]
Phys Abstr ... Physics Abstracts [*A publication*]
Phys Acoust ... Physical Acoustics. Principles and Methods [*A publication*]
Phys Act Coron Heart Dis Paavo Nurmi Symp ... Physical Activity and Coronary Heart Disease. Paavo Nurmi Symposium [*A publication*]
Phys Act Rep ... Physical Activities Report [*A publication*]
Phys Antiprotons LEAR ACOL Era Proc LEAR Workshop ... Physics with Antiprotons at LEAR [*Low Energy Antiproton Ring*] in the ACOL [*Antiproton Collector*] Era. Proceedings. LEAR Workshop [*A publication*]
Phys Appl .. Physics and Applications [*A publication*]
Phys Appl .. Physique Appliquee [*A publication*]
Phys Aspects Microsc Charact Mater Proc Pfefferkorn Conf ... Physical Aspects of Microscopic Characterization of Materials. Proceedings. Pfefferkorn Conference [*A publication*]
Phys Atoms and Molecules ... Physics of Atoms and Molecules [*A publication*]
Phys B .... Physica B. Europhysics Journal. Low Temperature and Solid State Physics [*A publication*]
PHYSBE ... Physiological Simulation Benchmark Experiment
Phys Belustigungen ... Physikalische Belustigungen [*A publication*]
Phys Ber .... Physikalische Berichte [*A publication*]
Phys Bioinorg Chem Ser ... Physical Bioinorganic Chemistry Series [*A publication*]
Phys Bl .... Physikalische Blaetter [*A publication*]
Phys Bohemoslov ... Physiologia Bohemoslovenica [*Later, Physiologia Bohemoslovaca*] [*A publication*]
Phys Briefs ... Physics Briefs [*West Germany*] [*A publication*]
Phys Bull ... Physics Bulletin [*A publication*]
Phys Bull (Peking) ... Physics Bulletin (Peking) [*A publication*]
Phys C .... Physica C. Europhysics Journal. Atomic, Molecular, and Plasma Physics Optics [*A publication*]
Phys Can .... Physics in Canada [*A publication*]
Phys C Glas ... Physics and Chemistry of Glasses [*A publication*]
Phys Chaos Relat Probl Proc Nobel Symp ... Physics of Chaos and Related Problems. Proceedings. Nobel Symposium [*A publication*]
Phys Chem ... Physical Chemistry [*A publication*]
Phys & Chem ... Physics and Chemistry [*A publication*]
Phys Chem ... Physik und Chemie [*A publication*]
Phys Chem Behav Atmos Pollut Proc Eur Symp ... Physico-Chemical Behaviour of Atmospheric Pollutants. Proceedings. European Symposium [*A publication*]
Phys Chem Biol ... Physico-Chemical Biology [*A publication*]
Phys-Chem Biol (Chiba) ... Physico-Chemical Biology (Chiba) [*A publication*]
Phys Chem Centralbl ... Physikalisch-Chemisches Centralblatt [*A publication*]
Phys Chem Earth ... Physics and Chemistry of the Earth [*A publication*]
Phys Chem Earth Sci Res Rep ... Physical, Chemical, and Earth Sciences Research Report [*A publication*]
Phys Chem Fast React ... Physical Chemistry of Fast Reactions [*A publication*]
Phys Chem Fission Proc IAEA Symp ... Physics and Chemistry of Fission. Proceedings. IAEA [*International Atomic Energy Agency*] Symposium. Physics and Chemistry of Fission [*A publication*]
Phys Chem Glasses ... Physics and Chemistry of Glasses [*A publication*]
Phys and Chem Glasses ... Physics and Chemistry of Glasses. Section B. Journal. Society of Glass Technology [*A publication*]
Phys Chem Liq ... Physics and Chemistry of Liquids [*A publication*]
Phys Chem Mater Layered Struct ... Physics and Chemistry of Materials with Layered Structures [*A publication*]
Phys Chem Miner ... Physics and Chemistry of Minerals [*A publication*]
Phys Chem (NY) ... Physical Chemistry (New York) [*A publication*]
Phys Chem Org Solvent Syst ... Physical Chemistry of Organic Solvent Systems [*Monograph*] [*A publication*]
Phys Chem (Peshawar Pak) ... Physical Chemistry (Peshawar, Pakistan) [*A publication*]
Phys Chem Phys ... Physiological Chemistry and Physics [*A publication*]
Phys Chem Sci Res Rep ... Physical and Chemical Sciences Research Report [*A publication*]
Phys Chem Ser Monogr ... Physical Chemistry. Series of Monographs [*A publication*]
Phys Chem Solids ... Physics and Chemistry of Solids [*A publication*]
Phys Chem Space ... Physics and Chemistry in Space [*A publication*]
Phys Chem (Washington DC) ... Physics and Chemistry (Washington, D. C.) [*A publication*]
PhySci .... Physical Sciences, Inc. [*Associated Press abbreviation*] (APAG)
Phys Collision ... Physics in Collision. High-Energy ee/ep/pp Interactions [*A publication*]
Phys Comp ... Physiologia Comparata et Oecologia [*A publication*]

Phys Condens Matter ... Physics of Condensed Matter [*A publication*]
Phys Con Matt ... Physics of Condensed Matter [*A publication*]
Phys Contemp Needs ... Physics and Contemporary Needs. Proceedings. International Summer College [*A publication*]
Phys D .... Physica D. Nonlinear Phenomena [*A publication*]
Phys Daten ... Physik Daten [*Physics Data*] [*A publication*]
Phys-Diaet Ther ... Physikalisch-Diaetetische Therapie [*West Germany*] [*A publication*]
Phys Didakt ... Physik und Didaktik [*A publication*]
Phys Earth Planetary Interiors ... Physics of the Earth and Planetary Interiors [*A publication*]
Phys Earth Planet Inter ... Physics of the Earth and Planetary Interiors [*A publication*]
PHYSEC ... Physical Security (MCD)
PHYS ED .. Physical Education
Phys Ed ...... Physical Educator [*A publication*]
Phys Ed Bul ... Physical Education Bulletin for Teachers in Secondary Schools [*A publication*] (APTA)
Phys Ed J ... Physical Education Journal [*A publication*] (APTA)
Phys Ed News ... Physical Education News [*A publication*]
Phys Educ ... Physical Education [*A publication*]
Phys Educ ... Physical Educator [*A publication*]
Phys Educ Index ... Physical Education Index [*A publication*]
Phys Educ Newsl ... Physical Education Newsletter [*A publication*]
Phys Electron At Collisions Invited Pap Int Conf ... Physics of Electronic and Atomic Collisions. Invited Papers. International Conference [*A publication*]
Phys Elem Part At Nucl ... Physics of Elementary Particles and Atomic Nuclei [*A publication*]
Phys Energ Fortis Phys Nucl ... Physica Energiae Fortis et Physica Nuclearis [*People's Republic of China*] [*A publication*]
Phys Energi Fort Phys Nuclear ... Physica Energiae Fortis et Physica Nuclearis [*People's Republic of China*] [*A publication*]
Phys Eng .... Physical Engineer
Phys Environ Rep Dep Archit Sci Syd Univ ... Physical Environment Report. Department of Architectural Science. University of Sydney [*A publication*] (APTA)
Phys E Plan ... Physics of the Earth and Planetary Interiors [*A publication*]
PHYSEXAM ... Physical Examination
Phys Failure Electron ... Physics of Failure in Electronics [*A publication*]
Phys Fenn .. Physica Fennica [*A publication*]
Phys Fit Newsl ... Physical Fitness Newsletter [*A publication*]
Phys Fit Res Dig ... Physical Fitness Research Digest [*A publication*]
Phys Flu A ... Physics of Fluids A. Fluid Dynamics [*A publication*]
Phys Flu B ... Physics of Fluids B. Plasma Physics [*A publication*]
Phys Fluids ... Physics of Fluids [*A publication*]
Phys Fluids A ... Physics of Fluids. A. Fluid Dynamics [*A publication*]
Phys Fluids B ... Physics of Fluids B. Plasma Physics [*A publication*]
Phys Fluids Suppl ... Physics of Fluids. Supplement [*A publication*]
Phys Grundlagen Med Abh Biophys ... Physikalische Grundlagen der Medizin. Abhandlungen aus der Biophysik [*A publication*]
Phys Hazards Dust Vap Occup Hyg ... Physical Hazards, Dust, and Vapours. Occupational Hygiene [*A publication*]
Physica A ... Physica A. Theoretical and Statistical Physics [*A publication*]
Physica B ... Physica B. Europhysics Journal. Low Temperature and Solid State Physics [*A publication*]
Physica C ... Physica C. Europhysics Journal. Atomic, Molecular, and Plasma Physics Optics [*A publication*]
Physical Educ J ... Physical Education Journal [*A publication*] (APTA)
Physica Status Solidi A ... Physica Status Solidi. Sectio A. Applied Research [*A publication*]
Physica Status Solidi B ... Physica Status Solidi. Sectio B. Basic Research [*A publication*]
Physician Assist ... Physician Assistant [*Later, Physician Assistant/Health Practitioner*] [*A publication*]
Physician Assist Health ... Physician Assistant/Health Practitioner [*A publication*]
Physician Assist Health Pract ... Physician Assistant/Health Practitioner [*A publication*]
Physician Comput Monthly ... Physician Computer Monthly [*A publication*]
Physician Exec ... Physician Executive [*A publication*]
Physicians Drug Man ... Physicians' Drug Manual [*A publication*]
Physicians Guide Pract Gastroenterol ... Physician's Guide to Practical Gastroenterology [*A publication*]
Physicians Manage ... Physicians Management [*A publication*]
Physician Sportsmed ... Physician and Sports Medicine [*A publication*]
Physician and Surg ... Physician and Surgeon [*A publication*]
Physicochem Hydrodyn ... Physicochemical Hydrodynamics [*England*] [*A publication*]
Physics & Chem ... Physics and Chemistry [*A publication*]
Physics Ed ... Physics Education [*A publication*]
Physics Med Biol ... Physics in Medicine and Biology [*A publication*]
Physics Teach ... Physics Teacher [*A publication*]
Physikertag Hauptvortr Jahrestag Verb Dtsch Phys Ges ... Physikertagung. Hauptvortraege der Jahrestagung des Verbandes Deutscher Physikalischer Gesellschaften [*A publication*]
Physikunterr ... Physikunterricht [*A publication*]
Phys Ind ..... Physics in Industry [*A publication*]
PHYSIO .... Physiotherapy [*Medicine*]
PHYSIOG ... Physiognomy [*Slang*] (DSUE)
PHYSIOG ... Physiographic

PHYSIOL ... Physiological (MSA)
PHYSIOL ... Physiology (ROG)
Physiol Abstr ... Physiological Abstracts [*A publication*]
Physiol Behav ... Physiology and Behavior [*A publication*]
Physiol Behav Mar Org Proc Eur Symp Mar Biol ... Physiology and Behaviour of Marine Organisms. Proceedings. European Symposium on Marine Biology [*A publication*]
Physiol Biochem Cultiv Plants ... Physiology and Biochemistry of Cultivated Plants [*A publication*]
Physiol Biochem Cult Plants (USSR) ... Physiology and Biochemistry of Cultivated Plants (USSR) [*A publication*]
Physiol Bohemoslov ... Physiologia Bohemoslovaca [*A publication*]
Physiol Can ... Physiology Canada [*A publication*]
Physiol Chem Phys ... Physiological Chemistry and Physics [*Later, Physiological Chemistry and Physics and Medical NMR*] [*A publication*]
Physiol Chem Phys Med NMR ... Physiological Chemistry and Physics and Medical NMR [*A publication*]
Physiol Dig Ruminant Pap Int Symp ... Physiology of Digestion in the Ruminant. Papers Presented. International Symposium on the Physiology of Digestion in the Ruminant [*A publication*]
Physiol Domest Fowl Br Egg Mark Board Symp ... Physiology of the Domestic Fowl. British Egg Marketing Board Symposium [*A publication*]
Physiol Ecol ... Physiology and Ecology [*A publication*]
Physiol Ecol (Jpn) ... Physiology and Ecology (Japan) [*A publication*]
Physiol Ent ... Physiological Entomology [*A publication*]
Physiol Entomol ... Physiological Entomology [*A publication*]
Physiol Menschen ... Physiologie des Menschen [*A publication*]
Physiol Mol Plant Pathol ... Physiological and Molecular Plant Pathology [*A publication*]
Physiologia Comp Oecol ... Physiologia Comparata et Oecologia [*A publication*]
Physiologia Pl ... Physiologia Plantarum [*A publication*]
Physiol Pathophysiol Skin ... Physiology and Pathophysiology of the Skin [*A publication*]
Physiol Pharmacol Physicians ... Physiology and Pharmacology for Physicians [*A publication*]
Physiol Physicians ... Physiology for Physicians [*A publication*]
Physiol Plant ... Physiologia Plantarum [*A publication*]
Physiol Plant Pathol ... Physiological Plant Pathology [*A publication*]
Physiol Plant Suppl ... Physiologia Plantarum. Supplementum [*A publication*]
Physiol Psychol ... Physiological Psychology [*A publication*]
Physiol Rev ... Physiological Reviews [*A publication*]
Physiol Soc Philadelphia Monogr ... Physiological Society of Philadelphia. Monographs [*A publication*]
Physiol Teach ... Physiology Teacher [*A publication*]
Physiol Veg ... Physiologie Vegetale [*A publication*]
Physiol Zool ... Physiological Zoology [*A publication*]
Physiother Can ... Physiotherapy Canada [*A publication*]
Physiother Pract ... Physiotherapy Practice [*A publication*]
Physis Secc A Oceanos Org ... Physis. Seccion A: Oceanos y Sus Organismos [*A publication*]
Physis Secc A Oceanos Sus Org ... Physis. Seccion A: Oceanos y Sus Organismos [*A publication*]
Physis Secc B Aguas Cont Org ... Physis. Seccion B: Aguas Continentales y Sus Organismos [*A publication*]
Physis Secc B Aguas Cont Sus Org ... Physis. Seccion B: Aguas Continentales y Sus Organismos [*A publication*]
Physis Secc C Cont Org Terr ... Physis. Seccion C: Continentes y Organismos Terrestres [*A publication*]
Phys Kondens Mater ... Physik der Kondensierten Materie [*A publication*]
PHYSL ...... Physiological (AFM)
Physl Behav ... Physiology and Behavior [*A publication*]
Physl Bohem ... Physiologia Bohemoslovaca [*A publication*]
Physl Chem ... Physiological Chemistry and Physics [*Later, Physiological Chemistry and Physics and Medical NMR*] [*A publication*]
Phys Lett.... Physics Letters [*Netherlands*] [*A publication*]
Phys Lett A ... Physics Letters. Section A [*A publication*]
Phys Lett B ... Physics Letters. Section B [*A publication*]
Phys Lett C ... Physics Letters. Section C [*Netherlands*] [*A publication*]
Phys Letters ... Physics Letters [*A publication*]
Physl Plant ... Physiologia Plantarum [*A publication*]
Physl Pl P .. Physiological Plant Pathology [*A publication*]
Physl Psych ... Physiological Psychology [*A publication*]
Physl Veget ... Physiologie Vegetale [*A publication*]
Physl Zool ... Physiological Zoology [*A publication*]
Phys Med Bi ... Physics in Medicine and Biology [*A publication*]
Phys Med Biol ... Physics in Medicine and Biology [*A publication*]
Phys Met .... Physics of Metals [*A publication*]
Phys Methods Chem Anal ... Physical Methods in Chemical Analysis [*A publication*]
Phys Methods Macromol Chem ... Physical Methods in Macromolecular Chemistry [*A publication*]
Phys Met Metallogr ... Physics of Metals and Metallography [*A publication*]
Phys Met (USSR) ... Physics of Metals (USSR) [*A publication*]
PHYSN ..... Physician
Phys News ... Physics News Bulletin. Indian Physics Association [*A publication*]
Phys Norv .. Physica Norvegica [*A publication*]

Phys Norveg ... Physica Norvegica [*A publication*]
Phys Occup Ther Geriatr ... Physical and Occupational Therapy in Geriatrics [*A publication*]
Phys Occup Ther Pediatr ... Physical and Occupational Therapy in Pediatrics [*A publication*]
PHYSOG .. Physiognomy [*Slang*] (DSUE)
Phys Pap.... Physics Papers [*A publication*]
Phys Pap Silesian Univ Katowice ... Physics Papers. Silesian University in Katowice [*Poland*] [*A publication*]
PHYSQUAL ... Physical Disqualification [*Military*] (DNAB)
Phys Quantum Electron ... Physics of Quantum Electronics [*A publication*]
Phys R .... Physical Review [*A publication*]
Phys Regelm Ber ... Physik in Regelmaessigen Berichten [*A publication*]
Phys Rep.... Physics Reports. Review Section of Physics Letters. Section C [*Netherlands*] [*A publication*]
Phys Rep Kumamoto Univ ... Physics Reports. Kumamoto University [*A publication*]
Phys Rep Phys Lett Sect C ... Physics Reports. Physics Letters. Section C [*A publication*]
Phys Rev.... Physical Review [*A publication*]
Phys Rev.... Physiological Reviews [*A publication*]
Phys Rev A ... Physical Review. Section A. General Physics [*A publication*]
Phys Rev A 3 ... Physical Review. Section A. General Physics. Third Series [*A publication*]
Phys Rev A Gen Phys ... Physical Review. Section A. General Physics [*A publication*]
Phys Rev B 3 ... Physical Review. Section B. Condensed Matter. Third Series [*A publication*]
Phys Rev B Conden Matt ... Physical Review. Section B. Condensed Matter [*A publication*]
Phys Rev B Condens Matter ... Physical Review. Section B. Condensed Matter [*A publication*]
Phys Rev C ... Physical Review. Section C. Nuclear Physics [*A publication*]
Phys Rev C 3 ... Physical Review. Section C. Nuclear Physics. Third Series [*A publication*]
Phys Rev D ... Physical Review. Section D. Particles and Fields [*A publication*]
Phys Rev D 3 ... Physical Review. Section D. Particles and Fields. Third Series [*A publication*]
Phys Rev L ... Physical Review. Letters [*A publication*]
Phys Rev Lett ... Physical Review. Letters [*A publication*]
Phys Rev Sect A ... Physical Review. Section A. General Physics [*A publication*]
Phys Rev Sect B ... Physical Review. Section B. Condensed Matter [*A publication*]
Phys Rev Suppl ... Physical Review. Supplement [*A publication*]
Phys Sci Data ... Physical Sciences Data [*Amsterdam*] [*A publication*]
Phys Scr..... Physica Scripta [*A publication*]
Phys Scripta ... Physica Scripta [*Stockholm*] [*A publication*]
Phys Sintering ... Physics of Sintering [*Yugoslavia*] [*A publication*]
Phys Soc Lond Proc ... Physical Society of London. Proceedings [*A publication*]
Phys Solariterr ... Physica Solariterrestris [*A publication*]
Phys Solid Earth (Engl Ed) ... Physics of the Solid Earth (English Edition) [*A publication*]
Phys Stat Sol A ... Physica Status Solidi. Sectio A. Applied Research [*A publication*]
Phys Stat Sol B ... Physica Status Solidi. Sectio B. Basic Research [*A publication*]
Phys Status Solidi ... Physica Status Solidi [*A publication*]
Phys Status Solidi A ... Physica Status Solidi. Sectio A. Applied Research [*A publication*]
Phys Status Solidi B ... Physica Status Solidi. Sectio B. Basic Research [*A publication*]
Phys St S-A ... Physica Status Solidi. Sectio A. Applied Research [*A publication*]
Phys St S-B ... Physica Status Solidi. Sectio B. Basic Research [*A publication*]
Phys Teach ... Physics Teacher [*A publication*]
Phys Tech Biol Res ... Physical Techniques in Biological Research [*A publication*]
Phys Technol ... Physics in Technology [*A publication*]
PHYSTER ... Physical Therapy (AABC)
Phys Ther ... Physical Therapy [*A publication*]
Phys Therapy ... Physical Therapy [*A publication*]
Phys Therapy Rev ... Physical Therapy Review [*A publication*]
Phys Thin Films ... Physics of Thin Films. Advances in Research and Development [*A publication*]
Phys Today ... Physics Today [*A publication*]
Phys Unserer Zeit ... Physik in Unserer Zeit [*A publication*]
PHYSY ...... Physiology
Phys Zool ... Physiological Zoology [*A publication*]
PHYT .... Physio Technology, Inc. [*NASDAQ symbol*] (NQ)
Phyt........... Phytopathology [*A publication*]
PHYTA ..... Phytopathology [*A publication*]
PHYTB ...... Physics in Technology [*A publication*]
Phytiat Phytopharm ... Phytiatrie-Phytopharmacie [*A publication*]
Phytochem ... Phytochemistry [*Oxford*] [*A publication*]
Phytochem Eff Environ Compd ... Phytochemical Effects of Environmental Compounds [*A publication*]
Phytochemistr (Oxf) ... Phytochemistry (Oxford) [*A publication*]

Phytochem Soc Annu Proc ... Phytochemical Society. Annual Proceedings [*A publication*]
Phytochem Soc Eur Symp Ser ... Phytochemical Society of Europe. Symposia Series [*A publication*]
Phytoma Def Cult ... Phytoma. Defense des Cultures [*France*] [*A publication*]
Phytomorph ... Phytomorphology [*A publication*]
Phytomorphol ... Phytomorphology [*A publication*]
Phyton Ann Rei Bot ... Phyton. Annales Rei Botanicae [*A publication*]
Phyton (Aust) ... Phyton. Annales Rei Botanicae (Austria) [*A publication*]
Phyton Int J Exp Bot ... Phyton. International Journal of Experimental Botany [*A publication*]
PHYTOPATH ... Phytopathology
Phytopathol ... Phytopathology [*A publication*]
Phytopathol Mediterr ... Phytopathologie Mediterranea [*A publication*]
Phytopathol News ... Phytopathology News [*A publication*]
Phytopathol ZJ Phytopathol ... Phytopathologische Zeitschrift/Journal of Phytopathology [*A publication*]
Phytoprot ... Phytoprotection [*A publication*]
Phytother R ... Phytotherapy Research [*A publication*]
Phytotronic Newsl ... Phytotronic Newsletter [*A publication*]
PHYVA ..... Physiologie Vegetale [*A publication*]
PHZ .... Ashland State General Hospital, Ashland, PA [*OCLC symbol*] (OCLC)
PHZAA ..... Pharmazeutische Zeitung. Vereinigt mit Apotheker-Zeitung [*A publication*]
PHZH .... Honolulu Air Traffic Control Center [*Hawaii*] [*ICAO location identifier*] (ICLI)
PHZIA ...... Pharamazeutische Zeitung [*A publication*]
PHZOA ..... Physiological Zoology [*A publication*]
pI .... Isoelectric Point (MAE)
PI .... Pacing Item (MCD)
PI .... Package Insert [*Instructional leaflet distributed with certain prescription drugs*] [*Also, PPI*]
PI .... Packaging Institute [*Later, PI/USA*] (EA)
PI .... Paducah & Illinois Railroad [*AAR code*]
PI .... Pagine Istriane [*A publication*]
PI .... Pancreatic Insufficiency [*Gastroenterology*]
Pi .... Pandectae (Pisanae) Florentinae [*A publication*] (DSA)
PI .... Panel Input
PI .... Pansophic Institute (EA)
PI .... Pantera International (EA)
PI .... Paper Insulated
PI .... Paracel Islands [*ANSI two-letter standard code*] (CNC)
PI .... Parallel Input [*Data processing*] (BUR)
PI .... Parental Investment [*Biology*]
PI .... Parity Index [*EEO*]
P & I .... Parole e le Idee [*A publication*]
PI .... Parti Independantiste [*Quebec*]
PI .... Particle Integration (CAAL)
PI .... Partido Independente [*Independent Party*] [*Costa Rica*] [*Political party*]
PI .... Partido Intransigente [*Intransigent Party*] [*Argentina*] [*Political party*] (PD)
P & I .... Passenger and Immigration Lists [*A publication*]
PI .... Passeport International [*International Passport*] [*An association*] [*France*] (EAIO)
PI .... Patient's Interests [*Medicine*]
PI .... Patrol Inspector [*Immigration and Naturalization Service*]
PI .... Payload Interrogator [*NASA*] (MCD)
PI .... Pen and Ink
PI .... Pepsin Inhibitor (OA)
PI .... Per Inquiry [*Advertising*]
PI .... Perceptions, Inc. (EA)
PI .... Perceptual Isolation
PI .... Perfect Initials [*Philately*]
PI .... Performance Improvement
PI .... Performance Index
PI .... Performance Indicator (MCD)
PI .... Performance Intensity (MAE)
P & I .... Performance and Interface [*Specification*] [*NASA*] (NASA)
PI .... Periodic Inspection [*Military*] (AFM)
PI .... Periodicals Institute (EA)
PI .... Peripheral Interface [*Data processing*] (PCM)
PI .... Peripheral Iridectomy [*Medicine*]
PI .... Perlite Institute (EA)
PI .... Permeability Index [*Clinical chemistry*]
PI .... Personal Identification
PI .... Personal Income
PI .... Personal Injury [*Insurance*]
PI .... Personal Injury Accident [*British police term*]
PI .... Personal Investment [*A publication*] (ADA)
PI .... Personality Inventory [*Psychology*]
PI .... Peru Indigena [*A publication*]
PI .... Petrol Injection [*British*]
PI .... Petroleum Information Corp. (IID)
PI .... Pharmacopoeia Internationalis [*International Pharmacopoeia*]
PI .... Phase-In
PI .... Phenanthroimidazole [*Organic chemistry*]
PI .... Phenyl Isocyanate [*Organic chemistry*]
PI .... Philippines [*Aircraft nationality and registration mark*] (FAAC)

PI .... Philosopher's Index [*A publication*]
Pi .... Phosphate, Inorganic [*Chemistry*]
PI .... Phosphatidylinositol [*Also, PtdIns*] [*Biochemistry*]
PI .... Photo International (EAIO)
P-I .... Photogrammetric Instrumentation (AAG)
PI .... Photographic Interpreter
PI .... Photointerpretation [*or Photointerpreter*]
PI .... Photoionization [*Physical chemistry*]
PI .... Physical Inventory (NRCH)
PI .... Physically Impaired
PI .... Physics International
PI .... Piaster [*Monetary unit*] [*Spain, Republic of Vietnam, and some Middle Eastern countries*]
PI .... Piedmont Aviation, Inc. [*ICAO designator*] (OAG)
PI .... Pig Iron
PI .... Pigeon Trainer [*Navy*]
Pi .... Pillius Medicinensis [*Flourished, 1165-1207*] [*Authority cited in pre-1607 legal work*] (DSA)
PI .... Pilot. Fort Smith and Simpson [*Northwest Territory, Canada*] [*A publication*]
PI .... Pilot International (EA)
PI .... Pilot Item (MCD)
PI .... Pilotless Intercepter [*Air Force*]
PI .... Pinedale [*Wyoming*] [*Seismograph station code, US Geological Survey*] [*Closed*] (SEIS)
PI .... Pink (ROG)
PI .... Pipe [*Freight*]
P & I .... Piping and Instrumentation [*Nuclear energy*] (NRCH)
PI .... Plant Introduction [*Botany*]
PI .... Plaque Index [*Dentistry*]
PI .... Plasma Iron [*Hematology*]
PI .... Plastochron Index [*Botany*]
PI .... Pneumatosis Intestinalis [*Medicine*]
PI .... Point of Impact (AFM)
PI .... Point Initiating
PI .... Point Insulating
PI .... Point of Interception [*Navigation*]
PI .... Point of Intersection
PI .... Poison Ivy [*Campers' slang*]
PI .... Polyimide [*Organic chemistry*]
PI .... Polyisoprene [*Organic chemistry*]
PI .... Polymer International (NS), Inc. [*Toronto Stock Exchange symbol*]
PI .... Pompeiiana, Inc. (EA)
PI .... Poni Iussit [*Ordered to Be Placed*] [*Latin*]
PI .... Popcorn Institute
PI .... Population Institute (EA)
PI .... Portfolio Insurance [*Finance*]
PI .... Position Indicator [*Army*]
PI .... Positive Identification Feature
PI .... Positive Interlace [*Television*]
P & I .... Postage and Insurance
PI .... Postimpressionist Movement [*Art*]
PI .... Postinoculation [*Medicine*]
PI .... Postischemic [*Medicine*]
PI .... Potash Institute [*Later, PPI*] (EA)
PI .... Potomac Institute (EA)
PI .... Power Injection
PI .... Power Input
PI .... Precision Instrument (NVT)
PI .... Predicted Impact (MCD)
PI .... Pregnancy Induced [*Gynecology*]
PI .... Preinduction [*Medicine*]
PI .... Preliminary Incubation (OA)
PI .... Preliminary Injunction [*Legal term*] (HGAA)
PI .... Preliminary Inspection (MCD)
PI .... Preliminary Investigation (NASA)
PI .... Preliminary Issue
PI .... Preparatory Interval [*Psychometrics*]
PI .... Prepositioned Instruction [*DoD*]
PI .... Present Illness [*Medicine*]
PI .... Pressure Indicator [*Nuclear energy*]
Pi .... Pressure of Inspiration [*Medicine*]
PI .... Primacord Interstage
PI .... Primary Infarction [*Medicine*]
PI .... Prime Interest Rate [*Banking*]
P & I .... Principal and Interest [*Banking*] (ADA)
PI .... Principal Investigator (MCD)
PI .... Printer [*Navy*]
PI .... Printers' Ink [*A publication*]
PI .... Priority Interrupt (IEEE)
PI .... Private Institution [*British*]
PI .... Private Investigator
PI .... Priviledged Information (SAA)
PI .... Proactive Inhibition [*Psychology*]
PI .... Problem Input (SAA)
PI .... Process Instrumentation [*Nuclear energy*] (NRCH)
PI .... Processor Interface
PI .... Procurement Inspection (MCD)
PI .... Procurement Item (NASA)
PI .... Product Improvement (MCD)

P/I .... Production Illustration   (MSA)
PI .... Production Interval
PI .... Productivity Index   (IEEE)
PI .... Program Indicator   (IEEE)
PI .... Program Information
PI .... Program Innovations   (ADA)
PI .... Program Instruction [*Data processing*]   (BUR)
PI .... Program of Instrumentation   (MUGU)
PI .... Program Interrupt
PI .... Program Introduction
PI .... Program Issuances [*Assistance Payments Administration, HEW*]
PI .... Programmed Information [*Data processing*]
PI .... Programmed Instruction
PI .... Programmed Introduction   (MCD)
PI .... Project Inform   (EA)
PI .... Project Intrex [*Massachusetts Institute of Technology*]   (EA)
PI .... Prolactin Inhibitor [*Endocrinology*]
P & I .... Properties and Installations
PI .... Property Index [*British police term*]
PI .... Propidium Iodide [*Fluorescent dye*]
PI .... Proportional-Plus Integral [*Digital control*]
PI .... Proprietary Information   (SAA)
PI .... Propyl Isome   (OA)
PI .... Protamine Insulin
Pi .... Protease Inhibitor
P & I .... Protection and Indemnity [*Insurance*]
PI .... Proteinase Inhibitor [*Biochemistry*]
PI .... Protocol Internationale
PI .... Psychiatric Institute
PI .... Psychosynthesis Institute   (EA)
PI .... Public Information
PI .... Publication Instructions
PI .... Puebla Institute   (EA)
PI .... Pulmonary Incompetence [*Medicine*]
PI .... Pulmonary Indices [*Medicine*]
PI .... Pulmonary Infarction [*Medicine*]
PI .... Pulmonary Intervertebral Disc [*Medicine*]
PI .... Pulse Induction   (ADA)
PI .... Purge Isolation [*Nuclear energy*]   (NRCH)
PI .... Pyritization Index [*Geoscience*]
PI .... Trademark for an ophthalmic drug
PI1 .... State Correctional Institute at Camp Hill, Camp Hill, PA [*OCLC symbol*]   (OCLC)
P2I .... Planned Product Improvement
PI2 .... State Correctional Institute at Dallas, Dallas, PA [*OCLC symbol*]   (OCLC)
P³I .... Preplanned Product Improvement [*DoD*]
PI3 .... State Correctional Institute at Grateford, Grateford, PA [*OCLC symbol*]   (OCLC)
PI4 .... State Correctional Institute at Huntingdon, Huntingdon, PA [*OCLC symbol*]   (OCLC)
PI5 .... State Correctional Institute at Muncy, Muncy, PA [*OCLC symbol*]   (OCLC)
PI6 .... State Correctional Institute at Pittsburgh, Pittsburgh, PA [*OCLC symbol*]   (OCLC)
PI7 .... State Regional Correctional Facility, Greensburg, PA [*OCLC symbol*]   (OCLC)
PIA............ Pacific Islands Association   (EA)
PIA............ Packaged Ice Association   (EA)
PIA............ Pakistan International Airlines Corp.
PIA............ Panel-Information-Air Operation
PIA............ Parapsychology Institute of America   (EA)
PIA............ Particle Impact Analyzer [*Astrophysics*]
PIA............ Passive Immunological Agglutination
PIA............ Payload Interface Adapter [*NASA*]   (SSD)
PIA............ Pensions and Investment Age [*A publication*]
PIA............ Peoria [*Illinois*] [*Airport symbol*]   (OAG)
PIA............ Perfumery Importers Association [*Defunct*]   (EA)
PIA............ Peripheral Interface Adapter [*Data processing*]
PIA............ Personal Investment Authority [*British*]   (ECON)
PIA............ Personnel Inventory Analysis [*Army*]
PIA............ Perspective Inversion Algorithm [*Data processing*]
PIA............ Petervin Information Associates [*Also, an information service or system*]   (IID)
PIA............ Petroleum Incentives Administration [*Canada*]
PIA............ Phenylisopropyladenosine [*Biochemistry*]
PIA............ Piano [*Softly*] [*Music*]
PIA............ Pilots International Association   (EA)
PIA............ Pitten [*Austria*] [*Seismograph station code, US Geological Survey*]   (SEIS)
PIA............ Place Indicator in Accumulators   (SAA)
PIA............ Plasma Insulin Activity [*Clinical chemistry*]
PIA............ Plastics Industries Association [*Ireland*]
PIA............ Plastics Institute of America   (EA)
PIA............ Plug-In Amplifier
PIA............ Polycultural Institution of America
PIA............ Positive Ion Accelerator
PIA............ Positron Intensity Accumulator   (MCD)
PIA............ Postal Inspectors' Association [*A union*] [*British*]
PIA............ Potentiometric Immunoassay [*Clinical chemistry*]

PIA............ Pre-Inspection Acceptance   (SAA)
PIA............ Preinstallation Acceptance
PIA............ Primary Inspection Agency [*Federal Manufactured Housing Construction and Safety Standards*] [*Department of Housing and Urban Development*]   (GFGA)
PIA............ Primary Insurance Account [*Social Security Administration*]   (OICC)
PIA............ Primary Insurance Amount
PIA............ Principal Industry Activity [*IRS*]
PIA............ Printing Industries of America   (EA)
PIA............ Proceedings. Irish Academy [*A publication*]
PIA............ Production Inventory Analysis   (AAG)
PIA............ Professional Insurance Agents [*Alexandria, VA*]   (EA)
PIA............ Program Initiation Agreement   (SSD)
PIA............ Project Impact Analysis   (NASA)
PIA............ Project Interface Adapter   (SSD)
PIA............ Psychiatric Institute of America [*For-profit network of private psychiatric hospitals*]   (EA)
PIA............ Public Information Act
PIA............ Public Information Adviser [*NATO*]   (NATG)
PIA............ Pumice Institute of America   (EA)
PIA............ White Haven Center, White Haven, PA [*OCLC symbol*]   (OCLC)
505 PIA...... 505th Parachute Infantry Association [*Later, 505th Regimental Combat Team Association*]   (EA)
PIAA......... Pre-Arrangement Interment Association of America [*Later, PAA*]   (EA)
PIAAD...... Proceedings. Indian Academy of Sciences. Series Chemical Sciences [*A publication*]
PIAC......... Partido de Integracion de America Central [*Nicaragua*] [*Political party*]   (EY)
PIAC......... Permanent International Altaistic Conference   (EA)
PIAC......... Petroleum Industry Advisory Committee [*British*]
PIAC......... Problem Identification and Correction [*DoD*]   (AFIT)
PIACA....... Proceedings. Indiana Academy of Science [*A publication*]
PIACCS.... Pacific Integrated Automatic Command and Control System [*Military*]   (DNAB)
PIACS ...... Pacific Integrated Automatic Communications Systems [*Military*]
PIACT ...... Program for the Introduction and Adaptation of Contraceptive Technology   (EA)
PIADC...... Plum Island Animal Disease Center [*Formerly, PIADL*]
PIADL....... Plum Island Animal Disease Laboratory [*of ARS, Department of Agriculture*] [*Later, PIADC*]
Piaget Theor Help Prof ... Piagetian Theory and the Helping Professions [*A publication*]
PIAH .... International Journal of African Historical Studies [*A publication*]
PIAL......... International Journal of American Linguistics [*A publication*]
PIAMA...... Professional Institute for the American Management Association   (OICC)
PIAMD...... Proceedings. Indian Academy of Sciences. Series Mathematical Sciences [*A publication*]
PIANC....... Permanent International Association of Navigation Congresses [*Brussels, Belgium*]   (EAIO)
PIand .... Papyri Iandanae [*A publication*]   (OCD)
PIAND ...... Proceedings. Indian Academy of Sciences. Series Animal Sciences [*A publication*]
PIANG ...... Piangendo [*Plaintive*] [*Music*]
PIANISS ... Pianissimo [*Very Softly*] [*Music*]
Piano Q ...... Piano Quarterly [*A publication*]
Piano Quart ... Piano Quarterly [*A publication*]
Piano Tech ... Piano Technician [*A publication*]
PIAP .... Psychologists Interested in the Advancement of Psychotherapy [*Later, APA*]   (EA)
PIAPACS .. Psychophysiological Information Acquisition, Processing, and Control System
PIAR......... Problem Identification and Analysis Report [*Military*]   (CAAL)
PIAR......... Project Impact Analysis Report   (MCD)
PIARC....... Permanent International Association of Road Congresses [*See also AIPCR*] [*Paris, France*]   (EAIO)
PIAS .... Photographic Inventory and Accountancy System
PIAS .... Piaster [*Monetary unit*] [*Spain, Republic of Vietnam, and some Middle Eastern countries*]
PIAS .... Precision Intelligence Augmentation System
PIAS .... Program Impact Analysis Scenario
PIASA .... Polish Institute of Arts and Sciences of America   (EA)
P I A Sci A ... Proceedings. Indian Academy of Sciences. Section A [*A publication*]
P I A Sci B ... Proceedings. Indian Academy of Sciences. Section B [*A publication*]
PIASH....... Proceedings. Israel Academy of Sciences and Humanities [*Jerusalem*] [*A publication*]
PIASS....... Paris International Aviation and Space Salon   (MCD)
PIAT......... Peabody Individual Achievement Test [*Education*]
PIAT .... Projector Infantry, Antitank [*British shoulder-controlled weapon*]
PIB............ George Junior Republic, Grove City, PA [*OCLC symbol*]   (OCLC)
PIB............ Laurel/Hattiesburg [*Mississippi*] [*Airport symbol*]   (OAG)
PIB............ Pacific Inland Tariff Bureau, Portland OR [*STAC*]

PIB............ Papuan Infantry Battalion
PIB............ Parachute Infantry Battalion [*Army*]
PIB............ Partial Ileal Bypass [*Medicine*]
PIB............ Partido Indio de Bolivia [*Political party*]
PIB............ Payload Integration Bay [*NASA*] (KSC)
PIB............ Pender Island [*British Columbia*] [*Seismograph station code, US Geological Survey*] (SEIS)
PIB............ Periodic Information Briefing (MCD)
PIB............ Personal Information Briefing [*of returning POW's*] [*Air Force*]
PIB............ Petroleum Information Bureau
PIB............ Photo Intelligence Brief (AFM)
PIB............ Photo Interpretation Brief (MCD)
PIB............ Plug-In Blank
PIB............ Polar Ionospheric Beacon
PIB............ Polyisobutylene [*Organic chemistry*]
PIB............ Polytechnic Institute of Brooklyn [*Later, PINY*] (MCD)
PIB............ Preliminary Instruction Book
PIB............ Prices and Incomes Board [*British*]
PIB............ Processor Interface Buffer [*Telecommunications*] (TEL)
PIB............ Product Improvement Bulletin
PIB............ Program Information Briefing
PIB............ Programmable Input Buffer
PIB............ Propellant Inspection Building [*NASA*] (KSC)
PIB............ Public Information Bulletin [*Australian Taxation Office*] [*A publication*] (APTA)
PIB............ Publishers Information Bureau [*New York, NY*] (EA)
PIB............ Publishing Information Bulletin [*A publication*]
PIB............ Pulse Interference Blanker
PIB............ Pyrotechnic Installation Building [*NASA*] (KSC)
PIBA.......... Primary Industry Bank of Australia Ltd. (ADA)
PIBAC........ Permanent International Bureau of Analytical Chemistry of Human and Animal Food
PIBAL........ Pilot Balloon Observation
PIBAL........ Polytechnic Institute of Brooklyn Aeronautical Laboratory (MCD)
PIBALS..... Pilot Balloon Soundings
PIBC.......... Pacific Inland Bancorp [*Anaheim, CA*] [*NASDAQ symbol*] (NQ)
PIBC.......... Pacific Institute of Bio-Organic Chemistry
PIBD.......... Point Initiating, Base Detonating Projectile [*Army*]
PIBL.......... PEMA Item Baseline List [*Army*] (AABC)
PIBMM..... Permanent International Bureau of Motorcycle Manufacturers
PIBMRI..... Polytechnic Institute of Brooklyn, Microwave Research Institute (IEEE)
PIBOL....... Pilot Back Up Control
PIBOL....... Pilot in Booster Loop (SAA)
PIBS .... Polar Ionospheric Beacon Satellite [*NASA*]
PIBSB........ Proceedings. Indian National Science Academy. Part B. Biological Sciences [*A publication*]
PIBTAD .... Proceedings. Congress of the International Society of Blood Transfusion [*A publication*]
PIBUC....... Pilot Back Up Control
PIC............ Calverton, NY [*Location identifier*] [*FAA*] (FAAL)
PIC............ Craig House Technoma Workshop, Pittsburgh, PA [*OCLC symbol*] (OCLC)
PIC............ Pacific Insurance Conference
PIC............ Pacific Intelligence Center (MCD)
PIC............ Paired-Ion Chromatography
PIC............ Para-iodoclonidine [*Biochemistry*]
PIC............ Parent Indicator Code (DNAB)
PIC............ Partially Incinerated Compound [*Furnace technology*]
PIC............ Particle in Cell [*Gas solid*]
PIC............ Partners in Change Program [*Department of Labor*]
PIC............ Payload Integration Center [*NASA*] (MCD)
PIC............ Payload Integration Committee [*NASA*] (NASA)
PIC............ Payload Integration Contractor (MCD)
PIC............ Peak Identification Computer
PIC............ People's Involvement Corp. (EA)
PIC............ Peripheral Interface Controller [*Data processing*]
PIC............ Pershing Instant Comment [*Donaldson, Lufkin & Jenrette*] [*Database*]
PIC............ Personal Identification Code [*Banking*]
PIC............ Personal Intelligent Communicator [*Data processing*] (PCM)
PIC............ Personality Inventory for Children [*Psychology*]
PIC............ Personnel Investigations Center
PIC............ Perspectives in Computing [*A publication*]
PIC............ Pesticides Information Center [*National Agricultural Library*] [*Terminated, 1969*]
PIC............ Petrochemical Investing Corp.
PIC............ Photographic Industry Council (EA)
PIC............ Photographic Interpretation Center (MCD)
PIC............ Physical Inorganic Chemistry [*Elsevier Book Series*] [*A publication*]
PIC............ Piccadilly Saloon [*London*] (DSUE)
PIC............ Piccolo [*Music*] (ROG)
PIC............ [*The*] Pickens Railroad Co. [*Later, PICK*] [*AAR code*]
Pic............ Picrotoxin [*Biochemistry*]
Pic .... Pictor [*Constellation*]
PIC............ Picture (AABC)
PIC............ Pig Improvement Co. [*British*] (ECON)
PIC............ Pilot in Command [*Aviation*] (FAAC)

PIC............ Pilot-Integrated Cockpit (AAG)
PIC............ Pine Cay [*British West Indies*] [*Airport symbol*] [*Obsolete*] (OAG)
PIC............ Pitch Impregnation Carbonization (MCD)
PIC............ Planned Insurance Coverage
PIC............ Plasma Insulin Concentration [*Clinical chemistry*]
PIC............ Plastic Insulated Conductor
PIC............ Policy Information Center [*Department of Health and Human Services*] [*Information service or system*] (IID)
PIC............ Polyethylene Insulated Conductor [*Telecommunications*]
PIC............ Polymer-Impregnated Concrete (KSC)
PIC............ Portable Imaging Computer
PIC............ Position Independent Code [*Telecommunications*] (TEL)
PIC............ Positive Ion Chamber
PIC............ Postinflammatory Corticoid [*Medicine*]
PIC............ Power Information Center [*Interagency Advanced Power Group*] [*DoD*] [*Washington, DC*]
PIC............ Power Integrated Circuit [*Data processing*]
PIC............ Predicted Intercept Contour
PIC............ Preinstallation Calibration (KSC)
PIC............ Preinstallation Checkout (NASA)
PIC............ Presbyterian Interracial Council (EA)
PIC............ Pressure Indicator Controller
PIC............ Primate Information Center [*University of Washington*] [*Seattle, WA*]
pic............. Prince Edward Island [*Canada*] [*MARC country of publication code*] [*Library of Congress*] (LCCP)
PIC............ Printer Interface Cartridge [*Epson America, Inc.*]
PIC............ Prior Informed Consent [*For use of pesticides*]
PIC............ Priority Interrupt Controller
PIC............ Private Industry Council [*Generic term for group that helps provide job training*]
PIC............ Procedures for Instrument Calibration
PIC............ Process Interface Control
PIC............ Processor Input Channel (NVT)
PIC............ Procurement Information Center
PIC............ Procurement Information for Contracts [*AFSC*]
PIC............ Product of Incomplete Combustion
PIC............ Product Information Center [*AgriData Resources, Inc.*] [*Information service or system*]
PIC............ Professional Instrument Course [*Aeronautics*]
PIC............ Professional Interfraternity Conference [*Later, PFA*] (EA)
PIC............ Program Identification Code (MUGU)
PIC............ Program for Improved Contract Management [*Military*] (AFIT)
PIC............ Program Information Center
PIC............ Program Initiations and Commitments (AAG)
PIC............ Program Instruction, Calibration [*Marine Corps*]
PIC............ Program Interrupt Control [*Data processing*]
PIC............ Programmable Interrupt Controller [*Data processing*]
PIC............ Programmable Interval Clock (NASA)
PIC............ Project Information Center
PIC............ Promotion Industry Club (EA)
PIC............ Pseudo-Isocytidine [*Antineoplastic compound*]
PIC............ Pseudoisocyanine [*Organic chemistry*]
PIC............ Public Information Center [*Nuclear energy*] (NRCH)
PIC............ Public Information Committee [*of the NATO Military Committee*] (NATG)
PIC............ Publishers' Information Card [*Later, IBIS*] [*British*]
PIC............ Pulsed Ionization Chamber
PIC............ Purpose Identification Code
PIC............ Pursuant to Instructions Contained In (MUGU)
PIC............ Pyrotechnic Ignition Control (NASA)
PIC............ Pyrotechnic Initiator Capacitor (NASA)
PIC............ Pyrotechnic Initiator Controller (NASA)
PICA.......... Palestine Israelite Colonisation Association
PICA.......... Participating Interest Contingency Agreement
PICA.......... Police Insignia Collector's Association (EA)
PICA.......... Porch Index of Communicative Ability [*Psychology*]
PICA.......... Posterior Inferior Cerebellar Artery [*Anatomy*]
PICA.......... Power Industry Computer Applications (MCD)
PICA.......... Primary Inventory Control Activity (MCD)
PICA.......... Printing Industry Computer Associates, Inc.
PICA.......... Private Investment Co. for Asia SA
PICA.......... Procedures for Inventory Control Afloat [*Navy*]
PICA.......... Professional Insurance Communicators of America (EA)
PICA.......... Programming Interpersonal Curricula for Adolescents [*Learning model*] [*Education*]
PICA.......... Project for Integrated Catalogue Automation [*Royal Netherlands Library*] [*Cataloging cooperative*] (IID)
PICA.......... Property Services Agency Information on Construction and Architecture [*Property Service Agency Library Service*] [*British*] [*Information service or system*]
PICA.......... Public Interest Computer Association (EA)
PICAC....... Porch Index of Communicative Ability in Children [*Psychology*]
PICAC....... Power Industry Computer Applications Conference (MCD)
PICADAD ... Place Identification/Characteristics and Area/Distance and Direction [*Bureau of the Census*]
PICAM...... Proceedings. International Congress of Americanists [*A publication*]

PICAO...... Provisional International Civil Aviation Organization [*Later, ICAO*]
Picardie Inform ... Picardie Information [*A publication*]
PICB.......... Peabody Institute of the City of Baltimore [*Maryland*]
PICC.......... Parts for Import Cars Coalition [*Inactive*]   (EA)
PICC.......... Peripherally-Inserted Central Catheter [*Medicine*]
PICC.......... Philadelphia International Convention Center [*Pennsylvania*]
PICC.......... Piccadilly Cafeterias, Inc. [*NASDAQ symbol*]   (NQ)
PICC.......... Piccolo
PICC.......... Plastics in Construction Council [*Later, CCS*]   (EA)
PICC.......... Professional Institutions Council for Conservation [*British*]
PICC.......... Provisional International Computation Center
PICCA........ Positive Ion Cluster Composition Analyzer [*Instrumentation*]
PICCED .... Pratt Institute Center for Community and Environmental Development [*Research center*]   (RCD)
PICCO...... Pennsylvania Industrial Chemical Corp. [*Trademark*]
PICD.......... Preliminary Interface Control Drawing
PICDG....... Polar Icebreaker Canadian Design Group
PICE.......... Product Improved Compatibility Electronics   (MCD)
PICE.......... Programmable Integrated Control Equipment
PICED....... Proceedings. International Conference on Noise Control Engineering [*A publication*]
PICEE....... President's Interagency Committee on Export Expansion [*Absorbed by President's Export Council in 1979*]   (EGAO)
PICE/PIA ... Printing Industry Credit Exchange/PIA [*of the Printing Industries of America*]   (EA)
PICESP ..... Put It in Corporate Executives' Swimming Pools [*Waste management slang*]
PICG.......... Programme International de Correlation Geologique [*International Geological Correlation Programme - IGCP*]   (EAIO)
PICGC....... Permanent International Committee for Genetic Congresses
PicGPA...... Picrylated Guinea Pig Albumin [*Immunochemistry*]
PICI.......... Polymer International Corp. [*Tampa, FL*] [*NASDAQ symbol*]   (NQ)
PICI.......... Publications. Institut de Civilisation Indienne [*A publication*]
P I Civ E 1 ... Proceedings. Institution of Civil Engineers. Part 1. Design and Construction [*A publication*]
P I Civ E 2 ... Proceedings. Institution of Civil Engineers. Part 2. Research and Theory [*A publication*]
PICJ.......... Pacific Islands Communication Journal [*A publication*]
PICK.......... Part Information Correlation Key
PICK.......... [*The*] Pickens Railroad Co. [*Formerly, PIC*] [*AAR code*]
Pick............ Pickering's Massachusetts Supreme Judicial Court Reports [*1822-39*] [*A publication*]   (DLA)
PICK.......... Pickwick [*Refers to an inferior quality cigar*]   (DSUE)
Picker Clin Scintil ... Picker Clinical Scintillator [*A publication*]
PICKFAIR ... [*Mary*] Pickford and [*Douglas*] Fairbanks [*Acronym is name of estate once owned by these early film stars*]
Pickle........ Pickle's Reports [*85-108 Tennessee*] [*A publication*]   (DLA)
PICKLE..... Preserving Individual Cultures and Knowledge in Lands Everywhere [*An association*]
PICKLE..... President's Intelligence Checklist [*Daily report prepared by CIA*]
Pickle Pak Sci ... Pickle Pak Science [*A publication*]
Pick (Mass) ... Pickering's Massachusetts Reports [*18-41 Massachusetts*] [*A publication*]   (DLA)
Pick Stat .... Pickering's English Statutes [*A publication*]   (DLA)
PICKUP .... Professional, Industrial and Commercial Updating [*Vocational training*] [*British*]
PICL.......... Proceedings. International Congress of Linguists [*A publication*]
PICM........ Master Chief Precision Instrumentman [*Navy rating*]
PICM........ Permanent International Committee of Mothers
PIC-MOD ... Purpose Identification Code - Month and Calendar Year of Detachment   (DNAB)
PIC-NF...... Picroindigocarmine-Nuclear Fast Red [*A biological stain*]
PICO.......... Partido Independiente de la Clase Obrera [*Panama*] [*Political party*]   (EY)
PICO.......... Person in Column One [*1980 census*]
PICO.......... Physicians Insurance Co. of Ohio [*NASDAQ symbol*]   (NQ)
PICO.......... Polar Ice Core Drilling Office [*National Science Foundation*]   (MSC)
PICO.......... Proceedings. International Congress of Orientalists [*A publication*]
PICO.......... Product Improvement Control Office   (AFM)
PICO.......... Purchasing Internal Change Order   (MCD)
PICOE....... Programmed Initiations, Commitments, Obligations, and Expenditures [*AFSC*]
PICOMM ... Potter Instrument Coordinated Measuring Machine
PICON ...... Process Intelligent Control [*A data processing system from LISP Machine, Inc.*]
PICOPD.... Pico Products, Inc. [*Associated Press abbreviation*]   (APAG)
PICORNAVIRUS ... Pico Ribonucleic Acid Virus
PICOST..... Probability of Incurring Estimated Costs [*Military*]   (MCD)
PICP.......... Prime Inventory Control Point   (DNAB)
PICP.......... Proceedings. International Congress of Philosophy [*A publication*]
PICP.......... Program Interface Control Plan   (NASA)
PICPAB..... Phenomena Induced by Charged Particle Beams

PICPS........ Proceedings. International Congress of Phonetic Sciences [*A publication*]
PICPSA..... Permanent International Commission for the Proof of Small-Arms   (EAIO)
PICRC .... Pesticide and Industrial Chemicals Research Center [*Public Health Service*]   (GRD)
PICRS........ Program Information Control and Retrieval System   (NASA)
PICRS........ Program Information Coordination and Review Service [*NASA*]   (NASA)
PICS .... Finest Hour, Inc. [*NASDAQ symbol*]   (NQ)
PICS .... International Journal of Comparative Sociology [*A publication*]
PICS .... Permit Imprint Collectors Society   (EA)
PICS .... Perpetual Inventory Control System
PICS .... Personnel Information Communication [*or Control*] System [*Data processing*]
PICS .... Pharmaceutical Information Control System   (DIT)
PICS .... Photo Index and Cataloging System   (NASA)
PICS .... Photographic Information Condensing System   (DNAB)
PICS .... Photography in Community Self-Development [*Program of Master Photo Dealers and Finishers Association*]
PICS .... Pioneer Image Converter System [*NASA*]
PICS .... Plastid Isolation Column System [*Analytical chemistry*]
PICS .... Plug-In Inventory Control System [*Bell System*]
PICS .... Predefined Input Control Sequence   (MCD)
PICS .... Procurement Information Control System [*NASA*]
PICS .... Production Information and Control System [*IBM Corp.*] [*Software package*]
PICS .... Production Inventory Control System
PICS .... Productivity Improvement and Control System   (BUR)
PICS .... Program Information and Control System   (MCD)
PICS/DCPR ... Plug-In Inventory Control System/Detailed Continuing Property Record [*Telecommunications*]   (TEL)
PICT .... Perceived Instrumentality of the College Test
Pict............ Pictor [*Constellation*]
PICT .... Pictorial   (ROG)
PICT .... Project on the Improvement of College Teaching
Pict Dict Rome ... Pictorial Dictionary of Ancient Rome [*A publication*]   (OCD)
PICTOMAP ... Photographic Image Conversion by Tonal Masking Procedures   (MCD)
PictR .... Pictorial Review [*A publication*]
PICTUREBALM ... [*A*] Programming Language [*1979*]   (CSR)
PICU.......... Parallel Instruction Control Unit
PICU.......... Pediatric Intensive Care Unit [*Medicine*]
PICU.......... Priority Interrupt Control Unit [*Data processing*]   (MDG)
PICU.......... Pulmonary Intensive Care Unit [*Medicine*]
PICUTPC ... Permanent and International Committee of Underground Town Planning and Construction
PID .... D. T. Watson Home for Crippled Children, Leetsdale, PA [*OCLC symbol*]   (OCLC)
PID .... Pain Intensity Differences [*Medicine*]
PID .... Parameter Identification [*Communications*]
PId .... Parole e le Idee [*A publication*]
PID .... Partial Initial Decision [*Nuclear energy*]   (NRCH)
PID .... Partido de Integracion Democrata [*Democratic Integration Party*] [*Argentina*] [*Political party*]   (PPW)
PID .... Partido Izquierda Democratica [*Democratic Left Party*] [*Political party*]   (EAIO)
PID .... Passenger Information Display
PID .... Patrol Input Device   (MCD)
PID .... Payload Insertion Device   (NASA)
PID .... Pelvic Inflammatory Disease [*Medicine*]
PID .... Perfect-Gas Isentropic Decompression [*Engineering*]
PID .... Personality and Individual Differences [*A publication*]
PID .... Personnel Inquiry/Death/Occupational Illness [*Report*]   (DNAB)
PID .... Phenindione [*or Phenylindandione*] [*Anticoagulant*]
PID .... Photointerpretation Department [*Military*]
PID .... Photoionization Detector
PID .... Photon-Induced Dissociation [*For spectral studies*]
PID .... Pictorial Information Digitizer [*Data processing*]   (DIT)
PID .... Pilot-Induced Deceleration
P & ID........ Piping and Instrumentation Diagram [*or Design or Drawing*] [*Calcomp Ltd.*] [*Software package*] [*Nuclear energy*]   (NRCH)
PID .... Plasma-Iron Disappearance [*Hematology*]   (MAE)
PID .... Political Intelligence Department [*British*] [*World War II*]
PID .... Port Identification [*Telecommunications*]   (TEL)
PID .... Prae-Italic Dialects of Italy [*A publication*]
PID .... Primary Immunodeficiency Disease [*Medicine*]
PID .... Prime Item Development   (MCD)
PID .... Process Identifier [*Data processing*]   (PCM)
P & ID........ Process and Instrumentation Diagram [*Nuclear energy*]   (NRCH)
PID .... Procurement Information Digest   (AFM)
PID .... Procurement Item/Identification Description [*DoD*]
PID .... Program Information Document [*NASA*]   (MCD)
PID .... Program Introduction Document   (NASA)
PID .... Project Implementation Directive [*Air Force*]
PID .... Prolapsed Intervertebral Disc [*Medicine*]

PID .... Proportional-Plus Integral-Plus Derivative [*Digital control algorithm*]
PID .... Protruded Intervertebral Disc [*Medicine*]
PID .... Pseudo Interrupt Device
PID .... Public Information Division [*Army*]
PIDA........ Payload Installation and Deployment Aid [*NASA*] (NASA)
PIDA........ Pet Industry Distributors Association (EA)
PIDAS ...... Portable Instantaneous Display and Analysis Spectrometer
PIDC......... Philadelphia Industrial Development Corp.
PIDC......... Procurement Intern Development Center (DNAB)
PIDCOM... Process Instruments Digital Communication System [*Beckman Industries*]
PIDD .... Passive Identification/Detection and Direction (MCD)
PI/DE .... Passive Identification/Direction Finding Equipment (MCD)
PI/DE .... Positive Identification and Direction Equipment
PIDEP ...... Preinterservice Data Exchange Program
PIDL......... Position Involves Intermittent Duty at Isolated Locations (FAAC)
PIDP .... Pacific Islands Development Program [*East-West Center*] [*Research center*] (RCD)
PIDP .... Pilot Information Display Panel
PIDP .... Programmable Indicator Data Processor [*Military*] (CAAL)
PIDR........ Product Inspection Discrepancy Report (MCD)
PIDRA....... Portable Insulin Dosage-Regulating Apparatus [*Medicine*]
PIDRS ...... Photographic Instrumentation Data Recording System (MCD)
PIDS .... Parameter Inventory Display System (DNAB)
PIDS .... Physical Intrusion Detection System (DWSG)
PIDS .... Portable Image Display System (NASA)
PIDS .... Prime Item Development Specification
PIDSA ...... Population Information Documentation System for Africa
PIDT......... Plasma-Iron Disappearance Time [*Hematology*] (MAE)
PIE........... Elwyn Institute, Elwyn, PA [*OCLC symbol*] (OCLC)
PIE........... Pacific Information Exchange [*Information service or system*] (IID)
PIE........... Pacific Islands Ecosystems [*Springfield, VA*] [*Department of the Interior*] [*Information service or system*] [*No longer available online*]
PIE........... Pacing Item Evaluation (MCD)
PIE........... Paedophile Information Exchange [*British*] (ILCA)
PIE........... Parallel Instruction Execution [*Data processing*] (BUR)
PIE........... Parallel Interface Element
PIE........... Patent Information Exploitation [*Canadian Patent Office*]
PIE........... Payload Integration Equipment [*NASA*] (MCD)
PIE........... Payroll Audit, Indexing, and Expiration
PIE........... Photo-Induced Electrochromism
PIE........... Piedmont Aviation, Inc. [*NYSE symbol*] (SPSG)
PIE........... Pietermaritzburg [*South Africa*] [*Seismograph station code, US Geological Survey*] [*Closed*] (SEIS)
PIE........... Pipestone Petroleums, Inc. [*Toronto Stock Exchange symbol*] [*Vancouver Stock Exchange symbol*]
PIE........... Plug-In Electronics
PIE........... Plume Interaction Experiment [*Army*] (RDA)
PIE........... Poly(iminoethylene) [*Organic chemistry*]
PIE........... Portable Information Evaluation
PIE........... Post-Irradiation Examination [*Nuclear energy*] (NRCH)
PIE........... Post-Irradiation Experiment [*Nuclear energy*] (NRCH)
PIE........... Preimplantation Embryo
PIE........... Price in Effect [*Military*]
PIE........... Program for Increased Education [*Military*]
PIE........... Program Interrupt Entry [*Data processing*]
PIE........... Programming and Instrumentation Environment [*Data processing*]
PIE........... Prolog Inference Engine [*Data processing*]
PIE........... Proposal Information Exchange [*Military*]
PIE........... Public Interest Economics Foundation [*Defunct*] (EA)
PIE........... Publications Indexed for Engineering [*A publication*]
PIE........... Pulmonary Infiltration with Eosinophilia [*Medicine*]
PIE........... Pulmonary Interstitial Emphysema [*Medicine*]
PIE........... Pulse Interference Eliminator [*RADAR*]
PIE........... Pulse Interference Emitting (MCD)
PIE........... St. Petersburg [*Florida*] [*Airport symbol*] (OAG)
3PIE......... Three-Pulse Image Photon Echo [*Spectroscopy*]
PIEA........ Pencil Industry Export Association [*Defunct*] (EA)
PIEA......... Petroleum Industry Electrical Association [*Later, ENTELEC*] (EA)
PIEA......... Pre-Arrangement Interment Exchange of America [*Later, PIAA*]
PIE-C........ Public Interest Economics Center (EA)
PIECOST ... Probability of Incurring Estimated Costs [*Military*]
PIECP........ Preliminary Impact Engineering Change Proposal (MCD)
PIED......... Piedmont Mining Co., Inc. [*NASDAQ symbol*] (NQ)
PiedNG...... Piedmont Natural Gas Co., Inc. [*Associated Press abbreviation*] (APAG)
PIEEA .... Proceedings. Institution of Electrical Engineers [*A publication*]
P IEEE....... Proceedings. Institute of Electrical and Electronics Engineers [*A publication*]
P IEE (Lond) ... Proceedings. Institution of Electrical Engineers (London) [*A publication*]
PIE-F .... Public Interest Economics Foundation [*Defunct*] (EA)
Pieleg Polozna ... Pielegniarka i Polozna [*A publication*]
Pienpuu Toimikun Julk ... Pienpuualan Toimikunnan Julkaisu [*A publication*]

PIEP .... Primary Irritation Evaluation Program
Pier 1......... Pier 1 Imports, Inc. [*Associated Press abbreviation*] (APAG)
Pierce RR... Pierce on Railroad Law [*A publication*] (DLA)
PIERS........ Port Import/Export Reporting Service [*Journal of Commerce, Inc.*] [*Information service or system*]
PIES .... Packaged Interchangeable Electronic System
PIES .... Penning Ionization Electron Spectroscopy
PIES .... Procurement and Inventory of Equipment System (DNAB)
PIES .... Project Independence Evaluation System [*Energy policy*]
PIESD ...... Proceedings. Indian Academy of Sciences. Series Earth and Planetary Sciences [*A publication*]
PIF .... Paris et Ile-De-France. Memoires [*A publication*]
P & IF .... Paris et Ile-De-France. Memoires [*A publication*]
PIF .... Partners in Friendship (EA)
PIF .... Payload Integration Facility [*NASA*] (KSC)
PIF .... Peak Inspiratory Flow [*Medicine*] (AAMN)
PIF .... Perpetual Inventory File (DNAB)
PIF .... Personnel Identification Feature [*Navy*] (NVT)
PIF .... Phase Inversion Formulation [*Chemistry*]
PIF .... Pilot Information File [*Army*]
PIF .... Place in Inactive File [*Army*]
PIF .... Point Initiating Fuze
PIF .... Positive Identification Feature (MCD)
PIF .... Predictive Influence Function [*Statistics*]
PIF .... Preparer Inventory File [*IRS*]
PIF .... Privatization Investment Fund Trust Units [*Toronto Stock Exchange symbol*]
PIF .... Productivity Investment Fund [*Program*] [*Air Force*]
PIF .... Program Information File
PIF .... Prolactin-Release Inhibiting Factor [*Also, PRIH*] [*Endocrinology*]
PIF .... Proliferation Inhibitory Factor [*Immunochemistry*]
PIF .... Provision of Industrial Facilities [*Army*] (AABC)
PIF .... Prudential Intermediate Income [*NYSE symbol*] (SPSG)
PIF .... Pseudo-Identification Feature (MCD)
PIF .... Punjab Irregular Force [*British military*] (DMA)
PIFAO .... Publications. Institut Francais d'Archeologie Orientale du Caire [*A publication*]
PIFAO BEC ... Publications. Institut Francais d'Archeologie Orientale. Bibliotheque d'Etudes Coptes [*A publication*]
PIFAS........ Publicaciones. Instituto de Filologia. Anejo de Sphinx [*A publication*]
PIFCM ...... Pitch Integrated Flight Control Module (MCD)
PIFEX........ Programmable Image Feature Extractor [*to provide real-time machine vision for the Martian Rover robot*] [*Jet Propulsion Laboratory*] (BYTE)
PIFF.......... Punjab Irregular Frontier Force [*British military*] (DMA)
PIFI .... Piemonte Foods, Inc. [*NASDAQ symbol*] (NQ)
PIFI .... Pressure-Induced Intracranial Focal Ischemia [*Medicine*]
PIFMLL...... Proceedings. International Federation for Modern Languages and Literatures [*A publication*]
PIFOV .... Planet in Field of View [*NASA*]
PIFR .... Peak Inspiratory Flow Rate [*Medicine*]
PIFS.......... Plume-Induced Flow Separation
PIFS.......... Post Infection Fatigue Syndrome [*Medicine*]
PIFS.......... Prime Item Fabrication Specification
PIFT .... Platelet Immunofluorescence Test [*Analytical biochemistry*]
PIFUA ...... Powerplant and Industrial Fuel Use Act of 1978
PIG .... Glenn Mills School, Glenn Mills, PA [*OCLC symbol*] (OCLC)
PIG .... Pacific Institute of Geography
PIG .... Passive-Income Generator [*Investment term*]
PIG .... Pendulous Integrating Gyro
PIG .... Phillips Ionization Gauge
PIG .... Phosphatidylinositol Glycan [*Biochemistry*]
PIG .... Photo-Island Grid
Pig............. Pig Iron [*A publication*]
Pig............. Pigott's Common Recoveries [*3 eds.*] [*1739-92*] [*A publication*] (DLA)
PIG .... Plasmatron Inert Gas (SAA)
PIG .... Pork Industry Gazette [*A publication*]
PIG .... Pride, Integrity, Guts [*Police alternative for the appellation applied to police by radical groups*]
PIG .... Process Ink Gamut [*Printing technology*]
PIG .... Production Image Generator (MCD)
PIG .... Production Installation Group [*Military*] (CAAL)
PIG .... Program Implementation Guideline (EG)
PIG .... Pulse Inert Gas
PIGA......... Pendulous Integrating Gyro Accelerometer
PIGBA .... Proceedings. Royal Institution of Great Britain [*A publication*]
PIGIT .... Putnam Intermediate Government Income Trust [*Associated Press abbreviation*] (APAG)
Pig Judg... Pigott's Foreign Judgments [*3rd ed.*] [*1908-09*] [*A publication*] (DLA)
PIGLET..... Purchase Information, Gifts, Loans, Exchanges Tracking [*Suggested name for the Library of Congress computer system*]
PIGM .... Pigmentum [*Paint*] [*Pharmacy*]
PIGM .... Putnam Investment Grade Municipal Trust [*Associated Press abbreviation*] (APAG)
PIGMA...... Pressurized Inert Gas Metal Arc (KSC)
Pigm Cell ... Pigment Cell [*A publication*]

Pigment Resin Tech ... Pigment and Resin Technology [*A publication*]
Pigment Resin Technol ... Pigment and Resin Technology [*A publication*]
PIGMI ...... Pion Generator for Medical Irradiation [*Radiology*]
PIGMI ...... Position Indicating General Measuring Instrument
Pig News Inf ... Pig News and Information [*A publication*]
PIGPA .... Pyruvate, Inosine, Glucose Phosphate, Adenine (AAMN)
Pig & R ...... Pigott and Rodwell's English Registration Appeal Cases [*1843-45*] [*A publication*] (DLA)
PIGR .... Polymeric Immunoglobulin Receptor [*Biochemistry*]
Pig Rec .... Pigott's Recoveries [*England*] [*A publication*] (DLA)
Pig Rsn Tech ... Pigment and Resin Technology [*A publication*]
PIGS .... PAFEC Interactive Graphics System [*PAFEC Ltd.*] [*Software package*] (NCC)
PIGS .... Passive Infrared Guidance System [*DoD*]
PIGS .... Pesticides in Groundwater Strategy [*Environmental Protection Agency*] (GFGA)
PIGS .... Poles, Italians, Greeks, and Slavs
PIGS .... Portable Inertial Guidance System
PIGU .... Pendulous Integrating Gyro Unit
PIH .... Permanent Income Hypothesis [*Economics*]
PIH .... Phenylisopropylhydrazine [*Pharmacology*]
PIH .... Pipeline Induction Heat [*Industrial firm*] [*British*]
PIH .... Pocatello [*Idaho*] [*Airport symbol*] (OAG)
PIH .... Pork Industry Handbook [*A publication*]
PIH .... Pregnancy-Induced Hypertension [*Gynecology*]
PIH .... Prolactin-Release Inhibiting Hormone [*Endocrinology*]
PIH .... Public and Indian Housing [*HUD*]
PIH .... St. Gabriel's Hall, Phoenixville, PA [*OCLC symbol*] (OCLC)
PIHANS .... Publications. Institut Historique et Archeologique Neerlandais de Stamboul [*Leiden*] [*A publication*]
PIHCA .... Polyisohexylcyanoacrylate [*Antibacterial*]
PIHI .... Journal of Interdisciplinary History [*A publication*]
PIHM .... Polish Institute of Hydrology and Meteorology
PII .... Fairbanks, AK [*Location identifier*] [*FAA*] (FAAL)
PII .... Pershing II [*Army*]
PII .... Phantom II [*Model of automobile*]
PII .... Plasma Inorganic Iodine [*Clinical chemistry*] (MAE)
PII .... Positive Immittance Inverter (IEEE)
PII .... Primary Irritation Indices [*for skin*]
PII .... Printing Industry Institute [*A graphic arts training school*]
PII .... Procurement Instrument Identification (NG)
PII .... Pueblo International, Inc. [*NYSE symbol*] (SPSG)
PII .... Sleighton School, Darling, PA [*OCLC symbol*] (OCLC)
PIIAA .... Proceedings. National Institute of Sciences (India). Part A. Physical Sciences [*A publication*]
PIIC .... Pergamon International Information Corp. [*Information service or system*] (IID)
PIIC .... Pilgrim Intergroup Investment Corp. [*NASDAQ symbol*] (NQ)
PIICAV ..... Convenio IICA-ZN-ROCAP [*Instituto Interamericano de Ciencias Agricolas-Zona Norte-Regional Organization for Central America and Panama*] Publicacion Miscelanea [*A publication*]
PIID .... Prediction Interval Initiation Date (DNAB)
PIID .... Publishers' International ISBN [*International Standard Book Number*] Directory [*A publication*]
PIIF .... Proteinase Inhibitor Inducing Factor [*Biochemistry*]
PIIM .... Planned Interdependency Incentive Method
PIIN .... Procurement Instruction Identification Number [*Army*] (AABC)
PIIN .... Procurement Instrument Identification Number [*Military*]
PI/INT'L ... Packaging Institute International [*Later, IoPP*] (EA)
PIJ .... Pickled-in-Jar [*Food technology*]
PIJAC .... Pet Industry Joint Advisory Council (EA)
PIJR .... Product Improvement Joint Review [*Military*]
PIK .... Glasgow-Prestwick [*Scotland*] [*Airport symbol*] (OAG)
PIK .... Payment in Kind
PIK .... Pic Prospectors [*Vancouver Stock Exchange symbol*]
PIK .... Portable Injection Kit
Pike .... Pike's Reports [*1-5 Arkansas*] [*A publication*] (DLA)
Pike & F Adm Law ... Pike and Fischer's Administrative Law [*A publication*] (DLA)
Pike & F Fed Rules Service ... Pike and Fischer's Federal Rules Service [*A publication*] (DLA)
Pike & Fischer Admin Law ... Pike and Fischer's Administrative Law [*A publication*] (DLA)
Pike H of L ... Pike's History of the House of Lords [*A publication*] (DLA)
PIKM .... PIK. Northern Magazine for Children [*Northwest Territory, Canada*] [*A publication*]
PIKS .... American Sports Advisors, Inc. [*NASDAQ symbol*] (NQ)
PIL .... Brazos Santiago, TX [*Location identifier*] [*FAA*] (FAAL)
PIL .... Pair Inter Langues [*Bourg La Reine, France*] (EAIO)
PIL .... Papers in Linguistics [*A publication*]
PIL .... Parti de l'Independance et de la Liberte [*Party for Independence and Liberty*] [*Congo*] [*Political party*]
PIL .... Payment in Lieu
PIL .... Percentage Increase in Loss [*Statistics*]
PIL .... Petroleum Investors Depositary Receipts Units [*NYSE symbol*] (SPSG)
PIL .... Pilar [*Argentina*] [*Geomagnetic observatory code*]
PIL .... Pilar [*Argentina*] [*Seismograph station code, US Geological Survey*] (SEIS)

PIL .... Pilot (WGA)
PIL .... Pilula [*Pill*] [*Pharmacy*]
PIL .... Pistol Petroleum [*Vancouver Stock Exchange symbol*]
PIL .... Pitt Interpretive Language [*Data processing*] (DIT)
PIL .... Plastic Impregnated Laminate
PIL .... Practice Instrument Landing (ADA)
PIL .... Preferred Item List (RDA)
PIL .... Processing Information List [*Data processing*]
PIL .... Procurement Information Letter (MCD)
PIL .... Publications International Ltd.
PIL .... Purple Indicating Light (MSA)
PIL .... Purpose in Life [*Personality development test*] [*Psychology*]
PILA .... Power Industry Laboratory Association (EA)
PILAC .... Pulsed Ion Linear Accelerator
PILB .... Passenger and Immigration Lists Bibliography [*A publication*]
PILC .... Paper-Insulated, Lead-Covered Cable [*Telecommunications*]
PILC .... Pilgrim Holdings Ltd. [*Formerly, Pilgrim Coal Corp.*] [*NASDAQ symbol*] (NQ)
PILC .... Pillared Interlayered Clays [*Catalysis technology*]
PILC .... Pregnancy and Infant Loss Center (EA)
PilgPr .... Pilgrims Pride Corp. [*Associated Press abbreviation*] (APAG)
PilgRg .... Pilgrim Regional Banc Shares, Inc. [*Associated Press abbreviation*] (APAG)
PILI .... Passenger and Immigration Lists Index [*A publication*]
PILL .... Newport Dock [*British depot code*]
PILL .... Programmed Instruction Language Learning [*Data processing*]
PILM .... Pillared Interlayered Montmorillonite [*Catalysis technology*]
PILO .... Public Information Liaison Officer [*Military*]
PILOT ...... Paton Lyall Tosh [*Rock music group*]
PILOT ...... Payment in Lieu of Taxes
PILOT ...... Permutation Indexed Literature of Technology (IEEE)
PILOT ...... Piloted Low-Speed Test [*Aerospace*]
PILOT ...... Printing Industry Language for Operations of Typesetting
PILP .... Parametric Integer Linear Program [*Data processing*]
PILP .... Program of Industry/Laboratory Projects [*National Research Council of Canada*]
PILP .... Pseudoinfinite, Logarithmically Periodic
PilPrm .... Pilgrim Prime Rate Trust [*Associated Press abbreviation*] (APAG)
PILS .... Payload Integration Library System [*NASA*] (SSD)
PILS .... Pilsener Lager (DSUE)
PILS .... Precision Instrument Landing System
PILSA .... Progress in Immunobiological Standardization [*A publication*]
PIL STA .... Pilot Station [*Nautical charts*]
PILT .... Payment in Lieu of Taxes Program [*Department of the Interior*]
PILTA .... Payment in Lieu of Taxes Act
PIm .... Immaculata College, Immaculata, PA [*Library symbol*] [*Library of Congress*] (LCLS)
PIM .... Pacem in Maribus [*Secondary name for the International Ocean Institute*] (MSC)
PIM .... Pacific Islands Monthly [*A publication*] (APTA)
PIM .... Pacific Rim Energy [*Vancouver Stock Exchange symbol*]
PIM .... Parallel Inference Machine [*Data processing*]
PIM .... Partners-in-Mission [*Church of England*]
PIM .... Penalties in Minutes [*Hockey*]
PIM .... Peripheral Interface Module
PIM .... Personal Information Manager
Pi M .... Pillius Medicinensis [*Flourished, 1165-1207*] [*Authority cited in pre-1607 legal work*] (DSA)
PIM .... Pine Mountain, GA [*Location identifier*] [*FAA*] (FAAL)
PIM .... Plan of Intended Movement (MUGU)
PIM .... Plated Interconnecting Matrix
PIM .... Plug-In Module (MCD)
PIM .... Point of Intended Movement [*Military*]
PIM .... Politica Internacional (Madrid) [*A publication*]
PIM .... Polyphase Induction Motor
PIM .... Position and Intended Movement [*or Maneuver*] (NATG)
PIM .... Position in Miles (MCD)
PIM .... Precision Indicator of the Meridian
PIM .... Precision Instrument Mount
PIM .... Presa Del Infiernillo [*Mexico*] [*Seismograph station code, US Geological Survey*] [*Closed*] (SEIS)
PIM .... Pricing Instructions Memorandum (MCD)
PIM .... Pro Independence Movement [*Puerto Rico*]
PIM .... Processor Interface Module
PIM .... Product Information Memoranda
PIM .... Program Integration Manual
PIM .... Program Interface Module
PIM .... Progress in Industrial Microbiology [*Elsevier Book Series*] [*A publication*]
PIM .... Provincial Institute of Mining
PIM .... Pulse Intensity Modulation
PIM .... Pulse Interval Modulation
PIM .... Putnam Master Intermediate Income Trust [*NYSE symbol*] (SPSG)
PIM .... South Mountain Restoration Center, South Mountain, PA [*OCLC symbol*] (OCLC)
PiMA .... Ateneo de Manila University, Manila, Philippines [*Library symbol*] [*Library of Congress*] (LCLS)
PIMA .... Paper Industry Management Association (EA)
PIMA .... Plug-In Module Assembly (MCD)

PIMA......... Polyisocyanurate Insulation Manufacturers Association (EA)
PIMA......... Prime Intermediate Maintenance Activity
PIMA......... Professional Insurance Mass-Marketing Association [*Bethesda, MD*] (EA)
PIMA Mag ... PIMA [*Paper Industry Management Association*] Magazine [*United States*] [*A publication*]
PIMA Yrb ... PIMA [*Paper Industry Management Association*] Yearbook [*A publication*]
PIMBel...... Pracy Instytuta Movaznaustva Akademii Nauk Belaruskaj SSR [*A publication*]
PIMCC...... Packards International Motor Car Club (EA)
PIMCO...... Poultry Industry Manufacturers Council [*Defunct*] (EA)
PIME........ Petrofi Irodalmi Muzeum Evkonyve [*A publication*]
PIME........ Pontifical Institute for Mission Extension [*Roman Catholic men's religious order*]
PIMGA...... Production and Inventory Management [*A publication*]
PIMI........ Preinactivation Material Inspection [*Military*] (NVT)
PIMIA....... Potentiometric Ionophore Modulated Immunoassay [*Electrochemistry*]
PIMIS....... Portable Integrated Maintenance Information System
PIMK........ Portable Injection Molding Kit
PIMMA..... Professional Insurance Mass-Marketing Association [*Bethesda, MD*] (EA)
PIMNY..... Printing Industries of Metropolitan New York
PIMO .... Presentation of Information for Maintenance and Operation [*DoD*]
PIMOS...... Parallel Inference Multiprocessor Operating System [*Data processing*]
PIMP........ Permissible Individual Maximum Pressure (SAA)
PIMP........ Peroxisomal Integral Membrane Protein [*Biochemistry*]
PIMP........ Pimperne [*England*]
PIMR........ International Migration Review. IMR [*A publication*]
PIMRA...... Pirmasens Missile Repair Activity [*Germany*] [*Army*]
PIMRA...... Progress in Industrial Microbiology [*A publication*]
PIMS........ Peacekeeper in Minuteman Silos (DWSG)
PIMS........ Personnel Inventory Management System [*AT & T*]
PIMS........ Photoionization Mass Spectrometry
PIMS........ Profit Impact of Marketing Strategy
PIMS........ Programmable Implantable Medication System
PIMSA ...... Prensa Independiente Mexicana Sociedad Anonima [*Press agency*] [*Mexico*]
PIMSST .... Pontifical Institute of Mediaeval Studies. Studies and Texts [*A publication*]
PIMST ...... Pontifical Institute of Mediaeval Studies. Studies and Texts [*A publication*]
PIMTB ...... Proceedings. Annual Technical Meeting. International Metallographic Society, Inc. [*A publication*]
Pim Ten ..... Pim on Feudal Tenures [*A publication*] (DLA)
Pi Mu Epsilon J ... Pi Mu Epsilon Journal [*A publication*]
PIMV......... Plantago Mottle Virus [*Plant pathology*]
PIN .... Jasper, TX [*Location identifier*] [*FAA*] (FAAL)
PIN .... P-Type Intrinsic N-Type [*or Positive-Intrinsic-Negative*]
PIN .... Page and Item Number
PIN .... Parallel Input
PIN .... Patriots Information Network (EA)
PIN .... Pennsylvania School for the Deaf, Philadelphia, PA [*OCLC symbol*] (OCLC)
PIN .... People in Need [*Food program sponsored by family of kidnapped heiress, Patricia Hearst, 1974*]
PIN .... Personal [*or Private*] Identification Number [*Banking*]
PIN .... Personal Information Network [*Indesys, Inc.*] [*Telecommunications service*] (TSSD)
PIN .... Personal Injury Notice (AAG)
PIN .... Piece Identification Number
PIN .... Pinedale [*Wyoming*] [*Seismograph station code, US Geological Survey*] [*Closed*] (SEIS)
PIN .... Pinion (MSA)
Pin............ Pinney's Wisconsin Supreme Court Reports [*1839-52*] [*A publication*] (DLA)
PIN .... Plan Identification Number (AFM)
PIN .... Plant Information Network [*Fish and Wildlife Service*] [*Ceased operation*] (IID)
PIN .... Plastics Industry Notes [*Later, CIN*]
PIN .... Police Information Network [*San Francisco Bay area, California*]
PIN .... Policy Review [*A publication*]
PIN .... Position Indicator
PIN .... Positive-Intrinsic-Negative [*or P-Type Intrinsic N-Type*]
PIN .... Preliminary Imagery Nomination File (MCD)
PIN .... Product Identification Number
PIN .... Product Information Network [*McGraw-Hill Information Systems Co.*] [*Information service or system*] (IID)
PIN .... Program Identification Number (MUGU)
PIN .... Program Integrated Network
PIN .... Property Inheritance Network Computer
PIN .... Proposal Identification Number (AAG)
PIN .... PSI Resources [*NYSE symbol*] (SPSS)
PIN .... Public Interest [*A publication*]
PIN .... Publication Identification Number [*Military*] (INF)
PINA .... International Affairs [*A publication*]
PINA .... Parallax in Altitude [*Navigation*]

PINA .... Parenting in a Nuclear Age (EA)
PINA .... Potash Institute of North America [*Later, PPI*] (EA)
PINC......... Property Income Certificate [*Investment term*] [*British*]
PINCCA .... Price Index Numbers for Current Cost Accounting [*Service in Information and Analysis*] [*British*] [*Information service or system*] (IID)
PIND .... Particle Impact Noise Detection
Pind......... Pindar [*518-438BC*] [*Classical studies*] (OCD)
PINE........ Passive Infrared Night Equipment (MCD)
Pineal Res Rev ... Pineal Research Reviews [*A publication*]
Pineapple Q ... Pineapple Quarterly [*A publication*]
PINEDV..... Annual Research Reviews. Pineal [*A publication*]
Pine Inst Am Abstr Chem Sect ... Pine Institute of America. Abstracts. Chemical Section [*A publication*]
Pine Inst Am Tech Bull ... Pine Institute of America. Technical Bulletin [*A publication*]
Pinell.......... [*Arius*] Pinellus [*Flourished, 1544-59*] [*Authority cited in pre-1607 legal work*] (DSA)
PINES .... Public Information on Nuclear Energy Service [*American Nuclear Society*]
PING .... Packet Internet Groper [*Computer program*] (PCM)
Ping Chat Mortg ... Pingrey's Treatise of Chattel Mortgages [*A publication*] (DLA)
PINGP....... Prairie Island Nuclear Generating Plant (NRCH)
PINH .... Health [*San Francisco*] [*A publication*]
PINH .... In Health [*A publication*]
PINH .... Pyridoxal Isonicotinoylhydrazone [*Biochemistry*]
PINHA3 .... Iraq Natural History Museum. Publication [*A publication*]
PINN .... Pinnacles National Monument
Pinn........... Pinney's Wisconsin Reports [*A publication*] (DLA)
PINN .... Proposed International Nonproprietary Name [*Drug research*]
Pinney .... Pinney's Wisconsin Reports [*A publication*] (DLA)
Pinney (sv) ... Pinney's Wisconsin Reports [*A publication*] (DLA)
PINO .... Positive Input - Negative Output [*Data processing*]
PINQ .... Inquiry [*A publication*]
PINS......... Personnel Information System [*Army*] (AABC)
PINS......... Persons in Need of Supervision [*Classification for delinquent children*]
PINS......... Point-in-Space (MCD)
PINS......... Political Information System [*Databank of political strategist Richard Wirthlin*]
PINS......... Portable Inertial Navigation System
PINS......... Precise Integrated Navigation System [*Offshore Systems of Vancouver*]
PINSAC .... PINS [*Portable Inertial Navigation System*] Alignment Console
PINSTD .... Preinserted
PINT........ Pioneer International Corp. [*NASDAQ symbol*] (NQ)
PINT........ Power Intelligence (DNAB)
PINT........ Purdue Interpretive Programming and Operating System (MCD)
Pint Acabados Ind ... Pinturas y Acabados Industriales [*A publication*]
PINTS .... Ported-Coax Intrusion Sensor [*Military*] (INF)
PInU .... Indiana University of Pennsylvania, Indiana, PA [*Library symbol*] [*Library of Congress*] (LCLS)
Pin (Wis).... Pinney's Wisconsin Reports [*A publication*] (DLA)
Pin Wis R... Pinney's Wisconsin Reports [*A publication*] (DLA)
PinWst .... Pinnacle West Capital Corp. [*Associated Press abbreviation*] (APAG)
PINX......... Pinxit [*He, or She, Painted It*] [*Latin*]
PINXT....... Pinxit [*He, or She, Painted It*] [*Latin*] (ROG)
PINY........ Polytechnic Institute of New York
PIO .... Palestine Information Office (EA)
PIO .... Parallel Input/Output
PIO .... Pheniminooxazolidinone [*Pharmacology*]
PIO .... Photo Interpretation Officer [*Air Force*]
PIO .... Pi Omicron National Sorority (EA)
PIO .... Pielago [*Ship's rigging*] (ROG)
PIO .... Pilot-Induced Oscillation
PIO .... Pilot Information Office
PIO .... Pinon, NM [*Location identifier*] [*FAA*] (FAAL)
PIO .... Pioneer Airlines, Inc. [*Denver, CO*] [*FAA designator*] (FAAC)
PIO .... Pioneer Electronic Corp. [*NYSE symbol*] (SPSS)
PIO .... Poets International Organisation [*Bangalore, India*] (EAIO)
PIO .... Position Iterative Operation
PIO .... Precision Interactive Operation [*Data processing*]
PIO .... Preliminary Inquiry Officer (DNAB)
PIO .... Private Input/Output [*Telecommunications*] (TEL)
PIO .... Processor Input-Output [*Data processing*] (MDG)
PIO .... Programmed Input/Output
PIO .... Provisioned Item Order (MCD)
PIO .... Public Information Office [*or Officer*]
PIO .... Western Pennsylvania School for the Deaf, Pittsburgh, PA [*OCLC symbol*] (OCLC)
PIOCA...... Progress in Inorganic Chemistry [*A publication*]
PIOCS .... Physical Input-Output Control System [*Data processing*] (BUR)
PIODCA.... Peruvian Inca Orchid Dog Club of America (EA)
PIOG .... [*The*] Pioneer Group, Inc. [*NASDAQ symbol*] (NQ)
PION .... Pioneer (AABC)
PION .... Pioneer Finance Corp. [*NASDAQ symbol*] (NQ)

Pioneering Concepts Mod Sci ... Pioneering Concepts in Modern Science [*A publication*]

Pioneers' Assoc of SA Pubs ... Pioneers' Association of South Australia. Publications [*A publication*] (APTA)

PionF .... Pioneer Financial Services, Inc. [*Associated Press abbreviation*] (APAG)

PionFS .... Pioneer Financial Services, Inc. [*Associated Press abbreviation*] (APAG)

PionrEl....... Pioneer Electronic Corp. [*Associated Press abbreviation*] (APAG)

PIOP.......... Pharmacists in Ophthalmic Practice (EA)

PIOPED .... Prospective Investigation of Pulmonary Embolism Diagnosis [*Medicine*]

PIOPIC ..... Protection and Indemnity of Oil Pollution Indemnity Clause [*Insurance*] (DS)

PIOR.......... International Organization [*A publication*]

PIOS.......... Pioneer-Standard Electronics, Inc. [*NASDAQ symbol*] (NQ)

PIOSA .... Pan-Indian Ocean Science Association (NOAA)

PIOTA....... Post-Irradiation Open Test Assembly [*Nuclear energy*] (NRCH)

PIOTA....... Proximity Instrumented Open Test Assembly [*Nuclear energy*] (NRCH)

PIOU .... Parallel Input-Output Unit [*Data processing*] (IEEE)

PIOUS....... Peripheral Integrated Off-Line Utility System (SAA)

PIP............ Pan-Iranist Party [*Political party*] (PPW)

PIP............ Paper Impact Printing (HGAA)

PIP............ Para-Isothiocyanatephenethylamine [*Biochemistry*]

PIP............ Participant Instrumentation Package (MCD)

PIP............ Participating Irredeemable Preference [*Shares*]

PIP............ Partido Independentista Puertorriqueno [*Puerto Rican Independence Party*] [*Political party*] (PPW)

PIP............ Partners in Progress [*Government*] [*Civil rights*]

PIP............ Pasuquin [*Philippines*] [*Seismograph station code, US Geological Survey*] (SEIS)

PIP............ Path Independent Protocol

PIP............ Payload Integration Plan [*NASA*] (NASA)

PIP............ Payload Interface Plan [*NASA*] (NASA)

PIP............ Payment in Part [*Business term*]

PIP............ Penny Illustrated Paper [*A publication*]

PIP............ Periodic Interim Payment Program [*Medicare*] (GFGA)

PIP............ Peripheral Interchange Program [*Data processing*]

PIP............ Peripheral Interface Programmer [*Circuit*] [*Data processing*]

PIP............ Persistent Internal Polarization

PIP............ Personal Identification Project [*Data processing*]

PIP............ Personal Injury Protection [*Insurance*]

PIP............ Personal Innovation Program

PIP............ Personnel Interface Processor (MCD)

PIP............ Petroleum Incentives Program [*Canada*]

PIP............ Phosphatidylinositol Phosphate [*Biochemistry*]

PIP............ Photo Image Processor (MCD)

PIP............ Photo Interpretive Program (BUR)

PIP............ Picture-in-a-Picture [*Multi-Vision Products*] [*Video technology*]

PIP............ Pilot Point [*Alaska*] [*Airport symbol*] (OAG)

PIP............ Piperacillin [*An antibiotic*]

PIP............ Plant Instrumentation Program

PIP............ Plant-in-Place

PIP............ Policy Improvement Program

PIPER........ Policy Integration Program

PIP............ Population Information Program [*Later, CCP*] (EA)

PIP............ Portable Instrumentation Package [*Military*] (CAAL)

PIP............ Position Indicating Probe (IEEE)

PIP............ Postal Instant Press [*AMEX symbol*] (SPSG)

PIP............ Power Input Panel

PIP............ Prearrival Inspection Procedure

PIP............ Precise Installation Position

PIP............ Predicted Impact Point [*Aerospace*] (AAG)

PIP............ Predicted Intercept Point

PIP............ Preliminary Information Pamphlet

PIP............ Preparatory Investment Protection [*For the consortia which invested in deep sea mining*]

PIP............ Preparedness and Industrial Planning

PIP............ Pretty Important Person

PIP............ Primary Indicating Position Data Logger (IEEE)

PIP............ Prior Immobilization and Positioning [*Roentgenology*]

PIP............ Probabilistic Information Processing

PIP............ Problem Identification Program (MCD)

PIP............ Problem Input Preparation [*Data processing*] (BUR)

PIP............ Procedural Information Pamphlet

PIP............ Proceedings in Print [*A bibliographic publication*]

PIP............ Product Improvement (MCD)

PIP............ Product Improvement Plan

PIP............ Product Improvement Program [*Military*]

PIP............ Product Improvement Program [*A publication*]

PIP............ Product Improvement Proposal (MCD)

PIP............ Product Introductory Presentation

PIP............ Production Implementation Program (AAG)

PIP............ Production Improvement Program [*Navy*] (NG)

PIP............ Production Instrumentation Package (NASA)

PIP............ Productivity Improvement Program [*Department of Labor*]

PIP............ Productivity Improvement Program [*Office of Management and Budget*] (GFGA)

PIP............ Profile Ignition Pick-Up [*Automotive engineering*]

PIP............ Profit Improvement Program

PIP............ Program Implementation Plan (MCD)

PIP............ Program Integration Plan

PIP............ Program in Process [*Data processing*] (BUR)

PIP............ Programmable Integrated Processor (IEEE)

PIP............ Programmable Interconnect Point [*Data processing*]

PIP............ Programs for the Improvement of Practice [*Washington, DC*] [*Department of Education*] (GRD)

PIP............ Progressive Independent Party [*South Africa*] [*Political party*] (EY)

PIP............ Progressive Inspection Plan [*Navy*] (NG)

PIP............ Project Implementation Plan

PIP............ Project on Information Processing (IEEE)

PIP............ Project Initiation Period

PIP............ Project Instrumentation Plan [*NASA*] (GFGA)

PIP............ Projected Impact Point [*Aviation*]

PIP............ Proof in Print

PIP............ Proposal Instruction Package (MCD)

PIP............ Proprietary Information Protection

PIP............ Prototypic Inlet Piping [*Nuclear energy*] (NRCH)

PIP............ Prove in Plan (MCD)

PIP............ Proximal Interphalangeal [*Joint*]

PIP............ Psychotic Inpatient Profile [*Psychology*]

PIP............ Public and Institutional Property [*Insurance*]

PIP............ Puerto Rican Independence Party [*Political party*] (PD)

PIP............ Pulse Input Proportional [*Electro-optical system*]

PIP............ Pulse Integrating Pendulum

PIP............ Western Psychiatric Institute and Clinic, University of Pittsburgh, Pittsburgh, PA [*OCLC symbol*] (OCLC)

PIPA .... Pacific Industrial Property Association (EA)

PIPA .... Pulse Integrating Pendulum Accelerometer

PIPA .... Pulse Integrating Pendulum Assembly (NASA)

PIPACE..... Peacetime Intelligence Plan, Allied Central Europe [*NATO*]

Pip & C Mil L ... Pipon and Collier's Military Law [*3rd ed.*] [*1865*] [*A publication*] (DLA)

PIPCST ..... Piping Cost and Weight Analysis Program (DNAB)

PIPE .... IPM, Inc. [*NASDAQ symbol*] (NQ)

PIPE .... Pipeline. Report of the Northern Pipeline Agency [*A publication*]

PIPE .... Pipestone National Monument

PIPE .... Plumbing Industry Progress and Education Fund

PIPECO .... Photoion-Photoelectron Coincidence [*Spectroscopy*]

Pipeline Contractors Assoc Can ... Pipeline Contractors Association of Canada [*A publication*]

Pipe Line D ... Pipeline Annual Directory and Equipment Guide [*A publication*]

Pipeline Eng ... Pipeline Engineer [*A publication*]

Pipeline Gas J ... Pipeline and Gas Journal [*A publication*]

Pipe Line Ind ... Pipe Line Industry [*A publication*]

Pipeline Manage Oper Eng Gas Distrib News ... Pipeline Management, Operations, Engineering, and Gas Distribution News [*A publication*]

Pipeline Underground Util Constr ... Pipeline and Underground Utilities Construction [*A publication*]

Pipeln Ind .. International Pipe Line Industry [*A publication*]

PIPER........ Pulsed Intense Plasma for Exploratory Research

PIPES........ Piperazinediethanesulfonic Acid [*A buffer*]

PIPES........ Program on International Politics, Economics, and Security [*University of Chicago*]

Pipes Pipelines Int ... Pipes and Pipelines International [*A publication*]

PIPICO ..... Panel on International Programs and International Cooperation in Oceans Affairs [*Department of State*] (NOAA)

PIPIDA ..... Para-Isopropylphenyl(iminodiacetic Acid)

Piping Eng ... Piping Engineering [*A publication*]

Piping Process Mach (Tokyo) ... Piping and Process Machinery (Tokyo) [*A publication*]

PIPJ.......... Proximal Interphalangeal Joint [*Anatomy*]

PIPLC .... Phosphatidylinositol-Specific Phospholipase C [*Biochemistry*]

PIPLD .... Proceedings. Indian Academy of Sciences. Series Plant Sciences [*A publication*]

PIPO .... Parallel-In Parallel-Out [*Telecommunications*] (TEL)

PIPO .... Phase-In, Phase-Out (MCD)

PIPPAP..... Pile for Producing Power and Plutonium [*Nuclear energy*] (NRCH)

PIPPS........ Publication Information Processing and Printing System

Pippy.......... Person Inheriting Parents' Property [*Lifestyle classification*] [*British*]

PIPR .... International Journal for Philosophy of Religion [*A publication*]

PIPR .... Piper Jaffray, Inc. [*Minneapolis, MN*] [*NASDAQ symbol*] (NQ)

PIPR .... Plant-in-Place Records

PIPR .... Polytechnic Institute of Puerto Rico

PIPR .... Public Interest Public Relations (EA)

PiprJf.......... Piper Jaffray, Inc. [*Minneapolis, MN*] (APAG)

PIPS.......... Paperless Item Processing System [*Banking*]

PIPS.......... Patient-Identified Physicians Survey [*Department of Health and Human Services*] (GFGA)

PIPS.......... Pattern Information Processing System

PIPS.......... Peabody Intellectual Performance Scale [*Education*]
PIPS.......... Postinjection Propulsion Subsystem [*NASA*]
PIPS.......... Preschool Interpersonal Problem Solving Test
PIPS.......... Professional Institute of the Public Service of Canada [*See also IPFP*]
PIPS.......... Properties of Irregular Parts System   (MCD)
PIPS.......... Science and Technology Policies Information Exchange Programme [*Superseded by SPINES*] [*UNESCO*] [*Information service or system*]   (IID)
PIPSAR..... Pipe Sizing Program - Air   (DNAB)
PIPSCR..... Philippine Islands Public Service Commission Reports [*A publication*]   (DLA)
PIPSD........ Preprint. Institut Prikladnoi Matematiki Akademii Nauk SSSR [*A publication*]
PIPSPK..... Pipe Sizing Program - Sprinkling   (DNAB)
PIPSST...... Pipe Sizing Program - Steam   (DNAB)
PIPUCR.... Philippine Islands Public Utility Commission Reports [*A publication*]   (DLA)
PIPWA...... Paper Industry and Paper World [*A publication*]
PIPYDX.... Proceedings. International Colloquium on Invertebrate Pathology [*A publication*]
PIQ .... Parallel Instruction Queue
PIQ .... Program Idea Quotient [*Study to determine audience receptivity to new TV program*]
PIQ .... Property in Question
PIQ .... State Regional Correctional Facility at Mercer, Mercer, PA [*OCLC symbol*]   (OCLC)
PIQA .... Proofing, Inspection, and Quality Assurance [*Military*]
PIQSY ...... Probes for the International Quiet Solar Year [*OSS*]
PIQUA ...... Pit and Quarry [*A publication*]
PIR .... Packaging Information Record   (MCD)
PIR............. Parachute Infantry Regiment [*Military*]
PIR............. Paragnostic Information Retrieval [*Parapsychology*]
PIR............. Partido de la Izquierda Revolucionaria [*Party of the Revolutionary Left*] [*Bolivia*] [*Political party*]   (PPW)
PIR............. Past in Review   (EA)
PIR............. Peak Intensity Ratio [*Spectroscopy*]
PiR............. Pecat' i Revoljucija [*A publication*]
PIR............. Pennsylvania International Raceway [*Auto racing*]
PIR............. Pennsylvania Rehabilitation Center, Johnstown, PA [*OCLC symbol*]   (OCLC)
PIR............. Periodic Incremental Release [*Physiology*]
PIR............. Periodic Intelligence Report
PIR............. Periodic Intelligence Review [*Supreme Allied Commander, Atlantic*]   (NATG)
PIR............. Personal Interview Record
PIR............. Personnel Information Roster [*Military*]
PIR............. Pesticide Ingredient Review Program [*Chemical Specialties Manufacturers Association*]
PIR............. Petrolite Irradiation Reactor
PIR............. Philippine Independence Ribbon [*Military decoration*]
PIR............. Phoenix International Raceway
PIR............. Photo Interpretation Report [*Air Force*]   (AFM)
PIR............. Photographic Intelligence Report [*Military*]
PIR............. Pier 1 Imports [*NYSE symbol*]   (SPSG)
PIR............. Pierre [*South Dakota*] [*Airport symbol*]   (OAG)
PIR............. Pilot Request   (SAA)
PIR............. Pirmasens [*Federal Republic of Germany*] [*Seismograph station code, US Geological Survey*]   (SEIS)
PIR............. Plug-In Relay
PIR............. Postinhibitory Rebound [*Physiology*]
PIR............. Precision Instrument Runway [*Aviation*]   (FAAC)
PIR............. Precision Instrumentation RADAR
PIR............. Predicted Intercept Range [*Military*]   (CAAL)
PIR............. Pressure Ignition Rocket   (NATG)
PIR............. Primary Intelligence Requirement [*Military*]   (INF)
PIR............. Priority Information Requirement [*Military intelligence*]   (INF)
PIR............. Priority Intelligence Requirement [*Military*]   (INF)
PIR............. Process and Indoctrinate Recruits
PIR............. Procurement Initiation Request   (MCD)
PIR............. Product Improvement Review
PIR............. Product Information Release
PIR............. Production Inspection Record
PIR............. Professional Investor Report [*A publication*]   (IT)
PIR............. Program Incident Report
PIR............. Program Information Report [*Head Start Program*] [*Department of Health and Human Services*]   (GFGA)
PIR............. Project Independence Report
PIR............. Prosopographia Imperii Romani [*A publication*]
PIR............. Protein Identification Resource [*National Biomedical Research Foundation*] [*Georgetown University Medical Center*] [*Information service or system*]   (IID)
PIR............. Protocol-Independent Routing [*Data processing*]
PIR............. Pure India Rubber [*Cables*]
PIRA.......... Prison Industries Reorganization Administration [*Terminated, 1940*]
PIRA.......... Provisional Irish Republican Army
PIRAD....... Proximity Information, Range, and Disposition
PIRAI .... PIRA International [*British*]   (EAIO)
PIRA Packag Abstr ... PIRA [*Printing Industry Research Association*] Packaging Abstracts [*A publication*]

PIRAZ....... Positive Identification RADAR Advisory Zone   (NVT)
PIRB.......... Position Indicating Radio Beacon
PIRC.......... Pier 1 Imports, Inc. [*NASDAQ symbol*]   (NQ)
PIRC.......... Portable Inflatable Recompression Chamber   (MCD)
PIRC.......... Preventive Intervention Research Center for Child Health [*Yeshiva University*] [*Research center*]   (RCD)
PIRCS....... Passive Infrared Confirming Sensor   (MCD)
PIRD.......... Program Instrumentation Requirements Document [*NASA*]
PIRE .... Pacific Institute for Research and Evaluation [*Research center*]   (RCD)
PIRED .... Power Industry Research [*A publication*]
PI Rep .... Philippine Island Reports [*A publication*]   (DLA)
PIREP....... Pilot Report [*Pertaining to meteorological conditions*] [*FAA*]
PIRF .... Perimeter-Insulated Raised Floor [*Residential construction*]
PIRFC .... Pilot Requests Forecast   (FAAC)
PIRG......... Public Interest Research Group [*Formed by consumer-advocate Ralph Nader*]
P-IRI .... Plasma Immunoreactive Insulin [*Hematology*]   (MAE)
PIRI .... Psychologists Interested in Religious Issues   (EA)
PIRID .... Passive Infrared Intrusion Detector   (NVT)
PIRINC ..... Petroleum Industry Research Foundation   (EA)
PIRM......... International Review of Mission [*A publication*]
PIRN......... Preliminary Interface Revision Notice [*NASA*]   (KSC)
PIRO......... People, Ideas, Resources, Objectives [*Management strategy*]   (DHSM)
PIRO......... Pictured Rocks National Lakeshore [*National Park Service designation*]
PIRP .... Provisional International Reference Preparation
PIRR .... Parts Installation and Removal Record [*NASA*]   (KSC)
PIRR .... Prepositioned War Reserve Interrogation and Readiness Reporting   (MCD)
PIRR .... Problem Investigation and Repair Record [*NASA*]   (KSC)
PIRR .... PWRS [*Prepositioned War Reserve Stock*] Interrogation and Readiness Reporting System [*Navy*]
PIRRB ...... Photo Intelligence Requirements Review Board [*Military*]
PIRS .... Passive Infrared Seeker
PIRS .... Personal Information Retrieval System
PIRS .... Perspectives in Religious Studies [*A publication*]
PIRS .... Philosopher's Information Retrieval System [*Bowling Green State University*]
PIRS .... Pollution Incident Reporting System [*Coast Guard*]
PIRS .... Poseidon Information Retrieval System [*Missiles*]
PIRS .... Project Information Retrieval System [*HEW*]
PIRT .... Precision Infrared Tracking
PIRT .... Precision Infrared Triangulation
PIRT .... Pretreatment Implementation Review Task Force [*Environmental Protection Agency*]   (EPA)
PIRU .... Public Information Reference Unit [*Environmental Protection Agency*]   (GFGA)
Pis .... In Pisonem [*of Cicero*] [*Classical studies*]   (OCD)
PIS .... Parts Identification Service
PIS .... Passenger Information System
PIS .... Passive Infrared System
PIS .... Photographic Interpretation Section
PIS .... Pisa [*Italy*] [*Seismograph station code, US Geological Survey*] [*Closed*]   (SEIS)
PIS .... Piscivorous
PIS .... Poitiers [*France*] [*Airport symbol*]   (OAG)
PIS .... Position Indicator System
PIS .... Positive Ion Source
PIS .... Postal Inspection Service
PIS .... Preinfarction Syndrome [*Cardiology*]
PIS .... Preinsert Sequencing
PIS .... Pressure-Indicating Switch [*Nuclear energy*]   (NRCH)
PIS .... Process Instrument Sheet
PIS .... Process Instrumentation System [*Nuclear energy*]   (NRCH)
PIS .... Product Information Specialist
PIS .... Provisional International Standard
PIS .... Pulse Integration System
PIS .... Pulsed Illumination Source
PiS .... Puskin i Ego Sovremenniki [*A publication*]
PIS .... Stevens Trade School, Lancaster, PA [*OCLC symbol*]   (OCLC)
PISA .... Persistent Information Space Architecture [*Data processing*]
PISA .... Polish Independent Student Association   (EA)
PISA .... Public Interest Satellite Association [*Defunct*]   (EA)
PISAA7 ..... Indian Academy of Sciences. Proceedings. Section A [*A publication*]
PISAB........ Pulse Interference Separation and Blanking [*RADAR*]
PISAD .... Proceedings. International Symposium on Automotive Technology and Automation [*A publication*]
PISBAA..... Indian Academy of Sciences. Proceedings. Section B [*A publication*]
PISC .... Impact of Science on Society [*A publication*]
PISC .... Pacific International Services Corp. [*NASDAQ symbol*]   (NQ)
PISC .... Parris Island, South Carolina [*Marine Corps*]
PISC .... Petroleum Industry Security Council   (EA)
Pisc............ Pisces [*Constellation*]
PISE .... No Pilot Balloon Observation Due to Unfavorable Sea Conditions [*National Weather Service*]   (FAAC)

PISEAJ ..... Proceedings. Research Institute of Pomology [*Skierniewice, Poland*]. Series E. Conferences and Symposia [*A publication*]
PISG .... Pitcairn Islands Study Group (EA)
PISGA .... Palestinian Interim Self-Government Authority [*Proposed*] (ECON)
PISH .... Program Instrumentation Summary Handbook [*NASA*] (KSC)
Pishch Pererabatyvayushchaya Promst ... Pishchevaya i Pererabatyvayushchaya Promyshlenost' [*A publication*]
Pishch Prom Kaz ... Pishchevaya Promyshlennost Kazakhstana [*A publication*]
Pishch Prom-St (Kiev 1965) ... Pishchevaya Promyshlennost (Kiev, 1965) [*A publication*]
Pishch Promst (Moscow) ... Pishchevaya Promyshlennost (Moscow) [*A publication*]
Pishch Promst Ser 6 Obz Inf ... Pishchevaya Promyshlennost. Seriya 6. Maslo-Zhirovaya Promyshlennost. Obzornaya Informatsiya [*A publication*]
Pishch Promst Ser 20 Obz Inf ... Pishchevaya Promyshlennost. Seriya 20. Maslo-Zhirovaya Promyshlennost. Obzornaya Informatsiya [*A publication*]
Pishch Promst SSSR ... Pishchevaya Promyshlennost SSSR [*A publication*]
Pism Pam Vostoka ... Pis'mennye Pamiatniki Vostoka [*A publication*]
PISMV ...... Plantago Severe Mottle Virus [*Plant pathology*]
PISO .... Parallel-In Serial-Out [*Telecommunications*] (TEL)
PISP .... Pipe Springs National Monument
PISQ .... International Studies Quarterly [*A publication*]
PISSC .... Programme International sur la Securite des Substances Chimiques [*International Programme on Chemical Safety*] (EAIO)
PIST .... Piston [*Automotive engineering*]
Pist .... Piston's Mauritius Reports [*A publication*] (DLA)
Piston .... Piston's Mauritius Reports [*A publication*] (DLA)
PISU .... Polyimidesulfone [*Organic chemistry*]
PISUKI ..... Pacific Islands Society of the United Kingdom and Ireland (EAIO)
PISW .... Journal of Interamerican Studies and World Affairs [*A publication*]
PISW .... Process Interrupt Status Word
PIT .... Pacific Investment Trust [*Finance*] [*British*]
PI/T .... Parallel Interface/Timer [*Motorola, Inc.*]
PIT .... Part-Time, Intermittent, Temporary [*Nuclear energy*]
PIT .... Parti de l'Independance et du Travail [*Party of Independence and Labor*] [*Senegal*] [*Political party*] (PPW)
PIT .... Parti Ivoirien des Travailleurs [*Ivorian Workers' Party*] [*The Ivory Coast*] [*Political party*] (EY)
PIT .... Partners in Transition [*Poland, Czechoslovakia, and Hungary*] (ECON)
PIT .... Passive Integrated Transponder
PIT .... Performance Improvement Tests
PIT .... Peripheral Input Tape [*Data processing*]
PIT .... Peripheral Interface Tests (MCD)
PIT .... Permanent Income Theory [*Econometrics*]
PIT .... Personal Income Tax
PIT .... Phase Inversion Temperature [*Physical Chemistry*]
PIT .... Photographic Interpretation Technique
PIT .... Picture Identification Test [*Psychology*]
PIT .... Picture Impressions Test [*Psychology*]
PIT .... Pilot Instructor Training [*Aviation*] (FAAC)
PIT .... Pirates Gold Corp. [*Vancouver Stock Exchange symbol*]
Pit .... Pitocin [*Trademark of Parke, Davis & Co. for Oxytocin, a labor-inducing drug*]
Pit .... Pitressin [*Trademark of Parke, Davis & Co. for Vasopressin, an antidiuretic hormone*]
PIT .... Pittsburgh [*Pennsylvania*] [*Seismograph station code, US Geological Survey*] [*Closed*] (SEIS)
PIT .... Pittsburgh [*Pennsylvania*] [*Airport symbol*]
PIT .... Pituitary [*Endocrinology*] (AAMN)
PIT .... Plasma Iron Transport [*Hematology*]
PIT .... Polar Ionospheric Trough
PIT .... Polaris Industrial Team [*Missiles*]
PIT .... Pre-Induction Training
PIT .... Preinstallation Test [*NASA*] (KSC)
PIT .... Prevailing-In Torque [*Automotive engineering*]
PIT .... Print Illegal and Trace
PIT .... Processing of Indexing Terms
PIT .... Product Improvement Test
PIT .... Program Instruction Tape [*Data processing*] (IEEE)
PIT .... Programmable Interval Timer
PIT .... Programmed Instruction Text
PIT .... Projected Inactive Time [*Data processing*]
PIT .... Provincial Institute of Textiles
PIT .... Psychological Insight Test [*Psychometrics*]
PIT .... University of Pittsburgh, Pittsburgh, PA [*OCLC symbol*] (OCLC)
PITA .... Pacific International Trapshooting Association (EA)
PITA .... Paper Industry Technical Association [*British*] (EAIO)
PITA .... Provincial Institute of Technology and Art
Pitanie Udobr Rast ... Pitanie i Udobrenie Rastenii [*A publication*]
PITB .... Pacific Inland Tariff Bureau

PITB .... PUSH [*People United to Save Humanity*] International Trade Bureau (EA)
PITBB .... Piano Teachers Journal [*A publication*]
Pitblado Lect ... Isaac Pitblado Lectures on Continuing Legal Education [*A publication*]
Pitblado Lect ... Isaac Pitblado's Lectures on Continuing Legal Education [*A publication*] (DLA)
PITC .... Phenylisothiocyanate [*Organic chemistry*]
PITC .... Photoinduced Tunnel Current
Pitc .... Pitcairn's Criminal Trials [*1488-1624*] [*Scotland*] [*A publication*] (DLA)
Pitc Crim Tr ... Pitcairn's Ancient Criminal Trials [*Scotland*] [*A publication*] (DLA)
Pitch Pine Nat ... Pitch Pine Naturalist [*A publication*]
PITCOM ... Parliamentary Information Technology Committee [*Political communications*] [*British*]
Pitc Tr .... Pitcairn's Criminal Trials [*3 Scotland*] [*A publication*] (DLA)
PITDSM ... Pittsburgh-Des Moines, Inc. [*Associated Press abbreviation*] (APAG)
PITE .... Project on Information Technology and Education (EA)
PITG .... Payload Integration Task Group [*NASA*] (NASA)
PITI .... Principal, Interest, Taxes, Insurance [*Real estate*]
Pitisc Lex ... Pitisci's Lexicon [*A publication*] (DLA)
PITKA ...... Proceedings. Institut Teknologi Bandung. Supplement [*A publication*]
Pit L .... University of Pittsburgh. Law Review [*A publication*]
Pitm Prin & Sur ... Pitman on Principal and Surety [*A publication*] (DLA)
PITN .... Polyisothianaphthene [*Organic chemistry*]
PitnB .... Pitney-Bowes, Inc. [*Associated Press abbreviation*] (APAG)
PitnyB .... Pitney-Bowes, Inc. [*Associated Press abbreviation*] (APAG)
Pit & Quar ... Pit and Quarry [*A publication*]
Pit Quarry ... Pit and Quarry [*A publication*]
PITR .... Plasma Iron Transport [*or Turnover*] Rate [*Hematology*]
PITS .... Passive Intercept Tracking System
PITS .... Payload Integration Test Set [*NASA*] (MCD)
PITS .... Photoinduced Transient Spectroscopy
PITS .... Primary Influent Treatment System
PITS .... Project Information Tracking System [*Environmental Protection Agency*] (GFGA)
PITS .... Propellant Injector Tube Simulator (MCD)
PITS .... Propulsion Integration Test Stand
Pit Sur .... Pitman on Principal and Surety [*1840*] [*A publication*] (DLA)
Pitt .... Pittsburgh, PA (DLA)
PITT .... Polaris Integrated Test Team [*Missiles*]
Pitt Bank .... Pitt's Bankruptcy Acts [*A publication*] (DLA)
Pitt CC Pr .. Pitt's County Court Practice [*A publication*] (DLA)
Pitt LJ .... Pittsburgh Legal Journal [*A publication*] (DLA)
Pitt Rivers Mus Univ Oxford Occas Pap Technol ... Pitt Rivers Museum. University of Oxford. Occasional Papers on Technology [*A publication*]
Pitts .... Pittsburgh, PA (DLA)
Pitts .... Pittsburgh Reports [*A publication*] (DLA)
Pittsb .... Pittsburgh, PA (DLA)
Pittsb .... Pittsburgh Reports [*A publication*] (DLA)
Pittsb Bs T ... Pittsburgh Business Times-Journal [*A publication*]
Pittsbg Bs ... Pittsburgh Business Review [*A publication*]
Pittsbg P .... Pittsburgh Press [*A publication*]
Pittsb Leg J ... Pittsburgh Legal Journal [*Pennsylvania*] [*A publication*] (DLA)
Pittsb Leg J NS ... Pittsburgh Legal Journal, New Series [*Pennsylvania*] [*A publication*] (DLA)
Pittsb Leg J (OS) ... Pittsburgh Legal Journal, Old Series [*A publication*] (DLA)
Pittsb Leg J (PA) ... Pittsburgh Legal Journal [*Pennsylvania*] [*A publication*] (DLA)
Pittsb LJ .... Pittsburgh Legal Journal [*Pennsylvania*] [*A publication*] (DLA)
Pittsb L Rev ... Pittsburgh Law Review [*A publication*] (DLA)
Pittsb R (PA) ... Pittsburgh Reporter [*Pennsylvania*] [*A publication*] (DLA)
Pittsburgh Bus R ... Pittsburgh Business Review [*A publication*]
Pittsburgh Leg J ... Pittsburgh Legal Journal [*Pennsylvania*] [*A publication*] (DLA)
Pittsburgh Leg Journal ... Pittsburgh Legal Journal [*Pennsylvania*] [*A publication*] (DLA)
Pittsburgh Sch ... Pittsburgh Schools [*A publication*]
Pittsburgh Univ Bull ... Pittsburgh University. Bulletin [*A publication*]
Pittsburgh Univ Sch Ed J ... Pittsburgh University. School of Education Journal [*A publication*]
Pitts Leg J ... Pittsburgh Legal Journal [*Pennsylvania*] [*A publication*] (DLA)
Pitts Leg J (NS) ... Pittsburgh Legal Journal, New Series [*Pennsylvania*] [*A publication*] (DLA)
Pitts Leg Jour ... Pittsburgh Legal Journal [*Pennsylvania*] [*A publication*] (DLA)
Pitts LJ ...... Pittsburgh Legal Journal [*A publication*] (DLA)
Pitts LJ (NS) ... Pittsburgh Legal Journal, New Series [*A publication*] (DLA)
Pitts L Rev ... University of Pittsburgh. Law Review [*A publication*]
Pitts R .... Pittsburgh Reports [*Pennsylvania*] [*A publication*] (DLA)
Pitts Rep ..... Pittsburgh Reports [*A publication*] (DLA)
Pitts Rep (PA) ... Pittsburgh Reports [*Pennsylvania*] [*A publication*] (DLA)
Pittstn .... [*The*] Pittston Co. [*Associated Press abbreviation*] (APAG)

Pitt Sym ..... Pittsburgh Symphony Orchestra. Program Notes [*A publication*]
Pitture Vern ... Pitture e Vernici [*A publication*]
PITTWAY ... Pittway Corp. [*Associated Press abbreviation*] (APAG)
Pittwy .... Pittway Corp. [*Associated Press abbreviation*] (APAG)
PITU .... Pipe or Tubing [*Freight*]
PITWVA ... Pittsburgh & West Virginia Railroad [*Associated Press abbreviation*] (APAG)
PITY-EM .. Principal, Interest, Taxes, Energy, and Maintenance [*Real estate*]
PIU .... East Pennsylvania Psychiatric Institute, Philadelphia, PA [*OCLC symbol*] (OCLC)
PIU .... Path Information Unit [*Data processing*]
PIU .... Photographic Interpretation Unit [*Marine Corps*]
PIU .... Pilot Information Utilization
PIU .... Piura [*Peru*] [*Airport symbol*] (OAG)
PIU .... Plug-In Unit
PIU .... Polymerase-Inducing Unit
PIU .... Power Integration Unit (SSD)
PIU .... Power Intercept Unit [*Military*] (CAAL)
PIU .... Power Interface Unit (MCD)
PIU .... Private Islands Unlimited (EA)
PIU .... Process Input Unit [*Data processing*] (BUR)
PIU .... Process Interface Unit
PIU .... Programmer Interface Unit (MCD)
PIU .... Pyrotechnic Initiator Unit (MCD)
PiU .... University of the Philippines, Quezon City, Philippines [*Library symbol*] [*Library of Congress*] (LCLS)
PIUG .... Parti Independantiste de l'Unite Guyanaise [*Pro-Independence Party of Guyanese Unity*] [*Political party*] (PPW)
PIUMP ...... Plug-In Unit Mounting Panel
PIUS .... Process Inherent Ultimately Safe [*Nuclear reactor*]
PI/USA ..... Packaging Institute, United States of America [*Later, PI/INT'L*] (EA)
PIUT .... Paiute Oil & Mining [*NASDAQ symbol*] (NQ)
PIV .... Parainfluenza Virus
PIV .... Peak Inverse Voltage [*RADAR*]
PIV .... Piva [*Solomon Islands*] [*Seismograph station code, US Geological Survey*] [*Closed*] (SEIS)
PIV .... Pivot [*Automotive engineering*]
PIV .... Planet in View [*NASA*]
PIV .... Plug-In Valve
PIV .... Positive Infinitely Variable
PIV .... Post Indicator Valve
PIV .... Product Inspection Verification
PIV .... Propellant Isolation Valve
PIV .... Scotland School for Veterans' Children, Scotland, PA [*OCLC symbol*] (OCLC)
PIV4 .... Plantago Virus 4 [*Plant pathology*]
PIVAD ...... Product Improvement Vulcan Air Defense (MCD)
PIVADS ... Product Improved Vulcan Air Defense System (MCD)
PIVD .... Protruded Intervertebral Disc [*Medicine*]
PIVED .... Plasma-Injection Vacuum Energy Diverter
PIVKA ...... Protein in Vitamin K Absence (AAMN)
PIVN .... Public Interest Video Network/New Voices Radio (EA)
PIVOT ...... Planning and Implementing Vocational Readiness in Occupational Therapy
PIVS .... Particle-Induced Visual Sensations
PivS .... Pivnicne Sjajvo [*A publication*]
PIVT .... Production Improvement Verification Test
PIVX .... Plantain Virus X [*Plant pathology*]
PIW .... Period of Incapacity for Work (DI)
PIW .... Petroleum Intelligence Weekly [*A publication*]
PIW .... Plastic Insulated Wire
PIW -......... Polski Instytut Wydawniczy [*A publication*]
PIW .... Ports and Inland Waterways
PIW .... Program Interrupt Word
PIW .... Woodhaven Center, Philadelphia, PA [*OCLC symbol*] (OCLC)
PIWC .... Petroleum Industry War Council
PIWCA ..... Proceedings. International Waste Conference [*A publication*]
PIWG .... Product Improvement Working Group [*Military*] (AFIT)
PIWI .... No Pilot Balloon Observation Due to High, or Gusty, Surface Wind [*National Weather Service*] (FAAC)
PIWSD ...... Proceedings. International Wire and Cable Symposium [*A publication*]
PIWWC ..... Planetary Initiative for the World We Choose (EA)
PIX .... Pico Island [*Azores*] [*Airport symbol*] (OAG)
PIX .... Picture
PIX .... Picture Rocks, PA [*Location identifier*] [*FAA*] (FAAL)
PIX .... Pinxit [*He, or She, Painted It*] [*Latin*] (ROG)
PIX .... Proton-Induced X-Ray Analysis
PIX .... School Pictures, Inc. [*AMEX symbol*] (SPSG)
PIX .... Youth Development Center, Loysville, Loysville, PA [*OCLC symbol*] (OCLC)
Pix Aud ..... Pixley on Auditors [*8th ed.*] [*1901*] [*A publication*] (DLA)
PIXE .... Particle [*or Proton*]-Induced X-Ray Emission
PIXEL .... Picture Element [*Single element of resolution in image processing*]
PIY .... Pembroke Imperial Yeomanry [*British military*] (DMA)
PIY .... Youth Development Center, New Castle, New Castle, PA [*OCLC symbol*] (OCLC)

PIZ .... Point Lay [*Alaska*] [*Airport symbol*] (OAG)
PIZ .... Point Lay, AK [*Location identifier*] [*FAA*] (FAAL)
PIZ .... Youth Development Center, Waynesville, Waynesburg, PA [*OCLC symbol*] (OCLC)
PIZA .... National Pizza Co. [*NASDAQ symbol*] (NQ)
PIZZ .... Pizzicato [*Plucked*] [*Music*]
PJ .... Bombay High Court Printed Judgments [*1869-1900*] [*India*] [*A publication*] (DLA)
PJ .... ICC [*Interstate Commerce Commission*] Practitioners' Journal [*A publication*]
PJ .... Netherlands Antilles [*Aircraft nationality and registration mark*] (FAAC)
PJ .... Pajamas
PJ .... Palastinajahrbuch. Deutsches Evangelische Institut fuer Altertumswissenschaft des Heiligen Landes zu Jerusalem [*Berlin*] [*A publication*]
PJ .... Panel Jack
PJ .... Parnelli Jones [*Race car driver*]
PJ .... Parteijargon [*Party Language*] [*German*]
PJ .... Participating Jurisdiction
PJ .... Peregrine Air Services Ltd. [*Great Britain*] [*ICAO designator*] (FAAC)
PJ .... Peripheral Jet (AAG)
PJ .... Personnel Journal [*A publication*]
PJ .... Petajoule (ADA)
PJ .... Pharmaceutical Journal [*A publication*]
PJ .... Philosophisches Jahrbuch [*A publication*]
PJ .... Philosophisches Jahrbuch der Goerres-Gesellschaft [*A publication*]
PJ .... Picojoule [*Logic gate efficiency measure*] (MDG)
PJ .... Plasma Jet (AAG)
PJ .... Plastic Jacket
P & J .... Plaza y Janes [*Publisher*] [*Spain*]
PJ .... Police Justice
PJ .... Poradnik Jezykowy [*A publication*]
PJ .... Possible Jobs [*Test*] [*Psychology*]
PJ .... Presiding Judge
PJ .... Presiding Probate Judge [*British*] (ROG)
PJ .... Preussische Jahrbuecher [*A publication*]
PJ .... Prince of Jerusalem [*Freemasonry*]
PJ .... Privacy Journal [*A publication*]
PJ .... Probate Judge
PJ .... Procurement Justification [*Navy*]
PJ .... Project Jonah (EA)
PJ .... Prudhoe Bay Journal [*A publication*]
PJ .... Pulsejet
PJ .... Purchases Journal [*Accounting*]
PJ's .... Pajamas [*Slang*]
PJ's .... Paramedic Jumpers
PJ's .... Physical Jerks [*Exercise*] [*Slang*] [*British*] (DSUE)
PJA .... Abington Library Society, Jenkintown, PA [*Library symbol*] [*Library of Congress*] [*Obsolete*] (LCLS)
PJa .... Papers on Japan [*A publication*]
PJAA .... Journal. American Academy of Religion [*A publication*]
PJAC .... Journal of American Culture [*A publication*]
PJACA ...... Proceedings. Japan Academy [*A publication*]
PJAFC ...... P. J. Allman Fan Club (EA)
PJAH .... Journal of African History [*A publication*]
PJAIA .... Philippine Journal of Animal Industry [*A publication*]
PJAIG .... Alverthorpe Gallery, Rosenwald Collection, Jenkintown, PA [*Library symbol*] [*Library of Congress*] (LCLS)
P Jap Acad ... Proceedings. Japan Academy [*A publication*]
PJAR .... Journal of Anthropological Research [*A publication*]
PJAS .... Journal of Asian and African Studies [*A publication*]
PJAY .... Journal of Asian History [*A publication*]
PJB .... Pad Journal Bearing
PJB .... Palastinajahrbuch. Deutsches Evangelische Institut fuer Altertumswissenschaft des Heiligen Landes zu Jerusalem [*Berlin*] [*A publication*]
PJB .... Premature Junctional Beat [*Cardiology*]
PJb .... Preussische Jahrbuecher [*A publication*]
PJBD .... Permanent Joint Board on Defense [*US, Canada*]
PJBL .... Journal of Biblical Literature [*A publication*]
PJBS .... Journal of British Studies [*A publication*]
PJBSA .... Pavlovian Journal of Biological Science [*A publication*]
PJC .... Jean Coutu Group (PJC), Inc. [*Toronto Stock Exchange symbol*]
PJC .... Paducah Junior College [*Kentucky*]
PJC .... Paris Junior College [*Texas*]
PJC .... Pensacola Junior College [*Florida*]
PJC .... Perkinston Junior College [*Mississippi*]
PJC .... Post Junior College [*Connecticut*]
PJC .... Poteau Junior College [*Oklahoma*]
PJC .... Pratt Junior College [*Kansas*]
PJC .... University of Pittsburgh, Johnstown, Johnstown, PA [*OCLC symbol*] (OCLC)
PJCA .... Journal of Contemporary Asia [*A publication*]
PJCE .... Journal of Comparative Economics [*A publication*]
PJCH .... Journal of Church and State [*A publication*]
PJCJ .... Journal of Criminal Justice [*A publication*]
PJCL .... Journal of Commonwealth Literature [*A publication*]

PJCP......... Journal of Comparative Psychology [*A publication*]
PJCR......... Journal of Confict Resolution [*A publication*]
PJCS......... Journal of Canadian Studies [*A publication*]
PJCTL....... Projectile　(MSA)
PJD........... Pedro Dome [*Alaska*] [*Seismograph station code, US Geological Survey*] [*Closed*]　(SEIS)
PJE........... Parachute Jumping Exercise
PJE........... Peabody Journal of Education [*A publication*]
PJE........... Project Engineer
PJE........... Pulse Jet Engine
PJEC........ Journal of Ecology [*A publication*]
PJEG........ JEGP. Journal of English and Germanic Philology [*A publication*]
PJEH........ Journal of American Ethnic History [*A publication*]
PJER........ Journal of the Early Republic [*A publication*]
PJES........ Photojet Edge Sensor
PJET......... Journal of Contemporary Ethnography [*A publication*]
PJF........... Peripheral Jet (Flat-Bottom)
PJF........... Pharmaceutical Journal Formulary　(ROG)
PJF........... Pin Jointed Framework
PJFH........ Journal of Family History [*A publication*]
PJFI.......... Journal of Family Issues [*A publication*]
PJFS......... Journal of Food Science [*A publication*]
PJFS......... Philip Jose Farmer Society　(EA)
PJG........... Panjgur [*Pakistan*] [*Airport symbol*]　(OAG)
PJG........... Potts Junction [*Guam*] [*Seismograph station code, US Geological Survey*]　(SEIS)
PJGG........ Philosophisches Jahrbuch der Goerres-Gesellschaft [*A publication*]
PJGNI....... Persica. Jaarboek van het Genootschap Nederland-Iran [*A publication*]
PJGP........ Journal of General Psychology [*A publication*]
PJGS........ Journal of Genetic Psychology [*A publication*]
PJH.......... Piper, Jr., H. E., Philadelphia PA [*STAC*]
PJH.......... PLRS/JTIDS [*Position Location Reporting System/Joint Tactical Information Distribution System*] Hybrid　(MCD)
PJHB........ Journal of Rehabilitation Research and Development [*A publication*]
PJHG........ Journal of Historical Geography [*A publication*]
PJHI......... PLRS/JTIDS [*Position Location Reporting System/Joint Tactical Information Distribution System*] Hybrid Interface
PJHP........ Journal of the History of Philosophy [*A publication*]
PJHS........ Journal of Hellenic Studies [*A publication*]
PJHX........ Journal of Homosexuality [*A publication*]
PJI........... Parachute Jump Instructor [*Military*] [*British*]　(INF)
PJI........... Pattern Jury Instructions [*A publication*]
PJI........... Personnel Journal Index [*Personnel Journal*] [*Information service or system*]　(CRD)
PJI........... Point Judith, RI [*Location identifier*] [*FAA*]　(FAAL)
PJIA......... Journal of International Affairs [*A publication*]
PJILMCC ... Philip C. Jessup International Law Moot Court Competition　(EA)
PJJ........... Provincial Judges Journal [*A publication*]
PJJQ......... James Joyce Quarterly [*A publication*]
PJJS......... Journal of Japanese Studies [*A publication*]
P JI.......... Pharmaceutical Journal [*A publication*]　(ROG)
PJL........... Philippine Journal of Linguistics [*A publication*]
PJLB........ Lower Burma Printed Judgments [*A publication*]　(DLA)
PJLN........ Journal of Linguistics [*A publication*]
PJLT......... Philippine Journal of Language Teaching [*A publication*]
PJM.......... Pennsylvania-Jersey-Maryland [*Electric power pool*]
PJM.......... Polymer Jell Material
PJM.......... Postjunctional Membrane
PJM.......... Power Jets Memorandum
PJM.......... Project Manager [*Military*]
PJMA........ Journal of Mammalogy [*A publication*]
PJME........ Journal of Medical Ethics [*A publication*]
PJMF........ Journal of Marital and Family Therapy [*A publication*]
PJMH........ Journal of Military History [*A publication*]
PJMP........ Journal of Medicine and Philosophy [*A publication*]
PJMR........ Journal of Medieval and Renaissance Studies [*A publication*]
PJMU........ Journal of Musicology [*A publication*]
PJN........... Fort Lauderdale, FL [*Location identifier*] [*FAA*]　(FAAL)
PJN........... Philippine Journal of Nursing [*A publication*]
PJNB........ Journal of Nonverbal Behavior [*A publication*]
PJNE........ Journal of Near Eastern Studies [*A publication*]
PJNEE5 .... Pakistan Journal of Nematology [*A publication*]
PJNU........ Journal of Nutrition Education [*A publication*]
PJNu........ Philippine Journal of Nutrition [*A publication*]
PJo........... Cambria County Library System, Johnstown, PA [*Library symbol*] [*Library of Congress*]　(LCLS)
PJO........... Pioneer Jupiter Orbit [*NASA*]
PJON........ Johnston Island/Johnston Atoll [*Johnston Island*] [*ICAO location identifier*]　(ICLI)
PJOP........ Preliminary Joint Operation Procedure　(KSC)
PJOPA....... Pakistan Journal of Psychology [*A publication*]
PJOS........ Journal. American Oriental Society [*A publication*]
PJOU........ Journalism History [*A publication*]
PJoU......... University of Pittsburgh at Johnstown, Johnstown, PA [*Library symbol*] [*Library of Congress*]　(LCLS)

PJP .... Philippine Journal of Pediatrics [*A publication*]
PJPA .... Journal of Parapsychology [*A publication*]
PJPA .... Philippine Journal of Public Administration [*A publication*]
PJPC......... Plug/Jack Patch Cord
PJPH........ Journal of Pacific History [*A publication*]
PJPI.......... Philippine Journal of Plant Industry [*A publication*]
PJPL......... Journal of Politics [*A publication*]
PJPM .... Journal of Policy Analysis and Management [*A publication*]
PJPR........ Journal of Peace Research [*A publication*]
PJPS......... Journal of Police Science and Admnistration [*A publication*]
PJPY......... Journal of Personality [*A publication*]
PJR .... Peoria, IL [*Location identifier*] [*FAA*]　(FAAL)
PJR .... Peterson, J. Robert, New York NY [*STAC*]
PJR .... Philadelphia Journalism Review [*A publication*]
PJR .... Pipe Joint Record　(DNAB)
PJR .... Port Jersey [*AAR code*]
PJR .... Power Jets Report
PJRC......... Journal of Research in Crime and Delinquency [*A publication*]
PJRCM .... Philippine Junior Red Cross Magazine [*A publication*]
PJRE......... Journal of Rehabilitation [*A publication*]
P Jr & H.... Patton, Jr., and Heath's Reports [*Virginia Special Court of Appeals*] [*A publication*]　(DLA)
PJRL......... Journal of Religion [*A publication*]
PJRM........ Journal of Recreational Mathematics [*A publication*]
PJRO........ Journal of Roman Studies [*A publication*]
PJRS......... Journal of Religious Ethics [*A publication*]
PJS .... Newport News, VA [*Location identifier*] [*FAA*]　(FAAL)
PJS .... Peripheral Jet (Skegs)
PJS .... Peutz-Jeghers Syndrome [*Oncology*]
PJS .... Philippine Journal of Science [*A publication*]
PJS .... Piezojunction Sensor
PJS .... Plug and Jack Set
PJS .... Production Job Sheet
PJ Schw E ... Politisches Jahrbuch der Schweizerischen Eidgenoessenschaft [*A publication*]
PJSE......... Journal of Southeast Asian Studies [*A publication*]
PJSG .... Journal of State Government [*A publication*]
PJSH .... Journal of Social History [*A publication*]
PJSN .... Journal of Southern History [*A publication*]
PJSP......... Journal of Social Policy [*A publication*]
PJSR......... Journal for the Scientific Study of Religion [*A publication*]
PJSRA...... Pakistan Journal of Scientific Research [*A publication*]
PJSS .... Journal of Social, Political, and Economic Studies [*A publication*]
PJSS .... PACAF [*Pacific Air Forces*] Jungle Survival School　(AFM)
PJSS .... Philippine Journal of Surgical Specialties [*A publication*]
PJST......... Journal of Modern African Studies [*A publication*]
PJSX......... Journal of Sex Research [*A publication*]
PJT .... Paroxysmal Junctional Tachycardia [*Cardiology*]
PJT .... Practical Job Training　(MCD)
PJT .... Pulse Jitter Tester
PJTN........ Projection　(MSA)
PJTP........ Planner Journal. Royal Town Planning Institute [*A publication*]
PJTR........ Projector　(MSA)
PJTS......... Journal of Theological Studies [*A publication*]
PJU.......... Juniata College, Huntingdon, PA [*OCLC symbol*]　(OCLC)
PJU.......... Physician's Journal Update [*Television program*]
PJUH .... Journal of Urban History [*A publication*]
P Jur Vj..... Prager Juristische Vierteljahrsschrift [*A publication*]
PJV .... Pump Jet Vehicle
PJWM...... Journal of Wildlife Management [*A publication*]
PJWT....... Journal of the West [*A publication*]
PJYA .... Journal of Youth and Adolescence [*A publication*]
PJZSAZ .... Agriculturae Conspectus Scientificus [*A publication*]
PK .... Indonesia [*Aircraft nationality and registration mark*]　(FAAC)
pK' .... Negative Log of the Dissociation Constant [*Medicine*]
PK .... Pack　(AAG)
PK .... Package [*Shipping*]　(MCD)
pk .... Pakistan [*IYRU nationality code*] [*MARC country of publication code*] [*Library of Congress*]　(LCCP)
PK .... Pakistan [*ANSI two-letter standard code*]　(CNC)
PK .... Pakistan International Airlines Corp. [*ICAO designator*]　(FAAC)
PK .... Park [*or Parking*]
PK .... Peak [*Maps and charts*]
pK .... Peak Value [*Data processing*]
PK .... Peck　(AAG)
P & K .... Perry and Knapp's English Election Cases [*1833*] [*A publication*]　(DLA)
PK .... Peter King [*Afro-jazz band*]
PK .... Phileleftheron Komma [*Liberal Party*] [*Greek*] [*Political party*]　(PPE)
PK .... Philologike Kypros [*A publication*]
PK .... Pike
PK .... Pink　(FAAC)
PK .... Pinkas ha-Kehilot [*Encyclopedia of Jewish Communities*] [*A publication*]
PK .... Plaste und Kautschuk [*A publication*]
PK .... Pole Cat [*Slang*]
PK .... Politicka Knihovna Ceskoslovenske Strany Lidove [*A publication*]

PK	Position Keeper
PK	Posta Kutusu [*Postbox*] [*Turkish*] (EY)
PK	Prausnitz-Kuestner [*Reaction*] [*Immunology*]
PK	Prawo Kanoniczne [*A publication*]
PK	Praxis-Kurier [*A publication*]
PK	Preacher's Kid [*Slang*]
PK	Pridie Kalendas [*The Day before the Calends*] [*Latin*]
PK	Principal Keeper [*Slang for a warden*]
PK	Probability of Kill (MCD)
PK	Prophets and Kings (BJA)
PK	Protein Kinase [*Also, PKase*] [*An enzyme*]
PK	Przeglad Klasyczny [*A publication*]
PK	Przeglad Koscielny [*A publication*]
PK	Przeglad Kulturalny [*A publication*]
PK	Psychokinesis
PK	Pyruvate Kinase [*An enzyme*]
P-K4	Pawn to King Four [*Standard opening to a game of chess. Pawn is moved to the fourth square in front of the king*]
PKA	Napaskiak [*Alaska*] [*Airport symbol*] (OAG)
PKA	Napaskiak, AK [*Location identifier*] [*FAA*] (FAAL)
PKA	Paul Kagan Associates, Inc. [*Information service or system*] [*Telecommunications*] (IID)
PKA	Pi Kappa Alpha [*Fraternity*]
PKA	Primary Knock-on-Atom (MCD)
PKA	Professional Karate Association (EA)
PKA	Prokininogenase [*An enzyme*] (MAE)
PKA	Protein Kinase A [*An enzyme*]
PkAF	Pakistani Air Force
PKAFA	PKA [*Professional Karate Association*] Fighters Association (EA)
PKAS	Parti Kadazan Asli Sabah [*Political party*] [*Malaysia*] (FEA)
PKase	Protein Kinase [*Also, PK*] [*An enzyme*]
PKAWA	Pocket Knife Ancillary Workers' Association [*A union*] [*British*]
PKB	Parkersburg [*West Virginia*] [*Airport symbol*] (OAG)
PKB	Parkersburg, WV [*Location identifier*] [*FAA*] (FAAL)
PKB	Photoelectric Keyboard
PKB	Portable Keyboard
PKC	Beijing Review [*A publication*]
PKC	Cocoa, FL [*Location identifier*] [*FAA*] (FAAL)
PKC	Pannill Knitting Co., Inc. [*NYSE symbol*] (SPSG)
PKC	Peckham Road [*California*] [*Seismograph station code, US Geological Survey*] (SEIS)
PKC	Position Keeping Computer
PKC	Protein Kinase C [*An enzyme*]
PKCVA	Promyshlennost Khimicheskikh Reaktivov i Osobo Chistykh Veshchestv [*A publication*]
PKD	Pac Ed Systems Corp. [*Vancouver Stock Exchange symbol*]
PKD	Park Rapids, MN [*Location identifier*] [*FAA*] (FAAL)
PKD	Parker Drilling Co. [*NYSE symbol*] (SPSG)
PKD	Partially Knocked Down [*Consignment*] [*Shipping*] (DS)
PKD	Philip K. Dick [*Science fiction writer*]
PKD	Pi Kappa Delta [*Society*]
PKD	Polycystic Kidney Disease [*Medicine*]
PKD	Programmable Keyboard and Display [*Data processing*] (NASA)
PKDB	Partai Kebang-Saan Demokratik Brunei [*Brunei National Democratic Party*] [*Political party*] (EY)
PKDOM	Pack for Domestic Use
PKD PDR	Packed Powder (WGA)
PKDR-B	Pakistan Development Review [*A publication*]
PKDS	Philip K. Dick Society (EA)
PKE	Pacific Kenridge [*Vancouver Stock Exchange symbol*]
PKE	Pakistan and Gulf Economist [*A publication*]
PKE	Park Electrochemical Corp. [*NYSE symbol*] (SPSG)
PKE	Parker, CA [*Location identifier*] [*FAA*] (FAAL)
PKE	Parkes [*Australia*] [*Airport symbol*] (OAG)
PKE	Public-Key Encryption [*Microcomputer technology*]
PKEN	Kenyon Review [*A publication*]
PKF	Park Falls, WI [*Location identifier*] [*FAA*] (FAAL)
PKF	Parkfield Array [*California*] [*Seismograph station code, US Geological Survey*] (SEIS)
PKF	Phagocytosis and Killing Function [*Immunology*] (AAMN)
PKF	Primary Kidney Fold
PKFC	Princess Kitty Fan Club (EA)
PKG	Package [*Shipping*] (AFM)
Pkg	Packing (DS)
Pkg instr	Packing Instruction (DS)
PKG	Parking (KSC)
PKG	Phonocardiogram [*Cardiology*]
PKG	Propylaeen Kunstgeschichte [*A publication*]
Pkg Abstr	Packaging Abstracts [*A publication*]
PKGE	Package
Pkg Eng	Package Engineering [*A publication*]
Pkg (India)	Packaging (India) [*A publication*]
P-K GL	[*A.*] Philippson and [*E.*] Kirsten, Die Griechischen Landschaften [*A publication*] (OCD)
Pkg (London)	Packaging (London) [*A publication*]
Pkg News	Packaging News [*A publication*]
Pkg Technol	Packaging Technology and Management [*A publication*]

PKH	Park Hill [*California*] [*Seismograph station code, US Geological Survey*] (SEIS)
PKH	Probability of a Kill Given a Hit [*Military*] (DNAB)
PKH	Publikatieblad van de Europese Gemeenschappen. Handelingen van het Europese Parlement [*A publication*]
PKHOW	Pack Howitzer [*Marine Corps*]
PKI	Parkland Industries Ltd. [*Toronto Stock Exchange symbol*]
PKI	Partai Katolik Indonesia [*Catholic Party of Indonesia*] [*Political party*]
PKI	Partai Komunis Indonesia [*Communist Party of Indonesia*] [*Political party*]
PKI	Partai Kristen Indonesia [*Christian Party of Indonesia*] [*Political party*]
P & KI	Promisel & Korn, Inc. [*Information service or system*] (IID)
PKI	Protein Kinase Inhibitor [*Biochemistry*]
PKIKA	Praxis der Kinderpsychologie und Kinderpsychiatrie [*A publication*]
PKJ	Pitanja Knjizevnosti a Jezika [*A publication*]
PKK	Kurdish Workers' Party [*Turkey*] [*Political party*] (PD)
PKK	Pakokku [*Myanmar*] [*Airport symbol*] (OAG)
PKK	Porkkala [*Finland*] [*Seismograph station code, US Geological Survey*] (SEIS)
PKK	Protein Kinase K [*An enzyme*]
PkKP	Pakistan National Scientific and Documentation Center, Karachi, Pakistan [*Library symbol*] [*Library of Congress*] (LCLS)
PKL	Parklane Technologies, Inc. [*Vancouver Stock Exchange symbol*]
PKL	Pi Kappa Lambda [*Society*]
PKLB	Pharmakinetics Laboratories, Inc. [*NASDAQ symbol*] (NQ)
PK-LT	Psychokinesis on Living Targets
PKM	Packmaster [*Army*] (WGA)
PKM	Perigee Kick Motor (MCD)
PKMA	Eniwetok [*Marshall Islands*] [*ICAO location identifier*] (ICLI)
PK-MB	Psychokinetic Metal-Bending [*Parapsychology*]
PKMJ	Majuro [*Marshall Islands*] [*ICAO location identifier*] (ICLI)
PKMKA	Prikladnaya Mekhanika [*A publication*]
PKMKCMD	Perhaps...Kids Meeting Kids Can Make a Difference (EA)
Pkmr	Packmaster [*Army*]
PKMS	Pertubohan Kebangsaan Melayu Singapura [*Singapore Malays' National Organization*] [*Political party*] (FEA)
PKN	Aspen, CO [*Location identifier*] [*FAA*] (FAAL)
PKN	Pangkalanbuun [*Indonesia*] [*Airport symbol*] (OAG)
PKN	Pauken [*Kettledrums*]
PKN	Perkin-Elmer Corp. [*NYSE symbol*] (SPSG)
PKNG HSE	Packing House [*Freight*]
PKO	Parakou [*Benin*] [*Airport symbol*] (OAG)
PKO	Peace-Keeping Operation (MCD)
PKO	Perdant par Knockout [*Losing by a Knockout*] [*French*]
PKOH	Park-Ohio Industries, Inc. [*NASDAQ symbol*] (NQ)
PKOM	Publicationen. Kaiserlich Osmanische Museen [*Constantinople*] [*A publication*]
PKOMA	Physik der Kondensierten Materie [*A publication*]
P Kon Ned A	Proceedings. Koninklijke Nederlandse Akademie van Wetenschappen. Series A. Mathematical Sciences [*A publication*]
P Kon Ned B	Proceedings. Koninklijke Nederlandse Akademie van Wetenschappen. Series B. Physical Sciences [*A publication*]
P Kon Ned C	Proceedings. Koninklijke Nederlandse Akademie van Wetenschappen. Series C. Biological and Medical Sciences [*A publication*]
PKOP	Piscovye Knigi Obonezskoj Pjatiny [*A publication*]
PKP	Palestiner Komunistische Partei [*Palestine Communist Party*] [*Political party*] (BJA)
PKP	Partido Komunista ng Pilipinas [*Communist Party of the Philippines*] [*Political party*] (PPW)
PKP	Penetrating Keratoplasty [*Ophthalmology*]
PKP	Perustuslaillinen Kansanpuolue [*Constitutional People's Party*] [*Finland*] [*Political party*] (PPE)
PKP	Polskie Koleje Panstwowe [*Polish State Railways*]
PKP	Preknock Pulse
PKP	Pukapuka [*French Polynesia*] [*Airport symbol*] (OAG)
PKP	Purple-K-Powder
PK/PK	Peak-to-Peak (MCD)
PKpP	Pennwalt Corp., King Of Prussia, PA [*Library symbol*] [*Library of Congress*] (LCLS)
PKPS	[*The*] Poughkeepsie Savings Bank FSB [*Poughkeepsie, NY*] [*NASDAQ symbol*] (NQ)
PKQ	Dallas-Fort Worth, TX [*Location identifier*] [*FAA*] (FAAL)
PKR	P. K. Le Roux Dam [*South Africa*] [*Seismograph station code, US Geological Survey*] (SEIS)
PKR	Packer (WGA)
PKR	Picker
PKR	Pokhara [*Nepal*] [*Airport symbol*] (OAG)
PKRDD	Pravitel'stvennaya Komissiya po Raketam Dalnego Deistviya [*State Commission for the Study of the Problems of Long-Range Rockets*] [*Former USSR*]
PKs	Bayard Taylor Memorial Library, Kennett Square, PA [*Library symbol*] [*Library of Congress*] (LCLS)
PKS	Packs of Cigarettes Smoked
PKS	Parti Kongres Sarawak [*Malaysia*] [*Political party*] (EY)

PKS............	Phi Kappa Sigma [*Fraternity*]
PKS............	Publikatieblad van de Europese Gemeenschappen. Serie C. Mededelingen en Bekendmakingen [*A publication*]
PKS............	Publikatieblad van de Europese Gemeenschappen. Supplement [*A publication*]
PKSCU......	PKS/Communications Uts [*NASDAQ symbol*] (NQ)
PKSEA	Pack for Overseas
PKSh........	Partia Komuniste e Shqiperise [*Communist Party of Albania*] [*Later, PPSh*] [*Political party*] (PPE)
PKsL..........	Longwood Gardens Library, Kennett Square, PA [*Library symbol*] [*Library of Congress*] (LCLS)
Pks & Rec ..	Parks and Recreation [*A publication*]
PKSS..........	Probability of Kill Single Shot (MCD)
PKSVAG ...	Pneumokoniosenavorsingseenheid Jaarverslag Pochvoznanie Agrokhimiya i Rastitelna Zashtita [*A publication*]
PKT............	Packet
PKT............	Phase Keying Technique
PKT............	Phi Kappa Tau [*Fraternity*]
PKT............	Pittsburgh Theological Seminary, Pittsburgh, PA [*OCLC symbol*] (OCLC)
PKT............	Pocket (MSA)
PKU	Pekanbaru [*Indonesia*] [*Airport symbol*] (OAG)
PKU	Phenylketonuria [*Congenital metabolism disorder*] [*Medicine*]
PKU	Pianoforte Keymakers' Union [*British*]
PKU	Unpublished Objects from Palaikastro Excavations, 1902-09 [*A publication*]
PKU-P	PKU [*Phenylketonuria*] Parents (EA)
PKuS........	Kutztown State College, Kutztown, PA [*Library symbol*] [*Library of Congress*] (LCLS)
PKV	Killed Poliomyelitis Vaccine [*Immunology*] (MAE)
PkV	Peak Kilovolts
PKV	Port Lavaka, TX [*Location identifier*] [*FAA*] (FAAL)
PKVJA	PKV [*Punjabrao Krishi Vidyapeeth*] Research Journal [*A publication*]
PKVL........	Pikeville National Corp. [*NASDAQ symbol*] (NQ)
PKVOA	Produktivnost [*A publication*]
PKV Res J ...	PKV [*Punjabrao Krishi Vidyapeeth*] Research Journal [*A publication*]
PKW	Kenosha, WI [*Location identifier*] [*FAA*] (FAAL)
PKW	Personenkraftwagen [*Automobile*] [*German*]
PKW	Selebi-Phikwe [*Botswana*] [*Airport symbol*] (OAG)
PKWA	Kwajalein [*Marshall Islands*] [*ICAO location identifier*] (ICLI)
PKWAY....	Parkway (MSA)
PKWY.......	Parkway (KSC)
PKWY.......	[*The*] Parkway Co. [*NASDAQ symbol*] (NQ)
PKY	Palangkaraya [*Indonesia*] [*Airport symbol*] (OAG)
PKY	Parkway (MCD)
PKY	Pecky (WGA)
PKy	Pneumatike Kypros [*A publication*]
PKY	Tri-City Air Taxi [*San Bernardino, CA*] [*FAA designator*] (FAAC)
PKZ............	Pensacola, FL [*Location identifier*] [*FAA*] (FAAL)
PL	Empresade Transporte Aere de Peru [*ICAO designator*] (FAAC)
PL	Front Line [*Revolutionary group*] [*Italy*]
PL	Lancaster County Library, Lancaster, PA [*Library symbol*] [*Library of Congress*] (LCLS)
PL	Packing List
PL	Padlock (AAG)
PL	Pail
PL	Palaeographia Latina [*A publication*]
PL	Palm Leaf [*Reaction*] [*Medicine*]
PL	Pamietnik Literacki [*A publication*]
PL	Pamphlet Laws [*A publication*] (DLA)
PL	Panel Left [*Nuclear energy*] (NRCH)
PL	Paper Life Ltd. [*British*]
PL	Paperleg [*A favored student*] [*Teen slang*]
PL	Papers in Linguistics [*A publication*]
PL	Parish Line R. R. [*AAR code*]
PL	Parti Liberal [*Liberal Party (1974-1979)*] [*Belgium*] [*Political party*] (PPE)
PL	Partial Loss [*Insurance*]
PL	Partido Liberal [*Liberal Party*] [*Paraguay*] [*Political party*] (PPW)
PL	Partido Liberal [*Liberal Party*] [*Honduras*] [*Political party*]
PL	Partido Liberal [*Liberal Party*] [*Colombia*] [*Political party*] (EY)
PL	Partido Liberal [*Liberal Party*] [*Portugal*] [*Political party*] (PPE)
PL	Partido Liberal [*Liberal Party*] [*Peru*] [*Political party*] (EY)
PL	Partido Liberal [*Liberal Party*] [*Spain*] [*Political party*] (PPE)
PL	Partido Liberal [*Liberal Party*] [*Panama*] [*Political party*] (PPW)
PL	Partido Libertador [*Liberating Party*] [*Brazil*] [*Political party*]
PL	Parting Line [*Castings*] (AAG)
PL	Parts List
PL	Path Loss [*Communications*]
PL	Patrol Land [*Aviation*]
PL	Patrologia Latina [*A publication*]
PL	Patrologiae Cursus. Series Latina [*A publication*] (OCD)
Pl................	Paul (BJA)
P & L..........	Paul and Lisa (EA)
PL	Paulist League (EA)
P de L........	Paulus de Liazaris [*Deceased, 1356*] [*Authority cited in pre-1607 legal work*] (DSA)
PL	Payload [*NASA*] (KSC)
PL	Paymaster-Lieutenant [*Navy*] [*British*]
PL	Peanut Leafspot [*Plant pathology*]
PL	Pectate Lyase [*An enzyme*]
Pl	Pelagius [*Deceased, 1232*] [*Authority cited in pre-1607 legal work*] (DSA)
PL	Pelusium Line [*Nile delta*] [*Geology*]
PL	People for Life (EA)
PL	People's Lobby (EA)
PL	Perceived Level [*Noise*]
PL	Perception of Light
P/L...........	Personal Lines
PL	Personnel Laboratory [*Air Research and Development Command*] [*Air Force*] (AAG)
PL	Petty Larceny
PL	Phase Line
PL	Philosophical Library [*A publication*]
PL	Philosophischer Literaturanzeiger [*A publication*]
P & L........	Philosophy and Literature [*A publication*]
PL	Phospholipid [*Biochemistry*]
PL	Photolocator (MCD)
PL	Photoluminescence
pl	Picoliter [*One trillionth of a liter*] (MAE)
PL	Pilatus Flugzeugwerke AG [*Switzerland*] [*ICAO aircraft manufacturer identifier*] (ICAO)
PL	Pile
PL	Pinelands, Inc. [*NYSE symbol*] (SPSG)
PL	Pipe Lines Act [*Town planning*] [*British*]
PL	Pipeline
PL	Piping Load [*Nuclear energy*] (NRCH)
PL	Pitch Line (MSA)
PL	Place
PL	Place [*Investment term*]
PL	Placebo [*Medicine*]
PL	Placental Lactogen [*Endocrinology*]
Pl	Plagioclase [*Lunar geology*]
PL	Plain (MSA)
PL	Plain Language [*As opposed to coded message*] [*Military*]
PL	Plans
Pl	Planta [*A publication*]
PL	Plantagenet [*Genealogy*] (ROG)
pl	Plasma
PL	Plaster (WGA)
PL	Plastic Laboratory [*Princeton University*] (MCD)
PL	Plastic Limit (IEEE)
PL	Plastic Surgery [*Medicine*]
pl	Plastid [*Botany*]
PL	Plate (KSC)
PL	Plateau Length
pl	Platelet [*Hematology*] (MAE)
PL	Platinum [*Chemistry*] (ROG)
Pl	Plato [*Fourth century BC*] [*Classical studies*] (OCD)
PL	Platoon (NATG)
PL	Platoon Leader [*Military*] (INF)
PL	Platz [*Square*] [*German*] (EY)
PL	Players League [*Major league in baseball, 1890*]
PL	Pleasure (ROG)
PL	[*The*] Plessey Co. Ltd. (MCD)
pl	Pleural [*Medicine*] (MAE)
PL	Plimsoll Line [*Shipping*] (DAS)
PL	Ploshchad [*Square*] [*Russian*] (EY)
Pl	Plowden's English King's Bench Commentaries [*or Reports*] [*1550-80*] [*A publication*] (DLA)
PL	Plug (AAG)
PL	Plume [*Numismatics*]
PL	Plural
PL	Poet Laureate
PL	Poet Lore [*A publication*]
PL	Poetry London [*A publication*] [*British*]
P & L........	Points and Lines [*Military*] (CAAL)
Pl	Poiseuille [*Unit of dynamic viscosity*]
pl	Poland [*MARC country of publication code*] [*Library of Congress*] (LCCP)
PL	Poland [*ANSI two-letter standard code*] (CNC)
PL	Polarized Light
PL	Policy Loan
P & L........	Politics and Letters [*A publication*]
PL	Poly-L-lysine [*Also, PLL*] [*Biochemical analysis*]
PL	Poor Law [*A publication*] (DLA)
P of L........	Port of London (ROG)
PL	Portable Low-Power [*Reactor*] (NRCH)
PL	Position Line [*Navigation*]
PL	Position Location [*DoD*]
PL	Post Landing [*NASA*] (KSC)
PL	Post Laundry [*Army*]
P & L..........	Power and Lighting (MSA)
P & L..........	Pratt & Lambert, Inc.

PL .... Prayers for Life (EA)
PL .... Prelaunch (NASA)
PL .... Preliminary Leaf [*Bibliography*]
P/L .... Presentation Label [*Publishing*]
PL .... Presley Labs [*Vancouver Stock Exchange symbol*]
PL .... Pressurizer Level (IEEE)
PL .... Price Level [*Economics*]
PL .... Price List
PL .... Primrose League [*British*] (DI)
PL .... Princess Louise's Sutherland and Argyll Highlanders [*Military*]
               [*British*] (ROG)
PL .... Private Label [*A publication*]
PL .... Private Label [*Business term*]
PL .... Private Library [*A publication*]
PL .... Private Line
PL .... Procedural Language (PCM)
PL .... Procedure Library [*Data processing*]
PL .... Product Liability [*Insurance*]
PL .... Product License
PL .... Production Language
PL .... Production List (AAG)
P/L .... Profit and Loss [*Accounting*]
P & L .... Profit and Loss [*Accounting*]
PL .... Program Library [*Data processing*]
PL .... Program Logic [*Data processing*] (TEL)
PL .... Programming Language [*Data processing*]
PL .... Programming Languages Series [*Elsevier Book Series*] [*A
               publication*]
PL .... Progressive Labor [*A faction of Students for a Democratic
               Society*]
PL .... Project Leader
PL .... Project Lighthawk [*Later, LH*] (EA)
PL .... Project Local [*Defunct*] (EA)
PL .... Projection Lens [*Microscopy*]
PL .... Prolymphocytic Leukemia [*Also, PLL*] [*Oncology*]
PL .... Propagation Loss
PL .... Propellant Loading [*NASA*] (KSC)
PL .... Property Line [*Real estate*] (MSA)
PL .... Proportional Limit
P/L .... Proprietary Limited (ADA)
PL .... Propulsion Laboratory [*Army*] (GRD)
PL .... Prospective Loss
PL .... Protected Location [*Shipping*] (DS)
PL .... Protectively Located [*Plant layout*]
PL .... Provisioning List (MCD)
PL .... Pseudolumina [*Anatomy*]
PL .... Psychological Laboratory (MCD)
PL .... Public Law [*An act of Congress*]
PL .... Public Liability [*Business term*]
PL .... Public Library
Pl .... Pulmonary Venous Pressure [*Medicine*] (MAE)
PL .... Pulpolingual [*Dentistry*]
PL .... Pulse Length (NVT)
P/L .... Purchased Labor (NASA)
PL .... Pyridoxal [*Also, Pxl*] [*Biochemistry*]
PL .... Radio Positioning Land Station [*ITU designation*] (CET)
PL/1 .... Programming Language, Version One [*Data
               processing*] (MCD)
PLA .... Pakistan Liberation Army (PD)
PLA .... Palau [*Palau Islands*] [*Seismograph station code, US Geological
               Survey*] [*Closed*] (SEIS)
PLA .... Palestine Liberation Army
PLA .... Parachute Location Aid (MCD)
PLA .... Parlamento Latinoamericano [*Latin American Parliament -
               LAP*] [*Bogota, Colombia*] (EAIO)
PLA .... Parlar Resources Ltd. [*Vancouver Stock Exchange symbol*]
PLA .... Partido Laborista Agrario [*Panama*] [*Political party*] (EY)
PLA .... Partido Liberal Autentico [*Panama*] [*Political party*] (EY)
PLA .... Party of Labor of Albania [*Political party*] (PPW)
PLA .... Passengers' Luggage in Advance [*Railway*] (ROG)
PLA .... Patriotic Liberation Army [*Myanmar*] (PD)
PLA .... Pedestrian League of America [*Later, APA*] (EA)
Pla .... Pelagius [*Deceased, 1232*] [*Authority cited in pre-1607 legal
               work*] (DSA)
PLA .... Pennilane Development [*Vancouver Stock Exchange symbol*]
PLA .... People's Liberation Army [*India*] (PD)
PLA .... People's Liberation Army [*China*]
PLA .... Pet Lovers Association (EA)
PLA .... Phase Locked Arrays [*Physics*]
PLA .... Philatelic Literature Association [*Later, APRL*] (EA)
PLA .... Philosophischer Literaturanzeiger [*A publication*]
PLA .... Physiological Learning Aptitude (KSC)
PLA .... Pitch Lock Actuator (MCD)
PLA .... Place (ADA)
PLA .... Placebo [*Medicine*]
Pla .... Placentinus [*Deceased, 1192*] [*Authority cited in pre-1607 legal
               work*] (DSA)
PLA .... Placitum [*or Placita*] [*Agreeable, Agreed Upon*] [*Latin*] [*Legal
               term*] (DLA)
PLA .... Plain Language Address [*Telecommunications*] (TEL)
PLA .... Plan of Launch Azimuth [*Aerospace*] (AAG)

PLA .... Planned Labor Application [*Military*] (AFIT)
PLA .... Planned Landing Area [*NASA*]
PLA .... Playboy Enterprises, Inc. [*NYSE symbol*] (SPSG)
PLA .... Plaza (ADA)
PLA .... Poetry League of America (EA)
PLA .... Poly-L-arginine [*Biochemistry*]
PLA .... Polylactic Acid [*Organic chemistry*] (RDA)
PLA .... Polynesian Airways [*Honolulu, HI*] [*FAA designator*] (FAAC)
PLA .... Popular Library of Art [*A publication*]
PLA .... Port of London Authority [*British*]
PLA .... Posterior Left Atrial Wall [*Cardiology*]
PLA .... Potential Leaf Area [*Botany*]
PLA .... Power Lever Angle
PLA .... Practice Landing Approach [*Aviation*]
PLA .... Practice Low Approach [*Aviation*] (FAAC)
PLA .... Price-Level-Adjusted Accounting (ADA)
PLA .... Print Load Analyzer
PLA .... Private Libraries Association [*British*]
PLA .... Product License Application [*FDA*]
PLA .... Professional Legal Assistants (EA)
PLA .... Programmable Line Adapter
PLA .... Programmable Logic Array [*Data processing*]
PLA .... Proton Linear Accelerator
PLA .... Psycholinguistic Age [*Education*]
PLA .... Psychological Learning Aptitude (MCD)
PLA .... Public Library Association (EA)
PLa .... Pulpolabial [*Dentistry*]
PLa .... Pulpolinguoaxial [*Dentistry*]
PLA .... Pulsed LASER Annealing [*Semiconductor technology*]
PLA .... Pulverized Limestone Association (EA)
PLA .... University of Pittsburgh, Law School, Pittsburgh, PA [*OCLC
               symbol*] (OCLC)
PLA$_2$ .... Phospholipase A$_2$ [*An enzyme*]
PLAA .... Positive Low Angle of Attack
PLA AEPS ... PLA [*Public Library Association*] Alternative Education
               Programs Section
PLAAF ...... People's Liberation Army Air Force
PLA AFLS ... PLA [*Public Library Association*] Armed Forces Library
               Section
PLAAR ...... Packaged Liquid Air-Augmented Rocket (MCD)
PLAAS ...... Plasma Atomic Absorption System [*Spectrometry*]
PLA AV ..... PLA [*Public Library Association*] Audiovisual
PLA AVC .. PLA [*Public Library Association*] Audiovisual Committee
PLAB .... Philadelphia Library Association. Bulletin [*A publication*]
PLAB .... Philippine Library Association. Bulletin [*A publication*]
PLAB .... Photronics, Inc. [*NASDAQ symbol*] (NQ)
PLABED ..... Plant Breeding [*A publication*]
PLA Bull .... PLA [*Pennsylvania Library Association*] Bulletin [*A
               publication*]
PLAC .... Placebo [*Medicine*]
Plac .... Placentinus [*Deceased, 1192*] [*Authority cited in pre-1607 legal
               work*] (DSA)
PLAC .... Post-Launch Analysis of Compliance [*NASA*]
Plac Abbrev . Placitorum Abbreviatio [*Latin*] [*A publication*] (DLA)
Plac Ang Nor ... Bigelow's Placita Anglo-Normanica [*A publication*] (DLA)
PLACE ...... Position Location and Aircraft Communication Equipment
PLACE ...... Position Location and Communications Experiment [*NASA*]
PLACE ...... Positioner Layout and Cell Evaluator [*Robotics*]
PLACE ...... Post-LANDSAT Advanced Concept Evaluation (MCD)
PLACE ...... Programa Latinoamericano de Cooperacion Energetica [*Latin
               American Energy Cooperation Program*] (EAIO)
PLACE ...... Programming Language for Automatic Checkout Equipment
Placenta Suppl ... Placenta. Supplement [*A publication*]
PlacerD ...... Placer Dome, Inc. [*Associated Press abbreviation*] (APAG)
Plac Gen ..... Placita Generalia [*Latin*] [*A publication*] (DLA)
PLACID ...... Payload Aboard, Caution in Descent [*NASA*]
PLA CIS .... PLA [*Public Library Association*] Community Information
               Section
PLACO ...... Planning Committee [*International Organization for
               Standardization*] (IEEE)
PLAD .... Parachute Low-Altitude Delivery [*Air Force*]
PLAD .... Plain Language Address Directory
PLAD .... Price-Level-Adjusted Deposit
PLADS ...... Parachute Low-Altitude Delivery System [*Military*]
PLADS ...... Pulsed LASER Airborne Depth Sounding System [*Naval
               Oceanographic Office*]
PLAFB .... Plattsburgh Air Force Base [*New York*] (AAG)
PLAFSEP ... Processing Libraries - Anecdotes, Facetia, Satire, Etc.,
               Periodicals [*A publication*]
Plag .... Plagioclase [*Lunar geology*]
PLAGM ..... Placid, Louisiana Land and Exploration, Amerada Hess, Getty,
               and Marathon [*Oil-and gas-holding bloc in Alaska*]
PLAH .... Labor History [*A publication*]
PLAI .... Preschool Language Assessment Instrument [*Child
               development test*]
PLAIC .... Purdue Laboratory for Applied Industrial Control [*Purdue
               University*] [*Research center*] (RCD)
PLAID .... Programmed Learning Aid
Plain Ra ..... Plain Rapper [*A publication*]
Plains Anthropol ... Plains Anthropologist [*A publication*]
PlainsP .... Plains Petroleum Co. [*Associated Press abbreviation*] (APAG)

PLAKA ...... Planovoe Khozyaistvo [*A publication*]
PLAL .... Latin American Literary Review [*A publication*]
PLAL .... Pro-Life Action League   (EA)
PLA LC ..... PLA [*Public Library Association*] Legislative Committee
PLAM .... Plastic Laminate [*Technical drawings*]
PLAM .... Practice Limpet Assembly Modular [*Navy*]   (CAAL)
PLAM .... Price-Level-Adjusted Mortgage
PLAMED .. Plantas Medicinales [*Ministerio de Sanidad y Consumo*]
   [*Spain*] [*Information service or system*]   (CRD)
PLA MLS ... PLA [*Public Library Association*] Metropolitan Libraries
   Section
PLA MPLSS ... PLA [*Public Library Association*] Marketing of Public
   Library Services Section
PLAN .... Parts Logistics Analysis Network
PLAN .... Payload Local Area Network [*NASA*]   (SSD)
PLAN .... People's Liberation Army of Namibia [*Political party*]   (PPW)
PLAN .... People's Liberation Army Navy
PLAN .... Planner Newsletter. NWT [*Northwest Territories, Canada*]
   Land Use Planning Commission [*A publication*]
Plan .... Planning   (DLA)
PLAN .... Polska Ludowa Akcja Niepodleglosci [*A publication*]
PLAN .... Positive Locator Aid to Navigation
PLAN .... Problem Language Analyzer [*Data processing*]
PLAN .... Program Language Analyzer [*Data processing*]   (IEEE)
PLAN .... Program for Learning in Accordance with Needs [*Westinghouse
   Learning Corp.*]
PLAN .... Programming Language Nineteen-Hundred [*Data processing*]
PLAN .... Protect Life in All Nations   (EA)
PLAN .... Public Libraries Automation Network [*California State Library*]
   [*Sacramento, CA*]
PLANA ...... Planta [*A publication*]
PLANAT ... North Atlantic Treaty Regional Planning Group
Planc .... Pro Plancio [*of Cicero*] [*Classical studies*]   (OCD)
Plan Can .... Plan Canada [*A publication*]
Plan Choz ... Planovoe Chozjajstvo [*A publication*]
PLANCODE ... Planning, Control, and Decision Evaluation System [*IBM
   Corp.*]
Plan & Comp ... Planning and Compensation Reports [*British*] [*A
   publication*]   (DLA)
Planeacion Reg ... Planeacion Regional [*A publication*]
Planen Pruef Investieren PPI ... Planen-Pruefen-Investieren. PPI [*West
   Germany*] [*A publication*]
PLANES ... Programmed Language-Based Enquiry System
PLANET ... Planned Logistics Analysis and Evaluation Technique [*Air
   Force*]
PLANET ... Planning Evaluation Technique   (MCD)
PLANET ... Private Local Area Network [*Racal LAN Systems, Inc.*] [*Boca
   Raton, FL*]   (TSSD)
Planet Assoc Clean Energy Newsl ... Planetary Association for Clean Energy.
   Newsletter [*Canada*] [*A publication*]
Planet Spac ... Planetary and Space Science [*A publication*]
Planet Space Sci ... Planetary and Space Science [*A publication*]
PLANEX ... [*The*] Planning Exchange Database [*Pergamon InfoLine*]
   [*Database*] [*Information service or system*]   (IID)
PLANEX ... Planning Exercise [*Military*]   (NVT)
Pl Ang-Norm ... Placita Anglo-Normannica Cases (Bigelow) [*A
   publication*]   (DLA)
Plan Higher Ed ... Planning for Higher Education [*A publication*]
Plan Higher Educ ... Planning for Higher Education [*A publication*]
Plan Hospod ... Planovane Hospodarstvi [*A publication*]
Plan Hoz .... Planovoe Hozjajstvo [*A publication*]
Planif Habitat Inform ... Planification, Habitat, Information [*A publication*]
Plan Inovtn ... Planned Innovation [*A publication*]
PLANIT .... Programming Language for Interaction and Teaching [*1966*]
   [*Data processing*]
Plan Khoz .. Planovoe Khozyaistvo [*A publication*]
PLANMAN ... Planned Maintenance [*Contract Data Research*] [*Software
   package*]   (NCC)
PLANN ..... Plant Location Assistance Nationwide Network
Plann Admin ... Planning and Administration [*A publication*]
Plann Build Dev ... Planning and Building Developments [*A publication*]
Planned Innov ... Planned Innovation [*England*] [*A publication*]
PLANNER ... [*A*] Programming Language   (CSR)
PLANNET ... Planning Network
Planning and Adm ... Planning and Administration [*A publication*]
Planning Bul ... Planning Bulletin [*A publication*]   (APTA)
Planning Develop Netherl ... Planning and Development in the Netherlands
   [*A publication*]
Planning History Bull ... Planning History Bulletin [*A publication*]
Plann News ... Planning News [*A publication*]   (APTA)
Plann Outlook ... Planning Outlook [*A publication*]
Plann Pam Nat Plann Ass ... Planning Pamphlets. National Planning
   Association [*A publication*]
Plann Parenthood Rev ... Planned Parenthood Review [*A publication*]
Plann Transp Abs ... Planning and Transportation Abstracts [*A publication*]
Plan Q .... Planning Quarterly [*A publication*]
Plan Rev .... Planning Review [*A publication*]
PLANS ...... Position Location and Navigation System
PLANS ...... Program Logistics and Network Scheduling System   (IEEE)
PLANS ...... Programming Language for Allocation and Network Scheduling
   [*1975*] [*Data processing*]   (CSR)

Planseeberichte ... Planseeberichte fuer Pulvermetallurgie [*A publication*]
Planseeber Pulvermet ... Planseeberichte fuer Pulvermetallurgie [*A
   publication*]
Plant .... De Plantatione [*Philo*]   (BJA)
Plant .... Plant Maintenance and Engineering [*A publication*]
PLANT ...... Program for Linguistic Analysis of Natural Plants   (IEEE)
Planta Med ... Planta Medica [*A publication*]
Plant Bibliogr ... Plant Bibliography [*A publication*]
Plant Biochem J ... Plant Biochemical Journal [*A publication*]
Plant Biol (NY) ... Plant Biology (New York) [*A publication*]
Plant Breed Abstr ... Plant Breeding Abstracts [*A publication*]
Plant Breed Rev ... Plant Breeding Reviews [*A publication*]
Plant Bull Rubber Res Inst Malays ... Planters' Bulletin. Rubber Research
   Institute of Malaysia [*A publication*]
Plant Cell Environ ... Plant Cell and Environment [*A publication*]
Plant Cell Physiol ... Plant and Cell Physiology [*A publication*]
Plant Cell Physiol (Kyoto) ... Plant and Cell Physiology (Kyoto) [*A
   publication*]
Plant Cell Physiol (Tokyo) ... Plant and Cell Physiology (Tokyo) [*A
   publication*]
Plant Cell Rep ... Plant Cell Reports [*A publication*]
Plant Cell Tissue Organ Cult ... Plant Cell Tissue and Organ Culture [*A
   publication*]
Plant Cel P ... Plant and Cell Physiology [*A publication*]
Plant Chron ... Planters' Chronicle [*A publication*]
Plant Cultiv Repub Argent Inst Bot Agric (B Aires) ... Plantas Cultivadas en la
   Republica Argentina. Instituto de Botanica Agricola
   (Buenos Aires) [*A publication*]
Plant Dis .... Plant Disease [*A publication*]
Plant Dis Adv Treatise ... Plant Disease. An Advanced Treatise [*A
   publication*]
Plant Dis Leafl Dept Agr Biol Br (NSW) ... Plant Disease Leaflet. Department
   of Agriculture. Biological Branch (New South Wales) [*A
   publication*]
Plant Dis R ... Plant Disease Reporter [*A publication*]
Plant Dis Rep ... Plant Disease Reporter [*A publication*]
Plant Dis Rep Suppl ... Plant Disease Reporter. Supplement [*A publication*]
Plant Energy Manage ... Plant Energy Management [*A publication*]
Plant Eng ... Plant Engineer [*A publication*]
Plant Eng ... Plant Engineering [*A publication*]
Plant & Eng Applications ... Plant and Engineering Applications [*A
   publication*]   (APTA)
Plant Eng (Lond) ... Plant Engineer (London) [*A publication*]
Plant Engng ... Plant Engineering [*A publication*]
Plant Engng & Maint ... Plant Engineering and Maintenance [*A publication*]
Plant Eng (Tokyo) ... Plant Engineer (Tokyo) [*A publication*]
Planter .... Planter and Sugar Manufacturer [*A publication*]
Planters' Bull ... Planters' Bulletin. Rubber Research Institute of Malaysia [*A
   publication*]
PLANTFACTS ... Steel Plants Information System [*German Iron and Steel
   Engineers Association*] [*Dusseldorf*] [*Information service
   or system*]   (IID)
Plant Field Lab Mimeo Rep Fla Univ ... Plantation Field Laboratory Mimeo
   Report. Florida University [*A publication*]
Plant Food Rev ... Plant Food Review [*A publication*]
Plant Foods Hum Nutr ... Plant Foods for Human Nutrition [*A publication*]
Plant Gard ... Plants and Gardens [*A publication*]
Plant Genet Resour Lett ... Plant Genetic Resources Newsletter [*A
   publication*]
Pl Anth .... Plains Anthropologist [*A publication*]
Plant Ind Dig (Manila) ... Plant Industry Digest (Manila) [*A publication*]
Plant Ind Ser Chin-Amer Joint Comm Rural Reconstr ... Plant Industry Series.
   Chinese-American Joint Commission on Rural
   Reconstruction [*A publication*]
Plant Ind Ser J Comm Rural Reconstr China (US Repub China) ... Plant
   Industry Series. Joint Commission on Rural
   Reconstruction in China (United States and Republic of
   China) [*A publication*]
Plant Info Bul ... Plant Information Bulletin [*A publication*]
Plant Maint ... Plant Maintenance [*A publication*]
Plant Maint Import Substitution ... Plant Maintenance and Import
   Substitution [*A publication*]
Plant Manage Eng ... Plant Management and Engineering [*A publication*]
Plant Med J Med Plant Res ... Planta Medica. Journal of Medicinal Plant
   Research [*A publication*]
Plant Med Phytother ... Plantes Medicinales et Phytotherapie [*A publication*]
Plant Mol Biol ... Plant Molecular Biology [*A publication*]
Plant Operations Prog ... Plant/Operations Progress [*A publication*]
Plant Oper Manage ... Plant Operating Management [*A publication*]
Plant Path ... Plant Pathology [*London*] [*A publication*]
Plant Pathol ... Plant Pathology [*A publication*]
Plant Pathol (Lond) ... Plant Pathology (London) [*A publication*]
Plant Physiol ... Plant Physiology [*A publication*]
Plant Physiol (Bethesda) ... Plant Physiology (Bethesda) [*A publication*]
Plant Physiol & Biochem ... Plant Physiology and Biochemistry [*A
   publication*]
Plant Physiol Commun (Shanghai) ... Plant Physiology Communications
   (Shanghai) [*A publication*]
Plant Physiol Suppl ... Plant Physiology. Supplement [*A publication*]
Plant Physl ... Plant Physiology [*A publication*]

Plant & Power Services Eng ... Plant and Power Services Engineer [*A publication*]
Plant Propagat ... Plant Propagator [*A publication*]
Plant Prot... Plant Protection [*A publication*]
Plant Prot Bull ... Plant Protection Bulletin [*A publication*]
Plant Prot Bull (Ankara) ... Plant Protection Bulletin (Ankara) [*A publication*]
Plant Prot Bull (New Delhi) ... Plant Protection Bulletin (New Delhi) [*A publication*]
Plant Prot Overseas Rev ... Plant Protection Overseas Review [*A publication*]
Plant Prot Q ... Plant Protection Quarterly [*A publication*]
Plant Sci Bull ... Plant Science Bulletin [*A publication*]
Plant Sci L ... Plant Science Letters [*A publication*]
Plant Sci Lett ... Plant Science Letters [*A publication*]
Plant Sci (Lucknow) ... Plant Science (Lucknow, India) [*A publication*]
Plant Sci (Lucknow India) ... Plant Science (Lucknow, India) [*A publication*]
Plant Sci (Shannon) ... Plant Science (Shannon) [*A publication*]
Plant Sci (Sofia) ... Plant Science (Sofia) [*A publication*]
Plants Gard ... Plants and Gardens [*A publication*]
Plant Sugar Manuf ... Planter and Sugar Manufacturer [*A publication*]
Plant Sys E ... Plant Systematics and Evolution [*A publication*]
Plant Syst Evol ... Plant Systematics and Evolution [*A publication*]
Plant Var Seeds ... Plant Varieties and Seeds [*A publication*]
PLANY ...... Protestant Lawyers Association of New York   (EA)
PLAO .... Parts List Assembly Order   (MCD)
PLAP .... Latin American Perspectives [*A publication*]
PLAP .... Placental Alkaline Phosphatase [*An enzyme*]
PLAP .... Power Lever Angle Position   (MCD)
Pla Par .... Placita Parliamentaria [*Latin*] [*A publication*]   (DLA)
PLapK .... Keystone Junior College, La Plume, PA [*Library symbol*] [*Library of Congress*]   (LCLS)
PLA PLSS ... PLA [*Public Library Association*] Public Library Systems Section
PLAQ .... Modern Language Quarterly [*A publication*]
PLAQ .... PLA [*Private Libraries Association*] Quarterly [*A publication*]
PLAR .... Latin American Research Review [*A publication*]
PLARA ...... Plastverarbeiter [*A publication*]
PLARS ...... Position Location and Reporting System [*Military*]   (INF)
PLAS .... Plaster   (AAG)
PLAS .... Private Line Assured Service [*Telecommunications*]   (TEL)
PLAS .... Program Logical Address Space
PLAS .... Programmable Link Adaptation System   (MCD)
PLASCAMS ... Plastics: Computer Aided Materials Selector [*Rapra Technology Ltd.*] [*Information service or system*]   (CRD)
Plas Compd ... Plastics Compounding [*A publication*]
Plas Com R ... Plastics Compounding Redbook [*A publication*]
Plas Desgn ... Plastics Design Forum [*A publication*]
Plas Eng..... Plastics Engineering [*A publication*]
Plas Ind ES ... Plastics Industry Europe. Special Report [*A publication*]
Plas Ind Eur ... Plastics Industry Europe [*A publication*]
Plas Ind N ... Plastics Industry News [*A publication*]
PLASMA .. Parents League of American Students of Medicine Abroad   (EA)
Plasma Chem ... Plasma Chemistry and Plasma Processing [*A publication*]
Plasma Chem Plasma Process ... Plasma Chemistry and Plasma Processing [*A publication*]
Plasma Phys ... Plasma Physics [*A publication*]
Plasma Phys Contr Nucl Fusion Res Conf Proc ... Plasma Physics and Controlled Nuclear Fusion Research. Conference Proceedings [*A publication*]
Plasma Phys Controlled Fusion ... Plasma Physics and Controlled Fusion [*A publication*]
Plasma Phys Index ... Plasma Physics Index [*West Germany*] [*A publication*]
Plas Massy ... Plasticheskie Massy [*A publication*]
PLASMEX ... International Plastics Exhibition
PLA SMLS ... PLA [*Public Library Association*] Small and Medium-Sized Libraries Section
Plas R Surg ... Plastic and Reconstructive Surgery [*A publication*]
Plas Rubbers Text ... Plastics, Rubbers, Textiles [*A publication*]
Plas Rub Int ... Plastics and Rubber International [*A publication*]
Plas Rubr ... Plastics and Rubber Weekly [*A publication*]
PLAST .... Propellant Loading and All Systems Test [*NASA*]   (KSC)
Plast Abstr ... Plastic Abstracts [*A publication*]
Plast Age.... Plastics Age [*A publication*]
Plast Aust .. Plastics in Australia [*A publication*]
Plast Bldg Constr ... Plastics in Building Construction [*A publication*]
Plast Build Constr ... Plastics in Building Construction [*A publication*]
Plast Bull (London) ... Plastics Bulletin (London) [*A publication*]
Plast Busin ... Plastics Business [*A publication*]
Plast Compd ... Plastics Compounding [*A publication*]
Plast Compounding ... Plastics Compounding [*A publication*]
Plast Des Process ... Plastics Design and Processing [*A publication*]
Plast Dig.... Plastics Digest [*A publication*]
PLASTEC ... Plastics Technical Evaluation Center [*Army*] [*Dover, NJ*]
PLASTEC Note ... PLASTEC [*Plastics Technical Evaluation Center*] Note [*A publication*]
PLASTEC Rep ... PLASTEC [*Plastics Technical Evaluation Center*] Report [*A publication*]
Plaste Kaut ... Plaste und Kautschuk [*A publication*]
Plaste und Kautsch ... Plaste und Kautschuk [*A publication*]
Plast Eng ... Plastics Engineering [*A publication*]
Plast Engng ... Plastics Engineering [*A publication*]

PLASTEUROTEC ... Groupement Europeen des Fabricants de Pieces Techniques Plastiques [*European Group of Fabricators of Technical Plastics Parts*]   (EAIO)
Plast Flash ... Plastiques Flash [*A publication*]
Plast Hmoty Kauc ... Plasticke Hmoty a Kaucuk [*A publication*]
Plastiche .... Materie Plastiche ed Elastomeri [*A publication*]
Plastic IN... Plastics Industry News [*A publication*]
Plastico ...... Noticiero del Plastico [*A publication*]
Plastic Prod ... Plastic Products [*A publication*]
Plastics in Aust ... Plastics in Australia [*A publication*]   (APTA)
Plastics Engng ... Plastics Engineering [*A publication*]
Plast Ind .... Plastic Industry [*India*] [*A publication*]
Plast Ind News ... Plastics Industry News [*A publication*]
Plast Ind News (Jap) ... Plastics Industry News (Japan) [*A publication*]
Plast Ind (NY) ... Plastics Industry (New York) [*A publication*]
Plast Ind (Paris) ... Plastiques et Industrie (Paris) [*A publication*]
Plast Inst Trans ... Plastics Institute. Transactions [*A publication*]
Plast Inst Trans J ... Plastics Institute. Transactions and Journal [*A publication*]
Plast Inst Trans J Conf Suppl ... Plastics Institute. Transactions and Journal. Conference Supplement [*A publication*]
Plast Kauc ... Plasty a Kaucuk [*A publication*]
Plast Massen Wiss Tech ... Plastische Massen in Wissenschaft und Technik [*A publication*]
Plast Massy ... Plasticheskie Massy [*A publication*]
Plast Mater (Tokyo) ... Plastics Materials (Tokyo) [*A publication*]
Plast M & E ... Plastics Machinery and Equipment [*A publication*]
Plast Mod .. Plasticos Modernos [*A publication*]
Plast Mod Elast ... Plastiques Modernes et Elastomeres [*A publication*]
Plast Mod Elastomeres ... Plastiques Modernes et Elastomeres [*A publication*]
Plast Molded Prod ... Plastics and Molded Products [*A publication*]
Plast News ... Plastics News [*A publication*]   (APTA)
Plast News (Aust) ... Plastics News (Australia) [*A publication*]
Plast News Briefs ... Plastics News. Briefs [*A publication*]
Plast Paint Rubber ... Plastics, Paint, and Rubber [*A publication*]
Plast Panorama ... Plast Panorama Scandinavia [*A publication*]
Plast Polym ... Plastics and Polymers [*A publication*]
Plast Polym Conf Suppl ... Plastics and Polymers. Conference Supplement [*A publication*]
Plast Prod .. Plastic Products [*A publication*]
Plast Prog India ... Plastics Progress in India [*A publication*]
Plast Reconstr Surg ... Plastic and Reconstructive Surgery [*A publication*]
Plast Reconstr Surg Transplant Bull ... Plastic and Reconstructive Surgery and the Transplantation Bulletin [*A publication*]
Plast Renf Fibres Verre Text ... Plastiques Renforces Fibres de Verre Textile [*A publication*]
Plast Resinas ... Plasticos y Resinas [*Mexico*] [*A publication*]
Plast Resins ... Plastics and Resins [*A publication*]
Plast Retail Packag Bull ... Plastics in Retail Packaging Bulletin [*A publication*]
Plast Rubber ... Plastics and Rubber [*Later, Plastics and Rubber International*] [*A publication*]
Plast Rubber Int ... Plastics and Rubber International [*A publication*]
Plast Rubber Mater Appl ... Plastics and Rubber. Material and Applications [*A publication*]
Plast Rubber News ... Plastics and Rubber News [*South Africa*] [*A publication*]
Plast Rubber Proc Appl ... Plastics and Rubber Processing and Applications [*A publication*]
Plast Rubber Process ... Plastics and Rubber Processing and Applications [*A publication*]
Plast & Rubber Process & Appl ... Plastics and Rubber Processing and Applications [*A publication*]
Plast Rubbers Text ... Plastics, Rubbers, Textiles [*A publication*]
Plast Rubber Wkly ... Plastics and Rubber Weekly [*England*] [*A publication*]
Plast Rubb Int ... Plastics and Rubber International [*A publication*]
Plast Rubb News ... Plastics and Rubber News [*South Africa*] [*A publication*]
Plast Rubb Process Appln ... Plastics and Rubber Processing and Applications [*A publication*]
Plast Rub Wkly ... Plastics and Rubber Weekly [*A publication*]
Plast (S Afr) ... Plastics (Southern Africa) [*A publication*]
Plast (S Africa) ... Plastics (Southern Africa) [*A publication*]
Plast (Sthn Afr) ... Plastics (Southern Africa) [*A publication*]
Plast Surg Nurs ... Plastic Surgical Nursing [*A publication*]
Plast Tech ... Plastics Technology [*A publication*]
Plast Technol ... Plastics Technology [*A publication*]
Plast Today ... Plastics Today [*A publication*]
Plast Trends ... Plastics Trends [*A publication*]
Plast Univers ... Plasticos Universales [*A publication*]
Plast World ... Plastics World [*A publication*]
PLAT .... Pilot-LOS [*Line of Sight*] Landing Aid Television   (NG)
PLAT .... Plateau [*Board on Geographic Names*]
PLAT .... Platelet [*Hematology*]
PLAT .... Platform   (KSC)
PLAT .... Platinum [*Chemical symbol is Pt*]   (AAG)
PLAT .... Platinum Technology [*NASDAQ symbol*]   (SPSG)
PLAT .... Platonic
PLAT .... Platoon
PLAT .... Platt National Park
PLAT .... Present Latitude [*Aviation*]   (FAAC)
PLATA ...... Plating [*A publication*]

Plateau Q Mus North Ariz ... Plateau. Quarterly of the Museum of Northern Arizona [*A publication*]
PLATF...... Platform (AAG)
Plating & Surface Finish ... Plating and Surface Finishing [*A publication*]
Platinum Met Rev ... Platinum Metals Review [*A publication*]
PLATLDR ... Platoon Leader [*Military*]
PLATN...... Platinum [*Chemistry*] (ROG)
PLATO...... Pennzoil Louisiana and Texas Offshore [*Oil industry group*]
PLATO...... Platform Observables Subassembly
PLATO...... Pollution Liability Agreement Among Tanker Owners [*Insurance*] (DS)
PLATO...... Programmed Logic for Automatic Teaching [*or Training*] Operations [*University of Illinois*] [*Programming language*]
Platoon Sch ... Platoon School [*A publication*]
PLATR ...... Pawling Lattice Test Rig [*United Nuclear Co.*]
PLATS...... Pilot Landing and Takeoff System (IIA)
PLatS......... Saint Vincent College, Latrobe, PA [*Library symbol*] [*Library of Congress*] (LCLS)
Plat Surf Finish ... Plating and Surface Finishing [*A publication*]
Platt .... Platt on the Law of Covenants [*1829*] [*A publication*] (DLA)
Platt .... Platt on Leases [*A publication*] (DLA)
Platt Cov ... Platt on the Law of Covenants [*A publication*] (DLA)
Platt Leas... Platt on Leases [*1847*] [*A publication*] (DLA)
PLAT/VLA ... Pilot Landing Aid Television / Visual Landing Aid [*System*] (DNAB)
Plaut......... Plautus [*Third century BC*] [*Classical studies*] (OCD)
PLAV........ Polish Legion of American Veterans, USA (EA)
PLAVA...... Polish Legion of American Veterans, USA, Ladies Auxiliary (EA)
PLAVLA ... Polish Legion of American Veterans, USA, Ladies Auxiliary (EA)
PLAWA..... Plastics World [*A publication*]
Plaxton....... Plaxton's Canadian Constitutional Decisions [*A publication*] (DLA)
PLAY........ Players International, Inc. [*NASDAQ symbol*] (NQ)
PLAY........ [*The*] Playgoer [*A publication*]
Playb.......... Playboy [*A publication*]
Playby........ Playboy Enterprises, Inc. [*Associated Press abbreviation*] (APAG)
Players Mag ... Players Magazine [*A publication*]
Playmate.... Children's Playmate Magazine [*A publication*]
PLAZ........ Plaza Communications [*NASDAQ symbol*] (NQ)
PLB........... Papyrologica Lugduno-Batava [*A publication*]
PLB........... Payload Bay [*NASA*] (MCD)
PLB........... Per Pound [*Freight*]
PLB........... Personal Locator Beacon [*Military*] (AFM)
PLB........... Plattsburgh [*New York*] [*Airport symbol*] (OAG)
PLB........... Plattsburgh, NY [*Location identifier*] [*FAA*] (FAAL)
PLB........... Plumbing Mart [*Vancouver Stock Exchange symbol*]
PLB........... Poor Law Board
PLB........... Proctolin-Like Bioactivity [*Neurobiology*]
PLB........... Public Light Bus [*British*]
PLB........... Publisher's Library Binding
PLB........... Pullbutton (AAG)
PLBD........ Payload Bay Door [*NASA*] (MCD)
PLBD........ Plugboard (MSA)
PLBG........ Plumbing (WGA)
Pl Biochem J ... Plant Biochemical Journal [*A publication*]
PLBK........ Playback (NASA)
PL-BL........ Plate Block [*Philately*]
PLBLK...... Pillow Block
PLBNDJ...... Faculte des Sciences Agronomiques. Laboratoire de Biochimie de la Nutrition. Publication [*A publication*]
PLBOL...... Position Launch/Bearing Only Launch
PLBPDP.... Contribution on the Paleolimnology of Lake Biwa and the Japanese Pleistocene [*A publication*]
PLBR........ Plumber (WGA)
PLBR........ Prototype Large Breeder Reactor [*Also, NCBR*] [*Nuclear energy*]
Pl Breed Abstr ... Plant Breeding Abstracts [*A publication*]
PLBYD...... Plan og Bygg [*A publication*]
PLC........... Pacific Logging Congress (EA)
PLC........... Palomares Road [*California*] [*Seismograph station code, US Geological Survey*] (SEIS)
PLC........... Parti de la Liberte du Citoyen [*Belgium*] [*Political party*] (EY)
PLC........... Partido Liberal Constitucionalista [*Constitutionalist Liberal Party*] [*Nicaragua*] [*Political party*] (PPW)
PLC........... Patrice Lumumba Coalition (EA)
PLC........... Paymaster-Lieutenant-Commander [*Navy*] [*British*]
PLC........... Periventricular Leukomalacia Complex [*Medicine*]
PLC........... Perry-Link Cubmarine [*A submersible vehicle*]
PLC........... Phospholipase C [*An enzyme*]
PLC........... Phospholysine C [*Biochemistry*]
PLC........... Pilot Laboratories Corp. [*Vancouver Stock Exchange symbol*]
PLC........... Placer Development Ltd. [*AMEX symbol*] (SPSG)
Pl C .... Placita Coronae [*Pleas of the Crown*] [*Latin*] [*Legal term*] (DLA)
PLC........... Planar Chromatography
PLC........... Platform Control
PLC........... Platoon Leader's Class [*Army*]

PLC........... PLC Systems [*Associated Press abbreviation*] (APAG)
PLC........... PLC Systems [*AMEX symbol*] (SPSG)
PLC........... Pneumatic Lead Cutter
PLC........... Poet Laureatus Caesareus [*Imperial Poet Laureate*] [*Latin*] (ROG)
PLC........... Point Loma College [*California*]
PLC........... Poor Law Commissioners [*British*]
PLC........... Power Lever Control (MCD)
PLC........... Power Line Carrier
PLC........... Power Line Communications
PLC........... Predictive Linguistic Constraint
PLC........... Presbyterian Lay Committee (EA)
PLC........... Primary Leadership Course [*Army*]
PLC........... Primary Location Code [*Data processing*]
PLC........... Prime Level Code
PLC........... Princeton University. Library. Chronicle [*A publication*]
PLC........... Process Liquid Chromatography
PLC........... Production Line Configured [*Military*] (CAAL)
PLC........... Products List Circular [*Patents*]
PLC........... Program-Length Commercial [*Television*]
PLC........... Program Level Change Tape [*Data processing*] (IBMDP)
PLC........... Programmable Logic Control [*Data processing*]
PLC........... Programming Language Committee [*CODASYL*]
PLC........... Proinsulin-Like Compound [*Endocrinology*]
PLC........... Pseudophase Liquid Chromatography
PLC........... Public Lands Council (EA)
PLC........... Public Lighting Commission
PLC........... Public Limited Co. [*British*]
PLCA........ Pipe Line Contractors Association (EA)
PLCAA..... Professional Lawn Care Association of America (EA)
PLCAI...... Pipe Line Contractors Association, International (EA)
PLCB........ Pseudoline Control Block [*Data processing*]
PLCC........ Plastic Leadless Chip Carrier [*Computer technology*] (PCM)
PLCC........ Primary Liver Cell Cancer [*Oncology*]
PLCC........ Propulsion Local Control Console (DNAB)
PLCD........ Product Liability Common Defense [*Later, PLPD*] [*An association*] (EA)
PLCEA ...... Part-Length Control Element Assembly [*Nuclear energy*] (NRCH)
PLCEDM .. Part-Length Control Element Drive Mechanism [*Nuclear energy*] (NRCH)
PLCEDV ... Plant Cell and Environment [*A publication*]
Pl Cell .... Plant Cell [*A publication*]
PLCH .... Kiritimati Island [*Christmas Islands*] [*Kiribati*] [*ICAO location identifier*] (ICLI)
PLCHB...... Physiological Chemistry and Physics [*Later, Physiological Chemistry and Physics and Medical NMR*] [*A publication*]
PLCLAS.... Propagation Loss Classification System [*Navy*] (NVT)
PLCM........ Propellant Loading Control Monitor [*NASA*] (KSC)
PLCMC ..... Public Library of Charlotte and Mecklenburg County [*North Carolina*]
PLCM & ND ... Proceedings. Linguistic Circle of Manitoba and North Dakota [*A publication*]
PLCN......... Parts List Change Notice (MCD)
PLCN-A .... Plan Canada [*A publication*]
PLCNY....... Publications. Linguistic Circle of New York [*A publication*]
Pl Com ...... Plowden's English King's Bench Commentaries [*or Reports*] [*1550-80*] [*England*] [*A publication*] (DLA)
PL Com ...... Poor Law Commissioner [*A publication*] (DLA)
PLCOP...... Prelaunch Checkout Plan [*NASA*] (KSC)
PLCP .... Law and Contemporary Problems [*A publication*]
PLCPB....... Plant and Cell Physiology [*A publication*]
Pl Cr Con Tr ... Plowden's Criminal Conversation Trials [*A publication*] (DLA)
PLCS .... Proceedings. London Classical Society [*A publication*]
PLCS .... Propellant Loading Control System [*NASA*] (AAG)
PLC Sys..... PLC Systems [*Associated Press abbreviation*] (APAG)
PLCU........ Propellant Level Control Unit [*NASA*] (KSC)
PLCV......... Pelargonium Leaf Curl Virus [*Plant pathology*]
PLCWTWU ... Power Loom Carpet Weavers' and Textile Workers' Union [*British*]
PLCY......... Policy (AFM)
PlcyMg ...... Policy Management Systems [*Associated Press abbreviation*] (APAG)
PLD .... All Pakistan Legal Decisions [*A publication*] (ILCA)
PLD .... Paid Land Diversion Program [*Department of Agriculture*] (GFGA)
PLD .... Parti Liberal-Democrate [*Cameroon*] [*Political party*] (EY)
PLD .... Partial Lipodystrophy [*Medicine*]
PLD .... Partido de la Liberacion Dominicana [*Dominican Liberation Party*] [*Dominican Republic*] [*Political party*] (PPW)
PLd .... Path Loss, Downlink [*Communications*]
PLD .... Payload [*NASA*]
PLD .... Personnel Letdown Device
PLD .... Phase Lock Demodulator
PLD .... Phospholipase D [*An enzyme*]
PLD .... Plaid (ADA)
PLD .... Plated (MSA)
PLD .... Platelet Defect [*Hematology*] (MAE)
PLD .... Played Matches [*Cricket*] (ROG)

PLD .... Portland, IN [*Location identifier*] [*FAA*] (FAAL)
PLD .... Posterior Latissimus Dorsi [*Anatomy*]
PLD .... Posterolateral Dendrite [*Neurology*]
PLD .... Potentially Lethal Damage [*Medicine*]
PLD .... Precision LASER Designator (RDA)
PLD .... Primary Layer Depth [*Military*] (CAAL)
PLD .... Principle of Limit Design
PLD .... Probable Line of Deployment [*Army*] (AABC)
PLD .... Procurement Legal Division [*Later, Office of General Counsel*] [*Navy*]
PLD .... Product Line Development
PLD .... Program Listing Document (MCD)
PLD .... Programmable Logic Device
PLD .... Protective LASER Devices (MCD)
PLD .... Public Libraries Division. Reporter [*A publication*]
PLD .... Pulse-Length Discriminator (IEEE)
PLD .... Pulse Level Detector (MCD)
PLdaC .... Calvary Baptist School of Theology, Lansdale, PA [*Library symbol*] [*Library of Congress*] (LCLS)
PLDAL ...... Pro-Life Direct Action League (EA)
PLDC .... Preliminary List of Design Changes
PLDC .... Primary Leadership Development Course [*Army*] (INF)
PLDC .... Primary Long-Distance Carrier [*Telephone service*]
PLDG .... Portuguese Language Development Group [*Modern Language Association of America*] (AEBS)
PLDH .... Plasma Lactic Dehydrogenase [*An enzyme*] (AAMN)
PLDI .... Payload Data Interleaver [*NASA*] (MCD)
PLDI .... Plastic Die [*Tool*] (AAG)
P & L Dig Laws ... Pepper and Lewis' Digest of Laws [*Pennsylvania*] [*A publication*] (DLA)
PLDK .... Peabody Language Development Kits [*Education*]
PLDM .... Payload Management [*NASA*] (MCD)
PLDMI ..... Precise LASER Distance Measuring Instrument
PLDP .... Parti Liberal Democrate et Pluraliste [*Belgium*] [*Political party*] (PPW)
PLDP .... Public Library Development Plan [*American Library Association, Public Library Association*]
PLD-PACOM ... Petroleum Logistical Data - Pacific Command (CINC)
PLDR .... Potentially Lethal Damage Repair [*Medicine*]
PLDRA ...... Plant Disease Reporter [*A publication*]
PLDS .... Payload Support [*NASA*] (MCD)
PLDS .... Public Library Data Service
PLDT .... Philippine Long Distance Telephone Co.
PLDTS ...... Propellant Loading Data Transmission System [*NASA*] (KSC)
PLE .... Encyclopedia of Pennsylvania Law [*A publication*] (DLA)
PLE .... Phased Loading Entry [*Data processing*]
PLE .... Photoluminescence Excitation [*Physics*]
PLE .... [*The*] Pittsburgh & Lake Erie Railroad Co. [*AAR code*]
PLE .... Planned Life Extension [*Pershing*] (MCD)
Ple .... Pleiade [*Record label*] [*France*]
PLE .... Plesetsk [*Satellite launch complex*] [*Former USSR*]
PLE .... Preliminary Logistics Evaluation
PLE .... Primary Loss Expectancy [*Insurance*]
PLE .... Prudent Limit of Endurance (NVT)
PLE .... Pulse Length Error (MCD)
PLE .... Pulsed LASER Experiment
PLEA .... Pacific Lumber Exporters Association (EA)
PLEA .... Poverty Lawyers for Effective Advocacy
PLEA .... Prototype Language for Economic Analysis [*Data processing*] (IID)
PLEAD ...... Place of Last Entered Active Duty [*Military*]
PLEADGS ... Pleadings [*Legal term*] (ROG)
PLEASE .... Parolees, Law-Enforcement Assist Student Education [*Project to reduce drug abuse among junior and senior high school students in California*]
PLeB .... Bucknell University, Lewisburg, PA [*Library symbol*] [*Library of Congress*] (LCLS)
PLEB .... Plebeian (WGA)
PLEB .... Plebiscitum [*A Decree of the People*] [*Latin*] (DLA)
PLebHi ...... Lebanon County Historical Society, Lebanon, PA [*Library symbol*] [*Library of Congress*] (LCLS)
PLebV .... United States Veterans Administration Hospital, Lebanon, PA [*Library symbol*] [*Library of Congress*] (LCLS)
PLED .... Periodic Lateralized Epileptiform Discharge [*Medicine*] (MAE)
PLEGA ...... Plant Engineering [*A publication*]
PLEGB ...... Plastics Engineering [*A publication*]
P Leg J .... Pittsburgh Legal Journal [*Pennsylvania*] [*A publication*] (DLA)
P Leg Jour ... Pittsburgh Legal Journal [*Pennsylvania*] [*A publication*] (DLA)
PLEI .... Journal of Leisure Research [*A publication*]
PLEI .... Public Law Education Institute (EA)
PLEN........ Plenipotentiary
PLEN........ Plenum Publishing Corp. [*NASDAQ symbol*] (NQ)
PLEN........ Public Leadership Education Network (EA)
PLENA ...... Plant Engineering [*A publication*]
PLENAPS ... Plans for the Employment of Naval and Air Forces of the Associated Powers in the Eastern Theatre in the Event of War with Japan
PLENCH... Pliers and Wrench [*Combination tool*]
PLEND...... Plumbing Engineer [*A publication*]
P & LERR ... [*The*] Pittsburgh & Lake Erie Railroad Co.

PLESA....... Programs for Persons with Limited English-Speaking Ability [*Department of Labor*]
Pleur Fl...... Pleural Fluid [*Medicine*] (MAE)
PLEURO... Pleuropneumonia [*Veterinary medicine*] (DSUE)
PLEVA ...... Pityriasis Lichenoides et Varioliformis Acuta [*Dermatology*] (MAE)
PLF .... Franklin and Marshall College, Lancaster, PA [*Library symbol*] [*Library of Congress*] (LCLS)
PLF .... Free Library of Philadelphia, Philadelphia, PA [*OCLC symbol*] (OCLC)
PLF .... Pacific Legal Foundation (EA)
PLF .... Page Length Field
PLF .... Palestine Liberation Front [*Political party*] (PD)
PLF .... Parachute Landing Fall [*Military*]
PLF .... Pastel Food [*Vancouver Stock Exchange symbol*]
PLF .... Patient Load Factor (AFM)
PLF .... People's Liberation Forces [*Ethiopia*] [*Political party*] (AF)
PLF .... Perilymph Fistula [*Medicine*]
PLF .... Phase Lock Frequency
PLF .... Phone Line Formatter
PLF .... Plaintiff
PLF .... Polar Lipid Fraction [*Biochemistry*]
PLF .... Positive Lock Fastener
PLF .... Power for Level Flight [*Aeronautics*]
PLF .... Private Line Telephone
PLF .... Proposition Letter Formula
PLF .... Public Administration [*A publication*]
PLFA .... Primary Level Field Activity [*Defense Supply Agency*]
PLFA .... Tabueran Island [*Fanning Islands*] [*Kiribati*] [*ICAO location identifier*] (ICLI)
Plf Adv ...... Plaintiff's Advocate [*A publication*]
PLFC .... Pulaski Furniture Corp. [*NASDAQ symbol*] (NQ)
PLFC & A ... Peggy Lee Fan Club and Archives [*Later, OOPLFC & A*] (EA)
PLFE .... Presidential Life Corp. [*NASDAQ symbol*] (NQ)
PLFF .... Plaintiff
PLFQ .... Literature/Film Quarterly [*A publication*]
PLFS........ Polarforschung [*A publication*]
PLFTR....... Please Furnish Transportation Requests (NOAA)
PLFUR....... Please Furnish (NOAA)
PLG .... Pakistan Labour Gazette [*A publication*]
PLG .... Piling (MSA)
PLG .... Place Resources Corp. [*Toronto Stock Exchange symbol*]
PLG .... Plane Guard (NVT)
PLG .... Plant Management and Engineering [*A publication*]
PLG .... Pleural Ganglion [*Medicine*]
PLG .... Plug (AAG)
PLG .... Poetae Lyrici Graeci [*A publication*] (OCD)
PLG .... PolyGram NV [*NYSE symbol*] (SPSG)
PLG .... Polygyros [*Greece*] [*Seismograph station code, US Geological Survey*] (SEIS)
PLG .... Poor Law Guardian [*British*]
PLG .... Private-Label and Generic Brands
PLG .... Probleme de Lingvistica Genarala [*A publication*]
PLG .... Progressive Librarians Guild [*American Library Association*]
PLG .... Prolyl(leucyl)glycinamide [*Biochemistry*]
PLG .... Pulsed Light Generator
PLGAA...... Plants and Gardens [*A publication*]
PLGC........ Presbyterians for Lesbian/Gay Concerns (EA)
PLGFA ...... Poligrafiya [*A publication*]
PLGJA ...... Pipeline and Gas Journal [*A publication*]
PLGL .... Plate Glass
PLGM....... NYC Parents of Lesbians and Gay Men (EA)
PLGR........ Plunger (MSA)
PLGS .... Partita Liberale Giovani Somali [*Somali Liberal Youth Party*] [*Political party*]
PLGSS....... Payload Ground Support Systems [*NASA*] (NASA)
PLGT........ Prototype Lunar Geologist Tool
P-LGV ...... Psittacosis-Lymphogranuloma Venereum [*Medicine*]
PLH .... Hamilton Watch Co., Lancaster, PA [*Library symbol*] [*Library of Congress*] [*Obsolete*] (LCLS)
PLH .... Palaemontes-Lightening Hormone
PLH .... Partido Liberal de Honduras [*Liberal Party of Honduras*] [*Political party*] (PPW)
PLH .... Payload Handling [*NASA*] (NASA)
PLH .... Plaser Light [*Vancouver Stock Exchange symbol*]
PLH .... Plymouth [*England*] [*Airport symbol*] (OAG)
PLH .... Punjab Light Horse [*British military*] (DMA)
PLHi .... Lancaster County Historical Society, Lancaster, PA [*Library symbol*] [*Library of Congress*] (LCLS)
PLHID....... Plant Hire [*A publication*]
PLHJA ...... Plumbing and Heating Journal [*A publication*]
PLhS......... Lock Haven State College, Lock Haven, PA [*Library symbol*] [*Library of Congress*] (LCLS)
PLI .... Leiner [*P.*] Nutritional Products Corp. [*AMEX symbol*] (SPSG)
PLI .... Ltd. Systems [*Vancouver Stock Exchange symbol*]
pli .... Pali [*MARC language code*] [*Library of Congress*] (LCCP)
PLI .... Panarea [*Lipari Islands*] [*Seismograph station code, US Geological Survey*] (SEIS)
PLI .... Partido Liberal Independiente [*Independent Liberal Party*] [*Nicaragua*] [*Political party*] (PPW)

PLI............ Partito Liberale Italiano [*Italian Liberal Party*] [*Political party*]   (PPW)
PLI............ Passenger and Immigration Lists Index [*A publication*]
PLI............ Payload Interrogator [*NASA*]   (MCD)
PLI............ Phone Line Interface [*IBM Corp.*]   (PCM)
PLI............ Pilot Location Indicator
PLI............ Power Level Indicator
PLI............ Practising Law Institute   (EA)
PLI............ Preload Indicating
PLI............ Private Line Interface
PLI............ Proctolin-Like Immunoactivity [*Neurobiology*]
PLI............ Public Lands Institute   (EA)
PLI............ Pulsed LASER Interferomètry
PLIA.......... Pollution Liability Insurance Association [*Downers Grove, IL*]   (EA)
PLIANT .... Procedural Language Implementing Analog Techniques [*Data processing*]   (IEEE)
PLIB......... Pacific Lumber Inspection Bureau   (EA)
PLIB......... Program Library [*Data processing*]
PLICK....... Pride, Loyalty, Integrity, Capability, Knowledge   (DNAB)
PLIE......... Phase Linear Interferometer Experiment   (MCD)
PLI F......... Polo Laico Liberali-Repubblicani Federalisti [*Italy*] [*Political party*]   (ECED)
PLIM........ Post Launch Information Message [*NASA*]   (KSC)
PLIMC...... Pipe Line Insurance Managers Conference [*Defunct*]   (EA)
PLimT....... Tyler Arboretum, Lima, PA [*Library symbol*] [*Library of Congress*]   (LCLS)
PLIN......... Power Line Impedance Network
PLINA...... Pipe Line Industry [*A publication*]
PLing .... Papers in Linguistics [*A publication*]
PLINK....... American People/Link [*American Design and Communication*] [*Information service or system*]   (IID)
PLIR......... Literary Review [*A publication*]
PLIRRA..... Pollution Liability Insurance and Risk Retention Act   (GFGA)
PLIS......... Preclinical Literature Information System [*Data processing*]
PLISN ...... Parts List Item Sequence Number   (MCD)
PLISN ...... Provisioning List Item Sequence Number   (NASA)
PLISP....... [*A*] Programming Language   (CSR)
PLISSIT.... Permission, Limited Information, Specific Suggestions, and Intensive Therapy [*Occupational therapy*]
PLIT .... Petrolite Corp. [*NASDAQ symbol*]   (NQ)
PLITTY..... Private Line Teletypewriter Service [*Telecommunications*]   (TEL)
PLIUN....... Partido Liberal Independiente de Unidad Nacional [*Nicaragua*] [*Political party*]   (EY)
PLIW........ Preload Indicating Washer
PLJ .... Pacific Law Journal [*A publication*]   (ILCA)
PLJ .... Parliamentary Lobby Journalists [*British*]
PLJ .... Pass Lake Resources Ltd. [*Vancouver Stock Exchange symbol*]
PLJ .... Patna Law Journal [*India*] [*A publication*]   (ILCA)
PLJ .... Pennsylvania Law Journal [*A publication*]   (DLA)
PLJ .... Philippine Law Journal [*A publication*]   (ILCA)
PLJ .... Philippine Library Journal [*A publication*]
PLJ .... Pittsburgh Legal Journal [*Pennsylvania*] [*A publication*]   (DLA)
PLJ .... Punjab Law Reporter [*India*] [*A publication*]   (DLA)
PLJ .... Pure Lemon Juice
PLJ NS...... Pittsburgh Legal Journal, New Series [*Pennsylvania*] [*A publication*]   (DLA)
PLK........... Branson, MO [*Location identifier*] [*FAA*]   (FAAL)
PLK........... Phi Lambda Kappa [*Fraternity*]
PLK........... Plank   (AAG)
PLK........... Ploecker-Lee-Kesler [*Equation of state*]
PLK........... Plucky Little King [*Used by Western diplomats in Amman in reference to King Hussein of Jordan*]
PLK........... Poincare-Lighthill-Kuo [*Method*]
PLKAA...... Plaste und Kautschuk [*A publication*]
PLKR........ Peacoat Locker
PLL........... Pall Corp. [*AMEX symbol*] [*NYSE symbol*]   (SPSG)
PLL........... Pallet [*Building construction*]
PLL........... Papers on Language and Literature [*A publication*]
PLL........... Parts Load List   (MCD)
PLL........... Passenger Legal Liability [*Insurance*]   (AIA)
PLL........... Peripheral Light Loss
PLL........... Permanent Logical Link [*Telecommunications*]
PLL........... Phase-Locked Loop [*NASA*]
Pl L........... Platt on Leases [*1841*] [*A publication*]   (DLA)
PLL........... Polo, IL [*Location identifier*] [*FAA*]   (FAAL)
PLL........... Poly-L-lysine [*Also, PL*] [*Biochemistry*]
PLL........... Positive Logic Level
PLL........... Prescribed Load List [*Vehicle maintenance operation*] [*Army*]
PLL........... Prolymphocytic Leukemia [*Also, PL*] [*Oncology*]
PLL........... Pseudoalcoholic Liver Lesions [*Medicine*]
PLLAA ...... Royal Society. Proceedings. Series A. Mathematical and Physical Sciences [*A publication*]
P & L Laws ... Private and Local Laws [*A publication*]   (DLA)
PLLE .... Prueba de Lectura y Lenguaje Escrito [*Standardized test of reading and writing in Spanish for students in grades 3 through 10*]
PLLL .... Parallel Petroleum Corp. [*NASDAQ symbol*]   (NQ)
PLLL .... Posterior Lateral Line Lobe [*Of electric fishes*]

PLLP .... Polish Literature/Litterature Polonaise [*A publication*]
PLLR .... Phase Lock Loop Receiver
PLLRC ...... Public Land Law Review Commission [*Terminated, 1970*]
PLLT .... Pallet   (NATG)
PLLTN ...... Pollution
PLLVM ..... Pennsylvania Farm Museum of Landis Valley, Lancaster, PA [*Library symbol*] [*Library of Congress*]   (LCLS)
PLM .... Pacific Law Magazine [*A publication*]   (DLA)
PLM .... Packaged Liquid Missile
PLM .... Pakistan Liberation Movement [*Political party*]   (PD)
PLM .... Palembang [*Indonesia*] [*Airport symbol*]   (OAG)
PLM .... Palomar [*California*] [*Seismograph station code, US Geological Survey*]   (SEIS)
PLM .... Papers in Linguistics of Melanesia [*A publication*]
PLM .... Passive Line Monitor [*Datapoint*]
PLM .... Passive Lunar Marker
PLM .... Payload Management [*NASA*]   (NASA)
PLM .... Payload Monitoring [*NASA*]   (NASA)
PLM .... People's Liberation Movement [*Montserrat*] [*Political party*]   (PPW)
PLM .... Percent Labeled Mitosis [*Cytology*]
PLM .... Phleomycin [*Biochemistry*]
PLM .... Plastic Laminating Mold   (MCD)
PLM .... PLM International, Inc. [*Associated Press abbreviation*]   (APAG)
PLM .... PLM International, Inc. [*AMEX symbol*]   (SPSG)
PLM .... Plymouth Financial [*Vancouver Stock Exchange symbol*]
PLM .... Poetae Latini Minores [*A publication*]   (OCD)
PLM .... Polarized Light Microscopy
PLM .... Poor Law Magazine [*A publication*]   (DLA)
PLM .... Power Line Modulation   (AABC)
PLM .... Prelaunch Monitor [*NASA*]   (KSC)
PLM .... Preliminary   (KSC)
PLM .... Product Line Manager
PLM .... Production Line Maintenance [*Air Force*]
PLM .... Production Line Manufacturing
PL/M........ Programming Language/Microcomputers [*Intel Corp.*] [*1973*] [*Data processing*]   (CSR)
PLM .... Programming Logic Manual
PLM .... Pulse-Length Modulation
PLMA........ Private Label Manufacturers Association   (EA)
PLMA........ Producers Livestock Marketing Association [*Later, IPLA*]   (EA)
PL Mag...... Poor Law Magazine [*1858-1930*] [*Scotland*] [*A publication*] [*A publication*]   (DLA)
PLMB........ Plumbing   (AAG)
PLMD .... Payload Mating Dolly [*NASA*]
PLME........ Peak Local Mean Error   (MCD)
PLMEA...... Planta Medica [*A publication*]
PLMG........ Plumbing   (WGA)
PLMG........ Publishers' Library Marketing Group   (EA)
PLMHi...... Lancaster Mennonite Conference Historical Society, Lancaster, PA [*Library symbol*] [*Library of Congress*]   (LCLS)
PLMN .... Partido Marxista Leninista de Nicaragua [*Political party*]   (EY)
PLMN .... Plasmine Corp. [*NASDAQ symbol*]   (NQ)
PLMP .... Program Logistic Management Plan   (MCD)
PLMPA ..... Permanent Labourers' Mutual Protective Association [*A union*] [*British*]
PLMR........ Paris, Lyons, and Mediterranean Railway   (ROG)
PLMR........ Post Launch Memorandum Report
PLMS .... Palms
PLMS .... Plastic Master [*Tool*]   (AAG)
PLMS .... Preservation of Library Materials Section [*Resources and Technical Services Division*] [*American Library Association*]
PLMS .... Program Logistics Master Schedule [*NASA*]   (NASA)
PLMS .... Public Land Mobile Service Data Base [*Comp Comm, Inc.*] [*Information service or system*]   (CRD)
PLMSA ..... Plasticheskie Massy [*A publication*]
PLMX........ PL/M Extended [*Programming language*]   (CSR)
PLMX........ PLM Financial Services [*NASDAQ symbol*]   (NQ)
PLN .... Flight Plan [*Aviation code*]
PLN .... Partido Liberacion Nacional [*National Liberation Party*] [*Costa Rica*] [*Political party*]   (PPW)
PLN .... Partido de Liberacion Nacional [*National Liberation Party*] [*El Salvador*] [*Political party*]   (EY)
PLN .... Partido Liberal Nacionalista [*Nationalist Liberal Party*] [*Nicaragua*]
PLN .... Pellston [*Michigan*] [*Airport symbol*]   (OAG)
PLN .... Pellston, MI [*Location identifier*] [*FAA*]   (FAAL)
PLN .... Phospholamban [*Biochemistry*]
PLN .... Plain
PLN .... Plan   (NASA)
PLN .... Plane   (MSA)
PLN .... Planning [*A publication*]
Pln............ Platoon [*British military*]   (DMA)
PLN .... Plauen [*German Democratic Republic*] [*Seismograph station code, US Geological Survey*]   (SEIS)
PLN .... Popliteal Lymph Node [*Anatomy*]
PLN .... Program Line Number [*DoD*]
PLN .... Program Logic Network   (NASA)
PLN .... Proteoliaisin [*Biochemistry*]

PLNAP...... Pro-Life Nonviolent Action Project   (EA)
Pln Dealr.... Plain Dealer [*A publication*]
PLNG........ Language [*A publication*]
PLNG .... Planning
PLNN .... Planning   (MCD)
PLNN-A .... Plan [*A publication*]
PLNO .... Plano Petroleum Corp. [*NASDAQ symbol*]   (NQ)
PLNP........ Literature and Psychology [*A publication*]
PLNR........ Planar   (MSA)
PLNRSC.... Plains Resources, Inc. [*Associated Press abbreviation*]   (APAG)
PLNS........ Plains   (MCD)
PLNSTD ... Planned Standard Equipment [*Navy*]   (AFIT)
PLNSW Staff News ... Public Library of New South Wales. Staff News [*A publication*]   (APTA)
PLNT........ Planet   (MSA)
PLNTY...... Planetary   (MSA)
PLO .... Pacific Launch Operations [*NASA*]
PLO .... Palestine Liberation Organization [*Political party*]   (PD)
PLO .... Parliamentary Liaison Officer   (ADA)
PLO .... Partial Lunar Orbit [*Planetary science*]
PLO .... Parts List Only   (MCD)
PLO .... Passenger Liaison Office [*Military*]   (AABC)
PLO .... Payload Officer [*NASA*]   (MCD)
PLO .... Pensiero e Linguaggio in Operazioni/Thought and Language in Operations [*A publication*]
PLO .... Pentagon Liaison Office   (MCD)
PLO .... Phase-Locked Oscillator
PLO .... Plans Officer
PLO .... Poly-L-ornithine
PLO .... Poor Law Office   (ROG)
PLO .... Port Liaison Officer
PLO .... Port Lincoln [*Australia*] [*Airport symbol*]   (OAG)
PLO .... Probability of Leakage through Overlay
PLO .... Product Line Organization
PLO .... Program Line Organization
PLO .... Programmed Local Oscillator
PLO .... Project Line Organization
PLO .... Public Land Order [*Interior*]
PLO .... Pulsed LASER Oscillator
PLO .... Pulsed Locked Oscillator
PLOA .... Proposed Letter of Agreement   (MCD)
PLOB........ Patrol Log Observations [*Aviation*]   (DSUE)
PLOB........ Place of Birth
PLOC........ Payload Operations Contractor [*NASA*]   (SSD)
PLOCAP ... Post Loss-of-Coolant Accident Protection [*Nuclear energy*]   (NRCH)
PLOCSA ... Personnel Liaison Officer, Chief of Staff, Army   (AABC)
PLOD .... Periodic List of Data [*Data processing*]
PLOD .... Planetary Orbit Determination   (IEEE)
Plodorodie Pochv Karelii Akad Nauk SSSR Karel'sk Filial ... Plodorodie Pochv Karelii. Akademiya Nauk SSSR. Karel'skii Filial [*A publication*]
P Lom........ Petrus Lombardi [*Flourished, 1154-59*] [*Authority cited in pre-1607 legal work*]   (DSA)
PLOM .... Prescribed Loan Optimization Model [*Army*]   (AABC)
PLOME..... Poor Little Old Me Syndrome [*British*]
P Lond Math ... Proceedings. London Mathematical Society [*A publication*]
PLondon .... Greek Papyri in the British Museum [*A publication*]   (OCD)
PLONEF ... Plates on Elastic Foundations [*Structures & Computers Ltd.*] [*Software package*]   (NCC)
PLONG ..... Present Longitude [*Aviation*]   (FAAC)
PLOO .... Pacific Launch Operations Office [*NASA*]
PLOP........ Planetary Landing Observation Package [*Aerospace*]
PLOP........ Policy Options/Options Politiques [*A publication*]
PLOP........ Pressure Line of Position [*Air Force*]
PLor .... Saint Francis College, Loretto, PA [*Library symbol*] [*Library of Congress*]   (LCLS)
PLOS........ Primary Line of Sight [*Sextants*]
PLOT........ People's Liberation Organization of Tamil Eelam [*Sri Lanka*] [*Political party*]
PLOT........ Plotting
PLOT........ Porous Layer, Open Tubular Column [*Gas chromatography*]
PLOT........ Probability of Launch on Time   (MCD)
Plot............ Vita Plotini [*of Porphyry*] [*Classical studies*]   (OCD)
PLOTE...... People's Liberation Organization of Tamil Eelam [*Sri Lanka*] [*Political party*]
Ploughs ...... Ploughshares [*A publication*]
Plovdiv Univ Naucn Trud ... Plovdivski Universitet. Naucni Trudove [*A publication*]
PLOW .... Petunia Lovers of the World
Plow .... Plowden's English King's Bench Commentaries [*or Reports*] [*A publication*]   (DLA)
Plowd .... Plowden's English King's Bench Commentaries [*or Reports*] [*A publication*]   (DLA)
PLOYREP ... Unit Deployment Report   (CINC)
PLP............ La Palma [*Panama*] [*Airport symbol*]   (OAG)
PLP............ Packet Level Procedure [*Computer programming*]   (PCM)
PLP............ Palo [*Philippines*] [*Seismograph station code, US Geological Survey*]   (SEIS)
PLP............ Palpus [*Arthropod anatomy*]
PLP............ Parliamentary Labour Party [*British*]

PLP........... Parti Liberal Progressiste [*Liberal Progressive Party*] [*Morocco*] [*Political party*]   (PPW)
PLP........... Parti pour la Liberation du Peuple [*People's Liberation Party*] [*Senegal*] [*Political party*]   (PPW)
PLP........... Parti de la Liberte et du Progres [*Party of Liberty and Progress*] [*See also PVV*] [*Belgium*]   (PPE)
PLP........... Partido de los Pobres [*Poor People's Party*] [*Mexico*] [*Political party*]   (PD)
PLP........... Partners for Livable Places   (EA)
PLP........... Parts List Page   (KSC)
PLP........... Pattern Learning Parser
PLP........... People's Liberation Party [*Pakistan*]
PLP........... Periodate Lysine-Paraformaldehyde
PLP........... Personal LASER Printer [*Data processing*]
PLP........... Phillips Petroleum Co. [*Toronto Stock Exchange symbol*]
PLP........... Plains Petroleum Co. [*NYSE symbol*]   (SPSG)
PLP........... Polyoma-Like Particle [*Genetics*]
PLP........... Post Launch Phase
PLP........... Preferred Lenders Program [*Small Business Administration*]
PLP........... Presentation Level Protocol [*AT & T Videotex System*]
PLP........... Principal Locating Point [*Automotive engineering*]
PLP........... Procedural Language Processor
PLP........... Process Layup Procedure
PLP........... Product Liability Prevention [*Conference*]
PLP........... Progressive Labor Party   (EA)
PLP........... Progressive Labour Party [*Saint Lucia*] [*Political party*]   (EAIO)
PLP........... Progressive Liberal Party [*Bahamas*] [*Political party*]   (PPW)
PLP........... Proteolipid [*Biochemistry*]
PLP........... Proteolipid Protein [*Biochemistry*]
PLP........... Pyridoxal Phosphate [*Also, PALP*] [*Biochemistry*]
PLPA .... Pageable Link-Pack Area
PLPA .... Palmyra, Palmyra Island [*Line Islands*] [*ICAO location identifier*]   (ICLI)
PLPA .... Permissive Low-Pressure Alarm   (IEEE)
Pl Par .... Placita Parliamentaria [*Latin*] [*A publication*]   (DLA)
Pl Path .... Plant Pathology [*A publication*]
PLPB .... Petroleum Labor Policy Board [*Abolished, 1936*]
PLPBD ...... Pulpboard
PLPD........ Product Liability Prevention and Defense [*An association*]   (EA)
PL & PD .... Public Liability and Property Damage [*Insurance*]
PLP FOR... Foramen of Labial Palpus [*Arthropod anatomy*]
PLPG .... Publishers' Library Promotion Group [*Later, PLMG*]   (EA)
PLP GRNDG ... Pulp Grinding [*Freight*]
PLPHA...... Plant Physiology [*A publication*]
PLPHB...... Plasma Physics [*A publication*]
Pl Physics .. Plasma Physics [*A publication*]
Pl Physiol (Lancaster) ... Plant Physiology (Lancaster) [*A publication*]
Pl Physiol (Wash) ... Plant Physiology (Washington) [*A publication*]
PLPLS....... Proceedings. Leeds Philosophical and Literary Society [*A publication*]
PLPLS-LHS ... Proceedings. Leeds Philosophical and Literary Society. Literary and Historical Section [*A publication*]
PLPLS-SS ... Proceedings. Leeds Philosophical and Literary Society. Scientific Section [*A publication*]
PLPP .... Position Location Post Processor   (MCD)
Pl & Pr Cas ... Pleading and Practice Cases [*1837-38*] [*England*] [*A publication*]   (DLA)
Pl Prot (Tokyo) ... Plant Protection (Tokyo) [*A publication*]
PLPS......... Packaged Liquid Propellant System
PLPS......... Propellant Loading and Pressurization System [*NASA*]
PLPSA....... Physiological Psychology [*A publication*]
PLPUA ...... Planseeberichte fuer Pulvermetallurgie (Austria) [*A publication*]
PLPV .... Pelargonium Line Pattern Virus [*Plant pathology*]
PLQ .... Plaque   (MSA)
PLQ .... Tallahassee, FL [*Location identifier*] [*FAA*]   (FAAL)
PLR .... LaRoche College, Pittsburgh, PA [*OCLC symbol*]   (OCLC)
PLR .... Pacific Law Reporter [*A publication*]   (DLA)
PLR .... Pakistan Law Reports [*A publication*]   (DLA)
PLR .... Pakistan Law Review [*A publication*]   (DLA)
PLR .... Palestine Law Reports [*A publication*]
PLR .... Parlake Resources Ltd. [*Toronto Stock Exchange symbol*]
PLR .... Partido Liberal Radical [*Radical Liberal Party*] [*Paraguay*] [*Political party*]   (PPW)
PLR .... Partido Liberal Radical [*Radical Liberal Party*] [*Ecuador*] [*Political party*]   (PPW)
PLR .... Patent Law Review [*A publication*]   (DLA)
PLR .... Patent Log Reading [*Navigation*]
PLR .... Patna Law Reporter [*India*] [*A publication*]   (DLA)
PLR .... Pell City, AL [*Location identifier*] [*FAA*]   (FAAL)
PLR .... Pennsylvania Law Record [*Philadelphia*] [*A publication*]   (DLA)
P-LR .... Pennsylvania Legislative Reference Bureau, Harrisburg, PA [*Library symbol*] [*Library of Congress*]   (LCLS)
PLR .... Periodic Logistical Report
PLR .... Philippine Liberation Ribbon [*Military decoration*]
PLR .... Pillar   (MSA)
PLR .... Planning Review [*A publication*]
PLR .... Pliers   (MSA)
PLR .... Plymouth Rubber Co., Inc. [*AMEX symbol*]   (SPSG)
PLR .... Portable LASER Range-Finder

PL & R .... Postal Laws and Regulations [*Later, Postal Manual*]
PLR............ Power Line Radiation [*Radioscience*]
PLR............ Presentation Loss Rate   (MCD)
PLR............ Pressure Level Recorder
PLR............ Primary Loss Retention [*Insurance*]
PLR............ Private Legislation Reports [*Scotland*] [*A publication*]   (DLA)
PLR............ Program Life Requirement   (NG)
PLR............ Psychological Laboratories [*Harvard University*]   (KSC)
PLR............ Public Law Review [*A publication*]
PLR............ Public Lending Right [*Royalty for books borrowed from public libraries*] [*British*]
PLR............ Puller   (MSA)
PLR............ Pulse Link Relay [*Telecommunications*]   (TEL)
PLR............ Pulse Link Repeater [*Telecommunications*]   (TEL)
PLR............ Punjab Law Reporter [*India*] [*A publication*]   (DLA)
PLR............ University of Pittsburgh. Law Review [*A publication*]
PLRA......... Partido Liberal Radical Autentico [*Authentic Liberal Radical Party*] [*Paraguay*] [*Political party*]   (PD)
PLRACTA ... Position Location, Reporting, and Control of Tactical Aircraft [*Military*]
PLRB......... Property Loss Research Bureau   (EA)
PLRC........ Pulsed LASER Remote Crosswind Sensor   (MCD)
PLRCA...... Pharmacological Research Communications [*A publication*]
PLRCAE.... Radio Corp. of America, Electron Tube Division, Engineering Section, Lancaster, PA [*Library symbol*] [*Library of Congress*] [*Obsolete*]   (LCLS)
PLRD........ Payload Requirements Document   (NASA)
PLRD........ Pull Rod
PLR Dacca ... Pakistan Law Reports, Dacca Series [*A publication*]   (DLA)
PLRE........ Prosopography of the Later Roman Empire [*A publication*]
PLRF .... Pediatric Liver Research Foundation [*Inactive*]   (EA)
pLRF......... Placental Luteinizing Hormone-Releasing Factor [*Endocrinology*]
PLRF .... Planer Fixture
PLRI .... Posterolateral Rotation Instability [*Sports medicine*]
PLRJ & K .. Punjab Law Reporter, Jammu and Kashmir Section [*India*] [*A publication*]   (DLA)
PLR Kar..... Pakistan Law Reports, Karachi Series [*1947-53*] [*A publication*]   (DLA)
PLR Lah .... Pakistan Law Reports, Lahore Series [*1947-55*] [*A publication*]   (DLA)
PLRPF....... Personnel Loss Rate Planning Factors   (MCD)
PLRS .... Pelorus
PLRS .... Phase Lock Receiving System
PLRS .... Position Location Reporting System [*Military*]
PLRSA .... Plasticos y Resinas [*A publication*]
Plrs' Bull Rubb Res Inst Malaya ... Planters' Bulletin. Rubber Research Institute of Malaya [*A publication*]
PLRS/TIDS ... Position Location Reporting System/Tactical Information Distribution Systems [*Military*]   (RDA)
PLRSTN.... Pelorus Stand
PLRT........ Polarity   (MSA)
PLRV........ Payload Launch Readiness Verification [*NASA*]   (MCD)
PLRV........ Potato Leafroll Virus
PLRWP ..... Pakistan Law Reports, West Pakistan Series [*A publication*]   (DLA)
PLS .... Palletized Load System [*Army*]   (RDA)
PLS .... Palomar-Leiden Survey
PLS .... Parcels   (MSA)
PLS .... Parsons Language Sample
PLS .... Parti Liberal Suisse [*Liberal Party of Switzerland*] [*Political party*]   (PPE)
PLS .... Partial Least Squares
PLS .... Patrol Locator System [*Army*]
PLS .... Payload Systems [*NASA*]   (MCD)
PLS .... Peerless Tube Co. [*AMEX symbol*]   (SPSG)
PLS .... Peninsula Library System [*Belmont, CA*] [*Library network*]
PLS .... People's Law School   (EA)
PLS .... Peralto Resources Corp. [*Vancouver Stock Exchange symbol*]
PLS .... Periodic Log System
PLS .... Pitch Limit Switch
PLS .... Plaisance [*Mauritius*] [*Geomagnetic observatory code*]
PLS .... Plasma Light Source
PLS .... Plates [*Classical studies*]   (OCD)
PLS .... Please   (AFM)
PLS .... Plugging Switch   (IEEE)
PLS .... Pneumatic Limit Switch
PLS .... Polson, MT [*Location identifier*] [*FAA*]   (FAAL)
PLS .... Polystyrene Latex Sphere
PLS .... Popular Low-Power Schottky [*Electronics*]   (MCD)
PLS .... Portable Laboratory Salinometer
PLS .... Position Location System [*Army*]
PLS .... Post Landing and Safing [*NASA*]   (NASA)
PLS .... Postsecondary Longitudinal Studies Program [*Department of Education*]   (GFGA)
PLS .... Precautions, Limitations, and Setpoints [*Nuclear energy*]   (NRCH)
PLS .... Preliminary Landing Site   (NASA)
PLS .... Preschool Language Scale [*Child development test*]
PLS .... President of the Linnaean Society [*British*]
PLS .... Primary Landing Site   (MCD)

PLS .... Private Line Service
PLS .... Product Line Simulator
PLS .... Professional Legal Secretary [*Designation awarded by National Association of Legal Secretaries*]
PLS .... Profit-and-Loss-Sharing Account [*Banking*]   (IMH)
PLS .... Programmable Logic Sequencer [*Data processing*]
PLS .... Progressive Learning Systems [*Potomac, MD*]   (TSSD)
PLS .... Propellant Loading Sequencer   (AAG)
PLS .... Propellant Loading System
PLS .... Prostaglandin-Like Substance [*Biochemistry*]   (MAE)
PLS .... Providenciales [*British West Indies*] [*Airport symbol*]   (OAG)
PLS .... Pulse   (MSA)
PLS .... Pulsed LASER System
PLS .... Pulsed Light Source
PLSC .... Purnell Library Service [*Commercial firm*]
PLSC .... Project Level Steering Committee   (HGAA)
PLSCB ...... Policy Sciences [*A publication*]
PLSCE4..... Plant Science [*Shannon*] [*A publication*]
PLSD......... Promotion List Service Date [*Air Force*]
PLSE .... Pulse Engineering [*NASDAQ symbol*]   (SPSG)
PLSFC....... Part Load Specific Fuel Consumption [*Gas turbine*]
Pls Gds....... Plants and Gardens [*A publication*]
PLSGT ...... Platoon Sergeant [*Marine Corps*]
PLSHD...... Polished [*Freight*]
PLSL......... Propellants and Life Support Laboratory [*NASA*]   (NASA)
PLSN........ Pulsation   (MSA)
PL/SNSR .. Payload Sensor [*NASA*]   (GFGA)
PLSO........ Propellant Life Support and Ordnance [*NASA*]   (KSC)
PLSOA ...... Plant and Soil [*A publication*]
PLSP......... Payload Signal Processor [*NASA*]   (MCD)
PLSP......... Prelaunch Survival Probability   (CINC)
PLSPS .... Performance Levels of a School Program Survey [*Teacher evaluation test*]
PLSR .... Law and Society Review [*A publication*]
PLSR .... Pulsar Oil & Gas [*NASDAQ symbol*]   (NQ)
PLSR .... Pulsator   (MSA)
PLSS......... Payload Support Structure [*NASA*]   (SSD)
PLSS......... Portable Life Support System [*or Subsystem*] [*NASA*]
PLSS......... Post-Landing Survival System [*NASA*]
PLSS......... Precision Location Strike System [*Air Force*]
PLSS......... Prelaunch Status Simulator
PLSS......... Primary Life Support System [*or Subsystem*]   (NASA)
PLSS......... Public Library Systems Section [*Public Library Association*]
PLSSA ...... Planetary and Space Science [*A publication*]
PLSSRS..... Plant and Soil Science Research Station [*Southern Illinois University at Carbondale*] [*Research center*]   (RCD)
PLSSU....... Portable Life Support Stretcher Unit [*Military*]   (CAAL)
PLSTC....... Plastic   (AAG)
PLSTR....... Plasterer   (ADA)
PLSTRER ... Plasterer   (WGA)
PLSV .... Propellant Latching Solenoid Valve
PLT........... Columbus, NE [*Location identifier*] [*FAA*]   (FAAL)
PLT........... Lancaster Theological Seminary of the United Church of Christ, Lancaster, PA [*Library symbol*] [*Library of Congress*]   (LCLS)
PLT........... Lutheran Theological Seminary, Philadelphia, PA [*OCLC symbol*]   (OCLC)
PLT........... Pallet   (AABC)
Plt............. Parliament
PLT........... Partido Liberal Teete [*Teete Liberal Party*] [*Paraguay*] [*Political party*]   (PPW)
PLT........... Patna Law Times [*India*] [*A publication*]   (DLA)
Plt............. Peltier's Orleans Appeals Decisions [*Louisiana*] [*A publication*]   (DLA)
PLT........... Photoluminescent Thermometer
PLT........... Pilot   (AFM)
PLT........... Pilot Knob [*California*] [*Seismograph station code, US Geological Survey*]   (SEIS)
PLT........... Pipeline Time [*Army*]
PLT........... Plaint [*Legal term*]   (ROG)
PLT........... Planar Tube
PLT........... Plant
PLT........... Plate
PLT........... Platelet [*Hematology*]
PLT........... Platoon [*Military*]   (AABC)
PLT........... Port Light
PLT........... Post Loading Test   (NG)
PLT........... Power Line Transient   (IEEE)
PLT........... Primed Lymphocyte Typing [*Hematology*]
PLT........... Princeton Large Torus [*Nuclear reactor*]
PLT........... Private Line Telephone
PLT........... Private Line Teletypewriter
PLT........... Procurement Lead Time [*Army*]
PLT........... Production Lead Time
PLT........... Program Library Tape [*Data processing*]   (IEEE)
PLT........... Programmed Learning Textbook
PLT........... Progress in Low Temperature Physics [*Elsevier Book Series*] [*A publication*]
PLT........... Progressive Lowering of Temperature
PLT........... Psittacosis-Lymphogranuloma Venereum Trachoma [*Microbiology*]

PLT .... Pulsed Light Theodolite
PLT .... Punjab Law Times [*India*] [*A publication*] (DLA)
PLT .... South Carolina Aeronautics Commission [*Columbia, SC*] [*FAA designator*] (FAAC)
PLTC .... Port Liner Terms Charges [*Shipping*] (DS)
PLTC .... Propellant Loading Terminal Cabinet (AAG)
PLTD .... Plated
PLTEA ...... Plastics Technology [*A publication*]
PLTF .... Par Leadership Training Foundation [*Defunct*] (EA)
PLTF .... Plaintiff [*Legal term*] (ROG)
PLTF .... Purple Loosestrife Task Force (EA)
PLTFF ...... Plaintiff
PLTFM ...... Platform
PLTG .... Plating
PLT GL ..... Plate Glass [*Freight*]
PLTHS ...... Pilothouse
PLT LT ...... Pilot Light (MSA)
Plt Off ...... Pilot Officer [*British military*] (DMA)
PLTP .... Phospholipid Transfer Protein [*Biochemistry*]
PLTPA ...... Progress in Low Temperature Physics [*A publication*]
PLTR .... Plan for Long-Range Technical Requirements
PLTR .... Plotter (MSA)
PLTR .... Procurement Lead Time Requirement
PLTRY ...... Poultry [*Freight*]
PLTS .... Precision LASER Tracking System (NASA)
PLTTNG ... Pilot Training [*Air Force*]
PLTTNGSq ... Pilot Training Squadron [*Air Force*]
PLTVA ...... Plastvaerlden [*A publication*]
PLTZ .... Pulitzer Publishing Co. [*St. Louis, MO*] [*NASDAQ symbol*] (NQ)
PLU .... Partido Liberal Unificado [*Unified Liberal Party*] [*Paraguay*] [*Political party*] (PPW)
PLu .... Path Loss, Uplink [*Communications*]
PLU .... People Like Us (IIA)
PLU .... Phi Lambda Upsilon [*Fraternity*]
PLU .... Platoon Leaders Unit [*Marine Corps*]
Pl U .... Plowden on Usury [*A publication*] (DLA)
PLU .... Pluggable Unit (SAA)
PLU .... Plural
PLU .... Plutonium [*Chemical symbol is Pu*] (AAG)
PLU .... Poor Law Union [*British*]
PLU .... Preservation of Location Uncertainty [*Strategy for protecting missiles*] [*Military*]
PLU .... Pressure Lubrication Unit
PLU .... Probability of Leakage through Underlay
PLU .... Propellant Loading and Utilization (AAG)
Plucne Bolesti Tuberk ... Plucne Bolesti i Tuberkuloza [*A publication*]
Plucne Boles Tuberk ... Plucne Bolesti i Tuberkuloza [*A publication*]
PLUCON .. Plutonium Decontamination Emergency Team [*Army*]
PLUDA ...... Plutonium-Dokumentation [*A publication*]
PLUG .... ComponentGuard, Inc. [*NASDAQ symbol*] (NQ)
PLUG .... Propellant Loading and Utilization Group (AAG)
PLUGE ...... Picture Line-Up Generator [*Television*]
PLuL .... Lincoln University, Lincoln University, PA [*Library symbol*] [*Library of Congress*] (LCLS)
PLUM .... Payload Launch Module
PLUM .... Payload Umbilical Mast (NASA)
PLUM .... Priority Low-Use Minimal
PLUMB ..... Plumbum [*Lead*] [*Pharmacy*]
Plumb Heat J ... Plumbing and Heating Journal [*A publication*]
Plumbing Eng ... Plumbing Engineer [*A publication*]
Plumbing Engr ... Plumbing Engineer [*A publication*]
Plumbing Heat Equip News ... Plumbing and Heating Equipment News [*A publication*]
Plum Contr ... Plumptre on Contracts [*2nd ed.*] [*1897*] [*A publication*] (DLA)
PlumCr .... Plum Creek Timber Co., Inc. [*Associated Press abbreviation*] (APAG)
PLUNA ..... Primeras Lineas Uruguayas de Navegacion Aerea [*Uruguayan National Airlines*]
PLund .... Papyri Lundenses [*A publication*] (OCD)
PLUP .... Pluperfect [*Grammar*]
PLUPF .... Pluperfect [*Grammar*]
PLUR .... Jarvis Island [*Line Islands*] [*ICAO location identifier*] (ICLI)
PLUR .... Photo Lab Usage Reporting (MCD)
PLUR .... Plural
Plural Soc .. Plural Societies [*The Hague*] [*A publication*]
PLUS .... Parent Loans to Undergraduate Students [*Later, ALAS*] [*Department of Education*]
PLUS .... PERT [*Program Evaluation and Review Technique*] Lifecycle Unified System
PLUS .... Plexus Resources Corp. [*NASDAQ symbol*] (NQ)
PLUS .... Portable Lightweight Upper Air Sounding System (MCD)
PLUS .... Potential Long Supply Utilization Screening (NATG)
PLUS .... Precision Loading and Utilization System (AAG)
PLUS .... Prima Leben und Sparen [*Quality Living and Saving*] [*Brand name and discount store chain in West Germany and US*]
PLUS .... Procedures for Long Supply Assets Utilization Screening [*DoD*]
PLUS .... Program Library Update System
PLUS .... Programmed Learning under Supervision
PLUS .... Programming Language for UNIVAC [*Universal Automatic Computer*] Systems [*Data processing*] (CSR)

PLUS .... Project Literacy US [*Joint project of American Broadcasting Co. and Public B roadcasting Service*]
Plut............ Plutarch [*First century AD*] [*Classical studies*] (OCD)
Plut............ Plutus [*of Aristophanes*] [*Classical studies*] (OCD)
PLUTA ...... Pollution [*A publication*]
PLUTHARCO ... Plutonium, Uranium, Thorium Assembly Reactivity Code
PLUTO ..... Pipeline under the Ocean [*British project*] [*World War II*]
PLUTO ..... Plutonium [*Loop-Testing*] Reactor [*British*] (DEN)
Plutonium-Dok ... Plutonium-Dokumentation [*West Germany*] [*A publication*]
PLUVUE... Plume Visibility Model [*Environmental Protection Agency*] (GFGA)
PLV............ Live Poliomyelitis Vaccine [*Immunology*] (MAE)
PLV............ Panleukopenia Virus [*Medicine*] (MAE)
PLV............ Peak Left Ventricular [*Pressure*] [*Cardiology*]
PLV............ Phenylalanine-Lysine-Vasopressin (MAE)
PLV............ Phu-Lien [*Kien-An*] [*Vietnam*] [*Seismograph station code, US Geological Survey*] (SEIS)
PLV............ Posterior Left Ventricular Wall [*Cardiology*]
PLV............ Postlanding Vent [*or Ventilation*] [*Apollo*] [*NASA*]
PLV............ Power Limiting Valve
PLV............ Presentation Level Video (PCM)
PLV............ Production Level Video
PLV............ Sterling Air Service, Inc. [*Sterling, CO*] [*FAA designator*] (FAAC)
PLVC........ Post-Landing Vent Control [*NASA*] (KSC)
PLVDA ..... Progress in Liver Diseases [*A publication*]
PLVRZD ... Pulverized (MSA)
PLW........... Palau [*ANSI three-letter standard code*] (CNC)
PLW........... Palu [*Indonesia*] [*Airport symbol*] (OAG)
PLW........... Patna Law Weekly [*India*] [*A publication*] (DLA)
PLW........... Plastic Engine Technology Corp. [*Toronto Stock Exchange symbol*]
PLW........... Plow (FAAC)
PLW........... Preload Washer
PL/WA ..... Plain Washer [*Automotive engineering*]
PLWG....... Photographic Laboratories Working Group [*Range Commanders Council*] [*White Sands Missile Range, NM*]
PLX........... Parallax Developments [*Vancouver Stock Exchange symbol*]
PLX........... Plains Resources, Inc. [*AMEX symbol*] (SPSG)
PLX........... Plantronics, Inc. [*NYSE symbol*] (SPSG)
PLX........... Plexus [*Medicine*]
PLX........... Position Launch [*Search mode wherein X signifies the launch mode number*] (MCD)
PLX........... Propellant Loading Exercise (MCD)
PLX........... Robinson, IL [*Location identifier*] [*FAA*] (FAAL)
PLXS .... Plexus Corp. [*NASDAQ symbol*] (NQ)
PLXX .... Polymerix, Inc. [*NASDAQ symbol*] (NQ)
PLY........... [*The*] Plessey Co. Ltd. [*NYSE symbol*] (SPSG)
Ply............ Plymouth [*Record label*]
PLY........... Plywood
PLY........... Polaris Energy [*Vancouver Stock Exchange symbol*]
PLY........... Polyphase Corp. [*AMEX symbol*] (SPSG)
PLY........... Prune Extract Lactose Yeast Medium [*Microbiology*]
PLYGA...... Psychologia: An International Journal of Psychology in the Orient [*A publication*]
PLYGEM .. Ply-Gem Industries, Inc. [*Associated Press abbreviation*] (APAG)
PLYHD ..... Polyhedron [*A publication*]
PLYINST .. Command Comply Current Instructions
PLYM........ Plymouth [*England*]
PLYMCHAN ... Plymouth Subarea Channel [*NATO*] (NATG)
Plymouth Miner Min Club J ... Plymouth Mineral and Mining Club. Journal [*A publication*]
PLYMP ..... Plympton [*England*]
PLYMT ..... Plymtree [*England*]
Plyn Voda Zdra Tech ... Plyn Voda a Zdravotni Technika [*A publication*]
PLYPASSPORT ... Application for Passport for Self and/or Dependents Accordance BUPERS Manual [*Navy*]
PlyR .... Plymouth Rubber Co., Inc. [*Associated Press abbreviation*] (APAG)
PLYWD.... Plywood (AAG)
Plyw Plyw Prod ... Plywood and Plywood Products [*A publication*] (APTA)
PLZ........... Plastics World [*A publication*]
PLZ........... Plaza (MCD)
PLZ........... Please
PLZ........... Polarize (MSA)
PLZ........... Port Elizabeth [*South Africa*] [*Airport symbol*] (OAG)
PLZ........... Programming Languages for the Zilog [*Data processing*] (CSR)
PLZA......... Plaza Commerce Bancorp [*NASDAQ symbol*] (NQ)
Plzen Lek Sb Suppl ... Plzensky Lekarsky Sbornik. Supplementum [*A publication*]
PLZN......... Polarization (MSA)
PLZT......... Pb-based Lanthanum-doped Zirconate Titanates
PM .... Brymon Airways [*British*] [*ICAO designator*] (FAAC)
PM .... [*The*] Chesapeake & Ohio Railway Co. (Pere Marquette District) [*AAR code*]
PM .... Ha-Po'el ha-Mizrahi (BJA)
PM .... International Journal of Psychiatry in Medicine [*A publication*]
P & M .... Law Reports, Probate and Matrimonial Cases [*England*] [*A publication*] (DLA)

PM .... Pacific Mail   (ROG)
PM .... Pad Mechanic [*Aerospace*]
PM .... Painting Machine
PM .... Pak [*or Phak*] Mai [*New Party*] [*Political party*]
PM .... Palace of Minos [*A publication*]
PM .... Paleographie Musicale [*A publication*]
PM .... Pamphlet
PM .... Panel Meter   (IEEE)
PM .... Paper Maker [*A publication*]
PM .... Paper Money [*A publication*]
PM .... Parachute Mine [*British military*]   (DMA)
PM .... Parameter [*Data processing*]
PM .... Paraxial Magnification   (SAA)
P M .... Paris Match [*A publication*]
PM .... Parlor Maid
PM .... Parole et Mission [*A publication*]
PM .... Particulate Matter
PM .... Partito Monarchico [*Monarchist Party*] [*Italy*] [*Political party*]   (PPE)
P/M .... Parts per Million   (IEEE)
PM .... Passed Midshipman
PM .... Passed Motion
PM .... Past Master [*Freemasonry*]
PM .... Patriotic Majority [*An association*]   (EA)
PM .... Patriotikon Metopon [*Patriotic Front*] [*Greek Cyprus*] [*Political party*]   (PPE)
PM .... Patternmaker [*Navy rating*]
PM .... Payload Management [*NASA*]   (NASA)
PM .... Payload Midbody [*NASA*]   (MCD)
PM .... Paymaster
PM .... Peace Museum   (EA)
PM .... Pectoralis Major [*Anatomy*]
PM .... Peculiar Meter
PM .... Penalty Minutes [*Hockey*]
PM .... Pension Mortgage [*British*]
PM .... People Meter [*TV ratings measuring device*] [*Advertising*]
PM .... Per Million
PM .... Per Month
PM .... Pere Marquette Railroad
PM .... Perfect Master [*Freemasonry*]
PM .... Performance Monitor [*NASA*]   (NASA)
PM .... Periodic Maintenance   (AFM)
PM .... Peritoneal Macrophage [*Immunology*]   (AAMN)
PM .... Permanent Magnet [*Loudspeaker*]
PM .... Petermanns Geographische Mitteilungen [*A publication*]
PM .... Petit Mal [*Epilepsy*]
PM .... Peuples Mediterraneens [*A publication*]
PM .... Phase Modulation [*Radio data transmission*]
PM .... Phased Maintenance   (MCD)
PM .... Philip Morris, Inc.
PM .... Philippine Manager [*A publication*]
PM .... Phorbol Monomyristate [*Organic chemistry*]
PM .... Phosphoramide Mustard [*Antineoplastic drug*]
PM .... Photo Marketing Magazine [*A publication*]   (EAAP)
PM .... Photo Master   (MCD)
PM .... Photomultiplier
PM .... Phyllosticta maydis [*A toxin-producing fungus*]
PM .... Physical Medicine
P/M .... Physical Medicine [*Medical Officer designation*] [*British*]
PM .... Piae Memoriae [*Of Pious Memory*] [*Latin*]
pm .... Picometer [*One trillionth of a meter*]
pM .... Picomoler [*One trillionth of a mole*]   (AAMN)
PM .... Pilot Motor   (MSA)
PM .... Pioneer Ministries   (EA)
PM .... Pit Membrane [*Paleobotany*]
PM .... Pitch Mark [*Shipfitting*]
PM .... Pitching Moment [*Physics*]
PM .... Placer Mining Times [*Whitehorse*] [*A publication*]
PM .... Planetary Mission [*NASA*]   (NASA)
PM .... Plasma Membrane [*Cytology*]
PM .... Plasmalemma [*Cytology*]
PM .... Plaster Master   (MSA)
PM .... Plastic Mold   (MCD)
P/M .... Player/Missile [*Atari computers*]
PM .... Plus Minus [*More or less*]
P or M .... Plus or Minus   (MSA)
PM .... PM. Pharmacy Management [*A publication*]
PM .... Pneumomediastinum [*Medicine*]   (AAMN)
PM .... Polarization Modulation   (MCD)
PM .... Police Magistrate
PM .... Police Mutual Assurance Society [*British*]
PM .... Policy Memorandum [*Military*]
PM .... Poliomyelitis [*Medicine*]
PM .... Pollen Mass [*Botany*]
P & M .... Pollock and Maitland's History of English Common Law [*A publication*]   (DLA)
PM .... Polymethacrylic [*Organic chemistry*]
PM .... Polymorph [*Hematology*]
PM .... Polymyositis [*Medicine*]
PM .... Pondus Medicinale [*Medicinal Weight*] [*Pharmacy*]   (ROG)
PM .... Pontifex Maximus [*Supreme Pontiff*] [*Latin*]

PM .... Poor Metabolism [*Medicine*]
PM .... Pope and Martyr [*Church calendars*]
PM .... Popular Mechanics [*A publication*]
PM .... Portable Magnetometer [*NASA*]
PM .... Portable Medium Power Plant [*Nuclear energy*]   (NRCH)
PM .... Post Magazine and Insurance Monitor [*A publication*]
PM .... Post Meridiem [*After Noon*] [*Latin*]
PM .... Post Mortem [*After Death*] [*Latin*]
PM .... Postal Manual
PM .... Posterior Mitral Leaflet [*Cardiology*]
PM .... Postmark [*Deltiology*]
PM .... Postmaster
PM .... Postmodernist [*Architecture*]
PM .... Potentiometer   (DEN)
PM .... Potting Mold   (MCD)
PM .... Pounds per Minute
PM .... Powder Metallurgy
PM .... Power Module   (MCD)
PM .... Powlesland & Mason [*Railway*] [*Wales*]
PM .... Pratt & Lambert, Inc. [*AMEX symbol*]   (SPSG)
PM .... Precious Metal
PM .... Prehistoric Macedonia [*A publication*]
PM .... Preincubation Mixture
PM .... Premium
PM .... Premolar [*Dentistry*]
PM .... Preparation Meetings [*Quakers*]
PM .... Prepared Message
PM .... Presbyterian Men   (EA)
PM .... Presentation Manager [*Data processing*]
PM .... Presidential Memo
PM .... Presse Medicale [*A publication*]
PM .... Pressure, Manifold
PM .... Pressure Multiplier [*Nuclear energy*]   (NRCH)
PM .... Pressurized Module   (SSD)
PM .... Presystolic Murmur [*Cardiology*]
PM .... Preventive Maintenance
PM .... Preventive Material
PM .... Preventive Medicine [*Also, PVNTMED*]   (AFM)
PM .... Priest and Martyr [*Church calendars*]
PM .... Primary Market [*Investment term*]
PM .... Primary Munition
PM .... Prime Minister
PM .... Prime Mover   (MCD)
PM .... Primitive Methodists   (ROG)
PM .... Principal Matron [*Navy*] [*British*]
PM .... Principle of Multiplying [*New math*]
PM .... Prize Money
PM .... Pro Memoria [*In Remembrance*] [*Latin*]
PM .... Pro Mense [*Per Month*] [*Latin*]
PM .... Pro Mille [*Per Thousand*] [*Latin*]
P & M .... Probate and Matrimonial [*Legal*] [*British*]
PM .... Procedures Manual   (IEEE)
PM .... Process Manual
PM .... Process Metallurgy [*Elsevier Book Series*] [*A publication*]
P & M .... Processes and Materials   (NASA)
PM .... Processing Modflow [*Computer program*] [*Scientific Software Group*]
PM .... Processing Module [*Data processing*]
PM .... Procurement and Material
PM .... Production Manager
PM .... Production Mode
PM .... Profit Motivated [*Housing*]
PM .... Program   (NG)
PM .... Program Manager [*or Management*]   (MCD)
PM .... Program Memorandum   (MCD)
PM .... Program Milestone [*NASA*]   (NASA)
PM .... Program Monitoring   (MUGU)
PM .... Project Magic   (EA)
PM .... Project Manager [*Military*]
Pm .... Promethium [*Chemical symbol*]
PM .... Propellant Management   (KSC)
PM .... Property Management   (OICC)
PM .... Propulsion Memorandum
PM .... Propulsion Module [*NASA*]   (KSC)
PM .... Prostatic Massage [*Medicine*]
PM .... Province du Maine [*A publication*]
PM .... Provost Marshal [*Army*]
PM .... Public Management [*A publication*]
PM .... Publicity Man [*Slang*]
PM .... Pulmonary Macrophages [*Medicine*]
PM .... Pulpomesial [*Dentistry*]
PM .... Pulse Modulation
Pm .... Pumice [*Quality of the bottom*] [*Nautical charts*]
PM .... Punjabi Muslim [*Pakistan*]
PM .... Purchase Memo   (MCD)
PM .... Purchase-Money Mortgage [*Real estate*]
PM .... Purchasing Manager
PM .... Purpose-Made [*Construction*]
PM .... Push Money [*Sales incentive*]
P/M .... Put of More [*Stock exchange term*]
PM .... Pyridoxamine [*Also, Pxm*] [*Biochemistry*]

PM .... St. Pierre and Miquelon [*ANSI two-letter standard code*] (CNC)
PM .... Sisters of the Presentation of Mary [*Roman Catholic religious order*]
PM1 .... Patternmaker, First Class [*Navy rating*]
PM2 .... Patternmaker, Second Class [*Navy rating*]
PM3 .... Patternmaker, Third Class [*Navy rating*]
PMA .... Allegheny College, Meadville, PA [*Library symbol*] [*Library of Congress*] (LCLS)
PMA .... Pacific Maritime Association (EA)
PMA .... Pan-Macedonian Association (EA)
PMA .... Panorama Resources Ltd. [*Vancouver Stock Exchange symbol*]
PMA .... Papillary, Marginal, Attached [*With reference to gingivae*] [*Dentistry*]
PMA .... Paramethoxyamphetamine
PMA .... Parts Manufacturer Approval [*FAA*] (MCD)
PMA .... Peat Moss Association (EA)
PMA .... Pemba Island [*Tanzania*] [*Airport symbol*] (OAG)
PMA .... Pencil Makers Association (EA)
PMA .... Performance Management Association (EAIO)
PMA .... Performance Monitor Annunciator [*NASA*] (MCD)
PMA .... Permanent Mailing Address
PMA .... Personal Money Allowance
PMA .... Personnel Management Abstracts [*A publication*]
PMA .... Personnel Management Advisor (NOAA)
PMA .... Personnel Management Assistance
PMA .... Petroleum Monitoring Agency [*Ministry of Energy, Mines, and Resources*] [*Canada*]
PMA .... Pharmaceutical Manufacturers Association (EA)
PMA .... Phenylmercuric Acetate [*Also, PMAC*] [*Herbicide and fungicide*]
PMA .... Philadelphia Musical Academy
PMA .... Philippine Mahogany Association [*Defunct*] (EA)
PMA .... Phonograph Manufacturers Association (EA)
PMA .... Phorbol Myristate Acetate [*Also, PTA, TPA*] [*Organic chemistry*]
PMA .... Phosphomolybdic Acid [*Organic chemistry*]
PMA .... Photo Marketing Association International (EA)
PMA .... Photonic Multichannel Analyzer
PMA .... Physical Memory Address
PMA .... Pine Manor College, Chestnut Hill, MA [*OCLC symbol*] (OCLC)
PMA .... Planetary Microbiological Assay [*Aerospace*]
PMA .... Plastic Mock-Up Assembly
PMA .... Pole-Mounted Amplifier
PMA .... Police Management Association (EA)
PMA .... Police Marksman Association (EA)
PMA .... Polish Museum of America (EA)
PMA .... Poly(methyl Acrylate) [*Organic chemistry*]
PMA .... Polyurethane Manufacturers Association (EA)
PMA .... Port Moller [*Alaska*] [*Seismograph station code, US Geological Survey*] (SEIS)
PMA .... Portable Maintenance Aid [*Army*]
PMA .... Positive Mental Attitude
PMA .... Power Marketing Administration [*Department of Energy*]
PMA .... Preamplifier Module Assembly
PMA .... Precious Metal Adder (Cost) (MCD)
PMA .... Precious Metal Anode
PMA .... Precision Measurements Association (EA)
PMA .... Precision Metalforming Association (EA)
PMA .... Premarket Approval Application [*Food and Drug Administration*]
PMA .... Preventive Maintenance Agreement
PMA .... Primary Market Area
PMA .... Primary Mental Abilities [*Test*] [*Education*]
PMA .... Priority Memory Access
PMA .... Prison Mission Association (EA)
PMA .... Probationary Medical Assistant [*British military*] (DMA)
P M A .... Proceedings. Musical Association [*A publication*]
PMA .... Proceedings. Royal Musical Association [*A publication*]
PMA .... Procurement and Management Assistance [*Small Business Administration*]
PMA .... Procurement Methods Analyst (AFM)
PMA .... Produce Marketing Association [*Newark, DE*] (EA)
PMA .... Production and Marketing Administration [*Department of Agriculture*] [*Functions dispersed, 1953*]
PMA .... Professional Managers Association (EA)
PMA .... Professional Manufacturers' Agents (EA)
PMA .... Professional Mariners Alliance (EA)
PMA .... Progressive Muscular Atrophy [*Medicine*]
PMA .... Project Manager, Air Systems Command [*Navy*]
PMA .... Project Military Adviser (NATG)
PMA .... Property Management Association of America (EA)
PMA .... Property Market Analysis [*Consulting firm*] [*British*]
PMA .... Prorated Mental Age [*Psychology*]
PMA .... Protected Memory Address
PMA .... Publications. Mediaeval Academy [*A publication*]
PMA .... Publishers Marketing Association (EA)
PMA .... Pulpomesioaxial [*Dentistry*]
PMA .... Pump-Motor Assembly
PMA .... Purchase Methods Analyst

PMA .... Pyridylmercuric Acetate [*Fungicide*] [*Organic chemistry*]
PMA .... Pyromellitic Acid [*Organic chemistry*]
PMAA .... Paper Makers Advertising Association (EA)
PMAA .... Petroleum Marketers Association of America (EA)
PMAA .... Promotion Marketing Association of America [*New York, NY*] (EA)
PMAA .... Property Management Association of America (EA)
PM-AAH... Project Manager, Advanced Attack Helicopter [*Military*]
PMAAR..... Papers and Monographs. American Academy in Rome [*A publication*]
PMAC ...... Parallel Memory Address Counter [*Data processing*]
PMAC ...... Phenylmercuric Acetate [*Also, PMA*] [*Herbicide and fungicide*]
PMAC ...... PMA Communications, Inc. [*Boston, MA*] (TSSD)
PMAC ...... Preliminary Maintenance Allocation Chart (MCD)
PMAC ...... Provisional Military Administrative Council [*Ethiopia*] [*Political party*] (PD)
PMAC ...... Purchasing Management Association of Canada
PMACODS ... Project Manager, Army Container Oriented Distribution System (MCD)
PM & ACS ... Procurement Management and Acquisition Control System [*Social Security Administration*]
PM ACS .... Product Manager, Army Communications System
PMAD ...... Performance Monitor Annunciation Driver [*NASA*] (MCD)
PMAD ...... Personnel Management Authorization Document [*Army*]
PMAD ...... Power Management and Distribution (NASA)
PMadW ..... Westinghouse Electric Corp., Waltz Mill Site Library, Madison, PA [*Library symbol*] [*Library of Congress*] (LCLS)
PMAESA .. Port Management Association of Eastern and Southern Africa (EA)
PMAF....... Polaris Missile Assembly Facility
PMAFS .... Public Members Association of the Foreign Service (EA)
PMAG ...... Program Manager Assistance Group [*Military*] (MCD)
PMAG ...... Provisional Military Advisory Group
PMAHD3 ... Annual Research Reviews. Peripheral Metabolism and Action of Thyroid Hormones [*A publication*]
PMAI........ Piano Manufacturers Association International (EA)
PMaine ...... Province du Maine [*A publication*]
PMAI News Lett ... PMAI [*Powder Metallurgy Association of India*] News Letter [*A publication*]
P/Maj .... Pipe-Major [*British military*] (DMA)
PMALS ..... Prototype Miniature Air-Launched System
PMAMA ... Prikladnaya Matematika i Mekhanika [*A publication*]
PMAN....... Man [*A publication*]
PMAN....... Piedmont Management Co., Inc. [*NASDAQ symbol*] (NQ)
PMA News ... PMA [*Pharmaceutical Manufacturers Association*] Newsletter [*A publication*]
PManM ..... Mansfield State College, Mansfield, PA [*Library symbol*] [*Library of Congress*] (LCLS)
PMANY .... Pattern Makers Association of New York (EA)
PMAODO ... Proceedings. American Society of Clinical Oncology. Annual Meeting [*A publication*]
PMAP....... Performance Monitor Annunciation Panel [*NASA*] (MCD)
PMAP....... Photomap
PMAPP..... Combined International Corp. Conv Pfd [*NASDAQ symbol*] (NQ)
PMAR ...... Massachusetts Review [*A publication*]
PMAR ...... Page Map Address Register
PMAR ...... Precious Metals Area Representative [*DoD*] (AFIT)
PMAR ...... Preliminary Maintenance Analysis Report [*Aerospace*] (AAG)
PMarhSO ... Sun Oil Co., Marcus Hook, PA [*Library symbol*] [*Library of Congress*] (LCLS)
PMARP..... Peacetime Manpower Allocation Requirements Plan (CINC)
PMARS..... Performance Management and Recognition System (MCD)
PMAS....... Police Mutual Assurance Society [*British*]
PMAS....... Purdue Master Attitude Scales [*Psychology*]
PMASAL .. Publications. Michigan Academy of Science, Arts, and Letters [*A publication*]
PM-ASE.... Project Manager, Aircraft Survivability Equipment [*Military*]
PM-ASH ... Project Manager, Advanced Scout Helicopter [*Military*]
PMAT....... Page Map Address Table [*NASA*] (NASA)
PMAT....... Portable Maintenance Access Terminal [*Data processing*]
PMAT....... Primary Mental Abilities Test [*Education*]
PMAT....... Purdue Mechanical Adaptability Test
PMAX ...... Petromax Energy Corp. [*NASDAQ symbol*] (NQ)
PMB .... Pacific Motor Tariff Bureau, Inc., Oakland CA [*STAC*]
PMB .... Para-Hydroxymercuribenzoate [*Biochemistry*] (MAE)
PMB .... Paranormal Metal Bending
PMB .... Pembina, ND [*Location identifier*] [*FAA*] (FAAL)
PMB .... Performance Measurement Baseline (MCD)
PMB .... Physical Metallurgy Branch
PMB .... Pilot Make Busy (IEEE)
PMB .... Plastic Media Blasting [*Coating technology*]
PMB .... Polish Maritime News [*A publication*]
PMB .... Polychrome Methylene Blue
PMB .... Polymethylbenzene [*Organic chemistry*]
PMB .... Polymorphonuclear Basophilic [*Leucocytes*] [*Hematology*]
PMB .... Postmenopausal Bleeding [*Medicine*]
PMB .... Potato Marketing Board [*British*]
PMB .... Practice Multiple Bomb (MCD)
PMB .... Precision Manned Bomber
PMB .... Prime Bancshares, Inc. [*AMEX symbol*] (SPSG)

PMB .... Print Measurement Bureau [*Founded in 1971*] [*Canada*] [*Also the name of a database*]
PMB .... Private Mail Bag
PMB .... Program Management Board   (AFM)
PMB .... PROM [*Programmable Read-Only Memory*] Memory Board
PMBAA..... Publications. Institut Royal Meteorologique de Belgique. Serie A [*A publication*]
PMBC........ Phuket Marine Biological Center [*Marine science*]   (MSC)
PMBIAS.... Percentage Median Bias [*Statistics*]
PMBIDB .. Plant Molecular Biology [*A publication*]
PMBK........ PrimeBank, Federal Savings Bank [*Grand Rapids, MI*] [*NASDAQ symbol*]   (NQ)
PMBR........ Practice Multiple Bomb Rack   (NG)
PMBRAZ.. Contributions. General Agricultural Research Station [*Bogor*] [*A publication*]
PMBS........ Pelican Man's Bird Sanctuary   (EA)
PMBS........ Prime Bancshares, Inc. [*NASDAQ symbol*]   (NQ)
PMBU .... Personal Member of the Baptist Union [*British*]
PMBX........ Private Manual Branch Exchange [*Communications*]
PMC .... Carnegie-Mellon University, Pittsburgh, PA [*OCLC symbol*]   (OCLC)
PMC .... Chief Patternmaker [*Navy rating*]
PMC .... Little Missionary Sisters of Charity [*Roman Catholic religious order*]
PMC .... Pacific Marine Center [*National Oceanic and Atmospheric Administration*]
PMC .... Pacific Missile Center [*Marine science*]   (MSC)
PMC .... Pan Metal [*formerly, Patton Morgan*] Corp. [*Ammunition manufacturer*]
PMC .... Parents of Murdered Children [*Later, POMC*]   (EA)
PMC .... Partially Mission Capable [*Maintenance and supply*]   (MCD)
PMC .... Patrol/Mine Countermeasure Craft [*British*]
PMC .... Payload Monitoring and Control [*NASA*]   (NASA)
PMC .... Penguin Modern Classics [*Book publishing*]
PMC .... Pennsylvania Military College
PMC .... Pentamethyl(hydroxy)chromane [*Organic chemistry*]
PMC .... People's Mandate Committee   (EA)
PMC .... Percent Modern Carbon [*In atmosphere*]
PMC .... Peripheral Mononuclear Cell [*Cytology*]
PMC .... Peritoneal Mast Cell
PMC .... Permanently Manned Capability   (SSD)
PMC .... Personnel Mobilization Center [*Military*]
PMC .... Phased Maintenance Checklist   (MCD)
PMC .... Phenolic Molding Compound
PMC .... Phenylmercuric Chloride [*Antiseptic*]
PMC .... Philatelic Music Circle   (EA)
PMC .... Piperidinomethylcyclohexane [*Organic chemistry*]
PM & C... Plant Monitoring and Control [*IBM Corp.*]
PMC .... Plaster-Molded Cornice [*Construction*]
PMC .... Plutona-Molybdenum CERMET [*Ceramic Metal Element*]   (NASA)
PMC .... PMC Capital, Inc. [*Associated Press abbreviation*]   (APAG)
PMC .... PMC Capital, Inc. [*AMEX symbol*]   (SPSG)
PMC .... Pollen Mother Cell [*Botany*]
PMC .... Pollution Engineering [*A publication*]
PMC .... Polymer Matrix Composite [*Materials science*]
PMC .... Post Maintenance Check   (MCD)
PMC .... Post Manufacturing Checkout   (KSC)
PMC .... Posterior Medial Corner of Knee [*Sports medicine*]
PMC .... Powdered Metal Cathode
PMC .... Precision Machining Commercialization   (MCD)
PMC .... Predictive Multisensor Correlation
PMC .... Premium Merchandising Club of New York   (EA)
PMC .... Premotor Cortex [*Neuroanatomy*]
PMC .... President of the Mess Committee [*Military*] [*British*]
PMC .... Pressurized Membrane Container
PMC .... Primary Mesenchyme Cell [*Cytology*]
PMC .... Prime Mover Control [*Valve*]
PMC .... Princeton Microfilm Corp.
PmC .... Princeton Microfilm Corporation, Princeton, NJ [*Library symbol*] [*Library of Congress*]   (LCLS)
PMC .... Private Mailing Card [*Deltiology*]
PMC .... Private Medical Communication
PMC .... Private Meter Check [*Telecommunications*]   (TEL)
PMC .... Pro Maria Committee   (EA)
PMC .... Processed Meats Committee [*Later, DPMC*]   (EA)
PMC .... Procurement Committee   (MCD)
PMC .... Procurement Management Code [*Military*]   (AFIT)
PMC .... Procurement, Marine Corps [*An appropriation*]
PMC .... Procurement Method Coding [*DoD*]
PMC .... Professional and Managerial Class [*British*]   (DI)
PMC .... Program Management Control
PMC .... Program Management Course [*Army*]   (RDA)
PMC .... Program Marginal Checking
PMC .... Programmable Machine Controller   (NRCH)
PMC .... Progress in Medicinal Chemistry [*Elsevier Book Series*] [*A publication*]
PMC .... Project Management Course [*Army*]
PMC .... Project Manufacturing Controller   (MCD)
PMC .... Propellant Monitor and Control   (AFM)
PMC .... Pseudo Machine Code [*Data processing*]   (BUR)

PMC .... Pseudomembranous Colitis [*Medicine*]
PMC .... Public Media Center   (EA)
PMC .... Puerto Montt [*Chile*] [*Airport symbol*]   (OAG)
PMC .... Pumice   (MSA)
PMCA .... Purple Martin Conservation Association   (EA)
PM-CAWS ... Project Manager for Cannon Artillery Weapon Systems   (RDA)
PMCB........ Partially Mission Capable Both [*Maintenance and supply*]   (MCD)
P/MCB .... Project/Miscellaneous Change Board   (MCD)
PMCC........ Peerless Motor Car Club   (EA)
PMCC........ Pensky-Martens Closed Cup [*Flash point test*]
PMCC........ Platform Mission Control Center [*NASA*]
PMCC........ Post Mark Collectors Club   (EA)
PMCD .... Post Mortem Core Dump [*Data processing*]
PMCF .... Partial Mission Capability Factor
PMCF .... Post Maintenance Check Flight   (MCD)
PMCHi...... Crawford County Historical Society, Meadville, PA [*Library symbol*] [*Library of Congress*]   (LCLS)
PM & C-HI ... Plant Monitoring and Control - Host Interface [*IBM Corp.*]
PMCI........ Phosphate Mining Corp. of Christmas Island   (EY)
PMC INC .. Precision Management of Concordville, Inc. [*Media, PA*]   (TSSD)
PMck .... Carnegie Free Library of McKeesport, McKeesport, PA [*Library symbol*] [*Library of Congress*]   (LCLS)
PMCL........ Periodica de Re Morali Canonica Liturgica [*A publication*]
PMCL........ Posterior Medial Collateral Ligament [*Anatomy*]
PMCL........ Proposed MILSTRIP Change Letters
PMCM ...... Master Chief Patternmaker [*Navy rating*]
PMCM ...... Partially Mission Capable Maintenance [*Maintenance and supply*]   (MCD)
PMCM ..... Permanent Mold Casting Mold   (MCD)
PMCM ..... Pulse Morse Code Modulation   (OA)
PMCO ...... Memory and Cognition [*A publication*]
PMCO ...... Pan American Mortgage Corp. [*Miami, FL*] [*NASDAQ symbol*]   (NQ)
PMCP........ Photo-Marker Corp. [*NASDAQ symbol*]   (NQ)
PMCR........ Mass Comm Review [*A publication*]
PMCS........ Media, Culture, and Society [*A publication*]
PMCS........ Partially Mission Capable Supply [*Maintenance and supply*]   (MCD)
PMCS........ Phoenix Materials [*NASDAQ symbol*]   (NQ)
PMCS........ Preventive Maintenance Checks and Services [*for Army vehicles*]   (INF)
PMCS........ Process Monitoring and Control System
PMCS........ Professional Military Comptroller School
PMCS........ Program [*or Project*] Management Control System [*Army*]
PMCS........ Pulse-Modulated Communications System
PMCS........ Senior Chief Patternmaker [*Navy rating*]
PMCT........ PAL [*Permissive Action Link*] Management Control Team [*Army*]   (AABC)
PMCU ...... Personal Member of the Congregational Union [*British*]
PMCV....... Programmed Multichannel Valve [*Chromatography*]
PMCX........ Polar Molecular Corp. [*NASDAQ symbol*]   (NQ)
PMD .... Palmdale, CA [*Location identifier*] [*FAA*]   (FAAL)
PMD .... Palmdale/Lancaster [*California*] [*Airport symbol*]   (OAG)
PMD .... Palmer Industries Ltd. [*Vancouver Stock Exchange symbol*]
PMD .... Panel-Mounted Display   (MCD)
PMD .... Part Manufacturing Design
PMD .... Payload Mating Dolly [*NASA*]
PMD .... Payload Module Decoder [*NASA*]
PMD .... Personnel Management Division [*Environmental Protection Agency*]   (GFGA)
PMD .... Pharmaco-Medical Documentation, Inc. [*Information service or system*]   (IID)
PMD .... Physical Medium Dependent [*Data processing*]
PMD .... Planning and Management Division [*Environmental Protection Agency*]   (GFGA)
PMD .... Pontiac Motor Division [*General Motors Corp.*]
PMD .... Post-Mortem Debugger [*Data processing*]   (PCM)
PMD .... Post Mortem Dump [*Data processing*]
PMD .... Preventive Maintenance, Daily   (MCD)
PMD .... Preventive Maintenance Division [*Air Force*]
PMD .... Primary Myeloproliferative Disease [*Medicine*]
PMD .... Primary Myocardial Disease [*Medicine*]
PMd .... Private Physician
PMD .... Processing, Marketing, and Distribution
PMD .... Program Management Directive [*Air Force*]
PMD .... Program Management Documentation [*Army*]
PMD .... Program Module Dictionary
PMD .... Program Monitoring and Diagnosis
PMD .... Programmed Multiple Development [*Analytical chemistry*]
PMD .... Progressive Muscular Dystrophy [*Medicine*]
PMD .... Project Manager Development   (MCD)
PMD .... Projected Map Display
PMD .... Psychiatric Military Duty
PMDA .... Peace Messenger. Diocese of Athabasca. Peace River [*A publication*]
PMDA .... Photographic Manufacturers and Distributors Association   (EA)
PMDA .... Plastics Machinery Distributors Association [*British*]   (EAIO)
PMDA .... Pyromellitic Dianhydride [*Organic chemistry*]

PMDAMT ... Pacific Mobile Depot Activity Maintenance Team (CINC)
PMDC .... Project Manager Development Course [*Military*] (RDA)
PMDC .... Project for Mathematical Development of Children [*National Science Foundation*]
PMDCA .... Progress in Medicinal Chemistry [*A publication*]
PMDD .... Personnel Management Development Directorate [*Military Personnel Center*] (AABC)
PMDF....... Project Master Data File [*For spacecraft*]
PMDG .... Pentamethylene Diguanidine [*Organic chemistry*]
PMDL .... Palmdale, CA (NASA)
PMDL .... Post M-Day Deployment List [*Military*] (AABC)
PMDL .... Provisional Military Demarcation Line (CINC)
PMDM ...... Polyhedra Molecular Demonstration Model
PMDM ...... Poly(mellitic Dianhydride Methacrylate) [*Organic chemistry*]
PMDO....... Phased Maintenance During Overhaul
PMDP .... Pavement Marking Demonstration Program [*Federal Highway Administration*]
PMDP .... Project Manager Development Program [*Army*] (RDA)
PMDR .... Parametric Monotone Decreasing Ratio [*Statistics*]
PMDR .... Phosphorescence-Microwave Double Resonance
PMDR .... Provisioning Master Data Record
PMDS....... (Phenylmercury)dodecenyl Succinate [*Antimicrobial agent*]
PMDS....... Pilot Map Display System
PMDS....... Point Missile Defense System (DNAB)
PMDS....... Projected Map Display System
PMDS....... Property Management and Disposal Service [*Abolished, 1973*] [*General Services Administration*]
PMDT .... Pentamethyldiethylenetriamine [*Organic chemistry*]
PMDU .... Projected Map Display Unit (DNAB)
PMDY .... Midway Naval Station [*Henderson Field*], Sand Island [*Midway Islands*] [*ICAO location identifier*] (ICLI)
PME .... Caltech Political Military Exercise [*International relations simulation game*]
PME .... Passive Microelectronic Element
PME .... Peace Movement of Ethiopia (EA)
PME .... Pectin Methylesterase [*Also, PE*] [*An enzyme*]
PME .... Pedal Mode Ergometer
PME .... Performance Management and Evaluation
PME .... Performance Monitoring Equipment (NVT)
PME .... Phosphatidylmonomethylethanolamine [*Biochemistry*]
PME .... Phosphomonoester [*Biochemistry*]
PME .... Phosphorylated Monester [*Organic chemistry*]
PME .... Photomagnetoelectric
PME .... Pinosylvin Methyl Ether [*Organic chemistry*]
PME .... Polymorphonuclear Eosinophile [*Hematology*]
PME .... Precision Measuring Equipment (AFM)
PME .... Primary Mission Equipment
PME .... Prime Ministers of England [*A publication*]
PME .... Process and Manufacturing Engineering (NRCH)
PME .... Processor Memory Enhancement
PME .... Professional Military Education (AFM)
PME .... Professional Military Ethic (MCD)
PME .... Project Manager, Electronics System Command [*Navy*]
PME .... Protective Multiple Earthing [*Electricity*]
PMEA....... Middle Eastern Studies [*A publication*]
PMEA....... (Phenyl)(methyl)ethanolamine [*Organic chemistry*]
PMEA....... Phosphonylmethoxyethyladenine [*Antiviral*]
PMEA....... Powder Metallurgy Equipment Association (EA)
P/MEA...... Probationary Marine Engineering Artificer [*British military*] (DMA)
PMEA....... Production and Maintenance Engineering Agent (MCD)
PMEA....... Publishing Manufacturers Executive Association (EA)
PMEAR...... Preliminary Maintenance Engineering Analysis Requirement (MCD)
PMED .... Pace Medical, Inc. [*NASDAQ symbol*] (NQ)
PMedS....... Delaware County Institute of Science, Media, PA [*Library symbol*] [*Library of Congress*] (LCLS)
PMEE....... Prime Mission Electronic Equipment [*NASA*] (KSC)
PMEF....... Petroleum Marketing Education Foundation (EA)
PMEL....... Pacific Marine Environmental Laboratory [*National Oceanic and Atmospheric Administration*] [*Seattle, WA*] (GRD)
PMEL....... Precision Measurements Equipment Laboratory [*NASA*]
PMELA...... Plastiques Modernes et Elastomeres [*A publication*]
PM-ENDOR ... Polarization Modulated Electron Nuclear Double Resonance [*Spectroscopy*]
PMer.......... Mercer Free Library, Mercer, PA [*Library symbol*] [*Library of Congress*] (LCLS)
PMER....... Mercury [*A publication*]
P Merton.... Descriptive Catalogue of the Greek Papyri in the Collection of Wilfred Merton [*A publication*]
PMES .... International Journal of Middle East Studies [*A publication*]
PMES .... Personnel Management Evaluation System [*Department of Labor*]
PMES .... Productivity Measurement and Evaluation System (MCD)
PMES .... Proposed Material Erection Schedule (MGD)
PMEST ..... Personality, Matter, Energy, Space, Time [*Colon classification, S. R. Ranganathan*] [*Library science*]
PMET....... Painter Metal (AAG)
PMEV....... Panel-Mounted Electronic Voltmeter
PMEXPO ... Property Management Exposition [*Bachner Communications*] (TSPED)

PMF.......... Paint and Resin News [*A publication*]
PMF.......... Parts Master File (MCD)
PMF.......... Patriot Maintenance Facility [*Army*]
PMF.......... Performance Monitor Function [*NASA*] (NASA)
PMF.......... Perigee Motor Firing [*Aerospace*] (MCD)
PMF.......... Permanent Magnetic Field
PMF.......... Permanent Military Force (ADA)
PMF.......... Personnel Master File [*Army*] (AABC)
PMF.......... Pilot Mortar Fire
PM of F...... Presidential Medal of Freedom [*Military decoration*] (AABC)
PMF.......... Price Master File (MCD)
PMF.......... Principle Management Facility (MCD)
PMF.......... Pro Media Foundation (EA)
PMF.......... Probable Maximum Flood [*Nuclear energy*] (NRCH)
PMF.......... Processed Message File (MCD)
PMF.......... Professional Medical Film (AABC)
PMF.......... Program Management Facility [*NASA*] (MCD)
PMF .... Progressive Massive Fibrosis
PMF.......... Project Management File (MCD)
PMF.......... Proton Motive Force [*Physics*]
PMFA....... Fireman Apprentice, Patternmaker, Striker [*Navy rating*]
PMFAA...... Pokroky Matematiky, Fyziky, a Astronomie [*A publication*]
PM-FAC.... Prednisone, Methotrexate, Fluorouracil, Adriamycin, Cyclophosphamide [*Antineoplastic drug regimen*]
PMFC....... Pacific Marine Fisheries Commission [*Later, PSMFC*] (EA)
PMFC........ Patsy Montana Fan Club (EA)
PMFG....... Peerless Manufacturing Co. [*NASDAQ symbol*] (NQ)
PM/FL....... Performance Monitor/Fault Locator [*Military*] (CAAL)
PMFLT ..... Pamphlet (MSA)
PMFN ...... Fireman, Patternmaker, Striker [*Navy rating*]
PMFPAC... Polaris Missile Facility, Pacific Fleet
PMFR....... Marriage and Family Review [*A publication*]
PMFS .... Pulsed Magnetic Field System
PMFWCMA ... Paper Mill Fourdrinier Wire Cloth Manufacturers Association [*Later, FWC*] (EA)
PMG.......... Pall Mall Gazette [*A publication*]
PMG.......... Paymaster General [*Navy*]
PMG.......... Permanent Magnet Generator
PMG.......... Phase Modulation Generator
PMG.......... Physiological Measurement Group
PMG.......... Phytophthora Megasperma F. Sp. Glycinea [*A fungus*]
PMG.......... Pinto Malartic [*Vancouver Stock Exchange symbol*]
PMG.......... Polymethylgalacturonase [*An enzyme*]
PMG.......... Ponta Pora [*Brazil*] [*Airport symbol*] (OAG)
PMG.......... Port Moresby [*Papua New Guinea*] [*Seismograph station code, US Geological Survey*] (SEIS)
PMG.......... Port Moresby [*Papua New Guinea*] [*Geomagnetic observatory code*]
PMG.......... Postmaster General
PMG.......... Poultry Marketing Guide
PMG.......... Prediction Marker Generator
PMG.......... Propodial Mucus Gland [*Zoology*]
PMG.......... Provisional Military Government [*Ethiopia*]
PMG.......... Provost Marshal General [*Army*]
PMG.......... Putnam Investment Grade Municipal Trade II [*NYSE symbol*] (SPSG)
P1MG........ P1 [*Code*] for Multigroup [*Method*] [*Nuclear energy*] (NRCH)
PMGDINYC ... Production Men's Guild of the Dress Industry of New York City (EA)
PMGFEL .. Preliminary Master Government-Furnished Equipment List (MCD)
PMGM ...... Program Manager's Guidance Memorandum
PMGO....... Office of the Provost Marshal General [*Army*]
PM-GPV .. Project Manager, General Purpose Vehicle (SAA)
PMGS....... Predictable Model Guidance Scheme (OA)
PMGS....... Provost Marshal General's School, United States Army
PMGW...... Primary Mission Gross Weight
PMH.......... Past Medical History
PMH.......... Phenylmercuric Hydroxide [*Organic chemistry*]
PMH.......... Portsmouth, OH [*Location identifier*] [*FAA*] (FAAL)
PMH.......... Probable Maximum Hurricane [*Nuclear energy*] (NRCH)
PMH.......... Production per Man-Hour
PMH.......... Putnam Tax-Free Health Care Fund [*NYSE symbol*] (SPSG)
PMHB .... Pennsylvania Magazine of History and Biography [*A publication*]
PMHBA .... Polish Medical Science and History Bulletin [*A publication*]
PMHC....... Pyridinylmethylethylene(hydrazinecarbothioamide) [*Organic chemistry*]
P & MHEL ... Pollock and Maitland's History of English Common Law [*A publication*] (DLA)
PMHL....... Preferred Measurement Hardware List [*NASA*] (NASA)
PMH/M.... Productive Man-Hours per Month [*Navy*] (NG)
PMHP ...... Para-Menthane Hydroperoxide [*Organic chemistry*]
PMHRON ... Patrol Combatant Missile Hydrofoil Squadron (DNAB)
PMHRON MLSG ... Patrol Combatant Missile Hydrofoil Squadron Mobile Logistics Support Group (DNAB)
PMHS .... Polymethylhydrosiloxane [*Organic chemistry*]
PMHS .... Proceedings. Massachusetts Historical Society [*A publication*]
PMHSA .... Polish Military History Society of America (EA)
PMi........... Milton Public Library, Milton, PA [*Library symbol*] [*Library of Congress*] (LCLS)

PMI .... Palma [*Mallorca Island*] [*Airport symbol*]   (OAG)
PMI .... Parmac Mines [*Vancouver Stock Exchange symbol*]
PMI .... Past [*or Previous*] Medical Illness
PMI .... Patient Medication Instruction
PMI .... Pearlitic Malleable Iron   (MCD)
PMI .... Pennsylvania Muscle Institute [*University of Pennsylvania*]
              [*Research center*]   (RCD)
PMI .... Pensions Management Institute [*British*]   (EAIO)
PMI .... Permanent Manufacturing Information   (MSA)
PMI .... Phenylmethylisoxazole [*Organic chemistry*]
PMI .... Phosphomannose Isomerase [*An enzyme*]   (MAE)
PMI .... Photo Methods for Industry [*A publication*]
PMI .... Photographic Microimage Master [*Reprography*]
PMI .... Plant Manager Instruction [*Nuclear energy*]   (NRCH)
PMI .... Plasma-Materials Interactions   (MCD)
PMI .... Plumbing Manufacturers Institute   (EA)
PMI .... Point of Maximal Impulse [*Medicine*]
PMI .... Point of Maximum Intensity
PMI .... Postmyocardial Infarction [*Syndrome*] [*Medicine*]
PMI .... Power Management Inventory [*Test*]
PMI .... Preliminary Maintenance Inspection   (MCD)
PMI .... Premark International, Inc. [*NYSE symbol*]   (SPSG)
PMI .... Prescriptive Math Inventory
PMI .... Present Medical Illness
PMI .... Presidential Management Incentives [*Office of Management
              and Budget*]
PMI .... Pressed Metal Institute [*Later, AMSA*]
PMI .... Preventive Maintenance Inspection   (AFM)
PMI .... Preventive Maintenance Instruction   (NASA)
PMI .... Primary Measurement Instrument
PMI .... Principal Maintenance Inspector   (NASA)
PMI .... Private Mortgage Insurance [*Insurance of mortgages by private
              insurers*]
PMI .... Probe Ministries International   (EA)
PMI .... Processor Monitoring Instrument [*Data processing*]   (ADA)
PMI .... Program Management Instruction
PMI .... Programmable Machine Interface   (MCD)
PMI .... Programmable Memory Interface [*Data processing*]
PMI .... Programmable MODEM Interface [*Data processing*]   (MCD)
PMI .... Project Management Institute   (EA)
PMI .... Proposed Military Improvement   (CAAL)
PMI .... Pseudomatrix Isolation
PMI .... Purchased Materials Inspection
PMIA........ Parallel Multiplexer Interface Adapter   (MCD)
PMIA........ Presidential Management Improvement Award
PMIC........ Parallel Multiple Incremental Computer
PMIC........ Payload Mission Integration Contract   (MCD)
PMIC........ Periodic Maintenance Information Cards   (MCD)
PMIC........ Personnel Management Information Center [*Air Force*]   (AFM)
PMIC........ Precious Metal Indicator Code
PMICA...... Proceedings. Institute of Medicine of Chicago [*A publication*]
P Mich ...... Michigan Papyri [*A publication*]
P Mich Zen ... Zenon Papyri in the University of Michigan Collection [*A
              publication*]
PMIG .... Programmers Minimal Interface to Graphics   (MCD)
PMIIT .... Putnam Master Intermediate Income Trust [*Associated Press
              abbreviation*]   (APAG)
PMIJ .... Pulse-Modulated Infrared Jammer
PMilan...... Papiri Milanesi [*A publication*]   (OCD)
PMilS .... Millersville State College, Millersville, PA [*Library symbol*]
              [*Library of Congress*]   (LCLS)
PMI/MO... Precedence Manual In / Manual Out   (DNAB)
PMIN .... Mathematical Intelligencer [*A publication*]
PM Iowa State Univ Sci Technol Coop Ext Serv ... PM. Iowa State University
              of Science and Technology. Cooperative Extension Service
              [*A publication*]
PMIP......... Pan Malayan Islamic Party
PMIP......... Postmaintenance Inspection Pilot
PMIP......... Presidential Management Intern Program [*Executive Office of
              the President*]   (GFGA)
PMIQ .... Midwest Quarterly [*A publication*]
PMIR........ Program Manager's Integration Review [*NASA*]   (NASA)
PMIR........ Psi-Mediated Instrumental Response [*Parapsychology*]
PMIRD...... Passive Microwave Intercept Receiver Display
PMIS....... Passive Microwave Imaging System [*NASA*]
PMIS........ Patient Medical Information System   (OA)
PMIS........ Personnel Management Information System
PMIS........ Plant Monitoring and Information System [*Nuclear
              energy*]   (NRCH)
PMIS .... Precision Mechanisms in Sodium [*Nuclear energy*]   (NRCH)
PMIS .... Printing Management Information Systems
PMIS........ Program Management Information System [*Army*]
PMIS........ Projects Management Information System
              [*UNESCO*]   (DUND)
PMIS........ PSRO [*Professional Standards Review Organization*]
              Management Information System   (DHSM)
PMIT........ Putnam Master Income Trust [*Associated Press
              abbreviation*]   (APAG)
PMITS ...... Post Mobilization Individual Training and Support   (MCD)
PMIZ........ PM Industries, Inc. [*NASDAQ symbol*]   (NQ)
PMJ .... Project Management Journal [*A publication*]

PMJ........... Pulse-Modulated Jammer
PMK .... Panel Marking Kit
PMK .... Pitch Mark [*Shipfitting*]   (AAG)
PMK .... Pointe Molloy [*Kerguelen Islands*] [*Seismograph station code,
              US Geological Survey*]   (SEIS)
PMK .... Portable Molding Kit
PMK .... Postmark
PMK .... Primark Corp. [*NYSE symbol*]   (SPSG)
PMK .... Primary Monkey Kidney [*Physiology*]
PMK .... Primary Rhesus Monkey Kidney   (AAMN)
PMKM ..... Past Master, Knights of Malta [*Freemasonry*]   (ROG)
PMKR .... Petromark Resources Co. [*Tulsa, OK*] [*NASDAQ
              symbol*]   (NQ)
PMKY .... Pittsburgh, McKeesport & Youghiogheny [*AAR code*]
PML .... Pakistan Muslim League [*Political party*]
PML .... Parts Material List
PML .... Pattern Makers' League of North America   (EA)
PML .... Physical Memory Level
PML .... PI Edit's Macro Language [*Iliad Group*] [*Data processing*]
PML .... [*The*] Pierpont Morgan Library   (BJA)
PML .... Plymouth Marine Laboratory [*Natural Environment Research
              Council*] [*British*] [*Information service or system*]   (IID)
PML .... Polymer Microdevice Laboratory [*Case Western Reserve
              University*] [*Research center*]   (RCD)
PML .... Polymorphonuclear Leukocyte [*Hematology*]
PML .... Port Moller [*Alaska*] [*Airport symbol*]   (OAG)
PML .... Port Moller, AK [*Location identifier*] [*FAA*]   (FAAL)
PML .... Posterior Mitral Leaflet [*Cardiology*]
PML .... Preliminary Materials List [*NASA*]
PML .... Probable Maximum Loss [*Insurance*]
PML .... Progressive Multifocal Leukoencephalopathy [*Oncology*]
PML .... Promotion Management List [*Pronounced "pemell"*] [*Air
              Force*]
PML .... University of Windsor, Paul Martin Law Library [*UTLAS
              symbol*]
PMLA........ Proceedings of the Modern Language Association [*A
              publication*]
PMLA........ Production Music Libraries Association   (EA)
PMLA........ Publications. Modern Language Association of America
              [*Database*] [*A publication*]
PMLAAm ... Publications. Modern Language Association of America [*A
              publication*]
PMLC........ Pooled Mixed Lymphocyte Culture [*Clinical chemistry*]
PMLC........ Programmed Multiline Controller
PMLE........ Polymorphous Light Eruption [*Medicine*]
PMLG........ Poly(methyl L-Glutamate) [*Organic chemistry*]
PMLM....... Photosensitive Membrane Light Modulator
PMLO .... Philippine Military Liaison Officer   (DNAB)
PMLO .... Principal Military Landing Offices [*British*]
PMLPC ..... Permanent Mass Layoffs and Plant Closings Program [*Bureau
              of Labor Statistics*]
PMLV....... Permanent Magnet Latch Valve
PMM .... Military Morale Division [*Coast Guard*]
PMM .... Pall Mall Magazine [*A publication*]
PMM .... Peace Mission Movement   (EA)
PMM .... Peat Marwick McLintock [*Accounting firm*] [*British*]
PMM .... Pedestal-Mounted Manipulator [*Nuclear energy*]   (NRCH)
PMM .... Penobscot Marine Museum   (EA)
PMM .... Personnel Management Manual [*A publication*]   (ADA)
PMM .... Petroleum Marketing Management [*Petroleum Marketers
              Association of America*] [*A publication*]
PMM .... Petroleum Marketing Monthly [*Department of Energy*]
              [*Information service or system*]   (CRD)
PMM .... Physical Memory Manager [*Data processing*]   (PCM)
PMM .... Phytophthora Megasperma F.Sp Medicaginia [*A fungus*]
PMM .... Poly(methyl Methacrylate) [*Also, PMMA*] [*Organic chemistry*]
PMM .... Pool Maintenance Module [*Telecommunications*]   (TEL)
PMM .... Portavideo [*Vancouver Stock Exchange symbol*]
PMM .... Presa Malpaso [*Mexico*] [*Seismograph station code, US
              Geological Survey*]   (SEIS)
PMM .... Procom Emerald [*Vancouver Stock Exchange symbol*]
PMM .... Professional Music Men, Inc.   (EA)
PMM .... Profile Milling Machine
PMM .... Programmable Microcomputer Module
PMM .... Property Management Manual [*NASA*]   (MCD)
PMM .... Pullman, MI [*Location identifier*] [*FAA*]   (FAAL)
PMM .... Pulse Mode Multiplex
PMM .... Purchase-Money Mortgage [*Real estate*]
PMM .... Putnam Managed Municipal Income [*NYSE symbol*]   (SPSG)
PMMA ...... Pere Marquette Memorial Association   (EA)
PMMA ...... Poly Methyl Methacrylate Association [*European Council of
              Chemical Manufacturers Federations*] [*Brussels,
              Belgium*]   (EAIO)
PMMA ...... Poly(methyl Methacrylate) [*Also, PMM*] [*Organic chemistry*]
PMMA ...... Publications. Metropolitan Museum of Art. Egyptian
              Expedition [*New York*] [*A publication*]
PMMAP...... Poly(methyl Methacrylate Peroxide) [*Organic chemistry*]
PMMAPA ... Poly Methyl Methacrylate Producers Association
              [*Belgium*]   (EAIO)
PMMB ...... Parallel Memory-to-Memory Bus
PMMC ...... Permanent Magnetic Movable Coil

PMMEA.... Prensa Medica Mexicana [*A publication*]
PM-MEP... Project Manager - Mobile Electric Power [*DoD*]
PMMF....... Precious Metals Master File [*DoD*]   (AFIT)
PMMF....... Presbyterian Medical Mission Fund [*A publication*]
PMMI .... Packaging Machinery Manufacturers Institute   (EA)
PMMI .... Putnam Managed Municipal Income Trust [*Associated Press abbreviation*]   (APAG)
PMMLA.... Papers. Midwest Modern Language Association [*A publication*]
PMMM ...... Pall Mall Money Management [*Investment group*] [*British*]
PMMP....... Preventive Maintenance Management Program
PMMR....... Panel-Mounted Microfilm Reader
PMMR ...... Passive Multichannel Microwave Radiometer [*NASA*]
PMMS....... Phrenicon Metabolic Monitoring System
PMMS....... Plainsong and Mediaeval Music Society   (EA)
PMMS....... Program Master Milestone Schedule   (MCD)
PMMU ...... Paged Memory Management Unit [*Computer chip*]   (BYTE)
PMMV ...... Pea Mild Mosaic Virus [*Plant pathology*]
PMN......... Pacific Mountain Network [*Television*]
PMN.......... Pahute Mesa [*Nevada*] [*Seismograph station code, US Geological Survey*] [*Closed*]   (SEIS)
PMN......... Permian Resources Ltd. [*Vancouver Stock Exchange symbol*]
PMN......... Phenylmercuric Nitrate [*Antiseptic*]
PMN......... Polymorphonuclear [*Hematology*]
PMN......... Polymorphonuclear Neutrophilic [*Hematology*]
PMN......... Postman   (DCTA)
PMN......... Premanufacture Notification [*Environmental Protection Agency*]
PMN......... Premarket Notification [*Requirement for introducing new chemicals into the EEC*]
PMN......... Program Management Network   (MCD)
PMN......... Proposed Material Need   (MCD)
PMN......... Pullman Co. [*NYSE symbol*]   (SPSG)
PMN......... Pumani [*Papua New Guinea*] [*Airport symbol*]   (OAG)
PMN......... Putnam New York Investment Grade Municipal [*AMEX symbol*]   (SPSG)
PM-NAVCON ... Project Manager, Navigation and Control [*Military*]
PMND....... Mind [*A publication*]
PMNF .... Premanufacture Notification Form [*Environmental Protection Agency*]   (GFGA)
PMNH....... Men's Health [*A publication*]
PMNK .... Mankind [*A publication*]
PMNL .... Polymorphonuclear Leukocyte [*Hematology*]
PMNP....... Platform-Mounted Nuclear Plant   (NRCH)
PMNR....... Periadenitis Mucosa Necrotica Recurrens [*Medicine*]
PMN/SFS ... People's Music Network for Songs of Freedom and Struggle   (EA)
PM-NUC... Project Manager for Nuclear Munitions [*Army*]   (RDA)
PMNV ...... Project Manager, Night Vision   (RDA)
PMNWA... Pressemitteilung Nordrhein-Westfalen [*A publication*]
PMo .... Monessen Public Library, Monessen, PA [*Library symbol*] [*Library of Congress*]   (LCLS)
PMO......... Palermo [*Italy*] [*Airport symbol*]   (OAG)
PMO......... Palermo Resources, Inc. [*Vancouver Stock Exchange symbol*]
PMO......... Perroni, Martin, O'Reilly [*Commercial firm*]
PMO......... Personnel Management Officer [*Army*]   (INF)
PMO......... Perturbation Molecular Orbital [*Theory*]
PMO......... Pianissimo [*Very Softly*] [*Music*]   (ROG)
PMO......... Pine Mountain Observatory
PMO......... Polaris Material Office [*Missiles*]
PMO......... Polaris Missile Office
PMO......... Pomariorio [*Tuamotu Archipelago*] [*Seismograph station code, US Geological Survey*]   (SEIS)
PMO......... Port Meteorological Office [*National Weather Service*]
PMO......... Postal Money Order [*Military*]
PMO......... Postmenopausal Osteoporosis [*Medicine*]
PMO......... Prime Minister's Office
PMO......... Principal Medical Officer
PMO......... Product Manager's Office   (RDA)
PMO......... Product Manufacturing Organization
PMO......... Profit Making Organization
PMO......... Program Management Office [*NASA*]   (KSC)
PMO......... Program Management Office [*Environmental Protection Agency*]   (GFGA)
PMO......... Project Management Office [*Army*]   (AABC)
PMO......... Property Movement Order
PMO......... Provisional [*Program Management*] Office [*Army*]
PMO......... Provost Marshal's Office
PMO......... Psychiatric Military Officer
PMOA ...... Modern Age [*A publication*]
PMOA ...... Prospectors and Mine Owners Association   (EA)
PMOC ...... Modern China [*A publication*]
PMOC ...... Pioneer Mission Operations Center [*NASA*]
PMOD...... Modern Drama [*A publication*]
PMODA.... Phenyl(mercapto)oxadiazole [*Reagent*]
PMOF ...... Presidential Medal of Freedom [*Military decoration*]   (GFGA)
PMOG....... Plutonium Maintenance and Operating Gallery [*Nuclear energy*]   (NRCH)
PMOG....... Proposed Material Ordering Guide   (MCD)
PMOGA.... Progress in Medical Genetics [*A publication*]
PMOJ........ Pesticides Monitoring Journal [*A publication*]
pmol .... Picomole [*One trillionth of a mole*]   (WGA)

PMOLANT ... Polaris Material Office, Atlantic Fleet [*Missiles*]
PMOM...... Performance Management Operations Manual [*NASA*]   (NASA)
PMON....... Performance Management Operations Network [*NASA*]   (NASA)
PMONDN ... Society of Economic Paleontologists and Mineralogists. Paleontological Monograph [*A publication*]
PMOP .... Modern Philology [*A publication*]
PMOPAC ... Polaris Material Office, Pacific Fleet [*Missiles*]
PMOS .... Modern Asian Studies [*A publication*]
PMOS .... Permanent Manned Orbital Station   (AAG)
PMOS .... Physical Movement of Spacecraft   (SAA)
PMOS .... Positive-Channel Metal-Oxide Semiconductor [*Telecommunications*]   (TEL)
PMOS .... Primary Military Occupational Specialty [*Army*]
PMOS .... Program Management and Operations Staff [*Environmental Protection Agency*]   (GFGA)
PMOSA..... Perceptual and Motor Skills [*A publication*]
PMOSC..... Primary Military Occupational Specialty Code [*Army*]   (AABC)
PMOT .... Modern Theology [*A publication*]
PMP .... Packed Main Parachute
PMP .... Parallel Microprogrammed Processor [*Data processing*]
PMP .... Parent Mass Peak
PMP .... Parents' Magazine Press
P & MP ..... Paris & Mount Pleasant Railroad   (IIA)
PMP .... Parti du Mouvement Populaire de la Cote Francaise des Somalis [*Popular Movement Party of French Somaliland*] [*Political party*]
PMP .... Partido ng Masang Pilipino [*Political party*]   (EY)
PMP .... Partito Monarchico Popolare [*Popular Monarchist Party*] [*Italy*] [*Political party*]   (PPE)
PMP .... Parts, Materials, and Packaging   (MCD)
PMP .... Parts, Materials, and Processes   (MCD)
PMP .... Passive Measurement Program
PMP .... Past Menstrual Period [*Medicine*]
PMP .... Patient Management Problem [*Gerontology*]
PMP .... Performance Management Package [*NASA*]   (NASA)
PmP .... Pergamon Press, Inc., Fairview Park, Elmsford, NY [*Library symbol*] [*Library of Congress*]   (LCLS)
PMP .... Permanent Manned Presence   (SSD)
PMP .... Persistent Mentoposterior [*A fetal position*] [*Obstetrics*]
PMP .... Peter Miller Apparel Group, Inc. [*Toronto Stock Exchange symbol*]
PMP .... Phenyl(methyl)pyrazolone [*An organic pigment*]
PMP .... Pimaga [*Papua New Guinea*] [*Airport symbol*]   (OAG)
PMP .... Planned Maintenance Plan   (MCD)
PMP .... Poly(metal Phosphinate) [*Organic chemistry*]
PMP .... Poly(methylpentene) [*Organic chemistry*]
PMP .... Pompano Beach, FL [*Location identifier*] [*FAA*]   (FAAL)
PMP .... Pompeii [*Italy*] [*Seismograph station code, US Geological Survey*] [*Closed*]   (SEIS)
PMP .... Pontifical Mission for Palestine   (EA)
PMP .... Position Management Program
PMP .... Powder Melting Process [*Physics*]
PMP .... Powdered Metal Part
PMP .... Power Management Profile [*Test*]
PMP .... Preliminary Mission Profile   (MCD)
PMP .... Premodulation Processor
PMP .... Preoperational Maintenance Plan
PMP .... Preoperational Monitoring Program [*Nuclear energy*]   (NRCH)
PMP .... Pressure Measurement Package
PMP .... Preventive Maintenance Plan   (KSC)
PMP .... Preventive Maintenance Procedure [*Nuclear energy*]   (NRCH)
PMP .... Previous Menstrual Period [*Medicine*]
PMP .... Prime Mission Project [*Military*]
PMP .... Prime Motor Inns LP [*NYSE symbol*]   (SPSG)
PMP .... Prism-Mirror-Prism [*For electron microscopy*]
PMP .... Probable Maximum Precipitation [*Nuclear energy*]   (NRCH)
PMP .... Professor of Moral Philosophy
PMP .... Program Management Plan [*NASA*]
PMP .... Program Monitor Panel
PMP .... Progressive Merger Procedure [*Econometrics*]
PMP .... Project Master Plan [*Army*]
PMP .... Project on Military Procurement [*Later, PGP*]   (EA)
PMP .... Protective Mobilization Plan
PMP .... Pulmonary Mean Pressure [*Medicine*]
PMP .... Pulsed Microwave Power
PMP .... Pump   (KSC)
PMP .... Pyridoxamine Phosphate [*Biochemistry*]
PMPA........ Permanent Magnet Producers Association [*Later, MMPA*]   (EA)
PMPA........ Petroleum Marketing Practices Act
PMPA........ Proximal Main Pulmonary Artery [*Anatomy*]
PMPA........ Publications. Missouri Philological Association [*A publication*]
PMPEA..... Professional Motion Picture Equipment Association [*Later, PFVEA*]   (EA)
PMPFR..... Program Manager's Preflight Review [*NASA*]   (KSC)
PMPH .... Pamphlet   (DLA)
PMPL........ Preferred Mechanical Parts List [*NASA*]   (NASA)
PMPM....... Perpetual Motion Poetry Machine
PMPM....... Phase Margin Performance Measure [*Manual control system*]

PMPM....... Programmable Multiple Position Machine   (MCD)
PMPM....... Pulse Mode Performance Model   (KSC)
PMPMA.... Plastic and Metal Products Manufacturers Association   (EA)
PMPO .... Postmenopausal Palpable Ovary [*Gynecology*]
PMPP........ Program Management Phase-Out Plan [*Military*]   (AFIT)
PMPPEZ... Physiological and Molecular Plant Pathology [*A publication*]
PMPPI....... Polymethylenepolyphenyl Polyisocyanate [*Organic chemistry*]
PMPQ .... Professional and Managerial Position Questionnaire [*Test*]
PMPR....... Program Management and Performance Review
PMPS .... Program Management Planning and Scheduling
              [*Military*]   (DNAB)
PMQ .... Perito Moreno [*Argentina*] [*Airport symbol*]   (OAG)
PMQ .... Permanent Married Quarters [*Canadian Forces*]
PMQ .... Phytylmenaquinone [*Vitamin K*] [*Also, K*] [*Biochemistry*]
PMQ .... Primitive Methodist Quarterly Review [*A publication*]   (ROG)
PMQR .... Michigan Quarterly Review [*A publication*]
PMR .... Micron Products, Inc. [*AMEX symbol*]   (SPSG)
PMR .... Pacific Missile Range [*Later, WTR*]
PMR .... Palmer [*Alaska*] [*Seismograph station code, US Geological
              Survey*]   (SEIS)
PMR .... Palmerston North [*New Zealand*] [*Airport symbol*]   (OAG)
PMR .... Parabolic Microwave Reflector
PMR .... Partido Mariateguista Revolucionario [*Peru*] [*Political
              party*]   (EY)
PMR .... Partidul Muncitoresc Roman [*Romanian Workers' Party*]
              [*Political party*]
PMR .... Parts Material Requirements File
PMR .... Payload Mass Ratio
PMR .... Paymaster
PMR .... Performance Measurement Report [*NASA*]   (NASA)
PMR .... Performance Monitoring Receiver
PMR .... Perinatal Mortality Rate [*Medicine*]
PMR .... Philippine Mining Record [*A publication*]
PM & R ..... Physical Medicine and Rehabilitation
PMR .... Planned Maintenance Requirements
PMR .... Pollutant Mass Rate [*Environmental science*]   (GFGA)
PMR .... Polymerization of Monomer Reactants [*Organic chemistry*]
PMR .... Polymyalgia Rheumatica [*Medicine*]
PMR .... Portable Microfiche Reader [*DASA Corp.*]
PMR .... Postmaster   (DCTA)
PMR .... Potential Military Relevance
PMR .... Power Monitor Relay
PMR .... Preliminary Materials Review
PMR .... Pressure Modulation Radiometer
PMR .... Preventive Maintenance and Repair [*Aviation*]   (MCD)
PMR .... Primary Mission Readiness
PMR .... Prime Resources Corp. [*Vancouver Stock Exchange symbol*]
PMR .... Priority Monitor Report
PMR .... Proceedings. Patristic, Mediaeval, and Renaissance Conference
              [*A publication*]
PMR .... Procurement Management Review [*DoD*]
PMR .... Profoundly Mentally Retarded
PMR .... Program Management Responsibility   (MCD)
PMR .... Program Manager's Review [*NASA*]   (NASA)
PMR .... Programmed Mixture Ratio   (KSC)
PMR .... Progress in Mutation Research [*Elsevier Book Series*] [*A
              publication*]
PMR .... Project Management Report
PMR .... Propellant Mass Ratio   (SAA)
PMR .... Property Movement Request   (MCD)
PMR .... Proportionate Mortality Rate [*or Ratio*]
PMR .... Protein Magnetic Resonance [*Medicine*]   (MAE)
PMR .... Proton Magnetic Resonance
PMR .... Provisioning Master Record   (MCD)
PMR .... Pulsational Magnetic Radiation [*Astronomy*]
PMRA .... Percent of Males Reproductively Active [*Ecology*]
PMRA .... Projected Manpower Requirements Account [*Navy*]
PMRAFNS ... Princess Mary's Royal Air Force Nursing Service [*British*]
PMRB........ Preliminary Materials Review Board
PMRC........ Parents' Music Resource Center   (EA)
PMRC........ Prepositioned Material Receipt Card [*DoD*]
PMRC........ Proctor Maple Research Center [*University of Vermont*]
              [*Research center*]   (RCD)
PMRD .... Prepositioned Material Receipt Documents   (MCD)
PMRDET .. Pacific Missile Range Detachment [*Obsolete*]   (MUGU)
PMRF........ Pacific Missile Range Facility [*Obsolete*]   (MSC)
PMRFAC .. Pacific Missile Range Facility [*Obsolete*]   (MUGU)
PMRG .... Preliminary Materials Review Group [*NASA*]   (KSC)
PMRI........ Posteromedial Rotation Instability [*Sports medicine*]
PMRL....... Pulp Manufacturers' Research League
PMRM....... Periodic Maintenance Requirements Manual [*Navy*]
PMRMO ... Protectable Mobilization Reserve Materiel Objective
              [*Army*]   (AABC)
PMRMR.... Protectable Mobilization Reserve Materiel Requirements
              [*Army*]
PMRN .... Parents' Music Resource Network   (EA)
PMR/NMC ... Pacific Missile Range / Naval Missile Center   (SAA)
PMRO .... Popular Magazine Review Online [*EBSCO Subscription
              Services*] [*Information service or system*]
PMRP........ Petroleum Material Requirements Plan   (MCD)
PMRP........ Precious Metals Recovery Program [*DoD*]   (AFIT)

PM-RPV.... Project Manager, Remotely Piloted Vehicle [*Military*]
PMRR........ Pacific Missile Range Representative [*Obsolete*]   (MUGU)
PMRR........ Pre-Mate Readiness Review [*NASA*]   (KSC)
PMRS........ Parachute Medical Rescue Service   (EA)
PMRS........ Performance Management and Recognition System
PMRS........ Physical Medicine and Rehabilitation Service
PMRS........ Progress of Medieval and Renaissance Studies in the United
              States and Canada [*A publication*]
PMRSG ...... Pacific Missile Range Study Group [*Obsolete*]
PMRT........ Peabody Mathematics Readiness Test [*Educational test*]
PMRT........ Program Management Responsibility Transfer   (MCD)
PMRT........ Progressive Muscle Relaxation Training [*Psychology*]
PMRTD..... Program Management Responsibility Transfer Date   (AFIT)
PMRTF ..... Pacific Missile Range Tracking Facility [*Obsolete*]   (MUGU)
PMRTP ..... Program Management Responsibility Transfer Plan   (AFIT)
PMRX........ Pharmaceutical Marketing Services [*NASDAQ
              symbol*]   (SPSG)
PMRY........ Presidio of Monterey [*Military*]   (AABC)
PMS........... Palmer - Arctic Valley [*Alaska*] [*Seismograph station code, US
              Geological Survey*]   (SEIS)
PMS........... Pantone Matching System [*Printing*]
PMS........... Paper Manifesting System
PMS........... Para-Methylstyrene [*Organic chemistry*]
PMS........... Parallel Mass Spectrometer
PMS........... Partial Metric System   (MCD)
PMS........... Particle Measuring Systems [*Aerosol measurement device*]
PMS........... Partido Mexicano Socialista [*Political party*]   (EY)
PMS........... Pedestal-Mounted Stinger [*Army*]
PMS........... People's Medical Society   (EA)
PMS........... People's Message System [*For Apple II computers*] [*Electronic
              bulletin board*]
PMS........... Perceptual and Motor Skills [*A publication*]
PMS........... Performance Management System
PMS........... Performance Measurement System [*Nuclear Regulatory
              Commission*]   (MCD)
PMS........... Performance Monitoring System [*Army*] [*Fort Belvoir,
              VA*]   (NASA)
PMS........... Permanent Magnet Speaker
PMS........... Personal Mailing System   (HGAA)
PMS........... Personnel Management Series [*Civil Service Commission*]
PMS........... Personnel Management Specialist   (GFGA)
PMS........... Personnel Management System [*Air Force*]   (AFM)
PMS........... Phenazine Methosulfate [*Biochemistry*]
PMS........... Phoenix Missile System
PMS........... Physiological Monitoring System   (SAA)
PMS........... Phytophthora Megasperma Var. Sojae [*A fungus*]
PMS........... Piccola Missione per il Sordomuti [*Little Mission for the Deaf-
              Mute - LMDM*] [*Rome, Italy*]   (EAIO)
PMS........... Picturephone Meeting Service [*AT & T*]
PMS........... Pitch Microwave System
PMS........... Planned Maintenance System [*SNMMS*]
PMS........... Planned Missile System
PMS........... Plant Monitoring System [*Nuclear energy*]   (NRCH)
PMS........... Plasmid Maintenance Sequence [*Genetics*]
PMS........... Plastic to Metal Seal
PMS........... PM Industries, Inc. [*Vancouver Stock Exchange symbol*]
PMS........... Polar Meteorological Satellite   (SSD)
PMS........... Polaris Missile System
PMS........... Policy Management Systems [*NYSE symbol*]   (SPSG)
PMS........... Pollution Monitoring Satellite
PMS........... Poor Miserable Soul [*Medical slang*]
PMS........... Popular Music and Society [*A publication*]
PMS........... Portable Monitoring Set   (MCD)
PMS........... Post-Marketing Surveillance
PMS........... Post-Merger Syndrome [*Business term*]
PMS........... Post-Mortem Survival [*Parapsychology*]
PMS........... Postmeiotic Segregation [*Genetics*]
PMS........... Postmenopausal Syndrome [*Medicine*]
PMS........... Postmitochondrial Supernatant [*Medicine*]   (MAE)
PMS........... Power Management System
PMS........... Prang-Mark Society   (EA)
PMS........... Pre-Midshipmen School
PMS........... Predicted Manning System [*Military*]
PMS........... Pregnant Mare's Serum [*Endocrinology*]
PMS........... Premature Start [*Yacht racing*]   (IYR)
PMS........... Premenstrual [*Stress*] Syndrome [*Medicine*]
PMS........... President of the Meteorological Society [*British*]
PMS........... President of the Miniature Society [*British*]   (DI)
PmS........... Preston Microfilming Services Ltd., Toronto, ON, Canada
              [*Library symbol*] [*Library of Congress*]   (LCLS)
PMS........... Preventive Maintenance System
PMS........... Probability of Mission Success [*Aerospace*]   (AAG)
PMS........... Probable Maximum Surge [*Nuclear energy*]   (NRCH)
PMS........... Processors, Memories, and Switches [*Programming
              language*]   (CSR)
PMS........... Product Management System
PMS........... Production Management System [*Safe Computing Ltd.*]
              [*Software package*]   (NCC)
PMS........... Professor of Military Science
PMS........... Program Management Staff [*Environmental Protection
              Agency*]   (GFGA)

PMS.......... Program Management Support [*Army*]
PMS.......... Program Management System [*Data processing*]
PMS.......... Program Master Schedule   (MCD)
PMS.......... Project Management System [*IBM Corp.*] [*Data processing*]
PMS.......... Project Manager, Ships
PMS.......... Projected Map System   (OA)
PMS.......... Proposal Management System
PMS.......... Public Management Sources [*A publication*]
PMS.......... Public Message Service [*Western Union Corp.*]
PMSA........ Mosaic [*A publication*]
PMSA........ Office of the Project Manager Selected Ammunition [*DoD*]
PMSA........ PM [*Product Management*] Materiel Systems Assessment   (RDA)
PMSA........ Posterior Middle Suprasylvian Area [*Anatomy*]
PMSA........ Primary Metropolitan Statistical Area [*Census Bureau*]
P/MSA...... Project/Major Subcontractor Affected   (MCD)
PMSA........ Project Manager for Selected Ammunition
PMSA........ Project Manager's System Assessment
PMSC........ Mosaic. A Journal for the Interdisciplinary Study of Literature [*A publication*]
PMSC........ Pluripotent Myeloid Stem Cell [*Cytology*]   (MAE)
PMSCD..... Proceedings. Microscopical Society of Canada [*A publication*]
PMSD........ Parti Mauricien Social-Democrate [*Mauritian Social Democratic Party*] [*Political party*]   (PPW)
PMSD........ Program Management and Support Division [*Environmental Protection Agency*]   (GFGA)
PMS/DOD ... Performance Measurement System/Department of Defense
PMSE........ Manchester School of Economic and Social Studies [*A publication*]
PMSE........ Percentage Mean Squared Error [*Statistics*]
PMSE........ Permanent Memory with Semi-Elastic Range   (MCD)
PMSE........ Program Management Simulation Exercise [*Aerospace*]
PMSF........ Phenylmethylsulfonyl Fluoride [*Analytical chemistry*]
PMSFN..... Planetary Manned Space Flight Network [*Aerospace*]   (MCD)
PMSG........ Peace Movement Study Group [*Colgate University*]   (EA)
PMSG........ Pregnant Mare's Serum Gonadotrophin [*Endocrinology*]
PMSGT..... Paymaster Sergeant [*Marine Corps*]
PMSI........ Prime Medical Services, Inc. [*NASDAQ symbol*]   (NQ)
PMSN........ Permission   (FAAC)
PMSO........ Project Management Staff Officer [*Military*]   (AFIT)
PMSO........ Project Management Support Office [*Army*]   (RDA)
PMSP........ Parallel Modular Signal Processor
PMSP........ Photon-Counting Microspectrophotometer
PMSP........ Preliminary Maintainability and Spare Parts
PMSPS..... Project Management Staffing Practices Study [*Navy*]   (NG)
PMS Public Manage Source ... PMS. Public Management Sources [*A publication*]
PMSQ........ Mississippi Quarterly [*A publication*]
PMSR........ Patternmaker, Ship Repair [*Navy rating*]
PMSR........ Physical, Mental, Social, Religious [*"Fourfold Life" symbol of American Youth Foundation*]
PMSRC..... Pittsburgh Mining and Safety Research Center [*Bureau of Mines*]
PMSRP..... Physical and Mathematical Sciences Research Paper   (IEEE)
PMSS........ Personnel Mobility Support System [*Military*]
PMSS........ Precision Measuring Subsystem   (KSC)
PMSS........ Program Management Support Staff [*Environmental Protection Agency*]   (GFGA)
PMSS........ Program Manager's Support System [*Defense Systems Management College*] [*Fort Belvoir, VA*]   (RDA)
PMSS........ Progress in Mathematical Social Sciences [*Elsevier Book Series*] [*A publication*]
PMS/SMS ... Planned Maintenance System for Surface Missile Ships
PMST........ Professor of Military Science and Tactics   (MUGU)
PMS & T .. Professor of Military Science and Tactics
PMSTA..... Promyshlennoe Stroitel'stvo [*A publication*]
PMSV........ Pilot-to-Metro Service
PMSX........ Processor Memory Switch Matrix
PMT.......... Medical Photography Technician [*Navy*]
PMT.......... Page Map Table [*NASA*]   (HGAA)
PMT.......... Para-Methoxytoluene [*Organic chemistry*]
PMT.......... Partido Mexicano de los Trabajadores [*Mexican Workers' Party*] [*Political party*]   (PPW)
PMT.......... Payment   (AFM)
PMT.......... Pennsylvania Motor Truck Association, Inc., Harrisburg PA [*STAC*]
PMT.......... Perceptual Maze Test [*Psychology*]
PMT.......... Performance Measuring Tool   (MCD)
PMT.......... Periodic Maintenance Team
PMT.......... Permanent Magnet Twistor [*Memory*] [*Bell Laboratories*]
PMT.......... Permit   (FAAC)
PMT.......... Personnel Management Team
PMT.......... Phase-Modulated Transmission
PMT.......... Philip Michael Thomas [*Co-star in TV series "Miami Vice"*]
PMT.......... Photomechanical Transfer [*Negative paper*] [*Eastman Kodak*]
PMT.......... Photomultiplier Tube [*Electronics*]
PMT.......... Physical Message Type [*Communications*]
PMT.......... Pilgrim Airlines [*New London, CT*] [*FAA designator*]   (FAAC)
PMT.......... Pine Mountain [*Oregon*] [*Seismograph station code, US Geological Survey*]   (SEIS)
PMT.......... Planning/Management Team [*NASA*]   (MCD)

PMT .... PMC Technologies Ltd. [*Vancouver Stock Exchange symbol*]
PMT .... Polaromicrotribrometry [*Analytical chemistry*]
PMT .... Portable Magnetic Tape
PMT .... Porteus Maze Test [*Medicine*]   (MAE)
PMT .... Post-Maastricht Tension [*Period after European Community's meeting at Maastricht, Netherlands*]   (ECON)
PMT .... Potteries Motor Traction Co. [*British*]
PMT .... Power Microwave Tube
PMT .... Premenstrual Tension [*Medicine*]
PMT .... Preparatory Marksmanship Training [*Military*]   (INF)
PMT .... Prepare Master Tape
PMT .... Preventive Maintenance Time   (MCD)
PMT .... Production Monitoring Test   (NG)
PMT .... Products, Marketing, and Technology [*Bank Administration Institute*] [*A publication*]
PMT .... Program Master Tape
PMT .... Programmed Math Tutorial [*National Science Foundation*]
PMT .... Pulse-Modulator Tube
PMT .... Pure Milk Tablet   (IIA)
PMT .... Putnam Master Income Trust [*NYSE symbol*]   (SPSG)
PMTA...... Page Map Table Address Register [*NASA*]   (HGAA)
PMTAS .... Pre-Menstrual Tension Advisory Service [*British*]
PMTC....... Pacific Missile Test Center [*Navy*] [*Point Mugu, CA*]
PMTC....... Parametric Technology Corp. [*NASDAQ symbol*]   (NQ)
PMTC....... Pittsburgh Mining Technology Center [*Department of Energy*]   (GRD)
PMTD ...... Post Mortem Tape Dump [*Data processing*]
PMT-EM... Project Manager, Training Devices Engineering Management [*Orlando, FL*] [*Army*]
PMTHP..... Project Mercury Technical History Program [*NASA*]
PM TMDS ... Program Manager - Test, Measurement, and Diagnostic Systems [*Army*]
PMTO .... Project Manager Test Offices [*Military*]
PMTP........ Production Missile Test Program
P/MTR..... Potentiometer [*Automotive engineering*]
PM TRADE ... Office of the Project Manager for Training Devices [*Military*]   (RDA)
PMTS .... Predetermined Motion Time Systems [*Management*]
PMTS .... Premenstrual Tension Syndrome [*Medicine*]
PMTT....... Phase-Modulated Telemetry Transmission
PMTT....... Pulmonary Mean Transit Time [*Medicine*]   (MAE)
PMTV....... Potato Mop-Top Virus [*Plant pathology*]
PMU.......... Paimiut, AK [*Location identifier*] [*FAA*]   (FAAL)
PMU.......... Performance Monitor Unit [*Communications*]
PMU.......... Permanently Medically Unfit
PMU.......... Physical Mock-Up
PMU.......... Pierce Mountain [*Vancouver Stock Exchange symbol*]
PMU.......... Plant Makeup [*Nuclear energy*]   (NRCH)
PMU.......... Pontifical Missionary Union [*Later, PMUPR*] [*See also OPM*]   (EA)
PMU.......... Portable Memory Unit [*Data processing*]
PMU.......... Pressure Measuring Unit   (KSC)
PMU.......... Preventive Medicine Unit [*Navy*]   (NVT)
PMU.......... Progress in Medical Ultrasound [*Elsevier Book Series*] [*A publication*]
PMU.......... Pulse Modulation Unit   (NASA)
PMUB .... Presbyterian, Methodist, and United Board [*British military*]   (DMA)
PMUCAH ... Memorias e Noticias Publicacoes. Museu e Laboratorio Mineralogico e Geologico. Universidade de Coimbra e Centro de Estudos Geologicos [*A publication*]
PMUN....... Notes [*A publication*]
PMUPR.... Pontifical Missionary Union of Priests and Religious   (EA)
PMUQ....... Musical Quarterly [*A publication*]
PMUR....... Music Review [*A publication*]
PMUS....... Music and Letters [*A publication*]
PMUS....... Permanently Mounted User Set [*Data processing*]   (ADA)
PMUS....... Polymuse, Inc. [*New York, NY*] [*NASDAQ symbol*]   (NQ)
PM-UTTAS ... Project Manager, Utility Tactical Transport Aircraft System [*Military*]
PMUW...... Muslim World [*A publication*]
PMUX ...... Programmable Multiplex [*Data processing*]   (TEL)
PMUX ...... Propulsion Multiplexer
PMv .... Monroeville Public Library, Monroeville, PA [*Library symbol*] [*Library of Congress*]   (LCLS)
PMV .... Panicum Mosaic Virus
PMV .... Papaya Mosaic Virus
PMV .... Paramyxovirus
PMV .... Parcel Mail Vans [*British railroad term*]
PMV .... Peanut Mottle Virus
PMV .... Plasma Membrane Vesicle [*Cytology*]
PMV .... Plate-Motion Vector [*Geology*]
PMV .... Plattsmouth, NE [*Location identifier*] [*FAA*]   (FAAL)
PMV .... Politically Motivated Violence   (ADA)
PMV .... Porlamar [*Venezuela*] [*Airport symbol*]   (OAG)
PMV .... Prime Mission Vehicle   (MCD)
PMV .... Private Motor Vehicle   (DNAB)
PMV .... Pro Mundi Vita [*Brussels, Belgium*]   (EAIO)
PMV .... Prolapsing Mitral Valve [*Cardiology*]

PMvAC......	Community College of Allegheny County, Boyce Campus, Monroeville, PA [*Library symbol*] [*Library of Congress*]　(LCLS)
PMVI........	Promovision Video Displays Corp. [*Jamaica, NY*] [*NASDAQ symbol*]　(NQ)
PMVIA......	Progress in Medical Virology [*A publication*]
PMvK	Koppers Co., Inc., Research Department, Monroeville, PA [*Library symbol*] [*Library of Congress*]　(LCLS)
PMVL........	Posterior Mitral Valve Leaflet [*Anatomy*]　(AAMN)
PMVR	Prime Mover [*Technical drawings*]
PMvS.........	United States Steel Corp., Research Center Library, Monroeville, PA [*Library symbol*] [*Library of Congress*]　(LCLS)
PMW........	Parts Manufacturing Workmanship
PMW........	Pole Mountain [*Wyoming*] [*Seismograph station code, US Geological Survey*] [*Closed*]　(SEIS)
PMW........	Private Microwave [*System*]
PMW........	Progressive Mine Workers of America
PMW........	Project Magic Wand [*Military*]　(MCD)
PMW........	Prompt Mobilization Designation Withdrawn
PMWI........	PACE Membership Warehouse, Inc. [*Aurora, CO*] [*NASDAQ symbol*]　(NQ)
PMWP.......	Probable Maximum Winter Precipitation [*Nuclear energy*]　(NRCH)
PMX	Packet Multiplexer
PMX	Palmer, MA [*Location identifier*] [*FAA*]　(FAAL)
PMX	Pamorex Minerals, Inc. [*Toronto Stock Exchange symbol*]
PMX	Private Manual Exchange
PMX	Protected Message Exchange
PMyE	Evangelical Congregational School of Theology, Myerstown, PA [*Library symbol*] [*Library of Congress*]　(LCLS)
PMYOB	Please Mind Your Own Business
PMZ	Plymouth, NC [*Location identifier*] [*FAA*]　(FAAL)
pn-----	North Pacific [*MARC geographic area code*] [*Library of Congress*]　(LCCP)
PN..............	North Pole [*Also, NP*]
PN..............	Pacific Communications Net [*Air Force*]
PN..............	Pakistan Navy
PN..............	Palace of Nestor at Pylos in Western Messenia [*A publication*]
PN..............	Palus Nebularum [*Lunar area*]
PN..............	Pan Am Corp. [*Formerly, Pan American Airways, Inc.*] [*See also PA, PAA, PAN-AM*] [*NYSE symbol*]　(SPSG)
pn	Panama [*MARC country of publication code*] [*Library of Congress*]　(LCCP)
PN..............	Papillary or Nodular Hyperplasia [*Medicine*]
PN..............	Parenteral Nutrition [*Medicine*]
PN..............	Part Number
PN..............	Partenavia Construzioni Aeronautiche SpA [*Italy*] [*ICAO aircraft manufacturer identifier*]　(ICAO)
PN..............	Parti Nationaliste [*Canada*]
PN..............	Partido Nacional [*National Party*] [*Dominican Republic*] [*Political party*]
PN..............	Partido Nacional [*National Party*] [*Uruguay*] [*Political party*]　(PPW)
PN..............	Partido Nacional [*National Party*] [*Honduras*] [*Political party*]　(PPW)
PN..............	Partit Nazzjonalista [*Nationalist Party*] [*Malta*] [*Political party*]　(EAIO)
Pn...............	Partition　(WGA)
PN..............	Perceived Noise
PN..............	Percussion Note [*Physiology*]
PN..............	Percussive Notes [*A publication*]
PN..............	Performance Number
PN..............	Periarteritis [*or Polyarteritis*] Nodosa [*Also, PAN*] [*Medicine*]
PN..............	Perigean Range
PN..............	Peripheral Nerve [*Anatomy*]
PN..............	Peripheral Neuropathy [*Medicine*]
PN..............	Personal Names from Cuneiform Inscriptions of the Cassite Period [*A publication*]　(BJA)
PN..............	Personnel Navigant
PN..............	Personnelman [*Navy rating*]
PN..............	Phenolic Nylon
PN..............	Philippine Aero Transport, Inc. [*Philippines*] [*ICAO designator*]　(FAAC)
PN..............	Philippine Navy
P/N.............	Phonogram [*British military*]　(DMA)
pN	Piconewton [*Unit of force*]
PN..............	Piedmont & Northern Railway Co. [*AAR code*]
P/N.............	Pin Number　(AAG)
PN..............	Pitcairn Islands [*ANSI two-letter standard code*]　(CNC)
PN..............	Place-Name
PN..............	Planners Network　(EA)
PN..............	Plant Normal [*Nuclear energy*]　(NRCH)
PN..............	Plasticity Number　(AAG)
PN..............	Please Note
PN..............	Pneumatic
PN..............	Pneumonia [*Medicine*]
PN..............	Poe Newsletter [*A publication*]
PN..............	Poesia Nuova [*A publication*]
PN..............	Poetry Northwest [*A publication*]
PN..............	Pontine Nuclei [*Neuroanatomy*]

PN..............	Portsmouth News [*United Kingdom*] [*A publication*]
PN..............	Position　(WGA)
PN..............	Position Number　(ADA)
PN..............	Position Pennant [*Navy*] [*British*]
PN..............	Positional Nystagmus [*Physiology*]　(MAE)
P/N.............	Positive/Negative
PN..............	Postal Note　(ADA)
PN..............	Postnatal [*Medicine*]
Pn...............	Poznan [*A publication*]
PN..............	Practical Nurse
PN..............	Preliminary Notification　(NRCH)
PN..............	Press Night
PN..............	Prior Notice Required　(FAAC)
PN..............	Pro Nervia [*A publication*]
PN..............	Processing Negativity [*Data processing*]
Pn...............	Production [*Economics*]
PN..............	Production Notice　(KSC)
PN..............	Program Notice　(KSC)
PN..............	Program Number [*Horse racing*]
PN..............	Programmable Network
PN..............	Project Note
PN..............	Project Number [*Data processing*] [*Online database field identifier*]
PN..............	Promissory Note [*Business term*]
PN..............	Pronuclei [*Embryology*]
PN..............	Pseudonoise
PN..............	Pseudorandom Number
PN..............	Psychiatric Nurse
P & N	Psychiatry and Neurology
PN..............	Psychic News [*A publication*]
PN..............	Psychoneurologist
PN..............	Psychoneurotic [*Cases, patients, etc.*]
PN..............	Public Network [*Telecommunications*]
PN..............	Publisher's Name [*Online database field identifier*]
PN..............	Publishing News [*A publication*]
PN..............	Pulse Network　(KSC)
PN..............	Punch On
PN..............	Pupil Nurse [*British*]　(DI)
PN..............	Putative Neurotransmitter [*Biochemistry*]
PN..............	Pyelonephritis [*Medicine*]　(MAE)
PN..............	Pyridoxine [*or Pyridoxol*] [*Also, Pxn*] [*Biochemistry*]
PN..............	Pyrrolnitrin [*Antifungal antibiotic*]
PN..............	Regular Pending Transaction [*IRS*]
PN1............	Personnelman, First Class [*Navy rating*]
PN2............	Personnelman, Second Class [*Navy rating*]
PN3............	Personnelman, Third Class [*Navy rating*]
PNA	Pa-O National Army [*Myanmar*] [*Political party*]　(EY)
PNA	Pakistan National Alliance　(PD)
PNA	Pamplona [*Spain*] [*Airport symbol*]　(OAG)
PNA	Paper Napkin Association
PNA	Para-Nitroaniline [*Organic chemistry*]
PNA	Parallel and Novel Architectures [*British*]
PNA	Parenting in a Nuclear Age　(EA)
PNA	Parisiensis Nomina Anatomica [*Paris Anatomical Nomenclature*] [*Medicine*]
PNA	Partacoona [*Australia*] [*Seismograph station code, US Geological Survey*]　(SEIS)
PNA	Parti Nationale Africain [*African National Party*] [*Chad*] [*Political party*]
PNA	Passed, but Not Advanced
PNA	Peanut Agglutinin [*Immunology*]
PNA	Pentosenucleic Acid [*Biochemistry*]
PNA	People's News Agency [*An association*]　(EA)
PNA	Pinedale, WY [*Location identifier*] [*FAA*]　(FAAL)
PNA	Pioneer Corp. [*Formerly, Pioneer Natural Gas Co.*] [*NYSE symbol*]　(SPSG)
PNA	Polish National Alliance of the United States of North America　(EA)
PNA	Polish Nobility Association　(EA)
PNA	Polyamide Nucleic Acid [*Biochemistry*]
PNA	Polynuclear Aromatic [*Organic chemistry*]
PNA	Price Not Available　(DNAB)
PNA	Processing Terminal Network Architecture [*Data processing*]　(BUR)
PNA	Project Network Analysis
PNAB	Percutaneous Needle Aspiration Biopsy [*Medicine*]
PNAC	Psychiatric Nurses' Association of Canada
PNAF........	Plan Name and Address File [*IRS*]
PNAF........	Potential Network Access Facility
PNAF........	Primary Nuclear Airlift Force
PNAH........	Polynuclear Aromatic Hydrocarbon [*Environmental chemistry*]
PNAP	Pro-Life Nonviolent Action Project　(EA)
PNAR	North American Review [*A publication*]
PNAS........	Palletized Night Attack System
PNAS........	Proceedings. National Academy of Sciences [*A publication*]
PNASA......	Para-Nitroaniline-o-sulfonic Acid [*Organic chemistry*]
P NAS (Ind) A ...	Proceedings. National Academy of Sciences (India). Section A. Physical Sciences [*A publication*]
P NAS (Ind) B ...	Proceedings. National Academy of Sciences (India). Section B. Biological Sciences [*A publication*]

P NAS (US) ... Proceedings. National Academy of Sciences (United States of America) [*A publication*]
PNAV .... Proportional Navigation
PNAvQ ...... Positive-Negative Ambivalent Quotient [*Psychology*]
PNazMHi ... Moravian Historical Society, Nazareth, PA [*Library symbol*] [*Library of Congress*] (LCLS)
PNB .... North Platte, NE [*Location identifier*] [*FAA*] (FAAL)
PNB .... Pacific Northwest Ballet
PNB .... Particle/Neutral Beam (MCD)
PNB .... Partido ng Bayan [*Party of the Nation*] [*Political party*] [*Philippines*]
PNB .... Permodalan Nasional Bank [*Malaysia*]
PNB .... Pomio [*New Britain*] [*Seismograph station code, US Geological Survey*] [*Closed*] (SEIS)
PNB .... Pottery Notebooks for Knossos [*A publication*]
PNBA .... Pennbancorp [*NASDAQ symbol*] (NQ)
PNBAS ...... ((Para-Nitrophenyl)azo)salicylic Acid [*A dye*] [*Organic chemistry*]
PNBC .... Pacific Northwest Bibliographic Center [*Library network*]
P²NBC² ...... Physiological and Psychological Effects of NBC [*Nuclear, Biological, and Chemical Warfare*] and Extended Operations [*Army study project*] (INF)
PNBF .... Peak Nucleate Boiling Flux
PNBMS ..... Pacific Northwest Bird and Mammal Society [*Later, SNUB*] (EA)
PNBS .... Pyridinium(nitro)benzenesulfonate [*Organic chemistry*]
PNBT .... Para-Nitroblue Tetrazolium
PNBT .... [*The*] Planters Corp. [*NASDAQ symbol*] (NQ)
PNC .... Chief Personnelman [*Navy rating*]
PNc .... New Castle Free Public Library, New Castle, PA [*Library symbol*] [*Library of Congress*] (LCLS)
PNC .... Northampton County Area Community College, Bethlehem, PA [*OCLC symbol*] (OCLC)
PNC .... Pakistan National Congress [*Political party*]
PNC .... Palestine National Council (PD)
PNC .... Parti National Caledonien [*Caledonian National Party*] [*Political party*] (PPW)
PNC .... Partido Nacional Ceuti [*Ceuta National Party*] [*Political party*] (PPW)
PNC .... Partido Nacional Conservador [*Nicaragua*] [*Political party*] (EY)
PNC .... Partido Nacional Cristiano [*National Christian Party*] [*Colombia*] [*Political party*] (EY)
PNC .... Partido Nacionalista Ceuti [*Political party*] (EY)
PNC .... Partidual Nationale Crestine [*National Christian Party*] [*Romania*] [*Political party*] (PPE)
PNC .... Passenger Name Check-In (MCD)
PNC .... Pencrude Resources, Inc. [*Vancouver Stock Exchange symbol*]
PNC .... Penicillin
PNC .... People's National Congress [*Guyana*] (PD)
PNC .... Peripheral Nucleated Cell (AAMN)
PNC .... Personal Names from Cuneiform Inscriptions of Cappadocia [*A publication*]
PNC .... Personal Number Calling [*Telecommunications*]
PNC .... Philatelic-Numismatic Combination [*or Commemorative*]
PNC .... Phosphonitrilic Chloride [*Inorganic chemistry*]
PNC .... Physitest Normalise Canadien [*Canadian Standardized Test of Fitness - CSTF*]
PNC .... Pine Canyon [*California*] [*Seismograph station code, US Geological Survey*] (SEIS)
PNC .... Plate Number Coil [*Philately*]
PNC .... PNC Financial Corp. [*NYSE symbol*] (SPSG)
PNC .... PNC Financial Corp. [*Associated Press abbreviation*] (APAG)
PNC .... Police National Computer [*British*]
PNC .... Ponca City [*Oklahoma*] [*Airport symbol*] (OAG)
PNC .... Ponca City, OK [*Location identifier*] [*FAA*] (FAAL)
PNC .... Postnatal Clinic
PNC .... Power Reactor and Nuclear Fuel Development Corp. [*Japan*] (PDAA)
PNC .... Premature Nodal Contraction [*Cardiology*]
PNC .... Programmed Numerical Control
PNC .... Prohibition National Committee (EA)
PNC .... Pseudonurse Cells [*Cytology*]
PNCB .... Pakistan Narcotics Control Board
PNCB .... Para-Nitrochlorobenzene [*Organic chemistry*]
PNCC .... Partial Network Control Center
PNCCA ...... Proceedings. National Cancer Conference [*United States*] [*A publication*]
PNCF .... PNC Financial Corp. [*NASDAQ symbol*] (NQ)
PNCFN ...... Permanent Nordic Committee on Food and Nutrition [*Copenhagen, Denmark*] (EAIO)
PNCH .... Partido Nacional Conservador de Honduras [*National Conservative Party of Honduras*] [*Political party*]
PNCH .... Pinch or Pound, Inc. [*Boca Raton, FL*] [*NASDAQ symbol*] (NQ)
PNCH .... Proceedings. National Conference on Health Education Goals [*A publication*]
PNCH .... Punch
PNCL .... Nineteenth-Century Literature [*A publication*]
PNCL .... Pinnacle Petroleum, Inc. [*NASDAQ symbol*] (NQ)
PNCM .... Master Chief Personnelman [*Navy rating*]

PNCOC ..... Primary Noncommissioned Officer Course [*Army*] (INF)
PNCR .... Pancretec, Inc. [*NASDAQ symbol*] (NQ)
PNCS .... Private Network Communication Systems (MCD)
PNCS .... Senior Chief Personnelman [*Navy rating*]
PNCTD ...... Proceedings. National Conference on Power Transmission [*A publication*]
PNCU .... Police National Computer Unit [*British*]
PND .... Paroxysmal Nocturnal Dyspnea [*Medicine*]
PND .... Parti National Democrate [*Morocco*] [*Political party*] (EY)
PND .... Parti des Nationalistes du Dahomey [*Dahomean Nationalists Party*] [*Political party*]
PND .... Partido Nacional Democratico [*National Democratic Party*] [*Costa Rica*] [*Political party*] (PPW)
PND .... Partido Nacional Democratico [*National Democratic Party*] [*Dominican Republic*] [*Political party*]
PND .... Partidul National-Democratic [*National Democratic Party*] [*Romania*] [*Political party*] (PPE)
PND .... Passive Navigation Device
PND .... Pending
PND .... Pictorial Navigation Display (OA)
PND .... Postnasal Drainage [*or Drip*] [*Medicine*]
pnd .... Pound (MAE)
PND .... Premodulation Processor - Near Earth Data (KSC)
PND .... Present Next Digit
PND .... Principal Neutralizing Determinant [*Immunology*]
PND .... Principal Neutralizing Domain [*Medicine*]
PND .... Program Network Diagram [*Telecommunications*] (TEL)
PND .... Pseudonyms and Nicknames Dictionary [*A publication*]
PND .... Punta Gorda [*Belize*] [*Airport symbol*] (OAG)
PNDB .... Pelerinage a Notre Dame de Beauraing [*An association*] (EAIO)
PNdB .... Perceived Noise Decibels
PNDC .... Parallel Network Digital Computer (IEEE)
PNDC .... Partido Nacional de Democracia Centrista [*Chile*] [*Political party*] (EY)
PNDC .... Progressive Neuronal Degeneration of Childhood [*Medicine*]
PNDC .... Provisional National Defence Council [*Ghana*] (PD)
PNDD .... Parti National pour la Democratie et le Developpement [*Benin*] [*Political party*] (EY)
PNDG .... Pending (AFM)
PNDI .... Pennsylvania Natural Diversity Inventory [*Bureau of Forestry*] [*Harrisburg*] [*Information service or system*] (IID)
PNDLR ...... Pendular
PNDM .... Project Nondesign Memo
PNDO .... Partial Neglect of Differential Overlap [*Physics*]
PNDT .... Parti Nationale pour la Developpement du Tchad [*National Party for the Development of Chad*]
PNE .... Pacific National Exhibition Home Show [*Southex Exhibitions*] (TSPED)
PNE .... Paine College, Warren A. Candler Library, Augusta, GA [*OCLC symbol*] (OCLC)
PNE .... Panhandle Eastern Corp. [*Toronto Stock Exchange symbol*]
PNE .... Peaceful Nuclear Explosion
PNE .... Philadelphia [*Pennsylvania*] North Philadelphia [*Airport symbol*] (OAG)
PNE .... Philadelphia, PA [*Location identifier*] [*FAA*] (FAAL)
PNE .... Practical Nurse's Education
PNEC .... Primary Navy Enlisted Classification [*Code*]
PNEC .... Proceedings. National Electronics Conference [*A publication*]
PNECA ...... Proceedings. National Electronics Conference [*United States*] [*A publication*]
PNed .... Pharmacopeia Nederlandsche [*Netherlands Pharmacopoeia*]
PNEM-APROME ... Partido Nacionalista Espanol de Melilla - Asociacion pro Melilla [*Political party*] [*Spanish North Africa*] (MENA)
PNEND ..... Progress in Nuclear Energy [*A publication*]
PNEQ .... New England Quarterly [*A publication*]
PNER .... New England Review and Bread Loaf Quarterly [*A publication*]
PNERL ...... Pacific Northwest Environmental Research Laboratory [*Environmental Protection Agency*] (MSC)
PNES .... Pines
PNET .... Peaceful Nuclear Explosions Treaty [*Officially, Treaty on Underground Nuclear Explosions for Peaceful Purposes*]
PNET .... Primitive Neuroectodermal Tumor [*Oncology*]
PNET .... ProNet, Inc. [*NASDAQ symbol*] (NQ)
PNEU .... Parents' National Educational Union [*British*]
PNEU .... Pneumatic (AAG)
pneu .... Pneumonia [*Medicine*] (MAE)
PNEUDZ .. Pneumoftiziologie [*Bucharest*] [*A publication*]
PNEUG ...... Pneumatic Pressure Generator (MCD)
PNEUM .... Pneumatic
Pneum Dig & Druckluft Prax ... Pneumatic Digest and Druckluft Praxis [*A publication*]
PNEUMO ... Pneumothorax [*Medicine*]
Pneumokoniosenavorsingseenheid Jaarversl ... Pneumokoniosenavorsingseenheid Jaarverslag [*A publication*]
Pneumolog Hung ... Pneumologia Hungarica [*Hungary*] [*A publication*]
Pneumol/Pneumol ... Pneumonologie/Pneumonology [*A publication*]
Pneumonol-P ... Pneumonologie/Pneumonology [*A publication*]
Pneumonol Pol ... Pneumonologia Polska [*A publication*]

PNEUROP ... European Committee of Manufacturers of Compressors, Vacuum Pumps, and Pneumatic Tools (EA)
PNEX .... Phonex, Inc. [*NASDAQ symbol*] (NQ)
PNF .... Pacific National Financial Corp. [*Toronto Stock Exchange symbol*] [*Vancouver Stock Exchange symbol*]
PNF .... Palestine National Front [*Political party*] (PD)
PNF .... Partito Nazionale Fascista [*National Fascist Party*] [*Italy*] [*Political party*] (PPE)
PNF .... Peierls-Nabarro Force [*Physics*]
PNF .... Penn Traffic Co. [*AMEX symbol*] (SPSG)
PNF .... Phosphonitrilic Fluoroelastomer [*Synthetic rubber*]
PNF .... Positive Neutral Finder [*Automotive engineering*]
PNF .... Postnuclear Fraction [*Biochemical tissue analysis*]
PNF .... Prenex Normal Form [*Logic*]
PNF .... Proprioceptive Neuromuscular Facilitation [*Neurology*]
PNFD .... Present Not for Duty [*Military*]
PNFI......... Petawawa National Forestry Institute [*Canadian Forestry Service*] [*Research center*] (RCD)
PNFI......... Pinnacle Financial Services, Inc. [*NASDAQ symbol*] (NQ)
PNG.......... Pacific Northern Gas Ltd. [*Toronto Stock Exchange symbol*] [*Vancouver Stock Exchange symbol*]
PNG.......... Papua New Guinea [*ANSI three-letter standard code*] (CNC)
PNG.......... Papua New Guinea Banking Corp.
PNG.......... Paranagua [*Brazil*] [*Airport symbol*] (OAG)
PNG.......... Partido Nacional Guevarista [*Ecuador*] [*Political party*] (PPW)
PNG.......... Penghu [*Hokoto*] [*Republic of China*] [*Seismograph station code, US Geological Survey*] (SEIS)
PNG.......... Persona Non Grata [*Unacceptable Person*] [*Latin*]
PNG.......... Philippine Natural Gum
PNG.......... Plant Nitrogen in Grain [*Harvest nitrogen index*]
PNG.......... Professional Numismatists Guild (EA)
PNG.......... Pseudonoise Generator
PNGCS...... Primary Navigation, Guidance and Control System (KSC)
PNGFA..... Pacific Northwest Grain and Feed Association (EA)
PNGL .... Papers in New Guinea Linguistics [*A publication*]
P & NGLR ... Papua and New Guinea Law Reports [*A publication*] (APTA)
PNGR .... Penguin Group, Inc. [*NASDAQ symbol*] (NQ)
PNGS........ Primary Navigation System
PNGUA8... Forest Research Institute [*Bogor*]. Communication [*A publication*]
PNH.......... North Hills School District Instructional Materials Center, Pittsburgh, PA [*OCLC symbol*] (OCLC)
PNH.......... Pan Head [*Design engineering*]
PNH.......... Paroxysmal Nocturnal Hemoglobinuria [*Medicine*]
PNH.......... Parti National d'Haiti [*National Party of Haiti*] [*Political party*]
PNH.......... Partido Nacional Hondureno [*Honduran National Party*] [*Political party*]
PNH.......... Phnom Penh [*Cambodia*] [*Airport symbol*] (OAG)
PNH.......... Pitcher Mountain [*New Hampshire*] [*Seismograph station code, US Geological Survey*] (SEIS)
PNH.......... Public Service Co. of New Hampshire [*NYSE symbol*] (SPSG)
PNHA....... Physicians National Housestaff Association [*Defunct*]
PNHDL.... Panhandle [*FAA*] (FAAC)
PNHS .... Pacific Northwest Heather Society [*Later, NAHS*] (EA)
PNHYD..... Perspectives in Nephrology and Hypertension [*A publication*]
PNI .... Part Number Index (MCD)
PNI .... Partai Nasionalis Indonesia [*Nationalist Party of Indonesia*] [*Political party*]
PNI .... Participate but Do Not Initiate [*Investment term*]
PNI .... Partido Nacional Independiente [*National Independent Party*] [*Costa Rica*] [*Political party*] (PPW)
PNI .... Pascoe Nally International [*British*]
PNI .... Peer Nomination Inventory [*Psychology*]
PNI .... Pensions and Investment Age [*A publication*]
PNI .... Peripheral Nerve Injury [*Medicine*]
PNI .... Pharmaceutical News Index [*UMI/Data Courier*] [*Information service or system*] [*A publication*]
PNI .... Pinerola [*Italy*] [*Seismograph station code, US Geological Survey*] (SEIS)
PNI .... Ponape [*Caroline Islands*] [*Airport symbol*] (OAG)
PNI .... Positive Noninterfering [*Alarm system*]
PNI .... Postnatal Infection [*Medicine*]
PNI .... Principal Neo-Tech, Inc. [*Toronto Stock Exchange symbol*]
PNI .... Protease Nexin I [*Biochemistry*]
PNI .... Psychoneuroimmunology
PNI .... Publications. Netherlands Institute of Archaeology and Arabic Studies [*Cairo*] [*A publication*]
PNIC......... Pleasure Navigation International Joint Committee [*See also CINP*] [*The Hague, Netherlands*] (EAIO)
PNID .... Peer Nomination Inventory of Depression [*Child development test*] [*Psychology*]
P-NID .... Precedence Network In-Dialing [*Telecommunications*] (TEL)
PNID/NOD ... Priority Network In-Dial / Network Out-Dial (DNAB)
PNII.......... Prentiss Normal and Industrial Institute [*Mississippi*]
PNII.......... Protease Nexin II [*Biochemistry*]
PNIO .... Priority National Intelligence Objectives (MCD)
PNIP......... Positive-Negative-Intrinsic-Positive [*Electron device*] (MSA)
PNIPAAM ... Poly-N-isopropylacrylamide [*Organic chemistry*]
PNIPAM... Poly-N-Isopropylacrylamide [*Organic chemistry*]
PNJ.......... Paterson [*New Jersey*] [*Seismograph station code, US Geological Survey*] (SEIS)

PNJ........... Paterson, NJ [*Location identifier*] [*FAA*] (FAAL)
PNJ........... Polar Night Jet Stream (ADA)
PNJALBB ... Peter Noone Just A Little Bit Better Promotion Club (EAIO)
PNJALBB ... Peter Noone Just a Little Bit Better Promotion Club (EA)
PNJHS...... Proceedings. New Jersey Historical Society [*A publication*]
PNK .... Pink Pages Publication [*Vancouver Stock Exchange symbol*]
PNK .... Pinkham Creek [*Montana*] [*Seismograph station code, US Geological Survey*] [*Closed*] (SEIS)
PNK .... Polynucleotide Kinase [*An enzyme*]
PNK .... Pontianak [*Indonesia*] [*Airport symbol*] (OAG)
PNkA........ Aluminum Co. of America, ALCOA Research Laboratories Library, New Kensington, PA [*Library symbol*] [*Library of Congress*] (LCLS)
pnksh .... Pinkish [*Philately*]
PNL .... Pacific Naval Laboratory [*Canada*]
PNL .... Pacific Northwest Laboratory [*Department of Energy*] [*Richland, WA*]
PNL .... Pakistan National League [*Political party*]
PNL .... Panel (KSC)
PNL .... Pantelleria [*Italy*] [*Airport symbol*] (OAG)
PNL .... Parti National Liberal [*National Liberal Party*] [*Lebanon*] [*Political party*] (PPW)
PNL .... Partidul National Liberal [*National Liberal Party*] [*Romania*] [*Political party*] (PPE)
PNL .... Passenger Name List [*Travel industry*]
PNL .... Peanut Lectin [*Immunochemistry*]
PNL .... Peninsula [*Alaska*] [*Seismograph station code, US Geological Survey*] (SEIS)
PNL .... Perceived Noise Level
PNL .... Pine Bell Mines [*Vancouver Stock Exchange symbol*]
PNL .... Polytechnic of North London, School of Librarianship, London, England [*OCLC symbol*] (OCLC)
PNL .... Prescribed Nuclear Load [*Military*] (AABC)
PNL .... Pressure Noise Level (MCD)
PNL .... Przewodnik Naukowy i Literacki [*A publication*]
PNL .... Pulsed Neodymium LASER
PNLA .... Pacific Northwest Library Association
PNLA .... Pacific Northwest Loggers Association (EA)
PNLAADA ... Programme National de Lutte Contre l'Abus de l'Alcohol et des Drogues chez les Autochtones [*Canada*]
PNLA Q..... Pacific Northwest Library Association. Quarterly [*A publication*]
pnlbd .... Panelboard [*National Electrical Code*] (IEEE)
PNLBRG... Panel Bridge (MUGU)
PNLG .... Phase Nulling LASER Gyroscope
PNLH .... New Literary History [*A publication*]
PNL/I .... Provisioning Numerical Listing/Index
PNLM .... Palestine National Liberation Movement [*Political party*] (BJA)
PNLO .... Principal Naval Liaison Officer [*British*]
PNLT........ Perceived Noise Level, Tone Corrected
PNM .... Pan-Somali Nationalist Movement [*Political party*]
PNM......... Partido Nacionalista de Mexicano [*Nationalist Party of Mexico*] [*Political party*]
PNM......... Partito Nazionale Monarchico [*National Monarchist Party*] [*Italy*] [*Political party*] (PPE)
PNM......... People's National Movement [*Trinidad and Tobago*] [*Political party*] (PD)
PNM......... Perinatal Mortality [*Medicine*]
PNM......... Perspectives of New Music [*A publication*]
Pnm........... Phantom [*A publication*]
PNM......... Phenolic Nylon with Microballoon
PNM......... Price Negotiation Memorandum (MCD)
PNM......... Public Service Co. of New Mexico [*NYSE symbol*] (SPSG)
PNM......... Pulse Number Modulation
PNM-Aprome ... Partido Nacionalista de Melilla - Asociacion Pro Melilla [*Political party*] (EY)
PNMBA .... Progress in Nucleic Acid Research and Molecular Biology [*A publication*]
PNMC....... Phenyl Methylcarbamate [*Organic chemistry*]
PNMO....... Provided No Military Objection Exists [*Army*]
PNMPA..... Psychiatrie, Neurologie, und Medizinische Psychologie [*A publication*]
PNMRA .... Progress in Nuclear Magnetic Resonance Spectroscopy [*A publication*]
PNMT .... Phenylethanolamine N-Methyltransferase [*An enzyme*]
PNMUB.... Perspectives of New Music [*A publication*]
PNMUD.... PNM Update [*A publication*]
PNN.......... Penn Engineering & Manufacturing Corp. [*AMEX symbol*] (SPSG)
PNN.......... Pinnacle Mountain [*Alaska*] [*Seismograph station code, US Geological Survey*] (SEIS)
PNN.......... Princeton, ME [*Location identifier*] [*FAA*] (FAAL)
PNNCF...... Pacific Northern Naval Coastal Frontier
PNNQ....... Notes and Queries [*A publication*]
PNNT....... Pennant (MSA)
PNo........... Montgomery County-Norristown Public Library, Norristown, PA [*Library symbol*] [*Library of Congress*] (LCLS)
PNO.......... Nashville, TN [*Location identifier*] [*FAA*] (FAAL)
PNO.......... Pa-O National Organization [*Myanmar*] [*Political party*] (EY)
PNO.......... Pancontinental Oil Ltd. [*Toronto Stock Exchange symbol*]

PNO.......... Parti Nationaliste Occitan [*Occitian Nationalist Party*] [*France*] [*Political party*] (PPE)
PNO.......... Party for National Order [*Turkey*] [*Political party*] [*Defunct*] (MENA)
PNO.......... Pendleton [*Oregon*] [*Seismograph station code, US Geological Survey*] (SEIS)
PNO.......... Piano [*Music*]
PNO.......... Preliminary Notification [*Nuclear energy*] (NRCH)
PNO.......... Premium Notice Ordinary [*Insurance*]
PNO.......... Principal Naval Overseer [*British*]
PNO.......... Principal Nursing Officer
PNOA....... Para-Nitro-ortho-anisidine [*Organic chemistry*]
pnob......... Pencil Note on Back [*Philately*]
PNOC....... Proposed Notice of Change
PNO-CI..... Pair Natural Orbital Configuration Interaction [*Atomic physics*]
PNoH........ Norristown State Hospital, Norristown, PA [*Library symbol*] [*Library of Congress*] (LCLS)
PNohM...... Mary Immaculate Seminary, Northampton, PA [*Library symbol*] [*Library of Congress*] (LCLS)
PNOK........ Primary Next of Kin [*Army*] (AABC)
PNOM....... Procedural Nomenclature (MCD)
PNOPO..... Parliament National Organisations and Public Offices [*British*]
PNortHi..... Historical Society of Montgomery County, Norristown, PA [*Library symbol*] [*Library of Congress*] [*Obsolete*] (LCLS)
PNOT....... Para-Nitro-o-toluidine [*Organic chemistry*]
PNOT....... Para-Nitro-ortho-toluidine [*Organic chemistry*]
PNotes ...... Pynchon Notes [*A publication*]
PNOU-A ... Planning Outlook [*A publication*]
PNOV........ Novel. A Forum on Fiction [*A publication*]
PNP .... Pakistan National Party [*Political party*] (PD)
PNP .... Panache Resources, Inc. [*Vancouver Stock Exchange symbol*]
PNP .... Para-Nitrophenol [*or Nitrophenyl*] [*Organic chemistry*]
PNP .... Parti National Populaire [*National Popular Party*] [*Canada*] [*Political party*] (PPW)
PNP .... Parti National du Progres [*National Progress Party*] [*Congo*] [*Political party*]
PNP .... Parti National Progressiste [*Haiti*] [*Political party*] (EY)
PNP .... Partido Nacionalista ng Pilipinas [*Philippine Nationalist Party*] [*Political party*] (EY)
PNP .... Partido Nacionalista Popular [*Popular Nationalist Party*] [*Panama*] [*Political party*] (PPW)
PNP .... Partido Nacionalista del Pueblo [*Bolivia*] [*Political party*] (PPW)
PNP .... Partido Nashonal di Pueblo [*National People's Party*] [*Netherlands Antilles*] [*Political party*] (EY)
PNP .... Partido Nuevo Progresista [*New Progressive Party*] [*Puerto Rico*] [*Political party*] (PPW)
PNP .... Partidul National Poporului [*National People's Party*] [*Romania*] [*Political party*] (PPE)
PNP .... Pay'n Pak Stores, Inc. [*NYSE symbol*] (SPSG)
PNP .... Peake's English Nisi Prius Cases [*1790-1812*] [*A publication*] (DLA)
PNP .... Pearl Necklace Polymer [*Organic chemistry*]
PNP .... Pediatric Nephrology [*Medical specialty*] (DHSM)
PNP .... Pediatric Nurse Practitioner
PNP .... Penuelas [*Puerto Rico*] [*Seismograph station code, US Geological Survey*] (SEIS)
PNP .... People's National Party [*Jamaica*] [*Political party*] (PPW)
PNP .... People's National Party [*Ghana*] [*Political party*] (PPW)
PNP .... Peripheral Neuropathy [*Medicine*]
PNP .... Popondetta [*Papua New Guinea*] [*Airport symbol*] (OAG)
PNP .... Popular Nationalist Party [*Panama*] [*Political party*] (PD)
PNP .... Positive-Negative-Positive [*Transistor*]
PNP .... Precision Navigation Project
PNP .... Preliminary Network Plan (SSD)
PNP .... Prenegotiation Position (MCD)
PNP .... Progressive National Party [*Turks and Caicos Islands*] [*Political party*] (PPW)
PNP .... Prototype Nuclear Process
PNP .... Psychogenic Nocturnal Polydipsia [*Medicine*]
PNP .... Purine-Nucleoside Phosphorylase [*An enzyme*]
PNP .... Pyridoxine Phosphate [*Biochemistry*]
PNPA........ Para-Nitrophenyl Acetate [*Organic chemistry*]
PNPDPP ... Para-Nitrophenyl Diphenyl Phosphate [*Organic chemistry*]
PNPF........ Piqua Nuclear Power Facility
PNPG .... P-Nitrophenyl-B-Galactoside [*Chemistry*] (MAE)
PNPG .... Para-Nitrophenylglycerine [*Biochemistry*]
PNPG .... Parti National Populaire Guyanais [*French Guiana*] [*Political party*] (EY)
PNPH........ Parti National Progressiste d'Haiti [*National Progressive Party of Haiti*] [*Political party*]
PNPL........ Para-Nitrophenyl Laurate [*Organic chemistry*]
PNPN .... Positive-Negative-Positive-Negative [*Transistor*] (MUGU)
P-NPNN... Para-Nitrophenyl Nitronyl Nitroxide
PNPP........ Para-Nitrophenyl Phosphate [*Organic chemistry*]
PNPP........ Perry Nuclear Power Plant (NRCH)
PNPR........ Positive-Negative Pressure Respiration
PNPRA...... Progress in Nuclear Energy. Series 3. Process Chemistry [*A publication*]
PNPS .... Palisades Nuclear Power Station (NRCH)
PNPS .... Plant Nitrogen Purge System (IEEE)

PNPSA ..... Progress in Neurology and Psychiatry [*A publication*]
PNQ.......... Pacific Northwest Quarterly [*A publication*]
PNQ.......... Pine Crest Resources [*Vancouver Stock Exchange symbol*]
PNQ.......... Poona [*India*] [*Airport symbol*] (OAG)
PNR .... Partido Nacional Republicano [*National Republican Party*] [*Paraguay*] [*Political party*]
PNR .... Partido Nacional Republicano [*National Republican Party*] [*Portugal*] [*Political party*] (PPE)
PNR .... Partido Nacional Revolucionario [*National Revolutionary Party*] [*Venezuela*] [*Political party*]
PNR .... Partido Nacionalista Renovador [*Nationalist Renewal Party*] [*Guatemala*] [*Political party*] (PPW)
PNR .... Partido Nacionalista Revolucionario [*Revolutionary Nationalist Party*] [*Ecuador*] [*Political party*] (PPW)
PNR .... Partij Nationalistische Republiek [*Nationalist Republic Party*] [*Surinam*] [*Political party*] (PPW)
PNR .... Passenger Name Record [*Airlines*]
PNR .... Peninsula Airlines, Inc. [*Port Angeles, WA*] [*FAA designator*] (FAAC)
PNR .... Pennant Resources Ltd. [*Toronto Stock Exchange symbol*]
PNR .... Penrod [*Nevada*] [*Seismograph station code, US Geological Survey*] [*Closed*] (SEIS)
PNR .... Philippine National Railways (DS)
PNR .... Pioneer
PNR .... Pittsburgh Naval Reactors Office [*Energy Research and Development Administration*]
PNR .... PN [*Poetry Nation*] Review [*A publication*]
PNR .... Point of No Return [*Aviation*]
PNR .... Pointe Noire [*Congo*] [*Airport symbol*] (OAG)
PNR .... Popular News and Review [*A publication*]
PNR .... Preliminary Negotiation Reports
PNR .... Primary Navigation Reference (AAG)
PNR .... Prior Notice Required (AFM)
PNR .... Prisoner
PNR .... Proximal Negative Response
PNR .... Pulse Nuclear Radiation (AAG)
PNRBC ..... Pacific Northwest River Basin Commission
PNRC .... Pacific Northwest Regional Commission [*Department of Commerce*]
PNRC .... Potomac Naval River Command (MCD)
PNRC .... Projet National de Coordination des Ressources dans le Domaine de la Statistiques et de l'Information Judiciaires [*Canada*]
P N Review ... Poetry Nation Review [*A publication*]
PNRG .... PrimeEnergy Corp. [*NASDAQ symbol*] (SPSG)
PNRHSL... Pacific Northwest Regional Health Science Library [*Library network*]
PNRL......... Penril Data Communication Networks [*NASDAQ symbol*] (SPSG)
PNRS........ Project Notification and Review System [*Department of Labor*]
PNRSV...... Prunus Necrotic Ringspot Virus
PNS .... Pansophic Systems, Inc. [*NYSE symbol*] (SPSG)
PNS .... Parabolized Navier-Stokes Modeling (MCD)
PNS .... Parasympathetic Nervous System
PNS .... Part Number Specification (MCD)
PNS .... Partial Niche Separation
PNS .... Peculiar and Nonstandard Items (AAG)
PNS .... Penas [*Bolivia*] [*Seismograph station code, US Geological Survey*] (SEIS)
PNS .... Pennington's Stores Ltd. [*Toronto Stock Exchange symbol*]
PNS .... Pensacola [*Florida*] [*Airport symbol*] (OAG)
PNS .... People's News Service [*British*]
PNS .... Peripheral Nerve Stimulator [*Medicine*] (MAE)
PNS .... Peripheral Nervous System [*Medicine*]
PNS .... Perkins Nuclear Station (NRCH)
PNS .... Philadelphia & Norfolk Steamship [*AAR code*]
PNS .... Philippines News Service
PNS .... Plate Number Society [*Defunct*] (EA)
PNS .... Portable Navigation System
PNS .... Portsmouth Naval Shipyard [*New Hampshire*]
PNS .... Positive-Negative Selection [*Genetic engineering technique*]
PNS .... Postnuclear Supernatant
PNS .... Prescribed Nuclear Stockage [*Military*] (AABC)
PNS .... Probability of Not Having a Space
PNS .... Professionals for National Security [*Inactive*] (EA)
PNS .... Professor of Naval Science
PNS .... Publishers Newspaper Syndicate
PNSA........ Pacific Northwest Ski Association (EA)
PNSA........ Peanut and Nut Salters Association [*Later, PBNPA*] (EA)
PNSA........ Seaman Apprentice, Personnelman, Striker [*Navy rating*]
PNSCEI..... National Museum of Natural Sciences [*Ottawa*]. Publications in Natural Sciences [*A publication*]
PNSCP ...... Plan for Navy Satellite Communications Plan
PNSD .... Parti National pour la Solidarite et le Developpement [*Algeria*] [*Political party*] (EY)
PNSFA ...... Proceedings. National Shellfisheries Association [*United States*] [*A publication*]
PNSI......... Polhemus Navigational Sciences, Inc. (MCD)
PNSL........ Peninsula Federal Savings & Loan [*NASDAQ symbol*] (NQ)
PNSN .... Seaman, Personnelman, Striker [*Navy rating*]
PNS & T .... Professor of Naval Science and Tactics [*Naval ROTC*]

PNSUS...... Placename Survey of the US   (EA)
PNSY........ Portsmouth Naval Shipyard [*New Hampshire*]
PNt............ Newtown Library Co., Newtown, PA [*Library symbol*] [*Library of Congress*] [*Obsolete*]   (LCLS)
PNT .... Paint   (MSA)
Pnt............. Panart [*Record label*] [*Cuba, USA*]
PNT .... Pantasote, Inc. [*AMEX symbol*]   (SPSG)
PNT .... Para-Nitrotoluene [*Organic chemistry*]
PNT .... Paroxysmal Nodal Tachycardia [*Cardiology*]
PNT .... Parti National du Travail [*Haiti*] [*Political party*]   (EY)
PNT .... Parti National du Travail [*Benin*] [*Political party*]   (EY)
PNT .... Partido Nacionalista de los Trabajadores [*Argentina*] [*Political party*]   (EY)
PNT .... Patient   (AABC)
PNT .... Pentagon
PNT .... Penticton [*British Columbia*] [*Seismograph station code, US Geological Survey*]   (SEIS)
PNT .... Petromet Resources Ltd. [*Toronto Stock Exchange symbol*]
PNT .... Point
PNT .... Pontiac, IL [*Location identifier*] [*FAA*]   (FAAL)
PNTA .... Pacific Northwest Trade Association
PNTA .... Pentair, Inc. [*NASDAQ symbol*]   (NQ)
PNtB .... Bucks County Community College, Newtown, PA [*Library symbol*] [*Library of Congress*]   (LCLS)
PNtC .... Council Rock High School, Newtown, PA [*Library symbol*] [*Library of Congress*]   (LCLS)
PNTC........ Panatech Research & Development Corp. [*NASDAQ symbol*]   (NQ)
PNTCENS ... Patient Census Report
PNTD .... Painted
PNTD .... Personnel Neutron Threshold Detector   (IEEE)
PN/TDMA ... Pseudo Noise/Time Division Multiple Access   (MCD)
PNtE .... Ellis College, Newtown, PA [*Library symbol*] [*Library of Congress*] [*Obsolete*]   (LCLS)
PNTEA...... Progress in Nuclear Energy. Series 4 [*A publication*]
PNTG .... Petromet Resources Ltd. [*NASDAQ symbol*]   (NQ)
PNTG .... Printing   (ROG)
PNTGN ..... Pentagon   (MSA)
PNTK .... Pentech International, Inc. [*NASDAQ symbol*]   (NQ)
PNTL........ Phonetel Technologies, Inc. [*NASDAQ symbol*]   (NQ)
PNTO .... Portuguese National Tourist Office   (EA)
PNTO .... Principal Naval Transport Officer [*British military*]   (DMA)
PNTOS..... Para-Nitrotoluene-ortho-sulfonic Acid [*Organic chemistry*]
PNTQ .... New Theatre Quarterly [*A publication*]
PNTR .... Painter   (FAAC)
PNTR .... Pinetree Computer Systems, Inc. [*NASDAQ symbol*]   (NQ)
PNTR .... Pointer   (MCD)
PNTS........ New Testament Studies [*A publication*]
PNts .... Newtown Public Library, Newtown Square, PA [*Library symbol*] [*Library of Congress*]   (LCLS)
PNU .... Panguitch [*Utah*] [*Airport symbol*]   (OAG)
PNU .... Peasants' National Unity [*Afghanistan*] [*Political party*]   (EY)
PNU .... Personennamen der Texte aus Ugarit [*A publication*]   (BJA)
PNU .... Platinum Communication System [*Vancouver Stock Exchange symbol*]
PNU .... Pneumatic Scale Corp. [*AMEX symbol*]   (SPSG)
PNU .... Protein Nitrogen Units [*Clinical chemistry*]
PNUA........ Partito Nazionale Unito Africa [*National Party of United Africans*] [*Somalia*] [*Political party*]
PNUA........ Polish National Union of America   (EA)
PNUD........ Programa de las Naciones Unidas para el Desarrollo [*United Nations Development Program - UNDP*] [*Spanish*]   (MSC)
PNUED ..... Preprint. Akademiya Nauk Ukrainskoi SSR Institut Elektrodinamiki [*A publication*]
PNUMA .... Programa de las Naciones Unidas para el Medio Ambiente [*United Nations Environmental Programme Regional Office for Latin America*]   (EAIO)
PNUPA ..... Progress in Nuclear Physics [*A publication*]
PNUT........ Nutrition Today [*A publication*]
PNUT........ Portable Nursing Unit Terminal
PNUT........ Possible Nuclear Underground Test
PNUT........ Specialty Retail Concepts, Inc. [*Winston-Salem, NC*] [*NASDAQ symbol*]   (NQ)
P Nutr Soc ... Proceedings. Nutrition Society [*A publication*]
PNUTS...... Possible Nuclear Test Site [*Pronounced "peanuts"*] [*Air Force intelligence*]
PNV .... National Velasquista Party [*Ecuador*] [*Political party*]   (PPW)
PNV .... Parti National Voltaique [*Voltaic National Party*] [*Political party*]
PNV .... Partido Nacional Velasquista [*National Velasquista Party*] [*Ecuador*] [*Political party*]   (PPW)
PNV .... Partido Nacionalista Vasco [*Basque Nationalist Party*] [*Spain*] [*Political party*]   (PPE)
PNV .... Patino N. V. [*Toronto Stock Exchange symbol*]
PNV .... Perini Investment Properties, Inc. [*AMEX symbol*] [*Later, Pacific Gateway Properties, Inc.*]   (SPSG)
PNVAL...... Previously Not Available [*Army*]   (AABC)
PNVD........ Passive Night Vision Devices [*Army*]   (AABC)
PNVS........ Pilot Night Vision System [*Army*]   (MCD)
PNVS........ Pilot's Night Vision Sensor

PNVTS...... Pyrotechnics No-Voltage Test Set
PNW......... Pacific Northwest
PNW......... Pinnacle West Capital Corp. [*NYSE symbol*]   (SPSG)
PNW......... [*The*] Prescott & Northwestern Railroad Co. [*AAR code*]
PNWC ...... Pacific Northwest Writers' Conference
PNwC........ Westminster College, New Wilmington, PA [*Library symbol*] [*Library of Congress*]   (LCLS)
PNWCSC .. Pacific Northwest Canadian Studies Consortium [*University of Oregon*]
PNWL .... Pacific Northwest Laboratory [*AEC*]
PNW Pac Northwest Ext Publ Oreg State Univ Coop Ext Serv ... PNW. Pacific Northwest Extension Publication. Oregon State University. Cooperative Extension Service [*A publication*]
PNWRBC ... Pacific Northwest River Basins Commission [*Water Resources Council*] [*Terminated, 1981*]   (NOAA)
PNX.......... Imperial Airways, Inc. [*St. Paul, MN*] [*FAA designator*]   (FAAC)
PNX.......... Phoenix Laser Systems, Inc. [*AMEX symbol*]   (SPSG)
PNX.......... Pneumothorax [*Medicine*]
PNXT .... Pinxit [*He, or She, Painted It*] [*Latin*]
PNY.......... Camp Parks, CA [*Location identifier*] [*FAA*]   (FAAL)
PNY.......... Piedmont Natural Gas Co., Inc. [*NYSE symbol*]   (SPSG)
PNY.......... Plattsburgh [*New York*] [*Seismograph station code, US Geological Survey*]   (SEIS)
PNY.......... Poetry New York [*A publication*]
PNY.......... Portuguese Navy
PNYA .... Port of New York Authority [*Later, PANYNJ*]
PNYMD .... Polytechnic Institute of New York. Department of Mechanical and Aerospace Engineering. Report POLY M/AE [*A publication*]
PNZ.......... Pennzoil Co., Exploration Library, Houston, TX [*OCLC symbol*]   (OCLC)
PNZ.......... Petrolina [*Brazil*] [*Airport symbol*]   (OAG)
PO............. Dust Devils [*Aviation code*]   (FAAC)
po----- .... Oceanica [*MARC geographic area code*] [*Library of Congress*]   (LCCP)
PO............. Officer Personnel Division [*Coast Guard*]
PO............. Oil City Library, Oil City, PA [*Library symbol*] [*Library of Congress*]   (LCLS)
PO............. Oscillopolarograph
PO............. Pacific Ocean
P & O .... Paints and Oil
PO............. Palomar Capital [*Vancouver Stock Exchange symbol*]
PO............. Parallel Output [*Data processing*]   (BUR)
P:O............ Parent Offspring [*Genetics*]
PO............. Parieto-Occipital [*Anatomy*]   (AAMN)
PO............. Parity Odd
PO............. Parking Orbit [*NASA*]
PO............. Parole Officer
P/O .... Part Of   (KSC)
PO............. Passport Office [*Department of State*]
PO............. Patent Office [*Later, PTO*] [*Department of Commerce*]
PO............. Patrologia Orientalis [*A publication*]
P & O .... Peninsular & Oriental Steam Navigation Co. [*Steamship line*]
PO............. Per Os [*By Mouth*] [*Pharmacy*]
PO............. Performance Objectives   (OICC)
P & O .... Performance and Operational [*Test or reports*]
PO............. Period of Onset [*Medicine*]
PO............. Permit Office [*British*]   (ROG)
PO............. Peroxidase [*Also, POD*] [*An enzyme*]
PO............. Personnel Office [*Kennedy Space Center Directorate*]   (NASA)
PO............. Personnel Officer
PO............. Pesticides Office [*Environmental Protection Agency*]
PO............. Petty Officer [*Navy*]
PO............. Phase-Out
PO............. Philharmonic Orchestra [*Music*]
P/O .... Phone Order [*Medicine*]
PO............. Phymatotrichum omnivorum [*A fungus*]
P & O .... Pickled and Oiled
PO............. Pilot Officer
P/O .... Pitch Over
PO............. Planetary Orbit
PO............. Planning Objectives
P & O .... Planning and Operations
P & O .... Planning and Organization
P & O .... Plans and Operations Division [*War Department*] [*World War II*]
PO............. Poco [*Somewhat*] [*Music*]
Po............. Poesie [*A publication*]
PO............. Point   (WGA)
PO............. Polarity   (AAG)
PO............. Pole [*Unit of measurement*]
Po............. Polet [*A publication*]
PO............. Police Officer
PO............. Political Officer [*NATO*]
P/O .... Pollen/Ovule Ratio [*Botany*]
Po............. Polonium [*Chemical element*]
PO............. Polskie Zaklady Lotnicze [*Poland*] [*ICAO aircraft manufacturer identifier*]   (ICAO)
PO............. Polymerizable Oligomer   (OA)
PO............. Polyolefin [*Organic chemistry*]

Po .... Polyzoa [*Quality of the bottom*] [*Nautical charts*]
PO .... Poona Orientalist [*A publication*]
PO .... Por Orden [*By Order*] [*Spanish*]
PO .... Port Flag [*Navy*] [*British*]
PO .... Port Officer
P & O .... Portland & Ogdensburgh Railroad
po .... Portugal [*MARC country of publication code*] [*Library of Congress*] (LCCP)
PO .... Portugal [*NATO*]
Po .... Portuguese [*Language, etc.*] (DLA)
PO .... Position Offered
P & O .... Positioning and Orientation
Po .... Possible
PO .... Post Flight Inspection [*Air Force*]
PO .... Post Office
PO .... Post Office Department [*Canada*]
PO .... Post Orbit [*NASA*]
PO .... Postal Officer (DCTA)
PO .... Postal Order
PO .... Posterior (MAE)
PO .... Postoperative [*Medicine*]
PO .... Postpay Coin Telephone [*Telecommunications*] (TEL)
PO .... Potential Officer [*British military*] (DMA)
PO .... Power-Operated
PO .... Power Oscillator [*Electronics*]
PO .... Power Output
PO .... Prairie Overcomer [*A publication*]
PO .... Pre-Authorization Order
PO .... Predominating Organism (AAMN)
PO .... Preoperational (MCD)
PO .... Preoptic [*Area of the brain*]
PO .... Presbyteri Oratorii [*Oratorians*] [*Roman Catholic religious order*]
PO .... Presbyterorum Ordinis [*Decree on the Ministry and Life of Priests*] [*Vatican II document*]
PO .... Preventive Officer [*British*] (ROG)
PO .... Previous Orders [*Military*]
PO .... Principal Officer [*Foreign Service*]
PO .... Principal Only Strip [*Mortgage security*]
PO .... Printout
PO .... Private Office [*Documents issued by the Secretary General, NATO*] (NATG)
PO .... Privately Owned (AFM)
PO .... Probation Officer
PO .... Processing Office [*Bureau of the Census*] (GFGA)
PO .... Procurement Objective (NVT)
PO .... Production Offset (AABC)
PO .... Production Order (KSC)
PO .... Professor Ordinarius [*Ordinary Professor*] [*Latin*] (ROG)
PO .... Program Objective
PO .... Program Office [*Air Force*] (CET)
PO .... Program Originator (AFM)
PO .... Programmed Oscillator
PO .... Project Office [*or Officer*] [*Military*]
PO .... Project ORBIS (EA)
PO .... Project Order [*DoD*]
PO .... Project Overcome (EA)
PO .... Proposals Outstanding
PO .... Proposition One (EA)
PO .... Propylene Oxide [*Organic chemistry*]
PO .... Protea Lugdiens [*South Africa*] [*ICAO designator*] (FAAC)
PO .... Province of Ontario [*Canada*]
PO .... Provisioning Order (AFM)
PO .... Przeglad Orientalistyczny [*A publication*]
PO .... Pseudoadiabatic Operation [*Chemical engineering*]
PO .... Psychological Operation [*Military*] (CINC)
PO .... Public Offering [*Investment term*]
PO .... Public Office [*British*] (ROG)
PO .... Public Official
PO .... Pulmonary Valve Opening [*Cardiology*]
PO .... Pulse Output
PO .... Pulsed Carrier without Any Modulation Intended to Carry Information (IEEE)
PO .... Punted Over [*Boating*] [*British*] (ROG)
PO .... Purchase Order
PO .... Purchasing Office [*DoD*] (AFIT)
PO .... Putout [*Baseball*]
PO .... Radio Positioning Mobile Station [*ITU designation*] [*Telecommunications*] (CET)
PO1 .... Petty Officer, First Class [*Navy*]
PO$_2$ .... Partial Pressure of Oxygen (AAMN)
PO2 .... Petty Officer, Second Class [*Navy*]
PO3 .... Petty Officer, Third Class [*Navy*]
PO'd .... Put Out [*i.e., angry*] [*Bowdlerized version*]
PO'ed .... Put Out [*i.e., angry*] [*Bowdlerized version*]
POA .... Pacific Ocean Area [*World War II*]
POA .... Pahoa, HI [*Location identifier*] [*FAA*] (FAAL)
POA .... Pancreatic Oncofetal Antigen [*Immunochemistry*]
POA .... Panel of Americans [*Defunct*] (EA)
POA .... Pay-on-Answer [*Telecommunications*] [*British*]
POA .... Peacetime Operating Assets [*DoD*] (AFIT)

POA .... Petroleum Operating Agreement (CINC)
POA .... Petty Officer Airman [*British military*] (DMA)
POA .... Phalangeal Osteoarthritis [*Medicine*]
POA .... Phenoxyacetic Acid [*Organic chemistry*]
POA .... Place of Acceptance [*Business term*] (DCTA)
POA .... Plan of Action (NASA)
POA .... Point of Application [*Medicine*] (MAE)
POA .... Pontifica Opera di Assistenza [*Pontifical Relief Organization*]
POA .... Port of Arrival
POA .... Porto Alegre [*Brazil*] [*Airport symbol*] (OAG)
POA .... Power of Attorney
POA .... Preoptic Area [*of the brain*]
POA .... Price on Application [*Business term*] (ADA)
POA .... Primary Optic Afferents
POA .... Primary Optic Atrophy
POA .... Prison Officers' Association [*A union*] [*British*] (DCTA)
POA .... Privately Owned Aircraft (FAAC)
POA .... Privately Owned Automobile
POA .... Proof of Accounts
POA .... Provisional Operating Authorization [*for nuclear power plant*]
POA .... Public Order Act
POA .... Purchase Order Authorization (SAA)
POA .... Purchased on Assembly (KSC)
POA .... Purgeable Organic Analyzer
POAA .... Planetary Operations Analysis Area [*NASA*]
POAA .... Problems of the Arctic and the Antarctic [*A publication*]
POAA .... Property Owners Association of America [*Defunct*] (EA)
POAC .... Pony of the Americas Club (EA)
POAC .... Port and Ocean Engineering Under Arctic Conditions International Committee (EAIO)
POAC .... Post Office Advisory Committee [*British*]
POAC .... Post Office Ambulance Centre [*British*] (DI)
POA Chronicle ... Professional Officers' Association Chronicle [*A publication*] (APTA)
POACMN ... Petty Officer Aircrewman [*British military*] (DMA)
POACS ...... Prior Other Active Commissioned Service [*Military*]
POADS...... Portland Air Defense Sector (SAA)
POAE .... Port of Aerial Embarkation [*Air Force*]
POAE .... Principal Officer of Aircraft Equipment [*Ministry of Aircraft Production*] [*British*] [*World War II*]
POAES...... Prior Other Active Enlisted Service [*Military*]
POAF........ Petty Officer Air Fitter [*British military*] (DMA)
POAG .... Petro Oil & Gas, Inc. [*NASDAQ symbol*] (NQ)
POAG .... Primary Open-Angle Glaucoma [*Ophthalmology*]
POAHEDPEARL ... Pacific Ocean Areas Headquarters Pearl Harbor
POAI .... Properties of America, Inc. [*NASDAQ symbol*] (NQ)
POALS ...... Petty Officers Advanced Leadership School [*Navy*] (MUGU)
POA & M .. Plan of Action and Milestones (NVT)
POAM .... Polar Ozone Aerosol Measurement
POAN....... Procurement of Ordnance and Ammunition - Navy
POAR .... Problem-Objective-Approach-Response [*System of planning patient care*] [*Medicine*]
POAR .... Project Order Action Request [*Navy*] (NG)
poas--- .... American Samoa [*MARC geographic area code*] [*Library of Congress*] (LCCP)
POAS........ Pankypria Omospondia Anexartiton Syntechnion [*Pancyprian Federation of Independent Trade Unions*] [*Cyprus*]
POAS........ Poems on Affairs of State [*A publication*]
POASP ...... Plans and Operations Automated Storage Program [*Military*]
POATSC ... Pacific Overseas Air Technical Service Command
POAU........ Protestants and Other Americans United [*for Separation of Church and State*]
POB .... Fayetteville, NC [*Location identifier*] [*FAA*] (FAAL)
POB .... Paris Opera Ballet
POB .... Parti Ouvrier Belge [*Belgian Workers' Party*] [*Later, Belgian Socialist Party*] [*Political party*] (PPE)
POB .... Penicillin, Oil, Beeswax [*Medicine*]
POB .... Perfluorooctyl Bromide [*Organic chemistry*]
POB .... Persons on Board [*Aviation*]
POB .... Phenoxybenzamine [*Later, PBZ*] [*Adrenergic blocking agent*]
POB .... Place of Birth
POB .... Point of Beginning
POB .... Point of Business
POB .... Polarboken [*A publication*]
POB .... Post Office Box
POB .... Postal Bulletin [*A publication*]
POB .... Power Outlet Box
POB .... Prevention of Blindness [*Medicine*] (MAE)
POB^2 .... Prepped Out Beyond Belief [*Book title*]
POBAL....... Powered Balloon [*System*]
POBATO... Propellant on Board at Takeoff
POBCOST ... Probabilistic Budgeting and Forward Costing (MCD)
POBI........ Polar Biology [*A publication*]
POBN....... Pyridyl Oxide-N-tert-butylnitrone [*Organic chemistry*]
POBN....... (Pyridyloxide)butylnitrone [*Organic chemistry*]
pobp---........ British Solomon Islands [*MARC geographic area code*] [*Library of Congress*] (LCCP)
POBR .... Problem-Oriented Basic Research [*National Science Foundation*]
POBS........ Portsmouth Bank Shares, Inc. [*NASDAQ symbol*] (NQ)
POBS........ Proceedings. Oxford Bibliographical Society [*A publication*]

POBSP ...... Pacific Ocean Biological Survey Program [*Smithsonian Institution*]   (GFGA)
POBUD ..... Polymer Bulletin [*A publication*]
POBY .... Prior Operating Budget Year [*Military*]   (AFIT)
POC .... Clarion State College, Oil City, PA [*Library symbol*] [*Library of Congress*]   (LCLS)
POC .... La Pocatiere [*Quebec*] [*Seismograph station code, US Geological Survey*]   (SEIS)
POC .... La Verne, CA [*Location identifier*] [*FAA*]   (FAAL)
POC .... Packaged Optimization Control [*Engineering*]
POC .... Parallel Optical Computer
POC .... Parti d'Opposition Congolais [*Congolese Opposition Party*] [*Political party*]
POC .... Particulate Organic Carbon
POC .... Particulate Organic Concentration [*Environmental science*]
POC .... Payload Operations Center [*NASA*]   (NASA)
P & OC ...... Peninsular & Oriental (Steam Navigation) Co. Ltd.   (ROG)
POC .... Performance Optimization Code
POC .... Personnel Operations Center
POC .... Peugeot Owners' Club   (EA)
POC .... Pick Off, Circuit
POC .... Planning Objective Coordinator
POC .... Plymouth Owners Club   (EA)
POC .... Poco Petroleums Ltd. [*Toronto Stock Exchange symbol*]
POC .... Pocono Air Lines, Inc. [*East Stroudsburg, PA*] [*FAA designator*]   (FAAC)
POC .... Poculum [*Cup*] [*Pharmacy*]
POC .... Point of Contact   (AABC)
POC .... Porsche Owners Club   (EA)
POC .... Port of Call
POc .... Porte-Oceane [*Record label*] [*France*]
POC ... Post of the Corps
POC .... Post Office Corps [*British military*]   (DMA)
POC .... Post Office Counters Ltd. [*British*]
POC .... Postoperative Care [*Medicine*]
POC .... Postoral Ciliary [*Gland*]
POC .... Power Control
POC .... Precision Oscillator Crystal
POC .... Preliminary Operational Capability [*Military*]   (AFIT)
POC .... Preservation of Capital [*Investment term*]
POC .... Principal Operating Component
POC .... Prisoners of Conscience [*File of persons imprisoned for political or religious beliefs kept by Amnesty International*]
POC .... Privately Owned Conveyance [*Army*]
PoC .... Problems of Communism [*A publication*]
POC .... Procarbazine, Oncovin [*Vincristine*], CCNU [*Lomustine*] [*Antineoplastic drug regimen*]
POC .... Proceed [*or Proceeding*] on Course [*Aviation*]   (FAAC)
POC .... Process Operator Console
POC .... Proche-Orient Chretien [*A publication*]
POC .... Production Operational Capability
POC .... Production Order Change   (KSC)
POC .... Professional Officer Course [*AFROTC*]   (AFM)
POC .... Programs of Cooperation   (MCD)
POC .... Proopiocortin [*Biochemistry*]
POC .... Purchase Order Closeout   (NASA)
POC .... Purchase Order Contract
POC .... Purgeable Organic Carbon [*Chemistry*]
POCA .... Association of Psychiatric Outpatient Centers of America [*Acronym is based on former name, Psychiatric Outpatient Centers of America*]   (EA)
POCA .... Petty Officer Caterer [*British military*]   (DMA)
POCA .... Post Office Clerks' Association [*A union*] [*Northern Ireland*]
POCA .... Prednisone, Oncovin [*Vincristine*], Cytarabine, Adriamycin [*Antineoplastic drug regimen*]
POCA .... Public Offender Counselors Association [*Later, IAAOC*]   (EA)
POCAL ...... Pre-Operational Common Age List
PO Cas .... Perry's Oriental Cases [*Bombay*] [*A publication*]   (DLA)
POCASEA ... Protection of Children Against Sexual Exploitation Act of 1977
POCB .... Plain Ol' Country Boy
POCC .... Payload Operations Control Center [*NASA*]   (NASA)
POCC .... Procarbazine, Oncovin [*Vincristine*], Cyclophosphamide, CCNU [*Lomustine*] [*Antineoplastic drug regimen*]
POCC .... Program Operation Control Center [*Space science*]
Poc Costs ... Pocock on Costs [*1881*] [*A publication*]   (DLA)
POCE .... Proof-of-Concept Experiment [*Solar thermal conversion*]
POCEL ...... Petty Officer Control Electrician [*British military*]   (DMA)
POCET ...... Proof-of-Concept Experiment Testbed [*Solar thermal conversion*]   (MCD)
POCH .... Progressiven Organisationen der Schweiz [*Progressive Organizations of Switzerland*] [*Political party*]   (PPE)
P-O Chr ..... Proche-Orient Chretien [*A publication*]
Poch Urozhai Latv Nauch-Issled Inst Zemled ... Pochva i Urozhai. Latviiskii Nauchno-Issledovatel'skii Institut Zemledeliya [*A publication*]
Pochv Issled Primen Udobr ... Pochvennye Issledovaniya i Primenenie Udobrenii [*A publication*]
Pochvoved .. Pochvovedenie [*A publication*]
Pochvozn Agrokhim ... Pochvoznanie i Agrokhimiya [*A publication*]
Pochv Usloviya Eff Udobr ... Pochvennye Usloviya i Effektivnost Udobrenii [*A publication*]

Pochvy Baskh Puti Ratsion Ikh Ispol'z ... Pochvy Baskhirii i Puti Ratsional'nogo Ikh Ispol'zovaniya [*Former USSR*] [*A publication*]
Pochvy Yuzhn Urala Povolzhya ... Pochvy Yuzhnogo Urala i Povolzh'ya [*A publication*]
poci--- .... Caroline Islands [*MARC geographic area code*] [*Library of Congress*]   (LCCP)
POCI .... Pontiac-Oakland Club International   (EA)
POCIBO .... Polar Circling Balloon Observatory
POCIC .... POCI, Inc. [*NASDAQ symbol*]   (SPSG)
POCIL .... Pocillum [*Little Cup*] [*Pharmacy*]   (ROG)
Pocill .... Pocillum [*Little Cup*] [*Pharmacy*]
POCK .... Petty Officer Cook [*British military*]   (DMA)
Pocket Pict Guides Clin Med ... Pocket Picture Guides to Clinical Medicine [*A publication*]
POCL .... Power on Clear [*Navy Navigation Satellite System*]   (DNAB)
POCL .... Project Office Change Letter
POCM .... Partido Obrero y Campesino de Mexico [*Mexico*] [*Political party*]
POCM .... Postal Contracting Manual [*Postal Service*]
POCN .... Purchase Order Change Notice
POCO .... European Political Cooperation [*EC*]   (ECED)
POCO .... Physiology of Chimpanzees in Orbit [*NASA*]
Poco .... Politically Correct
POCO .... Power On - Clock On [*Aerospace*]
POCO .... Purchase Order Change Order   (AAG)
POCO .... Purchase Order Closeout   (AAG)
POCOA ..... Post Office Controlling Officers' Association [*A union*] [*British*]
pocp--- .... Canton and Enderbury Islands [*MARC geographic area code*] [*Library of Congress*]   (LCCP)
POCP........ Program Objectives Change Proposal
POCR .... Program Objectives Change Request [*DoD*]
POCS .... Patent Office [*later, PTO*] Classification System
PO & CS .... Post Office and Civil Service Committee [*Obsolete*] [*US Senate*]
Po Ct .... Police Court   (DLA)
POCTA...... Prevention of Cruelty to Animals Society Member   (DSUE)
POCUL...... Poculum [*Cup*] [*Pharmacy*]   (ROG)
pocw--- ...... Cook Island [*MARC geographic area code*] [*Library of Congress*]   (LCCP)
POD .... Pacific Ocean Division [*Army Corps of Engineers*]
POD .... Parent Organization Designator   (MCD)
POD .... Parents of Diabetics
POD .... Pay on Delivery [*Shipping*]
POD .... Payable on Death [*Insurance*]
POD .... Payload Operations Division [*NASA*]   (MCD)
POD .... Permissible Operating Distance [*Army*]   (AFIT)
POD .... Peroxidase [*Also, PO*] [*An enzyme*]
POD .... Personal Orientation Dimensions [*Personality development test*] [*Psychology*]
POD .... Place of Death   (MAE)
POD .... Place of Delivery [*Shipping*]   (DS)
POD .... Place of Discharge
POD .... Plan of the Day
POD .... Pneumatically Operated Disconnect   (KSC)
POD .... Pocket Oxford Dictionary [*A publication*]
POD .... Podkamennaya [*Former USSR*] [*Geomagnetic observatory code*]
POD .... Podor [*Senegal*] [*Airport symbol*]   (OAG)
POD .... Point of Departure
POD .... Point of Discharge   (GFGA)
POD .... Point-of-Origin Device [*IEEE*]
POD .... Polycystic Ovarian Disease [*Medicine*]
POD .... Port of Debarkation [*Military*]
POD .... Port of Delivery [*Shipping*]
POD .... Port of Discharge [*Navy*]
POD .... Post of Duty
POD .... Post Office Department [*Later, United States Postal Service*]
POD .... Post Office Directory
POD .... Postoperative Day [*Medicine*]
POD .... Potential Ozone Depleter
POD .... Pounds-Out-the-Door [*Measure of industrial production*]
POD .... Precision Orbit Determination   (MCD)
POD .... Preflight Operation Division [*NASA*]
POD .... Professional and Organizational Development [*In association name Professional and Organizational Development Network in Higher Education*]   (EA)
POD .... Program Office Directive
POD .... Program Operation Description
POD .... Programmed Operational Date   (AFIT)
POD .... Proof of Debt [*Business term*]   (DCTA)
POD .... Proof of Delivery [*Shipping*]   (DS)
POD .... Proof of Deposit [*Banking*]
POD .... Proof of Design
POD .... Prosthetics and Orthotics Database [*University of Strathclyde*] [*Glasgow, Scotland*] [*Information service or system*]   (IID)
POD .... Proximity Optical Device   (NASA)
POD .... Pulse Omission Detector   (MCD)
POD .... Purchase Order Deviation   (KSC)
PODA .... Priority-Oriented Demand Assignment

PODAF...... Post Operation Data Analysis Facility
PODAF...... Power Density Exceeding a Specified Level over an Area with an Assigned Frequency Band (IEEE)
PODAPS... Portable Data Processing System
PODAS...... Portable Data Acquisition System
PODBCA... Post Office Department Board of Contract Appeals (AFIT)
PODCC ..... Plan, Organize, Direct, Coordinate, Control [*Principles of management*]
Pod D .... Doctor of Podiatry
PODE........ Pacific Ocean Division Engineers (CINC)
PODEX ..... [*Night*] Photographic Exercise [*Military*] (NVT)
PODF .... Post of Duty File
Podgot Koksovanie Uglei ... Podgotovka i Koksovanie Uglei [*A publication*]
Podgot Vosstanov Rud ... Podgotovka i Vosstanovlenie Rud [*A publication*]
PODIM ..... Poseidon Design Information Memo [*Missiles*]
P & O Div .. Planning and Operations Division [*Military*]
PODM........ Preliminary Orbit Determination Method [*Computer*] [*NASA*]
PODO....... Profit on Day One [*Classification for new newspaper*]
PODRS...... Patent Office [*later, PTO*] Data Retrieval System [*Department of Commerce*]
PODS .... Parents of Down's Syndrome (EA)
PODS .... Pilot Ocean Data System (MCD)
PODS .... Postoperative Destruct System (MCD)
PODSC...... Parents of Down's Syndrome Children (EA)
Podst Sterow ... Podstawy Sterowania [*A publication*]
PODU........ Praci Odes'koho Derzavnoho Universytetu [*A publication*]
PODUC..... Provided [*Following Named*] Officers Have Not Departed Your Command [*Amend Assignment Instructions as Indicated*] [*Army*] (AABC)
PODx........ Postoperative Diagnosis [*Medicine*]
PODx........ Preoperative Diagnosis [*Medicine*]
Podzemn Gazif Uglei ... Podzemnaya Gazifikatsiya Uglei [*Former USSR*] [*A publication*]
Podzemn Gazif Uglei (1934-35) ... Podzemnaya Gazifikatsiya Uglei (1934-35) [*A publication*]
Podzemn Gazif Uglei (1957-59) ... Podzemnaya Gazifikatsiya Uglei (1957-59) [*A publication*]
Podzemn Vody SSSR ... Podzemnye Vody SSSR [*A publication*]
POE .... Fort Polk [*Louisiana*] [*Airport symbol*] (OAG)
POE .... Fort Polk, LA [*Location identifier*] [*FAA*] (FAAL)
POE .... Panel on the Environment [*of President's Science Advisory Committee*]
POE .... Payment Option Election (MCD)
POE .... Peace on Earth [*Australia*] [*Political party*]
POE .... People of the Earth [*Also, RAN*] (EA)
POE .... Pilot Operational Equipment (MCD)
POE .... Plank-on-Edge
POE .... Pneumatically Operated Equipment (AAG)
Poe .... Poetik [*A publication*]
POE .... Point of Entry [*Accounts*]
POE .... Polyoxyethylene [*Organic chemistry*]
POE .... Port of Embarkation [*Shipping*]
POE .... Port of Entry [*Shipping*]
POE .... Post-Occupancy Evaluation
POE .... Post-Operations Evaluation (MCD)
POE .... Postoperative Endophthalmitis [*Ophthalmology*]
POE .... Predicted Operational Environment [*Military*] (CAAL)
POE .... Pretesting Orientation Exercises [*US Employment Service*] [*Department of Labor*]
POE .... Primary Organization Element (NOAA)
POE .... Print Out Effect
POE .... Projected Operational Environment (NVT)
POE .... Pull-Over Enrichment [*Automotive engineering*]
POE .... Pulsar Energy/Resources [*Vancouver Stock Exchange symbol*]
POE .... Pulse Oriented Electrophoresis [*Analytical biochemistry*]
poea---........ Easter Island [*MARC geographic area code*] [*Library of Congress*] (LCCP)
POEA .... Philippines Overseas Employment Administration (PDAA)
POEA .... Poe & Associates, Inc [*NASDAQ symbol*] (NQ)
POEA .... Protection of Offshore Energy Assets [*Navy*] (NVT)
P/OEA3..... Probationary Ordnance Electrical Artificer 3rd Class [*British military*] (DMA)
POEAS...... Planetary Orbiter Error Analysis Study Program
Poe Chpbk ... Poetry Chapbook [*A publication*]
POED........ Program Organization for Evaluation and Decision
POEER...... Pacific Oceanographic Equipment Evaluation Range (NOAA)
POEF........ Post Office Engineering Federation [*A union*] [*British*]
POEIT....... Provisional Organization for European Inland Transportation [*World War II*]
POEL(A) ... Petty Officer Electrician (Air) [*British military*] (DMA)
POEL(AW) ... Petty Officer Electrician (Air Weapon) [*British military*] (DMA)
P O Elect Engrs J ... Post Office Electrical Engineers. Journal [*A publication*]
P O Electr Eng J ... Post Office Electrical Engineers. Journal [*A publication*]
POEMS..... Polyneuropathy Associated with Organomegaly Endocrine Disorders, Myeloma, and Skin Modifications
POEMS..... Polyoxyethylene Monostearate [*Organic chemistry*]
POENIT..... Poenitentia [*Penance*] [*Latin*] (ADA)
POEOP...... Polyoxyethyleneoxypropylene [*Organic chemistry*]
Poe Pal...... Poetry Palisade [*A publication*]
Poe Pl......... Poe on Pleading and Practice [*A publication*] (DLA)

POERD ..... Power Engineer [*A publication*]
PoeS........... Poe Studies [*A publication*]
POES........... Polar Orbiting Environmental Satellite
POESID ..... Position of Earth Satellite in Digital Display (MCD)
Poe Stud..... Poe Studies [*A publication*]
Poet.......... De Poetis [*of Suetonius*] [*Classical studies*] (OCD)
POET........ Petty Officer Enroute Training [*Navy*] (NVT)
Poet .... Poetica [*A publication*]
Poet .... Poetica [*of Aristotle*] [*Classical studies*] (OCD)
Poet .... Poetry [*A publication*]
POET........ Primed Oscillator Expendable Transponder [*Military*] (CAAL)
POET......... Program Operation and Environment Transfer (SAA)
POET......... Psychological Operations Exploitation Team [*Vietnam*]
PoetC .... Poet and Critic [*A publication*]
Poet Crit..... Poet and Critic [*A publication*]
Poetics Tod ... Poetics Today [*A publication*]
Poet L......... Poet Lore [*A publication*]
Poet Mel Gr ... Poetae Melici Graeci [*A publication*] (OCD)
POETRI .... Programme on Exchange and Transfer of Information on Community Water Supply and Sanitation [*International Reference Center for Community Water Supply and Sanitation*] [*Information service or system*] (IID)
Poet Rom Vet ... Poetarum Romanorum Veterum Reliquiae [*A publication*] (OCD)
Poetry Aust ... Poetry Australia [*A publication*]
Poetry Mag ... Poetry Magazine [*A publication*] (APTA)
Poetry NW ... Poetry Northwest [*A publication*]
Poetry R..... Poetry Review [*London*] [*A publication*]
Poetry Wale ... Poetry Wales [*A publication*]
POETS ...... Phooey on Everything, Tomorrow's Saturday [*Bowdlerized version*]
Poets .... Poets in the South [*A publication*]
POETS ...... Push Off Early, Tomorrow's Saturday [*Bowdlerized version*]
PoetW .... Poetry Wales [*A publication*]
POEU .... Post Office Engineering Union [*British*]
Poeyana Inst Biol La Habana Ser A ... Poeyana Instituto de Biologia. La Habana. Serie A [*A publication*]
Poeyana Inst Biol La Habana Ser B ... Poeyana Instituto de Biologia. La Habana. Serie B [*A publication*]
Poeyana Inst Zool Acad Cienc Cuba ... Poeyana Instituto de Zoologia. Academia de Ciencias de Cuba [*A publication*]
POF .... American Jurisprudence Proof of Facts [*A publication*]
POF .... Pillar of Fire Church (IIA)
POF .... Pinhole Occulter Facility (SSD)
POF .... Planned Outage Factor [*Electronics*] (IEEE)
POF .... Point-of-Failure [*Data processing*] (IBMDP)
POF .... Police Officer, Female
POF .... Poplar Bluff [*Missouri*] [*Airport symbol*] (OAG)
POF .... Poplar Bluff, MO [*Location identifier*] [*FAA*] (FAAL)
POF .... Positive Opening Fin (MCD)
POF .... Postovulatory Follicle [*Endocrinology*]
POF .... Prilozi za Orijentalnu Filologiju [*A publication*]
POF .... Priority of Fire [*Military*] (INF)
POF .... Privately Owned Firearm (MCD)
POF .... Prolific Resources [*Vancouver Stock Exchange symbol*]
POF .... Pyruvate Oxidation Factor [*Biochemistry*]
POFA........ Programmed Operational Functional Appraisal [*Navy*]
POFI.......... Pacific Oceanic Fisheries Investigations (NOAA)
pofj--- .... Fiji [*MARC geographic area code*] [*Library of Congress*] (LCCP)
POFO .... Po Folks, Inc. [*NASDAQ symbol*] (NQ)
POFOOGUSA ... Protection of Foreign Officials and Official Guests of the United States Act
pofp .... French Polynesia [*MARC geographic area code*] [*Library of Congress*] (LCCP)
PO-FY .... Program Objectives for Fiscal Year (DNAB)
POG.......... Official Gazette. United States Patent Office [*A publication*]
POG........... Parents of Gays (EA)
POG........... Petty Officer's Guide [*A publication*] [*Navy*]
POG........... Piping Instrumentation and Operating Gallery [*Nuclear energy*] (NRCH)
POG........... Plant Operating Guide (DNAB)
Pog .... Pogledi [*A publication*]
POG........... Port Gentil [*Gabon*] [*Airport symbol*] (OAG)
POG........... Position of Germany [*British*] [*World War II*]
POG........... Post Office Guide [*Book of regulations*] [*British*]
POG........... Project Officer's Group
POG........... Propulsion Operating Guide (DNAB)
POG........... Provisional Ordnance Group [*Military*]
POG........... Tableware International [*A publication*]
POGASIS ... Planetary Observation Geometry and Science Instrument Sequence Program [*Aerospace*]
POGaz .... Post Office Gazette [*British*] [*A publication*] (DCTA)
POGCA ...... Progress in Organic Coatings [*A publication*]
POGE .... Planning Operational Gaming Experiment [*Game*]
POGE .... Polar Geography and Geology [*A publication*]
pogg---........ Galapagos Islands [*MARC geographic area code*] [*Library of Congress*] (LCCP)
Poggendorffs Ann ... Poggendorffs Annalen [*A publication*]
pogn---........ Gilbert and Ellice Islands [*Tuvalu*] [*MARC geographic area code*] [*Library of Congress*] (LCCP)

POGO........ Personal Objectives and Goals (MCD)
Pogo .... Pogonomyrinex Occidentalis [*A genus of ants*]
POGO........ Polar Orbiting Geophysical Observatory [*NASA*]
POGO........ Privately Owned/Government Operated (GFGA)
POGO........ Programmer-Oriented Graphics Operation (IEEE)
PogoPd....... Pogo Producing Co. [*Associated Press abbreviation*] (APAG)
POGR........ Poplar Grove National Cemetery
POGS .... National Association of Post Office and General Service Maintenance Employees [*Later, APWU*] [*AFL-CIO*]
POGSI....... Policy Group on Scientific Information [*Marine science*] (MSC)
POGT .... Power-Operated Gun Turret
pogu---........ Guam [*MARC geographic area code*] [*Library of Congress*] (LCCP)
pOH........... Hydroxyl Concentration [*Organic chemistry*] (MAE)
POH........... Placed off Hire
POH........... Planned Outage Hours [*Electronics*] (IEEE)
POH........... Pocahontas, IA [*Location identifier*] [*FAA*] (FAAL)
POH........... Pull-Out Harness
POHC........ Principal Organic Hazardous Constituent [*Environmental chemistry*]
POHI........ Physically or Otherwise Health Impaired
POHM....... Page-Oriented Holograph Memory [*Data processing*]
POHMA.... Project for the Oral History of Music in America
POHR........ Ohio Review [*A publication*]
POHS........ Presumed Ocular Histoplasmosis Syndrome [*Ophthalmology*]
POHWARO ... Pulsated, Overheated, Water Rocket [*Swiss space rocket*]
POHY........ Oral History Review [*A publication*]
POI .... Parking Orbit Injection [*NASA*]
POI .... Parti Oubanguien de l'Independance [*Ubangi Independence Party*] [*Political party*]
POI .... Period of Interest (MCD)
POI .... Personal Orientation Inventory [*Psychology*]
POI .... Personal Outlook Inventory [*Employment test*]
POI .... Plan of Instruction
POI .... Point of Impact
POI .... Point of Interface [*Telecommunications*]
POI .... Poison
POI .... Politique Etrangere [*A publication*]
POI .... Pre-Overhaul Inspection (MCD)
POI .... Pressure-Operated Initiator (MCD)
POI .... Product of Inertia (MCD)
POI .... Program of Instruction
POI .... Public Office of Information (MCD)
POI .... Purchase Order Item (KSC)
POIC........ Petty Officer in Charge [*Navy*] (NVT)
POIC........ Poly(octyl Isocyanate) [*Organic chemistry*]
POID .... Post Office Investigation/Intelligence Department [*British*] (DI)
POIF.......... Plan Organization Index File [*IRS*]
poik.......... Poikilocyte [*or Poikilocytosis*] [*Medicine*] (MAE)
Poimennye Pochvy Russ Ravniny ... Poimennye Pochvy Russkoi Ravniny [*A publication*]
POINT....... Pasadena Online Information Network [*Pasadena Public Library*] (OLDSS)
POINT....... Pursuing Our Italian Names Together (EA)
POINTER ... Particle Orientation Interferometer [*ASD*]
POINTERM ... Appointment Will Be Regarded as Having Terminated upon This Date
POINTMAIL ... Letter Appointment in Mail
Point Point Commun ... Point-to-Point Communication [*Later, Communication and Broadcasting*] [*A publication*]
Point Point Telecommun ... Point-to-Point Telecommunications [*A publication*]
Points Appui Econ Rhone-Alpes ... Points d'Appui pour l'Economie Rhone-Alpes [*A publication*]
Point Vet .... Point Veterinaire [*A publication*]
POIP.......... Potential Offender Identification Program
POIPCD .... Patent Office and Industrial Property and Copyright Department [*British*]
POIQT....... Performance-Oriented Infantry Qualification Test (INF)
POIR.......... Project Officers Interim Report [*Air Force*] (MCD)
POIS........ Poison (AAMN)
POIS........ Poisoning [*FBI standardized term*]
POIS.......... Post Office Insurance Society [*British*] (DI)
POIS.......... Procurement Operations Information System (MCD)
POIS.......... Prototype On-Line Instrument System [*Data processing*] (NRCH)
POIS.......... Purchase Order Information System (MCD)
POISE .... Panel on Inflight Scientific Experiments [*NASA*]
POISE .... Photosynthetic Oxygenation Illuminated by Solar Energy
POISE .... Pointing and Stabilization Platform Element [*Army*] (MCD)
POIT.......... Power of Influence Test [*Psychology*]
POJ............ Patent Office Journal [*India*] [*A publication*] (DLA)
POJ............ Selma, AL [*Location identifier*] [*FAA*] (FAAL)
poji--- .... Johnston Atoll [*MARC geographic area code*] [*Library of Congress*] (LCCP)
POK .... Sacramento, CA [*Location identifier*] [*FAA*] (FAAL)
poki--- .... Kermadec Islands [*MARC geographic area code*] [*Library of Congress*] (LCCP)
POKMV .... Pokeweed Mosaic Virus [*Plant pathology*]

Pokroky Mat Fyz Astron ... Pokroky Matematiky, Fyziky, a Astronomie [*A publication*]
Pokroky Praskove Metal ... Pokroky Praskove Metalurgie [*A publication*]
Pokroky Praskove Metal VUPM ... Pokroky Praskove Metalurgie VUPM [*Vyzkumny Ustav pro Praskovou Metalurgii*] [*A publication*]
Pokroky Vinohrad Vina- Vysk ... Pokroky vo Vinohradnickom a Vinarskom Vyskume [*A publication*]
Pol............. FS. Political Risk Letter [*A publication*]
POL .... Pacific Oceanographic Laboratories [*Later, Pacific Marine Environmental Laboratory*]
POL .... Pair Orthogonalized Lowdin [*Physics*]
POL .... Parents of Large Families
POL .... Paul Otchakovsky-Laurens [*Publishing imprint, named for imprint editor*]
POL .... Pemba [*Mozambique*] [*Airport symbol*] (OAG)
POL .... Petroleum, Oil, and Lubricants [*Military*]
POL .... Physician's Office laboratory
POL .... Pola [*Yugoslavia*] [*Seismograph station code, US Geological Survey*] [*Closed*] (SEIS)
POL .... Polacca [*Ship's rigging*] (ROG)
POL .... Poland [*ANSI three-letter standard code*] (CNC)
POL .... Polar Airways, Inc. [*Anchorage, AK*] [*FAA designator*] (FAAC)
POL .... Polarity [*or Polarize*] (KSC)
POL .... Police
POL .... Policy
POL .... Polish (AAG)
pol .... Polish [*MARC language code*] [*Library of Congress*] (LCCP)
Pol............. Politica [*of Aristotle*] [*Classical studies*] (OCD)
POL............ Political
POL .... Politician
Pol............. Politics [*A publication*]
Pol............. Pollexfen's English King's Bench Reports [*1669-85*] [*A publication*] (DLA)
POL .... Pollution
POL .... Polonium [*Chemical symbol is Po*] (AAG)
Pol............. Polonystyka [*Warsaw*] [*A publication*]
Pol............. [*Epistle of*] Polycarp (BJA)
Pol............. Polydor & Deutsche Grammophon [*Record label*] [*Germany, Europe, etc.*]
POL .... Polymerase [*An enzyme*]
Pol............. Polyphon [*Record label*] [*Denmark, etc.*]
POL .... Port of Loading [*Shipping*]
POL .... Problem-Oriented Language [*Data processing*]
POL .... Procedure-Oriented Language [*Data processing*]
POL .... Process-Oriented Language [*Data processing*] (IEEE)
POL .... Provisional Operating License [*for nuclear power plant*]
POL .... Public Opinion Laboratory [*Northern Illinois University*] [*Research center*] (RCD)
POLA .... Polaris Resources, Inc. [*NASDAQ symbol*] (NQ)
POLA .... Project on Linguistic Analysis
PolAb........ Pollution Abstracts [*A publication*]
Pol Acad Sci Bull Biol ... Polish Academy of Sciences. Bulletin. Biology [*A publication*]
Pol Acad Sci Bull Chem ... Polish Academy of Sciences. Bulletin. Chemistry [*A publication*]
Pol Acad Sci Bull Earth Sci ... Polish Academy of Sciences. Bulletin. Earth Sciences [*A publication*]
Pol Acad Sci Inst Ecol Rep Sci Act ... Polish Academy of Sciences. Institute of Ecology. Report on Scientific Activities [*A publication*]
Pol Acad Sci Inst Fundam Tech Res Nonlinear Vib Probl ... Polish Academy of Sciences. Institute of Fundamental Technical Research. Nonlinear Vibration Problems [*A publication*]
Pol Acad Sci Inst Fundam Tech Res Proc Vib Probl ... Polish Academy of Sciences. Institute of Fundamental Technical Research. Proceedings of Vibration Problems [*A publication*]
Pol Acad Sci Inst Geophys Publ Ser D ... Polish Academy of Sciences. Institute of Geophysics. Publications. Series D. Atmosphere Physics [*A publication*]
Pol Acad Sci Med Sect Ann ... Polish Academy of Sciences. Medical Section. Annals [*A publication*]
Pol Acad Sci Rev ... Polish Academy of Sciences. Review [*A publication*]
POLAD ...... Political Adviser
Pol Affairs ... Political Affairs [*A publication*]
Pol Akad Nauk Kom Ceram Pr Ser Ceram ... Polska Akademia Nauk. Komisja Ceramiczna. Prace. Serja Ceramika [*A publication*]
Pol Akad Nauk Kom Krystalogr Biul Inf ... Polska Akademia Nauk. Komisja Krystalografii. Biuletyn Informacyjny [*A publication*]
Pol Akad Nauk Rozpr Wydz Nauk Med ... Polska Akademia Nauk. Rozprawy Wydzialu Nauk Medycznych [*A publication*]
Polam LJ ... Polamerican Law Journal [*A publication*] (DLA)
Pol Am Stds ... Polish American Studies [*A publication*]
Poland China ... Poland China World [*A publication*]
Poland Inst Geol Biul ... Poland. Instytut Geologiczny. Biuletyn [*A publication*]
POLANG .. Polarization Angle [*Telecommunications*]
POLAR...... Production Order Location and Reporting [*NASA*] (NASA)
POLAR...... Projected Operational Logistics Analysis Requirements
Polar Biol... Polar Biology [*A publication*]

Pol Arch Hydrobiol ... Polskie Archiwum Hydrobiologii/Polish Archives of Hydrobiology [*A publication*]
Pol Arch Med Wewn ... Polskie Archiwum Medycyny Wewnetrznej [*A publication*]
Pol Arch Wet ... Polskie Archiwum Weterynaryjne [*A publication*]
Pol Arch Weter ... Polskie Archiwum Weterynaryjne [*A publication*]
POLARIS ... Polar-Motion Analysis by Radio Interferometric Surveying [*Geodetic measuring facilities*]
Polarogr Ber ... Polarographische Berichte [*A publication*]
Polaroid ..... Polaroid Corp. [*Associated Press abbreviation*]   (APAG)
Polar Rec ... Polar Record [*A publication*]
Polar Res ... Polar Research [*A publication*]
Pol Bildung ... Politische Bildung [*A publication*]
Pol C .... Political Code [*A publication*]   (DLA)
POLCAP ... Petroleum, Oils, and Lubricants Capabilities   (MCD)
POLCATS ... Pollution Characterization by Absorption on Spectroscopy   (SSD)
POLCOD .. Police Code [*INTERPOL*]
Pol Code ..... Political Code [*A publication*]   (DLA)
Pol Communication and Persuasion ... Political Communication and Persuasion [*A publication*]
Pol Cont ..... Pollock on Contracts [*A publication*]   (DLA)
POLDAM ... POL [*Petroleum, Oil, and Lubricants*] Installations Damage Report   (NATG)
Pol Dig Part ... Pollock's Digest of the Laws of Partnership [*A publication*]   (DLA)
Pol Diritto ... Politica del Diritto [*A publication*]
Pol Dokum ... Politische Dokumentation [*A publication*]
POLDPS ... Pioneer Off-Line Data-Processing System [*NASA*]
POLE .... Point-of-Last-Environment [*Data processing*]   (IBMDP)
POLEA ...... Polski Tygodnik Lekarski [*A publication*]
Pol Ecol Bibliogr ... Polish Ecological Bibliography [*A publication*]
Pol Ecol Stud ... Polish Ecological Studies [*A publication*]
Pol Endocrinol ... Polish Endocrinology [*A publication*]
Pol Endocrinol (Engl Transl Endokrynol Pol) ... Polish Endocrinology (English Translation of Endokrynologia Polska) [*A publication*]
Pol Eng ...... Polish Engineering [*A publication*]
Pol Eng Rev ... Polish Engineering Review [*A publication*]
Pol Etrang ... Politique Etrangere [*Paris*] [*A publication*]
Pol Etrangere ... Politique Etrangere [*A publication*]
POLEX ...... Polar Experiment
POLEX ...... Political Exercise [*International relations game*]
POLEX-NORTH ... Polar Experiment in the Northern Hemisphere   (MSC)
POLEX-SOUTH ... Polar Experiment in the Southern Hemisphere   (MSC)
POLFA ...... Polarforschung [*A publication*]
Pol Fedn Newsl ... Police Federation Newsletter [*A publication*]   (DLA)
POLGEN ... Problem-Oriented Language Generator [*Data processing*]   (BUR)
POLI .... Postal Life [*A publication*]
POLIA .... Polimery [*A publication*]
POLIC .... Petroleum Intersectional Command [*Army*]   (AABC)
Police Fedn Newsl ... Police Federation Newsletter [*A publication*]   (ILCA)
Police J ...... Police Journal [*A publication*]
Police J Ct ... Police Justice's Court [*A publication*]   (ILCA)
Police Lab Rev ... Police Labor Review [*A publication*]
Police LQ ... Police Law Quarterly [*A publication*]   (ILCA)
Police Mag ... Police Magazine [*A publication*]
Police Mag (Syria) ... Police Magazine (Syria) [*A publication*]
Police Res Bull ... Police Research Bulletin [*A publication*]
Police Rev .. Police Review [*A publication*]
Police Sc Abs ... Police Science Abstracts [*A publication*]
Police Sci Abstr ... Police Science Abstracts [*A publication*]
Policlinico Sez Chir ... Policlinico. Sezione Chirurgica [*A publication*]
Policlinico Sez Med ... Policlinico. Sezione Medica [*A publication*]
Policlinico Sez Prat ... Policlinico. Sezione Practica [*A publication*]
Policlin Infant ... Policlinico Infantile [*A publication*]
Policy Anal ... Policy Analysis [*Later, Journal of Policy Analysis and Management*] [*A publication*]
Policy Pol ... Policy and Politics [*A publication*]
Policy Polit ... Policy and Politics [*A publication*]
Policy Publ Rev ... Policy Publication Review [*England*] [*A publication*]
Policy R ...... Policy Review [*A publication*]
Policy Rev .. Policy Review [*A publication*]
Policy Sci ... Policy Sciences [*A publication*]
Policy Statement R Coll Gen Pract ... Policy Statement. Royal College of General Practitioners [*A publication*]
Policy Stud ... Policy Studies [*A publication*]
Policy Studies J ... Policy Studies Journal [*A publication*]
Policy Studies R ... Policy Studies Review [*A publication*]
Policy Stud J ... Policy Studies Journal [*A publication*]
Policy Stud Rev ... Policy Studies Review [*A publication*]
POLID .... Power Line [*A publication*]
Poligr Proizvod ... Poligraficheskoe Proizvodstvo [*A publication*]
Poligr Promst Obz Inf ... Poligraficheskaya Promyshlennost. Obzornaya Informatsiya [*A publication*]
Polim Mashinostr ... Polimery v Mashinostroenii [*Ukrainian SSR*] [*A publication*]
Polim Mater Ikh Issled ... Polimernye Materialy i Ikh Issledovanie [*A publication*]
Polim Med ... Polimery w Medycynie [*A publication*]

Polim Medziagos Ju Tyrimas ... Polimerines Medziagos ir Ju Tyrimas [*A publication*]
Polim Medziagu Panaudojimas Liaudies Ukyje ... Polimeriniu Medziagu Panaudojimas Liaudies Ukyje [*A publication*]
Polim Tworzwa ... Polimery Tworzywa [*Poland*] [*A publication*]
Polim Tworz Wielk ... Polimery-Tworzywa Wielkoczasteczkowe [*Poland*] [*A publication*]
Polim Tworz Wielkoczast ... Polimery-Tworzywa Wielkoczasteczkowe [*A publication*]
Polim Tworzywa Wielkoczasteczkowe ... Polimery Tworzywa Wielkoczasteczkowe [*A publication*]
Polim Vehomarim Plast ... Polimerim Vehomarim Plastiim [*A publication*]
Pol Inst Geol Bibliogr Geol Pol ... Poland. Instytut Geologiczny. Bibliografia Geologiczna Polski [*A publication*]
Pol Internat ... Politique Internationale [*A publication*]
POLIO .... Poliomyelitis [*Medicine*]
Poliplasti Mater Rinf ... Poliplasti e Materiali Rinforzati [*A publication*]
Poliplasti Plast Rinf ... Poliplasti e Plastici Rinforzati [*A publication*]
Poli Q .... Political Quarterly [*A publication*]
POLIS ...... Parliamentary On-Line Information System [*House of Commons Library*] [*Bibliographic database*] [*Information service or system*] [*British*]   (IID)
POLIS ...... Petroleum Intersectional Service [*Army*]
POLIS ...... Political Institutions Simulation [*Game*]
POLISARIO ... [*Frente*] Popular para la Liberacion de Saguia El Hamra y Rio De Oro [*Popular Front for the Liberation of Saguia El Hamra and Rio De Oro*] [*Morocco*]
Poli Sci ...... Political Science [*A publication*]
Poli Sci Q ... Political Science Quarterly [*A publication*]
Polish Acad Sci Fluid Flow ... Polish Academy of Sciences. Transactions. Institute of Fluid Flow Machinery [*Warsaw*] [*A publication*]
Polish Acad Sci Inst Philos Sociol Bull Sect Logic ... Polish Academy of Sciences. Institute of Philosophy and Sociology. Bulletin of the Section of Logic [*A publication*]
Polish Am Stud ... Polish American Studies [*A publication*]
Polish F ...... Polish Film [*A publication*]
Polish J Chem ... Polish Journal of Chemistry [*A publication*]
Polish J Pharmacol Pharmacy ... Polish Journal of Pharmacology and Pharmacy [*A publication*]
Polish Mus ... Polish Music [*A publication*]
Polish Perspect ... Polish Perspectives [*A publication*]
Polish R ...... Polish Review [*A publication*]
Polish Sociol B ... Polish Sociological Bulletin [*A publication*]
Polish Tech & Econ Abstr ... Polish Technical and Economic Abstracts [*A publication*]
Poli Societ ... Politics and Society [*A publication*]
POLIT .... Political   (EY)
Polit .... Politics [*A publication*]
Polit Aff ..... Political Affairs [*A publication*]
Polit Aujourd ... Politique d'Aujourd'hui [*A publication*]
Polit Belge ... Politique Belge [*A publication*]
POLITBUREAU ... Political Bureau [*of USSR*]
POLITBURO ... Politicheskoe Byuro [*Political Bureau of USSR*]
Polit Dir ..... Politica del Diritto [*A publication*]
Politech Rzeszowska Im Ignacego Lukasiewicza Rozpr ... Politechnika Rzeszowska Imienia Ignacego Lukasiewicza. Rozprawy [*A publication*]
Polit Eco ..... Review of Radical Political Economics [*A publication*]
Polit Econ .. Politica ed Economia [*A publication*]
Polit Ekon ... Politicka Ekonomie [*A publication*]
Polit Etr ..... Politique Etrangere [*A publication*]
Polit Foisk Kozlem ... Politikai Foiskola Kozlemenyei [*A publication*]
Polit Gazdasag Tanulmany ... Politikai Gazdasagtan Tanulmanyok [*A publication*]
Politic St .... Political Studies - London [*A publication*]
Polit Int (Roma) ... Politica Internazionale (Roma) [*A publication*]
Polit Meinung ... Politische Meinung [*A publication*]
Polit Methodol ... Political Methodology [*A publication*]
Polit Perspect ... Politiek Perspectief [*A publication*]
Polit Q .... Political Quarterly [*A publication*]
Polit Quart ... Political Quarterly [*A publication*]
Polit Rdsch ... Politische Rundschau [*A publication*]
Polit Sci ...... Political Science [*A publication*]
Polit Sci Ann ... Political Science Annual [*A publication*]
Polit Scientist ... Political Scientist [*A publication*]
Polit Sci Q ... Political Science Quarterly [*A publication*]
Polit Sci R ... Political Science Review [*A publication*]
Polit Sci R'er ... Political Science Reviewer [*A publication*]
Polit Sci (Wellington) ... Political Science (Wellington) [*A publication*]
Polit and Soc ... Politics and Society [*A publication*]
Polit Soc Econ Rev ... Political, Social, Economic Review [*A publication*]
Polit Spolecz ... Polityka Spoleczna [*A publication*]
Polit Stud ... Politische Studien [*Muenchen*] [*A publication*]
Polit Theor ... Political Theory [*A publication*]
Polit Today ... Politics Today [*A publication*]
Polit Vjschr ... Politische Vierteljahresschrift [*A publication*]
Polit Vjschr Sonderh ... Politische Vierteljahresschrift. Sonderheft [*A publication*]
Polit u Zeitgesch ... Politik und Zeitgeschichte [*A publication*]
Pol J .... Police Journal [*A publication*]   (ILCA)

Pol J Anim Sci Technol ... Polish Journal of Animal Science and Technology [*A publication*]
Pol J Chem ... Polish Journal of Chemistry [*A publication*]
Pol J Ecol... Polish Journal of Ecology [*A publication*]
Pol J Med Pharm ... Polish Journal of Medicine and Pharmacy [*A publication*]
Poljopriv Pregl ... Poljoprivredni Pregled [*A publication*]
Poljopriv Sumar ... Poljoprivredna i Sumarstvo [*A publication*]
Poljopriv Znan Smotra ... Poljoprivredna Znanstvena Smotra [*A publication*]
Poljopr Sumar ... Poljoprivredna i Sumarstvo [*A publication*]
Poljopr Znan Smotra ... Poljoprivredna Znanstvena Smotra [*A publication*]
Poljopr Znanst Smotra ... Poljoprivredna Znanstvena Smotra [*A publication*]
Pol J Phar ... Polish Journal of Pharmacology and Pharmacy [*A publication*]
Pol J Pharmacol Pharm ... Polish Journal of Pharmacology and Pharmacy [*A publication*]
Pol J Soil Sci ... Polish Journal of Soil Science [*A publication*]
POLK........ Polk Audio, Inc. [*Baltimore, MD*] [*NASDAQ symbol*]   (NQ)
POLK of A ... Polka Lovers Klub of America   (EA)
Poll............ Pollack's Ohio Unreported Judicial Decisions Prior to 1823 [*A publication*]   (ILCA)
POLL........ Pollex [*An Inch*] [*Pharmacy*]
Poll............ Pollexfen's English King's Bench Reports [*1669-85*] [*A publication*]   (ILCA)
PolL .... Polonista (Lublin) [*A publication*]
POLL........ Public Opinion Location Library [*The Roper Center for Public Opinion Research*] [*Information service or system*]   (CRD)
Poll Abstr... Pollution Abstracts [*A publication*]
Pollack Mihaly Muesz Foeisk Tud Koezl ... Pollack Mihaly Mueszaki Foeiskola Tudomanyos Koezlemenyei [*A publication*]
Pol Law of Nat ... Polson's Law of Nations [*1848*] [*A publication*]   (DLA)
Poll CC Pr ... Pollock's Practice of the County Courts [*A publication*]   (ILCA)
Poll Contr Guide ... Pollution Control Guide [*A publication*]   (DLA)
POLLD...... Pollimo [*A publication*]
Pollen Grain US For Serv Southeast Area ... Pollen Grain. United States Forest Service. Southeastern Area [*A publication*]
Pollex .... Pollexfen's English King's Bench Reports [*1669-85*] [*A publication*]   (ILCA)
Pollexf........ Pollexfen's English King's Bench Reports [*1669-85*] [*A publication*]   (ILCA)
Pollexfen.... Pollexfen's English King's Bench Reports [*1669-85*] [*A publication*]   (ILCA)
Pollock & Maitl ... Pollock and Maitland's History of English Common Law [*A publication*]   (DLA)
Poll Prod .... Pollock on the Production of Documents [*A publication*]   (DLA)
Pol LQ .... Police Law Quarterly [*A publication*]   (DLA)
POLLS ...... Parliamentary On-Line Library Study [*Atomic Energy Authority*] [*British*]
POLLUT ... Pollution
Pollut Abstr ... Pollution Abstracts [*A publication*]
Pollut Abstr Indexes ... Pollution Abstracts with Indexes [*A publication*]
Pollut Atmos ... Pollution Atmospherique [*A publication*]
Pollut Control ... Pollution Control [*Japan*] [*A publication*]
Pollut Control Mar Ind Proc Annu Int Conf ... Pollution Control in the Marine Industries. Proceedings. Annual International Conference [*A publication*]
Pollut Eng.. Pollution Engineering [*A publication*]
Pollut Eng Technol ... Pollution Engineering and Technology [*A publication*]
Pollution .... Pollution Equipment News [*A publication*]
Pollution Cont Guide (CCH) ... Pollution Control Guide (Commerce Clearing House) [*A publication*]   (DLA)
Pollut Monitor ... Pollution Monitor [*A publication*]
Pollut Tech ... Pollution Technology [*A publication*]
POLLY ...... [*A*] Programming Language [*1973*]   (CSR)
Pol Mach Ind ... Polish Machine Industry [*A publication*]
Pol Mach Ind Offers ... Polish Machine Industry Offers [*A publication*]
Pol Med J .. Polish Medical Journal [*A publication*]
Pol Med J (Engl Transl Pol Arch Med Wewn) ... Polish Medical Journal (English Translation of Polskie Archiwum Medycyny Wewnetrznej) [*A publication*]
Pol Med Sci Hist Bull ... Polish Medical Science and History Bulletin [*A publication*]
Pol Meinung ... Politische Meinung [*A publication*]
Pol Methodol ... Political Methodology [*A publication*]
Pol Mil Dig ... Poland's Digest of the Military Laws of the United States [*A publication*]   (DLA)
poln--- .... Central and Southern Line Islands [*MARC geographic area code*] [*Library of Congress*]   (LCCP)
POLNA ..... Polnohospodarstvo [*A publication*]
Polnohospod ... Polnohospodarstvo [*A publication*]
POLO .... Pacific Command Operations Liaison Office [*Army*]   (AABC)
POLO .... Plant and Office Layout   (MCD)
POLO .... Polar Orbiting Lunar Observatory [*Satellite*]
POLO .... Polaris Oil & Gas [*NASDAQ symbol*]   (NQ)
POLO .... Procurement Online Ordering System   (MCD)
Pologne Aff Occid ... Pologne et les Affaires Occidentales [*A publication*]
Pologne Contemp ... Pologne Contemporaine [*A publication*]
POLOPS ... Polynomial Operations [*Air Force*]
PolP .... Polish Perspectives [*A publication*]
Pol Pap Ser ... Policy Papers Series [*A publication*]

Pol Part...... Pollock's Digest of the Laws of Partnership [*A publication*]   (DLA)
Pol Perspect ... Polish Perspectives [*A publication*]
Pol Pismo Entomol ... Polskie Pismo Entomologiczne [*A publication*]
Pol Pismo Entomol Ser B Entomol Stosow ... Polskie Pismo Entomologiczne. Seria B. Entomologia Stosowana [*A publication*]
Pol and Polit ... Policy and Politics [*A publication*]
Pol Prod Doc ... Pollock on the Power of Courts to Compel the Production of Documents [*A publication*]   (DLA)
Pol Przegl Chir ... Polski Przeglad Chirurgiczny [*A publication*]
Pol Przegl Radiol ... Polski Przeglad Radiologii i Medycyny Nuklearnej [*A publication*]
Pol Przegl Radiol Med Nukl ... Polski Przeglad Radiologii i Medycyny Nuklearnej [*A publication*]
Pol Psych B ... Polish Psychological Bulletin [*A publication*]
Pol Q .... Political Quarterly [*A publication*]
Pol Quar..... Political Quarterly [*A publication*]
Pol R .... Policy Review [*A publication*]
PolR .... Polish Review [*New York*] [*A publication*]
POLR......... Polymeric Resources Corp. [*NASDAQ symbol*]   (NQ)
POLRA...... Polar Record [*A publication*]
Pol Rev Radiol Nucl Med ... Polish Review of Radiology and Nuclear Medicine [*A publication*]
POLRIN.... Polaris Industries Ltd. [*Associated Press abbreviation*]   (APAG)
Pol Sci........ Policy Sciences [*A publication*]
Pol Sci........ Political Science [*A publication*]
Pol Science Q ... Political Science Quarterly [*A publication*]
Pol Sci Q .... Political Science Quarterly [*A publication*]
Pol Sci Quar ... Political Science Quarterly [*A publication*]   (ILCA)
Pol Sci R .... Political Science Review [*Jaipur*] [*A publication*]
Polska Akad Nauk Met ... Polska Akademia Nauk. Metalurgia [*A publication*]
Polska Biblio Analit Mech ... Polska Bibliografia Analityczna. Mechanika [*A publication*]
Polska Gaz Lekar ... Polska Gazeta Lekarska [*A publication*]
Polskie Arch Med Wewnetrznej ... Polskie Archiwum Medycyny Wewnetrznej [*A publication*]
Polskie Archwm Wet ... Polskie Archiwum Weterynaryjne [*A publication*]
Polskie Pismo Entomol ... Polskie Pismo Entomologiczne [*A publication*]
Polskie Pismo Entomol Ser B Entomol Stosow ... Polskie Pismo Entomologiczne. Seria B. Entomologia Stosowana [*A publication*]
Polskie Tow Ent Klucze Oznaczania Owadow Pol ... Polskie Towarzystwo Entomologiczne. Klucze do Oznaczania Owadow Polski [*A publication*]
Polski Tygod Lek ... Polski Tygodnik Lekarski [*A publication*]
Pols Nat ..... Polson's Law of Nations [*1848*] [*A publication*]   (DLA)
Pol Soc .... Politics and Society [*A publication*]
Pol Soc B.... Polish Sociological Bulletin [*A publication*]
Pol Stud ..... Political Studies [*A publication*]
Pol Studien ... Politische Studien [*Muenchen*] [*A publication*]
Pol Studies ... Political Studies [*A publication*]
Pol Stud J ... Policy Studies Journal [*A publication*]
Pol Szt Lud ... Polska Sztuka Ludowa [*A publication*]
Pol Tech Abstr ... Polish Technical Abstracts [*A publication*]
Pol Tech Econ Abstr ... Polish Technical and Economic Abstracts [*A publication*]
Pol Technol News ... Polish Technological News [*A publication*]
Pol Tech Rev ... Polish Technical Review [*A publication*]
Pol Theory ... Political Theory [*A publication*]
POLTHN... Polyethylene [*Organic chemistry*]
POLTL...... Political   (AFM)
Pol Today... Politics Today [*A publication*]
Pol Tow Entomol Klucze Oznaczania Owadow Pol ... Polskie Towarzystwo Entomologiczne. Klucze do Oznaczania Owadow Polski [*A publication*]
Pol Tow Geol Rocz ... Polskie Towarzystwo Geologiczne. Rocznik [*A publication*]
Pol Trasporti ... Politica dei Trasporti [*A publication*]
Pol Tr Mar ... Poland's Law of Trade Marks [*A publication*]   (DLA)
Pol Tyg Lek ... Polski Tygodnik Lekarski [*A publication*]
Pol Tyg Lek Wiad Lek ... Polski Tygodnik Lekarski i Wiadomosci Lekarskie [*A publication*]
Poluch Strukt Svoistva Sorbentov ... Poluchenie, Struktura, i Svoistva Sorbentov [*A publication*]
Poluch Svoistva Tonkikh Plenok ... Poluchenie i Svoistva Tonkikh Plenok [*Ukrainian SSR*] [*A publication*]
Poluprovdn Prib Tekh Elektrosvyazi ... Poluprovodnikovye Pribory v Tekhnike Elektrosvyazi [*A publication*]
Poluprovodn Elektron ... Poluprovodnikovaya Elektronika [*A publication*]
Poluprovodn Ikh Primen Elektrotekh ... Poluprovodniki i Ikh Primenenie v Elektrotekhnike [*A publication*]
Poluprovodn Prib Ikh Primen ... Poluprovodnikovye Pribory i Ikh Primenenie [*A publication*]
Poluprovodn Prib Primen ... Poluprovodnikovye Pribory i Ikh Primenenie [*A publication*]
Poluprovodn Tekh i Mikroelektron ... Poluprovodnikovaya Tekhnika i Mikroelektronika [*A publication*]
Poluprov Tekh Mikroelektron ... Poluprovodnikovaya Tekhnika i Mikroelektronika [*Ukrainian SSR*] [*A publication*]
POLUT...... Pollution

Pol Vjschr .. Politische Vierteljahresschrift [*A publication*]
Pol VO ...... Polizeiverordnung [*A publication*]
POLWAR ... Political Warfare
POLWARADDIR ... Political Warfare Advisory Directorate
POLX .... Polydex Pharmaceuticals Ltd. [*NASDAQ symbol*]   (NQ)
Pol'y .... Policy   (DLA)
POLY .... Poly-Tech, Inc. [*NASDAQ symbol*]   (NQ)
POLY .... Polyester
POLY .... Polyethylene   (DEN)
POLY .... Polygamy [*FBI standardized term*]
POLY .... Polymorphonuclear Leukocyte [*Hematology*]
POLY .... Polytechnic
PolyA .... Polyadenylated
poly(A) .... Polyadenylic Acid [*Biochemistry*]   (MAE)
POLY-AE/AM Rep (Polytech Inst NY Dep Aerosp Eng Appl Mech) ...
          POLY-AE/AM Report (Polytechnic Institute of New York.
          Department of Aerospace Engineering and Applied
          Mechanics) [*A publication*]
Polyarn Siyaniya Svechenie Nochnogo Neba ... Polyarnye Siyaniya i Svechenie
          Nochnogo Neba [*A publication*]
Polyar Siyaniya ... Polyarnye Siyaniya [*Former USSR*] [*A publication*]
Polyb .... Polybius [*Second century BC*] [*Classical studies*]   (OCD)
Pol Yb of Internat L ... Polish Yearbook of International Law [*Warsaw*] [*A
          publication*]   (DLA)
Pol YB Int'l L ... Polish Yearbook of International Law [*Warsaw*] [*A
          publication*]   (DLA)
Polyc .... [*Epistle of*] Polycarp   (BJA)
POLYDOP ... Polystation Doppler Tracking System   (MCD)
POLYEST ... Polyester
Polygr .... PolyGram NV [*Associated Press abbreviation*]   (APAG)
Poly L Rev ... Poly Law Review [*A publication*]
Polym .... Polymusic [*Record label*]
Polym Age ... Polymer Age [*A publication*]
Polym Appl ... Polymer Application [*Japan*] [*A publication*]
POLYMAT ... Polymer Materials [*Deutsches Kunststoff-Institut*] [*Germany*]
          [*Information service or system*]   (CRD)
Polym Biol Med ... Polymers in Biology and Medicine [*A publication*]
Polym Bull ... Polymer Bulletin [*A publication*]
Polym Bull (Berlin) ... Polymer Bulletin (Berlin) [*A publication*]
Polym Commun ... Polymer Communications [*A publication*]
Polym Compos ... Polymer Composites [*A publication*]
Polym Composites ... Polymer Composites [*A publication*]
Polym Degradat Stabil ... Polymer Degradation and Stability [*A publication*]
Polym Eng Curric Proc Buhl Int Conf Mater ... Polymers in the Engineering
          Curriculum. Proceedings. Buhl International Conference on
          Materials [*A publication*]
Polym Engng News ... Polymer Engineering News [*A publication*]
Polym Engng Rev ... Polymer Engineering Reviews [*A publication*]
Polym Engng Sci ... Polymer Engineering and Science [*A publication*]
Polym Eng S ... Polymer Engineering and Science [*A publication*]
Polym Eng Sci ... Polymer Engineering and Science [*A publication*]
Polymer Engng Science ... Polymer Engineering and Science [*A publication*]
Polymer J ... Polymer Journal [*A publication*]
Polym J ...... Polymer Journal [*A publication*]
Polym J (Jap) ... Polymer Journal (Japan) [*A publication*]
Polym Mech ... Polymer Mechanics [*A publication*]
Polym Mech (Engl Transl) ... Polymer Mechanics (English Translation) [*A
          publication*]
Polym Monogr ... Polymer Monographs [*A publication*]
Polym News ... Polymer News [*A publication*]
POLYMODE ... Polygon-MODE [*Mid-Ocean Dynamics Experiment*]
          [*Soviet-US cooperative undersea weather exploration*]
Polym Paint Col J ... Polymers, Paint, and Colour Journal [*A publication*]
Polym Paint Colour J ... Polymers, Paint, and Colour Journal [*A publication*]
Polym Photochem ... Polymer Photochemistry [*A publication*]
Polym-Plast ... Polymer-Plastics Technology and Engineering [*A publication*]
Polym Plast Mater ... Polymers and Plastic Materials [*A publication*]
Polym-Plast Technol Eng ... Polymer-Plastics Technology and Engineering [*A
          publication*]
Polym Prepr Am Chem Soc Div Polym Chem ... Polymer Preprints. American
          Chemical Society. Division of Polymer Chemistry [*A
          publication*]
Polym Preprints ... Polymer Preprints [*A publication*]
Polym Rep ... Polymer Report [*A publication*]
Polym Rev ... Polymer Reviews [*A publication*]
Polym Sci Technol ... Polymer Science and Technology [*American Chemical
          Society*] [*Information service or system*] [*A publication*]
Polym Sci USSR ... Polymer Science. USSR [*English Translation of
          Vysokomolekulyarnye Soyedineniya. Series A*] [*A
          publication*]
Polym Solution ... Polymers in Solution [*Monograph*] [*A publication*]
Polym Test ... Polymer Testing [*A publication*]
Polym Theor Abst ... Polymer Theory Abstracts [*A publication*]
POLYN ..... Polynesia
Polyn Soc J ... Polynesian Society Journal [*A publication*]
POLYOX... Poly(ethylene Oxide) [*Trademark*]
POLYPH... Polyphase Instrument Corp. [*Associated Press
          abbreviation*]   (APAG)
Polysaccharides Biol Trans Conf ... Polysaccharides in Biology. Transactions
          of the Conference [*A publication*]
Polysar Prog ... Polysar Progress [*A publication*]

Polyscope Autom und Elektron ... Polyscope. Automatik und Elektronik [*A
          publication*]
Polyscope Comput und Elektron ... Polyscope. Computer und Elektronik [*A
          publication*]
Polytech Inst Brooklyn Microwave Res Inst Symp Ser ... Polytechnic Institute
          of Brooklyn. Microwave Research Institute. Symposia
          Series [*A publication*]
Polytech J ... Polytechnisches Journal [*A publication*]
Polytech Tijdschr Ed A ... Polytechnisch Tijdschrift. Editie A.
          Werktuigbouwkunde en Elektrotechniek [*A publication*]
Polytech Tijdschr Ed B ... Polytechnisch Tijdschrift. Editie B [*A publication*]
Polytech Tijdschr Elektrotech Elektron ... Polytechnisch Tijdschrift.
          Elektrotechniek. Elektronica [*A publication*]
Polytech Tijdschr Procestech ... Polytechnisch Tijdschrift. Procestechniek [*A
          publication*]
Polytech Tijdschr Werktuigbouw ... Polytechnisch Tijdschrift. Werktuigbouw
          [*A publication*]
Polytech Weekbl ... Polytechnisch Weekblad [*A publication*]
Polytek Revy ... Polyteknisk Revy [*Norway*] [*A publication*]
POLYTRAN ... Polytranslation Analysis and Programming   (IEEE)
Polyt Rv ..... Polytechnic Review [*A publication*]
poly(U) .... Polyuridylic Acid [*Biochemistry*]   (MAE)
POLY-WRI ... Polytechnic Institute of New York Weber Research Institute
          [*Farmingdale, NY*]
POM .... Operation: Peace of Mind [*Later, Runaway Hotline*] [*An
          association*]   (EA)
PoM .... Palace of Minos [*A publication*]
POM .... Pallet-Only Mode [*NASA*]   (NASA)
POM .... Particulate Organic Matter [*Environmental chemistry*]
POM .... Peritronics Med [*Vancouver Stock Exchange symbol*]
POM .... Personal Opinion Message [*Western Union*]   (IIA)
POM .... Personnel, Operations, Maintenance   (MCD)
POM .... Phenomenon of Man [*Project*]   (EA)
POM .... Police Officer, Male
POM .... Polycyclic Organic Matter
POM .... Poly(oxymethylene) [*Organic chemistry*]
POM .... Pomeranian Dog   (DSUE)
POM .... Pomona [*California*] [*Seismograph station code, US Geological
          Survey*] [*Closed*]   (SEIS)
POM .... Pomona, CA [*Location identifier*] [*FAA*]   (FAAL)
Pom .... Pompon [*Horticulture*]
Pom .... [*Sextus*] Pomponius [*Flourished, 2nd century*] [*Authority cited
          in pre-1607 legal work*]   (DSA)
POM .... Pool Operational Module [*Telecommunications*]   (TEL)
POM .... Port Moresby [*Papua New Guinea*] [*Airport symbol*]   (OAG)
POM .... Position Modulator   (NRCH)
POM .... Potential Officer Material [*British military*]   (DMA)
POM .... Potomac Electric Power Co. [*NYSE symbol*]   (SPSG)
POM .... Preparation for Overseas Movement [*Military*]
POM .... Prescription Only Medicine [*British*]
POM .... Printer Output Microfilm
POM .... Prior to Overseas Movement [*DoD*]
POM .... Priority of Movements [*Military*] [*British*]
POM .... Professional or Managerial   (WDMC)
POM .... Program Objectives Memorandum [*Military*]
POM .... Program Operation Mode
POM .... Project Office Memo
POM .... Project Officers Meeting
POMA .... Petty Officer Medical Assistant [*British military*]   (DMA)
POMA .... Petty Officer's Military Academy [*Navy*]
POMAR .... Position Operational, Meteorological Aircraft Report
POMAR .... Preventive Operational Maintenance and Repair
          [*Military*]   (NVT)
POMAS ..... Procurement Office for Military Automotive Supplies
POMBA .... Parents of Multiple Births Associations of Canada
POM/BES ... Program Objective Memorandum/Budget Estimate
          Submission   (MCD)
POMC .... Parents of Murdered Children   (EA)
POMC .... Pro-Opiomelanocortin [*Endocrinology*]
Pom Code Rem ... Pomeroy on Code Remedies [*A publication*]   (DLA)
Pom Const Law ... Pomeroy's Constitutional Law of the United States [*A
          publication*]   (DLA)
Pom Contr ... Pomeroy on Contracts [*A publication*]   (DLA)
POMCUS ... Prepositioning of Materiel Configured to Unit Sets
          [*Army*]   (AABC)
POMDA .... Postgraduate Medicine [*A publication*]
pome--- .... Melanesia [*MARC geographic area code*] [*Library of
          Congress*]   (LCCP)
POME .... Principal Ordnance Mechanical Engineer [*British
          military*]   (DMA)
POME .... Prisoner of Mother England [*Nineteenth-century convict in
          penal colony of Australia; term is said to have been
          shortened eventually to "pom" or "pommie" as a
          nickname for any Australian. A second theory maintains
          that the nickname is short for "pomegranate," a red fruit,
          and refers to the sunburn that fair-skinned Englishmen
          quickly acquire upon arrival in Australia.*]
POME .... Problems-Objectives-Methods-Evaluation [*Planning method*]
POMEM ... Petty Officer Marine Engineering Mechanic [*British
          military*]   (DMA)
Pom Eq Jur ... Pomeroy's Equity Jurisprudence [*A publication*]   (DLA)

Pom Eq Juris ... Pomeroy's Equity Jurisprudence [*A publication*]   (DLA)
POMERID ... Pomeridianus [*In the Afternoon*] [*Pharmacy*]
Pomeroy..... Pomeroy's Reports [*73-128 California*] [*A publication*]   (DLA)
POMF ...... Polaris Missile Facility
POMFE4... Ontario. Ministry of Agriculture and Food. Publication [*A publication*]
POMFLANT ... Polaris Missile Facility, Atlantic Fleet
POMFPAC ... Polaris Missile Facility, Pacific Fleet
POMG....... Omega [*A publication*]
POMGEN ... Program Objective Memorandum Generator [*Military*]
POMH....... National Association of Post Office Mail Handlers, Watchmen, Messengers, and Group Leaders [*Later, NPOMHWMGL*]
POMI .... Preliminary Operating and Maintenance Instructions [*Aerospace*]   (AAG)
Pomiary Autom Kontrola ... Pomiary Automatyka Kontrola [*A publication*]
POMINS.... Portable Mine Neutralization System   (MCD)
POMJA..... Polish Medical Journal [*A publication*]
POMM...... Preliminary Operating and Maintenance Manual [*Military*]   (AABC)
Pomme Terre Fr ... Pomme de Terre Francaise [*A publication*]
Pom Mun Law ... Pomeroy on Municipal Law [*A publication*]   (DLA)
POMNDR ... Museo Nacional de Historia Natural. Publicacion Ocasional [*Santiago, Chile*] [*A publication*]
POMO...... Partially Occupied Molecular Orbitals [*Physical chemistry*]
POMO...... Personnel Objectives Monitoring Operation
POMO...... Production-Oriented Maintenance Organization   (MCD)
POMO...... Program Operations and Management Office [*Environmental Protection Agency*]   (GFGA)
POMOL.... POMCUS [*Prepositioning of Materiel Configured to Unit Sets*] Objective Levels [*Military*]
POMOL .... Pomology
POMOLA ... Poor Man's Optical Landing System
Pomol Fr .... Pomologie Francaise [*A publication*]
Pomol Fruit Grow Soc Annu Rep ... Pomological and Fruit Growing Society. Annual Report [*A publication*]
Pomor Ant ... Pomorania Antiqua [*A publication*]
Pomp......... Epistula ad Pompeium [*of Dionysius Halicarnassensis*] [*Classical studies*]   (OCD)
Pomp......... Pompeius [*of Plutarch*] [*Classical studies*]   (OCD)
Pomp......... [*Sextus*] Pomponius [*Flourished, 2nd century*] [*Authority cited in pre-1607 legal work*]   (DSA)
POMP ...... Pomposo [*Grandly*] [*Music*]   (ROG)
POMP .... Prednisone, Oncovin [*Vincristine*], Methotrexate, Purinethol [*Mercaptopurine*] [*Antineoplastic drug regimen*]
POMP .... Principal Outer Membrane Protein
POMPA .... Publications. Mississippi Philological Association [*A publication*]
Pompebl ..... Pompebledon [*A publication*]
POMR....... Problem-Oriented Medical Record
Pom Rem .... Pomeroy on Civil Remedies [*A publication*]   (DLA)
Pom Rem & Rem Rights ... Pomeroy on Civil Remedies and Remedial Rights [*A publication*]   (DLA)
POMR/PST ... Partido Obrero Marxista Revolucionario/Partido Socialista de los Trabajadores [*Marxist Revolutionary Workers' Party/Socialist Workers' Party*] [*Peru*] [*Political party*]   (PPW)
POMS ...... Panel on Operational Meteorological Satellites
POMS ...... Profile of Mood States [*A questionnaire*]
POMS ...... Program Operations Manual System [*Social Security Administration*]
POMSA..... Post Office Management Staffs Association [*A union*] [*British*]   (DCTA)
POMS-BI.. Profile of Mood States-Bipolar Form
POMSEE .. Performance, Operating and Maintenance Standards for Electronic Equipment   (NG)
POMSIP .... Post Office Management and Service Improvement Program [*Obsolete*]
Pom Spec Perf ... Pomeroy on Specific Performance of Contracts [*A publication*]   (DLA)
POMT .... Planning and Operations Management Team   (MCD)
POMV .... National Federation Post Office Motor Vehicle Employees [*Later, APWU*]   (EA)
POMV .... Privately Owned Motor Vehicle   (NATG)
PON.......... Paraoxonase [*An enzyme*]
PON.......... Particulate Organic Nitrogen
PON.......... Ponce [*Puerto Rico*] [*Seismograph station code, US Geological Survey*]   (SEIS)
PON.......... Ponder Oils Ltd. [*Toronto Stock Exchange symbol*]
Pon .... Ponte [*A publication*]
Pon .... Pontius [*Authority cited in pre-1607 legal work*]   (DSA)
PON.......... Pontoon   (AAG)
PON.......... Pride of Newark [*Feigenspan beer*]
PON.......... Program Opportunity Notice [*Energy Research and Development Administration*]
PON.......... Public Opinion [*A publication*]
PONA........ Paraffins, Olefins, Naphthenes, Aromatics
Pon Ble....... Poncius Blegerii [*Flourished, 14th century*] [*Authority cited in pre-1607 legal work*]   (DSA)
PONBRG .. Pontoon Bridge   (MUGU)
POND........ Parents of Near Drownings [*An association*]   (EA)
POND........ Pondere [*By Weight*] [*Latin*]
POND........ Ponderosus [*Heavy*] [*Pharmacy*]

PONE........ Polar News. Japan Polar Research Association [*A publication*]
ponl--- .... New Caledonia [*MARC geographic area code*] [*Library of Congress*]   (LCCP)
ponn--- .... New Hebrides [*MARC geographic area code*] [*Library of Congress*]   (LCCP)
Po Now...... Poetry Now [*A publication*]
PONS .... Platt's Oilgram News Service
PONS .... Polar Notes [*A publication*]
PONS .... Profile of Nonverbal Sensitivity [*Psychology*]
PONSA ..... Platt's Oilgram News Service [*A publication*]
PONSE...... Personnel of the Naval Shore Establishment [*Report*]   (NG)
PONSI....... Program of Noncollegiate Sponsored Instruction   (OICC)
Pont.......... Epistulae ex Ponto [*of Ovid*] [*Classical studies*]   (OCD)
PONT .... Pontiac [*Automotive engineering*]
PONT .... Pontifex [*Bishop*] [*Latin*]   (WGA)
Pont.......... Pontoon   (WGA)
PONTA ..... Popular New Titles from Abroad [*Book acquisition program for libraries*]
Pontif Acad Sci Acta ... Pontificia Academia Scientiarum. Acta [*A publication*]
Pontif Acad Sci Comment ... Pontificia Academia Scientiarum. Commentarii [*A publication*]
Pontif Acad Sci Scr Varia ... Pontificia Academia Scientiarum. Scripta Varia [*A publication*]
ponu---........ Nauru [*MARC geographic area code*] [*Library of Congress*]   (LCCP)
PONUC..... Post Office National Users' Council [*British*]
PONY........ Pennsylvania, Ohio, New York Baseball League   (IIA)
PONY........ Pride of the Navy Yard   (DNAB)
PONY........ Prostitutes of New York
PONY........ Protect Our Nation's Youth [*Baseball league*] [*Name usually written Pony*]
PONY........ Purpose of Neighborhood Youth [*Foundation*]
PONYA ..... Port of New York Authority [*Later, PANYNJ*]
POO........... Panel on Oceanography
POO........... Payload Operations Office [*NASA*]
POO........... Platform of Opportunity Program [*National Oceanic and Atmospheric Administration*]   (MSC)
POO........... Pocos De Caldas [*Brazil*] [*Airport symbol*]   (OAG)
POO........... Poona [*India*] [*Seismograph station code, US Geological Survey*]   (SEIS)
POO........... Port Operations Officer   (DS)
POO........... Post Office Order
POO........... Priority Operational Objective [*Military*]
POO........... Program Operations Officer [*Social Security Administration*]
POOD........ Permanent Officer of the Day [*or Deck*] [*Navy*]
POOD........ Provisioning Order Obligating Document
POOEL...... Petty Officer Ordnance Electrician [*British military*]   (DMA)
POOFF...... Preservation of Our Femininity and Finances [*Women's group opposing below-the-knee fashions introduced in 1970*]
POOFF...... Professional Oglers of Female Figures [*Men's group opposing below-the-knee fashions introduced in 1970*]
POOL........ Poseidon Pools of America, Inc. [*NASDAQ symbol*]   (NQ)
Pooles Index Period Lit ... Poole's Index to Periodical Literature [*A publication*]
Poona Agr Col Mag ... Poona Agricultural College Magazine [*A publication*]
Poona Agric Coll Mag ... Poona Agricultural College Magazine [*A publication*]
POOP........ Process Oriented Observation Program [*NORPAX*]   (MSC)
POOR........ Prevention of Over-Radiation [*Military*]
Poore Const ... Poore's Federal and State Constitution [*A publication*]   (DLA)
Poor L & Local Gov't ... Poor Law and Local Government Magazine [*A publication*]   (DLA)
POOS .... Priority Order Output System [*Japan*]   (DIT)
POOW........ Petty Officer of the Watch [*Navy*]   (NVT)
POP .... Pacific Ocean Perch
POP .... Panoramic Office Planning
POP .... Parallel Output Platform
POP .... Parents of Punkers   (EA)
POP .... Paroxypropione [*or Paraoxypropiophenone*] [*Endocrinology*]
POP .... Parti Ouvrier et Paysan du Congo [*Congolese Workers' and Peasants' Party*] [*Political party*] [*Zaire*]
POP .... Parti Ouvrier-Progressiste [*Canada*]
POP .... Particulate Organic Phosphorus
POP .... Partido de Orientacion Popular [*Popular Orientation Party*] [*El Salvador*] [*Political party*]   (PPW)
POP .... Patrexes of the Panopticon   (EA)
POP .... Pay One Price
POP .... Payload Optimized Program [*NASA*]   (KSC)
POP .... Peak Overpressure [*Nuclear energy*]   (NRCH)
POP .... Period of Performance   (MCD)
POP .... Perpendicular Ocean Platform [*Oceanography*]
POP .... Perpendicular-to-Orbit Plane [*Aerospace*]   (KSC)
POP .... Persistent Occipit Posterior [*A fetal position*] [*Obstetrics*]
POP .... Pharmacists in Ophthalmic Practice [*Later, PIOP*]   (EA)
POP .... Pipeline Outfit, Petroleum   (MCD)
POP .... Plasma Oncotic Pressure [*Medicine*]   (MAE)
POP .... Plasma Osmotic Pressure [*Medicine*]
POP .... Plaster of Paris
PoP............ Point of Presence [*Telecommunications*]   (PCM)
POP .... Point of Purchase [*Advertising*]

POP .... Polar Orbiting Platform   (SSD)
PoP............. Political Psychology [*A publication*]
POP .... Pollution and Overpopulation
POP .... Pope & Talbot, Inc. [*NYSE symbol*]   (SPSG)
Pop .... Popham's English King's Bench Reports [*1592-1627*] [*A publication*]   (DLA)
POP .... Popliteal [*Artery*] [*Anatomy*]   (AAMN)
POP .... Popondetta [*Papua New Guinea*] [*Seismograph station code, US Geological Survey*] [*Closed*]   (SEIS)
POP .... Popping [*Mining engineering*]
POP .... Popular
Pop .... Populare [*Record label*] [*Romania*]
Pop .... Population [*A publication*]
POP .... Population   (AAG)
POP .... Population Division [*Bureau of the Census*]   (OICC)
POP .... Post Office Plan
POP .... Post Office Preferred   (DCTA)
POP .... Posterior Odds Processing [*Weather forecasting*] [*National Science Foundation*]
POP .... Postoperative [*Medicine*]
POP .... Power On/Off Protection
POP .... Practical Ordered Program   (OA)
POP .... Preburner Oxidizer Pump   (MCD)
POP .... Preflight Operations Procedure   (MCD)
POP .... Prelaunch Operations Plan [*NASA*]   (NASA)
POP .... Premanagement Orientation Program [*LIMRA*]
POP .... Pressurizer Overpressure Protection System [*Nuclear energy*]   (IEEE)
POP .... Primary Operation
pop .... Printer of Plates [*MARC relator code*] [*Library of Congress*]   (LCCP)
POP .... Printing-Out Paper
POP .... Profit Option Plan [*Retailing*]
POP .... Program Obligation Plan   (KSC)
POP .... Program Operating Plan
POP .... Programmed Operators and Primitives [*Data processing*]
POP .... Progressive Overload Program [*Weight training*]
POP .... Project Objective Plan   (NG)
POP .... Prompt Ordering Plan
POP .... Proof-Of Principle [*Test*]
POP .... Proof of Purchase
POP .... Puerto Plata [*Dominican Republic*] [*Airport symbol*]   (OAG)
POP .... Pump Optimizing Program
POP .... Purchase Outside Production   (SAA)
POPA .... Patent Office Professional Association   (EA)
POPA .... Payload Ordnance Processing Area   (NASA)
POPA .... Pet Owners' Protective Association
POPA .... Prevention of Oil Pollution Act [*1971*]
POPA .... Property Owners' Protection Association
POPAE...... Protons on Protons and Electrons [*Physics*]
POPAI....... Point-of-Purchase Advertising Institute [*Fort Lee, NJ*]   (EA)
POPAL...... Pre-Operational Peculiar Age List
Pop Astron ... Popular Astronomy [*A publication*]
Pop Astronomy ... Popular Astronomy [*A publication*]
Pop B....... Population Bulletin [*A publication*]
POP & B.... Proposed Operating Program and Budget [*Army*]
Pop Bul ...... Population Bulletin [*A publication*]
Pop Bull Colo State Univ Agr Exp Sta ... Popular Bulletin. Colorado State University. Agricultural Experiment Station [*A publication*]
popc---........ Pitcairn [*MARC geographic area code*] [*Library of Congress*]   (LCCP)
Pop Comput ... Popular Computing [*A publication*]
POP-CON ... Populist Conservative [*Wing of the Republican Party represented by Congressmen Gingrich, Kemp, and Lott*]
POPD .... Power-Operated
POPDA ..... Polish Psychological Bulletin [*A publication*]
POPDA ..... Polyoxypropylenediamine [*Organic chemistry*]
Pop Dev R ... Population and Development Review [*New York*] [*A publication*]
POPE........ Parents for Orthodoxy in Parochial Education [*Group opposing sex education in schools*]
Pope Cust... Pope on Customs and Excise [*11th ed.*] [*1828*] [*A publication*]   (DLA)
POP ED..... Popular Edition [*Publishing*]
Pop Educ.... Popular Educator [*A publication*]
Pop Electr .. Popular Electronics [*A publication*]
Pope Lun.... Pope on Lunacy [*A publication*]   (DLA)
PopeTal...... Pope & Talbot, Inc. [*Associated Press abbreviation*]   (APAG)
POPEZ...... Pope Resources Ltd. [*NASDAQ symbol*]   (SPSG)
Pop Gard ... Popular Gardening [*A publication*]
Pop Govt .... Popular Government [*A publication*]
POPGUN .. Policy and Procedure Governing the Use of Nicknames [*Army*]   (AABC)
Poph.......... Popham's English King's Bench Reports [*1592-1627*] [*A publication*]   (DLA)
Poph (2) ..... Cases at the End of Popham's Reports [*A publication*]   (DLA)
Popham...... Popham's English King's Bench Reports [*79 English Reprint*] [*1592-1626*] [*A publication*]   (DLA)
Poph Insol ... Popham's Insolvency Act of Canada [*A publication*]   (DLA)
POPI.......... Fast Food Operators, Inc. [*NASDAQ symbol*]   (NQ)

PopI .... Population Index [*A publication*]
POPI........ Post Office Position Indicator [*A form of long-range position indicator*] [*British*]
Pop Ind ..... Population Index [*A publication*]
Pop Index.... Population Index [*A publication*]
POPINFORM ... Population Information Network [*UNESCO*]
POPINS .... Population Information System [*UNESCO*]
POPLAB .. International Program of Laboratories for Population Statistics
Pop Lect Math ... Popular Lectures in Mathematics [*A publication*]
POPLER .... [*A*] Programming Language   (CSR)
POPLINE ... Population Information On-Line [*Bibliographic database*]   (IID)
POPLIT..... Popliteal [*Anatomy*]
Pop Mag Rev ... Popular Magazine Review [*A publication*]
Pop Mech... Popular Mechanics Magazine [*A publication*]
Pop Med (Tokyo) ... Popular Medicine (Tokyo) [*A publication*]
POPMIP ... Portable Ocean Platform Motion Instrumentation Package [*Marine science*]   (MSC)
Pop Mo L Tr ... Popular Monthly Law Tracts [*1877-78*] [*A publication*]   (DLA)
Pop Music Period Index ... Popular Music Periodicals Index [*A publication*]
Pop Music S ... Popular Music and Society [*A publication*]
Pop Mus Per Ind ... Popular Music Periodicals Index [*A publication*]
Pop Mus & Soc ... Popular Music and Society [*A publication*]
POPMV..... Poplar Mosaic Virus [*Plant pathology*]
Popn.......... Population
POPO .... Polar Post. Polar Postal History Society of Great Britain [*A publication*]
POPO .... Poured-On, Passed-Over [*Bowdlerized version*]
POPO .... Push-On, Pull-Off [*Data processing*]
POPOA ..... Phosphorus and Potassium [*A publication*]
POPPD ...... Plant/Operations Progress [*A publication*]
Pop Per Ind ... Popular Periodical Index [*A publication*]
Pop Phot .... Popular Photography [*A publication*]
Pop Photog ... Popular Photography [*A publication*]
Pop Plast.... Popular Plastics [*A publication*]
Pop Plast Annu ... Popular Plastics Annual [*A publication*]
POPQ .... Opera Quarterly [*A publication*]
POPR........ Pilot Overhaul Provisioning Review
POPR........ Prototype Organic Power Reactor [*Nuclear energy*]
POPS......... Free-Fall Pop-Up Ocean Bottom Seismometer [*Marine science*]   (MSC)
POPS......... Pantograph Optical Projection System   (IEEE)
POPS......... Parachute Opening Proximity Sensor   (MCD)
POPS......... People Opposed to Pornography in Schools [*Group opposing sex education in schools*]
POPS......... Platt's Oilgram Price Service
pops---........ Polynesia [*MARC geographic area code*] [*Library of Congress*]   (LCCP)
POPS......... Positioning Orbital Propulsion System   (MCD)
POPS......... Preserve Our Presidential Sites   (EA)
POPS......... Pressurizer Overpressure Protection System [*Nuclear energy*]   (NRCH)
POPS......... Process Operating System [*Toshiba Corp.*] [*Japan*]
POPS......... Procurers of Painted-Label Sodas   (EA)
POPS......... Program for Operator Scheduling [*Bell System computer program*]
POPS......... Project Operations [*Navy*]   (NVT)
POPS........ Protect Our Pelican Society [*Later, PMBS*]   (EA)
POPS......... Pyrotechnic Optical Plume Simulator   (MCD)
Pop Sci....... Popular Science Monthly [*A publication*]
POP SCI MO ... Popular Science Monthly [*A publication*]   (ROG)
Pop Sci (Peking) ... Popular Science (Peking) [*A publication*]
Pop Sci R ... Popular Science Review [*A publication*]
POPSE ...... Project Office for Physical Security Equipment [*Army*]   (RDA)
POPSER.... Polaris Operational Performance Surveillance Engineering Report [*Missiles*]
POPSI .... Precipitation and Off-Path Scattered Interference [*Report*] [*FCC*]
POPSIPT .. Project Operations in Port [*Navy*]   (NVT)
Pop Stud .... Population Studies [*London*] [*A publication*]
Pop Stud (Lo) ... Population Studies (London) [*A publication*]
Pop Stud (NY) ... Population Studies (New York) [*A publication*]
POPT......... Petty Officer Physical Trainer [*British military*]   (DMA)
POPT......... Pretesting Orientation on the Purpose of Testing [*US Employment Service*] [*Department of Labor*]
Pop Tech Tous ... Popular Technique pour Tous [*A publication*]
POPU .... Push Over Pull Up   (NASA)
Popul.......... Population [*A publication*]
Popular Govt ... Popular Government [*A publication*]
Popular M Soc ... Popular Music and Society [*A publication*]
Population Bul ... Population Bulletin [*A publication*]
Population Bul UN ... Population Bulletin. United Nations [*A publication*]
Population R ... Population Review [*A publication*]
Population Research and Policy R ... Population Research and Policy Review [*A publication*]
Popul et Avenir ... Population et Avenir [*A publication*]
Popul Bull .. Population Bulletin [*A publication*]
Popul Bull UN Econ Comm West Asia ... Population Bulletin. United Nations Economic Commission for Western Asia [*A publication*]

Popul B UN Econ Com West Asia ... Population Bulletin. United Nations Economic Commission for Western Asia [*A publication*]
Popul Counc Annu Rep ... Population Council. Annual Report [*A publication*]
Popul Data Inf Serv ... Population Data Information Service [*A publication*]
Popul Dev Rev ... Population and Development Review [*A publication*]
Popul Educ News ... Population Education News [*A publication*]
Popul Environ ... Population and Environment [*A publication*]
Popul et Famille ... Population et Famille [*A publication*]
Popul et Famille/Bevolk en Gezin ... Population et Famille/Bevolking en Gezin [*A publication*]
Popul Forum ... Population Forum [*A publication*]
Popul Geogr ... Population Geography [*A publication*]
Popul Ind ... Population Index [*A publication*]
Popul Index ... Population Index [*A publication*]
Popul Newsl ... Population Newsletter [*A publication*]
Popul Policy Compend ... Population Policy Compendium [*A publication*]
Popul Rep A ... Population Reports. Series A. Oral Contraceptives [*A publication*]
Popul Rep B ... Population Reports. Series B. Intrauterine Devices [*A publication*]
Popul Rep C ... Population Reports. Series C. Sterilization. Female [*A publication*]
Popul Rep D ... Population Reports. Series D. Sterilization (Male) [*A publication*]
Popul Rep E ... Population Reports. Series E. Law and Policy [*A publication*]
Popul Rep F ... Population Reports. Series F. Pregnancy Termination [*A publication*]
Popul Rep G ... Population Reports. Series G. Prostaglandins [*A publication*]
Popul Rep H ... Population Reports. Series H. Barrier Methods [*A publication*]
Popul Rep I ... Population Reports. Series I. Periodic Abstinence [*A publication*]
Popul Rep J ... Population Reports. Series J. Family Planning Programs [*A publication*]
Popul Rep K ... Population Reports. Series K. Injectables and Implants [*A publication*]
Popul Rep L ... Population Reports. Series L. Issues in World Health [*A publication*]
Popul Rep M ... Population Reports. Series M. Special Topics [*A publication*]
Popul Rep Spec Top Monogr ... Population Reports. Special Topics. Monographs [*A publication*]
Popul Rev ... Population Review [*A publication*]
Popul et Societes ... Population et Societes [*A publication*]
Popul Stud ... Population Studies [*A publication*]
Popul Today ... Population Today [*A publication*]
Populuxe .... Popular Luxury [*Coined by Thomas Hine, design critic for the Philadelphia Inquirer, to describe the period from the mid-1950's to the mid-1960's*]
POPUS ...... Post Office Processing Utility Subsystem [*Telecommunications*]   (TEL)
POPX .... POP Radio Corp. [*New York, NY*] [*NASDAQ symbol*]   (NQ)
POPYA ...... Portugaliae Physica [*A publication*]
POQ .... Production Offset Quantity [*Military*]
POQ .... Provided Otherwise Qualified [*Military*]   (AABC)
POQ .... Public Opinion Quarterly [*A publication*]
POQ .... Push Off Quickly [*i.e., Be quick about it*] [*British*]
POR .... Pacific Ocean Region
POR .... Pack Report. Fachzeitschrift fuer Verpackungs Marketing und Verpackungs (Technik) [*A publication*]
POR .... Parking Orbit Rendezvous [*NASA*]   (MCD)
POR .... Partido Obrero Revolucionario [*Revolutionary Workers Party*] [*Peru*] [*Political party*]
POR .... Partido Obrero Revolucionario [*Revolutionary Workers Party*] [*Argentina*] [*Political party*]
POR .... Partido Obrero Revolucionario [*Revolutionary Workers Party*] [*Bolivia*] [*Political party*]   (PPW)
POR .... Patent Office Reports [*A publication*]   (DLA)
POR .... Patrol Operations Report
POR .... Pay on Return [*Business term*]
POR .... Payable on Receipt [*Business term*]
POR .... Periodic Operation Report
POR .... Personnel Occurrence Report [*RAF*] [*British*]
POR .... Pilot Opinion Rating
POR .... Plutonium Organic Recycle [*Nuclear energy*]   (NRCH)
PoR .... Poetry Review [*London*] [*A publication*]
POR .... Pola Resources Ltd. [*Vancouver Stock Exchange symbol*]
POR .... Pori [*Finland*] [*Airport symbol*]   (OAG)
POR .... Port of Refuge [*Shipping*]
POr .... Porta Orientale [*A publication*]
POR .... Portec, Inc. [*NYSE symbol*]   (SPSG)
POR .... Portion
POR .... Portland [*Maine*] [*Seismograph station code, US Geological Survey*] [*Closed*]   (SEIS)
POR .... Portrait
Por .... Portugale [*A publication*]
POR .... Portuguese
por .... Portuguese [*MARC language code*] [*Library of Congress*]   (LCCP)
POR .... Position of Responsibility   (ADA)
POR .... Post Office Return
POR .... Post Office Rifles [*Military*] [*British*]   (ROG)

POR .... Preparation of Overseas Replacement [*Military*]   (RDA)
POR .... Press on Regardless [*Automotive marathon*]
POR .... Price on Request
POR .... Problem-Oriented Records [*Medicine*]
POR .... Problem-Oriented Routine   (IEEE)
POR .... Production Order Records   (SAA)
POR .... Production Order Request   (SAA)
POR .... Project Officers Report   (MCD)
POR .... Psychotherapy Outcome Research
POR .... Purchase Order Request
PORAC ...... Peace Officers Research Association of California
PORACC ... Principles of Radiation and Contamination Control [*Nuclear energy*]
PORADD .. Postgraduate Radiology [*A publication*]
Poradnik M ... Poradnik Muzyczny [*A publication*]
PORB .... Orbis [*A publication*]
PORB .... Production Operations Review Board [*NASA*]   (NASA)
PORC .... Partido Obrero Revolucionario-Combate [*Revolutionary Struggle Workers' Party*] [*Bolivia*] [*Political party*]   (PPW)
PORC .... Plant Operations Review Committee [*Nuclear energy*]   (NRCH)
PORC .... Porcelain   (AAG)
PORCD .... Population Reports. Series C [*United States*] [*A publication*]
PORCN ..... Production Order Records Change Notice   (KSC)
PORCO ..... Port Control Office
PORD .... Performance and Operations Requirements Document [*NASA*]   (NASA)
PORDA ..... Personnel Officers of Research and Development Agencies
PORDB ..... Ports and Dredging [*A publication*]
PORDIR .... Port Director
PORE .... Point Reyes National Seashore [*National Park Service designation*]
PORE .... Polar Record [*A publication*]
POREA ..... Post Office Regional Employees' Association [*Defunct*]   (EA)
POREEQ ... Polar Research [*A publication*]
POREL(A) ... Petty Officer Radio Electrician (Air) [*British military*]   (DMA)
POREP ...... Position Report [*Air Force*]
PORES ...... Purchase Order Receiving System   (MCD)
PORF .... Pacific Ocean Research Foundation   (EA)
P de Orfi ...... Petrus de Orfila [*Deceased, 1307*] [*Authority cited in pre-1607 legal work*]   (DSA)
Porg .... Person of Restricted Growth [*Lifestyle classification*] [*Slang term used to describe a person of limited cultural awareness*]
PORGIE .... Paperback Original [*Award for best original paperback books of the year*]
PORI .... Polaris Operational Readiness Instrumentation [*Missiles*]
PORI .... Preoperational Readiness Inspection   (MCD)
PORIS .... Post Office Radio Interference Service [*British*]   (DI)
Por Jez .... Poradnik Jezykowy [*A publication*]
PORK .... Sooner State Farms [*NASDAQ symbol*]   (NQ)
Pork Ind Gaz ... Pork Industry Gazette [*A publication*]
PORLA ..... Practica Oto-Rhino-Laryngologica [*A publication*]
PORM .... Plus or Minus
PORM-PST ... Partido Obrero Revolucionario Marxista-Partido Socialista de los Trabajadores [*Peru*] [*Political party*]   (EY)
PORN .... Pornography   (DSUE)
PORN .... Protect Our Responsibilities Now [*Book title*]
PORNO ...... Pornography   (DSUE)
Poroshk Metall ... Poroshkovaya Metallurgiya [*A publication*]
Poroshk Metall (Kiev) ... Poroshkovaya Metallurgiya (Kiev) [*A publication*]
Poroshk Metall (Kuibyshev) ... Poroshkovaya Metallurgiya (Kuibyshev) [*A publication*]
Porosh Met ... Poroshkovaya Metallurgiya [*A publication*]
PORP .... Partial Ossicular Replacement Prosthesis
Porph .... Porphyry [*Third century AD*] [*Classical studies*]   (OCD)
PORR .... Preliminary Operations Requirements Review [*NASA*]   (NASA)
PORR .... Purchase Order Revision Request
PORS .... Polar Research [*A publication*]
PORS .... Product Output Reporting System
PORS .... Publications in Operations Research Series [*Elsevier Book Series*] [*A publication*]
PORSE ...... Post Overhaul Reaction Safeguard Examination [*Navy*]   (NVT)
PORT .... Patient Outcome Research Team   (PCM)
PORT .... Photo-Optical Recorder Tracker
PORT .... Portable   (KSC)
PORT .... Porter   (DSUE)
Port .... Porter's Alabama Supreme Court Reports [*1834-39*] [*A publication*]   (DLA)
Port .... Porter's Indiana Reports [*3-7 Indiana*] [*A publication*]   (DLA)
PORT .... Portfolio   (WGA)
PORT .... Portland Railroad
PORT .... Portmanteau   (DSUE)
PORT .... Portrait
PORT .... Portugal
Port .... Portugale [*A publication*]
PORT .... Prescriptive Objective Reference Testing [*Vocational guidance*]
Port Acta Biol A ... Portugaliae Acta Biologica. A. Morfologia, Fisiologia, Genetica, e Biologia Geral [*A publication*]
Port Acta Biol Ser A ... Portugaliae Acta Biologica. Serie A [*A publication*]
Port Acta Biol Ser B ... Portugaliae Acta Biologica. Serie B [*A publication*]

PORTAGE ... Portage Industries Corp. [*Associated Press abbreviation*]   (APAG)
PORTAL ... Process-Oriented Real-Time Algorithmic Language [*1978*] [*Data processing*]   (CSR)
Port (Ala) ... Porter's Alabama Reports [*A publication*]   (DLA)
Port Ala R ... Porter's Alabama Reports [*A publication*]   (DLA)
PORTAPAK ... Portable, Self-Contained, Instrument Package
Portec .... Portec, Inc. [*Associated Press abbreviation*]   (APAG)
Port Electrochim Acta ... Portugaliae Electrochimica Acta [*A publication*]
Porter .... Porter's Alabama Reports [*A publication*]   (DLA)
Porter .... Porter's Indiana Reports [*3-7 Indiana*] [*A publication*]   (DLA)
Porter (Ala) ... Porter's Alabama Reports [*A publication*]   (DLA)
Porter R ...... Porter's Alabama Reports [*A publication*]   (DLA)
Porter's Ala R ... Porter's Alabama Reports [*A publication*]   (DLA)
Porter's R ... Porter's Alabama Reports [*A publication*]   (DLA)
Porter's Repts ... Porter's Alabama Reports [*A publication*]   (DLA)
Portfo .... Portfolio [*A publication*]
Portfo (Den) ... Portfolio (Dennie's) [*A publication*]
Port Gazette ... Melbourne Harbour Trust Port Gazette [*A publication*]   (APTA)
PortGC .... Portland General Corp. [*Associated Press abbreviation*]   (APAG)
Portia L J ... Portia Law Journal [*A publication*]
Port Ins ...... Porter's Laws of Insurance [*A publication*]   (DLA)
Port Junta Invest Cient Ultramar Estud Ensaios Doc ... Portugal. Junta de Investigacoes Cientificas do Ultramar. Estudos, Ensaios, e Documentos [*A publication*]
Port Lab Nac Eng Civ Mem ... Portugal. Laboratorio Nacional de Engenharia Civil. Memoria [*A publication*]
Portland Cem Ass Advanced Eng Bull ... Portland Cement Association. Advanced Engineering Bulletin [*A publication*]
Portland Cem Ass J PCA Res Develop Lab ... Portland Cement Association. Journal of the PCA Research and Development Laboratories [*A publication*]
Portland Cem Assoc Fellowship Natl Bur Stand Pap ... Portland Cement Association Fellowship at the National Bureau of Standards. Papers [*A publication*]
Portland Cem Assoc Res Dev Lab Dev Dep Bull D ... Portland Cement Association. Research and Development Laboratories. Development Department. Bulletin D [*A publication*]
Portland Soc N H Pr ... Portland Society of Natural History. Proceedings [*A publication*]
Portland UL Rev ... Portland University. Law Review [*A publication*]   (DLA)
Port Melb ... Port Of Melbourne [*A publication*]   (APTA)
Port Melbourne Quart ... Port Of Melbourne Quarterly [*A publication*]   (APTA)
Port Melb Q ... Port Of Melbourne Quarterly [*A publication*]   (APTA)
Port Minist Ultramar Junta Invest Ultramar Mem Ser Antropol ... Portugal. Ministerio do Ultramar. Junta de Investigacoes do Ultramar. Memorias. Serie Antropologica e Etnologica [*A publication*]
Port Minist Ultramar Junta Invest Ultramar Mem Ser Botanica ... Portugal. Ministerio do Ultramar. Junta de Investigacoes do Ultramar. Memorias. Serie Botanica [*A publication*]
Port Minist Ultramar Junta Invest Ultramar Mem Ser Geol ... Portugal. Ministerio do Ultramar. Junta de Investigacoes do Ultramar. Memorias. Serie Geologica [*A publication*]
Port Minist Ultramar Mem Junta Invest Ultramar ... Portugal. Ministerio do Ultramar. Memorias da Junta de Investigacoes do Ultramar [*A publication*]
PORTN ..... Portion   (ROG)
Port Of Melbourne Q ... Port Of Melbourne Quarterly [*A publication*]
Port Of Melbourne Quart ... Port Of Melbourne Quarterly [*A publication*]   (APTA)
Port Of Melb Q ... Port Of Melbourne Quarterly [*A publication*]   (APTA)
Port Of Melb Quart ... Port Of Melbourne Quarterly [*A publication*]   (APTA)
Port Of Syd ... Port Of Sydney [*A publication*]   (APTA)
Port Of Sydney J ... Port Of Sydney Journal [*A publication*]   (APTA)
PORTP ...... Partido Obrero Revolucionaria Trotskista Posadista [*Bolivia*] [*Political party*]   (PPW)
Port P .... Portuguese Pharmacopoeia [*A publication*]
Port Phillip Gaz ... Port Phillip Gazette [*A publication*]   (APTA)
Port Phy ..... Portugaliae Physica [*A publication*]
Port Phys ... Portugaliae Physica [*A publication*]
Port R .... Portland Review [*A publication*]
PORTREP ... Port [*or Anchorage*] Capacity Report [*Navy*]   (NVT)
PORTS .... Portsmouth [*City in England*]
Ports Dredging Oil Rep ... Ports and Dredging and Oil Report [*A publication*]
Port Serv Fom Min Estud Notas Trab ... Portugal. Servico de Fomento Mineiro. Estudos, Notas, e Trabalhos [*A publication*]
Port Serv Geol Mem ... Portugal. Servicos Geologicos. Memoria [*A publication*]
PORTSM .. Portsmouth [*County borough in England*]
Ports NSW Jl ... Ports of New South Wales Journal [*A publication*]
PORTSREP ... Ports Report File   (MCD)
PORTSUM ... Port [*or Anchorage*] Summary Report [*Navy*]   (NVT)
Port Syd ..... Port Of Sydney [*A publication*]   (APTA)
PORTSYS ... Porta Systems Corp. [*Associated Press abbreviation*]   (APAG)
Portug Acta Biol ... Portugaliae Acta Biologica [*A publication*]
Portugal Math ... Portugaliae Mathematica [*A publication*]
Portugal Phys ... Portugaliae Physica [*A publication*]

Portugl .... Portugal Fund [*Associated Press abbreviation*]   (APAG)
Port UL Rev ... Portland University. Law Review [*A publication*]   (DLA)
PORV .... Pilot-Operated Relief Valve [*Nuclear energy*]   (NRCH)
PORV .... Power-Operated Relief Valve [*Nuclear energy*]   (NRCH)
PORX .... Porex Technologies Corp. [*NASDAQ symbol*]   (NQ)
POS .... Catalina Marketing Corp. [*NYSE symbol*]   (SPSG)
POS .... Pacific Ocean Ship   (NASA)
POS .... Pacific Orchid Society of Hawaii   (EA)
POS .... Parent Operating Service   (MCD)
POS .... Partially Ordered Set   (OA)
POS .... Patent Office Society   (EA)
POS .... Peacetime Operating Stock [*Military*]   (CINC)
POS .... Period of Service [*Military*]
POS .... Photo Optic System
POS .... Pico Resources [*Vancouver Stock Exchange symbol*]
POS .... Piper Owner Society   (EA)
POS .... Plan of Service   (OICC)
POS .... Plant Operating System [*Nuclear energy*]   (NRCH)
P-O-S .... Point-of-Sale
POS .... Policy Statements [*Australian Broadcasting Tribunal*] [*A publication*]
POS .... Polycystic Ovarian Syndrome [*Also, PCOS*] [*Gynecology*]
POS .... Population Studies [*A publication*]
POS .... Port Of Spain [*Trinidad and Tobago*] [*Airport symbol*]   (OAG)
POS .... Portable Oxygen System   (MCD)
POS .... Position   (KSC)
POS .... Positive   (AFM)
POS .... Possession [*or Possessive*]   (WGA)
Pos .... Possible
POS .... Post Office Scheme [*Regulations*] [*British*]
POS .... Preferred Overseas Shore Duty
POS .... Pretoria Oriental Series [*A publication*]
POS .... Primary Operating System   (IEEE)
POS .... Primary Oxygen System
POS .... Probability of Survival [*Automotive componant analysis*]
POS .... Problem Oriented System
POS .... Production-Oriented Survey   (MCD)
POS .... Professions and Occupations Sourcebook [*A publication*]
POS .... Program Operations Staff [*Environmental Protection Agency*]   (GFGA)
POS .... Program Order Sequence
POS .... Programmable Option Select [*Data processing*]
POS .... Protein, Oil, and Starch [*Pilot manufacturing plant established by the Canadian government*]
POS .... Pskovskij Oblastnoj Slovar's Istoriceskimi Dannymi [*A publication*]
POS .... Pupil Observation Survey [*Education*]
POS .... Purchase Order Supplement
POSA .... Patriotic Order Sons of America   (EA)
POSA .... Payment Outstanding Suspense Accounts   (NATG)
POSA .... Petty Officer Stores Accountant [*British military*]   (DMA)
POSA .... Preliminary Operating Safety Analysis [*Nuclear energy*]   (NRCH)
POSARS ... Plan of Service Automated Reporting System [*Employment and Training Administration*] [*Department of Labor*]
POSB .... Polish Sociological Bulletin [*A publication*]
POSB .... Post Office Savings Bank
POSC .... Problem-Oriented System of Charting   (AAMN)
posc--- .... Santa Cruz Islands [*MARC geographic area code*] [*Library of Congress*]   (LCCP)
P & OSCC ... Plans and Operations for the Safeguard Communications Command [*Army*]   (RDA)
POSCH ..... Program of Surgical Control of Hyperlipidemia
POSCOR ... Position Correct   (CAAL)
POSCORB ... Planning, Organizing, Staffing, Coordinating, Reporting, and Budgeting [*Management*]
POSD .... Personnel on Station Date [*Army*]   (AABC)
POSD .... Program for Optical System Design
POSD .... Project Operation Support Division [*NASA*]
POSDCORB ... Planning, Organizing, Staffing, Directing, Coordinating, Reporting, and Budgeting [*Principles of management*]
POSDSPLT ... Positive Displacement
POSE .... Parents Opposed to Sex Education
POSE .... Photogrammetric Ocean Survey Equipment
POSE .... Power Operational Support Equipment
POSE .... Promotion of Social Education [*British*]   (DI)
POSEA ...... Peredovoi Opyt v Stroitel'stve i Ekspluatatsii Shakht [*A publication*]
Posebna Izdan ... Posebna Izdanja [*A publication*]
Posebna Izd Biol Inst N R Srb Beograd ... Posebna Izdanja Bioloski Institut N R Srbije Beograd [*A publication*]
Posebna Izd Geol Glas (Sarajevo) ... Posebna Izdanja Geoloskog Glasnika (Sarajevo) [*A publication*]
POSET ...... Partially Ordered Set   (HGAA)
Posey .... Posey's Unreported Cases [*Texas*] [*A publication*]   (ILCA)
Posey UC ... Texas Unreported Cases [*A publication*]   (DLA)
Posey Unrep Cas ... Posey's Unreported Cases [*Texas*] [*A publication*]   (DLA)
POSH .... Permuted on Subject Headings [*Indexing technique*]
POSH .... Personal & Organizational Security Handbook [*A publication*]

POSH........ Port Outwardbound, Starboard Homewardbound [*Some claim that this acronym describes the location of shaded cabins on ships carrying British officers to the Far East and back. Many etymologists, however, believe that the origin of the word "posh" is unknown*]

posh............ Samoa Islands [*MARC geographic area code*] [*Library of Congress*]   (LCCP)

POSI......... Personnel On-Site Integration   (SAA)

POSI......... Positech Corp. [*NASDAQ symbol*]   (NQ)

POSID...... Polyarnye Siyaniya [*A publication*]

POSIP...... Portable Ship's Instrumentation Package

POSIT...... Position   (NVT)

POSIT...... Positive

POSIT...... Positivism   (ROG)

POSITIVE ... Parents of Surrogate-Borne Infants and Toddlers in Verbal Exchange   (EA)

POSITREPS ... Position Reports

POSITRON ... Positive Electron

POSIX....... Portable Operating System Specification [*IEEE*]

POSK........ Polski Osrodek Spoleczno-Kulturalny [*Polish Social and Cultural Association - PSCA*]   (EAIO)

POSKP...... Polski Osrodek Spoleczno-Kulturalny Posk [*Polish Social and Cultural Association - PSCA*]   (EAIO)

POsl............ Papyri Osloenses [*A publication*]   (OCD)

POSL......... Parti Ouvrier Socialiste Luxembourgeois [*Luxembourg Socialist Workers' Party*]   (EAIO)

POSL......... Posi-Seal International [*NASDAQ symbol*]   (NQ)

PosLuth ... Positions Lutheriennes [*Paris*] [*A publication*]

POSM ...... National Association of Post Office and General Service Maintenance Employees [*Later, APWU*] [*AFL-CIO*]

POSM ...... Patient-Operated Selector Mechanism [*Pronounced "possum"*]

POSMA..... Postal Service Manual [*A publication*]

POSN .... Position   (AFM)

posn---........ Solomon Islands [*MARC geographic area code*] [*Library of Congress*]   (LCCP)

POSNA ..... Pediatric Orthopaedic Society of North America   (EA)

POS/NAV ... Position/Navigation [*System*] [*Military*]   (INF)

P & OSNCo ... Peninsular & Oriental Steam Navigation Co. [*Steamship line*]

POSP......... Pacific Ocean Stations Program   (SAA)

pos pr .... Positive Pressure   (MAE)

POSR........ Peacetime Operating Stock Requirement [*Military*]   (AFIT)

POS R....... Positive Review [*A publication*]   (ROG)

POSRIP..... People Organized to Stop Rape of Imprisoned Persons   (EA)

POSS .... Palomar Observatory Sky Survey [*NASA*]

POSS .... Passive Optical Satellite Surveillance [*System*]   (NATG)

POSS .... Photo-Optical Surveillance Subsystem

POSS .... Portable Oceanographic Survey System   (MCD)

POSS .... Possession [*or Possessive*]   (AFM)

POSS .... Possible

POSS .... Possis Corp. [*NASDAQ symbol*]   (NQ)

POSS .... Program Operations Support Staff [*Environmental Protection Agency*]   (GFGA)

POSS .... Prototype Optical Surveillance System

POSS .... Proximal Over-Shoulder Strap [*Medicine*]

POSSE ...... Parents Opposed to Sex and Sensitivity Education [*An association*]

POSSE ...... Police Operations Systems Support System Elementary

POSSE ...... Progressive Onslaught to Stamp out Stock Errors [*Navy*]   (NG)

POSSED ... Possessed   (ROG)

Posselt's Text J ... Posselt's Textile Journal [*A publication*]

POSSF........ Post Office Staff Superannuation Fund [*British*]   (DI)

POSSLQ ... Persons of Opposite Sex Sharing Living Quarters [*Bureau of the Census*]

POSSN ...... Possession   (WGA)

POSSNC ... Post Office Senior Staff Negotiating Council [*British*]

POSSON... Possession

POSSUB ... Possible Submarine [*Navy*]   (NVT)

POSSUM.. Polar Orbiting Satellite System - University of Michigan [*Designed by engineering students*]

Post .... De Posteritate Caini [*of Philo*]   (BJA)

POST........ Parliamentary Office of Science and Technology [*British*]

POST........ Passive Optical Scan Tracker   (MCD)

POST........ Passive Optical Seeker Technique

POST........ Payload Operations Support Team [*NASA*]   (MCD)

POST........ Peace Officer Standards and Training

POST........ Peritoneal Ovum Sperm Transfer [*Medicine*]

POST........ Piezoelectric-Oscillator Self-Tuned [*Electric system*]

POST........ Point-of-Sale Terminal [*Business term*]

POST........ Point-of-Sale Transaction

POST........ Polaris Operation Support Task Group [*Missiles*]

POST........ Polymer Science and Technology [*American Chemical Society*] [*Information service or system*] [*A publication*]

POST........ Positive   (AAG)

POST........ Postemergence [*Weed control*]

POST........ [*The*] Poster [*A publication*]   (ROG)

post............ Posterior

POST........ Postmortem   (AAMN)

Post .... Post's Reports [*23-26 Michigan*] [*A publication*]   (DLA)

Post .... Post's Reports [*42-64 Missouri*] [*A publication*]   (DLA)

POST........ Power-On Self Test [*IBM-PC feature*]

POST........ Production-Oriented Scheduling Techniques   (MCD)

POST........ Program to Operate Simulated Trajectories

POST........ Program to Optimize Shuttle [*or Simulated*] Trajectories [*NASA*]   (KSC)

POST........ Programmer Operating Standards Technique

POST-A..... Population Studies [*A publication*]

Post Accid Heat Removal Inf Exch Meet ... Post Accident Heat Removal Information Exchange Meeting [*A publication*]

Postal Bull ... Postal Bulletin. Weekly [*A publication*]

Postal Bull US Postal Serv ... Postal Bulletin. United States Postal Service [*A publication*]

Postal Spvr ... Postal Supervisor [*A publication*]

POST AUR ... Post Aurem [*Behind the Ear*] [*Pharmacy*]

PostB.......... Postilla Bohemica [*A publication*]

Post Bioch ... Postepy Biochemii [*A publication*]

POSTD..... Petty Officer Steward [*British military*]   (DMA)

Postdiplom Sem Fiz ... Postdiplomski Seminar iz Fizike [*A publication*]

Postdiplom Sem Mat ... Postdiplomski Seminar iz Matematike [*A publication*]

Post Dir...... Post's Paper Mill Directory [*A publication*]

POSTE...... Postage   (ROG)

POSTEC ... Powder Science and Technology Research Association [*Norway*]   (EAIO)

Postepy Astron ... Postepy Astronomii [*A publication*]

Postepy Astronaut ... Postepy Astronautyki [*A publication*]

Postepy Biochem ... Postepy Biochemii [*A publication*]

Postepy Biol Komorki ... Postepy Biologii Komorki [*A publication*]

Postepy Cybernet ... Postepy Cybernetyki [*A publication*]

Postepy Fiz ... Postepy Fizyki [*A publication*]

Postepy Fizjol ... Postepy Fizjologii [*A publication*]

Postepy Fiz Med ... Postepy Fizyki Medycznej [*A publication*]

Postepy Ftyz Pneumon ... Postepy Ftyzjatrii i Pneumonologii [*A publication*]

Postepy Hig Med Dosw ... Postepy Higieny i Medycyny Doswiadczalnej [*A publication*]

Postepy Med ... Postepy Medycyny [*A publication*]

Postepy Mikrobiol ... Postepy Mikrobiologii [*A publication*]

Postepy Nauk Roln ... Postepy Nauk Rolniczych [*A publication*]

Postepy Tech Jad ... Postepy Techniki Jadroweki [*A publication*]

Postepy Techn Jadr ... Postepy Techniki Jadrowej [*A publication*]

Postepy Technol Masz Urzadz ... Postepy Technologii Maszyn i Urzadzen [*A publication*]

Postepy Wied Med ... Postepy Wiedzy Medycznej [*A publication*]

Postepy Wiedzy Med ... Postepy Wiedzy Medycznej [*A publication*]

Postepy Wiedzy Roln ... Postepy Wiedzy Rolniczej [*A publication*]

POSTER ... Post Strike Emergency Reporting

Poste's Gai ... Poste's Translation of Gaius [*A publication*]   (ILCA)

Poste's Gaius Inst ... Poste's Translation of Gaius [*A publication*]   (DLA)

Poste Telecommun ... Poste e Telecommunicazioni [*A publication*]

POSTFAT ... Postfinal Acceptance Trials [*Navy*]   (NVT)

POSTFAX ... Post Office Facsimile [*British*]

Postg Med J ... Postgraduate Medical Journal [*A publication*]

Postgrad Courses Pediatr ... Postgraduate Courses in Pediatrics [*A publication*]

PostgradDipAgr ... Postgraduate Diploma in Agriculture

PostGradDipEdStud(IndArts) ... Postgraduate Diploma in Educational Studies (Industrial Arts)

Postgrad Med ... Postgraduate Medicine [*A publication*]

Postgrad Med J ... Postgraduate Medical Journal [*A publication*]

Postgrad Med J Suppl ... Postgraduate Medical Journal. Supplement [*A publication*]

Postgrad Med Ser ... Postgraduate Medicine Series [*A publication*]

Postgrad MJ ... Postgraduate Medical Journal [*A publication*]

Postgrad Paediatr Ser ... Postgraduate Paediatrics Series [*A publication*]

Postgrad Radiol ... Postgraduate Radiology [*A publication*]

Postgr Med ... Postgraduate Medicine [*A publication*]

POSTH...... Posthumous

Post Harvest Technol Cassava ... Post Harvest Technology of Cassava [*A publication*]

Post & Ins .. Postage and Insurance   (ILCA)

POST-J .... Polymer Science and Technology - Journals [*A publication*]

Postl Dict .... Postlethwaite's Dictionary of Trade and Commerce [*A publication*]   (DLA)

Postmasters Adv ... Postmasters Advocate [*A publication*]

Post-Medieval Arch ... Post-Medieval Archaeology [*A publication*]

Post-Medieval Archaeol ... Post-Medieval Archaeology [*A publication*]

post-obit ..... Post Obitum [*After Death*] [*Latin*]

Post O E E J ... Post Office Electrical Engineers. Journal [*A publication*]

Post Off Electr Eng J ... Post Office Electrical Engineers. Journal [*A publication*]

Post Off (GB) Res Dep Rep ... Post Office (Great Britain). Research Department Report [*A publication*]

Post Office Hist Soc Trans ... Post Office Historical Society. Transactions [*Queensland*] [*A publication*]   (APTA)

Post Off Telecommun J ... Post Office Telecommunications Journal [*A publication*]

POSTOP ... Postoperative [*Medicine*]

POST-P..... Polymer Science and Technology - Patents [*A publication*]

POSTP ...... Posterior Probability [*Computations*]

POSTP ...... Postprocessor [*Data processing*]

POSTPRO ... Postprocessor [*Data processing*]

Post & Reg ... Postage and Registration   (DLA)

Post S......... Post Script [*A publication*]

Post Sag D ... Posterior Sagittal Diameter [*Anatomy*] (MAE)
Post Scr....... Post Script [*A publication*]
POST SING SED LIQ ... Post Singulas Sedes Liquidas [*After Every Loose Stool*] [*Pharmacy*] (ROG)
POSWa...... Pozprawy Komisji Orientalistycznej Towarzystwa Naukowego Warszawskiego [*A publication*]
POSWG...... Poseidon Software Working Group [*Missiles*]
POT .... British Telecom Journal [*A publication*]
POT .... Papper och Trae [*A publication*]
POT .... Parallel Output
POT .... Pennsylvania-Ontario Transportation Co. [*AAR code*]
POT .... Physical Organization Table (HGAA)
POT .... Piston Operated Transducer
POT .... Pitch-Orthogonal Thrust
POT .... Plain Old Telephone [*Bell System's basic model*]
Po T.......... Poetics Today [*A publication*]
POT .... Port Antonio [*Jamaica*] [*Airport symbol*] (OAG)
POT .... Portable Outside Toilet [*A unit of mobility equipment*] [*Military*]
POT .... Post Office Telecommunications [*British*]
POT .... Potable
POT .... Potash Corp. of Saskatchewan [*NYSE symbol*] (SPSG)
pot .... Potassa [*Chemistry*] (MAE)
POT .... Potassium [*Chemical symbol is K*]
POT .... Potato (ROG)
POT .... Potentate
POT .... Potential (AFM)
POT .... Potentiometer [*or Potentiometric*]
Pot............. Potion
POT .... Potsdam [*German Democratic Republic*] [*Later, NGK*] [*Geomagnetic observatory code*]
POT .... Potsdam [*German Democratic Republic*] [*Seismograph station code, US Geological Survey*] (SEIS)
POT .... Pottle [*Unit of measure*] (ROG)
POT .... Pottsville Free Public Library, Pottsville, PA [*OCLC symbol*] (OCLC)
POT .... Potus [*A Drink*] [*Pharmacy*]
POT .... Prevailing-Out Torque [*Automotive engineering*]
POT .... Propeller Order Transmitter (OA)
PotAGT ..... Potential Abnormality of Glucose Tolerance [*Medicine*]
POTANN .. Potomac Annex [*Navy*]
Potash........ Potash Corp. of Saskatchewan, Inc. [*Associated Press abbreviation*] (APAG)
Potash 90 ... Potash 1990. Feast or Famine [*A publication*]
Potash J ..... Potash Journal [*A publication*]
Potash Rev ... Potash Review [*A publication*]
Potash Trop Agric ... Potash and Tropical Agriculture [*A publication*]
Potassium Inst Ltd Colloq Proc ... Potassium Institute Limited. Colloquium Proceedings [*A publication*]
Potassium Potasio Kalium Symp ... Potassium Potasio Kalium Symposium [*A publication*]
Potassium Symp ... Potassium. Symposium [*A publication*]
POTASWG ... Poseidon Test Analysis Software Working Group [*Missiles*]
Potato Abstr ... Potato Abstracts [*A publication*]
Potato Grow ... Potato Grower [*A publication*]
Potato Handb ... Potato Handbook [*A publication*]
Potato M .... Potato Magazine [*A publication*]
Potato Res ... Potato Research [*A publication*]
Pot Aust ..... Pottery in Australia [*A publication*] (APTA)
POTBI....... Places, Organizations, Things, Biographics, Intangibles
POTC .... PERT [*Program Evaluation and Review Technique*] Orientation and Training Center
POTCP...... Partially Oxidized Tetracyanoplatinate Compound [*Inorganic, one-dimensional conductor*]
POTD .... Player of the Decade [*Sports*]
Pot Dwar.... Potter's Edition of Dwarris on Statutes [*A publication*] (DLA)
PotEl.......... Potomac Electric Power Co. [*Associated Press abbreviation*] (APAG)
P O Telecommun J ... Post Office Telecommunications Journal [*A publication*]
POTEN ..... Potential (AAMN)
POTF.......... Polychromatic Optical Thickness Fringe (OA)
Potfuzetek Termeszettud Kozl ... Potfuzetek a Termeszettudomanyi Kozlonyhoz [*A publication*]
Poth Cont... Pothier's Contracts [*A publication*] (DLA)
Poth Contr Sale ... Pothier's Treatise on the Contract of Sale [*A publication*] (DLA)
Poth Cont Sale ... Pothier's Treatise on the Contract of Sale [*A publication*] (DLA)
Pothier Pand ... Pothier's Pandectae Justinianeae, Etc. [*A publication*] (DLA)
Poth Mar Cont ... Pothier's Treatise on Maritime Contracts [*A publication*] (DLA)
Poth Ob...... Pothier on the Law of Obligations [*A publication*] (DLA)
Poth Obl .... Pothier on the Law of Obligations [*A publication*] (DLA)
Poth Oblig ... Pothier on the Law of Obligations [*A publication*] (DLA)
Poth Oeuv .. Oeuvres de Pothier [*A publication*] (DLA)
Poth Pand ... Pothier's Pandects [*A publication*] (DLA)
Poth Part.... Pothier on Partnership [*A publication*] (DLA)
Poth Proc Civ ... Pothier. Procedure Civile [*A publication*] (DLA)
POT & I..... Preoverhaul Tests and Inspections [*Navy*] (NVT)
POTIB....... Polaris Technical Information Bulletin [*Missiles*]

potl--- .... Tokelau Islands [*MARC geographic area code*] [*Library of Congress*] (LCCP)
Pot LD .... Pott's Law Dictionary [*3rd ed.*] [*1815*] [*A publication*] (DLA)
Potltch........ Potlatch Corp. [*Associated Press abbreviation*] (APAG)
POTMC..... Protective Outfit Toxicological Microclimate Controlled (RDA)
PotmEl....... Potomac Electric Power Co. [*Associated Press abbreviation*] (APAG)
POTMLD ... Potential Mixed Layer Depth
POTN .... Problems of the North [*A publication*]
poto--- .... Tonga [*MARC geographic area code*] [*Library of Congress*] (LCCP)
POTOMAC ... Patent Office Techniques of Mechanized Access and Classification [*Automation project, shut down in 1972*]
Potomac Appalachian Trail Club Bull ... Potomac Appalachian Trail Club. Bulletin [*A publication*]
Potomac L Rev ... Potomac Law Review [*A publication*]
Potomac R ... Potomac Review [*A publication*]
Potravin Chladici Tech ... Potravinarska a Chladici Technika [*A publication*]
POTS........ Petty Officer Telegraphist Special (DSUE)
POTS........ Photo-Optical Terrain Simulator (MUGU)
POTS........ Plain Old Telephone Service [*Humorous term for Long Lines Department of AT & T*] [*See also PANS*]
POTS........ PORI [*Polaris Operational Readiness Instrumentation*] Operational Test System [*Missiles*]
POTS........ Precision Optical Tracking System (KSC)
POTS........ Preoverhaul Tests [*Navy*] (NVT)
POTS........ Purchase of Telephone Services Contracts
pott--- .... Trust Territory of the Pacific Islands [*MARC geographic area code*] [*Library of Congress*] (LCCP)
Pott Corp.... Potter on Corporations [*A publication*] (DLA)
Pott Dwarris ... Potter's Edition of Dwarris on Statutes [*A publication*] (DLA)
Potter .... Potter's Reports [*4-7 Wyoming*] [*A publication*] (DLA)
Potter Am Mo ... Potter's American Monthly [*A publication*]
Pottery .... Pottery in Australia [*A publication*] (APTA)
Pottery Aust ... Pottery in Australia [*A publication*]
Pottery Gaz Glass Trade Rev ... Pottery Gazette and Glass Trade Review [*A publication*]
Pottery Glass Rec ... Pottery and Glass Record [*A publication*]
Pottery Glass Trades J ... Pottery and Glass Trades Journal [*A publication*]
Potts LD..... Potts' Law Dictionary [*3rd ed.*] [*1815*] [*A publication*] (DLA)
POTUS....... President of the United States
POTV .... Personnel Orbit Transfer Vehicle (MCD)
Potvrda Valjanosti Broj Inst Meh Poljopr ... Potvrda o Valjanosti Broj-Institut za Mehanizaciju Poljoprivrede [*A publication*]
POTW .... Potable Water (KSC)
POTW .... Publically-Owned Treatment Works (DNAB)
POTW .... Publicly Owned Treatment Works (EG)
POTWA ..... Polimery Tworzywa [*A publication*]
POU.......... Paramount Resources Ltd. [*Toronto Stock Exchange symbol*]
POU.......... Placenta, Ovary, Uterus [*Medicine*]
POU.......... Poughkeepsie [*New York*] [*Airport symbol*] (OAG)
POU.......... Poughkeepsie, NY [*Location identifier*] [*FAA*] (FAAL)
POU.......... Pouilloux [*France*] [*Seismograph station code, US Geological Survey*] (SEIS)
POUCC ..... Post Office Users Coordination Committee [*British*]
POUDAY .. Poultry Digest [*A publication*]
POUF .... Projects of Optimum Urgency and Feasibility
Poughkeepsie Soc N Sc Pr ... Poughkeepsie Society of Natural Science. Proceedings [*A publication*]
POUL .... Poultry
Poult.......... Poultry Forum [*A publication*]
Poult Abstr ... Poultry Abstracts [*A publication*]
Poult Advis ... Poultry Adviser [*A publication*]
Poult Bull ... Poultry Bulletin [*A publication*]
Poult Dig.... Poultry Digest [*A publication*]
Poult Egg Situat PES US Dep Agric Econ Res Serv ... Poultry and Egg Situation. PES. United States Department of Agriculture. Economic Research Service [*A publication*]
Poult Health Symp ... Poultry Health Symposium [*A publication*]
Poult Ind .... Poultry Industry [*A publication*]
Poultry Dig ... Poultry Digest [*A publication*]
Poultry Livestock Comment ... Poultry and Livestock Comment [*A publication*]
Poultry Process ... Poultry Processing and Marketing [*A publication*]
Poultry Sci ... Poultry Science [*A publication*]
Poult Sci..... Poultry Science [*A publication*]
Poult Trib... Poultry Tribune [*A publication*]
Poult World ... Poultry World [*A publication*]
POUNC ...... Post Office Users' National Council [*British*] (ILCA)
POUP .... Post Overhaul Upkeep Period
poup---........ United States Miscellaneous Pacific Islands [*MARC geographic area code*] [*Library of Congress*] (LCCP)
Pour Sci (Paris) ... Pour la Science (Paris) (Edition Francaise de Scientific American) [*A publication*]
POUS .... Partido Operario de Unidade Socialista [*Workers' Party for Socialist Unity*] [*Portugal*] [*Political party*] (PPW)
POV.......... Peak Operated Valve (MCD)
POV.......... Peak Operating Voltage
POV.......... Personally Owned Vehicle
POV.......... Pinch-Off Voltage

POV .... Pittsburgh & Ohio Valley Railway Co. [*AAR code*]
POV .... Plane of Vibration
POV .... Pneumatically Operated Valve
POV .... Point of View
POV .... Pressure-Operated Valve (MCD)
POV .... Privately Owned Vehicle (NVT)
POV .... Proximity Operations Vehicle (SSD)
POV .... Purchase, Outside Vendors
POV .... Putting-On Voltage [*Doppler navigation*] (DEN)
Poverkhn Yavleniya Polim ... Poverkhnostnye Yavleniya v Polimerakh [*A publication*]
Poverkhn Yavleniya Zhidk Zhidk Rastvorakh ... Poverkhnostnye Yavleniya v Zhidkostyakh i Zhidkikh Rastvorakh [*A publication*]
POVEU ..... Program Operations Vocational Education Unit (OICC)
Pov & Human Resour Abstr ... Poverty and Human Resources Abstracts [*A publication*]
Pov Hum Resour ... Poverty and Human Resources [*A publication*]
Pov Hum Resour Abstr ... Poverty and Human Resources Abstracts [*A publication*]
Pov L Rep .. Poverty Law Reporter [*Commerce Clearing House*] [*A publication*] (DLA)
POVORTAD ... Positive Vorticity Advection [*Meteorology*] (FAAC)
POVT .... Puerperal Ovarian-Vein Thrombophlebitis [*Medicine*]
Povysh Plodorodiya Pochv Nechernozemn Polosy ... Povyshenie Plodorodiya Pochv Nechernozemnoi Polosy [*A publication*]
POW .... Pay Order of Withdrawal
POW .... Paying Their Own Way
POW .... Peoples of the World [*A publication*]
POW .... Perception of Ward [*Scales*] [*Psychology*]
POW .... Petty Officer of the Watch [*Navy*]
POW .... Powassan Encephalitis [*Medicine*]
POW .... Powder [*Navy*]
POW .... Power
POW .... Power Corp. of Canada [*Toronto Stock Exchange symbol*] [*Vancouver Stock Exchange symbol*]
POW .... Powhatan [*Arkansas*] [*Seismograph station code, US Geological Survey*] (SEIS)
POW .... Prince of Wales
POW .... Prisoner of War [*Also, PW*]
POW .... Progressive Order of the West [*Defunct*] (EA)
POW .... PSE, Inc. [*AMEX symbol*] (SPSG)
POWACO ... Portable Water Coolant Circulator
Pow App Proc ... Powell's Law of Appellate Proceedings [*A publication*] (DLA)
PoWBN ..... Biblioteka Narodowa [*National Library*], Warsaw, Poland [*Library symbol*] [*Library of Congress*] (LCLS)
PoWC .... Instytut Informacji Naukowej, Technicznej, i Ekonomicznej, Warsaw, Poland [*Library symbol*] [*Library of Congress*] (LCLS)
Pow Car ..... Powell's Inland Carriers [*2nd ed.*] [*1861*] [*A publication*] (DLA)
Pow Cont .... Powell on Contracts [*A publication*] (DLA)
Pow Conv ... Powell. Conveyancing [*1810*] [*A publication*] (ILCA)
POWD .... Powder [*England*]
POWD .... Powdered
Powder Coat ... Powder Coatings [*A publication*]
Powder Eng ... Powder Engineering [*Former USSR*] [*A publication*]
Powder Ind Res ... Powder Industry Research [*A publication*]
Powder Met ... Powder Metallurgy [*A publication*]
Powder Metall ... Powder Metallurgy [*A publication*]
Powder Metall Def Technol ... Powder Metallurgy in Defense Technology [*A publication*]
Powder Metall Int ... Powder Metallurgy International [*A publication*]
Powder Technol ... Powder Technology [*A publication*]
Powder Technol (Lausanne) ... Powder Technology (Lausanne) [*A publication*]
Powder Technol Publ Ser ... Powder Technology Publication Series [*A publication*]
Powder Technol (Tokyo) ... Powder Technology (Tokyo) [*A publication*]
Pow Dev ..... Powell's Essay upon the Learning of Devises, Etc. [*A publication*] (DLA)
Powd Metall ... Powder Metallurgy [*A publication*]
POWDR .... Protect Our Wetlands and Duck Resources [*Department of the Interior*] [*Washington, DC*]
Powd Tech ... Powder Technology [*A publication*]
POWER ..... Pension Opportunities for Workers' Expanded Retirement [*Plan proposed in 1991 by the Department of Labor*]
POWER ..... People Organized and Working for Economic Rebirth [*Program for black economic development*] [*Later, Nationway Ventures International Ltd.*]
POWER ..... Planning Operation With Enabling Resources
POWER ..... Professionals Organized for Women's Equal Rights [*Feminist group*]
POWER ..... Programmed Operational Warshot Evaluation and Review
POWER ..... Promote Our Wonderful Energy Resources (EA)
PowerConvers Int ... PowerConversion International [*A publication*]
Power Eng ... Power Engineering [*A publication*]
Power Eng (India) ... Power Engineer (India) [*A publication*]
Power Eng J Acad Sci (USSR) ... Power Engineering Journal. Academy of Sciences [*Former USSR*] [*A publication*]

Power Eng (NY Eng Transl) ... Power Engineering (New York, English Translation) [*A publication*]
Power Eqp ... Survey of Power Equipment Requirements of the United States Electric Utility Industry [*A publication*]
Power F ...... Power Farming [*A publication*]
Power Farming Aust ... Power Farming in Australia [*A publication*] (APTA)
Power Farming Better Farming Dig Aust NZ ... Power Farming and Better Farming Digest in Australia and New Zealand [*Later, Power Farming*] [*A publication*]
Power Farming Mag ... Power Farming Magazine [*A publication*] (APTA)
Power Fuel Bull ... Power and Fuel Bulletin [*A publication*]
Power Gener ... Power Generation [*A publication*]
Power Ind... Power Industry, Including Industrial Power and Industry Power [*A publication*]
Power Ind Res ... Power Industry Research [*England*] [*A publication*]
Power Plant Eng S Afr ... Power and Plant Engineering in South Africa [*A publication*]
Power Plant S Afr ... Power and Plant in Southern Africa [*A publication*]
Power Plant South Afr ... Power and Plant in Southern Africa [*A publication*]
Power Plant Sthn Afr ... Power and Plant in Southern Africa [*A publication*]
Power Pl Eng ... Power Plant Engineering [*A publication*]
Power Reactor Technol ... Power Reactor Technology [*Japan*] [*A publication*]
Power Reactor Technol Reactor Fuel Process ... Power Reactor Technology and Reactor Fuel Processing [*United States*] [*A publication*]
Power Reactor Technol (Tokyo) ... Power Reactor Technology (Tokyo) [*A publication*]
Power React Technol ... Power Reactor Technology [*A publication*]
Power React Technol React Fuel Process ... Power Reactor Technology and Reactor Fuel Processing [*A publication*]
Powers .... Powers' Reports, New York Surrogate Court [*A publication*] (DLA)
Power Sources Symp Proc ... Power Sources Symposium. Proceedings [*United States*] [*A publication*]
Power's Sur ... Powers' Reports, New York Surrogate Court [*A publication*] (DLA)
Power Trans Des ... Power Transmission Design [*A publication*]
Power Transm Des ... Power Transmission Design [*A publication*]
Power Works Eng ... Power and Works Engineering [*A publication*]
Power & Works Engng ... Power and Works Engineering [*A publication*]
Pow Ev .... Powell on Evidence [*10th ed.*] [*1921*] [*A publication*] (DLA)
powf--- .... Wallis and Futuna [*MARC geographic area code*] [*Library of Congress*] (LCCP)
Pow Inl Car ... Powell on the Law of Inland Carriers [*A publication*] (DLA)
powk--- .... Wake Island [*MARC geographic area code*] [*Library of Congress*] (LCCP)
POWL .... Powell Industries, Inc. [*NASDAQ symbol*] (NQ)
Powloki Ochr ... Powloki Ochronne [*A publication*]
POW/MIG ... Place of Work and Migration Sample [*Bureau of the Census*] (GFGA)
Pow Mort ... Powell on Mortgages [*6th ed.*] [*1826*] [*A publication*] (DLA)
Pow Mortg ... Powell on Mortgages [*A publication*] (DLA)
POWO .... Prince [*or Princess*] of Wales' Own [*Military unit*] [*British*] (DMA)
PoWP .... Biblioteka Golowna Politechniki Warszawskjej (Warsaw Technical University Central Library), Warsaw, Poland [*Library symbol*] [*Library of Congress*] (LCLS)
POWP .... Preliminary Overhaul Work Package (DNAB)
POWR .... Environmental Power Corp. [*NASDAQ symbol*] (NQ)
Pow R & D ... Power, Rodwell, and Drew's English Election Cases [*1847-56*] [*A publication*] (DLA)
POWRENAF ... Petty Officer WREN [*Women's Royal Naval Service*] Air Fitter [*British military*] (DMA)
POWRENCINE ... Petty Officer WREN [*Women's Royal Naval Service*] Cinema Operator [*British military*] (DMA)
POWRENCK ... Petty Officer WREN [*Women's Royal Naval Service*] Cook [*British military*] (DMA)
POWRENDHYG ... Petty Officer WREN [*Women's Royal Naval Service*] Dental Hygienist [*British military*] (DMA)
POWRENDSA ... Petty Officer WREN [*Women's Royal Naval Service*] Dental Surgery Assistant [*British military*] (DMA)
POWRENMET ... Petty Officer WREN [*Women's Royal Naval Service*] Meteorological Observer [*British military*] (DMA)
POWRENMT ... Petty Officer WREN [*Women's Royal Naval Service*] Motor Transport Driver [*British military*] (DMA)
POWRENPHOT ... Petty Officer WREN [*Women's Royal Naval Service*] Photographer [*British military*] (DMA)
POWRENQA ... Petty Officer WREN [*Women's Royal Naval Service*] Quarters Assistant [*British military*] (DMA)
POWREN(R) ... Petty Officer WREN [*Women's Royal Naval Service*] (RADAR) [*British military*] (DMA)
POWRENREL ... Petty Officer WREN [*Women's Royal Naval Service*] Radio Electrician [*British military*] (DMA)
POWRENRS(M) ... Petty Officer WREN [*Women's Royal Naval Service*] Radio Supervisor (Morse) [*British military*] (DMA)
POWRENSA ... Petty Officer WREN [*Women's Royal Naval Service*] Stores Accountant [*British military*] (DMA)
POWRENS(C) ... Petty Officer WREN [*Women's Royal Naval Service*] Stores Assistant (Clothes) [*British military*] (DMA)
POWRENS(S) ... Petty Officer WREN [*Women's Royal Naval Service*] Stores Assistant (Stores) [*British military*] (DMA)

POWRENSTD ... Petty Officer WREN [*Women's Royal Naval Service*] Steward [*British military*]   (DMA)
POWRENS(V) ... Petty Officer WREN [*Women's Royal Naval Service*] Stores Assistant (Victualling) [*British military*]   (DMA)
POWRENTEL ... Petty Officer WREN [*Women's Royal Naval Service*] Telephonist [*British military*]   (DMA)
POWRENTSA ... Petty Officer WREN [*Women's Royal Naval Service*] Training Support Assistant [*British military*]   (DMA)
POWRENWA ... Petty Officer WREN [*Women's Royal Naval Service*] Weapon Analyst [*British military*]   (DMA)
POWRENWTR(G) ... Petty Officer WREN [*Women's Royal Naval Service*] Writer (General) [*British military*]   (DMA)
POWRENWTR(P) ... Petty Officer WREN [*Women's Royal Naval Service*] Writer (Pay) [*British military*]   (DMA)
POWRENWW ... Petty Officer WREN [*Women's Royal Naval Service*] Welfare Worker [*British military*]   (DMA)
POWS .... Project Operating Work Statement [*NASA*]   (NASA)
POWS .... Pyrotechnic Outside Warning System   (IEEE)
pows--- .... Western Samoa [*MARC geographic area code*] [*Library of Congress*]   (LCCP)
POW-SIG ... Pagan/Occult/Witchcraft Special Interest Group   (EA)
Pow Surr .... Powers' Reports, New York Surrogate Court [*A publication*]   (DLA)
POWTECH ... International Powder and Bulk Solids Technology Exhibition and Conference
POWTR ..... Petty Officer Writer [*British military*]   (DMA)
POWU .... Post Office Work Unit [*Computer performance measure*] [*British Telecom*]
PoWU .... Uniwersytet Warszawski [*University of Warsaw*], Warsaw, Poland [*Library symbol*] [*Library of Congress*]   (LCLS)
POWWER ... Power of World Wide Energy Resources [*In organization name "Natural POWWER"*]   (EA)
Powys N ..... Powys Newsletter [*A publication*]
Powys Rev ... Powys Review [*A publication*]
POX .... Partial Oxidation [*Organic chemistry*]
POX .... Point of Exit
P-OX .... Pressure Oxidation
poxd--- .... Mariana Islands [*MARC geographic area code*] [*Library of Congress*]   (LCCP)
poxe--- .... Marshall Islands [*MARC geographic area code*] [*Library of Congress*]   (LCCP)
poxf--- .... Midway Islands [*MARC geographic area code*] [*Library of Congress*]   (LCCP)
P Oxf .... Some Oxford Papyri [*A publication*]
P Oxford .... Some Oxford Papyri [*A publication*]
poxh--- .... Niue [*MARC geographic area code*] [*Library of Congress*]   (LCCP)
POxy .... Oxyrhynchus Papyri [*A publication*]
POY .... Partially Oriented Yarns
POY .... Powell, WY [*Location identifier*] [*FAA*]   (FAAL)
POY .... Prairie Oil Royalties Co. Ltd. [*AMEX symbol*] [*Toronto Stock Exchange symbol*]   (SPSG)
Poynt M & D ... Poynter on Marriage and Divorce [*2nd ed.*] [*1824*] [*A publication*]   (DLA)
POZ .... Poznan [*Poland*] [*Airport symbol*]   (OAG)
POZBDM ... Folia Venatoria [*A publication*]
Pozharnaya Okhr ... Pozharnaya Okhrana [*A publication*]
Poznan Stud ... Poznan Studies [*A publication*]
Pozn St Teol ... Poznanskie Studie Teologiczne [*A publication*]
PP .... Brazil [*Aircraft nationality and registration mark*]   (FAAC)
PP .... Descent through Cloud [*Procedure*] [*Aviation code*]   (FAAC)
PP .... Die Palmyrenischen Personennamen [*A publication*]
PP .... Eisai Co. Ltd. [*Japan*] [*Research code symbol*]
PP .... Free Library of Philadelphia, Philadelphia, PA [*Library symbol*] [*Library of Congress*]   (LCLS)
P & P .... Packing and Preservation
PP .... Page Printer   (NVT)
PP .... Pages
PP .... Pages from the Past [*Later, PIR*] [*An association*]   (EA)
PP .... Palestine Post [*A publication*]
PP .... Palisades Plant [*Nuclear energy*]   (NRCH)
PP .... Palus Putretudinis [*Lunar area*]
P & P .... Pam and Peter Fisher [*Commercial firm*] [*British*]
PP .... Pan Pipes [*A publication*]
PP .... Pancreatic Polypeptide [*Biochemistry*]
PP .... Pandectes Periodiques [*A publication*]   (ILCA)
PP .... Panel Point [*Technical drawings*]
PP .... Pangu Pati [*Papua New Guinea*] [*Political party*]   (PPW)
PP .... Panstwo i Prawo [*A publication*]
PP .... Papa [*Pope*]
PP .... Paper Profit
P j P .... Paperi ja Puu [*A publication*]
pp .... Papua New Guinea [*MARC country of publication code*] [*Library of Congress*]   (LCCP)
PP .... Papyrusfunde und Papyrusforschung [*A publication*]
PP .... Paradigm Publishing Ltd. [*British*]
PP .... Parallel Processor
PP .... Parcel Post
PP .... Paris Publications, Inc.
PP .... Parish Priest
PP .... Parliamentary Paper [*A publication*]   (APTA)

PP .... Parliamentary Papers [*British*]
PP .... Parola del Passato [*A publication*]
PP .... Part Paid [*Business and trade*]
PP .... Parti du Peuple [*People's Party*] [*Burundi*] [*Political party*]
PP .... Partia Popullore [*Popular Party*] [*Albania*] [*Political party*]   (PPE)
P/P .... Partial Pay [*Air Force*]
PP .... Partial Pressure
PP .... Partial Program
PP .... Particular [*Named*] Port [*British*]   (ROG)
PP .... Partido Panamenista [*Panamanian Party*] [*Political party*]   (PPW)
PP .... Partido Popular [*Popular Party*] [*Spain*] [*Political party*]   (PPE)
PP .... Partido Populista [*Populist Party*] [*Argentina*] [*Political party*]
PP .... Partners in Politics   (EA)
PP .... Parts Per
PP .... [*The*] Passionate Pilgrim [*Shakespearean work*]
PP .... Passive Participle
PP .... Past Participle
PP .... Past Patriarch [*Freemasonry*]   (ROG)
P & P .... Past and Present [*A publication*]
PP .... Past President
PP .... Pastor Pastorum [*Shepherd of the Shepherds*] [*Latin*]   (ROG)
P/P .... Patch Panel   (NASA)
PP .... Pater Patriae [*The Father of His Country*] [*Latin*]
PP .... Patres [*Fathers*] [*Latin*]
PP .... Patriarchs and Prophets
PP .... Patriotic Party [*British*]
PP .... Patrol Vessels [*Navy symbol*]   (MUGU)
PP .... Pay Period   (FAAC)
P and P ...... Payments and Progress Committee [*NATO*]   (NATG)
PP .... Peace PAC   (EA)
P & P .... Peace and Prosperity Issue [*Politics*]
PP .... Peak-to-Peak
PP .... Peak Pressure
PP .... Peanut Pals   (EA)
PP .... Pedal Power
PP .... Pedal Pulse
PP .... Pellagra Preventive [*Factor*] [*See also PPF*] [*Biochemistry*]
PP .... Pension Plan
PP .... People's Party [*Halkci Partisi*] [*Turkey*] [*Political party*]   (PPW)
PP .... Pep Pill [*Slang*]
PP .... Per Procurationem [*By Proxy, By the Action Of*] [*Legal term*] [*Latin*]
P and P ...... Perception and Psychophysics [*A publication*]
PP .... Periodical Publications [*British Library shelf designation*]
PP .... Peripheral Processor [*Data processing*]
PP .... Periportal [*Anatomy*]
PP .... Periproct [*Invertebrate anatomy*]
PP .... Permanent Partial [*Dentistry*]   (MAE)
PP .... Permanent Party [*Military*]
PP .... Permanent Pasture [*Agriculture*]
PP .... Permanent Press   (ADA)
PP .... Permanent Professor
PP .... [*Length between*] Perpendiculars [*Shipbuilding*]
P-P .... Person to Person [*Word processing*]
PP .... Personal Property
PP .... Pet Pride   (EA)
PP .... Petroleum Point
PP .... Petrus Piccoli de Monteforte [*Flourished, 14th century*] [*Authority cited in pre-1607 legal work*]   (DSA)
PP .... Petticoat Peeping [*From one girl to another, in reference to dress disarrangement*]
PP .... Peyer's Patch [*Immunology*]
PP .... Philo-Phobe [*Psychological testing*]
PP .... Philologica Pragensia [*A publication*]
PP .... Philosophia Patrum [*A publication*]
PP .... Phoenix Project [*An association*]   (EA)
PP .... Phony Peach Bacteria [*Plant pathology*]
PP .... Photosynthetic Panel [*i.e., leaf*] [*Slang*]
PP .... Physical Profile
PP .... Physical Properties
PP .... Phytophthora Parasitica [*A fungus*]
PP .... Pianissimo [*Very Softly*] [*Music*]
PP .... Picked Ports
PP .... Pickpocket
PP .... Picture Peace [*Defunct*]   (EA)
P/P .... Pier to Pier   (ADA)
PP .... Piers Plowman [*Middle English poem*]
PP .... Piissimus [*Most Holy*] [*Latin*]
PP .... Pilot Parents   (EA)
PP .... Pilot Punch
PP .... Pilotless Plane
PP .... Pine Bark Mixed with Peat
PP .... Pinepointer [*A publication*]
PP .... Pink Puffer [*Emphysema*]   (MAE)
PP .... Pinpoint   (MAE)
PP .... Piping
PP .... Piscataqua Pioneers   (EA)
PP .... Pitt Press Series [*A publication*]

PP	Piu Piano [*More Softly*] [*Music*]
PP	PIXEL-Processing [*Data processing*]
PP	Placental Protein [*Gynecology*]
PP	Plan Profile
PP	Plane Parallel
PP	Plane Polarized [*Telecommunications*] (TEL)
PP	Planetary Programs [*NASA*]
PP	Planned Parenthood
PP	Planning Package [*NASA*] (NASA)
PP	Planning Purpose
P & P	Plans and Policies
P & P	Plans and Programs
PP	Plant Protection
PP	Plasma Protein
PP	Plasmapheresis [*Hematology*]
PP	Plaster of Paris
P to P	Plate to Plate (DEN)
PP	Play or Pay (ROG)
PP	Please Pay (ROG)
PP	Pleural Pressure [*Medicine*]
PP	Plot Points [*Data processing*]
PP	Pluvius Policy [*Insurance against rain*]
P a P	Poco a Poco [*Little by Little*] [*Music*]
PP	Poetry Project (EA)
P/P	Point-to-Point [*Air Force*]
PP	Polar Pacific [*American air mass*]
PP	Pole Piece (DEN)
PP	Polizei Pistole [*Police Pistol*] [*Walther Waffenfabrik, German arms manufacturer*]
PP	Polypeptide [*Biochemistry*]
PP	Polyphosphate [*Inorganic chemistry*] (AAMN)
PP	Polypropylene [*Organic chemistry*]
PP	Polypyrrole [*Photovoltaic energy systems*]
PP	Pom-Pom [*Gun*]
PP	Pontificum [*Of the Popes*] [*Latin*]
PP	Population (Paris) [*A publication*]
PP	Populist Party of America [*Political party*] (EA)
PP	Port Pipe (ADA)
P to P	Port to Port [*Shipping*] (DS)
PP	Posa Piano [*Handle with Care*] [*Italian*] [*Shipping*]
PP	Position Paper (MCD)
PP	Post Pagado [*Postage Paid*] [*Spanish*] [*Shipping*]
PP	Post Partum [*After Birth*] [*Latin*] (ADA)
PP	Post Position [*Racing*]
P & P	Postage and Packing [*Shipping*]
PP	Postage Paid [*Shipping*]
pp	Posted Price (MENA)
PP	Posterior Parietal Cortex [*Neuroanatomy*]
PP	Posterior Pituitary [*Medicine*]
pp	Postpaid
PP	Postpass
PP	Postponed
PP	Postprandial [*After Meals*] [*Pharmacy*]
PP	Pounds Pressure
PP	Power Package
PP	Power People
PP	Power Plant
PP	Power Play [*Hockey*]
PP	Power Pole (NASA)
PP	Power Supplies [*JETDS nomenclature*] [*Military*] (CET)
PP	Praemissis Praemittendis [*Omitting Preliminaries*] [*Latin*]
PP	Praepter Propter [*Approximately*] [*Pharmacy*]
PP	Prasa Polska [*A publication*]
Pp	Pratylenchus penetrans [*A nematode*]
PP	Prepaid
PP	Preparative Flag [*Navy*] [*British*]
PP	Preparing, Providing [*Pharmacy*] (ROG)
PP	Preposition [*Industrial engineering*]
PP	Prepositional Phrase (BYTE)
PP	Prepregnancy [*Medicine*]
PP	Preprinted
PP	Preprocessor
PP	Preproduction (KSC)
PP	Prescribed Period [*Social Security Administration*] (OICC)
PP	Present Participle [*Grammar*]
PP	Present Position [*Military*]
PP	Presocratic Philosophers [*A publication*]
PP	Press Packed
PP	Press Pressure (SSD)
PP	Pressure Pattern (MCD)
PP	Pressure-Proof [*Technical drawings*]
PP	Pretty Poor [*Slang*] [*Bowdlerized version*]
P & P	Pride and Prejudice [*Novel by Jane Austen*]
PP	Primary Pressure [*Nuclear energy*] (NRCH)
PP	Primary Producers (ADA)
PP	Princess Pat's [*Princess Patricia of Connaught's Light Infantry*] [*Military unit*] [*Canada*]
PP	Principal
PP	Principal Point
PP	Print Positions
PP	Print-Punch [*Data processing*] (BUR)
PP	Printer Page [*Data processing*]
P/P	Printer/Plotter (NASA)
PP	Prior Permission
PP	Priority Processor
PP	Private Jet Services AG [*Sweden*] [*ICAO designator*] (ICDA)
P/P	Private Passenger
PP	Private Patient [*Medicine*]
PP	Private Practice [*Chiropody*] [*British*]
PP	Private Property [*Military*]
PP	Privately Printed
pp	Pro Parte [*In Part*] [*Latin*]
PP	Procurement Plan (MCD)
P & P	Procurement and Production [*Military*]
PP	Producer Price
PP	Production Processes
P & P	Production and Procurement [*Military*]
PP	Professional Paper
PP	Professor Publicus [*Public Professor*] [*Latin*] (ROG)
PP	Program Package (MCD)
PP	Program Paper
PP	Program Performance (NASA)
PP	Program Product [*Data processing*]
PP	Programming Plan (AFM)
PP	Progress Payments [*Military procurement*]
PP	Project Priesthood (EA)
PP	Project Proposal (KSC)
PP	Proletarian Party
PP	Proodeftiki Parataxis [*Progressive Front*] [*Greek Cyprus*] [*Political party*] (PPE)
PP	Propeller Pitch
PP	Proportional Part
PP	Propria Persona [*In His or Her Own Person*] [*Latin*] (WGA)
PP	Propulsion Power (KSC)
PP	Protein Phosphatase [*An enzyme*]
PP	Prothrombin-Proconvertin [*Hematology*]
PP	Proton-Proton [*Nuclear physics*]
PP	Protoporphyria [*Medicine*]
PP	Protoporphyrin [*Biochemistry*]
PP	Provisioning Procedures [*Corps of Engineers*]
PP	Proximal Phalanx [*Anatomy*]
PP	Przeglad Powszechny [*A publication*]
PP	Psychic Phenomena
PP	Psychological Profile
PP	Psychologists and Psychiatrists [*in service*] [*British*]
P/P	Pterocephaliid-Ptychaspid [*Paleogeologic boundary*]
PP	Public Property
P or P	Publish or Perish [*Said of scholars, scientists, etc.*]
PP	Published Price [*of a book*]
PP	Pulse Polarography [*Analytical chemistry*]
PP	Pulse Pressure [*Medicine*]
PP	Pulvis Patrum [*The Fathers' Powder (or Jesuits' Powder)*] [*Pharmacy*] (ROG)
PP	Punctum Proximum [*Near Point*] [*Latin*]
PP	Purchase Power [*Commercial firm*] (EA)
PP	Purchase Price
PP	Purchased Parts
PP	Push-Pull [*Technical drawings*]
PP	Pusher Plane
PP	Pyrophosphate [*Chemistry*]
PPA	Athenaeum of Philadelphia, Philadelphia, PA [*Library symbol*] [*Library of Congress*] (LCLS)
PPA	National Plant Protection Association
PPA	Paleopathology Association (EA)
PP & A	Palpation, Percussion, and Auscultation [*Medicine*]
PPA	Palpation, Percussion, and Auscultation [*Medicine*]
PPA	Pampa, TX [*Location identifier*] [*FAA*] (FAAL)
PPA	Panamerican/Panafrican Association (EA)
PPA	Paper Pail Association [*Defunct*] (EA)
PPA	Paper Plate Association [*Later, SSI*] (EA)
PPA	Parcel Post Association [*Later, PSA*] (EA)
PPA	Parents for Private Adoption (EA)
PPa	Parola del Passato [*A publication*]
PPA	Partido Panamenista Autentico [*Panama*] [*Political party*] (EY)
PPA	Partido Patriotico Arubano [*Aruban Patriotic Party*] [*Netherlands Antilles*] [*Political party*] (PPW)
PPA	Partido Peronista Autentico [*Authentic Peronist Party*] [*Argentina*] [*Political party*] (EY)
PPA	Pathology Practice Association (EA)
PPA	Peat Producers Association [*British*] (EAIO)
PPA	Pension Protection Act (GFGA)
PPA	Pensioner Party of Australia [*Political party*]
PPA	Peppa Resources [*Vancouver Stock Exchange symbol*]
PPA	Per Power of Attorney [*Business term*]
PPA	Perennial Plant Association (EA)
PPA	Periodical Publishers Association [*Later, MCA*] (EA)
PPA	Permian Partnership LP [*NYSE symbol*] (SPSG)
PPA	Pesticide Producers Association (EA)
PPA	Pet Producers of America (EA)
PPA	Phenylpropanolamine [*Organic chemistry*]

PPA............ Phenylpropanolamine(hydrochloride) [*Also, PPH, PPM*] [*Decongestant*]
PPA............ Phenylpyruvic Acid [*Organic chemistry*]
PPA............ Phiala Prius Agitata [*Having First Shaken the Bottle*] [*Pharmacy*]
PPA............ Photo Peak Analysis   (IEEE)
PPA............ Pictorial Photographers of America   (EAIO)
PPA............ Pie De Palo [*Argentina*] [*Seismograph station code, US Geological Survey*]   (SEIS)
PPA............ Pilots and Passengers Association [*Defunct*]   (EA)
PPA............ Pitch Precession Amplifier
PPA............ Pittsburgh Pneumonia Agent [*Microbiology*]
PPA............ Plant Patent Act [*1930*]
PPA............ Plasminogen Proactivator [*Hematology*]
PPA............ Plutonium Preparation Area [*Nuclear energy*]   (GFGA)
PPA............ Policyholders Protective Association of America   (EA)
PPA............ Pollution Prevention Act [*1990*]
PPA............ Polymer Permeation Analyzer
PPA............ Poly(phosphoric Acid) [*Inorganic chemistry*]
PPA............ Popcorn Processors Association [*Later, PI*]
PPA............ Popski's Private Army [*Commando force led by Vladimir Peniakoff*] [*World War II*]
PPA............ Postpartum Amenorrhea [*Medicine*]
PPA............ Poultry Publishers Association   (EA)
PPA............ Power Plant Automation
PPA............ Powerplant Performance Analysis
PPA............ Preschool Playgrounds Association [*British*]
PPA............ Presidents' Professional Association [*Later, Presidents Association*]   (EA)
PPA............ Press and Publications Administration [*China*]
PPA............ Princeton-Pennsylvania Accelerator [*Closed, 1972*] [*AEC*]
PPA............ Principal Port Authority [*British*]   (ROG)
PPA............ Printing Platemakers Association [*Later, GPA*]
PPA............ Priority Problem Areas   (MCD)
PPA............ Process Plan Association [*British*]   (DS)
PPA............ Produce Packaging Association [*Later, PMA*]   (EA)
PPA............ Professional Panhellenic Association [*Later, PFA*]   (EA)
PP of A...... Professional Photographers of America   (EA)
PPA............ Professional Programmers Association   (EA)
PPA............ Professional Putters Association   (EA)
PPA............ Program Problem Area
PPA............ Progress Presse Agentur GmbH [*Press agency*] [*Germany*]
PPA............ Progressive Party of America [*Third party in 1948 Presidential race*]
PPA............ Propane-Precipitated Asphalt [*Petroleum technology*]
PPA............ Protestant Press Agency [*British*]
PPA............ Prudent Purchaser Arrangement [*Medical insurance*]
PPA............ Pseudopassive Array
PPA............ Public Personnel Association [*Later, IPMA*]   (EA)
PPA............ Publishers' Publicity Association   (EA)
PPA............ Pulmonary Artery Pressure [*Cardiology*]
PPA............ Pulse Plasma Accelerator
PPA............ Pulsed Power Amplifier
PPA............ Purple Plum Association [*Defunct*]   (EA)
PPAA........ Patres Amplissimi [*Cardinals*] [*Latin*]
PPAA........ Personal Protective Armor Association   (EA)
PPAB........ Program and Policy Advisory Board [*UN Food and Agriculture Organization*]
PPABP...... American Baptist Publication Society, Philadelphia, PA [*Library symbol*] [*Library of Congress*] [*Obsolete*]   (LCLS)
PPAC........ Penn-Pacific Corp. [*NASDAQ symbol*]   (NQ)
PPAC........ Pesticide Policy Advisory Committee [*Environmental Protection Agency*]
PPAC........ Primary Progress Assessment Chart [*Psychology*]
PPAC........ Private Planning Association of Canada
PPAC........ Product Performance Agreement Center [*Military*]
PPAC........ Progressive Political Action Committee [*Defunct*]
PPACE...... United States Army, Corps of Engineers, Philadelphia District Library, Custom House, Philadelphia, PA [*Library symbol*] [*Library of Congress*]   (LCLS)
PPACHi.... American Catholic Historical Society, Philadelphia, PA [*Library symbol*] [*Library of Congress*]   (LCLS)
PPAD........ Public Administration [*A publication*]
PPADS...... Parawing Precision Aerial Delivery System   (MCD)
PPAEM..... Albert Einstein Medical Center, Northern Division, Philadelphia, PA [*Library symbol*] [*Library of Congress*]   (LCLS)
PPAF........ Pacific Affairs [*A publication*]
PPAFA...... Pennsylvania Academy of the Fine Arts, Philadelphia, PA [*Library symbol*] [*Library of Congress*] [*Obsolete*]   (LCLS)
PPAG........ Personnel Profile - Age by Grade [*Army*]
PPAI........ Pinpoint Assignment Instructions [*Army*]   (INF)
PPAJ........ Performing Arts Journal [*A publication*]
PPAK........ Atwater Kent Museum, Philadelphia, PA [*Library symbol*] [*Library of Congress*]   (LCLS)
PPAL........ Principal   (ROG)
PPalZ......... New Jersey Zinc Co. [*of Pennsylvania*], Technical Library, Palmerton, PA [*Library symbol*] [*Library of Congress*]   (LCLS)
PPAmP...... American Philosophical Society, Philadelphia, PA [*Library symbol*] [*Library of Congress*]   (LCLS)

PPAmS...... American Sunday School Union, Philadelphia, PA [*Library symbol*] [*Library of Congress*] [*Obsolete*]   (LCLS)
PPAmSR ... American Sugar Refining Co., Philadelphia, PA [*Library symbol*] [*Library of Congress*] [*Obsolete*]   (LCLS)
PPAmSwM ... American Swedish Historical Foundation, Philadelphia, PA [*Library symbol*] [*Library of Congress*]   (LCLS)
PPAN .... Academy of Natural Sciences of Philadelphia, Philadelphia, PA [*Library symbol*] [*Library of Congress*]   (LCLS)
PPAN .... Pyrolyzed Polyacrylonitrile [*Organic chemistry*]
PPAp......... Apprentices' Free Library, Philadelphia, PA [*Library symbol*] [*Library of Congress*] [*Obsolete*]   (LCLS)
PPAP........ People's Party of Arunachal Pradesh [*India*] [*Political party*]   (PPW)
PPAP........ Precedents of Private Acts of Parliament [*A publication*]   (DLA)
PPAR........ Parabola [*A publication*]
PPAR........ Paterson Parchment Paper Co. [*Sunnyvale, CA*] [*NASDAQ symbol*]   (NQ)
PPAR........ Peroxisome Proliferator-Activated Receptor [*Genetics*]
PPAR........ Priority Problem Analysis Report [*Military*]   (DNAB)
PPAR........ Project Performance Audit Report
PPArmA .... Armstrong Association of Philadelphia, Philadelphia, PA [*Library symbol*] [*Library of Congress*] [*Obsolete*]   (LCLS)
PPAS .... Patti Page Appreciation Society   (EA)
PPAS .... Portable Public Address System   (MCD)
PPAS .... Potassium Picrate Active Substances [*Measure of detergent content of water*]
PPAS .... Probability Proportional to Aggregate Size [*Statistics*]
PPATDQ... Pediatric Pathology [*A publication*]
PPAtR....... Atlantic Refining Co., Philadelphia, PA [*Library symbol*] [*Library of Congress*]   (LCLS)
PPATY ...... Preparatory   (ROG)
PPAuC....... Automobile Club of Philadelphia, Philadelphia, PA [*Library symbol*] [*Library of Congress*] [*Obsolete*]   (LCLS)
PPA Univ KY Coop Ext Serv ... PPA. University of Kentucky. Cooperative Extension Service [*A publication*]
PPAUS ...... Peat Producers Association of the United States   (EA)
PPAW....... Public Policy Affecting Women Task Force   (EA)
PP & B ...... Paper, Printing, and Binding [*Publishing*]
PPB........... Parachute Paraglider Building [*NASA*]   (KSC)
PPB........... Parts per Billion
PPB........... Petro-Canada Products, Inc. [*Toronto Stock Exchange symbol*] [*Vancouver Stock Exchange symbol*]
PPB........... Philadelphia Bar Association, Philadelphia, PA [*Library symbol*] [*Library of Congress*]   (LCLS)
P-P-B .... Planning-Programming-Budgeting [*System*] [*Army*]
PPB........... Platelet-Poor Blood [*Hematology*]   (MAE)
PPB........... Political Party Broadcast [*Television*] [*British*]
PPB........... Polybiblion. Partie Litteraire [*A publication*]
PPB........... Poly(para-benzamide) [*Organic chemistry*]
PPB........... Positive Pressure Breathing [*Aerospace*]
PPB........... Power Plant Bulletin   (MCD)
PPB........... Precision Pressure Balance
PPB........... Pres Prudente [*Brazil*] [*Airport symbol*]   (OAG)
PPB........... Primary Propulsion Branch [*Manned Spacecraft Center*]
PPB........... Private Posting Box
PPB........... Production Parts Breakdown   (MCD)
PPB........... Program Performance Baseline   (NASA)
PPB........... Program Planning Budget   (NOAA)
PPB........... Program-Planning-Budgeting
PPB........... PROM [*Programmable Read-Only Memory*] Programmer Board
PPB........... Provisioning Parts Breakdown
PPB........... Purchasing Power Benefit   (ADA)
PPB........... Push-Pull Bearing
PPBB .... Partai Pesaka Bumiputra Bersatu [*United Traditional Bumiputra Party*] [*Malaysia*] [*Political party*]   (PPW)
PPBB .... Prime Power Brass Board   (MCD)
PPBC........ Pittsburgh Penguins Booster Club   (EA)
PPBC........ Plant Pathogenic Bacteria Committee   (EA)
PPBC-R ..... Portland Problem Behavior Checklist - Revised [*Educational test*]
P PBD....... Paper or Paperboard [*Freight*]
PPBD....... Port of Palm Beach District [*AAR code*]
PPBERS .... Program Performance and Budget Execution Review System [*Army*]
PPBES....... Planning, Programming, Budgeting, and Execution System [*Army*]   (RDA)
PPBES....... Program Planning and Budget Execution System [*Army*]
PPBES....... Program Planning-Budgeting-Evaluation System Project   (EA)
PPBESP .... Program Planning-Budgeting-Evaluation System Project   (EA)
PPBF........ Pan-American Pharmaceutical and Biochemical Federation
PPBFSPS .. Pen and Pocket Blade Forgers' and Smithers' Protective Society [*A union*] [*British*]
PPBG........ Preliminary Program and Budget Guidance
PPBI .... Balch Institute, Philadelphia, PA [*Library symbol*] [*Library of Congress*]   (LCLS)
PPBM....... Pulse Polarization Binary Modulation   (MCD)
PPBMIS.... Planning, Programming, and Budgeting Management Information System [*Army*]
PPBR .... Program Plan and Budget Request   (OICC)

PPBS .... Planning, Programming, and Budgeting System [*Army*]
PPBS .... Positive Pressure Breathing System [*Aerospace*]
PPBS .... Postprandial Blood Sugar [*Clinical chemistry*]
PPBS .... Program Planning and Budgeting Staff [*Environmental Protection Agency*] (GFGA)
PPBS .... Program, Planning, and Budgeting System [*Johnson Administration*] [*Executive Office of the President*] (GFGA)
PPBUA...... Personnel Practice Bulletin [*A publication*]
PPC........... College of Physicians of Philadelphia, Philadelphia, PA [*Library symbol*] [*Library of Congress*] [*OCLC symbol*] (LCLS)
PP-C .... Free Library of Philadelphia, Carson Collection, Philadelphia, PA [*Library symbol*] [*Library of Congress*] (LCLS)
PPC........... Journal of Pension Planning and Compliance [*A publication*]
PPC........... Pan Pacific Centers (EA)
PPC........... Paperboard Packaging Council (EA)
PPC........... Partial Pay Card
PPC........... Partido Popular Cristiano [*Christian Popular Party*] [*Peru*] [*Political party*] (PPW)
PPC........... Parting Post Calls (MCD)
PPC........... Partitu Populare Corsu [*Corsica*] [*Political party*] (PD)
PPC........... Parts Preference Code [*Military*] (AFIT)
PPC........... Patres Conscripti [*Senators*] [*Latin*] (ROG)
PPC........... Patrick Petroleum Co. [*NYSE symbol*] (SPSG)
PPC........... Patrol Plane Commander
PPC........... Peak Power Control [*Telecommunications*] (TEL)
PPC........... Per Pupil Cost (AFM)
PPC........... Permission to Photocopy (MCD)
PPC........... Persistent Photoconductivity [*Physics*]
PPC........... Personal Portable Computer
PPC........... Personal Productivity Center
PPC........... Petroleum Planning Committee [*Obsolete*] [*NATO*] (NATG)
PPC........... Phased Provisioning Code (NASA)
PPC........... Philatelic Press Club [*Later, IPPC*]
PPC........... Photographic Processing Cells (AFM)
PpC........... Pick Publishing Corporation, New York, NY [*Library symbol*] [*Library of Congress*] (LCLS)
PP & C ...... Pickpocket and Confidence [*Police term*]
PPC........... Picture Postcard
PPC........... Pierce's Perpetual Code [*1943*] [*A publication*] (DLA)
PPC........... Pine Pass [*British Columbia*] [*Seismograph station code, US Geological Survey*] [*Closed*] (SEIS)
PPC........... Plain Paper Copier [*Electrophotography*]
PPC........... Plain Plaster Cornice [*Construction*]
PPC........... Plant Pest Control Division [*of ARS, Department of Agriculture*]
PPC........... Plant Process Computer
PPC........... Platform Position Computer
PPC........... Plug Patch Cord
PPC........... Plutonium Process Cell [*Nuclear energy*] (NRCH)
PPC........... Plutonium Product Cell [*Nuclear energy*] (NRCH)
PPC........... Point-to-Point Correlation [*Graphing*]
PPC........... Point of Possible Collision [*Navigation*]
PPC........... Polyphthalate-Polycarbonate
PPC........... Positive Peer Control
PPC........... Posterior Parietal Cortex [*Brain anatomy*]
PPC........... Postpulmonary Complications
PPC........... Potential Points of Collision [*Navigation*]
PPC........... Pour Prendre Conge [*To Take Leave*] [*French*]
PPC........... Power Pack Charger
PPC........... Power Plant Change (NVT)
PPC........... PPC Oil & Gas Corp. [*Toronto Stock Exchange symbol*]
PPC........... Pre-Proposal Conference (MCD)
PPC........... Precision Photomechanical Corp.
PPC........... Preprocessing Center [*NASA*] (NASA)
PPC........... President of the Privy Council [*Canada*]
PPC........... Primary Power Control (MCD)
PPC........... Print Position Counter
PPC........... Priority Placement Certificate [*Military*] (AFM)
PPC........... Production Planning and Control
PP & C ...... Production Planning and Control [*Military*] (AABC)
PPC........... Professional Personal Computer
PPC........... Program Planning and Control (AAG)
PPC........... Program Planning Coordination Office [*United Nations*]
PPC........... Progressive Patient Care
PPC........... Project Parts Coordinator
PPC........... Project Physics Course [*National Science Foundation*]
PPC........... Project Planning Centre for Developing Countries [*Research center*] [*British*] (IRC)
PP & C ...... Project Planning and Control (NG)
PPC........... Prospect Creek, AK [*Location identifier*] [*FAA*] (FAAL)
PPC........... Prospective Parliamentary Candidate [*British*]
PPC........... Proximal Palmar Crease [*Anatomy*]
PPC........... Psychorotrophic Plate Count [*Bacteriology*]
PPC........... Publishers Publicity Circle
PPC........... Pulsed Power Circuit (IEEE)
PPCA........ Plasma [*or Proserum*] Prothrombin Conversion Accelerator [*Factor VII*] [*Also, SPCA*] [*Hematology*]
PPCAA...... Parole and Probation Compact Administrators Association (EA)
PPCAP ...... People to People Citizen Ambassador Program (EA)

PPCB .... Page Printer Control Block [*Data processing*]
PPCC........ Carpenters' Co., Philadelphia, PA [*Library symbol*] [*Library of Congress*] (LCLS)
PPCC........ Particles per Cubic Centimeter
PPCC........ Postmolded Plastic Chip Carrier [*Data processing*]
PPCCH...... Chestnut Hill College, Philadelphia, PA [*Library symbol*] [*Library of Congress*] (LCLS)
PPCE .... Portable Pneumatic Checkout Equipment (KSC)
PPCE .... Post-Proline Cleaving Enzyme [*Biochemistry*]
PPCF .... Plasmin Prothrombin Conversion Factor [*Factor V*] [*Hematology*]
PPCH .... People-to-People Committee for the Handicapped (EA)
PPCH .... Pilot Pouch [*Aviation*] (FAAC)
PPCI .... Curtis Institute of Music, Philadelphia, PA [*Library symbol*] [*Library of Congress*] (LCLS)
PPCI .... Pressure Piping Components, Inc. [*North Hills, NY*] [*NASDAQ symbol*] (NQ)
PPCiC .... Civic Club of Philadelphia, Philadelphia, PA [*Library symbol*] [*Library of Congress*] [*Obsolete*] (LCLS)
PPCIG .... Personal Property Consignment Instruction Guide (MCD)
PPC Jrl ..... Polymers, Paint, and Colour Journal [*A publication*]
PPCLI........ Princess Patricia of Connaught's Light Infantry [*Military unit*] [*Canada*]
PPCM........ Philadelphia County Medical Society, Philadelphia, PA [*Library symbol*] [*Library of Congress*] [*Obsolete*] (LCLS)
PPCO......... Philadelphia College of Osteopathic Medicine, Philadelphia, PA [*Library symbol*] [*Library of Congress*] (LCLS)
PPCO2...... Partial Pressure Carbon Dioxide
PPCoC .... Community College of Philadelphia, Philadelphia, PA [*Library symbol*] [*Library of Congress*] (LCLS)
PPColP ...... Colonial Penn Group, Inc., Marketing Research Library, Philadelphia, PA [*Library symbol*] [*Library of Congress*] (LCLS)
PPComm.... Commercial Museum, Philadelphia, PA [*Library symbol*] [*Library of Congress*] [*Obsolete*] (LCLS)
PPCP .... Propellant Pneumatic Control Panel (KSC)
PPCPC....... Philadelphia City Planning Commission, Philadelphia, PA [*Library symbol*] [*Library of Congress*] (LCLS)
PPCPSG.... Polish POW Camps Philatelic Study Group (EA)
PPCR .... Production Planning Change Request (SAA)
PPCS .... National Carl Schurz Memorial Foundation, Philadelphia, PA [*Library symbol*] [*Library of Congress*] [*Obsolete*] (LCLS)
PPCS .... Page Printer Control System [*Data processing*]
PPCS .... Person to Person: Collect and Special Instruction [*Telecommunications*] (TEL)
PPCS .... Precision Pointing Control System [*Engineering*]
PPCS .... Production Planning and Control System
PPCS .... Project Planning and Control System [*Social Security Administration*]
PPCuP .... Curtis Publishing Co., Research Library, Philadelphia, PA [*Library symbol*] [*Library of Congress*] [*Obsolete*] (LCLS)
PPD .... A Posteriori Probability Distribution [*Mathematics*]
PPD .... Drexel University, Philadelphia, PA [*Library symbol*] [*Library of Congress*] (LCLS)
PPD .... Humacao-Palmas [*Puerto Rico*] [*Airport symbol*] (OAG)
PPD .... Packs per Day [*Cigarettes*] [*Medicine*]
PPD .... Panel Power Distribution (MCD)
PPD .... Papered (ROG)
PPD .... Paraphenylenediamine [*Medicine*] (MAE)
PPD .... Parti Populaire Djiboutien [*Djibouti People's Party*] [*Political party*] (PPW)
PPD .... Parti Progressiste Dahomeen [*Dahomey Progressive Party*] [*Political party*]
PPD .... Partido por la Democracia [*Democratic Party*] [*Chile*] [*Political party*] (EY)
PPD .... Partido Popular Democratico [*Popular Democratic Party*] [*Puerto Rico*] [*Political party*] (PPW)
PPD .... Parts Provisioning Document
PPD .... Party for Peace and Democracy [*South Korea*] [*Political party*]
PPD .... Pay Packets Deficiency [*British*]
PPD .... Payload Position Data
PPD .... Pepsin Pancreatin Digest [*Food protein digestibility assay*]
P & PD ...... Percussion and Postural Drainage
PPD .... Permanent Partial Disability [*Dentistry*] (MAE)
PPD .... Personnel Planning Data [*Navy*]
PPD .... Personnel Priority Designator [*Military*] (AFM)
PPD .... Phenyldiphenyloxadiazole [*Organic chemistry*] (MAE)
PPD .... Pitch Phase Detector
PPD .... Plains Petroleum Co. [*Vancouver Stock Exchange symbol*]
PPD .... Plot Plan Drawing (SAA)
PPD .... Point Position Data
PPD .... Polish Perspectives [*A publication*]
PPD .... Politieke Partij Democraten 66 [*Political Party Democrats 66*] [*Netherlands*] (EAIO)
PPD .... Portuguese Popular Democrats
PPD .... Postpaid
PPD .... PostScript Printer Description [*Data processing*] (PCM)
PPD .... Pre-Paid Legal Services, Inc. [*AMEX symbol*] (SPSG)
PPD .... Prepaid
PPD .... Prepaid Dental Plan [*Insurance*] (MCD)
ppd .... Prepared (MAE)

PPD	Preprototype Demonstration
PPD	Presidential Protective Division [*US Secret Service*]
PPD	Prime Power Distribution
PPD	Processed Payment Document (GFGA)
PPD	Proficiency Pay Designator [*Military*] (AABC)
PPD	Prognostic Prediction Devices
PPD	Program Package Document
PPD	Program Planning Directives [*NASA*] (KSC)
PPD	Program Planning Document (NG)
PPD	Progressive Perceptive Deafness [*Medicine*]
PPD	Project Planning Directive (NG)
PPD	Projectile Pull and Drain [*Machine*] (MCD)
PPD	Propria Pecunia Dedicavit [*With His Own Money He Offered It*] [*Latin*] (ROG)
PPD	Propulsion and Power Division [*Manned Spacecraft Center*] [*NASA*]
PPD	Provisioning Procurement Data
PPD	Pulse-Type Phase Detector
PPD	Purified Protein Derivative [*Tuberculin*]
PPDA	Para-Phenylenediamine [*Organic chemistry*]
PPDA	Phenyl Phosphorodiamidate [*Fertilizer technology*]
PPDB	Personnel Planning Data Book [*Navy*]
PPDB	Point-Positioning Data Base [*Cartography*] (RDA)
PPD-B	Purified Protein Derivative - Battey [*Tuberculin*] (AAMN)
PPDC	Dental Cosmos Library, Philadelphia, PA [*Library symbol*] [*Library of Congress*] [*Obsolete*] (LCLS)
PPDC	Paraguayan People's Documentation Center [*Mestre, Italy*] (EAIO)
PPDC	Partido Popular Democratica Cristiana [*Popular Christian Democratic Party*] [*Spain*] [*Political party*] (PPE)
PPDC	Programming Panels and Decoding Circuits
PPDD	Plan Position Data Display
PPDD	Preliminary Project Design Description (NRCH)
PPDDS	Private Practice Dental Delivery System
PPDef-M ...	Defense Personnel Support Center, Directorate of Medical Material Library, Philadelphia, PA [*Library symbol*] [*Library of Congress*] (LCLS)
PPDF	Poisson Probability Distribution Function [*Mathematics*]
PPDG	Parti Progressiste Democratique Guadeloupeen [*Political party*] (EY)
PPDGF	Porcine Platelet-Derived Growth Factor [*Biochemistry*]
PPDI	Para-Phenylene Diisocyanate [*Organic chemistry*]
PPDIL	Pre-Power-Dependent Insertion Limit [*Nuclear energy*] (NRCH)
PPDio	Diocesan Library, Philadelphia, PA [*Library symbol*] [*Library of Congress*] [*Obsolete*] (LCLS)
PPDM	E. I. Du Pont de Nemours & Co., Marshall Laboratory, Philadelphia, PA [*Library symbol*] [*Library of Congress*] (LCLS)
PPDM	Pseudo-Pinch Design Method [*Heat exchange design*]
PPDMG......	Popular Priced Dress Manufacturers Group [*Later, AMA*] (EA)
PPDO	Personal Paid Days Off
PPDP	Preliminary Project Development Plan [*NASA*]
PPDP	Preprogram Definition Phase
PP-DPH	Free Library of Philadelphia, Library for the Blind and Physically Handicapped, Philadelphia, PA [*Library symbol*] [*Library of Congress*] (LCLS)
PPDR........	Pilot Performance Description Record
PPDR........	Population and Development Review [*A publication*]
PP/DR.......	Preliminary Performance Design Requirements
PPDR........	Production Packing Depth Range (NG)
PPDrop	Dropsie University, Philadelphia, PA [*Library symbol*] [*Library of Congress*] (LCLS)
PPDS	Personal Printer Data Stream [*IBM Corp.*] (PCM)
PPDS	Physical Property Data Service [*Institution of Chemical Engineers*] [*Databank*] [*Information service or system*] (IID)
PPDS	Planning Production Data Sheet
PPDS	Preservation and Packaging Data Sheet [*DoD*]
PPD-S........	Purified Protein Derivative-Standard [*Tuberculin*]
PPDSE	International Plate Printers, Die Stampers, and Engravers' Union of North America
PPDT........	(Phenylpyridyl)diphenyltriazine [*Analytical chemistry*]
PPDT........	Poly(phenyleneterephthalamide) [*Organic chemistry*]
PPE...........	Independent Union of Plant Protection Employees in the Electrical and Machine Industry
PPE...........	Parti Populaire Europeen [*European Peoples' Party - EPP*] (EAIO)
PPE...........	Personal Protective Equipment [*General Motors Corp.*]
PPE...........	Philosophy, Politics, Economics [*Oxford University*]
PPE...........	Pholbe Phillips Editions [*Publisher*] [*British*]
PPE...........	Pipette [*Chemistry*]
PPE...........	Platform Position Equipment
PPE...........	Polyphenylether (IEEE)
PPE...........	Polyphosphate Ester [*Inorganic chemistry*]
PPE...........	Porcine Pancreatic Elastase [*An enzyme*]
PPE...........	Portable Purge Equipment [*NASA*]
PPE...........	Potomac Pacific Engineering, Inc.
PPE...........	Predicted Period-of-Effect [*Meteorology*]
PPE...........	Premodulation Processing Equipment

PPE...........	Preproduction Engineering
PPE...........	Preproduction Evaluation (NG)
PPE...........	Preproduction Proposal Evaluation
PPE...........	Preproenkephalin [*Biochemistry*]
PPE...........	Print-Punch Editor [*Data processing*] (SAA)
PPE...........	Problem Program Efficiency (IEEE)
PPE...........	Problem Program Evaluator
PPE...........	Program Planning and Evaluation
PPE...........	Prototype Production Evaluation (NG)
PPE...........	Purchasing Power Equivalent
PPE...........	Pyridoxal Phosphate Effect [*Medicine*]
PPEA	Plant Performance Evaluation Activity [*Military*] (DNAB)
PPEB	Eastern Baptist Theological Seminary, Philadelphia, PA [*Library symbol*] [*Library of Congress*] (LCLS)
PPEB	[*The*] Pottery of Palestine from the Earliest Times to the End of the Early Bronze Age [*A publication*] (BJA)
PPeda........	Problemi della Pedagogia [*A publication*]
PPEF	Public Policy Education Fund (EA)
PPEFH	E. F. Hutton & Co., Philadelphia, PA [*Library symbol*] [*Library of Congress*] [*Obsolete*] (LCLS)
PPEMA	Portable Power Equipment Manufacturers Association (EA)
PPEN........	Purchased Parts Equipment Notice (SAA)
PPENA	Plant and Power Services Engineer [*A publication*]
PPEng.......	Engineers' Club, Philadelphia, PA [*Library symbol*] [*Library of Congress*] [*Obsolete*] (LCLS)
PPEP	Eastern Pennsylvania Psychiatric Institute, Philadelphia, PA [*Library symbol*] [*Library of Congress*] (LCLS)
PPEP	Plasma Physics and Environmental Perturbation (NASA)
P/PEP........	Progress Performance Evaluation Panel [*Job Corps*]
PPER........	Procurement Package Engineering Release (MCD)
PPERB	Progress in Pediatric Radiology [*A publication*]
PPES	Physical Performance Evaluation System [*Army*]
PPES	Pilot Performance Evaluation System [*Air Force*]
PPeSchw ...	Schwenkfelder Historical Library, Pennsburg, PA [*Library symbol*] [*Library of Congress*] (LCLS)
PPESD9	Proceedings. APRES [*American Peanut Research and Education Society*] [*A publication*]
PPET	Pangea Petroleum Co. [*NASDAQ symbol*] (NQ)
PPetr.........	Flinders Petrie Papyri [*A publication*]
PPEW........	Philosophy East and West [*A publication*]
PPF...........	Franklin Institute, Philadelphia, PA [*Library symbol*] [*Library of Congress*] [*OCLC symbol*] (LCLS)
PPF...........	Pacific Peace Fund (EA)
PPF...........	Parsons [*Kansas*] [*Airport symbol*] (OAG)
PPF...........	Parsons, KS [*Location identifier*] [*FAA*] (FAAL)
PPF...........	Parti Populaire Francais [*French Popular Party*] [*Political party*] (PPE)
PPF...........	Patriotic People's Front [*Hungary*] [*Political party*]
PPF...........	Payload Processing Facility [*Air Force*] (NASA)
PPF...........	Peacetime Planning Factors
PPF...........	Peak Power Frequency
PPF...........	Pellagra Preventive Factor [*See also PP*] [*Biochemistry*]
PPF...........	People's Police Force
PPF...........	Personal Property Floater [*Insurance*]
PPF...........	Phase Pushing Factor
PPF...........	Photophoretic Force [*Pressure exerted by light*]
PPF...........	Plasma Protein Fraction [*Hematology*]
PPF...........	Poetarum Philosophorum Graecorum Fragmenta [*A publication*] (OCD)
PPF...........	Polarization-Preserving Fiber
PPF...........	Poly(phenolformaldehyde) [*Organic chemistry*]
PPF...........	Porous Polyurethane Foam [*Also, PUF*] [*Plastics technology*]
PPF...........	Presbyterian Peace Fellowship (EA)
PPF...........	Primary Part Failure (DNAB)
PPF...........	Principal Profile Forms [*Soil classification*]
PPF...........	Privatefoeretagarnas Partioganisation i Finland [*Finnish Private Entrepreneurs' Party*] [*Political party*] (PPE)
PPF...........	Production Possibility Frontier [*Economics*]
PPF...........	Provision of Production Facilities [*Military*] (AABC)
PPF...........	United Association of Journeymen and Apprentices of the Plumbing and Pipe Fitting Industry of the United States and Canada
PPFA	Planned Parenthood Federation of America (EA)
PPFA	Plastic Pipe and Fittings Association (EA)
PPFA	Professional Picture Framers Association (EA)
PPFA	United States Army, Frankford Arsenal Library, Philadelphia, PA [*Library symbol*] [*Library of Congress*] (LCLS)
PPFAR	Federal Archives and Records Center, General Services Administration, Philadelphia, PA [*Library symbol*] [*Library of Congress*] (LCLS)
PPFAS.......	Past President of the Faculty of Architects and Surveyors [*British*] (DBQ)
PPFC	Philadelphia Fellowship Commission, Philadelphia, PA [*Library symbol*] [*Library of Congress*] [*Obsolete*] (LCLS)
PPFC	Priscilla Presley Fan Club (EA)
PPFCDY....	Proceedings. Southern Pasture and Forage Crop Improvement Conference [*A publication*]
PPFD........	Photosynthetically Active Photon Flux Density [*Botany*]
PPFF	Poisson Probability Frequency Function [*Mathematics*]
PPF-G........	Germantown Laboratories, Inc., Philadelphia, PA [*Library symbol*] [*Library of Congress*] (LCLS)

PPFHi........ Historical Society of Frankford, Philadelphia, PA [*Library symbol*] [*Library of Congress*] [*Obsolete*] (LCLS)
PPFJC .... Federation of Jewish Charities, Philadelphia, PA [*Library symbol*] [*Library of Congress*] [*Obsolete*] (LCLS)
PPFML...... Fidelity Mutual Life Insurance Co., Philadelphia, PA [*Library symbol*] [*Library of Congress*] (LCLS)
PPFO........ Paris Procurement Field Office
PPFPR....... F. P. Ristine & Co., Philadelphia, PA [*Library symbol*] [*Library of Congress*] [*Obsolete*] (LCLS)
PPFr.......... Friends' Free Library of Germantown, Philadelphia, PA [*Library symbol*] [*Library of Congress*] (LCLS)
PPFR .... Plutonium Product Filter Room [*Nuclear energy*] (NRCH)
PPFRB....... Federal Reserve Bank of Philadelphia, Philadelphia, PA [*Library symbol*] [*Library of Congress*] (LCLS)
PPFRT....... Prototype Preliminary Flight Rating Test
PPFS.......... Pergamon Professional and Financial Services [*Commercial firm*] [*British*]
PPG .... German Society of Pennsylvania, Philadelphia, PA [*Library symbol*] [*Library of Congress*] (LCLS)
PPG .... Pacific Proving Ground [*AEC*]
PPG .... Pago Pago [*Samoa*] [*Airport symbol*] (OAG)
PPG .... Pago Pago, AQ [*Location identifier*] [*FAA*] (FAAL)
PPG .... PEMA Policy and Guidance [*Military*] (AABC)
PPG .... Periodical Press Gallery [*US Senate*]
PPG .... Permanent Planning Group [*Military*] [*British*]
PPG .... Personnel Processing Group [*Army*]
PPG .... Phoenizisch-Punische Grammatik [*A publication*]
PPG .... Photoplethysmography [*Medicine*]
PPG .... Picopicogram [*One trillionth of one trillionth of a gram*]
PPG .... Piezoelectric Power Generation
PPG .... Pipe Plug
PPG .... Planned Procurement Guide
PPG .... Planning and Policy Guidance (MCD)
PPG .... Planning and Programming Guidance [*Army*] (AABC)
PPG .... Plasma Power Generator
PPG .... Player Piano Group (EAIO)
PPG .... Points per Game (WGA)
PPG .... Policies and Procedures Guide (SAA)
PPG .... Poly(propylene Glycol) [*Organic chemistry*]
ppg .... Pounds per Gallon
PPG .... Power-Play Goal [*Hockey*]
PPG .... PPG Industries, Inc. [*Formerly, Pittsburgh Plate Glass Co.*] [*NYSE symbol*] (SPSG)
PPG .... PPG Industries, Inc. [*Formerly, Pittsburgh Plate Glass Co.*] [*Associated Press abbreviation*] (APAG)
PPG .... PPG Industries, Inc., Coatings and Resins Division, Allison Park, PA [*OCLC symbol*] (OCLC)
PPG .... Predictive Proportional Guidance
PPG .... Primary Pattern Generator [*Bell Laboratories*]
PPG .... Program Planning Guide (OICC)
PPG .... Program Policy Guidelines
PPG .... Program Pulse Generator (IEEE)
PPG .... Propulsion and Power Generation
PPGA........ Personal Producing General Agent [*Insurance*]
PPGA........ Post Pill Galactorrhea-Amenorrhea [*Medicine*]
PPGA........ Preschool Play-Group Association [*British*] (DI)
PPGBL ...... Personal Property Government Bill of Lading (DNAB)
PPGE......... General Electric Co., Philadelphia, PA [*Library symbol*] [*Library of Congress*] (LCLS)
PPGE......... Partido del Progreso de Guinea Ecuatorial [*Progressive Party of Equatorial Guinea*] [*Political party*] (EY)
PPGE......... Professional Geographer [*A publication*]
PPGE-M..... General Electric Co., Missile and Space Vehicle Department, Aerosciences Laboratory, Philadelphia, PA [*Library symbol*] [*Library of Congress*] (LCLS)
PPGen........ Genealogical Society of Pennsylvania, Philadelphia, PA [*Library symbol*] [*Library of Congress*] (LCLS)
PPGenH .... Philadelphia General Hospital Laboratories, Philadelphia, PA [*Library symbol*] [*Library of Congress*] [*Obsolete*] (LCLS)
PPGeo........ Geographical Society of Philadelphia, Philadelphia, PA [*Library symbol*] [*Library of Congress*] [*Obsolete*] (LCLS)
PPGH .... Philadelphia General Hospital, Philadelphia, PA [*Library symbol*] [*Library of Congress*] (LCLS)
PPGi .... Girard College, Philadelphia, PA [*Library symbol*] [*Library of Congress*] [*Obsolete*] (LCLS)
PPGJW ..... Past Pro-Grand Junior Warden [*Freemasonry*] (ROG)
PPGM....... Past Provincial Grand Master [*Freemasonry*]
PPGM....... Planning-Programming Guidance Memo [*Navy*]
PPGO .... Past Pro-Grand Organist [*Freemasonry*] (ROG)
PPGO .... Past Pro-Grand Orient [*Freemasonry*] (ROG)
PPGP......... Past Pro-Grand Pursuivant [*Freemasonry*] (ROG)
PPGP......... Prepaid Group Practice [*Insurance*] (DHSM)
PPGraph.... Graphic Sketch Club, Philadelphia, PA [*Library symbol*] [*Library of Congress*] [*Obsolete*] (LCLS)
PPGratz ..... Gratz College, Philadelphia, PA [*Library symbol*] [*Library of Congress*] [*Obsolete*] (LCLS)
PPGRC...... Public Policy and Government Relations Council
PPGS......... Publications. Pennsylvania German Society [*A publication*]
PPGSB ...... Past Pro-Grand Sword Bearer [*Freemasonry*] (ROG)
PPGSN ...... Past Provincial Grand Senior [*Freemasonry*] (ROG)
PPGSW ..... Past Provincial Grand Senior Warden [*Freemasonry*]

PP Guide.... Prescription Proprietaries Guide [*A publication*] (APTA)
PPGW....... Past Pro-Grand Warden [*Freemasonry*] (ROG)
PPH .... Paid Personal Holiday
PPH .... Pamphlet
PPH .... Parts per Hundred
PPH .... Persistent Pulmonary Hypertension [*Medicine*]
PPH .... Petroleum Pipehead
PPH .... Phenylpropanolamine(hydrochloride) [*Also, PPA, PPM*] [*Decongestant*]
PPH .... Phosphopyruvate Hydratase [*An enzyme*]
PPH .... PHP Healthcare Corp. [*NYSE symbol*] (SPSG)
PPH .... Postpartum Hemorrhage [*Medicine*]
PPH .... Pounds per Hour (NG)
PPH .... Primary Pulmonary Hypertension [*Medicine*]
PPH .... Prophet Resources Ltd. [*Vancouver Stock Exchange symbol*]
PPH .... Protocollagen Proline Hydroxylase [*An enzyme*] (MAE)
PPH .... Pulses per Hour
PPHa .... Hahnemann Medical College and Hospital, Philadelphia, PA [*Library symbol*] [*Library of Congress*] (LCLS)
PPHA .... Peak Pulse Height Analysis
PPHA .... Private Proprietary Homes for Adults
PPHBA...... Peruvian Paso Half-Blood Association [*Later, PPPBR*] (EA)
PPHBD7..... Plant Physiology and Biochemistry [*A publication*]
PPHFC ...... Holy Family College, Philadelphia, PA [*Library symbol*] [*Library of Congress*] (LCLS)
PPHID...... Plasma Physics Index [*A publication*]
P Ph L........ Papers in Philippine Linguistics [*A publication*] (APTA)
PPHL......... Public Health Reports [*A publication*]
PPH/LB ... Pounds per Hour per Pound (SAA)
PPHM .... Parts per Hundred Million
P-PH-M..... Pulse Phase Modulation (DEN)
PPHN .... Persistent Pulmonary Hypertension of the Newborn [*Medicine*]
PPHOPT... Pseudo-Pseudohypoparathyroidism [*Also, PPHP*] [*Endocrinology*]
PPHor........ Pennsylvania Horticultural Society, Philadelphia, PA [*Library symbol*] [*Library of Congress*] (LCLS)
PPHP......... Pseudo-Pseudohypoparathyroidism [*Also, PPHOPT*] [*Endocrinology*]
PPHPI .... Henry Phipps Institute, Philadelphia, PA [*Library symbol*] [*Library of Congress*] [*Obsolete*] (LCLS)
PPHQ .... Pacific Philosophical Quarterly [*A publication*]
PPHR .... Pacific Historical Review [*A publication*]
PPHR .... Planned Parenthood Review [*A publication*]
PPHRA...... Philosophy and Phenomenological Research [*A publication*]
PPHRD ...... Photochemical and Photobiological Reviews [*A publication*]
PPHRII ..... Parents of Premature and High Risk Infants International (EA)
PPHRNA .. Peruvian Paso Horse Registry of North America (EA)
PPHS......... Partisan Prohibition Historical Society (EA)
PPHSL ...... Periodical Publication in Harvard Science Libraries
PPHT......... (Phenylethyl-propylamino)hydroxytetralin [*Biochemistry*]
PPHY .... Philosophy [*A publication*]
PPHYA...... Plant Physiology [*English Translation*] [*A publication*]
PPi .... Carnegie Library of Pittsburgh, Pittsburgh, PA [*Library symbol*] [*Library of Congress*] (LCLS)
PPI .... Institute for Psychosomatic and Psychiatric Research and Training [*Research center*] (RCD)
PPI............ Packing, Postage, and Insurance [*Shipping*]
PPI............ Padangpandjang [*Sumatra*] [*Seismograph station code, US Geological Survey*] (SEIS)
PPI............ Pages per Inch [*Publishing*]
PPI............ Pakistan Press International
PPI............ Parallel Peripheral Interface [*Data processing*]
PPI............ Parcel Post, Insured [*Shipping*]
PPI............ Park Practice Index [*A publication*]
PPI............ Particles per Inch
PPI............ Patient Package Insert [*Also, PI*] [*Instructional leaflet distributed with certain prescription drugs*]
PPI............ Pensioners for Peace International (EAIO)
PPI............ Pergamon Press, Inc.
PPI............ Personality and Personal Illness Questionnaires [*Psychology*]
PPI............ Personnel Planning Information
PPI............ Phoenix Precision Instrument Co.
PPI............ Pickle Packers International (EA)
PPI............ Pico Products, Inc. [*AMEX symbol*] (SPSG)
PPI............ Pictorial Position Indicator
PPI............ Pilgrim Holdings Ltd. [*Vancouver Stock Exchange symbol*]
PPI............ PIPA [*Pulsed Integrating Pendulous Accelerometer*] Pulse Integrator
PPI............ Piston Position Indicator
PPI............ PIXEL [*Picture Element*] per Inch [*Data processing*] (PCM)
PPI............ Plan Position Indicator Mode [*Data processing*] (ADA)
PPI............ Plane Position Indicator [*RADAR*]
PPI............ Planen-Pruefen-Investieren [*A publication*]
PPI............ Plasma Protein Isolate [*Food technology*]
PPI............ Plastics Pipe Institute (EA)
PPI............ Plot Position Indicator
PPI............ Policy Proof of Interest
PPI............ Polyphosphonositides
PPI............ Polyphthalimide [*Organic chemistry*]
PPI............ POM [*Program Objective Memorandum*] Preparation Instructions [*Military*]

PPI............ Popular Periodical Index [*A publication*]
ppi............. Pores per Inch
PPI............ Port Pirie [*Australia*] [*Airport symbol*]   (OAG)
PPI............ Postage Paid Impression [*Freight*]   (DCTA)
PPI............ Potash and Phosphate Institute   (EA)
PPI............ Pounds per Inch [*Lubrication load*]
PPI............ Pre Phase-In
PPI............ Preceding Preparatory Interval [*Psychometrics*]
PPI............ Preferred Parts Index
PPI............ Preplant Inc. [*Herbicides*] [*Agriculture*]
PPI............ Prepleading Investigation [*Law*]
PPI............ Present Pain Intensity
PPI............ Present Position Indicator [*Aviation*]
PPI............ Prices Paid Index [*Economics*]
PPI............ Primary Personal Interest [*Personnel study*]
PPI............ Prince Patrick Island [*Canada*]
PPI............ Producer Price Index [*Bureau of Labor Statistics*] [*Information service or system*]
PPI............ Program Position Indicator
PPI............ Programmable Peripheral Interface   (MCD)
PPI............ Progressive Policy Institute [*Political think-tank*]   (ECON)
PPI............ Project Procurement Instructions [*Jet Propulsion Laboratory, NASA*]
PPI............ Project Public Information [*Department of Education*]   (AEBS)
PPI............ Property Protection Insurance
PPI............ Proportional Plus Integral
PPI............ Public-Private Interface
PPI............ Pulp and Paper International [*A publication*]
PPI............ Pulse Position Indicator   (MCD)
PPI............ Pulses per Inch   (CMD)
PPI............ Pyrophosphate Index [*Agronomy*]
PPi............ Pyrophosphate, Inorganic [*Chemistry*]
PPi-A .... Carnegie Library of Pittsburgh, Allegheny Regional Branch, Monroeville, PA [*Library symbol*] [*Library of Congress*]   (LCLS)
PPIA .... Poultry Products Inspection Act   (GFGA)
PPIA .... Programme du Pipeline des Iles de l'Arctique [*Canada*]
PPiAC........ Community College of Allegheny County, Pittsburgh, PA [*Library symbol*] [*Library of Congress*]   (LCLS)
PPiAL........ Allegheny County Law Library, Pittsburgh, PA [*Library symbol*] [*Library of Congress*]   (LCLS)
PPiAM....... Pittsburgh Academy of Medicine, Pittsburgh, PA [*Library symbol*] [*Library of Congress*]   (LCLS)
PPIAS....... Parent-to-Parent Information on Adoption Services [*British*]   (DI)
PPIB .... Programmable Protocol Interface Board
PPiC........... Carnegie-Mellon University, Pittsburgh, PA [*Library symbol*] [*Library of Congress*]   (LCLS)
PPIC .... Pollution Prevention Information Clearinghouse [*Environmental Protection Agency*]
PPiCa......... Carlow College, Pittsburgh, PA [*Library symbol*] [*Library of Congress*]   (LCLS)
PPiCa-O .... Carlow College, Our Lady of Mercy Academy, Pittsburgh, PA [*Library symbol*] [*Library of Congress*]   (LCLS)
PPiCC........ Chatham College, Pittsburgh, PA [*Library symbol*] [*Library of Congress*]   (LCLS)
PPICR .... Institute for Cancer Research, Philadelphia, PA [*Library symbol*] [*Library of Congress*]   (LCLS)
PPiD .... Duquesne University, Pittsburgh, PA [*Library symbol*] [*Library of Congress*]   (LCLS)
PPID.......... Polaris-Poseidon Intelligence Digest   (MCD)
PPiD-L....... Duquesne University, School of Law, Pittsburgh, PA [*Library symbol*] [*Library of Congress*]   (LCLS)
PPiE........... E. D'Appolonia Consulting Engineers, Pittsburgh, PA [*Library symbol*] [*Library of Congress*]   (LCLS)
PPIE .... Pseudophase Ion Exchange [*Chemistry*]
PPIF .... Photo Processing Interpretation Facility
PPIFC....... Pauline Pinkney International Fan Club   (EA)
PPiGulf...... Gulf Research & Development Co., Pittsburgh, PA [*Library symbol*] [*Library of Congress*]   (LCLS)
PPiHB .... Carnegie-Mellon University, Hunt Institute for Botanical Documentation, Pittsburgh, PA [*Library symbol*] [*Library of Congress*]   (LCLS)
PPiHi......... Historical Society of Western Pennsylvania, Pittsburgh, PA [*Library symbol*] [*Library of Congress*]   (LCLS)
PPiI........... International Poetry Forum, Pittsburgh, PA [*Library symbol*] [*Library of Congress*]   (LCLS)
PPiK.......... Ketchum, McLeod & Grove, Inc., Pittsburgh, PA [*Library symbol*] [*Library of Congress*]   (LCLS)
PPiL.......... LaRoche College, Pittsburgh, PA [*Library symbol*] [*Library of Congress*]   (LCLS)
PPIL .... Priced Provisioned Item List   (MCD)
PPIL .... Problems in Private International Law [*Elsevier Book Series*] [*A publication*]
PPiM .... Carnegie-Mellon University, Mellon Institute, Pittsburgh, PA [*Library symbol*] [*Library of Congress*]   (LCLS)
PPiMS....... Mine Safety Appliances Co., Pittsburgh, PA [*Library symbol*] [*Library of Congress*]   (LCLS)
PPIn.......... Independence National Historical Park, Philadelphia, PA [*Library symbol*] [*Library of Congress*]   (LCLS)

PPINA....... Insurance Co., of North America, Corporate Archives, Philadelphia, PA [*Library symbol*] [*Library of Congress*]   (LCLS)
PPINICI.... Pulsed Positive Ion-Negative Ion Chemical Ionization [*Instrumentation*]
PPInstHE ... Past President of the Institution of Highway Engineers [*British*]   (DI)
P & P Intnl ... Pulp and Paper International Annual Review [*A publication*]
PPiPP .... Point Park College, Pittsburgh, PA [*Library symbol*] [*Library of Congress*]   (LCLS)
PPiPPG ..... PPG Industries, Inc., Glass Research Center, Information Services Library, Pittsburgh, PA [*Library symbol*] [*Library of Congress*]   (LCLS)
PPiPT .... Pittsburgh Theological Seminary, Pittsburgh, PA [*Library symbol*] [*Library of Congress*]   (LCLS)
PPIR .... Personnel Planning Information Report   (MCD)
PPiR.......... Rockwell International Corp., Pittsburgh, PA [*Library symbol*] [*Library of Congress*]   (LCLS)
PPIRO....... Planned Position Indicator Readout   (NVT)
PPIS.......... Pesticide Product Information System [*Environmental Protection Agency*]   (GFGA)
PPIS.......... Product Profile Information System [*Shell Oil Co.*]
PPIStructE ... Past President of the Institution of Structural Engineers [*British*]   (DI)
PPIU......... Programmable Peripheral Interface Unit
PPiU .... University of Pittsburgh, Pittsburgh, PA [*Library symbol*] [*Library of Congress*]   (LCLS)
PPiU-A ...... University of Pittsburgh, Henry Clay Frick Fine Arts Center, Pittsburgh, PA [*Library symbol*] [*Library of Congress*]   (LCLS)
PPiU-BL.... University of Pittsburgh, Blair-Lippincott Library, Eye and Ear Hospital of Pittsburgh, Pittsburgh, PA [*Library symbol*] [*Library of Congress*]   (LCLS)
PPiU-H...... University of Pittsburgh, Maurice and Laura Falk Library of the Health Professions, Pittsburgh, PA [*Library symbol*] [*Library of Congress*]   (LCLS)
PPiU-L ...... University of Pittsburgh, Law School, Pittsburgh, PA [*Library symbol*] [*Library of Congress*]   (LCLS)
PPiU-LS.... University of Pittsburgh, Graduate School of Library and Information Sciences, Pittsburgh, PA [*Library symbol*] [*Library of Congress*]   (LCLS)
PPiU-NS ... University of Pittsburgh, Natural Sciences Library, Pittsburgh, PA [*Library symbol*] [*Library of Congress*]   (LCLS)
PPiU-PH ... University of Pittsburgh, Graduate School of Public Health, Pittsburgh, PA [*Library symbol*] [*Library of Congress*]   (LCLS)
PPiU-PIA .. University of Pittsburgh, Graduate School of Public and International Affairs, Pittsburgh, PA [*Library symbol*] [*Library of Congress*]   (LCLS)
PPiUS........ United States Steel Corp., Pittsburgh, PA [*Library symbol*] [*Library of Congress*]   (LCLS)
PPiU-SF .... University of Pittsburgh, Stephen Collins Foster Memorial [*Music*] Library, Pittsburgh, PA [*Library symbol*] [*Library of Congress*]   (LCLS)
PPiUSM.... United States Department of the Interior, Bureau of Mines, Pittsburgh Research Center, Pittsburgh, PA [*Library symbol*] [*Library of Congress*]   (LCLS)
PPIV .... Per Person Interview Value [*Marketing*]   (WDMC)
PPiW .... Westinghouse Electric Corp., Research and Development Center, Pittsburgh, PA [*Library symbol*] [*Library of Congress*]   (LCLS)
PPiW-N..... Westinghouse Electric Corp., Nuclear Center Library, Pittsburgh, PA [*Library symbol*] [*Library of Congress*]   (LCLS)
PPiWP....... Western Psychiatric Institute and Clinic, University of Pittsburgh, Pittsburgh, PA [*Library symbol*] [*Library of Congress*]   (LCLS)
PPJ .... Philippine Planning Journal [*A publication*]
PPJ .... Pressure Plane Joint
PPJ .... Prilozi Proucavanju Jezika [*A publication*]
PPJ .... Pure Pancreatic Juice
PPJ .... Thomas Jefferson University, Philadelphia, PA [*Library symbol*] [*Library of Congress*]   (LCLS)
PPJea........ Jeanes Hospital, Philadelphia, PA [*Library symbol*] [*Library of Congress*] [*Obsolete*]   (LCLS)
PPJO .... Pli Premier Jour Officiel [*Official First Day Cover - OFDC*] [*Canada Post Corp.*]
P & P Jrl ... Pulp and Paper Journal [*A publication*]
PPJ-S........ Thomas Jefferson University, Scott Memorial Library, Philadelphia, PA [*Library symbol*] [*Library of Congress*]   (LCLS)
PPJW .... Past Pro-Junior Warden [*Freemasonry*]   (ROG)
PPK............ Paired Perpendicular Keratotomy [*Procedure to correct astigmatism*]
PPK........... Parametrized Post-Keplerian [*Physics*]
PPK........... Paramp Pump Klystron
PPK........... Parti Progressiste Katangais [*Political party*]
PPK............ Personal Preference Kit [*Small bag in which astronauts are allowed to take personal mementos*]

PPK........... Polizei Pistole Kriminal [*Pistol suitable for undercover police or detective use*] [*Walther Waffenfabrik, German arms manufacturer*]
PPK........... Punt, Pass, and Kick [*Youth competition sponsored by professional football*]
PPKB........ Partai Perpaduan Kebang-Saan Brunei [*Brunei National United Party*] [*Political party*]　(EY)
PPKCA ...... Pen and Pocket Knife Cutters' Association [*A union*] [*British*]
PPKG........ Power Package　(MSA)
PPKGA...... Ponpu Kogaku [*A publication*]
PPL........... Journal of Pension Planning and Compliance [*A publication*]
PPL........... Library Co. of Philadelphia, Philadelphia, PA [*Library symbol*] [*Library of Congress*]　(LCLS)
PPL........... Palach Press Ltd. [*British*]　(EAIO)
PPL........... Palmer Physical Laboratory [*Princeton University*]　(MCD)
PPL........... Participle [*Grammar*]　(WGA)
PPL........... Pembina Resources Ltd. [*Toronto Stock Exchange symbol*]
PPL........... Penicilloyl Polylysine [*Pharmacology*]
PPL........... Pennsylvania Power & Light Co. [*NYSE symbol*]　(SPSG)
PPL........... Per Pupil Limitation　(AFM)
PPL........... Peter Peregrinus Ltd. [*Publisher*]
PPL........... Phenylpropanolamine [*Organic chemistry*]
PPL........... Phonographic Performance Ltd. [*British*]
PPL........... Physical Properties Laboratory [*Oklahoma State University*] [*Research center*]　(RCD)
PPL........... Plan Position Landing　(DEN)
PPL........... Planning Parts List
PPL........... Plant Physiology Laboratory　(SSD)
PPL........... Plasma Physics Laboratory [*Also known as PPPL*]
PPL........... Plasma Propulsion Laboratory　(MCD)
PPL........... Plus Programming Language [*Data processing*]
PPL........... Plutonium Product Loadout [*Nuclear energy*]　(NRCH)
PPL........... Polybiblion. Partie Litteraire [*A publication*]
PPL........... Polymorphic Programming Language [*1971*] [*Data processing*]　(CSR)
PPL........... Populated Place [*Board on Geographic Names*]
PPL........... Porcine Pancreatic Lipase [*An enzyme*]
PPL........... Posterior Pole Plasm [*Insect embryology*]
PPL........... Power Plant Laboratory　(MUGU)
PPL........... Precise Participant Location
PPL........... Predictive Period LASER　(KSC)
PPL........... Preferential Planning List
PPL........... Preferred Parts List
PPL........... Preliminary Parts List
PPL........... Priced Parts List　(NASA)
P/PL........ Primary Payload [*NASA*]　(NASA)
PPL........... Princeton Polymer Laboratories
PPL........... Private Pilot's Licence [*British*]
PPL........... Program Production Library [*Data processing*]
PPL........... Project Priority List [*Environmental Protection Agency*]
PPL........... Provisioning Parts List　(AAG)
PPL........... Purchased Parts List
PPL........... Pure Prairie League [*Musical group*]
PPL........... Purple
PPL........... Puu Pili [*Hawaii*] [*Seismograph station code, US Geological Survey*]　(SEIS)
PpL........... W. & F. Pascoe Proprietory Ltd., Milsons Point, Australia [*Library symbol*] [*Library of Congress*]　(LCLS)
PPLA .... Practice Precautionary Landing Approach [*Aviation*]
PPLas .... La Salle College, Philadelphia, PA [*Library symbol*] [*Library of Congress*]　(LCLS)
PPlase........ Peptidylprolyl Cis-Trans Isomerase [*An enzyme*]
PPLD......... Pikes Peak Library District [*Internationally recognized computerized library system*]
PPLDF....... Professional Protector and Legal Defense Fund
PPLE .... Partial Preliminary Logistic Evaluation
PPLE .... Participle [*Grammar*]
PPLE .... Principle　(ROG)
PPLF......... Parliamentary Affairs [*A publication*]
PPLG........ Ploughshares [*A publication*]
PPL/H....... Private Pilot's Licence/Helicopters [*British*]　(AIA)
PPLI .... Precise Participant Location-Identification [*Navigation*]
PPLI .... Precise Position Location Information
PPLI .... Provisioning Parts List Index　(MCD)
PPLIF........ Pulsed Photolysis LASER-Induced Fluorescence [*Environmental science*]
PPLL .... Military Order of the Loyal Legion of the United States, [*Civil War Library and Museum, Philadelphia, PA [Library symbol*] [*Library of Congress*]　(LCLS)
PPLL .... Papers on Language and Literature [*A publication*]
PPLN........ Pipeline
PPLO......... Pleuropneumonia-Like Organisms [*Bacteriology*]
PPLP......... Photopolymers Lithograph Plate
P PLPBD... Paper or Pulpboard [*Freight*]
PPLS........ Precision Position Locator System [*Army*]
PPLS......... Preferred Parts List System　(MCD)
PPLS......... Propellant and Pressurant Loading System [*NASA*]　(KSC)
PPLT .... Lutheran Theological Seminary, Philadelphia, PA [*Library symbol*] [*Library of Congress*]　(LCLS)
PPLV .... Preliminary Pollutant Limit Value　(MCD)
PPLX .... Section of Populated Place [*Board on Geographic Names*]

PPM .... Aberdeen, MD [*Location identifier*] [*FAA*]　(FAAL)
PPM .... Mercantile Library, Philadelphia, PA [*Library symbol*] [*Library of Congress*] [*Obsolete*]　(LCLS)
P & PM...... Packing and Packaging Manual　(MCD)
PPM .... Pages per Minute [*Printer technology*]
PPM .... PaineWebber Premium Tax-Free, Inc. [*NYSE symbol*]　(SPSG)
ppm .... Papermaker [*MARC relator code*] [*Library of Congress*]　(LCCP)
PPM .... Part Program Manager
PPM .... Parti Pekerja-Pekerja Malaysia [*Workers' Party of Malaysia*] [*Political party*]　(PPW)
PPM .... Parti Progressiste Martiniquais [*Progressive Party of Martinique*] [*Political party*]　(PPW)
PPM .... Particuliere Participatiemaatschappy [*Private Joint Stock Company*] [*Dutch*]
PPM .... Partido del Pueblo Mexicano [*Mexican People's Party*] [*Political party*]　(PPW)
PPM .... Parts per Million
PPM .... Parts per Minute　(MCD)
PPM .... Pattani People's Movement [*Political party*] [*Thailand*]
PPM .... Peak Power Meter
PPM .... Peak Program Meter [*Television*]
PPM .... Periodic Permanent Magnet
PPM .... Periodic Pulse Metering [*Telecommunications*]　(TEL)
PPM .... Permanent Pacemaker [*Cardiology*]　(MAE)
PPM .... Pershing Project Manager
PPM .... Personnel Priority Model　(MCD)
PPM .... Personnel Program Manager [*Navy*]
PPM .... Phenylpropanolamine(hydrochloride) [*Also, PPA, PPH*] [*Decongestant*]
PPM .... Phosphopentomutase [*An enzyme*]
PPM .... Piecewise Parabolic Method [*Mathematical model of fluid flow*]
PPM .... Pilot Production Model [*Military*]　(CAAL)
PPM .... Pistol Prize Money [*British military*]　(DMA)
PPM .... Planned Preventive Maintenance　(IEEE)
PPM .... Popocatepetl [*Mexico*] [*Seismograph station code, US Geological Survey*]　(SEIS)
PPM .... Position and Pay Management [*Army*]　(AABC)
PPM .... Postage Prepaid in Money
PPM .... Postpass Message
PPM .... Pounds per Minute
PPM .... Prairie Print Makers [*Defunct*]　(EA)
PPM .... Previous Processor Mode
PPM .... Production Planning Memorandum
PPM .... Program, Project Management [*Army*]
PPM .... Project Profile Manual
PPM .... Prudential Portfolio Managers Ltd. [*British*]
PPM .... Public Personnel Management [*A publication*]
PPM .... Pulp and Paper Magazine of Canada [*Later, Pulp and Paper (Canada)*] [*A publication*]
PPM .... Pulse Position Modulation [*Radio data transmission*]
PPM .... Pulses per Minute
PPMA....... Plastic Products Manufacturers Association [*Later, Plastic and Metal Products Manufacturers Association*]　(EA)
PPMA....... Political Products Manufacturers Association　(EA)
PPMA....... Post-Poliomyelitis Muscular Atrophy [*Medicine*]
PPMA....... Precision Potentiometer Manufacturers Association [*Later, Variable Resistive Components Institute*]　(EA)
PPMA....... Pulp and Paper Manufacturers Association [*Later, PPMMA*]　(EA)
PPMAP..... Power Planning Modeling Application Procedure [*Environmental Protection Agency*]　(GFGA)
PPMC........ Parts per Million Carbon [*Automotive engineering*]
PPMC........ People to People Music Committee　(EA)
PPME........ Pacific Plate Motion Experiment　(NASA)
PPMFC ..... Preprints on Precision Measurement and Fundamental Constants [*National Institute of Standards and Technology*]
PPMG........ Professional Publishers Marketing Group　(EA)
PPMI........ Pilot Plant Meat Irradiator
PPMI........ Printed Paper Mat Institute　(EA)
PPMIN...... Pulses per Minute　(MSA)
PPMis........ Misericordia Hospital, Philadelphia, PA [*Library symbol*] [*Library of Congress*] [*Obsolete*]　(LCLS)
PPML....... Preferred Parts and Materials List [*NASA*]
PPMM....... Postpolycythemia Myeloid Metaplasia [*Medicine*]　(AAMN)
PPMMA.... Pulp and Paper Machinery Manufacturers Association [*Later, APMA*]　(EA)
PPMMB.... Periodica Polytechnica. Mechanical Engineering [*A publication*]
PPMN....... Preliminary Program Management Network [*Military*]
PPMNA..... Polski Przeglad Radiologii i Medycyny Nuklearnej [*A publication*]
PPMO .... Pershing Project Manager's Office　(RDA)
PPMO .... Provisional Program Management Office [*Army*]
PPMoI....... Moore College of Art, Philadelphia, PA [*Library symbol*] [*Library of Congress*]　(LCLS)
PPMPC .... Pilot Parachute Mortar Pyrotechnic Cartridge　(SAA)
PPMR....... Purchased Parts Material Requirements
PPMRC..... Pre-Positioned Materiel Receipt Card

PPMRC.....	Proceedings. PMR Conference. Annual Publication of the International Patristic, Mediaeval, and Renaissance Conference [*A publication*]
PPMS	Pitt Press Mathematical Series [*A publication*]
PPMS	Poly(para-Methylstyrene) [*Organic chemistry*]
PPMS	Professional Productivity Management System (HGAA)
PPMS	Program Performance Measurement Systems (IEEE)
PPMS	Programme and Project Management System [*United Nations Development Programme*] (DUND)
PPMS	Purdue Perceptual-Motor Survey [*Kephart Scale*]
PPMV.......	Parts per Million by Volume
PPMVA....	Pishchevaya Promyshlennost [*Kiev, 1965*] [*A publication*]
PPMW......	Parts per Million by Weight (MCD)
PPN	Numismatic and Antiquarian Society, Philadelphia, PA [*Library symbol*] [*Library of Congress*] [*Obsolete*] (LCLS)
PPN	Papenoo [*Society Islands*] [*Seismograph station code, US Geological Survey*] (SEIS)
PPN	Parameterized Post-Newtonian [*Gravity*]
PPN	Parametrized Post-Newtonian [*Physics*]
PPN	Parti Progressiste Nigerien [*Nigerian Progressive Party*] [*Political party*]
PPN	Partido Patriotico Nobo [*New Patriotic Party*] [*Aruba*] [*Political party*] (EY)
PPN	Partido Progreso Nacional [*National Progress Party*] [*Costa Rica*] [*Political party*] (PPW)
PPN	Patrol Plane Navigator (DNAB)
PPN	Peak-to-Peak Noise [*Instrumentation*]
PPN	Peroxyproprionyl Nitrate [*Organic chemistry*]
PPN	Polyphosphonate [*Organic chemistry*]
PPN	Popayan [*Colombia*] [*Airport symbol*] (OAG)
PPN	Portland Public Library, Portland, ME [*OCLC symbol*] (OCLC)
PPN	Precipitation (WGA)
PPN	Predictive Proportional Navigation
PPN	Procurement Program Number [*Military*]
PPN	Project, Programmer Number
PPN	Proportion (ROG)
PPNA	Peak Phrenic Nerve Activity [*Medicine*]
PP & NA....	Private Plants and Naval Activities
PPNADY...	Pitch Pine Naturalist [*A publication*]
PPNB........	Pre-Pottery Neolithic B Period [*Paleontology*]
PPNC........	Patrol Plane Navigator/Communicator (DNAB)
PPNC........	Pre-Pottery Neolithic C Phase [*Paleontology*]
PPNCFL....	Proceedings. Pacific Northwest Conference on Foreign Languages [*A publication*]
PPNDG	Petition Pending
PPNF........	Price-Pottenger Nutrition Foundation (EA)
PPNG	Penicillinase-Producing Neisseria gonorrhoeae
PPNICI.....	Pulsed Positive/Negative Ion Chemical Ionization
P/PNL.......	Pocket Panel [*Automotive engineering*]
PPNM	Perspectives of New Music [*A publication*]
PPNMC.....	United States Navy, Naval Regional Medical Center, Philadelphia, PA [*Library symbol*] [*Library of Congress*] (LCLS)
PPNP........	Past and Present. A Journal of Historical Studies [*A publication*]
PPNPD......	Progress in Particle and Nuclear Physics [*A publication*]
PPNS........	Politics and Society [*A publication*]
PPNSC	Preferred Procurement Number Selector Code [*Military*] (AFIT)
PPNSCA ...	Policy Plans and National Security Council Affairs
PPNT........	Proponent
PPNWA.....	N. W. Ayer & Son, Philadelphia, PA [*Library symbol*] [*Library of Congress*] [*Obsolete*] (LCLS)
PPO	Photographic Program Office [*NASA*] (KSC)
PPO	Platelet Peroxidase [*An enzyme*]
PPO	Pleuropneumonia Organisms [*Bacteriology*]
PPO	Police Petty Officer (DNAB)
PPO	Pollution Prevention Office [*Environmental Protection Agency*]
PPO	Polyphenol Oxidase [*An enzyme*]
PPO	Polyphenylene Oxide [*Organic chemistry*]
PPO	Poly(propylene Oxide) [*Organic chemistry*]
PPO	Port Postal Office (AFM)
PPO	Power Plant Operating
PPO	Pre Phase-Out
PPO	Preferred-Provider Option [*Insurance*]
PPO	Preferred-Provider Organization [*Insurance*]
PPO	Pressed Plutonium Oxide
PPO	Primary Party Organization [*Politics*]
PPO	Principal Priority Officer
PPO	Prior Permission Only (AFM)
PPO	Procurement Planning Officer
PPO	Program Printout (MCD)
PPO	Projected Program Objective (NG)
PPO	Public Pension Offset [*Federal Employees Retirement System*] (GFGA)
PPO	Publications and Printing Office [*Army*]
PPO	Pure Plutonium Oxide
PPO	Push-Pull Output (DEN)
PPO₂	Partial Pressure of Oxygen (CAAL)
PPOC........	Per Pupil Operating Cost (ADA)

PPol	Pensiero Politico [*A publication*]
PPol	Przeglad Polski [*A publication*]
PPOR........	Parnassus. Poetry in Review [*A publication*]
PPOS........	Philosophy of Science [*A publication*]
PPOS.........	Saint George United Methodist Church, Philadelphia, PA [*Library symbol*] [*Library of Congress*] (LCLS)
PPOSN......	Proposition (ROG)
PPOTA......	Prumysl Potravin [*A publication*]
PPOW......	Policy Review [*A publication*]
PPow.........	Przeglad Powszechny [*A publication*]
PPP	Pacific Peacemaker Project (EA)
PPP	Pakistan People's Party [*Political party*] (PD)
PPP	Pan Pacific Petroleum [*Vancouver Stock Exchange symbol*]
PPP	Paper, Printing, Publishing [*Department of Employment*] [*British*]
PPP	Parallel Pattern Processor
PPP	Pariser-Parr-Pople [*Physical chemistry*]
PPP	Partai Persatuan Pembangunan [*United Development Party*] [*Indonesia*] [*Political party*] (PPW)
PPP	Partido del Pueblo de Panama [*Panamanian People's Party*] [*Political party*] (PPW)
PPP	Peak Pulse Power
PPP	Pentose-Phosphate Pathway [*Metabolism*]
PPP	People's Patriotic Party [*Myanmar*] [*Political party*] (PD)
PPP	People's Political Party [*St. Vincent*] [*Political party*] (PPW)
PPP	People's Progress Party [*Papua New Guinea*] [*Political party*] (PPW)
PPP	People's Progressive Party [*Mauritania*] [*Political party*] (EY)
PPP	People's Progressive Party [*Gambia*] [*Political party*] (PPW)
PPP	People's Progressive Party [*Solomon Islands*] [*Political party*] (PPW)
PPP	People's Progressive Party [*Guyana*] [*Political party*] (PD)
PPP	People's Progressive Party [*Anguilla*] [*Political party*] (PPW)
PPP	Permanent Party Personnel (MCD)
PPP	Perpex Peristaltic Pump
PPP	Personal Property Policy [*Insurance*]
PPP	Personnel Performance Profile
PPP	Phased Project Planning [*NASA*] (KSC)
PPP	Pianississimo [*As Softly As Possible*] [*Music*]
PPP	Pickford Projective Pictures [*Psychology*]
PPP	Pipelines, Politics, and People. Capital Communications Ltd. [*A publication*]
PPP	Plan Position Presentation
PPP	Planning Purpose Proposal
PPP	Platelet-Poor Plasma [*Hematology*]
PPP	Pluripotent Progenitor [*Cytology*]
PPP	Pogo Producing Co. [*NYSE symbol*] (SPSG)
PPP	Point-to-Point Protocol [*Data processing*] (PCM)
PPP	Polluter Pays Principle
PPP	Poly(para-phenylene) [*Organic chemistry*]
PPP	Polypropylene-Paper-Polypropylene [*Biochemistry*]
PPP	Portable Plotting Package [*Nuclear energy*] (NRCH)
PPP	Positive Pressure Paradox
PPP	Powerful Permutation Procedure [*Meteorology*]
PPP	Preferred Pharmacy Program
PPP	Prescriptive Parent Programming [*Education*]
PPP	Prescriptive Program Plan [*Education*]
PPP	Pretty Poor Planning
PPP	Prison Pen Pals (EA)
PPP	Private Patients' Plan [*British*]
PPP	Production Part Pattern (MCD)
PPP	Profit and Performance Planning (DCTA)
PPP	Progressive People's Party [*Sierra Leone*] [*Political party*] (EY)
PPP	Progressive People's Party [*Sudan*] [*Political party*] (EY)
PPP	Progressive People's Party [*Liberia*] [*Political party*] (PPW)
PPow.........	Propria Pecunia Posuit [*Erected at His Own Expense*] [*Latin*]
PPP	Proserpine [*Australia*] [*Airport symbol*] (OAG)
PPP	Province Pacification Plan (CINC)
PPP	Provisioning Program Plan (MCD)
P & PP	Pull and Push Plate
PPP	Pulp and Paper International [*A publication*]
PPP	Purchasing Power Parity [*Economics*]
PPPA	Philosophy and Public Affairs [*A publication*]
PPPA	Poison Prevention Packaging Act
PPPA	Professional Pool Players Association (EA)
PPPA	Pulp and Paper Prepackaging Association [*Later, SSI*]
PPPBDD ...	Iran. Plant Pests and Diseases Research Institute. Department of Botany. Publication [*A publication*]
PPPBR.......	Peruvian Paso Part-Blood Registry (EA)
PPPC	Petroleum Pool Pacific Coast
PPPC	Pipe Plug Producers Council (EA)
PPPCA	Philadelphia College of Art Library, Philadelphia, PA [*Library symbol*] [*Library of Congress*] (LCLS)
PPPCity.....	Philadelphia City Institute Branch Free Library, Philadelphia, PA [*Library symbol*] [*Library of Congress*] [*Obsolete*] (LCLS)
PPPCO	Pennsylvania College of Optometry, Philadelphia, PA [*Library symbol*] [*Library of Congress*] (LCLS)
PPPCPh.....	Philadelphia College of Pharmacy and Science, Philadelphia, PA [*Library symbol*] [*Library of Congress*] (LCLS)

PPPE .... Pennsylvania Economy League, Inc., Eastern Division, Philadelphia, PA [*Library symbol*] [*Library of Congress*]   (LCLS)
PPPE .... People, Plans, and the Peace. Peace River Planning Commission [*A publication*]
PPPEA ...... Pulp, Paper, and Paperboard Export Association of the United States   (EA)
PPPEC....... Philadelphia Electric Co., Philadelphia, PA [*Library symbol*] [*Library of Congress*]   (LCLS)
PPPEE....... Pulsed Pinch Plasma Electromagnetic Engine   (AAG)
PPPF......... Positive Pregnancy and Parenting Fitness   (EA)
PPPFM...... Free and Accepted Masons of Pennsylvania, Grand Lodge Library, Philadelphia, PA [*Library symbol*] [*Library of Congress*]   (LCLS)
PPPG .... People's Progressive Party of Guyana [*Political party*]
PPPH......... Pennsylvania Hospital, Philadelphia, PA [*Library symbol*] [*Library of Congress*]   (LCLS)
PPPHA...... Philadelphia Housing Association, Philadelphia, PA [*Library symbol*] [*Library of Congress*] [*Obsolete*]   (LCLS)
PPPHC...... Philadelphia Tuberculosis and Health Association, Philadelphia, PA [*Library symbol*] [*Library of Congress*] [*Obsolete*]   (LCLS)
PPPH-I...... Institute of the Pennsylvania Hospital, Philadelphia, PA [*Library symbol*] [*Library of Congress*]   (LCLS)
PPPI .... Insurance Society of Philadelphia, Philadelphia, PA [*Library symbol*] [*Library of Congress*] [*Obsolete*]   (LCLS)
PPPI .... Personnel Performance Problems Inventory [*Test*]
PPPI .... Plan Positional Plot Indicator
PPPI .... Precision Plan Position Indicator
PPPI .... Preplanned Product Improvement [*DoD*]   (MCD)
PPPI .... Primary Private Practice Income [*Medicine*]   (MAE)
PPPI .... Private Pay Phones, Inc. [*NASDAQ symbol*]   (NQ)
PPPI .... Projection Plan Position Indicator
PPPI .... Pulp, Paper, and Paperboard Institute USA [*Later, API*]
PPPL .... Philadelphia Board of Public Education, Pedagogical Library, Philadelphia, PA [*Library symbol*] [*Library of Congress*]   (LCLS)
PPPL .... Planetary Physical Processes Laboratory   (SSD)
PPPL .... Princeton Plasma Physics Laboratory [*Also known as PPL - Plasma Physics Laboratory*] [*Department of Energy*] [*Princeton, NJ*]
PPPL .... Printed Planning Parts List
PPPL .... Program Preferred Parts List
PPPlanP .... Planned Parenthood of Southeast Pennsylvania, Philadelphia, PA [*Library symbol*] [*Library of Congress*]   (LCLS)
PPPlay....... Plays and Players Club, Philadelphia, PA [*Library symbol*] [*Library of Congress*] [*Obsolete*]   (LCLS)
PPPM....... Philadelphia Museum of Art, Philadelphia, PA [*Library symbol*] [*Library of Congress*]   (LCLS)
PPP & M ... Preservation, Packaging, Packing, and Marking
PPPMD.... Pishchevaya Promyshlennost. Seriya 12. Spirtavya i Likero-Vodochnaya Promyshlennost [*A publication*]
PPPM-I ..... Philadelphia Museum of Art, College of Art, Philadelphia, PA [*Library symbol*] [*Library of Congress*] [*Obsolete*]   (LCLS)
PPPP .... Past Performance and Present Posture   (AAG)
PPPP .... People's Peace and Prosperity Party [*Defunct*]   (EA)
PPPP .... Proposed Partial Package Program   (MUGU)
PPPPI....... Photographic Projection Plan Position Indicator   (DEN)
PPPR .... Philadelphia Transportation Co., Philadelphia, PA [*Library symbol*] [*Library of Congress*] [*Obsolete*]   (LCLS)
PPPRC ...... Poor Richard Club, Philadelphia, PA [*Library symbol*] [*Library of Congress*] [*Obsolete*]   (LCLS)
PPPres .... Presbyterian University of Pennsylvania, Scheie Eye Institute Library, Philadelphia, PA [*Library symbol*] [*Library of Congress*]   (LCLS)
PPPRF....... Pan Pacific Public Relations Federation [*Thailand*]
PPPrHi...... Presbyterian Historical Society, Philadelphia, PA [*Library symbol*] [*Library of Congress*]   (LCLS)
PPPrI........ Printing Institute, Philadelphia, PA [*Library symbol*] [*Library of Congress*] [*Obsolete*]   (LCLS)
PPProM..... Provident Mutual Life Insurance Co., Philadelphia, PA [*Library symbol*] [*Library of Congress*] [*Obsolete*]   (LCLS)
PPPS........ People's Press Printing Society [*British*]
PPPSB....... Philadelphia College of the Bible, Philadelphia, PA [*Library symbol*] [*Library of Congress*]   (LCLS)
PPPTe....... Philadelphia College of Textiles and Science, Philadelphia, PA [*Library symbol*] [*Library of Congress*]   (LCLS)
PPPYBC.... Physiological Plant Pathology [*A publication*]
PPQ .... Abandoned Police Post [*Board on Geographic Names*]
PPQ .... Parts per Quadrillion
PPQ .... Pittsfield, IL [*Location identifier*] [*FAA*]   (FAAL)
PPQ .... Planning Purpose Quote
PPQ .... Plant Protection and Quarantine Programs [*Department of Agriculture*]   (IMH)
PPQ .... Polyphenylquinoxaline [*Resin*]
PPQA........ Pageable Partition Queue Area [*Data processing*]
PPQN .... Parts per Quarter Note [*Data processing*]   (PCM)
PPQT........ Preproduction Qualification Test [*Army*]
PPQT & E ... Pre-Production Qualification Test and Evaluation [*Army*]
P & P Qtly ... Pulp and Paper Quarterly Statistics [*A publication*]
PPQU .... Philological Quarterly [*A publication*]

PPQUE8.... Plant Protection Quarterly [*A publication*]
PPr............ Paedagogische Provinz [*A publication*]
PPR........... Paid Pensioner Recruiter [*British military*]   (DMA)
PPR........... Palomino Pony Registry
PPR........... Paper
PPR........... Partido Panamenista Republicano [*Panama*] [*Political party*]   (EY)
PPR........... Partido Patriotico Revolucionario [*Mexico*] [*Political party*]   (EY)
PPR........... Partido Proletariano Revolucionario [*Proletarian Revolutionary Party*] [*Portugal*] [*Political party*]   (PPW)
PPR........... Payload Preparation Room [*VAFB*] [*NASA*]   (MCD)
PPR........... Peak Production Rate
PPR........... Periodic Personnel Report
PPR........... Periodicals Publishing Record [*Alberta Public Affairs Bureau*] [*Canada*] [*Information service or system*]   (CRD)
PPR........... Permanent Pay Record [*Military*]
PPR........... Peste des Petits Ruminants [*Rinderpest-like disease*] [*Veterinary medicine*]
PPR........... Philosophy and Phenomenological Research [*A publication*]
PPR........... Photo-Plastic-Recording
PPR........... Photographic Press Review [*A publication*] [*British*]
PPR........... Pilgrim Prime Rate Trust [*NYSE symbol*]   (SPSG)
PPR........... Pilot, Pressure Regulator   (MCD)
P Pr .... Pionerskaja Pravda [*A publication*]
PPR........... Polish People's Republic
PPR........... Politieke Partij Radikalen [*Radical Political Party*] [*Netherlands*] [*Political party*]   (PPE)
PPR........... Polska Partia Robotnicza [*Polish Workers' Party*] [*Political party*]
PPR........... Portable Propagation Recorder [*Bell System*]
PPR........... Potential Problem Report [*Navy*]   (CAAL)
PPR........... Present Participle [*Grammar*]
PPR........... Price. Procedural Regulation [*United States*] [*A publication*]   (DLA)
PPR........... Price's Precipitation Reaction [*Medicine*]
PPR........... Principal Private Residence [*Income tax*] [*British*]
PPR........... Principal Probate Registry   (DLA)
PPR........... Printed Paper Rate [*British*]   (ILCA)
PPR........... Prior Permission Required   (FAAC)
PPR........... Production Parts Release   (KSC)
PPR........... Production Progress Report   (MCD)
PPR........... Program Progress Review
PPR........... Program Proposal Request
PPR........... Project Progress Report   (OICC)
PPR........... Proper [*Heraldry*]
PPR........... Proprietary Procurement Request   (NG)
PPR........... Provisioning Preparedness Review [*Navy*]   (CAAL)
P & PR ...... Psychoanalysis and the Psychoanalytic Review [*A publication*]
PPR........... Public Productivity Review [*A publication*]
PPR........... Purchase Parts Request   (KSC)
PPRA .... Past President of the Royal Academy [*British*]   (EY)
PPRA .... Preliminary Personnel Requirements Analysis [*Navy*]
PPRAA ...... Polski Przeglad Radiologiczny [*A publication*]
PPRBD ...... Paperboard [*Freight*]
PPRC........ Personnel Program Review Committee [*Military*]
PPRC........ Prepositioned Receipt Card   (AABC)
PPRCl....... Rittenhouse Club, Philadelphia, PA [*Library symbol*] [*Library of Congress*] [*Obsolete*]   (LCLS)
PPRD........ Pontypool Road [*Welsh depot code*]
PPRDS ...... Products and Process Research and Development Support   (DCTA)
PPRE .... Paris Review [*A publication*]
PPRE .... Peroxisome Proliferator Response Element [*Biochemistry*]
PPREC ...... Pulp and Paper Research and Education Center [*Auburn University*] [*Research center*]   (RCD)
P Prehist S ... Proceedings. Prehistoric Society [*A publication*]
PPREPT.... Periodic Personnel Report [*Military*]   (AABC)
PPRETS .... Reformed Episcopal Seminary, Philadelphia, PA [*Library symbol*] [*Library of Congress*] [*Obsolete*]
PPRF .... Paramedian Pontine Reticular Formation [*Neuroanatomy*]
PPRF .... Pulse Pair Repetition Frequency   (MCD)
PPRF .... Rosenbach Foundation, Philadelphia, PA [*Library symbol*] [*Library of Congress*]   (LCLS)
PPRFA ...... Poliplasti e Plastici Rinforzati [*A publication*]
PPRG........ Precambrian Paleobiology Research Group
PPRGF ...... Richard Gimbel Foundation for Literary Research, Philadelphia, PA [*Library symbol*] [*Library of Congress*] [*Obsolete*]   (LCLS)
PPRI .... PACOM [*Pacific Command*] Priority Number   (CINC)
PPRI .... Poloron Products, Inc. [*NASDAQ symbol*]   (NQ)
PPRIBA.... Past President of the Royal Institute of British Architects   (EY)
PPRibP ...... Phosphoribose Diphosphate [*Biochemistry*]
PPRIC .... Pulp and Paper Research Institute of Canada
P Princet ... Papyri in the Princeton University Collections [*A publication*]
PPrIT........ Putnam Premier Income Trust [*Associated Press abbreviation*]   (APAG)
PPRL .... Poisonous Plant Research Laboratory [*Agricultural Research Service*] [*Research center*]   (RCD)
PPRM........ Population Protection and Resources Management [*Military*] [*British*]

PPRM........ Pure Premium Rating Method [*Insurance*]

PPRN........ Preliminary Publication Revision Notice

PPRN........ Purchased Parts Requirement Notice (KSC)

PPRNCM ... Professional Performance of the Royal Northern College of Music [*British*] (DBQ)

PPRNS ...... Pulse-Phased Radio Navigation System

PPRO........ Pattern Processing Technologies, Inc. [*NASDAQ symbol*] (NQ)

PPRO........ Per Procuration [*Business term*]

P Proc Hampshire Field Club ... Papers and Proceedings. Hampshire Field Club and Archaeological Society [*A publication*]

PProv .... Padova e la Sua Provincia [*A publication*]

PPRPA ...... Produits et Problemes Pharmaceutiques [*A publication*]

PPRPF....... Regional Planning Federation, Philadelphia, PA [*Library symbol*] [*Library of Congress*] [*Obsolete*] (LCLS)

PPRRD3.... Peptide and Protein Reviews [*A publication*]

PPRS .... Perceptions of Parental Role Scales

PPRS .... Pharmaceutical Price Regulation Scheme [*British*]

PPRS .... Program Planning and Review Staff [*Environmental Protection Agency*] (GFGA)

PPRS .... Promotions and Placements Referral System (MCD)

PPRSA ..... Past President of the Royal Society of Arts [*British*] (DI)

PPrStBrt.... Perspectives in Probability and Statistics: in Honor of M. S. Bartlett [*A publication*]

PPRV........ Peste des Petits Ruminants Virus [*Rinderpest-like disease*] [*Veterinary medicine*]

PPRV........ Physiological Reviews [*A publication*]

PPRWP ..... Poor Precordial R-Wave Progression [*Cardiology*]

PPS .... Packets per Second [*Data processing*] (PCM)

PPS .... Paco Pharmaceutical Services, Inc. [*NYSE symbol*] (SPSG)

PPS .... Page Printing System [*Honeywell, Inc.*] [*Data processing*]

PPS .... Paper Publications Society [*Amsterdam, Netherlands*] (EA)

PP & S ...... Papers on Poetics and Semiotics [*A publication*]

PPS .... Parallel Processing System [*Data processing*] (MDG)

PPS .... Parameter Processing System (CAAL)

PPS .... Parliamentary Private Secretary [*British*]

PPS .... Parti Populaire Senegalais [*Senegalese People's Party*] [*Political party*] (PPW)

PPS .... Parti Populaire Syrien [*Syrian People's Party*] [*Political party*] (BJA)

PPS .... Parti du Progres Social [*Burkina Faso*] [*Political party*] (EY)

PPS .... Parti du Progres et du Socialisme [*Party of Progress and Socialism*] [*Morocco*] [*Political party*] (PPW)

PPS .... Parti Progressiste Soudanais [*Sudanese Progressive Party*] [*Political party*]

PPS .... Partia e Punes e Shqiperise [*Party of Labor of Albania - PLA*] [*Political party*] (PPW)

PPS .... Partial Pressure Sensor

PPS .... Partido Popular Salvadoreno [*Salvadoran Popular Party*] [*Political party*] (PPW)

PPS .... Partido Popular Socialista [*Popular Socialist Party*] [*Argentina*] [*Political party*] (PPW)

PPS .... Partido Popular Socialista [*Popular Socialist Party*] [*Mexico*] [*Political party*]

PPS .... Partito Populare Somalo [*Somali People's Party*]

PPS .... Parts Provisioning System (KSC)

PPS .... Patchboard Programming System

PPS .... Payload Pointing System (SSD)

PPS .... Payload Power Switch

PPS .... Pension and Profit-Sharing Tax Journal [*A publication*]

PPS .... Peoples Oil Ltd. [*Vancouver Stock Exchange symbol*]

PPS .... Pepsin A [*Medicine*] (MAE)

PPS .... Personal Plane Service [*Aircraft restoration firm*] [*British*]

PPS .... Personal Preference Scale [*Psychology*]

PPS .... Personal Printer Series [*IBM Corp.*]

PPS .... Personal Printing System [*Data processing*]

PPS .... Personal Protection Squad [*of the London Metropolitan Police*]

PPS .... Personnel/Payroll System

PPS .... Personnel Processing Squadron

PPS .... Personnel Psychology [*A publication*]

PPS .... Petroleum Press Service

PPS .... Petroleum Production Survey [*Bureau of Mines*]

PPS .... Phantom Phanatics Society (EA)

PPS .... Phosphorous Propellant System (KSC)

PPS .... Photophoretic Spectroscopy

PPS .... Photopolarimeter Spectrometer

PPS .... Photovoltaic Power Supply

PPS .... Piece Part Specification (MCD)

PPS .... Pierpont [*South Carolina*] [*Seismograph station code, US Geological Survey*] (SEIS)

PPS .... Pitt Press Series [*A publication*]

PPS .... Plant Parasitic Systems

PPS .... Plant Protection System [*Nuclear energy*] (NRCH)

PPS .... Plasma Power Supply

PPS .... Plutonium Product Storage [*Nuclear energy*] (NRCH)

PPS .... Pneumatic Power Subsystem (NASA)

PPS .... Policy Processing Sheet [*Insurance*]

PPS .... Polonus Philatelic Society (EA)

PPS .... Polska Partia Socjalistyczna [*Polish Socialist Party*]

PPS .... Poly(para-phenylene Sulfide) [*Organic chemistry*]

PPS .... Post-Polio Sequelae [*Medicine*]

PPS .... Post-Postscriptum [*Further Postscript*] [*Latin*]

PPS .... Post Production Service (AAG)

PPS .... Post Production Support (MCD)

PPS .... Postpartum Sterilization [*Medicine*]

PPS .... Postperfusion Syndrome [*Medicine*]

PPS .... Postpump Syndrome [*Medicine*] (MAE)

PPS .... Pounds per Second (AAG)

PPS .... Precise Positioning Service [*Military*]

PPS .... Precision Power Supply

PPS .... Prepositioned Stock (NG)

PPS .... Prescribed Payments System (ADA)

PPS .... Primary Paraffin Sulfonate [*Organic chemistry*]

PPS .... Primary Power Standard

PPS .... Primary Power System [*Nuclear energy*] (NRCH)

PPS .... Primary Pressure Standard

PPS .... Primary Propulsion System [*Spacecraft*]

PPS .... Principal Private Secretary [*British*]

PPS .... Printer/Plotter System (MCD)

PPS .... Prior Preferred Stock

PPS .... Private Practice Section [*American Physical Therapy Association*] (EA)

PPS .... Probability Proportional to Size [*Statistics*]

PPS .... Proceedings. Prehistoric Society [*A publication*]

PPS .... Procurement Planning Schedule [*DoD*]

PPS .... Production Planning System [*TDS Business Systems Ltd.*] [*Software package*] (NCC)

PPS .... Program Performance Specification (CAAL)

PPS .... Program Planning Summary (OICC)

PPS .... Program Planning System [*DoD*]

PPS .... Program Policy Staff [*UN Food and Agriculture Organization*]

PPS .... Programmable Patch System

PPS .... Programmable Power Supply

PPS .... Programmed Processor System

PPS .... Programming Program Strela [*Data processing*]

PPS .... Progressive Pneumonia of Sheep

PPS .... Project for Public Spaces (EA)

PPS .... Propose (FAAC)

PPS .... Propulsion Pressurization Subsystem

PPS .... Propulsion and Propellant Section [*Picatinny Arsenal*] [*Dover, NJ*]

PPS .... Prospective Payment System [*For hospital care*]

PPS .... Provisioning Parts Schedule (MCD)

PPS .... Provisioning Performance Schedule (AFM)

PPS .... Provisioning Policy Statement (MCD)

PPS .... Prudential Property Services [*Prudential Group*] [*British*]

PPS .... Public and Private [*Nongovernment*] Schools [*Public-performance tariff class*] [*British*]

PPS .... Publications. Philological Society [*A publication*]

PPS .... Puerto Princesa [*Philippines*] [*Airport symbol*] (OAG)

PPS .... Pulses per Second [*Data transmission*]

PPSA .... Pan-Pacific Surgical Association (EA)

PPSA .... Prospect Park Savings & Loan Association [*NASDAQ symbol*] (NQ)

PPSAS...... Program Planning and Status Assessment System [*Nuclear energy*] (NRCH)

PPSB .... Personality and Social Psychology Bulletin [*A publication*]

PPSB .... Prothrombin, Proconvertin, Stuart Factor, Antihemophilic B Factor [*Blood coagulation factors*] [*Hematology*]

PPSC .... Physical Profile Serial Code [*Military*]

PPSC .... Prairie Schooner [*A publication*]

PPSC .... Privacy Protection Study Commission [*Government commission*]

PPSCA...... Partido Popular Social Cristiano Autentico [*Political party*] (EY)

PPSCI....... Seamen's Church Institute, Philadelphia, PA [*Library symbol*] [*Library of Congress*] [*Obsolete*] (LCLS)

PPSD .... Polska Partia Socialno-Demokratyczna [*Polish Social-Democrat Party*] [*Political party*]

PPSD .... Proposed

PPSE .... Petroleum Economist [*A publication*]

PPSE .... Purpose

PPSEAWA ... Pan-Pacific and South-East Asia Women's Association [*Tokyo, Japan*] (EAIO)

PPSEAWA-USA ... Pan Pacific and Southeast Asia Women's Association of the USA (EA)

PPSED3 .... Annual Research Reviews. Physiological and Pathological Aspects of Prolactin Secretion [*A publication*]

PPSEE4..... Postgraduate Paediatrics Series [*A publication*]

PPSF......... Palestinian Popular Struggle Front [*Political party*] (BJA)

PPS-FR...... Polska Partia Socjalistyczna - Frakcja Rewolucyjna [*Polish Socialist Party - Revolutionary Faction*] [*Political party*] (PPE)

PPSG .... Piston and Pin Standardization Group [*Later, NEPMA*] (EA)

PPSG .... Spring Garden College, Philadelphia, PA [*Library symbol*] [*Library of Congress*] (LCLS)

PPSh......... Partia e Punes e Shqiperise [*Labor Party of Albania*] [*Formerly, PKSh*] [*Political party*] (PPE)

PPSH......... Pseudovaginal Perineoscrotal Hypospadias [*Medicine*]

PPSI.......... Pacific Physician Services (SPSG)

PPSIA........ "Personal Property Shipping Information" [*Pamphlet*] Is Applicable [*Military*] (AABC)

PPSIAD.....   Past President of the Society of Industrial Artists and Designers [*British*]   (DI)
PPSJ.........   Policy Studies Journal [*A publication*]
PPSJ.........   Pressure Plane Swivel Joint
PPSJ.........   Saint Joseph's College, Philadelphia, PA [*Library symbol*] [*Library of Congress*]   (LCLS)
PPSJ-AF ...   Saint Joseph's College, Academy of Food Marketing, Philadelphia, PA [*Library symbol*] [*Library of Congress*]   (LCLS)
PPSKED....   Provisioning Performance Schedule   (MCD)
PPSKF.......   SmithKline Corp., Philadelphia, PA [*Library symbol*] [*Library of Congress*]   (LCLS)
PPSL........   Program Parts Selection List
PPSL........   Provisioning Parts Selection List   (MCD)
PPSMEC...   Procurement, Precedence of Supplies, Material and Equipment Committee [*Joint Communications Board*]
PPSN........   Present Position [*Aviation*]   (FAAC)
PPSN........   Public Packet Switched Network [*Telecommunications*]
PPSN........   Purchased Part Shortage Notice
PPSO........   Personal Property Shipping Office [*Military*]
PPSOPR....   Sun Oil Co., General Office Library, Philadelphia, PA [*Library symbol*] [*Library of Congress*] [*Obsolete*]   (LCLS)
PPSP.........   Page Printer Spooling System [*Data processing*]
PPSP.........   Ponderosa Pine or Sugar Pine [*Lumber*]
PPSP.........   Power Plant Siting Program [*Environmental Protection Agency*]   (GFGA)
PPSPS.......   Plutonium Product Shipping Preparation Station [*Nuclear energy*]   (NRCH)
PPSQ........   Presidential Studies Quarterly [*A publication*]
PPSR........   Periodic Personnel Strength Report [*Army*]   (AABC)
PPSR........   Philosophical Review [*A publication*]
PPSS.........   Foundation for the President's Private Sector Survey on Cost Control   (EA)
PPSS.........   Polyphenylene Sulfide Sulfone [*Organic chemistry*]
PPSSA.......   Proceedings. Nuclear Physics and Solid State Physics Symposium [*A publication*]
PPSSCC ....   Foundation for the President's Private Sector Survey on Cost Control   (EA)
PPST ....   Physics Teacher [*A publication*]
PPStarr......   Starr Center Association, Philadelphia, PA [*Library symbol*] [*Library of Congress*] [*Obsolete*]   (LCLS)
PPStCh......   Saint Charles Borromeo Seminary, Philadelphia, PA [*Library symbol*] [*Library of Congress*]   (LCLS)
PPSteph.....   William B. Stephens Memorial Library, Philadelphia, PA [*Library symbol*] [*Library of Congress*] [*Obsolete*]   (LCLS)
PPSU ....   Political Studies [*A publication*]
PPSV ....   Plutonium Product Storage Vault [*Nuclear energy*]   (NRCH)
PPS-WRN ...   Polska Partia Socjalistyczna - Wolnosc, Rownosc, Niepodleglosc [*Polish Socialist Party - Freedom, Equality, Independence*] [*Political party*]   (PPE)
PPSY ....   Psychiatry [*A publication*]
PPSYA ......   Personnel Psychology [*A publication*]
PP & T ....   Packaging, Preservation, and Transportation
PPT...........   Pamatai [*French Polynesia*] [*Geomagnetic observatory code*]
PPT...........   Papeete [*Society Islands*] [*Seismograph station code, US Geological Survey*]   (SEIS)
PPT...........   Papeete [*French Polynesia*] [*Airport symbol*]   (OAG)
PPT...........   Parti Progressiste Tchadien [*Progressive Party of Chad*] [*Political party*]
PPT...........   Partial Prothrombin Time [*Hematology*]
PPT...........   Parts per Thousand   (DNAB)
PPT...........   Parts per Trillion
p-p-t ....   Pay-per-Transaction [*Agreement between video cassette rental stores and owners of film rights*]
PPT...........   Pedunculopontine Tegmentum [*Neurology*]
PPT...........   Period Pulse Train
PPT...........   Periodic Programs Termination [*Data processing*]
PPT...........   Peripheral Performance Test   (CAAL)
PPT...........   Permanent Part-Time   (ADA)
PPT...........   Phosphinothricin [*Organic chemistry*]
PPT...........   Pine Point Mines Ltd. [*Toronto Stock Exchange symbol*] [*Vancouver Stock Exchange symbol*]
PPT...........   Pitch Precession Torquer
PPT...........   Plant Protease Test   (MAE)
PPT...........   Polypurine Tract [*Genetics*]
PPT...........   Pooh Property Trust [*A.A. Milne estate*] [*British*]
PPT...........   Poppet [*Engineering*]
PPT...........   Post Production Test
PPT...........   Practical Policy Test [*Psychology*]
PPT...........   Praecipitatus [*Precipitated*] [*Pharmacy*]
PPT...........   Praeparata [*Prepared*] [*Pharmacy*]   (ROG)
PPT...........   Precipitate   (MSA)
PPT...........   Preproduction Test [*Army*]
PPT...........   Preprotachykinin [*Biochemistry*]
PPT...........   Preprototype   (SAA)
PPT...........   Private Purchasing Tariff [*British*]
PPT...........   Process Page Table [*Telecommunications*]   (TEL)
PPT...........   Product Positioning Time   (AFM)
PPT...........   Production Prototype
PPT...........   Project Planning Technique   (MCD)
PPT...........   Prompt   (ROG)

PPT...........   Propyl(thio)uracil [*Biochemistry*]
PPT...........   Public and Private Transport
PPT...........   Pulse Plasma Thruster
PPT...........   Punched Paper Tape [*Data processing*]
PPT...........   Putnam Premier Income Trust [*NYSE symbol*]   (SPSG)
PPT...........   Temple University, Philadelphia, PA [*Library symbol*] [*Library of Congress*]   (LCLS)
PPT...........   Theosophical Society, Philadelphia, PA [*Library symbol*] [*Library of Congress*] [*Obsolete*]   (LCLS)
PPTA J ......   PPTA [*Post-Primary Teachers Association*] Journal [*A publication*]
PPTB ....   Pin-Pack Test Board
PPTBA ......   Pattern and Plastic Tool Builders Association   (EA)
PPTC ....   People-to-People Tennis Committee   (EA)
PPTC ....   Purchased Part Tab Card
PPTD........   Precipitated
PPT-D.......   Temple University, Dental-Pharmacy School, Philadelphia, PA [*Library symbol*] [*Library of Congress*]   (LCLS)
PPTEC ......   Polymer-Plastics Technology and Engineering [*A publication*]
PPTF ....   Public Policy Task Force [*Defunct*]   (EA)
PPTH........   Political Theory [*A publication*]
pPTH........   Porcine Parathyroid Hormone [*Endocrinology*]
PPTI ....   Passport Travel, Inc. [*NASDAQ symbol*]   (NQ)
PPT-ISA...   Picture Personality Test for Indian South Africans
PPTJ..........   Theodore F. Jenkins Memorial Law Library, Philadelphia, PA [*Library symbol*] [*Library of Congress*]   (LCLS)
PPTL ....   Postpartum Tubal Ligation [*Medicine*]
PPTL ....   Pulp and Paper Traffic League [*Defunct*]   (EA)
PPT-L........   Temple University, Law School, Philadelphia, PA [*Library symbol*] [*Library of Congress*]   (LCLS)
PPT-M......   Temple University, Medical School, Philadelphia, PA [*Library symbol*] [*Library of Congress*]   (LCLS)
PPTMR ....   Personal Property Traffic Management Regulation
PPTN........   Precipitation
PPTO........   Personal Property Transportation Officer
PPTO........   Principal Professional and Technology Officer [*British*]
PPTR ....   Partisan Review [*A publication*]
PPTR ....   Punched Paper Tape Reader [*Data processing*]
PPTri ....   Tri-Institutional Library, Philadelphia, PA [*Library symbol*] [*Library of Congress*]   (LCLS)
PPTS ....   Pianoforte Polishers' Trade Society [*A union*] [*British*]
PPTS ....   Portable Perishable Tool System   (MCD)
PPTS ....   Pre-Problem Training Situation   (SAA)
PPTS ....   Pyridinium Para-Toluenesulfonate [*Organic chemistry*]
PPTS ....   Pyridinium-para-Tosylate [*Organic chemistry*]
PPT-T ....   Temple University, School of Theology, Philadelphia, PA [*Library symbol*] [*Library of Congress*]   (LCLS)
PPTV ....   Parts per Trillion by Volume
PPTW.......   Permanent Part-Time Work
PPTY ....   Property   (AFM)
PPU ....   Cocoa, FL [*Location identifier*] [*FAA*]   (FAAL)
PPU ....   Papun [*Myanmar*] [*Airport symbol*]   (OAG)
PPU ....   Parti Populaire des Ueles [*Ueles People's Party*] [*Political party*]
PPU ....   Payment for Public Use [*Canada*]
PPU ....   Peace Pledge Union [*British*]
PPU ....   Peninsula Petroleum Corp. [*Vancouver Stock Exchange symbol*]
PPU ....   Peoria & Pekin Union Railway Co. [*AAR code*]
PPU ....   Peripheral Processing Unit [*Data processing*]
PPU ....   Platform Position Unit
PPU ....   Power Processing Unit   (MCD)
PPU ....   Preproduction Unit   (MCD)
PPU ....   Prime Power Unit
PPU ....   Professional Psychics United   (EA)
PPU ....   Promontory Point [*Utah*] [*Seismograph station code, US Geological Survey*] [*Closed*]   (SEIS)
PPUAES....   Publications. Princeton University Archaeological Expeditions to Syria in 1904-5 and 1909 [*A publication*]
PPUCA4....   Acta Scientiarum Naturalium. Academiae Scientiarum Bohemoslovacae [*Brno*] [*A publication*]
PPUG ....   United Gas Improvement Corp., Philadelphia, PA [*Library symbol*] [*Library of Congress*] [*Obsolete*]   (LCLS)
PPULC ......   Union Library Catalogue of Pennsylvania, Philadelphia, PA [*Library symbol*] [*Library of Congress*]   (LCLS)
PPUMD3 ..   Museum of Paleontology. Papers on Paleontology [*A publication*]
PPUNA .....   United States Naval Aircraft Factory, Philadelphia, PA [*Library symbol*] [*Library of Congress*] [*Obsolete*]   (LCLS)
PPUnC.......   University Club, Philadelphia, PA [*Library symbol*] [*Library of Congress*] [*Obsolete*]   (LCLS)
PPUNH.....   United States Naval Home, Philadelphia, PA [*Library symbol*] [*Library of Congress*] [*Obsolete*]   (LCLS)
PPUR-A ....   Population Review [*A publication*]
PPUSDA ...   United States Department of Agriculture, Agricultural Research Service, Eastern Utilization Research and Development Division, Philadelphia, PA [*Library symbol*] [*Library of Congress*]   (LCLS)
PPV...........   Pay-per-View [*Pay-television service*]
PPV...........   People-Powered Vehicle [*Recreational vehicle powered by pedaling*]

PPV............ Plum Pox Virus [*Plant pathology*]
PPV............ Polarized Platen Viewer   (OA)
PPV............ Positive Predictive Value [*Experimentation*]
PPV............ Positive Pressure Ventilation [*Medicine*]
PPV............ Preprogrammed Vehicles   (MCD)
PPV............ Primary Pressure Vessel   (MCD)
P/PV......... Public/Private Ventures [*Philadelphia, PA*] [*Research center*]   (RCD)
PPV............ United States Veterans Administration Hospital, Philadelphia, PA [*Library symbol*] [*Library of Congress*]   (LCLS)
PPVT........ Peabody Picture Vocabulary Test [*Education*]
PPVT-R..... Peabody Picture Vocabulary Test - Revised [*Education*]
PP-W......... Free Library of Philadelphia, H. Josephine Widener Memorial Branch, Philadelphia, PA [*Library symbol*] [*Library of Congress*] [*Obsolete*]   (LCLS)
PPW.......... PacifiCorp [*NYSE symbol*]   (SPSG)
PPW.......... Papa Westray [*Scotland*] [*Airport symbol*]   (OAG)
PPW.......... Parts per Weight
PPW.......... Petitions for Patent Waiver
PPW.......... Plane-Polarized Wave
PPW.......... Ponderosa Pine Woodwork Association [*Absorbed by NWWDA*]   (EA)
PPW.......... Potato Processing Waste
P & PW...... Publicity and Psychological Warfare
PPWA........ Ponderosa Pine Woodwork Association [*Absorbed by NWWDA*]
PPWa........ Wagner Free Institute of Science, Philadelphia, PA [*Library symbol*] [*Library of Congress*]   (LCLS)
PPWC........ Pulp, Paper, and Woodworkers of Canada
PPWD........ S. S. White Co., Philadelphia, PA [*Library symbol*] [*Library of Congress*] [*Obsolete*]   (LCLS)
PPWe........ Westminster Theological Seminary, Philadelphia, PA [*Library symbol*] [*Library of Congress*]   (LCLS)
PPWI........ Wistar Institute of Anatomy and Biology, Philadelphia, PA [*Library symbol*] [*Library of Congress*]   (LCLS)
PPWiH ..... Wills Eye Hospital, Philadelphia, PA [*Library symbol*] [*Library of Congress*]   (LCLS)
PPWM....... Medical College of Pennsylvania, Philadelphia, PA [*Library symbol*] [*Library of Congress*]   (LCLS)
PPWMA.... Progress in Powder Metallurgy [*A publication*]
PPWP .... Planned Parenthood - World Population [*Later, PPFA*]   (EA)
PPWQ .... Psychology of Women Quarterly [*A publication*]
PPWR........ Prepositioned War Reserves [*Army*]
PPWRS ..... Prepositioned War Reserve Stocks [*Army*]
PPX........... Packet Protocol Extension
PPX........... Port Moller, AK [*Location identifier*] [*FAA*]   (FAAL)
PPX........... Private Packet Exchange
PPY........... Pages per Year [*Facetious criterion for determining insignificance of Supreme Court Justices*] [*Proposed by University of Chicago professor David P. Currie*]
PPY........... Prophesy Development [*Vancouver Stock Exchange symbol*]
PPYH .... Young Men's and Young Women's Hebrew Association, Philadelphia, PA [*Library symbol*] [*Library of Congress*] [*Obsolete*]   (LCLS)
PPYSA ...... Plant Physiology. Supplement [*A publication*]
PPYU........ Party of Popular Yemenite Unity [*Political party*]   (PD)
PPZ........... Proton Polar Zone
PPZ........... Zoological Society of Philadelphia, PA [*Library symbol*] [*Library of Congress*] [*Obsolete*]   (LCLS)
PPZI .... Przeglad Pismiennictwa Zagadnien Informacji [*A publication*]
PQ.............. Pack Quickly [*Humorous interpretation for Parti Quebecois*] [*Canada*]
PQ.............. Pakistan Quarterly [*A publication*]
PQ.............. Panic in Quebec [*Humorous interpretation for Parti Quebecois*] [*Canada*]
PQ.............. Parliamentary Question [*British*]
PQ.............. Parti Quebecois [*Quebec separatist political party*]
P & Q .... Peace and Quiet
PQ.............. Performer Quotient [*TV-performer rating*]
PQ.............. Permeability Quotient
PQ.............. Personality Quotient [*Psychology*]
PQ.............. Philological Quarterly [*A publication*]
PQ.............. Philosophical Quarterly [*A publication*]
PQ.............. Physically Qualified
PQ.............. Physician's Questionnaire   (AAMN)
PQ.............. Piano Quarterly [*A publication*]
PQ.............. Planetary Quarantine [*NASA*]
PQ.............. Plant Quarantine Division [*of ARS, Department of Agriculture*]
PQ.............. Plasma Quad [*Instrumentation*]
PQ.............. Plastoquinone [*Biochemistry*]
PQ.............. Pollution Quotient
PQ.............. Polyquinoxaline [*Organic chemistry*]
P-Q........... Porphyrin-Quinone [*Photochemistry*]
PQ.............. PQ Corp. [*Formerly, Philadelphia Quartz Co.*]
PQ.............. Premium Quality   (MUGU)
PQ.............. Preparative Quencher [*Spectroscopy*]
PQ.............. Previous Question [*Parliamentary law*]
Pq.............. Primaquine [*Antimalarial*]
P and Q ...... Prime Quality [*Slang*]
pq .... Pro Querente [*For the Plaintiff*] [*Latin*] [*Legal term*]   (DLA)
PQ.............. Province Quebec [*Quebec*] [*Canadian province*] [*Postal code*]

PQ.............. Psi Quotient [*Parapsychology*]
PQ.............. Psychiatric Quarterly [*A publication*]
PQ.............. Public Quarters
PQ.............. Puerto Rico International Airlines, Inc. [*Prinair*] [*ICAO designator*]   (OAG)
PQ.............. Pyrimethamine-Quinine [*Organic chemistry*]   (MAE)
PQ.............. Quebec [*Postal code*]   (CDAI)
PQ.............. United States Patent Quarterly [*A publication*]   (DLA)
P's & Q's.... Of expression "Mind your P's and Q's." Exact origin unclear, but theories include: admonishment of pub-owners that British drinkers be aware of number of "Pints and Quarts" being marked on their accounts; warning to apprentice typesetters that "p" and "q" fonts be carefully restored to correct case, since each could so easily be mistaken for the other; cautioning of French dancing masters that pupils be aware of position of their "Pieds" [*feet*] and "Queues" [*wigs*] in executing the deep bow of a formal curtsey.
PQA .... Parts Quality Assurance
PQA .... Petroleum Quality Assurance
PQA .... Plant Quality Assurance
PQA .... Preliminary Quantitative Analysis
PQA .... Procurement Quality Assurance [*Program*] [*DoD*]
PQA .... Production Quality Assurance
PQA .... Project Quality Assurance
PQA .... Protected Queue Area [*Data processing*]   (BUR)
PQAD .... Plant Quality Assurance Director [*Nuclear energy*]   (NRCH)
PQAI .... Procurement Quality Assurance Instruction
PQAM ...... Project Quality Assurance Manager [*Nuclear energy*]   (NRCH)
PQAP....... Planned Quality Assurance Program [*Navy*]
PQAP....... Procurement Quality Assurance Program [*DoD*]
PQAR .... Petroleum Quality Assurance Representative
PQB .... Quebecor, Inc. [*AMEX symbol*]   (SPSG)
PQBOAK .. Pesquisas Botanica [*A publication*]
PQC .... Paul Quinn College [*Texas*]
PQC .... Paul Quinn College, Waco, TX [*OCLC symbol*]   (OCLC)
PQC .... Precision Quartz Crystal
PQC .... Production Quality Control
PQCS........ Philippine Quarterly of Culture and Society [*A publication*]
PQCS........ Process Quality Control System
PQCSD6... Commissione Internazionale per la Protezione delle Acque Italo-Svizzere. Rapporti [*A publication*]
PQD.......... Partido Quisqueyano Democrata [*Quisqueyan Democratic Party*] [*Dominican Republic*] [*Political party*]   (PPW)
PQD.......... Percentage Quartile Deviation [*Statistics*]
PQD.......... Predicted Quarterly Demand
PQD.......... Pyroelectric Quad Detector
PQDMB ... Percentage Quartile Deviation Median Bias [*Statistics*]
PQE .... Parents for Quality Education   (EA)
PQE .... Principal Quality Engineers [*British*]   (RDA)
PQE .... Project Quality Engineering
PQEP........ Product Quality Evaluation Plan [*Military*]   (AABC)
PQET........ Print Quality Enhancement Technology [*IBM*]   (PCM)
PQFP........ Plastic Quad Flat Package [*Data processing*]   (PCM)
PQGS........ Propellant Quantity Gauge [*or Gauging*] System [*Apollo*] [*NASA*]
PQI .... Presque Isle [*Maine*] [*Airport symbol*]   (OAG)
PQI .... Presque Isle, ME [*Location identifier*] [*FAA*]   (FAAL)
PQI .... Product Quality Improvement [*Program*] [*Chrysler Corp.*]
PQI .... Professional Qualification Index   (AFM)
PQI .... Propellant Quantity Indicator   (NASA)
PQL .... Prior Quarter Liability [*IRS*]
PQLI......... Physical Quality of Life Index [*Overseas Development Council*]
PQM .... Pacific Quarterly (Moana): An International Review of Arts and Ideas [*A publication*]
PQM .... Pilot Qualified in Model   (NVT)
PQM .... Post Quartermaster [*Marine Corps*]
PQM .... Pulse Quaternary Modulation
PQMC .... Philadelphia Quartermaster Center [*Merged with Defense Clothing and Textile Supply Center*] [*Military*]
PQMD....... Philadelphia Quartermaster Depot [*Military*]
PQMD....... Propellant Quantity Measuring Device
PQMDO.... Proposed Quality Material Development Objective   (NATG)
PQMR....... Preliminary Quantitative Material Requirements   (MCD)
PQMS........ Process Quality Measurement System [*Chemical process engineering*]
PQN.......... Consolidated Petroquin [*Vancouver Stock Exchange symbol*]
PQN.......... Pahaquarry [*New Jersey*] [*Seismograph station code, US Geological Survey*]   (SEIS)
PQN.......... Pipestone, MN [*Location identifier*] [*FAA*]   (FAAL)
PQN.......... Principal Quantum Number [*Atomic physics*]
PQO.......... Phoenix, AZ [*Location identifier*] [*FAA*]   (FAAL)
PQP.......... Planetary Quarantine Plan [*NASA*]
PQP.......... Prequalification Prototype   (KSC)
PQQ.......... Port Macquarie [*Australia*] [*Airport symbol*]   (OAG)
PQQ.......... Pyrroloquinoline Quinone [*Biochemistry*]
PQQPRI ... Provisional Qualitative and Quantitative Personnel Requirements Information [*Army*]   (AABC)
PQR.......... Pantan Resources [*Vancouver Stock Exchange symbol*]
PQR.......... Performance Qualification Requirement
PQR.......... Personnel Qualification Record [*Military*]   (INF)
PQR.......... Personnel Qualification Roster [*Military*]   (AABC)

PQR	Peruvian Quarterly Report [*A publication*]
PQR	Procedure Qualification Record [*Nuclear energy*] (NRCH)
PQRB	Quarterly Review of Biology [*A publication*]
PQRF	Quarterly Review of Film and Video [*A publication*]
PQRST	Personal Questionnaire Rapid Scaling Technique [*Personality development test*] [*Psychology*]
PQRST	Product-Quality-Routing-Service-Timing [*Industrial engineering*]
PQS	Palestine Exploration Fund. Quarterly Statement [*A publication*]
PQS	Personnel Qualification Standards [*Military*] (NVT)
PQS	Pilot Station [*Alaska*] [*Airport symbol*] (OAG)
PQS	Production Quotation Support
PQS	Progressive Qualification Scheme [*British*]
PQS	Promotion Qualification Score [*Military*]
PQSF	Preparative Quencher Stopped Flow [*Spectroscopy*]
PQT	Parquet Resources, Inc. [*Toronto Stock Exchange symbol*]
PQT	PC Quote, Inc. [*AMEX symbol*] (SPSG)
PQT	Performance Qualification Test (MCD)
PQT	Polyquinazolotriazole [*Organic chemistry*]
PQT	Preliminary Qualification Test (MCD)
PQT	Production Qualification and Testing
PQT	Professional Qualification Test [*of the National Security Agency*]
PQT	Prototype Qualification Testing (RDA)
PQT-C	Prototype Qualification Test - Contractor (MCD)
PQT & E	Production Qualification Test and Evaluation
PQT-G	Prototype Qualification Test - Government (MCD)
PQT/LOT ...	Production Qualification Test / Limited Operational Test
PQTR	Political Quarterly [*A publication*]
PQT-SE	Prototype Qualification Test - Service Evaluation (MCD)
P Qu	Philippines Quarterly [*A publication*]
PQU	Salisbury, MD [*Location identifier*] [*FAA*] (FAAL)
PQUE	Print Queue Processor [*Data processing*]
PQUEA	Progress in Quantum Electronics [*A publication*]
PQW	Placita de Quo Warranto, Record Commission [*England*] [*A publication*] (DLA)
PQX	Physically Qualified Except
PQZ	Premium Quality Zinc
PR	Abbott Laboratories [*Research code symbol*]
PR	Aircrew Survival Equipmentman [*Navy rating*]
PR	Pacific Reporter [*A publication*] (DLA)
P(R)	Packet (Receive)
PR	Painter (ADA)
PR	Pair (KSC)
PR	Pakistan Railways (DCTA)
PR	Panama Red [*Variety of marijuana*]
PR	Panel Receptacle
PR	Pangenesis Related [*Protein chemistry*]
PR	Panthere Rose [*An association*] [*France*] (EAIO)
PR	Paper Tape Reader
PR	Parachute Rigger [*Navy*] (KSC)
PR	Parallax and Refraction
PR	Parcel Receipt [*Shipping*]
PR	Parental Recommendation [*Movie rating*] (CDAI)
PR	Parents Rights (EA)
PR	Paris Review [*A publication*]
PR	Parish Register
P & R	Parks and Recreation [*A publication*]
PR	Parliamentary Report [*British*]
PR	Parrott Rifle
PR	Parti Republicain [*Republican Party*] [*Martinique*] [*Political party*] (PPW)
PR	Parti Republicain [*Republican Party*] [*France*] [*Political party*] (PPW)
PR	Parti Republicain [*Republican Party*] [*New Caledonia*] [*Political party*] (FEA)
PR	Parti Republicain [*Republican Party*] [*Reunion*] [*Political party*] (EY)
PR	Partial Remission [*Medicine*]
PR	Partial Response [*Oncology*]
PR	Partido Radical [*Radical Party*] [*Spain*] [*Political party*] (PPE)
PR	Partido Radical [*Radical Party*] [*Chile*] [*Political party*]
PR	Partido Reformista [*Reformist Party*] [*Dominican Republic*] [*Political party*] (PPW)
PR	Partido Republicano [*Republican Party*] [*Panama*] [*Political party*] (EY)
PR	Partido Republicano [*Republican Party*] [*Ecuador*] [*Political party*] (EY)
PR	Partido Revolucionario [*Revolutionary Party*] [*Guatemala*] [*Political party*] (PPW)
PR	Partido Riojano [*Spain*] [*Political party*] (EY)
PR	Partisan Review [*A publication*]
PR	Partito Radicale [*Radical Party*] [*Founded, 1955*] [*Italy*] [*Political party*] (PPE)
PR	Party Raayat [*Leftist organization in Singapore*]
PR	Passengers' Risk (ROG)
PR	Past in Review [*Later, PIR*] (EA)
PR	Pastor
PR	Pathogenesis Related [*Biology*]
PR	Patient Relations [*Medicine*]
PR	Patria Roja [*Red Fatherland*] [*Peru*] (PD)
PR	Patrol Vessel, River Gunboat [*Navy symbol*]
PR	Pattern Recognition (BUR)
PR	Payroll
PR	Peer Review
PR	Peking Review [*A publication*]
P & R	Pelvic and Rectal [*Medicine*]
PR	Pen Record (SAA)
PR	Peng-Robinson [*Equation of state*]
PR	Penicillium roqueforti [*Toxin*] [*Medicine*]
PR	Pennsylvania Reports (Penrose and Watts) [*A publication*] (DLA)
PR	Penny Resistance (EA)
PR	Per
PR	Per Price [*Business term*]
PR	Per Rectum [*Medicine*]
PR	Percent Recovery [*Plant pathology*]
PR	Percentage Rates
PR	Percentile Rank
PR	Performance Rating (OICC)
PR	Performance Ratio (AAG)
PR	Performance Report (AFM)
PR	Performance Requirement
P & R	Performance and Resources (NASA)
PR	Peripheral Resistance [*Medicine*]
PR	Perirenal [*Nephrology*]
PR	Permanens Rector [*Permanent Rector*]
PR	Permissive Reassignment [*Air Force*] (AFM)
PR	Pershing Rifles [*Honorary military organization*]
PR	Persistency Rater [*LIMRA*]
PR	Personality Record [*Psychological testing*]
PR	Personnel Resources (EA)
PR	Pesikta Rabbati (BJA)
PR	Petroleum Review [*A publication*]
PR	Pharmaceutical Record [*New York*] [*A publication*]
PR	Phenol Red
P & R	Philadelphia & Reading Railway
PR	Philadelphia Reports [*Pennsylvania*] [*A publication*] (DLA)
PR	Philanthropic Roundtable (EA)
PR	Philippine Airlines, Inc. [*PAL*] [*ICAO designator*] (FAAC)
PR	Philippine Island Reports [*A publication*] (DLA)
PR	Philosophical Review [*A publication*]
P & R	Philosophy and Rhetoric [*A publication*]
PR	Phosphate Rock [*Petrology*]
PR	Phosphorylase-Rupturing [*Biochemistry*]
PR	Photographic Reconnaissance [*Military*] (MCD)
PR	Photographic Recorder
PR	Photoreacting [*or Photoreactivation*] [*Biochemistry*]
PR	Photorecorder
PR	Photoresist
P/R	Photosynthesis/Respiration [*Biochemistry*]
PR	Physical Record [*Data processing*]
P & R	Picture and Resume [*Theatre slang*]
P & R	Pigott and Rodwell's Reports in Common Pleas [*1843-45*] [*A publication*] (DLA)
PR	Pilot Rating
PR	Pinch Runner [*Baseball*]
PR	Pineal Recess [*Neuroanatomy*]
PR	Pioneer [*Kumasi*] [*A publication*]
PR	Pipe Rail (AAG)
PR	Pitch Ratio
P/R	Pitch/Roll (MCD)
PR	Pittsburgh Reports [*1853-73*] [*Pennsylvania*] [*A publication*] (DLA)
PR	Pityriasis [*Dermatology*]
PR	Pityriasis Rosea [*Dermatology*] (MAE)
PR	Planetary RADAR [*Equipment box*]
P/R	Planned Requirements (DNAB)
PR	Planning Reference
P & R	Planning and Review (MCD)
PR	Plant Recovery [*Nuclear energy*] (NRCH)
PR	Plant Report
PR	Please Return
PR	Plotting and RADAR
PR	Ply Rating [*Tires*] (NATG)
PR	Pneumatic Retinopathy [*Ophthalmology*]
PR	Podravska Revija [*A publication*]
PR	Poetry Review [*A publication*]
PR	Policy Review (MCD)
PR	Polish Register [*Polish ship classification society*] (DS)
PR	Ponceau Red [*Biological stain*]
PR	Poor Rate [*British*] (ROG)
PR	Populus Romanus [*The Roman People*] [*Latin*]
PR	Position Record (NASA)
PR	Position Report [*Air Force*]
P & R	Post and Rail
PR	Post Request
PR	Post-Resuscitation
PR	Postal Regulations (DLA)
PR	Poste Recommandee [*Registered Post*]
PR	Posterior Ridge

PR	Pounder [*Gun*]
PR	Pour Remercier [*To Express Thanks*] [*French*]
PR	Power Range [*Nuclear energy*] (NRCH)
PR	Power Ratio
PR	Power Return
Pr	Practice Reports [*Various jurisdictions*] [*A publication*] (DLA)
Pr	Practitioner [*A publication*]
PR	Prairie (MCD)
Pr	Prandtl Number [*IUPAC*]
PR	Prandtl Number (SAA)
Pr	Praseodymium [*Chemical element*]
PR	Prayer
PR	Pre-Raphaelite
PR	Preacher
Pr	Preamble (ILCA)
Pr	Precancelled [*Philately*]
PR	Precedence Rating [*Military*] (AFIT)
Pr	Prednisone [*Also, P, PDN, Pred, Pro*] [*Antineoplastic drug*] [*Endocrinology*]
PR	Preferred [*Stock exchange term*] (SPSG)
PR	Prefix [*Indicating a private radiotelegram*] (BUR)
PR	Pregnancy Rate [*Medicine*]
PR	Preliminary Report
PR	Preliminary Review [*Army*]
PR	Premature Release [*Telecommunications*] (TEL)
PR	Prepare Reply
PR	Preposition
PR	Presbyopia [*Ophthalmology*]
PR	Presbyterian (ROG)
PR	Present
Pr	Presentation [*Gynecology*]
PR	Presidency (ROG)
Pr	Press [*Christchurch, New Zealand*] [*A publication*]
PR	Press Independent [*A publication*]
PR	Press Release
PR	Press Releases [*United Kingdom*] [*A publication*]
PR	Pressure
PR	Pressure Ratio
PR	Pressure Recorder (NRCH)
PR	Pressure Regulator (KSC)
Pr	Prevention [*A publication*]
PR	Price [*Online database field identifier*]
PR	Price Communications [*AMEX symbol*] (SPSG)
PR	Price Communications Corp. [*AMEX symbol*] (SPSG)
PR	Price Received
PR	Price Redetermination [*Economics*]
PR	Price Reduced [*of a book*]
Pr	Price's English Exchequer Reports [*1814-24*] [*A publication*] (DLA)
PR	Priest
PR	Primary (NASA)
PR	Primitive
PR	Prince
PR	Prince Regent (ROG)
PR	Princess Royal's [*Military unit*] [*British*]
Pr	Principal
PR	Principal Register [*Data processing*]
PR	Printed [*or Printer*]
PR	Printing Request (MCD)
PR	Prior
PR	Priority Regulation
PR	Priority Resolver
PR	Priory
PR	Prism
pr	Prismatic Tank [*Liquid gas carriers*]
Pr	Pristane [*Organic chemistry*]
pr	Private (DLA)
PR	Private Road [*Maps and charts*] [*British*] (ROG)
PR	Prize Ring [*Boxing*]
PR	Pro Rata
PR	Probabilistic Risk Assessment [*Computer-based technique for accident prediction*]
Pr	Probable
PR	Probate Reports [*A publication*] (DLA)
Pr	Probe [*A publication*]
PR	Problem Report (MCD)
Pr	Problemata [*of Aristotle*] [*Classical studies*] (OCD)
Pr	Procarbazine [*Also, P, PC, PCB*] [*Antineoplastic drug*]
PR	Procedural Regulations [*Civil Aeronautics Board*]
PR	Procedures Review [*DoD*]
PR	Proceedings. American Society of University Composers [*A publication*]
PR	Process-Reactive [*Scale*] [*Psychometrics*]
PR	Proctologist
PR	Procurement Regulation [*Military*]
PR	Procurement Request [*or Requisition*]
PR	Producing Region [*Agriculture*]
PR	Production Rate
PR	Production Requirements [*Military*] (AFIT)
P/R	Productivity/Respiration [*Physiology*]
PR	Profile Reliability (MCD)
PR	Profit Rate (WGA)
P-R	Progesterone Receptor [*Endocrinology*]
P-as-R	Program as Recorded [*Radio*] (DEN)
PR	Program Register [*Data processing*] (BUR)
PR	Program Requirements (KSC)
PR	Progress Report
PR	Progressive Resistance
Pr	Prohemio [*A publication*]
PR	Project Release (EA)
PR	Project Report
PR	Project Rover (SAA)
PR	Prolactin [*Also, LTH, PRL*] [*Endocrinology*]
PR	Prolonged-Release [*Pharmacy*]
Pr	Prometheus [*A publication*]
P-R	Pronominal [*Grammar*] (ROG)
PR	Pronoun
PR	Pronounced
PR	Proper
PR	Property
PR	Proportional Representation [*in legislatures, etc.*]
PR	Proposed Regulation
PR	Proposed Request
PR	Proposed Rule [*Federal government*] (GFGA)
PR	Propulsion Range
Pr	Propyl [*Organic chemistry*]
pr	Prose
PR	Prosthion [*Medicine*] (MAE)
Pr	Prostor [*Moscow*] [*A publication*]
PR	Protease [*Chemistry*]
PR	Protective Reaction [*Bombing raid*] [*Vietnam*]
PR	Protectorate Regiment [*British military*] (DMA)
PR	Protein (MAE)
PR	Protestant (ADA)
PR	Prototype
PR	Proved
PR	Provencal [*Language, etc.*]
Pr	Proverbs [*Old Testament book*] (BJA)
Pr	Proximal
PR	Pseudorandom
PR	Pseudoresidual
PR	Psychedelic Review [*A publication*]
PR	Psychoanalytic Review [*A publication*]
PR	Psychological Review [*A publication*]
PR	Public Relations
PR	Public Responsibility
PR	Public Roads [*A publication*]
PR	Puerto Rican [*Derogatory term*]
pr	Puerto Rico [*MARC country of publication code*] [*Library of Congress*] [*IYRU nationality code*] (LCCP)
PR	Puerto Rico [*Postal code*]
PR	Puerto Rico [*ANSI two-letter standard code*] (CNC)
PR	Puerto Rico Supreme Court Reports [*A publication*] (DLA)
PR	Pulse Rate
PR	Pulse Ratio (IEEE)
PR	Pulse Regenerator
P & R	Pulse and Respiration [*Medicine*]
PR	Punctum Remotum [*Far Point*] [*Latin*]
PR	Punjab Record [*India*] [*A publication*] (DLA)
PR	Purchase Request
PR	Purple (AAG)
PR	Purplish Red
PR	Pyke's Reports [*Canada*] [*A publication*] (DLA)
pr	Pyrite [*CIPW classification*] [*Geology*]
PR	Pyrogallol Red [*Also, PGR*] [*An indicator*] [*Chemistry*]
PR	Pyrolytic Release
PR+	Reactor Pressure Plus (NRCH)
PR	Reading Public Library, Reading, PA [*Library symbol*] [*Library of Congress*] (LCLS)
PR	River Gunboat [*Navy symbol*]
PR	Upper Canada Practice Reports [*1850-1900*] [*Ontario*] [*A publication*] (DLA)
PR1	Parachute Rigger, First Class [*Navy*]
PR2	Parachute Rigger, Second Class [*Navy*]
PR3	Parachute Rigger, Third Class [*Navy*]
PR's	Partial Responders [*to medication*]
PR's	Planning References (AAG)
PRA	Albright College, Reading, PA [*Library symbol*] [*Library of Congress*] (LCLS)
Pra	Die Praxis des Bundesgerichts [*Basel, Switzerland*] [*A publication*]
PRA	Division of Policy Research and Analysis [*National Science Foundation*]
PRA	Paint Research Association [*British*]
PRA	Paperwork Reduction Act (GFGA)
PRA	Parabolic Reflector Antenna
PRA	Parana [*Argentina*] [*Airport symbol*] (OAG)
PRA	Parool (Amsterdam) [*A publication*]
PRA	Parti du Regroupement Africain [*African Regroupment Party*] [*Banned, 1974*] [*Burkina Faso*] [*Political party*]
PRA	Parti du Regroupement Africain [*African Regroupment Party*] [*Niger*] [*Political party*] (PD)

PRA .... Partido Revolucionario Autentico [*Authentic Revolutionary Party*] [*Bolivia*] [*Political party*] (PPW)
PRA .... Pay Readjustment Act [*1942*]
PRA .... Pay Record Access
PRA .... Paymaster-Rear-Admiral [*Navy*] [*British*]
PRA .... Payroll Auditor [*Insurance*]
PRA .... Peak Recording Accelerograph [*Accelerometer*] (IEEE)
PRA .... Pendulous Reference Axis [*Accelerometer*] (IEEE)
PRA .... People's Revolutionary Army [*Grenada*]
PRA .... Permanent Restricted Area [*Former USSR*] (NATG)
PRA .... Personnel Research Activity [*Later, NPTRL*] [*Navy*]
PRA .... Petrol Retailers' Association [*British*]
PRA .... Phosphoribosylamine
PRA .... Pilots Rights Association (EA)
PRA .... Planetary Radio Astronomy
PRA .... Planned Regulatory Action [*Federal government*] (GFGA)
PRA .... Planned Restricted Availability [*Military*] (NVT)
PRA .... Plasma Renin Activity [*Hematology*]
PRA .... Plutonium Recycle Acid [*Nuclear energy*] (NRCH)
PRA .... Policy Research and Analysis
PRA .... Popular Rotocraft Association (EA)
PRA .... Praha [*Prague*] [*Czechoslovakia*] [*Seismograph station code, US Geological Survey*] (SEIS)
PRA .... Prairiefire Rural Action (EA)
pra .... Prakrit [*MARC language code*] [*Library of Congress*] (LCCP)
PRA .... Pre-Retirement Association [*British*] (DI)
PRA .... Precision Axis (KSC)
PRA .... Premium Audit
PRA .... Prerefund Audit [*IRS*]
PRA .... President of the Royal Academy [*British*]
PRA .... President's Re-Employment Agreement [*New Deal*]
PRA .... Primary Reviewing Authority
PrA............ Primer Acto [*Madrid*] [*A publication*]
PRA .... Print Alphanumerically [*Data processing*] (MDG)
PRA .... Probabilistic Risk Assessment [*Computer-based technique for accident prediction*]
PRA .... Probation and Rehabilitation of Airmen [*Air Force*] (AFM)
PRA .... Production Reader Assembly (KSC)
PRA .... Production Readiness Assessment [*Army*]
PRA .... Progesterone Receptor Assay [*Clinical chemistry*]
PRA .... Program Reader Assembly [*Data processing*]
PRA .... Projected Requisition Authority [*Army*] (AABC)
PRA .... Prompt Radiation Analysis (MCD)
PRA .... Proust Research Association (EA)
PRA .... Psoriasis Research Association (EA)
PRA .... Psychiatric Rehabilitation Association [*British*]
PRA .... Psychological Research Associates
PRA .... Public Resources Association [*Defunct*] (EA)
PRA .... Public Roads Administration
PRA .... Puerto Rico Area Office [*AEC*]
PRA .... US 1869 Pictorial Research Associates (EA)
PRAA.......... Airman Apprentice, Parachute Rigger, Striker [*Navy rating*]
PRAB........ Prab Robots, Inc. [*NASDAQ symbol*] (NQ)
Pra Bhar .... Prabuddha Bharata [*Calcutta*] [*A publication*]
Prac.......... Practical (DLA)
PRAC........ Practice (AABC)
PRAC........ Pressure Ratio Acceleration Control [*Gas turbine engine*]
PRAC........ Program Resource Advisory Committee [*TRADOC*] (MCD)
PRAC........ Public Relations Advisory Committee
PRACA...... Practitioner [*A publication*]
PRACA...... Problem Reporting and Corrective Action (MCD)
PRACA...... Puerto Rican Association for Community Affairs (EA)
Prac Acc..... Practical Accountant [*A publication*]
Prac Accnt ... Practical Accountant [*A publication*]
Prac Act..... Practice Act [*A publication*] (DLA)
Prac Anth... Practical Anthropology [*A publication*]
Prac Appr Pat TM and Copyright ... Practical Approach to Patents, Trademarks, and Copyrights [*A publication*]
Pra Cas ...... Prater's Cases on Conflict of Laws [*A publication*] (DLA)
Praca Zabezp Spolecz ... Praca i Zabezpieczenie Spoleczne [*A publication*]
Prac F.......... Practical Farmer [*A publication*]
Prac Forecast ... Practical Forecast for Home Economics [*A publication*]
Prac Home Econ ... Practical Home Economics [*A publication*]
PRACL...... Page-Replacement Algorithm and Control Logic [*Data processing*]
Prac Law.... Practical Lawyer [*A publication*]
Prac Lawyer ... Practical Lawyer [*A publication*]
Prac Lek..... Pracovni Lekarstvi [*A publication*]
PRACSATS ... Practical Satellites
PRACT...... Practical (ROG)
PRACT...... Practitioner
Pract Account ... Practical Accountant [*A publication*]
Pract Adm ... Practising Administrator [*A publication*] (APTA)
Pract Biotechnol ... Practical Biotechnology [*A publication*]
Pract Colloid Chem ... Practical Colloid Chemistry [*A publication*]
Pract Comput ... Practical Computing [*A publication*]
Pract Dig.... Practice Digest [*A publication*]
Pract Electron ... Practical Electronics [*A publication*]
Pract Electronics ... Practical Electronics [*A publication*]
Pract Energy ... Practical Energy [*A publication*]
Pract Eng (Chicago) ... Practical Engineer (Chicago) [*A publication*]

Pract Eng (London) ... Practical Engineering (London) [*A publication*]
Pract Gastroenterol ... Practical Gastroenterology [*A publication*]
Pract Genet ... Practical Genetics [*A publication*]
Pract House ... Practical Householder [*England*] [*A publication*]
Practical Comput ... Practical Computing [*A publication*]
Practition ... Practitioner [*A publication*]
Pract Law... Practical Lawyer [*A publication*] (DLA)
Pract M...... Practical Magazine [*A publication*]
Pract Med (Phila) ... Practice of Medicine (Philadelphia) [*A publication*]
Pract Metallogr Spec Issues ... Practical Metallography. Special Issues [*A publication*]
Pract Methods Electron Microsc ... Practical Methods in Electron Microscopy [*A publication*]
Pract Mot... Practical Motorist [*A publication*]
Pract Otol (Kyoto) ... Practica Otologica (Kyoto) [*A publication*]
Pract Otorhinolaryng ... Practica Oto-Rhinolaryngologica [*A publication*]
Pract Oto-Rhino-Laryngol ... Practica Oto-Rhino-Laryngologica [*A publication*]
Pract Pharm (Tokyo) ... Practical Pharmacy (Tokyo) [*A publication*]
Pract Plast ... Practical Plastics [*A publication*]
Pract Plast Aust NZ ... Practical Plastics in Australia and New Zealand [*A publication*]
Pract Power Farming ... Practical Power Farming [*A publication*]
Pract Reg ... Practical Register in the Common Pleas [*England*] [*A publication*] (DLA)
Pract Solar ... Practical Solar [*A publication*]
Pract Spectrosc ... Practical Spectroscopy [*A publication*]
Pract Spectrosc Ser ... Practical Spectroscopy Series [*A publication*]
Pract Surf Technol ... Practical Surface Technology [*Japan*] [*A publication*]
Pract Welder ... Practical Welder [*A publication*] (APTA)
Pract Wireless ... Practical Wireless [*A publication*]
Pract Woodworking ... Practical Woodworking [*England*] [*A publication*]
Prac Wel .... Practical Welder [*A publication*] (APTA)
PRAD .... Pitch Ratio Adjust Device (MCD)
PRADA...... Partido Revolucionario Dominicano Autentico [*Dominican Republic*] [*Political party*]
Pr Adm Dig ... Pritchard's Admiralty Digest [*3rd ed.*] [*1887*] [*A publication*] (DLA)
PRADOR .. PRF [*Pulse Repetition Frequency*] Ranging Doppler RADAR
PRADS...... Parachute Retrorocket Airdrop System (MCD)
PRAED...... Practical Energy [*A publication*]
praef.......... Praefatio [*Latin*] (OCD)
PrAeg........ Probleme der Aegyptologie [*Leiden*] [*A publication*]
Praem........ De Praemiis et Poenis [*of Philo*] (BJA)
Praep Evang ... Praeparatio Evangelica [*of Eusebius*] [*Classical studies*] (OCD)
Praepo........ Praepositus [*Deceased, 1509*] [*Authority cited in pre-1607 legal work*] (DSA)
Praep Pharmazie ... Praeparative Pharmazie [*A publication*]
PRAF........ Passenger-Reserved Air Freight
PRAG .... Pragma Bio-Tech, Inc. [*Bloomfield, NJ*] [*NASDAQ symbol*] (NQ)
PRAG .... Research on Aging [*A publication*]
PRAGA...... Probleme Agricole [*Romania*] [*A publication*]
Prager Med Wochenschr ... Prager Medizinische Wochenschrift [*A publication*]
Prag Micro ... Pragmatics Microficke [*A publication*]
PR Agric Exp Stn Bull ... Puerto Rico. Agricultural Experiment Station. Bulletin [*A publication*]
PR Agric Exp Stn Tech Pap ... Puerto Rico. Agricultural Experiment Station. Technical Paper [*A publication*]
Prague Bull Math Linguist ... Prague Bulletin of Mathematical Linguistics [*A publication*]
Prague St ... Studies in English by Members of the English Seminar of the Charles University, Prague [*A publication*]
Prague Stud Math Linguist ... Prague Studies in Mathematical Linguistics [*A publication*]
Pra H & W ... Prater on Husband and Wife [*2nd ed.*] [*1836*] [*A publication*] (DLA)
PRAI.......... Peer Review Analysis [*NASDAQ symbol*] (SPSG)
PRAI.......... Phosphoribosyl Anthranilate Isomerase
PRAIREO .. Prairie Oil Royalties Co. Ltd. [*Associated Press abbreviation*] (APAG)
Prairie Gard ... Prairie Garden [*A publication*]
Prairie Inst Environ Health PIEH ... Prairie Institute of Environmental Health. Report PIEH [*A publication*]
Prairie Nat ... Prairie Naturalist [*A publication*]
Prairie Sch ... Prairie Schooner [*A publication*]
Prairie Schoon ... Prairie Schooner [*A publication*]
Prairie Sch R ... Prairie School Review [*A publication*]
PRAIS ...... Passive Ranging Interferometer Sensor
PRAIS .... Pesticide Residue Analysis Information Service [*British*]
PRAJ .... Peace Research Abstracts Journal [*A publication*]
Prakla-Seismos Rep ... Prakla-Seismos Report [*West Germany*] [*A publication*]
Prakruti Utkal Univ J Sci ... Prakruti Utkal University Journal of Science [*A publication*]
Prakt Akad Athenon ... Praktika tes Akademias Athenon [*A publication*]
Prakt Ak Ath ... Praktika tes Akademias Athenon [*A publication*]
Prakt Anaesth ... Praktische Anaesthesie, Wiederbelebung, und Intensivtherapie [*A publication*]

Prakt Arzt ... Praktische Arzt [*A publication*]
Prakt Bl Pflanzenbau Pflanzenschutz ... Praktische Blaetter fuer Pflanzenbau und Pflanzenschutz [*A publication*]
Prakt Chem ... Praktische Chemie [*A publication*]
Prakt Desinfekt ... Praktische Desinfektor [*A publication*]
Prakt Energiek ... Praktische Energiekunde [*A publication*]
Prakt Hell Hydrobiol Inst ... Praktika. Hellenic Hydrobiological Institute [*A publication*]
Praktika ..... Praktika tes en Athenais Arkhaiologikes Hetairias [*A publication*]
Prakt Landtech ... Praktische Landtechnik [*A publication*]
Prakt Lek... Prakticky Lekar [*A publication*]
Prakt Metallogr ... Praktische Metallographie [*A publication*]
Prakt Metallogr Sonderb ... Praktische Metallographie. Sonderbaende [*A publication*]
Prakt Schadlingsbekampf ... Praktische Schadlingsbekampfer [*A publication*]
Prakt Sudebnopsikhiatr Ekspert ... Praktika Sudebnopsikhiatricheskoi Ekspertizy [*A publication*]
Prakt Tier .. Praktische Tieraerzt [*A publication*]
Prakt Tierarzt ... Praktische Tieraerzt [*German Federal Republic*] [*A publication*]
Prakt Tuberk Bl ... Praktische Tuberkulose Blaetter [*A publication*]
Prakt Vet (Moskva) ... Prakticheskaia Veterinariia (Moskva) [*A publication*]
Prakt Wegw Bienenz ... Praktischer Wegweiser fuer Bienenzuechter [*A publication*]
Prakt Yad Fiz ... Praktikum po Yadernoi Fizike [*A publication*]
PRAL........ Research in African Literatures [*A publication*]
PRAM .... Parallel Random Access Machine [*Data processing*]
PRAM .... Perambulator [*British*]
PRAM .... Poseidon Random Access Memory [*Missiles*]
PRAM .... Pre-Recorded Announcement and Boarding Music Reproducer
PRAM .... Product Reliability and Maintainability
PRAM .... Productivity, Reliability, Availability, and Maintainability Office [*Air Force*]
PRAM .... Program Requirements Analysis Method
PRAM .... Propelled Ascent Mine
PRAM .... Propelled Rapid Ascent Mine (MCD)
PRAMC..... Pramana [*A publication*]
PRAN .... Airman, Parachute Rigger, Striker [*Navy*]
PRAN .... Proust Research Association. Newsletter [*A publication*]
PRAND ..... Prandium [*Dinner*] [*Pharmacy*]
PRANDM ... Progress in Anesthesiology [*A publication*]
PRANG ..... Puerto Rico Air National Guard
PRAODP... Agricultural Research Organization. Preliminary Report (Bet-Dagan) [*A publication*]
PRAP........ Patient Resident Assessment Profile [*Geriatrics*]
PRAP........ Provincial/Regional Library Association Presidents [*Canada*]
PRAP........ Provisions of Following Reference Apply [*Army*] (AABC)
PRAR........ Partido Revolucionario Autentico Rios [*Bolivia*] [*Political party*] (PPW)
PRARE...... Precise Range and Range-Rate Experiment
PRARS ..... Pitch, Roll, Azimuth Reference System (NG)
PRAS........ Pacific Regional Advisory Service [*South Pacific Bureau for Economic Co-Operation*] (EY)
PRAS........ Pension and Retirement Annuity System
Pra S .... Prairie Schooner [*A publication*]
PRAS........ Prereduced, Anaerobically Sterilized [*Microbiology*]
PRASD...... Personnel Research Activity, San Diego [*California*] [*Navy*]
PRASD3 .... Alabama. Agricultural Experiment Station. Progress Report Series (Auburn University) [*A publication*]
Prat .... [*Pardulphus*] Pratteius [*Deceased, 1535*] [*Authority cited in pre-1607 legal work*] (DSA)
PRAT........ Predicted Range Against Target [*Military*] (NVT)
PRAT........ Pressure-Retaining Amphipod Trap [*Deep-sea biology*]
PRAT........ Production Reliability Acceptance Test
P RAT AET ... Pro Ratione Aetatis [*According to Age*] [*Pharmacy*] (ROG)
P RAT AETAT ... Pro Rata Aetatis [*According to Age*] [*Pharmacy*]
p rat aetat... Pro Ratione Aetatis [*In Proportion to Age*] [*Latin*] (MAE)
PRATHTL ... Pratt Hotel Corp. [*Associated Press abbreviation*] (APAG)
Pratica Med ... Pratica del Medico [*A publication*]
Prat Ind Mec ... Pratique des Industries Mecanique [*A publication*]
PRATLM .. Pratt & Lambert, Inc. [*Associated Press abbreviation*] (APAG)
Pratsi Inst Zool Akad Nauk Ukr RSR ... Pratsi Institutu Zoologii Akademiya Nauk Ukrains'koi RSR [*A publication*]
Pratsi Odes Derzh Univ Ser Biol Nauk ... Pratsi Odeskogo Derzhavnogo Universitetu. Seriya Biologichnikh Nauk [*A publication*]
Prat Soudage ... Pratique du Soudage [*A publication*]
Pratt .... Pratt's Contraband-of-War Cases [*A publication*] (DLA)
Pratt .... Pratt's Supplement to Bott's Poor Laws [*1833*] [*A publication*] (DLA)
Pratt BS ..... Pratt's Law of Benefit Building Societies [*A publication*] (DLA)
Pratt Cont .. Pratt's Contraband-of-War Cases [*A publication*] (DLA)
Pratt Cts Req ... Pratt's Statutes Establishing Courts of Request [*A publication*] (DLA)
Pratt Fr Soc ... Pratt on Friendly Societies [*15th ed.*] [*1931*] [*A publication*] (DLA)
Pratt High ... Pratt and Mackenzie on Highways [*21st ed.*] [*1967*] [*A publication*] (DLA)
Pratt PL ..... Pratt's Edition of Bott on the Poor Laws [*A publication*] (DLA)
Pratt Prop T ... Pratt on the Property Tax Act [*A publication*] (DLA)
Pratt Sav B ... Pratt on Savings Banks [*6th ed.*] [*1845*] [*A publication*] (DLA)

Pratt SL ..... Pratt on Sea Lights [*2nd ed.*] [*1858*] [*A publication*] (DLA)
Prat Vet Equine ... Pratique Veterinaire Equine [*A publication*]
PRAUD9 ... Agricultural Research Institute Ukiriguru. Progress Report [*A publication*]
PRAUS...... Programme de Recherche sur l'Amiante de l'Universite de Sherbrooke [*Asbestos Research Program*] [*University of Sherbrooke*] [*Quebec*] [*Information service or system*] (IID)
PRAVA...... Pravda [*A publication*]
PRAW .... Personnel Research Activity, Washington, DC [*Obsolete*] [*Navy*]
PRaW .... Wyeth Laboratories, Radnor, PA [*Library symbol*] [*Library of Congress*] (LCLS)
PRAWL...... Puerto Rican American Women's League
Prax .... Brown's Practice (Praxis) [*or Precedents*] in Chancery [*A publication*] (DLA)
PRAX........ Praxis Pharmaceuticals, Inc. [*Beverly Hills, CA*] [*NASDAQ symbol*] (NQ)
PRAXA...... Praxis [*A publication*]
Praxar........ Praxair, Inc. [*Associated Press abbreviation*] (APAG)
Prax Can.... Praxis Almae Curiae Cancellariae (Brown) [*A publication*] (DLA)
Prax Forsch ... Praxis und Forschung [*A publication*]
Praxis......... Praxis des Neusprachlichen Unterrichts [*A publication*]
Praxis Int ... Praxis International [*A publication*]
Praxis Math ... Praxis der Mathematik [*A publication*]
Prax Kinder ... Praxis der Kinderpsychologie und Kinderpsychiatrie [*A publication*]
Prax Kinderpsychol Kinderpsychiatr ... Praxis der Kinderpsychologie und Kinderpsychiatrie [*A publication*]
Prax Klin Pneumol ... Praxis und Klinik der Pneumologie [*A publication*]
Prax Naturw ... Praxis der Naturwissenschaften [*A publication*]
Prax Naturwiss Phy ... Praxis der Naturwissenschaften. Physik [*A publication*]
Prax Naturwiss Phys Unterr Sch ... Praxis der Naturwissenschaften. Physik im Unterricht der Schulen [*A publication*]
Prax Naturwiss Teil 3 ... Praxis der Naturwissenschaften. Teil 3. Chemie [*West Germany*] [*A publication*]
Prax Pneumol ... Praxis der Pneumologie [*A publication*]
Prax Psychother ... Praxis der Psychotherapie [*A publication*]
Prax Psychother Psychosom ... Praxis der Psychotherapie und Psychosomatik [*A publication*]
Prax Schriftenr Phys ... Praxis Schriftenreihe Physik [*A publication*]
Prax Vet..... Praxis Veterinaria [*A publication*]
PRAZ........ Prazosin [*A vasodilator*]
PRB........... Panel Review Board [*NASA*] (KSC)
PRB........... Parabola [*Mathematics*]
PRB........... Parachute Refurbishment Building [*NASA*] (NASA)
PRB........... Partido Republicano Brasileiro [*Brazil*] [*Political party*] (EY)
PRB........... Paso Robles, CA [*Location identifier*] [*FAA*] (FAAL)
PRB........... Pension Review Board [*Canada*]
PRB........... Personnel Reaction Blank [*Psychology*]
PRB........... Personnel Records Branch [*Army*] (AABC)
PRB........... Personnel Requirements Branch (MUGU)
PRB........... Personnel Research Branch [*Army*] (MCD)
PRB........... Planned Requirements - Bureau Directed
PRB........... Plant Review Board [*Nuclear energy*] (NRCH)
PRB........... Polar Research Board [*National Academy of Sciences*]
PRB........... Population Reference Bureau (EA)
PRB........... Pre-Raphaelite Brotherhood [*A publication*]
PRB........... Procedure Review Board [*Nuclear energy*] (NRCH)
PRB........... Procurement Review Board (MCD)
PRB........... Program Review Board
PRB........... Project Review Board [*NASA*] (NASA)
PRB........... Prosthetics Research Board
PRB........... Public Roads Bureau
PRBA........ Puerto Rican Bar Association (EA)
PRBA(AG) ... Personnel Research Board of the Army, Adjutant General
PrBayA ...... American Junior College of Puerto Rico, Bayamon, PR [*Library symbol*] [*Library of Congress*] (LCLS)
PrBayC ...... Bayamon Central University (Universidad Central de Bayamon), Bayamon, Puerto Rico [*Library symbol*] [*Library of Congress*] (LCLS)
PRBC......... Packed Red Blood Cells [*Medicine*]
PRBC......... Premier Bancorp, Inc. [*NASDAQ symbol*] (NQ)
PRBCA...... Process Biochemistry [*A publication*]
PRBCB ...... Preparative Biochemistry [*A publication*]
PRBD......... Paraboloid
PRBG........ Puerto Rican Board of Guardians [*Defunct*] (EA)
PRBK........ Provident Bancorp, Inc. [*NASDAQ symbol*] (NQ)
PRBL......... Probable (FAAC)
PRBLC ...... Parabolic
PRBLTY.... Probability (FAAC)
PRBMD...... Physical Review. Section B. Condensed Matter [*A publication*]
PRBMECAB ... Permanent Regional Bureau of the Middle East Committee for the Affairs of the Blind [*Riyadh, Saudi Arabia*] (EAIO)
PRBNT...... Prebent
Pr Bot Sadu Kiiv Derzh Univ ... Pratsi Botanichnogo Sadu Kiivs'kii Derzhavnii Universitet [*A publication*]
PRBP......... Review of Black Political Economy [*A publication*]
PRBS .... Pseudorandom Binary Sequence [*Data processing*]

PRBSG ...... Pseudorandom Binary Sequence Generator [*Data processing*] (NRCH)
PRBT .... Precision Remote Bathythermograph
PRBV .... Placental Residual Blood Volume [*Hematology*] (MAE)
PRC .... Chief Aircrew Survival Equipmentman [*Formerly, Chief Parachute Rigger*] [*Navy rating*]
PRC .... Packed Red Cell [*Hematology*] (MAE)
PRC .... Park Ridge Center (EA)
PRC .... Part Requirement Card
PRC .... Parti Republicain Caledonien [*Political party*] [*New Caledonia*] (FEA)
PRC .... Partial Response Coding (IEEE)
PRC .... Partido Regionalista de Cantabria [*Spain*] [*Political party*] (EY)
PRC .... Partido Republicano Calderonista [*Calderonista Republican Party*] [*Costa Rica*] [*Political party*] (PPW)
PRC .... Partido Revolucionario Comunista [*Brazil*] [*Political party*] (EY)
PRC .... Parts Release Card (KSC)
PRC .... Passaic River Coalition (EA)
PRC .... Passenger Reservation Center [*Army*]
PRC .... Penrose Resources Corp. [*Vancouver Stock Exchange symbol*]
PRC .... Pension Research Council (EA)
PRC .... Pension Rights Center [*Washington, DC*] (EA)
PRC .... People's Redemption Council [*Liberia*] (PD)
PRC .... People's Republic of China [*Mainland China*]
PRC .... People's Republic of the Congo
PRC .... Permanent Regular Commissions [*Army*] [*British*]
PRC .... Personality Research Center [*University of Texas at Austin*] [*Research center*] (RCD)
PRC .... Personnel Readiness Center [*Air Force*]
PRC .... Personnel Reception Centre [*British military*] (DMA)
PRC .... Personnel Recovery Center [*Military*]
PRC .... Personnel Reporting Code [*Army*] (AABC)
PRC .... Phase-Response Curve
PRC .... Philippine Resource Center [*An association*] (EA)
PRC .... Physical Review Council [*DoD*]
PRC .... Pierce (MSA)
PRC .... Pitch Rate Command (MCD)
PRC .... Pitch Ratio Controller (MCD)
PRC .... Planar Random Composite (MCD)
PRC .... Planned Requirements, Conversion (NG)
PRC .... Planning Research Corp. [*Telecommunications service*] (TSSD)
PRC .... Plant Records Center [*of the American Horticultural Society*] (IID)
PRC .... Plasma Renin Concentration [*Hematology*]
PRC .... Plastic Roller Conveyor
PRC .... Plutonium Rework Cell [*Nuclear energy*] (NRCH)
PRC .... Point of Reverse Curve (MSA)
PRC .... Point Reyes [*California*] [*Seismograph station code, US Geological Survey*] [*Closed*] (SEIS)
PRC .... Policy Review Committee [*Terminated, 1981*] [*National Security Council*] (EGAO)
PRC .... Polish Resettlement Corps [*British military*] (DMA)
PRC .... Population Research Center [*University of Chicago*] [*Research center*] (RCD)
PRC .... Population Resource Center (EA)
PRC .... Post Roman Conditam [*After the Founding of Rome*] [*Latin*]
PRC .... Postal Rate Commission [*Federal government*]
PRC .... Poultry Research Centre [*of the Agricultural Research Council*] [*British*] (ARC)
PRC .... Power Reflection Coefficient [*of RADAR signals*]
PRC .... Prattsburgh Railway Corp. [*AAR code*]
PRC .... Preoral Ciliary [*Gland*]
PRC .... Prescott [*Arizona*] [*Airport symbol*] (OAG)
PRC .... Prescott, AZ [*Location identifier*] [*FAA*] (FAAL)
PRC .... Pressure Recorder Controller [*Nuclear energy*] (NRCH)
PRC .... Pressure Response Cell [*For chemical kinetic studies*]
PRC .... Prevention Research Center [*Pacific Institute for Research and Evaluation*] [*Research center*] (RCD)
PRC .... Price Redetermination Contract (SAA)
PRC .... Primary Routing Center [*Telecommunications*] (TEL)
PRC .... Primate Research Center
PRC .... Printer Control
PRC .... Priory Cell
Pr C .... Prize Cases [*A publication*] (DLA)
PRC .... Problem Resolution Coordinator [*IRS*]
PRC .... Procaterol [*Pharmacology*]
PRC .... Procedure Review Committee (AAG)
PRC .... Procession Register Clock
PRC .... Proconsul
PRC .... Procurement Request Code [*Military*] (AFIT)
PRC .... Product Regional Center [*Department of Supply and Service*] [*Canada*] (IMH)
PRC .... Production Readjustments Committee [*WPB*]
PRC .... Products Research & Chemical Corp. [*NYSE symbol*] (SPSG)
PRC .... Professional Reference Center [*Los Angeles County Office of Education*] [*Downey, CA*] [*Library network*]
PRC .... Professional Relations Council [*American Chemical Society*]
PRC .... Program Rest Code (MCD)

PRC .... Program Review Committee (AFM)
PRC .... Propeller Change (MCD)
PrC .... Proster in Cas [*A publication*]
PRC .... Providence College, Phillips Memorial Library, Providence, RI [*OCLC symbol*] (OCLC)
PRC .... Pyrotechnic Rocket Container
PRC .... Revolutionary Socialist Party [*Peru*] [*Political party*] (PD)
Pr Ca .... Great War Prize Cases, by Evans [*England*] [*A publication*] (DLA)
PRCA .... Palomino Rabbit Co-Breeders Association (EA)
PRCA .... Parks, Recreation and Cultural Affairs Administration [*New York City*]
PRCA .... People's Republic of China Army (MCD)
PRCA .... Pitch and Roll Channel Assembly (MCD)
PRCA .... President of the Royal Canadian Academy
PRCA .... Problem Reporting and Corrective Action (NASA)
PRCA .... Professional Rodeo Cowboys Association (EA)
PRCA .... Public Relations Consultants Association (EAIO)
PRCA .... Puerto Rico Communications Authority
PRCA .... Pure Red Cell Agenesis [*Hematology*] (MAE)
PRCA .... Pure Red Cell Aplasia [*Hematology*]
PrCaC .... Colegio Universitario de Cayey, Cayey, PR [*Library symbol*] [*Library of Congress*] (LCLS)
PRCAD ..... Primary Care [*A publication*]
PRCAFL .... Publications. Research Center in Anthropology, Folklore, and Linguistics [*A publication*]
PRCB .... Program Requirements Change Board [*NASA*] (NASA)
PRCB .... Program Requirements Control Board [*NASA*]
PRCB .... Program Review Control Board [*NASA*] (NASA)
PRCBD ...... Program Requirements Control Board Directive [*NASA*] (NASA)
PRCBD ...... Program Review Control Board Directive [*NASA*] (NASA)
PRCC .... Peoria Record Club [*Record label*]
PRCC .... Puerto Rico Cancer Center [*University of Puerto Rico*] [*Research center*] (RCD)
PRCCh ...... Principal Roman Catholic Chaplain [*Navy*] [*British*]
PRCCOM ... Price Communications Corp. [*Associated Press abbreviation*] (APAG)
PRCE .... Pierce [*S. S.*] Co., Inc. [*NASDAQ symbol*] (NQ)
PR Cem ...... Puerto Rican Cement Co., Inc. [*Associated Press abbreviation*] (APAG)
PRCESSN ... Processing
PRCF .... Petroleum Resources Communications Foundation [*Canada*]
PRCF .... Plutonium Recycle Critical Facility [*Nuclear energy*]
PRCF .... Review of Contemporary Fiction [*A publication*]
PR Ch .... Practical Register in Chancery [*England*] [*A publication*] (DLA)
Pr Ch .... Precedents in Chancery, Edited by Finch [*1689-1722*] [*England*] [*A publication*] (DLA)
PRCH .... Precharge
PRCH .... Proprietary Chapel [*Church of England*]
PRCHT ...... Parachute (AFM)
Prcht Bad ... Parachutist Badge [*Military decoration*]
PRCI .... Parti Republicain de la Cote d'Ivoire [*Republicaqn Party of the Ivory Coast*] [*Political party*] (EY)
PRCI .... Policy Review Committee Intelligence [*Military*]
PRCI .... Production Reliability Cost Improvement (DWSG)
Pr CKB ...... Practice Cases, in the King's Bench [*England*] [*A publication*] (DLA)
PRCLS ...... Property Investors of Colorado [*NASDAQ symbol*] (NQ)
PRCM .... Master Chief Aircrew Survival Equipmentman [*Navy rating*] [*Formerly, Master Chief Parachute Rigger*]
PRCM .... Passive Radiation Countermeasure [*Military*]
PRCM .... Protocom Devices, Inc. [*Bronx, NY*] [*NASDAQ symbol*] (NQ)
PRCMC ..... Percussionist [*A publication*]
PRCMC ..... Protective Coatings on Metals [*English Translation*] [*A publication*]
PRCMT ..... Procurement (MSA)
PRCN .... Precision (MSA)
PR-CNTL ... Product Control Register
PRC & NW ... Pierre, Rapid City & Northwestern Railroad [*Nickname: Plenty Rough Country and No Women*]
PRCO .... Pacific Requisition Control Office [*Navy*]
Pr Co .... Prerogative Court (DLA)
PRCO .... Pricor, Inc. [*NASDAQ symbol*] (NQ)
PR/COM ... Vessel Delivered in Partially-Completed Status [*Navy*] (DNAB)
PR Commonw Water Resour Bull ... Puerto Rico Commonwealth. Water Resources Bulletin [*A publication*]
Pr Cont ...... Pratt's Contraband-of-War Cases [*1861*] [*A publication*] (DLA)
PRCP .... Personnel Readiness Capability Program [*Navy*] (DNAB)
PRCP .... Power Remote Control Panel (AAG)
PRCP .... Practical Register in the Common Pleas [*A publication*] (DLA)
PRCP .... President of the Royal College of Physicians [*British*]
PRCP .... President of the Royal College of Preceptors [*British*] (ROG)
PRCP .... Puerto Rican Communist Party [*Political party*]
PRCPTN ... Precipitin [*Test*] [*Immunology*]
PRCR .... Professional Health Care of America, Inc. [*NASDAQ symbol*] (NQ)
PRCR .... Protective Cover (AAG)
PRCS .... Passive and Remote Crosswind Sensor (MCD)

PRCS .... Personal Radio Communications System [*General Electric Co.*]
PRCS .... Personal Report of Confidence as a Speaker [*Psychology*]
PRCS .... Polish Red Cross Society
PRCS .... President of the Royal College of Surgeons [*British*]
PRCS .... Prevention and Removal of Corrosion and Scale [*Engineering*]
PRCS .... Process   (AFM)
P/RCS .... Propulsion and Reaction Control Subsystem [*NASA*]   (KSC)
PRCS .... Psychological Response Classification System
PRCS .... Purchase Requisition Change Supplement
PRCS .... Senior Chief Aircrew Survival Equipmentman [*Navy rating*] [*Formerly, Senior Chief Parachute Rigger*]
PRCSG ...... Processing   (MSA)
PRCST .... Precast   (AAG)
PRCT .... Pool Repair Cycle Time   (MCD)
517 PRCT A ... 517th Parachute Regimental Combat Team Association   (EA)
PRCTN ...... Precaution   (FAAC)
PRCU .... Power Regulating and Control Unit   (CET)
PRCUA .... Polish Roman Catholic Union of America   (EA)
PRCY .... ProCyte Corp. [*NASDAQ symbol*]   (NQ)
P and RD ... Decisions of the Department of the Interior, Pension and Retirement Claims [*United States*] [*A publication*]   (DLA)
PRD .... Part Reference Designator
PRD .... Parti Democratique Dahomeen [*Dahomey Democratic Party*] [*Political party*]
PRD .... Parti Radical-Democratique Suisse [*Radical Democratic Party of Switzerland*] [*Political party*]   (PPE)
PRD .... Parti du Renouveau Democratique [*Benin*] [*Political party*]   (EY)
PRD .... Partial Reaction of Degeneration
PRD .... Partido Reformista Democratico [*Democratic Reformist Party*] [*Spain*] [*Political party*]   (PPW)
PRD .... Partido de Renovacion Democratica [*Democratic Renewal Party*] [*Costa Rica*] [*Political party*]   (PPW)
PRD .... Partido de la Revolucion Democratica [*Mexico*] [*Political party*]   (EY)
PRD .... Partido Revolucionario Democratico [*Democratic Revolutionary Party*] [*Panama*] [*Political party*]   (PPW)
PRD .... Partido Revolucionario Dominicano [*Dominican Revolutionary Party*] [*Dominican Republic*] [*Political party*]   (PPW)
PRD .... Party of the Democratic Revolution [*Mexico*] [*Political party*]
PRD .... Payroll Deduction
PRD .... Period
PRD .... Periodontics and Restorative Dentistry
PRD .... Personal Radiation Dosimeter   (KSC)
PR & D ...... Personal Rest and Delay [*Air Force*]   (AFM)
PRD .... Personnel Readiness Date [*Army*]   (AABC)
PRD .... Personnel Records Division [*Army*]   (AABC)
PRD .... Personnel Requirements Data   (AAG)
PRD .... Personnel Research Division [*Navy*]   (MCD)
PRD .... Personnel Resources Data
PRD .... Piezoelectric Resonating Device
PRD .... Planned Residential Development
PRD .... Polaroid Corp. [*NYSE symbol*]   (SPSG)
PRD .... Political Resource Directory [*A publication*]
PRD .... Polytechnic Research & Development Co.   (AAG)
PRD .... Positive Regulatory Domain [*Genetics*]
PRD .... Postal Regulating Detachment [*Military*]
PRD .... Postradiation Dysplasia [*Medicine*]
PRD .... Potentially Reportable Deficiency [*Nuclear energy*]   (NRCH)
PRD .... Power Range Detector   (IEEE)
PRD .... Power Requirement Data
PR & D ...... Power, Rodwell, and Drew's English Election Cases [*1847-56*] [*A publication*]   (DLA)
PRD .... Predicted Range of the Day [*Military*]   (NVT)
PRD .... Preretro Update Display
PRD .... Pressing Direction
PRD .... Princeton Reference Design   (MCD)
PRD .... Printer Driver
PRD .... Printer Dump
PRD .... Pro Rate Distribution [*Clause*] [*Insurance*]
PRD .... Process Requirements Drawing   (MCD)
PRD .... Procurement Regulation Directive [*NASA*]   (NASA)
PRD .... Procurement Requirements Document [*NASA*]   (NASA)
PRD .... Production [*A publication*]
PRD .... Production Responsibilities Document   (MCD)
PRD .... Productivity Research Division [*Office of Personnel Management*]   (GRD)
PRD .... Proficiency Rating Designator [*Military*]
PRD .... Program [*or Project*] Requirement Data [*NASA*]   (KSC)
PRD .... Program Requirements Document
PRD .... Projected Rotation Date   (NG)
PR & D ...... Public Research and Development
PRD .... Puerto Rico, Decisiones [*A publication*]   (DLA)
PRD .... Push Rod [*Mechanical engineering*]
PRDA .... Program Research and Development Announcement [*Energy Research and Development Administration*]
PRDC .... Personnel Research and Development Center [*Office of Personnel Management*]   (GRD)
PRDC .... Polar Research and Development Center [*Army*]
PRDDO ...... Partial Retention of Diatomic Differential Overlap [*Physics*]

PRDE .... Preliminary Determination of Epicenters [*A publication*] [*National Oceanic and Atmospheric Administration*]
PRDE .... Pride Petroleum Services, Inc. [*NASDAQ symbol*]   (CTT)
PR & D El Cas ... Power, Rodwell, and Drew's English Election Cases [*A publication*]   (DLA)
PRDF .... Political Rights Defense Fund   (EA)
PRDG .... Princess Royal's Dragoon Guards [*Military unit*] [*British*]   (ROG)
PRDIAG .... Primary Diagnosis [*Medicine*]
Pr & Div ..... Law Reports, Probate and Divorce [*England*] [*A publication*]   (DLA)
PRDL .... Personnel Research and Development Laboratory [*Navy*]   (MCD)
PRDM .... Parti pour le Rassemblement Democratique des Mahorais [*Mayotte*] [*Political party*]   (EY)
PRDN .... Partido de Reconciliacion Democratica Nacional [*Party of National Democratic Reconciliation*] [*Guatemala*] [*Political party*]
PRDP .... Power Reactor Demonstration Program
PRDPEC ... Power Reactor Development Programme Evaluation Committee [*Canada*]   (HGAA)
PRDR .... Preproduction Reliability Design Review [*Navy*]   (CAAL)
PRDR .... Production Request Design Review
PRDV .... Peak Reading Digital Voltmeter
PRDX .... Prediction Program [*NASA*]
PRE .... Bureau for Private Enterprise
PRE .... Federation Europeenne des Fabricants de Produits Refractaires [*Zurich, Switzerland*]   (EAIO)
PRE .... Partido Republicano Evolucionista [*Republican Evolutionist Party*] [*Portugal*] [*Political party*]   (PPE)
PRE .... Partido Roldosista Ecuatoriano [*Ecuador*] [*Political party*]   (EY)
PRE .... Partner-Resisted Exercise [*Army*]   (INF)
PRE .... Personal Radio Exchange [*A publication*]
PRE .... Personal Rescue Enclosure   (NASA)
PRE .... Personnel Restraint Equipment   (SAA)
PRE .... Petroleum Refining Engineer
PRE .... Photoreactivating
PRE .... Pineridge Capital [*Vancouver Stock Exchange symbol*]
PRE .... Portable RADAR Equipment
PRE .... Precinct
PRE .... Precision Airlines [*North Springfield, VT*] [*FAA designator*]   (FAAC)
PRE .... Predecessor   (KSC)
PRE .... Prefect
PRE .... Prefix
PRE .... Preliminary
PRE .... Premier Industrial Corp. [*NYSE symbol*]   (SPSG)
PRE .... Prepayment Coin Telephone [*Telecommunications*]   (TEL)
PRE .... Presbyterian Historical Society, Philadelphia, PA [*OCLC symbol*]   (OCLC)
PRE .... President of the Royal Society of Painter-Etchers and Engravers [*British*]
PRE .... Pretoria [*South Africa*]   (KSC)
PRE .... Pretoria [*South Africa*] [*Seismograph station code, US Geological Survey*]   (SEIS)
PRE .... Problem Reproducer Equipment   (SAA)
PRE .... Processing Refabrication Experiment [*Nuclear energy*]   (NRCH)
PRE .... Progesterone [*A hormone*]
PRE .... Progesterone Response Element [*Endocrinology*]
PRE .... Progressive Resistive Exercise [*Medicine*]
PRE .... Protein Relaxation Enhancement   (OA)
PRE .... Proton Relaxation Enhancement [*Physics*]
PRE .... Public Relations Exchange [*Later, PRXI*]   (EA)
PRE .... Pulse Radiation Effect
PRE .... Realencyclopaedie fuer Protestantische Theologie und Kirche [*A publication*]
PRE .... Spanish Catalonian Battalion   (PD)
PREA .... Pension Real Estate Association   (EA)
P/REA .... Probationary Radio Electrical Artificer [*British military*]   (DMA)
PREA .... Reason [*A publication*]
PREAG ...... Photographic Reconnaissance Equipment Advisory Group [*Military*]
PREAMP .. Preamplifier   (AAG)
PREAP ...... Prison Research Education Action Project   (EA)
PRE-ARM ... People's Rights Enforced Against Riots and Murder [*Vigilante group in New Jersey*]
PREB .... Prebendary
PREB .... Pupil Record of Educational Behavior [*Aptitude test*]
PREBA3 .... Proceedings. Royal Society of Edinburgh. Section B. Biological Sciences [*A publication*]
PREBD ...... Population Reports. Series B [*United States*] [*A publication*]
Preb Dig..... Preble. Digest, Patent Cases [*A publication*]   (DLA)
Preb Pat Cas ... Preble. Digest, Patent Cases [*A publication*]   (DLA)
PREC .... Palestine Research and Educational Center   (EA)
PREC .... Precambrian [*Period, era, or system*] [*Geology*]
PREC .... Precedence   (AABC)
PREC .... Preceding
PREC .... Precentor   (ROG)

PREC .... Precious (ROG)
PREC .... Precision (AABC)
Prec .... Precite [*Supra, Cited Before*] [*French*] (ILCA)
PREC .... Propulsion Research Environmental Chamber
PREC .... Public Revenue Education Council (EA)
PRECA ...... Pauly-Wissowas Realencyclopaedie der Classischen Altertumswissenschaft [*A publication*]
Precamb Res ... Precambrian Research [*A publication*]
Precambrian Res ... Precambrian Research [*A publication*]
Precast Concr ... Precast Concrete [*A publication*]
Prec Ch ...... Precedents in Chancery, Edited by Finch [*24 English Reprint*] [*A publication*] (DLA)
Prec in Ch .. Precedents in Chancery, Edited by Finch [*24 English Reprint*] [*1689-1722*] [*A publication*] (DLA)
Prec in Ch (Eng) ... Precedents in Chancery, Edited by Finch [*24 English Reprint*] [*A publication*] (DLA)
PrecCst ...... Precision Castparts Corp. [*Associated Press abbreviation*] (APAG)
PRECD ..... Precede (FAAC)
PRECEDE ... Predisposing, Reinforcing, and Enabling Causes in Educational Diagnosis and Evaluation [*Occupational therapy*]
Pre Ch .... Precedents in Chancery, Edited by Finch [*A publication*] (DLA)
Precious Met ... Precious Metals [*A publication*]
PRECIP ..... Precipitation
PRECIS ..... Pre-Coordinate Indexing System
PRECIS ..... Preserved Context Index System [*British Library*] [*Information service or system*] [*London, England*]
Precis Eng ... Precision Engineering [*A publication*]
Precis Engng ... Precision Engineering [*A publication*]
Precis Met ... Precision Metal [*A publication*]
Precis Met Molding ... Precision Metal Molding [*A publication*]
PRECO ..... Preparatory Commission of the United Nations Organization
PRECOM ... Precommissioning [*Military*]
PRECOM ... Preliminary Communications Search [*Military*] (NVT)
PRECOMDET ... Precommissioning Detail [*Navy*] (NVT)
PRECOMG ... Precommissioning [*Military*] (NVT)
PRECOMM ... Preliminary Communications [*Military*] (NVT)
PRECOMMDET ... Precommissioning Detail [*Navy*]
PRECOMMSCOL ... Precommissioning School [*Navy*]
precomp ..... Precomputed Loan
PRECOMP ... Prediction of Contingency Maintenance and Parts Requirements (MCD)
PRECOMUNIT ... Precommissioning Unit [*Navy*] (DNAB)
PRECSA .... Precision Aerotech, Inc. [*Associated Press abbreviation*] (APAG)
PRED .... Predicate
PRED .... Predicted
PRED .... Prediction (AFM)
Pred .... Prednisone [*Also, P, PDN, Pr, Pro*] [*Antineoplastic drug*] [*Endocrinology*]
PREDECE ... Predecease (ROG)
Predel no Dopustimye Konts Atmos Zagryaz ... Predel no Dopustimye Kontsentratsii Atmosfernykh Zagryaznenii [*A publication*]
Predi .... Predicasts Special Study [*A publication*]
Predi 161 .... Predicasts. Recreational Vehicles Industry Study 161 [*A publication*]
Predi 162 .... Predicasts. World Rubber and Tire Markets Industry Study 162 [*A publication*]
Predi 163 .... Predicasts. Glass and Advanced Fibers Industry Study 163 [*A publication*]
Predi 165 .... Predicasts. Water Treatment Chemicals Industry Study 165 [*A publication*]
Predi 168 .... Predicasts. World Housing Industry Study 168 [*A publication*]
PredicadorEv ... El Predicador Evangelico [*Buenos Aires*] [*A publication*]
PREDICT ... Prediction of Radiation Effects by Digital Computer Techniques
Predi P55 .... Predicasts. Industrial Packaging Paper Trends P-55 [*A publication*]
Pr Edw I ..... Prince Edward Island (DLA)
Pr Edw I ..... Prince Edward Island Reports [*Canada*] [*A publication*] (DLA)
Pr Edw Isl .. Prince Edward Island (DLA)
Pr Edw Isl .. Prince Edward Island Reports [*Canada*] [*A publication*] (DLA)
PREEB ...... Presence [*A publication*]
PRE-EMPTN ... Pre-Emption (ROG)
PREF .... Preface
PREF .... Prefecture
PREF .... Preference [*or Preferred*] (AFM)
PREF .... Preferred (KSC)
PREF .... Prefix (AAG)
PREF .... Prefocused
PREF .... Propulsion Research Environmental Facility
PREFAB ... Prefabricated (KSC)
PREFACE ... Pre-Freshman and Cooperative Education for Minorities in Engineering
PREF-AP ... Prefect-Apostolic [*Roman Catholic*]
PREFAT .... Prepare Final Acceptance Trials [*Navy*] (NVT)
PREFCE .... Preface (ROG)
PREFLT .... Preflight (KSC)
PREFLTSCOL ... Preflight School [*Military*]
PREFMD .. Preformed

PREFRAM ... Prepare Fleet Rehabilitation and Modernization Overhaul [*Navy*] (NVT)
preft .... Prefecture
PREG .... Pregnancy [*or Pregnant*]
PREG .... Pregnenolone [*Endocrinology*]
PREGA ...... Promyshlennaya Energetika [*A publication*]
pregang ...... Preganglionic [*Anatomy*]
Pregled Naucnoteh Rad Inform Zavod Tehn Drveta ... Pregled Naucnotehnickih Radova i Informacija. Zavod za Tehnologiiu Drveta [*A publication*]
Pregl Probl Ment Retard Osoba ... Pregled Problema Mentalno Retardiranih Osoba [*A publication*]
PREGN ...... Pregnancy [*or Pregnant*] (AAMN)
Preh .... Prehistoire [*A publication*]
Prehist Arieg ... Prehistoire Ariegeoise [*A publication*]
Prehist Art Arch ... Prehistoric Art Archaeology [*A publication*]
Prehlad Lesnickej Lit ... Prehl'ad Lesnickej. Drevarskej. Celulozovej a Papierenskej Literatury [*A publication*]
Prehl Lesn Mysliv Lit ... Prehled Lesnicke a Myslivecke Literatury [*A publication*]
Prehl Zahr Zemed Lit ... Prehled Zahranicni Zemedelske Literatury [*A publication*]
Prehl Zemed Lit ... Prehled Zemedelske Literatury [*A publication*]
Prehl Zemed Lit Zahr Domaci ... Prehled Zemedelske Literatury Zahranicni i Domaci [*A publication*]
Prehrambeno Tehnol Rev ... Prehrambeno Tehnoloska Revija [*A publication*]
PREINACT ... Prepare Inactivation [*Navy*] (NVT)
PREINSURV ... Prepare for Board of Inspection and Survey [*Navy*] (NVT)
Preist Alp ... Preistoria Alpina [*Museo Tridentino di Scienze Naturali*] [*A publication*]
PREJ .... Prejudice (AABC)
PREL .... Pain Relief Level [*Medicine*]
PREL .... Preliminary
PREL .... Preliminary Evaluation [*Orbit identification*]
PREL .... Prelude [*Music*] (ROG)
PREL .... Priority Reconnaissance Exploitation List (CINC)
PREL .... Religion [*A publication*]
PRELA ...... Prensa Latina, Angencia Informativa Latinoamericana [*Press agency*] [*Cuba*]
PRELA ...... Przeglad Elektroniki [*Poland*] [*A publication*]
PRELIM .... Preliminary (AFM)
Prelim Rep Dir Gen Mines (Queb) ... Preliminary Report. Direction Generale des Mines (Quebec) [*A publication*]
Prelim Rep Rehovot Nat Univ Inst Agr ... Preliminary Report. Rehovot. National and University Institute of Agriculture [*A publication*]
prelims .... Preliminary Pages [*Frontmatter*] [*Publishing*]
PRELIMY ... Preliminary (ROG)
PRELOG ... People's Revolutionary League of Ghana [*Political party*] (PPW)
PRELORT ... Precision Long-Range Tracking RADAR
PREM .... Preliminary Reference Earth Model [*Geology*]
PREM .... Premature [*Medicine*]
PREM .... Premier (ROG)
PREM .... Premier Financial Services, Inc. [*Freeport, IL*] [*NASDAQ symbol*] (NQ)
PREM .... Premium (AFM)
PREM .... Probe-Microphone Real Ear Measurement [*Audiology*]
PREMA ...... Pulp Refining Equipment Manufacturers Association (EA)
PRE-MED ... Previous to Appearance in MEDLINE [*Latham, NY*] [*Bibliographic database*]
PREMEDU ... Preventive Medicine Unit
PREMES ... Premises (ROG)
Premium/Incentive Bus ... Premium/Incentive Business [*A publication*]
PREMOD ... Premodeling Data Output [*Environmental Protection Agency*]
PREMOD ... Premodulation (NASA)
PREMODE ... Preliminary Mid-Ocean Dynamics Experiment [*Marine science*] (MSC)
PremrI .... Premier Industrial Corp. [*Associated Press abbreviation*] (APAG)
Premrk .... Premark International, Inc. [*Associated Press abbreviation*] (APAG)
pre-mRNA ... Precursor-Messenger Ribonucleic Acid
PREMS ...... Premises (DSUE)
PREMSS ... Photographic Reconnaissance and Exploitation Management Support System (MCD)
PRENA ...... Product Engineering [*New York*] [*A publication*]
Pren Act ..... Prentice's Proceedings in an Action [*2nd ed.*] [*1880*] [*A publication*] (DLA)
prenat .... Prenatal
Prenatal Diagn ... Prenatal Diagnosis [*A publication*]
Prenat Diagn ... Prenatal Diagnosis [*A publication*]
PR Enferm ... Puerto Rico y Su Enferma [*A publication*]
PrEng .... Professional Engineer
Prensa Med Argent ... Prensa Medica Argentina [*A publication*]
Prensa Med Mex ... Prensa Medica Mexicana [*A publication*]
preocc .... Preoccupied [*Biology, taxonomy*]
PREOP ...... Preoperative [*Medicine*]
PREOS ...... Predicted Range for Electrooptical Systems [*Military*] (CAAL)
PREOVHL ... Prepare for Shipyard Overhaul [*Navy*] (NVT)
PREP .... Pacific Range Electromagnetic Platform (AAG)

PREP........ Parent Readiness Evaluation of Preschoolers [*Child development test*]
PREP........ Peace Research and Education Project
PREP........ Peacetime Requirements and Procedures [*Strategic Air Command*] (MUGU)
PREP........ Persons Responsive to Educational Problems (EA)
PREP........ Plan, Rehearse, Edit, and Psych [*Public speaking preparation technique*]
PREP........ Plasma Rotating Electrode Process [*Metallurgy*]
PREP........ Population, Resources, and Environment Program [*American Association for the Advancement of Science*]
PREP........ Predischarge Education Program [*DoD*]
PREP........ Preparation [*or Preparatory*]
PREP........ Prepare (AFM)
PREP........ Preposition
PREP........ Productivity Research and Extension Program [*North Carolina State University*] [*Research center*] (RCD)
PREP........ Programmed Educational Package
PREP........ Pupil Record of Educational Progress [*Education*] (AEBS)
PREP........ Purchasing, Receiving, and Payable System
PREP........ Putting Research into Educational Practice [*Information service of ERIC*]
PREPA...... Przeglad Epidemiologiczny [*A publication*]
Prepak........ People's Revolutionary Party of Kungleipak [*India*] [*Political party*] (PD)
PREPARE ... Premarital Personal and Relationship Evaluation
PREPARE ... Project for Retraining of Employable Persons as Relates to EDP
PREPAS.... Precise Personnel Assignment System [*Marine Corps*] (GFGA)
Prep Bioch ... Preparative Biochemistry [*A publication*]
Prep Biochem ... Preparative Biochemistry [*A publication*]
PrepCom.... Preparatory Committee [*United Nations Committee on Environment and Development*]
PREPD...... Prepared
PREPE...... Prepare (ROG)
Prep Food D ... Prepared Foods New Food Products Directory [*A publication*]
Prep Foods ... Prepared Foods [*A publication*]
PREPG...... Preparing
Prep Inorg React ... Preparative Inorganic Reactions [*A publication*]
PREPN...... Preparation
Prepo.......... Praepositus [*Deceased, 1509*] [*Authority cited in pre-1607 legal work*] (DSA)
Prepos........ Praepositus [*Deceased, 1509*] [*Authority cited in pre-1607 legal work*] (DSA)
PREPOS.... Preposition (AABC)
PREPOSTOR ... Prepositioned Storage [*Army*] (AABC)
Prep Prop Solid State Mat ... Preparation and Properties of Solid State Materials [*A publication*]
PREPPSA ... Prepare Postshakedown Availability [*Navy*] (NVT)
Preppy........ Preparatory School Alumnus [*Lifestyle classification*]
Prepr Am Chem Soc Div Fuel Chem ... Preprints. American Chemical Society. Division of Fuel Chemistry [*A publication*]
Prepr Amer Wood Pres Ass ... Preprint. American Wood Preservers' Association [*A publication*]
Prepr Am Soc Lubr Eng ... Preprints. American Society of Lubrication Engineers [*A publication*]
Prepr Annu Sci Meet Aerosp Med Assoc ... Preprints. Annual Scientific Meeting. Aerospace Medical Association [*A publication*]
Prepr Aust Miner Ind Annu Rev ... Preprints. Australian Mineral Industry. Annual Review [*A publication*]
Prepr Daresbury Lab ... Preprint. Daresbury Laboratory [*A publication*]
Prepr Div Pet Chem Am Chem Soc ... Preprints. American Chemical Society. Division of Petroleum Chemistry [*A publication*]
PREPREG ... Pre-Impregnated Glass Fibers [*Fiberglass production*]
Preprint Inst Eng Aust Conf ... Preprint. Institution of Engineers of Australia. Conference [*A publication*] (APTA)
PREPRO ... Preprocessor [*Computer*] [*Coast Guard*]
PREPROD ... Preproduction Model [*Military*] (AFIT)
Prepr Pap Annu Conf Australas Corros Assoc ... Australasian Corrosion Association. Preprinted Papers of the Annual Conference [*A publication*] (APTA)
Prepr Pap Natl Meet Div Environ Chem Am Chem Soc ... Preprints of Papers Presented at National Meeting. Division of Environmental Chemistry. American Chemical Society [*A publication*]
Prepr Pap Natl Meet Div Water Air Waste Chem Am Chem Soc ... Preprints of Papers Presented at National Meeting. Division of Water, Air, and Waste Chemistry. American Chemical Society [*A publication*]
Prepr Pap Oilseed Process Clin ... Preprints of Papers. Oilseed Processing Clinic [*A publication*]
Prepr Sci Program Aerosp Med Assoc ... Preprints. Scientific Program. Aerospace Medical Association [*A publication*]
Prepr Ser.... Preprint Series. University of Oslo. Institute of Mathematics [*A publication*]
Prepr Ser Inst Math Univ Oslo ... Preprint Series. Institute of Mathematics. University of Oslo [*Norway*] [*A publication*]
PREPS....... Predischarge Remedial Education Program [*For servicemen*]
PREPS....... Program of Research and Evaluation in Public Schools [*Mississippi State University*] [*Research center*] (RCD)
PREPSCOL ... Preparatory School
prepub........ Prepublication
PREQUAL ... Prequalified [*NASA*] (KSC)

Prer .... Prerogative Court (DLA)
PRER........ Prevention Resources [*A publication*]
PRER........ Putting Research into Educational Research
PRERECPAC ... Preplanned Reconnaissance Pacific (CINC)
PREREQ ... Prerequisite (WGA)
PRERLA ... Pupils Round, Equal, React to Light and Accommodation [*Medicine*] (MAE)
Prerog Ct.... Prerogative Court, New Jersey (DLA)
PRES........ Precision Resources, Inc. [*Whippany, NJ*] [*NASDAQ symbol*] (NQ)
PRES........ Premises (ROG)
Pres........... Presbyterian [*A publication*]
PRES........ Presbyterian
PRES........ Presence
PRES........ Present (AAG)
PRES........ Preserved
PRE-S........ Preshaving (MSA)
PRES........ President (EY)
PRES........ President of the Royal Entomological Society [*British*]
PRES........ Pressure (FAAC)
PRES........ Preston R. R. [*AAR code*]
PRES........ Presumptive [*Grammar*]
PRES........ Review of English Studies [*A publication*]
Pres Abs..... Preston's Abstracts of Title [*2nd ed.*] [*1823-24*] [*A publication*] (DLA)
PRESAC.... Photographic Reconnaissance System Analysis by Computer
PresAfr ...... Presence Africaine [*A publication*]
PRESAILEDREP ... Forecast Sailing Report [*Navy*] (NVT)
PRESAIR .. Pressurized Air Compressor (DNAB)
PRESB....... Presbyterian
PRESB....... Prescribe (AABC)
Presb Q...... Presbyterian Quarterly Review [*A publication*]
Presb R ..... Presbyterian Review [*A publication*]
Presb & Ref R ... Presbyterian and Reformed Review [*A publication*]
PRESBY.... Presbytery
Presbyt-St. Luke's Hosp Med Bull ... Presbyterian-St. Luke's Hospital. Medical Bulletin [*A publication*]
Presbyt-St. Luke's Hosp Res Rep ... Presbyterian-St. Luke's Hospital. Research Report [*A publication*]
Pres C of E Ch ... Presbyterian Church of England Chaplain [*Navy*] [*British*]
Pre-Sch Years ... Pre-School Years [*A publication*]
Pres Coll Physiol Inst J ... Presidency College. Physiological Institute Journal [*A publication*]
Pres Conv... Preston on Conveyancing [*5th ed.*] [*1819-29*] [*A publication*] (DLA)
PRESCORE ... Program for the Rapid Estimation of Construction Requirements
PRESCR.... Prescription (MSA)
Presd.......... Presidio Oil Co. [*Associated Press abbreviation*] (APAG)
PRESDL.... Presidential (WGA)
Presence Afr ... Presence Africaine [*A publication*]
PRESERV ... Preservation
Preserv Madeiras ... Preservacao de Madeiras [*A publication*]
Preserv Madeiras Bol Tec ... Preservacao de Madeiras. Boletim Tecnico [*A publication*]
Pres Est...... Preston on Estates [*3rd ed.*] [*1829*] [*A publication*] (DLA)
PRESET.... Preset Spin Echo Technique
Pres Fal...... Falconer's Decisions, Scotch Court of Session [*1744-51*] [*A publication*] (DLA)
Pres Fal...... Gilmour and Falconer's Reports, Scotch Court of Session [*A publication*] (DLA)
Pres Falc.... President Falconer's Scotch Session Cases (Gilmour and Falconer) [*1681-86*] [*A publication*] (DLA)
PRESFR.... Pressure Falling Rapidly [*Meteorology*] (FAAC)
Pres His S ... Presbyterian Historical Society. Journal [*A publication*]
Pres His SJ ... Presbyterian Historical Society. Journal [*A publication*]
PRESIG..... Pressurizing (KSC)
PRESIGN ... Procedure Sign
PRESINSURV ... Inspection and Survey Board [*Navy*]
Pres J........ Presbyterian Journal [*A publication*]
Pres Leg..... Preston on Legacies [*1824*] [*A publication*] (DLA)
Pres Life..... Presbyterian Life [*A publication*] (APTA)
Presly........ Presley Companies [*Associated Press abbreviation*] (APAG)
Pres Mer.... Preston on Merger [*A publication*] (DLA)
PRESNAVWARCOL ... Naval War College
PRESPROC ... Presidential Proclamation
PresR .... Presidential Realty Corp. [*Associated Press abbreviation*] (APAG)
PRESRR.... Pressure Rising Rapidly [*Meteorology*] (FAAC)
PRESS...... Pacific Range Electromagnetic Signature Studies [*or System*] [*Military*] (NG)
PRESS....... Parti Republicain Social du Senegal [*Social Republican Party of Senegal*] [*Political party*]
PRESS....... Prereading Expectancy Screening Scale [*Educational test*]
PRESS....... Pressure (MCD)
PRESS....... Prolog Equation Solving System (BYTE)
PRESS.... Property Record for Equipment Servicing and Sharing (MCD)
PRESSAR ... Presentation Equipment for Slow Scan RADAR
Presse Actual ... Presse Actualite [*A publication*]
Pressedienst Bundesminist Bild Wiss ... Pressedienst. Bundesministerium fuer Bildung und Wissenschaft [*A publication*]

Presse Med ... Presse Medicale [*A publication*]
Presse Med Belge ... Presse Medicale Belge [*A publication*]
Pressemitt Nordrh-Westfalen ... Pressemitteilung Nordrhein-Westfalen [*A publication*]
Presse Therm Clim ... Presse Thermale et Climatique [*A publication*]
Presse-Umsch ... Presse-Umschau [*A publication*]
Pressluft Ind ... Pressluft Industrie [*A publication*]
PRESSO.... Program for Elective Surgical Second Opinion [*Blue Cross/Blue Shield*]
Pres Studies Q ... Presidential Studies Quarterly [*A publication*]
Pres Stud Q ... Presidential Studies Quarterly [*A publication*]
Pressure Eng ... Pressure Engineering [*Japan*] [*A publication*]
PRESSURS ... Pre-Strike Surveillance/Reconnaissance System　(MCD)
PREST...... Present　(ROG)
PRES'T...... President
PRE-ST ..... Prestart　(AAG)
PREST...... Programme of Policy Research in Engineering Science and Technology [*British*]
Prest Conv ... Preston on Conveyancing [*A publication*]　(DLA)
Prestel D .... Prestel Directory and Magazine [*A publication*]
Prest Est .... Preston on Estates [*A publication*]　(DLA)
Prestige de la Photogr ... Prestige de la Photographie [*A publication*]
Prest Merg ... Preston on Merger [*A publication*]　(DLA)
PRESTMO ... Prestissimo [*Very Fast*] [*Music*]　(ROG)
PRESTO ... Personnel Response and Evaluation System for Target Obscuration [*Military*]　(RDA)
PRESTO ... Prestissimo [*Very Fast*] [*Music*]　(ROG)
PRESTO ... Program for Rapid Earth-to-Space Trajectory Optimization [*NASA*]
PRESTO ... Program Reporting and Evaluation System for Total Operations [*AFSC*]
Prest Shep T ... Sheppard's Touchstone by Preston [*A publication*]　(DLA)
PRET........ Periodic Reliability Evaluation Test　(MCD)
PRET........ Preterit [*Past tense*] [*Grammar*]　(ROG)
PRET........ Pretoria [*South Africa*]　(ROG)
PRETCHREP ... Preliminary Technical Report　(MCD)
PRETECHREP ... Preliminary Technical Report [*Army*]　(AABC)
PRETOS ... Proofreading Tests of Spelling [*Educational test*]
PRETTYBLUEBATCH ... Philadelphia Regular Exchange Tea Total Young Belles Lettres Universal Experimental Bibliographical Association To Civilize Humanity [*From Edgar Allan Poe essay "How to Write a Blackwood Article"*]
Preuss Jahrb ... Preussische Jahrbuecher [*A publication*]
Preuss Sitzb ... Preussische Akademie der Wissenschaften. Sitzungsbericht [*A publication*]
PREV........ Medical and Psychological Previews [*Database*] [*BRS Information Technologies*] [*Information service or system*]　(IID)
P Rev......... Powys Review [*A publication*]
PREV........ Prevention
PREV........ Previous　(AFM)
P Rev.......... Revenue Laws of Ptolemy Philadelphus [*A publication*]
PrevAGT ... Previous Abnormality of Glucose Tolerance
Prev Assist Dent ... Prevenzione e Assistenza Dentale [*A publication*]
PREVENT ... Precertification to Verify Necessary Treatment
Prev Fract Conf Aust Fract Group ... Prevention of Fracture. Conference of the Australian Fracture Group [*A publication*]　(APTA)
Prev Hum Serv ... Prevention in Human Services [*A publication*]
Previdenza Soc ... Previdenza Sociale [*A publication*]
Previd Soc ... Previdenza Sociale [*A publication*]
P Rev Laws ... Revenue Laws of Ptolemy Philadelphus [*A publication*]
Prev L Rep ... Preventive Law Reporter [*A publication*]
PREVLV.... Prevalve
Prev Med ... Preventive Medicine [*A publication*]
PREVMEDU ... Preventive Medicine Unit
Prev Stomatol ... Prevenzione Stomatologica [*A publication*]
PREVT ..... Preventative
Prev Vet M ... Preventive Veterinary Medicine [*A publication*]
Prev Vet Med ... Preventive Veterinary Medicine [*A publication*]
PREW........ Preway, Inc. [*NASDAQ symbol*]　(NQ)
PREWI...... Press Wireless [*A radio service for the transmission of news*]
PREXA ...... Personal Report for the Executive [*A publication*]
Pr Exch ...... Price's English Exchequer Reports [*1814-24*] [*A publication*]　(DLA)
PREXD...... Propellants and Explosives [*A publication*]
PRF........... Palestine Rejection Front　(BJA)
PRF........... Parachute Refurbishment Facility [*NASA*]　(NASA)
PRF........... Partial Reinforcement [*Training*]
PRF........... Partido Revolucionario Febrerista [*Febrerista Revolutionary Party*] [*Paraguay*] [*Political party*]　(PPW)
PRF........... Patient Record Form
PRF........... Penetration Room Filtration [*Nuclear energy*]　(NRCH)
prf.............. Performer [*MARC relator code*] [*Library of Congress*]　(LCCP)
PRF........... Personality Research Form [*Psychology*]
PRF........... Personnel Readiness File [*Army*]　(AABC)
PRF........... Petroleum Research Fund
PRF........... Phenol/Resorcinol/Formaldehyde [*Plastics technology*]
PRF........... Plant Response Fertilization [*Agriculture*]
PRF........... Plastics Recycling Foundation　(EA)
PRF........... Plutonium Reclamation Facility [*Nuclear energy*]
PRF........... Plymouth Rock Foundation　(EA)

PRF........... Plywood Research Foundation　(EA)
PRF........... Point Response Function [*Of a telescope*]
PRF........... Pontine Reticular Formation [*Neurophysiology*]
PRF........... Porpoise Rescue Foundation　(EA)
PRF........... Prefac Enterprises, Inc. [*Toronto Stock Exchange symbol*]
PRF........... Preformed [*Technical drawings*]
PRF........... Pride Companies LP [*NYSE symbol*]　(SPSG)
PRF........... Primary Reference Fuel [*Automotive engineering*]
PRF........... Pro-Air [*Mountain View, CA*] [*FAA designator*]　(FAAC)
PRF........... Processor Request Flag [*Telecommunications*]　(TEL)
PRF........... Progressive Renal Failure [*Medicine*]　(AAMN)
PRF........... Prolactin-Releasing Factor [*Endocrinology*]
PRF........... Proliferation Regulatory Factor [*Biochemistry*]
PRF........... Proof　(KSC)
PRF........... Protein Rich Fraction [*Food analysis*]
PRF........... Psychiatric Research Foundation
PRF........... Psychical Research Foundation　(EA)
PRF........... Psychosynthesis Research Foundation　(EA)
PRF........... Public Relations Foundation
PRF........... Public Residential Facility
PRF........... Publications Reference File [*Government Printing Office*] [*Washington, DC*] [*Database*]　(MCD)
PRF........... Publications Romanes et Francaises [*A publication*]
PRF........... Puerto Rico Federal Reports [*A publication*]　(DLA)
PRF........... Pulse Rate Frequency　(MUGU)
PRF........... Pulse Recurrence Frequency
PRF........... Pulse Repetition Frequency [*Data processing*]
PRF........... Purchase Rate Factor
PRF........... Purdue Research Foundation [*Purdue University*] [*Research center*]　(MCD)
PRFA........ Plasma Recognition Factor Activity [*Hematology*]　(AAMN)
Pr Falc .... President Falconer's Scotch Session Cases [*1744-51*] [*A publication*]　(DLA)
PRFAW ..... Personnel Research Field Activity, Washington [*Navy*]　(MUGU)
PRFBCP.... Professional Bancorp [*Associated Press abbreviation*]　(APAG)
PRFC........ Plymouth Rock Fanciers Club　(EA)
PRFC........ Potomac River Fisheries Commission [*Maryland and Virginia*]　(NOAA)
PRFCA ...... Products Finishing (Cincinnati) [*A publication*]
PRFCN...... Purification
PRFCS....... Prefocus
PRFD........ Pulse Recurrence Frequency Discrimination [*Telecommunications*]　(TEL)
PRFE .... Polar Reflection Faraday Effect
PR Fed .... Puerto Rico Federal Reports [*A publication*]　(DLA)
PRFG........ Proofing [*Freight*]
PRFI......... Portable Range-Finder/Illuminator
PRFI .... Puerto Rican Family Institute　(EA)
PRFIA .... Phase-Resolved Fluoroimmunoassay
PRFIA .... Product Finishing [*London*] [*A publication*]
PRFIC....... Plume RADAR Frequency Interference Code　(MCD)
PRFL .... Pressure Fed Liquid　(KSC)
PRFM....... Performance　(MSA)
PRFM....... Premature [*or Prolonged*] Rupture of Fetal Membrane [*Gynecology*]　(MAE)
PRFM....... Pseudorandom Frequency Modulated [*Data processing*]
PRFO........ Prairie Forum. Journal. Canadian Plains Research Centre [*A publication*]
PRFR .... Proofer [*Freight*]
PRFRD ..... Proofread　(MSA)
PRFS .... Phase-Resolved Fluorescence Spectroscopy
PRFS .... Pulse Recurrence Frequency Stagger　(OA)
PRFT........ Partially Relaxed Fourier Transform [*Mathematics*]
PRFT........ Press Fit
PRFT........ Presser Foot
PRFT........ Proffitt's, Inc. [*NASDAQ symbol*]　(NQ)
Prft Bldg St ... Profit-Building Strategies [*A publication*]
PRFU........ Processor Ready for Use [*Telecommunications*]　(TEL)
PRG .... Gilbert Associates, Inc., Reading, PA [*Library symbol*] [*Library of Congress*]　(LCLS)
PRG .... Parabolic Radius Gage　(MCD)
PRG .... Paris, IL [*Location identifier*] [*FAA*]　(FAAL)
PRG .... Peerless Carpet Corp. [*Toronto Stock Exchange symbol*]
PRG .... People's Revolutionary Government [*Grenada*]　(PD)
PRG .... Perennial Rye Grass [*Immunology*]
PRG .... Personnel Requirements Generator
PRG .... Personnel Resources Group [*Military*]
PRG .... Perugia [*Italy*] [*Seismograph station code, US Geological Survey*]　(SEIS)
PRG .... Pick Resources Guide [*ALLM Books*] [*England*] [*Information service or system*]　(IID)
PRG .... Plastic Radial Grating
PRG .... Prague [*Former Czechoslovakia*] [*Airport symbol*]　(OAG)
PRG .... Procedure Review Group [*Nuclear energy*]　(NRCH)
PRG .... Program Regulation Guide
PRG .... Program Review Group [*Military*]
PRG .... Psychological Readers' Guide [*A publication*]
PRG .... Purge　(AAG)
PRGC........ Past Royal Grand Cross [*Freemasonry*]　(ROG)
PRGEA...... Przeglad Geofizyczny [*A publication*]

PRG/I .... Pick Resources Guide/International [*ALLM Books*]
　　　　　 [*Information service or system*]   (IID)
PRGLB ...... Prostaglandins [*A publication*]
PRGM .... Program   (AFM)
PRGMG .... Programming   (MSA)
PRGMR..... Programmer   (AFM)
PRGO .... Perrigo Co. [*NASDAQ symbol*]   (SPSG)
Pr Gory Goretskaga Navuk Tav ... Pratsy Gory Goretskaga Navukov aga
　　　　　 Tavarystva [*A publication*]
PRGR......... ProGroup, Inc. [*NASDAQ symbol*]   (NQ)
PRGS........ President of the Royal Geographical Society [*British*]
PRGS........ Prognosis   (AABC)
PRGS........ Progress Software [*NASDAQ symbol*]   (SPSG)
PRGVB ..... Progressive [*A publication*]
PRH .... Partido Revolucionario Hondureno [*Honduras Revolutionary
　　　　　 Party*] [*Political party*]   (PPW)
PRH .... Petrol Railhead
PRH .... Phrae [*Thailand*] [*Airport symbol*]   (OAG)
PrH .... Prepositus Hypoglossi [*Neuroanatomy*]
PRH .... Program Requirements Handbook   (MUGU)
PRH .... Prolactin-Releasing Hormone [*Endocrinology*]
PRHA .... President of the Royal Hibernian Academy [*British*]
PRHBF...... Peak Reactive Hyperemia Blood Flow [*Hematology*]   (MAE)
Pr HC Ch... Practice of the High Court of Chancery [*A publication*]   (DLA)
PR Health Bull ... Puerto Rico Health Bulletin [*A publication*]
PR Health Sci J ... Puerto Rico Health Sciences Journal [*A publication*]
PRHi.......... Historical Society of Berks County, Reading, PA [*Library
　　　　　 symbol*] [*Library of Congress*]   (LCLS)
PrHsp .... Prime Hospitality Corp. [*Associated Press
　　　　　 abbreviation*]   (APAG)
PRI .... Farmington, MO [*Location identifier*] [*FAA*]   (FAAL)
PRI .... Pacific Research Institute for Public Policy   (EA)
PRI .... Pain Rating Index
PRI .... Paint Research Institute   (EA)
PRI .... Paleontological Research Institution   (EA)
PRI .... Partido Revolucionario Institucional [*Party of the
　　　　　 Institutionalized Revolution*] [*Mexico*] [*Political party*]
PRI .... Partito Repubblicano Italiano [*Italian Republican Party*]
　　　　　 [*Political party*]   (PPW)
PRI .... Partner Relationship Inventory [*Marital relations test*]
　　　　　 [*Psychology*]
PRI .... Peace Research Institute [*Later, Institute for Policy
　　　　　 Studies*]   (EA)
PRI .... Performance Registry International
PRI .... Personal Reaction Index [*Interpersonal skills and attitudes test*]
PRI .... Personnel Research, Inc. [*Information service or system*]   (IID)
PRI .... Personnel Research Institute Test   (AEBS)
PRI .... Petroleum Recovery Institute [*Research center*]   (RCD)
PRI .... Phosphate Rock Institute [*Defunct*]   (EA)
PRI .... Phosphoribose Isomerase [*An enzyme*]   (MAE)
PRI .... Photo RADAR Intelligence
PRI .... Photographic Reconnaissance and Interpretation   (NATG)
PRI .... Pineapple Research Institute of Hawaii   (EA)
PRI .... Plasticity Retention Index [*Rubber test method*]
PRI .... Plastics and Rubber Institute [*Formed by a merger of
　　　　　 Institution of the Rubber Industry and Plastics
　　　　　 Institute*]   (EAIO)
PRI .... Polymer Research Institute [*University of Massachusetts*]
　　　　　 [*Research center*]   (RCD)
PRI .... Polymer Research Institute [*Polytechnic Institute of New York*]
　　　　　 [*Research center*]   (RCD)
PRI .... Practice Training Index
PRI .... Praslin Island [*Seychelles Islands*] [*Airport symbol*]   (OAG)
PRI .... Preliminary Rifle Instruction [*Military*]
PRI .... Prescriptive Reading Inventory
PRI .... President Regimental Institutes [*British*]
PRI .... President of the Royal Institute (of Painters in Water Colours)
　　　　　 [*British*]   (ROG)
PRI .... President of the Royal Institution (London)   (ROG)
PRI .... Prevention Routiere Internationale [*International Road Safety
　　　　　 Organization*] [*Luxembourg*]   (EAIO)
Pri .... Price's English Exchequer Reports [*1814-24*] [*A
　　　　　 publication*]   (DLA)
Pri .... Price's English Mining Commissioners' Cases [*A
　　　　　 publication*]   (DLA)
PRI .... Priest [*California*] [*Seismograph station code, US Geological
　　　　　 Survey*]   (SEIS)
PRI .... Primary   (KSC)
PRI .... Primary Rate, Inc.
PRI .... Primary Rate Interface   (PCM)
PRI .... Primate Research Institute [*New Mexico State University*]
　　　　　 [*Hollman, NM*]
PRI .... Prime Computer Inc., Corporation Library, Framingham, MA
　　　　　 [*OCLC symbol*]   (OCLC)
PRI .... Princeville Airways, Inc. [*Honolulu, HI*] [*FAA
　　　　　 designator*]   (FAAC)
PRI .... Priority   (AFM)
PRI .... Priority Repair Induction [*Code*]
PRI .... Priority Requirement for Information   (AFM)
Pri .... Priscianus [*Authority cited in pre-1607 legal work*]   (DSA)
PRI .... Prison

PRI .... Private
PRI .... Prize [*or Prizeman*] [*British*]   (ROG)
PRI .... Processing Research Institute [*Carnegie Mellon University*]
PRI .... Production Rate Index   (OA)
PRI .... Production Records, Inc.   (EA)
PRI .... Program Revision Intent
PRI .... Projection Readout Indicator [*Aviation*]   (OA)
PRI .... Promus Companies [*NYSE symbol*]   (SPSG)
PRI .... Proteus Resources, Inc. [*Vancouver Stock Exchange symbol*]
PRI .... Psoriasis Research Institute   (EA)
PRI .... Puerto Rican Independence [*Later, GPRG*] [*An
　　　　　 association*]   (EA)
PRI .... Puerto Rico [*ANSI three-letter standard code*]   (CNC)
PRI .... Pulse Rate Increase [*Medicine*]
PRI .... Pulse Rate Indicator
PRI .... Pulse Recurrence [*or Repetition*] Interval   (NATG)
PRI .... Pulse Repetition Internal
PRI .... Pure Research Institute [*Later, BRINC*]   (EA)
PRIA .... Peer Review Improvement Act of 1982
PRIA .... President of the Royal Irish Academy
PRIA .... Priam Corp. [*NASDAQ symbol*]   (NQ)
PRIA .... Proceedings. Royal Irish Academy [*A publication*]
PRIA .... Public Rangelands Improvement Act of 1978
PRIA .... Society for Participatory Research in Asia [*India*]   (EAIO)
PRIAA ...... Proceedings. Royal Irish Academy. Section A. Mathematical
　　　　　 and Physical Sciences [*A publication*]
PRIAM...... Precision Range Information Analysis for Missiles   (MCD)
PrIAU-SJ .. Inter-American University of Puerto Rico, San Juan Campus,
　　　　　 San Juan, PR [*Library symbol*] [*Library of
　　　　　 Congress*]   (LCLS)
PRIB .... Private Brands, Inc. [*NASDAQ symbol*]   (NQ)
PRIBA ...... President of the Royal Institute of British Architects
PRIBA ...... Proceedings. Royal Irish Academy. Section B. Biological,
　　　　　 Geological, and Chemical Science [*A publication*]
PRIBAG .... Priority Baggage   (DNAB)
PRIBAN .... Proceedings. Royal Irish Academy. Section B. Biological,
　　　　　 Geological, and Chemical Science [*A publication*]
PRI BIL..... Primary Billet   (DNAB)
Pribliz Metod Resen Differencial Uravnen ... Priblizennye Metody Resenija
　　　　　 Differencial nyh Uravnenii [*A publication*]
Prib Metody Anal Izluch ... Pribory i Metody Analiza Izluchenii [*A
　　　　　 publication*]
Pribory i Sistemy Avtomat ... Pribory i Sistemy Avtomatiki [*A publication*]
Prib Sist Avtom ... Pribory i Sistemy Avtomatiki [*A publication*]
Prib Sist Upr ... Pribory i Sistemy Upravleniya [*A publication*]
Prib i Tekh Eksp ... Pribory i Tekhnika Eksperimenta [*A publication*]
Prib Tekhn ... Pribory i Tekhnika Eksperimenta [*A publication*]
Prib Ustroistva Sredstv Avtom Telemekh ... Pribory i Ustroistva Sredstv
　　　　　 Avtomatiki i Telemekhaniki [*A publication*]
PRIC Dec... Puerto Rico Industrial Commission Decisions [*A
　　　　　 publication*]   (DLA)
PRICE .... Physicians for Research in Cost-Effectiveness   (EA)
Price .... Price's English Exchequer Reports [*A publication*]   (DLA)
Price .... Price's English Mining Commissioners' Cases [*A
　　　　　 publication*]   (DLA)
PRICE .... Pricing Review to Intensify Competitive Environment [*Data
　　　　　 processing*]
PRICE .... Programmed Review of Information for Costing and
　　　　　 Evaluation   (MCD)
Price Gen Pr ... Price's General Practice [*A publication*]   (DLA)
Price Liens ... Price on Maritime Liens [*1940*] [*A publication*]   (DLA)
Price Min Cas ... Price's Mining Cases [*A publication*]   (DLA)
Price Notes PC ... Price's Notes of Practice Cases in Exchequer [*1830-31*]
　　　　　 [*England*] [*A publication*]   (DLA)
Price Notes PP ... Price's Notes of Points of Practice, English Exchequer Cases
　　　　　 [*A publication*]   (DLA)
Price PC..... Price's English Practice Cases [*1830-31*] [*A publication*]   (DLA)
Price Pr Cas ... Price's English Practice Cases [*A publication*]   (DLA)
Price R Est ... Price on Acts Relating to Real Estate [*A publication*]   (DLA)
Price & St... Price and Stewart's Trade Mark Cases [*A publication*]   (DLA)
Price Waterhouse R ... Price Waterhouse Review [*A publication*]
Price Waterhouse Rev ... Price Waterhouse Review [*A publication*]
Prickett...... Prickett's Reports [*1 Idaho*] [*A publication*]   (DLA)
PRICOM... Prison Commission [*British*]
PRID......... Pridie [*The Day Before*] [*Latin*]
PriD .... Princeton Datafilm, Inc., Princeton, NJ [*Library symbol*]
　　　　　 [*Library of Congress*]   (LCLS)
Prid & C ..... Prideaux and Cole's English Reports [*4 New Sessions Cases*]
　　　　　 [*1850-51*] [*A publication*]   (DLA)
Prid Ch W ... Prideaux's Directions to Churchwardens [*10th ed.*] [*1835*] [*A
　　　　　 publication*]   (DLA)
Prid & Co ... Prideaux and Cole's English Reports [*4 New Sessions Cases*]
　　　　　 [*1850-51*] [*A publication*]   (DLA)
PRIDCO... Puerto Rico Industrial Development Co.
Prid Conv... Prideaux's Forms and Precedents in Conveyancing [*24th ed.*]
　　　　　 [*1952*] [*A publication*]   (DLA)
PRIDE .... National Parents' Resource Institute for Drug Education   (EA)
PRIDE....... People for Rehabilitating and Integrating the Disabled through
　　　　　 Education [*New York City*]
PRIDE....... Perfection Requires Individual Defect Elimination

PRIDE....... Personal Responsibility in Daily Effort [*Military Airlift Command's acronym for the Zero Defects Program*]
PRIDE....... Preschool and Kindergarten Interest Descriptor [*Educational test*]
Pride.......... Pride Companies Ltd. [*Associated Press abbreviation*]   (APAG)
PRIDE....... Priority Receiving with Inter-Departmental Efficiency [*Data processing*]
PRIDE....... Production of Reliable Items Demands Excellence [*Navy*]   (NG)
PRIDE....... Productive Rehabilitation Institute of Dallas for Ergonomics [*Research center*]   (RCD)
PRIDE....... Productivity Improvements for the Decade of the Eighties
PRIDE....... Professional Results in Daily Effort [*Strategic Air Command's acronym for the Zero Defects Program*]
PRIDE....... Programmed Reliability in Design Engineering
PRIDE....... Promote Real Independence for the Disabled and Elderly   (EA)
PRIDE....... Prompt Response Insurance Delivery Express
PRIDE....... Protection of Reefs and Islands from Degradation and Exploitation
PRIDE....... Provisioning Review Input Data Evaluation   (MCD)
PRIDE....... Pulse RADAR Intelligent Diagnostic Environment [*US Army Missile Command*]   (RDA)
Pride Inst J Long Term Home Health Care ... Pride Institute. Journal of Long Term Home Health Care [*A publication*]
Prid Judg ... Prideaux's Judgments and Crown Debts [*4th ed.*] [*1854*] [*A publication*]   (DLA)
PRIF .... Prior Year Refund Information File [*IRS*]
PRI-FLY.... Primary Flight Control [*on an aircraft carrier*] [*Navy*]
PRIH .... Prolactin-Release Inhibiting Factor [*Also, PIF*] [*Endocrinology*]
PRIISM..... Pacific Research Institute for Information Systems and Management [*University of Hawaii at Manoa*] [*Research center*]   (RCD)
Prikladnaya Geofiz ... Prikladnaya Geofizika [*A publication*]
Prikl Biokhim Mikrobiol ... Prikladnaya Biokhimiya i Mikrobiologiya [*A publication*]
Prikl Geofiz ... Prikladnaya Geofizika [*A publication*]
Prikl Geom i Inzener Grafika ... Prikladnaja Geometrija i Inzenernaja Grafika [*A publication*]
Prikl Mat ... Prikladnaya Matematika i Mekhanika [*A publication*]
Prikl Mat Mekh ... Prikladnaya Matematika i Mekhanika [*A publication*]
Prikl Mat i Programmirovanie ... Prikladnaja Matematika i Programmirovanie [*A publication*]
Prikl Meh .. Akademija Nauk Ukrainskoi SSR. Otdelenie Matematiki. Mehaniki i Kibernetiki. Prikladnaja Mehanika [*A publication*]
Prikl Mekh ... Akademiya Nauk Ukrainskoi SSR. Otdelenie Matematiki. Mekhaniki i Kibernetiki. Prikladnaya Mekhanika [*A publication*]
Prikl Mekh ... Prikladnaya Mekhanika [*A publication*]
Prikl Mekh Priborostr ... Prikladnaya Mekhanika v Priborostroenii [*A publication*]
Prikl Problemy Proc i Plast ... Gor'kovskii Gosudarstvennyi Universitet Imeni N. I. Lobacevskogo. Prikladnye Problemy Procnosti i Plasticnosti [*A publication*]
Prikl Yad Fiz ... Prikladnaya Yadernaya Fizika [*A publication*]
Prikl Yad Spektrosk ... Prikladnaya Yadernaya Spektroskopiya [*A publication*]
PrilKJIF .... Prilozi za Knjizevnost, Jezik, Istoriju, i Folklor [*A publication*]
Prilozh Sb Nauchn Rab Med Fak Karlova Univ Gradtse Kralove ... Prilozhenie k Sborniku Nauchnykh Rabot Meditsinskogo Fakul'teta Karlova Universiteta v Gradtse Kralove [*A publication*]
Prilozi......... Prilozi za Knjizevnost, Jezik, Istoriju, i Folklor [*A publication*]
PrilPJ .... Prilozi Proucavanju Jezika [*A publication*]
PRIM......... Pac Rim Holding [*NASDAQ symbol*]   (SPSG)
PRIM......... Plans and Reports Improvement Memorandum [*Military*]   (CAAL)
PRIM......... Plume Radiation Intensity Measurement   (MUGU)
PRIM......... Primages, Inc. [*NASDAQ symbol*]   (NQ)
PRIM......... Primary   (AFM)
PRIM......... Primate
PRIM......... Primitive
PRIM......... Program for Information Managers [*Later, AIM*] [*An association*]
PRIM......... Programmed Instruction for Management Education   (HGAA)
PRIMA...... Pollutant Response in Marine Animals [*Marine science*]   (MSC)
PRIMA...... Public Risk and Insurance Management Association [*Washington, DC*]   (EA)
PRIMAR ... Program to Improve Management of Army Resources   (AABC)
Primary Cardiol ... Primary Cardiology [*A publication*]
Primary Ed ... Primary Education [*A publication*]
Primary Educ ... Primary Education [*A publication*]   (APTA)
Primary J... Primary Journal [*A publication*]   (APTA)
Primary Maths ... Primary Mathematics [*A publication*]
Primary Sci Bull ... Primary Science Bulletin [*A publication*]   (APTA)
PRIMATE ... Personal Retrieval of Information by Microcomputer and Terminal Ensemble
Primate Behav ... Primate Behavior [*A publication*]
Primates Med ... Primates in Medicine [*A publication*]
Primatolog ... Primatologia [*A publication*]

Primca........ Primerica Corp. [*Associated Press abbreviation*]   (APAG)
PRIME ...... Planning through Retrieval of Information for Management Extrapolation
PRIME ...... Precision Integrator for Meteorological Echoes   (IEEE)
PRIME ...... Precision Range Integrated Maneuver Exercise [*Army*]   (RDA)
PRIME ...... Precision Recovery Including Maneuvering Entry [*Air Force*]
PRIME ...... Preparedness of Resources in Mission Evaluation   (SAA)
PRIME ...... Prescribed Right to Income and Maximum Equity
PRIME ...... Priority Improved Management Effort   (KSC)
PRIME ...... Priority Improvement Effort [*DoD*]
PRIME ...... Priority Management Effort [*Army*]
PRIME ...... Priority Management Evaluation [*Navy*]
PRIME ...... Procarbazine, Ifosfamide, Methotrexate [*Antineoplastic drug regimen*]
PRIME ...... Processing, Research, Inspection, and Marine Extension Program [*National Oceanic and Atmospheric Administration*]   (MSC)
PRIME ...... Profession Related Intern-Mentorship Experience
PRIME ...... Program Independence, Modularity, Economy
PRIME ...... Program Research in Integrated Multiethnic Education [*Defunct*]   (EA)
PRIME ...... Programmed Instruction for Management Education [*American Management Association*]
Prim Ed-Pop Ed ... Primary Education - Popular Educator [*A publication*]
Prim Educ .. Primary Education [*A publication*]
Primenen Mat Ekonom ... Leningradskii Ordena Lenina Gosudarstvennyi Universitet Imeni A. A. Zdanova. Kafedra i Laboratorija Ekonomiko-Matematiceskih Metodov. Primenenie Matematikii v Ekonomike [*A publication*]
Primenen Mat Ekonom ... Primenenie Matematiki v Ekonomike [*A publication*]
Primenen Teor Verojatnost i Mat Statist ... Primenenie Teorii Verojatnostei i Matematiceskoi Statistiki [*A publication*]
PRIMENET ... Prime Network Software Package [*Prime Computer, Inc.*]
Primen Mat Metodov Biol ... Primenenie Matematicheskikh Metodov v Biologii [*A publication*]
Primen Mikroelem Sel-Khoz Akad Nauk UkrSSR ... Primenenie Mikroelementov Sel'skom Khozyaistve Akademiya Nauk Ukrainskoi SSR [*A publication*]
Primen Polim Mater Nar Khoz ... Primenenie Polimernykh Materialov v Narodnom Khozyaistve [*A publication*]
Primen Tsifrovykh Analogovykh Vychisl Mash Yad Fiz Tekh ... Primenenie Tsifrovykh i Analogovykh Vychislitel'nykh Mashin v Yadernoi Fizike i Tekhnike [*A publication*]
Primen Ul'traakust Issled Veshchestva ... Primenenie Ul'traakustiki k Issledovaniyu Veshchestva [*A publication*]
PRIMER ... Patient Record Information for Education Requirements [*Data processing*]
PRIMES.... Preflight Integration of Munitions and Electronic Systems   (MCD)
PRIMES.... Productivity Integrated Measurement System [*Army*]
PRIMEX ... Private Message Switching [*Telecommunications*] [*British*]
PRIMIP..... Primipara [*Woman bearing first child*] [*Medicine*]   (AAMN)
PRIMIR .... Product Improvement Management Information Report
PRIM LUC ... Prima Luce [*Early in the Morning*] [*Pharmacy*]
PRIM M..... Primo Mane [*Early in the Morning*] [*Pharmacy*]
PRIM METH ... Primitive Methodist [*A publication*]
PRIMO...... Programmable, Realtime, Incoherent, Matrix, Optical Processor [*Data processing*]
PRIMOS.... Prime Operating System [*Prime Computer, Inc.*]
PRIM & R .. Public Responsibility in Medicine and Research   (EA)
Primrk........ Primark Corp. [*Associated Press abbreviation*]   (APAG)
PRIMS ...... Product Requirement Information Management System   (MCD)
PRIMTEC ... Pacific Rim Interactive Multi-Media Technology
PRIMTRA ... Air Primary Training
PRIMUS ... Physician Reservists in Medical Universities and Schools [*Military*]
PRIMUS ... Primary Medical Care for the Uniformed Services [*DoD*]
PRIN......... Partido Revolucionario de la Izquierda Nacionalista [*National Leftist Revolutionary Party*] [*Bolivia*] [*Political party*]   (PPW)
·PRIN......... Performance Risk Index Number   (NG)
PRIN.......... Powerec International [*NASDAQ symbol*]   (NQ)
PRIN......... Princeton [*New Jersey*] [*Seismograph station code, US Geological Survey*]   (SEIS)
PRIN......... Principal
PRIN......... Principality   (ROG)
PRIN......... Principally   (ROG)
PRIN......... Principia [*Elements*] [*Latin*]   (ROG)
PRIN......... Principle   (ROG)
PRINAIR .. Puerto Rico National Airlines
Princ.......... Princeton Review [*A publication*]
PRINC....... Principal
PRINC....... Principle
Princ in Counc ... Principals in Council [*A publication*]
PRINCE .... Parts Reliability Information Center [*NASA*]
PRINCE .... Programmed International Computer Environment [*International relations simulation game*]
PRINCE .... Programmed Reinforced Instruction Necessary to Continuing Education

PRINCE/APIC ... Parts Reliability Information Center/Apollo Parts Information Center [*NASA*]
Prince NML ... Prince's New Mexico Laws [*A publication*]　(DLA)
Prince S B .. Princeton Seminary Bulletin [*A publication*]
Princeton Coll B ... Princeton College. Bulletin [*A publication*]
Princeton Conf Cerebrovasc Dis ... Princeton Conference on Cerebrovascular Diseases [*A publication*]
Princeton Conf Cereb Vasc Dis ... Princeton Conference on Cerebral Vascular Diseases [*Later, Princeton Conference on Cerebrovascular Diseases*] [*A publication*]
Princeton Math Ser ... Princeton Mathematical Series [*A publication*]
Princeton Mus Rec ... Princeton University. Museum of Historic Art. Record [*A publication*]
Princeton Stud Math Econom ... Princeton Studies in Mathematical Economics [*A publication*]
Princeton Univ Lib Chron ... Princeton University. Library. Chronicle [*A publication*]
Princ Food Rice ... Principal Food. Rice [*A publication*]
Principia Cardiol ... Principia Cardiologica [*A publication*]
Princ NS .... Princeton Review (New Series) [*A publication*]
Pr Incntv .... Premium/Incentive Business [*A publication*]
Princ Pract Pediatr Surg Spec ... Principles and Practice of the Pediatric Surgical Specialities [*A publication*]
PrincSB ...... Princeton Seminary Bulletin [*A publication*]
PrincSemB ... Princeton Seminary Bulletin [*Princeton, NJ*] [*A publication*]
Princ Tech Hum Res Ther ... Principles and Techniques of Human Research and Therapeutics [*A publication*]
Princ Theol R ... Princeton Theological Review [*A publication*]
Princ Univ Bull ... Princeton University. Bulletin [*A publication*]
Princ Viana ... Principe de Viana [*A publication*]
PRIND ...... Present Indications Are [*Aviation*]　(FAAC)
PRINDI ..... Princeton Diagnostic Laboratories of America, Inc. [*Associated Press abbreviation*]　(APAG)
PRINDUS ... Prison Industries [*Industries conducted in English prisons*]
PRINFO .... Printed Information Distribution　(SAA)
PRING .... Partido Revolucionario de Izquierda Nacional Gueiler [*Revolutionary Party of the National Left - Gueiler Wing*] [*Bolivia*] [*Political party*]　(PPW)
PRIN-L ...... Partido Revolucionario de la Izquierda Nacional Laboral [*Political party*]　(PPW)
PRINM ...... Partido Revolucionario de la Izquierda Nacional Moller [*Bolivia*] [*Political party*]　(PPW)
PRINMUS ... Principal Musician [*Marine Corps*]
PRINOBC/NEC ... Primary Navy Officer Billet Classification and Navy Enlisted Classification
Prin PL ...... Eden's Principles of Penal Law [*A publication*]　(DLA)
Prins & Conderlag ... Prins and Conderlag's Reports [*Ceylon*] [*A publication*]　(ILCA)
Pr Inst Geol Korisnikh Kopalin Akad Nauk Ukr ... Pratsi Institut Geologii Korisnikh Kopalin Akademiya Nauk Ukrains'koi [*A publication*]
Pr Inst Gidrobiol Akad Nauk Ukr RSR ... Pratsi Institutu Gidrobiologii Akademiya Nauk Ukrains'koi RSR [*A publication*]
PRINT .... Pre-Edited Interpretive System [*Data processing*]
PRINT .... Public Release of Information and Transcripts [*Student legal action organization*]
Print Abstr ... Printing Abstracts [*A publication*]
Print Art ..... Printing Art [*Massachusetts*] [*A publication*]
Print Art Q ... Printing Art Quarterly [*A publication*]
Print Bookbind Trade Rev ... Printing and Bookbinding Trade Review [*A publication*]
Print Coll Q ... Print Collector's Quarterly [*A publication*]
Print Equip Eng ... Printing Equipment Engineer [*A publication*]
Print Graph Arts ... Printing and Graphic Arts [*A publication*]　(APTA)
Printing ...... Printing Impressions [*A publication*]
Printing Abs ... Printing Abstracts [*A publication*]
Printing Abstr ... Printing Abstracts [*A publication*]
Printing Impr ... Printing Impressions [*A publication*]
Printing and Pub ... Printing and Publishing [*A publication*]
Printing Trades J ... Printing Trades Journal [*A publication*]
Print Mag .. Printing Magazine [*A publication*]
Print Mag Natl Lithogr ... Printing Magazine National Lithographer [*A publication*]
Print Manag ... Printing Management [*A publication*]
Print Prod .. Printing Production [*A publication*]
Print & Pub ... Printing and Publishing [*A publication*]
Print R .... Print Review [*A publication*]
Print Rev .... Print Review [*A publication*]
Printrn .... Printron, Inc. [*Associated Press abbreviation*]　(APAG)
Print Sales ... Printed Salesmanship [*A publication*]
Print Salesmanship ... Printed Salesmanship [*A publication*]
Print Technol ... Printing Technology [*A publication*]
Print Trades J ... Printing Trades Journal [*A publication*]　(APTA)
PRINUL .... Puerto Rico International Undersea Laboratory
PRIO .... International Peace Research Institution, Oslo [*Norway*]
PRIO .... Priority [*Telecommunications*]
PRIOR .... Program for In-Orbital Rendezvous [*Antisatellite system*] [*Air Force*]
PRIP .... Park Restoration and Improvement Program [*National Park Service*]
PRIP .... Parts Reliability Improvement Program

PRIP .... Planned Retirement Income Program [*Institute of Financial Management*]
PRIPACSEVOCAM ... Primary Pacific Secure Voice Communications [*Navy*]　(CAAL)
PRIPP .... Pacific Research Institute for Public Policy　(EA)
PRIRA .... Priroda [*Moscow*] [*A publication*]
P R Ir Ac A ... Proceedings. Royal Irish Academy. Section A. Mathematical, Astronomical, and Physical Science [*A publication*]
P R Ir Ac B ... Proceedings. Royal Irish Academy. Section B. Biological, Geological, and Chemical Science [*A publication*]
P R Ir Ac C ... Proceedings. Royal Irish Academy. Section C. Archaeology, Celtic Studies, History, Linguistics, Literature [*A publication*]
PRIRB ...... Priroda (Sofia, Bulgaria) [*A publication*]
Prir Gaz Sib ... Prirodnyi Gaz Sibiri [*A publication*]
Prir-Mat Fak Univ Kiril Metodij (Skopje) God Zb Biol ... Prirodno-Matematicka Fakultet na Univerzitetot Kiril i Metodij (Skopje). Godisen Zbornik. Biologija [*A publication*]
Prir Mat Fak Univ Kiril Metodij (Skopje) God Zb Sek A ... Prirodno-Matematicka Fakultet na Univerzitetot Kiril i Metodij (Skopje). Godisen Zbornik. Sekcja A. Matematika, Fizika, i Hemija [*A publication*]
Prir (Moscow) ... Priroda (Moscow) [*A publication*]
Prirodonauc Muz Skopje Posebno Izd ... Prirodonaucen Muzej Skopje Posebno Izdanie [*A publication*]
Prirodosl Istraz Acta Biol ... Prirodoslovna Istrazivanja Acta Biologica [*A publication*]
Prirodosl Istraz Acta Geol ... Prirodoslovna Istrazivanja Acta Geologica [*A publication*]
Prirodoved Cas Slezsky ... Prirodovedny Casopis Slezsky [*A publication*]
Prir (Sofia) ... Priroda (Sofia) [*A publication*]
Prir Tr Resur Levoberezhnoi Ukr Ikh Ispolz ... Prirodnye i Trudot ye Resursy Levoberezhnoi Ukrainy i Ikh Ispolzovanie [*A publication*]
Prir Usloviya Zapadn Sib ... Prirodnye Usloviya Zapadnoi Sibiri [*A publication*]
PRIS .... Pacific Range Instrumentation Satellite　(MUGU)
PRIS .... Pest Management Research Information System [*Agriculture Canada*] [*Information service or system*]　(IID)
PRIS .... Prison　(ROG)
PRIS .... Prisoner　(AFM)
PRIS .... Program Resource Information System [*Department of Agriculture*]
PRIS .... Propeller Revolution Indicator System　(MSA)
Prisadki Smaz Maslam ... Prisadki i Smazochnym Maslam [*A publication*]
PRISCO ...... Price Stabilization Corp.
PRISD .... Proceedings. Indian Academy of Sciences. Series Engineering Sciences [*A publication*]
PRISE .... Page Reader Input System with Editing　(NVT)
PRISE .... Pennsylvania Resources and Information Center for Special Education [*Montgomery County Intermediate Unit*] [*King of Prussia*] [*Information service or system*]　(IID)
PRISE .... Pennsylvania's Regional Instruction System for Education [*Network of colleges and universities*]
PRISE .... Program for Integrated Shipboard Electronics
PRISIC ...... Photographic Reconnaissance Interpretation Section [*Squadron*] Intelligence Center [*JICPOA*]
Pris Jrnl ..... Prisoners Journal [*A publication*]
PRISM ...... Parameter Related Internal Standard Method [*Statistical procedure*]
PRISM ...... Pattern Recognition Information Synthesis Modeling [*Market analysis*]
PRISM ...... Personnel Record Information Systems for Management
PRISM ...... Personnel Requirements Information System Methodology　(NVT)
PRISM ...... Power Reactor Inherently Safe Module [*Nuclear energy*]
PRISM ...... Prism Entertainment Corp. [*Associated Press abbreviation*]　(APAG)
PRISM ...... Program Reliability Information System for Management [*Polaris*]
PRISM ...... Programmable Integrated Scripts for MIRROR [*Management Information Reporting and review of Operational Resources Systems*][*Computer Language*]　(PCM)
PRISM ...... Programmed Integrated System Maintenance　(NG)
PRISM ...... Progressive Refinement of Integrated Supply Management　(AFM)
Prism Int .... Prism International [*A publication*]
PRISN .... Prime Stock Number
PRISNET ... Private Switching Network Service [*Telecommunications*]
Prison L Reptr ... Prison Law Reporter [*A publication*]　(ILCA)
Prison L Rptr ... Prison Law Reporter [*A publication*]　(DLA)
Prison Serv J ... Prison Service Journal [*A publication*]　(DLA)
PrisrAcSci&Hum ... Proceedings. Israel Academy of Sciences and Humanities [*Jerusalem*] [*A publication*]
PRISS .... Plaza Realty Investors SBI [*NASDAQ symbol*]　(NQ)
PRISS .... Post Deployment Software Support Real-Time Interactive Simulation System
PRIST .... Paper Radioimmunosorbent Test [*Analytical biochemistry*]
PRITA ...... Problems of Information Transmission [*A publication*]
Pritch Adm Dig ... Pritchard's Admiralty Digest [*3rd ed.*] [*1887*] [*A publication*]　(DLA)

Pritch M & D ... Pritchard's Divorce and Matrimonial Causes [*3rd ed.*] [*1874*] [*A publication*] (DLA)
Pritch Quar Sess ... Pritchard's Quarter Sessions [*A publication*] (DLA)
PRIV .... Private
PRIV .... Privative
PRIV .... Privilege
Privacy Rept ... Privacy Report [*A publication*]
Private Pract ... Private Practice [*A publication*]
PRIVAUTH ... Travel Authorized via Privately-Owned Vehicle with Understanding No Additional Cost to Government Involved
Priv C App ... Privy Council Appeals [*England*] [*A publication*] (DLA)
Priv CDI .... Indian Privy Council Decisions [*A publication*] (DLA)
Priv Counc App ... Privy Council Appeals [*England*] [*A publication*] (DLA)
Priv Counc DI ... Privy Council Decisions [*India*] [*A publication*] (DLA)
PRIVE .... Private (ROG)
Priv Hous Fin ... Private Housing Finance [*A publication*] (DLA)
Priv Lib ...... Private Library [*A publication*]
Priv Libr ..... Private Library [*A publication*]
Priv Lond ... Privilegia Londini [*A publication*] (DLA)
Priv Maintd ... Privately Maintained [*Nautical charts*]
PRIV PROP ... Private Property [*Military*] (DNAB)
PRIZE .... Program for Research in Information Systems Engineering [*University of Michigan*] [*Research center*] (RCD)
Prize CR ..... Prize Court Reports [*South Africa*] [*A publication*] (DLA)
PRIZM ...... Potential Rating Index by ZIP [*Zone Improvement Plan*] Market [*Advertising*]
PRJ .... American Junior College of Puerto Rico, Bayamon, PR [*OCLC symbol*] (OCLC)
PRJ .... Payroll Journal [*Accounting*]
PRJ .... Port Royal [*Jamaica*] [*Seismograph station code, US Geological Survey*] (SEIS)
PrJ .... Preussische Jahrbuecher [*A publication*]
PRJ .... Public Relations Journal [*A publication*]
PRJC .... Pearl River Junior College [*Poplarville, MS*]
PRJC .... Puerto Rico Junior College
PRJMP...... Pressure Jump (FAAC)
PR J Public Health Trop Med ... Puerto Rico Journal of Public Health and Tropical Medicine [*A publication*]
PRK .... Democratic People's Republic of Korea [*ANSI three-letter standard code*] (CNC)
PRK .... Paraskevi [*Lesbos*] [*Greece*] [*Seismograph station code, US Geological Survey*] (SEIS)
PRK .... Park
PRK .... Parkside Petroleum, Inc. [*Toronto Stock Exchange symbol*] [*Vancouver Stock Exchange symbol*]
PRK .... People's Republic of Kampuchea [*From 1979 to 1989*] [*Formerly, Cambodia*] [*Later, SOC*] (PD)
PRK .... Praktijkgids [*A publication*]
PRK .... Pridie Kalendas [*The Day before the Calends*] [*Latin*]
PRK .... Primary Rat Kidney [*Cells*]
PRKG .... Parking
PRKNA ..... Progress in Reaction Kinetics [*A publication*]
PRKPA ...... Probleme der Kosmichen Physik [*A publication*]
PRKRA ...... Parks and Recreation [*A publication*]
PRL .... Pacht, Ross et Al, Los Angeles, CA [*OCLC symbol*] (OCLC)
PRL .... Page Revision Log (NASA)
PRL .... Parallel (MSA)
PRL .... Parti Reformateur Liberal [*Liberal Reform Party*] [*Belgium*] [*Political party*] (PPW)
PRL .... Parti Republicain de la Liberte [*Republican Party for Liberty*] [*France*] [*Political party*] (PPE)
PRL .... Parti Republicain de la Liberte [*Republican Party for Liberty*] [*Burkina Faso*] [*Political party*]
PRL .... Partido Radical Liberal [*Radical Liberal Party*] [*Ecuador*] [*Political party*]
PRL .... Parts Requirement List (KSC)
PRL .... Peace Research Laboratory [*Later, LPRL*] [*An association*] (EA)
PRL .... Personnel Research Laboratory [*Lackland Air Force Base, TX*]
PRL .... Pesticide Research Laboratory and Graduate Study Center [*Pennsylvania State University*] [*Research center*] (RCD)
PRL .... Petroleum Refining Laboratory [*Pennsylvania State University*] (MCD)
PRL .... Philco Resources [*Vancouver Stock Exchange symbol*]
PRL .... Photoreactivating Light
PRL .... Physiological Research Laboratories [*University of California at San Diego*] [*Research center*]
PRL .... Pioneering Research Laboratory [*Massachusetts*] [*Army*]
PRL .... Planning Requirements List (MCD)
PRL .... Plastics Research Laboratory [*MIT*] (MCD)
PRL .... Political Risk Letter [*Database*] [*Frost & Sullivan, Inc.*] [*Information service or system*] (CRD)
PRL .... Preamble
PRL .... Precision Reduction Laboratory (AFM)
PRL .... Predicted Repair Level (MCD)
PRL .... Pressure Ratio Limiter (MCD)
PRL .... Priority Rate Limiting (MCD)
PRL .... Progressive Republican League
PRL .... Project Research Laboratory
PRL .... Prolactin [*Also, LTH, PR*] [*Endocrinology*]

PRL............ Properties Research Laboratory [*Purdue University*] [*Lafayette, IN*]
PRL............ Propulsion Research Laboratory
PRL............ Proton Reference Level [*Chemistry*]
PRL............ Publications Requirements List (NG)
PRLA......... Prairie Religious Library Association
PRLASR.... Population Research Laboratory. University of Alberta. Department of Sociology. Alberta Series Report [*A publication*]
PR Laws..... Laws of Puerto Rico [*A publication*]
PR Laws Ann ... Laws of Puerto Rico, Annotated [*A publication*] (DLA)
PRLC......... Pittsburgh Regional Library Center [*Chatham College*] [*Pittsburgh, PA*] [*Library network*]
PRLDEF.... Puerto Rican Legal Defense and Education Fund (EA)
PRLEA ...... Pracovni Lekarstvi [*A publication*]
PRLI .... Purchase Request Line Item [*DoD*]
PRLINK .... Public Relations Society of America Online Information Service (IID)
PRLKA ...... Przeglad Lekarski [*A publication*]
PRLP .... Planetary Rocket Launcher Platform (AAG)
PRLP .... Puerto Rico Legal Project [*of the National Lawyers Guild*] (EA)
PRLS .... Pima Regional Library Service [*Library network*]
PRLS .... Pulsed Ruby LASER System
PRLST ...... Price List
PRLTA ...... Physical Review. Letters [*A publication*]
PRLTRL & M ... Printer, Lithographer, and Multilith Operator [*Navy*]
PRLW........ Parti des Reformes et de la Liberte de Wallonie [*Belgium*] [*Political party*] (PPW)
PRLWCSR ... Population Research Laboratory. University of Alberta. Department of Sociology. Western Canada Series Report [*A publication*]
PRLX .... Parallax (AAG)
PRLX .... Parlex Corp. [*NASDAQ symbol*] (NQ)
PRM .... Panarim Resources, Inc. [*Vancouver Stock Exchange symbol*]
Prm .... Parmenides [*of Plato*] [*Classical studies*] (OCD)
PRM .... Parsons Mountain [*South Carolina*] [*Seismograph station code, US Geological Survey*] (SEIS)
PRM .... Partial Response Method
PRM .... Partially Reflecting Mirror
PRM .... Partially Regulated Module
PRM .... Payload Retention Mechanism [*NASA*] (NASA)
PRM .... Personal Radiation Monitor
PRM .... Petition [*or Proposal*] for Rule Making (NRCH)
PRM .... Phosphoribomutase [*An enzyme*] (MAE)
PRM .... Photoreceptor Membrane [*Of the eye*]
PRM .... Pilots Radio Manual
PRM .... Pit Rib Meristem [*Botany*]
PRM .... Polski Rocznik Muzykologiczny [*A publication*]
PRM .... Posigrade Rocket Motor (NASA)
PRM .... Power Range Monitor (IEEE)
PRM .... PR Magazin. Public Relations und Informationspolitik in Medien und Gesellschaft [*A publication*]
PRM .... Preformed Road Markings [*Road markings embedded in the pavement rather than painted on street's surface*]
PRM .... Preliminary Requirements Model [*NASA*]
PRM .... Premature [*or Prolonged*] Rupture of Membranes [*Gynecology*] (MAE)
PRM .... Premium
PRM .... Presbyterian Renewal Ministries (EA)
PRM .... Presidential Review Memorandum [*Jimmy Carter Administration*]
PRM .... Pressure Remanent Magnetization
PRM .... Preventive Medicine (MAE)
PRM .... Primary Reference Material [*Medicine*] (MAE)
PRM .... Prime (AAG)
PRM .... Prime Computer, Inc. [*NYSE symbol*] (SPSG)
PRM .... Process Radiation Monitor [*Nuclear energy*] (NRCH)
PRM .... Programmer Reference Manual [*Data processing*]
PRM .... Programming and Resources Management [*NASA*] (MCD)
PRM .... Promote (AABC)
PrM .... Protestantische Monatshefte [*A publication*]
PRM .... Publications Requirements Manager [*DoD*]
PRM .... Pulse Rate Modulation
PRMA ...... Permeator Corp. [*NASDAQ symbol*] (NQ)
PRMA ...... Proceedings. Royal Musical Association [*A publication*]
Pr Mac ...... Prehistoric Macedonia [*A publication*]
PrMan .... Prayer of Manasses [*Apocrypha*] (BJA)
PR of MAN ... [*The*] Prayer of Manasses, King of Judah [*Apocrypha*]
PRMAR...... Primary Mission Area [*Military*] (CAAL)
Pr Mater Pershogo Khark Derzh Med Inst ... Pratsi i Materiali Pershogo Kharkivs'kogo Derzhavnogo Medichnogo Institutu [*A publication*]
PrmBcs ...... Prime Bancshares, Inc. [*Associated Press abbreviation*] (APAG)
PRMC....... Periodically Replenished Magma Chambers [*Geology*]
PRMC....... Puerto Rican Migration Consortium (EA)
Prmca........ Primerica Corp. [*Associated Press abbreviation*] (APAG)
PRMCL...... Periodica de Re Morali Canonica Liturgica [*A publication*]
PRMCLS... Papers. Regional Meeting. Chicago Linguistics Society [*A publication*]

PRME........ Prime Capital Corp. [*Rolling Meadows, IL*] [*NASDAQ symbol*] (NQ)
PRMEA..... Presse Medicale [*A publication*]
Pr Med....... Presse Medicale [*A publication*]
PRMG .... Piston Ring Manufacturers Group [*Later, NEPMA*] (EA)
PRM GR.... Permanent Grade (DNAB)
PRMH ...... Parti Republicain Modere Haitien [*Political party*] (EY)
Prmian .... Permian Basin Royalty Trust [*Associated Press abbreviation*] (APAG)
Pr Min ...... Printed Minutes of Evidence [*A publication*] (DLA)
PR/MIPR ... Purchase Request/Military Interdepartmental Purchase Request (AFIT)
PRMIS ...... Printing Resources Management Information System (DNAB)
PRML........ Partial Response Maximum Likelihood [*Data processing*]
PRMLD..... Premolded [*Technical drawings*] (MSA)
PrMLtd...... Prime Motor Inns Ltd. [*Associated Press abbreviation*] (APAG)
PRMO .... Primo, Inc. [*Phoenix, AZ*] [*NASDAQ symbol*] (NQ)
Pr Molodikh Uch Ukr Akad Sil's'kogospod Nauk ... Pratsi Molodikh Uchenikh Ukrains'ka Akademiya Sil's'kogospodars'kikh Nauk [*A publication*]
PRMP........ Plutonium Recovery Modification Project [*Department of Energy*]
PRMP........ Review of Metaphysics [*A publication*]
PRMR........ Primer (MSA)
PRMSA..... Progress in Materials Science [*A publication*]
PRMSB ..... Proceedings. Royal Microscopical Society [*A publication*]
PRMSC ..... Proceedings. Annual Reliability and Maintainability Symposium [*A publication*]
PRMTR..... Parameter (AAG)
PRMV .... Peach Rosette Mosaic Virus [*Plant pathology*]
PRN .... Greenville, AL [*Location identifier*] [*FAA*] (FAAL)
PRN .... Pahrock Range [*Nevada*] [*Seismograph station code, US Geological Survey*] (SEIS)
PRN .... Partido de Reconstrucao Nacional [*Brazil*] [*Political party*] (EY)
PRN .... Partido Republicano Nacional [*National Republican Party*] [*Costa Rica*] [*Political party*] (EY)
PRN .... Partido de la Resistencia Nicaraguense [*Political party*] (EY)
PRN .... Partido de la Revolucion Nacional [*Party of the National Revolution*] [*Bolivia*] [*Political party*] (PPW)
PRN .... Parts Requirement Notice (KSC)
PRN .... Peace Research Network [*Later, PSA*] (EA)
PRN .... Physicians Radio Network
PRN .... Playfulness, Revelry, Nonsense [*Quarterly Newsletter of Nurses for Laughter*] [*Title is derived from the pharmaceutical term PRN (Pro Re Nata)*] [*A publication*]
PRN .... PR Newswire [*PR Newswire, Inc.*] [*Information service or system*] (IID)
PRN .... Pridie Nonas [*The Day before the Nones*] [*Latin*]
PRN .... Print Numerically (DEN)
PRN .... Printer [*Data processing*]
PRN .... Pristina [*Former Yugoslavia*] [*Airport symbol*] (OAG)
PRN .... Pro Re Nata [*Whenever Necessary*] [*Pharmacy*]
PRN .... Procurement Reallocation Notice
PRN .... Program Release Notice [*NASA*] (NASA)
PRN .... Prominent Resources Corp. [*Vancouver Stock Exchange symbol*]
PRN .... Pronasale [*Anatomy*]
PRN .... Pseudorandom Noise
PRN .... Pseudorandom Number
PRN .... Puerto Rican Cement Co., Inc. [*NYSE symbol*] (SPSG)
PRN .... Pulse Ranging Navigation
PRN .... Pulse Ranging Network (KSC)
PRN .... Purchase Request Number
pRNA........ Ribonucleic Acid, Polysomal [*Biochemistry, genetics*]
Pr Naturwiss Teil 3 ... Praxis der Naturwissenschaften. Teil 3. Chemie [*A publication*]
PRNBA..... Proceedings. Research Institute for Nuclear Medicine and Biology [*A publication*]
PRNC .... Potomac River Naval Command [*Washington, DC*]
PRNC .... Puerto Rico Nuclear Center
PRNC .... Renascence [*A publication*]
PrnDi .... Princeton Diagnostic Laboratories of America, Inc. [*Associated Press abbreviation*] (APAG)
PRNDL...... Park, Reverse, Neutral, Drive, Low [*Automotive term for automatic gearshift indicator in cars; pronounced "prindle"*]
PRNET...... Packet Radio Network
PRNG....... Purging (MSA)
PRNHA..... Professional Nursing Home [*A publication*]
PRNJ........ Project North Journal [*A publication*]
PRNN .... Project North Newsletter [*A publication*]
prnnl......... Perennial [*Botany*]
PRNQ .... Renaissance Quarterly [*A publication*]
PRNT .... Plaque Reduction Neutralization Test [*Immunochemistry*]
PRNTG..... Printing (MSA)
PRNTR..... Printer
PRNTV..... Preventive
PRNU .... Photoresponse Nonuniformity
PRO .... Pacific Research Office (CINC)

PRO .... Parallel Rod Oscillator
PRO .... Parents Rights Organization (EA)
PRO .... Particle Reduction Oven
PRO .... Parts Release Order
PRO .... Patients' Rights Organization (EA)
PRO .... Pay and Records Office [*British military*] (DMA)
PRO .... Peer Review Organization [*Medicare*]
PRO .... Pen Recorder Output (SAA)
PRO .... Performing Rights Organization [*Formerly, BMI-Canada Ltd.*] [*Canada*]
PRO .... Perry, IA [*Location identifier*] [*FAA*] (FAAL)
PRO .... Personnel Relations Officer [*for Shore Stations*] [*Navy*]
PRO .... Pitch Response Operator
PRO .... Planned Requirements, Outfitting [*Navy*] (NG)
PRO .... Planning Resident Order (KSC)
PRO .... Plant Representative Officer (MCD)
PRO .... Population Renewal Office (EA)
Pro............ Prednisone [*Also, P, PDN, PR, Pred*] [*Antineoplastic drug, Endocrinology*]
PRO .... Principal Public Library [*Library network*]
PRO .... Print Octal (DEN)
PRO .... Pro Musica [*A publication*]
PRO .... Probate
PRO .... Probation [*or Probationer*]
PRO .... Problem Resolution Office [*IRS*]
PRO .... Procedure (AABC)
Pro............ Proculus [*Flourished, 1st century*] [*Authority cited in pre-1607 legal work*] (DSA)
PRO .... Procurement Research Office [*Army*]
PRO .... Production Repair Order
PRO .... Produktnieuws voor Kantoor en Bedrijf. Investeringsinformatie voor Managers [*A publication*]
PRO .... Professional
PRO .... Professional Racing Organization of America [*Later, USCF*] (EA)
PRO .... Professional Report [*A publication*]
PRO .... Professional Resellers Organization (EA)
PRO .... Professional Review Organization [*Medicare*]
PRO .... Proficiency
PRO .... Proflavine [*An antiseptic*]
PRO .... Programmable Remote Operation [*Computer Devices, Inc.*]
PRO .... Progressive
Pro............ Proline [*Also, P*] [*An amino acid*]
Pro............ Prolyl [*Biochemistry*]
PRO .... Pronation [*Medicine*]
PRO .... Pronoun [*Grammar*] (WGA)
PRO .... Pronto Explorations Ltd. [*Toronto Stock Exchange symbol*]
PRO .... Propagation [*Military*]
PRO .... Propagation Prediction Report (SAA)
PRO .... Propeller Order
PRO .... Prophylactic (AABC)
PRO .... Prostitute (ADA)
Pro............ Protein
PRO .... Protest
Pro............ Prothrombin [*Factor II*] [*Hematology*]
PRO .... Proved
pro .... Provencal [*MARC language code*] [*Library of Congress*] (LCCP)
Pro............ Proverbs [*Old Testament book*] (BJA)
PRO .... Province (ROG)
PRO .... Provost
PRO .... Public Record Office [*British*]
PRO .... Public Relations Office [*or Officer*] [*Usually military*]
PRO .... Puchase Request Order
PROA .... Polymer Research Corp. of America [*NASDAQ symbol*] (NQ)
PROA .... Puerto Rico Operations Area
Pro Acad Pol Sci (USA) ... Proceedings. Academy of Political Science (USA) [*A publication*]
Pro Am Gas Inst ... Proceedings. American Gas Institute [*A publication*]
ProAOS ..... Proceedings. American Oriental Society [*Baltimore, MD*] [*A publication*]
PROAP...... Principal Regional Office for Asia and the Pacific [*UNESCO*]
Prob........... English Probate and Admiralty Reports for Year Cited [*A publication*] (DLA)
Prob........... Law Reports, Probate Division [*England*] [*A publication*] (DLA)
PROB .... Probability (KSC)
prob........... Probable
PROB .... Probably
Prob........... Probate [*Legal term*] (DLA)
PROB .... Probation [*FBI standardized term*]
PROB .... Problem
Prob........... Quod Omnis Probus Liber Sit [*of Philo*] (BJA)
PROB .... Teleprobe Systems, Inc. [*NASDAQ symbol*] (NQ)
Prob (1891) ... Law Reports, Probate Division [*1891*] [*England*] [*A publication*] (DLA)
Probab Math Stat ... Probability and Mathematical Statistics [*A publication*]
Probab Math Statist ... Probability and Mathematical Statistics [*A publication*]
Prob Actuels ORL ... Problemes Actuels d'Oto-Rhino-Laryngologie [*A publication*]

Prob & Adm Div ... Probate and Admiralty Division Law Reports [*A publication*] (DLA)
Prob Agric Ind Mex ... Problemas Agricolas e Industriales de Mexico [*A publication*]
Probat .... Probation [*Legal term*] (DLA)
Probation & Parole L Rep ... Probation and Parole Law Reports [*A publication*] (DLA)
Probation & Parole L Summ ... Probation and Parole Law Summaries [*A publication*] (DLA)
Probat J ..... Probation Journal [*A publication*] (ILCA)
Prob C .... Probate Code [*A publication*] (DLA)
Prob Com ... Problems of Communism [*A publication*]
Prob Commun ... Problems of Communism [*A publication*]
PROBCOST ... Probabilistic Budgeting and Forward Costing
Prob Ct Rep ... Probate Court Reporter [*Ohio*] [*A publication*] (DLA)
PROBDET ... Probability of Detection [*Navy*] (NVT)
Prob Div ..... Probate Division, English Law Reports [*A publication*] (DLA)
Prob & Div ... Probate and Divorce, English Law Reports [*A publication*] (DLA)
PROBE ...... Performance Review of Base Supply Effectiveness [*Air Force*] (AFM)
PROBE ...... Program Optimization and Budget Evaluation [*Military*]
PROBE ...... Program for Research on Objectives-Based Evaluation [*UCLA*]
Prob Econ .. Problems of Economics [*A publication*]
PROBES ... Processes and Resources of the Bering Sea Shelf [*University of Alaska*]
PROBFOR ... Probability Forecasting [*Computer program*] [*Bell System*]
PROBIT .... Probability Unit [*Statistics*]
Prob J .... Probation Journal [*A publication*] (DLA)
Prob Khig... Problemi na Khigienata [*A publication*]
Probl Actuels Biochim Appl ... Problemes Actuels de Biochimie Appliquee [*A publication*]
Probl Actuels Endocrinol Nutr ... Problemes Actuels d'Endocrinologie et de Nutrition [*A publication*]
Probl Actuels Ophthal ... Problemes Actuels d'Ophthalmologie [*A publication*]
Probl Actuels Otorhinolaryngol ... Problems Actuels d'Otorhinolaryngologie [*A publication*]
Probl Actuels Paediatr ... Problemes Actuels de Paediatrie [*A publication*]
Probl Actuels Phoniatr Logop ... Problemes Actuels de Phoniatrie et Logopedie [*A publication*]
Probl Actuels Psychotherap ... Problemes Actuels de Psychotherapie [*A publication*]
Probl Afr Centr ... Problemes d'Afrique Centrale [*A publication*]
Probl Agr (Bucharest) ... Probleme Agricole (Bucharest) [*A publication*]
Probl Agric ... Probleme Agricole [*A publication*]
Probl Attuali Sci Cult ... Problemi Attuali di Scienza e di Cultura [*A publication*]
Prob Law.... Probate Lawyer [*A publication*]
Probl Biocybern Biomed Eng ... Problems of Biocybernetics and Biomedical Engineering [*A publication*]
Probl Biol... Problems in Biology [*A publication*]
Probl Commu ... Problems of Communism [*A publication*]
Probl Control Inf Theor ... Problems of Control and Information Theory [*A publication*]
Probl Control and Inf Theory ... Problems of Control and Information Theory [*A publication*]
Probl Control and Inf Theory (Engl Transl Pap Rus) ... Problems of Control and Information Theory (English Translation of the Papers in Russian) [*A publication*]
Probl Cybern ... Problems of Cybernetics [*A publication*]
Probl Cybern (USSR) ... Problems of Cybernetics (USSR) [*A publication*]
Probl Desarr ... Problemas del Desarrollo [*A publication*]
Probl Drug Depend ... Problems of Drug Dependence [*A publication*]
Probl Ec ..... Problemes Economiques [*A publication*]
Probl Ecol Biocenol ... Problems of Ecology and Biocenology [*A publication*]
Probl Econ ... Problems of Economics [*A publication*]
Probl Econ (Bucharest) ... Probleme Economice (Bucharest) [*A publication*]
Problemas Bras ... Problemas Brasileiros [*A publication*]
Probleme de Automat ... Probleme de Automatizare [*A publication*]
Probleme Prot Plantelor ... Probleme de Protectia Plantelor [*A publication*]
Problemes Eur ... Problemes de l'Europe [*A publication*]
Problemi Sicurezza Soc ... Problemi della Sicurezza Sociale [*A publication*]
Problemi Tehn Kibernet ... Problemi na Tehniceskata Kibernetika [*Problems of Engineering Cybernetics*] [*A publication*]
Problemi Tekhn Kibernet Robot ... Problemi na Tekhnicheskata Kibernetika i Robotika [*Problems of Engineering Cybernetics and Robotics*] [*A publication*]
Problems Econ ... Problems of Economics [*A publication*]
Problems in Geometry ... Problems in Geometry in the Key Word Index [*Moscow*] [*A publication*]
Problems Inform Transmission ... Problems of Information Transmission [*A publication*]
Problemy Slucain Poiska ... Akademija Nauk Latviiskoi SSR. Institut Elektroniki i Vyceslitel'noi Tehniki. Problemy Slucainogo Poiska [*A publication*]
Probl Entrep Agric ... Problemes de l'Enterprise Agricole [*A publication*]
Probl Farine ... Problemes de Farine [*A publication*]
Probl Farmakol ... Problemi na Farmakologiyata [*A publication*]
Probl Festkoerperelektron ... Probleme der Festkoerperelektronik [*A publication*]

Probl Gestione ... Problemi di Gestione [*A publication*]
Probl Hematol Blood Transfus ... Problems of Hematology and Blood Transfusion [*A publication*]
Probl Hematol Blood Transfus (USSR) ... Problems of Hematology and Blood Transfusion (USSR) [*A publication*]
Probl Inf & Doc ... Probleme de Informare si Documentare [*A publication*]
Probl Inf Docum ... Probleme de Informare si Documentare [*A publication*]
Probl Infect Parasit Dis ... Problems of Infectious and Parasitic Diseases [*A publication*]
Probl Influenza Acute Respir Dis ... Problems of Influenza and Acute Respiratory Diseases [*A publication*]
Probl Inf Transm ... Problems of Information Transmission [*A publication*]
Probl Inf Transm (USSR) ... Problems of Information Transmission (USSR) [*A publication*]
Probl Khig ... Problemi na Khigienata [*A publication*]
Probl Kosm Phys ... Probleme der Kosmichen Physik [*West Germany*] [*A publication*]
Probl Low Temp Phys Thermodyn ... Problems of Low Temperature Physics and Thermodynamics [*A publication*]
Probl Mod Nucl Phys Proc Probl Symp Nucl Phys ... Problems of Modern Nuclear Physics. Proceedings. Problem Symposium on Nuclear Physics [*A publication*]
Probl Morfopatol ... Probleme de Morfopatologie [*A publication*]
Probl Nevrol Psikhiatr Nevrokhir ... Problemi na Nevrologiyata, Psikhiatriyata, i Nevrokhirurgiyata [*A publication*]
Probl North ... Problems of the North [*A publication*]
Probl Onkol (Sofia) ... Problemi na Onkologiyata (Sofia) [*A publication*]
Probl Patol Comp ... Probleme de Patologie Comparata [*A publication*]
Probl Ped ... Problemi della Pedagogia [*A publication*]
Probl Pnevmol Ftiziatr ... Problemi na Pnevmologiyata i Ftiziatriyata [*A publication*]
Probl Polit Soc ... Problemes Politiques et Sociaux [*A publication*]
Probl Prot Plant ... Probleme de Protectia Plantelor [*A publication*]
Probl Rentgenol Radiobiol ... Problemi na Rentgenologiyata i Radiobiologiyata [*A publication*]
Probl Sicur Soc ... Problemi della Sicurezza Sociale [*A publication*]
Probl Social (Milano) ... Problemi del Socialismo (Milano) [*A publication*]
Probl Soc Zair ... Problemes Sociaux Zairois [*A publication*]
Probl Soc Zairois ... Problemes Sociaux Zairois [*A publication*]
Probl Stellar Convect Proc Colloq ... Problems of Stellar Convection. Proceedings. Colloquium [*A publication*]
Probl Stomatol ... Problemi na Stomatologiyata [*A publication*]
Prob LT ...... Probyn on Land Tenure [*4th ed.*] [*1881*] [*A publication*] (DLA)
Probl Ter.... Probleme de Terapeutica [*A publication*]
Probl Zaraznite Parazit Bolesti ... Problemi na Zaraznite i Parazitnite Bolesti [*A publication*]
Probl Zooteh Vet ... Probleme Zootehnice si Veterinare [*A publication*]
Prob & Mat ... Probate and Matrimonial Cases [*A publication*] (DLA)
PROBO ..... Product/Ore/Bulk/Oil Carrier [*Shipping*] (DS)
PROBOUT ... Proceed On or About (MUGU)
Prob Pr Act ... Probate Practice Act [*A publication*] (DLA)
Prob and Prop ... Probate and Property [*A publication*]
Prob R .... Probate Reports [*A publication*] (DLA)
Prob Rep .... Probate Reports [*A publication*] (DLA)
Prob Rep Ann ... Probate Reports, Annotated [*A publication*] (DLA)
PROBSUB ... Probable Submarine (NVT)
PRO Bull Men ... PROSI [*Public Relations Office of the Sugar Industry*] Bulletin Mensuel [*Port Louis*] [*A publication*]
PROBUS... Program Budget System [*Military*]
Proby......... Probationary [*British military*] (DMA)
PROC .... Performing Rights Organization of Canada [*See also SDE*]
PROC .... Preliminary Required Operational Capability [*Military*]
PROC .... Pro-Cel International, Inc. [*NASDAQ symbol*] (NQ)
PROC .... Problems of Communism [*A publication*]
PROC .... Procedure (AAG)
PROC .... Proceedings
Proc............ Procellaria [*A publication*]
PROC .... Process (AABC)
PROC .... Procession (ROG)
PROC .... Processor [*or Processing*]
Proc............ Proclamation (DLA)
PROC .... Proctor
PROC .... Procure (AABC)
PROC .... Procurement (MSA)
PROC .... Programming Computer [*Data processing*]
PROC .... Proposed Required Operational Capability [*Military*] (AABC)
P6ROC ...... P6 Rover Owners Club (EAIO)
ProcAAAS ... Proceedings. American Association for the Advancement of Science [*A publication*]
Proc A Biol Colloq ... Proceedings. Annual Biology Colloquium [*A publication*]
Proc 31 A Blueberry Open House ... Proceedings. 31st Annual Blueberry Open House [*A publication*]
Proc Abstr Soc Biol Chem (Bangalore) ... Proceedings and Abstracts. Society of Biological Chemists (Bangalore) [*A publication*]
Proc Acad Man ... Proceedings. Academy of Management [*A publication*]
Proc Acad Nat Sci Phila ... Proceedings. Academy of Natural Sciences of Philadelphia [*A publication*]
Proc Acad Nat Sci Philadelphia ... Proceedings. Academy of Natural Sciences of Philadelphia [*A publication*]

Proc Acad Pol Sci ... Proceedings. Academy of Political Science [*A publication*]
Proc Acad Sci Armenian SSR ... Proceedings. Academy of Sciences of the Armenian SSR [*A publication*]
Proc Acad Sci Georgian SSR Biol Ser ... Proceedings. Academy of Sciences. Georgian SSR. Biological Series [*A publication*]
Proc Acad Sci United Prov Agra Oudh India ... Proceedings. Academy of Sciences. United Provinces of Agra and Oudh India [*A publication*]
Proc Acad Sci USSR Chem Technol Sect ... Proceedings. Academy of Sciences. USSR. Chemical Technology Section [*A publication*]
Proc Acad Sci USSR Geochem Sect ... Proceedings. Academy of Sciences of the USSR. Geochemistry Section [*A publication*]
Proc Acad Sci USSR Sect Agrochem ... Proceedings. Academy of Sciences of the USSR. Section Agrochemistry [*A publication*]
Proc Acad Sci USSR Sect Appl Phys ... Proceedings. Academy of Sciences of the USSR. Section Applied Physics [*A publication*]
Proc A Conv Am Cranberry Growers' Ass ... Proceedings. Annual Convention. American Cranberry Growers' Association [*A publication*]
Proc Afr Cl Ass ... Proceedings. African Classical Associations [*A publication*]
Proc Afr Classical Assoc ... Proceedings. African Classical Association [*A publication*]
Proc Agric Exp Stn (Palest) ... Proceedings. Agricultural Experiment Station (Palestine) [*A publication*]
Proc Agric Soc (Trinidad Tobago) ... Proceedings. Agricultural Society (Trinidad and Tobago) [*A publication*]
Proc Agron Soc NZ ... Proceedings. Agronomy Society of New Zealand [*A publication*]
Proc Agr Outlook Conf ... Proceedings. Agricultural Outlook Conference [*A publication*]
Proc Agr Pestic Tech Soc ... Proceedings. Agricultural Pesticide Technical Society [*A publication*]
Proc Air Pollut Contr Ass ... Proceedings. Air Pollution Control Association [*A publication*]
Proc Air Pollut Control Assoc ... Proceedings. Air Pollution Control Association [*A publication*]
Proc Alaska Sci Conf ... Proceedings. Alaska Science Conference [*A publication*]
Proc Alberta Sulphur Gas Res Workshop ... Proceedings. Alberta Sulphur Gas Research Workshop [*A publication*]
Proc Alfred Benzon Symp ... Proceedings. Alfred Benzon Symposium [*A publication*]
Proc All Pak Sci Conf ... Proceedings. All Pakistan Science Conference [*A publication*]
Proc Alumni Assoc (Malaya) ... Proceedings. Alumni Association (Malaya) [*A publication*]
Proc Am Acad ... Proceedings. American Academy of Arts and Sciences [*A publication*]
Proc Am Acad Arts Sci ... Proceedings. American Academy of Arts and Sciences [*A publication*]
ProcAmAcAS ... Proceedings. American Academy of Arts and Sciences [*A publication*]
Proc Am Ant Soc ... Proceedings. American Antiquarian Society [*A publication*]
Proc Am Ass Can Res ... Proceedings. American Association for Cancer Research [*A publication*]
Proc Am Assoc Cancer Res ... Proceedings. American Association for Cancer Research [*A publication*]
Proc Am Assoc Cancer Res Am Soc Clin Oncol ... Proceedings. American Association for Cancer Research and American Society of Clinical Oncology [*A publication*]
Proc Am Assoc Cancer Res Annu Meet ... Proceedings. American Association for Cancer Research. Annual Meeting [*A publication*]
Proc Am Assoc Econ Entomol North Cent States Branch ... Proceedings. American Association of Economic Entomologists. North Central States Branch [*A publication*]
Proc Am Assoc State Highw Off ... Proceedings. American Association of State Highway Officials [*A publication*]
Proc Am Chem Soc Symp Anal Calorim ... Proceedings. American Chemical Society Symposium on Analytical Calorimetry [*A publication*]
Proc Am Concr Inst ... Proceedings. American Concrete Institute [*A publication*]
Proc Am Congr Surv Mapp ... Proceedings. American Congress on Surveying and Mapping [*A publication*]
Proc Am Cotton Congr ... Proceedings. American Cotton Congress [*A publication*]
Proc Am Cranberry Grow Assoc ... Proceedings. American Cranberry Growers' Association [*A publication*]
Proc Am Cranberry Growers' Ass ... Proceedings. American Cranberry Growers' Association [*A publication*]
Proc Am Diabetes Assoc ... Proceedings. American Diabetes Association [*A publication*]
Proc Am Doc Inst ... Proceedings. American Documentation Institute [*A publication*]
Proc Am Drug Manuf Assoc Annu Meet ... Proceedings. American Drug Manufacturers Association. Annual Meeting [*A publication*]
Proc A Meet Coun Fertil Applic ... Proceedings. Annual Meeting. Council on Fertilizer Application [*A publication*]

Proc A Meeting Sugar Ind Technicians ... Proceedings. Annual Meeting of Sugar Industry Technicians [*A publication*]
Proc A Meet Pl Physiol Univ MD ... Proceedings. Annual Meeting. American Society of Plant Physiologists at the University of Maryland [*A publication*]
Proc Amer Acad Arts Sci ... Proceedings. American Academy of Arts and Sciences [*A publication*]
Proc Amer Ass State Highw Offic ... Proceedings. American Association of State Highway Officials [*A publication*]
Proc Amer Math Soc ... Proceedings. American Mathematical Society [*A publication*]
Proc Amer Phil Ass ... Proceedings and Addresses. American Philosophical Association [*A publication*]
Proc Amer Philosophical Soc ... Proceedings. American Philosophical Society [*A publication*]
Proc Amer Philos Soc ... Proceedings. American Philosophical Society [*A publication*]
Proc Amer Phil Soc ... Proceedings. American Philosophical Society [*A publication*]
Proc Amer Power Conf ... Proceedings. American Power Conference [*A publication*]
Proc Amer Soc Anim Pro W Sect ... Proceedings. American Society of Animal Production. Western Section [*A publication*]
Proc Amer Soc Anim Sci W Sect ... Proceedings. American Society of Animal Science. Western Section [*A publication*]
Proc Amer Soc Bakery Eng ... Proceedings. American Society of Bakery Engineers [*A publication*]
Proc Amer Soc Brew Chem ... Proceedings. American Society of Brewing Chemists [*A publication*]
Proc Amer Soc Hort Sci ... Proceedings. American Society for Horticultural Science [*A publication*]
Proc Amer Soc of Internat L ... Proceedings. American Society of International Law [*A publication*]   (DLA)
Proc Amer Soc Testing Materials ... Proceedings. American Society for Testing and Materials [*A publication*]
Proc Amer Soc U Composers ... Proceedings. American Society of University Composers [*A publication*]
Proc Amer Wood-Preserv Ass ... Proceedings. American Wood-Preservers' Association [*A publication*]
Proc Am Hortic Congr ... Proceedings. American Horticultural Congress [*A publication*]
Proc Am Inst Electr Eng ... Proceedings. American Institute of Electrical Engineers [*A publication*]
Proc Am Math Soc ... Proceedings. American Mathematical Society [*A publication*]
Proc Am Peanut Res Educ Assoc ... Proceedings. American Peanut Research and Education Association [*A publication*]
Proc Am Pet Inst Div Refining ... Proceedings. American Petroleum Institute. Division of Refining [*A publication*]
Proc Am Pet Inst Refin Dep ... Proceedings. American Petroleum Institute. Refining Department [*A publication*]
Proc Am Pet Inst Sect 1 ... Proceedings. American Petroleum Institute. Section 1 [*A publication*]
Proc Am Pet Inst Sect 2 ... Proceedings. American Petroleum Institute. Section 2. Marketing [*A publication*]
Proc Am Pet Inst Sect 3 ... Proceedings. American Petroleum Institute. Section 3. Refining [*A publication*]
Proc Am Pet Inst Sect 4 ... Proceedings. American Petroleum Institute. Section 4. Production [*A publication*]
Proc Am Pet Inst Sect 5 ... Proceedings. American Petroleum Institute. Section 5. Transportation [*A publication*]
Proc Am Pet Inst Sect 6 ... Proceedings. American Petroleum Institute. Section 6. Interdivisional [*A publication*]
Proc Am Pet Inst Sect 8 ... Proceedings. American Petroleum Institute. Section 8. Science and Technology [*A publication*]
Proc Am Pet Inst Sect 3 Refining ... Proceedings. American Petroleum Institute. Section 3. Refining [*A publication*]
Proc Am Pharm Manuf Assoc Annu Meet ... Proceedings. American Pharmaceutical Manufacturers' Association. Annual Meeting [*A publication*]
Proc Am Pharm Manuf Assoc Midyear East Sect Meet ... Proceedings. American Pharmaceutical Manufacturers' Association. Midyear Eastern Section Meeting [*A publication*]
Proc Am Philos Soc ... Proceedings. American Philosophical Society [*A publication*]
Proc Am Phil Soc ... Proceedings. American Philosophical Society [*A publication*]
Proc Am Phytopathol Soc ... Proceedings. American Phytopathological Society [*A publication*]
Proc Am Power Conf ... Proceedings. American Power Conference [*A publication*]
Proc Am Railw Eng Assoc ... Proceedings. American Railway Engineering Association [*A publication*]
Proc Am Soc Civ Eng ... Proceedings. American Society of Civil Engineers [*A publication*]
Proc Am Soc Civ Eng Transp Eng J ... Proceedings. American Society of Civil Engineers. Transportation Engineering Journal [*A publication*]
Proc Am Soc Clin Oncol Annu Meet ... Proceedings. American Society of Clinical Oncology. Annual Meeting [*A publication*]

Proc Am Soc Enol ... Proceedings. American Society of Enologists [*A publication*]

Proc Am Soc Hortic Sci ... Proceedings. American Society for Horticultural Science [*A publication*]

Proc Am Soc Hort Sci ... Proceedings. American Society for Horticultural Science [*A publication*]

Proc Am Soc Inf Sci ... Proceedings. American Society for Information Science [*A publication*]

Proc Am Soc Test & Mater ... Proceedings. American Society for Testing and Materials [*A publication*]

Proc Am Vet Med Ass ... Proceedings. American Veterinary Medical Association [*A publication*]

Proc Am Vet Med Assoc ... Proceedings. American Veterinary Medical Association [*A publication*]

Proc Am Water Works Assoc ... Proceedings. American Water Works Association [*A publication*]

Proc Am Water Works Assoc Annu Conf ... Proceedings. American Water Works Association Annual Conference [*A publication*]

Proc Am Wood-Preserv Assoc ... Proceedings. American Wood-Preservers' Association [*A publication*]

Proc Anal Div Chem Soc ... Proceedings. Analytical Division. Chemical Society [*A publication*]

Proc Anim Care Panel ... Proceedings. Animal Care Panel [*A publication*]

Proc Ann Conf High En Nucl Phys ... Proceedings. Annual Conference on High Energy Nuclear Physics [*A publication*]

Proc Ann Conf Rehab Eng ... Proceedings. Annual Conference on Rehabilitation Engineering [*A publication*]

Proc Annu AIChE Southwest Ohio Conf Energy Environ ... Proceedings. Annual AIChE [*American Institute of Chemical Engineers*] Southwestern Ohio Conference on Energy and the Environment [*A publication*]

Proc Annu Alberta Soil Sci Workshop ... Proceedings. Annual Alberta Soil Science Workshop [*A publication*]

Proc Annu Allerton Conf Circuit Syst Theory ... Proceedings. Annual Allerton Conference on Circuit and System Theory [*Later, Proceedings. Annual Allerton Conference on Communication, Control, and Computing*] [*A publication*]

Proc Annu Allerton Conf Commun Control Comput ... Proceedings. Annual Allerton Conference on Communication, Control, and Computing [*Formerly, Annual Allerton Conference on Circuit and System Theory*] [*United States*] [*A publication*]

Proc Annu Arkansas Water Works Pollut Control Conf Short Sch ... Proceedings. Annual Arkansas Water Works and Pollution Control Conference and Short School [*A publication*]

Proc Annu Battery Res Dev Conf ... Proceedings. Annual Battery Research and Development Conference [*A publication*]

Proc Annu Biochem Eng Symp ... Proceedings. Annual Biochemical Engineering Symposium [*United States*] [*A publication*]

Proc Annu Biol Colloq (Oreg State Univ) ... Proceedings. Annual Biology Colloquium (Oregon State University) [*A publication*]

Proc Annu Biomed Sci Instrum Symp ... Proceedings. Annual Biomedical Sciences Instrumentation Symposium [*A publication*]

Proc Annu Blueberry Open House ... Proceedings. Annual Blueberry Open House [*A publication*]

Proc Annu Calif Weed Conf ... Proceedings. Annual California Weed Conference [*A publication*]

Proc Annu Cli Spinal Cord Inj Conf ... Proceedings. Annual Clinical Spinal Cord Injury Conference [*A publication*]

Proc Annu Conf Adm Res ... Proceedings. Annual Conference on the Administration of Research [*A publication*]

Proc Annu Conf Agron Soc NZ ... Proceedings. Annual Conference. Agronomy Society of New Zealand [*A publication*]

Proc Annu Conf Autom Control Pet Chem Ind ... Proceedings. Annual Conference on Automatic Control in the Petroleum and Chemical Industries [*A publication*]

Proc Annu Conf Biol Sonar Diving Mamm ... Proceedings. Annual Conference on Biological Sonar and Diving Mammals [*A publication*]

Proc Annu Conf Biol Sonar Diving Mammals ... Proceedings. Annual Conference on Biological Sonar and Diving Mammals [*A publication*]

Proc Annu Conf Can Nucl Assoc ... Proceedings. Annual Conference. Canadian Nuclear Association [*A publication*]

Proc Annu Conf Can Soc Stud Educ Coop Assoc ... Proceedings. Annual Conference. Canadian Society for the Study of Education and Cooperating Associations [*A publication*]

Proc Annu Conf Eff Lithium Doping Silicon Sol Cells ... Proceedings. Annual Conference on Effects of Lithium Doping on Silicon Solar Cells [*A publication*]

Proc Annu Conf Energy Convers Storage ... Proceedings. Annual Conference on Energy Conversion and Storage [*A publication*]

Proc Annu Conf Environ Chem Hum Anim Health ... Proceedings. Annual Conference on Environmental Chemicals. Human and Animal Health [*A publication*]

Proc Annu Conf Ind Appl X Ray Anal ... Proceedings. Annual Conference on Industrial Applications of X-Ray Analysis [*A publication*]

Proc Annu Conf Int Symp N Am Lake Manage Soc ... Proceedings. Annual Conference and International Symposium. North American Lake Management Society [*A publication*]

Proc Annu Conf Kidney ... Proceedings. Annual Conference on the Kidney [*A publication*]

Proc Annu Conf Manitoba Agron ... Proceedings. Annual Conference of Manitoba Agronomists [*A publication*]

Proc Annu Conf MD Del Water Sewage Assoc ... Proceedings. Annual Conference. Maryland-Delaware Water and Sewage Association [*A publication*]

Proc Annu Conf Microbeam Anal Soc ... Proceedings. Annual Conference. Microbeam Analysis Society [*A publication*]

Proc Annu Conf Reinf Plast Compos Inst Soc Plast Ind ... Proceedings. Annual Conference. Reinforced Plastics/Composites Institute. Society of the Plastics Industry [*A publication*]

Proc Annu Conf Res Med Educ ... Proceedings. Annual Conference on Research in Medical Education [*A publication*]

Proc Annu Conf Restor Coastal Veg Fla ... Proceedings. Annual Conference on Restoration of Coastal Vegetation in Florida [*A publication*]

Proc Annu Conf Southeast Assoc Fish Wildl Agencies ... Proceedings. Annual Conference. Southeastern Association of Fish and Wildlife Agencies [*A publication*]

Proc Annu Conf Southeast Assoc Game Fish Comm ... Proceedings. Annual Conference. Southeastern Association of Game and Fish Commissioners [*A publication*]

Proc Annu Conf Steel Cast Res Trade Assoc ... Proceedings. Annual Conference. Steel Castings Research and Trade Association [*A publication*]

Proc Annu Congr S Afr Sugar Technol Assoc ... Proceedings. Annual Congress. South African Sugar Technologists Association [*A publication*]

Proc Annu Connector Symp ... Proceedings. Annual Connector Symposium [*A publication*]

Proc Annu Conv Assoc Am Pestic Control Off ... Proceedings. Annual Convention Association. American Pesticide Control Officials [*A publication*]

Proc Annu Conv Flavoring Ext Manuf Assoc US ... Proceedings. Annual Convention. Flavoring Extract Manufacturers' Association of the United States [*A publication*]

Proc Annu Conv Gas Process Assoc Meet Pap ... Proceedings. Annual Convention. Gas Processors Association. Meeting Papers [*A publication*]

Proc Annu Conv Gas Process Assoc Tech Pap ... Proceedings. Annual Convention. Gas Processors Association. Technical Papers [*A publication*]

Proc Annu Conv Indones Pet Assoc ... Proceedings. Annual Convention. Indonesian Petroleum Association [*A publication*]

Proc Annu Conv Milk Ind Found ... Proceedings. Annual Convention. Milk Industry Foundation [*A publication*]

Proc Annu Conv Nat Gasoline Assoc Am Tech Pap ... Proceedings. Annual Convention. Natural Gasoline Association of America. Technical Papers [*A publication*]

Proc Annu Conv Nat Gas Process Assoc Tech Pap ... Proceedings. Annual Convention. Natural Gas Processors Association. Technical Papers [*United States*] [*A publication*]

Proc Annu Conv Natur Gas Process Ass Tech Pap ... Proceedings. Annual Convention. Natural Gas Processors Association. Technical Papers [*A publication*]

Proc Annu Conv Oil Technol Assoc ... Proceedings. Annual Convention. Oil Technologists Association [*A publication*]

Proc Annu Conv Philipp Sugar Assoc ... Proceedings. Annual Convention. Philippine Sugar Association [*A publication*]

Proc Annu Conv Soc Leather Trades Chem ... Proceedings. Annual Convention. Society of Leather Trades Chemists [*A publication*]

Proc Annu Conv Sugar Technol Assoc India ... Proceedings. Annual Convention. Sugar Technologists' Association of India [*A publication*]

Proc Annu Conv West Can Water Sewage Conf ... Proceedings. Annual Convention. Western Canada Water and Sewage Conference (1960-1975) [*A publication*]

Proc Annu East Theor Phys Conf ... Proceedings. Annual Eastern Theoretical Physics Conference [*A publication*]

Proc Annu Eng Geol Soils Eng Symp ... Proceedings. Annual Engineering Geology and Soils Engineering Symposium [*A publication*]

Proc Annu Eng Geol Symp ... Proceedings. Annual Engineering Geology Symposium [*A publication*]

Proc Annu Environ Water Resour Eng Conf ... Proceedings. Annual Environmental and Water Resources Engineering Conference [*A publication*]

Proc Annu Fall Meet Am Physiol Soc ... Proceedings. Annual Fall Meeting Sponsored by the American Physiological Society [*A publication*]

Proc Annu Fall Meet Calif Nat Gasoline Assoc ... Proceedings. Annual Fall Meeting. California Natural Gasoline Association [*A publication*]

Proc Annu Fall Meet West Gas Process Oil Refin Assoc ... Proceedings. Annual Fall Meeting. Western Gas Processors and Oil Refiners Association [*A publication*]

Proc Annu Fall Meet West Gas Process Oil Refiners Assoc ... Proceedings. Annual Fall Meeting. Western Gas Processors and Oil Refiners Association [*A publication*]

Proc Annu Freq Control Symp ... Proceedings. Annual Frequency Control Symposium [*A publication*]

Proc Annu Hardwood Symp Hardwood Res Counc ... Proceedings. Annual Hardwood Symposium. Hardwood Research Council [*A publication*]

Proc Annu Highw Geol Symp ... Proceedings. Annual Highway Geology Symposium [*A publication*]

Proc Annu Holm Semin Electr Contacts ... Proceedings. Annual Holm Seminar on Electrical Contacts [*A publication*]

Proc Annu Ind Pollut Conf ... Proceedings. Annual Industrial Pollution Conference [*United States*] [*A publication*]

Proc Annu Instrum Conf ... Proceedings. Annual Instrumentation Conference [*A publication*]

Proc Annu Int Conf Can Nucl Assoc ... Proceedings. Annual International Conference. Canadian Nuclear Association [*A publication*]

Proc Annu Int Conf Fault Tolerant Comput ... Proceedings. Annual International Conference on Fault-Tolerant Computing [*A publication*]

Proc Annu Int Conf High Energy Phys ... Proceedings. Annual International Conference on High Energy Physics [*A publication*]

Proc Annu Int Conf Plasma Chem Technol ... Proceedings. Annual International Conference of Plasma Chemistry and Technology [*A publication*]

Proc Annu Int Game Fish Res Conf ... Proceedings. Annual International Game Fish Research Conference [*A publication*]

Proc Annu ISA Anal Instrum Symp ... Proceedings. Annual ISA Analysis Instrumentation Symposium [*A publication*]

Proc Annu Manage Conf Am Dent Assoc ... Proceedings. Annual Management Conference. American Dental Association [*A publication*]

Proc Annu Mar Coat Conf ... Proceedings. Annual Marine Coatings Conference [*A publication*]

Proc Annu Meat Sci Inst ... Proceedings. Annual Meat Science Institute [*A publication*]

Proc Annu Meet Agric Res Inst ... Proceedings. Annual Meeting. Agricultural Research Institute [*A publication*]

Proc Annu Meet Air Pollut Control Assoc ... Proceedings. Annual Meeting. Air Pollution Control Association [*A publication*]

Proc Annu Meet Am Assoc Vet Lab Diagn ... Proceedings. Annual Meeting. American Association of Veterinary Laboratory Diagnosticians [*A publication*]

Proc Annu Meet Am Coll Nutr ... Proceedings. Annual Meeting. American College of Nutrition [*A publication*]

Proc Annu Meet Amer Soc Hort Sci Caribbean Reg ... Proceedings. Annual Meeting. American Society for Horticultural Science. Caribbean Region [*A publication*]

Proc Annu Meet Am Pet Inst ... Proceedings. Annual Meeting. American Petroleum Institute [*A publication*]

Proc Annu Meet Am Psychopathol Assoc ... Proceedings. Annual Meeting. American Psychopathological Association [*A publication*]

Proc Annu Meet Am Sect Int Sol Energy Soc ... Proceedings. Annual Meeting. American Section. International Solar Energy Society [*A publication*]

Proc Annu Meet Am Soc Anim Sci West Sect ... Proceedings. Annual Meeting. American Society of Animal Science. Western Section [*A publication*]

Proc Annu Meet Am Soc Bak Eng ... Proceedings. Annual Meeting. American Society of Bakery Engineers [*A publication*]

Proc Annu Meet Am Soc Inf Sci ... Proceedings. Annual Meeting. American Society for Information Science [*A publication*]

Proc Annu Meet Am Soybean Assoc ... Proceedings. Annual Meeting. American Soybean Association [*A publication*]

Proc Annu Meet Biochem (Hung) ... Proceedings. Annual Meeting of Biochemistry (Hungary) [*A publication*]

Proc Annu Meet Can Nucl Assoc ... Proceedings. Annual Meeting. Canadian Nuclear Association [*A publication*]

Proc Annu Meet Can Soc Agron ... Proceedings. Annual Meeting. Canadian Society of Agronomy [*A publication*]

Proc Annu Meet Can Soc Biomech ... Proceedings. Annual Meeting. Canadian Society for Biomechanics [*A publication*]

Proc Annu Meet Chem Spec Manuf Assoc ... Proceedings. Annual Meeting. Chemical Specialties Manufacturers Association [*A publication*]

Proc Annu Meet Compressed Gas Assoc ... Proceedings. Annual Meeting. Compressed Gas Association [*A publication*]

Proc Annu Meet Conn Pomol Soc ... Proceedings. Annual Meeting. Connecticut Pomological Society [*A publication*]

Proc Annu Meet Contin Educ Lect ... Proceedings. Annual Meeting and Continuing Education Lectures [*A publication*]

Proc Annu Meet Electron Microsc Soc Am ... Proceedings. Annual Meeting. Electron Microscopy Society of America [*A publication*]

Proc Annu Meet Fert Ind Round Table ... Proceedings. Annual Meeting. Fertilizer Industry Round Table [*A publication*]

Proc Annu Meet Fla State Hortic Soc ... Proceedings. Annual Meeting. Florida State Horticultural Society [*A publication*]

Proc Annu Meet Hawaii Sugar Plant Assoc ... Proceedings. Annual Meeting. Hawaiian Sugar Planters Association [*A publication*]

Proc Annu Meeting Amer Soc Int Law ... Proceedings. Annual Meeting. American Society of International Law [*A publication*]

Proc Annu Meet Inst Nucl Mater Manage ... Proceedings. Annual Meeting. Institute of Nuclear Materials Management [*A publication*]

Proc Annu Meet Int Magnesium Assoc ... Proceedings. Annual Meeting. International Magnesium Association [*A publication*]

Proc Annu Meet Jpn Endocrinol Soc ... Proceedings. Annual Meeting. Japan Endocrinological Society [*A publication*]

Proc Annu Meet Lightwood Res Conf ... Proceedings. Annual Meeting. Lightwood Research Conference [*A publication*]

Proc Annu Meet Med Sect Am Counc Life Insur ... Proceedings. Annual Meeting. Medical Section. American Council of Life Insurance [*A publication*]

Proc Annu Meet Med Sect Am Life Conv ... Proceedings. Annual Meeting. Medical Section. American Life Convention [*A publication*]

Proc Annu Meet Med Sect Am Life Insur Assoc ... Proceedings. Annual Meeting. Medical Section. American Life Insurance Association [*A publication*]

Proc Annu Meet Met Powder Assoc ... Proceedings. Annual Meeting. Metal Powder Association [*A publication*]

Proc Annu Meet Nat Assoc Corros Eng ... Proceedings. Annual Meeting. National Association of Corrosion Engineers [*A publication*]

Proc Annu Meet Nat Ass Wheat Growers ... Proceedings. Annual Meeting. National Association of Wheat Growers [*A publication*]

Proc Annu Meet Natl Counc Radiat Prot Meas ... Proceedings. Annual Meeting. National Council on Radiation Protection and Measurements [*United States*] [*A publication*]

Proc Annu Meet Natl Jt Comm Fert Appl ... Proceedings. Annual Meeting. National Joint Committee on Fertilizer Application [*A publication*]

Proc Annu Meet Nat Res Counc Agr Res Inst ... Proceedings. Annual Meeting. National Research Council. Agricultural Research Institute [*A publication*]

Proc Annu Meet N Cent Weed Contr Conf ... Proceedings. Annual Meeting. North Central Weed Control Conference [*A publication*]

Proc Annu Meet NJ ... Proceedings. Annual Meeting. New Jersey Mosquito Extermination Association [*A publication*]

Proc Annu Meet Northeast Weed Sci Soc ... Proceedings. Annual Meeting. Northeastern Weed Science Society [*A publication*]

Proc Annu Meet NY State Hort Soc ... Proceedings. Annual Meeting. New York State Horticultural Society [*A publication*]

Proc Annu Meet Ohio State Hortic Soc ... Proceedings. Annual Meeting. Ohio State Horticultural Society [*A publication*]

Proc Annu Meet Pac Coast Fertil Soc ... Proceedings. Annual Meeting. Pacific Coast Fertility Society [*A publication*]

Proc Annu Meet Soc Promot Agric Sci ... Proceedings. Annual Meeting. Society for the Promotion of Agricultural Science [*A publication*]

Proc Annu Meet Upper Atmos Stud Opt Methods ... Proceedings. Annual Meeting on Upper Atmosphere Studies by Optical Methods [*A publication*]

Proc Annu Meet US Anim Health Assoc ... Proceedings. Annual Meeting. United States Animal Health Association [*A publication*]

Proc Annu Meet Utah Mosq Abatement Assoc ... Proceedings. Annual Meeting. Utah Mosquito Abatement Association [*A publication*]

Proc Annu Meet West Div Am Dairy Sci Assoc ... Proceedings. Annual Meeting. Western Division. American Dairy Science Association [*A publication*]

Proc Annu Meet West Soc Fr Hist ... Proceedings. Annual Meeting. Western Society for French History [*A publication*]

Proc Annu Meet W Farm Econ Ass ... Proceedings. Annual Meeting. Western Farm Economics Association [*A publication*]

Proc Annu Mid-Am Spectrosc Symp ... Proceedings. Annual Mid-America Spectroscopy Symposium [*A publication*]

Proc Annu Midwest Fert Conf ... Proceedings. Annual Midwest Fertilizer Conference [*A publication*]

Proc Annu Nat Dairy Eng Conf ... Proceedings. Annual National Dairy Engineering Conference [*A publication*]

Proc Annu Nat Dairy Food Eng Conf ... Proceedings. Annual National Dairy and Food Engineering Conference [*A publication*]

Proc Annu Northwest Wood Prod Clin ... Proceedings. Annual Northwest Wood Products Clinic [*A publication*]

Proc Annu NSF Trace Contam Conf ... Proceedings. Annual NSF [*National Science Foundation*] Trace Contaminants Conference [*A publication*]

Proc Annu Power Sources Conf ... Proceedings. Annual Power Sources Conference [*A publication*]

Proc Annu Pulp Paper Conf ... Proceedings. Annual Pulp and Paper Conference [*A publication*]

Proc Annu Purdue Air Qual Conf ... Proceedings. Annual Purdue Air Quality Conference [*A publication*]

Proc Annu Recipro Meat Conf Am Meat Sci Assoc ... Proceedings. Annual Reciprocal Meat Conference. American Meat Science Association [*A publication*]

Proc Annu Reliab Maintainability Symp ... Proceedings. Annual Reliability and Maintainability Symposium [*A publication*]

Proc Annu Reliab Maintain Symp ... Proceedings. Annual Reliability and Maintainability Symposium [*A publication*]

Proc Annu Rochester Conf High Energy Nucl Phys ... Proceedings. Annual Rochester Conference on High Energy Nuclear Physics [*A publication*]

Proc Annu Rocky Mount Bioeng Symp ... Proceedings. Annual Rocky Mountain Bioengineering Symposium [*A publication*]

Proc Annu Rocky Mt Bioeng Symp ... Proceedings. Annual Rocky Mountain Bioengineering Symposium [*A publication*]

Proc Annu San Franc Cancer Symp ... Proceedings. Annual San Francisco Cancer Symposium [*A publication*]

Proc Annu Sci Meet Comm Probl Drug Depend US Nat Res Counc ... Proceedings. Annual Scientific Meeting. Committee on Problems of Drug Dependence. United States National Research Council [*A publication*]

Proc Annu Senior Staff Conf USARS ... Proceedings. Annual Senior Staff Conference. United States Agricultural Research Service [*A publication*]

Proc Annu Sess Ceylon Assoc Adv Sci ... Proceedings. Annual Session. Ceylon Association for the Advancement of Science [*A publication*]

Proc Annu Southwest Pet Short Course ... Proceedings. Annual Southwestern Petroleum Short Course [*United States*] [*A publication*]

Proc Annu Stud Conf ... Proceedings. Annual Student Conference [*A publication*]

Proc Annu Symp Eng Geol Soils Eng ... Proceedings. Annual Symposium on Engineering Geology and Soils Engineering [*A publication*]

Proc Annu Symp Eugen Soc ... Proceedings. Annual Symposium of the Eugenics Society [*A publication*]

Proc Annu Symp Freq Control ... Proceedings. Annual Symposium on Frequency Control [*A publication*]

Proc Annu Symp Incremental Motion Control Syst Devices ... Proceedings. Annual Symposium. Incremental Motion Control Systems and Devices [*A publication*]

Proc Annu Symp Ind Waste Control ... Proceedings. Annual Symposium on Industrial Waste Control [*A publication*]

Proc Annu Tall Timbers Fire Ecol Conf ... Proceedings. Annual Tall Timbers Fire Ecology Conference [*A publication*]

Proc Annu Tech Conf Soc Vac Coaters ... Proceedings. Annual Technical Conference. Society of Vacuum Coaters [*A publication*]

Proc Annu Tech Manage Conf Soc Plast Ind Reinf Plast Div ... Proceedings. Annual Technical and Management Conference. Society of the Plastics Industry. Reinforced Plastics Division [*A publication*]

Proc Annu Tech Meet Inst Environ Sci ... Proceedings. Annual Technical Meeting. Institute of Environmental Sciences [*A publication*]

Proc Annu Tech Meet Int Metallogr Soc Inc ... Proceedings. Annual Technical Meeting. International Metallographic Society, Inc. [*A publication*]

Proc Annu Tech Meet Tech Assoc Graphic Arts ... Proceedings. Annual Technical Meeting. Technical Association. Graphic Arts [*A publication*]

Proc Annu Tex Nutr Conf ... Proceedings. Annual Texas Nutrition Conference [*A publication*]

Proc Annu Tung Ind Conv ... Proceedings. Annual Tung Industry Convention [*A publication*]

Proc Annu UMR DNR Conf Energy ... Proceedings. Annual UMR-DNR Conference on Energy [*A publication*]

Proc Annu UMR-MEC Conf Energy ... Proceedings. Annual UMR-MEC [*University of Missouri at Rolla - Missouri Energy Council*] Conference on Energy [*A publication*]

Proc Annu West Tex Oil Lifting Short Course ... Proceedings. Annual West Texas Oil Lifting Short Course [*A publication*]

Proc Annu World Conf Magnesium ... Proceedings. Annual World Conference on Magnesium [*A publication*]

Proc Annu WWEMA Ind Pollut Conf ... Proceedings. Annual WWEMA [*Water and Wastewater Equipment Manufacturers Association*] Industrial Pollution Conference [*United States*] [*A publication*]

Proc APCA Annu Meet ... Proceedings. APCA [*Air Pollution Control Association*] Annual Meeting [*A publication*]

PRO CAPILL ... Pro Capillis [*For the Hair*] [*Pharmacy*]

Proc APREA ... Proceedings. APREA [*American Peanut Research and Education Association*] [*A publication*]

Proc APRES (Am Peanut Res Educ Soc) ... Proceedings. APRES (American Peanut Research and Education Society) [*A publication*]

Proc Aris Soc ... Proceedings. Aristotelian Society [*A publication*]

Proc Ark Acad Sci ... Proceedings. Arkansas Academy of Science [*A publication*]

Proc Arkansas Acad Sci ... Proceedings. Arkansas Academy of Science [*A publication*]

Proc Arkansas Water Works Pollut Control Conf Short Sch ... Proceedings. Arkansas Water Works and Pollution Control Conference and Short School [*A publication*]

Proc ASA ... Proceedings ASA [*A publication*]

Proc Asian Pac Congr Antisepsis ... Proceedings. Asian/Pacific Congress on Antisepsis [*A publication*]

Proc Asian-Pac Congr Cardiol ... Proceedings. Asian-Pacific Congress of Cardiology [*A publication*]

Proc Asiat Soc (Bengal) ... Proceedings. Asiatic Society (Bengal) [*A publication*]

Proc ASIS Annu Meet ... Proceedings. ASIS [*American Society for Information Science*] Annual Meeting [*A publication*]

Proc Ass Asphalt Paving Technol ... Proceedings. Association of Asphalt Paving Technologists [*A publication*]

Proc Ass Econ Biol ... Proceedings. Association of Economic Biologists [*A publication*]

Proc Assoc Asphalt Paving Technol ... Proceedings. Association of Asphalt Paving Technologists [*A publication*]

Proc Assoc Clin Biochem ... Proceedings. Association of Clinical Biochemists [*A publication*]

Proc Assoc Off Seed Anal ... Proceedings. Association of Official Seed Analysts [*A publication*]

Proc Assoc Off Seed Anal (North Am) ... Proceedings. Association of Official Seed Analysts (North America) [*A publication*]

Proc Assoc Plant Prot Kyushu ... Proceedings. Association for Plant Protection of Kyushu [*A publication*]

Proc Assoc South Agric Work ... Proceedings. Association of Southern Agricultural Workers [*A publication*]

Proc Assoc Sugar Technol ... Proceedings. Association of Sugar Technologists [*A publication*]

Proc Ass Offic Seed Anal ... Proceedings. Association of Official Seed Analysts [*A publication*]

Proc Ass Plant Prot Hokuriku ... Proceedings. Association of Plant Protection of Hokuriku [*A publication*]

Proc Ass Plant Prot Kyushu ... Proceedings. Association for Plant Protection of Kyushu [*A publication*]

Proc Ass Res Nerv Ment Dis ... Proceedings. Association for Research in Nervous and Mental Diseases [*A publication*]

Proc Ass S Agr Workers ... Proceedings. Association of Southern Agricultural Workers [*A publication*]

Proc Ass Sth Agric Wkrs ... Proceedings. Association of Southern Agricultural Workers [*A publication*]

Proc ASTM ... Proceedings. American Society for Testing and Materials [*A publication*]

Proc Astron Soc Aust ... Proceedings. Astronomical Society of Australia [*A publication*]

Proc Astr Soc Aust ... Proceedings. Astronomical Society of Australia [*A publication*] (APTA)

Proc Aust Ass Clin Biochem ... Proceedings. Australian Association of Clinical Biochemists [*A publication*] (APTA)

Proc Aust Assoc Neurol ... Proceedings. Australian Association of Neurologists [*A publication*]

Proc Aust Biochem Soc ... Proceedings. Australian Biochemical Society [*A publication*]

Proc Aust Bldg Res Congr ... Australian Building Research Congress. Proceedings [*A publication*] (APTA)

Proc Aust Build Res Congr ... Australian Building Research Congress. Proceedings [*A publication*] (APTA)

Proc Aust Ceram Conf ... Australian Ceramic Conference. Proceedings [*A publication*] (APTA)

Proc Aust Ceramic Conf ... Australian Ceramic Conference. Proceedings [*A publication*] (APTA)

Proc Aust Clay Miner Conf ... Australian Clay Minerals Conference. Proceedings [*A publication*] (APTA)

Proc Aust Comput Conf ... Proceedings. Australian Computer Conference [*A publication*] (APTA)

Proc Aust Conf Nucl Tech Anal ... Australian Conference on Nuclear Techniques of Analysis. Proceedings [*A publication*] (APTA)

Proc Aust Grasslds Conf ... Proceedings. Australian Grasslands Conference [*A publication*] (APTA)

Proc Aust Inst Min and Metall ... Australasian Institute of Mining and Metallurgy. Proceedings [*A publication*] (APTA)

Proc Aust Inst Min Metall ... Proceedings. Australasian Institute of Mining and Metallurgy [*A publication*]

Proc Aust Physiol Pharmacol Soc ... Proceedings. Australian Physiological and Pharmacological Society [*A publication*]

Proc Aust Pulp Pap Ind Tech Assoc ... Proceedings. Australian Pulp and Paper Industry Technical Association [*A publication*]

Proc Australas Conf Radiat Biol ... Proceedings. Australasian Conference on Radiation Biology [*A publication*]

Proc Australasian Poultry Sci Conv ... Proceedings. Australasian Poultry Science Convention [*A publication*]

Proc Australas Inst Min Eng ... Proceedings. Australasian Institute of Mining Engineers [*A publication*]

Proc Australas Inst Min and Metall ... Australasian Institute of Mining and Metallurgy. Proceedings [*A publication*] (APTA)

Proc Australas Inst Min Metall ... Proceedings. Australasian Institute of Mining and Metallurgy [*A publication*]

Proc Aust Road Res Bd ... Australian Road Research Board. Proceedings [*A publication*] (APTA)

Proc Aust Road Research Board ... Australian Road Research Board. Proceedings [*A publication*] (APTA)

Proc Aust Soc Anim Prod ... Proceedings. Australian Society of Animal Production [*A publication*]

Proc Aust Soc Med Res ... Proceedings. Australian Society for Medical Research [*A publication*]

Proc Aust Soc Sugar Cane Technol ... Proceedings. Australian Society of Sugar Cane Technologists [*A publication*]

Proc Aust Weed Conf ... Proceedings. Australian Weed Conference [*A publication*]

Proc Auto Div Instn Mech Engrs ... Proceedings. Institution of Mechanical Engineers. Auto Division [*A publication*]

Proc AWWA Annu Conf ... Proceedings. AWWA [*American Water Works Association*] Annual Conference [*A publication*]

Proc Bakish Mater Corp Publ ... Proceedings. Bakish Materials Corp. Publication [*A publication*]

Proc B & B ... Proctor's Bench and Bar of New York [*A publication*] (DLA)

Proc Belg Congr Anesthesiol ... Proceedings. Belgian Congress of Anesthesiology [*A publication*]

Proc Beltwide Cotton Prod Res Conf ... Proceedings. Beltwide Cotton Production Research Conferences [*A publication*]

Proc Berkeley Symp Math Stat Probab ... Proceedings. Berkeley Symposium on Mathematical Statistics and Probability [*A publication*]

Proc Bewickwhire Nat Club ... Proceedings. Berwickshire Naturalists Club [*A publication*]

Proc Bienn Conf Inst Briquet Agglom ... Proceedings. Biennial Conference. Institute for Briquetting and Agglomeration [*A publication*]

Proc Bienn Conf Int Briquet Assoc ... Proceedings. Biennial Conference. International Briquiting Association [*A publication*]

Proc Bienn Gas Dyn Symp ... Proceedings. Biennial Gas Dynamics Symposium [*A publication*]

Proc Bienn Int Estuarine Res Conf ... Proceedings. Biennial International Estuarine Research Conference [*A publication*]

Proc Bienn Symp Turbul Liq ... Proceedings. Biennial Symposium on Turbulence in Liquids [*A publication*]

Proc Bihar Acad Agric Sci ... Proceedings. Bihar Academy of Agricultural Sciences [*A publication*]

Proc Bihar Acad Agr Sci ... Proceedings. Bihar Academy of Agricultural Sciences [*A publication*]

Proc Biol Soc Wash ... Proceedings. Biological Society of Washington [*A publication*]

Proc Bird Control Semin ... Proceedings. Bird Control Seminar [*A publication*]

Proc Bolton Landing Conf ... Proceedings. Bolton Landing Conference [*A publication*]

Proc Bos Soc ... Proceedings. Bostonian Society [*A publication*]

Proc Bot Soc Br Isles ... Proceedings. Botanical Society of the British Isles [*A publication*]

Proc Br Acad ... Proceedings. British Academy [*A publication*]

Proc Br Acoust Soc ... Proceedings. British Acoustical Society [*A publication*]

Proc Br Assoc Refrig ... Proceedings. British Association for Refrigeration [*A publication*]

Proc Br Ceram Soc ... Proceedings. British Ceramic Society [*A publication*]

Proc Br Crop Prot Conf ... Proceedings. 1980 British Crop Protection Conference. Weeds [*A publication*]

Proc Bristol Nat Soc ... Proceedings. Bristol Naturalists Society [*A publication*]

Proc Brit Ac ... Proceedings. British Academy [*A publication*]

Proc Brit Acad ... Proceedings. British Academy [*A publication*] (OCD)

Proc Brit Acad ... Proceedings. British Academy [*A publication*]

Proc Brit Ceram Soc ... Proceedings. British Ceramic Society [*A publication*]

Proc Brit Insectic Fungic Conf ... Proceedings. British Insecticide and Fungicide Conference [*A publication*]

Proc British Asso Ja Stud ... Proceedings. British Association for Japanese Studies [*A publication*]

Proc Brit Weed Contr Conf ... Proceedings. British Weed Control Conference [*A publication*]

Proc Brown Univ Symp Biol Skin ... Proceedings. Brown University Symposium on the Biology of Skin [*A publication*]

Proc Br Paedod Soc ... Proceedings. British Paedodontic Society [*A publication*]

Proc Br Soc Anim Prod ... Proceedings. British Society of Animal Production [*A publication*]

Proc Br Weed Control Conf ... Proceedings. British Weed Control Conference [*A publication*]

Proc Br West Indies Sugar Technol Conf ... Proceedings. British West Indies Sugar Technologists Conference [*A publication*]

Proc Buffalo Milan Symp Mol Pharmacol ... Proceedings. Buffalo-Milan Symposium on Molecular Pharmacology [*A publication*]

Proc Calif Acad Nat Sci ... Proceedings. California Academy of Natural Sciences [*A publication*]

Proc Calif Acad Sci ... Proceedings. California Academy of Sciences [*A publication*]

Proc Calif Ann Weed Conf ... Proceedings. California Annual Weed Conference [*A publication*]

Proc Calif Weed Conf ... Proceedings. California Weed Conference [*A publication*]

Proc Calif Zool Club ... Proceedings. California Zoological Club [*A publication*]

Proc Camb Philos Soc ... Proceedings. Cambridge Philosophical Society [*A publication*]

Proc Camb Phil Soc Math Phys Sci ... Proceedings. Cambridge Philosophical Society. Mathematical and Physical Sciences [*A publication*]

Proc Cambridge Antiq Soc ... Proceedings. Cambridge Antiquarian Society [*A publication*]

Proc Cambridge Ant Soc ... Proceedings. Cambridge Antiquarian Society [*A publication*]

Proc Cambridge Philos Soc ... Proceedings. Cambridge Philosophical Society [*A publication*]

Proc Cambridge Phil Soc ... Proceedings. Cambridge Philological Society [*A publication*]

Proc Cambr Phil Soc ... Proceedings. Cambridge Philological Society [*A publication*]

Proc Canad Oto Soc ... Proceedings. Canadian Otolaryngological Society [*A publication*]

Proc Can Cancer Res Conf ... Proceedings. Canadian Cancer Research Conference [*A publication*]

Proc Can Centen Wheat Symp ... Proceedings. Canadian Centennial Wheat Symposium [*A publication*]

Proc Can Fed Biol Soc ... Proceedings. Canadian Federation of Biological Societies [*A publication*]

Proc Can Natl Power Alcohol Conf ... Proceedings. Canadian National Power Alcohol Conference [*A publication*]

Proc Can Nat Weed Comm E Sect ... Proceedings. Canadian National Weed Committee. Eastern Section [*A publication*]

Proc Can Nat Weed Comm W Sect ... Proceedings. Canadian National Weed Committee. Western Section [*A publication*]

Proc Can Nucl Assoc Annu Int Conf ... Proceedings. Canadian Nuclear Association Annual International Conference [*A publication*]

Proc Can Phytopathol Soc ... Proceedings. Canadian Phytopathological Society [*A publication*]

Proc Can Rock Mech Symp ... Proceedings. Canadian Rock Mechanics Symposium [*A publication*]

Proc Can Soc Forensic Sci ... Proceedings. Canadian Society of Forensic Science [*A publication*]

Proc Can Soc Pl Physiol ... Proceedings. Canadian Society of Plant Physiologists [*A publication*]

Proc Cardiff Med Soc ... Proceedings. Cardiff Medical Society [*A publication*]

Proc Caribb Reg Am Soc Hort Sci ... Proceedings. Caribbean Region. American Society for Horticultural Science [*A publication*]

Proc Cath ... Proceedings. Catholic Theological Society of America [*A publication*]

Proc Cath Phil Ass ... Proceedings. American Catholic Philosophical Association [*A publication*]

Proc Cellul Conf ... Proceedings. Cellulose Conference [*A publication*]

Proc Ch ...... Proceedings in Chancery [*A publication*] (DLA)

Proc Chem Soc ... Proceedings. Chemical Society [*A publication*]

Proc Chem Soc (London) ... Proceedings. Chemical Society (London) [*A publication*]

Proc Chin Physiol Soc Chengtu Branch ... Proceedings. Chinese Physiological Society. Chengtu Branch [*A publication*]

PROCCIR ... Procurement Circular [*Air Force*] (AFIT)

Proc Clin Dial Transplant Forum ... Proceedings. Clinical Dialysis and Transplant Forum [*A publication*]

Proc Clin Res Cent Symp ... Proceedings. Clinical Research Centre Symposium [*A publication*]

Proc Coal Mining Inst Amer ... Proceedings. Coal Mining Institute of America [*A publication*]

Proc Coll Med Univ Philipp ... Proceedings. College of Medicine. University of the Philippines [*A publication*]

Proc Coll Nat Sci Sect 4 Biol Sci Seoul Natl Univ ... Proceedings. College of Natural Sciences. Section 4. Biological Sciences. Seoul National University [*A publication*]

Proc Coll Nat Sci Sect 2 Seoul Nat Univ ... Proceedings. College of Natural Sciences. Section 2. Physics, Astronomy. Seoul National University [*A publication*]

Proc Coll Nat Sci Sect 3 Seoul Nat Univ ... Proceedings. College of Natural Sciences. Section 3. Chemistry. Seoul National University [*A publication*]

Proc Coll Nat Sci Sect 4 Seoul Nat Univ ... Proceedings. College of Natural Sciences. Section 4. Life Sciences. Seoul National University [*A publication*]

Proc Coll Nat Sci Sect 5 Seoul Nat Univ ... Proceedings. College of Natural Sciences. Section 5. Geology, Meteorology, and Oceanography. Seoul National University [*A publication*]

Proc Coll Nat Sci (Seoul) ... Proceedings. College of Natural Sciences (Seoul) [*A publication*]

Proc Coll Nat Sci Seoul Natl Univ ... Proceedings. College of Natural Sciences. Seoul National University [*A publication*]

Proc Colloq Int Potash Inst ... Proceedings. Colloquium of the International Potash Institute [*A publication*]

Proc Colloq Spectrosc Int ... Proceedings. Colloquium Spectroscopicum Internationale [*A publication*]

Proc Commonw Min Metall Congr ... Proceedings. Commonwealth Mining and Metallurgical Congress [*A publication*]

Proc Conf Appl Small Accel ... Proceedings. Conference on Application of Small Accelerators [*A publication*]

Proc Conf Aust Road Res Board ... Proceedings. Conference of the Australian Road Research Board [*A publication*]

Proc Conf Aust Soc Sugar Cane Technol ... Australian Society of Sugar Cane Technologists. Proceedings of the Conference [*A publication*] (APTA)

Proc Conf Des Exp Army Res Dev Test ... Proceedings. Conference on the Design of Experiments in Army Research Development and Testing [*A publication*]

Proc Conf Eng Med Biol ... Proceedings. Conference of Engineering in Medicine and Biology [*A publication*]

Proc Conf Fluid Mach ... Proceedings. Conference on Fluid Machinery [*A publication*]

Proc Conf Great Lakes Res ... Proceedings. Conference on Great Lakes Research [*A publication*]

Proc Conf Hot Lab Equip ... Proceedings. Conference on Hot Laboratories and Equipment [*A publication*]

Proc Conf (Int) Solid State Devices ... Proceedings. Conference (International) on Solid State Devices [*A publication*]

Proc Conf Ion Plat Allied Tech ... Proceedings. Conference. Ion Plating and Allied Techniques [*A publication*]
Proc Conf NZ Grassl Assoc ... Proceedings. Conference. New Zealand Grassland Association [*A publication*]
Proc Conf Remote Syst Technol ... Proceedings. Conference on Remote Systems Technology [*A publication*]
Proc Conf Silic Ind ... Proceedings. Conference on the Silicate Industry [*A publication*]
Proc Conf Solid State Devices ... Proceedings. Conference on Solid State Devices [*A publication*]
Proc Conf Toxicol ... Proceedings. Conference on Toxicology [*A publication*]
Proc Congenital Anomalies Res Assoc Annu Rep ... Proceedings. Congenital Anomalies. Research Association. Annual Report [*A publication*]
Proc Cong Mediterr Phytopathol Union ... Proceedings. Congress of the Mediterranean Phytopathological Union [*A publication*]
Proc Congr Ann Corp Ingen For (Quebec) ... Proceedings. Congres Annuel. Corp. des Ingenieurs Forestiers (Quebec) [*A publication*]
Proc Congr Eur Organ Res Fluorine Dent Caries Prev ... Proceedings. Congress. European Organization for Research on Fluorine and Dental Caries Prevention [*A publication*]
Proc Congr Eur Soc Haematol ... Proceedings. Congress of the European Society of Haematology [*A publication*]
Proc Congr Fed Int Precontrainte ... Proceedings. Congress of the Federation Internationale de la Precontrainte [*A publication*]
Proc Congr Hung Assoc Microbiol ... Proceedings. Congress of the Hungarian Association of Microbiologists [*A publication*]
Proc Congr Int Assoc Sci Study Ment Defic ... Proceedings. Congress of the International Association for the Scientific Study of Mental Deficiency [*A publication*]
Proc Congr Int Comm Opt ... Proceedings. Congress of the International Commission for Optics [*A publication*]
Proc Congr Int Potash Inst ... Proceedings. Congress of the International Potash Institute [*A publication*]
Proc Congr Int Radiat Prot Soc ... Proceedings. Congress. International Radiation Protection Society [*A publication*]
Proc Congr Int Soc Blood Transf ... Proceedings. Congress of the International Society of Blood Transfusion [*A publication*]
Proc Congr Int Soc Blood Transfus ... Proceedings. Congress of the International Society of Blood Transfusion [*A publication*]
Proc Congr Int Soc Sugar Cane Technol ... Proceedings. Congress of the International Society of Sugar Cane Technologists [*A publication*]
Proc Congr Int Union For Res Organ ... Proceedings. Congress of the International Union of Forest Research Organizations [*A publication*]
Proc Congr Jpn Soc Cancer Ther ... Proceedings. Congress of the Japan Society for Cancer Therapy [*A publication*]
Proc Congr Obes ... Proceedings. Congress of Obesity [*A publication*]
Proc Congr S Afr Genet Soc ... Proceedings. Congress of the South African Genetic Society [*A publication*]
Proc Congr S Afr Sug Technol Ass ... Proceedings. Congress of the South African Sugar Technologists' Association [*A publication*]
Proc Conv Int Assoc Fish Wildl Agencies ... Proceedings. Convention. International Association of Fish and Wildlife Agencies [*A publication*]
Proc Cornell Nutr Conf Feed Mfr ... Proceedings. Cornell Nutrition Conference for Feed Manufacturers [*A publication*]
Proc Cosmic-Ray Res Lab Nagoya Univ ... Proceedings. Cosmic-Ray Research Laboratory. Nagoya University [*A publication*]
Proc Cotteswold Natur Fld Club ... Proceedings. Cotteswold Naturalists' Field Club [*A publication*]
Proc Cotton Dust Res Conf Beltwide Cotton Prod Res Conf ... Proceedings. Cotton Dust Research Conference. Beltwide Cotton Production Research Conferences [*A publication*]
Proc Counc Econ AIME ... Proceedings. Council of Economics. American Institute of Mining, Metallurgical, and Petroleum Engineers [*A publication*]
Proc Coventry Dist Natur Hist Sci Soc ... Proceedings. Coventry District Natural History and Scientific Society [*A publication*]
Proc Crayford Manor House Hist Archaeol Soc ... Proceedings. Crayford Manor House Historical and Archaeological Society [*A publication*]
Proc Crop Sci Chugoku Br Crop Sci Soc ... Proceedings. Crop Science. Chugoku Branch of the Crop Science Society [*A publication*]
Proc Crop Sci Soc Jap ... Proceedings. Crop Science Society of Japan [*A publication*]
Proc Crop Sci Soc Jpn ... Proceedings. Crop Science Society of Japan [*A publication*]
Proc Croydon Nat Hist Sci Soc ... Proceedings. Croydon Natural History Science Society [*A publication*]
ProcCTS .... Proceedings. College Theology Society [*A publication*]
ProcCTSA ... Proceedings. Catholic Theological Society of America [*A publication*]
Proc Cumberland Geol Soc ... Proceedings. Cumberland Geological Society [*A publication*]
PROCD ..... Procedure (AFM)
PROCD ..... Proceed (AFM)
PROCD ..... Processing [*Johannesburg*] [*A publication*]

Proc Dep Hortic Plant Health Massey Univ ... Proceedings. Department of Horticulture and Plant Health. Massey University [*A publication*]
Proc Devon Archaeol Soc ... Proceedings. Devon Archaeological Society [*A publication*]
Proc Devon Arch Expl Soc ... Proceedings. Devon Archaeological Exploration Society [*A publication*]
Proc Devon Arch Soc ... Proceedings. Devon Archaeological Society [*A publication*]
Proc Discuss Int Plast Congr ... Proceedings and Discussions. International Plastics Congress [*A publication*]
Proc Distill Feed Conf ... Proceedings. Distillers Feed Conference [*A publication*]
Proc Distill Feed Res Counc Conf ... Proceedings. Distillers Feed Research Council Conference [*A publication*]
Proc Divers' Gas Purity Symp ... Proceedings. Divers' Gas Purity Symposium [*A publication*]
Proc Div Refin Am Pet Inst ... Proceedings. Division of Refining. American Petroleum Institute [*A publication*]
Proc Dorset Natur Hist Archaeol Soc ... Proceedings. Dorset Natural History and Archaeological Society [*A publication*]
Proc Dorset Natur Hist Arch Soc ... Proceedings. Dorset Natural History and Archaeological Society [*A publication*]
Proc Dorset Soc ... Dorset Natural History and Archaeological Society. Proceedings [*A publication*]
PROCDRE ... Procedure (ROG)
Proc East Afr Acad ... Proceedings. East African Academy [*A publication*]
Proc Easter Sch Agric Sci Univ Nottingham ... Proceedings. Easter School in Agricultural Science. University of Nottingham [*England*] [*A publication*]
Proc Ecol Soc Aust ... Proceedings. Ecological Society of Australia [*A publication*]
PROCED ... Procedure
Proc Edinburgh Math Soc ... Proceedings. Edinburgh Mathematical Society [*A publication*]
Proc Edinburgh Math Soc 2 ... Proceedings. Edinburgh Mathematical Society. Series 2 [*A publication*]
Proc Edinburgh Math Soc Edinburgh Math Notes ... Proceedings. Edinburgh Mathematical Society. Edinburgh Mathematical Notes [*A publication*]
Proceedings of the IEEE ... Proceedings. Institute of Electrical and Electronics Engineers [*A publication*]
Proceedings NAPEHE ... Proceedings. National Association for Physical Education in Higher Education [*A publication*]
Proceedings NIRSA ... Proceedings. National Intramural Recreational Sports Association [*A publication*]
Proceedings SBA ... Proceedings. Society of Biblical Archaeology [*A publication*]
Proceedngs ... Proceedings. United States Naval Institute [*A publication*]
Proceed R Philos Soc of Glasgow ... Proceedings. Royal Philosophical Society of Glasgow [*A publication*]
Proc EGAS Conf Eur Group At Spectrosc ... Proceedings. EGAS Conference. European Group for Atomic Spectroscopy [*A publication*]
Proc Egypt Acad Sci ... Proceedings. Egyptian Academy of Sciences [*A publication*]
Proc Eighth Br Weed Control Conf ... Proceedings. Eighth British Weed Control Conference [*A publication*]
Proc Elec Assoc Aust ... Proceedings. Electrical Association of Australia [*A publication*]
Proc Elec Assoc NSW ... Proceedings. Electrical Association of New South Wales [*Australia*] [*A publication*]
Proc Electron Components Conf ... Proceedings. Electronic Components Conference [*A publication*]
Proc Electron Microsc Soc Am ... Proceedings. Electron Microscopy Society of America [*A publication*]
Proc Electron Microsc Soc South Afr ... Proceedings. Electron Microscopy Society of Southern Africa [*A publication*]
Proc Endoc Soc Aust ... Proceedings. Endocrine Society of Australia [*A publication*] (APTA)
Proc Energy Resour Conf ... Proceedings. Energy Resource Conference [*A publication*]
Proc Eng Assoc NSW ... Proceedings. Engineering Association of New South Wales [*Australia*] [*A publication*]
Proc Eng Soc Hong Kong ... Proceedings. Engineering Society of Hong Kong [*A publication*]
Proc Eng Soc West PA ... Proceedings. Engineers' Society of Western Pennsylvania [*A publication*]
Proc Entomol Soc Amer N Cent Br ... Proceedings. Entomological Society of America. North Central Branch [*A publication*]
Proc Entomol Soc BC ... Proceedings. Entomological Society of British Columbia [*A publication*]
Proc Entomol Soc Brit Columbia ... Proceedings. Entomological Society of British Columbia [*A publication*]
Proc Entomol Soc Manit ... Proceedings. Entomological Society of Manitoba [*A publication*]
Proc Entomol Soc Manitoba ... Proceedings. Entomological Society of Manitoba [*A publication*]
Proc Entomol Soc Ont ... Proceedings. Entomological Society of Ontario [*A publication*]
Proc Entomol Soc Ontario ... Proceedings. Entomological Society of Ontario [*A publication*]

Proc Entomol Soc Wash ... Proceedings. Entomological Society of Washington [*A publication*]

Proc Entomol Soc Wash DC ... Proceedings. Entomological Society of Washington, DC [*A publication*]

Proc Ent Soc Br Columb ... Proceedings. Entomological Society of British Columbia [*A publication*]

Proc Ent Soc Manitoba ... Proceedings. Entomological Society of Manitoba [*A publication*]

Proc Ent Soc Ont ... Proceedings. Entomological Society of Ontario [*A publication*]

Proc Ent Soc Wash ... Proceedings. Entomological Society of Washington [*A publication*]

Proc Environ Eng Sci Conf ... Proceedings. Environmental Engineering and Science Conference [*A publication*]

Proc ERDA Air Clean Conf ... Proceedings. ERDA [*Office of Exploratory Research and Problem Assessment*] Air Cleaning Conference [*A publication*]

Pro CERN Sch Comput ... Proceedings. CERN [*Conseil Europeen pour la Recherche Nucleaire*] School of Computing [*A publication*]

Process Archre ... Process Architecture [*A publication*]

Process Autom ... Process Automation [*A publication*]

Process Bio ... Process Biochemistry [*A publication*]

Process Biochem ... Process Biochemistry [*A publication*]

Process Chem Eng ... Process and Chemical Engineering [*A publication*]

Process Control Autom ... Process Control and Automation [*A publication*]

Process Des Dev ... Process Design and Development [*A publication*]

Process Econ Int ... Process Economics International [*A publication*]

Process Eng ... Process Engineering [*A publication*]

Process Eng Mag ... Process Engineering Magazine [*A publication*]

Process Engng ... Process Engineering [*A publication*]·

Process Eng Plant and Control ... Process Engineering. Plant and Control [*A publication*]

Process Engravers Mon ... Process Engravers Monthly [*A publication*]

Process Instrum ... Process Instrumentation [*A publication*]

Process Metall ... Process Metallurgy [*A publication*]

Process Ser Okla State Univ Agr Exp Sta ... Processed Series. Oklahoma State University. Agricultural Experimental Station [*A publication*]

Process St .. Process Studies [*A publication*]

Process Stud ... Process Studies [*A publication*]

Process Technol Int ... Process Technology International [*A publication*]

Proc Eur Conf Mixing ... Proceedings. European Conference on Mixing [*A publication*]

Proc Eur Conf Surf Sci ... Proceedings. European Conference on Surface Science [*A publication*]

Proc Eur Dial Transplant Assoc ... Proceedings. European Dialysis and Transplant Association [*A publication*]

Proc Eur Dial Transplant Assoc Eur Renal Assoc ... Proceedings. European Dialysis and Transplant Association - European Renal Association [*A publication*]

Proc Eur Mar Biol Symp ... Proceedings. European Marine Biology Symposium [*A publication*]

Proc Eur Prosthodontic Assoc ... Proceedings. European Prosthodontic Association [*A publication*]

Proc Eur Soc Artif Organs Annu Meet ... Proceedings. European Society for Artificial Organs. Annual Meeting [*A publication*]

Proc Eur Soc Toxicol ... Proceedings. European Society of Toxicology [*A publication*]

Proc Eur Symp Mar Biol ... Proceedings. European Symposium on Marine Biology [*A publication*]

Proc Fac Agric Kyushu Tokai Univ ... Proceedings. Faculty of Agriculture. Kyushu Tokai University [*A publication*]

Proc Fac Eng Keiogijuku Univ ... Proceedings. Faculty of Engineering. Keiogijuku University [*A publication*]

Proc Fac Eng Kyushu Univ ... Proceedings. Faculty of Engineering. Kyushu University [*A publication*]

Proc Fac Eng Tokai Univ ... Proceedings. Faculty of Engineering. Tokai University [*Japan*] [*A publication*]

Proc Fac Sci Tokai Univ ... Proceedings. Faculty of Science. Tokai University [*Japan*] [*A publication*]

Proc Farm Seed Conf ... Proceedings. Farm Seed Conference [*A publication*]

Proc FEBS Meet ... Proceedings. FEBS [*Federation of European Biochemical Societies*] Meeting [*A publication*]

Proc Fert Assoc India Tech Ser ... Proceedings. Fertiliser Association of India. Tech Series [*A publication*]

Proc Fertil Soc ... Proceedings. Fertilizer Society [*A publication*]

Proc Finn Dent Soc ... Proceedings. Finnish Dental Society of Washington [*A publication*]

Proc Finn US Jt Symp Occup Saf Health Swed Participation ... Proceedings. Finnish-US Joint Symposium on Occupational Safety and Healty with Swedish Participation [*A publication*]

Proc First Livest Ocean Conf ... Proceedings. First Livestock by Ocean Conference [*A publication*]

Proc Fla Acad Sci ... Proceedings. Florida Academy of Sciences [*A publication*]

Proc Fla Anti-Mosq ... Proceedings. Florida Anti-Mosquito Association [*A publication*]

Proc Fla Lychee Grow Ass ... Proceedings. Florida Lychee Growers Association [*A publication*]

Proc Fla State Hortic Soc ... Proceedings. Florida State Horticultural Society [*A publication*]

Proc Fla State Hort Soc ... Proceedings. Florida State Horticultural Society [*A publication*]

Proc Fla St Hort Soc ... Proceedings. Florida State Horticultural Society [*A publication*]

Proc Florida State Hortic Soc ... Florida. State Horticultural Society. Proceedings [*A publication*]

Proc Food ... Processed Prepared Food [*A publication*]

Proc For Microclim Symp Can Dep Fish For ... Proceedings. Forest Microclimate Symposium. Canada Department of Fisheries and Forestry [*A publication*]

Proc For Prod Res Soc ... Proceedings. Forest Products Research Society [*A publication*]

Proc For Symp LA Sch For ... Proceedings. Annual Forestry Symposium. Louisiana State University. School of Forestry and Wildlife Management [*A publication*]

Proc Forum Fundam Surg Probl Clin Congr Am Coll Surg ... Proceedings. Forum on Fundamental Surgical Problems. Clinical Congress of the American College of Surgeons [*A publication*]

Proc Found Orthod Res ... Proceedings. Foundation for Orthodontic Research [*A publication*]

Proc (Fourth) NZ Geogr Conf ... Proceedings. (Fourth) New Zealand Geographical Conference [*A publication*]

Proc FPLC Symp ... Proceedings. FPLC [*Fast Protein, Polypeptide, and Polynucleotide Liquid Chromatography*] Symposium [*A publication*]

Proc FRI Symp For Res Inst NZ For Serv ... Proceedings. FRI Symposium. Forest Research Institute. New Zealand Forest Service [*A publication*]

Proc Front Educ Conf ... Proceedings. Frontiers in Education Conference [*A publication*]

Proc Fujihara Mem Fac Eng Keio Univ ... Proceedings. Fujihara Memorial Faculty of Engineering. Keio University [*A publication*]

Proc Fujihara Mem Fac Eng Keio Univ (Tokyo) ... Proceedings. Fujihara Memorial Faculty of Engineering. Keio University (Tokyo) [*A publication*]

Proc Fusion Fission Energy Syst Rev Meet ... Proceedings. Fusion/Fission Energy Systems Review Meeting [*A publication*]

Proc Gas Cond Conf ... Proceedings. Gas Conditioning Conference [*United States*] [*A publication*]

Proc Genet Soc Can ... Proceedings. Genetics Society of Canada [*A publication*]

Proc Gen Meet Soc Ind Microbiol ... Proceedings. General Meeting of the Society for Industrial Microbiology [*A publication*]

Proc Geoinst ... Proceedings. Geoinstitut [*A publication*]

Proc Geol Ass ... Proceedings. Geological Association [*A publication*]

Proc Geol Ass Can ... Proceedings. Geological Association of Canada [*A publication*]

Proc Geol Assoc ... Proceedings. Geologists' Association [*A publication*]

Proc Geol Assoc Can ... Proceedings. Geological Association of Canada [*A publication*]

Proc Geol Assoc London ... Proceedings. Geologists' Association of London [*A publication*]

Proc Geol Soc China ... Proceedings. Geological Society of China [*Taipei*] [*A publication*]

Proc Geol Soc Lond ... Proceedings. Geological Society of London [*A publication*]

Proc Geol Soc S Afr ... Proceedings. Geological Society of South Africa [*A publication*]

Proc Geophys Soc Tulsa ... Proceedings. Geophysical Society of Tulsa [*A publication*]

Proc Geosci Inf Soc ... Proceedings. Geoscience Information Society [*A publication*]

Proc Ger Soc Neurosurg ... Proceedings. German Society of Neurosurgery [*A publication*]

Proc Ghana Acad Arts Sci ... Proceedings. Ghana Academy of Arts and Sciences [*A publication*]

Proc Grass Breeders Work Plann Conf ... Proceedings. Grass Breeders Work Planning Conference [*A publication*]

Proc Grassl Soc South Afr ... Proceedings. Grassland Society of Southern Africa [*A publication*]

Proc Great Plains Agr Conf ... Proceedings. Great Plains Agriculture Conference [*A publication*]

Proc Gulf Caribb Fish Inst ... Proceedings. Gulf and Caribbean Fisheries Institute [*A publication*]

Proc Hampshire Field Club ... Proceedings. Hampshire Field Club and Archaeological Society [*A publication*]

Proc Hampshire Fld Club Archaeol Soc ... Proceedings. Hampshire Field Club and Archaeological Society [*A publication*]

Proc Hamp Soc ... Proceedings. Hampshire Field Club and Archaeological Society [*A publication*]

Proc Hawaii Acad Sci ... Proceedings. Hawaiian Academy of Science [*A publication*]

Proc Hawaii Entomol Soc ... Proceedings. Hawaiian Entomological Society [*A publication*]

Proc Hawaii Ent Soc ... Proceedings. Hawaiian Entomological Society [*A publication*]

Proc Hawaii Int Conf Syst Sci ... Proceedings. Hawaii International Conference on System Science [*A publication*]

Proc Hawaii Top Conf Part Phys ... Proceedings. Hawaii Topical Conference in Particle Physics [*A publication*]

Proc Health Policy Forum ... Proceedings. Health Policy Forum [*A publication*]
Proc Heat Transfer Fluid Mech Inst ... Proceedings. Heat Transfer and Fluid Mechanics Institute [*A publication*]
Proc Helminthol Soc Wash ... Proceedings. Helminthological Society of Washington [*A publication*]
Proc Helminthol Soc (Wash DC) ... Proceedings. Helminthological Society (Washington, DC) [*A publication*]
Proc Helminth Soc Wash ... Proceedings. Helminthological Society of Washington [*A publication*]
Proc High Lysine Corn Conf ... Proceedings. High Lysine Corn Conference [*A publication*]
Prochn Deform Mater Neravnomernykh Fiz Polyakh ... Prochnost i Deformatsiya Materialov v Neravnomernykh Fizicheskikh Polyakh [*A publication*]
Prochnost Din Aviats Dvigatelei ... Prochnost i Dinamika Aviatsionnykh Dvigatelei [*Former USSR*] [*A publication*]
Proc Hokkaido Symp Plant Breed Crop Sci Soc ... Proceedings. Hokkaido Symposium of Plant Breeding and Crop Science Society [*A publication*]
Proc Hokuriku Br Crop Sci Soc (Jap) ... Proceedings. Hokuriku Branch of Crop Science Society (Japan) [*A publication*]
Proc Hortic Soc London ... Proceedings. Horticultural Society of London [*A publication*]
Proc Hoshi Coll Pharm ... Proceedings. Hoshi College of Pharmacy [*A publication*]
Proc Huguenot Soc Lond ... Proceedings. Huguenot Society of London [*A publication*]
Proc Hung Annu Meet Biochem ... Proceedings. Hungarian Annual Meeting for Biochemistry [*A publication*]
Proc Hydrol Symp ... Proceedings. Hydrology Symposium [*A publication*]
Proc I Cda ... Process Industries Canada [*A publication*]
Proc ICE .... Proceedings. Institution of Civil Engineers. Parts 1 and 2 [*A publication*]
Proc ICMR Semin ... Proceedings. ICMR [*International Center for Medical Research, Kobe University*] Seminar [*A publication*]
Proc IEE-A ... Institution of Electrical Engineers. Proceedings. A [*A publication*]
Proc IEE-B ... Institution of Electrical Engineers. Proceedings. B [*A publication*]
Proc IEE-C ... Institution of Electrical Engineers. Proceedings. C [*A publication*]
Proc IEE D ... Institution of Electrical Engineers. Proceedings. D [*A publication*]
Proc IEEE ... Proceedings. Institute of Electrical and Electronics Engineers [*A publication*]
Proc IEEE Conf Decis Control ... Proceedings. IEEE Conference on Decision and Control [*A publication*]
Proc IEEE Conf Decis Control Incl Symp Adapt Processes ... Proceedings. IEEE Conference on Decision and Control Including the Symposium on Adaptive Processes [*A publication*]
Proc IEEE Int Symp Circuits Syst ... Proceedings. IEEE International Symposium on Circuits and Systems [*A publication*]
Proc IEEE Minicourse Inertial Confinement Fusion ... Proceedings. IEEE [*Institute of Electrical and Electronics Engineers*] Minicourse on Inertial Confinement Fusion [*A publication*]
Proc IEE F ... Institution of Electrical Engineers. Proceedings. F [*A publication*]
Proc IEE G ... Institution of Electrical Engineers. Proceedings. G [*A publication*]
Proc IEE H ... Proceedings. Institution of Electrical Engineers. H [*A publication*]
Proc IEE I ... Proceedings. Institution of Electrical Engineers. I [*A publication*]
Proc III Natn Peanut Res Conf ... Proceedings. Third National Peanut Research Conference [*A publication*]
Proc Ill Mining Inst ... Proceedings. Illinois Mining Institute [*A publication*]
Proc Imp Acad Japan ... Proceedings. Imperial Academy of Japan [*A publication*]
Proc Imp Acad (Tokyo) ... Proceedings. Imperial Academy (Tokyo) [*A publication*]
Proc Indiana Acad Sci ... Proceedings. Indiana Academy of Science [*A publication*]
Proc Indian Acad Sci ... Proceedings. Indian Academy of Sciences [*A publication*]
Proc Indian Acad Sci A ... Proceedings. Indian Academy of Sciences. Section A [*A publication*]
Proc Indian Acad Sci Anim Sci ... Proceedings. Indian Academy of Sciences. Animal Sciences [*A publication*]
Proc Indian Acad Sci B ... Proceedings. Indian Academy of Sciences. Section B [*A publication*]
Proc Indian Acad Sci Chem Sci ... Proceedings. Indian Academy of Sciences. Chemical Sciences [*A publication*]
Proc Indian Acad Sci Earth Planetary Sci ... Proceedings. Indian Academy of Sciences. Earth and Planetary Sciences [*A publication*]
Proc Indian Acad Sci Earth Planet Sci ... Proceedings. Indian Academy of Sciences. Earth and Planetary Sciences [*A publication*]
Proc Indian Acad Sci Eng Sci ... Proceedings. Indian Academy of Sciences. Engineering Sciences [*A publication*]

Proc Indian Acad Sci Math Sci ... Proceedings. Indian Academy of Sciences. Mathematical Sciences [*A publication*]
Proc Indian Acad Sci Plant Sci ... Proceedings. Indian Academy of Sciences. Plant Sciences [*A publication*]
Proc Indian Acad Sci Sect A ... Proceedings. Indian Academy of Sciences. Section A [*A publication*]
Proc Indian Acad Sci Sect A Chem Sci ... Proceedings. Indian Academy of Sciences. Section A. Chemical Sciences [*A publication*]
Proc Indian Acad Sci Sect A Earth Planetary Sci ... Indian Academy of Sciences. Proceedings. Section A. Earth and Planetary Sciences [*A publication*]
Proc Indian Acad Sci Sect A Math Sci ... Proceedings. Indian Academy of Sciences. Section A. Mathematical Sciences [*A publication*]
Proc Indian Acad Sci Sect B ... Proceedings. Indian Academy of Sciences. Section B [*A publication*]
Proc Indian Acad Sci Sect C ... Proceedings. Indian Academy of Sciences. Section C. Engineering Sciences [*India*] [*A publication*]
Proc Indian Assoc Cultiv Sci ... Proceedings. Indian Association for Cultivation of Sciences [*A publication*]
Proc Indian Natl Sci Acad A ... Proceedings. Indian National Science Academy. Part A. Physical Sciences [*A publication*]
Proc Indian Natl Sci Acad Part A ... Proceedings. Indian National Science Academy. Part A [*A publication*]
Proc Indian Natl Sci Acad Part A Phys Sci ... Proceedings. Indian National Science Academy. Part A. Physical Sciences [*A publication*]
Proc Indian Natl Sci Acad Part B ... Proceedings. Indian National Science Academy. Part B. Biological Sciences [*A publication*]
Proc Indian Natl Sci Acad Part B Biol Sci ... Proceedings. Indian National Science Academy. Part B. Biological Sciences [*A publication*]
Proc Indian Nat Sci Acad Part A ... Proceedings. Indian National Science Academy. Part A. Physical Sciences [*A publication*]
Proc Indian Roads Congr ... Proceedings. Indian Roads Congress [*A publication*]
Proc Indian Sci Congr ... Proceedings. Indian Science Congress [*A publication*]
Proc Indo Pac Fish Counc ... Proceedings. Indo-Pacific Fisheries Council [*A publication*]
Proc Ind Waste Conf ... Proceedings. Industrial Waste Conference [*A publication*]
Proc Ind Waste Conf Purdue Univ ... Proceedings. Industrial Waste Conference. Purdue University [*A publication*]
Proc Ind Waste Util Conf ... Proceedings. Industrial Waste Utilization Conference [*A publication*]
Proc Inst Automob Eng (London) ... Proceedings. Institution of Automobile Engineers (London) [*A publication*]
Proc Inst Br Foundrymen ... Proceedings. Institute of British Foundrymen [*A publication*]
Proc Inst Chem (Calcutta) ... Proceedings. Institution of Chemists (Calcutta) [*A publication*]
Proc Inst Civ Eng ... Proceedings. Institution of Civil Engineers [*London*] [*A publication*]
Proc Inst Civ Eng (London) Suppl ... Proceedings. Institution of Civil Engineers (London). Supplement [*A publication*]
Proc Inst Civ Eng Part 1 ... Proceedings. Institution of Civil Engineers. Part 1. Design and Construction [*A publication*]
Proc Inst Civ Eng Part 2 ... Proceedings. Institution of Civil Engineers. Part 2. Research and Theory [*United Kingdom*] [*A publication*]
Proc Inst Criminol Univ Sydney ... University of Sydney. Institute of Criminology. Proceedings [*A publication*]
Proc Inst Elec Eng (London) ... Proceedings. Institution of Electrical Engineers (London) [*A publication*]
Proc Inst Elec Eng Pt B Elec Power Appl ... Proceedings. Institution of Electrical Engineers. Part B. Electric Power Applications [*A publication*]
Proc Inst Elec Eng Pt C Generation Transmission Distribution ... Proceedings. Institution of Electrical Engineers. Part C. Generation-Transmission-Distribution [*A publication*]
Proc Inst Elec Eng Pt E Computers Digital Tech ... Proceedings. Institution of Electrical Engineers. Part E. Computers and Digital Techniques [*A publication*]
Proc Inst Elec Eng Pt F Commun Radar Signal Process ... Proceedings. Institution of Electrical Engineers. Part F. Communications, Radar, and Signal Processing [*A publication*]
Proc Inst Elec Eng Pt G Electron Circuits Syst ... Proceedings. Institution of Electrical Engineers. Part G. Electronics Circuits and Systems [*A publication*]
Proc Inst Elec Eng Pt H Microwaves Opt Antennas ... Proceedings. Institution of Electrical Engineers. Part H. Microwaves, Optics, and Antennas [*A publication*]
Proc Inst Elec Engrs ... Proceedings. Institution of Electrical Engineers [*A publication*]
Proc Inst Elect ... Proceedings. Institution of Electrical Engineers [*A publication*]
Proc Inst Electr Eng ... Proceedings. Institution of Electrical Engineers [*A publication*]
Proc Inst Electr Eng (London) ... Proceedings. Institution of Electrical Engineers (London) [*A publication*]
Proc Inst Electr Eng Part 1 ... Proceedings. Institution of Electrical Engineers. Part 1. General [*A publication*]

Proc Inst Electr Eng Part 2 ... Proceedings. Institution of Electrical Engineers. Part 2. Power Engineering [*A publication*]

Proc Inst Electr Eng Part 3 ... Proceedings. Institution of Electrical Engineers. Part 3. Radio and Communication Engineering [*A publication*]

Proc Inst Electr Eng Part 4 ... Proceedings. Institution of Electrical Engineers. Part 4. Monographs [*A publication*]

Proc Inst Electr Eng Part A ... Proceedings. Institution of Electrical Engineers. Part A. Power Engineering [*A publication*]

Proc Inst Electr Eng Part A Suppl ... Proceedings. Institution of Electrical Engineers. Part A. Supplement [*A publication*]

Proc Inst Electr Eng Part B ... Proceedings. Institution of Electrical Engineers. Part B. Electronic and Communication Engineering Including Radio Engineering [*A publication*]

Proc Inst Electr Eng Part B Suppl ... Proceedings. Institution of Electrical Engineers. Part B. Supplement [*A publication*]

Proc Inst Electr Eng Part C ... Proceedings. Institution of Electrical Engineers. Part C. Monographs [*A publication*]

Proc Inst Environ Sci ... Proceedings. Institute of Environmental Sciences [*A publication*]

Proc Inst Fd Sci Technol ... Proceedings. Institute of Food Science and Technology [*A publication*]

Proc Inst Food Sci Technol UK ... Proceedings. Institute of Food Science and Technology of the United Kingdom [*A publication*]

Proc Inst Food Technol ... Proceedings. Institute of Food Technologists [*A publication*]

Proc Institute Med Chicago ... Proceedings. Institute of Medicine of Chicago [*A publication*]

Proc Inst Mech Eng ... Proceedings. Institution of Mechanical Engineers [*A publication*]

Proc Inst Mech Eng (London) ... Proceedings. Institution of Mechanical Engineers (London) [*A publication*]

Proc Inst Mech Eng Part A ... Proceedings. Institution of Mechanical Engineers. Part A. Power and Process Engineering [*A publication*]

Proc Inst Mech Eng Part B ... Proceedings. Institution of Mechanical Engineers. Part B. Management and Engineering Manufacture [*A publication*]

Proc Inst Mech Eng Part C ... Proceedings. Institution of Mechanical Engineers. Part C. Mechanical Engineering Science [*A publication*]

Proc Inst Mech Engrs ... Proceedings. Institution of Mechanical Engineers [*A publication*]

Proc Inst Med Chic ... Proceedings. Institute of Medicine of Chicago [*A publication*]

Proc Inst Med Chicago ... Proceedings. Institute of Medicine of Chicago [*A publication*]

Proc Inst Nat Sci Nihon Univ ... Proceedings. Institute of Natural Sciences. Nihon University [*A publication*]

Proc Instn CE ... Proceedings. Institution of Civil Engineers [*A publication*]

Proc Instn Civ Engrs ... Proceedings. Institution of Civil Engineers [*A publication*]

Proc Instn Civ Engrs 1 2 ... Proceedings. Institution of Civil Engineers. Parts 1 and 2 [*A publication*]

Proc Instn Elect Engrs ... Proceedings. Institution of Electrical Engineers [*A publication*]

Proc Instn Mech Engrs ... Proceedings. Institution of Mechanical Engineers [*A publication*]

Proc Instn Mech Engrs Pt B Mgmt Engng Mf ... Proceedings. Institution of Mechanical Engineers. Part B. Management and Engineering Manufacture [*A publication*]

Proc Instn Mech Engrs Pt C Mech Engng Sci ... Proceedings. Institution of Mechanical Engineers. Part C. Mechanical Engineering Science [*A publication*]

Proc Instn Mech Engrs Pt D Transp Engng ... Proceedings. Institution of Mechanical Engineers. Part D. Transport Engineering [*A publication*]

Proc Instn Radio Electron Engrs Aust ... Proceedings. Institution of Radio and Electronics Engineers of Australia [*A publication*] (APTA)

Proc Instn Radio Eng Aust ... Proceedings. Institution of Radio Engineers of Australia [*A publication*]

Proc Instn Radio Engrs Aust ... Proceedings. Institution of Radio Engineers of Australia [*A publication*] (APTA)

Proc Inst Oceanogr Fish Bulg Acad Sci ... Proceedings. Institute of Oceanography and Fisheries. Bulgarian Academy of Sciences [*A publication*]

Proc Inst Pomol (Skierniewice Pol) Ser E Conf Symp ... Proceedings. Research Institute of Pomology (Skierniewice, Poland). Series E. Conferences and Symposia [*A publication*]

Proc Inst Radio Electron Eng Aust ... Proceedings. Institution of Radio and Electronics Engineers of Australia [*A publication*] (APTA)

Proc Inst Railw Signal Eng ... Proceedings. Institution of Railway Signal Engineers [*A publication*]

Proc Inst Refrig ... Proceedings. Institute of Refrigeration [*A publication*]

Proc Inst Rubber Ind ... Proceedings. Institution of the Rubber Industry [*A publication*]

Proc Instrum Soc Am ... Proceedings. Instrument Society of America [*A publication*]

Proc Inst Sewage Purif ... Proceedings. Institute of Sewage Purification [*A publication*]

Proc Inst Statist Math ... Proceedings. Institute of Statistical Mathematics [*A publication*]

Proc Inst Teknol Bandung ... Proceedings. Institut Teknologi Bandung [*Indonesia*] [*A publication*]

Proc Inst Teknol Bandung Suppl ... Proceedings. Institut Teknologi Bandung. Supplement [*Indonesia*] [*A publication*]

Proc Inst Vitreous Enamellers ... Proceedings. Institute of Vitreous Enamellers [*A publication*]

Proc Int Acad Oral Pathol ... Proceedings. International Academy of Oral Pathology [*A publication*]

Proc Int Assoc Milk Dealers ... Proceedings. International Association of Milk Dealers [*A publication*]

Proc Int Assoc Test Mater ... Proceedings. International Association for Testing Materials [*A publication*]

Proc Int Assoc Theor Appl Limnol ... Proceedings. International Association of Theoretical and Applied Limnology [*A publication*]

Proc Int Assoc Vet Food Hyg ... Proceedings. International Association of Veterinary Food Hygienists [*A publication*]

Proc Int Astronaut Congr ... Proceedings. International Astronautical Congress [*A publication*]

Proc Int Barley Genet Symp ... Proceedings. International Barley Genetics Symposium [*A publication*]

Proc Int Bedding Plant Conf ... Proceedings. International Bedding Plant Conference [*A publication*]

Proc Int Bioclimatol Congr ... Proceedings. International Bioclimatological Congress [*A publication*]

Proc Int Bot Congr ... Proceedings. International Botanical Congress [*A publication*]

Proc Int Clean Air Congr ... Proceedings. International Clean Air Congress [*A publication*]

Proc Int Coelenterate Conf ... Proceedings. International Coelenterate Conference [*A publication*]

Proc Int Colloq Invertebr Pathol ... Proceedings. International Colloquium on Invertebrate Pathology [*A publication*]

Proc Int Colloq Plant Anal Fert Probl ... Proceedings. International Colloquium on Plant Analysis and Fertilizer Problems [*A publication*]

Proc Int Comm Glass ... Proceedings. International Commission on Glass [*A publication*]

Proc Int Conf Aquacult Nutr ... Proceedings. International Conference on Aquaculture Nutrition [*A publication*]

Proc Int Conf Beam Foil Spectrosc ... Proceedings. International Conference on Beam-Foil Spectroscopy [*A publication*]

Proc Int Conf Biochem Probl Lipids ... Proceedings. International Conference on Biochemical Problems of Lipids [*A publication*]

Proc Int Conf Cent High Energy Form ... Proceedings. International Conference. Center for High Energy Forming [*A publication*]

Proc Int Conf Cloud Phys ... Proceedings. International Conference on Cloud Physics [*A publication*]

Proc Int Conf Cosmic Rays ... Proceedings. International Conference on Cosmic Rays [*A publication*]

Proc Int Conf Cybern Soc ... Proceedings. International Conference on Cybernetics and Society [*A publication*]

Proc Int Conf Electrodeposition Met Finish ... Proceedings. International Conference on Electrodeposition and Metal Finishing [*A publication*]

Proc Int Conf Erosion Liq Solid Impact ... Proceedings. International Conference on Erosion by Liquid and Solid Impact [*A publication*]

Proc Int Conf Fire Saf ... Proceedings. International Conference on Fire Safety [*A publication*]

Proc Int Conf Fluid ... Proceedings. International Conference on Fluidization [*A publication*]

Proc Int Conf Fluid Sealing ... Proceedings. International Conference on Fluid Sealing [*A publication*]

Proc Int Conf Heat Treat Mater ... Proceedings. International Conference on Heat Treatment of Materials [*A publication*]

Proc Int Conf High Energy Phys ... Proceedings. International Conference on High Energy Physics [*A publication*]

Proc Int Conf High Energy Rate Fabr ... Proceedings. International Conference on High Energy Rate Fabrication [*A publication*]

Proc Int Conf Hydraul Transp Solids Pipes ... Proceedings. International Conference on the Hydraulic Transport of Solids in Pipes [*A publication*]

Proc Int Conf Int Assoc Water Pollut Res ... Proceedings. International Conference of the International Association on Water Pollution Research [*A publication*]

Proc Int Conf Ion Implant Semicond Other Mater ... Proceedings. International Conference on Ion Implantation in Semiconductors and Other Materials [*A publication*]

Proc Int Conf Lasers ... Proceedings. International Conference on Lasers [*A publication*]

Proc Int Conf Light Scattering Solids ... Proceedings. International Conference on Light Scattering in Solids [*A publication*]

Proc Int Conf Mech Bioenerg ... Proceedings. International Conference on Mechanisms in Bioenergetics [*A publication*]

Proc Int Conf Mycoses ... Proceedings. International Conference on the Mycoses [*A publication*]

Proc Int Conf New Front Hazard Waste Manage ... Proceedings. International Conference on New Frontiers for Hazardous Waste Management [*A publication*]

Proc Int Conf Noise Control Eng ... Proceedings. International Conference on Noise Control Engineering [*A publication*]

Proc Int Conf Nucl Photogr Solid State Track Detect ... Proceedings. International Conference on Nuclear Photography and Solid State Track Detectors [*A publication*]

Proc Int Conf Org Coat Sci Technol Technomic Publ ... Proceedings. International Conference in Organic Coatings Science and Technology. Technomic Publication [*A publication*]

Proc Int Conf Part Technol ... Proceedings. International Conference in Particle Technology [*A publication*]

Proc Int Conf Peaceful Uses Atomic Energy ... Proceedings. International Conference on the Peaceful Uses of Atomic Energy [*A publication*]

Proc Int Conf Pervaporation Processes Chem Ind ... Proceedings. International Conference on Pervaporation Processes in the Chemical Industry [*A publication*]

Proc Int Conf Photonucl React Appl ... Proceedings. International Conference on Photonuclear Reactions and Applications [*A publication*]

Proc Int Conf Plant Growth Regulat ... Proceedings. International Conference on Plant Growth Regulation [*A publication*]

Proc Int Conf Plant Pathog Bact ... Proceedings. International Conference on Plant Pathogenic Bacteria [*A publication*]

Proc Int Conf Prop Water Steam ... Proceedings. International Conference on the Properties of Water and Steam [*A publication*]

Proc Int Conf Rob Vision Sens Controls ... Proceedings. International Conference on Robot Vision and Sensory Controls [*A publication*]

Proc Int Conf Sci Aspects Mushroom Grow ... Proceedings. International Conference on Scientific Aspects of Mushroom Growing [*A publication*]

Proc Int Conf Spectrosc ... Proceedings. International Conference on Spectroscopy [*A publication*]

Proc Int Conf Synth Fibrinolytic Thrombolytic Agents ... Proceedings. International Conference on Synthetic Fibrinolytic-Thrombolytic Agents [*A publication*]

Proc Int Conf Thermoelectr Energy Convers ... Proceedings. International Conference on Thermoelectric Energy Conversion [*A publication*]

Proc Int Conf Waste Disposal Mar Environ ... Proceedings. International Conference on Waste Disposal in the Marine Environment [*A publication*]

Proc Int Conf Wildl Dis ... Proceedings. International Conference on Wildlife Disease [*A publication*]

Proc Int Cong Phot ... Proceedings. International Congress of Photography [*A publication*]

Proc Int Congr Anim Reprod Artif Insemin ... Proceedings. International Congress on Animal Reproduction and Artificial Insemination [*A publication*]

Proc Int Congr Aviat Space Med ... Proceedings. International Congress on Aviation and Space Medicine [*A publication*]

Proc Int Congr Biochem ... Proceedings. International Congress of Biochemistry [*A publication*]

Proc Int Congr Crop Prot ... Proceedings. International Congress on Crop Protection [*A publication*]

Proc Int Congr Deterior Conserv Stone ... Proceedings. International Congress on Deterioration and Conservation of Stone [*A publication*]

Proc Int Congr Ent ... Proceedings. International Congress of Entomology [*A publication*]

Proc Int Congr Entomol ... Proceedings. International Congress of Entomology [*A publication*]

Proc Int Congr Food Sci Technol ... Proceedings. International Congress of Food Science and Technology [*A publication*]

Proc Int Congr Genet ... Proceedings. International Congress of Genetics [*A publication*]

Proc Int Congr Geront ... Proceedings. International Congress on Gerontology [*A publication*]

Proc Int Congr Gerontol ... Proceedings. International Congress on Gerontology [*A publication*]

Proc Int Congr High Speed Photogr ... Proceedings. International Congress on High Speed Photography [*A publication*]

Proc Int Congr Hist Sci ... Proceedings. International Congress of the History of Science [*A publication*]

Proc Int Congr Hum Genet ... Proceedings. International Congress of Human Genetics [*A publication*]

Proc Int Congr Int Assoc Hydrogeol ... Proceedings. International Congress. International Association of Hydrogeologists [*A publication*]

Proc Int Congr Mar Corros Fouling ... Proceedings. International Congress on Marine Corrosion and Fouling [*A publication*]

Proc Int Congr Ment Retard ... Proceedings. International Congress on Mental Retardation [*A publication*]

Proc Int Congr Microbiol Stand ... Proceedings. International Congress for Microbiological Standardization [*A publication*]

Proc Int Congr Mushroom Sci ... Proceedings. International Congress on Mushroom Science [*A publication*]

Proc Int Congr Nephrol ... Proceedings. International Congress of Nephrology [*A publication*]

Proc Int Congr Neuropathol ... Proceedings. International Congress of Neuropathology [*A publication*]

Proc Int Congr Nutr (Hamburg) ... Proceedings. International Congress of Nutrition (Hamburg) [*A publication*]

Proc Int Congr Pharmacol ... Proceedings. International Congress on Pharmacology [*A publication*]

Proc Int Congr Pharm Sci ... Proceedings. International Congress of Pharmaceutical Sciences [*A publication*]

Proc Int Congr Photosynth Res ... Proceedings. International Congress on Photosynthesis Research [*A publication*]

Proc Int Congr Primatol ... Proceedings. International Congress of Primatology [*A publication*]

Proc Int Congr Protozool ... Proceedings. International Congress on Protozoology [*A publication*]

Proc Int Congr Psychother ... Proceedings. International Congress of Psychotherapy [*A publication*]

Proc Int Congr Pure Appl Chem ... Proceedings. International Congress of Pure and Applied Chemistry [*A publication*]

Proc Int Congr Radiat Prot ... Proceedings. International Congress of Radiation Protection [*A publication*]

Proc Int Congr Refrig ... Proceedings. International Congress of Refrigeration [*A publication*]

Proc Int Congr Rock Mech ... Proceedings. International Congress on Rock Mechanics [*A publication*]

Proc Int Congr Stereol ... Proceedings. International Congress for Stereology [*A publication*]

Proc Int Congr Virol ... Proceedings. International Congress for Virology [*A publication*]

Proc Int Congr Zool ... Proceedings. International Congress of Zoology [*A publication*]

Proc Int Conv Autom Instrum ... Proceedings. International Convention on Automation and Instrumentation [*A publication*]

Proc Int Dist Heat Assoc ... Proceedings. International District Heating Association [*A publication*]

Proc Int EMIS Conf Low Energy Ion Accel Mass Sep ... Proceedings. International EMIS [*Electromagnetic Isotope Separation*] Conference on Low Energy Ion Accelerators and Mass Separators [*A publication*]

Proc Internat School of Phys Enrico Fermi ... Proceedings. International School of Physics "Enrico Fermi" [*A publication*]

Proc Intersoc Energy Conver Eng Conf ... Proceedings. Intersociety Energy Conversion Engineering Conference [*A publication*]

Proc Intersoc Energy Convers Eng Conf ... Proceedings. Intersociety Energy Conversion Engineering Conference [*A publication*]

Proc Interuniv Fac Work Conf ... Proceedings. Interuniversity Faculty Work Conference [*A publication*]

Proc Int Gas Res Conf ... Proceedings. International Gas Research Conference [*A publication*]

Proc Int Grassland Congr ... Proceedings. International Grassland Congress [*A publication*]

Proc Int Gstaad Symp ... Proceedings. International Gstaad Symposium [*A publication*]

Proc Int Hort Congr ... Proceedings. International Horticultural Congress [*A publication*]

Proc Int Hortic Congr ... Proceedings. International Horticultural Congress [*A publication*]

Proc Int Iron Steel Congr ... Proceedings. International Iron and Steel Congress [*A publication*]

Proc Int ISA Biomed Sci Instrum Symp ... Proceedings. International ISA [*Instrument Society of America*] Biomedical Sciences Instrumentation Symposium [*A publication*]

Proc Int Leucocyte Conf ... Proceedings. International Leucocyte Conference [*A publication*]

Proc Int Meet Biol Stand ... Proceedings. International Meeting of Biological Standardization [*A publication*]

Proc Int Meet Future Trends Inflammation ... Proceedings. International Meeting on Future Trends in Inflammation [*A publication*]

Proc Int Microelectron Symp ... Proceedings. International Microelectronics Symposium [*A publication*]

Proc Int Microsc Symp ... Proceedings. International Microscopy Symposium [*A publication*]

Proc Int Neuropathol Symp ... Proceedings. International Neuropathological Symposium [*A publication*]

Proc Int Ornithol Congr ... Proceedings. International Ornithological Congress [*A publication*]

Proc Int Pharmacol Meet ... Proceedings. International Pharmacological Meeting [*A publication*]

Proc Int Pl Propag Soc ... Proceedings. International Plant Propagators' Society [*A publication*]

Proc Int Power Sources Symp (London) ... Proceedings. International Power Sources Symposium (London) [*A publication*]

Proc Intra Sci Res Found Symp ... Proceedings. Intra-Science Research Foundation Symposium [*A publication*]

Proc Int Rubber Conf ... Proceedings. International Rubber Conference [*A publication*]

Proc Int Sch Phys Enrico Fermi ... Proceedings. International School of Physics "Enrico Fermi" [*A publication*]

Proc Int Sci Congr Cultiv Edible Fungi ... Proceedings. International Scientific Congress on the Cultivation of Edible Fungi [*A publication*]

Proc Int Seaweed Symp ... Proceedings. International Seaweed Symposium [*A publication*]

Proc Int Seed Test Ass ... Proceedings. International Seed Testing Association [*A publication*]

Proc Int Seed Test Assoc ... Proceedings. International Seed Testing Association [*A publication*]

Proc Int Semin High Energy Phys Quantum Field Theory ... Proceedings. International Seminar on High Energy Physics and Quantum Field Theory [*A publication*]

Proc Int Shade Tree Conf ... Proceedings. Annual Meetings. International Shade Tree Conference [*A publication*]

Proc Int Soc Citric ... Proceedings. International Society of Citriculture [*A publication*]

Proc Int Soc Soil Sci ... Proceedings. International Society of Soil Science [*A publication*]

Proc Int Soc Sugar Cane Technol ... Proceedings. International Society of Sugar Cane Technologists [*A publication*]

Proc Int Spent Fuel Storage Technol Symp Workshop ... Proceedings. International Spent Fuel Storage Technology Symposium/ Workshop [*A publication*]

Proc Int Symp Adv Mater ULSI ... Proceedings. International Symposium on Advanced Materials for ULSI [*A publication*]

Proc Int Symp Anim Plant Microb Toxins ... Proceedings. International Symposium on Animal, Plant, and Microbial Toxins [*A publication*]

Proc Int Symp Automot Technol Autom ... Proceedings. International Symposium on Automotive Technology and Automation [*A publication*]

Proc Int Symp Biocybern ... Proceedings. International Symposium on Biocybernetics [*A publication*]

Proc Int Symp Can Soc Immunol ... Proceedings. International Symposium. Canadian Society for Immunology [*A publication*]

Proc Int Symp Chem Biol Aspects Pyridoxal Catal ... Proceedings. International Symposium on Chemical and Biological Aspects of Pyridoxal Catalysis [*A publication*]

Proc Int Symp Comp Res Leuk Relat Dis ... Proceedings. International Symposium on Comparative Research on Leukemia and Related Diseases [*A publication*]

Proc Int Symp Detect Prev Cancer ... Proceedings. International Symposium on Detection and Prevention of Cancer [*A publication*]

Proc Int Symp Electroslag Remelting Processes ... Proceedings. International Symposium on Electroslag Remelting Processes [*A publication*]

Proc Int Symp Enzyme Chem ... Proceedings. International Symposium on Enzyme Chemistry [*A publication*]

Proc Int Symp Exp Models Pathophysiol Acute Renal Failure ... Proceedings. International Symposium on Experimental Models and Pathophysiology of Acute Renal Failure [*A publication*]

Proc Int Symp Food Irradiation ... Proceedings. International Symposium on Food Irradiation [*A publication*]

Proc Int Symp Food Preserv Irradiat ... Proceedings. International Symposium on Food Preservation by Irradiation [*A publication*]

Proc Int Symp Fresh Water Sea ... Proceedings. International Symposium on Fresh Water from the Sea [*A publication*]

Proc Int Symp Gnotobiol ... Proceedings. International Symposium on Gnotobiology [*A publication*]

Proc Int Symp Inst Biomed Res Am Med Assoc Educ Res Found ... Proceedings. International Symposium of the Institute for Biomedical Research. American Medical Association Education and Research Foundation [*A publication*]

Proc Int Symp Isoelectr Focusing Isotachophoresis ... Proceedings. International Symposium on Isoelectric Focusing and Isotachophoresis [*A publication*]

Proc Int Symp Med Chem Main Lect ... Proceedings. International Symposium on Medicinal Chemistry. Main Lectures [*A publication*]

Proc Int Symp Med Mycol ... Proceedings. International Symposium on Medical Mycology [*A publication*]

Proc Int Symp Mult Valued Logic ... Proceedings. International Symposium on Multiple-Valued Logic [*A publication*]

Proc Int Symp Neurosecretion ... Proceedings. International Symposium on Neurosecretion [*A publication*]

Proc Int Symp Olfaction Taste ... Proceedings. International Symposium on Olfaction and Taste [*A publication*]

Proc Int Symp Phys Med Atmos Space ... Proceedings. International Symposium on the Physics and Medicine of the Atmosphere and Space [*A publication*]

Proc Int Symp Poll ... Proceedings. International Symposium on Pollination [*A publication*]

Proc Int Symp Princess Takamatsu Cancer Res Fund ... Proceedings. International Symposium of the Princess Takamatsu Cancer Research Fund [*A publication*]

Proc Int Symp Radiol Prot Adv Theory Pract ... Proceedings. International Symposium. Radiological Protection. Advances in Theory and Practice [*A publication*]

Proc Int Symp Remote Sens Environ ... Proceedings. International Symposium on Remote Sensing of Environment [*A publication*]

Proc Int Symp Remote Sensing Environ ... Proceedings. International Symposium on Remote Sensing of Environment [*A publication*]

Proc Int Symp Rickettsiae Rickettsial Dis ... Proceedings. International Symposium on Rickettsiae and Rickettsial Diseases [*A publication*]

Proc Int Symp Stress Alcohol Use ... Proceedings. International Symposium on Stress and Alcohol Use [*A publication*]

Proc Int Symp Water Rock Interact ... Proceedings. International Symposium on Water-Rock Interaction [*A publication*]

Proc Int Tech Conf APICS ... Proceedings. International Technical Conference. American Production and Inventory Control Society [*A publication*]

Proc Int Top Conf High Power Electron Ion Beam Res Technol ... Proceedings. International Topical Conference on High Power Electron and Ion Beam Research and Technology [*A publication*]

Proc Int Union Biol Sci Ser B ... Proceedings. International Union of Biological Sciences. Series B [*A publication*]

Proc Int Union Forest Res Organ ... Proceedings. International Union of Forest Research Organizations [*A publication*]

Proc Int Velsicol Symp ... Proceedings. International Velsicol Symposium [*A publication*]

Proc Int Vet Congr ... Proceedings. International Veterinary Congress [*A publication*]

Proc Int Water Qual Symp ... Proceedings. International Water Quality Symposium [*A publication*]

Proc Int Wheat Genet Symp ... Proceedings. International Wheat Genetics Symposium [*A publication*]

Proc Int Wheat Surplus Util Conf ... Proceedings. International Wheat Surplus Utilization Conference [*A publication*]

Proc Int Wire Cable Symp ... Proceedings. International Wire and Cable Symposium [*A publication*]

Proc Int Workshop Laser Velocimetry ... Proceedings. International Workshop on Laser Velocimetry [*A publication*]

Proc Int Workshop Nude Mice ... Proceedings. International Workshop on Nude Mice [*A publication*]

Proc Iowa Acad Sci ... Proceedings. Iowa Academy of Science [*A publication*]

Proc IPI Congr ... Proceedings. IPI [*International Potash Institute*] Congress [*A publication*]

Proc Iraqi Sci Soc ... Proceedings. Iraqi Scientific Societies [*A publication*]

Proc IRE .... Proceedings. IRE [*Institute of Radio Engineers*] [*United States*] [*A publication*]

Proc Irish Ac Section C ... Proceedings. Royal Irish Academy. Section C. Archaeology, Celtic Studies, History, Linguistics, Literature [*A publication*]

Proc Ironmaking Conf ... Proceedings. Ironmaking Conference [*A publication*]

Proc ISA .... Proceedings. Instrument Society of America [*A publication*]

Proc Isle Man Natur Hist Antiq Soc ... Proceedings. Isle of Man Natural History and Antiquarian Society [*A publication*]

Proc Isle Wight Natur Hist Archaeol Soc ... Proceedings. Isle of Wight Natural History and Archaeological Society [*A publication*]

Proc Ital Meet Heavy Forg ... Proceedings. Italian Meeting on Heavy Forgings [*A publication*]

Proc Jap Acad ... Proceedings. Japan Academy [*A publication*]

Proc Japan Acad ... Proceedings. Japan Academy [*A publication*]

Proc Japan Acad Ser A Math Sci ... Proceedings. Japan Academy. Series A. Mathematical Sciences [*A publication*]

Proc Japan Acad Ser B Phys Biol Sci ... Proceedings. Japan Academy. Series B. Physical and Biological Sciences [*A publication*]

Proc Jap Soc Civ Eng ... Proceedings. Japan Society of Civil Engineers [*A publication*]

ProcJPES .. Proceedings. Jewish Palestine Exploration Society [*A publication*]

Proc Jpn Acad ... Proceedings. Japan Academy [*A publication*]

Proc Jpn Acad Ser A ... Proceedings. Japan Academy. Series A. Mathematical Sciences [*A publication*]

Proc Jpn Acad Ser B ... Proceedings. Japan Academy. Series B. Physical and Biological Sciences [*A publication*]

Proc Jpn Acad Ser B Phys Biol Sci ... Proceedings. Japan Academy. Series B. Physical and Biological Sciences [*A publication*]

Proc Jpn At Ind Forum Inc ... Proceedings. Japan Atomic Industrial Forum, Inc. [*A publication*]

Proc Jpn Cem Eng Assoc ... Proceedings. Japan Cement Engineering Association [*A publication*]

Proc Jpn Conf Radioisot ... Proceedings. Japan Conference on Radioisotopes [*A publication*]

Proc Jpn Congr Mater Res ... Proceedings. Japan Congress on Materials Research [*A publication*]

Proc Jpn Congr Test Mater ... Proceedings. Japanese Congress for Testing Materials [*A publication*]

Proc Jpn Natl Congr Appl Mech ... Proceedings. Japan National Congress for Applied Mechanics [*A publication*]

Proc Jpn Pharmacol Soc ... Proceedings. Japanese Pharmacology Society [*A publication*]

Proc Jpn Soc Civ Eng ... Proceedings. Japan Society of Civil Engineers [*A publication*]

Proc Jpn Soc Clin Biochem Metab ... Proceedings. Japan Society of Clinical Biochemistry and Metabolism [*A publication*]

Proc Jpn Soc Med Mass Spectrom ... Proceedings. Japanese Society for Medical Mass Spectrometry [*A publication*]

Proc Jpn Soc Reticuloendothel Syst ... Proceedings. Japan Society of the Reticuloendothelial System [*A publication*]
Proc Jpn Symp Thermophys Prop ... Proceedings. Japan Symposium on Thermophysical Properties [*A publication*]
Proc J US Conf Compos Mater ... Proceedings. Japan-US Conference on Composite Materials [*A publication*]
Proc Kansai Plant Prot Soc ... Proceedings. Kansai Plant Protection Society [*A publication*]
Proc Kanto-Tosan Plant Prot Soc ... Proceedings. Kanto-Tosan Plant Protection Society [*A publication*]
Proc Kimbrough Urol Semin ... Proceedings. Kimbrough Urological Seminar [*A publication*]
Proc Kinki Symp Crop Sci Plant Breed Soc ... Proceedings. Kinki Symposium of Crop Science and Plant Breeding Society [*A publication*]
Proc K Ned Akad Wet ... Proceedings. Koninklijke Nederlandse Akademie van Wetenschappen [*A publication*]
Proc K Ned Akad Wet B ... Proceedings. Koninklijke Nederlandse Akademie van Wetenschappen. Series B. Physical Sciences [*A publication*]
Proc K Ned Akad Wet Ser A ... Proceedings. Koninklijke Nederlandse Akademie van Wetenschappen. Series A. Mathematical Sciences [*A publication*]
Proc K Ned Akad Wet Ser B ... Proceedings. Koninklijke Nederlandse Akademie van Wetenschappen. Series B. Physical Sciences [*A publication*]
Proc K Ned Akad Wet Ser B Palaeontol Geol Phys Chem ... Proceedings. Koninklijke Nederlandse Akademie van Wetenschappen. Series B. Palaeontology, Geology, Physics, and Chemistry [*Later, Proceedings. Koninklijke Nederlandse Akademie van Wetenschappen. Series B. Palaeontology, Geology, Physics, Chemistry, Anthropology*] [*A publication*]
Proc K Ned Akad Wet Ser B Phys Sci ... Proceedings. Koninklijke Nederlandse Akademie van Wetenschappen. Series B. Physical Sciences [*A publication*]
Proc K Ned Akad Wet Ser C ... Proceedings. Koninklijke Nederlandse Akademie van Wetenschappen. Series C. Biological and Medical Sciences [*A publication*]
Proc K Ned Akad Wet Ser C Biol Med Sci ... Proceedings. Koninklijke Nederlandse Akademie van Wetenschappen. Series C. Biological and Medical Sciences [*A publication*]
Proc LA Acad Sci ... Proceedings. Louisiana Academy of Sciences [*A publication*]
Proc LA Ass Agron ... Proceedings. Louisiana Association of Agronomists [*A publication*]
Proc Latin Int Biochem Meet ... Proceedings. Latin International Biochemical Meeting [*A publication*]
Proc Leatherhead Dist Local Hist Soc ... Proceedings. Leatherhead and District Local History Society [*A publication*]
Proc Lebedev Phys Inst ... Proceedings (Trudy). P. N. Lebedev Physics Institute [*A publication*]
Proc Leeds Phil Lit Soc Sci Sect ... Proceedings. Leeds Philosophical and Literary Society. Scientific Section [*A publication*]
Proc Leeds Philos & Lit Soc ... Proceedings. Leeds Philosophical and Literary Society [*A publication*]
Proc Leeds Philos Lit Soc Lit Hist Sect ... Proceedings. Leeds Philosophical and Literary Society. Literary and Historical Section [*A publication*]
Proc Leeds Philos Lit Soc Sci Sect ... Proceedings. Leeds Philosophical and Literary Society. Scientific Section [*A publication*]
Proc Leucocyte Cult Conf ... Proceedings. Leucocyte Culture Conference [*A publication*]
PROCLIB ... Procedure Library [*Data processing*]
Proc Lincoln Coll Farmers Conf ... Proceedings. Lincoln College. Farmer's Conference [*A publication*]
Proc Linnean Soc NSW ... Proceedings. Linnean Society of New South Wales [*A publication*]
Proc Linn Soc Lond ... Proceedings. Linnean Society of London [*A publication*]
Proc Linn Soc London ... Proceedings. Linnean Society of London [*A publication*]
Proc Linn Soc NSW ... Proceedings. Linnean Society of New South Wales [*A publication*] (APTA)
Proc Linn Soc NY ... Proceedings. Linnean Society of New York [*A publication*]
Proc Liverpool Geol Soc ... Proceedings. Liverpool Geological Society [*A publication*]
Proc London Math Soc ... Proceedings. London Mathematical Society [*A publication*]
Proc London Math Soc 3 ... Proceedings. London Mathematical Society. Third Series [*A publication*]
Proc Lunar Sci Conf ... Proceedings. Lunar Science Conference [*United States*] [*A publication*]
Proc Lund Int Conf Elem Part ... Proceedings. Lund International Conference on Elementary Particles [*A publication*]
Proc Malacol Soc Lond ... Proceedings. Malacological Society of London [*A publication*]
Proc Mark Milk Conf ... Proceedings. Market Milk Conference [*A publication*]
Proc Mar Safety Council USCG ... Proceedings. Marine Safety Council. United States Coast Guard [*A publication*]

Proc Mass Hist Soc ... Proceedings. Massachusetts Historical Society [*A publication*]
Proc Math Phys Soc (Egypt) ... Proceedings. Mathematical and Physical Society (Egypt) [*A publication*]
Proc Mayo Clin ... Proceedings. Staff Meetings of the Mayo Clinic [*A publication*]
Proc Mayo Clin Staff Meet ... Proceedings. Mayo Clinic Staff Meeting [*A publication*]
Proc MD Del Water Pollut Control Assoc ... Proceedings. Maryland-Delaware Water and Pollution Control Association [*A publication*]
Proc MD Nutr Conf Feed Manuf ... Proceedings. Maryland Nutrition Conference for Feed Manufacturers [*A publication*]
Proc Meat Ind Res Conf ... Proceedings. Meat Industry Research Conference [*A publication*]
Proc Medico-Legal Soc Vict ... Proceedings. Medico-Legal Society of Victoria [*A publication*] (APTA)
Proc Med-Leg Soc Vic ... Medico-Legal Society of Victoria. Proceedings [*A publication*]
Proc Meet Adrenergic Mech ... Proceedings. Meeting on Adrenergic Mechanisms [*A publication*]
Proc Meet Anim Husb Wing Board Agric Anim Husb India ... Proceedings. Meeting of the Animal Husbandry Wing. Board of Agriculture and Animal Husbandry in India [*A publication*]
Proc Meet Int Soc Artif Organs ... Proceedings. Meeting. International Society for Artificial Organs [*A publication*]
Proc Meet Jpn Soc Med Mass Spectrom ... Proceedings. Meeting of the Japanese Society for Medical Mass Spectrometry [*A publication*]
Proc Meet Text Inf Users Counc ... Proceedings. Meeting. Textile Information Users Council [*A publication*]
Proc Meet West Indies Sugar Technol ... Proceedings. Meeting of West Indies Sugar Technologists [*A publication*]
Proc Microbiol Res Group Hung Acad Sci ... Proceedings. Microbiological Research Group. Hungarian Academy of Science [*A publication*]
Proc Microscopical Soc Vic ... Proceedings. Microscopical Society of Victoria [*Australia*] [*A publication*]
Proc Microsc Soc Can ... Proceedings. Microscopical Society of Canada [*A publication*]
Proc Mid-Atl Ind Waste Conf ... Proceedings. Mid-Atlantic Industrial Waste Conference [*United States*] [*A publication*]
Proc Midwest Conf Fluid Mech ... Proceedings. Midwest Conference on Fluid Mechanics [*A publication*]
Proc Midwest Fert Conf ... Proceedings. Midwestern Fertilizer Conference [*A publication*]
Proc Mid Year Meet Am Pet Inst ... Proceedings. Mid-Year Meeting. American Petroleum Institute [*A publication*]
Proc Mine Med Off Assoc ... Proceedings. Mine Medical Officers Association [*A publication*]
Proc Mine Med Off Assoc SA ... Proceedings. Mine Medical Officers Association of South Africa [*A publication*]
Proc Minn Acad Sci ... Proceedings. Minnesota Academy of Sciences [*A publication*]
Proc Minn Nutr Conf ... Proceedings. Minnesota Nutrition Conference [*A publication*]
Proc Minutes Ann Meet Agric Res Inst ... Proceedings and Minutes. Annual Meeting of the Agricultural Research Institute [*A publication*]
Proc Mont Acad Sci ... Proceedings. Montana Academy of Sciences [*A publication*]
Proc Mont Nutr Conf ... Proceedings. Montana Nutrition Conference [*A publication*]
Proc Montpellier Symp ... Proceedings. Montpellier Symposium [*A publication*]
Proc Mtg Comm For Tree Breeding Can ... Proceedings. Meeting of the Committee on Forest Tree Breeding in Canada [*A publication*]
Proc Mtg Sect Int Union For Res Organ ... Proceedings. Meeting of Section. International Union of Forest Research Organizations [*A publication*]
Proc Nagano Pref Agr Exp Sta ... Proceedings. Nagano Prefectural Agricultural Experiment Station [*A publication*]
Proc NA Sci ... Proceedings. National Academy of Sciences [*A publication*]
Proc Nassau Cty Med Cent ... Proceedings. Nassau County Medical Center [*A publication*]
Proc NASSH ... Proceedings. North American Society for Sport History [*A publication*]
Proc Nat Acad Sc ... Proceedings. National Academy of Science [*A publication*]
Proc Nat Acad Sci ... Proceedings. National Academy of Sciences [*United States of America*] [*A publication*]
Proc Nat Acad Sci (India) Sect A ... Proceedings. National Academy of Sciences (India). Section A [*A publication*]
Proc Nat Acad Sci (India) Sect B ... Proceedings. National Academy of Sciences (India). Section B. Biological Sciences [*A publication*]
Proc Nat Acad Sci (USA) ... Proceedings. National Academy of Sciences (United States of America) [*A publication*]

Proc Nat Acad Sci (USA) Biol Sci ... Proceedings. National Academy of Sciences (United States of America). Biological Sciences [*A publication*]

Proc Nat Acad Sci (USA) Phys Sci ... Proceedings. National Academy of Sciences (United States of America). Physical Sciences [*A publication*]

Proc Nat Ass Wheat Growers ... Proceedings. National Association of Wheat Growers [*A publication*]

Proc Nat Conf AIAS ... Proceedings. National Conference. Australian Institute of Agricultural Science [*A publication*] (APTA)

Proc Nat Conf Fluid Power Annu Meet ... Proceedings. National Conference on Fluid Power. Annual Meeting [*A publication*]

Proc Nat Electron Conf ... Proceedings. National Electronics Conference [*A publication*]

Proc Nat Food Eng Conf ... Proceedings. National Food Engineering Conference [*A publication*]

Proc Nat Gas Process Assoc Tech Pap ... Proceedings. Natural Gas Processors Association. Technical Papers [*A publication*]

Proc Nat Gas Processors Assoc Annu Conv ... Proceedings. Natural Gas Processors Association. Annual Convention [*A publication*]

Proc Natl Acad Sci ... Proceedings. National Academy of Sciences [*United States of America*] [*A publication*]

Proc Natl Acad Sci (India) ... Proceedings. National Academy of Sciences (India) [*A publication*]

Proc Natl Acad Sci (India) Sect A ... Proceedings. National Academy of Sciences (India). Section A. Physical Sciences [*A publication*]

Proc Natl Acad Sci (India) Sect A Phys Sci ... Proceedings. National Academy of Sciences (India). Section A. Physical Sciences [*A publication*]

Proc Natl Acad Sci (India) Sect B ... Proceedings. National Academy of Sciences (India). Section B. Biological Sciences [*A publication*]

Proc Natl Acad Sci (India) Sect B Biol Sci ... Proceedings. National Academy of Sciences (India). Section B. Biological Sciences [*A publication*]

Proc Natl Acad Sci (USA) ... Proceedings. National Academy of Sciences (United States of America) [*A publication*]

Proc Natl Biomed Sci Instrum Symp ... Proceedings. National Biomedical Sciences Instrumentation Symposium [*A publication*]

Proc Natl Cancer Conf ... Proceedings. National Cancer Conference [*A publication*]

Proc Natl Conf Adm Res ... Proceedings. National Conference on the Administration of Research [*A publication*]

Proc Natl Conf Electron Probe Anal ... Proceedings. National Conference on Electron Probe Analysis [*A publication*]

Proc Natl Conf Fluid Power ... Proceedings. National Conference on Fluid Power [*United States*] [*A publication*]

Proc Natl Conf Fluid Power Annu Meet ... Proceedings. National Conference on Fluid Power. Annual Meeting [*A publication*]

Proc Natl Conf Individ Onsite Wastewater Syst ... Proceedings. National Conference for Individual Onsite Wastewater Systems [*A publication*]

Proc Natl Conf Methadone Treat ... Proceedings. National Conference on Methadone Treatment [*A publication*]

Proc Natl Conv Study Inf Doc ... Proceedings. National Convention for the Study of Information and Documentation [*Japan*] [*A publication*]

Proc Natl Counc Radiat Prot Meas ... Proceedings. National Council on Radiation Protection and Measurements [*A publication*]

Proc Natl Counc Sci Dev (Repub China) ... Proceedings. National Council on Science Development (Republic of China) [*A publication*]

Proc Natl Dist Heat Assoc ... Proceedings. National District Heating Association [*A publication*]

Proc Natl Electron Conf ... Proceedings. National Electronics Conference [*A publication*]

Proc Natl Food Eng Conf ... Proceedings. National Food Engineering Conference [*A publication*]

Proc Natl Incinerator Conf ... Proceedings. National Incinerator Conference [*A publication*]

Proc Natl Inst Sci (India) ... Proceedings. National Institute of Sciences (India) [*A publication*]

Proc Natl Inst Sci (India) A ... Proceedings. National Institute of Sciences (India). Part A. Physical Sciences [*A publication*]

Proc Natl Inst Sci (India) Part A ... Proceedings. National Institute of Sciences (India). Part A. Physical Sciences [*A publication*]

Proc Natl Inst Sci (India) Part A Phys Sci ... Proceedings. National Institute of Sciences (India). Part A. Physical Sciences [*A publication*]

Proc Natl Inst Sci (India) Part A Suppl ... Proceedings. National Institute of Sciences (India). Part A. Supplement [*A publication*]

Proc Natl Inst Sci (India) Part B ... Proceedings. National Institute of Sciences (India). Part B. Biological Sciences [*A publication*]

Proc Natl Inst Sci (India) Part B Biol Sci ... Proceedings. National Institute of Sciences (India). Part B. Biological Sciences [*A publication*]

Proc Natl Meet Biophys Biotechnol Finl ... Proceedings. National Meeting on Biophysics and Biotechnology in Finland [*A publication*]

Proc Natl Meet Biophys Med Eng Finl ... Proceedings. National Meeting on Biophysics and Medical Engineering in Finland [*A publication*]

Proc Natl Meet For Prod Res Soc ... Proceedings. National Meeting. Forest Products Research Society [*A publication*]

Proc Natl Open Hearth Basic Oxygen Steel Conf ... Proceedings. National Open Hearth and Basic Oxygen Steel Conference [*A publication*]

Proc Natl Sci Counc ... Proceedings. National Science Council [*A publication*]

Proc Natl Sci Counc (Repub China) ... Proceedings. National Science Council (Republic of China) [*A publication*]

Proc Natl Sci Counc (Repub China) Part A Appl Sci ... Proceedings. National Science Council (Republic of China). Part A. Applied Sciences [*A publication*]

Proc Natl Sci Counc (Repub China) Part A Phys Sci Eng ... Proceedings. National Science Council (Republic of China). Part A. Physical Science and Engineering [*A publication*]

Proc Natl Sci Counc (Repub China) Part B Basic Sci ... Proceedings. National Science Council (Republic of China). Part B. Basic Science [*A publication*]

Proc Natl Sci Counc (Repub China) Part B Life Sci ... Proceedings. National Science Council (Republic of China). Part B. Life Sciences[*A publication*]

Proc Natl Shade Tree Conf ... Proceedings. National Shade Tree Conference [*A publication*]

Proc Natl Shellfish Assoc ... Proceedings. National Shellfisheries Association [*A publication*]

Proc Natl Symp Desalin ... Proceedings. National Symposium on Desalination [*A publication*]

Proc Natl Symp Radioecol ... Proceedings. National Symposium on Radioecology [*A publication*]

Proc Natl Telecommun Conf ... Proceedings. National Telecommunications Conference [*A publication*]

Proc Natn Acad Sci (India) ... Proceedings. National Academy of Sciences (India) [*A publication*]

Proc Natn Acad Sci (USA) ... Proceedings. National Academy of Sciences (United States of America) [*A publication*]

Proc Natn Ent Soc (USA) ... Proceedings. National Entomological Society (United States of America) [*A publication*]

Proc Natn Inst Sci (India) ... Proceedings. National Institute of Sciences (India) [*A publication*]

Proc Nat Silo Ass ... Proceedings. National Silo Association [*A publication*]

Proc Nat Telemetering Conf ... Proceedings. National Telemetering Conference [*A publication*]

Proc Natur Gas Processors Ass ... Proceedings. Natural Gas Processors Association [*A publication*]

Proc N Cent Brch Am Ass Econ Ent ... Proceedings. North Central Branch. American Association of Economic Entomologists [*A publication*]

Proc N Cent Brch Ent Soc Am ... Proceedings. North Central Branch. Entomological Society of America [*A publication*]

Proc ND Acad Sci ... Proceedings. North Dakota Academy of Science [*A publication*]

Proc N Dak Acad Sci ... Proceedings. North Dakota Academy of Science [*A publication*]

Proc Near E S Afr Irrig Pract Semin ... Proceedings. Near East - South Africa Irrigation Practices Seminar [*A publication*]

Proc Nebr Acad Sci ... Proceedings. Nebraska Academy of Sciences [*A publication*]

Proc Nebr Acad Sci Affil Soc ... Proceedings. Nebraska Academy of Sciences and Affiliated Societies [*A publication*]

Proc Ned Akad Wet ... Proceedings. Koninklijke Nederlandse Akademie van Wetenschappen [*A publication*]

Proc N Engl Bioeng Conf ... Proceedings. New England Bioengineering Conference [*A publication*]

Proc N Engl Soils Discuss Grp ... Proceedings. North of England Soils Discussion Group [*A publication*]

Proc NewC ... Proceedings. Society of Antiquaries of Newcastle-upon-Tyne [*A publication*]

Proc News Aust Oil Colour Chem Assoc ... Proceedings and News. Australian Oil and Colour Chemists Association [*A publication*] (APTA)

Proc News Aust Oil Colour Chemists Assoc ... Proceedings and News. Australian Oil and Colour Chemists Association [*A publication*] (APTA)

Proc NH Acad Sci ... Proceedings. New Hampshire Academy of Science [*A publication*]

Proc Ninth Int Grassld Congr ... Proceedings. Ninth International Grassland Congress [*A publication*]

Proc NJ Hist Soc ... Proceedings. New Jersey Historical Society [*A publication*]

Proc NJ Mosq Control Assoc ... Proceedings. New Jersey Mosquito Control Association [*A publication*]

Proc NJ Mosq Control Assoc Suppl ... Proceedings. New Jersey Mosquito Control Association. Supplement [*A publication*]

Proc NJ Mosq Exterm Assoc ... Proceedings. New Jersey Mosquito Extermination Association [*A publication*]

Proc N Mex W Tex Phil Soc ... Proceedings. New Mexico-West Texas Philosophical Society [*A publication*]

Proc NMFA ... Procedure. National Microfilm Association [*A publication*]

Proc Nord Aroma Symp ... Proceedings. Nordic Aroma Symposium [*A publication*]

Proc North Am Metalwork Res Conf ... Proceedings. North American Metalworking Research Conference [*A publication*]

Proc North Cent Branch Entomol Soc Am ... Proceedings. North Central Branch. Entomological Society of America [*A publication*]

Proc North Cent Weed Control Conf ... Proceedings. North Central Weed Control Conference [*A publication*]

Proc Northeast Weed Contr Conf ... Proceedings. Northeastern Weed Control Conference [*A publication*]

Proc Northeast Weed Control Conf ... Proceedings. Northeastern Weed Control Conference [*A publication*]

Proc Northeast Weed Sci Soc ... Proceedings. Northeastern Weed Science Society [*A publication*]

Proc Northwest Conf Struct Eng ... Proceedings. Northwest Conference of Structural Engineers [*A publication*]

Proc Northwest Wood Prod Clin ... Proceedings. Northwest Wood Products Clinic [*A publication*]

Proc NS Inst Sci ... Proceedings. Nova Scotian Institute of Science [*A publication*]

Proc Ntheast For Tree Impr Conf ... Proceedings. Northeastern Forest Tree Improvement Conference [*A publication*]

Proc Nucl Conf Feed Manuf ... Proceedings. Nutrition Conference for Feed Manufacturers [*A publication*]

Proc Nucl Phys Solid State Phys Symp ... Proceedings. Nuclear Physics and Solid State Physics Symposium [*India*] [*A publication*]

Proc Nurs Theory Conf ... Proceedings. Nursing Theory Conference [*A publication*]

Proc Nutr Soc ... Proceedings. Nutrition Society [*A publication*]

Proc Nutr Soc Aust ... Proceedings. Nutrition Society of Australia [*A publication*] (APTA)

Proc Nutr Soc Aust Annu Conf ... Proceedings. Nutrition Society of Australia. Annual Conference [*A publication*]

Proc Nutr Soc South Afr ... Proceedings. Nutrition Society of Southern Africa [*A publication*]

Proc NY St Hist Assn ... Proceedings. New York State Historical Association [*A publication*]

Proc NY St Hort Soc ... Proceedings. New York State Horticultural Society [*A publication*]

Proc NZ Ecol Soc ... Proceedings. New Zealand Ecological Society [*A publication*]

Proc NZ Grassl Assoc ... Proceedings. New Zealand Grassland Association [*A publication*]

Proc NZ Grassl Assoc Conf ... Proceedings. New Zealand Grassland Association. Conference [*A publication*]

Proc NZ Grassld Ass ... Proceedings. New Zealand Grassland Association [*A publication*]

Proc NZ Inst Agr Sci ... Proceedings. New Zealand Institute of Agricultural Science [*A publication*]

Proc NZ Soc Anim Proc ... Proceedings. New Zealand Society of Animal Production [*A publication*]

Proc NZ Weed Conf ... Proceedings. New Zealand Weed and Pest Control Conference [*A publication*]

Proc NZ Weed Control Conf ... Proceedings. New Zealand Weed Control Conference [*A publication*]

Proc NZ Weed Pest Contr Conf ... Proceedings. New Zealand Weed and Pest Control Conference [*A publication*]

Proc NZ Weed & Pest Control Conf ... Proceedings. New Zealand Weed and Pest Control Conference [*A publication*]

PROCO ..... Procurement Officer [*Military*]

PROCO ..... Programmed Combustion [*Ford Motor Co.*]

PROCO ..... Projects for Continental Operations [*World War II*]

Proc Ocean Drill Program Init Rep ... Proceedings. Ocean Drilling Program. Initial Reports [*A publication*]

Proc Ohio State Hortic Soc ... Proceedings. Ohio State Horticultural Society [*A publication*]

Proc Ohio State Hort Soc ... Proceedings. Ohio State Horticultural Society [*A publication*]

Proc Oil Recovery Conf Tex Petrol Res Comm ... Proceedings. Oil Recovery Conference. Texas Petroleum Research Committee [*A publication*]

Proc Okla Acad Sci ... Proceedings. Oklahoma Academy of Science [*A publication*]

PROCOM ... Procedures Committee [*Institute of Electrical and Electronics Engineers*] (IEEE)

PROCOM ... Procurement Committee

PROCOMEXCHI ... Mexican-Chicano Cooperative Programs on Mexican-US-Chicano Futures (EA)

PROCOMP ... Process Computer [*Data processing*]

PROCOMP ... Program Compiler [*Data processing*] (IEEE)

PROCON .. Request Diagnosis, Prognosis, Present Condition, Probable Date and Mode of Disposition of Following Patient Reported in Your Hospital [*Military*]

Proc Ont Ind Waste Conf ... Proceedings. Ontario Industrial Waste Conference [*A publication*]

Procop .... Procopius [*Sixth century AD*] [*Classical studies*] (OCD)

Proc Oreg Acad Sci ... Proceedings. Oregon Academy of Science [*A publication*]

Proc Oreg Weed Conf ... Proceedings. Oregon Weed Conference [*A publication*]

Proc Organ Inst NSW ... Proceedings. Organ Institute of New South Wales [*A publication*]

Proc Osaka Prefect Inst Public Health Ed Food Sanit ... Proceedings. Osaka Prefecture Institute of Public Health. Edition of Food Sanitation [*A publication*]

Proc Osaka Prefect Inst Public Health Ed Ind Health ... Proceedings. Osaka Prefecture Institute of Public Health. Edition of Industrial Health [*A publication*]

Proc Osaka Prefect Inst Public Health Ed Ment Health ... Proceedings. Osaka Prefecture Institute of Public Health. Edition of Mental Health [*A publication*]

Proc Osaka Prefect Inst Public Health Ed Pharm Aff ... Proceedings. Osaka Prefecture Institute of Public Health. Edition of Pharmaceutical Affairs [*A publication*]

Proc Osaka Prefect Inst Public Health Ed Public Health ... Proceedings. Osaka Prefecture Institute of Public Health. Edition of Public Health [*A publication*]

Proc Osaka Public Health Inst ... Proceedings. Osaka Public Health Institute [*Japan*] [*A publication*]

PROCOTIP ... Promotion Cooperative du Transport Individuel Publique [*Public cars for private use to reduce traffic congestion*] [*Also known as TIP*] [*France*]

Proc PA Acad Sci ... Proceedings. Pennsylvania Academy of Science [*A publication*]

Proc Pac Chem Eng Congr ... Proceedings. Pacific Chemical Engineering Congress [*A publication*]

Proc Pac Coast Gas Ass ... Proceedings. Pacific Coast Gas Association, Inc. [*California*] [*A publication*]

Proc Pac Northwest Fert Conf ... Proceedings. Pacific Northwest Fertilizer Conference [*A publication*]

Proc Pac Northwest Ind Waste Conf ... Proceedings. Pacific Northwest Industrial Waste Conference [*A publication*]

Proc Pac Sci Congr ... Proceedings. Pacific Science Congress [*A publication*]

Proc PA Ger Soc ... Proceedings and Addresses. Pennsylvania-German Society [*A publication*]

Proc Pak Acad Sci ... Proceedings. Pakistan Academy of Sciences [*A publication*]

Proc Pakistan Statist Assoc ... Proceedings. Pakistan Statistical Association [*A publication*]

Proc Pakist Sci Conf ... Proceedings. Pakistan Science Conference [*A publication*]

Proc Pak Sci Conf ... Proceedings. Pakistan Science Conference [*A publication*]

Proc Panel Pract Appl Peaceful Uses Nucl Explos ... Proceedings. Panel on the Practical Applications of the Peaceful Uses of Nuclear Explosions [*A publication*]

Proc Pap Annu Conf Calif Mosq Control Assoc ... Proceedings and Papers. Annual Conference. California Mosquito Control Association [*A publication*]

Proc Pap Annu Conf Calif Mosq Vector Control Assoc ... Proceedings and Papers. Annual Conference. California Mosquito and Vector Control Association [*A publication*]

Proc Pap Graphic Arts Conf ... Proceedings and Papers. Graphic Arts Conference [*A publication*]

Proc Pap Int Union Conserv Nature Nat Resour ... Proceedings and Papers. International Union for the Conservation of Nature and Natural Resources [*A publication*]

Proc Path Soc Phila ... Proceedings. Pathological Society of Philadelphia [*A publication*]

Proc Paving Conf ... Proceedings. Paving Conference [*A publication*]

Proc Penn Acad Sci ... Proceedings. Pennsylvania Academy of Science [*A publication*]

Proc Peoria Acad Sci ... Proceedings. Peoria Academy of Science [*A publication*]

Proc Perugia Quadrenn Int Conf Cancer ... Proceedings. Perugia Quadrennial International Conference on Cancer [*A publication*]

Proc Pharm Soc Egypt ... Proceedings. Pharmaceutical Society of Egypt [*A publication*]

Proc Phil As ... Proceedings. American Philological Association [*A publication*]

Proc Phil Educ Soc Austl ... Proceedings. Philosophy of Education Society of Australasia [*A publication*]

Proc Phil Educ Soc GB ... Proceedings. Philosophy of Education Society of Great Britain [*A publication*]

Proc Phil Soc ... Proceedings. American Philosophical Society [*A publication*]

Proc Phys Math Soc Jpn ... Proceedings. Physico-Mathematical Society of Japan [*A publication*]

Proc Phys Semin Trondheim ... Proceedings. Physics Seminar in Trondheim [*Norway*] [*A publication*]

Proc Phys Soc ... Proceedings. Physics Society [*A publication*]

Proc Phys Soc Edinb ... Proceedings. Physical Society of Edinburgh [*A publication*]

Proc Phys Soc Jpn ... Proceedings. Physical Society of Japan [*A publication*]

Proc Phys Soc Lond ... Proceedings. Physical Society of London [*A publication*]

Proc Phys Soc London ... Proceedings. Physical Society of London [*A publication*]

Proc Phys Soc London Gen Phys ... Proceedings. Physical Society. London. General Physics [*A publication*]

Proc Phys Soc London Sect A ... Proceedings. Physical Society of London. Section A [*A publication*]

Proc Phys Soc London Sect B ... Proceedings. Physical Society of London. Section B [*A publication*]

Proc Phytochem Soc ... Proceedings. Phytochemical Society [*A publication*]

Proc Plant Growth Regul Work Group ... Proceedings. Plant Growth Regulator Working Group [*A publication*]

Proc Plant Propagators' Soc ... Proceedings. Plant Propagators' Society [*United States*] [*A publication*]
Proc PN Lebedev Phys Inst ... Proceedings. P. N. Lebedev Physics Institute [*A publication*]
Proc PN Lebedev Phys Inst Acad Sci USSR ... Proceedings. P. N. Lebedev Physics Institute. Academy of Sciences of the USSR [*A publication*]
Proc Porcelain Enamel Inst Tech Forum ... Proceedings. Porcelain Enamel Institute. Technical Forum [*A publication*]
Proc Power Plant Dyn Control Test Symp ... Proceedings. Power Plant Dynamics. Control and Testing Symposium [*A publication*]
Proc Pr .... Proctor's Practice [*A publication*] (DLA)
Proc Prac ... Proctor's Practice [*A publication*] (DLA)
Proc Prehist Soc ... Proceedings. Prehistoric Society [*A publication*]
Proc Pr Hist Soc ... Proceedings. Prehistoric Society [*A publication*]
Proc Process Inst Meet ... Proceedings. Processing Instructors' Meeting [*A publication*]
Proc Prod Liability Prev Conf ... Proceedings. Product Liability Prevention Conference [*A publication*]
Proc Pr Soc ... Proceedings. Prehistoric Society of East Anglia [*A publication*]
Proc PS ...... Proceedings. Prehistoric Society [*A publication*]
Proc Public Health Eng Conf ... Proceedings. Public Health Engineering Conference [*Loughborough University of Technology*] [*A publication*]
Proc QD Soc Sug Cane Tech ... Queensland Society of Sugar Cane Technologists. Proceedings [*A publication*] (APTA)
Proc QD Soc Sug Cane Technol ... Proceedings. Queensland Society of Sugar Cane Technologists [*A publication*]
Proc Quadrenn IAGOD Symp ... Proceedings. Quadrennial IAGOD [*International Association on the Genesis of Ore Deposits*] Symposium [*A publication*]
Proc Queensl Soc Sugar Cane Technol ... Proceedings. Queensland Society of Sugar Cane Technologists [*A publication*]
Proc Queensl Soc Sug Cane Technol ... Queensland Society of Sugar Cane Technologists. Proceedings [*A publication*] (APTA)
Proc Queens Soc Sugar Cane Technol ... Queensland Society of Sugar Cane Technologists. Proceedings [*A publication*] (APTA)
Proc Radio Club Am ... Proceedings. Radio Club of America [*A publication*]
Proc Radioisot Soc Philipp ... Proceedings. Radioisotope Society of the Philippines [*A publication*]
Proc R Agric Hort Soc S Aust ... Royal Agricultural and Horticultural Society of South Australia. Proceedings [*A publication*] (APTA)
Proc Rajasthan Acad Sci ... Proceedings. Rajasthan Academy of Sciences [*A publication*]
Proc R Aust Chem Inst ... Proceedings. Royal Australian Chemical Institute [*A publication*]
Proc R Can Inst ... Proceedings. Royal Canadian Institute [*A publication*]
Proc 3rd Int Conf Peaceful Uses Atom Energy ... Proceedings. Third International Conference on the Peaceful Uses of Atomic Energy [*A publication*]
Proc Refin Dep Am Pet Inst ... Proceedings. Refining Department. American Petroleum Institute [*A publication*]
Proc Reg Conf Int Potash Inst ... Proceedings. Regional Conference. International Potash Institute [*A publication*]
Proc Regge Cut Conf ... Proceedings. Regge Cut Conference [*A publication*]
Proc Relay Conf ... Proceedings. Relay Conference [*A publication*]
Proc Reliab Maint Conf ... Proceedings. Reliability and Maintainability Conference [*A publication*]
Proc Remote Syst Technol Div ANS ... Proceedings. Remote Systems Technology Division of the American Nuclear Society [*A publication*]
Proc Rencontre Moriond ... Proceedings. Rencontre de Moriond [*A publication*]
Proc R Entomol Soc Lond Ser A Gen Entomol ... Proceedings. Royal Entomological Society of London. Series A. General Entomology [*A publication*]
Proc R Entomol Soc Lond Ser B Taxon ... Proceedings. Royal Entomological Society of London. Series B. Taxonomy [*A publication*]
Proc R Ent Soc ... Proceedings. Royal Entomological Society [*A publication*]
Proc R Ent Soc Lond A ... Proceedings. Royal Entomological Society of London. A [*A publication*]
Proc Rep Belfast Nat Hist Philos Soc ... Proceedings and Reports. Belfast Natural History and Philosophical Society [*A publication*]
Proc Rep S Seedmen's Ass ... Proceedings and Reports. Southern Seedmen's Association [*A publication*]
Proc Res Conf Res Counc Am Meat Inst Found Univ Chicago ... Proceedings. Research Conference Sponsored by the Research Council of the American Meat Institute Foundation. University of Chicago [*A publication*]
Proc Res Inst Atmos Nagoya Univ ... Proceedings. Research Institute of Atmospherics. Nagoya University [*A publication*]
Proc Res Inst Nucl Med Biol ... Proceedings. Research Institute for Nuclear Medicine and Biology [*A publication*]
Proc Res Inst Nucl Med Biol Hiroshima Univ ... Proceedings. Research Institute for Nuclear Medicine and Biology. Hiroshima University [*Japan*] [*A publication*]
Proc Res Inst Oceanogr Fish (Varna) ... Proceedings. Research Institute of Oceanography and Fisheries (Varna) [*A publication*]

Proc Res Inst Pomol (Skierniewice Pol) Ser E Conf Symp ... Proceedings. Research Institute of Pomology (Skierniewice, Poland). Series E. Conferences and Symposia [*A publication*]
Proc Res Soc Jap Sugar Refin Technol ... Proceedings. Research Society of Japan Sugar Refineries' Technologists [*A publication*]
Proc Res Soc Jpn Sugar Refineries' Technol ... Proceedings. Research Society of Japan Sugar Refineries' Technologists [*A publication*]
Proc R Geogr Soc Australas S Aust Br ... Proceedings. Royal Geographical Society of Australasia. South Australian Branch [*A publication*] (APTA)
Proc R Geogr Soc Australas South Aust Branch ... Proceedings. Royal Geographical Society of Australasia. South Australian Branch [*A publication*] (APTA)
Proc R Geog Soc Aust S Aust Br ... Proceedings. Royal Geographical Society of Australasia. South Australian Branch [*A publication*] (APTA)
Proc RGS ... Proceedings. Royal Geographical Society [*A publication*]
Proc R Hortic Soc ... Proceedings. Royal Horticulture Society [*A publication*]
Proc R Inst GB ... Proceedings. Royal Institution of Great Britain [*A publication*]
Proc R Instn Gt Br ... Proceedings. Royal Institution of Great Britain [*A publication*]
Proc Rio Grande Val Hortic Inst ... Proceedings. Rio Grande Valley Horticultural Institute [*A publication*]
Proc R Ir Acad ... Proceedings. Royal Irish Academy [*A publication*]
Proc R Ir Acad A ... Proceedings. Royal Irish Academy. Section A. Mathematical, Astronomical, and Physical Science [*A publication*]
Proc R Ir Acad Sect B ... Proceedings. Royal Irish Academy. Section B. Biological, Geological, and Chemical Science [*A publication*]
Proc R Ir Acad Sect B Biol Geol Chem Sci ... Proceedings. Royal Irish Academy. Section B. Biological, Geological, and Chemical Science [*A publication*]
Proc R Irish Acad Sect A ... Proceedings. Royal Irish Academy. Section A. Mathematical, Astronomical, and Physical Science [*A publication*]
Proc R Irish Acad Sect B ... Proceedings. Royal Irish Academy. Section B. Biological, Geological, and Chemical Science [*A publication*]
Proc Risoe Int Symp Metall Mater Sci ... Proceedings. Risoe International Symposium on Metallurgy and Materials Science [*A publication*]
Proc R Microsc Soc ... Proceedings. Royal Microscopical Society [*England*] [*A publication*]
Proc RNS ... Proceedings. Royal Numismatic Society [*A publication*]
Proc Robert A Welch Found Conf Chem Res ... Proceedings. Robert A. Welch Foundation. Conferences on Chemical Research [*A publication*]
Proc Rochester Acad Sci ... Proceedings. Rochester Academy of Science [*A publication*]
Proc Rocky Mt Coal Min Inst ... Proceedings. Rocky Mountain Coal Mining Institute [*A publication*]
Proc Royal Aust Chem Inst ... Proceedings. Royal Australian Chemical Institute [*A publication*] (APTA)
Proc Royal Irish Acad ... Proceedings. Royal Irish Academy [*A publication*]
Proc Royal M Assoc ... Proceedings. Royal Musical Association [*A publication*]
Proc Royal Soc Canad ... Proceedings. Royal Society of Canada [*A publication*]
Proc Royal Soc London Ser A ... Proceedings. Royal Society of London. Series A. Mathematical and Physical Sciences [*A publication*]
Proc Royal Soc London Series A ... Proceedings. Royal Society of London. Series A [*A publication*]
Proc Roy Anthropol Inst ... Proceedings. Royal Anthropological Institute [*A publication*]
Proc Roy Anthropol Inst Gr Brit Ir ... Proceedings. Royal Anthropological Institute of Great Britain and Ireland [*A publication*]
Proc Roy Aust Chem Inst ... Proceedings. Royal Australian Chemical Institute [*A publication*] (APTA)
Proc Roy Entomol Soc Lond ... Proceedings. Royal Entomological Society of London [*A publication*]
Proc Roy Entomol Soc Lond C ... Proceedings. Royal Entomological Society of London. Series C. Journal of Meetings [*A publication*]
Proc Roy Entomol Soc London Ser A ... Proceedings. Royal Entomological Society of London. Series A [*A publication*]
Proc Roy Geog Soc Austral ... Proceedings. Royal Geographical Society of Australia. South Australian Branch [*A publication*]
Proc Roy Inst ... Proceedings. Royal Institution of Great Britain [*A publication*]
Proc Roy Inst Gr Brit ... Proceedings. Royal Institution of Great Britain [*A publication*]
Proc Roy Ir Acad B C ... Proceedings. Royal Irish Academy. Series B and C [*A publication*]
Proc Roy Irish Acad ... Proceedings. Royal Irish Academy [*A publication*]
Proc Roy Irish Acad Sect A ... Proceedings. Royal Irish Academy. Section A. Mathematical, Astronomical, and Physical Science [*A publication*]
Proc Roy Phys Soc Edinb ... Proceedings. Royal Physical Society of Edinburgh [*A publication*]
Proc Roy Soc ... Proceedings. Royal Society [*A publication*]

Proc Roy Soc B ... Proceedings. Royal Society of London. Series B. Biological Sciences [*A publication*]
Proc Roy Soc Can ... Proceedings. Royal Society of Canada [*A publication*]
Proc Roy Soc Canada ... Proceedings. Royal Society of Canada [*A publication*]
Proc Roy Soc Canada 4 ... Proceedings. Royal Society of Canada. Fourth Series [*A publication*]
Proc Roy Soc Edinb ... Proceedings. Royal Society of Edinburgh [*A publication*]
Proc Roy Soc Edinb B ... Proceedings. Royal Society of Edinburgh. Section B. Biological Sciences [*A publication*]
Proc Roy Soc Edinburgh Sect A ... Proceedings. Royal Society of Edinburgh. Section A. Mathematical and Physical Sciences [*A publication*]
Proc Roy Soc London ... Proceedings. Royal Society of London [*A publication*]
Proc Roy Soc London S B ... Proceedings. Royal Society of London. Series B. Biological Sciences [*A publication*]
Proc Roy Soc London Ser A ... Proceedings. Royal Society of London. Series A. Mathematical and Physical Sciences [*A publication*]
Proc Roy Soc Med ... Proceedings. Royal Society of Medicine [*A publication*]
Proc Roy Soc QD ... Royal Society of Queensland. Proceedings [*A publication*] (APTA)
Proc Roy Soc Qld ... Proceedings. Royal Society of Queensland [*Australia*] [*A publication*]
Proc Roy Soc Ser A ... Proceedings. Royal Society. Series A [*A publication*]
Proc Roy Soc Vic ... Proceedings. Royal Society of Victoria [*Australia*] [*A publication*]
Proc Roy Soc Vict ... Royal Society of Victoria. Proceedings [*A publication*] (APTA)
Proc Roy Zool Soc NSW ... Royal Zoological Society of New South Wales. Proceedings [*A publication*] (APTA)
Proc R Philos Soc Glasgow ... Proceedings. Royal Philosophical Society of Glasgow [*A publication*]
Proc R Physiogr Soc Lund ... Proceedings. Royal Physiograph Society at Lund [*A publication*]
Proc R Phys Soc Edinb ... Proceedings. Royal Physical Society of Edinburgh [*A publication*]
Proc R Soc A ... Proceedings. Royal Society of London. Series A. Mathematical and Physical Sciences [*A publication*]
Proc R Soc B ... Proceedings. Royal Society of London. Series B. Biological Sciences [*A publication*]
Proc R Soc Can ... Proceedings. Royal Society of Canada [*A publication*]
Proc R Soc Edinb Biol ... Proceedings. Royal Society of Edinburgh. Section B. Biology [*A publication*]
Proc R Soc Edinb Nat Environ ... Proceedings. Royal Society of Edinburgh. Section B. Natural Environment [*A publication*]
Proc R Soc Edinb Sect A ... Proceedings. Royal Society of Edinburgh. Section A. Mathematical and Physical Sciences [*Later, Proceedings. Royal Society of Edinburgh. Mathematics*] [*A publication*]
Proc R Soc Edinb Sect A Math Phys Sci ... Proceedings. Royal Society of Edinburgh. Section A. Mathematical and Physical Sciences [*Later, Proceedings. Royal Society of Edinburgh. Mathematics*] [*A publication*]
Proc R Soc Edinb Sect B ... Proceedings. Royal Society of Edinburgh. Section B. Biological Sciences [*A publication*]
Proc R Soc Edinb Sect B Biol ... Proceedings. Royal Society of Edinburgh. Section B. Biology [*A publication*]
Proc R Soc Edinb Sect B Nat Environ ... Proceedings. Royal Society of Edinburgh. Section B. Natural Environment [*A publication*]
Proc R Soc Edinburgh ... Proceedings. Royal Society of Edinburgh [*A publication*]
Proc R Soc Edinburgh B ... Proceedings. Royal Society of Edinburgh. Section B. Biological Sciences [*A publication*]
Proc R Soc Edinburgh Biol Sci ... Proceedings. Royal Society of Edinburgh. Section B. Biological Sciences [*A publication*]
Proc R Soc Edinburgh Sect A ... Proceedings. Royal Society of Edinburgh. Section A. Mathematical and Physical Sciences [*A publication*]
Proc R Soc Edinburgh Sect B Nat Environ ... Proceedings. Royal Society of Edinburgh. Section B. Natural Environment [*A publication*]
Proc R Soc Lond ... Proceedings. Royal Society of London. Series B. Biological Sciences [*A publication*]
Proc R Soc Lond B Biol Sci ... Proceedings. Royal Society of London. Series B. Biological Sciences [*A publication*]
Proc R Soc Lond Biol ... Proceedings. Royal Society of London. Series B. Biological Sciences [*A publication*]
Proc R Soc London A ... Proceedings. Royal Society of London. Series A. Mathematical and Physical Sciences [*A publication*]
Proc R Soc London Ser A ... Proceedings. Royal Society of London. Series A. Mathematical and Physical Sciences [*A publication*]
Proc R Soc Med ... Proceedings. Royal Society of Medicine [*A publication*]
Proc R Soc Med Suppl ... Proceedings. Royal Society of Medicine. Supplement [*England*] [*A publication*]
Proc R Soc NZ ... Proceedings. Royal Society of New Zealand [*A publication*]
Proc R Soc QD ... Proceedings. Royal Society of Queensland [*A publication*]
Proc R Soc Queensl ... Proceedings. Royal Society of Queensland [*A publication*]
Proc R Soc VIC ... Royal Society of Victoria. Proceedings [*A publication*] (APTA)

Proc R Soc Vict ... Proceedings. Royal Society of Victoria [*A publication*]
Proc R Soc Victoria ... Proceedings. Royal Society of Victoria [*A publication*]
Proc Ruakura Farmers Conf ... Proceedings. Ruakura Farmers' Conference [*A publication*]
Proc Ruakura Farmers Conf Week ... Proceedings. Ruakura Farmers' Conference Week [*A publication*]
Proc Rudolf Virchow Med Soc City NY ... Proceedings. Rudolf Virchow Medical Society in the City of New York [*A publication*]
Proc Rudolph Virchow Med Soc NY ... Proceedings. Rudolph Virchow Medical Society of New York [*A publication*]
Proc R Zool Soc NSW ... Proceedings. Royal Zoological Society of New South Wales [*A publication*]
PROCS ...... Proceedings
Proc S Afr Soc Anim Prod ... Proceedings. South African Society of Animal Production [*A publication*]
Proc S Afr Sugar Technol Assoc Annu Congr ... Proceedings. South African Sugar Technologists Association. Annual Congress [*A publication*]
Proc Sagamore Army Mater Res Conf ... Proceedings. Sagamore Army Materials Research Conference [*A publication*]
Proc San Diego Biomed Symp ... Proceedings. San Diego Biomedical Symposium [*A publication*]
Proc SA Scot ... Proceedings. Society of Antiquaries of Scotland [*A publication*]
Proc S Aust Brch R Geogr Soc Australas ... Royal Geographical Society of Australasia. South Australian Branch. Proceedings [*A publication*] (APTA)
Proc Scand Symp Surf Act ... Proceedings. Scandinavian Symposium on Surface Activity [*A publication*]
Proc SC Hist Assn ... Proceedings. South Carolina Historical Association [*A publication*]
Proc Sci Assoc Nigeria ... Proceedings. Science Association of Nigeria [*A publication*]
Proc Sci Inst Kinki Univ ... Proceedings. Science Institution. Kinki University [*A publication*]
Proc Sci Sect Toilet Goods Assoc ... Proceedings. Scientific Section of the Toilet Goods Association [*A publication*]
Proc Sci Soc Univ Adel ... Proceedings. Scientific Society. University of Adelaide [*A publication*]
Proc Scotts Turfgrass Res Conf ... Proceedings. Scotts Turfgrass Research Conference [*A publication*]
PROCSD ... Processed
Proc SD Acad Sci ... Proceedings. South Dakota Academy of Science [*A publication*]
Proc S Dak Acad Sci ... Proceedings. South Dakota Academy of Science [*A publication*]
Proc Sea Grant Conf ... Proceedings. Sea Grant Conference [*A publication*]
Proc Sec Int Symp Vet Epidemiol Econ ... Proceedings. Second International Symposium on Veterinary Epidemiology and Economics [*A publication*]
Proc Second Malays Soil Conf (Kuala Lumpur) ... Proceedings. Second Malaysian Soil Conference (Kuala Lumpur) [*A publication*]
Proc Sect Sci Is Acad Sci Humanit ... Proceedings. Section of Sciences. Israel Academy of Sciences and Humanities [*A publication*]
Proc Sect Sci K Ned Akad Wet ... Proceedings. Section of Sciences. Koninklijke Nederlandse Akademie van Wetenschappen [*A publication*]
Proc Seed Protein Conf ... Proceedings. Seed Protein Conference [*A publication*]
Proc Semin Biomass Energy City Farm Ind ... Proceedings. Seminar on Biomass Energy for City, Farm, and Industry [*A publication*]
Proc Semin Electrochem ... Proceedings. Seminar on Electrochemistry [*A publication*]
Proc Ser Am Water Resour Assoc ... Proceedings Series. American Water Resources Association [*A publication*]
Proc Serono Clin Colloq Reprod ... Proceedings. Serono Clinical Colloquia on Reproduction [*A publication*]
Proc Serono Symp ... Proceedings. Serono Symposia [*A publication*]
Proc SESA ... Proceedings. Society for Experimental Stress Analysis [*A publication*]
Proc Shikoku Br Crop Sci Soc (Jap) ... Proceedings. Shikoku Branch of Crop Science Society (Japan) [*A publication*]
Proc SID .... Proceedings. SID [*Society for Information Display*] [*A publication*]
Proc Sigatoka Workshop ... Proceedings. Sigatoka Workshop [*A publication*]
Proc Sigrid Juselius Found Symp ... Proceedings. Sigrid Juselius Foundation Symposium [*A publication*]
Proc Silvic Conf ... Proceedings. Silviculture Conference [*A publication*]
Proc Soc Agric Bacteriol ... Proceedings. Society of Agricultural Bacteriologists [*A publication*]
Proc Soc Am For ... Proceedings. Society of American Foresters [*A publication*]
Proc Soc Anal Chem ... Proceedings. Society for Analytical Chemistry [*A publication*]
Proc Soc Antiq Scot ... Proceedings. Society of Antiquaries of Scotland [*A publication*]
Proc Soc Antiq Scotland ... Proceedings. Society of Antiquaries of Scotland [*A publication*]
Proc Soc Antiqu London ... Proceedings. Society of Antiquaries of London [*A publication*]

Proc Soc Appl Bact ... Proceedings. Society for Applied Bacteriology [*A publication*]
Proc Soc Appl Bacteriol ... Proceedings. Society for Applied Bacteriology [*A publication*]
Proc Soc Biol Chem ... Proceedings. Society of Biological Chemists [*A publication*]
Proc Soc Biol Chem India ... Proceedings. Society of Biological Chemists of India [*A publication*]
Proc Soc Can ... Proceedings. Royal Society of Canada [*A publication*]
Proc Soc Chem Indust Vic ... Proceedings. Society of Chemical Industry of Victoria [*Australia*] [*A publication*]
Proc Soc Chem Ind (Victoria) ... Proceedings. Society of Chemical Industry (Victoria) [*A publication*]
Proc Soc Exp Biol Med ... Proceedings. Society for Experimental Biology and Medicine [*A publication*]
Proc Soc Exp Biol (NY) ... Proceedings. Society for Experimental Biology and Medicine (New York) [*A publication*]
Proc Soc Exper Biol Med ... Proceedings. Society for Experimental Biology and Medicine [*A publication*]
Proc Soc Exp Stress Anal ... Proceedings. Society for Experimental Stress Analysis [*A publication*]
Proc Soc Exp Stress Analysis ... Proceedings. Society for Experimental Stress Analysis [*A publication*]
Proc Soc Ind Microbiol ... Proceedings. Society for Industrial Microbiology [*A publication*]
Proc Soc Inf Disp ... Proceedings. Society for Information Display [*A publication*]
Proc Soc Lond ... Proceedings. Royal Society of London [*A publication*]
Proc Soc Med ... Proceedings. Royal Society of Medicine [*A publication*]
Proc Soc Photo Opt Instrum Eng ... Proceedings. Society of Photo-Optical Instrumentation Engineers [*A publication*]
Proc Soc Promot Agric Sci ... Proceedings. Society for the Promotion of Agricultural Science [*A publication*]
Proc Soc Protozool ... Proceedings. Society of Protozoologists [*A publication*]
Proc Soc Relay Eng ... Proceedings. Society of Relay Engineers [*A publication*]
Proc Soc Study Fertil ... Proceedings. Society for the Study of Fertility [*A publication*]
Proc Soc Study Ind Med ... Proceedings. Society for the Study of Industrial Medicine [*A publication*]
Proc Soc Vict ... Proceedings. Royal Society of Victoria [*A publication*]
Proc Soc Water Treat Exam ... Proceedings. Society for Water Treatment and Examination [*A publication*]
Proc Soil Crop Sci Soc Fla ... Proceedings. Soil and Crop Science Society of Florida [*A publication*]
Proc Soil Sci Soc Am ... Proceedings. Soil Science Society of America [*A publication*]
Proc Soil Sci Soc Amer ... Proceedings. Soil Science Society of America [*A publication*]
Proc Soil Sci Soc Fla ... Proceedings. Soil Science Society of Florida [*A publication*]
Proc Solvay Conf Phys ... Proceedings. Solvay Conference on Physics [*A publication*]
Proc Somerset Arch Natur Hist Soc ... Proceedings. Somerset Archaeology and Natural History Society [*A publication*]
Proc South Afr Electron Microsc Soc Verrigtings ... Proceedings. Southern African Electron Microscopy Society-Verrigtings [*A publication*]
Proc South Conf For Tree Improv ... Proceedings. Southern Conference on Forest Tree Improvement [*A publication*]
Proc Southeast Asian Reg Semin Trop Med Public Health ... Proceedings. Southeast Asian Regional Seminar on Tropical Medicine and Public Health [*A publication*]
Proc Southeastcon Reg 3 (Three) Conf ... Proceedings. Southeastcon Region 3 (Three) Conference [*United States*] [*A publication*]
Proc Southeast Pecan Grow Assoc ... Proceedings. Southeastern Pecan Growers Association [*US*] [*A publication*]
Proc South For Tree Improv Conf ... Proceedings. Southern Forest Tree Improvement Conference [*A publication*]
Proc South Lond Entom and Nat Hist Soc ... Proceedings. South London Entomological and Natural History Society [*A publication*]
Proc South Munic Ind Waste Conf ... Proceedings. Southern Municipal and Industrial Waste Conference [*A publication*]
Proc South Pasture Forage Crop Improv Conf ... Proceedings. Southern Pasture and Forage Crop Improvement Conference [*A publication*]
Proc South Wales Inst Eng ... Proceedings. South Wales Institute of Engineers [*A publication*]
Proc South Water Resour Pollut Control Conf ... Proceedings. Southern Water Resources and Pollution Control Conference [*A publication*]
Proc South Weed Conf ... Proceedings. Southern Weed Conference [*A publication*]
Proc South Weed Sci Soc ... Proceedings. Southern Weed Science Society [*A publication*]
Proc Southwest Agr Trade Farm Policy Conf ... Proceedings. Southwestern Agricultural Trade Farm Policy Conference [*A publication*]
Proc Space Congr ... Proceedings. Space Congress. Technology for the New Horizon [*A publication*]

Proc SPE Symp Form Damage Control ... Proceedings. Society of Petroleum Engineers. American Institute of Mining, Metallurgical, and Petroleum Engineers. Symposium on Formation Damage Control [*A publication*]
Proc SPE Symp Improv Oil Recovery ... Proceedings. Society of Petroleum Engineers. American Institute of Mining, Metallurgical, and Petroleum Engineers. Symposium on Improved Oil Recovery [*A publication*]
Proc SPI Annu Struct Foam Conf ... Proceedings. SPI [*Society of the Plastics Industry*] Annual Structural Foam Conference [*A publication*]
Proc SPI Int Tech Mark Conf ... Proceedings. SPI [*Society of the Plastic Industry*] International Technical/Marketing Conference [*A publication*]
Proc SPI Struct Foam Conf ... Proceedings. SPI [*Society of the Plastics Industry*] Structural Foam Conference [*A publication*]
Proc Sprinkler Irrig Assoc Tech Conf ... Proceedings. Sprinkler Irrigation Association. Technical Conference [*A publication*]
Proc SSSA ... Proceedings. Soil Science Society of America [*A publication*]
Proc St .... Process Studies [*A publication*]
Proc Staff Meetings Mayo Clin ... Proceedings. Staff Meetings of the Mayo Clinic [*A publication*]
Proc Staff Meet Mayo Clin ... Proceedings. Staff Meeting. Mayo Clinic [*A publication*]
Proc Staffs Iron Steel Inst ... Proceedings. Staffordshire Iron and Steel Institute [*A publication*]
Proc State Coll Wash Inst Dairy ... Proceedings. State College of Washington. Institute of Dairying [*A publication*]
Proc State Horti Assoc PA ... Proceedings. State Horticultural Association of Pennsylvania [*A publication*]
Proc State Secr Manage Conf Am Dent Assoc ... Proceedings. State Secretaries Management Conference. American Dental Association [*A publication*]
Proc Steel Treat Res Soc ... Proceedings. Steel Treating Research Society [*A publication*]
Proc Steenbock Symp ... Proceedings. Steenbock Symposium [*A publication*]
Proc Steklov Inst Math ... Proceedings. Steklov Institute of Mathematics [*A publication*]
Proc Sth Conf For Tree Impr ... Proceedings. Southern Conference on Forest Tree Improvement [*A publication*]
Proc Sth Weed Control Conf ... Proceedings. Southern Weed Control Conference [*A publication*]
Proc Sth Weed Sci Soc ... Proceedings. Southern Weed Science Society [*A publication*]
Proc Stream Workshop ... Proceedings. Streams Workshop [*A publication*]
Proc Study Fauna Flora USSR Sect Bot ... Proceedings on the Study of the Fauna and Flora of the USSR. Section of Botany [*A publication*]
Proc 1st Vic Weed Conf ... Proceedings. First Victorian Weed Conference [*A publication*] (APTA)
Proc Suff Inst A ... Proceedings. Suffolk Institute of Archaeology [*A publication*]
Proc Suffolk Inst Arch ... Proceedings. Suffolk Institute of Archaeology [*A publication*]
Proc Suffolk Inst Archaeol Hist ... Proceedings. Suffolk Institute of Archaeology and History [*A publication*]
Proc Sugar Beet Res Assoc ... Proceedings. Sugar Beet Research Association [*A publication*]
Proc Sugar Process Res Conf ... Proceedings. Sugar Processing Research Conference [*A publication*]
Proc Summer Comput Simul Conf ... Proceedings. Summer Computer Simulation Conference [*A publication*]
Proc Summer Conf Spectrosc Its Appl ... Proceedings. Summer Conference on Spectroscopy and Its Application [*A publication*]
Proc Summer Inst Part Phys ... Proceedings. Summer Institute on Particle Physics [*A publication*]
Proc S Wales Inst Eng ... Proceedings. South Wales Institute of Engineers [*A publication*]
Proc Symp Algol ... Proceedings. Symposium on Algology [*A publication*]
Proc Symp Appl Math ... Proceedings. Symposia in Applied Mathematics [*A publication*]
Proc Symp Biol Skin ... Proceedings. Symposium on the Biology of Skin [*A publication*]
Proc Symp Chem Biochem Prostanoids ... Proceedings. Symposium on the Chemistry and Biochemistry of Prostanoids [*A publication*]
Proc Symp Chem Data Append R Aust Chem Inst ... Proceedings. Symposium on Chemical Data. Royal Australian Chemical Institute [*A publication*] (APTA)
Proc Symp Chem Physiol Pathol ... Proceedings. Symposium on Chemical Physiology and Pathology [*A publication*]
Proc Symp Cosmic Rays Elem Part Phys Astrophys ... Proceedings. Symposium on Cosmic Rays, Elementary Particle Physics, and Astrophysics [*A publication*]
Proc Symp Effects Ionizing Radiat Seed Signific Crop Impr ... Proceedings. Symposium on the Effects of Ionizing Radiation on Seeds and Their Significance for Crop Improvement [*A publication*]
Proc Symp Eng Aspects Magnetohydrodyn ... Proceedings. Symposium. Engineering Aspects of Magnetohydrodynamics [*A publication*]

Proc Symp Eng Probl Fusion Res ... Proceedings. Symposium on Engineering Problems of Fusion Research [*A publication*]
Proc Symp Explos Pyrotech ... Proceedings. Symposium on Explosives and Pyrotechnics [*A publication*]
Proc Symp Fertil Indian Soils ... Proceedings. Symposium on Fertility of Indian Soils [*A publication*]
Proc Symp Ind Waste Control ... Proceedings. Symposium on Industrial Waste Control [*A publication*]
Proc Symp Isotop Plant Nutr Physiol (Vienna Austria) ... Proceedings. Symposium on Isotopes in Plant Nutrition and Physiology (Vienna, Austria) [*A publication*]
Proc Symp Mater Sci Res ... Proceedings. Symposium on Materials Science Research [*A publication*]
Proc Symp Neutron Dosim ... Proceedings. Symposium on Neutron Dosimetry [*A publication*]
Proc Sympos Appl Math ... Proceedings. Symposia in Applied Mathematics [*A publication*]
Proc Sympos Pure Math ... Proceedings. Symposia in Pure Mathematics [*A publication*]
Proc Symp Packag Electron Devices ... Proceedings. Symposium on Packaging of Electronic Devices [*A publication*]
Proc Symp Particleboard ... Proceedings. Symposium on Particleboard [*A publication*]
Proc Symp Photogr Sensitivity ... Proceedings. Symposium on Photographic Sensitivity [*A publication*]
Proc Symp Pract Treat Low Intermed Level Radioact Wastes ... Proceedings. Symposium on Practice in the Treatment of Low- and Intermediate-Level Radioactive Wastes [*A publication*]
Proc Symp Rock Mech ... Proceedings. Symposium on Rock Mechanics [*A publication*]
Proc Symp Soc Study Inborn Errors Metab ... Proceedings. Symposium. Society for the Study of Inborn Errors of Metabolism [*A publication*]
Proc Symp Spec Ceram ... Proceedings. Symposium on Special Ceramics [*A publication*]
Proc Symp Turbul Liq ... Proceedings. Symposium on Turbulence in Liquids [*A publication*]
Proc Symp Underwater Physiol ... Proceedings. Symposium on Underwater Physiology [*A publication*]
Proc Symp Use Isotop Weed Res ... Proceedings. Symposium on the Use of Isotopes in Weed Research [*Vienna, Austria*] [*A publication*]
Proc Symp Use Radioisotop Soil Plant Nutr Stud ... Proceedings. Symposium on the Use of Radioisotopes in Soil-Plant Nutrition Studies [*A publication*]
Proc Symp Waste Manage ... Proceedings. Symposium on Waste Management [*A publication*]
Proc Synth Pipeline Gas Symp ... Proceedings. Synthetic Pipeline Gas Symposium [*A publication*]
Proc Syst Symp ... Proceedings. Systems Symposium [*A publication*]
PROCT ...... Proctology
Proc Tall Timbers Conf Ecol Anim Control Habitat Manage ... Proceedings. Tall Timbers Conference on Ecological Animal Control by Habitat Management [*A publication*]
Proc Tall Timbers Fire Ecol Conf ... Proceedings. Tall Timbers Fire Ecology Conference [*A publication*]
Proc Tech Conf Soc Vac Coaters ... Proceedings. Technical Conference. Society of Vacuum Coaters [*A publication*]
Proc Tech Groups NZ Inst Eng ... Proceedings of Technical Groups. New Zealand Institution of Engineers [*A publication*]
Proc Tech Meet Soc Eng Sci ... Proceedings. Technical Meeting. Society of Engineering Science [*A publication*]
Proc Tech Mtg Int Union Conserv Nature ... Proceedings. Technical Meeting. International Union for Conservation of Nature and Natural Resources [*A publication*]
Proc Tech Program Electro-Opt Laser Conf Exp ... Proceedings. Technical Program. Electro-Optics/Laser Conference and Exposition [*A publication*]
Proc Tech Program Int Powder Bulk Solids Handl Process ... Proceedings. Technical Program. International Powder and Bulk Solids Handling and Processing [*A publication*]
Proc Tech Program Natl Electron Packag Prod Conf ... Proceedings. Technical Program. National Electronic Packaging and Production Conference [*A publication*]
Proc Tech Sess Cane Sugar Refin Res ... Proceedings. Technical Session on Cane Sugar Refining Research [*A publication*]
Proc Tex AM Annu Symp Instrum Process Ind ... Proceedings. Texas A & M Annual Symposium on Instrumentation for the Process Indtries [*A publication*]
Proc Tex Conf Comput Syst ... Proceedings. Texas Conference on Computing Systems [*A publication*]
Proc Tex Nutr Conf ... Proceedings. Texas Nutrition Conference [*A publication*]
Proc Tex Water Sewage Works Short Sch ... Proceedings. Texas Water and Sewage Works Short School [*A publication*]
Proc Tex Water Util Short Sch ... Proceedings. Texas Water Utilities Short School [*A publication*]
ProctG .... Procter & Gamble Co. [*Associated Press abbreviation*]   (APAG)
Proc Therm Power Conf ... Proceedings. Thermal Power Conference [*A publication*]
PROCTO ... Proctoscopy [*Medicine*]

Proc Top Conf RF Plasma Heat ... Proceedings. Topical Conference on RF Plasma Heating [*A publication*]
PROCTOR ... Priority Routine Organizer for Computer Transfers and Operations of Registers
PROCTOT ... Priority Routine Organizer for Computer Transfers and Operations and Transfers
Proc Trans Br Entomol Nat Hist Soc ... Proceedings and Transactions. British Entomological and Natural History Society [*A publication*]
Proc Trans Croydon Natur Hist Sci Soc ... Proceedings and Transactions. Croydon Natural History and Scientific Society [*A publication*]
Proc Trans Liverp Biol Soc ... Proceedings and Transactions. Liverpool Biological Society [*A publication*]
Proc and Trans Rhod Sci Assoc ... Proceedings and Transactions. Rhodesia Scientific Association [*A publication*]
Proc Trans R Soc Can ... Proceedings and Transactions. Royal Society of Canada [*A publication*]
Proc Tree Wardens Arborists Util Conf ... Proceedings. Tree Wardens, Arborists, and Utilities Conference [*A publication*]
Proc and Tr Liverpool Biol Soc ... Proceedings and Transactions. Liverpool Biological Society [*A publication*]
Proc Trop Reg ASHS ... Proceedings. Tropical Region ASHS [*American Society for Horticultural Science*] [*A publication*]
Proc Tr PN Lebedev Phys Inst ... Proceedings (Trudy). P. N. Lebedev Physics Institute [*A publication*]
Proc (Trudy) P N Lebedev Phys Inst ... Proceedings (Trudy). P. N. Lebedev Physics Institute [*A publication*]
ProCTS ...... Proceedings. College Theology Society [*A publication*]
Proc Tub Res Coun ... Proceedings. Tuberculosis Research Council [*A publication*]
Proc Turbomachinery Symp ... Proceedings. Turbomachinery Symposium [*A publication*]
Proc Turfgrass Sprinkler Irrig Conf ... Proceedings. Turfgrass Sprinkler Irrigation Conference [*A publication*]
PROCU ..... Processing Unit
Proc UNESCO Conf Radioisot Sci Res ... Proceedings. UNESCO Conference on Radioisotopes in Scientific Research [*A publication*]
Proc Univ Bristol Spelaeol Soc ... Proceedings. University of Bristol Spelaeological Society [*A publication*]
Proc Univ Durham Philos Soc Ser A ... Proceedings. University of Durham Philosophical Society. Series A. Science [*A publication*]
Proc Univ Durham Phil Soc ... Proceedings. University of Durham. Philosophical Society [*A publication*]
Proc Univ MD Nutr Conf Feed Mfr ... Proceedings. University of Maryland. Nutrition Conference for Feed Manufacturers [*A publication*]
Proc Univ MO Annu Conf Trace Subst Environ Health ... Proceedings. University of Missouri. Annual Conference on Trace Substances in Environmental Health [*A publication*]
Proc Univ Newcastle Upon Tyne Philos Soc ... Proceedings. University of Newcastle-Upon-Tyne Philosophical Society [*A publication*]
Proc Univ Otago Med Sch ... Proceedings. University of Otago Medical School [*A publication*]
PROCUP ... Partido Revolucionario Obrerista y Clandestino de Union Popular [*Mexico*] [*Political party*]   (EY)
Proc USAID Ghana Agr Conf ... Proceedings. USAID [*United States Agency for International Development*]. Ghana Agriculture Conference [*A publication*]
Proc US DOE Photovoltaics Technol Dev Appl Program Rev ... Proceedings. US DOE [*Department of Energy*] Photovoltaics Technology Development and Applications Program Review [*A publication*]
Proc US Natl Mus ... Proceedings. United States National Museum [*A publication*]
Proc US Nat Mus ... Proceedings. United States National Museum [*A publication*]
Proc US Nucl Regul Comm Water Reactor Saf Inf Meet ... Proceedings. US Nuclear Regulatory Commission Water Reactor Safety Information Meeting [*A publication*]
Proc Ussher Soc ... Proceedings. Ussher Society [*A publication*]
Proc Utah Acad Sci ... Proceedings. Utah Academy of Sciences, Arts, and Letters [*A publication*]
Proc Utah Acad Sci Arts Lett ... Proceedings. Utah Academy of Sciences, Arts, and Letters [*A publication*]
PROCVAL ... Validation Procedures Library [*Social Security Administration*]
Proc Vertebr Pest Conf ... Proceedings. Vertebrate Pest Conference [*A publication*]
Proc Veterans Adm Spinal Cord Inj Conf ... Proceedings. Veterans Administration Spinal Cord Injury Conference [*A publication*]
Proc Vib Probl ... Proceedings of Vibration Problems [*A publication*]
Proc VIC Weeds Conf ... Proceedings. Victorian Weeds Science Society [*A publication*]   (APTA)
Proc Virchow-Pirquet Med Soc ... Proceedings. Virchow-Pirquet Medical Society [*A publication*]
Proc Virgil Soc ... Proceedings. Virgil Society [*A publication*]
Proc Vol Bakish Mater Corp Publ ... Proceedings Volume. Bakish Materials Corporation. Publication [*A publication*]
Proc Vol Electrochem Soc ... Proceedings Volume. Electrochemical Society [*A publication*]

Proc WA Instn Eng ... Proceedings. Western Australian Institution of
　　Engineers [*A publication*]
Proc Wash Anim Nutr Conf ... Proceedings. Washington Animal Nutrition
　　Conference [*A publication*]
Proc Wash State Entomol Soc ... Proceedings. Washington State
　　Entomological Society [*A publication*]
Proc Wash State Univ Int Particleboard/Compos Mater Ser ... Proceedings.
　　Washington State University International Particleboard/
　　Composite Materials Series [*A publication*]
Proc Wash State Univ Int Symp Particleboard ... Proceedings. Washington
　　State University International Symposium on Particleboard
　　[*A publication*]
Proc Wash State Univ Symp Particleboard ... Proceedings. Washington State
　　University Symposium on Particleboard [*A publication*]
Proc Wash St Ent Soc ... Proceedings. Washington State Entomological
　　Society [*A publication*]
Proc Wash St Hort Ass ... Proceedings. Washington State Horticultural
　　Association [*A publication*]
Proc Water Borne Higher Solids Coat Symp ... Proceedings. Water-Borne and
　　Higher-Solids Coatings Symposium [*A publication*]
Proc Weed Soc NSW ... Proceedings. Weed Society of New South Wales [*A
　　publication*]   (APTA)
Proc West Can Weed Control Conf ... Proceedings. Western Canadian Weed
　　Control Conference [*A publication*]
Proc West Chapter Int Shade Tree Conf ... Proceedings. Western Chapter.
　　International Shade Tree Conference [*A publication*]
Proc West Eur Conf Photosyn ... Proceedings. Western Europe Conference on
　　Photosynthesis [*A publication*]
Proc West For Conserv Ass ... Proceedings. Western Forestry Conference.
　　Western Forestry and Conservation Association [*A
　　publication*]
Proc West Found Vertebr Zool ... Proceedings. Western Foundation of
　　Vertebrate Zoology [*A publication*]
Proc West Pharmacol Soc ... Proceedings. Western Pharmacology Society [*A
　　publication*]
Proc West Poult Dis Conf ... Proceedings. Western Poultry Disease
　　Conference [*A publication*]
Proc West Poult Dis Conf Poult Health Symp ... Proceedings. Western Poultry
　　Disease Conference and Poultry Health Symposia [*United
　　States*] [*A publication*]
Proc West Poult Dis Conf Poult Heath Symp ... Proceedings. Western Poultry
　　Disease Conference and Poultry Health Symposia [*A
　　publication*]
Proc West Snow Conf ... Proceedings. Western Snow Conference [*A
　　publication*]
Proc West Soc Weed Sci ... Proceedings. Western Society of Weed Science [*A
　　publication*]
Proc West Virginia Acad Sci ... Proceedings. West Virginia Academy of
　　Science [*A publication*]
Proc Wis Hist Soc ... Proceedings. Wisconsin State Historical Society [*A
　　publication*]
Proc Wkly Semin Neurol ... Proceedings. Weekly Seminar in Neurology [*A
　　publication*]
Proc Wld For Congr ... Proceedings. World Forestry Congress [*A publication*]
Proc Wld Orchid Conf ... Proceedings. World Orchid Conference [*A
　　publication*]
Proc Wood Pole Inst Colo State Univ ... Proceedings. Wood Pole Institute.
　　Colorado State University [*A publication*]
Proc World Conf Clin Pharmacol Ther ... Proceedings. World Conference on
　　Clinical Pharmacology and Therapeutics [*A publication*]
Proc World Congr Agr Res ... Proceedings. World Congress of Agricultural
　　Research [*A publication*]
Proc World Congr Fertil Steril ... Proceedings. World Congress on Fertility
　　and Sterility [*A publication*]
Proc World Congr Gastroenterol ... Proceedings. World Congress of
　　Gastroenterology [*A publication*]
Proc World Congr Pain ... Proceedings. World Congress on Pain [*A
　　publication*]
Proc World For Congr ... Proceedings. World Forestry Congress [*A
　　publication*]
Proc World Pet Congr ... Proceedings. World Petroleum Congress [*A
　　publication*]
Proc World Poultry Congr ... Proceedings. World Poultry Congress [*A
　　publication*]
Proc W Va Acad Sci ... Proceedings. West Virginia Academy of Science [*A
　　publication*]
Proc Yorks Geol Soc ... Proceedings. Yorkshire Geological Society [*England*]
　　[*A publication*]
Proc Yorkshire Geol Soc ... Proceedings. Yorkshire Geological Society [*A
　　publication*]
Proc Zool Soc ... Proceedings. Zoological Society [*A publication*]
Proc Zool Soc (Calcutta) ... Proceedings. Zoological Society (Calcutta) [*A
　　publication*]
Proc Zool Soc Lond ... Proceedings. Zoological Society of London [*A
　　publication*]
PROD .... Office of Production [*National Security Agency*]
PROD .... Photographic Retrieval from Optical Disk
PROD .... Prisoner Rehabilitation on Discharge [*A publication*]   (APTA)
PROD .... Produce
PROD .... Product [*or Production*]   (AABC)
PROD .... Professional Drivers Council for Safety and Health

PROD .... Professional Over-the-Road Drivers [*Part of Teamsters Union*]
PRODAC ... Programmed Digital Automatic Control [*Data processing*]
Prod Aggregates GB ... Production of Aggregates in Great Britain [*A
　　publication*]
Prod Agric Fr ... Producteur Agricole Francais [*A publication*]
PRODAN .. Propionyl(dimethylamino)naphthalene [*Organic chemistry*]
Prod Anim ... Produzione Animale [*A publication*]
PRODASE ... Protein Database
Prod Aust... Productivity Australia [*A publication*]
PRODC ..... Production Command [*Army*]
Proden........ Proyecto de Desarrollo Nacional [*Project for National
　　Development*] [*Chile*]   (PPW)
Prod Eng .... Product Engineering [*A publication*]
Prod Eng (Cleveland) ... Production Engineering (Cleveland) [*A publication*]
Prod Eng (Lond) ... Production Engineer (London) [*A publication*]
Prod Engng ... Production Engineering [*A publication*]
Prod Engr. ... Production Engineer [*London*] [*A publication*]
Pr Odes Gidrometeorol Inst ... Pratsi Odes'kogo Gidrometeorologichnogo
　　Institutu [*A publication*]
Prod Finish ... Product Finishing [*Cincinnati*] [*A publication*]
Prod Finish (Cinci) ... Product Finishing (Cincinnati) [*A publication*]
Prod Finish (Cincinnati) ... Products Finishing (Cincinnati) [*A publication*]
Prod Finish (Lond) ... Product Finishing (London) [*A publication*]
Prod G Am J ... Producers Guild of America. Journal [*A publication*]
Prod Invent Manage ... Production and Inventory Management [*A
　　publication*]
Prod and Inventory Manage ... Production and Inventory Management [*A
　　publication*]
PRODISCO ... Producers Distributing Corp.
Prod Lait Mod ... Production Laitiere Moderne [*A publication*]
Prod Liability Int ... Product Liability International [*A publication*]
Prod Liab Int ... Product Liability International [*A publication*]
Prod Liab Int'l ... Product Liability International [*A publication*]   (DLA)
Prod Liab Rep ... Product Liability Reporter [*Commerce Clearing House*] [*A
　　publication*]   (DLA)
Prod Liab Rep CCH ... Product Liability Reporter. Commerce Clearing House
　　[*A publication*]
Prod Manage ... Production Management [*A publication*]
Prod Market ... Product Marketing [*A publication*]
Prod Marketing ... Produce Marketing [*A publication*]
Prod Miner Serv Fom Prod Miner Avulso ... Producao Mineral Servico de
　　Fomento da Producao Mineral. Avulso [*A publication*]
Prod Miner Serv Fom Prod Miner Bol ... Producao Mineral Servico de
　　Fomento da Producao Mineral. Boletim [*A publication*]
Prod Mkt ... Product Marketing [*A publication*]
Prod Mktg ... Product Marketing [*A publication*]
Prod Mon... Producers Monthly [*United States*] [*A publication*]
Prodn .... Production
Prodn Engnr ... Production Engineer [*A publication*]
Prodn J ...... Production Journal [*A publication*]
ProDnt .... Professional Dental Technologies, Inc. [*Associated Press
　　abbreviation*]   (APAG)
PRODON ... Production
PRO DOS ... Pro Dose [*For a Dose*] [*Pharmacy*]
Prod Pharm ... Produits Pharmaceutiques [*France*] [*A publication*]
Prod Probl Pharm ... Produits et Problemes Pharmaceutiques [*A publication*]
Prod Prod Bull Natl Coal Board Min Dep ... Production and Productivity
　　Bulletin. National Coal Board. Mining Department [*A
　　publication*]
Prod Proj Trends Bldg ... Products, Projects, and Trends in Building [*A
　　publication*]   (APTA)
Prod Publ Assoc Off Seed Certifying Agencies ... Production Publication.
　　Association of Official Seed Certifying Agencies [*A
　　publication*]
Prod Publ Int Crop Impr Ass ... Production Publication. International Crop
　　Improvement Association [*A publication*]
PRODR ..... Producer
Prod Res Rep ... Production Research Report [*A publication*]
Prod Res Rep US Dep Agric ... Production Research Report. United States
　　Department of Agriculture [*A publication*]
Prod Res Rep US Dep Agric Sci Educ Adm ... Production Research Report.
　　United States Department of Agriculture. Science and
　　Education Administration [*A publication*]
Prod Rev .... Producers' Review [*A publication*]   (APTA)
Prod with Safety ... Production with Safety [*A publication*]   (APTA)
Prod Safety & Liab Rep ... Product Safety and Liability Reporter [*A
　　publication*]   (DLA)
Prod Safety & Liab Rep BNA ... Product Safety and Liability Reporter.
　　Bureau of National Affairs [*A publication*]
Prod Technol ... Productivity and Technology [*A publication*]
Prod Tech (Osaka) ... Production and Technique (Osaka) [*Japan*] [*A
　　publication*]
Prod Tech (Suita) ... Production and Technique (Suita) [*Japan*] [*A
　　publication*]
Produccion Anim ... Produccion Animal [*A publication*]
Producers R ... Producers' Review [*A publication*]   (APTA)
Producers' Rev ... Producers' Review [*A publication*]
Product Eng ... Product Engineering [*A publication*]
Product et Gestion ... Production et Gestion [*A publication*]
Production ... Production Engineering [*A publication*]
PRODUCTN ... Production

Product Res Dev ... Product Research and Development [*A publication*]
Produits Pharm ... Produits et Problemes Pharmaceutiques [*A publication*]
PRODUTAS ... Proceed on Duty Assigned [*Military*]
PRODVAL ... Product Validation   (MCD)
Prod Veg Cereale Plante Teh ... Productia Vegetala. Cereale si Plante Tehnice [*A publication*]
Prod Veg Mec Agric ... Productia Vegetala. Mecanizarea Agriculturii [*A publication*]
Prod Yb FAO ... Production Yearbook FAO [*Food and Agriculture Organization*] [*A publication*]
PROE .... Programme Regional Oceanien de l'Environnement [*South Pacific Regional Environmental Programme - SPREP*]   (EAIO)
Proefstn Akkerbouw Lelystad Versl Interprov Proeven ... Proefstation voor de Akkerbouw Lelystad. Verslagen van Interprovinciale Proeven [*A publication*]
Proefstn Akkerbouw (Wageningen) Versl Interprov Proeven ... Proefstation voor de Akkerbouw (Wageningen). Verslagen van Interprovinciale Proeven [*A publication*]
Pro Engr ..... Professional Engineer [*A publication*]   (APTA)
Pro Ex .... Protein Exchange [*Dietetics*]
PROF .... Peace Research Organization Fund
PROF .... Personal Radio Operators Federation [*Inactive*]   (EA)
PROF .... Profanity [*FBI standardized term*]
PROF .... Profession [*or Professional*]
PROF .... Professional Investors Insurance Group, Inc. [*NASDAQ symbol*]   (NQ)
PROF .... Professional Office System
PROF .... Professor   (EY)
Prof .... Profile
PROF .... Pupil Registering and Operational Filing [*Data processing*]
PROFAC ... Propulsive Fluid Accumulator
Prof Admin ... Professional Administration [*A publication*]
Prof Admin ... Professional Administrator [*A publication*]
PROFAGTRANS ... Proceed by First Available Government Transportation [*Military*]
Pro Fam Inf ... Pro Familia Informationen [*A publication*]
PROFAT ... Projet des Francophones de l'Atlantique [*Canada*]
Prof Build ... Professional Builder [*A publication*]
Prof Build Apartm Bus ... Professional Builder and Apartment Business [*A publication*]
Prof Builder/Apt Bus ... Professional Builder and Apartment Business [*A publication*]
Prof Burd ... Commemoratio Professorum Burdigalensium [*of Ausonius*] [*Classical studies*]   (OCD)
Prof Camera ... Professional Camera [*A publication*]
Prof Corp ... Proffatt on Private Corporations in California [*A publication*]   (DLA)
Prof Corp Guide (P-H) ... Professional Corporation Guide (Prentice-Hall, Inc.) [*A publication*]   (DLA)
PROFCY ... Proficiency
PROF-E ..... Programmed Review of Operator Functions - Elementary   (DNAB)
Prof Eng ..... Professional Engineer
Prof Eng (Pretoria) ... Professional Engineer (Pretoria) [*A publication*]
Prof Engr ... Professional Engineer [*A publication*]
Prof Eng (Wash DC) ... Professional Engineer (Washington, DC) [*A publication*]
Professional Eng ... Professional Engineer [*A publication*]   (APTA)
Profession Med ... Profession Medicale [*A publication*]
Professions et Entr ... Professions et Entreprises [*A publication*]
PROFESSL ... Professional
PROFFIS .. Professional Filler System [*Military*]
Prof Flashes ... Professional Flashes [*A publication*]
Prof Geog ... Professional Geographer [*A publication*]
Prof Geogr ... Professional Geographer [*A publication*]
Prof Geologist ... Professional Geologist [*A publication*]
Profile .... Profiles [*A publication*]
PROFILE ... Programmed Functional Indices for Laboratory Evaluation [*RAND Corp.*]
PROFILE ... [*A*] Programming Language   (CSR)
Profile Med Pract ... Profile of Medical Practice [*A publication*]
PROFILES ... Personal Reflection on Family Life and Employment Stressors [*Psychology*]
Profiles Hosp Mark ... Profiles in Hospital Marketing [*A publication*]
Profils Econ Nord-Pas-De-Calais ... Profils de l'Economie Nord-Pas-De-Calais [*A publication*]
Prof Inferm ... Professioni Infermieristiche [*A publication*]
PROFIS ..... Programminformationssystem Sozialwissenschaften [*Informationszentrum Sozialwissenschaften*] [*Germany*] [*Defunct*] [*Information service or system*]   (CRD)
PROFIT .... Program for Financed Insurance Techniques
PROFIT .... Programmed Reviewing, Ordering, and Forecasting Inventory Technique
PROFIT .... Propulsion Flight Control Integration Technology   (MCD)
Prof Jur ...... Proffatt on Trial by Jury [*A publication*]   (DLA)
PROFL ...... Professional
Prof Med Assist ... Professional Medical Assistant [*A publication*]
Prof Not ...... Proffatt on Notaries [*A publication*]   (DLA)
Prof Nurse ... Professional Nurse [*A publication*]
Prof Nurs Home ... Professional Nursing Home [*A publication*]

Prof Nutr .... Professional Nutritionist [*A publication*]
Prof Officer ... Professional Officer [*A publication*]
PROFP ...... Proficiency Pay [*Military*]
Prof Pap Deputy Minist Miner Resour (Saudi Arabia) ... Professional Papers. Deputy Ministry for Mineral Resources (Saudi Arabia) [*A publication*]
Prof Pap Geol Surv ... Professional Papers. United States Geological Survey [*A publication*]
Prof Pap Ser Fla Dep Nat Resour Mar Res Lab ... Professional Papers Series. Florida Department of Natural Resources. Marine Research Laboratory [*A publication*]
Prof Pap US Geol Surv ... Professional Papers. United States Geological Survey [*A publication*]
Prof Photogr ... Professional Photographer [*A publication*]
Prof Prac Man ... Professional Practice Management [*A publication*]
Prof Print ... Professional Printer [*A publication*]
Prof Psycho ... Professional Psychology [*A publication*]
Prof Regulation N ... Professional Regulation News [*A publication*]
Prof Rpt ..... Professional Report [*A publication*]
PROFS ...... Professional Office System [*IBM Corp.*]
PROFS ...... Program for Regional Observing and Forecasting Services [*Boulder, CO*] [*Department of Commerce*]   (GRD)
PROFS ...... Prototype Regional Observation and Forecasting Service [*National Oceanic and Atmospheric Administration*]   (GRD)
Prof Saf ...... Professional Safety [*A publication*]
Prof Safety ... Professional Safety [*A publication*]
Prof Sanit Manage ... Professional Sanitation Management [*A publication*]
Prof Wills .. Proffatt on Wills [*A publication*]   (DLA)
PROG .... Prognosis [*or Prognostication*]   (AAG)
PROG .... Program   (KSC)
PROG .... Programmer [*or Programming*]
PROG .... Progress   (AABC)
Prog .... Progressive [*A publication*]
Prog Aeronaut Sci ... Progress in Aeronautical Science [*A publication*]
Prog Aerosp Sci ... Progress in Aerospace Sciences [*A publication*]
Prog Agric ... Progresso Agricolo [*A publication*]
Prog Agric Ariz ... Progressive Agriculture in Arizona [*A publication*]
Prog Agric Vitic ... Progres Agricole et Viticole [*France*] [*A publication*]
Prog Agri Fr ... Progres Agricole de France [*A publication*]
Prog Allerg ... Progress in Allergy [*A publication*]
Prog Allergol Jpn ... Progress of Allergology in Japan [*A publication*]
Prog Allergy ... Progress in Allergy [*A publication*]
Prog Anal At Spectrosc ... Progress in Analytical Atomic Spectroscopy [*A publication*]
Prog Anal Chem ... Progress in Analytical Chemistry [*A publication*]
Prog Anat ... Progress in Anatomy [*A publication*]
Prog Androl ... Progres en Andrologie [*A publication*]
Prog Anesthesiol ... Progress in Anesthesiology [*A publication*]
Prog Anim Biometeorol ... Progress in Animal Biometeorology [*A publication*]
Prog Appl Mater Res ... Progress in Applied Materials Research [*A publication*]
Prog Appl Microcirc ... Progress in Applied Microcirculation [*A publication*]
Prog Arch ... Progressive Architecture [*A publication*]
Prog Archit ... Progressive Architecture [*A publication*]
Prog Astronaut Aeronaut ... Progress in Astronautics and Aeronautics [*A publication*]
Prog Astronaut Rocketry ... Progress in Astronautics and Rocketry [*A publication*]
Prog Astronaut Sci ... Progress in the Astronautical Sciences [*A publication*]
Prog At Med ... Progress in Atomic Medicine [*A publication*]
Prog Batteries Sol Cell ... Progress in Batteries and Solar Cells [*A publication*]
Prog Behav Modif ... Progress in Behavior Modification [*A publication*]
Prog Biochem Biophys ... Progress in Biochemistry and Biophysics [*People's Republic of China*] [*A publication*]
Prog Biochem Pharmacol ... Progress in Biochemical Pharmacology [*A publication*]
Prog Biochim ... Progressi in Biochimica [*A publication*]
Prog Biocybern ... Progress in Biocybernetics [*A publication*]
Prog Biol Sci Relat Dermatol ... Progress in the Biological Sciences in Relation to Dermatology [*A publication*]
Prog Biomass Convers ... Progress in Biomass Conversion [*A publication*]
Prog Biometeorol ... Progress in Biometeorology [*A publication*]
Prog Biometeorol Div A ... Progress in Biometeorology. Division A. Progress in Human Biometeorology [*Netherlands*] [*A publication*]
Prog Biometeorol Div B ... Progress in Biometeorology. Division B. Progress in Animal Biometeorology [*A publication*]
Prog Bioorg Chem ... Progress in Bioorganic Chemistry [*A publication*]
Prog Biophys Biophys Chem ... Progress in Biophysics and Biophysical Chemistry [*A publication*]
Prog Biophys Mol Biol ... Progress in Biophysics and Molecular Biology [*A publication*]
PROG BK ... Programmed Book [*Publishing*]
Prog Boron Chem ... Progress in Boron Chemistry [*A publication*]
Prog Bot ..... Progress in Botany [*A publication*]
Prog Bot Fortschr Bot ... Progress in Botany-Fortschritt der Botanik [*A publication*]
Prog Brain Res ... Progress in Brain Research [*A publication*]
Prog Build ... Progressive Builder [*A publication*]
Prog Cancer Res Ther ... Progress in Cancer Research and Therapy [*A publication*]

Prog Cardiol ... Progress in Cardiology [*A publication*]
Prog Cardiovasc Dis ... Progress in Cardiovascular Diseases [*A publication*]
Prog Catecholamine Res Part B Proc Int Catecholamine Symp ... Progress in Catecholamine Research. Part B. Central Aspects. Proceedings. International Catecholamine Symposium [*A publication*]
Prog Ceram Sci ... Progress in Ceramic Science [*A publication*]
Prog Chem Fats ... Progress in the Chemistry of Fats and Other Lipids [*A publication*]
Prog Chem Fats Other Lipids ... Progress in the Chemistry of Fats and Other Lipids [*A publication*]
Prog Chem Fibrinolysis Thrombolysis ... Progress in Chemical Fibrinolysis and Thrombolysis [*A publication*]
Prog Chem Toxicol ... Progress in Chemical Toxicology [*A publication*]
Prog Clin Biochem Med ... Progress in Clinical Biochemistry and Medicine [*A publication*]
Prog Clin Biol Res ... Progress in Clinical and Biological Research [*A publication*]
Prog Clin Cancer ... Progress in Clinical Cancer [*A publication*]
Prog Clin Immunol ... Progress in Clinical Immunology [*A publication*]
Prog Clin Neurophysiol ... Progress in Clinical Neurophysiology [*A publication*]
Prog Clin Pathol ... Progress in Clinical Pathology [*A publication*]
Prog Clin Pharm ... Progress in Clinical Pharmacy [*A publication*]
Prog Clin Pharmacol ... Progress in Clinical Pharmacology [*A publication*]
Prog Colloid Polym Sci ... Progress in Colloid and Polymer Science [*A publication*]
Prog Coll & Polym Sci ... Progress in Colloid and Polymer Science [*A publication*]
Prog Combus Sci Technol ... Progress in Combustion Science and Technology [*A publication*]
Prog Concept Control ... Progress in Conception Control [*A publication*]
Prog Contracep Delivery Syst ... Progress in Contraceptive Delivery Systems [*A publication*]
Prog Cosmic Ray Phys ... Progress in Cosmic Ray Physics [*A publication*]
ProgCp....... Progressive Corp. [*Associated Press abbreviation*]   (APAG)
Prog Crit Care Med ... Progress in Critical Care Medicine [*A publication*]
Prog Cryog ... Progress in Cryogenics [*A publication*]
Prog Cryst Growth Charact ... Progress in Crystal Growth and Characterization [*A publication*]
Prog Cryst Phys ... Progress in Crystal Physics [*A publication*]
PROGDEV ... Program Device   (KSC)
Prog Dielectr ... Progress in Dielectrics [*A publication*]
Prog Drug Metab ... Progress in Drug Metabolism [*A publication*]
Prog Drug Res ... Progress in Drug Research [*A publication*]
Prog Educ .. Progress in Education [*A publication*]   (APTA)
Prog Educ .. Progressive Education [*A publication*]
Prog Educ (Poona) ... Progress of Education (Poona) [*India*] [*A publication*]
Prog Elem Part Cosmic Ray Phys ... Progress in Elementary Particle and Cosmic Ray Physics [*A publication*]
Prog Endocr Res Ther ... Progress in Endocrine Research and Therapy [*A publication*]
Prog Energy Combust Sci ... Progress in Energy and Combustion Science [*A publication*]
Prog Explor Tuberc ... Progres de l'Exploration de la Tuberculose [*A publication*]
Prog Exp Pers Res ... Progress in Experimental Personality Research [*A publication*]
Prog Exp Tumor Res ... Progress in Experimental Tumor Research [*A publication*]
Prog Extr Metall ... Progress in Extractive Metallurgy [*A publication*]
Prog Ex Tum ... Progress in Experimental Tumor Research [*A publication*]
Prog F .... Progressive Farmer and Farm Woman [*A publication*]
Prog Farmer West ... Progressive Farmer for the West [*A publication*]
Prog Farming ... Progressive Farming [*A publication*]
Prog Farming/Farmer ... Progressive Farming/Farmer [*A publication*]
Prog Fire Retard Ser ... Progress in Fire Retardancy Series [*A publication*]
Prog Fish-C ... Progressive Fish-Culturist [*A publication*]
Prog Fish-Cult ... Progressive Fish-Culturist [*A publication*]
Prog Food Nutr Sci ... Progress in Food and Nutrition Science [*A publication*]
Prog Fotogr (Barcelona) ... Progresso Fotografico (Barcelona) [*A publication*]
Prog Fotogr (Milan) ... Progresso Fotografico (Milan) [*A publication*]
Prog Gastroenterol ... Progress in Gastroenterology [*A publication*]
Prog Geogr ... Progress in Geography [*A publication*]
Prog Groc... Progressive Grocer [*A publication*]
Prog Grocer ... Progressive Grocer [*A publication*]
Prog Gynecol ... Progress in Gynecology [*A publication*]
Prog Heat Mass Transf ... Progress in Heat and Mass Transfer [*A publication*]
Prog Heat Mass Transfer ... Progress in Heat and Mass Transfer [*A publication*]
Prog Hematol ... Progress in Hematology [*A publication*]
Prog Hemostasis Thromb ... Progress in Hemostasis and Thrombosis [*A publication*]
Prog Hemost Thromb ... Progress in Hemostasis and Thrombosis [*A publication*]
Prog High Polym ... Progress in High Polymers [*A publication*]
Prog High Temp Phys Chem ... Progress in High Temperature Physics and Chemistry [*A publication*]
Prog Histochem Cytochem ... Progress in Histochemistry and Cytochemistry [*A publication*]

Prog Horm Biochem Pharmacol ... Progress in Hormone Biochemistry and Pharmacology [*A publication*]
Prog Hort ... Progressive Horticulture [*India*] [*A publication*]
Prog Hortic ... Progressive Horticulture [*A publication*]
Prog Hum Biometeorol ... Progress in Human Biometeorology [*A publication*]
Prog Hum Nutr ... Progress in Human Nutrition [*A publication*]
Prog Immunobiol Stand ... Progress in Immunobiological Standardization [*A publication*]
Prog Ind Microbiol ... Progress in Industrial Microbiology [*A publication*]
Prog Infrared Spectrosc ... Progress in Infrared Spectroscopy [*A publication*]
Prog Inorg Chem ... Progress in Inorganic Chemistry [*A publication*]
Prog Instr Bul ... Programmed Instruction Bulletin [*A publication*]   (APTA)
Prog Instr & Ed Tech ... Programmed Instruction and Educational Technology [*A publication*]   (APTA)
Prog Learn ... Programmed Learning and Educational Technology [*A publication*]
Prog Learn Disabil ... Progress in Learning Disabilities [*A publication*]
Prog Leukocyte Biol ... Progress in Leukocyte Biology [*A publication*]
PROGLIB ... Production Program Library [*Social Security Administration*]
Prog Lipid Res ... Progress in Lipid Research [*A publication*]
Prog Liver Dis ... Progress in Liver Diseases [*A publication*]
Prog Low Temp Phys ... Progress in Low Temperature Physics [*A publication*]
PRO GM ... Pro Grand Master [*Freemasonry*]
Prog Mater Sci ... Progress in Materials Science [*A publication*]
Prog Mat Sc ... Progress in Materials Science [*A publication*]
Prog Med ... Progres Medical [*A publication*]
Prog Med Chem ... Progress in Medicinal Chemistry [*A publication*]
Prog Med Ge ... Progress in Medical Genetics [*A publication*]
Prog Med Genet ... Progress in Medical Genetics [*A publication*]
Prog Med (Istanbul) ... Progressus Medicinae (Istanbul) [*A publication*]
Prog Med Parasitol Jpn ... Progress in Medical Parasitology in Japan [*A publication*]
Prog Med Psychosom ... Progres en Medecine Psychosomatique [*A publication*]
Prog Med (Rome) ... Progresso Medico (Rome) [*A publication*]
Prog Med (Tokyo) ... Progress in Medicine (Tokyo) [*A publication*]
Prog Med Vi ... Progress in Medical Virology [*A publication*]
Prog Med Virol ... Progress in Medical Virology [*A publication*]
Prog Met Phys ... Progress in Metal Physics [*A publication*]
PROGMG ... Programming
Prog Migraine Res ... Progress in Migraine Research [*A publication*]
Prog Mol Subcell Biol ... Progress in Molecular and Subcellular Biology [*A publication*]
Prog Mutat Res ... Progress in Mutation Research [*A publication*]
PROGN ..... Prognosis   (AAMN)
Prog Neurobiol ... Progress in Neurobiology [*A publication*]
Prog Neurobiol (NY) ... Progress in Neurobiology (New York) [*A publication*]
Prog Neurobiol (Oxf) ... Progress in Neurobiology (Oxford) [*A publication*]
Prog Neurol Psychiatry ... Progress in Neurology and Psychiatry [*A publication*]
Prog Neurol Surg ... Progress in Neurological Surgery [*A publication*]
Prog Neuropathol ... Progress in Neuropathology [*A publication*]
Prog Neuro-Psychopharmacol ... Progress in Neuro-Psychopharmacology [*A publication*]
Prog Neuro-Psychopharmacol & Biol Psychiatry ... Progress in Neuro-Psychopharmacology and Biological Psychiatry [*A publication*]
Prog Neuropsychopharmacol Biol Psychiatry ... Progress in Neuropsychopharmacology and Biological Psychiatry [*A publication*]
PROGNO ... Prognosen-Trends-Entwicklungen [*Forecasts-Trends-Developments*] [*Society for Business Information*] [*Information service or system*]   (IID)
Prog Non Destr Test ... Progress in Non-Destructive Testing [*A publication*]
Prog Notes Walter Reed Army Med Cent ... Progress Notes. Walter Reed Army Medical Center [*A publication*]
Prog Nucleic Acid Res ... Progress in Nucleic Acid Research [*A publication*]
Prog Nucleic Acid Res Mol Biol ... Progress in Nucleic Acid Research and Molecular Biology [*A publication*]
Prog Nucl Energy ... Progress in Nuclear Energy [*England*] [*A publication*]
Prog Nucl Energy Anal Chem ... Progress in Nuclear Energy. Analytical Chemistry [*A publication*]
Prog Nucl Energy New Ser ... Progress in Nuclear Energy. New Series [*A publication*]
Prog Nucl Energy Ser 1 ... Progress in Nuclear Energy. Series 1. Physics and Mathematics [*A publication*]
Prog Nucl Energy Ser 2 ... Progress in Nuclear Energy. Series 2. Reactors [*A publication*]
Prog Nucl Energy Ser 3 ... Progress in Nuclear Energy. Series 3. Process Chemistry [*A publication*]
Prog Nucl Energy Ser 4 ... Progress in Nuclear Energy. Series 4. Technology, Engineering, and Safety [*A publication*]
Prog Nucl Energy Ser 5 ... Progress in Nuclear Energy. Series 5. Metallurgy and Fuels [*A publication*]
Prog Nucl Energy Ser 6 ... Progress in Nuclear Energy. Series 6 [*England*] [*A publication*]
Prog Nucl Energy Ser 8 ... Progress in Nuclear Energy. Series 8. The Economics of Nuclear Power Including Administration and Law [*A publication*]
Prog Nucl Energy Ser 9 ... Progress in Nuclear Energy. Series 9 [*England*] [*A publication*]

Prog Nucl Energy Ser 10 ... Progress in Nuclear Energy. Series 10. Law and Administration [*A publication*]
Prog Nucl Energy Ser 11 ... Progress in Nuclear Energy. Series 11. Plasma Physics and Thermonuclear Research [*A publication*]
Prog Nucl Energy Ser 12 ... Progress in Nuclear Energy. Series 12. Health Physics [*A publication*]
Prog Nucl Energy Ser 7 Med Sci ... Progress in Nuclear Energy. Series 7. Medical Sciences [*A publication*]
Prog Nucl Magn Reson Spectrosc ... Progress in Nuclear Magnetic Resonance Spectroscopy [*A publication*]
Prog Nucl Med ... Progress in Nuclear Medicine [*A publication*]
Prog Nucl Phys ... Progress in Nuclear Physics [*A publication*]
Prog Nucl Tech Instrum ... Progress in Nuclear Techniques and Instrumentation [*Netherlands*] [*A publication*]
Prog Nurse ... Progressive Nurse [*A publication*]
Prog Obstet Gynecol ... Progres en Obstetrique et Gynecologie [*A publication*]
Prog Oceanogr ... Progress in Oceanography [*A publication*]
Prog Odontostomatol ... Progres Odonto-Stomatologique [*A publication*]
PROGOFOP ... Program of Operation [*Data processing*]
Prog Ophtalmol ... Progres en Ophtalmologie [*A publication*]
Prog Ophthalmol Otolaryngol ... Progress in Ophthalmology and Otolaryngology [*A publication*]
Prog Opt .... Progress in Optics [*A publication*]
Prog Org Chem ... Progress in Organic Chemistry [*A publication*]
Prog Org Coat ... Progress in Organic Coatings [*A publication*]
Prog Org Coatings ... Progress in Organic Coatings [*A publication*]
Prog Oto-Rhino-Laryngol ... Progres en Oto-Rhino-Laryngologie [*A publication*]
Prog Part Nucl Phys ... Progress in Particle and Nuclear Physics [*England*] [*A publication*]
Prog Pass Sol Energy Syst ... Progress in Passive Solar Energy Systems [*A publication*]
Prog Pediatr Hematol/Oncol ... Progress in Pediatric Hematology/Oncology [*A publication*]
Prog Pediatr Pueric ... Progresos de Pediatria y Puericultura [*A publication*]
Prog Pediatr Radiol ... Progress in Pediatric Radiology [*Switzerland*] [*A publication*]
Prog Pediatr Surg ... Progress in Pediatric Surgery [*A publication*]
Prog Perfum Cosmet ... Progressive Perfumery and Cosmetics [*A publication*]
Prog Pharmacol ... Progress in Pharmacology [*A publication*]
Prog Photogr ... Progress in Photography [*A publication*]
Prog Phys .. Progress of Physics [*East Germany*] [*A publication*]
Prog Phys Geogr ... Progress in Physical Geography [*A publication*]
Prog Physiol Psychol ... Progress in Physiological Psychology [*A publication*]
Prog Physiol Sci (Engl Transl Usp Fiziol Nauk) ... Progress in Physiological Sciences (English Translation of Uspekhi Fiziologicheskikh Nauk) [*A publication*]
Prog Physiol Sci (USSR) ... Progress in Physiological Sciences (USSR) [*A publication*]
Prog Phys Org Chem ... Progress in Physical Organic Chemistry [*A publication*]
Prog Phys Sci (Moscow) ... Progress in Physical Sciences (Moscow) [*A publication*]
Prog Phys Ther ... Progress in Physical Therapy [*A publication*]
Prog Phytochem ... Progress in Phytochemistry [*A publication*]
Prog Plann ... Progress in Planning [*A publication*]
Prog Plast .. Progressive Plastics [*A publication*]
Prog Polym Sci ... Progress in Polymer Science [*A publication*]
Prog Powder Metall ... Progress in Powder Metallurgy [*A publication*]
Prog Protozool Proc Int Congr Protozool ... Progress in Protozoology. Proceedings. International Congress on Protozoology [*A publication*]
Prog Psychiatr Drug Treat ... Progress in Psychiatric Drug Treatment [*A publication*]
Prog Psychobiol Physiol Psychol ... Progress in Psychobiology and Physiological Psychology [*A publication*]
Prog Quantum Electron ... Progress in Quantum Electronics [*A publication*]
Prog Radiat Ther ... Progress in Radiation Therapy [*A publication*]
Prog Radiopharmacol ... Progress in Radiopharmacology [*A publication*]
Progr Agr ... Progresso Agricolo [*A publication*]
Progr Agr Ariz ... Progressive Agriculture in Arizona [*A publication*]
Progr Agr Vitic ... Progres Agricole et Viticole [*A publication*]
Progr Allergy ... Progress in Allergy [*A publication*]
Program Abstr Am Soc Parasitol Annu Meet ... Program and Abstracts. American Society of Parasitologists. Annual Meeting [*A publication*]
Program Aid US Dep Agric ... Program Aid. United States Department of Agriculture [*A publication*]
Program Am Dairy Sci Assoc Annu Meet Branch Abstr ... Program. American Dairy Science Association. Annual Meeting and Branch Abstracts [*A publication*]
Program Autom Libr Inf Syst ... Program. Automated Library and Information Systems [*England*] [*A publication*]
Program and Comput Software ... Programming and Computer Software [*A publication*]
Program Learn and Educ Technol ... Programmed Learning and Educational Technology [*A publication*]
Programmed Learning ... Programmed Learning and Educational Technology [*A publication*]
Programming and Comput Software ... Programming and Computer Software [*A publication*]

Programming Lang Ser ... Programming Languages Series [*A publication*]
Programmirovan ... Programmirovanie. Akademija Nauk SSSR [*A publication*]
Program News Comput Libr ... Program. News of Computers in Libraries [*A publication*]
Program Notes Assoc Univ Programs Health Adm ... Program Notes. Association of University Programs in Health Administration [*A publication*]
Program/Proc Natl Horsemen's Semin ... Program/Proceedings. National Horsemen's Seminar [*A publication*]
Progr Bull Alberta Univ Ext Dept ... Progress Bulletin. Alberta University Extension Department [*A publication*]
Progr Card ... Progress in Cardiovascular Diseases [*A publication*]
Progr Cardiovas Dis ... Progress in Cardiovascular Diseases [*A publication*]
Progr Clin Cancer ... Progress in Clinical Cancer [*A publication*]
Progr Contr Eng ... Progress in Control Engineering [*A publication*]
Progr Coop Centroamer Mejor Maiz ... Programa Cooperativo Centroamericano para el Mejoramiento del Maiz [*A publication*]
Prog React Kinet ... Progress in Reaction Kinetics [*A publication*]
Prog Rech Cancer ... Progres dans les Recherches sur le Cancer [*A publication*]
Prog Rech Exp Tumeurs ... Progres de la Recherche Experimentale des Tumeurs [*A publication*]
Prog Rech Pharm ... Progres des Recherches Pharmaceutiques [*A publication*]
Prog Refrig Sci Technol Proc Int Congr Refrig ... Progress in Refrigeration Science and Technology. Proceedings. International Congress of Refrigeration [*A publication*]
Prog Rep Agric Exp Stn Univ Idaho ... Progress Report. Agricultural Experiment Station. University of Idaho [*A publication*]
Prog Rep Ala Agric Exp Stn ... Progress Report. Alabama Agricultural Experiment Station [*A publication*]
Prog Rep Ariz Exp Stn ... Progress Report. Arizona Experiment Station [*A publication*]
Prog Rep Clovers Spec Purpose Legumes Res ... Progress Report. Clovers and Special Legumes Research [*A publication*]
Prog Rep Colo Exp Stn ... Progress Report. Colorado Experiment Station [*A publication*]
Prog Rep Dom Apiarist Canad Dep Agric ... Progress Report. Dominion Apiarist. Canadian Department of Agriculture [*A publication*]
Prog Rep Exp Stn Colorado State Univ ... Colorado State University. Experiment Station. Progress Report [*A publication*]
Prog Rep Exp Stns (Tanzania) ... Progress Reports. Experiment Stations (Tanzania) [*A publication*]
Prog Rep Gen Rev World Coal Ind ... Progress Report. General Review of the World Coal Industry [*A publication*]
Prog Rep KY Agric Exp Stn ... Progress Report. Kentucky Agricultural Experiment Station [*A publication*]
Prog Rep Minist Agric Fish Fd Exp Husb Fms Exp Hort Stns ... Progress Report. Ministry of Agriculture, Fisheries, and Food. Experimental Husbandry Farms and Experimental Horticulture Stations [*A publication*]
Prog Rep NM Bur Mines Miner Resour ... Progress Report. New Mexico Bureau of Mines and Mineral Resources [*A publication*]
Prog Rep Nucl Energy Res Jpn ... Progress Report. Nuclear Energy Research in Japan [*A publication*]
Prog Rep PA Agric Exp Stn ... Progress Report. Pennsylvania Agricultural Experiment Station [*A publication*]
Prog Reprod Biol ... Progress in Reproductive Biology [*A publication*]
Prog Reprod Biol Med ... Progress in Reproductive Biology and Medicine [*A publication*]
Prog Rep Texas Agric Exp Stn ... Progress Report. Texas Agricultural Experiment Station [*A publication*]
Prog Res ..... Progress thru Research [*A publication*]
Progres Arch ... Progressive Architecture [*A publication*]
Prog Res Clin Appl Corticosteroids Proc Annu Clin Symp ... Progress in Research and Clinical Applications of Corticosteroids. Proceedings. Annual Clinical Symposium [*A publication*]
Progres Ed ... Progressive Education [*A publication*]
Prog Res Emphysema Chronic Bronchitis ... Progress in Research in Emphysema and Chronic Bronchitis [*A publication*]
Progres Med (Paris) ... Progres Medical (Paris) [*A publication*]
Progreso Med (Habana) ... Progreso Medico (Habana) [*A publication*]
Prog Respir Res ... Progress in Respiration Research [*A publication*]
Progres Scientif ... Progres Scientifique [*A publication*]
Progressive Archit ... Progressive Architecture [*A publication*]
Progressive Archre ... Progressive Architecture [*A publication*]
Progress in Math ... Progress in Mathematics [*A publication*]
Progres Soc 3e Ser ... Progres Social. Troisieme Serie [*A publication*]
Progresso Fotogr ... Progresso Fotografico [*A publication*]
Progress Organic Coatings ... Progress in Organic Coatings [*A publication*]
Progress in Particle and Nuclear Phys ... Progress in Particle and Nuclear Physics [*A publication*]
Progress in Phys ... Progress in Physics [*A publication*]
Progress Phytochem ... Progress in Phytochemistry [*A publication*]
Progressv ... Progressive [*A publication*]
Progres Techn ... Progres Technique [*A publication*]
Progres Vet ... Progres Veterinaire [*A publication*]
Progr Hemat ... Progress in Hematology [*A publication*]
Progr Hum Geogr ... Progress in Human Geography. International Review of Current Research [*A publication*]

Progr Indust Microbiol ... Progress in Industrial Microbiology [*A publication*]
Progr Learn Educ Technol ... Programmed Learning and Educational Technology [*A publication*]
Progr Mater Sci ... Progress in Materials Science [*A publication*]
Progr Math (Allahabad) ... Progress of Mathematics (Allahabad) [*A publication*]
Progr Med (Paris) ... Progres Medical (Paris) [*A publication*]
Progr Med Virol ... Progress in Medical Virology [*A publication*]
Progr Neurol Psychiat ... Progress in Neurology and Psychiatry [*A publication*]
Progr Nucl Energy Ser 6 ... Progress in Nuclear Energy. Series 6. Biological Sciences [*A publication*]
Progr Nucl Energy Ser 8 Econ ... Progress in Nuclear Energy. Series 8. Economics [*A publication*]
Progr Nucl Energy Ser 10 Law Admin ... Progress in Nuclear Energy. Series 10. Law and Administration [*A publication*]
Progr Nucl Energy Ser 5 Met Fuels ... Progress in Nuclear Energy. Series 5. Metallurgy and Fuels [*A publication*]
Progr Nucl Energy Ser 1 Phys Math ... Progress in Nuclear Energy. Series 1. Physics and Mathematics [*A publication*]
Progr Nucl Energy Ser 11 Plasma Phys Thermonucl Res ... Progress in Nuclear Energy. Series 11. Plasma Physics and Thermonuclear Research [*A publication*]
Progr Nucl Energy Ser 3 Process Chem ... Progress in Nuclear Energy. Series 3. Process Chemistry [*A publication*]
Progr Nucl Energy Ser 2 Reactors ... Progress in Nuclear Energy. Series 2. Reactors [*A publication*]
Progr Nucl Energy Ser 4 Technol Eng ... Progress in Nuclear Energy. Series 4. Technology and Engineering [*A publication*]
Progr Offic Journee Interreg Recolte Mec Mais-Grain ... Programme Officiel. Journee Interregionale de Recolte Mechanique du Mais-Grain [*A publication*]
Progr Particle and Nuclear Phys ... Progress in Particle and Nuclear Physics [*A publication*]
Progr Phys ... Progress in Physics [*A publication*]
Progr Physiol Psych ... Progress in Physiological Psychology [*A publication*]
Progr Phys Sci ... Progress of Physical Sciences [*A publication*]
Progr Plast ... Progressive Plastics [*A publication*]
Progr Polymer Sci ... Progress in Polymer Science [*A publication*]
Progr Powder Met ... Progress in Powder Metallurgy [*A publication*]
Progr Prob Statist ... Progress in Probability and Statistics [*A publication*]
Progr Rep Cereal Breed Lab ... Progress Report. Cereal Breeding Laboratory [*A publication*]
Progr Rep Colo State Univ Agr Exp Sta ... Progress Report. Colorado State University. Agricultural Experiment Station [*A publication*]
Progr Rep Conn Agr Exp Sta ... Progress Report. Connecticut Agricultural Experiment Station [*A publication*]
Progr Rep Idaho Agr Res ... Progress Report. Idaho Agricultural Research [*A publication*]
Progr Rep KY Agr Exp Sta ... Progress Report. Kentucky Agricultural Experiment Station [*A publication*]
Progr Rep PA Agric Exp Sta ... Progress Report. Pennsylvania State University. Agricultural Experiment Station [*A publication*]
Progr Rep PA State Univ Agr Exp Sta ... Progress Report. Pennsylvania State University. Agricultural Experiment Station [*A publication*]
Progr Rep Ser Ala Agr Exp Sta ... Progress Report Series. Alabama Agricultural Experiment Station [*A publication*]
Progr Rep Tex Agr Exp Sta ... Progress Report. Texas Agricultural Experiment Station [*A publication*]
Progr Rep Tohoku Agr Exp Sta ... Progress Report. Tohoku Agricultural Experiment Station [*A publication*]
Progr Rep Univ Nebr Coll Agr Dept Agr Econ ... Progress Report. University of Nebraska. College of Agriculture. Department of Agricultural Economics [*A publication*]
Progr Rev For Prod Lab (Ottawa) ... Program Review. Forest Products Laboratory (Ottawa) [*A publication*]
Progr Rev For Prod Lab (Vancouver) ... Program Review. Forest Products Laboratory (Vancouver) [*British Columbia, Canada*] [*A publication*]
Progr Rubber Technol ... Progress of Rubber Technology [*A publication*]
Progr Sci Comput ... Progress in Scientific Computing [*A publication*]
Progr Soc ... Progres Social [*A publication*]
Progr Stiintei ... Progresele Stiintei [*A publication*]
Progr Surg ... Progress in Surgery [*A publication*]
Progr Ter Clin ... Progresos de Terapeutica Clinica [*A publication*]
Progr Theoret Phys ... Progress of Theoretical Physics [*A publication*]
Progr Theoret Phys Suppl ... Progress of Theoretical Physics. Supplement [*A publication*]
Prog Sci ... Progres Scientifique [*France*] [*A publication*]
Prog Sci Technol Rare Earths ... Progress in the Science and Technology of the Rare Earths [*A publication*]
Prog Semicond ... Progress in Semiconductors [*A publication*]
Prog Sens Physiol ... Progress in Sensory Physiology [*A publication*]
Prog Sep Purif ... Progress in Separation and Purification [*A publication*]
Prog Soil Sci (Nanjing Peoples Repub China) ... Progress in Soil Science (Nanjing, People's Republic of China) [*A publication*]
Prog Sol Energy ... Progress in Solar Energy [*A publication*]

Prog Solid State Chem ... Progress in Solid State Chemistry [*England*] [*A publication*]
Prog Stereochem ... Progress in Stereochemistry [*A publication*]
Prog Surf Membr Sci ... Progress in Surface and Membrane Science [*A publication*]
Prog Surf Sci ... Progress in Surface Science [*A publication*]
Prog Surg ... Progress in Surgery [*A publication*]
Prog Tech ... Progres Technique [*A publication*]
Prog Technol ... Progress in Technology [*United States*] [*A publication*]
Prog Tekhnol Mashinostr ... Progressivnaya Tekhnologiya Mashinostroeniya [*A publication*]
Prog Ter ... Progresso Terapeutico [*A publication*]
Prog Theor Biol ... Progress in Theoretical Biology [*A publication*]
Prog Theor Org Chem ... Progress in Theoretical Organic Chemistry [*A publication*]
Prog Theor Phys ... Progress of Theoretical Physics [*A publication*]
Prog Theor Phys Suppl ... Progress of Theoretical Physics. Supplement [*A publication*]
Prog Thin-Layer Chromatogr Relat Methods ... Progress in Thin-Layer Chromatography and Related Methods [*A publication*]
Prog Top Cytogenet ... Progress and Topics in Cytogenetics [*A publication*]
Prog T Phys ... Progress of Theoretical Physics [*A publication*]
Prog Underwater Sci ... Progress in Underwater Science [*A publication*]
Prog Vac Microbalance Tech ... Progress in Vacuum Microbalance Techniques [*A publication*]
PROGVAL ... Validation Program Library [*Social Security Administration*]
Progve Agric Ariz ... Progressive Agriculture in Arizona [*A publication*]
Progve Fmg ... Progressive Farming [*A publication*]
Prog Vet ... Progresso Veterinario [*A publication*]
Prog Vet Microbiol Immunol ... Progress in Veterinary Microbiology and Immunology [*A publication*]
Prog Virol Med ... Progres en Virologie Medicale [*A publication*]
Prog Water Technol ... Progress in Water Technology [*A publication*]
PROH........ Prohibit
PROH........ Prohibition [*FBI standardized term*]
PROH........ Promoting Health [*A publication*]
Prohib .... Prohibited
PROI......... President of the Royal Institute of Oil Painters [*British*]
PRO-IF...... Personal Radio Operators International Federation [*Formerly, ARC*] (EA)
PROIMREP ... Proceed Immediately - Report for Purpose Indicated [*Military*]
Pro Indian Soc of Internat L ... Proceedings of the Conference. Indian Society of International Law [*New Delhi, India*] [*A publication*] (DLA)
Proizv Obuc ... Proizvodstvennoe Obucenie [*A publication*]
Proizvod Elektrostali ... Proizvodstvo Elektrostali [*A publication*]
Proizvod Issled Stalei Splavov ... Proizvodstvo i Issledovanie Stalei i Splavov [*A publication*]
Proizvod Koksa ... Proizvodstvo Koksa [*A publication*]
Proizvod Krupnykh Mash ... Proizvodstvo Krupnykh Mashin [*A publication*]
Proizvod Smaz Mater ... Proizvodstvo Smazochnykh Materialov [*A publication*]
Proizvod Stochnye Vody ... Proizvodstvennye Stochnye Vody [*A publication*]
Proizvod Svarnykh Besshovnykh Trub ... Proizvodstvo Svarnykh i Besshovnykh Trub [*A publication*]
Proizvod Trub ... Proizvodstvo Trub [*A publication*]
Proizvod Vysokokach Prokata ... Proizvodstvo Vysokokachestvennogo Prokata [*A publication*]
Proizv Shin RTI i ATI ... Proizvodstvo Shin Rezinotekhnicheskikh i Asbestotekhnicheskikh Izdelii [*A publication*]
PROJ........ Project (AFM)
PROJ........ Projectile (AFM)
PROJ........ Projector
Proj Civ Trav Econ ... Projet. Civilisation, Travail, Economie [*France*] [*A publication*]
PROJECT ... Project Engineering Control
Project Hist Biobibliog ... Project for Historical Biobibliography [*A publication*]
Project IUCN/Wld Wildl Fund ... Project. International Union for Conservation of Nature. World Wildlife Fund. Joint Project Operations [*A publication*]
Projektrapp Grafiska Forskningslab ... Projektrapport. Grafiska Forskningslaboratoriet [*A publication*]
PROJENGR ... Project Engineer
PROJID .... Project Identification [*Data processing*]
PROJMGR ... Project Manager [*Military*]
PROJMGRASWS ... Project Manager, Antisubmarine Warfare Systems
PROJMGRFBM ... Project Manager, Fleet Ballistic Missile [*Navy*]
PROJMGRSMS ... Project Manager, Surface Missile Systems [*Navy*]
Proj RADAMBRAS Levantamento Recursos Nat ... Projeto RADAMBRASIL [*Radar da Amazonia, Brasil*]. Levantamento de Recursos Naturais [*A publication*]
Proj Rep Victoria Minist Conserv Environ Stud Program ... Victoria. Ministry for Conservation. Environmental Studies Program. Project Report [*A publication*] (APTA)
PROJTRNS ... Project Transition [*DoD*]
PROL........ Priority Requirement Objective List (AFM)
PROL........ Prologue
PRO L........ Province Laws (DLA)
PROLAMAT ... Programming Languages for Machine Tools [*Conference*]

PROLAN... Processed Language [*Data processing*]
PROLDI.... Annual Research Reviews. Prolactin [*A publication*]
Proler .... Proler International Corp. [*Associated Press abbreviation*] (APAG)
Prolif.......... Proliferative [*or Proliferation*]
PROLLAP ... Professional Library Literature Acquisition Program
PRO LOC et TEM ... Pro Loco et Tempore [*For the Place and Time*] [*Latin*] (ROG)
PROLOG .. Production of Onshore Lower 48 Oil and Gas Model [*Department of Energy*] (GFGA)
PROLOG .. Program Logistics (NG)
PROLOG .. Programming in Logic [*Programing language*] [*1970*]
Pro LR .... Professional Liability Reporter [*A publication*]
PROLT...... Procurement Lead Time
P Rom .... Papers in Romance [*A publication*]
PROM .... Passive Range of Motion [*Medicine*]
PROM .... Pockels Readout Optical Modulator
PROM .... Premature [*or Prolonged*] Rupture of Membranes [*Gynecology*]
PROM .... Program, Resources, Objectives, Management [*Air Force Systems Command technique*]
PROM .... Programmable Read-Only Memory [*Data processing*]
PROM .... Progressive Range of Motion [*Medicine*]
PROM .... Promenade [*Maps and charts*]
Prom dk ..... Promenade Deck [*of a ship*] (DS)
PROM ...... Prominent
Prom .... Promissory [*A publication*] (DLA)
PROM ...... Promontory
PROM .... Promote [*or Promotion*] (AFM)
Prom .... Promotion [*A publication*]
PROM ...... Promulgate (AABC)
PROM .... Romanic Review [*A publication*]
Pro-MACE ... Prednisone, Methotrexate with Leucovorin, Adriamycin, Cyclophosphamide, Epipodophyllin [*Etoposide, VP-16*] [*Antineoplastic drug regimen*]
PROMACE-MOPP ... Procarbazine, Methotrexate, Adriamycin, Cyclophosphamide, Etoposide, Mustargen [*Nitrogen mustard*], Oncovin [*Vincristine*], Procarbazine, Prednisone [*Antineoplastic drug regimen*]
PROMADATA ... Promotions Marketing and Advertising Data [*A publication*]
Prom Aerod ... Promyshlennaya Aerodinamika [*Former USSR*] [*A publication*]
PROMAG ... Production Management Action Group [*British*]
Pro Managr ... Program Manager [*A publication*]
PROMAP ... Program for the Refinement of the Materiel Acquisition Process [*Army*] (AABC)
Pro Med..... Pro Medico [*A publication*]
Prom Ekon Byull Sov Nar Khoz Ivanov Ekon Adm Raiona ... Promyshlenno-Ekonomicheskii Byulleten Sovet Narodnogo Khozyaistva Ivanovskogo Ekonomicheskogo Administrativnogo Raiona [*A publication*]
Prom Energ ... Promyshlennaya Energetika [*A publication*]
Pro Met...... Pro Metal [*A publication*]
PROMETHEUS ... Program for European Traffic with Highest Efficiency and Unprecedented Safety (ECON)
Promet-Meteorol Fortbild ... Promet-Meteorologische Fortbildung [*West Germany*] [*A publication*]
PROMEX ... Productivity Measurement Experiment [*National Institute of Standards and Technology*]
PROMIM ... Programmable Multiple Ion Monitor
PROMIS... Problem-Oriented Medical Information System [*Computerized patient-management system*]
PROMIS... Process Management and Information System [*I. P. Sharp Associates Ltd.*] [*Software package*] (NCC)
PROMIS... Project-Oriented Management Information System
PROMIS... Prosecutor's Management Information System [*Law Enforcement Assistance Administration*]
PROML..... Promulgate
PROMO.... Promotion [*Slang*] (DSUE)
Promoclim A Actual Equip Tech ... Promoclim A. Actualites, Equipement, Technique [*France*] [*A publication*]
Promoclim E ... Promoclim E. Etudes Thermiques et Aerauliques [*A publication*]
Promoclim Ind Therm Aerauliques ... Promoclim. Industries Thermiques et Aerauliques [*A publication*]
Prom Org Sint ... Promyslennyj Organiceskij Sintez [*A publication*]
Promot Dent ... Promotion Dentaire [*A publication*]
Promot Health ... Promoting Health [*A publication*]
Promozione Soc ... Promozione Sociale [*A publication*]
PROMPT ... Production, Reviewing, Organizing, and Monitoring of Performance Techniques (BUR)
PROMPT ... Program Monitoring and Planning Techniques (IEEE)
PROMPT ... Program to Record Official Mail Point-to-Point Times [*Postal Service program*]
PROMPT ... Project Management and Production Team Technique [*Data processing*]
PROMPT ... Project Reporting Organization and Management Planning Technique
PROMS..... Procurement Management System (MCD)
PROMS..... Program Monitoring System (MCD)
PROMS..... Programmable Read Only Memory System [*Data processing*]

PROMS..... Projectile Measurement System [*Data processing*] [*Army*]
Prom Sint Kauch ... Promyshlennost Sinteticheskogo Kauchuka [*A publication*]
PROMSS .. Procedures and Relationships for the Operation of Manual Stations and Spaces (DNAB)
Promst Arm ... Promyshlennost Armenii [*A publication*]
Prom-St Arm Sov Nar Khoz Arm SSR Tekh-Ekon Byull ... Promyshlennost Armenii Sovet Narodnogo Khozyajstva Armyanskoj SSR Tekhniko-Ekonomicheskij Byulleten [*A publication*]
PROM STAT ... Promotion Status (DNAB)
Promst Beloruss ... Promyshlennost Belorussii [*A publication*]
Prom-St Khim Reaktivov Osobo Chist Veshchestv ... Promyshlennost Khimicheskikh Reaktivov i Osobo Chistykh Veshchestv [*Former USSR*] [*A publication*]
Promst Khim Reakt Osobo Chist Veshchestv ... Promyshlennost Khimicheskikh Reaktivov i Osobo Chistykh Veshchestv [*A publication*]
Promst Lub Volokon ... Promyshlennost Lubyanykh Volokon [*A publication*]
Prom-St Org Khim ... Promyshlennost Organicheskoi Khimii [*Former USSR*] [*A publication*]
Prom Stroit ... Promyshlennoe Stroitel'stvo [*A publication*]
Prom Stroit Inzh Sooruzh ... Promyshlennoe Stroitel'stvo i Inzhenernye Sooruzheniya [*A publication*]
Promst Stroit Mater ... Promyshlennost Stroitel'nykh Materialov [*A publication*]
PROMT .... Precision Optimized Measurement Time [*Spectroscopy*]
PROMT .... Predicasts Overviews of Marketing and Technology [*Business database*]
PROMT .... Programmable Miniature Message Terminal (MCD)
Prom Teplotekh ... Promyshlennaya Teplotekhnika [*Ukrainian SSR*] [*A publication*]
Pro Mundi Vita ... Pro Mundi Vita Bulletin [*A publication*]
Pro Mundi Vita Africa Dossier ... Pro Mundi Vita Dossiers. Africa [*A publication*]
Pro Mundi Vita Asia-Australasia Dossier ... Pro Mundi Vita Dossiers. Asia and Australasia [*A publication*]
Pro Mundi Vita Europe N Am Dossier ... Pro Mundi Vita Dossiers. Europe/North America [*A publication*]
Promus....... Promus Companies [*Associated Press abbreviation*] (APAG)
PROMUS ... Provincial-Municipal Simulator [*Computer-based urban management system*]
PROMY .... Promissory (ROG)
Prom Zagryaz Vodoemov ... Promyshlennye Zagryazneniya Vodoemov [*A publication*]
PRON .... Patriotyczny Ruch Odrodzenia Narodowego [*Patriotic Movement for National Rebirth*] [*Poland*] (EY)
PRON .... Procurement Request Order Number [*Army*] (AABC)
PRON .... Pronation
PRON .... Pronominal (ADA)
PRON .... Pronoun
PRON .... Pronounced
PRON .... Pronunciation (ROG)
Pro Nat ...... Pro Natura [*A publication*]
Pro-Nica .... Professionals - Nicaragua (EA)
PRONTO .. Program for Numeric Tool Operation [*Data processing*]
PRONTO .. Programmable Network Telecommunications Operating System
prooem .... Prooemium (BJA)
PROOF...... Precision Recording (Optical) of Fingerprints
PROOF...... Projected Return on Open Office Facilities [*Computer program*]
proOLMC ... Pro-Opiolipomelanocortin [*Endocrinology*]
PROP........ Performance Review for Operating Programs (BUR)
PROP........ Pilot Repair Overhaul and Provisioning (MUGU)
PROP........ Planetary Rocket Ocean Platform
PROP........ Prerelease Orientation Program [*Reformatory program*]
PROP........ Preservation of the Rights of Prisoners [*An association*] [*British*]
PROP........ Prisoners' Right of Privacy [*British*] (DI)
PROP........ Production Operators Corp. [*NASDAQ symbol*] (NQ)
PROP........ Profit Rating of Projects
PROP........ Proof of Purchase (WDMC)
PROP........ Propaganda (AFM)
Prop .... Propagate [*Botany*]
PROP........ Propellant (KSC)
PROP........ Propeller
PROP........ Proper
PROP........ Propertius [*Roman poet, c. 29BC*] [*Classical studies*] (ROG)
PROP........ Property
Prop .... Property [*A publication*]
PROP........ Property Release Option Program [*HUD*]
PROP........ Proportional (KSC)
PROP........ Proposal (AAG)
PROP........ Proposed (AFM)
PROP........ Proposition
PROP........ Proprietor
PROP........ Propulsion (AAG)
PROP........ Propylthiouracil [*Also, PT, PTU*] [*Thyroid inhibitor*]
PROPA...... Propagation (FAAC)
PROPAC .. Progressive Political Action Committee [*Defunct*] (EA)
PROPAC .. Prospective Payment Assessment Commission [*Washington, DC*] (EGAO)

PROPAKASIA ... International Food Processing and Packaging Technology Exhibition and Conference for South East Asia
PROPAL ... Proportional
Propane Can ... Propane Canada [*A publication*]
PRO-PAY ... Proficiency Pay [*Military*]
Prop & Comp ... Property and Compensation Reports [*A publication*] (DLA)
Prop & Comp R ... Property and Compensation Reports [*A publication*] (DLA)
Propellants Explos ... Propellants and Explosives [*A publication*]
pro per .... Propria Persona [*In His or Her Own Person*] [*Latin*] (WGA)
PROPER COUNT ... Property Accountability (MCD)
Property Mthly Rev ... Property Monthly Review [*A publication*]
Property Tax J ... Property Tax Journal [*A publication*]
Prop & Ex ... Propellants, Explosives, and Pyrotechnics [*A publication*]
PROPH ... Prophylactic
PROPHET ... Proactive Rehabilitation of Outside Plant Using Heuristic Expert Techniques [*GTE computer software*]
Proph Sanit Mor ... Prophylaxie Sanitaire et Morale [*A publication*]
PROPIN.... Proprietary Information
Prop Law.... Property Lawyer [*1826-30*] [*A publication*] (DLA)
Prop Law Bull ... Property Law Bulletin [*A publication*] (DLA)
Prop Law NS ... Property Lawyer, New Series [*England*] [*A publication*] (DLA)
PROPLING ... Propelling
PROPLOSS ... Propagation Loss (NVT)
PROPLT ... Propellant (NASA)
PROPN ..... Proportion (MSA)
PROPON .. Proportion (MSA)
PROPORICH ... Proceed to Port in Which Unit is Located [*Navy*] (DNAB)
Proposte Soc ... Proposte Sociali
PROPR...... Proprietary (ROG)
PROPR...... Proprietor (EY)
Propr Agric ... Propriete Agricole [*A publication*]
PROPRE... Property Press (DLA)
PROPRSS ... Proprietress (ROG)
PROPTRY ... Proprietary [*Freight*]
PROPUL ... Propulsion
Pro Quer .... Pro Querente [*For the Plaintiff*] [*Latin*] (ILCA)
PROR .... Predicted Orbit
Pr Or .... Przeglad Orientalistyczny [*A publication*]
PRORA ..... Programs for Research on Romance Authors
PRORAT... Projected Rating
PRO RAT AET ... Pro Ratione Aetatis [*According to Age*] [*Pharmacy*]
PrOrChr ..... Proche-Orient Chretien [*Jerusalem*] [*A publication*]
PRO RECT ... Pro Recto [*Rectal*] [*Pharmacy*]
PROREP ... Proceed Ship, Command Station Reporting Duty or Purpose Indicated [*Military*]
Pr O S .... Princeton Oriental Series [*A publication*]
PROS......... Procurement Squadron
PROS......... Professional Reactor Operator Society (EA)
PROS......... Proscenium [*Theater term*] (DSUE)
PROS......... Prosecution (ROG)
PROS......... Prosody
PROS......... [*The*] Prospect Group, Inc. [*New York, NY*] [*NASDAQ symbol*] (NQ)
Pros........... Prospetti [*A publication*]
PROS......... Prosthetic (AABC)
PROS......... Prostitute (DSUE)
PROS......... Prostrate
PROSAM ... Programmed Single-Axis Mount [*Military camera*]
PROSAMO ... Planned Release of Selected and Modified Organisms [*British*]
Pros Atty ..... Prosecuting Attorney (DLA)
PRosC........ Rosemont College, Rosemont, PA [*Library symbol*] [*Library of Congress*] (LCLS)
PROSE ...... Problem Solution Engineering [*Programming language*] [*Data processing*] (CSR)
PROSE ...... Program System Example (SAA)
PROSEA ... Plant Resources of South-East Asia [*A publication*]
PROSECON ... Prosecution (ROG)
PROSI .... Procedure Sign [*Aviation*] (FAAC)
PROSI .... Public Relations Office of the Sugar Industry
PROSIG .... Procedure Signal [*Navy*]
PROSIGN ... Procedure Sign [*Military*] (AABC)
PROSIM ... Production System Simulator [*Data processing*]
PROSINE ... Procedure Sign [*Military*]
Pros J Natl Dist Att'y A ... Prosecutor. Journal of the National District Attorneys Association [*A publication*]
ProSoc........ Prometheus Society (EA)
Pro Soc Water Treat Exam ... Proceedings. Society for Water Treatment and Examination [*A publication*]
Prosop Att ... Prosopographia Attica [*A publication*] (OCD)
prosp .... Prospectively (DLA)
PROSPECT ... Proponent Sponsored Engineer Corps Training [*Army Corps of Engineers*]
Prospect West Aust ... Prospect Western Australia [*A publication*]
Prospett Merid ... Prospettive Meridionali [*A publication*]
Prosp R ...... Prospective Review [*A publication*]
PROSPRO ... Process Systems Program
ProsSt .... Prospect Street High Income Portfolio, Inc. [*Associated Press abbreviation*] (APAG)

PROST ...... Prostitute [*or Prostitution*] [*FBI standardized term*]
Prostagland ... Prostaglandins [*A publication*]
Prostaglandins Leukotrienes Med ... Prostaglandins, Leukotrienes, and Medicine [*A publication*]
Prostaglandins Med ... Prostaglandins and Medicine [*A publication*]
Prostaglandins Relat Lipids ... Prostaglandins and Related Lipids [*A publication*]
Prostaglandins Res Stud Ser ... Prostaglandins Research Studies Series [*A publication*]
Prostaglandins Ther ... Prostaglandins and Therapeutics [*A publication*]
PROSTAT ... Prostatic (AAMN)
PROSTH... Prosthesis
Prosthet and Orthotics Int ... Prosthetics and Orthotics International [*A publication*]
Prosthet Orthot Int ... Prosthetics and Orthotics International [*A publication*]
PROSY...... People's Republic of South Yemen (BJA)
PROT .... Protect [*or Protection*] (MSA)
PROT .... Protective Life Corp. [*NASDAQ symbol*] (NQ)
PROT .... Protein
PROT .... Protest (ROG)
PROT .... Protestant
Prot .... Protestantesimo [*A publication*]
PROT .... Proteus [*Bacterium*]
PROT .... Protinus [*Speedily*] [*Pharmacy*]
Prot .... Protocol (DLA)
PROT .... Prototype
PROT .... Protractor (AAG)
PROTA..... Protection Actual [*Probability for avoidance of ship*]
PROTA..... Protoplasma [*Austria*] [*A publication*]
ProTACA... Procurement Technical Assistance Cooperative Agreement Program [*DoD*]
Prot Aer ..... Protection Aerienne [*A publication*]
PROTAP... Professional Opportunities through Academic Partnership [*National War College*]
PROTAP... Protonotary Apostolic [*Roman Catholic*]
Prot Civ Secur Ind ... Protection Civile et Securite Industrielle [*A publication*]
Prot CJ....... Protocol on the Statute of the European Communities Court of Justice [*A publication*] (DLA)
Prot Coat Met ... Protective Coatings on Metals [*A publication*]
PROTCT... Protective (AAG)
PROTEC... Protection
Prot Ecol.... Protection Ecology [*A publication*]
PROTECON ... Process and Test Control [*Pendar Technical Association Ltd.*] [*Software package*] (NCC)
PROTECT ... Probabilities Recall Optimizing the Employment of Calibration Time (KSC)
Protein Abnorm ... Protein Abnormalities [*A publication*]
Protein Eng ... Protein Engineering [*A publication*]
Protein Nucl Acid Enzyme ... Protein Nucleic Acid Enzyme [*A publication*]
Protein Sequences Data Anal ... Protein Sequences and Data Analysis [*A publication*]
Proteins Iron Metab Proc Int Meet ... Proteins of Iron Metabolism. Proceedings. International Meeting [*A publication*]
Proteins Struct Funct Genet ... Proteins. Structure, Function, and Genetics [*A publication*]
Protein Struct ... Protein Structure [*A publication*]
Protein Synth ... Protein Synthesis [*A publication*]
Protein Synth Ser Adv ... Protein Syntheses: A Series of Advances [*A publication*]
Protein Targeting Proc John Innes Symp ... Protein Targeting. Proceedings. John Innes Symposium [*A publication*]
Proteinuria Symp Nephrol ... Proteinuria. Symposium of Nephrology [*A publication*]
PRO TEM ... Pro Tempore [*For the Time Being*] [*Latin*]
PRO TEM et LOC ... Pro Tempore et Loco [*For the Time and Place*] [*Latin*] (ROG)
Prot Epis His M ... Protestant Episcopal Church. Historical Magazine [*A publication*]
Protes Dent ... Protesista Dental [*A publication*]
Protet Stomatol ... Protetyka Stomatologiczna [*A publication*]
PROTEUS ... [*A*] Programming Language (CSR)
PROTEUS ... Project to Research Objects Theories, Extraterrrestrials, and Unusual Sightings (EA)
PROTEUS ... Propulsion Research and Open Water Testing of Experimental Underwater Systems (MCD)
PROTHROM ... Prothrombin [*Hematology*]
Proth Werkst Kd ... Prothetik und Werkstoffkunde [*A publication*]
Protides Biol Fluids Proc Colloq ... Protides of the Biological Fluids. Proceedings of the Colloquium [*Belgium*] [*A publication*]
Protides Biol Fluids Proc Colloq (Bruges) ... Protides of the Biological Fluids. Proceedings of the Colloquium (Bruges) [*A publication*]
PROTIMEREP ... Proceed in Time Report Not Later Than [*Hour and/or date indicated*] [*Military*]
Prot Met .... Protection of Metals [*A publication*]
Prot Metals ... Protection of Metals [*A publication*]
Prot Met (USSR) ... Protection of Metals (Union of Soviet Socialist Republics) [*A publication*]
PROTN ..... Procedure Turn [*Aviation*] (FAAC)
PROTO ..... Protoporphyrin [*Hematology*]
PROTO ..... Prototype (KSC)
Protok Fischereitech ... Protokolle zur Fischereitechnik [*A publication*]

Protok OS ... Protokoly Obscego Sobranija Akademii Nauk [*A publication*]
Protoplasma Suppl ... Protoplasma Supplementum [*A publication*]
Prot PI .... Protocol on Privileges and Immunities of the European Economic Community [*A publication*]   (DLA)
PROTR...... Protractor   (MSA)
Protr........... Protrepticus [*of Clemens Alexandrinus*] [*Classical studies*]   (OCD)
Protsessy Khromatogr Kolonkakh ... Protsessy v Khromatograficheskikh Kolonakh [*A publication*]
Prot Steel Zinc Dust Paints Pap Semin ... Protecting Steel with Zinc Dust Paints. Papers. Seminar [*A publication*]
Prot Vitae... Protectio Vitae [*A publication*]
Prouchvaniya Mikroelem Mikrotorovete Bulg ... Prouchvaniya vurkhu Mikroelementite i Mikrotorovete v Bulgariya [*A publication*]
Proud Dom Pub ... Proudhon's Domaine Public [*A publication*]   (DLA)
Proudf Land Dec ... United States Land Decisions (Proudfit) [*A publication*]   (DLA)
PROUS...... Proceed to a Port in Continental United States [*Military*]
PRO US EXT ... Pro Usu Externo [*For External Use*] [*Pharmacy*]
Prouty .... Prouty's Reports [*61-68 Vermont*] [*A publication*]   (DLA)
Prov........... De Providentia [*of Seneca the Younger*] [*Classical studies*]   (OCD)
PROV .... Provencal [*Language, etc.*]
PROV .... Provence [*France*]   (ROG)
PROV .... Proverb
Prov........... Proverbs [*Old Testament book*]
PROV .... Provide   (KSC)
PROV .... Providence Journal-Bulletin [*A publication*]
PROV .... Provident Institute for Savings of Boston [*NASDAQ symbol*]   (NQ)
PROV .... Province
Prov........... Provincia [*A publication*]
PROV .... Provincial
Prov........... Provincial [*A publication*]
PROV .... Provinciale [*Provincial*] [*Netherlands*]   (EY)
PROV .... Proving Ground [*Navy*]
PROV .... Provision [*or Provisional*]   (AFM)
Prov........... Provisional Light [*Navigation signal*]
PROV .... Provost
Prov Buenos Aires Com Invest Cient Inf ... Provincia de Buenos Aires. Comision de Investigaciones Cientificas. Informes [*A publication*]
Prov Buenos Aires Com Invest Cient Mem ... Provincia de Buenos Aires. Comision de Investigaciones Cientificas. Memoria [*A publication*]
Prov Can Stat ... Statutes of the Province of Canada [*A publication*]   (DLA)
Prov Cons... De Provinciis Consularibus [*of Cicero*] [*Classical studies*]   (OCD)
PROVCORPV ... Provisional Corps, Vietnam
PROVD ..... Provided
Provebruksmeld Nor Landbruksokonomiske Inst ... Provebruksmelding-Norges Landbruksokonomiske Institutt [*A publication*]
Prov Econ... Provincial Economies [*A publication*]
Provence Hist ... Provence Historique [*A publication*]
Provence Univ Ann Geol Mediterr ... Provence Universite. Annales. Geologie Mediterraneenne [*A publication*]
Provence Univ Lab Paleontol Hum Prehist Etud Quat Mem ... Provence Universite. Laboratoire de Paleontologie Humaine et de Prehistoire. Etudes Quaternaires. Memoire [*A publication*]
PROVER... Procurement for Minimum Total Cost through Value Engineering and Reliability
ProvGM..... Provincial Grand Master [*Freemasonry*]
PROVGR... Proving Grounds
Prov Hist.... Provence Historique [*A publication*]
PROVIB.... Propulsion System Decision and Vibration Analysis   (DNAB)
Provid........ De Providentia [*of Philo*]   (BJA)
Providence Hosp Detroit Med Bull ... Providence Hospital of Detroit. Medical Bulletin [*A publication*]
Providence Hosp (Southfield Mich) Med Bull ... Providence Hospital (Southfield, Michigan). Medical Bulletin [*A publication*]
Providen JB ... Providence Journal-Bulletin [*A publication*]
Providen SJ ... Providence Sunday Journal [*A publication*]
Providnc J ... Providence Journal [*A publication*]
Provincial Bank Can Econ R ... Provincial Bank of Canada. Economic Review [*A publication*]
Prov Inher & Gift Tax Rep CCH ... Provincial Inheritance and Gift Tax Reporter. Commerce Clearing House [*A publication*]
PROVIS .... Provision
Prov Judges J ... Provincial Judges Journal [*A publication*]
Prov Kaohsiung Teach Coll Chem Dep J ... Provincial Kaohsiung Teachers College Chemistry Department. Journal [*A publication*]
PROVMAAG ... Provisional Military Assistance Advisory Group   (CINC)
PROVMAAG-K ... Provisional Military Assistance Advisory Group, Korea   (CINC)
PROVMAIN ... Other Provisions Basic Orders Remain in Effect
PROVMAINTCO ... Provisional Maintenance Company [*Navy*]   (DNAB)
PROVMUSTCO ... Provisional Medical Unit Self-Contained Company [*Navy*]   (DNAB)
Prov Newfoundland Miner Dev Div Rep ... Province of Newfoundland. Mineral Development Division. Report [*A publication*]

provns .... Provisions   (DLA)
PROVO ...... Proviso [*Contract clause*]   (ROG)
PROVO ...... Provocateur   (DSUE)
PROVONS ... Provisions
PROVOST ... Priority Research Objectives for Vietnam Operations Support
Prov St .... Statutes, Laws, of the Province of Massachusetts [*A publication*]   (DLA)
PROWDELREP ... Proceed Without Delay Report Duty or Purpose Indicated [*Military*]
PROWLER ... Programmable Robot Observer with Logical Enemy Response [*Developed by Robot Defense Systems of Thornton, CO*]
PROWORD ... Procedure Word
PROX .... Proximity   (AABC)
PROX .... Proximo [*In Next Month*] [*Latin*]
PROX ACC ... Proxime Accessit [*Next in Order of Merit*] [*Latin*]
PRO-XAN ... Protein-Xanthophyll [*Alfalfa protein concentrate process*]
PROXI...... Projection by Reflection Optics of Xerographic Images   (IEEE)
prox luc ...... Proxima Luce [*Day Before*] [*Latin*]   (MAE)
Proyecto Desarrollo Pesq Publ ... Proyecto de Desarrollo Pesquero. Publicacion [*A publication*]
P Roy Music ... Proceedings. Royal Musical Association [*A publication*]
P Roy S Med ... Proceedings. Royal Society of Medicine [*A publication*]
P Roy Soc A ... Proceedings. Royal Society of London. Series A. Mathematical and Physical Sciences [*A publication*]
P Roy Soc B ... Proceedings. Royal Society of London. Series B. Biological Sciences [*A publication*]
PRP........... Pamjatniki Russkogo Prava [*A publication*]
PRP........... Panretinal Photocoagulation [*Ophthalmology*]
PRP........... Parent Rule Point   (MCD)
PRP........... Parti Republicain du Progres [*Republican Progress Party*] [*Central Africa*] [*Political party*]   (PD)
PRP........... Parti Republicain Progressif [*Algeria*] [*Political party*]   (EY)
PRP........... Parti de la Revolution Populaire [*People's Revolutionary Party*] [*Zaire*] [*Political party*]   (PD)
PRP........... Partido Renovacion Patriotica [*Honduras*] [*Political party*]   (EY)
PRP........... Partido de Renovacion Puertorriqueno [*Puerto Rican Renewal Party*] [*Political party*]   (EY)
PRP........... Partido de Representacao Popular [*Brazil*] [*Political party*]
PRP........... Partido Republicano Portugues [*Portuguese Republican Party*] [*Political party*]   (PPE)
PRP........... Partido Revolucionario Popular [*Popular Revolutionary Party*] [*Portugal*] [*Political party*]   (PPE)
PRP........... Peace Resource Project   (EA)
PRP........... Peak Radiated Power   (CET)
PRP........... People's Redemption Party [*Nigeria*] [*Political party*]   (PPW)
PRP........... People's Reform Party [*Philippines*] [*Political party*]   (EY)
PRP........... People's Revolutionary Party [*North Vietnam*] [*Political party*]
PRP........... People's Revolutionary Party [*Benin*] [*Political party*]
PRP........... Peptide Recognition Protein [*Biochemistry*]
PRP........... Performance-Related Pay   (ECON)
PRP........... Performance, Requirements, Practices [*Military*]
PRP........... Personnel Reliability Program [*Air Force*]
PRP........... Phantom Range Pod   (MCD)
PRP........... Phase Review Package   (MCD)
PRP........... Physical Readiness Program [*Navy*]   (DNAB)
PRP........... Pickup-Zone Release Point
PRP........... Pityriasis Rubra Pilaris [*Dermatology*]   (MAE)
PRP........... Platelet-Rich Plasma [*Hematology*]
PRP........... Pneumatically-Released Pilot   (DNAB)
PRP........... Polymer of Ribose Phosphate [*Organic chemistry*]   (MAE)
PRP........... Polyribitol Phosphate [*Organic chemistry*]
PRP........... Position Report Printout
PRP........... Postbuckled Rectangular Plate
PRP........... Potentially Responsible Party [*Environmental Protection Agency*]
PRP........... Power-Deployed Reserve Parachute   (MCD)
PRP........... Premature-Removal Period   (MCD)
PRP.......... Prepare   (FAAC)
PRP........... Prerigor Pressurization [*Meat processing*]
PR P.......... Present Participle   (WGA)
PRP........... President's Reorganization Project [*Carter Administration*] [*Executive Office of the President*]   (GFGA)
PRP........... Pressure Rate Product [*In treadmill test*]
PRP........... Primary Raynaud's Phenomenon [*Medicine*]
PRP........... Principal Responsible Party
PrP............ Prion Protein [*Biochemistry*]
PRP........... Problem Resolution Program [*IRS*]
PRP........... Procurement Requirements Package   (MCD)
PRP........... Production Readiness Plan
PRP........... Production Requirements Plan
PRP........... Production Reserve Policy
PRP........... Profit-Related Pay [*Economics*]
PRP........... Program Requirements Package [*Data processing*]
PRP........... Program Review Panel [*Army*]   (AABC)
PRP........... Progress in Radiopharmacology [*Elsevier Book Series*] [*A publication*]
PRP........... Progressive Rework Plan
PRP........... Progressive Rubella Panencephalitis [*Medicine*]
PRP........... Proliferative Retinopathy Photocoagulation
PRP........... Proline-Rich Protein [*Biochemistry*]

PRP............ Proper Return Port [*Shipping*]
PRP............ Prospective Reimbursement Plan [*Medicaid*]
PRP............ Protease-Resistant Prion [*Medicine*]
PrP............ Protease-Resistant Protein [*Microbiology*]
PrP............ Protein Phosphatase [*An enzyme*]
PRP............ Pseudorandom Pulse
PRP............ Psychotic Reaction Profile [*Psychology*]
PRP............ Public Relations Personnel [*Navy*]
PRP............ Pulse Recurrence [*or Repetition*] Period   (CET)
PRP............ Purchase Request Package [*Shipping*]   (MCD)
PRP............ Purple   (MSA)
PRP............ Purpose   (MSA)
PRP............ Reformed Presbyterian Theological Seminary, Pittsburgh, PA [*OCLC symbol*]   (OCLC)
PRPA........ Professional Race Pilots Association [*Later, USARA*]   (EA)
PRPB........ Parti de la Revolution Populaire du Benin [*Benin People's Revolutionary Party*] [*Political party*]   (PD)
PRPC........ Parti Republicain du Peuple Camerounais [*Political party*]   (EY)
PRPC........ Public Relations Policy Committee [*NATO*]   (NATG)
PRP-D....... Polyribosylribitol Phosphate-Diptheria Toxoid [*Medicine*]
PRPDLG ... Pre-Paid Legal Services, Inc. [*Associated Press abbreviation*]   (APAG)
PRPE........ Prairie Pacific Energy Corp. [*NASDAQ symbol*]   (NQ)
PRPF .... Planar Radial Peaking Factor [*Network analysis*]   (IEEE)
PRPG........ Proportioning
Pr/Ph........ Pristane/Phytane Ratio [*Environmental science*]
PRPH .... Research in Phenomenology [*A publication*]
PRPHL...... Peripheral
Pr Phys Soc L ... Proceedings. Physical Society of London [*A publication*]
PRPL........ PACOM [*Pacific Command*] Reconnaissance Priority List   (CINC)
PRPL .... People's Democratic Republic of Laos
PRPL .... Procurement Repair Parts List   (AAG)
PRPLN ...... Propulsion   (MSA)
PRPLNT ... Propellant   (KSC)
PRPLT....... Propellant   (MSA)
PRPNE...... Propane [*Organic chemistry*]
PRPO........ Review of Politics [*A publication*]
PRPOOS ... Plankton Rate Processes in Oligotrophic Oceans [*Cooperative research project*]
Pr Poznan Tow Przyj Nauk Wydz Nauk Roln Lesn ... Prace-Poznanskie Towarzystwo Przyjaciol Nauk. Wydzial Nauk Rolniczych i Lesnych [*A publication*]
PRPP .... Phosphoribosylpyrophosphate [*Biochemistry*]
PRPP .... Phosphorylribose Pyrophosphate [*Biochemistry*]
PRPP .... Pseudoresidual Plot Program
PRPQ........ Programming Request for Price Quotation [*Data processing*]
PR PR........ Praeter Propter [*About, Nearly*] [*Latin*]   (ROG)
Pr Preh Soc ... Proceedings. Prehistoric Society [*A publication*]
Pr Primer ... Prairie Primer [*A publication*]
PRPS .... Pressure Rise per Stage   (MCD)
PRPS .... Program Requirement Process Specification [*NASA*]   (KSC)
PRPSA ...... Petroleum Press Service [*A publication*]
PRPSB...... Progress in Polymer Science [*A publication*]
PRPSD ...... Proposed   (MSA)
PRPSL....... Proposal   (MSA)
PRPT........ Parti Revolutionnaire du Peuple Tunisien [*Revolutionary Party of the Tunisian People*] [*Political party*]   (PD)
PRPT .... Prescriptive Reading Performance Test [*Educational test*]
PRPT .... Probe Post [*A publication*]
PRPTA ...... Proceedings. Association of Asphalt Paving Technologists [*A publication*]
PR Publ Rep Aust Coal Ind Res Lab ... PR. Published Report. Australian Coal Industry Research Laboratories [*A publication*]
PRPUC...... Philippine Republic Presidential Unit Citation [*Military decoration*]
PRPUCE ... Philippine Republic Presidential Unit Citation Emblem [*Military decoration*]
PRPY........ Romance Philology [*A publication*]
PRPYA...... Praxis der Psychotherapie [*A publication*]
PRQ .... Houston, TX [*Location identifier*] [*FAA*]   (FAAL)
PRQ .... Problems of Communism [*A publication*]
PRQA .... Passenger Ride Quality Apparatus [*Public transportation*]
PRR .... Parts Replacement Request   (KSC)
PRR .... Passenger Reservation Request   (NVT)
PRR .... Passive Ranging RADAR
PRR .... Pawling Research Reactor
PRR .... Pennsylvania Railroad Co. [*AAR code*] [*Obsolete*]
PRR .... Performance-Related Remuneration   (ADA)
PRR .... Perrine, FL [*Location identifier*] [*FAA*]   (FAAL)
PRR .... Perris [*California*] [*Seismograph station code, US Geological Survey*] [*Closed*]   (SEIS)
PRR .... Personnel Requirements Report [*Army*]
PRR .... Philippine Research Reactor   (SAA)
PRR .... Placement Revision Request
PRR .... Planning Release Record   (AAG)
PRR .... Plans and Requirements Review
PRR .... Political Risk Review [*A publication*]   (EAAP)
Pr R.......... Practice Reports [*Quebec*] [*A publication*]   (DLA)
Pr R........... Practice Reports [*Ontario*] [*A publication*]   (DLA)

PRR .... Pre-Raphaelite Review [*A publication*]
PRR .... Preliminary Requirements Review [*NASA*]   (KSC)
PRR .... Premature Removal Rate
PRR .... Presbyterian and Reformed Renewal Ministries International [*Formerly, PCC*]   (EA)
PRR .... Presbyterian and Reformed Review [*A publication*]
PRR .... Pressure Rise Rate [*Nuclear energy*]   (NRCH)
PRR .... Prism Resources Ltd. [*Vancouver Stock Exchange symbol*]
PRR .... Producer's Reliability Risk
PRR .... Production Readiness Review
PRR .... Production Research Reports
PR & R...... Professional Rights and Responsibilities
PRR .... Program Requirements Review [*NASA*]   (NASA)
PRR .... Program Revision Report   (KSC)
PRR .... Proline-Rich Protein [*Biochemistry*]
PRR .... Proton Relaxation Rate
PRR .... Public Relations Review [*A publication*]
PRR .... Publication Revision Request   (AAG)
PRR .... Puerto Rico Reactor   (NRCH)
PRR .... Puerto Rico Reports [*A publication*]
PRR .... Puerto Rico Supreme Court Reports [*A publication*]   (DLA)
PRR .... Pulse Recurrence [*or Repetition*] Rate   (MUGU)
PrRA .... Academia Maria Reina, Rio Piedras, PR [*Library symbol*] [*Library of Congress*]   (LCLS)
PRRA........ Puerto Rico Reconstruction Administration [*Terminated, 1955*]
PRRB........ Physics Reports. Reprints Book Series [*Elsevier Book Series*] [*A publication*]
PRRB........ Provider Reimbursement Review Board [*Medicare*]
PRRC........ New Mexico Petroleum Recovery Research Center [*New Mexico Institute of Mining and Technology*] [*Research center*]   (RCD)
PRRC........ Pitch/Roll Rate Changer Assembly   (MCD)
PrRe........... Evangelical Seminary, Rio Piedras, PR [*Library symbol*] [*Library of Congress*]   (LCLS)
PRRE........ Pupils Round, Regular, and Equal [*Medicine*]   (MAE)
PRREA...... Philips Research Reports [*A publication*]
Pr Reg BC ... Practical Register in the Bail Court [*A publication*]   (DLA)
Pr Reg Ch .. Practical Register in Chancery [*1 vol.*] [*A publication*]   (DLA)
Pr Reg CP .. Practical Register in the Common Pleas [*1705-42*] [*A publication*]   (DLA)
Pr Rep .... Practice Reports [*England*] [*A publication*]   (DLA)
Pr Rep .... Practice Reports [*Ontario*] [*A publication*]   (DLA)
Pr Rep BC ... Lowndes, Maxwell, and Pollock's English Bail Court Practice Reports [*1850-51*] [*A publication*]   (DLA)
PR Rev Public Health Trop Med ... Porto Rico Review of Public Health and Tropical Medicine [*A publication*]
PRRFC ...... Planar Randomly Reinforced Fiber Composite
PRRI.......... Puerto Rico Rum Institute [*Later, PRRPA*]
PRRM........ Presbyterian and Reformed Renewal Ministries International   (EA)
PRRM........ Program Review and Resources Management [*NASA*]
PRRM........ Pulse Repetition Rate Modulation [*Data transmission*] [*Data processing*]   (TEL)
Pr Roy Soc ... Proceedings. Royal Society [*A publication*]
PRRPA...... Puerto Rico Rum Producers Association   (EA)
PRR & Regs ... Commonwealth of Puerto Rico Rules and Regulations [*A publication*]   (DLA)
PRRS .... Positioning Reporting Recording System   (RDA)
PRRS .... Problem Reporting and Resolution System [*Military*]   (CAAL)
Pr RS Med ... Proceedings. Royal Society of Medicine [*A publication*]
PR-RSV ..... Rous Sarcoma Virus, Prague Strain
PRS........... Pacific Railroad Society   (EA)
PRS........... Pacific Rocket Society   (EA)
PRS........... Padre Resources [*Vancouver Stock Exchange symbol*]
PRS........... Pairs
PRS........... Paraiso [*California*] [*Seismograph station code, US Geological Survey*]   (SEIS)
PRS........... Parametric Ruled Surface   (MCD)
PRS........... Parasi [*Solomon Islands*] [*Airport symbol*]   (OAG)
PRS........... Parliamentary Research Services [*British*]
PRS........... Partei fuer Renten-, Steuer-, und Soziale Gerechtigkeit [*Party for Equitable Pensions, Taxation, and Social Services*] [*Germany*] [*Political party*]   (PPW)
PRS........... Parti de la Revolution Socialiste [*Party of Socialist Revolution*] [*Benin*] [*Political party*]
PRS........... Parti de la Revolution Socialiste [*Party of Socialist Revolution*] [*Senegal*] [*Political party*]
PRS........... Partido para a Renovacao Social [*Party for Social Renovation*] [*Guinea-Bissau*] [*Political party*]   (EY)
PRS........... Partido de la Revolucion Socialista [*Party of the Socialist Revolution*] [*Cuba*] [*Political party*]
PRS........... Partido Revolucionario Socialista [*Mexico*] [*Political party*]   (EY)
PRS........... Partito Republicano Sammarinese [*Republican Party*] [*San Marino*] [*Political party*]   (EY)
PRS........... Passive RADAR Surveillance [*Military*]   (CAAL)
PRS........... Pattern Recognition Society   (EA)
PRS........... Pattern Recognition System
PRS........... Payload Retention Subsystem [*NASA*]   (NASA)

PRS........... Pennsylvania-Reading Seashore Lines [*Absorbed into Consolidated Rail Corp.*]
PRS........... Perceptual Respresentation System [*Memory*]
PRS........... Performance Rating System (OICC)
PRS........... Performing Right Society [*British*]
PRS........... Personal Recording System
PRS........... Personal Relations Survey [*Managerial skills test*]
PRS........... Personality Rating Scale [*Psychology*]
PRS........... Personnel Readiness System [*Air Force*]
PRS........... Personnel Rescue Service [*NASA*] (NASA)
PRS........... Personnel Rescue System [*NASA*] (MCD)
PRS........... Personnel Research Section [*Army*]
PRS........... Personnel Research Staff [*Department of Agriculture*]
PRS........... Perspectives in Religious Studies [*A publication*]
PRS........... Philatelic Research Society
PRS........... Philosophical Research Society (EA)
PRS........... Photo Resist Spinner
PRS........... Photographic Reconnaissance System
PRS........... Physically Restricted Status [*Military*]
PRS........... Pipe Roll Society (EA)
PRS........... Planar Rider System
PRS........... Planners Referral Service [*Information service or system*] (IID)
PRS........... Planning Record Sheet
PRS........... Planning Research & Systems Ltd. [*British*]
PRS........... Plasma Renin Substrate [*Hematology*]
PRS........... Pneumatic Reading System
PRS........... Pointing Reference System (KSC)
PRS........... Population Research Service [*Information service or system*] (IID)
PRS........... Power Reactant Subsystem [*NASA*] (NASA)
PRS........... Power Relay Satellite
PrS............. Prairie Schooner [*A publication*]
PRS........... Prayers (ROG)
PRS........... Precision Ranging System
PRS........... Precision Rotary Stripper
PRS........... Present (WGA)
PRS........... President of the Royal Society [*British*]
PRS........... Presidential Airways [*Philadelphia, PA*] [*FAA designator*] (FAAC)
PRS........... Presidio Oil Co. [*AMEX symbol*] (SPSG)
PRS........... Presidio, TX [*Location identifier*] [*FAA*] (FAAL)
PRS........... Press (MSA)
PRS........... Press Summary [*A publication*]
PRS........... Pressure Reducing Station
PRS........... Pressure Response Spectrum [*Nuclear energy*] (NRCH)
PR/S......... Prestrike (SAA)
PRS........... Primary Recovery Ship [*NASA*]
PRS........... Primary Recovery Site [*NASA*] (KSC)
PRS........... Primary Rescue Site [*NASA*] (NASA)
PRS........... Procedure Review Section [*Social Security Administration*]
PRS........... Process Radiation Sampler [*Nuclear energy*] (NRCH)
PRS........... Product Requirement Schedule (MCD)
PRS........... Production Recording System
PRS........... Production Release System (MCD)
PRS........... Program Requirements Summary (MUGU)
PRS........... Property Recovery Section
PRS........... Propodial Sinus [*Zoology*]
PRS........... Prospectors Air [*Vancouver Stock Exchange symbol*]
PRS........... Protestant Reformation Society (EA)
PRS........... Provide Repair Service [*Navy*] (NVT)
PRS........... Provisioning Requirements Statement
PRS........... Pseudorandom Sequence
PRS........... Psycholinguistic Rating Scale
PRS........... Public Relations Section [*Library Administration and Management Association*]
PRSA........ Pan-Rhodian Society of America (EA)
PRSA........ Power Reactant Storage Assembly [*NASA*] (MCD)
PRSA........ President of the Royal Scottish Academy
PRSA........ Public Relations Society of America (EA)
PRSA........ Puerto Rico Statehood Commission (EA)
PrSaC .... Colegio Universitario del Sagrado Corazon [*College of the Sacred Heart*], Santurce, PR [*Library symbol*] [*Library of Congress*] (LCLS)
Prsb Q........ Presbyterian Quarterly Review [*A publication*]
PRSC........ Plutonium Rework Sample Cell [*Nuclear energy*] (NRCH)
PRSC........ Puerto Rico Solidarity Committee (EA)
Pr Schae B ... Praktische Schaedlingsbekaempfer [*Braunschweig*] [*A publication*]
PRSCR ...... Puerto Rico Supreme Court Reports [*A publication*] (DLA)
PRSD........ Portable Rectilinear Scanning Device
PRSD........ Power Reactant Storage [*or Supply*] and Distribution [*NASA*] (NASA)
PRSD........ Pressed (AAG)
PRSDS ...... Power Reactant Storage and Distribution System (MCD)
PrSE .... El Mundo Publishing Co., San Juan, PR [*Library symbol*] [*Library of Congress*] (LCLS)
PRSE .... President of the Royal Society of Edinburgh
PRSE .... Proceedings. Royal Society of Edinburgh [*A publication*]
PRSEC....... Payroll Section

P RS Edin A ... Proceedings. Royal Society of Edinburgh. Section A. Mathematical and Physical Sciences [*A publication*]
P RS Edin B ... Proceedings. Royal Society of Edinburgh. Section B. Natural Environment [*A publication*]
Prsfdr .... Pressfeeder [*Printing*]
PRSG........ Personal Radio Steering Group [*Ann Arbor, MI*] [*Telecommunications service*] (TSSD)
PRSG........ Pulse-Rebalanced Strapdown Gyro (MCD)
PRSH........ President of the Royal Society for the Promotion of Health [*British*]
PRSL .... Pennsylvania-Reading Seashore Lines [*Absorbed into Consolidated Rail Corp.*] [*AAR code*]
PRSL .... Progressive Savings & Loan Association [*NASDAQ symbol*] (NQ)
PRSM .... Proceedings. Royal Society of Medicine [*A publication*]
PRSMA ...... Proceedings. Royal Society of Medicine [*A publication*]
PRSMN...... Pressman (AABC)
PRSN........ Provisional Relative Sunspot Number [*NASA*]
PRSNG...... Pressing
Prsnrs......... Prisoners [*A publication*]
PRSNT ...... Present (FAAC)
Pr Soc Exp Biol Med ... Proceedings. Society for Experimental Biology and Medicine [*A publication*]
PRSPL....... Planning and Role Setting for Public Libraries [*Public Library Association*] [*A publication*]
PRSR .... Presser (MSA)
PRSR .... Russian Review [*A publication*]
PRSRV ...... Preservative (AAG)
PRSRZ ...... Pressurize (MSA)
PRSS .... Pennsylvania-Reading Seashore Lines [*Absorbed into Consolidated Rail Corp.*]
PRSS .... Problem Report Squawk Sheet [*NASA*] (NASA)
PRSSA....... Philips Research Reports. Supplements [*A publication*]
PRSSA....... Public Relations Student Society of America (EA)
PRSSA....... Puerto Rico Mainland US Statehood Students Association (EA)
PRSSD ...... Pressed
PRST .... Persist (FAAC)
PRST .... Presstek, Inc. [*NASDAQ symbol*] (NQ)
PRST .... Probability Reliability Sequential Tests (MCD)
PRSTA ...... Progress in Stereochemistry [*A publication*]
Pr Stat....... Private Statutes [*Legal term*] (DLA)
PRSTB...... Progresele Stiintei [*A publication*]
PRSTC...... Prosthetic
PRSU........ Police Requirements Support Unit [*Home Office*] [*British*]
PRSU........ Religious Studies [*A publication*]
PRSUA...... Plastic and Reconstructive Surgery [*A publication*]
PRSUB...... Pribory i Sistemy Upravleniya [*A publication*]
PR Sugar Man ... Puerto Rico Sugar Manual [*A publication*]
PRSV........ Papaya Ringspot Virus [*Plant pathology*]
PRSVN...... Preservation (AABC)
PRSW........ President of the Royal Scottish Water Colour Society
PrSW .... World University, San Juan, PR [*Library symbol*] [*Library of Congress*] (LCLS)
PrSW-I ...... World University, International Institute of the Americas, Barbosa Esq. Guayama, San Juan, PR [*Library symbol*] [*Library of Congress*] (LCLS)
PRT........... Parr Terminal Railroad [*AAR code*]
PRT........... Part (AAG)
PRT........... Participating Research Teams [*Department of Energy*]
PRT........... Partido Revolucionario de los Trabajadores [*Workers' Revolutionary Party*] [*Peru*] [*Political party*] (PPW)
PRT........... Partido Revolucionario de los Trabajadores [*Workers' Revolutionary Party*] [*Uruguay*] [*Political party*] (PD)
PRT........... Partido Revolucionario de los Trabajadores [*Workers' Revolutionary Party*] [*Argentina*] [*Political party*] (PD)
PRT........... Partido Revolucionario de los Trabajadores [*Revolutionary Workers' Party*] [*Costa Rica*] [*Political party*] (EY)
PRT........... Partido Revolucionario de Trabajadores [*Revolutionary Worker's Party*] [*Colombia*] [*Political party*] (EY)
PRT........... Partido Revolucionario de los Trabajadores [*Revolutionary Workers Party*] [*Panama*] [*Political party*] (EY)
PRT........... Pattern Recognition Technique
PRT........... Payroll Tax (ADA)
PRT........... Periodic Reevaluation Tests
PRT........... Personal Rapid Transit [*Computer-guided transit system*]
PRT........... Personnel Research Test [*Military*]
PRT........... Petroleum Revenue Tax [*British*]
PRT........... Pharmaceutical Research and Testing [*Public Health Service*] (GRD)
PRT........... Philadelphia Reading Test [*Education*]
PRT........... Phosphoribosyltransferase [*Also, PRTase*] [*An enzyme*]
PRT........... Photoradiation Therapy [*Oncology*]
PRT........... Physical Readiness Training [*Army*] (INF)
P & RT...... Physical and Recreational Training [*Navy*] [*British*]
PRT........... Pictorial Reasoning Test [*Job screening test*]
PRT........... Platinum Resistance Thermometer
PRT........... Point Retreat, AK [*Location identifier*] [*FAA*] (FAAL)
PRT........... Port
PRT........... Portable Radiation Thermometer
PRT........... Portable Radio Telephone

PRT.......... Portable Remote Terminal
PRT.......... Portable Router Template   (MCD)
PRT.......... Portable Router Tool
PRT.......... Portugal [*ANSI three-letter standard code*]   (CNC)
PRT.......... Power Recovery Turbine
PRT.......... Prato [*Italy*] [*Seismograph station code, US Geological Survey*]   (SEIS)
PRT.......... Precision Radiation Thermometer
PRT.......... Preliminary Reference Trajectory [*NASA*]   (KSC)
PRT.......... Pressurized Relief Tank   (NRCH)
PRT.......... Primary Ranging Test   (OA)
PRT.......... Printer [*Data processing*]   (MDG)
prt............. Printer [*MARC relator code*] [*Library of Congress*]   (LCCP)
Prt .... Private [*British military*]   (DMA)
PRT.......... Problem Resolution Tasking System [*Army*]   (INF)
PRT.......... Procurement Review Team
PRT.......... Procurement Round Table   (EA)
PRT.......... Product Range Testing [*Business term*]
PRT.......... Production Reliability Test
PRT.......... Production Run Tape
PRT.......... Program Reference Table
PRT.......... Program Review Team [*Navy*]   (DNAB)
PRT.......... Prompt Relief Trip [*Nuclear energy*]   (NRCH)
Prt .... Protagoras [*of Plato*] [*Classical studies*]   (OCD)
PRT.......... Prova di Restituzione Termica [*Italy*] [*Medicine*]
PRT.......... Provost
PRT.......... Prudential Realty Trust [*NYSE symbol*]   (SPSG)
PRT.......... Psychiatric Rehabilitation Team   (EA)
PRT.......... Publications Requirements Tables   (AAG)
PRT.......... Pulse Recurrence [*or Repetition*] Time   (CET)
PRT.......... Pulsed RADAR Transmitter
PrTAm....... Property Trust of America [*Associated Press abbreviation*]   (APAG)
PRTB......... Partido Revolucionario de Trabajadores Bolivianos [*Bolivian Workers' Revolutionary Party*] [*Political party*]   (PD)
PRTBR ...... Partido Revolucionario de los Trabajadores de Bolivia Romero [*Bolivia*] [*Political party*]   (PPW)
PRTC......... Partido Revolucionario de los Trabajadores Centroamericanos [*Revolutionary Party of Central American Workers*] [*El Salvador*] [*Political party*]   (PD)
PRTC......... Pediatric Research and Training Center [*University of Connecticut*] [*Research center*]   (RCD)
PRTC......... Ports Canada
PRTC......... Precision Technologies [*NASDAQ symbol*]   (NQ)
PRTC......... Professional Rate Training Course   (DNAB)
PRTCD....... Progres Technique [*A publication*]
PRTCD....... Puerto Rico Tax Court Decisions [*A publication*]   (DLA)
PRTC-H .... Partido Revolucionario de los Trabajadores Centroamericanos -- Seccion de Honduras [*Revolutionary Party of Central American Workers -- Honduras*] [*Political party*]
PRTD......... Portland Traction Co. [*AAR code*]
PRTE......... Profit Technology, Inc. [*New York, NY*] [*NASDAQ symbol*]   (NQ)
PRTEA ...... Pribory i Tekhnika Eksperimenta [*A publication*]
PR Tex Agric Exp Stn ... PR. Texas Agricultural Experiment Station [*A publication*]
PRTF .... Pheromone and Receptor Transcription Factor [*Genetics*]
PRTF .... Psychiatric Review Technique Form [*Social Security Administration*]
PRTG......... Printing   (AFM)
PRTHA ...... Progress in Radiation Therapy [*A publication*]
PrThR .... Princeton Theological Review [*A publication*]
PRTHS...... Pennsylvania Railroad Technical and Historical Society   (EA)
PRTI .... Physical and Recreational Training Instructor [*British military*]   (DMA)
PRTK......... Presto-Tek Corp. [*NASDAQ symbol*]   (NQ)
PRTKT....... Parts Kit
PRTL......... Portable   (DNAB)
PRTLS....... Powered Return to Launch Site [*NASA*]   (MCD)
PRTLY ..... Partially
PRTM....... Printing Response-Time Monitor
PRTN .... Partition
PRTO .... Preservation Research and Testing Office [*Library of Congress*]   (EA)
PRTOT....... Prototype Real-Time Optical Tracker [*Data processing*]
PRT Plast Rubbers Text ... PRT. Plastics, Rubbers, Textiles [*A publication*]
PRT Polym Age ... PRT Polymer Age [*A publication*]
PRTR......... Plutonium Recycle Test Reactor [*Nuclear energy*]
PRTR......... Printer
Prt Rep....... Practice Reports [*A publication*]   (DLA)
PRTRL .... Printer, Lithographer [*Navy*]
PRTRM ..... Printer, Offset Process [*Navy*]
PRTRNS ... Programmable Transformer Converter   (MCD)
PRTS .... Personal Rapid Transit System [*Computer-guided transit system*]
PRTS .... Politisch-Religioese Texte aus der Sargonidenzeit [*A publication*]
PRTS .... Pretoria Theological Series [*A publication*]   (BJA)
PrtSc .... Print Screen [*Computer keyboard*]
Prtw............ Propeller Twist [*Genetics*]
PRTY .... Priority

PRU .... Packet Radio Unit
PRu .... Paedagogische Rundschau [*A publication*]
PRU .... Peripheral Resistance Unit [*Medicine*]
PRU .... Photographic Reconnaissance Unit [*Aircraft*] [*Marine Corps*]
PRU .... Pneumatic Regulation Unit   (AAG)
PRU .... Polarity Reversal Unit [*Electrochemistry*]
Pr U........... Pravda Ukrainy [*A publication*]
PRU .... Primary Replacement Unit
PRU .... Prisoner's Rights Union   (EA)
PRU .... Programs Research Unit   (KSC)
PRU .... Prome [*Myanmar*] [*Airport symbol*]   (OAG)
PRU .... Provincial Reconnaissance Unit [*Military*]
PRU .... Prudential Property & Casualty Insurance Co., Holmdel, NJ [*OCLC symbol*]   (OCLC)
PRU .... Pruhonice [*Czechoslovakia*] [*Seismograph station code, US Geological Survey*]   (SEIS)
PrU .... University of Puerto Rico, Rio Piedras, PR [*Library symbol*] [*Library of Congress*]   (LCLS)
PRUAA .... President of the Royal Ulster Academy of Arts
PRUC .... Partido Revolucionario de Union Civico [*Revolutionary Party for Civic Union*] [*Costa Rica*] [*Political party*]
PRUC .... Practice Reports [*1848-1900*] [*Upper Canada*] [*A publication*]   (DLA)
PRUD .... Partido Revolucionario de Unificacion Democratica [*Revolutionary Party of Democratic Unification*] [*El Salvador*]
PrU-H........ University of Puerto Rico, Humacao Regional College, Humacao, PR [*Library symbol*] [*Library of Congress*]   (LCLS)
PRUL......... Programs Unlimited [*NASDAQ symbol*]   (NQ)
PrU-L......... University of Puerto Rico, Law Library, San Juan, PR [*Library symbol*] [*Library of Congress*]   (LCLS)
PrU-M .... University of Puerto Rico, School of Medicine, San Juan, PR [*Library symbol*] [*Library of Congress*]   (LCLS)
PrU-MA .... University of Puerto Rico, Mayaguez Campus, Mayaguez, Puerto Rico [*Library symbol*] [*Library of Congress*]   (LCLS)
Prum Potravin ... Prumysl Potravin [*A publication*]
PrU-MS..... University of Puerto Rico, Department of Marine Sciences, Mayaguez, PR [*Library symbol*] [*Library of Congress*]   (LCLS)
PRUND ..... Plastics and Rubber News [*A publication*]
PrU-NS...... University of Puerto Rico, Natural Science Library, Rio Piedras, PR [*Library symbol*] [*Library of Congress*]   (LCLS)
PruRI .... Prudential Realty Trust [*Associated Press abbreviation*]   (APAG)
PruRtC....... Prudential Realty Trust [*Associated Press abbreviation*]   (APAG)
PRUS........ Prussia [*Obsolete*]
Prus........... Prussian [*Philately*]
PRUS........ Rural Sociology [*A publication*]
PRUSAF.... Puerto Rico, USA Foundation   (EA)
PRV .... Papaya Ringspot Virus
PRV .... Parsley Rhabdovirus [*Plant pathology*]
PRV .... Peak Reverse Voltage
PRV .... Pearl River Valley Railroad Co. [*AAR code*]
PRV .... Personnel Review [*A publication*]
PRv .... Philosophical Review [*A publication*]
PRV .... Polycythemia Rubra Vera [*Medicine*]
PRV .... Porvoo [*Finland*] [*Seismograph station code, US Geological Survey*] [*Closed*]   (SEIS)
PRV .... Pour Rendre Visite [*To Make a Call*] [*French*]
PRV .... Pressure Reducing [*or Regulation or Relief*] Valve
PRV .... Princess Ventures [*Vancouver Stock Exchange symbol*]
PRV .... Prior Record Variable [*Criminal sentencing*]
PRV .... Propeller Revolution
.Prv............ Proverbs [*Old Testament book*]
PRV .... Provincial
PRV .... Provisional Reconnaissance Unit
PRV .... Pseudorabies Virus
PRV .... Pseudorelative Velocity
Prv............. Pyruvenol [*Biochemistry*]
PRVD .... Procurement [*or Purchase*] Request for Vendor Data   (AAG)
PRVD .... Provide   (FAAC)
PRVENA.... Provena Foods, Inc. [*Associated Press abbreviation*]   (APAG)
PRVENG... Providence Energy Corp. [*Associated Press abbreviation*]   (APAG)
PRVEP ...... Pattern Reversal Visual Evoked Potential
Pr Vinnits'k Derzh Med Inst ... Pratsi Vinnits'kogo Derzhavnogo Medichnogo Institutu [*A publication*]
PrvLf......... Provident Life & Accident Insurance Co. of America [*Associated Press abbreviation*]   (APAG)
PRVNTV... Preventive
PRVOA ..... Pravda Vostoka [*A publication*]
PRVS........ Penetration Room Ventilation System [*Nuclear energy*]   (IEEE)
PRVT........ Product Reliability Validation Test   (MCD)
PRVT........ Production Readiness Verification Testing   (MCD)
Prvt Label .. Private Label [*A publication*]
PRVW........ Preview   (MSA)
PRVYD...... Polyteknisk Revy [*A publication*]

PRW .... Paired Wire [*Telecommunications*] (TEL)
PRW .... Percent Rated Wattage
PRW .... Polymerized Ragweed [*Immunology*]
Pr W .... Prawda Wostoka [*A publication*]
PRW .... Press Relations Wire [*Commercial firm*] (EA)
PRW .... Promark Software [*Vancouver Stock Exchange symbol*]
PRW .... Prosser [*Washington*] [*Seismograph station code, US Geological Survey*] (SEIS)
PRW .... Purchasing World [*A publication*]
PRW .... World University, San Juan, PR [*OCLC symbol*] (OCLC)
PRWAD .... Professional Rehabilitation Workers with the Adult Deaf [*Later, ADARA*] (EA)
PR Water Resour Bull ... Puerto Rico. Water Resources Bulletin [*A publication*]
PrWCJewSt ... Proceedings. World Congress of Jewish Studies [*Jerusalem*] [*A publication*]
PRWD .... Priority Regular World Day
PRWI........ Prince William Forest Park [*National Park Service designation*]
Pr Winter ... Probability Winter School. Proceedings of the Fourth Winter School on Probability [*A publication*]
PRWO .... Puerto Rican Revolutionary Workers Organization
PRWRA..... Puerto Rican Water Resources Authority
PRWS........ President of the Royal Society of Painters in Water Colours [*British*]
PRWV....... Peak Reserve Working Voltage
PRX .... Paris [*Texas*] [*Airport symbol*] (OAG)
PRX .... Paris, TX [*Location identifier*] [*FAA*] (FAAL)
PRX .... Pharmaceutical Resources [*NYSE symbol*] (SPSG)
PRX .... Pressure Regulation Exhaust
PRXI........ PRX [*Public Relations Exchange*] International (EA)
PRXS........ Praxis Biologics, Inc. [*NASDAQ symbol*] (NQ)
PRY .... Paraguay [*ANSI three-letter standard code*] (CNC)
PRY .... Parys [*South Africa*] [*Seismograph station code, US Geological Survey*] (SEIS)
PRY .... Pittway Corp. [*AMEX symbol*] (SPSG)
P Ryl .... Catalogue of the Greek Papyri in the John Rylands Library at Manchester [*A publication*] (OCD)
PRZ........... Portales, NM [*Location identifier*] [*FAA*] (FAAL)
PRZ........... Prism Entertainment Corp. [*AMEX symbol*] (SPSG)
PRZ........... Przhevalsk [*Former USSR*] [*Seismograph station code, US Geological Survey*] (SEIS)
Prz Arch..... Przeglad Archeologiczny [*A publication*]
Przegd St.... Przeglad Statystyczny [*A publication*]
Przegl A ..... Przeglad Archeologiczny [*A publication*]
Przeglad Bibliot ... Przeglad Biblioteczny [*A publication*]
Przeglad Geog ... Przeglad Geograficzny [*A publication*]
Przeglad Hist ... Przeglad Historyczny [*A publication*]
Przeglad Mech ... Przeglad Mechaniczny [*A publication*]
Przeglad Papier ... Przeglad Papierniczy [*A publication*]
Przeglad Statyst ... Przeglad Statystyczny [*A publication*]
Przeglad Wlok ... Przeglad Wlokienniczy [*A publication*]
Przegl Antrop ... Przeglad Antropologiczny [*A publication*]
Przegl Antropol ... Przeglad Antropologiczny [*A publication*]
Przegl Bibl ... Przeglad Biblioteczny [*A publication*]
Przegl Bibliogr Chem ... Przeglad Bibliograficzny Chemii [*A publication*]
Przegl Budow ... Przeglad Budowlany [*A publication*]
Przegl Dermatol ... Przeglad Dermatologiczny [*A publication*]
Przegl Dermatol Wenerol ... Przeglad Dermatologii i Wenerologii [*A publication*]
Przegl Derm Wener ... Przeglad Dermatologii i Wenerologii [*A publication*]
Przegl Dok Ceram Szlachetnej Szkla ... Przeglad Dokumentacyjny Ceramiki Szlachetnej i Szkla [*A publication*]
Przegl Dok Nafty ... Przeglad Dokumentacyjny Nafty [*A publication*]
Przegl Dokum Chem ... Przeglad Dokumentacyjny Chemii [*A publication*]
Przegl Dosw Roln ... Przeglad Doswiadezalnictwa Rolniczego [*A publication*]
Przegl Elektr ... Przeglad Elektroniki [*A publication*]
Przegl Elektron ... Przeglad Elektroniki [*A publication*]
Przegl Elektrotech ... Przeglad Elektrotechniczny [*A publication*]
Przegl Epidemiol ... Przeglad Epidemiologiczny [*A publication*]
Przegl Geofiz ... Przeglad Geofizyczny [*A publication*]
Przegl Geogr ... Przeglad Geograficzny [*A publication*]
Przegl Geogr Pol Geogr Rev ... Przeglad Geograficzny/Polish Geographical Review [*A publication*]
Przegl Geol ... Przeglad Geologiczny [*A publication*]
Przegl Gorn ... Przeglad Gorniczy [*A publication*]
Przegl Gorn Hutn ... Przeglad Gorniczo Hutniczy [*A publication*]
Przegl Hist ... Przeglad Historyczny [*A publication*]
Przegl Hodowlany ... Przeglad Hodowlany [*A publication*]
Przegl Kom ... Przeglad Komunikacyjny [*A publication*]
Przegl Komunik ... Przeglad Komunikacyjny [*A publication*]
Przegl Lek ... Przeglad Lekarski [*A publication*]
Przegl Mech ... Przeglad Mechaniczny [*A publication*]
Przegl Met Hydrol ... Przeglad Meteorologiczny i Hydrologiczny [*A publication*]
Przegl Morski ... Przeglad Morski [*A publication*]
Przegl Nauk Lit Zootech ... Przeglad Naukowej Literatury Zootechnicznej [*A publication*]
Przegl Nauk Tech Akad Gorn Hutn Krakowie Ser G ... Przeglad Naukowo Techniczny. Akademia Gorniczo Hutnicza w Krakowie. Seria G. Gornictwo [*A publication*]

Przegl Nauk Tech Akad Gorn Hutn Krakowie Ser H ... Przeglad Naukowo Techniczny. Akademia Gorniczo Hutnicza w Krakowie. Seria H. Hutnictwo [*A publication*]
Przegl Odlew ... Przeglad Odlewnictwa [*A publication*]
Przegl Organ ... Przeglad Organizacji [*A publication*]
Przegl Papiern ... Przeglad Papierniczy [*A publication*]
Przegl Przem Olejowego ... Przeglad Przemyslu Olejowego [*A publication*]
Przegl Skorzany ... Przeglad Skorzany [*A publication*]
Przegl Socjol ... Przeglad Socjologiczny [*A publication*]
Przegl Spawalnictwa ... Przeglad Spawalnictwa [*A publication*]
Przegl Stat ... Przeglad Statystyczny [*A publication*]
Przegl Telekomun ... Przeglad Telekomunikacyjny [*A publication*]
Przegl Wlok ... Przeglad Wlokienniczy [*A publication*]
Przegl Wojsk Ladowych ... Przeglad Wojsk Ladowych [*Poland*] [*A publication*]
Przegl Zachod ... Przeglad Zachodni [*A publication*]
Przegl Zboz Mlyn ... Przeglad Zbozowo Mlynarski [*A publication*]
Przegl Zbozowo Mlyn ... Przeglad Zbozowo Mlynarski [*A publication*]
Przegl Zool ... Przeglad Zologiczny [*A publication*]
Przekazy ... Przekazy/Opinie [*A publication*]
Przem Chem ... Przemysl Chemiczny [*A publication*]
Przem Drzew ... Przemysl Drzewny [*A publication*]
Przem Drzewny ... Przemysl Drzewny [*A publication*]
Przem Ferment ... Przemysl Fermentacyjny [*A publication*]
Przem Ferment Rolny ... Przemysl Fermentacyjny i Rolny [*A publication*]
Przem Naft ... Przemysl Naftowy [*A publication*]
Przem Roln Spozyw ... Przemysl Rolny i Spozywczy [*A publication*]
Przem Spozyw ... Przemysl Spozywczy [*A publication*]
Przem Spozywczy ... Przemysl Spozywczy [*A publication*]
Przem Wlok ... Przemysl Wlokienniczy [*A publication*]
Przemy Chem ... Przemysl Chemiczny [*A publication*]
PRZF .... Pyrazofurin [*Antineoplastic drug*]
PRZGA...... Przeglad Geologiczny [*A publication*]
PrzH .... Przeglad Humanistyczny [*A publication*]
PrzK .... Przeglad Kulturalny [*A publication*]
PrzKl .... Przeglad Klasyczny [*A publication*]
PrzOr .... Przeglad Orientalistyczny [*Cracow/Warsaw*] [*A publication*]
PRZPB ...... Przeglad Psychologiczny [*A publication*]
Prz Stat ...... Przeglad Statystyczny [*A publication*]
PrzZ .... Przeglad Zachodni [*A publication*]
PS.............. Abbott Laboratories [*Research code symbol*]
PS.............. American Political Science Association. Quarterly [*A publication*]
PS.............. Chloropicrin [*Poison gas*] [*Army symbol*]
PS.............. Pacific Southwest Airlines [*ICAO designator*] (OAG)
PS.............. Pacific Spectator [*A publication*]
PS.............. Pacific Star Communication [*Vancouver Stock Exchange symbol*]
P & S......... Packers and Stockyards
P(S)........... Packet (Send)
PS.............. Packet Switching [*Telecommunications*]
PS.............. Packing Sheet (MCD)
PS.............. Paddle Steamer (ADA)
PS.............. Paediatric Surgery
PS.............. Painting System
PS.............. Paleontological Society (EA)
PS.............. Palm Society [*Later, IPS*] (EA)
PS.............. Pamietnik Slowianski [*A publication*]
PS.............. Pan Salicornia Zone [*Ecology*]
P & S......... Paracentesis and Suction [*Medicine*]
PS.............. Parachute Subsystem [*NASA*] (NASA)
PS.............. Paradoxical Sleep
P/S............. Parallel to Serial Converter (MCD)
PS.............. Paramagnetic Scheromak
PS.............. Parents' Section of the Alexander Graham Bell Association for the Deaf (EA)
PS.............. Parents of Suicides (EA)
PS.............. Parity Switch
PS.............. Parliamentary Secretary [*British*]
PS.............. Parlor Snake [*Slang for "to escort visitors around post"*]
PS.............. Parochial School
PS.............. Parrot Society (EA)
ps.............. PARSEC [*Parallax Second*] [*See PARSEC*]
PS.............. Parti Socialiste [*Socialist Party*] [*Belgium*] [*Political party*] (PPW)
PS.............. Parti Socialiste - Federation de la Reunion [*Reunion Federation of the Socialist Party*] [*Political party*] (PPW)
PS.............. Partially Smutted [*Plant pathology*]
PS.............. Partially Synergistic [*Pharmacology*]
PS.............. Partido Socialista [*Socialist Party*] [*Chile*] [*Political party*]
PS.............. Partido Socialista [*Socialist Party*] [*Uruguay*] [*Political party*]
PS.............. Partido Socialista Portuguesa [*Portuguese Socialist Party*] [*Political party*] (PPE)
PS.............. Partido Socialista - Uno [*Socialist Party - One*] [*Also, PS-1*] [*Bolivia*] [*Political party*] (PPW)
PS.............. Partijnaja Shisn [*A publication*]
PS.............. Parts Shipper
PS.............. Passed School of Instruction [*of Officers*] [*British*]
PS.............. Passenger Service
PS.............. Passenger Steamer
PS.............. Passing Scuttle

PS............	Pastel Society [*British*]	
PS............	Pathologic Stage	
PS............	Pathological (Surgical) Staging [*For Hodgkin's Disease*]	
PS............	Patient's Serum [*Medicine*]	
PS............	Patrol Service [*British military*] (DMA)	
PS............	Patrol Ship (CINC)	
PS............	Patrologia Syriaca (BJA)	
PS............	Patton Society (EA)	
P/S............	Pause/Still [*Video technology*]	
P & S..........	Pay and Supply [*Coast Guard*]	
PS............	Payload Shroud (MCD)	
PS............	Payload Specialist [*NASA*] (MCD)	
PS............	Payload Station [*NASA*] (MCD)	
PS............	Payload Support [*NASA*] (NASA)	
PS............	Paymaster Sergeant	
PS............	Pedagogical Seminary and Journal of Genetic Psychology [*A publication*]	
PS............	Pedal Sinus	
PS............	Pellet Size	
PS............	Penal Servitude	
PS............	Penny Stock [*Investment term*]	
PS............	Pensiero e Scuola [*A publication*]	
PS............	Peperomia Society [*Later, PEPS*] (EA)	
PS............	Per Second (AAMN)	
PS............	Per Ship	
PS............	Per Speculum [*Medicine*]	
PS............	Perception Schedule	
PS............	Perceptual Speed (Test) [*Psychology*]	
PS............	Performance Score	
PS............	Performance Standard	
PS............	Performing Scale [*Medicine*] (MAE)	
PS............	Periodic Syndrome [*Medicine*]	
PS............	Peripheral Shock [*Psychology*]	
P & S..........	Perkins & Squier [*Paper manufacturer*]	
PS............	Permanent Secretary	
PS............	Permanent Signal [*Telecommunications*] (TEL)	
PS............	Personal Secretary (DCTA)	
PS............	Personal Skills	
PS............	Personal Survival	
PS............	Personal System [*IBM computer introduced in 1987*]	
PS............	Personnel Subsystem [*Army*]	
PS............	Peru Solidarity [*An association*] (EA)	
PS............	Pet Switchboard (EA)	
PS............	Petty Sessions (DLA)	
PS............	Phase Separation	
PS............	Phase-Shift	
P/S............	Phaser/Subarray	
PS............	Phasing System [*Telecommunications*] (OA)	
PS............	Phenix Society (EA)	
PS............	Phenomenally Speedy Ordinary [*Photographic plates*] (ROG)	
PS............	Philalethes Society (EA)	
PS............	Philippine Studies [*A publication*]	
PS............	Philnathean Society (EA)	
PS............	Philolexian Society (EA)	
PS............	Philological Society (EAIO)	
PS............	Philosophical Studies [*A publication*]	
PS............	Phosphate-Saline [*A buffer*] [*Cell culture*]	
PS............	Phosphatidylserine [*Biochemistry*]	
PS............	Photochemical System	
PS............	Photoemission Scintillation (MCD)	
PS............	Photographic Service	
PS............	Photographic Squadron	
PS............	Photometer System (KSC)	
PS............	Photosystems	
PS............	Phrase Structure (WGA)	
PS............	Phylaxis Society (EA)	
PS............	Physical Sciences	
PS............	Physical Security	
PS............	Physical Sequential (HGAA)	
PS............	Physical Status [*Medicine*]	
PS............	Picket Ships [*Navy*]	
ps............	Picosecond [*One trillionth of a second*]	
PS............	Pilgrim Power Station (NRCH)	
PS............	Pilgrim Society (EA)	
PS............	Pine Bark Mixed with Clay Loam Soil	
PS............	Pine Siskin [*Ornithology*]	
PS............	Pineal Stalk [*Neuroanatomy*]	
PS............	Pink Sheet [*Investment term*]	
PS............	Pirandello Society (EA)	
PS............	Pistol Sharpshooter [*Army*]	
PS............	Pitot/Static Tube (MCD)	
P & S..........	[*The*] Pittsburg & Shawmut Railroad Co.	
PS............	[*The*] Pittsburg & Shawmut Railroad Co. [*AAR code*]	
PS............	Pituitary Stalk [*Neuroanatomy*]	
PS............	Planet Stories [*A publication*]	
PS............	Planetary Society (EA)	
P & S..........	Planking and Strutting [*Construction*]	
PS............	Planning and Scheduling	
PS............	Planning Study (AAG)	
PS............	Plant Stress [*Horticulture*]	
P & S..........	Plant and Structures [*Aviation*] (FAAC)	

PS............	Plastic Surgery [*Medicine*]	
PS............	Platform (Sided) (DCTA)	
P/S............	Platoon/Section [*Army*]	
PS............	Plea Side (ROG)	
PS............	Pleural Sclerite [*Entomology*]	
PS............	Plotting System	
PS............	Plus	
PS............	Pneumatic System	
PS............	Poetry Society [*British*]	
P/S............	Point of Shipment	
PS............	Point of Switch	
PS............	Point of Symmetry	
PS............	Polanyi Society (EA)	
PS............	Polaris Standard [*Missiles*]	
PS............	Polarity Scale [*Psychology*]	
PS............	Police Sergeant [*Scotland Yard*]	
PS............	Policy Statement	
PS............	Polio Society (EA)	
PS............	Political Studies [*A publication*]	
Ps	Polyporus sulphureus [*A fungus*]	
PS............	Polystyrene [*Organic chemistry*]	
PS............	Polysulfone [*Also, PSO*] [*Organic chemistry*]	
P/S............	Polyunsaturated/Saturated [*Fatty acid ratio*]	
PS............	Pop Shop Magazine [*A publication*]	
PS............	Popular Science [*A publication*]	
PS............	Population Sample (MAE)	
PS............	Porlock Society (EA)	
PS............	Port Security	
P & S..........	Port and Starboard	
P/S............	Port or Starboard	
PS............	Port Store [*Telecommunications*] (TEL)	
PS............	Port Strobe [*Telecommunications*] (TEL)	
PS............	Porter-Silber Chromogen [*Medicine*] (MAE)	
PS............	Pos-Escrito [*Postscript*] [*Portuguese*]	
PS............	Position-Specific Antigen	
PS............	Post Script [*A publication*]	
PS............	Post Scriptum [*Written Afterwards, Postscript*] [*Latin*]	
PS............	Postal Satsang [*An association*] (EA)	
PS............	Postal Service [*US*]	
PS............	Poster Society (EA)	
PS............	Potassium Sorbate [*Food additive*]	
PS............	Potentiometer Synchro	
P/S............	Power Section (NG)	
PS............	Power Source	
PS............	Power-Specific (MCD)	
PS............	Power Station (MCD)	
PS............	Power Steering [*Automobile ads*]	
PS............	Power Supply	
PS............	Powys Society (EA)	
PS............	Prairie Schooner [*A publication*]	
PS............	Prairies Service [*Record series prefix*] [*Canada*]	
PS............	Pravoslavnyi Sobesiednik [*A publication*]	
PS............	Predictive Saccades [*Ophthalmology*]	
PS............	Preduzece Soko [*Former Yugoslavia*] [*ICAO aircraft manufacturer identifier*] (ICAO)	
PS............	Preferred Stock [*Investment term*]	
PS............	Prehistoric Society (EA)	
PS............	Preliminary Study	
PS............	Preparedness Staff [*Environmental Protection Agency*] (GFGA)	
Ps	Prescription (AAMN)	
PS............	Presentation Services [*Data processing*] (IBMDP)	
PS............	Press Secretary (ILCA)	
PS............	Press to Start (KSC)	
PS............	Pressure [*or Propellant*] Seal	
P-S............	Pressure-Sensitive	
PS............	Pressure Sensor	
PS............	Pressure Switch	
Ps	Pressure, Systolic [*Cardiology*]	
PS............	Price Spreading [*Business term*]	
PS............	Primary School (ADA)	
PS............	Prime Select (MCD)	
PS............	Prime Sponsor	
PS............	Principal Sojourner [*Freemasonry*] (ROG)	
PS............	Principal Subject [*In a sonata or rondo*] [*Music*] (ROG)	
PS............	Prior Service [*Military*]	
PS............	Private Screenings [*Cable TV programming service*]	
PS............	Private Secretary	
PS............	Private Security Program [*Association of Independent Colleges and Schools specialization code*]	
PS............	Private Siding [*Rail*] [*Shipping*] (DS)	
PS............	Privy Seal [*British*]	
PS............	Probability of Survival (MCD)	
PS............	Problem Specification	
PS............	Procambial Strand [*Botany*]	
PS............	Process Sheet	
PS............	Process Solution (MCD)	
PS............	Process Specification	
PS............	Process Studies [*A publication*]	
PS............	Process Subsystem [*Telecommunications*] (TEL)	
PS............	Processor Status	

PS.............. Procurement Specification (MCD)
PS.............. Product Software (MCD)
PS.............. Product Standards (MCD)
PS.............. Product Support
PS.............. Profit Sharing [*Business term*]
PS.............. Program Simulation (OICC)
PS.............. Program Specification (MCD)
PS.............. Program Start (KSC)
PS.............. Program Store [*Data processing*] (IEEE)
PS.............. Program Summary (NG)
PS.............. Programming System
PS.............. Project Slip
PS.............. Project Start [*Milestone chart*]
PS.............. Project Stock [*Military*] (AABC)
PS.............. Project Study [*British military*] (DMA)
PS.............. Proler International Corp. [*NYSE symbol*] (SPSG)
PS.............. Prolifers for Survival (EA)
PS.............. Prometheus Society (EA)
PS.............. Prompt Side [*of a stage*] [*i.e., the right side*] [*A stage direction*]
PS.............. Proof Shot [*Ammunition*]
PS.............. Proof Stress
PS.............. Propellant Supply (KSC)
PS.............. Propellant System
PS.............. Proportional Spacing [*Typography*] (WDMC)
PS.............. Propulsion Section
PS.............. Prose Studies 1800-1900 [*A publication*]
PS.............. Prostaglandin Synthetase [*An enzyme*]
PS.............. Protective Service
PS.............. Protective Shelter
PS.............. Protein Synthesis
PS.............. Proto-Semitic (BJA)
PS.............. Proton Synchrotron [*Nuclear energy*]
PS.............. Protoplasmic Surface [*Freeze etching in microscopy*]
PS.............. Provost-Sergeant
PS.............. Psalm
Ps .... Psalms [*Old Testament book*]
PS.............. Pseudo [*Classical studies*] (OCD)
Ps .... Pseudomonas [*Bacterium*] (MAE)
PS.............. Pseudomonas Stutzeri [*Bacterium*]
PS.............. Pseudonym (WGA)
PS.............. Psychiatric (MAE)
PS.............. Psychology Society (EA)
PS.............. Psychometric Society (EA)
PS.............. Psychonomic Society (EA)
PS.............. Psychotic
PS.............. Public Sale
PS.............. Public School
PS.............. Public Services
PS.............. Public Statutes [*Legal term*] (DLA)
PS.............. Public Stenographer
PS.............. Publication Standard
PS.............. Publishing Services [*American Library Association*]
PS.............. Puget Sound [*Also, Puget Sound Naval Shipyard*] [*Washington*]
PS.............. Pull Switch
PS.............. Pulmonary Stenosis [*Medicine*]
PS.............. Pulse Sensor (KSC)
PS.............. Pulse Shaper
PS.............. Pulse Stretcher
PS.............. Pulses per Second [*Data transmission*] (DEN)
PS.............. Pumping Station (NATG)
P & S .... Purchase and Sale [*Business term*]
PS.............. Purdon's Pennsylvania Statutes [*A publication*] (DLA)
PS.............. Purity-Supreme [*Supermarkets*]
PS.............. Pyloric Stenosis [*Medicine*]
ps----- .... South Pacific [*MARC geographic area code*] [*Library of Congress*] (LCCP)
PS.............. South Pole [*Also, SP*]
PS.............. Static Pressure
PS.............. Swarthmore Public Library, Swarthmore, PA [*Library symbol*] [*Library of Congress*] (LCLS)
PS.............. Transport [*Russian aircraft symbol*]
PS-1 .... Partido Socialista - Uno [*Socialist Party - One*] [*Also, PS*] [*Bolivia*] [*Political party*] (PD)
PS/2 .... Personal System/2 [*IBM Corp.*]
PS2.............. Picture System 2 [*Evans & Sutherland Computer Corp.*] (MCD)
PS² .... Profound Sensitivity Syndrome [*Psychology*]
PS3............. PROBE [*Program Optimization and Budget Evaluation*] Staff Support System [*Military*]
PS2000....... Public Service 2000 Program [*Canada*]
PSA........... Pacific Science Association (EA)
PSA........... Pacific Southwest Airlines
P & SA ...... Packers and Stockyards Administration [*Department of Agriculture*]
PSA........... Papeles de Son Armadans [*A publication*]
PSA........... Parametric Semiconductor Amplifier
PSA........... Parametric Sound Amplifier [*Blaupunkt*]
PSA........... Parcel Shippers Association (EA)
PSA........... Part Stress Analysis (MCD)
PSA........... Parti Socialiste Autonome [*Autonomous Socialist Party*] [*France*] [*Political party*] (PPE)

PSA........... Parti Solidaire Africain [*African Solidarity Party*] [*Congo*] [*Political party*]
PSA........... Particle Size Analyzer
PSA........... Partido Socialista Aponte [*Bolivia*] [*Political party*] (PPW)
PSA........... Partido Socialista Argentino [*Socialist Party of Argentina*] [*Political party*]
PSA........... Partito Socialista Autonomo [*Autonomous Socialist Party*] [*Switzerland*] [*Political party*] (PPW)
PSA........... Past Shakedown Availability [*Military*]
PSA........... Pastel Society of America (EA)
PSA........... Path Selection Algorithm [*Telecommunications*] (TEL)
PSA........... Path of Steepest Ascent [*Statistical design of experiments*]
PSA........... Payload Service Area [*NASA*] (NASA)
PSA........... Payload Support Avionics [*NASA*] (NASA)
PSA........... Peace and Solidarity Alliance (EA)
PSA........... Peace Studies Association (EA)
PSA........... People's Supreme Assembly [*Yemen*] [*Political party*] (PPW)
PSA........... Personal Service Agreements (MCD)
PSA........... Personal Statement Analyzer (HGAA)
PSA........... Personnel and Service Area [*Nuclear energy*] (NRCH)
PSA........... Petersburg [*Alaska*] [*Seismograph station code, US Geological Survey*] (SEIS)
PSA........... Petites Soeurs de l'Assumption [*Little Sisters of the Assumption - LSA*] [*Paris, France*] (EAIO)
PSA........... Philippine Sugar Association [*Later, PSC*] (EA)
PSa............ Philippiniana Sacra [*A publication*]
PSA........... Philosophy of Science Association (EA)
PSA........... Phobia Society of America [*Later, ADAA*] (EA)
PSA........... Photographic Society of America (EA)
PSA........... Phycological Society of America (EA)
PSA........... Pirandello Society of America (EA)
PSA........... Pisa [*Italy*] [*Airport symbol*] (OAG)
PsA .... Pisces Austrinus [*Constellation*]
PSA........... Pisces Society of America
PSA........... Play Schools Association (EA)
PSA........... Pleasant Sunday Afternoons
PSA........... Plumeria Society of America (EA)
PSA........... Pneumatic Sensor Assembly
PSA........... Poe Studies Association (EA)
PSA........... Poetry Society of America (EA)
PSA........... Police Science Abstracts [*A publication*]
PSA........... Political Studies Association [*British*]
P Sa .... Polotitscheskoje Samoorbrasowanije [*A publication*]
PSA........... Polyethylene Sulfonic Acid [*Organic chemistry*] (MAE)
PSA........... Polysilicic Acid [*Organic chemistry*]
PSA........... Port Storage Area [*Telecommunications*] (TEL)
PSA........... Portable Sanitation Association (EA)
PSA........... Portable Sound Analyzer
PSA........... Post Shakedown Availability
PSA........... Post-Sleep Activity
PSA........... Potential Surface Analysis (ADA)
PSA........... Poultry Science Association (EA)
PSA........... Power Servo Amplifier (KSC)
PSA........... Power Servo Assembly (MCD)
PSA........... Power Supply Assembly
PSA........... Power Switching Amplifier
PSA........... Power Switching Assembly
PSA........... Pre/Post Sleep Activity (NASA)
PSA........... Prefabricated Surfacing Aluminum
PSA........... Preferred Storage Area (MCD)
PSA........... Prefix Storage Area [*Data processing*] (OA)
PSA........... Preliminary Safety Analysis [*NASA*] (SSD)
PSA........... President of the Society of Antiquaries [*British*]
PSA........... Pressure Sensitive Adhesive [*Trademark*]
PSA........... Pressure Suit Assembly
PSA........... Pressure-Swing Adsorption [*Chemical engineering*]
PSA........... Pressure Switch Assembly (NASA)
PSA........... Presunrise Authority
PSA........... Private Schools Association [*British*]
PSA........... Probabilistic Safety Analysis (NRCH)
PSA........... Procurement Seminar for Auditors [*Army*]
PSA........... Product Safety Association (EA)
PSA........... Product Support Administration (MCD)
PSA........... Professional Salespersons of America [*Albuquerque, NM*] (EA)
PSA........... Professional Skills Alliance (EA)
PSA........... Professional Stringers Association (EA)
PSA........... Program Study Authorization (KSC)
PSA........... Prolonged Sleep Apnea
PSA........... Property Services Agency [*Department of the Environment*] [*British*]
PSA........... Prostate-Specific Antigen [*Immunochemistry*]
PSA........... Provisional Site Acceptance (NATG)
PSA........... Provisions Stowage Assembly (NASA)
PSA........... Psalm
Psa .... Psalms [*Old Testament book*]
PSA........... Pseudomonic Acid [*Biochemistry*]
PSA........... Psychological Operations Support Activity [*Military*] (MCD)
PSA........... Psychologists for Social Action [*Defunct*] (EA)
PSA........... Psychopharmacology Abstracts [*A publication*]
PSA........... Public Securities Association [*Database producer*] (EA)
PSA........... Public Service Announcement

PSA............ Publication Systems Associates, Inc. [*Information service or system*] (IID)
PSA............ Push Down Stack Automaton [*Data processing*]
PSA............ Storage Properties, Inc. [*AMEX symbol*] (SPSG)
PSAA......... Pacific Special Activities Area [*Military*]
PSAA......... Pakistan Students' Association of America
PSAA......... Polish Singers Alliance of America (EA)
PSAA......... Poststimulatory Auditory Adaptation
PSAB........ Prime Bancorp, Inc. [*NASDAQ symbol*] (CTT)
PSAB........ Production Systems Acceptance Branch [*Social Security Administration*]
PSAC........ Passive Satellite Attitude Control
PSAC........ Personnel Service Company [*Army*] (AABC)
PSAC........ Policy Signing and Accounting Centre [*Insurance firm*] [*British*]
PSAC........ Preferred Stock Advisory Committee [*New Deal*]
PSAC........ President's Science Advisory Committee [*Terminated, 1973*] [*Executive Office of the President*]
PSAC........ Private Security Advisory Council [*Terminated, 1977*] [*Department of Justice*] (EGAO)
PSAC........ Product Safety Advisory Council [*Consumer Product Safety Commission*]
PSAC........ Professional Skating Association of Canada
PSAC........ Public Service Alliance of Canada [*Labor union of federal government employees*]
PSACN...... Process Specification Advance Change Notice (SAA)
PSAcPh..... Prostate-Specific Acid Phosphatase [*An enzyme*]
PSACPOO ... President's Scientific Advisory Committee Panel on Oceanography [*Marine science*] (MSC)
PSAD........ Predicted Site Acquisition Data [*NASA*]
PSAD........ Prediction, Simulation, Adaptation, Decision [*Data processing*]
PSAF........ Private Sector Adjustment Factor [*Banking*]
Ps Af........ Psychopathologie Africaine [*A publication*]
PSAF......... Studies in American Fiction [*A publication*]
PSAGN...... Poststreptococcal Acute Glomerulonephritis [*Medicine*]
PSAIR....... Priority Specific Air Information Request [*Defense Mapping Agency*] (MCD)
PSA J........ PSA [*Photographic Society of America*] Journal [*A publication*]
PSA Jl........ Photographic Society of America. Journal [*A publication*]
PSA Journal ... Photographic Society of America. Journal [*A publication*]
PSA J Sect B ... PSA [*Photographic Society of America*] Journal. Section B. Photographic Science and Technique [*A publication*]
PSA J Suppl ... PSA [*Photographic Society of America*] Journal. Supplement [*A publication*]
P de Sal...... Petrus de Salinis [*Flourished, 13th century*] [*Authority cited in pre-1607 legal work*] (DSA)
PSAL........ Proceedings. Society of Antiquaries of London [*A publication*]
PSAL........ Programming System Activity Log [*Data processing*]
PSAL........ Public Schools Athletic League
PSALI....... Permanent Supplementary Artificial Lighting of Interiors (IEEE)
P Salin .... Petrus de Salinis [*Flourished, 13th century*] [*Authority cited in pre-1607 legal work*] (DSA)
PSALM ..... Project Structured Analysis of LOGEX [*Logistical Exercise*] Methodology (MCD)
PSAM....... Partitioned Sequence Access Method
P de Sam .... Petrus de Sampsone [*Flourished, 1246-58*] [*Authority cited in pre-1607 legal work*] (DSA)
PSAM....... Point Source Ambient Monitoring [*Environmental Protection Agency*] (GFGA)
PSAM....... Publications. Service des Antiquites du Maroc [*A publication*]
P de Samp ... Petrus de Sampsone [*Flourished, 1246-58*] [*Authority cited in pre-1607 legal work*] (DSA)
PSAN........ Phase Stabilized Ammonium Nitrate (MCD)
PSANDT... Pay, Subsistence, and Transportation [*Military*]
PSANP...... Phenol-Soluble Acidic Nuclear Protein[s] [*Biochemistry*]
PSAO........ Pharmacy Services Administrative Organization
PSAO........ Primary Staff Action Officer [*Military*]
PSAP........ Plane Stress Analysis and Plot [*Data processing*]
PSAP........ Public Safety Answering Point [*Telecommunications*] (TEL)
PSAP........ Pulmonary Surfactant Apoprotein [*Biochemistry*]
PSA/PS ..... Political Studies. Political Studies Association [*United Kingdom*] [*A publication*]
PsaQ .... Psychoanalytic Quarterly [*A publication*]
PSAQ........ South Atlantic Quarterly [*A publication*]
PSAR........ Platform Shock Attenuation and Realignment System (MCD)
PSAR........ Pneumatic [*or Pressure*] System Automatic Regulator (AAG)
PSAR........ Preliminary Safety Analysis Report
PSAR........ Programmable Synchronous/Asynchronous Receiver (IEEE)
PSAR........ Propulsion Systems Analysis Report (SAA)
PsaR........ Psychoanalytic Review [*A publication*]
PSarg........ Pre-Sargonic (BJA)
PSAS .... Papers in International Studies. Africa Series. Ohio University [*A publication*]
PSAS .... Prespeech Assessment Scale [*Occupational therapy*]
PSAS .... Proceedings. Society of Antiquaries of Scotland [*A publication*]
PSAS .... Production Systems Acceptance Section [*Social Security Administration*]
PSAS .... Program Support and Advanced Systems (SAA)
PSASS....... Perishable Subsistence Automated Supply System [*DoD*]
PSASV...... Phase-Sensitive Anodic Stripping Voltammetry
PSAT .... Predicted Site Acquisition Table [*NASA*]

PSAT .... Preliminary Scholastic Aptitude Test
PSAT .... Programmable Synchronous/Asynchronous Transmitter (IEEE)
PSAUK..... Political Studies Association of the United Kingdom
PSAUSA ... Polish Socialist Alliance of the United States of America (EA)
PSAVA...... Pribory i Sistemy Avtomatiki [*A publication*]
PSAX........ Pacific Southwest Airlines [*Air carrier designation symbol*]
PSB........... Pacific Science Board [*National Academy of Sciences*]
PSB........... Personeelbeleid [*A publication*]
PSB........... Philatelic Sales Branch [*Later, PSD*] [*US Postal Service*]
PSB........... Philipsburg, PA [*Location identifier*] [*FAA*] (FAAL)
PSB........... Phosphorus-Solubilizing Bacteria [*Microbiology*]
PSB........... Plant Safety Bureau
PSB........... Plant Service Building [*Nuclear energy*] (NRCH)
PSB........... Polski Slownik Biograficzny [*A publication*]
PSB........... Polytechnic of the South Bank [*London, England*]
PS & B ...... Power Steering and Brakes [*Automotive engineering*] (IIA)
PSB........... Premium Savings Bond [*British*] (DCTA)
PSB........... Program Specification Block [*IBM Corp.*]
PSB........... Program Station Basis [*Rating system*] (WDMC)
PSB........... Protected Specimen Brush [*Medicine*]
PSB........... PS Business Parks, Inc. [*AMEX symbol*] (SPSG)
PSB........... Psychiatric BioScience, Inc. [*AMEX symbol*] (SPSG)
PsB........... Psychological Bulletin [*A publication*]
PSB........... Psychological Services Bureau (AEBS)
Ps B .... Psychologische Beitraege fuer alle Gebiete der Psychologie [*A publication*]
PSBA........ Power-Specific Biological Activity [*Engine emissions testing*]
PSBA .... Proceedings. Society of Biblical Archaeology [*A publication*]
PSBBF...... Pearl S. Buck Birthplace Foundation (EA)
PSBF........ Pearl S. Buck Foundation (EA)
PSBF........ Pioneer Savings Bank FSB [*NASDAQ symbol*] (NQ)
PSBG........ Pregnancy-Specific beta-Glycoprotein [*Gynecology*]
PSBH........ Pad Safety in Blockhouse
PSBH........ Proceedings. Society of Biblical Archaeology [*A publication*]
PSBI .... Performance Standardization Branch Instruction (SAA)
PSBK........ Progressive Bank, Inc. [*Pawling, NY*] [*NASDAQ symbol*] (NQ)
PSBL........ Possible (FAAC)
PSBLS....... Permanent Space Based Logistics System
PSBMA ..... Professional Services Business Management Association [*Later, PSMA*] (EA)
PSBN........ Pioneer Bancorp, Inc. [*Formerly, Pioneer Savings Bank, Inc.*] [*NASDAQ symbol*] (NQ)
PSBNDY ... Sociedade Brasileira de Nematologia. Publicacao [*A publication*]
PSBP .... PS Business Parks, Inc. [*Associated Press abbreviation*] (APAG)
PSBR .... Pennsylvania State University Breazeale Nuclear Reactor [*Research center*] (RCD)
PSBR .... Public Sector Borrowing Requirement
PSBRA9 .... International Committee for Bird Preservation. Pan American Section. Research Report [*A publication*]
PSBS........ Policy Sciences Book Series [*Elsevier Book Series*] [*A publication*]
PSBT .... Pilot Self-Briefing Terminal (FAAC)
PSBU........ Propeller Shaft Bearing Unit [*Truck engineering*]
PSBU......... Psychopharmacology Bulletin [*A publication*]
PSBUA ...... Psychological Bulletin [*A publication*]
Ps Bull....... Psychological Bulletin [*A publication*]
PSBX .... Peoples Savings Bank FSB [*NASDAQ symbol*] (NQ)
PSC........... Congolese Socialist Party [*Zaire*] [*Political party*] (PD)
PSC........... Isla De Pascua [*Easter Island*] [*Seismograph station code, US Geological Survey*] [*Closed*] (SEIS)
PSC........... Pacific Salmon Commission (EA)
PSC........... Pacific Science Center
PSC........... Pacific Science Council
PSC........... Pacific South Coast Freight Bureau, San Francisco CA [*STAC*]
PSC........... Pacific Studies Center (EA)
PSC........... Palestine Solidarity Committee [*Defunct*] (EA)
PSC........... Palmer Skin Conductance
PSC........... Parallel to Serial Converter
PSC........... Parallel Switch Control (MCD)
PSC........... Parents Sharing Custody (EA)
PSC........... Parti Socialiste Caledonien [*New Caledonia*] [*Political party*] (FEA)
PSC........... Parti Socialiste Camerounais [*Cameroon Socialist Party*] [*Political party*]
PSC........... Parti Socialiste Centrafricain [*Central African Socialist Party*] [*Political party*] (PD)
PSC........... Partido Social Conservador Colombiano [*Colombian Social Conservative Party*] [*Political party*] (EY)
PSC........... Partido Social Cristiano [*Social Christian Party*] [*Guatemala*] [*Political party*] (PPW)
PSC........... Partido Social Cristiano [*Social Christian Party*] [*Bolivia*] [*Political party*]
PSC........... Partido Social Cristiano [*Social Christian Party*] [*Ecuador*] [*Political party*] (PPW)
PSC........... Partido Socialcristiano Nicaraguense [*Nicaraguan Social Christian Party*] [*Political party*] (PPW)

PSC............ Partido Socialista de Catalunya [*Catalan Socialist Party*] [*Spain*] [*Political party*] (PPE)
PSC............ Pasco [*Washington*] [*Airport symbol*] (OAG)
PSC............ Pasco, WA [*Location identifier*] [*FAA*] (FAAL)
PSC............ Passed Staff College [*British*]
PSC............ Passenger Services Conference [*IATA*] (DS)
PSC............ Patriot Steering Committee
PSC............ Paul Smiths College [*New York*]
PSC............ Peacetime Subcontract
PSC............ Pembroke State College [*North Carolina*]
PSC............ Per Standard Compass [*Navigation*]
PSC............ Percentage of Successful Collisions [*Obstetrics*]
PSC............ Personal Computing [*A publication*]
PSC............ Personal Supercomputer [*Culler Scientific Systems Corp.*]
PSC............ Personnel Service Center [*or Company*] [*Military*] (INF)
PSC............ Personnel Status Change (KSC)
PSC............ Personnel Subsystem Cost
PSC............ Petty Sessional Court [*British*] (ROG)
PSC............ Phase-Sensitive Converter
PSC............ Philadelphia Service Center [*IRS*]
PSC............ Philadelphia Suburban Corp. [*NYSE symbol*] (SPSG)
PSC............ Philander Smith College [*Little Rock, AR*]
PSC............ Philippine Sugar Commission (EA)
PSC............ Phonemic Spelling Council (EA)
PSC............ Photosensitive Cell (IEEE)
PSC............ Physical Sciences Center
PSC............ Physical Sciences Committee [*Terminated, 1977*] [*NASA*] (EGAO)
PSC............ Physical Security/Pilferage Code (MCD)
Psc............ Pisces [*Constellation*]
PSC............ Pittsburgh Supercomputing Center [*National Science Foundation*] [*Research center*] (RCD)
PSC............ Pittsburgh Superconducting Center [*Pennsylvania*] (GRD)
pSC............ Plasmid Stanley Cohen [*Molecular biology*]
PSC............ Platform Support Center [*NASA*] (SSD)
PSC............ Pluripotent Stem Cell [*Cytology*]
PSC............ Plutonium Stripping Concentrate [*Nuclear energy*] (NRCH)
PSC............ Polar Science Center [*University of Washington*] [*Research center*] (RCD)
PSC............ Polar Stratospheric Cloud [*Meteorology*]
PSC............ Polaroid Stereoscopic Chroncyclegraph
PSC............ Population Studies Center [*University of Michigan*] [*Research center*] (RCD)
PSC............ Porcelain on Steel Council [*Defunct*] (EA)
PSC............ Porter-Silber Chromogen [*Medicine*] (MAE)
PSC............ Portland Society for Calligraphy (EA)
PSC............ Post-Storage Checkout [*NASA*] (KSC)
PSC............ Postal Service Center (AFM)
PSC............ Posterior Subcapsular Cataracts [*Ophthalmology*]
PSC............ Potentiometer Strip Chart
PSC............ Potomac State College [*of West Virginia University*]
PSC............ Power Supply Calibrator
PSC............ Pressure Suit Circuit (KSC)
PSC............ Pressure System Control (AAG)
PSC............ Prestressed Concrete (ADA)
PSC............ Presumptive Hematopoietic Stem Cell
PSC............ Price Signal Code [*Military*] (AABC)
PSC............ Primary Sclerosing Cholangitis [*Medicine*]
PSC............ Principal Subordinate Command (NATG)
PSC............ Private Secretary's Certificate [*British*] (DI)
PSC............ Private Sector Council (EA)
PS & C .... Private Siding and Collected One End
PSC............ PROBE [*Program Optimization and Budget Evaluation*] Steering Committee [*Military*]
PSC............ Processing Service Centers [*Social Security Administration*]
PSC............ Processing and Spectral Control
PSC............ Procurement Source Code (AFM)
PSC............ Product Support Confidential (AAG)
PSC............ Professional Services Council [*Washington, DC*] (EA)
PSC............ Program Schedule Chart (NASA)
PSC............ Program Service Center [*Social Security Administration*] (OICC)
PSC............ Program Standards Checker [*Data processing*]
PSC............ Program Status Chart [*Data processing*]
PSC............ Program Structure Code (AFM)
PSC............ Program Support Contract (SSD)
PSC............ Programmable Sample Changer [*Spectroscopy*]
PSC............ Project Systems Control (MCD)
PSC............ Prototype System Characteristics
PSC............ Public Service Careers [*Program*] [*Department of Labor*]
PSC............ Public Service Commission [*Usually, of a specific state*]
PSC............ Public Service Co.
PSC............ Pulse Synchronized Contraction [*In the vascular system*] [*Medicine*]
PSC............ Sandoz AG [*Switzerland*] [*Research code symbol*]
PSc............ Scranton Public Library, Scranton, PA [*Library symbol*] [*Library of Congress*] (LCLS)
PSC............ Swarthmore College, Swarthmore, PA [*Library symbol*] [*Library of Congress*] [*OCLC symbol*] (LCLS)
PSCA......... Parliamentary Select Committee on Agriculture [*British*]
PscA........... Pisces Austrinus [*Constellation*]

PSCA......... Polish Social and Cultural Association [*British*] (EAIO)
PSCA......... Pressure Suit Conditioning Assembly (MCD)
PSCA......... Profit Sharing Council of America (EA)
PSCAN...... Purchase Order Scan
PSCB........ Padded Sample Collection Bag [*NASA*]
PSCBG ...... Paper Shipping-Containers Buyers Group
PS & CC ..... Packaging, Storage, and Containerization Center [*DARCOM*] (MCD)
PSCC......... Photo Systems Controller Console (KSC)
PSCC......... Projets de Services Communautaires du Canada
PSCC......... Studies in Comparative Communism [*A publication*]
PSCD......... Plutonium Stripping Concentration Distillate [*Nuclear energy*] (NRCH)
PSCD......... Program for the Study of Crime and Delinquency [*Ohio State University*] [*Research center*] (RCD)
PSCEC...... Planning Status of Committed Engineering Changes (SAA)
PSCF .... Personal Security Clearance File
PSCF .... Processor Storage Control Function
PSCFB..... Pacific South Coast Freight Bureau
PSCG........ Power Supply and Control Gear
PSCG........ Power Supply Control Group [*Military*] (CAAL)
PSCH....... Postoperative Suprachoroidal Hemorrhage [*Medicine*]
P Sch.......... Prairie Schooner [*A publication*]
PSC-Hi ...... Friends Historical Library of Swarthmore College, Swarthmore, PA [*Library symbol*] [*Library of Congress*] (LCLS)
PSCHO ..... Psychopharmacology [*A publication*]
PSCI .... Plastic Shipping Container Institute (EA)
PSCI .... Sciences [*A publication*]
PSCJ......... Perseverance Society of Carpenters and Joiners [*A union*] [*British*]
PSCJ......... Progressive Society of Carpenters and Joiners [*A union*] [*British*]
PSCKAR.... Bulletin of National Fisheries. University of Pusan. Natural Sciences [*A publication*]
PSCL .... Papers and Studies in Contrastive Linguistics [*A publication*]
PSCL .... Programmed Sequential Control Language
PSCL .... Propellant Systems Cleaning Laboratory [*NASA*] (NASA)
PSCL .... Propellants System Components Laboratory [*Kennedy Space Center*] [*NASA*]
PScLL........ Lackawanna Bar Association Law Library, Scranton, PA [*Library symbol*] [*Library of Congress*] (LCLS)
PScM .... Marywood College, Scranton, PA [*Library symbol*] [*Library of Congress*] (LCLS)
PSCM....... Process Steering and Control Module [*Telecommunications*] (TEL)
PSCN........ Partido Socialcristiano Nicaraguense [*Nicaraguan Social Christian Party*] [*Political party*] (PPW)
PSCN........ Permanent System Control Number (MCD)
PSCN........ Preliminary Specification Change Notice [*NASA*] (NASA)
PSCN....... Program Support Communications Network (SSD)
PSCN........ Proposed Specification Change Notice
PSCNET.... Pittsburgh Superconducting Center Network
PSCO........ Pennsylvania State College of Optometry
PSCO........ Personnel Survey Control Officer [*Military*] (AABC)
PSCOB ...... Psychiatric Communications [*A publication*]
PSCol......... Public Service Co. of Colorado [*Associated Press abbreviation*] (APAG)
P S Conf Co ... Proceedings. Southern Conference on Corrections [*A publication*]
PSCP .... Palestine Symphonic Choir Project (EA)
P/S CP....... Platoon/Section Command Post
PSCP .... Polar Continental Shelf Project [*Canada*]
PSCP .... Public Service Careers Program [*Department of Labor*]
PSC-P........ Swarthmore College Peace Collection, Swarthmore, PA [*Library symbol*] [*Library of Congress*] (LCLS)
PSCPD ...... Philadelphia Signal Corps Procurement District [*Army*]
PSC-PSOE ... Partit dels Socialistes de Catalunya [*Party of Socialists of Catalonia*] [*Political party*] (PPW)
PSCPT....... Preschool Self-Concept Picture Test [*Psychology*]
PScQ.......... Political Science Quarterly [*A publication*]
PSCR .... Permanent Scratch File [*Data processing*]
PSCR .... Photo-Selective Copper Reduction [*For circuit board manufacture*]
PSCR .... Priority System Change Request
PSCR .... Production Schedule Completion Report [*DoD*]
PSCR .... Programmable Scanning Receiver (DWSG)
PSCR .... Public Service Commission Reports [*A publication*] (DLA)
PSCRD ...... Program Support Communications Requirements Document (SSD)
P Scribe...... Portland Scribe [*A publication*]
PSCRT....... Passive Satellite Communications Research Terminal (SAA)
PSCS......... Pacific Scatter Communications System [*Air Force*] (CET)
PSCS......... Program Support Control System
PSCT .... Scandinavian Studies [*A publication*]
PSCU........ Power Supply Control Unit (CET)
PSCU........ Speculum. Journal of Medieval Studies [*A publication*]
PScU......... University of Scranton, Scranton, PA [*Library symbol*] [*Library of Congress*] (LCLS)
PSCUS ...... Peters' United States Supreme Court Reports [*26-41 United States*] [*A publication*] (DLA)

PSCX .... PSC, Inc. [*Formerly, Photographic Sciences Corp.*] [*NASDAQ symbol*]   (NQ)
PSD .... Destour Socialist Party [*Tunisia*] [*Political party*]   (PD)
PSD .... Doctor of Political Science
Ps D .... Doctor of Psychology
Ps D .... Doctor of Psychology in Metaphysics
PSD .... Doctor of Public Service
PSD .... Packed Switched Data
PSD .... Parti Social-Democrate [*Social Democratic Party*] [*France*] [*Political party*]   (PPW)
PSD .... Parti Social-Democrate [*Algeria*] [*Political party*]   (EY)
PSD .... Parti Social Democrate de Madagascar et des Comores [*Social Democratic Party of Madagascar and Comores*]
PSD .... Parti Social-Democratie [*Benin*] [*Political party*]   (EY)
PSD .... Parti Socialiste Democratique [*Cameroon*] [*Political party*]   (EY)
PSD .... Particle Size Distribution
PSD .... Partido Social Democrata [*Social Democratic Party*] [*Mexico*] [*Political party*]   (PPW)
PSD .... Partido Social Democrata [*Social Democratic Party*] [*Spain*] [*Political party*]   (PPE)
PSD .... Partido Social Democrata [*Social Democratic Party*] [*Bolivia*] [*Political party*]   (PPW)
PSD .... Partido Social Democratico [*Social Democratic Party*] [*Brazil*] [*Political party*]
PSD .... Partido Social Democratico [*Social Democratic Party*] [*El Salvador*] [*Political party*]
PSD .... Partido Social Democratico [*Social Democratic Party*] [*Nicaragua*] [*Political party*]   (PPW)
PSD .... Partido Socialdemocracia [*Social Democratic Party*] [*Chile*] [*Political party*]   (EY)
PSD .... Partido Socialista Democratico [*Social Democratic Party*] [*Guatemala*] [*Political party*]   (PD)
PSD .... Partido Socialista Democratico [*Social Democratic Party*] [*Argentina*] [*Political party*]   (PPW)
PSD .... Passed   (ROG)
PSD .... Passing Scene Display
PSDN .... Past Start Date
PSD .... Paternal Sister Dam   (OA)
PSD .... Patient Symptom Diary
PSD .... Peptone-Starch-Dextrose [*Microbiology*]   (MAE)
PSD .... Permanent Signal Detection [*Telecommunications*]   (TEL)
PSD .... Personal Services Department [*Navy*] [*British*]
PSD .... Personnel Services Division [*Army*]
PSD .... Personnel System [*or Subsystem*] Development   (AAG)
PSD .... Pescadero [*California*] [*Seismograph station code, US Geological Survey*]   (SEIS)
PSD .... Petroleum Safety Data [*American Petroleum Institute*]
PSD .... Petty Session Division [*Legal term*]   (DLA)
PSD .... Phase-Sensitive Demodulator [*or Detector*]
PSD .... Phase Shifter Driver
PSD .... Philatelic Sales Division [*Formerly, PSB*] [*US Postal Service*]
PSD .... Photoconductive, Semiconductive Device
PSD .... Photon Stimulated Desorption [*For analysis of surfaces*]
PSD .... Physical Sciences Data [*Elsevier Book Series*] [*A publication*]
PSD .... Pictorialized Scatter Diagram [*Botany*]
PSD .... Pitch Servo Drive
PSD .... Polystyrene, Deuterated [*Organic chemistry*]
PSD .... Pore Size Distribution
PSD .... Port Security Detachment [*Military*]   (GFGA)
PSD .... Post Sending Delay
Ps D .... Postsynaptic Density [*Neurophysiology*]
PSD .... Power Spectral [*or Spectrum*] Density
PSD .... Power Spectrum Distribution [*Electronics*]
PSD .... Preferred Sea Duty
PSD .... Pressure-Sensitive Devices   (MCD)
PSD .... Prevention of Significant Deterioration [*Environmental Protection Agency*]
PSD .... Private-Sector Development   (ECON)
PS & D .... Private Siding and Delivered One End
PSD .... Procedural Support Data
PSD .... Process Specification Departure   (SAA)
PSD .... Processing Status Display [*NASA*]
PSD .... Procurement Surveys Division [*NASA*]   (MCD)
PSD .... Professional Service Dates [*Formerly, ADBD*]
PSD .... Professional Systems Division [*American Institute of Architects Service Corp.*] [*Information service or system*]   (IID)
PSD .... Program Status Documents [*Data processing*]
PSD .... Program Status Doubleword
PSD .... Program Support Document   (MUGU)
PSD .... Program System Description   (SAA)
PSD .... Program Systems Division [*Environmental Protection Agency*]   (GFGA)
PSD .... Programme Support and Development [*British*]
PSD .... Programmed Slip Differential [*Automotive engineering*]
PSD .... Promotion Service Date
PSD .... Propellant Slosh Dynamics
PSD .... Propellant Storage Depot [*NASA*]
PSD .... Proportional Stock Density [*Pisciculture*]
PSD .... Protective Serum Dilution
PSD .... Protective Structures Division [*Office of Civil Defense*]

PSD .... Pseudo Stow Document   (DNAB)
PSD .... Pseudosingle Domain [*Behavior of grains in rocks*] [*Geophysics*]
PSD .... Puget Sound Power & Light Co. [*NYSE symbol*]   (SPSG)
PSD .... Pulse Shape Discriminator
PSD .... Pure Screw Dislocation
PSDA .... Partial Source Data Automation   (NVT)
PSDA .... Particle Size Distribution Analysis [*Statistics*]
P/SDA .... Power/Signal Distribution Assembly
PSDB .... Partido da Social Democracia Brasiliera [*Brazilian Social Democratic Party*] [*Political party*]   (EY)
PSDC .... Pennsylvania State Data Center [*Middletown*] [*Information service or system*]   (IID)
PSDC .... Plant Sciences Data Center [*Formerly, Plant Records Center*] [*American Horticultural Society*] [*Mt. Vernon, VA*]
PSDC .... Power Sprayer and Duster Council   (EA)
PSDC .... Protective Structures Development Center [*Military*]
PSDD .... Preliminary System Design Description [*Nuclear energy*]   (NRCH)
PSDDS ...... Pilot [*or Public*] Switched Digital Data Service [*Telecommunications*]   (TEL)
Psdepgr ...... Pseudepigrapha   (BJA)
PSDF .... Popular Self-Defense Force [*Local armed units protecting Vietnamese hamlets*]
PSDF .... Propulsion Systems Development Facility   (KSC)
PSDI .... Partido Social Democratico Independente [*Independent Social Democratic Party*] [*Portugal*] [*Political party*]   (PPE)
PSDI .... Partito Socialista Democratico Italiano [*Italian Social Democratic Party*] [*Political party*]
PSDIAD .... Photostimulated Desorption Ion Angular Distribution [*Surface analysis*]
PSDIS .... Partito Socialista Democratico Indipendente Sammarinese [*Independent Social Democratic Party of San Marino*] [*Political party*]   (PPE)
PSdM .... Mennonite Publishing House, Scottsdale, PA [*Library symbol*] [*Library of Congress*]   (LCLS)
PSD(MS) ... Photon Stimulated Desorption (Mass Spectroscopy)   (MCD)
PSDN .... Packet Switched Data Network [*Telecommunications*]
PSDP .... Payload Station Distribution Panel [*NASA*]   (MCD)
PSDP .... Personnel Subsystem Development Plan
PSDP .... Phrase Structure and Dependency Parser   (DIT)
PSDP .... Professional Skills Development Program [*Bureau of the Census*]   (GFGA)
PSDP .... Programmable Signal Data Processor   (MCD)
PSDR .... Planning and Scheduling Document Record [*NASA*]   (NASA)
PSDR .... Public Sector Debt Repayment [*British*]   (ECON)
PSDS .... Packet Switch Data System [*Information retrieval*]   (IID)
PSDS .... Packet Switched Data Service [*Telecommunications*]   (TEL)
PSDS .... Partito Socialista Democratico Sammarinese [*Social Democratic Party of San Marino*] [*Political party*]   (PPE)
PSDS .... Passing Scene Display System
PSDS .... Permanently Separated from Duty Station [*Military*]
PS & DS ..... Program Statistics and Data Systems
PSDS .... Public Switched Data Service [*Telecommunications*]
PSDSP ...... Pious Society of the Daughters of Saint Paul [*See also FSP*] [*Rome, Italy*]   (EAIO)
PSDT .... President   (ROG)
PSDTC ..... Pacific Securities Depository Trust Co.
PSDU .... Polish Social Democratic Union [*Political party*]
PSDU .... Power Switching Distribution Unit
PSDVB ...... Poly(styrene-Divinylbenzene) [*Organic chemistry*]
PSE .... Pacific Stock Exchange   (EA)
PSE .... Packet-Switching Exchange
PSE .... Pale Soft Exudative [*Pork*]
PSE .... Partido Socialista Ecuatoriano [*Ecuadorean Socialist Party*] [*Political party*]   (PPW)
PSE .... Partido Socialista de Euskadi [*Basque Socialist Party*] [*Spain*] [*Political party*]   (EY)
PSE .... Passive Seismic Experiment [*NASA*]
PSE .... Payload Service Equipment [*NASA*]   (MCD)
PSE .... Payload Support Equipment [*NASA*]   (MCD)
PSE .... Peculiar Support Equipment [*NASA*]   (NASA)
PSE .... Personnel Subsystem Elements [*Army*]   (AABC)
PSE .... Perth Stock Exchange [*Australia*]
PSE .... Phase-Shifter, Electronic
PSE .... Philadelphia Stock Exchange
PS and E .... Photographic Science and Engineering [*A publication*]
PSE .... Photosensitive Epilepsy
PSE .... Physical Security Equipment [*Army*]   (RDA)
PSE .... Phytochemical Society of Europe   (EA)
PSE .... Pitch Steering Error
PS & E ...... Plans, Specifications, and Estimates [*Construction*]
PSE .... Pleasant Saturday Evenings
PSE .... Pleasant Sunday Evenings   (ROG)
PSE .... Please   (MDG)
PSE .... Point of Subjective Equality [*Psychology*]
PSE .... Polestar Exploration, Inc. [*Vancouver Stock Exchange symbol*]
PSE .... Ponce [*Puerto Rico*] [*Airport symbol*]   (OAG)
PSE .... Portal Systemic Encephalopathy [*Medicine*]
PSE .... Postshunt Encephalopathy [*Medicine*]
PSE .... Power Spectrum Equalization [*Electronics*]

PSE .... Power System Engineering (MCD)
PSE .... Prague Studies in English [*A publication*]
PSE .... Pre-Stamped Envelope
PSE .... Pressurized Subcritical Experiment [*Nuclear energy*]
PSE .... Prevention of Stripping Equipment (NATG)
PSE .... Princeton Studies in English [*A publication*]
PSE .... Principal Staff Element [*Defense Supply Agency*]
PSE .... Priority Standardization Effort [*Army*] (AABC)
PSE .... Probability of Successful Engagement [*Military*] (CAAL)
PSE .... Process Systems Engineering
PSE .... Producer Subsidy Equivalent [*OECD model for the study of farm-support policies in the EC, Japan, America, Canada, Australia, and New Zealand*]
PSE .... Product Support Engineering (MCD)
PSE .... Programmed System Evolution (MCD)
PSE .... Protein Separation Efficiency [*Food technology*]
PSE .... Psychological Stress Evaluator [*Lie detector*]
PSE .... Public Sector [*or Service*] Employment
PSE .... Public Service Electric & Gas Co., Newark, NJ [*OCLC symbol*] (OCLC)
PSE .... Pulse Sense
3PSE .... Three-Pulse Stimulated Photon Echo [*Spectroscopy*]
PSEA .... Pacific and Southeast Asia (DNAB)
PSEA .... Physical Security Equipment Agency [*Army*]
PSEA .... Pleaters, Stitchers, and Embroiderers Association (EA)
PSEAL ...... Papers in South East Asian Linguistics [*A publication*]
PSEB .... Poisoning Surveillance and Epidemiology Branch (EA)
PSEBA ...... Proceedings. Society for Experimental Biology and Medicine [*A publication*]
PSEBM ..... Proceedings of the Society for Experimental Biology and Medicine [*A publication*]
PSEC .... International Security [*A publication*]
P/SEC .... Personal Secretary (DCTA)
PSEC .... Picosecond [*One trillionth of a second*]
PSE & C .... Power Supply Engineering and Construction [*Nuclear energy*] (NRCH)
PSED .... Preliminary Systems Engineering Design
PSEE .... Slavic and East European Journal [*A publication*]
PSEF .... Pennsylvania Science and Engineering Foundation
PSEF .... Plastic Surgery Educational Foundation (EA)
PSE & G .... Public Service Electric & Gas Co.
PSEG .... Public Service Electric & Gas Co. [*Associated Press abbreviation*] (APAG)
PSEG .... Public Service Enterprise Group, Inc. [*Associated Press abbreviation*] (APAG)
PSEKUT ... Paar Sammukest Eesti Kirjanduse Uurimise Teed [*A publication*]
PSelS .... Susquehanna University, Selinsgrove, PA [*Library symbol*] [*Library of Congress*] (LCLS)
PSEMA ..... Parti Social d'Education des Masses Africaines [*African Party for Social Education of the Masses*] [*Burkina Faso*]
PSENA ..... Photographic Science and Engineering [*A publication*]
PSEP .... Passive Seismic Experiments Package [*NASA*]
PSEP .... Physical Security Evaluation Procedure [*US Army Construction Engineering Research Laboratory*] (RDA)
PSEPB ...... Progress in Separation and Purification [*A publication*]
PSEQ .... Pupil Services Expectation Questionnaire
PS & ER ..... Production Support and Equipment Replacement [*Military*] (AABC)
PSER .... Slavonic and East European Review [*A publication*]
PSERC ...... Public Sector Economics Research Centre [*University of Leicester*] [*British*] (CB)
PSES .... Pretreatment Standards for Existing Sources [*Environmental Protection Agency*]
PSEU .... Production Support Equipment Unit (MCD)
Pseud .... Pseudepigrapha (BJA)
PSEUD ..... Pseudonym
Pseudep ..... Pseudepigrapha (BJA)
PSEW .... Project on the Status and Education of Women (EA)
PSEW .... Sewanee Review [*A publication*]
PSewD ...... Dixmont State Hospital, Sewickley, PA [*Library symbol*] [*Library of Congress*] (LCLS)
PSF .... Pakistan Science Foundation
PSF .... Panama Sea Frontier
PSF .... Panhandle & Santa Fe Railway Co. [*AAR code*]
P & SF .... Panhandle & Santa Fe Railway Co.
PSF .... Parti Social Francais [*French Social Party*] [*Political party*] (PPE)
PSF .... Passive Solar Foundation (EA)
PSF .... Payload Structure Fuel [*Ratio*]
PSF .... Peptide Supply Factor [*Biochemistry*]
PSF .... Per Square Foot (ADA)
PSF .... Permanent Signal Finder
PSF .... Philippine Sea Frontier
PSF .... Pittsfield, MA [*Location identifier*] [*FAA*] (FAAL)
PSF .... Plutonium Stripper Feed [*Nuclear energy*] (NRCH)
PSF .... Point Spread Function
PSF .... Popular Struggle Front [*Palestine*] [*Political party*] (PD)
PSF .... Port Stanley [*Falkland Islands*] [*Seismograph station code, US Geological Survey*] [*Closed*] (SEIS)
PSF .... Pounds per Square Foot

PSF .... Preservation Services Fund
PSF .... Presidio of San Francisco [*Military*] (AABC)
PSF .... Prime Subframe (MCD)
PSF .... Private Source Funds (DNAB)
PSF .... Probability Sample File [*Human Relations Area Files*] [*Information retrieval*]
PSF .... Probability of Spurious Fire [*Military*] (CAAL)
PSF .... Processing and Staging Facility [*Solid rocket booster*] (NASA)
PSF .... Processing and Storage Facility [*NASA*] (NASA)
PSF .... Program for the Study of the Future (EA)
PSF .... Progres Social Francais [*French Social Progress*] [*Political party*] (PPE)
PSF .... Progressive Space Forum (EA)
PSF .... Provisional Sinn Fein [*Northern Ireland*]
PSF .... Provisional System Feature [*Telecommunications*] (TEL)
PSF .... Prudential Strategic Income [*NYSE symbol*] (SPSG)
PSF .... Pseudosarcomatous Fasciitis [*Medicine*]
PSF .... Public Storage Properties VI [*AMEX symbol*] (SPSG)
PSF .... Saint Francis College, Loretto, PA [*OCLC symbol*] (OCLC)
PSFADF .... Proceedings. Annual Conference. Southeastern Association of Fish and Wildlife Agencies [*A publication*]
PSFAM ..... Parameter Sensitive Frequency Assignment Method (MCD)
PS/FC .... Power Supply / Frequency Converter (DWSG)
PS/FC .... Power Supply/Fuel Cell (MCD)
PSFC .... Process Supercritical Fluid Chromatography
PSFC .... Provisional Special Forces Co. (CINC)
PSFC/HIMH ... Pete Shelley Fan Club/Harmony in My Head (EA)
PSFD .... Public Sector Financial Deficit
PSFF .... Science-Fiction Studies [*A publication*]
PSFL........... Puget Sound Freight Lines [*AAR code*]
PSFQ .... Pupil Services Fulfillment Questionnaire
PSFS.......... Philadelphia Savings Fund Society [*NASDAQ symbol*] · (NQ)
PSFS.......... Studies in Formative Spirituality [*A publication*]
PSG........... Pacific Seabird Group (EA)
PSG........... Palestine Study Group (EA)
PSG........... Parachute Study Group (EA)
PSG........... Parti Socialiste Guyanais [*Guiana Socialist Party*] [*Political party*] (PPW)
PS de G ...... Partido dos Socialistas de Galicia [*Spain*] [*Political party*] (EY)
PSG........... Passage (FAAC)
PSG........... Passing (FAAC)
PSG........... Peak Systolic Gradient [*Medicine*] (MAE)
PSG........... Pershing [*Missile*] (GFGA)
PSG........... Personnel Subsystem Group (SAA)
PSG........... Petersburg [*Alaska*] [*Airport symbol*] (OAG)
PSG........... Petersburg, AK [*Location identifier*] [*FAA*] (FAAL)
PSG........... Phenol Sector Group [*European Council of Chemical Manufacturers Federations*] [*Belgium*] (EAIO)
PSG........... Phosphate-Saline-Glucose [*A buffer*] [*Cell culture*]
PSG........... Phosphosilicate Glass (IEEE)
PSG........... Phrase-Structure Grammar [*Data processing*]
PSG........... Planning Systems Generator
PSG........... Platoon Sergeant [*Army*] (AABC)
PSG........... Polysomnogram [*Medicine*] (MAE)
PSG........... Post Stall Gyration (MCD)
PSG........... Power Subsystem Group [*NASA*] (MCD)
PSG........... Presystolic Gallop [*Cardiology*]
PSG........... Production System Generator
PSG........... Professional Specialty Group
PSG........... Programmable Sound Generator [*Chip*] [*Atari, Inc.*]
PSG........... Programmable Symbol Generator
PSG........... PS Group, Inc. [*NYSE symbol*] (SPSG)
PSG........... Pseudomonas Syringae PV Glycinea [*Plant pathology*]
PSG........... Psychogalvanometer
PSG........... Publishing Systems Group [*Later, CPSUG*] (EA)
PSG........... Pulse Sequence Generation [*Instrumentation*]
PSGA........ Parkinson Support Groups of America (EA)
PSGA........ Pedal Steel Guitar Association (EA)
PSGA........ Professional Skaters Guild of America (EA)
PSGA........ Sociological Analysis [*A publication*]
PSGB .... Pharmaceutical Society of Great Britain
PSGD........ Past Senior Grand Deacon [*Freemasonry*]
PSGE .... Partido Socialdemocrata de Guinea Ecuatorial [*Social Democratic Party of Equatorial Guinea*] [*Political party*] (EY)
PSGE......... Photosynthetic Gas Exchanger (SAA)
PSG-EG..... Partido Socialista Galego - Esquerda Galega [*Spain*] [*Political party*] (EY)
PSGH .... Sociology and Social Research [*A publication*]
PSGI .... Sociological Inquiry [*A publication*]
PSGM....... Past Supreme Grand Master [*Freemasonry*]
PSGN........ Post-Streptococcal Glomerulonephritis [*Medicine*]
PSGQ........ Sociological Quarterly [*A publication*]
PSGR........ Passenger (AFM)
PSGR........ Sociological Review [*A publication*]
PS Grp ...... PS Group, Inc. [*Associated Press abbreviation*] (APAG)
PSGT .... Platoon Sergeant [*Military*]
PSGTCAEI ... Permanent Secretariat of the General Treaty on Central American Economic Integration (EAIO)
PSGW........ Past Senior Grand Warden [*Freemasonry*]

PSGY......... Sociology. Journal. British Sociological Association [*A publication*]
PSH .... Friends Historical Library of Swarthmore College, Swarthmore, PA [*OCLC symbol*]   (OCLC)
PSH .... Parshall, ND [*Location identifier*] [*FAA*]   (FAAL)
PSH .... Permanent Shift of Hearing
PSH .... Peshawar [*Pakistan*] [*Seismograph station code, US Geological Survey*]   (SEIS)
PSH .... Phase Shift   (MSA)
PSH .... Polystyrene, Hydrogenous [*Organic chemistry*]
PSH .... Post-Stimulus Histogram [*Psychometrics*]
PSH .... Postspinal Headache   (AAMN)
PSH .... Preselect Heading   (NG)
PSH .... Pressure Switch, High [*Nuclear energy*]   (NRCH)
PSH .... Program Support Handbook
PSH .... Proximity Sensing Head
PSH .... Public Storage Canadian Properties IIIa Ltd. [*Toronto Stock Exchange symbol*]
PSH .... Public Storage Properties VII [*AMEX symbol*]   (SPSG)
PSH .... Publications Statistiques Hongroises [*Hungary*]
P Shaw .... Patrick Shaw's Justiciary Cases [*1819-31*] [*Scotland*] [*A publication*]   (DLA)
PSHC........ Permanent Secretariat of the Hemispheric Congress   (EA)
PSHC........ Public Speaking and Humor Club   (EA)
PSHCJ ...... Philanthropic Society of House Carpenters and Joiners [*A union*] [*British*]
PSHD .... Phase-Shift Driver   (MSA)
PSHED...... Psychologie Heute [*A publication*]
PSHF........ Polysulfone Hollow Fiber [*Filtration membrane*]
PSHIGDL ... Publications. Section Historique. Institut Grand-Ducal de Luxembourg [*A publication*]
PSHIL .... Publications. Section Historique. Institut Grand-Ducal de Luxembourg [*A publication*]
PSHP........ Pennsylvania Journal for Health, Physical Education, and Recreation [*A publication*]
PSHP........ Studies in History and Philosophy of Science [*A publication*]
PSHPZ ...... PSH Master LP I [*NASDAQ symbol*]   (SPSG)
PSHQ .... Southwestern Historical Quarterly [*A publication*]
PSHR........ Pusher [*Freight*]
PSHR........ Southern Humanities Review [*A publication*]
PSHS........ Shakespeare Studies [*A publication*]
PShS .... Shippensburg State College, Shippensburg, PA [*Library symbol*] [*Library of Congress*]   (LCLS)
PSHT........ Powys Self-Help Trust [*British*]
PSHU .... Shakespeare Survey [*A publication*]
PSI .... Pacific Semiconductors, Inc.   (MCD)
PSI .... Paid Service Indication [*Telecommunications*]   (TEL)
PSI .... Paper Stock Institute of America   (EA)
PSI .... Parapat [*Sumatra*] [*Seismograph station code, US Geological Survey*]   (SEIS)
PSI .... Parapsychological Services Institute   (EA)
PSI .... Parenting Stress Index [*Psychology*]
PSI .... Partai Socialis Indonesia [*Socialist Party of Indonesia*]
PSI .... Parti Socialiste Ivoirien [*Ivorian Socialist Party*] [*The Ivory Coast*] [*Political party*]   (EY)
PSI .... Participation Systems, Inc. [*Electronics Communications Co.*] [*Winchester, MA*] [*Telecommunications*]   (TSSD)
PSI .... Particle-Sizing Interferometer   (MCD)
PSI .... Partito Socialista Italiano [*Italian Socialist Party*] [*Political party*]   (PPE)
PSI .... Pasni [*Pakistan*] [*Airport symbol*]   (OAG)
PSI .... Passive Solar Institute   (EA)
P & SI .... Pay and Supply Instruction [*Coast Guard*]
PSI .... Per Square Inch   (ADA)
PSI .... Percent Similarity Index
PSI .... Performance Systems International, Inc.
PSI .... Peripherally Synapsing Interneuron [*Neurology*]
PSI .... Permanent Staff Instructor [*Military*] [*British*]
PSI .... Permuterm Subject Index [*Institute for Scientific Information*] [*A publication*]   (IID)
PsI .... Perpetual Storage, Inc., Salt Lake City, UT [*Library symbol*] [*Library of Congress*]   (LCLS)
PSI .... Person of Special Importance [*British military*]   (DMA)
PSI .... Personal Sequential-Inference Machine [*Data processing*]
PSI .... Personal Service Income
PSI .... Personalized System of Instruction
PSI .... Personnel Security Investigation [*Military*]
PSI .... Personnel Selection Inventory [*Test*]
PSI .... Phenomenological Systems, Inc.
PSI .... Photo Services Industrial Ltd. [*British*]
PSI .... Photographic Society International   (EA)
PSI .... Photometric Sunspot Index
PSI .... Physical, Sensitivity, Intellectual [*Biorhythmics*]
PSI .... Piccole Storie Illustrate [*A publication*]
PSI .... Plan Speed Indicator [*Military*]
PSI .... Planned Start Installation [*Telecommunications*]   (TEL)
PSI .... Platoon Sector Indicator [*Army*]
PSI .... Play Skills Inventory
PSI .... Policy Studies Institute [*Research center*] [*British*]   (IRC)
PSI .... Pollutant Standards Index [*Environmental Protection Agency*]
p-Si............ Polycrystalline Silicon [*Photovoltaic energy systems*]

PSI .... Porta Systems Corp. [*AMEX symbol*]   (SPSG)
PSI .... Positive Self-Image [*Psychology*]
PSI .... Posterior Sagittal Index [*Anatomy*]   (AAMN)
PSI .... Postpartum Support, International   (EA)
PSI .... Pounds per Square Inch
PSI .... Power per Square Inch
PSI .... Power Static Inverter   (NASA)
PSI .... Praed Street Irregulars   (EA)
PSI .... Pre-Sentence Investigation   (OICC)
PSI .... Preprogrammed Self-Instruction [*Data processing*]   (IEEE)
PSI .... Present Serviceability Index   (IEEE)
PSI .... Preservice Inspection [*Nuclear energy*]   (NRCH)
PSI .... Preshipment Inspection [*International trade*]
PSI .... Pressure Sensitive Identification
PSI .... Pressurized Sphere Injection   (DNAB)
PSI .... Prime System Indicator
PSI .... Probe Systems, Inc.
PSI .... Problem-Solving Information [*Apparatus*]
PSI .... Problem-Solving Interpreter [*Computer language*]
PSI .... Process System Index
PSI .... Process Systems, Inc.
PSI .... Proctorial System of Instruction   (IEEE)
PSI .... Product Support Instructions   (AAG)
PSI .... Production Stock Item   (MCD)
PSI .... Professional Secretaries International [*Kansas City, MO*]   (EA)
PSI .... Program Status Information [*Data processing*]   (MCD)
PSI .... Program Supply Interest   (MCD)
PSI .... Programmed School Input   (NVT)
PSI .... Project Starlight International   (EA)
PSI .... Protosynthex Index
PSI .... PSI Energy [*Associated Press abbreviation*]   (APAG)
PSI .... PSI Resources [*Associated Press abbreviation*]   (APAG)
PSI .... Psychological Screening Inventory [*Personality development test*]
PSI .... Psychosomatic Inventory [*Psychology*]
PSI .... Pubblicazioni. Societa Italiana per la Ricerca dei Papiri Greci e Latini in Egitto [*Florence*] [*A publication*]
PSI .... Public Services International [*See also ISP*] [*Ferney Voltaire, France*]   (EAIO)
PSI .... Publications Standing Instruction   (AAG)
PSI .... Pulse Sciences, Inc.
PSIA .... Paper Stock Institute of America   (EA)
PSIA .... Pounds per Square Inch Absolute
PSIA .... President of the Society of Industrial Artists [*British*]
PSIA .... Production System Integration Area
PSIA .... Professional Ski Instructors of America   (EA)
PSIA .... Public Security Investigation Agency [*Japan*]   (CINC)
PSI Ber ..... PSI [*Paul Scherrer Institut*] Bericht [*A publication*]
PSIC .... Passenger Service Improvement Corp.
PSIC .... Passive Solar Industries Council   (EA)
PSIC .... Process Signal Interface Controller
PSIC .... Production Scheduling and Inventory Control
PSICD ...... Proceedings. IEEE Computer Society's International Computer Software and Applications Conference [*A publication*]
PSICP .... Program Support Inventory Control Point
PSID .... Partial Seismic Intrusion Device   (MCD)
PSID .... Patrol Seismic Intrusion Detector [*DoD*]
PSID .... Pounds per Square Inch Differential   (MCD)
PSID .... Preliminary Safety Information Document [*Nuclear energy*]   (NRCH)
PS/IDS ...... Physical Security/Intrusion Detection System   (MCD)
PSIEP........ Project on Scientific Information Exchange in Psychology [*Superseded by Office of Communication*]
PSIG .... Pounds per Square Inch Gauge
PSIG .... Propulsion Systems Integration Group [*NASA*]   (NASA)
PSIL......... Potential Selected Item List   (MCD)
PSIL.......... Preferred Speech Interference Level
PSI-LOGO ... Listing of Oil and Gas Opportunities [*Online Resource Exchange, Inc.*] [*Database*]
PSIM .... Power System Instrumentation and Measurement   (MCD)
PSIM .... Problem-Solving Instructional Material [*National Science Foundation project*]
PSIP.......... Private Sector Initiative Program [*Department of Labor*]
PSIR Bull Monogr ... PSIR [*Pakistan Council of Scientific and Industrial Research*] Bulletin Monograph [*A publication*]
PSIS.......... Pounds per Square Inch Sealed   (NASA)
PSIS.......... Programme for Strategic and International Security Studies [*Switzerland*]   (PDAA)
PSISIG ...... Psychic Science International Special Interest Group   (EA)
PSIT .... Property Security Investment Trust [*British*]
PSIU .... Power/Sequence Interface Unit   (MCD)
PSIUP .... Partito Socialista Italiano di Unita Proletaria [*Italian Socialist Party of Proletarian Unity (1945-1947)*] [*Political party*]   (PPE)
PSIV .... Passive
PSIX .... Peripheral Systems, Inc. [*Portland, OR*] [*NASDAQ symbol*]   (NQ)
PSJ .... Parallel Swivel Joint
PSJ .... Petites Soeurs de Jesus [*Little Sisters of Jesus*] [*Italy*]   (EAIO)
PSJ .... Philosophical Studies of Japan [*A publication*]
PSJ .... Plane Swivel Joint

PSJ .... Poso [*Indonesia*] [*Airport symbol*]   (OAG)
PSJ .... Pressure Switch Joint
PSJ .... Public Service Job   (OICC)
PSJS .... Pier and Span Junction Set   (MCD)
PSJT .... Scottish Journal of Theology [*A publication*]
PSK .... Dublin, VA [*Location identifier*] [*FAA*]   (FAAL)
PSK .... Phase-Shift Keying [*Data processing*]
PSK .... PostSparKasse [*Post Office Savings Bank*] [*Austria*]
PSK .... Power Supply Kit
PSK .... Private Secretary to the King [*British*]
PSK .... Program Selection Key [*Data processing*]   (BUR)
PSK .... Protection Survey Kit
PSK .... Pulse Shift Keying   (CAAL)
PSKAD ..... Promyshlennost Sinteticheskogo Kauchuka [*A publication*]
PSKI .... Pikes Peak Ski Corp. [*NASDAQ symbol*]   (NQ)
PSKI .... Skeptical Inquirer [*A publication*]
PSKJ .... Pitanja Savremenog Knjizevnog Jezika [*A publication*]
PSKM .... Phase-Shift Keying MODEM
PSK-PCM ... Phase-Shift Keying - Pulse Code Modulation
PSL .... Palouse Silt Loam [*Agronomy*]
PSL .... Parallel Strand Lumber
PSL .... Parasternal Line [*Anatomy*]   (MAE)
PSL .... Parti Social-Liberal [*Algeria*] [*Political party*]   (EY)
PSL .... Paymaster-Sub-Lieutenant [*Navy*] [*British*]
PSL .... Peabody Short Line R. R. [*Army*]
PSL .... Personnel Management [*A publication*]
PSL .... Personnel Skill Levels   (AAG)
PSL .... Petroleum Ether-Soluble Lipid
PSL .... Photographic Science Laboratory [*Navy*]
PSL .... Photostimulated Luminescence [*Physics*]
PSL .... Physical Sciences Laboratory [*Bethesda, MD*] [*National Institutes of Health*]   (GRD)
PSL .... Physical Sciences Laboratory [*University of Wisconsin - Madison, New Mexico State University*] [*Research center*]
PSL .... Pipe Sleeve
PSL .... Pocket Select Language [*Burroughs Corp.*]
PSL .... Polskie Stronnictwo Ludowe [*Polish Peasant Party*] [*Political party*]   (PPE)
PSL .... Polymer Science Library [*Elsevier Book Series*] [*A publication*]
PSL .... Portable Standard List Processing [*Data processing*]
PSL .... Potassium, Sodium Chloride, Sodium Lactate [*Solution*]   (AAMN)
PSL .... Potential Source List   (MCD)
PSL .... Power and Signal List [*Telecommunications*]   (TEL)
PSL .... Power Source Logic
PS & L ...... Power Switching and Logic
PSL .... Practical Storage Life
PSL .... Pressure Seal [*NASA*]
PSL .... Pressure-Sensitive Label
PSL .... Primary Standards Laboratory
PSL .... Private Sector Liquidity
PSL .... Problem-Solving Language
PSL .... Problem Specification Language
PSL .... Process Simulation Language [*Data processing*]   (TEL)
PSL .... Process Status Longword [*Number*] [*Data processing*]   (BYTE)
PSL .... Program Support Library   (MCD)
PSL .... Project Support Laboratory [*Military*]   (CAAL)
PSL .... Propellant Seal
PSL .... Propulsion Systems Laboratory [*USATACOM*]   (RDA)
PSL .... Public School League [*Sports*]
PSL .... Pycnocline Scattering Layer   (DNAB)
PSL .... South Hills Library Association, Pittsburgh, PA [*OCLC symbol*]   (OCLC)
PSLA .... Palaung State Liberation Army [*Myanmar*] [*Political party*]   (EY)
PSLA .... Polish Sea League of America   (EA)
PSLA .... Preferred Savings Bank, Inc. [*NASDAQ symbol*]   (NQ)
Psl Admr.... Personnel Administrator [*A publication*]
PSLC .... Pawathy Stare Literary Ceske [*A publication*]
PSLC .... Post-Schistosomal Liver Cirrhosis [*Medicine*]
PSLC .... Private Security Liaison Council   (EA)
Psl Exec ..... Personnel Executive [*A publication*]
PSLG .... Public Service and Local Government [*A publication*]
Psl & Guid J ... Personnel and Guidance Journal [*A publication*]
PSLI........... Packet Switch Level Interface
PSLI........... Partito Socialista dei Lavoratori Italiani [*Socialist Party of Italian Workers*] [*Political party*]   (PPE)
PSLI.......... Penta Systems International, Inc. [*NASDAQ symbol*]   (NQ)
PSLI.......... Physalaemin-Like Immunoreactivity [*Medicine*]
PSLI.......... Studies in the Literary Imagination [*A publication*]
Psl J .... Personnel Journal [*A publication*]
PSLJ.......... Southern Literary Journal [*A publication*]
PSL-Lewica ... Polskie Stronnictwo-Lewica [*Polish Peasant Party-Left (1947-1949)*] [*Political party*]   (PPE)
PSL-Lewica ... Polskie Stronnictwo Ludowe-Lewica [*Polish Peasant Party-Left (1913-1920)*] [*Political party*]   (PPE)
PSLLS .... Pulsed Solid-State LASER Light Source
PSL-NW.... Polskie Stronnictwo Ludowe-Nowe Wyzwolenie [*Polish Peasant Party-New Liberation*] [*Political party*]   (PPE)
PSLO .... Palaung State Liberation Organization [*Myanmar*] [*Political party*]   (EY)

PSL-Piast .. Polskie Stronnictwo Ludowe-Piast [*Polish Peasant Party-Piast*] [*Political party*]   (PPE)
PSL/PSA... Problem Statement Language/Problem Specification Analyzer [*Data processing*]
Psl Psy .... Personnel Psychology [*A publication*]
Psl R.......... Personnel Review [*A publication*]
PSLR .... Product Safety and Liability Reporter [*A publication*]
PSLS.......... Pan Stock Line Station   (MCD)
PSLT .... Picture Story Language Test
PSLT .... Pressurized Sonobuoy Launch Tube [*Navy*]   (CAAL)
PSLV .... Poa Semilatent Virus
PSL-Wyzwolenie ... Polskie Stronnictwo Ludowe-Wyzwolenie [*Polish Peasant Party-Liberation*] [*Political party*]   (PPE)
PSM........... Pagine di Storia della Medicina [*A publication*]
PSM........... Parallel Slit Map   (OA)
PSM........... Parc Saint-Maur [*France*] [*Later, CLF*] [*Geomagnetic observatory code*]
PSM........... Parcel Sorting Machine [*Freight*]   (DCTA)
PSM........... Parti Socialiste Mauricien [*Mauritian Socialist Party*] [*Political party*]   (EY)
PSM........... Parti Socialiste Monegasque [*Monaco Socialist Party*] [*Political party*]   (PPW)
PSM........... Particle Size Monitor [*Instrumentation*]
PSM........... Passenger Service Manager [*Travel industry*]
PSM........... Past Savio Movement   (EA)
PSM........... Peak Selector Memory [*Data processing*]
PSM........... Pennwalt Corp. [*Formerly, Pennsalt Chemicals Corp.*] [*NYSE symbol*]   (SPSG)
PSM........... Personal Skills Map [*Career effectiveness test*]
PSM........... Personnel Subsystem Manager [*Army*]   (AABC)
PS & M ...... Personnel Supervision and Management Division of ASTSECNAV's Office [*Absorbed into SECP, 1944*]
PSM........... Personnel Systems Management [*Air Force*]   (AFM)
PSM........... Petroleum Supply Monthly [*Database*] [*Department of Energy*] [*Information service or system*]   (CRD)
PSM........... Phase-Sensitive Modulator   (MCD)
PSM........... Phase-Shifter Module
PSM........... Philippine Studies (Manila) [*A publication*]
PSM........... Pia Societas Missionum [*Fathers of the Pious Society of Missions, Pallotini*] [*Roman Catholic religious order*]
PSM........... Pioneer Metals Corp. [*Toronto Stock Exchange symbol*] [*Vancouver Stock Exchange symbol*]
PSM........... Platyschisma Shale Member [*Geology*]
PSM........... Please See Me
PSM........... Plymouth State College of the University of New Hampshire, Plymouth, NH [*OCLC symbol*]   (OCLC)
PSM........... Point Source Monitoring [*Environmental Protection Agency*]   (GFGA)
PSM........... Portsmouth, NH [*Location identifier*] [*FAA*]   (FAAL)
PSM........... Postal Service Manual [*A publication*]   (AFM)
PSM........... Postsynaptic Membrane [*Neurology*]
PSM........... Power Strapping Machine
PSM........... Power System Module
PSM........... Preservation Security Manager
PSM........... Presystolic Murmur [*Cardiology*]
PSM........... Prism   (MSA)
PSM........... Pro Sanctity Movement   (EA)
P & SM ...... Procurement and Subcontract Management [*NASA*]   (NASA)
PSM........... Product Support Manual   (AAG)
PSM........... Program-Sensitive Malfunction
PSM........... Program Support Management [*NASA*]   (KSC)
PSM........... Programming Support Monitor [*Texas Instruments, Inc.*]
PSM........... Project Safety Management
PSM........... Propellant Storage Module [*NASA*]
PSM........... Public School Magazine [*A publication*]
PSM........... Pyro Substitute Monitor [*NASA*]   (NASA)
PSM........... Pytannja Slov'jans'koho Movoznavstva [*A publication*]
PSm........... Thesaurus Syriacus [*R. Paine Smith*] [*A publication*]   (BJA)
PSMA....... Power Saw Manufacturers Association [*Later, CSMA*]   (EA)
PSMA....... President of the Society of Marine Artists [*British*]
PSMA....... Professional Services Management Association [*Alexandria, VA*]   (EA)
PSMA....... Progressive Spinal Muscular Atrophy [*Medicine*]
PSMA....... Pyrotechnic Signal Manufacturers Association   (EA)
PSMD....... Photo Selective Metal Deposition
PSMDC..... Psychological Medicine [*A publication*]
PSMDEQ ... Psychiatric Medicine [*A publication*]
PSME .... Partido Socialista de Melilla [*Political party*] [*See also PSOE*] [*Spanish North Africa*]   (MENA)
PSMEA ..... Psychosomatic Medicine [*A publication*]
PSME-PSOE ... Partido Socialista de Melilla - Partido Socialista Obrero Espanol [*Political party*]   (EY)
PSMF .... Protein Sparing Modified Fast
PSMFC...... Pacific States Marine Fisheries Commission
PSMI........ Phase-Shift Modal Interference
PSMI........ Precise Ship Motion Instrument
PSMIT ...... Programming Services for Multimedia Industry Terminals [*IBM Corp.*]
PSML........ Prague Studies in Mathematical Linguistics [*A publication*]
PSML........ Processor System Modeling Language [*1976*] [*Data processing*]   (CSR)

PSMM....... Multimission Patrol Ship [*Symbol*]
PSMMA.... Plastic Soft Materials Manufacturers Association (EA)
PSMMAF ... Proceedings. Staff Meeting of the Mayo Clinic [*A publication*]
PSMP....... Project Software Management Plan (SSD)
PSMR....... Parts Specification Management for Reliability
PSMR....... Pneumatic [*or Pressure*] System Manifold [*or Manual*]
            Regulator (AAG)
PSMS .... Permanent Section of Microbiological Standardization (MCD)
PSMSC...... Psychotherapie und Medizinische Psychologie [*A publication*]
PSMSL...... Permanent Service for Mean Sea Level [*of the Federation of*
            Astronomical and Geophysical Data Analysis Services]
            [*Birkenhead, Merseyside, England*] (EAIO)
PSMT....... Perishable Sheet Metal Tool (MCD)
PSMU....... Power Supply and Multiplexer Unit
            [*Telecommunications*] (TSSD)
PSMUD..... Psychology of Music [*A publication*]
PSMV....... Paspalum Striate Mosaic Virus [*Plant pathology*]
PSMV....... Pea Seed-Borne Mosaic Virus [*Plant pathology*]
PSN .... Package Sequence Number
PSN .... Packet Switched Network
PSN .... Packet Switching Node
PSN .... Palestine, TX [*Location identifier*] [*FAA*] (FAAL)
PSN .... Parti de la Solidarite Nationale [*Party of National Solidarity*]
            [*Luxembourg*] [*Political party*] (PPE)
PSN .... Partial Shipment Number [*DoD*]
PSN .... Partido Socialista Nicaraguense [*Nicaraguan Socialist Party*]
            [*Political party*] (PPW)
PSN .... Permanent Sort Number [*Data processing*]
PSN .... Position
PSN .... Private Satellite Network, Inc. [*New York, NY*]
            [*Telecommunications*] (TSSD)
PSN .... Proceedings. Society of Antiquaries of Newcastle-upon-Tyne [*A*
            publication]
PSN .... Processing Serial Number (MCD)
PSN .... Program Summary Network (MCD)
PSN .... Progressive Student Network (EA)
PSN .... Provisioning Sequence Number (MCD)
PSN .... Public Switched Network (BUR)
PSNA........ Phytochemical Society of North America (EA)
PSNA........ Powys Society of North America (EA)
PSNB........ Puget Sound Bancorp [*NASDAQ symbol*] (NQ)
PSNC........ Parti Socialiste de la Nouvelle Caledonie [*Socialist Party of New*
            Caledonia] [*Political party*] (PPW)
PSNC........ Public Service Co. of North Carolina, Inc. [*NASDAQ*
            symbol] (NQ)
PSNCF ...... Pacific Southern Naval Coastal Frontier
PSNCO...... Personnel Staff Noncommissioned Officer [*Military*]
PSNEB...... Psychiatric Annals [*A publication*]
PSNG........ Simulation and Gaming [*A publication*]
PSNL........ Personnel (FAAC)
PSNO .... Studies in the Novel [*A publication*]
P & SNP .... Pay and Subsistence of Naval Personnel [*Budget appropriation*
            title]
PSNP........ Pebble Springs Nuclear Plant (NRCH)
PSNR........ Positioner
PSNR........ Power Signal-to-Noise Ratio
PSNRP...... Position Report [*Aviation*] (FAAC)
PSNS........ Physical Science for Nonscience Students
PSNS........ Pretreatment Standards for New Indirect Sources
            [*Environmental Protection Agency*]
PSNS........ Programmable Sampling Network Switch
PSNS........ Puget Sound Naval Shipyard [*Bremerton, WA*] (MCD)
PSNS........ Science and Society [*A publication*]
PSNS-MATLABS ... Puget Sound Naval Shipyard Material Laboratories
            [*Bremerton, WA*]
PSNSR ...... Position Sensor (MCD)
PSNSY ...... Puget Sound Naval Shipyard [*Bremerton, WA*]
PSNT........ Pismo Swiete Nowego Testamentu [*Posen*] [*A publication*]
PSNT........ Present [*Legal term*] (ROG)
PSNTA...... Progres Scientifique [*A publication*]
PSO .... Pad Safety Officer [*Aerospace*] (MCD)
PSO .... Paint Spray Outfit
PSO .... Pasto [*Colombia*] [*Seismograph station code, US Geological*
            Survey] (SEIS)
PSO .... Pasto [*Colombia*] [*Airport symbol*] (OAG)
PSO .... Pauli Spin Operator [*Physics*]
PSO .... Peacetime Stockage Objective [*DoD*] (AFIT)
PSO .... Penobscot Shoe Co. [*AMEX symbol*] (SPSG)
PSO .... Personnel Security Officer [*Military*]
PSO .... Personnel Selection Officer [*British military*] (DMA)
PSO .... Piano-Shaped Object
PSO .... Pilot Systems Operator
PSO .... Planet Sensor Output
PSO .... Point Surface Origin
PSO .... Polaris Systems Officer [*British military*] (DMA)
PSO .... Policy Studies Organization (EA)
PSO .... Political Survey Officers [*Navy*]
PSO .... Polysulfone [*Also, PS*] [*Organic chemistry*]
PSO .... Port Services Office [*or Officer*] (DNAB)
PSO .... Primary Standardization Office [*Military*] (AABC)
PSO .... Principal Scientific Officer [*British*]

PSO .... Principal Staff Officer [*British military*] (DMA)
PSO .... Procurement Services Office
PSO .... Product Support Organization
PSO .... Profco Resources Ltd. [*Vancouver Stock Exchange symbol*]
PSO .... Program Staff Officer
PSO .... Prospective Supply Officer (DNAB)
PSO .... Provisions Supply Office [*Military*]
PSO .... Public Safety Officer
PSO .... Public Service Organisation [*Government grant*] [*British*]
PSO .... Publications Supply Officer [*Military*]
PSO .... Publicity Security Officer [*Navy*]
PSOA......... Pro Stock Owners Association (EA)
PSOB......... Paper Society for the Overseas Blind [*Defunct*] (EA)
PSOB......... Social Biology [*A publication*]
PSOC......... Preliminary System Operational Concept (MCD)
PSoc.......... Przeglad Socjologiczny [*A publication*]
P Soc Exp M ... Proceedings. Society for Experimental Biology and Medicine
            [*A publication*]
PSOE......... Partido Socialista Obrero Espanol [*Spanish Socialist Workers'*
            Party] [*See also PSME*] [*Political party*] (PPE)
PSOH .... Social History [*A publication*]
P Sol......... Partly Soluble (WGA)
PSOLMHT ... Pious Society of Our Lady of the Most Holy Trinity (EA)
PSom.......... Mary S. Biesecker Public Library, Somerset, PA [*Library*
            symbol] [*Library of Congress*] (LCLS)
PSomHi ..... Somerset County Historical and Genealogical Society,
            Somerset, PA [*Library symbol*] [*Library of*
            Congress] (LCLS)
PSON .... Person (ROG)
PSONAL... Personal (ROG)
PSOP......... Parti Socialiste des Ouvriers et Paysans [*Socialist Party of*
            Workers and Peasants] [*France*] [*Political party*]
PSOP......... Payload Systems Operating Procedures [*NASA*] (NASA)
PSOP......... Power System Optimization Program [*Data processing*]
PSOP......... Social Psychology Quarterly [*A publication*]
PSOR......... Preliminary System of Requirements
PSOR......... Social Research [*A publication*]
Psoriasis Proc Int Symp ... Psoriasis. Proceedings. International Symposium
            [*A publication*]
PSOS......... Social Science Journal [*A publication*]
PSP........... Pace-Setting Potential [*Physiology*]
PSp........... Pacific Spectator [*A publication*]
PSP........... Pacifistische Socialistische Partij [*Pacific Socialist Party*]
            [*Political party*] [*Netherlands*]
PSP........... Package Size Proneness [*Marketing*]
PSP........... Packaging Shipping Procedures
PSP........... Packet Switching Processor
PSP........... Pad Safety Plan
PSP........... Palm Springs [*California*] [*Airport symbol*] (OAG)
PSP........... Palm Springs, CA [*Location identifier*] [*FAA*] (FAAL)
PSP........... Pancreatic Spasmolytic Peptide [*Biochemistry*]
PSP........... Paralytic Shellfish Poisoning [*Marine biology*]
PSP........... Parathyroid Secretory Protein [*Biochemistry*]
PSP........... Parti Social pour le Progres [*Tunisia*] [*Political party*] (EY)
PSP........... Parti Socialiste Polynesien [*Polynesian Socialist Party*]
            [*Political party*] (PPW)
PSP........... Parti de la Solidarite du Peuple [*Cameroon*] [*Political*
            party] (EY)
PSP........... Parti Soudanais Progressiste [*Sudanese Progressive Party*]
            [*Political party*]
PSP........... Partido Social Progresista [*Social Progressive Party*] [*Brazil*]
            [*Political party*]
PSP........... Partido Socialista del Peru [*Socialist Party of Peru*] [*Political*
            party] (PPW)
PSP........... Partido Socialista Popular [*Popular Socialist Party*] [*Pre-1965*]
            [*Cuba*] [*Political party*] (PPW)
PSP........... Partido Socialista Popular [*Popular Socialist Party*] [*Peru*]
            [*Political party*] (PPW)
PSP........... Partido Socialista Popular [*Popular Socialist Party*] [*Spain*]
            [*Political party*] (PPE)
PSP........... Partido Socialista Portuguesa [*Portuguese Socialist Party*]
            [*Political party*] (PPW)
PSP........... Parts Screening Program
PSP........... Patrol Seaplane
PSP........... Payload Signal Processor [*NASA*] (NASA)
PSP........... Payload Specialist Panel [*NASA*] (NASA)
PSP........... Payload Support Plan [*NASA*] (MCD)
PSP........... Payroll Savings Plan (GFGA)
PSP........... Peak Sideband Power (DEN)
PSP........... Perforated Steel Planking (SAA)
PSP........... Perforated Steel Plating (DNAB)
PSP........... Performance Shaping Parameters (IEEE)
PSP........... Performance Standards Program
PSP........... Periodic Short Pulse (MAE)
PSP........... Personal Success Program
PSP........... Personnel Subsystem Process [*Army*] (AABC)
PSP........... Pharmacological Sciences Program [*Bethesda, MD*] [*National*
            Institute of General Medical Sciences] (GRD)
PSP........... Phenolsulfonephthalein [*Chemical indicator*]
PSP........... Pierced Steel Planking [*Military*]
PSP........... Plane Strain Plastometer

PSP	Planet Scan Platform [*NASA*] (KSC)
PSP	Planned Standard Programming [*Data processing*]
PSP	Plasma Spraying [*Welding*]
PSP	Plasmon Surface Polariton [*Physics*]
PSP	Platform Sensor Package
PSP	Pointed Soft Point [*Ammunition*]
PSP	Pointed Soft Point Bullet
PSP	Policies, Systems, and Procedures
PSP	Polyfactorial Study of Personality [*Psychology*]
PSP	Poly(styrene peroxide) [*Organic chemistry*]
PSP	Portable Service Processor (IEEE)
PSP	Positive Spike Pattern (MAE)
PSP	Post-Shoring-Polyethylene [*Method of constructing underground homes*]
PSP	Post-Surgical Pain [*Medicine*]
PSP	Postipankki [*National savings bank*] [*Finland*]
PSP	Postsynaptic Potential [*Neurophysiology*]
PSP	Potential for Successful Performance [*Test*]
PSP	Power System Planning
PSP	Praja Socialist Party [*India*] [*Political party*] (PPW)
PSP	Precision Spot Positioning
PSP	Predictable System Performance (SAA)
PSP	Predictive Smooth Pursuit [*Ophthalmology*]
PSP	Presensitized Photoplate
PSP	Prestart Panel [*Aerospace*] (AAG)
PSP	Priced Spare Parts [*Military*] (AFIT)
PSP	Primary Sodium Pump [*Nuclear energy*] (NRCH)
PSP	Primary Supply Point [*Military*] (AFM)
PSP	Primary Support Point [*Military*] (AFM)
PSP	Priority Strike Program
PSP	Product Service Publication [*General Motors Corp.*]
PSP	Product Support Program (NG)
PSP	Program Segment Prefix [*Data processing*]
PSP	Program Support Plan [*NASA*]
PSP	Programmable Signal Processor (MCD)
PSP	Progressive Socialist Party [*Lebanon*] [*Political party*] (BJA)
PSP	Progressive Supranuclear Palsy [*Neurology*]
PSP	Project Schedule Plan (NASA)
PSP	Project Standard Practice (DNAB)
PSP	Protective Shielding Program
PSP	Protocol for Specific Purpose
PSP	Provincia de Sao Pedro [*Brazil*] [*A publication*]
PSP	Pseudopregnancy [*Gynecology*]
PSP	Public Storage Canadian Properties [*Limited Partnership Units*] [*Toronto Stock Exchange symbol*]
PSP	Public Storage Properties [*AMEX symbol*] (SPSG)
PSP	Puerto Rican Socialist Party [*Political party*] (PD)
PSP	Swarthmore College Peace Collection, Swarthmore, PA [*OCLC symbol*] (OCLC)
PSPA	Pacific Seafood Processors Association (EA)
PSPA	Passive Solar Products Association (EA)
PSPA	Pennview Savings Association [*NASDAQ symbol*] (NQ)
PSPA	Pressure Static Probe Assembly (MCD)
PSPA	Professional School Photographers of America (EA)
PSPAEW...	Psychotherapy Patient [*A publication*]
PSPC	Partido Socialista del Pueblo de Ceuta [*Political party*] (EY)
PSPC	Physical Security / Pilferage Code
PSPC	Polystyrene Packaging Council (EA)
PSPC	President's Soviet Protocol Committee [*World War II*]
PSPCD	Proceedings. Annual Southwestern Petroleum Short Course [*A publication*]
PSPCE4.....	Proceedings. Sugar Processing Research Conference [*A publication*]
PSPD	Permits and State Programs Division [*Environmental Protection Agency*] (GFGA)
PSPD	Position-Sensitive Proportional Detector [*For X-ray diffraction*]
PSP & E.....	Product Support Planning and Estimating (AAG)
PSPEN	Primary/Secondary Peace Education Network [*Later, PEN*] (EA)
PSPF.........	Potential Single Point Failures [*NASA*] (KSC)
PSPF.........	Prostacyclin Stimulating Plasma Factor [*Endocrinology*]
PSPFLI....	Pulsed Single Photon Fluorescence Lifetime Instrumentation
PSPGV	Primary Sodium Pump Guard Vesel [*Nuclear energy*] (NRCH)
PSPH........	Studies in Philology [*A publication*]
PSPHA......	Psychophysiology [*A publication*]
PSPHDI	Psychopharmacology Series [*A publication*]
PSphR.......	Rohm & Haas Co., Research Library Services, Spring House, PA [*Library symbol*] [*Library of Congress*] (LCLS)
PSPI..........	Psychosocial Pain Inventory [*Psychology*]
PSPL.........	Priced Spare Parts List
PSPL.........	Progressive Socialist Party of Lebanon
PSPLR.......	Priced Spare Parts List Revision
PSPM........	Procurement Seminar for Project Management [*Army*]
PSPMW	International Brotherhood of Pulp, Sulphite, and Paper Mill Workers [*Later, UPIU*]
PSPOB	Psychiatria Polska [*A publication*]
PSPOS.......	Philological Society. Publications. Occasional Studies [*A publication*]
PSPP.........	Preliminary System Package Plan
PSPP.........	Program System Package Plan
PSPP.........	Proposed System Package Plan [*Military*]
PSPR........	Personnel Subsystem Products [*Army*] (AABC)
PSPR........	Programmable Signal Processor RADAR
PSPS.........	Paddle Steamer Preservation Society [*High Wycombe, Buckinghamshire, England*]
PSPS.........	Pesticides Safety Precautions Scheme [*British*]
PSPS.........	Planar Silicon Photoswitch (IEEE)
PSPS.........	Power-Steering Pressure Sensor [*Automotive engineering*]
PSPS.........	Power Steering Pressure Switch [*Automotive engineering*]
PS to PS.....	Private Siding to Private Siding
PSPS.........	Product Support Procurement Summary (MCD)
PSPS.........	Program Support Plan Summary
PSPSB	Psychotherapy and Psychosomatics [*A publication*]
PSPT	Passport (AABC)
PSPT	Planar Silicon Power Transistor
PSPV	Partido Socialista del Pais Valenciano [*Spain*] [*Political party*] (EY)
PSQ...........	Personnel Security Questionnaire
PSQ...........	Personnel Squadron
PSQ...........	Philologische Studien und Quellen [*A publication*]
PSQ...........	Political Science Quarterly [*A publication*]
PSQ...........	Protein Sequence Query
PSQ...........	Public Storage Properties XV [*AMEX symbol*] (SPSG)
PSQA........	Pageable System Queue Area [*Data processing*] (MCD)
PSQAA......	Psychoanalytic Quarterly [*A publication*]
PSQSA......	Psychiatric Quarterly. Supplement [*A publication*]
PSQUA......	Psychiatric Quarterly [*A publication*]
PSR...........	Pacific Security Region
PSR...........	Pacific-Sierra Research Corp.
PSR...........	Pacific Sociological Review [*A publication*]
PSR...........	Packed Snow on Runway [*Aviation*] (FAAC)
PSR...........	Pad Safety Report [*NASA*]
PSR...........	Page Send-Receive [*Teletypewriter*]
PSR...........	Pain Sensitivity Range [*Biometrics*]
PSR...........	Panoramic Stereo Rectification
PSR...........	Parachute Status Report [*Army*] (AABC)
PSR...........	Partido Socialista Revolucionario [*Revolutionary Socialist Party*] [*Peru*] [*Political party*] (PPW)
PSR...........	Partido Socialista Revolucionario [*Revolutionary Socialist Party*] [*Portugal*] [*Political party*] (PPE)
PSR...........	Partido Socialista Revolucionario [*Revolutionary Socialist Party*] [*Mexico*] [*Political party*] (PPW)
PSR...........	Party Socialiste Revolutionnaire [*Socialist Revolutionary Party*] [*Lebanon*] [*Political party*] (PPW)
psr	Paternal Sex Ratio Gene [*Genetics*]
PSR...........	Paul's Scarlet Rose [*Plant cell line*]
PSR...........	Pennsylvania State Reports [*A publication*] (DLA)
PSR...........	Pennsylvania State University Reactor (NRCH)
PSR...........	Perfectly Stirred Reactor
PSR...........	Performance Summary Report (NG)
PSR...........	Peripheral Shim Rod [*Nuclear energy*] (NRCH)
PSR...........	Personnel Status Report [*Military*]
PSR...........	Pescara [*Italy*] [*Airport symbol*] (OAG)
PSR...........	Petaluma & Santa Rosa Railroad Co. [*AAR code*]
PSR...........	Petrostates Resource Corp. [*Vancouver Stock Exchange symbol*]
PSR...........	Petty Sessions Review [*A publication*] (APTA)
PSR...........	Phase Sequence Relay
PSR...........	Philatelic Societies' Record [*A publication*] [*British*]
PSR...........	Philippine Sociological Review [*A publication*]
PSR...........	Photo Scale Reciprocal (DNAB)
PSR...........	Physical Sciences Research Program [*North Carolina State University*] [*Research center*] (RCD)
PSR...........	Physicians for Social Responsibility (EA)
PSR...........	Plow-Steel Rope
PSR...........	Point of Safe Return (MCD)
PSR...........	Policy Status Report [*Insurance*]
PSR...........	Political Science Review [*A publication*]
PSR...........	Political and Social Reform Movement [*British*]
PSR...........	Portable Seismic Recorder
PSR...........	[*Extrahepatic*] Portal-Systemic Resistance [*Medicine*] (MAE)
PSR...........	Positive Support Review, Inc. [*Telecommunications service*] (TSSD)
PSR...........	Post-Sinusoidal Resistance
PSR...........	Postal Service Representative [*British*] (DCTA)
PSR...........	Power System Relaying (MCD)
PSR...........	Predicted SONAR Range [*Military*] (NVT)
PSR...........	Price-Sales Ratio [*Economics*]
PSR...........	Primary Surveillance RADAR
PSR...........	Problem Status Report (MCD)
PSR...........	Processor State Register
PSR...........	Procurement Status Report (IEEE)
PSR...........	Program Status Register
PSR...........	Program Status Report [*or Review*]
PSR...........	Program Status Review [*NASA*] (NASA)
PSR...........	Program Study Request (AAG)
PSR...........	Program Summary Record [*Military*] (AFIT)
PSR...........	Program Support Requirements (KSC)
PSR...........	Programming Status Report [*Data processing*]
PSR...........	Programming Support Representative [*IBM Corp.*]
PSR...........	Progress Summary Report

PSR............ Project Scan Record
PSR............ Project Summary Report (MCD)
PSR............ Propeller Shaft Rate [*Navy*] (CAAL)
PSR............ Proton Storage Ring [*Nuclear physics*]
PSR............ Prototype Systems Review
PSR............ Provisioning Support Request [*Military*] (CAAL)
PsR............ Psychoanalytic Review [*A publication*]
PsR............ Psychological Review [*A publication*]
PSR............ Public Service Co. of Colorado [*NYSE symbol*] (SPSG)
PSR............ Public Social Responsibility [*Unit of the Anglican Church of Canada General Synod*]
PSR............ Pulmonary Stretch Receptors [*Medicine*]
PSRA........ Problem Status Report Analysis (SAA)
PSRA........ Professional Soccer Reporter's Association (EA)
PSRAA...... Progress in the Science and Technology of the Rare Earths [*A publication*]
PSRAAALAA ... President's Special Representative and Adviser on African, Asian, and Latin American Affairs [*Department of State*]
PSRAM..... Physical Security Requirements Assessment Methodology [*Civil Engineering Research Laboratory*] [*Navy*] (RDA)
PSRC........ Plastic Surgery Research Council (EA)
PSRC........ Pretrial Services Resource Center (EA)
PSRC........ Public Service Research Council (EA)
PSRCA..... Professional Standards Review Council of America (EA)
PSRD........ Personnel Shipment Ready Date [*Army*] (AABC)
PSRD........ Program Support Requirements Document [*NASA*] (KSC)
PSRE........ Partido Socialista Revolucionario Ecuatoriano [*Socialist Revolutionary Party of Ecuador*] [*Political party*] (PPW)
PSRE........ Propulsion System Rocket Engine (MCD)
PSREA...... Psychoanalytic Review [*A publication*]
PSRED...... Psychological Research [*A publication*]
PSRF........ Product Support Reports and Functions
PSRF........ Profit Sharing Research Foundation (EA)
PSRI......... Particulate Solid Research Institute
PSRI......... Personnel Specialities and Record Inventory (SAA)
PSRI......... Position Subject Return of Incumbent (FAAC)
PSRI......... Psycho-Social Rehabilitation International (EAIO)
PSRIA....... Papers. Ship Research Institute [*A publication*]
PSRL........ Post Strike Reconnaissance List [*Military*] (CINC)
PSRM........ Parti Sosialis Rakyat Malaya [*People's Socialist Party of Malaya*]
PSRM........ Post-Scram Reactivity Monitor [*Nuclear energy*] (NRCH)
PSRM........ Pressurization Systems Regulator Manifold (AAG)
PSRM........ Processor State Register Main [*Data processing*]
PSRMA..... Pacific Southwest Railway Museum Association [*Later, SDRM*] (EA)
PSR-ML/MIR ... Partido Socialista Revolucionario (Marxista-Leninista)/ Movimiento de Izquierda Revolucionaria [*Revolutionary Socialist Party (Marxist-Leninist)/Militant Movement of the Revolutionary Left*] [*Peru*] [*Political party*] (PPW)
PSRMLS... Pacific Southwest Regional Medical Library [*Library network*]
PSRMT..... Piecewise-Sinusoidal Reaction Matching Technique [*Antenna*] [*Navy*]
PSRO........ Passenger Standing Route Order [*Army*] (AABC)
PSRO........ Professional Standards Review Organization [*Generic term for groups of physicians who may review the policies and decisions of their colleagues*]
PSRO........ Studies in Romanticism [*A publication*]
PSR-P........ Packed Snow on Runway - Patchy [*Aviation*] (DNAB)
PSRP........ Physical Sciences Research Papers [*Air Force*] (MCD)
PSRP........ Production Support Repair Plan (SAA)
PSRPD...... Prakla-Seismos Report [*A publication*]
PSRR........ Parachute Supported Radio Relay
PSRR........ Product and Support Requirements Request [*Data processing*] (IBMDP)
PSRS........ Pictographic Self-Rating Scale [*Psychology*] (AEBS)
PSRS........ Portable Seismic Recording System
PSRS........ Position Subject to Rotating Shifts (FAAC)
PSrS........... Slippery Rock State College, Slippery Rock, PA [*Library symbol*] [*Library of Congress*] (LCLS)
PSRT........ Passive Satellite Research Terminal
PS-RTP..... Paper-Substrate Room-Temperature Phosphorescence [*Analytical chemistry*]
PSRU........ Processor State Register Utility [*Data processing*]
PSRU........ Production Support Repair Unit (SAA)
PSRV........ Southern Review [*A publication*]
PSRVA...... Psychological Review [*A publication*]
PSRWD..... Policy Studies Review [*A publication*]
PSS............ Hastings, NE [*Location identifier*] [*FAA*] (FAAL)
PSS............ International Production, Service, and Sales Union
PSS............ Packet Switching Service [*Telecommunications*] [*Information service or system*] [*British*] (IID)
PSS............ Packet SwitchStream [*British Telecommunications Plc*] [*London*] [*Information service or system*] (IID)
PSS............ Pad Safety Supervision [*Aerospace*] (AAG)
PSS............ Palomar Sky Survey [*NASA*]
PSS............ Parti Socialiste Suisse [*Social Democratic Party of Switzerland*] [*Political party*] (PPE)
PSS............ Parti de Solidarite Senegalaise [*Senegalese Solidarity Party*] [*Political party*]

PSS .... Partia Socialiste e Shqiperise [*Socialist Party of Albania*] [*Political party*] (EAIO)
PSS .... Partially Sighted Society [*British*]
PSS .... Partito Socialista Sammarinese [*Socialist Party of San Marino*] [*Political party*] (PPE)
PSS .... Partito Socialista Somalo [*Somali Socialist Party*] [*Political party*]
PSS .... Passenger Service Supervisor [*Travel industry*]
PSS .... Passenger Service Systems [*Airlines*]
PSS .... Patent Search System [*Pergamon*] [*Database*] [*Data processing*] [*British*]
PSS .... Pauli Spin Susceptibility [*Physics*]
PSS .... Payload Specialist Station [*NASA*] (NASA)
PSS .... Payload Support System [*NASA*] (MCD)
PSS .... Performance Standard Sheet
PSS .... Periscope Simulation System [*Navy*]
PSS .... Personal Signaling System
PSS .... Personnel Staffing Specialist (GFGA)
PSS .... Personnel Subsystem [*Air Force*] (AFM)
PSS .... Personnel Support System [*Army*] (AABC)
PSS .... Phase-System Switching [*Physical chemistry*]
PSS .... Physical Security Subsystem
PSS .... Physiological Saline Solution [*Physiology*]
PSS .... Planetary Scan System [*or Subsystem*]
PSS .... Planned Systems Schedule (AAG)
PSS .... Planning Summary Sheets (AAG)
PSS .... Plant Science Seminar [*Later, ASP*]
PS/S.......... Plumbing Supervisor/Specialist (AAG)
PSS .... Plunger Snap Switch
PSS .... Pneumatic Supply Subsystem (AAG)
PSS .... Polar Subsurface Sounder (SSD)
PSS .... Poly(styrenesulfonate) [*Organic chemistry*]
PSS .... Porcine Stress Syndrome [*Veterinary medicine*]
PSS .... Portable Simulation System (MCD)
PSS .... Posadas [*Argentina*] [*Airport symbol*] (OAG)
PSS .... Postal Savings System [*Terminated, 1966*]
PSS .... Postal Separation System (SAA)
PSS .... Postscripts
PSS .... Power Supply Section
PSS .... Power System Synthesizer
PSS .... Precancel Stamp Society (EA)
PSS .... Premature Separation Switch (SAA)
PSS .... Presbyteri Sancti Sulpicii [*Sulpicians*] [*Roman Catholic men's religious order*]
P/S/S......... Price/Stern/Sloan Publishers, Inc.
PSS .... Primary Sampling System [*Nuclear energy*] (NRCH)
PSS .... Princess (ROG)
PS to S .... Private Siding to Station
PSS .... Probabilistic Safety Study [*Nuclear energy*] (NRCH)
PSS .... Process Sampling System [*Nuclear energy*] (NRCH)
PSS .... Professor of Sacred Scripture
PSS .... Program Support Staff [*Environmental Protection Agency*] (GFGA)
PSS .... Programming Support System (SAA)
PSS .... Progressive Science Series [*A publication*]
PSS .... Progressive Systemic Sclerosis [*Medicine*]
PSS .... Propellant Supply System [*or Subsystem*]
PSS .... Proposed Sale of Securities (GFGA)
PSS .... Proprietary Software Systems [*Data processing*] (IEEE)
PSS .... Propulsion Subsystem Structure
PSS .... Propulsion Support System (KSC)
PSS .... Protective Security Service
PSS .... Protective Signature Service (MCD)
PSS .... Psalms [*Old Testament book*]
PSS .... Pseudo Spread Spectrum (MCD)
Pss............ Pseudomonas Syringae Syringae [*Plant pathology*]
PSS .... Psychiatric Services Section [*of the American Hospital Association*] [*Later, SCSMHPS*] (EA)
PSS .... Psychiatric Status Schedules [*Psychology*]
PSS .... Pubblicazioni. Seminario de Semitistica. Istituto Orientale di Napoli [*A publication*]
PSS .... Public Services Satellite
PSS .... Public Storage Canadian Properties II [*Limited Partnership Units*] [*Toronto Stock Exchange symbol*]
PSS .... Push-Button Selection Station
PSSA .... Pilot Signal Selector Adaptor (SAA)
PSSA .... Pitch Starting Synchro Assembly
PSSA .... Pseudo-Steady-State Approximation [*Chemical engineering*]
PSSAANDPS ... Permanent Secretariat of the South American Agreement on Narcotic Drugs and Psychotropic Substances (EAIO)
PSSAB....... Physica Status Solidi. Sectio A. Applied Research [*A publication*]
PSSB.......... Palm Springs Savings Bank [*Palm Springs, CA*] [*NASDAQ symbol*] (NQ)
PSSB.......... Passing Stopped School Bus [*Traffic offense charge*]
PSSBB....... Public School System Blanket Bond [*Insurance*]
PSSC......... Parachute Subsystem Sequence Controller [*NASA*] (SAA)
PSSC......... Personal Social Services Council [*British*] (DI)
PSSC......... Petroleum Security Subcommittee [*of Foreign Petroleum Supply Committee*] [*Terminated, 1976*] (EGAO)

PSSC......... Physical Science Study Committee [*National Science Foundation*]
PSSC......... Pious Society of Missionaries of St. Charles [*Later, CS*] [*Roman Catholic men's religious order*]
PSSC......... Public Service Satellite Consortium   (EA)
PSSCC..... Peter Symonds School Cadet Corps [*British military*]   (DMA)
PSSD........ Parallel-Serial Scan Design [*Electronics*]
PSSEAS .... Papers in International Studies. Southeast Asia Series. Ohio University [*A publication*]
PSSEP...... Preliminary System Safety Engineering Plan
PSSF......... Petites Soeurs de la Sainte-Famille [*Little Sisters of the Holy Family*] [*Sherbrooke, PQ*]   (EAIO)
PSSFB....... Progress in Surface Science [*A publication*]
PSSG .... Physical Science Study Group
PSSGL....... Penn State Series in German Literature [*A publication*]
PSSHR ...... Philippine Social Sciences and Humanities Review [*A publication*]
PSS-I .... Peace Science Society (International)   (EA)
PSSI.......... Primary Specialty Skill Identifier [*Military*]   (AABC)
PSSIIS....... Partito Socialista: Sezione Italiana del Internazionale Socialista [*Socialist Party: Italian Section of International Socialism*] [*Political party*]   (PPE)
PSS(Int)..... Peace Science Society (International)
PSSJ .... International Social Science Journal [*A publication*]
PSSK .... Probability of Single Shot Kill [*Of a guided missile*]
PSSL.......... Princeton University Solid State and Materials Laboratory [*New Jersey*]
PSSM .... Preliminary Science Meeting [*NASA*]
PSSMA ..... Paper Shipping Sack Manufacturers Association   (EA)
PSSMDE... Proceedings. Symposium of the Society for the Study of Inborn Errors of Metabolism [*A publication*]
PSSMLF ... Provincial Society of Spanish and Moroccan Leather Finishers [*A union*] [*British*]
PSSO .... Pass Slip Stitch Over [*Knitting*]
PsSol.......... Psalms of Solomon [*Pseudepigrapha*]   (BJA)
PSSP.......... Payload Specialist Station Panel [*NASA*]   (MCD)
PSSP.......... Phone Center Staffing and Sizing Program [*Telecommunications*]   (TEL)
PSSP.......... Price/Stern/Sloan, Inc. [*Formerly, Price/Stern/Sloan Publishers, Inc.*] [*NASDAQ symbol*]   (NQ)
PSSR .... Parallel-Shaft Speed Reducer
PSSR .... Philippine Social Science Review [*A publication*]
PSSR .... Problem Status and Summary Report [*NASA*]   (KSC)
PSSR .... Provisioning Supply Support Requests [*DoD*]
PSSR .... Social Science Research [*A publication*]
PSSRA....... Public Service Staff Relations Act [*Canada*]
PSSRB ...... Public Service Staff Relations Board [*Canada*]
PSSS......... Philosophic Society for the Study of Sport   (EA)
PSSS.......... Proceedings. Shevchenko Scientific Society. Philological Section [*A publication*]
PSSSP .... Proceedings. Shevchenko Scientific Society. Philological Section [*A publication*]
PSST.......... Periodic Significant Scheduled Tasks [*NASA*]   (NASA)
PSSTA....... Port Security Station [*Coast Guard*]
PSSTA....... Progress in Solid State Chemistry [*A publication*]
PSSU .... Patch Survey and Switching Unit   (MCD)
PSSUE5..... Psychopharmacology. Supplementum [*A publication*]
PSSV .... Social Service Review [*A publication*]
PST........... Pacific Standard Time
PST........... Pacific Summer Time
PST........... Pair Selected Ternary [*Data processing*]
PST........... Pancreatic Suppression Test [*Medicine*]   (AAMN)
PST........... Partido Socialista de los Trabajadores [*Socialist Workers Party*] [*Panama*] [*Political party*]   (EY)
PST........... Partido Socialista de los Trabajadores [*Socialist Workers' Party*] [*Colombia*] [*Political party*]   (PPW)
PST........... Partido Socialista de los Trabajadores [*Socialist Workers' Party*] [*Mexico*] [*Political party*]   (PPW)
PST........... Pass Time [*Military*]
PST........... Paste
PST........... Pastry   (MSA)
PST........... Pasture Canyon [*Utah*] [*Seismograph station code, US Geological Survey*] [*Closed*]   (SEIS)
PS & T .... Pay, Subsistence, and Transportation [*Military*]
PST........... Penicillin, Streptomycin, and Tetracycline [*Antibiotics*]   (MAE)
PSt .... Pennsylvania State University, University Park, PA [*Library symbol*] [*Library of Congress*]   (LCLS)
PST........... Performance Specification Tree
PST........... Periodic Self-Test [*Data processing*]
PST........... Peristimulus Time [*Neurophysiology*]
PST........... Personnel Subsystem Team [*Military*]   (AFIT)
PST........... Peseta [*Monetary unit*] [*Spain and Latin America*]
PST........... Petrie Stores Corp. [*NYSE symbol*]   (SPSG)
PST........... Phase Space Theory [*Physical chemistry*]
PST........... Phenol Sulfotransferase [*An enzyme*]
PST........... Philadelphia Suburban Transportation [*AAR code*]
PST........... Philological Society. Transactions [*A publication*]
PST........... Piston Shock Tunnel
PST........... Planetary Spectroscopy Telescope   (SSD)
PST........... Point of Spiral Tangent   (KSC)
PST........... Polaris Star Tracker [*Missiles*]

PST........... Policy Studies Journal. Policy Studies Institute [*London*] [*A publication*]
PST........... Polished Surface Technique   (IEEE)
PST........... Pontifical Institute of Mediaeval Studies. Studies and Texts [*A publication*]
PST........... Porcine Somatotropin [*Gene-spliced animal hormone*] [*Monsanto Co.*]
PST........... Post-Stimulus Time
PST........... Pressure-Sensitive Tape
PST........... Primary Surge Tank [*Nuclear energy*]   (NRCH)
PST........... Prior Service Training [*US Army Reserve*]   (INF)
PST........... Priority Selection Table [*Data processing*]   (IBMDP)
PST........... Product Support Technician
PST........... Production Special Tooling   (MCD)
PST........... Production Surveillance Test   (MCD)
PST........... Professional, Scientific, and Technical
PST........... Profit Sharing Trustee   (DLA)
PST........... Program Synchronization Table   (CMD)
PST........... Project ST [*Later, NSTA*]   (EA)
PST........... Propeller STOL [*Short Takeoff and Landing*] Transport
PSt............ Prose Studies [*A publication*]
PST........... Shepard's Preparing for Settlement and Trial [*A publication*]
3PST......... Triple-Pole, Single-Throw [*Switch*]   (MUGU)
4PST......... Four-Pole, Single-Throw [*Switch*]
PSTA .... Packaging Science and Technology Abstracts [*International Food Information Service*] [*Germany*] [*Information service or system*]
PSTA .... Partido Socialista Tito Atahuichi [*Bolivia*] [*Political party*]   (PPW)
PSt-A .... Pennsylvania State University, Agricultural Library, University Park, PA [*Library symbol*] [*Library of Congress*]   (LCLS)
PSta .... Philippine Statistician [*A publication*]
PSTA .... Pre-Sea Trial Audit   (MCD)
PSt-All....... Pennsylvania State University, Allentown Campus, Allentown, PA [*Library symbol*] [*Library of Congress*]   (LCLS)
PSt-Alt....... Pennsylvania State University, Altoona Campus, Altoona, PA [*Library symbol*] [*Library of Congress*]   (LCLS)
PSTAU ..... Pastabilities Food Uts [*NASDAQ symbol*]   (NQ)
PSt-B .... Pennsylvania State University, Berks Campus, Wyomissing, PA [*Library symbol*] [*Library of Congress*]   (LCLS)
PSTB .... Picture Story Test Blank [*Psychology*]
PSTB .... Propulsion System Test Bed [*for ABC helicopters*]   (RDA)
PSTB .... Puget Sound Tug & Barge [*AAR code*]
PSt-Be....... Pennsylvania State University, Beaver Campus, Monaca, PA [*Library symbol*] [*Library of Congress*]   (LCLS)
PS & TC..... Population Studies and Training Center [*Brown University*] [*Research center*]   (RCD)
PSTC .... Pressure Sensitive Tape Council   (EA)
PSTC .... Product Support Task Control   (AAG)
PSTC .... Public Switched Telephone Circuits [*Telecommunications*]   (TEL)
PStcA........ American Philatelic Research Library, State College, PA [*Library symbol*] [*Library of Congress*]   (LCLS)
PSt-Ca ...... Pennsylvania State University, Capitol Campus, Middletown, PA [*Library symbol*] [*Library of Congress*]   (LCLS)
PSTCA ...... Public Services Temporary Clerks' Association [*A union*] [*British*]
PStcH .... HRB-Singer, Inc., Science Park, State College, PA [*Library symbol*] [*Library of Congress*]   (LCLS)
PSTCO ...... Per Steering Compass [*Navigation*]   (DNAB)
PSt-D......... Pennsylvania State University, DuBois Campus, DuBois, PA [*Library symbol*] [*Library of Congress*]   (LCLS)
PSTD .... Potato Spindle Tuber Disease
PSTD .... Promotable Second-Tier Debt [*Economics*]
PstdE .... Eastern College, St. Davids, PA [*Library symbol*] [*Library of Congress*]   (LCLS)
PSt-De .... Pennsylvania State University, Delaware Campus, Chester, PA [*Library symbol*] [*Library of Congress*]   (LCLS)
PSt-E .... Pennsylvania State University, Behrend Campus, Erie, PA [*Library symbol*] [*Library of Congress*]   (LCLS)
PSTE .... Personnel Subsystem Test and Evaluation [*Military*]
PST-E........ Priority Selection Table Extension [*Data processing*]   (IBMDP)
PSTE .... Production Special Testing Equipment   (MCD)
PSTEP....... Pre-Service Teacher Education Program [*National Science Foundation*]
PSTF......... Payload Spin Test Facility   (MCD)
PSt-F......... Pennsylvania State University, Fayette Campus, Uniontown, PA [*Library symbol*] [*Library of Congress*]   (LCLS)
PSTF......... Pioneer Station Training Facility [*NASA*]
PSTF......... Pressure Suppression Test Facility [*Nuclear energy*]   (IEEE)
PSTF......... Privately-Owned Sewage Treatment Facility
PSTF......... Profit Sharing Trust Fund
PSTF......... Proximity Sensor Test Facility [*Nuclear energy*]   (NRCH)
PSTF......... Pump Seal Test Facility [*Nuclear energy*]   (NRCH)
PSTG .... Postage   (WGA)
PSTGC ...... Per Steering Compass [*Navigation*]
PSt-H......... Pennsylvania State University, Hazelton Campus, Hazelton, PA [*Library symbol*] [*Library of Congress*]   (LCLS)
PSTH........ Peristimulus Time Histogram
PSTH........ Posthumously
PSTH......... Poststimulus Time Histogram [*Medical statistics*]

PSTH......... Professional Sports Teams Histories [*A publication*]
PSTI .... Pancreatic Secretory Trypsin Inhibitor [*Biochemistry*]
PSTIAC..... Pavements and Soil Trafficability Information Analysis Center [*Army Corps of Engineers*] (IID)
PSt-KP....... Pennsylvania State University, King of Prussia Graduate Center, King of Prussia, PA [*Library symbol*] [*Library of Congress*] (LCLS)
PSTL .... Pastoral
PSTL .... Pistol (MSA)
PSTL .... Postal (AFM)
PSTL .... Pressure Model Static and Transient Launch Configuration (SAA)
PSTM .... Persistent Standoff Target Marker (MCD)
PSTM .... Photon Scanning Tunnelling Microscope
PSTMA..... Paper Stationery and Tablet Manufacturers Association [*Later, PCA*] (EA)
PSt-MA ..... Pennsylvania State University, Mont Alto Campus, Mont Alto, PA [*Library symbol*] [*Library of Congress*] (LCLS)
PSt-McK.... Pennsylvania State University, McKeesport Campus, McKeesport, PA [*Library symbol*] [*Library of Congress*] (LCLS)
PS & TN ... Pay, Subsistence, and Transportation, Navy
PSTN......... Piston (MSA)
PSTN......... Public Switched Telephone Network
PSt-NK...... Pennsylvania State University, New Kensington Campus, New Kensington, PA [*Library symbol*] [*Library of Congress*] (LCLS)
PSt-O......... Pennsylvania State University, Ogontz Campus, Abington, PA [*Library symbol*] [*Library of Congress*] (LCLS)
PSTO......... Principal Sea Transport Officer
PSTO......... Purdue Student-Teacher Opinionaire [*Test*]
PSTOA...... Psychology Today [*A publication*]
PSTP .... Social Theory and Practice [*A publication*]
PSt-PiN ..... Pennsylvania State University, School of Nursing, Allegheny General Hospital, Pittsburgh, PA [*Library symbol*] [*Library of Congress*] (LCLS)
PSTR .... Pacesetter Corp. [*NASDAQ symbol*] (NQ)
PSTR .... Penn State TRIGA [*Training Reactor, Isotopes General Atomic*] Reactor
P/STRG..... Power Steering [*Automotive engineering*]
PSTS......... Passive SONAR Tracking System
PSt-S......... Pennsylvania State University, Scranton Campus, Scranton, PA [*Library symbol*] [*Library of Congress*] (LCLS)
PSt-Sk .... Pennsylvania State University, Schuylkill Campus, Schuylkill Haven, PA [*Library symbol*] [*Library of Congress*] (LCLS)
PSt-SV ...... Pennsylvania State University, Shenango Valley Campus, Sharon, PA [*Library symbol*] [*Library of Congress*] (LCLS)
PStu .... Philippine Studies [*A publication*]
PSTV .... Potato Spindle Tuber Virus
PSTV .... Private Screening, Inc. [*NASDAQ symbol*] (NQ)
PSTVd .... Potato Spindle Tuber Viroid [*Plant pathology*]
PSt-WB ..... Pennsylvania State University, Wilkes-Barre Campus, Wilkes-Barre, PA [*Library symbol*] [*Library of Congress*] (LCLS)
PSt-WS...... Pennsylvania State University, Worthington Scranton Campus, Dunmore, PA [*Library symbol*] [*Library of Congress*] (LCLS)
PSt-Y .... Pennsylvania State University, York Campus, York, PA [*Library symbol*] [*Library of Congress*] (LCLS)
PSTY .... Style [*A publication*]
PSTYY ...... President Steyn Gold Mining ADR [*NASDAQ symbol*] (NQ)
PSTZG ...... Pasteurizing [*Freight*]
PSu............ John R. Kaufman, Jr., [*Sunbury*] Public Library, Sunbury, PA [*Library symbol*] [*Library of Congress*] (LCLS)
PSU........... Package Size Unspecified
PSU........... Packet Switching Unit
PSU........... Parti Socialiste Unifie [*Unified Socialist Party*] [*France*] [*Political party*] (PPW)
PSU........... Partido Socialista Unificado [*Socialist Unification Party*] [*Argentina*] [*Political party*] (PPW)
PSU........... Partido Socialista Uruguayo [*Uruguayan Socialist Party*] [*Political party*] (PD)
PSU........... Partidul Socialist Unitar [*Unitary Socialist Party*] [*Romania*] [*Political party*] (PPE)
PSU........... Partito Socialista Unificato [*Unified Socialist Party*] [*Italy*] [*Political party*] (PPE)
PSU........... Partito Socialista Unitario [*Socialist Unity Party*] [*Italy*] [*Political party*] (PPE)
PSU........... Path Setup [*Telecommunications*] (TEL)
PSU........... Pennsylvania State University
PSU........... Pet Services, Unlimited [*Commercial firm*] (EA)
PSU........... Philatelic Sales Unit
PSU........... Photosynthetic Unit
PSU........... Plasma Spray Unit
PSU........... Polyphenylene Sulfone [*Organic chemistry*]
PSU........... Port Storage Utility [*Telecommunications*] (TEL)
PSU........... Portland State University
PSU........... Power Supply Unit (MSA)
PSU........... Power Switching Unit (MCD)
PSU........... Pressure Status Unit (AAG)

PSU........... Primary Sampling Unit [*Statistics*]
PSU........... Probability Sampling Unit (WDMC)
PSU........... Processor Speed Up [*Computer memory core*]
PSU........... Program Storage Unit [*Data processing*] (MDG)
PSU........... Public Storage Properties XVI [*AMEX symbol*] (SPSG)
PSU........... Tatoo-a-Pet [*Commercial firm*] (EA)
PSU-ADA ... Pennsylvania State University-Abstracts of Doctoral Dissertations [*A publication*]
PSUB......... Piston-Supported Upper Bearing
PSUC........ Partit Socialista Unificat de Catalunya [*Unified Socialist Party of Catalonia*] [*Spain*] [*Political party*] (PPE)
PSUI......... Suicide and Life-Threatening Behavior [*A publication*]
PSU/IRL... Pennsylvania State University Ionosphere Research Laboratory
PSULI .... Partito Socialista Unitario de Lavoratori Italiani [*Unitary Socialist Party of Italian Workers*] [*Political party*] (PPE)
PSUN .... Piper Hydro, Inc. [*NASDAQ symbol*] (NQ)
PSUPB ...... Pribory i Sistemy Upravleniya [*A publication*]
PSuQ........ Philologische Studien und Quellen [*A publication*]
PSUR........ Pennsylvania State University Reactor
PSURA ..... Progress in Surgery [*A publication*]
PSURAO.... Pennsylvania State University Radio Astronomy Observatory
PSurg .... Plastic Surgery [*Medicine*]
PSUSAM .. Philippine Statehood USA Movement [*An association*] (EA)
PSV........... Peanut Stunt Virus
PSV........... Photographic-Spatial Volume (SAA)
PSV........... Pictorial Study of Values [*Psychology*]
PSV........... Planetary Space Vehicle [*NASA*] (NASA)
PSV........... Portable Sensor Verifier (AAG)
PSV........... Positive Start Voltage
PSV........... Preserve (MSA)
PSV........... Probability State Variable [*Statistics*]
PSV........... Progressive Surinaamse Volkspartij [*Progressive Suriname People's Party*] [*Political party*] (PPW)
PSV........... Psychological, Social, and Vocational [*Adjustment factors*]
PSV........... Public Service Vehicle
PSV........... Public Storage Properties XVII [*AMEX symbol*] (SPSG)
PSV........... Saint Vincent College, Latrobe, PA [*OCLC symbol*] (OCLC)
PSVB .... Penn Savings Bank FSB [*Wyomissing, PA*] [*NASDAQ symbol*] (NQ)
PSvcBad.... Presidential Service Badge [*Military decoration*] (AABC)
PSvCol ...... Public Service Co. of Colorado [*Associated Press abbreviation*] (APAG)
PSVD........ Polystyrene-Divinylbenzene Copolymer [*Organic chemistry*]
PSVM .... Phase-Sensitive Voltmeter
PSvNM...... Public Service Co. of New Mexico [*Associated Press abbreviation*] (APAG)
PSVOA ..... Purse Seine Vessel Owners Association (EA)
PSVOMA ... Purse Seine Vessel Owners Marketing Association [*Later, PSVOA*] (EA)
PSVP .... Pilot Secure Voice Project [*NATO Integrated Communications System*] (NATG)
PSVS .... Soviet Studies [*A publication*]
PSVT .... Paroxysmal Supraventricular Tachycardia [*Cardiology*]
PSVT .... Passivate [*Metallurgy*]
PSVTN ...... Preservation (MSA)
PSVTV ...... Preservative (MSA)
PS & W ...... Pacific, Southern & Western Railroad [*Nickname: Play Safe and Walk*]
PSW........... Pacific Southwest Forest and Range Experiment Station [*Berkeley, CA*] [*Department of Agriculture*] (GRD)
PSW........... Pinetree Software Canada Ltd. [*Vancouver Stock Exchange symbol*]
PSW........... Plasma Spray Welder
PSW........... Politically Simulated World [*Computer-assisted political science game*]
PSW........... Potential Switch
PSW........... Potentiometer Slidewire
PSW........... Powerplant Specific Weight
PSW........... Primary Shield Water (DNAB)
PSW........... Processor Status Word
PSW........... Program Status Word [*Data processing*]
PSW........... Psychiatric Social Worker [*British*]
PSW........... Public Storage Properties XVIII [*AMEX symbol*] (SPSG)
4PSW........ Four-Pole Switch
PSWA........ Pacific Southwest Airlines [*San Diego, CA*] [*NASDAQ symbol*] (NQ)
PSWA .... Partially Smooth Water Area (DS)
PSWAD.... Perspective Study of World Agricultural Development [*FAO*] [*United Nations*] (MSC)
PSWB .... Public School Word-Book [*A publication*]
PSWBD..... Power Switchboard
PSWBS..... Project Summary Work Breakdown Structure
PSWEA ..... Proceedings. South Wales Institute of Engineers [*A publication*]
PSWFRES ... Pacific Southwest Forest and Range Experiment Station [*Berkeley, CA*] (SAA)
PSWG........ Pressure Sine Wave Generator
PSWMOW ... Psychiatric Social Work in Mental Observation Wards [*British*]
PSWO....... Picture and Sound World Organization
PSWO........ Princess of Wales' Own [*Military unit*] [*British*] (ROG)
PSWO........ Product Support Work Order

PSWOPC .. Psychiatric Social Work in Out-Patient Clinics [*British*]
PSWP .... Plant Service Water Pump   (IEEE)
PSWR .... Powell Sport Wagon Registry   (EA)
PSWR .... Power Standing Wave Ratio
PSWS .... Potable and Sanitary Water System [*Nuclear energy*]   (NRCH)
PSwS .... Smith, Kline & French Co. [*Later, SmithKline Corp.*], Swedeland, PA [*Library symbol*] [*Library of Congress*]   (LCLS)
PSWT .... Polysonic Wind Tunnel   (MCD)
PSWT .... Psychiatric Social Work Training [*British*]
PSWTUF... Public Service Workers' Trade Union Federation [*Ceylon*]
PSWV .... Southwest Review [*A publication*]
PSWYA ..... Psychologia Wychowawcza [*A publication*]
PSX .... Pacific Scientific Co. [*NYSE symbol*]   (SPSG)
PSX .... Palacios, TX [*Location identifier*] [*FAA*]   (FAAL)
PSXJ .... Sixteenth Century Journal [*A publication*]
PSY .... Persky Air Service [*Valdosta, GA*] [*FAA designator*]   (FAAC)
PSY .... Pillsbury Co. [*NYSE symbol*]   (SPSG)
PSY .... Port Stanley [*Falkland Islands*] [*Airport symbol*]
PSY .... PSM Technologies, Inc. [*Vancouver Stock Exchange symbol*]
PSY .... Psychiatry
PSY .... Psychological   (CINC)
PsyAb .... Psychological Abstracts [*A publication*]
Psy B .... Psychological Bulletin [*A publication*]
PSYBB...... Psychopharmacology Bulletin [*A publication*]
PSYC .... Psych Systems, Inc. [*NASDAQ symbol*]   (NQ)
PSYC .... Psychology
PSYCA ..... Psychiatry [*A publication*]
PSYCD ...... Psychendocrinology [*A publication*]
PSYCH ..... Psychiatrist   (DSUE)
PSYCH ..... Psychiatry
PSYCH ..... Psychic   (ROG)
PSYCH ..... Psychology   (AFM)
Psych Bull ... Psychological Bulletin [*A publication*]
Psych Depend Bayer Symp ... Psychic Dependence. Definition, Assessment in Animals and Man. Theoretical and Clinical Implications. Bayer-Symposium [*A publication*]
Psychedelic Rev ... Psychedelic Review [*A publication*]
PSYCHEM ... Psychiatric Chemistry
Psychiat ..... Psychiatry [*A publication*]
Psychiat Cl ... Psychiatria Clinica [*A publication*]
Psychiat Digest ... Psychiatry Digest [*A publication*]
Psychiat Fo ... Psychiatric Forum [*A publication*]
Psychiat Me ... Psychiatry in Medicine [*A publication*]
Psychiat Opin ... Psychiatric Opinion [*A publication*]
Psychiat Q ... Psychiatric Quarterly [*A publication*]
Psychiatr Ann ... Psychiatric Annals [*A publication*]
Psychiatr Annals ... Psychiatric Annals [*A publication*]
Psychiatr Clin ... Psychiatria Clinica [*A publication*]
Psychiatr Clin (Basel) ... Psychiatria Clinica (Basel) [*A publication*]
Psychiatr Commun ... Psychiatric Communications [*A publication*]
Psychiatr Dev ... Psychiatric Developments [*A publication*]
Psychiatr Enfant ... Psychiatrie de l'Enfant [*A publication*]
Psychiatr Fenn ... Psychiatria Fennica [*A publication*]
Psychiatr Fenn Monogr ... Psychiatria Fennica. Monografiasarja [*A publication*]
Psychiatr Forum ... Psychiatric Forum [*A publication*]
Psychiatr Hosp ... Psychiatric Hospital [*A publication*]
Psychiatr J Univ Ottawa ... Psychiatric Journal. University of Ottawa [*A publication*]
Psychiatr Med ... Psychiatric Medicine [*A publication*]
Psychiatr Neurol ... Psychiatria et Neurologia [*A publication*]
Psychiatr Neurol Jpn ... Psychiatria et Neurologia Japonica [*A publication*]
Psychiatr Neurol Med Psychol ... Psychiatrie, Neurologie, und Medizinische Psychologie [*A publication*]
Psychiatr Neurol Med Psychol (Leipz) ... Psychiatrie, Neurologie, und Medizinische Psychologie (Leipzig) [*A publication*]
Psychiatr Neurol Neurochir ... Psychiatria, Neurologia, Neurochirurgia [*A publication*]
Psychiatr Neurol Wochenschr ... Psychiatrisch Neurologische Wochenschrift [*A publication*]
Psychiatr News ... Psychiatric News [*A publication*]
Psychiatr Nurs Forum ... Psychiatric Nursing Forum [*A publication*]
Psychiatr Opinion ... Psychiatric Opinion [*A publication*]
Psychiatr Pol ... Psychiatria Polska [*A publication*]
Psychiatr Prax ... Psychiatrische Praxis [*A publication*]
Psychiatr Q ... Psychiatric Quarterly [*A publication*]
Psychiatr Q (NY) ... Psychiatric Quarterly (New York) [*A publication*]
Psychiatr Q Suppl ... Psychiatric Quarterly. Supplement [*A publication*]
Psychiatr Res Rep ... Psychiatric Research Reports [*A publication*]
Psychiatr Res Rep Am Psychiatr Assoc ... Psychiatric Research Reports. American Psychiatric Association [*A publication*]
Psychiatr Soc ... Psychiatrie Sociale [*A publication*]
Psychiatry Dig ... Psychiatry Digest [*A publication*]
Psychiatry Med ... Psychiatry in Medicine [*A publication*]
Psychiatry Res ... Psychiatry Research [*A publication*]
Psychiatry Ser (Berlin) ... Psychiatry Series (Berlin) [*A publication*]
Psychic R ... Psychical Review [*A publication*]
PSYCHL ... Psychological   (AFM)
Psych & MLJ ... Psychological and Medico-Legal Journal [*A publication*]   (DLA)

Psych of Music ... Psychology of Music [*A publication*]
PSYCHO... Psychoanalysis   (DSUE)
Psychoanal Contemp Sci ... Psychoanalysis and Contemporary Science [*A publication*]
Psychoanal Contemp Thought ... Psychoanalysis and Contemporary Thought [*A publication*]
Psychoanal Q ... Psychoanalytic Quarterly [*A publication*]
Psychoanal R ... Psychoanalytic Review [*A publication*]
Psychoanal Rev ... Psychoanalytic Review [*A publication*]
Psychoanal Stud Child ... Psychoanalytic Study of the Child [*A publication*]
Psychoanal Study Child ... Psychoanalytic Study of the Child [*A publication*]
Psychoanal Study Child Monogr Ser ... Psychoanalytic Study of the Child. Monograph Series [*A publication*]
Psychoan Q ... Psychoanalytic Quarterly [*A publication*]
Psychoan Re ... Psychoanalytic Review [*A publication*]
Psychobiol Psychopathol ... Psychobiology and Psychopathology [*A publication*]
Psychocultural R ... Psychocultural Review [*A publication*]
Psychohist Rev ... Psychohistory Review [*A publication*]
PSYCHOL ... Psychology
Psychol Abstr ... Psychological Abstracts [*A publication*]
Psychol Absts ... Psychological Abstracts [*A publication*]
Psychol Afr ... Psychologia Africana [*A publication*]
Psychol Africana ... Psychologia Africana [*A publication*]
Psychol Afr Monogr Suppl ... Psychologie Africana. Monograph and Supplement [*A publication*]
Psychol B ... Psychological Bulletin [*A publication*]
Psychol Be ... Psychologische Beitraege [*A publication*]
Psychol Beitr ... Psychologische Beitraege [*A publication*]
Psychol Bel ... Psychologica Belgica [*A publication*]
Psychol Belg ... Psychologica Belgica [*A publication*]
Psychol Bul ... Psychological Bulletin [*A publication*]
Psychol Bull ... Psychological Bulletin [*A publication*]
Psychol Can ... Psychologie Canadienne [*A publication*]
Psychol Clinic ... Psychological Clinic [*A publication*]
Psychol Erz ... Psychologie in Erziehung und Unterricht [*A publication*]
Psychol Forsch ... Psychologische Forschung [*A publication*]
Psychol Fr ... Psychologie Francaise [*A publication*]
Psychol Iss ... Psychological Issues [*A publication*]
Psychol Issues ... Psychological Issues [*A publication*]
Psychol Issues Monogr ... Psychological Issues. Monographs [*A publication*]
Psychol Learn & Motiv ... Psychology of Learning and Motivation [*A publication*]
Psychol Med ... Psychological Medicine [*A publication*]
Psychol Med ... Psychologie Medicale [*A publication*]
Psychol Med Monogr Suppl ... Psychological Medicine. Monograph Supplement [*A publication*]
Psychol Monogr Gen Appl ... Psychological Monographs. General and Applied [*A publication*]
Psychology M ... Psychology of Music [*A publication*]
Psychol Prax ... Psychologische Praxis [*A publication*]
Psychol R ... Psychological Review [*A publication*]
Psychol Read Guide ... Psychological Reader's Guide [*A publication*]
Psychol Rec ... Psychological Record [*A publication*]
Psychol Rep ... Psychological Reports [*A publication*]
Psychol Res ... Psychological Research [*A publication*]
Psychol Rev ... Psychological Review [*A publication*]
Psychol Rundsch ... Psychologische Rundschau [*A publication*]
Psychol Sch ... Psychology in the Schools [*A publication*]
Psychol in the Schs ... Psychology in the Schools [*A publication*]
Psychol Stu ... Psychological Studies [*A publication*]
Psychol Tod ... Psychology Today [*A publication*]
Psychol Today ... Psychology Today [*A publication*]
Psychol Women Q ... Psychology of Women Quarterly [*A publication*]
Psychometri ... Psychometrika [*A publication*]
Psychometrika Monogr Suppl ... Psychometrika. Monograph Supplement [*A publication*]
Psycho Mycol Stud ... Psycho-Mycological Studies [*A publication*]
Psychon Sci ... Psychonomic Science [*A publication*]
Psychon Sci Sect Anim Physiol Psychol ... Psychonomic Science. Section on Animal and Physiological Psychology [*A publication*]
Psychon Sci Sect Hum Exp Psychol ... Psychonomic Science. Section on Human Experimental Psychology [*A publication*]
Psychop Afr ... Psychopathologie Africaine [*A publication*]
Psychopathol Afr ... Psychopathologie Africaine [*A publication*]
Psychopathol Expression Suppl Encephale ... Psychopathologie de l'Expression. Supplement de l'Encephale [*A publication*]
Psychopathol Pict Expression ... Psychopathology and Pictorial Expression [*A publication*]
Psychopharm ... Psychopharmacologia [*A publication*]
Psychopharmacol Abstr ... Psychopharmacology Abstracts [*A publication*]
Psychopharmacol Bull ... Psychopharmacology Bulletin [*A publication*]
Psychopharmacol Commun ... Psychopharmacology Communications [*A publication*]
Psychopharmacol Front Proc Psychopharmacol Symp ... Psychopharmacology Frontiers. Proceedings. Psychopharmacology Symposium [*A publication*]
Psychopharmacology Suppl ... Psychopharmacology. Supplementum [*A publication*]
Psychopharmacol Ser ... Psychopharmacology Series [*A publication*]

Psychopharmacol Ser (Dekker) ... Psychopharmacology Series (Dekker) [*A publication*]
Psychopharmacol Serv Cent Bull ... Psychopharmacology Service Center. Bulletin [*A publication*]
Psychopharmacol Suppl ... Psychopharmacology. Supplementum [*A publication*]
Psychopharmacol Suppl Encephale ... Psychopharmacologie. Supplement de l'Encephale [*A publication*]
Psychoph C ... Psychopharmacology Communications [*A publication*]
Psychophysl ... Psychophysiology [*A publication*]
Psychos Med ... Psychosomatic Medicine [*A publication*]
Psychosocial Rehabil J ... Psychosocial Rehabilitation Journal [*A publication*]
Psychosoc Proc Iss Child Ment Health ... Psychosocial Process. Issues in Child Mental Health [*A publication*]
Psychosoc Rehabil J ... Psychosocial Rehabilitation Journal [*A publication*]
Psychosomat ... Psychosomatics [*A publication*]
Psychosom Med ... Psychosomatic Medicine [*A publication*]
Psychotherapy (NY) ... Psychotherapy (New York) [*A publication*]
Psychother Med Psychol ... Psychotherapie und Medizinische Psychologie [*A publication*]
Psychother Patient ... Psychotherapy Patient [*A publication*]
Psychother Psychosom ... Psychotherapy and Psychosomatics [*A publication*]
Psychother Psychosom Med Psychol ... Psychotherapie, Psychosomatik, Medizinische Psychologie [*A publication*]
Psychother Theory Res Pract ... Psychotherapy: Theory, Research, and Practice [*A publication*]
Psychoth MP ... Psychotherapie und Medizinische Psychologie [*A publication*]
Psychoth Ps ... Psychotherapy and Psychosomatics [*A publication*]
Psychoth/TR ... Psychotherapy: Theory, Research, and Practice [*A publication*]
Psych Prax ... Psychologische Praxis [*A publication*]
Psych Soc... Psychology and Social Theory [*A publication*]
Psych Stud ... Psychological Studies [*Mysore*] [*A publication*]
Psych Teaching ... Psychology Teaching [*A publication*]
Psych Today ... Psychology Today [*A publication*]
PsycINFO ... Psychological Abstracts Information Services [*American Psychological Association*] (IID)
PSYCTRC ... Psychiatric
PSYCTRY ... Psychiatry
Psycul R..... Psychocultural Review [*A publication*]
PsyD ... Doctor of Psychology
PsyETA ..... Psychologists for the Ethical Treatment of Animals (EA)
PSYM....... Symposium [*A publication*]
PSYOP...... Psychological Operation [*Military*]
PSY-OPS.. Psychological Warfare Operations (DNAB)
Psy R......... Proceedings. Society for Psychical Research [*A publication*]
PsyR.......... Psychoanalytic Review [*A publication*]
PSYR........ Psychological Record [*A publication*]
Psy Rund... Psychologische Rundschau [*A publication*]
PSYS.......... Programming and Systems, Inc. [*NASDAQ symbol*] (NQ)
PsyS.......... Psychonomic Science [*A publication*]
PSYSA....... Psyche [*A publication*]
PSY-SDIV ... Psychological Sciences Division [*Office of Naval Research*] (DNAB)
PsySR .... Psychologists for Social Responsibility (EA)
P Sy St Carletn ... Proceedings. Symposium on Statistics and Related Topics. Carleton University [*A publication*]
Psy T......... Psychology Today [*A publication*]
PSYU........ Public Sustained Yield Unit [*Forestry*]
PSYWAR .. Psychological Warfare
PSYWPN .. Psychological Weapon [*Military*] (AFM)
PSZ........... Partially-Stabilized Zirconia [*Ceramics*]
PSZ........... Piszkesteto [*Hungary*] [*Seismograph station code, US Geological Survey*] (SEIS)
PSZ........... Pressure Sealing Zipper
PSZ........... Pro Air Services [*Miami, FL*] [*FAA designator*] (FAAC)
PSZ........... Public Storage Properties XX [*AMEX symbol*] (SPSG)
PSZ........... Puerto Suarez [*Bolivia*] [*Airport symbol*] (OAG)
PSzL .... Polska Sztuka Ludowa [*A publication*]
PSZN........ Pubblicazioni. Stazione Zoologica di Napoli [*A publication*]
PT .... Advanced Planning and Technology Office [*Kennedy Space Center Directorate*] (NASA)
PT .... Brazil [*Aircraft nationality and registration mark*] (FAAC)
PT .... Duffryn Yard [*Welsh depot code*]
PT .... Motor Torpedo Boat [*Navy symbol*] [*Obsolete*]
PT .... Pacific Time
PT .... Pain Threshold
PT .... Pallet Truck (DCTA)
P-T .... Palomero Toluqueno [*Race of maize*]
PT .... Pamietnik Teatralny [*A publication*]
PT .... Paper Tape
PT .... Paper Title [*Business term*]
PT .... Paper Trooper [*One who salvaged paper for war effort*] [*World War II*]
PT .... Para-Terphenyl [*Organic chemistry*]
PT .... Parathyroid [*Medicine*]
PT .... Parcel Ticket [*Freight*]
PT .... Paroxysmal Tachycardia [*Cardiology*]
PT .... Part [*Online database field identifier*]
pt................ Part [*of a deck*] (DS)

PT .... Part Throttle [*Engines*]
P-T .... Part-Time [*Employment*]
PT .... Part Total [*Earnings less than weekly benefit amount*] [*Unemployment insurance*] (OICC)
PT .... Participative Teams (MCD)
PT .... Partido Trabajador [*Mexico*] [*Political party*] (EY)
PT .... Partido de los Trabajadores [*Paraguay*] [*Political party*] (EY)
PT .... Paschale Tempore [*Easter Time*] [*Latin*]
PT .... Passenger Transport
PT .... Passing Title [*Real estate*]
PT .... Passive Track [*Military*] (CAAL)
PT .... Past Tense
PT .... Pataca [*Monetary unit*] [*Macau*]
PT .... Patellar Tendon [*Anatomy*]
PT .... Patient
PT .... Patrol Torpedo Boat [*Later, PTF*] [*Navy symbol*]
PT .... Pay Tone [*Telecommunications*] (TEL)
PT .... Paying Teller [*Banking*]
PT .... Payment
PT .... Pencil Tube
PT .... Penetrant Test [*Nuclear energy*] (NRCH)
PT .... Penetration Test (NATG)
PT .... Peninsula Terminal Co. [*AAR code*]
PT .... Pennant [*British naval signaling*]
PT .... Pension Trustee (DLA)
PT .... Per Truck
PT .... Perfect Title [*Business term*]
PT .... Performance Test
PT .... Periodic Test [*Nuclear energy*] (NRCH)
P & T .... Permanent and Total [*Disability*] [*Medicine*]
PT .... Persepolis Texts (BJA)
PT .... Persistent Tease [*Slang*] [*Bowdlerized version*]
P/T............. Personal Time [*Employment*]
PT .... Personal Trade [*In some retail establishments, customers are assigned to salesmen in rotation. A customer who is the "PT" or personal client of a salesman is not counted as part of the salesman's share of customers*]
PT .... Personal Transporter
P & T .... Personnel and Training [*Military*] (MUGU)
PT .... Perstetur [*Let It Be Continued*] [*Pharmacy*]
PT .... Perturbation Theory [*Physical chemistry*]
PT .... Pertussis Toxin [*Pharmacology*]
PT .... Peseta [*Monetary unit*] [*Spain and Latin America*]
PT .... Pet, Inc. [*NYSE symbol*] (SPSG)
Pt................ Peter [*New Testament book*]
PT .... Petrol Tractor [*British*]
PT .... Petroleum Times [*A publication*]
PT .... Petty Theft
P & T .... Pharmacy and Therapeutics
PT .... Pheasant Trust (EA)
PT .... Phoenix Theatre [*Defunct*] (EA)
PT .... Photoconductive Thermoplastic [*Materials science*]
PT .... Photographic Intelligenceman [*Navy rating*]
PT .... Phototherapy [*Medicine*]
PT .... Phototoxity [*Medicine*]
PT .... Phototransistor (NRCH)
PT .... Physical Teardown (MCD)
PT .... Physical Therapy [*or Therapist*]
PT .... Physical Training [*Military*]
PT .... Physiotherapy [*Medicine*]
PT .... Piaster [*Monetary unit*] [*Spain, Republic of Vietnam, and some Middle Eastern countries*] (IMH)
PT .... Pine Tar [*Medicine*]
PT .... Pint
PT .... Pipe Tap (MSA)
PT .... Pitch Trim (MCD)
PT .... Placebo Treated [*Medicine*]
PT .... Plain Talk (EA)
PT .... Plain Test (MCD)
PT .... Planning and Timing [*of Investments*]
P & T .... Plans and Training [*Military*] (IIA)
PT .... Planum Temporale [*Brain anatomy*]
P-T .... Plasma Thermocouple Reactor [*Nuclear energy*] (NRCH)
PT .... Plastic Tube
PT .... Plastics Technology [*A publication*]
Pt................ Platinum [*Chemical element*]
PT .... Platoon Truck [*British*]
PT .... Pleno Titulo [*With Full Title*] [*Latin*]
PT .... Plenty Tough [*Slang*]
PT .... Plenty Trouble [*Slang*]
PT .... Plonia Technica
PT .... Plot Titles [*Test*] [*Psychology*]
PT .... Plotting Equipment [*JETDS nomenclature*] [*Military*] (CET)
PT .... Pneumatic Tube [*Technical drawings*]
PT .... Pneumothorax [*Medicine*]
PT .... Poetry Treasury [*An association*] [*Inactive*] (EA)
PT .... Point
PT .... Point [*Maps and charts*]
PT .... Point of Tangency
PT .... Point of Turn [*Navigation*]
P/T............. Pointer/Tracker (MCD)

PT .... Polar Times [*A publication*]
PT .... Poll-Tax Rolls [*British*]
PT .... Pollen Tube [*Botany*]
PT .... Polythiophene [*Organic chemistry*]
PT .... Pool Temperature [*Nuclear energy*]   (NRCH)
PT .... Popliteal Tendon [*Anatomy*]
PT .... Port
PT .... Port Number [*Telecommunications*]   (TEL)
PT .... Port Talbot Railway [*Wales*]
PT .... Portal Tract [*Anatomy*]
PT .... Portugal [*ANSI two-letter standard code*]   (CNC)
pt .... Portuguese Timor [*io (Indonesia) used in records cataloged after January 1978*] [*MARC country of publication code*] [*Library of Congress*]   (LCCP)
PT .... Positional Tolerancing
PT .... Post Town
PT .... Postal Telegraph Co. [*Terminated*]
PT .... Poste e Telegrafi [*Post and Telegraph Service*] [*Italy*]
PT .... Posterior Tibial [*Anatomy*]
P & T .... Posts and Timbers [*Technical drawings*]
PT .... Potential Transformer
PT .... Power Transfer   (KSC)
PT .... Prachakorn Thai [*Thai Citizens Party*] [*Political party*]
PT .... Precision Teaching
PT .... Precision Time Fuze
PT .... Preferential Treatment   (OICC)
PT .... Prehistoric Thessaly [*A publication*]
PT .... Preoperational Test [*Nuclear energy*]   (NRCH)
PT .... Press Test [*Psychology*]
P/T............ Pressure/Temperature   (KSC)
PT .... Pressure Test   (AAG)
PT .... Pressure Time Fuel System [*Cummins Engine Co., Inc.*]
PT .... Pressure Transducer   (KSC)
PT .... Pressure Transmitter   (NRCH)
PT .... Pressure Tubing
PT .... Pretectal [*Neuroanatomy*]
pt .... Preterit [*Past tense*] [*Grammar*]
PT .... Previous Operating Time   (AFIT)
PT .... Primal Therapy
PT .... Primary Target [*Army*]
PT .... Primary Trainer [*Aircraft*]
PT .... Print   (MSA)
PT .... Printed Text
PT .... Printer Terminal
PT .... Prior Treatment [*Medicine*]
PT .... Priority Telegram
PT .... Private Terms
PT .... Pro Tempore [*For the Time Being*] [*Latin*]
PT .... Procedure Turn [*Aviation*]   (FAAC)
PT .... Processing Tax Division [*United States Internal Revenue Bureau*]   (DLA)
PT .... Processing Time
PT .... Production Techniques   (MCD)
PT .... Production Test [*Military*]
PT .... Productive Time [*Computer order entry*]
P & T .... Professional and Technology [*Category*] [*British*]
PT .... Proficiency Testing
PT .... Profile Template
PT .... Profit Taking [*Investment term*]
PT .... Program (Exercise) on Treadmill
PT .... Programmable Terminal [*Data processing*]
PT .... Programmer and Timer
PT .... Progress in Technology [*Automotive industry*]
PT .... Prohibited Telegrams
PT .... Project Tibet   (EA)
PT .... Project Transition [*DoD*]   (OICC)
PT .... Project Trust   (EAIO)
PT .... Prolong Tablets [*Pharmacy*]
PT .... Proof Test   (AAG)
PT .... Propellant Transfer
PT .... Propeller Torpedo [*Boat*]
PT .... Property Transfer [*Real estate*]   (KSC)
PT .... Prophet
PT .... Propylthiouracil [*Also, PROP, PTU*] [*Thyroid inhibitor*]
PT .... Prothrombin Time [*Hematology*]
PT .... Provascular Tissue [*Botany*]
PT .... Provincetown-Boston Airlines, Inc. and Naples Airlines, Inc. [*ICAO designator*]   (FAAC)
PT .... Provisioning Team   (AAG)
PT .... Przeglad Teologiczny [*A publication*]
Pt............... Pseudoword Target [*Psychology*]
PT .... Psychology Today [*A publication*]
Pt............... Pteropods [*Quality of the bottom*] [*Nautical charts*]
PT .... PTP Resource Corp. [*Formerly, Petrologic Petroleum Ltd.*] [*Vancouver Stock Exchange symbol*]
PT .... Public Trustee
PT .... Publication Type [*Online database field identifier*]
P & T .... Pugsley and Trueman's New Brunswick Reports [*A publication*]   (DLA)
PT .... Pull-Through [*Gun cleaning*]
PT .... Pulmonary Tuberculosis [*Medicine*]

PT .... Pulp Testing [*Dentistry*]
PT .... Pulse Timer
PT .... Pulse Train
PT .... Punched Tape [*Data processing*]
PT .... Pupil Teacher
PT .... Purchase Tax [*British*]
PT .... Pure Telepathy [*Psychical research*]
P & T .... Purge-and-Trap [*Technique*] [*Environmental Protection Agency*]
PT .... Pyramid Texts   (BJA)
PT .... Pyramidal Tract [*Anatomy*]
PT .... Pytannja Tekstolohiji [*A publication*]
PT .... Total Pressure
PT1 .... Photographic Intelligenceman, First Class [*Navy rating*]
PT2 .... Photographic Intelligenceman, Second Class [*Navy rating*]
PT3 .... Photographic Intelligenceman, Third Class [*Navy rating*]
PTA .... CareerCom Corp. [*NYSE symbol*]   (SPSG)
PTA .... Kunststofen Rubber [*A publication*]
PTA .... National Postal Transport Association [*Later, APWU*]
PTA .... Palatines to America   (EA)
PTA .... Pantorama Industries, Inc. [*Toronto Stock Exchange symbol*]
PTA .... Paper and Twine Association   (EA)
PTA .... Parallel Tubular Array [*Cytology*]
PTA .... Parent-Teacher Association
PTA .... Part Throttle Acceleration [*Engines*]   (EG)
PTA .... Passenger Transport Authorities [*British*]
PTA .... People Taking Action
PTA .... Percent Time Active   (CAAL)
PTA .... Percutaneous Transluminal Angioplasty [*Medicine*]
PTA .... Periodical Title Abbreviations [*A publication*]
PTA .... Persistent Truncus Arteriosus [*Medicine*]   (MAE)
PTA .... Personnel and Training Abstracts [*A publication*]
PTA .... Peseta [*Monetary unit*] [*Spain and Latin America*]
PTA .... Petaluma Aero, Inc. [*Petaluma, CA*] [*FAA designator*]   (FAAC)
PTA .... Phenyltrimethylammonium [*Also, PTM, PTMA*] [*Organic chemistry*]
PTA .... Phorbol Tetradecanoyl Acetate [*Also, PMA, TPA*] [*Organic chemistry*]
PTA .... Phosphoryl Triamide [*Organic chemistry*]
PTA .... Phosphotransacetylase [*An enzyme*]
PTA .... Phosphotungstic Acid [*Inorganic chemistry*]
PTA .... Photographers' Telegraph Association
PTA .... Phototransistor Amplifier
PTA .... Physical Therapy Assistant
PTA .... Picatinny Arsenal [*New Jersey*] [*Later, Armament Development Center*] [*Army*]
PTA .... Pitch Trim Adjustment
PTA .... Pitch Trim Angle
PTA .... Planar Turbulence Amplifier   (IEEE)
PTA .... Plasma Thromboplastin Antecedent [*Factor XI*] [*Hematology*]
PTA .... Plasma Transferred Arc [*Metallurgy*]
PTA .... Platinized Titanium Anode
PTA .... Point of Total Assumption   (MCD)
PTA .... Port Alsworth [*Alaska*] [*Airport symbol*]   (OAG)
PTA .... Post-Test Analysis [*NASA*]   (NASA)
PTA .... Post-Traumatic Amnesia [*Medicine*]
PTA .... Potential Toxic Area   (NASA)
PTA .... Practical Accountant [*A publication*]
PTA .... Preferential Trade Arrangements [*ASEAN*]   (IMH)
PTA .... Premium Transportation Authorization   (AAG)
PTA .... Prepaid Ticket Advice [*Travel industry*]
PTA .... Preparation through Acceptance
PTA .... Pressure Transducer Assembly
PTA .... Price-Tag Awareness [*See also PTS*]
PTA .... Primary Target Area [*Military*]
PTA .... Primary Tungsten Association [*British*]   (EAIO)
PTA .... Prior to Admission [*Medicine*]
PTA .... Prior to Arrival [*Medicine*]   (MAE)
PTA .... Program Time Analyzer
PTA .... Programmable Translation Array
PTA .... Proposed Technical Approach
PTA .... Propulsion Test Article [*NASA*]   (NASA)
PTA .... Prothrombin Activity [*Hematology*]
PTA .... Proton Target Area
PTA .... Pulse Torquing Assembly   (KSC)
PTA .... Punta Arenas [*Chile*] [*Seismograph station code, US Geological Survey*] [*Closed*]   (SEIS)
PTA .... Purchase Transaction Analysis
PTA .... Purified Terephthalic Acid [*Organic chemistry*]
PTAA......... Airman Apprentice, Photographic Intelligenceman, Striker [*Navy rating*]
PTA-A .... Periodical Title Abbreviations: by Abbreviation [*A publication*]
PTAB........ Photographic Technical Advisory Board [*American National Standards Institute*]
PTAC........ Penn Treaty American Corp. [*NASDAQ symbol*]   (NQ)
PTAC........ Plant Transportation Advisory Committee
PTAC........ Professional and Technical Advisory Committee [*JCAH*]
PTACV ...... Prototype Tracked Air-Cushion Vehicle
PTAD .... (Phenyl)triazolinedione [*Organic chemistry*]
PTAD .... Productivity and Technical Assistance Division [*Mutual Security Agency*] [*Abolished, 1953*]

PT AEQ ..... Partes Aequales [*Equal Parts*] [*Pharmacy*]
PTAG .... Professional Tattoo Artists Guild (EA)
PTAH .... Phosphotungstic Acid-Hematoxylin [*A stain*]
PTAIOC .... Proceedings and Transactions. All-India Oriental Conferences [*A publication*]
PTAL .... Para-Tolualdehyde [*Organic chemistry*]
PTA Mag ... PTA [*Parent-Teacher Association*] Magazine [*A publication*]
PTAN .... Airman, Photographic Intelligenceman, Striker [*Navy rating*]
PTANYC... Protestant Teachers Association of New York City (EA)
PTAP .... Phenyltrimethylammonium Perbromide [*Organic chemistry*]
PTAP .... Purified Diphtheria Toxoid Precipitated by Aluminum Phosphate (AAMN)
PTAR .... Prime Time Access Rule [*Television*]
PTASB ...... Photographic Applications in Science, Technology, and Medicine [*A publication*]
PTASE ...... Phosphatase [*An enzyme*] (DHSM)
PTA-T .... Periodical Title Abbreviations: by Title [*A publication*]
PTAVE ..... Parents and Teachers Against Violence in Education (EA)
PTAWT ..... Atlantic Wind Test Site, Tignish, Prince Edward Island [*Library symbol*] [*National Library of Canada*] (NLC)
PTB .... Paragon Trade Brands [*NYSE symbol*] (SPSG)
ptB .... Part Bunkers [*Shipping*] (DS)
PTB .... Parti du Travail de Belgique [*Belgian Labour Party*] [*Political party*] (EY)
PTB .... Parti du Travail du Burkina [*Burkina Faso*] [*Political party*] (EY)
PTB .... Partido Trabalhista Brasileiro [*Brazilian Labor Party*] [*Political party*] (PPW)
PTB .... Patellar Tendon Bearing [*Medicine*]
PTB .... Payload Timing Buffer [*NASA*] (NASA)
PTB .... Perishables Tariff Bureau, Atlanta GA [*STAC*]
PTB .... Personnel Test Battery
PTB .... Petersburg, VA [*Location identifier*] [*FAA*] (FAAL)
PTB .... Physical Transaction Block
PTB .... Point Barrow [*Alaska*] [*Later, BRW*] [*Geomagnetic observatory code*]
PTB .... Point Barrow [*Alaska*] [*Seismograph station code, US Geological Survey*] [*Closed*] (SEIS)
PTB .... Pounds per Thousand Barrels [*Petroleum technology*]
PTB .... Pressure Test Barrel
PTB .... Prior to Birth [*Medicine*]
PTB .... Process Technical Bulletin (MCD)
PTB .... Program Time Base [*Military*] (AFIT)
PTB .... PT Boats, Inc. (EA)
PTBA .... Proud to be Australian [*Political party*]
PTBB .... Para-tertiary-butylbenzaldehyde [*Organic chemistry*]
PTBBA ..... Para-tertiary-butylbenzoic Acid [*Organic chemistry*]
PTBC .... Pittsburgh Brewing Co. [*NASDAQ symbol*] (NQ)
PTBD .... Percutaneous Transhepatic Biliary Drainage [*Medicine*]
PTBF .... Portal Tributary Blood Flow [*Physiology*]
PTBI .... PT Boats, Inc. (EAIO)
PTBK .... Partbook [*Music*]
PTBL .... Portable (AABC)
PTB Mitt ... PTB [*Physikalisch-Technische Bundesanstalt*] Mitteilungen. Amts- und Mitteilungsblatt der Physikalisch- Technische Bundesanstalt [*Braunschweig-Berlin*] [*A publication*]
PTB Mitt Forsch Pruefen ... PTB [*Physikalisch-Technische Bundesanstalt*] Mitteilungen. Forschen und Pruefen [*A publication*]
PTBR .... Processing Tax Board of Review Decisions [*United States Internal Revenue Bureau*] [*A publication*] (DLA)
PTBR .... Punched Tape Block Reader [*Data processing*]
PtBS .... Poly(tertiary-butylstyrene) [*Organic chemistry*]
PTBT .... Para-tertiary-butyltoluene [*Organic chemistry*]
PTBT .... Partial Test-Ban Treaty
PTBT .... Pretransplant Blood Transfusion [*Medicine*]
PTC .... Chief Photographic Intelligenceman [*Navy rating*]
PTC .... Motor Boat Subchaser [*Navy symbol*] [*Obsolete*]
PTC .... Pacific Telecommunications Council (EA)
PTC .... Pacific Tuna Conference
PTC .... Packung und Transport in der Chemischen Industrie [*A publication*]
PTC .... PAR Technology Corp. [*NYSE symbol*] (SPSG)
PTC .... Part Through Crack [*Alloy tension*]
PTC .... Parti Travailliste Congolais [*Congolese Labor Party*] [*Political party*]
Ptc .... Participating [*Business term*]
PTC .... Passive Thermal Control
PTC .... Patent, Trademark, and Copyright Institute [*Franklin Pierce College*] (IID)
PTC .... Patrol Vessel, Motor Torpedo Boat, Submarine Chaser [*Navy symbol*]
PTC .... Pentagon Telecommunications Center (MCD)
PTC .... Peoria Terminal Co. [*AAR code*]
PTC .... Percutaneous Cholangiography [*Medicine*]
PTC .... Percutaneous Transhepatic Cholangiogram [*Medicine*]
PTC .... Performance Test Chamber (MCD)
PTC .... Performance Test Code
PTC .... Permission to Take Classes [*Education*]
PTC .... Personnel Transfer Capsule [*Undersea technology*]
PTC .... Personnel Transport Carrier
PTC .... Phase Transfer Catalysis [*Physical chemistry*]

PTC .... Phenylisothiocyanate [*Organic chemistry*]
PTC .... Phenylthiocarbamide [*or Phenylthiocarbamyl*] [*Organic chemistry*]
PTC .... Pheochromocytoma, Thyroid Carcinoma Syndrome [*Oncology*] (MAE)
PTC .... Photographic Training Centre [*British*] (CB)
PTC .... Photographic Type Composition (ADA)
PTC .... Pipe Tobacco Council (EA)
PTC .... Pipe and Tobacco Council of America [*Defunct*] (EA)
PTC .... Pitch Trim Compensator
PTC .... Pitch Trim Controller (MCD)
PTC .... Plan to Clear [*Aviation*] (FAAC)
PTC .... Plasma Thromboplastin Component [*Factor IX*] [*Also, CF*] [*Hematology*]
PTC .... Plastic Training Cartridge [*Army*] (INF)
PTC .... Pneumatic Temperature Control
PTC .... Pneumatic Test Console
PTC .... Police Training Centre [*British*]
PTC .... Portable Tele-Transaction Computer [*Telxon*]
PTC .... Portable Temperature Control (KSC)
PTC .... Porto Cannone [*Italy*] [*Seismograph station code, US Geological Survey*] (SEIS)
PTC .... Portuguese Trade Commission (EA)
PTC .... Positive Target Control (FAAC)
PTC .... Positive Temperature Coefficient
PTC .... Positive Transmitter Control
PTC .... Post-Tensioned Concrete [*Technical drawings*]
PTC .... Post-Turnover Change [*Nuclear energy*] (NRCH)
PTC .... Postal Telegraph Cable
PTC .... Posterior Trabeculae Carneae [*Heart anatomy*]
PTC .... Power Testing Code (MCD)
PTC .... Power Transfer Coefficient
PTC .... Power Transmission Council
PTC .... Preoperative Testing Center
PTC .... Pressure and Temperature Control (KSC)
PTC .... Pressure Transducer Calibrator
PTC .... Primary Technical Course [*Military*]
PTC .... Primary Training Centre [*British military*] (DMA)
PTC .... Princeton Resources Corp. [*Vancouver Stock Exchange symbol*]
PTC .... Programmable Temperature Controls
PTC .... Programmable Test Console
PTC .... Programmed Transmission Control (BUR)
PTC .... Programmer Training Center
PTC .... Promotional Telephone Call [*Marketing*] (OICC)
PTC .... Proof Test Capsule [*NASA*]
PTC .... Propellant Tanking Console (AAG)
PTC .... Propulsion Test Complex (KSC)
PTC .... Prothrombin Complex [*Hematology*]
PTC .... Pseudotumor Cerebri [*Medicine*] (AAMN)
PTC .... Psychophysical Timing Curve
PTC .... Publishing Technology Corp. [*Information service or system*] (IID)
PTC .... Pulse Time Code
PTCA .... Patience T'ai Chi Association (EA)
PTCA .... Percutaneous Transluminal Coronary Angioplasty [*Medicine*]
PTCA .... Plains Tribal Council of Assam [*India*] [*Political party*] (PPW)
PTCA .... Postal Telegraph Clerks' Association [*A union*] [*British*]
PTCA .... Pressure Technology Corp. of America
PTCA .... Private Truck Council of America (EA)
PTCAA ...... Professional Turkey Calling Association of America (EA)
PTCAD ...... Provisional Troop Carrier Airborne Division
PTCC .... Pacific Division Transport Control Center
PT/CC .... Problem Tracking and Change Control [*Data processing*]
PTCCS .... Polaris Target Card Computing System [*Missiles*]
PtcD .... Phosphatidylcholine [*Biochemistry*]
PTCEDJ ..... Plant Cell Tissue and Organ Culture [*A publication*]
PTCH ...... Pacer Technology [*NASDAQ symbol*] (NQ)
PTCH ...... Patch (FAAC)
PTCI .... Programmable Telecommunications Interface (MCD)
PTCI .... Programmable Terminal Communications Interface (MCD)
PTCI .... Pullman Transportation [*NASDAQ symbol*] (NQ)
PTC J .... Patent, Trademark, and Copyright Journal [*A publication*]
PTCJB ...... Postepy Techniki Jadrowej [*A publication*]
PTCL .... Peripheral T-Cell Lymphoma [*Oncology*]
PTCLA ..... Presse Thermale et Climatique [*A publication*]
PTCLD ...... Part Called [*Stock exchange term*] (SPSG)
PTCM .... Master Chief Photographic Intelligenceman [*Navy rating*]
PTCM .... Pacific Telecom, Inc. [*NASDAQ symbol*] (NQ)
PTCO .... Petroleum Equipment Tools Co. [*NASDAQ symbol*] (NQ)
Pt Copyright & TM Cas ... Patent, Copyright, and Trade Mark Cases [*United States*] [*A publication*] (DLA)
PTCP .... Participate (FAAC)
PTCP .... Positive Turnaround Control Point (MCD)
PTCR .... Pad Terminal Connection Room [*NASA*]
PTCR .... Payload Terminal Connector Room [*NASA*] (MCD)
PTCR .... Positive Temperature Coefficient Resistance [*Materials science and technology*]
PTCRM ..... Partial Thermochemical Remanent Magnetization
PTCS .... Passive Thermal Control Section [*NASA*] (NASA)
PTCS .... Passive Thermal Control System (NASA)
PTCS .... Pax Tibi cum Sanctis [*Peace to Thee with the Saints*] [*Latin*]

PTCS .... Phenyltrichlorosilane [*Organic chemistry*]
PTCS .... Planning, Training, and Checkout System [*NASA*] (MCD)
PTCS .... Powertrain Control Signal [*Automotive engineering*]
PTCS .... Pressure Transducer Calibration System
PTCS .... Propellant Tanking Computer System (KSC)
PTCS .... Senior Chief Photographic Intelligenceman [*Navy rating*]
PTCT .... Protect (MSA)
PTCV .... Pilot-Operated Temperature Control Valve
PTCV .... Plowright Tissue Culture Vaccine [*Against rinderpest*]
PTD .... Painted (AAG)
PTD .... Paper Towel Dispenser [*Technical drawings*]
PTD .... Parallel Transfer Disk [*Data processing*]
PTD .... Part Throttle Deceleration [*Engines*] (EG)
PTD .... Particle Transfer Device
P & TD ...... Parts and Tool Disposition (SAA)
PTD .... Permanent Total Disability [*Medicine*]
PTD .... Phenyltriazolinedione [*Organic chemistry*]
Ptd............. Phosphatidyl
PTD .... Photodiode Detector [*Instrumentation*]
PTD .... Photothermal Deflection
PTD .... Physical Teardown (MCD)
PTD .... Pilot to Dispatcher
PTD .... Plant Test Date [*Telecommunications*] (TEL)
PTD .... Pointed (WGA)
PTD .... Portland [*Oregon*] [*Seismograph station code, US Geological Survey*] (SEIS)
PTD .... Posttuning Drift
PTD .... Potsdam, NY [*Location identifier*] [*FAA*] (FAAL)
PTD .... Potter Distilleries Ltd. [*Toronto Stock Exchange symbol*] [*Vancouver Stock Exchange symbol*]
PTD .... Printed
PTD .... Prior to Discharge [*Medicine*] (MAE)
PTD .... Programmable Threshold Detector (MCD)
PTD .... Programmed Thermal Desorber
PTD .... Provisioning Technical Documentation
PTD .... Provisioning Transcript Documentation (MCD)
PTDA .... Per Task Data Area [*Data processing*] (BYTE)
PTDA .... Power Transmission Distributors Association (EA)
PTDB .... Point Target Data Base (SAA)
PTDC .... Pacific Trade and Development Conference [*OPTAD*] (FEA)
PTDDSS.... Provisioning Technical Documentation Data Selection Sheet [*NASA*] (NASA)
PTDF .... Pacific Tuna Development Foundation (EA)
PTDF .... Procurement Technical Data File [*DoD*]
PTDIA .... Professional Truck Driver Institute of America (EA)
PtdIns .... Phosphatidylinositol [*Also, PI*] [*Biochemistry*]
P & T Div ... Plans and Training Division [*Military*]
PTDOS ...... Processor Technology Disk Operating System
PTDP......... Preliminary Technical Development Plan (AFM)
PTDP......... Proposed Technical Development Plan
PTDQ .... Polymerized Trimethyldihydroquinoline [*Organic chemistry*]
PtdS .... Phosphatidylserine [*Biochemistry*]
PTDS .... Photo Target Detection System
Ptd Salesmanship ... Printed Salesmanship [*A publication*]
PTDTL ...... Pumped Tunnel Diode Transistor Logic
PTDU .... Pointing and Tracking Demonstration Unit (MCD)
PTe............. Indian Valley Public Library, Telford, PA [*Library symbol*] [*Library of Congress*] (LCLS)
PTE........... International Federation of Professional and Technical Engineers
PTE........... Packet Transfer Engine [*Newbridge Networks Corp.*]
PTE........... Packet Transport Equipment [*Data processing*] (PCM)
PTE........... Page Table Entry
PTE........... Parathyroid Extract [*Medicine*]
PTE........... Partido de Trabajadores Espanoles [*Spanish Workers' Party*] [*Political party*] (PPE)
PTE........... Passenger Transport Executive [*British*]
PTE........... Pectin transeliminase [*or Pectate Lyase*] [*An enzyme*]
PTE........... Peculiar Test Equipment
PTE........... Photographic Tasks and Equipment [*NASA*]
PT & E ...... Physical Teardown and Evaluation (MCD)
PTE........... Plate (ROG)
PTE........... Port Stephens [*Australia*] [*Airport symbol*] (OAG)
PTE........... Portable Test Equipment (AAG)
PTE........... Portage [*Alaska*] [*Seismograph station code, US Geological Survey*] (SEIS)
PTE........... Power Transport Equipment
PTE........... Pressure Test Equipment (MCD)
PTE........... Pressure-Tolerant Electronics (IEEE)
PTE........... Pretax Earnings [*Employment*]
PTE........... Primrose Technology Corp. [*Vancouver Stock Exchange symbol*]
PTE........... Private [*British*]
PTE........... Private Trade Entity
PTE........... Problem Trend Evaluation (MCD)
PTE........... Production Test Equipment (MCD)
PT & E ...... Progress Tests and Examinations
PTE........... Proxylem Tracheary Element [*Botany*]
Pte .... Pteroyl [*Biochemistry*]
PTE........... Pulmonary Thromboembolism [*Medicine*]
PTEA......... Preliminary Training Effectiveness Analysis

PTEAR ...... Physical Teardown
PTEAR ...... Physical Teardown and Maintenance Allocation Review (MCD)
PTeb........... Tebtunis Papyri [*A publication*] (OCD)
PTEC .... Petrotech, Inc. [*NASDAQ symbol*] (NQ)
PTEC .... Phoenix Technologies Ltd. [*NASDAQ symbol*] (NQ)
PTEC .... Plastics Technical Evaluation Center [*Military*]
PTED......... Pulmonary Thromboembolic Disease [*Medicine*]
PteGlu........ Pteroylmonoglutamic Acid [*Folic acid*] [*Also, FA, PGA*] [*Biochemistry*]
PTEK........ Protectaire Systems Co. [*NASDAQ symbol*] (NQ)
PTEKAA ... Klucze do Oznaczania Owadow Polski [*A publication*]
PTEL .... People's Telephone Co., Inc. [*NASDAQ symbol*] (NQ)
PTER .... Physical Teardown and Evaluation Review (MCD)
PT & ER .... Physical Teardown and Evaluation Review (MCD)
Pteridine Chem Proc Int Symp ... Pteridine Chemistry. Proceedings. International Symposium [*A publication*]
Ptero........... Pterodactyl [*A publication*]
PTES .... Productivity Trend Evaluation System (MCD)
PTES .... Purdue Teacher Evaluation Scale
PTETD ...... Production Test Engineering Task Description (MCD)
PTETPC.... Party to Expose the Petrov Conspiracy [*Australia*] [*Political party*]
PTETS....... Pioneer Television and Electronic Technicians Society [*Defunct*] (EA)
PTEV......... Primrose Technology Corp. [*Vancouver, BC*] [*NASDAQ symbol*] (NQ)
PText .... Papiere zur Textlinguistik [*Papers in Textlinguistics*] [*A publication*]
PTF............ Malololailai [*Fiji*] [*Airport symbol*] (OAG)
PTF............ Paralemniscal Tegmental Field [*Neuroanatomy*]
PTF............ Parts Transfer Form (SAA)
PTF............ Patch and Test Facility
PTF............ Patrol Torpedo Boat, Fast [*Formerly, PT*] [*Navy symbol*]
PTF............ Payload Test Facility [*VAFB*] [*NASA*] (MCD)
PTF............ Permit to Fly [*Aviation*] (AIA)
PTF............ Petersfield Oil & Minerals [*Vancouver Stock Exchange symbol*]
PTF............ Phase Transfer Function (MCD)
PTF............ Plaintiff [*Legal term*] (ROG)
PTF........... Plasma Thromboplastin Factor [*Factor VIII*] [*Also, AHF, AHG, TPC*] [*Hematology*]
PTF............ Police Training Foundation
PTF............ Polymer Thick Film
PTF............ Port Task Force
PTF............ Power Test Fail
PTF............ Production Tabulating Form (AAG)
PTF............ Program Temporary Fix [*Data processing*]
PTF............ Programmable Transversal Filter [*SMP*]
PTF............ Proof Test Facility [*Nuclear energy*]
PTF............ Propellant Tank Flow
PTF............ Pulse Transfer Function
PTFA .... Preliminary Tool and Facility Analysis (MCD)
PTFC .... Pretty Things Fan Club (EA)
PTFD......... Personnel, Training and Force Development [*Army*]
PTFDA ...... Professional Travel Film Directors Association [*Later, Professional Travelogue Sponsors - PTS*] (EA)
PTFE .... Polytetrafluoroethylene [*Organic chemistry*]
PTFG......... Large Guided Missile Motorboat [*Navy symbol*] (DNAB)
PTFHA ...... Physician Task Force on Hunger in America (EA)
PTFHC...... Putnam Tax Free Health Care Fund [*Associated Press abbreviation*] (APAG)
PTFM........ Platform (AAG)
PTFMA .... Peacetime Force Material Assets [*Navy*] (AFIT)
PTFMA ..... Public Telecommunications Financial Management Association (EA)
PTFMO...... Peacetime Force Materiel Objective [*Army*]
PTFMPO .. Peacetime Force Materiel Procurement Objective [*Army*]
PTFMR .... Peacetime Force Materiel Requirements [*Army*]
PTFMR-A ... Peacetime Force Materiel Requirements - Acquisition [*Army*] (AABC)
PTFMR-R ... Peacetime Force Materiel Requirements - Retention [*Army*] (AABC)
PTFP .... Public Telecommunications Facilities Program [*Department of Commerce*]
PTFS.......... Pilot-to-Forecaster Service (NOAA)
PTFS.......... Publications. Texas Folklore Society [*A publication*]
PTFT .... Production Temporary Facility Tool (SAA)
PTFUR ...... President's Task Force on Urban Renewal (EA)
PTFX .... Plating Fixture (AAG)
PTG .... Parent-Teacher Group
PTG .... Pennington Gap, VA [*Location identifier*] [*FAA*] (FAAL)
PTG .... Piano Technicians Guild (EA)
PTG .... Pietersburg [*South Africa*] [*Airport symbol*] (OAG)
PTG .... Polaris Task Group [*Missiles*]
PTG .... Portage Industries [*AMEX symbol*] (SPSG)
PTG .... Portageville [*Missouri*] [*Seismograph station code, US Geological Survey*] [*Closed*] (SEIS)
PTG .... Portugal, Belgique, Luxembourg. Informations Economiques [*A publication*]
PTG .... Portuguese (ROG)
PTG .... Precise Tone Generator [*Telecommunications*] (TEL)

PTG .... Pressure Test Gauge
PTG .... Pressure Transfer Gauge
PTG .... Printing
PTG .... Professional Technical Group
PTG .... Prothoracic Gland [*Insect anatomy*]
PTG .... Pulse Target Generator
PTG .... Small Guided Missile Motorboat [*Navy symbol*] (DNAB)
PTGA........ Pteroyltriglutamic Acid [*Pharmacology*]
PTGAP ...... Professional Technical Group on Antennas and Propagation [*of the IEEE*]
Ptg Art .... Printing Art [*A publication*]
PTGBD...... Percutaneous Transhepatic Gallbladder Drainage [*Medicine*]
PTGC........ Programmed Temperature Gas Chromatography
PTGEC ...... Professional Technical Group on Electronic Computers [*Later, IEEE Computer Society*]
PT GEO..... Posted to Geographics
PTGEWS .. Professional Technical Group on Engineering Writing and Speech [*of the IEEE*]
pTGF .... Porcine Transforming Growth Factor
PTGL........ Pyrolysis to Gases and Liquids [*Chemical processing*]
PTGMA...... Photogrammetria [*A publication*]
PTGS .... Paper Trade Golfing Society [*British*]
PTGS........ Portable Telemetry Ground Station
PTGT .... Primary Target [*Military*]
PTH .... Hydrofoil Motor Torpedo Boat [*Ship symbol*] (NATG)
PTH .... Pallet Torque Hook
PTH .... Panther Mines Ltd. [*Vancouver Stock Exchange symbol*]
PTH .... Paper Tape Half-Duplex
PTH .... Parathormone [*Medicine*] (MAE)
PTH .... Parathyroid Hormone [*Endocrinology*]
PTH .... Pathology [*Medical specialty*] (DHSM)
PTH .... Peak Tanning Hours [*Supposedly occurring between 10am and 2pm*] [*See also BROTS, SROTS*]
PTH .... Phenylthiohydantoin [*Organic chemistry*]
PTH .... Plated through Hole
PTH .... Port Heiden [*Alaska*] [*Airport symbol*] (OAG)
PTH .... Port Heiden, AK [*Location identifier*] [*FAA*] (FAAL)
PTH .... Post-Transfusion Hepatitis [*Medicine*]
PTH .... Project Top Hat (EA)
PtHA......... Pinto Horse Association of America (EA)
P Th B........ Bachelor of Practical Theology
PTHEA...... Physical Therapy [*A publication*]
PTHEAT... Petroleum Heat & Power Co. [*Associated Press abbreviation*] (APAG)
PTHF........ Polytetrahydrofuran [*Organic chemistry*]
PTH-LP..... Parathyroid Hormone-Like Peptide [*Endocrinology*]
PTHO........ Thought [*A publication*]
PThR .... Princeton Theological Review [*A publication*]
PTHrP .... Parathyroid Hormone-Related Protein [*Biochemistry*]
PTHS........ Parathyroid Hormone Secretion Rate [*Endocrinology*] (MAE)
PTHS........ Theological Studies [*A publication*]
PTI............ Package Turn In (MCD)
PTI............ Pancreatic Trypsin Inhibitor [*Biochemistry*]
PTI............ Parkes-Tidbinbilla Interferometer [*Astronomy*]
PTI............ Party Identity [*Telecommunications*] (TEL)
PTI............ Pathways to Independence [*An association*] (EA)
PTI............ Penn Telecom, Inc. [*Gibsonia, PA*] (TSSD)
PTI............ Pennsylvania Transportation Institute [*Pennsylvania State University*] [*Research center*] (RCD)
PTI............ Persistent Tolerant Infection
PTI............ Personnel Tests for Industry
PTI............ Personnel Transaction Identifier [*Air Force*] (AFM)
PTI............ Petroleum Times [*A publication*]
PTI............ Philadelphia Textile Institute
PTI............ Physical-Technical Institute [*Former USSR*]
PTI............ Physical Training Instructor [*British*]
PTI............ Pictorial Test of Intelligence [*Education*]
PTI............ Pipe Test Insert [*Liquid Metal Engineering Center*] [*Energy Research and Development Administration*] (IEEE)
PTI............ Plugging Temperature Indicator [*Nuclear energy*] (NRCH)
PTI............ Poetry Therapy Institute (EA)
PTI............ Porous Tungsten Ionizer
PTI............ Post-Tensioning Institute (EA)
PTI............ Power Tool Institute (EA)
PTI............ Pre-Trial Investigation (DNAB)
PTI............ Pre-Trip Inspection [*Shipping*]
PTI............ Precision Technology, Inc. (AAG)
PTI............ Preliminary Test Information (KSC)
PTI............ [*The*] Press Trust of India
PTI............ Production Training Indicator [*Data processing*]
PTI............ Program Transfer Interface
PTI............ Programmed Test Input (MCD)
PTI............ Programming Tools and Information [*IBM Corp.*] [*Data processing*]
PTI............ Promethean Technologies, Inc. [*Vancouver Stock Exchange symbol*]
PTI............ Public Technology, Inc. [*Research center*] (RCD)
PTI............ Publicacoes Tecnicas Internacionais Ltda. [*International Technical Publications Ltd.*] [*Information service or system*] (IID)
PTI............ Puntilla Lake, AK [*Location identifier*] [*FAA*] (FAAL)

PTIA......... Pet Trade and Industry Association (EAIO)
PTIC......... Patent and Trade Mark Institute of Canada
PTIE......... Pet Trade and Industry Exhibition [*British*] (ITD)
PTIG......... Presentation of Technical Information Group (SAA)
PTIL......... Parts Test Information List (KSC)
PTIND....... Paper Technology and Industry [*A publication*]
PTI-ODT... Personnel Tests for Industry - Oral Directions Test
PTIP......... Physical Therapist in Independent Practice (GFGA)
PTIS .... Pacific Triangle Information Services [*Information service or system*] (IID)
PTIS .... Plasma-Therm, Inc. [*NASDAQ symbol*] (NQ)
PTIS .... Powertrain Input Signal [*Automotive engineering*]
PTIS .... Programmed Test Input System (MCD)
PTIS .... Propulsion Test Instrumentation System (KSC)
PTIWU...... Posts and Telegraphs Industrial Workers' Union [*India*]
PTJ .... Part-Time Job
PTJ .... Piano Technician's Journal [*A publication*]
PTJ .... Portland [*Australia*] [*Airport symbol*] (OAG)
PTJ .... Property Tax Journal [*A publication*]
PTJA .... Plan to Join Airways (FAAC)
PTJO .... Theatre Journal [*A publication*]
PTK........... Polishing Tool Kit
PTK........... Pontiac, MI [*Location identifier*] [*FAA*] (FAAL)
PTK........... Potentiometer Tapping Kit
PTK........... Prehistoric Tombs at Knossos [*A publication*]
PTK........... Protein-Tyrosine Kinase [*An enzyme*]
PTKK........ Truk [*Caroline Islands*] [*ICAO location identifier*] (ICLI)
PTL........... Part Time Legislature
PTL........... Partial Total Loss [*Insurance*] (DS)
PTL........... Patrol [*or Patrolman*] (AABC)
PTL........... Peacetime Losses [*Military*]
PTL........... Penteli [*Greece*] [*Seismograph station code, US Geological Survey*] (SEIS)
PTL........... People That Love [*Of television's "PTL Club"*] [*Facetious translations: "Pass the Loot" and "Pay the Lady"*]
PTL........... Perinatal Telencephalic Leukoencephalopathy [*Medicine*]
PTL........... Peripheral T-Cell Lymphoma [*Oncology*]
PTL........... Petroleum Testing Laboratory
PTL........... Phase Tracking Loop (MCD)
PTL........... Photographic Technology Laboratory (KSC)
PTL........... Pintle [*Design engineering*]
PTL........... Planning Test List
PTL........... Pocket Testament League (EA)
PTL........... Power Transmission Line (OA)
PTL........... Praise the Lord [*Of television's "PTL Club"*] [*Facetious translations: "Pass the Loot" and "Pay the Lady"*]
PTL........... Pre-Test Laboratory (DNAB)
PTL........... Pressure, Torque, and Load
PTL........... Pretty Tough Lawyer [*Refers to Melvin Belli, attorney for Tammy and Jim Bakker of the PTL Club*]
PTL........... Primary Target Line [*Military*]
PTL........... Process and Test Language
PTL........... Providence Airline [*Coventry, RI*] [*FAA designator*] (FAAC)
PTL........... Public Television Library
PTLA .... Praise the Lord Anyway
PTLA .... Publishers' Trade List Annual
PTLC .... Piedmont Triad Library Council [*Library network*]
PT-LD....... Physical Teardown - Logistics Demonstration (MCD)
PTLD........ Post-Transfusion Liver Disease [*Medicine*]
PTLD........ Prescribed Tumor Lethal Dose [*Oncology*]
PTLEF...... Peace through Law Education Fund (EA)
PTLEN...... Petal Length [*Botany*]
PTLF .... Pressure, Temperature, Level, and Flow [*Chemical engineering*]
PTLRS....... Publications and Technical Literature Research Section [*Environmental Protection Agency*] (IID)
PTLV .... Primate T-Lymphotropic Viruses
PTLX .... Patlex Corp. [*NASDAQ symbol*] (NQ)
PTLY .... Partly (FAAC)
PTM .... Palmarito [*Venezuela*] [*Airport symbol*] (OAG)
PTM .... Pancake Torquer Motor (SAA)
PTM .... Passenger Traffic Manager
PTM .... Pattern Transformation Memory
PTM .... Performance Test Model (OA)
PTM .... Petromac Energy, Inc. [*Vancouver Stock Exchange symbol*]
PTM .... Phase Time Modulation
PTM .... Phenyltrimethylammonium [*Also, PTA, PTMA*] [*Organic chemistry*]
PTM .... Physical Teardown and Maintenance (MCD)
PTM .... Pietermaritzburg [*South Africa*] [*Seismograph station code, US Geological Survey*] (SEIS)
PTM .... Pneumatic Telescope Mast
PTM .... Polaris Tactical Missile
PTM .... Portable Traffic Monitor [*Telecommunications*] (TEL)
PTM .... Portland Terminal Co. [*AAR code*]
PTM .... Posttransfusion Mononucleosis [*Medicine*]
PTM .... Practising Manager [*A publication*]
PTM .... Pressure-Transmitting Medium [*Engineering*]
PTM .... Preterm Milk [*Medicine*]
PTM .... Primary Thickening Meristem [*Botany*]
PTM .... Program Timing and Miscellaneous [*Electronics*]
PTM .... Programmable Terminal Multiplexer [*Texas Instruments, Inc.*]

PTM .... Programmable Timer Module
PTM .... Proof Test Model [*NASA*]
PTM .... Pulse Time Modulation [*Radio*]
PTM .... Pulse Time Multiplex
PTM .... Pulse Transmission Mode   (MCD)
PTM .... Southeastern Airways Corp. [*Double Springs, AL*] [*FAA designator*]   (FAAC)
PTMA....... Phenyltrimethylammonium [*Also, PTA, PTM*] [*Organic chemistry*]
PTMA....... Phosphotungstomolybdic Acid [*Inorganic chemistry*]
PTMAS.... Professional, Technical, Managerial, and Administrative Staff
PTMC....... Polaris Tender Management Computer [*Missiles*]
PTMD .... Propellant Toxicity Monitoring Devices   (KSC)
PTMDF.... Pupils, Tension, Media, Disc, Fundus [*Medicine*]
PT & ME ... Physical Teardown and Maintenance Evaluation [*Army*]
PTMEG..... Polytetramethylene Ether Glycol [*Organic chemistry*]
PTMI........ Precision Target Marketing, Inc. [*New Hyde Park, NY*] [*NASDAQ symbol*]   (NQ)
PTML....... PNP [*Positive-Negative-Positive*] Transistor Magnetic Logic   (IEEE)
PTMRA..... Platinum Metals Review [*A publication*]
PTMS....... Para-Toluidine-meta-sulfonic Acid [*Also, PTMSA*] [*Organic chemistry*]
PTMS....... Pattern Transformation Memory System
PTMS....... Precision Torque Measuring System   (NASA)
PTMS....... Publication Text Management System   (MCD)
PTMSA..... Para-Toluidine-meta-sulfonic Acid [*Also, PTMS*] [*Organic chemistry*]
PTMT....... Poly(tetramethylene Terephthalate) [*Organic chemistry*]
PTMTLG .. Pitometer-Log [*Engineering*]
PTMU .... Power and Temperature Monitor Unit   (KSC)
PTMUD .... Postepy Technologii Maszyn i Urzadzen [*A publication*]
PTMUX..... Pulse Time Multiplex   (MSA)
PTN .... Morgan City/Patterson [*Louisiana*] [*Airport symbol*]   (OAG)
PTN .... Particulate Total Nitrogen [*Analytical chemistry*]
PTN .... Partido Trabalhista Nacional [*National Workers' Party*] [*Brazil*]
PTN .... Partition   (KSC)
PTN .... Patterson, LA [*Location identifier*] [*FAA*]   (FAAL)
PTN .... Phenotemperature Normogram [*Phenology*]
PTN .... Phenytoin [*Anticonvulsant*]
PTN .... Plant Test Number [*Telecommunications*]   (TEL)
PTN .... Pluton Industries Ltd. [*Vancouver Stock Exchange symbol*]
PTN .... Portion   (FAAC)
PTN .... Potsdam [*New York*] [*Seismograph station code, US Geological Survey*]   (SEIS)
PTN .... Procedure Turn [*Aviation*]   (FAAC)
Ptn............. Pterin [*Biochemistry*]
PTNC........ Technology and Culture [*A publication*]
PTNM .... [*The*] Putnam Trust Co. of Greenwich [*NASDAQ symbol*]   (NQ)
PTNMA .... Protection of Metals [*English Translation*] [*A publication*]
PTNR .... Partner   (ROG)
PTNRA8.... Pattern Recognition [*A publication*]
PTNRSHIP ... Partnership   (ROG)
PTNX .... Printronix, Inc. [*NASDAQ symbol*]   (NQ)
PTO .... Pacific Theater of Operations [*World War II*]
PTO .... Packard Truck Organization   (EA)
PTO .... Participating Test Organization [*Air Force*]
PTO .... Partners Oil & Mining [*Vancouver Stock Exchange symbol*]
PTO .... Patent and Trademark Office [*Formerly, PO*] [*Department of Commerce*]
PTO .... Pato Branco [*Brazil*] [*Airport symbol*]   (OAG)
PTO .... People, Topics, Opinions [*A publication*] [*British*]
PTO .... Perlsucht Tuberculin Original [*Medicine*]   (MAE)
PTO .... Please Turn Over [*the page*]
PTO .... Port Transportation Officer
PTO .... Porto [*Serro Do Pilar*] [*Portugal*] [*Seismograph station code, US Geological Survey*]   (SEIS)
PTO .... Power Takeoff [*Automotive engineering*]
PTO .... Power Test Operations   (MCD)
PTO .... Professional and Technology Officer [*British*]
PTO .... Project Technical Office [*Military*]   (DNAB)
PTO .... Project Type Organization   (AAG)
PTO .... Proof Test Orbiter [*NASA*]
PTO .... Propellant Transfer Operation   (AFM)
PTO .... Public Trustee Office   (DLA)
PTO .... Purdue Teacher Opinionaire [*Test*]
PTO .... Pyridinethiol Oxide [*Pharmacology*]
PTOA .... Projective Tests of Attitudes
PTobA........ United States Army, Tobyhanna Army Depot Library, Tobyhanna, PA [*Library symbol*] [*Library of Congress*]   (LCLS)
PTOC........ Progress in Theoretical Organic Chemistry [*Elsevier Book Series*] [*A publication*]
PToG .... General Telephone & Electronics, GTE Sylvania, Inc., Towanda, PA [*Library symbol*] [*Library of Congress*]   (LCLS)
PTOL........ Peacetime Operating Level   (AFM)
Ptol............ Ptolemaeus Mathematicus [*Second century AD*] [*Classical studies*]   (OCD)

Ptol............ Ptolemaic   (BJA)
PTOMAIN ... Project to Optimize Many Individual Numbers   (SAA)
PTON........ Proteon, Inc. [*NASDAQ symbol*]   (SPSG)
PTOP........ Program Test and Operations Plan
PTOS........ Paper Tape Oriented Operating System
PTOS........ Patent and Trademark Office Society   (EA)
PTOS........ Patriot Tactical Operations Simulator [*Army*]
PTOS........ Peacetime Operating Stock [*Military*]
PTOUT ..... Printout   (MSA)
PTP........... Paper Tape Perforator [*or Punch*]
PTP........... Parameter Test Program   (SAA)
PTP........... Parti Togolais du Progres [*Party for Togolese Progress*]
PTP........... Peak-to-Peak [*Nuclear energy*]
PTP........... Pensions for Technical Professionals [*An association*]
PTP........... People to People International   (EA)
PTP........... Percutaneous Transhepatic Selective Portography [*Roentgenography*]
PTP........... Petrologic Petroleum [*Vancouver Stock Exchange symbol*]
PTP........... Phase Transition Phenomena [*Elsevier Book Series*] [*A publication*]
PTP........... Phenyltetrahydropyridine [*Biochemistry*]
PTP........... Platinum Temperature Probe
PTP........... Point Park College, Pittsburgh, PA [*OCLC symbol*] [*Inactive*]   (OCLC)
PTP........... Point-to-Point [*Robotics*] [*Telecommunications*]
PTP........... Pointe-A-Pitre [*Guadeloupe*] [*Airport symbol*]   (OAG)
PTP........... Pollution Transfer Program [*Marine science*]   (MSC)
PTP........... Porous Tungsten Plug
PTP........... Post-Tetanic Potentiation [*Neurology*]
PTP........... Post-Transfusion Purpura [*Medicine*]
PTP........... Posto Telefonico Pubblico [*Public Telephone*] [*Italy*]
PTP........... Posttetanic Potentiation [*Neurophysiology*]
PTP........... Potato Tuber Peroxidase [*An enzyme*]
PTP........... Preferred Target Point   (KSC)
PTP........... Preliminary Task Plan   (MCD)
PTP........... Pretransmission Precautionary Answer to Nature's Call [*Especially before a long program*] [*Television*]
PTP........... Primary Target Point [*NASA*]
PTP........... Prior to Program [*Medicine*]   (MAE)
PTP........... Production Test Plan   (MCD)
PTP........... Production Test Procedure   (NATG)
PTP........... Professional Tax Planner
PTP........... Program Task Planning   (MCD)
PTP........... Programmable Text Processor [*Programming language*]   (CSR)
PTP........... Programmable Touch Panel [*Electronics*]
PTP........... Programmed Turn Phase
PTP........... Protect the Planet [*Manual*]
PTP........... Proximity Test Plug [*Nuclear energy*]   (NRCH)
PTP........... Pueblo to People   (EA)
Ptp............ Transpulmonary Pressure   (MAE)
PTPase ..... Protein Tyrosine Phosphatase [*An enzyme*]
PTPC .... Professional Teaching Practices Commission   (OICC)
PTPD........ Part Paid [*Business term*]
PTPE .... Powertrain Product Engineering [*Automotive*]
PTP'er........ Prime Time Performer [*In book title, "Vitale: Just Your Average Bald, One-Eyed Basketball Wacko Who Beat the Ziggy and Became a PTP'er"*]
PTPF .... Payee TIN [*Taxpayer Identification Number*] Perfection File [*IRS*]
Pt Phil Gaz ... Port Phillip Gazette [*A publication*]   (APTA)
PTPI .... People to People International   (EAIO)
PTPI .... Professional and Technical Programs, Inc.
PTPKA ...... Progress of Theoretical Physics (Kyoto) [*A publication*]
PTPL .... PTP Resource Corp. [*Formerly, Petrologic Petroleum Ltd.*] [*NASDAQ symbol*]   (NQ)
PTPN........ Ponape Island [*Caroline Islands*] [*ICAO location identifier*]   (ICLI)
PTPN........ Poznanskie Towarzystwo Przyjaciol Nauk [*A publication*]
PT/Procestech ... PT/Procestechniek [*A publication*]
PTPS .... Package Test Power Supply
PTPS .... Propellant Transfer Pressurization System   (KSC)
PTPS .... Pumped Two-Phase System   (SSD)
PTPSC....... People-to-People Sports Committee   (EA)
P-TPT........ Portable Tactual Performance Test [*Child development test*] [*Psychology*]
PTPU........ Program Tape Preparation Unit
PTQ .... Poly(tolyquinoxaline) [*Organic chemistry*]
PTQ .... Pulse-Taking Questionnaire
PTQR........ Triquarterly [*A publication*]
PTR........... Pacific Test Range   (MUGU)
PTR........... Painter
PTR........... Paper Tape Reader
PTR........... Paper Towel Receptor [*Technical drawings*]
PTR........... Part Throttle Reheat [*Aviation*]   (OA)
PTR........... Partido Tercera Republica [*Chile*] [*Political party*]   (EY)
PTR........... Partner
PTR........... Parts Tool Requirements File
PTR........... Parts Transfer Record   (SAA)
PTR........... Patuxent River [*Navy*]   (MCD)
PTR........... Perforated Tape Reader
PTR........... Peripheral Total Resistance [*Medicine*]   (MAE)

PTR........... Perlsucht Tuberculin Rest [*Medicine*]   (MAE)
P/Tr.......... Permian/Triassic [*A geological period boundary*]
PTR........... Personality Tests and Reviews [*A publication*]
PTR........... Peterson [*Alabama*] [*Seismograph station code, US Geological Survey*]   (SEIS)
Ptr .... Petrine [*Of, or relating to, Peter the Apostle or Peter the Great*]   (BJA)
PTR........... Photoelectric Tape Reader
PTR........... Physikalisch-Technische Reichsanstalt
PTR........... Pilot Training Rate [*Navy*]
PTR........... Pleasant Harbor [*Alaska*] [*Airport symbol*]   (OAG)
PTR........... Plug-Type Receptacle
PTR........... Pointer [*Data processing*]
PTR........... Polar to Rectangular   (SAA)
PTR........... Pool Test Reactor [*Nuclear energy*]
PTR........... Pool Training Reactor [*Nuclear energy*]
PTR........... Poor Transmission [*Telecommunications*]   (TEL)
PTR........... Portable Tape Recorder
PTR........... Position Track RADAR
PTR........... Positive Termination Rate [*Job Training and Partnership Act*]   (OICC)
PTR........... Post-Trip Review
PTR........... Power Transformers   (MCD)
PTR........... Pre-Trial Release   (OICC)
PTR........... Precision Transmitter Receiver
PTR........... Preliminary Technical Report
PTR........... Preliminary Test Report [*NASA*]   (KSC)
PTR........... Pressure Test Record
PTR........... Pressure-Tube Reactor [*Nuclear energy*]
PTR........... Pretransmit Receiving
PTR........... Princeton Theological Review [*A publication*]
PTR........... Printer   (MSA)
P Tr .... Private Trust [*Includes testamentary, investment, life insurance, holding title, etc.*] [*Legal term*]   (DLA)
PTR........... Processor Tape Read
PTR........... Production Test Record
PTR........... Production Test Requirements   (KSC)
PTR........... Professional Tennis Registry, USA   (EA)
PTR........... Proficiency Testing Research   (EA)
PTR........... Program Technical Review   (MCD)
PTR........... Program Trouble Report [*NASA*]   (KSC)
PTR........... Programmer Trouble Report [*Nuclear energy*]   (GFGA)
PTR........... Proof Test Reactor [*Nuclear energy*]
PTR........... Property Trust of America SBI [*NYSE symbol*]   (SPSG)
PTR........... Publishing Trade [*A publication*]
PTR........... Punched Tape Reader [*Data processing*]
PTR........... Pupil-Teacher Ratio
PTRA........ Port Terminal Railroad Association
PTRA........ Power Transmission Representatives Association   (EA)
P/TRAC ... Positraction [*Automotive engineering*]
PTrB .... Betz Laboratories, Inc., Trevose, PA [*Library symbol*] [*Library of Congress*]   (LCLS)
PTRC........ Personnel and Training Research Center [*Air Force*]
PTRC........ PTRC. Planning and Transport Research and Computation [*A publication*]
PTRD........ Part Redeemed [*Stock exchange term*]   (SPSG)
PTREA ...... Philips Technical Review [*A publication*]
PTREDQ ... Proceedings. Technical Session on Cane Sugar Refining Research [*A publication*]
PTRF .... Peacetime Rate Factor [*Military*]   (AABC)
PTRF .... Peacetime Replacement Factor [*Military*]
PTRI .... Pharmaceutical and Toxicological Research Institute [*Ohio State University*] [*Research center*]   (RCD)
PTRI .... Theatre Research International [*A publication*]
Ptr Ink........ Printers' Ink [*A publication*]
Ptr Ink Mo ... Printers' Ink Monthly [*A publication*]
PTRJ .... Powered Thermocouple Reference Junction
PTRK........ Preston Corp. [*NASDAQ symbol*]   (NQ)
PTRL........ Petrol Industries, Inc. [*NASDAQ symbol*]   (NQ)
PTRM....... Partial Thermoremanent Magnetization [*Geophysics*]
PTRNMKR ... Patternmaker   (WGA)
PTRO .... Koror [*Caroline Islands*] [*ICAO location identifier*]   (ICLI)
PTRO .... Personnel Transaction Register by Originator [*Military*]   (AABC)
PTRO .... Petrominerals Corp. [*NASDAQ symbol*]   (NQ)
PTRO .... Preoverhaul Test Requirement Outline
PTRR .... Port Townsend Railroad, Inc. [*Formerly, PTS*] [*AAR code*]
PTRS .... Philosophical Transactions. Royal Society of London [*A publication*]
PTRSC....... Proceedings and Transactions. Royal Society of Canada [*A publication*]
PT Rulings ... Pay-Roll Tax Rulings [*Australia*] [*A publication*]
PTRY........ Pottery [*Freight*]
PTS........... Painful Tonic Seizure   (AAMN)
PTS........... Pali Text Society   (EA)
PTS........... Paper Tape-to-Magnetic Tape Conversion System   (DIT)
PTS........... Paper Tape Sender
PTS........... Papiertechnische Stiftung [*Database producer*]
PTS........... Para-Toluenesulfonic Acid
PTS........... Parachute Training School [*British military*]   (DMA)
PTS........... Parameter Test Setup

PTS........... Parts
PTS........... Patellar-Tendon Supracondylar [*Anatomy*]
PTS........... Payload Test Set [*NASA*]   (NASA)
PTS........... Payload Transportation System [*NASA*]   (MCD)
PTS........... People's Translation Service   (EA)
PTS........... Performance Tracking System
PTS........... Permanent Threshold Shift [*Hearing evaluation*]
PTS........... Petro-Sun International, Inc. [*Toronto Stock Exchange symbol*]
PTS........... Photogrammetric Target System [*Air Force*]
PTS........... Photothermal Spectroscopy
PTS........... Pi Tau Sigma [*Society*]
PTS........... Pilot Training Squadron [*Air Force*]
PTS........... Pittsburg, KS [*Location identifier*] [*FAA*]   (FAAL)
PTS........... Planning Tracking System   (MCD)
PTS........... Player Trade Society [*A union*] [*British*]
PTS........... Pneumatic Test Sequencer   (AFM)
PTS........... Pneumatic Test Set   (KSC)
PTS........... Pneumatic Tube System
PTS........... Pod Tail Section
PTS........... Pointing and Tracking Scope
PTS........... Port Townsend Railroad, Inc. [*Later, PTRR*] [*AAR code*]
PTS........... Post-Traumatic Stress [*Medicine*]
PTS........... Power Transfer Switch
PTS........... Power Transient Suppressor   (IEEE)
PTS........... Precision Timing System
PTS........... Predicasts Terminal Systems [*Predicasts, Inc.*] [*Cleveland, OH*] [*Database*]
PTS........... Predicasts Time Series [*Series of databases*] [*Predicasts, Inc.*] [*Cleveland, OH*]
PTS........... Preflight Test Set   (DNAB)
PTS........... Pressure Test Station   (DNAB)
PTS........... Pressurized Thermal Shock [*Nuclear energy*]
PTS........... Price-Tag Shock [*See also PTA*]
PTS........... Prime Time Sunday [*TV program*]
PTS........... Princeton Theological Seminary, Princeton, NJ [*OCLC symbol*]   (OCLC)
PTS........... Private Telecommunications Systems [*Radio-Suisse Ltd.*] [*Switzerland*] [*Telecommunications*]
PTS........... Proactive TMDE Support   (RDA)
PTS........... Proceed to Select [*Telecommunications*]   (TEL)
PTS........... Proceed to Send [*Telecommunications*]   (TEL)
PTS........... Production Test Specification
PTS........... Professional Travelogue Sponsors   (EA)
PTS........... Program of Technology and Society [*Later, DTS*]   (EA)
PTS........... Program Test System [*Data processing*]   (IEEE)
PTS........... Program Triple Store
PTS........... Programmer Test Station
PTS........... Propellant Transfer System
PTS........... Public Telephone Service [*or System*] [*Telecommunications*]   (TEL)
PTS........... Pure Time Sharing [*Data processing*]   (IEEE)
PTSA .... Kusaie [*Caroline Islands*] [*ICAO location identifier*]   (ICLI)
PTSA .... Para-Toluenesulfonic Acid [*Organic chemistry*]
PTSA .... Parent-Teacher-Student Association [*Nickname: "Pizza"*]
PTSA .... Professional Trucking Services Association   (EA)
PT-S/C ...... Proof Test Spacecraft [*NASA*]
PTSD .... Pesticides and Toxic Substances Division [*Environmental Protection Agency*]   (GFGA)
PTSD .... Post-Traumatic Stress Disorder [*Psychiatry*]
PTSE .... Paper Tape Splicing Equipment
PTSI .... PAM Transportation Services, Inc. [*NASDAQ symbol*]   (NQ)
PTSI .... Para-Toluene Sulfonylisocyanate [*Organic chemistry*]
PTSLA....... Plant Science Letters [*A publication*]
PTSO .... Personnel Transaction Summary by Originator [*Photographer*] [*Military*]   (AABC)
PTSP .... Peacetime Support Period [*DoD*]
PT/SP........ Pressure Tube to Spool Piece [*Nuclear energy*]   (NRCH)
PTS PROMT ... Predicasts Overview of Markets and Technology [*Predicasts, Inc.*] [*Cleveland, OH*] [*Bibliographic database*]
PTSR .... Performance Technical Survey Report
PTSR .... Preliminary Technical Survey Report [*Military*]   (AFIT)
PTSR .... Pressure-Tube Superheat Reactor [*Nuclear energy*]
PTSS......... Photon Target Scoring System   (AAG)
PTSS......... Princeton Time Sharing Services, Inc.
PTSSD5..... US National Park Service. Transactions and Proceedings [*A publication*]
PTST .... Personnel Transaction Summary by Type Transaction [*Military*]   (AABC)
PTST .... Pretransfusion Serologic Testing
PTST .... Prime Time School Television   (EA)
PTSU .... Theatre Survey [*A publication*]
PTT........... Pacific Telephone & Telegraph Co.   (FAAC)
PTT........... Part Task Trainer   (MCD)
PTT........... Partial Thromboplastin Time [*Hematology*]
PTT........... Particle Transport Time   (MAE)
PTT........... Party Test [*Telecommunications*]   (TEL)
PTT........... Peak Twitch Tension [*Physiology*]
PTT........... Petrotex Resources [*Vancouver Stock Exchange symbol*]
PTT........... Physical Therapist Technician
PTT........... Platform Transmitter Terminal [*Satellite-based tracking system*]

PTT........... Post und Telegraphenverwaltung [*Postal and Telegraph Administration*] [*Austria*] [*Telecommunications*]
PTT........... Post, Telephon und Telegraphenbetriebe [*Switzerland*] [*Telecommunications*]
PTT........... Post Ten Tumblers [*Pseudonym used by William Maginn*]
PTT........... Postal, Telegraph, and Telephone Administration (NATG)
PTT........... Postes, Telegraphes, et Telediffusion [*Post, Telegraph, and Telephone*] [*General Post Office*] [*Facetious translation: Prostitution Telematique et Telephonique*] [*France*]
PTT........... Pratt, KS [*Location identifier*] [*FAA*] (FAAL)
PTT........... Press to Transmit
PTT........... Private Tombs at Thebes [*Oxford*] [*A publication*] (BJA)
PTT........... Production Type Test
PTT........... Program Technical Training (AFM)
PTT........... Program Test Tape [*Data processing*] (IEEE)
PTT........... Prothrombin Time [*Hematology*] (AAMN)
PTT........... Public Telecommunications Trust [*Proposed replacement for Corporation for Public Broadcasting*]
PTT........... Pulmonary Transit Time [*Physiology*]
PTT........... Push to Talk
PTTC........ Pacific Transportation Terminal Command [*Army*]
PTTC........ Paper Tape and Transmission Code
PTTDA...... Petroleum Today [*A publication*]
PTTDAR ... Personnel Training and Training Devices Analysis Report (MCD)
PTTH .... Prothoracicotropic Hormone
PTTI .... Postal, Telegraph, and Telephone International [*See also IPTT*] [*Geneva, Switzerland*] (EAIO)
PTTI .... Precise Time and Time Interval (AFM)
PTTI Stud ... PTTI [*Postal, Telegraph, and Telephone International*] Studies [*A publication*]
PTTK........ Kosrae Island [*Caroline Islands*] [*ICAO location identifier*] (ICLI)
PTTK........ Partial Thromboplastin Time with Kaolin [*Hematology*]
PTTL......... Press-to-Test Light
PTTMC..... PACOM [*Pacific Command*] Tactical Target Materials Catalog (CINC)
PTTPD ...... Bandaoti Xuebao [*A publication*]
PTTS .... Pressure Temperature Test Set (DWSG)
PTU .... Package Transfer Unit
PTU .... Pallet Transporter Unit [*Military*] (CAAL)
PTU .... Parallel Transmission Unit (AAG)
PTU .... Part-Throttle Unlock [*Automotive engineering*]
PTU .... Pathology Transcription Unit
PTU .... Phenylthiourea [*Organic chemistry*]
PTU .... Pilot Test Unit [*Air Force*]
PTU .... Planning Tracking Unit (MCD)
PTU .... Platinum [*Alaska*] [*Airport symbol*] (OAG)
PTU .... Platinum, AK [*Location identifier*] [*FAA*] (FAAL)
PTU .... Plumbing Trades Union [*British*]
PTU .... Portable Test Unit
PTU .... Power Transfer Unit
PTU .... Propylthiouracil [*Also, PROP, PT*] [*Thyroid inhibitor*]
PTUC........ Pacific Trade Union Community [*Australia*] (EAIO)
PTV........... Parachute Test Vehicle
PTV........... Paratransit Vehicle
PTV........... Passenger Transfer Vehicle [*Airport transportation*]
PTV........... Passenger Transport Vehicle
PTV........... Pathfinder Test Vehicle [*NASA*] (MCD)
PTV........... Pay Television
PTV........... Peach Tree Valley [*California*] [*Seismograph station code, US Geological Survey*] (SEIS)
PTV........... Peak-to-Valley
PTV........... Penetration Test Vehicle [*Aerospace*]
PTV........... Pietas Tutissima Virtus [*Piety Is the Safest Virtue*] [*Latin*] [*Motto of Ernst, Margrave of Brandenburg (1583-1613)*]
PTV........... Pitch Thrust Vector (KSC)
PTV........... Porous Tungsten Vaporizer
PTV........... Porterville, CA [*Location identifier*] [*FAA*] (FAAL)
PTV........... Predetermined Time Value (IEEE)
PTV........... Programmable Temperature Vaporizer
PTV........... Programmed-Temperature Vaporizing [*Analytical chemistry*]
PTV........... Propulsion Technology Validation (MCD)
PTV........... Propulsion Test Vehicle
PTV........... Prototype Test Vehicle (MCD)
PTV........... Public Television
PTV........... Punched Tape Verifier [*Data processing*]
PTVA........ Propulsion Test Vehicle Assembly [*NASA*]
PTVC........ Pitch Thrust Vector Control (KSC)
PTVD........ Portable Toxic Vapor Detector
PTVE........ Propulsion Test Vehicle Engineering [*NASA*] (MCD)
PTVST....... Port Visit [*Navy*] (NVT)
PTVV........ Peak-to-Valley Variation (MCD)
PT & W..... Physical Training and Welfare [*British military*] (DMA)
PTW .... Physikalisch-Technische-Werkstatten [*Roentgenology*]
PTW .... Pilot Training Wing [*Air Force*]
PTW .... Playing to Win (EA)
PTW .... Point Target Weapon
PTW .... Pottstown, PA [*Location identifier*] [*FAA*] (FAAL)
PTW .... Pressure-Treated Wood
PTW .... Pressure-Type Window

PTWC....... Pacific Tsunami Warning Center [*National Weather Service*] (MSC)
PTWC....... Project on Technology, Work, and Character (EA)
PTWF....... Pakistan Transport Workers' Federation
PTWG ...... Provisioning Technical Working Group
PTWL....... Tulsa Studies in Women's Literature [*A publication*]
PTWM...... Power Transformation Weighting Method [*Mathematics*]
P-TWP...... Post-Township
PTWT....... Photo-Type Traveling Wave Tube (NG)
PTX........... Pacific Trans-Ocean Resources Ltd. [*Toronto Stock Exchange symbol*]
PTX........... Palytoxin [*Organic chemistry*]
PTx........... Parathyroidectomy [*Medicine*]
PTX........... Pertussis Toxin [*Pharmacology*]
PTX........... Picrotoxin [*Biochemistry*]
PTX........... Pneumothorax [*Medicine*] (AAMN)
PTX........... Polythiazide [*Organic chemistry*]
PTX........... Pressure-Temperature Composition
PTXB........ Pumiliotoxin B [*Organic chemistry*]
PTXS .... Texas Studies in Literature and Language [*A publication*]
PTY........... Panama City [*Panama*] [*Airport symbol*] (OAG)
PTY........... Party (AAG)
PTY........... Proprietary
PTYA........ Yap [*Caroline Islands*] [*ICAO location identifier*] (ICLI)
PTZ........... Pentylenetetrazole [*CNS stimulant*]
PU............. Pack Unit [*Single title, multiple orders*] [*Publishing*] [*British*]
PU............. Paid Up [*Insurance*] (EY)
PU............. Parents United (EA)
PU............. Participating Unit (NVT)
PU............. Parts Used [*Medicine*]
PU............. Passed Urine [*Medicine*]
PU............. Paste Up (ADA)
PU............. Peptic Ulcer [*Medicine*]
PU............. Per Urethra [*Medicine*]
PU............. Perbonate Unit [*Analytical biochemistry*]
PU............. Percent Utilization [*Anesthesiology*]
PU............. Peripheral Unit [*Computers*] (MSA)
PU............. Personnel, Utility [*British military*] (DMA)
PU............. Peru [*IYRU nationality code*] (IYR)
PU............. Physical Unit [*Data processing*] (IBMDP)
PU............. Pick Up [*Business term*]
PU............. Plant Unit
PU............. Players' Union [*Football*] [*British*]
PU............. Pluggable Unit (SAA)
Pu............. Plutonium [*Chemical element*]
PU............. Polyurethane [*Also, PUR*] [*Organic chemistry*]
PU............. Power Equipment [*JETDS nomenclature*] [*Military*] (CET)
PU............. Power Unit
PU............. Pregnancy Urine [*Medicine*]
PU............. Prilled Urea [*A fertilizer*]
PU............. Primeras Lineas Uruguayas [*ICAO designator*] (FAAC)
PU............. Princeton University
PU............. Prisoner's Union [*Later, PRU*] (EA)
PU............. Problemi di Ulisse [*A publication*]
PU............. Processing Unit [*Data processing*]
PU............. Processor Utility [*Telecommunications*] (TEL)
PU............. Production Unit (CAAL)
PU............. Propellant Unit (NASA)
PU............. Propellant Utilization [*Aerospace*]
PU............. Propulsion Unit (KSC)
PU............. Propyleneurea [*Organic chemistry*]
PU............. Proutist Universal (EA)
PU............. Publications (MCD)
PU............. Publisher [*Online database field identifier*]
PU............. Puetzer [*Germany*] [*ICAO aircraft manufacturer identifier*] (ICAO)
PU............. Pump Unit (AAG)
Pu............. Punic (BJA)
Pu............. Punjab Regiment [*Army*] [*India*]
PU............. Purdue University
Pu............. Purine [*Biochemistry*]
PU............. Purple (ROG)
PU............. University of Pennsylvania, Philadelphia, PA [*Library symbol*] [*Library of Congress*] (LCLS)
PUA .... Partido de Unificacion Anticomunista [*Anti-Communist Unification Party*] [*Guatemala*] [*Political party*] (PPW)
PUA .... Plant-Unique Analysis [*Nuclear energy*] (NRCH)
PUA .... Polish Union of America (EA)
PUA .... Pride Users' Association [*Defunct*] (EA)
PUA .... Public Administration [*A publication*]
PU-A......... University of Pennsylvania, Morris Arboretum, Philadelphia, PA [*Library symbol*] [*Library of Congress*] (LCLS)
PUAA .... Public Utilities Advertising Association [*Later, PUCA*] (EA)
PUAC .... Propellant Utilization Acoustical Checkout (AAG)
PU-AC....... University of Pennsylvania, Annenberg School of Communications, Philadelphia, PA [*Library symbol*] [*Library of Congress*] (LCLS)
PUAD........ Pueblo Army Depot [*Colorado*] (AABC)
PUADA ..... Pueblo Army Depot Activity (AABC)
PUAHC..... Proceedings. Union of American Hebrew Congregations [*A publication*]

PUAID ...... Parti d'Unite Arabe Islamique-Democratique [*Algeria*] [*Political party*]   (EY)
PUAQ .... Urban Affairs Quarterly [*A publication*]
PUAR .... Pulse Acquisition RADAR [*Military*]   (MSA)
PUAS .... Postal Union of the Americas and Spain [*See also UPAE*] [*Montevideo, Uruguay*]   (EAIO)
PUASAL ... Proceedings. Utah Academy of Sciences, Arts, and Letters [*A publication*]
PUASP ...... Postal Union of the Americas, Spain, and Portugal [*Uruguay*]   (EAIO)
PUB .... Pacific University Bulletin [*A publication*]
PUB .... Partido Union Boliviana [*Bolivian Unity Party*] [*Political party*]   (PPW)
PUB .... Phycourobilin [*Biochemistry*]
PUB .... Physical Unit Block [*Data processing*]
PUB .... Puale Bay [*Alaska*] [*Seismograph station code, US Geological Survey*]   (SEIS)
PUB .... Public
PUB .... Public House [*A drinking establishment*] [*British*]
PUB .... Publication   (AFM)
PUB .... Publicity
PUB .... Published   (AABC)
PUB .... Publisher
Pub .... Publisher [*A publication*]
PUB .... Pueblo [*Colorado*] [*Airport symbol*]   (OAG)
PUB .... Pueblo, CO [*Location identifier*] [*FAA*]   (FAAL)
Pub Adm .... Public Administration [*A publication*]
Pub Admin ... Public Administration [*A publication*]   (APTA)
Pub Admin Abstr ... Public Administration Abstracts and Index of Articles [*A publication*]
Pub Admin Survey ... Public Administration Survey [*A publication*]
Pub Adm R ... Public Administration Review [*A publication*]
Pub Adm Rev ... Public Administration Review [*A publication*]
Pub Ad Rev ... Public Administration Review [*A publication*]
PUBAFF .... Public Affairs   (DNAB)
PUBAFFRRU ... Public Affairs Ready Reserve Unit   (DNAB)
Pub Am Stat Assn ... Publications. American Statistical Association [*A publication*]
Pub Archives Can Report ... Public Archives of Canada. Report [*A publication*]
Pub Ast S J ... Publications. Astronomical Society of Japan [*A publication*]
Pub Ast S P ... Publications. Astronomical Society of the Pacific [*A publication*]
Pub Bargaining Cas (CCH) ... Public Bargaining Cases (Commerce Clearing House) [*A publication*]   (DLA)
Pubbl (Bergamo) Sta Sper Maiscoltura ... Pubblicazioni (Bergamo) Stazione Sperimentale di Maiscoltura [*A publication*]
Pubbl Centro Sper Agr Forest ENCC ... Pubblicazioni. Centro di Sperimentazione Agricola e Forestale. Ente Nazionale per la Cellulosa e per la Carta [*A publication*]
Pubbl Cent Sper Agric For ... Pubblicazioni. Centro di Sperimentazione Agricola e Forestale [*A publication*]
Pubbl Cent Sper Agric For (Rome) ... Pubblicazioni. Centro di Sperimentazione Agricola e Forestale (Rome) [*A publication*]
Pubbl Cent Stud Citogenet Veg CNR ... Pubblicazioni. Centro di Studio per la Citogenetica Vegetale. Consiglio Nazionale della Ricerche [*A publication*]
Pubbl Chim Biol Med Ist "Carlo Erba" Ric Ter ... Pubblicazioni Chimiche, Biologiche, e Mediche. Istituto "Carlo Erba" per Ricerche Terapeutiche [*A publication*]
Pubbl Ente Naz Cellulosa Carta ... Pubblicazioni. Ente Nazionale per la Cellulosa e per la Carta [*A publication*]
Pubbl Fac Sci Ing Univ Trieste Ser A ... Pubblicazioni. Facolta di Scienze e d'Ingegneria. Universita di Trieste. Serie A [*A publication*]
Pubbl Fac Sci Ing Univ Trieste Ser B ... Pubblicazioni. Facolta di Scienze e d'Ingegneria. Universita di Trieste. Serie B [*A publication*]
Pubbl IAC ... Pubblicazioni. Istituto per le Applicazioni del Calcolo. Consiglio Nazionale delle Ricerche [*A publication*]
Pubbl Ist Chim Agrar Sper Gorizia Nuovi Ann ... Pubblicazione. Istituto Chimico Agrario Sperimentale di Gorizia. Nuovi Annali [*A publication*]
Pubbl Ist Geol Mineral Univ Ferrara ... Pubblicazioni. Istituto di Geologia e Mineralogia. Universita di Ferrara [*A publication*]
Pubbl Ist Sper Selv (Arezzo) ... Pubblicazioni. Istituto Sperimentale per la Selvicoltura (Arezzo, Italy) [*A publication*]
Pubbl Oss Geofis Trieste ... Pubblicazioni. Osservatorio Geofisico di Trieste [*A publication*]
Pubbl Ser III ... Pubblicazione. Serie III [*A publication*]
Pubbl Stn Zool Napoli ... Pubblicazioni. Stazione Zoologica di Napoli [*A publication*]
PUBC .... Presbyterians United for Biblical Concerns [*Later, PBC*]   (EA)
PUBC .... Pubcoa, Inc. [*NASDAQ symbol*]   (NQ)
Pubcaster ... Public Broadcaster [*Radio or TV station affiliated with NPR or PBS*]
Pub Circ ..... Publishers' Circular and Booksellers' Record [*A publication*]
Pub Col Soc Mass ... Publications. Colonial Society of Massachusetts [*A publication*]
Pub Cont LJ ... Public Contract Law Journal [*A publication*]
Pub Cont Newsl ... Public Contract Newsletter [*A publication*]
Pub Contract L J ... Public Contract Law Journal [*A publication*]

PUBD .... Published   (ROG)
PUB DOC ... Public Documents   (ROG)
Pub Dom Ast ... Publications. Dominion Astrophysical Observatory [*A publication*]
Pub Emp .... Public Employee [*A publication*]
Pub Employee Bargaining CCH ... Public Employee Bargaining. Commerce Clearing House [*A publication*]
Pub Employee Bargaining Rep (CCH) ... Public Employee Bargaining Reports (Commerce Clearing House) [*A publication*]   (DLA)
Pub Employee Rel Rep ... Public Employee Relations Reports [*A publication*]   (DLA)
Pub Ent Advert & Allied Fields LQ ... Publishing, Entertainment, Advertising, and Allied Fields Law Quarterly [*A publication*]   (DLA)
Pub Ent Adv LQ ... Publishing, Entertainment, Advertising, and Allied Fields Law Quarterly [*A publication*]
Pub Gen Laws ... Public General Laws [*A publication*]   (DLA)
PUB HA .... Public Hall [*Freemasonry*]   (ROG)
Pub Health ... United States Public Health Service, Court Decisions [*A publication*]   (DLA)
Pub Health Monogr ... Public Health Monographs [*A publication*]
Pub Health Nurs ... Public Health Nursing [*A publication*]
Pub Health Rep ... Public Health Reports [*A publication*]
Pub Health Rept ... Public Health Reports [*A publication*]
Pub Health Rep US Pub Health and Mar Hosp Serv ... Public Health Reports. United States Surgeon-General. Public Health and Marine Hospital Service [*A publication*]
Pub Health Rep US Pub Health Serv ... Public Health Reports. United States Public Health Service [*A publication*]
Pub Health Soc B ... Public Health Society. Bulletin [*Kuala Lumpur*] [*A publication*]
Pub Hist Inst Luxembourg ... Publications. Section Historique. Institut Grand-Ducal de Luxembourg [*A publication*]
PUBINFO ... Office of Public Information [*Formerly, OPR*] [*Navy*]
Pub Interest ... Public Interest [*A publication*]
Pub Intl L .... Public International Law [*A publication*]   (DLA)
PUBL .... Public   (WGA)
Pub L .... Public Law [*A publication*]
PUBL .... Publication [*or Published or Publisher*]   (EY)
Publ Adm ... Public Administration [*A publication*]   (APTA)
Publ Admin ... Public Administration [*A publication*]
Publ Adm R ... Public Administration Review [*A publication*]
Publ Adm Re ... Public Administration Review [*A publication*]
Publ Aff B .. Public Affairs Bulletin [*A publication*]
Publ Agric (Can) ... Publication. Agriculture (Canada) [*A publication*]
Publ Agric Ext Serv N Carol St Univ ... Publication. Agricultural Extension Service. North Carolina State University [*A publication*]
Publ Agric Res Serv US Dep Agric ... Publication. Agricultural Research Service. United States Department of Agriculture [*A publication*]
Publ Alberta Dept Agr ... Publication. Alberta Department of Agriculture [*A publication*]
Publ Allegheny Obs Univ Pittsburgh ... Publications. Allegheny Observatory. University of Pittsburgh [*A publication*]
Publ Amakusa Mar Biol Lab Kyushu Univ ... Publications. Amakusa Marine Biological Laboratory. Kyushu University [*A publication*]
Publ Am Assoc Adv Sci ... Publication. American Association for the Advancement of Science [*A publication*]
Publ Am Concr Inst ... Publication. American Concrete Institute [*A publication*]
Publ Amer Ass Advan Sci ... Publication. American Association for the Advancement of Science [*A publication*]
Publ Amer Univ Beirut Fac Agr Sci ... Publication. American University of Beirut. Faculty of Agricultural Sciences [*A publication*]
Publ Am Inst Biol Sci ... Publication. American Institute of Biological Sciences [*A publication*]
Publ Am Inst Hist Pharm ... Publication. American Institute of the History of Pharmacy [*A publication*]
Publ Am Pet Inst ... Publication. American Petroleum Institute [*A publication*]
Publ Am Univ Beirut Fac Agric Sci ... Publication. American University of Beirut. Faculty of Agricultural Sciences [*A publication*]
Publ ANARE Data Rep Ser ... Publications. ANARE [*Australian National Antarctic Research Expeditions*] Data Reports Series [*A publication*]   (APTA)
Pub Land L Rev ... Public Land Law Review [*A publication*]   (DLA)
Pub Land & Res L Dig ... Public Land and Resources Law Digest [*A publication*]
Pub Lands Dec ... Department of the Interior, Decisions Relating to Public Lands [*A publication*]   (DLA)
Publ Ass For-Cell ... Publication. Association Foret-Cellulose [*A publication*]
Publ Assoc Etude Paleontol Stratigr Houilleres ... Publication. Association pour l'Etude de la Paleontologie et de la Stratigraphie Houilleres [*A publication*]
Publ Assoc Ing Fac Polytech Mons ... Publications. Association des Ingenieurs. Faculte Polytechnique de Mons [*A publication*]
Publ Astron Soc Jpn ... Publications. Astronomical Society of Japan [*A publication*]
Publ Astron Soc Pac ... Publications. Astronomical Society of the Pacific [*A publication*]

Publ Aust Natl Univ Res Sch Phys Sci Dep Eng Phys ... Australian National University. Research School of Physical Sciences. Department of Engineering Physics. Publication [*A publication*]   (APTA)
Publ Avulsa FZB Fund Zoobot Rio Grande Sul ... Publicacao Avulsa FZB. Fundacao Zoobotanica do Rio Grande Do Sul [*A publication*]
Publ Avulsas Cent Pesqui Aggeu Magalhaes (Recife Braz) ... Publicacoes Avulsas. Centro de Pesquisas Aggeu Megalhaes (Recife, Brazil) [*A publication*]
Publ Avulsas Inst Aggeu Magalhaes (Recife Braz) ... Publicacoes Avulsas. Instituto Aggeu Magalhaes (Recife, Brazil) [*A publication*]
Publ Avulsas Mus Nac (Rio De J) ... Publicacoes Avulsas. Museu Nacional (Rio De Janeiro) [*A publication*]
Pub Law For ... Public Law Forum [*A publication*]
Publ BC Minist Agric ... Publications. British Columbia Ministry of Agriculture [*A publication*]
Publ BC Minist Agric Food ... Publications. British Columbia Ministry of Agriculture and Food [*A publication*]
Publ Beaverlodge Res Stn ... Publication. Beaverlodge Research Station [*A publication*]
Publ Bot ..... Publications in Botany [*A publication*]
Publ Bot Univ Calif Berkeley ... Publications in Botany. University of California, Berkeley [*A publication*]
Publ Brit Columbia Dept Agr ... Publication. British Columbia Department of Agriculture [*A publication*]
Publ Bur Etud Geol Minieres Colon (Paris) ... Publications. Bureau d'Etudes Geologiques et Minieres Coloniales (Paris) [*A publication*]
Publ Bur Rech Geol Geophys Minieres (Fr) ... Publications. Bureau de Recherches Geologiques, Geophysiques, et Minieres (France) [*A publication*]
Publ Cairo Univ Herb ... Publications. Cairo University Herbarium [*A publication*]
Publ Calif Dep Agric ... Publication. California Department of Agriculture [*A publication*]
Publ Calif State Water Resour Control Board ... Publication. California State Water Resources Control Board [*A publication*]
Publ Canada Dep Agric ... Publication. Canada Department of Agriculture [*A publication*]
Publ Canada Dep For ... Publication. Canada Department of Forestry [*A publication*]
Publ Can Dep Agric ... Publication. Canada Department of Agriculture [*A publication*]
Publ Can Dept Agr ... Publication. Canada Department of Agriculture [*A publication*]
Publ Can For Serv ... Publication. Canadian Forestry Service [*A publication*]
Publ Carnegie Inst Washington ... Publication. Carnegie Institution of Washington [*A publication*]
Publ Cent Adv Study Geol (Chandigarh India) ... Publication. Centre of Advanced Study in Geology (Chandigarh, India) [*A publication*]
Publ Center Medieval Ren Stud UCLA ... Publications. Center for Medieval and Renaissance Studies. UCLA [*University of California at Los Angeles*] [*A publication*]
Publ Cent Estud Leprol ... Publicacoes. Centro de Estudos Leprologicos [*A publication*]
Publ Cent Etude Util Sciures de Bois ... Publication. Centre d'Etude pour l'Utilisation des Sciures de Bois [*A publication*]
Publ Cent Natl Exploit Oceans Actes Colloq ... Publications. Centre National pour l'Exploitation des Oceans. Actes de Colloques [*A publication*]
Publ Cent Natl Exploit Oceans Result Campagnes Mer ... Publications. Centre National pour l'Exploitation des Oceans. Resultats des Campagnes a la Mer [*A publication*]
Publ Cent Natl Exploit Oceans Ser Rapp Sci Tech (Fr) ... Publications. Centre National pour l'Exploitation des Oceans. Serie. Rapport Scientifique et Technique (France) [*A publication*]
Publ Cent Natl Geol Houillere ... Publication. Centre National de Geologie Houillere [*A publication*]
Publ Cent Quim Ind (Buenos Aires) ... Publicacion. Centro de Quimicos Industriales (Buenos Aires) [*A publication*]
Publ Cent Rech Zootech Univ Louvain ... Publication. Centre de Recherches Zootechniques. Universite de Louvain [*A publication*]
Publ Centre Recherches Math Pures Ser 3 ... Publications. Centre de Recherches en Mathematiques Pures. Serie 3 [*A publication*]
Publ Centre Rech Math Pures ... Publications. Centre de Recherches en Mathematiques Pures [*A publication*]
Publ Centre Rech Math Pures 1 ... Publications. Centre de Recherches en Mathematiques Pures. Serie 1 [*A publication*]
Publ Centre Rech Math Pures Ser 3 ... Publications. Centre de Recherches en Mathematiques Pures. Serie 3 [*A publication*]
Publ Centre Tech For Trop ... Publication. Centre Technique Forestier Tropical [*A publication*]
Publ Cent Tech For Trop (Nogent-Sur-Marne Fr) ... Publication. Centre Technique Forestier Tropical (Nogent-Sur-Marne, France) [*A publication*]
Publ Chile Univ Cent Estud Entomol ... Publicaciones. Chile Universidad. Centro de Estudios Entomologicos [*A publication*]
Publ Choice ... Public Choice [*A publication*]

Publ Clark ... Publications. Clark Library Professorship. University of California at Los Angeles [*A publication*]
Publ Cleans ... Public Cleansing [*A publication*]
Publ CMMI Congr ... Publications. CMMI [*Council of Mining and Metallurgical Institutions*] Congress [*A publication*]
Publcoes Avuls Mus Parana ... Publicacoes Avulsas. Museu Paranaense [*A publication*]
Publcoes Cult Co Diam Angola ... Publicacoes Culturais. Companhia de Diamantes de Angola [*A publication*]
Publcoes Dir Ger Servs Flor Aquic ... Publicacoes. Direccao Geral dos Servicos Florestais e Aqueicolas [*A publication*]
Publ Coffee Brew Inst ... Publication. Coffee Brewing Institute [*A publication*]
Publ Com Nac Energ At (Argent) Misc ... Publicaciones. Comision Nacional de Energia Atomica (Argentina). Miscelanea [*A publication*]
Publ Com Nac Energ At (Argent) Ser Fis ... Publicaciones. Comision Nacional de Energia Atomica (Argentina). Serie Fisica [*A publication*]
Publ Com Nac Energ At (Argent) Ser Geol ... Publicaciones. Comision Nacional de Energia Atomica (Argentina). Serie Geologia [*A publication*]
Publ Com Nac Energ At (Argent) Ser Mat ... Publicaciones. Comision Nacional de Energia Atomica (Argentina). Serie Matematica [*A publication*]
Publ Com Nac Energ At (Argent) Ser Quim ... Publicaciones. Comision Nacional de Energia Atomica (Argentina). Serie Quimica [*A publication*]
Publ Cons Recur Nat No Renov (Mex) ... Publicacion. Consejo de Recursos Naturales No Renovables (Mexico) [*A publication*]
Publ Cons Recursos Miner ... Publicacion. Consejo de Recursos Minerales [*A publication*]
Publ Contr LJ ... Public Contract Law Journal [*A publication*]
Publ Coop Ext Serv Miss State Univ ... Publication. Cooperative Extension Service. Mississippi State University [*A publication*]
Publ Coop Ext Serv Wash St Univ ... Publication. Cooperative Extension Service. Washington State University [*A publication*]
Publ Co-Op Ext Univ Calif ... Publication. Cooperative Extension. University of California [*A publication*]
Publ Cult Cia Diamantes Angola ... Publicacoes Culturais. Companhia de Diamantes de Angola [*A publication*]
PUBLD ...... Published   (ROG)
Publ Dep Agric (Can) ... Publication. Department of Agriculture (Ottawa, Canada) [*A publication*]
Publ Dep Cristalogr Miner CSIC (Spain) ... Publicaciones. Departamento de Cristalografia y Mineralogia. Consejo Superior de Investigaciones Cientificas (Spain) [*A publication*]
Publ Dep Eng Phys Res Sch Phys Sci Aust Natl Univ ... Publication. Department of Engineering Physics. Research School of Physical Sciences. Australian National University [*A publication*]
Publ Dep Math Lyon ... Publications. Departement de Mathematiques. Faculte des Sciences de Lyon [*A publication*]
Publ Dept Agr (Can) ... Publications. Department of Agriculture (Canada) [*A publication*]
Publ Dept Agr Conserv (Manitoba) ... Publications. Department of Agriculture and Conservation (Manitoba) [*A publication*]
Publ Dep Zool (Barc) ... Publicaciones. Departamento de Zoologia (Barcelona) [*A publication*]
Publ Dir Gen Geol Minas Repub Ecuador ... Publicacion. Direccion General de Geologia y Minas. Republica del Ecuador [*A publication*]
Publ Dir Gen Invent Nac For (Mex) ... Publicacion. Direccion General del Inventario Nacional Forestal (Coyoacan, Mexico) [*A publication*]
Publ Diverses Mus Natl Hist Nat ... Publications Diverses. Museum National d'Histoire Naturelle [*A publication*]
Publ Dom Astrophys Obs ... Publications. Dominion Astrophysical Observatory [*Victoria, British Columbia*] [*A publication*]
Publ Dom Astrophys Obs (Victoria BC) ... Publications. Dominion Astrophysical Observatory (Victoria, British Columbia) [*A publication*]
Publ Dom Obs (Ottawa) ... Publications. Dominion Observatory (Ottawa) [*A publication*]
Publ Dushanb Inst Epidemiol Gig ... Publikatsiya Dushanbinskogo Instituta Epidemiologii i Gigieny [*A publication*]
Publ Earth Phys Branch (Can) ... Publications. Earth Physics Branch (Canada) [*A publication*]
Publ Earth Phys Branch Dep Energy Mines & Resour ... Publications. Earth Physics Branch. Department of Energy, Mines, and Resources [*A publication*]
Publ Econometriques ... Publications Econometriques [*A publication*]
Publ EE Univ Toronto Inst Environ Stud ... Publication EE. University of Toronto. Institute for Environmental Studies [*A publication*]
Publ Elektrote Fak Univ Beogradu Ser Mat Fiz ... Publikacije Elektrotehnickog Fakulteta Univerziteta u Beogradu. Serija Matematika i Fizika [*A publication*]
Publ Elektroteh Fak Ser Elektroenerg ... Publikacije Elektrotehnickog Fakulteta. Serija Elektroenergetika [*A publication*]

Publ Elektroteh Fak Ser Elektron Telekommun Autom ... Publikacije Elektrotehnickog Fakulteta. Serija Elektronika Telekommunikacije. Automatika [*A publication*]
Publ Elektroteh Fak Ser Mat & Fiz ... Publikacije Elektrotehnickog Fakulteta. Serija Matematika i Fizika [*A publication*]
Publ Elektroteh Fak Univ Beogr Ser Mat Fiz ... Publikacije Elektrotehnickog Fakulteta Univerziteta u Beogradu. Serija Matematika i Fizika [*A publication*]
Publ Energ ... Publicacion sobre Energia [*A publication*]
Publ Eng Exp St State Univ Agric Appl Sci (Okla) ... Publication. Engineering Experiment Station. State University of Agriculture and Applied Science (Oklahoma) [*A publication*]
Publ Ent Adv A ... Publishing, Entertainment, Advertising, and Allied Fields Law Quarterly [*A publication*]
Publ E Purdue Univ Coop Ext Serv ... Publication E. Purdue University. Cooperative Extension Service [*A publication*]
Publ Espec Inst Nac Invest Forest (Mex) ... Publicacion Especial. Instituto Nacional de Investigaciones Forestal (Mexico) [*A publication*]
Publ Espec Inst Oceanogr (San Paulo) ... Publicacao Especial. Instituto Oceanografico (San Paulo) [*A publication*]
Publ Ethnol ... Publications in Ethnology [*A publication*]
Publ Eur Assoc Ani Prod ... Publication. European Association for Animal Production [*A publication*]
Publ Eur Gem ... Publicatieblad van de Europese Gemeenschappen [*A publication*]
Publ Ext Serv Israel Min Agric ... Israel. Ministry of Agriculture. Extension Service Publication [*A publication*]
Pub LF .... Public Law Forum [*A publication*] (DLA)
Publ Fac Agron Univ Teheran ... Publications. Faculte d'Agronomie. Universite de Teheran [*A publication*]
Publ Fac Agr Sci Amer Univ (Beirut) ... Publications. Faculty of Agricultural Sciences. American University (Beirut) [*A publication*]
Publ Fac Dr Econ Amiens ... Publications. Faculte de Droit et d'Economie d'Amiens [*A publication*]
Publ Fac Dr Sci Polit Soc Amiens ... Publications. Faculte de Droit et des Sciences Politiques et Sociales d'Amiens [*A publication*]
Publ Fac Sci Univ Clermont Geol Mineral ... Publications. Faculte des Sciences. Universite de Clermont. Geologie et Mineralogie [*A publication*]
Publ FAO/ECE Jt Comm Working Tech ... Publication. FAO [*Food and Agriculture Organization of the United Nations*]/ECE [*Economic Commission for Europe*] Joint Committee on Forest Working Techniques and Training Forest Workers [*A publication*]
Publ Far East Reg Inst Sci Res Vladivostok ... Publications. Far Eastern Regional Institute for Scientific Research. Vladivostok [*A publication*]
Publ Far East State Univ (Vladivostok) ... Publications. Far Eastern State University (Vladivostok) [*A publication*]
Publ Farm (Sao Paulo) ... Publicacoes Farmaceuticas (Sao Paulo) [*A publication*]
Publ Fert Soc S Afr ... Publication. Fertilizer Society of South Africa [*A publication*]
Publ Finan ... Public Finance [*A publication*]
Publ Finance ... Public Finance [*A publication*]
Publ Finn State Agric Res Board ... Publications. Finnish State Agricultural Research Board [*A publication*]
Publ Fin Q ... Public Finance Quarterly [*A publication*]
Publ Fond Agathon de Potter ... Publications. Foundation Agathon de Potter [*A publication*]
Publ For Commn NSW ... Publication. Forestry Commission of New South Wales [*A publication*]
Publ Foreign Agric Serv US Dep Agric ... Publication. Foreign Agricultural Service. United States Department of Agriculture [*A publication*]
Publ Forest Res Brch Canada Dep For ... Publication. Forest Research Branch. Canada Department of Forestry [*A publication*]
Publ For Res Inst Finl ... Publications. Forest Research Institute in Finland [*A publication*]
Publ For Sci ... Publications of Forestry Science [*A publication*]
Publ For Serv (Can) ... Publication. Forestry Service. Department of Fisheries and Forestry (Ottawa, Canada) [*A publication*]
Publ Found Sci Res Surinam Neth Antilles ... Publications. Foundation for Scientific Research in Surinam and the Netherlands Antilles [*A publication*]
Publ Geol Dep Ext Serv Univ West Aust ... Publication. Geology Department and the Extension Service. University of Western Australia [*A publication*]
Publ Geol Dep Victoria Univ Wellington ... Publication. Geology Department. Victoria University of Wellington [*A publication*]
Publ Geol Sci Univ Calif ... Publications in Geological Sciences. University of California [*A publication*]
Publ Geol Surv Queensl ... Publication. Geological Survey of Queensland [*A publication*] (APTA)
Publ Great Lakes Res Div Univ Mich ... Publication. Great Lakes Research Division. University of Michigan [*A publication*]
Publ Great Plains Agric Coun ... Great Plains Agricultural Council. Publication [*A publication*]
Publ Group Adv Psychiatry ... Publication. Groups for the Advancement of Psychiatry [*A publication*]

Publ Group Av Methodes Spectrogr ... Publication. Groupement pour l'Avancement des Methodes Spectrographiques [*A publication*]
Publ Gulf Coast Res Lab Mus ... Publications. Gulf Coast Research Laboratory. Museum [*A publication*]
Publ Haewundae Mar Lab Pusan Fish Coll ... Publications. Haewundae Marine Laboratory. Pusan Fisheries College [*A publication*]
Publ Hannah Inst Hist Med ... Publication. Hannah Institute for the History of Medicine [*A publication*]
Publ Heal ... Public Health: The Journal of the Society of Community Medicine [*A publication*]
Publ Heal R ... Public Health Reviews [*A publication*]
Publ Health Lab ... Public Health Laboratory [*A publication*]
Publ Hea Re ... Public Health Reports [*A publication*]
Publ Heb Univ (Jerusalem) ... Publications. Hebrew University (Jerusalem) [*A publication*]
Publ Hlth ... Public Health [*A publication*]
Publ Hlth Ne ... Public Health News [*A publication*]
Publ Hlth Rep (Wash) ... Public Health Reports (Washington, DC) [*A publication*]
Publ Hung Cent Inst Dev Min ... Publications. Hungarian Central Institute for the Development of Mining [*A publication*]
Publ Hung Min Res Inst ... Publications. Hungarian Mining Research Institute [*A publication*]
Publ Hung Res Inst Mining ... Publications. Hungarian Research Institute for Mining [*A publication*]
Pub Lib ...... Public Libraries [*A publication*]
Pub Lib Op ... Public Library Opinion [*A publication*] (APTA)
Pub Lib Trustee ... Public Library Trustee [*A publication*]
public .... Publicist
Publicaciones Dept Agric Costa Rica ... Publicaciones. Departamento de Agricultura de Costa Rica [*A publication*]
Public Adm ... Public Administration [*A publication*]
Public Adm Abstr Index Artic (India) ... Public Administration Abstracts and Index of Articles (India) [*A publication*]
Public Adm Bull ... Public Administration Bulletin [*A publication*]
Public Admin ... Public Administration [*A publication*] (APTA)
Public Admin Bull ... Public Administration Bulletin [*A publication*]
Public Admin and Development ... Public Administration and Development [*A publication*]
Public Admin J (Kathmandu) ... Public Administration Journal (Kathmandu) [*A publication*]
Public Admin R ... Public Administration Review [*A publication*]
Public Admin Survey ... Public Administration Survey [*A publication*]
Public Adm R ... Public Administration Review [*A publication*]
Public Adm Rev ... Public Administration Review [*A publication*]
Public Affairs Rept ... Public Affairs Report [*A publication*]
Public Aff Inf Serv Bull ... Public Affairs Information Service Bulletin [*A publication*]
Public Aff Rep ... Public Affairs Report [*A publication*]
Public Anal Assoc J ... Public Analysts Association. Journal [*England*] [*A publication*]
Public Budgeting and Fin ... Public Budgeting and Finance [*A publication*]
Public Clean Tech Rep ... Public Cleansing Technical Report [*A publication*]
Public Fin ... Public Finance [*A publication*]
Public Fin Account ... Public Finance and Accountancy [*A publication*]
Public Fin (Berlin) ... Public Finance (Berlin) [*A publication*]
Public Fin Q ... Public Finance Quarterly [*A publication*]
Public Health Eng ... Public Health Engineer [*England*] [*A publication*]
Public Health Eng Abstr ... Public Health Engineering Abstracts [*A publication*]
Public Health Eng Conf Proc ... Public Health Engineering Conference. Proceedings [*A publication*]
Public Health Eur ... Public Health in Europe [*A publication*]
Public Health J ... Public Health Journal [*A publication*]
Public Health J (Peking) ... Public Health Journal (Peking) [*A publication*]
Public Health Lab ... Public Health Laboratory [*United States*] [*A publication*]
Public Health Monogr ... Public Health Monograph [*A publication*]
Public Health Nurs ... Public Health Nursing [*A publication*]
Public Health Pap ... Public Health Papers [*A publication*]
Public Health Rep ... Public Health Reports [*A publication*]
Public Health Rev ... Public Health Reviews [*A publication*]
Public Health Revs ... Public Health Reviews [*A publication*]
Public Health Soc Med Hyg ... Public Health. Social Medicine and Hygiene [*A publication*]
Public Hlth Engr ... Public Health Engineer [*A publication*]
Public Inf Circ Geol Surv Wy ... Public Information Circular. Geological Survey of Wyoming [*A publication*]
Public Inf Circ Iowa Geol Surv ... Public Information Circular. Iowa Geological Survey [*A publication*]
Publick .... Publicker Industries, Inc. [*Associated Press abbreviation*] (APAG)
Public Land Resour Law Dig ... Public Land and Resources Law Digest [*United States*] [*A publication*]
Public Lib .. Public Libraries [*A publication*]
Public Light ... Public Lighting [*A publication*]
Public Manage Source ... Public Management Sources [*A publication*]
Public Mgt ... Public Management [*A publication*]
Public Opin ... Public Opinion [*A publication*]

Public Opinion Q ... Public Opinion Quarterly [*A publication*]
Public Opin Q ... Public Opinion Quarterly [*A publication*]
Public Pers Manage ... Public Personnel Management [*A publication*]
Public Prod Rev ... Public Productivity Review [*A publication*]
Public Rel... Public Relations Journal [*A publication*]
Public Relations R ... Public Relations Review [*A publication*]
Public Relat J ... Public Relations Journal [*A publication*]
Public Relat Q ... Public Relations Quarterly [*A publication*]
Public Relat Rev ... Public Relations Review [*A publication*]
Public Sect ... Public Sector. New Zealand Institute of Public Administration [*A publication*]
Public Sector Health Care Risk Manage ... Public Sector. Health Care Risk Management [*A publication*]
Public Serv Action ... Public Service Action [*A publication*]
Public TC Review ... Public Telecommunications Review [*A publication*]
Public Util Fortn ... Public Utilities Fortnightly [*A publication*]
Public Water Supply Eng Conf Proc ... Public Water Supply Engineers Conference. Proceedings [*A publication*]
Public Welf ... Public Welfare [*A publication*]
Public Works Congr Proc ... Public Works Congress. Proceedings [*A publication*]
Public Works Eng Yearb ... Public Works Engineers' Yearbook [*A publication*]
Public Works Local Gov Eng ... Public Works and Local Government Engineering [*A publication*]
Public Works Rev ... Public Works Review [*Japan*] [*A publication*]
Public Works Roads Transp ... Public Works, Roads, and Transport [*A publication*]
Public Works Ser ... Public Works and Services [*A publication*] (APTA)
Public Work (Syd) ... Public Works and Services (Sydney) [*A publication*] (APTA)
Publ Ill Inst Technol ... Publications. Illinois Institute of Technology [*A publication*]
Publ INCAR ... Publicacion INCAR [*Instituto Nacional del Carbon y Sus Derivados "Francisco Pintado Fe"*] [*A publication*]
Publ INED ... Publications INED [*Institut National d'Etudes Demographiques*] [*A publication*]
Publ Inst Antart Argent (B Aires) ... Publicacion. Instituto Antartico Argentino (Buenos Aires) [*A publication*]
Publ Inst Biol Apl (Barc) ... Publicaciones. Instituto de Biologia Aplicada (Barcelona) [*A publication*]
Publ Inst Biol Apl (Barcelona) ... Publicaciones. Instituto de Biologia Aplicada (Barcelona) [*A publication*]
Publ Inst Bot "Dr Goncalo Sampaio" Fac Cienc Univ Porto ... Publicacoes. Instituto de Botanica "Dr. Goncalo Sampaio." Faculdade de Ciencias. Universidade do Porto [*A publication*]
Publ Inst Fis "Alonso De St Cruz" ... Publicaciones. Instituto de Fisica "Alonso De Santa Cruz" [*A publication*]
Publ Inst Florestal ... Publicacao. Instituto Florestal [*A publication*]
Publ Inst Found Engng Soil Mech Rock Mech Waterways Constr ... Publications. Institute of Foundation Engineering, Soil Mechanics, Rock Mechanics, and Waterways Construction [*A publication*]
Publ Inst Fr Pet Collect Colloq Semin ... Publications. Institut Francais du Petrole. Collection Colloques et Seminaires [*France*] [*A publication*]
Publ Inst Geogr (Bogota) ... Publicacion. Instituto Geografico Agustin Codazzi (Bogota) [*A publication*]
Publ Inst Geol (Barcelona) ... Publicaciones. Instituto Geologico (Barcelona) [*A publication*]
Publ Inst Geol Topogr ... Publicaciones. Instituto Geologico Topografico [*A publication*]
Publ Inst Geol Univ Chile ... Publicaciones. Instituto de Geologia del Universidade de Chile [*A publication*]
Publ Inst Geophys Pol Acad Sci ... Publication. Institute of Geophysics. Polish Academy of Sciences [*A publication*]
Publ Inst Geophys Pol Acad Sci D ... Publications. Institute of Geophysics. Polish Academy of Sciences D. Physics of the Atmosphere [*A publication*]
Publ Inst Geophys Pol Acad Sci Ser A ... Publications. Institute of Geophysics. Polish Academy of Sciences. Series A. Physics of the Earth Interior [*A publication*]
Publ Inst Geophys Pol Acad Sci Ser B ... Publications. Institute of Geophysics. Polish Academy of Sciences. Series B. Seismology [*A publication*]
Publ Inst Geophys Pol Acad Sci Ser C ... Publications. Institute of Geophysics. Polish Academy of Sciences. Series C. Earth Magnetism [*A publication*]
Publ Inst Geophys Pol Acad Sci Ser E ... Publications. Institute of Geophysics. Polish Academy of Sciences. Series E. Ionosphere Physics [*A publication*]
Publ Inst Geophys Pol Acad Sci Ser F ... Publications. Institute of Geophysics. Polish Academy of Sciences. Series F. Planetary Geodesy [*A publication*]
Publ Inst Geophys Ser D Pol Acad Sci ... Publications. Institute of Geophysics. Polish Academy of Sciences. Series D. Atmosphere Physics [*A publication*]
Publ Inst Invest Geol Diputacion Barcelona ... Publicaciones. Instituto de Investigaciones Geologicas. Diputacion de Barcelona [*A publication*]

Publ Inst Invest Geol Diputacion Prov Barcelona ... Publicaciones. Instituto de Investigaciones Geologicas. Diputacion Provincial de Barcelona [*A publication*]
Publ Inst Mar Sci Nat Fish Univ Busan ... Publications. Institute of Marine Sciences. National Fisheries. University of Busan [*A publication*]
Publ Inst Mar Sci Natl Fish Univ Busan ... Publications. Institute of Marine Sciences. National Fisheries University of Busan [*A publication*]
Publ Inst Mar Sci Univ Tex ... Publications. Institute of Marine Science. University of Texas [*A publication*]
Publ Inst Mar Sci Univ Texas ... Publications. Institute of Marine Science. University of Texas [*A publication*]
Publ Inst Math (Belgrade) ... Publications. Institut Mathematique. Nouvelle Serie (Belgrade) [*A publication*]
Publ Inst Math (Belgrad) NS ... Institut Mathematique. Publications. Nouvelle Serie (Belgrade) [*A publication*]
Publ Inst Math Univ Nancago ... Publications. Institut Mathematique. Universite de Nancago [*Paris*] [*A publication*]
Publ Inst Math Univ Strasbourg ... Publications. Institut de Mathematiques. Universite de Strasbourg [*A publication*]
Publ Inst Mex Recursos Nat Renov ... Publicacion. Instituto Mexicano de Recursos Naturales Renovables [*A publication*]
Publ Inst Mineral Paleontol Quat Geol Univ Lund ... Publications. Institutes of Mineralogy, Paleontology, and Quaternary Geology. University of Lund [*A publication*]
Publ Inst Musee Voltaire ... Publications. Institut et Musee Voltaire [*A publication*]
Publ Inst Nac Carbon Sus Deriv "Francisco Pintado Fe" ... Publicacion. Instituto Nacional del Carbon y Sus Derivados "Francisco Pintado Fe" [*A publication*]
Publ Inst Nat Etude Agron Congo ... Publications. Institut National pour l'Etude Agronomique du Congo [*A publication*]
Publ Inst Nat Etude Agron Congo (INEAC) Serie Scientifique ... Publications. Institut National pour l'Etude Agronomique du Congo (INEAC). Serie Scientifique [*A publication*]
Publ Inst Natl Etude Agron Congo Belge Ser Sci ... Publications. Institut National pour l'Etude Agronomique du Congo Belge. Serie Scientifique [*A publication*]
Publ Inst Natl Etude Agron Congo Ser Sci ... Publications. Institut National pour l'Etude Agronomique du Congo. Serie Scientifique [*A publication*]
Publ Inst Natl Etude Agron Congo Ser Tech ... Publications. Institut National pour l'Etude Agronomique du Congo. Serie Technique [*A publication*]
Publ Inst Opt Madrid ... Publicaciones. Instituto de Optica Daza de Valdes de Madrid [*A publication*]
Publ Inst Pesqui Mar ... Publicacao. Instituto de Pesquisas da Marinha [*A publication*]
Publ Inst Quim Fis Rocasolano ... Publicaciones. Instituto de Quimica Fisica "Rocasolano" [*A publication*]
Publ Inst Rech Sider Ser B ... Publications. Institut de Recherches de la Siderurgie. Serie B [*A publication*]
Publ Inst Rech Siderurg Ser A ... Publications. Institut de Recherches de la Siderurgie [*Saint-Germain-En-Laye*]. Serie A [*A publication*]
Publ Inst R Meteorol Belg A ... Publications. Institut Royal Meteorologique de Belgique. Serie A. Format in-4 [*A publication*]
Publ Inst R Meteorol Belg B ... Publications. Institut Royal Meteorologique de Belgique. Serie B. Format in-8 [*A publication*]
Publ Inst R Meteorol Belg Ser A ... Publications. Institut Royal Meteorologique de Belgique. Serie A. Format in-4 [*A publication*]
Publ Inst R Meteorol Belg Ser B ... Publications. Institut Royal Meteorologique de Belgique. Serie B [*A publication*]
Publ Inst Soil Rock Mech Univ Fridericiana (Karlsruhe) ... Publications. Institute for Soil and Rock Mechanics. University of Fridericiana (Karlsruhe) [*A publication*]
Publ Inst Statist Univ Paris ... Publications. Institut de Statistique. Universite de Paris [*A publication*]
Publ Inst Suflos Agrotec (B Aires) ... Publicacion. Instituto de Suflos y Agrotecnia (Buenos Aires) [*A publication*]
Publ Inst Tecnol Estud Super Monterrey Ser Cienc Biol ... Publicaciones. Instituto Tecnologico y de Estudios Superiores de Monterrey. Serie Ciencias Biologicas [*A publication*]
Publ Inst Zool "Dr Augusto Nobre" Fac Cienc Porto ... Publicacoes. Instituto de Zoologia "Dr. Augusto Nobreda." Faculdade de Ciencias. Universidade do Porto [*A publication*]
Publ Inst Zootec (Rio De J) ... Publicacao. Instituto de Zootecnia (Rio De Janeiro) [*A publication*]
Publ Int...... Public Interest [*A publication*]
Publ Int Ass Scient Hydrol Symp (Budapest) ... Publication. International Association of Scientific Hydrology. Symposium (Budapest) [*A publication*]
Publ Inter... Public Interest [*A publication*]
Publ Int Inst Land Reclam Improv ... Publication. International Institute for Land Reclamation and Improvement [*A publication*]
Publ Int Tin Res Inst ... Publication. International Tin Research Institute [*A publication*]
PUBLINX ... Public Links [*Amateur golf*]

Publ IOM Natl Acad Sci Inst Med ... Publication IOM [*Institute of Medicine*]. National Academy of Sciences. Institute of Medicine [*A publication*]
Publishers ... Publishers' Weekly [*A publication*]
Publ Istanbul Univ Obs ... Publications. Istanbul University Observatory [*A publication*]
Publius J F ... Publius. Journal of Federalism [*A publication*]
Publ Jefferson Med Coll Hosp ... Publications. Jefferson Medical College Hospital [*A publication*]
Publ Jpn Med Res Found ... Publication. Japan Medical Research Foundation [*A publication*]
Publ Junta Nac Prod Pecu Ser A Ser Cient Invest ... Publicacoes. Junta Nacional dos Produtos Pecuarios. Serie A. Serie Cientifica e de Investigacao [*A publication*]
Publ Korean Natl Astron Obs ... Publications. Korean National Astronomical Observatory [*Republic of Korea*] [*A publication*]
Publ L .... Public Law [*A publication*]
Publ Lab Biochim Nutr Univ Cathol Louvain Fac Sci Agron ... Publication. Laboratoire de Biochimie de la Nutrition. Universite Catholique de Louvain. Faculte des Sciences Agronomiques [*A publication*]
Publ Lab Cent Ensayo Mater Constr (Madrid) ... Publication. Laboratorio Central de Ensayo de Materiales de Construccion (Madrid) [*A publication*]
Publ Lab Jefferson Med Coll Hosp ... Publications. Laboratories of the Jefferson Medical College Hospital [*A publication*]
Publ Lab Photoelasticite Ecole Polytech Fed (Zurich) ... Publications. Laboratoire de Photoelasticite. Ecole Polytechnique Federale (Zurich) [*A publication*]
Publ Lab Physiol Chem Univ Amsterdam ... Publications. Laboratory of Physiological Chemistry. University of Amsterdam [*A publication*]
Publ Law (London) ... Public Law (London) [*A publication*]
Publ Ld Capability Surv Trinidad & Tobago ... Publication. Land Capability Survey of Trinidad and Tobago [*A publication*]
Publ Ltg ..... Public Lighting [*A publication*]
Publ Manit Dep Mines Nat Resour Mines Branch ... Publication. Manitoba Department of Mines and Natural Resources. Mines Branch [*A publication*]
Publ Manit Dep Mines Resour Environ Manage Mines Branch ... Publication. Manitoba. Department of Mines, Resources, and Environmental Management. Mines Branch [*A publication*]
Publ Manitoba Beekprs Ass ... Publication. Manitoba Beekeepers' Association [*A publication*]
Publ Mar Biol Stn (Al Ghardaqa) ... Publications. Marine Biological Station (Al Ghardaqa, Red Sea) [*A publication*]
Publ Mar Biol Stn (Ghardaqa Red Sea) ... Publications. Marine Biological Station (Al Ghardaqa, Red Sea) [*A publication*]
Publ Mar Biol Stn Stalin ... Publications. Marine Biological Station of Stalin [*A publication*]
Publ Mar Lab Pusan Fish Coll ... Publications. Marine Laboratory. Pusan Fisheries College [*South Korea*] [*A publication*]
Publ Math Debrecen ... Publicationes Mathematicae. Universitatis Debreceniensis [*A publication*]
Publ Math Orsay 80 ... Publications Mathematiques d'Orsay 80 [*A publication*]
Publ Math Orsay 81 ... Publications Mathematiques d'Orsay 81 [*A publication*]
Publ Math Orsay 82 ... Publications Mathematiques d'Orsay 82 [*A publication*]
Publ Math Res Center Univ Wisconsin ... Publications. Mathematics Research Center. University of Wisconsin [*A publication*]
Publ Math Res Cent Univ Wis ... Publication. Mathematics Research Center. University of Wisconsin [*A publication*]
Publ Math Res Cent Univ Wis Madison ... Publication. Mathematics Research Center. University of Wisconsin-Madison [*A publication*]
Publ Math Res Cent US Army Univ Wis ... Publication. Mathematics Research Center. United States Army. University of Wisconsin [*A publication*]
Publ Math Res Inst (Istanbul) ... Publications. Mathematical Research Institute (Istanbul) [*A publication*]
Publ Math Soc Japan ... Publications. Mathematical Society of Japan [*A publication*]
Publ Math Univ Bordeaux ... Publications Mathematiques. Universite de Bordeaux [*A publication*]
Publ Math Univ Paris VII ... Publications Mathematiques. Universite de Paris. VII [*A publication*]
Publ Math Univ Pierre et Marie Curie ... Publications Mathematiques. Universite Pierre et Marie Curie [*A publication*]
Publ Med ... Publicacoes Medicas [*A publication*]
Publ Metaalinst TNO ... Publikatie. Metaalinstituut TNO [*Nederlands Centrale Organisatie voor Toegepast-Natuurwetenschappelijk Onderzoek*] [*A publication*]
Publ Mich State Univ Mus Biol Ser ... Publications. Michigan State University Museum. Biological Series [*A publication*]
Publ Mid South Neurosci Dev Group ... Publication. Mid-South Neuroscience Development Group [*A publication*]

Publ Min Agr Ser Premios Nac Invest Agr ... Publicaciones. Ministerio de Agricultura. Serie. Premios Nacionales de Investigacion Agraria [*A publication*]
Publ Miner Res Explor Inst Turk ... Publications. Mineral Research and Exploration Institute of Turkey [*A publication*]
Publ Miner Resour Div (Winnipeg) ... Publication. Mineral Resources Division (Winnipeg) [*A publication*]
Publ Minist Agric (Can) ... Publication. Ministry of Agriculture (Canada) [*A publication*]
Publ Miss State Univ Agr Ext Serv ... Publication. Mississippi State University. Agricultural Extension Service [*A publication*]
Publ Mod Lang Ass ... Publications. Modern Language Association of America [*A publication*]
Publ Mus Hist Nat "Javier Prado" Ser A Zool ... Publicaciones. Museo de Historia Natural "Javier Prado." Series A. Zoologia [*A publication*]
Publ Mus Hist Nat "Javier Prado" Ser B Bot ... Publicaciones. Museo de Historia Natural "Javier Prado." Series B. Botanica [*A publication*]
Publ Mus Hist Nat Javier Prado Ser C Geol ... Publicaciones. Museo de Historia Natural "Javier Prado." Series C. Geologia [*A publication*]
Publ Mus Lab Mineral Geol Fac Cienc Porto ... Publicacoes. Museu e Laboratorio Mineralogico e Geologico. Faculdade de Ciencias do Porto [*A publication*]
Publ Mus Mich State Univ Biol Ser ... Publications. Museum. Michigan State University. Biological Series [*A publication*]
Publ Nat Acad Sci Nat Res Counc ... Publication. National Academy of Sciences. National Research Council [*A publication*]
Publ Natn Acad Sci Natn Res Coun (Wash) ... Publication. National Academy of Sciences. National Research Council (Washington) [*A publication*]
Publ Natuurhist Genoot Limburg ... Publicaties. Natuurhistorisch Genootschap in Limburg [*A publication*]
Publn Inst Nac Tec Agropec (B Aires) ... Publicacion. Instituto Nacional de Tecnologia Agropecuaria (Buenos Aires) [*A publication*]
Publn Inst Suelos Agrotec ... Publicacion. Instituto de Suelos y Agrotecnia [*A publication*]
Publ NMAB Natl Mater Advis Board (US) ... Publication. NMAB. National Materials Advisory Board (US) [*A publication*]
Publ Nor Inst Kosm Fys ... Publikasjoner. Norske Institutt foer Kosmisk Fysikk [*A publication*]
Publ Obs Astr Univ Belgr ... Publications. Observatoire Astronomique. Universite de Belgrade [*A publication*]
Publ Obs Univ Mich ... Publications. Observatory. University of Michigan [*A publication*]
Publ OECD (Paris) ... Publication. OECD [*Organization for Economic Cooperation and Development*] (Paris) [*A publication*]
Publ Okla State Univ Agr Inform Serv ... Publication. Oklahoma State University. Agricultural Information Service [*A publication*]
Publ Ont Dep Agric ... Publication. Ontario Department of Agriculture and Food [*A publication*]
Publ Ont Fish Res Lab ... Publications. Ontario Fisheries Research Laboratory [*A publication*]
Publ Opin Q ... Public Opinion Quarterly [*A publication*]
Publ Pacif Nth-West Co-Op Ext Serv ... Publication. Pacific Northwest Cooperative Extension Service [*A publication*]
Publ Palaeontol Inst Univ Upps Spec Vol ... Publications. Palaeontological Institution. University of Uppsala. Special Volume [*A publication*]
Publ Pers M ... Public Personnel Management [*A publication*]
Publ Personnel Manag ... Public Personnel Management [*A publication*]
Publ Phil Soc ... Publications. Philological Society [*A publication*]
Publ Pol ..... Public Policy [*A publication*]
Publ Policy ... Public Policy [*A publication*]
Publ Puget Sound Biol St Univ Wash ... Publications. Puget Sound Biological Station. University of Washington [*A publication*]
Publ Puget Sound Mar Stn Univ Wash ... Publications. Puget Sound Marine Station. University of Washington [*A publication*]
Publ Purdue Univ Sch Civ Eng ... Publication. Purdue University. School of Civil Engineering [*A publication*]
PUBLR ...... Publisher
Publ Ramanujan Inst ... Publications. Ramanujan Institute [*A publication*]
Publ Rapeseed Assoc Can ... Publication. Rapeseed Association of Canada [*A publication*]
Publ R Coll Physicians Edinburgh ... Publication. Royal College of Physicians of Edinburgh [*A publication*]
Publ Relat Congo Belg Reg Voisines ... Publications Relatives au Congo Belge et aux Regions Voisines [*A publication*]
Publ Rel J .. Public Relations Journal [*A publication*]
Publ Rep Aust Coal Ind Res Lab ... Published Reports. Australian Coal Industry Research Laboratories [*A publication*]
Publ Res Inst Aabo Akad Found ... Publication. Research Institute. Aabo Akademi Foundation [*A publication*]
Publ Res Inst Math Sci ... Publications. Kyoto University. Research Institute for Mathematical Sciences [*A publication*]
Publ Res Inst Math Sci Ser A ... Publications. Research Institute for Mathematical Sciences. Series A [*Japan*] [*A publication*]
Publ Res Inst Math Sci Ser B ... Publications. Research Institute for Mathematical Sciences. Series B [*Japan*] [*A publication*]

Publ Rev..... Publications Review [*A publication*]
Publ Rev Manage Technol Policy ... Publications Review. Management and Technology and Policy [*A publication*]
Publ Roads ... Public Roads [*A publication*]
Publ R Obs (Edinburgh) ... Publications. Royal Observatory (Edinburgh) [*A publication*]
Publ Rom Fr ... Publications Romanes et Francaises [*A publication*]
Publ R Trop Inst Amsterdam ... Publication. Royal Tropical Institute. Amsterdam [*A publication*]
Publ S Afr Inst Med Res ... Publications. South African Institute for Medical Research [*A publication*]
Publs ANARE Data Rep Ser ... Publications. ANARE [*Australian National Antarctic Research Expeditions*] Data Reports Series [*A publication*]   (APTA)
Publs ANARE Interim Rep Ser ... Publications. ANARE [*Australian National Antarctic Research Expeditions*] Interim Reports Series [*A publication*]   (APTA)
Publs ANARE Sci Rep Ser ... Publications. ANARE [*Australian National Antarctic Research Expeditions*] Scientific Reports Series [*A publication*]   (APTA)
Publs Aust Soc Soil Sci ... Publications. Australian Society of Soil Science [*A publication*]   (APTA)
Publs Aust Soc Soil Science ... Publications. Australian Society of Soil Science [*A publication*]   (APTA)
Publ Scient Univ Alger Ser B ... Publications Scientifiques. Universite d'Alger. Serie B. Sciences Physiques [*A publication*]
Publ Sci For Bois ... Publications Scientifiques Forestieres et du Bois [*A publication*]
Publ Sci Tech Min Air ... Publications Scientifiques et Techniques. Ministere de l'Air [*France*] [*A publication*]
Publ Sci Tech Min Air Bull Serv Tech ... Publications Scientifiques et Techniques. Ministere de l'Air. Bulletins des Services Techniques [*France*] [*A publication*]
Publ Sci Tech Min Air Notes Tech ... Publications Scientifiques et Techniques. Ministere de l'Air [*France*]. Notes Techniques [*A publication*]
Publ Sci Tech Minist Air (Fr) ... Publications Scientifiques et Techniques. Ministere de l'Air (France) [*A publication*]
Publ Sci Tech Minist Air (Fr) Bull Serv Tech ... Publications Scientifiques et Techniques. Ministere de l'Air (France). Bulletin des Services Techniques [*A publication*]
Publ Sci Tech Res Comm Organ Afr Unity ... Publication. Scientific, Technical, and Research Commission. Organization of African Unity [*A publication*]
Publs Co-Op Ext Univ Mass Coll Agric ... Publications. Co-Operative Extension Service. University of Massachusetts. College of Agriculture [*A publication*]
Publs Dep Agric (Alberta) ... Publications. Department of Agriculture (Alberta) [*A publication*]
Publs Dep Agric (Can) ... Publications. Department of Agriculture (Canada) [*A publication*]
Publ Sem Geom Univ Neuchatel Ser 2 ... Publications. Seminaire de Geometrie. Universite de Neuchatel. Serie 2 [*A publication*]
Publ Sem Geom Univ Neuchatel Ser 3 ... Publications. Seminaire de Geometrie. Universite de Neuchatel. Serie 3 [*A publication*]
Publ Sem Mat Garcia De Galdeano ... Publicaciones. Seminario Matematico Garcia De Galdeano [*A publication*]
Publ Ser Eur Fed Chem Eng ... Publication Series. European Federation of Chemical Engineering [*A publication*]
Publ Serv Agric (Mozambique) ... Publicacoes. Seryicos de Agricultura. Servicos de Veterinaria (Lourenco Marques, Mozambique) [*A publication*]
Publ Serv Flor Aqueic (Portugal) ... Publicacoes. Direccao Geral dos Servicos Florestais e Aqueicolas (Lisbon, Portugal) [*A publication*]
Publ Serv Geol Alger Bull ... Publications. Service Geologique de l'Algerie. Bulletin [*A publication*]
Publ Serv Geol Luxemb ... Publications. Service Geologique de Luxembourg [*A publication*]
Publ Serv Met Madag ... Publications. Service Meteorologique de Madagascar [*A publication*]
Publ Serv Piscic Ser I-C ... Publicacao. Servico de Piscicultura. Serie I-C [*A publication*]
Publ Serv Plagas For (Madrid) ... Publicacion. Servicio de Plagas Forestales (Madrid) [*A publication*]
Publ Serv Rev ... Public Service Review [*A publication*]
Publ Seto Mar Biol Lab ... Publications. Seto Marine Biological Laboratory [*A publication*]
Publ Seto Mar Biol Lab Spec Publ Ser ... Publications. Seto Marine Biological Laboratory. Special Publication Series [*A publication*]
Publs Geol Surv QD ... Publications. Geological Survey of Queensland [*A publication*]   (APTA)
Publs Geol Surv QD Palaeont Pap ... Publications. Geological Survey of Queensland. Palaeontological Papers [*A publication*]   (APTA)
PUBLSHG ... Publishing   (DCTA)
Publ Shirley Inst ... Publication. Shirley Institute [*A publication*]
Publ S Ill Univ Sch Agr ... Publication. Southern Illinois University. School of Agriculture [*A publication*]

Publs Indiana Dep Conserv ... Publications. Indiana Department of Conservation [*A publication*]
Publs Inst Natn Etude Agron Congo Ser Sci ... Publications. Institut National pour l'Etude Agronomique du Congo. Serie Scientifique [*A publication*]
Publs Manitoba Dep Agric ... Publications. Manitoba Department of Agriculture [*A publication*]
Publs Maria Moors Cabot Fdn Bot Res ... Publications. Maria Moors Cabot Foundation for Botanical Research [*A publication*]
Publs Met Dep Melb Univ ... Publications. Meteorology Department. University of Melbourne [*A publication*]   (APTA)
Publ Smithson Inst ... Publication. Smithsonian Institution [*A publication*]
Publs Mktg Bd ... Publications. Empire Marketing Board [*A publication*]
Publs Mus Natn Hist Nat ... Publications. Museum National d'Histoire Naturelle [*A publication*]
Publ Soil Bur (NZ) ... Publication. Soil Bureau. Department of Scientific and Industrial Research (New Zealand) [*A publication*]
Publs Osaka Mus Nat Hist ... Publications. Osaka Museum of Natural History [*A publication*]
Publ SP Am Concr Inst ... Publication SP. American Concrete Institute [*A publication*]
Publs Petrol Search Subsidy Acts ... Publications. Petroleum Search Subsidy Acts. Bureau of Mineral Resources, Geology, and Geophysics [*Australia*] [*A publication*]   (APTA)
Publ Sta Fed Essais Agr (Lausanne) ... Publications. Stations Federales d'Essais Agricoles (Lausanne) [*A publication*]
Publ State Inst Agric Chem (Finl) ... Publications. State Institute of Agricultural Chemistry (Finland) [*A publication*]
Publ State Inst Tech Res ... Publications. State Institute for Technical Research [*A publication*]
Publ Stn Fed Essais Agric (Lausanne) ... Publication. Stations Federales d'Essais Agricoles (Lausanne) [*A publication*]
Publ SUG... Publikace. Statni Ustav Geofysikalni [*A publication*]
Publ Systematics Ass ... Publication. Systematics Association [*A publication*]
Publ Tallinn Inst Technol Ser A ... Publications. Tallinn Institute of Technology. Series A [*A publication*]
Publ Tartu Astrofiz Obs ... Publikatsii Tartuskoi Astrofizicheskoi Observatorii [*Estonian SSR*] [*A publication*]
Publ Tech Charbon Fr Inf Tech ... Publications Techniques des Charbonnages de France. Informations Techniques [*A publication*]
Publ Tech Inst Belge Amelior Betterave Tirlemont ... Publications Techniques. Institut Belge pour l'Amelioration de la Betterave Tirlemont [*A publication*]
Publ Technion Israel Inst Technol Agric Eng Fac ... Publication-Technion. Israel Institute of Technology. Agricultural Engineering Faculty [*A publication*]
Publ Tech Pap Proc Annu Meet Sugar Ind Technol Inc ... Publication of Technical Papers and Proceedings. Annual Meeting of Sugar Industry Technologists, Inc. [*A publication*]
Publ Tech Res Cen Finl Mater Process Technol ... Publication. Technical Research Centre of Finland. Materials and Processing Technology [*A publication*]
Publ Tech Res Cent Finl ... Publications. Technical Research Centre of Finland [*A publication*]
Publ Tech Res Cent Finl Electr Nucl Technol ... Publications. Technical Research Centre of Finland. Electrical and Nuclear Technology [*A publication*]
Publ Tech Sci Pap Tech Univ (Brno) A ... Publications of Technical and Scientific Papers. Technical University (Brno). A [*A publication*]
Publ Tech Sci Pap Tech Univ Brno B ... Publications of Technical and Scientific Papers. Technical University. Brno. B [*A publication*]
Publ Tech Univ Est Tallinn Ser A ... Publications. Technical University of Estonia at Tallinn. Series A [*A publication*]
Publ Tech Univ Heavy Ind (Miskoic) Ser B Metall ... Publications. Technical University for Heavy Industry (Miskoic). Series B. Metallurgy [*Hungary*] [*A publication*]
Publ Tech Univ Heavy Ind (Miskolc Hung) ... Publications. Technical University for Heavy Industry (Miskolc, Hungary) [*A publication*]
Publ Tech Univ Heavy Ind (Miskolc Hung) Foreign Lang Ed ... Publications. Technical University for Heavy Industry (Miskolc, Hungary). Foreign Language Edition [*A publication*]
Publ Tech Univ Heavy Ind Ser A (Miskolc Hung) ... Publications. Technical University for Heavy Industry. Series A. Mining (Miskolc, Hungary) [*A publication*]
Publ Tech Univ Heavy Ind Ser B (Miskolc Hung) ... Publications. Technical University for Heavy Industry. Series B. Metallurgy (Miskolc, Hungary) [*A publication*]
Publ Tec Inst Patol Veg (B Aires) ... Publicacion Tecnica. Instituto de Patologia Vegetal (Buenos Aires) [*A publication*]
Publ Tehn Fak u Sarajevu ... Publikacije Tehnickog Fakulteta u Sarajevu [*A publication*]
Publ Thoresby Soc ... Publications. Thoresby Society [*A publication*]
Publ UER Math Pures Appl IRMA ... Publications. Unites d'Enseignement et de Recherche de Mathematiques Pures et Appliquees. Institut de Recherche de Mathematiques Avancees [*A publication*]
Publ Univ Calif Agric Ext Serv ... Publication. University of California. Agricultural Extension Service [*A publication*]

Publ Univ Europ ... Publications Universitaires Europeennes [*Frankfurt Am Main*] [*A publication*]
Publ Univ Fl Inst Food Agric Sci ... Publication. University of Florida. Institute of Food and Agricultural Sciences [*A publication*]
Publ Univ Innsbruck ... Publications. University of Innsbruck [*A publication*]
Publ Univ Joensuu Ser B ... Publications. University of Joensuu. Series B [*Finland*] [*A publication*]
Publ Univ Joensuu Ser B-I ... Publications. University of Joensuu. Series B-I [*A publication*]
Publ Univ Joensuu Ser B-II ... Publications. University of Joensuu. Series B-II [*A publication*]
Publ Univ Kuopio Community Health Ser Orig Rep ... Publications. University of Kuopio. Community Health Series. Original Reports [*A publication*]
Publ Univ Laval ... Publications. Universite Laval [*A publication*]
Publ Univ Mass Water Resour Res Cent ... Publication. University of Massachusetts. Water Resources Research Center [*A publication*]
Publ Univ Off Congo Elisabethville ... Publications. Universite Officielle du Congo a Elisabethville [*A publication*]
Publ Univ Off Congo Lubumbashi ... Publications. Universite Officielle du Congo a Lubumbashi [*A publication*]
Publ Univ Pretoria ... Publikasies. Universiteit van Pretoria [*A publication*]
Publ Univ Tech Sci Budapest ... Publications. University of Technical Sciences. Budapest [*A publication*]
Publ Univ Tex Bur Econ Geol ... Publication. University of Texas. Bureau of Economic Geology [*A publication*]
Publ Univ Toronto Dep Civ Eng ... Publication. University of Toronto. Department of Civil Engineering [*A publication*]
Publ Univ Toronto Inst Environ Stud ... Publication. University of Toronto. Institute for Environmental Studies [*A publication*]
Publ Univ Toulouse-Le Mirail Ser A ... Publications. Universite de Toulouse-Le Mirail. Serie A. [*A publication*]
Publ Univ Wis Ext ... Publication. University of Wisconsin Extension [*A publication*]
Publ Univ Wyo ... Publications. University of Wyoming [*A publication*]
Publ Univ Zululand Ser 3 ... Publications. University of Zululand. Series 3. Specialized Publications
Publ US Agric Res Serv ... Publication. United States Agricultural Research Service [*A publication*]
Publ US Agric Res Serv East Reg Res Cent ... Publication. United States Agricultural Research Service. Eastern Regional Research Center [*A publication*]
Publ US Int Trade Commn ... Publication. United States International Trade Commission [*A publication*]
Publ US Natl Tech Inf Serv ... United States. National Technical Information Service. Publication [*A publication*]
Publ Utah Geol Assoc ... Publication. Utah Geological Association [*A publication*]
Publ Va Div Miner Resour ... Publication. Virginia Division of Mineral Resources [*A publication*]
Publ Virginia Div Miner Resour ... Publication. Virginia Division of Mineral Resources [*A publication*]
Publ Vulkaninst Immanuel Friedlaender ... Publikationen Herausgegeben von der Stiftung Vulkaninstitut Immanuel Friedlaender [*A publication*]
Publ W ... Publishers' Weekly [*A publication*]
Publ Wagner Free Inst Sci Philadelphia ... Publications. Wagner Free Institute of Science of Philadelphia [*A publication*]
Publ Water Environ Res Inst ... Publications. Water and Environment Research Institute [*A publication*]
Publ Water Res Inst ... Publications. Water Research Institute [*A publication*]
Publ Welfar ... Public Welfare [*A publication*]
Publ West Tex Geol Soc ... Publication. West Texas Geological Society [*A publication*]
Publ Wiss Filmen Sekt Tech Wiss Naturwiss ... Publikationen zu Wissenschaftlichen Filmen. Sektion Technische Wissenschaften. Naturwissenschaften [*A publication*]
Publ W J Barrow Res Lab ... Publication. W. J. Barrow Research Laboratory [*A publication*]
Publ Wkly ... Publishers' Weekly [*A publication*]
Publ Wks ... Public Works [*A publication*]   (APTA)
Publ Wks Local Govt Engng ... Public Works and Local Government Engineering [*A publication*]   (APTA)
Publ W Va Univ Eng Exp Stn ... Publication. West Virginia University. Engineering Experiment Station [*A publication*]
Publ Zoo .... Publications in Zoology [*A publication*]
Pub Manag ... Public Management [*A publication*]
Pub Mgt ..... Public Management [*A publication*]
PUBN .... Publication (MSA)
PUBNET ..... American Association of Publishers' electronic ordering system
PUBO .... Pubco Corp. [*NASDAQ symbol*]   (NQ)
Pub Opin .... Public Opinion [*A publication*]
Pub Opinion Q ... Public Opinion Quarterly [*A publication*]
Pub Opn Q ... Public Opinion Quarterly [*A publication*]
Pub Op Q ... Public Opinion Quarterly [*A publication*]
Pub Papers ... Public Papers of the President [*A publication*]   (DLA)
Pub Pers Mgt ... Public Personnel Management [*A publication*]
Pub Pol .... Public Policy [*A publication*]
Pub Rel ...... Public Relations

Pub Rel Bull ... Public Relations Bulletin [*American Bar Association*] [*A publication*]   (DLA)
Pub Rel J ... Public Relations Journal [*A publication*]
Pub Rel Q .. Public Relations Quarterly [*A publication*]
Pub Rel Rv ... Public Relations Review [*A publication*]
Pub Res C .. Public Resources Code [*California*] [*A publication*]   (ILCA)
Pub Res No ... Public Resolution Number [*Congress*]   (ILCA)
Pub Roads ... Public Roads [*A publication*]
Pub Roch Hist Soc ... Publication Fund Series. Rochester Historical Society [*A publication*]
PUBS .... Percutaneous Umbilical Blood Sampling [*Medicine*]
PUBS .... Pop-Up Bottom Seismograph [*Marine science*]   (MSC)
PUBS .... Publication Series
PUBS .... Publications (CDAI)
PUBSAT ... Publications Special Assistance Team [*Military*]
Pub Sector ... Public Sector [*New Zealand*] [*A publication*]
Pub Ser Comm ... Public Service Commission [*Usually, of a specific state*]   (DLA)
Pub Service J Vic ... Public Service Journal of Victoria [*A publication*]   (APTA)
Pub Serv Management ... Public Service Management [*A publication*]
Pub Soc Bras Nematol ... Publicacao. Sociedade Brasileira de Nematologia [*A publication*]
Pubs Petrol Search Subsidy Acts ... Publications. Petroleum Search Subsidy Acts. Bureau of Mineral Resources, Geology, and Geophysics [*Australia*] [*A publication*]   (APTA)
Pub St .... Public Statutes [*A publication*]   (DLA)
Pub Technol N ... Public Technology News [*A publication*]
Pub U Rep ... Public Utilities Reports [*A publication*]   (DLA)
Pub Util ..... Public Utilities Fortnightly [*A publication*]
Pub Util C ... Public Utilities Code [*A publication*]   (DLA)
Pub Util Fort ... Public Utilities Fortnightly [*A publication*]
Pub Util Fortnightly ... Public Utilities Fortnightly [*A publication*]
Pub Util L Anthol ... Public Utilities Law Anthology [*A publication*]   (DLA)
Pub Util Rep ... Public Utilities Reports [*A publication*]   (DLA)
Pub W ..... Publishers' Weekly [*A publication*]
Pub Wel ..... Public Welfare [*A publication*]
PU-BZ .... University of Pennsylvania, Biology Library, Philadelphia, PA [*Library symbol*] [*Library of Congress*]   (LCLS)
PUC .... Pacific Unicorn [*Vancouver Stock Exchange symbol*]
PUC .... Pacific Union College [*Angwin, CA*]
PUC .... Papers under Consideration
PUC .... Parti de l'Unite Congolaise [*Congolese Unity Party*] [*Political party*]
PUC .... Pediatric Urine Collector [*Medicine*]
PUC .... Permanent Unit Code   (NG)
PUC .... Pick-Up Car
PUC .... Planification d'Urgence Canada [*Emergency Planning Canada - EPC*]
PUC .... Player Unit Component   (MCD)
PUC .... Pontificia Universidade Catolica [*Rio de Janeiro*]
PUC .... Popular Unity of Chile [*Political party*]
PUC .... Port Utilization Committee
PUC .... Post Urbem Conditam [*After the Building of the City of Rome*] [*Latin*]
PUC .... Presidential Unit Citation [*Military decoration*]
PUC .... Price [*Utah*] [*Airport symbol*]   (OAG)
PUC .... Price, UT [*Location identifier*] [*FAA*]   (FAAL)
PUC .... Processing Unit Cabinet [*Data processing*]
PUC .... Production Urgency Committee [*WPB*]
PUC .... Program Unit Code [*Military*]   (AFIT)
PUC .... Provided You Concur [*Army*]
PUC .... Pubblicazioni. Universita Cattolica del Sacro Cuore [*A publication*]
PUC .... Public Utilities Commission
PUC .... Public Utility Co.
PU-C .... University of Pennsylvania, Chemistry Library, Philadelphia, PA [*Library symbol*] [*Library of Congress*]   (LCLS)
PUCA .... Partido Unionista Centro Americana [*Nicaragua*] [*Political party*]   (EY)
PUCA .... Public Utilities Communicators Association [*Later, UCI*] [*New Castle, PA*]   (EA)
PUCalLL ... Publications. University of California. Languages and Literature [*A publication*]
PUCC .... Port Utilities [*AAR code*]
PUCK .... Propellant Utilization Checkout Kit   (KSC)
PUCK .... Pucklechurch [*England*]
PUCM .... Progressive Union of Cabinet Makers [*British*]
PUCODM ... Conseil Scientifique International de Recherches sur les Trypanosomiases et leur Controle [*A publication*]
PUCS .... Propellant Utilization Control System   (KSC)
PUCU .... Propellant Utilization Control Unit
PUD .... Partido Union Democratica [*Guatemala*] [*Political party*]
PUD .... Peptic Ulcer Disease
PU & D ..... Pick Up and Delivery [*Business term*]
PUD .... Pick Up and Delivery [*Business term*]
PUD .... Planned Unit Development [*Housing*]
PUD .... Planned Urban Development
PUD .... Preretro Update Display
PUD .... Prisoner under Detention   (ADA)
PUD .... Public Utility District [*Bonds*]

PUD.......... Puerto Deseado [*Argentina*] [*Airport symbol*]   (OAG)
PUD.......... Pulmonary Disease [*Medicine*]
PU-D.......... University of Pennsylvania, Evans Dental Library, Philadelphia, PA [*Library symbol*] [*Library of Congress*]   (LCLS)
PUDA........ Pueblo Depot Activity [*Colorado*] [*Army*]
PUDCPAHM ... Poona University and Deccan College Publications in Archaeology and History of Maharashtra [*A publication*]
PUDD........ Programmable Universal Direct Drive
PUDN........ Perpetuation of Unit Documentation Number   (MCD)
PUDOC..... Centrum voor Landbouwpublikaties en Landbouwdocumentatie [*Center for Agricultural Publishing and Documentation*] [*Ministry of Agriculture and Fisheries*] [*Information service or system*]   (IID)
PUDOC Annu Rep ... PUDOC [*Centre for Agricultural Publishing and Documentation*] Annual Report [*A publication*]
PUDOC (Cent Landbouwpubl Landbouwdoc) Literatuuroverz ... PUDOC (Centrum voor Landbouwpublikaties en Landbouwdocumentatie) Literatuuroverzicht [*A publication*]
PU-DPL..... Princeton University Device Physics Laboratory [*New Jersey*]
PUDT........ Propellant Utilization Data Translator   (AAG)
PUDVM.... Pulsed Ultrasound Doppler Velocity Meter
PUE.......... Phosphorus Utilization Efficiency [*Ecology*]
PUE.......... Pre-Stock Unit Equipment [*Military*] [*British*]
PUE.......... Presidential Unit Emblem [*Military decoration*]   (AABC)
PUE.......... Propellant Utilization Exerciser
PUE.......... Puebla [*Mexico*] [*Seismograph station code, US Geological Survey*] [*Closed*]   (SEIS)
PUE.......... Puerto Obaldia [*Panama*] [*Airport symbol*]   (OAG)
PUE.......... Pyrexia of Unknown Etiology [*Medicine*]
PUEE........ Publications. Universite de l'Etat a Elisabethville [*A publication*]
PU-EI........ University of Pennsylvania, Moore School of Electrical Engineering, Philadelphia, PA [*Library symbol*] [*Library of Congress*]   (LCLS)
Puer Rico ... Puerto Rico Libre [*A publication*]
Puerto Rico ... Puerto Rico Reports [*A publication*]   (DLA)
Puerto Rico Bus R ... Puerto Rico Business Review [*A publication*]
Puerto Rico Dept Indus Research Bull ... Puerto Rico. Department of Industrial Research. Bulletin [*A publication*]
Puerto Rico F ... Puerto Rico Federal Reports [*A publication*]   (DLA)
Puerto Rico Fed ... Puerto Rico Federal Reports [*A publication*]   (DLA)
Puerto Rico J Publ Hlth ... Puerto Rico Journal of Public Health and Tropical Medicine [*A publication*]
Puerto Rico Rep ... Puerto Rico Supreme Court Reports [*A publication*]   (DLA)
Puerto Rico Univ Agr Expt Sta Tech Paper ... Puerto Rico University. Agricultural Experiment Station. Technical Paper [*A publication*]
Puerto Rico Water Resources Authority Water Resources Bull ... Puerto Rico. Water Resources Authority. Water Resources Bulletin [*A publication*]
PUF.......... Partido Union Federal [*Federal Union Party*] [*Argentina*] [*Political party*]
PUF.......... Pau [*France*] [*Airport symbol*]   (OAG)
PUF.......... People's United Front [*Bangladesh*] [*Political party*]
PUF.......... People's United Front [*Papua New Guinea*] [*Political party*]   (PPW)
PUF.......... Percent Unaccounted For
PUF.......... Pluimveehouderij [*A publication*]
PUF.......... Polyurethane Film [*Plastics technology*]
PUF.......... Polyurethane Foam
PUF.......... Porous Polyurethane Foam [*Also, PPF*] [*Plastics technology*]
PUF.......... Prime Underwriting Facility [*Banking*]
PUF.......... Public Utilities Fortnightly [*A publication*]
Puf........... Puffendorf's Law of Nature and Nations [*A publication*]   (DLA)
PU-F.......... University of Pennsylvania, H. H. Furness Memorial Library, Philadelphia, PA [*Library symbol*] [*Library of Congress*]   (LCLS)
PUFA........ Polyunsaturated Fatty Acid [*Nutrition*]
PU-FA .... University of Pennsylvania, School of Fine Arts, Philadelphia, PA [*Library symbol*] [*Library of Congress*]   (LCLS)
PUFF........ People United to Fight Frustrations   (EA)
PUFF........ Picofarad   (MDG)
PUFF........ Proposed Uses of Federal Funds [*Health Planning and Resource Development Act of 1974*]
PUFFS...... Passive Underwater Fire Control Feasibility Study
PUFFS...... Passive Underwater Fire Control Feasibility System
PUFFT ...... Purdue University Fast FORTRAN [*Formula Translation*] Translator [*Data processing*]
PUFI......... Packed under Federal Inspection
PUFL......... Pump Fed Liquid   (KSC)
PUFO .... Pack Up and Fade Out [*End of military exercise*] [*British*]   (DSUE)
PU Fort...... Public Utilities Fortnightly [*A publication*]
PUFS......... Programmer's Utility Filing System   (DIT)
PUFS......... Proposed Underwater Fire Control Feasibility Study   (SAA)
PUG.......... Partially Underground [*Military*]
PUG.......... PASCAL Users' Group   (EA)
PUG.......... Penta Users Group   (EA)

PUG.......... Port Augusta [*Australia*] [*Airport symbol*]   (OAG)
PUG.......... Porzellan und Glas [*A publication*]
PUG.......... PRIME Users Group   (EA)
PUG.......... Print under Glaze [*Ceramics*]
PUG.......... Propellant Utilization and Gauging [*Apollo*] [*NASA*]
PUG.......... Przeglad Ustawodawstwa Gospodarczego [*A publication*]
PUG.......... Publications. Universite de Grenoble [*A publication*]
PUG.......... Pugilist
PUG.......... Pugillus [*A Handful*] [*Pharmacy*]   (ROG)
Pug.......... Pugsley's New Brunswick Reports [*14-16 New Brunswick*] [*A publication*]   (DLA)
PUG.......... Pulsed Universal Grid
PUG.......... Pure Gold Resources, Inc. [*Toronto Stock Exchange symbol*]
PugetP....... Puget Sound Power & Light Co. [*Associated Press abbreviation*]   (APAG)
Puget Snd... Puget Sound Business Journal [*A publication*]
Puglia Chir ... Puglia Chirurgica [*A publication*]
PUGS........ Propellant Utilization and Gauging System [*Apollo*] [*NASA*]   (KSC)
Pugs.......... Pugsley's New Brunswick Reports [*14-16 New Brunswick*] [*A publication*]   (DLA)
Pugs & Bur ... Pugsley and Burbridge's New Brunswick Reports [*17-20 New Brunswick*] [*A publication*]   (DLA)
Pugs & Burg ... Pugsley and Burbridge's New Brunswick Reports [*17-20 New Brunswick*] [*A publication*]   (DLA)
Pugs & T .... Pugsley and Trueman's New Brunswick Reports [*A publication*]   (DLA)
Pugs & Tru ... Pugsley and Trueman's New Brunswick Reports [*1882-83*] [*A publication*]   (DLA)
PUH.......... Pauahi [*Hawaii*] [*Seismograph station code, US Geological Survey*]   (SEIS)
PUH.......... Pregnancy Urine Hormone [*Endocrinology*]
PUH.......... Purchasing [*A publication*]
PUHCA .... Public Utility Holding Co. Act of 1935
PUHS .... Proceedings. Unitarian Historical Society [*A publication*]
PUI........... Pen User Interface [*Data processing*]
PUI........... Pilot-under-Instruction [*Navy*]
PUI........... Platelet Uptake Index [*Clinical chemistry*]
PUIAA7..... Atas. Instituto de Micologia da Universidade Federal de Pernambuco [*A publication*]
PU-Ind ...... University of Pennsylvania, Industrial Research Department, Philadelphia, PA [*Library symbol*] [*Library of Congress*] [*Obsolete*]   (LCLS)
PUIWP...... People for a United India and World Peace   (EA)
PUJ.......... Punta Cana [*Dominican Republic*] [*Airport symbol*]   (OAG)
PUK.......... Pack-Up Kit   (MCD)
PUK.......... Parti d'Unite Katangaise [*Katanga Unity Party*] [*Political party*]
PUK.......... Patriotic Union of Kurdistan [*Iraq*] [*Political party*]   (PD)
PUK.......... Pechiney-Ugine-Kuhlmann [*Commercial firm*] [*France*]
PUK.......... Prourokinase [*An enzyme*] [*Thrombolytic*]
PUK.......... Pukarua [*French Polynesia*] [*Airport symbol*]   (OAG)
PUKO....... Pan-American Union of Karatedo Organizations   (EA)
PUKOD.... Puresutoresuto Konkurito [*A publication*]
PUKS........ Pivotal Unknowables
PUL.......... Percutaneous Ultrasonic Lithotripsy [*Medicine*]
PUL.......... Preconfiguration Unit Load
PUL.......... Press Union of Liberia
PUL.......... Princeton University, Princeton, NJ [*OCLC symbol*] [*Inactive*]   (OCLC)
PUL.......... Program Update Library
PUL.......... Propellant Utilization and Loading
PUL.......... Public Ledger [*A publication*]
PUL.......... Publicker Industries, Inc. [*NYSE symbol*]   (SPSG)
PUL.......... Pulkovo [*Former USSR*] [*Seismograph station code, US Geological Survey*]   (SEIS)
PUL.......... Pulley   (AAG)
PUL.......... Pulmonary
PUL.......... Pulse Resources [*Vancouver Stock Exchange symbol*]
PU-L......... University of Pennsylvania, Biddle Law Library, Philadelphia, PA [*Library symbol*] [*Library of Congress*]   (LCLS)
PULA........ Public Laws
PULC........ Princeton University. Library. Chronicle [*A publication*]
PULHES ... Physical Capacity, Upper Extremities, Lower Extremities, Hearing, Eyes, and Psychiatric System   (DNAB)
PULL........ Power for Underwater Logistics and Living
PULL........ Pullman-Peabody Co. [*Princeton, NJ*] [*NASDAQ symbol*]   (NQ)
Pull Acc...... Pulling on Mercantile Accounts [*1846*] [*A publication*]   (DLA)
Pull Accts... Pulling's Law of Mercantile Accounts [*A publication*]   (DLA)
Pull Att ...... Pulling on Attorneys and Solicitors [*3rd ed.*] [*1862*] [*A publication*]   (DLA)
Pull Groupe Etud Rythmes Biol ... Bulletin. Groupe d'Etude des Rythmes Biologiques [*A publication*]
Pull Laws & Cust Lond ... Pulling's Treatise on the Laws, Customs, and Regulations of the City and Port of London [*A publication*]   (DLA)
Pull Port of London ... Pulling's Treatise on the Laws, Customs, and Regulations of the City and Port of London [*A publication*]   (DLA)
pulm.......... Pulmentum [*Gruel Pulmonary*] [*Latin*]   (MAE)

PULM .... Pulmonary
Pulm Hypertens Proc Int Symp ... Pulmonary Hypertension. Proceedings. International Symposium on Pulmonary Circulation [*A publication*]
Pulm Macrophage Epithelial Cells Proc Annu Hanford Biol Symp ... Pulmonary Macrophage and Epithelial Cells. Proceedings. Annual Hanford Biology Symposium [*A publication*]
Pulm Pharm ... Pulmonary Pharmacology [*A publication*]
Pulm Pharmacol ... Pulmonary Pharmacology [*A publication*]
PULO .... Pattani United Liberation Organization [*Thailand*] [*Political party*] (PD)
PULP......... Kingston Systems, Inc. [*NASDAQ symbol*] (NQ)
PULP......... Premium Unleaded Petrol
Pulping Conf Proc ... Pulping Conference. Proceedings [*A publication*]
Pulp & Pa... Pulp and Paper [*A publication*]
Pulp & Pa Can ... Pulp and Paper Magazine of Canada [*Later, Pulp and Paper (Canada)*] [*A publication*]
Pulp Pap ... Pulp and Paper [*A publication*]
Pulp Pap & Board ... Pulp, Paper, and Board [*A publication*]
Pulp Pap (Can) ... Pulp and Paper (Canada) [*A publication*]
Pulp & Pap Eng ... Pulp and Paper Engineering [*A publication*]
Pulp Paper Mag Can ... Pulp and Paper Magazine of Canada [*Later, Pulp and Paper (Canada)*] [*A publication*]
Pulp Paper Manual Can ... Pulp and Paper Manual of Canada [*A publication*]
Pulp Pap Ind ... Pulp and Paper Industry [*A publication*]
Pulp Pap Ind Corros Probl Int Semin ... Pulp and Paper Industry Corrosion Problems. International Seminar on Pulp and Paper Industry Corrosion Problems [*A publication*]
Pulp Pap Ind Corros Probl Proc Int Symp Corros Pulp Pap Ind ... Pulp and Paper Industry Corrosion Problems. Proceedings. International Symposium on Corrosion in the Pulp and Paper Industry [*A publication*]
Pulp Pap Int ... Pulp and Paper International [*A publication*]
Pulp Pap Mag Can ... Pulp and Paper Magazine of Canada [*A publication*]
Pulp Pap (Sofia) ... Pulp and Paper (Sofia) [*A publication*]
Pulpudeva .. Pulpudeva. Semaines Philippopolitaines de l'Histoire et de la Culture Thrace [*A publication*]
Pulpwood Annu ... Pulpwood Annual [*United States*] [*A publication*]
Pulpwood Prodn ... Pulpwood Production and Sawmill Logging [*A publication*]
PULS .... Poseidon Undersea Launching System (NOAA)
PULS .... Propellant Utilization Loading System (AAG)
PULS .... Pulawski Savings & Loan Association [*South River, NJ*] [*NASDAQ symbol*] (NQ)
PULSAR ... Pulsating Star
PULSAR ... Pulsed Uniform LASER-Stimulated Artificial Radiation [*Proposed acronymic designation for pulsars, in the event they are found to be artificially caused by intelligent life from outer space*]
PULSE ...... Public Urban Locator Service
Pulse .... Pulse. Montana State Nurses Association [*A publication*]
PULSES .... Physical Condition, Upper Extremity Function, Lower Extremity Function, Sensory and Communication Abilities, Excretory Control, Social Support [*A neurological disability profile*]
Pulsifer (ME) ... Pulsifer's Reports [*35-68 Maine*] [*A publication*] (DLA)
PULSTAR ... Pulse Training Assembled Reactor [*Nuclear energy*] (NRCH)
Pult............. Pulton. De Pace Regis [*A publication*] (DLA)
PULV......... Pulverized
PULV......... Pulvis [*Powder*] [*Pharmacy*]
PULV CONSPER ... Pulvis Conspersus [*Dusting Powder*] [*Pharmacy*]
pulv gros..... Pulvis Grossus [*Coarse Powder*] [*Latin*] [*Pharmacy*] (MAE)
pulv subtil .. Pulvis Subtilis [*Smooth Powder*] [*Latin*] [*Pharmacy*] (MAE)
PUM .... Partido Unificado Mariateguista [*Peru*] [*Political party*] (EY)
PUM .... Pennsylvania University Museum
PUM .... Per Unit Monthly (DNAB)
PUM .... Pomalaa [*Indonesia*] [*Airport symbol*] (OAG)
PUM .... President of the United Mineworkers
PUM .... Processor Utility Monitor [*Telecommunications*] (TEL)
PUM .... PW. Maandblad voor Personeelswerk en Arbeidsverhoudingen [*A publication*]
PUM .... Pytannja Ukrajins'koho Movoznavstva [*A publication*]
PUMA ...... Powered Ultralight Manufacturers Association (EA)
PUMA ...... Processor-Upgradable Microcomputer Architecture [*DFI, Inc.*] (PCM)
PUMA ...... Programmable Universal Manipulator for Assembly [*General Motors Corp. assembly robot*]
PUMA ...... Prostitutes' Union of Massachusetts
PU-Math ... University of Pennsylvania, Mathematics-Physics Library, Philadelphia, PA [*Library symbol*] [*Library of Congress*] (LCLS)
PUMCODOXPURSACOMLOPAR ... Pulse-Modulated Coherent Doppler-Effect X-Band Pulse-Repetition Synthetic-Array Pulse Compression Side Lobe Planar Array
PU-Med..... University of Pennsylvania, Medical School, Philadelphia, PA [*Library symbol*] [*Library of Congress*] (LCLS)
PU-Med-TS ... University of Pennsylvania, Medical School, Hospital Nurses Library, Philadelphia, PA [*Library symbol*] [*Library of Congress*] (LCLS)
PUMF........ Peaceful Uses of Military Forces

PUMGC .... Pious Union of Our Mother of Good Counsel [*See also SMBC*] [*Genazzano, Italy*] (EAIO)
PUMP .... Production Upgrade Management Program (DNAB)
PUMP .... Protesting Unfair Marketing Practices [*Student legal action organization*]
Pump Eng (Tokyo) ... Pump Engineering (Tokyo) [*A publication*]
Pumpen & Verdichter Inf ... Pumpen und Verdichter Information [*A publication*]
Pumps .... Pumps-Pompes-Pumpen [*England*] [*A publication*]
Pumps Their Appl ... Pumps and Their Applications [*England*] [*A publication*]
PUMRL..... Purdue University. Monographs in Romance Languages [*A publication*]
PUMS....... Permanently Unfit for Military Service [*British*]
PUMS....... Public Use Microdata Sample [*Bureau of the Census*] (GFGA)
PUMST.... Polish Underground Movement (1939-1945) Study Trust (EA)
PUMTA .... Trace Substances in Environmental Health [*A publication*]
PU-Mu...... University of Pennsylvania, University Museum, Philadelphia, PA [*Library symbol*] [*Library of Congress*] (LCLS)
PU-Music .. University of Pennsylvania, School of Music, Philadelphia, PA [*Library symbol*] [*Library of Congress*] (LCLS)
Pun .... All India Reporter, Punjab [*A publication*] (DLA)
Pun .... Indian Law Reports, Punjab Series [*A publication*] (DLA)
PUN .... Parti de l'Unite Nationale [*Party of National Unity*] [*Haiti*] [*Political party*] (PPW)
PUN .... Partido Union Nacional [*National Union Party*] [*Costa Rica*] [*Political party*]
PUN .... Plasma Urea Nitrogen (AAMN)
PUN .... Plutonyl Nitrate [*Inorganic chemistry*]
PUN .... Precision Underwater Navigation
PUN .... Prepare a New Perforated Tape for Message [*Communications*] (FAAC)
PUN .... Punch
PUN .... Puncheon [*Unit of measurement*]
Pun .... Punica [*of Silius Italicus*] [*Classical studies*] (OCD)
PUN .... Punishment (DSUE)
PUN .... Puno [*Peru*] [*Seismograph station code, US Geological Survey*] (SEIS)
PUN .... Punta [*Flamenco dance term*]
PUNA .... Parti de l'Unite Nationale [*National Unity Party*] [*Congo*]
PUNC .... Partido de Unidad Nacional Conservadora [*Nicaragua*] [*Political party*] (EY)
PUNC .... Practical, Unpretentious, Nomographic Computer
PUNC .... Probable Ultimate Net Cost [*Accounting*]
PUNC .... Program Unit Counter
PUNC .... Punctuation
PUNCT ..... Punctuation (ROG)
PUNGA ..... Parti de l'Unite Nationale Gabonaise [*Party for Gabonese National Unity*] [*Political party*]
Punjab Fruit J ... Punjab Fruit Journal [*A publication*]
Punjab Hortic J ... Punjab Horticultural Journal [*A publication*]
Punjab Irrig Res Inst Annu Rep ... Punjab Irrigation Research Institute. Annual Report [*A publication*]
Punjab Irrig Res Inst Mem ... Punjab Irrigation Research Institute. Memoirs [*A publication*]
Punjab Irrig Res Inst Res Publ ... Punjab Irrigation Research Institute. Research Publication
Punjab Irrig Res Lab Mem ... Punjab Irrigation Research Laboratory. Memoirs [*A publication*]
Punjab Med J ... Punjab Medical Journal [*A publication*]
Punjabrao Krishi Vidyapeeth Coll Agric (Nagpur) Mag ... Punjabrao Krishi Vidyapeeth. College of Agriculture (Nagpur). Magazine [*A publication*]
Punjabrao Krishi Vidyapeeth Res J ... Punjabrao Krishi Vidyapeeth. Research Journal [*A publication*]
Punjab Univ J Math (Lahore) ... Punjab University. Journal of Mathematics (Lahore) [*A publication*]
Punj Med J ... Punjab Medical Journal [*A publication*]
Punj Rec..... Punjab Record [*India*] [*A publication*] (DLA)
PUNS .... Partido de Union Nacional del Sahara [*Western Sahara*] [*Political party*]
PUNS .... Permanently Unfit for Naval Service [*British*]
PUO.......... Placed under Observation [*Medicine*]
PUO.......... Princeton University Observatory [*New Jersey*]
PUO.......... Prudhoe Bay [*Arkansas*] [*Airport symbol*] (OAG)
PUO.......... Prudhoe Bay, AK [*Location identifier*] [*FAA*] (FAAL)
Puo .... [*A*] Purine Nucleoside [*Also, R*]
PUO.......... Pyrexia [*fever*] of Unknown Origin [*Commonly called Trench Fever*]
P U Otago M ... Proceedings. University of Otago Medical School [*A publication*]
PUOW....... Proposed Units of Work
PUP .... Paid-Up Policy [*Insurance*] (DSUE)
PUP .... Parti de l'Unite du Peuple Gabonais [*Political party*] (EY)
PUP .... Parti de l'Unite Populaire [*Tunisia*] [*Political party*] (EY)
PUP .... Partido Union Patriotica [*Patriotic Union Party*] [*Dominican Republic*] [*Political party*] (PPW)
PUP .... Peak Underpressure [*Nuclear energy*] (NRCH)
PUP .... People's United Party [*Belize*] [*Political party*] (PPW)
PUP .... Peripheral Unit Processor [*Data processing*]
PUP .... Pick Up (FAAC)

PV .... Princess Victoria's Royal Irish Fusiliers [*Military*] [*British*]   (ROG)
PV .... Principe de Viana [*A publication*]
PV .... Private Varnish [*Privately owned railroad cars*]
PV .... Production Validation [*Military*]   (AABC)
PV .... Professional Virgin   (DSUE)
PV .... Professional Volunteer
P/V............. Profit/Volume Ratio
PV .... Project Volunteer   (EA)
PV .... Prometheus Vinctus [*of Aeschylus*] [*Classical studies*]   (OCD)
PV .... Proteus Vulgaris [*Bacterium*]
PV .... Public Volunteer
PV .... Public Voucher
PV .... Pull and Void   (MCD)
PV .... Pulmonary Valvotomy [*Cardiology*]
PV .... Pulmonary Vascularity [*Medicine*]
PV .... Pulmonary Vein [*Medicine*]
PV .... Pulse Voltammetry [*Analytical chemistry*]
P & V......... Pyloroplasty and Vagotomy [*Medicine*]
PV .... Pyrocatechol Violet [*Also, PCV*] [*An indicator*] [*Chemistry*]
Pv.............. Ventral Pressure Neurons [*of a leech*]
PV .... Villanova University, Villanova, PA [*Library symbol*] [*Library of Congress*]   (LCLS)
PV1 .... Private E-1 [*Army*]
PV2 .... Private E-2 [*Army*]
PV 4 .... Pickup Trucks, Vans, and Four-Wheel-Drive Vehicles [*Initialism used as title of a publication*]
PVA .... Paralyzed Veterans of America   (EA)
PVA .... Personal Values Abstract [*Scale*]
PVA .... Platinova Resources Ltd. [*Toronto Stock Exchange symbol*]
PVA .... Poly(vinyl Alcohol) [*Also, PVAL*] [*Organic chemistry*]
PVA .... Positive Vorticity Advection [*Meteorology*]   (FAAC)
PVA .... Potato Virus A [*Plant pathology*]
PVA .... Preburner Valve Actuator [*NASA*]   (NASA)
PVA .... Present Value Analysis   (MCD)
PVA .... Privacy Act   (MCD)
PVA .... Propellant Valve Actuator   (MCD)
PVA .... Providencia [*Colombia*] [*Airport symbol*]   (OAG)
PVA .... Provident Life Accident Insurance Co. of America [*NYSE symbol*]   (SPSG)
PVAC........ Peak Volts Alternating Current   (KSC)
PVAC........ Poly(vinyl Acetate) [*Organic chemistry*]
PVAC........ Present Value of Annual Charges
PVAE........ Poly(vinyl Acetate) [*Organic chemistry*]
PVAGA...... Pochvoznanie i Agrokhimiya [*A publication*]
PVAHI ...... Augustinian Historical Institute, Villanova University, Villanova, PA [*Library symbol*] [*Library of Congress*]   (LCLS)
PVAL........ Poly(vinyl Alcohol) [*Also, PVA*] [*Organic chemistry*]
PVAM .... Virginia Magazine of History and Biography [*A publication*]
PVAQ .... Virginia Quarterly Review [*A publication*]
PVAR........ Percentage Variance [*Statistics*]
PVAS........ Primary Voice Alert System [*NORAD*]   (MCD)
PVat II ...... Il Papiro Vaticano Greco II [*A publication*]   (OCD)
PVB........... Platinol [*Cisplatin*], Vinblastine, Bleomycin [*Antineoplastic drug regimen*]
PVB........... Platteville, WI [*Location identifier*] [*FAA*]   (FAAL)
PVB........... Poly(vinyl Butyral) [*Safety glass laminating material*] [*Organic chemistry*]
PVB........... Portametric Voltmeter Bridge
PVB........... Premature Ventricular Beat [*Cardiology*]
PVB........... Provident Life & Accident Insurance Co. of America [*NYSE symbol*]   (SPSG)
PV-B .... Villanova University, Business and Finance Library, Villanova, PA [*Library symbol*] [*Library of Congress*]   (LCLS)
PVBPA ..... Proceedings of Vibration Problems [*Poland*] [*A publication*]
PVBRDX ... Pesquisa Veterinaria Brasileira [*Brazilian Journal of Veterinary Research*] [*A publication*]
PVC .... Pacvest Capital, Inc. [*Toronto Stock Exchange symbol*]
PVC .... Partido de Veteranos Civiles [*Civilian Veterans' Party*] [*Dominican Republic*] [*Political party*]   (PPW)
PVC .... Peripheral Vasoconstriction [*Medicine*]
PVC .... Periscope Viewer/Controller   (MCD)
PVC .... Permanent Virtual Circuit
PVC .... Pigment Volume Concentration
PVC .... Point of Vertical Curve
PVC .... Points de Vente. Le Magazine des Magasins [*A publication*]
PVC .... Poly(vinyl Chloride) [*Organic chemistry*]
PVC .... Port Vila [*New Hebrides*] [*Seismograph station code, US Geological Survey*]   (SEIS)
PVC .... Position and Velocity Computer
PVC .... Postvoiding Cystogram [*Medicine*]   (MAE)
PVC .... Potential Volume Change
PVC .... Premature Ventricular Contraction [*Cardiology*]
PVC .... Pressure Vacuum Chamber
PVC .... Pressure Volume Compensator   (KSC)
pvc .... Price Variation Clause   (DS)
PVC .... Primary Visual Cortex [*Anatomy*]
PVC .... Private Virtual Circuit [*Telecommunications*]
PVC .... Prosthetic Valve (Disk) Closing [*Cardiology*]
PVC .... Provincetown [*Massachusetts*] [*Airport symbol*]   (OAG)

PVC .... Provincetown, MA [*Location identifier*] [*FAA*]   (FAAL)
PVC .... Pulmonary Venous Congestion [*Medicine*]
PVC .... Pulse Voltage Converter   (OA)
PVCA........ Polyvinylchloride Acetate [*Organic chemistry*]
PVCBMA.. PVC [*Polyvinylchloride*] Belting Manufacturers Association   (EA)
PVCC........ PVC Container Corp. [*Eatontown, NJ*] [*NASDAQ symbol*]   (NQ)
PVCF .... Present Value Cash Flow [*Finance*]
PVCI .... Peripheral Vision Command Indicator
PVCN .... Poly(vinyl Cinnamate) [*Organic chemistry*]
PVco₂ .... Venous Carbon Dioxide Pressure [*Medicine*]   (MAE)
PVCP........ Victorian Poetry [*A publication*]
PVCS .... Portable Voice Communications System
PVCS .... Victorian Studies [*A publication*]
PVCV........ Pelargonium Vein Clearing Virus [*Plant pathology*]
PVD .... Pancreatic Ventral Duct [*Anatomy*]
PVD .... Paravisual Director [*British*]
PVD .... Peripheral Vascular Disease [*Medicine*]
PVD .... Physical Vapor Deposition [*Coating technology*]
PVD .... Physical Vulnerability Division [*Air Force*]
PVD .... Plan [*or Planned*] View Display [*RADAR*]   (AFM)
PVD .... Planned Variations Demonstration [*HUD*]
PVD .... Portable Vapor Detector
PVD .... Posterior Vitreous Detachment [*Ophthalmology*]
PVD .... Product Verification Demonstration   (MCD)
PVD .... Protective Vehicle Division [*US Secret Service*]
PVD .... Providence [*Rhode Island*] [*Airport symbol*]   (OAG)
PVD .... Pulmonary Vascular Disease [*Medicine*]
PV & D....... Purge, Vent, and Drain   (NASA)
PVD .... Purge, Vent, Drain System   (MCD)
PvdA .... Partij van de Arbeid [*Labor Party*] [*Netherlands*] [*Political party*]   (PPE)
PvdA/PTA ... Partij van de Arbeid van Belgiee/Parti du Travail de Belgique [*Belgian Labor Party*] [*Political party*]   (PPW)
PVDC .... Poly(vinylidene Chloride) [*Organic chemistry*]
PVDC .... Princeville Corp. [*NASDAQ symbol*]   (NQ)
PVDF........ Poly(vinylidene Difluoride) [*Organic chemistry*]
PVDF........ Poly(vinylidene Fluoride) [*Organic chemistry*]
PVDL........ Precision Variable Delay Line
PVDS........ Physical Vulnerability Data Sheets   (MCD)
PvdV .... Partij van de Vrijheid [*Party of Freedom*] [*Netherlands*] [*Political party*]   (PPE)
PVE........... Pine Valley Explorers [*Vancouver Stock Exchange symbol*]
PVE........... Polyvinyl Ether [*Organic chemistry*]
PVE........... Porvenir [*Panama*] [*Airport symbol*]   (OAG)
PVE........... Premature Ventricular Extrasystole [*Cardiology*]   (AAMN)
PVE........... Prolonged Vacuum Exposure
P & VE....... Propulsion and Vehicle Engineering [*A Marshall Space Flight Center laboratory*]   (MCD)
PVE........... Prosthetic Valve Echogram [*Cardiology*]
PVE........... Prosthetic Valve Endocarditis [*Medicine*]
PVE........... Provisioning Engineer
PVE........... Pulmonary Vascular Effect [*Physiology*]
P & VE-ADM ... Propulsion and Vehicle Engineering - Administrative [*Marshall Space Flight Center Laboratory*]   (SAA)
PVED......... Parity Violating Energy Difference [*Physical chemistry*]
P & VE-DIR ... Propulsion and Vehicle Engineering - Director [*Marshall Space Flight Center Laboratory*]   (SAA)
P & VE-E... Propulsion and Vehicle Engineering - Vehicle Engineering [*Marshall Space Flight Center Laboratory*]   (SAA)
P & VE-F... Propulsion and Vehicle Engineering - Advanced Flight Systems [*Marshall Space Flight Center Laboratory*]   (SAA)
P & VE-M ... Propulsion and Vehicle Engineering - Engineering Materials [*Marshall Space Flight Center Laboratory*]   (SAA)
P & VE-N... Propulsion and Vehicle Engineering - Nuclear Vehicle Projects [*Marshall Space Flight Center Laboratory*]   (SAA)
P & VE-P... Propulsion and Vehicle Engineering - Propulsion and Mechanics [*Marshall Space Flight Center Laboratory*]   (SAA)
P & VE-PC ... Propulsion and Vehicle Engineering - Program Coordination [*Marshall Space FlightCenter Laboratory*]   (SAA)
PVEPP....... Preliminary Value Engineering Program Plan   (MCD)
P & VE-REL ... Propulsion and Vehicle Engineering - Reliability [*Marshall Space Flight Center Laboratory*]   (SAA)
P & VE-S... Propulsion and Vehicle Engineering - Structures [*Marshall Space Flight Center Laboratory*]   (SAA)
P & VE-TS ... Propulsion and Vehicle Engineering - Technical and Scientific Staff [*Marshall Space Flight Center Laboratory*]   (SAA)
P & VE-V... Propulsion and Vehicle Engineering - Vehicle Systems Integration [*Marshall Space Flight Center Laboratory*]   (SAA)
PVF........... Peak Visibility Factor
PVF........... Peripheral Visual Field [*Optics*]
PVF........... Placerville, CA [*Location identifier*] [*FAA*]   (FAAL)
PVF........... Political Victory Fund [*National Rifle Association*]
PVF........... Poly(vinyl Fluoride) [*Organic chemistry*]
PVF........... Polyvinyl Formal [*Organic chemistry*]
PVF........... Portal Venous Flow [*Physiology*]
PVF₂ .... Poly(vinylidene Fluoride) [*Organic chemistry*]
PVFD......... Pipe Ventilated, Forced Draught

PVfHi......... Valley Forge Historical Society, Valley Forge, PA [*Library symbol*] [*Library of Congress*] (LCLS)
PVFHP...... Public Voice for Food and Health Policy (EA)
PVFM........ Polyvinyl Formal [*Organic chemistry*]
PVfP .... Philadelphia Quartz Co., Valley Forge, PA [*Library symbol*] [*Library of Congress*] (LCLS)
PVG .... Periventricular Gray [*Neurobiology*]
PVG .... Personalvertretungsgesetz [*A publication*]
PVG .... Portsmouth, VA [*Location identifier*] [*FAA*] (FAAL)
PVG .... Programmable Variations Generator [*Data processing*]
PVG .... Project on the Vietnam Generation [*Later, II*] (EA)
PVGC........ Pioneer Venus Gas Chromatograph [*NASA*]
PVH.......... Paraventricular Hypothalmic Nucleus [*Neuroanatomy*]
PVH.......... Periventricular Hemorrhage [*Medicine*]
PVH.......... Phillips-Van Heusen Corp. [*NYSE symbol*] (SPSG)
PVH.......... Pope Valley Holding [*Vancouver Stock Exchange symbol*]
PVH.......... Porto Velho [*Brazil*] [*Airport symbol*] (OAG)
PVH.......... Pulmonary Venous Hypertension [*Medicine*]
PVHO........ Pressure Vessel for Human Occupancy [*Deep-sea diving*]
PVHS........ Photorefractive Volume Holographic Storage
PVI........... Pacific Vocational Institute Library [*UTLAS symbol*]
PVI........... Peripheral Vascular Insufficiency [*Medicine*]
PVI........... Perpendicular Vegetation Index [*Botany*]
PVI........... Personal Values Inventory [*Psychology*]
PVI........... Picture Vocational Interest Questionnaire for Adults [*Vocational guidance test*]
PVI........... Pilot-Vehicle Interface [*Search technology*]
PVI........... Point of Vertical Intersection
PVI........... Poly(vinyl Isobutyl Ether) [*Organic chemistry*]
PVI........... Portal Vein Inflow [*Physiology*]
PVI........... Premature Vulcanization Inhibitor (MCD)
PVI........... Prevulcanization Inhibitor
PVI........... Primary Vocational Interest [*Personnel study*]
PVI........... Product Verification Inspection [*DoD*]
PVI........... Programmable Video Interface
PVID........ Pipe Ventilated, Induced Draught
PVIF .... Present Value Interest Factor [*Finance*]
PVIFA ...... Present Value Interest Factor of an Annuity [*Real estate*]
PVIR........ Penn Virginia Corp. [*NASDAQ symbol*] (NQ)
P & VIR ... Pure and Vulcanized Rubber Insulation
PVIZT ...... Phenyl(vinyl)imidazolidinethione [*Organic chemistry*]
PvJ .... Paleis van Justitie. Nieuwsblad Gewijd aan Binnen- en Buitenlandse Rechtspleging [*A publication*]
PVJ .... Pauls Valley, OK [*Location identifier*] [*FAA*] (FAAL)
PVJC .... Palo Verde Junior College [*California*]
PVK .... Packaged Ventilation Kit [*Civil Defense*]
PVK .... Polyvinylcarbazol [*Organic chemistry*] (IEEE)
PVK .... Preveza/Lefkas [*Greece*] [*Airport symbol*] (OAG)
P-VL .... Panton-Valentine Leukocidin
PVL........... Pavlikeny [*Bulgaria*] [*Seismograph station code, US Geological Survey*] (SEIS)
PVL........... Periventricular Leukomalacia [*Medicine*]
PVL........... Povest' Vremennych Let [*A publication*]
PVL........... Pressure to Vertical Locks
PVL........... Prevail (FAAC)
PV-L .... Villanova University, Law School, Villanova, PA [*Library symbol*] [*Library of Congress*] (LCLS)
PV-2(L)..... Poliovirus Type 2, Lansing
PVLT .... Prevalent (FAAC)
PVM .... Pneumonia Virus of Mice
PVM .... Poly(vinyl Methyl Ether) [*Organic chemistry*]
PVM .... Posterior Ventral Microtubule [*Anatomy*]
PVM .... Potato Virus M [*Plant pathology*]
PVM .... Potentiometric Voltmeter
PVM .... Power Vacuum Module [*Automotive engineering*]
PVM .... Pressure Vessel Material
PVM .... Progressive Minerals [*Vancouver Stock Exchange symbol*]
PVM .... Projection Video Monitor
PVM .... Protein, Vitamins, Minerals [*J. B. Williams Co. brand of liquid protein*]
PVM .... Proton Vector Magnetometer (NOAA)
PV-1(M) .... Poliovirus Type 1, Maloney
PVMA .... Pressure Vessel Manufacturers Association (EA)
PVMB....... Potential Variation Mixed Basis [*Photovoltaic energy systems*]
PVME........ Poly(vinyl Methyl Ether) [*Organic chemistry*]
PVMI........ Parish Visitors of Mary Immaculate [*Roman Catholic women's religious order*]
PVMT....... Pavement [*Technical drawings*]
PVMTD..... Preservation Method
PVMV .... Pepper Veinal Mottle Virus [*Plant pathology*]
PVN .... Paraventricular Nucleus [*Brain anatomy*]
PVN .... Peters Valley [*New Jersey*] [*Seismograph station code, US Geological Survey*] [*Closed*] (SEIS)
PVN .... Proven Resources Ltd. [*Vancouver Stock Exchange symbol*]
PVNGS...... Palo Verde Nuclear Generating Station (NRCH)
PVNO........ Polyvinylpyridine-N-Oxide [*Organic chemistry*]
PVNPS...... Post-Vietnam Psychiatric Syndrome
PVNS........ Pigmented Villonodular Synovitis [*Also, PVS*] [*Medicine*]
PVNT .... Prevent (AAG)
PVNTMED ... Preventive Medicine [*Also, PM*]
PVO.......... Atlantic City, NJ [*Location identifier*] [*FAA*] (FAAL)

PVO .... Phosphorus Vanadium Oxide [*Inorganic chemistry*]
PVO .... Pioneer Venus Orbiter [*NASA*]
PVO .... Portoviejo [*Ecuador*] [*Airport symbol*] (OAG)
PVO .... Principal Veterinary Officer (ROG)
PVO .... Private Voluntary Organization
PVO .... Project Vietnam Orphans [*British*] (DI)
PVO .... Prosthetic Valve (Disk) Opening [*Cardiology*]
PVO .... Protivo-Voxdushnaia Oborona [*Antiaircraft Defense*] [*Former USSR*]
PVOA .... Public Vehicle Operators' Association [*Later, CBRPT*] [*British*] (DI)
PVOD....... Peripheral Vascular Occlusive Disease [*Medicine*]
PVOR....... Precision VHF Omnirange
PVOUVS... Pioneer Venus Orbiter Ultraviolet Spectrometer [*NASA*]
PVP........... Modern Paint and Coatings [*A publication*]
PV-P .... Past Vice-President
PVP........... Penicillin V Potassium [*Biochemistry*] (MAE)
PVP........... Peripheral Vein Plasma [*Cardiology*] (MAE)
PVP........... Peripheral Venous Pressure [*Cardiology*]
PVP........... Plasma Vaporization Process
PVP........... Poly(vinylpyrrolidone) [*Organic chemistry*]
PVP........... Portal Venous Pressure [*Physiology*]
PVP........... Preferred Vision Provider
PVP........... President's Veterans Program [*Employment*]
PVP........... Professional Video Productions, Inc. [*Telecommunications service*] (TSSD)
PVP........... Pueblo Viejo [*Peru*] [*Seismograph station code, US Geological Survey*] [*Closed*] (SEIS)
PVPA........ Plant Variety Protection Act [*1970*]
PVPDC...... Poly(vinylpyridinium) Dichromate [*Organic chemistry*]
PVP-I........ Poly(vinylpyrrolidone) Iodine Complex
PVPMPC .. Perpetual Vice-President-Member Pickwick Club [*From "The Pickwick Papers" by Charles Dickens*]
PVPO........ Plant Variety Protection Office [*Department of Agriculture*]
P & V Prod ... Paint and Varnish Production [*A publication*]
PVPS .... Plasma Varactor Phase Shifter
PVQ .... Deadhorse, AK [*Location identifier*] [*FAA*] (FAAL)
PVQ .... Personal Value Questionnaire [*Navy*]
PVR .... Palos Verdes [*California*] [*Seismograph station code, US Geological Survey*] [*Closed*] (SEIS)
PVR .... Peripheral Vascular Resistance [*Cardiology*]
PVR .... Phase Volume Ratio [*Physical chemistry*]
PVR .... Platte Valley Review [*A publication*]
PVR .... Pontefract Volunteer Rifles [*British military*] (DMA)
PVR .... Postvoiding Residual [*Medicine*]
PVR .... Precision Voltage Reference (MDG)
PVR .... Premature Voluntary Release [*British military*] (DMA)
PVR .... Procedure Validation Report (AAG)
PVR .... Process Variable Record
PVR .... Profit/Volume Ratio
PVR .... Proliferative Vitreoretinopathy [*Ophthalmology*]
PVR .... Puerto Vallarta [*Mexico*] [*Airport symbol*] (OAG)
PVR .... Pulmonary Vascular Resistance [*Physiology*]
PVR .... Pulse Volume Rate [*Physiology*]
PVR .... Pulse Volume Recording [*Medicine*]
PVRC........ Pressure Vessel Research Committee [*National Institute of Standards and Technology*]
PVRD .... Purge, Vent, Repressurize, and Drain (NASA)
PVRO .... Plant Variety Rights Office [*Ministry of Agriculture, Fisheries, and Food*] [*British*]
PVS........... [*The*] Pecos Valley Southern Railway Co. [*AAR code*]
PVS........... Performance Verification System
PVS........... Peritoneovenous Shunt [*Medicine*]
PVS........... Persistent Vegetative State [*Medicine*]
PVS........... Personal Videoconferencing Station [*Widcom, Inc.*] [*Los Gatos, CA*] [*Telecommunications service*] (TSSD)
PVS........... Photovoltaic System
PVS........... Pigmented Villonodular Synovitis [*Also, PVNS*] [*Medicine*]
PVS........... Plant Vent Stack [*Nuclear energy*] (NRCH)
PVS........... Plexus Visibility Score [*Medicine*]
PVS........... Politische Vierteljahresschrift [*A publication*]
PVS........... Polyvinylsulfonate [*Organic chemistry*]
PVS........... Ported Vacuum Switch [*Automotive engineering*]
PVS........... Post-Vietnam Syndrome
PVS........... Postal Vehicle Service
PVS........... Potato Virus S [*Plant pathology*]
PVS........... Premature Ventricular Systole [*Cardiology*] (MAE)
PVS........... Present Value Service [*LIMRA*]
PVS........... Pressure Vacuum System
PVS........... Principal Veterinary Surgeon [*British*]
PVS........... Priority Ventures [*Vancouver Stock Exchange symbol*]
PVS........... Private Viewdata System [*Data processing*]
PVS........... Proceedings. Virgil Society [*A publication*]
PVS........... Professional Video Services Corp. [*Telecommunications service*] (TSSD)
PVS........... Program Validation Services [*Data processing*]
PVS........... Propellant Venting System
PVS........... Pulmonary Valve Stenosis [*Cardiology*]
PVSA........ Parkvale Financial Corp. [*NASDAQ symbol*] (NQ)
PVSC .... Professional Video Services Corp. [*Telecommunications service*] (TSSD)

PVSCA ...... Proceedings. Veterans Administration Spinal Cord Injury Conference [*A publication*]
PVSCD5 .... Perspectives in Vertebrate Science [*A publication*]
P-V Seances Com Int Poids Mes ... Proces-Verbaux des Seances. Comite International des Poids et Mesures [*A publication*]
PVSG .... Paravertebral Sympathetic Ganglion [*Neuroanatomy*]
PVSG .... Periscope Visual Scene Generation
PV SIg .... Polyvalent Surface Immunoglobulin [*Immunology*]
PV/ST....... Premate Verification/System Test [*NASA*]   (KSC)
PVT........... Pacific Vending Technology Ltd. [*Vancouver Stock Exchange symbol*]
PVT........... Page View Terminal [*Typography*] [*Videotex terminal*]
PVT........... Par Voie Telegraphique [*By Telegraph*] [*French*]
PVT........... Paroxysmal Ventricular Tachycardia [*Medicine*]
PVT........... Performance Verification Test
PV/T......... Photovoltaic/Thermal
PVT........... Physical Vapor Transport [*Materials processing*]
PVT........... Pivot   (MSA)
PVT........... Point of Vertical Tangent
PVT........... Polyvalent Tolerance [*Immunology*]
PVT........... Poly(vinyltoluene) [*Organic chemistry*]
PVT........... Portal Vein Thrombosis [*Physiology*]
PVT........... Position Velocity-Time
PVT........... Potato Virus T [*Plant pathology*]
PVT........... Precision Verification Team
PVT........... Precision Verification Test   (MCD)
PVT........... Preflight Verification Test   (NASA)
PVT........... Pressure, Volume, Temperature
PVT........... Private [*Military*]   (AFM)
PVT........... Probe Velocity Transducer   (KSC)
PVT........... Product Verification Test   (MCD)
PVT........... Prototype Validation Test   (MCD)
PVT........... Provisioning Technician
PVT........... Pulse Video Thermography [*Nondestructive testing technique*]
PVT........... Pyrotechnic Verification Test [*NASA*]   (NASA)
PVTAP ..... Photovoltaic Transient Analysis Computer Program
PVT-C....... Product Verification Test - Contractor   (MCD)
PVT-C....... Production Validation Test - Contractor   (MCD)
PVT-C....... Prototype Validation Test - Contractor   (MCD)
PVTE........ Private
PVT-G ...... Production Validation Test - Government
PVT-G ...... Prototype Validation Test - Government
PVTI......... Piping and Valve Test Insert [*Nuclear energy*]   (NRCH)
PVTM...... Physical Vulnerability Technical Memorandum   (MCD)
PVTM....... Victimology [*A publication*]
PVTMA.... Preventive Medicine [*A publication*]
PVTOS...... Physical Vapor Transport of Organic Solutions [*Materials processing*]
PVTR........ Portable Video Tape Recorder
PVU .... Perimeter Ventures Ltd. [*Vancouver Stock Exchange symbol*]
PVU .... Precision Velocity Update   (MCD)
PVU .... Provo [*Utah*] [*Airport symbol*]   (OAG)
PVU .... Provo, UT [*Location identifier*] [*FAA*]   (FAAL)
PVU .... Villanova University, Villanova, PA [*OCLC symbol*]   (OCLC)
PV Ue........ Pariser Verbandsuebereinkunft zum Schutze des Gewerblichen Eigentums [*A publication*]
PVV .... Fondation Europeenne "Pro Venetia Viva" [*European Foundation "Pro Venetia Viva"*]   (EAIO)
PVV .... Partij voor Vrijheid en Vooruitgang [*Freedom and Progress Party*] [*See also PLP*] [*Belgium*] [*Political party*]   (PPW)
PVV .... Portal Venous Velocity [*Physiology*]
PVV .... Pressure, Vent, and Vacuum
PVW .... Plainview, TX [*Location identifier*] [*FAA*]   (FAAL)
PVW .... Wilson College, Chambersburg, PA [*OCLC symbol*]   (OCLC)
PVWA ...... Plan Value Work Accounting   (MCD)
PVWA ...... Planned Value of Work Accomplished
PVWS....... Planned Value of Work Scheduled   (MCD)
PVX .... Potato Virus X [*Plant pathology*]
PVY .... Pope Vanoy [*Alaska*] [*Airport symbol*]   (OAG)
PVY .... Potato Virus Y
PVY .... Providence Energy Corp. [*AMEX symbol*]   (SPSG)
PVYV........ Pittosporum Vein Yellowing Virus [*Plant pathology*]
PVZ.......... Painesville, OH [*Location identifier*] [*FAA*]   (FAAL)
PVZTA...... Plyn [*A publication*]
PW............ Citizens Library, Washington, PA [*Library symbol*] [*Library of Congress*]   (LCLS)
PW............ Pacific Western Airlines Ltd. [*Canada*] [*ICAO designator*]   (OAG)
PW............ Packed Weight
PW............ Paedagogische Welt [*A publication*]
PW............ Palau [*ANSI two-letter standard code*]   (CNC)
PW............ Paper Wrapper   (ADA)
PW............ Paraguay Watch   (EA)
PW............ Passing Window   (MSA)
PW............ Password [*Data processing*]
PW............ [*A.*] Pauly, [*G.*] Wissowa, and [*W.*] Kroll, Real-Encyclopaedie der Klassischen Altertumswissenschaft [*A publication*]   (OCD)
PW............ Peere-Williams' English Chancery Reports [*1695-1736*] [*A publication*]   (DLA)

P & W .... Penrose and Watts' Pennsylvania Reports [*1829-32*] [*A publication*]   (DLA)
P & W .... Pension and Welfare   (WDMC)
PW .... Pension World [*A publication*]
PW .... Pension for Wounds [*Navy*] [*British*]   (ROG)
PW .... Per Week
PW .... Pericardium Wall [*Medicine*]
PW .... Petroleum Week [*A publication*]
PW .... Philadelphia & Western Railroad [*AAR code*] [*Terminated*]
PW .... Philologische Wochenschrift [*A publication*]
pW .... Picowatt
PW .... Pilot Wire   (MSA)
PW .... Pine Bark Mixed with Weblite and Peat
PW .... Pittsburgh & West Virginia Railroad [*AMEX symbol*]   (SPSG)
PW .... Pivoted Window   (AAG)
PW .... Plain Washer   (MSA)
PW .... Platoon Weapons [*British military*]   (DMA)
PW .... Poetry Wales [*A publication*]
PW .... Poets and Writers   (EA)
PW .... Ports and Waterways
PW .... Position Wanted [*Employment*]
P & W .... Post and Wire   (ADA)
PW .... Posterior Wall [*Medicine*]
PW .... Postwar
PW .... Potable Water [*Nuclear energy*]   (NRCH)
PW .... Power
PW .... Power Wagon [*Military vehicle*]
PW .... Power Windows [*Automobile ads*]
P-W .... Prader-Willi [*Syndrome*] [*Medicine*]   (AAMN)
P & W .... Pratt & Whitney [*Aircraft*]
PW .... Present Worth [*Economics*]
PW .... Pressurized Water
PW .... Prime Western [*Zinc*]
PW .... Prince of Wales [*Military unit*] [*British*]
PW .... Printed Wiring   (MSA)
PW .... Prisoner of War [*Also, POW*]
PW .... Private Wire   (NATG)
PW .... Progesterone Withdrawal [*Endocrinology*]
PW .... Projected Window   (MSA)
PW .... Projection Welding
PW .... Protestant World [*A publication*]   (APTA)
PW .... Providence & Worcester Co. [*AAR code*]
PW .... Psychological Warfare
PW .... Public Welfare
PW .... Public Works
PW .... Publishers' Weekly [*A publication*]
PW .... Pulpwash [*Byproduct of citrus processing*]
PW .... Pulse Width [*RADAR*]
PW .... Purlwise [*Knitting*]
PW .... Royal Warrant for Pay and Promotion [*British military*]   (DMA)
PW2........... Personal Workstation 2 [*Computer hardware*] [*Unisys Corp.*]   (PCM)
PWA .... Oklahoma City, OK [*Location identifier*] [*FAA*]   (FAAL)
PWA .... Pacific Western Airlines Ltd. [*Toronto Stock Exchange symbol*] [*Vancouver Stock Exchange symbol*]
PWA .... Palmer-Houston [*Alaska*] [*Seismograph station code, US Geological Survey*]   (SEIS)
PWA .... People with AIDS Coalition   (EA)
PWA .... Performance Warehouse Association   (EA)
PWA .... Person with AIDS [*Acquired Immune Deficiency Syndrome*] [*Medicine*]
PWA .... Pharmaceutical Wholesalers Association [*Later, DWA*]
PWA .... Please Wait Awhile [*Humorous interpretation for Pacific Western Airlines Corp.*]
PWA .... Portuguese West Africa [*Angola*]
PWA .... Pratt & Whitney Aircraft   (MCD)
P & WA..... Pratt & Whitney Aircraft   (KSC)
PWA .... Pray while Aloft [*Humorous interpretation for Pacific Western Airlines Corp.*]
PWA .... Printed Wire Assembly [*Data processing*]
PWA .... Private Write Area [*NASA*]   (NASA)
PWA .... Probably Won't Arrive [*Humorous interpretation for Pacific Western Airlines Corp.*]
PWA .... Product Work Authorization   (NASA)
PWA .... Project Work Authorization
PWA .... Public Works Administration [*All functions transferred to office of Federal Works Agency, 1943*]
PWA .... Publishers' Weekly Announcements [*Title changed to Forthcoming Books*] [*A publication*]
PWA .... PWA Corp. [*Toronto Stock Exchange symbol*] [*Vancouver Stock Exchange symbol*]
PWa .... Warren Library Association and County Division, Warren, PA [*Library symbol*] [*Library of Congress*]   (LCLS)
PWA .... Waynesburg College, Waynesburg, PA [*OCLC symbol*]   (OCLC)
PWAA .... Paint and Wallpaper Association of America [*Later, NDPA*]   (EA)
PWAA .... Polish Western Association of America   (EA)
PWAA .... Polish Women's Alliance of America   (EA)
PWAA .... Professional Women's Appraisal Association   (EA)
PWAC .... Periodical Writers Association of Canada

PWAC .... Pratt & Whitney Aircraft (AAG)
PWAC .... Present Worth of Annual Charges [*Pronounced "p-wack"*] [*Bell System*]
PWacD ...... David Library of the American Revolution, Washington Crossing, PA [*Library symbol*] [*Library of Congress*] (LCLS)
PWAF........ Polish Workers' Aid Fund (EA)
PWAF........ World Affairs [*A publication*]
PWAFRR .. Present Worth of All Future Revenue Requirements [*Finance*]
PWAK .... Wake Island Air Force Base [*Wake Island*] [*ICAO location identifier*] (ICLI)
PWal .... Helen Kate Furness Free Library, Wallingford, PA [*Library symbol*] [*Library of Congress*] (LCLS)
PWalPH .... Pendle Hill Library, Wallingford, PA [*Library symbol*] [*Library of Congress*] (LCLS)
PWAP........ Public Works of Art Projects [*New Deal*]
PWAR .... World Archaeology [*A publication*]
PWA Rep... PWA. Report fuer Mitarbeiter und Freunde der Papierwerke "Waldhof-Aschaffenburg" [*A publication*]
P Warren ... Warren Papyri [*A publication*]
PWAS........ Washingtonian [*A publication*]
PWayC ...... Waynesburg College, Waynesburg, PA [*Library symbol*] [*Library of Congress*] (LCLS)
PWB .... Directorate of Post War Building [*British*] (DAS)
PWb.......... Osterhout Free Library, Wilkes-Barre, PA [*Library symbol*] [*Library of Congress*] (LCLS)
PWB .... Pacific Western Bancshares [*AMEX symbol*] (SPSG)
PWB .... Partial Weight Bearing [*Medicine*]
PWB .... Pencil Writing on Back [*Deltiology*]
PWB .... Permanent Water Ballast (DS)
PW & B..... Philadelphia, Wilmington & Baltimore Railroad
PWB .... Pilot Weather Briefing (FAAC)
PWB .... Printed Wiring Board
PWB .... Programmer's Workbench [*Microsoft, Inc.*] (PCM)
PWB .... Psychological Warfare Branch [*Allied Forces*] [*World War II*]
PWB .... Pulling Whaleboat
PWBA........ Pension and Welfare Benefits Administration [*Department of Labor*]
PWBA........ Plane-Wave Born Approximation
PWBA........ Printed Wiring Board Assembly (MCD)
PWBA........ Professional Women Bowlers Association [*Later, LPBT*] (EA)
PWBC........ Peripheral White Blood Cells [*Medicine*]
PWbH........ Wyoming Historical and Geological Society, Wilkes-Barre, PA [*Library symbol*] [*Library of Congress*] (LCLS)
PWBI........ Posterior Wall of Bronchus Intermedius [*Anatomy*]
PWbK .... King's College, Wilkes-Barre, PA [*Library symbol*] [*Library of Congress*] (LCLS)
PWBP........ Pension and Welfare Benefit Programs [*Labor-Management Services Administration*]
PWBQ .... Wilson Quarterly [*A publication*]
PWBS........ Program Work Breakdown Structure (NASA)
PWBU .... Wilson Bulletin [*A publication*]
PWbW .... Wilkes College, Wilkes-Barre, PA [*Library symbol*] [*Library of Congress*] (LCLS)
PWC .... Chester County District Library Center, Exton, PA [*OCLC symbol*] (OCLC)
PWC .... Pacific War Council [*World War II*]
PWC .... Peak Work Capacity
PWC .... Pentecostal World Conference [*Emmetten, Switzerland*] (EA)
PWC .... Personal Watercraft
PWC .... Physical Work Capacity
PWC .... Physicians Who Care (EA)
PWC .... Poland Watch Center (EA)
PWC .... Port Workers' Committee [*British*]
PWC .... Pratt & Whitney Canada, Inc. [*Montreal, PQ, Canada*] [*FAA designator*] (FAAC)
PWC .... Primary Work Code (SSD)
PWC .... Printed Wiring Cards [*Telecommunications*]
PWC .... Prisoner of War Cage
PWC .... Prisoner of War Camp
PWC .... Prisoner of War Command
PWC .... Prisoner of War Compound
PWC .... Process Water Cooler (MSA)
PWC .... Professional Women in Construction (EA)
PWC .... Professional Women's Caucus (EA)
PWC .... Provincial Warning Center [*NATO*] (NATG)
PWC .... Public Works Canada [*See also TPC*]
PWC .... Public Works Center [*Navy*]
PWC .... Pulse-Width Coded
PWCACE .. Public Works Center Activity Civil Engineer [*Navy*] (DNAB)
PWcC........ Chester County District Library Center, West Chester, PA [*Library symbol*] [*Library of Congress*] (LCLS)
PWCC........ Political Warfare Coordination Committee [*London*] [*World War II*]
PWCCA..... Pembroke Welsh Corgi Club of America (EA)
PWCDET.. Public Works Center Detachment [*Navy*] (DNAB)
PWCEN..... Public Works Center [*Navy*]
PWcHi .... Chester County Historical Society, West Chester, PA [*Library symbol*] [*Library of Congress*] (LCLS)
PW/CI/DET ... Prisoner of War/Civilian Internees/Detainees (MCD)

PWCJS...... Proceedings. Fifth World Congress of Jewish Studies [*1969*] [*A publication*]
PWCLANT ... Public Works Center, Atlantic [*Navy*]
PWCMIS .. Public Works Center Management Information System [*Navy*] (DNAB)
PWCMS.... Public Works Center Management System [*Navy*]
PWCOU .... Public Workers and Constructional Operatives' Union [*British*]
PWCPAC .. Public Works Center, Pacific [*Navy*]
PWcS......... West Chester State College, West Chester, PA [*Library symbol*] [*Library of Congress*] (LCLS)
PWD.......... Pan World Ventures, Inc. [*Vancouver Stock Exchange symbol*]
PWD.......... Permanent Wants Directory [*A publication*]
PWD.......... Petroleum Warfare Department [*Ministry of Fuel and Power*] [*British*] [*World War II*]
PWD.......... Plentywood, MT [*Location identifier*] [*FAA*] (FAAL)
PWD.......... Plywood [*Technical drawings*]
PWD.......... Powder (KSC)
PWD.......... Power Distributor (KSC)
PWD.......... Procurement Work Directive [*Army*] (AABC)
PWD.......... Proximity Warning Device (MCD)
PWD.......... Psychological Warfare Division [*SHAEF*] [*World War II*]
PWD.......... Public Works Department [*Navy*]
PWD.......... Pulse-Width Detector [*or Discriminator*] [*RADAR*]
PWDC........ Philippine War Damage Commission [*Post-World War II*]
PWDCA .... Portuguese Water Dog Club of America (EA)
PWDEPT .. Public Works Department [*Navy*]
PWDG....... Prince of Wales' Dragoon Guards [*Military*] [*British*] (ROG)
PWDI .... Program with Developing Institutions (EA)
PWDMS.... Public Works Developmental Management System [*Navy*]
PWDP........ Powder Passing
PWDR .... Partial Wave Dispersing Relation
PWDRD .... Powdered [*Freight*]
PWDS........ Protected Wireline Distribution System (CET)
PWE .... Pauli-Weisskopf Equation [*Physics*]
PWE .... Pawnee City, NE [*Location identifier*] [*FAA*] (FAAL)
PWE .... Political Warfare Executive [*World War II*]
PWE .... Present Worth Expenditures [*Telecommunications*] (TEL)
PWE .... Primary Weapons and Equipment
PWE .... Prisoner of War Enclosure
PWE .... Pulse-Width Encoder
PWEA........ Printed Wiring and Electronic Assemblies [*NASA*]
PW/ED...... Pratt & Whitney Engineering Division
PWEDA.... Public Works and Economic Development Act
PWEDA.... Public Works and Economic Development Association (EA)
PWEHC .... Public Works Emergency Housing Corp. [*New Deal*]
P'well .... Planwell [*A publication*]
PWER........ Power Recovery Systems, Inc. [*Cambridge, MA*] [*NASDAQ symbol*] (NQ)
PWesAC .... Community College of Allegheny County, South Campus, West Mifflin, PA [*Library symbol*] [*Library of Congress*] (LCLS)
PWesD....... Dresser Industries, Inc., Harbison-Walker Refractories Co., West Mifflin, PA [*Library symbol*] [*Library of Congress*] (LCLS)
P West Ph S ... Proceedings. Western Pharmacology Society [*A publication*]
PWF.......... Pacific Whale Foundation (EA)
PWF.......... Package Will Follow [*Birthday-card notation*]
PWF.......... Pax World Foundation (EA)
PWF.......... Permanent Wood Foundation [*Building term*]
PWF.......... Photoelectric Work Function
PWF.......... Pop Warner Football (EA)
PWF.......... Power Financial Corp. [*Toronto Stock Exchange symbol*]
PWF.......... Present Worth Factor [*Real estate*]
PWF.......... Propellant Weight Fraction (NATG)
PWF.......... Pulse Wave Form
PWFG....... Primary Waveform Generator [*Telecommunications*] (TEL)
PWFK....... Western Folklore [*A publication*]
PWFN....... Projection Weld Flange Nut
PWFND..... Publikationen zu Wissenschaftlichen Filmen. Sektion Technische Wissenschaften. Naturwissenschaften [*A publication*]
PWFR....... Plantwide Failure Reporting (MCD)
PWFU....... World Futures [*A publication*]
PWG......... Panzerwagen [*Tank*] [*German military - World War II*]
PWG......... Permanent Working Group (NATG)
PWG......... Photoelectric Web Guide
PWG......... Plastic Wire Guide
PWG......... Powergem Resources Corp. [*Vancouver Stock Exchange symbol*]
PWH......... Pellet Warhead
PWH......... Poliokeawe [*Pali*] [*Hawaii*] [*Seismograph station code, US Geological Survey*] (SEIS)
PWH......... Precision Welding-Head
PWH......... Proprietor of Copyright on a Work Made for Hire
PWH......... Prototype Wave Height
PWHA....... Plutonium Waste Handling Area [*Nuclear energy*] (NRCH)
Pwhe .... Person Who Has Everything [*Lifestyle classification*]
PWhi.......... Whitehall Township Public Library, Whitehall, PA [*Library symbol*] [*Library of Congress*] (LCLS)
PWHQ....... Peace War Headquarters (NATG)
PWHQ....... Western Historical Quarterly [*A publication*]

PWHS	Public Works Historical Society (EA)
PWHT	Post-Weld Heat Treatment [*Nuclear energy*] (NRCH)
PWI	PACOM [*Pacific Command*] Warning Intelligence [*Army*]
PWI	Permanent Ware Institute [*Defunct*] (EA)
PWI	Permanent Way Institution [*Fleet, Hampshire, England*] (EAIO)
PWI	Physiological Workload Index [*Aviation*]
PWI	Pilot Warning Indicator [*or Instrument*] [*Aviation*]
PWI	Plasma Wave Instrument [*Physics*]
PWI	Platoon Weapons Instructor [*British military*] (DMA)
PWI	Posterior Wall Infarct [*Anatomy*] (MAE)
PWI	Potable Water Intake
PWI	Precedence Work Item
PWI	Prince of Wales' Island (ROG)
PWI	Prisoner of War Interrogation
PWI	Projects with Industry Program [*Department of Education*]
PWI	Proximity Warning Indicator [*or Instrument*] [*Aviation*]
PWIA........	Personal Watercraft Industry Association (EA)
PWIB........	Prisoner of War Information Bureau [*Post-World War II*]
PWIF	Plantation Workers' International Federation [*Later, IFPAAW*]
PWIFC	Porter Wagoner International Fan Club (EA)
PWIN	Prototype WWMCCS Intercomputer Network (MCD)
PWJ	PaineWebber Group, Inc. [*NYSE symbol*] (SPSG)
PWJ	Pulsating Water-Jet Lavager [*Medicine*] (RDA)
PWJC	Paine, Webber, Jackson & Curtis [*Later, Paine Webber, Inc.*]
PWJR	WJR. Washington Journalism Review [*A publication*]
PWK	Chicago/Wheeling, IL [*Location identifier*] [*FAA*] (FAAL)
PWL...........	Piecewise-Linear
PWL...........	Piecework Linear
PWL..........	Port Wells [*Alaska*] [*Seismograph station code, US Geological Survey*] (SEIS)
PWL..........	Poughkeepsie, NY [*Location identifier*] [*FAA*] (FAAL)
PWL..........	Power Level
PWL..........	Printed Wiring Laboratory (MCD)
PWLB.......	Public Works Loan Board [*British*]
PWLBD.....	PaineWebber Group, Inc. [*Associated Press abbreviation*] (APAG)
PWLBI	PaineWebber Group, Inc. [*Associated Press abbreviation*] (APAG)
PWLT........	World Literature Today [*A publication*]
PWLV........	Posterior Wall of Left Ventricle [*Anatomy*] (AAMN)
PWM.........	Planar Wing Module (MCD)
PWM.........	Plated Wire Memory
PWM.........	Pokeweed Mitogen [*Genetics*]
PWM.........	Portable Welding Machine
PWM.........	Portland [*Maine*] [*Airport symbol*] (OAG)
PWM.........	Portland, ME [*Location identifier*] [*FAA*] (FAAL)
PWM........	Printed Wiring Master
PWM.........	Pulse-Width Modulation [*Electronic instrumentation*]
PWM.........	Pulse-Width Multiplier (IEEE)
PWMA	Portable Wear Metal Analyzer [*Air Force*]
PWMD	Printed Wiring Master Drawing (NASA)
PWM-FM ...	Pulse-Width Modulation - Frequency Modulation [*RADAR*]
PWMIB.....	Powder Metallurgy International [*A publication*]
PWmL....	Lycoming College, Williamsport, PA [*Library symbol*] [*Library of Congress*] (LCLS)
PWML.......	Patchy White Matter Lesion [*Medicine*]
PWMO......	World Monitor [*A publication*]
PWmP	James V. Brown Library of Williamsport and Lycoming County, Williamsport, PA [*Library symbol*] [*Library of Congress*] (LCLS)
PWMQ	William and Mary Quarterly [*A publication*]
P Wms	Peere-Williams' English Chancery Reports [*1695-1736*] [*A publication*] (DLA)
PWMS......	Public Works Management System [*Navy*]
PWMSCM ...	Pokeweed Mitogen-Stimulated Spleen-Cell-Conditioned Medium [*For growing cells*]
P Wms (Eng) ...	Peere-Williams' English Chancery Reports [*1695-1736*] [*A publication*] (DLA)
PWN..........	Cash America International, Inc. [*NYSE symbol*] (SPSG)
PWN..........	Panstwowe Wydawnictwo Naukowe [*A publication*]
PWN..........	Patna Weekly Notes [*India*] [*A publication*] (ILCA)
PWN..........	Pinewood Nematode
PWN..........	Polskie Wydawnictwe Naukowe [*A publication*]
PWN..........	Pulsar Wind Nebula [*Astronomy*]
PWN..........	West Plains, MO [*Location identifier*] [*FAA*] (FAAL)
PWNE.......	Women and Environments [*A publication*]
PWNH.......	Women and Health [*A publication*]
PW-NWLZOA ...	Pioneer Women/Na'amat, the Women's Labor Zionist Organization of America [*Later, MWWV*] (EA)
PWO.........	Parliamentarians for World Order (EA)
PWO.........	Prince of Wales' Own [*Military unit*] [*British*]
PWO.........	Principal Welfare Officer [*Navy*] [*British*]
PWO.........	Principle Warfare Officer [*British*]
PWO.........	Production Work Order (MCD)
PWO.........	Public Works Officer [*Navy*]
PWOC.......	Protestant Women of the Chapel
PWOM......	Working Mother [*A publication*]
PWOP	Pregnant without Permission [*Military*] [*World War II*]
PWOQD...	Psychology of Women Quarterly [*A publication*]
PWOR	Prince of Wales' Own Royal [*Military unit*] [*British*]

PWP...........	Barrio Florida [*Puerto Rico*] [*Seismograph station code, US Geological Survey*] (SEIS)
PWP...........	Parents without Partners (EA)
PWP...........	Past Worthy Patriarch
PWP...........	Peasants' and Workers' Party [*India*] [*Political party*] (PPW)
PWP...........	Picowatt Power (CET)
pWp	Picowatts, Psophometrically Weighted
PWP...........	Planning Work Package (MCD)
PWP...........	Plastic Waste Processor (DWSG)
PWP...........	Plasticized White Phosphorus
PWP...........	Polish Workers' Party
PWP...........	Postwar Planning [*World War II*]
PWP...........	Prelaunch Wind Profile (SAA)
P-W-P........	Product-with-Purchase (WDMC)
PWP...........	Professional Women Photographers (EA)
PWP...........	Public Watering Place (ADA)
PWP...........	Public Works Planning (GFGA)
PWP...........	Pulmonary Wedge Pressure [*Medicine*]
PWP...........	Purchase-with-Purchase [*Sales promotion*]
pW0p	Picowatts, Psophometrically Weighted at a Point of Zero Reference Level
PWpM	Merck, Sharp & Dohme [*Later, Merck & Co., Inc.*] Research Laboratories, Library Services, West Point, PA [*Library symbol*] [*Library of Congress*] (LCLS)
PWPP	Professionwide Pension Plan [*American Chemical Society*]
PWPQ	Western Political Quarterly [*A publication*]
PWPS	Pure Water Preservation Society [*British*]
PWQ..........	Petersburg, WV [*Location identifier*] [*FAA*] (FAAL)
PWQ..........	Preferred and Well Qualified [*Candidate designation*]
PWQM	Protection Water Quality Management
PWR	International Power Machines Corp. [*AMEX symbol*] (SPSG)
PWR	Peak Watt Rating [*Electrical engineering*]
PWR	Pilot Wire Regulator
PWR	Police War Reserve [*British*] (DAS)
PWR	Port Walter, AK [*Location identifier*] [*FAA*] (FAAL)
PWR	Power (KSC)
PWR	Power Explorations, Inc. [*Toronto Stock Exchange symbol*]
PWR	Power Wirewound Resistor
PWR	Pressurized-Water Reactor [*Nuclear energy*]
PWR	Prevailing Wage Rate [*US Employment Service*] [*Department of Labor*]
PWR	Prince of Wales' Royal [*Military unit*] [*British*]
PWR	Program Work Request
PWR	Program Work Requirement (MCD)
PWR	Project Work Review [*Army*] (AFIT)
PWR	Public Worship Regulation Act [*1874*] [*British*] (ROG)
PWR	Publication Work Request (MCD)
PWR	Punjab Weekly Reporter [*India*] [*A publication*] (ILCA)
PWRC.......	Power Conversion [*NASDAQ symbol*] (NQ)
PWRCB.....	President's War Relief Control Board [*World War II*]
PWRE.......	Prepositioned War Reserve Equipment [*Army*]
PWREMR ...	Prepositioned War Reserve Material Requirements [*Navy*] (MCD)
PWREMS ...	Prepositioned War Reserve Material Stocks [*Navy*] (MCD)
P W Rev	Price Waterhouse Review [*A publication*]
Pwr Fmg.....	Power Farming [*A publication*]
Pwr Fmg Aust NZ ...	Power Farming in Australia and New Zealand and Better Farming Digest [*A publication*] (APTA)
Pwr Fmg Mag ...	Power Farming Magazine [*A publication*] (APTA)
Pwr Frmg ...	Power Farming in Australia and New Zealand [*A publication*] (APTA)
Pwr Frmg Aust NZ ...	Power Farming in Australia and New Zealand [*A publication*] (APTA)
PWRH.......	Powerhouse (MSA)
PWRIMC..	Prince of Wales Royal Indian Military College [*British military*] (DMA)
PWRM	Prepositioned War Reserve Materiel (MCD)
PWRMR....	Prepositioned War Reserve Materiel Requirement (NVT)
PWRMRB ...	Prepositioned War Reserve Materiel Requirement Balance (AFIT)
PWRMS....	Prepositioned War Reserve Materiel Stock (NVT)
PWRNO.....	Power Failure (FAAC)
PWRO.......	Pending Work Release Order (MCD)
PWROK	Power Restored (FAAC)
PWRR.......	Prepositioned War Reserve Requirements [*Army*] (NG)
PWRR.......	Providence and Worcester Railroad Co. [*NASDAQ symbol*] (NQ)
PWRR-MF ...	Prepositioned War Reserve Requirements for Medical Facilities [*Army*] (AABC)
PWRS.......	Prepositioned War Reserve Stocks [*Army*]
PWRS.......	Programmable Weapons Release System (IEEE)
PWRS-MF ...	Prepositioned War Reserve Stocks for Medical Facilities [*Army*] (AABC)
Pwr Wks Engng ...	Power and Works Engineering [*A publication*]
PWS...........	Paddle-Wheel Steamer [*Shipping*] (ROG)
PWS...........	Parallel Working System
PWS...........	Pattern Weavers' Society [*A union*] [*British*] (DCTA)
PWS...........	Performance Work Standard
PWS...........	Performance Work Statement [*DoD*]
PWS...........	Peter Warlock Society (EA)
PWS...........	Petrified Wood Society (EA)

PWS........... Petroleum and Water Systems [*Army*] (RDA)
PWS........... Phoenix Weapons System
PWS........... Plane-Wave Spectrum
PWS........... Plasma Wave Source [*Physics*]
PWS........... Plasma Wave System [*Instrumentation*]
PWS........... Port-Wine Stain
PWS........... Potable Water System (KSC)
PWS........... Prader-Willi Syndrome Association (EA)
PWS........... Predicted Wave Signaling
PWS........... Preliminary Work Statement (MCD)
PWS........... Pressure Wave Supercharger [*Automotive engineering*]
PWS........... Pricing Work Statement (MCD)
PWS........... Private Wire Service
PWS........... Private Wire System (AAG)
PWS........... Program Work Statement (MCD)
PWS........... Programmer Work Station
PWS........... Project Work Schedule [*Data processing*]
PWS........... Psychological Warfare Service [*Allied Forces*] [*World War II*]
PWS........... Psychological Warfare Society [*Birmingham, England*] (EA)
PWS........... Public Water System (GFGA)
PWS........... Pulau-Weh [*Sumatra*] [*Seismograph station code, US Geological Survey*] [*Closed*] (SEIS)
PWSA......... Ports and Waterways Safety Act (GFGA)
PWSB........ Peoples Westchester Savings Bank [*Hawthorne, NY*] [*NASDAQ symbol*] (NQ)
PWSC........ Post-War Scientific Collaboration [*British*]
PWSCC..... Prince William Sound Community College [*Alaska*]
PWSO........ Pilot Weapons System Officer
PWSP........ Power Spectra, Inc. [*NASDAQ symbol*] (NQ)
PWsp......... Przeglad Wspotczesny [*A publication*]
PWSPP...... Payne Whitney Suicide Prevention Program [*New York Hospital*] (EA)
PWSS........ Port War Signal Station [*British military*] (DMA)
PWSS........ Public Water Supply System (GFGA)
PWST........ Pacwest Bancorp [*NASDAQ symbol*] (NQ)
PWST........ Protected Water Storage Tank [*Nuclear energy*] (NRCH)
PWSU........ Women's Studies [*A publication*]
PWT.......... Bremerton, WA [*Location identifier*] [*FAA*] (FAAL)
PWT.......... Panstwowe Wydawnictwo Techniczne [*A publication*]
PWT.......... Penn West Petroleum Ltd. [*Toronto Stock Exchange symbol*]
PWT.......... Pennyweight
PWT.......... Picture World Test [*Psychology*]
PWT.......... Progressive Wave Tube
PWT.......... Propulsion Wind Tunnel Facility [*Air Force*] [*Arnold Air Force Base, TN*]
PWTC........ Powertec, Inc. [*NASDAQ symbol*] (NQ)
PWTC........ Public Works Training Center [*Navy*]
PWTC........ Public Works Transportation Center (MCD)
PWTCA..... Powder Technology [*A publication*]
PWTCVA.. Procurement of Weapons and Tracked Combat Vehicles, Army (AABC)
PWTF........ Polish Workers Task Force (EA)
PWTN....... Power Train (AABC)
PWTP....... Process Waste Treatment Plant [*Engineering*]
PWTR....... Pewter (MSA)
PWTR....... Philadelphia War Tax Resistance (EA)
PWTVA..... Procurement of Weapons and Tracked Vehicles, Army (AABC)
PWU.......... Political World Union (EA)
PWV......... Passionfruit Woodiness Virus [*Plant pathology*]
PWV......... Pittsburgh & West Virginia Railroad [*AAR code*]
P & WV.... Pittsburgh & West Virginia Railroad
PWV......... Precipitable Water Vapor
PWV......... Pressure Wave Velocity [*Cardiology*]
PWV......... Prince of Wales' Volunteers [*Military unit*] [*British*]
PWV......... Pulse Wave Velocity
PWVA....... Pacific War Veterans of America [*Defunct*]
PWVS........ Prince of Wales' Volunteer Service [*British*]
PWW......... Plannar Wing Weapon (MCD)
PWW......... Point Weather Warning
PWW......... Project West Wing (MCD)
PWW......... Washington and Jefferson College, Washington, PA [*Library symbol*] [*Library of Congress*] (LCLS)
PWWC...... Post War World Council [*Defunct*] (EA)
PW-WLZOA ... Pioneer Women, the Women's Labor Zionist Organization of America [*Later, PW-MWLZOA*] (EA)
PWWR...... Power Wirewound Resistor
PWX......... Permanent Working Staff [*NATO*] (NATG)
PWX......... Prisoners of War Executive [*Branch of SHAEF*] [*World War II*]
PX............. Air Niugini [*New Guinea*] [*ICAO designator*] (FAAC)
PX............. Pancreatectomized [*Medicine*]
PX............. Pedro Ximenez [*A blending sherry*]
PX............. Peroxidase [*Also, PO, POD*] [*An enzyme*]
PX............. Physical Examination
PX............. Piroxicam [*Anti-inflammatory*]
Px............. Plantwax [*A fungicide*]
PX............. Please Exchange
PX............. Pneumothorax [*Medicine*]
PX............. Post Exchange [*Military*]
PX............. Praxair, Inc. [*NYSE symbol*] (SPSG)
PX............. Private Exchange
PX............. Production Executive of the War Cabinet [*World War II*]

Px............. Prognosis [*Medicine*] (WGA)
PX............. Pyroxene [*Also, PYX*] [*A mineral*]
PXA........... Place Index in Address (SAA)
PXA .... Pulsed Xenon Arc
PXC........... Proximity Computer (MCD)
PXCMD..... Phoenix Contract Management District (SAA)
PXD........... Place Index in Decrement
PXD .... Post-Exercise Discussion [*NATO*] (NATG)
PXD .... Price Ex-Dividend [*Stock market*]
PXE........... Phenylxylylethane [*Organic chemistry*]
PXE........... Poly(xylenyl ether) [*Organic chemistry*]
PXE........... Provinces X Explorations [*Vancouver Stock Exchange symbol*]
PXE........... Pseudoxanthoma Elasticum [*Medicine*]
PXF........... Primex Forest Industries Ltd. [*Toronto Stock Exchange symbol*] [*Vancouver Stock Exchange symbol*]
PXG .... Phoenix Gold Mines Ltd. [*Toronto Stock Exchange symbol*]
PXI........... Pax Christi International (EA)
PXI........... Pulsed Xenon Illuminator
PxIMP...... Peroxisomal Integral Membrane Protein [*Biochemistry*]
PX In........ Arrival Time [*Aviation*]
PXL........... Poney Explorations Ltd. [*Vancouver Stock Exchange symbol*]
PXL........... Pulsed Xenon LASER
Pxl........... Pyridoxal [*Also, PL*] [*Biochemistry*]
PXLS......... Phoenix Laser Systems, Inc. [*NASDAQ symbol*] (NQ)
PXLS......... Pulsed Xenon Light Source
PXLSS...... Pulsed Xenon Light Source System
PXM......... Projection X-Ray Microscope
Pxm......... Pyridoxamine [*Also, PM*] [*Biochemistry*]
PX Me....... Report My Arrival or Departure [*Aviation slang*]
PXN .... Panoche, CA [*Location identifier*] [*FAA*] (FAAL)
Pxn........... Pyridoxine [*Also, PN*] [*Biochemistry*]
PXO........... Porto Santo [*Portugal*] [*Airport symbol*] (OAG)
PXO........... Prospective Executive Officer
PX Out...... Takeoff Time [*Aviation*]
PXPA .... Journal of Experimental Psychology. Animal Behavior Processes [*A publication*]
PXPG........ Journal of Experimental Psychology. General [*A publication*]
PXPH .... Journal of Experimental Psychology. Human Perception and Performance [*A publication*]
PXPL .... Journal of Experimental Psychology. Learning, Memory, and Cognition [*A publication*]
PXPPL...... Pull and Push Plate
PXR........... Paxar Corp. [*AMEX symbol*] [*NYSE symbol*] (SPSG)
PXR .... Plus-X-Reversal
PXR .... Praxis Resources Ltd. [*Vancouver Stock Exchange symbol*]
PXRE......... Phoenix Re Corp. [*NASDAQ symbol*] (NQ)
PXS........... Plexus Resources Corp. [*Toronto Stock Exchange symbol*]
PXS........... Pulsed Xenon System
PXSC .... Proximity Sensing Computer (MCD)
PXSS .... Pulsed Xenon Solar Simulator
PXSTR ..... Phototransistor (IEEE)
PXT........... Patuxent River, MD [*Location identifier*] [*FAA*] (FAAL)
PXT........... Pinxit [*He, or She, Painted It*] [*Latin*]
PXT........... Praxis Technologies Corp. [*Toronto Stock Exchange symbol*]
PXU .... Portable X-Ray Unit
PXV .... Evansville, IN [*Location identifier*] [*FAA*] (FAAL)
PXV .... Pedro Ximenez Viejo [*A blending sherry*]
PXXP .... Pacific Express Holding [*NASDAQ symbol*] (NQ)
PXY .... Milwaukee, WI [*Location identifier*] [*FAA*] (FAAL)
Pxy........... Pyridoxyl [*Biochemistry*]
PY .... Martin Memorial [*York City and County*] Library, York, PA [*Library symbol*] [*Library of Congress*] (LCLS)
py .... Paraguay [*MARC country of publication code*] [*Library of Congress*] [*IYRU nationality code*] (LCCP)
PY .... Paraguay [*ANSI two-letter standard code*] (CNC)
PY .... Patrol Vessel, Yacht [*Navy symbol*]
PY .... Pembroke Yeomanry [*British military*] (DMA)
PY .... Person Years [*After radiation exposure*]
PY .... Physical Year
P/Y........... Pitch or Yaw
PY .... Polysar Ltd. [*Toronto Stock Exchange symbol*] [*Vancouver Stock Exchange symbol*]
PY .... Preferred Health Care [*AMEX symbol*] (SPSG)
PY .... Prior Year (AABC)
PY .... Program Year (AFM)
PY .... Project Yedid (EA)
PY .... Proto Yiddish (BJA)
PY .... Publication Year [*Online database field identifier*]
Py............. Pyrene [*Organic chemistry*] (AAMN)
Py............. Pyridine [*Organic chemistry*]
Py............. Pyrogen [*Medicine*]
PY .... Pyrometer (IEEE)
PY .... Pyronin Y [*A biological dye*]
PY .... Pythium [*A fungus*]
PY .... Surinaamse Luchtvaart Maatschappij NV [*Surinam*] [*ICAO designator*] (FAAC)
PYA .... Penn Yan, NY [*Location identifier*] [*FAA*] (FAAL)
PYA .... Pioneer Youth of America (EA)
PYA .... Pittsburgh, Youngstown & Ashland Railway Co. (IIA)
PYA .... Plan, Year, and Age [*Insurance designations*]
PYA .... Psychoanalysis [*Medicine*]

PYA .... Pyatigorsk [*Former USSR*] [*Seismograph station code, US Geological Survey*] (SEIS)
PYA .... Pyroair Tech [*Vancouver Stock Exchange symbol*]
PYACA...... Psychoanalytic Study of the Child [*A publication*]
PYAFB ..... Psychologia Africana [*A publication*]
PYAIA ...... Postepy Astronomii [*A publication*]
PYarE .... Electric Storage Battery Co., Yardley, PA [*Library symbol*] [*Library of Congress*] (LCLS)
Py B .... Bachelor of Pedagogy
PYB.......... Borg-Warner Corp., York Division, York, PA [*Library symbol*] [*Library of Congress*] (LCLS)
PYB.......... [*The*] Palestine Year Book [*New York*] [*A publication*] (BJA)
PYB.......... Problems of Economics. A Journal of Translations [*A publication*]
PYBT........ [*The*] Prince's Youth Business Trust [*British*]
PYC.......... Kuparuk, AK [*Location identifier*] [*FAA*] (FAAL)
PYC.......... Pale Yellow Candle [*Baltic coffee-house*] [*London*] (DSUE)
PYC.......... Patrol Vessel, Yacht, Coastal [*Navy symbol*] [*Obsolete*]
PYC.......... Pembroke Yeomanry Cavalry [*British military*] (DMA)
PYC.......... Perishability Code [*Military*] (AFIT)
PYC.......... Playon Chico [*Panama*] [*Airport symbol*] (OAG)
PYC.......... Pope and Young Club (EA)
PYC.......... Proteose-Yeast Castione Medium [*Microbiology*] (MAE)
PyC .... Pyogenic Culture [*Medicine*] (MAE)
PYC.......... York College of Pennsylvania, York, PA [*Library symbol*] [*Library of Congress*] (LCLS)
PYCG........ Pyrochromatogram [*Analytical chemistry*]
PYCHB..... Psychology [*A publication*]
PYCOA...... Phycologia [*A publication*]
Pyd............ [*A*] Pyrimidine Nucleoside [*Also, Y*]
PYDV .... Potato Yellow Dwarf Virus [*Plant pathology*]
PYE.......... Point Reyes, CA [*Location identifier*] [*FAA*] (FAAL)
PYE.......... Progressive Incorporated Equity [*NYSE symbol*] (SPSG)
PYE.......... Protect Your Environment [*Groups*]
PYE.......... Pryme Energy Resources [*Vancouver Stock Exchange symbol*]
PYF.......... French Polynesia [*ANSI three-letter standard code*] (CNC)
PYF.......... Pay-Fone Systems, Inc. [*AMEX symbol*] (SPSG)
PYF.......... Pyrenees [*France*] [*Seismograph station code, US Geological Survey*] (SEIS)
Py-FD-MS ... Pyrolysis Field Desorption Mass Spectrometry
PYFS .... Yale French Studies [*A publication*]
PYFV........ Parsnip Yellow Fleck Virus [*Plant pathology*]
PYG .... Peptone-Yeast-Glucose [*Medium*] [*Microbiology*]
PYGC........ Pyrolysis Gas Chromatography
PYGM .... Peptone-Yeast Glucose Maltose Agar [*Microbiology*] (MAE)
PYGN .... Pyrogen Unit [*Biochemistry*]
PYGS........ Church of Jesus Christ of Latter-Day Saints, Genealogical Society Library, Gettysburg Branch, York, PA [*Library symbol*] [*Library of Congress*] (LCLS)
PYH.......... Puerto Ayacucho [*Venezuela*] [*Airport symbol*] (OAG)
PYH.......... York Hospital, York, PA [*Library symbol*] [*Library of Congress*] (LCLS)
PYHi......... Historical Society of York County, York, PA [*Library symbol*] [*Library of Congress*] (LCLS)
Py-HRMS ... Pyrolysis High-Resolution Mass Spectrometry
PYI............ Presidential Young Investigator Program [*National Science Foundation*]
PYJ .... Louisville, KY [*Location identifier*] [*FAA*] (FAAL)
Pyke .... Pyke's Lower Canada King's Bench Reports [*1809-10*] [*A publication*] (ILCA)
Pyke LC ..... Pyke's Lower Canada King's Bench Reports [*1809-10*] [*A publication*] (ILCA)
Pyke's R ..... Pyke's Lower Canada King's Bench Reports [*1809-10*] [*A publication*] (ILCA)
PYL.......... Perry Island, AK [*Location identifier*] [*FAA*] (FAAL)
PYLR........ Peach Yellow Leaf Roll [*Plant pathology*]
PYM .... Martin Memorial [*York City and County*] Library, York, PA [*OCLC symbol*] (OCLC)
PYM .... Pan-African Youth Movement (EA)
PYM .... Plymouth, MA [*Location identifier*] [*FAA*] (FAAL)
PYM .... Psychosomatic Medicine
PYM .... Putnam High Yield Municipal [*NYSE symbol*] (SPSG)
PYMOA .... Psychological Monographs. General and Applied [*A publication*]
Py-MS .... Pyrolysis Mass Spectrometry
Pymt.......... Payment
PYMV .... Peanut Yellow Mottle Virus [*Plant pathology*]
PYN.......... Chicago, IL [*Location identifier*] [*FAA*] (FAAL)
PYN.......... Poneloya [*Nicaragua*] [*Seismograph station code, US Geological Survey*] (SEIS)
PYNC .... Prior Year Notice [*IRS*]
PYNNA..... Psychiatria, Neurologia, Neurochirurgia [*A publication*]
PYNS........ Youth and Society [*A publication*]
PYO .... Pick Your Own [*Fruits and vegetables*] (DSUE)
PYO .... Pyongyang [*Heizo*] [*North Korea*] [*Seismograph station code, US Geological Survey*] [*Closed*] (SEIS)
PYOL........ Pyramid Oil Co. [*NASDAQ symbol*] (NQ)
PYoW .... Westmoreland County Community College, Youngwood, PA [*Library symbol*] [*Library of Congress*] (LCLS)
PYP.......... Pyrophosphate [*Scintiscanning*]
PYPER ...... Promote Yard Performance Efficiency and Reliability (DNAB)

PYPH .... Polyphase
PYPYB ..... Psychophysiology (Baltimore) [*A publication*]
P-Y-R......... Pitch-Yaw-Roll (AAG)
PYR .... Player Resources, Inc. [*Vancouver Stock Exchange symbol*]
PYR .... Prior Year Report
PYR .... Prior Year's Return [*IRS*]
Py R .... Pyke's Lower Canada King's Bench Reports [*1809-10*] [*A publication*] (ILCA)
Pyr............ Pyralidae [*Entomology*]
PYR .... Pyramid [*California*] [*Seismograph station code, US Geological Survey*] (SEIS)
PYR .... Pyramid (MSA)
Pyr............ Pyramidal Tract [*Neuroanatomy*]
PYR .... Pyridine [*Organic chemistry*]
Pyr............ [*A*] Pyrimidine [*Biochemistry*]
PYR .... Pyrometer (AAG)
PYR .... Pyruvate [*Biochemistry*]
PYRCA...... Psychological Record [*A publication*]
PYRD .... Pyramid Technology Corp. [*NASDAQ symbol*] (NQ)
PYRETH ... Pyrethrum [*Pellitory*] [*Pharmacology*] (ROG)
Pyridine Its Deriv ... Pyridine and Its Derivatives [*A publication*]
PYRM........ Pyramid Magnetics, Inc. [*Chatsworth, CA*] [*NASDAQ symbol*] (NQ)
PYRMD..... Pyramid [*Freight*]
PYRO .... Pyrogallic Acid (ROG)
PYRO .... Pyrotechnic
PYROM .... Pyrometer [*Engineering*]
PYROTECH ... Pyrotechnical (ROG)
PYROX GN ... Pyroxene Gneisses [*Agronomy*]
PYRR........ Pyrrolidine [*Organic chemistry*]
PYRREC ... Pyrrolidinoethyl Chloride [*Organic chemistry*]
Pyrrh......... Pyrrhus [*of Plutarch*] [*Classical studies*] (OCD)
PYRS .... Pyramids [*Board on Geographic Names*]
PYRTA...... Psychological Reports [*A publication*]
PYS........... Partial Yield Spectroscopy (MCD)
PYS........... Primitive Yolk Sac [*Embryology*]
PYSCB ...... Psychology in the Schools [*A publication*]
PYSOA...... Physiologist [*A publication*]
PYSSB ...... Psychoanalytic Study of Society [*A publication*]
PYT........... Payment (DCTA)
PYT........... Playitas [*Nicaragua*] [*Seismograph station code, US Geological Survey*] (SEIS)
PYT........... Prentiss, MS [*Location identifier*] [*FAA*] (FAAL)
PYT........... Pretty Young Thing [*In song title from the Michael Jackson album "Thriller"*]
PYT........... Pyng Tech [*Vancouver Stock Exchange symbol*]
PYTCA...... Phytochemistry [*A publication*]
Pyth........... Pythian [*of Pindar*] [*Classical studies*] (OCD)
Py-TRMS.. Pyrolysis Time-Resolved Mass Spectrometry
PYV .... Payton Ventures [*Vancouver Stock Exchange symbol*]
PyV .... Polyoma Virus
PYV .... Yaviza [*Panama*] [*Airport symbol*] (OAG)
PYX .... Perryton, TX [*Location identifier*] [*FAA*] (FAAL)
PYX .... Pyroxene [*Also, PX*] [*A mineral*]
Pyx............ Pyxis [*Constellation*]
Pyxi........... Pyxis [*Constellation*]
PZ .... Canal Zone [*ANSI two-letter standard code*] [*Obsolete*] (CNC)
PZ .... Lineas Aereas Paraguayas [*ICAO designator*] (FAAC)
PZ .... Pancreozymin [*Also, CCK*] [*Endocrinology*]
PZ .... Panzerbrechend [*Armor-Piercing*] [*German military - World War II*]
PZ .... Partiinaya Zhizn [*A publication*]
PZ .... Past Z
PZ .... Pastural Zone [*Agriculture*]
PZ .... Paterson Zochonis [*Commercial firm*] [*British*]
PZ .... Penzance [*British depot code*]
PZ .... Peripheral Zone [*Botany*] [*Anatomy*]
PZ .... Phase Zero
Pz .... Phenylazobenzyloxycarbonyl [*Biochemistry*]
PZ .... Pick Up Zone [*Shipping*]
PZ .... Pie Zeses [*May You Live Piously*] [*Italian*]
pz.............. Pieze [*Unit of pressure*]
PZ .... Poland [*IYRU nationality code*] (IYR)
PZ .... Potez [*Etablissements Henri Potez*] [*France*] [*ICAO aircraft manufacturer identifier*] (ICAO)
PZ .... Prazosin [*A vasodilator*]
PZ .... Pregnancy Zone Protein (AAMN)
PZ .... Primary Zone [*Military*]
PZ .... Prisoner of Zion (BJA)
PZ .... Protective Zone
PZ .... Prozone Phenomenon [*Immunology*]
PZ .... Przeglad Zachodni [*A publication*]
PZ .... Psychic Zodiac
PZ .... Pyrazine [*Organic chemistry*]
PZA .... Patrol Zone Area (MCD)
PZA .... Paz De Ariporo [*Colombia*] [*Airport symbol*] (OAG)
PZA .... Piasa Commuter Airlines, Inc. [*St. Louis, MO*] [*FAA designator*] (FAAC)
PZA .... Pizza Inn, Inc. [*AMEX symbol*] (SPSG)
PZA .... Provena Foods, Inc. [*AMEX symbol*] (SPSG)
PZA .... Pyrazinamide [*Antibacterial compound*]

PZAA......... Polarized Zeeman Atomic Absorption
PZB............ Pietermaritzburg [*South Africa*] [*Airport symbol*]   (OAG)
PZBUA...... Przeglad Budowlany [*Poland*] [*A publication*]
PZC............ Pezamerica Resources Corp. [*Vancouver Stock Exchange symbol*]
PZC............ Point of Zero Charge [*Electrochemistry*]
PZC............ Progressive Zionist Caucus   (EA)
PZ-CCK..... Pancreozymin-Cholecystokinin [*Endocrinology*]   (MAE)
PZCO .... Pickup-Zone Control Officer [*Military*]   (INF)
PZD .... Phase Zero Defense
PZDV........ Panzer-Division [*Armored Division*] [*German military*]
PZE............ Pamietniki Zjazdow Polskiego Zwiazku Entomologicznego [*A publication*]
PZE............ Penzance [*England*] [*Airport symbol*]   (OAG)
PZE............ Piezoelectric
PZELA ...... Przeglad Elektrotechniczny [*A publication*]
PZFC........ Pia Zadora Fan Club   (EA)
PZH............ Zhob [*Pakistan*] [*Airport symbol*]   (OAG)
PZI............ Indiana University of Pennsylvania, Indiana, PA [*OCLC symbol*]   (OCLC)
PZI............ Protamine Zinc Insulin
PZKPFW... Panzerkampfwagen [*German tank*] [*World War II*]
PZKW....... Panzerkampfwagen [*German tank*] [*World War II*]
PZL............ Pennzoil Co. [*NYSE symbol*] [*Toronto Stock Exchange symbol*]   (SPSG)
PZL............ Progressive Zionist League-Hashomer Hatzair   (EA)
PZM .... Pod Znamenem Marksizma [*A publication*]
PZM .... Pressurized Zone Microphone
PZMEA..... Przeglad Mechaniczny [*A publication*]
PZO .... Peebles, OH [*Location identifier*] [*FAA*]   (FAAL)
PZO .... Puerto Ordaz [*Venezuela*] [*Airport symbol*]   (OAG)
PZP............ Phase Zero Program
PZP............ Pregnancy Zone Protein
PZPR........ Polska Zjednoczona Partia Robotnicza [*Polish United Workers' Party - PUWP*] [*Political party*]   (PPW)
PZQ .... Rogers City, MI [*Location identifier*] [*FAA*]   (FAAL)
PZ(R)........ Penetration Zone (Radius)   (MCD)
PZR............ Pressurizer   (NRCH)
PZR LCS ... Pressurizer Level Control System [*Nuclear energy*]   (GFGA)
PZR PCS ... Pressurizer Pressure Control System [*Nuclear energy*]   (GFGA)
PZS............ President of the Zoological Society [*British*]
PZS............ Przeglad Zagadnien Socjalnych [*A publication*]
PZSV .... Pelargonium Zonate Spot Virus [*Plant pathology*]
PZT............ Lead [*Plumbum*] Zirconate-Titanate [*Piezoelectric transducer*]
PZT............ Photographic Zenith Tube
PZT............ Piezoelectric Transducer [*or Translator*]
PZT............ Piezoelectric Zirconate Titanate
PZT............ Polycrystalline Lead Zirconate Titanate [*Piezoelectricity*]
PZU .... Port Sudan [*Sudan*] [*Airport symbol*]   (OAG)
PZV............ New York, NY [*Location identifier*] [*FAA*]   (FAAL)
PZWS........ Panstwowe Zaklady Wydawnictwo Szkolnych [*A publication*]
PZX............ Paragould, AR [*Location identifier*] [*FAA*]   (FAAL)
PZY............ Piestany [*Former Czechoslovakia*] [*Airport symbol*]   (OAG)
PZYG........ Zygon [*A publication*]
PZZ............ Pizza Patio Ltd. [*Vancouver Stock Exchange symbol*]

Q

Q .... Chicago, Burlington & Quincy Railroad [*Also known as Burlington Route*] [*Slang*]
Q .... Codex Marchalianus (BJA)
Q .... Coefficient of Association [*Statistics*]
Q .... Coenzyme Q [*Ubiquinone*] [*Also, CoQ, U, UQ*] [*Biochemistry*]
Q .... Combination of Purpose [*JETDS nomenclature*]
Q .... Drone [*Designation for all US military aircraft*]
Q .... Dynamic Pressure [*NASA*]
Q .... Glutamine [*One-letter symbol; see Gln*]
Q .... Heat [*or q*] [*Symbol*] [*IUPAC*]
Q .... Kuwait [*IYRU nationality code*] (IYR)
Q .... Merit of a Coil or Capacitor [*Electronics*]
q .... Partition Function, Particle [*Symbol*] [*IUPAC*]
Q .... Partition Function, System [*Symbol*] [*IUPAC*]
Q .... Polaris Correction [*Missiles*]
Q .... Promotional Fare [*Also, K, L, V*] [*Airline fare code*]
Q .... Proportion Not in a Specific Class
Q .... Q-Factor (DEN)
Q .... Qere (BJA)
Q .... Quadragesms [*Year Books of Edward III*] [*A publication*] (ILCA)
Q .... Quadrans [*A Farthing*] [*Monetary unit*] [*British*]
Q .... Quadriceps [*Anatomy*]
Q .... Quadrillion BTU's [*Also known as "quads"*]
Q .... Quadrivium [*A publication*]
Q .... Quadruple
Q .... Quadruple Expansion Engine
Q .... Quaere [*Inquire*] [*Latin*]
Q .... Qualifier [*Linguistics*]
Q .... Quality Factor
q .... Quality of Output [*Economics*]
Q .... Quantity
Q .... Quantity of Electricity [*Symbol*] [*IUPAC*]
Q .... Quaque [*Each or Every*] [*Latin*]
Q .... Quark [*Physics*]
Q .... Quart
Q .... Quarter
Q .... Quarter Word Designator [*Data processing*]
Q .... Quarterback [*Football*]
Q .... Quartering [*Military*] [*British*]
Q .... Quarterly
Q .... Quartermaster [*Military*]
Q .... Quarternary [*Geology*]
Q .... Quarters [*Officer's rating*] [*British Royal Navy*]
Q .... Quartile
Q .... Quarto [*Book from 25 to 30 centimeters in height*]
Q .... Quarto Edition [*Shakespearean work*]
Q .... Quartz [*CIPW classification*] [*Geology*]
Q .... Quasi [*Almost, As It Were*] [*Latin*]
Q .... Quebec [*Phonetic alphabet*] [*International*] (DSUE)
Q .... Queen [*Phonetic alphabet*] [*Pre-World War II*] [*World War II*] (DSUE)
Q .... Queen [*Chess*]
Q .... Queen
Q .... Queenie [*Phonetic alphabet*] [*Royal Navy*] [*World War I*] (DSUE)
Q .... Queen's Quarterly [*A publication*]
Q .... Queensway [*Furniture store chain*] [*British*]
Q .... Queer [*Homosexual*] [*Slang*] (DSUE)
Q .... Quercetin [*Botany*]
Q .... Query
Q .... Query Language [*1975*] (CSR)
Q .... Question
q .... Questioned [*Soundness of decision or reasoning in cited case questioned*] [*Used in Shepard's Citations*] [*Legal term*] (DLA)
Q .... Questionnaire
Q .... Quetzal [*Monetary unit*] [*Guatemala*]
Q .... Queue
Q .... Quick
Q .... Quick [*Flashing*] Light [*Navigation signal*]

Q .... Quiescent [*Cytology*]
Q .... Quiescit [*He Rests*] [*Latin*]
Q .... Quiller-Couch [*Sir Arthur, 1863-1944, English man of letters*] [*Letter used as pen name*]
Q .... Quiller Press [*Publisher*] [*British*]
Q .... Quilting
Q .... Quinacrine [*Fluorescent method*] [*Chromosome stain*]
Q .... Quintal [*Unit of weight*]
Q .... Quintar [*Monetary unit*] [*Albania*]
Q .... Quintus [*Fifth*] [*Latin*]
Q .... Quinzaine [*A publication*]
Q .... Quire [*Measure of paper*]
Q .... Quisque [*Each, Every*] [*Pharmacy*]
Q .... Qumran (BJA)
Q .... Quorum (DLA)
Q .... Quotient (ADA)
Q .... Radiant Energy [*Symbol*] [*IUPAC*]
Q .... Receivership [*or Bankruptcy*] [*Designation used with NYSE symbols*] (SPSG)
Q .... Respiratory Quotient [*Also, RQ*] [*Physiology*]
Q .... San Quentin [*Prison*]
Q .... Semi-Interquartile Range or Quartile Deviation [*Statistics*]
Q .... Sonar [*JETDS nomenclature*]
Q .... Special Purpose [*JETDS nomenclature*]
Q .... Squall [*Meteorology*] (FAAC)
Q .... Volume Rate [*Heat transmission symbol*]
Q (Car)....... Chrysler car made by Maserati
QA........... Bibliotheque Municipale, Alma, Quebec [*Library symbol*] [*National Library of Canada*] (NLC)
QA............. Inter City Airlines [*Great Britain*] [*ICAO designator*] (FAAC)
QA............. National Restaurant Association Quality Assurance Study Group (EA)
QA............. QANTAS Airways Ltd. [*Australia*] (DS)
QA............. Qatar [*ANSI two-letter standard code*] [*IYRU nationality code*] (CNC)
qa............... Qatar [*MARC country of publication code*] [*Library of Congress*] (LCCP)
QA............. Quadrans [*A Farthing*] [*Monetary unit*] [*British*] (ROG)
QA............. Quadripartite Agreement
QA............. Quality Assurance
QA............. Quantum Access, Inc. [*Database producer*] (IID)
QA............. Quarternary Ammonium [*Chemistry*]
QA............. Quarters Allowance
QA............. Quarters Armourer [*British military*] (DMA)
QA............. Quarters Assistant [*British military*] (DMA)
QA............. Quasi Algorithm (OA)
QA............. Query Analyzer (IEEE)
QA............. Query Author [*Proofreader's notation*]
Q & A .... Question and Answer (MSA)
QA............. Quick-Acting
QA............. Quick Assembly [*Furniture*]
QA............. Quick Asset [*Finance*]
QA............. Quiescent Aerial [*or Antenna*]
QA............. Quinic Acid [*Organic chemistry*]
QA............. Quisqualic Acid [*Biochemistry*]
QAA........... ALCAN International Ltee. [*ALCAN International Ltd.*] Jonquiere, Quebec [*Library symbol*] [*National Library of Canada*] (NLC)
QAA........... Quality Assurance Assistant [*DoD*]
QAA........... Quality Assurance Audit (MCD)
QAA......... Quinoline Amino Alcohol [*Organic chemistry*]
QAAS .... Quality Assurance Ammunition Specialist [*or Speciality*] (MCD)
QAB........... Queen Anne's Bounty
QAB........... Quick Action Button [*Military*] (CAAL)
QABA .... Bibliotheque et Audiovisuel, Alma, Quebec [*Library symbol*] [*National Library of Canada*] (NLC)
Q Abh Mittelrh Kg ... Quellen und Abhandlungen zur Mittelrheinischen Kirchengeschichte [*A publication*]
QAC........... Quadrant Aimable Charge Warhead (MCD)
QAC........... Quadripartite Agreements Committee [*Military*]

2919

QAC.......... Quality Assurance Chart (MCD)
QAC.......... Quality Assurance Checklist (NRCH)
QAC.......... Quality Assurance Code
QAC.......... Quality Assurance Coordinator [*Environmental Protection Agency*] (GFGA)
QAC.......... Quality Assurance Criterion [*Nuclear energy*] (NRCH)
QAC.......... Quarternary Ammonium Compound [*Chemistry*]
QAC.......... Quebec Appeal Cases [*Maritime Law Book Co. Ltd.*] [*Canada*] [*Information service or system*] (CRD)
QAC.......... Quick-Acting Choke [*Automotive engineering*]
QACAD..... Quality Assurance Corrective Action Document (NASA)
QACC Mot Trader ... QACC [*Queensland Automobile Chamber of Commerce*] Motor Trader [*A publication*] (APTA)
QACHL..... Centre de Documentation, Centre Hospitalier des Laurentides et Centre d'Accueil et de Readaptation des Hautes-Vallees, L'Annonciation, Quebec [*Library symbol*] [*National Library of Canada*] (BIB)
Qad .... Qadmoniot [*Jerusalem*] (BJA)
QAD.......... Quadriceps Active Displacement [*Sports medicine*]
QAD.......... Quality Assurance Data
QAD.......... Quality Assurance Directive
QAD.......... Quality Assurance Directorate [*Materials*] [*British*]
QAD.......... Quality Assurance Division [*Picatinny Arsenal*] [*Dover, NJ*]
QAD.......... Quick Attach-Detach [*Engine*]
QADC....... Queen's Aide-de-Camp [*Military*] [*British*]
QADK....... Quick Attach-Detach Kit
QAD(MATS) ... Quality Assurance Directorate (Materials) [*British*]
QADS....... Quality Assurance Data System
QAE......... Quality Assurance Engineering
QAE......... Quality Assurance Evaluator [*Military*]
QAE......... Queen's Awards for Export [*British*]
QAES........ Quality Assurance and Expert Systems [*Data processing*]
QAET .... Quality Assurance Environment Testing [*Military*] (CAAL)
QAET .... Quality Assurance Evaluation Test (NG)
QAF......... Quality Assurance Function
QAFA....... Quality Assurance Field Activity
QAFM...... Quality Assurance Forms Guide Manual (SAA)
QAFO....... Quality Assurance Field Operations
Q Ag J....... Queensland Agricultural Journal [*A publication*] (APTA)
QAHD ...... Centre de Documentation, Hotel-Dieu d'Arthabaska, Quebec [*Library symbol*] [*National Library of Canada*] (BIB)
QAHI........ American Healthcare Management, Inc. [*AMEX symbol*] (SPSG)
QAI.......... Quality Assurance Index (MCD)
QAI.......... Quality Assurance Inspection
QAI.......... Quality Assurance Instruction (NRCH)
QAIA .... Queen Alia International Airport [*Jordan*]
QAIL .... Quality Assurance Information Letter (MCD)
QAIMNS... Queen Alexandra's Imperial Military Nursing Service [*British*]
QAIMNSR ... Queen Alexandra's Imperial Military Nursing Service Reserve [*British military*] (DMA)
QAIP .... Quality Assurance Inspection Procedure
QAIRG ...... Quality Assurance Installation Review Group [*Nuclear energy*] (NRCH)
QA + IS .... Quality Association and Inspection Service [*British*]
QAK.......... Quick Attach Kit
QAL.......... Q Allowance List [*Aviation*] (DNAB)
QAL.......... Quaderni di Archeologia della Libia [*A publication*]
QAL.......... Quality Assurance Laboratory
QAL.......... Quarterly Acceptance List (AFIT)
QAL.......... Quarterly Accession List
QAL.......... Quartz Aircraft Lamp
QAL.......... Quebec Airways Ltd. (MCD)
QAL.......... Quebec Aviation Ltd. [*Quebec City, PQ, Canada*] [*FAA designator*] (FAAC)
QALAS...... Qualified Associate of the Land Agents' Society [*British*]
QALC........ College d'Alma, Lac St.-Jean, Quebec [*Library symbol*] [*National Library of Canada*] (NLC)
QALI .... Quality Assurance Letter of Instructions
QALL........ Quartz Aircraft Landing Lamp
QALTR...... Quality Assurance Laboratory Test Request (MCD)
QALY's..... Quality Adjusted Life Years
QAM......... Quadrature Amplitude Modulation
QAM......... Quality Assurance Manager
QAM......... Quality Assurance Manual
QAM......... Quaque Aente Meridiem [*Every Morning*] [*Pharmacy*]
QAM......... Queued Access Method [*Data processing*]
QAMAA.... Quarterly of Applied Mathematics [*A publication*]
QAMDO ... Quadripartite Agreed Materiel Development Objective [*Military*]
QAMFNS ... Queen Alexandra's Military Family Nursing Service [*British military*] (DMA)
QAMIS...... Quality Assurance Management and Information System [*Environmental Protection Agency*] (GFGA)
QAML....... Centre de Documentation, Musee Laurier, Arthabaska, Quebec [*Library symbol*] [*National Library of Canada*] (NLC)
QAMM...... Quality Assurance Management Meeting [*DoD*]
QAMR....... Quadripartite Agreed Materiel Requirement [*Military*]
QAMR....... Quality Assurance Management Review [*DoD*]
QA Mrh K ... Quellen und Abhandlungen zur Mittelrheinischen Kirchengeschichte [*A publication*]

QAMS....... Quality Assurance Management Staff [*Environmental Protection Agency*] (GFGA)
QAN .... Queensland Air Navigation Co. Ltd. [*Australia*] (ADA)
QANT....... Quantech Electronics Corp. [*NASDAQ symbol*] (NQ)
Qantas....... Quantas Empire Airways [*A publication*] (APTA)
QANTAS... Queensland & Northern Territory Aerial Service [*Later, QANTAS Airways Ltd.*] [*Australia*]
Qantas E Air ... Qantas Empire Airways [*A publication*] (APTA)
QAO .... Quality Assurance Office [*Navy*]
QAO .... Quality Assurance Officer [*Environmental Protection Agency*] (GFGA)
QAO .... Quality Assurance Operation
QA & O...... Quality Assurance and Operations [*Nuclear Regulatory Commission*] (GFGA)
QAO .... Quality Assurance Outline
QAO .... Queen's Awards Office [*British*]
QAOGR.... Queen Alexandra's Own Gurkha Rifles [*British military*] (DMA)
QAOP....... Quality Assurance Operating Plan
QAP.......... Department of Antiquities in Palestine. Quarterly [*A publication*]
QAP.......... Quadratic Assignment Problem [*Mathematics*]
QAP.......... Qualifications Appraisal Panel (OICC)
QAP.......... Quality Assurance Plan
QAP.......... Quality Assurance Procedure
QAP.......... Quality Assurance Program [*Nuclear energy*]
QAP.......... Quality Assurance Provision
QAP.......... Quanah, Acme & Pacific Railway Co. [*AAR code*]
QAP.......... Quinine, Atabrine, Plasmoquine [*Treatment for malaria*]
QAPED ..... Quadripartite Agreed Plans of Engineering Design [*Military*]
QAPET..... Quadripartite Agreed Plans of Engineering Tests [*Military*]
QAPI........ Quality Assurance Program Index [*Nuclear energy*] (NRCH)
QAPL........ Queensland Airlines Party Ltd.
Q Ap Math ... Quarterly of Applied Mathematics [*A publication*]
1QApoc..... [*The*] Genesis Apocryphon from Qumran. Cave One (BJA)
QAPP........ Quality Assurance Program Plan [*Nuclear energy*] (NRCH)
Q Appl Math ... Quarterly of Applied Mathematics [*A publication*]
Q App Math ... Quarterly of Applied Mathematics [*A publication*]
QAPST...... Quadripartite Agreed Plans of Service Tests [*Military*]
QAR.......... Quaderni di Archeologia Reggiana [*A publication*]
QAR.......... Quality Assurance Record
QA & R...... Quality Assurance and Reliability
QAR.......... Quality Assurance Representative
QAR.......... Quality Assurance Requirements (NRCH)
QAR.......... Quality Assurance Responsible/Witness (MCD)
QAR.......... Quantitative Autoradiography [*Medicine*]
QAR.......... Quasi-Adiabatic Representation
QAR.......... Questionable Activity Report [*Employment and Training Administration*] [*Department of Labor*]
QAR.......... Quick Access Recording
QARANC.. Queen Alexandra's Royal Army Nursing Corps [*British*]
QARC....... Quality Assurance Record Center (MCD)
QARC....... Quality Assurance Review Center [*National Cancer Institute*]
QARI .... Quality Assurance Receipt Inspection [*Military*] (DNAB)
QARM....... Bibliotheque Municipale, Arthabaska, Quebec [*Library symbol*] [*National Library of Canada*] (NLC)
QARNNS .. Queen Alexandra's Royal Navy Nursing Service [*British*]
QARNNSR ... Queen Alexandra's Royal Naval Nursing Service Reserve [*British military*] (DMA)
QAR-R...... Quality Assurance Record - Receiving (MCD)
QAR-T...... Quality Assurance Record - Tooling (MCD)
QAS .... Quality Assurance Service [*Medicine*]
QAS .... Quality Assurance Specialist [*DoD*]
QAS .... Question-Answering System
QAS .... Quick Action Shuttle
QASAC...... Quality Assurance Spacecraft Acceptance Center (MCD)
QASAG ..... Experimental Farm, Agriculture Canada [*Ferme Experimentale, Agriculture Canada*] L'Assomption, Quebec [*Library symbol*] [*National Library of Canada*] (NLC)
QASAR..... Quality Assurance Systems Analysis Review (FAAC)
QASAS...... Quality Assurance Specialist, Ammunition Surveillance (MCD)
QASB........ Bibliotheque Municipale, Asbestos, Quebec [*Library symbol*] [*National Library of Canada*] (NLC)
QASC .... Quadripartite Armaments Standardization Committee [*Military*] (AABC)
QASDM .... Quality Assurance, Sample, and Data Management
QASK .... Quadrature Amplitude Shift Keying
QASL........ Quality Assurance Systems List (IEEE)
QASP....... Quality Assurance Standard Practice (MCD)
QASPR...... QUALCOMM, Inc. Automatic Satellite Position Reporting
Q Assoc Lig Arch Stor Nav ... Quaderni. Associazione Ligure di Archeologia e Storia Navale [*A publication*]
QAST........ Quality Assurance Service [*or Serviceability*] Test [*Nuclear energy*] (NG)
Qat .... Qatabanian (BJA)
QAT.......... Qatar [*ANSI three-letter standard code*] (CNC)
QAT.......... Quaker Oats Co. [*Toronto Stock Exchange symbol*]
QAT.......... Qualification Approval Test (NATG)
QAT.......... Quality Assurance Team (MCD)
Qatar Univ Sci Bull ... Qatar University. Science Bulletin [*A publication*]
QATIP....... Quality Assurance Test and Inspection Procedures (MCD)

QATP .... Quality Assurance Technical Publications (AAG)
QATS........ Quarterly Advanced Training Schedule [*Navy*] (DNAB)
QATT .... Qualification for Acceptance Thermal Testing [*NASA*] (NASA)
QAU .... Quality Assurance Unit
QAVC .... Quiet Automatic Volume Control
QAVP .... Quality Assurance Verification Procedures [*Military*] (DNAB)
QAVT .... Qualification Acceptance Vibration Test [*NASA*] (NASA)
QAWT ...... Quick-Acting Water-Tight (DNAB)
QAY .... Bibliotheque Municipale, Aylmer, Quebec [*Library symbol*] [*National Library of Canada*] (NLC)
QB............ Bibliotheque Municipale, Brossard, Quebec [*Library symbol*] [*National Library of Canada*] (BIB)
QB............. Qualified Bidder (FAAC)
QB............. Qualified Buyer
QB............. Quarterback [*Football*]
QB............. Quebecair, Inc. [*Airlines*] [*ICAO designator*] (OAG)
QB............. Queen's Bays [*Later, QDG*] [*Military unit*] [*British*]
QB............. Queen's Bench [*Legal*] [*British*]
QB............. Queen's Bench Reports, by Adolphus and Ellis, New Series [*A publication*] (DLA)
QB............. Queen's Bishop [*Chess*]
QB............. Quick Break (MSA)
QB............. Quickbrew [*Brand of tea*] [*British*]
QB............. Quiet Birdmen [*An association*] (EA)
Qb............. Total Body Clearance (MAE)
QBA .... Quality Bakers of America Cooperative (EA)
QBA .... Quality Brands Associates of America [*Defunct*] (EA)
QBA .... Quantitative Budget Analysis (MCD)
QBA .... Quebecair, Inc. [*Airlines*]
QBAC .... Quality Bakers of America Cooperative (EA)
QBAN........ Qui Bixit Annos [*Who Lived ____ Years*] [*Latin*]
Q Bar News ... Queensland Bar News [*A publication*] (APTA)
QBB .... Queen's Bad Bargain [*Undesirable serviceman*] [*Slang*] [*British*] (DSUE)
QBC .... Bella Coola [*Canada*] [*Airport symbol*] (OAG)
QBCB .... Quarterly Bulletin of Chinese Bibliography [*A publication*]
QBCCL...... Centre de Documentation, CLSC de l'Aquilon, Baie-Comeau, Quebec [*Library symbol*] [*National Library of Canada*] (BIB)
QBCDP...... Quarterly Bibliography of Computers and Data Processing [*A publication*]
QBCH........ Centre de Documentation, Pavillon St.-Joseph, Centre Hospitalier Regional de Beauceville, Quebec [*Library symbol*] [*National Library of Canada*] (BIB)
QBD.......... Quasi Birth and Death [*Statistics*]
QBD.......... Queen's Bench Division [*Military unit*] [*British*]
QBD.......... Queen's Bench Division, Law Reports [*A publication*]
QB Div .... English Law Reports, Queen's Bench Division [*1865-75*] [*A publication*] (DLA)
QBE .... Beaconsfield Public Library, Quebec [*Library symbol*] [*National Library of Canada*] (NLC)
QBE .... Query by Example [*Data processing search method*]
QBEAU ..... Bibliotheque Municipale, Beauport, Quebec [*Library symbol*] [*National Library of Canada*] (BIB)
QBEC .... Bibliotheque Municipale, Becancour, Quebec [*Library symbol*] [*National Library of Canada*] (NLC)
QBEHBI.... H. Bergstrom International Ltd., Beaconsfield, Quebec [*Library symbol*] [*National Library of Canada*] (NLC)
QBF .... Query-by-Forms [*Data processing search method*]
QBFJOTF ... [*The*] Quick Brown Fox Jumped over the Fence [*Typing exercise*]
QBFJOTLD ... [*The*] Quick Brown Fox Jumped over the Lazy Dogs [*Typing exercise*]
QBI .... Quite Bloody Impossible [*British slang, applied particularly to flying conditions*]
QBib.......... Quarterly Bibliography of Computers and Data Processing [*A publication*]
Q Bibliogr Comput Data Process ... Quarterly Bibliography of Computers and Data Processing [*A publication*]
QBID .... Queensland Business and Industry Directory [*Australia*] [*A publication*]
QBIO .... Quest Biotechnology, Inc. [*Detroit, MI*] [*NASDAQ symbol*] (NQ)
QBIR .... Quarterly Printing Industry Business Indicator Report [*A publication*] (EAAP)
QBIX .... Qubix Graphic Systems, Inc. [*NASDAQ symbol*] (NQ)
QBJ........... Juniorat des Freres du Sacre-Coeur, Bramptonville, Quebec [*Library symbol*] [*National Library of Canada*] (NLC)
QBKI .... Beker Industries Corp. [*NYSE symbol*] (SPSG)
QBL .... Qualified Bidders List
QBLC........ Queen's Bench Reports, Lower Canada [*A publication*] (DLA)
QBMS .... Mitel Semiconductor, Bromont, Quebec [*Library symbol*] [*National Library of Canada*] (NLC)
QBO.......... Bibliotheque Municipale, Boucherville, Quebec [*Library symbol*] [*National Library of Canada*] (NLC)
QBO.......... Mail Advertising Service Association International. Quarterly Business Outlook [*A publication*]
QBO.......... Quarterly Business Outlook [*A publication*] (EAAP)
QBO.......... Quasi-Biennial Oscillation [*Earth science*]
Q-BOP....... Quick Basic Oxygen Process [*Steelmaking*]
Q Bottling Suppl ... Quarterly Bottling Supplement [*A publication*]

QBP .... Queen's Bishop's Pawn [*Chess*] (IIA)
QBPL........ Queens Borough Public Library [*New York, NY*]
QBR .... Quebecor, Inc. [*Toronto Stock Exchange symbol*]
QBR .... Queen's Bench Reports [*Legal*] [*British*]
QBR .... Queen's Bench Reports, by Adolphus and Ellis, New Series [*A publication*] (DLA)
QBRA .... ACS Biblio-information, Inc., Brossard, Quebec [*Library symbol*] [*National Library of Canada*] (BIB)
QBRG .... Centre Hospitalier Robert Giffard, Beauport, Quebec [*Library symbol*] [*National Library of Canada*] (NLC)
QBSA........ Centre Hospitalier St.-Augustin, Beauport, Quebec [*Library symbol*] [*National Library of Canada*] (BIB)
QBSM .... Que Besa Sus Manos [*Kissing Your Hands*] [*Spanish*]
QBSPH...... Centre Hospitalier de Charlevoix, Baie St.-Paul, Quebec [*Library symbol*] [*National Library of Canada*] (BIB)
QBU.......... Bibliotheque Municipale, Buckingham, Quebec [*Library symbol*] [*National Library of Canada*] (NLC)
QBUC .... Queen's Bench Reports, Upper Canada [*A publication*] (DLA)
Q Building Yrbk ... Queensland Building Yearbook [*A publication*] (APTA)
Q Bull Alp Gdn Soc ... Quarterly Bulletin. Alpine Garden Society [*A publication*]
Q Bull Am Rhodod Soc ... Quarterly Bulletin. American Rhododendron Society [*A publication*]
Q Bull Ass Fd Drug Off (US) ... Quarterly Bulletin. Association of Food and Drug Officials (United States) [*A publication*]
Q Bull Assoc Food Drug Off ... Quarterly Bulletin. Association of Food and Drug Officials [*A publication*]
Q Bull Assoc Food Drug Off US ... Quarterly Bulletin. Association of Food and Drug Officials of the United States [*Later, Quarterly Bulletin. Association of Food and Drug Officials*] [*A publication*]
Q Bull Fac Sci Tehran Univ ... Quarterly Bulletin. Faculty of Science. Tehran University [*A publication*]
Q Bull Fac Sci Univ Tehran ... Quarterly Bulletin. Faculty of Science. University of Tehran [*A publication*]
Q Bull Geo-Heat Util Cent ... Quarterly Bulletin. Geo-Heat Utilization Center [*United States*] [*A publication*]
Q Bull Health Organ League Nations ... Quarterly Bulletin. Health Organisation. League of Nations [*A publication*]
Q Bull IAALD ... Quarterly Bulletin. International Association of Agricultural Librarians and Documentalists [*A publication*]
Q Bull Indiana Univ Med Cent ... Quarterly Bulletin. Indiana University. Medical Center [*A publication*]
Q Bull Int Ass Agric Libr ... Quarterly Bulletin. International Association of Agricultural Librarians and Documentalists [*A publication*]
Q Bull Int Assoc Agric Libr & Doc ... Quarterly Bulletin. International Association of Agricultural Librarians and Documentalists [*A publication*]
Q Bull Mich St Univ Agric Exp Stn ... Quarterly Bulletin. Michigan State University. Agricultural Experiment Station [*A publication*]
Q Bull Mon Auth Sing ... Quarterly Bulletin. Monetary Authority of Singapore [*A publication*]
Q Bull Natl Res Counc Can Div Mech Eng ... Quarterly Bulletin. National Research Council of Canada. Division of Mechanical Engineering [*A publication*]
Q Bull Natn Counc Women Aust ... National Council of Women of Australia. Quarterly Bulletin [*A publication*]
Q Bull Northwest Univ Med Sch ... Quarterly Bulletin. Northwestern University. Medical School [*A publication*]
Q Bull NWest Univ Med Sch ... Quarterly Bulletin. Northwestern University. Medical School [*A publication*]
Q Bull S Afr Libr ... Quarterly Bulletin. South African Library [*A publication*]
Q Bull S Afr Natl Gall ... Quarterly Bulletin. South African National Gallery [*A publication*]
Q Bull Sea View Hosp ... Quarterly Bulletin. Sea View Hospital [*A publication*]
QC............. Air Zaire SA [*Zaire*] [*ICAO designator*] (ICDA)
QC............. Bibliotheque Municipale, Cowansville, Quebec [*Library symbol*] [*National Library of Canada*] (BIB)
QC............. QC Explorations [*Vancouver Stock Exchange symbol*]
QC............. Quad Center [*Typography*]
QC............. Quaderni della Critica [*A publication*]
QC............. Qualification Course
QC............. Quality Certificate
QC............. Quality Circle [*Labor-management team organized to increase industrial productivity*]
QC............. Quality Control [*or Controller*]
QC............. Quantek Corp. [*Trademark*]
QC............. Quantitative Command
QC............. Quantum Counter
QC............. Quarter of Coverage [*Social Security Administration*] (OICC)
QC............. Quarterly Credit
QC............. Quartermaster Corps [*Army*] (WGA)
QC............. Quarters of Coverage [*Social Security Administration*] (GFGA)
QC............. Quartz Crystal
QC............. Quasi-Contract [*Business term*]
QC............. Quaternary Carrier [*Biochemistry*]
QC............. Quebec Central Railway Co. [*AAR code*]
QC............. Queen Consort [*British*] (ROG)
QC............. Queen's College [*Oxford and Cambridge Universities*] (ROG)

QC.............. Queen's Counsel [*British*]
QC.............. Quench Correction
QC.............. Quick Charge [*Airplane*]   (IIA)
QC.............. Quick Cleaning   (MSA)
QC.............. Quick Connect
QC.............. Quick Curl [*Refers to Barbie doll hair*] [*Doll collecting*]
QC.............. Quickchange [*Aviation*]
QC.............. Quiesce-Completed [*Data processing*]   (IBMDP)
QC.............. Quiescent Center [*Plant root growth*]
QC.............. Quinine-Colchicine [*Medicine*]   (MAE)
QC.............. Quixote Center   (EA)
QC.............. Societe Air-Zaire [*ICAO designator*]   (FAAC)
QCA.......... Bibliotheque Municipale, Candiac, Quebec [*Library symbol*] [*National Library of Canada*]   (BIB)
QCA.......... Quality Control Analysis
QCA.......... Quarterly Compilation of Abstracts [*A publication*]
QCA.......... Queen Charlotte Airlines Ltd.
QCA.......... Quiet Communities Act   (GFGA)
QCAG....... Ministere de l'Agriculture, des Pecheries et de l'Alimentation, Chateauguay, Quebec [*Library symbol*] [*National Library of Canada*]   (NLC)
QCAI........ Quality Conformance Acceptance Inspection   (MCD)
QCAL....... Centre de Documentation, Centre Hospitalier Anna-Laberge, Chateauguay, Quebec [*Library symbol*] [*National Library of Canada*]   (BIB)
Q Can Studies ... Quarterly of Canadian Studies [*A publication*]
QCAR....... Queensland Criminal Reports [*A publication*]
Q Case Note ... Queensland Law Reporter Case Note [*A publication*]   (APTA)
QCB.......... Bibliotheque Municipale, Coaticook, Quebec [*Library symbol*] [*National Library of Canada*]   (NLC)
QCB.......... Quality Control Board   (MCD)
QCB.......... Queue Control Block [*Data processing*]
QCBC....... Quick Change Boost Control [*Automotive engineering*]
QCBK....... [*The*] Quincy Co-Operative Bank [*Quincy, MA*] [*NASDAQ symbol*]   (NQ)
QCC.......... Bibliotheque Gaspesienne, Cap-Chat, Quebec [*Library symbol*] [*National Library of Canada*]   (NLC)
QCC.......... Quaderni di Cultura Contemporanea [*A publication*]
QCC.......... Qualification Correlation Certification
QCC.......... Quality Communications Circle   (MCD)
QCC.......... Quality Control Committee   (MCD)
QCC.......... Queen Charlotte [*British Columbia*] [*Seismograph station code, US Geological Survey*]   (SEIS)
QCC.......... Quenched Carbonaceous Composite [*Plasma technology*]
QCC.......... Quick Connect Coupling
QCC.......... Quinsigamond Community College [*Worchester, MA*]
QCCA....... Quality Control Council of America   (EA)
QCCARS... Quality Control Collection Analysis and Reporting System
QCCB....... Queen's College Cadet Battalion [*Taunton*] [*British military*]   (DMA)
QCCL....... CLSC Albert Samson, Coaticook, Quebec [*Library symbol*] [*National Library of Canada*]   (NLC)
QCCR....... Quality Control Change Request   (SAA)
QCCRS...... Conseil Regional de la Sante et des Services Sociaux, Chicoutimi, Quebec [*Library symbol*] [*National Library of Canada*]   (NLC)
QCCS........ Cree School Board, Chisasibi, James Bay, Quebec [*Library symbol*] [*National Library of Canada*]   (BIB)
QCD.......... Quality Control Data
QCD.......... Quality Control Directive   (MCD)
QCD.......... Quantum Chromodynamics [*Nuclear physics*]
QCD.......... Quick Control Dial [*Photography*]
QCDPA..... Quality Chekd Dairy Products Association   (EA)
QCDR....... Quality Control Deficiency Report   (AFM)
QCDSU..... Quality Control Directive Supplement   (SAA)
QCE.......... Quality Control Engineers
QCE.......... Quality Control and Evaluation   (MCD)
QCEA....... Quaker Council for European Affairs   (EA)
Q Census & Statistics Bul ... Australia. Commonwealth Bureau of Census and Statistics. Queensland Office. Bulletin [*A publication*]   (APTA)
QCF.......... Quality Control [*Tabulating*] Form   (AAG)
QCF.......... Quarterly Control Contract Factor   (MCD)
QCF.......... Quartz Crystal Filter
QCF.......... Quench Compensation Factor
QCFO....... Quartz Crystal Frequency Oscillator
QCG.......... Quartz Creek Gold Mines (BC), Inc. [*Vancouver Stock Exchange symbol*]
QCGAT..... Quiet, Clean, General Aviation Turbofan [*NASA*]
QCH.......... Hopital de Chicoutimi, Inc., Quebec [*Library symbol*] [*National Library of Canada*]   (NLC)
QCH.......... Quick Connect Handle
Q Chicago Med Sch ... Quarterly. Chicago Medical School [*A publication*]
QCHJC...... Health Sciences Information Centre, Jewish Rehabilitation Hospital [*Centre d'Information sur les Sciences de la Sante, Hopital Juif de Readaptation*] Chomedey, Quebec [*Library symbol*] [*National Library of Canada*]   (NLC)
QCHM...... Quaker Chemical Corp. [*NASDAQ symbol*]   (NQ)
QCHR....... Quality Control History Record
QCI........... Quality Conformance Inspection   (MSA)

QCI........... Quality Control Index [*Environmental Protection Agency*]   (GFGA)
QCI........... Quality Control Information   (AABC)
QCI........... Quality Control Inspection
QCI........... Quarto Castello [*Italy*] [*Seismograph station code, US Geological Survey*] [*Closed*]   (SEIS)
QCI........... Queen's College, Ireland   (ROG)
QCI........... Quota Club International [*Later, QI*]
QCI's........ Queen Charlotte Islands
QCID........ Quality Control and Inspection Department [*Navy*]   (DNAB)
QCIE........ Quality Control Inspection Element   (AFIT)
QCIM....... Quarterly Cumulative Index Medicus [*A publication*]
QCIP......... Quality Control Inspection Procedure [*Nuclear energy*]   (NRCH)
QCIR........ Queen's University at Kingston Centre for International Relations [*Canada*] [*Research center*]   (RCD)
Q Circ Rubber Res Inst Ceylon ... Quarterly Circular. Rubber Research Institute of Ceylon [*A publication*]
QCJ........... Quality Circles Journal [*A publication*]
QCJJ......... Quaker Committee on Jails and Justice [*Canada*]
QCK.......... Quick Connect Kit
Qckslv....... Quicksilver Times [*A publication*]
QCL.......... Logilab, Inc., Charlebois, Quebec [*Library symbol*] [*National Library of Canada*]   (NLC)
QCL.......... Quality Characteristics List   (MSA)
QCL.......... Quality Checklist
QCL.......... Quality Control Level
QCL.......... Queensland Conveyancing Library [*A publication*]   (APTA)
QCLBS....... Quarterly Check-List of Biblical Studies [*A publication*]
QCLC........ CLC of America, Inc. [*Formerly, Consolidated Leasing Corp. of America*] [*NYSE symbol*]   (SPSG)
QCLCS...... Quarterly Checklist of Classical Studies [*A publication*]
QCLLR..... Queensland Crown Lands Law Reports [*A publication*]   (APTA)
QCLM...... Quarterly Checklist of Medievalia [*A publication*]
QCLPC..... National Historic Park, Parks Canada [*Parc Historique National, Parcs Canada*] Coteau-du-Lac, Quebec [*Library symbol*] [*National Library of Canada*]   (NLC)
QCLRS..... Quarterly Check-List of Renaissance Studies [*A publication*]
QCM........ Bibliotheque Municipale, Chateauguay, Quebec [*Library symbol*] [*National Library of Canada*]   (BIB)
QCM........ Quality Control Manager
QCM........ Quality Control Manual
QCM........ Quality Courts Motels [*Later, QM*]
QCM........ Quantitative Computer Management   (IEEE)
QCM........ Quantum Conformal Fluctuation [*Theoretical physics*]
QCM........ Quartz Crystal Microbalance
QCM........ Quartz Crystal Monitor
QCMB...... Centre de Documentation, Musee Beaulne, Coaticook, Quebec [*Library symbol*] [*National Library of Canada*]   (NLC)
QCMM...... Bibliotheque Municipale, Cap-De-La-Madeleine, Quebec [*Library symbol*] [*National Library of Canada*]   (NLC)
QCMPE..... Quantum Chemistry Microcomputer Program Exchange
QCO.......... Quality Control Officer   (AAG)
QCO.......... Quality Control Organization
QCO.......... Quantity at Captain's Option [*Shipping*]   (DS)
QCO.......... Quartz Crystal Oscillator
QCOA........ QCOA: Journal of the Queensland Council on the Ageing [*A publication*]   (APTA)
Q Coal Rpt ... Quarterly Coal Report [*A publication*]
Q Colorado Sch Mines ... Quarterly. Colorado School of Mines [*A publication*]
Q Colo Sch Mines ... Quarterly. Colorado School of Mines [*A publication*]
QCOM...... Qualcomm, Inc. [*NASDAQ symbol*]   (SPSG)
Q Conv R ... Queensland Conveyancing Cases [*Australia*] [*A publication*]
Q Coop ...... Queensland Co-Operator [*A publication*]   (APTA)
QCOP....... Quality Control Operating Procedure
Q Countrywoman ... Queensland Countrywoman [*A publication*]   (APTA)
QCP.......... Quality Check Program [*DoD*]
QCP.......... Quality Continuation Plan [*BMW manufacturer's warranty*]
QCP.......... Quality Control Procedure
QCP.......... Quezon City [*Philippines*] [*Seismograph station code, US Geological Survey*]   (SEIS)
QCP.......... Quiet Community Program [*Environmental Protection Agency*]   (GFGA)
QCPC....... Quality Control Property Clearance   (SAA)
QCPE........ Quantum Chemistry Program Exchange
QCPI......... Queen's College of Physicians, Ireland   (ROG)
QCPM...... Quality Control Procedures Manual   (SAA)
QCPMS..... Quality Control and Performance Monitoring System   (MCD)
QCPSA..... Quaker Center for Prisoner Support Activities   (EA)
QCPSK..... Quaternary Coherent Phase-Shift Keying
QCQ.......... Quebec [*Quebec*] [*Seismograph station code, US Geological Survey*]   (SEIS)
QCR.......... Qualitative Construction Requirement [*Army*]
QCR.......... Quality Control/Reliability
QCR.......... Quality Control Report
QCR.......... Quality Control Reports: the Gold Sheet [*A publication*]
QCR.......... Quality Control Representative [*Military*]   (AABC)
QCR.......... Quality Control Review
QCR.......... Quality Control Room

QCR........... Queensland Criminal Reports [*A publication*]   (APTA)
QCR........... Quick Change Response [*System*]
QCR........... Quick Connect Relay
QCRCN ..... Campus Notre-Dame-De-Foy, Cap-Rouge, Quebec [*Library symbol*] [*National Library of Canada*]   (NLC)
QCRI .... Quality Control Reliability Investigator   (SAA)
QCRM .... Bibliotheque Municipale, Cap-Rouge, Quebec [*Library symbol*] [*National Library of Canada*]   (BIB)
QCRS........ Seminaire St-Augustin, Cap-Rouge, Quebec [*Library symbol*] [*National Library of Canada*]   (NLC)
QCS .... Quad-Cities Station [*Nuclear energy*]   (NRCH)
QCS .... Quality Control Standard   (AAG)
QCS .... Quality Control Survey   (SAA)
QCS .... Quality Control System
QCS .... Quality Cost System
QCS .... Query Control Station   (MCD)
QCS .... Service de la Bibliotheque de Ville de Laval, Chomedey, Quebec [*Library symbol*] [*National Library of Canada*]   (BIB)
QCSC........ Quadripartite Chemical, Biological, Radiological Standardization Committee [*Military*]   (AABC)
QCSEE...... Quiet, Clean, Short-Haul Experimental Engine [*NASA*]
QCSEL...... Quality Control Select Vendor   (MCD)
QCSH........ Societe Historique du Saguenay, Chicoutimi, Quebec [*Library symbol*] [*National Library of Canada*]   (NLC)
QCSM ...... Quiescent Command/Service Module   (MCD)
QCSMA..... Quarterly. Colorado School of Mines [*A publication*]
QCSR........ Quality Control Service Request   (SAA)
QCSS........ Quaderni di Cultura e Storia Sociale [*A publication*]
QCSSP ...... Quality Control Single Source Procurement   (MCD)
QCSTL...... Cote St. Luc Public Library, Quebec [*Library symbol*] [*National Library of Canada*]   (NLC)
QC & T ...... Quality Control and Techniques   (SAA)
QCT........... Quantitative Computerized Tomography [*Biomedical engineering*]
QCT........... Quasiclassical Trajectory [*Chemical physics*]
QCT........... Questionable Corrective Task
QCTE .... Quality Control Test Engineering   (SAA)
QCTR .... Quality Control Test Report
QCTT .... Quality Control Test Team [*Military*]
QCU.......... Quality Courts United [*Later, QM*]   (EA)
QCU.......... Quartz Crystal Unit
QCU.......... Quick Change Unit   (MCD)
QCU.......... Universite du Quebec, Chicoutimi, Quebec [*Library symbol*] [*National Library of Canada*]   (NLC)
QCUG........ Departement de Geographie, Universite du Quebec, Chicoutimi, Quebec [*Library symbol*] [*National Library of Canada*]   (NLC)
QCUGC..... Cartotheque, Universite du Quebec, Chicoutimi, Quebec [*Library symbol*] [*National Library of Canada*]   (NLC)
Q Cum Index Med ... Quarterly Cumulative Index Medicus [*A publication*]
QCUS .... Quartz Crystal Unit Set
QCVC .... Quick Connect Valve Coupler
QCVTI...... Quality Control Verification Test Inspection   (SAA)
QCW.......... Quadrant Continuous Wave
QCW.......... Quality Criteria for Water   (EG)
QCWA....... Quarter Century Wireless Association   (EA)
QD .... Bibliotheque Municipale, Dorval, Quebec [*Library symbol*] [*National Library of Canada*]   (BIB)
QD .... QData Systems, Inc. [*Vancouver Stock Exchange symbol*]
QD .... Quaderni Dannunziani [*A publication*]
QD .... Quaestiones Disputatae   (BJA)
QD .... Quantity Distance [*Explosives*]
QD .... Quantum Design, Inc.
QD .... Quaque Die [*Every Day*] [*Pharmacy*]
QD .... Quarter Distribution [*Parapsychology*]
QD .... Quarterdeck
QD .... Quartile Deviation [*Statistics*]
QD .... Quasi Dicat [*As If One Should Say, or As Though One Should Say*] [*Latin*]
QD .... Quasi Dictum [*As If Said, or As Though It Had Been Said*] [*Latin*]
QD .... Quasi Dixisset [*As If One Had Said*] [*Latin*]
QD .... Quater in Die [*Four Times a Day*] [*Pharmacy*]
QD .... Questioned Document [*Criminology*]
Q & D........ Quick and Dirty [*Data processing*]
QD .... Quick Disconnect
QD .... Quicksilver Data [*Information service or system*]   (IID)
QD .... Transbrasil SA Linhas Aereas [*Brazil*] [*ICAO designator*]   (ICDA)
6QD .... Damascus Document [*or Sefer Berit Damesek*] from Qumran. Cave Six   (BJA)
QDA.......... Qualifying Dividend Account
QDA.......... Quantitative Descriptive Analysis
QDA.......... Quantity Discount Agreement
QDA.......... Quarterly. Department of Antiquities in Palestine [*Jerusalem*] [*A publication*]
Qd Ag J...... Queensland Agricultural Journal [*A publication*]   (APTA)
Qd Agric J ... Queensland Agricultural Journal [*A publication*]   (APTA)
QDAP........ Quarterly. Department of Antiquities in Palestine [*Jerusalem*] [*A publication*]

QDA Pal .... Quarterly. Department of Antiquities in Palestine [*A publication*]
Qd Bur Invest Tech Bull ... Queensland. Department of Public Lands. Bureau of Investigation. Technical Bulletin [*A publication*]   (APTA)
Qd Bur Sug Exp Stat Tech Commun ... Queensland. Bureau of Sugar Experiment Stations. Technical Communication [*A publication*]   (APTA)
Qd Bur Sug Exp Stn Tech Commun ... Queensland. Bureau of Sugar Experiment Stations. Technical Communication [*A publication*]   (APTA)
QDC.......... Quick Dependable Communications
QDC.......... Quick Die Change [*Automotive engineering*]
QDC.......... Quick Disconnect Cap
QDC.......... Quick Disconnect Connector
QDCC....... Quick Disconnect Circular Connector
QDCE .... College Bourgchemin (CEGEP), Drummondville, Quebec [*Library symbol*] [*National Library of Canada*]   (NLC)
QDC & E ... Quartz Devices Conference and Exhibition
Qd Chamber Manufacturers Yb ... Queensland Chamber of Manufacturers. Yearbook [*A publication*]   (APTA)
QDD .... Qualified for Deep Diving Duties [*Navy*] [*British*]
QDD .... Quantized Decision Detection
Qd Dent J .. Queensland Dental Journal [*A publication*]   (APTA)
Qd Dent Mag ... Queensland Dental Magazine [*A publication*]   (APTA)
QDE.......... Etablissement Donnacona, Quebec [*Library symbol*] [*National Library of Canada*]   (BIB)
QDE.......... Qualified Designated Entities [*Independent counseling groups and churches involved with aiding aliens*] [*Immigration and Naturalization Service term*]
QDE.......... Quality Data Evaluation   (MCD)
QDEAS....... Quality Deficiency Evaluation and Action System   (MCD)
QDEK........ Quarterdeck Office Systems [*NASDAQ symbol*]   (SPSG)
QDEL .... Quidel Corp. [*NASDAQ symbol*]   (SPSG)
Q Dent Rev ... Quarterly Dental Review [*A publication*]
4QDeut32 .. Manuscript of Deuteronomy 32 from Qumran. Cave 4   (BJA)
QDF.......... Quantum Distribution Function
Qd For Dep Adv Leafl ... Queensland. Department of Forestry. Advisory Leaflet [*A publication*]   (APTA)
Qd For Dep Pamph ... Queensland. Department of Forestry. Pamphlet [*A publication*]   (APTA)
Qd Forest Bull ... Queensland Forest Bulletin [*A publication*]   (APTA)
QDG .... Queen's Dragoon Guards [*Formerly, KDG, QB*] [*Military unit*] [*British*]
Qd Geogr J ... Queensland Geographical Journal [*A publication*]   (APTA)
Qd Geol Surv 1:250 000 Geol Ser ... Queensland. Geological Survey. 1:250,000 Geological Series [*A publication*]   (APTA)
Qd Geol Surv Rep ... Queensland. Geological Survey. Report [*A publication*]   (APTA)
Qd Govt Mining J ... Queensland Government Mining Journal [*A publication*]
Qd Govt Min J ... Queensland Government Mining Journal [*A publication*]
Qd Graingrower ... Queensland Graingrower [*A publication*]
QDH .... Quick Disconnect Handle
Qd Heritage ... Queensland Heritage [*A publication*]   (APTA)
QDHSC..... Hopital Sainte-Croix, Drummondville, Quebec [*Library symbol*] [*National Library of Canada*]   (NLC)
Q Digger .... Queensland Digger [*A publication*]   (APTA)
Qd Ind........ Queensland Industry [*A publication*]
QDISC....... Quick Disconnect
Qd J Agric Anim Sci ... Queensland Journal of Agricultural and Animal Sciences [*A publication*]
Qd J Agric Sci ... Queensland Journal of Agricultural Science [*Later, Queensland Journal of Agricultural and Animal Sciences*] [*A publication*]   (APTA)
QDK.......... Quick Disconnect Kit
QDL........... Quick Disconnect, Large
Qd Law Soc J ... Queensland Law Society. Journal [*A publication*]
QDLC .... Quadlogic Controls Corp. [*NASDAQ symbol*]
QDM .... Centre d'Information Documentaire Come-Saint-Germain, Drummondville, Quebec [*Library symbol*] [*National Library of Canada*]   (NLC)
QDM .... Magnetic Heading (Zero Wind) [*to steer to reach me*] [*Aviation code*]   (FAAC)
QDM .... Quad Driver Module [*Electronics*]
QDM .... Quick Disconnect, Miniature
1QDM .... [*The*] Words of Moses from Qumran. Cave One   (BJA)
QDMBPT ... Quasi-Degenerate Many-Body Perturbation Theory [*Physics*]
QDMC....... Quadratic Matrix Control [*Chemical engineering*] [*Data processing*]
QDN .... Quick Disconnect Nipple
Qd Nat .... Queensland Naturalist [*A publication*]   (APTA)
QDO .... Quadripartite Development Objective [*Military*]   (AABC)
QDO .... Quantitative Design Objective
QDO .... Quick Delivery Order
QDOPH .... Office des Personnes Handicapees du Quebec, Drummondville, Quebec [*Library symbol*] [*National Library of Canada*]   (NLC)
QDOS........ Quick and Dirty Operating System [*Microsoft Corp.*]   (ECON)
QDP.......... Quick Disconnect Pivot
Qd Police J ... Queensland Police Journal [*A publication*]

Qd Prod......	Queensland Producer [*A publication*] (APTA)
QDPSK......	Quaternary Differential Phase-Shift Keying (TEL)
QDR..........	Dubai Riyal [*Monetary unit*]
QDR..........	Magnetic Bearing [*from me*] [*Aviation code*] (FAAC)
QDR..........	Qualification Design Review [*NASA*] (MCD)
QDR..........	Quality Data and Reporting (MCD)
QDR..........	Quality Deficiency Record [*DoD*]
QDR..........	Quality Deficiency Report [*DoD*]
Qd R..........	Queensland Reports [*A publication*] (APTA)
QDRI........	Qualitative Development Requirement Information
QDRL........	Questionnaire Design Research Laboratory [*Department of Health and Human Services*] (GFGA)
QDRNT.....	Quadrant (MSA)
QDRT........	Qadrant Corp. [*NASDAQ symbol*] (NQ)
QDRT........	Quadrant
QDRTR......	Quadrature
QDRX........	Quadrax Corp. [*NASDAQ symbol*] (NQ)
QDS..........	Quality Data System (NASA)
QDS..........	Quarantine Document System [*Information retrieval*] [*NASA*]
QDS..........	Quick Disconnect Series
QDS..........	Quick Disconnect, Small
QDS..........	Quick Disconnect Swivel
QDSB........	Quadrature Double Sideband (MCD)
Qd Surv......	Queensland Surveyor [*A publication*] (APTA)
QDT..........	Qualified Domestic Trust
QDT..........	Quintessence of Dental Technology
QDTA........	Quantitative Differential Thermal Analysis
QDTAA.....	Queensland Dive Tourism Association of Australia
Qd Teach J ...	Queensland Teachers' Journal [*A publication*]
QDU..........	Dusseldorf-Main RR [*Germany*] [*Airport symbol*] (OAG)
Qd Univ Agric Dep Pap ...	University of Queensland. Agriculture Department. Papers [*A publication*] (APTA)
Qd Univ Bot Dep Pap ...	University of Queensland. Botany Department. Papers [*A publication*] (APTA)
Qd Univ Civ Engng Dep Bull ...	University of Queensland. Department of Civil Engineering. Bulletin [*A publication*] (APTA)
Qd Univ Comput Centre Pap ...	University of Queensland. Computer Centre. Papers [*A publication*] (APTA)
Qd Univ Ent Dep Pap ...	University of Queensland. Entomology Department. Papers [*A publication*] (APTA)
Qd Univ Fac Vet Sci Pap ...	University of Queensland. Faculty of Veterinary Science. Papers [*A publication*] (APTA)
Qd Univ Geol Dep Pap ...	University of Queensland. Geology Department. Papers [*A publication*] (APTA)
Qd Univ Pap Zool Dep ...	University of Queensland. Zoology Department. Papers [*A publication*] (APTA)
Qd Univ Zool Dep Pap ...	University of Queensland. Zoology Department. Papers [*A publication*] (APTA)
QDV..........	Quick Disconnect Valve
Qd Vet Proc ...	Queensland Veterinary Proceedings [*A publication*] (APTA)
QDX..........	Quick Decision Exercise [*Training simulation*] [*Army*]
QDXR........	Quadriplexer
QE..............	Air Tahiti [*ICAO designator*] (FAAC)
QE..............	Bibliotheque Municipale, St.-Eustache, Quebec [*Library symbol*] [*National Library of Canada*] (BIB)
QE..............	Journal of Quantum Electronics [*A publication*] (MCD)
QE..............	Quadrant Elevation
QE..............	Quadruple Expansion (DS)
QE..............	Quaestiones et Salutationes in Exodum [*Philo*] (BJA)
QE..............	Quality Engineer [*or Engineering*]
QE..............	Quality Evaluation (NG)
QE..............	Quality Excellence [*Chrysler Corp.*]
QE..............	Quantum Efficiency
QE..............	Quantum Electronics [*A publication*]
QE..............	Queue Entry
QE..............	Quod Est [*Which Is*] [*Latin*]
QE..............	Quotation Estimate (MCD)
QE..............	Quoted Exhibit (SAA)
QE 2..........	Queen Elizabeth 2 [*Luxury liner*]
QEA..........	QANTAS Empire Airways Ltd. [*Later, QANTAS Airways Ltd.*]
QeA..........	Questo e Alto [*A publication*]
QEAD..........	Quality Engineering and Assurance Division [*Navy*] (DNAB)
QEAE........	Quarternary Ethylaminoethyl [*Organic chemistry*]
QEAM......	Quick Erecting Antenna Mast [*Army*] (RDA)
QEAS........	Quantum Electronics and Applications Society (MCD)
QEAV........	Quick Exhaust Air Valve
QEB..........	Quality Engineering Bulletin [*NASA*]
QEBG........	Quellen und Eroerterungen zur Bayerischen Geschichte [*A publication*]
QEC..........	Quantum Electronics Council
QEC..........	Quantum Energy [*Vancouver Stock Exchange symbol*]
QEC..........	Queen Elizabeth College [*British*]
QEC..........	Quick Engine Change
QEC..........	Quiesce-at-End-of-Chain [*Data processing*] (IBMDP)
QECA......	Quick Engine Change Assembly (NG)
QECCH.....	Compton County Historical and Museum Society [*Societe d'Histoire et du Musee du Comte de Compton*] Eaton Corner, Quebec [*Library symbol*] [*National Library of Canada*] (NLC)
QECK........	Quick Engine Change Kit (NG)
Q Econ Comment ...	Quarterly Economic Commentary [*A publication*]
Q Economic Rev of UK ...	Quarterly Economic Review of the United Kingdom [*A publication*]
Q Econ R....	Quarterly Economic Review [*Seoul*] [*A publication*]
Q Econ Rev Chile ...	Quarterly Economic Review of Chile [*A publication*]
Q Econ Rev Iran ...	Quarterly Economic Review of Iran [*A publication*]
Q Econ Rev Oil West Eur ...	Quarterly Economic Review. Oil in Western Europe [*A publication*]
QECS........	Quick Engine Change Stand (NG)
QECU........	Quick Engine Change Unit
QED..........	Quality Education Data [*Information service or system*] (IID)
QED..........	Quantitative Evaluative Device (AEBS)
QED..........	Quantum Electrodynamics [*Theory*]
QED..........	Quentin E. Deverill [*Protagonist in TV series; initialism also used as title of the series*]
QED..........	Quick Erection Dome
QED..........	Quick Text Editor
QED..........	Quod Erat Demonstrandum [*Which Was the Thing to Be Proved*] [*Latin*]
QEDL........	Quality Engineering Diagnostic Laboratory (MCD)
Q Ed Off Gaz ...	Education Office Gazette. Queensland Department of Education [*A publication*] (APTA)
QEDX........	QED Exploration, Inc. [*NASDAQ symbol*] (NQ)
QEEL........	Quality Evaluation and Engineering Laboratory [*Navy*]
QEEL/CO ...	Quality Evaluation and Engineering Laboratory, Concord [*California*] [*Navy*]
QEF..........	Quod Erat Faciendum [*Which Was to Be Made, or Done*] [*Latin*]
QEH..........	Queen Elizabeth Hall [*London, England*]
QEH..........	Queen Elizabeth's Hospital School [*England*]
QEI..........	Quod Erat Inveniendum [*Which Was to Be Found Out*] [*Latin*]
QEIC........	Quicksilver Enterprises, Inc. [*NASDAQ symbol*] (NQ)
QE/K........	Quality Evaluation and Engineering Laboratory, Keyport [*Washington*] [*Naval Torpedo Station*]
QEKG........	Q-Med, Inc. [*Clark, NJ*] [*NASDAQ symbol*] (NQ)
QEL..........	Quality Evaluation Laboratory
QEL..........	Queue Element [*Data processing*]
QEL..........	Quiet Extended Life
Q Elec Contractor ...	Queensland Electrical Contractor [*A publication*] (APTA)
QElecSC....	Quadripartite Electronic Standardization Committee [*Military*] (AABC)
QELS........	Quantitative Evaluation of Library Searching [*Spectra matching technique*]
QELS........	Quasi-Elastic Light Scattering [*Also, QLS, QUELS*] [*Physics*]
QEM..........	Quadrant Electrometer
QEM..........	Qualified Export Manager [*Designation awarded by American Society of International Executives*]
QEM..........	Quality Education for Minorities Project (EA)
QEMM......	Quarterdeck Expanded Memory Manager [*Data processing*]
QEN..........	Quare Executionem Non [*Wherefore Execution Should Not Be Issued*] [*Latin*] [*Legal term*] (DLA)
Q Engl J Tech Assoc Refract Jpn ...	Quarterly English Journal. Technical Association of Refractories. Japan [*A publication*]
QEngrSC ...	Quadripartite Engineer Standardization Committee [*Military*] (AABC)
QEO..........	Quality Engineering Operations
QEO..........	Queen Elizabeth's Own [*British military*] (DMA)
QEOP........	Quartermaster Emergency Operation Plan [*Army*]
QEP..........	Quality Evaluation Program [*College of American Pathologists*]
QEP..........	Quality Examination Program (AFM)
QEPL........	Quality Engineering Planning List (MCD)
QER..........	Qualitative Equipment Requirements [*Army*] (AABC)
QER..........	Quarterly Economic Review [*A publication*]
QER..........	Queen's Edinburgh Rifles [*British military*] (DMA)
QES..........	Quadrant Eleventh-Gram Second
QES..........	Quaker Esperanto Society (EA)
QESCP......	Quality Engineering Significant Control Points (MCD)
QEST........	Quality Evaluation System Tests (NG)
QEST........	Query, Update Entry, Search, Time-Sharing System (NVT)
QET..........	Quality Expo TIME-International (ITD)
QET..........	Quasi-Equilibrium Theory [*Physical chemistry*]
QEV..........	Quick Exhaust Valve
QEVY........	Evans Products Co. [*NYSE symbol*] (SPSG)
QEW..........	Queen Elizabeth Way [*Canada*]
QEW..........	Quick Early Warning Test [*Medicine*] (MAE)
QF..............	Qabel Foundation (EA)
QF..............	QANTAS Airways Ltd. [*Australia*] [*ICAO designator*]
QF..............	Qualifying Facility [*Electric power*]
QF..............	Quality Factor [*Nuclear energy*]
QF..............	Quality Form [*Nuclear energy*] (NRCH)
QF..............	Quarterfinals (WGA)
QF..............	Quellen und Forschungen aus Italienischen Archiven und Bibliotheken [*A publication*]
QF..............	Quellen und Forschungen zur Sprach- und Kulturgeschichte der Germanischen Voelker [*A publication*]
QF..............	Quench Frequency (DEN)
QF..............	Queue Full
QF..............	Quick-Firing [*Gun*]
QF..............	Quick Fix (MCD)
QF..............	Quick Freeze
QFA..........	Qualification Firings Alignment (DNAB)

QFA .... Quantitative Fibrinogen Assay [*Clinical chemistry*]
QFAB........ Quellen und Forschungen aus Italienischen Archiven und Bibliotheken [*A publication*]
QFB .... Quiet Fast Boat [*Navy symbol*]
QF-BH....... Quick Fix - Black Hawk
QFC .... Quantitative Flight Characteristics
QFCC........ Quantitative Flight Characteristics Criteria
QFCI......... Quality Food Centers, Inc. [*NASDAQ symbol*] (NQ)
QFCI.......... Quartermaster Food and Container Institute for the Armed Forces
QFD .... Quality Function Deployment [*Automotive engineering*]
QFD .... Quantum Flavor Dynamics
QFD .... Quarterly Forecast Demand
QFE .... Atmospheric Pressure at Aerodrome Elevation [*or Runway Threshold*] [*Aviation code*] (FAAC)
QFE .... Columbus [*Georgia*] Fort Benning [*Airport symbol*] (OAG)
QFE .... Query Formulation and Encoding
QFF........... Atmospheric Pressure Converted to Mean Sea Level Elevation [*Aviation code*] (AIA)
QFF........... Quadrupole Flip-Flop [*Data processing*]
QFG .... Quaderni di Filologia Germanica. Facolta di Lettere e Filosofia. Universita di Bologna [*A publication*]
QFI .... Qualified Flight Instructor
QFI .... Quellen und Forschungen aus Italienischen Archiven und Bibliotheken [*A publication*]
QFIA......... Quantitative Fluorescence Image Analysis [*Medicine*]
QFIA......... Quantitative Fluorescence Image Analysis
QFIAB....... Quellen und Forschungen aus Italienischen Archiven und Bibliotheken [*A publication*]
Q Film Radio TV ... Quarterly of Film, Radio, and Television [*A publication*]
QFINBL .... Queensland. Department of Harbours and Marine. Fisheries Notes [*A publication*]
QFIRC....... Quick Fix Interference Reduction Capability (AFM)
QFL .... Quasi-Fermi Level
4QFlor .... Florilegium. A Miscellany from Qumran. Cave Four (BJA)
QFLOW .... Quota Flow Control Procedures (FAAC)
QFM .... Quantized Frequency Modulation
QFM .... Quartz-Fayalite-Magnetite [*Geology*]
QFMR ...... Quantized Frequency Modulation Repeater
QFO .... Quartz Frequency Oscillator
QFP .... Quartz Fiber Product
QFP .... Quick Fix Program
QFr .... Epistulae ad Quintum Fratrem [*of Cicero*] [*Classical studies*] (OCD)
QFR .... Quarterly Financial Report for Manufacturing, Mining, and Trade Companies [*Information service or system*] [*A publication*]
QFR .... Quarterly Force Revision [*Military*] (NVT)
QFRNAV... Queensland. Department of Forestry. Research Note [*A publication*]
QFRT........ Quarterly of Film, Radio, and Television [*A publication*]
Q Fruit & Veg News ... Queensland Fruit and Vegetable News [*A publication*] (APTA)
QFS........... Quick-Fit Sea (DNAB)
QFSK........ Quellen und Forschungen zur Sprach- und Kulturgeschichte der Germanischen Voelker [*A publication*]
QFSM........ Queen's Fire Service Medal for Distinguished Service [*British*]
QFSR........ Quartus Foundation for Spiritual Research (EA)
QFT .... Quantized Field Theory
QFU........... Magnetic Orientation of Runway [*Aviation code*] (FAAC)
Q Fuel Energy Summ ... Quarterly Fuel and Energy Summary [*United States*] [*A publication*]
QG .... Bibliotheque Municipale, Gatineau, Quebec [*Library symbol*] [*National Library of Canada*] (NLC)
QG .... Quadrature Grid
QG .... Quaestiones et Salutationes in Genesin [*Philo*] (BJA)
QG .... Qualified in Gunnery [*British military*] (DMA)
QG .... Quartermaster General [*Military*]
QG .... Seychelles-Kilimanjaro Air Transport Ltd. [*Kenya*] [*ICAO designator*] (FAAC)
QGAH .... Hotel-Dieu de Gaspe, Quebec [*Library symbol*] [*National Library of Canada*] (NLC)
QGAP........ Centre de Documentation, Peches Maritimes, Ministere de l'Agriculture, des Pecheries, et de l'Alimentation du Quebec, Gaspe, Quebec [*Library symbol*] [*National Library of Canada*] (NLC)
QGBF .... Quasi-Grain Boundary Free [*Photovoltaic energy systems*]
QGC........... College de la Gaspesie, Gaspe, Quebec [*Library symbol*] [*National Library of Canada*] (NLC)
QGCH .... Centre Hospitalier de Gatineau, Quebec [*Library symbol*] [*National Library of Canada*] (NLC)
QGE........... Queen's Gurkha Engineers [*British military*] (DMA)
1QGen........ [*The*] Genesis Apocryphon from Qumran. Cave One (BJA)
Q Geog J ... Queensland Geographical Journal [*A publication*] (APTA)
Q Geol Notes ... Quarterly Geological Notes [*Australia*] [*A publication*]
Q Geol Notes Geol Surv South Aust ... South Australia. Geological Survey. Quarterly Geological Notes [*A publication*] (APTA)
QGG .... Queensland Government Gazette [*A publication*] (APTA)
QGHR .... Quellen zur Geschichte des Humanismus und der Reformation in Facsimile-Ausgaben [*A publication*]

QGI............ Grosse Ile Library, Magdalen Islands, Quebec [*Library symbol*] [*National Library of Canada*] (NLC)
QGIG .... Queensland Government Industrial Gazette [*A publication*] (APTA)
QGJD .... Quellen zur Geschichte der Juden in Deutschland [*A publication*]
QGL........... Granby Leader Mail Office, Quebec [*Library symbol*] [*National Library of Canada*] (NLC)
QGM .... Bibliotheque Municipale, Granby, Quebec [*Library symbol*] [*National Library of Canada*] (NLC)
QGM .... Queen's Gallantry Medal [*British*]
QGM .... Quellen und Studien zur Geschichte der Mathematik [*A publication*]
QGMath .... Quellen und Studien zur Geschichte der Mathematik [*A publication*]
QGMG....... Musee de la Gaspesie, Gaspe, Quebec [*Library symbol*] [*National Library of Canada*] (BIB)
QGMJA .... Queensland Government Mining Journal [*A publication*]
QGMM...... Bibliotheque Municipale, Grand'Mere, Quebec [*Library symbol*] [*National Library of Canada*] (NLC)
QGNG .... Ecole Secondaire Nicolas-Gatineau, Gatineau, Quebec [*Library symbol*] [*National Library of Canada*] (BIB)
QGO .... Queen's Gurkha Officer [*Military*] [*British*]
Q Gov Indus Gaz ... Queensland Government Industrial Gazette [*A publication*] (APTA)
Q Govt Min J ... Queensland Government Mining Journal [*A publication*] (APTA)
Q Govt PRB News Bul ... Queensland Government. Public Relations Bureau. News Bulletin [*A publication*] (APTA)
QGP........... Queensland Government Publications [*A publication*] (APTA)
Q Graingrower ... Queensland Graingrower [*A publication*] (APTA)
QGS........... Quantity Gauging System (NASA)
QGSH........ Societe Historique du Comte de Shefford, Granby, Quebec [*Library symbol*] [*National Library of Canada*] (NLC)
QGV........... Quantized Gate Video [*RADAR*]
QH .... Air Florida, Inc. [*ICAO designator*] (FAAC)
QH .... Bibliotheque Municipale, Hull, Quebec [*Library symbol*] [*National Library of Canada*] (NLC)
QH .... Quaker History [*A publication*]
QH .... Quaque Hora [*Every Hour*] [*Pharmacy*]
QH .... Quartz Halogen
QH .... Quartz Helix
QH .... Queensland Heritage [*A publication*] (APTA)
QH .... Quorn Hounds
1QH .... Hodayot. Hymns of Thanksgiving from Qumran. Cave One (BJA)
Q2H .... Quaque Secunda Hora [*Every Second Hour*] [*Pharmacy*]
Q3H .... Quaque Tertia Hora [*Every Third Hour*] [*Pharmacy*]
Q4H .... Quaque Quartus Hora [*Every Fourth Hour*] [*Pharmacy*]
QHAC....... CEGEP [*College d'Enseignement General et Professionnel*] de Hauterive, Baie Comeau, Quebec [*Library symbol*] [*National Library of Canada*] (NLC)
QHACR..... Conseil Regional de la Sante et des Services Sociaux de la Region Cote-Nord, Hauterive, Quebec [*Library symbol*] [*National Library of Canada*] (NLC)
QHB .... Economics Information Centre, Bell Canada, Hull, Quebec [*Library symbol*] [*National Library of Canada*] (NLC)
QHB .... Queen's Hard Bargain [*Undesirable serviceman*] [*Slang*] [*British*] (DSUE)
QHBC........ Bibliotheque Centrale de Pret d'Outaouais, Hull, Quebec [*Library symbol*] [*National Library of Canada*] (BIB)
QHBEER .. Headquarters Engineering Economics Reference Centre, Bell Canada, Hull, Quebec [*Library symbol*] [*National Library of Canada*] (NLC)
QHBRM.... Bell Canada Headquarters, Regulatory Matters-Regulatory Information Bank, Hull, Quebec [*Library symbol*] [*National Library of Canada*] (NLC)
QHC .... CEGEP [*College d'Enseignement General et Professionnel*] de l'Outaouais, Hull, Quebec [*Library symbol*] [*National Library of Canada*] (NLC)
QHC .... Queen's Honorary Chaplain [*British*]
QHCH .... Heritage Campus, CEGEP de l'Outaouais, Hull, Quebec [*Library symbol*] [*National Library of Canada*] (NLC)
QHCL........ Centre de Documentation, CLSC de Hull, Quebec [*Library symbol*] [*National Library of Canada*] (NLC)
QHCRS ..... Conseil Regional de la Sante et des Services Sociaux de la Region Outaouais-Hull, Hull, Quebec [*Library symbol*] [*National Library of Canada*] (NLC)
QHDS........ Queen's Honorary Dental Surgeon [*British*]
QHE .... E. B. Eddy Co., Hull, Quebec [*Library symbol*] [*National Library of Canada*] (NLC)
QHE .... Quantum Hall Effect [*Physics*]
Q Health .... Queensland's Health [*A publication*] (APTA)
Q Her .... Queensland Heritage [*A publication*]
QHESJ...... Ecole Secondaire St.-Joseph, Hull, Quebec [*Library symbol*] [*National Library of Canada*] (BIB)
Q Hist Soc J ... Queensland Historical Society. Journal [*A publication*]
QHM .... Quartz Horizontal Magnetometer (NOAA)
QHM .... Queen's Harbour Master [*British*]
QHMML... Micromedia Ltee., Hull, Quebec [*Library symbol*] [*National Library of Canada*] (BIB)

QHNS....... Queen's Honorary Nursing Sister [*British*]
QHO........... Queen's Hall Orchestra
QHP........... Queen's Honorary Physician [*British*]
QHP........... Quiet Helicopter Program (RDA)
QHPJ .... Centre Hospitalier Pierre Janet, Hull, Quebec [*Library symbol*] [*National Library of Canada*] (NLC)
QHQAR .... Centre Regional de l'Outaouais, Archives Nationales du Quebec, Hull, Quebec [*Library symbol*] [*National Library of Canada*] (BIB)
QHR .... Quality History Record [*Nuclear energy*] (NRCH)
q hr............ Quaque Hora [*Every Hour*] [*Latin*] [*Pharmacy*] (WGA)
QHR .... Queensland Historical Review [*A publication*] (APTA)
QHRI........ Quantum Health Resources [*NASDAQ symbol*] (SPSG)
QHS......... Qinghaosu [*Antimalarial drug*]
qhs............. Quaque Hora Somni [*Every Hour of Sleep*] [*Latin*] [*Pharmacy*] (MAE)
QHS........... Queen's Honorary Surgeon [*British*]
QHSA .... Societe d'Amenagement de l'Outaouais, Hull, Quebec [*Library symbol*] [*National Library of Canada*] (NLC)
QHSC....... Centre Hospitalier Regional de l'Outaouais, Hull, Quebec [*Library symbol*] [*National Library of Canada*] (NLC)
QHTA Bull ... QHTA [*Queensland History Teachers Association*] Bulletin [*A publication*] (APTA)
QHU .... Universite du Quebec, Hull, Quebec [*Library symbol*] [*National Library of Canada*] (NLC)
QHV .... Quiet Heavy Vehicle [*Automotive engineering*]
QI.............. Cimber Air [*Denmark*] [*ICAO designator*] (FAAC)
QI.............. Quaderni Ibero-Americani [*A publication*]
QI.............. Quaderni d'Italianistica [*A publication*]
QI.............. Qualified Instructor [*British military*] (DMA)
QI.............. Quality Increase (AABC)
QI.............. Quality Index
QI.............. Quantity Indicator (KSC)
QI.............. Quart Imperial (DNAB)
QI.............. Quarterly Index [*A publication*]
QI.............. Quartz Iodine
QI.............. Quasi-Inertial
QI.............. Quota International (EA)
QIA .... Quaderni Ibero-Americani [*A publication*]
QIA .... Quantitative Infrared Analysis
QIAET....... Quartzsite Integrated Acoustic and Engine Test Site
1QIaIQIsa ... Complete Isaiah Scroll from Qumran. Cave One (BJA)
QIB .... Quarterly Information Bulletin [*Navy*] (DNAB)
QIB .... Queensland Imperial Bushmen [*British military*] (DMA)
QIB .... Quick Is Beautiful [*NASA project philosophy*]
QIBA .... Quaderni Italiani di Buenos Aires [*A publication*]
QIC .... Quality Information Center
QIC .... Quality Inspection Criteria
QIC .... Quarter Inch Cartridge [*Data processing*]
QIC .... Quarter-Inch Compatibility [*Format*]
QIC .... Quartz Iodine Crystal
QID........... Quater in Die [*Four Times a Day*] [*Pharmacy*]
QIDN........ Queen's Institute of District Nursing [*British*]
QIE .... Quantitative Immunoelectrophoresis Methods [*Analytical biochemistry*]
QIE-AF...... Qualified International Executive - Air Forwarding [*Designation awarded by American Society of International Executives, Inc.*]
QIE-EM .... Qualified International Executive - Export Management [*Designation awarded by American Society of International Executives, Inc.*]
QIE-F........ Qualified International Executive - Forwarding [*Designation awarded by American Society of International Executives, Inc.*]
QIER J ...... QIER [*Queensland Institute for Educational Research*] Journal [*A publication*] (APTA)
QIE-TM .... Qualified International Executive - Traffic Management [*Designation awarded by American Society of International Executives, Inc.*]
QIF .... Quartz-Iron-Fayalite [*Geology*]
QIFL.......... Quaderni. Istituto di Filologia Latina. Universita di Padova [*A publication*]
QIFMA...... Archives des Freres Maristes, Iberville, Quebec [*Library symbol*] [*National Library of Canada*] (NLC)
QIG........... Quaderni. Istituto di Glottologia [*Bologna*] [*A publication*]
QIG........... Queensland Industrial Gazette [*A publication*]
QIGB .... Quaderni. Istituto di Glottologia (Bologna) [*A publication*]
QIK........... Quick (MSA)
QIL .... Quad In-Line
QIL .... Quartz Incandescent Lamp
QIL .... Quartz Iodine Lamp
Q Illust....... Quarterly Illustrator [*A publication*]
QILS......... Quantification of Integrated Logistics Support
QILT......... Pathe Computer Control Systems Corp. [*NASDAQ symbol*] (NQ)
QIMA .... QIMA. Institute of Municipal Administration, Queensland Division [*A publication*] (APTA)
Q Ind......... Queensland Industry [*A publication*] (APTA)
Q Industry ... Queensland Industry [*A publication*] (APTA)
3QInv .... [*The*] Copper Treasure Inventory Scroll from Qumran. Cave Three (BJA)

QIO............ Queue Input/Output
QIP .... PALINET [*Pennsylvania Area Library Network*] Central, Philadelphia, PA [*OCLC symbol*] (OCLC)
QIP .... Quality Improvement Process [*Chrysler Corp.*]
QIP .... Quality Inspection Point (KSC)
QIP .... Quarterly Intercession Paper [*A publication*] (ROG)
QIP .... Quarters Improvement Program (MCD)
QIP .... Quartz Insulation Part
QIP .... Query Interpretation Program (SAA)
QIP .... Quiescat in Pace [*May He, or She, Rest in Peace*] [*Latin*]
QIP Rep Natl Asphalt Pavement Assoc ... QIP Report. National Asphalt Pavement Association [*A publication*]
QISAM...... Queued Indexed Sequential Access Method [*IBM Corp.*] [*Data processing*]
Q Isr Inst Metals ... Quarterly. Israel Institute of Metals [*A publication*]
QIT .... Quality Information and Test [*System*]
QITLJ........ Queensland Institute of Technology. Law Journal [*A publication*]
QJ .... Bibliotheque Municipale, Jonquiere, Quebec [*Library symbol*] [*National Library of Canada*] (BIB)
QJ .... Jordanian World Airways [*ICAO designator*] (FAAC)
QJ .... Quarterly Journal. Library of Congress [*A publication*]
QJ .... Quarterly Journal. University of North Dakota [*A publication*]
QJ .... Quick Junction [*Electronics*]
QJAAA...... Queensland Journal of Agricultural and Animal Sciences [*A publication*]
QJ Agric Econ ... Quarterly Journal of Agricultural Economy [*A publication*]
Q Japan Com'l Arb Ass'n ... Quarterly. Japan Commercial Arbitration Association [*A publication*] (DLA)
QJBE........ Quarterly Journal of Business and Economics [*A publication*]
QJC........... College de Joliette, Quebec [*Library symbol*] [*National Library of Canada*] (NLC)
QJCA .... Quarterly Journal of Current Acquisitions [*A publication*]
QJCH .... Centre de Documentation, Departement de Sante Communautaire de Lanaudiere, Joliette, Quebec [*Library symbol*] [*National Library of Canada*] (BIB)
Q J Chem Soc London ... Quarterly Journal. Chemical Society. London [*A publication*]
Q J Crude Drug Res ... Quarterly Journal of Crude Drug Research [*A publication*]
QJCSVA.... Archives Provinciales des Clercs de Saint-Viateur, Joliette, Quebec [*Library symbol*] [*National Library of Canada*] (NLC)
QJE........... Quarterly Journal of Economics [*A publication*]
Q J Econ .... Quarterly Journal of Economics [*A publication*]
QJ Eng Geol ... Quarterly Journal of Engineering Geology [*A publication*]
QJEPs .... Quarterly Journal of Experimental Psychology [*A publication*]
Q/JET .... Quadrajet Carburetor [*Automotive engineering*]
QJewR .... Quarterly Jewish Review [*A publication*]
QJewSt ...... Quarterly of Jewish Studies. Jewish Chronicle [*A publication*]
Q J Exp Physiol ... Quarterly Journal of Experimental Physiology and Cognate Medical Sciences [*A publication*]
Q J Exp Physiol Cogn Med Sci ... Quarterly Journal of Experimental Physiology and Cognate Medical Sciences [*A publication*]
Q J Exp Psy ... Quarterly Journal of Experimental Psychology [*A publication*]
Q J Exp Psychol ... Quarterly Journal of Experimental Psychology [*A publication*]
QJ Exp Psychol A Hum Exp Psychol ... Quarterly Journal of Experimental Psychology. A. Human Experimental Psychology [*A publication*]
Q J Exp Psychol B ... Quarterly Journal of Experimental Psychology. B. Comparative and Physiological Psychology [*A publication*]
QJ Exp Psychol B Comp Physiol Psychol ... Quarterly Journal of Experimental Psychology. B. Comparative and Physiological Psychology [*A publication*]
Q J Fla Acad Sci ... Quarterly Journal. Florida Academy of Sciences [*A publication*]
Q J For....... Quarterly Journal of Forestry [*A publication*]
Q J Forestry ... Quarterly Journal of Forestry [*A publication*]
Q J Geol Min Metall Soc (India) ... Quarterly Journal. Geological, Mining, and Metallurgical Society (India) [*A publication*]
Q J Geol Soc Lond ... Quarterly Journal. Geological Society of London [*A publication*]
Q J Geol Soc London ... Quarterly Journal. Geological Society of London [*A publication*]
QJH .... Centre Hospitalier Regional de Lanaudiere, Joliette, Quebec [*Library symbol*] [*National Library of Canada*] (NLC)
Q J Hist Sci Technol ... Quarterly Journal of the History of Science and Technology [*A publication*]
Q J Indian Chem Soc ... Quarterly Journal. Indian Chemical Society [*A publication*]
Q J Indian Inst Sci ... Quarterly Journal. Indian Institute of Science [*A publication*]
Q J Indones At Energy Agency ... Quarterly Journal. Indonesian Atomic Energy Agency [*A publication*]
QJ Int Agric ... Quarterly Journal of International Agriculture [*A publication*]
QJJ .... Seminaire de Joliette, Quebec [*Library symbol*] [*National Library of Canada*] (NLC)
Q J Jpn Weld Soc ... Quarterly Journal. Japan Welding Society [*A publication*]
QJL........... Querner, J. L., San Antonio TX [*STAC*]

QJLC .... Quarterly Journal. Library of Congress [*A publication*]
Q J Lib Con ... Quarterly Journal. Library of Congress [*A publication*]
Q J Lit Sci Arts ... Quarterly Journal of Literature, Science, and the Arts [*A publication*]
Q J Liverpool Univer Inst Commer Res Trop ... Quarterly Journal. Liverpool University Institute of Commercial Research in the Tropics [*A publication*]
Q Jl Microsc Sci ... Quarterly Journal of Microscopical Science [*A publication*]
Q J Local Self Govt Inst ... Quarterly Journal. Local Self-Government Institute [*Bombay*] [*A publication*]
Q Jl R Met Soc ... Quarterly Journal. Royal Meteorological Society [*A publication*]
Q Jl Rubb Res Inst Ceylon ... Quarterly Journal. Rubber Research Institute of Ceylon [*later, Sri Lanka*] [*A publication*]
QJLSGI ..... Quarterly Journal. Local Self-Government Institute [*Bombay*] [*A publication*]
QJLSI .... Quarterly Journal. Local Self-Government Institute [*Bombay*] [*A publication*]
QJMA .... Musee d'Art de Joliette, Quebec [*Library symbol*] [*National Library of Canada*]   (NLC)
Q J Math ... Quarterly Journal of Mathematics [*A publication*]
Q J Mech Ap ... Quarterly Journal of Mechanics and Applied Mathematics [*A publication*]
QJ Mech Appl Math ... Quarterly Journal of Mechanics and Applied Mathematics [*A publication*]
Q J Med..... Quarterly Journal of Medicine [*A publication*]
Q J Micro Sc ... Quarterly Journal of Microscopical Science [*A publication*]
Q J Microsc Sci ... Quarterly Journal of Microscopical Science [*A publication*]
QJMP........ Queue Jump Command
QJMS........ Quarterly Journal. Mythic Society [*A publication*]
Q Jnl Speech ... Quarterly Journal of Speech [*A publication*]
QJOC .... College de Jonquiere, Quebec [*Library symbol*] [*National Library of Canada*]   (NLC)
Q J Pakistan Lib Assn ... Quarterly Journal. Pakistan Library Association [*Karachi*] [*A publication*]
QJ Pharm Allied Sci ... Quarterly Journal of Pharmacy and Allied Sciences [*A publication*]
Q J Pharm Pharmacol ... Quarterly Journal of Pharmacy and Pharmacology [*A publication*]
QJP (Mag Cas) ... Queensland Justice of the Peace (Magisterial Cases) [*A publication*]   (APTA)
QJPR........ Queensland Justice of the Peace. Reports [*A publication*]   (APTA)
Q J Pub Speak ... Quarterly Journal of Public Speaking [*A publication*]
QJRAA...... Quarterly Journal. Royal Astronomical Society [*A publication*]
Q J R Astro ... Quarterly Journal. Royal Astronomical Society [*A publication*]
QJR Astron Soc ... Quarterly Journal. Royal Astronomical Society [*A publication*]
QJRMA..... Quarterly Journal. Royal Meteorological Society [*A publication*]
Q J R Meteo ... Quarterly Journal. Royal Meteorological Society [*A publication*]
Q J R Meteorol Soc ... Quarterly Journal. Royal Meteorological Society [*A publication*]
Q J R Neth Soc Agric Sci ... Quarterly Journal. Royal Netherlands Society for Agricultural Science [*A publication*]
Q J Rubber Res Inst Ceylon ... Quarterly Journal. Rubber Research Institute of Ceylon [*A publication*]
Q J Rubber Res Inst Sri Lanka ... Quarterly Journal. Rubber Research Institute of Sri Lanka [*formerly, Ceylon*] [*A publication*]
QJS............ Quarterly Journal of Speech [*A publication*]
Q J Sc .... Quarterly Journal of Science [*A publication*]
Q J Sc .... Quarterly Journal of Science, Literature, and the Arts [*A publication*]
Q J Sci Arts ... Quarterly Journal of Science and the Arts [*A publication*]
QJ Sci Lit Arts ... Quarterly Journal of Science, Literature, and the Arts [*A publication*]
QJ Seismol ... Quarterly Journal of Seismology [*A publication*]
QJSp......... Quarterly Journal of Speech [*A publication*]
QJSPA ...... Quarterly Journal of Speech [*A publication*]
Q J Speech ... Quarterly Journal of Speech [*A publication*]
Q J Stud Al ... Quarterly Journal of Studies on Alcohol [*A publication*]
Q J Stud Alcohol ... Quarterly Journal of Studies on Alcohol [*A publication*]
Q J Stud Alcohol Part A ... Quarterly Journal of Studies on Alcohol. Part A [*A publication*]
QJ Stud Alcohol Suppl ... Quarterly Journal of Studies on Alcohol. Supplement [*A publication*]
QJ Surg Sci ... Quarterly Journal of Surgical Sciences [*A publication*]
Q J Taiwan Mus (Taipei) ... Quarterly Journal. Taiwan Museum (Taipei) [*A publication*]
QJXPA ...... Quarterly Journal of Experimental Psychology [*A publication*]
QK.............. Compagnie Aeromaritime [*France*] [*ICAO designator*]   (FAAC)
QK.............. Kirkland Municipal Library [*Bibliotheque Municipale de Kirkland*] Quebec [*Library symbol*] [*National Library of Canada*]   (NLC)
QK.............. Queen's Knight [*Chess*]
QK.............. Quick   (FAAC)
QKB .... Brome County Historical Society, Knowlton, Quebec [*Library symbol*] [*National Library of Canada*]   (NLC)

QKBW .... Burroughs Wellcome & Co., Kirkland, Quebec [*Library symbol*] [*National Library of Canada*]   (NLC)
QKC.......... Aero Taxi Aviation, Inc. [*Lester, PA*] [*FAA designator*]   (FAAC)
QKFL......... Quick Flashing Light [*Navigation signal*]
Qk Froz Fd ... Quick Frozen Foods [*A publication*]
QKITA....... Institut de Technologie Agricole, Kamouraska, Quebec [*Library symbol*] [*National Library of Canada*]   (NLC)
QKL.......... Cologne/Bonn-Main RR [*Germany*] [*Airport symbol*]   (OAG)
QKLN .... Laboratoires Nordic, Inc., Kirkland, Quebec [*Library symbol*] [*National Library of Canada*]   (BIB)
QKPC .... Medical Library, Pfizer Canada, Inc., Kirkland, Quebec [*Library symbol*] [*National Library of Canada*]   (NLC)
QkReily...... Quick & Reilly Group, Inc. [*Associated Press abbreviation*]   (APAG)
QKT .... Queen's Knight [*Chess*]
QKTP .... Queen's Knight's Pawn [*Chess*]   (IIA)
QL............. Ethyl 2-(Diisopropylamino)ethylmethylphosphonite [*See EDMP*] [*Army symbol*]
QL............. Lesotho Airways [*ICAO designator*]   (FAAC)
QL............. Quad Left [*Typography*]
QL............. Quaderni Linguistici [*A publication*]
QL............. Quality of Living
QL............. Quantum Libet [*As Much as Is Desired*] [*Pharmacy*]
QL............. Quarrel   (ROG)
QL............. Quartz-Locked
QL............. Quebec Law [*A publication*]   (DLA)
QL............. Queen's Lancers [*Military unit*] [*British*]
QL............. Queensland Lawyer [*A publication*]   (APTA)
QL............. Query Language [*Data processing*]   (DIT)
QL............. Queue Length [*Telecommunications*]   (TEL)
Q/L............. Quick Look   (KSC)
QL............. Quintal [*Unit of weight*]
QL............. Quinzaine Litteraire [*A publication*]
QL............. Qumran Literature   (BJA)
QLA .... Bibliotheque Municipale, Laval, Quebec [*Library symbol*] [*National Library of Canada*]   (NLC)
QLA .... Lasham [*England*] [*Airport symbol*]
QLA/ABO ... Quebec Library Association/Association des Bibliothecaires du Quebec [*Canada*]
QLAB .... Quick Like a Bunny
QLAC .... CEGEP [*College d'Enseignement General et Professionnel*] Montmorency, Laval, Quebec [*Library symbol*] [*National Library of Canada*]   (NLC)
QLACS ...... Cite de la Sante de Laval, Quebec [*Library symbol*] [*National Library of Canada*]   (NLC)
QLACW .... Canadian Workplace Automation Research Centre [*Centre Canadien de Recherche sur l'Informatisation du Travail*] Laval, Quebec [*Library symbol*] [*National Library of Canada*]   (NLC)
QLAG .... Research Station, Agriculture Canada [*Station de Recherches, Agriculture Canada*] Lennoxville, Quebec [*Library symbol*] [*National Library of Canada*]   (NLC)
QLAH....... Lennoxville-Ascot Historical Society Museum, Lennoxville, Quebec [*Library symbol*] [*National Library of Canada*]   (NLC)
QLAID ...... Ateliers d'Ingenierie Dominion, Lachine, Quebec [*Library symbol*] [*National Library of Canada*]   (NLC)
QLAP......... Quick Look Analysis Program
QLAR .... Canadian Arsenals Ltd. [*Arsenaux Canada Ltee.*], Le Gardeur, Quebec [*Library symbol*] [*National Library of Canada*]   (BIB)
QLASC ...... College de l'Assomption, Quebec [*Library symbol*] [*National Library of Canada*]   (NLC)
QLASGPT ... Federal Training Centre, Penitentiary, Ministry of the Solicitor General [*Centre Federal de Formation, Penitencier, Ministere du Solliciteur General*] Laval, Quebec [*Library symbol*] [*National Library of Canada*]   (NLC)
QLAVD ..... Centre de Documentation, Assurance-Vie Desjardins, Levis, Quebec [*Library symbol*] [*National Library of Canada*]   (NLC)
Q Law Soc J ... Queensland Law Society. Journal [*A publication*]   (APTA)
QLB .... Bishop's University, Lennoxville, Quebec [*Library symbol*] [*National Library of Canada*]   (NLC)
QL Beor ..... Beor's Queensland Law Reports [*A publication*]   (APTA)
QLBG .... Department of Geography, Bishop's University, Lennoxville, Quebec [*Library symbol*] [*National Library of Canada*]   (NLC)
QLC .... College de Levis, Quebec [*Library symbol*] [*National Library of Canada*]   (NLC)
QLC .... Quasi-Liquid Crystal [*Organic chemistry*]
QLCCP...... Service de Documentation et de Reference, Confederation des Caisses Populaires et d'Economie Desjardins du Quebec, Levis, Quebec [*Library symbol*] [*National Library of Canada*]   (NLC)
QLCLL ...... CEGEP [*College d'Enseignement General et Professionnel*] de Levis-Lauzon, Lauzon, Quebec [*Library symbol*] [*National Library of Canada*]   (BIB)
QLCR .... Queensland Land Court Reports [*A publication*]   (APTA)

QLCRS...... Conseil Regional de la Sante et des Services Sociaux, Longueuil, Quebec [*Library symbol*] [*National Library of Canada*] (NLC)
QLCS........ Quick Look and Checkout System
QLD.......... Queen's Light Dragoons [*British military*] (DMA)
QLD.......... Quillo Resources, Inc. [*Vancouver Stock Exchange symbol*]
QLDC........ Delmar Chemicals, La Salle, Quebec [*Library symbol*] [*National Library of Canada*] (NLC)
Qld Geog J ... Queensland Geographical Journal [*A publication*] (APTA)
Qld Govt Indust Gaz ... Queensland Government Industrial Gazette [*A publication*] (APTA)
Qld Health ... Queensland's Health [*A publication*] (APTA)
Qld Heritage ... Queensland Heritage [*A publication*] (APTA)
Qld Ind...... Queensland Industry [*A publication*]
Qld Law ..... Queensland Lawyer [*A publication*]
Qld Mus Mem ... Queensland Museum. Memoirs [*A publication*] (APTA)
Qld Nat..... Queensland Naturalist [*A publication*] (APTA)
Qld Nurs.... Queensland Nurse [*A publication*]
Qld Parl Deb ... Queensland Parliamentary Debates [*A publication*] (APTA)
QLDR........ Quick Look Data Reference (NASA)
QLDS........ Quick Look Data Station [*NASA*] (KSC)
Qld Sci Teach ... Queensland Science Teacher [*A publication*] (APTA)
Qld Teach J ... Queensland Teachers' Journal [*A publication*] (APTA)
Qld Univ Law J ... University of Queensland. Law Journal [*A publication*]
QLE .... Bibliotheque Municipale, Levis, Quebec [*Library symbol*] [*National Library of Canada*] (NLC)
QLFCAE ... Fonds de Recherches Forestieres. Universite Laval. Contribution [*A publication*]
QLFCP...... Federation des Caisses Populaires Desjardins, Levis, Quebec [*Library symbol*] [*National Library of Canada*] (NLC)
QLFD .... Qualified (KSC)
QLFECA ... Archives des Freres des Ecoles Chretiennes, Ville de Laval, Quebec [*Library symbol*] [*National Library of Canada*] (NLC)
QLFY........ Qualify (FAAC)
QLG.......... Quick-Look Guide
QLHD....... Hotel-Dieu de Levis, Quebec [*Library symbol*] [*National Library of Canada*] (NLC)
QLI .... Quality of Life Index
Q Lib......... Quantum Libet [*As Much as You Please*] [*Pharmacy*]
Q Liberal.... Queensland Liberal [*A publication*] (APTA)
QLing........ Quantitative Linguistics [*A publication*]
Q-Link .... QuantumLink [*Quantum Computer Services, Inc.*] [*Vienna, VA*] [*Information service or system*] (IID)
QLISP .... [*A*] Programming Language (CSR)
QLit.......... Quebec. Litteraire [*A publication*]
QLIT......... Quick Look Intermediate Tape
Q LJ......... Queen's Law Journal [*A publication*]
QLJ.......... Queensland Law Journal [*A publication*] (APTA)
QLJ (NC) .. Queensland Law Journal (Notes of Cases) [*A publication*] (APTA)
QLL .... Quaderni di Lingue e Letterature [*A publication*]
QLL .... Quartz Landing Lamp [*Aviation*]
QLLC........ Qualified Logical Link Control [*Telecommunications*]
QLM......... Bibliotheque Municipale de Lachine, Quebec [*Library symbol*] [*National Library of Canada*] (NLC)
QLM......... Quasi-Linear Machine
QLMD....... Qual-Med, Inc. [*NASDAQ symbol*] (SPSG)
QLNLB...... Institut Nazareth et Louis-Braille, Longueuil, Quebec [*Library symbol*] [*National Library of Canada*] (NLC)
QLO.......... Bibliotheque Municipale, Longueuil, Quebec [*Library symbol*] [*National Library of Canada*] (NLC)
QLOCE ..... College Edouard-Montpetit, Longueuil, Quebec [*Library symbol*] [*National Library of Canada*] (NLC)
QLOCSS ... Centre de Services Sociaux Richelieu, Longueuil, Quebec [*Library symbol*] [*National Library of Canada*] (NLC)
QLOPB...... Centre de Documentation, Centre Hospitalier Pierre Boucher, Longueuil, Quebec [*Library symbol*] [*National Library of Canada*] (NLC)
QLOU....... Pratt & Whitney Aircraft Ltd., Longueuil, Quebec [*Library symbol*] [*National Library of Canada*] (NLC)
QLP .... Quality Low-Priced [*Art series*]
QLP .... Query Language Processor [*Data processing*]
QLP .... Questions Liturgiques et Paroissiales [*A publication*]
QLP .... Quinoxaline Ladder Polymer [*Organic chemistry*]
QLPED...... Pylon Electronic Development Co. Ltd., Lachine, Quebec [*Library symbol*] [*National Library of Canada*] (NLC)
QLPS........ Petro-Sun International, Inc., Longueuil, Quebec [*Library symbol*] [*National Library of Canada*] (NLC)
QLR .... Quebec Law Reports
QLR .... Queen's Lancashire Regiment [*Military unit*] [*British*]
QLR .... Queensland Law Reporter [*A publication*] (APTA)
QLR .... Queensland Law Reports [*A publication*] (APTA)
QL(R)........ Quick Look (Report)
QLR (Beor) ... Queensland Law Reports (Beor) [*A publication*] (APTA)
QL Rev....... Quarterly Law Review [*A publication*] (DLA)
QLS.......... Bibliotheque Municipale, La Salle, Quebec [*Library symbol*] [*National Library of Canada*] (NLC)
QLS.......... Quasi-Elastic Light Scattering [*Also, QELS, QUELS*] [*Physics*]
QLS.......... Quick Look Station [*NASA*] (MCD)

QLSA........ Queue Line Sharing Adapter [*Data processing*]
QLSAA...... Archives des Soeurs de Sainte-Anne, Lachine, Quebec [*Library symbol*] [*National Library of Canada*] (NLC)
QLSD........ Societe de Developpement International Desjardins, Levis, Quebec [*Library symbol*] [*National Library of Canada*] (BIB)
QLSE........ ESSO Building Products of Canada Ltd., La Salle, Quebec [*Library symbol*] [*National Library of Canada*] (NLC)
QLSHG ..... Bibliotheque Medicale, Hopital General La Salle, Quebec [*Library symbol*] [*National Library of Canada*] (NLC)
QLSJ .... Queensland Law Society. Journal [*A publication*] (APTA)
QLSM....... Quasi-Linear Sequential Machine
QLSO .... L'Octogone, Centre de la Culture, La Salle, Quebec [*Library symbol*] [*National Library of Canada*] (NLC)
QL Soc J .... Queensland Law Society. Journal [*A publication*]
QLSS .... Research Department, J. E. Seagram & Sons Ltd., La Salle, Quebec [*Library symbol*] [*National Library of Canada*] (NLC)
QLT .... Bibliotheque Municipale, La Tuque, Quebec [*Library symbol*] [*National Library of Canada*] (NLC)
QLT .... Quadra Logic Technologies, Inc. [*Vancouver Stock Exchange symbol*] [*Toronto Stock Exchange symbol*]
QLT .... Quantitative Leak Test
QLT .... Quasi-Linear Theory
QLTI......... Quadra Logic Technologies, Inc. [*NASDAQ symbol*] (NQ)
QLTV .... LTV Corp. [*Formerly, Ling-Temco-Vought, Inc.*] [*NYSE symbol*] (SPSG)
QLTY .... Quality (AFM)
QLTY........ Quality Mills, Inc. [*NASDAQ symbol*] (NQ)
QLTYCONO ... Quality Control Officer [*Military*]
Qly Land R ... Fitzgibbon's Irish Land Reports [*A publication*] (DLA)
QM .... Air Malawi [*ICAO designator*] (FAAC)
QM .... Bulgaria [*License plate code assigned to foreign diplomats in the US*]
QM .... Quadrature Modulation
QM .... Qualification Motor (MCD)
QM .... Quality Manual [*A publication*] (MCD)
QM .... Quality Memorandum
QM .... Quality of Merit
QM .... Quality Motels (EA)
QM .... Quantitative Methods
QM .... Quantum Mechanics
QM .... Quaque Matin [*Every Morning*] [*Pharmacy*]
QM .... Quarterly Meetings [*Quakers*]
QM .... Quarterly Memorandum
QM .... Quartermaster [*Military*] (AFM)
QM .... Queen Mother [*British*]
QM .... Queen's Messenger [*British*]
QM .... Query Module (MCD)
QM .... Queue Manager [*Data processing*] (CMD)
QM .... Quinacrine Mustard [*Chromosome stain*]
QM .... Quinonemethide [*Organic chemistry*]
QM .... Qumran Manuscripts (BJA)
QM .... Quo Modo [*In What Manner*] [*Latin*]
1QM .... Milchemet, the War of the Sons of Light and the Sons of Darkness from Qumran. Cave One (BJA)
QM1 .... Quartermaster, First Class [*Navy rating*]
QM2 .... Quartermaster, Second Class [*Navy rating*]
QM3 .... Quartermaster, Third Class [*Navy rating*]
QMA .... Group Information Centre, Alcan Aluminum Ltd. [*Centre d'Information du Groupe, Alcan Aluminium Ltee*] Montreal, Quebec [*Library symbol*] [*National Library of Canada*] (NLC)
QMA........ Qualified Military Available
QMA.......... Qualitative Materiel Approach [*Army*] (AABC)
QMA.......... Quartermasters Association [*Later, ALA*]
QMAA....... Archives de la Chancellerie, L'Archeveche de Montreal, Quebec [*Library symbol*] [*National Library of Canada*] (NLC)
QMAAC.... Queen Mary's Army Auxiliary Corps [*The WAAC*] [*British*]
QMAB...... Montreal Association for the Blind, Quebec [*Library symbol*] [*National Library of Canada*] (NLC)
QMABB .... TECSULT, Montreal, Quebec [*Library symbol*] [*National Library of Canada*] (NLC)
QMAC....... Macdonald College Library, Ste-Anne-De-Bellevue, Quebec [*Library symbol*] [*National Library of Canada*] (NLC)
QMAC....... Quadripartite Materiel and Agreements Committee [*Military*] (AABC)
QMACL .... Quebec Association for Children with Learning Disabilities [*Association Quebecoise pour les Enfants Souffrant de Troubles d'Apprentissage*] Montreal, Quebec [*Library symbol*] [*National Library of Canada*] (NLC)
QMACM... Centre des Dossiers et de Documentation, Direction de Montreal, Ministere des Affaires Culturelles du Quebec [*Library symbol*] [*National Library of Canada*] (BIB)
QMACN.... Archives de la Congregation de Notre-Dame, Montreal, Quebec [*Library symbol*] [*National Library of Canada*] (NLC)
QMADMA ... Archives, Diocese of Montreal, Anglican Church of Canada, Quebec [*Library symbol*] [*National Library of Canada*] (NLC)
QMAE....... Aviation Electric Ltd., Montreal, Quebec [*Library symbol*] [*National Library of Canada*] (NLC)

QMAEC .... Atomic Energy of Canada [*L'Energie Atomique du Canada*] Montreal, Quebec [*Library symbol*] [*National Library of Canada*] (NLC)

QMAGB.... Bibliotheque Municipale, Magog, Quebec [*Library symbol*] [*National Library of Canada*] (NLC)

Q(Maint) ... Quartermaster Maintenance [*World War II*]

QMAL .... Air Liquide Canada Ltee., Montreal, Quebec [*Library symbol*] [*National Library of Canada*] (NLC)

QMALL..... Abbott Laboratories Ltd., Montreal, Quebec [*Library symbol*] [*National Library of Canada*] (NLC)

QMAM...... Allan Memorial Institute, Montreal, Quebec [*Library symbol*] [*National Library of Canada*] (NLC)

QMAMA... Lavalin Environnement, Montreal, Quebec [*Library symbol*] [*National Library of Canada*] (NLC)

QMAMI .... Minerais LAC Ltee., Malartic, Quebec [*Library symbol*] [*National Library of Canada*] (NLC)

QMAO ...... Qualified for Mobilization Ashore Only [*Navy*]

QMAPO.... Centre de Documentation, APO Quebec, Montreal, Quebec [*Library symbol*] [*National Library of Canada*] (NLC)

QMAPS..... Quebec Aid for the Partially-Sighted [*Aide aux Insuffisants Visuels du Quebec*] Montreal, Quebec [*Library symbol*] [*National Library of Canada*] (NLC)

QMARC .... Archives Provinciales des Capucins, Montreal, Quebec [*Library symbol*] [*National Library of Canada*] (NLC)

QMAS .... Archives du Seminaire de Saint-Sulpice, Montreal, Quebec [*Library symbol*] [*National Library of Canada*] (NLC)

QMASBB .. ASEA [*Allmaenna Svenska Elektriska Aktiebolaget*] Brown Boveri, Inc., Montreal, Quebec [*Library symbol*] [*National Library of Canada*] (BIB)

QMASC..... Bibliotheque Municipale, Mascouche, Quebec [*Library symbol*] [*National Library of Canada*] (BIB)

QMASRC ... Space Research Corp., Mansonville, Quebec [*Library symbol*] [*National Library of Canada*] (NLC)

QMASSAS ... Centre de Documentation, Secteur Affaires Sociales, Association pour la Sante et la Securite du Travail, Montreal, Quebec [*Library symbol*] [*National Library of Canada*] (NLC)

Q Master Plumber ... Queensland Master Plumber [*A publication*] (APTA)

QMATC .... College de Matane, Quebec [*Library symbol*] [*National Library of Canada*] (NLC)

QMAV....... Bibliotheque des Avocats, Barreau de Montreal, Quebec [*Library symbol*] [*National Library of Canada*] (NLC)

QMAX....... Qmax Technology Group, Inc. [*Dayton, OH*] [*NASDAQ symbol*] (NQ)

QMAY....... Ayerst, McKenna & Harrison, Inc. Montreal, Quebec [*Library symbol*] [*National Library of Canada*] (NLC)

QMB......... Information Resource Centre, Bell Canada [*Centre d'Information Specialisee, Bell Canada*] Montreal, Quebec [*Library symbol*] [*National Library of Canada*] (NLC)

QMB......... Qualified Mortgage Bond

QMB.......... Quarterly Management Bulletin [*A publication*] (DNAB)

QMB......... Queensbury [*England*] [*Seismograph station code, US Geological Survey*] (SEIS)

QMB......... Quick Make-and-Break [*Contact*] (DEN)

QMBA....... Ecole des Beaux-Arts, Montreal, Quebec [*Library symbol*] [*National Library of Canada*] (NLC)

QMBAE .... Bristol Aero Engines Ltd., Montreal, Quebec [*Library symbol*] [*National Library of Canada*] (NLC)

QMBAN.... Centre de Documentation, Banque Nationale du Canada, Montreal, Quebec [*Library symbol*] [*National Library of Canada*] (NLC)

QMBB .... College Bois-De-Boulogne, Montreal, Quebec [*Library symbol*] [*National Library of Canada*] (NLC)

QMBBL..... Beauchemin, Beaton, Lapointe, Inc., Montreal, Quebec [*Library symbol*] [*National Library of Canada*] (NLC)

QMBC....... Byers, Casgrain, Montreal, Quebec [*Library symbol*] [*National Library of Canada*] (BIB)

QMBD....... Translation Bureau, Canada Department of the Secretary of State [*Bureau des Traductions, Secretariat d'Etat*] Montreal, Quebec [*Library symbol*] [*National Library of Canada*] (NLC)

QMBE .... Centre de Documentation, Bureau des Economies d'Energie du Quebec, Montreal, Quebec [*Library symbol*] [*National Library of Canada*] (NLC)

QMBGC.... Bibliotheque d'Ingenierie, BG Checo International Ltee., Montreal, Quebec [*Library symbol*] [*National Library of Canada*] (NLC)

QMBIM ... Bio-Mega, Inc., Montreal, Quebec [*Library symbol*] [*National Library of Canada*] (NLC)

QMBL .... Law Library, Bell Canada, Montreal, Quebec [*Library symbol*] [*National Library of Canada*] (NLC)

QMBM...... Bibliotheque de la Ville de Montreal, Quebec [*Library symbol*] [*National Library of Canada*] (NLC)

QMBMO... Bank of Montreal [*Banque de Montreal*], Quebec [*Library symbol*] [*National Library of Canada*] (NLC)

QMBMS ... Management Sciences Library, Bell Canada, Montreal, Quebec [*Library symbol*] [*Obsolete*] [*National Library of Canada*] (NLC)

QMBN....... Bibliotheque Nationale du Quebec, Montreal, Quebec [*Library symbol*] [*National Library of Canada*] (NLC)

QMBNR.... Bell Northern Research, Montreal, Quebec [*Library symbol*] [*National Library of Canada*] (NLC)

QMBP .... Building Products Ltd., Montreal, Quebec [*Library symbol*] [*National Library of Canada*] (NLC)

QMBR .... Bio-Research Laboratories Ltd., Pointe-Claire, Quebec [*Library symbol*] [*National Library of Canada*] (NLC)

QMBT .... Montreal Board of Trade [*Chambre de Commerce du District de Montreal*] Quebec [*Library symbol*] [*National Library of Canada*] (NLC)

QMC......... Chief Quartermaster [*Navy rating*]

QMC......... College de Montreal, Quebec [*Library symbol*] [*National Library of Canada*] (NLC)

QMC......... James Carson Breckinridge Library, Quantico, VA [*OCLC symbol*] (OCLC)

QMC......... Quadripartite Materiel Committee [*Military*]

QMC......... Quartermaster Clerk [*Marine Corps*]

QMC......... Quartermaster Corps [*Army*]

QMC......... Queen Mary College [*London*]

QMC......... Quick Modification Concept (MCD)

QMCA...... Engineering Library, Canadair Ltd., Montreal, Quebec [*Library symbol*] [*National Library of Canada*] (NLC)

QMCAD.... Centre d'Animation, de Developpement, et de Recherche en Education, Montreal, Quebec [*Library symbol*] [*National Library of Canada*] (NLC)

QMCADM ... Centre d'Accueil Domremy-Montreal, Ste.-Genevieve, Quebec [*Library symbol*] [*National Library of Canada*] (NLC)

QMCADQ ... Conservatoire d'Art Dramatique de Montreal, Quebec [*Library symbol*] [*National Library of Canada*] (NLC)

QMCAE .... CAE Electronics Ltd., Montreal, Quebec [*Library symbol*] [*National Library of Canada*] (NLC)

QMCAG.... College Andre Grasset, Montreal, Quebec [*Library symbol*] [*National Library of Canada*] (NLC)

QMCAI ..... Canadian Asbestos Information Centre [*Centre Canadien d'Information sur l'Amiante*] Montreal, Quebec [*Library symbol*] [*National Library of Canada*] (NLC)

QMCAR .... Carmel de Montreal, Quebec [*Library symbol*] [*National Library of Canada*] (NLC)

QMCAT .... Commission de la Sante et de la Securite du Travail du Quebec, Montreal [*Library symbol*] [*National Library of Canada*] (NLC)

QMCAV .... Direction Generale du Cinema et de l'Audio-Visuel, Ministere des Communications du Quebec, Montreal, Quebec [*Library symbol*] [*National Library of Canada*] (NLC)

QMCB .... Canadian Broadcasting Corp. [*Societe Radio-Canada*] Montreal, Quebec [*Library symbol*] [*National Library of Canada*] (NLC)

QMCBE .... Engineering Headquarters, Canadian Broadcasting Corp. [*Service de l'Ingenierie, Societe Radio-Canada*] Montreal, Quebec [*Library symbol*] [*National Library of Canada*] (NLC)

QMCBH ... Catherine Booth Hospital, Montreal, Quebec [*Library symbol*] [*National Library of Canada*] (NLC)

QMCBM ... Music Library, Canadian Broadcasting Corp. [*Musicotheque et Discotheque, Societe Radio-Canada*], Montreal, Quebec [*Library symbol*] [*National Library of Canada*] (BIB)

QMCC....... Canada Cement Co., Montreal, Quebec [*Library symbol*] [*National Library of Canada*] (NLC)

QMCCA .... Centre Canadien d'Architecture [*Canadian Centre for Architecture*] Montreal, Quebec [*Library symbol*] [*National Library of Canada*] (NLC)

QMCCL..... Currie, Coopers & Lybrand Ltd., Montreal, Quebec [*Library symbol*] [*National Library of Canada*] (NLC)

QMCCR .... Canadian Council of Resource Ministers [*Conseil Canadien des Ministres des Ressources*] Montreal, Quebec [*Library symbol*] [*National Library of Canada*] (NLC)

QMCCS..... Centraide, Montreal, Quebec [*Library symbol*] [*National Library of Canada*] (NLC)

QMCD....... Centre Documentaire, Centrale des Bibliotheques, Montreal, Quebec [*Library symbol*] [*National Library of Canada*] (NLC)

QMCDM... College de Maisonneuve, Montreal, Quebec [*Library symbol*] [*National Library of Canada*] (NLC)

QMCDP .... Caisse de Depot et Placement du Quebec, Montreal, Quebec [*Library symbol*] [*National Library of Canada*] (NLC)

QMCE .... Celanese Canada Ltd., Montreal, Quebec [*Library symbol*] [*National Library of Canada*] (NLC)

QMCEA .... Canadian Export Association [*Association Canadienne d'Exportation*] Montreal, Quebec [*Library symbol*] [*National Library of Canada*] (NLC)

QMCEC .... Catholic School Commission [*Commission des Ecoles Catholiques*] Montreal, Quebec [*Library symbol*] [*National Library of Canada*] (NLC)

QMCECI... Centre Canadien d'Etudes et de Cooperation Internationale, Montreal, Quebec [*Library symbol*] [*National Library of Canada*] (NLC)

QMCED .... Centre de Documentation, Ministere du Commerce Exterieur et du Developpement Technologique du Quebec, Montreal, Quebec [*Library symbol*] [*National Library of Canada*] (BIB)

QMCF .... Merck Frosst Laboratories [*Laboratoires Merck Frosst*] Montreal, Quebec [*Library symbol*] [*National Library of Canada*] (NLC)

QMCFH .... Centre de Documentation, Charette, Fortier, Hawey, Touche, Ross, Montreal, Quebec [*Library symbol*] [*National Library of Canada*] (NLC)

QMCGW ... Clarkson, Gordon, Woods, Gordon, Montreal, Quebec [*Library symbol*] [*National Library of Canada*] (NLC)

QMCHC .... Montreal Chest Hospital Centre [*Centre Hospitalier Thoracique de Montreal*] Quebec [*Library symbol*] [*National Library of Canada*] (NLC)

QMCHF .... Centre de Documentation, Centre Hospitalier Fleury, Montreal, Quebec [*Library symbol*] [*National Library of Canada*] (NLC)

QMCHL .... Centre Hospitalier de Lachine, Montreal, Quebec [*Library symbol*] [*National Library of Canada*] (NLC)

QMCICM ... Centre Interculturel Monchanin, Montreal, Quebec [*Library symbol*] [*National Library of Canada*] (NLC)

QMCIH ..... Bibliotheque de Documentation des Archives, Ville de Montreal, Quebec [*Library symbol*] [*National Library of Canada*] (NLC)

QMCIM .... Canadian Institute of Mining and Metallurgy [*Institut Canadien des Mines et de la Metallurgie*] Montreal, Quebec [*Library symbol*] [*National Library of Canada*] (NLC)

QMC-IRL ... Queen Mary College Industrial Research Ltd. [*Research center*] [*British*] (IRUK)

QMCJ .... Canadian Jewish Congress [*Congres Juif Canadien*] Montreal, Quebec [*Library symbol*] [*National Library of Canada*] (NLC)

QMCL .... CanAtom Ltd., Montreal, Quebec [*Library symbol*] [*National Library of Canada*] (NLC)

QMCLG .... College Lionel Groulx, Ste-Therese, Quebec [*Library symbol*] [*National Library of Canada*] (NLC)

QMCLK .... Quartermaster Clerk [*Navy rating*]

QMCM ...... Canadian Marconi Co., Montreal, Quebec [*Library symbol*] [*National Library of Canada*] (NLC)

QMCM ...... Master Chief Quartermaster [*Navy rating*]

QMCM ...... Quartermaster Corporal-Major [*British military*] (DMA)

QMCN .... Canadian National Railways [*Chemins de fer Nationaux du Canada*] Montreal, Quebec [*Library symbol*] [*National Library of Canada*] (NLC)

QMCNC .... Chemical Library, Canadian National Railways [*Bibliotheque Chimique, Chemins de fer Nationaux du Canada*] Montreal, Quebec [*Library symbol*] [*Obsolete*] [*National Library of Canada*] (NLC)

QMCOM ... Conservatoire de Musique de Montreal, Quebec [*Library symbol*] [*National Library of Canada*] (NLC)

QMCP .... Canadian Pacific Ltd. [*Le Canadien Pacifique*] Montreal, Quebec [*Library symbol*] [*National Library of Canada*] (NLC)

QMCQ .... Cinematheque Quebecoise, Montreal, Quebec [*Library symbol*] [*National Library of Canada*] (BIB)

QMCR .... Canadian Copper Refiners Ltd., Montreal, Quebec [*Library symbol*] [*National Library of Canada*] (NLC)

QMCR .... Quartermaster Corps Regulations [*Army*]

QMCRI ..... Centre de Recherche Industrielle du Quebec, Montreal, Quebec [*Library symbol*] [*National Library of Canada*] (NLC)

QMCRIM ... Centre de Documentation, Centre de Recherche Informatique de Montreal, Quebec [*Library symbol*] [*National Library of Canada*] (BIB)

QMCRP .... Conference des Recteurs et des Principaux des Universites du Quebec, Montreal, Quebec [*Library symbol*] [*National Library of Canada*] (NLC)

QMCS .... Christian Science Reading Room, Montreal, Quebec [*Library symbol*] [*National Library of Canada*] (NLC)

QMCS .... Quality Monitoring Control System [*Military*] (CAAL)

QMCS .... Senior Chief Quartermaster [*Navy rating*]

QMCSCA ... Archives de la Congregation de Sainte-Croix, Montreal, Quebec [*Library symbol*] [*National Library of Canada*] (NLC)

QMC & SO ... Quartermaster Cataloging and Standardization Office [*Army*]

QMCSSMM ... CSSMM [*Centre de Services Sociaux du Montreal Metropolitain*], Montreal, Quebec [*Library symbol*] [*National Library of Canada*] (NLC)

QMCSSS ... Service de Reference, Conseil de la Sante et des Services Sociaux de la Region de Montreal Metropolitain, Montreal, Quebec [*Library symbol*] [*National Library of Canada*] (NLC)

QMCSVA ... Archives des Clercs de Saint-Viateur, Province de Montreal, Outremont, Quebec [*Library symbol*] [*National Library of Canada*] (NLC)

QMCT .... Commission de Transport de la Communaute Urbaine de Montreal, Quebec [*Library symbol*] [*National Library of Canada*] (NLC)

QMCT .... QMC Technology, Inc. [*NASDAQ symbol*] (NQ)

QMCTC .... Quartermaster Corps Technical Committee [*Army*]

QMCTM ... Canadian Tobacco Manufacturers' Council [*Conseil Canadien des Fabricants des Produits du Tabac*] Montreal, Quebec [*Library symbol*] [*National Library of Canada*] (NLC)

QMCVDDH ... Que Me - Comite Vietnam pour la Defense des Droits de l'Homme [*Que Me - Vietnam Committee on Human Rights*] (EAIO)

QMCVM ... Commission des Valeurs Mobilieres du Quebec, Montreal, Quebec [*Library symbol*] [*National Library of Canada*] (NLC)

QMCW ...... Canada Wire & Cable Co. Ltd., Montreal, Quebec [*Library symbol*] [*National Library of Canada*] (NLC)

QMD .... Institut Genealogique Drouin, Montreal, Quebec [*Library symbol*] [*National Library of Canada*] (NLC)

QMDA .... Daniel Arbour & Associes, Montreal, Quebec [*Library symbol*] [*National Library of Canada*] (NLC)

QMDB .... College Jean-De-Brebeuf, Montreal, Quebec [*Library symbol*] [*National Library of Canada*] (NLC)

QMDC .... Dawson College, Montreal, Quebec [*Library symbol*] [*National Library of Canada*] (NLC)

QMDE .... Dominion Engineering Works Ltd., Montreal, Quebec [*Library symbol*] [*National Library of Canada*] (NLC)

QMDEP .... Quartermaster Depot [*Army*]

QMDH ...... Douglas Hospital Centre [*Centre Hospitalier Douglas*] Montreal, Quebec [*Library symbol*] [*National Library of Canada*] (NLC)

QMDK .... Quick Mechanical Disconnect Kit

QMDL .... Domtar Ltd., Montreal, Quebec [*Library symbol*] [*National Library of Canada*] (NLC)

QMDM ..... Montreal Association for the Mentally Retarded [*Association de Montreal pour les Deficients Mentaux*] Quebec [*Library symbol*] [*National Library of Canada*] (NLC)

QMDMR .... Groupe DMR, Inc., Montreal, Quebec [*Library symbol*] [*National Library of Canada*] (BIB)

QMDO ...... Qualitative Materiel Development Objective [*Army*]

QMDOM ... Dominion Bridge Co. Ltd., Montreal, Quebec [*Library symbol*] [*National Library of Canada*] (NLC)

QMDPC .... Quartermaster Data Processing Center [*Army*]

QMDT .... Dominion Textile, Montreal, Quebec [*Library symbol*] [*National Library of Canada*] (NLC)

QME .... Quarber Merkur [*A publication*]

QMEA .... Atmospheric Environment Service, Environment Canada [*Service de l'Environnement Atmospherique, Environnement Canada*] Dorval, Quebec [*Library symbol*] [*National Library of Canada*] (NLC)

QMEC .... Monenco Consultants Ltd., Montreal, Quebec [*Library symbol*] [*National Library of Canada*] (NLC)

QMECB .... Centrale des Bibliotheques, Services Documentaires Multimedia, Inc., Montreal, Quebec [*Library symbol*] [*National Library of Canada*] (NLC)

QMECS ..... Experts-Conseils Shawinigan, Montreal, Quebec [*Library symbol*] [*National Library of Canada*] (NLC)

QMED .... Quest Medical, Inc. [*NASDAQ symbol*] (NQ)

Q Med Rev ... Quarterly Medical Review [*A publication*]

QMEE .... Environmental Protection Service, Environment Canada [*Service de la Protection de l'Environnement, Environnement Canada*] Montreal, Quebec [*Library symbol*] [*National Library of Canada*] (NLC)

QMEM ...... Bibliotheque Municipale de la Ville de Montreal-Est, Quebec [*Library symbol*] [*National Library of Canada*] (BIB)

QMEN .... Ministere de l'Environnement, Montreal, Quebec [*Library symbol*] [*National Library of Canada*] (NLC)

QMENT .... National Theatre School [*Ecole Nationale de Theatre*] Montreal, Quebec [*Library symbol*] [*National Library of Canada*] (NLC)

QMEP .... Ecole Polytechnique, Montreal, Quebec [*Library symbol*] [*National Library of Canada*] (NLC)

QMEPCC ... Quartermaster Equipment and Parts Commodity Center [*Army*]

QMERS ..... E. R. Squibb & Sons Ltd., Montreal, Quebec [*Library symbol*] [*National Library of Canada*] (NLC)

QMES .... Ecole Secondaire Saint-Stanislas, Montreal, Quebec [*Library symbol*] [*National Library of Canada*] (NLC)

QMF .... Fraser-Hickson Institute, Montreal, Quebec [*Library symbol*] [*National Library of Canada*] (NLC)

QMF .... Query Management Facility [*Database*] (BYTE)

QMFA .... Montreal Museum of Fine Arts [*Musee des Beaux-Arts de Montreal*] Quebec [*Library symbol*] [*National Library of Canada*] (NLC)

QMFAC .... Farinon Canada, Dorval, Quebec [*Library symbol*] [*National Library of Canada*] (NLC)

QMFBD .... Federal Business Development Bank [*Banque Federale de Developpement*] Montreal, Quebec [*Library symbol*] [*National Library of Canada*] (NLC)

QMFC .... First Church of Christ, Scientist, Montreal, Quebec [*Library symbol*] [*National Library of Canada*] (NLC)

QMFCIAF ... Quartermaster Food and Container Institute for the Armed Forces

QMFCJ ..... Bibliotheque de Theologie, les Facultes de la Compagnie de Jesus, Montreal, Quebec [*Library symbol*] [*National Library of Canada*] (NLC)

QMFER ..... Forest Engineering Research Institute of Canada [*Institut Canadien de Recherches en Genie Forestier*] Pointe-Claire, Quebec [*Library symbol*] [*National Library of Canada*] (NLC)

QMFH .... Frank W. Horner Ltd., Montreal, Quebec [*Library symbol*] [*National Library of Canada*] (NLC)

QMFMO... Federation des Medecins Omnipraticiens du Quebec, Montreal, Quebec [*Library symbol*] [*National Library of Canada*] (NLC)

QMFMS.... Federation des Medecins Specialistes du Quebec, Montreal, Quebec [*Library symbol*] [*National Library of Canada*] (NLC)

QMFR .... Arctic Biological Station, Fisheries and Oceans Canada [*Station Biologique de l'Arctique, Peches et Oceans Canada*] Ste-Anne-De-Bellevue, Quebec [*Library symbol*] [*National Library of Canada*] (NLC)

QMFRA .... Archives des Franciscains, Montreal, Quebec [*Library symbol*] [*National Library of Canada*] (NLC)

QMFRAN ... Studium Franciscain de Theologie, Montreal, Quebec [*Library symbol*] [*National Library of Canada*] (NLC)

QMFSGA ... Archives des Freres de Saint-Gabriel, Montreal, Quebec [*Library symbol*] [*National Library of Canada*] (NLC)

QMG .... QMG Holdings, Inc. [*Toronto Stock Exchange symbol*]

QMG .... Quartermaster General [*Army*]

QMG .... Quench Melt Growth [*Physics*]

QMG .... Sir George Williams Campus, Concordia University, Montreal, Quebec [*Library symbol*] [*National Library of Canada*] (NLC)

QMGA....... Montreal Gazette, Quebec [*Library symbol*] [*National Library of Canada*] (NLC)

QMGB .... Grands Ballets Canadiens, Montreal, Quebec [*Library symbol*] [*National Library of Canada*] (NLC)

QMGDH ... Grace Dart Hospital Center, Montreal, Quebec [*Library symbol*] [*National Library of Canada*] (NLC)

QM Gen..... Quartermaster General [*Military*] (GFGA)

QMGF....... Quartermaster-General to the Forces [*Military*] [*British*]

QMGG....... Department of Geography, Sir George Williams Campus, Concordia University, Montreal, Quebec [*Library symbol*] [*National Library of Canada*] (NLC)

QMGGM... University Map Collection, Department of Geography, Sir George Williams Campus, Concordia University, Montreal, Quebec [*Library symbol*] [*National Library of Canada*] (NLC)

QMGH ...... Montreal General Hospital [*Hopital General de Montreal*] Quebec [*Library symbol*] [*National Library of Canada*] (NLC)

QMGHC ... Community Health Department, Montreal General Hospital [*Departement de Sante Communautaire, Hopital General de Montreal*], Quebec [*Library symbol*] [*National Library of Canada*] (NLC)

QMGHN ... Nurses' Library, Montreal General Hospital [*Bibliotheque des Infirmieres, Hopital General de Montreal*], Quebec [*Library symbol*] [*National Library of Canada*] (NLC)

QMGL....... Genstar Ltd., Montreal, Quebec [*Library symbol*] [*National Library of Canada*] (NLC)

QMGLS..... Library Studies Program, Concordia University, Montreal, Quebec [*Library symbol*] [*National Library of Canada*] (NLC)

QMGM...... Gaz Metropolitain, Montreal, Quebec [*Library symbol*] [*National Library of Canada*] (BIB)

QMGMC... Quartermaster-General of the Marine Corps

QMGO ...... Quartermaster-General's Office [*Military*] [*British*] (ROG)

QMGP....... Gerard Parizeau Ltee, Montreal, Quebec [*Library symbol*] [*National Library of Canada*] (NLC)

QMGPA .... Quarry Management and Products [*Later, Quarry Management*] [*A publication*]

QMGS .... Grand Seminaire, Montreal, Quebec [*Library symbol*] [*National Library of Canada*] (NLC)

QMH .... Hydro-Quebec, Montreal, Quebec [*Library symbol*] [*National Library of Canada*] (NLC)

QMH .... Queens Moat Houses [*Hoteller*] [*British*]

QMHC ...... Medical Library, Hoechst Canada, Inc., Montreal, Quebec [*Library symbol*] [*National Library of Canada*] (BIB)

QMHCL.... Bibliotheque Medicale, Hopital Charles Lemoyne, Greenfield Park, Quebec [*Library symbol*] [*National Library of Canada*] (NLC)

QMHCLC ... Departement de Sante Communautaire, Hopital Charles Lemoyne, Greenfield Park, Quebec [*Library symbol*] [*National Library of Canada*] (NLC)

QMHD ...... Hotel-Dieu de Montreal, Quebec [*Library symbol*] [*National Library of Canada*] (NLC)

QMHDE.... Centre de Documentation, Direction de l'Environnement, Hydro-Quebec, Montreal, Quebec [*Library symbol*] [*National Library of Canada*] (NLC)

QMHE....... Ecole des Hautes Etudes Commerciales, Montreal, Quebec [*Library symbol*] [*National Library of Canada*] (NLC)

QMHGC ... Centre Hospitalier de Verdun, Quebec [*Library symbol*] [*National Library of Canada*] (NLC)

QMHGF.... Hopital General Fleury, Montreal, Quebec [*Library symbol*] [*National Library of Canada*] (NLC)

QMHI........ Centre de Documentation, Hydro-Quebec International, Montreal, Quebec [*Library symbol*] [*National Library of Canada*] (BIB)

QMHJR .... Centre de Documentation du Personnel, Hopital de Convalescents Julius Richardson [*Staff Library, Julius Richardson Convalescent Hospital, Inc.*], Montreal, Quebec [*Library symbol*] [*National Library of Canada*] (NLC)

QMHJT .... Hopital Jean Talon, Montreal, Quebec [*Library symbol*] [*National Library of Canada*] (NLC)

QMHM ..... Centre Hospitalier Jacques Viger, Montreal, Quebec [*Library symbol*] [*National Library of Canada*] (NLC)

QMHME... Hopital Marie-Enfant, Montreal, Quebec [*Library symbol*] [*National Library of Canada*] (NLC)

QMHMR .. Hopital Maisonneuve-Rosemont, Montreal, Quebec [*Library symbol*] [*National Library of Canada*] (NLC)

QMHND ... Hopital Notre-Dame, Montreal, Quebec [*Library symbol*] [*National Library of Canada*] (NLC)

QMHNDI ... Bibliotheque des Services Infirmiers, Hopital Notre-Dame, Montreal, Quebec [*Library symbol*] [*National Library of Canada*] (NLC)

QMHP...... Qualified Mental Health Professional

QMHRP.... Hopital Riviere-Des-Prairies, Montreal, Quebec [*Library symbol*] [*National Library of Canada*] (NLC)

QMHRT.... Centre de Documentation, Redaction et Terminologie, Hydro-Quebec, Montreal, Quebec [*Library symbol*] [*National Library of Canada*] (BIB)

QMHSC .... Hopital du Sacre-Coeur, Montreal, Quebec [*Library symbol*] [*National Library of Canada*] (NLC)

QMHSCA ... Hopital Santa Cabrini, Montreal, Quebec [*Library symbol*] [*National Library of Canada*] (NLC)

QMHSJ..... Hopital Louis H. LaFonataine, Montreal, Quebec [*Library symbol*] [*National Library of Canada*] (NLC)

QMHSJA ... Hopital Ste-Jeanne-D'Arc, Montreal, Quebec [*Library symbol*] [*National Library of Canada*] (NLC)

QMHSL .... Hopital Saint-Luc, Montreal, Quebec [*Library symbol*] [*National Library of Canada*] (NLC)

QMHSLC ... Departement de Sante Communautaire, Hopital Saint-Luc, Montreal, Quebec [*Library symbol*] [*National Library of Canada*] (NLC)

QMHVG ... Centre de Documentation, Verification Generale, Hydro-Quebec, Montreal, Quebec [*Library symbol*] [*National Library of Canada*] (BIB)

QMI.......... Insurance Institute of the Province of Quebec [*Insitut d'Assurance du Quebec*] Montreal, Quebec [*Library symbol*] [*National Library of Canada*] (NLC)

QMI.......... Qualification Maintainability Inspection

QMIA........ International Air Transport Association [*Association du Transport Aerien International*] Montreal, Quebec [*Library symbol*] [*National Library of Canada*] (NLC)

QMIA........ Quartermaster Intelligence Agency [*Merged with Defense Intelligence Agency*]

QMIAA ..... Institut des Arts Appliques, Montreal, Quebec [*Library symbol*] [*National Library of Canada*] (NLC)

QMIAG ..... Institut des Arts Graphiques, Montreal, Quebec [*Library symbol*] [*National Library of Canada*] (NLC)

QMIAP...... Pavillon Albert Prevost, Montreal, Quebec [*Library symbol*] [*National Library of Canada*] (NLC)

QMIC .... International Civil Aviation Organization [*Organisation de l'Aviation Civile Internationale*] Montreal, Quebec [*Library symbol*] [*National Library of Canada*] (NLC)

QMICA ..... Institute of Chartered Accountants of Quebec [*Institut Canadien des Comptables Agrees du Quebec*] Montreal, Quebec [*Library symbol*] [*National Library of Canada*] (NLC)

QMICAV... Institut Culturel Avataq, Montreal, Quebec [*Library symbol*] [*National Library of Canada*] (BIB)

QMICE...... Canadian Institute of Adult Education [*Institut Canadien d'Education des Adultes*] Montreal, Quebec [*Library symbol*] [*National Library of Canada*] (NLC)

QMICM .... Institut de Cardiologie de Montreal, Quebec [*Library symbol*] [*National Library of Canada*] (NLC)

QMIF .... Imasco Foods Ltd., Montreal, Quebec [*Library symbol*] [*National Library of Canada*] (NLC)

QMIFQ ..... Informatech France-Quebec, Montreal, Quebec [*Library symbol*] [*National Library of Canada*] (NLC)

QMIG........ Industrial Grain Products Ltd., Montreal, Quebec [*Library symbol*] [*National Library of Canada*] (NLC)

QMII .... Istituto Italiano di Cultura, Montreal, Quebec [*Library symbol*] [*National Library of Canada*] (NLC)

QMIIS....... Islamic Studies Library, McGill University, Montreal, Quebec [*Library symbol*] [*National Library of Canada*] (NLC)

QMIIST .... International Institute of Stress [*Institut International du Stress*] Montreal, Quebec [*Library symbol*] [*Obsolete*] [*National Library of Canada*] (NLC)

QMIKES ... Quadrupole Mass Analyzed Ion Kinetic Energy Spectroscopy

QMILO ..... International Labour Office [*Bureau International du Travail*] Montreal, Quebec [*Library symbol*] [*National Library of Canada*] (NLC)

QMIM .... Institut Armand-Frappier, Universite du Quebc, Laval, Quebec [*Library symbol*] [*National Library of Canada*] (NLC)

QMIMM... Ministere des Communautes Culturelles et de l'Immigration, Montreal, Quebec [*Library symbol*] [*National Library of Canada*] (NLC)

QMIMSO ... Quartermaster Industrial Mobilization Services Offices [*Army*]

QMINC ..... Institut du Cancer de Montreal, Quebec [*Library symbol*] [*National Library of Canada*] (NLC)

QMINCA .. Institut National Canadien pour les Aveugles, Montreal, Quebec [*Library symbol*] [*National Library of Canada*] (NLC)

QMINP ..... Institut National de Productivite, Montreal, Quebec [*Library symbol*] [*National Library of Canada*] (NLC)

QMIP .... Institute of Parasitoloy, Macdonald College, Ste-Anne-De-Bellevue, Quebec [*Library symbol*] [*National Library of Canada*] (NLC)

QMIPP ...... Institut Philippe Pinel de Montreal, Quebec [*Library symbol*] [*National Library of Canada*] (NLC)

QMIRC ..... Institut de Recherches Cliniques, Montreal, Quebec [*Library symbol*] [*National Library of Canada*] (NLC)

QMIRP ...... Institute for Research on Public Policy [*Institut de Recherches Politiques*] Montreal, Quebec [*Library symbol*] [*National Library of Canada*] (NLC)

QMIRS ..... Informatheque IRSST [*Institut de Recherche en Sante et Securite au Travail*] Montreal, Quebec [*Library symbol*] [*National Library of Canada*] (NLC)

QMIS .... Quality Review Management Information System [*IRS*]

QMISM ..... Centre de Documentation, Institut Raymond-Dewar, Montreal, Quebec [*Library symbol*] [*National Library of Canada*] (NLC)

QMIST ...... Centre d'Information, IST [*Industriel Services Techniques*], Montreal, Quebec [*Library symbol*] [*National Library of Canada*] (BIB)

QMIT .... Imperial Tobacco Co. of Canada Ltd., Montreal, Quebec [*Library symbol*] [*National Library of Canada*] (NLC)

QMITR ...... Research Library, Imperial Tobacco Co. of Canada Ltd., Montreal, Quebec [*Library symbol*] [*National Library of Canada*] (NLC)

QMJ .... Jewish Public Library [*Bibliotheque Juive Publique, Montreal*] Quebec [*Library symbol*] [*National Library of Canada*] (NLC)

QMJB .... Jardin Botanique, Montreal, Quebec [*Library symbol*] [*National Library of Canada*] (NLC)

QMJES ..... Technical Services, Joseph E. Seagram & Sons Ltd., La Salle, Quebec [*Library symbol*] [*National Library of Canada*] (NLC)

QMJG .... Jewish General Hospital, Montreal, Quebec [*Library symbol*] [*National Library of Canada*] (NLC)

QMJGI ...... Institute of Community and Family Psychiatry, Jewish General Hospital, Montreal, Quebec [*Library symbol*] [*National Library of Canada*] (NLC)

QMJGL ..... Lady Davis Institute for Medical Research, Jewish General Hospital, Montreal, Quebec [*Library symbol*] [*National Library of Canada*] (NLC)

QMJH .... Hopital de Mont-Joli, Inc., Quebec [*Library symbol*] [*National Library of Canada*] (NLC)

QMJHW ... Johnson & Higgins, Willis, Faber Ltd., Montreal, Quebec [*Library symbol*] [*National Library of Canada*] (NLC)

QMJJ .... Johnson & Johnson Ltd., Montreal, Quebec [*Library symbol*] [*National Library of Canada*] (NLC)

QMJL .... John Lovell & Son City Directories Ltd., Montreal, Quebec [*Library symbol*] [*National Library of Canada*] (NLC)

QMJLP ..... Laboratoire de Police Scientifique, Montreal, Quebec [*Library symbol*] [*National Library of Canada*] (NLC)

QMJM ...... Canada Department of Justice [*Ministere de la Justice*] Montreal, Quebec [*Library symbol*] [*National Library of Canada*] (NLC)

QMJRH .... James R. Hay & Associates, Pointe Claire, Quebec [*Library symbol*] [*National Library of Canada*] (BIB)

QMJSJ ...... Commission des Services Juridiques du Quebec, Montreal, Quebec [*Library symbol*] [*National Library of Canada*] (NLC)

QML .... Loyola Campus, Concordia University, Montreal, Quebec [*Library symbol*] [*National Library of Canada*] (NLC)

QML .... Qayyum Moslem League [*Pakistan*] (PD)

QML .... Qualified Manufacturers List [*DoD*]

QMLA .... Laboratoires Abbott Ltee, Montreal, Quebec [*Library symbol*] [*National Library of Canada*] (NLC)

QMLAV .... Lavalin, Inc., Montreal, Quebec [*Library symbol*] [*National Library of Canada*] (BIB)

QMLAVE ... Lavalin Environment, Inc., Montreal, Quebec [*Library symbol*] [*National Library of Canada*] (BIB)

QMLBD .... Lafleur, Brown & De Granpre, Montreal, Quebec [*Library symbol*] [*National Library of Canada*] (BIB)

QMLCA .... Lower Canada Arms Collectors Association, Montreal, Quebec [*Library symbol*] [*National Library of Canada*] (NLC)

QMLCC ..... Lower Canada College Montreal, Quebec [*Library symbol*] [*National Library of Canada*] (NLC)

QMLCPF .. Bibliotheque de la Faune, Ministere du Loisir, de la Chasse et de la Peche, Montreal, Quebec [*Library symbol*] [*National Library of Canada*] (NLC)

QMLF .... Librairies Flammarion, Montreal, Quebec [*Library symbol*] [*National Library of Canada*] (NLC)

QMLG .... Lakeshore General Hospital [*Hopital General du Lakeshore*] Pointe-Claire, Quebec [*Library symbol*] [*National Library of Canada*] (NLC)

QMLGC .... Community Health Department, Lakeshore General Hospital [*Departement de Sante Communautaire, Hopital General du Lakeshore*], Pointe-Claire, Quebec [*Library symbol*] [*National Library of Canada*] (NLC)

QMLM ...... Bibliotheque Municipale, Mont-Laurier, Quebec [*Library symbol*] [*National Library of Canada*] (NLC)

QMLP .... Centre de Documentation, La Presse Ltee., Montreal, Quebec [*Library symbol*] [*National Library of Canada*] (NLC)

QMLPT ..... Librairie Pointe-Aux-Trembles, Quebec [*Library symbol*] [*National Library of Canada*] (NLC)

QMLQ .... Centre de Documentation, Loto-Quebec, Montreal, Quebec [*Library symbol*] [*National Library of Canada*] (NLC)

QMLR .... Constance-Lethbridge Rehabilitation Centre [*Centre de Readaptation Constance-Lethbridge*] Montreal, Quebec [*Library symbol*] [*National Library of Canada*] (NLC)

QMM .... McLennan Library, McGill University, Montreal, Quebec [*Library symbol*] [*National Library of Canada*] (NLC)

QMMAC ... Musee d'Art Contemporain, Montreal, Quebec [*Library symbol*] [*National Library of Canada*] (NLC)

QMMAQ ... La Magnetotheque, Montreal, Quebec [*Library symbol*] [*National Library of Canada*] (NLC)

QMMAR ... Marianapolis College, Montreal, Quebec [*Library symbol*] [*National Library of Canada*] (NLC)

QMMB ...... Blackader/Lauterman Library of Architecture and Art, McGill University, Montreal, Quebec [*Library symbol*] [*National Library of Canada*] (NLC)

QMMBC ... Molson Breweries of Canada Ltd., Montreal, Quebec [*Library symbol*] [*Obsolete*] [*National Library of Canada*] (NLC)

QMMBG ... Botany-Genetics Library, McGill University, Montreal, Quebec [*Library symbol*] [*National Library of Canada*] (BIB)

QMMBZ ... Blacker-Wood Library of Zoology and Ornithology, McGill University, Montreal, Quebec [*Library symbol*] [*National Library of Canada*] (NLC)

QMMC ...... Miron Co. Ltd., Montreal, Quebec [*Library symbol*] [*National Library of Canada*] (NLC)

QMMCH .. Montreal Children's Hospital, Quebec [*Library symbol*] [*National Library of Canada*] (NLC)

QMMCR ... Musee du Chateau de Ramezay, Montreal, Quebec [*Library symbol*] [*National Library of Canada*] (NLC)

QMMD ..... Religious Studies Library, McGill University, Montreal, Quebec [*Library symbol*] [*National Library of Canada*] (NLC)

QMME ...... Physical Sciences and Engineering Library, McGill University, Montreal, Quebec [*Library symbol*] [*National Library of Canada*] (NLC)

QMMG ...... Map and Air Photo Library, McGill University, Montreal, Quebec [*Library symbol*] [*National Library of Canada*] (NLC)

QMMGS ... Department of Geological Sciences, McGill University, Montreal, Quebec [*Library symbol*] [*National Library of Canada*] (NLC)

QMMH ..... Mental Hygiene Istitute [*Institut de l'Hygiene Mentale*] Montreal, Quebec [*Library symbol*] [*National Library of Canada*] (NLC)

QMMHH ... Maimonides Hospital Geriatric Center [*Centre Hospitalier Geriatrique Maimonides*], Montreal, Quebec [*Library symbol*] [*National Library of Canada*] (NLC)

QMMI .... Atwater Library [*Formerly, Mechanics Institute Library*] Montreal, Quebec [*Library symbol*] [*National Library of Canada*] (NLC)

QMMIQ .... Quebec Regional Office, Employment and Immigration Canada [*Bureau Regional du Quebec, Emploi et Immigration Canada*] Montreal, Quebec [*Library symbol*] [*National Library of Canada*] (NLC)

QMML ...... Law Library, McGill University, Montreal, Quebec [*Library symbol*] [*National Library of Canada*] (NLC)

QMMLS .... Library Science Library, McGill University, Montreal, Quebec [*Library symbol*] [*National Library of Canada*] (NLC)

QMMM ..... Medical Library, McGill University, Montreal, Quebec [*Library symbol*] [*National Library of Canada*] (NLC)

QMMMCM ... McCord Museum, McGill University, Montreal, Quebec [*Library symbol*] [*National Library of Canada*] (NLC)

QMMMDM ... Marvin Duchow Music Library, McGill University, Montreal, Quebec [*Library symbol*] [*National Library of Canada*] (NLC)

QMMMM ... Montreal Military and Maritime Museum, Quebec [*Library symbol*] [*National Library of Canada*] (NLC)

QMMN ..... Nursing/Social Work Library, McGill University, Montreal, Quebec [*Library symbol*] [*National Library of Canada*] (NLC)

QMMO ..... Osler Library, McGill University, Montreal, Quebec [*Library symbol*] [*National Library of Canada*] (NLC)

QMMOC ... Monsanto Canada Ltd., Montreal, Quebec [*Library symbol*] [*National Library of Canada*] (NLC)

QMMOS ... Montreal Star, Quebec [*Library symbol*] [*National Library of Canada*] (NLC)

QMMPB ... MPB Technologies, Dorval, Quebec [*Library symbol*] [*National Library of Canada*] (NLC)

QMMRB ... Department of Rare Books and Special Collections, McGill University, Montreal, Quebec [*Library symbol*] [*National Library of Canada*] (NLC)

QMMRS ... Mendelsohn Rosentzveig Shacter, Montreal, Quebec [*Library symbol*] [*National Library of Canada*]   (BIB)

QMMSC ... Howard Ross Library of Management, McGill University, Montreal, Quebec [*Library symbol*] [*National Library of Canada*]   (NLC)

QMMSR ... Centre de Documentation, Ministere de la Main-d'Oeuvre et de la Securite du Revenu du Quebec, Montreal, Quebec [*Library symbol*] [*National Library of Canada*]   (NLC)

QMN .... Centres Biblio-Culturels de Montreal-Nord, Quebec [*Library symbol*] [*National Library of Canada*]   (NLC)

QMNA ...... Canadian Pulp and Paper Asssociation [*Association Canadienne des Producteurs dePates et Papiers*] Montreal, Quebec [*Library symbol*] [*National Library of Canada*]   (NLC)

QMNB...... Biotechnology Branch, CISTI [*Canada Institute for Scienctific and Technical Information*] [*Annexe de Biotechnologie, ICIST*], Montreal, Quebec [*Library symbol*] [*National Library of Canada*]   (BIB)

QMNDE.... Hopital Notre-Dame-De-L'Esperance-De-St-Laurent, Montreal, Quebec [*Library symbol*] [*National Library of Canada*]   (NLC)

QMNE...... Northern Electric Co. Ltd., Montreal, Quebec [*Library symbol*] [*National Library of Canada*]   (NLC)

QMNF...... National Film Board, Montreal [*Formerly, Ottawa*] [*Office National du Film, Montreal (Anciennement Ottawa)*] Quebec [*Library symbol*] [*National Library of Canada*]   (NLC)

QMNFNI .. National Information/Distribution System, National Film Board [*Systeme d'Information et de Distribution pour les Produits Audio-Visuels Canadiens, Office National du film*] Montreal, Quebec [*Library symbol*] [*National Library of Canada*]   (NLC)

QMNHH... Health Protection Branch, Canada Department of National Health and Welfare [*Direction Generale de la Protection de la Sante, Ministere de la Sante Nationale et du Bien-Etre Social*] Montreal, Quebec [*Library symbol*] [*National Library of Canada*]   (NLC)

QMNIH .... Montreal Neurological Institute and Hospital [*Institut et Hopital Neurologiques de Montreal*] Quebec [*Library symbol*] [*National Library of Canada*]   (NLC)

QMNOT.... Northern Telecom Canada Ltd., Montreal, Quebec [*Library symbol*] [*National Library of Canada*]   (NLC)

QMNR...... Noranda Research Centre, Pointe-Claire, Quebec [*Library symbol*] [*National Library of Canada*]   (NLC)

QMNT...... Nesbitt, Thomson & Co. Ltd., Montreal, Quebec [*Library symbol*] [*National Library of Canada*]   (NLC)

QMO .... Oratoire Saint-Joseph, Montreal, Quebec [*Library symbol*] [*National Library of Canada*]   (NLC)

QMO .... Qualitative Materiel Objective [*Army*]   (AABC)

QMO .... Quartz Mountain State Park [*Oklahoma*] [*Seismograph station code, US Geological Survey*]   (SEIS)

QMO .... Queen Mary's Own [*British military*]   (DMA)

QMOB...... Office de Biologie, Ministere du Loisir, de la Chasse et de la Peche, Montreal, Quebec [*Library symbol*] [*Obsolete*] [*National Library of Canada*]   (NLC)

QMobSC ... Quadripartite Mobility Standardization Committee [*Military*]   (AABC)

QMOCP.... Canadian Livestock Feed Board [*Office Canadien des Provendes*] Montreal, Quebec [*Library symbol*] [*National Library of Canada*]   (NLC)

QMOCQ... Office de la Construction du Quebec, Montreal, Quebec [*Library symbol*] [*National Library of Canada*]   (NLC)

QMOF...... Ogilvie Flour Mills Co. Ltd., Montreal, Quebec [*Library symbol*] [*National Library of Canada*]   (NLC)

QMOFJ..... Office Franco-Quebecois pour la Jeunesse, Montreal, Quebec [*Library symbol*] [*National Library of Canada*]   (NLC)

QMOI........ Ordre des Infirmieres et Infirmiers du Quebec, Montreal, Quebec [*Library symbol*] [*National Library of Canada*]   (NLC)

QMOLF .... Office de la Langue Francaise, Montreal, PQ, Canada [*Library symbol*] [*National Library of Canada*]   (NLC)

QMO & O ... Quebec, Montreal, Ottawa & Occidental [*Railway*]

QMOP...... Centre de Documentation, Office de Planification et de Developpement du Quebec, Montreal, Quebec [*Library symbol*] [*National Library of Canada*]   (BIB)

QMOR...... Ogilvy, Renaud Law Library, Montreal, Quebec [*Library symbol*] [*National Library of Canada*]   (BIB)

QMORC.... Quartermaster Officers' Reserve Corps [*Military*]

Q(Mov)...... Quartermaster Movements [*World War II*]

QMOW ..... Quartermaster of the Watch [*Navy*]   (DNAB)

QMP......... Qualitative Management Program [*Army*]   (INF)

QMP......... Quarry, Mine, and Pit [*A publication*]   (APTA)

QMPA ...... Centre de Documentation, Projet Archipel de Montreal, Quebec [*Library symbol*] [*National Library of Canada*]   (NLC)

QMPA ...... Quartermaster Purchasing Agency [*Army*]

QMPAE .... Paramax Electronics, Montreal, Quebec [*Library symbol*] [*National Library of Canada*]   (BIB)

QMPC ...... Presbyterian College, Montreal, Quebec [*Library symbol*] [*National Library of Canada*]   (NLC)

QMPC ...... Quartermaster Petroleum Center [*Army*]   (MUGU)

QMPCA .... Agriculture Canada, Montreal, Quebec [*Library symbol*] [*National Library of Canada*]   (NLC)

QMPCG .... Documentation Centre, George Etienne Cartier House, Parks Canada [*Centre de Documentation, Maison George-Etienne Cartier, Parcs Canada*], Montreal, Quebec [*Library symbol*] [*National Library of Canada*]   (NLC)

QMPCUSA ... Quartermaster Petroleum Center, United States Army

QMPE .... Pezaris Electronics Co., Montreal, Quebec [*Library symbol*] [*National Library of Canada*]   (NLC)

QMPI .... Polish Institute of Arts and Sciences in Canada [*Institut Polonais des Arts et des Sciences au Canada*] Montreal, Quebec [*Library symbol*] [*National Library of Canada*]   (NLC)

QMPM...... Peat, Marwick, Mitchell et Cie., Montreal, Quebec [*Library symbol*] [*National Library of Canada*]   (NLC)

QMPM...... Quantitative Methods for Public Management [*Course*]

QMPP .... Pulp and Paper Research Institute of Canada [*Institut Canadien de Recherches sur les Pates et Papiers*] Pointe-Claire, Quebec [*Library symbol*] [*National Library of Canada*]   (NLC)

QMPPM ... Montreal Branch, Pulp and Paper Research Institute of Canada [*Succursale de Montreal, Centre Canadien de Recherche sur les Pates et Papiers*], Quebec [*Library symbol*] [*National Library of Canada*]   (BIB)

QMPRA .... Archives Providence, Montreal, Quebec [*Library symbol*] [*National Library of Canada*]   (NLC)

QMPSB..... Protestant School Board of Greater Montreal, Quebec [*Library symbol*] [*National Library of Canada*]   (NLC)

QMPSR..... P. S. Ross & Partners, Montreal, Quebec   (NLC)

QMPTI...... Potton Technical Industries, Mansonville, Quebec [*Library symbol*] [*National Library of Canada*]   (NLC)

QMPWQ... Quebec Region Library, Public Works Canada [*Bibliotheque de la Region du Quebec, Travaux Publics Canada*] Montreal, Quebec [*Library symbol*] [*National Library of Canada*]   (NLC)

QMQ .... Queen Mary Veterans Hospital [*Hopital Reine-Marie (Anciens combattants)*] Montreal, Quebec [*Library symbol*] [*National Library of Canada*]   (NLC)

QMQAR.... Centre Regional de Montreal, Archives Nationales du Quebec, Quebec [*Library symbol*] [*National Library of Canada*]   (NLC)

QMQAR.... Quebec Archives, Montreal, Quebec [*Library symbol*] [*National Library of Canada*]   (NLC)

QMQB....... Quick-Make, Quick-Break

QMQDP.... Commission des Droits de la Personne du Quebec, Montreal, Quebec [*Library symbol*] [*National Library of Canada*]   (NLC)

QMQE....... Queen Elizabeth Hospital, Montreal, Quebec [*Library symbol*] [*National Library of Canada*]   (NLC)

QMR......... Qualitative Material Report

QMR......... Qualitative Materiel Requirement [*Army*]

QMR......... Qualitative Military Requirements [*NATO*]   (NATG)

QMR......... Quartermaster

QMR......... Queen Mary's Regiment [*British military*]   (DMA)

QMR......... Royal Bank of Canada [*Banque Royale du Canada*] Montreal, Quebec [*Library symbol*] [*National Library of Canada*]   (NLC)

QMRA ...... Railway Association of Canada, Montreal, Quebec [*Library symbol*] [*National Library of Canada*]   (NLC)

QMRAD.... Centre de Documentation, Institut de Recherche Appliquee sur le Travail, Montreal, Quebec [*Library symbol*] [*National Library of Canada*]   (NLC)

QMRAQ.... Recherches Amerindiennes au Quebec, Montreal, Quebec [*Library symbol*] [*National Library of Canada*]   (NLC)

QMRC ...... Quartermaster Reserve Corps [*Military*]

QMRC .... Royal Canadian Air Force [*Corps d'Aviation Royale du Canada*] Montreal, Quebec [*Library symbol*].[*National Library of Canada*]   (NLC)

QMRCH.... Richmond County Historical Society [*Societe d'Histoire du Comte de Richmond*] Melbourne, Quebec   (NLC)

QMRCM ... Raymond, Chabot, Martin, Pare, Montreal, Quebec [*Library symbol*] [*National Library of Canada*]   (NLC)

QMRD...... Reader's Digest of Canada Ltd., Montreal, Quebec [*Library symbol*] [*National Library of Canada*]   (NLC)

QMRE .... Revenue Canada [*Revenu Canada*] Montreal, Quebec [*Library symbol*] [*National Library of Canada*]   (NLC)

QMREC .... Quartermaster Research and Engineering Command [*Army*]

QMREFEA ... Quartermaster Research and Engineering Field Evaluation Agency [*Merged with Troop Evaluation Test*]

QMREG .... Regie de l'Electricite et du Gaz, Montreal, Quebec [*Library symbol*] [*National Library of Canada*]   (NLC)

QMREX .... Canada Department of Regional Industrial Expansion [*Ministere de l'Expansion Industrielle Regionale*] Montreal, Quebec [*Library symbol*] [*National Library of Canada*]   (NLC)

QMRH ...... Centre de Recherches en Relations Humaines, Montreal, Quebec [*Library symbol*] [*National Library of Canada*]   (NLC)

QMRI........ Rehabilitation Institute of Montreal [*Institut de Rehabilitation de Montreal*] Quebec [*Library symbol*] [*National Library of Canada*]   (NLC)

QMRL .... Quartermaster Radiation Laboratory [*Army*]
QMRL .... Regie du Logement, Montreal, Quebec [*Library symbol*] [*National Library of Canada*] (NLC)
QMRM....... Reddy Memorial Hospital, Montreal, Quebec [*Library symbol*] [*National Library of Canada*] (NLC)
QMROS ..... Robinson-Sheppard, Montreal, Quebec [*Library symbol*] [*National Library of Canada*] (BIB)
QMRP .... Qualified Mental Retardation Professional
QMRP .... Rhone-Poulenc Pharma, Inc., Montreal, Quebec [*Library symbol*] [*National Library of Canada*] (NLC)
QMRPA .... Quartermaster Radiation Planning Agency [*Army*]
QMRQ...... Societe de Radio-Television du Quebec, Montreal, Quebec [*Library symbol*] [*National Library of Canada*] (NLC)
QMRR...... Rolls-Royce of Canada Ltd., Montreal, Quebec [*Library symbol*] [*National Library of Canada*] (NLC)
QMRRD..... Reginald P. Dawson Library, Town of Mount Royal, Quebec [*Library symbol*] [*National Library of Canada*] (NLC)
QMRS .... Information Centre, Canadian Security Intelligence Service [*Centre d'Information, Service Canadien du Renseignement de Securite*], Montreal, Quebec [*Library symbol*] [*National Library of Canada*] (BIB)
QMRSJA .. Archives des Religieuses Hospitalieres de Saint-Joseph, Montreal, Quebec [*Library symbol*] [*National Library of Canada*] (NLC)
QMRV....... Royal Victoria Hospital, Montreal, Quebec [*Library symbol*] [*National Library of Canada*] (NLC)
QMRVW ... Women's Pavilion, Royal Victoria Hospital, Montreal, Quebec [*Library symbol*] [*National Library of Canada*] (NLC)
QMS .... QMS, Inc. [*Associated Press abbreviation*] (APAG)
QMS .... Quadrupole Mass Spectrometer
QMS .... Quality Management System
QMS .... Quality Micro Systems [*Trademark*]
QMS .... Quality Monitoring System (MCD)
QMS .... Quarterly Journal. Mythic Society [*Bangalore*] [*A publication*]
QMS .... Quarterly Meteorological Summary [*Navy*] (DNAB)
QMS .... Quartermaster School [*Army*]
QMS .... Quartermaster Sergeant [*Military*]
QMS .... Quartermaster Stores [*Military*]
QMS .... Quicksilver Messenger Service [*Pop music group*]
QMS .... Sun Life of Canada [*Sun Life du Canada*] Montreal, Quebec [*Library symbol*] [*National Library of Canada*] (NLC)
QMSA ...... Seaman Apprentice, Quartermaster, Striker [*Navy rating*]
QMSA ...... Service de la Documentation, Ministere de la Sante et des Services Sociaux du Quebec, Montreal, Quebec [*Library symbol*] [*National Library of Canada*] (NLC)
QMSAC..... Sandoz Canada, Inc., Dorval, Quebec [*Library symbol*] [*National Library of Canada*] (NLC)
QMSAP..... Societe des Artistes Professionnels du Quebec, Montreal, Quebec [*Library symbol*] [*National Library of Canada*] (NLC)
QMSC ...... Southern Canada Power Co., Montreal, Quebec [*Library symbol*] [*National Library of Canada*] (NLC)
QMSCA..... Statistics Canada [*Statistique Canada*] Montreal, Quebec [*Library symbol*] [*National Library of Canada*] (NLC)
QMSCC..... Queen Mary's School Cadet Corps [*British military*] (DMA)
QMSCM ... Canadian Microfilming Co. Ltd. [*Societe Canadienne du Microfilm, Inc.*] Montreal, Quebec [*Library symbol*] [*National Library of Canada*] (NLC)
QMSD .... Information Resource Centre, Systems Development [*Centre d'Information Specialise, Systemes-Applications Pratiques*], Montreal, Quebec [*Library symbol*] [*National Library of Canada*] (BIB)
QMSDB .... Societe de Developpement de la Baie James, Montreal, Quebec [*Library symbol*] [*National Library of Canada*] (NLC)
QMSDI...... Centre de Documentation, SOGIC [*Societe Generale des Industries Culturelles du Quebec*], Montreal, Quebec [*Library symbol*] [*National Library of Canada*] (BIB)
QMSDL..... Sidbec-Dosco Ltd./Ltee., Montreal, Quebec [*Library symbol*] [*National Library of Canada*] (NLC)
QM Segt .... Quartermaster-Sergeant [*British military*] (DMA)
QMSG .... Queue Message [*Data processing*] (PCM)
QMSGA .... Archives Generales des Soeurs Grises, Montreal, Quebec [*Library symbol*] [*National Library of Canada*] (NLC)
QMSGE .... Office des Services de Garde a l'Enfance, Montreal, Quebec [*Library symbol*] [*National Library of Canada*] (NLC)
QMSGME ... Service General des Moyens d'Enseignement, Ministere de l'Education du Quebec, Montreal, Quebec [*Library symbol*] [*National Library of Canada*] (NLC)
QMSGT .... Quartermaster Sergeant [*Marine Corps*]
QMSH....... Societe Historique de Montreal, Quebec [*Library symbol*] [*National Library of Canada*] (NLC)
QMSHE .... Stadler Hurter, Montreal, Quebec [*Library symbol*] [*National Library of Canada*] (NLC)
QMSHQ.... Centre de Documentation, Societe d'Habitation du Quebec, Montreal, Quebec [*Library symbol*] [*National Library of Canada*] (BIB)
QMSI........ Quality Micro Systems [*NASDAQ symbol*] (NQ)
QMSI........ Quartermaster-Sergeant Instructor [*British military*] (DMA)
QMSI........ Scolasticat de l'Immaculee-Conception, Montreal, Quebec [*Library symbol*] [*National Library of Canada*] (NLC)

QMSIL...... Silicart, Inc., Montreal, Quebec [*Library symbol*] [*National Library of Canada*] (NLC)
QMSJ........ St. Joseph's Teachers' College, Montreal, Quebec [*Library symbol*] [*National Library of Canada*] (NLC)
QMSMA ... St. Mary's Hospital, Montreal, Quebec [*Library symbol*] [*National Library of Canada*] (NLC)
QMSN .... Seaman, Quartermaster, Striker [*Navy rating*]
QMSNC .... SNC, Inc., Montreal, Quebec [*Library symbol*] [*National Library of Canada*] (NLC)
QMSO ...... Quartermaster Supply Officer [*Army*]
QMSO .... Shell Oil Co. of Canada, Montreal, Quebec [*Library symbol*] [*National Library of Canada*] (NLC)
QMSOB ... Le Groupe SOBECO, Montreal, Quebec [*Library symbol*] [*National Library of Canada*] (NLC)
QMSQC .... Squibb Canada, Inc., Montreal, Quebec [*Library symbol*] [*National Library of Canada*] (NLC)
QMST .... Legal Department, Steinberg, Inc., Montreal, Quebec [*Library symbol*] [*National Library of Canada*] (NLC)
QMSTJ ..... Centre d'Information sur la Sante de l'Enfant, Hopital Sainte-Justine, Montreal, Quebec [*Library symbol*] [*National Library of Canada*] (NLC)
QMSTJS... Departement de Sante Communautaire, Hopital Sainte-Justine, Montreal, Quebec [*Library symbol*] [*National Library of Canada*] (NLC)
QMSU .... Surete du Quebec, Montreal, Quebec [*Library symbol*] [*National Library of Canada*] (NLC)
QMSVM ... Centre de Service Social Ville-Marie [*Ville-Marie Social Service Centre*] Montreal, Quebec [*Library symbol*] [*National Library of Canada*] (NLC)
QMSW ...... Quartz Metal Sealed Window
QMSW ...... Sherwin-Williams Co. of Canada Ltd., Montreal, Quebec [*Library symbol*] [*National Library of Canada*] (NLC)
QMSWP.... Shawinigan Engineering Ltd. Co., Montreal, Quebec [*Library symbol*] [*National Library of Canada*] (NLC)
QMT......... Montreal Trust Co., Quebec [*Library symbol*] [*National Library of Canada*] (NLC)
QMT......... Quantitative Muscle Testing [*Medicine*] (MAE)
QM-T........ Quartermaster-Trainee [*Navy*] (DNAB)
QMTA ...... Tomenson Alexander Ltd., Montreal, Quebec [*Library symbol*] [*National Library of Canada*] (NLC)
QMTC ...... Air Canada, Montreal, Quebec [*Library symbol*] [*National Library of Canada*] (NLC)
QMTD...... Transportation Development Centre, Transport Canada [*Centre de Developpement des Transports, Transports Canada*] Montreal, Quebec [*Library symbol*] [*National Library of Canada*] (NLC)
QMTGC .... Teleglobe Canada, Montreal, Quebec [*Library symbol*] [*National Library of Canada*] (NLC)
QMTH....... Institut de Tourisme et d'Hotellerie du Quebec, Montreal, Quebec [*Library symbol*] [*National Library of Canada*] (NLC)
QMTMO... Centre de Documentation, Ministere du Travail du Quebec, Montreal, Quebec [*Library symbol*] [*National Library of Canada*] (NLC)
QMTOE .... Quartermaster Table of Organization and Equipment [*Units*] [*Military*]
QMTQ....... Direction des Communications, Tourisme Quebec, Montreal, Quebec [*Library symbol*] [*National Library of Canada*] (BIB)
QMTQM... Trans Quebec & Maritimes, Montreal, Quebec [*Library symbol*] [*National Library of Canada*] (NLC)
QMTR....... Waterways Development, Transport Canada [*Developpement des vois Navigables, Transports Canada*] Montreal, Quebec [*Library symbol*] [*National Library of Canada*] (NLC)
QMTRA .... Centre de Documentation, Ministere des Transports du Quebec, Montreal, Quebec [*Library symbol*] [*National Library of Canada*] (NLC)
QMU .... Universite de Montreal, Quebec [*Library symbol*] [*National Library of Canada*] (NLC)
QMUA...... Service des Archives de l'Universite de Montreal, Quebec [*Library symbol*] [*National Library of Canada*] (NLC)
QMUC....... Union Carbide Canada Ltd., Pointe-Aux-Trembles, Quebec [*Library symbol*] [*National Library of Canada*] (NLC)
QMUDD ... Departement de Demographie, Universite de Montreal, Quebec [*Library symbol*] [*National Library of Canada*] (NLC)
QMUE....... Bibliotheque de l'Institut d'Etudes Medievales, Universite de Montreal, Quebec [*Library symbol*] [*National Library of Canada*] (NLC)
QMUEB .... Ecole de Bibliotheconomie, Universite de Montreal, Quebec [*Library symbol*] [*National Library of Canada*] (NLC)
QMUEC .... L'Ecole de Criminologie, Universite de Montreal, Quebec [*Library symbol*] [*National Library of Canada*] (NLC)
QMUGC.... Cartotheque, Departement de Geographie, Universite de Montreal, Quebec [*Library symbol*] [*National Library of Canada*] (NLC)
QMUGL.... Cartotheque, Institut de Geologie, Universite de Montreal, Quebec [*Library symbol*] [*National Library of Canada*] (NLC)
QMUQ ..... Universite de Quebec, Montreal, Quebec [*Library symbol*] [*National Library of Canada*] (NLC)

QMUQA ... Service des Archives de l'Universite du Quebec a Montreal [*Library symbol*] [*National Library of Canada*] (BIB)
QMUQC.... Cartotheque, Universite du Quebec, Montreal, Quebec [*Library symbol*] [*National Library of Canada*] (NLC)
QMUQEN ... Ecole Nationale d'Administration Publique, Universite du Quebec, Montreal, Quebec [*Library symbol*] [*National Library of Canada*] (NLC)
QMUQET ... Ecole de Technologie Superieure, Universite de Quebec, Montreal, Quebec [*Library symbol*] [*National Library of Canada*] (NLC)
QMUQIC .. Cartotheque, INRS-Urbanisation, Montreal, Quebec [*Library symbol*] [*National Library of Canada*] (NLC)
QMUQIS .. Centre de Documentation, INRS [*Institut National de la Recherche Scientifique*]-Sante, Montreal, Quebec [*Library symbol*] [*National Library of Canada*] (NLC)
QMUQIU ... Centre de Documentation INRS [*Institut National de la Recherche Scientifique*]-Urbanisation, Montreal, Quebec [*Library symbol*] [*National Library of Canada*] (NLC)
QMUQPA ... Pavillon des Arts, Universite du Quebec, Montreal, Quebec [*Library symbol*] [*National Library of Canada*] (NLC)
QMUQS.... Bibliotheque des Sciences, Universite du Quebec, Montreal [*Library symbol*] [*National Library of Canada*] (BIB)
QMUQTM ... Tele-Universite, Universite du Quebec, Montreal, Quebec [*Library symbol*] [*National Library of Canada*] (NLC)
Q Museum Memoirs ... Memoirs. Queensland Museum [*A publication*] (APTA)
QMV......... Qualified Majority Voting [*Napoleonic Code*]
QMV......... RCA Victor Co. Ltd., Montreal, Quebec [*Library symbol*] [*National Library of Canada*] (NLC)
QMVC....... Media Resource Centre, Vanier College, Montreal, Quebec [*Library symbol*] [*National Library of Canada*] (NLC)
QMVR....... Resource Centre, VIA Rail Canada, Inc. [*Centre de Documentation, VIA Rail Canada, Inc.*] Montreal, Quebec [*Library symbol*] [*National Library of Canada*] (NLC)
QMVRM ... Centre de Maintenance, VIA Rail, Montreal, Quebec [*Library symbol*] [*National Library of Canada*] (BIB)
QMW........ Quartz Metal Window
QMW........ Warnock Hersey Co. Ltd., Montreal, Quebec [*Library symbol*] [*National Library of Canada*] (NLC)
QMWM..... William M. Mercer, Montreal, Quebec [*Library symbol*] [*National Library of Canada*] (NLC)
QMY......... Queen Mary's Yeomanry [*British military*] (DMA)
QMY......... YWCA, Montreal, Quebec [*Library symbol*] [*National Library of Canada*] (NLC)
QMYH ...... YM - YWHA, Montreal, Quebec [*Library symbol*] [*National Library of Canada*] (NLC)
QN .... Kabo Air Travels [*Nigeria*] [*ICAO designator*] (FAAC)
QN .... Quantifier Negation [*Principle of logic*]
QN .... Quantum Number
QN .... Quaque Nocte [*Every Night*] [*Pharmacy*]
QN .... Quarterly Newsletter. American Bar Association [*A publication*] (DLA)
QN .... Quarterly Notes (ILCA)
QN .... Quarternote [*A publication*] (EAAP)
QN .... Queen (ADA)
QN .... Queen's Knight [*Chess*] (IIA)
QN .... Query Normalization
QN .... Question (FAAC)
QN .... Quetzalcoatlus Northropi [*Pterosaur, a model constructed for the Smithsonian Institution and referred to by these initials*]
QN .... Quintuple Screw (DS)
QN .... Quotation [*Investment term*]
QNA .... Quinuclidinol Atrolactate [*Organic chemistry*]
QNaN .... Quiet Not a Number [*Computer programming*] (BYTE)
QNat......... Quaestiones Naturales [*of Seneca the Younger*] [*Classical studies*] (OCD)
Q Nat Acc Bull ... Quarterly National Accounts Bulletin [*A publication*]
Q Natl Dent Assoc ... Quarterly. National Dental Association [*US*] [*A publication*]
Q Natl Fire Prot Assoc ... Quarterly. National Fire Protection Association [*A publication*]
QNB.......... Quinuclidinyl Benzilate [*Also, BZ*] [*Hallucinogen*]
QNC.......... New Castle Free Public Library, New Castle, PA [*OCLC symbol*] (OCLC)
QNCCR ..... Quarterly Notes on Christianity and Chinese Religion [*A publication*]
QNCH .... Quenched (MSA)
QNCHRN ... Centre Hospitalier Rouyn-Noranda, Noranda, Quebec [*Library symbol*] [*National Library of Canada*] (NLC)
QNCR........ Quarterly Noncompliance Report [*Environmental Protection Agency*] (GFGA)
QNCRS ..... Conseil Regional de la Sante et des Services Sociaux Rouyn-Noranda, Rouyn-Noranda, Quebec [*Library symbol*] [*National Library of Canada*] (NLC)
QND .... Quantum Nondemolition [*Method of measurement*]
QNE.......... Height Altimeter Set to 1013.2 Millibars Will Read on Landing [*Aviation code*] (AIA)
Q Newl-Spec Comm Env L ... Quarterly Newsletter. Special Committee on Environmental Law [*A publication*] (DLA)

Q News Bull Geol Soc S Afr ... Quarterly News Bulletin. Geological Society of South Africa [*A publication*]
Q Newsl Rhod Nurses Assoc ... Quarterly Newsletter. Rhodesia Nurses Association [*A publication*]
QNH......... Altimeter Subscale Setting to Obtain Elevation When on the Ground [*Aviation code*] (FAAC)
QNI........... Queen's Nursing Institute [*British*]
QNICA ...... Soeurs de L'Assomption, Nicolet, Quebec [*Library symbol*] [*National Library of Canada*] (NLC)
QNICS....... Seminaire de Nicolet, Quebec [*Library symbol*] [*National Library of Canada*] (NLC)
QNIP .... Institut de Police du Quebec, Nicolet, Quebec [*Library symbol*] [*National Library of Canada*] (NLC)
QNL.......... Quarterly News Letter [*Book Club of California*] [*A publication*]
QNM .... Quilter's Newsletter Magazine [*A publication*]
QN MAG... Quilter's Newsletter Magazine [*A publication*]
QNMC....... Quadripartite Nonmateriel Committee [*Military*] (AABC)
QNO........ Quinidine-N-oxide [*Organic chemistry*]
QNOAG .... Experimental Farm, Agriculture Canada [*Ferme Experimentale, Agriculture Canada*] Normandin, Quebec [*Library symbol*] [*National Library of Canada*] (NLC)
QNP.......... Queen's Knight's Pawn [*Chess*] (IIA)
QNS.......... Quantity Not Sufficient [*Pharmacy*]
QNSC........ Qui Nhon Support Command [*Vietnam*]
QNST .... Quick Neurological Screening Test
QNT.......... Quantizer (MDG)
QNT.......... Quintet [*Music*]
QNTJB...... Queensland and Northern Territory Judgements Bulletin [*Australia*] [*A publication*]
QNTL .... Quintel Corp. [*Tempe, AZ*] [*NASDAQ symbol*] (NQ)
QNTM....... Quantum Corp. [*NASDAQ symbol*] (NQ)
QNTY .... Quantity (AFM)
QO .... Otrag Range Air Service [*Zaire*] [*ICAO designator*] (FAAC)
QO .... Quaker Oats [*Trade name*]
QO .... Qualified Optician [*British*]
QO .... Qualified in Ordnance [*Obsolete*] [*Navy*]
QO .... Quartermaster Operation [*Military*]
QO .... Quarters Officer [*British military*] (DMA)
QO .... Queen's Own [*Military unit*] [*British*]
QO .... Quick Opening [*Nuclear energy*] (NRCH)
QO .... Quinoline Oxide [*Biochemistry*] (OA)
QO$_2$ .... Oxygen Quotient (AAMN)
QOBV....... Quick-Opening Blowdown Valve [*Nuclear energy*] (NRCH)
QOC.......... Quality of Conformance
QOC.......... Quasi-Optical Circuit
QOCG....... Queen's Own Corps of Guides [*British military*] (DMA)
QOCH....... Queen's Own Cameron Highlanders [*Military unit*] [*British*]
QOD .... Quality of Design
QOD .... Quantitative Oceanographic Data
QOD .... Quaque Otra Die [*Every Other Day*] [*Pharmacy*]
QOD .... Quick-Opening Device
QOD & WSY ... Queen's Own Dorset and West Somerset Yeomanry [*British military*] (DMA)
QODY....... Queen's Own Dorsetshire Yeomanry [*British military*] (DMA)
QOH .... Quantity on Hand
QOH .... Quaque Otra Hora [*Every Other Hour*] [*Pharmacy*]
QOH .... Queen's Own Hussars [*Military unit*] [*British*]
QOI........... Quality Operating Instruction
Q Oil Stat .. Quarterly Oil Statistics [*France*] [*A publication*]
QOL.......... Quality of Life [*Program*] [*Army*]
QOLCPF ... Bibliotheque de la Faune, Ministere du Loisir, de la Chasse, et de la Peche, Orsainville, Quebec [*Library symbol*] [*National Library of Canada*] (NLC)
QOLY .... Queen's Own Lowland Yeomanry [*Military unit*] [*British*] (DMA)
QOMAC.... Quarter Orbit Magnetic Attitude Control
QOMY....... Queen's Own Mercian Yeomanry [*Military unit*] [*British*]
QON .... Quaque Otra Nocte [*Every Other Night*] [*Pharmacy*]
QON .... Quarter Ocean Net
QONR .... Queen's Own Nigeria Regiment [*British military*] (DMA)
QOOH....... Queen's Own Oxfordshire Hussars [*British military*] (DMA)
Q(Ops)....... Quartermaster Operations [*World War II*]
QOR......... Qualitative Operational Requirement [*Military*]
QOR......... Quarterly Operating Report
QOR......... Quebec Official Reports [*A publication*] (DLA)
QOR......... Queen's Own Rifles [*Military unit*] [*British*]
QOR......... Queen's Own Royal [*Military unit*] [*British*]
QORC....... Queen's Own Rifles, Canada [*Military*] (ROG)
QORGIY ... Queen's Own Royal Glasgow Imperial Yeomanry [*British military*] (DMA)
QORGS ..... Quasi-Optimal Rendezvous Guidance System
QORGY..... Queen's Own Royal Glasgow Yeomanry [*British military*] (DMA)
QORR........ Queen's Own Royal Regiment [*British military*] (DMA)
QORWKR ... Queen's Own Royal West Kent Regiment [*Military unit*] [*British*]
QOS.......... Quality of Service [*Telecommunications*] (TEL)
QOT.......... Quasi-Optical Technique
QOT.......... Quote (FAAC)
QOT & E .. Qualification, Operational Test, and Evaluation

QOWH ...... Queen's Own Worcestershire Hussars [*British military*] (DMA)
QOWVR .... Queen's Own Westminster Volunteer Rifles [*Military*] [*British*] (ROG)
QOY .... Queen's Own Yeomanry [*British military*] (DMA)
QP .... Caspair Ltd. [*Kenya*] [*ICAO designator*] (FAAC)
QP .... Quaderni Portoghesi [*A publication*]
QP .... Quadratic Programming [*Data processing*] (BUR)
QP .... Quadruple Play (DEN)
QP .... Qualification Proposal
QP .... Qualified Psychiatrist (MAE)
QP .... Quality People
QP .... Quanti-Pirquet [*Reaction or test for tuberculin*] (AAMN)
QP .... Quantum Placet [*As Much as You Please*] [*Pharmacy*]
QP .... Quartered Partition
QP .... Quasi-Peak
QP .... Quasiparticle [*Physics*]
QP .... Queen Post
QP .... Queen's Pawn [*Chess*] (ADA)
QP .... Queen's Pleasure [*British*]
QP .... Query Processing (MCD)
QP .... Quest for Peace (EA)
QP .... Quick Processing [*Chemicals*]
QP .... Quoted Price [*Investment term*]
QPA .... Bibliotheque Municipale, Port-Alfred, Quebec [*Library symbol*] [*National Library of Canada*] (NLC)
QPA .... Quality Product Assurance
Q/PA .... Quality/Productivity Assessment (MCD)
QPA .... Quantity per Application (MCD)
QPA .... Quantity per Assembly (MCD)
QPAA .... Quality Planning and Administration (MCD)
QPAG .... Experimental Farm, Agriculture Canada [*Ferme Experimentale, Agriculture Canada*] La Pocatiere, Quebec [*Library symbol*] [*National Library of Canada*] (NLC)
QPAM ...... Quantized Pulsed Amplitude Modulation
QPB .... Quality Paperback Book Club [*Trademark of Book-of-the-Month Club, Inc.*]
QPBC........ Quality Paperback Book Club [*Trademark of Book-of-the-Month Club, Inc.*] (CDAI)
QPC .... College de Ste.-Anne, La Pocatiere, Quebec [*Library symbol*] [*National Library of Canada*] (NLC)
QPC .... Quality Performance Chart (SAA)
QPC .... Quantity per Equipment/Component
QPC .... Quasi-Propulsive Coefficient (DS)
QPC .... Quasi-Public Company
QPCAI Report ... Queensland Parliamentary Commissioner for Administration. Investigations Report [*Australia*] [*A publication*]
QPCB........ Quench Particle Collection Bomb (MCD)
QPCE......... CEGEP [*College d'Enseignement General et Professionnel*] de La Pocatiere, Quebec [*Library symbol*] [*National Library of Canada*] (NLC)
QPCM ...... Bibliotheque Municipale, Port-Cartier, Quebec [*Library symbol*] [*National Library of Canada*] (BIB)
QPD .... Bibliotheque Intermunicipale de Pierrefonds et Dollard-Des-Ormeaux, Pierrefonds, Quebec [*Library symbol*] [*National Library of Canada*] (NLC)
QPD .... Quadrature Phase Detection [*Physics*]
QPD .... Queensland Parliamentary Debates [*A publication*] (APTA)
QPDM ...... Quadpixel Data-Flow Manager [*Data processing*]
QPDOLL... Quarterly Payment Demand on Legal Loan
Q Pediatr Bull ... Quarterly Pediatric Bulletin [*A publication*]
QPEI .... Quantity per End Item (MCD)
QPES .... Centre de Documentation, Institut de Technologie Agro-Alimentaire de La Pocatiere, Quebec [*Library symbol*] [*National Library of Canada*] (NLC)
QPF .... Quantitative Precipitation Forecast (NOAA)
QPH.......... Queen's Park Harriers [*British*] (ROG)
1QpHab .... Commentary [*or Pesher on Habakkuk*] from Qumran. Cave One (BJA)
Q Philipp Sugar Inst ... Quarterly. Philippine Sugar Institute [*A publication*]
1QpHos ..... Commentary on Hosea from Qumran. Cave One (BJA)
1QPhyl...... Phylacteries [*or Tefillin*] from Qumran. Cave One (BJA)
QPI .... Quadratic Performance Index
QPI .... Quality Productivity Improvement (MCD)
QPIMC...... Quadratic Programming Internal Model Control [*Chemical engineering*] [*Data processing*]
QPIR.......... EBRI [*Employee Benefit Research Institute*] Quarterly Pension Investment Report [*A publication*]
QPIS .... Quality Planning Instruction Sheet (MCD)
QPIT......... Quantitative Pilocarpine Ionophoresis Test
QPL .... Qualified Parts List (AAG)
QPL .... Qualified Products List [*Military*]
Q PL.......... Quantum Placet [*As Much as You Please*] [*Pharmacy*]
QPLM .... Bibliotheque Municipale, Plessisville, Quebec [*Library symbol*] [*National Library of Canada*] (NLC)
QPLR........ Queensland Planning Law Reports [*A publication*] (APTA)
QPL & S .... Qualified Products Lists and Sources
QPLT .... Quiet Propulsion Lift Technology [*NASA*]
QPM......... Quality Practice Manual [*A publication*]
QPM .... Quality Program Manager [*Nuclear energy*] (NRCH)
QPM......... Quality-Protein Maize

QPM.......... Quantized Pulse Modulation
QPM.......... Queen's Police Medal [*British*]
QPM.......... Queen's [*Victoria*] Prime Ministers [*A publication*]
1QpMi .... Pesher [*or Commentary on Micah*] from Qumran. Cave One (BJA)
QPMV .... Quail Pea Mosaic Virus [*Plant pathology*]
1QpNah ..... Pesher [*or Commentary on Nahum*] from Qumran. Cave One (BJA)
4QpNah ..... Pesher [*or Commentary on Nahum*] from Qumran. Cave Four (BJA)
Q/PNL....... Quarter Panel [*Automotive engineering*]
QPO .... Quasi-Periodic Oscillation [*Astronomy*]
QPOC....... Pointe-Claire Public Library [*Bibliotheque Publique de Pointe-Claire*] Quebec [*Library symbol*] [*National Library of Canada*] (NLC)
QPOCQ ..... Quebec Family History Society, Pointe Claire, Quebec [*Library symbol*] [*National Library of Canada*] (BIB)
Q Police J .. Queensland Police Journal [*A publication*] (APTA)
QPON........ Seven Oaks International, Inc. [*NASDAQ symbol*] (NQ)
Q Population Bul NZ ... Quarterly Population Bulletin (New Zealand) [*A publication*]
Q Poul Bull ... Quarterly Poultry Bulletin [*A publication*]
Q Poult Bull ... Quarterly Poultry Bulletin [*A publication*]
QPP .... Quality Program Plan (MCD)
QPP .... Quality Program Provision
QPP .... Quantized Pulse Position
QPP .... Quebec Pension Plan [*Canada*]
QPP .... Queensland Parliamentary Papers [*A publication*] (APTA)
QPP .... Queensland People's Party [*Australia*] [*Political party*]
QPP .... Quiescent Push-Pull [*Electronics*] (DEN)
QPPC........ Quarterly Production Progress Conference [*Navy*] (NG)
4QpPs37 .... Pesher [*or Commentary on Psalm 37*] from Qumran. Cave Four (BJA)
QPQ.......... Quid Pro Quid
QPR .... Pittsburgh Regional Library Center - Union List, Pittsburgh, PA [*OCLC symbol*] (OCLC)
QPR .... Qualitative Personnel Requirements [*NASA*] (KSC)
QPR .... Quality Progress [*A publication*]
QPR .... Quality Progress Review (MCD)
QPR .... Quarterly Process Review
QPR .... Quarterly Progress Report
QPR .... Quebec Practice Reports [*A publication*] (DLA)
QPR .... Queen's Park Ranger [*British*] (DI)
QPR .... Queensland Practice Reports [*A publication*] (APTA)
1QPrayers ... Liturgical Fragments from Qumran. Cave One (BJA)
QPRD .... Quality Planning Requirements Document [*NASA*] (NASA)
Q Predict.... Quarterly Predictions of National Income and Expenditure [*New Zealand*] [*A publication*]
QPRF........ Quantitative Precipitation Ratio Forecasts [*National Weather Service*]
QPRI......... Qualitative Personnel Requirements Information [*NASA*] (MCD)
QPRI......... Qualitative Personnel Requirements Inventory (MCD)
QPRM ...... Bibliotheque Municipale, Princeville, Quebec [*Library symbol*] [*National Library of Canada*] (NLC)
4QPrNab ... [*The*] Prayer of Nabonidus from Qumran. Cave Four (BJA)
QPRS........ Quadrature Partial-Response System [*Telecommunications*] (TEL)
QPRS........ Quarterly Project Reliability Summary [*Navy*] (NG)
QPS........... Quaker Peace and Service [*An association*] (EAIO)
QPS........... Qualified Process Supplies (MCD)
QPS........... Qualified Processing Source
QPS........... Quality Planning Specification [*NASA*] (NASA)
QPS........... Quantitative Physical Science
QPS........... Quantity Planning Specification (NASA)
QPS........... Quiescent Power Supply
QPSC......... Quiescent Power Supply Current
QPSII .... Qualified Possession Source Investment Income [*IRS*]
QPSK........ Quadrature-Phase Shift Key
QPSL .... Qualified Parts and Suppliers List (MCD)
QPT .... Quadrant Power Tilt (IEEE)
Q Publ Am Stat Assoc ... Quarterly Publications. American Statistical Association [*A publication*]
QPW......... Quattro Pro for Windows [*Data processing*] [*Borland International*] (PCM)
QPX .... QPX Minerals, Inc. [*Vancouver Stock Exchange symbol*]
QQ .... Aerovias Quisqueyana [*Airlines*] [*Dominican Republic*] [*ICAO designator*] (OAG)
QQ .... Bibliotheque de Quebec, Quebec [*Library symbol*] [*National Library of Canada*] (NLC)
QQ .... Potential Hijacker [*Airline notation*]
QQ .... Qualitate Qua [*In the Capacity Of*] [*Latin*]
Q-Q .... Quantile-Quantile [*Data processing*]
QQ .... Quaque [*Each or Every*] [*Pharmacy*]
QQ .... Queen's Quarterly [*A publication*]
QQ .... Questionable Questionnaires
QQ .... Questions
Q and Q .... Quill and Quire [*A publication*]
QQ .... Quisque [*Each, Every*] [*Pharmacy*]
QQ .... Quoque [*Also*] [*Pharmacy*]

QQA .... Archives Nationales du Quebec, Quebec [*Library symbol*] [*National Library of Canada*] (NLC)

QQA .... Quarterly Quality Assurance [*Environmental Protection Agency*]

QQAA .... Archives de l'Archeveche de Quebec, Quebec [*Library symbol*] [*National Library of Canada*] (NLC)

QQAC .... Ministere des Affaires Culturelles du Quebec, Quebec, Quebec [*Library symbol*] [*National Library of Canada*] (NLC)

QQACJ ...... Archives de la Compagnie de Jesus, Province du Canada - Francais, Saint-Jerome, Quebec, Quebec [*Library symbol*] [*National Library of Canada*] (NLC)

QQAG .... Centre de Documentation du 200, Ministere de l'Agriculture, des Pecheries, et de l'Alimentation, Quebec, Quebec [*Library symbol*] [*National Library of Canada*] (NLC)

QQAI .... Bibliotheque Administrative, Ministere des Affaires Inter-Gouvernementales du Quebec, Quebec, Quebec [*Library symbol*] [*Obsolete*] [*National Library of Canada*] (NLC)

QQAM .... Centre de Documentation, Ministere des Affaires Municipales du Quebec, Quebec, Quebec [*Library symbol*] [*National Library of Canada*] (NLC)

QQAND .... Archives du Monastere Notre-Dame-Des-Anges, Quebec, Quebec [*Library symbol*] [*National Library of Canada*] (NLC)

QQAPC ..... Cerebral Palsy Association of Quebec, Inc. [*L'Association de Paralysie Cerebrale du Quebec, Inc.*] Quebec, Quebec [*Library symbol*] [*National Library of Canada*] (NLC)

QQAQ .... Bibliotheque des Services Diocesains, Archeveche de Quebec, Quebec [*Library symbol*] [*National Library of Canada*] (BIB)

QQAQS ..... Synod Office, Diocese of Quebec, Anglican Church of Canada, Quebec, Quebec [*Library symbol*] [*National Library of Canada*] (NLC)

QQAS .... Archives du Seminaire de Quebec, Quebec, Quebec [*Library symbol*] [*National Library of Canada*] (NLC)

QQASF ..... Conseil des Affaires Sociales et de la Famille, Quebec, Quebec [*Library symbol*] [*National Library of Canada*] (NLC)

QQBJNQ .. Bureau de la Baie James et du Nord Quebecois, Ste.-Foy, Quebec [*Library symbol*] [*National Library of Canada*] (NLC)

QQBL .... Bibliotheque des Freres des Ecoles Chretiennes, Quebec [*Library symbol*] [*National Library of Canada*] (NLC)

QQBMC .... Bibliotheque Municipale, Charlesbourg, Quebec [*Library symbol*] [*National Library of Canada*] (BIB)

QQBS .... Bureau de la Statistique du Quebec, Quebec, Quebec [*Library symbol*] [*National Library of Canada*] (NLC)

QQBST ...... Centre de Documentation, Ministere de l'Enseignement Superieur et de la Science du Quebec, Ste.-Foy, Quebec [*Library symbol*] [*National Library of Canada*] (NLC)

QQC .... Defence Research Establishment Valcartier, Canada Department of National Defence [*Centre de Recherches pour la Defense Valcartier, Ministere de la Defense Nationale*] Courcelette, Quebec [*Library symbol*] [*National Library of Canada*] (NLC)

QQC .... Quantitative Quality Characteristics

QQCAD ..... Conservatoire d'Art Dramatique du Quebec, Quebec [*Library symbol*] [*National Library of Canada*] (NLC)

QQCAI ...... Centre de Documentation, Commission d'Acces a l'Information, Quebec, Quebec [*Library symbol*] [*National Library of Canada*] (NLC)

QQCAT ..... Commission de la Sante et de la Securite du Travail du Quebec, Quebec, Quebec [*Library symbol*] [*National Library of Canada*] (NLC)

QQCC .... Centre de Documentation, Conseil des Colleges du Quebec, Quebec, Quebec [*Library symbol*] [*National Library of Canada*] (BIB)

QQCDP ..... Commission des Droits de la Personne du Quebec, Quebec, Quebec [*Library symbol*] [*National Library of Canada*] (NLC)

QQCDT ..... Centre de Documentation, Commission des Normes du Travail, Quebec [*Library symbol*] [*National Library of Canada*] (NLC)

QQCE .... CEGEP [*College d'Enseignement General et Professionnel*] de Limoilou, Quebec, Quebec [*Library symbol*] [*National Library of Canada*] (NLC)

QQCF .... Centre Francois Charron, Quebec, Quebec [*Library symbol*] [*National Library of Canada*] (BIB)

QQCFP ...... Centre de Documentation, Commission de la Fonction Publique du Quebec, Quebec, Quebec [*Library symbol*] [*National Library of Canada*] (BIB)

QQCFX ..... CEGEP [*College d'Enseignement General et Professionnel*] F. X. Garneau, Sillery, Quebec [*Library symbol*] [*National Library of Canada*] (NLC)

QQCGI ...... Centre de Documentation, CGI [*Conseillers en Gestion et Informatique*], Inc., Quebec [*Library symbol*] [*National Library of Canada*] (NLC)

QQCH .... Departement des Archives et Statistiques de la Ville de Quebec, Quebec, Quebec [*Library symbol*] [*National Library of Canada*] (NLC)

QQCHJH ... Centre Hospitalier Jeffery Hale, Quebec, Quebec [*Library symbol*] [*National Library of Canada*] (BIB)

QQCLF ...... Conseil de la Langue Francaise, Quebec, Quebec [*Library symbol*] [*National Library of Canada*] (NLC)

QQCM ...... College Merici, Quebec, Quebec [*Library symbol*] [*National Library of Canada*] (NLC)

QQCMQ .... Service de la Documentation et de l'Audiovisuel, Conservatoire de Musique de Quebec, Quebec [*Library symbol*] [*National Library of Canada*] (NLC)

QQCOC ..... Centre de Documentation - DGTI [*Direction Generale des Technologies de l'Information*], Ministere des Communications du Quebec, Ste.-Foy, Quebec [*Library symbol*] [*National Library of Canada*] (BIB)

QQCOM .... Centre de Documentation, Direction Generale des Medias, Ministere des Communications du Quebec, Quebec [*Library symbol*] [*National Library of Canada*] (BIB)

QQCPQ ..... Parks Service, Environment Canada [*Service des Parcs, Environnement Canada*], Quebec [*Library symbol*] [*National Library of Canada*] (BIB)

QQCPS ...... Centre de Documentation, Conseil de la Science et de la Technologie du Quebec, Ste.-Foy, Quebec [*Library symbol*] [*National Library of Canada*] (NLC)

QQCR .... Centre Hospitalier Christ-Roi, Quebec, Quebec [*Library symbol*] [*National Library of Canada*] (BIB)

QQCRS ...... Conseil Regional de la Sante et des Services Sociaux, Quebec, Quebec [*Library symbol*] [*National Library of Canada*] (NLC)

QQCS .... Service de Documentation et de Bibliotheque, Complexe Scientifique, Ste.-Foy, Quebec [*Library symbol*] [*National Library of Canada*] (NLC)

QQCSF ...... Conseil du Statut de la Femme, Quebec, Quebec [*Library symbol*] [*National Library of Canada*] (NLC)

QQCSS ...... Centre de Documentation, Centre de Services Sociaux de Quebec, Quebec [*Library symbol*] [*National Library of Canada*] (BIB)

QQCT .... Commission de Toponymie du Quebec, Quebec, Quebec [*Library symbol*] [*National Library of Canada*] (NLC)

QQCU .... Conseil des Universites du Quebec, Ste.-Foy, Quebec [*Library symbol*] [*National Library of Canada*] (NLC)

QQCUQ .... Communaute Urbaine de Quebec [*Library symbol*] [*National Library of Canada*] (BIB)

QQE .... Wildlife and Inland Waters Library, Environment Canada [*Bibliotheque de la Faune et des Eaux Interieures, Environement Canada*] Ste-Foy, Quebec [*Library symbol*] [*National Library of Canada*] (NLC)

QQED .... Centre de Documentation, Ministere de l'Education du Quebec, Quebec, Quebec [*Library symbol*] [*National Library of Canada*] (BIB)

QQEDOP .. Centre de Documentation, Office des Professions du Quebec, Quebec [*Library symbol*] [*National Library of Canada*] (NLC)

QQEN .... Ministere de l'Environnement, Ste-Foy, Quebec [*Library symbol*] [*National Library of Canada*] (NLC)

QQERE ..... Centre de Documentation-Energie, Ministere de l'Energie et des Ressources du Quebec, Quebec, Quebec [*Library symbol*] [*National Library of Canada*] (NLC)

QQERM .... Centre de Documentation-Mines, Ministere de l'Energie et des Ressources du Quebec, Quebec, Quebec [*Library symbol*] [*National Library of Canada*] (NLC)

QQERT ..... Centre de Documentation-Terres et Forets, Ministere de l'Energie et des Ressources du Quebec, Quebec, Quebec [*Library symbol*] [*National Library of Canada*] (NLC)

QQESE ...... Centre de Documentation, Direction Generale de l'Enseignement et de la Recherche Universitaires, Ministere de l'Enseignement Superieur et de la Science du Quebec, Quebec, Quebec [*Library symbol*] [*National Library of Canada*] (BIB)

QQF .... Bibliotheque Franciscaine, Quebec, Quebec [*Library symbol*] [*National Library of Canada*] (NLC)

QQFPCE ... Direction de la Classification et de l'Evaluation des Emplois, Ministere de la Fonction Publique, Quebec, Quebec [*Library symbol*] [*National Library of Canada*] (NLC)

QQFTI .... Service du Traitement de l'Information, Ministere des Finances, Duberger, Quebec [*Library symbol*] [*National Library of Canada*] (NLC)

QQGR .... Bibliotheque Gabrielle-Roy, Quebec, Quebec [*Library symbol*] [*National Library of Canada*] (BIB)

QQH .... Quaque Hora [*Every Hour*] [*Pharmacy*]

QQH .... Quaque Quarta Hora [*Every Fourth Hour*] [*Pharmacy*]

QQHD .... Hotel-Dieu de Quebec, Quebec [*Library symbol*] [*National Library of Canada*] (NLC)

QQHDM ... Musee des Augustines de l'Hotel-Dieu de Quebec, Quebec [*Library symbol*] [*National Library of Canada*] (NLC)

QQHDS ..... Hotel-Dieu du Sacre-Coeur, Quebec, Quebec [*Library symbol*] [*National Library of Canada*] (NLC)

QQHEJ ..... Hopital de l'Enfant-Jesus, Quebec, Quebec [*Library symbol*] [*National Library of Canada*] (NLC)

QQHFA ..... Hopital St-Francois d'Assise, Quebec, Quebec [*Library symbol*] [*National Library of Canada*] (NLC)

QQ HOR ... Quaque Hora [*Every Hour*] [*Pharmacy*]

QQHSS ..... Hopital du Saint-Sacrement, Quebec, Quebec [*Library symbol*] [*National Library of Canada*] (NLC)

QQHSSC...   Centre de Documentation, Departement de Sante Communautaire, Hopital du Saint-Sacrement, Quebec, Quebec [*Library symbol*] [*National Library of Canada*]   (BIB)

QQIAS.......   Service de la Documentation, Ministere de la Sante et des Services Sociaux du Quebec, Quebec, Quebec [*Library symbol*] [*National Library of Canada*]   (NLC)

QQIC.........   Ministere de l'Industrie, du Commerce et du Tourisme, Quebec, Quebec [*Library symbol*] [*National Library of Canada*]   (NLC)

QQIF ....   Inspecteur General des Institutions Financieres, Quebec, Quebec [*Library symbol*] [*National Library of Canada*]   (NLC)

QQIN.........   Indian and Northern Affairs Canada [*Affaires Indiennes et du Nord Canada*], Quebec [*Library symbol*] [*National Library of Canada*]   (BIB)

QQIQRC ...   Institut Quebecois de Recherche sur la Culture, Quebec, Quebec [*Library symbol*] [*National Library of Canada*]   (NLC)

QQJ ....   Ministere de la Justice du Quebec, Ste-Foy, Quebec [*Library symbol*] [*National Library of Canada*]   (NLC)

QQL..........   Bibliotheque de l'Assemblee Nationale, Quebec, Quebec [*Library symbol*] [*National Library of Canada*]   (NLC)

QQLA........   Universite Laval, Quebec, Quebec [*Library symbol*] [*National Library of Canada*]   (NLC)

QQLAAA ..   Secteur Art et Architecture, Universite Laval, Quebec, Quebec [*Library symbol*] [*National Library of Canada*]   (NLC)

QQLAAV ..   Ecole des Arts Visuels, Universite Laval, Quebec, Quebec [*Library symbol*] [*National Library of Canada*]   (NLC)

QQLACA ..   Cartotheque, Universite Laval, Quebee, Quebec [*Library symbol*] [*National Library of Canada*]   (NLC)

QQLACH ...   Centre Hospitalier de l'Universite Laval, Quebec, Quebec [*Library symbol*] [*National Library of Canada*]   (NLC)

QQLACHC ...   Centre de Documentation, Departement de Sante Communautaire, Centre Hospitalier, Universite Laval, Quebec [*Library symbol*] [*National Library of Canada*]   (NLC)

QQLACHR ...   Centre de Recherche, Centre Hospitalier, Universite Laval, Quebec, Quebec [*Library symbol*] [*National Library of Canada*]   (BIB)

QQLACHT ...   Centre de Toxicologie, Centre Hospitalier, Universite Laval, Quebec, Quebec [*Library symbol*] [*National Library of Canada*]   (BIB)

QQLACI....   Centre International de Recherches sur le Bilinguisme, Universite Laval, Quebec, Quebec [*Library symbol*] [*National Library of Canada*]   (NLC)

QQLAD.....   Faculte de Droit, Universite Laval, Quebec, Quebec [*Library symbol*] [*National Library of Canada*]   (NLC)

QQLAG.....   Institut de Geographie, Universite Laval, Quebec, Quebec [*Library symbol*] [*National Library of Canada*]   (NLC)

QQLAGM ...   Departement de Geologie et de Mineralogie, Universite Laval, Quebec, Quebec [*Library symbol*] [*National Library of Canada*]   (NLC)

QQLAI ......   Societa Dante Alighieri, Universite Laval, Quebec, Quebec [*Library symbol*] [*National Library of Canada*]   (NLC)

QQLAS......   Bibliotheque Scientifique, Universite Laval, Quebec, Quebec [*Library symbol*] [*National Library of Canada*]   (NLC)

QQLCP......   Ministere du Loisir, de la Chasse et de la Peche, Quebec, Quebec [*Library symbol*] [*National Library of Canada*]   (NLC)

QQLH........   Literary and Historical Society of Quebec [*Societe Litteraire et Historique de Quebec*] Quebec [*Library symbol*] [*National Library of Canada*]   (NLC)

QQLM.......   Centre de Documentation, Laurentienne Mutuelle d'Assurance, Quebec, Quebec [*Library symbol*] [*National Library of Canada*]   (BIB)

QQMAA....   Archives du Monastere des Augustines, Quebec, Quebec [*Library symbol*] [*National Library of Canada*]   (NLC)

QQMAB....   Bibliotheque du Monastere des Augustines, Quebec, Quebec [*Library symbol*] [*National Library of Canada*]   (NLC)

QQMAGA ...   Archives des Augustines du Monastere de l'Hopital General de Quebec, Quebec [*Library symbol*] [*National Library of Canada*]   (NLC)

QQMC......   Forestry Canada [*Forets Canada*], Ste.-Foy, Quebec [*Library symbol*] [*National Library of Canada*]   (NLC)

QQMCH ...   Bibliotheque Administrative, (Edifice H), Ministere des Communications du Quebec, Quebec [*Library symbol*] [*National Library of Canada*]   (NLC)

QQMF.......   Laurentian Forestry Centre, Canadian Forestry Service [*Centre de Foresterie des Laurentides, Service Canadien des Forets*] Ste.-Foy, Quebec [*Library symbol*] [*National Library of Canada*]   (NLC)

QQMQ......   Musee du Quebec, Quebec [*Library symbol*] [*National Library of Canada*]   (NLC)

QQMR.......   Le Mussee du Royal 22e Regiment et la Regie du Royal 22e Regiment, Quebec, Quebec [*Library symbol*] [*National Library of Canada*]   (NLC)

QQM & R..   Quantitative, Qualitative, Maintainability, and Reliability

QQMSRD ...   Centre de Documentation, Direction Generale des Ressources Informationnelles, Ministere de la Main d'Oeuvre et de la Securite du Revenu du Quebec, Quebec, Quebec [*Library symbol*] [*National Library of Canada*]   (NLC)

QQMSRP ...   Centre de Documentation, Direction Generale de la Planification, Ministere de la Main-d'Oeuvre et de la Securite du Revenu du Quebec, Quebec [*Library symbol*] [*National Library of Canada*]   (BIB)

QQMUC....   Centre de Documentation, Musee de la Civilisation, Quebec [*Library symbol*] [*National Library of Canada*]   (BIB)

QQO ....   Quasiquadrennial Oscillation [*Astronomy*]

QQOLF .....   Office de la Langue Francaise, Quebec, Quebec [*Library symbol*] [*National Library of Canada*]   (NLC)

QQOPC .....   Office de la Protection du Consommateur, Quebec, Quebec [*Library symbol*] [*National Library of Canada*]   (NLC)

QQOPD.....   Direction de la Documentation, Office des Promotions du Quebec, Quebec, Quebec [*Library symbol*] [*National Library of Canada*]   (NLC)

QQP..........   Quick Query Program

QQPCQ.....   Canadian Park Service, Environment Canada [*Service Canadien des Parcs, Environnement Canada*], Quebec, Quebec [*Library symbol*] [*National Library of Canada*]   (NLC)

QQPEA .....   Archives des Peres Eudistes, Charlesbourg, Quebec [*Library symbol*] [*National Library of Canada*]   (NLC)

QQPR.......   Quantitative and Qualitative Personnel Requirements

QQPRI.......   Quantitative and Qualitative Personnel Requirements Information [*Military*]

QQPSM ....   Maurice Lamontagne Institute, Fisheries and Oceans Canada [*Institut Maurice Lamontagne, Peches et Oceans Canada*], Mont-Joli, Quebec [*Library symbol*] [*National Library of Canada*]   (NLC)

QQQE.......   Centre Quebecois des Sciences de l'Eau, Universite du Quebec, Quebec, Quebec [*Library symbol*] [*National Library of Canada*]   (NLC)

QQR..........   Technical Information Centre, Reed Ltd., Quebec, Quebec [*Library symbol*] [*National Library of Canada*]   (NLC)

QQRA.......   Roche Associes Ltee., Group-Conseil, Ste.-Foy, Quebec [*Library symbol*] [*National Library of Canada*]   (NLC)

QQRAA .....   Regie de l'Assurance Automobile du Quebec, Sillery, Quebec [*Library symbol*] [*National Library of Canada*]   (NLC)

QQRAMQ ...   Regie de l'Assurance-Maladie du Quebec, Sillery, Quebec [*Library symbol*] [*National Library of Canada*]   (NLC)

QQRE........   Ministere du Revenu, Ste.-Foy, Quebec [*Library symbol*] [*National Library of Canada*]   (NLC)

QQRRQ.....   Regie des Rentes du Quebec, Ste.-Foy, Quebec [*Library symbol*] [*National Library of Canada*]   (NLC)

QQRSP......   Regie des Services Publics, Ste.-Foy, Quebec [*Library symbol*] [*National Library of Canada*]   (NLC)

QQS..........   Quality Quest System [*Vancouver Stock Exchange symbol*]

QQS..........   Seminaire de Quebec, Quebec [*Library symbol*] [*National Library of Canada*]   (NLC)

QQSAA .....   Centre de Documentation, Secretariat aux Affaires Autochtones, Quebec [*Library symbol*] [*National Library of Canada*]   (BIB)

QQSAJ......   Secretariat a la Jeunesse, Conseil Executif, Quebec, Quebec [*Library symbol*] [*National Library of Canada*]   (NLC)

QQSC........   Quadripartite Quartermaster Standardization Committee [*Military*]   (AABC)

QQSCA......   Archives des Soeurs de la Charite de Quebec, Quebec, Quebec [*Library symbol*] [*National Library of Canada*]   (NLC)

QQSCF......   Centre de Documentation, Secretariat a la Condition Feminine du Quebec, Quebec, Quebec [*Library symbol*] [*National Library of Canada*]   (BIB)

QQSHQ.....   Centre de Documentation, Societe d'Habitation du Quebec, Quebec [*Library symbol*] [*National Library of Canada*]   (BIB)

QQSIP.......   Societe Quebecoise d'Initiatives Petrolieres, Ste.-Foy, Quebec [*Library symbol*] [*National Library of Canada*]   (NLC)

QQSP ....   Centre de Documentation, Syndicat de Professionnels et de Professionnelles du Gouvernement du Quebec, Quebec [*Library symbol*] [*National Library of Canada*]   (BIB)

QQSS.........   Quebec Library, Translation Bureau, Secretary of State Canada [*Bibliotheque de Quebec, Bureau des Traductions, Secretariat d'Etat*], Ste.-Foy, Quebec [*Library symbol*] [*National Library of Canada*]   (NLC)

QQST ....   Centre de Documentation, Conseil de la Science et de la Technologie, Quebec [*Library symbol*] [*National Library of Canada*]   (NLC)

QQTCG .....   Canadian Coast Guard [*Garde Cotiere Canadienne*] Quebec, Quebec [*Library symbol*] [*National Library of Canada*]   (NLC)

QQTE........   Tecrad, Inc., Ancienne-Lorette, Quebec [*Library symbol*] [*National Library of Canada*]   (NLC)

QQTO........   Ministere du Tourisme du Quebec, Quebec [*Library symbol*] [*National Library of Canada*]   (NLC)

QQTQ........   Centre de Documentation, Ministere du Travail du Quebec, Quebec [*Library symbol*] [*National Library of Canada*]   (BIB)

QQTR ....   Ministere des Transports, Quebec, Quebec [*Library symbol*] [*National Library of Canada*]   (NLC)

QQTRD.....   Centre de Documentation, Ministere des Transports - Rue Dorchester, Quebec [*Library symbol*] [*National Library of Canada*]   (NLC)

QQU .... Couvent des Ursulines, Quebec, Quebec [*Library symbol*] [*National Library of Canada*]   (NLC)

QQUA .... Archives du Monastere des Ursulines de Merici, Quebec, Quebec [*Library symbol*] [*National Library of Canada*]   (NLC)

QQUIE ...... Centre de Documentation, INRS [*Institut National de la Recherche Scientifique*]-Eau, Quebec, Quebec [*Library symbol*] [*National Library of Canada*]   (NLC)

QQUQ .... Universite du Quebec, Quebec, Quebec [*Library symbol*] [*National Library of Canada*]   (NLC)

QQUQEN ... Ecole Nationale d'Administration Publique, Universite du Quebec, Quebec, Quebec [*Library symbol*] [*National Library of Canada*]   (NLC)

QQUQT..... Tele-Universite, Universite du Quebec, Quebec, Quebec [*Library symbol*] [*National Library of Canada*]   (NLC)

QQV.......... Centre de Documentation, le Verificateur General du Quebec, Quebec, Quebec [*Library symbol*] [*National Library of Canada*]   (BIB)

QQ V .... Quae Vide [*Which See*] [*Plural form*] [*Latin*]

QQV.......... Quantum Vis [*As Much as You Wish*] [*Pharmacy*]   (ADA)

Q-QY .... Question or Query   (AAG)

QQZ.......... Jardin Zoologique de Quebec, Charlesbourg, Quebec [*Library symbol*] [*National Library of Canada*]   (NLC)

QR............. Inter RCA [*Central African Republic*] [*ICAO designator*]   (FAAC)

QR............. Qatar Riyal [*Monetary unit*]   (BJA)

Qr.............. Qere   (BJA)

QR............. Quad Right [*Typography*]

QR............. Quadrans [*A Farthing*] [*Monetary unit*] [*British*]   (ROG)

QR............. Qualifications Record   (AEBS)

Q & R .... Quality and Reliability

QR............. Quality Review

QR............. Quantitative Restrictions [*International trade*]

QR............. Quantity Requested

QR............. Quantity Required

QR............. Quantum Rectum [*The Quantity Is Correct*] [*Pharmacy*]

QR............. Quantum Resources [*Vancouver Stock Exchange symbol*]

QR............. Quarantine Report [*HEW*]

QR............. Quart

QR............. Quarter

QR............. Quarterly   (ROG)

QR............. Quarterly Replenishment

QR............. Quarterly Report   (OICC)

QR............. Quarterly Review [*A publication*]

QR............. Quarters Rating [*British military*]   (DMA)

QR............. Quaternary Research [*A publication*]

QR............. Quebec Official Reports [*A publication*]   (DLA)

QR............. Queen's Rangers [*British military*]

QR............. Queen's Regulation [*Military*] [*British*]

QR............. Queen's Rook [*Chess*]   (ADA)

QR............. Queen's Royal [*Military unit*] [*British*]

Q/R .... Query/Response   (MCD)

QR............. Quick Reaction

QR............. Quieting Reflex [*In book title "Q-R: The Quieting Reflex" by Charles F. Stroebel*]

QR............. Quire [*Measure of paper*]

QR............. Quotation Request

QR............. Sources Public Library [*Bibliotheque Municipale des Sources*] Roxboro, Quebec [*Library symbol*] [*National Library of Canada*]   (NLC)

QRA.......... Archeveche de Rimouski, Quebec [*Library symbol*] [*National Library of Canada*]   (NLC)

QRA.......... Quality and Reliability Assurance   (NG)

Q & RA ...... Quality and Reliability Assurance

QRA.......... Quantified Risk Analysis

QRA.......... Quarterly Review and Analysis

QRA.......... Quick Reaction Acquisition   (MCD)

QRA.......... Quick Reaction Aircraft   (MCD)

QRA.......... Quick Reaction Alert [*Military*]   (AFM)

QRA.......... Quick Reaction Area   (MCD)

QRA.......... Quick Replaceable Assembly

QRAAT ..... Centre de l'Abitibi-Temiscamingue, Archives Nationales du Quebec, Rouyn-Noranda, Quebec [*Library symbol*] [*National Library of Canada*]   (BIB)

QRAC .... Quality and Reliability Assessment Council

QRADA..... Quaderni di Radiologia [*A publication*]

QR Ag Econ ... Quarterly Review of Agricultural Economics [*A publication*]   (APTA)

Q R Agric Econ ... Quarterly Review of Agricultural Economics [*A publication*]

QRAH....... Robins [*A. H.*] Co., Inc. [*NYSE symbol*]   (SPSG)

QR & AI..... Queen's Regulations and Admiralty Instructions [*Obsolete*] [*Navy*] [*British*]

QR Air .... Queen's Regulations and Orders for the Royal Canadian Air Force

QRAL .... Quality and Reliability Assurance Laboratory [*NASA*]   (KSC)

QRAN....... Archives Nationales du Quebec, Rimouski, Quebec [*Library symbol*] [*National Library of Canada*]   (BIB)

QR Aust Educ ... Quarterly Review of Australian Education [*A publication*]   (APTA)

QRB .... Quality Review Bulletin [*A publication*]

QRB.......... Quarterly Review of Biology [*A publication*]

QRBC .... Bibliotheque Centrale de Pret d'Abitibi-Temiscamingue, Rouyn-Noranda, Quebec [*Library symbol*] [*National Library of Canada*]   (NLC)

QRBIA...... Quarterly Review of Biology [*A publication*]

Q R Biol ..... Quarterly Review of Biology [*A publication*]

Q R Biophys ... Quarterly Review of Biophysics [*A publication*]

QRBM .... Quasi-Random Band Model

QRC.......... Quaker Resources Canada Ltd. [*Vancouver Stock Exchange symbol*]

QRC.......... Quick Reaction Capability [*Military*]

QRC.......... Quick Reaction Change   (MCD)

QRC.......... Quick Response Capability [*Military*]

QRCA .... Qualitative Research Consultants Association   (EA)

QRCB .... College Bourget, Rigaud, Quebec [*Library symbol*] [*National Library of Canada*]   (NLC)

QRCC .... Quadripartite Research Coordination Committee [*Military*]   (AABC)

QRCC .... Query Response Communications Console

QRCG .... Quasi-Random Code Generator   (CET)

QRCH....... Centre de Documentation, Centre Hospitalier Regional de Rimouski, Quebec [*Library symbol*] [*National Library of Canada*]   (NLC)

QRCN .... College de l'Abitibi-Temiscamingue, Rouyn, Quebec [*Library symbol*] [*National Library of Canada*]   (NLC)

QRCN .... Queen's Regulations and Orders for the Royal Canadian Navy

QRCR .... Quality Reliability Consumption Reports

QRCRS..... Conseil Regional de la Sante et des Services Sociaux, Rimouski, Quebec [*Library symbol*] [*National Library of Canada*]   (NLC)

QRD.......... Quick Reaction Development

QRDC .... Quartermaster Research and Development Center [*or Command*] [*Natick, MA*]

QRDEA .... Quartermaster Research and Development Evaluation Agency [*Army*]

QRDN....... Quality Requirement Discrepancy Notice   (SAA)

QRDS .... Quarterly Review of Drilling Statistics [*American Petroleum Institute*]

QRE.......... Bibliotheque Municipale, Repentigny, Quebec [*Library symbol*] [*National Library of Canada*]   (NLC)

QRE.......... Quarterly Review of Economics and Business [*A publication*]

QRE.......... Quick Reaction [*or Response*] Estimate

QREB .... Quarterly Review of Economics and Business [*A publication*]

QREBA...... Quarterly Review of Economics and Business [*A publication*]

QREC .... Quartermaster Research and Engineering Center [*or Command*] [*Natick, MA*]

Q R Econ Bu ... Quarterly Review of Economics and Business [*A publication*]

Q R Econ & Bus ... Quarterly Review of Economics and Business [*A publication*]

QRECS...... Centre Regional de Documentation Pedagogique, Commission Scolaire de Le Gardeur, Repentigny, Quebec [*Library symbol*] [*National Library of Canada*]   (BIB)

Q Rep Railw Tech Res Inst (Tokyo) ... Quarterly Report. Railway Technical Research Institute (Tokyo) [*A publication*]

Q Rep Sulfur Chem ... Quarterly Reports on Sulfur Chemistry [*A publication*]

Q Rep Univ W Indies Sch Agric ... Quarterly Report. University of the West Indies. School of Agriculture [*A publication*]

QRESA...... Quaternary Research [*New York*] [*A publication*]

Q Res Rep Southeast Asian Fish Dev Cent Aquacult Dep ... Quarterly Research Report. Southeast Asian Fisheries Development Center. Aquaculture Department [*A publication*]

Q Rev .... Quarterly Review [*A publication*]

Q Rev Ag Economics ... Quarterly Review of Agricultural Economics [*A publication*]   (APTA)

Q Rev Agric Econ ... Quarterly Review of Agricultural Economics [*A publication*]   (APTA)

Q Rev Allergy Appl Immunol ... Quarterly Review of Allergy and Applied Immunology [*A publication*]

Q Rev Am Electroplat Soc ... Quarterly Review. American Electroplaters' Society [*A publication*]

Q Rev Aust Ed ... Quarterly Review of Australian Education [*A publication*]   (APTA)

Q Rev Biol ... Quarterly Review of Biology [*A publication*]

Q Rev Bioph ... Quarterly Reviews of Biophysics [*A publication*]

Q Rev Biophys ... Quarterly Reviews of Biophysics [*A publication*]

Q Rev Chem Soc ... Quarterly Reviews. Chemical Society [*A publication*]

Q Rev Chem Soc (Lond) ... Quarterly Reviews. Chemical Society (London) [*A publication*]

Q Rev DC Nurses Assoc ... Quarterly Review. District of Columbia Nurses Association [*A publication*]

Q Rev Drill Stat US ... Quarterly Review. Drilling Statistics for the United States [*A publication*]

Q Rev Drug Metab Drug Interact ... Quarterly Reviews on Drug Metabolism and Drug Interactions [*A publication*]

Q Rev Econ Bus ... Quarterly Review of Economics and Business [*A publication*]

Q Rev Environ ... Quarterly Review on Environment [*Japan*] [*A publication*]

Q Rev Evan Luth Ch ... Quarterly Review. Evangelical Lutheran Church [*A publication*]

Q Rev Film ... Quarterly Review of Film Studies [*A publication*]

Q Rev F Studies ... Quarterly Review of Film Studies [*A publication*]

Q Rev Harefuah ... Quarterly Review of the Harefuah [*A publication*]
Q Rev Hist S ... Quarterly Review of Historical Studies [*A publication*]
Q Review of F Studies ... Quarterly Review of Film Studies [*A publication*]
Q Rev Intern Med Dermatol ... Quarterly Review of Internal Medicine and Dermatology [*A publication*]
Q Rev Juris ... Quarterly Review of Jurisprudence [*1887-88*] [*A publication*]   (DLA)
Q Rev Lit.... Quarterly Review of Literature [*A publication*]
Q Rev Med ... Quarterly Review of Medicine [*A publication*]
Q Rev NAAS ... Quarterly Review NAAS [*National Agriculture Advisory Service, London*] [*A publication*]
Q Rev Obstet Gynecol ... Quarterly Review of Obstetrics and Gynecology [*A publication*]
Q Rev Pediatr ... Quarterly Review of Pediatrics [*A publication*]
Q Rev Rural Econ ... Quarterly Review of the Rural Economy [*A publication*]
Q Rev Soil Assoc ... Quarterly Review. The Soil Association [*A publication*]
Q Rev Surg ... Quarterly Review of Surgery [*A publication*]
Q Rev Surg Obstet Gynecol ... Quarterly Review of Surgery. Obstetrics and Gynecology [*A publication*]
Q Rev Surg Surg Spec ... Quarterly Review of Surgery and Surgical Specialities [*A publication*]
Q Rev Urol ... Quarterly Review of Urology [*A publication*]
QRF .... Quadrature Rejection Frequency
QRF .... Quality Review File [*IRS*]
QRF .... Quick Reaction Force [*Military*]   (CINC)
Q R Film S ... Quarterly Review of Film Studies [*A publication*]
QRG.......... Quadrupole Residual Gas
QRG.......... Quick Reaction Grooming
QRG.......... Quick Response Graphic
QRGA .... Quadrupole Residual Gas Analyzer
QRGAS ..... Quadrupole Residual Gas Analyzer System
QRGS .... Grand Seminaire de Rimouski, Quebec [*Library symbol*] [*National Library of Canada*]   (NLC)
QRH .... Rosemere High School, Quebec [*Library symbol*] [*National Library of Canada*]   (BIB)
QRHD .... Bibliotheque Medicale, Hotel-Dieu de Roberval, Quebec [*Library symbol*] [*National Library of Canada*]   (NLC)
Q R Higher Ed Among Negroes ... Quarterly Review of Higher Education among Negroes [*A publication*]
QR Higher Ed Negroes ... Quarterly Review of Higher Education among Negroes [*A publication*]
Q R Hist Stud ... Quarterly Review of Historical Studies [*A publication*]
QRI .... Qualitative Requirements Information [*Army*]
QRI .... Quick Reaction Integration   (NASA)
QRIA .... Quick Reaction Integration Activity   (NASA)
QRIB .... Haskell Free Library, Rock Island, Quebec [*Library symbol*] [*National Library of Canada*]   (NLC)
QRIC .... CEGEP [*College d'Enseignement General et Professionnel*] de Rimouski, Quebec [*Library symbol*] [*National Library of Canada*]   (NLC)
QRIC .... Quick Reaction Installation Capability   (CET)
QRICC....... Quick Reaction Inventory Control Center [*Army*]   (MCD)
QRIH........ Queen's Royal Irish Hussars [*Military unit*] [*British*]
QRIM .... Institut Maritime, CEGEP de Rimouski, Quebec [*Library symbol*] [*National Library of Canada*]   (NLC)
QR J........... QR Journal. Indian Association for Quality and Reliability [*A publication*]
QRJOD ..... QR [*Quality and Reliability*] Journal [*A publication*]
QRKB .... Quebec King's Bench Reports [*A publication*]   (DLA)
QRKB .... Rapports Judiciaires de Quebec, Cour du Banc du Roi [*Quebec Law Reports, King's Bench*] [*A publication*]   (DLA)
QRL .... Bibliotheque Municipale, Riviere-Du-Loup, Quebec [*Library symbol*] [*National Library of Canada*]   (BIB)
QRL .... Q-Switch Ruby LASER
QRL .... Quadripartite Research List [*Military*]   (AABC)
QRL .... Quarterly Review of Literature [*A publication*]
QRL .... Quaternary Research Laboratory [*University of Michigan*] [*Research center*]   (RCD)
QRL .... Quick Reference List
QRL .... Quick Relocate and Link
QRLC .... CEGEP [*College d'Enseignement General et Professionnel*] de Riviere-Du-Loup, Quebec [*Library symbol*] [*National Library of Canada*]   (BIB)
QRLH....... Centre de Documentation DSC, Hotel-Dieu de Riviere-Du-Loup, Quebec [*Library symbol*] [*National Library of Canada*]   (BIB)
QR of Lit.... Quarterly Review of Literature [*A publication*]
QRLP........ Centre de Recherche, Tourbieres Premier Ltee., Riviere-Du-Loup, Quebec [*Library symbol*] [*National Library of Canada*]   (BIB)
QRLY .... Quarterly
QRM.......... Artificial Interference to Transmission or Reception [*Broadcasting*]
QRM.......... Bibliotheque Municipale, Rimouski, Quebec [*Library symbol*] [*National Library of Canada*]   (NLC)
QRM......... Quarterly Review of Marketing [*A publication*]
QRM......... Quorum Resource Corp. [*Vancouver Stock Exchange symbol*]
QRMC....... Quadrennial Review of Military Compensation [*DoD*]
QRMC ...... Quick Response Multicolor Copier   (MCD)
QRMF .... Quick Reacting, Mobile Force [*Military*] [*NATO*]   (NATG)
QRMP .... Quick-Response Multicolor Printer   (RDA)

Qr Mr......... Quartermaster [*British military*]   (DMA)
QRN.......... Soeurs de Notre-Dame du Saint-Rosaire, Rimouski, Quebec [*Library symbol*] [*National Library of Canada*]   (NLC)
QROA....... Quarter Racing Owners of America   (EA)
QR & O (Can) ... Queen's Regulations and Orders for the Canadian Army
QRosc .... Pro Roscio Comoedo [*of Cicero*] [*Classical studies*]   (OCD)
QRP .... Queen's Rook's Pawn [*Chess*]   (IIA)
QRP .... Query and Reporting Processor
QRP .... Quick Reaction Program [*Army*]
QRP .... Quick Response Proposal [*Navy*]
QRPAO .... Qualified Radium Plaque Adaptometer Operator [*Navy*]
QRPS........ Quick Reaction Procurement System [*Army*]   (AABC)
QRQB .... Quebec Queen's Bench Reports [*Canada*] [*A publication*]   (DLA)
QRR .... Quadrature Rejection Ratio
QRR .... Quadrupole Resonance Response
QRR .... Qualitative Research Requirement for Nuclear Weapons Effects Information   (AABC)
QRR .... Quality Readiness Review   (MCD)
QRR .... Quarterly Research Review
QRR .... Queen's Royal Regiment [*Military unit*] [*British*]
QRR .... Queen's Royal Rifles [*British military*]   (DMA)
QRR .... Quincy Railroad Co. [*AAR code*]
QRRB .... Qualified Railroad Retirement Beneficiary
QRRF....... Master Quality Review Report File [*IRS*]
QRRI .... Qualitative Research Requirements Information [*Army*]
QRRK .... Quantum Rice-Ramsperger-Kassel [*Chemical kinetics methodology*]
QRRR .... Distress call for emergency use only by amateur radio stations in an emergency situation
Q R Rural Economy ... Quarterly Review of the Rural Economy [*A publication*]
QRS .... Natural Interference to Transmission or Reception [*Broadcasting*]
QRS .... Qualification Review Sheet   (KSC)
QRS .... Qualified Repair Source   (AFIT)
QRS .... Quantum Readout System [*Method of measurement*]
QRS .... Quarters
QRS .... Queen's Row Spare
QRS .... Quick Reaction Sortie   (NASA)
QRSC .... Quebec Superior Court Reports [*A publication*]   (DLA)
QRSC........ Rapports Judiciaires de Quebec, Cour Superieure [*Quebec Law Reports, Superior Court*] [*A publication*]   (DLA)
QRSL........ Qualified Repair Source List   (AFIT)
QRSL........ Quick Reaction Space Laboratory [*NASA*]   (NASA)
QRT .... Queue Run-Time [*Data processing*]
QRT .... Quick Reaction Task   (MCD)
QRT .... Quick Reaction Team [*Military*]
QRT .... Quiet Radio Transmission   (DNAB)
QRTIA...... Quarterly Report. Railway Technical Research Institute [*A publication*]
QRTLY...... Quarterly   (ROG)
QRTP........ Quick Response Targeting Program [*Lunar*]
QRTZ .... Quartz Engineering & Materials, Inc. [*NASDAQ symbol*]   (NQ)
QRU .... Quarterly Review of Urology [*A publication*]
QRU .... Queen's Row Unit
QRU.......... Universite du Quebec, Rimouski, Quebec [*Library symbol*] [*National Library of Canada*]   (NLC)
QRUC....... Cartotheque, Universite du Quebec, Rimouski, Quebec [*Library symbol*] [*National Library of Canada*]   (NLC)
QRUQR..... Universite du Quebec en Abitibi-Temiscamingue, Rouyn, Quebec [*Library symbol*] [*National Library of Canada*]   (NLC)
QRUS .... Queen's Row Unit Spare
QRV.......... Queenstown Rifle Volunteers [*British military*]   (DMA)
QRV.......... Quick Release Valve
QRV.......... Quinn River Valley [*Nevada*] [*Seismograph station code, US Geological Survey*] [*Closed*]   (SEIS)
QRVB .... Queen's Rifle Volunteer Brigade [*British military*]   (DMA)
QRW......... Quail Ridge Winery [*Vancouver Stock Exchange symbol*]
QRXI .... Quarex Industries, Inc. [*NASDAQ symbol*]   (NQ)
QRY .... Quality and Reliability Year
QRY .... Quarry   (KSC)
QRZ .... Quaddel Reaktion Zeit [*Wheal Reaction Time*] [*German*]
QS.............. African Safari Airways [*ICAO designator*]   (FAAC)
QS.............. Les Quatre Saisons [*Record label*] [*France*]
QS.............. Quaderni di Semitistica [*Florence*] [*A publication*]
QS.............. Quaderni di Storia [*A publication*]
QS.............. Quadrupole Splitting   (OA)
QS.............. Quality Standard
QS.............. Quality Stock
QS.............. Quality Surveillance [*Navy*]   (DNAB)
QS.............. Quantity Share [*Economics*]
QS.............. Quantity Surveying
QS.............. Quantum Sufficit [*A Sufficient Quantity*] [*Pharmacy*]   (ADA)
QS.............. Quarantine Station
QS.............. Quarter Section
QS.............. Quarter Sessions
QS.............. Quartermaster Sergeant [*Military*]
QS.............. Queen's Scarf   (ADA)
QS.............. Queen's Scholar [*British*]

QS .... Queen's Serjeant [*Military*] [*British*]   (ROG)
Q-S .... Queneau-Schuhmann [*Lead process*]
QS .... Query System [*Data processing*]
QS .... Question Standard   (NATG)
QS .... Queue Select [*Data processing*]
QS .... Quick Service
QS .... Quick Sweep [*Construction*]
QS .... Quiet Sleep [*Physiology*]
QS .... Quota Source   (AABC)
1QS .... Community Rule, Rule of the Congregation [*or Manual of Discipline, Serekh ha-Yahad*] from Qumran. Cave One   (BJA)
1QS .... Divrei Berakhot [*or Blessings*] from Qumran. Cave One   (BJA)
QSA .... Quad Synchronous Adapter [*Perkin-Elmer*]
QSA .... Qualification Site Approval [*NASA*]   (NASA)
QSA .... Qualified in Small Arms [*British military*]   (DMA)
QSA .... Quick Service Assistant   (MCD)
QSABS .... Laboratoire de Sante Publique du Quebec, Ste.-Anne-De-Bellevue, Quebec [*Library symbol*] [*National Library of Canada*]   (NLC)
QS AD .... Quantum Sufficiat Ad [*To a Sufficient Quantity*] [*Pharmacy*]
QSAL......... Quadripartite Standardization Agreements List [*Military*]
QSAM .... Quadrature Sideband Amplitude Modulation
QSAM .... Queued Sequential Access Method [*IBM Corp.*] [*Data processing*]
(Q)SAR...... Quantitative Structure-Activity Relationship [*Pharmacochemistry*]
QSAR .... Quantitative Structure-Activity Relationships [*A publication*]
QSAR Drug Des Toxicol Proc Eur Symp Quan Struct Act Relat ... QSAR [*Quantitative Structure-Activity Relationships*] in Drug Design and Toxicology. Proceedings. European Symposium on Quantitative Structure-Activity Relationships [*A publication*]
QSATS ...... Quiet Short-Haul Air Transportation System
1QSb .... Divrei Berakhot [*or Blessings*] from Qumran. Cave One   (BJA)
QSBR......... Bio-Research Laboratory, Senneville, Quebec [*Library symbol*] [*National Library of Canada*]   (NLC)
QSC .... Al-Ahli Bank of Qatar   (MENA)
QSC .... College de Shawinigan, Quebec [*Library symbol*] [*National Library of Canada*]   (NLC)
QSC .... Quality, Service, Cleanliness [*McDonald's Hamburger stands motto*]
QSC .... Quasi-Sensory Communication [*Parapsychology*]
QSC .... Queen Street Camera, Inc. [*Toronto Stock Exchange symbol*]
QSC .... Questionnaire Service Co. [*Information service or system*]   (IID)
QSC .... Quick Set Compound
QSCR........ Queensland. Supreme Court. Reports [*A publication*]
QSCV......... Quality, Service, Cleanliness, and Value [*Formula for successful fast-food restaurants as taught by McDonald's Corp. at its Hamburger University*]
QSD .... Quality Surveillance Division [*Navy*]
QSDC .... Quantitative Structural Design Criteria [*NASA*]
QSE .... Qualified Scientists and Engineers
QSED .... Research Centre, Domtar Ltd., Senneville, Quebec [*Library symbol*] [*National Library of Canada*]   (NLC)
QSEE......... Quiet STOL [*Short Takeoff and Landing*] Experimental Engine [*Aviation*]   (OA)
QSem .... Quaderni di Semantica [*A publication*]
QSEMH .... Missisquoi Historical Society [*Societe d'Histoire de Missisquoi*] Stanbridge-East, Quebec [*Library symbol*] [*National Library of Canada*]   (NLC)
QSF........... Bibliotheque Municipale, Ste.-Foy, Quebec [*Library symbol*] [*National Library of Canada*]   (NLC)
QSF........... Quasi-Static Field
QSF........... Quasi-Stationary Front
QSFAG...... Research Station, Agriculture Canada [*Station de Recherches, Agriculture Canada*] Ste-Foy, Quebec [*Library symbol*] [*National Library of Canada*]   (NLC)
QSFB......... Biorex, Ste.-Foy, Quebec [*Library symbol*] [*National Library of Canada*]   (BIB)
QSFBP ...... Maison Generalice des Soeurs du Bon Pasteur, Ste-Foy, Quebec [*Library symbol*] [*National Library of Canada*]   (NLC)
QSFC......... Centre des Medias, CEGEP [*College d'Enseignement General et Professionnel*] de Ste.-Foy, Quebec [*Library symbol*] [*National Library of Canada*]   (NLC)
QSFC......... College d'Enseignement, Ste.-Foy, Quebec [*Library symbol*] [*National Library of Canada*]   (NLC)
QSFCAE ... Clinique d'Aide a l'Enfance, Ste.-Foy, Quebec [*Library symbol*] [*National Library of Canada*]   (NLC)
QSFCD...... Societe de Cooperation pour le Developpement International, Ste.-Foy, Quebec [*Library symbol*] [*National Library of Canada*]   (BIB)
QSFCM..... College Marguerite d'Youville, Ste.-Foy, Quebec [*Library symbol*] [*National Library of Canada*]   (NLC)
QSFCP ...... Commission de Police du Quebec, Ste.-Foy, Quebec [*Library symbol*] [*National Library of Canada*]   (NLC)
QSFCR ...... Centre de Recherche Industrielle du Quebec, Ste.-Foy, Quebec [*Library symbol*] [*National Library of Canada*]   (NLC)

QSFCRO ... Centre de Documentation, Commission Rochon, Ste.-Foy, Quebec [*Library symbol*] [*National Library of Canada*]   (BIB)
QSFCSE.... Centre de Documentation, Conseil Superieur de l'Education du Quebec, Ste.-Foy, Quebec [*Library symbol*] [*National Library of Canada*]   (BIB)
QSFE......... Centre de Documentation, Directeur General des Elections du Quebec, Ste.-Foy, Quebec [*Library symbol*] [*National Library of Canada*]   (BIB)
QSFHL....... Hopital Laval, Ste.-Foy, Quebec [*Library symbol*] [*National Library of Canada*]   (NLC)
QSFIG .... Centre de Documentation, INRS [*Institut National de la Recherche Scientifique*]-Georessources, Ste.-Foy, Quebec [*Library symbol*] [*National Library of Canada*]   (NLC)
QSFIO .... Institut National d'Optique, Ste.-Foy, Quebec [*Library symbol*] [*National Library of Canada*]   (BIB)
QSFPC ...... Centre de Documentation, Bureau de la Protection Civile du Quebec, Ste.-Foy, Quebec [*Library symbol*] [*National Library of Canada*]   (BIB)
QSFS .... SOQUEM [*Societe Quebecoise d'Exploration Miniere*] Documentation, Ste.-Foy, Quebec [*Library symbol*] [*National Library of Canada*]   (NLC)
QSG .... Quasi-Steady Glide [*NASA*]
QSG .... Quasi-Stellar Galaxy
QSGLL...... Queensland Studies in German Language and Literature [*A publication*]
QSGVT...... Quarter Scale Ground Vibration Test   (MCD)
QSH.......... Stanstead Historial Society, Quebec [*Library symbol*] [*National Library of Canada*]   (NLC)
QSHAG..... Saint-Hyacinthe Food Research Centre, Agriculture Canada [*Centre de Recherches Alimentaires de Saint-Hyacinthe, Agriculture Canada*] Quebec [*Library symbol*] [*National Library of Canada*]   (NLC)
QSHC........ CEGEP [*College d'Enseignement General et Professionnel*] de Shawinigan, Quebec [*Library symbol*] [*National Library of Canada*]   (NLC)
QSHCH..... Centre Hospitalier Regional de La Mauricie, Shawinigan, Quebec [*Library symbol*] [*National Library of Canada*]   (NLC)
QSHCHS .. Departement de Sante Communautaire, Centre Hospitalier Regional de la Mauricie, Shawinigan, Quebec [*Library symbol*] [*National Library of Canada*]   (BIB)
QSHCP...... Hopital Communautaire du Pontiac [*Pontiac Community Hospital*], Shawville, Quebec [*Library symbol*] [*National Library of Canada*]   (NLC)
QSHERAN ... Centre Regional de l'Estrie, Archives Nationales du Quebec, Sherbrooke, Quebec [*Library symbol*] [*National Library of Canada*]   (NLC)
QSHERB... Bibliotheque Centrale de Pret de l'Estrie, Sherbrooke, Quebec [*Library symbol*] [*National Library of Canada*]   (BIB)
QSHERC... Bibliotheque des Sciences de la Sante, Universite de Sherbrooke, Quebec [*Library symbol*] [*National Library of Canada*]   (NLC)
QSHERCR ... Conseil Regional de la Sante et des Services Sociaux des Cantons de l'Est, Sherbrooke, Quebec [*Library symbol*] [*National Library of Canada*]   (NLC)
QSHERD .. Sherbrooke Daily Record, Quebec [*Library symbol*] [*National Library of Canada*]   (NLC)
QSHERE... College de Sherbrooke (CEGEP) [*College d'Enseignement General et Professionnel*], Quebec [*Library symbol*] [*National Library of Canada*]   (NLC)
QSHERG .. Bibliotheque du Grand Seminaire, Sherbrooke, Quebec [*Library symbol*] [*National Library of Canada*]   (NLC)
QSHERH.. Huntingdon Gleaner, Quebec [*Library symbol*] [*National Library of Canada*]   (NLC)
QSHERHD ... Centre Hospitalier Hotel-Dieu, Sherbrooke, Quebec [*Library symbol*] [*National Library of Canada*]   (NLC)
QSHERM ... Monastere des Peres Redemptoristes, Sherbrooke, Quebec [*Library symbol*] [*Obsolete*] [*National Library of Canada*]   (NLC)
QSHERN .. Bibliotheque Municipale, Sherbrooke, Quebec [*Library symbol*] [*National Library of Canada*]   (NLC)
QSHERS... Seminaire de Sherbrooke, Quebec [*Library symbol*] [*National Library of Canada*]   (NLC)
QSHERSB ... Les Conseillers Samson Belair, Inc., Sherbrooke, Quebec [*Library symbol*] [*National Library of Canada*]   (NLC)
QSHERSC ... College du Sacre-Coeur, Sherbrooke, Quebec [*Library symbol*] [*National Library of Canada*]   (NLC)
QSHERSF ... Ecole Secondaire St.-Francois, Sherbrooke, Quebec [*Library symbol*] [*National Library of Canada*]   (NLC)
QSHERSG ... Societe de Genealogie des Cantons de l'Est, Sherbrooke, Quebec [*Library symbol*] [*National Library of Canada*]   (NLC)
QSHERSH ... La Societe d'Histoire des Cantons de l'Est, Sherbrooke, Quebec [*Library symbol*] [*National Library of Canada*]   (NLC)
QSHERSV ... Centre Hospitalier St.-Vincent-De-Paul, Sherbrooke, Quebec [*Library symbol*] [*National Library of Canada*]   (NLC)
QSHERU .. Bibliotheque Generale, Universite de Sherbrooke, Quebec [*Library symbol*] [*National Library of Canada*]   (NLC)

QSHERUA ... Galerie d'Art et Centre Culturel, Universite de Sherbrooke, Quebec [*Library symbol*] [*National Library of Canada*] (NLC)
QSHERUD ... Bibliotheque de Droit, Universite de Sherbrooke, Quebec [*Library symbol*] [*National Library of Canada*] (NLC)
QSHERUG ... Departement de Geographie, Universite de Sherbrooke, Quebec [*Library symbol*] [*National Library of Canada*] (NLC)
QSHERUGC ... Cartotheque, Departement de Geographie, Universite de Sherbrooke, Quebec [*Library symbol*] [*National Library of Canada*] (NLC)
QSHERURA ... Centre de Documentation, Programme de Recherche sur l'Amiante, Universite de Sherbrooke, Quebec [*Library symbol*] [*National Library of Canada*] (NLC)
QSHERUS ... Bibliotheque des Sciences, Universite de Sherbrooke, Quebec [*Library symbol*] [*National Library of Canada*] (NLC)
QSHERY... Centre de Documentation et d'Audio-Visuel, Hopital d'Youville de Sherbrooke, Quebec [*Library symbol*] [*National Library of Canada*] (NLC)
QSHM...... Municipal Library [*Bibliotheque Municipale*] Shawinigan, Quebec [*Library symbol*] [*National Library of Canada*] (NLC)
QSHS .... Seminaire Ste-Marie, Shawinigan, Quebec [*Library symbol*] [*National Library of Canada*] (NLC)
QSI .... Bibliotheque Municipale, Sept-Iles, Quebec [*Library symbol*] [*National Library of Canada*] (NLC)
QSI .... Quality Salary Increase (AFM)
QSI .... Quality Service Indicator
QSI .... Quality Step Increase (GFGA)
QSI .... Quantum Scalar Irradiance [*Instrumentation*]
QSI .... Quarterly Survey of Intentions [*Became Consumer Buying Expectations Survey*] [*Bureau of the Census*]
QSIA......... Centre Regional de la Cote-Nord, Archives Nationales du Quebec, Sept-Iles, Quebec [*Library symbol*] [*National Library of Canada*] (BIB)
QSIBCP..... Bibliotheque Centrale de Pret de la Cote-Nord, Sept-Iles, Quebec [*Library symbol*] [*National Library of Canada*] (NLC)
QSIC......... CEGEP [*College d'Enseignement General et Professionnel*] de Sept-Iles, Quebec [*Library symbol*] [*National Library of Canada*] (BIB)
QSIC......... Quality Standard Inspection Criteria
QSIH .... Hopital des Sept-Iles, Quebec [*Library symbol*] [*National Library of Canada*] (NLC)
QSII.......... Quality Systems, Inc. [*NASDAQ symbol*] (NQ)
QSIIOM.... Mineralogy Laboratory, Iron Ore Co., Sept-Iles, Quebec [*Library symbol*] [*National Library of Canada*] (NLC)
QSILC .... College Jesus-Marie de Sillery, Quebec [*Library symbol*] [*National Library of Canada*] (NLC)
QSJ .... Stanstead Journal, Quebec [*Library symbol*] [*National Library of Canada*] (NLC)
QSJHD...... Hotel-Dieu de Saint-Jerome, Quebec [*Library symbol*] [*National Library of Canada*] (NLC)
QSK .... Quadriphase Shift Keying (MCD)
QSL........... Q-Switch LASER
QSL........... Qualification Status List (KSC)
QSL........... Qualified Source List [*NASA*] (NASA)
QSL........... Quality of School Life Scale [*Educational test*]
QSL........... Quarterly Stock List
QS & L....... Quarters, Subsistence, and Laundry [*Military*]
QSL........... Queue Search Limit [*Data processing*]
QSLCR ...... Campus 1, Champlain Regional College, St.-Lambert, Quebec [*Library symbol*] [*National Library of Canada*] (NLC)
QSLE......... Bibliotheque Municipale, Saint-Leonard, Quebec [*Library symbol*] [*National Library of Canada*] (NLC)
QSM .... Quality Systems Management [*DoD*]
QSM .... Quarter Scale Model (MCD)
QSM .... Quarter Square Multiplier
QSM .... Quasi-Linear Sequential Machine
QSM .... Southmark Corp. [*NYSE symbol*] (SPSG)
QSMVT..... Quarter Scale Model Vibration Testing (NASA)
QSNDF...... Archer Communications, Inc. [*NASDAQ symbol*] (SPSG)
QSNT .... (Quinolinesulfonyl)nitrotriazole [*Organic chemistry*]
QSO .... Bibliotheque Municipale, Sorel, Quebec [*Library symbol*] [*National Library of Canada*] (NLC)
QSO .... Quasi-Biennial Stratospheric Oscillation
QSO .... Quasi-Stellar [*or QUASAR*] Object
QSOCS...... C. Stroemgren, Sorel, Quebec [*Library symbol*] [*National Library of Canada*] (NLC)
QSOCS...... QIT - Fer et Titane, Inc., Sorel, Quebec [*Library symbol*] [*National Library of Canada*] (NLC)
QSOP .... Quadripartite Standing Operating Procedures [*Military*]
QSP........... Quench Spray Pump (IEEE)
QSP........... Quick Search Procedure
QSPS .... Qualification Standards for Postal Field Service
QSR .... Quality Status Review (MCD)
QSR .... Quality Strike Reconnaissance
QSR .... Quality System Review
QSR .... Quarterly Statistical Report (NRCH)
QSR .... Quarterly Status Report
QSR .... Quarterly Summary Report

QSR .... Quasi-Stellar Radio Source
QSR .... Quebec Sturgeon River Mines Ltd. [*Toronto Stock Exchange symbol*]
QSR .... Quick-Start Recording [*Video technology*]
QSR .... Quick Strike Reconnaissance (MCD)
QSR .... Quien Sabe Ranch [*California*] [*Seismograph station code, US Geological Survey*] (SEIS)
QSR .... Quinoline Still Residue [*Coal tar technology*]
QSR .... State Reports (Queensland) [*A publication*] (APTA)
QSRA .... Quiet Short-Haul Research Aircraft [*NASA*]
QSRI......... QSR, Inc. [*NASDAQ symbol*] (NQ)
QSRMC.... Quality Scheme for Ready Mixed Concrete (EAIO)
QSRS........ Quasi-Stellar Blue Galaxies (SAA)
QSRS........ Quasi-Stellar Radio Source
QSRT........ Quebec Sturgeon River Mines Ltd. [*NASDAQ symbol*] (NQ)
QSS........... Quadratic Score Statistic [*Test*]
QSS........... Quadrupole Screw Ship
QSS........... Quasi-Steady State
QSS........... Quasi-Stellar Source
QSS........... Quench Spray Subsystem (IEEE)
QSS........... Quick Service Supervisor (MCD)
QSS........... Quick Supply Store [*Military*] (AABC)
QSS........... Quill and Scroll Society (EA)
QSS........... Quindar Scanning System (NASA)
QSSA .... Quasi-Stationary State Approximation
QSSI .... Quarterly Surprise Security Inspection [*Navy*] (DNAB)
QSSP .... Quasi-Solid State Panel
QSSR........ Quarterly Stock Status Report
QST .... QSA Tech, Inc. [*Vancouver Stock Exchange symbol*]
QST .... Quarterly Statement [*A publication*]
QST .... Quarterly Statements. Palestine Exploration Fund [*A publication*]
QST .... Questmont Mines [*Vancouver Stock Exchange symbol*]
QSTAG...... Quadripartite Standardization Agreement [*Military*]
QSTAG...... Quality Standardization Agreements (MCD)
QSTAH ..... Ste-Anne's Hospital, Ste-Anne-De-Bellevue, Quebec [*Library symbol*] [*National Library of Canada*] (NLC)
QSTAJ ...... John Abbott College, Ste-Anne-De-Bellevue, Quebec [*Library symbol*] [*National Library of Canada*] (NLC)
QSTAMP.. Quality Stamp
QSTAR...... Quantitative Structure-Time-Activity Relationship [*Chemistry*]
QSTAS ...... Spar Technology Ltd., Ste-Anne-De-Bellevue, Quebec [*Library symbol*] [*National Library of Canada*] (NLC)
QSTB........ Bibliotheque Municipale, Saint-Bruno-De-Montarville, Quebec [*Library symbol*] [*National Library of Canada*] (BIB)
QSTBL ...... Abbaye de Saint-Benoit-Du-Lac, Comte De Brome, Quebec [*Library symbol*] [*National Library of Canada*] (NLC)
QSTC........ Tioxide Canada, Inc., Sorel, Quebec [*Library symbol*] [*National Library of Canada*] (NLC)
QSTFAG ... Centre de Documentation, Ministere de l'Agriculture, des Pecheries, et de l'Alimentation, Ste.-Foy, Quebec [*Library symbol*] [*National Library of Canada*] (NLC)
QSTFCE.... Centre de Documentation, Centrale de l'Enseignement du Quebec, Ste.-Foy, Quebec [*Library symbol*] [*National Library of Canada*] (NLC)
QSTFCR.... Resource Centre, St. Lawrence Campus, Champlain Regional College, Ste.-Foy, Quebec [*Library symbol*] [*National Library of Canada*] (NLC)
QSTFP ...... Protecteur du Citoyen du Quebec, Ste.-Foy [*Library symbol*] [*National Library of Canada*] (BIB)
QSTFR ...... Rexfor, Ste.-Foy, Quebec [*Library symbol*] [*National Library of Canada*] (NLC)
QSTFRA ... Centre de Documentation, Roche Associes Ltee., Ste.-Foy, Quebec [*Library symbol*] [*National Library of Canada*] (NLC)
QSTHHR.. Societe d'Histoire Regionale de St-Hyacinthe, Quebec [*Library symbol*] [*National Library of Canada*] (NLC)
QSTHS...... Seminaire de St-Hyacinthe, Quebec [*Library symbol*] [*National Library of Canada*] (NLC)
QSTHTA... Institut de Technologie Agricole et Alimentaire de St.-Hyacinthe, Quebec [*Library symbol*] [*National Library of Canada*] (NLC)
QSTHUM ... Headquarters Mobile Command, Canada Department of National Defence [*Quartier-General du Commandement de la Defense Nationale*] St-Hubert, Quebec [*Library symbol*] [*National Library of Canada*] (NLC)
QSTHV ..... Faulte de Medecine Veterinaire de l'Universite de Montreal, Saint-Hyacinthe, Quebec [*Library symbol*] [*National Library of Canada*] (NLC)
QSTING.... Quasi-Spectral Time Integration on Nested Grids
QSTJ .... College Militaire Royal de Saint-Jean, Quebec [*Library symbol*] [*National Library of Canada*] (NLC)
QSTJA ...... Bibliotheque Adelard-Berger, St.-Jean-Sur-Richelieu, Quebec [*Library symbol*] [*National Library of Canada*] (BIB)
QSTJAG ... Research Station, Agriculture Canada [*Station de Recherches, Agriculture Canada*] Saint-Jean, Quebec [*Library symbol*] [*National Library of Canada*] (NLC)
QSTJB....... Bibliotheque Municipale, Saint-Jean, Quebec [*Library symbol*] [*National Library of Canada*] (NLC)
QSTJC....... College Saint-Jean-Sur-Richelieu, Saint-Jean, Quebec [*Library symbol*] [*National Library of Canada*] (NLC)

QSTJCF .... Canadian Forces Base St. Jean [*Base des Forces Canadiennes St.-Jean*], Quebec [*Library symbol*] [*National Library of Canada*] (NLC)
QSTJE .... Bibliotheque Municipale, Saint-Jerome, Quebec [*Library symbol*] [*National Library of Canada*] (NLC)
QSTJEC .... CEGEP [*College d'Enseignement General et Professionnel*] de St.-Jerome, Quebec [*Library symbol*] [*National Library of Canada*] (BIB)
QSTJECR ... Conseil Regional de la Sante et des Services Sociaux Laurentides-Lanaudiere, Saint-Jerome, Quebec [*Library symbol*] [*National Library of Canada*] (NLC)
QSTJEJ .... Jesuites/Bibliotheque, Saint-Jerome, Quebec [*Library symbol*] [*National Library of Canada*] (NLC)
QSTJH ...... Bibliotheque Medicale, Hopital du Haut-Richelieu, St.-Jean-Sur-Richelieu, Quebec [*Library symbol*] [*National Library of Canada*] (BIB)
QSTJSC .... Centre de Documentation, Departement de Sante Communautaire du Haut-Richelieu, St.-Jean, Quebec [*Library symbol*] [*National Library of Canada*] (NLC)
QSTL .... Bibliotheque Municipale, Saint-Laurent, Quebec [*Library symbol*] [*National Library of Canada*] (NLC)
QSTLD ...... Dominion Yarn Co., St. Laurent, Quebec [*Library symbol*] [*National Library of Canada*] (BIB)
QSTNRY ... Quasi-Stationary (FAAC)
QSTOL ...... Quiet-Short-Takeoff-and-Landing [*Airplane*] [*Japan*]
QSTR .... Bibliotheque Municipale de Saint-Raphael-De-L'Ile-Bizard, Quebec [*Library symbol*] [*National Library of Canada*] (NLC)
QSTTB ...... Engineering Library, Bell Helicopter Textron, Ste. Therese, Quebec [*Library symbol*] [*National Library of Canada*] (NLC)
QSTTH ..... Les Industries Harnois, St-Thomas-De-Joliette, Quebec [*Library symbol*] [*National Library of Canada*] (NLC)
QstV .... Quest for Value Fund [*Associated Press abbreviation*] (APAG)
QSTX .... Questronics, Inc. [*NASDAQ symbol*] (NQ)
qsuff .... Quantum Sufficit [*As Much As Will Suffice*] [*Latin*] (MAE)
QS Wkly .... Quantity Surveyor Weekly [*A publication*]
QSY .... Quiet Sun Year
QT .... Aer Turas Teoranta [*Ireland*] [*ICAO designator*] (FAAC)
QT .... Bibliotheque Municipale, Trois-Rivieres, Quebec [*Library symbol*] [*National Library of Canada*] (NLC)
QT .... Quadruple Thermoplastic (SAA)
QT .... Qualification Test
QT .... Quantity
QT .... Quarry Tile [*Technical drawings*]
QT .... Quart (AFM)
QT .... Quarters
QT .... Quartet [*Music*]
Qt .... Quartet [*A publication*]
QT .... Quebec-Telephone [*Toronto Stock Exchange symbol*]
QT .... Quenched and Tempered (MCD)
QT .... Questioned Trade [*on a stock exchange*]
QT .... Queuing Theory [*Telecommunications*]
QT .... Queuing Time [*Telecommunications*] (TEL)
QT .... Qui Tam [*Who as Well*] [*Latin*] (ILCA)
QT .... Quick Tan [*Trademark of Plough, Inc.*]
QT .... Quick Test
QT .... Quiet [*or sub rosa, as, "On the QT"*]
QT .... Quotation Ticker [*Business term*]
QT .... Quotient
QTA .... Archives Nationales du Quebec, Trois-Rivieres, Quebec [*Library symbol*] [*National Library of Canada*] (NLC)
QTA .... Quadrant Transformer Assembly
QTAM .... Quadrature Amplitude Modulation (MCD)
QTAM .... Queued Telecommunications Access Method [*IBM Corp.*] [*Data processing*]
QTAM .... Queued Terminal Access Method [*Data processing*]
QTB .... Le Boreal Express, Montreal, Quebec [*Library symbol*] [*National Library of Canada*] (NLC)
QTB .... Quarry-Tile Base [*Technical drawings*]
QTBC .... Bibliotheque Centrale de Pret de la Mauricie, Trois-Rivieres, Quebec [*Library symbol*] [*National Library of Canada*] (NLC)
QTC .... Quick Transmission Change (MCD)
QTC .... Quick Turnaround Cell [*Engineering*] (RDA)
QTCE .... CEGEP [*College d'Enseignement General et Professionnel*], Trois-Rivieres, Quebec [*Library symbol*] [*National Library of Canada*] (NLC)
QTCHC ..... Centre Hospitalier Cooke, Trois-Rivieres, Quebec [*Library symbol*] [*National Library of Canada*] (NLC)
QTCL .... College Lafleche, Trois-Rivieres, Quebec [*Library symbol*] [*National Library of Canada*] (NLC)
QTCO .... Communication-Quebec, Trois-Rivieres, Quebec [*Library symbol*] [*National Library of Canada*] (NLC)
QTCPB ...... Corporation Pierre Boucher, Trois-Rivieres, Quebec [*Library symbol*] [*National Library of Canada*] (NLC)
QTCRD ..... Conseil Regional de Developpement, Trois-Rivieres, Quebec [*Library symbol*] [*National Library of Canada*] (NLC)
QTCRS ...... Conseil Regional de la Sante et des Services Sociaux, Trois-Rivieres, Quebec [*Library symbol*] [*National Library of Canada*] (NLC)

QTCSRV ... Commission Scolaire Regionale des Vieilles-Forges, Trois-Rivieres, Quebec [*Library symbol*] [*National Library of Canada*] (NLC)
QTCSS ...... Centre de Services Sociaux, Trois-Rivieres, Quebec [*Library symbol*] [*National Library of Canada*] (NLC)
QTD .... Quadruple Terminal Digits (AABC)
QTD .... Quartered
QTD .... Quasi-Two-Dimensional
QTDG .... Quaker Theological Discussion Group (EA)
QTDM .... Qazaq Tili Tarychy Men Dyalektology Jasinin Moseleleri [*A publication*]
QT DX .... Quantitas Duplex [*Double Quantity*] [*Pharmacy*]
QTE .... Ecole Normale M. L. Duplessis, Trois-Rivieres, Quebec [*Library symbol*] [*National Library of Canada*] (NLC)
QT & E .... Qualification Test and Evaluation [*Military*]
QTE .... Qualite [*Quality*] [*French*] (ROG)
QTE .... Quote
QTE .... True Bearing [*from me*] [*Aviation code*] (FAAC)
Q Teachers J ... Queensland Teachers' Journal [*A publication*] (APTA)
QTEC .... QuesTech, Inc. [*NASDAQ symbol*] (NQ)
Q-TECH .... Quality-Technology
QTER .... Bibliotheque Municipale, Terrebonne, Quebec [*Library symbol*] [*National Library of Canada*] (NLC)
4QTest .... [*The*] Testimonia from Qumran. Cave Four (BJA)
QTEV .... Quadruple Turbo-Electric Vessel (DS)
QTF .... Quarry-Tile Floor [*Technical drawings*]
QTH .... Queued Transaction Handling [*Data processing*]
QTHSJ ...... Hopital Saint-Joseph, Trois-Rivieres, Quebec [*Library symbol*] [*National Library of Canada*] (NLC)
QTHSM .... Hopital Sainte-Marie, Trois-Rivieres, Quebec [*Library symbol*] [*National Library of Canada*] (NLC)
QTI .... Institut Albert Tessier, Trois-Rivieres, Quebec [*Library symbol*] [*National Library of Canada*] (NLC)
QTIA .... Queensland Tourism Industry Authority [*Australia*]
Q Tic Num Ant Clas ... Quaderni Ticinesi. Numismatica e Antichita Classiche [*A publication*]
Q-TIP .... Qualified Terminable Interest Property [*Plan*] [*Tax law*]
QTL .... Qualified Thrift Lender
QTL .... Quantitative Trait Loci [*Genetics*]
QTL .... Quantum Theory of LASERS
QTL .... Quarterly Title List
QTL .... Quintel Industries Ltd. [*Vancouver Stock Exchange symbol*]
4QTLevi.... Testament of Levi from Qumran. Cave Four (BJA)
Qtly .... Quarterly
QTM.......... Qualification Test Model
QTMC .... College de la Region de l'Amiante (CEGEP), Thetford-Mines, Quebec [*Library symbol*] [*National Library of Canada*] (NLC)
QTMC .... Quantum Diagnostics Ltd. [*Hauppauge, NY*] [*NASDAQ symbol*] (NQ)
QTME .... Ministere de l'Energie et des Ressources du Quebec, Trois-Rivieres, Quebec [*Library symbol*] [*National Library of Canada*] (BIB)
QTMH....... Hopital General de la Regie de l'Amiante, Inc., Thetford Mines, Quebec [*Library symbol*] [*National Library of Canada*] (BIB)
QTNT .... QT & T, Inc. [*Brentwood, NY*] [*NASDAQ symbol*] (NQ)
QTO .... Qualified Testing Officer [*British military*] (DMA)
QTO .... Quarto [*Book from 25 to 30 centimeters in height*]
QTOD........ Todd Shipyards Corp. [*NYSE symbol*] (SPSG)
QTOL .... Quiet Takeoff and Landing [*Aviation*]
QTOPDQ .. Centre de Documentation, Office de Planification et de Developpement du Quebec, Trois-Rivieres, Quebec [*Library symbol*] [*National Library of Canada*] (NLC)
QTOW....... Towle Manufacturing Co. [*NYSE symbol*] (SPSG)
QTP .... Qualification Test Plan [*NASA*] (NASA)
QTP .... Qualification Test Procedure
QTP .... Qualification Test Program
QTP .... Quality Test Plan [*Nuclear energy*] (NRCH)
QTP .... Quantum Theory of Paramagnetism
QTP .... Quantum Theory Project [*University of Florida*] [*Research center*] (RCD)
QTPC......... Quadripartite Technical Procedures Committee [*Military*] (AABC)
QTPR........ Quarterly Technical Progress Report
QTR .... Qualification Test Report
QTR .... Qualified Tuition Reduction [*IRS*]
QTR .... Quarry-Tile Roof [*Technical drawings*]
QTR .... Quarter (AFM)
QTR .... Quarterly (AFM)
QTR .... Quarterly Technical Report
QTR .... Quarterly Technical Review [*Jet Propulsion Laboratory publication*]
QTR .... Queenstake Resources Ltd. [*Toronto Stock Exchange symbol*]
Q Trans Am Inst Electr Eng ... Quarterly Transactions. American Institute of Electrical Engineers [*A publication*]
QTRLY...... Quarterly
QTRRSS.... Centre de Documentation, Regie de la Securite dans les Sports du Quebec, Trois-Rivieres, Quebec [*Library symbol*] [*National Library of Canada*] (NLC)
QTRS........ Quarters

QTS .... Qualification Test Specification
QTS .... Quartz Thermometer Sensor
QTS .... Seminaire de Trois-Rivieres, Quebec [*Library symbol*] [*National Library of Canada*] (NLC)
QTT .... Quartet [*Music*]
QTT .... Trois-Rivieres High School, Quebec [*Library symbol*] [*National Library of Canada*] (NLC)
QTTA .... Quaderni Triestini sul Teatro Antico [*A publication*]
QTTE....... Quartette [*Music*]
QTTF........ Temifibre, Inc., Temiscaming, Quebec [*Library symbol*] [*National Library of Canada*] (NLC)
QTTP........ Q-Tags Test of Personality [*Psychology*]
QTU.......... Qualification Test Unit
QTU.......... Universite du Quebec, Trois-Rivieres, Quebec [*Library symbol*] [*National Library of Canada*] (NLC)
QTUAH..... Archives Historiques, Universite du Quebec, Trois-Rivieres, Quebec [*Library symbol*] [*National Library of Canada*] (NLC)
QTUGC..... Cartotheque, Departement de Geographie, Universite du Quebec, Trois-Rivieres, Quebec [*Library symbol*] [*National Library of Canada*] (NLC)
QTUIH...... Imprimes Historiques, Universite du Quebec, Trois-Rivieres, Quebec [*Library symbol*] [*National Library of Canada*] (NLC)
QTURA ..... Archives des Ursulines, Trois-Rivieres, Quebec [*Library symbol*] [*National Library of Canada*] (NLC)
QTUTH..... Centre de Documentation en Theatre Quebecois, Trois-Rivieres, Quebec [*Library symbol*] [*National Library of Canada*] (NLC)
QTV .... Qualification Test Vehicle
Qty .... Quality (DS)
QTY .... Quantity (KSC)
QTYDESREQ ... Quantity Desired as Requested [*Military*]
QTZ.......... Quartz (AAG)
QTZ.......... Quartzite [*Lithology*]
QU .... Nicaragua [*License plate code assigned to foreign diplomats in the US*]
QU .... Quaderni dell'Umanesimo [*A publication*]
QU .... Quadrantectomy [*Medicine*]
QU .... Quail Unlimited (EA)
QU .... Quart (WGA)
QU .... Quarter (ADA)
QU .... Quartermaster (ROG)
QU .... Quartern (ROG)
QU .... Quasi [*Almost, As It Were*] [*Latin*]
QU .... Quay (ROG)
QU .... Queen
QU .... Queen's University [*Canada*]
QU .... Query
QU .... Question
QU .... Questionnaire
QU .... Quina [*Quinine*] [*Pharmacy*] (ROG)
QU .... Quinto Mining [*Vancouver Stock Exchange symbol*]
QU .... Quotation (ROG)
QU .... Uganda Airlines Corp. [*ICAO designator*] (FAAC)
QUA .... Quabbin [*Massachusetts*] [*Seismograph station code, US Geological Survey*] (SEIS)
QUA .... Quality [*A publication*]
QUA .... Quinterra Resources, Inc. [*Toronto Stock Exchange symbol*] [*Vancouver Stock Exchange symbol*]
QUAC....... Quadriatic Arc Computer
QUAD .... Quadrajet Carburetor [*Automotive engineering*]
QUAD .... Quadrangle (AAG)
QUAD .... Quadrant (KSC)
QUAD ...... Quadraphonic
QUAD ...... Quadrature (NASA)
QUAD ...... Quadrex Corp. [*NASDAQ symbol*] (NQ)
QUAD ...... Quadrilateral (WGA)
QUAD ...... Quadrillion
Quad .... Quadriplegic
Quad .... Quadrivium [*A publication*]
QUAD ...... Quadruple
Quad Acta Neurol ... Quaderni di Acta Neurologica [*A publication*]
Quad A Libia ... Quaderni di Archeologia della Libia [*A publication*]
Quad Anat Prat ... Quaderni di Anatomia Pratica [*A publication*]
Quad Azione Soc ... Quaderni di Azione Sociale [*A publication*]
Quad Chim CNR (Italy) ... Quaderni di Chimica. Consiglio Nazionale delle Ricerche (Italy) [*A publication*]
Quad Clin Ostet ... Quaderni di Clinica Ostetrica e Ginecologica [*A publication*]
Quad Clin Ostet Ginecol ... Quaderni de Clinica Ostetrica e Ginecologica [*A publication*]
Quad Coagulazione Argomenti Connessi ... Quaderni della Coagulazione e Argomenti Connessi [*A publication*]
Quad Criminol Clin ... Quaderni di Criminologia Clinica [*A publication*]
Quad Econ (Sarda) ... Quaderni dell'Economia (Sarda) [*A publication*]
Quad Emiliani ... Quaderni Emiliani [*A publication*]
Quad Ente Naz Semen Elette ... Quaderno. Ente Nazionale Sementi Elette [*A publication*]
Quad Formaz ... Quaderni di Formazione [*A publication*]
Quad Geofis Appl ... Quaderni di Geofisica Applicata [*A publication*]

Quad G Fis ... Quaderni del Giornale di Fisica [*Italy*] [*A publication*]
Quad Ing Chim Ital ... Quaderni dell'Ingegnere Chimico Italiano [*A publication*]
Quad Ist Bot Univ Lab Crittogam (Pavia) ... Quaderni. Istituto Botanico. Universita Laboratorio Crittogamico (Pavia) [*A publication*]
Quad Ist Fil Gr ... Quaderni dell'Istituto di Filologia Greca [*A publication*]
Quad Mathesis Cosenza ... Mathesis di Cosenza. Quaderni [*A publication*]
Quad Merceol Ist Merceol Univ Bari ... Quaderni di Merceologia. Istituto di Merceologia. Universita Bari [*A publication*]
Quad Nutr ... Quaderni della Nutrizione [*A publication*]
Quad Nutr (Bologna) ... Quaderni della Nutrizione (Bologna) [*A publication*]
QUADPAN ... Quadrilateral Element Panel Method [*Aerospace propulsion*]
Quad Pignone ... Quaderni Pignone [*A publication*]
Quadr......... Quadragesms [*Yearbooks of Edward III*] [*A publication*] (DLA)
Quadr......... Quadrant [*A publication*]
QUADR..... Quadruple
QUADRADAR ... Four-Way RADAR Surveillance
Quad Radiol ... Quaderni di Radiologia [*A publication*]
Quadrangle Rep Conn State Geol Nat Hist Surv ... Quadrangle Report. Connecticut. State Geological and Natural History Survey [*A publication*]
Quadrangle Ser 1:50000 Geol Surv Jap ... Quadrangle Series 1:50,000. Geological Survey of Japan [*A publication*]
Quadrenn Meet Int Assoc Study Liver ... Quadrennial Meeting. International Association for the Study of the Liver [*A publication*]
Quad Ricerca Sci ... Quaderni de la Ricerca Scientifica [*A publication*]
Quad Ric Progettazione ... Quaderni di Ricerca e Progettazione [*A publication*]
Quad Ric Sci ... Quaderni de la Ricerca Scientifica [*A publication*]
Quadrupl.... Quadruplicato [*Four Times as Much*] [*Pharmacy*]
QUADS..... Quality Achievement Data System (NASA)
Quad Sardi Econ ... Quaderni Sardi di Economia [*A publication*]
Quad Sclavo Diagn ... Quaderni Sclavo di Diagnostica Clinica e di Laboratorio [*A publication*]
Quad Sclavo Diagn Clin Lab ... Quaderni Sclavo di Diagnostica Clinica e di Laboratorio [*A publication*]
Quad Ser III ... Quaderni. Serie III [*A publication*]
Quad Sez Perugina Soc Ital Biol Sper ... Quaderni. Sezione Perugina. Societa Italiana di Biologia Sperimentale [*A publication*]
Quad Sociol ... Quaderni di Sociologia [*A publication*]
Quad Stor ... Quaderni di Storia [*A publication*]
Quad Stor... Quaderni Storici [*A publication*]
Quad Stor Univ Padova ... Quaderni per la Storia. Universita di Padova [*A publication*]
Quad Tec Sint Spec Org ... Quaderni di Tecniche e Sintesi Speciali Organiche [*A publication*]
Quad Top Ant ... Quaderni. Istituto di Topografia Antica. Universita di Roma [*A publication*]
Quad Urb C ... Quaderni Urbinati di Cultura Classica [*A publication*]
Quad Urbin ... Quaderni Urbinati di Cultura Classica [*A publication*]
Quaest Conv ... Quaestiones Convivales [*of Plutarch*] [*Classical studies*] (OCD)
Quaest Ent ... Quaestiones Entomologicae [*A publication*]
Quaest Entomol ... Quaestiones Entomologicae [*A publication*]
Quaest Geobiol ... Quaestiones Geobiologicae [*A publication*]
Quaest Graec ... Quaestiones Graecae [*of Plutarch*] [*Classical studies*] (OCD)
Quaest Inf.. Quaestiones Informaticae [*A publication*]
Quaestiones Math ... Quaestiones Mathematicae [*A publication*]
Quaest Plat ... Quaestiones Platonicae [*of Plutarch*] [*Classical studies*] (OCD)
Quaest Rom ... Quaestiones Romanae [*of Plutarch*] [*Classical studies*] (OCD)
QuakerH.... Quaker History [*A publication*]
QuakrO...... Quaker Oats Co. [*Associated Press abbreviation*] (APAG)
QuakSC.... Quaker State Corp. [*Associated Press abbreviation*] (APAG)
QUAL....... Qualification (NG)
QUAL....... Qualitative
Qual .... Qualiton & MHV [*Record label*] [*Hungary*]
QUAL....... Quality (KSC)
Qual Assur ... Quality Assurance [*A publication*]
Qual Contr Appl Stat ... Quality Control and Applied Statistics [*A publication*]
Qual Control Appl Stat ... Quality Control and Applied Statistics [*A publication*]
Qual Control Clin Chem Trans Int Symp ... Quality Control in Clinical Chemistry. Transactions. International Symposium [*A publication*]
Qual Control Med Proc Int Congr Pharm Sci ... Quality Control of Medicines. Proceedings. International Congress of Pharmaceutical Sciences [*A publication*]
Qual Control Rem Site Invest Hazard Ind Solid Waste Test ... Quality Control in Remedial Site Investigation. Hazardous and Industrial Solid Waste Testing [*A publication*]
Qual Eng.... Quality Engineer [*A publication*]
Qual Eval... Quality Evaluation [*A publication*]
Qual Foods Beverages Chem Technol Proc Symp Int Flavor Conf ... Quality of Foods and Beverages. Chemistry and Technology. Proceedings. Symposium. International Flavor Conference [*A publication*]
QUALGO ... Quasi-Autonomous Local Government Organisation [*British*] (DI)

Qual Groundwater Proc Int Symp ... Quality of Groundwater. Proceedings. International Symposium [*A publication*]

Qualitas Pl Pl Fds Human Nutr ... Qualitas Plantarum/Plant Foods for Human Nutrition [*A publication*]

Quality .... Quality of Sheffield and South Yorkshire [*A publication*]

Quality Prog ... Quality Progress [*A publication*]

QUALN ..... Qualification   (ROG)

Qual Plant ... Qualitas Plantarum/Plant Foods for Human Nutrition [*A publication*]

Qual Plant Mater Veg ... Qualitas Plantarum et Materiae Vegetabiles [*Later, Qualitas Plantarum/Plant Foods for Human Nutrition*] [*A publication*]

Qual Plant Plant Foods Hum Nutr ... Qualitas Plantarum/Plant Foods for Human Nutrition [*A publication*]

Qual Poult Meat Proc Eur Symp ... Quality of Poultry Meat. Proceedings. European Symposium on Poultry Meat Quality [*A publication*]

Qual Prog... Quality Progress [*A publication*]

Qual Publ Malting Barley Improv Assoc ... Quality Publication. Malting Barley Improvement Association [*A publication*]

Qual Quant ... Quality and Quantity [*A publication*]

Qual Reliab J ... Quality and Reliability Journal [*India*] [*A publication*]

QUALT ..... Queensland University Aphasia and Language Test

QUALTIS ... Quality Technology Information Service [*Atomic Energy Authority*] [*British*]   (IID)

Qual Today ... Quality Today [*A publication*]

Qual Zuverlaessigk ... Qualitaet und Zuverlaessigkeit [*A publication*]

Qual und Zuverlassigkeit ... Qualitaet und Zuverlaessigkeit [*A publication*]

QUAM...... Quadrature Amplitude Modulation   (IEEE)

QUAN .... Quantity   (KSC)

QUAN .... Quantronix Corp. [*NASDAQ symbol*]   (NQ)

Quanex...... Quanex Corp. [*Associated Press abbreviation*]   (APAG)

QUANGO ... Quasi-Autonomous Non-Governmental [*or National Governmental*] Organisation [*British*]

Quan Sociol ... Quantitative Sociology [*A publication*]

QUANT ..... Quantitative [*or Quantity*]

Quant Approaches Drug Des ... Quantitative Approaches to Drug Design [*A publication*]

Quant Aspects Risk Assess Chem Carcinog Symp ... Quantitative Aspects of Risk Assessment in Chemical Carcinogenesis. Symposium [*A publication*]

Quant Chem Symp ... Quantum Chemistry Symposia [*A publication*]

Quantitative Appl in the Social Sciences ... Quantitative Applications in the Social Sciences [*A publication*]

Quantitative Meth Unternehmungsplanung ... Quantitative Methoden der Unternehmungsplanung [*A publication*]

Quantity Surv ... Quantity Surveyor [*A publication*]

Quantm...... Quantum Chemical Corp. [*Associated Press abbreviation*]   (APAG)

Quant Mass Spectrom Life Sci ... Quantitative Mass Spectrometry in Life Sciences. Proceedings. International Symposium [*A publication*]

Qu Ant Pal ... Quarterly. Department of Antiquities in Palestine [*A publication*]

QUANTRAS ... Question Analysis Transformation and Search [*Data processing*]

Quant Struct Act Relat ... Quantitative Structure-Activity Relationships [*A publication*]

QUANT SUFF ... Quantum Sufficiat [*A Sufficient Quantity*] [*Pharmacy*]

Quant Suff ... Quantum Sufficit [*A Sufficient Quantity*] [*Pharmacy*]

Quantum Biol Symp Int J Quantum Chem ... Quantum Biology Symposium. International Journal of Quantum Chemistry [*A publication*]

Quantum Chaos Stat Nucl Phys Proc ... Quantum Chaos and Statistical Nuclear Physics. Proceedings [*A publication*]

Quantum Chem Symp ... Quantum Chemistry Symposia [*A publication*]

Quantum Electron Opt Proc Nat Quantum Electron Conf ... Quantum Electronics and Electro-Optics. Proceedings. National Quantum Electronics Conference [*A publication*]

Quantum Electron (New York) ... Quantum Electronics (New York) [*A publication*]

Quantum Electron Proc Int Congr ... Quantum Electronics. Proceedings. International Congress [*A publication*]

Quantum Opt Proc Int Symp ... Quantum Optics. Proceedings. International Symposium [*A publication*]

Quantum Stat Many Body Probl Proc Symp ... Quantum Statistics and the Many-Body Problem. Proceedings. Symposium on Quantum Statistics and Many-Body Problems [*A publication*]

Quantum Stat Mech Nat Sci ... Quantum Statistical Mechanics in the Natural Sciences [*A publication*]

Quanx .... Quanex Corp. [*Associated Press abbreviation*]   (APAG)

QUAOPS .. Quarantine Operations [*Military*]   (NVT)

QUAP........ Quality Assurance Procedures

QUAPP ..... Qu'Appelle [*Canadian river*]   (ROG)

QUAPS...... Quality Assurance Publications [*Navy*]

QUAR........ Quarantine   (AABC)

QUAR........ Quarter [*Business term*]

QUAR........ Quarterly

Quar .... Quarterly Review [*A publication*]

QUARAM ... Quality and Reliability Management [*DoD*]

Quar Crim Dig ... Quarles' Tennessee Criminal Digest [*A publication*]   (DLA)

Quar Jour Econ ... Quarterly Journal of Economics [*A publication*]

QUARK ..... Quantizer, Analyzer, and Record Keeper [*Telecommunications*]   (TEL)

Quarks Mesons Isobars Nucl Proc Top Sch ... Quarks, Mesons, and Isobars in Nuclei. Proceedings. Topical School [*A publication*]

Quarks Nucl Struct Proc Klaus Erkelenz Symp ... Quarks and Nuclear Structure. Proceedings. Klaus Erkelenz Symposium [*A publication*]

Quar Law Journal ... Quarterly Law Journal [*Virginia*] [*A publication*]   (DLA)

Quar L Rev ... Quarterly Law Review [*Virginia*] [*A publication*]   (DLA)

QUARLY .. Quarterly   (ROG)

QUARPEL ... Quartermaster Water-Repellent Clothing [*Military*]

Quar R Biol ... Quarterly Review of Biology [*A publication*]

Quar Rev.... Quarterly Review [*A publication*]

Quarries Mines Coal Health Saf ... Quarries and Mines Other than Coal. Health and Safety [*A publication*]

Quarry Manage Prod ... Quarry Management and Products [*Later, Quarry Management*] [*A publication*]

Quarry Mgmt ... Quarry Management [*A publication*]

Quarry Mgmt Products ... Quarry Management and Products [*Later, Quarry Management*] [*A publication*]

Quarry Min News ... Quarry and Mining News [*A publication*]

QUART ..... Quadrantectomy, Axillary Dissection, Radiotherapy [*Oncology*]

QUART ..... Quality Assurance and Reliability Team

QUART ..... Quarterly

QUART ..... Quartetto [*Quartet*] [*Music*]   (ROG)

QUART ..... Quartus [*Fourth*] [*Pharmacy*]

Quart Appl Math ... Quarterly of Applied Mathematics [*A publication*]

Quart Bul Ass Food Drug Offic US ... Quarterly Bulletin. Association of Food and Drug Officials of the United States [*Later, Quarterly Bulletin. Association of Food and Drug Officials*] [*A publication*]

Quart Bull Instn Eng Aust ... Quarterly Bulletin. Institution of Engineers of Australia [*A publication*]

Quart Bull Int Ass Agric Libr Docum ... Quarterly Bulletin. International Association of Agricultural Librarians and Documentalists [*A publication*]

Quart Bull Mich Agric Exp Sta ... Quarterly Bulletin. Michigan State University. Agricultural Experiment Station [*A publication*]

Quart Bull Mich State Univ Agr Exp Sta ... Quarterly Bulletin. Michigan State University. Agricultural Experiment Station [*A publication*]

Quart Bull Northwestern Univ M School ... Quarterly Bulletin. Northwestern University Medical School [*A publication*]

Quart Colo Sch Mines ... Quarterly. Colorado School of Mines [*A publication*]

Quarter Horse Dig ... Quarter Horse Digest [*A publication*]

Quarterly Appl Math ... Quarterly of Applied Mathematics [*A publication*]

Quarterly of F R TV ... Quarterly of Film, Radio, and Television [*A publication*]

Quartermaster Food Container Inst Armed Forces Act Rep ... Quartermaster Food and Container Institute for the Armed Forces. Activities Report [*A publication*]

Quart J Adm ... Quarterly Journal of Administration [*A publication*]

Quart J Agr Econ ... Quarterly Journal of Agricultural Economy [*A publication*]

Quart J Chin For (Taipei) ... Quarterly Journal of Chinese Forestry (Taipei) [*A publication*]

Quart J Crude Drug Res ... Quarterly Journal of Crude Drug Research [*A publication*]

Quart J Econ ... Quarterly Journal of Economics [*A publication*]

Quart J Econom ... Quarterly Journal of Economics [*A publication*]

Quart J Exp Physiol ... Quarterly Journal of Experimental Physiology [*A publication*]

Quart J Exp Psychol ... Quarterly Journal of Experimental Psychology [*A publication*]

Quart J For ... Quarterly Journal of Forestry [*A publication*]

Quart J Indian Inst Sci ... Quarterly Journal. Indian Institute of Science [*A publication*]

Quart J Libr Congress ... Quarterly Journal. Library of Congress [*A publication*]

Quart J Math Oxford Ser 2 ... Quarterly Journal of Mathematics. Oxford. Second Series [*A publication*]

Quart J Mech Appld Math ... Quarterly Journal of Mechanics and Applied Mathematics [*A publication*]

Quart J Mech Appl Math ... Quarterly Journal of Mechanics and Applied Mathematics [*A publication*]

Quart J Med ... Quarterly Journal of Medicine [*A publication*]

Quart J Microsc Sci ... Quarterly Journal of Microscopical Science [*A publication*]

Quart J Micr Sc ... Quarterly Journal of Microscopical Science [*A publication*]

Quart J Roy Meteorol Soc ... Quarterly Journal. Royal Meteorological Society [*A publication*]

Quart J Taiwan Mus ... Quarterly Journal. Taiwan Museum [*A publication*]

Quart J Vet Sc India ... Quarterly Journal of Veterinary Science in India and Army Animal Management [*A publication*]

Quart LJ (VA) ... Quarterly Law Journal [*Virginia*] [*A publication*]   (DLA)

Quart L Rev (VA) ... Quarterly Law Review [*Virginia*] [*A publication*]   (DLA)

QUARTM ... Quartermaster (ROG)
Quart Nat Dent Ass ... Quarterly. National Dental Association [*A publication*]
Quart Nebr Agr Exp Sta ... Quarterly. Nebraska Agricultural Experiment Station [*A publication*]
Quart Newsl (Dehra Dun) ... Quarterly News Letter. Forest Research Institute and Colleges (Dehra Dun) [*A publication*]
Quart Philippine Sugar Inst ... Quarterly. Philippine Sugar Institute [*A publication*]
Quart R ...... Quarterly Review [*A publication*]
Quart R ...... Quarterly Reviews. Chemical Society [*A publication*]
Quart R Agric ... Quarterly Review of Agricultural Economics [*A publication*] (APTA)
Quart R Agric Econ ... Quarterly Review of Agricultural Economics [*A publication*]
Quart R Centr Bank Ireland ... Quarterly Review. Central Bank of Ireland [*A publication*]
Quart R Econ Busin ... Quarterly Review of Economics and Business [*A publication*]
Quart Rep Ry Tech Res Inst ... Quarterly Report. Railway Technical Research Institute [*Tokyo*] [*A publication*]
Quart Rev... Quarterly Review [*A publication*]
Quart Rev... Quarterly Reviews. Chemical Society [*A publication*]
Quart Rev Agr Econ ... Quarterly Review of Agricultural Economics [*A publication*]
Quart Rev Agric Econ ... Quarterly Review of Agricultural Economics [*A publication*] (APTA)
Quart Rev Allergy ... Quarterly Review of Allergy and Applied Immunology [*A publication*]
Quart Rev Biol ... Quarterly Review of Biology [*A publication*]
Quart Rev Chem Soc ... Quarterly Reviews. Chemical Society [*A publication*]
Quart Rev Guernsey Soc ... Quarterly Review. Guernsey Society [*A publication*]
Quart Revs ... Quarterly Reviews. Chemical Society [*A publication*]
Quart Trans Soc Autom Eng ... Quarterly Transactions. Society of Automotive Engineers [*A publication*]
Quart Univ Nebr Coll Agr Home Econ Agr Exp Sta ... Quarterly. University of Nebraska. College of Agriculture and Home Economics. Agricultural Experiment Station [*A publication*]
QUARTZ GR ... Quartzite Granite [*Agronomy*]
QUASAR... Quasi-Stellar [*Astronomy*]
QUASAT... Quasar Satellite [*Proposed observatory in space*]
QUASD ..... Quality Assurance [*A publication*]
QUASER... Quantum Amplification by Stimulated Emission of Radiation
QUASS...... Quassia [*Pharmacology*] (ROG)
QUAT........ Quater [*Four Times*] [*Pharmacy*]
QUAT........ Quaternary [*Period, era, or system*] [*Geology*]
QUAT........ Quaternary Ammonium Compound [*Class of antimicrobial agents*]
QUAT........ Quaternion (NASA)
QUAT........ Quatrefoil [*Numismatics*]
Quaternary Res ... Quaternary Research [*A publication*]
Quatern Res ... Quaternary Research [*A publication*]
QUATIP.... Quality Assurance Test and Inspection Plan [*Military*] (CAAL)
Quat Res (Jap Assoc Quat Res) ... Quaternary Research (Japan Association of Quaternary Research) [*A publication*]
Quat Res (NY) ... Quaternary Research (New York) [*A publication*]
Quat Res (Tokyo) ... Quaternary Research (Tokyo) [*A publication*]
Quat Sci R ... Quaternary Science Reviews [*A publication*]
QUB.......... Queen's University, Belfast [*Ireland*]
QUBMIS... Quantitatively Based Management Information System
Qu Bull....... Quarterly Bulletin [*A publication*]
quc............. Quebec [*MARC country of publication code*] [*Library of Congress*] (LCCP)
QUCA........ Quality Care, Inc. [*NASDAQ symbol*] (NQ)
QUCC........ Quaderni Urbinati di Cultura Classica [*A publication*]
QUE.......... Albuquerque Public Library, Albuquerque, NM [*OCLC symbol*] (OCLC)
QUE.......... Quebec [*Canadian province*]
que............. Quechua [*MARC language code*] [*Library of Congress*] (LCCP)
QUE.......... Queenston Gold Mines Ltd. [*Toronto Stock Exchange symbol*]
QUE.......... Quetta [*Pakistan*] [*Seismograph station code, US Geological Survey*] (SEIS)
QUE.......... Quetta [*Pakistan*] [*Geomagnetic observatory code*]
QUEBCOR ... Quebecor, Inc. [*Associated Press abbreviation*] (APAG)
Quebec Dept Nat Resources Prelim Rept ... Quebec. Department of Natural Resources. Preliminary Report [*A publication*]
Quebec Dept Nat Resources Spec Paper ... Quebec. Department of Natural Resources. Special Paper [*A publication*]
Quebec Dept Trade and Commerce Geog Service Pub ... Quebec. Department of Trade and Commerce. Geographical Service. Publication [*A publication*]
Quebec L (Can) ... Quebec Law Reports [*Canada*] [*A publication*] (DLA)
Quebec Pr (Can) ... Quebec Practice [*Canada*] [*A publication*] (DLA)
Queb KB .... Quebec Official Reports, King's Bench [*Canada*] [*A publication*] (DLA)
Queb Pr...... Quebec Practice Reports [*1897-1943*] [*A publication*] (DLA)
Que BR ...... Quebec Rapports Judiciaires Officiels (Banc de la Reine, Cour Superieure) [*A publication*] (DLA)
Que C A ..... Quebec Official Reports, Court of Appeals [*A publication*]

Que CA ...... Rapports Judiciaires Officiels, Cour d'Appel [*1892-date*] [*Official Law Reports, Court of Appeal*] [*Quebec*] [*A publication*] (DLA)
Que CBR.... Rapports Judiciaires Officiels, Cour du Banc du Roi [*ou de la Reine*] [*Official Law Reports, Court of King's, or Queen's, Bench*] [*Quebec*] [*A publication*] (DLA)
Que Cons Rech Dev For Rapp ... Quebec. Conseil de la Recherche et du Developpement Forestiers. Rapport [*A publication*]
Que Cons Rech Dev For Rapp Annu ... Quebec. Conseil de la Recherche et du Developpement Forestiers. Rapport Annuel [*A publication*]
Que CS....... Rapports Judiciaires Officiels, Cour Superieure [*Official Law Reports, Superior Court*] [*Quebec*] [*A publication*] (DLA)
Que Dep Ind Commer Annu Rep ... Quebec. Department of Industry and Commerce. Annual Report [*A publication*]
Que Dep Lands For Res Serv Res Pap ... Quebec. Department of Lands and Forest Research Service. Research Paper [*A publication*]
Que Dep Natur Resour Geol Rep ... Quebec. Department of Natural Resources. Geological Report [*A publication*]
Que Dep Natur Resour Prelim Rep ... Quebec. Department of Natural Resources. Preliminary Report [*A publication*]
Que Dp Col Mines Br Rp ... Quebec. Department of Colonization, Mines, and Fisheries. Mines Branch. Report on Mining Operations [*A publication*]
Queen Q..... Queen's Quarterly [*A publication*]
Queens .... Queensland [*Australia*]
Queens .... Queensway Studios [*Record label*] [*Great Britain*]
Queens B Bull ... Queens Bar Bulletin [*United States*] [*A publication*] (DLA)
Queens CBA Bull ... Queens County Bar Association. Bulletin [*United States*] [*A publication*] (DLA)
Queens Intra LJ ... Queen's Intramural Law Journal [*1968-70*] [*Canada*] [*A publication*] (DLA)
Queen's Intramural LJ ... Queen's Intramural Law Journal [*A publication*] (DLA)
Queens JP & Loc Auth Jo ... Queensland Justice of the Peace and Local Authorities' Journal [*A publication*] (DLA)
Queensl ...... Queensland Reports [*A publication*]
Queensl Acts ... Queensland Public Acts [*A publication*] (DLA)
Queensl Agric J ... Queensland Agricultural Journal [*A publication*]
Queensland Ag J ... Queensland Agricultural Journal [*A publication*]
Queensland Agr J ... Queensland Agricultural Journal [*A publication*]
Queensland Dent Mag ... Queensland Dental Magazine [*A publication*] (APTA)
Queensland Gov Min J ... Queensland Government Mining Journal [*A publication*] (APTA)
Queensland Govt Min Jour ... Queensland Government Mining Journal [*A publication*]
Queensland Hist R ... Queensland Historical Review [*A publication*]
Queensland J Agr Anim Sci ... Queensland Journal of Agricultural and Animal Sciences [*A publication*]
Queensland J Ag Sci ... Queensland Journal of Agricultural Science [*Later, Queensland Journal of Agricultural and Animal Sciences*] [*A publication*] (APTA)
Queensland Land Court Rep ... Queensland Land Court Reports [*A publication*] (APTA)
Queensland L Soc'y J ... Queensland Law Society. Journal [*A publication*]
Queensland Pap in Econ Policy ... Queensland Papers in Economic Policy [*A publication*] (APTA)
Queens Law ... Queensland Lawyer [*Australia*] [*A publication*] (DLA)
Queensl Cr Lands LR ... Queensland Crown Lands Law Reports [*A publication*] (DLA)
Queensl Dent J ... Queensland Dental Journal [*A publication*] (APTA)
Queensl Dep Agric Stock ... Queensland. Department of Agriculture and Stock. Annual Report [*A publication*] (APTA)
Queensl Dep Mines Geol Surv Queensl Publ ... Queensland. Department of Mines. Geological Survey of Queensland. Publication [*A publication*] (APTA)
Queensl Dep Mines Geol Surv Queensl Rep ... Queensland. Department of Mines. Geological Survey of Queensland. Report [*A publication*] (APTA)
Queensl Dep Primary Ind Agric Chem Branch Tech Rep ... Queensland. Department of Primary Industries. Agricultural Chemistry Branch. Technical Report [*A publication*]
Queensl Dep Primary Ind Div Anim Ind Bull ... Queensland. Department of Primary Industries. Division of Animal Industry. Bulletin [*A publication*]
Queensl Dep Primary Ind Div Dairy Bull ... Queensland. Department of Primary Industries. Division of Dairying. Bulletin [*A publication*]
Queensl Dep Primary Ind Div Plant Ind Bull ... Queensland. Department of Primary Industries. Division of Plant Industry. Bulletin [*A publication*]
Queensl Dep Primary Ind Inf Ser ... Queensland. Department of Primary Industries. Information Series [*A publication*]
Queensl Fish Serv Res Bull ... Queensland. Fisheries Service. Research Bulletin [*A publication*]
Queensl Fish Serv Tech Rep ... Queensland. Fisheries Service. Technical Report [*A publication*]
Queensl Geogr J ... Queensland Geographical Journal [*A publication*] (APTA)
Queensl Geol ... Queensland Geology [*A publication*]

Queensl Geol Surv 1:250000 Geol Ser ... Queensland. Geological Survey. 1:250,000 Geological Series [*A publication*]   (APTA)
Queensl Geol Surv Publ ... Queensland. Geological Survey. Publication [*A publication*]
Queensl Geol Surv Rep ... Queensland. Geological Survey. Report [*A publication*]
Queensl Gov Min J ... Queensland Government Mining Journal [*A publication*]
Queensl Herit ... Queensland Heritage [*A publication*]   (APTA)
Queen's L J ... Queen's Law Journal [*A publication*]
Queens LJ ... Queensland Law Journal and Reports [*A publication*]   (APTA)
Queensl J Agric Anim Sci ... Queensland Journal of Agricultural and Animal Sciences [*A publication*]
Queensl J Agric Sci ... Queensland Journal of Agricultural Science [*Later, Queensland Journal of Agricultural and Animal Sciences*] [*A publication*]
Queensl JPR ... Queensland Justice of the Peace. Reports [*A publication*]   (DLA)
Queensl JP Rep ... Queensland Justice of the Peace. Reports [*A publication*]   (DLA)
Queensl L... Queensland Law [*A publication*]   (DLA)
Queensl LJ (Austr) ... Queensland Law Journal (Australia) [*A publication*]
Queensl LJ & R ... Queensland Law Journal and Reports [*A publication*]
Queensl LR ... Queensland Law Reports [*A publication*]
Queensl LSJ ... Queensland Law Society. Journal [*A publication*] [*A publication*]
Queensl L Soc'y J ... Queensland Law Society. Journal [*A publication*]
Queensl Nat ... Queensland Naturalist [*A publication*]
Queensl Nurses J ... Queensland Nurses Journal [*A publication*]
Queensl Pub Acts ... Queensland Public Acts [*A publication*]   (DLA)
Queens LR ... Queensland Law Reports (Beor) [*A publication*]   (APTA)
Queensl R .. Queensland State Reports [*A publication*]   (DLA)
Queensl SC (Austr) ... Queensland. Supreme Court. Reports (Australia) [*A publication*]
Queensl SCR ... Queensland. Supreme Court. Reports [*A publication*]   (DLA)
Queensl S Ct R ... Queensland. Supreme Court. Reports [*A publication*]
Queensl Soc Sugar Cane Technol Proc ... Queensland Society of Sugar Cane Technologists. Proceedings [*A publication*]   (APTA)
Queens L Soc'y J ... Queensland Law Society. Journal [*A publication*]   (DLA)
Queensl St R ... Queensland State Reports [*Australia*] [*A publication*]   (DLA)
Queensl St Rep ... Queensland State Reports [*Australia*] [*A publication*]   (DLA)
Queensl Univ Dep Civ Eng Bull ... Queensland University. Department of Civil Engineering. Bulletin [*A publication*]
Queensl Univ Dep Geol Pap ... Queensland University. Department of Geology. Papers [*A publication*]
Queensl Vet Proc ... Queensland Veterinary Proceedings (Australian Veterinary Association, Queensland Division) [*A publication*]   (APTA)
Queen's Nurs J ... Queen's Nursing Journal [*A publication*]
Queen's Papers in Pure and Appl Math ... Queen's Papers in Pure and Applied Mathematics [*A publication*]
Queen's Q .. Queen's Quarterly [*A publication*]
Queen's Quart ... Queen's Quarterly [*A publication*]
Queens St R ... Queensland State Reports [*A publication*]   (DLA)
Queens Univ Therm Fluid Sci Group Rep ... Queen's University. Thermal and Fluid Science Group. Report [*A publication*]
Que KB ... Quebec Official Reports, King's Bench [*A publication*]   (DLA)
Que L ... Quebec Law [*A publication*]   (DLA)
Quellen Stud Philos ... Quellen und Studien zur Philosophie [*A publication*]
Que LR ... Quebec Law Reports [*Canada*] [*A publication*]   (DLA)
QUELS ... Quasi-Elastic Light Scattering [*Also, QELS, QLS*] [*Physics*]
Que Minist Agric Pech Aliment Dir Gen Pech Marit Cah Inf ... Quebec. Ministere de l'Agriculture, des Pecheries, et de l'Alimentation. Direction General des Peches Maritimes. Cahier d'Information [*A publication*]
Que Minist Chasse Pech Contrib ... Quebec. Ministere de la Chasse et des Pecheries. Contributions [*A publication*]
Que Minist Energ Ressour Serv Rech For Mem ... Quebec. Ministere de l'Energie et des Ressources. Service de la Recherche Forestiere. Memoire [*A publication*]
Que Minist Energ Ressour Serv Rech Mem ... Quebec. Ministere de l'Energie et des Ressources. Service de la Recherche. Memoire [*A publication*]
Que Minist Ind Commer Dir Rech Cah Inf ... Quebec. Ministere de l'Industrie et du Commerce. Direction de la Recherches Cahiers d'Information [*A publication*]
Que Minist Ind Commer Rapp Pech ... Quebec. Ministere de l'Industrie et du Commerce. Rapport sur les Pecheries [*A publication*]
Que Minist Ind Commer Serv Biol Rapp Annu ... Quebec. Ministere de l'Industrie et du Commerce. Service de Biologie. Rapport Annuel [*A publication*]
Que Minist Richesses Nat Etude Spec ... Quebec. Ministere des Richesses Naturelles. Etude Speciale [*A publication*]
Que Minist Terres For Serv Rech Note ... Quebec. Ministere des Terres et Forets. Service de la Recherche. Note [*A publication*]
Que Pr ... Quebec Practice [*A publication*]   (DLA)
Que PR ... Quebec Practice Reports [*A publication*]   (DLA)
Que Prac .... Quebec Practice Reports [*A publication*]   (DLA)

Que (Prov) Dep Mines Gen Rep Minist Mines ... Quebec (Province). Department of Mines. General Report of the Minister of Mines [*A publication*]
Que (Prov) Minist Richesses Nat Rapp Prelim ... Quebec (Province). Ministere des Richesses Naturelles. Rapport Preliminaire [*A publication*]
Que QB ...... Quebec Official Reports, Queen's Bench [*A publication*]   (DLA)
QUERC ..... Quercus [*Oak*] [*Pharmacology*]   (ROG)
Que Rev Jud ... Quebec Revised Judicial [*A publication*]   (DLA)
Que Rev Regs ... Revised Regulations of Quebec [*A publication*]
Que Rev Stat ... Quebec Revised Statutes [*Canada*] [*A publication*]   (DLA)
Que Rev Stat ... Revised Statutes of Quebec [*A publication*]
Query File Commonw Bur Hortic Plant Crops ... Query File. Commonwealth Bureau of Horticulture and Plantation Crops [*A publication*]
QUES .... Question   (AAG)
QUES .... Question Mark   (AABC)
Que SC ...... Quebec Official Reports, Superior Court [*A publication*]   (DLA)
Que Sci ...... Quebec Science [*A publication*]
Que Serv Faune Rapp ... Quebec. Service de la Faune. Rapport [*A publication*]
Que Soc Prot Plants Rep ... Quebec Society for the Protection of Plants. Report [*A publication*]
QUEST ...... Qualitative Experimental Stress Tomography
QUEST ...... Quality Electrical Systems Test [*Interpreter*]
QUEST ...... Quality Utilization Effectiveness Statistically Qualified
QUEST ...... Quantitative Environmental Science and Technology [*ULDECO Ltd.*] [*British*]   (IRUK)
QUEST ...... Quantitative Understanding of Explosive Stimulus Transfer
QUEST ...... Quantitative Utility Estimates for Science and Technology [*RAND Corp.*]
QUEST ...... Query Evaluation and Search Technique
QUEST ...... Question
Quest Act Soc ... Questions Actuelles du Socialisme [*A publication*]
Quest Act Socialisme ... Questions Actuelles du Socialisme [*A publication*]
Questar ...... Questar Corp. [*Associated Press abbreviation*]   (APAG)
Que Stat ..... Quebec Statutes [*Canada*] [*A publication*]   (DLA)
QUESTER ... Quick and Effective System to Enhance Retrieval [*Data processing*]
Quest For ... Questions of Forestry [*A publication*]
QUESTIIO ... Quaderns d'Estadistica. Sistemes. Informatica i Investigacio Operativa [*A publication*]
QUESTN ... Question
Questn .... Questionnaire   (ADA)
QUESTOL ... Quiet Experimental Short Takeoff and Landing [*Program*] [*NASA*]
Que Super .. Quebec Official Reports, Superior Court [*A publication*]   (DLA)
Que Tax Rep (CCH) ... Quebec Tax Reporter (Commerce Clearing House) [*A publication*]   (DLA)
Quetico-Super Wilderness Res Cent Annu Rep ... Quetico-Superior Wilderness Research Center. Annual Report [*A publication*]
Quetico-Super Wilderness Res Cent Tech Note ... Quetico-Superior Wilderness Research Center. Technical Note [*A publication*]
QUF .... National Bank of Yugoslavia. Quarterly Bulletin [*A publication*]
QU Gazette ... Queensland University. Gazette [*A publication*]   (APTA)
QUH .... Queen's University Highland Battalion [*British military*]   (DMA)
QUI .... Queen's University, Ireland
QUI .... Quincy Railroad Co. [*Later, QRR*] [*AAR code*]
QUI .... Quito [*Ecuador*] [*Seismograph station code, US Geological Survey*] [*Closed*]   (SEIS)
QUI .... Quito, Ecuador, Tracking Station [*NASA*]   (NASA)
QUI .... Thomas Crane Public Library, Quincy, MA [*OCLC symbol*]   (OCLC)
QUIBA ...... Quimica e Industria [*Madrid*] [*A publication*]
QUIC .... Quality Data Information and Control   (NASA)
QUICHA ... Quantitative Inhalation Challenge Apparatus [*Medicine*]   (MAE)
QUICK ...... Quotation Information Center KK [*Nihon Keizai Shimbun, Inc.*] [*Information service or system*]   (IID)
QUICKTRAN ... Quick FORTRAN [*Programming language*] [*1979*]
QUID .... Quantified Intrapersonal Decision-Making [*In book title*]
QUIES .... Quiescent
QUIJA .... Quintessence International [*A publication*]
QUIK .... Quiksilver, Inc. [*Costa Mesa, CA*] [*NASDAQ symbol*]   (NQ)
QUIL .... Quad in Line [*Electronics*] [*Telecommunications*]   (TEL)
QUILL .... Queen's University Interrogation of Legal Literature [*Queen's University of Belfast*] [*Northern Ireland*] [*Information service or system*]   (IID)
QUILL .... QUILL: Queensland Inter-Library Liaison [*A publication*]   (APTA)
Quill & Q ... Quill and Quire [*A publication*]
Quim Anal ... Quimica Analitica [*A publication*]
Quim Farm ... Quimica y Farmica [*A publication*]
Quim Ind .... Quimica e Industria [*A publication*]
Quim Ind (Barcelona) ... Quimica e Industria (Barcelona) [*A publication*]
Quim Ind (Bogota) ... Quimica e Industria (Bogota) [*A publication*]
Quim Ind (Madrid) ... Quimica e Industria (Madrid) [*A publication*]
Quim Ind (Montevideo) ... Quimica Industrial (Montevideo) [*A publication*]

Quim Ind (Sao Paulo) ... Quimica e Industria (Sao Paulo) [*A publication*]
Quim Nova ... Quimica Nova [*A publication*]
QUIN......... Quina [*Quinine*] [*Pharmacy*]　(ROG)
QUIN......... Quincy Savings Bank [*Formerly, Excel Bancorp. Inc.*] [*NASDAQ symbol*]　(SPSG)
Quin .... Quincy's Massachusetts Reports [*A publication*]　(DLA)
QUIN......... Quintuple
Quin Bank ... Quin on Banking [*1833*] [*A publication*]　(DLA)
Quinct .... Pro Quinctio [*of Cicero*] [*Classical studies*]　(OCD)
Quincy........ Quincy's Massachusetts Reports [*A publication*]　(DLA)
quinq .... Quinque [*Five*] [*Latin*]　(MAE)
QUINT...... Quintetto [*Quintet*] [*Music*]　(ROG)
Quint......... Quintilian [*First century AD*] [*Classical studies*]　(OCD)
QUINT...... Quintuple
QUINT...... Quintus [*Fifth*] [*Latin*]　(WGA)
Quintessence Dent Technol ... Quintessence of Dental Technology [*A publication*]
Quintessence Int ... Quintessence International [*A publication*]
Quintessence Int Dent Dig ... Quintessence International Dental Digest [*A publication*]
Quintessencia Protese Lab ... Quintessencia de Protese de Laboratorio [*A publication*]
Quintessenz J ... Quintessenz Journal [*A publication*]
Quintessenz Zahntech ... Quintessenz der Zahntechnik [*A publication*]
Quinti Quinto ... Year Book 5 Henry V [*England*] [*A publication*]　(DLA)
Quint Smyrn ... Quintus Smyrnaeus [*Classical studies*]　(OCD)
Quinz Lit.... Quinzaine Litteraire [*A publication*]
QUIP .... Quad In-Line Package
QUIP .... Quantum-Well Infrared Photodetector [*Physics*]
QUIP .... Query Interactive Processor　(IEEE)
QUIP .... Quipp, Inc. [*NASDAQ symbol*]　(NQ)
QUIP .... QUOTA [*Query Online Terminal Assistance*] Input Processor [*Data processing*]
QUIV .... Quiver　(ROG)
Quix .... Quixote [*A publication*]
QUIX .... Quixote Corp. [*NASDAQ symbol*]　(NQ)
Qu Jour Int-Amer Rel ... Quarterly Journal of Inter-American Relations [*A publication*]　(DLA)
QUK.......... Quaker Resources, Inc. [*Vancouver Stock Exchange symbol*]
QUL.......... Quillagua [*Chile*] [*Seismograph station code, US Geological Survey*]　(SEIS)
Qu Lait...... Quebec Laitier [*A publication*]
QU Law J .. University of Queensland. Law Journal [*A publication*]　(APTA)
Qu LJ........ Quarterly Law Journal [*A publication*]　(DLA)
QULJ........ Queensland University. Law Journal [*A publication*]　(APTA)
Qu L Rev.... Quarterly Law Review [*A publication*]　(DLA)
QUM .... Queen's University, Medical Library [*UTLAS symbol*]
QUM .... Quillmana [*Peru*] [*Seismograph station code, US Geological Survey*] [*Closed*]　(SEIS)
QUMDO .. Qualitative Materiel Development Objective [*Army*]　(AFIT)
QUME....... Qume Corp. [*NASDAQ symbol*]　(NQ)
Qu Minist Ind Commer Serv Rech Cah Inf ... Quebec. Ministere de l'Industrie et du Commerce. Service de la Recherche. Cahiers d'Information [*A publication*]
Qu Minist Terres For Serv Rech Mem ... Quebec. Ministere des Terres et Forets. Service de la Recherche. Memoire [*A publication*]
Qu Minist Terres For Serv Rech Note ... Quebec. Ministere des Terres et Forets. Service de la Recherche. Note [*A publication*]
QUMR...... Quality Unsatisfactory Material Report　(MCD)
QUMS....... Quasar Microsystems [*NASDAQ symbol*]　(NQ)
Q Univ Gaz ... University of Queensland. Gazette [*A publication*]　(APTA)
QUNJA ...... Queensland Nurses Journal [*A publication*]
QUNO ...... Quaker United Nations Office　(EAIO)
QUO .... Quadex Users' Organization　(EA)
QUO .... Quote Resources, Inc. [*Vancouver Stock Exchange symbol*]
QUODD .... Quodlibet [*Newsletter of the Southeastern Region*] [*A publication*]
Quomodo Adul ... Quomodo Adulescens Poetas Audire Debeat [*of Plutarch*] [*Classical studies*]　(OCD)
QUON ...... Question　(ROG)
Quon Attach ... Quoniam Attachiamenta [*A publication*]　(DLA)
QUONBLE ... Questionable　(ROG)
QUOR .... Quorum [*Of Which*] [*Pharmacy*]
QUOT....... Quotation
quot .... Quoted In [*or Quoting*] [*Legal term*]　(DLA)
QUOT....... Quotient　(MSA)
QUOT....... Quoties [*As Often as Needed*] [*Pharmacy*]
QUOT....... Quotron Systems [*NASDAQ symbol*]　(NQ)
QUOTA..... Query Online Terminal Assistance [*Data processing*]
QUOTID... Quotidie [*Daily*] [*Pharmacy*]
QUOT OP SIT ... Quoties Opus Sit [*As Often as Necessary*] [*Pharmacy*]
QUP.......... Quality Unit Pack
QUP.......... Quantity Unit Pack
QUP.......... Quonset Point [*Navy*]
Qu (Prov) Dep Mines Gen Rep Minist Mines ... Quebec (Province). Department of Mines. General Report. Minister of Mines [*A publication*]
Qu (Prov) Dep Mines Prelim Rep ... Quebec (Province). Department of Mines. Preliminary Report [*A publication*]

Qu (Prov) Dep Nat Resour Spec Pap ... Quebec (Province). Department of Natural Resources. Special Paper [*A publication*]
QUR.......... Quinstar Resources [*Vancouver Stock Exchange symbol*]
QURBA .... Quarterly Reviews of Biophysics [*A publication*]
QUREA ..... Quarterly Reviews. Chemical Society [*A publication*]
QURZ........ Quartz, Inc. [*NASDAQ symbol*]　(NQ)
QuSAR ...... Quantitative Structure Activity Relationships [*National Institute on Drug Abuse*]
Qu Serv Faune Bull ... Quebec. Service de la Faune. Bulletin [*A publication*]
Qu Serv Faune Rapp ... Quebec. Service de la Faune. Rapport [*A publication*]
QUSZA ...... Quintessenz Journal [*A publication*]
QUTLJ ...... Queensland University of Technology. Law Journal [*A publication*]
QUX.......... Quinella Exploration Ltd. [*Vancouver Stock Exchange symbol*]
QUY.......... Quest Energy Corp. [*Vancouver Stock Exchange symbol*]
QV............. Bibliotheque Municipale, Victoriaville, Quebec [*Library symbol*] [*National Library of Canada*]　(NLC)
QV............. Lao Aviation [*Laos*] [*ICAO designator*]　(ICDA)
QV............. Qualification and Validation Board [*Army*]　(RDA)
QV............. Quality Verification [*Nuclear energy*]　(NRCH)
QV............. Quantum Vis [*or Voleris*] [*As Much as You Wish*] [*Pharmacy*]
QV............. Quatro Ventos [*A publication*]
QV............. Quattrovalvole [*Four valves per cylinder*] [*Italian*]
QV............. Queen Victoria [*British*]
QV............. Qui Vixit [*Who Lived*] [*Latin*]
QV............. Quo Vadis [*A publication*]
QV............. Quod Vide [*or Videte*] [*Which See*] [*Latin*]
Q4V........... Quicker for Victory [*World War II*]
QVAH .... Institut de Recherche d'Hydro-Quebec, Varennes, Quebec [*Library symbol*] [*National Library of Canada*]　(NLC)
QVAI .... Centre de Documentation, INRS [*Institut National de la Recherche Scientifique*]-Energie, Varennes, Quebec [*Library symbol*] [*National Library of Canada*]　(NLC)
Q Van Weyt ... Q. Van Weytson on Average [*A publication*]　(DLA)
QVBFL...... Bibliotheque Felix-Leclerc, Val-Belair, Quebec [*Library symbol*] [*National Library of Canada*]　(NLC)
QVC........... College de Victoriaville, Quebec [*Library symbol*] [*National Library of Canada*]　(NLC)
QVC........... Qualification, Validation, and Certification Board [*Army*]　(RDA)
QVC........... Quality Value Convenience Network, Inc. [*Television*]
QVCEMBO ... Ecole Quebecoise du Meuble et du Bois Ouvre, College de Victoriaville, Quebec [*Library symbol*] [*National Library of Canada*]　(NLC)
QVCN....... QVC Network, Inc. [*West Chester, PA*] [*NASDAQ symbol*]　(NQ)
QVCSF...... Queen Victoria's Clergy Sustentation Fund [*British*]
QVE........... Bibliotheque Municipale, Verdun, Quebec [*Library symbol*] [*National Library of Canada*]　(BIB)
QVEC .... Cultural Centre [*Centre Culturel*] Verdun, Quebec [*Library symbol*] [*National Library of Canada*]　(NLC)
QVEC .... Qualified Voluntary Employee Contribution
QVGCCQ .. Cree Regional Authority, Grand Council of the Crees (of Quebec) [*Administration Regionale Crie, Grand Conseil des Cris (du Quebec)*] Val D'Or, Quebec [*Library symbol*] [*National Library of Canada*]　(NLC)
QVI........... Quality Verification Inspection
Q Vic.......... Statutes of Quebec in the Reign of Victoria [*A publication*]　(DLA)
Q Vit .... Quaderni del Vittoriale [*A publication*]
QVJVVNW ... Quellenverzeichnis der Justizverwaltungsvorschriften des Landes Nordrhein-Westfalen [*A publication*]
QVL........... Qualified Vendors List
QVLBI....... Quasi-Very-Long-Baseline Interferometry
QVO .... Queen Victoria's Own [*British military*]　(DMA)
QVP........... Quality Verification Plan
QVPL......... Qualified Verification Procedures List
QVR.......... Quality Verification Report
QVR.......... Queen Victoria's Rifles [*Military unit*] [*British*]
QVS........... Queen Victoria's School [*British military*]　(DMA)
QVSLEA ... Atmospheric Environment Service, Environment Canada [*Service de l'Environnement Atmospherique, Environnement Canada*] Ville St-Laurent, Quebec [*Library symbol*] [*National Library of Canada*]　(NLC)
QVT.......... Qualified Verification Testing [*NASA*]
QVVT .... Qualified Verification Vibration Testing [*NASA*]　(NASA)
QW .... Inter-Island Air Services Ltd. [*Grenada*] [*ICAO designator*]　(FAAC)
QW .... Poland [*License plate code assigned to foreign diplomats in the US*]
QW .... Quantum Well [*Physics*]
QW .... Quarter Wave
Q W .... Quarterly West [*A publication*]
QW .... Waterloo Public Library, Quebec [*Library symbol*] [*National Library of Canada*]　(NLC)
QWA......... Quarter-Wave Antenna
QWAM...... Qualified for Warrant Air Mechanic [*British military*]　(DMA)
Q WAR ...... Quo Warranto [*Latin*] [*Legal term*]　(DLA)
QWASP..... Quebec White Anglo-Saxon Protestant
QWBI........ Quality of Well Being Index
QWBP .... Qualification Standards for Wage Board Positions

QWC.......... West Chester State College, West Chester, PA [*OCLC symbol*]   (OCLC)
QWD .... Quarterly World Day
Q/WDO..... Quarter Window [*Automotive engineering*]
QWE.......... Qualified for Warrant Engineer [*British military*]   (DMA)
QWERTY ... First six keys in the upper row of letters of a standard typewriter's keyboard [*Sometimes used as an informal name for a standard keyboard typewriter*]
QWG.......... Quadripartite Working Group [*Military*]
QWG/CD .. Quadripartite Working Group on Combat Developments   (MCD)
QWG/ENG ... Quadripartite Working Group on Engineering   (MCD)
QWG/EW ... Quadripartite Working Group on Electronic Warfare   (MCD)
QWG/LOG ... Quadripartite Working Group on Logistics [*Military*]   (RDA)
QWG/PIQA ... Quadripartite Working Group on Proofing Inspection Quality Assurance   (MCD)
QWG/STANO ... Quadripartite Working Group on Surveillance and Target Acquisition/Night Observation   (MCD)
QWIKTRAN ... Quick FORTRAN [*Programming language*] [*1979*]   (CSR)
QWL.......... Quality of Work Life [*Anti-recession program of Ford Motor Co.*]
QWL.......... Quality of Working Life [*Labour Canada program*]
QWL.......... Quick Weight Loss
QWLD....... Quality of Worklife Database [*Management Directions*] [*Information service or system*]   (IID)
QWM........ Qualified for Warrant Mechanician [*British military*]   (DMA)
QWMP...... Quadruped Walking Machine Program [*Army*]
QWN .... Weekly Notes. Queensland [*A publication*]   (APTA)
QWP.......... Quarter-Wave Plate
QWR.......... Quarterly Weight Report   (DNAB)
QWR.......... Que West Resources Ltd. [*Toronto Stock Exchange symbol*]
QWR.......... Queen's Westminster Rifles [*British military*]   (DMA)
QWRV....... Queen's Westminster Rifle Volunteers [*British military*]   (DMA)
QWSH....... Congregation Shaar Hashomayim Library-Museum, Westmount, Quebec [*Library symbol*] [*National Library of Canada*]   (NLC)
QWSMM .. Westmount Public Library, Quebec [*Library symbol*] [*National Library of Canada*]   (NLC)
QX............. Qatar Amiri Flight [*Qatar*] [*ICAO designator*]   (ICDA)
QXE.......... Horizon Airlines, Inc. [*Seattle, WA*] [*FAA designator*]   (FAAC)
QY............. Air Limousin T A [*France*] [*ICAO designator*]   (FAAC)
QY............. Quantum Yield
QY............. Quay   (ROG)
QY............. Query
QY............. Quota Year [*Pisciculture*]
QYM......... SOLINET [*Southeastern Library Network*] Center, Atlanta, GA [*OCLC symbol*]   (OCLC)
QZ............. Quartz [*Quality of the bottom*] [*Nautical charts*]
QZ............. Stockholm University Computing Center [*Sweden*]   (TSSD)
QZ............. Zambia Airways [*ICAO designator*]   (FAAC)
QZE.......... Quadratic Zeeman Effect [*Physics*]
QZM......... Quartz Mountain Gold Corp. [*Vancouver Stock Exchange symbol*] [*Toronto Stock Exchange symbol*]
QZMG....... Quartz Mountain Gold Corp. [*NASDAQ symbol*]   (NQ)
QZN.......... Quan Zhou [*Republic of China*] [*Seismograph station code, US Geological Survey*]   (SEIS)

R

R...............	Abstracted Reappraisement Decisions [*A publication*] (DLA)
R...............	Acknowledgment of Receipt [*Message handling*] [*Telecommunications*]
R...............	All India Reporter, Rajasthan [*A publication*] (DLA)
r...............	Angular Yaw Velocity (AAG)
R...............	Antenna with Reflector
r------	Arctic Ocean and Region [*MARC geographic area code*] [*Library of Congress*] (LCCP)
R...............	Arginine [*One-letter symbol; see Arg*]
R...............	Army [*Military aircraft identification prefix*] (FAAC)
R...............	Cilag-Chemie AG [*Switzerland*] [*Research code symbol*]
R...............	Denver Laboratories [*Great Britain*] [*Research code symbol*]
R...............	Janssen [*Belgium*] [*Research code symbol*]
R...............	Kentucky Law Reporter [*A publication*] (DLA)
R...............	Molar Gas Constant [*Symbol*] [*IUPAC*] (NASA)
R...............	Nicolaus Rufulus [*Flourished, 13th century*] [*Authority cited in pre-1607 legal work*] (DSA)
R...............	Parti Republicain Radical et Radical-Socialiste [*France*] [*Political party*] (ECED)
R...............	Product Moment Coefficient of Correlation [*Statistics*]
R...............	[*A*] Purine Nucleoside [*One-letter symbol; see Puo*]
R...............	R-Register [*Data processing*]
R...............	Rabba (BJA)
R...............	Rabbanite (BJA)
R...............	Rabbi
R...............	Race
r...............	Racemic [*Also, dl, rac*] [*Chemistry*]
R...............	RACON [*RADAR Beacon*]
R...............	RADAR Contact [*A diagonal line through R indicates RADAR service terminated; a cross through R indicates RADAR contact lost*] [*Aviation*] (FAAC)
R...............	Radfahrabteilung [*Bicycle Battalion*] [*German military - World War II*]
R...............	Radial [*Followed by three digits; for use on instrument approach charts*] [*Aviation*]
R...............	Radial (FAAC)
R...............	Radian
R...............	Radiancy
R...............	Radiation
R...............	Radical
R...............	Radio
R...............	Radio (BBC Monitoring) [*A publication*]
R...............	Radioactive Mineral (MAE)
R...............	Radiographer [*British military*] (DMA)
R...............	Radiology [*or Radiologist*] (ADA)
R...............	Radiotelegram
R...............	Radium [*Chemical symbol is Ra*] (KSC)
r...............	Radius [*Symbol*] [*IUPAC*]
R...............	Radius
r...............	Radius of Gyration (AAG)
R...............	Rail (MSA)
R...............	Railroad [*or Railway*]
R...............	Railway [*A publication*]
R...............	Rain [*Meteorology*]
R dk...........	Raised Deck [*of a ship*] (DS)
R...............	Ram
R...............	Rand [*Monetary unit*] [*Botswana, Lesotho, South Africa, and Swaziland*]
R...............	Random Number
R...............	Range
R...............	Rank
R...............	Rankine [*Temperature scale*]
R...............	Raphe Nucleus [*Neuroanatomy*]
R...............	Rare [*When applied to species*] [*Biology*]
R...............	Rare [*Numismatics*]
R...............	Rate
R...............	Ratio
R...............	Rational Number (MDG)
R...............	Rationing [*British*]
R...............	Rawle's Pennsylvania Reports [*1828-35*] [*A publication*] (DLA)
R...............	Rayleigh Wave [*Seismology*]
R...............	Raymundus de Pennafort [*Deceased, 1275*] [*Authority cited in pre-1607 legal work*] (DSA)
R...............	Raymundus de Sabanacho [*Authority cited in pre-1607 legal work*] (DSA)
R...............	Rays
R...............	Reaction (AAG)
R...............	Read (AAG)
R...............	Readiness Count
R...............	Real
R...............	Realites [*A publication*]
R...............	Ream (ADA)
R...............	Rear
R...............	Reasoning Factor [*or Ability*] [*Psychology*]
R...............	Reaumur [*Temperature scale*] [*German*]
R...............	Rebounds [*Basketball, hockey*]
R...............	Receipt (ROG)
R...............	Received (FAAC)
R...............	Received Solid [*Amateur radio*]
R...............	Receiver
R...............	Receptor [*Biochemistry*]
R...............	Recessed [*Electrical outlet symbol*]
R...............	Recht [*Law*] [*German*]
R...............	Rechtsstrijd [*A publication*]
R...............	Recipe [*Take*] [*Pharmacy*]
R...............	Reciprocating
R...............	Recite [*Swell Organ*] [*Music*]
R...............	Recluse
R...............	Recognition [*Experimentation*]
R...............	Reconditioned (DCTA)
R...............	Reconnaissance [*Designation for all US military aircraft*]
R...............	Reconstruction Committee [*British*] [*World War II*]
R...............	Record
R...............	Recreations
R...............	Recruit (ROG)
R...............	Rectal [*or Rectum*] [*Medicine*]
r...............	Rectangular Tank [*Liquid gas carriers*]
R...............	Rectilinear Polarization [*Physics*] (ECON)
R...............	Recto [*Also, RO*]
R...............	Rector [*or Rectory*]
(R)............	Rectus [*Clockwise configuration*] [*Biochemistry*] [*See RS*]
R...............	Recurrence [*Medicine*]
R...............	Red
R...............	Redemption Fee [*Finance*]
R...............	Redetermination
R...............	Redundancy [*Used in correcting manuscripts, etc.*]
R...............	Referee [*Football*]
R...............	Referred (OICC)
R...............	Refill [*of bract liquid*] [*Botany*]
R...............	Reflectance
R...............	Reflection [*Angle of*]
R...............	Reflector Lamp
R...............	Reflexive
R...............	Reform [*Judaism*]
R...............	Refraction
R...............	Refrigerated [*Shipping*] (DS)
R...............	Refrigerated Tank [*Liquid gas carriers*]
R...............	Refrigerator
R...............	Refuse Disposal [*British Waterways Board sign*]
R...............	Refused
R...............	Regenerated [*Biology*]
R...............	Regiment
R...............	Regina [*Queen*] [*Latin*]
R...............	Register [*Data processing*]
R...............	Registered
R...............	Registrar (ROG)
R...............	Regna [*Queen*] [*Latin*] (DLA)
R...............	Regression Coefficient (AAMN)
R...............	Regular (ADA)
R...............	Regulating
R...............	Reigned

R	Reiz [*Stimulus*] [*German*] [*Psychology*]
R	Relation [*Data processing*]
R	Relative Humidity
R	Relaxed
R	Relay (DNAB)
R	Reliability (MCD)
R	Religious (DNAB)
R	Reluctance
R	Remote [*Telecommunications*] (TEL)
R	Remotum [*Far Respiration*] [*Latin*] (MAE)
R	Repair (DNAB)
R	Repeal [*Legal term*] (DLA)
R	Repetitive [*Electronics*]
R	Replaceability (AAG)
R	Replaced [*Dentistry*]
R	Reply (ADA)
R	Reports
R	[*The*] Reports, Coke's English King's Bench [*A publication*] (DLA)
R	Repressor [*Psychology*] (MAE)
R	Reprint
R	Reproducible (DNAB)
R	Republic
R	Republican
R	Republika [*Zagreb*] [*A publication*]
R	Request
R	Requiescat [*He, or She Rests*] [*Latin*]
R	Rerun [*of a television show*]
R	Rescinded [*Legal term*] (DLA)
R	Research
R	Resentment [*Psychology*]
R	Reserve
R	Reset (MDG)
R	Reside [*or Resident*]
R	Resistance [*Symbol*] [*IUPAC*]
R	Resistor
R	Resolution
R	Resolved [*Legal term*] (DLA)
R	Respectfully [*Letter closing*]
R	Respiration
R	Respond [*or Response*]
R	Responder [*Strain of mice*]
R	Responsorium [*Responsory*]
R	Respublica [*Commonwealth*] [*Latin*]
R	Restricted [*Immunology*]
R	Restricted [*Military document classification*]
R	Restricted [*Persons under eighteen (sixteen in some localities) not admitted unless accompanied by parent or adult guardian*] [*Movie rating*]
R	Restricted Area [*Followed by identification*]
R	Retarder [*Slow*] [*On clock-regulators*] [*French*]
R	Reticular [*Nucleus of thalamus*] [*Neuroanatomy*]
R	Retired [*or Retiree*]
R	Rettie's Scotch Court of Session Reports, Fourth Series [*A publication*] (DLA)
R	Returning
R	Revenue
R	Reverse [*Giemsa method*] [*Chromosome stain*]
R	Reverse
R	Review (AAMN)
R	Revised (MCD)
R	Revision [*Legal term*] (DLA)
R	Revoked [*Legal term*] (DLA)
R	Reward
R	Rex [*King*] [*Latin*]
R	Reynolds Number [*Viscosity*]
R	Rhinitis [*Medicine*]
R	Rhizoctonia [*A fungus*]
R	Rhode Island State Library, Providence, RI [*Library symbol*] [*Library of Congress*] (LCLS)
R	Rhodesia [*Later, Zimbabwe*] (ROG)
R	Rhodium [*Chemical element*] [*Symbol is Rh*] (ROG)
R	Rhodopsin [*Visual purple*]
R	Rhythm
R	Rial [*Monetary unit*] [*Iran, Saudi Arabia, etc.*]
r	Ribose [*One-letter symbol; see Rib*]
R	Ricardus Anglicus [*Deceased, 1242*] [*Authority cited in pre-1607 legal work*] (DSA)
R	Richard (King of England) (DLA)
R	Richtkreis [*Aiming Circle*] [*Gunnery term*] [*German military - World War II*]
R	Rickettsia
R3	Riffle
R	Rifle
R	Rigger [*British military*] (DMA)
R	Right [*Direction*]
R	Right [*Politics*]
R	Right [*side of a stage*] [*A stage direction*]
R	Right Edge [*Skating*]
R	Right-Hand [*Music*] (DAS)
R	Riker Laboratories, Inc. [*Research code symbol*]
R	Rimus (BJA)
R	Ring [*Technical drawings*]
r	Ring Chromosome [*Medicine*] (MAE)
R	Ring Lead [*Telecommunications*] (TEL)
R	Ring Road [*Traffic sign*] [*British*]
-R	Rinne's Test Negative [*Hearing test*]
+R	Rinne's Test Positive [*Hearing test*]
R	Rio [*River*] [*Spanish*] (ROG)
R	Rio De Janeiro [*A publication*]
R	Rise [*Electronics*]
R	Riser [*Technical drawings*]
R	Rises
R	Risk
R	River [*Maps and charts*]
R	Riveted (DS)
R	Road
R	Road-Holding [*In automobile name Rolls-Royce Bentley Turbo R*]
R	Roan (Leather) [*Bookbinding*] (ROG)
R	Robert [*Phonetic alphabet*] [*Royal Navy*] [*World War I*] [*Pre-World War II*] (DSUE)
R	Robertus [*Authority cited in pre-1607 legal work*] (DSA)
R	Robin Avions [*Pierre Robin*] [*France*] [*ICAO aircraft manufacturer identifier*] (ICAO)
R	Robotics
R	Rocket [*Missile vehicle type symbol*]
R	Rod [*Measurement*]
r	Roentgen [*Also, RU*] [*Unit measuring X and gamma radiations*]
R	Roger [*All right or OK*] [*Communications slang*]
R	Roger [*Phonetic alphabet*] [*World War II*] (DSUE)
R	Roll
R	Roller-Skating Rinks [*Public-performance tariff class*] [*British*]
R	Rollout (KSC)
R	Roman
R	Roman Catholic School [*British*]
R	Romania [*A publication*]
R	Romania
R	Romans [*New Testament book*] (BJA)
R	Romeo [*Phonetic alphabet*] [*International*] (DSUE)
R	Rood [*Unit of measurement*]
R	Rook [*Chess*]
R	Rosary
R	Roscoe's Cape Of Good Hope [*A publication*] (DLA)
R	Rosin [*Standard material for soldering*]
R	Rostral [*Anatomy*]
R	Rotary Wing [*Aircraft designation*]
R	Rotor
R	Rough [*Appearance of bacterial colony*]
R	Rough Sea [*Navigation*]
R	Roussel [*France*] [*Research code symbol*]
R	Route
R	Routine (KSC)
R	Royal
R	Royalty Monthly [*A publication*]
R	Rub [*Medicine*] (MAE)
R	Rubber
R	Rubidomycin [*See also D, Daunorubicin*] [*Antineoplastic drug*]
R	Ruble [*Monetary unit*] [*Former USSR*]
R	Rue [*Street*] [*French*]
R	Rule
R	Ruled [*Followed by the dates of a monarch's reign*]
r	Ruler
R	Rum (ROG)
R	Run [*Distance sailed from noon to noon*] [*Navy*] [*British*] (ROG)
R	Run [*Deserted*] [*Nautical*] [*British*] (ROG)
R	Runic
R	Runs [*scored*] [*Baseball or cricket*]
R	Rupee [*Monetary unit*] [*Ceylon, India, and Pakistan*]
R	Rural (MCD)
R	Rydberg Constant [*Spectroscopy*] [*Symbol*] (DEN)
R	Ryder System, Inc. [*NYSE symbol*] (SPSG)
R	Rydge's [*A publication*] (APTA)
R	Ryman [*Office equipment and furniture store chain*] [*British*]
R	Ship [*Missile launch environment symbol*]
R	Stauffer Chemical Co. [*Research code symbol*]
R	Transfer Payments [*Economics*]
R	Transport [*Naval aircraft designation*]
R	Yaw Control Axis [*Symbol*]
R2	Reporting Responsibility [*DoD*]
R2	Richard II [*Shakespearean work*]
R3	Rearm, Resupply, Refuel [*Army*]
R³	Relay, Reporter, Responder [*Military*] (CAAL)
3R	Request, Retrieve, and Report [*Data processing*]
3R	Resurfacing, Restoration, and Rehabilitation [*Also, RRR*] [*Later, 4R*] [*Federal Highway Administration*]
3R	Rheingold-Rotary-Reciprocating [*Motor*]
R3	Richard III [*Shakespearean work*]
4R	Resurfacing, Restoration, Rehabilitation, and Reconstruction [*Formerly, 3R, RRR*] [*Federal Highway Administration*]

5R	Madagascar [*Aircraft nationality and registration mark*] (FAAC)
3R's	Readin', Ritin', and Rithmetic [*Also, RRR*]
3R's	Recognition, Reassurance, and Relaxation [*Military mental health technique*] (INF)
3R's	Reduction, Refinement, and Replacement [*Animal research*]
3R's	Reference and Research Library Resources Systems [*New York State Library*] [*Albany*] [*Information service or system*] (IID)
3R's	Relief, Recovery, Reform [*Elements of the New Deal*]
6R's	Remedial Readin', Remedial Ritin', and Remedial Rithmetic [*Also, RRRRRR*] [*Humorous interpretation of the three R's*]
R (Count)	Readiness Count (MCD)
R (Day)	Redeployment Day [*Military*]
Ra	Airway Resistance [*Medicine*] (MAE)
RA	Coast RADAR Station [*Maps and charts*]
RA	High-Powered Radio Range (Adcock)
RA	Rabbinical Assembly (EA)
RA	RADAR Altimeter [*Aviation*] (KSC)
Ra	RADAR Station
RA	Radio Altimeter
RA	Radio Antenna
RA	Radio Authority [*Government regulatory agency*] [*British*]
RA	Radioactive
RA	Radionic Association (EA)
Ra	Radium [*Chemical element*]
RA	Radius of Action (AAG)
Ra	Raduga [*Moscow*] [*A publication*]
RA	Ragweed Antigen [*Immunology*]
RA	Rain [*Meteorology*] (FAAC)
Ra	Rainerius [*Authority cited in pre-1607 legal work*] (DSA)
RA	Rainforest Alliance (EA)
RA	Raise (AAG)
RA	Ramp Actuator
RA	Random Access [*Data processing*] (AAG)
RA	Range [*Aviation*]
RA	Range Area (NASA)
RA	Range Assessor [*British military*] (DMA)
RA	Rape [*Division in the county of Sussex*] [*British*]
RA	Rapid-American Corp.
RA	Rapid Anastigmatic (Lens) [*Photography*] (ROG)
RA	Raritan Arsenal (AAG)
Ra	Rastell's Entries [*A publication*] (DSA)
RA	Rate Action (AAG)
RA	Rate of Application
RA	Rate of Approach (IIA)
RA	Ratepayers' Association [*British*] (ILCA)
R & A	Rates and Allotments [*Eight-Sheet Outdoor Advertising Association*] [*A publication*]
RA	Rating Appeals [*United Kingdom*] [*A publication*]
RA	Ratio Actuator (MCD)
RA	Ration
RA	Ration Allowance [*British military*] (DMA)
Ra	Rayleigh Number [*IUPAC*]
Ra	Raymundus de Pennafort [*Deceased, 1275*] [*Authority cited in pre-1607 legal work*] (DSA)
RA	Raynaud's Phenomenon [*Medicine*]
RA	Rayon (AAG)
RA	Read Amplifier
RA	Ready-Access [*Telecommunications*] (TEL)
RA	Ready Alert [*Navy*] (NVT)
RA	Rear Admiral [*Also, RADM, RADML*]
RA	Rear Artillery
R/A	Rear Axle [*Automotive engineering*]
RA	Rebuild America (EA)
RA	Receiver Attenuation
RA	Rechtsgeleerde Adviezen [*A publication*]
RA	Recipient Agency [*Federal government*] (GFGA)
RA	Recipient Rights Adviser
RA	Reconnaissance Aircraft (DNAB)
R/A	Recorded Announcement [*Telecommunications*] (TEL)
RA	Records Administration (MCD)
RA	Recreation Aide [*Red Cross*]
RA	Redevelopment Act (OICC)
RA	Redstone Arsenal [*Huntsville, AL*] [*Army*]
RA	Reduced Aperture (MCD)
RA	Reduction of Area
RA	Refer to Accepter [*Banking*]
RA	Refractory Anemia [*Medicine*]
RA	Refugee Agency [*NATO*] (NATG)
RA	Regional Administrator
RA	Regional Associations [*Marine science*] (MSC)
RA	Registered Architect (IIA)
RA	Registration Act
RA	Registration Appeals [*A publication*] (DLA)
RA	Regular Army
RA	Regulation Appeals [*A publication*] (DLA)
RA	Regulatory Alternative [*Federal government*] (GFGA)
RA	Regulatory Analysis [*Federal government*] (GFGA)
RA	Rehabilitation Act (OICC)
RA	Reimbursement Authorization (AFM)
RA	Reims Aviation [*France*] [*ICAO aircraft manufacturer identifier*] (ICAO)
RA	Reinforced Alert (NATG)
RA	Relative Abundance [*Chemistry*]
RA	Relative Activity [*Physiology*]
RA	Relative Address
RA	Release Authorization
RA	Released-Action [*Pharmacy*]
RA	Reliability Analysis (AAG)
RA	Reliability Assessment (KSC)
RA	Reliability Assurance (MCD)
R & A	Reliability and Availability
RA	Religious of the Apostolate of the Sacred Heart [*Roman Catholic women's religious order*]
RA	Religious of the Assumption [*Roman Catholic women's religious order*]
RA	Relocation Address
RA	Relocation Assistance [*HUD*]
RA	Remedial Action [*Navy*]
RA	Remittance Advice (MCD)
RA	Remote Area
RA	Renal Artery [*Anatomy*]
RA	Renin Activity (AAMN)
RA	Rental Agreement
RA	Repair Assignment (AAG)
RA	Repeat Action [*Medicine*]
R/A	Repeat Attempt [*Telecommunications*] (TEL)
RA	Repeated Attacks [*Medicine*]
Ra	Repertorio Americano [*A publication*]
RA	Replacement Algorithm
RA	Reporting Activity (MCD)
R & A	Reports and Analysis
RA	Representative Assembly
RA	Republicans Abroad (EA)
RA	Requesting Agency (MUGU)
RA	Requirements Analysis
R & A	Rescue and Assistance
RA	Research Abstracts [*University Microfilms International*] [*A publication*]
R & A	Research and Analysis
RA	Resident Agent (AFM)
RA	Resident Alien
RA	Resident Assistant [*College housing*]
RA	Resident Auditor
RA	Residual Air
RA	Resistor Assembly
RA	Resource Allocation (MCD)
RA	Respiratory Allergy [*Immunology*]
RA	Respiratory Arrest [*Medicine*]
R-A	Response Errors [*Statistics*]
R & A	Responsibility and Action
RA	Restaurant Associates Industries, Inc. [*AMEX symbol*] (SPSG)
RA	Restricted Account [*Banking*]
RA	Resume-Accelerate [*Automotive engineering*]
RA	Retinal Anlage [*Ophthalmology*]
RA	Retinoic Acid [*Biochemistry*]
RA	Retrograde Amnesia [*Medicine*]
RA	Return Address
RA	Return Air [*Technical drawings*]
R/A	Return to Author [*Bookselling*]
RA	Revenue Act [*1962, 1964, 1971, 1976, 1978*]
RA	Revenue Agent [*IRS*]
RA	Reverendus Admodum [*Very Reverend*] [*Latin*]
R & A	Review and Analysis
R & A	Review and Approval
RA	Reviewing Activity (MCD)
RA	Reviewing Authority
RA	Reviews in Anthropology [*A publication*]
RA	Revue Administrative [*A publication*] (ILCA)
RA	Rheinisches Archiv [*A publication*]
RA	Rheumatoid Agglutinins [*Clinical chemistry*]
RA	Rheumatoid Arthritis [*Medicine*]
RA	Riders Association [*Commercial firm*] (EA)
RA	Right Aft (MCD)
RA	Right Angle (DEN)
RA	Right Arch [*Freemasonry*]
RA	Right Arm [*Medicine*]
RA	Right Ascension [*Navigation*]
RA	Right Atrium [*Cardiology*]
RA	Right Auricle [*Anatomy*]
RA	Right Axilla (KSC)
RA	Ripple Adder
RA	Risk Analysis (MCD)
RA	Risk Assessment (GFGA)
RA	Road America [*Automotive raceway*]
RA	Robbery Armed
RA	Robustus Archistriatalis [*Bird brain anatomy*]
RA	Rocket Assist (RDA)
RA	Rokitansky-Aschoff [*Sinus*] [*Gastroenterology*]
RA	Romanistische Arbeitshefte [*A publication*]

RA	Root Apex [Botany]
RA	Roquefort Association (EA)
RA	Rosin Acid [Organic chemistry]
RA	Rosin Activated [Standard material for soldering]
RA	Rotary Assembly
RA	Rotogravure Association
RA	Royal Academician [or Academy] [British]
RA	Royal Academy of Arts in London [British]
R & A	Royal and Ancient Golf Club of St. Andrews [Recognized as the game's legislative authority in all countries except the US] [British]
RA	Royal Arch [Freemasonry]
RA	Royal Armouries [Tower of London]
RA	Royal Art
RA	Royal Artillery [British]
RA	Royal Artist
RA	Royal Nepal Airlines Corp. [ICAO designator] (FAAC)
RA	Royal Regiment of Artillery [Military] [British]
RA	Rueckwaertiges Armeegebiet [Rear area of an army] [German military]
R & A	Rules and Administration Committee [US Senate]
RA	Rules on Appeal [A publication] (DLA)
RA	Russian Air [To distinguish call-signs and frequencies] [World War II] [British]
RA	Russian American
RA	Thermal Resistance of Unit Area [Heat transmission symbol]
RAA	Rabbinical Alliance of America (EA)
RAA	Reagan Alumni Association (EA)
RA(A)	Rear-Admiral of Aircraft Carriers [Obsolete] [British]
RA(A)	Recueil des Arrets et Avis du Conseil d'Etat [A publication]
RAA	Reeve Aleutian Airways, Inc. [Air carrier designation symbol]
RAA	Regenerative Agriculture Association [Later, RI] (EA)
RAA	Regional Administrative Assistant (ADA)
RAA	Regional Airline Association (EA)
RAA	Regional Arts Association [British]
RAA	Reinsurance Association of America [Washington, DC] (EA)
RAA	Relational Algebra Accelerator [Computer board]
RAA	Rendiconti. Accademia di Archeologia, Lettere, e Belle Arti [Napoli] [A publication]
RAA	Renewal Assistance Administration [HUD]
RAA	Renin-Angiotensin-Aldosterone [Clinical nephrology]
RAA	Research Animal Alliance (EA)
RAA	Respiratory Aid Apparatus
RAAC	Revue. Academie Arabe [A publication]
RAA	Right Angle Adapter
RAA	Right Ascension Angle
RAA	Right Atrial Appendage [Medicine]
RAA	Rockette Alumnae Association (EA)
RAA	Royal Academy of Arts [British] (ROG)
RAA	Rynes Aviation, Inc. [Melrose Park, IL] [FAA designator] (FAAC)
RAAA	Red Angus Association of America (EA)
RAAA	Relocation Assistance Association of America (EA)
RAAAS	Remote Antiarmor Assault System (MCD)
RAAB	Remote Amplifier and Adaption Box (NASA)
RAAB	Remote Application and Advisory Box (MCD)
RAABF	Royal Artillery Association Benevolent Fund [British military]
RAAC	Rhodesian Air Askari Corps [British military] (DMA)
RAAC	Rome Allied Area Command [World War II]
RAACA	Radiochimica Acta [A publication]
RAACC	Robotics and Automation Applications Consulting Center [Ford Motor Co.]
RAACEF	Rear-Admiral of Aircraft Carriers, Eastern Fleet [British]
RAACT	Radioactive
RAAD	Radford Army Ammunition Depot [Virginia] (MCD)
RAAD	Restructured Air Assault Division (MCD)
RAAD	Revue. Academie Arabe de Damas [A publication]
RAADC	Regional Accounting and Disbursing Center (DNAB)
RAADES	Relative Antiair Defense Effectiveness Simulation [Military] (CAAL)
RAAEAV	South Africa. Department of Agriculture. Entomology Memoir [A publication]
RAAEC Nletter	Royal Australian Army. Educational Corps. Newsletter [A publication] (APTA)
RA(A)EF	Rear-Admiral (Administration) Eastern Fleet [British]
RAAF	Redstone Army Airfield [Huntsville, AL]
RAAFA	Royal Australian Air Force Association
RAAF Reserve	Royal Australian Air Force Reserve. Magazine [A publication] (APTA)
RAAG	Regional Aviation Assistance Group [FAA]
RAAGA	Railway Age [New York] [A publication]
RAAG Res Notes	Research Notes and Memoranda of Applied Geometry for Prevenient Natural Philosophy [Tokyo] [A publication]
RAAM	Race Across America [Annual cycling event]
RAAM	Remote Antiarmor Mine (RDA)
RAAM	Residual-Area-Analysis Method [Spectrometry]
RAAMS	Remote Antiarmor Mine System [Military] (AABC)
RAAN	Rendiconti. Accademia di Archeologia, Lettere, e Belle Arti (Napoli) [A publication]
RAAN	Repair Activity Accounting Number [Navy]
RAANES	Recent Advances in Animal Nutrition [A publication]
RAAP	Radford Army Ammunition Plant (AABC)
RAAP	Residue Arithmetic Associative Processor [Data processing] (OA)
RAAQ	Recherches Amerindiennes au Quebec. Bulletin d'Information [A publication]
RAAR	RAM Address Register
RAAS	Royal Amateur Art Society [British]
RAAT	Recombinant Alpha 1-Antitrypsin [Biochemistry]
RAAWS	RADAR Altimeter and Altitude Warning System [Military] (CAAL)
RAAWS	Ranger Antiarmor, Antipersonnel Weapon System [Army] (INF)
RAB	Rabaul [New Britain] [Seismograph station code, US Geological Survey] (SEIS)
RAB	Rabaul [Papua New Guinea] [Airport symbol] (OAG)
RAB	Rabbet (MSA)
RAB	Rabbinical
RAB	Rabbit Oil & Gas [Vancouver Stock Exchange symbol]
RAB	Rabelais [French author, 1494-1553] (ROG)
RAB	Radio Advertising Bureau [New York, NY] (EA)
RAB	Reactor Auxiliary Building [Nuclear energy] (NRCH)
RAB	Regional Advisory Board [American Hospital Association]
RAB	Rent Advisory Board [Cost of Living Council]
RAB	Richard Austen Butler [1902-1982] [In book title "RAB: The Life of R. A. Butler"]
RAB	Rotating Arm Basin
Raba	[Januarius] Rabaca [Flourished, 1342-48] [Authority cited in pre-1607 legal work] (DSA)
RABA	Radioantigen-Binding Assay [Medicine]
RABAC	Real Americans Buy American Cars [An association] [Defunct]
RABAL	Radiosonde Balloon
RABAR	Radiosonde Balloon Release (FAAC)
RABAR	Raytheon Advanced Battery Acquisition RADAR
Rab Azovsko-Chernomorsk Nauchn Rybokhoz Stn	Raboty Azovsko-Chernomorskoi Nauchnoi Rybokhozyaistvennoi Stantsii [A publication]
RABB	Rabbinical
RABBAR	Revista. Museo Argentino de Ciencias Naturales Bernardino Rivadavia e Instituto Nacional de Investigacion de las Ciencias Naturales. Ciencias Botanicas [A publication]
RABBI	Rapid Access Blood Bank Information (MAE)
RABET	RADAR Beacon Transponder
RABFAC	RADAR Beacon, Forward Air Controller
RABFAC-TDC	RADAR Beacon Forward Air Controller - Target Data Communicator (MCD)
Rab Fiz Tverd Tela	Raboty po Fizike Tverdogo Tela [A publication]
RABH	Reported Altitude Block Height (SAA)
RABI	Royal Agricultural Benevolent Institution [Church of England]
Rab Issled Inst Meteorol Gidrol Chast 2	Raboty i Issledovaniya. Institut Meteorologii i Gidrologii. Chast 2. Gidrologiya [A publication]
Rab Khim Rastvorov Kompleksn Soedin	Raboty po Khimii Rastvorov i Kompleksnykh Soedinenii [A publication]
RABMA	Radiobiologia si Biologia Moleculara [A publication]
Rab Molodykh Uch Vses Akad Skh Nauk	Raboty Molodykh Uchenykh Vsesoyuznaya Akademiya Sel'skokhozyaistvennykh Nauk [A publication]
Rab Neft	Rabochii Neftyanik [A publication]
RABNVS	Reactor Auxiliary Building Normal Ventilation System [Nuclear energy] (NRCH)
RABOA	Radiation Botany [A publication]
Rabocij Klass Sovrem Mir	Rabocij Klass i Sovremennyj Mir [A publication]
RABol	Rendiconto. Accademia delle Scienze. Istituto di Bologna [A publication]
RABP	Renal Artery Bypass [Medicine]
Rab Post	Pro Rabirio Postumo [of Cicero] [Classical studies] (OCD)
RABR	Rainbow Bridge National Monument
RABR	Right Angle Bulkhead Receptacle
RABS	Rear-Wheel Antilock Brake System [Automotive engineering]
RABS	Remote Air Battle Station
RABT	Rabbit Software Corp. [Malvern, PA] [NASDAQ symbol] (NQ)
Rab Tyan-Shan Fiz-Geogr Sta	Raboty Tyan-Shan'skoi Fiziko-Geograficheskoi Stantsii. Akademiya Nauk Kirgizskoi SSR [A publication]
Rab Tyan Shan'skoi Fiz Geogr Stn Akad Nauk Kirg SSR	Raboty Tyan-Shan'skoi Fiziko-Geograficheskoi Stantsii. Akademiya Nauk Kirgizskoi SSR [A publication]
RABV	Reflood Assist Bypass Valve [Nuclear energy] (NRCH)
RABVAL	RADAR Bomb Evaluation (MCD)
RAC	IEEE Robotics and Automation Council (EA)
rac	Racemic [Also, dl, r] [Chemistry]
RAC	Racer Resources Ltd. [Vancouver Stock Exchange symbol]
RAC	Raciborz [Poland] [Seismograph station code, US Geological Survey] (SEIS)
RAC	Racine, WI [Location identifier] [FAA] (FAAL)
RAC	RADAR Address Counter
R & AC	RADAR and Air Communications
RAC	RADAR Area Correlator

RAC .... RADAR Azimuth Converter
RAC .... Radio Adaptive Communications
RAC .... Radiological Assessment Coordinator [*Nuclear energy*]　(NRCH)
RAC .... Radiometric Area Correlator　(MCD)
RAC .... RAI Research Corp. [*AMEX symbol*]　(SPSG)
RAC .... Raisin Administrative Committee　(EA)
RAC .... Ram Air Charters Ltd. [*Inuvik, NT, Canada*] [*FAA designator*]　(FAAC)
RAC .... Ram Air Cushion [*Aerospace*]　(AAG)
RAC .... Ramsay's Appeal Cases [*Canada*] [*A publication*]　(DLA)
RAC .... Random Access Capability [*Microscopy*]
RAC .... Random Access Computer　(IIA)
RAC .... Rangefinder with Automatic Compensator [*Firearms*]
RAC .... Rapid Action Change [*DoD*]
RAC .... Ration Accessory Convenience [*World War II*]
RAC .... Rational Activity Coefficient
RAC .... Reactor Accident Calculation
RAC .... Read Address Counter
RAC .... Reallexikon fuer Antike und Christentum [*A publication*]　(OCD)
RAC .... Rear-Admiral Commanding [*British*]
RAC .... Receptor-Affinity Chromatography
RAC .... Recessed Annular Connector
RAC .... Recombinant DNA Advisory Committee [*National Institutes of Health*]
RAC .... Recreation Advisory Council [*Bureau of Outdoor Recreation*]
RAC .... Rectified Alternating Current [*Radio*]
RAC .... Reflect Array Pulse Compressor　(RDA)
RAC .... Refrigerant-Air Condition　(DNAB)
RAC .... Release and Approval Center　(MCD)
RAC .... Reliability Action Center [*NASA*]　(NASA)
RAC .... Reliability Analysis Center [*Griffiss Air Force Base, NY*] [*DoD*]　(GRD)
RAC .... Reliability Assessment of Components　(KSC)
RAC .... Renal Arterial Constriction [*Medicine*]
RAC .... Repair, Alignment, and Calibration　(NVT)
RAC .... Reparable Assets Control　(AFM)
RAC .... Representation des Artistes Canadiens
RAC .... Request Altitude Change [*Aviation*]　(FAAC)
RAC .... Request for Authority to Contract [*Military*]
RAC .... Requisition Advice Care [*Military*]
RAC .... Research Advisory Committee
RAC .... Research Advisory Council
RAC .... Research Analysis Corp. [*Nonprofit contract agency*] [*Army*]
RAC .... Responsibility Analysis Chart　(DNAB)
RAC .... Retail Advertising Conference　(EA)
RAC .... Rework After Completion　(SAA)
RAC .... Risk Assessment Code　(MCD)
RAC .... Royal Academician (of Canada)　(ROG)
RAC .... Royal Aero Club [*British*]
RAC .... Royal Agricultural College [*British*]
RAC .... Royal Arch Chapter [*Freemasonry*]
RAC .... Royal Armoured Corps [*British*]
RAC .... Royal Artillery Committee [*British military*]　(DMA)
RAC .... Royal Automobile Club [*Controlling body of motor racing in Britain*]
RAC .... Rubber Allocation Committee
RAC .... Rules of the Air and Air Traffic Control [*ICAO Air Navigation Commission*]
Ra Ca .... English Railway and Canal Cases [*A publication*]　(DLA)
RACA .... Recovered Alcoholic Clergy Association　(EA)
RACA .... Regroupement d'Artistes des Centres Alternatifs [*Association of National Non-Profit Artists' Centres - ANNPAC*] [*Canada*]
RACA .... Requiring Activity Contract Administrator [*DoD*]
RACA .... Rural Arts and Crafts Association　(EA)
RACAA ...... Radiocarbon [*A publication*]
R Acad Cienc y Artes Barcelona Mem ... Real Academia de Ciencias y Artes de Barcelona. Memorias [*A publication*]
R Acad Farm Barcelona Discursos Recepcion ... Real Academia de Farmacia de Barcelona. Discursos de Recepcion [*A publication*]
R Acad Farm Barcelona Ses Inaug ... Real Academia de Farmacia de Barcelona. Sesion Inaugural [*A publication*]
RACAS ...... Radiation Automatic Casualty Assessment System [*Military*]
RACathHS ... Records. American Catholic Historical Society of Philadelphia [*A publication*]
RACC .... Radiation and Contamination Control
RACC .... Regional Agricultural Credit Corp.
RACC .... Remote ARIA [*Apollo Range Instrumentation Aircraft*] Control Center [*NASA*]
RACC .... Remotely Activated Command and Control [*Military*]　(CAAL)
RACC .... Reporting Activity Control Card [*Army*]　(AABC)
RACC .... Research Aviation Coordinating Committee
RACC .... Rituels Acadiens [*A publication*]　(BJA)
RACC .... Royal Armoured Corps Centre [*British*]　(MCD)
RACC .... Royal Automobile Club of Canada
RACCA ...... Refrigeration and Air Conditioning Contractors Association - National [*Later, National Environmental Systems Contractors Association*]　(EA)
Racc Fis-Chim Ital ... Raccolta Fisico-Chimica Italiana [*A publication*]

R Ac Cienc Habana An ... Real Academia de Ciencias Medicas, Fisicas, y Naturales de la Habana. Anales [*A publication*]
Raccoglitore Med Forli ... Raccoglitore Medico Fano Forli [*A publication*]
Raccolta Mem Turin Univ Fac Sci Agr ... Raccolta di Memorie. Turin. Universita. Facolta di Scienze Agrarie [*A publication*]
Racc Opuscoli Sci Filol ... Raccolta d'Opuscoli Scientifici e Filologici [*A publication*]
RACD .... Royal Army Chaplains' Department [*British*]
RACD .... Royal Army Clothing Department [*British*]
RACE........ Mid-America Racing Stables, Inc. [*NASDAQ symbol*]　(NQ)
Race .... Race and Class [*A publication*]
RACE........ Racial Attitudes and Consciousness Exam [*Two-part television program broadcast in 1989*]
RACE........ Radiation Adaptive Compression Equipment
RACE........ Random Access Computer Equipment
RACE........ Random Access Control Equipment　(IEEE)
RACE........ Rapid Amplification of CDNA [*Complementary Deoxyribonucleic Acid*] Ends [*Genetics*]
RACE........ Rapid Automatic Checkout Equipment
RACE........ Request Altitude Changes En Route [*Aviation*]
RACE........ Research in Advanced Communications in Europe [*European Commission*]
RACE........ Research on Automatic Computation Electronics
RACE........ Resource Assessment and Conservation Engineering [*Environmental protection*]
RACE........ Restoration of Aircraft to Combat Effectivity [*Army*]
Race Clas ... Race and Class [*A publication*]
Race Hyg ... Race Hygiene [*Japan*] [*A publication*]
RACEL...... Record of Access/Eligibility [*DoD*]
RACEP...... Random Access and Correlation for Extended Performance [*Telecommunications*]
Race Rela L R ... Race Relations Law Reporter [*A publication*]
Race Rela L Sur ... Race Relations Law Survey [*A publication*]
Race Rel L Rep ... Race Relations Law Reporter [*A publication*]　(DLA)
RACES ...... Radio Amateur Civil Emergency Service [*Civil defense*]
RACES ...... Remote Arming Common Element System
RACF........ Resource Access Control Facility [*IBM Corp.*]
RACFI ...... Radio and Communication Facilities Inoperative
RACFOE.... Research Analysis Corporation Field Office, Europe [*Army*]　(AABC)
RACG .... Radiometric Area Correlation Guidance
RAChD...... Royal Army Chaplains' Department [*British*]
RACHS...... Records. American Catholic Historical Society of Philadelphia [*A publication*]
RACHSP... Records. American Catholic Historical Society of Philadelphia [*A publication*]
RACIC....... Remote Area Conflict Information Center [*Battelle Memorial Institute*]
RAC In...... RAC Income Fund [*Associated Press abbreviation*]　(APAG)
RACIS ...... RADAR Computer Interaction Simulator
RACM .... Raycomm Transworld Industries, Inc. [*NASDAQ symbol*]　(NQ)
RACM .... Reasonable Available Control Measures [*Environmental Protection Agency*]　(GFGA)
RACMSC.. Royal Automobile Club Motor Sports Council [*British*]　(DI)
RACND3... Annual Research Reviews. Rheumatoid Arthritis and Related Conditions [*A publication*]
RACNE ..... Regional Advisory Committee on Nuclear Energy
RACNSC... Religious Activities Committee, National Safety Council　(EA)
RACO....... RADAR-Absorbing Coating [*Military*]　(RDA)
RACO....... RealAmerica Co. [*NASDAQ symbol*]　(NQ)
RACO....... Rear Area Combat Operations　(INF)
RACOB(WA) ... Rear-Admiral Commanding Combined Operational Bases (Western Approaches) [*British*]
RACOMS ... Rapid Combat Mapping Service [*or System*] [*Military*]
RACON..... RADAR Responder Beacon
Ra (Conspic) ... RADAR Conspicuous Object
RACOON ... Radiation Controlled Balloon [*Meteorology*]
RACP........ Royal Australasian College of Physicians
RACPAS ... RADAR Coverage Penetration Analysis
RACR .... Resources Allocation Change Request
Rac Rel L Survey ... Race Relations Law Survey [*A publication*]　(DLA)
RAC/RJ..... Religious Action Center of Reform Judaism　(EA)
RACS........ Random Access Communications System
RACS........ Recruit Allocation Control System [*Navy*]　(NVT)
RACS........ Redundant Attitude Control System　(MCD)
RACS........ Regenerable Affinity Chromatography Support
RACS........ Remote Access Computing System [*Data processing*]
RACS........ Remote Automatic Calibration System　(NASA)
RACS........ Remote Automatic Control System　(KSC)
RACS........ Request for Approval of Contractual Support
RACS........ Rotation Axis Coordinate System　(MCD)
RACS........ Royal Australasian College of Surgeons
RACT........ Reasonable Available Control Technology [*Environmental Protection Agency*]
RACT........ Remote Access Computer Technique [*Data processing*]　(IEEE)
RACT........ Reverse-Acting
RACU .... Remote Acquisiton and Command Unit [*NASA*]　(NASA)
RACUAHC ... Religious Action Center of the Union of American Hebrew Congregations [*Later, RAC/RJ*]　(EA)

Rac Uff....... Raccolta Ufficiale delle Leggi e dei Decreti della Repubblica Italiana [*A publication*]
RACYA...... Reviews in Analytical Chemistry [*A publication*]
RACZA...... Revista. Academia de Ciencias Exactas, Fisico-Quimicas, y Naturales de Zaragoza [*A publication*]
RAD.......... Parti Radical [*Radical Party*] [*France*] [*Political party*] (EAIO)
Rad............ Rad Jugoslavenski Akademija Znanosti i Umjetnosti [*A publication*]
RAD.......... RADAR
RAD.......... RADAR Augmentation Device
RAD.......... Radford Army Ammunition Plant [*Virginia*]
RAD.......... Radford Arsenal [*Army*] (AAG)
RAD.......... RADIAC [*Radiation Detection, Indication, and Computation*] Equipment (NATG)
RAD.......... Radial
rad............. Radian [*Symbol*] [*SI unit of plane angle*]
RAD.......... Radian (MCD)
RAD.......... Radiation (KSC)
RAD.......... Radiation Absorbed Dose [*Unit of measurement of radiation energy*]
RAD.......... Radiator (AAG)
RAD.......... Radical
Rad............ Radical Teacher [*A publication*]
RAD.......... Radio (AAG)
RAD.......... Radioactivity Detection
RAD.......... Radiogram
Rad............ Radiola [*Record label*] [*Australia*]
RAD.......... Radiology [*or Radiologist*] (ADA)
Rad............ Radiotherapist (MAE)
RAD.......... Radium [*Chemical symbol is Ra*]
RAD.......... Radius (AAG)
RAD.......... Radix [*Root*] [*Latin*]
RAD.......... Radnorshire [*County in Wales*] (ROG)
RAD.......... Raised Afterdeck [*of a ship*] (DS)
RAD.......... Random Access Data (BUR)
RAD.......... Random Access Device
RAD.......... Random Access Disc (MCD)
RAD.......... Rapid Access Data [*Xerox Corp.*]
RAD.......... Rapid Access Device
RAD.......... Rapid Access Disk
RAD.......... Rapid Access Drive (BUR)
RADN........ Rapid Automatic Drill
RAD.......... Ratio Adjust Device (MCD)
RAD.......... Ratio Analysis Diagram [*Metallurgy*]
RAD.......... Reactive Airway Disease [*Medicine*] (MAE)
RA(D)........ Rear-Admiral (Destroyers) [*Obsolete*] [*Navy*] [*British*]
RAD.......... Recommendation Approval Document (MCD)
RAD.......... Records Arrival Date [*Bell System*] (TEL)
RAD.......... Recruiting Aids Department [*Navy*]
RAD.......... Reference Attitude Display
RAD.......... Reflex Anal Dilatation [*Medicine*]
RAD.......... Regional Accountable Depot [*Military*]
RADAT...... Regional Administrative Directors
RAD.......... Relative Air Density (OA)
RAD.......... Released from Active Duty [*Navy*]
RAD.......... Repair at Depot (MCD)
RAD.......... Reported for Active Duty [*Navy*]
RAD.......... Request for Apollo Documents [*NASA*] (KSC)
RAD.......... Required Availability Date [*Military*]
RAD.......... Requirements Action Directive (AFM)
R & AD...... Research and Advanced Development
RAD.......... Research and Advanced Development (MCD)
RAD.......... Reservists on Active Duty [*Navy*]
RAD.......... Resource Allocation Display [*Navy*]
RAD.......... Resource Availability Determination (MCD)
RAD.......... Respect voor Arbeid en Democratie [*Belgium*] [*Political party*] (EY)
RAD.......... Restricted Activity Days [*Veterans Administration*] (GFGA)
RAD.......... Restricted Shipyard Availability Requiring Drydocking [*Navy*] (NVT)
RAD.......... Return to Active Duty [*Military*]
RAD.......... Review and Approval Document (MCD)
RAD.......... Right Anterior Digestive [*Gland*]
RAD.......... Right Axis Deviation [*Medicine*]
RAD.......... Rite Aid Corp. [*NYSE symbol*] (SPSG)
RAD.......... Roentgen Administered Dose
RAD.......... Royal Academy of Dancing [*British*] (EAIO)
RAD.......... Royal Academy of Dancing, United States Branch (EA)
RAD.......... Royal Albert Dock [*British*]
RAD.......... Rural Areas Development
RAD.......... Warroad, MN [*Location identifier*] [*FAA*] (FAAL)
RadA........ Radical Alliance [*British*]
RADA........ Radioactive
RADA........ Random Access Discrete Address [*Army division-level battlefield radio communications system*]
RADA........ Realignment of Airdrop Activities (MCD)
RADA........ Right Acromio-Dorsoanterior [*A fetal position*] [*Obstetrics*]
RADA........ Royal Academy of Dramatic Art [*British*]
RADAC..... RADAR Analog Digital Data and Control (KSC)
RADAC..... Rapid Digital Automatic Computing
RADAC...... Raytheon Automatic Drafting Artwork Compiler

RADACS... Random Access Discrete Address Communications System [*Army*]
RaDaK....... Rabbi David Kimhi [*Biblical scholar, 1160-1235*] (BJA)
RADAL...... Radio Detection and Location
RADALT.. RADAR Altimeter [*Aviation*] (SSD)
Rad Am...... Radical America [*A publication*]
Rad Amer... Radical America [*A publication*]
RADAN...... RADAR Analysis System (MCD)
RADAN..... RADAR Doppler Automatic Navigator
RADAN..... RADAR Navigation
RADANT.. RADOME [*RADAR Dome*] Antenna (NVT)
Radar........ Radar's Reports [*138-163 Missouri*] [*A publication*] (DLA)
RADAR.... Radio Association Defending Airwave Rights (EA)
RADAR.... Radio Detection and Ranging
RADAR..... Rassemblement des Democrates pour l'Avenir de la Reunion [*Rally of Democrats for the Future of Reunion*] [*Political party*] (PPW)
RADAR..... Repertoire Analytique d'Articles de Revues de Quebec [*Database*] [*A publication*]
RADAR..... Reseau d'Approvisionnement et de Debouches d'Affaires [*Business Opportunities Sourcing System - BOSS*] [*Canada*]
RAD-AR.... Risk/Benefit Assessment of Drugs - Analysis and Response [*Post-marketing surveillance*]
RADAR..... Royal Association for Disability and Rehabilitation [*British*]
RADARC... Radially Distributed Annular Rocket Chamber
RADAREVALSq ... RADAR Evaluation Squadron [*Air Force*]
RADARSAT ... RADAR Satellite [*Canada*]
RADAS..... Random Access Discrete Address System
RADAT..... RADAR Alignment Designation Accuracy Test (MCD)
RADAT..... RADAR Data Transmission
RADAT..... Radio Direction and Track
RADAT..... Radiosonde Observation Data
RADATA... RADAR Data Transmission and Assembly (IEEE)
RADATAC ... Radiation Data Acquisition Chart
RADAUS... Radio-Austria AG
RADAY..... Radio Day (CET)
RADB........ Radiometric Age Data Bank [*Geological Survey*] [*Information service or system*] [*Defunct*] (IID)
RADBA..... Radiobiology [*English Translation*] [*A publication*]
RADBIOL ... Radiobiology
RADBN..... Radio Battalion [*Marine Corps*]
RAD(BPF) ... Rear-Admiral Commanding Destroyers (British Pacific Fleet)
RADC....... RADAR Countermeasures and Deception [*Military*] (MCD)
RADC....... Regiment Air Defense Center (NATG)
RADC....... Review, Approve or Disapprove, and Comment (MCD)
RADC....... Rome Air Development Center [*Griffiss Air Force Base, NY*] [*Air Force*]
RADC........ Royal Army Dental Corps [*British*]
RADCAP... Research and Development Contributions to Aviation Progress [*Air Force*]
RADCAS... Radiation Casualty [*Criteria for battlefield targets*] (MCD)
RADCAT... RADAR Calibration Target (MCD)
RADCC..... Radiation Control Center
RADCC..... Radiological Control Center [*Army*] (KSC)
RADCC..... Rear Area Damage Control Center (AABC)
RADC/ETR ... Rome Air Development Center Deputy for Electronic Technology [*ESD*]
RADCHM ... Radiochemistry
Rad Clinica ... Radiologia Clinica [*A publication*]
Rad Clin NA ... Radiologic Clinics of North America [*A publication*]
RADCM..... RADAR Countermeasures and Deception [*Military*]
RADCOL... RADC [*Rome Air Development Center*] Automatic Document Classification On-Line [*Air Force*] [*Information service or system*] (IID)
RADCOM ... Radio Communications (MCD)
RADCOM ... Radiometric Contrast Matching (MCD)
RADCOM ... Research and Development Command (MCD)
RADCON ... RADAR Control
RADCON ... RADAR Data Converter (AFM)
RADCON ... Radiological Control [*Military*] (AABC)
RADCOT .. Radial Optical Tracking Theodolite (MUGU)
RADCS...... RADAR Control Squadron
RADDEF... Radiological Defense [*To minimize the effect of nuclear radiation on people and resources*]
Rad Diagn ... Radiologia Diagnostica [*A publication*]
RADDOL.. Raddolcendo [*Gradually Softer*] [*Music*]
RADDS...... RADAR Display Distribution System (DWSG)
RADE........ Research and Development Division [*Obsolete*] [*National Security Agency*]
RADEC...... Radiation Detection Capability (MCD)
RADEF...... Radiological Defense [*To minimize the effect of nuclear radiation on people and resources*]
RADEM.... Random Access Delta Modulation
Rad Eng (London) ... Radio Engineering (London) [*A publication*]
RADEP...... RADAR Departure (FAAC)
RADER...... Rassemblement Democratique du Ruanda [*Democratic Rally of Rwanda*]
RADES...... RADAR Evaluation Squadron [*Air Force*]
RADES...... Realistic Air Defense Engagement System [*Army*] (RDA)
RADEX...... RADAR Exercise (NVT)

RADEX...... Radiation Exclusion Plot [*Chart of actual or predicted fallout*]
Radex Rundsch ... Radex Rundschau [*A publication*]
Radex Runsch ... Radex Rundschau [*A publication*]
RADFAC... Radiating Facility
RADFAL... Radiological Prediction Fallout Plot
RADFET ... Radiation-Sensing Field Effect Transistor [*Instrumentation*]
RADFO ..... Radiological Fallout [*Army*]
Rad Geoinst ... Radovi - Geoinstitut [*A publication*]
RADHAZ... Radiation Hazards
Rad Hist ... Radical History Review [*A publication*]
Rad Humanist ... Radical Humanist [*A publication*]
RADI .... Rada Electronic Industries Ltd. [*New York, NY*] [*NASDAQ symbol*]   (NQ)
RADI .... Radiographic Inspection [*NASA*]   (AAG)
Radi........... Radium [*Record label*] [*France*]
RADIA ...... Radiography [*A publication*]
RADIAC.... Radiation Detection, Indication, and Computation [*Radiological measuring instruments*]
RADIAC.... Radioactive Detection and Measurement
RADIAT.... Radiation
Radiata Pine Tech Bull ... Radiata Pine Technical Bulletin (Radiata Pine Association of Australia) [*A publication*]   (APTA)
Radiat Biol ... Radiation Biology [*England*] [*A publication*]
Radiat Bot ... Radiation Botany [*A publication*]
Radiat Data Rep ... Radiation Data and Reports [*A publication*]
Radiat Eff .. Radiation Effects [*A publication*]
Radiat Effects ... Radiation Effects [*A publication*]
Radiat Eff Express ... Radiation Effects Express [*A publication*]
Radiat Eff Lett ... Radiation Effects. Letters Section [*A publication*]
Radiat Eff Lett Sect ... Radiation Effects. Letters Section [*A publication*]
Radiat Env ... Radiation and Environmental Biophysics [*A publication*]
Radiat Environ Biophys ... Radiation and Environmental Biophysics [*A publication*]
Radiat Med ... Radiation Medicine [*A publication*]
Radiat Phys Chem ... Radiation Physics and Chemistry [*A publication*]
Radiat Prot ... Radiation Protection [*Republic of Korea*] [*A publication*]
Radiat Prot Aust ... Radiation Protection in Australia [*A publication*]
Radiat Prot Dosim ... Radiation Protection Dosimetry [*A publication*]
Radiat Prot ICRP Publ ... Radiation Protection. ICRP [*International Commission on Radiological Protection*] Publication [*A publication*]
Radiat Prot (Seoul) ... Radiation Protection (Seoul) [*A publication*]
Radiat Prot (Taiyuan People's Repub China) ... Radiation Protection (Taiyuan, People's Republic of China) [*A publication*]
Radiat Rep ... Radiation Report [*A publication*]
Radiat Res ... Radiation Research [*A publication*]
Radiat Res Polym ... Radiation Research on Polymers [*Japan*] [*A publication*]
Radiat Res Rev ... Radiation Research Reviews [*A publication*]
Radiat Res Suppl ... Radiation Research. Supplement [*A publication*]
Radiats Fiz ... Radiatsionnaya Fizika [*A publication*]
Radiats Fiz Akad Nauk Latv SSR Inst Fiz ... Radiatsionnaya Fizika. Akademiya Nauk Latviiskoi SSR. Institut Fiziki [*Latvian SSR*] [*A publication*]
Radiats Fiz Nemet Krist ... Radiatsionnaya Fizika Nemetallicheskikh Kristallov [*A publication*]
Radiats Fiz Tverd Tela Radiats Materialoved ... Radiatsionnaya Fizika Tverdogo Tela i Radiatsionnoe Materialovedenie [*A publication*]
Radiats Gig ... Radiatsionnaya Gigiena [*Former USSR*] [*A publication*]
Radiat Shielding Inf Cent Rep ... Radiation Shielding Information Center. Report [*A publication*]
Radiats Tekh ... Radiatsionnaya Tekhnika [*A publication*]
Radiaz Alta Energ ... Radiazioni di Alta Energia [*A publication*]
Radiaz Radioisot ... Radiazioni e Radioisotopi [*A publication*]
RADIC...... Radical   (ROG)
RADIC...... Radio Interior Communications
RADIC...... Redifon Analog-Digital Computer [*British*]
RADIC...... Research and Development Information Center   (AFM)
Radical Am ... Radical America [*A publication*]
Radical Commun Med ... Radical Community Medicine [*A publication*]
Radical Ed ... Radical Education [*A publication*]
Radical Ed Dossier ... Radical Education Dossier [*A publication*]
Radical Educ Dossier ... Radical Education Dossier [*A publication*]   (APTA)
Radical His ... Radical History Review [*A publication*]
Radical Scot ... Radical Scotland [*A publication*]
RADIC-LIB ... Radical Liberal
RADIL....... Research Animal Diagnostic and Investigative Laboratory [*University of Missouri-Columbia*] [*Research center*]   (RCD)
Rad Imunol Zavoda (Zagreb) ... Radovi Imunoloskog Zavoda (Zagreb) [*A publication*]
RADINJCLRDS ... Radiation Injury Claims Record   (DNAB)
Rad Inst Geol-Rud Istraz Ispit Nukl Drugih Miner Sirovina ... Radovi Instituta za Geolosko-Rudarska Istrazivanja i Ispitivanja Nuklearnih i Drugih Mineralnih Sirovina [*Yugoslavia*] [*A publication*]
Rad Inst Proucavanje Suzbijanje Alkohol Drugih Narkomanija ... Radovi Instituta za Proucavanje i Suzbijanje Alkoholizma i Drugih Narkomanija u Zagrebu [*A publication*]

Rad Inst Prouc Suzbijanje Alkohol Drugih Narkomanija Zagrebu ... Radovi Instituta za Proucavanje i Suzbijanje Alkoholizma i Drugih Narkomanija u Zagrebu [*A publication*]
Rad Inst Sum Istraz ... Radovi Institut za Sumarska Istrazivanja. Sumarskog Fakulteta. Sveucilista u Zagrebu [*A publication*]
RADINT.... RADAR Intelligence
RADIO ...... Radiotherapy
Radioact Sea ... Radioactivity in the Sea [*Austria*] [*A publication*]
Radioact Surv Data Jap ... Radioactivity Survey Data in Japan [*A publication*]
Radioact Waste Disposal Res Ser Inst Geol Sci ... Radioactive Waste Disposal. Research Series. Institute of Geological Sciences [*A publication*]
Radioact Waste Manage ... Radioactive Waste Management [*A publication*]
Radioact Waste Manage Nucl Fuel Cycle ... Radioactive Waste Management and the Nuclear Fuel Cycle [*A publication*]
Radioact Waste Manage (Oak Ridge Tenn) ... Radioactive Waste Management (Oak Ridge, Tennessee) [*A publication*]
Radioact Waste Technol ... Radioactive Waste Technology [*A publication*]
Radioaktiv Zivotn Prostr ... Radioaktivita a Zivotne Prostredie [*A publication*]
Radiobiol.... Radiobiologiya [*A publication*]
RADIOBIOL ... Radiobiology
Radiobiol Biol Mol ... Radiobiologia si Biologia Moleculara [*Romania*] [*A publication*]
Radiobiol Inf Byull ... Radiobiologiya Informatsionnyi Byulleten' [*A publication*]
Radiobiol Lat ... Radiobiologica Latina [*Italy*] [*A publication*]
Radiobiol Proc All Union Sci Tech Conf Appl Radioact Isot ... Radiobiology. A Portion of the Proceedings. All-Union Scientific and Technical Conference on the Application of Radioactive Isotopes [*A publication*]
Radiobiol Radioter Fis Med ... Radiobiologia, Radioterapia, e Fisica Medica [*A publication*]
Radiobiol-Radiother ... Radiobiologia-Radiotherapia [*A publication*]
Radiobiol-Radiother (Berl) ... Radiobiologia-Radiotherapia (Berlin) [*A publication*]
Radiobiol-Radiother (Berlin) ... Radiobiologia-Radiotherapia (Berlin) [*A publication*]
Radioch Act ... Radiochimica Acta [*A publication*]
RADIOCHEM ... Radiochemistry
Radiochem Radioanal Lett ... Radiochemical and Radioanalytical Letters [*A publication*]
Radiochim Acta ... Radiochimica Acta [*A publication*]
Radioch Rad ... Radiochemical and Radioanalytical Letters [*A publication*]
Radio Commun ... Radio Communication [*A publication*]
Radioekol Vodn Org ... Radioekologiya Vodnykh Organizmov [*A publication*]
Radio Elec ... Radio-Electronics [*A publication*]
Radio-Electr ... Radio-Electronics [*A publication*]
Radio Electron ... Radio Electronica [*Netherlands*] [*A publication*]
Radio-Electron ... Radio-Electronics [*A publication*]
Radio Electron Commun Syst ... Radio Electronics and Communications Systems [*A publication*]
Radioelectron and Commun Syst ... Radioelectronics and Communication Systems [*A publication*]
Radio & Electron Constructor ... Radio and Electronics Constructor [*A publication*]
Radio Electron Eng ... Radio and Electronic Engineer [*A publication*]
Radio Electron Eng (London) ... Radio and Electronic Engineer (London) [*A publication*]
Radio & Electronic Eng ... Radio and Electronic Engineer [*A publication*]
Radio and Electron World ... Radio and Electronics World [*A publication*]
Radio Elec W ... Radio Electrical Weekly [*A publication*]   (APTA)
Radio Elektron ... Radio Elektronica [*A publication*]
Radio Elektroniikkalab Tek Korkeakoulu Kertomus ... Radio- ja Elektroniikkalaboratoriot. Teknillinen Korkeakoulu. Kertomus [*A publication*]
Radio Elektron Schau ... Radio Elektronik Schau [*A publication*]
Radio El En ... Radio and Electronic Engineer [*A publication*]
Radio Eng .. Radio Engineering [*A publication*]
Radio Eng Electron Phys ... Radio Engineering and Electronic Physics [*A publication*]
Radio Eng Electron (USSR) ... Radio Engineering and Electronic Physics (USSR) [*A publication*]
Radio Engrg Electron Phys ... Radio Engineering and Electronic Physics [*A publication*]
Radio Eng (USSR) ... Radio Engineering (USSR) [*A publication*]
Radio Fernsehen Elektron ... Radio Fernsehen Elektronik [*A publication*]
Radiogr ...... Radiographer [*A publication*]   (APTA)
Radiogr Today ... Radiography Today [*A publication*]
Radio Hobbies Aust ... Radio and Hobbies Australia [*A publication*]
Radio Ind ... Radio Industria [*A publication*]
Radioind Elettron-Telev ... Radioindustria Elettronica-Televisione [*A publication*]
Radioisot (Praha) ... Radioisotopy (Praha) [*A publication*]
Radioisot (Tokyo) ... Radioisotopes (Tokyo) [*A publication*]
Radiol......... Radiology
Radio Lab Tech Univ Helsinki Intern Rep ... Radio Laboratory. Technical University of Helsinki. Internal Report [*A publication*]
Radiol Austriaca ... Radiologia Austriaca [*A publication*]
Radiol Bras ... Radiologia Brasileira [*A publication*]

Radiol Cancer Sel Pap Int Congr Radiol ... Radiology of Cancer. Selected Papers. International Congress of Radiology [*A publication*]
Radiol Clin ... Radiologia Clinica [*A publication*]
Radiol Clin (Basel) ... Radiologia Clinica (Basel) [*A publication*]
Radiol Clin Biol ... Radiologia Clinica et Biologica [*A publication*]
Radiol Clin N Am ... Radiologic Clinics of North America [*A publication*]
Radiol Clin North Am ... Radiologic Clinics of North America [*A publication*]
Radiol Clin North America ... Radiologic Clinics of North America [*A publication*]
Radiol Diagn ... Radiologia Diagnostica [*A publication*]
Radiol Diagn (Berlin) ... Radiologia Diagnostica (Berlin) [*A publication*]
Radiol Health Data ... Radiological Health Data [*A publication*]
Radiol Health Data Rep ... Radiological Health Data and Reports [*A publication*]
Radiol Iugosl (Ljubljana) ... Radiologia Iugoslavica (Ljubljana) [*A publication*]
Radiol Kozl ... Radiologiai Kozlemenyek [*A publication*]
Radiol Manage ... Radiology Management [*A publication*]
Radiol Med ... Radiologia Medica [*A publication*]
Radiol Med (Torino) ... Radiologia Medica (Torino) [*A publication*]
Radiological Protect Bull ... Radiological Protection Bulletin [*A publication*]
Radiol Prat ... Radiologia Pratica [*Italy*] [*A publication*]
Radiol Prot Bull ... Radiological Protection Bulletin [*A publication*]
Radiol Rev Miss Val Med J ... Radiological Review and Mississippi Valley Medical Journal [*A publication*]
Radiol Technol ... Radiologic Technology [*A publication*]
Radio Mentor Electron ... Radio Mentor Electronic [*A publication*]
Radio Mntr ... Radio Mentor Electronic [*A publication*]
Radiom Polarogr ... Radiometer Polarographics [*A publication*]
Radio N ...... Radio News [*A publication*]
Radiophysiol Radiother ... Radiophysiologie et Radiotherapie [*A publication*]
Radiophys Quantum Electron ... Radiophysics and Quantum Electronics [*A publication*]
Radio Rev Aust ... Radio Review of Australia [*A publication*]
Radio Sci .... Radio Science [*A publication*]
Radio Serv Bul ... Radio Service Bulletin [*A publication*]
Radio T ...... Radio Times [*United Kingdom*] [*A publication*]
Radiotehn i Elektron ... Akademija Nauk SSSR. Radiotehnika i Elektronika [*A publication*]
Radiotehn (Kharkov) ... Radiotehnika (Kharkov) [*A publication*]
Radiotek El ... Radiotekhnika i Elektronika [*A publication*]
Radiotekh .. Radiotekhnika [*A publication*]
Radiotekh Elektron ... Radiotekhnika i Elektronika [*A publication*]
Radiotekhn ... Khar'kovskii Ordena Trudovogo Krasnogo Znameni Gosudarstvennyi Universitet Imeni A.M. Gor'kogo Radiotekhnika [*A publication*]
Radiotekhn i Elektron ... Radiotekhnika i Elektronika. Akademiya Nauk SSSR [*A publication*]
Radiotekh Proizvod ... Radiotekhnicheskoe Proizvodstvo [*A publication*]
Radio Telev ... Radio Television [*A publication*]
Radio Telev Int Rev ... Radio - Television International Review [*A publication*]
Radio Tel & Hobbies ... Radio, Television, and Hobbies [*A publication*] (APTA)
Radioter Radiobiol Fis Med ... Radioterapia, Radiobiologia, e Fisica Medica [*A publication*]
Radiother Oncol ... Radiotherapy and Oncology [*A publication*]
Radioth Onc ... Radiotherapy Oncology [*A publication*]
Radio-TV-Electron ... Radio-TV-Electronic [*Later, RTE. Radio-TV-Electronic*] [*A publication*]
Radio-TV-Electron Serv ... Radio-TV-Electronic Service [*Later, RTE. Radio-TV-Electronic*] [*Switzerland*] [*A publication*]
Radio TVH ... Radio, Television, and Hobbies [*A publication*] (APTA)
Radio & TV N ... Radio and Television News [*A publication*]
Radio es TV Szle ... Radio es TV Szemle [*A publication*]
RADIQUAD ... Radio Quadrangle [*Military*]
RADIR ...... Random Access Document Indexing and Retrieval
RADIST .... RADAR Distance Indicator
RADIT .... Radio Teletype (IEEE)
RADIUS .... Research and Development Institute of the United States [*Research center*] (RCD)
RadJA .... Radovi Jugoslavenske Akademije Znanosti i Umjetnosti [*A publication*]
Rad Jugosl Akad Znan Umjet ... Radovi Jugoslavenske Akademije Znanosti i Umjetnosti [*A publication*]
Rad Jugoslav Akad Znan Umjet ... Radovi Jugoslavenske Akademije Znanosti i Umjetnosti [*A publication*]
Rad Jugoslav Akad Znan Umjet Odjel Prir Nauke ... Radovi Jugoslavenske Akademije Znanosti i Umjetnosti. Odjel za Prirodne Nauke [*A publication*]
RADKA ..... Radiokhimiya [*A publication*]
RADL .... Radial (AAG)
RADL .... Radiological [*or Radiology*] (AAG)
RadL .... Radyans'ske Literaturoznavstvo [*Kiev*] [*A publication*]
RADLA ...... Radiology [*A publication*]
RADLAB ... Radiation Laboratory (AAG)
RADLAC ... Radial Pulse Line Accelerators (MCD)
RADLCEN ... Radiological Center
RADLDEF ... Radiological Defense [*To minimize the effect of nuclear radiation on people and resources*]

RADLDEFLAB ... Radiological Defense Laboratory [*NASA*]
RADLFO ... Radiological Fallout [*Army*] (AABC)
RADLGC ... Radiologic
RADLGCL ... Radiological
RADLGY ... Radiology
RADLMON ... Radiological Monitor [*or Monitoring*] [*Military*]
RADLO ..... Radiological Officer
RADLO ..... Regional Air Defense Liaison Officer (FAAC)
RADLOPS ... Radiological Operations [*Military*] (AABC)
RADLSAFE ... Radiological Safety [*Military*]
RADLSO ... Radiological Survey Officer [*Military*]
RADLSV ... Radiological Survey [*Military*]
RadLV ...... Radiation Leukemia Virus
RADLWAR ... Radiological Warfare
RADM .... RADARman (GFGA)
RADM .... Random Walk Advection and Dispersion Model [*Environmental Protection Agency*] (GFGA)
RADM .... Rear Admiral [*Also, RA, RADML*] (AAG)
RADM .... Regional Acid Deposition Model [*for acid rain*] [*Environmental Protection Agency*]
Rad Med Fak Rijeka ... Radovi Medicinskogo Fakulteta. Rijeka [*A publication*]
Rad Med Fak Zagrebu ... Radovi Medicinskogo Fakulteta u Zagrebu [*A publication*]
RADMIS ... Research Activities Designators Management Information System
RADML .... Rear Admiral [*Also, RA, RADM*] (FAAC)
RADMON ... Radiological Monitoring (AFM)
RADN .... Radiation (AAG)
RADN .... Radnorshire [*County in Wales*]
RADN .... Radyne Corp. [*NASDAQ symbol*] (NQ)
RADNORS ... Radnorshire [*County in Wales*] (ROG)
RADNOS .. No Radio [*Military*]
RADNOTE ... Radio Note [*Military*]
RADOA ..... Radiobiologiya [*A publication*]
RADOC ..... Regional Air Defense Operations Center (NATG)
RADOC ..... Remote Automatic Detection Contingencies
RADOD ..... Research and Development Objectives Document (MCD)
RADOME ... RADAR Dome [*NASA*]
RADON ..... RADAR Beacon
RADON ..... Research and Development Operational Needs (MCD)
RADOP ..... RADAR Doppler [*Missile-tracking system*] (AAG)
RADOP ..... RADAR Operator (CET)
RADOP ..... RADAR/Optical Weapons [*Military*]
RADOP ..... Radio Operator [*Navy*]
RADOPR .. Radio Operator (AAG)
RADOPWEAP ... RADAR Optical Weapons (IEEE)
RADOSE ... Radiation Dosimeter Satellite [*NASA*]
RADOT ..... Real-Time [*or Recording*] Automatic Digital Optical Tracker
RADP .... Right Acromio-Dorsoposterior [*A fetal position*] [*Obstetrics*]
Rad Phil ..... Radical Philosophy [*A publication*]
Rad Phil News ... Radical Philosopher's Newsjournal [*A publication*]
RADPLANBD ... Radio Planning Board [*Navy*]
Rad Poljopriv Fak Univ Saraj ... Radovi Poljoprivrednog Fakulteta Univerziteta u Sarajevu [*A publication*]
Rad Poljopriv Fak Univ Sarajevu ... Radovi Poljoprivrednog Fakulteta Univerziteta u Sarajevu [*A publication*]
RADPROPCAST ... Radio Propagation Forecast
RADREF ... RADAR Refraction (MCD)
Rad Reg P & F ... Radio Regulation. Pike and Fischer [*A publication*]
Rad Rel ...... Radical Religion [*A publication*]
RADREL ... Radio Relay [*Military*]
Rad Relig ... Radical Religion [*A publication*]
RADRON ... RADAR Squadron [*Air Force*]
RADS .... RADAR Squadron [*Air Force*]
RAD/S ...... Radians per Second
RADS .... Radiation and Dosimetry Services (NRCH)
RADS .... Radiation Systems, Inc. [*NASDAQ symbol*] (NQ)
RADS .... Radius (AAG)
RADS .... Rapid Area Distribution Support [*Air Force*]
RADS .... Raw Data System
RADS .... Ryukyu Air Defense System
RAD/S² ...... Radians per Second Squared
RADSAFE ... Radiological Safety [*Military*]
Rad Sarajevo Univ Poljopr Fak ... Radovi Sarajevo Univerzitet. Poljoprivredni Fakultet [*A publication*]
RADSCAT ... Radiometer/Scatterometer [*Sensor*] [*Meteorology*]
Rad Scien ... Radical Science Journal [*A publication*]
RADSO ..... Radiological Survey Officer (IEEE)
RADSOC ... Request for Authority to Develop a System or Change [*Military*] (AFIT)
RADSTA ... Radio Station
Rad Sumar Fak Inst Sumar Sarajevo ... Radovi Sumarskog Fakulteta i Instituta za Sumarstvo u Sarajevo [*A publication*]
Rad Sum Fak i Inst Sum ... Radovi Sumarski Fakultet i Institut za Sumarstvo [*A publication*]
RadT .... Radiola-Telefunken [*Record label*] [*Australia*]
RADT .... Radtech, Inc. [*Albuquerque, NM*] [*NASDAQ symbol*] (NQ)
R/ADT .... Registration/Admission, Disposition and Transfer [*Tri-Service Medical Information System*] (DNAB)
Rad Teach ... Radical Teacher [*A publication*]

Rad Ther .... Issues in Radical Therapy [*A publication*]
Rad Thera ... Issues in Radical Therapy [*A publication*]
RADTS ...... Rabbit Antidog Thymus Serum [*Immunology*]   (MAE)
RADTT ...... Radio Teletypewriter   (CET)
RADU .... RADAR Analysis and Development Unit [*National Severe Storms Forecast Center*]   (NOAA)
RADU .... Ram Air-Driven Unit
RAD-UDRT ... Respect voor Arbeid en Democratie/Union Democratique pour le Respect du Travail [*Respect for Labor and Democracy/Democratic Union for the Respect of Labor*] [*Belgium*] [*Political party*]   (PPE)
Rad Ul .... Radius-Ulna [*Medicine*]   (MAE)
Rad Voj Muz ... Rad Vojvodanskich Muzeja [*A publication*]
RADVS ..... RADAR Altimeter and Doppler Velocity Sensor
RADWAR ... Radiological Warfare
RADWASTE ... Radioactive Waste
RADX .... Radionics, Inc. [*NASDAQ symbol*]   (NQ)
Rad Zavoda Fiz ... Radovi Zavoda za Fiziku [*A publication*]
RadZSF ..... Radovi Zavoda za Slavensku Filologiju [*A publication*]
RAE .... Arar [*Saudi Arabia*] [*Airport symbol*]   (OAG)
RA(E) .... Engineer Rear-Admiral [*Navy*] [*British*]   (DMA)
RAE .... RADAR Altimeter Equipment
RAE .... Radio Astronomy Explorer [*Satellite*]
RAE .... Radiodifusion Argentina al Exterior [*Broadcasting organization*] [*Argentina*]
RAE .... Range, Azimuth, and Elevation   (MCD)
RAE .... Real Academia Espanola. Boletin [*A publication*]
RAE .... Review of Applied Entomology [*Database*] [*Commonwealth Institute of Entomology*] [*Information service or system*]   (CRD)
RAE .... Right Arithmetic Element
RAE .... Right Ascension Encoder
RAE .... Right Atrial Enlargement [*Cardiology*]
RAE .... Royal Aircraft Establishment [*British Ministry of Defense*] [*Research center*]
RAE .... Royal Army Establishment [*British*]
RAEA .... Regroupement des Auteurs-Editeurs Autonomes [*Canada*]
RAEB .... Refractory Anemia with Excess of Blasts [*Hematology*]
RAEB-T ..... Refractory Anemia with Excess of Blasts in Transformation [*Hematology*]
RAEC .... Rabbit Aortic Endothelial Cells
RAEC .... Royal Army Educational Corps [*British*]
RAECO ...... Rare-Earth Cobalt
RAEDOT .. Range, Azimuth, and Elevation Detection of Optical Targets
RAEFB ...... Radiation Effects [*A publication*]
RAELA ...... Radiotekhnika i Elektronika [*A publication*]
RAEM .... Refractory Anemia with Excess Myeloblast [*Hematology*]   (MAE)
RAEN .... Radio Amateur Emergency Network   (IEEE)
Ra Ent .... [*Lord*] Raymond's Entries [*A publication*]   (DLA)
RaeRG .... Reallexikon der Aegyptischen Religionsgeschichte [*Berlin*] [*A publication*]   (BJA)
RAES .... Radio Astronomy Experiment Selection Panel
RAES .... Rapid Access with Extensive Search [*Algorithm*]
RAES .... Ratios for Automotive Executives [*Computer software*]
RAES .... Remote Access Editing System [*Data processing*]   (IEEE)
RAeS .... Royal Aeronautical Society [*British*]   (EAIO)
RAET .... Range, Azimuth, Elevation, and Time
RAETDS ... Reciprocating Aircraft Engine Type Designation System
RAETU ...... Reserve Airborne Electronics Training Unit   (DNAB)
Raevar .... [*Jacobus*] Raevardus [*Deceased, 1568*] [*Authority cited in pre-1607 legal work*]   (DSA)
RAF .... Racial Awareness Facilitator [*School*] [*Navy*]   (NVT)
Ra F .... Raphael Fulgosius [*Deceased, 1427*] [*Authority cited in pre-1607 legal work*]   (DSA)
RAF .... Regular Air Force
RAF .... Requirements Allocation Form
RAF .... Requirements Analysis Form [*NASA*]   (NASA)
RAF .... Research Aviation Facility [*National Center for Atmospheric Research*]
RAF .... Reserved Air Freight
RAF .... Resource Allocation Formula
RAF .... Reynolds Analogy Factor [*Physics*]
RAF .... Rheumatoid Arthritis Factor [*Medicine*]   (MAE)
RAF .... Rote Armee Faktion [*Red Army Faction (Baader-Meinhof Group)*] [*Terrorist group*] [*Germany*]
RAF .... Royal Air Force [*British*]
RAF .... Royal Aircraft Factory [*World War I*] [*British*]
RAF .... Sacramento, CA [*Location identifier*] [*FAA*]   (FAAL)
RAFA .... Rank Annihilation Factor Analysis [*Data processing*]
RAFA .... Royal Air Forces Association   (EAIO)
Ra Fab .... Raymundus Fabri [*Flourished, 14th century*] [*Authority cited in pre-1607 legal work*]   (DSA)
Rafair .... Royal Air Force [*Airline call sign*] [*British*]
RAFAR ...... Radio Automated Facsimile and Reproduction
RAFAX ...... RADAR Facsimile
RAFB .... Randolph Air Force Base [*Texas*]
RAFB .... Rickenbacker Air Force Base [*Formerly, Lockbourne Air Force Base*] [*Ohio*]
RAFB .... Royal Air Force Base [*British*]
RAFBF ...... Royal Air Force Benevolent Fund [*British military*]   (DMA)

RAFC .... Richmond Area Film Cooperative [*Library network*]
RAFC .... Royal Air Force Club [*British*]
RAFC .... Royal Air Force College [*British*]
RAFC .... Royal Artillery Flying Club [*British military*]   (DMA)
RAFCC ...... Royal Air Force Cinema Corp. [*British military*]   (DMA)
RAFCC ...... Royal Air Force Coastal Command [*British*]
RAFD .... Rome Air Force Depot
RAFES ...... Royal Air Force Educational Service [*British military*]   (DMA)
RAFFC ...... Royal Air Force Fighter Command [*British*]
Raff Pens Man ... Raff's Pension Manual [*A publication*]   (DLA)
RAFG .... Royal Air Force, Germany [*British military*]   (DMA)
RAFI .... Ravenswood Finance Corp. [*NASDAQ symbol*]   (NQ)
RAFI .... Rural Advancement Fund International [*Later, RAFI-USA*]   (EA)
RAFIA .... Radiatsionnaya Fizika. Akademiya Nauk Latviiskoi SSR. Institut Fiziki [*A publication*]
RAFL .... Rainfall   (FAAC)
RAFLO ...... Radio Frequency Liaison Office [*Navy*]   (DNAB)
RAFME ..... Royal Air Force, Middle East [*British military*]   (DMA)
RAFMS ..... Royal Air Force Medical Service [*British*]
RAFNS ..... Royal Air Force Nursing Service [*British military*]   (DMA)
RAFO .... Reserve Air Force Officers [*Later, RAFRO*] [*British*]
RAFR .... Royal Air Force Regiment [*British*]
RAFRC ...... Revolutionary Armed Forces of the Republic of Cuba
R African Pol Economy ... Review of African Political Economy [*A publication*]
RAFRO ...... Royal Air Force Reserve of Officers [*Formerly, RAFO*] [*British*]
RAFRZ ...... Radiosonde Observation - Freezing Levels   (FAAC)
RAFS .... R. Austin Freeman Society   (EA)
RAFS .... Regional Analysis and Forecast System [*National Meteorological Center*]
RAFS .... Royal Air Force Station [*British*]   (MCD)
RAFSAA ... Royal Air Force Small Arms Association [*British military*]   (DMA)
RAFSC ...... Royal Air Force Staff College [*British*]
RAFSC ...... Royal Air Force Support Command [*British*]
RAFSP ...... Royal Air Force Service Police [*British military*]   (DMA)
RAFSTN ... Royal Air Force Air Station
RAFT .... Racial Awareness Facilitator Training [*Navy program*]
RAFT .... Radially Adjustable Facility Tube   (IEEE)
RAFT .... Rear-Admiral Fleet Train [*British Pacific Fleet*]
RAFT .... Recomp Algebraic Formula Translator [*Data processing*]
RAFT .... Regional Accounting and Finance Test [*Military*]   (AFM)
RAFT .... Resource Allocation for Transportation   (DNAB)
RAFT .... Reunion des Amateurs de Fox Terriers [*An association*]   (EAIO)
RAFTC ...... Royal Air Forces Transport Command [*British*]
Ra Fulgo ..... Raphael Fulgosius [*Deceased, 1427*] [*Authority cited in pre-1607 legal work*]   (DSA)
RAFVR ...... Royal Air Force Volunteer Reserve [*British*]
RAG .... Ragged   (FAAC)
Rag .... Ragland's California Superior Court Decisions [*A publication*]   (DLA)
RAG .... Raina un Aspazijas Gadagramata [*A publication*]
RAG .... Readiness Analysis Group
RAG .... Recombination-Activating Gene
RAG .... Regimental Artillery Group [*OPFOR*]   (GFGA)
RAG .... Regional Advisory Group [*Generic term*]   (DHSM)
RAg .... Related Antigen [*Immunology*]
RAG .... Religious Arts Guild [*Defunct*]   (EA)
RAG .... Replacement Air Group
RAG .... Requirements Advisory Group [*Air Force*]   (MCD)
RAG .... Resource Appraisal Group [*US Geological Survey*]
RAG .... Retail Associates Group, Inc. [*Homesewing industry trade group*]
RAG .... Returned Ammunition Group   (NATG)
RAG .... Reusable Agena [*NASA*]   (NASA)
RAG .... Ring Airfoil Grenade [*Army*]
RAG .... River Assault Group [*Military*]
RAG .... ROM [*Read-Only Memory*] Address Gate [*Data processing*]
RAG .... Runway Arresting Gear [*Aviation*]
RAG-1 .... Rosenberg, Avraham, and Gutnick [*Strain of bacteria named for its researchers: Eugene Rosenberg, Avraham Reisfield, and David Gutnick*]
RAGAN ..... Ragan [*Brad*], Inc. [*Associated Press abbreviation*]   (APAG)
RAGBRAI ... [*Des Moines*] Register Annual Great Bicycle Race Across Iowa [*Pronounced "ragbray"*]
RAGC .... Rainbows for All God's Children [*Later, RFAGC*]   (EA)
RAGC .... Relief General Communications Vessel
RAGC .... Royal and Ancient Golf Club [*Scotland*]
RAGE .... Radio Amplification of Gamma Emissions [*Antiguerrilla weapon*]
RAGEA ..... Razvedochnaya Geofizika [*A publication*]
RAGEMS ... Radioactive Gaseous Effluent Monitoring System
RAGES ...... Rail Armed Guard Escort Service [*Military Traffic Management Command*]
RAGF .... Remote Air-Ground Facility [*Aviation*]
Ragg .... Rheumatoid Agglutinator [*Immunology*]
RagL .... Raguaglio Librario [*A publication*]
RAGN .... Ragen Corp. [*NASDAQ symbol*]   (NQ)

R Agr Econ Mal ... Review of Agricultural Economics of Malaysia [*A publication*]
R Agric Soc (Cairo) Bull Tech Sect ... Royal Agricultural Society (Cairo). Bulletin. Technical Section [*A publication*]
R Agric Soc Kenya QJ ... Royal Agricultural Society of Kenya. Quarterly Journal [*A publication*]
RAGS........ Coated Sales, Inc. [*Laurence Harbor, NJ*] [*NASDAQ symbol*] (NQ)
Rag Super Ct Dec (Calif) ... Ragland's California Superior Court Decisions [*A publication*] (DLA)
RAH.......... Rabbit Anti-Human [*Immunology*]
RAH.......... Radiation-Anneal Hardening [*Alloy*]
RAH.......... Rafha [*Saudi Arabia*] [*Airport symbol*] (OAG)
RAH.......... Receipt, Excess, Adjustment, Due-In History File [*Army*]
RAH.......... Receiving Array Hydrophone
RAH.......... Reconnaissance Attack Helicopter
RAH.......... Regressing Atypical Histiocytosis [*Medicine*]
RAH.......... Reviews in American History [*A publication*]
RAH.......... Right Anterior Hemiblock [*Medicine*] (AAMN)
RAH.......... Right Atrial Hypertrophy [*Cardiology*]
RAH.......... Royal Albert Hall [*London, England*]
Ra de Hacur ... Raoul d'Harcourt [*Deceased, 1307*] [*Authority cited in pre-1607 legal work*] (DSA)
RAHBol..... Real Academia de la Historia. Boletin [*A publication*]
RAHE........ Review of Allied Health Education [*A publication*]
RAHF .... Research Animal Holding Facility [*NASA*] (NASA)
RaHGBM ... Rabbit Anti-Human Glomerular Basement Membrane [*Immunology*]
RAHO .... Rabbits Against Human Ovary [*Immunology*]
RAHO .... Royal Albert Hall Orchestra
RAHS .... Royal Australian Historical Society. Journal [*A publication*] (APTA)
RAHSJ ...... Royal Australian Historical Society. Journal and Proceedings [*A publication*] (APTA)
RAHTG ..... Rabbit Anti-Human Thymocyte Globulin [*Immunology*] (AAMN)
RAHTS...... Rabbit Anti-Human Thymocyte Serum [*Immunology*] (OA)
RAI .... Praia [*Cape Verde Islands*] [*Airport symbol*] (OAG)
RAI .... Racquetball Association of Ireland (EAIO)
RAI .... RADAR Altimeter Indicator (MCD)
RAI .... Radiation Applications, Inc.
RAI .... Radioactive Interference [*NASA*]
RAI .... Radioactive Iodine [*Medicine*]
RAI .... Radioactive Isotope [*Roentgenology*]
Rai............ Rainerius [*Authority cited in pre-1607 legal work*] (DSA)
RAI .... Random Access and Inquiry [*Data processing*]
RAI .... Range Azimuth Indicator
RAI .... Raspberry Island [*Alaska*] [*Seismograph station code, US Geological Survey*] (SEIS)
RAI .... Rassemblement Arabique-Islamique [*Algeria*] [*Political party*] (EY)
RAI .... Reliability Assurance Instructions (KSC)
RAI .... Rencontre Assyriologique Internationale [*A publication*]
RAI .... Rendiconti. Classe di Scienze Morali e Storiche. Accademia d'Italia [*A publication*]
RAI .... Repair at Intermediate (MCD)
RAI .... Request for Additional Information (NRCH)
RAI .... Research Advisory Institute, Inc.
RAI .... Resource Analysts, Inc.
RAI .... Roll Attitude Indicator [*NASA*]
RAI .... Rounders Association of Ireland (EAIO)
RAI .... Royal Albert Institution [*British*] (DAS)
RAI .... Royal Anthropological Institute [*British*]
RAI .... Royal Archaeological Institute [*British*]
RAI .... Royal Artillery Institution [*British military*] (DMA)
RAI .... Runway Alignment Indicator [*Aviation*]
RAI .... Rural America, Inc. (EA)
RAIAD ...... Reverse Acronyms, Initialisms, and Abbreviations Dictionary [*Formerly, RAID*] [*A publication*]
RAIAM...... Random Access Indestructive Advanced Memory [*Data processing*] (MSA)
RAIB.......... Rendiconti. Accademia delle Scienze. Istituto di Bologna [*A publication*]
RAIC.......... Radiological Accident and Incident Control
RAIC.......... Red Andina de Informacion Comercial [*Andean Trade Information Network*] (EAIO)
RAIC.......... Redstone Arsenal Information Center [*Army*]
RAIC.......... Royal Architectural Institute of Canada
RAICG...... Radiosonde Observation Icing at _____ (FAAC)
RAID .... RADAR Identification and Direction System (NG)
RAID .... Ram Air-Inflated Drogue [*Military*] (CAAL)
RAID .... Ram-Air Inflation Decelerator [*Munitions*] (RDA)
RAID .... Real-Time Applications Interactive Debugger (MCD)
RAID .... Recallable Airborne Infrared Display
RAID .... Redundant Arrays of Inexpensive Disks [*Data processing*]
RAID .... Remote Access Interactive Debugger [*Data processing*] (IEEE)
RAID .... Reverse Acronyms and Initialisms Dictionary [*Later, RAIAD*] [*A publication*]
RAID .... River Assault Interdiction Division [*Navy*] (NVT)
RAIDERS ... Remote Automated Issue, Document Entry, and Register System [*Army*]

RAIDEX.... Antisurface Raiders Exercise [*NATO*] (NATG)
RAIDS...... Rapid Acquisition and Identification System
RAIDS...... Rapid Availability of Information and Data for Safety [*NASA*] (KSC)
RAIDS...... Recently Acquired Income Deficiency Syndrome
RAIDS...... Reduced Annual Income Deficiency Syndrome [*British*]
RAIF .... Reseau d'Action et d'Information pour les Femmes [*Canada*]
Raiffeisen-Rundsch ... Raiffeisen-Rundschau [*A publication*]
RAIL.......... Railroad Advancement through Information and Law Foundation
RAIL.......... Railroad Financial Corp. [*NASDAQ symbol*] (NQ)
RAIL.......... Railway (ROG)
RAIL Ca...... Runway Alignment Indicator Light [*or Lighting*] [*Aviation*]
Rail Ca ..... Railway and Canal Cases [*1835-54*] [*A publication*] (DLA)
Rail & Can Cas ... English Railway and Canal Cases [*A publication*] (DLA)
Rail & Can Cas ... Railway and Canal Traffic Cases [*A publication*] (DLA)
Rail Cas ..... Railway Cases [*A publication*] (DLA)
Rail Clerk .. Railway Clerk Interchange [*A publication*]
Rail Eng .... Railway Engineer [*Later, Railway Engineer International*] [*A publication*]
Rail Eng Int ... Rail Engineering International [*A publication*]
RAILFN .... Railroad Financial Corp. [*Associated Press abbreviation*] (APAG)
Rail Int....... Rail International [*A publication*]
Rail M........ Railway Magazine [*A publication*]
Railroad Gaz ... Railroad Gazette [*A publication*]
Railroad Res Bul ... Railroad Research Bulletin [*A publication*]
RAILS .... Remote Area Instrument Landing Sensor [*Army*]
RAILS .... Remote Area Instrument Landing System [*Army*]
RAILS .... Report of Assets in Long Supply
RAILS .... Runway Alignment Indicator Light [*or Lighting*] System [*Aviation*] (MCD)
Rail Syst Contr ... Railway Systems Control [*A publication*]
Rail Transport Proc ... Rail Transportation Proceedings [*A publication*]
Railw Age... Railway Age [*A publication*]
Railway & Corp Law J ... Railway and Corporation Law Journal [*A publication*] (DLA)
Railway R... Railway Review [*A publication*] (APTA)
Railways in Aust ... Railways in Australia [*A publication*] (APTA)
Railways Union Gaz ... Railways Union Gazette [*A publication*] (APTA)
Railway Trans ... Railway Transportation [*A publication*] (APTA)
Railw Cas... Railway Cases [*A publication*] (DLA)
Railw Dev News ... Railway Development News [*A publication*]
Railw Eng .. Railway Engineer [*Later, Railway Engineer International*] [*A publication*]
Railw Eng Int ... Railway Engineer International [*A publication*]
Railw Eng J ... Railway Engineering Journal [*Incorporated in Railway Engineer International*] [*A publication*]
Railw Eng Maint ... Railway Engineering and Maintenance [*A publication*]
Railw Engr ... Railway Engineer [*Later, Railway Engineer International*] [*A publication*]
Railw Gaz... Railway Gazette [*Later, Railway Gazette International*] [*England*] [*A publication*]
Railw Gaz Int ... Railway Gazette International [*A publication*]
Railw Locomot Cars ... Railway Locomotives and Cars [*A publication*]
Railw Manage Rev ... Railway Management Review [*A publication*]
Railw Mech Eng ... Railway Mechanical Engineer [*United States*] [*A publication*]
Railw Q...... Railway Quarterly [*A publication*]
Railw Rev... Railway Review [*A publication*]
Railw Signal Commun ... Railway Signalling and Communications [*United States*] [*A publication*]
Railw South Afr ... Railways Southern Africa [*A publication*]
Railw Syst Control ... Railway Systems Control [*A publication*]
Railw Track Struct ... Railway Track and Structures [*A publication*]
RAIM .... Receiver Autonomous Integrity Monitoring [*Computer software*]
RAIN .... Relational Algebraic Interpreter
RAIN .... Relief for Africans in Need (EA)
RAIN .... Reversing Acidification in Norway
RAIN .... Royal Anthropological Institute News [*Later, Anthropology Today*] [*A publication*]
RAIN .... Royal Anthropological Institute. Newsletter [*A publication*]
RAINB....... Radio Industria [*A publication*]
RAINBO ... Research and Instrumentation for National Bio-Science Operations (MUGU)
RAINPAL ... Recursive Aided Inertial Navigation for Precision Approach and Landing [*NASA*]
RAINS...... Regional Acidification Information and Simulation [*International Institute for Applied Systems Analysis*]
RAIP.......... Rapport d'Activites. Institut de Phonetique [*A publication*]
RAIP.......... Recruiting Advertising Improvement Program [*Navy*] (DNAB)
RAIP.......... Requester's Approval in Principle (NRCH)
RAIR.......... Random Access Information Retrieval [*Data processing*] (IEEE)
RAIR.......... Rapid Advancement in Reading [*Education*]
RAIR.......... Recordak Automated Information Retrieval [*System*]
RAIR.......... Reflection Absorption Infrared Spectroscopy [*Also, IRAS, IRRAS, RAIRS, RAIS*]
RAIR.......... Regent Air Corp. [*NASDAQ symbol*] (NQ)
RAIR.......... Remote Access Immediate Response [*Data processing*]

R Aircr Establ List Reports ... Royal Aircraft Establishment. List of Reports [*A publication*]
RAIRS .... Railroad Accident/Incident Reporting System [*Department of Transportation*]
RAIRS .... Reflection Absorption Infrared Spectroscopy [*Also, IRAS, IRRAS, RAIR, RAIS*]
RAIS .... Range Automated Information System   (KSC)
RAIS .... Reflection Absorption Infrared Spectroscopy [*Also, IRAS, IRRAS, RAIR, RAIRS*]
RAISA .... Radioisotopes [*Tokyo*] [*A publication*]
RAISE .... Reliability Accelerated In-Service Echelon   (MCD)
RAISE .... Rigorous Approach to Industrial Software Engineering [*British*]
RAIST .... Reseau Africain d'Institutions Scientifiques et Technologiques [*African Network of Scientific and Technological Institutions*]   (EAIO)
RAIT .... Radioimmunotherapy [*Medicine*]
RAIT .... Rendiconti. Reale Accademia d'Italia [*A publication*]
Raith St ...... Raithby's English Statutes at Large [*A publication*]   (DLA)
Raith St ...... Raithby's Study of the Law [*A publication*]   (DLA)
RAI-TV ...... Radio Audizioni Italiana-Televisione [*Italian Radio Broadcasting and Television Company*]
RAIU .... Radioiodide Uptake [*Endocrinology*]
RAIX .... Rosenbalm Aviation [*Air carrier designation symbol*]
Raj .... All India Reporter, Rajasthan [*A publication*]   (DLA)
Raj .... Rajaratam Revised Reports [*Ceylon*] [*A publication*]   (DLA)
raj .... Rajasthani [*MARC language code*] [*Library of Congress*]   (LCCP)
RAJ .... Rajkot [*India*] [*Airport symbol*]   (OAG)
Ra JAH ...... Rackham Journal of the Arts and Humanities [*A publication*]
RAJAM ..... RADAR Jamming   (FAAC)
Rajasthan .. Indian Law Reports, Rajasthan Series [*A publication*]   (DLA)
Rajasthan Agric ... Rajasthan Agriculturist [*A publication*]
Rajasthan J Agric Sci ... Rajasthan Journal of Agricultural Sciences [*A publication*]
Rajasthan Med J ... Rajasthan Medical Journal [*A publication*]
Rajasthan Univ Studies Statist ... Rajasthan University. Studies in Statistics. Science Series [*A publication*]
Rajasthan Univ Stud Statist ... Rajasthan University. Studies in Statistics. Science Series [*A publication*]
RAJB .... Recueil Annuel de Jurisprudence Belge [*A publication*]
RAJFC .... Rex Allen, Jr. Fan Club   (EA)
RAJPO ...... Range Applications Joint Program Office
RAJ Tech Bull ... RAJ [*Rhodesia Agricultural Journal*] Technical Bulletin [*A publication*]
RAK .... Marrakech [*Morocco*] [*Airport symbol*]   (OAG)
RAK .... Rakhov [*Former USSR*] [*Seismograph station code, US Geological Survey*] [*Closed*]   (SEIS)
RAK .... Read Access Key
RAK .... Remote Access Key
RaKet .... Rahnema-Ye Ketab [*A publication*]
Raketentech Raumfahrtforsch ... Raketentechnik und Raumfahrtforschung [*A publication*]
RAKO .... Rawson-Koenig, Inc. [*NASDAQ symbol*]   (NQ)
Rakstu Krajums Daugavpils Pedagog Inst ... Rakstu Krajums. Daugavpils Pedagogiskais Instituts [*A publication*]
RAKTP ...... Royal Arch Knight Templar Priest [*Freemasonry*]
RAL .... Rabalanakaia [*New Britain*] [*Seismograph station code, US Geological Survey*]   (SEIS)
RAL .... Radio Annoyance Level   (OA)
RAL .... Radio Astronomy Laboratory [*Research center*]   (RCD)
RAL .... Ralston Purina Co. [*NYSE symbol*]   (SPSG)
RAL .... Rapid Access Loop
RAL .... Rear-Admiral, Alexandria [*British*]
RAL .... Reenlistment Allowance [*Military*]
RAL .... Register of Additional Locations [*Library of Congress*]
RAL .... Remote Area Landing   (NG)
RAL .... Rendiconti. Classe di Scienze Morali e Storiche. Accademia dei Lincei [*A publication*]
RAL .... Reports and Analysis Letter   (OICC)
RAL .... Required Average Life   (MCD)
RAL .... Research in African Literatures [*A publication*]
RAL .... Resorcylic Acid Lactone [*Veterinary pharmacology*]
RAL .... Responsibility Assignment List [*NASA*]   (NASA)
RAL .... Revista. Academias de Letras [*A publication*]
RAL .... Reynold's Aluminum Co. of Canada Ltd. [*Toronto Stock Exchange symbol*]
RAL .... Riverband Acoustical Laboratory   (KSC)
RAL .... Riverside [*California*] [*Airport symbol*]   (OAG)
RAL .... Riverside, CA [*Location identifier*] [*FAA*]   (FAAL)
RAL .... Robotics & Automation Research Laboratory [*University of Toronto*] [*Research center*]   (RCD)
RAL .... Roswell Airlines [*Roswell, NM*] [*FAA designator*]   (FAAC)
RAL .... Rubber-Air-Lead [*Tile*]
RAL .... Rutherford and Appleton Laboratory [*Observatory*] [*British*]
RALAC ..... RADAR Altimeter Low-Altitude Control [*Military*]   (CAAL)
RALACS ... RADAR Altimeter Low-Altitude Control System [*Military*]   (NG)
RALA-EHF ... Roycrofters-at-Large Association/Elbert Hubbard Foundation   (EA)
RALD .... Richmond Area Library Directors [*Library network*]
RALF .... Relocatable Assembly Language Floating Point

RALF .... Repertoire Analytique de Litterature Francaise [*Bordeaux*] [*A publication*]
RALF .... Robotic Assistant Labor Facilitator [*In the movie "Flight of the Navigator" (1986)*]
RALFH ...... Random Access Logical File Handler   (MCD)
RALI .... Regimento de Artilharia Ligeira [*Light Artillery Regiment*] [*Portuguese*]
RALI .... Remarried Association of Long Island   (EA)
RALI .... Resource and Land Investigation [*Program*] [*Department of the Interior*]   (GRD)
R Alicante .. Revista. Instituto de Estudios Alicantinos [*A publication*]
RALinc ...... Rendiconti. Classe di Scienze Morali e Storiche. Accademia dei Lincei [*A publication*]
RALincei ... Rendiconti. Classe di Scienze Morali e Storiche. Accademia dei Lincei [*A publication*]
RALL .... Rallentando [*Gradually Slower*] [*Music*]
RALLA ...... Regional Allied Long-Lines Agency [*Formerly, RELLA*]   (NATG)
RALLEN ... Rallentando [*Gradually Slower*] [*Music*]   (ROG)
RALLO ...... Rallentando [*Gradually Slower*] [*Music*]   (ROG)
RALPH ...... Reduction and Acquisition of Lunar Pulse Heights [*NASA*]   (NASA)
RALPH ...... Royal Association for the Longevity and Preservation of the Honeymooners   (EA)
RALRend ... Rendiconti. Classe di Scienze Morali e Storiche. Accademia dei Lincei [*A publication*]
RALS .... Remote Augmented Lift System   (MCD)
RALS .... Resources for American Literary Study [*A publication*]
RALS .... Right Add, Left Subtract [*Army field artillery technique*]   (INF)
RALS .... Robotic Ammunition Landing System
RALSA ...... Restraint and Life Support Assembly   (MCD)
RAL Scav ... Reale Accademia dei Lincei. Atti. Notizie degli Scavi [*A publication*]
RalsPu .... Ralston Purina Co. [*Associated Press abbreviation*]   (APAG)
RALT .... RADAR Altimeter [*Aviation*]   (NASA)
RALT .... Range Light   (AAG)
RALT .... Ranging Airborne LASER Tracker   (MCD)
RALT .... Regardless of Altitude [*Aviation*]   (FAAC)
RALT .... Routine Admission Laboratory Tests [*Medicine*]
RALU .... Register and Arithmetic/Logic Unit [*Data processing*]
RALU .... Rotary Analog Logic Unit   (MCD)
RALV .... Random Access Light Valve
RaLV .... Rasheed (Rat) Leukemia Virus
RALW .... Radioactive Liquid Waste   (IEEE)
Ralw & Corp LJ ... Railway and Corporation Law Journal [*A publication*]   (DLA)
RAM .... Rabbit Alveolar Macrophage [*Clinical chemistry*]
RAM .... Rabbit Antimouse [*Hematology*]
RAM .... RADAR-Absorbing Material
RAM .... Radiation Attenuation Measurement   (CET)
RAM .... Radio-Active Magazine [*A publication*]
RAM .... Radio Attenuation Measurement [*Spacecraft for testing communications*]
RAM .... Radioactive Material
RAM .... RAID Assessment Mode   (MCD)
RAM .... Ramada, Inc. [*NYSE symbol*]   (SPSG)
RAM .... Raman [*Turkey*] [*Seismograph station code, US Geological Survey*]   (SEIS)
Ram .... Ramanathan's Reports [*Ceylon*] [*A publication*]   (DLA)
RAM .... Ramcor Resources, Inc. [*Vancouver Stock Exchange symbol*]
RAM .... Ramingining [*Australia*] [*Airport symbol*]   (OAG)
Ram .... Ramsey's Quebec Appeal Cases [*A publication*]   (DLA)
RAM .... Random Access Measurement [*System*] [*Data processing*]
RAM .... Random Access Memory [*Data processing*]
RAM .... Random Angle Modulation
RAM .... Range-Altitude Monitor
RAM .... Range Assessment Mode   (MCD)
RAM .... Rapid Alternating Movement
RAM .... Rapid Amortization Mortgage
RAM .... Rapid Area Maintenance [*Air Force*]
RAM .... Raytheon Airborne Microwave   (MCD)
RAM .... Readiness and Money   (DNAB)
RAM .... Recent Advances in Manufacturing [*Information service or system*]   (IID)
RAM .... Recovery Aids Material   (MUGU)
RAM .... Red Artillery Model [*Military*]
RAM .... Redeye Air Missile [*System*]   (RDA)
RAM .... Reentry Antimissile
RAM .... Reentry Attenuation Measurement [*NASA*]
RAM .... Reform the Armed Forces Movement [*Philippines*]
RAM .... Regional Audit Manager
RAM .... Registered Apartment Manager [*Designation awarded by National Association of Home Builders*]
RAM .... Regular Army and Militia [*British*]
RAM .... Releasable Asset Program [*Military*]   (AFIT)
RAM .... Reliability Assessment for Management
RAM .... Reliability, Availability, and Maintainability [*Army*]
RAM .... Religions, Ancient and Modern [*A publication*]
RAM .... Remote Access Monitor   (MCD)
RAM .... Remote Area Monitoring   (KSC)
RAM .... Repeater Amplitude Modulation   (MCD)

RAM......... Repeating Antipersonnel Mine
RAM......... Research and Applications Module [*NASA*]
RAM......... Research Aviation Medicine [*Navy program of research into aerospace medical techniques*]
RAM......... Reserve Adjustment Magnitude
RAM......... Resident Access Methods (MCD)
RAM......... Resident Aerospace Medicine [*Physician in specialty training*] [*Military*]
RAM......... Resources Analysis and Management
RAM......... Responsibility Assignment Matrix [*NASA*] (NASA)
RAM......... Restricted Access Memory [*Data processing*] (MCD)
RAM......... Returned Account Mechanical [*Aviation*] (FAAC)
RAM......... Reverse Annuity Mortgage
RAM......... Revolutionary Action Movement
RAM......... Right Ascension of the Meridian [*Navigation*]
RAM......... Rock Australia Magazine [*A publication*] (APTA)
RAM......... Rocket and Missile System [*Army*]
RAM......... Rolling Airframe Missile
RAM......... Royal Academy of Music [*British*]
RAM......... Royal Air Maroc [*Morocco*]
RAM......... Royal Appliance Manufacturing [*NYSE symbol*] (SPSG)
RAM......... Royal Arch Mason [*Freemasonry*]
RAM......... Royal Ark Mariners
RAMA....... Railway Automotive Management Association (EA)
RAMA....... Recap and Movement Authorization [*NASA*] (NASA)
RAMA....... Region of Assured Mission Abort [*Military*] (CAAL)
RAMA....... Rome Air Materiel Area [*Deactivated*] [*Air Force*]
RAMAB ... Ready Afloat Marine Amphibious Brigade (CINC)
RAMAC .... Random Access Method of Accounting and Control [*Data processing*]
Ramachandrier A ... Ramachandrier's Cases on Adoption [*1892*] [*India*] [*A publication*] (DLA)
Ramachandrier DG ... Ramachandrier's Cases on Dancing Girls [*1892*] [*India*] [*A publication*] (DLA)
Ramachandrier HML ... Ramachandrier's Cases on Hindu Marriage Law [*1891*] [*India*] [*A publication*] (DLA)
RAMADCS ... Reliability, Availability, and Maintainability Automated Data Collection System [*Army*]
RAMAIDB ... RAM [*Radioactive Materials*] Accident/Incident Database [*Nuclear energy*]
Raman Res Inst Mem ... Raman Research Institute. Memoirs [*A publication*]
RAMARK ... RADAR Marker [*Military*]
Ram Ass..... Ram on Assets, Debts, and Incumbrances [*2nd ed.*] [*1837*] [*A publication*] (DLA)
RAMAZ .... Rabbi Moses Zacuto (BJA)
RAMB .... Random Access Memory Buffer [*Data processing*]
RaM-BaM ... Rabbi Moses ben Maimon [*Maimonides*] [*Jewish philosopher, 1135-1204*]
RAMBAN ... Rabbi Moses ben Nahman [*Spanish Talmudist, 1195-1270*] (BJA)
RAMBO .... Real-Time Acquisitions Management and Bibliographic Order System [*Suggested name for the Library of Congress computer system*]
RAMBO .... Remove Aquino from Malacanang before October [*Operation proposed by rebel military leader "Gringo" Honasan*] [*1987*] [*Philippines*]
RAMBO .... Restore a More Benevolent Order Coalition [*Later, NCAN*] (EA)
RAMC .... Resource Allocation and Mine Costing Model [*Department of Energy*] (GFGA)
RAMC .... Royal Army Medical College [*British*] (MCD)
RAMC .... Royal Army Medical Corps [*Initialism also facetiously translated during World War I as "Rats after Moldy Cheese," "Rob All My Comrades," or "Run Away, Matron's Coming!"*] [*British*]
Ram Cas P & E ... Ram's Cases of Pleading and Evidence [*A publication*] (DLA)
RA/MCC... Restricted Area/Military Climb Corridor [*Aviation*] (FAAC)
RAMCT..... Royal Army Medical Corps, Territorials [*British*] (ROG)
RAMD....... Random Access Memory Device [*Data processing*]
RAMD....... Receiving Agency Materiel Division [*Military*]
RAMD....... Reliability, Availability, and Maintainability Demonstration
RAM-D...... Reliability, Availability, Maintainability, and Durability [*Army*] (AABC)
RAMEA .... Radiologia Medica [*A publication*]
RAMEC..... Rapid Action Maintenance Engineering Change [*Navy*] (MCD)
RAMEC..... Rapid Action Minor Engineering Change
RAMED .... Reine und Angewandte Metallkunde in Einzeldarstellungen [*A publication*]
Ram F .... Ram on Facts [*A publication*] (DLA)
RAMFAS .. Reliability Analysis of Microcircuit Failure in Avionic Systems (MCD)
R Am Hist ... Reviews in American History [*A publication*]
RamHO..... Ramsay-HMO, Inc. [*Associated Press abbreviation*] (APAG)
RAMHR..... Risk-Adjusted Multiple Hurdle Rates (ADA)
RAMIG ..... Rabbit Antimouse Immunoglobulin G [*Immunology*]
RAMIS...... Rapid Access Management Information System [*Data processing*]
RAMIS...... Rapid Automatic Malfunction Isolation System
RAMIS...... Receiving, Assembly Maintenance, Inspection, Storage [*Military*]

RAMIS...... Repair, Assemble, Maintain, Issue, and Supply (MUGU)
RAMIT...... Rate-Aided Manually Implemented Tracking (NATG)
Ram Leg J ... Ram's Science of Legal Judgment [*2nd ed.*] [*1834*] [*A publication*] (DLA)
Ram Leg Judgm (Towns Ed) ... Ram's Science of Legal Judgment, Notes by Townshend [*A publication*] (DLA)
RAM/LOG ... Reliability, Availability, Maintainability, and Logistics (MCD)
RAMM...... Random Access Memory Module [*Data processing*]
RAMM...... Recording Ammeter (MSA)
RAMMIT ... Reliability, Availability, and Maintenance Management Improvements Technique
RAMMIT ... Reliability and Maintainability Management Improvement Techniques [*Army*]
Ram & Mor ... Ramsey and Morin's Montreal Law Reporter [*A publication*] (DLA)
RAMMS.... Responsive Automated Materiel Management System [*Army*] (AABC)
RAMNAC ... Radio Aids to Marine Navigation Committee [*British*]
RAMOGE ... Regional Pollution Studies in the Ligurian Sea [*Marine science*] (MSC)
RAMONT ... Radiological Monitoring
RAMOS .... Remote Automatic Meteorological Observing Station
RAMP ...... RADAR Mapping of Panama
RAMP ...... RADAR Modification Program (NG)
RAMP ...... Radiation Airborne Measurement Program
RAMP ...... Radio Attenuation Measurement Project
Ramp......... Ramparts Magazine [*A publication*]
RAMP ...... Random Access Mechanization of Phosphorus
RAMP ...... Rapid Acquisition of Manufactured Parts [*Military*]
RAMP ...... Raytheon Airborne Microwave Platform [*Sky station*]
RAMP ...... Records and Archives Management Programme [*UNESCO*]
RAMP ...... Recovered Allied Military Personnel
RAMP ...... Regional Administrative Management Plan [*Department of Labor*]
RAMP ...... Reliability and Maintainability Program
RAMP ...... Research Association of Minority Professors (EA)
RAMP ...... Reserve Associate Manning Program [*Military*]
RAMP ...... Review of Army Mobilization Planning (MCD)
R/AMP...... Rifampin [*Also, RF, RIF, RMP*] [*Bactericide*]
RAMP ...... Ring Airfoil Munition Projectile [*Army*]
RAMP ...... Rural Abandoned Mine Program [*Department of Agriculture*]
RAMPAC ... Radioactive Materials Packaging [*Nuclear energy*]
RAMPART ... RADAR Advanced Measurements Program for Analysis of Reentry Techniques [*ARPA - Raytheon*]
RAMPART ... Route to Airlift Mobility through Partnership (MCD)
Ramp Mag ... Ramparts Magazine [*A publication*]
RAMPS.... Rapid Message Preparation System (NATG)
RaMPS...... Rapid Multiple Peptide System [*Biotechnology*]
RAMPS..... Repatriated American Military Personnel [*World War II*]
RAMPS..... Resources Allocation and Multiproject Scheduling
Ram Rep .... Ramanathan's Supreme Court Reports [*Ceylon*] [*A publication*] (ILCA)
RAMS....... RADAR Target Scattering Advanced Measurement System
RAMS....... Random Access Measurement System [*Data processing*]
RAMS....... Random Access Memory Store [*Data processing*] (TEL)
RAMS....... Rapid Munitions Assembly System (DWSG)
RAMS....... Rascal Avionics Management System (MCD)
RAMS....... Record Archival Management System (HGAA)
RAMS....... Recovery and Modification Services (MCD)
RAMS....... Recruiting Advertising Management System [*Navy*] (DNAB)
RAMS....... Reduced-Size Antenna Monopulse System
RAMS....... Regional Air Monitoring Station [*or System*] [*Environmental Protection Agency*]
RAMS....... Regulatory Activities Manpower System [*Nuclear energy*] (NRCH)
RAM-S ...... Reliability, Availability, Maintainability - Supportability (MCD)
RAMS....... Reliability and Maintainability Studies [*Army*] (RDA)
RAMS....... Remote Area Mobility Study (MCD)
RAMS....... Remote Automatic Multipurpose Station
RAMS....... Remotely Accessible Management Systems [*Data processing*]
RAMS....... Repairables Asset Management System [*Military*] (CAAL)
RAMS....... Requirements Analysis Material Sheet [*or Study*] (MCD)
RAMS....... Right Ascension Mean Sun [*Navigation*]
RAMS....... Rocket and Missile System [*Army*]
RAMSA..... Radio Aeronautica Mexicana, Sociedad Anonima
Rams App .. Ramsey's Quebec Appeal Cases [*1873-86*] [*A publication*] (DLA)
Ramsay App Cas ... Ramsay's Appeal Cases [*Canada*] [*A publication*] (DLA)
Ramsay App Cas (Can) ... Ramsay's Appeal Cases [*Canada*] [*A publication*] (DLA)
Ram SC...... Ramanathan's Supreme Court Reports [*Ceylon*] [*A publication*] (DLA)
RAMSES... Reprogrammable Advanced Multimode Shipborne ECM System [*Canadian Navy*]
RAMSEZ .. Records. Australian Museum. Supplement [*A publication*]
RAMSH .... Reliability, Availability, Maintainability, Safety, and Human Factors [*Telecommunications*] (TEL)
RAMSIM .. Reliability, Availability, Maintainability, Simulation [*Navy*] (DNAB)
RAMSS..... Royal Alfred Merchant Seamen's Society [*British*]

RAMT .... Rabbit Antimouse Thymocyte [*Immunology*]
RAMT .... Rudder Angle Master Transmitter
RAMTAC ... Reentry Analysis and Modeling of Target Characteristics
RAMTIP ... Reliability and Maintainability Technology Insertion Program [*DoD*]
RAMTRA ... Reserve Air Maintenance Training　(DNAB)
RAMUS .... Remote Access Multi-User System　(DNAB)
RAMV .... Radish Mosaic Virus [*Plant pathology*]
RAMVAN ... Reconnaissance Aircraft Maintenance Van
Ram W .... Ram on Exposition of Wills of Landed Property [*1827*] [*A publication*]　(DLA)
RAN........... RADAR Navigation　(DNAB)
RAN........... Railway Abidjan-Niger
RAN........... Rainforest Action Network　(EA)
Ran............. Ranae [*Frogs*] [*of Aristophanes*] [*Classical studies*]　(OCD)
RAN........... Random　(DNAB)
RAN........... Rangifer. Nordisk Organ foer Reinforskning [*A publication*]
RAN........... Rangoon [*Burma*] [*Seismograph station code, US Geological Survey*] [*Closed*]　(SEIS)
RAN........... Ranitidine [*An antiulcer drug*]
RAN........... Ransome Air, Inc. [*Philadelphia, PA*] [*FAA designator*]　(FAAC)
RAN........... Read around Number
RAN........... Reconnaissance/Attack Navigator
RAN........... Regional Air Navigation [*ICAO*]
RAN........... Remote Area Nurse
RAN........... Rendiconti. Accademia di Archeologia, Lettere, e Belle Arti (Napoli) [*A publication*]
RAN........... Repair Activity Accounting Number [*Navy*]
RAN........... Reporting Accounting Number　(NG)
RAN........... Request for Authority to Negotiate
RAN........... Requirement Action Number
RAN........... Requisition Account Number
RAN........... Resource-Adjacent Nation [*Ocean fishery management*]
RAN........... Revenue Anticipation Note
RANA....... Rheumatoid Arthritis Nuclear Antigen [*Immunology*]
RANA....... Rhodesia & Nyasaland Airways
RANAM .... Recherches Anglaises et Americaines [*A publication*]
RANAS..... Rear-Admiral, Naval Air Stations [*British military*]　(DMA)
RANBDM ... Institut des Sciences Agronomiques du Burundi [*ISABU*]. Rapport Annuel et Notes Annexes [*A publication*]
RANC........ RADAR Absorption Noise and Clutter　(NASA)
RANCA ..... Retired Army Nurse Corps Association　(EA)
Ranchi Univ J Agric Res ... Ranchi University. Journal of Agricultural Research [*A publication*]
Ranchi Univ Math J ... Ranchi University. Mathematical Journal [*A publication*]
Ranch Mag ... Ranch Magazine [*A publication*]
RANCID... Real and Not Corrected Input Data [*Data processing*]
RANCIN ... Retrieval and Analysis of Navy Classified Information　(DNAB)
RANCOM ... Random Communication Satellite
RAND....... Rand Capital Corp. [*NASDAQ symbol*]　(NQ)
Rand........... Randall's Reports [*62-71 Ohio State*] [*A publication*]　(DLA)
Rand........... Randolph's Reports [*21-56 Kansas*] [*A publication*]　(DLA)
Rand........... Randolph's Reports [*22-27 Virginia*] [*1821-28*] [*A publication*]　(DLA)
Rand........... Randolph's Reports [*7-11 Louisiana*] [*A publication*]　(DLA)
RAND....... Research and No Development [*Origin of name of RAND Corporation, a nonprofit national defense research organization*]
Rand........... Selected Rand Abstracts [*A publication*]
RANDAM ... Random Access Nondestructive Advanced Memory [*Data processing*]
Rand Ann... Randolph Annual [*A publication*]　(DLA)
Rand Com Paper ... Randolph on Commercial Paper [*A publication*]　(DLA)
Rand Corp Pap ... Rand Corporation. Papers [*A publication*]
Rand Corp Rep ... Rand Corporation. Report [*A publication*]
Rand Em Dom ... Randolph on Eminent Domain [*A publication*]　(DLA)
Randers...... Randers Group, Inc. [*Associated Press abbreviation*]　(APAG)
Rand & Fur Poi ... Rand and Furness on Poisons [*A publication*]　(DLA)
RANDID.... Rapid Alphanumeric Digital Indicating Device
RANDO.... Radiotherapy Analog Dosimetry
Rand Peak ... Randall's Edition of Peake on Evidence [*A publication*]　(DLA)
Rand Perp ... Randall on Perpetuities [*A publication*]　(DLA)
Rand Revw ... Rand Research Review [*A publication*]
Rane........... Rainerius de Forlivio [*Deceased, 1358*] [*Authority cited in pre-1607 legal work*]　(DSA)
Raney........ Raney's Reports [*16-20 Florida*] [*A publication*]　(DLA)
RANF Rev ... RANF [*Royal Australian Nursing Federation*] Review [*A publication*]
RANG........ Range Group [*Military*]
RANG........ Rangoon [*City in Burma*]　(ROG)
Rang Cr LJ ... Rangoon Criminal Law Journal [*A publication*]　(DLA)
Rang Dec.... Sparks' Rangoon Decisions [*British Burma*] [*A publication*]　(DLA)
RANGECO ... Range Company　(DNAB)
Range Improv Notes US For Serv Intermt Reg ... Range Improvement Notes. United States Forest Service. Intermountain Region [*A publication*]

Range Improv Studies Calif Dep Conserv Div For ... Range Improvement Studies. California Department of Conservation. Division of Forestry [*A publication*]
Range Impr Stud Calif Div For ... Range Improvement Studies. California Division of Forestry [*A publication*]
Range Sci Dep Ser Colo State Univ ... Range Science Department Series. Colorado State University [*A publication*]
Rang LR..... Rangoon Law Reports [*India*] [*A publication*]　(DLA)
RangrO ...... Ranger Oil Ltd. [*Associated Press abbreviation*]　(APAG)
RANK........ [*The*] Rank Organisation Ltd. [*NASDAQ symbol*]　(NQ)
Rank P .... Rankin on Patents [*1824*] [*A publication*]　(DLA)
Rank & S Comp L ... Ranking and Spicer's Company Law [*11th ed.*] [*1970*] [*A publication*]　(DLA)
Rank S & P Exec ... Ranking, Spicer, and Pegler on Executorship [*21st ed.*] [*1971*] [*A publication*]　(DLA)
RANL .... Rendiconti. Reale Accademia Nazionale dei Lincei [*A publication*]
RANN........ Research Applied to National Needs [*Formerly, IRRPOS*] [*National Science Foundation*] [*Obsolete*]
Rannsoknastofnun Fiskidnadarins Arsskyrs ... Rannsoknastofnun Fiskidnadarins Arsskyrsla [*A publication*]
RANOSP... Radiological North Sea Project [*British*]
rANP .... Rat Atrial Natriuretic Peptide [*Biochemistry*]
RANS .... Range Squadron
RANS .... Report. Australian Numismatic Society [*A publication*]
RANS .... Revenue Anticipation Notes
RANSA...... Rutas Aereas Nacionales Sociedad Anonima [*Cargo airline*] [*Venezuela*]
RANT .... Reentry Antenna Test
R Anthrop .. Reviews in Anthropology [*A publication*]
RANXPE... Resident Army Nike-X Project Engineer　(AABC)
RAO........... National Radio Astronomy Observatory, Charlottesville, VA [*OCLC symbol*]　(OCLC)
RAO........... RADAR Operator
RAO........... Radio Astronomy Observatory [*University of Michigan*] [*Research center*]
RAO........... Rado Reef Resources [*Vancouver Stock Exchange symbol*]
RAO........... Raoul [*Raoul Island*] [*Seismograph station code, US Geological Survey*]　(SEIS)
RAO........... Recueil d'Archeologie Orientale [*A publication*]
RAO........... Regimental Amalgamation Officer [*British military*]　(DMA)
RAO........... Regional Accounting Office [*Telecommunications*]　(TEL)
RAO........... Regional Administrative Office
RAO........... Regional Agricultural Officer [*Ministry of Agriculture, Fisheries, and Food*] [*British*]
RAO........... Retired Affairs Officers　(EA)
RAO........... Ribeirao Preto [*Brazil*] [*Airport symbol*]　(OAG)
RAO........... Right Anterior Oblique [*Medicine*]
RAO........... Rudder Angle Order　(MSA)
RAOA........ Railway Accounting Officers Association [*Later, AAR*]
RAOB........ Radiosonde Observation
RAOB........ Royal Antediluvian Order of Buffaloes
RAOC........ Rear Area Operations Center　(MCD)
RAOC........ Regional Air Operations Center　(NATG)
RAOC........ Royal Army Ordnance Corps [*Formerly, AOC*] [*British*]
RAOC(E).. Royal Army Ordnance Corps (Engineering) [*British military*]　(DMA)
Rao DHL ... Rao's Decisions on Hindu Law [*1893*] [*India*] [*A publication*]　(DLA)
RAOMP .... Report of Accrued Obligations, Military Pay　(AFM)
RAONDT .. Radiotherapy and Oncology [*A publication*]
RAOP .... Regional Air Operations Plan　(NATG)
RAOU Newsl ... RAOU [*Royal Australasian Ornithologists Union*] Newsletter [*A publication*]　(APTA)
RAP .... RADAR-Absorbing Paint [*Military*]　(RDA)
RAP .... RADAR Aim Point
RAP .... Radical Alternatives to Prison [*British*]
RAP .... Radio Access Point　(MCD)
RAP .... Radio Air Play
RAP .... Radiological Assistance Plan [*AEC*]
RAP .... Random Access Program [*Data processing*]
RAP .... Random Access Projector
RAP .... Ranger Assessment Phase [*Army*]　(INF)
RAP .... Rapid　(AAG)
RAP .... Rapid Assessment Program [*Environmental evaluation strategy*]
RAP .... Rapid City [*South Dakota*] [*Airport symbol*]　(OAG)
RAP .... Rapid City, SD [*Location identifier*] [*FAA*]　(FAAL)
RAP .... Rapindik [*New Britain*] [*Seismograph station code, US Geological Survey*] [*Closed*]　(SEIS)
RAP .... Reactive Atmosphere Process
RAP .... Readiness Action Proposal　(MCD)
RAP .... Readiness Assessment Program [*Navy*]
RAP .... Rear Area Protection [*Military*]　(AABC)
RAP .... Recognize All Potential　(DNAB)
RAP .... Recruiter Assistance [*or Assistant*] Program [*Navy*]　(DNAB)
RAP .... Reduced Acreage Program [*Agriculture*]
RAP .... Redundancy Adjustment of Probability　(IEEE)
RAP .... Regimental Aid Post [*British*]
RAP .... Regional Acceleratory Phenomenon [*Physiology*]
RAP .... Regression Analysis Program [*Military*]

RAP .... Regression-Associated Protein [*Biochemistry*]
RAP .... Regulatory Accounting Practices [*or Principles*] [*Business term*]
RAP .... Regulatory Analysis Program [*Federal government*]
RAP .... Relational Associative Processor   (IEEE)
RAP .... Relationship Anecdotes Paradigm Method [*Psychology*]
RAP .... Relative Accident Probability
RAP .... Releasable Assets Program
RAP .... Reliability Assessment Prediction
RAP .... Reliability Assessment Program
RAP .... Reliable Acoustic Path
RAP .... Remedial Action Program [*or Projects*]   (MCD)
RAP .... Remote Access Point [*Telecommunications*]
RAP .... Renal Artery Pressure [*Medicine*]
RAP .... Rental Assistance Payment Program [*HUD*]
RAP .... Requirements Analysis Package [*Data processing*]
RAP .... Resident Assembler Program
RAP .... Resident Assessment Protocol [*Occupational therapy*]
RAP .... Resident Associate Program [*Smithsonian Institution*]
RAP .... Residual Analysis Program [*Space Flight Operations Facility, NASA*]
RAP .... Resource Allocation Processor   (CMD)
RAP .... Response Analysis Program [*Data processing*]   (IBMDP)
RAP .... Restricted Access Processor   (SSD)
RAP .... Results Analysis Plan   (MCD)
RAP .... Review and Analysis Process
RAP .... Revised Accounting Procedures
RAP .... Revolutionary Action Power [*A publication*]   (APTA)
RAP .... Right Angle Plug
RAP .... Right Atrial Pressure [*Cardiology*]
RAP .... Ring-Around Programming   (CAAL)
RAP .... Rocket-Assisted Projectile   (RDA)
RAP .... "Round Up" Administration Planning Staff [*for the invasion of France*] [*World War II*]
RAP .... Rubidium Acid Phthalate [*Organic chemistry*]
RAP .... Rules for Admission to Practice [*A publication*]   (DLA)
RA-P .... Rumex Acetosa Polysaccharide [*Antineoplastic drug*]
RAP .... Rupees, Annas, Pies [*Monetary units*] [*India*]
RAP .... Smithsonian Resident Associate Program   (EA)
RAPAC ...... Research Applications Policy Advisory Committee [*National Science Foundation*]   (EGAO)
RAPAD ...... Research Association for Petroleum Alternative Development
Rapalje & L ... Rapalje and Lawrence's Law Dictionary [*A publication*]   (DLA)
Rapal & L ... Rapalje and Lawrence's American and English Cases [*A publication*]   (DLA)
RAPBPPI .. Research Association for the Paper and Board, Printing, and Packaging Industries [*Research center*] [*British*]   (IRC)
Rap Bur Nutr Anim Elev ... Rapport. Bureau de la Nutrition Animale et de l'Elevage [*A publication*]
RAPC .... Radio Administration Plenipotentiary Conference
RAPC .... Right Angle Pressure Cartridge
RAPC .... Royal Army Pay Corps [*Formerly, APC*] [*British*]
RAPCAP ... RADAR Picket Combat Air Patrol   (NVT)
RAPCC ...... RADAR Approach Control Center   (MCD)
RAPCO ...... Regional Air Priorities Control Office [*Army*]   (AABC)
RAPCOE ... Random Access Programming and Checkout Equipment
RAPCON .. RADAR Approach Control [*Air Force*]
Rap Contempt ... Rapalje on Contempt [*A publication*]   (DLA)
RAPD .... Random Amplified Polymorphic DNA [*Deoxyribonucleic Acid*][*Genetics*]
RAPD .... Relatively Afferent Pupillary Defect [*Ophthalmology*]
RAPD .... Response Amplitude Probability Data
RAPE .... RADAR Arithmetic Processing Element [*Navy*]
RAPEC ...... Rocket-Assisted Personnel Ejection Catapult
RAPECA ... Rassemblement du Peuple Camerounais [*Camerounese People's Rally*]
RAP-EX ..... Rear Area Protection Operations Extended   (MCD)
Rap Fed Ref Dig ... Rapalje's Federal Reference Digest [*A publication*]   (DLA)
Raph .... Raphael Fulgosius [*Deceased, 1427*] [*Authority cited in pre-1607 legal work*]   (DSA)
RAPH .... Recherches d'Archeologie, de Philologie,et d'Histoire [*Cairo*] [*A publication*]
Raph Cum ... Raphael Cumanus [*Deceased, 1427*] [*Authority cited in pre-1607 legal work*]   (DSA)
RAPIC .... Remedial Action Program Information Center [*Department of Energy*] [*Also, an information service or system*]   (IID)
RAPID ...... Random Access Personnel Information Dissemination
RAPID ...... Reactor and Plant Integrated Dynamics [*Data processing*]   (KSC)
RAPID ...... Reader-to-Advertiser Phone Inquiry Delivery System [*Chilton Corp.*]
RAPID ...... Real-Time Acquisition and Processing of Inflight Data
RAPID ...... Relative Address Programming Implementation Device [*Data processing*]
RAPID ...... Reliability Assessment Program with In-Plant Data
RAPID ...... Remote Access Planning for Institutional Development [*Data processing*]
RAPID ...... Remote Access Procedure for Interactive Design [*General Motors Corp.*]
RAPID ...... Research in Automatic Photocomposition and Information Dissemination

RAPID ...... Retrieval through Automated Publication and Information Digest [*Data processing*]   (DIT)
RAPID ...... Retrieval and Processing Information for Display
RAPID ...... Retrorocket-Assisted Parachute in Flight Delivery
RAPID ...... Rocketdyne Automatic Processing of Integrated Data [*Data processing*]
RAPID ...... Ryan Automatic Plot Indicator Device
RAPIDS .... Random Access Personnel Information Dissemination System [*Army*]   (AABC)
RAPIDS .... Rapid Automated Problem Identification System [*DoD*]
RAPIDS .... Real-Time Automated Personnel Identification System [*DoD*]
RAPIER .... Rapid Emergency Reconstitution Team [*Military*]
Rap Inst Fiz Tech Jad AGH ... Raport. Instytut Fizyki i Techniki Jadrowej AGH [*Akademia Gorniczo-Hutnicza*] [*A publication*]
Rap Inst Nat Etude Agron Congo (INEAC) ... Rapport. Institut National pour l'Etude Agronomique du Congo (INEAC)
Rap Inst Tech Jad AGH ... Raport. Instytut Techniki Jadrowej AGH [*Akademia Gorniczo-Hutnicza*] [*A publication*]
Rap Jud QBR ... Rapports Judiciaires de Quebec, Cour du Banc de la Reine [*Quebec Law Reports, Queen's Bench*] [*A publication*]
Rap Jud QCS ... Rapports Judiciaires de Quebec. Cour Superieure [*Quebec Law Reports, Superior Court*] [*A publication*]
Rap Jud Quebec CS (Can) ... Rapports Judiciaires de Quebec [*Quebec Law Reports*] [*Canada*] [*A publication*]   (DLA)
Rap Jud Quebec KB (Can) ... Rapports Judiciaires de Quebec [*Quebec Law Reports*] [*Canada*] [*A publication*]   (DLA)
Rap Jud Quebec QB (Can) ... Rapports Judiciaires de Quebec [*Quebec Law Reports*] [*Canada*] [*A publication*]   (DLA)
Rap & L ...... Rapalje and Lawrence's American and English Cases [*A publication*]   (DLA)
Rap Lar ...... Rapalje on Larceny [*A publication*]   (DLA)
Rap & Law ... Rapalje and Lawrence's American and English Cases [*A publication*]   (DLA)
Rap & L Law Dict ... Rapalje and Lawrence's Law Dictionary [*A publication*]   (DLA)
RAPLOC ... Rapid Passive Localization   (MCD)
RAPLOC-LSI ... Rapid Passive Localization - Low-Ship Impact [*Navy*]   (CAAL)
RAPLOC-WAA ... Rapid Passive Localization - Wide Aperture Array [*Military*]   (CAAL)
RAPM .... Reliability Assessment Prediction Model
RAPM .... Risk-Adjusted Profitability Measure [*Banking*]   (ECON)
Rap NY Dig ... Rapalje's New York Digest [*A publication*]   (DLA)
RAPO .... Rabbit Antibodies to Pig Ovary [*Immunology*]
RAPO .... Resident Apollo Project Office [*NASA*]   (KSC)
RAPP .... Racial Awareness Pilot Project [*University of Cincinnati*]
Rapp .... Rapport [*A publication*]
RAPP .... Reconciliation and Purification Program [*Air Force*]
RAPP .... Registered Air Parcel Post
RAPP's ...... Radiologists, Anesthesiologists, Pathologists, and Physiatrists
Rapp Act Bur Voltaique Geol Mines ... Rapport. Activite du Bureau Voltaique de la Geologie et des Mines [*A publication*]
Rapp Act Serv Geol (Madagascar) ... Rapport d'Activite. Service Geologique (Madagascar) [*A publication*]
Rapp Act Serv Geol (Malagasy) ... Rapport d'Activite. Service Geologique (Malagasy) [*A publication*]
Rapp Act Stn Amelior Plant Maraicheres ... Rapport d'Activite. Station d'Amelioration des Plants Maraicheres [*A publication*]
Rapp Anal Phys Chim Eau Rhin ... Rapport sur les Analyses Physico-Chimiques de l'Eau du Rhin [*A publication*]
Rapp Annu AFOCEL (Assoc For Cellul) ... Rapport Annuel. AFOCEL (Association Foret-Cellulose) [*A publication*]
Rapp Annu Fed Chambres Synd Miner Met Non Ferreux ... Rapport Annuel. Federation des Chambres Syndicales des Minerais et des Metaux Non Ferreux [*A publication*]
Rapp Annu Serv Geol (Malagasy) ... Rapport Annuel. Service Geologique (Malagasy) [*A publication*]
Rapp Assoc Int Chim Cerealiere ... Rapports. Association Internationale de Chimie Cerealiere [*A publication*]
Rapp BIPM ... Rapport. BIPM [*Bureau International des Poids et Mesures*] [*A publication*]
Rapp Bount ... Rapp on the Bounty Laws [*A publication*]   (DLA)
Rapp Comm Int Mer Mediter ... Rapport. Commission Internationale pour la Mer Mediterranee [*France*] [*A publication*]
Rapp Commissar Energie Atom ... Rapport. Commissariat a l'Energie Atomique [*France*] [*A publication*]
Rapp Cons Exp Rech Agron Insp Gen Agric (Algeria) ... Rapport. Conseil de l'Experimentation et des Recherches Agronomiques. Inspection Generale de l'Agriculture (Algeria) [*A publication*]
Rapp Final Conf Tech OCEAC ... Rapport Final. Conference Technique. OCEAC [*Organisation de Coordination pour la Lutte Contre les Endemies en Afrique Centrale*] [*A publication*]
Rapp Fonct Tech Inst Pasteur Dakar ... Rapport sur le Fonctionnement Technique. Institut Pasteur de Dakar [*A publication*]
Rapp Geol Minist Energie Ressour (Quebec) ... Rapport Geologique. Ministere de l'Energie et des Ressources (Quebec) [*A publication*]
Rapp Gronl Geol Unders ... Rapport. Gronlands Geologiske Undersogelse [*A publication*]

RAPPI .... Random Access Plan-Position Indicator [*Air Force*]
Rapp Inst Bodemvruchtbaar ... Rapport. Instituut voor Bodemvruchtbaarheid [*A publication*]
Rapp Instn Virkeslara Skogshogsk ... Rapporter. Institutionen for Virkeslara. Skogshogskolan [*A publication*]
Rapp Inter Etude Lab J Dedek Raffinerie Tirlemontoise ... Rapport Interieur d'une Etude Effectuee au Laboratoire J. Dedek Raffinerie Tirlemontoise [*A publication*]
Rapp ISTISAN ... Rapporti ISTISAN [*Istituto Superiore di Sanita*] [*A publication*]
Rapp Korrosionsinst ... Rapport. Korrosionsinstitutet [*A publication*]
Rapp Lab Prod For Est (Can) ... Rapport. Laboratoire des Produits Forestiers de l'Est (Canada) [*A publication*]
Rapp Off Int Epizoot ... Rapport. Office International des Epizooties [*A publication*]
Rapport Conjonct ... Rapport de Conjoncture [*A publication*]
Rapp Prelim Minist Richesses Nat (Que) ... Rapport Preliminaire. Ministere des Richesses Naturelles (Quebec) [*A publication*]
Rapp Proefstn Groenteteelt Vollegrond Ned ... Rapport. Proefstation voor de Groenteteelt in de Vollegrond in Nederland [*A publication*]
Rapp P-V Reun Cons Int Explor Mer ... Rapports et Proces-Verbaux des Reunions. Conseil International pour l'Exploration de la Mer [*A publication*]
Rapp Rech Lab Cent Ponts Chaussees ... Rapport de Recherche. Laboratoire Central des Ponts et Chaussees [*A publication*]
Rapp Sci Tech CNEXO (Fr) ... Rapports Scientifiques et Techniques. CNEXO [*Centre National pour l'Exploitation des Oceans*] (France) [*A publication*]
Rapp Stat Can Hydrogr Sci Oceaniques ... Rapport Statistique Canadien sur l'Hydrographie et les Sciences Oceaniques [*A publication*]
Rapp Sven Livsmedel-Sinstitutet ... Rapport. Svenska Livsmedelsinstitutet [*A publication*]
Rapp Uppsats Avd Skogsekol Skogshogsk ... Rapporter och Uppsatser. Avdelningen foer Skogsekologi. Skogshogskolan [*A publication*]
Rapp Uppsats Instn Skoglig Mat Statist Skogshogsk ... Rapporter och Uppsatser. Institutionen foer Skoglig Matematisk Statistik. Skogshogskolan [*A publication*]
Rapp Uppsats Instn Skogsforyngr Skogshogsk ... Rapporter och Uppsatser. Institutionen foer Skogsforyngring. Skogshogskolan [*A publication*]
Rapp Uppsats Instn Skogsgenet Skogshogsk ... Rapporter och Uppsatser. Institutionen foer Skogsgenetik. Skogshogskolan [*A publication*]
Rapp Uppsats Instn Skogsprod Skogshogsk ... Rapporter och Uppsatser. Institutionen foer Skogsproduktion. Skogshogskolan [*A publication*]
Rapp Uppsats Instn Skogstax Skogshogsk ... Rapporter och Uppsatser. Institutionen foer Skogstaxering. Skogshogskolan [*A publication*]
Rapp Uppsats Instn Skogstek Skogshogsk ... Rapporter och Uppsatser. Institutionen foer Skogsteknik. Skogshogskolan [*A publication*]
RAPR .... RADAR Processor   (CET)
RAPR .... Right Angle Panel Receptacle
RAPRA ...... RAPRA Technology [*Formerly, Rubber and Plastics Research Association*]   (EA)
RAPRA Abst ... RAPRA [*Rubber and Plastics Research Association*] Abstract [*A publication*]
RAPRA Abstr ... RAPRA [*Rubber and Plastics Research Association*] Abstracts [*A publication*]
RAPRA Members J ... RAPRA [*Rubber and Plastics Research Association*] Members Journal [*England*] [*A publication*]
RAPRB ...... Radioprotection [*A publication*]
RAPRENOx ... Rapid Reduction of Nitrogen Oxides [*Automotive engineering*]
RAPS .... RADAR-Absorbing Primary Structure   (MCD)
RAPS .... RADAR Prediction System   (MCD)
RAPS .... RADAR Proficiency Simulator
RAPS .... Radioactive Argon Processing System   (NRCH)
RAPS .... Regional Air Pollution Study [*Environmental Protection Agency*]
RAPS .... Regulated Air Pressure System   (MCD)
RAPS .... Regulatory Affairs Professionals Society   (EA)
RAPS .... Reliable Acoustic Path SONAR   (MCD)
RAPS .... Remote Area Power Supply
RAPS .... Retired Army Personnel System
RAPS .... Retiree Annuitant Pay System
RAPS .... Retrieval Analysis and Presentation System [*Data processing*]
RAPS .... Right Aft Propulsion System [*Aerospace*]   (GFGA)
RAPS .... Risk Appraisal of Programs System
RAPS .... Role Activity Performance Scale [*Mental health*]
RAPSAG ... Rapid Sealift Acquisition Group [*Navy*]
RAPSG ...... Rapsgate [*England*]
RAPT .... Reusable Aerospace Passenger Transport   (MCD)
RAPTAP ... Random Access Parallel Tape
RAP-TAP .. Releasable Assets Program - Transferable Assets Program [*Navy*]   (NG)
RAPTN ...... RAPRA Trade Names [*RAPRA Technology Ltd.*] [*Information service or system*]   (IID)
Raptor Res ... Raptor Research [*A publication*]

RAPTS ...... Resource Accounting Project Tracking System   (DNAB)
RAPTUS ... Rapid Thorium-Uranium System [*Nuclear energy*]
RAPUD ..... Revenue Analysis from Parametric Usage Descriptions [*Telecommunications*]   (TEL)
RAPWI ...... Organization for the Recovery of Allied Prisoners of War and Internees [*Initially in Headquarters of Allied Land Forces, Southeast Asia*] [*World War II*]
Rap Wit ...... Rapalje's Treatise on Witnesses [*A publication*]   (DLA)
RAQ .... Raha [*Indonesia*] [*Airport symbol*]   (OAG)
RAQ .... Regional Air Quality
RAQ .... Wirtschaft und Produktivitaet [*A publication*]
R Aquat Sci ... Reviews in Aquatic Sciences [*A publication*]
RAR .... RADAR Augmentation Reliability   (MCD)
RAR .... Radio Acoustic Ranging
RAR .... Random Age Replacement
RAR .... Rapid Access Recording   (IEEE)
Rar .... Rare Records [*Record label*]
RAR .... Rarotonga [*Cook Islands*] [*Seismograph station code, US Geological Survey*]   (SEIS)
RAR .... Rarotonga [*Cook Islands*] [*Airport symbol*]   (OAG)
RAR .... Read around Ratio
RAR .... Real Aperture RADAR
RAR .... Reallexikon der Aegyptischen Religionsgeschichte [*Berlin*] [*A publication*]   (BJA)
RAR .... Reasonable Assumed [*or Assured*] Resources [*Minerals*]
RAR .... Record and Report
RAR .... Redevelopment Area Resident
RAR .... Reduced Aspect Ratio
RAR .... Regular Army Reserve
RAR .... Relative Accumulation Rate [*Ecology*]
RAR .... Reliability Action Report [*or Request*]
RAR .... Remote Arm Reset   (MCD)
RAR .... Remove Audible Ring
RAR .... Renaissance and Reformation [*A publication*]
RAR .... Repair as Required   (AAG)
RAR .... Report Authorization Record [*or Request*]   (AAG)
RAR .... Request RADAR Blip Identification Message [*Communications*]   (FAAC)
RAR .... Reserve Asset Ratio [*Banking*]   (ADA)
RAR .... Resource Allocation Recommendations [*Military*]
RAR .... Restricted Articles Regulation   (DS)
RAR .... Retinoic Acid Receptor [*Biochemistry*]
RAR .... Return Address Register
RAR .... Revenue Agent's Report [*IRS*]
RAR .... Revise as Required   (MCD)
R-Ar .... Rhode Island State Archives, Providence, RI [*Library symbol*] [*Library of Congress*]   (LCLS)
RAR .... Rhodesian African Rifles [*Military unit*]
RAR .... Right Arm Recumbent [*Medicine*]   (AAMN)
RAR .... ROM [*Read-Only Memory*] Address Register
RAR .... Royal Army Reserve [*British*]
RAR .... Rural Area Redevelopment
RARAD ..... RADAR Advisory   (FAAC)
RARAF ...... Radiological Research Accelerator Facility [*Department of Energy*]
R Ar Av C Et ... Recueil des Arrets et Avis du Conseil d'Etat [*A publication*]
RARB .... Raritan Bancorp, Inc. [*NASDAQ symbol*]   (NQ)
R Arb .... Recht der Arbeit [*Right to Work*] [*German*]   (DLA)
RARC .... Revoked Appointment and Returned to Civilian Status [*Navy*]
RARDE ...... Royal Armament Research and Development Establishment [*British*]
RARDEN .. Royal Armament Research and Development Establishment, Enfield [*British military*]   (DMA)
RARE .... Associated Networks for European Research [*EC*]   (ECED)
RARE .... Ram Air Rocket Engine
RARE .... Rare Animal Relief Effort
RARE .... Rare Antigen/Antibody Resource Exchange Program [*American Association of Blood Banks*]
RARE .... Rehabilitation of Addicts by Relatives and Employers
RARE .... Reinforcement and Resupply of Europe   (MCD)
RARE .... Reseaux Associes pour la Recherche Europeene [*Associated Networks for European Research*]
RARE .... Retinoic Acid Responsive Element [*Biochemistry*]
RARE .... Roadless Area Resource Evaluation
RARE .... Ronne Antarctic Research Expedition [*1947-48*]
RAREA ...... Radiation Research [*A publication*]
Ra Ref .... RADAR Reflector
RAREF ...... Radiation and Repair Engineering Facility [*Nuclear energy*]   (NRCH)
Rarefied Gas Dyn ... Rarefied Gas Dynamics [*A publication*]
Rarefied Gas Dyn Proc Int Symp ... Rarefied Gas Dynamics. Proceedings of the International Symposium [*A publication*]
RAREP ...... RADAR Report [*FAA*]
RARF .... RADOME [*RADAR Dome*], Antenna, and Radio Frequency [*Array*] [*Electronics*]
RARG .... Regulatory Analysis Review Group [*Comprising several federal agencies*]
RARI .... Reporting and Routing Instructions [*Navy*]
RARLS ...... Rabbit Antirat Lymphocyte Serum [*Immunology*]   (MAE)
RARMB .... Razrabotka Rudnykh Mestorozhdenii [*A publication*]
RARNEB ... Recent Achievements in Restorative Neurology [*A publication*]

RARO .... Regular Army Reserve of Officers [*British*]
RAROC ..... Risk-Adjusted Return on Capital [*Economics*]
RAR OCC ... Raro Occurrit [*Rarely Occurs*] [*Latin*]   (ROG)
RARP .... Radio Affiliate Replacement Plan [*Canadian Broadcasting Corporation*]
RARP .... Reverse Address Resolution Protocol [*Data processing*]   (PCM)
RARR .... Reinstallation and Removal Record   (KSC)
RARS .... Refractory Anemia with Ringed Sideroblasts [*Hematology*]
RARSA .... Radiation Research. Supplement [*A publication*]
RArt .... Royal Artillery [*British*]
RARU .... Rackham Arthritis Research Unit [*University of Michigan*] [*Research center*]   (RCD)
RARU .... Radio Range Station Reported Unreliable [*Message abbreviation*]
RAS .... Rabbonim Aid Society
RAS .... RADAR-Absorbing Structures
RAS .... RADAR Advisory Service
RAS .... RADAR Assembly Spares   (NG)
RAS .... RADAR Augmentation System   (MCD)
RAS .... Radio Science [*A publication*]
RAS .... RADOME [*RADAR Dome*] Antenna Structure
RAS .... Radula Sinus
RAS .... Rasht [*Iran*] [*Airport symbol*]   (OAG)
RAS .... Rassegna. Archivi di Stato [*A publication*]
ras .... Rasurae [*Scrapings or Filings*] [*Latin*]   (MAE)
RAS .... Reaction Augmentation System
RAS .... Reactor Alarm System   (IEEE)
RAS .... Reactor Analysis and Safety [*Nuclear energy*]   (NRCH)
RAS .... Readers Advisory Service [*A publication*]
RAS .... Rear Area Security [*Army*]   (AABC)
RAS .... Recirculation Actuation Signal [*Nuclear energy*]   (NRCH)
RAS .... Record Assigned System   (MCD)
RAS .... Records and Analysis Subsystem   (TEL)
RAS .... Recruiting Analysis Service [*LIMRA*]
RAS .... Rectified Air Speed [*Navigation*]
RAS .... Recurrent Aphthous Stomatitis [*Medicine*]
RAS .... Reflector Antenna System
RASA .... Refractory Anemia with Ringed Sideroblasts [*Hematology*]
RAS .... Regional Automated Systems
RAS .... Relay Antenna Subsystem [*NASA*]
RAS .... Reliability, Availability, and Serviceability [*IBM Corp. slogan*]   (MCD)
RAS .... Remote Acquisition Station [*Nuclear energy*]   (NRCH)
RAS .... Remote Active Spectrometer
RAS .... Remote Area Support   (MCD)
RAS .... Remote Arm Set   (MCD)
RAS .... Renal Artery Stenosis [*Medicine*]   (MAE)
RAS .... Renin-Angiotensin System [*Endocrinology*]
RAS .... Replenishment at Sea [*Navy*]
RAS .... Report Audit Summary   (AAG)
RAS .... Reproduction Assembly Sheet   (MCD)
RAS .... Requirements Allocation Sheet
RAS .... Requirements Analysis Sheet [*NASA*]   (KSC)
RAS .... Requirements Audit System
RAS .... Reserve Advisory Squadron
RAS .... Resource Analysis System   (HGAA)
RAS .... Reticular Activating System [*Diffuse network of neurons in the brain*]
RAS .... Rheumatoid Arthritis Serum [*Factor*] [*Medicine*]
RAS .... River Assault Squadron [*Navy*]   (NVT)
RAS .... Riverside Air Service [*Riverside, CA*] [*FAA designator*]   (FAAC)
RAS .... Rockhampton Aerial Services [*Australia*]
RAS .... Route Accounting Subsystem [*Telecommunications*]   (TEL)
RAS .... Row-Address Strobe   (IEEE)
RAS .... Royal Accounting System [*United States Geological Survey*]
RAS .... Royal Aeronautical Society [*British*]
RAS .... Royal African Society   (EAIO)
RAS .... Royal Agricultural Society [*British*]   (DAS)
RAS .... Royal Asiatic Society [*British*]
RAS .... Royal Astronomical Society [*British*]
RAS .... Royal International Agricultural Show [*British*]   (ITD)
RASA .... Railway and Airline Supervisors Association [*AFL-CIO*]
RASA .... Realignment of Supply Activities   (MCD)
RASA .... Redstone Arsenal Support Activity   (MCD)
RASA .... Regional Aeronautical Support Activity   (AFIT)
RASAU ...... Reserve Antisubmarine Warfare Systems Analysis Mobilization Unit   (DNAB)
RASC .... Radiological Affairs Safety Committee   (DNAB)
RASC .... Rear Area Security Controller [*Military*]
RASC .... Religious Altered State of Consciousness [*Psychology*]
RASC .... Rome Air Service Command [*Air Force*]
RASC .... Royal Agricultural Society of the Commonwealth   (EAIO)
RASC .... Royal Army Service Corps [*Formerly, ASC; later, RCT*] [*British*]
RASC .... Royal Astronomical Society of Canada
RASCA ...... Radio Science [*A publication*]
RASCAL ... Random Access Secure Communications Antijam Link
RASCAL ... Rotorcraft-Aircrew Systems Concepts Airborne Laboratory   (RDA)

RASCAL ... Royal Aircraft Establishment Sequence Calculator [*British*]   (DEN)
RASCAP ... Replenishment at Sea Corrective Action Program   (MCD)
RASCC ...... Rear Area Security Control Center [*Military*]
RASC/DC ... Rear Area Security and Area Damage Control [*Military*]
Raschet Konstr Issled Oborud Proizvod Istochnikov Toka ... Raschet. Konstruirovanie i Issledovanie Oborudovaniya Proizvodstva Istochnikov Toka [*A publication*]
Raschet Konstr Neftezavod Oborud ... Raschet i Konstruirovanie Neftezavodskogo Oborudovaniya [*A publication*]
Raschet Konstr Neftezvod Oborudovaniya ... Raschet i Konstruirovanie Neftezavodskogo Oborudovaniya [*A publication*]
Raschety Prochn ... Raschety na Prochnost [*A publication*]
RASCOM ... Regional African Satellite Communication System for the Development of Africa [*ITU*] [*United Nations*]   (DUND)
RASCORE ... RADAR Scorer   (MCD)
RASC/RCT ... Royal Army Service Corps/Royal Corps of Transport [*British*]
RASD .... Reference and Adult Services Division [*American Library Association*]   (EA)
RASD BRASS ... RASD [*Reference and Adult Services Division*] Business Reference Services Section
RASD CODES ... RASD [*Reference and Adult Services Division*] Collection Development and Evaluation Section
RASD HS ... RASD [*Reference and Adult Services Division*] History Section
RASD ILC ... RASD [*Reference and Adult Services Division*] Interlibrary Loan Committee [*American Library Association*]
RASD MARS ... RASD [*Reference and Adult Services Division*] Machine-Assisted Reference Section
RASDS ...... Regional Advisory Service in Demographic Statistics [*United Nations*]   (EY)
RASE .... Rapid Automatic Sweep Equipment [*Air Force*]
RASE .... Royal Agricultural Society of England
RASER ...... Radio Amplification by Stimulated Emission of Radiation
RASER ...... Random-to-Serial Converter
RASER ...... Range and Sensitivity Extending Resonator [*Electronics*]
RASGN ...... Reassignment
RASH .... Rain Showers [*Meteorology*]
RASHA ...... RAS. Rohr-Armatur-Sanitaer-Heizung [*A publication*]
RASHI .... Rabbi Shlomo Yitzhaqi [*Medieval Jewish commentator*]
RaSHI .... Rabbi Solomon Bar Isaac   (BJA)
RASIB .... Rendiconto. Accademia delle Scienze. Istituto di Bologna [*A publication*]
RASIDS ..... Range Safety Impact Display System
RASILA ..... Rannikko- ja Sisaevesiliikenteen Tvoenantajaliitto [*Employers' Federation of Coastal and Inland Waterways Transportation*] [*Finland*]   (EY)
RASL .... Royal Apex Silver, Inc. [*NASDAQ symbol*]   (NQ)
RASM .... Remote Analog Submultiplexer   (MCD)
rASMC ..... Rat Aortic Smooth Muscle Cells
RASN .... Rain and Snow [*Sleet*] [*Meteorology*]
RASO .... Radiological Affairs Support Office [*Obsolete*] [*Navy*]
RASO .... Rear Airfield Supply Organization [*Military*]
RASO .... Regional Aviation Supply Officer [*Navy*]   (AFIT)
RASONDE ... Radiosonde Observation
RASP .... Receiver Active Signal Processor [*Military*]   (CAAL)
RASP .... Refined Aeronautical Support Program   (NG)
RASP .... Reliability and Aging Surveillance Program [*Air Force*]
RASP .... Remote Access Switching and Patching
RASP .... Retrieval and Sort Processor [*Data processing*]
RASPE ...... Resident Army SENSCOM [*Sentinel Systems Command*] Project Engineer   (AABC)
RASPO ...... Resident Apollo Spacecraft Program Office [*NASA*]   (KSC)
RASR .... Regular Army Special Reserve   (ADA)
RASS .... RADAR Acoustic Sounding System [*National Oceanic and Atmospheric Administration*]
RASS .... RADAR Attitude Sensing System   (MCD)
RASS .... Radio Acoustic Sounding System
RASS .... Rapid Area Supply Support [*Military*]   (AFM)
RASS .... Remote Activated Stores System   (MCD)
RASS .... Rock Analysis Storage System [*United States Geological Survey*] [*Information service or system*]   (IID)
RASS .... Rotating Acoustic Stereo-Scanner [*Telecommunications*]   (OA)
RASS .... Ruggedized Airborne Seeker Simulator   (MCD)
RASSAN ... RADAR Sea State Analyzer [*Marine science*]   (MSC)
RASSAS .... Radio Astronomical Space System of Aperture Synthesis   (MCD)
RASSH ...... Radiosondes Shipped From   (NOAA)
R Assoc Canad Educ Langue Franc ... Revue. Association Canadienne d'Education de Langue Francaise [*A publication*]
RASSR ...... Reliable Advanced Solid-State RADAR
RAS-STADES ... Records Association System - Standard Data Elements System   (MCD)
RASSW ..... Radical Alliance of Social Service Workers   (EA)
RAST .... Radioallergosorbent Test [*Immunochemistry*]
Rast .... Rastell's Entries and Statutes [*England*] [*A publication*]   (DLA)
RAST .... Recovery, Assist, Secure, and Traverse System [*Navy*]
RAST .... Reliability and System Test
RASTA ...... Radiant Augmented Special Test Apparatus   (MCD)
RASTA ...... Radio Station [*Coast Guard*]
Rast Abr ..... Rastell's Abridgment of the Statutes [*A publication*]   (DLA)
RASTAC ... Random Access Storage and Control [*Data processing*]

RASTAD ... Random Access Storage and Display [*Data processing*]
RASTAS .... Radiating Site Target Acquisition System   (MCD)
Rasteniev'd Nauki ... Rasteniev'dni Nauki [*A publication*]
Rastenievud Nauk ... Rastenievudni Nauki [*A publication*]
Rastenievud Nauki ... Rastenievudni Nauki [*A publication*]
Rast Ent ..... Rastell's Entries and Statutes [*A publication*]   (DLA)
RASTI .... Rapid Speech Transition Index [*Acoustics*]
RASTIC ..... Rail, Automatic Straightening, Intrinsically Controlled
    [*Railroad maintenance device*] [*British*]
Rastit Belki ... Rastitel'nye Belki [*A publication*]
Rastit Krainego Sev Ee Osvoenie ... Rastitel'nost Krainego Severa i Ee
    Osvoenie [*A publication*]
Rastit Krainego Sev SSSR Ee Osvoenie ... Rastitel'nost Krainego Severa SSSR
    i Ee Osvoenie [*A publication*]
Rastit Latv SSR ... Rastitel'nost Latviiskoi SSR [*A publication*]
Rastit Resur ... Rastitel'nye Resursy [*A publication*]
Rastit Zasht ... Rastitelna Zashtita [*Plant Protection*] [*A publication*]
Rastit Zasht Plant Prot ... Rastitelna Zashtita/Plant Protection [*A*
    publication]
Rast Nauki ... Rastenievudni Nauki [*A publication*]
RASTR ...... Recorded Acoustic Signal Target Repeater
Rast Resursy ... Rastitel'nye Resursy [*A publication*]
R Astron Soc Can Pr ... Royal Astronomical Society of Canada. Selected
    Papers and Proceedings [*A publication*]
Rast Zashch ... Rastitelna Zashchita [*A publication*]
RaSV .... Rasheed (Rat) Sarcoma Virus
RASV .... Reusable Aerodynamic Space Vehicle
RAT .... Radiatively-Active Trace [*Analytical chemistry*]
RAT .... Radiological Assessment Team [*Nuclear energy*]   (NRCH)
RAT .... Ram Air Temperature
RAT .... Ram Air Turbine   (MCD)
RAT .... Ranges, Ammunition, and Targets   (MCD)
RAT .... Rat Island [*Alaska*] [*Seismograph station code, US Geological
    Survey*] [*Closed*]   (SEIS)
RAT .... Rat Resources [*Vancouver Stock Exchange symbol*]
RAT .... Rated
RAT .... Rating   (AABC)
RAT .... Ratio   (AAG)
RAT .... Rations [*Military*]   (AABC)
RAT .... Raynaud's Association Trust   (EA)
RAT .... Receipt Account Title File [*Office of Management and
    Budget*]   (GFGA)
RAT .... Regular Associated Troupers   (EA)
RAT .... Relative Accuracy Test   (GFGA)
RAT .... Reliability Assurance Test
RAT .... Remote Area Terminal
RAT .... Remote Associates Test [*Psychology*]
RAT .... Repeat Action Tablet [*Pharmacology*]
R & AT ...... Research and Advanced Technology
RAT .... Reseau des Amis de la Terre [*Network of Friends of the Earth*]
    [*France*] [*Political party*]   (PPE)
RAT .... Reserve Auxiliary Transformer   (IEEE)
RAT .... Resistance Armee Tunisienne [*Tunisian Armed
    Resistance*]   (PD)
RAT .... Restricted Articles Tariff
RAT .... Revue. Academie Internationale du Tourisme [*A publication*]
RAT .... Right Anterior Thigh [*Anatomy*]
RAT .... Rocket-Assisted Torpedo [*Antisubmarine warfare*]
RAT .... Rotational Autonomic Tester
RATA .... Rankine Cycle Air Turboaccelerator
RA/TA ...... Restricted Availability/Technical Availability   (NVT)
RATAC ..... RADAR Analog Target Acquisition Computer
RATAC ..... Raytheon Acoustic Telemetry and Control
RATAC ..... Remote Airborne Television Display of Ground RADAR
    Coverage via TACAN   (CET)
RATAN ..... RADAR and Television Aid to Navigation
RATAV ..... RADAR Terrain Avoidance
RATBP ..... Revised Appendix to Be Published   (MCD)
RATC .... Rate-Aided Tracking Computer
RATC .... Rhodesian Air Training Centre [*British military*]   (DMA)
RATCC ..... RADAR Air Traffic Control Center [*Later, RATCF*] [*Navy*]
RATCC ..... Regional Air Traffic Control Center   (NATG)
RATCF ..... RADAR Air Traffic Control Facility [*Formerly, RATCC*]
    [*Navy*]   (FAAC)
RATCON .. RADAR Terminal Control
RATD .... RADAR Automatic Target Detection [*Military*]   (CAAL)
RATDA ..... Regional African Telecommunication Database [*International
    Telecommunication Union*]   (DUND)
RATE........ Rate Analysis and Transportation Evaluation [*Student legal
    action organization*]
RATE......... Record and Tape Exchange   (EA)
RATE......... Remote Automatic Telemetry Equipment
RATE......... Retention and Transfer Enhancement [*Military*]
RATEA ..... Radiotekhnika [*Moscow*] [*A publication*]
RATEL ...... Radiotelephone
RATEL ...... Raytheon Automatic Test Equipment Language [*Data
    processing*]   (CSR)
RATELO... Radiotelephone Operator   (AABC)
RATER ..... Response Analysis Tester [*NASA*]
RATES ...... Rapid Access Tariff Expediting Service [*Journal of Commerce,
    Inc.*] [*Database*]

RATEX ...... Rational Expectations [*Economics*]
RATF .... Radio Aids Training Flight [*British military*]   (DMA)
RATFOR... Rational FORTRAN [*Data processing*]
RA-TFR..... RADAR Altimeter - Terrain Following RADAR   (MCD)
RATG .... Rabbit Antithymocyte Globulin [*Immunochemistry*]
RATG .... Radiotelegram [*or Radiotelegraph*]
RATG .... Rhodesian Air Training Group [*British military*]   (DMA)
RATHAS..... Rat Thymus Antiserum [*Biochemistry*]   (MAE)
RATHQ..... Rath Packing [*NASDAQ symbol*]   (NQ)
RATIB ...... Radiologic Technology [*A publication*]
RATIG ...... Robert A. Taft Institute of Government [*Later, TTI*]   (EA)
RATIO...... Radio Telescope in Orbit   (IEEE)
Rationalisierung ... Monatsschrift des Rationalisierungs [*A publication*]
Ration Drug Ther ... Rational Drug Therapy [*A publication*]
RATLER ... Robotic All-Terrain Lunar Exploration Rover [*NASA*]
RATN .... Ratners Group Ltd. [*NASDAQ symbol*]   (NQ)
Rat News Lett ... Rat News Letter [*A publication*]
RATO .... Rocket-Assisted Takeoff [*Aerospace*]
RATO .... Rocket-Assisted Takeoff [*Aerospace*]
RATOG ..... Rocket-Assisted Takeoff Gear [*Aviation*]   (IEEE)
RATPAC ... RADAR Acquisition Tracking Probe for Active
    Calibration   (DNAB)
RATR .... Reliability Abstracts and Technical Reviews [*NASA*]
RATS........ RADAR Acquisition and Tracking System   (MCD)
RATS........ RADAR Altimeter Target Simulator   (MCD)
RATS........ Radio Amateur Telecommunications Society   (EA)
RATS........ Ram Air Turbine System
RATS........ Rapid Area Transportation Support [*Air Force*]   (MCD)
RATS........ Rate and Track Subsystem
RATS........ Reconnaissance and Tactical Security [*Teams*] [*Military*]
RATS........ Reform of the Australian Taxation System [*1985*] [*A
    publication*]
RATS........ Remote Alarm Transmission System
RATS........ Remote Area Tactical [*Location and Landing*] System
RATS........ Remote Area Terminal System
RATS........ Resolver Alignment Test Set
RATS........ Restricted Articles Terminal System [*IATA*]   (DS)
RATSC...... Rome Air Technical Service Command [*Air Force*]
RATSCAT ... RADAR Target Scatter [*RADAR program*]
RATSEC.... Robert A. Taft Sanitary Engineering Center   (AABC)
Rat Sel Cas ... Rattigan's Select Hindu Law Cases [*A publication*]   (DLA)
RATT........ Radio Airborne Teletype   (MCD)
RATT........ Radio Telephone/Teleprinter   (INF)
RATT........ Radioteletype
RATTC...... Radio and Teletype Control Center
Rattigan ..... Rattigan's Select Hindu Law Cases [*India*] [*A
    publication*]   (DLA)
Ratt LC ...... Rattigan's Leading Cases on Hindu Law [*A publication*]   (DLA)
Rat Unrep Cr ... Ratanlal's Unreported Criminal Cases [*India*] [*A
    publication*]   (DLA)
RATWUS ... Research and Technology Work Unit Summary
RATx .... Radiation Therapy [*Medicine*]   (MAE)
RAU........... Radion Access Unit [*Army*]
RAU........... Recurrent Aphthous Ulceration [*Medicine*]
RAU........... Regional Acquisition Unit [*NASA*]   (NASA)
RAU........... Remote Acquisition Unit [*NASA*]   (NASA)
RAU........... River Assault Unit [*Navy*]
Rauch Pnt .. Rauch Guide to the United States Paint Industry Data [*A
    publication*]
RA-UDAA ... Robbery Armed - Unlawful Driving Away of an Automobile
    [*Police code*]
RAUIC....... Repair Activity Unit Identification Code   (MCD)
RAUIS....... Remote Acquisition Unit Interconnecting Station
    [*NASA*]   (NASA)
RAUK........ Rear-Admiral of the United Kingdom [*Navy*] [*British*]   (ROG)
Raumforsch u-Ordnung ... Raumforschung und Raumordnung [*A
    publication*]
Raumforsch und Raumordnung ... Raumforschung und Raumordnung [*A
    publication*]
R Aust Chem Inst ... Royal Australian Chemical Institute [*A publication*]
R Aust Chem Inst J Proc ... Royal Australian Chemical Institute. Journal and
    Proceedings [*A publication*]   (APTA)
R Aust Chem Inst J Proc Suppl ... Royal Australian Chemical Institute.
    Journal and Proceedings. Supplement [*A
    publication*]   (APTA)
R Aust Chem Inst Proc ... Royal Australian Chemical Institute. Proceedings
    [*A publication*]
R Aust Plan Inst J ... Royal Australian Planning Institute. Journal [*A
    publication*]
R Aust Plann Inst J ... RAPIJ: Royal Australian Planning Institute. Journal [*A
    publication*]   (APTA)
RAUT .... Republic Automotive Parts, Inc. [*NASDAQ symbol*]   (NQ)
RAUU........ [*The*] Renabie Gold Trust [*NASDAQ symbol*]   (NQ)
R Aux AF... Royal Auxiliary Air Force [*Formerly, AAF*] [*British*]
RAV .... Cravo Norte [*Colombia*] [*Airport symbol*]   (OAG)
RAV .... Ramm Venture [*Vancouver Stock Exchange symbol*]
RAV .... Random Access Viewer
RAV .... Raven Industries, Inc. [*AMEX symbol*]   (SPSG)
RAV .... Ravensburg [*Federal Republic of Germany*] [*Seismograph
    station code, US Geological Survey*]   (SEIS)
RAV .... Ravine, PA [*Location identifier*] [*FAA*]   (FAAL)
RAV .... Reduced Availability   (MCD)

RAV .... Remotely Augmented Vehicle [*Aircraft*]
RAV .... Restricted Availability (NG)
RAV .... Rous-Associated Virus (MAE)
RAVC .... Royal Army Veterinary Corps [*Formerly, AVC*] [*British*]
RAVE .... RADAR Acquisition Visual-Tracking Equipment
RAVE .... Random Access Video Editing [*Computerized film editing*]
RAVE .... Random Access Viewing Equipment
RAVE .... Readjustment Assistance Act 74 for Vietnam Era
                Veterans (OICC)
RAVE .... Research Aircraft for the Visual Environment [*Helicopters*]
                [*Army*]
RAVEC .... RADAR Vector
RAVEN ..... Ranging and Velocity Navigation
Ravena .... [*Petrus*] Ravennas [*Flourished, 1468-1508*] [*Authority cited in
                pre-1607 legal work*] (DSA)
RAVES ...... Rapid Aerospace Vehicle Evaluation System [*Grumman Corp.*]
RAVIR .... RADAR Video Recorder (NVT)
RAVPRO..... Resource Allocation and Validation Program
R-AVR .... Ruggedized Airborne Video Recorder
RAVU .... Radiosonde Analysis and Verification Unit
RAW .... Airway Resistance [*Medicine*]
RAW .... Arawa [*Papua New Guinea*] [*Airport symbol*] (OAG)
RAW .... Raad van Advies voor het Wetenschapsbeleid. Informatiebank.
                Tweekbericht [*A publication*]
RAW .... Rapid American Withdrawal [*Antiwar march sponsored by
                Vietnam Veterans Against the War*] (EA)
Raw .... Rawle's Pennsylvania Reports [*5 vols.*] [*A publication*] (DLA)
RAW .... Read Alter Wire
RAW .... Read after Write
RAW .... Ready and Waiting [*or Willing*] [*Slang*]
RAW .... Rear Axle Weight [*Automotive engineering*]
RAW .... Reconnaissance Attack Wing [*Navy*] (NVT)
RAW .... Record of the Arab World [*Beirut*] [*A publication*]
RAW .... Redmond, OR [*Location identifier*] [*FAA*] (FAAL)
RAW .... Reliability Assurance Warranty (MCD)
RAW .... Rent-a-Wreck Industries Corp. [*Vancouver Stock Exchange
                symbol*]
RAW .... Request for Additional Work [*Navy*] (DNAB)
RAW .... Return America to Work [*Also translated as "Reaganomics
                Ain't Working"*] [*UAW bumper sticker slogan*]
RAW .... Rifleman's Assault Weapon (MCD)
RAW .... Right Attack Wing [*Women's lacrosse position*]
RAW .... Rural American Women (EA)
RAWA .... Rail-Water [*Shipping*]
RAWA .... Renaissance Artists and Writers Association (EA)
RAWA .... Rent-a-Wreck of America, Inc. [*Los Angeles, CA*] [*NASDAQ
                symbol*] (NQ)
RAWA .... Revolutionary Association of the Women of Afghanistan
RAWARA ... Rail-Water-Rail [*Shipping*]
RAWARC ... RADAR and Warning Coordination [*Teletypewriter circuit*]
RAWB .... Railroad and Airline Wage Board [*Terminated, 1953*]
RAWC .... Republic American Corp. [*Encino, CA*] [*NASDAQ
                symbol*] (NQ)
Raw Const ... Rawle on the Constitution of the United States [*A
                publication*]
Raw Cov ..... Rawle on Covenants for Title [*A publication*] (DLA)
RAWEB..... Refractory Anemia without Excess of Blasts [*Hematology*]
Raw Eq .... Rawle's Equity in Pennsylvania [*A publication*] (DLA)
RAWIE .... Radio Weather Intercept Element
RAWIN ...... RADAR Wind [*Upper air observation*]
RAWIND .. RADAR Wind [*Upper air observation*]
RAWINDS ... RADAR Wind Sounding [*Upper air observation*] (MSA)
RAWINS ... RADAR Winds [*Upper air observation*]
RAWINSONDE ... RADAR Wind Sounding and Radiosonde [*Upper air
                observation*]
RAWIT ...... RNA [*Ribonucleic Acid*] Amplification with In/Vitro
                Translation [*Genetics*]
Rawle .... Rawle's Pennsylvania Supreme Court Reports [*1828-35*] [*A
                publication*] (DLA)
Rawle Const US ... Rawle on the Constitution of the United States [*A
                publication*] (DLA)
Rawle Cov .. Rawle on Covenants for Title [*A publication*] (DLA)
Rawle Pen & W ... Rawle, Penrose, and Watts' Pennsylvania Reports [*1828-
                40*] [*A publication*] (DLA)
Rawl Mun Corp ... Rawlinson's Municipal Corporations [*10th ed.*] [*1910*] [*A
                publication*] (DLA)
Raw Mater ... Raw Material [*A publication*]
Raw Materials Survey Res Rept ... Raw Materials Survey. Resource Report [*A
                publication*]
Raw Mater Rep ... Raw Materials Report [*Sweden*] [*A publication*]
RAWO....... Reliability Assurance Work Order (MCD)
RAWOOP-SNAP ... Ramo-Wooldridge One-Pass Assembly Program (SAA)
RAWP .... Resource Allocation Working Party [*British*]
RAWS....... RADAR Altimeter Warning Set (MCD)
RAWS....... RADAR Automatic Weather System
RAWS....... Remote Area Weather Station (MCD)
RAWS....... Remote Automatic Weather Station
RAWS....... Role Adaptable Weapons System [*Military*]
RAWSII .... Raw Statement of Intelligence Interest (MCD)
RAWTS..... RNA [*Ribonucleic Acid*] Amplification with Transcript
                Sequencing [*Genetics*]

RAWX .... Returned Account Weather [*Aviation*] (FAAC)
RAX .... Remote Access [*Data processing*] [*Telecommunications*]
RAX .... Rio Alto Exploration Ltd. [*Toronto Stock Exchange symbol*]
RAX .... Rosenbalm Aviation, Inc. [*Ypsilanti, MI*] [*FAA
                designator*] (FAAC)
RAX .... Rural Automatic Exchange (DEN)
RAXR .... Rax Restaurants, Inc. [*NASDAQ symbol*] (NQ)
RAXRA..... Radex Rundschau (Austria) [*A publication*]
Ray .... Raymundus de Pennafort [*Deceased, 1275*] [*Authority cited in
                pre-1607 legal work*] (DSA)
Ray .... Raynerius de Forlivio [*Deceased, 1358*] [*Authority cited in pre-
                1607 legal work*] (DSA)
RAY .... Rayrock Yellowknife Resources, Inc. [*Toronto Stock Exchange
                symbol*]
RAY .... Raytech Corp. [*NYSE symbol*] (SPSG)
RAY .... Rothesay [*Scotland*] [*Airport symbol*] (OAG)
RAY .... Royale Airlines, Inc. [*Shreveport, LA*] [*FAA
                designator*] (FAAC)
Ray B Ex ... Raymond's Bill of Exceptions [*A publication*] (DLA)
RAYCI...... Raytheon Controlled Inventory [*Data processing*]
Raycm .... Raychem Corp. [*Associated Press abbreviation*] (APAG)
RAY-COM ... Raytheon Communications Equipment [*Citizens band radio*]
RAYDAC... Raytheon Digital Automatic Computer (MUGU)
Rayden....... Rayden on Divorce [*A publication*] (DLA)
RAYDIST ... Ray-Path Distance (MUGU)
Ray de For ... Raynerius de Forlivio [*Deceased, 1358*] [*Authority cited in pre-
                1607 legal work*] (DSA)
Ray Ins....... Ray's Medical Jurisprudence of Insanity [*A publication*] (DLA)
RAYM ...... [*The*] Raymond Corp. [*NASDAQ symbol*] (NQ)
Raym.......... [*Sir Thomas*] Raymond's King's Bench Reports [*83 English
                Reprint*] [*1660-84*] [*A publication*] (DLA)
Raym B Ex ... Raymond's Bill of Exceptions [*A publication*] (DLA)
Raym Ch Dig ... Raymond's Digested Chancery Cases [*A publication*] (DLA)
Ray Med Jur ... Ray's Medical Jurisprudence of Insanity [*A
                publication*] (DLA)
Ray Men Path ... Ray's Mental Pathology [*A publication*] (DLA)
Raym Ent... [*Lord*] Raymond's Entries [*A publication*] (DLA)
Raym Ld ... Lord Raymond's English King's Bench Reports [*3 vols.*] [*A
                publication*] (DLA)
Raymond.... Raymond's Reports [*81-89 Iowa*] [*A publication*] (DLA)
Raymond W Brink Selected Math Papers ... Raymond W. Brink Selected
                Mathematical Papers [*A publication*]
Raym Sir T ... [*Sir Thomas*] Raymond's English King's Bench Reports [*A
                publication*] (DLA)
Raym T ...... [*Sir Thomas*] Raymond's English King's Bench Reports [*A
                publication*] (DLA)
Rayn.......... Rayner's English Tithe Cases [*3 vols.*] [*A publication*] (DLA)
Rayn Ti Cas ... Rayner's English Tithe Cases [*1575-1782*] [*A
                publication*] (DLA)
RAYOF...... Raymac Oil Corp. [*NASDAQ symbol*] (NQ)
Rayon........ Rayon and Synthetic Textiles [*A publication*]
Rayon J ...... Rayon Journal [*A publication*]
Rayon J Cellul Fibers ... Rayon Journal and Cellulose Fibers [*A publication*]
Rayon Melliand Text Mon ... Rayon and Melliand Textile Monthly [*A
                publication*]
Rayonne Fibres Synth ... Rayonne et Fibres Synthetiques [*A publication*]
Rayonnem Ionis ... Rayonnements Ionisants [*A publication*]
Rayonnem Ionis Tech Mes Prot ... Rayonnements Ionisants. Techniques de
                Mesures et de Protection [*A publication*]
Rayonr .... Rayonier Timberlands Ltd. [*Associated Press
                abbreviation*] (APAG)
Rayon Rayon J ... Rayon and the Rayon Journal [*A publication*]
Rayon Rec ... Rayon Record [*A publication*]
Rayon Synth Text ... Rayon and Synthetic Textiles [*A publication*]
Rayon Synth Yarn J ... Rayon and Synthetic Yarn Journal [*A publication*]
Rayon Text Mon ... Rayon Textile Monthly [*A publication*]
RAY/RD.... Raytheon Co./Research Division
Ray de Saba ... Raymundus de Sabanacho [*Authority cited in pre-1607 legal
                work*] (DSA)
Ray Sir T.... [*Sir Thomas*] Raymond's English King's Bench Reports [*83
                English Reprint*] [*1660-84*] [*A publication*] (DLA)
RAYSISTOR ... Raytheon Resistor [*Electro-optical control device*]
RAYSPAN ... Raytheon Spectrum Analyzer
RAY-TEL.. Raytheon Telephone [*Citizens band radio*]
Raythn....... Raytheon Co. [*Associated Press abbreviation*] (APAG)
Ray Ti Cas ... Rayner's English Tithe Cases [*1575-1782*] [*A
                publication*] (DLA)
RAZ .... Rolled Alloyed Zinc
RAZEL...... Range, Azimuth, and Elevation
RazFe........ Razon y Fe [*Madrid*] [*A publication*]
Raziskave Stud Kmetijski Inst Slov ... Raziskave in Studije-Kmetijski Institut
                Slovenije [*A publication*]
RAZON..... Range and Azimuth Only
RAZPE...... Resident ARGMA [*Army Rocket and Guided Missile Agency*]
                Zeus Project Engineer (AAG)
Razpr Slov Akad Znan Umet IV ... Razprave. Slovenska Akademija Znanosti
                in Umetnosti. IV [*A publication*]
Razpr Slov Akad Znan Umet Razred Mat Fiz Teh Vede Ser A ... Razprave.
                Slovenska Akademija Znanosti in Umetnosti. Razred za
                Matematicne, Fizikalne, in Tehnicne Vede. Serija A.
                Matematicne, Fizikalne, in Kemicne Vede [*A publication*]

Razrab Ehkspl Gazov Gazokondens Mestorozhd ... Razrabotka i
　　Ehksplutatsiya Gazovykh i Gazokondensatnykh
　　Mestorozhdenij [*A publication*]
Razrab Mestorozhd Polezn Iskop (Kiev) ... Razrabotka Mestorozhdenii
　　Poleznykh Iskopaemykh (Kiev) [*A publication*]
Razrab Mestorozhd Polezn Iskop (Tiflis) ... Razrabotka Mestorozhdenii
　　Poleznykh Iskopaemykh (Tiflis) [*A publication*]
Razrab Neft Gazov Mestorozhd ... Razrabotka Neftyanykh i Gazovykh
　　Mestorozhdenii [*A publication*]
Razrab Rudn Mestorozhd ... Razrabotka Rudnykh Mestorozhdenii [*Ukrainian
　　SSR*] [*A publication*]
Razred Mat Fiz Teh Vede Dela ... Razred za Matematicne, Fizikalne in
　　Tehnicne Vede Dela [*Ljubliana*]
RAZS........ Rolled Alloyed Zinc Sheet
Raz SAZU ... Razprave Razreda za Filoloske in Literarne vede Slovenske
　　Akademije Znanoste in Umetnosti [*A publication*]
Razved Geofiz ... Razvedochnaya Geofizika [*A publication*]
Razved Geofiz (Leningrad) ... Razvedochnaya Geofizika (Leningrad) [*A
　　publication*]
Razved Nedr ... Razvedka Nedr [*Former USSR*] [*A publication*]
Razved Okhr Nedr ... Razvedka i Okhrana Nedr [*A publication*]
Razved Promysl Geofiz ... Razvedochnaya i Promyslovaya Geofizika [*A
　　publication*]
Razved Razrab Neft Gazov Mestorozhd ... Razvedka i Razrabotka Neftyanykh
　　i Gazovykh Mestorozhdenii [*A publication*]
R/B .... ASE [*National Institute for Automotive Service Excellence*]
　　Test Registration Booklet [*A publication*]　(EAAP)
RB .... Botswana [*IYRU nationality code*]　(IYR)
RB .... RADAR Beacon
R/B .... Radio Beacon
RB .... Radio Bearing　(DEN)
RB .... Radio Brenner [*Radio network*] [*Germany*]
RB .... Rate Beacon　(AAG)
RB .... Rated Boost
RB .... Rating Board [*Medicine*]　(MAE)
RB .... Ration Book
RB .... Reactor Building [*Nuclear energy*]　(NRCH)
RB .... Read Back [*Communications*]　(FAAC)
RB .... Read Backward
RB .... Read Buffer
RB .... Reading & Bates Corp. [*NYSE symbol*]　(SPSG)
RB .... Reasons to Believe [*An association*]　(EA)
RB .... Recherches Bibliques [*A publication*]
RB .... Rechtsgeleerd Bijblad [*A publication*]
RB .... Recirculating Ball [*Automotive engineering*]
RB .... Reconnaissance Bomber
RB .... Recovery Beacon
R & B......... Red and Blue　(KSC)
RB .... Red Book [*Full name is "Drug Topics Red Book," a
　　pharmacist's guide*] [*A publication*]
RB .... Red Brigades [*Revolutionary group*] [*Italy*]
RB .... Redeemable Bond [*Investment term*]
RB .... Reentry Body
RB .... Regular Budget [*United Nations*]
RB .... Relative Bearing [*Navigation*]
RB .... Relay Block　(MSA)
RB .... Religious Broadcasting [*A publication*]
R & B......... Remington and Ballinger's Code [*1910*] [*A publication*]　(DLA)
RB .... Renaut's Bodies [*Neurology*]
R/B .... Renegotiation Board [*Terminated, 1979*] [*Federal government*]
RB .... Renegotiation Bulletins [*A publication*]　(DLA)
RB .... Repeated Back [*Communications*]　(FAAC)
RB .... Report Bibliography
RB .... Request Block
RB .... Rescue Boat　(FAAC)
RB .... Research Bulletin
RB .... Reserve Bank　(ADA)
RB .... Resistance Brazing
RB .... Respiratory Bronchiole [*Medicine*]　(MAE)
RB .... Restiform Body [*Neuroanatomy*]
RB .... Restricted Bulletin
RB .... Retail Business [*A publication*]
Rb.............. Retinoblastoma [*Oncology*]
RB .... Retractable Boom
RB .... Retraining Benefits [*Employment*]　(OICC)
RB.............. Return to Bias
RB .... Revenue Bond [*Investment term*]
RB .... Reverse Blocked
RB .... Revision Block　(MSA)
R & B......... Rhythm and Blues [*Music*]
RB .... Rich Bitch [*Slang*]
R/B .... Rifle Brigade
RB .... Right Border [*Genetics*]
RB .... Right Buttock [*Anatomy*]
RB .... Right Fullback [*Soccer*]
RB .... Rigid Boat
RB .... Rigid Body
Rb.............. Risicobank [*A publication*]
Rb.............. Ritzaus Bureau [*Press agency*] [*Denmark*]
RB .... Road Bend
RB .... Road Buffer　(SAA)

RB .... Roast Beef [*Restaurant slang*]
Rb.............. Rock Bass [*Ichthyology*]
RB .... Rocket Branch　(AAG)
RB .... Rohon-Beard (Cells) [*Neurology*]
RB .... Rollback [*Telecommunications*]　(TEL)
RB .... Rollback Disability Claims [*Social Security
　　Administration*]　(OICC)
RB .... Roller Bearing
RB .... Roman-British
R & B......... Room and Board
RB .... Rose Bengal [*A dye*]
RB .... Round Bobbin [*A publication*]　(EAAP)
RB .... Royal Burgh
RB .... Rubber Band　(ADA)
RB .... Rubber Base [*Technical drawings*]
RB .... Rubber Bearing　(DS)
RB .... Rubber Block　(DNAB)
Rb.............. Rubidium [*Chemical element*]
RB .... Ruble [*Monetary unit*] [*Former USSR*]
RB .... Run Back [*Typography*]
RB .... Running Back [*Football*]
RB .... Rural Bank　(ADA)
RB .... Russell Bodies [*Medicine*]
RB .... Russet-Burbank Potato
RB .... Syrian Arab Airlines [*Syrian Arab Republic*] [*ICAO
　　designator*]　(FAAC)
RBa .... Barrington Public Library, Barrington, RI [*Library symbol*]
　　[*Library of Congress*]　(LCLS)
RBA .... Rabat [*Morocco*] [*Seismograph station code, US Geological
　　Survey*]　(SEIS)
RBA .... Rabat [*Morocco*] [*Airport symbol*]　(OAG)
RBA .... RADAR Beacon Antenna
RBA .... Radial Blanket Assembly [*Nuclear energy*]　(NRCH)
RBA .... Radio Beacon Array
RBA .... Radiobinding Assay [*Analytical chemistry*]
RBA .... Raisin Bargaining Association　(EA)
RBA .... Ranger Battalions Association　(EA)
RBA .... Recovery Beacon Antenna [*NASA*]　(KSC)
RBA .... Reentry Body Assembly
RBA .... Rehoboth Baster Association [*Namibia*]　(PPW)
RBA .... Relative Binding Affinity [*Chemistry*]
RBA .... Relative Byte Address [*Data processing*]　(MCD)
RBA .... Religious Booksellers Association　(EA)
RBA .... Rescue Breathing Apparatus
RBA .... Retail Bakers of America　(EA)
RBA .... Retail, Book, Stationery, and Allied Trades Employees'
　　Association [*A union*] [*British*]
RBA .... Roadside Business Association　(EA)
RBA .... Rose Bengal Antigen　(MAE)
RBA .... Rotary Beam Antenna
RBA .... Rotor Blade Antenna
RBA .... Royal Brunei Airlines　(DS)
RBA .... Royal Society of British Architects
RBA .... Royal Society of British Artists
RBAADT... Ain Shams University. Faculty of Agriculture. Research Bulletin
　　[*A publication*]
RBAAP...... Riverbank Army Ammunition Plant　(AABC)
RBaB.......... Barrington College, Barrington, RI [*Library symbol*] [*Library of
　　Congress*]　(LCLS)
RBAF........ Royal Belgian Air Force
RBAF........ Royal Brunei Armed Forces
RBAL......... Reprocessing Building Analytical Laboratory [*Nuclear
　　energy*]　(NRCH)
RBAM .... Revista. Biblioteca, Archivo, y Museo del Ayuntamiento de
　　Madrid [*A publication*]
RBAMM ... Revista. Biblioteca, Archivo, y Museo del Ayuntamiento de
　　Madrid [*A publication*]
RBAN .... Rainier Bancorporation [*NASDAQ symbol*]　(NQ)
R Banco Republ ... Revista. Banco de la Republica [*A publication*]
RBAP......... Repetitive Bursts of Action Potential [*Electrophysiology*]
RBAUSC... Romanian Baptist Association of United States and Canada
　　[*Inactive*]　(EA)
RBA WWII ... Ranger Battalions Association World War II　(EA)
RBB .... Reference Books Bulletin [*A publication*]
RBB .... Right Bundle Branch [*Cardiology*]　(AAMN)
RBBB .... Right Bundle-Branch Block [*Cardiology*]
RBBS......... Remote Bulletin Board System [*For IBM computers*]
　　[*Telecommunications*]
RBBSB ...... Right Bundle-Branch System Block [*Cardiology*]
RBBT........ Rebabbit
RBBX........ Right Breast Biopsy Examination [*Medicine*]　(AAMN)
RBC .... Radio Beam Communications
RBC .... Radio Bureau of Canada
RBC .... Rail-Borne Crane [*British*]
RBC .... Reactive Bias Circuit　(MCD)
RBC .... Real Estate Brokerage Council　(EA)
RBC .... Red Badge of Courage　(EA)
RBC .... Red Blood Cell [*or Corpuscle*] [*Medicine*]
RBC .... Red Blood Count [*Medicine*]
RBC .... Redundant Battery Charger　(KSC)
RBC .... Regal-Beloit Corp. [*AMEX symbol*]　(SPSG)

RBC .... Regional Blood Center [*Red Cross*]
RBC .... Regulations of British Columbia [*Attorney General's Ministry*] [*No longer available online*] [*Information service or system*]   (CRD)
RBC .... Remote Balance Control
RBC .... Retortable Barrier Container [*For food*]
RBC .... Return Beam Camera
RBC .... Rhodesia Broadcasting Corp.
RBC .... Rio Blanco [*Colorado*] [*Seismograph station code, US Geological Survey*] [*Closed*]   (SEIS)
RBC .... Roller Bearing Corp.   (MCD)
RBC .... Ropec Industries, Inc. [*Vancouver Stock Exchange symbol*]
RBC .... Rotating Beam Ceilometer [*Aviation*]
RBC .... Rotating Biological Contractors [*Processing equipment*]
RBC .... Royal Bank of Canada [*UTLAS symbol*]
RBC .... Royal British Colonial Society of Artists
RBCA .... Rhodes Bantam Class Association   (EA)
RBC-ADA ... Red Blood Cell Adenosine Deaminase [*An enzyme*]   (AAMN)
R du B Can ... Revue. Barreau Canadien [*A publication*]   (DLA)
RBCC........ Reentry Body Coordination Committee
RBCCW ..... Reactor Building Closed Cooling Water [*Nuclear energy*]   (NRCH)
RBC/hpf .... Red Blood Cells per High Power Field [*Hematology*]   (MAE)
RBCM ...... Red Blood Cell Mass [*in circulation*]
RBCM ...... Reference Book of Corporate Managements [*Dun's Marketing Services*] [*Information service or system*]   (CRD)
RBCN .... Rubicon Corp. [*Richardson, TX*] [*NASDAQ symbol*]   (NQ)
RBCNO ..... Rotating Beam Ceilometer Inoperative [*Aviation*]   (FAAC)
RBCO .... Ryan, Beck & Co., Inc. [*West Orange, NJ*] [*NASDAQ symbol*]   (NQ)
RBCPDG ... Canadian Forestry Service. Pacific Forest Research Centre. Report BC-X [*A publication*]
RBCR........ Reprocessing Building Control Room [*Nuclear energy*]   (NRCH)
RBCS .... Radio Beam Communications Set
RBCS .... Reactor Building Cooling System [*Nuclear energy*]   (NRCH)
RBCU .... Reactor Building Cooling Unit [*Nuclear energy*]   (NRCH)
RBCV .... Red Blood Cell Volume [*Hematology*]
RBCWS ..... Reactor Building Cooling Water System   (IEEE)
RBD .... Dallas, TX [*Location identifier*] [*FAA*]   (FAAL)
RBD .... Recurrent Brief Depression [*Psychology*]   (ECON)
RBD .... Refined, Bleached, and Deodorized [*Vegetable oil technology*]
RBD .... Reliable Block Diagram   (MCD)
RBD .... REM [*Rapid Eye Movement*] Behavior Disorder [*Medicine*]
RBD .... Reserve Bank of India. Bulletin [*A publication*]
RBD .... Rice Blast Disease [*Fungal disease of crop plants*]
RBD .... Right Border of Dullness [*Cardiology*]
RBD .... Rubbermaid, Inc. [*NYSE symbol*]   (SPSG)
RBDE .... RADAR Bright Display Equipment [*FAA*]
RBDNRQ .. Received but Did Not Return Questionnaire   (AABC)
RBDP........ Rehoboth Bevryde Demokratiese Party [*Rehoboth Free Democratic Party or Liberation Front*] [*Namibia*] [*Political party*]   (EY)
RBDP........ Rocket Booster Development Program [*Aerospace*]   (AAG)
RBDS........ RADAR Bomb Directing Systems
RBDV .... Raspberry Bushy Dwarf Virus [*Plant pathology*]
RBE .... Bassett, NE [*Location identifier*] [*FAA*]   (FAAL)
RBE .... Radiation Biological Equivalent
RBE .... Red Ball Express [*Military*]
RBE .... Relative Biological Effectiveness [*or Efficiency*] [*of stated types of radiation*]
RBE .... Remote Batch Entry   (CMD)
RBE .... Renabie Mines (1981) Ltd. [*Toronto Stock Exchange symbol*]
RBE .... Replacement Battery Equipment
RBE .... Review of Business and Economic Research [*A publication*]
RBEB........ Ribbon Bridge Erection Boat   (MCD)
RBEC........ Roller Bearing Engineers Committee   (EA)
RBEDT..... Reactor Building Equipment Drain Tank [*Nuclear energy*]   (NRCH)
RB/ER ...... Reduced Blast/Enhanced Radiation
RBER........ Review of Business and Economic Research [*A publication*]
RBESI....... Reactor Building Exhaust System Isolation [*Nuclear energy*]   (NRCH)
RBF .... Radial Basis Function [*Mathematics*]
RBF .... Red Lake Buffalo Resources Ltd. [*Toronto Stock Exchange symbol*]
RBF .... Regional Blood Flow [*Physiology*]
RBF .... Remote Batch Facility
RBF .... Renal Blood Flow [*Medicine*]
RBF .... Retarded Bomb Fuze
RBF .... Roberson, Fred, Louisville KY [*STAC*]
RBFC .... Razzy Bailey Fan Club   (EA)
RBFC .... Retract Before Firing Contractor   (NG)
RBFI .... Richard Barrie Fragrances, Inc. [*NASDAQ symbol*]   (NQ)
RBFPP...... Rocket Booster Fuel Pod Pickup   (MUGU)
RBFT .... Romanian Bank of Foreign Trade   (IMH)
RBG .... British Guiana Reports of Opinions [*A publication*]   (DLA)
RBG .... Ransburg Corp. [*AMEX symbol*]   (SPSG)
RBG .... Right Buccal Ganglion [*Dentistry*]
RBG .... Roseburg, OR [*Location identifier*] [*FAA*]   (FAAL)
RBGd .... Rocznik Biblioteki Gdanskiej Pan [*A publication*]

RBGED3.... Brazilian Journal of Genetics [*A publication*]
RBGM .... Real Beam Ground Map   (MCD)
RBGS .... Radio Beacon Guidance System   (AAG)
RBH .... Regimental Beachhead [*Army*]
RBH .... Royal Bucks Hussars [*British military*]   (DMA)
RBH .... Rutherford Birchard Hayes [*US president, 1822-1893*]
RBHA .... Rotor Blade Homing Antenna
RBHB .... Red and Black Horizontal Bands [*Navigation markers*]
RBHC .... Regional Bell Holding Co.   (BYTE)
RBHGPV... Rheinische Beitraege und Hilfsbuecher zur Germanischen Philologie und Volkskunde [*A publication*]
RBHPC..... Rutherford B. Hayes Presidential Center   (EA)
RBHPF..... Reactor Building Hydrogen Purge Fan   (IEEE)
RBHS .... Reactor Building Heating System [*Nuclear energy*]   (NRCH)
RBI............ Rabi [*Fiji*] [*Airport symbol*]   (OAG)
RBI............ RADAR Blip Identification Message
RBI............ Radio Berlin International
RBI............ Railway Benevolent Institution [*British*]
RBI............ Range Bearing Indicator   (MCD)
RBI............ RB Industries, Inc. [*NYSE symbol*]   (SPSG)
RBI............ Recherches Bibliques [*A publication*]
RBI............ Remote Bus Isolator   (SSD)
RBI............ Reply by Indorsement
RBI............ Reserve Bank of India   (ECON)
RBI............ Ripple-Blanking Input   (IEEE)
RBI............ Root Beer Institute [*Defunct*]
RBI............ Runs Batted In [*Baseball*]
RBIB .... Reserve Bank of India. Bulletin [*Bombay*] [*A publication*]
R Bibl Nac (Cuba) ... Revista. Biblioteca Nacional de Cuba [*A publication*]
RBiCalz...... Revista Biblica. Rafael Calzada [*Argentina*] [*A publication*]   (BJA)
RBIF .... Red Basic Intelligence File   (MCD)
RBIMBZ ... Bio-Mathematics [*A publication*]
RBIN .... R & B, Inc. [*NASDAQ symbol*]   (SPSG)
RBJ .... Rebun [*Japan*] [*Airport symbol*] [*Obsolete*]   (OAG)
RBJ .... Tucson, AZ [*Location identifier*] [*FAA*]   (FAAL)
RBK .... RBK NT Corp. [*Toronto Stock Exchange symbol*]
RBK .... Reebok International Ltd. [*NYSE symbol*]   (SPSG)
RBK .... Right Bank
RBK & C ... Royal Borough of Kensington and Chelsea [*England*]
RBKr .... Rocznik Biblioteki Pan w Krakowie [*A publication*]
R Bk Rel.... Review of Books and Religion [*A publication*]
RBL............ Radiation Biology Laboratory [*Smithsonian Institution*]
RBL............ Range and Bearing Launch [*Navy*]   (CAAL)
RBL............ Rat Basophilic Leukemia [*Cell line*]
RBL............ Reasonable Benefit Limit [*Superannuation*]
RBL............ Rebroadcast Link [*Aerial*]
RBL............ Recommended Buy List
RBL............ Red Bluff, CA [*Location identifier*] [*FAA*]   (FAAL)
RBL............ Reid's Base Line [*Neuroanatomy*]
RBL............ Resource Based Learning   (ADA)
RBL............ Rifled Breech-Loading [*Gun*]
RBL............ Right Buttock Line   (MCD)
RBL............ Rio Blanco Resources Ltd. [*Vancouver Stock Exchange symbol*]
RBL............ Royal British Legion [*British military*]   (DMA)
RBL............ Rubblestone [*Technical drawings*]
RBL............ Ruble [*Monetary unit*] [*Former USSR*]
RBL............ Ruch Biblijny i Liturgiczny   (BJA)
R Black Pol Econ ... Review of Black Political Economy [*A publication*]
R Black Pol Economy ... Review of Black Political Economy [*A publication*]
RBLC......... Renaissance Business and Law Center, Inc. [*Detroit, MI*]   (TSSD)
RBLR........ Red-Banded Leaf Roller [*Entomology*]
RBLS .... River Bend Library System [*Library network*]
RBM .... Range Betting Method
RBM .... Real-Time Batch Monitor [*Xerox Corp.*]
RBM .... Regional Battle Manager [*DoD*]
RBM .... Regional Bone Mass
R-B-M........ Reinforced Brick Masonry
RBM .... Remote Batch Module
RBM .... Resistance to Bending Moment [*Automotive engineering*]
RBM .... Retractor Bulb Motoneuron [*Neurology*]
RBM .... Rifleman's Breaching Munition Program [*Military*]   (INF)
RBM .... Rod-Block Monitor [*Nuclear energy*]   (NRCH)
RBMA .... Radiologists Business Managers Association   (EA)
RBME........ Richard [*Cragun*], Birgit [*Keil*], Marcia [*Haydee*], Egon [*Madsen*] [*In ballet title, "Initials RBME." Refers to the four starring dancers.*]
RBMECAB ... Regional Bureau of the Middle East Committee for the Affairs of the Blind [*An association*]   (EAIO)
RBML....... Rare Books and Manuscripts Librarianship [*A publication*]
RBML....... Repertorium fuer Biblische und Morgenlaendische Litteratur [*Leipzig*] [*A publication*]
RBMR....... Rotating Bubble Membrane Radiator [*Battelle Pacific Northwest Laboratories*]
RBMS........ Rare Books and Manuscripts Section [*Association of College and Research Libraries*]
RBMS........ Remote Bridge Management Software   (HGAA)
RBMT....... Retrospective Bibliographies on Magnetic Tape   (NASA)
RBMU .... Regions Beyond Missionary Union [*Later, Regions Beyond Missionary Union International*]   (EA)

RBMUDD ... Research Bulletin. Marathwada Agricultural University [*A publication*]
RBN .... Brown University, Providence, RI [*OCLC symbol*]   (OCLC)
RBN .... PTS [*Predicasts*] Regional Business News [*Cleveland, OH*] [*Database*] [*Information service or system*]   (IID)
RBN .... Radiobeacon [*Maps and charts*]
RBN .... Random Block Number [*Data processing*]
R B v N .... Rechtskundig Blad voor het Notairs-Ambt [*A publication*]
R Bn .... Red Beacon [*Nautical charts*]
RBN .... Retrobulbar Neuritis [*Medicine*]
RBN .... Ribbon   (MSA)
RBN .... Rybnik [*Poland*] [*Seismograph station code, US Geological Survey*]   (SEIS)
RBNC .... Republic Bancorp, Inc. [*NASDAQ symbol*]   (NQ)
RBNC .... Revista. Biblioteca Nacional de Cuba [*A publication*]
RBNH .... Revista. Biblioteca Nacional de Cuba [*A publication*]
RBNH .... Rockingham Bancorp [*NASDAQ symbol*]   (NQ)
RBNK .... Regent Bancshares Corp. [*NASDAQ symbol*]   (NQ)
RBNZ .... Reserve Bank of New Zealand
RBO .... RBO Royalty [*Associated Press abbreviation*]   (APAG)
RBO .... Relationship by Objective [*Management technique*]
RBO .... Ripple-Blanking Output   (IEEE)
RBO .... Russian Brotherhood Organization of the United States of America
RBOA .... Richardson Boat Owners Association   (EA)
RBOBDY... Bardsey Observatory Report [*A publication*]
RBOC .... Rapid Bloom Offboard Chaff [*Navy ship system*]
RBOC .... Regional Bell Operating Co.
RBOD .... Required Beneficial Occupancy Data   (SAA)
RBOF........ Receiving Basin for Off-Site Fuel [*Nuclear energy*]
RBOK .... Rinderpest Bovine Old Kabete [*A virus*]
R Bolsa Comer Rosario ... Revista. Bolsa de Comercio de Rosario [*A publication*]
RBOT .... Robotics Information [*EIC/Intelligence, Inc.*] [*Information service or system*]   (IID)
R Bot Garden Edinb Notes ... Royal Botanical Garden of Edinburgh. Notes [*A publication*]
R Bot Gard (Kew) Notes Jodrell Lab ... Royal Botanic Gardens (Kew). Notes from the Jodrell Laboratory [*A publication*]
RBOUSA... Russian Brotherhood Organization of the USA   (EA)
RBP........... Raba Raba [*Papua New Guinea*] [*Airport symbol*]   (OAG)
RBP........... Ratio Balance Panel
RBP........... Ration Breakdown Point [*Military*]   (AABC)
RBP........... Reactor Building Protection [*Nuclear energy*]   (NRCH)
RBP........... Registered Business Programmer [*Offered earlier by Data Processing Management Association, now discontinued*]   (IEEE)
RBP........... Retinol-Binding Protein [*Biochemistry*]
RBP........... Retractable Bow Propeller
RBP........... Return Battery Pack   (KSC)
RBP........... Riboflavin-Binding Protein [*Biochemistry*]
RBP........... Ribose Binding Protein [*Biochemistry*]
RBP........... Rocket Branch Panel   (AAG)
RBP........... RUBISCO [*Ribulosebisphosphate Carboxylase/Oxygenase*] Binding Protein [*Biochemistry*]
RBPA........ Royal Bank of Pennsylvania [*NASDAQ symbol*]   (NQ)
RBPC........ Revised Behavior Problem Checklist [*Test*]
RBPCA ...... Rare Breeds Poultry Club of America   (EA)
RBPCase.... Ribulosebisphosphate Carboxylase [*Also, RUBISCO*] [*An enzyme*]
RBPD........ Religious Book Publishing Division [*of Association of American Publishers*] [*Superseded by RPG*]
RBPP .... Rotor Burst Protection Program [*NASA*]
RBPT .... Rose Bengal Plate Test [*Agriculture*]   (OA)
RBQ.......... Rurrenabaque [*Bolivia*] [*Airport symbol*]   (OAG)
RBR .... RADAR Boresight Range   (KSC)
RBR .... Rambler Exploration [*Vancouver Stock Exchange symbol*]
RBR .... Refracted Bottom-Reflected Ray
RBR .... Renegotiation Board Regulation [*or Ruling*]
RBR .... Research Branch [*Naval Technical Training Command*] [*Millington, TN*]
RBR .... Ricerche Bibliche e Religiose [*A publication*]
RBR .... Rio Branco [*Brazil*] [*Airport symbol*]   (OAG)
RBr............ Rogers Free Library, Bristol, RI [*Library symbol*] [*Library of Congress*]   (LCLS)
RBR .... Rotor Blade RADAR
RBR .... Rubber
rbr .... Rubricator [*MARC relator code*] [*Library of Congress*]   (LCCP)
RBRC........ RB Robot Corp. [*NASDAQ symbol*]   (NQ)
RBrHi .... Bristol Historical and Preservation Society, Bristol, RI [*Library symbol*] [*Library of Congress*]   (LCLS)
RBRI......... Reference Book Review Index [*A publication*]
RBRIZED ... Rubberized
RBRRS ...... Rhythm and Blues Rock and Roll Society [*Later, RBRRSI*]   (EA)
RBRRSI..... Rhythm and Blues Rock and Roll Society, Inc.   (EA)
RBrRW...... Roger Williams College, Bristol, RI [*Library symbol*] [*Library of Congress*]   (LCLS)
RBRV........ Resource-Based Relative Value [*Health insurance*]
RBRVS ...... Resource-Based Relative Value Scale [*Medicare*]
RBS........... RADAR Beacon Sequencer

RBS........... RADAR Beacon System
RBS........... RADAR Beam Sharpening
RBS........... RADAR Bomb Scoring
RBS........... RADAR Bombardment System   (NATG)
RBS........... RADAR Bombsight
RBS........... Raise-Bottom-Slightly [*Definition of a gentleman*] [*Slang*] [*British*]   (DI)
RBS........... Random Barrage System [*Military*]
RBs........... Random Blood Sugar [*Medicine*]   (MAE)
RBS........... Rare Books Section [*Association of College and Research Libraries*]
RBS........... Reactor Building Spray [*Nuclear energy*]   (NRCH)
RBS........... Recoverable Booster System
RBS........... Reformer's Book Shelf [*A publication*]
RBS........... Regional Briefing Station
RBS........... Remote Batch System
RBS........... Remote Battle System
RBS........... Research for Better Schools, Inc. [*Department of Education*] [*Philadelphia, PA*]
RBS........... Resources Breakdown Structure [*Data processing*]   (PCM)
RBS........... River Bend Station [*Nuclear energy*]   (NRCH)
RBS........... Roberts, IL [*Location identifier*] [*FAA*]   (FAAL)
RBS........... Royal Ballet School [*British*]   (DI)
RBS........... Royal Bank of Scotland [*NYSE symbol*]   (SPSG)
RBS........... Royal Society of British Sculptors
RBS........... Rutherford Backscattering Spectroscopy
RBSA .... [*Member of the*] Royal Birmingham Society of Artists [*British*]
RBSC .... RADAR Bomb Scoring Central   (NG)
RBSc .... Royal Bank of Scotland Group Ltd. [*Associated Press abbreviation*]   (APAG)
RBSc .... Royal Society of British Sculptors
RBSCD ...... Rare Book and Special Collections Division [*Library of Congress*]
RBSct........ Royal Bank of Scotland Group Ltd. [*Associated Press abbreviation*]   (APAG)
RBSDV ...... Rice Black-Streaked Dwarf Virus [*Plant pathology*]
RBSE .... RADAR Beam Sharpening Element
RBSEBR.... Radiologia [*Madrid*] [*A publication*]
rBSF......... Recombinant B-Cell Stimulatory Factor [*Biochemistry*]
RBSF .... Retail Branch Stores Forum   (EA)
RBSL .... Regensburger Beitrage zur Deutschen Sprach- und Literaturwissenschaft [*A publication*]
RBSN........ Reaction Bonded Silicon Nitride [*Materials science and technology*]
RBSN........ Robeson Industries Corp. [*NASDAQ symbol*]   (NQ)
RBSP .... Religious Books and Serials in Print [*A publication*]
RBSR .... Reprocessing Building (Cable) Spreading Room [*Nuclear energy*]   (NRCH)
RBSRA ...... Red Berkshire Swine Record Association   (EA)
RBSS .... Recoverable Booster Support System
RBST .... Rare Breeds Survival Trust [*British*]
RBST .... Remedial and Basic Skills Training   (OICC)
R & B Supp ... Remington and Ballinger's Code, Supplement [*1913*] [*A publication*]   (DLA)
R v B S V .... Raad van Beroep. Sociale Verzekering [*A publication*]
RBT .... Rabbet [*Technical drawings*]
RBT .... Radial Beam Tube [*Electronics*]
RBT .... Rainbow Trout
RBT .... Random Breath Testing   (ADA)
RBT .... Rational Behavior Therapy
RBT .... Rebate [*Technical drawings*]
RBT .... Rebuilt   (DS)
RBT .... Remote Batch Terminal
RBT .... Resistance Bulb Thermometer
RBT .... Reviews in Biochemical Toxicology [*Elsevier Book Series*] [*A publication*]
RBT .... Ribbon Bridge Transporter   (MCD)
RBT .... Ringback Tone [*Telecommunications*]   (TEL)
RBT .... Rough Blanking Template   (MCD)
RBT .... Rubber Tile [*Technical drawings*]
RBT .... Rutland Biotech Ltd. [*Vancouver Stock Exchange symbol*]
RBTA........ Road Builders Training Association   (EA)
RbtCec .... Robertson-Ceco Corp. [*Associated Press abbreviation*]   (APAG)
RBTE........ Replacement Battery Terminal Equipment
RbtHlf........ Robert Half International, Inc. [*Associated Press abbreviation*]   (APAG)
RBTL........ RADAR Beacon Tracking Level [*FAA*]
RBTS .... Rider Block Tagline System [*Military*]   (CAAL)
RBTWT .... Radial Beam Traveling Wave Tube [*Electronics*]
RBU .... Red Butte Canyon [*Utah*] [*Seismograph station code, US Geological Survey*]   (SEIS)
Rbu........... Ribulose [*Biochemistry*]
RB Ue .... Revidierte Berner Uebereinkunft [*A publication*]
RBUPC...... Research in British Universities, Polytechnics, and Colleges [*Formerly, SRBUC*] [*British Library*]
R Bus & Econ Res ... Review of Business and Economic Research [*A publication*]
R Bus and Econ Research ... Review of Business and Economic Research [*A publication*]
R Bus St John's Univ ... Review of Business. St. John's University [*A publication*]

RBV	Reactor Building Vent (IEEE)
RBV	Relative Biological Value [*Food science*]
RBV	Return Beam Vidicon [*Satellite camera*]
RBV	Robbinsville, NJ [*Location identifier*] [*FAA*] (FAAL)
RBVC	Return Beam Vidicon Camera
RBVI	Reactor Building Ventilation Isolation [*Nuclear energy*] (NRCH)
RBVPRM ..	Reactor Building Vent Process Radiation Monitor [*Nuclear energy*] (NRCH)
RBW	RB & W Corp. [*Associated Press abbreviation*] (APAG)
RBW	RB & W Corp. [*Formerly, Russell, Burdsaw & Ward Corp.*] [*AMEX symbol*] (SPSG)
RBW	Walterboro, SC [*Location identifier*] [*FAA*] (FAAL)
RBWCD9 ..	Washington State University. Agricultural Research Center. Research Bulletin [*A publication*]
RBX	Manteo, NC [*Location identifier*] [*FAA*] (FAAL)
Rby	Ribitol [*or Ribityl*] [*Biochemistry*]
RBY	Rotterdam Europoort Delta [*A publication*]
RBY	Royal Bucks Yeomanry [*British military*] (DMA)
RBY	Ruby [*Alaska*] [*Airport symbol*] (OAG)
RBY	Ruby Resources Ltd. [*Vancouver Stock Exchange symbol*]
RBYC	Royal Berkshire Yeomanry Cavalry [*British*] (ROG)
RBYOA	Rinsho Byori [*A publication*]
RBZ	Rabat Zaers [*Morocco*] [*Seismograph station code, US Geological Survey*] (SEIS)
RBZ	Rotterdam [*A publication*]
RBZ	Rubidazone [*An antibiotic*]
RC	Circular Radio Beacon
RC	Congregation de Notre Dame de la Retraite au Cenacle [*Congregation of Our Lady of the Retreat in the Cenacle*] (EAIO)
RC	Congregation of Our Lady of the Retreat in the Cenacle [*Roman Catholic women's religious order*] [*Italy*]
RC	Cuba [*IYRU nationality code*] (IYR)
RC	[*The*] Item Requested Has Been Rescinded. All Stock Has Been Destroyed. Copies Are Not Available [*Advice of supply action code*] [*Army*]
RC	Missouri Revised Statutes [*1855*] [*A publication*] (DLA)
RC	Nicholl, Hare, and Carrow's Railway Cases [*1835-55*] [*A publication*] (DLA)
RC	Nondirectional Radio Beacon [*ITU designation*] (CET)
RC	RADAR Computer (MCD)
RC	RADAR Control (DEN)
RC	Radio Car [*British*]
RC	Radio Code Aptitude Area [*Military*]
R/C	Radio Command [*or Control*] (KSC)
RC	Radio Compass
R/C	Radio Control [*British military*] (DMA)
RC	Radix Complement [*Mathematics*]
R & C	Rail and Canal
RC	Railway Cases [*A publication*] (DLA)
RC	Rainbow Coalition [*Named for the 1984 political campaign of Rev. Jesse Jackson*] [*Later, NRCI*] (EA)
RC	Rainform Compressed (MCD)
R/C	Range Clearance [*NASA*] (KSC)
RC	Range Command [*NASA*] (NASA)
RC	Range Contractor [*NASA*] (KSC)
RC	Range Control [*NASA*] (KSC)
RC	Range Correction
RC	Rapid Change (MCD)
RC	Rapid Curing [*Asphalt grade*]
RC	Rate Center [*Telecommunications*] (TEL)
RC	Rate of Change
R/C	Rate of Climb [*Aviation*]
RC	Rate Command
R/C	Ratio Command (MCD)
RC	Ray Control
RC	Rayon and Cotton [*Freight*]
RC	Reaction Center
RC	Reaction Chamber
RC	Reaction Control
RC	Reactor Cavity [*Nuclear energy*] (NRCH)
RC	Reactor Compartment (MSA)
RC	Reactor Coolant [*Nuclear energy*] (NRCH)
RC	Read and Compute
RC	Reader Code
RC	Ready Calendar
RC	Real Circuit
RC	Rear Commodore [*Navy*] (NVT)
RC	Rear Connection (MSA)
RC	Rearwin Club (EA)
R & C	Reasonable and Customary [*Refers to medical charges*] [*Insurance*]
RC	Receipt
RC	Receiver Card
RC	Reception Center [*Army*]
RC	Receptor-Chemoeffector [*Biochemistry*]
RC	Recirculating Cooler
RC	Recirculatory Air (AAG)
RC	Recognition Context [*Data processing*] (PCM)
RC	Reconnaissance Car [*British*]
R/C	Reconsign
RC	Reconstruction Committee [*British*] [*World War II*]
RC	Record Change [*or Changer*] (AAG)
RC	Record Commissioners [*British*] (DLA)
RC	Record Count [*Data processing*]
RC	Recording Completing [*Trunk*] [*Telecommunications*] (TEL)
RC	Recording Controller [*Nuclear energy*] (NRCH)
RC	Records Check (AFM)
RC	Records Communication Program [*Army*]
R & C	Records and Control
R/C	Recovered
RC	Recovery Code
RC	Recovery Controller [*NASA*] (MCD)
R/C	Recredited
RC	Recruiting Center
RC	Recurring Cost (NASA)
RC	Red Cell [*or Corpuscle*] [*Hematology*]
RC	Red Cell Cast [*Hematology*] (MAE)
RC	Red China
RC	Red Cross
RC	Reduced Capability (MCD)
RC	Reduced Cuing
RC	Reels [*JETDS nomenclature*] [*Military*] (CET)
RC	Reference Cavity
RC	Reference Clock [*Telecommunications*] (TEL)
RC	Reference Configuration (SSD)
RC	Referred Care [*Medicine*]
RC	Reformed Church
RC	Refrigerated Centrifuge
RC	Regiment of Cavalry [*British military*] (DMA)
RC	Regional Center
RC	Regional Commandant [*Air Force*] [*British*]
RC	Regional Commissioner [*Social Security Administration*]
RC	Regional Council
RC	Register Containing (SAA)
RC	Register of Copyrights [*US*]
RC	Registered Check
RC	Registered Criminologist
RC	Registration Cases [*A publication*] (DLA)
RC	Regulatory-Catalytic Unit [*Physiology*]
RC	Regulatory Council [*FAA*] (MCD)
RC	Rehabilitation Center
RC	Rehabilitation Counselor
RC	Reinforced Concrete [*Technical drawings*]
RC	Rekishi Chiri [*A publication*]
RC	Relative [*Force*] Cost (MCD)
RC	Relative Covariance [*Statistics*]
RC	Relay Computer (BUR)
RC	Release Card
RC	Release Clause [*Real estate*]
RC	Relief Claim
R & C	Religion y Cultura [*A publication*]
R & C	Religioni e Civitia [*A publication*]
RC	Remington's Code [*A publication*] (DLA)
RC	Remote Component
RC	Remote Computer
RC	Remote Concentrator
R/C	Remote Control
RC	Rent Charge
RC	Reopened Claim [*Unemployment insurance*] (OICC)
RC	Reorder Cycle
RC	Repair Costs [*Technical drawings*]
RC	Replacement Cost [*Insurance*]
RC	Replication Controller [*Data processing*]
RC	Reply Coupon [*Advertising*]
RC	Report of Contact [*Social Security Administration*] (OICC)
RC	Republic Airlines, Inc. [*ICAO designator*] (FAAC)
RC	Republic of China (CDAI)
R/C	Request for Checkage [*Navy*]
R & C	Requirements and Configuration
RC	Requirements Contract
RC	Rescriptum [*Counterpart*] [*Latin*]
RC	Research Center (IEEE)
RC	Research-Cottrell, Inc. [*NYSE symbol*] (SPSG)
RC	Reserve Components [*Military*]
RC	Reserve Corps
RC	Reserve Currency
RC	Resin Coated (MCD)
RC	Resistance-Capacitance
RC	Resistance Coupled
R-C	Resistor-Capacitor
RC	Resolver Control
RC	Resource Capital International Ltd. [*Toronto Stock Exchange symbol*]
RC	Resources Council (EA)
RC	Respiration Ceased [*Medicine*]
RC	Respiratory Care [*A publication*]
RC	Respiratory Care [*Medicine*]
RC	Respiratory Center [*Medicine*]
RC	Responsibility Center [*Air Force*] (AFM)
RC	Rest Camp

R & C .... Rest and Convalescence (ADA)
RC .... Rest Cure
RC .... Restrictive Cardiomyopathy [Cardiology]
RC .... Retail Consortium [British]
RC .... Retention Catheter [Medicine]
RC .... Retrograde Cystogram [Medicine] (MAE)
r/c .... Return Cargo [Shipping] (DS)
RC .... Revenue Canada
RC .... Revenue Cutter [Coast Guard]
RC .... Reverse Course [Aviation]
RC .... Reverse Current
RC .... Reversing Gear Clutch (DS)
RC .... Review of the Churches [A publication]
R & C .... Review and Comment [Aerospace]
RC .... Review Cycle [Military] (AFIT)
RC .... Revised Code
RC .... Revue Critique de Legislation et de Jurisprudence de Canada [A
                  publication] (DLA)
RC .... Rib Cage [Anatomy]
RC .... Ribbon-Frame Camera (MUGU)
RC .... Richard of Cashel [Pseudonym used by Richard Laurence]
RC .... Rider Club [Commercial firm] (EA)
RC .... Right Center [A stage direction]
RC .... Right Center [Position in soccer, hockey]
RC .... Right Chest [Medicine]
RC .... Ring Counter
RC .... Risk Capital [Finance]
RC .... Road Reconnaissance (FAAC)
RC .... Robert & Carriere [France] [Research code symbol]
R & C .... Rod and Custom [A publication]
RC .... Roll Center [Automotive engineering]
RC .... Roll Channel
RC .... Roller Chock [Shipfitting]
RC .... Roller Coating
RC .... Rolling Chassis [Automotive engineering]
RC .... Rolls Court [Legal] [British]
RC .... ROM [Rough Order of Magnitude] Control
RC .... Roman Catholic
RC .... Root Canal [Dentistry]
rc .... Root Cast [Archaeology]
RC .... Rosin Core [Foundry technology]
RC .... Rosslyn Connecting Railroad Co. [AAR code]
RC .... Rotary Combustion [Automobile]
RC .... Rotation Control (NASA)
RC .... Rough Cast (ADA)
RC .... Rough Cutting [Construction]
RC .... Round Corners [Bookselling]
RC .... Rounding Control [Computer programming] (BYTE)
R/C .... Routing and Clipping (MCD)
RC .... Royal Commission [British]
RC .... Royal Correspondence in the Hellenistic Period [A publication]
RC .... Royal Crest [British]
RC .... Royal Crown [Soft drink brand]
R/C .... Rubber-Capped
RC .... Rudder Club (EA)
RC .... Rules Committee [House of Representatives] (OICC)
RC .... Ruling Cases [A publication] (DLA)
RC .... Ruperto-Carola [A publication]
RC .... Rural Coalition (EA)
RC .... Rural Construction
RC .... Rushlight Club (EA)
R & C .... Russell and Chesley's Nova Scotia Equity Reports [A
                  publication] (DLA)
R & C .... Russell and Chesley's Nova Scotia Reports [A
                  publication] (DLA)
RCA .... Rabbinical Council of America (EA)
RCA .... RADAR Controlled Approach (NVT)
RCA .... Radiative-Convective-Atmospheric [Meteorology]
RCA .... Radio Club of America (EA)
RCA .... Radio Collectors of America (EA)
RCA .... Radio Corp. of America (NASA)
RCA .... Radiological Control Area (MCD)
RCA .... Rapid City, SD [Location identifier] [FAA] (FAAL)
RCA .... Rate Change Authorization (NVT)
RCA .... Ration Cash Allowance [British military] (DMA)
RCA .... Reach Cruising Altitude [Aviation] (FAAC)
RCA .... Reaction Control Assembly
RCA .... Red Cell Aggregate [or Aggregation] [Hematology]
RCA .... Red Cross Act
RCA .... Reformed Church in America (ROG)
RCA .... Refugee Cash Assistance [Office of Refugee Resettlement]
                  [Department of Health and Human Services] (GFGA)
RCA .... Regulator of Complement Activation [Biochemistry]
RCA .... Remote Control Amplifier (MCD)
RCA .... Renault Club of America (EA)
RCA .... REO [Rawson E. Olds] Club of America (EA)
RCA .... Replacement Cost Accounting (ADA)
RCA .... Republican Communications Association (EA)
RCA .... Request for Corrective Action (AAG)
RCA .... Resident Care Aide
RCA .... Residential Care Alternatives

RCA .... Residential Care Association [British]
RCA .... Review and Concurrence Authority
RCA .... Ricinus communis Agglutinin [Immunology]
RCA .... Right Coronary Artery [Anatomy]
RCA .... Riot Control Agent (NVT)
RCA .... Rocket Cruising Association (EA)
RCA .... Rodeo Cowboys Association [Later, PRCA] (EA)
RCA .... Root Canal Anterior [Dentistry]
RCA .... Root Cause Analysis (MCD)
RCA .... Royal Cambrian Academy [British]
RCA .... Royal Cambrian Academy of Art [British]
RCA .... Royal Canadian Academy
RCA .... Royal Canadian Academy of Arts
RCA .... Royal Canadian Army (MCD)
RCA .... Royal Canadian Artillery
RCA .... Royal College of Art [British]
RCA .... Royal Co. of Archers [British] (DI)
RCA .... Ruger Collectors Association (EA)
RCA .... Soil and Water Resources Conservation Act [1977]
R-19/CA .... Rhodes 19 Class Association (EA)
RCAA .... Rocket City Astronomical Association [Later, VBAS] (EA)
RCAB........ Review and Concurrence Advisory Board
RCAC .... Radio Corp. of America Communications (MCD)
RCAC .... Remote Computer Access Communications Service
RCAC .... Reserve Component Assistance Coordinator (MCD)
RCAC .... Royal Canadian Armoured Corps
Rc Accad Lincei Cl di Sci Mor Stor Fil ... Rendiconti. Accademia Nazionale
                  dei Lincei. Classe di Scienze Morali. Storiche e Filologiche
                  [A publication]
RCACS ...... USREDCOM [United States Readiness Command] Command
                  and Control System (AABC)
RCADI....... Recueil des Cours. Academie de Droit International de La Haye
                  [A publication]
RCADV ..... Reverse Course and Advise [Aviation] (FAAC)
RCAE........ Royal Correspondence of the Assyrian Empire [A
                  publication] (BJA)
RCAEB...... RCA [Radio Corp. of America] Engineer [A publication]
RCA Eng.... RCA [Radio Corp. of America] Engineer [A publication]
RCAF........ Rail Cost Adjustment Factor [Interstate Commerce
                  Commission]
RCAF........ Royal Canadian Air Force
RCAFA...... Royal Canadian Air Force Association
RCAF(WD) ... Royal Canadian Air Force, Women's Division
RCAG .... Remote Center Air/Ground Facility [NASA]
RCAG .... Remote-Controlled Air-Ground Communication Site (MCD)
RCAG .... Replacement Carrier Air Group [Military] (AFIT)
RCAI........ Railroadiana Collectors Association Inc. (EA)
RCAJ........ Royal Central Asian Society. Journal [A publication]
R/CAL....... Resistance Calibration (MCD)
RCALT ...... Reach Cruising Altitude [Aviation] (FAAC)
RCamA ...... [Member of the] Royal Cambrian Academy [Formerly, RCA]
                  [British]
RCAMC..... Royal Canadian Army Medical Corps
RCAN .... Recorded Announcement [Telecommunications] (TEL)
R & Can Cas ... Railway and Canal Cases [England] [A publication] (DLA)
R Can Dent Corps Q ... Royal Canadian Dental Corps. Quarterly [A
                  publication]
R & Can Tr ... Railway and Canal Traffic Cases [England] [A
                  publication] (DLA)
R & Can Tr Cas ... Railway and Canal Traffic Cases [England] [A
                  publication] (DLA)
RCAP........ Rural Community Assistance Program (EA)
RCAPC...... Royal Canadian Army Pay Corps
RCAPDR... Revolutionary Council of the Algerian People's Democratic
                  Republic
RCAPS ..... Roosevelt Center for American Policy Studies (EA)
RCA R....... RCA [Radio Corp. of America] Review [A publication]
RCAR .... Religious Coalition for Abortion Rights (EA)
RCARC...... RCA [Radio Corp. of America] Review [A publication]
RCA Rev .... RCA [Radio Corp. of America] Review [A publication]
RCAS........ Journal. Royal Central Asian Society [A publication]
RCAS........ Requirements for Close Air Support [Army] (MCD)
RCAS........ Research Center for Advanced Study [University of Texas at
                  Arlington] [Research center]
RCAS........ Reserve Component Automation System [DoD]
RCAS........ Royal Central Asian Society [British]
RCASC...... Royal Canadian Army Service Corps
RCAT........ Radio Code Aptitude Test
RCAT........ Radio-Controlled Aerial Target [Military]
RCAT........ Remote-Controlled Aerial Target (NATG)
RCAT........ Ridgetown College of Agricultural Technology [Canada] (ARC)
RCA Tech Not ... RCA [Radio Corp. of America] Technical Notes [A
                  publication]
RCA Tech Notes ... RCA [Radio Corp. of America] Technical Notes [A
                  publication]
RCAV .... Rozpravy Ceskoslovenske Akademie Ved [A publication]
RCAVA...... Rozpravy Ceskoslovenske Akademie Ved. Rada
                  Matematickych a Prirodnich Ved [A publication]
RCAY .... Gangshan [China] [ICAO location identifier] (ICLI)
RCB .... Radiation Control Board (AAG)
RCB .... Randomized Complete Block [Statistical design]

RCB	Reactor Containment Building [*Nuclear energy*] (NRCH)
RCB	Ready Crew Building (NATG)
RCB	Reflection Coefficient Bridge
RCB	Region Control Block [*Data processing*] (BUR)
RCB	Regular Commissions Board [*British military*] (DMA)
RCB	Regulations of the Civil Aeronautics Board
RCB	Releases Control Branch [*Edison, NJ*] [*Environmental Protection Agency*] (GRD)
RCB	Remote Circuit Breaker (MCD)
RCB	Remote Control Bandwidth
RCB	Representative Church Body [*Ireland*] [*Church of England*]
RCB	Requirements Control Board (MCD)
RCB	Resource Control Block [*Data processing*] (IBMDP)
RCB	Richards Bay [*South Africa*] [*Airport symbol*] (OAG)
RCB	Right Cornerback [*Football*]
RCB	Root Canal Bicuspid [*Dentistry*]
RCB	Rubber Control Board
RCBA........	Ratio Changers and Boosters Assembly (MCD)
RCBA........	Relative Basal Area of Conifer Species [*Ecology*]
RCBA........	Royal Crown Bottlers Association (EA)
RCBC........	Red Cross Blood Center
rCBF	Regional Cerebral Blood Flow [*Medicine*]
RCBHT	Reactor Coolant Bleed Holdup Tank [*Nuclear energy*] (NRCH)
RCBI.........	Brown [*Robert C.*] & Co., Inc. [*NASDAQ symbol*] (NQ)
RCBOA	Radiologia Clinica et Biologica [*A publication*]
RCBPEJ	Reviews in Clinical and Basic Pharmacology [*A publication*]
RCBR........	Rotating Catalytic Basket Reactor [*Chemical engineering*]
RCBS	Jinmen [*China*] [*ICAO location identifier*] (ICLI)
RCBT........	Reactor Coolant Bleed Tank [*Nuclear energy*] (NRCH)
RCBV........	Regional Cerebral Blood Volume [*Medicine*] (MAE)
RCBW	Radiological-Chemical-Biological Warfare
RCC	Belleville, IL [*Location identifier*] [*FAA*] (FAAL)
RCC	International Society of Reply Coupon Collectors (EA)
RCC	Rachel Carson Council (EA)
RCC	Rack Clearance Center [*Association of American Publishers*]
RCC	RADAR Control Clouds
RCC	RADAR Control Computer (MCD)
RCC	RADAR Control Console [*Military*] (CAAL)
RCC	Radiation Coordinating Council [*Environmental Protection Agency*] (GFGA)
RCC	Radio Common Carrier
RCC	Radio Common Channels
RCC	Radio Communications Center
RCC	Radiochemical Centre [*United Kingdom*] (NRCH)
RCC	Radiological Control Center [*Army*]
RCC	Rag Chewers' Club [*Amateur radio*]
R & CC......	Railway and Canal Cases [*1835-54*] [*A publication*] (DLA)
RCC	Range Commanders Council [*White Sands Missile Range*] (KSC)
RCC	Range Communications Component (MCD)
RCC	Range Control Center [*NASA*]
RCC	Rape Crisis Center (EA)
RCC	Ratio of Charges to Costs
RCC	RCA Corp. Communications
RCC	Re Capital Corp. [*AMEX symbol*] (SPSG)
RCC	Reaction Control Center (KSC)
RCC	Reactor Closed Cooling [*Nuclear energy*] (NRCH)
RCC	Read Channel Continue
RCC	Reader Common Contact
RCC	Real-Time Computer Complex
RCC	Recco Corp. [*Vancouver Stock Exchange symbol*]
RCC	Receptor-Chemoeffector Complex [*Biochemistry*]
RCC	Record Collectors' Club (EA)
R & CC......	Recorder and Communications Control (NASA)
RCC	Recovery Control Center
RCC	Rectangular Concrete Columns [*Jacys Computing Services*] [*Software package*] (NCC)
RCC	Red Carpet Clubs [*United Airlines' club for frequent flyers*] (EA)
RCC	Red Cell Count [*Hematology*] (MAE)
RCC	Red Cross of Constantine (EA)
RCC	Reduced Crude Conversion [*Petroleum refining*]
RCC	Regional Census Center [*Bureau of the Census*] (GFGA)
RCC	Regional Control Center [*North American Air Defense*] (FAAC)
RCC	Regional Coordination Committee [*Department of Health and Human Services*]
RCC	Reinforced Carbon-Carbon (MCD)
RCC	Relative Casein Content [*Food analysis*]
RCC	Remote Center Compliance [*Data processing*]
RCC	Remote Combat Center (SAA)
RCC	Remote Communications Central
RCC	Remote Communications Complex
RCC	Remote Communications Concentrator
RCC	Remote Communications Console
RCC	Remote Computer Center (MCD)
RCC	Remote Control Complex (SAA)
RCC	Renal Cell Carcinoma [*Medicine*]
RCC	Representative Church Council [*Episcopalian*]
RCC	Rescue Control Center
RCC	Rescue Coordination Center [*Coast Guard*]

RCC	Rescue Crew Commander (AFM)
RCC	Research Computing Center [*University of New Hampshire*] [*Research center*] (RCD)
RCC	Reset Control Circuit
RCC	Resistance-Capacitance Coupling (DNAB)
RCC	Resistor Color Code (DEN)
RCC	Resource Category Code [*Military*] (CAAL)
RCC	Resource Control Center [*Military*] (AFIT)
RCC	Resources for Community Change [*Defunct*] (EA)
RCC	Reusable Carbon-Carbon (MCD)
RCC	Rio Carpintero [*Cuba*] [*Seismograph station code, US Geological Survey*] (SEIS)
R & CC......	Riot and Civil Commotion
RCC	Riverside City College [*California*]
RCC	Robotic Command Center [*Army*]
RCC	Rochester Community College, Rochester, MN [*OCLC symbol*] (OCLC)
RCC	Rockefeller Center Cable
RCC	Rocket Combustion Chamber (SAA)
RCC	Rod Cluster Control [*Nuclear energy*] (NRCH)
RCC	Roller-Compacted Concrete
RCC	Roman Catholic Church
RCC	Roman Catholic Church Curate (ROG)
RCC	Rough Combustion Cutoff [*NASA*]
RCC	Rubber Covered Cable (MSA)
RCC	Rural Construction Cadre [*Military*]
RCC	Russian Corps Combatants (EA)
RCCA	Race Car Club of America [*An association*]
R & C Ca...	Railway and Canal Cases [*England*] [*A publication*] (DLA)
RCCA	Record Carrier Competition Act [*1981*]
RCCA	Recovery Control Center, Atlantic (DNAB)
RCCA	Rickenbacker Car Club of America (EA)
RCCA	Rod Cluster Control Assembly [*Nuclear energy*] (NRCH)
RCCA	Rogers Cablesystems of America, Inc. [*NASDAQ symbol*] (NQ)
RCCA	Rough Combustion Cutoff Assembly [*NASA*] (KSC)
RCCA	Route Capacity Control Airline (DS)
R & C Cas .	Railway and Canal Cases [*England*] [*A publication*] (DLA)
RCCB........	Remote Control Circuit Breaker (NASA)
RCCC........	Range Communications Control Center [*Military*] (MCD)
RCCC........	Regional Communications Control Center [*FAA*] (FAAC)
RCCC........	Regular Common Carrier Conference (EA)
RCCC........	Reserve Component Career Counselor [*Military*] (AABC)
RCCC........	Reserve Component Coordination Council (MCD)
RC/CC.......	Responsibility Center/Cost Center [*Military*] (AFIT)
RCCC........	Return Critical Control Circuit
RCCC........	Royal Caledonia Curling Club
RCCC........	Royal Commission on Corporate Concentration [*Canada*]
RCCC........	Royal Curling Club of Canada
RC/CCI	Resource Code/Cost Category Input (SAA)
RCCDF......	Remote Control Center Development Facility (SSD)
RCCE........	Regional Congress of Construction Employers (EA)
RC-CE	Revenue Canada, Customs and Excise
RCCE........	Rotating Cylinder-Collector Electrode [*Electrochemistry*]
RCCES	Research Centre for Canadian Ethnic Studies [*University of Calgary*] [*Research center*] (RCD)
RCCF........	Reserve Components Contingency Force [*Military*]
RCCh	Roman Catholic Chaplain [*Navy*] [*British*]
RCCH	Roman Catholic Church
RCCL........	Royal Caribbean Cruise Line
RCCLS	Resource Center for Consumers of Legal Services [*Later, NRCCLS*] (EA)
RCCM	Research Council for Complementary Medicine [*British*] (IRUK)
RCC/MG...	Range Commanders Council Meteorological Group [*White Sands Missile Range*]
RCCO........	RADAR Control Console Operator [*Military*] (CAAL)
RCCOL......	Reinforced Concrete Column [*Camutek*] [*Software package*] (NCC)
RCCOW	Return Channel Control Orderwire [*Military*] (CAAL)
RCCP........	Recorder and Communications Control Panel (NASA)
RCCP........	Recovery Control Center, Pacific (DNAB)
RCCP........	Reinforced Concrete Culvert Pipe [*Technical drawings*]
RCCPDS ...	Reserve Component Common Personnel Data System [*Marine Corps*] (GFGA)
RCCPLD ...	Resistance-Capacitance Coupled
RC & CR....	Revenue, Civil, and Criminal Reporter [*Calcutta*] [*A publication*] (DLA)
RCCRA......	Rough Combustion Cutoff Replaceable Assembly [*NASA*] (KSC)
RCCS........	Rate Command Control System (AAG)
RCCS........	Reactor Cavity Cooling System [*Nuclear energy*]
RCCS........	Remote Communicatios Central Set (SAA)
RCC & S	Riots, Civil Commotions, and Strikes [*Insurance*]
RCCS........	Royal Canadian Corps of Signals
RCC/TG....	Range Commanders Council Telemetry Group [*White Sands Missile Range, NM*]
RCCUS......	Republican Citizens Committee of the United States (EA)
RCCV........	Red Clover Cryptic Virus [*Plant pathology*]
RCD	RADAR Cloud Detection Report [*Meteorology*] (FAAC)

RCD .... Rapid City [*South Dakota*] [*Seismograph station code, US Geological Survey*]   (SEIS)
RCD .... Rassemblement Constitutionnel Democratique [*Tunisia*] [*Political party*]   (ECON)
RCD .... Rassemblement pour la Culture et la Democratie [*Algeria*] [*Political party*]   (EY)
RCD .... Received
RCD .... Receiver-Carrier Detector
RCD .... Reconnaissance Cockpit Display
RCD .... Record
RCD .... Redox Chemiluminescence Detector [*Instrumentation*] [*Sievers*]
RCD .... Reduced Crude Desulfurization [*Petroleum refining*]
RCD .... Reference Configuration Description   (SSD)
RCD .... Regent's Canal Dock [*British*]
RCD .... Reinforcement Control Depot [*Air Force*]
RCD .... Relative Cardiac Dullness [*Medicine*]
RCD .... Research and Acquisition Communications Division [*Military*]
RCD .... Research Centers Directory [*A publication*]
RCD .... Residual Current Device [*Electrical circuits*]
RC & D ...... Resource Conservation and Development [*Department of Agriculture*]
RCD .... Retrofit Configuration Drawing   (MCD)
RCD .... Reverse Circulation Drilling [*Mining technology*]
RCD .... Reverse Current Device [*Electronics*]   (MSA)
RCD .... Rock Coring Device
RCD .... Rocket Cushioning Device   (NG)
RCD .... Route Control Digit [*Telecommunications*]   (TEL)
RCD .... Royal Canadian Dragoons [*Military*]
RCD .... Rural Civil Defense
RCD .... Sisters of Our Lady of Christian Doctrine [*Roman Catholic religious order*]
RCDA .... Religion in Communist Dominated Areas [*A publication*]
RCDA .... Research Career Development Awards [*Department of Health and Human Services*]
RCDC .... Pingdong (South) [*China*] [*ICAO location identifier*]   (ICLI)
RCDC .... RADAR Course-Directing Central [*Military*]
RCDC .... RADAR Course-Directing Control   (MUGU)
RCDC .... Radiation Chemistry Data Center [*Notre Dame, IN*] [*Department of Commerce*]
RCDC .... Ross Cosmetics Distribution Centers, Inc. [*NASDAQ symbol*]   (NQ)
RCDC .... Royal Canadian Dental Corps
RCDCB..... Regional Civil Defense Coordination Boards [*DoD*]   (AABC)
RCDD........ Registered Communications Distribution Designer [*Designation awarded by Building Industry Consulting Service International*]   (TSSD)
RCDEP...... Rural Civil Defense Education Program
RCDG........ Recording   (MSA)
RCDHS ..... Rehabilitation and Chronic Disease Hospital Section [*American Hospital Association*]   (EA)
RCDI .... Longtan [*China*] [*ICAO location identifier*]   (ICLI)
RCDIW...... Royal Commission on the Distribution of Income and Wealth [*British*]
RCDMB .... Regional Civil and Defense Mobilization Boards
RCDMS..... Reliability Central Data Management System [*Air Force*]   (DIT)
RCDNA ..... RADAR Cloud Detection Report Not Available [*Meteorology*]   (FAAC)
RCDNE ..... RADAR Cloud Detection Report No Echoes Observed [*Meteorology*]   (FAAC)
RCDNO..... RADAR Cloud Detector Inoperative Due to Breakdown Until [*Followed by time*] [*Meteorology*]   (FAAC)
RCDO........ Regional Case Development Officer [*Environmental Protection Agency*]   (GFGA)
RCDOM.... RADAR Cloud Detector Inoperative Due to Maintenance Until [*Followed by time*] [*Meteorology*]   (FAAC)
RCDP........ Record Parallel   (MCD)
RCDR .... Recorder   (KSC)
RCDS........ Records
RCDS........ Royal College of Defence Studies [*British*]
RCDS........ Rural Community Development Service [*Abolished, 1970*] [*Department of Agriculture*]
RCDT .... Reactor Coolant Drain Tank [*Nuclear energy*]   (NRCH)
RCE .... Radio Communications Equipment
RCE .... Railway Construction Engineer [*British military*]   (DMA)
RCE .... Rapid Changing Environment   (AAG)
RCE .... Rapid Circuit Etch
RC de l'E.... Rapports de la Cour de l'Echiquier [*Exchequer Court Reports*] [*Canada*] [*A publication*]   (DLA)
RCE .... Reaction Control Engine
RCE .... Reactor Compatibility Experiment [*Nuclear energy*]   (NRCH)
rce.............. Recording Engineer [*MARC relator code*] [*Library of Congress*]   (LCCP)
RCE .... Reece Corp. [*NYSE symbol*]   (SPSG)
RCE .... Reentry Control Electronics
RCE .... Reliability Control Engineering   (AAG)
RCE .... Religious of Christian Education [*Roman Catholic women's religious order*]
RCE .... Remote Control Equipment   (DIT)

RCE .... Repertoire Canadien sur l'Education [*See also CEI*] [*A publication*]
RCE .... Reviews in Cancer Epidemiology [*Elsevier Book Series*] [*A publication*]
RCE .... Rice University, Fondren Library, Houston, TX [*OCLC symbol*]   (OCLC)
RCE .... Roche Harbor [*Washington*] [*Airport symbol*]   (OAG)
RCE .... Ross Consumer Electronics [*British*]
RCE .... Royal Canadian Engineers
RCE .... Union Restaurants Collectifs Europeens [*European Catering Association*]   (EAIO)
RCEA........ Recreational Coach and Equipment Association [*Later, MHI*]
RCEA........ Research Council Employees' Association [*Canada*]
RCEAC...... Regional Civil Emergency Advisory Committee [*Formerly, JRCC*] [*Civil defense*]
RCEE........ Revista. Centro de Estudios Extemoenos [*A publication*]
RCEEA...... Radio Communications and Electronic Engineers Association
RCEI........ Range Communications Electronics Instructions [*NASA*]   (KSC)
RCEME.... Royal Canadian Electrical and Mechanical Engineers
RCEP........ Royal Commission on Environmental Pollution [*British*]
RCEP........ Rural Concentrated Employment Program [*Department of Labor*]
RCERA...... Religious Committee for the ERA [*Equal Rights Amendment*]   (EA)
RCERB...... Ricerche di Termotecnica [*A publication*]
RCERIP..... Reserve Component Equipment Readiness Improvement Program [*Military*]   (AABC)
RCEUSA ... Romanian Catholic Exarchy in the United States of America   (EA)
RCEVH ..... Research Centre for the Education of the Visually Handicapped [*University of Birmingham*] [*British*]   (CB)
RCF........... Radcliffe Resources Ltd. [*Vancouver Stock Exchange symbol*]
RCF........... Radiocommunication Failure Message [*Aviation*]
RCF........... Ratio Correction Factor
RCF........... Reader's Comment Form   (IBMDP)
RCF........... Recall Finder
RCF........... Red Cell Folate [*Hematology*]   (AAMN)
RCF........... Refractory Ceramic Fiber [*Materials science*]
RCF........... Regenerated Cellulose Film [*Organic chemistry*]
RCF........... Relative Centrifugal Force
RCF........... Relative Cumulative Frequency
RCF........... Remain on Company Frequency [*Aviation*]   (FAAC)
RCF........... Remote Call Forwarding [*Bell System*]
RCF........... Repair Cost Factor [*Navy*]
RCF........... Repair Cycle Float [*Military*]   (AABC)
RCF........... Retail Computer Facilities
RCF........... Review of Contemporary Fiction [*A publication*]
RCF........... River Conservation Fund [*Later, ARCC*]   (EA)
RCF........... Rosicrucian Fellowship   (EA)
RCF........... Rotating Cylinder Flap
RCF........... Royal Carmarthen Fusiliers [*British military*]   (DMA)
RCFA........ Religious Communities for the Arts   (EA)
RCFA........ Royal Canadian Field Artillery [*Military*]
RCFC........ Ray Coble Fan Club [*Defunct*]   (EA)
RCFC........ Reactor Containment Fan Cooler [*Nuclear energy*]   (NRCH)
RCFC........ Ron Craddock Fan Club   (EA)
RCFC........ Rosanne Cash Fan Club   (EA)
RCFC........ Roy Clark Fan Club   (EA)
RCFC........ Roy Clayborne Fan Club   (EA)
RCFC(U) ... Reactor Core Fan Cooling (Unit)   (IEEE)
RCFF .... Repair Cycle Float Factor   (MCD)
RCFN........ Taidong/Fengnian [*China*] [*ICAO location identifier*]   (ICLI)
RCFNA...... Revista. Real Academia de Ciencias Exactas, Fisicas, y Naturales de Madrid [*A publication*]
RCFP........ Reporters Committee for Freedom of the Press   (EA)
RCFR........ Red Cross Field Representative
RCFR........ Royal Canadian Fleet Reserve
RCFS........ Jiadong [*China*] [*ICAO location identifier*]   (ICLI)
RCFT........ Randomized Controlled Field Trial [*Statistics*]
RCFU........ Rotary Carton Feed Unit
RCFZ........ Fengshan [*China*] [*ICAO location identifier*]   (ICLI)
RCG .... Radiation Concentration Guide [*Formerly, MPC*]
RCG .... Radio Command Guidance   (AAG)
RCG .... Radioactivity Concentration Guide   (KSC)
rCG .... Rat Chorionic Gonadotropin
RCG .... Reaction Cured Glass [*Ceramic technology*]
RCG .... Receiving   (AAG)
RCG .... Recommended Concentration Guide [*Nuclear energy*]   (NRCH)
RCG .... Reference Concept Group   (SSD)
RCG .... Restricted Categorical Grammar
RCG .... Resurgens Communications Group [*AMEX symbol*]   (SPSG)
RCG .... Retail Credit Group [*British*]
RCG .... Reverberation Control of Gain
RCG .... Right Cerebral Ganglion [*Anatomy*]
RCGA .... Royal Canadian Garrison Artillery [*Military*]
RCGD .... Research Center for Group Dynamics [*University of Michigan*] [*Research center*]   (RCD)
RCGI.......... Ludao [*China*] [*ICAO location identifier*]   (ICLI)
RCGJA...... Royal College of General Practitioners. Journal [*A publication*]

RCGM ...... Reactor Cover Gas Monitor [*Nuclear energy*]   (NRCH)
RCGM ...... Taoyuan [*China*] [*ICAO location identifier*]   (ICLI)
RCGP........ Royal College of General Practitioners [*British*]
rCGRP ...... Rat Calcitonin Gene-Related Peptide [*Biochemistry*]
RCGS........ RADAR Correlation Guidance Study
RCGS........ Recent College Graduates Survey [*Department of Education*]   (GFGA)
RCH.......... Reach   (FAAC)
RCH.......... Rich Resources Ltd. [*Vancouver Stock Exchange symbol*]
RCH.......... Riohacha [*Colombia*] [*Airport symbol*]   (OAG)
RCH.......... Rotary Clothes Hoist   (ADA)
RCH.......... Rural Cooperative Housing
RCHA........ Rachel Carson Homestead Association   (EA)
RCHA........ Royal Canadian Horse Artillery
R Ch Com Franc Canada ... Revue. Chambre de Commerce Francaise au Canada [*A publication*]
R Ch Comm Marseille ... Revue. Chambre de Commerce de Marseille [*A publication*]
RCHCS...... Regenerable Carbon Dioxide and Humidity Control System   (NASA)
RCHE .... Recherche [*A publication*]
RCHF .... Richfood Holdings, Inc. [*NASDAQ symbol*]   (NQ)
RCHG........ Reduced Charge   (AAG)
RCHI .... Rauch Industries, Inc. [*NASDAQ symbol*]   (NQ)
R Ch J .... Rencontre. Chretiens et Juifs [*A publication*]
RCHM....... Royal Commission on Historical Monuments [*British*]
RCHRA ...... Regional Council on Human Rights in Asia   (EAIO)
RchScR ...... Recherches de Science Religieuse [*A publication*]
RCHT .... Ratchet [*Design engineering*]
RCH/TCH ... Receive Channel/Transmit Channel [*Telecommunications*]   (MCD)
RCI .... RADAR Coverage Indication [*or Indicator*]
RCI .... Radio Canada International
RCI .... Radio Communications Instruction   (MUGU)
RCI .... Range Communications Instructions [*NASA*]   (KSC)
RCI .... Read Channel Initialize
RCI .... Recommended Course Indicator
RCI .... Regesta Chartarum Italiae [*A publication*]
RCI .... Reggio Calabria [*Italy*] [*Seismograph station code, US Geological Survey*]   (SEIS)
RCI .... Reichhold Chemicals, Inc. [*NYSE symbol*]   (SPSG)
RCI .... Religious of Christian Instruction [*Roman Catholic religious order*]
RCI .... Remote Control Indicator   (CAAL)
RCI .... Remote Control Interface
RC/I........... Request for Change and/or Information   (SAA)
RCI .... Request for Contract Investigation   (MCD)
RCI .... Resident Classification Index
RCI .... Resident Cost Inspector
RCI .... Resort Condominiums International   (EA)
RCI .... Respiratory Control Index [*Biochemistry*]
RCI .... Retail Confectioners International   (EA)
RCI .... Rochester Commercial and Industrial [*Database*]
RCI .... Rogers Communications, Inc. [*Toronto Stock Exchange symbol*] [*Vancouver Stock Exchange symbol*]
RCI .... Roof Consultants Institute   (EA)
RCI .... Routing Control Indicator [*Telecommunications*]   (TEL)
RCI .... Royal Colonial Institute [*British*]
RCIA........ Retail Clerks International Association [*Later, UFCWIU*]   (EA)
RCIA........ Retail Credit Institute of America [*Later, NFCC*]
RCIC........ Reactor Core Isolation Cooling [*Nuclear energy*]   (NRCH)
RCIC........ Red Cross International Committee
RCIC........ Regional Coastal Information Center [*National Marine Advisory Service*]   (MSC)
RCIC........ Reserve Component Issues Conference [*Military*]   (MCD)
RCIC........ Royal Canadian Infantry Corps
RCICDE .... International Whaling Commission. Report of the Commission [*A publication*]
RCICS .... Reactor Core Isolation Cooling System [*Nuclear energy*]   (NRCH)
RCID .... Recruiter Code Identification [*Army*]   (AABC)
RCIE .... Regional Council for International Education [*University of Pittsburgh*]
RCIL.......... Reliability Critical Item List   (AAG)
RCIRR .... Reserve Components, Individual Ready Reserve [*Military*]
RCIS .... Research Conference on Instrumentation Science
Rc Ist Lomb Sci Lett ... Rendiconti. Istituto Lombardo di Scienze e Lettere [*A publication*]
Rc Ist Sup Sanita ... Rendiconti. Istituto Superiore di Sanita [*A publication*]
RCITR....... Red Cell Iron Turnover Rate [*Hematology*]   (MAE)
RCIU .... Remote Computer Interface Unit
RCIVS .... Regional Conference on International Voluntary Service [*Commercial firm*]   (EAIO)
RCJ........... RCJ Resources Ltd. [*Vancouver Stock Exchange symbol*]
RCJ........... Reaction Control Jet
RCJ........... Reinforced Composite Joint
RCJ........... Reports of Certain Judgments of the Supreme Court, Vice-Admiralty Court, and Full Court of Appeal, Lagos [*1884-92*] [*Nigeria*] [*A publication*]   (DLA)
RC(J) .... Rettie, Crawford, and Melville's Session Cases, Fourth Series [*1873-98*] [*Scotland*] [*A publication*]   (DLA)

RCJ........... Royal Courts of Justice [*British*]
RCK .... Radio Check [*Aviation*]   (FAAC)
RCK .... Ramp Check [*Aviation*]   (FAAC)
RCK .... Rockdale, TX [*Location identifier*] [*FAA*]   (FAAL)
RckCtr .... Rockefeller Center Properties, Inc. [*Associated Press abbreviation*]   (APAG)
RCKH........ Gaoxiong [*China*] [*ICAO location identifier*]   (ICLI)
RCKT........ Rocket   (FAAC)
RCKU .... Jiayi [*China*] [*ICAO location identifier*]   (ICLI)
RCKW .... Hengchun [*China*] [*ICAO location identifier*]   (ICLI)
RCKY........ Rockies [*FAA*]   (FAAC)
RCKY........ Rocky Mountain Exploration [*NASDAQ symbol*]   (NQ)
RCL........... Radial Collateral Ligament [*Anatomy*]
RCL........... Radiation Counter Laboratories, Inc.
RCL........... Radio Command Linkage   (AAG)
RC & L....... Rail, Canal, and Lake [*Transportation*]
RCL........... Ramp Craft Logistic [*Navy*] [*British*]
RCL........... Ramped Cargo Lighter
RCL........... Ramsey County Public Library, St. Paul, MN [*OCLC symbol*]   (OCLC)
RCL........... Rationalist Concept of Logic
RCL........... Reactor Coolant Loop [*Nuclear energy*]   (NRCH)
RCL........... Reading-Canada-Lecture [*A publication*]
RCL........... Recall   (MSA)
RCL........... Recleared [*Aviation*]   (FAAC)
RCL........... Recoil   (MSA)
RCL........... Redcliff [*Vanuatu*] [*Airport symbol*]   (OAG)
RCL........... Reichhold Ltd. [*Toronto Stock Exchange symbol*]
RCL........... Reliability Component List   (MCD)
RCL........... Reliability Control Level   (KSC)
RCL........... Religion in Communist Lands [*A publication*]
RCL........... Remote Control Location
RCL........... Repair Cycle Level
RCL........... Research Computation Laboratory [*University of Houston*] [*Research center*]   (RCD)
RCL........... Reserved Commodity List [*World War II*]
RCL........... Review of Contemporary Law [*A publication*]
RCL........... Royal Canadian Legion
RCL........... Rubber Continuous Liner   (DS)
RCL........... Ruby Crystal LASER
RCL........... Ruling Case Law
RCL........... Runway Centerline [*Aviation*]
RCLA........ Regis College Lay Apostolate   (EA)
RCLAD...... Ricerca in Clinica e in Laboratorio [*A publication*]
RCLADN... Investigacion en la Clinica y en el Laboratorio [*A publication*]
RCLB........ Revolutionary Communist League of Britain [*Political party*]   (PPW)
RCLC........ Reactor Coolant Leakage Calculation   (IEEE)
RCLC........ Reactor Coolant Letdown Cooler [*Nuclear energy*]   (NRCH)
RCLC........ Republican Congressional Leadership Council   (EA)
RCLC........ Xiao Liu Qiu [*China*] [*ICAO location identifier*]   (ICLI)
RCLD........ Reclined   (MSA)
RCLG........ Recoilless Gun   (AABC)
RCLG........ Taizhong [*China*] [*ICAO location identifier*]   (ICLI)
RCLGGL... Royal Commission on Local Government in Greater London [*British*]
RCLJ .... Revue Critique de Legislation et de Jurisprudence [*A publication*]   (DLA)
RCLM....... Reclaim   (AABC)
RCLM....... Runway Centerline Marking [*Aviation*]
RCLMG...... Reclaiming
RCLO .... Reports Control Liaison Officer [*Army*]   (AABC)
RCLR........ Radio Communications Link Repeater   (FAAC)
RCLR........ Recoilless Rifle   (AABC)
RCLS .... Lishan [*China*] [*ICAO location identifier*]   (ICLI)
RCLS .... Ramapo Catskill Library System [*Library network*]
RCLS .... Recoilless
RCLS .... Runway Centerline Lights System [*Aviation*]   (FAAC)
RCLT........ Radio Communications Link Terminal   (FAAC)
RCLU .... Jilong [*China*] [*ICAO location identifier*]   (ICLI)
RCLWUNE ... Regional Commission on Land and Water Use in the Near East   (EA)
RCLY........ Lanyu [*China*] [*ICAO location identifier*]   (ICLI)
RCM .... ARCO Chemical Co. [*NYSE symbol*]   (SPSG)
RCM .... Aviation Radio and RADAR Countermeasures Technician [*Navy*]
RCM .... La Republique des Citoyens du Monde [*Commonwealth of World Citizens*]
RCM .... RADAR [*or Radio*] Countermeasures [*Military*]   (AAG)
RCM .... Radial Compression Model [*Chromatography*]
RCM .... Radiative-Convective Model [*Meteorology*]
RCM .... Radio-Controlled Mine [*Military*]
RCM .... Radio Counter-Measures [*British military*]   (DMA)
RCM .... Radiocontrast Media [*Clinical chemistry*]
RCM .... Random Coefficient Model [*Mathematics*]
RCM .... Random Coincidence Monitor [*Beckman Instruments, Inc.*] [*Instrumentation*]
RCM .... Range Change Method [*Aircraft*]
RCM .... Rassemblement Chretien de Madagascar [*Christian Rally of Madagascar*]
RCM .... Reactor Materials [*A publication*]

RCM .... Receipt of Classified Material   (AAG)
RCM .... Recent Crustal Movements [*Geology*]   (NOAA)
RCM .... Red Cell Mass [*Hematology*]
RCM .... Reduced Casualties and Mishaps
RCM .... Refurbished Command Module [*NASA*]   (KSC)
RCM .... Regimental Corporal-Major [*British*]
RCM .... Regimental Court-Martial
RCM .... Reinforced Clostridial Medium [*Microbiology*]
RCM .... Reliability-Centered Maintenance [*DoD*]
RCM .... Reliability Corporate Memory   (IEEE)
RCM .... Religious Conceptionist Missionaries [*Roman Catholic women's religious order*]
RCM .... Repair Cycle Monitor
RCM .... Replacement Culture Medium [*Microbiology*]
RCM .... Revised Code of Montana [*A publication*]
RCM .... Rhode Island College, Providence, RI [*OCLC symbol*]   (OCLC)
RCM .... Richmond [*Australia*] [*Airport symbol*]   (OAG)
RCM .... Right Costal Margin [*Medicine*]
RCM .... Root Canal Molar [*Dentistry*]
RCM .... Rosmac Resources Ltd. [*Vancouver Stock Exchange symbol*]
RCM .... Rotor Current Meter
RCM .... Rous Conditioned Medium
RCM .... Royal Canadian Mint
RCM .... Royal College of Midwives [*British*]
RCM .... Royal College of Music [*British*]
RCM .... Royal College of Music. Magazine [*A publication*]
RCM .... Royal Conservatory of Music [*Leipzig*]
RCMA .... Radio Communications Monitoring Association   (EA)
RCMA .... Railroad Construction and Maintenance Association [*Later, NRC/MAI*]   (EA)
RCMA .... Religious Conference Management Association   (EA)
RCMA .... Reservist Clothing Maintenance Allowance [*Military*]
RCMA .... Roof Coatings Manufacturers Association   (EA)
RCMASA.. Russian Consolidated Mutual Aid Society of America   (EA)
RCMAT..... Radio-Controlled Miniature Aerial Target [*Military*]   (MCD)
RCMD....... Recommend   (FAAC)
RCMD....... Rice Council for Market Development   (EA)
RCM and E ... Radio Control Models and Electronics [*A publication*]
RCME .... Russian Commodity and Raw Materials Exchange [*Russian Federation*]   (EY)
RCMF........ Royal Commonwealth Military Forces   (ADA)
RCMI........ Research Centers in Minority Institutions Program [*Bethesda, MD*] [*National Institutes of Health*]   (GRD)
RCMIS...... Reserve Components Management Information System [*Army*]
RCMJ........ Donggang [*China*] [*ICAO location identifier*]   (ICLI)
RCMLDR ... Australia. Commonwealth Scientific and Industrial Research Organisation. Marine Laboratories. Report [*A publication*]
RCMM ...... Registered Competitive Market Maker [*Stock exchange term*]   (SPSG)
RCMP........ RCMP [*Royal Canadian Mounted Police*] Quarterly [*A publication*]
RCMP........ Recompute Last Fix [*Navy Navigation Satellite System*]   (DNAB)
RCMP........ Royal Canadian Mounted Police [*Formerly, RNWMP*]
RCMPQ .... Royal Canadian Mounted Police Quarterly [*A publication*]
RCMPRS .. Recompression
RCMQ .... Qingquangang [*China*] [*ICAO location identifier*]   (ICLI)
rCMR....... Regional Cerebral Metabolic Rate [*Brain research*]
RCMS........ Ilan [*China*] [*ICAO location identifier*]   (ICLI)
RCMS........ Reliability Centered Maintenance Strategy   (MCD)
RCMS........ Research Careers for Minority Scholars [*National Science Foundation*]
RCMT .... RCM Technologies, Inc. [*NASDAQ symbol*]   (NQ)
RCMTA..... Ricerche di Matematica [*A publication*]
RCMUH.... Ruperto-Carola. Mitteilungen der Vereinigung der Freunde der Studentenschaft der Universitaet Heidelberg [*A publication*]
RCMV .... Red Clover Mottle Virus [*Plant pathology*]
RCN .... Energiespectrum [*A publication*]
RCN .... Receipt of Change Notice
RCN .... Reconnaissance
RCN .... Record Control Number [*Military*]   (AFM)
RCN .... Record Number [*Online database field identifier*]
RCN .... Recovery Communications Network
RCN .... Recreation   (MSA)
RCN .... Report Change Notice   (MCD)
RCN .... Report Control Number   (MCD)
RCN .... Requirements Change Notice [*NASA*]   (NASA)
RCN .... Resource Center for Nonviolence   (EA)
RCN .... Reticulum-Cell Neoplasia [*Oncology*]
RCN .... Rimacan Resources Ltd. [*Vancouver Stock Exchange symbol*]
RCN .... Royal Canadian Navy [*Obsolete*]
RCN .... Royal College of Nursing [*British*]
RCNAA ..... Radiologic Clinics of North America [*A publication*]
RCNAS...... Royal Canadian Naval Air Station
RCN Bull ... RCN [*Reactor Centrum Nederland*] Bulletin [*A publication*]
RCNC .... Royal Canadian Naval College [*1943-1948*]
RCNC .... Royal Corps of Naval Constructors [*British*]
RCNCOES ... Reserve Components Noncommissioned Officer Education System [*Army*]
RCNDT ..... Recondition

RCNLR...... Reconnaissance Long Range [*Army*]
RCN Meded ... Reactor Centrum Nederland. Mededeling [*A publication*]
RCNMR .... Royal Canadian Navy. Monthly Review [*A publication*]
RCNMV .... Red Clover Necrotic Mosaic Virus [*Plant pathology*]
RCNN....... Tainan [*China*] [*ICAO location identifier*]   (ICLI)
RCNO....... Dongshi [*China*] [*ICAO location identifier*]   (ICLI)
RCNR .... Royal Canadian Naval Reserve
RCN Rep.... Reactor Centrum Nederland. Report [*A publication*]
RCNSC...... Reserve Component National Security Course [*National Defense University*]   (INF)
R & C N Sc ... Russell and Chesley's Nova Scotia Reports [*A publication*]   (DLA)
RCNSS ...... Reserve Component National Security Seminar   (MCD)
RCNTR..... Ring Counter   (MSA)
RCNV .... Resource Center for Nonviolence   (EA)
RCNVR .... Royal Canadian Naval Volunteer Reserve [*1923-1945*]
RCO.......... RADAR Control Officer
RCO.......... Radio Control Operator
RCO.......... Range Control Office [*or Officer*] [*NASA*]   (KSC)
RCO.......... Range Cutoff   (MCD)
RCO.......... Reactor Core   (IEEE)
RCO.......... Receiver Cuts Out [*Telecommunications*]   (TEL)
RCO.......... Reclamation Control Officer [*Military*]   (AFIT)
RCO.......... Regional Catering Officer [*British*]   (DCTA)
RCO.......... Remote Communication Outlet [*ATCS*]
RCO.......... Remote Control Office
RCO.......... Remote Control Operator
RCO.......... Remote Control Oscillator
RCO.......... Rendezvous Compatible Orbit [*Aerospace*]
RCO.......... Reports Control Officer [*Army*]   (AABC)
RCO.......... Representative Calculating Operation
RCO.......... Requisition Control Office
RCO.......... Research Contracting Officer
RCO.......... Resistance-Controlled Oscillator
RCo.......... Ristocetin Cofactor
RCO.......... Rococco Resources Ltd. [*Vancouver Stock Exchange symbol*]
RCO.......... Royal College of Organists [*British*]
RCOA .... Radio Club of America
RCOA .... Record Club of America [*Defunct*]
RCOA .... Retailing Corp. of America [*NASDAQ symbol*]   (NQ)
RC-OAC .... Reserve Component Infantry Officer Advance Course [*Military*]   (INF)
RCOC .... Regional Communications Operations Center [*Military*]   (MCD)
RC/OC....... Reverse Current/Overcurrent   (KSC)
RCOC .... Royal Canadian Ordnance Corps
RCOCB...... Research Communications in Chemical Pathology and Pharmacology [*A publication*]
RCOG .... Royal College of Obstetricians and Gynaecologists [*British*]
R Coll For Dep Refor Res Notes ... Royal College of Forestry. Department of Reforestation. Research Notes [*A publication*]
R Coll Sci Technol (Glasg) Res Rep ... Royal College of Science and Technology (Glasgow). Research Report [*A publication*]
RCOMD6 ... Recent Advances in Community Medicine [*A publication*]
R Comitato G Italia B ... Reale Comitato Geologico d'Italia. Bolletino [*A publication*]
RCON....... Reconfiguration   (FAAC)
RCOND..... Resources and Conservation [*A publication*]
R/CONT ... Remote Control [*Automotive engineering*]
RCONT ..... Rod Control
R Contemp Sociol ... Review of Contemporary Sociology [*A publication*]
RCOR .... Remote Computer Output Room   (MCD)
RCOT .... Recoton Corp. [*NASDAQ symbol*]   (NQ)
RCOT .... Rolling Contour Optimization Theory [*Bridgestone Corp.*]
RCP........... Racal Communications Processor [*Racal Datacom, Inc.*]
RCP........... RADAR Chart Protector   (DNAB)
RCP........... RADAR Control Panel   (MCD)
RCP........... RADAR Conversion Program
RCP........... Radiation Constraints Panel [*NASA*]   (MCD)
RCP........... Radiative-Convective-Photochemical [*Meteorology*]
RCP........... Radical Caucus in Psychiatry   (EA)
RCP........... Radio Control Panel [*Aviation*]
RCP........... Radiological Control Program [*Nuclear energy*]   (NRCH)
RCP........... Random Close-Packed [*Granular physics*]
RCP........... Rapid City Public Library, Rapid City, SD [*OCLC symbol*]   (OCLC)
RCP........... Reactor Characterization Program [*Nuclear energy*]   (NRCH)
RCP........... Reactor Coolant Pump [*Nuclear energy*]   (NRCH)
RCP........... Receive Clock Pulse
rcp .... Recipient [*MARC relator code*] [*Library of Congress*]   (LCCP)
RCP........... Recognition and Control Processor [*Data processing*]   (IBMDP)
RCP........... Reconciling Congregation Program   (EA)
RCP........... Recording Control Panel
RCP........... Recovery Command Post
RCP........... Recrea Plus [*A publication*]
RCP........... Recruiting Command Post
RCP........... Rectangular Coordinate Plotter
RCP........... Reflector-cum-Periscope [*British military*]   (DMA)
RCP........... Regimental Command Post
RCP........... Regional Conservation Program
RCP........... Register Clock Pulse

RCP........... Registry of Comparative Pathology (EA)
RCP........... Reinforced Concrete Pavement
RCP........... Reinforced Concrete Pipe [*Technical drawings*]
RCP........... Relative Competitive Preference [*Marketing*]
RCP........... Reliability Critical Problem (AAG)
RCP........... Remote Control Panel
RCP........... Request for Contractual Procurement
RCP........... Requirements Change Proposal
RCP........... Restartable Cryogenic Propellant
RCP........... Restoration Control Point [*Telecommunications*] (TEL)
RCP........... Retention Control Point [*Military*] (INF)
RCP........... Returns Compliance Program [*Internal Revenue Service*]
RCP........... Revolutionary Communist Party of India [*Political party*] (PPW)
RCP........... Riboflavin Carrier Protein [*Immunology*]
RCP........... Right Circular Polarization
RCP........... Rockefeller Center Properties, Inc. [*NYSE symbol*] (SPSG)
RCP........... Roll Centering Pickoff (SAA)
RCP........... Roman Catholic Priest (ROG)
RCP........... Romanian Communist Party [*Political party*]
RCP........... Rotation Combat Personnel
RCP........... Royal College of Pathologists [*British*]
RCPB........ Royal College of Physicians of London [*British*]
RCP........... Royal College of Preceptors [*British*] (ROG)
RCP........... Royal Commission on the Press [*British*]
RCPA........ Reserve Components Program of the Army (AABC)
RCPA........ Rural Cooperative Power Association
RCPAC...... Reserve Components Personnel and Administration Center [*Army*] (AABC)
RCPath...... Royal College of Pathologists [*British*]
RCPB........ Reactor Coolant Pressure Boundary [*Nuclear energy*] (NRCH)
RCP(B)...... Romanian Communist Party (Bolshevik) [*Political party*]
RCP(b)....... Russian Communist Party (Bolsheviks) [*Political party*]
RCPBO...... Research Communications in Psychology, Psychiatry, and Behavior [*A publication*]
RCPC........ Regional Check Processing Centers
RCPC........ Royal Canadian Postal Corps [*Formerly, CPC*]
RCPCR...... Recombinant Circle Polymerase Chain Reaction [*Genetics*]
RCPD........ Reserve Components Personnel Directorate [*Office of Personnel Operations*] [*Army*]
RCPE........ Radiological Control Practices Evaluation (MCD)
RCPE........ Royal College of Physicians, Edinburgh
RCPEd....... Royal College of Physicians, Edinburgh
RCPGlas.... Royal College of Physicians and Surgeons of Glasgow
RCPI......... Revolutionary Communist Party of India [*Political party*] (PPW)
RCPI......... Royal College of Physicians, Ireland
RCPJA...... Royal College of Physicians of London. Journal [*A publication*]
RCPL........ Right Circularly Polarized Light
RCPL........ Royal College of Physicians, London (ROG)
RCPO....... Regional Contract Property Officer
RCPO....... Xinzhu [*China*] [*ICAO location identifier*] (ICLI)
RCPP........ Refrigeration, Compressor and Electrical Power, Airborne Pod Enclosure (DNAB)
RCPP........ Reinforced Concrete Pressure Pipe
RCPRA...... Record of Chemical Progress [*A publication*]
RCPS........ Royal College of Physicians and Surgeons of Glasgow
RCPS........ Royal College of Physicians and Surgeons (of United States of America) (EA)
RCPS(C).... Royal College of Physicians and Surgeons of Canada
RCPS(Glasg) ... Royal College of Physicians and Surgeons of Glasgow (DBQ)
RCPT........ Receipt (AFM)
RCPT........ Receptacle (MSA)
RCPT........ Reception (AABC)
RCPT........ Refrigeration, Compressor and Electrical Power, Trailer-Mounted (DNAB)
RCPT........ Registered Cardiopulmonary Technologist [*Medicine*] (WGA)
RCPTN...... Reception (MSA)
RCPV....... Riot Control Patrol Vehicle
RCQ.......... Reconquista [*Argentina*] [*Airport symbol*] (OAG)
RCQ.......... Rich Capital Corp. [*Vancouver Stock Exchange symbol*]
RCQC........ Magong [*China*] [*ICAO location identifier*] (ICLI)
RCQS......... Taidong/Zhihang [*China*] [*ICAO location identifier*] (ICLI)
RCR.......... Rabbinical Council Record [*New York*] [*A publication*]
RCR .... RADAR Control Room
RCR .... Ramsbottom Carbon Residue [*Analysis of petroleum products*]
RCR .... Rated Capacity Report [*Army*]
RCR .... Reactor Control Room
RCR .... Reader Control Relay
RCR .... Reciprocating Cryogenic Refrigerator
RCR .... Regenerative Cyclic Reactor [*Chemical engineering*]
RCR .... Relative Citation Rate [*Bibliography*]
RCR .... Relative Consumption Rate [*Entomology*]
RCR .... Required Carrier Return Character [*Data processing*]
RCR .... Respiratory Control Ratio [*Medicine*]
RCR .... Restitution of Conjugal Rights [*Legal*] [*British*] (ROG)
RCR .... Retrofit Configuration Record [*NASA*] (NASA)
RCR .... Rochester, IN [*Location identifier*] [*FAA*] (FAAL)
RCR .... Room Cavity Ratio [*Lighting*]
RCR .... Royal Canadian Regiment [*Military*]
RCR .... Royal Canadian Rifles [*Military unit*]

RCR .... Royal College of Radiologists [*British*]
RCR .... Runway Condition Reading [*or Report*] [*Aviation*] (FAAC)
RCRA .... Radiologically-Controlled Radiation Area (DNAB)
RCRA .... Refrigeration Compressor Rebuilders Association (EA)
RCRA .... Resort and Commercial Recreation Association (EA)
RCRA .... Resource Conservation and Recovery Act [*Pronounced "rickra"*] [*1976*]
RCRA .... Rural Cooperative and Recovery Act (OICC)
RCRA .... Zouying [*China*] [*ICAO location identifier*] (ICLI)
R-CRAS..... Rogers Criminal Responsibility Assessment Scales [*Personality development test*] [*Psychology*]
RCRBSJ .... Research Council on Riveted and Bolted Structural Joints [*Later, RCSC*] (EA)
RCRC........ Rabbinic Center for Research and Counseling (EA)
RCRC........ Reinforced Concrete Research Council (EA)
RCRC........ Revoked Commission, Returned to Civilian Status [*Navy*]
RCRD........ Record (AFM)
RCRF........ Rei Cretariae Romanae Fautorum Acta [*A publication*]
RCRHRCS ... Research Center for Religion and Human Rights in Closed Societies (EA)
RCRL........ Reliability Critical Ranking List (AAG)
R1 Cro........ Croke's English King's Bench Reports Tempore Elizabeth [*1582-1603*] [*A publication*] (DLA)
R2 Cro....... Croke's English King's Bench Reports Tempore James [*Jacobus*] I [*A publication*] (DLA)
R3 Cro........ Croke's English King's Bench Reports Tempore Charles I [*1625-41*] [*A publication*] (DLA)
RCRP........ Regional Centers for Radiological Physics [*National Cancer Institute*]
RCRR........ Roster Chaplain - Ready Reserve [*Army*]
RCRS........ Regenerative Carbon-Dioxide Removal System (MCD)
RCRS........ Reserve Combat Replacement Squadron (DNAB)
RcRt.......... Romantic Reassessment [*A publication*]
RCRUA ..... Revista. Consejo de Rectores. Universidades Chilenas [*A publication*]
RCRVA...... Russian Chemical Reviews [*English Translation*] [*A publication*]
RCS........... Rabbit Aorta Contracting Substance [*TA_2 - see TA, Thromboxane*] [*Biochemistry*]
RCS........... RADAR Calibration Sphere
RCS........... RADAR Collimator System
RCS........... RADAR Control Ship
RCS........... RADAR Cross Section
RCS........... Radio Command System
RCS........... Radio Communications Set
RCS........... Radio Communications System [*Military*] (CAAL)
RCS........... Radio Control System
R & CS....... Radiological and Chemical Support [*Nuclear energy*] (NRCH)
RCS........... Range Calibration Satellite (SAA)
RCS........... Range Control Station [*or System*] [*Army*]
RCS........... Rapports de la Cour Supreme du Canada [*Database*] [*Federal Department of Justice*] [*Information service or system*] (CRD)
RCS........... Rate Command System (AAG)
RCS........... Reaction Control System [*or Subsystem*] [*Steering system in spacecraft*] [*NASA*]
RCS........... Reactive Current Sensing (MCD)
RCS........... Reactor Coolant System [*Nuclear energy*] (NRCH)
RCS........... Rearward Communications System (MDG)
RCS........... Recurrent Change of Station (SAA)
RCS........... Recurrent Change of Status (SAA)
RCS........... Reentry Control System [*Aerospace*] (AFM)
RCS........... Refurbishment Cost Study (KSC)
RCS........... Regional Control Station [*Military*] (MCD)
RCS........... Reliability Control Specification
RCS........... Reliable Corrective Action Summary (AAG)
RCS........... Reloadable Control Storage [*Data processing*]
RCS........... Remington's Compiled Statutes [*1922*] [*A publication*] (DLA)
RCS........... Remote Computing Service
RCS........... Remote Control Set
RC(S)........ Remote Control (System) (DEN)
R/CS........ Repeat Cesarean Section [*Obstetrics*] (MAE)
RCS........... Reports Control Symbol [*Military*]
RCS........... Reports Creation System
RCS........... Representative Conflict Situations [*Army*]
RCS........... Request for Consultation Service (WGA)
RCS........... Requirement Clearance Symbol [*Military*] (AFM)
RCS........... Requirements Control Symbol [*Military*] (MCD)
RCS........... Requirements Control System
RCS........... Residential Conservation Service [*Offered by major electric and gas utilities*]
Rcs .... Resources [*Army*]
RCS........... Reticulum Cell Sarcoma [*Medicine*]
RCS........... Retrofit Configuration System (MCD)
RCS........... Revenue Cutter Service [*Coast Guard*]
RCS........... Rich Coast Sulphur Ltd. [*Vancouver Stock Exchange symbol*]
RCS........... Ride-Control Segment [*or System*] [*Aviation*]
RCS........... Right Coronary Sinus [*Cardiology*] (AAMN)
RCS........... Rip-Out Control Sheet (DNAB)
RCS........... Rizzoli Corriere della Sera [*Publisher*]
RCS........... Royal College of Science [*British*]

RCS............ Royal College of Surgeons [*British*]
RCS............ Royal Commonwealth Society [*British*]
RCS............ Royal Corps of Signals [*British*]
RCSADO... Research Communications in Substances of Abuse [*A publication*]
RCSAV...... Rozpravy Ceskoslovenske Akademie Ved [*A publication*]
RCSB......... [*The*] Rochester Community Savings Bank [*Rochester, NY*] [*NASDAQ symbol*]　(NQ)
RCSBP....... Reserve Components Survivor Benefits Plan [*Military*]
RCSC......... Huwei [*China*] [*ICAO location identifier*]　(ICLI)
RCSC......... Radio Component Standardization Committee [*British*]
RCSC......... Reaction Control System [*or Subsystem*] Controller [*Apollo*] [*NASA*]　(NASA)
RCSC......... Research Council on Structural Connections　(EA)
RCSC......... Royal Canadian Sea Cadets
RCSC...... Royal Canadian Sea Cadets Corps
RCSCSPL ... Russian, Croatian and Serbian, Czech and Slovak, Polish Literature [*A publication*]
RCSDE...... Reactor Coolant System Dose Equivalent　(IEEE)
RCSDP...... League of Red Cross Societies Development Program
RCSE......... Remote Control and Status Equipment　(MCD)
RCSE......... Royal College of Surgeons, Edinburgh
R2CSE....... Relaxed Two-Color Stimulated Echo [*Spectroscopy*]
RCSEd....... Royal College of Surgeons, Edinburgh
RCSEL....... Recommended Common Support Equipment List　(MCD)
RCSEng..... Royal College of Surgeons, England
RCSHSB ... Red Cedar Shingle and Handsplit Shake Bureau [*Later, CSSB*]　(EA)
RCSI......... Receipt for [*or of*] Classified Security Information　(AAG)
RCSI......... Rede CONSISDATA de Servicos Integrados [*CONSISDATA Integrated Services Network*] [*Consultoria, Sistemas, e Processamento de Dados Ltda.*] [*Brazil*] [*Information service or system*]　(CRD)
RCSI......... Royal College of Surgeons, Ireland
RCSIS....... Radio/Cable Switching Integration System　(MCD)
RCSL........ Rich Coast Sulphur Ltd. [*NASDAQ symbol*]　(NQ)
RCSM....... Ri Yue Tan [*China*] [*ICAO location identifier*]　(ICLI)
RCSMC.... Recent Advances in Studies on Cardiac Structure and Metabolism [*A publication*]
RCSO........ Research Contract Support Office
RCSQ........ Pingdong (North) [*China*] [*ICAO location identifier*]　(ICLI)
RCSS........ Radial Compression Separation System [*Chromatography*]
RCSS........ Random Communication Satellite System
RCSS........ Recruiting Command Support System [*Navy*]　(DNAB)
RCSS........ Reduced Chi-Square Statistic
RCSS........ Taibei/Songshan [*China*] [*ICAO location identifier*]　(ICLI)
RCSSA...... Regional Centre for Seismology for South America　(EAIO)
RCSSMRS ... Regional Centre for Services in Surveying, Mapping, and Remote Sensing [*West Africa*]
RCS Supp .. Remington's Compiled Statutes, Supplement [*A publication*]　(DLA)
RCSU........ Repair Cycle Support Unit
RCSX........ North American Car Corp. [*AAR code*]
RCT .... RADAR Control Trailer [*Military*]　(AABC)
RCT .... Radiation/Chemical Technician　(IEEE)
RCT .... Radiobeacon Calibration Transmitter
RCT .... Randomized Clinical Trial [*Medicine*]
RCT .... Randomized Control Trial [*Statistics*]
RCT .... Real Estate Investment Trust, California [*NYSE symbol*]　(SPSG)
RCT .... Receipts [*Stock exchange term*]　(SPSG)
RCT .... Received Copy of Temporary Pay Record
RCT .... Recruit
RCT .... Reed City, MI [*Location identifier*] [*FAA*]　(FAAL)
RCT .... Regimental Combat Team
RCT .... Region Control Task [*Data processing*]　(BUR)
RCT .... Registered Care Technician [*Proposed by American Medical Association to alleviate nursing shortage*]
RCT .... Regular Care Technologist
RCT .... Rehabilitation and Research Center for Torture Victims　(EAIO)
RCT .... Remote Control [*Systems*]　(MCD)
RCT .... Remote Control Terminal　(MCD)
RCT .... Renal Cortical Tumor [*Oncology*]
RCT .... Repair Cycle Time　(MCD)
RCT .... Repeat Cycle Timer
RCT .... Resolver Control Transformer
RCT .... Resource Consulting Teacher
RCT .... Response Coordination Team [*Nuclear energy*]　(NRCH)
RCT .... Retention Control Training [*Medicine*]
RC-T .... Revenue Canada, Taxation
RCT .... Reversible Counter
RCT .... Rework/Completion Tag [*Nuclear energy*]　(NRCH)
RCT .... Ridgecrest Resources [*Vancouver Stock Exchange symbol*]
RCT .... Roll Call Training
RCT .... Root Canal Therapy [*Dentistry*]
RCT .... Rorschach Content Test [*Psychology*]
RCT .... Royal Clinical Teacher [*British*]
RCT .... Royal Corps of Transport [*Army*] [*British*]
RCT .... Royal Cosmic Theology [*British*]

RCTA......... Retail Confectionery and Tobacconists' Association [*British*]　(DI)
RCTB......... Reserve Components Troop Basis [*Army*]　(AABC)
RCTC........ Regeneratively-Cooled Thrust Chamber
RCTC........ Reserve Components Training Center [*Military*]
RCTC........ Union of Rail Canada Traffic Controllers [*See also CCFC*]
RCTCA...... Recherche Technique [*A publication*]
RCTDPOVALCAN ... Request Concurrent Travel of Dependents by Privately Owned Vehicle [*ALCAN Highway or Via Route Required*] [*Army*]　(AABC)
RCTEA...... Rubber Chemistry and Technology [*A publication*]
RCTG .... Recruiting　(AABC)
RCTI......... Rajawali Citra Televisi Indonesia　(EY)
RCTL......... Resistance-Coupled Transistor Logic
RCTL......... Resistor-Capacitor Transistor Logic
RCTM .... Regional Center for Tropical Meteorology [*National Hurricane Center*]
RCTN .... Reaction　(MSA)
RCTP........ Reserve Components Troop Program [*Army*]
RCTP........ Taibei City/Taibei International Airport [*China*] [*ICAO location identifier*]　(ICLI)
RCTPA...... Russian Castings Production [*English Translation*] [*A publication*]
RCTPS....... Revue Canadienne de Theorie Politique et Sociale [*A publication*]
RCTRANSMOD ... Reserve Components Transition to Modernization
R & C Tr Cas ... Railway and Canal Traffic Cases (Neville) [*England*] [*A publication*]　(DLA)
RCTS........ Railway Correspondence and Travel Society [*British*]
RCTS......... Reactor Coolant Treatment System [*Nuclear energy*]　(NRCH)
R (Ct of Sess) ... Rettie, Crawford, and Melville's Session Cases, Fourth Series [*1873-98*] [*Scotland*] [*A publication*]　(DLA)
RCTSR ...... Radio Code Test, Speed of Response [*Military*]
RCTV........ Radio Caracas Television [*Venezuela*]　(EY)
RCTV........ RCA Cable and Rockefeller Center Cable Pay-TV Program Service
RCTV........ Remote Controlled Target Vehicle [*Military*]　(INF)
RCU .... Rack Controller Unit [*Data processing*]　(PCM)
RCU .... RADAR Calibration Unit
RCU .... RADAR Control Unit [*Military*]　(CAAL)
RCU .... Rate Construction Unit [*Hypothetical basic currency unit*]　(DCTA)
RCU .... Reference Control Unit　(MCD)
RCU .... Regional Coordinating Unit [*Advisory Committee on Pollution of the Sea*]
RCU .... Relay Control Unit　(AAG)
RCU .... Remote Control Unit
RCU .... Requisition Control Unit
RCU .... Research into Chronic Unemployment [*British*]
RCU .... Research Coordinating Unit [*Oklaholma State Department of Vocational and Technical Education*] [*Stillwater, OK*]
R/CU .... Research and Curriculum Unit [*Mississippi State University*] [*Research center*]　(RCD)
RCU .... Reserve Component Unit [*Army*]　(AABC)
RCU .... Respiratory Care Unit [*Medicine*]
RCU .... Revolution Control Unit [*Automotive engineering*]
RCU .... Rio Cuarto [*Argentina*] [*Airport symbol*]　(OAG)
RCU .... Rocket Countermeasure Unit
RCUA .... Remote Checkout Umbilical Array
RCUEP...... Research Center for Urban and Environmental Planning [*Princeton University*]
RCUK .... Bakuai [*China*] [*ICAO location identifier*]　(ICLI)
RCUL .... Reference Control Unit Launch　(MCD)
RCUR .... Recurrent　(MSA)
R Current Activities Tech Ed ... Review of Current Activities in Technical Education [*A publication*]　(APTA)
RCV .... RADAR Control Van　(NATG)
RCV .... Radiation Control Valve [*Nuclear energy*]　(NRCH)
RCV .... Reaction-Control Valve
RCV .... Receive　(AFM)
RCV .... Receiver
RCV .... Receiver/Exciter Subsystem [*Deep Space Instrumentation Facility, NASA*]
RCV .... Recreatievoorzieningen. Maandblad voor Recreatie, Milieu, en Landschap [*A publication*]
RCV .... Red Cell Volume [*Hematology*]
RCV .... Relative Conductor Volume
RCV .... Remote-Controlled Vehicle　(MCD)
RCV .... Replacement Cost Valuation [*Insurance*]
RCV .... Restartable Cryogenic Vehicle
RCV .... Reversed Circular Vection [*Optics*]
RCV .... Revised Claim Valuation [*Insurance*]
RCV .... Rich Cut Virginia [*Tobacco*]　(ROG)
RCV .... Riot Control Vehicle
RCV .... Robotic Combat Vehicle [*Army*]　(RDA)
RCV .... Routine Coefficient of Variation [*Statistics*]
RCV .... Ryegrass Cryptic Virus [*Plant pathology*]
RCV-COMMZ ... Rear Combat Vehicle/Communications Zone　(MCD)
RCVD .... Reactive Chemical Vapor Deposition [*Coating technology*]
RCVD .... Received　(MSA)
RCVG .... Receiving　(MSA)

RCVG .... Replacement Carrier Fighter Group [*V is Navy code for Fighter*]
RCVMV..... Red Clover Vein Mosaic Virus
RCVR........ Receiver (AAG)
RCVRB...... Royal Military College of Canada. Civil Engineering Research Report [*A publication*]
RCVS........ Remote Control Video Switch (MCD)
RCVS........ Royal College of Veterinary Surgeons [*British*]
RCVSG...... Readiness Antisubmarine Warfare Carrier Air Wing [*Navy*] (NVT)
RCVT........ Registered Cardiovascular Technologist [*Medicine*] (WGA)
RCVTA...... Rozpravy Ceskoslovenske Akademie Ved. Rada Technickych Ved [*A publication*]
RCVTB...... Recherches Veterinaires [*A publication*]
RCVV .... Rear Compressor Variable Vane
RCVW....... Readiness Attack Carrier Air Wing [*Navy*] (NVT)
RCVY........ Recovery (MSA)
RCW .... Raw Cooling Water [*Nuclear energy*] (NRCH)
RCW .... Reactor Cooling Water [*Nuclear energy*] (NRCH)
RCW .... Record Control Word [*Data processing*]
RCW .... Reformed Church Women [*An association*] (EA)
RCW .... Register Containing Word
RCW .... Research Center on Women (EA)
RCW .... Resident Careworker
RCW .... Return Control Word
RCWA ...... Revised Code of Washington Annotated [*A publication*] (DLA)
RCWI........ Right Ventricular Cardiac Work Index [*Cardiology*]
RCWK...... Xinshe [*China*] [*ICAO location identifier*] (ICLI)
RCWP....... Rural Clean Water Program [*Department of Agriculture*]
RCWS....... Remote Control Water Sampler
RCWS....... Russian Children's Welfare Society - Outside of Russia (EA)
RCX .... Ladysmith, WI [*Location identifier*] [*FAA*] (FAAL)
RCXY........ Guiren [*China*] [*ICAO location identifier*] (ICLI)
RCY .... Recovery (NASA)
RCY .... Red Cross and Red Crescent Youth [*Geneva, Switzerland*]
RCY .... Remaining Cycles (MCD)
RCY .... Rotating Coil Yoke
RCY .... Royal Crystal [*Vancouver Stock Exchange symbol*]
RCYRA...... Rooster Class Yacht Racing Association (EA)
RCYU .... Hualian [*China*] [*ICAO location identifier*] (ICLI)
RCZ .... Radiation Control Zone
RCZ .... Rear Combat Zone (NATG)
RCZ .... Rockingham, NC [*Location identifier*] [*FAA*] (FAAL)
RD............. Airlift International, Inc. [*ICAO designator*]
Rd............. Albert Rolland [*France*] [*Research code symbol*]
RD............. Boots Pure Drug Co. [*Great Britain*] [*Research code symbol*]
RD............. Directional Radio Beacon [*ITU designation*] (CET)
RD............. Distribution Is Restricted to Government Agencies Only [*Advice of supply action code*] [*Army*]
RD............. Indian Revenue Decisions [*A publication*] (DLA)
rd............... Rad [*Non-SI unit; preferred unit is Gy, Gray*]
RD............. RADAR (DEN)
RD............. RADAR Data
RD............. RADAR Display
RD............. RADARman [*Also, RDM*] [*Navy rating*]
RD............. Radiation Damage [*Nucleonics*] (OA)
RD............. Radiation Detection
Rd............. Radiolaria [*Quality of the bottom*] [*Nautical charts*]
RD............. Radiological Defense [*To minimize the effect of nuclear radiation on people and resources*]
Rd............. Rainbow Darter [*Ichthyology*]
RD............. Random Drift
RD............. Random Driver [*Nuclear energy*] (NRCH)
RD............. Range Development (MUGU)
R/D .... Rate of Descent [*Aviation*] (MCD)
RD............. Raynaud's Disease [*Medicine*]
RD............. Reaction of Degeneration [*Physiology*]
RD............. Read (AAG)
RD............. Read Data
R & D .... Read and Destroy
RD............. Read Direct
RD............. Reader's Digest [*A publication*]
RD............. Readiness Data
RD............. Readiness Date
RD............. Reappraisement Decisions [*A publication*] (DLA)
RD............. Rear Door
RD............. Receipt Day (NRCH)
RD............. Received Data (IEEE)
RD............. Recemment Degorgee [*Recently Disgorged*] [*Refers to aging of wine*] [*French*]
RD............. Recognition Differential
RD............. Record Description [*Data processing*]
RD............. Recorders-Reproducers [*JETDS nomenclature*] [*Military*] (CET)
RD............. Recording Demand (DEN)
RD............. Red
RD............. Red Pennant [*Navy*] [*British*]
Rd............. Reduce [*Army*]
RD............. Refer to Drawer [*Banking*]
RD............. Reference Designator (NASA)
RD............. Reference Document

RD............. Reference Drawing (NATG)
RD............. Regio Decreto [*Royal Decree*] [*Latin*] (DLA)
RD............. Regional Director
RD............. Register Drive (MSA)
RD............. Registered (ROG)
RD............. Registered Dietitian
RD............. Registration Division [*Environmental Protection Agency*] (EPA)
RD............. Reinforcement Designee [*Air Force*] (AFM)
RD............. Relative Density
RD............. Relaxation Delay
RD............. Relay Drawer
RD............. Relay Driver
RD............. Remedial Design (EPA)
RD............. Remove Directory [*Data processing*]
RD............. Renaissance Drama [*A publication*]
RD............. Renal Disease [*Medicine*]
RD............. Rendered (ROG)
RD............. Replacement Detachment [*Army*]
RD............. Replenishable Demand
RD............. Reply Delay (MUGU)
R of D........ Reporter of Debate [*US Senate*]
RD............. Required Date
R & D .... Requirements and Distribution (AFM)
RD............. Requirements Document [*NASA*] (KSC)
R & D .... Research and Demonstration [*Labor training*]
R & D .... Research and Development
RD............. Research and Development
RD............. Reserve Decoration [*Navy*] [*British*]
RD............. Resistance Determinant [*Medicine*] (MAE)
RD............. Resource Development
RD............. Respiratory Disease
RD............. Restricted Data [*Security classification*]
RD............. Retention and Disposal
RD............. Retinal Detachment [*Ophthalmology*]
RD............. Revision Directive [*Drawings*]
RD............. Revolutionary Development [*South Vietnam*]
R du D........ Revue du Droit [*A publication*] (DLA)
RD............. Reye's Disease [*Medicine*]
RD............. Right Defense
RD............. Right Deltoid [*Medicine*]
RD............. Right Door [*Theater*]
RD............. Right Dorso Anterior [*Medicine*] (MAE)
RD............. Rights in Data (OICC)
RD............. Ringdown [*Telecommunications*] (TEL)
RD............. Rive Droite [*Right Bank*] [*French*]
RD............. Rix-Dollar
RD............. Road [*Maps and charts*] (AAG)
RD............. Rod
RD............. Romanovsky Dye [*Biological stain*]
RD............. Rood [*Unit of measurement*]
RD............. Roof Drain (AAG)
RD............. Root Diameter (MSA)
R/D .... Rotary to Digital (MCD)
RD............. Rotodrome
RD............. Round (AAG)
RD............. Royal Dragoons [*British*]
RD............. Royal Dutch Petroleum Co. [*NYSE symbol*] (SPSG)
RD............. Royal Naval Reserve Decoration [*British*]
RD............. Ruling Date [*IRS*]
RD............. Run Down [*Typography*]
RD............. Running Days
RD............. Rupture Disk (KSC)
RD............. Rural Deacon [*or Deaconry*] [*Church of England*]
RD............. Rural Dean [*Church of England*]
RD............. Rural Delivery
RD............. Rural Development
RD............. Rural District
rd............... Rutherford [*Unit of strength of a radioactive source*]
RD1........... RADARman, First Class [*Navy rating*]
RD2........... RADARman, Second Class [*Navy rating*]
rd²............ Square Rod (CDAI)
RD3........... RADARman, Third Class [*Navy rating*]
RDA........... Radioactive Dentin Abrasion [*Dentistry*]
RDA........... Railway Development Association [*British*]
RDA........... Ranging Demodulator Assembly [*Deep Space Instrumentation Facility, NASA*]
RDA........... Rassemblement Democratique Africain [*Ivory Coast*] [*Political party*] (PPW)
RDA........... Rassemblement Democratique Africain [*Niger*] [*Political party*] (PD)
RDA........... Read Data Available
RDA........... Reader's Digest Association [*NYSE symbol*] (SPSG)
RDA........... Readers Digest Association [*Commercial firm*] (EA)
RDA........... Real-Time Debugging Aid
RDA........... Recirculation Duct Assembly
RDA........... Recommended Daily Allowance [*Dietary*]
RDA........... Recommended Duty Assignment (AFM)
RDA........... Regional Dance America (EA)
RDA........... Regional Dance Association

RDA .... Regional Data Associates [*Information service or system*] (IID)
RDA .... Regional Dental Activity (AABC)
RDA .... Register Display Assembly
RDA .... Reliability Design Analysis (MCD)
RDA .... Remote Data Access (NASA)
RDA .... Request for Deviation Approval (MCD)
RDA .... Research and Development Abstracts [*A publication*]
RD & A ...... Research, Development, and Acquisition [*A publication*]
RD & A ...... Research, Development, and Acquisition [*DoD*]
RDA .... Research and Development, Army
R & DA ...... Research and Development Associates for Military Food and Packaging Systems (EA)
RDA .... Resent, Demand, Appreciate [*In Sidney Simon, Leland Howe, and Howard Kirschenbaum's book "Values Clarification"*]
RDA .... Resident Data Area (NASA)
RDA .... Retail Display Agreement (WDMC)
RDA .... Reverse Diels-Alder [*Organic chemistry*]
RDA .... Riding for the Disabled Association (EAIO)
RDA .... Right Dorso Anterior [*Medicine*] (ROG)
RDA .... Rod Drop Accident (IEEE)
RDA .... Rome Daily American [*An English-language newspaper in Italy*] [*A publication*]
RDA .... Royal Danish Army (NATG)
RDA .... Royal Defence Academy [*British*]
RDA .... Rules for the Discipline of Attorneys [*A publication*] (DLA)
RDA .... Rural Development Abstracts [*Database*] [*Commonwealth Bureau of Agricultural Economics*] [*Information service or system*] (CRD)
RDA .... Rural Development Act [*1972*] (OICC)
RdAc .... Radioactinium [*Nuclear physics*] (WGA)
RDAC .... Recruiting District Assistance Council [*Navy*] (DNAB)
RDAC .... Report. Department of Antiquities of Cyprus [*A publication*]
RDAC .... Research and Development Acquisition Committee [*Military*]
RDAF .... Revue de Droit Administratif et de Droit Fiscal [*Lausanne, Switzerland*] [*A publication*] (DLA)
RDAF .... Royal Danish Air Force
RDAFCI .... Research and Development Associates, Food and Container Institute (EA)
RDAISA .... Research, Development, and Acquisition Information Systems Agency [*Army*] (AABC)
RDAL .... Representation Dependent Accessing Language
RDAR .... Reliability Design Analysis Report (AAG)
RDARA ...... Regional and Domestic Air Route Area
RDAS........ Reflectivity Data Acquisition System
RDAT .... RADAR Data (FAAC)
RDAT .... Registered Designs Appeal Tribunal (DLA)
RDAT .... Remote Data Acquisition Terminal (NRCH)
RDAT .... Research and Development Acceptance Test
RDAT .... Research, Development, and Test
RDAT .... Rotary Digital Audio Tape
RDAU....... Remote Data Acquisition Unit
RDAVS...... Recovered Doppler Airborne Vector Scorer
RDB .... RADAR Decoy Balloon [*Air Force*]
RDB .... Ramped Dump Barge
RDB .... Rapidly Deployable Barge [*Military*] (MCD)
RDB .... Rare Disease Database [*National Organization for Rare Disorders*] [*Information service or system*] (IID)
RDB .... Reference Data and Bias (SAA)
RDB .... Relational Database
RDB .... Requirements Data Bank [*Air Force*] (GFGA)
RDB .... Requirements and Design Branch (SAA)
RDB .... Research and Development Board [*Abolished, 1953, functions transferred to Department of Defense*]
RDB .... Resistance Decade Box
RDB .... Round Die Bushing
RDB .... Royal Danish Ballet
RDB .... Rural Development Board [*British*]
RDBA .... Roll Drive and Brake Assembly
RDBGA ..... Radiobiologia-Radioterapia [*A publication*]
RDBL........ Readable
RDBMD .... Review on the Deformation Behavior of Materials [*A publication*]
RDBMS..... Relational Database Management System [*Data processing*] (BYTE)
Rdbr Kraftanl ... Rundbrief Kraftanlagen [*A publication*]
RDC .... Chief RADARman [*Navy rating*]
RDC .... RADAR Data Converter (MCD)
RDC .... RADAR Design Corp.
RDC .... RADAR Display Console
RDC .... Radiac [*Nucleonics*]
RDC .... Radiation Density Constant
RDC .... Radioactivity Decay Constant
RDC .... Rail Diesel Car
RDC .... Rapaport Diamond Corp. [*Information service or system*] (IID)
RDC .... Rapid Development Capability [*Military*] (NG)
RDC .... Rassemblement Democratique Caledonien [*Caledonian Democratic Rally*] [*Political party*] (PPW)
RDC .... Rassemblement Democratique Centrafricain [*Central African Republic*] [*Political party*]

RDC .... Rate Damping Control
RDC .... Read Data Check (CMD)
RDC .... Real Decisions Corp. [*Information service or system*] (IID)
RDC .... Recording Doppler Comparator [*Astronomy*] (OA)
RDC .... Reduce (MSA)
RDC .... Reference Designator Code (NASA)
RDC .... Reflex Digital Control
RDC .... Refugee Documentation Centre [*Information service or system*] (IID)
RDC .... Regional Data Center [*Marine science*] (MSC)
RDC .... Regional Dissemination Center [*NASA*]
RDC .... Regional Distribution Center [*TRW Automotive Aftermarket Group*]
RDC .... Reliability Data Center (KSC)
RDC .... Remote Data Collection (MCD)
RDC .... Remote Data Concentrator
RDC .... Remote Detonation Capability
RDC .... Reply Delay Compensation (MUGU)
RDC .... Request for Document Change (NASA)
RDC .... Research and Development Command [*Military*]
RDC .... Research Diagnostic Criteria [*Medicine, psychiatry*]
RdC .... Resto del Carlino [*A publication*]
RDC .... Revolutionary Development Cadre [*South Vietnam*]
RDC .... Rochester Diocesan Chronicle [*A publication*]
RDC .... Rotary Dispersion Colorimeter
RDC .... Rotating Diffusion Cell [*Chemistry*]
RDC .... Rotating Disk Contractor [*Chemical engineering*]
RDC .... Rowan Companies, Inc. [*NYSE symbol*] (SPSG)
RDC .... Royal Defence Corps [*British*]
RDC .... Rubber Development Corp. [*Expired, 1947*]
RDC .... Running-Down Clause [*Business term*]
RDC .... Rural Development and Conservation [*Department of Agriculture*]
RDC .... Rural District Council [*British*]
RDC .... Sisters of Divine Compassion [*Roman Catholic religious order*]
R2DC3 ...... Rapid Reaction, Deployable Command, Control, and Communications
RDCA .... Rural District Councils Association [*British*]
RDCC .... Regional Distributors and Carriers Conference (EA)
RD-CCSA ... Reciprocal Derivative Constant-Current Stripping Analysis [*Analytical electrochemistry*]
RDCEHCY ... Research and Demonstration Center for the Education of Handicapped Children and Youth (EA)
RDCEO ..... Rural District Council Executive Officer [*British*]
RDCF........ Restricted Data Cover Folder (AAG)
RDCHE ..... Rene Dubos Center for Human Environments (EA)
RDCM ...... Master Chief RADARman [*Navy rating*]
RDCM ...... Reduced Delta Code Modulation [*Digital memory*]
RDCN....... Reduction (MSA)
RDCO........ Reliability Data Control Office (AAG)
R & D Con Mn ... Research and Development Contracts Monthly [*A publication*]
RDCP........ Remote Display Control Panel (MCD)
RDCR .... Reducer (MSA)
RDCRIT .... Read Criteria (SAA)
RDCS........ Reconfiguration Data Collection System [*or Subsystem*] (MCD)
RDCS........ Senior Chief RADARman [*Navy rating*]
RDCTD8 ... Australia. Commonwealth Scientific and Industrial Research Organisation. Division of Chemical Technology. Research Review [*A publication*]
R & DCTE ... Research and Development Center for Teacher Education [*Department of Education*] (GRD)
RDCU........ Receipt Delivery Control Unit [*Social Security Administration*]
RDD.......... Random Digit Dialing [*Telecommunications*]
RDD.......... Rapid Demolition Device
RDD.......... Rassemblement Democratique Dahomeen [*Dahomean Democratic Rally*]
RDD.......... Reactor Development Division [*of AEC*]
RDD.......... Redding [*California*] [*Airport symbol*] (OAG)
RDD.......... Reference Design Document (KSC)
RDD.......... Required Delivery Date (AABC)
RDD.......... Requirements Definition Document [*NASA*] (NASA)
RDD.......... Requisition Due Date (TEL)
RD & D ...... Research, Development, and Demonstration
RDD.......... Research and Development Directorate [*Army*]
RDD.......... Return Due Date [*IRS*]
RDD.......... Routine Dynamic Display (MCD)
RDDA........ Recommended Daily Dietary Allowance
RDDCS...... Range Drone Data Control System [*Military*] (CAAL)
RDD & E.... Research, Development, Diffusion [*or Dissemination*], and Evaluation
RDDM....... Reactor Deck Development Mock-Up [*Nuclear energy*] (NRCH)
RDDMI ..... Radio Digital Distance Magnetic Indicator (MCD)
RDDP .... RNA [*Ribonucleic Acid*]-Directed DNA [*Deoxyribonucleic Acid*] Polymerase [*Formerly, RIDP*] [*An enzyme*]
RDDR........ Rod Drive
RDDS .... RADAR Data Distribution Switchboard [*Military*] (CAAL)
RDDS .... Retail Dental Delivery System [*Dentistry*]
RDE .... RADAR Display Equipment

RDE .... Radial Defect Examination   (IEEE)
RDE .... Receptor-Destroying Enzyme [*A neuraminidase*]
            [*Immunochemistry*]
RDE .... Recommended Distribution of Effort [*Civil defense*]
RDE .... Relational Database Engine   (PCM)
RDE .... Reliability Data Extractor   (MCD)
RD & E ...... Research, Development, and Engineering
RDE .... Research, Development, and Engineering   (RDA)
RDE .... Research and Development Establishment [*British*]
RDE .... Research Development Exchange   (OICC)
RDE .... Rotating Disc Electrode
RDE & A .... Research, Development, Engineering, and Acquisition   (RDA)
RDEB .... Recessive Dystrophic Epidermolysis Bullosa [*Also, EBDR*]
            [*Dermatology*]
RDEC .... Research, Development, and Engineering Center   (RDA)
RDEEA ...... Radio and Electronic Engineer [*A publication*]
R & DELSEC ... Research and Development Electronic Security
            [*Military*]   (AABC)
RDEP .... Recruit Depot [*Navy*]
RDES .... Requirement and Determination Execution System
RD & ES .... Requirements Determination and Exercise System
            [*Military*]   (MCD)
RDF .... RADAR Direction Finder [*or Finding*]   (CET)
RDF .... Radial Distribution Function [*X-ray diffraction*]
RDF .... Radio Direction Finder [*or Finding*]   (AABC)
RDF .... Rapid Deployment Force [*Military*]
RDF .... Record Definition Field [*Data processing*]   (BUR)
RDF .... Redford Resources, Inc. [*Vancouver Stock Exchange symbol*]
RDF .... Reflection Direction Finding
RDF .... Refuse-Derived Fuel
RDF .... Repeater Distribution Frame   (NATG)
RDF .... Research, Development, and Facilities   (NOAA)
RDF .... Reserve Defense Fleet [*Navy*]
RDF .... Resource Data File   (MCD)
RDF .... Robotech Defense Force   (EA)
RDF .... Roger Wyburn-Mason and Jack M. Blount Foundation for the
            Eradication of Rheumatoid Disease   (EA)
RDF .... Royal Dublin Fusiliers [*British*]
RDF-A .... Rapid Deployment Force - Army
RDFDF ...... Redford Resources, Inc. [*NASDAQ symbol*]   (NQ)
RDFI .... Receiving Depository Financial Institution
RDFL .... Reflection Direction Finding, Low Angle   (MCD)
RDF/LT.... Rapid Deployment Force/Light Tank [*Military*]   (MCD)
RDFQ .... Recueil de Droit Fiscal Quebecois [*A publication*]   (DLA)
RDFSTA ... Radio Direction Finder Station
RDFU .... Research and Development Field Unit [*Military*]
RDFU-V .... Research and Development Field Unit - Vietnam
            [*Military*]   (MCD)
RDG.......... Reading [*British depot code*]
RDG.......... Reading
RDG.......... Reading [*Pennsylvania*] [*Airport symbol*]   (OAG)
Rdg........... Reducing   (WGA)
RDG.......... Reference Drawing Group [*NATO*]   (NATG)
RDG.......... Regional Development Grant [*British*]   (DCTA)
RDG.......... Registrar Data Group [*Information service or system*]   (IID)
RDG.......... Relative Disturbance Gain [*Control engineering*]
RDG.......... Research Discussion Group   (EA)
RDG.......... Resolver Differential Generator
RDG.......... Resource Development Group Ltd. [*British*]
RDG.......... Ridge   (MSA)
RDG.......... Right Digestive Gland
RDG.......... Rounding
RDG.......... Rover P4 Drivers Guild [*An association*]   (EAIO)
RdgBte .... Reading & Bates Corp. [*Associated Press
            abbreviation*]   (APAG)
RDGC .... Reading Co. [*NASDAQ symbol*]   (NQ)
RDGE .... Resorcinol Diglycidyl Ether [*Organic chemistry*]
RDGF .... Retina-Derived Growth Factor [*Biochemistry*]
RDGNA ..... Radiologia Diagnostica [*A publication*]
RDGRA ..... Radiographer [*A publication*]
RDGT .... Reliability Development Growth Testing   (RDA)
RDGTA ..... Rational Drug Therapy [*A publication*]
RDH .... Radioactive Drain Header [*Nuclear energy*]   (NRCH)
RDH .... Rapid Displacement Heating [*Pulp and paper technology*]
RDH .... Red Hill Marketing Group Ltd. [*Vancouver Stock Exchange
            symbol*]
RDH .... Registered Dental Hygienist
RDH .... Resource Dispersion Hypothesis [*Animal ecology*]
RDH .... Round Head
RDH .... Royal Deccan Horse [*British military*]   (DMA)
RDHER ..... Revolutionary Development Hamlet Evaluation Report [*South
            Vietnam*]
RDI .... Radio Doppler Inertial
RDI .... Rassemblement des Democrates Liberaux pour la
            Reconstruction Nationale [*Benin*] [*Political party*]   (EY)
RDI .... Rassemblement Democratique pour l'Independance [*Quebec*]
RDI .... Recommended Daily Intake [*Dietary*]
RDI .... Reference Daily Intake [*FDA*]
RDI .... Reference Designation Index   (MCD)
RDI .... Rejection and Disposition Item
RDI .... Released Data Index

RDI .... Reliability Design Index   (DNAB)
RDI .... Relief and Development Institute [*Formerly, International
            Disaster Institute*]   (EA)
RDI .... Remote Data Input
RDI .... Research and Development Institute, Inc. [*Montana State
            University*] [*Research center*]   (RCD)
RDI .... Research and Development of Instrumentation [*Program*]
            [*Army*]
RDI .... Riley's Datashare International Ltd. [*Toronto Stock Exchange
            symbol*]
RDI .... Route Digit Indicator [*Telecommunications*]   (TEL)
RDI .... Royal Designer for Industry [*British*]
RDI .... Rupture Delivery Interval [*Obstetrics*]
RDIA .... Regional Development Incentives Act
RDIF .... Rural Development Insurance Fund [*Farmers Home
            Administration*] [*Department of Agriculture*]   (GFGA)
RDIGA ..... Reader's Digest [*A publication*]
RDIPP .... Rivista di Diritto Internazionale Privato e Processuale [*A
            publication*]   (DLA)
RDIS........ Radiation Disposal Systems, Inc. [*Charlotte, NC*] [*NASDAQ
            symbol*]   (NQ)
RDIS........ Replenishment Demand Inventory System
RDIS........ Research and Development Information System [*Later, EPD/
            RDIS*] [*Electric Power Research Institute*] [*Information
            service or system*]   (IID)
RDISSS ..... Royal Dockyard Iron and Steel Shipbuilders' Society [*A union*]
            [*British*]
RDIU .... Remote Device Interface Unit
R 1 DIY ...... Royal 1st Devon Imperial Yeomanry [*British military*]   (DMA)
RDJ........... Readjustment
RDJ........... Rio De Janeiro [*Brazil*] [*Later, VSS*] [*Geomagnetic observatory
            code*]
RDJ........... Rio De Janeiro [*Brazil*] [*Seismograph station code, US
            Geological Survey*]   (SEIS)
RDJCT ..... Register, Department of Justice and the Courts of the United
            States [*A publication*]
RDJTF....... Rapid Deployment Joint Task Force [*Military*]   (RDA)
RDK .... Red Oak, IA [*Location identifier*] [*FAA*]   (FAAL)
RDK .... Research and Development Kit
RDK .... Ruddick Corp. [*NYSE symbol*]   (SPSG)
RDKN....... Redken Laboratories, Inc. [*NASDAQ symbol*]   (NQ)
RDL .... Radial   (MSA)
RDL .... Radioactive Decay Law
RDL .... Radiological Defense Laboratory [*NASA*]   (KSC)
RDL .... Rail Dynamics Laboratory
RDL .... Random Dynamic Load
RDL .... Rapid Draft Letter   (DNAB)
RDL .... [*The*] Reactor Development Laboratory [*UKAEA*] [*British*]
RDL .... Reallexikon der Deutschen Literaturgeschichte [*A publication*]
RDL .... Rear Defence Locality [*British military*]   (DMA)
RDL .... Reciprocal Detection Latency
RDL .... Recurring Document Listing   (MCD)
RDL .... Redlaw Industries, Inc. [*AMEX symbol*] [*Toronto Stock
            Exchange symbol*]   (SPSG)
RDL .... Regional Development Laboratory [*Philadelphia, PA*]
RDL .... Reliable Detection Limit [*Analytical chemistry*]
RDL .... Remote Display Link
RDL .... Replaceable Display Light
RDL .... Resistor Diode Logic
RDL .... Rim of Dorsal Lip
RDL .... Rocket Development Laboratory [*Air Force*]
RDLGB...... Radiologe [*A publication*]
RDLGE...... Reunion Democratica para la Liberacion de Guinea Ecuatorial
            [*Democratic Movement for the Liberation of Equatorial
            Guinea*] [*Political party*]   (PD)
RDLI .... Royal Durban Light Infantry [*British military*]   (DMA)
RD-LMXB ... Radiation-Driven Low-Mass X-Ray Binary [*Cosmology*]
RDLN .... Retrodorsolateral Nucleus [*Neuroanatomy*]
RDLP........ Research and Development Limited Partnership [*Tax-shelter
            investment*]
RDLX .... Airlift International, Inc. [*Air carrier designation symbol*]
RdM......... Die Religionen der Menschheit [*A publication*]   (BJA)
RDM........ RADARman [*Also, RD*]
RDM........ Radial Distribution Method
RDM........ Random   (WGA)
RDM........ Random Dimer Model [*Physics*]
RDM........ Real-Time Data Manager   (MCD)
RDM........ Recording Demand Meter
RDM........ Redmond [*Oregon*] [*Airport symbol*]   (OAG)
RDM........ Relay Driver Module
RDM........ Remote Data Management
RDM........ Remote Digital Multiplexer   (MCD)
RDM........ Retail and Distribution Management [*A publication*]
RDMAA .... R and D [*Research and Development*] Management [*A
            publication*]
R and D Manage ... R and D [*Research and Development*] Management [*A
            publication*]
R & D Mangt ... R and D [*Research and Development*] Management [*A
            publication*]
RDMC .... Research and Development Management Course [*Army*]
R de D McGill ... Revue de Droit de McGill [*A publication*]   (DLA)

RDME .... Range and Distance Measuring Equipment
RDMF .... Rapidly Deployable Medical Facilities
RDMGA .... Railway Dock and Marine Grades Association [*A union*] [*British*]
RDMI .... Roof Drainage Manufacturers Institute [*Defunct*]   (EA)
RDMS .... Range Data Measurement Subsystem   (MCD)
RDMS .... Registered Diagnostic Medical Sonologist
RDMS .... Retail Development Management Services [*British*]
RDMS .... Retrospective Data Management System
RDMSS ..... Rapidly Deployable Mobile SIGINT [*Signal Intelligence*] System   (MCD)
RDMTR .... Radiometer   (NASA)
RDMU .... Range-Drift Measuring Unit
RDN.......... Real de Minas Mine [*Vancouver Stock Exchange symbol*]
RDN.......... Rejection Disposition Notice
RDN.......... Royal Danish Navy   (NATG)
RDN.......... Rural Deanery [*Church of England*]
rDNA .... Deoxyribonucleic Acid, Recombinant [*Biochemistry, genetics*]
rDNA .... Deoxyribonucleic Acid, Ribosomal [*Biochemistry, genetics*]
RDNA........ Recombinant DNA [*Deoxyribonucleic Acid*]   (MCD)
R & DNET ... Research and Development Network [*Formerly, ARPANET*]
RDNG........ Reading   (MSA)
RDNGB..... Ryukyu Daigaku Nogakubu Gakujutsu Hokoku [*A publication*]
RDNP .... Rassemblement Democratique Nationaliste et Progressiste [*Progressive Nationalist and Democratic Assembly*] [*Haiti*]   (PD)
RDNS .... Readiness   (MSA)
RDNU........ Rally for Democracy and National Unity [*Mauritania*] [*Political party*]   (EY)
RDO.......... Radio   (AABC)
RDO.......... Radio Readout
RDO.......... Radiological Defense Officer [*Civil defense*]
RDO.......... Range Development Officer   (MUGU)
RDO.......... Rechnungswesen, Datentechnik, Organisation [*A publication*]
RDO.......... Reconnaissance Duty Officer
RDO.......... Redistribution Order [*Military*]   (AFM)
RDO.......... Regional Defense Organization   (DNAB)
RDO.......... Regional Disbursing Office
RDO.......... Research and Development Objectives [*Military*]   (AFM)
RDO.......... Research, Development, and Operation [*Military appropriation*]
R & DO...... Research and Development Operations [*Marshall Space Flight Center*] [*NASA*]   (NASA)
RDO.......... River District Office [*National Weather Service*]
RDO.......... Rodeo Resources Ltd. [*Vancouver Stock Exchange symbol*]
RDO.......... Runway Duty Officer [*Aviation*]   (MCD)
RDOC....... Reference Designation Overflow Code   (NASA)
RDOC....... Residential Distillate Oil Combustion [*Industrial medicine*]
RDOM...... Restructured Division Operations Manual   (MCD)
RDON .... Radon Testing Corp. of America, Inc. [*NASDAQ symbol*]   (NQ)
RDON .... Road Octane Number [*Fuel technology*]
RDOS .... Real-Time Disk-Operating System [*Data processing*]
RDOUT..... Readout
RDP .... RADAR Data Processing
RDP .... RADAR Digital Probe
RDP .... Radiation Degradation Product
RDP .... Radiodifusao Portuguesa [*State Broadcasting Service*]
RDP .... Range Data Processor   (MCD)
RDP .... Range Deflection Protractor [*Weaponry*]   (INF)
RDP .... Rassemblement pour la Democratie et le Progres [*Mali*] [*Political party*]   (EY)
RDP .... Ration Distributing Point [*Military*]
RDP .... Reactor Development Program [*Nuclear Regulatory Commission*]   (NRCH)
RDP .... Receiver and Data Processor   (MCD)
RDP .... Rectifying-Demodulating Phonopneumograph [*Medicine*]
RDP .... Redeployment Point [*Military*]   (INF)
RDP .... Remote Data Processor
RDP .... Requirements Data Plan   (NASA)
RDP .... Requirements Development Plan [*NASA*]   (NASA)
RDP .... Research Data Publication [*Center*]
RDP .... Research and Development Plan
RD & P....... Research, Development, and Production [*NATO*]   (NATG)
RDP .... Reunification Democracy Party [*Political party*] [*South Korea*]
RDP .... Revolutionary Development Program [*South Vietnam*]
RDP .... Ribulosediphosphate [*Also, RuBP*] [*Biochemistry*]
RDP .... Right Dorso Posterior [*Medicine*]   (ROG)
RDP .... Rocca Di Papa [*Italy*] [*Seismograph station code, US Geological Survey*]   (SEIS)
RDPB........ RADAR Data Plotting Board
RDPB........ Research and Development Planning and Budgeting   (AFIT)
RD/PBM ... Research and Development/Programming Budget Memorandum   (MCD)
RDPC....... RADAR Data Processing Center [*Military*]
RDPE........ RADAR Data Processing Equipment   (AABC)
RDPJ .... Rail Discharge Point Jet   (NATG)
RDPM....... Rail Discharge Point Mogas   (NATG)
RDPM .... Revised Draft Presidential Memorandum
RDPM .... Rotary Drive Piston Motor

R & DPP .... Research and Development Program Planning [*Database*] [*DTIC*]
RDPR .... Refer to Drawer Please Represent [*Business term*]   (DCTA)
RDPS........ RADAR Data Processing System
RDPS........ Remote Docking Procedures Simulator   (MCD)
RDPS........ Research and Development Planning Summary
RdQ........... Reading Quotient
RDR .... Grand Forks, ND [*Location identifier*] [*FAA*]   (FAAL)
RDR .... RADAR   (AAG)
RDR .... Raider
RDR .... Rapid Canadian Resource Corp. [*Vancouver Stock Exchange symbol*]
RDR .... Raw Data Recorder   (NASA)
RDR .... Reader   (MSA)
R/DR .... Rear Door [*Automotive engineering*]
RDR .... Receive Data Register [*Data processing*]   (MDG)
RDR .... Rejection Disposition Report [*NASA*]   (KSC)
RDR .... Relative Digestion Rate [*Nutrition*]
RDR .... Reliability Design Review
RDR .... Reliability Diagnostic Report   (AAG)
RDR .... Remote Digital Readout
RDR .... Repeat Discrepancy Report   (MCD)
RDR .... Research and Development Report
RDR .... Research Division Report
RDR .... Ribonucleoside Diphosphate Reductase [*An enzyme*]
RDR .... Risk Data Report [*Insurance*]
RDR .... Risk-Driven Remediation
RDR .... Rudder   (NASA)
RDR .... Ryukoku Daigaku Ronshu [*A publication*]
RDRBCN... RADAR Beacon   (KSC)
RDRC .... Road Design and Road Costs [*British*]
RdrD .... Readers Digest Association [*Associated Press abbreviation*]   (APAG)
RDRD .... Remote Digital Readout
RdrDg .... Reader's Digest Association [*Associated Press abbreviation*]   (APAG)
RDR/EO.... RADAR/Electro-Optical   (MCD)
R/D Res/Develop ... R/D. Research/Development [*A publication*]
RD Res Dev (Kobe Steel Ltd) ... R & D. Research and Development (Kobe Steel Ltd.) [*A publication*]
RDRIA .... Radiazioni e Radioisotopi [*A publication*]
RDRINT.... RADAR Intermittent   (IEEE)
RDRKB..... Ritsumeikan Daigaku Rikogaku Kenkyusho Kiyo [*A publication*]
RDRM .... Return Data Relay Measurement   (SSD)
RDRSMTR ... RADAR Transmitter   (AAG)
RDRT .... Read-Rite Corp. [*NASDAQ symbol*]   (SPSG)
RDRV .... Rhesus Diploid-Cell-Strain Rabies Vaccine
RDR XMTR ... RADAR Transmitter
RDS .... RADAR Distribution Switchboard
RDS .... RADAUS [*Radio-Austria AG*] Data-Service [*Telecommunications*]
RDS .... Radio Digital System [*Telecommunications*]   (TEL)
RDS .... Radius   (FAAC)
RDS .... Random Dot Stereogram
RDS .... Range Destruct System
RDS .... Rate-Determining Step [*Chemical kinetics*]
RDS .... Rate of Dispersal Success [*Ecology*]
RDS .... Raytheon Data Systems Co.
RDS .... Read Select   (SAA)
RDS .... Read Strobe
RDS .... Reeds [*Music*]
RDS .... Relative Detector Sensitivity [*Robotics technology*]
RDS .... Rendezvous Docking Simulator [*Aerospace*]
RDS .... Reperimento Documentazione Siderurgica [*Iron and Steel Documentation Service*] [*Information service or system*]   (IID)
RDS .... Request for Data Services
RDS .... Required Number of Days of Stock
RDS .... Requisition Distribution System
RDS .... Research Defence Society [*British*]
RDS .... Research and Development Service [*Army-Ordnance*]
RDS .... Research, Development, and Standardization [*Groups*] [*Army*]   (RDA)
RD & S....... Research, Development, and Studies [*Marine Corps*]
RDS .... Research and Development Survey
RDS .... Research Documentation Section [*Public Health Service*] [*Information service or system*]   (IID)
RDS .... Research Documents Search [*Information service or system*]   (IID)
RDS .... Residuum Desulfurization [*Petroleum technology*]
RDS .... Resistive Divider Standard
RDS .... Resource Development Services   (EA)
RDS .... Respiratory Distress Syndrome [*Formerly, HMD*] [*Medicine*]
RdS .... Responsabilita del Sapere [*A publication*]
RDS .... Retail Distribution Station [*Military*]   (AFM)
RDS .... Reticuloendothelial Depressing Substance [*Medicine*]   (AAMN)
RDS .... Revolutionary Development Support [*South Vietnam*]
RDS .... Revolving Discussion Sequence
RDS .... Rhode Island Department of State Library Services, Providence, RI [*OCLC symbol*]   (OCLC)

RDS .... Richard D. Siegrest [*Alaska*] [*Seismograph station code, US Geological Survey*] (SEIS)
RDS .... Robotic Deriveter System
RDS .... Robust Detection Scheme [*Navigation*] (OA)
RDS .... Rocket Development Section [*Picatinny Arsenal*] [*Dover, NJ*]
RDS .... Rocketdyne Digital Simulator [*NASA*] (NASA)
RDS .... Rokeach Dogmatism Scale
RDS .... Rounds [*of ammunition*] [*Military*]
RDS .... Royal Drawing Society [*British*]
RDS .... Royal Dublin Society
RDS .... Rural Development Service [*Department of Agriculture*]
RDS .... Russkaja Demokraticeskaja Satira XVII Veka [*A publication*]
RDSA....... Seaman Apprentice, RADARman Striker [*Navy rating*]
RD/SB .... Rudder Speed Brake [*Aviation*] (MCD)
RDSD .... Reliability Design Support Document [*Nuclear energy*] (NRCH)
RDSD .... Revolutionary Development Support Division [*South Vietnam*]
Rds Eng Constr ... Roads and Engineering Construction [*A publication*]
RDSM ...... Remote Digital Submultiplexer (KSC)
RDSM ...... Research Development Safety Management [*Air Force*]
RDS/M...... Rounds per Minute [*Military*]
RDSN .... RADARman, Seaman [*Navy rating*]
RDSN .... Seaman, RADARman, Striker [*Navy rating*]
RDSO .... Research, Design, and Standardization Organization [*Indian Railways*] [*India*] (PDAA)
RDSP........ Revolutionary Development Support Plan [*or Program*] [*South Vietnam*]
Rds Rd Constn ... Roads and Road Construction [*A publication*]
RDSS .... Radio Determination Satellite Service [*Geostar Corp.*]
RDSS .... Rapid Deployable Surveillance Systems [*Military*] (NVT)
RD Sup ...... Revenue Decisions, Supplement [*India*] [*A publication*] (DLA)
RDT .... Radio Digital Terminal [*Bell System*]
RDT .... Rapid Decompression Test
RDT .... Reactor Development and Technology [*Nuclear energy*] (MCD)
RDT .... Reactor Drain Tank [*Nuclear energy*] (NRCH)
RDT .... Recreatie-Documentatie. Literatuuroverzicht Inzake Dagrecreatie, Verblijfsrecreatie, en Toerisme [*A publication*]
RDT .... Redoubt [*Alaska*] [*Seismograph station code, US Geological Survey*] (SEIS)
RDT .... Regular Dialysis Treatment [*Medicine*]
RDT .... Reliability Demonstration Test
RDT .... Reliability Design Test
RDT .... Reliability Development Testing (CAAL)
RDT .... Remote Data Transmitter
RDT .... Renal Dialysis Treatment [*Nephrology*]
RDT .... Repertory Dance Theatre [*Salt Lake City, UT*]
RD & T...... Research, Development, and Testing
RDT .... Reserve Duty Training [*Military*]
RDT .... Resource Definition Table [*Data processing*] (IBMDP)
RDT .... Retinal Damage Threshold [*Ophthalmology*]
RDT .... Revue de Droit du Travail [*A publication*] (DLA)
RDT .... Richard-Toll [*Senegal*] [*Airport symbol*] (OAG)
RDT .... Rotational Direction Transmission
RDT & E.... Research, Development, Test, and Engineering (SSD)
RDTE .... Research, Development, Test, and Evaluation [*DoD*]
RDT & E.... Research, Development, Test, and Evaluation [*DoD*]
RDTEA...... Research, Development, Test, and Evaluation, Army
RDT & EN ... Research, Development, Test, and Evaluation, Navy
RDTF........ Revolutionary Development Task Force [*South Vietnam*]
RdTh........ Radiothorium [*Nuclear physics*] (WGA)
RDTL........ Resistor Diode Transistor Logic (IEEE)
RDTLC...... Rotating Disc Thin-Layer Chromatography
RDTM .... Rated Distribution and Training Management
RDTR .... Radiator (MSA)
RDTR .... Research Division Technical Report
RDTSR...... Rapid Data Transmission System for Requisitioning [*Navy*]
RDU.......... RADAR Display Unit
RDU.......... Raleigh/Durham [*North Carolina*] [*Airport symbol*]
RDU.......... Receipt and Despatch Unit [*Aircraft*]
RDU.......... Refrigerated Detector Unit (SAA)
RDU.......... Remote Display Unit [*American Solenoid Co.*] [*Somerset, NJ*]
RDU.......... Rideau Resources Corp. [*Vancouver Stock Exchange symbol*]
R Dublin Soc J Life Sci ... Royal Dublin Society. Journal of Life Sciences [*A publication*]
R Dublin Soc J Sc Pr ... Royal Dublin Society. Journal. Scientific Proceedings [*A publication*]
R Dublin Soc Rep ... Royal Dublin Society. Report [*A publication*]
RDUC........ Receiver Data from Unit Control (MCD)
RDV......... Rechentechnik-Datenverarbeitung [*A publication*]
RDV.......... Recoverable Drop Vehicle (MCD)
RDV.......... Red Devil [*Alaska*] [*Airport symbol*] (OAG)
RDV.......... Rice Dwarf Virus [*Plant pathology*]
RDV.......... Rotary Disk Valve [*Automotive engineering*]
RDV.......... Rotating Dome Valve [*Military*] (RDA)
RDVA .... Radva Corp. [*Radford, VA*] [*NASDAQ symbol*] (NQ)
RDVT .... Reliability Design Verification Test
RDVU....... Rendezvous (AABC)
RDW.......... Red Cell Size Distribution Width [*Hematology*]

RDW.......... Redwood Resources, Inc. [*Vancouver Stock Exchange symbol*]
RDW.......... Response Data Word (MCD)
RDW.......... Return Data Word (MCD)
RDW.......... Right Defense Wing [*Women's lacrosse position*]
RDWA....... Returned Development Workers Association (EAIO)
RDWCA .... Royal Dockyard Wood Caulkers' Association [*A union*] [*British*]
RDWI .... Roadway Motor Plazas, Inc. [*Rochester, NY*] [*NASDAQ symbol*] (NQ)
RDWND.... RADAR Dome Wind [*Meteorology*] (FAAC)
RDWS .... Radiological Defense Warning System
RDWW...... United Slate Tile and Composition Roofers, Damp and Waterproof Workers Association [*Later, UURWAW*]
RDX .... Cocoa, FL [*Location identifier*] [*FAA*] (FAAL)
RDX .... Research Department Explosive [*Cyclonite*]
RDY .... Aspen, CO [*Location identifier*] [*FAA*] (FAAL)
RDY .... Ready (AAG)
RDY .... Roadway
RDY .... Royal Devon Yeomanry [*British military*] (DMA)
RDY .... Royal Dockyard [*British*]
RDYA .... Royal Devon Yeomanry Artillery [*British military*] (DMA)
RDZ .... Ringier Dokumentationszentrum [*Ringier Documentation Center*] [*Switzerland*] [*Information service or system*] (IID)
RDZ .... Rodez [*France*] [*Airport symbol*] (OAG)
Re .... Earth or Geocentric Radius (AAG)
RE .... Fellow of the Royal Society of Painter-Etchers and Engravers [*British*]
RE .... Nordeste Linhas Aereas Regionais SA [*Brazil*] [*ICAO designator*] (FAAC)
Re .... Ohio Decisions Reprint [*A publication*] (DLA)
RE .... Radiated Emission (IEEE)
RE .... Radiation Effects (AAG)
RE .... Radiation Equipment (NRCH)
RE .... Radio-Eireann [*Eire*] [*Record label*]
RE .... Radio Electrician
RE .... Radio Exposure (AAG)
RE .... Radium Emanation
RE .... Railway Executive [*British*]
Re .... Rainerius [*Authority cited in pre-1607 legal work*] (DSA)
RE .... Rainform Expanded (MCD)
RE .... Ram Effect [*Mechanical engineering*] (OA)
RE .... Rare Earth
RE .... Rate Effect (IEEE)
RE .... Rate of Exchange
R of E .... Rate of Exchange
RE .... Rational Expectations [*Economics*] (ECON)
RE .... Rattus Exulans [*The Polynesian rat*]
RE .... Raw End (OA)
RE .... Reactive Evaporation [*Coating technology*]
RE .... Reading-Ease [*Score*] [*Advertising*]
Re .... Real [*Mathematics*]
RE .... Real-Encyclopaedie der Klassischen Altertumswissenschaft [*A publication*]
RE .... Real Estate
RE .... Real Estate Program [*Association of Independent Colleges and Schools specialization code*]
RE .... Real Number (DEN)
Re .... Realidad [*A publication*] (MCD)
RE .... Receiver/Exciter
RE .... Recent [*Used to qualify weather phenomena*]
RE .... Reconnaissance Experimental [*British military*] (DMA)
RE .... Rectal Examination [*Medicine*]
RE .... Red Edges
RE .... Redman Industries, Inc. [*NYSE symbol*] (SPSG)
RE .... Reel (MSA)
R/E .... Reentry [*Aerospace*] (KSC)
RE .... Reference [*Online database field identifier*]
RE .... Reference Equivalent [*Telecommunications*] (TEL)
RE .... Reflux
Re .... Reforme [*A publication*]
RE .... Reformed Episcopal [*Church*]
RE .... Refrigeration Effect
RE .... Regarding
RE .... Regional Enteritis [*Medicine*]
RE .... Rehearsal Engineer (MCD)
RE .... Reinforced [*Technical drawings*]
Re .... Reinsurance [*A publication*]
RE .... Relative Effectiveness [*or Efficiency*] (MCD)
RE .... Relay Assemblies [*JETDS nomenclature*] [*Military*] (CET)
RE .... Release
RE .... Religious Education [*A publication*]
RE .... Religious Education [*Secondary school course*] [*British*]
RE .... Religious of the Eucharist [*Roman Catholic women's religious order*]
RE .... Renewal Registration [*US Copyright Office class*]
RE .... Renovacion Espanola [*Spanish Renovation*] (PPE)
RE .... Repair Equipment [*Navy*]
RE .... Repair Equipment for F-15 and Subsequent Programs [*Military*] (MCD)
RE .... Repayable to Either

RE .... Repetitive Extrasystole [*Cardiology*]
RE .... Reportable Event   (EPA)
Re .... Republic [*Quezon City*] [*A publication*]
RE .... Republication [*NASA*]
RE .... Request for Estimate
R & E .... Research and Education   (MAE)
RE .... Research and Engineering
R & E .... Research and Engineering
RE .... Research and Experiments Department [*Ministry of Home
                    Security*] [*British*] [*World War II*]
RE .... Reset   (MDG)
RE .... Resolution Enhancement [*Computer graphics*]
Re .... Respiratory Exchange Ratio [*Medicine*]   (MAE)
Re .... Response [*A publication*]
RE .... Responsible Engineer   (NASA)
RE .... Rest [*or Resting*] Energy [*Medicine*]
RE .... Restriction Endonuclease [*An enzyme*]
RE .... Reticuloendothelial [*or Reticuloendothelium*] [*Medicine*]
RE .... Retinal Equivalent [*For Vitamin A*]
RE .... Retinyl Ester [*Organic chemistry*]
re .... Reunion [*MARC country of publication code*] [*Library of
                    Congress*]   (LCCP)
RE .... Reunion [*ANSI two-letter standard code*]   (CNC)
RE .... Reversal of Prior Entry [*Banking*]
RE .... Review of Ethnology [*A publication*]
RE .... Review and Expositor [*A publication*]
RE .... Revised Edition [*Publishing*]
Re .... Reynolds Number [*Viscosity*] [*IUPAC*]
Re .... Rhenium [*Chemical element*]
RE .... Rifle Expert
RE .... Right Eminent [*Freemasonry*]
RE .... Right End
RE .... Right Excellent
RE .... Right Eye
RE .... Risk Evaluation [*Insurance*]
RE .... Risk Exercise
RE .... Riviera Explorations Ltd. [*Vancouver Stock Exchange symbol*]
RE .... Rotary Engine [*Automotive engineering*]
RE .... Royal Engineers [*Military*] [*British*]
RE .... Royal Exchange [*British*]
RE .... Royal Society of Painter-Etchers and Engravers [*British*]
RE .... Rupee [*Monetary unit*] [*Ceylon, India, and Pakistan*]
RE .... Rural Electrification
R2E .... Realisations et Etudes Electronique [*Computer manufacturer*]
                    [*France*]
REA .... RADAR Echoing Area
REA .... Radiation Emergency Area
REA .... Radiative Energy Attenuation [*Analytical chemistry*]
REA .... Radio Electrical Artificer [*British military*]   (DMA)
REA .... Radioenzymatic Assay [*Analytical biochemistry*]
REA .... Railroad Evangelistic Association   (EA)
REA .... Railway Express Agency [*Later, REA Express*] [*Defunct*]
REA .... Range Error Average   (MUGU)
REA .... Rare-Earth Alloy
R & EA ...... Readiness and Emergency Action [*Red Cross Disaster Services*]
REA .... Realcap Holdings Ltd. [*Toronto Stock Exchange symbol*]
REA .... Reao [*French Polynesia*] [*Airport symbol*]   (OAG)
REA .... Recycle Acid [*Nuclear energy*]   (NRCH)
REA .... Reentry Angle
REA .... Religious Education Association   (EA)
REA .... Renaissance Educational Associates   (EA)
REA .... Renal Anastomosis [*Medicine*]
REA .... Request for Engineering Authorization
REA .... Request for Equitable Adjustment [*Navy*]
REA .... Research and Education Association
REA .... Research Engineering Authorization   (AAG)
REA .... Reserve Enlisted Association   (EA)
REA .... Responsible Engineering Activity
REA .... Rice Export Association
REA .... Ridihalgh, Eggers & Associates, Columbus, OH [*OCLC
                    symbol*]   (OCLC)
REA .... Rocket Engine Assembly
REA .... Rubber Export Association [*Defunct*]   (EA)
REA .... Rural Education Association [*Later, NREA*]   (EA)
REA .... Rural Electrification Administration [*Department of
                    Agriculture*]
REA et A.... Rite Ecossais Ancien et Accepte [*Ancient and Accepted Scottish
                    Rite*] [*French*] [*Freemasonry*]
REA Bull ... REA [*Rural Electrification Administration*] Bulletin [*A
                    publication*]
REA Bull ... Rural Electrification Administration. Bulletin [*A
                    publication*]   (DLA)
REAC........ Radiation Equipment and Accessories Corporation   (SAA)
REAC........ Reaction   (AAG)
REAC........ Reactive
REAC........ Reactor   (AAG)
REAC........ Real Estate Aviation Chapter   (EA)
REAC........ Reeves Electronic Analog Computer
REAC........ Regional Educational Advisory Council [*British*]
REACCS ... Reaction Access System [*Computer program*]
REACDU .. Recalled to Active Duty

REACH ..... Reassurance to Each [*To help families of the mentally ill*]
REACH ..... Recognizing Exceptional Achievement in Community Help
                    Award [*Association of Personal Computer User
                    Groups*]   (PCM)
REACH ..... Research, Education, and Assistance for Canadians with Herpes
REACH ..... Responsible Educated Adolescents Can Help   (EA)
REACH ..... Retired Executives Action Clearing House [*British*]   (DI)
REACH ..... Rural Employment Action and Counseling Help [*Project*]
REACK...... Receipt Acknowledged
REACOT... Remove Errors and Complete on Time   (DNAB)
REACQ ..... Reacquire
REACT...... RADAR Electrooptical Area Correlation Tracker
                    [*Military*]   (CAAL)
REACT...... Radio Emergency Associated Citizens Teams [*Acronym alone is
                    now used as official association name*]   (EA)
RE ACT .... Rapid Execution and Combat Targeting [*Air Force*]
RE ACT .... Reconnaissance/Reaction   (MCD)
REACT...... Register Enforced Automated Control Technique [*Cash register-
                    computing system*]
REACT...... Reliability Evaluation and Control Technique
REACT...... Rese Engineering Automatic Core Tester
REACT...... Resource Allocation and Control Technique [*Management*]
React Cent Ned Rep ... Reactor Centrum Nederland. Report [*A publication*]
React Fuel Process ... Reactor Fuel Processing [*A publication*]
React Fuel-Process Technol ... Reactor and Fuel-Processing Technology [*A
                    publication*]
React Intermed ... Reactive Intermediates [*A publication*]
React Kin C ... Reaction Kinetics and Catalysis Letters [*A publication*]
React Kinet ... Reaction Kinetics [*Later, Gas Kinetics and Energy Transfer*] [*A
                    publication*]
React Kinet Catal Lett ... Reaction Kinetics and Catalysis Letters [*A
                    publication*]
Reactor Fuel Process ... Reactor Fuel Processing [*A publication*]
Reactor Mater ... Reactor Materials [*A publication*]
React Polym ... Reactive Polymers [*The Netherlands*] [*A publication*]
React Polym Ion Exch Sorbents ... Reactive Polymers, Ion Exchangers.
                    Sorbents [*A publication*]
React Res Soc News ... Reaction Research Society. News [*A publication*]
React Res Soc Rep ... Reaction Research Society. Report [*A publication*]
REAC/TS ... Radiation Emergency Assistance Center/Training Site
                    [*Department of Energy*]
REACTS.... Reader Action Service [*ZIP code computer*]
REACTS.... Regional Educators Annual Chemistry Teaching Symposium
React Struct Concepts Org Chem ... Reactivity and Structure Concepts in
                    Organic Chemistry [*A publication*]
React Technol ... Reactor Technology [*A publication*]
REACTVT ... Reactivate
READ .... American Learning Corp. [*Chicago, IL*] [*NASDAQ
                    symbol*]   (NQ)
READ .... RADAR Echo Augmentation Device
READ .... Readability Ease Assessment Device   (MCD)
READ .... Reading [*County borough in England*]
READ .... Reading Efficiency and Delinquency [*Program*]
READ .... Real-Time Electronic Access and Display [*System*] [*Data
                    processing*]
READ .... Remedial Education for Adults
READ .... Remote Electronic Alphanumeric Display [*Data
                    processing*]   (IEEE)
READ .... Research and Economic Analysis Division [*Office of
                    Transportation*]   (GRD)
READ .... Reserve on Extended Active Duty [*Military*]
Read Abstr ... Reading Abstracts [*A publication*]
Read Dec.... Read's Declarations and Pleadings [*A publication*]   (DLA)
Read Dig .... Reader's Digest [*A publication*]
Read Digest ... Reader's Digest [*A publication*]
Read Disabil Dig ... Reading Disability Digest [*A publication*]
READE...... Reduce Errors and Decrease Expense   (DNAB)
Read Educ ... Reading Education [*A publication*]   (APTA)
READEF ... Reason for Deficiency   (SAA)
Reader....... Reader Magazine [*A publication*]
Readers D .. Reader's Digest [*A publication*]   (APTA)
Reader's Dig ... Reader's Digest [*A publication*]
Readex .... Readex Microprint Corp., New York, NY [*Library symbol*]
                    [*Library of Congress*]   (LCLS)
Read Geog ... Reading Geographer [*A publication*]
Read Glass Hist ... Readings in Glass History [*A publication*]
Read Guide Period Lit ... Readers' Guide to Periodical Literature [*A
                    publication*]
READI....... Rocket Engine Analyzer and Decision Instrumentation
READIMP ... Readiness Improvement   (MCD)
Read Improv ... Reading Improvement [*A publication*]
Reading Educ ... Reading Education [*A publication*]
Reading Univ Geol Rep ... Reading University. Geological Reports [*A
                    publication*]
READJ ...... Readjusted
READJP.... Readjustment Pay [*Military*]
READL...... Railway Employers' Association Defence League [*British*]
Read Man ... Reading Manitoba [*A publication*]
Read PL ..... Read's Declarations and Pleadings [*A publication*]   (DLA)
Read Psychol ... Reading Psychology [*A publication*]

READR...... Remain in Effect after Discharge and Reenlistment [*Refers to orders*] [*Army*]
Read Res Q ... Reading Research Quarterly [*A publication*]
READS...... Reader Enrollment and Delivery System [*Library of Congress*] [*Washington, DC*] [*Information service or system*]   (IID)
READS...... Reentry Air Data System   (ADA)
READS...... Reno Air Defense Sector [*ADC*]
READSUPPGRUDET ... Readiness Support Group Detachment   (DNAB)
Read Teach ... Reading Teacher [*A publication*]
Read Time ... Reading Time [*A publication*]   (APTA)
Read Today Int ... Reading Today International [*A publication*]
READTRAFAC ... Readiness Training Facility   (DNAB)
READU ..... Ready Duty   (NVT)
READU ..... Ready Unit   (NVT)
Read World ... Reading World [*A publication*]
READYREP ... Ready-to-Sail Report [*Navy*]   (NVT)
REAF........ Reorganization of Engineer Active Forces   (MCD)
REAF........ Resources Exchange Association Foundation [*Also known as REA Foundation*]   (EA)
REAF........ Revised Engineer Active Force   (MCD)
REAG .... Reproductive Effects Assessment Group [*Environmental Protection Agency*]   (EPA)
Reakt Bull ... Reaktor Bulletin [*A publication*]
Reaktortag (Fachvortr) ... Reaktortagung (Fachvortraege) [*West Germany*] [*A publication*]
Reakt Osobo Chist Veshchestva ... Reaktivy i Osobo Chistye Veshchestva [*A publication*]
Reakts Metody Issled Org Soedin ... Reaktsii i Metody Issledovaniya Organicheskikh Soedinenii [*Former USSR*] [*A publication*]
Reakts Sposobn Koord Soedin ... Reaktsionnaya Sposobnost' Koordinatsionnykh Soedinenii [*A publication*]
Reakts Sposobn Mekh Reakts Org Soedin ... Reaktsionnaya Sposobnost' i Mekhanizmy Reaktsii Organicheskikh Soedinenii [*A publication*]
Reakts Sposobn Org Soedin ... Reaktsionnaya Sposobnost' Organicheskikh Soedinenij [*A publication*]
Reakts Sposobnost' Org Soedin Tartu Gos Univ ... Reaktsionnaya Sposobnost' Organicheskikh Soedinenij. Tartuskij Gosudarstvennyj Universitet [*A publication*]
ReAL......... Re Artes Liberales [*A publication*]
REAL........ Re: Arts and Letters [*A publication*]
R/EAL....... Reading/Everyday Activities in Life [*Educational test*]
REAL........ Realistic, Equal, Active, for Life Women of Canada [*An association*]
REAL........ Reliability, Inc. [*NASDAQ symbol*]   (NQ)
REAL........ Research-Extension Analytical Laboratory [*Ohio State University*] [*Research center*]   (RCD)
REAL........ Routine Economic Air Lift [*Army*]
Real Anal Exchange ... Real Analysis Exchange [*A publication*]
REALB ...... REAL. The Yearbook of Research in English and American Literature [*A publication*]
REALCOM ... Real-Time Communications [*RCA*]
Real Econ... Realta Economica [*A publication*]
Real-Encycl Ges Heilk ... Real-Encyclopaedie der Gesammten Heilkunde Medicinisch-Chirurgisches Handwoerterbuch fuer Praktische Aerzte [*A publication*]
Real Estate Appraiser & Anal ... Real Estate Appraiser and Analyst [*A publication*]
Real Estate J ... Real Estate Journal [*A publication*]   (APTA)
Real Estate L J ... Real Estate Law Journal [*A publication*]
Real Estate R ... Real Estate Review [*A publication*]
Real Estate Rev ... Real Estate Review [*A publication*]
Real Estate & Stock J ... Real Estate and Stock Journal [*A publication*]   (APTA)
Real Est L .. Real Estate Law Journal [*A publication*]
Real Est LJ ... Real Estate Law Journal [*A publication*]
Real Est L Rep ... Real Estate Law Report [*A publication*]   (DLA)
Real Est Re ... Real Estate Review [*A publication*]
Real Est Rec ... Real Estate Record [*New York*] [*A publication*]   (DLA)
Real Est Rev ... Real Estate Review [*A publication*]
REAL FAMMIS ... Real-Time Finance and Manpower Management Information System [*Marine Corps*]   (MCD)
Realidad Econ ... Realidad Economica [*A publication*]
Real Ist Veneto Mem ... Reale Istituto Veneto di Scienze, Lettere, ed Arti. Memorie [*A publication*]
REALIZN ... Realization   (ROG)
Reallexikon ... Reallexikon der Aegyptischen Religionsgeschichte [*A publication*]
Real M .... Realta del Mezzogiorno. Mensile di Politica, Economia, Cultura [*A publication*]
REALM..... Remote Access Line Monitor [*Cornet, Inc.*]
RealN......... Realta Nuova [*A publication*]
Real Pr Cas ... Real Property Cases [*England*] [*A publication*]   (DLA)
Real Prop Acts ... Real Property Actions and Proceedings [*A publication*]   (DLA)
Real Prop Cas ... Real Property Cases [*1843-47*] [*A publication*]   (DLA)
Real Prop P ... Real Property, Probate, and Trust Journal [*A publication*]
Real Prop Probate & Trust J ... Real Property, Probate, and Trust Journal [*A publication*]
Real Prop Prob and Tr J ... Real Property, Probate, and Trust Journal [*A publication*]

Real Prop Prob & Trust J ... Real Property, Probate, and Trust Journal [*A publication*]   (DLA)
Real Prop Rep ... Real Property Reports [*A publication*]
Realta Econ ... Realta Economica [*A publication*]
Realta Mezzogiorno ... Realta del Mezzogiorno [*A publication*]
Real Wr... Realist Writer [*A publication*]   (APTA)
REAM .... Rapid Excavation and Mining [*Project*] [*Bureau of Mines*]
REAMS..... Resources Evaluation and Management System [*Army*]
REAN .... Royal East African Navy [*British military*]   (DMA)
Reanim Med Urgence ... Reanimation et Medecine d'Urgence [*A publication*]
Reanim Organes Artif ... Reanimation et Organes Artificiels [*A publication*]
REAP........ Read, Encode, Annotate, Ponder [*Reading improvement method*]
REAP........ Remote Entry Acquisition Package
REAP........ Research and Engineering Apprenticeship Program [*Army*]   (RDA)
REAP........ Resource Engineering & Planning Co.
REAP........ Reutilization Expedite Assets Program [*DoD*]
REAP........ Rural Environmental Assistance Program [*Department of Agriculture*]
Reap Dec.... United States Customs Court Reports, Reappraisement Decision [*A publication*]   (DLA)
REAPOR... Real Estate Accounts Payable and Operating Reports
Reapp Dec ... United States Customs Court Reports, Reappraisement Decision [*A publication*]   (DLA)
REAPS ..... Rotary Engine Antipollution System
REAPT...... Reappoint   (AFM)
REAPTD... Reappointed   (WGA)
REAR....... Reliability Engineering Analysis Report   (IEEE)
REARA..... Recherche Aerospatiale [*A publication*]
REARM..... Renovation of Armament Manufacturing Program [*Army*]   (MCD)
REARM.... Underway Rearming [*Navy*]   (NVT)
REART...... Restricted Articles [*IATA*]   (DS)
REA (Rural Electr Adm) Bull (US) ... REA (Rural Electrification Administration) Bulletin (United States) [*A publication*]
REAS........ Real Estate Appraisal School [*Federal Home Loan Bank Board*]
REAS........ Reasonable   (ROG)
REAS........ Register of Environment Assessments and Statements   (MCD)
REAS........ Resources, Entities Accounting Subsystem   (MCD)
REASM..... Reassemble   (AAG)
REASN...... Reason   (ROG)
REASSCE ... Reassurance   (ROG)
REASSEM ... Reassemble   (MSA)
REASSN ... Reassign   (ROG)
REASSND ... Reassigned   (ROG)
REASST .... Reassignment   (ROG)
REASSY.... Reassembly   (MSA)
REASTAN ... Renton Electrical Analog for Solution of Thermal Analogous Networks
REAT........ Radiological Emergency Assistance Team [*AEC*]
REAT........ Realty Industries [*NASDAQ symbol*]   (NQ)
REAUM .... Reaumur   (ROG)
REB .... R. E. Blake [*Record label*]
REB .... RADAR Evaluation Branch [*ADC*]
REB .... Real Estate Business [*Realtors National Marketing Institute*] [*A publication*]
REB .... Reba Resources Ltd. [*Vancouver Stock Exchange symbol*]
REB .... Rebecca/Eureka [*Navigation*]   (AIA)
REB .... Rebel
REB .... Rebounds [*Basketball, hockey*]
Reb............. [*Petrus*] Rebuffus [*Deceased, 1557*] [*Authority cited in pre-1607 legal work*]   (DSA)
REB .... Rebuilt
REB .... Redwood Empire Bancorp [*AMEX symbol*]   (SPSG)
REB .... Reentry Body
REB .... Regional Education Board of the Christian Brothers   (EA)
REB .... Regional Examining Bodies [*British*]   (DI)
REB .... Relativistic Electron Beam   (MCD)
REB .... Research Earth Borer
REB .... Resultaten van de Conjunctuurenquete bij het Bedrijfsleven in de Gemeenschap [*A publication*]
REB .... Review of Regional Economics and Business [*A publication*]
REB .... Rocket Engine Band
REB .... Rod End Bearing [*Army helicopter*]
REB .... Roentgen-Equivalent-Biological [*Irradiation unit*]
REBA .... Relativistic Electron Beam Accelerator
REBAR...... Reinforcing Bar   (AAG)
REBAT...... Restricted Bandwidth Techniques   (NG)
REBC....... Real Estate Brokerage Council   (EA)
R-EBD-HS ... Recessive Epidermolysis Bullosa Dystrophia-Hallopeaun Siemens [*Dermatology*]
REBE....... Recovery Beacon Evaluation
REBECCA ... RADAR Responder Beacon [*System*]   (MUGU)
REBIA .... Regional Educational Building Institute for Africa
REBK........ Repertoire des Banques de Donnees en Conversationnel [*Association Nationale de la Recherche Technique*] [*Information service or system*]
REBS .... Royal Engineers Balloon School [*British military*]   (DMA)
REBUD ..... Rehabilitation Budgeting Program [*Telecommunications*]   (TEL)

REBUD ..... Renewable Energy Bulletin [*A publication*]
Rebuf .... [*Petrus*] Rebuffus [*Deceased, 1557*] [*Authority cited in pre-1607 legal work*] (DSA)
Rebuff .... [*Petrus*] Rebuffus [*Deceased, 1557*] [*Authority cited in pre-1607 legal work*] (DSA)
REBUS ...... Reseau des Bibliotheques Utilisant SIBIL [*Library Network of SIBIL Users*] [*University of Lausanne*] [*Switzerland*] [*Information service or system*] (IID)
REBUS ...... Routine for Executing Biological Unit Simulations [*Computer program*]
REC .... Clarion State College, Clarion, PA [*OCLC symbol*] (OCLC)
REC .... Radiant Energy Conversion
REC .... Radio Electronic Combat [*Communications*]
REC .... Radioelectrocomplexing [*Clinical chemistry*] (AAMN)
REC .... Railway Executive Committee [*British*]
REC .... Rain Erosion Coating
REC .... Rare-Earth Catalyst [*Automotive engineering*]
REC .... Reactor Engineer Console
REC .... Real Estate Council
REC .... Receipt
REC .... Received (DS)
REC .... Receiver (AAG)
REC .... Recens [*Fresh*] [*Pharmacy*]
REC .... Recent (ROG)
REC .... Receptacle (WGA)
REC .... Reception
REC .... Recess (MSA)
REC .... Recherches sur l'Origine de l'Ecriture Cuneiforme [*A publication*] (BJA)
REC .... Recife [*Brazil*] [*Airport symbol*] (OAG)
REC .... Recipe
REC .... Reclamation (WGA)
REC .... Recognition Equipment, Inc. [*NYSE symbol*] (SPSG)
REC .... Recommendation (AFM)
REC .... Record (AAG)
Rec .... Recordati [*Italy*] [*Research code symbol*]
REC .... Recorder
REC .... Recover [*or Recovery*]
REC .... Recreation
REC .... Recreational and Educational Computing [*A publication*]
REC .... Recreo [*Guatemala*] [*Seismograph station code, US Geological Survey*] (SEIS)
Rec .... Recruiter [*British military*] (DMA)
REC .... Rectifier (IEEE)
Rec .... Recueil (BJA)
Rec .... Recurrence [*A publication*]
rec .... Recurrence [*or Recurrent*] [*Medicine*] (MAE)
REC .... Recurring (MCD)
REC .... Regiment Etranger de Cavalerie [*Foreign Cavalry Regiment*] [*French*]
REC .... Regional Electronics Centers [*British*]
REC .... Regional Evaluation Center (NVT)
REC .... Rehabilitation Engineering Center for the Hearing Impaired [*Gallaudet College*] [*Research center*] (RCD)
REC .... Rehabilitation Engineering Centers [*Department of Health and Human Services*]
REC .... REM [*Roentgen-Equivalent-Man*] Equivalent Chemical [*Irradiation unit*]
REC .... Request for Engineering Change (MCD)
REC .... Reserve Equalization Committee [*Military*]
REC .... Residual Evaluation Center (MCD)
REC .... Retail Control [*A publication*]
REC .... Revloc, PA [*Location identifier*] [*FAA*] (FAAL)
REC .... Ripling Electrochemical
REC .... Rudge Enthusiasts Club (EA)
RECA .... Residual Capabilities Assessment (MCD)
RECA .... Revenue and Expenditure Control Act of 1968
Rec Agric Res ... Record of Agricultural Research [*A publication*]
Rec Agric Res (Belfast) ... Record of Agricultural Research (Belfast) [*A publication*]
Rec Agric Res Minist Agric (Nth Ire) ... Record of Agricultural Research. Ministry of Agriculture (Northern Ireland) [*A publication*]
Rec Agr Res (N Ireland) ... Record of Agricultural Research (Northern Ireland) [*A publication*]
Rec Ak Inst Mus ... Records. Auckland Institute and Museum [*New Zealand*] [*A publication*]
RECALC ... Recalculated
Rec Am Cath Hist Soc ... Records. American Catholic Historical Society of Philadelphia [*A publication*]
Rec Annu Conv Br Wood Preserv Assoc ... Record of the Annual Convention. British Wood Preserving Association [*A publication*]
RECAP ...... Re Capital Corp. [*Associated Press abbreviation*] (APAG)
RECAP ...... Real Estate Cost Analysis Program
RECAP ...... Recapitulation (AABC)
RECAP ...... Reliability Engineering and Corrective Action Program
RECAP ...... Reliability Evaluation Continuous Analysis Program
RECAP ...... Research and Education Center for Architectural Preservation [*University of Florida*] [*Research center*] (RCD)
RECAP ...... Resource and Capabilities Model (KSC)
RECAP ...... Review and Command Assessment of Project [*Military*]
RECAPS .... Regionalized Civilian Automated Pay System [*Air Force*]

Rec Art Mus ... Record. Art Museum. Princeton University [*A publication*]
Rec Asilomar Conf Circuits Syst Comput ... Record. Asilomar Conference on Circuits, Systems, and Computers [*A publication*]
Rec Ass'n Bar City of NY ... Record. Association of the Bar of the City of New York [*A publication*]
RECAT ...... Ad Hoc Committee on the Cumulative Regulatory Effects on the Cost of Automotive Transportation [*Terminated, 1972*] (EGAO)
RECAU ..... Receipt Acknowledged and Understood
Rec Auckland Inst ... Records. Auckland Institute and Museum [*A publication*]
Rec Auckl Inst Mus ... Records. Auckland Institute and Museum [*A publication*]
RecAug .... Recherches Augustiniennes [*A publication*]
Rec Aust Acad Sci ... Records. Australian Academy of Science [*A publication*]
Rec Aust Mus ... Records. Australian Museum [*A publication*]
Rec Aust Museum ... Records. Australian Museum [*A publication*] (APTA)
Rec Aust Mus Suppl ... Records. Australian Museum. Supplement [*A publication*]
RECBAD ... United States Army Recruiter Badge [*Military decoration*] (GFGA)
RECBKS .... Receiving Barracks
Rec Bot Surv India ... Records. Botanical Survey of India [*A publication*]
Rec Buckinghamshire ... Records of Buckinghamshire [*A publication*]
RECC .... Rhine Evacuation and Control Command [*NATO*] (NATG)
Rec Canterbury Mus ... Records. Canterbury Museum [*Christchurch, New Zealand*] [*A publication*]
RECCB ...... Regional Education Committee of the Christian Brothers [*Later, REB*] (EA)
RECCE ...... Reconnaissance (CINC)
Rec CEDH ... Recueil des Decisions de la Commission Europeenne de Droits de l'Homme [*A publication*]
RECCEXREP ... Reconnaisance Exploitation Report (MCD)
RECCFO ... Received in Connection with Fitting Out (DNAB)
Rec Changer ... Record Changer [*A publication*]
Rec Chem Prog ... Record of Chemical Progress [*A publication*]
RECCO ...... Reconnaissance (NVT)
Rec Coll ...... Record Collector [*A publication*]
REC COM ... Record Commissioner [*British*] (DLA)
Rec Conv Brit Wood Pres Ass ... Record of the Annual Convention. British Wood Preserving Association [*A publication*]
RECD .... Received (AAG)
Rec Dec ...... Vaux's Recorder's Decisions [*1841-45*] [*Philadelphia, PA*] [*A publication*] (DLA)
Rec Dom Mus (Wellington) ... Records. Dominion Museum (Wellington, New Zealand) [*A publication*]
Recd Res Fac Agr Univ Tokyo ... Records of Researches. Faculty of Agriculture. University of Tokyo [*A publication*]
RECDUINS ... Received for Duty under Instruction
RECDUT ... Received for Duty
RECE .... Cuban Representation of Exiles [*Also known as Representacion Cubana del Exilio*] (EA)
RECE .... Relativistic Electron Coil Experiment (MCD)
Rec Electr Commun Eng Conversat Tohoku Univ ... Record of Electrical and Communication Engineering Conversation. Tohoku University [*Japan*] [*A publication*]
Rec Eng N ... Recovery Engineering News [*A publication*]
RECENT ... Recentis [*Fresh*] [*Pharmacy*] (ROG)
Recent Achiev Restorative Neurol ... Recent Achievements in Restorative Neurology [*A publication*]
Recent Adv Aerosp Med ... Recent Advances in Aerospace Medicine [*A publication*]
Recent Advanc Bot ... Recent Advances in Botany [*A publication*]
Recent Advanc Invert Physiol ... Recent Advances in Invertebrate Physiology [*A publication*]
Recent Adv Anim Nutr ... Recent Advances in Animal Nutrition [*A publication*]
Recent Adv Avian Endocrinol ... Recent Advances of Avian Endocrinology [*A publication*]
Recent Adv Biol Psychiatry ... Recent Advances in Biological Psychiatry [*A publication*]
Recent Adv Capillary Gas Chromatogr ... Recent Advances in Capillary Gas Chromatography [*A publication*]
Recent Adv Clin Nucl Med ... Recent Advances in Clinical Nuclear Medicine [*A publication*]
Recent Adv Clin Pathol ... Recent Advances in Clinical Pathology [*A publication*]
Recent Adv Clin Pharmacol ... Recent Advances in Clinical Pharmacology [*A publication*]
Recent Adv Community Med ... Recent Advances in Community Medicine [*A publication*]
Recent Adv Endocrinol Metab ... Recent Advances in Endocrinology and Metabolism [*A publication*]
Recent Adv Eng Sci ... Recent Advances in Engineering Science [*A publication*]
Recent Adv Food Sci ... Recent Advances in Food Science [*A publication*]
Recent Adv Gastroenterol ... Recent Advances in Gastroenterology [*A publication*]
Recent Adv Geriatr Med ... Recent Advances in Geriatric Medicine [*A publication*]

Recent Adv Gut Horm Res ... Recent Advances in Gut Hormone Research [*A publication*]
Recent Adv Med ... Recent Advances in Medicine [*A publication*]
Recent Adv Nucl Med ... Recent Advances in Nuclear Medicine [*A publication*]
Recent Adv Physiol ... Recent Advances in Physiology [*A publication*]
Recent Adv Phytochem ... Recent Advances in Phytochemistry [*A publication*]
Recent Adv Renal Dis ... Recent Advances in Renal Disease [*A publication*]
Recent Adv RES Res ... Recent Advances in RES [*Reticuloendothelial System*] Research [*A publication*]
Recent Adv Stud Card Struct Metab ... Recent Advances in Studies on Cardiac Structure and Metabolism [*A publication*]
Recent Adv Treat Depression ... Recent Advances in the Treatment of Depression [*A publication*]
Recent Dev Alcohol ... Recent Developments in Alcoholism [*A publication*]
Recent Dev Chem Nat Carbon Compd ... Recent Developments in the Chemistry of Natural Carbon Compounds [*A publication*]
Recent Dev Hist Chem ... Recent Developments in the History of Chemistry [*A publication*]
Recent Dev Neurobiol Hung ... Recent Developments of Neurobiology in Hungary [*A publication*]
Recenti Prog Med ... Recenti Progressi in Medicina [*A publication*]
Recent Lit Hazard Environ Ind ... Recent Literature on Hazardous Environments in Industry [*A publication*]
Recent Med ... Recentia Medica [*A publication*]
Recent Prog Horm Res ... Recent Progress in Hormone Research [*A publication*]
Recent Prog Kinins ... Recent Progress on Kinins [*A publication*]
Recent Prog Med (Roma) ... Recenti Progressi in Medicina (Roma) [*A publication*]
Recent Prog Microbiol ... Recent Progress in Microbiology [*A publication*]
Recent Prog Nat Sci Jap ... Recent Progress of Natural Sciences in Japan [*A publication*]
Recent Prog Psychiatry ... Recent Progress in Psychiatry [*A publication*]
Recent Progr Hormone Res ... Recent Progress in Hormone Research [*A publication*]
Recent Progr Natur Sci Japan ... Recent Progress of Natural Sciences in Japan [*A publication*]
Recent Prog Surf Sci ... Recent Progress in Surface Science [*A publication*]
Recent Publ Artic ... Recently Published Articles. American Historical Association [*A publication*]
Recent Publ Gov Probl ... Recent Publications on Governmental Problems [*United States*] [*A publication*]
Recent Pubns Governmental Problems ... Recent Publications on Governmental Problems [*A publication*]
Recent Res Carnitine ... Recent Research on Carnitine [*A publication*]
Recent Results Cancer Res ... Recent Results in Cancer Research [*A publication*]
Recent Results Pept Horm Androg Steroid Res Proc Congr Hung ... Recent Results in Peptide, Hormone, and Androgenic Steroid Research. Proceedings. Congress. Hungarian Society of Endocrinology and Metabolism [*A publication*]
RECEP ...... Reception (ADA)
Recept Biochem Methodol ... Receptor Biochemistry and Methodology [*A publication*]
Recept Horm Action ... Receptors and Hormone Action [*A publication*]
Recept Ligands Intercell Commun ... Receptors and Ligands in Intercellular Communication [*A publication*]
RECERT ... Recertification (NASA)
RECETED ... Receipted (ROG)
RecFIN ...... Recreational Fisheries Information Network [*Database*] [*National Marine Fisheries Service*]
RECFM ..... Record Format [*Data processing*]
RECG .... Radioelectrocardiograph
RECG .... Reciting
RECGA ...... Research and Engineering Council of the Graphic Arts Industry
RECGAI .... Research and Engineering Council of the Graphic Arts Industry (EA)
Rec Gen Enr et Not ... Recueil General de l'Enregistrement et du Notariat [*A publication*]
Rec Geol Surv Br Guiana ... Records. Geological Survey of British Guiana [*A publication*]
Rec Geol Surv Dep North Rhod ... Records. Geological Survey Department. Northern Rhodesia [*A publication*]
Rec Geol Surv Guyana ... Records. Geological Survey of Guyana [*A publication*]
Rec Geol Surv India ... Records. Geological Survey of India [*A publication*]
Rec Geol Surv Malawi ... Records. Geological Survey of Malawi [*A publication*]
Rec Geol Surv New South Wales ... Records. Geological Survey of New South Wales [*A publication*]
Rec Geol Surv Niger ... Records. Geological Survey of Nigeria [*A publication*]
Rec Geol Surv NSW ... Records. Geological Survey of New South Wales [*A publication*]
Rec Geol Surv Pak ... Records. Geological Survey of Pakistan [*A publication*]
Rec Geol Surv Tanganyika ... Records. Geological Survey of Tanganyika [*A publication*]
Rec Geol Surv Tasm ... Tasmania. Geological Survey. Record [*A publication*] (APTA)

Rec Geol Surv (Zambia) ... Records. Geological Survey (Zambia) [*A publication*]
RECGP ...... Recovery Group [*Air Force*]
Rech .... Recherche [*A publication*]
RecH .... Recusant History [*A publication*]
RECH .... Reformed Episcopal Church
RechA .... Recherches Augustiniennes [*A publication*]
Rech A Crac ... Recherches Archeologiques. Institut d'Archeologie. Universite de Cracovie [*A publication*]
Rech Aeronaut ... Recherche Aeronautique [*A publication*]
Rech Aerosp ... Recherche Aerospatiale [*A publication*]
Rech Aerospat ... Recherche Aerospatiale [*A publication*]
Rech Aerospat English ... La Recherche Aerospatiale. English Edition [*A publication*]
Rech Agron ... Recherches Agronomiques [*A publication*]
Rech Agron (Quebec) ... Recherches Agronomiques (Quebec) [*A publication*]
Rech Amerind ... Recherches Amerindiennes [*A publication*]
RECHAR... Recombiner Charcoal Adsorber [*Nuclear energy*] (NRCH)
RechBib ..... Recherches Bibliques. Journees du Colloque Biblique de Louvain [*A publication*]
RechBibl .... Recherches Bibliques. Journees du Colloque Biblique de Louvain [*A publication*]
Rech Chir Eur ... Recherches Chirurgicales Europeennes [*A publication*]
Rech Clin Lab ... Recherche dans la Clinique et le Laboratoire [*A publication*]
Rech Econ Louvain ... Recherches Economiques de Louvain [*A publication*]
Rechentech Datenverarb ... Rechentechnik-Datenverarbeitung [*A publication*]
Recherche Aerospat ... La Recherche Aerospatiale [*A publication*]
Recherches ... Recherches sur la Musique Francaise Classique [*A publication*]
Recherche Soc (Paris) ... Recherche Sociale (Paris) [*A publication*]
Recher Sc Rel ... Recherches de Science Religieuse [*A publication*]
RECHG ..... Recharge (NASA)
Rech Geol Afr ... Recherches Geologiques en Afrique [*A publication*]
Rech Graphique ... Recherche Graphique [*A publication*]
Rech Graphique Commun ... Recherche Graphique. Communications [*A publication*]
Rech Hydrobiol Cont ... Recherches d'Hydrobiologie Continentale [*A publication*]
Rech Int ..... Recherches Internationales a la Lumiere du Marxism [*A publication*]
Rech Invent ... Recherches et Inventions [*A publication*]
Rechn Transp ... Rechnoi Transport [*A publication*]
Rech Prod Foret ... Recherches sur les Produits de la Foret [*A publication*]
RECHRG .. Recharger
Rech Sci Rel ... Recherches de Science Religieuse [*A publication*]
Rech Sci Relig ... Recherches de Science Religieuse [*A publication*]
RechScR ... Recherches de Science Religieuse [*A publication*]
Rech Sociogr ... Recherches Sociographiques [*A publication*]
Rech Sociographiques ... Recherches Sociographiques [*A publication*]
Rech Sociol ... Recherches Sociologiques [*A publication*]
Rech Soc (Paris) ... Recherche Sociale (Paris) [*A publication*]
Rech Spat ... Recherche Spatiale [*A publication*]
Rech Spatiale ... Recherche Spatiale [*A publication*]
RechSR ...... Recherches de Science Religieuse [*A publication*]
Rech Tech .. Recherche Technique [*A publication*]
Recht Elektrizitaetswirtsch ... Recht der Elektrizitaetswirtschaft [*West Germany*] [*A publication*]
RechTh ...... Recherches de Theologie Ancienne et Medievale [*A publication*]
Recht Landwirtsch ... Recht der Landwirtschaft [*A publication*]
Recht Steuern Gas-Wasserfach ... Recht und Steuern im Gas- und Wasserfach [*West Germany*] [*A publication*]
Rec Hung Agric Exp Stn A ... Records. Hungarian Agricultural Experiment Stations. A. Plant Production [*A publication*]
Rec Hung Agric Exp Stn C ... Records. Hungarian Agricultural Experiment Stations. C. Horticulture [*A publication*]
Rec Huntingdonshire ... Records of Huntingdonshire [*A publication*]
Rech Vet ..... Recherches Veterinaires [*A publication*]
Rech Vet (Paris) ... Recherches Veterinaires (Paris) [*A publication*]
RECIFS ..... Recherches et Etudes Comparatistes Ibero-Francaises de la Sorbonne Nouvelle [*A publication*]
Rec Indian Mus ... Records. Indian Museum [*A publication*]
Rec Indian Mus (Calcutta) ... Records. Indian Museum (Calcutta) [*A publication*]
Rec Intersoc Energy Convers Eng Conf ... Records. Intersociety Energy Conversion Engineering Conference [*A publication*]
RECIP .... Recipient
RECIP .... Reciprocate (AAG)
RECIP .... Reciprocating Gas-Fueled Engine
RECIPE ..... Recomp Computer Interpretive Program Expediter [*Data processing*]
Recipe Period Index ... Recipe Periodical Index [*A publication*]
RECIR .... Recirculating [*Automotive engineering*]
RECIRC .... Recirculate (AAG)
RECIT .... Recitation
RECIT .... Recitative [*Music*]
Rec Jur T A Ni ... Recueil de Jurisprudence des Tribunaux de l'Arrondissement de Nivelles [*A publication*]
REC L .... Recent Law (DLA)
RECL .... Recital (ROG)
RECL .... Reclamation
RECL .... Reclose

Rec L.......... Recovering Literature [*A publication*]
Reclam Era ... Reclamation Era [*A publication*]
Reclam Rev ... Reclamation Review [*A publication*]
Reclam Reveg Res ... Reclamation and Revegetation Research [*A publication*]
Rec Laws.... Recent Laws in Canada [*A publication*] (DLA)
Recl J R Neth Chem Soc ... Recueil. Journal. Royal Netherlands Chemical Society [*A publication*]
Recl Med Vet ... Recueil de Medecine Veterinaire [*A publication*]
Recl Med Vet Ec Alfort ... Recueil de Medecine Veterinaire. Ecole d'Alfort [*A publication*]
Recl Trav Inst Biol (Beogr) ... Recueil des Travaux. Institut Biologique (Beograd) [*A publication*]
Recl Trav Inst Ecol Biogeogr Acad Serbe Sci ... Recueil des Travaux. Institut d'Ecologie et de Biogeographie. Academie Serbe des Sciences [*A publication*]
Recl Trav Inst Rech Struct Matiere (Belgrade) ... Recueil de Travaux. Institut de Recherches sur la Structure de la Matiere (Belgrade) [*A publication*]
Recl Trav Stn Mar Endoume Fac Sci Mars ... Recueil des Travaux. Station Marine d'Endoume. Faculte des Sciences de Marseille [*A publication*]
Recl Trav Stn Mar Endoume Marseille Fasc Hors Ser Suppl ... Recueil des Travaux. Station Marine d'Endoume-Marseille. Fascicule Hors Serie. Supplement [*A publication*]
Recl Trav Stn Mar Endoume-Mars Fasc Hors Ser Suppl ... Recueil des Travaux. Station Marine d'Endoume-Marseille. Fascicule Hors Serie. Supplement [*A publication*]
RECM .... Recommend (KSC)
Rec Malar Surv India ... Records of the Malaria Survey of India [*A publication*]
REC MAN ... Recreation Management Exhibition [*British*] (ITD)
RECMD .... Recommend (AAG)
Recmd .... Recommissioned (DS)
RECMECH ... Recoil Mechanism (AAG)
Rec Med Vet ... Recueil de Medecine Veterinaire [*A publication*]
Rec Med Vet Ecole Alfort ... Recueil de Medecine Veterinaire. Ecole d'Alfort [*A publication*]
Rec Med Vet Exot ... Recueil de Medecine Veterinaire Exotique [*A publication*]
Rec Mem Med Mil ... Recueil des Memoires de Medecine, de Chirurgie, et de Pharmacie Militaires [*A publication*]
Rec Mem et Obs Hyg et Med Vet Mil ... Recueil des Memoires et Observations sur l'Hygiene et la Medecine Veterinaires Militaires [*A publication*]
RECMF..... Radio and Electronic Component Manufacturers' Federation
RECMN .... Recommendation
RECMOP ... Received [*Payment under Provisions of the*] Mustering Out Payment Act [*Military*] (DNAB)
RECMPT .. Recomputation
RECN .... Reconnaissance
RECNCLN ... Reconciliation (AABC)
RecnEq....... Recognition Equipment, Inc. [*Associated Press abbreviation*] (APAG)
RECNO ..... This Office Has No Record Of [*Army*] (AABC)
RECNUM ... Record Number [*Online database field identifier*]
RECO .... Remote Command and Control (MCD)
Rec Obs Med Hop Mil ... Recueil des Observations de Medecine des Hopitaux Militaires [*A publication*]
Rec Obs Scripps Inst Oceanogr ... Records of Observations. Scripps Institution of Oceanography [*A publication*]
Rec Oceanogr Works Jpn ... Records of Oceanographic Works in Japan [*A publication*]
Rec Oceanogr Works Jpn Sp Number ... Records of Oceanographic Works in Japan. Special Number [*A publication*]
RECODEX ... Report Collection Index [*Studsvik Energiteknik AB*] [*Database*] [*Nykoping, Sweden*]
RECOG ..... Recognition [*or Recognize*] (AAG)
RECOGE... Recognisance (ROG)
RECOGN .. Recognizance
RECOGS... Recognisances (ROG)
RECOGSIG ... Recognition Signal [*Navy*]
RECOL...... Retrieval Command Language [*Computer search language*]
Recomb DNA Tech Bull ... Recombinant DNA Technical Bulletin [*A publication*]
Recomb DNA Tech Bull Suppl ... Recombinant DNA Technical Bulletin. Supplement [*A publication*]
RECOMMTRANSO ... Upon Receipt of These Orders Communicate with Transportation Officer for Priority Designator via Government Air If Available to _____
RECOMP ... Recommended Completion
RECOMP ... Recomplement
RECOMP ... Redstone Computer
RECOMP ... Repairs Completed [*Military*] (NVT)
RECOMP ... Retrieval and Composition (DIT)
RECON ..... Readiness Condition [*Military*]
RECON ..... Reconciliation
RECON ..... Reconnaissance (NATG)
RECON ..... Reference Conversation (FAAC)
RECON ..... Reliability and Configuration Accountability System
RECON ..... Remote Console [*NASA computer*]
RECON ..... Remote Control (KSC)

RECON ..... Resources Conservation (MCD)
RECON ..... Retrospective Conversion of Bibliographic Records [*Library of Congress*]
RECONATKRON ... Reconnaissance Attack Squadron [*Navy*] (DNAB)
RECONATKWING ... Reconnaissance Attack Wing [*Navy*] (DNAB)
RECONBN ... Reconnaissance Battalion [*Navy*] (DNAB)
RECONCE ... Reconveyance (ROG)
Reconciliation Quart ... Reconciliation Quarterly [*A publication*]
RECONCO ... Reconnaissance Co. [*Military*]
R Econ Conditions Italy ... Review of the Economic Conditions in Italy [*A publication*]
R Econ Condit Italy ... Review of the Economic Conditions in Italy [*A publication*]
RECOND.. Recondition (AABC)
RECONDO ... Reconnaissance Commando Doughboy [*Military*] (AABC)
RECONEX ... Raid/Reconnaissance Exercise [*Military*] (NVT)
RECONFIG ... Reconfiguration (NASA)
RECONN.. Reconnaissance (AAG)
R Econ S .... Royal Economic Society [*British*]
Recons Surg ... Reconstruction Surgery and Traumatology [*A publication*]
RECONST ... Reconstruct (AABC)
R Econ Stat ... Review of Economics and Statistics [*A publication*]
R Econ Statist ... Review of Economics and Statistics [*A publication*]
R Econ Statistics ... Review of Economics and Statistics [*A publication*]
Reconstr Surg Traumatol ... Reconstruction Surgery and Traumatology [*A publication*]
R Econ Stud ... Review of Economic Studies [*A publication*]
Recontr Surg Traumatol ... Reconstruction Surgery and Traumatology [*A publication*]
RECONVCE ... Reconveyance (ROG)
Record........ Record. Association of the Bar of the City of New York [*A publication*]
Record Broward County Med Assoc ... Record. Broward County Medical Association [*Florida*] [*A publication*]
Recorder Columbia Med Soc ... Recorder. Columbia Medical Society of Richland County [*South Carolina*] [*A publication*]
Recorder M Magazine ... Recorder and Music Magazine [*A publication*]
Recorder and Mus ... Recorder and Music [*A publication*]
Recorder & Mus Mag ... Recorder and Music Magazine [*A publication*]
Record of NYCBA ... Record. Association of the Bar of the City of New York [*A publication*]
Records Buck ... Records of Buckinghamshire [*A publication*]
Records Queen Museum ... Records. Queen Victoria Museum [*A publication*] (APTA)
Records SA Museum ... Records. South Australian Museum [*A publication*] (APTA)
RECOV ..... Recovery (KSC)
RECOVER ... Remote Continual Verification [*Telephonic monitoring system*]
RECOVER ... Remote Control Verification [*Nuclear safeguards*]
Recovery Eng News ... Recovery Engineering News [*A publication*]
Recovery Pulping Chem ... Recovery of Pulping Chemicals [*A publication*]
RECOVY... Recovery
RECP........ International College of Real Estate Consulting Professionals [*Minneapolis, MN*] (EA)
RECP........ International College of Real Estate Consulting Professionals (EAIO)
RECP........ Real Estate Consulting Professional [*Designation awarded by International College of Real Estate Consulting Professionals*]
RECP........ Receptacle
RECP........ Receptech Corp. [*NASDAQ symbol*] (NQ)
RECP........ Reception (WGA)
RECP........ Reciprocal (AAG)
RECP........ Release Engineering Change Proposal (MCD)
RECP........ Request for Engineering Change Proposal [*NASA*]
RECP........ Rural Environmental Conservation Program
RecPap....... Recherches de Papyrologie [*A publication*]
Rec Papua New Guinea Mus ... Records. Papua New Guinea Museum [*A publication*]
Rec Past ..... Records of the Past [*A publication*]
Recp Cen.... Reception Center [*Army*]
RecPh......... Recherches Philosophiques [*A publication*]
RecPhL...... Recherches de Philologie et de Linguistique [*Louvain*] [*A publication*]
RECPOM ... Resource Constrained Procurement Objectives for Munitions Model [*Army*]
RECPST.... Receptionist (WGA)
RECPT ...... Receipt
RECPT ...... Receptacle (AAG)
RECPT ...... Reception (AAG)
Rec Queen Vic Mus ... Records. Queen Victoria Museum [*A publication*] (APTA)
Rec Queen Vict Mus ... Records. Queen Victoria Museum [*A publication*] (APTA)
Rec Queen Victoria Mus ... Records. Queen Victoria Museum [*A publication*]
Rec Queen Victoria Mus Launceston ... Records. Queen Victoria Museum of Launceston [*A publication*]
Rec Q Vict Mus ... Records. Queen Victoria Museum [*A publication*] (APTA)
RECR......... Receiver
RECR........ Reclamation Review [*A publication*]

Rec R.......... Record Review [*A publication*]
RECR......... Recreation (AABC)
RECRAS ... Retrieval System for Current Research in Agricultural Sciences [*Japan*]
RECRC...... Recirculate (NASA)
RECRE...... Recreation
Rec Res ...... Record Research [*A publication*]
Rec Res Annu Rep East Afr Agric For Res Organ ... Record of Research. Annual Report. East African Agriculture and Forestry Research Organisation [*A publication*]
Rec Res Fac Agric Univ Tokyo ... Records of Researches. Faculty of Agriculture. University of Tokyo [*A publication*]
Rec Rev ...... Records in Review [*A publication*]
RECRN...... Recreation
Recr Sci...... Recreative Science [*A publication*]
RECRT...... Recruit (AFM)
RECRYST ... Recrystallized
RECS......... Radiological Emergency Communications System [*Nuclear energy*] (NRCH)
RECS......... Rear Echelon COMINT [*Communications Intelligence*] System [*Military*] (MCD)
RECS......... Reconfigurable EC System (MCD)
RECS......... Reconstitutable Emergency Communications System
RecS.......... Recorded Sound [*A publication*]
RECS......... Representative Shuttle Environmental Control System [*NASA*] (MCD)
RECS......... Residential Energy Consumption Survey [*Department of Energy*] (GFGA)
RECSAM .. Southeast Asian Regional Center for Education in Science and Mathematics [*Malaysia*]
RECSAT.... Reconnaissance Satellite (NVT)
RECSATSUM ... Reconnaissance Satellite Summary (DNAB)
Rec S Aust Mus ... Records. South Australian Museum [*A publication*] (APTA)
Rec S Aust Mus (Adelaide) ... Records. South Australian Museum (Adelaide) [*A publication*]
Rec Sci Rel ... Recherches de Science Religieuse [*A publication*]
Rec Scott Church Hist Soc ... Records. Scottish Church History Society [*A publication*]
rec sec......... Recording Secretary (WGA)
RECSG...... Renewable Energy Congressional Staff Group (EA)
RECSHIP ... Receiving Ship
Rec Sound .. Recorded Sound [*A publication*]
Rec South Aust Mus ... Records. South Australian Museum [*A publication*] (APTA)
Rec South Aust Mus (Adelaide) ... Records. South Australian Museum (Adelaide) [*A publication*]
RECSQUAD ... Reconnaissance Squadron [*Military*]
RecSR........ Recherches de Science Religieuse [*A publication*]
RECSTA.... Receiving Station [*Military*]
RECSYS.... Recreation Systems Analysis [*Data processing*]
RECT......... Receipt
RECT......... Rectangle (AAG)
RECT......... Rectificatus [*Rectified*] [*Pharmacy*]
RECT......... Rectify (AAG)
RECT......... Rectisel Corp. [*NASDAQ symbol*] (NQ)
RECT......... Rector
rect .... Rectum [*Medicine*] (MAE)
RECT......... Rectus [*Muscle*] [*Anatomy*]
RECTAD... Received for Temporary Additional Duty
RECTADINS ... Received for Temporary Additional Duty under Instruction
RECTAS.... Regional Centre for Training in Aerial Surveys (EAIO)
RECTD...... Received for Temporary Duty
RECTD...... Recited (ROG)
RECTEMDUINS ... Received for Temporary Duty under Instruction
RECTENNA ... Rectifying Antenna [*Microwave power transmission*]
RECTG...... Reciting (ROG)
RecTh......... Recherches de Theologie Ancienne et Medievale [*A publication*]
RECTIFON ... Rectification (ROG)
RECTIL..... Rectilineal [*Geometry*] (ROG)
RECTON... Reduction (ROG)
RECTR...... Recommend Transfer Of (NOAA)
RECTR...... Rectifier
RECTR...... Restoration and Eighteenth Century Theatre Research [*A publication*]
Rec Trav Inst Nat Hyg ... Recueil des Travaux. Institut National d'Hygiene [*A publication*]
Rec Trav Lab Physiol Veg Fac Sci Bordeaux ... Recueil des Travaux. Laboratoire de Physiologie Vegetale. Faculte des Sciences de Bordeaux [*A publication*]
RECTREAT ... Received for Treatment
Recueil .... Recueil des Cours. Academie de Droit International [*A publication*]
RECUR...... Recurrence [*or Recurrent*] [*Medicine*]
Recur Hidraul ... Recursos Hidraulicos [*A publication*]
Recursos Hidraul ... Recursos Hidraulicos [*Mexico*] [*A publication*]
Recursos Min ... Recursos Minerales [*A publication*]
Rec US Dep State ... Record. United States Department of State [*A publication*]
RECV......... Receive (NASA)

RECVD...... Received
RECVG..... Receiving
RECVR..... Receiver (NASA)
Rec West Aust Mus Suppl ... Records. Western Australian Museum. Supplement [*A publication*]
RECY......... Recovery (AAG)
Recycling Waste Disposal ... Recycling and Waste Disposal [*A publication*]
Recycl Weltkongr Konf Niederschr ... Recycling Weltkongress. Konferenz-Niederschriften [*A publication*]
Recycl World Congr Congr Proc ... Recycling World Congress. Congress Proceedings [*A publication*]
Rec Zool Surv India ... Records. Zoological Survey of India [*A publication*]
Rec Zool Surv Pak ... Records. Zoological Survey of Pakistan [*A publication*]
RED .... A'Beckett's Reserved Judgements [*New South Wales*] [*A publication*] (APTA)
RED .... New South Wales Reserved Equity Decisions [*A publication*] (DLA)
RED .... R and D (Research and Development) Management [*A publication*]
RED .... Radian Energy Distribution
RED .... Radiation Experience Data [*Food and Drug Administration*] [*Database*]
RED .... Radical Education Dossier [*A publication*] (ADA)
RED .... Radio Equipment Department [*British military*] (DMA)
RED .... Railroad Employees' Department [*of AFL-CIO*]
RED .... Range Error Detector
RED .... Rapid Excess Disposal [*Military*] (AABC)
RED .... Rare-Earth Device
RED .... RCRA [*Resource Conservation and Recovery Act*] Enforcement Division [*Environmental Protection Agency*] (GFGA)
RED .... Red Lion Inns Ltd. [*AMEX symbol*] (SPSG)
RED .... Red Lodge, MT [*Location identifier*] [*FAA*] (FAAL)
RED .... Redactor (WGA)
RED .... Redeemed
Red .... Redfield's New York Surrogate Reports [*A publication*] (DLA)
Red .... Redington's Reports [*31-35 Maine*] [*A publication*] (DLA)
RED .... Redoubt Volcano [*Alaska*] [*Seismograph station code, US Geological Survey*] (SEIS)
RED .... Reduce [*or Reduction*] (AAG)
RED .... Redundant (KSC)
Red .... Redwar's Comments on Ordinances of the Gold Coast Colony [*1889-1909*] [*Ghana*] [*A publication*] (DLA)
RED .... Reflection Electron Diffraction [*For surface structure analysis*]
RED .... Registered Expected Death
R Ed .... Religious Education [*A publication*]
RED .... Repairable Equipment Depot [*British military*] (DMA)
RE & D....... Research, Engineering, and Development
RED .... Restructured Expanded Data (MCD)
RED .... Resume Entry Device
RED .... Review, Evaluation, Disposition Board (AAG)
RED .... Ritchie's Equity Decisions (Russell) [*Canada*] [*A publication*] (DLA)
REDA........ Rural Educational and Development Association [*Canada*]
REDAC....... Real-Time Data Acquisition
Red Am R Cas ... Redfield's American Railway Cases [*A publication*] (DLA)
Red Am RR Cas ... Redfield's Leading American Railway Cases [*A publication*] (DLA)
REDAP...... Reentrant Data Processing
REDAS...... Reduced to Apprentice Seaman [*Navy*]
REDB .... Redbourne [*England*]
REDBA....... Redbook [*A publication*]
Red Bail ..... Redfield on Carriers and Bailments [*A publication*] (DLA)
Red & Big Cas B & N ... Redfield and Bigelow's Leading Cases on Bills and Notes [*A publication*] (DLA)
REDBR...... Redbridge [*England*]
REDC .... Regional Economic Development Center [*Memphis State University*] [*Research center*] (RCD)
REDCAP ... Real-Time Electromagnetic Digitally Controlled Analyser and Processor
REDCAPE ... Readiness Capability [*Military*]
Red Car...... Redfield on Carriers and Bailments [*A publication*] (DLA)
Red Cas RR ... Redfield's Leading American Railway Cases [*A publication*] (DLA)
Red Cas Wills ... Redfield's Leading Cases on Wills [*A publication*] (DLA)
REDCAT ... Racial and Ethnic Category [*Army*] (INF)
REDCAT ... Range-Extended Directionally-Controlled Antitank Missile (MCD)
REDCAT ... Readiness Category [*Military*]
REDCN...... Reducing (ROG)
REDCOM ... Readiness Command [*Army*]
REDCON .. Readiness Condition [*Military*]
Red Cross M ... Red Cross Magazine [*A publication*]
REDD......... Reduced (ROG)
REDEA...... Research/Development [*A publication*]
Redem .... Redemption (DLA)
REDEMP .. Redwood Empire Bancorp [*Associated Press abbreviation*] (APAG)
Redes Pl..... Redesdale's Treatise upon Equity Pleading [*A publication*] (DLA)
Redf............ Redfield's New York Surrogate Reports [*A publication*] (DLA)

Redf Am Railw Cas ... Redfield's American Railway Cases [*A publication*] (DLA)
Redf & B .... Redfield and Bigelow's Leading Cases [*England*] [*A publication*] (DLA)
Redf Carr ... Redfield on Carriers and Bailments [*A publication*] (DLA)
Redf (NY) .. Redfield's New York Surrogate Reports [*A publication*] (DLA)
Redf Railways ... Redfield on Railways [*A publication*] (DLA)
Redf R Cas ... Redfield's Railway Cases [*England*] [*A publication*] (DLA)
Redf Sur (NY) ... Redfield's New York Surrogate Court Reports [*A publication*] (DLA)
Redf Surr ... Redfield's New York Surrogate Reports [*A publication*] (DLA)
Redf Surr (NY) ... Redfield's New York Surrogate Court Reports [*5 vols.*] [*A publication*] (DLA)
Redf Wills ... Redfield's Leading Cases on Wills [*A publication*] (DLA)
RED HORSE ... Rapid Engineer Development, Heavy Operational Repair Squadron, Engineering [*Air Force*] (AFM)
REDI......... ReadiCare, Inc. [*NASDAQ symbol*] (NQ)
REDI......... Real Estate Data, Inc. [*Information service or system*] (IID)
REDI......... Remote Electronic Delivery of Information [*Library science*]
Redia G Zool ... Redia Giornale di Zoologia [*A publication*]
REDICORT ... Readiness Improvement through Correspondence Training (MCD)
REDICR.... ReadiCare, Inc. [*Associated Press abbreviation*] (APAG)
REDIG IN PULV ... Redigatur In Pulverent [*Let It Be Reduced to Powder*] [*Pharmacy*] (ROG)
Redington... Redington's Reports [*31-35 Maine*] [*A publication*] (DLA)
Red Int L.... Reddie's Inquiries in International Law [*2nd ed.*] [*1851*] [*A publication*] (DLA)
REDIS....... Reference Dispatch (NOAA)
REDISC .... Rediscount [*Banking*]
REDIST..... Redistilled
REDISTR ... Redistribution (AFM)
Redk Elem ... Redkie Elementy [*A publication*]
Redk Met... Redkie Metally [*A publication*]
REDL........ Redlane [*England*]
REDLAW ... Redlaw Industries, Inc. [*Associated Press abbreviation*] (APAG)
REDLN ..... Red Lion Inns Ltd. [*Associated Press abbreviation*] (APAG)
REDLOG .. Logistic Readiness Report [*Navy*] (CINC)
REDLW..... Redlaw Industries, Inc. [*Associated Press abbreviation*] (APAG)
Redman...... Redman on Landlord and Tenant [*A publication*] (DLA)
Redm Arb... Redman on Arbitration [*A publication*] (DLA)
Red Mar Com ... Reddie's Law of Maritime Commerce [*1841*] [*A publication*] (DLA)
Red Mar Int L ... Reddie's Researches in Maritime International Law [*1844-45*] [*A publication*] (DLA)
Red Menac ... Red Menace [*A publication*]
REDN........ Reduction
REDNON ... Operational Readiness Report (Nonatomic) (CINC)
REDNT ..... Redundant (AAG)
REDO........ RADAR Engineering Design Objectives (NG)
REDO........ Red Documental [*Ministerio de Educacion Publica*] [*Chile*] [*Information service or system*] (CRD)
Redog ForsknStift Skogsarb ... Redogorelse. Forskningsstiftelsen Skogsarbeten [*A publication*]
REDOPS ... Ready for Operations [*Reporting system*] [*DoD*]
REDOX ..... Reduction and Oxidation
REDP........ Redondo Peak [*New Mexico*] [*Seismograph station code, US Geological Survey*] (SEIS)
Red Pop...... Post Reditum ad Populum [*of Cicero*] [*Classical studies*] (OCD)
Red Pr .... Redfield's New York Practice Reports [*A publication*] (DLA)
RED in PULV ... Redactus in Pulverem [*Reduce to a Powder*] [*Pharmacy*]
REDR .... Redruth [*England*]
REDRAT ... Readiness Rating
REDREP ... Redeployment Report [*Military*]
R Ed Res .... Review of Educational Research [*A publication*]
Red RL....... Reddie's Roman Law [*A publication*] (DLA)
Red RR....... Redfield on the Law of Railroads [*A publication*] (DLA)
Red RR Cas ... Redfield's Leading American Railway Cases [*A publication*] (DLA)
REDS........ Revised Engine-Delivery Schedule (DNAB)
REDS........ Royal Engineers Diving School [*British military*] (DMA)
Red Sc L....... Reddie's Science of Law [*2nd ed.*] [*A publication*] (DLA)
Red Sen...... Post Reditum in Senatu [*of Cicero*] [*Classical studies*] (OCD)
REDSG...... Redesignate (AFM)
redsh.......... Reddish [*Philately*]
REDSO...... Regional Economic Development Services Office [*USAID*]
REDSOD... Repetitive Explosive Device for Soil Displacement
REDSO/ESA ... Regional Economic Development Services Office for East and Southern Africa
RED-T .... Remote Electric Drive Turret
REDTOP... Reactor Design from Thermal-Hydraulic Operating Parameters [*NASA*]
REDTRAIN ... Readiness Training (MCD)
REDUC ..... Red Latinoamericana de Documentacion en Educacion [*Latin American Education Documentation Network*] (PDAA)
REDUC ..... Reduction (KSC)
R Educ........ Review of Education [*A publication*]

REDUCE... Reduction of Electrical Demand Using Computer Equipment [*Energy management system designed by John Helwig of Jance Associates, Inc.*]
R Educ Res ... Review of Educational Research [*A publication*]
REDUN..... Redundancy (NASA)
REDUPL.... Reduplication
REDV .... Resource Development. Incorporating Northern Development and Oceanic Industries [*A publication*]
REDW .... Redwood National Park
Redwar....... Redwar's Comments on Ordinances of the Gold Coast Colony [*1889-1909*] [*Ghana*] [*A publication*] (DLA)
Red Wills ... Redfield on the Law of Wills [*A publication*] (DLA)
REDWN.... Redrawn
REDX .... Red Eagle Resources Corp. [*NASDAQ symbol*] (NQ)
REDY .... Recirculating Dialyzate [*Artificial kidney dialysis system*]
REDYP...... Reentry Dynamics Program
REE .... Lubbock, TX [*Location identifier*] [*FAA*] (FAAL)
REE .... Radio Exterior Espana (EY)
REE .... Rapid Extinction Effect [*Electrophysiology*]
REE .... Rare-Earth Element [*Chemistry*]
REE .... Rational Expectations Equilibrium [*Economics*]
REE .... Red Earth Energy Ltd. [*Vancouver Stock Exchange symbol*]
REE .... [*Department of*] Regional Economic Expansion [*Canada*]
REE .... Reliance Electric Co. [*NYSE symbol*] (SPSG)
REE .... Resources and Energy [*A publication*]
REE .... Respiratory Energy Expenditure [*Physiology*]
REE .... Resting Energy Expenditure
REEA........ Real Estate Educators Association [*Chicago, IL*] (EA)
Reebok .... Reebok International Ltd. [*Associated Press abbreviation*] (APAG)
REEC........ Regional Export Expansion Council [*Department of Commerce*]
Reece.......... Reece Corp. [*Associated Press abbreviation*] (APAG)
REECO..... Reynolds Electrical & Engineering Co.
Reed .... Reed on Bills of Sale [*A publication*] (DLA)
REED .... Reeds Jewelers, Inc. [*Wilmington, NC*] [*NASDAQ symbol*] (NQ)
REED .... Resources on Educational Equity for the Disabled
Reed Am LS ... Reed's American Law Studies [*A publication*] (DLA)
Reed BS ... Reed on Bills of Sale [*A publication*] (DLA)
Reed Car .... Reed on Railways as Carriers [*A publication*] (DLA)
Reed Fraud ... Reed's Leading Cases on Statute of Frauds [*A publication*] (DLA)
REEDN ..... Records of Early English Drama. Newsletter [*A publication*]
Reed PA Black ... Reed's Pennsylvania Blackstone [*A publication*] (DLA)
Reed Pr Sug ... Reed's Practical Suggestions for the Management of Lawsuits [*A publication*] (DLA)
Reed's Mar Equip News Mar Dig ... Reed's Marine and Equipment News and Marine Digest [*A publication*]
Reeduc Orthophon ... Reeducation Orthophonique [*A publication*]
REEF........ Rocket Exhaust Effects Facility (MCD)
REEFER.... Refrigerator, Refrigerated, or Cold Storage [*Airplane, railway car, truck*]
REEG........ Radioelectroencephalograph
REEGT...... Registered Electroencephalographic Technician [*Medicine*] (AAMN)
REEI.......... Russian and East European Institute [*Indiana University*] [*Research center*] (RCD)
REEL........ Radiation Exposure Evaluation Laboratory (DNAB)
REEL........ Recessive-Expressive Emergent Language Scores [*For the hearing-impaired*]
REEM........ Reserves Embarked [*Navy*] (NVT)
REEN .... Regional Energy Education Network [*National Science Teachers Association*]
REENA...... Refrigerating Engineering [*A publication*]
REENL...... Reenlist [*Military*] (AFM)
REENLA.... Reenlistment Allowance [*Military*]
REENL ALLOW ... Reenlistment Allowance [*Military*] (DNAB)
REENLB... Reenlistment Bonus [*Military*]
Reenlmt..... Re-Enlistment [*Army*]
REEP........ Range Estimating and Evaluation Procedure [*Data processing*]
REEP........ Regression Estimation of Event Probabilities (IEEE)
REEP........ Review of Environmental Effects of Pollutants [*Environmental Protection Agency*] (GFGA)
REEP........ Revista. Escuela de Estudios Penitenciarios [*A publication*]
REES .... Center for Russian and East European Studies [*University of Pittsburgh*] [*Research center*] (RCD)
REES .... Reactive Electronic Equipment Simulator (RDA)
REES .... Russian and East European Studies Area Program [*University of Pittsburgh*] [*Research center*] (RCD)
Rees' Cyclopaedia ... [*Abraham*] Rees' English Cyclopaedia [*A publication*] (DLA)
Reese.......... Reporter of Vols. 5 and 11, Heiskell's Tennessee Reports [*A publication*] (DLA)
REETA ...... Rural Extension, Education and Training Abstracts [*Database*] [*Commonwealth Bureau of Agricultural Economics*] [*Information service or system*] (CRD)
REETS ...... Radiological Effluent and Environmental Technical Specifications [*Nuclear Regulatory Commission*] (NRCH)
Reeve Des .. Reeve on Descents [*A publication*] (DLA)
Reeve Dom Rel ... Reeve on Domestic Relations [*A publication*] (DLA)

Reeve Eng L ... Reeve's History of the English Law [*A publication*] (DLA)
Reeve Eng Law ... Reeve's History of the English Law [*A publication*] (DLA)
Reeve Hist Eng Law ... Reeve's History of the English Law [*A publication*] (DLA)
Reeve Sh .... Reeve on the Law of Shipping [*A publication*] (DLA)
Reeves HEL ... Reeve's History of the English Law [*A publication*] (DLA)
Reeves Hist Eng Law ... Reeve's History of the English Law [*A publication*] (DLA)
Reeves J ..... Reeves Journal [*A publication*]
REF .... Range Error Function [*Aerospace*] (AAG)
REF .... Rat Embryo Fibroblast [*Cells*]
REF .... Refectory (DSUE)
REF .... Refer (EY)
REF .... Referee
REF .... Reference [*Online database field identifier*] (NATG)
REF .... Referendum
REF .... Refinery [*or Refining*]
REF .... Reflection Resources [*Vancouver Stock Exchange symbol*]
REF .... Reflector
Ref. .... Reformatio [*A publication*]
REF .... Reformation
REF .... Reformed
REF .... Refrain (WGA)
REF .... Refresher (AABC)
REF .... Refrigerant [*Cooling*] [*Medicine*] [*British*] (ROG)
REF .... Refrigerator (WGA)
REF .... Refugee Coordinator [*Department of State*] (GFGA)
REF .... Refund [*or Refunding*]
REF .... Refurbishment (NASA)
REF .... Refused (ADA)
REF .... Release of Excess Funds
REF .... Renal Erythropoietic Factor [*Medicine*]
REF .... Unclear Pronoun Reference [*Used in correcting manuscripts, etc.*]
REFA .... Real Estate Fund of America
REFAA4 .... Research and Farming [*North Carolina Agricultural Research Service*] [*A publication*]
REFA Nachr ... REFA [*Reichsausschuss fuer Arbeitsstudien*] Nachrichten [*A publication*]
Ref Aust ..... Reference Australia [*A publication*]
Ref Book Rev Index ... Reference Book Review Index [*A publication*]
REFC .... REFAC Technology Development Corp. [*NASDAQ symbol*] (NQ)
REFC .... Reference (ROG)
REFC .... Reflections of Elvis Fan Club (EA)
REFC .... Richard Eden Fan Club (EA)
REFCD ...... Research and Education Foundation for Chest Disease (EA)
Ref Chem Ind ... Referate aus dem Gebiet der Chemischen Industrie [*A publication*]
Ref Ch R .... Reformed Church Review [*A publication*]
REFCO ...... Resolution Funding Corp. [*Established by the Financial Institutions Reform , Recovery, and Enforcement Act of 1989*]
REFCON ... Reference Configuration (SSD)
RefCorp ...... Resolution Funding Corp. [*Established by the Financial Institutions Reform , Recovery, and Enforcement Act of 1989*]
REFD .... Referred
REFD .... Refined
REFD .... Reformed (WGA)
REFD .... Refund (AFM)
REFD CON ... Reinforced Concrete [*Freight*]
Ref Dec ...... Referee's Decision [*Legal term*] (DLA)
REF/DES .. Reference Designator Number (MCD)
REFD MTL ... Reinforced Metal [*Freight*]
ref doc .... Referring Doctor [*Medicine*] (AAMN)
Ref Dokl Nauchno-Issled Rab Aspir Ukr Skh Akad ... Referaty Dokladov o Nauchno-Issledovatel'skoi Rabote Aspirantov. Ukrainskaya Sel'skokhozyaistvennaya Akademiya [*A publication*]
Ref Dok Mosk Skh Akad ... Referaty Dokladov Moskovskaya Sel'skokhozyaistvennaya Akademiya Imeni K. A. Timiryazeva [*A publication*]
Ref Dopov Nauk Dosl Rob Aspir Ukr Akad Sil's'kogospod Nauk ... Referati Dopovidei pro Naukovo-Doslidnu Robotu Aspirantiv. Ukrains'ka Akademiya Sil's'kogospodars'kikh Nauk [*A publication*]
REFD PLYWD ... Reinforced Plywood [*Freight*]
REFEC ...... Refectory (DSUE)
RefEgyhaz ... Reformatus Egyhaz [*Budapest*] [*A publication*]
Referatebl zur Raumentwicklung ... Referateblatt zur Raumentwicklung [*A publication*]
Referatebl zur Raumordnung ... Referateblatt zur Raumordnung [*A publication*]
Referat Zh Biol ... Referativnyi Zhurnal. Biologiya [*A publication*]
Referat Zh Zhivot Vet ... Referativnyi Zhurnal. Zhivotnovodstvo i Veterinariya [*A publication*]
REFF .... References (WGA)
REFG .... Refrigerating [*or Refrigeration*]
Ref Girl ...... Refractory Girl [*A publication*]
REFGR ...... Refrigerator

REFIC .... Research Fire Control (SAA)
Refin Eng ... Refining Engineer [*A publication*]
Refiner Nat Gasoline Manuf ... Refiner and Natural Gasoline Manufacturer [*A publication*]
Ref J .... National Association of Referees in Bankruptcy. Journal [*A publication*]
Ref J .... Reformed Journal [*A publication*]
REFL .... Reference Librarian [*A publication*]
REFL .... Reference Line (AAG)
REFL .... Reflectance [*or Reflector*] (AAG)
REFL .... Reflex
REFL .... Reflexive
REFLD ...... Reflected
REFLES .... Reference Librarian Enhancement System [*University of California*] [*Online microcomputer system*]
Reflets Econ Franc-Comtoise ... Reflets de l'Economie Franc-Comtoise [*A publication*]
Reflets et Perspectives ... Reflets et Perspectives de la Vie Economique [*A publication*]
Reflets Perspect Vie Econ ... Reflets et Perspectives de la Vie Economique [*A publication*]
REFLEX .... Reserve Flexibility [*Military*] (MCD)
Ref Libr ...... Reference Librarian [*A publication*]
Ref Lit Music ... Reformed Liturgy and Music [*A publication*]
Refl Persp Vie Ec ... Reflets et Perspectives de la Vie Economique [*A publication*]
Ref Mag ..... Referee Magazine [*A publication*]
REFMCHY ... Refrigerating Machinery
Ref Med ..... Reforma Medica [*A publication*]
REFMS ..... Recreation and Education for Multiple Sclerosis
REFMT ..... Reinforcement
REFNA ...... REFA [*Reichsausschuss fuer Arbeitsstudien*] Nachrichten [*A publication*]
REFNO ..... Reference Number (CINC)
Ref NRE ... Refused, Not Reversible Error [*Legal term*] (DLA)
REFONE .... Reference Our Telephone Conversation (FAAC)
REFORGER ... Return of Forces to Germany [*Military*]
REFORM ... Reference Form (FAAC)
REFORM ... Reformatory (ROG)
REFORMA ... National Association to Promote Library Services to the Spanish-Speaking
Refor Mon ... Reforestation Monthly [*A publication*]
REFP .... Reference Papers [*Army*] (AABC)
Ref Pres W ... Reformed and Presbyterian World [*A publication*]
Ref Q .... Reformed Quarterly Review [*A publication*]
Ref R .... Reformed Review [*A publication*]
REFR .... Refractory (AAG)
REFR .... Refrigerate (KSC)
REFR .... Research Frontiers, Inc. [*NASDAQ symbol*] (NQ)
REFRA ...... Refractories [*English Translation*] [*A publication*]
REFRACDUTRA ... Release from Active Duty for Training [*Army*] (AABC)
Refract Inst Tech Bull ... Refractories Institute. Technical Bulletin [*A publication*]
Refract J .... Refractories Journal [*A publication*]
Refract Mater ... Refractory Materials [*A publication*]
Refractor J ... Refractories Journal [*A publication*]
REFRAD ... Release from Active Duty [*Army*]
REFRADT ... Release from Active Duty for Training [*Army*] (AABC)
REFRANACDUTRA ... Release from Annual Active Duty for Training [*Army*] (AABC)
REFRAT ... Release from Annual Training [*Army*] (AABC)
REFRD ...... Refrigerated (AAG)
Refr G .... Refractory Girl [*A publication*]
REFRG ...... Refrigerate (AAG)
REFRIG .... Refrigerated Service [*Shipping*] [*British*]
Refrig .... Refrigeration [*A publication*]
REFRIG .... Refrigerator
Refrig A ..... Refrigeration Annual [*A publication*] (APTA)
Refrig Air ... Refrigeration and Air Conditioning [*A publication*]
Refrig Air Cond & Heat ... Refrigeration Journal, Incorporating Air Conditioning and Heating [*A publication*] (APTA)
Refrig Air Condit ... Refrigeration and Air Conditioning [*A publication*]
Refrig Air Condit Heat Recovery ... Refrigeration, Air Conditioning, and Heat Recovery [*A publication*]
Refrig Ann ... Refrigeration Annual [*A publication*] (APTA)
Refrig Annual ... Refrigeration Annual [*A publication*] (APTA)
Refrig Cold Stor ... Refrigeration, Cold Storage, and Air-Conditioning [*A publication*] (APTA)
Refrig Cold Storage ... Refrigeration and Cold Storage [*A publication*]
Refrig Cold Storage Air Cond ... Refrigeration, Cold Storage, and Air-Conditioning [*A publication*] (APTA)
Refrig Eng ... Refrigerating Engineering [*A publication*]
Refrigeration J ... Refrigeration Journal [*A publication*] (APTA)
Refrig J .... Refrigeration Journal [*A publication*]
REFRIGN ... Refrigeration
Refrig Sci Technol ... Refrigeration Science and Technology [*A publication*]
Refrig W .... Refrigerating World [*A publication*]
Ref Sc Lit Fire ... References to Scientific Literature on Fire [*A publication*]
Ref Serv R ... Reference Services Review [*A publication*]
Ref Serv Rev ... Reference Services Review [*A publication*]
Ref Shelf .... Reference Shelf [*A publication*]

REFSMMAT ... Reference Stable Member Matrix (KSC)
Ref Source ... Reference Sources [*A publication*]
REFSRV .... [*The*] Reference Service [*Mead Data Central, Inc.*] [*Information service or system*] (IID)
REFT .... Release for Experimental Flight Test (NG)
REFTEL .... Reference Telegram (NATG)
Ref Theol R ... Reformed Theological Review [*A publication*]
Ref Th R .... Reformed Theological Review [*A publication*]
REFTO ..... Reference Travel Order (NOAA)
RefTR .... Reformed Theological Review [*Australia*] [*A publication*]
REFTRA ... Refresher Training (NVT)
REFTS ...... Resonant Frequency Tracking System
REFUL ...... Refueling
REFURB ... Refurbished
REFURDIS ... Reference Your Dispatch
REFURLTR ... Reference Your Letter
Refu Vet ..... Refuah Veterinarith [*A publication*]
Ref W .... Reformed World [*A publication*]
RefWID ..... Refugee Women in Development (EA)
Ref WM ..... Refused, Want of Merit [*Legal term*] (DLA)
REFY .... Refinery
Ref Zh Astron ... Referativnyi Zhurnal. Astronomiya [*A publication*]
Ref Zh Astron Geod ... Referativnyi Zhurnal. Astronomiya. Geodeziya [*A publication*]
Ref Zh Biol ... Referativnyi Zhurnal. Biologiya [*A publication*]
Ref Zh Biol Khim ... Referativnyi Zhurnal. Biologicheskaya Khimiya [*A publication*]
Ref Zh Faramakol Khimioter Sredstva Toksikol ... Referativnyi Zhurnal. Farmakologiya. Khimioterapeuticheskie Sredstva. Toksikologiya [*A publication*]
Ref Zh Fiz ... Referativnyi Zhurnal. Fizika [*A publication*]
Ref Zh Fiz-Khim Biol Biotekhnol ... Referativnyi Zhurnal. Fiziko-Khimicheskaya Biologiya i Biotekhnologiya [*A publication*]
Ref Zh Fotokinotekh ... Referativnyi Zhurnal. Fotokinotekhnika [*A publication*]
Ref Zh Geod ... Referativnyi Zhurnal. Geodeziya [*A publication*]
Ref Zh Geod Aerosemka ... Referativnyi Zhurnal. Geodeziya i Aeros'emka [*A publication*]
Ref Zh Geof ... Referativnyi Zhurnal. Geofizika [*A publication*]
Ref Zh Geol ... Referativnyi Zhurnal. Geologiya [*A publication*]
Ref Zh Inf .. Referativnyi Zhurnal. Informatika [*A publication*]
Ref Zh Khim ... Referativnyi Zhurnal. Khimiya [*A publication*]
Ref Zh Khim Biol Khim ... Referativnyi Zhurnal. Khimiya. Biologicheskaya Khimiya [*A publication*]
Ref Zh Korroz ... Referativnyi Zhurnal. Korroziya [*A publication*]
Ref Zh Legk Promst ... Referativnyi Zhurnal. Legkaya Promyshlennost [*A publication*]
Ref Zh Mekh ... Referativnyi Zhurnal. Mekhanika [*A publication*]
Ref Zh Metall ... Referativnyi Zhurnal. Metallurgiya [*Former USSR*] [*A publication*]
Ref Zh Metrol Izmer Tekh ... Referativnyi Zhurnal. Metrologiya i Izmeritel'naya Tekhnika [*A publication*]
Ref Zh Nasosostr Kompressorostr Kholod Mashinostr ... Referativnyi Zhurnal. Nasosostroenie i Kompressorostroenie. Kholodil'noe Mashinostroenie [*A publication*]
Ref Zh Okhr Prir Vosproizvod Prir Resur ... Referativnyi Zhurnal. Okhrana Prirody i Vosproizvodstvo Prirodnykh Resursov [*Former USSR*] [*A publication*]
Ref Zh Pochvoved Agrokhim ... Referativnyi Zhurnal. Pochvovedenie i Agrokhimiya [*A publication*]
Ref Zh Radiats Biol ... Referativnyi Zhurnal. Radiatsionnaya Biologiya [*Former USSR*] [*A publication*]
Ref Zh Rastenievod ... Referativnyi Zhurnal. Rastenievodstvo [*A publication*]
Ref Zh Teploenerg ... Referativnyi Zhurnal. Teploenergetika [*A publication*]
Ref Zh Yad Reakt ... Referativnyi Zhurnal. Yadernye Reaktory [*A publication*]
Ref Zh Zhivotnovod Vet ... Referativnyi Zhurnal. Zhivotnovodstvo i Veterinariya [*A publication*]
RefZtg .... Reform Zeitung [*Berlin*] [*A publication*]
REG .... Aircraft Nationality and Registration Marks
Reg .... Daily Register [*New York City*] [*A publication*] (DLA)
REG .... Radiation Exposure Guide
REG .... Radioencephalogram
REG .... Random Event Generator [*Psychology*]
REG .... Range Extender with Gain [*Bell System*]
REG .... Reeves Entertainment Group [*Television*]
Reg .... Regal, Branch of EMI [*Record label*] [*Spain*]
REG .... Regardie's Magazine [*A publication*]
REG .... Regarding
REG .... Regency Resources [*Vancouver Stock Exchange symbol*]
REG .... Regent
REG .... Regina [*Queen*] [*Latin*]
REG .... Reggio Calabria [*Italy*] [*Airport symbol*] (OAG)
REG .... Regiment
REG .... Region (AAG)
REG .... Regional Science and Urban Economics [*A publication*]
REG .... Regis College, Weston, MA [*OCLC symbol*] (OCLC)
REG .... Register (AAG)
REG .... Registered [*Stock exchange term*] (SPSG)
REG .... Registrar (ROG)

Reg .... Registration Cases [*A publication*] (DLA)
Reg .... Registrum Omnium Brevium [*Register of Writs*] [*Latin*] [*A publication*] (DSA)
REG .... Registry
REG .... Regular (AAG)
REG .... Regulate (AAG)
REG .... Regulating [*Duties*] [*Navy*] [*British*]
REG .... Regulation
REG .... Regulator (DEN)
REG .... Repair-Evacuator Group [*Former USSR*]
REG .... Rheoencephalography [*Medicine*]
REG .... Rock Eagle [*Georgia*] [*Seismograph station code, US Geological Survey*] (SEIS)
REGAF ..... Regular Air Force
REGAL ...... Range and Elevation Guidance for Approach and Landing [*Aviation*] (FAAC)
Regal .... Regal International, Inc. [*Associated Press abbreviation*] (APAG)
REGAL ...... Remotely Guided Autonomous Lightweight Torpedo (MCD)
REGALBL ... Regal-Beloit Corp. [*Associated Press abbreviation*] (APAG)
Reg Anaesth ... Regional Anaesthesia [*A publication*]
Regan Rep Nurs Law ... Regan Report on Nursing Law [*A publication*]
Reg App ..... Registration Appeals [*England*] [*A publication*] (DLA)
Reg Arch .... Registered Architect
REGARD ... Ruby, Emerald, Garnet, Amethyst, Ruby, Diamond [*Jewelry*]
REGB .... Regional Bancorp, Inc. [*NASDAQ symbol*] (NQ)
Reg Brev ..... Registrum Omnium Brevium [*Register of Writs*] [*Latin*] [*A publication*] (DLA)
REGC .... Right Eminent Grand Commander [*Freemasonry*]
REG/CAN ... Registry Number/Chemical Abstracts Number [*American Chemical Society information file*]
Reg Cas ...... Registration Cases [*England*] [*A publication*] (DLA)
Reg Cat Earthquakes ... Regional Catalogue of Earthquakes [*A publication*]
Reg Conf Ser Appl Math ... Regional Conference Series in Applied Mathematics [*A publication*]
REGD .... Registered (EY)
Reg Deb ..... Gales and Seaton's Register of Debates in Congress [*1824-37*] [*A publication*] (DLA)
Reg Deb (Gales) ... Register of Debates in Congress (Gales) [*1789-91*] [*A publication*] (DLA)
Reg Deb (G & S) ... Gales and Seaton's Register of Debates in Congress [*1824-37*] [*A publication*] (DLA)
Reg Dev ...... Regional Development News [*New Zealand*] [*A publication*]
Reg Dolg .... Regeszeti Dolgozatok az Eoetvoes Lorand Tudomanyegyetem Regeszeti Lutezeteboel [*A publication*]
Regelungstech ... Regelungstechnik [*A publication*]
Regelungstech Prax ... Regelungstechnische Praxis [*A publication*]
Regelungstech Prax Prozess-Rechentech ... Regelungstechnische Praxis und Prozess-Rechentechnik [*A publication*]
Regelungstech Prozess-Datenverarb ... Regelungstechnik und Prozess-Datenverarbeitung [*A publication*]
Regelungstech Prozess-Datenverarbeitung ... Regelungstechnik und Prozess-Datenverarbeitung [*A publication*]
Regelungstech RT ... Regelungstechnik. RT [*West Germany*] [*A publication*]
REGEM ..... Release of Genetically Engineered Microorganisms [*A conference*]
REGEN ..... Regeneration (AAG)
Regensb Univ-Ztg ... Regensburger Universitaets-Zeitung [*A publication*]
Regensburger Math Schriften ... Regensburger Mathematische Schriften [*A publication*]
REGENT ... Reduce Geography in No Time (SAA)
Reger .... Mitteilungen. Max Reger Institut [*Bonn*] [*A publication*]
Reg Erzb Koeln ... Regesten der Erzbischoefe von Koeln im Mittelalter [*A publication*]
Reg Fuez .... Regeszeti Fuezetek [*A publication*]
Reg Gen ..... Regulae Generales [*A publication*] (DLA)
Reg Genet Mineral ... Regional'naya i Geneticheskaya Mineralogiya [*A publication*]
Reg Geol Ser NC Div Resour Plann Eval Miner Resour Sect ... Regional Geology Series. North Carolina Division of Resource Planning and Evaluation. Mineral Resources Section [*A publication*]
Reg Geol Ser NC Miner Resour Sect ... Regional Geology Series. North Carolina Mineral Resources Section [*A publication*]
RegHlt .... Regency Health Services [*Associated Press abbreviation*] (APAG)
REGI .... [*The*] Regina Co., Inc. [*Rahway, NJ*] [*NASDAQ symbol*] (NQ)
Regia Soc Sci Upsal Nova Acta ... Regia Societas Scientiarum Upsaliensis. Nova Acta [*A publication*]
Regia Stn Chim Agrar Sper Roma Pubbl ... Regia Stazione Chimico-Agraria Sperimentale di Roma. Pubblicazione [*A publication*]
Regia Stn Sper Seta Boll Uffic (Italy) ... Regia Stazione Sperimentale per la Seta. Bollettino Ufficiale (Italy) [*A publication*]
REGIM ..... Regimental (ROG)
REGING .... Registering (ROG)
Regional Development J ... Regional Development Journal [*A publication*] (APTA)
Regional Rail Reorg Ct ... Special Court Regional Railroad Reorganization Act [*A publication*] (DLA)
Regional Science and Urban Econ ... Regional Science and Urban Economics [*A publication*]

Regional Stud ... Regional Studies [*Oxford*] [*A publication*]
Region Develop J ... Regional Development Journal [*A publication*]   (APTA)
Region Urb Econ ... Regional and Urban Economics Operational Methods [*A publication*]
REGIS .... Regency Investors [*NASDAQ symbol*]   (NQ)
REGIS .... Register   (AABC)
REGIS .... Relational General Information System
ReGIS .... Remote Graphics Instruction Set   (HGAA)
Register of Kentucky Hist Soc ... Register. Kentucky Historical Society [*A publication*]
Regist KY Hist Soc ... Register. Kentucky Historical Society [*A publication*]
Reg Jb Aerztl Fortbild ... Regensburger Jahrbuch fuer Aerztliche Fortbildung [*A publication*]
Reg J Energy Heat Mass Transfer ... Regional Journal of Energy, Heat, and Mass Transfer [*India*] [*A publication*]
Reg J Social Issues ... Regional Journal of Social Issues [*A publication*]
REGL .... Regimental
Regl .... Reglement [*Administrative Ordinance or Rule of Procedure*] [*French*]   (ILCA)
Reg Lib ...... Register Book [*A publication*]   (DLA)
Reg Lib ...... Registrar's Book, Chancery [*A publication*]   (DLA)
REGLN ...... Regulation   (AAG)
REGLON .. Regulation   (ROG)
REGLOS ... Reserve and Guard Logistic Operations-Streamline [*Army*]   (AABC)
Reg Maj ..... Books of Regiam Majestatem [*Scotland*] [*A publication*]   (DLA)
REGN .... Regeneron Pharmaceuticals [*NASDAQ symbol*]   (SPSG)
REGN .... Registry Number
REG-NEG ... Regulatory Negotiation
Regnum Veg ... Regnum Vegetabile [*A publication*]
Reg Om Brev ... Registrum Omnium Brevium [*Register of Writs*] [*Latin*] [*A publication*]   (DLA)
Reg Orig ..... Registrum Originale [*Latin*] [*A publication*]   (DLA)
REGPOWREN ... Regulating Petty Officer WREN [*Women's Royal Naval Service*] [*British military*]   (DMA)
RegProf ...... Regius Professor [*The King's Professor*] [*British*]
REGR .... Register   (ROG)
REGR .... Registrar
REGR .... Regulator   (AAG)
REGR .... Resources Group Review. Suncor, Inc. [*A publication*]
Reg Rep New Hebrides Geol Surv ... Regional Report. New Hebrides Geological Survey [*A publication*]
REGS .... Regulations
REGS-A ..... Regional Studies [*A publication*]
Reg Soc Sci Upsal Nova Acta ... Regia Societas Scientiarum Upsaliensis. Nova Acta [*A publication*]
REGSTD ... Registered
REGSTR ... Registrar
REGSTRTN ... Registration
Reg Stud .... Regional Studies [*A publication*]
Reg Stud Assoc Newsl ... Regional Studies Association. Newsletter [*A publication*]
REGT .... Regent
REGT .... Regiment   (AABC)
REGT .... Regulator
Reg Tech Conf Soc Plast Eng ... Regional Technical Conference. Society of Plastics Engineers [*A publication*]
Reg Tech Meet Am Iron Steel Inst ... Regional Technical Meetings. American Iron and Steel Institute [*A publication*]
REGTL ...... Regimental
REGUL ...... Regular   (ROG)
REGULAT ... Regulation
Regulatory Action Net ... Regulatory Action Network [*A publication*]
Regul Bull KY Agr Exp Sta ... Regulatory Bulletin. Kentucky Agricultural Experiment Station [*A publication*]
Regul Bull Ky Agric Exp Stn ... Regulatory Bulletin. Kentucky Agricultural Experiment Station [*A publication*]
Regul Bull Univ KY Coll Agric Agric Exp Stn ... Regulatory Bulletin. University of Kentucky. College of Agriculture. Agricultural Experiment Station [*A publication*]
Regul y Mando Autom ... Regulacion y Mando Automatico [*A publication*]
Regul Pept ... Regulatory Peptides [*A publication*]
Regul Pept Suppl ... Regulatory Peptides. Supplement [*A publication*]
Regul Toxicol Pharmacol ... Regulatory Toxicology and Pharmacology [*A publication*]
Regul Tox P ... Regulatory Toxicology and Pharmacology [*A publication*]
Reg Umb .... Regio Umbilici [*Region of the Umbilicus*] [*Pharmacy*]
Reg Urban Econ ... Regional and Urban Economics [*Netherlands*] [*A publication*]
Reg Urb Econ ... Regional Science and Urban Economics [*A publication*]
Reg Writ .... Register of Writs [*A publication*]   (DLA)
REGY .... Registry   (ROG)
REH .... Random Evolutionary Hits
REH .... Rational Expectations Hypothesis [*Economics*]
REH .... Rehoboth Beach, DE [*Location identifier*] [*FAA*]   (FAAL)
REHAB ..... Rehabilitate [*or Rehabilitation*]   (AFM)
Rehab .... Rehabilitation [*A publication*]
Rehab Aust ... Rehabilitation in Australia [*A publication*]
Rehab Couns ... Rehabilitation Counseling Bulletin [*A publication*]
REHABIL ... Rehabilitation

Rehabil Aust ... Rehabilitation in Australia [*A publication*]   (APTA)
Rehabil Lit ... Rehabilitation Literature [*A publication*]
Rehabil Nurs ... Rehabilitation Nursing [*A publication*]
Rehabil Psychol ... Rehabilitation Psychology [*A publication*]
Rehabil Rec ... Rehabilitation Record [*A publication*]
Rehabil SA ... Rehabilitation in South Africa [*A publication*]
Rehabil S Afr ... Rehabilitation in South Africa [*A publication*]
Rehabil Suppl (Bratisl) ... Rehabilitacia Supplementum (Bratislava) [*A publication*]
REHABIT ... Reitan Evaluation of Hemispheric Abilities and Brain Improvement Training [*Neuropsychology test*]
Rehab Lit ... Rehabilitation Literature [*A publication*]
Reh Allowed ... Rehearing Allowed [*Used in Shepard's Citations*] [*Legal term*]   (DLA)
REHC .... Random Evolutionary Hits per Codon
Reh Den ..... Rehearing Denied [*Used in Shepard's Citations*] [*Legal term*]   (DLA)
Reh Dis ...... Rehearing Dismissed [*Used in Shepard's Citations*] [*Legal term*]   (DLA)
Reh'g .... Rehearing [*Legal term*]   (DLA)
REHID ...... Recursos Hidraulicos [*A publication*]
REHIS .... Royal Environmental Health Institute of Scotland [*British*]
REHNRAP ... Recreational, Entertainment, and Health Naturally Radioactive Products   (NRCH)
REHT .... Reheat   (KSC)
REHVA ..... Representatives of European Heating and Ventilating Associations
REI .... Range from Entry Interface   (NASA)
REI .... Rat der Europaeischen Industrieverbaende [*Council of European Industrial Federations*]
REI .... Real Estate Issues [*American Society of Real Estate Counselors*] [*A publication*]
REI .... Recycling [*Den Haag*] [*A publication*]
REI .... Regiment Etranger d'Infanterie [*Foreign Infantry Regiment*] [*French*]
REI .... Reidovoe [*Former USSR*] [*Seismograph station code, US Geological Survey*]   (SEIS)
REI .... Religion and Ethics Institute   (EA)
REI .... Request for Engineering Information   (NG)
REI .... Request for Engineering Investigation [*Nuclear energy*]   (NRCH)
REI .... Research-Engineering Interaction   (IEEE)
REI .... Reusable External Insulation [*of space shuttle*] [*NASA*]
REI .... Runway-End Identification [*Aviation*]   (NASA)
REI .... Rural Economics Institute   (OICC)
REIC .... Radiation Effects Information Center [*Defunct*] [*Battelle Memorial Institute*]
REIC .... Renewable Energy Info Center   (EA)
REIC .... Research Industries Corp. [*NASDAQ symbol*]   (NQ)
Reichhold-Albert-Nachr ... Reichhold-Albert-Nachrichten [*A publication*]
Reichsber Phys ... Reichsberichte fuer Physik [*A publication*]
Reichstoff Ind Kosmet ... Reichstoff Industrie und Kosmetik [*A publication*]
ReichTg ..... Reich & Tang Ltd. [*Associated Press abbreviation*]   (APAG)
REIC (Radiat Eff Inf Cent) Rep ... REIC (Radiation Effects Information Center) Report [*A publication*]
Rei Cret Rom Faut Acta ... Rei Cretariae Romanae Fautorum Acta [*A publication*]
REID .... Reid-Provident Laboratories [*NASDAQ symbol*]   (NQ)
Reid PL Dig ... Reid's Digest of Scotch Poor Law Cases [*A publication*]   (DLA)
Reihe Informat ... Reihe Informatik [*A publication*]
REIL .... Real Estate Investing Letter [*Harcourt Brace Jovanovich, Inc.*] [*No longer available online*] [*Information service or system*]   (CRD)
REIL .... Runway-End Identification Lights [*Aviation*]
Reilly .... Reilly's English Arbitration Cases [*A publication*]   (DLA)
Reilly EA ... Reilly's European Arbitration. Lord Westbury's Decisions [*A publication*]   (DLA)
REI(M) ...... Regiment Etranger d'Infanterie (de Marche) [*Foreign Marching Infantry Regiment*] [*French*]
REIM .... Reimburse   (AABC)
REIMB ...... Reimburse   (MSA)
REIMBJTR ... Reimbursement [*in Accordance with*] Joint Travel Regulations [*Military*]   (DNAB)
REIN .... Raymond Engineering [*NASDAQ symbol*]   (NQ)
REIN .... Real Estate Information Network [*Database*]
REIN .... Reinforce
Rein .... Reinstated [*Regulation or order reinstated*] [*Used in Shepard's Citations*] [*Legal term*]   (DLA)
Reine Angew Metallkd Einzeldarst ... Reine und Angewandte Metallkunde in Einzeldarstellungen [*A publication*]
REINET ...... Real Estate Information Network [*National Association of Realtors*] [*Information service or system*]   (IID)
REINF .... Refund Information File [*IRS*]
REINF .... Reinforce   (AAG)
REINFD ... Reinforced   (AAG)
REINFG .... Reinforcing   (AAG)
REINFM .... Reinforcement   (AAG)
Rein Foie Mal Nutr ... Rein et Foie. Maladies de la Nutrition [*France*] [*A publication*]
Reinf Plast ... Reinforced Plastics [*A publication*]

Reinf Plast (Boston) ... Reinforced Plastics (Boston) [*A publication*]
Reinf Plast Compos World ... Reinforced Plastics and Composites World [*A publication*]
Reinf Plast (London) ... Reinforced Plastics (London) [*A publication*]
REINIT ..... Reinitialize (MCD)
REINS .... RADAR-Equipped Inertial Navigation System
REINS .... Requirements Electronic Input System [*NASA*] (KSC)
REINSR .... Reinsurance
REINV .... Reference Invoice (FAAC)
REIPS .... Real Estate Investment Properties [*NASDAQ symbol*] (NQ)
REIQ .... Refrigeration Installation Equipment (SAA)
REIS .... Readiness Information System [*Army*]
REIS .... Reconstitutable and Enduring Intelligence System
REIS .... Regional Economic Information System [*Department of Commerce*] [*Information service or system*] (IID)
REIS .... Regional Energy Information System [*Minnesota State Department of Energy and Economic Development*] [*St. Paul*] [*Information service or system*] (IID)
REIS .... Research and Engineering Information Services [*Exxon Research & Engineering Co.*] (IID)
REIS .... Reseau Europeen Integre d'Image et de Services [*European Integrated Network of Image and Services*] (EAIO)
Reiss-Davis Clin Bull ... Reiss-Davis Clinic. Bulletin [*A publication*]
REIT .... Real Estate Investment Trust [*Generic term*]
REIT .... Real Estate Investment Trust [*California*] [*Associated Press abbreviation*] (APAG)
REIT .... REIT of California [*Los Angeles, CA*] [*NASDAQ symbol*] (NQ)
REIT .... Reiteration [*Printing*] (ROG)
REIV .... Rocket Engine Injector Valve
REJ .... Redig, SD [*Location identifier*] [*FAA*] (FAAL)
REJ .... Reject (MSA)
REJ .... Religious Education Journal of Australia [*A publication*] (APTA)
Re de J .... Revue de Jurisprudence [*Montreal*] [*A publication*] (DLA)
REJASE .... Reusing Junk as Something Else [*Conversion of junk into reusable items*]
REJD .... Rejoined (WGA)
REJIS .... Regional Justice Information Service [*St. Louis, MO*]
REJN .... Rejoin (AABC)
REJO .... Rod Easterling and Jim Osburn [*Automobile named for designers*]
REJOD ...... Reeves Journal [*A publication*]
REJU .... Reject Unit [*IRS*]
REK .... Reykjavik [*Iceland*] [*Airport symbol*] (OAG)
REKY .... Royal East Kent Yeomanry [*Military unit*] [*British*]
REL .... Radiation Evaluation Loop [*Nuclear energy*] (NRCH)
REL .... Radio Electrician [*Navy*] [*British*]
REL .... Radio Engineering Laboratories
REL .... Rapidly Extensible Language System [*Data processing*] (CSR)
REL .... Rare-Earth LASER
REL .... Rassemblement Europeen de la Liberte [*European Liberty Rally*] [*France*] [*Political party*] (PPE)
REL .... Rate of Energy Loss
REL .... Reactor Equipment Ltd. [*Nuclear energy*] (NRCH)
REL .... Real Estate Law Journal [*A publication*]
REL .... Recommended Exposure Limit
REL .... Regional Education Laboratory
REL .... Related
REL .... Relations
REL .... Relative
REL .... Relativity
Rel .... Relatore [*Reporter*] [*Italian*] (ILCA)
REL .... Relay (AAG)
REL .... Release (AAG)
REL .... Reliability
REL .... Reliance Group Holdings, Inc. [*Formerly, Leasco Corp.*] [*NYSE symbol*] (SPSG)
REL .... Relic
REL .... Relie [*Bound*] [*Publishing*] [*French*]
REL .... Relief (AAG)
REL .... Religion
Rel .... Religion [*A publication*]
REL .... Reliquary and Illustrated Archaeologist [*A publication*] (ROG)
Rel .... Reliquiae [*of Suetonius*] [*Classical studies*] (OCD)
REL .... Reliquiae [*Remains*] [*Latin*]
REL .... Relizane [*Algeria*] [*Seismograph station code, US Geological Survey*] [*Closed*] (SEIS)
REL .... Relocatable [*Data processing*]
REL .... Reluctance (DEN)
REL .... Rescue Equipment Locker (AAG)
REL .... Restricted Energy Loss
REL .... Review of English Literature [*A publication*]
Re de L .... Revue de Jurisprudence et Legislation [*Montreal*] [*A publication*] (DLA)
REL .... Trelew [*Argentina*] [*Airport symbol*] (OAG)
RELA .... Real Estate Leaders of America [*Montgomery, AL*] (EA)
RELAA ..... Recht der Landwirtschaft [*A publication*]
RelAb .... Religious and Theological Abstracts [*A publication*]
RELACDU ... Released from Active Duty [*Navy*] (DNAB)
Relac Int ..... Relaciones Internacionales [*A publication*]

RELACS .... RADAR Emission Location Attack Control System
Relais .... Relais Statistiques de l'Economie Picarde [*A publication*]
Relais Econ Picarde ... Relais Statistiques de l'Economie Picarde [*A publication*]
RELAT ...... Related
Relat .... Relativity [*A publication*]
Relat Annu Inst Geol Publ Hung ... Relationes Annuae. Instituti Geologici Publicii Hungarici [*A publication*]
Relata Tech Chim Biol Appl ... Relata Technica di Chimica e Biologia Applicata [*A publication*]
Relat Cient Esc Super Agric Luiz Queiroz Dep Inst Genet ... Relatorio Cientifico. Escola Superior de Agricultura Luiz de Queiroz. Departamento e Instituto de Genetica [*A publication*]
Relat DNOCS ... Relatoria. DNOCS [*Departamento Nacional de Obras Contra as Secas*] [*A publication*]
Relat Ind .... Relations Industrielles [*A publication*]
Relat Industr ... Relations Industrielles [*A publication*]
Relat Int ..... Relations Internationales [*A publication*]
Relat Int (Geneve) ... Relations Internationales (Geneve) [*A publication*]
Relations Inds (Quebec) ... Relations Industrielles (Quebec) [*A publication*]
RELATN ... Relation (ROG)
Relay Eng ... Relay Engineer [*A publication*]
Relaz Attiv Stn Sper Pratic Lodi ... Relazione sull'Attivita della Stazione Sperimentale di Praticoltura di Lodi [*A publication*]
Relaz Clin Sci ... Relazione Clinico Scientifiche [*A publication*]
Relazione Comm Dirett Ist Zootec Laziale (Roma) ... Relazione. Commissione Direttiva. Istituto Zootecnico Laziale (Roma) [*A publication*]
Relaz Soc ... Relazioni Sociali [*A publication*]
RelB .... Religion och Bibel [*Uppsala*] [*A publication*]
RelBib .... Religion och Bibel [*Uppsala*] [*A publication*]
RELBL ..... Reliability
RELBY ...... When Relieved By [*Army*]
RELC .... Regional Language Centre [*SEAMEO*] [*Research center*] [*Singapore*] (IRC)
RELC .... RELC [*Regional English Language Centre*] Journal [*Singapore*] [*A publication*]
RELC .... Reliability Committee [*NASA*]
Rel Cab ...... Religious Cabinet [*A publication*]
Rel Comm Lands ... Religion in Communist Lands [*A publication*]
RELCT ...... Relocate (FAAC)
RELCTD ... Relocated
RELCV ..... Regional Educational Laboratory for the Carolinas and Virginia
RELD .... Rare-Earth LASER Device
RELD .... Relieved (WGA)
RELDET ... When Relieved Detached [*Duty Indicated*]
RELDIRDET ... When Relieved and When Directed Detached [*Duty Indicated*]
RELE .... Radio Electrician
RELE .... Release (ROG)
Rel Ed .... Religious Education [*A publication*]
RelElc .... Reliance Electric Co. [*Associated Press abbreviation*] (APAG)
RELET ...... Reference Letter (FAAC)
Relevance Logic Newslett ... Relevance Logic Newsletter [*A publication*]
Relev Log News ... Relevance Logic Newsletter [*A publication*]
RELF .... ReLife, Inc. [*NASDAQ symbol*] (SPSG)
Rel d Griech ... Die Religion der Griechen [*A publication*] (OCD)
RelGrp .... Reliance Group Holdings, Inc. [*Formerly, Leasco Corp.*] [*Associated Press abbreviation*] (APAG)
RELI .... Religion Index [*American Theological Library Association*] [*Information service or system*]
RELIA .... Rehabilitation Literature [*A publication*]
Reliab Eng ... Reliability Engineering [*A publication*]
Reliability Eng ... Reliability Engineering [*A publication*]
Reliable P J ... Reliable Poultry Journal [*A publication*]
RELIG .... Religion [*or Religious*]
Relig Ed ..... Religious Education [*A publication*]
Relig Educ ... Religious Education [*A publication*]
Relig Hum ... Religious Humanism [*A publication*]
Relig Index One Period ... Religion Index One. Periodicals [*A publication*]
Relig in Life ... Religion in Life [*A publication*]
Relig Soc .... Religion and Society [*A publication*]
Relig Sthn Afr ... Religion in Southern Africa [*A publication*]
Relig Stud ... Religious Studies [*A publication*]
Relig Theol Abstr ... Religious and Theological Abstracts [*A publication*]
Relig T J .... Religion Teacher's Journal [*A publication*]
Rel Ind .... Relations Industrielles [*A publication*]
Rel Ind One ... Religion Index One [*A publication*]
RELIP .... Radially Extended Linear Impeller Propulsion [*Submarine technology*]
RELIQ .... Reliquiae [*Remains*] [*Latin*]
RELIQ .... Reliquum [*The Remainder*] [*Pharmacy*]
RELL .... Reinforced Education Learning Laboratory (EA)
RELL .... Richardson Electronics Ltd. [*NASDAQ symbol*] (NQ)
RELLA ...... Regional European Long-Lines Agency [*Later, RALLA*] (NATG)
Rel Life ...... Religion in Life [*A publication*]
RELMA ...... Robert E. Lee Memorial Association (EA)
RELMAT .. Relative Matrix (MCD)
RELO .... Revue. International Organization for Ancient Languages Analysis by Computer [*A publication*]

RELO .... Revue. Organisation Internationale pour l'Etude des Langues Anciennes par Ordinateur [*A publication*]
RELOC ...... Relocate   (AAG)
RELP .... Real Estate Limited Partnership
RELPAS .... Restricted Express Lists/Physiological Activity Section [*National Science Foundation*]
RelPerI ...... Religious Periodicals Index [*A publication*]
Rel & Pub Order ... Religion and the Public Order [*A publication*]   (DLA)
RELQ .... Release-Quiesce [*Data processing*]
REL-R .... Reliability Report   (AAG)
RELR .... Revised and Expurgated Law Reports [*India*] [*A publication*]   (DLA)
RELS .... Real Estate Listing Service [*Database*] [*MDR Telecom*] [*Information service or system*]   (CRD)
RELS .... Redeye Launch Simulator   (MCD)
RELS .... Relations
RelS .... Religious Studies [*A publication*]
RELSA ...... Radio Elektronik Schau [*A publication*]
Rel So Africa ... Religion in Southern Africa [*A publication*]
Rel Soc .... Religion and Society [*A publication*]
Rel St .... Religious Studies [*A publication*]
Rel St R ... Religious Studies Review [*A publication*]
Rel St Rev .. Religious Studies Review [*A publication*]
Rel Stud ..... Religious Studies [*London*] [*A publication*]
RELT .... Reltron Corp. [*NASDAQ symbol*]   (NQ)
RelTAbstr ... Religious and Theological Abstracts [*Myerstown, PA*] [*A publication*]
RELTD ...... Related
Rel & Theol Abstr ... Religious and Theological Abstracts [*A publication*]
Rel Trad ..... Religious Traditions [*A publication*]
RELX .... Realex Corp. [*NASDAQ symbol*]   (NQ)
RELY .... Ingres Corp. [*NASDAQ symbol*]   (NQ)
REM .... C & M Aviation, Inc. [*Inyokern, CA*] [*FAA designator*]   (FAAC)
REM .... Radio Electrical Mechanic [*British military*]   (DMA)
REM .... Radioactivity Environmental Monitoring [*Information service or system*]   (IID)
REM .... Random Entry Memory   (ADA)
REM .... Range Evaluation Missile
REM .... Rapid Eye Movement
REM .... Rare Earth Metal [*Inorganic chemistry*]
REM .... Raumbildentfernungsmesser [*Stereoscopic range-finder*] [*German military - World War II*]
REM .... Reaction Engine Module [*NASA*]   (KSC)
REM .... Recognition Memory [*Semionics Associates*] [*Data processing*]
REM .... Recovery Exercise Module   (MCD)
REM .... Reentry Module
REM .... Reflection Electron Microscopy
REM .... Registered Equipment Management [*Air Force*]   (AFM)
REM .... Release-Engage [*or Engagement*] Mechanism   (NASA)
REM .... Release Engine Mechanism   (NASA)
REM .... Release Engine Module   (MCD)
REM .... Release Escape Mechanism   (MCD)
REM .... Reliability Engineering Model   (KSC)
REM .... Remainder   (MSA)
REM .... Remark
Rem .... Remigius [*Flourished, 841-908*] [*Authority cited in pre-1607 legal work*]   (DSA)
Rem .... Remington [*Record label*] [*USA, Europe, etc.*]
REM .... Remit   (AABC)
Rem .... Remittance   (DLA)
REM .... Remote [*Alaska*] [*Seismograph station code, US Geological Survey*]   (SEIS)
REM .... Remote Event Module [*Data processing*]
REM .... Remove [*or Removal*]   (AAG)
REM .... Repertoire d'Epigraphie Meroitique [*A publication*]
REM .... Research Management [*A publication*]
REM .... Reserves Embarked [*Navy*]   (NVT)
REM .... Rocket Engine Module   (MCD)
REM .... Roentgen-Equivalent-Mammal [*Irradiation unit*]
REM .... Roentgen-Equivalent-Man [*Later, Sv*] [*Irradiation unit*]
REMA .... Refrigeration Equipment Manufacturers Association [*Later, ARI*]   (MCD)
REMAB .... Radiation Equivalent Manikin Absorption
REMAB ..... Remote Marshalling Base   (MCD)
Rem Actual ... Remedes-Actualites [*A publication*]
REMAD .... Remote Magnetic Anomaly Detection
Rem Am ..... Remedia Amoris [*of Ovid*] [*Classical studies*]   (OCD)
REMAP ..... Record Extraction, Manipulation, and Print
REMARC ... Retrospective Machine Readable Catalog [*Carrollton Press, Inc.*] [*Arlington, VA*] [*Bibliographic database*] [*Online version of the US Library of Congress Shelflist*]
Remarques Afr ... Remarques Africaines [*A publication*]
REMAS ..... Radiation Effects Machine Analysis System   (AAG)
REMAT ..... Research Centre for Management of New Technology [*Wilfrid Laurier University*] [*Canada*] [*Research center*]   (RCD)
REMBASS ... Remotely Monitored Battlefield Area Sensor System   (MCD)
REMBJTR ... Reimbursement in Accordance with Joint Travel Regulations
REMC .... Radio and Electronics Measurements Committee [*London, England*]   (DEN)
REMC .... Resin-Encapsulated Mica Capacitor

REMCA ..... Reliability, Maintainability, Cost Analysis   (MCD)
REMCAL .. Radiation Equivalent Manikin Calibration
REMCE ..... Remittance   (ROG)
REMCO .... Committee on Reference Materials [*ISO*]   (DS)
REMCO .... Rear Echelon Maintenance Combined Operation [*Military*]
Rem Corps Ames ... Remedes des Corps et des Ames [*A publication*]
Rem Cr Tr ... Remarkable Criminal Trials [*A publication*]   (DLA)
REMD .... Rapid Eye Movement Deprivation
Rem'd .... Remanded [*Legal term*]   (DLA)
REME .... Royal Electrical and Mechanical Engineers [*Military*] [*British*]
REMED ...... Remedium [*Remedy*] [*Pharmacy*]   (ROG)
Remedial Ed ... Remedial Education [*A publication*]
Remedial Educ ... Remedial Education [*A publication*]
Rem Educ ... Remedial Education [*A publication*]
REMES ...... Reference Message   (FAAC)
REMG ...... Radioelectromyograph
Rem'g .... Remanding [*Legal term*]   (DLA)
REMI .... Reliability Engineering and Management Institute   (EA)
REMI .... Remington Diversified Industries Corp. [*NASDAQ symbol*]   (NQ)
REMIC ...... Real Estate Mortgage Investment Conduit [*Federal National Mortgage Association*]
REMIDS ... Remote Minefield Identification and Deployment [*or Display*] System   (MCD)
Remigi .... Remigius de Gonni [*Deceased, 1554*] [*Authority cited in pre-1607 legal work*]   (DSA)
REMILOC ... Required Inservice Manyears in Lieu of Controls [*Military*]
REMIS ...... Real Estate Management Information System   (BUR)
REMIS ...... Reliability and Maintainability Information System [*Air Force*]   (GFGA)
REMIT ...... Remittance   (DSUE)
REMIT ...... Research Effort Management Information Tabulation
Remitt .... Remittance   (DLA)
REML .... Radiation Effects Mobile Laboratory
REML .... Removal   (ROG)
REML .... Restricted Maximum Likelihood [*Statistics*]
REM-M ..... Rapid Eye Movement-Movement Period
Remma ...... Reese, "Musik in the Middle Ages" [*A publication*]
REMMPS ... Reserve Manpower Management and Pay System [*Marine Corps*]
REMN .... Radio Electrical Mechanician [*British military*]   (DMA)
REMN .... Remain   (ROG)
REMOA .... Revista. Escola de Minas [*Brazil*] [*A publication*]
REMOBE ... Readiness for Mobilization Evaluation   (MCD)
REMOS ..... Real-Time Event Monitor [*Data processing*]   (IEEE)
REMOS ..... Resources Management Online System   (HGAA)
REMOSS .. Reliability Monitoring of Subcontractors/Suppliers   (MCD)
Remote Sens Earth Resour Environ ... Remote Sensing of Earth Resources and Environment [*A publication*]
Remote Sens Environ ... Remote Sensing of Environment [*A publication*]
Remote Sensing Earth Resour ... Remote Sensing of Earth Resources [*A publication*]
Remote Sensing Environ ... Remote Sensing of Environment [*A publication*]
REMP .... Radiological Environmental Monitoring Program [*Nuclear energy*]   (NRCH)
REMP .... Research, Engineering, Mathematics, and Physics Division [*Obsolete*] [*National Security Agency*]
REMP .... Research and Evaluation Methods Program [*University of Massachusetts*] [*Research center*]   (RCD)
REMP .... Research Group for European Migration Problems
REMP .... Roentgen-Equivalent-Man Period [*Irradiation Unit*]   (MAE)
REMPAC .. Reflectivity Measurements Pacific
REMPI ...... Resonance Enhanced Multiple Photon Ionisation [*Physics*]
REMPI ...... Resonant Enhanced Multiphoton Ionization [*Spectroscopy*]
REMPI ...... Resonant Multiphoton Ionization [*Physics*]
REM-Q ..... Rapid Eye Movement - Quiescent Period
REMR .... Remainder
REMR .... Remington Rand Corp. [*NASDAQ symbol*]   (NQ)
Rem R .... Remington Review [*A publication*]
REMR .... Repair, Evaluation, Maintenance, Rehabilitation
REM-RAND ... Remington Rand Corp. [*Later, a division of Sperry-Rand*]
REMRO .... Remote RADAR Operator   (MCD)
REMS .... Rapid Excavation and Maintenance System [*for gas piping repair*]
REMS .... Rapid Eye Movement State
REMS .... Reentry Measurement System
REMS .... Refinery Evaluation Modeling System [*Department of Energy*]   (GFGA)
REMS .... Registered Equipment Management System [*Air Force*]
REMS .... Remotely Employed Sensor [*Military*]   (GFGA)
ReMS .... Renaissance and Modern Studies [*A publication*]
REMS .... Robust Expert Maintenance System [*US Army Tank-Automotive Command*]   (RDA)
REMSA ..... Railway Engineering Maintenance Suppliers Association   (EA)
REMSTA .. Remote Electronic Microfilm Storage Transmission and Retrieval
REMT .... Radiological Emergency Medical Team [*Military*]   (AABC)
REMT .... Relief Electronic Maintenance Technician
REMT .... Remote
REMTDS .. Rocket Engine and Motor Type Designation System

Rem Tr....... Cummins and Dunphy's Remarkable Trials [*A publication*]   (DLA)
Rem Tr No Ch ... Benson's Remarkable Trials and Notorious Characters [*A publication*]   (DLA)
REMUDY ... Records. Western Australian Museum [*A publication*]
Remy......... Remy's Reports [*145-162 Indiana*] [*15-33 Indiana Appellate*] [*A publication*]   (DLA)
REN.......... Real Estate Newsletter [*A publication*]
REN.......... Religion and Ethics Network   (EA)
REN.......... Remote Enable   (IEEE)
REN.......... Renaissance
Ren............ Renaissance [*Record label*]
Ren............ Renaissance [*A publication*]
ren............. Renal [*Medicine*]   (MAE)
REN.......... Rename File [*Data processing*]
Ren............. Renascence [*A publication*]
REN.......... Rencon Mining Co. [*Vancouver Stock Exchange symbol*]
REN.......... Renewable
REN.......... Renewal
REN.......... Renin [*An enzyme*]
Ren............ Renner's Gold Coast Colony Reports [*A publication*]   (DLA)
REN.......... Reno [*Nevada*] [*Seismograph station code, US Geological Survey*] [*Closed*]   (SEIS)
ren............. Renovetur [*Renew*] [*Latin*] [*Pharmacy*]   (MAE)
REN.......... Ringer Equivalence Number [*Telephones*]
REN.......... Rollins Environmental Services, Inc. [*NYSE symbol*]   (SPSG)
REN.......... Rural Equipment News [*A publication*]   (APTA)
Rena.......... Renascence [*A publication*]
Renais News ... Renaissance News [*A publication*]
Renaissance Q ... Renaissance Quarterly [*A publication*]
Renaiss Dr ... Renaissance Drama [*A publication*]
Renaiss Q... Renaissance Quarterly [*A publication*]
Renaiss Ref ... Renaissance and Reformation [*A publication*]
Renal Funct Trans Conf ... Renal Function. Transactions. Conference [*A publication*]
Renal Physiol ... Renal Physiology [*A publication*]
Renal Physiol Biochem ... Renal Physiology and Biochemistry [*A publication*]
RENAMO ... Resistencia Nacional Mocambicana [*Mozambique*]
RENAT...... Revolutsiya, Nauka, Trud [*Revolution, Science, Labor*] [*Given name popular in Russia after the Bolshevik Revolution*]
Ren B .... Renaissance Bulletin [*A publication*]
RenBib....... Rencontres Biblique [*A publication*]
RencAssyrInt ... Recontre Assyriologique Internationale. Compte Rendu [*A publication*]
Rencontre Biol ... Rencontre Biologique [*A publication*]
RenD.......... Renaissance Drama [*A publication*]
REND........ Rendered   (ADA)
Rend.......... Rendezvous [*A publication*]
Rend Accad Naz 40 (Quaranta) ... Rendiconti. Accademia Nazionale dei 40 (Quaranta) [*A publication*]
Rend Accad Naz XL ... Rendiconti. Accademia Nazionale dei XL [*A publication*]
Rend Accad Naz XL 4 ... Accademia Nazionale dei XL. Rendiconti. Serie 4 [*A publication*]
Rend Accad Naz XL 5 ... Accademia Nazionale dei XL. Rendiconti. Serie 5 [*A publication*]
Rend Accad Sci Fis Mat (Napoli) ... Rendiconto. Accademia delle Scienze Fisiche e Matematiche (Napoli) [*A publication*]
Rend Accad Sci Fis Mat Napoli 4 ... Societa Nazionale di Scienze, Lettere, ed Arti in Napoli. Rendiconto dell'Accademia delle Scienze Fisiche e Matematiche. Serie 4 [*A publication*]
Rend Acc It ... Atti. Reale Accademia d'Italia. Rendiconti. Classe di Scienze Morali [*A publication*]
Rend Acc (Napoli) ... Rendiconti. Accademia di Archeologia, Lettere, e Belle Arti (Napoli) [*A publication*]
Rend Circ Mat Palermo ... Rendiconti. Circolo Matematico di Palermo [*A publication*]
Rend Circ Mat Palermo 2 ... Rendiconti. Circolo Matematico di Palermo. Serie II [*A publication*]
RENDD..... Rendered   (ROG)
Rendic Accad Sc Fis e Mat (Napoli) ... Rendiconto. Accademia delle Scienze Fisiche e Matematiche (Napoli) [*A publication*]
Rendic R Accad Sc Ist Bologna ... Rendiconto. Reale Accademia delle Scienze. Istituto di Bologna [*A publication*]
Rend Istit Mat Univ Trieste ... Rendiconti. Istituto di Matematica. Universita di Trieste [*A publication*]
Rend Ist Lomb ... Rendiconti. Istituto Lombardo. Accademia di Scienze e Lettere [*A publication*]
Rend Ist Lomb Accad Sci Lett A ... Rendiconti. Istituto Lombardo. Accademia di Scienze e Lettere. Sezione A. Scienze Matematiche, Fisiche, e Geologiche [*Italy*] [*A publication*]
Rend Ist Lomb Accad Sci Lett A Sci Mat Fis Chim Geol ... Rendiconti. Istituto Lombardo. Accademia di Scienze e Lettere. Sezione A. Scienze Matematiche, Fisiche, Chimiche, e Geologiche [*A publication*]
Rend Ist Lomb Accad Sci Lett B ... Rendiconti. Istituto Lombardo. Accademia di Scienze e Lettere. Sezione B. Scienze Biologiche e Mediche [*Italy*] [*A publication*]
Rend Ist Lomb Accad Sci Lett Parte Gen Atti Uffic ... Rendiconti. Istituto Lombardo. Accademia di Scienze e Lettere. Parte Generale e Atti Ufficiali [*A publication*]

Rend Ist Lomb Sci Lett A ... Rendiconti. Istituto Lombardo di Scienze e Lettere. Sezione A. Scienze Matematiche, Fisiche, Chimiche, e Geologiche [*A publication*]
Rend Ist Lomb Sci Lett A Sci Mat Fis Chim Geol ... Rendiconti. Istituto Lombardo di Scienze e Lettere. Sezione A. Scienze Matematiche, Fisiche, Chimiche, e Geologiche [*A publication*]
Rend Ist Lomb Sci Lett Parte Gen Atti Uffic ... Rendiconti. Istituto Lombardo. Accademia di Scienze e Lettere. Parte Generale e Atti Ufficiali [*A publication*]
Rend Ist Mat Univ Trieste ... Rendiconti. Istituto di Matematica. Universita di Trieste [*A publication*]
Rend Ist Sanita Pubblica ... Rendiconti. Istituto di Sanita Pubblica [*A publication*]
Rend Ist Sci Univ Camerino ... Rendiconti. Istituti Scientifici. Universita di Camerino [*A publication*]
Rend Ist Super Sanita ... Rendiconti. Istituto Superiore di Sanita [*A publication*]
Rend Linc... Rendiconti. Reale Accademia dei Lincei [*A publication*]
Rend (Nap) ... Rendiconti. Reale Accademia di Archeologia, Lettere, ed Arti (Naples) [*A publication*]
RENDOCK ... Rendezvous and Docking [*Aerospace*]   (MCD)
Rend Pont .. Rendiconti. Pontificia Accademia Romana di Archeologia [*A publication*]
Rend Pont Acc ... Rendiconti. Pontificia Accademia Romana di Archeologia [*A publication*]
Rend R Ist Lomb Sci Lett ... Rendiconti. Reale Istituto Lombardo di Scienze e Lettere [*A publication*]
Rend Riun Annu Assoc Elettrotec Ital ... Rendiconti. Riunione Annuale. Associazione Elettrotecnica Italiana [*Italy*] [*A publication*]
Rend Riunione Assoc Elettrotec Ital ... Rendiconti. Riunione Annuale. Associazione Elettrotecnica Italiana [*A publication*]
Rend Sc Int Fis Enrico Fermi ... Rendiconti. Scuola Internazionale di Fisica "Enrico Fermi" [*A publication*]
Rend Sc Int Fis Fermi ... Rendiconti. Scuola Internazionale di Fisica "Enrico Fermi" [*A publication*]
Rend Scu Int Fis Enrico Fermi ... Rendiconti. Scuola Internazionale di Fisica "Enrico Fermi" [*Italy*] [*A publication*]
Rend Sem Fac Sci Univ Cagliari ... Rendiconti. Seminario della Facolta di Scienze. Universita di Cagliari [*A publication*]
Rend Semin Fac Sci Univ Cagliari ... Rendiconti. Seminario della Facolta di Scienze. Universita di Cagliari [*A publication*]
Rend Semin Mat Fis Milano ... Rendiconti. Seminario Matematico e Fisico di Milano [*A publication*]
Rend Sem Mat Brescia ... Rendiconti. Seminario Matematico di Brescia [*A publication*]
Rend Sem Mat Fis Milano ... Rendiconti. Seminario Matematico e Fisico di Milano [*A publication*]
Rend Sem Mat Univ Padova ... Rendiconti. Seminario Matematico. Universita di Padova [*A publication*]
Rend Sem Mat Univ Politec Torino ... Rendiconti. Seminario Matematico gia Conferenze di Fisica e di Matematica. Universita e Politecnico di Torino [*A publication*]
Rend Sem Mat Univ e Politec Torino ... Rendiconti. Seminario Matematico. Universita e Politecnico di Torino [*A publication*]
Rend Soc Chim Ital ... Rendiconti. Societa Chimica Italiana [*A publication*]
Rend Soc Ital Mineral Petrol ... Rendiconti. Societa Italiana di Mineralogia e Petrologia [*A publication*]
Rend Soc Ital Sci Accad XL ... Rendiconti. Societa Italiana delle Scienze detta Accademia dei XL [*A publication*]
Rend Soc Mineral Ital ... Rendiconti. Societa Mineralogica Italiana [*A publication*]
RENDZ ..... Rendezvous   (KSC)
RenE .... Reinare en Espana [*A publication*]
RENE .... Rocket Engine/Nozzle Ejector
Renew........ Renewal [*A publication*]
Renew Energy Bull ... Renewable Energy Bulletin [*England*] [*A publication*]
RENFE...... Red Nacional de los Ferrocariles Espanoles [*Spanish National Railways*]   (EY)
Ren Funct... Renal Function [*A publication*]
R ENG .... Royal Engineers [*Military*] [*British*]   (ROG)
R Eng J ...... Royal Engineers Journal [*A publication*]
R Engl Lit .. Review of English Literature [*A publication*]
R Engl Stud ... Review of English Studies [*A publication*]
REngS........ Review of English Studies [*A publication*]
R Eng Stud .. Review of English Studies [*A publication*]
R Eng Stud NS ... Review of English Studies. New Series [*A publication*]
RENID3 .... Annual Research Reviews. Renin [*A publication*]
RENJA...... Russian Engineering Journal [*A publication*]
RENL .... REN Corp - USA [*Formerly, Renal System, Inc.*] [*NASDAQ symbol*]   (NQ)
RENLO ..... Revue. Ecole Nationale des Langues Orientales [*A publication*]
Ren M .... Renaissance Monographs [*A publication*]
RENM .... Request for Next Message
Ren Mod St ... Renaissance and Modern Studies [*A publication*]
Ren Mod Stud ... Renaissance and Modern Studies [*A publication*]
RENMR .... Reconnaissance Medium Range [*Army*]
Ren MS....... Renaissance and Modern Studies [*A publication*]
RenN.......... Renaissance News [*A publication*]
Renn.......... Renner's Reports, Notes of Cases, Gold Coast Colony and Colony of Nigeria [*1861-1914*] [*A publication*]   (DLA)

Ren News... Renaissance News [*A publication*]
RENO........ Research on Norway [*A publication*]
RENOT..... Regional Notice [*FAA*]
RENOVAND ... Renovandus [*To Be Renewed*] [*Pharmacy*] (ROG)
RenP......... Renaissance Papers [*A publication*]
RENPA...... Radio Engineering and Electronic Physics [*English Translation*]
      [*A publication*]
RENPE...... Rare and Endangered Native Plant Exchange   (EA)
RenQ......... Renaissance Quarterly [*A publication*]
Ren & R..... Renaissance and Reformation [*A publication*]
RENRA...... Rentgenologiya i Radiologiya [*A publication*]
RENRAD .. Rendezvous RADAR [*NASA*]   (NASA)
Ren & Ref... Renaissance and Reformation [*A publication*]
RENS........ Radiation Effects on Network Systems
RENS........ Reconnaissance, Electronic Warfare, and Naval Intelligence
      System
REN SEM ... Renovetur Semel [*Renew Once*] [*Pharmacy*]
RENSONIP ... Reconnaissance Electronic Warfare, Special Operations, and
      Naval Intelligence Processing   (MCD)
Rensselaer Polytech Inst Eng Sci Ser ... Rensselaer Polytechnic Institute.
      Engineering and Science Series [*A publication*]
RENT .... Reentry Nose Tip [*Air Force*]
RENT .... Rentrak Corp. [*NASDAQ symbol*]   (NQ)
Rental........ Rental Product News [*A publication*]
Rent Equip ... Rental Equipment Register [*A publication*]
Rentgenogr Miner Syr'ya ... Rentgenografiya Mineral'nogo Syr'ya [*A
      publication*]
Rentgenol Radiol ... Rentgenologiya i Radiologiya [*A publication*]
R Entomol Soc London Symp ... Royal Entomological Society of London.
      Symposia [*A publication*]
RENU........ Reconstruction Education for National Understanding [*An
      association*]   (EA)
RENUNCN ... Renunciation   (ROG)
RENV .... Renovate   (AABC)
RENX .... Renaissance GRX, Inc. [*NASDAQ symbol*]   (NQ)
REO .... Ransom Eli Olds [*Acronym used as name of automobile
      manufactured by Ransom E. Olds Co.*]
REO .... Rare-Earth Oxide
REO .... Rea Gold Corp. [*Toronto Stock Exchange symbol*] [*Vancouver
      Stock Exchange symbol*]
REO .... Real Estate Owned [*Banking*]
REO .... Receptive-Expressive Observation [*Sensorimotor skills test*]
REO .... Regenerated Electrical Output
REO .... Regional Executive Officer [*British*]
REO .... Reinforcements   (DSUE)
REO .... Respiratory and Enteric Orphan [*Virus*]   (MAE)
REO .... Responsible Engineering Office [*Military*]   (AFIT)
REO .... Rio Airways [*Killeen, TX*] [*FAA designator*]   (FAAC)
REO .... Rome, OR [*Location identifier*] [*FAA*]   (FAAL)
Reo .... Te Reo. Linguistic Society of New Zealand [*A publication*]
REOC .... Report When Established on Course [*Aviation*]   (FAAC)
REOC .... Royal Enfield Owners Club   (EA)
REOG .... Rea Gold Corp. [*Vancouver, BC*] [*NASDAQ symbol*]   (NQ)
REON .... Rocket Engine Operations - Nuclear   (IEEE)
REOP .... Reopening [*Investment term*]
ReOpt........ Remedial Option [*Data processing*]
REOPT...... Reorder Point [*Army*]
REORG ..... Reorganize   (EY)
REOS........ Racal Electronic Optical System [*Software package*] [*Racal
      Imaging Systems*]
REOS........ Rare-Earth Oxysulfide
REOS........ Reflective Electron Optical System
REOT .... Right-End-of-Tape
REOU........ Radio and Electronic Officers' Union [*British*]   (DCTA)
Rep............ Coke's English King's Bench Reports [*1572-1616*] [*A
      publication*]   (DLA)
Rep............ De Republica [*of Cicero*] [*Classical studies*]   (OCD)
REP........... Die Republikaner [*Republican Party*] [*Germany*] [*Political
      party*]   (PPW)
Rep............ Knapp's Privy Council Reports [*England*] [*A
      publication*]   (DLA)
REP........... RADAR Effects Processor   (MCD)
REP........... RADAR Evaluation Pod [*Spacecraft*]
REP........... Radical Education Project [*Students for a Democratic Society*]
REP........... Radiological Emergency Plan [*Nuclear energy*]   (NRCH)
REP........... Railway Equipment and Publication Co., The, New York NY
      [*STAC*]
REP........... Range Error Probable [*Military*]
REP........... Range Estimation Program   (MCD)
REP........... Rapid Electrophoresis
REP........... Reaction Energy Profile
REP........... Reasonable Efforts Program [*Environmental Protection
      Agency*]   (EPA)
REP........... Recovery and Evacuation Program [*Marine Corps*]
REP........... Reentrant Processor [*Telecommunications*]
REP........... Reentry Physics Program
REP........... Regional Employment Premium [*British*]
REP........... Relativistic Electron Precipitation [*Meteorology*]
REP........... Rendezvous Evaluation Pad [*NASA*]   (KSC)
REP........... Rendezvous Exercise Pod   (SAA)
REP........... Repair   (AAG)

REP........... Repeal   (ROG)
REP........... Repeat   (AAG)
Rep............ Repertoire   (DLA)
REP........... Repertory   (ADA)
REP........... Repertory Theater   (DSUE)
REP........... Repetatur [*Let It Be Repeated*] [*Pharmacy*]
REP........... Repetition   (DSUE)
REP........... Replace   (NVT)
REP........... Replication [*Telecommunications*]   (TEL)
REP........... Report   (AAG)
REP........... Report Evaluation Program   (SAA)
REP........... Reporter
REP........... Reporting Point [*Aviation*]
REP........... Representative   (AAG)
Rep............ Representing   (DLA)
REP........... Reprimand   (DSUE)
Rep............ Reprint   (DLA)
REP........... Reproducing Programs [*Data processing*]
REP........... Reproductive Endocrinology Program [*University of Michigan*]
      [*Research center*]   (RCD)
REP........... Repsol SA ADS [*NYSE symbol*]   (SPSG)
REP........... Republic   (EY)
REP........... Republican
Rep............ Republika [*Zagreb*] [*A publication*]
REP........... Repulsion
REP........... Reputation   (DSUE)
REP........... Request for Proposal   (MUGU)
REP........... Research and Economic Programs [*Department of the
      Treasury*]   (GRD)
REP........... Research Expenditure Proposal
REP........... Research Project   (FAAC)
REP........... Reserve Enlisted Program [*Military*]
REP........... Resonance Escape Probability [*Nuclear energy*]   (NRCH)
REP........... Retrograde Pyelogram [*Medicine*]
REP........... Rework Excellence Program [*Navy*]   (DNAB)
REP........... Richardson Emergency Psychodiagnostic Summary
      [*Psychology*]
REP........... Rocket Engine Processor
REP........... Roentgen-Equivalent-Physical [*Irradiation unit*]
REP........... Unnecessary Repetition [*Used in correcting manuscripts, etc.*]
Rep............ Wallace's "The Reporters" [*A publication*]   (DLA)
REP 63....... Reserve Enlistment Program 1963   (MCD)
Rep AAS (Austral) ... Report. Meeting. Association for the Advancement of
      Science (Australia) [*A publication*]
Rep Acad Sci (Lemberg Pol) ... Reports. Academy of Science (Lemberg,
      Poland) [*A publication*]
Rep Acad Sci Ukr SSR ... Reports. Academy of Sciences of the Ukrainian SSR
      [*A publication*]
Rep Acad Sci Ukr SSR (Engl Transl Dopov Akad Nauk Ukr RSR) ... Reports.
      Academy of Sciences. Ukrainian SSR (English Translation
      of Dopovidi Akademii Nauk Ukrains'koi RSR) [*A
      publication*]
Rep Acc Natl Coal Board ... Report and Accounts. National Coal Board
      [*British*] [*A publication*]
Rep Activ Dan Atom Energy Commn ... Report. Activities of the Danish
      Atomic Energy Commission [*A publication*]
Rep Act Res Inst Water Resour Budapest ... Report. Activities. Research
      Institute for Water Resources. Budapest [*A publication*]
Rep Advis CSIR Alberta ... Report. Advisory Council of Scientific and
      Industrial Research of Alberta [*A publication*]
Rep Aeromed Lab ... Reports. Aeromedical Laboratory [*A publication*]
Rep Aeronaut Res Inst ... Report. Aeronautical Research Institute [*A
      publication*]
Rep Aeronaut Res Inst Univ Tokyo ... Report. Aeronautical Research
      Institute. University of Tokyo [*A publication*]
Rep AFL Univ Cincinnati Dep Aerosp Eng ... Report AFL. University of
      Cincinnati. Department of Aerospace Engineering [*A
      publication*]
Rep Agric Coll Swed Ser A ... Reports. Agricultural College of Sweden. Series
      A [*A publication*]
Rep Agric Coll Swed Ser B ... Reports. Agricultural College of Sweden. Series
      B [*A publication*]
Rep Agric Hort Res Stn Univ Bristol ... Report. Agricultural and Horticultural
      Research Station. University of Bristol [*A publication*]
Rep Agric Res Coun Radiobiol Lab ... Report. Agricultural Research Council.
      Radiobiological Laboratory [*A publication*]
Rep Agron Branch Dep Agric South Aust ... Report. Agronomy Branch.
      Department of Agriculture and Fisheries. South Australia
      [*A publication*]   (APTA)
Rep Aichi Inst Public Health ... Report. Aichi Institute of Public Health
      [*Japan*] [*A publication*]
Rep Aichi Prefect Inst Public Health ... Report. Aichi Prefectural Institute of
      Public Health [*A publication*]
REPAIRS.. Readiness Evaluation Program for Avionics Intermediate
      Repair Simulation   (MCD)
Rep Akita Prefect Inst Public Health ... Report. Akita Prefecture. Institute of
      Public Health [*Japan*] [*A publication*]
Rep Alaska Div Mines Geol ... Report. Alaska Division of Mines and Geology
      [*A publication*]
Rep Alaska Div Mines Miner ... Report. Alaska Division of Mines and
      Minerals [*A publication*]

Rep Alberta Res Counc ... Report. Alberta Research Council [*A publication*]
Rep Alfalfa Improv Conf ... Report. Alfalfa Improvement Conference [*A publication*]
REPAML .. Reply by Airmail (FAAC)
Rep Am Mus Nat Hist ... Report. American Museum of Natural History [*A publication*]
Rep Am Univ Field Staff ... Reports. American Universities Field Staff [*A publication*]
Rep Anal Chem Unit Inst Geol Sci ... Report. Analytical Chemistry Unit. Institute of Geological Sciences [*A publication*]
Rep Anim Breed Res Organ ... Report. Animal Breeding Research Organisation [*A publication*]
Rep Anim Hlth Serv G Br ... Report on Animal Health Services in Great Britain [*A publication*]
Rep Anim Res Div (NZ) ... Report. Animal Research Division. Department of Agriculture (New Zealand) [*A publication*]
Rep Annu Conf Hawaii Sugar Technol ... Reports. Annual Conference. Hawaiian Sugar Technologists [*A publication*]
Rep Annu Conf Ontario Dept Agr Ext Br ... Report. Annual Conference. Ontario Department of Agriculture. Extension Branch [*A publication*]
Rep Annu Date Grow Inst ... Report. Annual Date Growers Institute [*A publication*]
Rep Annu Gen Meet Scott Soc Res Plant Breed ... Report. Annual General Meeting. Scottish Society for Research in Plant Breeding [*A publication*]
Rep Annu Meet Wash State Hortic Assoc ... Report. Annual Meeting. Washington State Horticultural Association [*A publication*]
Rep Appl Geophys Unit Inst Geol Sci ... Report. Applied Geophysics Unit. Institute of Geological Sciences [*A publication*]
Rep Archit Sci Unit Univ Queensl ... Report. Architectural Science Unit. University of Queensland [*A publication*] (APTA)
Rep Ariz Agr Exp Sta ... Report. Arizona Agricultural Experiment Station [*A publication*]
Rep Ariz Agric Exp Stn ... Report. Arizona Agricultural Experiment Station [*A publication*]
Rep Ark Agric Exp Stn ... Report. Arkansas Agricultural Experiment Station [*A publication*]
Rep Army Res Test Lab ... Report. Army Research and Testing Laboratory [*South Korea*] [*A publication*]
REPAS ...... Research, Evaluation, and Planning Assistance Staff [*AID*]
Rep Asahi Glass Found Ind Technol ... Reports. Asahi Glass Foundation for Industrial Technology [*A publication*]
Rep Ass Occup Ther ... Report. Association of Occupational Therapists [*A publication*]
Rep Assoc Hawaii Sugar Technol ... Reports. Association of Hawaiian Sugar Technologists [*A publication*]
Rep Assoc Trimeresurus Res Kagoshima Univ ... Reports. Association of Trimeresurus Research. Kagoshima University [*A publication*]
Rep Ass Y .. Clayton's English Reports, York Assizes [*A publication*] (DLA)
REPAT ...... Repatriate (AABC)
Rep Aust Acad Sci ... Reports. Australian Academy of Science [*A publication*]
Rep Aust At Energy Comm ... Report. Australian Atomic Energy Commission [*A publication*] (APTA)
Rep Aust CSIRO Div Text Ind ... Australia. Commonwealth Scientific and Industrial Research Organisation. Division of Textile Industry. Report [*A publication*] (APTA)
Rep Aust CSIRO Div Text Ind ... Report. Australia Commonwealth Scientific and Industrial Research Organisation. Division of Textile Industry [*A publication*]
Rep Aust Def Stand Lab ... Report. Australia Defence Standards Laboratories [*A publication*]
Rep Aust Gov Anal Lab ... Report. Australian Government Analytical Laboratories [*A publication*]
Rep Aust Mater Res Lab ... Report. Australia. Materials Research Laboratory [*A publication*]
Rep Aust NZ Assoc Adv Sci ... Report. Australian and New Zealand Association for the Advancement of Science [*A publication*]
Rep Aust Road Res Board ... Report. Australian Road Research Board [*A publication*]
REPB .... Republic (MSA)
REPB .... Republic Resources Corp. [*NASDAQ symbol*] (NQ)
Rep Basic Sci Chungnam Nat Univ ... Reports of Basic Sciences. Chungnam National University [*A publication*]
Rep BC-X Can For Serv Pac For Res Cent ... Report BC-X. Canadian Forestry Service. Pacific Forest Research Centre [*A publication*]
Rep Bd Health Calif ... Reports. State Board of Health of California [*A publication*]
Rep Bd Health Ohio ... Reports. State Board of Health of Ohio [*A publication*]
Rep Bibl Phil ... Repertoire Bibliographique de la Philosophie [*A publication*]
RepBibPhil ... Repertoire Bibliographique de la Philosophie [*A publication*]
Rep Biochem Res Found Franklin Inst ... Reports. Biochemical Research Foundation. Franklin Institute [*A publication*]
Rep Biomed ... Repertoire Biomed [*A publication*]
Rep BISRA ... Report. BISRA [*British Iron and Steel Research Association*] [*A publication*]
Rep Bot Inst Univ Aarhus ... Reports. Botanical Institute. University of Aarhus [*A publication*]
Rep Bot Surv Ind ... Report. Botanical Survey of India [*A publication*]

Rep Bot Surv India ... Report. Botanical Survey of India [*A publication*]
Rep Br Beekprs Ass ... Report. British Beekeepers Association [*A publication*]
Rep Brit Ass Adv Sc ... Report. British Association for the Advancement of Science [*A publication*]
Rep Brit Assoc Adv Sci ... Report. British Association for the Advancement of Science [*A publication*]
Rep Brit Canc Camp ... Report. British Empire Cancer Campaign [*A publication*]
Rep Brit El All Ind Res Ass ... Report. British Electrical and Allied Industries Research Association [*A publication*]
Rep Brit Mus Natur Hist ... Report. British Museum. Natural History [*A publication*]
Rep Br Palaeobot & Palynol ... Report on British Palaeobotany and Palynology [*A publication*]
Rep Bull Agr Exp Sta S Manchuria Ry Co ... Research Bulletin. Agricultural Experiment Station. South Manchuria Railway Company [*A publication*]
Rep Bur Miner Resour Geol Geophys ... Report. [*Australia*] Bureau of Mineral Resources. Geology and Geophysics [*A publication*] (APTA)
Rep Bur Miner Resour Geol Geophys (Aust) ... Report. Bureau of Mineral Resources, Geology, and Geophysics (Australia) [*A publication*]
Rep Bur Mines Miner Resour Geol Geophys Microform ... Report. Bureau of Mines and Mineral Resources. Geology and Geophysics Microform [*A publication*]
Rep BWRA ... Report BWRA [*British Welding Research Association*] [*A publication*]
REPBX ...... Reference Private Branch Exchange Message (SAA)
REPC .... Regional Economic Planning Council [*British*]
REPC .... Representation Commissioner [*Canada*]
REPC .... Research and Educational Planning Center [*University of Nevada - Reno*] [*Research center*] (RCD)
REPC .... Research and Engineering Policy Council [*DoD*]
Rep in CA .. Court of Appeal Reports [*New Zealand*] [*A publication*] (DLA)
Rep in C of A ... Reports in Courts of Appeal [*New Zealand*] [*A publication*] (DLA)
Rep Cacao Res Imp Coll Trop Agric (St Augustine Trinidad) ... Report on Cacao Research. Imperial College of Tropical Agriculture (St. Augustine, Trinidad) [*A publication*]
Rep Cacao Res Reg Cent Br Caribb ... Report on Cacao Research. Regional Research Centre of the British Caribbean [*A publication*]
Rep Calif Water Resour Cent ... Report. California Water Resources Center [*A publication*]
Rep in Can ... Reports in Chancery [*21 English Reprint*] [*A publication*] (DLA)
Rep Cant Agric Coll ... Report. Canterbury Agricultural College [*A publication*]
Rep Cas Eq ... Gilbert's English Chancery Reports [*1705-27*] [*A publication*] (DLA)
Rep Cas Inc Tax ... Reports of Cases Relating to Income Tax [*1875*] [*A publication*] (DLA)
Rep Cas Madr ... Reports of Cases, Diwani Adalat, Madras [*A publication*] (DLA)
Rep Cas Pr ... Cooke's Practice Cases [*1706-47*] [*England*] [*A publication*] (DLA)
Rep Cast Res Lab ... Report. Castings Research Laboratory [*A publication*]
Rep Cast Res Lab Waseda Univ ... Report. Castings Research Laboratory. Waseda University [*A publication*]
REPCAT ... Report Corrective Action Taken [*Military*]
Rep CC-X Chem Control Res Inst ... Report CC-X. Chemical Control Research Institute [*A publication*]
Rep Cent Adv Instrum Anal Kyushu Univ ... Report. Center of Advanced Instrumental Analysis. Kyushu University [*A publication*]
Rep Cent Customs Lab (Jpn) ... Reports. Central Customs Laboratory (Japan) [*A publication*]
Rep Cent Insp Inst Weights Meas Tokyo ... Report. Central Inspection Institute of Weights and Measures. Tokyo [*A publication*]
Rep Cent Inst Met (Leningrad) ... Reports. Central Institute of Metals (Leningrad) [*A publication*]
Rep CENTO Sci Programme ... Report. CENTO [*Central Treaty Organization*] Scientific Programme [*A publication*]
Rep Cent Res Inst Chem Hung Acad Sci ... Reports. Central Research Institute for Chemistry. Hungarian Academy of Sciences [*A publication*]
Rep Cent Res Inst Electr Power Ind Agric Lab ... Report. Central Research Institute. Electric Power Industry Agricultural Laboratory [*A publication*]
Rep Cent Res Inst Electr Power Ind Tech Lab ... Report. Central Research Institute. Electric Power Industry Technical Laboratory [*A publication*]
Rep Cent Res Inst Phys (Budapest) ... Reports. Central Research Institute for Physics (Budapest) [*A publication*]
Rep Cent Res Lab Nippon Suisan Co ... Reports. Central Research Laboratory. Nippon Suisan Co. [*A publication*]
Rep CE Technion-Isr Inst Technol Dep Chem Eng ... Report CE. Technion-Israel Institute of Technology. Department of Chemical Engineering [*A publication*]
Rep CG D US Coast Guard Off Res Dev ... Report CG-D. United States Coast Guard. Office of Research and Development [*A publication*]

Rep Ch .... Reports in Chancery [*1615-1710*] [*England*] [*A publication*] (DLA)
Rep in Ch ... Reports in Chancery [*21 English Reprint*] [*A publication*] (DLA)
Rep in Cha ... Bittleston's Chamber Cases [*1883-84*] [*A publication*] (DLA)
Rep Chem Branch Mines Dep (West Aust) ... Report. Chemical Branch. Mines Department (Western Australia) [*A publication*]
Rep Chem Eng Dep Monash Univ ... Report. Chemical Engineering Department. Monash University [*A publication*]
Rep Chem Fiber Res Inst Kyoto Univ ... Report. Chemical Fiber Research Institute. Kyoto University [*A publication*]
Rep Chem Lab Am Med Assoc ... Reports. Chemical Laboratory. American Medical Association [*A publication*]
Rep Chem Lab (West Aust) ... Report. Chemical Laboratory (Western Australia) [*A publication*]
Rep in Ch (Eng) ... Reports in Chancery [*21 English Reprint*] [*A publication*] (DLA)
Rep Chiba Inst Technol ... Report. Chiba Institute of Technology [*A publication*]
Rep Chiba Inst Technol Sci Ser ... Report. Chiba Institute of Technology. Scientific Series [*A publication*]
Rep Chiba Prefect Ind Res Inst ... Reports. Chiba Prefectural Industrial Research Institute [*A publication*]
Rep Chief US Forest Serv ... Report of the Chief. United States Forest Service [*A publication*]
Rep Ch Pr .. Reports on Chancery Practice [*England*] [*A publication*] (DLA)
Rep Class Research ... Reporting Classroom Research [*A publication*]
Rep Clemson Univ Water Resour Res Inst ... Report. Clemson University. Water Resources Research Institute [*A publication*]
Rep CLM R UKAEA Culham Lab ... Report CLM-R. United Kingdom Atomic Energy Authority. Culham Laboratory [*A publication*]
Rep CLM R UKAEA Res Group Culham Lab ... Report CLM-R - UKAEA [*United Kingdom Atomic Energy Authority*] Research Group. Culham Laboratory [*A publication*]
Rep CLM R UK At Energy Auth Res Group Culham Lab ... Report CLM-R. United Kingdom Atomic Energy Authority. Research Group. Culham Laboratory [*A publication*]
Rep Cocoa Res Inst (Tafo Ghana) ... Report. Cocoa Research Institute (Tafo, Ghana) [*A publication*]
Rep Coll Eng Hosei Univ ... Report. College of Engineering. Hosei University [*A publication*]
Rep Com Cas ... Commercial Cases, Small Cause Court [*1851-60*] [*Bengal, India*] [*A publication*] (DLA)
Rep Com Cas ... Report of Commercial Cases [*1895-1941*] [*A publication*] (DLA)
REPCOMDESPAC ... Representative of Commander Destroyers, Pacific Fleet
Rep Comm Accredit Rehabil Facil ... Report. Commission on Accreditation of Rehabilitation Facilities [*A publication*]
Rep Commonw Conf Plant Pathol ... Report. Commonwealth Conference on Plant Pathology [*A publication*]
Rep Commonwealth Entomol Conf ... Report. Commonwealth Entomological Conference [*A publication*]
Rep Commonwealth Mycol Conf ... Report. Commonwealth Mycological Conference [*A publication*]
Rep Commonw Mycol Conf ... Report. Commonwealth Mycological Conference [*A publication*]
Rep Comput Centre Univ Tokyo ... Report. Computer Centre. University of Tokyo [*A publication*]
Rep Comput Cent Univ Tokyo ... Report. Computer Centre. University of Tokyo [*A publication*]
Rep CONCAWE ... Report. CONCAWE [*Conservation of Clean Air and Water, Europe*] [*A publication*]
Rep Concr Silic Lab Tech Res Cent Finl ... Report. Concrete and Silicate Laboratory. Technical Research Centre of Finland [*A publication*]
Rep Conf Role Wheat World Food Supply ... Report. Conference on the Role of Wheat in the World's Food Supply [*A publication*]
Rep Congr Eur Ass Res Plant Breed ... Report. Congress of the European Association for Research on Plant Breeding [*A publication*]
Rep Congr Eur Orthod Soc ... Report. Congress. European Orthodontic Society [*A publication*]
Rep Const Ct ... South Carolina Constitutional Court Reports [*A publication*] (DLA)
Rep Constr Eng Res Inst Found (Kobe) ... Reports. Construction Engineering Research Institute Foundation (Kobe) [*Japan*] [*A publication*]
Rep Coop Res Chugoku Reg ... Report of the Cooperative Research in Chugoku Region [*A publication*]
Rep Coop Res Kinki Chugoku Reg ... Report. Cooperative Research in Kinki-Chugoku Region [*A publication*]
Rep Coord Res Counc Inc ... Report. Coordinating Research Council, Inc. [*A publication*]
Rep Counc Miner Technol (Randburg S Afr) ... Report. Council for Mineral Technology (Randburg, South Africa) [*A publication*]
Rep Cr L Com ... Reports of Criminal Law Commissioners [*England*] [*A publication*] (DLA)
Rep Crop Res Lesotho ... Report on Crop Research in Lesotho [*A publication*]

Rep CSIRO Div Fish Oceanogr ... Australia. Commonwealth Scientific and Industrial Research Organisation. Division of Fisheries and Oceanography. Report [*A publication*] (APTA)
Rep CSIRO Div Fish Oceanogr (Aust) ... Report. Commonwealth Scientific and Industrial Research Organisation. Division of Fisheries and Oceanography (Australia) [*A publication*]
Rep CSIRO Div Miner Eng (Aust) ... Report. Commonwealth Scientific and Industrial Research Organisation. Division of Mineral Engineering (Australia) [*A publication*]
Rep CSIRO Div Text Ind Aust ... Australia. Commonwealth Scientific and Industrial Research Organisation. Division of Textile Industry. Report [*A publication*] (APTA)
Rep CSIRO Div Text Ind (Aust) ... Report. Commonwealth Scientific and Industrial Research Organization. Division of Textile Industry (Australia) [*A publication*]
Rep CSIRO Mar Lab ... Report. CSIRO [*Commonwealth Scientific and Industrial Research Organisation*] Marine Laboratories [*A publication*]
Rep CSIRO Sol Energy Stud ... Report. Commonwealth Scientific and Industrial Research Organisation. Solar Energy Studies [*A publication*] (APTA)
Rep Culham Lab UK At Energy Auth ... Report. Culham Laboratory. United Kingdom Atomic Energy Authority [*A publication*]
REPCY ...... Repair Cycle
Rep Czech Foundry Res ... Reports of Czechoslovak Foundry Research [*A publication*]
Rep Def Stand Lab Aust ... Australia. Defence Standards Laboratories. Report [*A publication*] (APTA)
Rep Deir-Alla Res Sta ... Report. Deir-Alla Research Station [*Jordan*] [*A publication*]
Rep Del Nurses Assoc ... Reporter. Delaware Nurses Association [*A publication*]
Rep Dep Agric Econ Univ Nebr Agric Exp Stn ... Report. Department of Agricultural Economics. University of Nebraska. Agricultural Experiment Station [*A publication*]
Rep Dep Agric NSW ... Report. Department of Agriculture of New South Wales [*A publication*]
Rep Dep Chem Eng Monash Univ ... Report. Department of Chemical Engineering. Monash University [*A publication*]
Rep Dep Fish Fauna West Aust ... Report. Department of Fisheries and Fauna. Western Australia [*A publication*] (APTA)
Rep Dep Fish Wildl West Aust ... Report. Department of Fisheries and Wildlife. Western Australia [*A publication*] (APTA)
Rep Dep Mines Energy Gov Newfoundland Labrador ... Report. Department of Mines and Energy. Government of Newfoundland and Labrador [*A publication*]
Rep Dep Mines (NSc) ... Report. Department of Mines (Nova Scotia) [*A publication*]
Rep Dep Mines West Aust ... Report. Department of Mines. Western Australia [*A publication*]
Rep Dep Nucl Tech Univ Oulu (Finl) ... Reports. Department of Nuclear Technics. University of Oulu (Finland) [*A publication*]
Rep Dep Phys Univ Oulu ... Report. Department of Physics. University of Oulu [*A publication*]
Rep Dept Agric (Brit East Africa) ... Report. Department of Agriculture (British East Africa) [*A publication*]
Rep Dept Antiquities Cyprus ... Report. Department of Antiquities of Cyprus [*A publication*]
Rep Director Vet Serv Dept Agric (Union South Africa) ... Report. Director of Veterinary Services and Animal Industry. Department of Agriculture (Union of South Africa) [*A publication*]
Rep Dir Gov Chem Lab (West Aust) ... Report. Director of Government Chemical Laboratories (Western Australia) [*A publication*]
Rep Dir Mines (Tasmania) ... Report. Director of Mines (Tasmania) [*A publication*]
Rep Dir Vet Serv Anim Ind (Onderstepoort) ... Report. Director of Veterinary Services and Animal Industry (Onderstepoort) [*A publication*]
Rep Diss Agric Coll Swed Dep Plant Husb ... Reports and Dissertations. Agricultural College of Sweden. Department of Plant Husbandry [*A publication*]
Rep Div Bldg Res CSIRO ... Report. Division of Building Research. Commonwealth Scientific and Industrial Research Organisation [*A publication*] (APTA)
Rep Div Build Res CSIRO ... Report. Division of Building Research. Commonwealth Scientific and Industrial Research Organisation [*A publication*] (APTA)
Rep Div Chem Eng CSIRO ... Report. Division of Chemical Engineering. Commonwealth Scientific and Industrial Research Organisation [*A publication*] (APTA)
Rep Div Chem Engng CSIRO ... Report. Division of Chemical Engineering. Commonwealth Scientific and Industrial Research Organisation [*A publication*] (APTA)
Rep Div Fish Oceanogr CSIRO ... Report. Division of Fisheries and Oceanography. Commonwealth Scientific and Industrial Research Organisation [*A publication*] (APTA)
Rep Div Hort Res CSIRO ... Report. Division of Horticultural Research. Commonwealth Scientific and Industrial Research Organisation [*A publication*] (APTA)

Rep Div Mech Engng CSIRO ... Report. Division of Mechanical Engineering. Commonwealth Scientific and Industrial Research Organisation [*A publication*]   (APTA)

Rep Div Miner CSIRO ... Report. Division of Mineralogy. Commonwealth Scientific and Industrial Research Organisation [*A publication*]   (APTA)

Rep Div Nutr Food Res TNO ... Report. Division for Nutrition and Food Research TNO [*A publication*]

Rep Div Text Ind CSIRO ... Report. Division of Textile Industry. Commonwealth Scientific and Industrial Research Organisation [*A publication*]   (APTA)

Rep Div Water Land Dev Hawaii ... Report. Division of Water and Land Development. Hawaii [*A publication*]

Rep DL NZ Dep Sci Ind Res Dom Lab ... Report DL. New Zealand Department of Scientific and Industrial Research. Dominion Laboratory [*A publication*]

REPDN ..... Reproduction   (AFM)

REPDU ...... Report for Duty [*Military*]

Rep Dudley Obs ... Reports. Dudley Observatory [*A publication*]

REPEA ...... Research and Engineers Professional Employees Association

Rep Earth Sci Coll Gen Educ Kyushu Univ ... Reports on Earth Science. College of General Education. Kyushu University [*A publication*]

Rep Earth Sci Dep Gen Educ Kyushu Univ ... Reports on Earth Science. Department of General Education. Kyushu University [*A publication*]

Rep East For Prod Lab (Can) ... Report. Eastern Forest Products Laboratory (Canada) [*A publication*]

Rep East Malling Res Stn (Maidstone Engl) ... Report. East Malling Research Station (Maidstone, England) [*A publication*]

Rep ED Eng Sect CSIRO ... Report ED. Engineering Section. Commonwealth Scientific and Industrial Research Organisation [*A publication*]   (APTA)

Rep Eg Expl Soc ... Report for the Year. Egypt Exploration Society [*A publication*]

Rep Ehime Prefect Res Inst Environ Sci ... Report. Ehime Prefectural Research Institute for Environmental Science [*A publication*]

Rep E Malling Res Stn ... Annual Report. East Malling Research Station [*A publication*]

REPEM- CEAAL ... Red de Educacion Popular Entre Mujeres Afiliada al Consejo de Educacion de A dultos de America Latino [*Women's Network of the Council for Adult Education in Latin American*] [*Ecuador*]   (EAIO)

Rep EM Ont Minist Transp Commun Eng Mater Off ... Report EM. Ontario Ministry of Transportation and Communications. Engineering Materials Office [*A publication*]

Rep Eng Inst Fac Eng Tokyo Univ ... Report. Engineering Institute. Faculty of Engineering. Tokyo University [*Japan*] [*A publication*]

Rep Eng Res Lab Obayashi-Gumi Ltd ... Report. Engineering Research Laboratory. Obayashi-Gumi Ltd. [*Japan*] [*A publication*]

Rep Ent Soc Ont ... Report. Entomological Society of Ontario [*A publication*]

Rep Environ Prot Serv Ser EPS 3 (Can) ... Report. Environmental Protection Service. Series EPS-3 (Canada) [*A publication*]

Rep Environ Prot Serv Ser EPS 4 (Can) ... Report. Environmental Protection Service. Series EPS-4 (Canada) [*A publication*]

Rep Environ Radiat Surveill Wash Dep Soc Health Serv ... Report. Environmental Radiation Surveillance. Washington Department of Social and Health Services [*A publication*]

Rep Environ Res Organ Chiba Univ ... Report. Environmental Research Organization. Chiba University [*A publication*]

Rep Environ Sci Inst Hyogo Prefect ... Report. Environmental Science Institute of Hyogo Prefecture [*A publication*]

Rep Environ Sci Inst Kinki Univ ... Report. Environmental Science Institute. Kinki University [*A publication*]

Rep Environ Sci Inst Mie Prefect ... Report. Environment Science Institute. Mie Prefecture [*A publication*]

Rep Environ Sci Mie Univ ... Report of Environmental Science. Mie University [*A publication*]

Rep Environ Sci Res Cent Shiga Prefect ... Report. Environmental Science Research Center of Shiga Prefecture [*A publication*]

Rep Environ Sci Res Inst Kinki Univ ... Report. Environmental Science Research Institute. Kinki University [*A publication*]

Rep Environ Sci Tech Lab Nippon Bunri Univ ... Reports. Environmental Science and Technology Laboratory. Nippon Bunri University [*A publication*]

Rep Environ Sci Technol Lab Nippon Bunri Univ ... Reports. Environmental Science and Technology Laboratory. Nippon Bunri University [*A publication*]

Rep Environ Sci Technol Lab Oita Inst Technol ... Reports. Environmental Science and Technology Laboratory. Oita Institute of Technology [*A publication*]

Rep EPS Can Environ Prot Serv Solid Waste Manage Branch ... Report EPS. Canada. Environmental Protection Service. Solid Waste Management Branch [*A publication*]

Rep Eq .... Gilbert's Reports in Equity [*England*] [*A publication*]   (DLA)

Reperes-Econ Languedoc-Roussillon ... Reperes-Economie du Languedoc-Roussillon [*A publication*]

REPERF .... Reperforator [*Telecommunications*]   (TEL)

REPERMSG ...... Report in Person or by Message to Command or Person Indicated

Rep ERP/PMRL Phys Metall Res Lab (Can) ... Report ERP/PMRL. Physical Metallurgy Research Laboratories (Canada) [*A publication*]

Repertoire Anal Litt Francaise ... Repertoire Analytique de Litterature Francaise [*Bordeaux*] [*A publication*]

Repertorium der Phot ... Repertorium der Photographie [*A publication*]

Repert Pharm ... Repertoire de Pharmacie [*A publication*]

Repert Plant Succulentarum ... Repertorium Plantarum Succulentarum [*A publication*]

REPET ...... Repetatur [*Let It Be Repeated*] [*Pharmacy*]

Rep Europe ... Report from Europe [*A publication*]

Rep Evol Comm Roy Soc Lond ... Report to the Evolution Committee. Royal Society of London [*A publication*]

Rep Exp Res Stn (Cheshunt) ... Report. Experimental and Research Station. Nursery and Market Garden Industries Development Society, Ltd. (Cheshunt) [*A publication*]

Rep F .... Repertoire Fiscal [*A publication*]

Rep Fac Agr Shizuoka Univ ... Reports. Faculty of Agriculture. Shizuoka University [*A publication*]

Rep Fac Anim Husb Hung Univ Agric Sci (Godollo) ... Reports. Faculty for Animal Husbandry. Hungarian University of Agricultural Science (Godollo) [*A publication*]

Rep Fac Eng Kanagawa Univ ... Reports. Faculty of Engineering. Kanagawa University [*A publication*]

Rep Fac Eng Kinki Univ Kyushu Sci Technol Sect ... Reports. Faculty of Engineering. Kinki University in Kyushu. Science and Technology Section [*A publication*]

Rep Fac Eng Nagasaki Univ ... Reports. Faculty of Engineering. Nagasaki University [*A publication*]

Rep Fac Engrg Kanagawa Univ ... Kanagawa University. Faculty of Engineering. Reports [*A publication*]

Rep Fac Engrg Oita Univ ... Oita University. Faculty of Engineering. Reports [*A publication*]

Rep Fac Eng Shizuoka Univ ... Reports. Faculty of Engineering. Shizuoka University [*A publication*]

Rep Fac Eng Tottori Univ ... Reports. Faculty of Engineering. Tottori University [*A publication*]

Rep Fac Eng Yamanashi Univ ... Reports. Faculty of Engineering. Yamanashi University [*A publication*]

Rep Fac Fish Prefect Univ Mie ... Report. Faculty of Fisheries. Prefectural University of Mie [*A publication*]

Rep Fac Sci Engrg Saga Univ Math ... Reports. Faculty of Science and Engineering. Saga University. Mathematics [*A publication*]

Rep Fac Sci Kagoshima Univ ... Reports. Faculty of Science. Kagoshima University [*A publication*]

Rep Fac Sci Kagoshima Univ (Earth Sci Biol) ... Reports. Faculty of Science. Kagoshima University. Earth Sciences and Biology [*A publication*]

Rep Fac Sci Kagoshima Univ Math Phys Chem ... Reports. Faculty of Science. Kagoshima University. Mathematics, Physics, and Chemistry [*A publication*]

Rep Fac Sci Shizuoka Univ ... Reports. Faculty of Science. Shizuoka University [*A publication*]

Rep Fac Sci Technol Meijyo Univ ... Reports. Faculty of Science and Technology. Meijyo University [*A publication*]

Rep Fac Tech Kanagawa Univ ... Kanagawa University. Faculty of Technology. Reports [*A publication*]

Rep Fac Technol Kanagawa Univ ... Reports. Faculty of Technology. Kanagawa University [*A publication*]

Rep Fam L ... Reports of Family Law [*A publication*]

Rep FAO/IAEA Tech Meet (Brunswick-Volkenrode) ... Report. FAO [*Food and Agriculture Organization of the United Nations*]/IAEA [*International Atomic Energy Agency*] Technical Meeting (Brunswick-Volkenrode) [*A publication*]

Rep Far East State Univ (Vladivostok) ... Reports. Far Eastern State University (Vladivostok) [*A publication*]

Rep Fd Res Inst (Tokyo) ... Report. Food Research Institute (Tokyo) [*A publication*]

Rep Fed Railroad Adm ... Report. Federal Railroad Administration [*United States*] [*A publication*]

Rep Fermented Foods Exp Stn Kagawa Prefect ... Report. Fermented Foods Experimental Station. Kagawa Prefecture [*A publication*]

Rep Ferment Ind ... Report on the Fermentation Industries [*A publication*]

Rep Ferment Res Inst ... Report. Fermentation Research Institute [*A publication*]

Rep Ferment Res Inst (Chiba) ... Report. Fermentation Research Institute (Chiba) [*A publication*]

Rep Ferment Res Inst (Tsukuba-Gun Jpn) ... Report. Fermentation Research Institute (Tsukuba-Gun, Japan) [*A publication*]

Rep Ferment Res Inst (Yatabe) ... Report. Fermentation Research Institute (Yatabe) [*A publication*]

Rep Field Act Miner Resour Div (Manitoba) ... Report of Field Activities. Mineral Resources Division (Manitoba) [*A publication*]

Rep Finn Acad Sci Lett Sodankyla Geophys Obs ... Report. Finnish Academy of Science and Letters. Sodankyla Geophysical Observatory [*A publication*]

Rep Fire Res Inst Jpn ... Report. Fire Research Institute of Japan [*A publication*]

Rep Fire Technol Lab Tech Res Cent Finl ... Reports. Fire Technology Laboratory. Technical Research Centre of Finland [*A publication*]

Rep Fish Board Swed Inst Mar Res ... Report. Fishery Board of Sweden. Institute of Marine Research [*A publication*]

Rep Fish Board Swed Ser Hydrogr ... Reports. Fishery Board of Sweden. Series Hydrography [*A publication*]

Rep Fish Res Lab Kyushu Univ ... Report. Fishery Research Laboratory. Kyushu University [*A publication*]

Rep Fla Agric Exp Stn ... Report. Florida Agricultural Experiment Station [*A publication*]

Rep FM Univ Calif Berkeley ... Report FM. University of California, Berkeley [*A publication*]

Rep Food Ind Exp Stn Hiroshima Prefect ... Report. Food Industrial Experiment Station. Hiroshima Prefecture [*A publication*]

Rep Food Res Inst Niigata Prefect ... Report. Food Research Institute. Niigata Prefecture [*A publication*]

Rep Food Res Inst (Tokyo) ... Report. Food Research Institute (Tokyo) [*A publication*]

Rep Food Res Inst Yamanashi Prefect ... Report. Food Research Institute. Yamanashi Prefecture [*A publication*]

Rep Forest Dep (Tanganyika) ... Report. Forest Department (Tanganyika Territory) [*A publication*]

Rep Forest Exp Stn Hokkaido ... Annual Report. Hokkaido Branch. Government Forest Experiment Station [*A publication*]

Rep For Game Manage Res Inst ... Reports. Forestry and Game Management Research Institute [*A publication*]

REPFORMAINT ... Representative of Maintenance Force

Rep For Prod Res Inst (Bogor Indones) ... Report. Forest Products Research Institute (Bogor, Indonesia) [*A publication*]

Rep For Prod Res Inst (Hokkaido) ... Report. Hokkaido Forest Products Research Institute (Asahikawa, Hokkaido) [*A publication*]

Rep For Res ... Report on Forest Research [*A publication*]

Rep For Resour Reconn Surv Malaya ... Report. Forest Resources Reconnaissance Survey of Malaya [*A publication*]

Rep Forsknstift Skogsarb ... Report. Redogorelse. Forskningsstiftelsen Skogsarbeten [*A publication*]

Rep FPM-X For Pest Manage Inst ... Report FPM-X. Forest Pest Management Institute [*A publication*]

Rep Freedom Hunger Campaign ... Report. Freedom from Hunger Campaign. FAO [*Food and Agriculture Organization of the United Nations*] [*A publication*]

Rep Fuel Res Inst ... Report. Fuel Research Institute [*A publication*]

Rep Fukushima Prefect Inst Public Health ... Report. Fukushima Prefectural Institute of Public Health [*A publication*]

Rep Fukushima Prefect Public Health Inst ... Report. Fukushima Prefectural Public Health Institute [*Japan*] [*A publication*]

Rep Fukushima Seric Exp Stn ... Report. Fukushima Sericultural Experimental Station [*A publication*]

Rep Fys Lab I Tek Hoejsk (Lyngby) ... Report. Fysisk Laboratorium I. Danmarks Tekniske Hoejskole (Lyngby) [*A publication*]

REPGA ...... Reprographics [*A publication*]

Rep GA For Res Coun ... Report. Georgia Forest Research Council [*A publication*]

Rep Gen Fish Counc Mediterr ... Report. General Fisheries Council for the Mediterranean [*A publication*]

Rep Geod Inst (Den) ... Report. Geodetic Institute (Denmark) [*A publication*]

Rep Geol Miner Explor (Seoul) ... Report of Geological and Mineral Exploration (Seoul) [*A publication*]

Rep Geol Min Explor ... Report of Geological and Mineral Exploration [*South Korea*] [*A publication*]

Rep Geol Min Surv Iran ... Report. Geological and Mining Survey of Iran [*A publication*]

Rep Geol Surv Borneo Reg Malays ... Report. Geological Survey of the Borneo Region, Malaysia [*A publication*]

Rep Geol Surv Dep Br Guiana ... Report. Geological Survey Department. British Guiana [*A publication*]

Rep Geol Surv Dep (Guyana) ... Report. Geological Survey Department (Guyana) [*A publication*]

Rep Geol Surv Dep (Zambia) ... Report. Geological Survey Department (Zambia) [*A publication*]

Rep Geol Surv East Malays ... Report. Geological Survey of East Malaysia [*A publication*]

Rep Geol Surv Greenl ... Report. Geological Survey of Greenland [*A publication*]

Rep Geol Surv Hokkaido ... Report. Geological Survey of Hokkaido [*Japan*] [*A publication*]

Rep Geol Surv Hokkaido ... Report. Geological Survey of Hokkaido [*A publication*]

Rep Geol Surv Iran ... Report. Geological Survey of Iran [*A publication*]

Rep Geol Surv Jpn ... Report. Geological Survey of Japan [*A publication*]

Rep Geol Surv Kenya ... Report. Geological Survey of Kenya [*A publication*]

Rep Geol Surv Malays ... Report. Geological Survey of Malaysia [*A publication*]

Rep Geol Surv Mines Dep (Uganda) ... Report. Geological Survey and Mines Department (Uganda) [*A publication*]

Rep Geol Surv NSW ... Report. Geological Survey of New South Wales [*A publication*]   (APTA)

Rep Geol Surv NZ ... Report. Geological Survey of New Zealand [*A publication*]

Rep Geol Surv Papua New Guinea ... Report. Geological Survey of Papua, New Guinea [*A publication*]

Rep Geol Surv Qd ... Report. Geological Survey of Queensland [*A publication*]   (APTA)

Rep Geol Surv Queensl ... Report. Geological Survey of Queensland [*A publication*]   (APTA)

Rep Geol Surv Tasm ... Report. Geological Survey of Tasmania [*A publication*]   (APTA)

Rep Geol Surv Uganda ... Report. Geological Survey of Uganda [*A publication*]

Rep Geol Surv Vic ... Report. Geological Survey of Victoria [*A publication*]   (APTA)

Rep Geol Surv Vict ... Report. Geological Survey of Victoria [*A publication*]   (APTA)

Rep Geol Surv West Aust ... Report. Geological Survey of Western Australia [*A publication*]

Rep Geol Surv West Aust ... Western Australia. Geological Survey. Report [*A publication*]   (APTA)

Rep Geol Surv Zambia ... Report. Geological Survey of Zambia [*A publication*]

Rep Geophys Geochem Explor Geol Surv Korea ... Report of Geophysical and Geochemical Exploration. Geological Survey of Korea [*A publication*]

Rep Geophys Res Stn Kyoto Univ ... Reports. Geophysical Research Station. Kyoto University [*A publication*]

Rep Geosci Miner Resour ... Report on Geoscience and Mineral Resources [*Republic of Korea*] [*A publication*]

Rep Geosci Miner Resour Korea Inst Energy Resour ... Report on Geoscience and Mineral Resources. Korea Institute of Energy and Resources [*A publication*]

Rep Geosci Miner Resour Korea Res Inst Geosci Miner Resour ... Report on Geoscience and Mineral Resources. Korea Research Institute of Geoscience and Mineral Resources [*A publication*]

Rep Ghana Geol Surv ... Report. Ghana Geological Survey [*A publication*]

Rep Gifu Prefect Inst Public Health ... Report. Gifu Pefectural Institute of Public Health [*A publication*]

Rep Glasshouse Crops Res Inst ... Report. Glasshouse Crops Research Institute [*A publication*]

Rep Glass Res Inst Tohoku Univ ... Report. Glass Research Institute. Tohoku University [*A publication*]

REPGLD ... Republic Goldfields Corp. [*Associated Press abbreviation*]   (APAG)

Rep Gov Chem Ind Res Inst (Tokyo) ... Reports. Government Chemical Industrial Research Institute (Tokyo) [*A publication*]

Rep Gov Chem Lab (West Aust) ... Report. Government Chemical Laboratories (Western Australia) [*A publication*]

Rep Gov For Exp Stn ... Report. Government Forest Experiment Station [*A publication*]

Rep Gov Ind Dev Lab (Hokkaido) ... Reports. Government Industrial Development Laboratory (Hokkaido) [*A publication*]

Rep Gov Ind Res Inst (Kyushu) ... Reports. Government Industrial Research Institute (Kyushu) [*Japan*] [*A publication*]

Rep Gov Ind Res Inst (Nagoya) ... Reports. Government Industrial Research Institute (Nagoya) [*A publication*]

Rep Gov Ind Res Inst (Osaka) ... Reports. Government Industrial Research Institute (Osaka) [*A publication*]

Rep Gov Ind Res Inst (Shikoku) ... Reports. Government Industrial Research Institute (Shikoku) [*A publication*]

Rep Gov Ind Res Inst (Tohoku) ... Reports. Government Industrial Research Institute (Tohoku) [*A publication*]

Rep Gov Mech Lab Tokyo ... Report. Government Mechanical Laboratory. Tokyo [*A publication*]

Rep Gov Mineral Anal Chem (West Aust) ... Report. Government Mineralogist, Analyst, and Chemist (Western Australia) [*A publication*]

Rep Gov Sugar Exp Stn (Tainan Formosa) ... Report. Government Sugar Experiment Station (Tainan, Formosa) [*A publication*]

Rep Govt Inst Vet Research (Fusan Chosen) ... Report. Government Institute for Veterinary Research (Fusan, Chosen) [*A publication*]

Rep Govt Mech Lab (Tokyo) ... Report. Government Mechanical Laboratory (Tokyo) [*A publication*]

Rep Gr Brit Agr Res Counc ... Report. Great Britain Agricultural Research Council [*A publication*]

Rep Gr Brit Colon Pestic Res Unit CPRU/Porton ... Report. Great Britain Colonial Pesticides Research Unit. CPRU/Porton [*A publication*]

Rep Greenkeep Res NZ Inst Turf Cult Greenkeep Res Comm ... Report on Greenkeeping Research. New Zealand Institute for Turf Culture. Greenkeeping Research Committee [*A publication*]

Rep Group Adv Psychiatry ... Report. Group for the Advancement of Psychiatry [*A publication*]

Rep Gt Brit Trop Pestic Res Unit TPRU/Porton ... Report. Great Britain Tropical Pesticides Research Unit. TPRU/Porton [*A publication*]

RepGyp ...... Republic Gypsum Co. [*Associated Press abbreviation*]   (APAG)

Rep Hawaii Att'y Gen ... Hawaii Attorney General Report [*A publication*]   (DLA)

Rep Hawaii Div Water Land Dev ... Report. Hawaii. Division of Water and Land Development [*A publication*]

Rep Hawaii Sugar Technol ... Reports. Hawaiian Sugar Technologists [*A publication*]

Rep Health Soc Subj (Lond) ... Reports. Health and Social Subjects (London) [*A publication*]

Rep Helsinki Univ Technol Radio Lab ... Report. Helsinki University of Technology. Radio Laboratory [*A publication*]

Rep Himeji Inst Technol ... Reports. Himeji Institute of Technology [*A publication*]

Rep Himeji Tech Coll ... Reports. Himeji Technical College [*A publication*]

REPHO ..... Reference Telephone Conversation (NOAA)

Rep Hokkaido Fish Hatchery ... Reports. Hokkaido Fish Hatchery [*A publication*]

Rep Hokkaido For Prod Res Inst ... Report. Hokkaido Forest Products Research Institute [*Japan*] [*A publication*]

Rep Hokkaido Ind Res Inst ... Reports. Hokkaido Industrial Research Institute [*A publication*]

Rep Hokkaido Inst Public Health ... Report. Hokkaido Institute of Public Health [*A publication*]

Rep Hokkaido Nat Agr Exp Sta ... Report. Hokkaido National Agricultural Experiment Station [*A publication*]

Rep Hokkaido Natn Agric Exp Stn ... Report. Hokkaido National Agricultural Experiment Station [*A publication*]

Rep Hokkaido Pref Agr Exp Sta ... Report. Hokkaido Prefectural Agricultural Experiment Station [*A publication*]

Rep Hokkaido Prefect Agric Exp Stn ... Report. Hokkaido Prefectural Agricultural Experiment Stations [*A publication*]

Rep Hokkaido Res Inst Environ Pollut ... Report. Hokkaido Research Institute for Environmental Pollution [*A publication*]

Rep Horace Lamb Inst Oceanogr ... Report. Horace Lamb Institute of Oceanography [*A publication*] (APTA)

Rep Hort Exp Sta (Ontario) ... Report. Horticultural Experiment Station (Ontario) [*A publication*]

Rep Hort Exp Stn Prod Lab (Vineland) ... Report. Horticultural Experiment Station and Products Laboratory (Vineland Station) [*Ontario*] [*A publication*]

Rep H Phipps Inst Tuberc ... Report. Henry Phipps Institute for the Study, Treatment, and Prevention of Tuberculosis [*A publication*]

Rep Hung Acad Sci Cent Res Inst Phys ... Report. Hungarian Academy of Sciences. Central Research Institute for Physics. Koezponti Fizikai Kutato Intezet [*A publication*]

Rep Hung Agric Exp Stn ... Reports. Hungarian Agricultural Experiment Station [*A publication*]

Rep Hung Biol Stn Tihany ... Reports. Hungarian Biological Station at Tihany [*A publication*]

Rep Hybrid Corn Ind Res Conf ... Report. Hybrid Corn Industry. Research Conference [*A publication*]

Rep Hyg Lab Shiga Prefect ... Report. Hygiene Laboratory of Shiga Prefecture [*A publication*]

Rep Hyogo Prefect For Exp Stn ... Report. Hyogo Prefectural Forest Experiment Station [*A publication*]

Rep IA St Apiar ... Report of Iowa State Apiarist [*A publication*]

Rep ICJ ...... International Court of Justice. Reports of Judgements, Advisory Opinions, and Orders [*A publication*]

Rep ICTIS/ER IEA Coal Res ... Report ICTIS/ER [*IEA Coal Research Technical Information Service/Executive Review*] IEA [*International Energy Agency*] Coal Research [*A publication*]

Rep ICTIS/TR IEA Coal Res ... Report ICTIS/TR [*IEA Coal Research Technical Information Service/Technical Report*]. IEA [*International Energy Agency*] Coal Research [*A publication*]

REPIDISCA ... Red Panamericana de Informacion y Documentacion en Ingenieria Sanitaria y Ciencias del Ambiente [*Pan American Network for Information and Documentation in Sanitary Engineering and Environmental Sciences*] [*WHO*] [*United Nations*] (DUND)

Rep Ill Beekeep Ass ... Report. Illinois Beekeeping Association [*A publication*]

Rep Imp Coun Agric Res ... Report. Imperial Council of Agricultural Research [*A publication*]

Rep Imp Fuel Res Inst (Jpn) ... Reports. Imperial Fuel Research Institute (Japan) [*A publication*]

Rep Imp Mycol Conf ... Report. Imperial Mycological Conference [*A publication*]

REPIN .... Reply If Negative [*Military*]

Rep Ind Coun Agric Res ... Report. Indian Council of Agricultural Research [*A publication*]

Rep Ind Educ Res Cent Chungnam Natl Univ ... Report. Industrial Education Research Center. Chungnam National University [*Republic of Korea*] [*A publication*]

Rep Ind Hlth Res Bo ... Report. Industrial Health Research Board [*A publication*]

Rep India Min Rur Dev ... Report. India Ministry of Rural Development [*A publication*]

Rep Ind Res Cent Shiga Prefect ... Reports. Industrial Research Center. Shiga Prefecture [*A publication*]

Rep Ind Res Inst Aichi Prefect Gov ... Reports. Industrial Research Institute. Aichi Prefectural Government [*A publication*]

Rep Ind Res Inst Hyogo Prefect ... Reports. Industrial Research Institute. Hyogo Prefecture [*A publication*]

Rep Ind Res Inst Ishikawa ... Report. Industrial Research Institute of Ishikawa [*A publication*]

Rep Ind Res Inst Kanagawa Prefect ... Report. Industrial Research Institute of Kanagawa Prefecture [*A publication*]

Rep Ind Res Inst Kumamoto Prefect ... Report. Industrial Research Institute. Kumamoto Prefecture [*A publication*]

Rep Ind Res Inst Nagano Technol Dev Cent Nagano ... Reports. Industrial Research Institute of Nagano and Technology Development Center of Nagano [*A publication*]

Rep Ind Res Inst Osaka Prefect ... Reports. Industrial Research Institute. Osaka Prefecture [*Japan*] [*A publication*]

Rep Ind Tech Res Inst ... Report. Osaka Industrial Technical Research Institute [*A publication*]

Rep Inf Cent Jt Inst Lab Astrophys ... Report. Information Center. Joint Institute for Laboratory Astrophysics [*A publication*]

Rep Inst Agric Res Tohoku Univ ... Reports. Institute for Agricultural Research. Tohoku University [*A publication*]

Rep Inst Agr Res (Korea) ... Report. Institute of Agricultural Research (Korea) [*A publication*]

Rep Inst Anim Physiol ... Report. Institute of Animal Physiology [*A publication*]

Rep Inst Appl Microbiol Univ Tokyo ... Reports. Institute of Applied Microbiology. University of Tokyo [*A publication*]

Rep Inst Bas Med Sci ... Report. Institute of Basic Medical Sciences [*A publication*]

Rep Inst Chem Res Kyoto Univ ... Reports. Institute for Chemical Research. Kyoto University [*A publication*]

Rep Inst Clin Res Exp Med ... Report. Institute of Clinical Research and Experimental Medicine. Middlesex Hospital Medical School [*A publication*]

Rep Inst Fish Biol Minist Econ Aff Natl Taiwan Univ ... Report. Institute of Fishery Biology. Ministry of Economic Affairs. National Taiwan University [*A publication*]

Rep Inst Freshwater Res (Drottningholm) ... Report. Institute of Freshwater Research (Drottningholm) [*A publication*]

Rep Inst Geol Sci ... Report. Institute of Geological Sciences [*A publication*]

Rep Inst Geol Sci (UK) ... Report. Institute of Geological Sciences (United Kingdom) [*A publication*]

Rep Inst High Speed Mech Tohoku Univ ... Reports. Institute of High Speed Mechanics. Tohoku University [*A publication*]

Rep Inst Ind Sci Univ Tokyo ... Report. Institute of Industrial Science. University of Tokyo [*A publication*]

Rep Inst Ind Technol Yeung Nam Univ ... Report. Institute of Industrial Technology. Yeung Nam University [*A publication*]

Rep Inst Jpn Chem Fibers Kyoto Univ ... Reports. Institute of Japanese Chemical Fibers. Kyoto University [*A publication*]

Rep Inst Ld Wat Mgmt Res ... Report. Institute for Land and Water Management Research [*A publication*]

Rep Inst Mar Res Fish Board Swed ... Report. Institute of Marine Research. Fishery Board of Sweden [*A publication*]

Rep Inst Med Dent Eng Tokyo Med Dent Univ ... Reports. Institute for Medical and Dental Engineering. Tokyo Medical and Dental University [*A publication*]

Rep Inst Med Vet Sci (SA) ... Report. Institute of Medical and Veterinary Science (South Australia) [*A publication*]

Rep Inst Met (Leningrad) ... Reports. Institute of Metals (Leningrad) [*A publication*]

Rep Inst Min Res Univ Rhod ... Report. Institute of Mining Research. University of Rhodesia [*A publication*]

Rep Inst Min Res Univ Zimbabwe ... Report. Institute of Mining Research. University of Zimbabwe [*A publication*]

Rep Inst Nat Prod Yeungnam Univ ... Report. Institute of Natural Products. Yeungnam University [*A publication*]

Rep Inst Nucl Phys (Krakow) ... Report. Institute of Nuclear Physics (Krakow) [*A publication*]

Rep Inst Opt Res (Tokyo) ... Reports. Institute for Optical Research (Tokyo) [*A publication*]

Rep Inst Phys Chem Acad Sci Ukr SSR ... Reports. Institute of Physical Chemistry. Academy of Sciences. Ukrainian SSR [*A publication*]

Rep Inst Phys Chem Res ... Reports. Institute of Physical and Chemical Research [*A publication*]

Rep Inst Phys Chem Res (Jpn) ... Reports. Institute of Physical and Chemical Research (Japan) [*A publication*]

Rep Inst Phys Warsaw Tech Univ ... Reports. Institute of Physics. Warsaw Technical University [*A publication*]

Rep Inst Pulp Pap Ind Shizuoka Prefect ... Reports. Institute of the Pulp and Paper Industry. Shizuoka Prefecture [*A publication*]

Rep Inst Sci Labour (Tokyo) ... Reports. Institute for Science of Labour (Tokyo) [*A publication*]

Rep Inst Sci Technol ... Report. Institute of Science and Technology [*Republic of Korea*] [*A publication*]

Rep Inst Sci Technol Sung Kyun Kwan Univ ... Report. Institute of Science and Technology. Sung Kyun Kwan University [*A publication*]

Rep Inst Sci Technol Tokyo Univ ... Report. Institute of Science and Technology. Tokyo University [*A publication*]

Rep Inst Soc Med ... Report. Institute of Social Medicine [*A publication*]

Rep Inst Space Astronaut Sci (Tokyo) ... Report. Institute of Space and Astronautical Science (Tokyo) [*A publication*]

Rep Inst Syst Des Optim Kans State Univ ... Report. Institute for Systems Design and Optimization. Kansas State University [*A publication*]

Rep Inst Theor Astrophys Univ Oslo ... Report. Institute of Theoretical Astrophysics. University of Oslo [*A publication*]

Rep Inst Wine Food Technol Yamanashi Prefect ... Report. Institute for Wine and Food Technology. Yamanashi Prefecture [*A publication*]
Rep Int Assoc Cereal Chem ... Reports. International Association of Cereal Chemistry [*A publication*]
Rep Int Conf Ironmaking ... Reports. International Conference on Ironmaking [*A publication*]
Rep Int Counc Scient Un ... Report. International Council of Scientific Unions [*A publication*]
Rep Int Hortic Congr ... Report. International Horticultural Congress [*A publication*]
Rep Int Pac Halibut Comm ... Report. International Pacific Halibut Commission [*A publication*]
Rep Int Whaling Comm ... Report. International Whaling Commission [*A publication*]
Rep Int Whaling Comm Spec Issue ... Report. International Whaling Commission. Special Issue [*A publication*]
Rep Int Workshop Int Histocompat Conf ... Report. International Workshop. International Histocompatibility Conference [*A publication*]
Rep Inventory Minn Off Iron Range Resour Rehabil ... Report of Inventory. Minnesota Office of Iron Range Resources and Rehabilitation [*A publication*]
Rep Invest Aust Gov Anal Lab ... Australian Government Analytical Laboratories. Report of Investigations [*A publication*] (APTA)
Rep Invest Bur Econ Geol (Texas) ... Report of Investigations. Bureau of Economic Geology (Texas) [*A publication*]
Rep Invest Bur Mines Philipp ... Report of Investigations. Bureau of Mines of the Philippines [*A publication*]
Rep Invest Conn State Geol Nat Hist Surv ... Report of Investigations. Connecticut State Geological and Natural History Survey [*A publication*]
Rep Invest Delaware Geol Surv ... Report of Investigations. Delaware Geological Survey [*A publication*]
Rep Invest Del Geol Surv ... Report of Investigations. Delaware. Geological Survey [*A publication*]
Rep Invest Div Miner Resour (VA) ... Report of Investigations. Division of Mineral Resources (Virginia) [*A publication*]
Rep Invest Fla Bur Geol ... Report of Investigations. Florida Bureau of Geology [*A publication*]
Rep Invest Geol Surv Div Mich ... Report of Investigations. Geological Survey Division of Michigan [*A publication*]
Rep Invest Geol Surv Finl ... Report of Investigation. Geological Survey of Finland [*A publication*]
Rep Invest Geol Surv MO ... Report of Investigations. Geological Survey of Missouri [*A publication*]
Rep Invest Geol Surv S Aust ... Report of Investigations. Geological Survey of South Australia [*A publication*]
Rep Invest Geol Surv South Aust ... Report of Investigations. Geological Survey of South Australia [*A publication*] (APTA)
Rep Invest Geol Surv Wyo ... Report of Investigations. Geological Survey of Wyoming [*A publication*]
Rep Invest Geol Surv Wyoming ... Report of Investigations. Geological Survey of Wyoming [*A publication*]
Rep Invest Gov Chem Labs West Aust ... Report of Investigations. Government Chemical Laboratories. Western Australia [*A publication*] (APTA)
Rep Invest Ill State Geol Surv ... Report of Investigations. Illinois State Geological Survey [*A publication*]
Rep Invest Ill State Water Surv ... Report of Investigation. Illinois State Water Survey [*A publication*]
Rep Invest Iowa Geol Surv ... Report of Investigations. Iowa Geological Survey [*A publication*]
Rep Invest Ky Geol Surv ... Report of Investigations. Kentucky. Geological Survey [*A publication*]
Rep Invest Md Geol Surv ... Report of Investigations. Maryland Geological Survey [*A publication*]
Rep Invest Mich Geol Surv Div ... Report of Investigation. Michigan Geological Survey Division [*A publication*]
Rep Invest Minnesota Geol Surv ... Report of Investigations. Minnesota Geological Survey [*A publication*]
Rep Invest Mo Div Geol Land Surv ... Report of Investigations. Missouri Division of Geology and Land Survey [*A publication*]
Rep Invest Mo Geol Surv ... Report of Investigations. Missouri Geological Survey [*A publication*]
Rep Invest Mo Geol Surv Water Resources ... Report of Investigations. Missouri Geological Survey and Water Resources [*A publication*]
Rep Invest N B Miner Resour Branch ... Report of Investigation. New Brunswick. Mineral Resources Branch [*A publication*]
Rep Invest NC Div Ground Water ... Report of Investigations. North Carolina Division of Ground Water [*A publication*]
Rep Invest ND Geol Surv ... Report of Investigations. North Dakota Geological Survey [*A publication*]
Rep Invest Ohio Div Geol Surv ... Report of Investigations. Ohio Division of Geological Survey [*A publication*]
Rep Invest Philipp Bur Mines ... Report of Investigation. Philippines. Bureau of Mines [*A publication*]
Rep Invest Philipp Bur Mines Geo Sci ... Report of Investigation. Philippines Bureau of Mines and Geo-Sciences [*A publication*]

Rep Invest SD Geol Surv ... Report of Investigations. South Dakota Geological Survey [*A publication*]
Rep Invest South Aust Geol Surv ... Report of Investigations. South Australia Geological Survey [*A publication*]
Rep Invest State Water Surv Ill ... Report of Investigation. State Water Survey of Illinois [*A publication*]
Rep Invest Tenn Div Geol ... Report of Investigations. Tennessee Division of Geology [*A publication*]
Rep Invest Univ Tex Austin Bur Econ Geol ... Report of Investigations. University of Texas at Austin. Bureau of Economic Geology [*A publication*]
Rep Invest US Bur Mines ... Report of Investigations. United States Bureau of Mines [*A publication*]
Rep Invest Va Div Miner Resour ... Report of Investigations. Virginia Division of Mineral Resources [*A publication*]
Rep Invest WA Govt Chem Labs ... Report of Investigations. Government Chemical Laboratories. Western Australia [*A publication*] (APTA)
Rep Invest West Aust Gov Chem Lab ... Report of Investigations. Western Australia. Government Chemical Laboratories [*A publication*]
Rep Invest W Va Geol Econ Surv ... Report of Investigations. West Virginia Geological and Economic Survey [*A publication*]
Rep Ionos Res Jpn ... Report of Ionosphere Research in Japan [*Later, Report of Ionosphere and Space Research in Japan*] [*A publication*]
Rep Ionos & Space Res Jap ... Report of Ionosphere and Space Research in Japan [*A publication*]
Rep Ionos and Space Res Jpn ... Report of Ionosphere and Space Research in Japan [*A publication*]
Rep Ion Spa ... Report of Ionosphere and Space Research in Japan [*A publication*]
Rep Iowa State Univ Eng Res Inst ... Report. Iowa State University. Engineering Research Institute [*A publication*]
Rep Iowa St Hort Soc ... Report. Iowa State Horticultural Society [*A publication*]
REPISIC ... Report Immediate Superior in Command [*Navy*]
Rep Jpn Inst Baking ... Report. Japan Institute of Baking [*A publication*]
Rep Jpn Mar Prod Co Res Lab ... Reports. Japan Marine Products Co.. Research Laboratory [*A publication*]
Rep Jpn Spinners Insp Found ... Report. Japan Spinners' Inspecting Foundation [*A publication*]
Rep Jt Inst Lab Astrophys ... Report. Joint Institute for Laboratory Astrophysics [*A publication*]
Rep Jur ... Repertorium Juridicum [*Latin*] [*A publication*] (DLA)
Rep de Jur Com ... Repertoire de Jurisprudence Commerciale [*Paris*] [*A publication*] (DLA)
Rep Kagawa Ken Shoyu Exp Stn ... Report. Kagawa-Ken Shoyu Experiment Station [*A publication*]
Rep Kagawa Prefect Inst Public Health ... Report. Kagawa Prefectural Institute of Public Health [*A publication*]
Rep Kagawa Prefect Res Cent Environ Pollut Control ... Report. Kagawa Prefectural Research Center for Environmental Pollution Control [*A publication*]
Rep Kagoshima Prefect Inst Environ Pollut Public Health ... Report. Kagoshima Prefectural Institute of Environmental Pollution and Public Health [*A publication*]
Rep Kagoshima Prefect Inst Public Health ... Report. Kagoshima Prefectural Institute of Public Health [*A publication*]
Rep Kansas Agric Exper Station ... Report. Kansas Agricultural Experiment Station [*A publication*]
Rep Kans State Board Agr ... Report. Kansas State Board of Agriculture [*A publication*]
Rep Kans State Univ Cent Energy Stud ... Report. Kansas State University. Center for Energy Studies [*A publication*]
Rep Kans State Univ Inst Syst Des Optim ... Report. Kansas State University. Institute for Systems Design and Optimization [*A publication*]
Rep Kans Water Sewage Works Assoc ... Report. Kansas Water and Sewage Works Association [*A publication*]
Rep Kenya Mines Geol Dep ... Report. Kenya. Mines and Geological Department [*A publication*]
Rep Kevo Subarct Res Stn ... Reports. Kevo Subarctic Research Station [*A publication*]
Rep Kihara Inst Biol Res ... Reports. Kihara Institute for Biological Research [*Japan*] [*A publication*]
Rep Kochi Univ Nat Sci ... Reports. Kochi University. Natural Science [*A publication*]
Rep Kumamoto Prefect Seric Exp Stn ... Report. Kumamoto Prefecture Sericulture Experiment Station [*A publication*]
Rep Kunst W ... Repertorium fuer Kunstwissenschaft [*A publication*]
Rep KY Agric Exp Stat ... Report. Kentucky Agricultural Experiment Station. University of Kentucky [*A publication*]
Rep Kyoto Coll Pharm ... Report. Kyoto College of Pharmacy [*A publication*]
Rep Kyoto Univ For ... Reports. Kyoto University Forests [*A publication*]
Rep Kyushu Br Crop Sci Soc Jap ... Report. Kyushu Branch. Crop Science Society of Japan [*A publication*]
Rep Kyushu Univ For ... Reports. Kyushu University Forests [*A publication*]
REPL ... Replace (AAG)
repl ... Replacement (DLA)
REPLAB ... Responsive Environment Programmed Laboratory (IEEE)

Rep Lab Clin Stress Res Karolinska Inst ... Reports. Laboratory for Clinical Stress Research. Karolinska Institute [*A publication*]

Rep Lab Soils Fert Fac Agric Okayama Univ ... Reports. Laboratory of Soils and Fertilizers. Faculty of Agriculture. Okayama University [*A publication*]

Rep Lawrence Livermore Lab ... Report. Lawrence Livermore Laboratory. University of California [*Livermore*] [*A publication*]

Rep Lib Arts Fac Shizuoka Univ Nat Sci ... Reports. Liberal Arts Faculty. Shizuoka University. Natural Science [*A publication*]

Rep Lib Arts Sci Fac Shizuoka Univ ... Report. Liberal Arts and Science Faculty. Shizuoka University [*A publication*]

Rep Lib Arts Sci Fac Shizuoka Univ Nat Sci ... Reports. Liberal Arts and Science Faculty. Shizuoka University. Natural Science [*A publication*]

Rep Liberal Arts Sci Fac Shizuoka Univ Nat Sci ... Reports. Liberal Arts and Science Faculty. Shizuoka University. Natural Science [*Japan*] [*A publication*]

Rep Liv Med Inst ... Report. Liverpool Medical Institution [*A publication*]

REPLN ...... Replenish   (AABC)

Rep Local Govt Bd (London) ... Reports. Local Government Board (London) [*A publication*]

Rep Long Ashton Res Stn ... Report. Long Ashton Research Station. University of Bristol [*A publication*]

REPLTR .... Report by Letter   (NVT)

REPM .... Rare Earth Permanent Magnet

REPM .... Repairman   (NATG)

REPM .... Representatives of Electronic Products Manufacturers [*Later, ERA*]

Rep Malta ... Report on the Working of the Museum Department for the Year. Malta Department of Information [*A publication*]

Rep Mar Anal Chem Stand Program Natl Res Counc (Can) ... Report. Marine Analytical Chemistry Standards Program. National Research Council (Canada) [*A publication*]

Rep Mar Pollut Lab ... Report. Marine Pollution Laboratory [*A publication*]

Rep Mass Att'y Gen ... Report of the Attorney General of the State of Massachusetts [*A publication*]   (DLA)

Rep Mater Res Lab Aust ... Australia. Materials Research Laboratories. Report [*A publication*]   (APTA)

Rep Mathematical Phys ... Reports on Mathematical Physics [*A publication*]

Rep Math Log ... Reports on Mathematical Logic [*A publication*]

Rep Math Logic ... Reports on Mathematical Logic [*Warsaw/Krakow*] [*A publication*]

Rep Math Phys ... Reports on Mathematical Physics [*A publication*]

Rep Maurit Sug Ind Res Inst ... Report. Mauritius Sugar Industry Research Institute [*A publication*]

Rep MC ..... Reports of Municipal Corporations [*A publication*]   (DLA)

REPMC ..... Representative to the Military Committee [*NATO*]

Rep MD Agr Soc ... Report. Maryland Agricultural Society [*A publication*]

Rep MD Beekprs Ass ... Report. Maryland Beekeepers' Association [*A publication*]

Rep Mech Developm Comm For Comm (Lond) ... Report. Mechanical Development Committee. Forestry Commission (London) [*A publication*]

Rep Mech Eng Lab (Tokyo) ... Report. Mechanical Engineering Laboratory (Tokyo) [*A publication*]

Rep Mech Lab Tokyo ... Report. Mechanical Laboratory. Tokyo [*A publication*]

Rep Med and Health Dept (Mauritius) ... Report. Medical and Health Department (Mauritius) [*A publication*]

Rep Med and Health Work Sudan ... Report on Medical and Health Work in the Sudan [*A publication*]

Rep Med Res Probl Jpn Anti-Tuberc Assoc ... Reports on Medical Research Problems of the Japan Anti-Tuberculosis Association [*A publication*]

Rep Med Res Soc Min Smelting Ind ... Report. Medical Research Society for Mining and Smelting Industries [*A publication*]

Rep Meet Aust NZ Assoc Adv Sci ... Report. Meeting. Australian and New Zealand Association for the Advancement of Science [*A publication*]

Rep Melb Metrop Board Works ... Report. Melbourne and Metropolitan Board of Works [*A publication*]   (APTA)

REPMES ... Reply by Message   (FAAC)

Rep Mich Dept Conserv Game Div ... Report. Michigan Department of Conservation. Game Division [*A publication*]

Rep Miner Bur (S Afr) ... Report. Minerals Bureau. Department of Mines (South Africa) [*A publication*]

Rep Miner Dev Div (Newfoundland) ... Report. Mineral Development Division. Department of Mines (Newfoundland) [*A publication*]

Rep Miner Ind Res Lab Univ Alaska ... Report. Mineral Industry Research Laboratory. University of Alaska [*A publication*]

Rep Miner Res Lab CSIRO ... Report. Division of Mineralogy. Minerals Research Laboratory. Commonwealth Scientific and Industrial Research Organisation [*A publication*]   (APTA)

Rep MINTEK ... Report. MINTEK [*Council for Mineral Technology*] [*A publication*]

REPMIS .... Reserve Personnel Management Information System [*Military*]

Rep Miss Agr Exp Sta ... Report. Mississippi Agricultural Experiment Station [*A publication*]

REPML ..... Reply by Mail   (FAAC)

Rep Mont Univ Jt Water Resour Res Cent ... Report. Montana University Joint Water Resources Research Center [*A publication*]

Rep MRL NC State Univ Miner Res Lab ... Report MRL. North Carolina State University. Minerals Research Laboratory [*A publication*]

Rep MRP MSL Can Cent Miner Energy Technol Miner Res Program ... Report MRP/MSL. Canada Centre for Mineral Energy Technology. Minerals Research Program/Mineral Sciences Laboratories [*A publication*]

Rep MRP PMRL (Phys Metall Res Lab) Can ... Report MRP/PMRL (Physical Metallurgy Research Laboratories). Canada [*A publication*]

REPMSG .. Report by Message   (DNAB)

Rep Musc Dyst Assoc Can ... Reporter. Muscular Dystrophy Association of Canada [*A publication*]

Rep Nagano Prefect Ind Res Inst ... Reports. Nagano Prefectural Industrial Research Institute [*A publication*]

Rep Nankai Reg Fish Res Lab ... Report. Nankai Regional Fisheries Research Laboratory [*A publication*]

Rep Nat Inst Nutr ... Report. National Institute of Nutrition [*A publication*]

Rep Natl Food Res Inst ... Report. National Food Research Institute [*A publication*]

Rep Natl Food Res Inst (Tokyo) ... Report. National Food Research Institute (Tokyo) [*A publication*]

Rep Natl Gas Turbine Establ UK ... Report. National Gas Turbine Establishment. United Kingdom [*A publication*]

Rep Natl Ind Res Inst (Korea) ... Report. National Industrial Research Institute (Korea) [*A publication*]

Rep Natl Ind Stand Res Inst (Korea) ... Report. National Industrial Standards Research Institute (Korea) [*A publication*]

Rep Natl Inst Health (Repub Korea) ... Report. National Institute of Health (Republic of Korea) [*A publication*]

Rep Natl Inst Metall ... Report. National Institute for Metallurgy [*A publication*]

Rep Natl Inst Metall (S Afr) ... Report. National Institute for Metallurgy (South Africa) [*A publication*]

Rep Natl Inst Vet Res (Pusan South Korea) ... Report. National Institute for Veterinary Research (Pusan, South Korea) [*A publication*]

Rep Natl Mus Victoria ... Reports. National Museum of Victoria [*A publication*]

Rep Natl Radiol Prot Board ... Report. National Radiological Protection Board [*A publication*]

Rep Natl Res Counc Can Mar Anal Chem Stand Program ... Report. National Research Council Canada. Marine Analytical Chemistry Standards Program [*A publication*]

Rep Natl Res Inst Met ... Report. National Research Institute for Metals [*Tokyo*] [*A publication*]

Rep Natl Res Inst Police Sci (Jpn) Res Forensic Sci ... Reports. National Research Institute of Police Science (Japan). Research on Forensic Science [*A publication*]

Rep Natl Res Inst Pollut Resour (Kawaguchi Jpn) ... Report. National Research Institute for Pollution and Resources (Kawaguchi, Japan) [*A publication*]

Rep Natl Res Lab Metrol ... Report. National Research Laboratory of Metrology [*A publication*]

Rep Natl Swed Environ Prot Board ... Report. National Swedish Environment Protection Board [*A publication*]

Rep Natl Water Resour Counc Repub Philipp ... Report. National Water Resources Council. Republic of the Philippines [*A publication*]

Rep Natn Fd Res Inst (Jap) ... Report. National Food Research Institute (Japan) [*A publication*]

Rep Natn Inst Genet (Misima) ... Report. National Institute of Genetics (Misima) [*A publication*]

Rep Natn Inst Metall (S Afr) ... Report. National Institute of Metallurgy (South Africa) [*A publication*]

Rep Nat Res Inst Police Sci ... Reports. National Research Institute of Police Science [*A publication*]

Rep Nat Res Inst Police Sci Res Traffic Saf Regul ... Reports. National Research Institute of Police Science. Research on Traffic Safety and Regulation [*A publication*]

Rep Nat Res Inst Pollut Resour (Jpn) ... Report. National Research Institute for Pollution and Resources (Japan) [*A publication*]

Rep Natto Res Cent ... Reports. Natto Research Center [*A publication*]

REPNAVRESCEN ... Report to Naval Reserve Center   (DNAB)

Rep Nav Res Lab Prog ... Report of Naval Research Laboratory Progress [*A publication*]

Rep NC Att'y Gen ... North Carolina Attorney General Reports [*A publication*]   (DLA)

Rep Neb Att'y Gen ... Report of the Attorney General of the State of Nebraska [*A publication*]   (DLA)

Rep N Engl Assoc Chem Teach ... Report. New England Association of Chemistry Teachers [*A publication*]

Rep Neth Indian Civ Med Serv ... Reports. Netherlands-Indian Civil Medical Service [*A publication*]

Rep Nevada Bur Mines Geol ... Report. Nevada Bureau of Mines and Geology [*A publication*]

Rep Nev Bur Mines ... Report. Nevada Bureau of Mines [*A publication*]

Rep Nev Bur Mines Geol ... Report. Nevada Bureau of Mines and Geology [*A publication*]

Rep Newfoundland Miner Dev Div ... Report. Newfoundland. Mineral Development Division [*A publication*]
Rep New Hebrides Geol Surv ... Report. New Hebrides Geological Survey [*A publication*]
Rep Niigata Agric Exp Stn ... Report. Niigata Agricultural Experiment Station [*A publication*]
Rep Niigata Food Res Inst ... Report. Niigata Food Research Institute [*A publication*]
Rep NIM ... Report NIM [*National Institute of Metallurgy, South Africa*] [*A publication*]
Rep NJ St Agric Exp Stat ... Report. New Jersey State Agricultural Experiment Station [*A publication*]
Rep Noda Inst Sci Res ... Report. Noda Institute for Scientific Research [*A publication*]
Rep Nord PAH Proj ... Report. Nordic PAH [*Polycyclic Aromatic Hydrocarbons*] Project [*A publication*]
Rep Northeast Corn Impr Conf ... Report. Northeastern Corn Improvement Conference [*A publication*]
Rep Norw Fish Mar Invest Rep Technol Res ... Reports on Norwegian Fishery and Marine Investigation. Reports on Technological Research [*A publication*]
Rep Norw For Res Inst ... Reports. Norwegian Forest Research Institute [*A publication*]
Rep de Not ... Repertoire de Notariae [*Paris*] [*A publication*]   (DLA)
Rep Nottingham Univ Sch Agr ... Report. Nottingham University. School of Agriculture [*A publication*]
Rep Nova Scotia Dep Mines Energy ... Report. Nova Scotia Department of Mines and Energy [*A publication*]
Rep NRL Prog ... Report of NRL [*Naval Research Laboratory*] Progress [*A publication*]
Rep NS Dep Mines ... Report. Nova Scotia Department of Mines [*A publication*]
RepNY .... Republic New York Corp. [*Associated Press abbreviation*]   (APAG)
Rep NY State Vet Coll Cornell Univ ... Report. New York State Veterinary College at Cornell University [*A publication*]
Rep NZ Dep Sci Ind Res Dom Lab ... Report. New Zealand. Department of Scientific and Industrial Research. Dominion Laboratory [*A publication*]
Rep NZ Energy Res Dev Comm ... Report. New Zealand Energy Research and Development Committee [*A publication*]
Rep NZ Geol Surv ... Report. New Zealand Geological Survey [*A publication*]
Rep NZGS ... Report. New Zealand Geological Survey [*A publication*]
Rep NZ Sci Cong ... Report. New Zealand Science Congress [*A publication*]
REPO .... Reporting Officer [*Navy*]
REPO .... Repossess
REPO .... Repurchase Agreement [*Also, RP*] [*Investment term*]
Rep Ohara Inst Agr Biol ... Report. Ohara Institute of Agricultural Biology [*A publication*]
Rep Ohara Inst Agric Biol ... Report. Ohara Institute of Agricultural Biology [*A publication*]
Rep Ontario Geol Surv ... Report. Ontario Geological Survey [*A publication*]
Rep Ont Dep Agric ... Report. Ontario Department of Agriculture [*A publication*]
Rep Ont Dep Mines ... Reports. Ontario Department of Mines [*A publication*]
Rep Ont Geol Surv ... Report. Ontario Geological Survey [*A publication*]
Rep Ont Minist Environ ... Report. Ontario Ministry of the Environment [*A publication*]
Rep Ont Vet Coll ... Report. Ontario Veterinary College [*A publication*]
REP-OP ..... Repetitive Operation [*Data processing*]   (MDG)
Rep & Ops Atty Gen Ind ... Indiana Attorney General Reports [*A publication*]   (DLA)
Rep Ore For Res Lab ... Report. Oregon State University. Forest Research Laboratory [*A publication*]
Rep Oreg Agric Exp Stat ... Report. Oregon Agricultural Experiment Station [*A publication*]
Rep Oreg Wheat Comm ... Report. Oregon Wheat Commission [*A publication*]
Rep Orient Cann Inst ... Report. Oriental Canning Institute [*A publication*]
Rep ORO US Dep Energy ... Report ORO [*Oak Ridge Operations Office*] US Department of Energy [*A publication*]
Reporter Aust Inst of Crim Qrtly ... Reporter. Australian Institute of Criminology. Quarterly [*A publication*]   (APTA)
Report of Invest Wash Div Mines Geol ... Report of Investigations. Washington Division of Mines and Geology [*A publication*]
Reportr D ... Reporter Dispatch [*A publication*]
Reports .... Coke's English King's Bench Reports [*1572-1616*] [*A publication*]   (DLA)
Reports Inst High Speed Mech Tohoku Univ ... Reports. Institute of High Speed Mechanics. Tohoku University [*A publication*]
Reports Res Inst Appl Mech Kyushu Univ ... Reports. Research Institute for Applied Mechanics. Kyushu University [*A publication*]
Report TNO Div Nutr Food Res TNO ... Report. TNO. Division for Nutrition and Food Research TNO [*A publication*]
Rep Osaka City Inst Hyg ... Report. Osaka City Institute of Hygiene [*A publication*]
Rep Osaka City Inst Public Health Environ Sci ... Report. Osaka City Institute of Public Health and Environmental Sciences [*A publication*]

Rep Osaka Ind Res Inst ... Report. Osaka Industrial Research Institute [*A publication*]
Rep Osaka Munic Hyg Lab ... Report. Osaka Municipal Hygienic Laboratory [*A publication*]
Rep Osaka Munic Inst Domest Sci ... Report. Osaka Municipal Institute for Domestic Science [*A publication*]
Rep Osaka Prefect Ind Res Inst ... Reports. Osaka Prefectural Industrial Research Institute [*Japan*] [*A publication*]
Repos Trab LNIV Port Lab Nac Inves Vet ... Repositorio de Trabalhos do LNIV-Portugal. Laboratorio Nacional de Investigacao Veterinaria [*A publication*]
Rep Overseas Div Inst Geol Sci ... Report. Overseas Division. Institute of Geological Sciences [*A publication*]
REPPAC.... Repetitively Pulsed Plasma Accelerator
Rep Pap Northamptonshire Antiq Soc ... Reports and Papers. Northamptonshire Antiquarian Society [*A publication*]
Rep Pat Cas ... Reports of Patent, Design, and Trade Mark Cases [*England*] [*A publication*]   (DLA)
Rep Pat Des & Tr Cas ... Reports of Patent, Design, and Trade Mark Cases [*A publication*]   (DLA)
Rep Phil ..... Reports on Philosophy [*A publication*]
Rep Plann Conf Strategy Virus Manage Potato II ... Report. Planning Conference on the Strategy for Virus Management in Potatoes. II [*A publication*]
Rep Popul-Fam Plann ... Reports on Population-Family Planning [*A publication*]
Rep Prat ..... Repertoire Pratique du Droit Belge [*A publication*]
Rep Prefect Ind Res Inst (Shizuoka) ... Reports. Prefectural Industrial Research Institute (Shizuoka) [*Japan*] [*A publication*]
Rep Proc Annu Conf Int Iron Steel Inst ... Report of Proceedings. Annual Conference. International Iron and Steel Institute [*A publication*]
Rep Proc Annu Conv Am Electroplat Soc ... Report of Proceedings. Annual Convention. American Electroplaters' Society [*A publication*]
Rep Proc Annu Conv Natl Pecan Assoc ... Report. Proceedings. Annual Convention. National Pecan Association [*A publication*]
Rep Proc Assoc Shellfish Comm ... Report. Proceedings. Association of Shellfish Commissioners [*A publication*]
Rep Proc Belfast Nat Hist Philos Soc ... Reports and Proceedings. Belfast Natural History and Philosophical Society [*A publication*]
Rep Proc Br Soc Anim Prod ... Report of Proceedings. British Society of Animal Production [*A publication*]
Rep Proc Int Assoc Ice Cream Manuf ... Report of Proceedings. International Association of Ice Cream Manufacturers [*A publication*]
Rep Proc Natl Assoc Ice Cream Manuf ... Report. Proceedings. National Association of Ice Cream Manufacturers [*A publication*]
Rep Proc ORAU IEA (Oak Ridge Assoc Univ Inst Energy Anal) ... Report and Proceedings. ORAU/IEA (Oak Ridge Associated Universities. Institute for Energy Analysis) [*A publication*]
Rep Prog Appl Chem ... Reports on the Progress of Applied Chemistry [*A publication*]
Rep Prog Indiana Geol Surv ... Report of Progress. Indiana. Geological Survey [*A publication*]
Rep Prog Phys ... Reports on Progress in Physics [*A publication*]
Rep Prog Polym Phys (Jpn) ... Reports on Progress in Polymer Physics (Japan) [*A publication*]
Rep Progr Appl Chem ... Reports on the Progress of Applied Chemistry [*A publication*]
Rep Progr Chem ... Report on the Progress of Chemistry [*A publication*]
Rep Progr Kans Agr Exp Sta ... Report of Progress. Kansas Agricultural Experiment Station [*A publication*]
Rep Progr Kansas Agric Exp Stn ... Report of Progress. Kansas Agricultural Experiment Station [*A publication*]
Rep Progr Phys ... Reports on Progress in Physics [*A publication*]
Rep Proj LA Agr Exp Sta Dept Agron ... Report of Projects. Louisiana Agricultural Experiment Station. Department of Agronomy [*A publication*]
Rep Prov NS Dep Mines ... Report. Province of Nova Scotia Department of Mines [*A publication*]
Rep Prov NS Dep Mines Energy ... Report. Province of Nova Scotia Department of Mines and Energy [*A publication*]
Rep Pr Ph .. Reports on Progress in Physics [*A publication*]
Rep Pr Phys ... Reports on Progress in Physics [*A publication*]
Rep Publ Hlth Comm Ind ... Report. Public Health Commissioner, India [*A publication*]
Rep Public Health Med Subj (Lond) ... Reports on Public Health and Medical Subjects (London) [*A publication*]
Rep Punjab Irrig Res Inst ... Report. Punjab Irrigation Research Institute [*A publication*]
Rep QA ...... Reports Tempore Queen Anne [*11 Modern*] [*A publication*]   (DLA)
Rep Quebec Soc Prot Plant ... Report. Quebec Society for the Protection of Plants [*A publication*]
Rep Que Soc Prot Plants ... Report. Quebec Society for the Protection of Plants [*A publication*]
REPR........ Real Estate Planning Report [*Military*]   (AABC)
REPR........ Repair   (ROG)
REPR........ Reports on Polar Research. Berichte zur Polarforschung [*A publication*]
REPR........ Representative

REPR......... Repressurization (MCD)
REPR......... Reprinted
REPR......... Repro Med Systems, Inc. [*NASDAQ symbol*] (NQ)
Rep Radiat Chem Res Inst Tokyo Univ ... Reports. Radiation Chemistry Research Institute. Tokyo University [*A publication*]
Rep R Agric Coll Swed Ser A ... Reports. Royal Agricultural College of Sweden. Series A [*A publication*]
Rep Rain Making Jpn ... Report of Rain-Making in Japan [*A publication*]
Repr BRA .. Reprint. Bee Research Association [*A publication*]
Repr Bull Bk R ... Reprint Bulletin. Book Reviews [*A publication*]
Rep Rd Res Lab Minist Transp ... Report. Road Research Laboratory. Ministry of Transport [*A publication*]
Rep React Cent (Ned) ... Report. Reactor Centrum (Nederlandse) [*A publication*]
Rep Reelfoot Lake Biol Stn Tenn Acad Sci ... Report. Reelfoot Lake Biological Station. Tennessee Academy of Science [*A publication*]
Rep Reg Res Cent ICTA (Trinidad) ... Report. Regional Research Centre of the British Caribbean. Imperial College of Tropical Agriculture (Trinidad) [*A publication*]
Repr Eng Exp Stn Oreg State Coll ... Reprint. Engineering Experiment Station. Oregon State College [*A publication*]
Rep Repr Sci Pap Saranac Lab Study Tuberc ... Report and Reprints of Scientific Papers. Saranac Laboratory for the Study of Tuberculosis [*A publication*]
Rep Res Cent Assoc Am Railroads ... Report. Research Center. Association of American Railroads [*A publication*]
Rep Res Cent Ion Beam Technol Hosei Univ ... Report. Research Center of Ion Beam Technology. Hosei University [*A publication*]
Rep Res Cent Ion Beam Technol Hosei Univ Suppl ... Report. Research Center of Ion Beam Technology. Hosei University. Supplement [*A publication*]
Rep Res Comm North Cent Weed Control Conf ... Report. Research Committee. North Central Weed Control Conference [*A publication*]
Rep Res Counc Alberta ... Report. Research Council of Alberta [*A publication*]
Rep Res Dept Kyushu Electr Power Co Inc ... Report. Research Department. Kyushu Electric Power Co., Inc. [*Japan*] [*A publication*]
Rep Res Grantees Minist Educ (Jpn) ... Reports on Researches by Grantees. Ministry of Education (Japan) [*A publication*]
Rep Res Inst Appl Mech ... Reports. Research Institute for Applied Mechanics [*A publication*]
Rep Res Inst Appl Mech Kyushu Univ ... Reports. Research Institute for Applied Mechanics. Kyushu University [*A publication*]
Rep Res Inst Basic Sci Chungnam Nat Univ ... Reports. Research Institute of Basic Sciences. Chungnam National University [*A publication*]
Rep Res Inst Brew ... Report. Research Institute of Brewing [*A publication*]
Rep Res Inst Ceram Tokyo Inst Technol ... Reports. Research Institute of Ceramics. Tokyo Institute of Technology [*A publication*]
Rep Res Inst Chem Spectrosc Chungnam Natl Univ ... Reports. Research Institute of Chemical Spectroscopy. Chungnam National University [*A publication*]
Rep Res Inst Dent Mater Tokyo Med Dent Univ ... Report. Research Institute of Dental Materials. Tokyo Medical and Dental University [*A publication*]
Rep Res Inst Electr Commun Tohoku Univ ... Reports. Research Institute of Electrical Communication. Tohoku University [*A publication*]
Rep Res Inst Gunze Silk Manuf Co Ltd ... Reports. Research Institute. Gunze Silk Manufacturing Co. Ltd. [*A publication*]
Rep Res Inst Ind Saf ... Reports. Research Institute of Industrial Safety [*Japan*] [*A publication*]
Rep Res Inst Ind Sci Kyushu Univ ... Reports. Research Institute of Industrial Science. Kyushu University [*A publication*]
Rep Res Inst Nat Resour Min Coll Akita Univ ... Report. Research Institute of Natural Resources. Mining College. Akita University [*A publication*]
Rep Res Inst Nat Sci ... Report. Research Institute of Natural Sciences [*Republic of Korea*] [*A publication*]
Rep Res Inst Nat Sci Chungnam Natl Univ ... Reports. Research Institute of Natural Sciences. Chungnam National University [*A publication*]
Rep Res Inst Phys Chem Chungnam Natl Univ ... Reports. Research Institute of Physics and Chemistry. Chungnam National University [*A publication*]
Rep Res Inst Sci Ind Kyushu Univ ... Reports. Research Institute of Science and Industry. Kyushu University [*Japan*] [*A publication*]
Rep Res Inst Sci Technol Nihon Univ ... Report. Research Institute of Science and Technology. Nihon University [*A publication*]
Rep Res Inst Strength and Fract Mater ... Reports. Research Institute for Strength and Fracture of Materials [*A publication*]
Rep Res Inst Strength Fract Mater Tohoku Univ ... Reports. Research Institute for Strength and Fracture of Materials. Tohoku University [*A publication*]
Rep Res Inst Strength Fracture Mater Tohoku Univ (Sendai) ... Reports. Research Institute for Strength and Fracture of Materials. Tohoku University (Sendai) [*Japan*] [*A publication*]
Rep Res Inst Technol Nihon Univ ... Report. Research Institute of Technology. Nihon University [*A publication*]

Rep Res Inst Underground Resour Min Coll Akita Univ ... Report. Research Institute of Underground Resources. Mining College. Akita University [*Japan*] [*A publication*]
Rep Res Kagawa-Ken Meizen Jr Coll ... Reports of Research. Kagawa-Ken Meizen Junior College [*A publication*]
Rep Res Lab Asahi Glass Co Ltd ... Report. Research Laboratory. Asahi Glass Co. Ltd. [*A publication*]
Rep Res Lab Eng Mater Tokyo Inst Technol ... Report. Research Laboratory of Engineering Materials. Tokyo Institute of Technology [*A publication*]
Rep Res Lab Hydrotherm Chem (Kochi Jpn) ... Reports. Research Laboratory of Hydrothermal Chemistry (Kochi, Japan) [*A publication*]
Rep Res Lab Imp Iron Works (Jpn) ... Report. Research Laboratory. Imperial Iron Works (Japan) [*A publication*]
Rep Res Lab Kirin Brew Co ... Report. Research Laboratories of Kirin Brewery Co. [*A publication*]
Rep Res Lab Kirin Brewery Co Ltd ... Report. Research Laboratories of Kirin Brewery Co. Ltd. [*Japan*] [*A publication*]
Rep Res Lab Nippon Seitetsu Yawata Steel Works ... Report. Research Laboratory. Nippon Seitetsu. Yawata Steel Works [*A publication*]
Rep Res Lab Nippon Suisan Co ... Reports. Research Laboratory. Nippon Suisan Co. [*A publication*]
Rep Res Lab Shimizu Constr Co Ltd ... Reports. Research Laboratory of Shimizu Construction Co. Ltd. [*Japan*] [*A publication*]
Rep Res Lab Snow Brand Milk Prod Co ... Reports. Research Laboratory. Snow Brand Milk Products Co. [*A publication*]
Rep Res Lab Surf Sci Okayama Univ ... Reports. Research Laboratory for Surface Science. Okayama University [*A publication*]
Rep Res Lab Tohoku Electr Power Co Ltd ... Report. Research Laboratory. Tohoku Electric Power Co. Ltd. [*Japan*] [*A publication*]
Rep Res Matsuyama Shinonome Jr Coll ... Reports of Research. Matsuyama Shinonome Junior College [*A publication*]
Rep Res Mishimagakuen Women's Jr Sr Coll ... Reports. Researches. Mishimagakuen Women's Junior and Senior College [*A publication*]
Rep Res Nippon Inst Technol ... Report of Researches. Nippon Institute of Technology [*A publication*]
Rep Resour Res Inst (Kawaguchi) ... Report. Resource Research Institute (Kawaguchi) [*Japan*] [*A publication*]
Rep Res Progr Ill Agr Exp Sta ... Report. Research Progress at the Illinois Agricultural Experiment Station [*A publication*]
Rep Res Proj Dis Ornam Pl ... Report. Research Project for Diseases of Ornamental Plants (Victorian Plant Research Institute) [*A publication*] (APTA)
Rep Results Bacteriol Chem Biol Exam London Waters ... Report on the Results of the Bacteriological, Chemical, and Biological Examination of the London Waters [*A publication*]
Rep Res Worcester Found Exp Biol ... Report of Research. Worcester Foundation for Experimental Biology [*A publication*]
Repr For Prod (Aust) ... Reprint. Division of Forest Products (Melbourne, Australia) [*A publication*]
Rep Rheum Dis ... Reports on Rheumatic Diseases [*A publication*]
Rep Rheum Dis Ser 2 Pract Probl ... Reports on Rheumatic Diseases. Series 2. Practical Problems [*A publication*]
Rep Rheum Dis Ser 2 Top Rev ... Reports on Rheumatic Diseases. Series 2. Topical Reviews [*A publication*]
Reprint....... English Reports, Full Reprint [*A publication*] (DLA)
Reprint Bull Bk R ... Reprint Bulletin. Book Reviews [*A publication*]
Repr Kans State Univ Kans Eng Exp Stn ... Reprint. Kansas State University. Kansas Engineering Experiment Station [*A publication*]
Repr NZ For Serv ... Reprint. New Zealand Forest Service [*A publication*]
REPRO...... Reproduce (KSC)
REPROC... Reprocess (MCD)
Reprocess Newsl ... Reprocessing Newsletter [*A publication*]
Rep Rock Found ... Report. Rockefeller Foundation [*A publication*]
REPROD... Receiver Protective Device (DEN)
REPROD... Reproduction
Reprod Contracept ... Reproduction and Contraception [*A publication*]
Reprod Fert ... Reproduction Fertility and Development [*A publication*]
Reprod Fertil Dev ... Reproduction, Fertility, and Development [*A publication*]
Reprodn Paper News Bull ... Reproduction Paper News. Bulletin [*A publication*]
Reprodn Rev ... Reproductions Review and Methods [*A publication*]
Reprod Nutr Dev ... Reproduction, Nutrition, Developpement [*A publication*]
Reprod Perinat Med ... Reproductive and Perinatal Medicine [*A publication*]
Reprod Rev ... Reproductions Review [*A publication*]
Reprod Tox ... Reproductive Toxicology [*A publication*]
Reprod Toxicol ... Reproductive Toxicology [*A publication*]
Reproduccio ... Reproduccion [*A publication*]
Reproduction Eng ... Reproduction Engineering [*A publication*]
Reprographics Q ... Reprographics Quarterly [*A publication*]
Reprography Newsl ... Reprography Newsletter [*A publication*]
Reprogr Q .. Reprographics Quarterly [*A publication*]
REPROM ... Reprogrammable Programmable Read-Only Memory [*Data processing*] (TEL)
REPRON... Representation (ROG)
Rep Ross Conf Med Res ... Report. Ross Conference on Medical Research [*A publication*]

Rep Ross Conf Obstet Res ... Report. Ross Conference on Obstetric Research [*A publication*]

Rep Ross Conf Pediatr Res ... Report. Ross Conference on Pediatric Research [*A publication*]

Rep Ross Pediatr Res Conf ... Report. Ross Pediatric Research Conference [*A publication*]

Rep Rothamsted Exp Sta ... Report. Rothamsted Experimental Station [*A publication*]

Rep Rothamsted Exp Stn ... Report. Rothamsted Experimental Station [*A publication*]

REPROTOX ... Reproductive Toxicology Center [*Database*] [*Washington, DC*]

Rep Rowett Inst ... Report. Rowett Institute [*A publication*]

Repr Res SP ... Representative Research in Social Psychology [*A publication*]

Rep RRL GB Dep Sci Ind Res Road Res Lab ... Report RRL. Great Britain Department of Scientific and Industrial Research. Road Research Laboratory [*A publication*]

Repr Stat NZ ... Reprint of the Statutes of New Zealand [*A publication*] (DLA)

Rep R Swed Acad Agric Sci Sect ... Report. Royal Swedish Academy of Agriculture. Scientific Section [*A publication*]

Repr Wis Eng Exp Stn ... Reprint. Wisconsin Engineering Experiment Station [*A publication*]

Rep Ryojun Coll Eng ... Reports. Ryojun College of Engineering [*A publication*]

REPS .... Regional Economic Projections Series [*NPA Data Services, Inc.*] [*Information service or system*] (CRD)

REPS .... Regional Emissions Projection System [*Environmental Protection Agency*]

REPS .... Repetitive Electromagnetic Pulse Simulator [*Army*] (RDA)

REPS .... Representative

REPS .... Royal Engineers Postal Section [*British military*] (DMA)

Rep SA Ass Adv Sci ... Report. South African Association for the Advancement of Science [*A publication*]

Rep Sado Mar Biol Stn Niigata Univ ... Report. Sado Marine Biological Station. Niigata University [*A publication*]

Rep Saf Mines Res Establ (GB) ... Report. Safety in Mines Research Establishment (Great Britain) [*A publication*]

Rep S Afr Ass Adv Sci ... Report. South African Association for the Advancement of Science [*A publication*]

Rep S Afr Assoc Adv Sci ... Report. South African Association for the Advancement of Science [*A publication*]

Rep S Afr Inst Med Res ... Report. South African Institute for Medical Research [*A publication*]

Rep Saitama Inst Environ Pollut ... Report. Saitama Institute of Environmental Pollution [*A publication*]

Rep Saitama Prefect Brew Inst ... Report. Saitama Prefectural Brewery Institute [*A publication*]

Rep Saskatchewan Energy Mines ... Report. Saskatchewan Energy and Mines [*A publication*]

Rep Sask Dep Miner Resour ... Report. Saskatchewan Department of Mineral Resources [*A publication*]

Rep Sask Res Counc ... Report. Saskatchewan Research Council [*A publication*]

Rep Sask Res Counc Geol Div ... Report. Saskatchewan Research Council. Geology Division [*A publication*]

Rep SCAT ... Report SCAT [*Sewage Collection and Treatment*] [*A publication*]

Rep Sch Agric Univ Nottingham ... Report. School of Agriculture. University of Nottingham [*A publication*]

Rep Sci Ind Forum ... Report. Science and Industry Forum. Australian Academy of Science [*A publication*] (APTA)

Rep Sci Indust Forum ... Report. Science and Industry Forum. Australian Academy of Science [*A publication*] (APTA)

Rep Sci Indust Forum Aust Acad Sci ... Report. Science and Industry Forum. Australian Academy of Science [*A publication*] (APTA)

Rep Sci Living ... Reports of the Science of Living [*A publication*]

Rep Sci Res Inst ... Reports. Scientific Research Institute [*A publication*]

Rep Sci Res Inst Tokyo ... Reports. Scientific Research Institute. Tokyo [*A publication*]

Rep Sci Sess Jpn Dent Assoc ... Reports. Scientific Session. Japan Dental Association [*A publication*]

Rep Scott Beekprs Ass ... Report. Scottish Beekeepers Association [*A publication*]

Rep SC Water Resour Comm ... Report. South Carolina Water Resources Commission [*A publication*]

Rep Sea Fish Inst Ser B (Gdynia Pol) ... Reports. Sea Fisheries Institute. Series B. Fishing Technique and Fishery Technology (Gdynia, Poland) [*A publication*]

Rep Sel Cas Ch ... [*William*] Kelynge's English Chancery Reports [*A publication*] (DLA)

Rep of Sel Cas in Ch ... [*William*] Kelynge's Select Cases in Chancery [*A publication*] (DLA)

Rep Sendai Munic Inst Public Health ... Report. Sendai Municipal Institute of Public Health [*A publication*]

Rep Sendai Public Health Cent ... Report. Sendai Public Health Center [*A publication*]

Rep Ser Ark Agr Exp Sta ... Report Series. Arkansas Agricultural Experiment Station [*A publication*]

Rep Ser Ark Agric Exp Stn ... Report Series. Arkansas Agricultural Experiment Station [*A publication*]

Rep Ser Arkansas Agric Exp Stn ... Report Series. Arkansas Agricultural Experiment Station [*A publication*]

Rep Ser Chem Univ Oulu ... Report Series in Chemistry. University of Oulu [*A publication*]

Rep Ser Geol Surv Irel ... Report Series. Geological Survey of Ireland [*A publication*]

Rep Ser Inland Waters Branch (Can) ... Report Series. Inland Waters Branch (Canada) [*A publication*]

Rep Ser Inland Waters Dir (Can) ... Report Series. Inland Waters Directorate (Canada) [*A publication*]

Rep Ser Phys Univ Helsinki ... Report Series in Physics. University of Helsinki [*A publication*]

Rep Ser Univ Inst Phys ... Report Series. University of Oslo. Institute of Physics [*A publication*]

Rep Ser Univ Oslo Dep Phys ... Report Series. University of Oslo. Department of Physics [*A publication*]

Rep Sess Gen Fish Counc Mediterr ... Report of the Session. General Fisheries Council for the Mediterranean [*A publication*]

Rep Shiga Prefect Inst Public Health ... Report. Shiga Prefectural Institute of Public Health [*A publication*]

Rep Shiga Prefect Inst Public Health Environ Sci ... Report. Shiga Prefectural Institute of Public Health and Environmental Science [*A publication*]

Rep Shikoku Eng Assoc ... Report. Shikoku Engineering Association [*A publication*]

Rep Shimane Prefect Inst Public Health Environ Sci ... Report. Shimane Prefectural Institute of Public Health and Environmental Science [*A publication*]

Rep Shinshu-Miso Res Inst ... Reports. Shinshu-Miso Research Institute [*A publication*]

Rep Ship Res Inst (Tokyo) ... Report. Ship Research Institute (Tokyo) [*A publication*]

REPSHIPS ... Reports of Shipments [*Military*]

Rep Shizuoka Prefect Ind Res Inst ... Reports. Shizuoka Prefectural Industrial Research Institute [*A publication*]

Rep Shizuoka Prefect Ind Technol Cent ... Reports. Shizuoka Prefectural Industrial Technology Center [*A publication*]

Rep Silk Sci Res Inst ... Reports. Silk Science Research Institute [*Japan*] [*A publication*]

Rep SIPRE ... Report SIPRE [*Snow, Ice, and Permafrost Research Establishment*] [*A publication*]

Rep (Sixth) Conf Int Ass Quatern Res ... Report. Sixth Conference. International Association on Quaternary Research [*A publication*]

Rep Smithson Instn ... Report. Smithsonian Institution [*A publication*]

REPSNO ... Report through Senior Naval Officer

Rep Soc Lib St ... Society of Libyan Studies. Annual Report [*A publication*]

Rep Soc Naut Res ... Report. Society for Nautical Research [*A publication*]

Rep Soc Res City Futu ... Report of the Social Research on the City of Futu [*A publication*]

Repsol .... Repsol SA [*Associated Press abbreviation*] (APAG)

Rep Sol Energy Stud CSIRO ... Report. Solar Energy Studies. Commonwealth Scientific and Industrial Research Organisation [*A publication*] (APTA)

Rep South Conf Geront ... Report. Southern Conference on Gerontology [*A publication*]

Rep South Corn Impr Conf ... Report. Southern Corn Improvement Conference [*A publication*]

Rep Spec Res Natl Inst Environ Stud (Jpn) ... Report of Special Research. National Institute for Environmental Studies (Japan) [*A publication*]

Rep Spec Res Proj Natl Inst Environ Stud (Jpn) ... Report. Special Research Project. National Institute for Environmental Studies (Japan) [*A publication*]

Rep Stanford Univ John A Blume Earthquake Eng Cent ... Report. Stanford University. John A. Blume Earthquake Engineering Center [*A publication*]

Rep Stat Appl Res UJSE ... Reports of Statistical Application Research. Union of Japanese Scientists and Engineers [*A publication*]

Rep Stat Appl Res Union Jpn Sci Eng ... Reports of Statistical Application Research. Union of Japanese Scientists and Engineers [*A publication*]

Rep State Bd Health Iowa ... Report. State Board of Health of Iowa [*A publication*]

Rep State Biol Surv Kans ... Reports. State Biological Survey of Kansas [*A publication*]

Rep State Energy Comm WA ... Report. State Energy Commission of Western Australia [*A publication*] (APTA)

Rep Statist Appl Res Un Japan Sci Engrs ... Reports of Statistical Application Research. Union of Japanese Scientists and Engineers [*A publication*]

Rep Steno Mem Hosp Nord Insulinlab ... Reports. Steno Memorial Hospital and the Nordisk Insulinlaboratorium [*A publication*]

Rep Sticht CONCAWE ... Report. Stichting CONCAWE [*Conservation of Clean Air and Water, Europe*] [*A publication*]

Rep Stud GESAMP ... Reports and Studies. GESAMP (Joint Group of Experts on the Scientific Aspects of Marine Pollution) [*A publication*]

Rep Stud Tokyo Coll Domest Sci ... Reports of Studies. Tokyo College of Domestic Science [*A publication*]

Rep Yamanashi Ind Technol Cent ... Report. Yamanashi Industrial Technology Center [*A publication*]
Rep Yamanouchi Cent Res Lab ... Report. Yamanouchi Central Research Laboratories [*A publication*]
REPYB ...... Research Policy [*Netherlands*] [*A publication*]
Rep Yeungnam Univ Inst Ind Technol ... Report. Yeungnam University. Institute of Industrial Technology [*A publication*]
Rep Yeungnam Univ Inst Nat Prod ... Report. Yeungnam University. Institute of Natural Products [*A publication*]
Rep York Ass ... Clayton's English Reports, York Assizes [*A publication*] (DLA)
Rep Yr Dublin Univ Coll Agr Dept ... Report of the Year. Dublin University College. Agricultural Department [*A publication*]
REQ .... Request (AAG)
REQ .... Require (AAG)
REQ .... Requisition
REQAFA ... Request Advise as to Further Action [*Army*] (AABC)
REQANA .. Requirements Analysis (MCD)
REQANS ... Request Answer By [*Date*] [*Military*]
REQAURQN ... Request Authority to Requisition [*Army*] (AFIT)
REQCAPS ... Requirements and Capabilities Automated Planning System (MCD)
REQD .... Required (AAG)
REQDI ...... Request Disposition Instructions [*Army*] (AABC)
REQED ..... Required Execution Date (MCD)
REQFOLINFO ... Request Following Information Be Forwarded This Office [*Army*] (AABC)
REQIBO .... Request Item Be Placed on Back Order [*Army*]
REQID ...... Request If Desired (FAAC)
REQINT .... Request Interim Reply By [*Date*] [*Military*] (AABC)
REQMAD ... Request Mailing Address (FAAC)
REQMNT ... Requirement (NVT)
REQMT ... Requirement
REQN .... Requisition (AAG)
REQNOM ... Request Nomination
REQON ..... Request Consideration (SAA)
REQPER ... Request Permission [*Navy*] (NVT)
REQRCM ... Request Recommendation (FAAC)
REQRE ..... Require (ROG)
REQREC ... Request Recommendation (NVT)
REQS .... Requires
REQSI ...... Request Shipping Instructions [*Military*]
REQSSD ... Request Supply Status and Expected Delivery Date [*Army*] (AABC)
REQSTD ... Requested (FAAC)
REQSUPSTAFOL ... Request Supply Status of Following [*Army*] (AABC)
REQT .... Request (ROG)
REQT .... Requirement (AAG)
REQTAT ... [*It Is*] Requested That [*Military*] (AABC)
REQTRAC ... Request Tracer Be Initiated [*Military*]
REQUAL ... Requalify
REQUCHRD ... Request Unit of Issue Be Changed to Read [*Army*] (AABC)
REQUEST ... Restricted English Question-Answering (HGAA)
REQUONS ... Requisitions
REQVER ... Requirements Verification (IEEE)
RER .... RADAR Effects Reactor
RER .... Radiation Effects Reactor [*Nuclear energy*]
RER .... Railway Equipment Register
RER .... Real Estate Review [*A publication*]
RER .... Receiver/Exciter Ranging [*NASA*]
ReR .... Remington Rand Corp., Blue Bell, PA [*Library symbol*] [*Library of Congress*] (LCLS)
RER .... Renal Excretion Rate [*Medicine*] (MAE)
RER .... Representatives for Experiment Review [*Nuclear energy*] (NRCH)
RER .... Rerun (AAG)
RER .... Residual Error Rate
RER .... Resource Evaluation Report (MCD)
RER .... Respiratory Exchange Rate
RER .... Retlaw Resources, Inc. [*Vancouver Stock Exchange symbol*]
RER .... Reusable-Expendable-Reusable
RER .... Review of Educational Research [*A publication*]
RER .... Rough [*Surfaced*] Endoplasmic Reticulum [*Cytology*]
RER .... Rubberized Equipment Repair
RERA .... Reclamation Era [*A publication*]
RERA .... RERA: Official Monthly Journal. Radio and Electrical Retailers' Association of New South Wales [*A publication*] (APTA)
RERAA ...... Reclamation Era [*A publication*]
RERAD ..... Reference Radio
RERAD ..... Reradiation
RERC .... Radiological Emergency Response Coordination [*Nuclear energy*] (NRCH)
RERC .... Rare Earth Research Conference (EA)
RERC .... Real Estate Research Corp.
RER & D .... Rehabilitative Engineering Research and Development Service [*Veterans Administration*] (GRD)
REREPS .... Repair and Rehabilitation of Paved Surfaces (MCD)
REREQ ...... Reference Requisition (NOAA)
REREX ...... Remote Readout Experiment
RERF .... Radiation Effects Research Foundation [*Formerly, ABCC*]

RERI .... Radiation Effect Research Institute
RERIC .... Regional Energy Resources Information Center [*Asian Institute of Technology*] [*British*] [*Information service or system*] (IID)
RERIF .... Rainier Energy Resources [*NASDAQ symbol*] (NQ)
RERL .... Residual Equivalent Return Loss
Rer Nat Scr Graec Min ... Rerum Naturalium Scriptores Graeci Minores [*A publication*] (OCD)
RERO .... Radiological Emergency Response Operation [*Nuclear energy*] (NRCH)
RERO .... Royal Engineers Reserve of Officers [*British*]
RERP .... Radiological Emergency Response Planning (NRCH)
RERTD ..... Regelungstechnik. RT [*A publication*]
RERTR ..... Reduced Enrichment in Research and Test Reactions [*Department of Energy*]
RERTR ..... Research Enrichment in Research and Test Reactors Program [*Department of Energy*]
RES .... Eastman School of Music, Rochester, NY [*OCLC symbol*] (OCLC)
RES .... Hawaiian Air Tour Service [*Honolulu, HI*] [*FAA designator*] (FAAC)
RES .... Office of Nuclear Regulatory Research [*Nuclear Regulatory Commission*]
RES .... Office of Research [*Washington, DC*] [*Bureau of Intelligence and Research*] [*Department of State*] (GRD)
RES .... On Reserved List [*Army*] [*British*] (ROG)
RES .... RADAR Environment Simulation (NATG)
RES .... RADAR Evaluation Squadron [*Military*]
RES .... Radiation Exposure State (NATG)
RES .... Radio-Echo Sounding [*Geophysics*]
RES .... Readiness Estimation System (MCD)
RES .... Recent Economic Developments [*Jerusalem*] [*A publication*]
RES .... Record Element Specification [*Data processing*]
RES .... Record Evaluation System
RES .... Reentry System (ADA)
RES .... Rehabilitation Evolution System [*Medicine*]
ReS .... Reinare en Espana [*A publication*]
RES .... Relative Electric Strength (MCD)
RES .... Relief Electronics Specialist
ReS .... Religion et Societes [*A publication*]
RES .... Remote Entry Services (MCD)
RES .... Renaissance Energy Ltd. [*Toronto Stock Exchange symbol*]
RES .... Repertoire d'Epigraphie Semitique [*Paris*] [*A publication*]
RES .... Reprint Expediting Service
RES .... Resawed (WGA)
RES .... Research (AAG)
Res .... Researcher [*Samar*] [*A publication*]
RES .... Reserve (EY)
RES .... Reservoir (AAG)
RES .... Reset
RES .... Residence
RES .... Resident
RES .... Residual (KSC)
RES .... Residue
RES .... Resigned
RES .... Resilient [*Technical drawings*]
RES .... Resistance [*or Resistor*] (AAG)
RES .... Resistencia [*Argentina*] [*Airport symbol*] (OAG)
RES .... Resistor
Res .... Resolu [*Resolved, Decided*] [*French*] (ILCA)
RES .... Resolute [*Northwest Territories*] [*Seismograph station code, US Geological Survey*] (SEIS)
RES .... Resolute Bay [*Northwest Territories*] [*Geomagnetic observatory code*]
RES .... Resolution
Res .... Resolved [*Legal term*] (DLA)
RES .... Resonator [*Automotive engineering*]
RES .... Resources
RES .... Restaurant (DSUE)
RES .... Restore
Res .... Resurrection (BJA)
RES .... Reticuloendothelial Society (EA)
RES .... Reticuloendothelial System [*Medicine*]
RES .... Review of Economics and Statistics [*A publication*]
RES .... Review of English Studies [*A publication*]
RES .... Romance of Empire Series [*A publication*]
RES .... Royal Economic Society [*British*]
RES .... Royal Empire Society [*British*]
RES .... Royal Entomological Society [*British*]
RES .... RPC Energy Services, Inc. [*NYSE symbol*] (SPSG)
ResA .... R & E Research Associates, Palo Alto, CA [*Library symbol*] [*Library of Congress*] (LCLS)
RESA .... Regional Education Service Agency
RESA .... Ring-Infected Erythrocyte Surface Antigen [*Immunochemistry*]
RESA .... Scientific Research Society of America (EA)
Res Abstr Reclassif Not Nat Advis Comm Aeronaut (US) ... Research Abstracts and Reclassification Notice. National Advisory Committee for Aeronautics (United States) [*A publication*]
Res/Accel ... Research/Accelerators [*A publication*]

Res Act Fac Sci Engrg Tokyo Denki Univ ... Research Activities. Faculty of Science and Engineering of Tokyo Denki University [*A publication*]

Res Act For Comm (Victoria Aust) ... Research Activity. Forests Commission (Victoria, Australia) [*A publication*]

Res Adv Alcohol Drug Probl ... Research Advances in Alcohol and Drug Problems [*A publication*]

RESAF ...... Reserve of the Air Force

Res African Lit ... Research in African Literatures [*A publication*]

Res Afric Lit ... Research in African Literatures [*A publication*]

Res Afr Lit ... Research in African Literatures [*A publication*]

Res Aging... Research on Aging [*A publication*]

RESALIFT ... Reserve Airlift   (NVT)

Res Annu Nihon Nosan Kogyo ... Research Annual. Nihon Nosan Kogyo [*A publication*]

RESANTISUBCARIARGRU ... Reserve Antisubmarine Warfare Carrier Air Group [*Navy*]   (DNAB)

Res Appl Ind ... Research Applied in Industry [*A publication*]

Res Appl Natl Needs Rep NSF/RA (US) ... Research Applied to National Needs. Report. NSF/RA [*National Science Foundation/Research Applied*] (United States) [*A publication*]

Res Appl Technol Symp Mined-Land Reclam Pap ... Research and Applied Technology Symposium on Mined-Land Reclamation. Papers [*A publication*]

RESAR ...... Reference Safety Analysis Report [*Nuclear energy*]   (NRCH)

Res Assoc Br Paint Colour Varn Manuf Bull ... Research Association of British Paint, Colour, and Varnish Manufacturers. Bulletin [*A publication*]

RESASWCARAIREGRU ... Reserve Antisubmarine Warfare Carrier Air Group [*Navy*]   (DNAB)

RESASWTRACEN ... Reserve Antisubmarine Warfare Training Center [*Navy*]   (DNAB)

Res Bib....... Research Service Bibliographies [*A publication*]   (APTA)

Res Bk........ Reserve Bank Bulletin [*New Zealand*] [*A publication*]

Res Bk NZ ... Reserve Bank of New Zealand. Bulletin [*A publication*]

Res Brch Rep Can Dep Agric ... Research Branch Report. Canada Department of Agriculture [*A publication*]

Res Briefs... Research Briefs [*A publication*]

Res Briefs Fish Comm Oreg ... Research Briefs. Fish Commission of Oregon [*A publication*]

Res Briefs Sch For Resour PA St Univ ... Research Briefs. School of Forest Resources. Pennsylvania State University [*A publication*]

Res Bull Agr Home Econ Exp Sta Iowa State Coll ... Research Bulletin. Agricultural and Home Economics Experiment Station. Iowa State College [*A publication*]

Res Bull Agric Exp Stn (Ga) ... Research Bulletin. Agricultural Experiment Stations (Georgia) [*A publication*]

Res Bull Agric Exp Stn (Iowa) ... Research Bulletin. Agricultural Experiment Station (Iowa) [*A publication*]

Res Bull Agric Exp Stn Univ Idaho ... Research Bulletin. Agricultural Experiment Station. University of Idaho [*A publication*]

Res Bull Agric Exp Stn Univ Nebr ... Research Bulletin. Agricultural Experiment Station. University of Nebraska [*A publication*]

Res Bull Agric Exp Stn Univ Wis ... Research Bulletin. Agricultural Experiment Station. College of Agriculture. University of Wisconsin [*A publication*]

Res Bull Agric Home Econ Exp Stn (Iowa) ... Research Bulletin. Agricultural and Home Economics Experiment Station (Iowa) [*A publication*]

Res Bull Aichi-Ken Agric Res Cent ... Research Bulletin. Aichi-Ken Agricultural Research Center [*A publication*]

Res Bull Aichi-Ken Agric Res Cent Ser A ... Research Bulletin. Aichi-Ken Agricultural Research Center. Series A. Food Crop [*A publication*]

Res Bull Aichi-Ken Agric Res Cent Ser B ... Research Bulletin. Aichi-Ken Agricultural Research Center. Series B. Horticulture [*A publication*]

Res Bull Aichi-Ken Agric Res Cent Ser B Hortic ... Research Bulletin. Aichi-Ken Agricultural Research Center. Series B. Horticulture [*Japan*] [*A publication*]

Res Bull Aichi-Ken Agric Res Cent Ser C ... Research Bulletin. Aichi-Ken Agricultural Research Center. Series C. Poultry [*A publication*]

Res Bull Aichi-Ken Agric Res Cent Ser D ... Research Bulletin. Aichi-Ken Agricultural Research Center. Series D. Sericulture [*A publication*]

Res Bull Aichi-Ken Agric Res Cent Ser E ... Research Bulletin. Aichi-Ken Agricultural Research Center. Series E. Animal Industry [*A publication*]

Res Bull BCSIR Lab (Chittagong) ... Research Bulletin. BCSIR [(*Bangladesh Council of Scientific and Industrial Research*)] Laboratories (Chittagong) [*A publication*]

Res Bull Birla Archaeol Cult Res Inst ... Research Bulletin. Birla Archaeological and Cultural Research Institute [*A publication*]

Res Bull Bunda Coll Agric Univ Malawi ... Research Bulletin. Bunda College of Agriculture. University of Malawi [*A publication*]

Res Bull Cem Res Inst India ... Research Bulletin. Cement Research Institue of India [*A publication*]

Res Bull CIMMYT ... Research Bulletin. Centro Internacional de Mejoramiento de Maiz y Trigo [*A publication*]

Res Bull Coll Exp For Hokkaido Univ ... Research Bulletins. College Experiment Forests. Hokkaido University [*A publication*]

Res Bull Coll Expt Forest Hokkaido Univ ... Research Bulletins. College Experiment Forests. Hokkaido University [*A publication*]

Res Bull Coll Gen Educ Nagoya Univ Nat Sci Psychol ... Research Bulletin. College of General Education. Nagoya University. Natural Sciences and Psychology [*A publication*]

Res Bull East Panjab Univ ... Research Bulletin. East Panjab University [*A publication*]

Res Bull Egypt Sugar Distill Co Sugar Cane Dep ... Research Bulletin. Egyptian Sugar and Distillation Co.. Sugar-Cane Department [*A publication*]

Res Bull Electr Power Dev Co Ltd ... Research Bulletin. Electric Power Development Co. Ltd. [*Japan*] [*A publication*]

Res Bull Exp For Hokkaido Univ ... Research Bulletin. College Experiment Forests. Hokkaido University [*A publication*]

Res Bull Fac Agr Gifu Univ ... Research Bulletin. Faculty of Agriculture. Gifu University [*A publication*]

Res Bull Fac Agric Ain Shams Univ ... Research Bulletin. Faculty of Agriculture. Ain Shams University [*A publication*]

Res Bull Fac Agric Gifu-Ken Prefect Univ ... Research Bulletin. Faculty of Agriculture. Gifu-Ken Prefectural University [*A publication*]

Res Bull Fac Agric Gifu Univ ... Research Bulletin. Faculty of Agriculture. Gifu University [*A publication*]

Res Bull Fac Ed Oita Univ ... Research Bulletin. Faculty of Education. Oita University [*A publication*]

Res Bull Fac Educ Oita Univ Nat Sci ... Research Bulletin. Faculty of Education. Oita University. Natural Science [*A publication*]

Res Bull Fac Lib Arts Oita Univ ... Research Bulletin. Faculty of Liberal Arts. Oita University [*A publication*]

Res Bull For Res Lab Oreg State Univ ... Research Bulletin. Forest Research Laboratory. Oregon State University [*A publication*]

Res Bull Ga Agric Exp Stn ... Research Bulletin. Georgia Agricultural Experiment Stations [*A publication*]

Res Bull Gangweon Natl Univ ... Research Bulletin. Gangweon National University [*A publication*]

Res Bull Geol Mineral Inst Tokyo Univ Educ ... Research Bulletin. Geological and Mineralogical Institute. Tokyo University of Education [*A publication*]

Res Bull Gifu Imp Coll Agr ... Research Bulletin. Gifu Imperial College of Agriculture [*A publication*]

Res Bull Gifu Imp Coll Agric ... Research Bulletin. Gifu Imperial College of Agriculture [*A publication*]

Res Bull Gov Print Bur ... Research Bulletin. Government Printing Bureau [*Japan*] [*A publication*]

Res Bull Hawaii Agric Exp Stn ... Research Bulletin. Hawaii Agricultural Experiment Station [*A publication*]

Res Bull Hiroshima Inst Technol ... Research Bulletin. Hiroshima Institute of Technology [*A publication*]

Res Bull Hokkaido Nat Agr Exp Sta ... Research Bulletin. Hokkaido National Agricultural Experiment Station [*A publication*]

Res Bull Hokkaido Natl Agric Exp Stn ... Research Bulletin. Hokkaido National Agricultural Experiment Station [*A publication*]

Res Bull Hokkaido Natn Agric Exp Stn ... Research Bulletin. Hokkaido National Agricultural Experiment Station [*A publication*]

Res Bull Idaho Agric Exp Stn ... Research Bulletin. Idaho Agricultural Experiment Station [*A publication*]

Res Bull Iida Women's Jr Coll ... Research Bulletin. Iida Women's Junior College [*A publication*]

Res Bull Indiana Agr Exp Sta ... Research Bulletin. Indiana Agricultural Experiment Station [*A publication*]

Res Bull Int Cent Impr Maize Wheat ... Research Bulletin. International Center for the Improvement of Maize and Wheat [*A publication*]

Res Bull Iowa Agric Exp Stn ... Research Bulletin. Iowa Agricultural Experiment Station [*A publication*]

Res Bull Iowa Agric Home Econ Exp Stn ... Research Bulletin. Iowa Agricultural and Home Economics Experiment Station [*A publication*]

Res Bull Iowa State Univ Sci Technol Agric Home Econ Exp Stn ... Research Bulletin. Iowa State University of Science and Technology. Agriculture and Home Economics Experiment Station [*A publication*]

Res Bull Iowa St Univ Agric Home Econ Exp Stn ... Research Bulletin. Iowa State University Agricultural and Home Economics Experiment Station [*A publication*]

Res Bull Kangweon Natl Univ ... Research Bulletin. Kangweon National University [*Republic of Korea*] [*A publication*]

Res Bull Korean Soc Anim Sci ... Research Bulletin. Korean Society of Animal Science [*A publication*]

Res Bull Marathwada Agric Univ ... Research Bulletin. Marathwada Agricultural University [*A publication*]

Res Bull Mass Agric Exp Stn ... Research Bulletin. Massachusetts Agricultural Experiment Station [*A publication*]

Res Bull Matsumoto Dent Coll Gen Educ ... Research Bulletin. Matsumoto Dental College. General Education [*A publication*]

Res Bull Meguro Parasitol Mus ... Research Bulletin. Meguro Parasitological Museum [*A publication*]

Res Bull Meisei Univ ... Research Bulletin. Meisei University [*A publication*]

Res Bull Meisei Univ Phys Sci Eng ... Research Bulletin. Meisei University. Physical Sciences and Engineering [*A publication*]

Res Bull Missouri Agric Exp Stn ... Research Bulletin. Missouri Agricultural Experiment Station [*A publication*]

Res Bull MO Agric Exp Sta ... Research Bulletin. Missouri Agricultural Experiment Station [*A publication*]

Res Bull Mo Agric Exp Stn ... Research Bulletin. Missouri Agricultural Experiment Station [*A publication*]

Res Bull Nat Hist Parks Site Branch ... Research Bulletin. National Historic Parks and Site Branch [*A publication*]

Res Bull Neb Agric Exp Stn ... Research Bulletin. Nebraska Agricultural Experiment Station [*A publication*]

Res Bull Nebr Agric Exp Stn ... Research Bulletin. Nebraska Agricultural Experiment Station [*A publication*]

Res Bull NJ Zinc Co ... Research Bulletin. New Jersey Zinc Co. [*A publication*]

Res Bull Obihiro Univ Ser I ... Research Bulletin. Obihiro University. Series I [*A publication*]

Res Bull Obihiro Zootech Univ ... Research Bulletin. Obihiro Zootechnical University. Series I [*A publication*]

Res Bull Obihiro Zootech Univ Ser I ... Research Bulletin. Obihiro Zootechnical University. Series I [*A publication*]

Res Bull Ohio Agric Res Dev Center ... Research Bulletin. Ohio Agricultural Research and Development Center [*A publication*]

Res Bull Ohio Agric Res Developm Cent ... Research Bulletin. Ohio Agricultural Research and Development Center [*A publication*]

Res Bull Oita Res Stn Agric Util Hotspring ... Research Bulletin. Oita Research Station for Agricultural Utilization of Hotspring [*A publication*]

Res Bull Ore For Res Lab ... Research Bulletin. Oregon State University. Forest Research Laboratory [*A publication*]

Res Bull Pak CSIR Lab (Rajshahi) ... Research Bulletin. Pakistan Council of Scientific and Industrial Research Laboratories (Rajshahi) [*A publication*]

Res Bull Panjab Univ ... Research Bulletin. Panjab University [*A publication*]

Res Bull Panjab Univ NS ... Research Bulletin. Panjab University. New Series [*A publication*]

Res Bull Panjab Univ Sci ... Research Bulletin. Panjab University. Science [*A publication*]

Res Bull PCSIR Lab ... Research Bulletin. PCSIR [*Pakistan Council of Scientific and Industrial Research*] Laboratories [*A publication*]

Res Bull PCSIR Lab (Rajshahi) ... Research Bulletin. PCSIR [*Pakistan Council of Scientific and Industrial Research*] Laboratories (Rajshahi) [*A publication*]

Res Bull Plant Prot Serv (Jap) ... Research Bulletin. Plant Protection Service (Japan) [*A publication*]

Res Bull Plant Prot Serv (Jpn) ... Research Bulletin. Plant Protection Service (Japan) [*A publication*]

Res Bull PN Bio Farma ... Research Bulletin. PN [*Perusahaan Negara*] Bio Farma [*A publication*]

Res Bull Print Bur Minist Finance ... Research Bulletin. Printing Bureau. Ministry of Finance [*A publication*]

Res Bull Printing Bur (Tokyo) ... Research Bulletin. Printing Bureau. Ministry of Finance (Tokyo) [*A publication*]

Res Bull Purdue Univ Agr Exp Sta ... Research Bulletin. Purdue University. Agricultural Experiment Station [*A publication*]

Res Bull Purdue Univ Agric Exp Stn ... Research Bulletin. Purdue University. Agricultural Experiment Station [*A publication*]

Res Bull Reg Eng Coll (Warangal) ... Research Bulletin. Regional Engineering College (Warangal) [*A publication*]

Res Bull Saitama Agr Exp Sta ... Research Bulletin. Saitama Agricultural Experiment Station [*A publication*]

Res Bull Sugar-Cane Dep Egypt Sugar Distill Co ... Research Bulletin. Sugar-Cane Department. Egyptian Sugar and Distillation Co. [*A publication*]

Res Bull Tokushima Bunri Univ ... Research Bulletin. Tokushima Bunri University [*A publication*]

Res Bull Toyama Prefect Coll Technol ... Research Bulletin. Toyama Prefectural College of Technology [*A publication*]

Res Bull Univ Calcutta ... Research Bulletin. University of Calcutta [*A publication*]

Res Bull Univ Farm Hokkaido Univ ... Research Bulletin. University Farm. Hokkaido University [*A publication*]

Res Bull Univ Ga Coll Agric Exp Stn ... Research Bulletin. University of Georgia. College of Agriculture Experiment Stations [*A publication*]

Res Bull Univ GA Exp Stn ... Research Bulletin. University of Georgia. Experiment Stations [*A publication*]

Res Bull Univ Idaho Agric Exp Stn ... Research Bulletin. University of Idaho. Agricultural Experiment Station [*A publication*]

Res Bull Univ MO Coll Agr Exp Sta ... Research Bulletin. University of Missouri. College of Agriculture. Experiment Station [*A publication*]

Res Bull Univ Nebr Coll Agr Home Econ Agr Exp Sta ... Research Bulletin. University of Nebraska. College of Agriculture and Home Economics. Agricultural Experiment Station [*A publication*]

Res Bull Univ Nebr Lincoln Agric Exp Stn ... Research Bulletin. University of Nebraska-Lincoln. Agricultural Experiment Station [*A publication*]

Res Bull Univ Wis Madison Coll Agric Life Sci Res Div ... Research Bulletin. University of Wisconsin-Madison. College of Agricultural and Life Sciences. Research Division [*A publication*]

Res Bull Univ Wis Madison Res Div Coll Agric Life Sci ... Research Bulletin. University of Wisconsin-Madison. Research Division. College of Agricultural and Life Sciences [*A publication*]

Res Bull West Scotl Agric Coll ... Research Bulletin. West of Scotland Agricultural College [*A publication*]

Res Bull Wis Agr Exp Sta ... Research Bulletin. Wisconsin Agricultural Experiment Station [*A publication*]

Res Bull Wis Agric Exp Stn ... Research Bulletin. Wisconsin Agricultural Experiment Station [*A publication*]

Res Bull W Scotl Coll Agric ... Research Bulletin. West of Scotland College of Agriculture [*A publication*]

RESC .... Regional Educational Service Center

RESC .... Rescind   (AAG)

RESC .... Rescue   (AFM)

RESC .... Resource

RESC .... Roanoke Electric Steel Corp. [*NASDAQ symbol*]   (NQ)

RESCAN ... Reflecting Satellite Communication Antenna

RESCAP .... Rescue Combat Air Patrol [*Army*]

Res Cas ...... Reserved Cases [*Ireland*] [*A publication*]   (DLA)

RESCEN ... Reserve Center [*Navy*]   (DNAB)

Res Cent Ion Beam Technol Hosei Univ Rep Suppl ... Research Center of Ion Beam Technology. Hosei University. Report. Supplement [*A publication*]

Res Chem In ... Research on Chemical Intermediates [*A publication*]

Res Chem Intermed ... Research on Chemical Intermediates [*A publication*]

Res Circ Ohio Agric Exp Stn ... Research Circular. Ohio Agricultural Experiment Station [*A publication*]

Res Circ Ohio Agric Res Dev Cent ... Research Circular. Ohio Agricultural Research and Development Center [*A publication*]

Res Circ Ohio Agr Res Develop Cent ... Research Circular. Ohio Agricultural Research and Development Center [*A publication*]

Res Circ Wash State Univ Agric Res Cent ... Research Circular. Washington State University. Agricultural Research Center [*A publication*]

Res Clin Forums ... Research and Clinical Forums [*A publication*]

Res Clin L ... Research in Clinic and Laboratory [*A publication*]

Res Clin Lab ... Research in Clinic and Laboratory [*A publication*]

Res Clin Stud Headache ... Research and Clinical Studies in Headache [*A publication*]

Res Coat ..... Research for Coatings [*A publication*]

Res Comm C P ... Research Communications in Chemical Pathology and Pharmacology [*A publication*]

RESCOMMIS ... Reserve Command Management Information System   (DNAB)

Res Commun Chem Pathol Pharmacol ... Research Communications in Chemical Pathology and Pharmacology [*A publication*]

Res Commun Inst Ferment (Osaka) ... Research Communications. Institute for Fermentation (Osaka) [*A publication*]

Res Commun Psychol Psychiatry Behav ... Research Communications in Psychology, Psychiatry, and Behavior [*A publication*]

Res Communs Chem Path Pharmac ... Research Communications in Chemical Pathology and Pharmacology [*A publication*]

Res Commun Subst Abuse ... Research Communications in Substances of Abuse [*A publication*]

Res Constructs Peaceful Uses Nucl Energy ... Research Constructs on Peaceful Uses of Nuclear Energy [*Japan*] [*A publication*]

Res Corresp ... Research Correspondence [*A publication*]

Res Counc Alberta Bull ... Research Council of Alberta. Bulletin [*A publication*]

Res Counc Alberta (Can) Inform Ser ... Research Council of Alberta (Canada). Information Series [*A publication*]

Res Counc Alberta Econ Geol Rep ... Research Council of Alberta. Economic Geology Report [*A publication*]

Res Counc Alberta Geol Div Bull ... Research Council of Alberta. Geological Division. Bulletin [*A publication*]

Res Counc Alberta Geol Div Mem ... Research Council of Alberta. Geological Division. Memoir [*A publication*]

Res Counc Alberta Geol Div Rep ... Research Council of Alberta. Geological Division. Report [*A publication*]

Res Counc Alberta Inf Ser ... Research Council of Alberta. Information Series [*A publication*]

Res Counc Alberta Mimeogr Circ ... Research Council of Alberta. Mimeographed Circular [*A publication*]

Res Counc Alberta Mimeogr Ser ... Research Council of Alberta. Mimeographed Series [*A publication*]

Res Counc Alberta Rep ... Research Council of Alberta. Report [*A publication*]

Res Counc Isr Annu Rep ... Research Council of Israel. Annual Report [*A publication*]

RESCRU ... Reserve Cruise [*Navy*]   (NVT)

RESCU ...... Radio Emergency Search Communications Unit

RESCU ...... Rocket-Ejection Seat Catapult Upward [*Aviation*]
RESCUE ... Recovery Employing Storage Chute Used in Emergencies [*Inflatable aircraft wing*]
RESCUE ... Referring Emergency Service for Consumers' Ultimate Enjoyment [*Service plan of Recreational Vehicle Dealers of America*] (EA)
RESCUE ... Remote Emergency Salvage and Clean Up Equipment
Rescue Archaeol Hampshire ... Rescue Archaeology in Hampshire [*A publication*]
R Escuela Def Nac ... Revista. Escuela de Defensa Nacional [*A publication*]
RESCUER ... Rocket Escape System with Cruise Using Electric Rotor (MCD)
RESD......... Reentry Environmental Systems Division [*General Electric Co.*] (MCD)
RESD......... Resigned
RESD......... Resolved (ROG)
RESDAT ... Restricted Data [*Atomic Energy Act of 1954*]
Res Dep Rep Post Off Res Cent (UK) ... Research Department Report. Post Office Research Centre (United Kingdom) [*A publication*]
Res Des ...... Research and Design [*A publication*]
RESDESDIV ... Reserve Destroyer Division (DNAB)
RESDESRON ... Reserve Destroyer Squadron (DNAB)
Res Dev ...... Research/Development [*A publication*]
Res Dev Assoc Mil Food Packag Syst Act Rep ... Research and Development Associates for Military Food and Packaging Systems. Activities Report [*A publication*]
Res Dev Assoc Mil Food Packag Syst Act Rep R & D Assoc ... Research and Development Associates for Military Food and Packaging Systems. Activities Report. R and D Associates [*A publication*]
Res Dev Bull Portland Cem Assoc ... Research and Development Bulletin. Portland Cement Association [*A publication*]
Res/Develop ... Research/Development [*A publication*]
Res Developm Pap For Comm (Lond) ... Research and Development Paper. Forestry Commission (London) [*A publication*]
Res Dev Ind ... Research and Development for Industry [*A publication*]
Res Dev Lab Portland Cem Assoc Res Dep Bull ... Research and Development Laboratories. Portland Cement Association. Research Department Bulletin [*A publication*]
Res Dev Pap For Comm (GB) ... Research and Development Paper. Forestry Commission (Great Britain) [*A publication*]
Res Dev Pap UK For Comm ... Research and Development Paper. United Kingdom Forestry Commission [*A publication*]
Res Dev Rep Br Libr ... Research and Development Reports. British Library [*A publication*]
Res Dev Rep Monsanto Res Corp Mound Lab ... Research and Development Report. Monsanto Research Corp. Mound Laboratory [*A publication*]
Res Dev Rep US Dep Inter Off Coal Res ... Research and Development Report. United States Department of the Interior. Office of Coal Research [*A publication*]
Res Dev Rep US Off Coal Res ... Research and Development Report. United States Office of Coal Research [*A publication*]
Res Dev Rev Mitsubishi Chem ... Research and Development Review. Mitsubishi Chemical [*A publication*]
Res Dev Rev Mitsubishi Kasei Corp ... Research and Development Review. Mitsubishi Kasei Corp. [*A publication*]
Res Dev Tech Rep ECOM US Army Electron Command ... Research and Development Technical Report ECOM. United States Army Electronics Command [*A publication*]
Res Dev Tech Rep US Army Electron Command ... Research and Development Technical Report. United States Army Electronics Command [*A publication*]
Res Discl.... Research Disclosure [*A publication*]
Res Disclosure ... Research Disclosure [*A publication*]
RESDIST .. Reserve District
Res Div Bull Va Polytech Inst State Univ ... Research Division Bulletin. Virginia Polytechnic Institute and State University [*A publication*]
Res Div Rep Va Polytech Inst State Univ ... Research Division Report. Virginia Polytechnic Institute and State University [*A publication*]
Res Drug Actions Interact ... Research on Drug Actions and Interactions [*A publication*]
RESE......... Reseaux [*A publication*]
Research Bul ... Liberal Party of Australia. New South Wales Division. Research Bulletin [*A publication*] (APTA)
Research Council Alberta Bull ... Research Council of Alberta. Bulletin [*A publication*]
Research Council Alberta Rept ... Research Council of Alberta. Report [*A publication*]
Research in Ed ... Research in Education [*A publication*]
Researches Popul Ecol Kyoto Univ ... Researches on Population Ecology. Kyoto University [*A publication*]
Research F ... Research Film [*A publication*]
Research L & Econ ... Research in Law and Economics [*A publication*] (DLA)
Research Mgt ... Research Management [*A publication*]
RESEB ...... Resources in Education [*A publication*]
RESEC ...... Real Estate Securities Income Fund, Inc. [*Associated Press abbreviation*] (APAG)

Res Econ Hist ... Research in Economic History [*A publication*]
Res Educ .... Research in Education [*England*] [*A publication*]
ResEduc ..... Resources in Education [*A publication*]
Res Electrotech Lab ... Researches. Electrotechnical Laboratory [*Japan*] [*A publication*]
Res Electrotech Lab (Tokyo) ... Researches. Electrotechnical Laboratory (Tokyo) [*A publication*]
Res Eng ...... Research Engineer [*A publication*]
Res Eng Jeonbug Natl Univ ... Research of Engineering. Jeonbug National University [*Republic of Korea*] [*A publication*]
Res Eng Res Inst Ind Technol Jeonbug Natl Univ ... Research of Engineering. Research Institute of Industrial Technology. Jeonbug National University [*Republic of Korea*] [*A publication*]
Res Environ Disruption Interdiscip Coop ... Research on Environmental Disruption toward Interdisciplinary Cooperation [*Japan*] [*A publication*]
RESEP....... Reentry System Environmental Protection
Res & Eq J ... Reserved and Equity Judgements [*New South Wales*] [*A publication*] (APTA)
Res & Eq Jud ... Reserved and Equity Judgements [*New South Wales*] [*A publication*]
Res & Eq Judg ... A'Beckett's Reserved Judgements [*New South Wales*] [*A publication*]
Res & Eq Judgm ... Reserved and Equity Judgements [*New South Wales*] [*A publication*]
RESER ...... Reentry Systems Evaluation RADAR [*Aerospace*]
reserva........ Reservation
Reserv Cas ... Reserved Cases [*1860-64*] [*A publication*] (DLA)
Reserve Bank Australia Statis Bul ... Reserve Bank of Australia. Statistical Bulletin [*A publication*]
Reserve Bank India B ... Reserve Bank of India. Bulletin [*A publication*]
Reserve Bank NZ Bul ... Reserve Bank of New Zealand. Bulletin [*A publication*]
RESERVON ... Reservation (ROG)
Res Essent Oils Aust Flora ... Researches on Essential Oils of the Australian Flora [*A publication*]
Res Esst Oils Aust Flora ... Researches on Essential Oils of the Australian Flora [*A publication*]
Res Establ Risoe Rep Risoe-M (Den) ... Research Establishment Risoe. Report. Risoe-M (Denmark) [*A publication*]
Res Establ Risoe Risoe Rep (Den) ... Research Establishment Risoe. Risoe Report (Denmark) [*A publication*]
RESET ...... Regression Specification Error Test [*Statistics*]
Res Exp Econ ... Research in Experimental Economics [*A publication*]
Res Exp Med ... Research in Experimental Medicine [*A publication*]
Res Exp Med (Berlin) ... Research in Experimental Medicine (Berlin) [*A publication*]
Res Exp Rec Minist Agric North Irel ... Research and Experimental Record. Ministry of Agriculture. Northern Ireland [*A publication*]
Res Exp Rec Minist Agric (Nth Ire) ... Research and Experimental Record. Ministry of Agriculture (Northern Ireland) [*A publication*]
Res Ext Ser Hawaii Inst Trop Agric Hum Resour ... Research Extension Series. Hawaii Institute of Tropical Agriculture and Human Resources [*A publication*]
RESF .... Research and Engineering Support Facility (MCD)
RESFAC.... Reserve Facility (DNAB)
Res & Farm ... Research and Farming [*North Carolina Agricultural Experiment Station*] [*A publication*]
Res Farmers ... Research for Farmers [*A publication*]
Res Farming ... Research and Farming [*North Carolina Agricultural Experiment Station*] [*A publication*]
Res Farming (NC Agric Exp Stn) ... Research and Farming (North Carolina Agricultural Experiment Station) [*A publication*]
Res Farming NC Agric Res Serv ... Research and Farming. North Carolina Agricultural Research Service [*A publication*]
Res Film..... Research Film [*A publication*]
Res Fish Annu Rep Coll Fish Univ Wash ... Research in Fisheries. Annual Report. College of Fisheries. University of Washington [*A publication*]
Res Fish Annu Rep Sch Fish Univ Wash ... Research in Fisheries. Annual Report. School of Fisheries. University of Washington [*A publication*]
Res Fish (Seattle) ... Research in Fisheries (Seattle) [*A publication*]
RESFLD.... Residual Field (AAG)
RESFLY.... Respectfully (ROG)
Res Food Sci ... Research in Food Science [*A publication*]
Res Food Sci Nutr ... Research in Food Science and Nutrition [*A publication*]
RESFOR ... AUTODIN CRT for Secure Reserve Force (MCD)
RESFORON ... Reserve Force Squadron (DNAB)
Res Front Fertil Regul ... Research Frontiers in Fertility Regulation [*A publication*]
Res Future Res Pap ... Resources for the Future Research Paper [*A publication*]
Res Futures ... Research Futures [*A publication*]
RESFV....... Renaissance Editions. San Fernando Valley State College [*A publication*]
RESG......... Research Engineering Standing Group [*DoD*]
Res Gamma Eta Gamma ... Rescript of Gamma Eta Gamma [*A publication*] (DLA)
RESGD...... Resigned
RESGND... Resigned

RESHAPE ... Resource Self-Help/Affordability Planning Effort [*Program*] [*Federal government*] (RDA)
Res Health Econ ... Research in Health Economics [*A publication*]
Res High Educ Abstr ... Research into Higher Education. Abstracts [*A publication*]
Res Higher Educ ... Research in Higher Education [*A publication*]
RESHUS... Reseau Documentaire en Sciences Humaines de la Sante [*Network for Documentation in the Human Sciences of Health*] [*Institut de l'Information Scientifique et Technique*] [*Information service or system*] (IID)
RES I .... Research EMP [*Electromagnetic Pulse*] Simulator I [*Air Force*]
RESIC .... Redstone Scientific Information Center [*Army*]
RES/IC...... Reserve - In Commission [*Vessel status*]
resid .... Residency
RESID ...... Residual (AAG)
Resid Group Care & Treat ... Residential Group Care and Treatment [*A publication*]
Resid Staff Physician ... Resident and Staff Physician [*A publication*]
Residual Gases Electron Tubes Proc Int Conf ... Residual Gases in Electron Tubes. Proceedings. International Conference [*A publication*]
Residuals Trace Elem Iron Steel Int Conf ... Residuals and Trace Elements in Iron and Steel. International Conference [*A publication*]
Residue Rev ... Residue Reviews [*A publication*]
RESIG .... Resignation (AFM)
RESIL .... Resilient
Res Immunochem Immunobiol ... Research in Immunochemistry and Immunobiology [*A publication*]
Res Immunol ... Research in Immunology [*A publication*]
RESIN .... Resina [*Resin*] [*Pharmacy*] (ROG)
Res Ind....... Research and Industry [*A publication*]
Res Indicat Petrol ... Resumos Indicativos do Petroleo [*A publication*]
Res Ind (New Delhi) ... Research and Industry (New Delhi) [*A publication*]
Res Indus... Research and Industry [*A publication*]
Resin Rev... Resin Review [*A publication*]
Resin Rev (Philadelphia) ... Resin Review (Philadelphia) [*A publication*]
Resin Rev (Richmond Engl) ... Resin Review (Richmond, England) [*A publication*]
Res Inst Appl Electr Hokkaido Univ Monogr Ser ... Research Institute of Appled Electricity. Hokkaido University. Monograph Series [*A publication*]
Res Inst Appl Mech Kyushu Univ Report ... Research Institute for Applied Mechanics. Kyushu University. Reports [*A publication*]
Res Inst Fund Information Sci Res Rep ... Research Institute of Fundamental Information Science. Research Report [*A publication*]
Res Inst Fund Inform Sci Res Rep ... Kyushu University. Research Institute of Fundamental Information Science. Research Report [*A publication*]
Res Inst Ind Technol Chungnam Natl Univ Rep ... Research Institute of Industrial Technology. Chungnam National University. Report [*A publication*]
Res Inst Nedri As (Hveragerdi Icel) Rep ... Research Institute Nedri As (Hveragerdi, Iceland). Report [*A publication*]
Res Inst Phys Annu Rep (Swed) ... Research Institute of Physics. Annual Report (Sweden) [*A publication*]
Res Inst Sumatra Plant Assoc Bull ... Research Institute. Sumatra Planters Association. Bulletin [*A publication*]
Res Inst Sumatra Plant Assoc Commun Rubber Ser ... Research Institute. Sumatra Planters Association. Communications. Rubber Series [*A publication*]
Res Int........ Residential Interiors [*A publication*]
Res Intell News ... Research and Intelligence News [*A publication*]
Res & Invt .. Research and Invention [*A publication*]
Res Ipsa ..... Res Ipsa Loquitur [*The Thing Speaks for Itself*] [*Latin*] (DLA)
RES/IS ...... Reserve - In Service [*Vessel status*]
RESIS....... Resistance
RESIST ..... Replace Essential Supplies in Sufficient Time [*Navy*] (NVT)
RESIST ..... Resistant
RESIST ..... Reusable Surface Insulation Stresses [*NASA computer program*]
Resistencia (Ser Econ e Gestao) ... Resistencia (Serie de Economia e Gestao) [*A publication*]
RESJA....... RES. Journal of the Reticuloendothelial Society [*A publication*]
Res J Agric Anim Sci (Karnal India) ... Research Journal of Agriculture and Animal Sciences (Karnal, India) [*A publication*]
Res J Dir Gen Higher Educ Indones ... Research Journal. Directorate General of Higher Education. Indonesia [*A publication*]
Res J Dir Higher Educ (Indones) ... Research Journal. Directorate of Higher Education (Indonesia) [*A publication*]
Res J Fac Agric Andalas Univ ... Research Journal. Faculty of Agriculture. Andalas University [*A publication*]
Res J Fac Sci Kashmir Univ ... Research Journal. Faculty of Science. Kashmir University [*A publication*]
Res J Hindi Sci Acad ... Research Journal. Hindi Science Academy [*A publication*]
Res J Kanpur Agr Coll ... Research Journal. Kanpur Agricultural College [*A publication*]
Res J Living Sci ... Research Journal of Living Science [*A publication*]
Res J Mahatma Phule Agric Univ ... Research Journal. Mahatma Phule Agricultural University [*A publication*]

Res J Philo Soc Sci ... Research Journal of Philosophy and Social Sciences [*Meerut Cantt, India*] [*A publication*]
Res J Phys Educ ... Research Journal of Physical Education [*A publication*]
RES J Reticuloendothel Soc ... RES. Journal of the Reticuloendothelial Society [*A publication*]
Res J Sci .... Research Journal of Sciences [*A publication*]
Res J Sci Univ Indore ... Research Journal: Science. University of Indore [*A publication*]
Res Jud ...... Res Judicatae [*A publication*] (APTA)
Res Judic ... Res Judicatae [*A publication*] (DLA)
Res J Univ Wyo Agric Exp Stn ... Research Journal. University of Wyoming. Agricultural Experiment Station [*A publication*]
Res J Water ... Research Journal. Water Pollution Control Federation [*A publication*]
Res J Water Pollut Control Fed ... Research Journal. Water Pollution Control Federation [*A publication*]
Res J West Mindanao State Univ Univ Res Cent ... Research Journal. Western Mindanao State University. University Research Center [*A publication*]
RESL .... Radiological and Environmental Sciences Laboratory [*Nuclear energy*] (NRCH)
RESLAB.... Research Laboratory
Res Lab Commun Sci Univ Electro-Commun Annu Rep ... Research Laboratory of Communication Science. University of Electro-Communications. Annual Report [*A publication*]
Res Lab Eng Mater Tokyo Inst Technol Rep ... Research Laboratory of Engineering Materials. Tokyo Institute of Technology. Report [*A publication*]
Res Lab Gen Mot Corp Res Publ ... Research Laboratories. General Motors Corporation. Research Publication [*A publication*]
Res Lab Portland Cem Assoc Bull ... Research Laboratories. Portland Cement Association. Bulletin [*A publication*]
Res Lab Precis Mach Electron ... Research Laboratory Precision Machinery and Electronics [*A publication*]
Res Lab Rec ... Research Laboratory Record [*A publication*]
Res L Deviance and Soc Control ... Research in Law, Deviance, and Social Control [*A publication*]
Res Leafl For Res Inst NZ For Serv ... Research Leaflet. Forest Research Institute. New Zealand Forest Service [*A publication*]
Res Leafl Oreg For Prod Lab ... Research Leaflet. Oregon Forest Products Laboratory [*A publication*]
Res Leafl Sav For Res Sta ... Research Leaflet. Savanna Forestry Research Station [*A publication*]
Res L & Econ ... Research in Law and Economics [*A publication*]
Res Lett Atmos Electr ... Research Letters on Atmospheric Electricity [*A publication*]
Res Libnship ... Research in Librarianship [*A publication*]
Res Librarianship ... Research in Librarianship [*A publication*]
Res Life Sci ... Research in Life Sciences [*A publication*]
Res Life Sci Maine Life Sci Agric Exp Stn ... Research in the Life Sciences. Maine Life Sciences and Agriculture Experiment Station [*A publication*]
Res Lit........ Respublica Literaria [*A publication*]
Res L and Soc ... Research in Law and Sociology [*A publication*]
RESLV ...... Resolve (KSC)
RESM........ Restaurant Management Services, Inc. [*Macon, GA*] [*NASDAQ symbol*] (NQ)
RESMA ..... Railway Electric Supply Manufacturers Association [*Later, RSA*]
RESMA ..... Research Management [*A publication*]
Res Manag ... Research Management [*A publication*]
Res Management ... Research Management [*A publication*]
Res McGill ... Research McGill [*A publication*]
Res Mech... Res Mechanica [*A publication*]
Res Mech Lett ... Res Mechanica Letters [*A publication*]
Res Memo Int Inst Appl Syst Anal ... Research Memorandum. International Institute for Applied Systems Analysis [*A publication*]
Res Memor Int Inst Appl Syst Anal ... Research Memorandum. International Institute for Applied Systems Analysis [*A publication*]
Res Meth Neurochem ... Research Methods in Neurochemistry [*A publication*]
Res Methods Neurochem ... Research Methods in Neurochemistry [*A publication*]
Res Mgt ..... Research Management [*A publication*]
Res Microb ... Research in Microbiology [*A publication*]
Res Microbiol ... Research in Microbiology [*A publication*]
RESMILCON ... Reserve Military Construction (DNAB)
Res Mol Biol ... Research in Molecular Biology [*A publication*]
Res Monogr Cell Tissue Physiol ... Research Monographs in Cell and Tissue Physiology [*A publication*]
Res Monogr Immunol ... Research Monographs in Immunology [*A publication*]
Res Monogr Natl Inst Alcohol Abuse Alcohol ... Research Monograph. National Institute on Alcohol Abuse and Alcoholism [*A publication*]
Res Monogr Ser Natl Inst Drug Abuse (US) ... Research Monograph Series. National Institute on Drug Abuse (United States) [*A publication*]
Res Monogr Tex A & M Univ Tex Agric Exp Stn ... Research Monograph. Texas A and M University. Texas Agricultural Experiment Station [*A publication*]

RESN......... Resonant
RESNA...... RESNA [*Rehabilitation Engineering Society of North America*]: Association for the Advancement of Rehabilitation Technology [*Association retains acronym from former name*] (EA)
Res Natl Mus (Bloemfontein) ... Researches. National Museum (Bloemfontein) [*A publication*]
RESND...... Resources and Energy [*A publication*]
Res News Off Res Adm Univ Mich (Ann Arbor) ... Research News. Office of Research Administration. University of Michigan (Ann Arbor) [*A publication*]
Res Norw Agric ... Research in Norwegian Agriculture [*A publication*]
Res Note BC For Serv ... Research Notes. British Columbia Forest Service [*A publication*]
Res Note Bur For (Philippines) ... Research Note. Bureau of Forestry (Philippines) [*A publication*]
Res Note Colo Coll For Nat Resour ... Research Note. Colorado State University. College of Forestry and Natural Resources [*A publication*]
Res Note Div For Res (Zambia) ... Research Note. Division of Forest Research (Zambia) [*A publication*]
Res Note Fac For Univ BC ... Research Note. Faculty of Forestry. University of British Columbia [*A publication*]
Res Note For Comm NSW ... Research Note. Forestry Commission of New South Wales [*A publication*]
Res Note For Mgmt Res Ore For Res Lab ... Research Note. Forest Management Research. Oregon State University. Forest Research Laboratory [*A publication*]
Res Note FPL For Prod Lab ... Research Note FPL. Forest Products Laboratory [*United States*] [*A publication*]
Res Note NB Res Prod Counc ... Research Note. New Brunswick Research and Productivity Council [*A publication*]
Res Note N Cent Forest Exp Stn US Dep Agric ... Research Note. North Central Forest Experiment Station. US Department of Agriculture [*A publication*]
Res Note NC US For Serv ... Research Note NC. US Forest Service [*A publication*]
Res Note NE US Dep Agric For Serv ... Research Note NE. US Department of Agriculture. Forest Service [*A publication*]
Res Note Oreg State Univ Sch For For Res Lab ... Research Notes. Oregon State University. School of Forestry. Forest Research Laboratory [*A publication*]
Res Note Pacif SW For Exp Stn ... Research Note. Pacific Southwest Forest and Range Experiment Station. US Department of Agriculture [*A publication*]
Res Note Prov BC Minist For ... Research Note. Province of British Columbia. Ministry of Forests [*A publication*]
Res Note Qd For Serv ... Research Notes. Queensland Forest Service [*A publication*]
Res Note Res Prod Counc (NB) ... Research Note. Research and Productivity Council (New Brunswick) [*A publication*]
Res Notes in Math ... Research Notes in Mathematics [*A publication*]
Res Notes Memoranda Appl Geom Post-RAAG ... Research Notes and Memoranda of Applied Geometry in Post-RAAG [*Research Association of Applied Geometry*] [*A publication*]
Res Notes NSW For Comm ... New South Wales. Forestry Commission. Research Notes [*A publication*] (APTA)
Res Notes Qd Dep For ... Research Notes. Queensland Department of Forestry [*A publication*] (APTA)
Res Note Tex For Serv ... Research Note. Texas Forest Service [*A publication*]
Res Note UBC For Club ... Research Notes. University of British Columbia. Forest Club [*A publication*]
Res Note Univ Tex Austin Bur Econ Geol ... Research Note. University of Texas at Austin. Bureau of Economic Geology [*A publication*]
Res Not Ford For Cent ... Research Note. Ford Forestry Center [*A publication*]
RESNS...... Review of English Studies. New Series [*A publication*]
Res Nurs Health ... Research in Nursing and Health [*A publication*]
Res Nurs Hlth ... Research in Nursing and Health [*A publication*]
RESO......... Regional Environmental Support Office (DNAB)
RESO......... Resoluta [*Music*] (ROG)
RESO......... Resources Bulletin. Man and Resources Conference Program [*A publication*]
RESOC...... Research Sonobuoy Configuration (NG)
RES/OC.... Reserve - Out of Commission [*Vessel status*]
Resoconti Assoc Min Sarda ... Resoconti. Associazione Mineraria Sarda [*A publication*]
RESOJET ... Resonant Pulse Jet
RESOLN... Resolution (MSA)
RESORS ... Remote Sensing On-Line Retrieval System [*Canada Centre for Remote Sensing*] [*Department of Energy, Mines, and Resources*] [*Database*] [*Information service or system*] (IID)
RES/OS..... Reserve - Out of Service [*Vessel status*]
Resour Am L ... Resources for American Literary Study [*A publication*]
Resour Atlas Univ Nebr Lincoln Conserv Surv Div ... Resource Atlas. University of Nebraska-Lincoln. Conservation and Survey Divsion [*A publication*]

Resour Biomed Res Educ ... Resources for Biomedical Research and Education [*A publication*]
Resour Biosphere (USSR) ... Resources of the Biosphere (USSR) [*A publication*]
Resour Book Publ ... Resources for Book Publishers [*United States*] [*A publication*]
Resources Conserv ... Resources and Conservation [*Netherlands*] [*A publication*]
Resources Pol ... Resources Policy [*A publication*]
Resour Conserv ... Resources and Conservation [*A publication*]
Resour Conserv Recycl ... Resources, Conservation, and Recycling [*A publication*]
Resour Educ ... Resources in Education [*A publication*]
Resour Energy ... Resources and Energy [*Netherlands*] [*A publication*]
Resour Ind ... Resources Industry [*A publication*]
Resour Manage Optim ... Resource Management and Optimization [*United States*] [*A publication*]
Resour Manage and Optimiz ... Resource Management and Optimization [*A publication*]
Resour Manage Optimization ... Resource Management and Optimization [*A publication*]
Resour Policy ... Resources Policy [*A publication*]
Resour Recovery Conserv ... Resource Recovery and Conservation [*Netherlands*] [*A publication*]
Resour Recovery Energy Rev ... Resource Recovery and Energy Review [*A publication*]
Resour Rep Coop Ext Univ Wis ... Resource Report. Cooperative Extension. University of Wisconsin [*A publication*]
Resour Sharing and Libr Networks ... Resource Sharing and Library Networks [*A publication*]
Res Outlook ... Research Outlook [*A publication*]
Resp .... De Respiratione [*of Aristotle*] [*Classical studies*] (OCD)
RESP .... Registered Education Savings Plan [*Canada*]
RESP .... Regulated Electrical Supply Package
ResP........... Research and Progress [*A publication*]
ResP........... Research Publications, Inc., New Haven, CT [*Library symbol*] [*Library of Congress*] (LCLS)
RESP .... Respectively
RESP .... Respiration (KSC)
RESP .... Respirator
RESP .... Respironics, Inc. [*NASDAQ symbol*] (NQ)
RESP .... Respondent
RESP .... Response (AAG)
RESP .... Responsible (AFM)
Resp .... Republica [*of Plato*] [*Classical studies*] (OCD)
RESPA ...... Real Estate Settlement Procedures Act of 1974
Res Pam (Div For Res Zambia) ... Research Pamphlet (Division of Forest Research, Zambia) [*A publication*]
Res Pam For Res Inst (Kepong) ... Research Pamphlet. Forest Research Institute (Kepong) [*A publication*]
Res Pamphl For Res Inst (Malaya) ... Research Pamphlet. Forest Research Institute (Malaya) [*A publication*]
Res Pap Dep For (Qd) ... Research Paper. Department of Forestry (Queensland) [*A publication*] (APTA)
Res Pap Dep For (Queensl) ... Research Paper. Department of Forestry (Queensland) [*A publication*] (APTA)
Res Paper Horace Lamb Centre Oceanogr Res ... Research Paper. Horace Lamb Centre for Oceanographical Research. Flinders University [*South Australia*] [*A publication*] (APTA)
Res Pap Fac For Univ BC ... Research Paper. Faculty of Forestry. University of British Columbia [*A publication*]
Res Pap For Dep (West Aust) ... Research Paper. Forests Department (Western Australia) [*A publication*] (APTA)
Res Pap Forests Dep (West Aust) ... Research Paper. Forests Department (Western Australia) [*A publication*] (APTA)
Res Pap (Forest Ser) Fed Dep Forest Res (Niger) ... Research Paper (Forest Series). Federal Department of Forest Research (Nigeria) [*A publication*]
Res Pap For Res Lab Oreg State Univ ... Research Paper. Forest Research Laboratory. Oregon State University [*A publication*]
Res Pap FPL For Prod Lab (US) ... Research Paper FPL. Forest Products Laboratory (US) [*A publication*]
Res Pap GA For Res Coun ... Research Paper. Georgia Forest Research Council [*A publication*]
Res Pap Geogr Univ Newcastle ... Research Papers in Geography. University of Newcastle [*A publication*] (APTA)
Res Pap Helsinki Univ Technol ... Research Papers. Helsinki University of Technology [*A publication*]
Res Pap Horace Lamb Centre Oceanogrl Res ... Research Paper. Horace Lamb Centre for Oceanographical Research. Flinders University [*South Australia*] [*A publication*] (APTA)
Res Pap Natl Build Stud ... Research Paper. National Building Studies [*A publication*]
Res Pap Ore For Res Lab ... Research Paper. Oregon State University. Forest Research Laboratory [*A publication*]
Res Pap Oreg State Univ For Res Lab ... Research Paper. Oregon State University. Forest Research Lab [*A publication*]
Res Pap Phys Educ ... Research Papers in Physical Education [*A publication*]
Res Pap PNW (Pac Northwest For Range Exp Stn) ... Research Paper PNW (Pacific Northwest Forest and Range Experiment Station) [*A publication*]

Res Pap PNW US For Serv ... Research Paper PNW [*Pacific Northwest Forest and Range Experiment Station*] . US Forest Service [*A publication*]

Res Pap Resour Future ... Research Paper. Resources for the Future [*A publication*]

Res Pap Sav For Res Sta ... Research Paper. Savanna Forestry Research Station [*A publication*]

Res Pap Sch For Resour PA St Univ ... Research Paper. School of Forest Resources. Pennsylvania State University [*A publication*]

Res Pap Ser Int Rice Res Inst ... Research Paper Series. International Rice Research Institute [*A publication*]

Res Pap Tob Res Counc ... Research Paper. Tobacco Research Council [*A publication*]

Res Pap US Forest Serv Lake St Forest Exp Stn ... Research Paper. United States Forest Service. Lake States Forest Experiment Station [*A publication*]

Res Pap (West Aust) For Dep ... Research Paper (Western Australia). Forests Department [*A publication*]

Resp C........ Respiratory Care [*A publication*]

Resp Care... Respiratory Care [*A publication*]

Res Phenomenol ... Research in Phenomenology [*A publication*]

Res Photobiol Proc Int Congr ... Research in Photobiology. Proceedings. International Congress on Photobiology [*A publication*]

Respiration Suppl ... Respiration. Supplement [*Switzerland*] [*A publication*]

Respir Care ... Respiratory Care [*A publication*]

Respir Circ ... Respiration and Circulation [*A publication*]

Respir Med ... Respiratory Medicine [*A publication*]

Respir Physiol ... Respiration Physiology [*A publication*]

Respir Res ... Respiration Research [*A publication*]

Respir Technol ... Respiratory Technology [*A publication*]

Respir Ther ... Respiratory Therapy [*A publication*]

RESPLY .... Respectively

Resp Med... Respiratory Medicine [*A publication*]

RESPO ...... Responsible Property Officer [*Army*] (AABC)

Res Pol....... Research Policy [*A publication*]

RESPOND ... Respondere [*To Answer*] [*Pharmacy*] (ROG)

RESPONSA ... Retrieval of Special Portions from Nuclear Science Abstracts (DIT)

Res Popul Ecol ... Researches on Population Ecology [*A publication*]

Res Popul Ecol (Kyoto) ... Researches on Population Ecology (Kyoto) [*A publication*]

Resp Physl ... Respiration Physiology [*A publication*]

Res Pract Forensic Med ... Research and Practice in Forensic Medicine [*A publication*]

Res Preview ... Research Previews [*A publication*]

Res Prog Lithogr Tech Found ... Research Progress. Lithographic Technical Foundation [*A publication*]

Res Prog Org-Biol Med Chem ... Research Progress in Organic-Biological and Medicinal Chemistry [*A publication*]

Res Program Rep Wash State Highw Dep ... Research Program Report. Washington State Highway Department [*A publication*]

Res Prog Rep Purdue Univ Agric Exp Stn ... Research Progress Report. Purdue University. Agricultural Experiment Station [*Indiana*] [*A publication*]

Res Prog Rep Tokai-Kinki Natn Agric Exp Stn ... Research Progress Report. Tokai-Kinki National Agricultural Experiment Station [*A publication*]

Res Prog Rep UK At Energy Res Establ Health Phys Med Div ... Research Progress Report. United Kingdom Atomic Energy Research Establishment. Health Physics and Medical Division [*A publication*]

Res Progr Rep Indiana Agr Exp Sta ... Research Progress Report. Indiana Agricultural Experiment Station [*A publication*]

Res Progr Rep Purdue Agric Exp Sta ... Research Progress Report. Purdue University. Agricultural Experiment Station [*Indiana*] [*A publication*]

Res Progr Rep Purdue Univ Agr Exp Sta ... Research Progress Report. Purdue University. Agricultural Experiment Station [*Indiana*] [*A publication*]

Res Progr Rep Tokai-Kinki Nat Agr Exp Sta ... Research Progress Report. Tokai-Kinki National Agricultural Experiment Station [*A publication*]

Res Progr Rep West Weed Control Conf ... Research Progress Report. Western Weed Control Conference [*A publication*]

Res Proj Ser Victoria Dep Agric ... Victoria. Department of Agriculture. Research Project Series [*A publication*] (APTA)

Res Prostaglandins ... Research in Prostaglandins [*A publication*]

RESPT....... Respondent

Resp Technol ... Respiratory Technology [*A publication*]

Resp Ther .. Respiratory Therapy [*A publication*]

Res Pub...... Res Publica [*A publication*] (ILCA)

Res Publ..... Res Publica [*A publication*]

Res Publ Assoc Res Nerv Ment Dis ... Research Publications Association for Research in Nervous and Mental Disease [*A publication*]

Res Publ Gen Mot Corp Res Lab ... Research Publication. General Motors Corporation. Research Laboratories [*A publication*]

Res Publ Kan Agric Exp Stn ... Research Publication. Kansas Agricultural Experiment Station [*A publication*]

RESPY ...... Respectfully (ROG)

Res Q .... Research Quarterly [*A publication*]

Res Q (AAHPER) ... Research Quarterly. American Association for Health, Physical Education, and Recreation [*A publication*]

Res Q Am Alliance Health Phys Educ Recreat ... Research Quarterly. American Alliance for Health, Physical Education, and Recreation [*A publication*]

Res Q Am Assoc Health Phys Educ Recreat ... Research Quarterly. American Association for Health, Physical Education, and Recreation [*A publication*]

Res Q Am Assoc Health Phys Educ Recreation ... Research Quarterly. American Association for Health, Physical Education, and Recreation [*A publication*]

Res Q Exercise Sport ... Research Quarterly for Exercise and Sport [*A publication*]

Res Q Exerc Sport ... Research Quarterly for Exercise and Sport [*A publication*]

Res Q Ont Hydro ... Research Quarterly. Ontario Hydro [*A publication*]

Res Quart... Research Quarterly [*A publication*]

ReSR......... Recherches de Science Religieuse [*A publication*]

RESR .... Research, Inc. [*NASDAQ symbol*] (NQ)

Res R .... Research in Review [*A publication*]

RESR .... Resources (AABC)

RESRC ...... Resources

Resrce Recv ... Resource Recovery Update [*A publication*]

RESRCL.... Resource Recycling Technologies, Inc. [*Associated Press abbreviation*] (APAG)

Res Rec Malawi For Res Inst ... Research Record. Malawi Forest Research Institute [*A publication*]

Res Relat Child ... Research Relating to Children [*A publication*]

RESREP.... Resident Representative (MUGU)

Res Rep Agric Exp Stn Mich St Univ ... Research Report. Agricultural Experiment Station. Michigan State University [*A publication*]

Res Rep Agric Exp Stn Univ Wisc ... Research Report. Agricultural Experiment Station. University of Wisconsin [*A publication*]

Res Rep Agric Exp Stn Utah St Univ ... Research Report. Agricultural Experiment Station. Utah State University [*A publication*]

Res Rep Akita Tech Coll ... Research Reports. Akita Technical College [*A publication*]

Res Rep Anan Tech College ... Research Reports. Anan Technical College [*A publication*]

Res Rep Autom Control Lab Fac Eng Nagoya Univ ... Research Reports. Automatic Control Laboratory. Faculty of Engineering. Nagoya University [*A publication*]

Res Rep Biotech Fac Univ Edvard Kardelj (Ljublj) Vet Issue ... Research Reports. Biotechnical Faculty. University of Edvard Kardelj (Ljubljana). Veterinary Issue [*A publication*]

Res Rep Biotech Fac Univ Ljublj Agric Issue ... Research Reports. Biotechnical Faculty. University of Ljubljana. Agricultural Issue [*A publication*]

Res Rep Can Dept Agr Nat Weed Comm West Sect ... Research Report. Canada Department of Agriculture. National Weed Committee. Western Section [*A publication*]

Res Rep Cent Highw Res Univ Tex Austin ... Research Report. Center for Highway Research. University of Texas at Austin [*A publication*]

Res Rep Coll Agric Korea Univ ... Research Reports. College of Agriculture. Korea University [*A publication*]

Res Rep Coll Agric Univ Wis ... Research Report. Experiment Station. College of Agriculture. University of Wisconsin [*A publication*]

Res Rep Coll Agric Vet Med Nihon Univ ... Research Reports. College of Agriculture and Veterinary Medicine. Nihon University [*Japan*] [*A publication*]

Res Rep Coll Eng Busan Natl Univ ... Research Report. College of Engineering. Busan National University [*A publication*]

Res Rep Conn Storrs Agric Res Stn ... Research Report. Connecticut. Storrs Agricultural Research Station [*A publication*]

Res Rep DAE LA St Univ Agric Exp Stn ... Research Report. Department of Agricultural Economics and Agri-Business. Louisiana State University and Agricultural Experiment Station [*A publication*]

Res Rep Dep Crop Sci NC State Univ ... Research Report. Department of Crop Science. North Carolina State University. Agricultural Experiment Station [*A publication*]

Res Rep Dep Electl Engng Melb Univ ... Research Report. Department of Electrical Engineering. University of Melbourne [*A publication*] (APTA)

Res Rep Dep Electr Eng Melb Univ ... Research Report. Department of Electrical Engineering. University of Melbourne [*A publication*] (APTA)

Res Rep Div Appl Org Chem CSIRO ... Research Report. Division of Applied Organic Chemistry. Commonwealth Scientific and Industrial Research Organisation [*A publication*] (APTA)

Res Rep East Sect Nat Weed Comm Can ... Research Report. Eastern Section. National Weed Committee of Canada [*A publication*]

Res Rep Electron Gen Res Inst ... Research Report. Electronics General Research Institute [*Japan*] [*A publication*]

Res Rep Fac Biotech Univ Ljublj Vet Issue ... Research Reports. Faculty of Biotechnics. University of Ljubljana. Veterinary Issue [*A publication*]

Res Rep Fac Eng Kagoshima Univ ... Research Reports. Faculty of Engineering. Kagoshima University [*Japan*] [*A publication*]

Res Rep Fac Eng Meiji Univ ... Research Reports. Faculty of Engineering. Meiji University [*A publication*]

Res Rep Fac Eng Nagoya Univ ... Research Reports. Faculty of Engineering. Nagoya University [*A publication*]

Res Rep Fac Eng Niigata Univ ... Research Report. Faculty of Engineering. Niigata University [*A publication*]

Res Rep Fac Engrg Tokyo Denki Univ ... Research Reports. Faculty of Engineering. Tokyo Denki University [*A publication*]

Res Rep Fac Eng Tokyo Denki Univ ... Research Reports. Faculty of Engineering. Tokyo Denki University [*A publication*]

Res Rep Fac Eng Toyo Univ ... Research Reports. Faculty of Engineering. Toyo University [*A publication*]

Res Rep Fac Sci and Technol Meijyo Univ ... Research Reports. Faculty of Science and Technology. Meijyo University [*A publication*]

Res Rep Fac Text Seric Shinshu Univ ... Research Reports. Faculty of Textiles and Sericulture. Shinshu University [*A publication*]

Res Rep Fish Comm Oreg ... Research Reports. Fish Commission of Oregon [*A publication*]

Res Rep Fish Wildl Serv (US) ... Research Report. Fish and Wildlife Service (United States) [*A publication*]

Res Rep Fla Agric Exp Stn ... Research Report. Florida Agricultural Experiment Station [*A publication*]

Res Rep Fla Sch For ... Research Report. University of Florida. School of Forestry [*A publication*]

Res Rep Flinders Inst Atmos Mar Sci ... Research Report. Flinders Institute of Atmospheric and Marine Sciences. Flinders University [*A publication*] (APTA)

Res Rep Food Ind Res Dev Inst (Taiwan) ... Research Report. Food Industry Research and Development Institute (Taiwan) [*A publication*]

Res Rep For Prod Util Lab Miss St Univ ... Research Report. Forest Products Utilization Laboratory. Mississippi State University [*A publication*]

Res Rep For Res Inst ... Research Reports. Forest Research Institute [*A publication*]

Res Rep Fukui Tech Coll Nat Sci Eng ... Research Reports. Fukui Technical College. Natural Science and Engineering [*Japan*] [*A publication*]

Res Rep Fukuoka Agr Exp Sta ... Research Report. Fukuoka Agricultural Experiment Station [*A publication*]

Res Rep Fukuoka Agric Exp Stn ... Research Report. Fukuoka Agricultural Experiment Station [*A publication*]

Res Rep GA Agr Exp Sta ... Research Report. Georgia Agricultural Experiment Station [*A publication*]

Res Rep Hanyang Res Inst Ind Sci ... Research Reports. Hanyang Research Institute of Industrial Sciences [*A publication*]

Res Rep Hawaii Agric Exp Stn ... Research Report. Hawaii Agricultural Experiment Station [*A publication*]

Res Rep Helsinki Univ Technol Lab Phys ... Research Report. Helsinki University of Technology. Laboratory of Physics [*A publication*]

Res Rep Hokkaido Natl Agric Exp Stn ... Research Report. Hokkaido National Agricultural Experiment Station [*A publication*]

Res Rep Hunter Valley Res Fdn ... Research Report. Hunter Valley Research Foundation [*A publication*] (APTA)

Res Rep Hunter Valley Res Found ... Research Report. Hunter Valley Research Foundation [*A publication*] (APTA)

Res Rep Inst For Genet ... Research Report. Institute of Forest Genetics [*A publication*]

Res Rep Inst For Genet (Korea) ... Research Report. Institute of Forest Genetics (Suwon, Korea) [*A publication*]

Res Rep Inst For Genet (Suwon) Imop Sihomjang ... Research Report. Institute of Forest Genetics (Suwon). Imop Sihomjang [*A publication*]

Res Rep Inst Industr Res (Nigeria) ... Research Report. Federal Institute of Industrial Research (Lagos, Nigeria) [*A publication*]

Res Rep Inst Inform Sci Tech Tokyo Denki Univ ... Tokyo Denki University. Institute of Information Science and Technology. Research Reports [*A publication*]

Res Rep Inst Inf Sci and Technol Tokyo Denki Univ ... Research Reports. Institute of Information Science and Technology. Tokyo Denki University [*A publication*]

Res Rep Inst Plasma Phys Nagoya Univ ... Research Report. Institute of Plasma Physics. Nagoya University [*A publication*]

Res Rep Int Food Policy Res Inst ... Research Report. International Food Policy Research Institute [*A publication*]

Res Rep IPPCZ Czech Acad Sci Inst Plasma Phys ... Research Report IPPCZ. Czechoslovak Academy of Sciences. Institute of Plasma Physics [*A publication*]

Res Rep Kasetsart Univ ... Research Reports. Kasetsart University [*A publication*]

Res Rep Kitakyushu Tech Coll ... Research Report. Kitakyushu Technical College [*A publication*]

Res Rep Kochi Univ Agric Sci ... Research Reports. Kochi University. Agricultural Science [*A publication*]

Res Rep Kogakuin Univ ... Research Reports. Kogakuin University [*Japan*] [*A publication*]

Res Rep Korea Min Agr Forest Office Rural Develop ... Research Reports. Republic of Korea Ministry of Agriculture and Forestry. Office of Rural Development [*A publication*]

Res Rep Kurume Tech Coll ... Research Reports. Kurume Technical College [*A publication*]

Res Rep Kushiro Tech College ... Research Reports. Kushiro Technical College [*A publication*]

Res Rep Lab Nucl Sci Tohoku Univ ... Research Report. Laboratory of Nuclear Science. Tohoku University [*A publication*]

Res Rep Lab Nucl Sci Tohoku Univ Suppl ... Research Report. Laboratory of Nuclear Science. Tohoku University. Supplement [*Japan*] [*A publication*]

Res Rep MAFES ... Research Report. MAFES [*Mississippi Agricultural and Forestry Experiment Station*] [*A publication*]

Res Rep Maizuru Tech Coll ... Research Reports. Maizuru Technical College [*A publication*]

Res Rep Mich State Univ Agric Exp Stn ... Research Report. Michigan State University. Agricultural Experiment Station [*A publication*]

Res Rep Miss Agric For Exp Stn ... Research Report. Mississippi Agricultural and Forestry Experiment Station [*A publication*]

Res Rep Miyagi Natl Coll Technol ... Research Reports. Miyagi National College of Technology [*A publication*]

Res Rep Miyagi Tech College ... Research Reports. Miyagi Technical College [*A publication*]

Res Rep Miyakonojo Tech Coll ... Research Report. Miyakonojo Technical College [*A publication*]

Res Rep Mont Agric Exp Stn ... Research Report. Montana Agricultural Experiment Station [*A publication*]

Res Rep Nagano Tech Coll ... Research Report. Nagano Technical College [*Japan*] [*A publication*]

Res Rep Nagaoka Tech Coll ... Research Reports. Nagaoka Technical College [*A publication*]

Res Rep Nagoya Ind Sci Res Inst ... Research Reports. Nagoya Industrial Science Research Institute [*Japan*] [*A publication*]

Res Rep Nara Tech Coll ... Research Reports. Nara Technical College [*Japan*] [*A publication*]

Res Rep Natl Geogr Soc ... Research Reports. National Geographic Society [*A publication*]

Res Rep Natl Inst Nutr ... Research Report. National Institute of Nutrition [*Japan*] [*A publication*]

Res Rep Nat Sci Council Math Res Center ... Research Reports. National Science Council. Mathematics Research Center [*A publication*]

Res Rep NC Agr Exp Sta Dept Crop Sci ... Research Report. North Carolina Agricultural Experiment Station. Department of Crop Science [*A publication*]

Res Rep NC Agr Exp Sta Dept Field Crops ... Research Report. North Carolina Agricultural Experiment Station. Department of Field Crops [*A publication*]

Res Rep N Cent Weed Contr Conf ... Research Report. North Central Weed Control Conference [*A publication*]

Res Rep N Dak Agr Exp Sta ... Research Report. North Dakota Agricultural Experiment Station [*A publication*]

Res Rep New Mex Agric Exp Stn ... Research Report. New Mexico Agricultural Experiment Station [*A publication*]

Res Rep NH Agric Exp Stn ... Research Report. New Hampshire Agricultural Experiment Station [*A publication*]

Res Rep Niger Fed Inst Ind Res ... Research Report. Nigeria. Federal Institute of Industrial Research [*A publication*]

Res Rep N Mex Agr Exp Sta ... Research Report. New Mexico Agricultural Experiment Station [*A publication*]

Res Rep Norfolk Agr Exp Sta ... Research Report. Norfolk Agricultural Experiment Station [*A publication*]

Res Rep North Cent Weed Control Conf ... Research Report. North Central Weed Control Conference [*A publication*]

Res Rep Nth Cent Weed Control Conf ... Research Report. North Central Weed Control Conference [*A publication*]

Res Rep Numazu Tech Coll ... Research Reports. Numazu Technical College [*A publication*]

Res Rep Office Rur Dev Minist Agric For (Korea) ... Research Reports. Office of Rural Development. Ministry of Agriculture and Forestry (Suwon, South Korea) [*A publication*]

Res Rep Off Rural Dev Agric Eng Farm Manage & Seric (Suweon) ... Research Reports. Office of Rural Development. Agricultural Engineering, Farm Management, and Sericulture (Suweon) [*A publication*]

Res Rep Off Rural Dev Crop (Suwon) ... Research Reports. Office of Rural Development. Crop (Suwon, South Korea) [*A publication*]

Res Rep Off Rural Dev Hortic Agric Eng (Korea Repub) ... Research Reports. Office of Rural Development. Horticulture and Agricultural Engineering (Korea Republic) [*A publication*]

Res Rep Off Rural Dev Hortic (Suwon) ... Research Reports. Office of Rural Development. Horticulture (Suwon, South Korea) [*A publication*]

Res Rep Off Rural Dev Livest (Korea Republic) ... Research Reports. Office of Rural Development. Livestock (Korea Republic) [*A publication*]

Res Rep Off Rural Dev Livest Seric (Suwon) ... Research Reports. Office of Rural Development. Livestock, Sericulture (Suwon, South Korea) [*A publication*]

Res Rep Off Rural Dev Livest (Suwon) ... Research Reports. Office of Rural Development. Livestock (Suwon, South Korea) [*A publication*]

Res Rep Off Rural Dev Livest & Vet (Suweon) ... Research Reports. Office of Rural Development. Livestock and Veterinary (Suweon) [*A publication*]

Res Rep Off Rural Dev Plant Environ (Suwon) ... Research Reports. Office of Rural Development. Plant Environment (Suwon, South Korea) [*A publication*]

Res Rep Off Rural Dev Seric-Vet (Suwon) ... Research Reports. Office of Rural Development. Sericulture-Veterinary (Suwon, South Korea) [*A publication*]

Res Rep Off Rural Dev (Suwon) ... Research Reports. Office of Rural Development (Suwon, South Korea) [*A publication*]

Res Rep Off Rural Dev (Suwon) Livestock ... Research Reports. Office of Rural Development (Suwon, South Korea). Livestock [*A publication*]

Res Rep Off Rural Dev Vet Seric (Korea Republic) ... Research Reports. Office of Rural Development. Veterinary and Sericulture (Korea Republic) [*A publication*]

Res Rep Off Rural Dev Vet (Suwon) ... Research Reports. Office of Rural Development. Veterinary (Suwon, South Korea) [*A publication*]

Res Rep Oklahoma Agric Exp St ... Oklahoma. Agricultural Experiment Station. Research Report [*A publication*]

Res Rep Ore St Univ Forest Res Lab ... Research Report. Oregon State University. Forest Research Laboratory [*A publication*]

Res Reports Fac Engng Meiji Univ ... Research Reports. Faculty of Engineering. Meiji University [*A publication*]

Res Rep Oyama Natl Coll Technol ... Research Reports. Oyama National College of Technology [*A publication*]

Res Rep Oyama Tech Coll ... Research Reports. Oyama Technical College [*A publication*]

Res Rep P Agric Exp Stn Okla State Univ ... Research Report P. Agricultural Experiment Station. Oklahoma State University [*A publication*]

Res Rep Res Inst Ind Saf ... Research Report. Research Institute of Industrial Safety [*A publication*]

Res Rep Res Program Abatement Munic Pollut Provis Can Ont Ag ... Research Report. Research Program for the Abatement of Municipal Pollution under Provisions of the Canada-Ontario Agreement on Great Lakes Water Quality [*A publication*]

Res Reprod ... Research in Reproduction [*A publication*]

Res Rep Rural Dev Adm (Suweon) ... Research Reports. Rural Development Administration (Suweon) [*A publication*]

Res Rep Sasebo Tech Coll ... Research Reports. Sasebo Technical College [*A publication*]

Res Rep Sch Civ Engng Syd Univ ... Research Report. School of Civil Engineering. University of Sydney [*A publication*]   (APTA)

Res Rep Shibaura Inst Technol ... Research Reports. Shibaura Institute of Technology [*Japan*] [*A publication*]

Res Rep Taiwan Sugar Exp Stn ... Research Report. Taiwan Sugar Experiment Station [*A publication*]

Res Rep Timber Dev Assoc (London) ... Research Report. Timber Development Association (London) [*A publication*]

Res Rep Timb Res Developm Ass ... Research Report. Timber Research and Development Association [*A publication*]

Res Rep Tokyo Denki Univ ... Research Reports. Tokyo Denki University [*A publication*]

Res Rep Tokyo Electr Eng Coll ... Research Reports. Tokyo Electrical Engineering College [*A publication*]

Res Rep Tokyo Electr Engrg College ... Research Reports. Tokyo Electrical Engineering College [*A publication*]

Res Rep Tokyo Electrical Engrg College ... Research Reports. Tokyo Electrical Engineering College [*A publication*]

Res Rep Tokyo Natl Tech Coll ... Research Reports. Tokyo National Technical College [*A publication*]

Res Rep Toyama Natl Coll Technol ... Research Reports. Toyama National College of Technology [*A publication*]

Res Rep Univ Arkansas Eng Exp Stn ... Research Report. University of Arkansas. Engineering Experiment Station [*A publication*]

Res Rep Univ Fla Sch For Resour Conserv ... Research Report. University of Florida. School of Forest Resources and Conservation [*A publication*]

Res Rep Univ GA Coll Agric Exp Stn ... Research Report. University of Georgia. College of Agriculture. Experiment Stations [*A publication*]

Res Rep Univ Tex Austin Cent Highw Res ... Research Report. University of Texas at Austin. Center for Highway Research [*A publication*]

Res Rep US Army Eng Waterw Exp Stn ... Research Report. US Army Engineers. Waterways Experiment Station [*A publication*]

Res Rep US Army Mater Command Cold Reg Res Engng Lab ... Research Report. United States Army Material Command. Cold Regions Research and Engineering Laboratory [*A publication*]

Res Rep US Bur Sport Fish Wildl ... Research Report. United States Bureau of Sport Fisheries and Wildlife [*A publication*]

Res Rep US Fish Wildl Serv ... Research Report. United States Fish and Wildlife Service [*A publication*]

Res Rep VA Agr Exp Sta ... Research Report. Virginia Agricultural Experiment Station [*A publication*]

Res Rep Vet Issue ... Research Reports. Veterinary Issue [*A publication*]

Res Rep West Sect Nat Weed Comm Can ... Research Report. Western Section. National Weed Committee of Canada [*A publication*]

Res Rep Winnipeg Manitoba Res Sta ... Research Report. Winnipeg, Manitoba Research Station [*A publication*]

Res Rep Wis Agr Exp Sta ... Research Report. Wisconsin Agricultural Experiment Station [*A publication*]

Res Rep Yonago Tech Coll ... Research Reports. Yonago Technical College [*A publication*]

Res Results Dig ... Research Results Digest [*A publication*]

ResRev .... Research Review [*A publication*]

Res Rev Bur Hort Plantat Crops ... Research Review. Commonwealth Bureau of Horticulture and Plantation Crops [*A publication*]

Res Rev Can Res Stn (Agassiz BC) ... Research Review. Canada Research Station. (Agassiz, British Columbia) [*A publication*]

Res Rev Chung-Buk Natl Univ ... Research Review. Chung-Buk National University [*A publication*]

Res Rev CSIRO Div Chem Technol ... Australia. Commonwealth Scientific and Industrial Research Organisation. Division of Chemical Technology. Research Review [*A publication*]   (APTA)

Res Rev Div Chem Technol CSIRO ... Research Review. Division of Chemical Technology. Commonwealth Scientific and Industrial Research Organisation [*A publication*]

Res Rev Florida State Univ Bull ... Research in Review. Florida State University. Bulletin [*A publication*]

Res Rev Kyungpook Univ ... Research Review. Kyungpook University [*A publication*]

Res Rev (Off Aerosp Res) ... Research Review (Office of Aerospace Research) [*A publication*]

RESRG ...... Resurgens Communications Group [*Associated Press abbreviation*]   (APAG)

RESRT ...... Resort

RESRT ...... Restart [*Data processing*]

RESS .... RADAR Echo Simulation Study [*or Subsystem*]

RESS .... Recruiting Enlisted Selection System [*Military*]   (DNAB)

Res Ser Appl Geogr New Engl Univ ... Research Series in Applied Geography. University of New England [*A publication*]   (APTA)

Res Ser Fowlers Gap Arid Zone Res Stn ... Research Series. Fowlers Gap Arid Zone Research Station. University of New England [*A publication*]   (APTA)

Res Ser ICAR ... Research Series ICAR. Indian Council of Agricultural Research [*A publication*]

RESSI .... Real Estate Securities and Syndication Institute   (EA)

Res Stat Note ... Research and Statistics Note. Social Security Administration. Office of Research and Statistics [*A publication*]

Res Stat Note Health Care Financ Adm Off Policy Plann Res ... Research and Statistics Note. Health Care Financing Administration. Office of Policy, Planning, and Research [*A publication*]

Res Steroids ... Research on Steroids [*A publication*]

Res Stud ..... Research Studies [*A publication*]

Res Stud Udaipur Univ Coll Agr ... Research Studies. Udaipur University. College of Agriculture [*A publication*]

Res Stud Wash State Univ ... Research Studies. Washington State University [*Pullman*] [*A publication*]

Res Sum Ohio Agr Res Develop Cent ... Research Summary. Ohio Agricultural Research and Development Center [*A publication*]

REST .... RADAR Electronic Scan Technique

REST .... Rain Erosion Seed Test

REST .... Range Endurance Speed and Time [*Computer*]

REST .... Reentry Environment and Systems Technology

REST .... Reentry System Test Program

REST .... Reporting System for Training [*Navy*]   (NG)

REST .... Residence in Science and Technology

REST .... Restaurant   (ROG)

REST .... Restored

REST .... Restrict   (AAG)

REST .... Restricted Environmental Stimulation Technique

RESt .... Review of English Studies [*A publication*]

RESTA ...... Reconnaissance, Surveillance, and Target Acquisition [*Military*]   (AABC)

RESTAS ...... Reception Station System [*Army*]

RESTAT .... Reserve Components Status Reporting [*Army*]   (AABC)

RESTAT .... Review of Economics and Statistics [*A publication*]

Restau Bus ... Restaurant Business [*A publication*]

Restau & Inst ... Restaurants and Institutions [*A publication*]

Restau Bus ... Restaurant Business and Economic Research [*A publication*]

Restaurnt B ... Restaurant Business [*A publication*]

RESTD ...... Real Estate Today [*A publication*]

RESTD ...... Restricted [*Security classification*] [*Military*]

Res Teach Engl ... Research in the Teaching of English [*A publication*]

Res Tech Instrum ... Research Techniques and Instrumentation [*A publication*]

Rest Inst ..... Restaurants and Institutions [*A publication*]

R Est LJ ..... Real Estate Law Journal [*A publication*]

RESTO ...... Restaurant

Res Today .. Research Today [*A publication*]

Res Topics Physiol ... Research Topics in Physiology [*A publication*]

Restoration Q ... Restoration Quarterly [*A publication*]
Restorative Dent ... Restorative Dentistry [*A publication*]
Restor Eigh ... Restoration and Eighteenth Century Theatre Research [*A publication*]
RESTR ...... Restaurant (WGA)
RESTR ...... Restorer
RESTR ...... Restrict (AABC)
RESTRACEN ... Reserve Training Center
RESTRAFAC ... Reserve Training Facility
Res Trends ... Research Trends [*A publication*]
Restric Prac ... Reports of Restrictive Practices Cases [*A publication*] (DLA)
Restr Mgt ... Restaurant Management [*A publication*]
Restrnt H ... Restaurant Hospitality [*A publication*]
RESTS ...... Restoration Survey
R E Stud ..... Review of Economic Studies [*A publication*]
RESUB ...... Resources [*A publication*]
RESUB ...... Resublimed
RESUDU ... Records. Western Australian Museum. Supplement [*A publication*]
Resultate Math ... Resultate der Mathematik [*A publication*]
Resultats .... Resultats Statistiques du Poitou-Charentes [*A publication*]
Result Exped Cient Buque Oceanogr "Cornide de Saavedra" ... Resultados Expediciones Cientificas del Buque Oceanografico "Cornide de Saavedra" [*A publication*]
Results Norw Sci Exped Tristan Da Cunha 1937-1938 ... Results of the Norwegian Scientific Expedition to Tristan Da Cunha 1937-1938 [*A publication*]
Results Probl Cell Differ ... Results and Problems in Cell Differentiation [*A publication*]
Results Res Annu Rep Univ KY Agr Exp Sta ... Results of Research. Annual Report. University of Kentucky. Agricultural Experiment Station [*A publication*]
Resumenes Invest INP-CIP ... Resumenes de Investigacion. INP-CIP [*Instituto Nacional de la Pesca-Centro de Investigaciones Pesqueras*] [*A publication*]
RESUP ...... Resupply (AABC)
RESUPSHIP ... Resident Supervisor of Shipbuilding Conversion and Repair (DNAB)
Resur Biosfery ... Resursy Biosfery [*A publication*]
RESURR ... Resurrection
RESUS ...... Resuscitation
RESV .... Reserve Fleet [*Navy*]
RESVD ...... Reserved (ROG)
Res Vet Sci ... Research in Veterinary Science [*United Kingdom*] [*A publication*]
Res Virol .... Research in Virology [*A publication*]
Res Voc Educ ... Resources in Vocational Education [*A publication*]
Res Vol Surrey Archaeol Soc ... Research Volumes. Surrey Archaeological Society [*A publication*]
RESVON ... Reservation (ROG)
RESVR ...... Reservoir (AAG)
Res Wks Georgian Beekeep Res Stn (Tbilisi) ... Research Works. Georgian Beekeeping Research Station (Tbilisi) [*A publication*]
Res Works Grad Sch Dong A Univ ... Research Works of the Graduate School. Dong-A University [*A publication*]
RESY .... Residuary (ROG)
RET .... Rad-Equivalent Therapy [*Radiology*]
RET .... RADAR Equipment Trailer (MCD)
R-ET .... Rational-Emotive Psychotherapy [*Also known as R-EP, RT*]
RET .... Readiness Enhancement Technology [*Military*]
RET .... Reiteration [*Printers' term*] (DSUE)
RET .... Reitman's (Canada) Ltd. [*Toronto Stock Exchange symbol*]
RET .... Relay Extractor Tool
RET .... Reliability Evaluation Test
RET .... Repetitive Extrasystole Threshold [*Cardiology*]
RE & T ...... Research Engineering and Test (NASA)
RET .... Resolution Enhancement Technology [*Printer feature*] [*Hewlett-Packard Co.*] [*Data processing*] (PCM)
RET .... Resonance Energy Transfer [*Physical chemistry*]
RET .... Retain (AAG)
RET .... Retard (AAG)
Ret .... Reticulum [*Constellation*]
RET .... Retired (AFM)
RET .... Retired after Finishing [*Yacht racing*] (IYR)
RET .... Retract
RET .... Return [*or Returnable*] (AAG)
RET .... Right Esotropia [*Ophthalmology*]
RET .... Ring Emitter Transistor
RET .... Road Equivalent Tariff [*To finance ferries*] [*British*] (DI)
RET .... Rost [*Norway*] [*Airport symbol*] (OAG)
RET .... Roster of Employees Transferred [*Army*]
RETA .... Reactor Environmental Test Apparatus (MCD)
RETA .... Refrigerating Engineers and Technicians Association (EA)
RETA .... Retrieval of Enriched Textual Abstracts [*Information retrieval program*]
RET-ABSTEE ... Returned Absentee (DNAB)
RETAC ...... Regional Educational Television Advisory Council
RETACT ... Real-Time Advanced Core and Thermohydraulic
RETAI .... Real Estate Trainers Association, International (EA)
Retail Dist Mgmt ... Retail and Distribution Management [*A publication*]
Retailer of Q ... Retailer of Queensland [*A publication*] (APTA)

Retail Packag ... Retail Packaging [*A publication*]
Retail Pkg .. Retail Packaging [*A publication*]
RETAIN .... Remote Technical Assistance and Information Network [*Data processing*]
RETAT ...... [*It Is*] Requested That (NVT)
RET BREV ... Retorna Brevium [*The Return of Writs*] [*Latin*] [*Legal term*] (DLA)
RETC .... Railroad Equipment Trust Certificate
RETC .... Rat Embryo Tissue Culture
RETC .... Regional Emergency Transportation Center [*Military*]
RETCO ..... Regional Emergency Transportation Coordinator [*Military*]
RETD .... Recueil d'Etudes Theologiques et Dogmatiques [*A publication*]
RETD .... Retained
RETD .... Retired (EY)
RETD .... Returned
RETEN ..... Retention [*Insurance*] (MCD)
RETEST ... Reinforcement Testing for System Training (SAA)
RETF .... Retired Document File [*IRS*]
RETG .... Retaining
R Ethnol ..... Review of Ethnology [*A publication*]
RETI .... Communaute de Travail des Regions Europeennes de Tradition Industrielle [*Association of Traditional Industrial Regions of Europe*] [*Lille, France*] (EAIO)
Reti .... Reticulum [*Constellation*]
RETIC .... Reticulocyte [*Hematology*]
Reticuloendothel Soc J ... Reticuloendothelial Society. Journal [*A publication*]
RETIMP ... Raleigh-Edwards Tensile Impact Machine Pendulum
Retina Found Inst Biol Med Sci Monogr Conf ... Retina Foundation. Institute of Biological and Medical Sciences. Monographs and Conferences [*A publication*]
RETIREX ... Retirement Exhibition [*British*] (ITD)
RETL .... Retail
RETL .... Rocket Engine Test Laboratory [*Air Force*]
Ret Liv .... Retirement Living [*A publication*]
RETMA ..... Radio-Electronics-Television Manufacturers Association [*Later, Electronic Industries Association*]
RETMOB ... Requirements for Total Mobilization Study
RETN .... Return (ROG)
RETNA ...... Reactor Technology [*A publication*]
RETNDU .. Return to Duty [*Military*] (DNAB)
Ret News .... Retail News [*A publication*]
RETNG ..... Retraining
RETNN ...... Retention [*Insurance*]
RETNR ...... Retainer (ADA)
RETO .... Review of Education and Training for Officers [*Military*] (RDA)
RETORC ... Research Torpedo Configuration (NG)
RETP .... Reliability Evaluation Test Procedure
RETP .... Reserve Entry Training Plan [*Canada*]
RETP .... Retape
RETR .... Retainer (ROG)
RETR .... Retention Register [*Data processing*]
RETR .... Retraced
RETR .... Retract (AAG)
RETR .... Retrieve (KSC)
RETRA ...... Radio, Electrical, and Television Retailers' Association [*British*]
Retract .... Retractationes [*of Augustine*] [*Classical studies*] (OCD)
RETRAN ... Refined Trajectory Analysis
RETRANS ... Retransmit
RETRANS ... [*For*] Return Transportation [*To*]
RETRD ..... Retarded
RETREAD ... Retiree Training for Extended Active Duty [*Military*] (MCD)
RETREP .... Regional Emergency Transportation Representative
RETRF ...... Rural Electrification and Telephone Revolving Fund [*Department of Agriculture*]
RETRG ...... Retracting (WGA)
RETRO ...... Regional Environmental Training and Research Organization [*Retraining program for unemployed space-industry workers*]
RETRO ...... Retro-Rocket (AAG)
RETRO ...... Retroactive (AAG)
RETRO ...... Retrofire (KSC)
RETRO ...... Retrofire Officer
RETRO ...... Retrofit
RETRO ...... Retrograde
RETROF ... Retrofire (SAA)
RETRO FA ... Retroactive Family Allowance [*Military*] (DNAB)
RETROG ... Retrogressive
Retros .... Retrospective Review [*A publication*]
Retrosp .... Retrospectively (DLA)
RETRV ...... Retrieve (MCD)
RETS .... Radiological Environmental Technical Specifications [*Nuclear energy*] (NRCH)
RETS .... Real-Time Sonobuoy (MCD)
RETS .... Reconfigurable Electrical Test Stand (NASA)
RETS .... Remoted Targets System (MCD)
RETS .... Renaissance English Text Society (EA)
RETSCP .... Rocket Engine Thermal Strains with Cyclic Plasticity [*Propellant*]
RETSER .... Retained in Service [*Military*] (DNAB)
Ret Serv Lab Rep ... Retail/Services Labor Report [*A publication*]

RETSIE..... Renewable Energy Technologies Symposium and International Exposition [*Renewable Energy Institute*] (TSPED)
RETSPL.... Reference Equivalent Threshold Sound Pain [*or Pressure*] Level
RETT........ Relatively Easy to Test [*Audiology*]
Rett .... Rettie's Scotch Court of Session Cases, Fourth Series [*A publication*] (DLA)
Rettie......... Rettie's Scotch Court of Session Cases, Fourth Series [*A publication*] (DLA)
RETULSIGN ... Retain on Board until Ultimate Assignment Received
RETX........ Retix [*NASDAQ symbol*] (SPSG)
RETXEB ... Reviews in Environmental Toxicology [*A publication*]
REU........... AREUEA [*American Real Estate and Urban Economics Association*] Journal [*A publication*]
REU.......... Rectifier Enclosure Unit [*Power supply*] [*Telecommunications*] (TEL)
REU.......... Requesting Expeditor Unit (DNAB)
REU........... Reunion [*ANSI three-letter standard code*] (CNC)
REU........... Reunion Island [*Seismograph station code, US Geological Survey*] (SEIS)
REU.......... Reus [*Spain*] [*Airport symbol*] (OAG)
REUMA .... Reumatismo [*A publication*]
Reun Annu Sci Terre (Programme Resumes) ... Reunion Annuelle des Sciences de la Terre (Programme et Resumes) [*A publication*]
Reun A Soc Bras Genet ... Reuniao Anual. Sociedade Brasileira de Genetica [*A publication*]
Reunion Latinoam Prod Anim ... Reunion Latinoamericana de Produccion Animal [*A publication*]
Reun Latinoamer Fitotec Actas ... Reunion Latinoamericana de Fitotecnia. Actas [*A publication*]
REUR .... Reference Your
REURAD .. Reference Your Radio
REURD ..... Reuse/Recycle [*A publication*]
REURTWX ... Reference Your TWX [*Teletypewriter communications*] (AAG)
REUSE...... Revitalize Effective Utilization of Supply Excess [*Navy*] (NG)
REV .... Ratio of Earth-to-Vehicle Radii
REV .... Reentry Vehicle [*Aerospace*]
REV .... Regulator of Virion-Protein Expression [*Genetics*]
REV .... Representative Elementary Volume [*Sampling for analysis*]
REV .... Reticuloendotheliosis Virus
Rev .... Revelation [*New Testament book*]
REV .... Revelstoke Companies Ltd. [*Toronto Stock Exchange symbol*]
REV .... Reventador [*Race of maize*]
REV .... Revenue
REV .... Reverend (EY)
REV .... Reverse (AAG)
REV .... Review (AFM)
Rev .... Review [*A publication*]
REV .... Revise [*or Revision*] (AAG)
REV .... Revlon Group, Inc. [*NYSE symbol*] (SPSG)
REV .... Revocable [*Business term*]
REV .... Revolution (AAG)
REV .... Rotor Entry Vehicle [*Aerospace*]
REVA .... Recommended Vehicle Adjustment [*Military*] (AABC)
REVAB ...... Relief Valve Augmented Bypass [*Nuclear energy*] (NRCH)
Rev ABIA/SAPRO ... Revista. ABIA/SAPRO [*Associacao Brasileira das Industrias da Alimentacao/Setor de Alimentos Calorico-Proteicos*] [*A publication*]
Rev Acad Cienc Exactas Fis-Quim Nat Zaragoza ... Revista. Academia de Ciencias Exactas, Fisico-Quimicas, y Naturales de Zaragoza [*A publication*]
Rev Acad Cienc (Zaragoza) ... Revista. Academia de Ciencias (Zaragoza) [*A publication*]
Rev Acad Cienc Zaragoza 2 ... Revista. Academia de Ciencias Exactas, Fisico-Quimicas, y Naturales de Zaragoza. Serie 2 [*A publication*]
Rev Acad Ci Zaragoza ... Revista. Academia de Ciencias Exactas, Fisico-Quimicas, y Naturales de Zaragoza [*A publication*]
Rev Acad Colomb Cienc Exactas Fis Nat ... Revista. Academia Colombiana de Ciencias Exactas Fisicas y Naturales [*A publication*]
Rev Act Metallges ... Review of Activities. Metallgesellschaft [*A publication*]
Rev Act Metallges AG ... Review of Activities. Metallgesellschaft AG [*A publication*]
Rev Adm Nac Agua (Argent) ... Revista. Administracion Nacional del Agua (Argentina) [*A publication*]
Rev Agric Econ Hokkaido Univ ... Review of Agricultural Economics. Hokkaido University [*A publication*]
Rev Allergy ... Review of Allergy and Applied Immunology [*A publication*]
Rev Allergy Appl Immunol ... Review of Allergy and Applied Immunology [*A publication*]
Rev Amersham Corp ... Review. Amersham Corp. [*A publication*]
Rev Am Hist ... Reviews in American History [*A publication*]
Rev AMRIGS ... Revista. AMRIGS [*Associacao Medica do Rio Grande Do Sul*] [*A publication*]
Rev Anal Chem ... Reviews in Analytical Chemistry [*A publication*]
Rev Anal Chem Euroanal ... Reviews on Analytical Chemistry. Euroanalysis [*A publication*]
Rev Anat Morphol Exp ... Revues d'Anatomie et de Morphologie Experimentale [*A publication*]
Rev Appl Ent ... Review of Applied Entomology [*A publication*]
Rev Appl Mycol ... Review of Applied Mycology [*A publication*]
Rev Aquat Sci ... Reviews in Aquatic Sciences [*A publication*]

REVAR...... Authorized Revisit Above-Mentioned Places and Vary Itinerary as Necessary
Rev Archit Sci Unit Univ Queensl ... Review. Architectural Science Unit. University of Queensland [*A publication*] (APTA)
Revard........ [*Jacobus*] Raevardus [*Deceased, 1568*] [*Authority cited in pre-1607 legal work*] (DSA)
Rev Asoc Argent Criad Cerdos ... Revista. Asociacion Argentina Criadores de Cerdos [*A publication*]
Rev Asoc Argent Dietol ... Revista. Asociacion Argentina de Dietologia [*A publication*]
Rev Asoc Argent Microbiol ... Revista. Asociacion Argentina de Microbiologia [*A publication*]
Rev Asoc Bioquim Argent ... Revista. Asociacion Bioquimica Argentina [*A publication*]
Rev Asoc Cienc Nat Litoral ... Revista. Asociacion de Ciencias Naturales del Litoral [*A publication*]
Rev Asoc Geol Argent ... Revista. Asociacion Geologica Argentina [*A publication*]
Rev Asoc Med Argent ... Revista. Asociacion Medica Argentina [*A publication*]
Rev Asoc Med Mex ... Revista. Asociacion Medica Mexicana [*A publication*]
Rev Asoc Odontol Argent ... Revista. Asociacion Odontologica Argentina [*A publication*]
Rev Asoc Odontol Costa Rica ... Revista. Asociacion Odontologica de Costa Rica [*A publication*]
Rev Asoc Prof Hosp Nac Odontol ... Revista. Asociacion de Profesionales. Hospital Nacional de Odontologia [*A publication*]
Rev Asoc Rural Urug ... Revista. Asociacion Rural del Uruguay [*A publication*]
Rev Asoc Rural Uruguay ... Revista. Asociacion Rural del Uruguay [*A publication*]
Rev Assoc Fr Tech Pet ... Revue. Association Francaise des Techniciens du Petrole [*A publication*]
Rev Assoc Med Bras ... Revista. Associacao Medica Brasileira [*A publication*]
Rev Assoc Med Minas Gerais ... Revista. Associacao Medica de Minas Gerais [*A publication*]
Rev Assoc Med Rio Grande Do Sul ... Revista. Associacao Medica do Rio Grande Do Sul [*A publication*]
Rev Assoc Paul Cir Dent ... Revista. Associacao Paulista de Cirurgioes Dentistas [*A publication*]
Rev Ateneo Catedra Tec Oper Dent ... Revista. Ateneo de la Catedra de Tecnica de Operatoria Dental [*A publication*]
Rev At Ind ... Review of Atomic Industries [*Japan*] [*A publication*]
Rev du B..... Revue. Barreau de la Province de Quebec [*A publication*]
RevBAM.... Revista. Biblioteca, Archivo, y Museo del Ayuntamiento de Madrid [*A publication*]
Rev Bank London South Am ... Review. Bank of London and South America [*A publication*]
Rev Bank NSW ... Review. Bank of New South Wales [*A publication*]
Rev Barreau Que ... Revue. Barreau de Quebec [*A publication*]
Rev Biochem Toxicol ... Reviews in Biochemical Toxicology [*A publication*]
Rev Biol Res Aging ... Review of Biological Research in Aging [*A publication*]
Rev Bl Pol .. Review of Black Political Economy [*A publication*]
Rev Bolsa Cereal ... Revista. Bolsa de Cereales [*A publication*]
Rev Bolsa Comer Rosario ... Revista. Bolsa de Comercio de Rosario [*A publication*]
Rev Bulg Geol Soc ... Review. Bulgarian Geological Society [*A publication*]
Rev Bus Econ Res ... Review of Business and Economic Research [*A publication*]
Rev C Abo PR ... Revista. Colegio de Abogados de Puerto Rico [*A publication*]
Rev C Abo PR ... Revista de Derecho. Colegio de Abogados de Puerto Rico [*A publication*] (DLA)
Rev Can...... Revue Canadienne [*Quebec*] [*A publication*] (DLA)
Rev Can D Fam ... Revue Canadienne de Droit Familial [*A publication*] (DLA)
Rev Can Dr Com ... Revue Canadienne de Droit Communautaire [*A publication*] (DLA)
Rev Cas ...... Revenue Cases [*A publication*] (DLA)
Rev Cas (Ind) ... Revised Cases [*India*] [*A publication*] (DLA)
Rev C & C Rep ... Revenue, Civil, and Criminal Reporter [*Calcutta*] [*A publication*] (DLA)
Rev Cent Cienc Biomed Univ Fed Santa Maria ... Revista. Centro de Ciencias Biomedicas. Universidade Federal de Santa Maria [*A publication*]
Rev Cent Cienc Rurais ... Revista. Centro de Ciencias Rurais [*A publication*]
Rev Cent Ed ... Revista. Centro de Estudios Educativos [*A publication*]
Rev Cent Estud Cabo Verde Ser Cienc Biol ... Revista. Centro de Estudos de Cabo Verde. Serie de Ciencias Biologicas [*A publication*]
Rev Cent Nac Patol Anim ... Revista. Centro Nacional de Patologia Animal [*A publication*]
Rev Centr Estud Med Vet ... Revista. Centro de Estudiantes de Medicina Veterinaria [*A publication*]
Rev CETHEDEC ... Revue. Centre d'Etudes Theoriques de la Detection et des Communications [*A publication*]
Rev CETHEDEC Cahier ... Revue. Centre d'Etudes Theoriques de la Detection et des Communications. Cahier [*Paris*] [*A publication*]
Rev Chem En ... Reviews in Chemical Engineering [*A publication*]
Rev Cie Gen Electr ... Review of Compagnie Generale d'Electricite [*France*] [*A publication*]

Rev Circ Argent Odontol ... Revista. Circulo Argentino de Odontologia [*A publication*]
Rev Circ Eng Mil ... Revista. Circulo de Engenharia Militar [*Brazil*] [*A publication*]
Rev Circ Odontol Sur ... Revista. Circulo Odontologico del Sur [*A publication*]
Rev Civ Code ... Revised Civil Code [*A publication*] (DLA)
Rev Civ St .. Revised Civil Statutes [*A publication*] (DLA)
Rev Clin Basic Pharm ... Reviews in Clinical and Basic Pharmacology [*A publication*]
Rev Clin Basic Pharmacol ... Reviews in Clinical and Basic Pharmacology [*A publication*]
Rev Clin Pharmacol Pharmacokinet ... Review of Clinical Pharmacology and Pharmacokinetics [*A publication*]
Revco.......... Revco DS, Inc. [*Associated Press abbreviation*] (APAG)
Rev Coat Corros ... Reviews on Coatings and Corrosion [*A publication*]
Rev Code Civ Proc ... Revised Code of Civil Procedure [*A publication*] (DLA)
Rev Code Cr Proc ... Revised Code of Criminal Procedure [*A publication*] (DLA)
Rev Col Med Guatem ... Revista. Colegio Medico de Guatemala [*A publication*]
Rev Col Nac Enferm ... Revista. Colegio Nacional de Enfermeras [*A publication*]
Rev Col Quim Ing Quim Costa Rica ... Revista. Colegio de Quimicos e Ingenieros Quimicos de Costa Rica [*A publication*]
REVCOM ... Revolutionary Committee [*China*]
REVCON .. Review Conference
Rev Confed Med Panam ... Revista. Confederacion Medica Panamericana [*A publication*]
Rev Consor Cent Agr Manabi ... Revista. Consorcio de Centros Agricolas de Manabi [*A publication*]
Rev Cons Rectores Univ Chilenas ... Revista. Consejo de Rectores. Universidades Chilenas [*A publication*]
Rev Contemp L ... Review of Contemporary Law [*A publication*] (DLA)
Rev Cont L ... Review of Contemporary Law [*A publication*]
Rev Cr Code ... Revised Criminal Code [*A publication*] (DLA)
Rev CREA (Asoc Argent Consorcios Reg Exp Agric) ... Revista. CREA (Asociacion Argentina de Consorcios Regionales de Experimentacion Agricola) [*A publication*]
Rev Crit...... Revue Critique de Legislation et de Jurisprudence de Canada [*A publication*] (DLA)
Rev Crit de Leg ... Revue Critique de Legislation [*Paris*] [*A publication*] (DLA)
Rev Crit de Legis et Jur ... Revue Critique de Legislation et de Jurisprudence [*Montreal*] [*A publication*] (DLA)
Rev Cubana de Derecho ... Revista Cubana de Derecho [*Havana, Cuba*] [*A publication*] (DLA)
REVCUR... Reverse Current (AAG)
Rev Current Activities Tech Ed ... Review of Current Activities in Technical Education [*A publication*] (APTA)
Rev Czech Med ... Review of Czechoslovak Medicine [*A publication*]
REVD .... Reverend (ROG)
Rev'd .... Reversed [*Legal term*] (DLA)
Rev Data Sci Resour ... Reviews of Data on Science Resources [*United States*] [*A publication*]
Rev Data Sci Resour Natl Sci Found ... Reviews of Data on Science Resources. National Sciences Foundation [*A publication*]
Rev Deform Behav Mater ... Reviews on the Deformation Behavior of Materials [*A publication*]
Rev de Derecho Esp y Amer ... Revista de Derecho Espanol y Americano [*Madrid, Spain*] [*A publication*] (DLA)
Rev de Derecho Jurispr y Cienc Soc ... Revista de Derecho, Jurisprudencia, y Ciencias Sociales y Gaceta de los Tribunales [*A publication*] (DLA)
REV DEV.. Revolutionary Development [*South Vietnam*]
Rev Dir Gen Geol Minas (Ecuador) ... Revista. Direccion General de Geologia y Minas (Ecuador) [*A publication*]
Rev du Dr... Revue du Droit [*Quebec*] [*A publication*] (DLA)
Rev de Droit Contemp ... Revue de Droit Contemporain [*Brussels, Belgium*] [*A publication*] (DLA)
Rev de Droit Hong ... Revue de Droit Hongrois [*A publication*] (DLA)
Rev Droit Int'l Moyen-Orient ... Revue de Droit International pour le Moyen-Orient [*A publication*] (DLA)
Rev de Droit Penal Mil et de Droit de la Guerre ... Revue de Droit Penal Militaire et de Droit de la Guerre [*A publication*] (DLA)
Rev Droit Penal Militaire et Dr de la Guerre ... Revue de Droit Penal Militaire et de Droit de la Guerre [*A publication*] (DLA)
Rev de Droit Unif ... Revue de Droit Uniforme [*A publication*] (DLA)
Rev de Droit Uniforme ... Revue de Droit Uniforme [*A publication*] (DLA)
Rev Drug Metabol Drug Interact ... Reviews on Drug Metabolism and Drug Interactions [*A publication*]
Rev D US... Revue de Droit. Universite de Sherbrooke [*A publication*]
Rev East Med Sci ... Review of Eastern Medical Sciences [*A publication*]
Rev Econ Co ... Review of the Economic Conditions in Italy [*A publication*]
Rev Econom Statist ... Review of Economics and Statistics [*A publication*]
Rev Econom Stud ... Review of Economic Studies [*A publication*]
Rev Economy Emplyment ... Review of the Economy and Employment [*A publication*]
Rev Econ S ... Review of Economic Studies [*A publication*]
Rev Econ St ... Review of Economics and Statistics [*A publication*]

Rev Econ Stat ... Review of Economic Statistics [*A publication*]
Rev Econ Stat ... Review of Economics and Statistics [*A publication*]
Rev Econ Stud ... Review of Economic Studies [*A publication*]
Rev Educational Res ... Review of Educational Research [*A publication*]
Rev Educ Re ... Review of Educational Research [*A publication*]
Rev Educ Res ... Review of Educational Research [*A publication*]
REVEL ...... Reverberation Elimination
Rev El Comm ... Review. Electrical Communication Laboratory [*Tokyo*] [*A publication*]
Rev Elec Commun Lab (Tokyo) ... Review. Electrical Communication Laboratory (Tokyo) [*A publication*]
Rev Electr Commun Lab ... Review. Electrical Communication Laboratory [*A publication*]
Rev Electr Commun Lab (Tokyo) ... Review. Electrical Communication Laboratory (Tokyo) [*A publication*]
Rev Endocr Relat Cancer Suppl ... Reviews on Endocrine-Related Cancer. Supplement [*A publication*]
Rev Eng Geol ... Reviews in Engineering Geology [*United States*] [*A publication*]
Rev Engl St ... Review of English Studies [*A publication*]
Rev Engl Stu ... Review of English Studies [*A publication*]
Rev Engl Stud ... Review of English Studies [*A publication*]
Rev Environ Health ... Reviews on Environmental Health [*A publication*]
Rev Environ Toxicol ... Reviews in Environmental Toxicology [*A publication*]
REVERB ... Reverberator [*Automotive engineering*]
REVERSY ... Reversionary (ROG)
Rev Esc Agron Vet Univ Rio Grande Do Sul (Porto Alegre) ... Revista. Escola de Agronomia e Veterinaria da Universidade do Rio Grande Do Sul (Porto Alegre) [*A publication*]
Rev Esc Enferm USP ... Revista. Escola de Enfermagem. Universidade de Sao Paulo [*A publication*]
Rev Esc Minas ... Revista. Escola de Minas [*A publication*]
Rev Et Anc ... Revue des Etudes Anciennes [*A publication*] (OCD)
Rev Et Grec ... Revue des Etudes Grecques [*A publication*] (OCD)
Rev Et Lat ... Revue des Etudes Latines [*A publication*] (OCD)
Rev Exist Psychol Psychiat ... Review of Existential Psychology and Psychiatry [*A publication*]
Rev Exist Psych Psychiat ... Review of Existential Psychology and Psychiatry [*A publication*]
RevExp ...... Review and Expositor [*A publication*]
Rev and Expositor ... Review and Expositor [*A publication*]
Rev Fac Agron Alcance (Maracay) ... Revista. Facultad de Agronomia Alcance (Maracay) [*A publication*]
Rev Fac Agron (Maracay) ... Revista. Facultad de Agronomia (Maracay) [*A publication*]
Rev Fac Agron Univ Fed Rio Grande Sul ... Revista. Faculdade de Agronomia. Universidade Federal do Rio Grande Do Sul [*A publication*]
Rev Fac Agron Vet (Buenos Aires) ... Revista. Facultad de Agronomia y Veterinaria (Buenos Aires) [*A publication*]
Rev Fac Agron Vet Univ Rio Grande Do Sul ... Revista. Faculdade de Agronomia e Veterinaria. Universidade do Rio Grande Do Sul [*A publication*]
Rev Fac Agron Vet Univ Rio Grande Sul ... Revista. Faculdade de Agronomia e Veterinaria. Universidade do Rio Grande Do Sul [*A publication*]
Rev Fac Cienc 2a Ser A Cienc Mat ... Revista. Faculdade de Ciencias. Universidade de Lisboa. 2a Serie A. Ciencias Matematicas [*Portugal*] [*A publication*]
Rev Fac Cienc Med Buenos Aires ... Revista. Facultad de Ciencias Medicas de Buenos Aires [*A publication*]
Rev Fac Cienc Med Cordoba ... Revista. Facultad de Ciencias Medicas de Cordoba [*A publication*]
Rev Fac Cienc Med Univ Catol Parana ... Revista. Faculdade de Ciencias Medicas. Universidade Catolica do Parana [*A publication*]
Rev Fac Cienc Univ Coimbra ... Revista. Faculdade de Ciencias. Universidade de Coimbra [*A publication*]
Rev Fac Cienc Univ Lisboa B ... Revista. Faculdade de Ciencias. Universidade de Lisboa. Serie B. Ciencias Fisico-Quimicas [*A publication*]
Rev Fac Cienc Univ Lisboa Ser B ... Revista. Faculdade de Ciencias. Universidade de Lisboa. Serie B. Ciencias Fisico-Quimicas [*A publication*]
Rev Fac Cienc Univ Lisboa Ser C ... Revista. Faculdade de Ciencias. Universidade de Lisboa. Serie C. Ciencias Naturais [*A publication*]
Rev Fac Cienc Univ Lisb Ser C Cienc Nat ... Revista. Faculdade de Ciencias. Universidade de Lisboa. Serie C. Ciencias Naturais [*A publication*]
Rev Fac Cienc Vet La Plata ... Revista. Facultad de Ciencias Veterinarias de La Plata [*A publication*]
Rev de la Fac de Derecho (Caraboba) ... Revista. Facultad de Derecho. Universidad de Caraboba [*Valencia, Venezuela*] [*A publication*] (DLA)
Rev de la Fac de Derecho (Caracas) ... Revista. Facultad de Derecho. Universidad Catolica Andres Bello (Caracas) [*A publication*] (DLA)
Rev de la Fac de Derecho y Cienc Soc ... Revista. Facultad de Derecho y Ciencias Sociales [*Montevideo, Uruguay*] [*A publication*] (DLA)

Rev de la Fac de Derecho de Mex ... Revista. Facultad de Derecho de Mexico [*A publication*]
Rev da Fac de Direito (Lisbon) ... Revista. Faculdade de Direito. Universidade de Lisboa (Lisbon) [*A publication*] (DLA)
Rev de Fac de Direito (Sao Paulo) ... Revista. Faculdade de Direito. Universidade de Sao Paulo [*Sao Paulo, Brazil*] [*A publication*] (DLA)
Rev Fac Eng Univ Porto ... Revista. Faculdade de Engenharia. Universidade do Porto [*A publication*]
Rev Fac Farm Bioquim Univ Fed St Maria ... Revista. Faculdade de Farmacia e Bioquimica. Universidade Federal de Santa Maria [*A publication*]
Rev Fac Farm Bioquim Univ Sao Paulo ... Revista. Faculdade de Farmacia e Bioquimica. Universidade de Sao Paulo [*A publication*]
Rev Fac Farm Odontol Araraquara ... Revista. Faculdade de Farmacia e Odontologia de Araraquara [*A publication*]
Rev Fac Farm Odontol Ribeirao Preto ... Revista. Facultade de Farmacia e Odontologia de Ribeirao Preto [*A publication*]
Rev Fac Med (Maracaibo) ... Revista. Facultad de Medicina (Maracaibo) [*A publication*]
Rev Fac Med (Mex) ... Revista. Facultad de Medicina (Mexico) [*A publication*]
Rev Fac Med (Tucuman) ... Revista. Facultad de Medicina (Tucuman) [*A publication*]
Rev Fac Med Univ Fed Ceara ... Revista. Faculdade de Medicina. Universidade Federal do Ceara [*A publication*]
Rev Fac Med Univ Fed Santa Maria ... Revista. Faculdade de Medicina. Universidade Federal de Santa Maria [*A publication*]
Rev Fac Med Vet Univ Sao Paulo ... Revista. Faculdade de Medicina Veterinaria. Universidade de Sao Paulo [*A publication*]
Rev Fac Med Vet Zootec (Bogota) ... Revista. Facultad de Medicina, Veterinaria, y Zootecnia (Bogota) [*A publication*]
Rev Fac Med Vet Zootec Univ Sao Paulo ... Revista. Faculdade de Medicina Veterinaria e Zootecnia. Universidade de Sao Paulo [*A publication*]
Rev Fac Nac Agron (Medellin) ... Revista. Facultad Nacional de Agronomia (Medellin) [*A publication*]
Rev Fac Odontol Aracatuba ... Revista. Faculdade de Odontologia de Aracatuba [*A publication*]
Rev Fac Odontol (P Alegre) ... Revista. Faculdade de Odontologia (Porto Alegre) [*A publication*]
Rev Fac Odontol Pernambuco ... Revista. Faculdade de Odontologia de Pernambuco [*A publication*]
Rev Fac Odontol Port Alegre ... Revista. Faculdade de Odontologia de Port Alegre [*A publication*]
Rev Fac Odontol Sao Jose Dos Campos ... Revista. Faculdade de Odontologia de Sao Jose Dos Campos [*A publication*]
Rev Fac Odontol Sao Paulo ... Revista. Faculdade de Odontologia. Universidade de Sao Paulo [*A publication*]
Rev Fac Odontol Univ Fed Bahia ... Revista. Faculdade de Odontologia. Universidade Federal da Bahia [*A publication*]
Rev Fac Odontol Univ Sao Paulo ... Revista. Faculdade de Odontologia. Universidade de Sao Paulo [*A publication*]
Rev Fac Sci Univ Istanbul C ... Revue. Faculte des Sciences. Universite d'Istanbul. Serie C [*A publication*]
Rev Fac Sci Univ Istanbul Ser B Sci Nat ... Revue. Faculte des Sciences. Universite d'Istanbul. Serie B. Sciences Naturelles [*A publication*]
Rev Fac Sci Univ Istanbul Ser C ... Review. Faculty of Science. University of Istanbul. Series C [*Istanbul Universitesi fen Fakultesi Mecmuasi. Serie C*] [*A publication*]
Rev Fed Am Health Syst ... Review. Federation of American Health Systems [*A publication*]
Rev Fed Am Hosp ... Review. Federation of American Hospitals [*A publication*]
Rev Fed Doct Cienc Filos Let (Havana) ... Revista. Federacion de Doctors en Ciencias y en Filosofia y Letras (Havana) [*A publication*]
Rev Fed Fr Soc Sci Nat ... Revue. Federation Francaise des Societes de Sciences Naturelles [*A publication*]
Rev Fed Odontol Colomb ... Revista. Federacion Odontologica Colombiana [*A publication*]
Rev Food Sci Technol (Mysore) ... Reviews in Food Sciences and Technology (Mysore) [*A publication*]
Rev Food Technol (Mysore) ... Reviews in Food Technology (Mysore) [*A publication*]
Rev Fund Serv Saude Publica (Braz) ... Revista. Fundacao Servicos de Saude Publica (Brazil) [*A publication*]
Rev Fund SESP ... Revista. Fundacao Servicos de Saude Publica [*Brazil*] [*A publication*]
Rev Fund SESP (Braz) ... Revista. Fundacao Servicos de Saude Publica (Brazil) [*A publication*]
rev'g ... Reversing [*Legal term*] (DLA)
Rev Gastroenterol ... Review of Gastroenterology [*A publication*]
Rev Gen ... Revue Generale de Droit [*A publication*] (DLA)
Rev Gen D ... Revue Generale de Droit [*A publication*] (DLA)
Rev Gen de Legis y Jurispr ... Revista General de Legislacion y Jurisprudencia [*Madrid, Spain*] [*A publication*] (DLA)
Rev Gen Reg ... Revised General Regulation, General Accounting Office [*United States*] [*A publication*] (DLA)
Rev Geophys ... Reviews of Geophysics [*Later, Reviews of Geophysics and Space Physics*] [*A publication*]

Rev Geophys ... Reviews of Geophysics and Space Physics [*A publication*]
Rev Geophysics ... Reviews of Geophysics [*Later, Reviews of Geophysics and Space Physics*] [*A publication*]
Rev Geophys Space Phys ... Reviews of Geophysics and Space Physics [*A publication*]
Rev Ghana L ... Review of Ghana Law [*A publication*] (DLA)
REVHA ... Reviews on Environmental Health [*A publication*]
Rev High-Temp Mater ... Reviews on High-Temperature Materials [*A publication*]
Rev Hist Rel ... Revue de l'Histoire des Religions [*A publication*] (OCD)
Rev Hosp Clin Fac Med Univ Sao Paulo ... Revista. Hospital das Clinicas. Faculdade de Medicina. Universidade de Sao Paulo [*A publication*]
Rev Hosp Clin Fac Med Univ Sao Paulo Supl ... Revista. Hospital das Clinicas. Faculdade de Medicina. Universidade de Sao Paulo. Suplemento [*A publication*]
Rev Hosp Clin Sao Paulo ... Revista. Hospital das Clinicas. Faculdade de Medicina. Universidade de Sao Paulo [*A publication*]
Rev Hosp Nino (Lima) ... Revista. Hospital del Nino (Lima) [*A publication*]
Rev Hosp Ninos (B Aires) ... Revista. Hospital de Ninos (Buenos Aires) [*A publication*]
Rev Hosp Psiquiatr Habana ... Revista. Hospital Psiquiatrico de la Habana [*A publication*]
Rev Hosp San Juan De Dios (Bogota) ... Revista. Hospital de San Juan de Dios (Bogota) [*A publication*]
Rev Hosp S Juan ... Revista. Hospital de San Juan de Dios [*Bogota*] [*A publication*]
Rev/I ... Revista/Review Interamericana [*A publication*]
Rev IBYS ... Revista. IBYS [*Instituto de Biologia y Sueroterapia*] [*A publication*]
Rev ICIDCA ... Revista. ICIDCA [*Instituto Cubano de Investigaciones de los Derivados de la Cana de Azucar*] [*A publication*]
Rev IDIEM ... Revista. IDIEM [*Instituto de Investigaciones de Engoyes de Materiales*] [*A publication*]
REVIEW ... Recording and Video Playback of Electronic Warfare Information
Review ... Weekly Review [*A publication*]
Review Inst Nucl Power Oper ... Review. Institute of Nuclear Power Operations [*A publication*]
Rev I F Pet ... Revue. Institut Francais du Petrole [*A publication*]
Rev Ig ... Revista. Igiena, Bacteriologie, Virusologie, Parazitologie, Epidemiologie, Pneumoftiziologie [*A publication*]
Rev Ig Bacteriol Virusol Parazitol Epidemiol Pneumoftiziol ... Revista. Igiena, Bacteriologie, Virusologie, Parazitologie, Epidemiologie, Pneumoftiziologie [*A publication*]
RevIMA ... Review of Indonesian and Malayan Affairs [*A publication*]
Rev IMESC (Inst Med Soc Criminol Sao Paulo) ... Revista. IMESC (Instituto de Medicina Social e de Criminologia de Sao Paulo) [*A publication*]
Rev Immunoassay Technol ... Reviews on Immunoassay Technology [*A publication*]
Rev Indon & Malayan Affairs ... Review of Indonesian and Malayan Affairs [*A publication*] (APTA)
Rev Infect Dis ... Review of Infectious Diseases [*A publication*]
Rev Inst Adolfo Lutz ... Revista. Instituto Adolfo Lutz [*A publication*]
Rev Inst Agr Catalan San Isidro ... Revista. Instituto Agricola Catalan de San Isidro [*A publication*]
Rev Inst Antibiot (Recife) ... Revista. Instituto de Antibioticos. Universidade Federal de Pernambuco (Recife) [*A publication*]
Rev Inst Antibiot Univ Fed Pernambuco ... Revista. Instituto de Antibioticos. Universidade Federal de Pernambuco [*A publication*]
Rev Inst Antibiot Univ Recife ... Revista. Instituto de Antibioticos. Universidade do Recife [*A publication*]
Rev Inst Bacteriol Dep Nac Hig (Argent) ... Revista. Instituto Bacteriologico. Departamento Nacional de Higiene (Argentina) [*A publication*]
Rev Inst Bacteriol Malbran ... Revista. Instituto Bacteriologico Malbran [*A publication*]
Rev Inst Colomb Agropecu ... Revista. Instituto Colombiano Agropecuario [*A publication*]
Rev del Inst de Derecho Comparado ... Revista. Instituto de Derecho Comparado [*Barcelona, Spain*] [*A publication*] (DLA)
Rev Inst Franc Petrol ... Revue. Institut Francais du Petrole [*A publication*]
Rev Inst Fr Pet ... Revue. Institut Francais du Petrole [*A publication*]
Rev Inst Fr Pet ... Revue. Institut Francais du Petrole et Annales des Combustibles Liquides [*Later, Revue. Institut Francais du Petrole*] [*A publication*]
Rev Inst Fr Pet Ann Combust Liq ... Revue. Institut Francais du Petrole et Annales des Combustibles Liquides [*Later, Revue. Institut Francais du Petrole*] [*A publication*]
Rev Inst Geogr Geol (Sao Paulo) ... Revista. Instituto Geografico e Geologico (Sao Paulo) [*A publication*]
Rev Inst Hist Geogr Bras ... Revista. Instituto Historico e Geografico Brasileiro [*A publication*]
Rev Inst Hyg Mines ... Revue. Institut d'Hygiene des Mines [*A publication*]
Rev Inst Hyg Mines (Hasselt) ... Revue. Institut d'Hygiene des Mines (Hasselt) [*A publication*]
Rev Inst Invest Tecnol (Bogota) ... Revista. Instituto de Investigaciones Tecnologicas (Bogota) [*A publication*]
Rev Inst Malbran ... Revista. Instituto Malbran [*A publication*]

Rev Inst Med Leg Estado Guanabara ... Revista. Instituto Medico-Legal do Estado da Guanabara [*A publication*]
Rev Inst Med Trop Sao Paulo ... Revista. Instituto de Medicina Tropical de Sao Paulo [*A publication*]
Rev Inst Mex Pet ... Revista. Instituto Mexicano del Petroleo [*A publication*]
Rev Inst Mex Petrol ... Revista. Instituto Mexicano del Petroleo [*A publication*]
Rev Inst Munic Bot (B Aires) ... Revista. Instituto Municipal de Botanica (Buenos Aires) [*A publication*]
Rev Inst Nac Geol Min (Argent) ... Revista. Instituto Nacional de Geologia y Mineria (Argentina) [*A publication*]
Rev Inst Nac Hig ... Revista. Instituto Nacional de Higiene [*A publication*]
Rev Inst Nacl Cancerol (Mex) ... Revista. Instituto Nacional de Cancerologia (Mexico) [*A publication*]
Rev Inst Nac Med Leg Colombia ... Revista. Instituto Nacional de Medicina Legal de Colombia [*A publication*]
Rev Inst Napoleon ... Revue. Institut Napoleon [*A publication*]
Rev Inst Pasteur Lyon ... Revue. Institut Pasteur de Lyon [*A publication*]
Rev Inst Salubr Enferm Trop ... Revista. Instituto de Salubridad y Enfermedades Tropicales [*A publication*]
Rev Inst Sociol ... Revue. Institut de Sociologie [*A publication*]
Rev Int Biol Prog ... Review. International Biological Programme [*A publication*]
Rev Internac y Diplom ... Revista Internacional y Diplomatica. Publicacion Mensual [*Mexico*] [*A publication*]   (DLA)
Rev Internat Franc du Droit des Gens ... Revue Internationale Francaise du Droit des Gens [*A publication*]   (DLA)
Rev Int'l Comm Jur ... Review. International Commission of Jurists [*A publication*]   (DLA)
Rev Int'l Comm Jurists ... Review. International Commission of Jurists [*A publication*]   (DLA)
Rev Int'l Dr Auteur ... Revue Internationale du Droit d'Auteur [*A publication*]   (DLA)
Rev Int'l Droit Comp ... Revue Internationale de Droit Compare [*A publication*]   (DLA)
Rev Int'l des Droits de l'Antiquite ... Revue Internationale des Droits de l'Antiquite [*A publication*]   (DLA)
Rev Int'l Dr Penal ... Revue Internationale de Droit Penal [*A publication*]   (DLA)
Rev IRE ..... Revue. IRE [*Institut National des Radioelements*] [*A publication*]
Revised Rep ... Revised Reports [*England*] [*A publication*]   (DLA)
Rev I Soc ... Revue. Institut de Sociologie [*A publication*]
Rev Ivoirienne de Droit ... Revue Ivoirienne de Droit [*A publication*]   (DLA)
Rev J Phil Soc Sci ... Review Journal of Philosophy and Social Science [*A publication*]
Rev J & PJ ... Revenue, Judicial, and Police Journal [*Bengal*] [*A publication*]   (DLA)
Rev Jud & Police J ... Revenue, Judicial, and Police Journal [*A publication*]   (DLA)
Rev de Jur ... Revue de Jurisprudence [*Quebec*] [*A publication*]   (DLA)
Rev Jur d'Alsace et de Lorraine ... Revue Juridique d'Alsace et de Lorraine [*A publication*]   (DLA)
Rev Jur de Buenos Aires ... Revista Juridica de Buenos Aires [*A publication*]   (DLA)
Rev Jur du Congo ... Revue Juridique du Congo [*A publication*]   (DLA)
Rev Kobe Univ Merc Mar Part 2 ... Review. Kobe University of Mercantile Marine. Part 2 [*Japan*] [*A publication*]
Rev Kobe Univ Merc Mar Part 2 Marit Stud Sci Eng ... Review. Kobe University of Mercantile Marine. Part 2. Maritime Studies, and Science and Engineering [*A publication*]
Rev Laser Eng ... Review of Laser Engineering [*Japan*] [*A publication*]
Rev Leg ...... Revue Legale [*Canada*] [*A publication*]   (DLA)
Rev de Leg ... Revue de Legislation et de Jurisprudence [*Montreal*] [*A publication*]   (DLA)
Rev Leg ...... Revue de Legislation et de Jurisprudence [*Quebec*] [*A publication*]   (DLA)
Rev Legale ... Revue Legale [*A publication*]   (DLA)
Rev de Legis ... Revue de Legislation [*Canada*] [*A publication*]   (DLA)
Rev Leg NS ... Revue Legale. New Series [*Canada*] [*A publication*]   (DLA)
Rev Leg (OS) ... Revue Legale (Old Series) [*A publication*]   (DLA)
Rev Litigation ... Review of Litigation [*A publication*]
Revln .... Revlon, Inc. [*Associated Press abbreviation*]   (APAG)
Rev L & Soc ... Review of Law and Social Change [*A publication*]   (DLA)
Rev Macromol Chem ... Reviews in Macromolecular Chemistry [*A publication*]
Rev Market & Ag Econ ... Review of Marketing and Agricultural Economics [*A publication*]   (APTA)
Rev Market Agric Econ ... Review of Marketing and Agricultural Economics [*A publication*]   (APTA)
Rev Market Agric Econ (Sydney) ... Review of Marketing and Agricultural Economics (Sydney) [*A publication*]   (APTA)
Rev Marketing Agr Econ ... Review of Marketing and Agricultural Economics [*A publication*]
Rev Med Normandes ... Revues Medicales Normandes [*A publication*]
Rev Med Pharmacol ... Review of Medical Pharmacology [*A publication*]
Rev Med Vet Mycol ... Review of Medical and Veterinary Mycology [*A publication*]
Rev Metaph ... Review of Metaphysics [*A publication*]
Rev Metaphy ... Review of Metaphysics [*A publication*]
Rev Met Lit ... Review of Metal Literature [*A publication*]

Rev Met Technol ... Review of Metals Technology [*A publication*]
RevMex ..... Revolutionary Mexican Historical Society   (EA)
REV/MIN ... Revolutions per Minute [*e.g., in reference to phonograph records*]
Rev Mineral ... Reviews in Mineralogy [*A publication*]
Rev Mktg Agric Econ (Sydney) ... Review of Marketing and Agricultural Economics (Sydney) [*A publication*]
REVMN .... Revell-Monogram Industries [*Associated Press abbreviation*]   (APAG)
Rev Modern Phys ... Reviews of Modern Physics [*A publication*]
Rev Mod Phys ... Reviews of Modern Physics [*A publication*]
Rev M Phys ... Reviews of Modern Physics [*A publication*]
Rev Mus Hist Nat Mendoza ... Revista. Museo de Historia Natural de Mendoza [*A publication*]
Rev Mus La Plata ... Revista. Museo de La Plata [*A publication*]
Rev Mus La Plata Secc Antropol ... Revista. Museo de La Plata. Seccion Antropologia [*A publication*]
Rev Mus La Plata Secc Bot ... Revista. Museo de La Plata. Seccion Botanica [*A publication*]
Rev Mus La Plata Secc Geol ... Revista. Museo de La Plata. Seccion Geologia [*A publication*]
Rev Mus La Plata Secc Paleontol ... Revista. Museo de La Plata. Seccion Paleontologia [*A publication*]
Rev Mus La Plata Secc Zool ... Revista. Museo de La Plata. Seccion Zoologia [*A publication*]
REVN .... Reversion   (ROG)
Rev Nat Lit ... Review of National Literatures [*A publication*]
Rev Nat Res Counc Can ... Review. National Research Council of Canada [*A publication*]
Rev Neurosci ... Reviews of Neuroscience [*A publication*]
REVNRY ... Revolutionary
REVO .... Revoke   (AABC)
REVO .... Revolution   (DSUE)
Rev Oak Ridge Natl Lab (US) ... Review. Oak Ridge National Laboratory (United States) [*A publication*]
REVOCN ... Revocation   (ROG)
REVOCON ... Remote Volume Control
REVOCON ... Revocation
REVOL ...... Revolution   (WGA)
Revol Wld .. Revolutionary World [*A publication*]
Revol World ... Revolutionary World [*A publication*]
REVON ..... Reversion
REVOP ...... Random Evolutionary Operation
Rev Ord ...... Revised Ordinances [*A publication*]   (DLA)
Rev Ord NWT ... Revised Ordinances, Northwest Territories [*1888*] [*Canada*] [*A publication*]   (DLA)
Rev Palaeobot Palynol ... Review of Palaeobotany and Palynology [*A publication*]
Rev Palaeobot Palynology ... Review of Palaeobotany and Palynology [*A publication*]
Rev Palae P ... Review of Palaeobotany and Palynology [*A publication*]
Rev Pen Code ... Revised Penal Code [*A publication*]   (DLA)
Rev Perinat Med ... Reviews in Perinatal Medicine [*A publication*]
Rev Perspect ... Review and Perspective [*A publication*]
Rev Petrol Technol ... Review of Petroleum Technology [*A publication*]
Rev Pet Technol (London) ... Reviews of Petroleum Technology (London) [*A publication*]
Rev Ph Ch J ... Review of Physical Chemistry of Japan [*A publication*]
Rev Phys B ... Reviews of Physiology, Biochemistry, and Pharmacology [*A publication*]
Rev Phys Chem Jpn ... Review of Physical Chemistry of Japan [*A publication*]
Rev Physiol Biochem Exp Pharmacol ... Reviews of Physiology, Biochemistry, and Experimental Pharmacology [*A publication*]
Rev Physiol Biochem Pharmacol ... Reviews of Physiology, Biochemistry, and Pharmacology [*A publication*]
Rev Phys Technol ... Review of Physics in Technology [*United Kingdom*] [*A publication*]
Rev Plant Path ... Review of Plant Pathology [*A publication*]
Rev Plant Pathol ... Review of Plant Pathology [*A publication*]
Rev Plant Prot Res ... Review of Plant Protection Research [*A publication*]
Rev Plasma Phys ... Reviews of Plasma Physics [*A publication*]
Rev Pol .... Review of Politics [*A publication*]
Rev Pol Acad Sci ... Review. Polish Academy of Sciences [*A publication*]
Rev Polarogr ... Review of Polarography [*A publication*]
Rev Polarogr (Jpn) ... Review of Polarography (Japan) [*A publication*]
Rev Pol Code ... Revised Political Code [*A publication*]   (DLA)
Rev of Polish Law and Econ ... Review of Polish Law and Economics [*Warsaw, Poland*] [*A publication*]   (DLA)
Rev Polit .... Review of Politics [*A publication*]
Rev Pol L ... Review of Polish Law [*A publication*]   (DLA)
Rev Polym Technol ... Reviews in Polymer Technology [*A publication*]
Rev Powder Metall Phys Ceram ... Reviews on Powder Metallurgy and Physical Ceramics [*A publication*]
REV PROC ... Revenue Procedure [*Internal Revenue Service*]
Rev Prog Color Relat Top ... Review of Progress in Coloration and Related Topics [*A publication*]
Rev Pub Dat ... Review of Public Data Use [*A publication*]
Rev Pub Data Use ... Review of Public Data Use [*A publication*]
Rev Pure Appl Chem ... Reviews of Pure and Applied Chemistry [*A publication*]

Rev Pure Appl Pharmacol Sci ... Reviews in Pure and Applied Pharmacological Sciences [*A publication*]
REVR........ Receiver (AAG)
REVR........ Reversioner (ROG)
REVR........ Reviewer (AFM)
Rev R......... Revised Reports [*1759-1866*] [*England*] [*A publication*] (DLA)
Rev R Acad Cienc Exactas Fis Nat Madr ... Revista. Real Academia de Ciencias Exactas, Fisicas, y Naturales de Madrid [*A publication*]
Rev R Acad Farm Barcelona ... Revista. Real Academia de Farmacia de Barcelona [*A publication*]
Rev Radic Polit Econ ... Review of Radical Political Economics [*A publication*]
Rev Radiochem Cent (Amersham Eng) ... Review. Radiochemical Centre (Amersham, England) [*A publication*]
Rev Radio Res Lab ... Review. Radio Research Laboratories [*A publication*]
Rev React Species Chem React ... Reviews on Reactive Species in Chemical Reactions [*A publication*]
Rev Real Acad Ci Exact Fis Natur Madrid ... Revista. Real Academia de Ciencias Exactas, Fisicas, y Naturales de Madrid [*A publication*]
Rev Reh...... Reversed [*or Reversing*] on Rehearing [*Used in Shepard's Citations*] [*Legal term*] (DLA)
Rev Relig.... Review for Religious [*A publication*]
Rev Rel Res ... Review of Religious Research [*A publication*]
Rev Rep...... Revised Reports [*England*] [*A publication*] (DLA)
Rev Rep Inf Cent Pol AEC ... Review Report Information Center. Polish Atomic Energy Commission [*A publication*]
Rev Res Vis Arts Educ ... Review of Research in Visual Arts Education [*A publication*]
Rev Rev (A) ... Review of Reviews. Australian Edition [*A publication*]
Rev Revs Australas Ed ... Review of Reviews. Australasian Edition [*A publication*] (APTA)
Rev River Plate ... Review of the River Plate [*A publication*]
REV RUL.. Revenue Ruling [*Internal Revenue Service*]
REVS........ Reconnaissance Electro-Optical Viewing System
REVS........ Requirements Engineering and Validation System
REVS........ Reverse Shot [*Photography*] (WDMC)
REV/S....... Revolutions per Second
REVS........ Rotor Entry Vehicle System [*Aerospace*]
Rev Sao Paulo Braz Univ Fac Med Vet Zootec ... Revista. Sao Paulo Universidade. Faculdade de Medicina Veterinaria e Zootecnia [*A publication*]
Rev de Sci Criminelle et de Droit Penal Compare ... Revue de Science Criminelle et de Droit Penal Compare [*Paris, France*] [*A publication*] (DLA)
Rev Sci Ins ... Review of Scientific Instruments [*A publication*]
Rev Sci Instr ... Review of Scientific Instruments [*A publication*]
Rev Sci Instrum ... Review of Scientific Instruments [*A publication*]
RevScR ...... Regue des Sciences Religieuses [*Strasbourg/Paris*] [*A publication*]
Rev Sec Reg ... Review of Securities Regulation [*A publication*]
Rev Sel Code Leg ... Review of Selected Code Legislation [*A publication*] (DLA)
Rev Ser IAEA ... Review Series. International Atomic Energy Agency [*A publication*]
Rev Serv Espec Saude Publica ... Revista. Servicio Especial de Saude Publica [*A publication*]
Rev Serv Nac Min Geol (Argent) ... Revista. Servicio Nacional Minero Geologico (Argentina) [*A publication*]
Rev Serv Nac Salud ... Revista. Servicio Nacional de Salud [*A publication*]
Rev SESP .. Revista. Servicio Especial de Saude Publica [*A publication*]
Revs Geophys Space Phys ... Reviews of Geophysics and Space Physics [*A publication*]
Rev Silicon Germanium Tin Lead Compd ... Reviews on Silicon, Germanium, Tin, and Lead Compounds [*A publication*]
Rev Soc Argent Biol ... Revista. Sociedad Argentina de Biologia [*A publication*]
Rev Soc Argent Neurol y Psiquiat ... Revista. Sociedad Argentina de Neurologia y Psiquiatria [*A publication*]
Rev Soc Boliv Hist Nat ... Revista. Sociedad Boliviana de Historia Natural [*A publication*]
Rev Soc Bras Agron ... Revista. Sociedade Brasileira de Agronomia [*A publication*]
Rev Soc Bras Med Trop ... Revista. Sociedade Brasileira de Medicina Tropical [*A publication*]
Rev Soc Bras Quim ... Revista. Sociedade Brasileira de Quimica [*A publication*]
Rev Soc Bras Zootec ... Revista. Sociedade Brasileira de Zootecnia [*A publication*]
Rev Soc Cient Parag ... Revista. Sociedad Cientifica del Paraguay [*A publication*]
Rev Soc Colomb Endocrinol ... Revista. Sociedad Colombiana de Endocrinologia [*A publication*]
Rev Soc Cubana Bot ... Revista. Sociedad Cubana de Botanica [*A publication*]
Rev Soc Cubana Ing ... Revista. Sociedad Cubana de Ingenieros [*A publication*]
Rev Soc Cub Hist Med ... Revista. Sociedad Cubana de la Historia de Medicina [*A publication*]
Rev Soc Ec ... Review of Social Economy [*A publication*]
Rev Soc Econ ... Review of Social Economy [*A publication*]

Rev Soc Entomol Argent ... Revista. Sociedad Entomologica Argentina [*A publication*]
Rev Soc Geol Argent ... Revista. Sociedad Geologica Argentina [*A publication*]
Rev Soc L ... Review of Socialist Law [*A publication*]
Rev Soc Lun Int ... Revista. Sociedad Lunar Internacional [*A publication*]
Rev Soc Malacol Carlos Torre ... Revista. Sociedad Malacologica Carlos de la Torre [*A publication*]
Rev Soc Med Argent ... Revista. Sociedad Medica Argentina [*A publication*]
Rev Soc Med Cir Sao Jose Rio Preto ... Revista. Sociedade de Medicina e Cirurgia de Sao Jose Do Rio Preto [*A publication*]
Rev Soc Med Int ... Revista. Sociedad de Medicina Interna [*A publication*]
Rev Soc Med Vet (Buenos Aires) ... Revista. Sociedad de Medicina Veterinaria (Buenos Aires) [*A publication*]
Rev Soc Med Vet Chile ... Revista. Sociedad de Medicina Veterinaria de Chile [*A publication*]
Rev Soc Mex Hig ... Revista. Sociedad Mexicana de Higiene [*A publication*]
Rev Soc Mex Hist Nat ... Revista. Sociedad Mexicana de Historia Natural [*A publication*]
Rev Soc Mex Hist Natur ... Revista. Sociedad Mexicana de Historia Natural [*A publication*]
Rev Soc Mex Lepid AC ... Revista. Sociedad Mexicana de Lepidopterologia. AC [*A publication*]
Rev Soc Mex Lepidopterol AC ... Revista. Sociedad Mexicana de Lepidopterologia. AC [*A publication*]
Rev Soc Obstet Ginec ... Revista. Sociedad de Obstetricia y Ginecologia de Buenos Aires [*A publication*]
Rev Soc Pediat ... Revista. Sociedad de Pediatria [*A publication*]
Rev Soc Pediatr Litoral ... Revista. Sociedad de Pediatria del Litoral [*A publication*]
Rev Soc Peru Endocrinol ... Revista. Sociedad Peruana de Endocrinologia [*A publication*]
Rev Soc Quim Mex ... Revista. Sociedad Quimica de Mexico [*A publication*]
Rev Soc Rural Rosario ... Revista. Sociedad Rural de Rosario [*A publication*]
Rev Soc Venez Cardiol ... Revista. Sociedad Venezolana de Cardiologia [*A publication*]
Rev Soc Venez Hist Med ... Revista. Sociedad Venezolana de Historia de la Medicina [*A publication*]
Rev Soc Venez Quim ... Revista. Sociedad Venezolana de Quimica [*A publication*]
Rev Solid State Sci ... Reviews of Solid State Science [*A publication*]
Rev Sov Med ... Review of Soviet Medicine [*A publication*]
Rev Sov Med Sci ... Review of Soviet Medical Sciences [*A publication*]
Rev Sport Leisure ... Review of Sport and Leisure [*A publication*]
Rev St........ Revised Statutes [*A publication*] (DLA)
Rev Stat...... Revised Statutes [*Various jurisdictions*] [*A publication*] (DLA)
Rev Suisse Dr Int'l Concurrence ... Revue Suisse du Droit International de la Concurrence [*Swiss Review of International Antitrust Law*] [*A publication*] (DLA)
Rev Surg..... Review of Surgery [*A publication*]
Rev Sw Dig ... Revision of Swift's Digest of Connecticut Laws [*A publication*] (DLA)
Revta Fac Farm Bioquim S Paulo ... Revista. Faculdade de Farmacia e Bioquimica. Universidade de Sao Paulo [*A publication*]
Revta Mus Argent Cienc Nat Bernardina Rivadavia Zool ... Revista. Museo Argentino de Ciencias Naturales Bernardino Rivadavia. Zoologia [*A publication*]
RevTar ...... Revenue Tariff [*Australia*] [*Political party*]
Rev Tax Indiv ... Review of Taxation of Individuals [*A publication*]
Rev Tax'n Indiv ... Review of Taxation of Individuals [*A publication*] (DLA)
Rev & TC ... Revenue and Taxation Code [*A publication*] (DLA)
Rev Textile Progr ... Review of Textile Progress [*A publication*]
Rev Text Progr ... Review of Textile Progress [*A publication*]
Rev Trimestr de Jurispr ... Revista Trimestral de Jurisprudencia [*Rio De Janeiro, Brazil*] [*A publication*] (DLA)
Rev Tunisienne de Droit ... Revue Tunisienne de Droit [*Tunis, Tunisia*] [*A publication*] (DLA)
Rev Tussock Grassl Mt Lands Inst ... Review. Tussock Grasslands and Mountain Lands Institute [*A publication*]
Rev Un B.... Revue. Universite de Bruxelles [*A publication*]
Rev Union Mat Argent ... Revista. Union Matematica Argentina [*A publication*]
Rev Union Mat Argent Asoc Fis Argent ... Revista. Union Matematica Argentina y Asociacion Fisica Argentina [*A publication*]
Rev Univ Brux ... Revue. Universite de Bruxelles [*A publication*]
Rev Univ Burundi ... Revue. Universite du Burundi [*A publication*]
Rev Univ Fed Para Ser II ... Revista. Universidade Federal do Para. Serie II [*A publication*]
Rev Univ Natl Zaire Campus Lubumbashi Ser B ... Revue. Universite Nationale du Zaire. Campus de Lubumbashi. Serie B. Sciences [*A publication*]
Rev Univ Ottawa ... Revue. Universite d'Ottawa [*A publication*]
Rev Un Mat Argentina ... Revista. Union Matematica Argentina [*A publication*]
REVW .... Review (NVT)
Rev Warren Spring Lab (UK) ... Review. Warren Spring Laboratory (United Kingdom) [*A publication*]
Rev World ... Revolutionary World [*A publication*]
REVY........ Reversionary (ROG)
REW .... Recycle Water [*Nuclear energy*] (NRCH)
REW .... Redwood Valley, CA [*Location identifier*] [*FAA*] (FAAL)

REW	Reward (AFM)
REW	Rewind (MDG)
REW	Russisch-Etymologisches Woerterbuch [*A publication*]
REWDAC ...	Retrieval by Title Words, Descriptors, and Classification (DIT)
REWK	Rework (MSA)
REWRC.....	Report When Established Well to Right of Course [*Aviation*] (FAAC)
REWS.......	Radio Electronic Warfare Service (MCD)
REWSON ...	Reconnaissance, Electronic Warfare, Special Operations, and Naval Intelligence Processing Systems
REX	Ram Air Freight, Inc. [*Hillsborough, NC*] [*FAA designator*] (FAAC)
REX	Rapid Text Search [*Data processing*] (IT)
REX	Rare-Earth Exchanged [*Faujasite, a zeolite*]
REX	Reactor Experimental [*Former USSR*] (DEN)
REX	Real-Time Executive Routine [*Data processing*]
REX	Rechtswissenschaftliche Experten und Gutachter [*NOMOS Datapool*] [*Database*]
REX	Reduced Exoatmospheric Cross Section
REX	Reentry Experiment
REX	Reflector Erosion Experiment [*NASA*]
REX	Regression Expert [*Data processing*]
REX	Related Experience (SAA)
REX	Requisition Exception Code [*Air Force*] (AFIT)
REX	Research, Evaluation, and Experimental Program [*Bureau of the Census*] (GFGA)
R EX........	Review and Expositor [*A publication*]
REX	Rex Silver Mines [*Vancouver Stock Exchange symbol*]
REX	Rexburg [*Idaho*] [*Seismograph station code, US Geological Survey*] (SEIS)
REX	Rexnord [*NYSE symbol*] (SPSG)
REX	Reynosa [*Mexico*] [*Airport symbol*] (OAG)
REX	Robot Excavation [*Carnegie-Mellon Robotics Institute*]
REX	Run Executive [*Data processing*]
REXC.......	Reserve Exploration Co. [*NASDAQ symbol*] (NQ)
Rexene	Rexene Corp. [*Associated Press abbreviation*] (APAG)
REXI........	Resource Exploration, Inc. [*NASDAQ symbol*] (NQ)
R Exist Psych Psych ...	Review of Existential Psychology and Psychiatry [*A publication*]
REXL........	Rexhall Industries, Inc. [*NASDAQ symbol*] (NQ)
REXMIT ...	Retransmitted (AABC)
REXN	Rexon, Inc. [*NASDAQ symbol*] (NQ)
Rexnrd	Rexnord Corp. [*Associated Press abbreviation*] (APAG)
Rexroth Inf ...	Rexroth Informationen [*A publication*]
REXS........	Radio Exploration Satellite [*Japan*]
REXW	Rexworks, Inc. [*NASDAQ symbol*] (NQ)
REY	Reentry
REY	Reyes [*Bolivia*] [*Airport symbol*] (OAG)
REY	Reykjavik [*Iceland*] [*Seismograph station code, US Geological Survey*] (SEIS)
REY	Reynolds & Reynolds Co. [*NYSE symbol*] (SPSG)
REY	Rush Ventures, Inc. [*Vancouver Stock Exchange symbol*]
ReyMtl......	Reynolds Metals Co. [*Associated Press abbreviation*] (APAG)
Reyn.........	Reynolds, Reports [*40-42 Mississippi*] [*A publication*] (DLA)
REYN	[*The*] Reynolds and Reynolds Co. [*NASDAQ symbol*] (NQ)
Reyn L Ins ...	Reynold's Life Insurance [*A publication*] (DLA)
Reynolds	Reynolds, Reports [*40-42 Mississippi*] [*A publication*] (DLA)
Reynolds' Land Laws ...	Reynolds' Spanish and Mexican Land Laws [*A publication*] (DLA)
Reyon Synth Zellwolle ...	Reyon, Synthetica, Zellwolle [*A publication*]
Reyon Zellwolle Andere Chem Fasern ...	Reyon, Zellwolle, und Andere Chemie Fasern [*A publication*]
ReyRey.......	Reynolds & Reynolds Co. [*Associated Press abbreviation*] (APAG)
Reyrolle Parsons Rev ...	Reyrolle Parsons Review [*A publication*]
REZ	Mary Esther, FL [*Location identifier*] [*FAA*] (FAAL)
Rezanie Instrum ...	Rezanie i Instrument [*A publication*]
Re Zh Khim Neftepererab Polim Mashinostr ...	Referativnyi Zhurnal. Khimicheskoe. Neftepererabatyuayushchee i Polimerjnoe Mashinostroenie [*A publication*]
Rezul't Issled Mezhdunar Geofiz Proektam ...	Rezul'taty Issledovanyi po Mezhdunarodny Geofizicheskim Proektam [*Former USSR*] [*A publication*]
RF	Fournier [*France*] [*ICAO aircraft manufacturer identifier*] (ICAO)
RF	Franc [*Monetary unit*] [*Rwanda*]
RF	Radial Fibers [*Ear anatomy*]
RF	Radial Flow (AAG)
RF	Radical Force (EA)
RF	Radio Facility
RF	Radio Frequency [*Transmission*]
RF	Railroad Financial Corp. [*AMEX symbol*] (SPSG)
RF	Rainfed [*Agriculture*]
RF	Rainform (MCD)
RF	Raised Face (MSA)
RF	Range-Finder [*Gunnery*]
R & F........	Rank and File
RF	Rapeseed Flour [*Food technology*]
RF	Rapid-Fire
RF	Rapports des Fouilles [*A publication*]
Rf	Rate of Flow [*Medicine*] (MAE)

RF	Rating Factor (IEEE)
RF	Razon y Fe [*A publication*]
R & F.........	Reach and Frequency [*Advertising*] (WDMC)
RF	Read Forward
RF	Reason Foundation (EA)
RF	Reception Fair [*Radio logs*]
RF	Receptive Field [*of visual cortex*]
RF	Reconnaissance Fighter (MUGU)
RF	Reconnaissance Force
RF	Recovery Forces
RF	Recovery Forecast
RF	Recruitment for the Armed Forces [*British*]
RF	Rectus Femoris [*A muscle*] [*Anatomy*]
RF	Red Fumes (NATG)
RF	Reducing Flame
RF	Reef
RF	Reference [*Online database field identifier*]
RF	Reference Fuel
RF	Reflight
RF	Refunding
RF	Regional Forces [*ARVN*]
RF	Register File
RF	Register Finder
RF	Reitland-Franklin Unit (AAMN)
RF	Relative Flow [*Rate*]
Rf	Relative Fluorescence [*Analytical chemistry*] (MAE)
Rf	Relative to the Solvent Front [*Paper chromatography*] [*Analytical chemistry*]
RF	Release Factor (NRCH)
RF	Releasing Factor [*Also, RH*] [*Endocrinology*]
RF	Reliability Factor
RF	Renal Failure [*Medicine*]
RF	Rent Free
RF	Replacement Factor [*Military*]
RF	Replicative Factor [*or Form*] [*Genetics*]
RF	Reply Finding [*Nuclear energy*] (NRCH)
RF	Reporting File
RF	Representative Fraction
RF	Republique Francaise [*A publication*]
RF	Republique Francaise [*French Republic*]
RF	Reserve Flight [*British military*] (DMA)
RF	Reserve Force
RF	Resistance Factor
RF	Resorcinol-Formaldehyde [*Organic chemistry*]
RF	Respectable Frere [*Worshipful Brother*] [*French*] [*Freemasonry*] (ROG)
RF	Respiratory Failure [*Medicine*]
RF	Response Factor
RF	Retardation Factor
RF	Retention File [*IRS*]
RF	Reticular Formation [*Sleep*]
RF	Retroperitoneal Fibromatosis [*Oncology*]
RF	Reverse Free
RF	Revolving Fund [*Finance*]
RF	Rex Francorum [*King of the Franks*] [*Latin*]
RF	RFG Reiseflug und Industrieflug GmbH [*West Germany*] [*ICAO designator*] (FAAC)
RF	Rheumatic Fever [*Medicine*]
RF	Rheumatoid Factor [*Also known as IgM*] [*Immunology*]
RF	Rhinal Fissure [*Anatomy*]
RF	Rhodesian Front [*Later, Republican Front*]
RF	Riboflavin [*Biochemistry*]
RF	Rice Flour (OA)
RF	Richmond Fellowship (EAIO)
RF	Rifampin [*Also, R/AMP, RIF, RMP*] [*Bactericide*]
RF	Riffle Frequency
RF	Rigging Fixtures (MCD)
RF	Right Field [*or Fielder*] [*Baseball*]
RF	Right Foot
RF	Right Forward [*Football*]
RF	Right Front
RF	Right Fullback [*Soccer*]
RF	Rinforzando [*With Special Emphasis*] [*Music*]
RF	Ring Frame
RF	Ripple Factor
rf...............	Rise of Floor (DS)
RF	Rockefeller Foundation
RF	Rodeo Foundation (EA)
RF	Roll Film [*Photography*]
RF	Romanische Forschungen [*A publication*]
RF	Roof (WGA)
RF	Roof Fan (OA)
RF	Rosicrucian Fellowship (EA)
RF	Rosicrucian Fraternity (EA)
RF	Rough Finish
RF	Royal Fusiliers [*Military unit*] [*British*]
RF	Royal Windsor Foresters [*British military*] (DMA)
RF	Ruch Filozoficzny [*A publication*]
RF	Running Forward
Rf	Rutherfordium [*Proposed name for chemical element 104*] [*See also Ku*]

RF .... Sisters of St. Philip Neri Missionary Teachers [*Roman Catholic religious order*]
RF1 .... Federal Reserve Bank of Boston, Boston, MA [*OCLC symbol*]   (OCLC)
RFA .... RADAR Filter Assembly
RFA .... Radiation Field Analyzer
RFA .... Radio Frequency Allocation   (MCD)
RFA .... Radio Frequency Amplifier
RFA .... Radio Frequency Attenuator   (MCD)
RFA .... Radio Frequency Authorizations [*Air Force*]
RFA .... Raleigh Flying Service, Inc. [*Morrisville, NC*] [*FAA designator*]   (FAAC)
RFA .... Rapid Flow Analysis
RFA .... RCRA [*Resource Conservation and Recovery Act*] Facility Assessment
RFA .... Recommendation for Acceptance   (AAG)
RFA .... Recurrent Fault Analysis [*Telecommunications*]   (TEL)
RFA .... Registered Fitness Appraiser [*Canadian Association of Sports Sciences*]
RFA .... Regulatory Flexibility Act
RFA .... Relieved from Assigned [*Military*]
RFA .... Remote File Access
RFA .... Renewable Fuels Association   (EA)
RFA .... Request for Action   (KSC)
RFA .... Request for Alteration   (AAG)
RFA .... Request for Analysis
RFA .... Request for Application
RFA .... Request for Assistance   (GFGA)
RFA .... Request Further Airways [*Aviation*]   (FAAC)
RFA .... Request for Grant Applications
RFA .... Reserve Forces Act
RFA .... Restrictive Fire Area [*Military*]   (AABC)
RFA .... Retarding Field Analyzer [*Surface analysis*]
RFA .... Right Femoral Artery [*Anatomy*]
RFA .... Right Frontoanterior [*A fetal position*] [*Obstetrics*]
RFA .... Rimfire Adapter   (MCD)
RFA .... Risley Family Association   (EA)
RFA .... Rocky Flats Area Office   (SAA)
RFA .... Roll Follow-Up Amplifier
RFA .... Royal Field Artillery [*Military*] [*British*]
RFA .... Royal Fleet Auxiliary [*British*]
RFA .... Rural Forestry Assistance [*Program*] [*Forest Service*]
RFAA .... Relieved from Attached and Assigned [*Army*]
RFAC .... Royal Fine Art Commission [*British*]
R Fac Cienc Ec Com ... Revista. Facultad de Ciencias Economicas y Comerciales [*A publication*]
R Fac Der (Caracas) ... Revista. Facultad de Derecho (Caracas) [*A publication*]
R Fac Der Mexico ... Revista. Facultad de Derecho de Mexico [*A publication*]
RFAD .... Released from Active Duty Not Result of Demobilization [*Navy*]
RFAD .... Request for Accelerated Delivery   (MCD)
RFAED ...... Readiness Forecast Authorization Equipment Data [*Air Force*]   (AFM)
RFAF .... Request for Additional Fire   (MCD)
RF/AFG .... Radio Frequency/Acoustic Firing Group [*Military*]   (CAAL)
RFAGB ...... Riforma Agraria [*A publication*]
RFAGC ...... Rainbows for All God's Children   (EA)
RFALROU ... Request Follow-Up Action on Listed Requisitions Indicated Still Outstanding in Unit [*Army*]   (AABC)
RFAO .... Rocky Flats Area Office [*Energy Research and Development Administration*]
RFAS .... Radio Frequency Attitude Sensor
RFASIX ..... Reserve Forces Act of 1955, Six Months Trainee
RFASS .... Rapid Fire Artillery Support System   (MCD)
RFAT .... Relieved from Attached [*Army*]   (AABC)
RFATE ...... Radio Frequency Automatic Test Equipment   (MCD)
RFATHREE ... Reserve Forces Act of 1955, Three Months Trainee
RFB .... Air-Cushion Vehicle built by Rhein Flugzeugbau [*Germany*] [*Usually used in combination with numerals*]
RFB .... Rabobank [*A publication*]
RFB .... Ready for Baseline   (NASA)
RFB .... Reason for Backlog [*Telecommunications*]   (TEL)
RFB .... Recording for the Blind   (EA)
RFB .... Recording for the Blind, Bethesda, MD [*OCLC symbol*]   (OCLC)
RFB .... Reliability Functional Block
RFB .... Request for Bid   (AFM)
RFB .... Retained Foreign Body [*Medicine*]
RFB .... Right Fullback [*Soccer*]
RFBA .... Reserve Forces Benefit Association [*Later, REA*]   (EA)
RFBABQ ... Anais. Reuniao de Fitossanitarisatas do Brasil [*A publication*]
RFBC .... River Forest Bancorp [*NASDAQ symbol*]   (NQ)
RFBI .... Regional Federal Bancorp, Inc. [*NASDAQ symbol*]   (NQ)
RFBK .... RS Financial Corp. [*Formerly, Raleigh Federal Savings Bank*] [*NASDAQ symbol*]   (NQ)
RFC .... Radio Facility Charts   (MCD)
RFC .... Radio Frequency Chart   (AAG)
RFC .... Radio Frequency Choke   (AAG)
RFC .... Radio Frequency Communications
RFC .... Radio Frequency Compatibility

RFC .... Radio Frequency Crystal
RFC .... Railroad Freight Classification
RFC .... Ranger Fan Club   (EA)
RFC .... Rare Fruit Council [*Later, RFCI*]   (EA)
RFC .... Ravan Fan Club   (EA)
RFC .... Reason for Change   (MCD)
RFC .... Recirculation Flow Control [*Nuclear energy*]   (NRCH)
RFC .... Reconstruction Finance Corp. [*Abolished, 1957*]
RFC .... Reduced Function Computer [*Data processing*]
RFC .... Reference Concentration [*Toxicology*]
RFC .... Regenerative Fuel Cell
RFC .... Relative Force Capability   (NATG)
RFC .... Religious Formation Conference   (EA)
RFC .... Remote Food Carriers [*Army*]   (INF)
RFC .... Request for Change   (KSC)
RFC .... Request for Comment [*Telecommunications*]   (PCM)
RFC .... Request for Confirmation   (MCD)
RFC .... Request for Contract   (GFGA)
RFC .... Required Functional Capability [*Navy*]
RFC .... Research Facilities Center [*National Oceanic and Atmospheric Administration*]   (GRD)
RFC .... Residual Functional Capacity [*Social Security Administration*]   (OICC)
RFC .... Residuum Fluid Cracking [*Petroleum refining*]
RFC .... Resolution Funding Corp. [*Established by the Financial Institutions Reform, Recovery, and Enforcement Act of 1989*]
RFC .... Resources for Communication [*Information service or system*]   (IID)
RFC .... Retirement-for-Cause [*Program*] [*Air Force*]
RFC .... RFC Resource Finance Corp. [*Toronto Stock Exchange symbol*]
RFC .... RFC Resources Corp. [*Vancouver Stock Exchange symbol*]
RFC .... River Forecast Center [*National Weather Service*]   (NOAA)
RFC .... Rosette-Forming Cell [*Immunochemistry*]
RFC .... Royal Flying Corps [*Later, RAF*] [*British*]
RFC .... Royal Flying Cross [*British*]   (IIA)
RFC .... Rugby Football Club
RFCA .... Racing Fans Club of America   (EA)
RFCA .... Reconstruction Finance Corporation Act [*Obsolete*]
RFCA .... Residual Functional Capacity Assessment [*Social Security Administration*]   (GFGA)
RFCEA ...... Revival Fires (Christian Evangelizers Association)   (EA)
RFCFDE .... Revista. Faculdade de Ciencias Farmaceuticas [*Araraquara*] [*A publication*]
RFCG .... Radio Frequency Command Generator   (MCD)
RFCI .... Rare Fruit Council International   (EA)
RFCI .... Resilient Floor Covering Institute   (EA)
RFCM .... Radio Frequency Control Monitor [*Formerly, RFU*]   (MCD)
RFCMC ..... Reconstruction Finance Corporation Mortgage Co.
RFCO .... Radio Frequency Checkout   (AAG)
RFCP .... Radio Frequency Compatibility Program
RFCP .... Request for Computer Program   (NASA)
RFCP .... Requests for Contractual Procurement   (MUGU)
RFCR .... Refacer
RFCS .... Radio Frequency Carrier Shift   (NVT)
RFCS .... Recirculation Flow Control System [*Nuclear energy*]   (NRCH)
RFCS .... Regenerative Fuel Cell Subsystem
RFCSEUSG ... Retirement Federation of Civil Service Employees of the United States Government [*Defunct*]   (EA)
RFCT .... Report of Federal Cash Transactions   (OICC)
RFCVET .... Revista. Facultad de Ciencias Veterinarias [*A publication*]
RFD .... Radiation Flux Density
RFD .... Radio Frequency Demodulator
RFD .... Radio Frequency Display   (MCD)
RFD .... Raised Face Diameter   (MSA)
RFD .... Raised Foredeck [*of a ship*]   (DS)
RFD .... Reactor Flight Demonstration
RFD .... Ready for Data   (IEEE)
RFD .... Ready for Delivery   (MUGU)
RFD .... Ready for Duty
RFD .... Reentry Flight Demonstration
RfD .... Reference Dose [*Environmental science*]
RFD .... Refurbish for Delivery   (MCD)
RFD .... Released for Delivery   (NG)
RFD .... Remote Frequency Display   (MCD)
RFD .... Reporting for Duty [*Air Force*]
RFD .... Request for Delivery
RFD .... Request for Deviation
RFD .... Request for Parts Disposition   (MCD)
RFD .... Requirements Formulation Document [*NASA*]   (NASA)
RFD .... Reserve Forces Duty [*Military*]   (MCD)
RFD .... Residual Flux Density
RFD .... Reverse-Flux Diverter [*Engineering*]
RFD .... Rockford [*Illinois*] [*Airport symbol*]   (OAG)
RFD .... Rockford Minerals, Inc. [*Toronto Stock Exchange symbol*]
RFD .... Rural Free Delivery [*of mail*]
RFDA .... Request for Deviation Approval
RFDB .... Red Flag Database [*Air Force*]   (GFGA)
RFDL .... Radio Frequency Data Link   (MCD)
RFDT .... Reliability Failure Diagnostic Team   (AAG)
RFDU .... Reconfiguration and Fault Detection Unit

RFE............ Radio Free Europe [*A publication*]
RFE............ Radio Free Europe
R Fe............ Razon y Fe [*A publication*]
RFE............ Request for Effectivity   (MCD)
RFE............ Request for Estimate   (KSC)
RFE............ Request for Expenditure
RFE............ Rotating Field Electrophoresis [*Analytical biochemistry*]
RFE............ Rutherfordton, NC [*Location identifier*] [*FAA*]   (FAAL)
RFEA......... Radio Frequency Equipment Analyzer
RFEA......... Regular Forces Employment Association [*British military*]   (DMA)
RFECM..... Revised for Engineering Change Memorandum   (SAA)
RFED........ Radio Frequency Expandable Decoy   (DWSG)
RFED........ Research Facilities and Equipment Division [*NASA*]   (MCD)
RFED........ Roosevelt Financial Group, Inc. [*NASDAQ symbol*]   (NQ)
R Fed Am Hosp ... Review. Federation of American Hospitals [*A publication*]
RFEHB...... Retired Federal Employees Health Benefits Program   (MCD)
RFEI......... Request for Engineering Information   (KSC)
RFELB...... Radio Fernsehen Elektronik [*A publication*]
RF/EMI.... Radio Frequency and Electromagnetic-Interference [*Telecommunications*]
RFEN........ Reef Energy Corp. [*NASDAQ symbol*]   (NQ)
RFEP........ Reserve Female Enlistment Program [*Military*]   (DNAB)
RFER........ Reefer [*Military*]   (DNAB)
RFERB...... Radio Free Europe. Research Bulletin [*A publication*]
RFE/RL..... Radio Free Europe/Radio Liberty   (EA)
RFF............ Radio Frequency Filter
RFF............ Radio Frequency Finder   (NVT)
RFF............ Radio Frequency Fuze
RFF............ Random Force Field
RFF............ Ready for Ferry [*Navy*]   (NVT)
RFF............ Recirculative Fluid Flow
RFF............ REFF, Inc. [*Toronto Stock Exchange symbol*]
RFF............ Refuge from Flood   (ADA)
RFF............ Regular Federal Funds [*Medicaid*]   (GFGA)
RFF............ Relative Failure Frequency
RFF............ Relief from Face to Face [*Education*]
RFF............ Remote Fiber Fluorometer [*Instrumentation*]
RFF............ Request for Fire [*Military*]
RFF............ Request for Form
RFF............ Research Flight Facility [*Air Force*]
RFF............ Resources for the Future
RFF............ Rift-Fracture-Fracture [*Geology*]
RFF............ Royal Filling Factory [*British military*]   (DMA)
RFFC........ Randy Floyd Fan Club   (EA)
RFFD........ Radio Frequency Fault Detection
RFFH........ Revista. Facultad de Filosofia y Humanidades [*A publication*]
RFFID4 ..... Canadian Forestry Service. Forest Pest Management Institute. Information Report. FPM-X [*A publication*]
RFFLUP.... Revista. Faculdade de Filosofia e Letras. Universidade do Parana [*A publication*]
RFFO........ Request for Factory Order   (MCD)
RFFSA...... Rede Ferroviaria Federal Sociedade Anonima [*Federal Railway Corporation*] [*Brazil*]   (EY)
RFG .... RADAR Field Gradient   (IEEE)
RFG .... Radio Frequency Generator
RFG .... Rapid-Fire Gun
RFG .... Rate and Free Gyro
RFG .... Receive Format Generator
RFG .... Reformulated Gasoline
RFG .... Refugio, TX [*Location identifier*] [*FAA*]   (FAAL)
RFG .... Refunding [*Business term*]
RFG .... Reise und Industrieflug [*Airline*] [*Germany*]
RFG .... Report Format Generator
RFG .... Rhodesian Financial Gazette [*A publication*]
RFG .... Rifle Fine Grain [*British military*]   (DMA)
RFG .... Roofing   (AAG)
RFG .... Royscot Finance Group [*Royal Bank of Scotland*]
RFGN .... Refrigeration [*Charges*]
RFGND ..... RoeFo. Fortschritte auf dem Gebiete der Roentgenstrahlen und der Nuklearmedizin [*A publication*]
RFGT........ Refrigerant   (MSA)
RFH.......... Radio Frequency Heating
RFH.......... Raised Face Height   (MSA)
RFH.......... Reichsfinanzhof [*Reich Finance Court*] [*German*]   (ILCA)
RFH.......... Roof Hatch [*Technical drawings*]
RFH.......... Royal Festival Hall [*London*]
RFH.......... Royal Free Hospital
RFHC........ Revista. Facultad de Humanidades y Ciencias [*A publication*]
RFHCO ..... Rocket Fuel Handler Clothing Outfit [*Protective suit*]
RFHI .... Real Fire Heating International Exhibition [*British*]   (ITD)
RFHT........ Radio Frequency Horn Technique
RFI........... RADAR Frequency Interferometer   (MCD)
RFI........... Radio Frequency Indicator
RFI........... Radio Frequency Interchange   (MDG)
RFI........... Radio Frequency Interface   (MCD)
RFI........... Radio Frequency Interference
RFI........... Rajneesh Foundation International   (EA)
RFI........... RCRA [*Resource Conservation and Recovery Act*] Facility Investigation
RFI........... Ready for Installation   (MCD)

RFI............ Ready for Issue [*Military*]
RFI............ Regionalism and the Female Imagination [*A publication*]
RFI............ Relative Fluorescent Intensity [*Analytical chemistry*]
RFI............ Release for Issue   (MCD)
RFI............ Remote Facility Inquiry [*NASA*]   (KSC)
RFI............ Remote File Inquiry [*NASA*]   (NASA)
RFI............ Report/File Language   (HGAA)
RFI............ Representative of a Foreign Interest
RFI............ Request for Information
RFI............ Request for Investigation
RFI............ Request for Issue
RFI............ Requested for Information
RFI............ Retail Floorcovering Institute [*Later, AFA*]   (EA)
RFI............ Richmond Fellowship International [*British*]   (EAIO)
RFID......... Radio Frequency Identification
RFID......... Request for Implementation Date
RFIF .... Refund Information File [*IRS*]
RFIFO ...... Receive, First-In, First-Out [*Communications engineering*]
RFil.......... Russkaja Filologija [*A publication*]
RF Illus... RF [*Rockefeller Foundation*] Illustrated [*A publication*]
RFIM....... Radio Frequency Interference Meter
RFIN........ Rock Finance Corp. [*NASDAQ symbol*]   (NQ)
RFIP .... Radio Frequency Impedance Probe
RF/IR .... RADAR Frequency/Infrared Frequency   (IEEE)
RFIT .... Radio Frequency Interference Tests   (KSC)
RFIT .... THE Fitness Centers, Inc. [*Coral Springs, FL*] [*NASDAQ symbol*]   (NQ)
RFJ .... Radio Free Jazz [*A publication*]
RFJ .... Radio Frequency Joint
RFJI......... Research Foundation for Jewish Immigration   (EA)
RFK......... Anguilla, MS [*Location identifier*] [*FAA*]   (FAAL)
RFK......... Radio Free Kabul [*British*]   (EAIO)
RFK......... Reflets et Perspectives de la Vie Economique [*A publication*]
RFK......... Robert Francis Kennedy [*American politician, 1925-68*]
RFKM....... Robert F. Kennedy Memorial   (EA)
RFL......... Radio Frequency Laboratories
RFL......... Radio Frequency Lens
RFL......... Radio-Frequency LINAC   (SDI)
RFL......... Reduced Focal Length
RFil......... Reflect   (NASA)
RFL......... Reflector [*or Reflected*]
RFL......... Refuel   (AAG)
RFL......... Reports of Family Law [*A publication*]
RFL......... Requested Flight Level
RFL......... Reset Flux Level
RFL......... Resorcinol-Formaldehyde-Latex
RFL......... Restrictive Fire Line [*Military*]   (AABC)
RFL......... Revista. Faculdade de Letras. Universidade de Lisboa [*A publication*]
RFL......... Right Frontolateral [*Anatomy*]   (AAMN)
RFL......... Rough Field Landing
RFLA....... Rheumatoid Factor-Like Activity [*Immunology*]   (MAE)
RFLD....... Radio Frequency Leakage Detector
RFL 2d...... Reports of Family Law. Second Series [*A publication*]
RFLHGA... Revue. Faculte de Langues, d'Histoire, et de Geographie. Universite d'Ankara [*A publication*]
RFLL....... Revista. Faculdade de Letras. Universidade de Lisboa [*A publication*]
RFLMN.... Rifleman   (AABC)
RFLP........ Restriction Fragment Length Polymorphism [*Genetics*]
R/FLR ...... Rear Floor [*Automotive engineering*]
RFLS .... Rheumatoid Factor-Like Substance [*Immunology*]   (MAE)
RFLT .... Right Front Lining Temperature [*Automotive engineering*]
RFLUL ...... Revista. Faculdade de Letras. Universidade de Lisboa [*A publication*]
RFLX .... Reflex   (MSA)
RFM .... Radio Frequency Management   (NOAA)
RFM .... Radio Frequency Monitoring [*Military*]   (CAAL)
RFM .... Reactive Factor Meter
RFM .... Red Fox Minerals [*Vancouver Stock Exchange symbol*]
RFM .... Refueling Mission [*Air Force*]
RFM .... Release for Manufacture   (DNAB)
RFM .... Reserve Forces Modernization   (MCD)
RFM .... Roll Follow-Up Motor
RFM .... Roll Forming Machine
RFM .... Runway Friction Measurement [*Aviation*]
RFM .... Rural Financial Market
RFMA....... Reliability Figure of Merit Analysis
RFMC....... Regional Fishery Management Council [*National Oceanic and Atmospheric Administration*]   (MSC)
RFMNB.... Rein et Foie. Maladies de la Nutrition [*A publication*]
RFMO ...... Radio Frequency Management Office   (MCD)
RFMS .... Remote File Management System
RFMT....... Runway Friction Measurement Test [*Aviation*]
RFN .... Radio Frequency Noise
RFN .... Raufarhofn [*Iceland*] [*Airport symbol*]   (OAG)
RFN .... Registered Fever Nurse
RFN .... Remote Filter Niche [*Nuclear energy*]   (NRCH)
RFN .... Rifleman
RFNA .... Radio Frequency Noise Analyzer   (DNAB)
RFNA .... Red Fuming Nitric Acid

RFNCC...... Regional Nuclear Fuel Cycle Centers
RFND........ Refined (MSA)
RFNG........ Roofing
RFNM....... Ready for Next Message
RFNRE...... Revolving Fund for Natural Resources Exploration [*United Nations*] (EY)
RFO.......... Radio Frequency Oscillator
RFO .... Ready for Occupancy (MCD)
RFO .... Reason for Outage (FAAC)
RFO .... Regional Field Officer [*Civil Defense*]
RFO .... Request for Factory Order (MCD)
RFO .... Request for Orders [*Military*]
RFO .... Research Fiscal Office (SAA)
RFO .... Retrofire Officer [*NASA*] (KSC)
RFO .... Roll Follow-Up Operation
RFOA .... Reasonable Factors Other than Age [*Equal Employment Opportunity Commission*]
RFOB........ Rear Face of Block [*Automotive engineering*]
RFOFD6.... Revista. Faculdade de Odontologia de Araraquara [*A publication*]
RFOFM..... Records for Our Fighting Men [*Collected phonograph records during World War II*]
RFOG .... Resonant Fiber Optic Gyroscope
RF & OOA ... Railway Fuel and Operating Officers Association [*Later, IAROO*] (EA)
RFOP........ Regional Financial Operating Plan
RForsch ..... Romanische Forschungen [*A publication*]
RFP........... Radio Finger Printing [*Identification of wireless radio operators by individual keying characteristics*]
RFP........... Radio Free People [*An association*] [*Defunct*]
RFP........... Radio Frequency Plasma
RFP........... Radio Frequency Pulse (MCD)
RFP........... Raiatea [*French Polynesia*] [*Airport symbol*] (OAG)
RFP........... Rapid Filling Period [*Cardiology*]
RFP........... Reactor Feed Pump [*Nuclear energy*] (NRCH)
RFP........... Registered Financial Planner [*Designation awarded by International Association of Registered Financial Planners*]
RFP........... Relative Frass Production [*Ecology*]
RFP........... Remaining Force Potential (MCD)
RFP........... Reproductive Freedom Project [*ACLU*] [*Attempts to enforce the Supreme Court decisions guaranteeing a woman's right to choose abortion*] (EA)
RFP........... Republicans for Progress [*Defunct*]
RFP........... Request for Price Quotation
RFP........... Request for Programming [*Data processing*]
RFP........... Request for Proposal
RFP........... Request for Purchase
RFP........... Requirements and Formulation Phase (MCD)
RFP........... Requirements for Production [*Army*] (RDA)
RFP........... Requisition for Procurement [*DoD*]
RFP........... Retired on Full Pay [*Military*] [*British*]
RFP........... Reversed Field Pinch [*Plasma physics*] (NRCH)
RFP........... Reviews for Physicians [*Elsevier Book Series*] [*A publication*]
RFP........... Richmond, Fredericksburg & Potomac Railroad Co. [*AAR code*]
RFP........... Right Frontoposterior [*A fetal position*] [*Obstetrics*]
RFPA........ Request for Part Approval (MCD)
RFPA........ Request for Proposal Authorization [*NASA*] (NASA)
RFPA........ Right to Financial Privacy Act
RFPB........ Reserve Forces Policy Board [*DoD*]
RFPC........ Reserve Flag Officer Policy Council [*Navy*]
RFPC......... RF & P Corp. [*NASDAQ symbol*] (NQ)
RF/PF........ Regional Forces - Popular Forces [*Republic of Vietnam*] [*Army*]
RFPI .... Registered Financial Planners Institute (EA)
RFPP .... Radio Frequency Propagation Program (NG)
RFPR........ Radiant Flash Pyrolysis Reactor [*Chemical engineering*]
RFPRA...... Reactor Fuel Processing [*A publication*]
RFPRS...... Retail Food Price-Reporting System
RFPS .... Request for Proposal Supplement (DNAB)
RFPS .... Royal Faculty of Physicians and Surgeons of Glasgow
RFPT........ Reactor Feed Pump Turbine [*Nuclear energy*] (NRCH)
RFQ .... Radio-Frequency Quadrupole [*Accelerator for subatomic physics study*]
RFQ .... Request for Qualifications (OICC)
RFQ .... Request for Quotation
RFR........... Radial Flow Reactor [*Chemical engineering*]
RFR........... Radio Frequency Receiver
RFR........... Radio Frequency Relay
RFR........... Rear Engine, Front and Rear Drive [*Automotive design*]
RFR........... Redfern Resources [*Vancouver Stock Exchange symbol*]
RFR........... Reduced Frequency Response [*Telecommunications*] (OA)
RFR........... Refraction (AAMN)
RFR........... Reject Failure Rate
RFr........... Required Freight Rate (DS)
RFr........... Revolution Francaise [*A publication*]
RFR........... Rio Frio [*Costa Rica*] [*Airport symbol*] (OAG)
RFR........... Roofer (WGA)
RFR........... Royal Fleet Reserve [*British*]
RFRC........ Refractory (MSA)

RFRJ .... Radio Frequency Rotary Joint
RFRO .... Raumforschung und Raumordnung [*A publication*]
RFRR-A.... Raumforschung und Raumordnung [*A publication*]
RFRSH...... Refresh [*Computer graphics*]
RFS........... R. F. Scientific, Inc. [*Telecommunications service*] (TSSD)
RFS............ Radio Frequency Seal
RFS............ Radio-Frequency Shift (IEEE)
RFS............ Radio Frequency Subsystem [*NASA*]
RFS............ Random Filing System
RFS............ Range Frequency Synthesizer
RFS............ Ready for Sea [*Navy*]
RFS............ Ready for Service
RFS............ Reduced Friction Strut [*Suspension system*] [*Automotive engineering*]
RFS............ Refuse (FAAC)
RFS............ Regardless of Feature Size [*Manufacturing term*]
RFS............ Regional Field Specialist [*Civil Defense*]
RFS............ Regional Frequency Supplies [*Telecommunications*] (TEL)
RFS............ Registry of Friendly Societies [*British*] (ILCA)
RFS............ Relapse-Free Survival [*Oncology*]
RFS............ Religion and Family Life Section (EA)
RFS............ Remote Fiber Spectroscopy
RFS............ Remote File Service [*or System*] [*Data processing*] (PCM)
RFS............ Remote File Sharing [*Data processing*]
RFS............ Renal Function Studies [*Medicine*]
RFS............ Render, Float, and Set [*Construction*]
RFS............ Request for Services [*Social Security Administration*]
RFS............ Request for Shipment (MCD)
RFS............ Resources Forecasting System
RFS............ Response Feedback System [*NASA*]
RFS............ Roll Follow-Up System
RFS............ Rossendorfer Forschungs-Reaktor [*Rossendorf Research Reactor*] [*German*]
RFS............ Rotational Flight Simulator [*Air Force*]
RFS............ Rover Flight Safety
RFS............ Royal Forestry Society of England [*British*]
RFSB .... Regional Forward Scatter Branch [*Supreme Allied Commander, Europe*] (NATG)
RFSB .... Reisterstown Federal Savings Bank [*NASDAQ symbol*] (NQ)
RFSE .... Radio Frequency Shielded Enclosure
RFS/ECM ... Radio Frequency Surveillance/Electronic Countermeasures (MCD)
RFSEDN ... French Journal of Water Science [*A publication*]
RFSH .... Refresh [*Computer graphics*]
RFSHA ...... Reports. Liberal Arts and Science Faculty. Shizuoka University. Natural Science [*A publication*]
RFS/ISE.... Ready for Sea/Individual Ship Exercise (MCD)
RFSMS...... Radio Frequency Signal Management System [*Aviation*] (GFGA)
RFSP .... Radioactive Fallout Study Program [*Canada*]
RFSP .... Rigid Frame Selection Program
RFSS......... Radio Frequency Simulation System (MCD)
RFSS......... Radio Frequency Surveillance Subsystem
RFSS......... Reliability Failure Summary Support (SAA)
RFST .... Research Foundation for the Study of Terrorism [*British*]
RFSTF .... Radio Frequency Systems Test Facility (KSC)
RFSU .... Rugby Football Schools Union [*British*]
RFT........... Rapid Fermentation Technique
RFT........... Ready for Training [*Military*]
RFT........... Ready for Typesetter [*Publishing*]
RFT........... Real Fourier Transform
RFT........... Reflectance, Fluorescence, Transmittance [*Densitometer*] [*Instrumentation*]
RFT........... Refresher Training [*Navy*] (NVT)
RFT........... Regge Field Theory [*Particle Physics*]
RFT........... Regional Film Theatre [*British*]
RFT........... Reinforcement
RFT........... Request for Tender (ADA)
RFT........... Revisable Form Text [*Data processing*] (PCM)
RFT........... Right Frontotransverse [*A fetal position*] [*Obstetrics*]
RFT........... Rod-and-Frame Test (MAE)
RFT........... Rotary Feed-Through
RFTC........ Radio Frequency Test Console
RFTD........ Radial Flow Torr Deposition System (IEEE)
RFT:DCA .. Revisable Form Text: Document Content Architecture [*IBM Corp.*] [*Data processing*]
RFTDS ...... RADAR Frequency Target Discrimination System (MCD)
RFTF .... Radio Frequency Test Facility [*Oak Ridge National Laboratory*]
RF-TK........ Radio Frequency Tracking [*Military*] (MCD)
RFTL .... Radio Frequency Transmission Line
RFTN......... Reflectone, Inc. [*NASDAQ symbol*] (NQ)
RFTO......... Ready for Takeoff [*Aviation*]
RFTOI .... Request for Test or Inspection (MCD)
RFTP .... Request for Technical Proposal
RFTS .... Radio Frequency Test Set (AABC)
RFTS .... Return Free Tax System [*Internal Revenue Service*] (GFGA)
RFTW .... Ready for the World [*Rhythm and Blues recording group*]
RFTY........ Reformatory (AABC)
RFU .... Radio Frequency Unit [*Later, RFCM*] (MCD)
RFU .... Ready-for-Use (NG)

RFU .... Reference Frequency Unit [*Telecommunications*]   (OA)
RFU .... Reliability Field Unit
RFU .... Remote Firing Unit   (MCD)
RFU .... Returns File Unit [*IRS*]
RFU .... Rugby Football Union [*British*]
RFUA .... Roll Follow-Up Amplifier
RFUDL...... Radio Frequency Update Link
RFUM .... Roll Follow-Up Motor
RFUO .... Roll Follow-Up Operation
RFUS .... Reversible Follow-Up System
RFUS .... Roll Follow-Up System
RFUSA4 .... Clinical Gynecology and Obstetrics [*Tokyo*] [*A publication*]
RFV........... RADAR Film Viewer
RFV........... Ragado Fino Virus
RFV........... Regressing Friend Virus
RFV........... Resonant Frequency Vibration
RFVC .... Reason for Visit Classification [*Medicine*]   (DHSM)
R-FVII .... Reading Free Vocational Interest Inventory [*Vocational guidance test*]
RFVM .... Radio Frequency Voltmeter
RFW .... Radio Free Women   (EA)
RFW .... Radio Frequency Wave
RFW .... Rapid Filling Wave [*Cardiology*]
RFW .... Reactor Feedwater [*Nuclear energy*]   (NRCH)
RFW .... Refrigerated Fresh Water Medium [*Microbiology*]
RFW .... Request for Waiver   (MCD)
RFW .... Reserve Feed Water [*Technical drawings*]
RFW .... Reversible Full Wave
RFWAC ..... Reversible Full-Wave Alternating Current
RFWAR..... Requirements for Work and Resources   (MUGU)
RFWDC..... Reversible Full-Wave Direct Current
RFWF .... Radio Frequency Wave Form
RFX........... East Hartford, CT [*Location identifier*] [*FAA*]   (FAAL)
RFX........... Reversed Field Experiment [*Nuclear energy*]   (NRCH)
RFZ........... Restrictive Fire Zone [*Military*]
RFZ........... Rinforzando [*With Special Emphasis*] [*Music*]
RG............. Radial Glial Guide [*Neurology*]
R/G .... Radiation Guidance   (MUGU)
RG............. Radio Direction Finding Station [*ITU designation*]   (CET)
RG............. Radio Frequency Cables; Bulk [*JETDS nomenclature*] [*Military*]   (CET)
RG............. Radio Guidance   (AAG)
RG............. Radiogram   (DEN)
R-G .... Radiologist-General
RG............. Range   (AAG)
RG............. Ranging Gun [*British military*]   (DMA)
RG............. Rate [*Loop*] Gain
RG............. Rate Grown
RG............. Rate Gyroscope   (KSC)
RG............. Readers' Guide to Periodical Literature [*A publication*]
RG............. Readiness Group [*Military*]   (AABC)
RG............. Reagent Grade
RG............. Real Gas
R/G .... Rear Gunner [*British military*]   (DMA)
RG............. Rebuilding Grade [*Automotive engineering*] [*Polymer Steel Corp.*]
RG............. Reception Good [*Radio logs*]
RG............. Recherches Germaniques [*A publication*]
RG............. Rechtsgeschichte [*German*]   (ILCA)
RG............. Rectangular Guide   (DEN)
R/G .... Red and Gold (Edges) [*Bookbinding*]   (ROG)
RG............. Red-Green
RG............. Reduction Gear [*or Gearbox*]   (NG)
RG............. Register   (CET)
RG............. Regula Generalis [*General Rule or Order of Court*] [*Latin*] [*A publication*]   (DLA)
RG............. Regulated Gallery [*Nuclear energy*]   (NRCH)
RG............. Regulatory Guide [*Nuclear energy*]   (NRCH)
RG............. Regummed [*Philately*]
RG............. Reichsgericht [*Reich Supreme Court*] [*German*]   (ILCA)
RG............. Release Guard [*Telecommunications*]   (TEL)
RG............. Remak's Ganglion [*Neurology*]
RG............. Remedial Gymnast [*British*]
RG............. Renabie Gold Trust [*Formerly, Barrick-Cullation Gold Trust*] [*Toronto Stock Exchange symbol*]
RG............. Report Generator   (CMD)
RG............. Report Guide
RG............. Reserve Grade [*Military*]
RG............. Reset Gate
RG............. Resettlement Grants [*British*] [*World War II*]
RG............. Resolving Gel [*Biochemistry*]
RG............. Reticle Generator
RG............. Reticulated Grating   (AAG)
RG............. Reverse Gate
RG............. Revolutionary Government [*Vietnam*]
RG............. Right Gluteus [*Anatomy*]
RG............. Right Guard [*Football*]
RG............. Right Gun
RG............. Ringing Generator [*Telecommunications*]   (TEL)
R-G .... [*Alain*] Robbe-Grillet [*French author and film director*]

RG............. Robert Graham [*Designer's mark on US 1984 $1 Olympic commemorative coin*]
RG............. Rogers Group   (EA)
RG............. Rogue's Gallery   (EA)
RG............. Rolled Gold
RG............. Romana Gens [*A publication*]
RG............. Rueckgang [*Return*] [*Music*]
R & G .... Russell and Geldert's Nova Scotia Reports [*A publication*]   (DLA)
RG............. VEB Fahlberg-List [*East Germany*] [*Research code symbol*]
RG............. Viacao Aerea Rio-Grandense [*VARIG*] [*Brazil*] [*ICAO designator*]   (FAAC)
RGA .... Range-Gemini to Agena   (SAA)
RGA .... Rate Gyro Assembly
RGA .... Readers' Guide Abstracts [*A publication*]
RGA .... Reduction Gearbox Assembly   (DNAB)
RGA .... Regal Petroleum Ltd. [*Vancouver Stock Exchange symbol*]
RGA .... Relative Gain Array [*Control engineering*]
RGA .... Republican Governors Association   (EA)
RGA .... Request for Graphic Arts Service
RGA .... Residual Gas Analyzer
RGA .... Ring Guild of America [*Defunct*]   (EA)
RGA .... Rio Grande [*Argentina*] [*Airport symbol*]   (OAG)
RGA .... Royal Garrison Artillery [*British*]
RGA .... Royal Guernsey Artillery [*British military*]   (DMA)
RGA .... Rubber Growers' Association [*Later, TGA*]   (EAIO)
RGAA .... Radiochemical Gamma Activation Analysis
R Gad .... Raina Gadagramata [*A publication*]
RGAL .... Rate Gyro Assembly - Left Solid Rocket Booster   (MCD)
RGAL .... Reference Guide to American Literature [*A publication*]
RGand........ Romanica Gandensia [*A publication*]
RGAO .... Rate Gyro Assembly - Orbiter   (MCD)
RGAP .... Rate Gyro Accelerometer Package   (MCD)
RGAR .... Rate Gyro Assembly - Right Solid Rocket Booster   (MCD)
RGAS......... Rocky Mountain Natural Gas Co. [*NASDAQ symbol*]   (NQ)
RGB .... Barry [*R. G.*] Corp. [*AMEX symbol*]   (SPSG)
RGB .... Red Green Blue [*Video monitor*]
RGB .... Refractory Grade Bauxite [*Geology*]
RGB .... River Gunboat
RGBI......... Red Green Blue Intensity [*Video monitor*]
RGB-MB ... Resistencia da Guine-Bissau Movimento Bafata [*Political party*]   (EY)
RGC .... Radio-Gas Chromatography
RGC .... Rangely [*Colorado*] [*Seismograph station code, US Geological Survey*]   (SEIS)
RGC .... Reconstructed Gas Chromatogram
RGC .... Reigate Resources (Canada) Ltd. [*Toronto Stock Exchange symbol*]
RGC .... Repair Group Category [*Military*]   (AFIT)
RGC .... Repository for Germinal Choice [*A sperm bank*]
RGC .... Republic Gypsum Co. [*NYSE symbol*]   (SPSG)
RGC .... Retinal Ganglion Cell [*Neurochemistry*]
RGC .... Rio Grande College [*Ohio*]
RGC .... Rio Grande College, Rio Grande, OH [*OCLC symbol*]   (OCLC)
RGC .... Royal Greenwich Conservatory [*British*]
RGC .... Rural Governments Coalition [*Defunct*]   (EA)
RGCR .... Renner's Gold Coast Colony Reports [*1868-1914*] [*Ghana*] [*A publication*]   (DLA)
RGCT .... Residential Group Care and Treatment [*A publication*]
RGCY .... RELM Communications, Inc. [*Formerly, Regency Electronics, Inc.*] [*NASDAQ symbol*]   (NQ)
RGD.......... Ragged   (FAAC)
RGD.......... Rarefied Gas Dynamics
RGD.......... Regis Development Corp. [*Vancouver Stock Exchange symbol*]
RGD.......... Regular Geophysical Day
RGD.......... Revue de Geomorphologie Dynamique [*A publication*]
RGD.......... Rigid   (MSA)
RGda......... Radio Grenada
RGDT .... Reliability Growth/Development Test
RGDV .... Rice Gall Dwarf Virus [*Plant pathology*]
RGE .... Porgera [*Papua New Guinea*] [*Airport symbol*]   (OAG)
RGE .... Range [*Maps and charts*]   (MDG)
RGE .... Rat der Gemeinden Europas [*Council of European Municipalities*]
RGE .... Red under Gold Edges [*Books*]
RGE .... Reduced Gravity Environment
RGE .... Regroupement des Guineens a l'Exterieur [*Rally of Guineans Abroad*]   (PD)
RGE .... Relative Gas Expansion   (AAMN)
RGE .... Rotating Gel Electrophoresis
RGEA .... Rate Gyro Electronics Assembly   (MCD)
RGEN .... Repligen Corp. [*Cambridge, MA*] [*NASDAQ symbol*]   (NQ)
RGenBelge ... Revue General Belge [*A publication*]   (BJA)
R Geog Soc Pr ... Royal Geographical Society. Proceedings [*A publication*]
RGEPS .... Rucker-Gable Educational Programming Scale [*Psychology*]
RGEQ .... Regency Equities Corp. [*NASDAQ symbol*]   (NQ)
RGer.......... Recherches Germaniques [*A publication*]
RGF .... Range Gated Filter
RGF .... Rarefied Gas Field [*or Flow*]
RGF .... Republic Goldfields [*AMEX symbol*]   (SPSG)
RGF .... Roemisch-Germanische Forschungen [*A publication*]

RGF .... Royal Gun Factory [*British military*]   (DMA)
RGFC........ Ray Griff Fan Club   (EA)
RGFC........ Remote Gas Filter Correlation   (KSC)
RGFC........ Robin George Fan Club   (EA)
RGFil .... Romano-Germanskaja Filologija [*A publication*]
RGFRD4... Ghana. Fishery Research Unit. Information Report [*A publication*]
RGG........... Religion in Geschichte und Gegenwart [*A publication*]
RGG........... Rotating Gravity Gradiometer
RGG........... Royal Grenadier Guards [*British*]
RGH .... Rare Gas Halogen [*Inorganic chemistry*]
RGH .... Rat Growth Hormone [*Endocrinology*]
RGH .... Rough   (AAG)
R Ghana Law ... Review of Ghana Law [*A publication*]
RGHSDH ... Annual Research Reviews. Regulation of Growth Hormone Secretion [*A publication*]
RGI .... Rangiroa [*French Polynesia*] [*Airport symbol*]   (OAG)
RGI .... Royal Glasgow Institute of Fine Arts [*Scotland*]
RGICC....... Region Internal Computer Code [*Data processing*]
RGIFA....... Royal Glasgow Institute of Fine Arts [*Scotland*]
RGIS.......... Regis Corp. [*NASDAQ symbol*]   (NQ)
RGIT......... Representative for German Industry and Trade [*An association*]   (EA)
RGIT......... Robert Gordon Institute of Technology [*Scotland*]
RGJ............ Richmond, VA [*Location identifier*] [*FAA*]   (FAAL)
RGJ............ Royal Green Jackets [*Military unit*] [*British*]
RGJLond ... Royal Green Jackets, London [*Military unit*] [*British*]
RGJTAVR ... Royal Green Jackets Territorial and Army Volunteer Reserve [*Military unit*] [*British*]
RGK .... Red Wing, MN [*Location identifier*] [*FAA*]   (FAAL)
RGK .... Reserv Glavnogo Komandovaniia [*Reserve of the High Command*] [*Former USSR*]
RGKAI....... Roemisch-Germanische Kommission des Archaeologischen Instituts [*A publication*]
RGKNA ..... Rikagaku Kenkyusho Kenkyu Nempo [*A publication*]
RGL .... Rate Gyroscope Limit
RGL .... Reading Grade Level
RGL .... Regal International, Inc. [*NYSE symbol*]   (SPSG)
RGL .... Regional Resources Ltd. [*Toronto Stock Exchange symbol*] [*Vancouver Stock Exchange symbol*]
RGL .... Regulate   (MSA)
RGL .... Reihe Germanistische Linguistik [*A publication*]
RGL .... Report Generator Language [*Data processing*]   (IEEE)
RGL .... Resources Policy [*A publication*]
RGL .... Review of Ghana Law [*A publication*]
RGL .... Rio Gallegos [*Argentina*] [*Airport symbol*]   (OAG)
RGL .... Wrangell, AK [*Location identifier*] [*FAA*]   (FAAL)
RGLD .... Royal Gold, Inc. [*NASDAQ symbol*]   (NQ)
RGLR........ Regular   (MSA)
RGLT........ Regulating   (MSA)
RGLTD...... Regulated   (MSA)
RGLTR...... Regulator   (MSA)
RGM.......... Radiogas Monitor [*Nuclear energy*]   (NRCH)
RGM.......... Recorder Group Monitor
RGM.......... Redundant Gyro Monitor   (NASA)
RGM.......... Reliability Growth Management   (MCD)
RGM.......... Remote Geophysical Monitor   (MCD)
RGM.......... Reversible Gelatin Matrix
RGM.......... Rounds per Gun per Minute
RGM.......... Royex Gold Mining Corp. [*Toronto Stock Exchange symbol*] [*Vancouver Stock Exchange symbol*]
RGMI .... Regulations Governing the Meat Inspection [*of the USDA*]
RGMNA.... Chijil Kwangmul Chosa Yongu Pokoso [*A publication*]
RGMS ...... Reversible Gelatin Matrix System
RGMV....... Ryegrass Mosaic Virus [*Plant pathology*]
RGN.......... Rangoon [*Myanmar*] [*Airport symbol*]   (OAG)
RGN.......... Region   (AFM)
RG(N)........ Register (N) Stages   (MCD)
RGN.......... Registered General Nurse
RGN.......... Riggins Resources [*Vancouver Stock Exchange symbol*]
RGNEB ..... Review of Compagnie Generale d'Electricite [*A publication*]
RGNG....... Rigging   (MSA)
RGNL........ Regional
R & G N Sc ... Russell and Geldert's Nova Scotia Reports [*A publication*]   (DLA)
RGO.......... Akron, OH [*Location identifier*] [*FAA*]   (FAAL)
RGO.......... Radio Guidance Operation   (DNAB)
RGO.......... Ranger Oil Ltd. [*NYSE symbol*] [*Toronto Stock Exchange symbol*]   (SPSG)
RGO.......... Regulation [*A publication*]
RGo.......... Romanica Gothoburgensia [*A publication*]
RGO.......... Royal Greenwich Observatory [*British*]
RGP .... Rate Gyro Package
RGP .... Regina Public Library [*UTLAS symbol*]
RGP .... Remote Graphics Processor
RGP .... Retired Greyhounds as Pets   (EA)
RGP .... Rhodesian Government Party
RGP .... Rigid Gas Permeable [*Contact lens*]
RGP .... Rijks Geschiedkundige Publicaties [*A publication*]
RGP .... Rocketdyne Gun Propellant   (MCD)
RGP .... Rolled Gold Plate [*Metallurgy*]

RGPF......... Royal Gunpowder Factory [*British*]
RG PH ...... Registered Pharmacist
RGPO........ Range Gate Pull Off   (NVT)
RGPS........ Razor Grinders' Protection Society [*A union*] [*British*]
RGR .... Oklahoma City, OK [*Location identifier*] [*FAA*]   (FAAL)
RGR .... Range Gated Receiver
RGR .... Ranger
RGR .... Rare-Gas Recovery [*Nuclear energy*]   (NRCH)
RGR .... Rassemblement des Gauches Republicaines [*Assembly of the Republican Left*] [*France*] [*Political party*]
RGR .... Receipt of Goods Received
RGR .... Regionair, Inc. [*Canada*] [*FAA designator*]   (FAAC)
RGR .... Regulus Resources, Inc. [*Vancouver Stock Exchange symbol*]
RGR .... Relative Growth Rate [*Entomology*]
RGR .... Ringer   (WGA)
RGR .... Royal Garrison Regiment [*Military*] [*British*]   (ROG)
RGR .... Royal Gurkha Regiment [*British military*]   (DMA)
RGR .... Sturm Ruger & Co. [*NYSE symbol*]   (SPSG)
RGRCD ..... Geothermal Resources Council. Special Report [*A publication*]
R Greenwich Obs Bull ... Royal Greenwich Observatory. Bulletins [*A publication*]
RGRMA .... Rate Gyro Redundancy Management Algorithm   (NASA)
RgrT.......... Ranger Tab [*Military decoration*]
RGS .... RADAR Ground Stabilization
RGS .... Radio Guidance System
RGS .... Rate Gyro System
RGS .... Refined Gigabit System [*High purity hydrogen peroxide*]
RGS .... Remote Ground Switching
RGS .... Rene Guyon Society   (EA)
RGS .... Research Grants Staff [*Environmental Protection Agency*]   (GFGA)
RGS .... Restructured General Support [*Military*]
RGS .... Rio Grande Southern Railroad   (IIA)
RGS .... River Gauging Station
RGS .... Rochester Gas & Electric Corp. [*NYSE symbol*]   (SPSG)
RGS .... Rocket Guidance System   (KSC)
RGS .... Royal Geographical Society [*British*]
RGS .... Royal Gold Enterprises, Inc. [*Toronto Stock Exchange symbol*]
RGS .... Ruffed Grouse Society   (EA)
RGS .... Sisters of Our Lady of Charity of the Good Shepherd [*Roman Catholic religious order*]
RGSAT ...... Radio Guidance Surveillance and Automatic Tracking   (AAG)
RGS Austsia SA Br Proc ... Royal Geographical Society of Australasia. South Australian Branch. Proceedings [*A publication*]   (APTA)
RGSC......... Ramp Generator and Signal Converter   (IEEE)
RGSDLR ... Rigsdaler [*Numismatics*]
RGSF .... Reference Guide to Short Fiction [*A publication*]
RGSIA ...... Records. Geological Survey of India [*A publication*]
R G Soc Cornwall Tr ... Royal Geological Society of Cornwall. Transactions [*A publication*]
R G Soc Ireland J ... Royal Geological Society of Ireland. Journal [*A publication*]
RGSSA ...... Royal Geographical Society of Australasia, South Australian Branch
RGSTV ...... Rice Grassy Stunt Virus [*Plant pathology*]
RGSU .... Restructured General Support Unit   (MCD)
RGSWA..... Records. Geological Survey of New South Wales [*A publication*]
Rgt.............. Regent [*Record label*]
RGT .... Regent College Library [*UTLAS symbol*]
RGT .... Regiment
RGT .... Rengat [*Indonesia*] [*Airport symbol*]   (OAG)
RGT .... Resonant Gate Transistor [*Data processing*]
RGT .... Reverse Garbage Truck   (ADA)
RGT .... Rigging Template   (MCD)
RGT .... Right
RGTF......... Royal General Theatrical Fund [*British*]   (DI)
RGTM .... Regional Government Technical Monitor [*Department of Housing and Urban Development*]   (GFGA)
RGTP........ Reseau Gouvernemental de Transmission par Paquets [*Government Packet Network - GPN*] [*Canada*]
RGTP........ Rough Template   (AAG)
RGTR .... Register
RGU.......... Rate Gyroscope Unit
RGUMD.... Argument [*A publication*]
RGV.......... Relative Gas Vacuolation [*In algae*]
RGV.......... Rio Grande Ventures Ltd. [*Vancouver Stock Exchange symbol*]
R-GVB ...... Resonating-Generalized Valence Bond [*Physical chemistry*]
RGVV .... Religionsgeschichtliche Versuche und Vorarbeiten [*A publication*]
RGW .... Ramp Gross Weight [*Aviation*]
RGW .... Reagent Grade Water
RGWS ...... RADAR Guided Weapon System   (MCD)
RGY .... Regency Airlines [*Chicago, IL*] [*FAA designator*]   (FAAC)
RGZ .... Recommended Ground Zero [*Military*]   (AABC)
RGZM .... Roemisch-Germanische Zentralmuseum (Mainz) [*A publication*]
RGZTA...... Railway Gazette [*Later, Railway Gazette International*] [*A publication*]
RH .... 1st Nottinghamshire (Robin Hood) Rifle Volunteer Corps [*British military*]   (DMA)

RH .... Air Rhodesia [*ICAO designator*]   (FAAC)
RH .... Air Zimbabwe [*Zimbabwe*] [*ICAO designator*]   (ICDA)
RH .... Rabbinic Hebrew   (BJA)
RH .... Radiant Heat
RH .... Radiation Homing   (AAG)
RH .... Radiation Hybrid Mapping [*Biochemistry*]
RH .... Radiological Health   (KSC)
r/h .... RADs [*Radiation Absorbed Doses*] per Hour   (DEN)
RH .... Railhead [*British military*]   (DMA)
RH .... Rankine-Hugoniot [*Physics*]
RH .... Reactive Hyperemia [*Medicine*]
RH .... Receive Hub [*Telegraph*] [*Telecommunications*]   (TEL)
RH .... Red Herring [*Investment term*]
RH .... Regional Headquarters   (NOAA)
RH .... Relative Humidity
RH .... Releasing Hormone [*Also, RF*] [*Endocrinology*]
RH .... Religious Humanism [*A publication*]
RH .... Remotely Handled
r/h .... REMs [*Roentgen Equivalents, Man*] per Hour   (DEN)
RH .... Report Heading   (BUR)
RH .... Request-Response Header [*Data processing*]   (BUR)
RH .... Requesta Regni Hierosolymitani [*A publication*]   (BJA)
RH .... Research Highlights [*A publication*]   (DIT)
RH .... Residential Hotels [*Public-performance tariff class*] [*British*]
RH .... Restaurant Hospitality [*A publication*]
RH .... Revisionist History [*Taby, Sweden*]   (EAIO)
R/H .... Revolutions per Hour   (DEN)
RH .... Rheostat   (IEEE)
Rh .... Rhesus [*Blood factor*]
Rh .... Rhetorica [*of Aristotle*] [*Classical studies*]   (OCD)
rh .... Rheumatic [*Medicine*]   (MAE)
Rh .... Rheumatism [*Medicine*]
RH .... Rhinitis [*Medicine*]
RH .... Rhinoceros   (ROG)
rh .... Rhodesia [*Southern Rhodesia*] [*MARC country of publication code*] [*Library of Congress*]   (LCCP)
Rh .... Rhodium [*Chemical element*]
Rh .... Rhodopsin [*Visual Purple*]
rh .... Rhonchi [*Rales*] [*Latin*]   (MAE)
RH .... Right Halfback [*Soccer*]
RH .... Right Hand
RH .... Right Hyperphoria [*Medicine*]
RH .... Road Haulage
RH .... Rochester History [*A publication*]
RH .... Rockwell Hardness
r/h .... Roentgens per Hour   (DEN)
RH .... Roger Houghton Ltd. [*Publisher*] [*British*]
RH .... Rosh Hashanah [*New Year*]   (BJA)
RH .... Rotuli Hundredorum [*Latin*] [*A publication*]   (DLA)
RH .... Round Head
RH .... Round House [*Maps and charts*]
RH .... Royal Highlanders [*Military unit*] [*British*]
RH .... Royal Highness
RH .... Royal Hospital [*London*]
RH .... Royal Hospital [*Chelsea*] [*British military*]   (DMA)
RH .... Royal Hussars [*Military unit*] [*British*]
RH .... Rueckwaertiges Heeresgebiet [*Rear area of a group of armies*] [*German military*]
RH .... Runaway Hotline   (EA)
RH .... Running Head [*Printing*]   (WDMC)
RH .... Ryan's Hope [*Television program*]
RH .... Southern Rhodesia [*ANSI two-letter standard code*] [*Obsolete*]   (CNC)
RHA .... Ranching Heritage Association   (EA)
RHA .... Records Holding Area [*Military*]
RHA .... Regional Health Authority [*British*]
RHA .... Reichold [*Alabama*] [*Seismograph station code, US Geological Survey*]   (SEIS)
RHA .... Reindeer Herders Association   (EA)
RHA .... Religious Heritage of America   (EA)
RHA .... Renewal and Housing Assistance Report [*HUD*]
RHA .... Respiratory Health Association   (EA)
RHA .... Reykholar [*Iceland*] [*Airport symbol*] [*Obsolete*]   (OAG)
RHA .... Road Haulage Association [*British*]
RHA .... Rohm & Haas Co., Spring House, PA [*OCLC symbol*]   (OCLC)
RHA .... Rolled Homogeneous Armor [*Weaponry*]   (INF)
RHA .... Roman High Avoidance [*Behavior trait*]
RHA .... Rose Hybridizers Association   (EA)
RHA .... Royal Hawaiian Air Service [*Honolulu, HI*] [*FAA designator*]   (FAAC)
RHA .... Royal Hellenic Army   (NATG)
RHA .... Royal Hibernian Academy
RHA .... Royal Horse Artillery [*British*]
RHA .... Rural Housing Alliance [*Later, RAI*]   (EA)
RHAB .... Random House AudioBooks [*Publisher*]
RHAB .... Rehab Hospital Services [*NASDAQ symbol*]   (NQ)
RHAF .... Royal Hellenic Air Force
Rh Al .... Rhetorica ad Alexandrum [*of Aristotle*] [*Classical studies*]   (OCD)
RHAM ...... Rhammus [*Pharmacology*]   (ROG)
R Hanazono Coll ...   Review of Hanazono College [*A publication*]

RHAP .... Rhapsody   (WGA)
RHASS ...... Royal Highland and Agricultural Society of Scotland [*British*]
RHA(T) ..... Regional Health Authority (Teaching) [*British*]
RHAV .... Rat Hepatoma-Associated Virus
RHAW ...... RADAR Homing and Warning   (MCD)
RHAWR ... RADAR Homing and Warning Receiver   (MCD)
RHAWS ... RADAR Homing and Warning System
RHB .... RADAR Homing Bomb [*Air Force*]
RHB .... Regional Hospital Boards [*British*]
RhB .... Rheinische Blaetter [*A publication*]
RHB .... Rheinische Heimatblaetter [*A publication*]
RHB .... Right Halfback [*Soccer*]
RHB .... Right Heart Bypass [*Medicine*]   (MAE)
RHB .... Round Hole Broach
RHBA .... Racking Horse Breeders Association of America   (EA)
R & H Bank ... Roche and Hazlitt's Bankruptcy Practice [*2nd ed.*] [*1873*] [*A publication*]   (DLA)
RHBC .... RehabCare Corp. [*NASDAQ symbol*]   (SPSG)
RHBF .... Reactive Hyperemia Blood Flow [*Medicine*]   (MAE)
RHBNA ..... Rehabilitation [*A publication*]
RHBV .... Rice Hoja Blanca Virus [*Plant pathology*]
RHC .... Reactive Hydrocarbon [*Environmental science*]
RHC .... Reactor Head Cooling [*Nuclear energy*]   (NRCH)
RHC .... Regional Holding Co.
RHC .... Resetting Half-Cycle
RHC .... Resin Hemoperfusion Column
RHC .... Respirations Have Ceased [*Medicine*]
RHC .... Right-Hand Circular [*NASA*]   (KSC)
RHC .... Right-Hand Console
RHC .... Right Hypochondrium [*Medicine*]
RHC .... Riverside Methodist Hospital Library, Columbus, OH [*OCLC symbol*]   (OCLC)
RHC .... Road Haulage Cases [*1950-55*] [*England*] [*A publication*]   (DLA)
RHC .... Rosary Hill College [*New York*]
RHC .... Rotational Hand Controller [*NASA*]
RHC .... Royal Highlanders of Canada [*Military unit*] [*World War I*]
RHC .... Royal Holloway College [*British*]   (DI)
RHC .... Rubber Hydrocarbon
RHC .... Rural Health Clinic [*Department of Health and Human Services*]   (GFGA)
RHCA .... Red Hills Conservation Association   (EA)
Rh CA .... Rhodesian Court of Appeal Law Reports [*1939-46*] [*A publication*]   (DLA)
RHCA .... Roller Hockey Coaches Association   (EA)
RHCC .... Reproductive Health Care Center
RHCC .... Rocking Horse Child Care Centers of America, Inc. [*NASDAQ symbol*]   (NQ)
RHCC/PP ... Reproductive Health Care Center/Planned Parenthood
RHCF .... Residential Health Care Facility [*Medicine*]   (DHSM)
RHCFA ..... Revista. Hospital das Clinicas. Faculdade de Medicina. Universidade de Sao Paulo [*A publication*]
RHCG .... Research for Health Charities Group [*British*]
RHCI .... Radiant Heating and Cooling Institute
RHCI .... Ramsay Health Care, Inc. [*NASDAQ symbol*]   (NQ)
RHCM ...... Relative Humidity Control/Monitor   (NASA)
RHCP .... Right-Hand Circularly Polarized [*LASER waves*]
RHCS .... Rocznik Historii Czasopismiennictwa Polskiego [*A publication*]
RHCSA ..... Regional Hospitals Consultants' and Specialists' Association
RHD .... Archangelos [*Greece*] [*Seismograph station code, US Geological Survey*]   (SEIS)
RHD .... Radiological Health Data
RHD .... Railhead
RHD .... Random House Dictionary [*A publication*]
RHD .... Regional Health Director [*HEW*]
RHD .... Relative Hepatic Dullness [*Medicine*]
RHD .... Renal Hypertensive Disease [*Medicine*]
RHD .... Required Hangar Depth   (MCD)
RHD .... Return Head
RHD .... Rheumatic Heart Disease [*Medicine*]
RHD .... Rhodes, Inc. [*NYSE symbol*]   (SPSG)
RHD .... Right Hand Drive [*Automotive engineering*]
RHD .... Rural Housing Disaster
RHDEL-II ... [*The*] Random House Dictionary of the English Language: Second Edition - Unabridged [*A publication*]
R & H Dig ... Robinson and Harrison's Digest [*Ontario*] [*A publication*]   (DLA)
RHD-II ...... [*The*] Random House Dictionary of the English Language: Second Edition - Unabridged [*A publication*]
RHD & R ... Radiological Health Data and Reports [*A publication*]
RHDRA ..... Radiological Health Data and Reports [*A publication*]
RHE .... Radiation Hazard Effects   (KSC)
RHE .... Random House Encyclopedia [*A publication*]
RHE .... Record Handling Electronics
RHE .... Reims [*France*] [*Airport symbol*]   (OAG)
RHE .... Reliability Human Engineering   (AAG)
RHE .... Remote Hellfire Electronics [*Army*]
RHE .... Reversible Hydrogen Electrode
RHE .... RHI Entertainment, Inc. [*AMEX symbol*]   (SPSG)
RHEA .... Reentry Heating Energies Analyzer [*Air Force*]
RHEA .... Research into Higher Education. Abstracts [*A publication*]

RHEAA ..... Rheologica Acta [*A publication*]
RHEB .... Right-Hand Equipment Bay [*Apollo*] [*NASA*]
RHEED ...... Reflected High-Energy Electron Diffraction [*Spectroscopy*]
Rhein Bienenztg ... Rheinische Bienenzeitung [*A publication*]
RHEINHYP ... Rheinische Hypothekenbank AG [*Germany*] (EY)
Rheinisches Mus Philol ... Rheinisches Museum fuer Philologie [*A publication*]
Rheinisch-Westfael Akad Wiss Nat- Ing- Wirtschaftswiss Vort ... Rheinisch-Westfaelische Akademie der Wissenschaften Natur-, Ingenieur-, und Wirtschaftswissenschaften. Vortraege [*A publication*]
Rhein Mus (Bonn) ... Rheinische Landesmuseum (Bonn) [*A publication*]
Rheinstahl Tech ... Rheinstahl Technik [*A publication*]
Rhein Vb .... Rheinische Vierteljahresblaetter [*A publication*]
Rhein Viert Jbl ... Rheinische Vierteljahrsblaetter [*A publication*]
Rhein-Westfael Akad Wiss Vortr N ... Rheinisch-Westfaelische Akademie der Wissenschaften Natur-, Ingenieur-, und Wirtschaftswissenschaften. Vortraege [*A publication*]
RHel .... Romanica Helvetica [*A publication*]
RHEL .... Rutherford High Energy Laboratory (MCD)
RHEM ...... Rheometrics, Inc. [*Piscataway, NJ*] [*NASDAQ symbol*] (NQ)
RHEO .... Rheostat (AAG)
Rheol Abstr ... Rheology Abstracts [*A publication*]
Rheol Act ... Rheologica Acta [*A publication*]
Rheol Acta ... Rheologica Acta [*A publication*]
Rheol Bull ... Rheology Bulletin [*A publication*]
Rheol Leafl ... Rheology Leaflet [*A publication*]
Rheol Mem ... Rheological Memoirs [*A publication*]
Rheol Texture Food Qual ... Rheology and Texture in Food Quality [*A publication*]
Rhes .... Rhesus [*of Euripides*] [*Classical studies*] (OCD)
Rhet .... Ars Rhetorica [*of Dionysius Halicarnassensis*] [*Classical studies*] (OCD)
Rhet .... De Rhetoribus [*of Suetonius*] [*Classical studies*] (OCD)
Rhet .... Rhetores Graeci [*A publication*] (OCD)
RHET .... Rhetoric
Rhet Her .... Rhetorica ad Herennium [*First century BC*] [*Classical studies*] (OCD)
Rhet Lat Min ... Rhetores Latini Minores [*A publication*] (OCD)
RHEUM ...... Rheumatism [*Medicine*]
Rheumatol Balneo Allergol ... Rheumatologia, Balneologia, Allergologia [*A publication*]
Rheumatol Int ... Rheumatology International [*A publication*]
Rheumatol Phys Med ... Rheumatology and Physical Medicine [*A publication*]
Rheumatol Rehabil ... Rheumatology and Rehabilitation [*A publication*]
Rheum Intl ... Rheumatology International [*A publication*]
RHF .... Rarefied Hypersonic Flow
RHF .... Remembrance of the Holocaust Foundation (EA)
RHF .... Restricted Hartree-Fock [*Quantum mechanics*]
RHF .... Retired History File [*Army*]
RHF .... Right Heart Failure [*Medicine*]
RHF .... Roller Hockey Federation (EA)
RHF .... Royal Highland Fusiliers [*Military unit*] [*British*]
RHFC .... Richard Hatch Fan Club (EA)
RHFC .... Robyn Hitchcock Fan Club (EA)
RHFEB ...... Right-Hand Forward Equipment Bay [*NASA*] (KSC)
RHFF .... Richard Hatch Fan Fellowship (EAIO)
RHFS .... Receiving Hospital Field Station
RHFS .... Round Hill Field Station [*MIT*] (MCD)
RHG .... Royal Horse Guards [*British*]
RHG-CSF ... Recombinant Human Granulocyte, Colony Stimulating Factor [*Hematology*]
RHG1D ..... Royal Horse Guards and 1st Dragoons [*British military*] (DMA)
RHGH ...... Recombinant Human Growth Hormone [*Biochemistry*]
rhGRF .... Rat Hypothalamus Growth Hormone-Releasing Factor [*Endocrinology*]
RHGSA ..... Russian Historical and Genealogical Society in America [*Later, RNAA*] (EA)
RHH .... Right-Hand Head
RHH .... Robertson-Ceco Corp. [*NYSE symbol*] (SPSG)
RHI .... Halmi [*Robert*], Inc. [*AMEX symbol*] (SPSG)
RHI .... RADAR Height Indicator (CET)
RHI .... Range-Height Indicator [*RADAR*]
RHI .... Real Hazard Index
RHI .... Relative Humidity Indicator (AAG)
RHI .... Responsible Hospitality Institute (EA)
RHI .... Rhinelander [*Wisconsin*] [*Airport symbol*] (OAG)
RHI .... Rhinology [*Medicine*] (DHSM)
RHI .... Rhode Island
RHI .... Rhode Island Historical Society Library, Providence, RI [*OCLC symbol*] (OCLC)
RHi .... Rhode Island Historical Society, Providence, RI [*Library symbol*] [*Library of Congress*] (LCLS)
Rh I .... Rhode Island Reports [*A publication*] (DLA)
Rh I .... Rhode Island Supreme Court Reports [*A publication*] (DLA)
RHI .... Rigid-Hull Inflatable [*US Coast Guard vessel*]
RHI .... Robert Half International, Inc. [*NYSE symbol*] (SPSG)
RHI .... Round Hill Installation (SAA)
RHIA .... Radiation-Hardened Interfacing Amplifier

RHIB .... Rain and Hail Insurance Bureau [*Defunct*] (EA)
RHIC .... Relativistic Heavy Ion Collider [*Nuclear physics*]
RHIDEC .... [*The*] Restaurant/Hotel International Design Exposition (ITD)
RHI En ...... RHI Entertainment, Inc. [*Associated Press abbreviation*] (APAG)
RHIF .... Rural Housing Insurance Fund [*Department of Agriculture*] (GFGA)
RHIFC .... Ray Heatherton Irish Friends Club (EA)
RHIG .... RH [*or Rhesus*] Immune Globulin [*Immunology*]
RHIMO ..... Agency for Navigation on the Rhine and the Moselle (NATG)
Rhin .... Rhinology [*Medicine*]
RHINO ...... Range-Height Indicator Not Operating [*Aviation*] (FAAC)
Rhino .... Really Here in Name Only [*Education*] [*British*]
RHINO .... Rhinoceros (DSUE)
RHINOL ... Rhinology [*Medicine*]
RHIO .... Rank Has Its Obligations [*Military slang*]
RHIP .... Radiation Health Information Project (EA)
RHIP .... Rank Has Its Privileges [*Military slang*]
RHIR .... Rank Has Its Responsibilities [*Military slang*]
RHi-Sh ...... Rhode Island Historical Society, George L. Shepley Collection, Providence, RI [*Library symbol*] [*Library of Congress*] (LCLS)
RHistM ...... Roemische Historische Mitteilungen [*A publication*]
RHistS .... Royal Historical Society [*British*]
RhITC .... Rhodamine Isothiocyanate [*Biochemistry*]
RHittAs ..... Revue Hittite et Asianique [*Paris*] [*A publication*] (BJA)
RHJ .... Rubber Hose Jacket (MSA)
Rh.JbV .... Rheinisches Jahrbuch fuer Volkskunde [*A publication*]
RHK .... Radio Hong Kong
RHK .... Reefing Hook
RHL .... Radiological Health Laboratory
RHL .... Rat Hepatic Lectin [*Biochemistry*]
RHL .... Residual Hazards List [*NASA*] (NASA)
RHL .... Rettie's Scotch Court of Session Cases, Fourth Series [*House of Lords' Part*] [*A publication*] (DLA)
RHL .... Reverse Half-Line [*Feed*]
RHL .... Richland Mine, Inc. [*Vancouver Stock Exchange symbol*]
RHL .... Right Hepatic Lobe [*Anatomy*]
RHLG .... Radiometric Homing Level Gauge
RHLI .... Royal Hamilton Light Infantry [*British military*] (DMA)
Rh LJ .... Rhodesian Law Journal [*A publication*] (DLA)
RHLK .... Reihe Hanser Literature-Kommentare [*A publication*]
RHLN .... Right Hilar Lymph Node [*Anatomy*] (MAE)
RHM .... Ranks Hovis McDougall [*Commercial firm*] [*British*] (ECON)
RHM .... Refractory Heavy Minerals [*In sands used for glass making*]
RHM .... Relative Humidity Monitor (GFGA)
RHM .... Renewal and Housing Management [*HUD*]
RHM .... Rhabdomyosarcoma [*Also, RMS*] [*Oncology*]
RhM .... Rheinische Merkur [*A publication*]
RhM .... Rheinisches Museum fuer Philologie [*A publication*]
RHM .... Rio Hardy [*Mexico*] [*Seismograph station code, US Geological Survey*] (SEIS)
RHM .... Roemische Historische Mitteilungen [*A publication*]
RHM .... Roentgen per Hour at One Meter
RHMII .... Right Hand Man II [*Computer package*] [*Futurus, Inc.*] (PCM)
RhMP .... Rheinisches Museum fuer Philologie [*A publication*]
Rh M Ph ..... Rheinisches Museum fuer Philologie [*A publication*]
RHMS ...... Royal Hibernian Military School [*Dublin*]
RHMTA ...... Rhumatologie [*Paris*] [*A publication*]
Rh Mus ...... Rheinisches Museum fuer Philologie [*A publication*] (OCD)
RHN .... Royal Hellenic Navy [*Obsolete*] (NATG)
RHNB .... RHNB Corp. [*Rock Hill, SC*] [*NASDAQ symbol*] (NQ)
Rh Neg .... Rhesus Factor Negative [*Hematology*] (MAE)
RHNL .... Reindeer Herders Newsletter. Institute of Arctic Biology. University of Alaska [*A publication*]
RHNP .... Rhone-Poulenc, Inc. [*Associated Press abbreviation*] (APAG)
RhnPl .... Rhone-Poulenc, Inc. [*Associated Press abbreviation*] (APAG)
RHO .... Railhead Officer [*Military*] [*Obsolete*]
RHO .... Remanufactured High Output
RHO .... Rhodes [*Greece*] [*Seismograph station code, US Geological Survey*] [*Closed*] (SEIS)
RHO .... Rhodes Island [*Greece*] [*Airport symbol*] (OAG)
RHO .... Rhodesia [*Later, Zimbabwe*]
RHO .... Rhombic [*Antenna*]
RHO .... Southern Rhodesia [*ANSI three-letter standard code*] [*Obsolete*] (CNC)
RHOB .... Rayburn House Office Building [*Washington, DC*] (DLA)
Rhod .... Rhodesia
RHOD .... Rhodium [*Chemistry*]
RHODA .... Rhodora [*A publication*]
Rhod Agric J ... Rhodesia Agricultural Journal [*A publication*]
Rhod Agric J Tech Handb ... Rhodesia Agricultural Journal. Technical Handbook [*A publication*]
Rhod Beekeeping ... Rhodesian Beekeeping [*A publication*]
Rhod Bee News ... Rhodesian Bee News [*A publication*]
Rhod Bull For Res ... Rhodesia. Bulletin of Forestry Research [*A publication*]
Rhod Chibero Coll Agric Annu Rep ... Rhodesia. Chibero College of Agriculture. Annual Report [*A publication*]
Rhod Cotton Res Inst Annu Rep ... Rhodesia Cotton Research Institute. Annual Report [*A publication*]

Rhod Div Livest Pastures Annu Rep ... Rhodesia. Division of Livestock and Pastures. Annual Report [*A publication*]
Rhode Isl Agric ... Rhode Island Agriculture [*A publication*]
Rhode Island ... Bulletin. Rhode Island School of Design. Museum Notes [*A publication*]
Rhode Island Med J ... Rhode Island Medical Journal [*A publication*]
Rhode Island Rep ... Rhode Island Reports [*A publication*]   (DLA)
Rhod Eng ... Rhodesian Engineer [*A publication*]
Rhodesia Ag J ... Rhodesia Agricultural Journal [*A publication*]
Rhodesia Agric J ... Rhodesia Agricultural Journal [*A publication*]
Rhodesia Agr J ... Rhodesia Agricultural Journal [*A publication*]
Rhodesian J Agr Res ... Rhodesian Journal of Agricultural Research [*A publication*]
Rhodesian J Econ ... Rhodesian Journal of Economics [*A publication*]
Rhodesian LJ ... Rhodesian Law Journal [*A publication*]   (DLA)
Rhodesian Min Jour ... Rhodesian Mining Journal [*A publication*]
Rhodesian Tob J ... Rhodesian Tobacco Journal [*A publication*]
Rhodesia Zambia Malawi J Agr Res ... Rhodesia, Zambia, and Malawi Journal of Agricultural Research [*A publication*]
Rhod Esigodini Agric Inst Annu Rep ... Rhodesia. Esigodini Agricultural Institute. Annual Report [*A publication*]
Rhodes Univ Dep Ichthyol Ichthyol Bull ... Rhodes University. Department of Ichthyology. Ichthyological Bulletin [*A publication*]
Rhodes Univ Dep Ichthyol Occas Pap ... Rhodes University. Department of Ichthyology. Occasional Paper [*A publication*]
Rhodes Univ J L B Smith Inst Ichthyol Spec Publ ... Rhodes University. J. L. B. Smith Institute of Ichthyology. Special Publication [*A publication*]
Rhod Fmr ... Rhodesian Farmer [*A publication*]
Rhod Geol Surv Bull ... Rhodesia. Geological Survey. Bulletin [*A publication*]
Rhod Geol Surv Miner Resour Ser ... Rhodesia. Geological Survey. Mineral Resources Series [*A publication*]
Rhod Geol Surv Short Rep ... Rhodesia. Geological Survey. Short Report [*A publication*]
Rhod Grassl Res Stn Annu Rep ... Rhodesia Grasslands Research Station. Annual Report [*A publication*]
Rhod Hist .. Rhodesian History [*A publication*]
Rhod J Agric Res ... Rhodesia Journal of Agricultural Research [*A publication*]
Rhod Jl Agric Res ... Rhodesian Journal of Agricultural Research [*A publication*]
Rhod Librn ... Rhodesian Librarian [*A publication*]
Rhod Lowveld Res Stn Annu Rep ... Rhodesia. Lowveld Research Station. Annual Report [*A publication*]
Rhod Minist Agric Dep Res Spec Serv Seed Serv Annu Rep ... Rhodesia. Ministry of Agriculture. Department of Research and Specialist Services. Seed Services. Annual Report [*A publication*]
Rhod Minist Agric Gatooma Res Stn Annu Rep ... Rhodesia. Ministry of Agriculture. Gatooma Research Station. Annual Report [*A publication*]
Rhod Minist Agric Grassl Res Stn Annu Rep ... Rhodesia. Ministry of Agriculture. Grasslands Research Station. Annual Report [*A publication*]
Rhod Nurse ... Rhodesian Nurse [*A publication*]
Rhod Prehist ... Rhodesian Prehistory [*A publication*]
Rhod Salisbury Res Stn Annu Rep ... Rhodesia. Salisbury Research Station. Annual Report [*A publication*]
Rhod Sci News ... Rhodesia Science News [*A publication*]
Rhod Tob ... Rhodesian Tobacco [*A publication*]
Rhod Zambia Malawi J Agric Res ... Rhodesia, Zambia, and Malawi Journal of Agricultural Research [*A publication*]
RHOGI ...... RADAR Homing Guidance Investigation   (MCD)
RHOJ .... RADAR Home on Jam
Rho L .... Rhodian Law [*A publication*]   (DLA)
RHOMB ..... Rhomboid [*Mathematics*]
RHOSA ...... Rinsho Hoshasen [*A publication*]
RHOSP ..... Registered Home Ownership Savings Plan
RHP .... Radiant Heat Pump
RHP .... Rated Horsepower
RHP .... Reduced Hard Pressure   (MSA)
RHP .... Resource Holding Potential
RHP .... Resource Holding Power [*Fighting ability - animal defense*]
RhP .... Rhone-Poulenc, Inc. [*Associated Press abbreviation*]   (APAG)
RHP .... Right-Hand Page   (WDMC)
RHP .... Right Hand Panel   (MCD)
RHP .... Right-Handed Pitcher [*Baseball*]
RHP .... Rural Health Program [*Military*]   (CINC)
RHPA .... Reverse Hemolytic Plaque Assay [*Clinical chemistry*]
RHPC .... Rapid-Hardening Portland Cement
rhPF .... Recombinant Human Platelet Factor [*Biochemistry*]
RH PL .... Rhodium Plate   (MSA)
RHPLC ...... Radio-High-Performance Liquid Chromatography
Rh Pos .... Rhesus Factor Positive [*Hematology*]   (MAE)
RHPS .... Radiation-Hardened Power Supply
RHPS .... Rapid Housing Payment System [*Department of Housing and Urban Development*]   (GFGA)
RHQ .... Regimental Headquarters
RHR .... Rear Headrest
RHR .... Receiver Holding Register
RHR .... Reheater   (AAG)

RHR .... Rejectable Hazard Rate   (IEEE)
RHR .... Residual Heat Removal [*Nuclear energy*]   (NRCH)
RHR .... Resting Heart Rate [*Cardiology*]
r/hr .... Roentgens per Hour   (AABC)
RHR .... Rohr, Inc. [*NYSE symbol*]   (SPSG)
RHR .... Roughness Height Rating   (MSA)
RHR .... Royal Highland Regiment [*Military unit*] [*British*]
RHRCA ..... Rehabilitation Record [*A publication*]
RHRP .... Residual Heat Removal Pump [*Nuclear energy*]   (NRCH)
RHRS .... Residual Heat Removal System [*Nuclear energy*]   (NRCH)
RHRSW .... Residual Heat Removal Service Water [*Nuclear energy*]   (NRCH)
RHS .... Rectangular Hollow Section [*Metal industry*]
RHS .... Regency Health Services [*AMEX symbol*]   (SPSG)
RHS .... Retirement History Survey
RHS .... Right-Hand Side
RHS .... Rocketdyne Hybrid Simulator [*NASA*]   (NASA)
RHS .... Rodeo Historical Society   (EA)
RHS .... Rolled Hollow Section
RHS .... Rough Hard Sphere [*Model of liquids*]
RHS .... Royal Historical Society [*British*]
RHS .... Royal Historical Society. Transactions [*A publication*]
RHS .... Royal Horticultural Society [*British*]   (ARC)
RHS .... Royal Humane Society [*British*]
RHSC .... Richmond Hill School Company [*British military*]   (DMA)
RHSC .... Right-Hand-Side by Centroid
RHSC .... Right-Hand Side Console [*NASA*]   (KSC)
RHSCH ..... Rhodes Scholar
RhSh .... Rosh Hashanah [*New Year*]   (BJA)
RHSI .... Rubber Heel and Sole Institute [*Defunct*]   (EA)
RHSJ .... Religious Hospitallers of St. Joseph [*Roman Catholic women's religious order*]
RhSNA ...... National Archives of Rhodesia, Salisbury, Rhodesia [*Library symbol*] [*Library of Congress*]   (LCLS)
RHSQ .... Royal Historical Society of Queensland. Journal [*A publication*]   (APTA)
RHSQJ ...... Royal Historical Society of Queensland. Journal [*A publication*]   (ADA)
RHSTr .... Royal Historical Society. Transactions [*A publication*]
RHT .... Radiant Heat Temperature   (NASA)
RHT .... Reynolds Hydrodynamic Theory [*Physics*]
RHT .... Richton International Corp. [*AMEX symbol*]   (SPSG)
RHT .... Right Hypertropia [*Ophthalmology*]
RHTKA ..... Rheinstahl Technik [*A publication*]
RHTM ...... Regional Highway Traffic Model [*Database*] [*Obsolete*]
RHTMA .... Reviews on High-Temperature Materials [*A publication*]
RHTPS ...... Razor Hafters' Trade Protection Society [*A union*] [*British*]
RHTS .... Reactor Heat Transport System   (NRCH)
RHU .... Radioisotope Heater Unit   (NASA)
RHU .... Registered Health Underwriter [*NAHU*]
RHU .... Requisition Held Up   (DNAB)
RHU .... Residuum Hydrocracking Unit [*Petroleum refining*]
RHU .... Rheumatology [*Medical specialty*]   (DHSM)
RHUEA ..... Rheumatism [*England*] [*A publication*]
rHuEPO .... Recombinant Human Erythropoietin [*Biochemistry*]
RHUMA .... Rhumatologie [*A publication*]
RHV .... Registered Health Visitor [*British*]
RHV .... Remnant Hepatic Volume [*Hematology*]
RhV .... Rheinische Vierteljahresblaetter [*A publication*]
RhV .... Rheinische Vorzeit in Wort und Bild [*A publication*]
RHV .... RHYS Industries Ltd. [*Vancouver Stock Exchange symbol*]
RHV .... Road Haulage Vehicle   (DCTA)
RHV .... San Jose, CA [*Location identifier*] [*FAA*]   (FAAL)
RhVJ .... Rheinische Vierteljahresblaetter [*A publication*]
RHW .... Required Hangar Width   (MCD)
RHW .... Reversible Half-Wave
RHW .... Right Half Word
RHW .... Router Header Word   (NASA)
RHWAC .... Reversible Half-Wave Alternating Current
RHWACDC ... Reversible Half-Wave Alternating Current - Direct Current
RHWB .... [*The*] Reverend Henry Ward Beecher [*American clergyman, 1813-1887*]
RHWDC .... Reversible Half-Wave Direct Current
RHWR .... RADAR Homing and Warning Receiver   (MCD)
RHX .... Atlanta, GA [*Location identifier*] [*FAA*]   (FAAL)
RHX .... Regenerative Heat Exchanger [*Nuclear energy*]   (NRCH)
RHY .... Rhyolite Resources [*Vancouver Stock Exchange symbol*]
RHYTHM ... Remember How You Treat Hazardous Materials [*E. I. Du Pont De Nemours & Co. program*]
Rhythm ...... Rhythmica [*of Aristoxenus*] [*Classical studies*]   (OCD)
Rhythmes Monde ... Rhythmes du Monde [*A publication*]
RI .... Indonesia [*JYRU nationality code*]   (IYR)
RI .... Member of the Royal Institute of Painters in Water Colours [*British*]
RI .... RADAR Input
RI .... Radiation Indicator [*Nuclear energy*]   (NRCH)
RI .... Radiation Intensity   (AABC)
R & I .... Radical and Intense [*Extremely great*] [*Slang*]
RI .... Radicalist International   (EA)
RI .... Radio Inertial   (MCD)
RI .... Radio Influence

RI	Radio Inspector
RI	Radio Interference (MCD)
RI	Radioisotope
RI	Radix Institute (EA)
RI	Rampart Institute (EA)
RI	Random Interlace [*Television*]
RI	Random Interval (AEBS)
RI	Range Instrumentation (MCD)
RI	Ranger Instructor [*Army*] (INF)
R/I.............	Rate of Interest [*Economics*]
RI	REACT International (EA)
RI	Reactor Island [*Nuclear energy*] (NRCH)
RI	Read-In (DEN)
RI	Readers International [*Subscription book club*] [*British*]
RI	Reallocation Inventory (AFIT)
RI	Receiver Interface
RI	Receiving Inspection (AAG)
R & I..........	Receiving and Inspection (KSC)
RI	Recipe Index [*A publication*]
RI	Recombinant Inbred [*Genetics*]
RI	Reconnaissance Inspection [*Military*] (GFGA)
RI	Recovery, Inc.
RI	Recruit Induction [*Military*]
RI	Recruit Instruction [*Navy*]
RI	Redheads International (EA)
RI	Reflective Insulation [*Technical drawings*]
RI	Refractive Index
RI	Refugees International (EA)
RI	Regimental Institute [*British military*] (DMA)
RI	Regina Imperatrix [*Queen Empress*] [*Latin*]
R et I	Regina et Imperatrix [*Queen and Empress*] [*Latin*]
RI	Regional Ileitis [*Medicine*]
RI	Registro Italiano [*Italian ship classification society*] (DS)
RI	Rehabilitation International (EA)
RI	Reimplantation [*Dentistry*]
RI	Reinitiate (SAA)
RI	Reinsurance (ADA)
RI	Reissue [*of a book or periodical*] [*Publishing*]
RI	Relative Intensity
RI	Relaxation Instruction [*Psychology*]
RI	Release-Inhibiting Factor [*Endocrinology*] (MAE)
RI	Reliability Index
RI	Religion Indexes [*A publication*]
RI	Religious Instruction (ADA)
RI	Remission Induction [*Oncology*]
R & I..........	Removal and Installation (NRCH)
RI	Repeat Indication [*Telecommunications*] (TEL)
RI	Replaceable Item
RI	Replicative Intermediate [*Medicine*] (MAE)
RI	Report of Investigation
RI	Repulsion Induction [*Motor*]
RI	Request for Information (MCD)
RI	Require Identification
RI	Rescue, Inc. (EA)
RI	Research Institute [*Fort Belvoir, VA*] [*United States Army Engineer Topographic Laboratories*] (GRD)
RI	Resistance Index
RI	Resistance Inductance (IEEE)
RI	Resistance International (EA)
RI	Resolve, Inc. (EA)
RI	Resonance Integral [*Nuclear energy*] (NRCH)
RIAM	Respiratory Illness [*Medicine*]
R & I..........	Restaurants and Institutions [*A publication*]
RI	Retention Index
RI	Retirement Income
RI	Retreats International (EA)
RI	Retroactive Inhibition [*Psychology*]
RI	Reunite, Inc. (EA)
RI	Reverberation Index
R et I	Rex et Imperator [*King and Emperor*] [*Latin*]
RI	RHEMA [*Restoring Hope through Educational and Medical Aid*] International (EA)
RI	Rhode Island [*Postal code*]
RI	Rhode Island Music Educators Review [*A publication*]
RI	Rhode Island Reports [*A publication*]
RI	Rhode Island Supreme Court Reports [*A publication*] (ILCA)
RI	Ribosomal [*Protein*] [*Cytology*]
Ri................	Ricardus Anglicus [*Deceased, 1242*] [*Authority cited in pre-1607 legal work*] (DSA)
RI	Rice Institute Pamphlet [*A publication*]
Ri................	Richardson Number [*Physics*]
RI	Rigorous Imprisonment [*British military*] (DMA)
RI	Ring Index [*of chemical compounds*] [*A publication*]
RI	Ring Indicator [*MODEM*] (PCM)
RI	Rio-Sul, Servicos Aereos Regionais SA [*Brazil*] [*ICAO designator*] (ICDA)
RI	Risorgimento Italiano [*A publication*]
RI	Rock Island Lines [*Railroad*]
RI	Rockwell International Corp. (MCD)
RI	Rodale Intstitute (EA)
RI	Rolf Institute (EA)

RI	Rotary International (EA)
RI	Routing Identifier [*or Indicator*] (AFM)
RI	Royal Institution [*British*]
RI	Royal Irish [*Military unit*] [*British*]
RI	Rubber Insulation [*Technical drawings*]
RI	Rulers of India [*A publication*]
RI	Rutherford Institute (EA)
RIA	Radioimmunoassay [*Clinical chemistry*]
RIA	Rain in Area (ADA)
RIA	Reactivity Initiated Accident [*Nuclear energy*] (NRCH)
RIA	Registered Industrial and Cost Accountant
RIA	Registered Investment Adviser [*Securities*]
RIA	Regulatory Impact Analysis [*or Assessment*]
RIA	Religious Instruction Association [*Later, PERSC*]
RIA	Remote Intelligence Acquisition
RIA	Removable Instrument Assembly [*Nuclear energy*] (NRCH)
RIA	Research Institute of America [*New York, NY*] [*Information service or system*] (IID)
RIA	Rich International Airways, Inc. [*Miami, FL*] [*FAA designator*] (FAAC)
RIA	Rivista. Istituto Nazionale d'Archeologia e Storia dell'Arte [*A publication*]
RÍA	Robotic Industries Association (EA)
RIA	Rock Island Arsenal [*Illinois*] [*Army*]
RIA	Royal Irish Academy
RIA	Santa Maria [*Brazil*] [*Airport symbol*] (OAG)
RIAA	Recording Industry Association of America (EA)
RIAC..........	Regional Industry Advisory Committee [*Civil Defense*]
RIAC..........	Royal Irish Automobile Club (EAIO)
RIACS	Research Institute for Advanced Computer Science [*University Space Research Association*] [*Research center*] (RCD)
RI Acts & Resolves ...	Acts and Resolves of Rhode Island and Providence Plantations [*A publication*]
RIAD	Rencontres Internationales des Assureurs Defense [*Genoa, Italy*] (EA)
RIA-DA	Radioimmunoassay Double Antibody [*Test*] [*Clinical chemistry*]
RIADAG....	Radovi Instituta za Proucavanje i Suzbijanje Alkoholizma i Drugih Narkomanija u Zagrebu [*A publication*]
RIAEC.......	Rhode Island Atomic Energy Commission
RIAES	Rhode Island Agricultural Experiment Station [*University of Rhode Island*] [*Research center*] (RCD)
RIAF.........	Royal Indian Air Force
RIAF.........	Royal Iraqi Air Force
RI Ag.........	Rhode Island Agriculture [*A publication*]
RI Ag Exp ...	Rhode Island. Agricultural Experiment Station. Publications [*A publication*]
RI Agr	Rhode Island Agriculture. Rhode Island Agricultural Experiment Station [*A publication*]
RI Agric	Rhode Island Agriculture [*A publication*]
RI Agric Exp Stn Bull ...	Rhode Island. Agricultural Experiment Station. Bulletin [*A publication*]
RI Agric Exp Stn Res Q Rev ...	Rhode Island. Agricultural Experiment Station. Research Quarterly Review [*A publication*]
RIAI..........	Royal Institute of the Architects of Ireland
RIAIAD	Reverse International Acronyms, Initialisms, and Abbreviations Dictionary [*A publication*]
RIAL.........	Religion in American Life (EA)
RIAL.........	Revised Individual Allowance List [*Navy*] (NVT)
RIAL.........	Rock Island Arsenal Laboratories [*Illinois*] (MCD)
RIALF	Flair Resources Ltd. [*NASDAQ symbol*] (NQ)
RIAM	Royal Irish Academy of Music
RIAND	Risk Analysis [*A publication*]
RIAP.........	Research Institute for Asia and the Pacific [*Australia*]
RIAR.........	Requirements Inventory Analysis Report (AFM)
RIA-R	Rock Island Arsenal General Thomas J. Rodman Laboratory [*Army*]
RIAS.........	Radio in American Sector (SAA)
RIAS.........	Readiness Information Access System (MCD)
RIAS.........	Research Initiation and Support [*National Science Foundation program*]
RIAS.........	Research Institute for Advanced Studies [*Martin Marietta Corp.*]
RIAS.........	Royal Incorporation of Architects in Scotland
RIAS.........	Rundfunk im Amerikanischen Sektor Berlins [*Radio in American Sector*] [*Germany*]
RIASB	Richerche Astronomiche [*A publication*]
RIASC	Royal Indian Army Service Corps [*British*]
RIA/SE......	Rock Island Arsenal/Science and Engineering Directorate [*Illinois*]
RIA Tax.....	Research Institute of America Tax Coordinator [*A publication*] (DLA)
RIAX.........	Rich International Airways, Inc. [*Air carrier designation symbol*]
RIB............	Racing Information Bureau [*British*] (CB)
RIB............	Railway Information Bureau
RIB............	Receiver Interface Board [*Navy Navigation Satellite System*] (DNAB)
RIB............	Recoverable Item Breakdown
RIB............	Recyclable, Incineratable, Biodegradable [*Food packaging*]

RIB............ Review of International Affairs. Politics, Economics, Law, Science, Culture [*A publication*]
RIB............ Review of International Broadcasting [*A publication*]
RIB............ Ribbed   (AAG)
RIB............ Riberalta [*Bolivia*] [*Airport symbol*]   (OAG)
Rib............ Ribose [*Also, r*] [*A sugar*]
RIB............ Right Inboard   (MCD)
RIB............ Right Intermediate Bronchus [*Anatomy*]
RIB............ [*The*] Roman Inscriptions of Britain [*A publication*]   (OCD)
RIB............ Rural Industries Bureau
RIBA......... Recombinant Immunobioassay
RIBA......... Royal Institute of British Architects   (IID)
RIBA J....... Royal Institute of British Architects. Journal [*A publication*]
RIBA Journal ... Journal. Royal Institute of British Architects [*A publication*]
RI Bd RC ... Rhode Island Board of Railroad Commission Reports [*A publication*]   (DLA)
RIBE.......... Reactive Ion Beam Etching
RIBI........... Ribi Immunochem Research, Inc. [*NASDAQ symbol*]   (NQ)
RIBIT......... Read in Bed - It's Terrific
RIBJ......... Rhode Island Bar Journal [*A publication*]
RIBJD....... RIBA [*Royal Institute of British Architects*] Journal [*A publication*]
RIBLIM..... Reduction in Benefit Limitation
RIBS.......... Restructured Infantry Battalion System   (AABC)
RIBS.......... Royal Institute of British Sculptors
RIBSS....... Research Institute for the Behavioral and Social Sciences [*Army*]
RI Bur Industrial Statistics An Rp Nat Res S B ... Rhode Island Bureau of Industrial Statistics. Annual Report. Natural Resources Survey. Bulletin [*A publication*]
RIC .... RADAR Indicating Console [*FAA*]
RIC .... RADAR Input Control
RIC .... RADAR Intercept Calculator
RIC .... RADAR Intercept Control
RIC .... Radio Industry Council [*British*]
RIC .... Radioimmunoconjugate
RIC .... Rafter Input Converter
RIC .... Rainforest Information Centre [*Australia*]   (EAIO)
RIC .... Range Instrumentation Conference   (MUGU)
RIC .... Range Instrumentation Coordination   (KSC)
RIC .... Raptor Information Center   (EA)
RIC .... Rare-Earth Information Center   (EA)
RIC .... Read-In Counter
RIC .... Reconstituted Ion Current [*Chromatography*]
RIC .... Reconstructed Ion Chromatogram
RIC .... Record Identification Code [*Navy*]
RIC .... Recruiter Identification Code [*Military*]
RIC .... Regolamento Internazionale Carrozze [*International Carriage and Van Union*]
RIC .... Relocation Instruction Counter [*Data processing*]   (OA)
RIC .... Remote Information Center
RIC .... Remote Interactive Communications [*Xerox Corp.*]
RIC .... Repair Induction Code [*Module Maintenance Facility*]
RIC .... Repairable Identification Code
RIC .... Repairable Item Code
RIC .... Repertoire Bibliographique des Institutions Chretiennes [*Bibliographical Repertory of Christian Institutions*] [*Centre de Recherche et de Documentation des Institutions Chretiennes*] [*France*] [*Information service or system*]   (CRD)
RIC .... Replaceable Item Code
RIC .... Request for Instrumentation Clarification [*NASA*]   (KSC)
RIC .... Resident Inspector-in-Charge
RIC .... Resistance, Inductance, and Capacitance   (NASA)
RIC .... Resource Identification Code [*Navy*]
RIC .... Resource Information Center System [*Search system*]
RIC .... Retirement Income Credit
RIC .... Review of International Cooperation [*A publication*]
Ric............ Ricardus Malumbra [*Deceased, 1334*] [*Authority cited in pre-1607 legal work*]   (DSA)
Ric............ Richard (King of England)   (DLA)
RIC .... Richmond [*Florida*] [*Seismograph station code, US Geological Survey*] [*Closed*]   (SEIS)
RIC .... Richmond [*Virginia*] [*Airport symbol*]
RIC .... Ricks College, David O. McKay Learning Resources Center, Rexburg, ID [*OCLC symbol*]   (OCLC)
RIC .... Road Information Center [*Arab Contractors Co.*]   (IID)
RIC .... Rockwell International Corp.   (NASA)
RIC .... Rodeo Information Commission   (EA)
RIC .... Roman Imperial Coinage [*A publication*]   (OCD)
RIC .... Routing Identification Code   (NATG)
RIC .... Royal Institute of Chemistry [*Later, RSC*] [*British*]
RIC .... Royal Irish Constabulary
RIC .... Rural Information Center [*Department of Agriculture*] [*Information service or system*]   (IID)
RICA......... Railway Industry Clearance Association   (EA)
RICA......... Research Institute for Consumer Affairs [*British*]
RICAL....... Research Information Center and Library [*Foster Wheeler Corp.*] [*Information service or system*]   (IID)
Ricar.......... Ricardus [*Authority cited in pre-1607 legal work*]   (DSA)

RICASIP ... Research Information Center and Advisory Service on Information Processing [*National Bureau of Standards - National Science Foundation*]
Ric Autom .. Ricerche di Automatica [*A publication*]
RICB......... Research into Child Blindness [*British*]   (DI)
RicBibRel... Ricerche Bibliche e Religiose [*Milan*] [*A publication*]
Ric Biol Selvaggina ... Ricerche di Biologia della Selvaggina [*A publication*]
RICC......... Regional Interagency Coordinating Committee [*Department of Labor*]
RICC......... Remote Intercomputer Communications Interface   (MCD)
RICC......... Reportable Item Control Code [*Army*]   (AABC)
Ric Clin Lab ... Ricerca in Clinica e in Laboratorio [*A publication*]
Ric Demos ... Ricerche Demoscopiche [*A publication*]
Ric Doc Tess ... Ricerca e Documentazione Tessile [*A publication*]
RICE.......... American Rice, Inc. [*NASDAQ symbol*]   (NQ)
RICE.......... Recreational Industries Council on Exporting   (EA)
RICE.......... Regional Information and Communications Exchange [*Rice University Library*] [*Houston, TX*]
RICE.......... Relative Index of Combat Effectiveness [*Military*] [*British*]
RICE.......... Research and Information Centre on Eritrea   (EA)
RICE.......... Resources in Computer Education [*Northwest Regional Educational Laboratory Microcomputer Software and Information for Teachers*] [*Information service or system*] [*No longer available online*]
RICE.......... Rest, Ice, Compression, Elevation [*Medicine*]
Rice .... Rice's South Carolina Law Reports [*1838-39*] [*A publication*]   (DLA)
RICE.......... Right to a Comprehensive Education   (EAIO)
Rice Ch ...... Rice's South Carolina Equity Reports [*A publication*]   (DLA)
Ric Econ..... Ricerche Economiche [*A publication*]
Rice Dig .... Rice's Digest of Patent Office Decisions [*A publication*]   (DLA)
Rice Eq...... Rice's South Carolina Equity Reports [*1838-39*] [*A publication*]   (DLA)
Rice Ev....... Rice's Law of Evidence [*A publication*]   (DLA)
Rice Inst P ... Rice Institute Pamphlet [*A publication*]
Rice Inst Pam ... Rice Institute Pamphlet [*A publication*]
Rice J .... Rice Journal [*A publication*]
Rice L (SC) ... Rice's South Carolina Law Reports [*A publication*]   (DLA)
Ricerca Scient ... Ricerca Scientifica [*A publication*]
Ricerche Automat ... Ricerche di Automatica [*A publication*]
Ricerche Mat ... Ricerche di Matematica [*A publication*]
Rice's Code ... Rice's Code of Practice [*Colorado*] [*A publication*]   (DLA)
Rice Univ Aero-Astronaut Rep ... Rice University. Aero-Astronautic Report [*A publication*]
Rice Univ Stud ... Rice University. Studies [*A publication*]
Rice Univ Studies ... Rice University. Studies [*A publication*]
RiceUS....... Rice University. Studies [*A publication*]
RicF........... Ricerche Filosofiche [*A publication*]
RICH .... Radiation-Induced Color Halo [*Physics*]
Rich............ Richard (King of England)   (DLA)
Rich............ Richardson's Reports [*2-5 New Hampshire*] [*A publication*]   (DLA)
Rich............ [*J. S. G.*] Richardson's South Carolina Law Reports [*A publication*]   (DLA)
RICH .... Richmond Hill Savings Bank [*Floral Park, NY*] [*NASDAQ symbol*]   (NQ)
RICH .... Richmond National Battlefield Park
Richardson Law Practice ... Richardson's Establishing a Law Practice [*A publication*]
Richardson's S Ca Rep ... [*J. S. G.*] Richardson's South Carolina Law Reports [*A publication*]   (DLA)
Rich Cas..... [*J. S. G.*] Richardson's South Carolina Cases [*1831-32*] [*A publication*]   (DLA)
Rich Cas (SC) ... [*J. S. G.*] Richardson's South Carolina Equity Cases [*A publication*]   (DLA)
Rich Ch ...... [*J. S. G.*] Richardson's South Carolina Equity Reports [*A publication*]   (DLA)
Rich Ch Pr ... Richardson's Chancery Practice [*1838*] [*A publication*]   (DLA)
Rich CP...... Richardson's Practice Common Pleas [*England*] [*A publication*]   (DLA)
Rich Ct Cl .. Richardson's Court of Claims Reports [*A publication*]   (DLA)
RICHD ...... Reviews in Inorganic Chemistry [*A publication*]
Richd E Repts ... [*J. S. G.*] Richardson's South Carolina Equity Reports [*A publication*]   (DLA)
Rich Dict.... Richardson's New Dictionary of the English Language [*A publication*]   (DLA)
Rich'd Law R ... [*J. S. G.*] Richardson's South Carolina Law Reports [*A publication*]   (DLA)
RICHEL.... Richmond - Cape Henry Environmental Laboratory [*NASA/USGS*]
Rich Eq ...... [*J. S. G.*] Richardson's South Carolina Equity Reports [*1844-46, 1850-68*] [*A publication*]   (DLA)
Rich Eq Cas ... [*J. S. G.*] Richardson's South Carolina Equity Reports [*A publication*]   (DLA)
Rich Eq Ch ... [*J. S. G.*] Richardson's South Carolina Equity Reports [*A publication*]   (DLA)
Rich & H .... Richardson and Hook's Street Railway Decisions [*A publication*]   (DLA)
Rich Land A ... Richey's Irish Land Act [*A publication*]   (DLA)
Rich Law (SC) ... [*J. S. G.*] Richardson's South Carolina Law Reports [*A publication*]   (DLA)

Rich L (SC) ... [*J. S. G.*] Richardson's South Carolina Law Reports [*A publication*]   (DLA)

Richmd T-D ... Richmond Times-Dispatch [*A publication*]

Richmond Cty Hist ... Richmond County History [*A publication*]

Rich NH..... Richardson's Reports [*3-5 New Hampshire*] [*A publication*]   (DLA)

Rich NS ..... [*J. S. G.*] Richardson's South Carolina Reports, New Series [*A publication*]   (DLA)

Rich PRCP ... Richardson's Practical Register of English Common Pleas [*A publication*]   (DLA)

Rich Pr KB ... Richardson's Attorney's Practice in the Court of King's Bench [*8th ed.*] [*1792*] [*A publication*]   (DLA)

Rich Pr Reg ... Richardson's Practical Register of English Common Pleas [*A publication*]   (DLA)

Rich & S..... Richardson and Sayles' Select Cases of Procedure without Writ [*Selden Society Publication 60*] [*A publication*]   (DLA)

RICHTON ... Richton International Corp. [*Associated Press abbreviation*]   (APAG)

Rich & W ... Richardson and Woodbury's Reports [*2 New Hampshire*] [*A publication*]   (DLA)

Rich Wills ... Richardson's Law of Testaments and Last Wills [*A publication*]   (DLA)

RICJA .... Rice Journal [*A publication*]

Rick Eng St ... Rickard's English Statutes [*A publication*]   (DLA)

Rickia Arq Bot Estado Sao Paulo Ser Criptogam ... Rickia. Arquivos de Botanica do Estado de Sao Paulo. Serie Criptogamica [*A publication*]

Rickia Arq Bot Estado Sao Paulo Ser Criptogam Supl ... Rickia. Arquivos de Botanica do Estado de Sao Paulo. Serie Criptogamica [*A publication*]

Rickia Supl ... Rickia. Suplemento [*A publication*]

Rick & M ... Rickards and Michael's English Locus Standi Reports [*A publication*]   (DLA)

Rickmansworth Hist ... Rickmansworth Historian [*A publication*]

Rick & S..... Rickards and Saunders' English Locus Standi Reports [*A publication*]   (DLA)

RICL.......... Receipt Inspection Checklist   (DNAB)

RicLing ...... Ricerche Linguistiche [*A publication*]

RICM........ Registre International des Citoyens du Monde [*International Registry of World Citizens*]

RicM .... Ricerche Musicali [*A publication*]

RICM........ Right Intercostal Margin [*Medicine*]

Ric Mat...... Ricerche di Matematica [*A publication*]

RICMD..... Richmond Contract Management District   (SAA)

RICMO ..... RADAR Input Countermeasures Officer [*Air Force*]

Ric Morfol ... Ricerche di Morfologia [*A publication*]

RICMT...... RADAR Input Countermeasures Technician [*Air Force*]

RICO .... Racketeer-Influenced and Corrupt Organizations [*Nickname of a 1970 law used by federal prosecutors to indict organized crime leaders*]

RI Comp of Rules of St Agencies ... Rhode Island Compilation of Rules of State Agencies [*A publication*]   (DLA)

RI Const..... Rhode Island Constitution [*A publication*]   (DLA)

RICP.......... Revista. Instituto de Cultura Puertorriquena [*A publication*]

RicR .... Ricerche Religiose [*A publication*]

RicRel .... Ricerche Religiose [*A publication*]

RICRS .... Rockford Institute Center on Religion and Society   (EA)

Ric Ruf....... Ricardus Rufulus [*Authority cited in pre-1607 legal work*]   (DSA)

RICS .... Range Instrumentation Control System

RICS .... Remote Image Confirming Sensor   (MCD)

RICS .... Reports Index Control   (MCD)

RICS .... Respiratory Intensive Care System [*Medicine*]

Ric & S....... Rickards and Saunders' English Locus Standi Reports [*1890-94*] [*A publication*]   (DLA)

RICS .... Royal Institution of Chartered Surveyors [*British*]

RICS Abs Rev ... RICS [*Royal Institution of Chartered Surveyors*] Abstracts and Review [*A publication*]

Ric Sci........ Ricerca Scientifica [*A publication*]

Ric Sci Parte 2 Sez A ... Ricerca Scientifica. Parte 2. Rendiconti. Sezione A. Biologica [*A publication*]

Ric Sci Parte 2 Sez B ... Ricerca Scientifica. Parte 2. Rendiconti. Sezione B. Biologica [*A publication*]

Ric Sci Prog Tec ... Ricerca Scientifica ed il Progresso Tecnico [*A publication*]

Ric Sci Quad ... Ricerca Scientifica. Quaderni [*A publication*]

Ric Sci Rend Sez B ... Ricerca Scientifica. Serie Seconda. Parte II. Rendiconti. Sezione B. Biologica [*A publication*]

Ric Sci Ricostr ... Ricerca Scientifica e Ricostruzione [*A publication*]

Ric Sci Suppl ... Ricerca Scientifica. Supplemento [*A publication*]

RicSL......... Ricerche Slavistiche [*A publication*]

Ric Spettrosc ... Ricerche Spettroscopiche [*A publication*]

Ric Spettros Lab Astrofis Specola ... Ricerche Spettroscopiche. Laboratorio Astrofisico della Specola Vaticana [*A publication*]

RicSRel..... Ricerche di Storia Religiosa [*A publication*]

Ric St (Brindisi) ... Ricerche e Studi. Museo Provinciale Francesco Ribezzo (Brindisi) [*A publication*]

RicStRel..... Ricerche di Storia Religiosa [*Rome*] [*A publication*]

Ric Termotecnica ... Ricerche di Termotecnica [*Italy*] [*A publication*]

RI Ct Rec ... Rhode Island Court Records [*A publication*]   (DLA)

RICU .... Respiratory Intensive Care Unit [*Medicine*]

Ric Zool Appl Caccia ... Ricerche di Zoologia Applicata alla Caccia [*A publication*]

Ric Zool Appl Caccia Suppl ... Ricerche di Zoologia Applicata alla Caccia. Supplemento [*A publication*]

RID .... RADAR Input Drum

RID .... Radial Immunodiffusion [*Analytical biochemistry*]

RID .... Radio Intelligence Division [*of the Federal Communications Commission*]

RID .... Radioisotope Detection

RID .... Range Instruments Development   (MCD)

RID .... Real-Fluid Isentropic Decompression [*Engineering*]

RID .... Record Identity [*Military*]   (AFIT)

RID .... Records Issue Date [*Bell System*]   (TEL)

RID .... Reduced Ignition Relay   (MCD)

RID .... Refractive Index Detector [*Instrumentation*]

RID .... Regimented Inmate Discipline [*Mississippi State Penitentiary*]

RID .... Registry of Interpreters for the Deaf   (EA)

RID .... Reglement International Concernant le Transport des Marchandises Dangereuses [*International Regulation Governing the Carriage of Dangerous Goods*]

RID .... Regulatory Integration Division [*Environmental Protection Agency*]   (GFGA)

RID .... Released to Inactive Duty

RID .... Reliability Index Determination   (MCD)

RID .... Remove Intoxicated Drivers [*An association*]

RID .... Research Institutes and Divisions [*of National Institutes of Health*]

RID .... Reset Inhibit Drive

RID .... Reset Inhibit Drum

RID .... Retrofit Installation Data   (MCD)

RID .... Reversible Intravas Device

RID .... Review Item Discrepancy   (MCD)

RID .... Review Item Disposition [*NASA*]   (NASA)

RID .... Richmond, IN [*Location identifier*] [*FAA*]   (FAAL)

RID .... Rider College Library, Lawrenceville, NJ [*OCLC symbol*]   (OCLC)

Rid.............. Ridotto [*A publication*]

RID .... Royal Irish Dragoons [*British military*]   (DMA)

RIDA .... Raster Image Device Accelerator [*Printer technology*]

RIDA .... Reverse Isotope Dilution Assay [*Chemical analysis*]

RIDAC...... Range Interference Detecting and Control

RIDAURA ... Remission Inducing Drug, Au [*Chemical symbol for gold*], Rheumatoid Arthritis [*Gold-based drug manufactured by SmithKline Beckman Corp.*]

RIDB........ Readiness Intergrated Database

RIDC .... Ryerson International Development Centre [*Ryerson Polytechnical Institute*] [*Canada*] [*Research center*]   (RCD)

RIDD .... Range Instrumentation Development Division   (SAA)

Riddle's Lex ... Riddle's Lexicon [*A publication*]   (DLA)

RIDDOR ... Reporting of Injuries, Diseases, and Dangerous Occurrences Regulations [*British*]

RIDE.......... People Ridesharing Systems, Inc. [*Newark, NJ*] [*NASDAQ symbol*]   (NQ)

RIDE.......... Research Institute for Diagnostic Engineering

RI Dec........ Rhode Island Decisions [*A publication*]   (DLA)

RI Dent J ... Rhode Island Dental Journal [*A publication*]

RIDES .... Rockford Infant Developmental Scales [*Child development test*]

RI Dev Counc Geol Bull ... Rhode Island Development Council. Geological Bulletin [*A publication*]

RI Devel Council Geol Bull Sci Contr ... Rhode Island Development Council. Geological Bulletin. Scientific Contribution [*A publication*]

RIDEX....... Ridexchange   (EA)

RIDF......... Random Input Describing Function [*Data processing*]

Ridg........... Ridgeway's Reports Tempore Hardwicke, Chancery and English King's Bench [*A publication*]

RIDG .... Royal Inniskilling Dragoon Guards [*Military unit*] [*British*]

RIDG .... Royal Irish Dragoon Guards [*British military*]   (DMA)

Ridg Ap...... Ridgeway's Irish Appeal (or Parliamentary) Cases [*A publication*]   (DLA)

Ridg App.... Ridgeway's Irish Appeal (or Parliamentary) Cases [*A publication*]   (DLA)

Ridg Cas..... Ridgeway's Reports Tempore Hardwicke, Chancery and English King's Bench [*A publication*]   (DLA)

RIDGE....... Ridge Interdisciplinary Global Experiments [*NOAA, NSF, ONR, and USGS*]

Ridgew .... Ridgeway's Reports Tempore Hardwicke, Chancery and English King's Bench [*A publication*]   (DLA)

Ridgew Ir PC ... Ridgeway's Irish Parliamentary Reports [*1784-96*] [*A publication*]   (DLA)

Ridgew L & S (Ir) ... Ridgeway, Lapp, and Schoales' Irish Term Reports [*A publication*]   (DLA)

Ridgew L & S (Ire) ... Ridgeway, Lapp, and Schoales' Irish Term Reports [*A publication*]   (DLA)

Ridgew T Hardw ... Ridgeway's Reports Tempore Hardwicke, Chancery [*27 English Reprint*] [*1744-46*] [*A publication*]   (DLA)

Ridgew T Hardw (Eng) ... Ridgeway Tempore Hardwicke [*27 English Reprint*] [*A publication*]   (DLA)

Ridg & Hard ... Ridgeway's Reports Tempore Hardwicke, Chancery and English King's Bench [*A publication*]   (DLA)

Ridg L & S ... Ridgeway, Lapp, and Schoales' Irish Term Reports [*A publication*] (DLA)
Ridg Parl Rep ... Ridgeway's Irish Parliamentary Reports [*1784-96*] [*A publication*] (DLA)
Ridg PC ..... Ridgeway's Irish Appeal (or Parliamentary) Cases [*A publication*] (DLA)
Ridg Pr Rep ... Ridgeway's Irish Appeal (or Parliamentary) Cases [*A publication*] (DLA)
Ridg Rep .... Ridgeway's Reports of State Trials in Ireland [*A publication*] (DLA)
Ridg St Tr .. Ridgeway's (Individual) Reports of State Trials in Ireland [*A publication*] (DLA)
Ridg Temp H ... Ridgeway's Reports Tempore Hardwicke, Chancery [*27 English Reprint*] [*1744-46*] [*A publication*] (DLA)
Ridg T H .... Ridgeway's Reports Tempore Hardwicke, Chancery [*27 English Reprint*] [*1744-46*] [*A publication*] (DLA)
Ridg T Hard ... Ridgeway's Reports Tempore Hardwicke, Chancery and English King's Bench [*27 English Reprint*] [*A publication*] (DLA)
Ridg T Hardw ... Ridgeway's Reports Tempore Hardwicke, Chancery and English King's Bench [*27 English Reprint*] [*A publication*] (DLA)
Ridgw Ir PC ... Ridgeway's Irish Parliamentary Cases [*A publication*] (DLA)
RIDI.......... Receiving Inspection Detail Instruction [*NASA*] (NASA)
RIDIC....... Radiopharmaceutical Internal Dose Information Center [*Oak Ridge, TN*] [*Department of Energy*] (GRD)
RIDIT....... Relative to an Identified Distribution Transformation [*Pharmacology*]
RIDL......... Radiation Instrument Development Laboratory
RIDL......... Riddell Sports [*NASDAQ symbol*] (SPSG)
RIDL......... Ridge Instrument Development Laboratory [*Navy*]
Ridley Civil & Ecc Law ... Ridley's Civil and Ecclesiastical Law [*A publication*] (DLA)
RIDP......... RADAR-IFF Data Processor (MCD)
RIDP......... RNA [*Ribonucleic Acid*]-Instructed DNA [*Deoxyribonucleic Acid*] Polymerase [*Later, RDDP*] [*An enzyme*]
RIDPE3..... Bulletin of Fisheries Research and Development [*A publication*]
RIDS......... Radio Information Distribution System (MCD)
RIDS......... Range Information Display System (MCD)
RIDS......... Receiving Inspection Data Status [*Report*] [*Nuclear energy*] (NRCH)
RIDS......... Regional Operations Control Centre Information Display System [*NORAD*]
RIDS......... Regulatory Information Distribution System [*Nuclear energy*] (NRCH)
Rid Sup Proc ... Riddle's Supplementary Proceedings [*New York*] [*A publication*] (DLA)
RIE............ RADAR Intercept Event
RIE............ Range of Incentive Effectiveness
RIE............ Reactive Ion Etching [*Semiconductor technology*]
RIE............ Recognised Investment Exchange [*British*]
RIE............ Refrigeration Installation Equipment (SAA)
RIE............ Research in Education [*Monthly publication of ERIC*]
RIE............ Resources in Education [*Formerly, Research in Education*] [*National Institute of Education*] [*Database*]
RIE............ Retirement Income Endowment [*Insurance*]
RIE............ Rice Lake [*Wisconsin*] [*Airport symbol*] (OAG)
RIE............ Riedel EnvironTech, Inc. [*AMEX symbol*] (SPSG)
RIE............ Right Inboard Elevon [*Aviation*] (MCD)
RIE............ Royal Institute of Engineers [*British*]
RIEB......... Revista. Instituto de Estudos Brasileiros [*A publication*]
RIEC......... Royal Indian Engineering College [*British*]
Riech Aromen Kosmet ... Riechstoffe, Aromen, Kosmetica [*A publication*]
Riechst Aromen ... Riechstoffe und Aromen [*A publication*]
Riechst Aromen Koerperpflegem ... Riechstoffe, Aromen, Koerperpflegemittel [*Later, Riechstoffe, Aromen, Kosmetica*] [*A publication*]
Ried............ Riedell's Reports [*68, 69 New Hampshire*] [*A publication*] (DLA)
RIEDA...... Reseau d'Innovations Educatives pour le Developpement en Afrique [*Network of Educational Innovation for Development in Africa*] (EAIO)
RIEDAC.... Research in International Economics of Disarmament and Arms Control [*A program of Columbia University School of International Affairs*]
RIEDEL.... Riedel EnvironTech, Inc. [*Associated Press abbreviation*] (APAG)
RIEEC....... Research Institute for the Education of Exceptional Children [*A publication*]
RIEF.......... Recycling Isoelectric Focusing [*Preparative electrophoresis*]
RIEI.......... Roofing Industry Educational Institute (EA)
RIEM........ Research Institute for Environmental Medicine [*Army*] (MCD)
RIEMA...... Rapports et Proces-Verbaux des Reunions. Conseil International pour l'Exploration de la Mer [*A publication*]
RIES.......... Research Institute for Engineering Sciences [*Wayne State University*] [*Research center*] (RCD)
RIES.......... Resonance Ionization Emission Spectroscopy
RIETCOM ... Regional Interagency Emergency Transportation Committee
RIETDJ..... Institut d'Elevage et de Medecine Veterinaire des Pays Tropicaux. Rapport d'Activite [*A publication*]
RIEtnN...... Revista. Instituto Etnologico Nacional [*A publication*]

RIF............ Radio-Influence Field (IEEE)
RIF............ Radio Interference Filter
RIF............ Rate Input Form (NVT)
RIF............ Readiness Index Factor
RIF............ Reading Is Fundamental (EA)
RIF............ Real Estate Securities Income Fund, Inc. [*AMEX symbol*] (CTT)
RIF............ Receipt Inspection Form [*Military*] (DNAB)
RIF............ Reduced Injury Factor Baseball
RIF............ Reduction in Force [*Military*]
RIF............ Refund Information File [*IRS*]
RIF............ Relative Importance Factor (NASA)
RIF............ Release-Inhibiting Factor [*Endocrinology*]
RIF............ Reliability Improvement Factor
RIF............ Reportable Item File [*Military*] (AFIT)
RIF............ Resistance Inducing Factor (ADA)
RIF............ Richfield [*Utah*] [*Airport symbol*] (OAG)
RIF............ Richfield, UT [*Location identifier*] [*FAA*] (FAAL)
RIF............ Rifampin [*Also, R/AMP, RF, RMP*] [*Bactericide*]
RIF............ Rifle
RIF............ Right Iliac Fossa [*Medicine*]
RIF............ Rodeo Information Foundation [*Later, Rodeo News Bureau*]
RIF............ Royal Inniskilling Fusiliers [*Military unit*] [*British*]
RIF............ Royal Irish Fusiliers [*Military unit*] [*British*]
RIFA......... Radioiodinated Fatty Acid [*Medicine*] (MAE)
RIFBAZ..... Ching Chi Pu Kuo Li Taiwan Ta Hsueh Ho Pan Yu Yeh Sheng Wu Shih Yen So Yen Chiu Pao Kao [*A publication*]
RIFC......... Radio In-Flight Correction
RIFC......... Radioactive Illuminated Fire Control (MCD)
RIFC......... Rat Intrinsic Factor Concentrate
RIFCM...... Roll Integrated Flight Control Module (MCD)
RIFF......... Resource Interchange File Format [*Data processing*] (PCM)
RIFFED.... Forced Out by a Reduction in Force
RIFFI......... Riksforbundet Internationella Foereningen foer Invandrarkvinnor [*Sweden*]
RIFI.......... Radio Interference Field Intensity [*Meter*] (NG)
RIFI.......... Radio-Interference-Free Instrument
RIFIM....... Radio Interference Field Intensity Meter
RIFL......... Random Item File Locater
RIFM........ Research Institute for Fragrance Materials (EA)
RIFMA...... Roentgen-Isotope-Fluorescent Method of Analysis
RIFN........ Recombinant Interferon [*Biochemistry*]
Riforma Agrar ... Riforma Agraria [*Italy*] [*A publication*]
Riforma Med ... Riforma Medica [*A publication*]
RIFPA....... Revue. Institut Francais du Petrole et Annales des Combustibles Liquides [*Later, Revue. Institut Francais du Petrole*] [*A publication*]
RIFRAF..... Institute of Freshwater Research (Drottningholm). Report [*A publication*]
RIFS......... Radioisotope Field Support
RI/FS........ Remedial Investigation and Feasibility Study [*Environmental Protection Agency*]
RIFT......... Reactor-in-Flight Test [*NASA*]
RIFT/S...... Reactor-in-Flight Test/System [*NASA*] (AAG)
RIG............ Bouwadviseur Opinievormend Beroepstijdschrift voor Adviseurs [*A publication*]
RIG............ Rabies Immune Globulin [*Immunology*]
RIG............ Radio Inertial Guidance (AAG)
RIG............ Radio Interference Guard
RIG............ Rate Integrating Gyro
RIG............ Ridgeling [*Horse racing*]
RIG............ Rigging (ROG)
RIG............ Rio Grande [*Brazil*] [*Airport symbol*] (OAG)
RIG............ Roll-Imitation Gold
RIGAA....... Rinsho Ganka [*A publication*]
Rigasche Ind Ztg ... Rigasche Industrie Zeitung [*A publication*]
Rigas Med Inst Zinat Rakstu Krajums ... Rigas Medicinas Instituta Zinatnisko Rakstu Krajums [*A publication*]
Rigas Politeh Inst Zinat Raksti ... Rigas Politehniskais Instituts. Zinatniskie Raksti [*A publication*]
RIGB......... Royal Institution of Great Britain
RI Gen Laws ... General Laws of Rhode Island [*A publication*] (DLA)
RIGFET..... Resistive Insulated-Gate Field Effect Transistor
Rigg............ Select Pleas, Starrs, and Other Records from the Rolls of the Exchequer of the Jews, Edited by J. M. Riggs [*Selden Society Publications, Vol. 15*] [*A publication*] (DLA)
RIGGS....... Ross Ice Shelf Geophysical and Glaciological Survey [*Ross Ice Shelf Project*]
RIGH......... Rabies Immune Globulin, Human [*Immunology*] (MAE)
RIGHTS.... Reforming Institutions to Guarantee Humane Treatment Standards [*Student legal action organization*]
RIGI.......... Receiving Inspection General Instruction [*NASA*] (NASA)
RiGI.......... Romanskoe i Germanskoe Iazykoznanie [*Minsk*] [*A publication*]
RIGIB........ Radovi Instituta za Geolosko-Rudarska Istrazivanja i Ispitivanja Nuklearnih i Drugih Mineralnih Sirovina [*A publication*]
RIGPA....... Rezul'taty Issledovanyi po Mezhdunarodny Geofizicheskim Proektam [*A publication*]
RI Grad Sch Oceanogr Occas Publ ... Rhode Island Graduate School of Oceanography. Occasional Publication [*A publication*]

RIGS......... Radio Inertial Guidance System
RIGS......... Resonant Infrasonic Gauging System
RIGS......... Riggs National Corp. [*NASDAQ symbol*]   (NQ)
RIGS......... Runway Identifiers with Glide Slope [*Aviation*]
RIH........... Rhode Island History [*A publication*]
RIH........... Rhode Island Hospital, Providence, RI [*OCLC symbol*]   (OCLC)
RIH........... Right Inguinal Hernia [*Medicine*]
RIHAA...... Rivers and Harbors [*A publication*]
Rihaknonjip Res Inst Appl Sci Kon-Kuk Univ ... Rihaknonjip. Research Institute of Applied Science. Kon-Kuk University [*Republic Of Korea*] [*A publication*]
RIHANS... River and Harbor Aid to Navigation System [*Coast Guard*]
RIHED...... Regional Institute of Higher Education and Development
RIHGSP.... Revista. Instituto Historico e Geografico de Sao Paulo [*A publication*]
RI His S.... Rhode Island Historical Society. Collections [*A publication*]
RI Hist...... Rhode Island History [*A publication*]
RI Hist Soc Coll ... Rhode Island Historical Society. Collections [*A publication*]
RiHM .... Riemann, "Handbuch der Musikgeschichte" [*A publication*]
RIHS......... Royal International Horse Show [*British*]
RIHSA...... Radioactive Iodinate Human Serum Albumin [*Clinical chemistry*]   (AAMN)
RIHT .... RIHT Financial Corp. [*NASDAQ symbol*]   (NQ)
RIHYA ...... Rinsho Hinyokika [*A publication*]
RII............. RADAR Intelligence Information
RII............. Receiving Inspection Instruction [*Nuclear energy*]   (NRCH)
RII............. Resort Income Investors, Inc. [*AMEX symbol*]   (CTT)
RIIA.......... Royal Institute of International Affairs [*British*]
RIIA/IA..... International Affairs. Royal Institute of International Affairs [*A publication*]
RIIA/WT... World Today. Royal Institute of International Affairs [*A publication*]
RIIC.......... Research Institute on International Change [*Columbia University*]
RIIES........ Research Institute on Immigration and Ethnic Studies [*Smithsonian Institution*]
RIISA .... Report. Institute of Industrial Science. University of Tokyo [*A publication*]
RIISE........ Research Institute for Information Science and Engineering, Inc. [*Information service or system*]   (IID)
Riista-Kalataloudes Tutkimuslaitos Kalantutkimusosasto Tied ... Riista- ja Kalataloudes Tutkimuslaitos Kalantutkimusosasto Tiedonantoja [*A publication*]
Riistatiet Julkaisuja ... Riistatieteellisia Julkaisuja [*A publication*]
RIIXS........ Remote Interrogation Information Exchange System   (DNAB)
RIJ .... Right Internal Jugular [*Vein*] [*Anatomy*]
RIJ .... Rioja [*Peru*] [*Airport symbol*]   (OAG)
RIJ .... Romano Internacionalno Jekhethanibe [*International Romani Union*]   (EA)
RIJAZ .... Radovi Instituta Jugoslavenske Akademije Znanosti i Umjetnosti u Zadru [*A publication*]
RIJAZUZ ... Radovi Instituta Jugoslavenske Akademije Znanosti i Umjetnosti u Zadru [*A publication*]
RIJC .... Rhode Island Junior College [*Later, CCRI*]
RI Jew Hist Note ... Rhode Island Jewish Historical Notes [*A publication*]
RI Jewish Historical Notes ... Rhode Island Jewish Historical Notes [*A publication*]
RIJHN....... Rhode Island Jewish Historical Notes [*A publication*]
Rijks Geol Dienst Meded Nieuwe Ser (Neth) ... Rijks Geologische Dienst. Mededelingen. Nieuwe Serie (Netherlands) [*A publication*]
Rijksuniv Utrecht Jaarversl Wet Deel ... Rijksuniversiteit Utrecht. Jaarverslag Wetenschappelijk Deel [*A publication*]
Rijkswaterstaat Commun ... Rijkswaterstaat Communications [*A publication*]
Rijksw Commun ... Rijkswaterstaat Communications [*A publication*]
RIJU......... Riistatieteellisia Julkaisuja. Finnish Game Research [*A publication*]
RIK .... Replacement in Kind   (NG)
RIKAA...... Rinsho Kagaku [*A publication*]
RIKEB....... Rinsho Ketsueki [*A publication*]
RIKES ...... Raman-Induced Kerr Effect Scattering [*Spectroscopy*]
RIL............ Radio Influence Level
RIL............ Radio Interference Level
RIL............ Radiology and Imaging Letter [*A publication*]
RIL............ Recombinant Interleukin [*Immunotherapy*]
RIL............ Recoverable Item List
RIL............ Red Indicator Light
RIL............ Reduction in Leadtime   (MCD)
RIL............ Reliability Intensity Level   (CAAL)
RIL............ Religion in Life [*A publication*]
RIL............ Rendiconti. Istituto Lombardo di Scienze e Lettere [*A publication*]
RIL............ Repairable Item List   (CAAL)
RIL............ Rifle, CO [*Location identifier*] [*FAA*]   (FAAL)
Ril .... Riley's South Carolina Chancery Reports [*1836-37*] [*A publication*]   (DLA)
Ril .... Riley's South Carolina Equity Reports [*A publication*]   (DLA)
RIL............ University of Rhode Island, Graduate Library School, Kingston, RI [*OCLC symbol*]   (OCLC)

RILA......... Repertoire International de la Litterature de l'Art [*International Repertory of the Literature of Art*] [*Information service or system*] [*A publication*]
RILAMAC ... Research in Laboratory Animal Medicine and Care
RILEM...... Reunion Internationale des Laboratoires d'Essais et de Recherches sur les Materiaux et les Constructions [*International Union of Testing and Research Laboratories for Materials and Structures*]   (EAIO)
Riley.......... Riley's Reports [*37-42 West Virginia*] [*A publication*]   (DLA)
Riley.......... Riley's South Carolina Chancery Reports [*A publication*]   (DLA)
Riley.......... Riley's South Carolina Law Reports [*A publication*]   (DLA)
Riley Ch .... Riley's South Carolina Equity Reports [*A publication*]   (DLA)
Riley Eq .... Riley's South Carolina Equity Reports [*A publication*]   (DLA)
Riley Eq (SC) ... Riley's South Carolina Equity Reports [*A publication*]   (DLA)
Riley L (SC) ... Riley's South Carolina Law Reports [*A publication*]   (DLA)
RILFC....... Rhode Island Library Film Cooperative [*Library network*]
Ril Harp..... Riley's Edition of Harper's South Carolina Reports [*A publication*]   (DLA)
RILKO...... Research into Lost Knowledge Organisation Trust   (EAIO)
RILM........ RILM [*Repertoire International de la Litterature Musicale*] Abstracts of Music Literature [*City University of New York*] [*Database*] [*A publication*]
RILOB...... Recherches Publiees sous la Direction de l'Institut de Lettres Orientales de Beyrouth [*A publication*]
RILOP ...... Reclamation in Lieu of Procurement [*Navy*]   (NG)
RILPG ...... Regenerative Injection Liquid Propellant Gun   (MCD)
RILS .... Ranging Integration Location System
RILS .... Rapid Integrated Logistic Support System [*Military*]   (AABC)
RILSA ...... Resident Integrated Logistics Support Activity [*Military*]   (AFIT)
RILSD ...... Resident Integrated Logistics Support Detachment [*Military*]   (MCD)
RILSL........ Rendiconti. Istituto Lombardo. Classe di Lettere, Scienze Morali, e Storiche [*A publication*]
RILST....... Remote Integrated Logistics Support Team [*Military*]   (MCD)
RILT .... Rabbit Ileal Loop Test [*for enterotoxins*]
RILWAS.... Regionalized Integrated Lake-Watershed Acidification Study [*Adirondack mountains*]
RIM .... RADAR Input Mapper
RIM .... RADAR Input Monitor   (CET)
RIM .... RADAR Intelligence Map
RIM .... Radial Inlet Manifold
RIM .... Radiant Intensity Measurements   (MUGU)
RIM .... Radioisotope Medicine
RIM .... Radioisotope Method [*Analytical chemistry*]
RIM .... Railroad Interdiction Mine [*DoD*]
RIM .... Rate Improvement Mortgage [*Banking*]
RIM .... Reaction Injection Molding [*Plastics technology*]
RIM .... Read-In Mode
RIM .... Read Interrupt Mask [*Data processing*]
RIM .... Readiness Indicator Model   (MCD)
RIM .... Receipt, Inspection, and Maintenance [*Military*]
RIM .... Receiver Intermodulation [*Telecommunications*]   (TEL)
RIM .... Recreation Information Management System [*Department of Agriculture*] [*Washington, DC*] [*Information service or system*]   (IID)
RIM .... Refractive Index Matching [*Coal technology*]
RIM .... Regulation Interpretation Memorandum [*Environmental Protection Agency*]
RIM .... Relational Information Management [*Acronym is title of a book by Wayne Erickson*]   (PCM)
RIM .... Relative Intensity Measures [*of nursing care*]
RIM .... Research in Marketing [*A publication*]
RIM .... Resident Industrial Manager
RIM .... Resource Interface Module [*Datapoint*]
RIM .... Rim [*Hawaii*] [*Seismograph station code, US Geological Survey*]   (SEIS)
RIM .... Rimrock Airlines, Inc. [*Spokane, WA*] [*FAA designator*]   (FAAC)
RIM .... Rockridge Mining [*Vancouver Stock Exchange symbol*]
RIM .... Rotors in Motion [*Aviation*]   (AIA)
RIM .... Royal Indian Marine
RIM .... RSU [*Remote Subscriber Unit*] Interface Module [*Telecommunications*]
RIM .... Rubber Insulation Material
RIMA .... Right Internal Mammary Artery [*Anatomy*]   (AAMN)
RIMAD ..... Refractive Index Matched Anomalous Diffraction [*Light measurement*]
RIMAS...... Russian Independent Mutual Aid Society   (EA)
RiMB........ Riemann, "Musikgeschichte in Beispielen" [*A publication*]
RIMB........ Roche Institute of Molecular Biology
Rimba Indones ... Rimba Indonesia [*A publication*]
RIMC........ Reparable Item Movement Control [*Military*]   (AFIT)
RIMC........ Reportable Items of Major Combinations [*Army*]   (AABC)
RIMCS...... Reparable Item Movement Control System [*Military*]   (AFIT)
RIMD .... Regulation and Information Management Division [*Environmental Protection Agency*]   (EPA)
RIMD .... Resources and Institutional Management Division [*NASA*]
RIME........ Radio Inertial Missile Equipment

RIME......... Radio Inertial Monitoring Equipment (KSC)
RIME......... Relaynet International Message Exchange [*Information network*] [*Data processing*] (PCM)
RIME......... Research Institute for Management Executives [*Washington, DC*]
RI Med J.... Rhode Island Medical Journal [*A publication*]
RIMF......... Reportable Item Master File [*Military*] (AFIT)
RIMI......... Research Improvement in Minority Institutions [*Program*] [*National Science Foundation*]
Rimini Stor Art Cult ... Rimini Storia Arte e Cultura [*A publication*]
RIMJA...... Rhode Island Medical Journal [*A publication*]
RiML........ Riemann, "Musik Lexikon" [*A publication*]
RIMLF...... Rostral Interstitial Nucleus of Medial Longitudinal Fasciculus [*Neuroanatomy*]
RIMM....... Report on Improved Manpower Management
RIMMS..... RVNAF [*Republic of Vietnam Air Force*] Improvement and Modernization Management System
RIMOB ..... Reserve Indication of Mobilization [*Army*] (AABC)
RIMP........ Minimum Range to Avoid Plumb Impingement (MCD)
RIMP........ Remote Input Message Processor
RIMP......... Risk Management Program (MCD)
RIMPAC ... Rim of the Pacific [*Naval exercise; name refers to the four participating countries: Australia, Canada, New Zealand, and the United States*]
RIMPTF.... Recording Industries Music Performance Trust Funds [*Later, MPTF*] (EA)
RIMR .... Rockefeller Institute for Medical Research
RIMRASP ... Reserve Intelligence Mobilization Readiness and Support Projects (MCD)
RIMS........ RADAR In-Flight Monitoring System
RIMS........ Radiant Intensity Measuring System
RIMS........ Radio Interference Measuring System
RIMS........ Record Information Movement Study (KSC)
RIMS........ Remote Information Management System
RIMS........ Replacement Inertial Measurement System
RIMS........ Requirements Inventory Management System (MCD)
RIMS........ Resonance Ionization Mass Spectrometry
RIMS........ Retarding Ion Mass Spectrometer [*Instrumentation*]
RIMS........ Risk and Insurance Management Society [*Database producer*] (EA)
RIMSE...... Relative Integrated Mean Square Error [*Statistics*]
RIMSTOP ... Retail Inventory Management/Stockage Policy [*DoD*]
RIMTech... Research Institute for the Management of Technology [*Southern California Technology Executives Network*] [*Research center*] (RCD)
RIN........... Radio Inertial (MSA)
RIN........... Rassemblement pour l'Independance Nationale [*Quebec separatist party, 1960-1968*] [*Canada*]
RIN........... Rat Insulinoma [*A cell line*]
RIN........... Record Identification Number
RIN........... Redpath Industries Ltd. [*Toronto Stock Exchange symbol*]
RIN........... Reference Indication Number
RIN........... Regular Inertial Navigator (MCD)
RIN........... Regulatory Identifier Number [*Environmental Protection Agency*]
RIN........... Report Identification Number [*Military*] (AABC)
Rin............. Rinascimento [*A publication*]
Rin............. Rinascita [*A publication*]
Rin............. Riner's Reports [*2 Wyoming*] [*A publication*] (DLA)
RIN........... Ringi Cove [*Solomon Islands*] [*Airport symbol*] (OAG)
RIN........... Rotor Impulsive Noise [*Helicopters*]
RIN........... Royal Indian Navy
RIN........... Royal Institute of Navigation (DS)
RIN........... Springfield, MO [*Location identifier*] [*FAA*] (FAAL)
RINA .... Resident Inspector of Naval Aircraft
RINA .... Royal Institution of Naval Architects [*British*]
RINAB...... Research Institute Nedri As (Hveragerdi, Iceland). Bulletin [*A publication*]
RINAL...... RADAR Inertial Altimeter
RINASA .... Rivista. Istituto Nazionale d'Archeologia e Storia dell'Arte [*A publication*]
Rinascenza Med ... Rinascenza Medica [*A publication*]
RINC .... Recruiter-in-Charge (DNAB)
R Income Wealth ... Review of Income and Wealth [*A publication*]
RIND........ Reversible Ischemic Neurological Deficit [*or Disability*] [*Medicine*]
Rindertuberk Brucell ... Rindertuberkulose und Brucellose [*A publication*]
R Indo Mal Aff ... Review of Indonesian and Malayan Affairs [*Australia*] [*A publication*]
R Indones Malay Aff ... Review of Indonesian and Malayan Affairs [*A publication*]
R Indones Malayan Aff ... Review of Indonesian and Malayan Affairs [*A publication*]
Riner .... Riner's Reports [*2 Wyoming*] [*A publication*] (DLA)
RINF........ Rinforzando [*With Special Emphasis*] [*Music*]
RINFZ....... Rinforzando [*With Special Emphasis*] [*Music*]
RING .... Ringer
Ring Bank ... Ringwood's Principles of Bankruptcy [*18th ed.*] [*1947*] [*A publication*] (DLA)

RINGDOC ... Pharmaceutical Literature Documentation [*Derwent Publications Ltd.*] [*British*] [*Information service or system*] (IID)
Ringing Migr ... Ringing and Migration [*A publication*]
Ring Int Ornithol Bull ... Ring. International Ornithological Bulletin [*A publication*]
RINM .... Resident Inspector of Naval Material
RINN......... Recommended International Nonproprietary Name [*Drug research*]
RINR .... Royal Indian Naval Reserve [*British military*] (DMA)
RINRBM... Berichte aus der Forschungsstelle Nedri As Hveragerdi Island [*A publication*]
RINS......... Rand Information Systems, Inc. [*NASDAQ symbol*] (NQ)
RINS......... Research Institute for the Natural Sciences
RINS......... Resident Inspector
Rin S .... Rinascenza Salentina [*A publication*]
RINS......... Rotorace Inertial Navigation System (MCD)
RINSMAT ... Resident Inspector of Naval Material (MUGU)
RINSORD ... Resident Naval Inspector of Ordnance
RINSPOW ... Resident Naval Inspector of Powder
R Ins (Solv) ... Revue. Institut de Sociologie (Solvay) [*A publication*]
R Inst Chem Lect Monogr Rep ... Royal Institute of Chemistry. Lectures, Monographs, and Reports [*A publication*]
R Inst Chem Lect Ser ... Royal Institute of Chemistry. Lecture Series [*A publication*]
R Inst Cienc Soc ... Revista. Instituto de Ciencias Sociales [*A publication*]
R Inst Nav Archit (London) Suppl Pap ... Royal Institution of Naval Architects (London). Supplementary Papers [*A publication*]
R Inst Nav Archit Q Trans ... Royal Institution of Naval Architects [*London*]. Quarterly Transactions [*A publication*]
R Inst Nav Archit Suppl Pap ... Royal Institution of Naval Architects [*London*]. Supplementary Papers [*A publication*]
R Inst Pr .... Royal Institution of Great Britain. Proceedings [*A publication*]
R Inst Public Health Hyg J ... Royal Institute of Public Health and Hygiene. Journal [*A publication*]
R Inst Sociol ... Revue. Institut de Sociologie [*A publication*]
RINSUL.... Rubber Insulation
RINT .... RADAR Intermittent (MSA)
RINT .... Radiation Intelligence
RINT .... Revista. Instituto Nacional de la Tradicion [*A publication*]
R Int Commiss Jurists ... Review. International Commission of Jurists [*A publication*]
R Int Coop ... Review of International Cooperation [*A publication*]
RINTDU ... Reactive Intermediates [*A publication*]
R Internat Affairs ... Review of International Affairs [*A publication*]
R Int'l Arb Awards ... United Nations Reports of International Arbitral Awards [*A publication*] (DLA)
RINV .... Reliable Investors Corp. [*NASDAQ symbol*] (NQ)
RINVR....... Royal Indian Naval Volunteer Reserve [*British military*] (DMA)
RIO .... RADAR Intercept Officer [*Navy*]
RIO .... RADAR-Intercept Operator
RIO .... Radio Intercept Operator (MCD)
RIO .... Ramus Infraorbitalis [*Anatomy*]
RIO .... Registry of Italian Oddities (EA)
RIO .... Relocatable Input/Output
RIO .... Remain Intact Organization (EA)
RIO .... Reporting In and Out [*Military*]
RIO .... Research Industry Office (MCD)
RIO .... Reshaping the International Order [*Title of Club of Rome report*]
RIO .... Resident Inspector Office [*Coast Guard*]
RIO .... Resident Inspector of Ordnance (AAG)
RIO .... Resin-in-Pulp [*Process for uranium ore treatment*] (IIA)
RIO .... Retail Issue Outlets (NG)
RIO........... Ride-It-Out
RIO .... Rio De Janeiro [*Brazil*] [*Airport symbol*] (OAG)
RIO .... Rio Grant [*Caja Del Rio*] [*New Mexico*] [*Seismograph station code, US Geological Survey*] [*Closed*] (SEIS)
RIO .... Rio Sierra Silver [*Vancouver Stock Exchange symbol*]
RIO .... Royal International Optical Corp. [*NYSE symbol*] (SPSG)
RIO........... Royal Italian Opera
RIO........... Russkoe Istoriceskoe Obscestvo [*A publication*]
RIOAL....... Revue. International Organization for Ancient Languages Analysis by Computer [*A publication*]
RIOAL....... Rio Algom Ltd. [*Associated Press abbreviation*] (APAG)
Rio De Janeiro Univ Federal Inst Geociencias Bol Geologia ... Universidade Federal do Rio De Janeiro. Instituto de Geociencias. Boletim Geologia [*A publication*]
RIOE .... Research in Ocean Engineering. University Sources and Resources [*A publication*]
RIOGD ...... Rio Grande [*FAA*] (FAAC)
Rio Grande Do Sul Inst Geocien Mapa Geol ... Universidade Federal do Rio Grande Do Sul. Instituto de Geociencias. Mapa Geologico da Folha de Morretes [*A publication*]
Rio Grande Do Sul Inst Pesqui Zootec Bol Tec ... Rio Grande Do Sul. Instituto de Pesquisas Zootecnicas. Boletim Tecnico [*A publication*]
RIOH........ Rio Hotel & Casino [*Formerly, MarCor Resorts, Inc.*] [*NASDAQ symbol*] (SPSG)

RIOJ......... Recurrent Intrahepatic Obstructive Jaundice [*Medicine*] (MAE)
RIOMETER ... Relative Ionospheric Opacity Meter
RIOPR....... Rhode Island Open Pool Reactor
RIO-RIT-RIM ... Religion Index Database - Religion Index One; Religion Index Two; Research in Ministry [*American Theological Library Association*] [*Information service or system*] (CRD)
RIOS......... Joint Working Group on River Inputs to Ocean Systems [*Marine science*] (MSC)
RIOS......... Receiving Inspection Operating Sheet (MCD)
RIOS......... ROM [*Read-Only Memory*] BIOS [*Pronounced "rye-ose"*] [*Data processing*]
RIOS......... Rotating Image Optical Scanner
RIOT .... RAM Input/Output Timer
RIOT .... Real-Time Input-Output Transducer [*or Translator*] [*Data processing*]
RIOT .... Remote Input/Output Terminal [*Data processing*]
RIOT ...., Resolution of Initial Operational Techniques
RIOT .... Retrieval of Information by On-Line Terminal [*Atomic Energy Authority*] [*Data processing*] [*British*]
RIOTEX.... Riot Exercise (DNAB)
RIOV .... Rio Verde Energy Corp. [*NASDAQ symbol*] (NQ)
RIP........... RADAR Identification Point (AFM)
RIP........... RADAR Improvement Plan (NATG)
RIP........... RADAR Improvement Program
RIP........... Radioimmunoprecipitation [*Clinical chemistry*]
RIP........... Radioisotopic Pathology [*Medical specialty*] (DHSM)
RIP........... Radiological Information Plot (NATG)
RIP........... Random Input Sampling [*Data processing*]
RIP........... Rapid Ignition Propagation (MCD)
RIP........... Rapid Installation Plan
RIP........... Raster Image Processor [*Printer technology*]
RIP........... Rate-Invariant Path [*Economic theory*]
RIP........... Rays Initiating from a Point (MCD)
RIP........... RCRA [*Resource Conservation and Recovery Act*] Implementation Plan [*Environmental Protection Agency*] (GFGA)
RIP........... Reactive Ion Plating [*Coating technology*]
RIP........... Reactor Instrument Penetration Valve (IEEE)
RIP........... Readiness Improvement Program [*Military*] (CAAL)
RIP........... Rearrangement Induced Premeiotically [*Genetics*]
RIP........... Receiving Inspection Plan [*Nuclear energy*] (NRCH)
RIP........... Recoverable Item Program [*Marine Corps*]
RIP........... Reduction Implementation Panel [*DoD*]
RIP........... Reduction in Paperwork (SAA)
RIP........... Reenlistment Incentive Program (DNAB)
RIP........... Refractive Index Profile
RIP........... Register Indicator Panel
RIP........... Register of Intelligence Publications (MCD)
RIP........... Relationship Improvement Program (SAA)
RIP........... Reliability Improvement Program
RIP........... Remain in Place (MCD)
RIP........... Remote Indicator Panel (CAAL)
RIP........... Renin Inhibitory Peptide [*Biochemistry*]
RIP........... Repeat-Induced Point Mutation [*Genetic engineering technique*]
RIP........... Report on Individual Personnel (MCD)
RIP........... Requiescat [*or Requiescant*] in Pace [*May He (She, or They) Rest in Peace*] [*Latin*] (GPO)
RIP........... Research in Parapsychology [*A publication*]
RIP........... Research in Progress (MCD)
RIP........... Respiratory Inversion Point [*Physiology*]
RIP........... Rest in Proportion [*Printing*] (WDMC)
RIP........... Retired in Place [*Telecommunications*] (TEL)
RIP........... Retirement Improvement Program [*Air Force*] (AFM)
RIP........... Retirement Income Plan [*Insurance*] (MCD)
RIP........... Ribosome Inactivating [*or Inhibiting*] Protein [*Biochemistry*]
RIP........... Rice Institute Pamphlet [*A publication*]
RIP........... Ring Index Pointer [*Data processing*] (OA)
Rip............ [*Johannes Franciscus de*] Ripa [*Deceased, 1534*] [*Authority cited in pre-1607 legal work*] (DSA)
RIP........... Ripieno [*Additional*] [*Music*]
RIP........... Ripple Resources Ltd. [*Vancouver Stock Exchange symbol*]
RIP........... Routing Information Process [*or Protocol*] [*Telecommunications*] (TEL)
RIP........... Rural Industrialization Program [*Department of Agriculture*]
RIPA........ Radioimmunoprecipitation Assay [*Clinical chemistry*]
RIPA........ Royal Institute of Public Administration [*British*]
RIPC......... Regroupement des Independants et Paysans Camerounais [*Regrouping of Independents and Farmers of the Cameroons*]
RIPCO....... Receiving Inspection and Preparation for Checkout (SAA)
RIPD......... RLG [*Research Libraries Group, Inc.*] Research-in-Progress Database [*Information service or system*] (CRD)
RIPE......... Range Instrumentation Performance Evaluation (MUGU)
RIPEH....... Review of Iranian Political Economy and History [*A publication*]
RIPFCOMTF ... Rapid Item Processor to Facilitate Complex Operations on Magnetic Tape Files [*Data processing*]
RIPH & H ... Royal Institute of Public Health and Hygiene [*British*]

RIPILS ...... Recently Immigrated Professional Irish Legals [*Lifestyle classification*]
RIPIS........ Rhode Island Pupil Identification Scale [*Psychology*]
RIPL......... Representation-Independent Programming Language
RIPOM...... Report [*command indicated*] If Present, Otherwise by Message [*Navy*]
RI Port Indus Devel Comm Geol Bull Sci Contr ... Rhode Island. Port and Industrial Development Commission. Geological Bulletin. Scientific Contribution [*A publication*]
RIPOSTE ... Restitution Incentive Program Operationalized as a Strategy Toward an Effective Learning Environment [*HEW*]
RIPP .... RADAR Intelligence Photo Producer
RIPP .... Regulatory Information on Pesticide Products [*Database*] (IT)
RIPPLE .... Radioactive Isotope-Powered Pulse Light Equipment (IEEE)
RIPPLE .... Radioisotope-Powered Prolonged Life Equipment (IEEE)
RIPPLE ..... Ripplesmere [*England*]
RIPR......... Recommended Immediate Procurement Records (MCD)
RIPRS ...... Recovery Improvement Program Reporting System
RIPS .... RADAR Impact Prediction System (CET)
RIPS .... Radio-Isotope Power Supply [*or System*] [*Nuclear energy*] (NG)
RIPS .... Range Instrumentation Planning Study [*AFSC*]
RIPS .... Raster Image Processor System (PCM)
RIPS .... Remote Image Processing System
RIPSD3 ..... Annual Report. Institute of Physics. Academia Sinica [*A publication*]
RI Pub Laws ... Public Laws of Rhode Island [*A publication*] (DLA)
RI Pub Laws ... Public Laws of Rhode Island and Providence Plantations [*A publication*]
RIPV......... Reactor Isolation Pressure Valve (IEEE)
RIPWC...... Royal Institute of Painters in Water-Colours [*British*]
RIPY......... Ripley Co., Inc. [*NASDAQ symbol*] (NQ)
RIQAP....... Reduced Inspection Quality Assurance Program
RIQS......... Remote Information Query System [*Information retrieval service*] [*Data processing*]
RIR .... RADAR Interface Recorder (MCD)
RIR .... Range Illumination RADAR
RIR .... Receiving Inspection Report
RIR .... Redgrave Information Resources Corp. [*Publisher*]
RiR .... Redgrave Information Resources Corp., Westport, CT [*Library symbol*] [*Library of Congress*] (LCLS)
RIR .... Reduction in Requirement [*Air Force*] (AFM)
RIR .... Regimental Inquiry Regulations [*British military*] (DMA)
RIR .... Rehabilitation Information Round Table (EA)
RIR .... Reliability Investigation Requests (KSC)
RIR .... Reportable Item Report [*NASA*] (NASA)
RIR .... Resonant Internal Reflection
RIR .... Rhode Island Red [*Poultry*]
RIR .... Right Iliac Region [*Medicine*] (MAE)
RIR .... Riverside/Rubidoux, CA [*Location identifier*] [*FAA*] (FAAL)
RIR .... ROM [*Read-Only Memory*] Instruction Register
RIR .... Royal Irish Rifles [*British military*] (DMA)
RIRAA...... Russian Immigrants' Representative Association In America
R Ir Acad Proc Sect B ... Royal Irish Academy. Proceedings. Section B [*A publication*]
RIRAP ...... Recombinant Interleukin Receptor Antagonist Protein [*Biochemistry*]
RIRB........ Radioiodinated Rose Bengal [*Medicine*] (MAE)
RIRB........ Railway Insurance Rating Bureau [*Defunct*] (EA)
RIRCA...... Rhode Island Red Club of America (EA)
RI/RD....... Rockwell International/Rocketdyne Division
RIRED...... Revue. IRE [*Institut National des Radioelements*] [*Belgium*] [*A publication*]
RI Rep........ Rhode Island Reports [*A publication*] (DLA)
RI Resour... Rhode Island Resources [*A publication*]
RIrF........ Royal Irish Fusiliers [*Military unit*] [*British*] (DMA)
RIRIG....... Reduced-Excitation Inertial Reference Integrating Gyro
R Irish Ac Pr ... Royal Irish Academy. Proceedings [*A publication*]
RIRJ .... Research Institute of Religious Jewry (EA)
RIRMA...... Revisers, Ink and Roller Makers' Auxiliaries [*A union*] [*British*] (DI)
RIRMS ...... Remote Information Retrieval and Management System [*Data processing*] (BUR)
RIRO .... Roll-In/Roll-Out [*Storage allocation*] [*Data processing*]
RIRS......... Reliability Information Retrieval System (MCD)
RIRT........ Rehabilitation Information Round Table (EA)
RIRT........ Rhodium-Iron Resistance Thermometer
RIRTI .... Recording Infrared Tracking Instrument
RIS........... Kansas City, MO [*Location identifier*] [*FAA*] (FAAL)
RIS........... RADIAC [*Radiation Detection, Indication, and Computation*] Instrument System
RIS........... Radio Interference Service [*Department of Trade*] [*British*]
RIS........... Radiology Information System [*Data processing*]
RIS........... Ramjet Inlet System
RIS........... Range Information System [*For aircraft*] (MCD)
RIS........... Range Instrumentation Ship
RIS........... Range Instrumentation Station
RIS........... Reblooming Iris Society (EA)
RIS........... Receipt Inspection Segment (OA)
RIS........... Receiving Inspection Segment
RIS........... RECON Information System (MCD)

RIS............ Record Input Subroutine
RIS............ Recorded Information Service [*Telecommunications*]   (TEL)
RIS............ Redwood Inspection Service   (EA)
RIS............ Regulatory Impact Statement
RIS............ Regulatory Information Service [*Congressional Information Service, Inc.*] [*Information service or system*] [*Defunct*]
RIS............ Reliability Information System
RIS............ Remote Information System
RIS............ Reports Identification Symbol
RIS............ Research Information Service [*John Crerar Library*] [*Information service or system*]   (IID)
RIS............ Research Information Services [*Georgia Institute of Technology*] [*Atlanta*] [*Information service or system*]   (IID)
RIS............ Research Information System [*Rehabilitation Services Administration*]   (IID)
RIS............ Resonance Ionization Spectroscopy
RIS............ Retail Information System   (BUR)
RIS............ Retarded Infants Services [*Later, CFS*]   (EA)
RIS............ Retransmission Identity Signal [*Telecommunications*]   (TEL)
RIS............ Revolution Indicating System   (MSA)
RIS............ Revue. Institut de Sociologie [*A publication*]
RIS............ Rise Resources, Inc. [*Vancouver Stock Exchange symbol*]
RIS............ Rishiri [*Japan*] [*Airport symbol*] [*Obsolete*]   (OAG)
Ris............. Risorgimento [*A publication*]
RIS............ Rock Island Southern Railroad   (IIA)
RIS............ Rotatable Initial Susceptibility
RIS............ Rotating Image Scanner
RIS............ Routine Interest Shipping   (MCD)
RIS............ Russian Intelligence Service
RISA......... Radioimmunosorbent Assay [*Clinical chemistry*]
RISA......... Radioiodinated Serum Albumin [*Medicine*]
RISA......... Railway and Industrial Spring Association [*Later, RISRI*]
RISA......... Romani Imperii Semper Auctor [*Continual Increaser of the Roman Empire*] [*Latin*]
RIS-ALEX ... Research Information Services - Alexander Library
RISB......... Rotter Incomplete Sentences Blank [*Psychology*]
RISC......... Reduced Instruction Set Computer
RISC......... Refractive Index Sounding Central
RISC......... Regulatory Information Service Center [*Office of Management and Budget*]   (GFGA)
RISC......... Remote Information Systems Center
RISC......... Research Institute of Scripps Clinic [*Research center*]   (RCD)
RISC......... Rockwell International Science Center
RISCA....... Ricerca Scientifica [*A publication*]
RI Sch Des Bul ... Rhode Island School of Design. Bulletin [*A publication*]
RISD......... Requisition and Invoice Shipping Document
RISD......... Rhode Island School of Design
RISD......... Rural Institutions and Services Division [*FAO*]
RISE......... Catch a Rising Star, Inc. [*NASDAQ symbol*]   (NQ)
RISE......... National Institute for Resources in Science and Engineering   (EA)
RISE......... Radiation-Induced Surface Effect
RISE......... RAM [*Reliability, Availability, and Maintainability*] Improvement of Selected Equipment [*Military*]   (MCD)
RISE......... Readiness Improvement Status Evaluation   (MCD)
RISE......... Readiness Improvement Summary Evaluation   (MCD)
RISE......... Reform of Intermediate and Secondary Education   (OICC)
RISE......... Register for International Service in Education [*Institute of International Education*]   (IID)
RISE......... Reliability Improvement Selected Equipment   (AABC)
RISE......... Research and Information Services for Education [*Montgomery County Intermediate Unit*] [*King of Prussia, PA*]
RISE......... Research Institute for Studies in Education [*Iowa State University*] [*Research center*]   (RCD)
RISE......... Research in Science Education [*National Science Foundation*]   (GRD)
RISE......... Research in Supersonic Environment
RISE......... Reusable Inflatable Salvage Equipment
RISE......... Rulings Information System, Excise [*Revenue Canada - Customs and Excise*] [*Information service or system*]   (CRD)
RISEAP..... Regional Islamic Da'Wah Council of Southeast Asia and the Pacific   (EAIO)
RISEB8...... Clinical Orthopaedic Surgery [*A publication*]
Riser......... Riser Foods, Inc. [*Associated Press abbreviation*]   (APAG)
RISH......... Research Initiative into Silicon Hybrids [*British*]
RISHB....... Rinsho Shinkeigaku [*A publication*]
RISHBH.... Clinical Neurology [*Tokyo*] [*A publication*]
RISHE....... Research Institute for Supersensonic Healing Energies
RISI......... Review. International Statistical Institute [*A publication*]
RISIC........ Rubber-Insert Sound Isolation Coupling   (DNAB)
Rising Up... Rising Up Angry [*A publication*]
RISK........ George Risk Industries, Inc. [*NASDAQ symbol*]   (NQ)
RISK......... Rock Is Stoning Kids [*Defunct*]   (EA)
RISKAC .... Risk Acceptance   (NASA)
Risk Anal... Risk Analysis [*A publication*]
Risk Bk Ser ... Risk. Book Series [*A publication*]
Risk Manage ... Risk Management [*A publication*]
Risk Mgmt ... Risk Management [*A publication*]
Risk Mgt.... Risk Management [*A publication*]

RISL......... Residual Item Selection List
RiSL......... Rossija i Slavjanstvo [*A publication*]
RISM........ Reference Interaction Site Model [*Chemical physics*]
RISM........ Repertoire International des Sources Musicales [*A publication*]
RISM........ Research Institute for the Study of Man [*Army*]   (MCD)
RI/SME..... Robotics International of SME [*Society of Manufacturing Engineers*]   (EA)
RISO......... Range Instrumentation Systems Office [*White Sands Missile Range*]
RISoc .... Revue. Institut de Sociologie [*Solvay*] [*A publication*]
Risoe Inf..... Risoe Information [*Denmark*] [*A publication*]
Risoe Natl Lab Rep Risoe-M (Den) ... Risoe National Laboratory. Report Risoe-M (Denmark) [*A publication*]
Risoe Rep (Den) Res Establ Risoe ... Risoe Report. (Denmark) Research Establishment Risoe [*A publication*]
RISOL....... Risoluto [*Resolutely*] [*Music*]   (ROG)
RISOP....... Red Integrated Strategic Offensive Plan [*Army*]   (AABC)
Riso Rep..... Risoe Report [*A publication*]
Risorgiment ... Risorgimento [*A publication*]
RISP......... Robotics and Intelligent Systems Program [*Oak Ridge National Laboratory*]
RISP......... Ross Ice Shelf Project [*International cooperative research project*]
RISPT....... Ross Ice Shelf Project. Technical Reports [*A publication*]
RI-SR........ Removal Item - Ship's Record   (MCD)
RiSR.......... Ricerche di Storia Religiosa [*A publication*]
RISRA .... Report of Ionosphere and Space Research in Japan [*A publication*]
RISRI........ Railway and Industrial Spring Research Institute [*Defunct*]   (EA)
RISS .... Range Instrumentation and Support Systems
RISS .... Recommended Initial System Stockage
RISS .... Refractive Index Sounding System
RISS .... Regional Information Sharing System [*Department of Justice*]
RISS .... Rockwell International Suspension Systems Co.
RISSB........ Research Institute on the Sino-Soviet Bloc   (EA)
RIST .... RADAR Installed System Tester   (KSC)
RIST .... Radioimmunosorbent Technique [*or Test*] [*Clinical chemistry*]
RIST .... Radioisotopic Sand Tracer [*Marine science*]   (MSC)
R Istituto Veneto Memorie ... Reale Istituto Veneto di Scienze, Lettere, ed Arti. Memorie [*A publication*]
R Ist Lomb ... Rendiconti. Istituto Lombardo di Scienze e Lettere [*A publication*]
Ri St V .... Richtlinien fuer das Strafverfahren [*A publication*]
RISULB..... Revue. Institut de Sociologie. Universite Libre de Bruxelles [*A publication*]
RISVD....... Risvegliato [*Reanimated*] [*Music*]   (ROG)
RISW........ Registered Industrial Social Worker [*Designation awarded by the American Association of Industrial Social Workers*]
RISW........ Royal Institution of South Wales [*British*]
RISWR...... Regional Institute of Social Welfare Research   (EA)
RIT............ RADAR Inputs Test
RIT............ Radio Information Test
RIT............ Radio Network for Inter-American Telecommunications
RIT............ Radioiodinated Triolein [*Medicine*]   (MAE)
RIT............ Railway Inclusive Tour   (DCTA)
RIT............ Rate of Information Throughput [*Data processing*]   (BUR)
R & IT........ Rating and Income Tax Reports [*England*] [*A publication*]   (DLA)
RIT............ Readiness Initiative Team [*Military*]
RIT............ Receiver Incremental Tuning
RIT............ Reclamation Insurance Type [*Military*]   (AFIT)
RIT............ Refining in Transit
RIT............ Relative Ignition Temperature
RIT............ Request for Interface Tool [*NASA*]   (NASA)
RIT............ Retrieval Injury Threshold
RIT............ Rio Tigre [*Panama*] [*Airport symbol*]   (OAG)
RIT............ Ritardando [*Gradually Slower*] [*Music*]
RIT............ Ritenuto [*Immediately Slower*] [*Music*]
rit.............. Ritual   (BJA)
RIT............ Rochester Institute of Technology [*New York*]
RIT............ Rochester Institute of Technology Library [*UTLAS symbol*]
RIT............ Rocket Interferometer Tracking
RIT............ Rod-in-Tube
RIT............ Rotary Indexing Table
RIT............ Rothschild Investment Trust
RITA......... Rand Intelligent Terminal Agent
RITA......... Recoverable Interplanetary Transport Approach
RITA......... Refundable Income Tax Account
RITA......... Reservation, Information, Tourist Accommodation [*Computerized system for booking hotel rooms*] [*British*]
RITA......... Resist Inside the Army [*Peace-movement slang*]
RITA......... Reusable Interplanetary Transport Approach Vehicle
RITA......... Rivera and Tamayo Fault Exploration [*Marine science*]   (MSC)
RITA......... Romance Is Treasured Always [*Annual award bestowed by Romance Writers of America. Acronym selected to honor cofounder, Rita Clay Estrada*]
RITA......... Rural Industrial Technical Assistance [*Latin American building program*]
RITA......... Russian Information Telegraph Agency [*Formerly, TASS*]

RITAC....... Retail Industry Trade Action Coalition [*Washington, DC*] (EA)
RitAcc....... Rituels Accadiens [*A publication*] (BJA)
RITAD....... Radiation-Induced Thermally Activated Depolarization [*Radiation dosimetry technique*]
RITAR...... Ritardando [*Gradually Slower*] [*Music*]
RITARD.... Ritardando [*Gradually Slower*] [*Music*]
RITARO.... Ritardando [*Gradually Slower*] [*Music*] (ROG)
RITB......... Road Transport Industry Training Board [*British*]
RITC......... Rhodamine Isothiocyanate [*Biochemistry*]
Ritch.......... Ritchie's Cases Decided by Francis Bacon [*1617-21*] [*A publication*] (DLA)
Ritch.......... Ritchie's Equity Reports [*1872-82*] [*Nova Scotia*] [*A publication*] (DLA)
Ritch Eq Dec ... Ritchie's Equity Decisions [*Nova Scotia*] [*A publication*] (DLA)
Ritch Eq Rep ... Ritchie's Equity Reports [*Nova Scotia*] [*A publication*] (DLA)
Ritchie....... Ritchie's Equity [*Canada*] [*A publication*] (DLA)
RITE......... Rapid Information Technique for Evaluation
RITE......... Rapidata Interactive Text Editor (IEEE)
RITE......... Regenerative Intercooled Turbine Engine (MCD)
RITE......... Rent Rite Reservation Network, Inc. [*NASDAQ symbol*] (NQ)
RITE........ Research Institute for Innovative Technolgies for the Earth
RITEA....... Rock Island Railroad Transportation and Employee Assistance Act [*1980*]
RiteAid...... Rite Aid Corp. [*Associated Press abbreviation*] (APAG)
RITEN...... Ritenuto [*Immediately Slower*] [*Music*]
RITENA..... Reunion Internacional de Tecnicos de la Nutricion Animal [*International Meeting of Animal Nutrition Experts*] (EAIO)
RITENO.... Ritenuto [*Immediately Slower*] [*Music*] (ROG)
RITG......... Radiatively Important Trace Gas
RITI.......... Resident Inspection Test Instruction
RITLS....... Rhode Island Test of Language Structure
RITMB....... Rayonnements Ionisants [*A publication*]
RITOP....... Red Integrated Tactical Operational Plan (CINC)
RITQ .... Revised Infant Temperament Questionnaire
RITR......... Rework Inspection Team Report
RITRC...... RIT Research Corp.
RITREAD ... Rapid Iterative Reanalysis for Automated Design [*Computer program*]
RITS .... Radiatively Important Trace Substances
RITS .... Rapid Information Transmission System
RITS .... Reconnaissance Intelligence Technical Squadron
Rits Cts Leet ... Ritson's Jurisdiction of Courts-Leet [*A publication*] (DLA)
Rits Int....... Ritso's Introduction to the Science [*A publication*] (DLA)
RITSL........ Reconfigured Integrated Two-Stage Liquefaction [*Chemical engineering*]
RITSq .... Reconnaissance Intelligence Technical Squadron [*Air Force*]
RITU .... Research Institute of Temple University (KSC)
RITZ .... Ritzy's [*G.*], Inc. [*NASDAQ symbol*] (NQ)
RIU .... Andalusia, AL [*Location identifier*] [*FAA*] (FAAL)
RIU .... RADAR Interface Unit [*Military*] (CAAL)
RIU .... Radioactive Iodine Uptake [*Medicine*]
RIU .... Railroad Insurance Underwriters [*Later, RTI*] (EA)
RIU .... Refractive Index Unit
RIU .... Remote Interface Unit [*NASA*] (NASA)
riu.............. Rhode Island [*MARC country of publication code*] [*Library of Congress*] (LCCP)
RIU .... University of Rhode Island, Kingston, RI [*OCLC symbol*] (OCLC)
Riun Annu Assoc Elettrot Elettron Ital Rend ... Riunione Annuale della Associazione Elettrotecnica ed Elettronica Italiana. Rendiconti [*A publication*]
RI Univ Agric Exp Stn Bull ... Rhode Island University. Agricultural Experiment Station. Bulletin [*A publication*]
RI Univ Div Eng Res Dev Eng Repr ... Rhode Island University. Division of Engineering. Research and Development Engineering Reprint [*A publication*]
RI Univ Div Eng Res Dev Leafl ... Rhode Island University. Division of Engineering. Research and Development Leaflet [*A publication*]
RI Univ Eng Exp Stn Bull ... Rhode Island University. Engineering Experiment Station. Bulletin [*A publication*]
RI Univ Eng Exp Stn Eng Repr ... Rhode Island University. Engineering Experiment Station. Engineering Reprint [*A publication*]
RI Univ Mar Tech Rep ... Rhode Island University. Marine Technical Report [*A publication*]
RIUPDJ .... US National Institute on Drug Abuse. Research Issues [*A publication*]
RIUSA....... Rehabilitation International USA
RIV .... Radio Influence Voltage
RIV .... Ramus Interventricularis [*First-order branch of coronary artery*] [*Medicine*]
RIV .... Recirculation Isolation Valve (NASA)
RIV .... Regolamento Internazionale Veicoli [*Italian generic term meaning "International Regulation of Vehicles"*] [*Initialism also refers to International Wagon Union*]
RIV .... River
RIV .... Riverbend International [*AMEX symbol*] (SPSG)

RIV .... Riverside, CA [*Location identifier*] [*FAA*] (FAAL)
RIV .... Riverview [*Australia*] [*Seismograph station code, US Geological Survey*] (SEIS)
RIV .... Rivet (AAG)
Riv.............. Riviera [*Record label*] [*France*]
Riv.............. Rivista [*Review*] [*Italian*] (BJA)
Riv Ann Reg ... Rivington's Annual Register [*A publication*] (DLA)
Riv d Arch Crist ... Rivista di Archeologia Cristiana [*A publication*] (OCD)
Riv Bas Bull ... River Basin Bulletin [*A publication*]
RIVBEA .... [*Sam*] Rivers and Bea [*Rivers*] [*As in Rivbea Festival, jazz event named for saxophonist Sam Rivers and his wife, Bea*]
Riv Dir Int e Comp del Lavoro ... Rivista di Diritto Internazionale e Comparato del Lavoro [*Bologna, Italy*] [*A publication*] (DLA)
Riv Dir Int'le Priv & Proc ... Rivista di Diritto Internazionale Privato e Processuale [*Padova, Italy*] [*A publication*] (DLA)
Riv di Diritto Internaz e Comparato del Lavoro ... Rivista di Diritto Internazionale e Comparato del Lavoro [*Padua, Italy*] [*A publication*] (DLA)
RIVDIV ..... River Assault Division [*Military*]
RIVE......... Resources in Vocational Education [*Database*] [*National Center for Research in Vocational Education*] [*Information service or system*] (CRD)
RIVE......... Riverside Properties [*NASDAQ symbol*] (NQ)
River Plat... Review of the River Plate [*A publication*]
RIVFLOT ... River Flotilla [*Military*]
RIVFLOTONE ... River Flotilla One [*Military*]
Riviera Sci ... Riviera Scientifique [*A publication*]
Riv Ist Arch ... Rivista. Reale Istituto d'Archeologia e Storia dell'Arte [*A publication*]
Riv Ist Sieroter Ital ... Rivista. Istituto Sieroterapico Italiano [*A publication*]
Riv Ist Vaccinogeno Consorzi Prov Antituberc ... Rivista. Istituto Vaccinogeno e Consorzi Provinciali Antitubercolari [*A publication*]
Riv Ital per le Sc Giur ... Rivista Italiana per le Scienze Giuridiche [*A publication*] (OCD)
RIVL......... Regesten van de Aanwinsten van het Institut voor Vergelijkend Literatuuronderzoek aan de Rijksuniversiteit te Utrecht [*A publication*]
RIVL......... Rival Manufacturing [*NASDAQ symbol*] (NQ)
Rivoluzione Ind ... Rivoluzione Industriale [*Italy*] [*A publication*]
RIVPATFLOT ... River Patrol Flotilla [*Navy*] (DNAB)
RIVPATFOR ... River Patrol Force [*Navy*] (DNAB)
RIVRON ... River Assault Squadron [*Navy*] (DNAB)
RIVS......... Ruptured Interventricular Septum [*Medicine*] (AAMN)
RIVSEC..... River Section (DNAB)
RIVSUPPRON ... River Support Squadron [*Navy*] (DNAB)
RIVT......... RECO International [*AMEX symbol*] (SPSG)
RIVT......... Rivulet (ADA)
Rivwdl....... Riverwood International Corp. [*Associated Press abbreviation*] (APAG)
Riv World .. River World [*A publication*]
RIW .... Reliability Improvement Warranty [*Navy*]
RIW .... Repaired in Works [*British military*] (DMA)
RIW .... Review of Income and Wealth [*A publication*]
RIW .... Riverton [*Wyoming*] [*Airport symbol*] (OAG)
RI Water Res Coordinating Board Geol Bull Hydrol Bull ... Rhode Island. Water Resources Coordinating Board. Geological Bulletin. Hydrologic Bulletin [*A publication*]
RI Water Resour Board Hydrol Bull ... Rhode Island. Water Resources Board. Hydrologic Bulletin [*A publication*]
RI Water Resour Cent Annu Rep ... Rhode Island. Water Resources Center. Annual Report [*A publication*]
RI Water Resour Coord Board Geol Bull ... Rhode Island. Water Resources Coordinating Board. Geological Bulletin [*A publication*]
RI Water Resour Coordinating Board Geol Bull ... Rhode Island. Water Resources Coordinating Board. Geological Bulletin [*A publication*]
RIWC........ Royal Institute of Painters in Water-Colours [*British*] (ROG)
Riwt............ Rich International White Trash [*Lifestyle classification*]
RIX .... Riga [*Former USSR*] [*Airport symbol*] (OAG)
RIX .... University of Rhode Island, Extension Division Library, Providence, RI [*OCLC symbol*] (OCLC)
RIXT......... Remote Information Exchange Terminal (MCD)
RIY .... Renaissance of Italian Youth (EA)
Riyad Univ Fac Sci Bull ... Riyad University. Faculty of Science. Bulletin [*A publication*]
Riyad Univ Fac Sci J ... Riyad University. Faculty of Science. Journal [*A publication*]
RIZ............ Radio Industry Zagreb [*Former Yugoslavia*]
RIZ............ Rio Alzucar [*Panama*] [*Airport symbol*] (OAG)
Riz Rizi ...... Riz et Riziculture [*A publication*]
Riz Rizicult Cult Vivr Trop ... Riz et Riziculture et Cultures Vivrieres Tropicales [*A publication*]
Rizsk Inst Inz Grazdan Aviacii ... Rizskii Institut Inzenerov Grazdanskoi Aviacii Imeni Leninskogo Komsomola [*A publication*]
RJ.............. A'Beckett's Reserved Judgements [*Port Phillip*] [*A publication*] (ILCA)
R(J)........... Justiciary Cases [*Scotland*] [*A publication*] (DLA)
RJ.............. La Reveil Juif. Sfax [*A publication*] (BJA)

R & J......... Rabkin and Johnson's Federal, Income, Gift, and Estate Taxation [*A publication*]   (DLA)
RJ.............. RADAR/Jimsphere
R & J......... Rafique and Jackson's Privy Council Decisions [*India*] [*A publication*]   (DLA)
RJ.............. Ramjet
RJ.............. Reform Judaism   (BJA)
RJ.............. Reformed Journal [*A publication*]
RJ.............. Reject
RJ.............. Revue Judiciaire, by Bruzard [*1843-44*] [*Mauritius*] [*A publication*]   (DLA)
RJ.............. Revue de Jurisprudence [*A publication*]   (DLA)
R de J........ Revue de Jurisprudence [*Quebec*] [*A publication*]   (DLA)
RJ.............. [*The*] River Jordan [*A publication*]   (BJA)
RJ.............. Road Junction [*Maps and charts*]
RJ.............. Romanistisches Jahrbuch [*A publication*]
R & J......... Romeo and Juliet [*Shakespearean work*]
RJ.............. Rotary Joint
RJ.............. Royal Jordanian Airlines Co. [*Arab Air Cargo*] [*Jordan*] [*ICAO designator*]   (FAAC)
RJ.............. Rusky Jazyk [*A publication*]
RJ11........... Standard modular telephone jack for a single line instrument   (TSSD)
RJ 500........ Rolls-Japan 500 [*Type of Rolls-Royce engine*]
RJA........... Ramjet Addition   (AAG)
RJA........... Reform Jewish Appeal   (EA)
RJA........... Retail Jewelers of America [*Later, JA*]   (EA)
RJA........... Rotary Joint Assembly
RJA........... Royal Jersey Artillery [*Military unit*] [*British*]
RJA........... Russko-Jewrejsky Archiw [*A publication*]   (BJA)
RJAA........ Tokyo/New Tokyo International [*Japan*] [*ICAO location identifier*]   (ICLI)
RJAF........ Matsumoto [*Japan*] [*ICAO location identifier*]   (ICLI)
RJAF........ Royal Jordanian Air Force
RJAH........ Hyakuri [*Japan*] [*ICAO location identifier*]   (ICLI)
RJAI......... Ichigaya [*Japan*] [*ICAO location identifier*]   (ICLI)
RJAK........ Kasumigaura [*Japan*] [*ICAO location identifier*]   (ICLI)
RJAM....... Minamitorishima [*Japan*] [*ICAO location identifier*]   (ICLI)
RJamF....... Raymond James Financial, Inc. [*Associated Press abbreviation*]   (APAG)
RJAO........ Chichijima [*Japan*] [*ICAO location identifier*]   (ICLI)
RJaS......... Russkij Jazyk v Skole [*A publication*]
RJAT........ Takigahara [*Japan*] [*ICAO location identifier*]   (ICLI)
RJAW....... Iwo Jima [*Japan*] [*ICAO location identifier*]   (ICLI)
RJaz......... Rusky Jazyk [*A publication*]
RJB........... Rajbiraj [*Nepal*] [*Airport symbol*] [*Obsolete*]   (OAG)
RJB........... Relay Junction Box   (KSC)
RJb........... Romanistisches Jahrbuch [*A publication*]
RJB........... Ruby Jewel Bearing
RJBD........ Nanki-Shirahama [*Japan*] [*ICAO location identifier*]   (ICLI)
RJBE........ Relative Jostle Biological Effectiveness
RJC........... Ranger Junior College [*Texas*]
RJC........... Reaction Jet Control [*NASA*]   (NASA)
RJC........... Robinson Jeffers Committee   (EA)
RJC........... Rochester Junior College [*Minnesota*] [*Later, Rochester Community College*]
RJCA........ Asahikawa [*Japan*] [*ICAO location identifier*]   (ICLI)
RJCB........ Obihiro [*Japan*] [*ICAO location identifier*]   (ICLI)
RJCC........ Sapporo/Chitose [*Japan*] [*ICAO location identifier*]   (ICLI)
RJCG........ Sapporo [*Japan*] [*ICAO location identifier*]   (ICLI)
RJCH........ Hakodate [*Japan*] [*ICAO location identifier*]   (ICLI)
RJCK........ Kushiro [*Japan*] [*ICAO location identifier*]   (ICLI)
RJCM........ New Memanbetsu [*Japan*] [*ICAO location identifier*]   (ICLI)
RJCN........ Nakashibetsu [*Japan*] [*ICAO location identifier*]   (ICLI)
RJCO........ Sapporo/Okadama [*Japan*] [*ICAO location identifier*]   (ICLI)
RJCR........ Rebun [*Japan*] [*ICAO location identifier*]   (ICLI)
RJCS........ Kushiro/Kenebetsu [*Japan*] [*ICAO location identifier*]   (ICLI)
RJCT........ Tokachi [*Japan*] [*ICAO location identifier*]   (ICLI)
RJCW....... Wakkanai [*Japan*] [*ICAO location identifier*]   (ICLI)
RJCY........ Muroran/Yakumo [*Japan*] [*ICAO location identifier*]   (ICLI)
RJD........... Reaction Jet Device [*NASA*]   (NASA)
RJD........... Reaction Jet Driver [*NASA*]   (NASA)
RJDA........ Rassemblement des Jeunesses Democratiques Africaines [*Rally of African Democratic Youth*]
RJDA........ Reaction Jet Driver - Aft [*NASA*]   (NASA)
RJDB........ Iki [*Japan*] [*ICAO location identifier*]   (ICLI)
RJDC........ Yamaguchi-Ube, Honshu Island [*Japan*] [*ICAO location identifier*]   (ICLI)
RJDF........ Reaction Jet Driver - Forward [*NASA*]   (NASA)
RJDG........ Fukuoka [*Japan*] [*ICAO location identifier*]   (ICLI)
R & J Dig... Robinson and Joseph's Digest [*Ontario*] [*A publication*]   (DLA)
RJDK........ Kamigoto [*Japan*] [*ICAO location identifier*]   (ICLI)
RJDM....... Metabaru [*Japan*] [*ICAO location identifier*]   (ICLI)
RJDO........ Ojika [*Japan*] [*ICAO location identifier*]   (ICLI)
RJDT........ Tsushima [*Japan*] [*ICAO location identifier*]   (ICLI)
RJE........... Ramjet Engine
RJE........... Rayleigh-Jeans Equation [*Physics*]
RJE........... Remote Job Entry [*Data processing*]
RJEB........ Monbetsu [*Japan*] [*ICAO location identifier*]   (ICLI)
RJEC........ Asahikawa [*Japan*] [*ICAO location identifier*]   (ICLI)
RJ/EC........ Reaction Jet/Engine Control [*NASA*]   (NASA)

RJEO........ Okushiri [*Japan*] [*ICAO location identifier*]   (ICLI)
RJER........ Rishiri Island [*Japan*] [*ICAO location identifier*]   (ICLI)
RJETS....... Remote Job Entry Terminal System [*Data processing*]   (MCD)
RJF........... Les Rejaudoux [*France*] [*Seismograph station code, US Geological Survey*]   (SEIS)
RJF........... Raymond James Financial, Inc. [*NYSE symbol*]   (SPSG)
RJFA .... Ashiya [*Japan*] [*ICAO location identifier*]   (ICLI)
RJFA .... Roumanian Jewish Federation of America   (EA)
RJFB........ Gannosu/Brady [*Japan*] [*ICAO location identifier*]   (ICLI)
RJFC........ Yakushima [*Japan*] [*ICAO location identifier*]   (ICLI)
RJFE........ Fukue [*Japan*] [*ICAO location identifier*]   (ICLI)
RJFF......... Fukuoka [*Japan*] [*ICAO location identifier*]   (ICLI)
RJFG........ Tanegashima [*Japan*] [*ICAO location identifier*]   (ICLI)
RJFK........ Kagoshima [*Japan*] [*ICAO location identifier*]   (ICLI)
RJFM........ Miyazaki [*Japan*] [*ICAO location identifier*]   (ICLI)
RJFN........ Nyutabaru [*Japan*] [*ICAO location identifier*]   (ICLI)
RJFN........ RJ Financial Corp. [*NASDAQ symbol*]   (NQ)
RJFO........ Oita [*Japan*] [*ICAO location identifier*]   (ICLI)
RJFR........ Kitakyushu [*Japan*] [*ICAO location identifier*]   (ICLI)
RJFT......... Kumamoto [*Japan*] [*ICAO location identifier*]   (ICLI)
RJFU........ Nagasaki [*Japan*] [*ICAO location identifier*]   (ICLI)
RJFY........ Kanoya [*Japan*] [*ICAO location identifier*]   (ICLI)
RJFZ .... Tsuiki [*Japan*] [*ICAO location identifier*]   (ICLI)
RJICA ...... Russian Journal of Inorganic Chemistry [*English Translation*] [*A publication*]
RJIS.......... Regional Justice Information System
RJK........... Rijeka [*Former Yugoslavia*] [*Airport symbol*]   (OAG)
RJKA........ Amami [*Japan*] [*ICAO location identifier*]   (ICLI)
RJKB........ Okierabu [*Japan*] [*ICAO location identifier*]   (ICLI)
RJKI......... Kikai/Kikaigashima Island [*Japan*] [*ICAO location identifier*]   (ICLI)
RJKN........ Tokunoshima Island [*Japan*] [*ICAO location identifier*]   (ICLI)
RJLI .... Royal Jersey Light Infantry [*Military unit*] [*British*]
RJM......... Reed, John M., San Antonio TX [*STAC*]
RJM......... Religious of Jesus-Mary [*Roman Catholic women's religious order*]
RJM......... Royal Jersey Militia [*Military unit*] [*British*]
RJM......... Warner Robins, GA [*Location identifier*] [*FAA*]   (FAAL)
RJN.......... Robinson Jeffers Newsletter [*A publication*]
RJNF........ Fukui [*Japan*] [*ICAO location identifier*]   (ICLI)
RJNG .... Gifu [*Japan*] [*ICAO location identifier*]   (ICLI)
RJNH .... Hamamatsu [*Japan*] [*ICAO location identifier*]   (ICLI)
RJNK........ Kanazawa/Komatsu [*Japan*] [*ICAO location identifier*]   (ICLI)
RJNN .... Nagoya [*Japan*] [*ICAO location identifier*]   (ICLI)
RJNO .... Oki [*Japan*] [*ICAO location identifier*]   (ICLI)
RJNT........ Toyama [*Japan*] [*ICAO location identifier*]   (ICLI)
RJNY........ Yaizu/Shizuhama [*Japan*] [*ICAO location identifier*]   (ICLI)
RJO .... Rapports Judiciaires Officiels de Quebec [*Quebec Official Law Reports*] [*A publication*]   (ILCA)
RJO .... Remote Job Output [*Data processing*]
RJO .... Revolutionary Justice Organization [*Lebanese terrorist group*]
RJOA........ Hiroshima [*Japan*] [*ICAO location identifier*]   (ICLI)
RJOB........ Okayama [*Japan*] [*ICAO location identifier*]   (ICLI)
RJOC........ Izumo [*Japan*] [*ICAO location identifier*]   (ICLI)
RJOD........ Reaction Jet OMS [*Orbital Maneuvering Subsystem*] Driver [*NASA*]   (NASA)
RJOE........ Akeno [*Japan*] [*ICAO location identifier*]   (ICLI)
RJOF........ Hofu [*Japan*] [*ICAO location identifier*]   (ICLI)
RJOH........ Miho [*Japan*] [*ICAO location identifier*]   (ICLI)
RJOI .... Iwakuni [*Japan*] [*ICAO location identifier*]   (ICLI)
RJOK........ Kochi [*Japan*] [*ICAO location identifier*]   (ICLI)
RJOM .... Matsuyama [*Japan*] [*ICAO location identifier*]   (ICLI)
RJOO .... Osaka/International [*Japan*] [*ICAO location identifier*]   (ICLI)
RJOP........ Komatsujima [*Japan*] [*ICAO location identifier*]   (ICLI)
RJOQ (BR) ... Rapports Judiciaires Officiels de Quebec, Cour du Banc du Roi [*Quebec Official Law Reports, King's Bench*] [*A publication*]   (ILCA)
RJOQ (CS) ... Rapports Judiciaires Officiels de Quebec, Cour Superieure [*Quebec Official Law Reports, Superior Court*] [*A publication*]   (ILCA)
RJOR........ Tottori [*Japan*] [*ICAO location identifier*]   (ICLI)
RJOS........ Tokushima [*Japan*] [*ICAO location identifier*]   (ICLI)
RJOT........ Takamatsu [*Japan*] [*ICAO location identifier*]   (ICLI)
RJOY........ Osaka/Yao [*Japan*] [*ICAO location identifier*]   (ICLI)
RJOZ........ Ozuki [*Japan*] [*ICAO location identifier*]   (ICLI)
RJP........... Reaction Jet Pipe
RJP........... Realistic Job Preview
RJP........... Remote Job Processing [*Data processing*]
RJP........... RJP Electronics [*Vancouver Stock Exchange symbol*]
RJP........... Rocket Jet Plume
RJPA .... Ramjet Performance Analysis   (MCD)
RJPCA ...... Russian Journal of Physical Chemistry [*English Translation*] [*A publication*]
RJ & PJ ..... Revenue, Judicial, and Police Journal [*Calcutta*] [*A publication*]   (DLA)
RJQ .... Rapports Judiciaires [*Quebec Law Reports*] [*A publication*]   (DLA)
RJQ BR ..... Rapports Judiciaires de Quebec, Cour du Banc du Roi [*Quebec Law Reports, King's Bench*] [*A publication*]   (DLA)
RJQ CS...... Rapports Judiciaires de Quebec, Cour Superieure [*Quebec Law Reports, Superior Court*] [*A publication*]   (DLA)

RJR............ Mathieu's Quebec Revised Reports [*A publication*]   (DLA)
RJR............ R. J. Reynolds Tobacco Co.
RJR............ RJR Nabisco Holding Corp. [*Associated Press abbreviation*]   (APAG)
RJR............ Rotary Joint Reed
RJR............ Russkij Jazyk za Rubezom [*A publication*]
RJRA......... Rotary Joint Reed Assembly
RJR Nab.... RJR Nabisco Holding Corp. [*Associated Press abbreviation*]   (APAG)
RJRQ......... Mathieu's Quebec Revised Reports [*A publication*]   (DLA)
RJS............ Reaction Jet System   (KSC)
RJS............ Remote Job System [*Data processing*]   (MCD)
RJS............ Richard Jeffries Society   (EAIO)
RJS............ Roberta Jo Society   (EA)
RJS............ Rocket and JATO [*Jet-Assisted Takeoff*] Section [*Picatinny Arsenal*] [*Dover, NJ*]
RJS............ Russkij Jazyk v Skole [*A publication*]
RJS............ Ruth Jackson Society   (EA)
RJSA......... Aomori [*Japan*] [*ICAO location identifier*]   (ICLI)
RJSC......... Yamagata [*Japan*] [*ICAO location identifier*]   (ICLI)
RJSD......... Sado [*Japan*] [*ICAO location identifier*]   (ICLI)
RJSFC....... R. J. Sutton Fan Club   (EA)
RJSH........ Hachinohe [*Japan*] [*ICAO location identifier*]   (ICLI)
RJSHDQ... Jugoslovanski Simpozij za Hmeljarstvo Referati [*A publication*]
RJSI.......... Hanamaki [*Japan*] [*ICAO location identifier*]   (ICLI)
RJSK........ Akita [*Japan*] [*ICAO location identifier*]   (ICLI)
RJSM........ Misawa [*Japan*] [*ICAO location identifier*]   (ICLI)
RJSN........ Niigata [*Japan*] [*ICAO location identifier*]   (ICLI)
RJSO......... Ominato [*Japan*] [*ICAO location identifier*]   (ICLI)
RJSS......... Sendai [*Japan*] [*ICAO location identifier*]   (ICLI)
RJST........ Matsushima [*Japan*] [*ICAO location identifier*]   (ICLI)
RJSU........ Kasuminome [*Japan*] [*ICAO location identifier*]   (ICLI)
RJT........... Rassemblement des Jeunes Togolais [*Togolese Youth Rally*]
RJT........... Reference Jet Transport
RJT........... Rejection Message [*Communications*]   (FAAC)
RJT........... Royal Jubilee Trust [*Provides financial aid to start new businesses*] [*British*]
RJTA......... Atsugi [*Japan*] [*ICAO location identifier*]   (ICLI)
RJTC......... Tachikawa [*Japan*] [*ICAO location identifier*]   (ICLI)
RJTD........ Tokyo [*Japan*] [*ICAO location identifier*]   (ICLI)
RJTE........ Tateyama [*Japan*] [*ICAO location identifier*]   (ICLI)
RJTF........ Chofu [*Japan*] [*ICAO location identifier*]   (ICLI)
RJTG........ Tokyo [*Japan*] [*ICAO location identifier*]   (ICLI)
RJTH........ Hachijojima [*Japan*] [*ICAO location identifier*]   (ICLI)
RJTI......... Tokyo [*Japan*] [*ICAO location identifier*]   (ICLI)
RJTJ......... Iruma [*Japan*] [*ICAO location identifier*]   (ICLI)
RJTK........ Kisarazu [*Japan*] [*ICAO location identifier*]   (ICLI)
RJTL........ Shimofusa [*Japan*] [*ICAO location identifier*]   (ICLI)
RJTO........ Oshima [*Japan*] [*ICAO location identifier*]   (ICLI)
RJTQ........ Miyakejima [*Japan*] [*ICAO location identifier*]   (ICLI)
RJTR........ Zama/Rankin [*Japan*] [*ICAO location identifier*]   (ICLI)
RJTT........ Tokyo/International [*Japan*] [*ICAO location identifier*]   (ICLI)
RJTU........ Utsunomiya [*Japan*] [*ICAO location identifier*]   (ICLI)
RJTV........ Ramjet Test Vehicle
RJTW....... Zama [*Japan*] [*ICAO location identifier*]   (ICLI)
RJTY........ Yokota [*Japan*] [*ICAO location identifier*]   (ICLI)
RJTZ........ Fuchu [*Japan*] [*ICAO location identifier*]   (ICLI)
R de Jur..... Revue de Jurisprudence [*Quebec*] [*A publication*]   (DLA)
RJV........... Rheinisches Jahrbuch fuer Volkskunde [*A publication*]
RK............. Air Afrique [*Ivory Coast*] [*ICAO designator*]   (ICDA)
RK............. Ark Restaurants Corp. [*AMEX symbol*]   (SPSG)
RK............. Rabbit Kidney
RK............. Rack
RK............. Radial Keratotomy [*Ophthalmology*]
RK............. Rassemblement Katangais [*Katanga Rally*]
RK............. Rat Kidney
RK............. Realkatalog der Aegyptologie [*A publication*]   (BJA)
R-K............ Redlich-Kwong [*Physics*]
RK............. Republic of Korea [*IYRU nationality code*]   (IYR)
RK............. Rhodopsin Kinase [*An enzyme*]
RK............. Right Kidney
RK............. Right to Know   (EA)
RK............. Rock [*Maps and charts*]   (MCD)
RK............. Royal Knight [*British*]
RK............. Rubbing Keel [*of a ship*]   (DS)
RK............. Run of Kiln
RK............. Societe Air Afrique [*Cameroon*] [*ICAO designator*]   (FAAC)
RKA......... Rockdale, NY [*Location identifier*] [*FAA*]   (FAAL)
RKAF....... Royal Khmer Air Force [*Cambodia*]
RKANA..... Rost Kristallov [*A publication*]
RKB......... Red Kidney Bean
RKCC....... Right to Know Committee of Correspondence [*Defunct*]   (EA)
RKCLA..... Reaction Kinetics and Catalysis Letters [*A publication*]
RKCSN...... Rospravy Kralovske Ceske Spolecnosti Nauk [*A publication*]
RKD......... Rockland [*Maine*] [*Airport symbol*]   (OAG)
RKE......... Roskilde [*Denmark*] [*Airport symbol*]   (OAG)
RKFC....... Ray Kirkland Fan Club   (EA)
RKFJ .... Rad Kongresa Folklorista Jugoslavije [*A publication*]
RKG......... Radiocardiogram
RKG......... Rockingham R. R. [*AAR code*]
RKG.......... Royal Khmer Government [*Cambodia*]

RKH........... Rock Hill [*South Carolina*] [*Airport symbol*]   (OAG)
RKH........... Rockingham Resources, Inc. [*Vancouver Stock Exchange symbol*]
RKHLit...... Rocznik Komisji Historycznoliterackiej Pan [*A publication*]
RKHS .... Reducing Kernel Hilbert Space [*Electronics*]   (OA)
RKHS .... Register. Kentucky Historical Society [*A publication*]
RK II .... Runge-Kutta Second Order [*Mathematics*]
RkInt......... Rockwell International Corp. [*Associated Press abbreviation*]   (APAG)
RKJ............ Ramsey, Kenneth J., Pittsburgh PA [*STAC*]
RKJ............ Rozprawy Komisji Jezykowej Lodzkiego Towarzystwa Naukowego [*A publication*]
RKJJ.......... Kwangju [*South Korea*] [*ICAO location identifier*]   (ICLI)
RKJK........ Kunsan [*South Korea*] [*ICAO location identifier*]   (ICLI)
RKJL .... Rozprawy Komisji Jezykowej Lodzkiego Towarzystwa Naukowego [*A publication*]
RKJM....... Mokpo [*South Korea*] [*ICAO location identifier*]   (ICLI)
RKJO........ Hongjungri [*South Korea*] [*ICAO location identifier*]   (ICLI)
RKJU........ Jhunju [*South Korea*] [*ICAO location identifier*]   (ICLI)
RKJW....... Rozprawy Komisji Jezykowej Wroclawskiego Towarzystwa Naukowego [*A publication*]
RKJY........ Yeosu [*South Korea*] [*ICAO location identifier*]   (ICLI)
RKKA....... Raboche-Krest'ianskaia Krasnaia Armiia [*Workers' and Peasants' Red Army*] [*Redesignated Soviety Army*] [*Former USSR*]
RKKHA ..... Rikagaku Kenkyusho Hokoku [*A publication*]
RKL .... Right Knee Left [*Guitar playing*]
RKL .... Ruskin Developments Ltd. [*Vancouver Stock Exchange symbol*]
RKLM .... Ruskin Developments Ltd. [*NASDAQ symbol*]   (NQ)
RKM .... Risk Management [*A publication*]
RKM .... Runge-Kutta Method [*Mathematics*]
RKN.......... Root Knot Nematode [*Plant pathology*]
RKN.......... Runge-Kutta-Nystroem [*Formula*] [*Mathematics*]
RKNC........ Chunchon [*South Korea*] [*ICAO location identifier*]   (ICLI)
RKND........ Sokcho [*South Korea*] [*ICAO location identifier*]   (ICLI)
RKNFSYS ... Rock Information System [*National Science Foundation*] [*Carnegie Institution*] [*Databank*]   (IID)
RKNH........ Heongsung [*South Korea*] [*ICAO location identifier*]   (ICLI)
RKNI .... Injae [*South Korea*] [*ICAO location identifier*]   (ICLI)
RKNK........ Kwandaeri [*South Korea*] [*ICAO location identifier*]   (ICLI)
RKNKA ..... Rakuno Kagaku No Kenkyu [*A publication*]
RKNN........ Kangnung [*South Korea*] [*ICAO location identifier*]   (ICLI)
RKNW...... Wonju [*South Korea*] [*ICAO location identifier*]   (ICLI)
RKNY .... Yangku [*South Korea*] [*ICAO location identifier*]   (ICLI)
RKO.......... Radio-Keith-Orpheum [*Motion picture production and exhibition firm, also active in broadcasting*]
RKO.......... Range Keeper Operator [*Navy*]
RKP .... Rockport, TX [*Location identifier*] [*FAA*]   (FAAL)
RKP .... Routledge & Kegan Paul [*British publisher*]
RKPC........ Cheju/International [*South Korea*] [*ICAO location identifier*]   (ICLI)
RKPD........ Chedong [*South Korea*] [*ICAO location identifier*]   (ICLI)
RKPE........ Chinhae [*South Korea*] [*ICAO location identifier*]   (ICLI)
RKPK........ Kimhae/International [*South Korea*] [*ICAO location identifier*]   (ICLI)
RKPM .... Cheju/Mosulpo [*South Korea*] [*ICAO location identifier*]   (ICLI)
RKPN .... Rooms Katholieke Partij Nederland [*Roman Catholic Party of the Netherlands*] [*Political party*]   (PPE)
RKPP........ Busan [*South Korea*] [*ICAO location identifier*]   (ICLI)
RKPS........ Sachon [*South Korea*] [*ICAO location identifier*]   (ICLI)
RKPU........ Ulsan [*South Korea*] [*ICAO location identifier*]   (ICLI)
RKR .... Poteau, OK [*Location identifier*] [*FAA*]   (FAAL)
RKr .... Rakstu Krajums [*A publication*]
RKR .... Rocker   (AAG)
RKR .... Rockspan Resources [*Vancouver Stock Exchange symbol*]
RKRA .... Rocker Arm [*Mechanical engineering*]
RKS........... Reko [*Solomon Islands*] [*Seismograph station code, US Geological Survey*]   (SEIS)
RKS........... Rock Springs [*Wyoming*] [*Airport symbol*]   (OAG)
RKS........... Rocket Stories [*A publication*]
RKSA........ Ascom City [*South Korea*] [*ICAO location identifier*]   (ICLI)
RKSB........ Uijeongbu [*South Korea*] [*ICAO location identifier*]   (ICLI)
RKSC........ Cheongokri [*South Korea*] [*ICAO location identifier*]   (ICLI)
RKSD........ Kanamni [*South Korea*] [*ICAO location identifier*]   (ICLI)
RKSE........ Paekryoungdo Beach [*South Korea*] [*ICAO location identifier*]   (ICLI)
RKSF........ Republic of Korea Air Force Headquarters [*South Korea*] [*ICAO location identifier*]   (ICLI)
RKSG........ Pyongtaek [*South Korea*] [*ICAO location identifier*]   (ICLI)
RKSH........ Kwanak [*South Korea*] [*ICAO location identifier*]   (ICLI)
RKSI......... Chajangni [*South Korea*] [*ICAO location identifier*]   (ICLI)
RKSK........ Susaek [*South Korea*] [*ICAO location identifier*]   (ICLI)
RKSL........ Seoul City [*South Korea*] [*ICAO location identifier*]   (ICLI)
RKSM........ Seoul East [*Sinchonri*] [*South Korea*] [*ICAO location identifier*]   (ICLI)
RKSO .... Osan [*South Korea*] [*ICAO location identifier*]   (ICLI)
RKSP........ Paekryoungdo Site [*South Korea*] [*ICAO location identifier*]   (ICLI)

RKSP......... Rooms Katholieke Staatspartij [*Roman Catholic State Party*] [*Netherlands*] [*Political party*] (PPE)
RKSR......... Yeongdongri [*South Korea*] [*ICAO location identifier*] (ICLI)
RKSS......... Seoul/Kimpo International [*South Korea*] [*ICAO location identifier*] (ICLI)
RKST......... Tongoucheon [*South Korea*] [*ICAO location identifier*] (ICLI)
RKSU......... Yeoju [*South Korea*] [*ICAO location identifier*] (ICLI)
RKSW......... Suwon [*South Korea*] [*ICAO location identifier*] (ICLI)
RKSX......... Song San-Ri [*South Korea*] [*ICAO location identifier*] (ICLI)
RKSY......... Seoul/Yungsan [*South Korea*] [*ICAO location identifier*] (ICLI)
RKT.......... Ras Al Khaymah [*United Arab Emirates*] [*Airport symbol*] (OAG)
RKT.......... Rikitea [*Tuamotu Archipelago*] [*Seismograph station code, US Geological Survey*] (SEIS)
RKT.......... Rocket (AAG)
RKTA........ Andong [*South Korea*] [*ICAO location identifier*] (ICLI)
RKTC........ Chungju [*South Korea*] [*ICAO location identifier*] (ICLI)
RKTD........ Taejon [*South Korea*] [*ICAO location identifier*] (ICLI)
RKTEA...... Rakennusteknikka [*A publication*]
RKTH........ Pohang [*South Korea*] [*ICAO location identifier*] (ICLI)
RKTJ......... Kyungju [*South Korea*] [*ICAO location identifier*] (ICLI)
RKTM....... Seosan [*South Korea*] [*ICAO location identifier*] (ICLI)
RKTN........ Taegu [*South Korea*] [*ICAO location identifier*] (ICLI)
RKTO........ Nonsan [*South Korea*] [*ICAO location identifier*] (ICLI)
RKTR........ Rocketeer
RKTS........ Sangju [*South Korea*] [*ICAO location identifier*] (ICLI)
RKTSTA ... Rocket Station
RKTT........ Taegu [*South Korea*] [*ICAO location identifier*] (ICLI)
RKTY........ Yechon [*South Korea*] [*ICAO location identifier*] (ICLI)
RKU.......... Yule Island [*Papua New Guinea*] [*Airport symbol*] (OAG)
RKV.......... Rabbit Kidney Vacuolating Virus
RKV.......... Rose Knot Victor [*Gemini tracking ship*]
RKVA........ Reactive Kilovolt-Ampere
RKVAM .... Recording Kilovolt-Ampere Meter (MSA)
RKVP......... Rooms Katholieke Volkspartij [*Roman Catholic People's Party*] [*Netherlands*] [*Political party*] (PPE)
RKW.......... Renal Potassium Wasting (MAE)
RKW.......... Repertorium fuer Kunstwissenschaft [*A publication*]
RKW.......... Rockwood, TN [*Location identifier*] [*FAA*] (FAAL)
RKWD........ Rockwood Holding Co. [*NASDAQ symbol*] (NQ)
Rk Wkbl ... Rechtskundig Weekblad [*A publication*]
RKX.......... Maxton, NC [*Location identifier*] [*FAA*] (FAAL)
RKY.......... Rockaway Corp. [*NYSE symbol*] (SPSG)
Rky.......... Rocky [*Quality of the bottom*] [*Nautical charts*]
RKY.......... Roentgen Kymography
RKY.......... Rokeby [*Australia*] [*Airport symbol*] [*Obsolete*] (OAG)
RKZ.......... Reformierte Kirchenzeitung [*A publication*]
R & L......... Bureau for Reference and Loan Services [*Library network*]
RL............. LAR [*Liniile Aeriene Romane*] [*ICAO designator*] (FAAC)
RL............. Master Cross-Reference List
RL............. Radiation Laboratory
RL............. Radiation Level [*Nuclear energy*]
RL............. Radio Liberty [*Board for International Broadcasting*]
RL............. Radio Liberty [*A publication*]
RL............. Radio Link (OA)
RL............. Radiolocation
RL............. Radioluminescent
RL............. Radionavigation land station using two separate loop antennas, and a single transmitter, and operating at a power of 150 watts or more [*ITU designation*] (CET)
RL............. Ragged Left [*Printing*] (WDMC)
RL............. Rahmana Litslan (BJA)
RL............. Rail (AAG)
R & L......... Rail and Lake
RL............. Ralph Lauren [*Fashion designer, 1939-*]
RL............. Raman LASER
RL............. Random Lengths [*Lumber*]
RL............. Random Logic
R/L............. Rate/Limited (MCD)
RL............. Rated Load
RL............. Reactor Licensing [*Nuclear energy*] (NRCH)
RL............. Reader's Library [*A publication*]
RL............. Reading List
RL............. Receive Leg [*Telecommunications*] (TEL)
RL............. Receptor-Ligand Complex
R d L.......... Recht der Landwirtschaft [*A publication*]
RL............. Record Length
R/L............. Redline (KSC)
RL............. Reduced [*or Reduction*] Level
RL............. Reel
RL............. Reeling Machines [*JETDS nomenclature*] [*Military*] (CET)
RL............. Reference Library
RL............. Reference List
RL............. Reflection Loss [*Telecommunications*] (TEL)
RL............. Reiz-Limen [*Stimulus threshold*] [*Psychology*]
RL............. Relay Logic
RL............. Release Load
RL............. Religion in Life [*A publication*]
R and L...... Religion and Literature [*A publication*]
RL............. Relocation Library (HGAA)

R/L............. Remote/Local (NASA)
RL............. Report Immediately upon Leaving [*Aviation*] (FAAC)
RL............. Research Laboratory
RL............. Reserve List (ADA)
RL............. Residential Lease [*Real estate*] (ADA)
RL............. Resistor Logic (IEEE)
RL............. Respectable Loge [*Worshipful Lodge*] [*French*] [*Freemasonry*] (ROG)
RL............. Restaurant Liquor [*License*]
RL............. Restricted Line Officer
RL............. Retarded Learner [*Education*]
RL............. Reticular Lamina [*Ear anatomy*]
RL............. Retired List
RL............. Retirement Loss
R/L............. Return Link (MCD)
RL............. Return Loss
RL............. Revised Laws [*A publication*] (DLA)
RL............. Revue Legale [*Canada*] [*A publication*] (DLA)
R de L........ Revue de Legislation et de Jurisprudence [*Canada*] [*A publication*] (DLA)
RL............. Rhumb Line
RL............. Rial [*Monetary unit*] [*Iran, Saudi Arabia, etc.*]
RL............. Ricerche Linguistiche [*A publication*]
RL............. Richland Operations Office [*Energy Research and Development Administration*]
RL............. Richtlinien [*Instructions, Directions*] [*German*] (ILCA)
RL............. Right to Left
R/L............. Right and Left
RL............. Right Leg
RL............. Right Line
RL............. Right Lower [*Medicine*]
RL............. Right Lung
RL............. Ring Level (BUR)
RL............. Ringer Lactated [*Medicine*]
RL............. Rive'on Le-Khalkalah [*Tel Aviv*] (BJA)
RL............. River Lines, Inc. [*AAR code*]
RL............. Road Locomotive [*British*]
RL............. Rocket Launcher
RL............. Roll
RL............. Roll Lift [*NASA*] (KSC)
RL............. Rolland, Inc. [*Toronto Stock Exchange symbol*]
RL............. Roman Law (DLA)
RL............. Roof Leader (MSA)
RL............. Round Lot [*Unit of trading*]
RL............. Royal (ROG)
RL............. Royal Lancers [*British military*] (DMA)
RL............. Royal Licence [*British*]
RL............. Ruch Literacki [*Krakow*] [*A publication*]
RL............. Rugby League [*British*] (DI)
RL............. Run Length [*Data processing*]
RL............. Running Losses [*Automotive engineering*]
RL............. Russian Literature [*A publication*]
RLA.......... Aeronautical Marker Beacon [*ITU designation*] (CET)
RLA.......... Reallexikon der Assyriologie [*Berlin*] [*A publication*] (BJA)
RLA.......... Receptive Language Age [*of the hearing-impaired*]
RLA.......... Redevelopment Land Agency [*Washington, DC*]
RLA.......... Regional Land Agent [*Ministry of Agriculture, Fisheries, and Food*] [*British*]
RLA.......... Regional Letter of Acceptance [*Department of Housing and Urban Development*] (GFGA)
RLA.......... Relay (FAAC)
RLA.......... Religious Leaders of America [*A publication*]
RLA.......... Remote Line Adapter
RLA.......... Remote Loop Adapter [*Telecommunications*]
RLA.......... Repair Level Analysis [*Military*] (AFIT)
RLA.......... Repair Line Agreement (NASA)
RLA.......... Research Laboratory for Archeology [*British*]
RLA.......... Responsible Local Agencies (OICC)
RLA.......... Restricted Landing Area [*Aviation*]
RLA.......... Roll Lock Actuator (MCD)
RLA.......... Royal Lao Army [*Laos*]
RLA.......... Rui Lopes Associates, Inc. [*Sunnyvale, CA*] [*Telecommunications*] (TSSD)
RLA.......... Rural Land Alliance (EA)
RLAB........ Royce Laboratories, Inc. [*Miami, FL*] [*NASDAQ symbol*] (NQ)
RLAC........ Reallexikon fuer Antike und Christentum [*A publication*]
RLAC........ Recycling Legislation Action Coalition (EA)
RLADD .... RADAR Low-Angle Drogue Delivery (AFM)
RLAF........ Royal Laotian Air Force
RLANO...... Relay Equipment Out of Operation [*Aviation*] (FAAC)
RLAOK...... Relay Equipment Resumed Operation [*Aviation*] (FAAC)
RLAS........ Rocket Lunar Attitude System
RLAss........ Reallexikon der Assyriologie [*Berlin*] [*A publication*] (BJA)
RLB.......... RACON Station [*ITU designation*] (CET)
RLB.......... Reliability [*or Reliable*] (AAG)
RLB.......... Right Linebacker (WGA)
RLB.......... United States Railroad Labor Board Decisions [*A publication*] (DLA)
RLBCD...... Right Lower Border of Cardiac Dullness [*Cardiology*]
RLB Dec .... Railroad Labor Board Decisions [*A publication*] (DLA)

RLBG......... Relative Bearing [*Navigation*]   (FAAC)
RLBL.......... Regional Laser and Biotechnology Laboratories [*University of Pennsylvania*] [*Research center*]   (RCD)
RLBM........ Rearward Launched Ballistic Missile
RLC........... Radio Launch Control System   (IEEE)
RLC........... Radio Liberty Committee [*Later, RFE/RL*]   (EA)
RLC........... Receive Logic Chassis
RLC........... Refund Litigation Coordinator [*IRS*]
RLC........... Regulatory Light Chain [*Physiology*]
RLC........... Remote Line Concentrator
RLC........... Remote Load Controller [*NASA*]   (MCD)
RLC........... Report Landing Completed [*Aviation*]   (FAAC)
RLC........... Republican Liberty Caucus   (EA)
RLC........... Residual Lung Capacity [*Medicine*]
RLC........... Resistance Inductance Capacitance   (MSA)
RLC........... Ribosome-Lamella Complex [*Physiology*]
RLC........... Right Line Contactor   (MCD)
RLC........... Right Line Contractor
RLC........... Robinson Little & Co. Ltd. [*Toronto Stock Exchange symbol*]
RLC........... Rollins Truck Leasing [*NYSE symbol*]   (SPSG)
RLC........... ROM [*Read-Only Memory*] Location Counter
RLC........... Rotating Litter Chair [*NASA*]   (KSC)
RLC........... Run Length Coding
RLCA......... National Rural Letter Carriers' Association
RLCA......... Reaction-Limited Cluster Aggregation
RLCA......... Religion and Labor Council of America [*Defunct*]   (EA)
RLCAA...... Railway Locomotives and Cars [*A publication*]
RLCD........ Relocated
RLCM........ Rat Lung-Conditioned Medium [*Culture media*]
RLCR........ Railcar   (MSA)
RLCS......... Radio Launch Control System
RLCU .... Reference Link Control Unit [*Telecommunications*]   (TEL)
RLD .... RADAR Laydown Delivery   (AFM)
RLD .... Related Living Donor [*Medicine*]
RLD .... Relocation Dictionary
RLD .... Relocation List Directory
RLD .... Repetitive LASER Desorption
RLD .... Retail Liquor Dealer
RLD .... Richland [*Washington*] [*Airport symbol*] [*Obsolete*]   (OAG)
RLD .... Rolled   (AAG)
RLD .... Run Length Discriminator   (MCD)
RLD .... Ruptured Lumbar Disc [*Medicine*]
RLDS........ Reorganized Church of Jesus Christ of Latter-Day Saints
RLE........... Raleigh Energy [*Vancouver Stock Exchange symbol*]
RLE........... Relative Luminous Efficiency   (NATG)
RLE........... Request Loading Entry [*Data processing*]
RLE........... Research Laboratory of Electronics [*MIT*] [*Research center*]
RLE........... Resorts Leisure Exchange [*Commercial firm*] [*British*]
RLE........... Right Lower Extremity [*Medicine*]
RLE........... Run-Length Encoding [*Data processing*]
RLEA......... Railway Labor Executives' Association   (EA)
RLEO .... Request Liaison Engineering Order [*NASA*]   (NASA)
RLETFL.... Report Leaving Each Thousand-Foot Level [*Aviation*]   (FAAC)
RLEW........ Research Library for Edward Woodward   (EA)
RLF........... Relevant Labor Force   (DNAB)
RLF........... Relief   (AAG)
RLF........... Religion and Labor Foundation
RLF........... Religious Liberty Foundation   (EA)
RLF........... Remote Lift Fan [*Aviation*]
RLF........... Retrograde Lipid Flow [*Hypothesis for biological cell movement*]
RLF........... Retrolental Fibroplasia [*Eye disease in premature babies*]
RLF........... Rhizoctonia-Like Fungus
RLF........... Right Lateral Femoral [*Site of injection*] [*Medicine*]
RLF........... Royal Laotian Forces
RLF........... Royal Literary Fund [*British*]
RLFC........ Rebel Lee Fan Club   (EA)
RLFE .... Revista. Laboratorio de Fonetica Experimental [*A publication*]
RLG .... Glidepath [*Slope*] Station [*ITU designation*]   (CET)
RLG .... Kremmling, CO [*Location identifier*] [*FAA*]   (FAAL)
RLG .... Railing   (AAG)
RLG .... Regimental Landing Group
RLG .... Regional Liaison Group   (CINC)
RLG .... Release Guard [*Telecommunications*]   (TEL)
RLG .... Relief Landing Ground [*British military*]   (DMA)
RLG .... Research Libraries Group [*An association*] [*Also, an information service or system*]   (EA)
RLG .... Rifle Large Grain [*British military*]   (DMA)
RLG .... Ring LASER Gyro [*Navy*]
RLG .... Royal Laotian Government
RLG .... Royal Lepage Ltd. [*Toronto Stock Exchange symbol*] [*Vancouver Stock Exchange symbol*]
RLGD .... Realigned
RLGM .... Remote Look Group Multiplexer   (MCD)
RLGM-CD ... Remote Look Group Multiplexer Cable Drive   (MCD)
RLGN .... Ring LASER Gyro Navigation   (MCD)
R & LH ..... Right and Left Hands [*Work-factor system*]
RLH .... Run Like Hell [*Slang*]
RLHIT....... Royal Life High Income Trust [*British*]
RLHS......... Railway and Locomotive Historical Society   (EA)

RLHTE....... Research Laboratory of Heat Transfer in Electronics [*MIT*]   (MCD)
RLI............ Anniston, AL [*Location identifier*] [*FAA*]   (FAAL)
RLI............ Radiation Level Indicator
RLI............ Rand Light Infantry [*British military*]   (DMA)
RLI............ Realtors Land Institute   (EA)
RLI............ Retirement Life Item
RLI............ Rhodesian Light Infantry [*Military unit*]
RLI............ Right/Left Indicator   (NVT)
RLI............ RLI Corp. [*NYSE symbol*]   (SPSG)
RLI............ Rostral Length Index
RLIB .... Relocatable Library [*Data processing*]
RLIBD6 .... Swedish University of Agricultural Sciences. Department of Farm Buildings. Report [*A publication*]
RLI Cp ...... RLI Corp. [*Associated Press abbreviation*]   (APAG)
RLIEVDP ... Request Line Items Be Expedited for Vehicles [*or Equipment*] Deadlined for Parts [*Army*]   (AABC)
RLIF .... [*The*] Reliable Life Insurance Co. [*NASDAQ symbol*]   (NQ)
R Lim E...... Roll-Limiting Engine
RLIN.......... Research Libraries Information Network [*Pronounced "arlen"*] [*Formerly, BALLOTS*] [*Research Libraries Group, Inc.*] [*Stanford, CA*] [*Library network*] [*Information service or system*]
RLing .... Ricerche Linguistiche [*A publication*]
RLing .... Russian Linguistics [*A publication*]
RLir........... Realismo Lirico [*A publication*]
RLit........... Russkaja Literatura [*A publication*]
RLitC .... Readings in Literary Criticism [*A publication*]
RLITDQ .... Swedish University of Agricultural Sciences. Department of Agricultural Engineering. Report [*A publication*]
RLIV .... Retirement Living Tax-Exempt Mortgage Fund LP [*NASDAQ symbol*]   (NQ)
R de L et de J ... Revue de Legislation et de Jurisprudence [*A publication*]   (DLA)
RLJ .... Rhodes-Livingstone Journal [*A publication*]
RLJ .... Rhodesian Law Journal [*A publication*]   (DLA)
RLJ .... Russian Language Journal [*A publication*]
RLKBAD... Report. Research Laboratories of Kirin Brewery Co. Ltd. [*A publication*]
RLL............ Localizer Station [*ITU designation*]   (CET)
RLL............ Religion in Literature and Life [*A publication*]
RLL............ Relocating Linking Loader
RLL............ Representation-Language Language [*Data processing*]
RLL............ Reviews in Leukemia and Lymphoma [*Elsevier Book Series*] [*A publication*]
RLL........... Right Lower Limb [*Medicine*]
RLL........... Right Lower Lobe [*Lungs*]
RLL........... Rim of Lateral Lip
RLL........... Rocket Launcher Locator
RLL........... Rolla, ND [*Location identifier*] [*FAA*]   (FAAL)
RLL........... Run-Length-Limited [*Data processing*]
RLLB .... Right Long Leg Brace [*Medicine*]
RLLB .... Right Lower Leg Brace [*Medicine*]
RLLD........ Registered Laundry and Linen Director [*Designation awarded by National Association of Institutional Linen Management*]
RLLSC....... Right to Life League of Southern California   (EA)
R & LL & T ... Redman and Lyon on Landlord and Tenant [*8th ed.*] [*1924*] [*A publication*]   (DLA)
RLLY .... Rally's, Inc. [*NASDAQ symbol*]   (NQ)
RLM .... Marine Radio Beacon Station [*ITU designation*]   (CET)
RLM .... Rearward Launched Missile
RLM .... Regional Library of Medicine [*Pan American Health Organization*]
RLM .... Reichsleftfahrt Ministerium [*German Air Ministry*] [*World War II*]
RLM .... Remote Line Module [*Telecommunications*]
RLM .... Return to Land and Management [*Agriculture*]
RLM .... Reynolds Metals Co. [*NYSE symbol*]   (SPSG)
RLM .... Roy-L Merchant Group, Inc. [*Toronto Stock Exchange symbol*]
RLM .... Royal American Airways [*Tucson, AZ*] [*FAA designator*]   (FAAC)
RLM .... Royal Lancashire Militia [*British military*]   (DMA)
RLM .... Royal London Militia
RLMA .... Roll Label Manufacturers Association   (EA)
RLMBA..... Rendiconti. Istituto Lombardo. Accademia di Scienze e Lettere. Sezione B. Scienze Biologiche e Mediche [*A publication*]
RLMD....... Rat Liver Mitochondria   (MAE)
RLME....... Rapid Liquid Metal Embrittlement   (MCD)
RLMM ...... Research Laboratory for Mechanics of Materials   (MCD)
RLMPB ..... Proceedings. Reliability and Maintainability Conference [*A publication*]
RLMS....... RADAR Land Mass Simulation
RLMS....... Reproduction of Library Materials Section [*Resources and Technical Services Division of ALA*]
RLN .... LORAN Station [*ITU designation*]   (CET)
RLN .... Recurrent Laryngeal Nerve [*Medicine*]   (MAE)
RLN .... Remote LAN [*Linked Access Network*] Node [*DCA, Inc.*]   (PCM)
RLND....... Regional Lymph Node Dissection [*Medicine*]
RLNS........ Revue Legale. New Series [*Canada*] [*A publication*]   (DLA)

RLO .... Omnidirectional Range Station [*ITU designation*] (CET)
RLO .... RADAR Lock-On
RLO .... Regional Liaison Office [*Military*] (AFM)
R & LO ..... Reliability and Launch Operations (MCD)
RLO .... Repairs Liaison Officer [*Landing craft and barges*] [*Navy*]
R/LO .... Response/Lockout (MCD)
RLO .... Restricted Line Officer (DNAB)
RLO .... Returned Letter Office
RLO .... Richland Operations Office [*Energy Research and Development Administration*]
RLO .... Rose Lookout Tower [*Oklahoma*] [*Seismograph station code, US Geological Survey*] (SEIS)
RLO .... Rudder Lock-Out (MCD)
RLOCK...... Record Lock
RLOE .... Roemische Limes in Oesterreich [*A publication*]
RLOP........ Reactor Licensing Operating Procedure [*Nuclear energy*] (NRCH)
RLOS........ Retention Level of Supply [*Navy*] (NG)
RLOS........ Revue Legale (Old Series) [*Canada*] [*A publication*] (DLA)
RLP........... Radiation-Leukemia-Protection (MAE)
RLP........... Rail Loading Point (NATG)
RLP........... Random Loose-Packed [*Granular physics*]
RLP........... Remote Line Printer (MCD)
RLP........... Ribosome-Like Particle [*Cytology*]
RLP........... Roads and Landscape Planning [*British*]
RLP........... Rosella Plains [*Australia*] [*Airport symbol*] [*Obsolete*] (OAG)
RLP........... Rotatable Log Periodic Antenna (MCD)
RLP........... Rotating Linear Polarization
RLP........... Ruby LASER Pulse
RLPA......... Retail Loss Prevention Association [*New York, NY*] (EA)
RLPA......... Rotating Log Periodic Antenna
RLPG........ Regenerative Liquid Propellant Gun (MCD)
RLPH .... Reflected Light Photohead
RlphSu ...... Ralphs Supermarkets [*Associated Press abbreviation*] (APAG)
RLPL .... Railway Labor's Political League
RLPNLP.... Retired League Postmasters of the National League of Postmasters (EA)
RLQ .... Right Lower Quadrant [*of abdomen*] [*Medicine*]
RLQB........ Revue Legale Reports, Queen's Bench [*Canada*] [*A publication*] (DLA)
RLR .... Radio Range Station [*ITU designation*] (CET)
RLR .... Radioactive Lighting Rod [*Nuclear energy*] (NRCH)
RL & R...... Rail, Lake, and Rail
RLR .... Record Length Register
RLR .... Retired Lives Reserve [*Insurance*]
RLR .... Right Larval Retractor
RLR .... Right Lateral Rectus [*Eye anatomy*]
RLR .... Right Lateral Rotation [*Medicine*]
RLR .... Riverina Library Review [*A publication*]
RLR .... Roller (MSA)
RLR .... Rutgers Law Review [*A publication*]
RLRB .... Radio Liberty Research Bulletin [*A publication*]
RLRF........ RLR Financial Services, Inc. [*Lauderhill, FL*] [*NASDAQ symbol*] (NQ)
RLRIU ...... Radio Logic Routing Interface Unit (MCD)
RLRS .... Regional Learning Resources Services [*Veterans Administration*] (GFGA)
RLS........... Person who stammers, unable to enunciate the letters R, L, and S
RLS........... RADAR Line of Sight
RLS........... Radius of Landing Site [*NASA*] (KSC)
RLS........... Raman LASER Source
RLS........... Ranfurly Library Service [*An association*] (EAIO)
RLS........... Recursive Least Squares [*Mathematics*]
RLS........... Regional Language Studies [*Newfoundland*] [*A publication*]
RLS........... Release (FAAC)
RLS........... Remote Line Switch [*Telecommunications*] (TEL)
RLS........... Research in the Life Sciences Committee [*National Academy of Sciences*]
RLS........... Reservoir Level Sensor (MCD)
RLS........... Resonance Light Scattering [*Physics*]
RLS........... Restless Legs Syndrome [*Medicine*]
RLS........... Restricted Least Squares [*Statistics*]
RL & S ...... Ridgeway, Lapp, and Schoales' Irish King's Bench Reports [*1793-95*] [*A publication*] (DLA)
RLS........... Rim Latch Set
RLS........... Ringer's Lactate Solution [*Physiology*]
RLS........... Riolos of Patras [*Greece*] [*Seismograph station code, US Geological Survey*] (SEIS)
RLS........... Robert Louis Stevenson [*Nineteenth-century Scottish author*]
RLS........... Rocket Launching System
RLS........... Roll Limit Switch
RLS........... Rotary Limit Switch
RLS........... Ruby LASER System
RLS........... Surveillance RADAR Station [*ITU designation*] (CET)
RLS........... Westerly, RI [*Location identifier*] [*FAA*] (FAAL)
RLSA .... Republican Law Students Association of New York (EA)
RLSA NY .. Republican Law Students Association of New York (EA)
RLSC .... Revue Legale Reports, Supreme Court [*Canada*] [*A publication*] (DLA)
RLSCA ...... Research in Life Sciences [*A publication*]

RLSD........ Received Line Signal Detector
RLSD........ Research and Laboratory Services Division [*Health and Safety Executive*] [*British*] (IRUK)
RLSE .... Release (MSA)
RLSP .... Ruby LASER Single Pulse
RLSS .... Regenerative Life Support System [*NASA*] (NASA)
RLSS .... Royal Life Saving Society [*Studley, Warwickshire, England*] (EAIO)
R L St........ Rackham Literary Studies [*A publication*]
RLST .... Realist, Inc. [*NASDAQ symbol*] (NQ)
RLST .... Release Timer [*Telecommunications*] (TEL)
RLSTA ...... Regelungstechnik [*A publication*]
RLSTN ...... Relay Station (FAAC)
RLT........... Arlit [*Niger*] [*Airport symbol*] (OAG)
RLT........... Redeemable Listed Trust
RLT........... Regimental Landing Team [*Military*]
RLT........... Registered Laboratory Technician [*Medicine*] (WGA)
RLT........... Relating To (AABC)
RLT........... Reliability Life Test
RLT........... Reorder Lead Time [*Navy*] (NG)
RLT........... Repair Lead Time
RLT........... Research & Laser Technology, Inc.
RLT........... Return Line Tether [*NASA*] (MCD)
RLT........... Right Lateral Thigh [*Medicine*]
RLT........... Ring LASER Technique
RLT........... Rolling Liquid Transporter [*Army*]
RLT........... Russian Literature Triquarterly [*A publication*]
RLTA........ Reenlistment Leave Travel Allowance [*Military*]
RLTA........ Rhodesian Lawn Tennis Association
RLTK........ Rhumb Line Track (FAAC)
RLTM....... Research Laboratories Technical Memorandum
RLTN .... Relation (MSA)
RLTO .... Regional Lime Technical Officer [*Ministry of Agriculture, Fisheries, and Food*] [*British*]
Rltr............ Realtor (WGA)
RltRef........ Realty Refund Trust [*Associated Press abbreviation*] (APAG)
RLTS .... Radio Linked Telemetry System
RLTV........ Relative (AFM)
RLU .... RADAR Logic Unit (MCD)
RLU .... Relative Light Units [*Analysis of light intensity*]
RLU .... Remote Line Unit [*Telecommunications*]
RLU .... Reserve Liaison Unit (DNAB)
RLU .... Waterville, ME [*Location identifier*] [*FAA*] (FAAL)
RLub .... Rocznik Lubelski [*A publication*]
RLV .... Rauscher [*Murine*] Leukemia Virus
RLV .... Reallexikon der Vorgeschichte [*Berlin*] [*A publication*] (BJA)
RLV .... Relieve (AFM)
RLV .... Reusable Launch Vehicle [*Aerospace*]
RLV .... Roving Lunar Vehicle (AAG)
RLVD .... Relieved
RLVDT...... Rotary Linear Variable Differential Transformer
RLVS .... Recoverable Launch Vehicle Structure (KSC)
RLW .... Rajasthan Law Weekly [*India*] [*A publication*] (DLA)
RLW .... Real West Airlines [*Fargo, ND*] [*FAA designator*] (FAAC)
RL & W ..... Roberts, Leaming, and Wallis' County Court Reports [*1849-51*] [*A publication*] (DLA)
RLW-30 ..... Ration Lightweight-30 Day [*Military*] (RDA)
RLWL....... Reactor Low-Water Level (IEEE)
RLWY....... Railway (AAG)
RLXN .... Relaxation (MSA)
Rly............. Railway [*A publication*]
RLY .... Railway
RLY .... Relay (AAG)
RLY .... Worland, WY [*Location identifier*] [*FAA*] (FAAL)
Rly Engng .. Railway Engineering Journal [*Incorporated in Railway Engineer International*] [*A publication*]
Rly Gaz ...... Railway Gazette [*Later, Railway Gazette International*] [*A publication*]
Rly Mag .... Railway Magazine [*A publication*]
R Lz........... Radjans'ke Literaturoznavstvo. Naukovo-Teoretycnyj Zurnal [*A publication*]
RM............. Journal of Recreational Mathematics [*A publication*]
RM............. Lab. Roland-Marie [*France*] [*Research code symbol*]
R & M .... Law Reporter, Montreal [*Canada*] [*A publication*] (DLA)
RM............. Maritime Radionavigation Mobile Station [*ITU designation*] (CET)
RM............. McAlpine Aviation [*Great Britain*] [*ICAO designator*] (FAAC)
RM............. Mitteilungen des Deutschen Archaeologischen Instituts. Roemische Abteilung [*A publication*]
RM............. Office of Resource Management [*Nuclear energy*] (NRCH)
RM............. RADAR Mapper
RM............. RADAR Missile (MUGU)
RM............. Radiation Measurement
R/M........... Radiation/Meteoroid [*NASA satellite*]
RM............. Radiation Monitor (NRCH)
RM............. Radical Mastectomy [*Medicine*]
RM............. Radio Marti [*Cuba*]
RM............. Radio Material Officer (MCD)
RM............. Radio Monitor
RM............. Radioman [*Navy rating*]
RM............. Range Marks

RM............	Range of Movement [*Medicine*]
RM............	Raven's Matrices [*Intelligence test*]
RM............	Raw Material
RM............	Reaction Mass
RM............	Reactor Manufacturer [*Nuclear energy*] (NRCH)
R/M..........	Read/Mostly [*Data processing*] (TEL)
RM............	Readiness Manager [*DARCOM*] [*Army*]
RM............	Readout Matrix
RM............	Ready Money (ROG)
RM............	Ream
RM............	Reasoning Module [*Data processing*]
RM............	Receiver, Mobile
RM............	Receiving Memo
RM............	Rechtsgeleerd Magazijn [*A publication*]
RM............	Record Mark (BUR)
RM............	Record Mirror [*A publication*]
RM............	Red Marrow [*Hematology*]
R & M	Redistribution and Marketing (AFM)
RM............	Redundancy Management (MCD)
RM............	Reference Material
RM............	Reference Memory [*Psychology*]
RM............	Reference Method
RM............	Reference Mission [*NASA*] (NASA)
RM............	Refresh Memory (MCD)
R & M	Refurbishment and Modification
RM............	Regeneration Medium [*Biology*]
RM............	Regional Manager
RM............	Regional Meetings [*Quakers*]
RM............	Register Memory
RM............	Registered Midwife [*British*] (DBQ)
RM............	Reichsmark [*Later, DM*] [*Monetary unit*] [*German*]
RM............	Relais Musique [*Phonorecord series*] [*Canada*]
RM............	Relative Mobility [*of ions*] [*Chemistry*]
R & M	Release and Material (MCD)
R & M	Reliability and Maintainability [*Navy*]
RM............	Religionen der Menschheit [*A publication*]
RM............	Remedial Maintenance (AFM)
Rm............	Remission [*Medicine*]
RM............	Remote Manipulator [*NASA*] (NASA)
RM............	Remote Manual (NRCH)
RM............	Remote Multiplexer [*Data processing*] (CAAL)
RM............	Rendezvous Maneuver (MCD)
RM............	Repair Manual
RM............	Repetition Maximum [*Medicine*]
RM............	Replaceable Module
R & M	Reports and Memorandum (MCD)
RM............	Rescue Module [*NASA*] (NASA)
RM............	Research Materials [*National Institute of Standards and Technology*]
RM............	Research Memorandum
RM............	Resident Magistrate
RM............	Residential Member [*Designation awarded by American Institute of Real Estate Appraisers of the National Association of Realtors*]
RM............	Resource Manager
RM............	Resource Module (SSD)
RM............	Respiratory Movement
RM............	Response Memoranda [*Jimmy Carter administration*]
RM............	Retail Manager
RM............	Retrospective Method [*Insurance*]
RM............	Return Material [*Navy*] (NG)
RM............	Review of Metaphysics [*A publication*]
R/M	Revolutions per Minute
RM............	Rheinisches Museum fuer Philologie [*A publication*]
RM............	Rhesus Monkey
RM............	Richmark Resources Ltd. [*Vancouver Stock Exchange symbol*]
RM............	Riding Master [*British*]
RM............	Right Mid
RM............	Ring Micrometer
RM............	Risk Management [*A publication*]
RM............	Rocket Management (MCD)
RM............	Rocket Motor
RM............	Rocky Mountains
RM............	Rollback Module [*Telecommunications*] (TEL)
RM............	Rolling Moment [*Physics*]
RM............	Roman Martyrology
rm..............	Romania [*MARC country of publication code*] [*Library of Congress*] (LCCP)
RM............	Romans [*New Testament book*]
RM............	Room (AAG)
RM............	Roumania [*IYRU nationality code*] (IYR)
RM............	Routine Maintenance (AAG)
RM............	Routing Manager
RM............	Rowley Mile [*Horseracing*] [*British*]
RM............	Rowohlts Monographien [*A publication*]
RM............	Royal Mail [*British*]
RM............	Royal Marines [*British*]
RM............	Royal Mint [*British*] (DAS)
RM............	Rubber Mold (MCD)
RM............	Rule Making [*Nuclear energy*] (NRCH)
RM............	Ruptured Membrane [*Medicine*]

RM............	Rural Municipality (DLA)
R & M	Russell and Mylne's English Chancery Reports [*A publication*] (DLA)
RM............	Russian Military [*World War II*]
RM............	Russkaja Mysl' [*A publication*]
R & M	Ryan and Moody's English Nisi Prius Reports [*A publication*] (DLA)
RM............	RYMAC Mortgage Investment Corp. [*AMEX symbol*] (CTT)
RM1..........	Radioman, First Class [*Navy rating*]
RM2..........	Radioman, Second Class [*Navy rating*]
R & M/2.....	RON [*Research Octane Number*] and MON [*Motor Octane Number*] Averaged [*Antiknock index*] [*Fuel technology*]
RM3..........	Radioman, Third Class [*Navy rating*]
RM³	Remote Multimedia Mode [*Army*]
RMA	Racquetball Manufacturers Association (EA)
RMA	Radio-Labeled Monoclonal Antiglobulin [*Clinical chemistry*]
RMA	Radio Manufacturers Association [*Later, Electronic Industries Association*]
RMA	Radiometric Microbiological Assay
RMA	Random Multiple Access
RMA	Reactive Modulation Amplifier
RMA	Rear Maintenance Area [*Military*] [*British*]
RMA	Receiver Measurement Adapter (MCD)
RMA	Reclaim Managers Association [*Defunct*] (EA)
RMA	Regiment de Marche d'Afrique [*African Marching Regiment*] [*French*]
RMA	Regional Manpower Administration
RMA	Registered Medical Assistants [*Later, ARMA*] (EA)
RMA	Reliability, Maintainability, and Availability [*Standards*]
RMA	Reliability and Maintenance Analysis (CAAL)
RMA	Remote Manipulator Arm [*NASA*] (MCD)
RMA	Research and Marketing Act [*1946*]
RMA	Reserve Military Aviator
RMA	Retail Merchants' Association of Canada
RMA	Rhythmic Motor Activity [*Physiology*]
RMA	Rice Millers' Association (EA)
RMA	Right Mentoanterior [*A fetal position*] [*Obstetrics*]
RMA	Robert Morris Associates [*National Association of Bank Loan and Credit Officers*] [*Philadelphia, PA*] (EA)
RMA	Rockefeller Mountains [*Antarctica*] [*Seismograph station code, US Geological Survey*] [*Closed*] (SEIS)
RMA	Rocky Mountain Airways [*Denver, CO*] [*FAA designator*] (FAAC)
RMA	Rocky Mountain Arsenal [*Army*] (AABC)
RMA	Rodeo Media Association (EA)
RMA	Roma [*Australia*] [*Airport symbol*] (OAG)
RMA	Rosin Mildly Activated [*Standard material for soldering*]
RMA	Royal Malta Artillery [*Military unit*] [*British*]
RMA	Royal Marine Academy [*British*]
RMA	Royal Marine Artillery [*Obsolete*] [*British*]
RMA	Royal Marines Association [*British military*] (DMA)
RMA	Royal Military Academy [*For cadets of Royal Engineers and Royal Artillery; frequently referred to as Woolwich*] [*British*]
RMA	Royal Military Asylum [*British*]
RMA	Royal Musical Association [*British*]
RMA	Royal Musical Association. Proceedings [*A publication*]
RMA	Rubber Manufacturers Association (EA)
RMAAS.....	Reactivity Monitoring and Alarm System [*Nuclear energy*] (NRCH)
RMAB	Royal Marines Auxiliary Brigade [*British military*] (DMA)
RMAC	Remote Master Aircraft (MCD)
RMACHA ...	Rocky Mountain Automated Clearing House Association
R-MAD......	Reactor Maintenance, Assembly, and Disassembly
RMAF.......	Royal Moroccan Air Force
RMAFA.....	Revista. Union Matematica Argentina y Asociacion Fisica Argentina [*A publication*]
RMAL	Revised Master Allowance List [*Military*] (AFIT)
RMALAN ...	Royal Malaysian Navy
RMAO.......	Resources Management and Administration Office [*Environmental Protection Agency*] (GFGA)
RMA Proc ...	Royal Musical Association. Proceedings [*A publication*]
RMARC	Royal Musical Association. Research Chronicle [*A publication*]
RMA Res Chron ...	RMA [*Royal Musical Association*] Research Chronicle [*A publication*]
RMA Research ...	Royal Musical Association. Research Chronicle [*A publication*]
RMA Research Chron ...	RMA [*Royal Musical Association*] Research Chronicle [*A publication*]
R Mark Agric Econ ...	Review of the Marketing and Agricultural Economy [*A publication*]
R Marketing & Ag Econ ...	Review of Marketing and Agricultural Economics [*A publication*] (APTA)
R Marketing and Agric Econ ...	Review of Marketing and Agricultural Economics [*A publication*]
RMA Rubber ...	RMA [*Rubber Manufacturers Association*] Industry Rubber Report [*A publication*]
RMAS.......	Royal Military Academy Sandhurst [*British*]
R MAST	Radio Mast
RMAT	Royal Marine Advisory Team [*British military*] (DMA)

RMA Tire .. RMA [*Rubber Manufacturers Association*] Tire and Innertube Statistical Report [*A publication*]
RMATS-1 ... Remote Maintenance, Administration, and Traffic System-1 [*Telecommunications*] (TEL)
RMAX .... Range, Maximum
RMAZDB ... Revista. Museo Argentino de Ciencias Naturales Bernardino Rivadavia e Instituto Nacional de Investigacion de las Ciencias Naturales. Zoologia [*A publication*]
RMB .... Radio Marker Beacon
RMB .... Radio Marketing Bureau [*British*] (CB)
RMB .... Rambler Oil Co. [*Toronto Stock Exchange symbol*]
RMB .... Rand Merchant Bank [*South Africa*]
RMB .... Raw Materials Board [*of the Reconstruction Finance Corp.*]
RMB .... Renminbi [*Monetary unit*] [*China*]
RMB .... Roadside Mailbox (ADA)
RMB .... Rocky Mountain Motor Tariff Bureau, Inc., Denver CO [*STAC*]
RMB .... Rombauer [*Missouri*] [*Seismograph station code, US Geological Survey*] (SEIS)
RMB .... Royal Marine Bands [*British military*] (DMA)
RMB .... Royal Marines Badge [*British*]
RMBC .... Regional Marine Biological Centre [*UNESCO*] (MSC)
RMBC .... Rocky Mountain Beverage Co. [*NASDAQ symbol*] (NQ)
RMBF .... Required Myocardial Blood Flow [*Cardiology*]
RMBI .... Canadian Risk Management and Business Insurance [*A publication*]
RM Bl .... Reichministerialblatt [*A publication*]
R-MBP-A .. Rat-Mannose-Binding Protein A
R-MBP-C .. Rat-Mannose-Binding Protein C
RMBPD .... Royal Marine Boom Patrol Detachment [*World War II*]
RMC .... American Restaurant Partners Ltd. [*AMEX symbol*] (SPSG)
RMC .... Captain of Royal Marines [*Military*] [*British*]
RMC .... [*Robert M.*] Charlton's Georgia Reports [*1811-37*] [*A publication*] (DLA)
RMC .... Chief Radioman [*Navy rating*]
RMC .... Radiation Management Corp. (NRCH)
RMC .... Radiation Material Corp.
RMC .... Radio Management Control (MCD)
RMC .... Radio Monte Carlo [*Monaco*] (EY)
RMC .... Randolph-Macon College [*Virginia*]
RMC .... Rat Mast Cell
RMC .... Raytheon Manufacturing Co. (MCD)
RM & C .... Reactor Monitoring and Control [*Nuclear energy*] (NRCH)
RMC .... Ready Mixed Cement [*Commercial firm*] [*British*]
RMC .... Ready Mixed Concrete (ADA)
RMC .... Recursive Monte Carlo Method
RMC .... Reduced Material Condition (NVT)
RMC .... Redundancy Management Control (MCD)
RMC .... Regional Media Center
RMC .... Regular Military Compensation (AABC)
RMC .... Regulated Motor Carriers
RMC .... Relative-Motion Control [*Microcopy*]
RMC .... Remote Manual Control (NRCH)
RMC .... Remote Multiplexer Combiner (MCD)
RMC .... Rendezvous Mercury Capsule [*NASA*] (AAG)
RMC Tire ... Repair Manufacturer Codes
RMC .... Representative in Medical Council [*Royal College of Physicians*] [*British*] (ROG)
RMC .... Republican Mainstream Committee (EA)
RMC .... Republican Majority Coalition [*Republican party faction*]
RMC ... Resident Management Corp. [*Public housing*]
RMC .... Residential Manpower Center [*Job Corps*]
RMC .... Resource Management Consultants [*Salem, NH*] [*Telecommunications*] (TSSD)
RMC .... Resource Management Corp.
RMC .... Return to Military Control (AABC)
RMC .... Revolutionary Military Council [*Grenada*]
RMC .... Revue du Marche Commun [*Review of the Common Market*] [*French*]
RMC .... Revue Musicale [*A publication*]
RMC .... Rocket Motor Case
RMC .... Rocky Mountain College [*Billings, MT*]
RMC .... Rod Memory Computer [*NCR Corp.*]
RMC .... Rosemont College, Rosemont, PA [*OCLC symbol*] (OCLC)
RMC .... Rotary Mirror Camera
RMC .... Rotating Modulation Collimator
RMC .... Royal Marine Commandos [*British*]
RMC .... Royal Military College [*For army cadets; often referred to as Sandhurst*] [*British*]
RMC .... Rural Manpower Center [*Michigan State University*]
RMCA ...... Right Middle Cerebral Artery [*Anatomy*]
RMCAT ..... Ralph Mayer Center for Artists' Techniques [*University of Delaware*] [*Newark*] [*Information service or system*] (IID)
RMCB ...... Registered Mail Central Bureau [*Later, RMIA*] (EA)
RMCB ...... Reserve Mobile Construction Battalion
RMCB ...... Royal Marine Commando Brigade [*British*]
RMCC ...... RADAR Monitor and Control Console [*Military*] (CAAL)
RMCC ...... Rotating Map, Cursor Centered [*Automotive engineering*]
RMCC .... Royal Military College of Canada [*British military*] (DMA)

RMCC .... Ryan and Moody's English Crown Cases [*A publication*] (DLA)
R & MCC... Ryan and Moody's English Crown Cases Reserved [*A publication*] (DLA)
RMCCR ..... Ryan and Moody's English Crown Cases [*A publication*] (DLA)
RMCCSC .. Raw Materials Committee of the Commonwealth Supply Council [*British*] [*World War II*]
RMCDC .... Rocky Mountain Child Development Center [*University of Colorado*] [*Research center*] (RCD)
RM-CEAAL ... Red de Mujeres del Consejo de Educacion de Adultos de Americana Latina [*Women's Network of the Council for Adult Education in Latin America - WN-CAELA*] [*Quito, Ecuador*] (EAIO)
RMCF .... Rocky Mountain Chocolate Factory, Inc. [*Durango, CO*] [*NASDAQ symbol*] (NQ)
R & McG.... Income Tax Decisions of Australasia (Ratcliffe and McGrath) [*A publication*] (APTA)
R & McG Ct of Rev ... Court of Review Decisions (Ratcliffe and McGrath) [*A publication*]
R M Ch ...... [*Robert M.*] Charlton's Georgia Reports [*1811-37*] [*A publication*] (DLA)
R M Charlt (GA) ... [*Robert M.*] Charlton's Georgia Reports [*1811-37*] [*A publication*] (DLA)
RMCI........ Right Management Consultants, Inc. [*Philadelphia, PA*] [*NASDAQ symbol*] (NQ)
RMCL........ Recommended Maximum Contaminant Level [*Environmental Protection Agency*]
RMCM ...... Master Chief Radioman [*Navy rating*]
RMCM ...... Reduced Material Condition Maintenance (MCD)
RMCM ...... Return Material Credit Memo
RMCM ...... Rotating Map, Cursor Moving [*Automotive engineering*]
RMCM ...... Royal Manchester College of Music [*British*]
RMCMI..... Rocky Mountain Coal Mining Institute (EA)
RMCO .... Raymond Manufacturing Co.
RMCOEH ... Rocky Mountain Center for Occupational and Environmental Health [*University of Utah*] [*Research center*] (RCD)
RMCP........ Rat Mast Cell Protease [*An enzyme*]
RMCPA...... Rocky Mountain College Placement Association (AEBS)
RMCS........ Range Monitoring and Control Subsystem (MCD)
RMCS........ Reactor Manual Control System [*Nuclear energy*] (NRCH)
RMCS........ Remote Monitoring and Control System [*Telecommunications*]
RMCS........ Royal Medical and Chirurgical Society [*British*] (ROG)
RMCS........ Royal Military College of Science [*British*]
RMCS........ Senior Chief Radioman [*Navy rating*]
RMCSF ...... Recombinant Macrophage Colony-Stimulating Factor [*Biochemistry*]
RMCT .... Research Monographs in Cell and Tissue Physiology [*Elsevier Book Series*] [*A publication*]
RMCUSA ... Riley Motor Club USA (EA)
RMD......... Raw Materials Department [*Ministry of Supply*] [*British*]
RMD......... Reaction Motors Division (SAA)
RMD......... Ready Money Down [*Immediate payment*]
RMD......... Repair and Modification Directive (AAG)
RMD......... Retromanubrial Dullness [*Medicine*]
RMD......... Right Manubrial Dullness [*Anatomy*] (MAE)
RMDA ...... Request for Manufacturing Development Authorization (AAG)
RMDHS...... Regional Model Data Handling System [*Environmental Protection Agency*] (GFGA)
RMDI .... Radio Magnetic Deviation Indicator (AAG)
RM Dig...... Rapalje and Mack's Digest of Railway Law [*A publication*] (DLA)
RMDIR ...... Remove Directory [*Data processing*]
RMDP .... Rural Manpower Development Program
Rmdr .... Remainder (DLA)
RMDU....... Remote Multiplexer/Demultiplexer Unit (SSD)
RME .... Radiation Monitoring Equipment
RME .... Railway Age [*A publication*]
RME .... Raw Materials (MCD)
RME .... Receptor Mediated Endocytosis [*Biochemistry*]
RME .... Reflex Milk Ejection (OA)
RME .... Relay Mirror Experiment
RME .... Request Monitor Entry [*Data processing*]
RME .... Resident Maintenance Engineer (NATG)
RME .... Rocket Mission Evaluator (MCD)
RME .... Rocky Mountain Energy [*Vancouver Stock Exchange symbol*]
RME .... Rome, NY [*Location identifier*] [*FAA*] (FAAL)
RME .... Royal Marine Engineers [*British*]
RMEC .... Refractory Metals Electrofinishing Corp.
RMEC .... Regional Medical Education Center [*Veterans Administration*] (GFGA)
RMED .... R-Med International, Inc. [*NASDAQ symbol*] (NQ)
RMED .... Recruit, Retrain, Reemploy Medics [*Program*]
RMED .... Rocky Mountain Medical Corp. [*Greenwood Village, CO*] [*NASDAQ symbol*] (NQ)
RMedSoc ... Royal Medical Society, Edinburgh
RMEF........ Rocky Mountain Elk Foundation (EA)
RMEL....... Rocky Mountain Educational Laboratory [*Closed*]
RMELB ...... Radio Mentor Electronic [*A publication*]
R Melb Hosp Q ... Royal Melbourne Hospital. Quarterly [*A publication*]

R Melbourne Hosp Clin Rep ... Royal Melbourne Hospital. Clinical Reports [*A publication*]
RMEPDZ ... Romanian Journal of Morphology, Embryology, and Physiology [*A publication*]
RMER ...... Resource Management Expense Reporting System (MCD)
RMERA..... Rumanian Medical Review [*A publication*]
R Metaphys ... Review of Metaphysics [*A publication*]
R Met S...... Royal Meteorological Society [*British*]
RMF .... RAC Income Fund [*NYSE symbol*] (SPSG)
RMF .... Raw Materials Finance Department [*Ministry of Supply*] [*British*]
RMF .... RCS [*Reaction Control System*] Module Forward [*NASA*] (NASA)
RMF .... Reactivity Measurement Facility [*Nuclear energy*]
RMF .... Reamfixture (MCD)
RMF .... Reduced Magnetic Field [*Data processing*] (PCM)
RMF .... Reflectivity Measuring Facility
RMF .... Research Management. The International Journal of Research Management [*A publication*]
RMF .... Residual Master File [*Data processing*]
RMF .... Resource Measurement Facility [*Data processing*]
RMF .... Reymann Memorial Farms [*West Virginia University*] [*Research center*] (RCD)
RMF .... Royal Munster Fusiliers [*Military unit*] [*British*]
RMFA....... Royal Malta Fencible Artillery [*British military*] (DMA)
RMFC....... Rachel Minke Fan Club (EA)
R M F C..... Recherches sur la Musique Francaise Classique [*A publication*]
RMFC....... Ronnie McDowell Fan Club (EA)
RMFC....... Ronnie Milsap Fan Club (EA)
RMFFA ..... Raumfahrtforschung [*A publication*]
RMFMA.... Rock Mechanics [*A publication*]
RMFVR..... Royal Marine Forces Volunteer Reserve [*Obsolete*] [*British*]
RMFZA ..... Radovi Medicinskogo Fakulteta u Zagrebu [*A publication*]
RMG.......... RADAR Mapper Gapfiller
RMG.......... RAL Marketing Group, Inc. [*Vancouver Stock Exchange symbol*]
RMG.......... Ranging Machine Gun [*British military*] (DMA)
RMG.......... Recommended for Medal and Gratuity [*British*]
RMG.......... Relative-Motion Gauge
RMG.......... Resource Management Group [*Military*]
RMG.......... Right Main Gear (MCD)
RMG.......... Rome [*Georgia*] [*Seismograph station code, US Geological Survey*] (SEIS)
RMG.......... Rome [*Georgia*] [*Airport symbol*] [*Obsolete*] (OAG)
RMG.......... Ronald Martin Groome [*Commercial firm*] [*British*]
RMG.......... Royal Marine Gunner [*British*]
RMG.......... Russkaya Muzikal'naya Gazeta [*A publication*]
RMGCA .... Rocky Mountain Association of Geologists. Field Conference [*A publication*]
RMGF .... RADAR Mapper, Gap Filler (MSA)
RMGO....... Regional Military Government Officer [*World War II*]
RMGQA.... Records Management Quarterly [*A publication*]
RMH .... Rabbit-Mouse Hybridomas [*Immunochemistry*]
RMH .... Refrigerator Mechanical Household (MSA)
RMH .... Reserve Bank of Malawi. Financial and Economic Review [*A publication*]
RMH .... Riemann's Metrical Hypothesis [*Mathematics*]
RMHA....... Rocky Mountain Horse Association (EA)
RMHCSDI ... Robert Maynard Hutchins Center for the Study of Democratic Institutions (EA)
RMHDDHG ... Regiere Mich Herr durch Deinen Heiligen Geist [*Rule Me, Lord, Through Thy Holy Spirit*] [*German*] [*Motto of Ann, Margravine of Brandenburg (1575-1612)*]
RMHF....... Rat, Mouse, and Hamster Fanciers (EA)
RMHI........ Religious and Mental Health Inventory
RMHI........ Rocky Mountain Helicopters [*NASDAQ symbol*] (SPSG)
RMHPB ... Reports on Mathematical Physics [*A publication*]
RMI.......... Merrell-National Laboratories [*Research code symbol*]
RMI.......... Rack Manufacturers Institute (EA)
RMI.......... Radio Magnetic Indicator
RMI.......... Radiological Monitoring for Instructors [*Civil Defense*]
RMI.......... Reich Ministry of Interior
RMI.......... Release of Material for Issue
RMI.......... Reliability Maturity Index [*Polaris*]
RMI.......... Reliability Monitoring Index
RMI.......... Religious of Mary Immaculate [*Roman Catholic women's religious order*]
RMI.......... Remote Magnetic Indication
RMI.......... Renewable Materials Institute [*College of Environmental Science and Forestry at Syracuse*] [*Research center*] (RCD)
RMI.......... Repair and Maintenance Instruction [*Military*]
RMI.......... Repairs, Maintenance, and Improvements
RMI.......... Republic of the Marshall Islands
RMI.......... Research Monographs in Immunology [*Elsevier Book Series*] [*A publication*]
RMI.......... Residential Mortgage Investments, Inc. [*AMEX symbol*] (SPSG)
RMI.......... Richardson-Merrell, Inc. [*Later, Richardson-Vicks, Inc.*]
RMI.......... Rocket Motor Igniter
RMI.......... Roll Manufacturers Institute (EA)

RMI .... Rotonics Manufacturing [*Formerly, Koala Technologies*] [*AMEX symbol*] (SPSG)
RMI .... Route Monitoring Information [*Telecommunications*] (TEL)
RMI .... Rural Ministry Institute (EA)
RMIA .... Rattan Manufacturers and Importers Association
RMIA .... Registered Mail Insurance Association (EA)
RMIC........ Research Materials Information Center [*ORNL*]
RMICBM ... Road Mobile Intercontinental Ballistic Missile
RMIFC....... Reba McEntire International Fan Club (EA)
RMII......... Reference Method Item Identification [*DoD*]
R Mil Coll Can Civ Eng Res Rep ... Royal Military College of Canada. Civil Engineering Research Report [*A publication*]
RMIM ...... Repeater Media Interface Module [*Telecommunications*]
RMIMDC ... Research Monographs in Immunology [*Elsevier Book Series*] [*A publication*]
RMI/MO .. Routine Manual In / Manual Out [*Military*] (DNAB)
R/MIN ...... Revolutions per Minute
RMIND...... Reviews in Mineralogy [*A publication*]
RMIP........ Reentry Measurements Instrumentation Package
RMIS........ Readiness Management Information System [*Military*] (AABC)
RMIS........ Resource Management Information System [*Environmental Protection Agency*]
RMIT........ Remittance Technologies Corp. [*NASDAQ symbol*] (NQ)
RMIT........ Rolland Maintenance Institutional Trainer [*Army*]
RMI Ti....... RMI Titanium Co. [*Associated Press abbreviation*] (APAG)
RMJ.......... Ramjet (MSA)
RMJ.......... Rumoi [*Japan*] [*Seismograph station code, US Geological Survey*] (SEIS)
RMJM....... Recluse Missionaries of Jesus and Mary [*Roman Catholic women's religious order*]
RMJMA.... Rocky Mountain Journal of Mathematics [*A publication*]
RMK......... Remark (AFM)
RMK......... Renmark [*Australia*] [*Airport symbol*] (OAG)
RMK......... Retrofit Modification Kit
RMK......... Rhesus Monkey Kidney [*Medicine*]
RMK......... Robert-Mark [*AMEX symbol*] (SPSG)
RMK....... Roxmark Mines Ltd. [*Toronto Stock Exchange symbol*]
R Mkting Agric Econ ... Review of Marketing and Agricultural Economics [*A publication*]
RMKUA .... Report. Research Institute for Applied Mechanics (Kyushu University) [*A publication*]
RML .... Lieutenant, Royal Marines [*Navy*] [*British*] (ROG)
RML .... RADAR Mapper, Long Range
RML .... RADAR Microwave Link (IEEE)
RML .... Range Measurements Laboratory [*Air Force*]
RML .... Refresher Maintenance Lab
RML .... Regional Medical Library
RML .... Relational Machine Language
RML .... Remote Maintenance Line [*Bell Laboratories*]
RML .... Remote Measurements Laboratory
RML .... Rescue Motor Launch [*Air/sea rescue*] [*Navy*]
RML .... Restricted Maximum Likelihood [*Statistics*]
RML .... Review of Metal Literature [*American Society for Metals*] [*A publication*]
RML .... Rifled Muzzle-Loading [*Gun*]
RML .... Right Mediolateral [*Episiotomy*] [*Obstetrics*]
RML .... Right Mentolateral [*Episiotomy*] [*Obstetrics*]
RML .... Right Middle Lobe [*Lungs*]
RML .... Rock Mechanics Laboratory [*Pennsylvania State University*] [*Research center*] (RCD)
RML .... Rocky Mountain Laboratories [*National Institutes of Health*]
RML .... Rotating Mirror LASER
RML .... Russell Corp. [*NYSE symbol*] (SPSG)
RMLA .... Rocky Mountain Lama Association (EA)
RMLC....... Royal Marine Labour Corps [*British military*] (DMA)
RMLE........ Regiment de Marche de la Legion Etrangere [*Foreign Legion Marching Regiment*] [*French*]
RMLI........ Royal Marine Light Infantry [*Obsolete*] [*British*]
RML IV ..... Mid-Atlantic Regional Medical Library Program [*Library network*]
RMLO ...... Reports Management Liaison Officer [*Defense Supply Agency*]
RMLP........ Regional Medical Library Program [*Department of Health and Human Services*]
RMLR....... RADAR Mapper, Long Range (MSA)
RMLR....... RADAR Microwave Link Repeater (FAAC)
RMLR....... Rocky Mountain Law Review [*Later, University of Colorado. Law Review*] [*A publication*]
RMLT........ RADAR Microwave Link Terminal (FAAC)
RMM........ RADAR Map Matching
RMM........ Rapid Micromedia Method [*Analytical biochemistry*]
RMM Ti...... Read-Mostly Memory [*Data processing*]
RMM........ Read-Mostly Mode [*Data processing*]
RMM........ Remote Maintenance Monitor [*Data processing*] (MCD)
RMM........ Rifle Marksman
RMM........ Ripple Mark Meter
RMM........ Rosedale Mennonite Missions (EA)
RMMC...... Regiment Materiel Management Center [*Military*] (AABC)
RMMC...... Rocky Mountain Mapping Center [*Colorado*]
RMMDBO ... Royal Marine Mobile Defended Base Organisation [*British military*] (DMA)

RMMEA ... Rolling Mill Machinery and Equipment Association [*Defunct*] (EA)
RMMI .... Rocky Mountain Minerals, Inc. [*NASDAQ symbol*] (NQ)
RMMJA.... Rocky Mountain Medical Journal [*A publication*]
RMMLF... Rocky Mountain Mineral Law Foundation (EA)
RMMLR... Rocky Mountain Mineral Law Review [*A publication*] (DLA)
RMMND... Rocky Mountain Mineral Law Newsletter [*A publication*]
RMMP ...... Riceland Mosquito Management Plan [*Department of Agriculture*]
RM/MS & C ... Redundancy Management/Moding, Sequencing, and Control (MCD)
RMMTB.... Rocky Mountain Motor Tariff Bureau, Inc.
RMMU...... Removable Media Memory Units
RMN......... Registered Mental Nurse
RMN......... Remain (FAAC)
RMN......... Reserve Material [*Account*] Navy
RMN......... Richard Milhous Nixon [*US president, 1913-*]
RMN......... Roman Corp. Ltd. [*Toronto Stock Exchange symbol*]
RMNac...... Revista. Museo Nacional [*A publication*]
R & MNP... Ryan and Moody's English Nisi Prius Reports [*A publication*] (DLA)
RMNS .... Royal Malayan Navy Ship [*British military*] (DMA)
RMNUBP ... Research Methods in Neurochemistry [*A publication*]
RMNZA .... Rudy i Metale Niezelazne [*A publication*]
RMO......... RADAR Master Oscillator
RMO......... RADAR Material Office [*Navy*] (MCD)
RMO......... Radio Material Office [*or Officer*] [*Navy*] (IEEE)
RMO......... Ramsey-HMO, Inc. [*NYSE symbol*] (SPSG)
RMO......... Records Management Office [*or Officer*] [*Military*] (AFM)
RMO......... Recruitment and Manning Organization [*WSA*]
RMO......... Refined Menhaden Oil [*Food science*]
RMO......... Regimental Medical Officer (NATG)
RMO......... Regimental Munitions Officer [*Army*]
RMO......... Regional Management Officer [*Social Security Administration*]
RMO......... Regional Medical Officer [*British*]
RMO......... Reports Management Officer [*DoD*]
RMO......... Resident Medical Officer [*British*]
RMO......... Resources Management Office [*NASA*] (KSC)
RMO......... Rochester-Mercier [*New York*] [*Seismograph station code, US Geological Survey*] [*Closed*] (SEIS)
RMO......... Rocket Management Office [*Army*] (RDA)
RMO......... Royal Marine Office [*British*]
RM Obs .... Royal Marine Observer [*British military*] (DMA)
RMOC....... Reaction Mechanisms in Organic Chemistry [*Elsevier Book Series*] [*A publication*]
RMOC....... Recommended Maintenance Operation Chart [*Army*] (AABC)
RMOGA.... Rocky Mountain Oil and Gas Association
RMOKHS ... Religious and Military Order of Knights of the Holy Sepulchre (EA)
RMON....... Resident Monitor
RMON MIB ... Remote Network Monitoring Management Information Base [*Telecommunications*]
R MON RE(M) ... Royal Monmouthshire Royal Engineers (Militia) [*British military*] (DMA)
RMOS .... Refractory Metal-Oxide Semiconductor (IEEE)
RMP .... International Migration [*A publication*]
RMP .... Radio Motor Patrol [*New York police cars*]
RMP .... Rainform Message Processing (MCD)
RMP .... Raman Microprobe [*Spectrometer*]
RMP .... Rampart [*Alaska*] [*Airport symbol*] (OAG)
RMP .... Rampart Resources Ltd. [*Vancouver Stock Exchange symbol*]
RMP .... Range Maintenance Plan (MCD)
RMP .... Rapidly Miscible Pool [*Medicine*] (MAE)
RMP .... Rate Measuring Package (MCD)
RMP .... Rated Maximum Pressure (SAA)
RMP .... Receptor-Mediated Permeabilizer [*Medicine*]
RMP .... Reduction of the Membrane Potential
RMP .... Reentry Measurement Program [*Military*]
RMP .... Refiner Mechanical Pulp [*Papermaking*]
RMP .... Regional Medical Program
RMP .... Registered Medical Practitioner [*British*] (ROG)
RMP .... Reprogrammable Microprocessor
RMP .... Research Management Plan
RMP .... Research and Microfilm Publications
RMP .... Resident Manufacturing Plan (SAA)
RMP .... Resting Membrane Potential [*Neuroelectrochemistry*]
RMP .... Revised Management Procedure
RMP .... Rheinisches Museum fuer Philologie [*A publication*]
RMP .... Rifampin [*Also, R/AMP, RF, RIF*] [*Bactericide*]
RMP .... Right Mentoposterior [*A fetal position*] [*Obstetrics*]
RMP .... RMP: Rural Marketing and Policy [*A publication*]
RMP .... Rocket Motor Plume
RMP .... Rocket Motor Propellant (MUGU)
RMP .... Rocketdyne Mortar Propellant (MCD)
RMP .... Rome [*Monte Porzio Catone*] [*Italy*] [*Seismograph station code, US Geological Survey*] (SEIS)
RMP .... Round Maximum Pressure (NATG)
RMP .... Royal Marine Police [*British military*] (DMA)
RMP .... Royal Military Police [*British*]
RMPA .... Rocky Mountain Psychological Association (MCD)
RMPA .... Royal Medico-Psychological Association [*British*]

RMPaul ..... Revista. Museu Paulista [*A publication*]
RMPE........ Root Mean Percentage Error [*Statistics*]
RMPF........ Rocky Mountain Poison Foundation
RMPI......... Remote Memory Port Interface
RMPIA...... Razrabotka Mestorozhdenii Poleznykh Iskopaemykh [*A publication*]
RMPM ...... Rich Man, Poor Man [*Book title*]
RMPM ...... Royal Mail Parcels Marketing [*British Post Office*]
RMPO....... Ramapo Financial Corp. [*NASDAQ symbol*] (NQ)
RM & PP ... Raw Material and Purchase Parts (MCD)
RMPP........ Risk Management and the Prevention Plan [*Hazardous materials*]
RMPR....... Rassemblement Mahorais pour la Republique [*Mayotte Rally for the Republic*] [*Political party*] (PPW)
RMPR....... Rated Mobilization and Professional Resource (MUGU)
RMPR....... Revised Maximum Price Regulation [*World War II*]
RMPS........ Regional Medical Programs Service [*Health Services and Mental Health Administration, HEW*]
RMPTC..... Royal Military Police Training Centre [*British*]
RMQ......... Records Management Quarterly [*A publication*]
RMQM....... Quarter-Master, Royal Marines [*Navy*] [*British*] (ROG)
RMR......... Malraux Society (EAIO)
RMR......... Rapid Memory Reload (MCD)
RMR......... Reamer [*Design engineering*]
RMR......... Reference Mixture Radio (KSC)
RMR......... Reflector Moderated Reactor (AAG)
RMR......... Regional Maintenance Representative [*Military*]
RMR......... Remote Map Reader
RMR......... Reserve Minority Report [*Army*]
RMR......... Resource Management Review [*Military*]
RMR......... Resource Mortgage Capital [*Formerly, RAC Mortgage Investment*] [*NYSE symbol*] (SPSG)
RMR......... Resting Metabolic Rate [*Physiology*]
RMR......... Right Medial Rectus [*Eye anatomy*]
RMR......... Rock-Mass Rating [*Mining technology*]
RMR......... Rocky Mountain Law Review [*Later, University of Colorado. Law Review*] [*A publication*]
RMR......... Rocky Mountain Review [*A publication*]
RMR......... Rocky Mountain Review of Language and Literature [*A publication*]
RMR......... Rotation Magnitude Ratio
RMR......... Rotational Magnetic-Dipole Radiation [*Astronomy*]
RMR......... Royal Malayan Regiment [*British military*] (DMA)
RMR......... Royal Marines Reserve [*British*]
RMR......... Royal Montreal Regiment [*Military unit*]
RMRA...... Royal Marines Rifle Association [*British military*] (DMA)
RMREL..... Rocky Mountain Regional Education Laboratory (AEBS)
RMRHB.... Rheumatology and Rehabilitation [*A publication*]
RMRM ..... Radioactive Materials Reference Manual (NRCH)
RMRO....... Royal Marine Routine Orders [*British military*] (DMA)
RMROCK ... Rocket Motors Records Office Center [*Navy*]
RMRS........ Remote Meter Resetting System [*Postage meter*]
RMRS........ Repeatable Maintenance and Recall System (NASA)
RMS .... RADAR Maintenance Spares (NG)
RMS .... RADAR Manual System (DNAB)
RMS .... RADAR Mapping Set [*or System*]
RMS .... Radian Means per Second (NASA)
RMS .... Radiation and Meteoroid Satellite [*NASA*]
RMS .... Radio Marker Station
RMS .... Radio and Microwave Systems [*British*]
RMS .... Radiological Monitoring System
RMS .... Radiology Management System
RMS .... Radiometric Sextant Subsystem
RMS .... Rail Mail Steamer
RMS .... Railway Mail Service
RMS .... Random Mass Storage [*Data processing*]
RMS .... Random Motion Simulator [*NASA*] (NASA)
RMS .... Range Measuring System [*Air Force*]
RMS .... Range Modification System
RMS .... Rapid Multistream
RMS .... Rathkamp Matchcover Society (EA)
RMS .... Reactor Monitor System (IEEE)
RMS .... Reconnaissance Management System
RMS .... Record Management System
RMS .... Recovery Management Support [*Data processing*]
RMS .... Recruiting Main Station [*Military*]
RMS .... Redundancy Management System [*NASA*] (MCD)
RMS .... Reentry Measurement System
RMS .... Regulatory Manpower System [*Nuclear energy*] (NRCH)
RMS .... Regulatory Monitoring System (NRCH)
RMS .... Rehabilitation Medicine Service [*Veterans Administration*]
RMS .... Reliability and Maintainability Simulator
RMS .... Remote Maintenance System
RMS .... Remote Manipulator Subsystem [*NASA*] (NASA)
RMS .... Remote Manual Switch [*Nuclear energy*] (NRCH)
RMS .... Remote Master Station (MCD)
RMS .... Remote Missile Select
RMS .... Remote Monitor System
RMS .... Renaissance and Modern Studies [*A publication*]
RMS .... Reports Management System [*Office of Management and Budget*] [*Database*]

RMS .... Resource Management Squadron [*Military*]
RMS .... Resources Management Staff [*Environmental Protection Agency*] (GFGA)
RMS .... Resources Management System [*Army*]
RMS .... Respiratory Muscle Strength [*Physiology*]
RMS .... Retromotor Simulator
RMS .... Reusable Multipurpose Spacecraft [*Aerospace*] (IIA)
RMS .... Revenue Management System (ECON)
RMS .... Revised Magnetic Standard
RMS .... Rhabdomyosarcoma [*Also, RHM*] [*Oncology*]
RMS .... Rheometrics Mechanical Spectrometer
RMS .... RMS International [*Later, Diversified Communications Industries*] [*AMEX symbol*] (SPSG)
RMS .... Rocket Management System (MCD)
RMS .... Roll Microwave Sensor
RMS .... Romanian Missionary Society (EA)
RMS .... Root Mean Square [*Physics, statistics*]
RMS .... Royal Mail Service [*British*]
RMS .... Royal Mail Steamship [*British*]
RMS .... Royal Marine Signaller [*British military*] (DMA)
RMS .... Royal Meteorological Society [*British*]
RMS .... Royal Microscopical Society [*British*]
RMS .... Royal Museum of Scotland
RMS .... Royal Society of Miniature Painters, Sculptors, and Gravers [*British*]
RMS .... Rural Manpower Services (OICC)
RMSA....... Rural Music Schools Association [*British*]
RMSA....... Seaman Apprentice, Radioman, Striker [*Navy rating*]
RM/SAD... Remote Motor/Safe and Arming Device
RMSchMus ... Royal Marines School of Music [*British*]
RMSD ...... Root Mean Square Deviation [*Statistics*]
RMSD ...... Royal Mail Special Delivery [*British Post Office facility*] (DCTA)
RMSDS..... Reserve Merchant Ship Defense System [*Navy*] (MCD)
RMSE....... Relative Mean Square Error [*Statistics*]
RMSE....... Root Mean Square Error
RMSF....... Rocky Mountain Spotted Fever
RMSG ...... Resource Management Study Group [*Military*]
RMSI....... Royal Marine Signalling Instructor [*British military*] (DMA)
RMSM ...... Royal Military School of Music [*British*]
RMSN .... Seaman, Radioman, Striker [*Navy rating*]
RMSP....... Refractory Metal Sheet Program [*Navy*] (NG)
RMSP....... Resource and Mission Sponsor Plan [*Navy*]
RMSP....... Royal Mail Steam Packet Co.
RMSP....... Rubber Modified Silica Phenolie
RMSS .... Range Meteorological Sounding System (MCD)
RMSS........ Religious Mercedarians of the Blessed Sacrament [*Roman Catholic women's religious order*]
RMSSJ...... Rocky Mountain Social Science Journal [*A publication*]
RMSt .... Reading Medieval Studies [*A publication*]
RMSU ...... Remote Monitoring Sensor Unit (MCD)
RMSU .... Rocket Motor Switching Unit (MCD)
RMSVP ..... Remote Manipulation Subsystem Verification Plan [*NASA*] (MCD)
RMT .... Radiometric Moon Tracer
RMT .... Rapid Mass Transfer [*Physics*]
RMT .... Rapidly Moving Telescope [*Astronomy*]
RMT .... Rectangular Midwater Trawl (ADA)
RMT .... Registered Massage Therapist
RMT .... Registered Music Teacher
RMT .... Registered Music Therapist
RMT .... Registry of Medical Technologists
RMT .... Remote [*Telecommunications*] (MSA)
RMT .... Remount (WGA)
RMT .... Renal Mesenchymal Tumor [*Oncology*]
RMT .... Research Methods and Techniques
RMT .... Reserve Mechanical Transport [*British military*] (DMA)
RMT .... Resource Management Team (MCD)
RMT .... Retromolar Trigone [*Dentistry*] (MAE)
RMT .... Rework Monitoring Test
RMT .... Right Mentotransverse [*A fetal position*] [*Obstetrics*]
RMTB....... Reconfiguration Maximum Theoretical Bandwidth
RMTC ...... RADAR Maintenance and Test Control (MCD)
RMTC .... Regional Medical Training Center
RMTC .... Rider Motorcycle Touring Club [*Commercial firm*] [*Later, RC*] (EA)
RMTE....... Remote (AAG)
RMTF........ Ready Missile Test Facility [*Military*] (CAAL)
RM Th .... Rechtsgeleerd Magazijn Themis [*A publication*]
RMTH....... Regular Member of the Third House [*Pseudonym used by Dr. Francis Bacon*]
RMTH....... River Mouth [*Board on Geographic Names*]
RMTK ...... Ramtek Corp. [*NASDAQ symbol*] (NQ)
RMTO ...... Regional Motor Transport Officer [*British*] (DCTA)
RMTR .... Redesigned Missile Tracking RADAR [*Army*] (AABC)
RMTS....... Research Member of the Technical Staff
RMTSA..... Revista. Instituto de Medicina Tropical de Sao Paulo [*A publication*]
RMTSDH ... Texas. Agricultural Experiment Station. Research Monograph [*A publication*]
RMU .... Radio Maintenance Unit (DEN)

RMU .... Rainbow Monument [*Utah*] [*Seismograph station code, US Geological Survey*] (SEIS)
RMU......... Reference Measuring Unit (MCD)
RMU......... Remote Maneuvering Unit [*NASA*]
RMU......... Remote Monitoring Unit [*Telecommunications*]
RMU......... Remote Multiplexer Unit [*Data processing*] (KSC)
RMUC...... Reference Measuring Unit Computer
RMUC....... Rocky Mount Undergarment Co., Inc. [*Rocky Mount, NC*] [*NASDAQ symbol*] (NQ)
R-MuLV .... Rauscher Murine Leukemia Virus
R Mus Art Archeol ... Revue. Musee d'Art et d'Archeologie [*A publication*]
R Mus La Plata Antropol ... Revista. Museo de La Plata. Seccion Antropologia [*A publication*]
R Mus Nac ... Revista. Museo Nacional [*A publication*]
RMV .... Reentry Measurement Vehicle [*Military*]
RMV .... Remotely Manned Vehicle
RMV .... Remove (AAG)
RMV .... Respiratory Minute Volume [*Physiology*]
RMV .... Ribgrass Mosaic Virus [*Plant pathology*]
RMVBL..... Removable (AAG)
RMVD....... Removed (AAG)
RMVE .... Regiment de Marche de Volontiers Etrangers [*Foreign Volunteers Marching Regiment*] [*French*]
RMVG....... Removing (AAG)
RMVL .... Removal (AAG)
RMVM...... Review of Medical and Veterinary Mycology [*Database*] [*Commonwealth Mycological Institute*] [*Information service or system*] (CRD)
RMVT .... Repetitive Monomorphic Ventricular Tachycardia [*Cardiology*]
RMW......... Rattlesnake Mountain [*Washington*] [*Seismograph station code, US Geological Survey*] (SEIS)
RMW......... Reactor Makeup Water [*Nuclear energy*] (NRCH)
R/M/W...... Read/Modify/Write
RMW......... Resource Management Wing [*Military*]
RMWAA ... Roadmasters and Maintenance of Way Association of America (EA)
RMWC ...... Randolph-Macon Woman's College [*Virginia*]
RMWO..... Warrant Officer, Royal Marines [*Navy*] [*British*] (ROG)
RMWR..... Religious, Morale, Welfare, and Recreation [*Military*] (AFM)
RMWS ...... Reactor Makeup Water Storage [*Nuclear energy*] (NRCH)
RMWT ..... Reactor Makeup Water Tank [*Nuclear energy*] (NRCH)
RMX .... Resource Management Executive (MCD)
R & My ...... Russell and Mylne's English Chancery Reports [*A publication*] (DLA)
RN............. Compagnia d'Exploitation de Lignes Aeriennes Interieures - Royal Air Inter [*Morocco*] [*ICAO designator*] (FAAC)
RN............. Neptune Radii [*Astronomy*]
RN............. Newport Public Library, Newport, RI [*Library symbol*] [*Library of Congress*] (LCLS)
RN............. Rada Narodowa [*A publication*]
RN............. Radio National [*Australian Broadcasting Corp.*]
RN............. Radio Navigation
RN............. Radionuclide [*Radiology*]
Rn............. Radon [*Chemical element*]
RN............. Random Number (IEEE)
RN............. Rassemblement National [*Canada*] [*Political party*] (PPW)
RN............. Rattus Norvegicus [*The Norway or brown rat*]
RN............. Real Name [*British Library indexing for pseudonymous author*]
RN............. Realta Nuova [*A publication*]
RN............. Reception Nil [*Radio logs*]
RN............. Reception Node
RN............. Record Number [*Online database field identifier*]
RN............. Red Nucleus [*Brain anatomy*]
RN............. Reference Noise [*Telecommunications*]
RN............. Reference Number
RN............. Registered Nurse
RN............. Registered Nurse [*A publication*]
RN............. Registry Number
RN............. Rejection Notice (AAG)
RN............. Release Note [*Shipping*] (DS)
RN............. Removable Needle [*Medicine*]
RN............. Renaissance News [*A publication*]
RN............. Renastera Noastra [*Rumania*] [*A publication*] (BJA)
RN............. Renovacion Nacional [*National Renovation*] [*Chile*] [*Political party*] (EY)
Rn............. Renumbered [*Existing article renumbered*] [*Used in Shepard's Citations*] [*Legal term*] (DLA)
RN............. Research Note
RN............. Revision Notice (KSC)
RN............. Revolucion Nacional [*Spain*] [*Political party*] (EY)
RN............. Reynolds Number [*Viscosity*]
R & N .... Rhodesia and Nyasaland Law Reports [*1956*] [*A publication*] (DLA)
RN............. Richard Nixon [*In book title "RN - The Memoirs of Richard Nixon"*]
RN............. River Name (BJA)
RN............. RJR Nabisco Holdings [*NYSE symbol*] (SPSG)
RN............. Roan (Leather) [*Bookbinding*] (ROG)
RN............. Root Tip Necrosis [*Plant pathology*]
RN............. Rough Notes [*A publication*]
RN............. Royal Name (BJA)

RN............. Royal Navy [British]
RN............. Rubber Non-Continuous Liner (DS)
RN............. Ruin (ROG)
RN............. Ruritan National (EA)
RNA.......... Radio Naval Association [British]
RNA.......... Radio Navigational Aids (NATG)
RNA.......... Radionuclide Angiography [Medicine]
RNA.......... Rassemblement National Arabe [Arab National Rally] [Tunisia] (PD)
RNA.......... Rations Not Available [Military] (AABC)
RNA.......... Recurring Nuisances Act [British]
RNA.......... Regina Resources [Vancouver Stock Exchange symbol]
RNA.......... Registered Nurse Anesthetist
RNA.......... Registered Nursing Assistant
RNA.......... Religion Newswriters Association (EA)
RNA.......... Republic of New Africa (EA)
RNA.......... Research Natural Area [National Science Foundation]
RNA.......... Ribonucleic Acid [Biochemistry, genetics]
RNA.......... Robbery Not Armed
RNA.......... Romantic Novelists' Association [British]
RNA.......... Rotatable Nozzle Assembly
RNA.......... Rough, Noncapsulated, Avirulent [With reference to bacteria]
RNA.......... Royal Naval Association [British military] (DMA)
RNA.......... Royal Neighbors of America (EA)
RNA.......... Royal Netherlands Army
RNA.......... Royal Norwegian Army (MCD)
RNAA....... Radiochemical Neutron Activation Analysis
RNAA....... Radiometric Neutron Activation Analysis
R/NAA ...... Rocketdyne - North American Aviation [Later, Rockwell International Corp.] (AAG)
RNAA....... Russian Nobility Association in America (EA)
RNAAC.... Reference Number Action Activity Code (MCD)
RNAAF..... Royal Norwegian Army and Air Force
RNABC News ... RNABC (Registered Nurses Association of British Columbia) News [A publication]
RNAC....... Remote Network Access Controller
RNAC....... Royal Nepal Airlines Corp.
RNAD....... Royal Naval Armament Depot [British]
RNAEC ..... Rhodesia and Nyasaland Army Educational Corps [British military] (DMA)
RNAF .... Royal Naval Air Force [British]
RNAF .... Royal Netherlands Air Force
RNAF .... Royal Norwegian Air Force
RNAH ...... Royal Naval Auxiliary Hospital [British military] (DMA)
RNAL .... Radionuclear Applications Laboratory [Pennsylvania State University] [Research center] (RCD)
RNAM...... Regional Network for Agricultural Machinery [Institute of Agricultural Engineering and Technology] [Philippines]
RNAMY .... Royal Naval Aircraft Maintenance Yard [British]
RNAO News ... RNAO (Registered Nurses Association of Ontario) News [A publication]
RNAP .... Ribonucleic Acid Polymerase [An enzyme]
RNAPII..... Ribonucleic Acid Polymerase II [An enzyme]
RNar .... Ragioni Narrative [A publication]
RNAS .... Royal Naval Air Service [Precursor of Fleet Air Arm] [British] [Initialism also facetiously translated during World War I as "Really Not a Sailor"]
RNAS .... Royal Naval Air Station [British]
RNASBR... Royal Naval Auxiliary Sick Berth Reserve [British military] (DMA)
RNase .... Ribonuclease [An enzyme]
RNaseP..... Ribonuclease-P [An enzyme]
RNasin ...... Ribonuclease Inhibitor [Biochemistry]
RNATE...... Royal Naval Air Training Establishment [British]
RNAV....... Area Navigation
R-NAV....... Random Navigation
RNAV....... Royal Naval Artillery Volunteers [British]
RNAW...... Royal Naval Aircraft Workshop [British]
RNAY ...... Royal Naval Aircraft Yard [British]
RNB.......... Millville, NJ [Location identifier] [FAA] (FAAL)
RNB.......... Received, Not Billed (AFM)
RNB.......... Renegotiation Board [Terminated, 1979] [Federal government]
RNB.......... Republic New York Corp. [NYSE symbol] (SPSG)
RNB.......... Resonant Nuclear Battery
RNB.......... Ronneby [Sweden] [Airport symbol] (OAG)
RNB.......... Royal Naval Barracks [British]
RNBC....... Royal Naval Beach Commando [British]
RNBD....... Royal North British Dragoons [British military] (DMA)
RNBF....... Royal North British Fusiliers [British military] (DMA)
RNBM...... Radio Noise Burst Monitor (MCD)
RNBM...... Royal Navy Ballistic Missile [British]
RNBO....... Rainbow Technologies, Inc. [NASDAQ symbol] (NQ)
RNBT .... Royal Naval Benevolent Trust [British]
RNBWS..... Royal Naval Bird Watching Society [British]
RNC.......... Little Raleigh [North Carolina] [Seismograph station code, US Geological Survey] (SEIS)
RNC.......... McMinnville, TN [Location identifier] [FAA] (FAAL)
RNC.......... Radio Noncontingent
RNC.......... Rainbow Network Communications [Floral Park, NY] [Telecommunications] (TSSD)
RNC.......... Republican National Committee (EA)

RNC.......... Request Next Character
RNC.......... Romanian National Council (EA)
RNC.......... Royal Naval College [For future officers; often spoken of as Dartmouth] [British]
RNC.......... Rumanian National Committee [Later, Romanian National Tourist Office] (EA)
RNCA .... Rhodesia and Nyasaland Court of Appeal Law Reports [A publication] (DLA)
RNCBC...... Reserve Naval Construction Battalion Center (DNAB)
RNCBCDET ... Reserve Naval Construction Battalion Center Detachment (DNAB)
RNCBMU ... Reserve Naval Construction Battalion Maintenance Unit (DNAB)
RNCC .... Reference Number Category Code (MCD)
RNCC .... Royal Naval College of Canada [1911-1922]
RNCF........ Read Natural Childbirth Foundation (EA)
RNCH....... Ranch (MCD)
RNCM....... Royal Northern College of Music [British]
RNColl...... Royal Naval College, Greenwich [British]
RNCR .... Reserve Naval Construction Regiment (DNAB)
RN & CR... Ryde, Newport & Cowes Railway [British]
RNCSIR .... Royal Norwegian Council for Scientific and Industrial Research (EAIO)
RNCT .... Reports of the Working Committees. Northeast Conference on the Teaching of Foreign Languages [A publication]
RNCV .... Radio Nacional de Cabo Verde [National Radio of Cape Verde] (EY)
RNCV .... Royal Navy Coast Volunteers [British military] (DMA)
RNCVR .... Royal Naval Canadian Volunteer Reserve [World War I]
RND.......... Radical Neck Dissection [Medicine]
RND.......... Random
RND......... Rassemblement National pour la Democratie [Benin] [Political party] (EY)
RND.......... Rassemblement National Democratique [National Democratic Rally] [Senegal] [Political party] (PPW)
RND.......... Real-Fluid Nonisentropic Decompression [Engineering]
RND.......... Rocznik Naukowo-Dydaktyczny [A publication]
RND.......... Round
RND.......... Royal Naval Division [British]
RND.......... San Antonio, TX [Location identifier] [FAA] (FAAL)
RNDH ...... Royal North Devon Hussars [British military] (DMA)
RNDM...... Random (MSA)
RNDM...... Random Access, Inc. [NASDAQ symbol] (NQ)
RNDPD..... Roundup [United States] [A publication]
RNDQ....... Royal Naval Detention Quarter [British] (DI)
RNDr .... Doctor of Natural Sciences
RNDZ....... Rendezvous (KSC)
RNE........... Aspen, CO [Location identifier] [FAA] (FAAL)
RNE........... Roanne [France] [Airport symbol] (OAG)
RNEC .... Royal Naval Engineering College [British]
RNEColl ... Royal Naval Engineering College [British]
RNEE .... Royal Navy Equipment Exhibition [British]
RNEIA....... Royal Netherlands East Indies Army
RNEIAF ... Royal Netherlands East Indies Air Force
RNEIN ...... Royal Netherlands East Indies Navy
RNERL...... Radiochemistry and Nuclear Engineering Research Laboratory [National Environmental Research Center]
RNES........ Royal Naval Engineering Service [British]
RNETA...... Royal Naval Endurance Triathlon Association [British]
RNEW ...... Religious Network for Equality for Women (EA)
RNF .... Radial Nerve Factor [of sea urchin]
RNF .... Radio Noise Figure (CET)
RNF .... Receiver Noise Figure
RNF .... Refounded National Party [South Africa] [Political party] (EAIO)
RNF .... Refracted Near Field [Optics]
RNF .... Royal Naval Fund [British] (DAS)
RNF .... Royal Northumberland Fusiliers [Military unit] [British]
RNFC....... Reference Number Format Code (MCD)
RNFC....... Royal Naval Film Corp. [British military] (DMA)
RNFL....... Rainfall (FAAC)
RNFL....... Retinal Nerve Fiber Layer [Anatomy]
RNFP....... RADAR Not Functioning Properly [Military] (AFIT)
RNG.......... Army National Guard (FAAC)
RNG.......... Radio Range
RNG.......... Random Number Generator [Parapsychology]
RNG.......... Range [or Ranging] (AAG)
RNG.......... Ranging Noise Generator
RNG.......... Reference Noise Generator
RNG.......... Regulations under the Natural Gas Act
RNG.......... Running
RNGG....... Ringing (MSA)
RNGHQ .... Royal Navy General Headquarters [British]
RNGLND.. Rangeland
RNGM...... Royal North Gloucestershire Militia [British military] (DMA)
RNGMA.... Refiner and Natural Gasoline Manufacturer [A publication]
RNG RT .... Range Rate (MCD)
RNGT....... Renegotiate
RNGYA..... Rhinology [A publication]
RNH .... New Richmond, WI [Location identifier] [FAA] (FAAL)
RNH .... Royal Naval Hospital [British]

RNHA .... Republican National Hispanic Assembly of the United States (EA)
RNHi .... Newport Historical Society, Newport, RI [*Library symbol*] [*Library of Congress*] (LCLS)
RN-HSG.... Radionuclide Hysterosalpingogram [*Medicine*]
RNI .... Kansas City, MO [*Location identifier*] [*FAA*] (FAAL)
RNI .... Research Notes (Ibadan) [*A publication*]
RNI .... Research Policy. A Journal Devoted to Research Policy, Research Management, and Planning [*A publication*]
RNI .... Resident Navy Inspector
RNIB .... Royal National Institute for the Blind [*British*]
RNIC .... Robinson Nugent, Inc. [*NASDAQ symbol*] (NQ)
RN ID .... RN Idaho [*A publication*]
RNID......... Routine Network-In-Dial (DNAB)
RNID......... Royal National Institute for the Deaf [*British*]
RNID/NOD ... Routine Network-In-Dial / Network-Out-Dial (DNAB)
RNIE .... Royal Netherlands Institute of Engineers
RNIM .... Rotors Not in Motion [*Aviation*] (AIA)
RNIO .... Resident Naval Inspector of Ordnance
RNIR .... Reduction to Next Inferior Rank
RNIT .... Radio Noise Interference Test
RNJ .... Ramapo College of New Jersey, Mahwah, NJ [*OCLC symbol*] (OCLC)
RNJ .... Rektorskommitten for de Nordiska Journalist Hogskolorna [*Committee for Nordic Universities of Journalism - CNUJ*] (EAIO)
RNJ .... Yoron-Jima [*Japan*] [*Airport symbol*] (OAG)
RNk .... North Kingstown Free Library, North Kingstown, RI [*Library symbol*] [*Library of Congress*] (LCLS)
RNKID ...... Rikuyo Nainen Kikan [*A publication*]
RNL.......... Rainelle, WV [*Location identifier*] [*FAA*] (FAAL)
RNL.......... Renewal (MSA)
RNL.......... Rennell Island [*Solomon Islands*] [*Airport symbol*] (OAG)
RNL.......... Retail Newsletter [*A publication*]
RNL.......... Review of National Literatures [*A publication*]
RNLA .... Royal Netherlands Army
RNLAF..... Royal Netherlands Air Force
RNLBI...... Royal National Life-Boat Institution [*British*]
RNLC .... Rosary Novena for Life Committee (EA)
RNLI......... Royal National Life-Boat Institution [*British*]
RNLJ .... Rhodesia and Nyasaland Law Journal [*A publication*] (DLA)
RNLO........ Royal Naval Liaison Officer [*British*]
R & NLR.... Rhodesia and Nyasaland Law Reports [*1956-64*] [*A publication*] (DLA)
RNLT .... Running Light
RNM.......... Radio-Navigation Mobile
RNM.......... Radionuclide Migration
RNM.......... Resistencia Nacional Mocambicana [*Mozambican National Resistance*] (PD)
RNM.......... University of Rochester, Miner Medical Library, Rochester, NY [*OCLC symbol*] (OCLC)
RN Mag..... RN Magazine [*A publication*]
RNMBR ... Royal Naval Motor Boat Reserve [*British military*] (DMA)
RNMC....... Regional Nursing Midwifery Committee [*National Health Service*] [*British*] (DI)
RNMC....... Royal Netherlands Marine Corps
RNMCB .... Reserve Naval Mobile Construction Battalion (DNAB)
RNMCBDET ... Reserve Naval Mobile Construction Battalion Detachment (DNAB)
RNMCC .... Reference Number Mandatory Category Code [*DoD*]
RNMD....... Registered Nurse for Mental Defectives
RNMDSF ... Royal National Mission to Deep Sea Fishermen [*British*]
RNMH ...... Registered Nurse for the Mentally Handicapped [*British*] (DBQ)
RNMI .... Realtors National Marketing Institute [*Chicago, IL*] (EA)
RNMS .... Registered Nurse for the Mentally Subnormal [*British*]
RNMS .... Royal Naval Minewatching Service [*British military*] (DMA)
RNMV....... Rice Necrosis Mosaic Virus [*Plant pathology*]
RNMVDW ... Reports. National Museum of Victoria [*A publication*]
RNN.......... Naval War College, Newport, RI [*Library symbol*] [*Library of Congress*] (LCLS)
RNN.......... Ronne [*Denmark*] [*Airport symbol*] (OAG)
RNN.......... Royal Netherlands Navy
RNN.......... Royal Norwegian Navy
RNNAS .... Royal Netherlands Naval Air Service
RNNU .... United States Navy, Naval Underwater Systems Center, Technical Library, Newport, RI [*Library symbol*] [*Library of Congress*] (LCLS)
RN and O... Raleigh News and Observer [*A publication*]
RNO .... Regional Nuclear Option (MCD)
RNO .... Regional Nursing Officer [*British*]
RNO .... Reno [*Nevada*] [*Airport symbol*] (OAG)
RNO .... Resident Naval Officer [*Followed by place name*] (NATG)
RNO .... Results Not Observed (DNAB)
RNO .... Rhino Resources [*Vancouver Stock Exchange symbol*]
RNO .... Roan Selection Trust Ltd. [*Formerly, RHO; later, RST*] [*NYSE symbol*] (SPSG)
RNO .... Rough Notes [*A publication*]
RNOA........ Royal Norwegian Army (NATG)
RNOAF ..... Royal Norwegian Air Force

RNOC........ Resistencia Nicaraguense de Organizacion Civica [*Political party*] (EY)
RNOC........ Royal Naval Officers Club [*Defunct*] (EA)
RNODC..... Responsible National Oceanographic Data Center [*Marine science*] (MSC)
RNON ...... Royal Norwegian Navy (NATG)
RNORA.... Royal Norwegian Army
RNORN..... Royal Norwegian Navy
RNP .... Radio Navigation Point [*Military*] (MCD)
RNP .... Rassemblement National Populaire [*National People's Rally*] [*France*]
RNP .... Registered Nurse Practitioner (AAMN)
RNP .... Remote Network Processor
RNP .... Ribonucleoprotein [*Biochemistry*]
RNP .... RNA [*Ribonucleic Acid*] Nuclear Protein
RNP .... Rongelap [*Marshall Islands*] [*Airport symbol*] (OAG)
RNP .... Roscoe's Nisi Prius Evidence [*20th ed.*] [*1934*] [*A publication*] (DLA)
RNP .... Royal Naval Personnel Research Committee [*British*]
RNPA .... Regional Nuclear Power Authority
RNPC .... Regional Nuclear Power Co.
RNPC .... Required Navigation Performance Capability
RNPL......... Royal Naval Physiological Laboratory [*Later, AMTE (PL)*] [*British*]
RNPR .... Relative Net Protein Ratio [*Nutrition*]
RNPRC..... Royal Naval Personnel Research Committee [*British*] (MCD)
RNPS........ Royal Naval Patrol Service [*Obsolete*] [*British*]
RNPS........ Royal Navy Polaris School [*British*]
RNQ.......... Waycross, GA [*Location identifier*] [*FAA*] (FAAL)
RNR.......... Rate Not Reported (DS)
RNR.......... Receive Not Ready [*Data processing*] (IEEE)
RNR.......... Redwood Library and Athenaeum, Newport, RI [*Library symbol*] [*Library of Congress*] (LCLS)
RNR.......... Renewable Natural Resources (DI)
RNR.......... Renewal Not Required (AIA)
RNR.......... Resonant Nuclear Reaction [*Physics*]
RNR.......... Ribonucleotide Reductase [*An enzyme*]
RNR.......... Robinson River [*Papua New Guinea*] [*Airport symbol*] (OAG)
RNR.......... Royal Naval Reserve [*British*]
RNR.......... Runner (MSA)
RNRA .... Resonant Nuclear Reaction Analysis [*Physics*]
RNRA .... Royal Naval Rifle Association [*British military*] (DMA)
RNRB .... Relative Navigational Reference Beacon [*Military*] (CAAL)
RNRC .... Riverside National Bank [*NASDAQ symbol*] (NQ)
RNRE .... Refused, Not Reversible Error [*Legal term*] (ILCA)
RNRF .... Renewable Natural Resources Foundation (EA)
RNRLA..... Report of Naval Research Laboratory Progress [*United States*] [*A publication*]
RNRS........ Royal National Rose Society [*British*] (EAIO)
RNR(T)..... Royal Naval Reserve (Trawlers) [*British military*] (DMA)
RNRVAK .. Feddes Repertorium. Specierum Novarum Regni Vegetabilis [*A publication*]
RNS .... Race, National Origin, and Sex (DNAB)
RNS .... RADAR Netting Station [*Military*] (AABC)
RNS .... Ransom Resources Ltd. [*Vancouver Stock Exchange symbol*]
RNS .... Reference Normal Serum [*Clincial chemistry*] (AAMN)
RNS .... Religious News Service (EA)
RNS .... Rennes [*France*] [*Airport symbol*] (OAG)
RNS .... Reusable Nuclear Shuttle [*NASA*]
RNS .... Reusable Nuclear Stage [*Aerospace*]
RNS .... Ribonuclease S [*An enzyme*]
RNS .... Royal Naval School [*British*]
RNS .... Royal Numismatic Society [*British*]
RNS .... Russian Numismatic Society (EA)
RNSA .... Royal Naval Sailing Association [*British*]
RNSAC..... Range Surveillance Aircraft (MCD)
RNSC........ Reference Number Status Code (MCD)
RNSC........ Rocket/Nimbus Sounder Comparison [*NASA*]
RNSC........ Royal Naval Staff College [*British*]
RNSD .... Royal Naval Stores Depot [*British*]
RNSG .... Reserve Naval Security Group (DNAB)
RNSGC..... Reserve Naval Security Group Course (DNAB)
RNSH........ Royal National Scottish Hospital
RNSJA ...... Rinsho Seijinbyo [*A publication*]
RNS of M .. Royal Naval School of Music [*British military*] (DMA)
RNSP........ Round-Nose Soft-Point Bullet
RNSQ........ Royal Naval Sick Quarters [*British*]
RNSR........ Royal Naval Special Reserve [*British military*] (DMA)
RNSR........ Royal Nova Scotia Regiment [*Military unit*]
RNSS........ Royal Naval Scientific Service [*British*] (DEN)
RNSS........ Royal Norwegian Society of Sciences
RNSTS ..... Royal Naval Supply and Transport Service [*British*]
RNSYS..... Royal Nova Scotia Yacht Squadron
RNT .... Regensburger Neues Testament [*A publication*] (BJA)
RNT .... Registered Nurse Tutor [*British*]
RNT .... Renton, WA [*Location identifier*] [*FAA*] (FAAL)
RNTE .... Royal Naval Training Establishment [*British military*] (DMA)
RNTL .... Rockwood National Corp. [*NASDAQ symbol*] (NQ)
rNTP .... Ribonucleoside Triphosphate [*Biochemistry*]
RNTU........ Royal Naval Training Unit [*British military*] (DMA)
RNTWPA ... Radio-Newsreel-Television Working Press Association (EA)

RNU.......... RADAR Netting Unit [*Military*] (AABC)
RNU.......... Ranau [*Malaysia*] [*Airport symbol*] (OAG)
R Numis Soc Spec Publ ... Royal Numismatic Society. Special Publication
RNV.......... Cleveland, MS [*Location identifier*] [*FAA*] (FAAL)
RNV.......... Radio Noise Voltage
RNV.......... Radionuclide Venography [*Clinical chemistry*] (AAMN)
RNV.......... Radionuclide Ventriculography [*Medicine*]
RNV.......... Random Noise Voltmeter
RNV.......... Relative Nutritive Value [*Nutrition*]
RNV.......... Replacement Naval Vessels
RNV.......... Resistive Null Voltage
RNV.......... Reusable Nuclear Vehicle [*Aerospace*] (KSC)
RNV.......... Royal Naval Volunteer (Reserve) [*British*] (ROG)
RNVC........ Reference Number Variation Code (MCD)
RN(V)R...... Royal Naval (Volunteer) Reserve [*Obsolete*] [*World War II*]
          [*British*]
RNVR(A)... Royal Naval Volunteer Reserve (Air) [*British military*] (DMA)
RNVSDY... Kongelige Norske Videnskabers Selskab. Museet. Botanisk
          Avdeling Rapport [*A publication*]
RNVSR...... Royal Naval Volunteer Supplementary Reserve [*Obsolete*]
          [*World War II*] [*British*]
RNV(W)R ... Royal Naval Volunteer (Wireless) Reserve [*British
          military*] (DMA)
RNWAR .... Royal Naval Wireless Auxiliary Reserve [*British
          military*] (DMA)
RNWBL..... Renewable . (MSA)
RNWMP ... Royal North West Mounted Police [*Later, RCMP*] [*Canada*]
RNWSD .... Research News [*A publication*]
RNWY .... Runway (AABC)
RNX.......... Renox Creek Resources [*Vancouver Stock Exchange symbol*]
RNX.......... Rex-Noreco, Inc. [*AMEX symbol*] (SPSG)
RNXS........ Royal Naval Auxiliary Service [*British*]
RNY.......... Rainier Energy Resources [*Vancouver Stock Exchange symbol*]
RNY.......... Republic New York Corp. [*Associated Press
          abbreviation*] (APAG)
RNY.......... Runway Lights [*Aviation*] (AIA)
RNYPO ..... Regional Navy Youth Programs Officer (DNAB)
RNZ.......... Radio New Zealand
RNZ.......... Reserve Bank of New Zealand. Bulletin [*A publication*]
RNZ.......... Rhein-Neckar-Zeitung [*A publication*]
RNZ.......... Royal New Zealand
RNZAF...... Royal New Zealand Air Force
RNZE .... Royal New Zealand Engineers
RNZN .... Royal New Zealand Navy
RNZN(V)R ... Royal New Zealand Naval (Volunteer) Reserve
RNZOD8... Polish Journal of Animal Science and Technology [*A
          publication*]
Ro .... Hoffmann-La Roche, Inc. [*Switzerland, USA*] [*Research code
          symbol*]
RO............. Observer (Radio) [*British military*] (DMA)
RO............. Omani Rial [*Monetary unit*] (IMH)
RO............. RADAR Observer
RO............. RADAR Operator
RO............. Radiation Office [*Environmental Protection Agency*]
RO............. Radio Operator
RO............. Radio Orchestra
RO............. Radionavigation Mobile Station [*ITU designation*] (CET)
RO............. Radioopaque
R & O .... Rail and Ocean
RO............. Railway Office [*British*] (ROG)
RO............. Range Only (CAAL)
RO............. Range Operation (AAG)
RO............. Rank Organisation Ltd. [*Toronto Stock Exchange symbol*]
RO............. Reactor Operator [*Nuclear energy*] (NRCH)
RO............. Read Only [*Data processing*] (IBMDP)
RO............. Readout (KSC)
RO............. Reality Orientation
RO............. Receive Only
RO............. Receiving Office [*or Officer*]
RO............. Receiving Order [*Business term*] (DCTA)
RO............. Reconnaissance Officer
RO............. Recorders [*JETDS nomenclature*] [*Military*] (CET)
RO............. Records Office [*or Officer*] [*Air Force*] (AFM)
RO............. Recovery Operations [*NASA*]
RO............. Recruiting Officer [*Military*]
RO............. Recto [*Also, R*]
RO............. Recueil Officiel des Lois et Ordonnances de la Confederation
          Suisse [*A publication*]
RO............. Reddish Orange
RO............. Redistribution Order [*Military*] (DNAB)
RO............. Reference Oscillator [*Telecommunications*] (OA)
RO............. Referral Order [*Military*] (DNAB)
RO............. Regimental Orders [*Army*]
RO............. Regional Office [*or Officer*]
RO............. Register Output
R/O............ Regular Order
RO............. Regulated Output (FAAC)
RO............. Relieving Officer (ROG)
RO............. Relocatable Output [*Data processing*]
RO............. Rent Officer [*British*] (ILCA)
RO............. Repair Order

R/O........... Repair and Overhaul (MCD)
RO............. Reportable Occurrence [*Nuclear energy*] (NRCH)
RO............. Reporting Officer [*Army*] (AABC)
RO............. Reproducible Ozalid (DNAB)
RO............. Requirements Objective
R & O .... Requirements and Objectives
RO............. Requisitioning Objective [*Military*] (AABC)
R/O........... Requisitions/Objectives (CINC)
RO............. Research Objective (MCD)
RO............. Research Officer [*British*]
R of O .... Reserve of Officers [*British*]
RO............. Reserve of Officers [*British*]
RO............. Reserve Order
RO............. Responding Officer [*Police term*]
RO............. Restriction Orifice [*Nuclear energy*] (NRCH)
RO............. Retired Officer [*Military*] [*British*]
RO............. Retrofit Order [*Navy*] (NG)
RO............. Retrofit Order [*Navy*] (DNAB)
RO............. Returning Officer (ROG)
RO............. Revenue Officer [*IRS*]
RO............. Reverse-Osmosis [*Physical chemistry*]
RO............. Rework Order (MCD)
R/O........... Rewritable/Optical
Ro............. Rhodium [*Correct symbol is Rh*] [*Chemical element*]
RO............. Right Outboard (MCD)
RO............. Rimoil Corp. [*Toronto Stock Exchange symbol*]
RO............. Rip Out (DNAB)
RO............. Ritter-Oleson Technique [*Medicine*] (MAE)
RO............. Road (WGA)
RO............. Roan [*Thoroughbred racing*]
RO............. Rock [*Germany*] [*ICAO aircraft manufacturer
          identifier*] (ICAO)
RO............. Rocznik Orientalistyczny [*A publication*]
Ro............. Rodoicus [*Authority cited in pre-1607 legal work*] (DSA)
RO............. Roemisches Oesterreich. Jahresschrift der Oesterreichischen
          Gesellschaft fuer Archaeologie [*A publication*]
Ro............. Roffredus Beneventanus [*Flourished, 1215-43*] [*Authority cited
          in pre-1607 legal work*] (DSA)
Ro............. Rolandus Bandinelli [*Deceased, 1181*] [*Authority cited in pre-
          1607 legal work*] (DSA)
RO............. Roll
Ro............. Rolle's Abridgment [*A publication*] (DLA)
R/O........... Rollout (MCD)
R/O........... Rollover
R & O .... Roma e l'Oriente [*A publication*]
Ro............. Romania [*A publication*]
RO............. Romania [*ANSI two-letter standard code*] (CNC)
RO............. Romanian Air Transport [*ICAO designator*] (FAAC)
RO............. Romans [*Old Testament book*]
RO............. Rood [*Unit of measurement*]
RO............. Room Only
RO............. Roper Organization (EA)
RO............. Rose (ROG)
RO............. Rough
RO............. Rough Opening [*Technical drawings*]
RO............. Route Order [*Military*]
RO............. Routine Order
RO............. Routing Office [*or Officer*] [*Navy*]
RO............. Rowed Over [*Rowing*] [*British*] (ROG)
RO............. Royal Observatory [*British*]
RO............. Royal Octavo
RO............. Royal Ordnance Factory [*British*]
R/O........... Rule Out [*Medicine*]
R-O .... Run-On [*Used in correcting manuscripts, etc.*]
RO............. Runoff Election
RO............. Runout (MSA)
RO............. Runover [*Publishing*]
RO............. Russian Obuckhoff Rifle
RO............. Rust and Oxidation (DNAB)
ROA.......... Altimeter Station [*ITU designation*] (CET)
ROA.......... Radiation Oncology Administrators [*Later, SROA*] (EA)
ROA.......... Radio Operator's Aptitude Test [*Military*]
ROA.......... Radius of Action (CAAL)
ROA.......... Raman Optical Activity [*Spectrometry*]
ROA.......... RAS. Rohr-Armatur-Sanitaer-Heizung Informationsblatt fuer
          den Fachhandel und das Sanitaerfach und Heizungsfach [*A
          publication*]
ROA.......... Recorder Announcement (DNAB)
ROA.......... Reference Optical Alignment
ROA.......... Rehabilitation of Offenders Act [*1974*] [*British*] (DCTA)
ROA.......... Reinsurance Offices Association [*British*] (AIA)
ROA.......... Report on the ORT Activities [*Paris/Geneva*] [*A publication*]
ROA.......... Reserve Officers Association of the United States (EA)
ROA.......... Return on Assets [*Finance*]
ROA.......... Right Occipitoanterior [*A fetal position*] [*Obstetrics*]
ROA.......... Roanoke [*Virginia*] [*Airport symbol*]
ROA.......... Robert Owen Association (EA)
roa .... Romance [*MARC language code*] [*Library of
          Congress*] (LCCP)
ROA.......... Rules of the Air (AFM)
ROA.......... Russian Orchestra of the Americas

Ro Abr........ Rolle's Abridgment [*A publication*] (ILCA)

ROAD....... Inroads [*Database*] [*Australia*]

ROAD....... Reorganization Objectives, Army Division [*Military*]

ROAD....... Retires on Active Duty [*Military*] (MCD)

ROAD....... Roadway Services, Inc. [*NASDAQ symbol*] (NQ)

ROAD....... Ruch Obywatelski-Akcja Demokratyczna [*Civil Movement for Democratic Action*] [*P oland*] [*Political party*]

Road Abstr ... Road Abstracts [*A publication*]

Road A R.... Road Apple Review [*A publication*]

Road Maps ... Economic Road Maps [*A publication*]

Road Note Road Res Lab (UK) ... Road Note. Road Research Laboratory (United Kingdom) [*A publication*]

Road Res Bull ... Road Research Bulletin [*A publication*]

Road Res Lab (UK) RRL Rep ... Road Research Laboratory (United Kingdom). RRL Report [*A publication*]

Road Res Monogr ... Road Research Monographs [*A publication*]

Road Res Notes ... Road Research Notes [*A publication*]

Road Res Pap ... Road Research Papers [*A publication*]

Road Res Techn Pap ... Road Research Technical Papers [*A publication*]

ROADS ..... Real-Time Optical Alignment and Diagnostic System [*Module*]

ROADS ..... Roadway Analysis and Design System [*Data processing*]

Road Saf .... Road Safety [*A publication*] (APTA)

Roads & Bridges ... Roads and Bridges [*A publication*]

Roads & Constr ... Roads and Construction [*A publication*]

Roads Construct ... Roads and Construction [*A publication*]

Roads & Eng Constr ... Roads and Engineering Construction [*A publication*]

Roads Road Constr ... Roads and Road Construction [*A publication*]

Roads St..... Roads and Streets [*A publication*]

Road Transp Aust ... Road Transporter of Australia [*A publication*] (APTA)

ROAH .... Naha [*Ryukyu Islands*] [*ICAO location identifier*] (ICLI)

ROAM....... RAN Energy, Inc. [*NASDAQ symbol*] (NQ)

ROAM....... Return on Assets Managed [*Finance*]

ROAMA..... Rome Air Materiel Area [*Deactivated*] [*Air Force*]

ROANA..... Rover Owners' Association of North America [*Defunct*] (EA)

ROAP .... Rubidazone [*Zorubicin*], Oncovin [*Vincristine*], ara-C [*Cytarabine*], Prednisone [*Antineoplastic drug regimen*]

ROAR .... Radio Operated Auto Racing

ROAR .... Recovery and Overpayment Accounting and Reporting System [*Social Security Administration*] (GFGA)

ROAR .... Regional Organization for Airways Restudy

ROAR .... Restore Our Alienated Rights [*Boston antibusing group*]

ROAR .... Return of Army Repairables (AABC)

ROAR .... Royal Optimizing Assembly Routing [*Royal McBee Corp.*] [*Data processing*]

ROARE ..... Reduction of Attitudes and Repressed Emotions [*Treatment given to sex offenders*] [*Psychology*]

ROARS...... Rutgers Online Automated Retrieval Service [*Rutgers University*] (OLDSS)

ROAT .... Radio Operator's Aptitude Test [*Military*]

ROB........... Monrovia [*Liberia*] Roberts International Airport [*Airport symbol*] (OAG)

ROB........... RADAR Order of Battle

ROB........... RADAR Out of Battle (CET)

ROB........... Recovery Operations Branch [*NASA*] (KSC)

ROB........... Regional Office Building

ROB........... Relieve of Booty [*Crime term*]

RoB .... Religion och Bibel [*A publication*]

ROB........... Remaining on Board

ROB........... Report on Board [*Navy*]

ROB........... Report on Business (IT)

ROB........... Reserve on Board

ROB........... Reserveoffizier-Bewerber [*Reserve officer applicant*] [*German military - World War II*]

ROB........... Review of Business [*A publication*]

ROB........... Right of Baseline (MCD)

ROB........... Right Outboard (MCD)

ROB........... Rijksdienst voor het Oudheidkundig Bodemonderzoek [*A publication*]

Rob........... Robards' Reports [*12, 13 Missouri*] [*A publication*] (DLA)

Rob........... Robards' Texas Conscript Cases [*A publication*] (DLA)

ROB........... Robert Morris College, Coraopolis, PA [*OCLC symbol*] (OCLC)

ROB........... Roberts Airways [*Dallas, TX*] [*FAA designator*] (FAAC)

Rob........... Roberts' Reports [*29-31 Louisiana Annual*] [*A publication*] (DLA)

ROB........... Robertsfield [*Liberia*] [*Airport symbol*]

Rob........... Robertson's English Ecclesiastical Reports [*A publication*] (DLA)

Rob........... Robertson's Reports [*24-30 New York Superior Court*] [*1863-68*] [*A publication*] (DLA)

Rob........... Robertson's Reports [*1 Hawaii*] [*A publication*] (DLA)

Rob........... Robertson's Scotch Appeal Cases [*1707-27*] [*A publication*] (DLA)

ROB........... Robin International, Inc. [*Toronto Stock Exchange symbol*]

Rob........... Robinson's English Admiralty Reports [*1799-1809, 1838-1852*] [*A publication*] (DLA)

Rob........... Robinson's English Ecclesiastical Reports [*1844-53*] [*A publication*] (DLA)

Rob........... Robinson's Louisiana Reports [*1-4 Louisiana Annual*] [*1841-46*] [*A publication*] (DLA)

Rob........... Robinson's Reports [*1-8 Ontario*] [*A publication*] (DLA)

Rob............ Robinson's Reports [*2-9, 17-23 Colorado Appeals*] [*A publication*] (DLA)

Rob............ Robinson's Reports [*1 Nevada*] [*A publication*] (DLA)

Rob............ Robinson's Reports [*38 California*] [*A publication*] (DLA)

Rob............ Robinson's Reports [*40, 41 Virginia*] [*A publication*] (DLA)

Rob............ Robinson's Scotch Appeal Cases [*1840-41*] [*A publication*] (DLA)

Rob............ Robinson's Upper Canada Reports [*A publication*] (DLA)

ROB.......... Roborough [*England*]

ROB.......... Robotic Operating Buddy [*Nintendo video game system accessory*]

ROB.......... Robotics Age [*A publication*]

ROB.......... Roburent [*Italy*] [*Geomagnetic observatory code*]

ROB.......... Roburent [*Italy*] [*Seismograph station code, US Geological Survey*] (SEIS)

ROB.......... Round of Beam (DS)

ROB.......... Run of Book [*Advertising*] (WDMC)

ROB.......... Waco, TX [*Location identifier*] [*FAA*] (FAAL)

RoBA .... Academia R.S. Romania [*Academy of Romania*], Bucharest, Romania [*Library symbol*] [*Library of Congress*] (LCLS)

Rob A .... [*C.*] Robinson's Admiralty Reports [*1799-1809*] [*A publication*] (DLA)

Rob Adm .... [*C.*] Robinson's Admiralty Reports [*England*] [*A publication*] (DLA)

Rob Adm .... [*W.*] Robinson's English Admiralty Reports [*A publication*] (DLA)

Rob Adm & Pr ... Roberts on Admiralty and Prize [*A publication*] (DLA)

ROBAMP ... Rotational Base for Aviation Maintenance Personnel

Rob App..... Robinson's Scotch Appeal Cases [*1840-41*] [*A publication*] (DLA)

Robards...... Robards' Reports [*12, 13 Missouri*] [*A publication*] (DLA)

Robards...... Robards' Texas Conscript Cases [*1862-65*] [*A publication*] (DLA)

Robards & Jackson ... Robards and Jackson's Reports [*26-27 Texas*] [*A publication*] (DLA)

ROBAT ..... Robotic Obstacle-Breaching Assault Tank

Robb........... Robbins' New Jersey Equity Reports [*67-70 New Jersey*] [*A publication*] (DLA)

Robb........... Robb's United States Patent Cases [*A publication*] (DLA)

Rob Bank ... Robertson's Handbook of Bankers' Law [*A publication*] (DLA)

Rob Bank ... Robson on Law and Practice in Bankruptcy [*7th ed.*] [*1894*] [*A publication*] (DLA)

RoBBC....... Biblioteca Centrala de Stat a R.S. Romania [*Central State Library of Romania*], Bucharest, Romania [*Library symbol*] [*Library of Congress*] (LCLS)

Robb (NJ).. Robbins' New Jersey Equity Reports [*A publication*] (DLA)

Robb Pat Cas ... Robb's United States Patent Cases [*A publication*] (DLA)

ROBC .... Robec, Inc. [*NASDAQ symbol*] (NQ)

Rob Cal ...... Robinson's Reports [*38 California*] [*A publication*] (DLA)

Rob Car V .. Robertson's History of the Reign of the Emperor Charles V [*A publication*] (DLA)

Rob Cas...... Robinson's Scotch Appeal Cases [*1840-41*] [*A publication*] (DLA)

Rob Chr...... Robinson's Reports [*2-9, 17-23 Colorado Appeals*] [*A publication*] (DLA)

ROBCO ..... Readiness Objective Code [*Military*] (AABC)

ROBCO ..... Requirement Objective Code

Rob Colo .... Robinson's Reports [*2-9, 17-23 Colorado Appeals*] [*A publication*] (ILCA)

Rob Cons Cas (Tex) ... Robards' Texas Conscript Cases [*A publication*] (DLA)

Rob Consc Cas ... Robards' Texas Conscript Cases [*A publication*] (DLA)

ROBD........ Robot Defense Systems [*NASDAQ symbol*] (NQ)

Rob Dig...... Robert's Digest [*Lower Canada*] [*A publication*] (DLA)

Rob Dig...... Robert's Digest of Vermont Reports [*A publication*] (DLA)

Rob E .... Robertson's English Ecclesiastical Reports [*2 vols.*] [*1844-53*] [*A publication*] (DLA)

Rob Ecc ...... Robertson's English Ecclesiastical Reports [*2 vols.*] [*1844-53*] [*A publication*] (DLA)

Rob Eccl ..... Robertson's English Ecclesiastical Reports [*2 vols.*] [*1844-53*] [*A publication*] (DLA)

Rob El Law ... Robinson's Elementary Law [*A publication*] (DLA)

Rob Ent ...... Robinson's Book of Entries [*A publication*] (DLA)

ROBEPS ... RADAR Operating below Prescribed Standards (FAAC)

Rob Eq ...... Roberts' Principles of Equity [*A publication*] (DLA)

Rober......... Robertus [*Authority cited in pre-1607 legal work*] (DSA)

Rober Maran ... Robertus Maranta [*Flourished, 16th century*] [*Authority cited in pre-1607 legal work*] (DSA)

Robert .... Robertson's Scotch Appeal Cases [*1707-27*] [*A publication*] (DLA)

Robert App ... Robertson's Scotch House of Lords Appeals [*A publication*] (DLA)

Robert App Cas ... Robertson's Scotch House of Lords Appeals [*A publication*] (DLA)

Robert A Taft Sanit Eng Cent Tech Rep ... Robert A. Taft Sanitary Engineering Center. Technical Report [*A publication*]

Robert A Taft Water Res Cent Rep ... Robert A. Taft Water Research Center. Report [*A publication*]

Robert A Welch Found Conf Chem Res Proc ... Robert A. Welch Foundation. Conferences on Chemical Research. Proceedings [*A publication*]

Robert A Welch Found Res Bull ... Robert A. Welch Foundation. Research Bulletin [*A publication*]
Robert Morris Associates Bull ... Robert Morris Associates. Bulletin [*A publication*]
Roberts...... Roberts' Reports [*29-31 Louisiana Annual*] [*A publication*] (DLA)
Roberts Emp Liab ... Roberts on Federal Liabilities of Carriers [*A publication*] (DLA)
Robertson... Robertson's English Ecclesiastical Reports [*A publication*] (DLA)
Robertson... Robertson's Reports [*New York Marine Court*] [*A publication*] (DLA)
Robertson... Robertson's Reports [*1 Hawaii*] [*A publication*] (DLA)
Robertson... Robertson's Reports [*24-30 New York Superior Court*] [*A publication*] (DLA)
Robertson... Robertson's Scotch Appeal Cases [*1707-27*] [*A publication*] (DLA)
Robertson's Rep ... Robertson's Reports [*24-30 New York Superior Court*] [*A publication*] (DLA)
Rob Forms ... Robinson's Virginia Forms [*A publication*] (DLA)
Rob Fr...... Roberts on Frauds [*1805*] [*A publication*] (DLA)
Rob Fr Conv ... Roberts on Fraudulent Conveyances [*A publication*] (DLA)
Rob Gav ..... Robinson's Common Law of Kent, or Custom on Gavelkind [*5th ed.*] [*1897*] [*A publication*] (DLA)
Rob Hawaii ... Robinson's Reports [*1 Hawaii*] [*A publication*] (DLA)
ROBIN ...... Remote On-Line Business Information Network [*Data processing*] (IEEE)
ROBIN ...... Rocket Balloon Instrument [*Air Force*]
Robin App ... Robinson's Scotch House of Lords Appeals [*A publication*] (DLA)
ROBINS.... Roberts Information Services, Inc. [*Information service or system*] (IID)
Robin Sc App ... Robinson's Scotch Appeal Cases [*1840-41*] [*A publication*] (DLA)
Robinson.... [*W.*] Robinson's English Admiralty Reports [*A publication*] (DLA)
Robinson.... Robinson's English Ecclesiastical Reports [*1844-53*] [*A publication*] (DLA)
Robinson.... Robinson's Louisiana Reports [*1-12 Louisiana*] [*A publication*] (DLA)
Robinson.... Robinson's Ontario Reports [*A publication*] (DLA)
Robinson.... Robinson's Reports [*1 Nevada*] [*A publication*] (DLA)
Robinson.... Robinson's Reports [*38 California*] [*A publication*] (DLA)
Robinson.... Robinson's Reports [*17-23 Colorado*] [*A publication*] (DLA)
Robinson.... Robinson's Reports [*40-41 Virginia*] [*A publication*] (DLA)
Robinson.... Robinson's Scotch House of Lords Appeals [*A publication*] (DLA)
Robinson.... [*J. L.*] Robinson's Upper Canada Reports [*A publication*] (DLA)
Robinson Sc App Cas ... Robinson's Scotch Appeal Cases [*1840-41*] [*A publication*] (DLA)
Rob & J ...... Robards and Jackson's Reports [*26, 27 Texas*] [*A publication*] (DLA)
Rob Jun...... William Robinson's English Admiralty Reports [*1838-52*] [*A publication*] (DLA)
Rob Jus...... Robinson's Justice of the Peace [*1836*] [*A publication*] (DLA)
Rob LA....... Robinson's Louisiana Reports [*1-4 Louisiana Annual*] [*1841-46*] [*A publication*] (DLA)
Rob (LA Ann) ... Robinson's Louisiana Reports [*1-4 Louisiana Annual*] [*A publication*] ·(DLA)
Rob Leg...... Robertson's Legitimation by Subsequent Marriage [*1829*] [*A publication*] (DLA)
Rob Louis... Robinson's Louisiana Reports [*1-12 Louisiana*] [*A publication*] (DLA)
Rob L & W ... Roberts, Leaming, and Wallis' County Court Reports [*1849-51*] [*A publication*] (DLA)
Rob Mar (NY) ... Robertson and Jacob's New York Marine Court Reports [*A publication*] (DLA)
Rob MO..... Robards' Reports [*12, 13 Missouri*] [*A publication*] (DLA)
ROBMV ...... Robinia Mosaic Virus [*Plant pathology*]
ROBN........ Robbins & Myers, Inc. [*NASDAQ symbol*] (NQ)
Rob Nev ..... Robinson's Reports [*1 Nevada*] [*A publication*] (DLA)
Rob (NY).... Robertson's Reports [*24-30 New York Superior Court*] [*A publication*] (DLA)
ROBO........ Robotool Ltd. [*NASDAQ symbol*] (NQ)
ROBO........ Rocket Orbital Bomber
ROBOMB ... Robot Bomb [*Air Force*]
Rob Ont ..... Robinson's Reports [*1-8 Ontario*] [*A publication*] (DLA)
Robot Age .. Robotics Age [*A publication*]
Robot Eng .. Robotics Engineering [*A publication*]
Robotics T ... Robotics Today [*A publication*]
Robotron Tech Commun ... Robotron Technical Communications [*A publication*]
Robot Wld ... Robotics World [*A publication*]
Rob Pat ...... Robinson on Patents [*A publication*] (DLA)
Rob Per Suc ... Robertson's Law of Personal Succession [*1836*] [*A publication*] (DLA)
Rob Pr........ Robinson's Practice [*A publication*] (DLA)
Rob Prior ... Robertson's Law of Priority of Incumbrances [*A publication*] (DLA)
R Obs Ann ... Royal Observatory. Annals [*A publication*]

Robs Bank ... Robson on Law and Practice in Bankruptcy [*7th ed.*] [*1894*] [*A publication*] (DLA)
Robs Bankr ... Robertson's Handbook of Bankers' Law [*A publication*] (DLA)
R Obs Bull ... Royal Observatory. Bulletins [*A publication*]
Rob Sc App ... Robinson's Scotch Appeal Cases [*A publication*] (DLA)
Rob SI .... Robertson's Sandwich Island Reports [*1 Hawaii*] [*A publication*] (DLA)
Robson .... Robson on Law and Practice in Bankruptcy [*7 eds.*] [*1870-94*] [*A publication*] (DLA)
Rob Sr Ct ... Robertson's New York Superior Court Reports [*24-30*] [*A publication*] (DLA)
Rob Succ .... Roberts on the Law of Personal Succession [*A publication*] (DLA)
Rob Super Ct ... Robertson's Reports [*24-30 New York Superior Court*] [*A publication*] (DLA)
Robt Eccl.... Robertson's English Ecclesiastical Reports [*163 English Reprint*] [*1844-53*] [*A publication*] (DLA)
Robt Eccl (Eng) ... Robertson's English Ecclesiastical Reports [*163 English Reprint*] [*A publication*] (DLA)
Robt (NY) .. Robertson's Reports [*24-30 New York Superior Court*] [*A publication*] (DLA)
Robt Sc App Cas ... Robertson's Scotch Appeal Cases [*A publication*] (DLA)
Rob UC ...... Robinson's Upper Canada Reports [*A publication*] (DLA)
ROBV .... Robotic Vision Systems, Inc. [*NASDAQ symbol*] (NQ)
Rob VA ...... Robinson's Reports [*40, 41 Virginia*] [*A publication*] (DLA)
Rob W .... Roberts. Wills and Codicils [*1826*] [*A publication*] (ILCA)
Rob Wm Adm ... [*William*] Robinson's English Admiralty Reports [*3 vols.*] [*1838-50*] [*A publication*] (DLA)
Roc .... New Hampshire Reports [*A publication*] (DLA)
ROC.......... Radius of Curvature
ROC.......... Railton Owners Club (EA)
ROC.......... Range Operations Center [*Western Test Range*] (MCD)
ROC.......... Range Operations Conference [*NASA*] (KSC)
ROC.......... Rapid Omnidirectional Compaction [*Materials technology*] [*Dow Chemical Co.*]
ROC.......... Rate of Climb [*Aviation*]
ROC.......... Rate of Convergence (IEEE)
R/OC .... Receive-Only Center (FAAC)
ROC.......... Receiver [*or Relative*] Operating Characteristics [*Signal detection*] [*Graph for assessing diagnostic tests*]
ROC.......... Recommended Operating Condition [*Data processing*]
ROC.......... Reconnaissance and Operations Center (NATG)
ROC.......... Reconnaissance Optique de Caracteres [*Optical Character Recognition*] [*French*]
ROC.......... Record of Changes (DNAB)
ROC.......... Record of Comments (NASA)
ROC.......... Redeem Our Country (EA)
ROC.......... Reduce Operating Costs [*Air Force project*]
ROC.......... Reduced Operational Capability Program [*Navy*] (NVT)
ROC.......... Reduced Oxygen Concentration (MCD)
ROC.......... Region One Cooperative Library Service Unit [*Library network*]
ROC.......... Regional Operating Center [*NATO Integrated Communications System*] (NATG)
ROC.......... Regroupement des Officiers Communistes [*Burkina Faso*] [*Political party*] (EY)
ROC.......... Relative Operating Characteristics (MCD)
ROC.......... Reliability Operating Characteristic
ROC.......... Remote Operator's Console
ROC.......... Republic of China
ROC.......... Republican Organizing Committee [*Political organization in opposition to the NPL of North Dakota*]
ROC.......... Request of Change (NASA)
ROC.......... Required Operational Capability [*Military*] (RDA)
ROC.......... Requirements Document [*Army*] (RDA)
ROC.......... Reserve Officer Candidate
RO in C...... Resident Officer-in-Charge [*Navy*]
ROC.......... Return on Capital [*Finance*]
ROC.......... Reusable Orbital Carrier [*Aerospace*] (MCD)
ROC.......... ROC Taiwan Fund SBI [*NYSE symbol*] (SPSG)
ROC.......... Rochester [*New York*] [*Airport symbol*] (OAG)
ROC.......... Rochester-Odenbach [*New York*] [*Seismograph station code, US Geological Survey*] (SEIS)
ROC.......... Rochester Public Library, Rochester, MN [*OCLC symbol*] (OCLC)
Roc .... Rochus Curtius [*Flourished, 1470-1515*] [*Authority cited in pre-1607 legal work*] (DSA)
Roc .... Rococo Records [*Record label*] [*Canada, USA*]
ROC.......... Rotatable Optical Cube
ROC.......... Rothmans Inc. [*Formerly, Rothmans of Pall Mall Canada*] [*Toronto Stock Exchange symbol*] [*Vancouver Stock Exchange symbol*]
ROC.......... Royal Observer Corps [*British civilian aircraft observers*] [*World War II*]
ROC.......... Royal Ordnance Corps [*British*]
ROCAF...... Republic of China Air Force
Rocaf.......... [*Bernardus de*] Rocafixa [*Flourished, 14th century*] [*Authority cited in pre-1607 legal work*] (DSA)
ROCALDIS ... Routine Calls May Be Dispensed With

ROCAP...... Regional Office [*or Officer*] for Central American Programs [*Department of State*]

ROCAPPI ... Research on Computer Applications for the Printing and Publishing Industries

Rocas Miner ... Rocas y Minerales [*A publication*]

ROCAT ..... Rocket Catapult

ROCC .... Range Operations Conference Circuit (MUGU)

ROCC .... Range Operations Control Center (MCD)

ROCC .... Receptor-Operated Calcium Channel [*Physiology*]

ROCC .... Regional Oil Combating Center [*United Nations Environment Programme*] (MSC)

ROCC .... Regional Operations Control Center [*AT & T*]

ROCC .... Remote Operational Control Center

Rocc............ Roccus. De Navibus et Naulo [*Maritime law*] [*A publication*] (DLA)

ROCC .... Russell's Owl Collectors Club (EA)

Rocc De Nav et Nau ... Roccus. De Navibus et Naulo [*Maritime law*] [*A publication*] (DLA)

Roccus Ins ... Roccus on Insurance [*A publication*] (DLA)

ROCE .... Return on Capital Employed [*Accounting term*]

ROCF .... [*The*] Rockies Fund, Inc. [*NASDAQ symbol*] (NQ)

ROC Fd...... ROC Taiwan Fund [*Associated Press abbreviation*] (APAG)

ROCH....... Rochester [*Municipal borough in England*] (ROG)

Roch .... Rochus Curtius [*Flourished, 1470-1515*] [*Authority cited in pre-1607 legal work*] (DSA)

ROCH....... Ruch Oporu Chlopskiego [*Movement of Peasant Resistance*] [*Poland*] [*Political party*] (PPE)

Roch Curt... Rochus Curtius [*Flourished, 1470-1515*] [*Authority cited in pre-1607 legal work*] (DSA)

Roche D & K ... Roche, Dillon, and Kehoe's Irish Land Reports [*1881-82*] [*A publication*] (DLA)

Roche & H Bank ... Roche and Hazlitt's Bankruptcy Practice [*2nd ed.*] [*1873*] [*A publication*] (DLA)

Roche Image Med Res ... Roche Image of Medicine and Research [*A publication*]

Roche Med Image Comment ... Roche Medical Image and Commentary [*A publication*]

Rochester Acad Sci Proc ... Rochester Academy of Science. Proceedings [*A publication*]

Rochester Conf Coherence Quantum Opt Proc ... Rochester Conference on Coherence and Quantum Optics. Proceedings [*A publication*]

Rochester Conf Data Acquis Processing Biol Med Proc ... Rochester Conference on Data Acquisition and Processing in Biology and Medicine. Proceedings [*A publication*]

Rochester Conf Toxic ... Rochester Conference on Toxicity [*A publication*]

Rochester Hist ... Rochester History [*A publication*]

Rochester Hist Soc Publ Fund Ser ... Rochester Historical Society. Publication Fund Series [*A publication*]

Rochester Int Conf Environ Toxic ... Rochester International Conference on Environmental Toxicity [*A publication*]

Rochester Univ Lib Bul ... University of Rochester. Library Bulletin [*A publication*]

RochG .... Rochester Gas & Electric Corp. [*Associated Press abbreviation*] (APAG)

Roch Patr ... Rochester Patriot [*A publication*]

Roch Phil ... Rochester Philharmonic Orchestra. Program Notes [*A publication*]

RochTl .... Rochester Telephone Corp. [*Associated Press abbreviation*] (APAG)

ROCI .... Rahim Organizational Conflict Inventories [*Interpersonal skills and attitudes test*]

ROCI .... Rauschenberg Overseas Cultural Interchange [*Retrospective exhibit of artist Robert Rauschenberg's work*]

ROCI .... Rickman Owners Club International (EA)

ROCIA ...... Rozhledy v Chirurgii [*A publication*]

ROCID ...... Reorganization of Combat Infantry Division [*Army*] (AABC)

Roc Ins .... Roccus on Insurance [*A publication*] (DLA)

Rock .... New Hampshire Reports [*A publication*] (DLA)

Rock .... Rocket (MCD)

ROCK .... Rockor, Inc. [*NASDAQ symbol*] (NQ)

Rock .... Smith's New Hampshire Reports [*A publication*] (DLA)

ROCKET... Rand's Omnibus Calculator of the Kinetics of Earth Trajectories

Rocket News Lett ... Rocket News Letter [*A publication*]

Rocket News Lett J Space Flight ... Rocket News Letter and Journal of Space Flight [*A publication*]

Rocket Propul Technol ... Rocket Propulsion Technology [*A publication*]

ROCKEX... Rocket Exercise [*Military*] (NVT)

ROCKF...... Rockford [*England*]

Rock Form Miner Proc Gen Meet IMA ... Rock-Forming Minerals. Proceedings. General Meeting of IMA [*International Mineralogical Association*] [*A publication*]

Rockingham ... Smith's New Hampshire Reports [*A publication*] (DLA)

Rock Magn Paleogeophys ... Rock Magnetism and Paleogeophysics [*A publication*]

Rock Mech ... Rock Mechanics [*A publication*]

Rock Mech Am Northwest Congr Exped Guide ... Rock Mechanics. The American Northwest. Congress Expedition Guide [*A publication*]

Rock Mech Eng Geol ... Rock Mechanics and Engineering Geology [*A publication*]

Rock Mech Felsmech Mec Roches ... Rock Mechanics/Felsmechanik/Mecanique des Roches [*A publication*]

Rock Min ... Rockwell on Mines [*A publication*] (DLA)

Rock Miner Anal ... Rock and Mineral Analysis [*A publication*]

Rock Oil Ind ... Rock Oil Industry [*A publication*]

ROCKOON ... Rocket Balloon [*Navy*]

Rock Prod .. Rock Products [*A publication*]

Rocks Miner ... Rocks and Minerals [*A publication*]

Rock Sp Law ... Rockwell's Spanish and Mexican Law Relating to Mines [*A publication*] (DLA)

ROCKSTORE ... Rock Storage [*Storage in excavated rock caverns*]

Rockwl .... Rockwell International Corp. [*Associated Press abbreviation*] (APAG)

Rocky Mountain J Math ... Rocky Mountain Journal of Mathematics [*A publication*]

Rocky Mountain MJ ... Rocky Mountain Medical Journal [*A publication*]

Rocky Mount Med J ... Rocky Mountain Medical Journal [*A publication*]

Rocky Mt Assoc Geol ... Rocky Mountain Association of Geologists [*A publication*]

Rocky Mt B ... Rocky Mountain Business Journal [*A publication*]

Rocky Mt Bioeng Symp Proc ... Rocky Mountain Bioengineering Symposium. Proceedings [*A publication*]

Rocky Mt J Math ... Rocky Mountain Journal of Mathematics [*A publication*]

Rocky Mt L Rev ... Rocky Mountain Law Review [*Later, University of Colorado. Law Review*] [*A publication*]

Rocky Mt Med J ... Rocky Mountain Medical Journal [*A publication*]

Rocky Mt Miner Law Inst Annu Inst Proc ... Rocky Mountain Mineral Law Institute. Annual Institute. Proceedings [*A publication*]

Rocky Mt Miner L Rev ... Rocky Mountain Mineral Law Review [*A publication*] (DLA)

Rocky Mt Min L Inst ... Rocky Mountain Mineral Law Institute. Proceedings [*A publication*]

Rocky Mt Min L Inst Proc ... Rocky Mountain Mineral Law Institute. Proceedings [*A publication*]

Rocky Mtn L Rev ... Rocky Mountain Law Review [*Later, University of Colorado. Law Review*] [*A publication*]

Rocky Mtn Med J ... Rocky Mountain Medical Journal [*A publication*]

Rocky Mtn Oil Reporter ... Rocky Mountain Oil Reporter [*A publication*]

Rocky Mtn Soc Sci J ... Rocky Mountain Social Science Journal [*A publication*]

Rocky Mt R ... Rocky Mountain Review of Language and Literature [*A publication*]

Rocky Mt So ... Rocky Mountain Social Science Journal [*A publication*]

Rocky Mt Soc Sci J ... Rocky Mountain Social Science Journal [*A publication*]

Rocky Mt Spectrosc Conf Program Abstr ... Rocky Mountain Spectroscopy Conference. Program and Abstracts [*A publication*]

ROCL .... Rockwell Drilling Co. [*NASDAQ symbol*] (NQ)

Rocla Pipes Ltd Tech J ... Rocla Pipes Ltd. Technical Journal [*A publication*] (APTA)

ROCMAGV ... Republic of China, Military Assistance Group, Vietnam

ROCMAS ... Russian Orthodox Catholic Mutual Aid Society of USA (EA)

ROCMC ... Republic of China Marine Corps

ROCMM... Regional Office of Civilian Manpower Management

ROCN....... Reclamation Order Control Number

ROCN........ Republic of China Navy

ROCN........ Retraining Objective Control Number [*Air Force*] (AFM)

RocO .... Rocznik Orientalistyczny [*Warszawa*] [*A publication*]

ROCOA ..... Renault Owners Club of America (EA)

ROCOB ..... Rocketsonde Observation (NOAA)

ROCOCO ... Rocailles, Coquilles, et Cordeau [*Rocks, Shells, and String*] [*French*]

ROCOMP ... Radio or Computer Operated Mobile Platform [*Army*]

ROCOZ..... Rocket-Borne Ozonesonde (SAA)

ROCP .... RADAR Out of Commission for Parts [*ADC*]

ROCP .... Regional Occupation Center Program (OICC)

ROCPEX... Republic of China Philatelic Exhibition

ROCR .... Recovery Operations Control Room [*NASA*] (KSC)

ROCR .... Remote Optical Character Recognition [*Data processing*]

ROCS........ Range Operations Control System (SAA)

ROCU .... Remote Operational Control Unit [*Military*] (CAAL)

ROCWMAS ... Russian Orthodox Catholic Women's Mutual Aid Society (EA)

Rocz Bial.... Rocznik Bialostocki [*A publication*]

Rocz Bialostocki ... Rocznik Bialostocki [*A publication*]

Rocz Jeleniogorski ... Rocznik Jeleniogorski [*A publication*]

Rocz Krakowski ... Rocznik Krakowski [*A publication*]

Rocz Muz Etnogr ... Rocznik Muzeum Etnograficznego w Krakowie [*A publication*]

Rocz Muz Narod Warszawie ... Rocznik Muzeum Narodowego w Warszawie [*A publication*]

Rocz Muz Swiet ... Rocznik Muzeum Swietokrzyskiego [*A publication*]

Rocz Muz Toruniu ... Rocznik Muzeum w Toruniu [*A publication*]

Rocz Muz Warsz ... Rocznik Muzeum Narodowego w Warszawie [*A publication*]

Rocz Nauk Zootech Pol J Anim Sci Technol ... Rocznik Naukowe Zootechniki. Polish Journal of Animal Science and Technology [*A publication*]

Roczn Bibliot Narodowe ... Rocznik Bibliotek Narodowe [*A publication*]

Roczn Dendrol Polsk Tow Bot ... Rocznik Sekcji Dendrologicznej Polskiego Towarzystwa Botanicznego [*A publication*]
Roczn Wyz Szk Roln Poznan ... Rocznik Wyzszej Szkoly Rolniczej Poznaniu [*A publication*]
RoczOr .... Rocznik Orientalistyczny [*Warsaw*] [*A publication*]
Rocz Pol Tow Geol ... Rocznik Polskiego Towarzystwa Geologicznego [*A publication*]
Rocz Pomor Akad Med Szczecinie ... Rocznik Pomorskiej Akademii Medycznej Imienia Generala Karola Swierczewskiego w Szczecinie [*Poland*] [*A publication*]
Rocz Sekc Dendrol Pol Tow Bot ... Rocznik Sekcji Dendrologicznej Polskiego Towarzystwa Botanicznego [*A publication*]
RoczSl .... Rocznik Slawistyczny [*A publication*]
Rocz Stat Pow Zot ... Rocznik Statystyczny Powiatu Zotow [*A publication*]
Rocz Wojsk Inst Hig Epidemiol ... Rocznik Wojskowego Instytutu Higieny i Epidemiologii [*Poland*] [*A publication*]
ROD.......... Railway Operating Department [*British military*]   (DMA)
ROD.......... Range of the Day [*Military*]   (CAAL)
ROD.......... Range Operations Directorate [*White Sands Missile Range*]
ROD.......... Rate of Descent   (KSC)
ROD.......... Record of Decision [*Environmental Protection Agency*]
ROD.......... Record of Discussion   (MCD)
ROD.......... Recorder on Demand
ROD.......... Release Order Directive [*Later, ERO*]   (NRCH)
ROD.......... Remote Operated Door   (MCD)
ROD.......... Repair and Overhaul Directive   (AAG)
ROD.......... Report of Discrepancies
ROD.......... Required on Dock   (KSC)
ROD.......... Required Operational Date
ROD.......... Reverse-Osmosis Desalination
R-O-D .... Rise-Off-Disconnect   (AAG)
ROD.......... Roddy Resources, Inc. [*Toronto Stock Exchange symbol*]
Rod............. Rodericus Suarez [*Flourished, 15th century*] [*Authority cited in pre-1607 legal work*]   (DSA)
ROD.......... Rosewood, OH [*Location identifier*] [*FAA*]   (FAAL)
ROD.......... Route Opening Detachment   (MCD)
RODA .... Regardless of Destination Airport   (FAAC)
RODA .... Sisters Oblates to Divine Love [*Roman Catholic religious order*]
RODAC ..... Reorganization Objectives, Army Division, Army and Corps [*Military*]   (AABC)
ROD/AC ... Rotary Dual Input for Analog Computation   (SAA)
RODATA .. Registered Organization Data Bank
RODC .... Regional Oceanographic Data Center [*Marine science*]   (MSC)
RODC .... Registered Organization Development Consultant [*Designation awarded by Organization Development Institute*]
Rodds Chem Carbon Comp ... Rodd's Chemistry of Carbon Compounds [*Monograph*] [*A publication*]
RODE .... Iejima United States Air Force Base [*Ryukyu Islands*] [*ICAO location identifier*]   (ICLI)
Rod and Gun and Canad Silver Fox News ... Rod and Gun and Canadian Silver Fox News [*A publication*]
RO-DI .... Reverse Osmosis - Deionization System [*Water purification*]
RODIAC ... Rotary Dual Input for Analog Computation
R-O Dis ...... Reality-Oriented Discussion
RODM .... Rodime Ltd. [*NASDAQ symbol*]   (NQ)
Rodm .... Rodman's Reports [*78-82 Kentucky*] [*A publication*]   (DLA)
Rodman ...... Rodman's Reports [*78-82 Kentucky*] [*A publication*]   (DLA)
RODN .... Kadena Air Base [*Ryukyu Islands*] [*ICAO location identifier*]   (ICLI)
RODO .... Range Operations Duty Officer   (MUGU)
Rodo............ Rodoicus [*Authority cited in pre-1607 legal work*]   (DSA)
Rodo Kenky Kenky ... Rodoeisei Kenkyujo Kenkyuhokoku [*A publication*]
RodRen ...... Rodman & Renshaw Capital Group [*Associated Press abbreviation*]   (APAG)
RODS .... American Steel & Wire Corp. [*NASDAQ symbol*]   (CTT)
RODS .... Real-Time Operations, Dispatching, and Scheduling [*System*] [*TRW, Inc.*]
ROE .... Birmingham, AL [*Location identifier*] [*FAA*]   (FAAL)
ROE .... Rate of Exchange [*Finance*]
ROE .... Reflector Orbital Equipment
ROE .... Reflector Orbital Experiment   (MCD)
ROE .... Return on Equity [*Finance*]
ROE .... Review of Economics and Statistics [*A publication*]
ROE .... Roemisches Oesterreich [*A publication*]
ROE .... Roster of Exception [*Military*]   (AABC)
ROE .... Round Off Error
ROE .... Royal Observatory, Edinburgh [*Scotland*]
ROE .... Rules of Engagement [*Military*]   (AABC)
ROED .... Ridgeway Exco, Inc. [*NASDAQ symbol*]   (NQ)
ROEFEX ... Rotterdam Energy Futures Exchange [*Netherlands*]   (EY)
RoeFo Fortschr Geb Roentgenstr Nuklearmed ... RoeFo. Fortschritte auf dem Gebiete der Roentgenstrahlen und der Nuklearmedizin [*West Germany*] [*A publication*]
Roelk Man ... Roelker's Manual for Notaries and Bankers [*A publication*]   (DLA)
Roemische Quartalschrift ... Roemische Quartalschrift fuer Christliche Altertumskunde und fuer Kirchengeschichte [*A publication*]
Roem Jahr Kunstges ... Roemisches Jahrbuch fuer Kunstgeschichte [*A publication*]

Roem Mitt ... Mitteilungen. Deutsches Archaeologische Institut. Abteilung Rome [*A publication*]
Roem Oe .... Roemisches Oesterreich. Jahresschrift der Oesterreichischen Gesellschaft fuer Archaeologie [*A publication*]
Roem Q ...... Roemische Quartalschrift fuer Christliche Altertumskunde und fuer Kirchengeschichte [*A publication*]
Roem Qu .... Roemische Quartalschrift fuer Christliche Altertumskunde und fuer Kirchengeschichte [*A publication*]
ROEND ..... Roentgenstrahlen [*A publication*]
Roent........... Roentgenology [*Radiology*]
Roentgen Ber ... Roentgen Berichte [*A publication*]
Roentgen-Bl ... Roentgen-Blaetter [*A publication*]
Roentgen Laboratoriumsprax ... Roentgen Laboratoriumspraxis [*A publication*]
Roentgenprax ... Roentgenpraxis [*A publication*]
Roentgen Technol ... Roentgen Technology. Official Journal of the Indian Association of Radiological Technologists [*A publication*]
Roent M ..... Master of Roentgenology
Roe Q .... Roemische Quartalschrift fuer Christliche Altertumskunde und fuer Kirchengeschichte [*A publication*]
ROESY ...... Rotating-Frame Overhauser Enchancement Spectroscopy [*Organic chemistry*]
Roe US Com ... Roe's Manual for United States Commissioners [*A publication*]   (DLA)
ROF .... Rate of Fire [*In rounds per minute*] [*Military*]
ROF .... Reformed Ogboni Fraternity [*Nigeria*]
ROF .... Remote Operator Facility [*Honeywell, Inc.*]
ROF .... Reporting Organizational File [*Military*]   (AFM)
Rof............. Roffredus Beneventanus [*Flourished, 1215-43*] [*Authority cited in pre-1607 legal work*]   (DSA)
ROF .... Romanische Forschungen [*A publication*]
ROF .... Royal Oak Foundation   (EA)
ROF .... Royal Ordnance Factory [*British*]   (NATG)
ROF-B ...... Royal Ordnance Factory, Bishopton [*Scotland*]
Rof Bn .... Roffredus Beneventanus [*Flourished, 1215-43*] [*Authority cited in pre-1607 legal work*]   (DSA)
ROFF......... Retail Office Furniture Forum   (EA)
ROFF......... Roffler Industries [*NASDAQ symbol*]   (NQ)
Roffe Be ..... Roffredus Beneventanus [*Flourished, 1215-43*] [*Authority cited in pre-1607 legal work*]   (DSA)
ROFFEN ... Roffensis [*Signature of Bishop of Rochester*] [*Latin*]   (ROG)
ROFL......... Russian Orthodox Fraternity Lubov   (EA)
ROFOR ..... Route Forecast [*Aviation*]   (FAAC)
ROFR .... Repair of Repairables   (MCD)
ROFT........ RADAR Off Target
ROFT........ Rapid Optics Fabrication Technology   (MCD)
RofThPh ... Review of Theology and Philosophy [*A publication*]
ROG.......... Reactive Organic Gas [*Environmental chemistry*]
ROG.......... Receipt of Goods
ROG.......... Recruiting Operations Group [*Military*]
ROG.......... Residency Operations Group
R-O-G .... Rise-Off-Ground [*Model airplane*]   (AAG)
ROG.......... Rodale's Organic Gardening [*A publication*]
Rog............ Rogerius Beneventanus [*Flourished, 12th century*] [*Authority cited in pre-1607 legal work*]   (DSA)
ROG.......... Rogers, AR [*Location identifier*] [*FAA*]   (FAAL)
ROG.......... Rogers Corp. [*AMEX symbol*]   (SPSG)
ROG.......... Roggianite [*A zeolite*]
ROG.......... Rothchild Gold [*Vancouver Stock Exchange symbol*]
RO1(G) ..... Radio Operator (General) 1st Class [*British military*]   (DMA)
RO2(G) ..... Radio Operator (General) 2nd Class [*British military*]   (DMA)
ROGAR ..... Review of Guard and Reserve Task Force   (MCD)
Rog CHR ... Rogers' City Hall Recorder [*1816-22*] [*New York*] [*A publication*]   (DLA)
Rog Ecc L... Rogers' Ecclesiastical Law [*5th ed.*] [*1857*] [*A publication*]   (DLA)
Rog Ecc Law ... Rogers' Ecclesiastical Law [*A publication*]   (DLA)
Rog Elec..... Rogers on Elections and Registration [*A publication*]   (DLA)
ROGERS... Rogers Corp. [*Associated Press abbreviation*]   (APAG)
Rogers .... Rogers on Elections [*A publication*]   (DLA)
Rogers .... Rogers' Reports [*47-51 Louisiana Annual*] [*A publication*]   (DLA)
Rog Hov .... Roger De Hoveden's Chronica [*A publication*]   (DLA)
ROGI .... Roberts Oil & Gas, Inc. [*NASDAQ symbol*]   (NQ)
Rog Jud Acts ... Rogers on the Judicature Acts [*A publication*]   (DLA)
Rog Min ..... Rogers on Mines and Minerals [*A publication*]   (DLA)
Rog Min ..... Rogers. Mines, Minerals, and Quarries [*A publication*]   (ILCA)
ROGOPAG ... Rossellini, Jr.; Godard, Pasolini, Gregoretti [*Title of episodic motion picture formed from surnames of its directors*]
Rog Rec ...... Rogers' New City Hall Recorder [*A publication*]   (DLA)
Rog Trav .... Rogers' Wrongs and Rights of a Traveller [*A publication*]   (DLA)
ROH .... Rat Ovarian Hyperemia [*Test*]   (MAE)
ROH .... Ray of Hope [*An association*]   (EA)
R-O-H .... Receiver Off the Hook
ROH .... Regular Overhaul [*Navy*]   (NG)
ROH .... Returned on Hire
roh .... Rhaeto-Romance [*MARC language code*] [*Library of Congress*]   (LCCP)
ROH .... Robinhood [*Australia*] [*Airport symbol*] [*Obsolete*]   (OAG)
ROH .... Rohm & Haas Co. [*NYSE symbol*]   (SPSG)

ROH .... Rohtak [*India*] [*Seismograph station code, US Geological Survey*] [*Closed*] (SEIS)
RoH............ Roumeliotiko Hemerologio [*A publication*]
ROH .... Royal Opera House [*Covent Garden, London*]
RoHaas...... Rohm & Haas Co. [*Associated Press abbreviation*] (APAG)
Rohm Haas Rep ... Rohm and Haas Reporter [*A publication*]
Rohm & Haas Reptr ... Rohm and Haas Reporter [*A publication*]
Rohr .... Rohr Industries, Inc. [*Associated Press abbreviation*] (APAG)
ROHRA..... Rohre, Rohrleitungsbau, Rohrleitungstransport [*A publication*]
Rohre Rohrleitungsbau Rohrleitungstransp ... Rohre, Rohrleitungsbau, Rohrleitungstransport [*West Germany*] [*A publication*]
Rohst Landerber ... Rohstoffwirtschaftliche Landerberichte [*A publication*]
ROI .... Member of the Royal Institute of Oil Painters [*British*]
ROI .... Radio, Optical, Inertial
ROI .... Range Operations Instruction [*NASA*] (KSC)
ROI .... Reactive Oxygen Intermediate [*Biochemistry*]
ROI .... Region of Interest [*Nuclear energy*] (NRCH)
ROI .... Registration of Interest
ROI .... Relevant, Original, Impact [*Advertising*] (WDMC)
ROI .... Reliability Organization Instruction (AAG)
ROI .... Religious Observance Index (BJA)
ROI .... Remnant of Israel (EA)
ROI .... Rendezvous Orbit Insertion [*Aerospace*]
ROI .... Report of Investigation [*Military*] (AFM)
ROI .... Resource Objectives, Inc. [*Ridgewood, NJ*] (TSSD)
ROI .... Return on Investment [*Finance*]
ROI .... River Oaks Industries, Inc. [*NYSE symbol*] (SPSG)
ROI .... Rotating Optical Interferometer
ROI .... Royal Institute of Oil Painters [*British*]
ROIC .... Resident Officer-in-Charge [*Military*]
ROICC...... Resident Officer-in-Charge of Construction [*Military*]
ROICM ..... Resident Officer-in-Charge of Material [*Navy*] (DNAB)
ROID .... Report of Item Discrepancy [*Army*] (AABC)
ROIG .... Ishigaki Jima [*Ryukyu Islands*] [*ICAO location identifier*] (ICLI)
ROIL.......... Reserve Industries Corp. [*NASDAQ symbol*] (NQ)
ROINST.... Range Operations Instruction [*NASA*] (MUGU)
ROIP......... Remaining Oil in Place [*Petroleum industry*]
ROIS.......... Radio Operational Intercom System (KSC)
ROITL....... Reports of Interest to Lawyers [*Merton Allen Associates*] [*Information service or system*] (CRD)
ROJ .... Range of Jamming
ROJ .... Romanistisches Jahrbuch [*A publication*]
ROJ .... Royal Order of Jagie Ilo [*Later, SHOSJ*] (EA)
ROK.......... Republic of Korea
ROK.......... Rockhampton [*Australia*] [*Airport symbol*] (OAG)
ROK .... Rockwell International Corp. [*NYSE symbol*] [*Toronto Stock Exchange symbol*] (SPSG)
ROKA .... Republic of Korea Army
ROKAA ..... Rodo Kagaku [*A publication*]
ROKAF..... Republic of Korea Air Force
ROKAP ..... Republic of Korea Civic Action Program
ROKDTF.. Republic of Korea Division Task Force
ROKF .... Republic of Korea Forces
ROKFV..... Republic of Korea Forces in Vietnam
ROKG....... Republic of Korea Government
ROKG........ Rocking
ROKIT....... Republic of Korea Indigenous Tank Program (MCD)
ROKJ........ Kume Jima [*Ryukyu Islands*] [*ICAO location identifier*] (ICLI)
ROKMC .... Republic of Korea Marine Corps
ROKN....... Republic of Korea Navy
ROKOA5... Folia Entomologica Hungarica [*A publication*]
ROKPTN.. Rockhampton (ROG)
ROKPUC... Republic of Korea Presidential Unit Citation Badge [*Military decoration*]
ROKPUCE ... Republic of Korea Presidential Unit Citation [*Military decoration*]
ROKUSCFC ... Republic of Korea and US Combined Forces Command (MCD)
ROKW....... Yomitan [*Ryukyu Islands*] [*ICAO location identifier*] (ICLI)
ROL.......... RADAR Observer License
ROL.......... Record of Oral Language (ADA)
ROL.......... Reduction-Option Loan [*Banking*]
ROL.......... Remote Operating Location (MCD)
ROL.......... Reordering Level
ROL.......... Right Occipitolateral [*Obstetrics*]
ROL.......... Rolla [*Missouri*] [*Seismograph station code, US Geological Survey*] (SEIS)
Rol.............. Rolle's Abridgment [*A publication*] (DLA)
Rol.............. Rolle's English King's Bench Reports [*2 vols.*] [*A publication*] (DLA)
ROL .... Rollins, Inc. [*NYSE symbol*] (SPSG)
ROL.......... Rotate Left [*Data processing*]
ROL .... Royal Oak Resources Ltd. [*Toronto Stock Exchange symbol*]
ROL.......... Royal Overseas League [*British*] (EAIO)
Rol Ab .... Rolle's Abridgment [*A publication*] (DLA)
ROLAC...... Regional Office for Latin America and the Caribbean [*United Nations Environment Programme*] (EAIO)
ROLAC...... Regional Organization of Liaison for Allocation of Circuit (NATG)

ROLAC...... Registry of Life Assurance Commission [*British*]
ROLADES ... Roland Air Defense System (MCD)
ROLE .... Receive Only Link Eleven [*Naval datalink system*] [*British*]
Role Fert Intensif Agric Prod Proc Congr Int Potash Inst ... Role of Fertilization in the Intensification of Agricultural Production. Proceedings. Congress. International Potash Institute [*A publication*]
Role Immunol Factors Viral Oncog Processes Int Symp ... Role of Immunological Factors in Viral and Oncongenic Processes. International Symposium [*A publication*]
Role Membr Secretory Processes Proc Meet Int Conf Biol Membr ... Role of Membranes in Secretory Processes. Proceedings. Meeting. International Conference on Biological Membranes [*A publication*]
Role Pharmacokinet Prenatal Perinat Toxicol Symp Prenatal De ... Role of Pharmacokinetics in Prenatal and Perinatal Toxicology. Symposium on Prenatal Development [*A publication*]
ROLET...... Reference Our Letter (NOAA)
ROLF........ Remotely Operated Longwall Face (IEEE)
ROLF........ Rolfite Co. [*NASDAQ symbol*] (NQ)
RoLit.......... Romania Literara [*A publication*]
Roll............ Rolle's Abridgment [*A publication*] (DLA)
Roll............ Rolle's English King's Bench Reports [*2 vols.*] [*A publication*] (DLA)
Roll Abr ..... Rolle's Abridgment [*A publication*] (DLA)
Rolle........... Rolle's Abridgment [*A publication*] (DLA)
Rolle........... Rolle's English King's Bench Reports [*2 vols.*] [*1614-25*] [*A publication*] (DLA)
Rolle Abr.... Rolle's Abridgment of the Common Law [*A publication*] (DLA)
RolLeas...... Rollins Truck Leasing [*Associated Press abbreviation*] (APAG)
Rolle R .... Rolle's English King's Bench Reports [*2 vols.*] [*1614-25*] [*A publication*] (DLA)
RollinE....... Rollins Environmental Services, Inc. [*Associated Press abbreviation*] (APAG)
Rollins........ Rollins, Inc. [*Associated Press abbreviation*] (APAG)
Roll Rep ..... Rolle's English King's Bench Reports [*2 vols.*] [*1614-25*] [*A publication*] (DLA)
Rolls Ct Rep ... Rolls' Court Reports [*A publication*] (DLA)
Roll Stone .. Rolling Stone [*A publication*]
Ro/Lo .... Roll-On, Roll-Off/Lift-On, Lift-Off [*Shipping*] (DS)
ROLR .... Receiving Objective Loudness Rating [*Telephones*] (IEEE)
ROLS......... Recoverable Orbital Launch System
ROLSIM ... Roland Simulation (MCD)
ROM.......... Priest, CA [*Location identifier*] [*FAA*] (FAAL)
ROM.......... Radiopaque Contrast Material (WGA)
ROM.......... Range of Motion [*or Movement*]
ROM.......... Reactive Oxygen Metabolites [*Biochemistry*]
ROM.......... Read-Only Memory [*Computer memory*] [*Data processing*]
ROM.......... Read-Only Men [*On Board car window sign's version of the computer term, Read-Only Memory*]
ROM.......... Readout Memory (IEEE)
ROM.......... Recruiter of the Month [*Navy*] (DNAB)
ROM.......... Regional Oxidant Model [*Environmental Protection Agency*] (GFGA)
ROM.......... Register of Merit (WGA)
ROM.......... Return on Market Value [*Finance*]
ROM.......... Rio Algom Ltd. [*AMEX symbol*] [*Toronto Stock Exchange symbol*] (SPSG)
Rom............ Roemisch [*Roman*] [*German*]
Rom............ [*Ludovicus Pontanus de*] Roma [*Deceased, 1439*] [*Authority cited in pre-1607 legal work*] (DSA)
ROM.......... Roman [*Type*] [*Publishing*]
ROM.......... Romance
Rom............ Romania [*A publication*]
ROM.......... Romania [*ANSI three-letter standard code*] (CNC)
Rom............ Romans [*New Testament book*]
rom............. Romany [*MARC language code*] [*Library of Congress*] (LCCP)
Rom............ Romany Records [*Record label*]
ROM.......... Romberg [*Medicine*]
ROM.......... Rome [*Italy*] [*Seismograph station code, US Geological Survey*] [*Closed*] (SEIS)
ROM.......... Rome [*Italy*] [*Airport symbol*] (OAG)
Rom............ Romeo and Juliet [*Shakespearean work*]
Rom............ Romilly's Notes of English Chancery Cases [*1767-87*] [*A publication*] (DLA)
Rom............ Romulus [*of Plutarch*] [*Classical studies*] (OCD)
ROM.......... Rough Order of Magnitude [*Army*] (AABC)
ROM.......... Royal Ontario Museum [*Toronto, ON*] [*Research center*]
ROM.......... Run of Mine
ROM.......... Rupture of Membranes [*Medicine*]
ROMA....... Return on Managed Assets [*Business term*]
ROMAA..... Rom-Amer Pharmaceuticals [*NASDAQ symbol*] (NQ)
ROMAC .... Range Operations Monitor Analysis Center (MCD)
ROMAC .... Range Operations Monitoring and Control
ROMAC .... Robotic Muscle Activator
ROMACC ... Range Operational Monitoring and Control Center
ROMAD .... Radio Operator/Maintenance Driver
Rom Adelsparteien ... Roemische Adelsparteien und Adelsfamilien [*A publication*] (OCD)
Roma Econ ... Roma Economica [*A publication*]

Romagna Med ... Romagna Medica [*A publication*]
Romance Philol ... Romance Philology [*A publication*]
Roman Forsc ... Romanische Forschungen [*A publication*]
Roman Forsch ... Romanische Forschungen [*A publication*]
Romanian F ... Romanian Film [*A publication*]
Romanian R ... Romanian Review [*A publication*]
Romania P ... Romania during the 1981-1985 Development Plan [*A publication*]
Roman Note ... Romance Notes [*A publication*]
Romanobarbar ... Romanobarbarica. Contributi allo Studio dei Rapporti Culturali tra il Mondo Latino e Mondo Barbarico [*A publication*]
Roman Phil ... Romance Philology [*A publication*]
Roman Philol ... Romance Philology [*A publication*]
Roman R .... Romanic Review [*A publication*]
Roman Rev ... Romanic Review [*A publication*]
ROMANS ... Range-Only Multiple Aircraft Navigation System [*Air Force*]
ROMANS ... Remote Manipulation Systems [*NASA*]
Romant Move ... Romantic Movement [*A publication*]
RO(M)B .... Reduction of (Military) Budgets
ROMBI ..... Results of Marine Biological Investigations [*Marine science*] (MSC)
ROMBUS ... Reusable Orbital Module Booster and Utility Shuttle [*Aerospace*]
Rom Cas ..... Romilly's Notes of English Chancery Cases [*1767-87*] [*A publication*] (DLA)
ROMCOE ... Rocky Mountain Center on Environment (EPA)
Rom Com Geol Dari Seama Sedin ... Romania Comitetul de Stat al Geologiei. Institutul Geologic. Dari de Seama ale Sedintelor [*A publication*]
Rom Cr Law ... Romilly's Observations on the Criminal Law [*3rd ed.*] [*1813*] [*A publication*] (DLA)
ROMD .... Minami Daito Jima [*Ryukyu Islands*] [*ICAO location identifier*] (ICLI)
ROMD .... Remote Operations and Maintenance Demonstration [*Nuclear energy*]
ROME .... Resource Organizations and Meetings for Educators [*National Center for Research in Vocational Education*] [*Information service or system*] [*Defunct*] (CRD)
ROMEMO ... Reference Our Memorandum (FAAC)
ROMES ..... Reference Our Message (FAAC)
RomF .... Romanische Forschungen [*A publication*]
Rom Fgn Tr ... Romanian Foreign Trade [*A publication*]
Rom Forsch ... Roemische Forschungen [*A publication*] (OCD)
Rom G .... Romanica Gandensia [*A publication*]
Rom Gesch ... Grundriss der Romischen Geschichte [*A publication*] (OCD)
Rom Gesch ... Romische Geschichte bis zum Beginn der Punischen Kriege [*A publication*] (OCD)
ROMI .... Rule Out Myocardial Infarction [*Medicine*]
Romilly NC (Eng) ... Romilly's Notes of English Chancery Cases [*A publication*] (DLA)
Rom Inst Geol Dari Seama Sedin ... Romania Institutul Geologic. Dari de Seama ale Sedintelor [*A publication*]
Rom Inst Geol Mem ... Romania Institutul Geologic. Memorii [*A publication*]
RomJ .... Romanistisches Jahrbuch [*A publication*]
Rom J Chem ... Romanian Journal of Chemistry [*A publication*]
Rom J Gerontol Geriatr ... Romanian Journal of Gerontology and Geriatrics [*A publication*]
Rom J Med Endocrinol ... Romanian Journal of Medicine. Endocrinology [*A publication*]
Rom J Med Intern Med ... Romanian Journal of Medicine. Internal Medicine [*A publication*]
Rom J Med Neurol Psychiatry ... Romanian Journal of Medicine. Neurology and Psychiatry [*A publication*]
Rom J Med Virol ... Romanian Journal of Medicine. Virology [*A publication*]
Rom J Morphol ... Romanian Journal of Morphology, Embryology, and Physiology. Morphology and Embryology [*A publication*]
Rom J Morphol Embryol Physiol Physiol ... Romanian Journal of Morphology, Embryology, and Physiology. Physiology [*A publication*]
Rom J Tech Sci Appl Mech ... Romanian Journal of Technical Sciences. Applied Mechanics [*A publication*]
Rom Law .... Mackeldey's Handbook of the Roman Law [*A publication*] (DLA)
RomLit .... Romania Literara [*Bucharest*] [*A publication*]
ROMM ...... Read-Only Memory Module [*Data processing*]
Rom Med Rev ... Romanian Medical Review [*A publication*]
RomN .... Romance Notes [*A publication*]
ROMO ...... Rocky Mountain National Park
ROMON ... Receiving-Only Monitor
ROMOSS ... Revised Officer Military Occupational Speciality System (MCD)
ROMOTAR ... Range-Only Measurement of Trajectory and Recording
ROMP .... Radiotelephone Operator Maintenance Proficiency (DNAB)
ROMP .... Recovery of Male Potency (EA)
ROMP .... Report of Obligation Military Pay (AFM)
ROMP .... Review of Management Practices [*or Processes*]
ROMP .... Ring Opening Metathesis Polymerization [*Organic chemistry*]
Rom Pat Doc ... Romania. Patent Document [*A publication*]
RomPh .... Romance Philology [*A publication*]
Rom Pol ... Roman Politics 220-150BC [*A publication*] (OCD)

ROMPS ..... Regional Office Monthly Personnel Status [*Department of Labor*]
RomR .... Romanic Review [*A publication*]
Rom Rev ..... [*The*] Roman Revolution [*1939*] [*A publication*] (OCD)
Rom Rule Asia Min ... Roman Rule in Asia Minor [*A publication*] (OCD)
ROMS .... Remote Ocean Surface Measuring System [*Navy*] (CAAL)
RomSl .... Romanoslavica [*A publication*]
Rom Staatsr ... Roemisches Staatsrecht [*A publication*] (OCD)
Rom Strafr ... Roemisches Strafrecht [*A publication*] (OCD)
Rom Stud ... Roemische Studien [*A publication*] (OCD)
Rom Today ... Romania Today [*A publication*]
ROMY .... Miyako [*Ryukyu Islands*] [*ICAO location identifier*] (ICLI)
RON .... Receiving Only (FAAC)
RON .... Remaining [*or Rest*] Overnight [*Aviation*]
RON .... Remote [*Alaska*] [*Seismograph station code, US Geological Survey*] [*Closed*] (SEIS)
RON .... Report of NAC/ENTAC (MCD)
RON .... Research-Octane-Number [*Fuel technology*]
RON .... Rest Overnight [*or Rest-of-Night*] [*Pronounced "ron"*] [*Chance for a candidate to catch some sleep during a traveling political campaign*]
RoN .... Romance Notes [*A publication*]
RON .... Rondon [*Colombia*] [*Airport symbol*] [*Obsolete*] (OAG)
RON .... Squadron (MUGU)
RONA .... Naha United States Naval Base [*Ryukyu Islands*] [*ICAO location identifier*] (ICLI)
RONA .... Return on Net Assets
RONAG ..... Reserve Officers Naval Architecture Group
RONB .... Research-Octane-Number-Barrels [*Fuel technology*]
RONC .... Ronson Corp. [*Somerset, NJ*] [*NASDAQ symbol*] (NQ)
Ronchegall ... [*Johannes*] Ronchegallus [*Flourished, 1559-80*] [*Authority cited in pre-1607 legal work*] (DSA)
RONCO ...... Rock-Oldies-News-Commercials Operation [*Formula radio*]
RONCOM ... Ronald Como, Inc. [*Perry Como's production firm; Ronald is his son*]
ROND ...... Remote Ordnance Neutralization Device (DWSG)
RONEO ..... Rotary and Neostyle [*Duplicating machine*] [*Acronym is trademark*]
RONLY ..... Receiver Only [*Radio*]
RONS .... Reserve Officers of the Naval Service [*Later, ROA*]
R Ont Mus J ... Royal Ontario Museum. Journal [*A publication*]
R Ont Mus Life Sci Contrib ... Royal Ontario Museum. Life Sciences. Contributions [*A publication*]
R Ont Mus Life Sci Misc Publ ... Royal Ontario Museum. Life Sciences. Miscellaneous Publications [*A publication*]
R Ont Mus Life Sci Occas Pap ... Royal Ontario Museum. Life Sciences. Occasional Paper [*A publication*]
R Ont Mus Zool Paleontol Contrib ... Royal Ontario Museum of Zoology and Paleontology. Contributions [*A publication*]
RONWT .... Revised Ordinances, Northwest Territories [*Canada*] [*A publication*] (DLA)
ROO .... Radio Optical Observatory
ROO .... Railhead Ordnance Officer
ROO .... Range Operations Officer
ROO .... Reserve of Officers [*British*]
ROO .... Resident Obstetric Officer [*British*]
ROO .... Richland Operations Office [*Energy Research and Development Administration*]
ROO .... Rondonopolis [*Brazil*] [*Airport symbol*] (OAG)
ROOPH ..... Readily Operative Overhead Protection by Hippos [*Facetious proposal for protection against nuclear attack*]
ROORD3 ... Radiologia [*Bucharest*] [*A publication*]
Roorkee Univ Res J ... Roorkee University. Research Journal [*A publication*]
ROOS .... Roosevelt National Investment Co. [*NASDAQ symbol*] (NQ)
ROOSCH .. Royal Order of Sputnik Chasers
Roosevelt Wild Life Bull ... Roosevelt Wild Life Bulletin [*A publication*]
ROOST ...... Reusable One-Stage Orbital Space Truck [*Aerospace*]
ROOT .... Mr. Rooter Corp. [*Oklahoma City, OK*] [*NASDAQ symbol*] (NQ)
ROOT .... Relaxation Oscillator Optically Tuned
Root .... Root's Connecticut Reports [*1774-89*] [*A publication*] (DLA)
Root .... Root's Connecticut Supreme Court Reports [*1789-98*] [*A publication*] (DLA)
Root Bt Laws ... Root's Digest of Law and Practice in Bankruptcy [*1818*] [*A publication*] (DLA)
Root R .... Root's Connecticut Reports [*A publication*] (DLA)
Roots .... Root's Connecticut Reports [*A publication*] (DLA)
Root's Rep ... Root's Connecticut Reports [*A publication*] (DLA)
ROP .... Raster Operation
ROP .... Rate of Pay [*British military*] (DMA)
ROP .... Rate of Penetration [*Drilling technology*]
ROP .... Receive-Only Printer [*Data processing*]
ROP .... Receiving Operations Package [*DoD*]
ROP .... Record of Performance
ROP .... Record of Production
ROP .... Record of Purchase (NRCH)
ROP .... Refined Oil Products
ROP .... Regional Operating Plan [*Department of Labor*]
ROP .... Regional Oversight Policy [*Environmental Protection Agency*] (GFGA)
ROP .... Registered Options Principal

ROP..........	Reorder Point [*Navy*]　(NG)
ROP..........	Reorder Price
ROP..........	Repeat Offenders Project
ROP..........	Republic of Panama
ROP..........	Republic of the Philippines
ROP..........	Requirements Objectives Period
ROP..........	Retinopathy of Prematurity [*Medicine*]
ROP..........	Right Occipitoposterior [*A fetal position*] [*Obstetrics*]
ROP..........	Right Outside Position [*Dancing*]
ROP..........	Rites of Passage
ROP..........	Robson Petroleum Ltd. [*Toronto Stock Exchange symbol*]
ROP..........	Roll-Over Protection Equipment　(MCD)
ROP..........	Romance Philology [*A publication*]
ROP..........	Roper Corp. [*NYSE symbol*]　(SPSG)
Rop.............	Roper on Legacies [*4 eds.*] [*1799-1847*] [*A publication*]　(DLA)
ROP..........	Rota [*Mariana Islands*] [*Airport symbol*]　(OAG)
ROP..........	Royal Order of Piast　(EA)
ROP..........	Run of Paper [*Business term*]
ROP..........	Run of Press [*i.e., on an unspecified page or plate in web press set-up*] [*Printing*]
ROP₃.........	Revision of Procurement Policy and Procedures
ROPA	Reserve Officer Personnel Act of 1954
ROPAR	Regional Operators Program for Aircraft Reliability
ROPB	Reserve Officers Promotion Board [*Air Force*]
ROPBX.....	Reference Our Private Branch Exchange Message　(SAA)
ROPE	Remotely Operated Platform Electronic [*Submarine technology*]
ROPE	Reunion of Professional Entertainers　(EA)
ROPER.....	Regional Operators Program for Engine Reliability
ROPES.....	Remote Online Print Executive System
ROPEVAL ...	Readiness/Operational Evaluation　(NVT)
ROPEVAL ...	Rim of the Pacific Evaluation　(MCD)
ROPF.......	Research into One-Parent Families [*British*]
ROPHO.....	Reference Our Telephone Call　(NOAA)
Rop Husb & Wife ...	Roper's Law of Property between Husband and Wife [*A publication*]　(DLA)
Rop H & W ...	Roper's Law of Property between Husband and Wife [*2nd ed.*] [*1826*] [*A publication*]　(DLA)
ROPIS.......	Response of Plants to Interacting Stress Program [*Electric Power Research Institute*]
ROPK	Ropak Corp. [*NASDAQ symbol*]　(NQ)
Rop Leg......	Roper on Legacies [*A publication*]　(DLA)
ROPM	Revue. Ordre de Premontre et de Ses Missions [*A publication*]
ROPMA	Reserve Officers Personnel Management Act [*Proposed*]
ROPME	Regional Organization for the Protection of the Marine Environment [*Safat, Kuwait*]　(EAIO)
ROPP........	Receive-Only Page Printer
ROPP........	Review of Plant Pathology [*Database*] [*Commonwealth Mycological Institute*] [*Information service or system*]　(CRD)
Rop Prop....	Roper's Law of Property between Husband and Wife [*2nd ed.*] [*1826*] [*A publication*]　(DLA)
ROPRA	Reserve Officer Performance Recording Activity
ROPRA	Rock Products [*A publication*]
Rop Rev......	Roper on Revocation of Wills [*A publication*]　(DLA)
ROPS........	Range Operation Performance Summary
ROPS........	Roll-Over Protection System [*for tractors*]
ROPS........	Roll Over Protective Structures [*NASA*]　(KSC)
ROPT	Remaining Number of Operations
ROPT	Robson Petroleum Ltd. [*NASDAQ symbol*]　(NQ)
ROPU	RADAR Overheat Protection Unit　(MCD)
ROPXA	Roentgenpraxis [*A publication*]
ROQ..........	Houghton Lake, MI [*Location identifier*] [*FAA*]　(FAAL)
ROQ..........	Recruiter of the Quarter [*Navy*]　(DNAB)
ROQ..........	Reordering Quality
ROR	Koror [*Palau Islands*] [*Airport symbol*]　(OAG)
ROR	Range-Only RADAR [*Military*]　(AABC)
ROR	Rate of Read
ROR	Rate of Return　(MCD)
ROR	Released on Own Recognizance [*Law*]
ROR	Repair, Overhaul, Restoration　(MCD)
ROR	Repair of Repairables　(MCD)
ROR	Residual Oil Remover [*Lens cleaner*] [*V-Vax Products*]
ROR	Return of Repairables
RoR	Review of Religion [*A publication*]
ROR	Right of Rescission [*Business term*]
ROR₃.........	Rochester Minerals [*Vancouver Stock Exchange symbol*]
ROR	Rocket on Rotor
ROR	Rockton & Rion Railway [*AAR code*]
RoR	Romanian Review [*A publication*]
ROR	Romanic Review [*A publication*]
ROR	Rorschach [*Test*]
ROR	Rotate Right [*Data processing*]
RORA	Aguni [*Ryukyu Islands*] [*ICAO location identifier*]　(ICLI)
RORA	Reliable Operate RADAR Altimeter
RORA	Reserve Officer Recording Activity
RORC	Royal Ocean Racing Club [*British*]
RORCE......	Rate of Return on Capital Employed　(DS)
RORD........	Research Opportunities in Renaissance Drama [*A publication*]
RORD........	Return on Receipt of Document [*Business term*]
RORE	Iejima [*Ryukyu Islands*] [*ICAO location identifier*]　(ICLI)

ROREF......	Rosmac Resources Ltd. [*NASDAQ symbol*]　(NQ)
Ro Rep	Robards' Texas Conscript Cases [*1862-65*] [*A publication*]　(DLA)
Ro Rep	Rolle's English King's Bench Reports [*A publication*]　(DLA)
ROREQ	Reference Our Requisition　(NOAA)
Rorer Jud Sales ...	Rorer on Void Judicial Sales [*A publication*]　(DLA)
Rorer RR....	Rorer on Railways [*A publication*]　(DLA)
RORET.......	Authorized Rotational Retention [*Navy*]
RORG........	Naha [*Ryukyu Islands*] [*ICAO location identifier*]　(ICLI)
RORH........	Hateruma [*Ryukyu Islands*] [*ICAO location identifier*]　(ICLI)
RO/RI.......	Redistribution Out/Redistribution In　(CINC)
Ror Int St L ...	Rorer on Inter-State Law [*A publication*]　(DLA)
RORIS.......	Remote Operated Radiographic Inspection System
Ror Jud Sal ...	Rorer on Void Judicial Sales [*A publication*]　(DLA)
RORK........	Kitadaito [*Ryukyu Islands*] [*ICAO location identifier*]　(ICLI)
RO/RO	Roll-On/Roll-Off [*Shipping*]　(AFM)
RO-RO	Rolls Royce [*Automobile*] [*Slang*]　(DSUE)
RORQN.....	Reference Our Requisition　(FAAC)
RORS	Realignment of Resources and Services　(MCD)
RORS	Shimojishima [*Ryukyu Islands*] [*ICAO location identifier*]　(ICLI)
RORSAT ...	RADAR Ocean Reconnaissance Satellite　(MCD)
RORT	Report on Reimbursable Transactions [*DoD*]
RORT	Tarama [*Ryukyu Islands*] [*ICAO location identifier*]　(ICLI)
RORU	Rest of Route Unchanged　(FAAC)
RORY	Yoron [*Ryukyu Islands*] [*ICAO location identifier*]　(ICLI)
ROS	RADAR Order Switch
ROS	Radius of Suspension
ROS	Range Operation Station
ROS	Range Operations Supervisor　(MUGU)
ROS	Range of Spares　(MCD)
ROS	Rat Osteosarcoma [*Cell line*]
ROS	Rate of Speed　(MCD)
ROS	Reactive Oxygen Species
ROS	Read-Only Storage [*Data processing*]
ROS	Ready Operating Status　(DNAB)
ROS	Reduced Operational Status [*Military*]
ROS	Reed Organ Society　(EA)
ROS	Registration Offering Statistics System [*Securities and Exchange Commission*]　(GFGA)
ROS	Regulated Oxygen Supply　(MCD)
ROS	Regulated Oxygen System　(NASA)
ROS	Remote Optical Sight [*Military*]　(CAAL)
ROS	Remote Optical System
ROS	Removable Overhead Structure　(MCD)
ROS	Report Originator System [*Military*]　(CAAL)
ROS	Representative Observation Site [*Weather observing facility*] [*Air Force*]
ROS	Requisition on Stores [*Nuclear energy*]　(NRCH)
ROS	Research Optical Sensor　(MCD)
ROS	Resident Operating System
ROS	Residual Oil Saturation [*Petroleum technology*]
ROS	Restored Oil Shales
ROS	Return from Overseas [*Military*]
ROS	Return on Sales
ROS	Review of Systems [*Medicine*]
ROS	Robotics Operating System
ROS	Rod Outer Segments [*of the retina*]
ROS	Rosa [*Rose*] [*Pharmacology*]　(ROG)
ROS	Rosario [*Argentina*] [*Airport symbol*]　(OAG)
ROS	Rosary
Ros	Roscommon [*County in Ireland*]　(WGA)
ROS	Rose Resources Corp. [*Vancouver Stock Exchange symbol*]
ROS	Roseneath [*New Zealand*] [*Seismograph station code, US Geological Survey*] [*Closed*]　(SEIS)
ROS	Ross Aviation, Inc. [*Tulsa, OK*] [*FAA designator*]　(FAAC)
ROS	Roswell Public Library, Roswell, NM [*OCLC symbol*]　(OCLC)
ROS	Rotary on Stamps Fellowship　(EA)
ROS	Rotating Optical Scanner
ROS	Royal Order of Scotland　(EA)
ROS	Run of Schedule [*Commercial announcement to be broadcast throughout the program schedule*] [*Advertising*]
ROS	Rush Order Service
ROSA	Record One Stop Association [*Defunct*]　(EA)
ROSA	Recording Optical Spectrum Analyzer　(MCD)
ROSA	Report of Supply Activity　(MCD)
ROSAR.....	Read-Only Storage Address Register
ROSAT.....	RADAR Ocean Surveillance Satellite　(NVT)
ROSAT.....	Roentgen Satellite [*Space research*]
ROSC........	Reserve Officers Sanitary Corps
ROSC........	Restoration of Spontaneous Circulation
ROSC........	Review of Scottish Culture [*A publication*]
ROSC........	Road Operators Safety Council [*British*]
Rosc...........	Roscoe's Reports of the Supreme Court [*1861-78*] [*South Africa*] [*A publication*]　(DLA)
ROSC........	Roscommon [*County in Ireland*]　(ROG)
Rosc Act.....	Roscoe on Actions [*1825*] [*A publication*]　(DLA)
Rosc Adm....	Roscoe's Admiralty Jurisdiction and Practice [*A publication*]　(DLA)
Rosc Am.....	Pro Sexto Roscio Amerino [*of Cicero*] [*Classical studies*]　(OCD)

Rosc Bdg Cas ... Roscoe's Digest of Building Cases [*4th ed.*] [*1900*] [*A publication*]　(DLA)
Rosc Bills ... Roscoe's Bills of Exchange [*2nd ed.*] [*1843*] [*A publication*]　(DLA)
Rosc Civ Pr ... Roscoe's Outlines of Civil Procedure [*2nd ed.*] [*1880*] [*A publication*]　(DLA)
Rosc Cr ...... Roscoe's Law of Evidence in Criminal Cases [*16 eds.*] [*1835-1952*] [*A publication*]　(DLA)
Rosc Crim Ev ... Roscoe's Law of Evidence in Criminal Cases [*16 eds.*] [*1835-1952*] [*A publication*]　(DLA)
Rosc Ev ...... Roscoe's Nisi Prius Evidence [*20th ed.*] [*1934*] [*A publication*]　(DLA)
Rosc Jur ..... Roscoe's Jurist [*England*] [*A publication*]　(DLA)
Rosc Light ... Roscoe's Law of Light [*4th ed.*] [*1904*] [*A publication*]　(DLA)
Rosc NP ..... Roscoe's Law of Evidence at Nisi Prius [*20 eds.*] [*1827-1934*] [*A publication*]　(DLA)
ROSCO ..... Rotating Stratified Combustion [*Automotive engineering*]
ROSCOE ... RADAR and Optical Systems Code
Roscoe .... Roscoe's Reports of the Supreme Court of Cape Of Good Hope [*South Africa*] [*A publication*]　(DLA)
Roscoe Bldg Cas ... Roscoe's Digest of Building Cases [*England*] [*A publication*]　(DLA)
Roscoe Cr Ev ... Roscoe's Law of Evidence in Criminal Cases [*16 eds.*] [*1835-1952*] [*A publication*]　(DLA)
Roscoe's BC ... Roscoe's Digest of Building Cases [*England*] [*A publication*]　(DLA)
ROSCOM ... Roscommon [*County in Ireland*]
ROSCOP ... Report of Observations/Samples Collected by Oceanographic Programs [*Intergovernmental Oceanographic Commission*]　(MSC)
Rosc PC ..... Roscoe's English Prize Cases [*1745-1859*] [*A publication*]　(DLA)
Rosc Pl .... Roscoe's Pleading [*1845*] [*A publication*]　(DLA)
ROSDR ..... Read-Only Storage Data Register
ROSE .... Reconstruction by Optimized Series Expansion [*Of large molecules*]
ROSE .... Remote Optical Sensing of Emissions [*Instrumentation*]
ROSE .... Remotely Operated Special Equipment [*Nuclear energy*]
ROSE .... Resident Operational Support Equipment
ROSE .... Residuum Oil Supercritical Extraction [*Petroleum refining*]
ROSE .... Retrieval by Online Search [*Data processing*]
ROSE .... Rising Observational Sounding Equipment
ROSE .... Rivera Ocean Seismic Experiment
Rose .... Rose's English Bankruptcy Reports [*A publication*]　(DLA)
Rose Annu R Natl Rose Soc ... Rose Annual. Royal National Rose Society [*A publication*]
Rose Bankr ... Rose's English Bankruptcy Reports [*1810-16*] [*A publication*]　(DLA)
Rose Bankr (Eng) ... Rose's English Bankruptcy Reports [*A publication*]　(DLA)
Rose BC ..... Rose's English Bankruptcy Reports [*A publication*]　(DLA)
Rose Dig ..... Rose's Digest of Arkansas Reports [*A publication*]　(DLA)
Rosenberger ... Street Railway Law [*United States*] [*A publication*]　(DLA)
Rosenberger Pock LJ ... Rosenberger's Pocket Law Journal [*A publication*]　(DLA)
Rose Notes ... Rose's Notes on United States Reports [*A publication*]　(DLA)
Rose RA ..... Roscoe on Real Actions [*A publication*]　(DLA)
Rose St D ... Roscoe on Stamp Duties [*A publication*]　(DLA)
ROSET ...... Register of Solicitors Employing Trainees　(ILCA)
Rose WC ..... Rose. Will Case [*New York*] [*A publication*]　(DLA)
ROSIE .... Reconnaissance by Orbiting Ship-Identification Equipment
ROSIE .... Rooters Organized to Stimulate Interest and Enthusiasm [*Women baseball fans, Cincinnati*]
ROSIE .... Rule Oriented System for Implementing Expertise　(MCD)
Roskills Lett China ... Roskill's Letter from China [*A publication*]
ROSL .... Royal Overseas League [*British*]　(DI)
RoSlaw ...... Rocznik Slawistyczny [*A publication*]
ROSMAR ... Rosmarinus [*Rosemary*] [*Pharmacology*]　(ROG)
ROSO .... Relay-Operated Sampling Oscilloscope
RoSPA ...... Royal Society for the Prevention of Accidents [*British*]
ROSR .... Radio On-Scene Report　(WDMC)
ROSS .... Ross Systems [*NASDAQ symbol*]　(SPSG)
Ross Conf Med Res Rep ... Ross Conference on Medical Research. Report [*A publication*]
Ross Conf Pediatr Res Rep ... Ross Conference on Pediatric Research. Report [*A publication*]
Ross Cont ... Ross on Contracts [*A publication*]　(DLA)
Ross Conv .. Ross' Lectures on Conveyancing, Etc. [*Sc.*] [*A publication*]　(DLA)
Ross LC ..... Ross's Leading Cases on Commercial Law [*England*] [*A publication*]　(DLA)
Ross LC ..... Ross's Leading Cases in the Law of Scotland (Land Rights) [*1638-1840*] [*A publication*]　(DLA)
Ross Ldg Cas ... Ross's Leading Cases on Commercial Law [*A publication*]　(DLA)
Ross Ldg Cas ... Ross's Leading Cases in the Law of Scotland (Land Rights) [*A publication*]　(DLA)
Ross Lead Cas ... Ross' Leading Cases [*England*] [*A publication*]　(DLA)
Ross Lead Cas ... Ross's Leading Cases in the Law of Scotland (Land Rights) [*1638-1840*] [*A publication*]　(DLA)

Ross V & P ... Ross on Vendors and Purchasers [*2nd ed.*] [*1826*] [*A publication*]　(DLA)
ROST .... Regional Office of Science and Technology [*UNESCO*]　(MSC)
ROST .... Ross Stores, Inc. [*Newark, CA*] [*NASDAQ symbol*]　(NQ)
ROSTA ...... Regional Office for Science and Technology in Africa [*UNESCO*] [*See also BRUSTA*] [*Nairobi, Kenya*]　(EAIO)
ROSTA ...... Roads and Streets [*A publication*]
ROSTA Bull ... ROSTA [*Victoria. Road Safety and Traffic Authority*] Bulletin [*A publication*]　(APTA)
ROSTE ...... Regional Office for Science and Technology for Europe [*UNESCO*] [*Italy*]　(EAIO)
Roster Organ Field Autom Comput Mach ... Roster of Organizations in the Field of Automatic Computing Machinery [*A publication*]
Rost Krist ... Rost Kristallov [*A publication*]
Rostl Vyroba ... Rostlinna Vyroba [*A publication*]
Rostl Vyroba Cesk Akad Zemed Ustav Vedeckotech Inf Zemed ... Rostlinna Vyroba-Ceskoslovenska Akademie Zemedelska. Ustav Vedeckotechnickych Informaci pro Zemedelstvi [*A publication*]
Rostocker Phys Manuskr ... Rostocker Physikalische Manuskripte [*A publication*]
Rostock Math Kolloq ... Rostocker Mathematisches Kolloquium [*A publication*]
Rostov-Na-Donu Gos Univ Ucen Zap ... Rostovskii-Na-Donu Gosudarstvennyi Universitet. Ucenyi Zapiski [*A publication*]
ROSTSCA ... Regional Office of Science and Technology for South and Central Asia [*UNESCO*]　(IRC)
ROSTSEA ... Regional Office of Science and Technology for Southeast Asia [*UNESCO*]　(IRC)
Rost Ustoich Rast ... Rost i Ustoichivost Rastenii [*A publication*]
ROSX .... Ross Industries, Inc. [*Midland, VA*] [*NASDAQ symbol*]　(NQ)
ROT .... RADAR on Target
ROT .... Range on Target
ROT .... Rate of Turn
ROT .... Rechtsinformation. Berichte und Dokumente zum Auslaendischen Wirtschafts- und Steuerrecht [*A publication*]
ROT .... Red Oak Tannins [*in leaves*]
ROT .... Reference Our Telex　(DS)
ROT .... Remaining Operating Time　(NASA)
ROT .... Remedial Occupation Therapy
ROT .... Reserve Oil Tank　(MSA)
ROT .... Reusable Orbital Transport [*Aerospace*]
ROT .... Right Occipitotransverse [*A fetal position*] [*Obstetrics*]
ROT .... Right Outer Thigh [*Injection site*]
ROT .... Rotary　(AAG)
ROT .... Rotate　(AAG)
ROT .... Rotating Light [*Navigation signal*]
ROT .... Rotor　(ADA)
ROT .... Rotorua [*New Zealand*] [*Seismograph station code, US Geological Survey*] [*Closed*]　(SEIS)
ROT .... Rotorua [*New Zealand*] [*Airport symbol*]　(OAG)
ROT .... Rule of Thumb
ROTAA ...... Road Tar [*A publication*]
ROTAB ..... Rotable Table
ROT ABCCC ... Rotational Airborne Command and Control Center　(CINC)
ROTAC ..... Rotary Oscillating Torque Actuators
ROTAD ..... Required Overseas Terminal Arrival Date　(DNAB)
ROTAD ..... Round Table [*A publication*]
ROTAS ...... Rotate and Slide　(DNAB)
Rotation Method Crystallogr ... Rotation Method in Crystallography [*A publication*]
Rotavapor .. Rotary Evaporator
ROT AWS ... Rotational Air Weather Squadron　(CINC)
ROT BS ..... Rotational Bomb Squadron　(CINC)
ROTC .... Reserve Officers' Training Corps [*Separate units for Army, Navy, Air Force*]
ROTC .... RoTech Medical Corp. [*Orlando, FL*] [*NASDAQ symbol*]　(NQ)
ROTCC ...... Receiver-Off-Hook Tone Connecting Circuit
Rot Chart ... Rotulus Chartarum [*Charter Roll*] [*Latin*] [*A publication*]　(DLA)
Rot Claus ... Rotuli Clause [*Close Roll*] [*Latin*] [*A publication*]　(DLA)
ROTCM .... Reserve Officers' Training Corps Manual　(AABC)
ROTCR ...... Reserve Officers' Training Corps Region　(AABC)
Rot Cur Reg ... Rotuli Curiae Regis [*1194-99*] [*Latin*] [*A publication*]　(DLA)
ROTE .... Range Optical Tracking Equipment　(AAG)
ROTE .... Role of Occupational Therapy with the Elderly [*Project*]
ROTE AREFS ... Rotating Air Refueling Squadron　(CINC)
ROTEL ...... Reference Our Telegram　(FAAC)
ROTEL ...... Rolling Hotel [*European bus-tour system*]
ROTEL ...... Rotational Telemetry
Rotenburger Symp ... Rotenburger Symposium [*A publication*]
Rotenburg Ferment Symp ... Rotenburg Fermentation Symposium [*A publication*]
Rotenburg Schr ... Rotenburger Schriften [*A publication*]
ROTERO .. Roterodamum [*Rotterdam*]　(ROG)
ROTF .... Russian Orthodox Theological Fund　(EA)
ROT FIS ...... Rotating Fighter Interceptor Squadron　(CINC)
ROT FIS DET ... Rotating Fighter Interceptor Squadron Detachment　(CINC)

Rot Flor...... Rotae Florentine [*Reports of the Supreme Court of Florence*] [*Latin*] [*A publication*] (DLA)
ROTG........ Rotating (FAAC)
ROTH........ Read-Only Tape Handler
Rothamsted Exp Stn Rep ... Rothamsted Experimental Station. Report [*A publication*]
Rothamsted Exp Stn Rep Part 1 ... Rothamsted Experimental Station. Report. Part 1 [*A publication*]
Rothamsted Exp Stn Rep Part 2 ... Rothamsted Experimental Station. Report. Part 2 [*A publication*]
Rothmill Q ... Rothmill Quarterly [*A publication*]
ROTHR..... Relocatable Over-the-Horizon RADAR
ROTI .... Range Optical Tracking Instrument
ROTI .... Recording Optical Tracking Instrument [*Missiles*]
ROTI .... Reinforced Oxide Throat Insert
ROTL .... Remote Office Test Line [*Bell Laboratories*]
ROTLT/BCN ... Rotating Light or Beacon
ROTM........ Futema [*Ryukyu Islands*] [*ICAO location identifier*] (ICLI)
ROTMH.... Raised Oil-Tight Manhole [*Shipfitting*]
ROTN........ Rotation (ROG)
ROTO........ Roto-Rooter, Inc. [*Cincinnati, OH*] [*NASDAQ symbol*] (NQ)
ROTOB ..... Romania Today [*A publication*]
ROTOMT ... Rotometer
Rotonc........ Rotonics Manufacturing [*Associated Press abbreviation*] (APAG)
ROTOR..... Rotorcraft Helicopter [*Pilot rating*] (AIA)
Rotor & W ... Rotor and Wing International [*A publication*]
ROTP .... Regular Officer Training Plan [*Canada*]
Rot Parl...... Rotulae Parliamentariae [*Latin*] [*A publication*] (DLA)
Rot Pat ...... Rotuli Patenes [*Latin*] [*A publication*] (DLA)
Rot Plac ..... Rotuli Placitorum [*Latin*] [*A publication*] (DLA)
ROT PROJ ... Rotation Project (DNAB)
ROTR........ Receive-Only Typing Reperforator
ROTR .... Rotator [*Electromagnetics*]
ROT RCS .. Rotational RADAR Calibration Squadron (CINC)
ROTR-S/P ... Receive-Only Typing Reperforator - Series to Parallel
ROTS......... RADAR Observer Testing System
ROTS........ Range on Target Signal
ROTS........ Remote Operator Task Station [*Air Force*]
ROTS........ Rotary Out Trunk Switch [*Telecommunications*] (TEL)
ROTSAL ... Rotate and Scale [*Data processing*]
ROTT .... Rate of Turntable
ROTT .... Reorder Tone Trunks [*Telecommunications*] (TEL)
ROT TAS .. Rotational Tactical Assault Squadron (CINC)
ROT TBS .. Rotational Tactical Bomber Squadron (CINC)
ROT TCS .. Rotational Troop Carrier Squadron (CINC)
ROTTER.... Rotterdam (ROG)
ROT TX..... Rotating Transformer
Rotuli Curiae Reg ... Rotuli Curiae Regis [*1194-99*] [*Latin*] [*A publication*] (DLA)
ROTV .... Reusable Orbital Transport Vehicle [*Aerospace*]
ROTWX .... Reference Our TWX [*Teletypewriter communications*] (FAAC)
ROU.......... Radio Officers Union [*British*]
ROU.......... Rougiers [*France*] [*Seismograph station code, US Geological Survey*] [*Closed*] (SEIS)
ROU.......... Rouyn Ressources Minieres, Inc. [*Toronto Stock Exchange symbol*]
ROU.......... Russe [*Bulgaria*] [*Airport symbol*] (OAG)
ROUHA .... Ropa a Uhlie [*A publication*]
ROUL........ Rouletted (ROG)
Roum P ...... Roumanian Pharmacopoeia [*A publication*]
Round Dom ... Round's Law of Domicil [*1861*] [*A publication*] (DLA)
Round L & A ... Round's Right of Light and Air [*1868*] [*A publication*] (DLA)
Round Lien ... Round's Law of Lien [*1863*] [*A publication*] (DLA)
Round Tab ... Round Table [*A publication*]
Round Table Semin Int Miner Process Congr ... Round Table Seminar. International Mineral Processing Congress [*A publication*]
ROUS........ [*The*] Rouse Co. [*NASDAQ symbol*] (NQ)
Rouse Conv ... Rouse's Practical Conveyancer [*3rd ed.*] [*1867*] [*A publication*] (DLA)
Rouse Cop ... Rouse's Copyhold Enfranchisement Manual [*3rd ed.*] [*1866*] [*A publication*] (DLA)
Rouse Pr Mort ... Rouse's Precedents and Conveyances of Mortgaged Property [*A publication*] (DLA)
R-OUT....... Rollout (NASA)
ROUT........ Routine (AABC)
Roux Archiv EntwMech Organ ... Roux Archiv fuer Entwicklungsmechanik der Organismen [*A publication*]
Roux's Arch Dev Biol ... Roux's Archives of Developmental Biology [*A publication*]
ROV.......... Refined Oil of Vitriol
ROV.......... Remote Operated Valve (KSC)
ROV.......... Remote Optical Viewing
ROV........ Remotely Operated Vehicle [*Underwater robot*]
ROV.......... Repairs to Other Vessels
ROV.......... Report Over (FAAC)
ROV.......... Report of Visit [*LIMRA*]
ROV.......... Restricted Overhaul (MCD)

ROV.......... Risk, Originality, and Virtuousity [*Scoring considerations in gymnastics competition*]
ROV.......... Rostov [*Former USSR*] [*Airport symbol*] (OAG)
ROVAC ..... Rotary Vane Air Cycle (MCD)
ROVD........ Relay-Operated Voltage Divider
Rov Koezlem ... Rovartani Koezlemenyek [*A publication*]
ROVNITE ... Remaining Overnight
ROVS........ Remote Optical Viewing System
ROVYA ..... Rostlinna Vyroba [*A publication*]
ROW.......... Randstrom Manufacturing Corp. [*Vancouver Stock Exchange symbol*]
ROW.......... Relocate Out of Washington [*Navy*] (NG)
ROW.......... Requisition on Warehouse [*Nuclear energy*] (NRCH)
ROW.......... Rest of World [*Newly industrialized countries of Asia*]
ROW.......... Right of Way
ROW.......... Risk of War
ROW.......... Roll Welding
ROW.......... Romanian Engineering [*A publication*]
ROW.......... Roswell [*New Mexico*] [*Airport symbol*] (OAG)
ROW.......... Rowe Furniture Corp. [*AMEX symbol*] (SPSG)
ROW.......... Rowesville [*South Carolina*] [*Seismograph station code, US Geological Survey*] (SEIS)
RO1(W).... Radio Operator (Warfare) 1st Class [*British military*] (DMA)
RO2(W).... Radio Operator (Warfare) 2nd Class [*British military*] (DMA)
ROWA....... Read Once, Write All [*Data processing*]
Rowan .... Rowan Companies, Inc. [*Associated Press abbreviation*] (APAG)
ROWB....... Rowberrow [*England*]
Rowe........ Rowe's Interesting Cases [*England and Ireland*] [*1798-1823*] [*A publication*] (DLA)
Rowe........... Rowe's Interesting Parliamentary and Military Cases [*A publication*] (DLA)
ROWEF..... Rowe Furniture Corp. [*Associated Press abbreviation*] (APAG)
Rowell .... Rowell's Reports [*45-52 Vermont*] [*A publication*] (DLA)
Rowell El Cas ... Rowell's Contested Election Cases [*A publication*] (DLA)
Row Eng Const ... Rowland's Manual of the English Constitution [*1859*] [*A publication*] (DLA)
Rowe Rep ... Rowe's Irish Reports [*A publication*] (DLA)
Rowe Sci Jur ... Rowe's Scintilla Juris [*A publication*] (DLA)
Rowett Res Inst Annu Rep Stud Anim Nutr Allied Sci ... Rowett Research Institute. Annual Report. Studies in Animal Nutrition and Allied Sciences [*A publication*]
ROW/FEPA ... Riders of the Wind, the Field Events Player's Association (EA)
ROWJ .... Records of Oceanographic Works in Japan [*A publication*]
ROWJA..... Records of Oceanographic Works in Japan [*A publication*]
ROWP....... Reference Overhaul Work Package (DNAB)
ROWPE..... Reverse Osmosis Water Purification Equipment (MCD)
ROW & PF ... Rake Out, Wedge, and Point Flashings [*Construction*]
ROWPS..... Reverse Osmosis Water Purification System (MCD)
ROWPU..... Reverse Osmosis Water Purification Unit [*Army*] (RDA)
ROWPVT ... Receptive One-Word Picture Vocabulary Test [*Educational test*]
ROWS .... RADAR Ocean Wave Spectrometer
ROX.......... Roseau, MN [*Location identifier*] [*FAA*] (FAAL)
ROX.......... Roxburgh [*New Zealand*] [*Seismograph station code, US Geological Survey*] (SEIS)
ROXB .... Roxburghe [*Style of bookbinding*] (ROG)
ROXB .... Roxburghshire [*County in Scotland*]
ROXL .... Rotate through X Left [*Data processing*]
ROXR .... Rotate through X Right [*Data processing*]
ROY.......... Moultonboro, NH [*Location identifier*] [*FAA*] (FAAL)
ROY.......... Rest of You (IIA)
ROY.......... Rio Mayo [*Argentina*] [*Airport symbol*] (OAG)
ROY.......... Rookie of the Year
ROY.......... Royal
Roy............. Royale & Allegro-Royale [*Record label*]
Roy Aeronaut Soc J ... Royal Aeronautical Society. Journal [*A publication*]
Royal.......... [*The*] Royal Magazine [*A publication*]
Royal Agric Soc England J ... Journal. Royal Agricultural Society of England [*A publication*]
Royal Astron Soc Canada Jour ... Royal Astronomical Society of Canada. Journal [*A publication*]
Royal Astron Soc Geophys Jour ... Royal Astronomical Society. Geophysical Journal [*A publication*]
Royal Astron Soc Monthly Notices Geophys Supp ... Royal Astronomical Society. Monthly Notices. Geophysical Supplements [*A publication*]
Royal Astron Soc Quart Jour ... Royal Astronomical Society. Quarterly Journal [*A publication*]
Royal Aust Army Ed Corps News ... Royal Australian Army. Educational Corps. Newsletter [*A publication*] (APTA)
Royal Aust Chem Inst J & Proc ... Royal Australian Chemical Institute. Journal and Proceedings [*A publication*] (APTA)
Royal Aust Chem Inst Proc ... Royal Australian Chemical Institute. Proceedings [*A publication*] (APTA)
Royal Aust Hist Soc J ... Royal Australian Historical Society. Journal and Proceedings [*A publication*] (APTA)
Royal Aust Hist Soc J Proc ... Royal Australian Historical Society. Journal and Proceedings [*A publication*]
Royal Australian Planning Inst Jnl ... Royal Australian Planning Institute. Journal [*A publication*]

Royalauto... Royalauto [*Royal Automobile Club of Victoria*] Journal [*A publication*] (APTA)

Royal Bank Can Mo Letter ... Royal Bank of Canada. Monthly Letter [*A publication*]

Royal Empire Soc News ... Royal Empire Society. News [*A publication*] (APTA)

Royal Geog Soc Asia SA Branch Proc ... Royal Geographical Society of Australasia. South Australian Branch. Proceedings [*A publication*] (APTA)

Royal Hist Soc Q Hist Misc ... Royal Historical Society of Queensland. Historical Miscellanea [*A publication*] (APTA)

Royal Hist Soc QJ ... Royal Historical Society of Queensland. Journal [*A publication*] (APTA)

Royal Hist Soc Trans ... Royal Historical Society. Transactions [*A publication*]

Royal Hort Soc J ... Royal Horticultural Society. Journal [*A publication*]

Royal Inst of British Archts Trans ... Royal Institute of British Architects. Transactions [*A publication*]

Royal Microscopical Soc Proc ... Royal Microscopical Society. Proceedings [*A publication*]

ROYALO .. Royal Oak Mines [*Associated Press abbreviation*] (APAG)

Royal Ontario Mus Div Zoology and Palaeontology Contr ... Royal Ontario Museum. Division of Zoology and Palaeontology. Contributions [*A publication*]

Royal Perth Hospital J ... Royal Perth Hospital. Journal [*A publication*] (APTA)

Royal Prince Alfred Hospital J ... Royal Prince Alfred Hospital. Journal [*A publication*] (APTA)

Royal Soc Arts Jnl ... Royal Society of Arts. Journal [*A publication*]

Royal Soc Canada Proc ... Royal Society of Canada. Proceedings [*A publication*]

Royal Soc of Health Jnl ... Royal Society of Health. Journal [*A publication*]

Royal Soc Hlth J ... Royal Society of Health. Journal [*A publication*]

Royal Soc NSW J & Proc ... Royal Society of New South Wales. Journal and Proceedings [*A publication*] (APTA)

Royal Soc Q Proc ... Royal Society of Queensland. Proceedings [*A publication*] (APTA)

Royal Soc SA Trans ... Royal Society of South Australia. Transactions [*A publication*] (APTA)

Royal Soc Tasmania Papers and Proc ... Royal Society of Tasmania. Papers and Proceedings [*A publication*]

Royal Soc Tas Papers & Proc ... Royal Society of Tasmania. Papers and Proceedings [*A publication*] (APTA)

Royal Soc Vic Proc ... Royal Society of Victoria. Proceedings [*A publication*] (APTA)

Royal Soc Victoria Proc ... Royal Society of Victoria. Proceedings [*A publication*]

Royal Statis Soc J Ser A Gen ... Journal. Royal Statistical Society. Series A. General [*A publication*]

Royalton R ... Royalton Review [*A publication*]

Royal Zoological Soc NSW Proc ... Royal Zoological Society of New South Wales. Proceedings [*A publication*] (APTA)

RoyApl....... Royal Appliance Manufacturing [*Associated Press abbreviation*] (APAG)

Roy Arch Inst Can J ... Royal Architectural Institute of Canada. Journal [*A publication*]

Roy Astron Soc Mem ... Royal Astronomical Society. Memoirs [*A publication*]

Roy Aust Hist J ... Royal Australian Historical Society. Journal [*A publication*]

Roy Aust Hist Soc J Proc ... Royal Australian Historical Society. Journal and Proceedings [*A publication*] (APTA)

Roy Can Inst Trans ... Royal Canadian Institute. Transactions [*A publication*]

Royce.......... Royce Value Trust, Inc. [*Associated Press abbreviation*] (APAG)

Roy Dig...... Royall's Digest Virginia Reports [*A publication*] (DLA)

Roy Eng J .. Royal Engineers Journal [*A publication*]

ROYG........ Royal Business Group, Inc. [*NASDAQ symbol*] (NQ)

ROYGBIV ... Red, Orange, Yellow, Green, Blue, Indigo, Violet [*Primary Colors*] [*Mnemonic aid*]

Roy His S... Royal Historical Society. Transactions [*A publication*]

Roy Hist Soc Qld Hist Misc ... Royal Historical Society of Queensland. Historical Miscellanea [*A publication*] (APTA)

Roy Hist Soc Qld J ... Royal Historical Society of Queensland. Journal [*A publication*] (APTA)

Roy Hist Soc Trans ... Royal Historical Society. Transactions [*A publication*]

Roy Hist Soc Vic News ... Royal Historical Society of Victoria. Newsletter [*A publication*] (APTA)

Roy Hort Soc J ... Royal Horticultural Society. Journal [*A publication*]

Roy Inst Brit Arch J ... Royal Institute of British Architects. Journal [*A publication*]

Roy Inst Nav Architects Quart Trans ... Royal Institution of Naval Architects [*London*]. Quarterly Transactions [*A publication*]

Roy Inst Ph ... Royal Institute of Philosophy. Lectures [*A publication*]

ROYL .... Royalpar Industries, Inc. [*NASDAQ symbol*] (NQ)

RoylD......... Royal Dutch Petroleum Co. [*Associated Press abbreviation*] (APAG)

Royle Stock Sh ... Royle on the Law of Stock Shares, Etc. [*A publication*] (DLA)

Roy Meteorol Soc Q J ... Royal Meteorological Society. Quarterly Journal [*A publication*]

Roy Microscop Soc Proc ... Royal Microscopical Society. Proceedings [*A publication*]

Roy Micros Soc J ... Royal Microscopical Society. Journal [*A publication*]

ROYN....... Yonagunijima [*Ryukyu Islands*] [*ICAO location identifier*] (ICLI)

ROYPLM ... Royal Palm Beach Ltd. [*Associated Press abbreviation*] (APAG)

Roy Soc Arts J ... Royal Society of Arts. Journal [*A publication*]

Roy Soc Can ... Royal Society of Canada. Proceedings and Transactions [*A publication*]

Roy Soc of Canada Trans ... Royal Society of Canada. Proceedings and Transactions [*A publication*]

Roy Soc Edinb Trans ... Royal Society of Edinburgh. Transactions [*A publication*]

Roy Soc of Edinburgh Trans ... Royal Society of Edinburgh. Transactions [*A publication*]

Roy Soc Hea ... Royal Society of Health. Journal [*A publication*]

Roy Soc of London Philos Trans ... Royal Society of London. Philosophical Transactions [*A publication*]

Roy Soc Lond Philos Trans ... Royal Society of London. Philosophical Transactions [*A publication*]

Roy Soc of New South Wales Jour and Proc ... Royal Society of New South Wales. Journal and Proceedings [*A publication*]

Roy Soc NSW J ... Royal Society of New South Wales. Journal [*A publication*] (APTA)

Roy Soc NSW J & Proc ... Royal Society of New South Wales. Journal and Proceedings [*A publication*]

Roy Soc NZ Bull ... Royal Society of New Zealand. Bulletin [*A publication*]

Roy Soc NZ J ... Royal Society of New Zealand. Journal [*A publication*]

Roy Soc NZ Proc ... Royal Society of New Zealand. Proceedings [*A publication*]

Roy Soc NZ Trans ... Royal Society of New Zealand. Transactions [*A publication*]

Roy Soc NZ Trans Bot ... Royal Society of New Zealand. Transactions. Botany [*A publication*]

Roy Soc NZ Trans Earth Sci ... Royal Society of New Zealand. Transactions. Earth Sciences [*A publication*]

Roy Soc NZ Trans Gen ... Royal Society of New Zealand. Transactions. General [*A publication*]

Roy Soc NZ Trans Geol ... Royal Society of New Zealand. Transactions. Geology [*A publication*]

Roy Soc NZ Trans Zool ... Royal Society of New Zealand. Transactions. Zoology [*A publication*]

Roy Soc Proc ... Proceedings. Royal Society [*A publication*]

Roy Soc Qld Proc ... Royal Society of Queensland. Proceedings [*A publication*] (APTA)

Roy Soc SA Trans ... Royal Society of South Australia. Transactions [*A publication*] (APTA)

Roy Soc Tas Papers ... Royal Society of Tasmania. Papers and Proceedings [*A publication*] (APTA)

Roy Soc Vic Proc ... Royal Society of Victoria. Proceedings [*A publication*] (APTA)

Roy Soc WA J ... Royal Society of Western Australia. Journal [*A publication*] (APTA)

Roy Stat Soc J ... Royal Statistical Society. Journal [*A publication*]

Roy Telev Soc J ... Royal Television Society. Journal [*A publication*]

Roy Town Plan Inst ... Royal Town Planning Institute. Journal [*A publication*]

Roy West Aust Hist Soc J Proc ... Royal Western Australian Historical Society. Journal and Proceedings [*A publication*] (APTA)

Roy Zool Soc NSW Proc ... Royal Zoological Society of New South Wales. Proceedings [*A publication*] (APTA)

Roz Cesk Akad ... Rozpravy Ceskoslovenske Akademie Ved [*A publication*]

Rozhl Chir ... Rozhledy v Chirurgii [*A publication*]

Rozhl Tuberk Nemocech Plicn ... Rozhledy v Tuberkulose a v Nemocech Plicnich [*A publication*]

Roz Narod Tech Muz Praze ... Rozpravy Narodniho Technickeho Muzea v Praze [*A publication*]

Rozpr Akad Roln Szczecinie ... Rozprawy. Akademia Rolnicza w Szczecinie [*A publication*]

Rozpravy CSAV ... Rozpravy Ceskoslovenske Akademie Ved [*A publication*]

Rozprawy Elektrotech ... Rozprawy Elektrotechniczne. Polska Akademia Nauk. Instytut Technologii Elektronowej. [*A publication*]

Rozprawy Politech Poznan ... Rozprawy. Politechnika Poznanska [*A publication*]

Rozpr Cesk Akad Rada Tech Ved ... Rozpravy Ceskoslovenske Akademie Ved. Rada Technickych Ved [*Czechoslovakia*] [*A publication*]

Rozpr Cesk Akad Ved Rada Mat Prir Ved ... Rozpravy Ceskoslovenske Akademie Ved. Rada Matematickych a Prirodnich Ved [*A publication*]

Rozpr Cesk Akad Ved Rada Tech Ved ... Rozpravy Ceskoslovenske Akademie Ved. Rada Technickych Ved [*A publication*]

Rozpr Elektrotech ... Rozprawy Elektrotechniczne [*A publication*]

Rozpr Hydrotech ... Rozprawy Hydrotechniczne [*A publication*]

Rozpr Inz ... Rozprawy Inzynierskie [*A publication*]

Rozpr Politech Poznan ... Rozprawy. Politechnika Poznanska [*A publication*]

Rozpr Politech Rzeszowska Im Ignacego Lukasiewicza ... Rozprawy. Politechnika Rzeszowska Imienia Ignacego Lukasiewicza [*A publication*]

Rozpr Ustred Ustavu Geol ... Rozpravy Ustredniho Ustavu Geologickeho [*A publication*]

Rozpr Wydz 3 Nauk Mat Przyr Gdansk Tow Nauk ... Rozprawy Wydziału 3. Nauk Matematyczno-Przyrodniczych. Gdanskie Towarzystwo Naukowe [*A publication*]

Rozpr Wydz Nauk Med Pol Akad Nauk ... Rozprawy Wydziału Nauk Medyczynch Polska Akademia Nauk [*A publication*]

RP .... Bristol-Myers Co. [*Research code symbol*]
RP .... Problems of Reconstruction [*British*] [*World War II*]
RP .... Providence Public Library, Providence, RI [*Library symbol*] [*Library of Congress*]   (LCLS)
Rp............. Pulmonary Resistance [*Cardiology*]   (MAE)
RP .... RADAR Plot   (DEN)
RP .... Radial Artery Pressure [*Medicine*]
RP .... Radial Pulse [*Medicine*]
RP .... Radiation Pressure
RP .... Radiation Protection
RP .... Radio Phone   (DS)
R-P............. Radiologist-Pediatric
RP .... Raid Plotter
RP .... Rally Point [*Air Force*]
RP .... Ranchers for Peace   (EA)
RP .... Range Pulse
RP .... Raphe Pallidus [*Anatomy*]
RP .... Rapid Processing [*Film*]   (MAE)
RP .... Rappen [*Monetary unit*] [*Switzerland*]
RP .... Rate Package   (AAG)
RP .... Rated Pressure   (NATG)
RP .... Raynaud's Phenomenon [*Medicine*]
RP .... Re-Geniusing Project   (EA)
RP .... Reactive Protein [*Clinical chemistry*]   (MAE)
RP .... Reactor Pressure [*Nuclear energy*]   (NRCH)
RP .... Reactor Project [*Nuclear energy*]   (NRCH)
RP .... Reader Printer
RP .... Reader Punch
RP .... Readiness Potential
RP .... Real Part [*of complex number*]   (DEN)
RP .... Real Property
RP .... Rear Projection [*Television*]
RP .... Receipt Pass   (AAG)
RP .... Receive Processor
RP .... Received Pronunciation [*of the English language*]
RP .... Reception Poor [*Radio logs*]
RP .... Receptor Potential
RP .... Recommended Practice
RP .... Record Processor [*Data processing*]   (OA)
RP .... Recorder Point   (MCD)
RP .... Records of the Past [*A publication*]   (BJA)
RP .... Recovery Phase   (IEEE)
R & P......... Recruitment and Placement   (MCD)
RP .... Red Phosphorus [*Military*]   (RDA)
RP .... Reddish Purple
RP .... Reference Paper
RP .... Reference Pattern   (NATG)
RP .... Reference Point
RP .... Reference Publication   (MCD)
RP .... Reference Pulse
RP .... Refilling Point
RP .... Reformed Presbyterian
RP .... Refractory Period [*Medicine*]
RP .... Regeneration Project [*Later, CR*]   (EA)
RP .... Regimental Paymaster [*British military*]   (DMA)
RP .... Regimental Police [*British*]
RP .... Registered Plumbers [*British*]
RP .... Regius Professor [*The King's Professor*] [*British*]
RP .... Regulatory Peptides [*A publication*]
RP .... Reinforced Plastic [*Packaging*]
RP .... Relative Pressure   (KSC)
RP .... Relay Panel
RP .... Release Point [*Ground traffic*] [*Military*]
RP .... Relief Pitcher [*Baseball*]
RP .... Religious Program Specialist [*Navy*]   (DNAB)
RP .... Remote Pickup
RP .... Remote Printer   (BUR)
RP .... Renaissance Papers [*A publication*]
RP .... Rent Regulation (Office of Price Stabilization) [*Economic Stabilization Agency*] [*A publication*]   (DLA)
RP .... Reorder Point [*Army*]
RP .... Repair Period   (NASA)
RP .... Repeater
RP .... Repetitively Pulsed   (MCD)
RP .... Replaceable Pad   (MCD)
RP .... Replacement Pilot [*Navy*]
RP .... Replenishment Park [*British*]
RP .... Reply Paid
RP .... Report Immediately upon Passing [*Fix altitude*] [*Aviation*]   (FAAC)
RP .... Reporting Post [*RADAR*]
RP .... Reprint
RP .... Reproducers [*JETDS nomenclature*] [*Military*]   (CET)
RP .... Republic of Panama

RP .... Republic of the Philippines
RP .... Republican Party [*Iraq*] [*Political party*]   (BJA)
RP .... Republikeinse Party van Suidwesafrika [*Republican Party of South West Africa*] [*Namibia*] [*Political party*]   (PPW)
RP .... Repurchase Agreement [*Also, REPO*] [*Investment term*]
RP .... Research Paper
RP .... Research Publications
RP .... Reserve Personnel [*Air Force*]   (AFM)
R & P......... Reserve and Process   (NASA)
RP .... Reserve Purchase
RP .... Resist Pressure [*Industrial engineering*]
RP .... Resistance Plate   (AAG)
RP .... Resolving Power [*of a lens*]
RP .... Resource Processor [*Telecommunications*]   (TSSD)
RP .... Respirable Particulate [*Environmental science*]   (GFGA)
RP .... Respiratory Rate:Pulse Rate [*Index*] [*Medicine*]
RP .... Rest Pain [*Medicine*]   (MAE)
RP .... Resting Pressure [*Physiology*]   (MAE)
RP .... Resting Pulse [*Physiology*]
RP .... Restoration Priority   (CET)
RP .... Restriction of Privileges [*British military*]   (DMA)
RP .... Resupply Provisions [*NASA*]   (KSC)
RP .... Retained Personnel [*Military*]
RP .... Retinitis Pigmentosa [*Eye disease*] [*Ophthalmology*]
RP .... Retinyl Palmitate [*Organic chemistry*]
RP .... Retrograde Pyelography [*Medicine*]
RP .... Retroperitoneal [*Medicine*]
R/P............. Return to Port [*for Orders*]   (DS)
RP .... Return of Post
RP .... Return Premium
RP .... Revealed Preference Analysis [*Economics*]
RP .... Reverend Pere [*Reverend Father*] [*French*]
RP .... Reverendus Pater [*Reverend Father*] [*Latin*]
R-P............. Reversed Phase [*Chromatography*]
RP .... Revertive Pulsing
RP .... Review of Politics [*A publication*]
RP .... Revision Proposal   (NG)
Rp............. Revoked or Rescinded in Part [*Existing regulation or order abrogated in part*] [*Used in Shepard's Citations*] [*Legal term*]   (DLA)
R/P............. Reward/Penalty
RP .... Rhone-Poulenc [*France*] [*Research code symbol*]
RP .... Right Traffic Pattern [*Aviation*]   (FAAC)
R & P......... Ring and Pinion [*Automotive engineering*]
R/P............. Rise/Passive   (MCD)
RP .... Ristocetin-Polymyxin [*Antibacterial mixture*]
RP .... Rocket Projectile
RP .... Rocket Propellant
RP .... Rockland and Pollin [*Scale*] [*Psychology*]
RP .... Rodent Potency Dose
RP .... Roll Pad   (MCD)
RP .... Rollback Process [*Telecommunications*]   (TEL)
RP .... Romance Philology [*A publication*]
RP .... Ron Pair!
RP .... Room and Pillar [*Coal mining*]
RP .... Root Primordia [*Botany*]
RP .... Rotatable Pool Quantity
RP .... Rotuli Parliamentorum [*1278-1533*] [*Latin*] [*A publication*]   (DLA)
RP .... Round Punch
RP .... Route Package   (CINC)
RP .... Royal Panopticon   (ROG)
RP .... Royal Provincials [*British military*]   (DMA)
RP .... [*Member of*] Royal Society of Portrait Painters [*British*]
RP .... Rules of Procedure
R & P......... Rules and Procedures   (MSA)
RP .... Rupiah [*Monetary unit*] [*Indonesia*]
RP .... Russow Aviation GmbH & Co. Luftfahrtunternehmen, Frankfurt [*West Germany*] [*ICAO designator*]   (FAAC)
RP .... Rust Preventive
RP .... Specia [*France*] [*Research code symbol*]
R-5-P......... Ribose-5-Phosphate [*Biochemistry*]   (MAE)
R2P2 .... Rapid Retargeting and Precision Pointing [*Strategic Defense Initiative*]
RPA .... British Plastics and Rubber [*A publication*]
RPA .... Executive Air Travel [*Denver, CO*] [*FAA designator*]   (FAAC)
RPA .... Providence Athenaeum, Providence, RI [*Library symbol*] [*Library of Congress*]   (LCLS)
RPA .... RADAR Performance Analyzer
RPA .... Radium Plaque Adaptometer [*Navy*]
RPA .... Random Phase Approximation
RPA .... Rationalist Press Association [*British*]   (EAIO)
RPA .... Real Property Administrator [*Designation awarded by Building Owners and Managers Institute*]
RPA .... Record and Playback Assembly   (MCD)
RPA .... Record of Procurement Action   (MCD)
RPA .... Redundancy Payments Act [*1965*] [*British*]   (DCTA)
RPA .... Reentrant Process Allocator [*Telecommunications*]   (TEL)
RPA .... Regional Plan Association   (EA)
RPA .... Regional Ports Authority [*British*]
RPA .... Registered Public Accountant

RPA .... Relative Peak Area [*Medicine*]
RPA .... Renal Physicians Association (EA)
RPA .... Renewal Projects Administration [*HUD*]
RPA .... Replacement Price Accounting (ADA)
RPA .... Republican Party of Australia [*Political party*]
RPA .... Request Present Altitude [*Aviation*] (FAAC)
RPA .... Request for Procurement Action [*Authorization*] [*NASA*] (NASA)
RPA .... Reserve Personnel Appropriation
RPA .... Reserve Personnel, Army
RPA .... Resident Programmer Analyst [*Data processing*]
RPA .... Resource Planning Associates, Cambridge, MA [*OCLC symbol*] (OCLC)
RPA .... Response Profile Analysis [*National Demographics & Lifestyles, Inc.*]
RPA .... Resultant Physiological Acceleration
RPA .... Retarding Potential Analyzer [*NASA*]
RPA .... Retinoylphorbolacetate [*Biochemistry*]
RPA .... Retired Philosphers Association (EA)
RPA .... Right Pulmonary Artery [*Medicine*]
RPA .... Rolpa [*Nepal*] [*Airport symbol*] (OAG)
RPA .... Royal Pakistan Artillery [*British military*] (DMA)
RPA .... RPA [*Royal Prince Alfred Hospital*] Magazine [*A publication*] (APTA)
RPA .... Rubber Peptizing Agent
RPA .... Rural Preservation Association [*British*]
RPA .... Rust Prevention Association [*Later, Crop Quality Council*]
RPAA .... Rendiconti. Pontificia Accademia di Archeologia [*A publication*]
RPAA .... Rotating Phase Array Antenna
RPAB .... Brown University, Annmary Brown Memorial Library, Providence, RI [*Library symbol*] [*Library of Congress*] (LCLS)
RPACA ...... Reports on the Progress of Applied Chemistry [*A publication*]
RPACDV ... Australia. Commonwealth Scientific and Industrial Research Organisation. Division of Applied Organic Chemistry. Research Report [*A publication*]
RPAE .... Retarding Potential Analyzer Experiment [*NASA*]
RPAG .... Retired Professionals Action Group [*Later, Gray Panthers*]
RPAL .... Royal Palm Savings Bank [*NASDAQ symbol*] (NQ)
R Palaeobot & Palynol ... Review of Palaeobotany and Palynology [*A publication*]
RPAM .... American Mathematical Society, Providence, RI [*Library symbol*] [*Library of Congress*] (LCLS)
RPAM .... Regional Public Affairs Manager [*Nuclear energy*] (NRCH)
RPAM .... Research in Public Administration and Management [*British*]
RPAO .... Radium Plaque Adaptometer Operator [*Navy*]
RPAODS... Remotely Piloted Aerial Observation Detection System (MCD)
RPAP........ Repap Enterprises Corp., Inc. [*NASDAQ symbol*] (NQ)
RPAPC ...... Religious Press Associations Postal Coalition (EA)
RPAPL ...... Real Property Actions and Proceedings Law [*New York, NY*] [*A publication*]
RPAR........ Rebuttable Presumption Against Regulation [*of pesticides*] [*Environmental Protection Agency*]
RPAS .... Audubon Society of Rhode Island, Providence, RI [*Library symbol*] [*Library of Congress*] (LCLS)
RPAS .... Reactor Protection Actuating Signal [*Nuclear energy*] (NRCH)
RPAS .... Review. Polish Academy of Sciences [*A publication*]
RPASC ...... Royal Pakistan Army Service Corps [*British military*] (DMA)
RPASDB ... Reviews in Pure and Applied Pharmacological Sciences [*A publication*]
RPASMC .. Rubber and Plastic Adhesive and Sealant Manufacturers Council [*Later, Adhesive and Sealant Council*] (EA)
R Pat Cas ... Reports of Patent, Design, and Trade Mark Cases [*A publication*] (DLA)
RP-ATLF... Roscoe Pound - American Trial Lawyers Foundation (EA)
RPaw......... Pawtucket Public Library, Pawtucket, RI [*Library symbol*] [*Library of Congress*] (LCLS)
RPB........... Belleville, KS [*Location identifier*] [*FAA*] (FAAL)
RPB........... Brown University, Providence, RI [*Library symbol*] [*Library of Congress*] (LCLS)
RPB........... RADAR Plotting Board
RPB........... Recognised Professional Body [*Marketing of Investments Board Organising Committee, London Stock Exchange*] [*Finance*]
RPB........... Regional Preparedness Board [*Military*] (AABC)
RPB........... Research to Prevent Blindness (EA)
RPB........... Resources Protection Board
RPB........... River Purification Board [*British*] (DCTA)
RPB........... Royal Palm Beach Ltd. [*AMEX symbol*] (SPSG)
RPB........... Royal Protection Branch [*of the London Metropolitan Police*]
Rp B Bk R ... Reprint Bulletin. Book Reviews [*A publication*]
RPBG........ Revised Program and Budget Guidance [*Military*]
RPBH .... Butler Health Center, Providence, RI [*Library symbol*] [*Library of Congress*] (LCLS)
RPB-JH..... Brown University, John Hay Library of Rare Books annd Special Collections, Providence, RI [*Library symbol*] [*Library of Congress*] (LCLS)
RPB-S........ Brown University, Sciences Library, Providence, RI [*Library symbol*] [*Library of Congress*] (LCLS)

RPBSC....... Rules Peculiar to the Business of the Supreme Court [*A publication*] (DLA)
RPC........... Baltimore Regional Planning Commission [*Library network*]
RPC........... RADAR Planning Chart
RPC........... RADAR Processing Center
RPC........... Radiological Physics Center [*National Cancer Institute*]
RPC........... Rapeseed Protein Concentrate [*Food technology*]
RPC........... Readers per Copy [*Newspapers and magazines*]
RPC........... Real Property Cases [*1843-48*] [*England*] [*A publication*] (DLA)
RPC........... Real Property Commissioner's Report [*1832*] [*England*] [*A publication*] (DLA)
RPC........... Records Processing Center [*Veterans Administration*]
RPC........... Recruiting Publicity Center [*Military*]
RPC........... Reefed Parachute Canopy
RPC........... Refugee Processing Center (MCD)
RPC........... Regional Personnel Center
RPC........... Regional Planning Commission
RPC........... Regional Preparedness Committee [*Civil Defense*]
RPC........... Registered Protective Circuit
RPC........... Registered Publication Clerk [*or Custodian*] [*Navy*]
RPC........... Reliability Policy Committee (AAG)
RPC........... Remote Parameter Control [*Automotive engineering*]
RPC........... Remote Position Control
RPC........... Remote Power Controller
RPC........... Remote Procedure Call [*Data processing*]
RPC........... Remote Process Cell [*Nuclear energy*] (NRCH)
RPC........... Remotely Piloted Craft [*Navy*]
RPC........... Remount Purchasing Commission [*British military*] (DMA)
RPC........... Renopericardial Canal [*Medicine*]
RPC........... Repair Parts Catalog
RPC........... Repair Parts Cost (MCD)
RPC........... Repairable Provisioning Center (MCD)
RPC........... Reparable Processing Center (AFM)
RPC........... Reply Postcard
RPC........... Report to Commander [*Military*]
RPC........... Reported Post Coastal (NATG)
RPC........... Reports of English Patent Cases [*A publication*] (DLA)
RPC........... Reports of Patent Cases [*Legal*] [*British*]
RPC........... Reports of Patent, Design, and Trade Mark Cases [*A publication*] (DLA)
RPC........... Republican Policy Committee
RPC........... Request the Pleasure of Your Company [*On invitations*] (DSUE)
RPC........... Requisition Processing Cycle (MCD)
RPC........... Research Planning Conference [*LIMRA*]
RPC........... Resource Policy Center [*Dartmouth College*] [*Research center*] (RCD)
RPC........... Ressources Phytogenetiques du Canada [*Plant Gene Resources of Canada - PGRC*]
RPC........... Restrictive Practices Court [*Legal*] [*British*]
RPC........... Restructured Pork Chop [*Food industry*]
RPC........... Reticularis Pontis Caudalis [*Brain anatomy*]
RPC........... Revenue Properties Ltd. [*AMEX symbol*] [*Toronto Stock Exchange symbol*] (SPSG)
RPC........... Reverse-Phase Chromatography
RPC........... Reverse-Phase Column
RPC........... Rice Polishing Concentrate (OA)
RPC........... River Patrol Craft [*Military*] (CINC)
RPC........... Romanian Philatelic Club (EA)
RPC........... Row Parity Check (IEEE)
RPC........... Royal Parks Constabulary [*British*]
RPC........... Royal Pioneer Corps [*British*]
RPC........... RPC Energy Services, Inc. [*Associated Press abbreviation*] (APAG)
RPC........... Rules of Practice in Patent Cases [*A publication*]
RPC........... Rural Political Cadre [*Vietnam*]
RPC........... Russian People's Center (EA)
RPC........... Russian Privatization Center (ECON)
RPCA......... Remotely Programmable Conference Arranger [*Telecommunications*] (TSSD)
RPCA......... Reverse Passive Anaphylaxis [*Immunology*]
RPCAS ...... Requisition Priority Code Analysis System [*Army*]
RPCC........ Reactor Physics Constants Center [*Argonne National Laboratory*]
RPCC........ Remote Process Crane Cave [*Nuclear energy*] (NRCH)
RPCCA ...... Red Poll Cattle Club of America [*Later, ARPA*] (EA)
RPCF .... Reiter Protein Complement Fixation [*Obsolete test for syphilis*]
RPCH .... Ameriwood Industries International [*NASDAQ symbol*] [*Formerly, Rospatch Corp.*] (SPSG)
RPCH .... Reformed Presbyterian Church
RPCH .... Rural Primary Care Hospital
RPCI......... Regroupement des Partis de la Cote-D'Ivoire [*Regroupment of the Parties of the Ivory Coast*]
RP/CI .... Reinforced Plastics/Composites Institute [*Later, SPICI*] (EA)
RPCK......... Renopericardial Canal, Kidney [*Medicine*]
RP/CL .... Reporting Post, Coastal Low [*RADAR*]
RPCM........ Rassemblement Populaire Caledonien et Metropolitain [*Caledonian and Metropolitan Popular Rally*] [*Political party*] (PPW)
RP/CM...... Reporting Post, Coastal Medium [*RADAR*]

RPCO .... Reclamation Program Control Officer [*Military*]   (AFIT)
RPCO .... Repco, Inc. [*NASDAQ symbol*]   (NQ)
RPCP .... Radioisotope-Powered Cardiac Pacemaker   (MCD)
RPCP .... Renopericardial Canal, Pericardium [*Medicine*]
RPCR .... Rassemblement pour la Caledonie dans la Republique [*Popular Caledonian Rally for the Republic*] [*Political party*]   (PPW)
RPCRAAIO ... Receive and Process Complaints and Requests for Assistance, Advice, or Information Only [*Army*]   (AABC)
RPC Rep .... Real Property Commissioner's Report [*1832*] [*England*] [*A publication*]   (DLA)
RPCRS ...... Reactor Protection Control Rod System   (IEEE)
RPCS .... Reactor Plant Control System [*Nuclear energy*]   (NRCH)
RPCV .... Returned Peace Corps Volunteer
RPCVCCA ... Returned Peace Corps Volunteers Committee on Central America   (EA)
RPCVD ...... Remote Plasma Chemical Vapor Deposition [*Coating technology*] [*Semiconductor technology*]
RPD .... RADAR Planning Device
RPD .... RADAR Prediction Device
RPD .... Radiation Protection Dosimetry [*A publication*]
RPD .... Radioisotope Power Device
RPD .... Rapid   (AAG)
RPD .... Reactive Plasma Deposition
RPD ...... Reactor Plant Designer [*Nuclear energy*]   (NRCH)
RPD .... Reflex Plasma Discharge
RPD .... Regius Professor of Divinity   (ROG)
RPD .... Regulatory Policy Division [*Environmental Protection Agency*]   (EPA)
RPD .... Relative Power Density
RPD .... Renewal Parts Data   (MSA)
RPD .... Repadre Resources Ltd. [*Vancouver Stock Exchange symbol*]
RPD .... Repatriation Pension Decisions [*Australia*] [*A publication*]
RPD .... Rerum Politicarum Doctor [*Doctor of Political Science*]
RPD .... Reserves Available to Support Private, Noninterbank Deposits [*Federal Reserve System*]
RPD .... Resistance Pressure Detector
RPD .... Respiratory Protective Device [*Medicine*]
RPD .... Retarding Potential Difference   (IEEE)
RPD .... Retired Pay Defense   (NVT)
RPD .... Review of Public Data Use [*A publication*]
RPD .... Rhode Island School of Design, Providence, RI [*Library symbol*] [*Library of Congress*]   (LCLS)
RPD .... Rocket Propulsion Department [*Royal Aircraft Establishment*] [*British*]
RPDB........ Repertoire Pratique de Droit Belge [*A publication*]   (ILCA)
RPDES ...... Research Program Development and Evaluation Staff [*Department of Agriculture*]
RPDF........ Radiation Protection Design Features   (NRCH)
RPDH........ Reserve Shutdown Planned Derated Hours [*Electronics*]   (IEEE)
RPDL........ Radioisotope Process Development Laboratory [*ORNL*]
RPDL........ Rensselaer Polytechnic Institute Plasma Dynamics Laboratory [*Research center*]   (RCD)
RPDL........ Repair Parts Decision List [*Military*]   (CAAL)
RPDMRC ... Reference or Partial Description Method Reason Code   (MCD)
RPDO .... Repair Parts Directive Order
RPDP........ Recoverable Plasma Diagnostics Package   (SSD)
RPDQDK .. Queensland. Department of Forestry. Research Paper [*A publication*]
RPDR .... Reproducer   (MSA)
RPDR .... Rotating Packed Disk Reactor [*Chemical engineering*]
RPDS........ Rapids   (MCD)
RPDS........ Retired Personnel Data System [*Air Force*]
RPDt.......... Registered Professional Dietitian
RPD & TM ... Reports of Patent, Design, and Trade Mark Cases [*United Kingdom*] [*A publication*]
RPDTMC ... Reports of Patent, Design, and Trade Mark Cases [*Australia*] [*A publication*]
RPD & TM Cas ... Reports of Patent Design and Trade Mark Cases [*United Kingdom*] [*A publication*]   (DLA)
RPDWR..... Revised Primary Drinking Water Regulations
RPE........... Elmwood Public Library, Providence, RI [*Library symbol*] [*Library of Congress*]   (LCLS)
RPE........... Radial Probable Error   (IEEE)
RPE........... Range Planning Estimate   (MUGU)
RPE........... Range Probable Error [*Formerly, Range Error Probable*] [*Air Force*]   (NATG)
RPE........... Rating of Perceived Exertion
RPE........... Reformed Protestant Episcopal
RPE........... Registered Professional Engineer   (IEEE)
RPE........... Related Payroll Expense
RPE........... Related Production Equipment   (SAA)
RPE........... Relative Price Effect
RPE........... Reliability Project Engineer   (NASA)
RPE........... Remote Peripheral Equipment   (IEEE)
RPE........... Repair Parts Estimate   (MCD)
RPE........... Report of Patients Evacuated [*Aeromedical evacuation*]
RPE........... Required Page-End Character [*Data processing*]
RPE........... Resource Planning and Evaluation [*Nuclear energy*]   (NRCH)
RPE........... Retinal Pigment Epithelium

RPE........... Rocket Propulsion Establishment [*British*]   (KSC)
RPE........... Ron Pair Enterprises [*Division of Wilson, Inc.*]
RPE........... Rotating Platinum Electrode [*Electrochemistry*]
RPE........... Royal Pakistan Engineers [*British military*]   (DMA)
RPEA........ Regional Planning and Evaluation Agency [*California State Board of Education*]
RP/ED...... Rapid Prototyping/Evolutionary Design   (MCD)
RPEN ...... Retry Pending   (SSD)
RPEng........ Providence Engineering Society, Providence, RI [*Library symbol*] [*Library of Congress*]   (LCLS)
RPEP .... Register of Planned Emergency Procedures [*Military*]
RPET .... Royal Dutch Petroleum Co. [*NASDAQ symbol*]   (NQ)
RPEV........ Roadway Powered Electric Vehicle
RPF........... Radio Position Finding [*A term for RADAR before early 1942*]
RPF........... Radio Proximity Fuze
RPF........... Radiometer Performance Factor
RPF........... Real Property Facilities [*Army*]   (AABC)
RPF........... Reduced Physical Fidelity   (MCD)
RPF........... Reference Point Foundation   (EA)
RPF........... Reformatorische Politieke Federatie [*Reformist Political Federation*] [*Netherlands*] [*Political party*]   (PPE)
RPF........... Region Peaking Factor [*Nuclear energy*]   (NRCH)
RPF........... Registered Professional Forester
RPF........... Relaxed Pelvic Floor [*Medicine*]
RPF........... Remote Personnel Facility
RPF........... Remote Processing Facility   (MCD)
RPF........... Renal Plasma Flow [*Medicine*]
RPF........... Repair Parts Facility   (MCD)
rpf............ Reperforated [*Philately*]
RPF........... Right Panel Front [*Nuclear energy*]   (NRCH)
RPF........... Rotable Pool Factor   (MCD)
RPF........... Royal Pacific Sea Farms Ltd. [*Toronto Stock Exchange symbol*] [*Vancouver Stock Exchange symbol*]
RPFADG ... Forests Department of Western Australia. Research Paper [*A publication*]
RPFC .... Ray Price Fan Club   (EA)
RPFC .... Recurrent Peak Forward Current
RPFFB....... RP [*Retinitis Pigmentosa*] Foundation Fighting Blindness   (EA)
RPFOD...... Reported for Duty   (FAAC)
RPFS .... Rudder Pedal Force Sensor   (MCD)
RPFT .... Rudder Pedal Force Transducer   (MCD)
RPFUB ...... Radovi Poljoprivrednog Fakulteta Univerziteta u Sarajevu [*A publication*]
RPFWDE .. US Fish and Wildlife Service. Resource Publication [*A publication*]
RPG .... Radiation Protection Guide [*AEC*]
RPG .... Radioisotopic Power Generator [*Navy*]
RPG .... Rampage Resources Ltd. [*Vancouver Stock Exchange symbol*]
RPG .... Random Pulse Generator [*Telecommunications*]   (OA)
RPG .... Rebounds per Game [*Basketball, hockey*]
RPG .... Reflection Phase Grating [*Acoustics*]
RPG .... Refugee Policy Group   (EA)
RPG .... Regional Planning Group   (NATG)
RPG .... Register Program Generator   (HGAA)
RPG .... Religion Publishing Group   (EA)
RPG .... Report Processor Generator   (MCD)
RPG .... Report Program Generator [*Programming language*] [*1962*]
RPG .... Research Planning Guide   (MCD)
RPG .... Retrograde Pyelogram [*Medicine*]
RPG .... Right Pedal Ganglion
RPG .... Rocket-Propelled Grenade
RPG .... Role-Playing Game [*Video game*]
RPG .... Rotary Pulse Generator
RPG .... Rounds per Gun
RPGAN ...... Role-Playing Game Association Network   (EA)
RPGN .... Rapidly Progressive Glomerular Nephritis [*Medicine*]
RPGPA...... Recent Publications on Governmental Problems [*A publication*]
RPGPM..... Rounds per Gun per Minute
RPH .... Raypath Resources Ltd. [*Vancouver Stock Exchange symbol*]
RPH .... Registered Pharmacist
RPH .... Relative Pulse Height   (OA)
RPH .... Remember Pearl Harbor [*Group*] [*World War II*]
RPH .... Remotely Piloted Helicopter
RP/H .... Repairs, Heavy
RPH .... Revolutions per Hour   (MCD)
RPH .... Rhode Island Hospital, Peters House Medical Library, Providence, RI [*Library symbol*] [*Library of Congress*]   (LCLS)
RPH .... Rideout Pyrohydrolysis
RPh............ Romance Philology [*A publication*]
RPHA .... Reverse Passive Hemagglutination [*Clinical chemistry*]
RPhilS .... Royal Philharmonic Society [*British*]   (DI)
RPHJ .... Royal Perth Hospital. Journal [*A publication*]   (ADA)
RPhO .... Regional Pharmaceutical Officer [*National Health Service*] [*British*]   (DI)
RP-HPLC ... Reversed-Phase High-Performance Liquid Chromatography
RPHRA ...... Recent Progress in Hormone Research [*A publication*]
RPHST ...... Research Participation for High School Teachers [*National Science Foundation*]

R Phys Soc Edinb Pr ... Royal Physical Society of Edinburgh. Proceedings [*A publication*]
RPI............ RADAR Precipitation Integrator [*National Weather Service*]
RPI............ Railway Progress Institute (EA)
RPI............ Rapeseed Protein Isolate [*Food technology*]
RPI............ Rassemblement Populaire pour l'Independance [*People's Rally for Independence*] [*Djibouti*] [*Political party*] (PPW)
RPI............ Rated Position Identifier (AFM)
RPI............ Read, Punch, and Interpret
RPI............ Real Property Inventory [*Military*]
RPI............ Recover Processor Improvement (DWSG)
RPI............ Registro de la Propiedad Industrial [*Spanish Patent Office*] [*Information service or system*] (IID)
RPI............ Relative Position Indication (NRCH)
RPI............ Relay Position Indicator
RPI............ Remarried Parents, Inc. (EA)
RPI............ Rensselaer Polytechnic Institute [*Troy, NY*] (MCD)
RPI............ Republican Party of India [*Political party*] (PPW)
RPI............ Research Price Index
RPI............ Resource Policy Institute (EA)
RPI............ Responsive Production Inventory
RPI............ Retail Prices Index [*British*]
RPI............ Reticulocyte Production Index [*Hematology*]
RPI............ Richmond Professional Institute [*Virginia*]
RPI............ Rimpac Industries [*Vancouver Stock Exchange symbol*]
RPI............ Rod Position Indicator [*Nuclear energy*] (NRCH)
RPI............ Roll Position Indicator (MCD)
RPI............ Rose Polytechnic Institute [*Indiana*]
RPI............ Royal Polytechnic Institute (ROG)
R & PI........ Rubber and Plastics Industry (MCD)
RPIA.......... Rocket Propellant Information Agency (MCD)
RPIA.......... Roll Position Indicator Assembly
RPIAC....... Retail Prices Index Advisory Committee [*Department of Employment*] [*British*]
RPIC.......... Reagan Political Items Collectors (EA)
RPIC.......... Republic Pictures Corp. [*Los Angeles, CA*] [*NASDAQ symbol*] (NQ)
RPIC.......... Rock Properties Information Center [*Purdue University*] [*National Science Foundation*] (IID)
RPI/CIE .... Rensselaer Polytechnic Institute/Center for Integrated Electronics [*Troy, NY*]
RPIE.......... Real Property Installed Equipment [*Air Force*] (MCD)
RPIE.......... Replacement of Photography Imagery Equipment (RDA)
RPIF......... Real Property Industrial Fund
RPIFC........ Robert Plant International Fan Club (EA)
RPIFC....... Ronnie Prophet International Fan Club (EA)
RPI/MA .... Rensselaer Polytechnic Institute/Microwave Acoustics Laboratory [*Troy, NY*]
RPIO.......... Registered Publication Issuing Office [*Military*]
RPIS......... Rod Position Indication System [*Nuclear energy*] (NRCH)
RPIS......... Rod Position Information System [*Nuclear energy*] (NRCH)
RPIT.......... Related-Party International Transaction
RPJ............ [*The*] Rise of Provincial Jewry [*A publication*] (BJA)
RPJ............ Rotary Pressure Joint
RPJCB....... John Carter Brown Library, Providence, RI [*Library symbol*] [*Library of Congress*] (LCLS)
RPK .... Revenue Passenger Kilometer (AIA)
RPK .... Ribophosphate Pyrophosphokinase [*An enzyme*]
RPK .... Roosevelt [*Washington*] [*Seismograph station code, US Geological Survey*] (SEIS)
RPL............ RADAR Processing Language [*Data processing*] (IEEE)
RPL............ Radiation Physics Laboratory [*National Institute of Standards and Technology*] (MCD)
RPL............ Radio-Photo Luminescent [*Dosimetry*]
RPL............ Ram Petroleums Ltd. [*Toronto Stock Exchange symbol*]
RPL............ Ramped Powered Lighter [*British military*] (DMA)
RPL............ Ramseur Pilot Light Teaching System
RPL............ Rapid Pole Line [*A type of pole line construction*]
RPL............ Rated Power Level (NASA)
RPL............ Reactor Primary Loop
RPL............ Reading Public Library, Reading, PA [*OCLC symbol*] (OCLC)
RPL............ Receive Replenishment From [*Navy*] (NVT)
RPL............ Recommended Provisioning List
RPL............ Reemployment Priority List [*DoD*]
RPL............ Remote Program Load
RPL............ Renewal Parts Leaflet (MSA)
RPL............ Repair Parts List [*Army*] (AABC)
RP/L.......... Repairs, Light
RPL............ Repetitive Flight Plan [*Aviation*] (FAAC)
RPL............ Replenish (NVT)
RPL............ Request Parameter List [*Data processing*] (BUR)
RPL............ Requested Privilege Level [*Data processing*]
RPL............ Resident Programming Language [*Data processing*]
RPL............ Resident Pulmonary Lymphocyte [*Immunology*]
RPL............ Review of the River Plate [*A publication*]
RPL............ Rhode Island State Law Library, Providence, RI [*Library symbol*] [*Library of Congress*] (LCLS)
RPL............ Richmond Public Library [*UTLAS symbol*]
RPL............ Ripe Pulp Liquid [*A banana substrate*]
RPL............ Ripple
RPL............ Robot Programming Language [*Data processing*]

RPL............ Rocket Propulsion Laboratory [*Air Force*]
RPL............ Rodent and Primate Laboratory (SSD)
RPL............ Running Program Language [*Data processing*]
RPLAA...... Reinforced Plastics [*A publication*]
RPLC......... Replace (FAAC)
RPLC......... Reversed-Phase Liquid Chromatography
RPLit .... Res Publica Litterarum [*A publication*]
RPLN......... Retroperitoneal Lymph Nodes [*Medicine*]
RPLNG...... Replenishing
RPLO........ Regal Petroleum Ltd. [*NASDAQ symbol*] (NQ)
RPLPA ...... Reviews of Plasma Physics [*English Translation*] [*A publication*]
RPLR......... Repeller (MSA)
RPLS .... Radionuclide Perfusion Lung Scan
RPLS .... Reactor Protection Logic System (IEEE)
RPLSN ...... Repulsion (MSA)
RPLT .... Repellent (MSA)
RPLV........ Reentry Payload Launch Vehicle
RPM .... RADAR Performance Monitor
RPM .... Radial-Burning Pulse Motor (MCD)
RPM .... Radiation Polarization Measurement
RPM .... Random Phase Model (OA)
RPM .... Rapid Processing Mode [*Medicine*] (MAE)
RPM .... Rate per Minute
RPM .... Reactive Plume Model [*Environmental Protection Agency*] (GFGA)
RPM .... Read Program Memory [*Data processing*] (MDG)
RPM .... Real Property Management
RPM .... Reclamation Program Manager [*Military*] (AFIT)
RPM .... Registered Publications Manual [*Navy*]
RPM .... Registered Publications Memorandum
RPM .... Registrants Processing Manual [*Selective Service System*]
RPM .... Regulated Power Module
RPM .... Relaxation Potential Model [*Physics*]
RPM .... Reliability Performance Measure [*QCR*]
RPM .... Reliability Planning and Management (MCD)
RPM .... Remedial Project Manager [*Navy*]
RPM .... Remote Performance Monitoring (CET)
RPM .... Remote Program Management
RPM .... Remotely Piloted Munitions [*Army*]
RPM .... Resale Price Maintenance
R & PM...... Research and Program Management [*NASA*]
RPM......... Research and Program Management [*NASA*]
RPM .... Resident Process Manager [*Data processing*] (PCM)
RPM .... Resistant Plant Material [*Soil science*]
R & PM...... Resources and Program Management [*NASA*]
RPM .... Response-per-Thousand [*Marketing*]
RPM .... Resupply Provisions Module [*NASA*] (KSC)
RPM .... Retail Price Maintenance (DCTA)
RPM .... Returns Program Manager [*IRS*]
RPM .... Revenue per Mile
RPM .... Revenue Passenger Mile
RPM .... Revolutions per Minute [*e.g., in reference to phonograph records*]
RPM .... Rhode Island Medical Society, Providence, RI [*Library symbol*] [*Library of Congress*] (LCLS)
RPM .... Rifle Prize Money [*British military*] (DMA)
RPM .... Rocket-Propelled Mines (NATG)
RPM .... Roll Position Mechanism (MCD)
RPM .... Rotations per Minute
RPM .... Rounds per Minute [*Military*] (INF)
RPM .... Royalty Payment Mechanism
RPMa .... Masonic Temple Library, Providence, RI [*Library symbol*] [*Library of Congress*] (LCLS)
RPMA .... Real Property Maintenance Activities [*or Administration*] [*Army*] (AABC)
RPMB........ Cubi Naval Air Station, Bataan [*Philippines*] [*ICAO location identifier*] (ICLI)
RPMC........ Cebu/Lahug, Cebu [*Philippines*] [*ICAO location identifier*] (ICLI)
RPMC........ Remote Performance Monitoring and Control
RPMC........ Reserve Personnel, Marine Corps (MCD)
RPMD .... Resources Planning and Mobilization Division [*of OEP*]
RPMDA .... Recenti Progressi in Medicina [*A publication*]
RPMDDQ ... Malaysia. Ministry of Agriculture and Rural Development. Risalah Penerangan [*A publication*]
RPMF........ Reserve Personnel Master File [*Military*]
RPMI........ Radiant Power Measuring Instrument [*Geophysics*]
RPMI........ Revolutions-per-Minute Indicator
RPMI......... Roswell Park Memorial Institute [*State University of New York at Buffalo*] [*Research center*] (RCD)
RPMIO...... Registered Publication Mobile Issuing Office [*Military*]
RPMK .... Clark Air Base, Pampanga [*Philippines*] [*ICAO location identifier*] (ICLI)
RPMKA..... Rocznik Pomorskiej Akademii Medycznej Imienia Generala Karola Swierczewskiego w Szczecinie [*A publication*]
RPMKAA ... Annales Academiae Medicae Stetinensis [*A publication*]
RPML........ Laoag/International, Ilocos Norte [*Philippines*] [*ICAO location identifier*] (ICLI)
RPMM ...... Manila/International [*Philippines*] [*ICAO location identifier*] (ICLI)

RPMN .... Repairman (AABC)
RPMO .... Radio Projects Management Office
RPMOR .... Rounds per Mortar
RPMORPM ... Rounds per Mortar per Minute
RPMP........ Legazpi, Albay [Philippines] [ICAO location identifier] (ICLI)
RPMP........ Register of Plan Mobilization Producers
RPMR........ Romblon, Tablas Island [Philippines] [ICAO location identifier] (ICLI)
RPMS....... Real Property Management System (MCD)
RPM/S...... Revolutions per Minute/Second (DEN)
RPMS........ Royal Postgraduate Medical School [British]
RPMS........ Sangley Point Naval Station, Cavite [Philippines] [ICAO location identifier] (ICLI)
RPMT........ Lapu-Lapu/Mactan International [Philippines] [ICAO location identifier] (ICLI)
RPMZ........ Zamboanga/International [Philippines] [ICAO location identifier] (ICLI)
RPN .... Registered Professional Nurse
RPN .... Reserve Personnel, Navy [An appropriation]
RPN .... Reverse Polish Notation [Arithmetic evaluation] [Data processing] (IEEE)
RPN .... Rosh-Pina [Israel] [Airport symbol] (OAG)
RPN .... Royal Pakistan Navy [British military] (DMA)
RPND .... Reprinting, No Date [Publishing]
R & P News ... Rubber and Plastics News [A publication]
R & P News 2 ... Rubber and Plastics News. 2 [A publication]
RPNSM..... Replenishment
RPNVR...... Royal Pakistan Naval Volunteer Reserve [British military] (DMA)
RPO .... Radiation Protection Officer [NASA] (NASA)
RPO .... Radiophare Omnidirectionnel [Omnidirectional Radio Beacon] (NATG)
RPO .... Railway Post Office
RPO .... Range Planning Office (MUGU)
RPO .... Readiness Project Officer
RPO .... Regional Personnel Officer [Social Security Administration]
RPO .... Regional Pests Officer [Ministry of Agriculture, Fisheries, and Food] [British]
RPO .... Regional Program [or Project] Officer (OICC)
RPO .... Regional Purchasing Office [Defense Supply Agency]
RPO .... Registered Publications Officer [Navy] (DNAB)
RPO .... Regular Production Option [Automotive engineering]
RPO .... Regulating Petty Officer [British]
RPO .... Rejection Purchase Order (MCD)
RPO .... Repair Parts Order [Navy]
RPO .... Replacement Purchase Order
RPO .... Responsible Property Officer [Military] (AFIT)
RPO .... Retired Pay Operations [Army]
RPO .... Revolution per Orbit
RPO .... Rotor Power Output
RPO .... Royal Philharmonic Orchestra [British]
RPOA .... Recognized Private Operating Agencies (NATG)
RPOC .... Remote Payload Operations Center [NASA] (MCD)
RPOC .... Report Proceeding on Course [Aviation] (FAAC)
RPOC .... Residual Particulate Organic Carbon [Environmental science]
RPOCC..... Remote Payload Operations Control Center [NASA] (SSD)
RPOCN ..... Request for Purchase Order Change Notice (AAG)
R Pol .... Review of Politics [A publication]
R Polit....... Review of Politics [A publication]
R Politics.... Review of Politics [A publication]
RPOOK..... Receive Pulse On/Off Keyed (MCD)
RPOP........ Rover Preflight Operations Procedures [NASA] (KSC)
RPorP .... Portsmouth Priory, Portsmouth, RI [Library symbol] [Library of Congress] (LCLS)
R Porto....... Revista. Faculdade de Letras. Serie de Historia. Universidade do Porto [A publication]
RPOW .... RPM, Inc. [NASDAQ symbol] (NQ)
RPP.......... RADAR Power Programmer
RPP.......... Radiation Protection Plan [Nuclear energy] (NRCH)
RPP.......... Radiochemical Processing Plant [Oak Ridge National Laboratory]
RPP.......... Rassemblement Populaire pour le Progres [Popular Rally for Progress] [Djibouti] [Political party] (PPW)
RPP.......... Rate Pressure Product [Cardiology]
RPP.......... Reactor Plant Planning (DNAB)
RPP.......... Real Property Practice [A publication]
RPP.......... Real Property, Probate, and Trust Journal [A publication]
RPP.......... Rechargeable Power Pack
RPP.......... Recovered Polypropylene [Organic chemistry]
R & PP ...... Recreation and Public Purposes Act
RPP.......... Reductive Pentose Phosphate [Photosynthesis cycle]
RPP.......... Regional Priority Program [Army] (AABC)
RPP.......... Regional Promotion Plan [FAA] (FAAC)
RPP.......... Registered Postal Packet
RPP.......... Reinforced Pyrolytic Plastic (NASA)
RPP.......... Reliability Program Plan (MCD)
RPP.......... Removable Patch Panel
RPP.......... Rendezvous Point Position [Aerospace]
RPP.......... Repair Parts Provisioning
RPP.......... Repap Enterprises Corp., Inc. [Toronto Stock Exchange symbol] [Vancouver Stock Exchange symbol]

RPP........... Reply Paid Postcard
RPP........... Republican People's Party [Cumhuriyet Halk Partisi - CHP] [Turkey] [Political party] (PPW)
RPP........... Request Present Position [Aviation] (FAAC)
RPP........... Request for Proposal Preparation (SAA)
RPP........... Requisition Processing Point [Military]
RPP........... Retrograde Processing Point (MCD)
RPP........... Retropubic Prostatectomy [Medicine]
RPP........... Reverse Pulse Polarography [Analytical chemistry]
RPP........... Review of Public Personnel Administration [A publication]
RPP........... Rivers Pollution Prevention (ROG)
RPP........... Roll-Pitch Pickoff
RP and P .... Romanticism Past and Present [A publication]
RPP........... Rules of Practices and Procedure
RPP........... Rural Practice Project [An association] [Defunct] (EA)
RPPA .... Republican Postwar Policy Association [Encouraged Republican Party to drop its isolationist viewpoint and take a stand for an American share in international collaboration after the war] [World War II]
RPPC .... Providence College, Providence, RI [Library symbol] [Library of Congress] (LCLS)
RPPE........ Research, Program, Planning, and Evaluation
RPPHA...... Reports on Progress in Physics [A publication]
RPPI .... Remote Plan Position Indicator (MCD)
RPPI .... Repeater Plan Position Indicator (NVT)
RPPI .... Role Perception Picture Inventory
RPPJA....... Reports on Progress in Polymer Physics (Japan) [A publication]
RPPL .... Repair Parts Price List
RPPL .... Repair Parts Provisioning List
RPPM........ Park Museum Reference Library, Providence, RI [Library symbol] [Library of Congress] (LCLS)
RPPMP .... Repair Parts Program Management Plans
RPPO........ Regional Printing Procurement Office [Army]
RPPP .... Repair Parts Program Plan [Army]
RPPP .... Rules of Pleading, Practice, and Procedure [A publication] (DLA)
RPPR........ Rooney, Pace Group, Inc. [NASDAQ symbol] (NQ)
RPPS .... Retired Pay / Personnel System [Military] (DNAB)
RPPS .... Robotnicza Partia Polskich Socjalistow [Workers Party of Polish Socialists] [Political party] (PPE)
RPPS-Lewica ... Robotnicza Partia Polskich Socjalistow - Lewica [Workers Party of Polish Socialists - Left] [Political party] (PPE)
RPPTF....... Rotatable Porous-Prism Test Fixture
RPPY .... Reactor Plant Planning Year (DNAB)
RPQ .... Rapports de Pratique de Quebec [Quebec Practice Reports] [Canada] [A publication] (DLA)
RPQ .... Request for Price Quotation
RPQ .... Rutter Parent Questionnaire
RPQEA...... Radiophysics and Quantum Electronics [English Translation] [A publication]
RPR .... Federation Guadeloupeenne du Rassemblement pour la Republique [Guadeloupe Federation of the Rally for the Republic] [Political party] (PPW)
RPR .... Radio Physics Research
RPR .... Railway Pioneer Regiment [British military] (DMA)
RPR .... Raipur [India] [Airport symbol] (OAG)
RPR .... Rapid Plasma Reagin [Card test for venereal disease]
RPR .... Rapid Power Reduction (IEEE)
RPR .... Rassemblement pour la Republique [Rally for the Republic] [French Guiana] [Political party] (PPW)
RPR .... Rassemblement pour la Republique [Rally for the Republic] [Mayotte] [Political party] (EY)
RPR .... Rassemblement pour la Republique [Rally for the Republic] [France] [Political party] (ECON)
RPR .... Rassemblement pour la Republique [Rally for the Republic] [French Polynesia] [Political party] (PPW)
RPR .... Rassemblement pour la Republique [Rally for the Republic] [Wallis and Futuna Islands] [Political party] (PD)
RPR .... Rassemblement pour la Republique [Rally for the Republic] [Reunion] [Political party] (PPW)
RPR .... Rassemblement pour la Republique [Rally for the Republic] [Martinique] [Political party] (PPW)
RPR .... Rated Pressure Ratio (EG)
RPR .... Read Printer
RPR .... Real Property Reports [A publication]
RPR .... Rear Projection Readout
RPR .... Rectangular Parallelepiped Resonant Method [Crystal elasticity]
RPR .... Red Blood Cell Precursor Production Rate [Hematology]
RPR .... Rent Procedural Regulation (Office of Rent Stabilization) [Economic Stabilization Agency] [A publication] (DLA)
RPR .... Repair (MSA)
RPR .... Repair Parts Requisition
RPR .... Research Project Report [A publication] (EAAP)
RPR .... Rhone-Poulenc Rorer [NYSE symbol] (SPSG)
RPR .... Rhone-Poulenc Rorer [Associated Press abbreviation] (APAG)
RPR .... Rockport Resources Ltd. [Vancouver Stock Exchange symbol]
RPR .... Roger Williams College, Providence Campus, Providence, RI [Library symbol] [Library of Congress] (LCLS)
RPR .... Roll-Pitch Resolver
RPR .... Rotatable Pool Rate (MCD)

RPRA......... Railroad Public Relations Association (EA)
R Prac Patent Cases ... Rules of Practice in Patent Cases [*A publication*] (DLA)
RPrag......... Romanistica Pragensia [*A publication*]
RPRC......... Regional Primate Research Centers
RPRC......... Religious Public Relations Council (EA)
RPRC......... Retired and Pioneer Rural Carriers of United States (EA)
RPRC......... Rhode Island College, Providence, RI [*Library symbol*] [*Library of Congress*] (LCLS)
RPR-CT..... Rapid Plasma Reagin Card Test [*Clinical chemistry*]
RPRD......... Research Policy and Review Division [*of OEP*]
rPRL......... Rat Prolactin [*Biochemistry*]
RPRL......... Regional Parasite Research Laboratory [*US Department of Agriculture*] [*Research center*] (RCD)
RPRL......... Regional Poultry Research Laboratory [*East Lansing, MI*] [*Department of Agriculture*] (GRD)
RPRMN .... Repairman
RPRO .... ReproTech, Inc. [*Sweetwater, TN*] [*NASDAQ symbol*] (NQ)
RPRODG .. Annual Research Reviews. Renal Prostaglandins [*A publication*]
RPROM .... Reprogrammable Read-Only Memory [*Data processing*] (HGAA)
RPROP...... Receiving Proficiency Pay [*Military*]
R Prop Prob and Tr J ... Real Property, Probate, and Trust Journal [*A publication*]
RPRRB ...... Real Property Resource Review Board (AFM)
RPRS......... Random-Pulse RADAR System (AAG)
RPRS......... Roll-Pitch Resolver System
RPRT......... Report (AFM)
RPRV......... Remotely Piloted Research Vehicle [*NASA*]
RPRWP..... Reactor Plant River Water Pump (IEEE)
RPS........... Racial Preservation Society [*British*]
RPS........... RADAR Plotting Sheet (OA)
RPS........... RADAR Position Symbol (FAAC)
RPS........... Radiation Protection Standards (SAA)
RPS........... Radical Philosophy Society [*British*]
RPS........... Radio Program Standard [*Australian Broadcasting Tribunal*]
RPS........... Radiological Protection Service (DEN)
RPS........... Range Pad Service
RPS........... Range Positioning System
RPS........... Rapid Patent Service [*Research Publications, Inc.*] [*Information service or system*] (IID)
RPS........... Rapid Photo Screening
RPS........... Rare Poultry Society [*British*]
RPS........... Reactor Protection System [*Nuclear energy*] (NRCH)
RPS........... Real-Time Programming System [*Data processing*] (IEEE)
RPS........... Record and Playback Subsystem (NASA)
RPS........... Records per Sector [*Data processing*]
RPS........... Registered Publications System
RPS........... Regulated Power Supply
RPS........... Regulatory Performance Summary [*Report*] [*Nuclear energy*] (NRCH)
RPS........... Reinforced Porcelain System [*Dentistry*]
RPS........... Relative Performance Score [*Telecommunications*] (TEL)
RPS........... Relay Power Supply (MCD)
RPS........... Remittance Processing Systems [*IRS*]
RPS........... Remote Printing System
RPS........... Remote Processing Service (BUR)
RPS........... Remote Programming System (MCD)
RPS........... Renal Pressor Substance [*Medicine*]
RPS........... Requirements Planning System [*Data processing*]
RPS........... Response-Produced Stimulation
RPS........... Retired Persons Services (EA)
RPS........... Return Pressure Sensing (MCD)
RPS........... Revolutions per Second (AFM)
rps .... Rhodopseudomonas Virides [*A bacterium*]
RPS........... Right Pedal Sinus
RPS........... Rigid Proctosigmoidoscopy [*Proctoscopy*]
RPS........... Ripe Pulp Solid [*A banana substrate*]
RPS........... RMS [*Remote Manipulator System*] Planning System (SSD)
RPS........... Rochester Public Schools, Library Processing Center, Rochester, MN [*OCLC symbol*] (OCLC)
RPS........... Role Performance Scale [*Occupational therapy*]
RPS........... Rotary Precision Switch
RPS........... Rotating Passing Scuttle
RPS........... Rotational Position Sensing [*Data processing*]
RPS........... Royal Philharmonic Society (EAIO)
RPS........... Royal Photographic Society of Great Britain (DEN)
RPS........... RPS Realty Trust [*NYSE symbol*] (SPSG)
RPS........... RPS Realty Trust [*Associated Press abbreviation*] (APAG)
RPS........... Rutile-Paper-Slurry [*Grade of titanium dioxide*]
RPSA .... Religious Program Specialist Seaman Apprentice [*Navy rating*] (DNAB)
RPSA .... Resources Pension Shares 1 [*New York, NY*] [*NASDAQ symbol*] (NQ)
RPSA .... Rudder Pedal Sensor Assembly (MCD)
RPSB .... Resources Pension Shares 2 [*NASDAQ symbol*] (NQ)
RPSC .... Resources Pension Shares 3 [*New York, NY*] [*NASDAQ symbol*] (NQ)
RPSC .... Royal Philatelic Society of Canada

RPSCTDY ... Return to Proper Station Upon Completion of Temporary Duty [*Military*]
RPS-DL..... Registered Publications Section - District Library [*Navy*]
R & P SEC ... Radio and Panel Section [*Navy*]
RPSEL....... Recommended Peculiar Support Equipment List (MCD)
RPSGB ...... Royal Pharmaceutical Society of Great Britain (EAIO)
RPSGB ...... Royal Photographic Society of Great Britain (EAIO)
RP (Ships) ... Registered Ships' Plumbers [*British*]
RPSI .... Roche Psychiatric Service Institute
RPSIO ...... Registered Publications Subissuing Office [*Military*] (NVT)
RPSL .... Repair Parts Selective List
RPSL .... Rhode Island Department of State Library Services, Providence, RI [*Library symbol*] [*Library of Congress*] (LCLS)
RPSM....... Registered Publication Shipment Memorandum
RPSM....... Resources Planning and Scheduling Method
RPSMG..... Reactor Protective System Motor Generator (IEEE)
RPSML ..... Repair Parts Support Material List
RPSN........ Religious Program Specialist Seaman [*Navy rating*] (DNAB)
RPSP .... RADAR Programmable Signal Processor
RPS-PL...... Registered Publications Section - Personnel Library [*Navy*]
RPSS .... Ryukyu Philatelic Specialist Society (EA)
RPS Subj Cat ... Royal Photographic Society of Great Britain. Library Catalogue. Part 2. Subject Catalogue [*A publication*]
RPST .... Reaction Products Separator Tank [*Nuclear energy*] (NRCH)
RPST .... Recombinant Porcine Somatotropin
RPSTL ...... Repair Parts and Special Tools List [*Army*] (AABC)
RPSY .... Rapitech Systems, Inc. [*Suffern, NY*] [*NASDAQ symbol*] (NQ)
R Psych...... Reading Psychology [*A publication*]
RPT........... Congregation Sons of Israel and David, Temple Beth-El, Providence, RI [*Library symbol*] [*Library of Congress*] (LCLS)
RPT........... Raluana Point [*New Britain*] [*Seismograph station code, US Geological Survey*] (SEIS)
RPT........... Rapid Pull Through [*Gastroenterology*]
RPT........... Rassemblement du Peuple Togolais [*Rally of the Togolese People*] [*Political party*] (PPW)
RPT........... Reactor for Physical and Technical Investigations [*Former USSR*] [*Nuclear energy*]
RPT........... Reactor Plant Test (DNAB)
RPT........... Recirculation Pump Trip [*Nuclear energy*] (NRCH)
RPT........... Recruit Performance Test (OA)
RPT........... Reference Point Tracking
RPT........... Registered Physical Therapist
RPT........... Regular Public Transport (ADA)
RPT........... Relative Prime Transform
RPT........... Repair Parts Transporter (MCD)
RPT........... Repeat (AAG)
RPT........... Reply Paid Telegram
RPT........... Report
RPT........... Reprint
RPT........... Request Programs Termination [*Data processing*]
RPT........... Resident Provisioning Team [*NASA*]
R & PT....... Rifle and Pistol Team [*Navy*]
RPT........... Rocket-Powered Target
RPT........... Rocket Propulsion Technician [*Air Force*]
RPT........... Rotary Power Transformer
RPT........... Rudder Pedal Transducer (NASA)
RPTA......... Rudder Pedal Transducer Assembly (NASA)
RPTC........ Repeating Coil (MSA)
RPTD........ Repeated
RPTD........ Reported
RPTD........ Reprinted (WGA)
RPTD........ Ruptured
RPTEA ...... Reviews of Petroleum Technology [*A publication*]
RPTF .... Republican Presidential Task Force (EA)
RPTF .... Rotatable Porro-Mirror Test Fixture
RPTGA...... Rocznik Polskiego Towarzystwa Geologicznego [*A publication*]
RPTL........ Real Property Tax Law [*New York, NY*] [*A publication*]
RPTLC....... Reverse Phase Thin-Layer Chromatography
RPTN........ Repetition (AAG)
RPTOW..... Rocznik Polskiego Towarzystwa [*A publication*]
RPTR........ Repeater (MSA)
RPTS........ Reactor Plant Test Section (DNAB)
RPTS........ Roadway-Powered Transporter System [*Experimental vehicle*]
RPTSO...... Reactor Plant Test Support Organization (DNAB)
RPU.......... RADAR Prediction Uncertainty
RPU.......... Radio Phone Unit [*Navy*]
RPU.......... Radio Propagation Unit [*Army*] (MCD)
RPU.......... Railway Patrolmen's International Union [*Later, BRAC*] (EA)
RPU.......... Receiver Processor Unit [*Electronics*]
RPU.......... Rectifier Power Unit
RPU.......... Regional Planning Unit (OICC)
RPU.......... Regional Processing Unit
RPU.......... Registered Publication Unit
RPU.......... Release Program Unit (DWSG)
RPU.......... Remote Pickup Unit
RPU.......... Remote Processing Unit (KSC)
RPU.......... Retention Pending Use [*Air Force*]
RPU.......... Rhone-Poulenc, Inc. [*NYSE symbol*] (SPSG)
RPU.......... Rotatable Pool Unit (DNAB)

RPUA .... Aparri, Cagayan [*Philippines*] [*ICAO location identifier*]   (ICLI)

RPUB .... Baguio, Benguet [*Philippines*] [*ICAO location identifier*]   (ICLI)

R Public Data Use ... Review of Public Data Use [*A publication*]

RPUC .... Cabanatuan, Nueva Ecija [*Philippines*] [*ICAO location identifier*]   (ICLI)

RPUC .... Reprint under Consideration [*Publishing*]

RPUD .... Daet, Camarines Norte [*Philippines*] [*ICAO location identifier*]   (ICLI)

RPUE .... Lucena, Quezon [*Philippines*] [*ICAO location identifier*]   (ICLI)

RPUF .... Floridablanca Air Base, Pampanga [*Philippines*] [*ICAO location identifier*]   (ICLI)

RPUG .... Lingayen, Pangasinan [*Philippines*] [*ICAO location identifier*]   (ICLI)

RPUH .... San Jose, Occidental Mindoro [*Philippines*] [*ICAO location identifier*]   (ICLI)

RPUI .... Iba, Zambales [*Philippines*] [*ICAO location identifier*]   (ICLI)

RPUJ .... Castillejos, Zambales [*Philippines*] [*ICAO location identifier*]   (ICLI)

RPUK .... Calapan, Oriental Mindoro [*Philippines*] [*ICAO location identifier*]   (ICLI)

RPUL .... Lipa/Fernando Air Base, Batangas [*Philippines*] [*ICAO location identifier*]   (ICLI)

RPUM .... Mamburao, Occidental Mindoro [*Philippines*] [*ICAO location identifier*]   (ICLI)

RPUN .... Naga, Camarines Sur [*Philippines*] [*ICAO location identifier*]   (ICLI)

RPUO .... Basco, Batanes Island [*Philippines*] [*ICAO location identifier*]   (ICLI)

RPUP .... Jose Panganiban/PIM, Camarines Norte [*Philippines*] [*ICAO location identifier*]   (ICLI)

RPUQ .... Vigan, Ilocos Sur [*Philippines*] [*ICAO location identifier*]   (ICLI)

RPUR .... Baler, Aurora Sub-Province [*Philippines*] [*ICAO location identifier*]   (ICLI)

RPUS .... San Fernando, La Union [*Philippines*] [*ICAO location identifier*]   (ICLI)

RPUSSR .... Research Program of the USSR. New York Series [*A publication*]

RPUT .... Tuguegarao, Cagayan [*Philippines*] [*ICAO location identifier*]   (ICLI)

RPUU .... Bulan, Sorsogon [*Philippines*] [*ICAO location identifier*]   (ICLI)

RPUV .... Virac, Catanduanes [*Philippines*] [*ICAO location identifier*]   (ICLI)

RPUW .... Marinduque/Gasan, Marinduque [*Philippines*] [*ICAO location identifier*]   (ICLI)

RPUX .... Plaridel, Bulacan [*Philippines*] [*ICAO location identifier*]   (ICLI)

RPUY .... Cauayan, Isabela [*Philippines*] [*ICAO location identifier*]   (ICLI)

RPUZ .... Bagabag, Neuva Viscaya [*Philippines*] [*ICAO location identifier*]   (ICLI)

RPV .... Reactor Pressure Vessel [*Nuclear energy*]   (NRCH)

RPV .... Real Program Value   (CAAL)

RPV .... Recorder Processor Viewer

RPV .... Reduced Product Verification [*DoD*]

RPV .... Remote Positioning Valve

RPV .... Remotely Piloted Vehicle [*Aircraft*]

RPV .... Residual Pressure Valve [*Automotive engineering*]

RPV .... Rhopalosiphum padi Virus

RPV .... Right Pulmonary Vein [*Medicine*]

RPV .... Rinderpest Virus

RPV .... United States Veterans Administration Hospital, Davis Park, Providence, RI [*Library symbol*] [*Library of Congress*]   (LCLS)

RPVA .... Tacloban/Daniel Z. Romualdez, Leyte [*Philippines*] [*ICAO location identifier*]   (ICLI)

RPVB .... Bacolod, Negros Occidental [*Philippines*] [*ICAO location identifier*]   (ICLI)

RPVC .... Calbayog, Western Samar [*Philippines*] [*ICAO location identifier*]   (ICLI)

RPVD .... Dumaguete/Sibulan Negros Oriental [*Philippines*] [*ICAO location identifier*]   (ICLI)

RPVE .... Caticlan, Aklan [*Philippines*] [*ICAO location identifier*]   (ICLI)

RPVF .... Catarman, Northern Samar [*Philippines*] [*ICAO location identifier*]   (ICLI)

RPVG .... Guiuan, Eastern Samar [*Philippines*] [*ICAO location identifier*]   (ICLI)

RPVH .... Hilongos, Leyte Del Norte [*Philippines*] [*ICAO location identifier*]   (ICLI)

RPVI .... Iloilo, Iloilo [*Philippines*] [*ICAO location identifier*]   (ICLI)

RPVI-AIAF ... Remotely Piloted Vehicle Investigation - Adjustment of Indirect Artillery Fire

RPVI-ES.... Remotely Piloted Vehicle Investigation - Emerging Sensors   (MCD)

RPVIO...... Registered Publication Van Issuing Office [*Military*]   (NVT)

RPV-IT...... Remotely Piloted Vehicle - Institutional Trainer [*Military*]

RPVK .... Kalibo, Aklan [*Philippines*] [*ICAO location identifier*]   (ICLI)

RPVL......... Roxas/Del Pilar, Palawan [*Philippines*] [*ICAO location identifier*]   (ICLI)

RPVM .... Masbate [*Philippines*] [*ICAO location identifier*]   (ICLI)

RPVN .... Medellin, Cebu [*Philippines*] [*ICAO location identifier*]   (ICLI)

RPVNTV... Rust Preventative

RPVO .... Ormoc, Leyte [*Philippines*] [*ICAO location identifier*]   (ICLI)

RPVP......... Puerto Princesa, Palawan [*Philippines*] [*ICAO location identifier*]   (ICLI)

RPVR......... Roxas, Capiz [*Philippines*] [*ICAO location identifier*]   (ICLI)

RPVS .... San Jose De Buenavista/Antique [*Philippines*] [*ICAO location identifier*]   (ICLI)

RPVT........ Relative Position Velocity Technique

RPVT........ Tagbilaran, Bohol [*Philippines*] [*ICAO location identifier*]   (ICLI)

RPVX .... Remote-Piloted Vehicle Experiment

RPW .... Rawle, Penrose, and Watts' Pennsylvania Reports [*1828-40*] [*A publication*]   (DLA)

RP & W ...... Rawle, Penrose, and Watts' Pennsylvania Reports [*1828-40*] [*A publication*]   (DLA)

RPW .... Resistance Projection Welding [*Manufacturing term*]

RPWA .... Surallah/Allah Valley, Cotabato (South) [*Philippines*] [*ICAO location identifier*]   (ICLI)

RPWB........ Buayan/General Santos, Cotabato (South) [*Philippines*] [*ICAO location identifier*]   (ICLI)

RPWC........ Cotabato, North Cotabato [*Philippines*] [*ICAO location identifier*]   (ICLI)

RPWD .... Davao/Francisco Bangoy International [*Philippines*] [*ICAO location identifier*]   (ICLI)

RPWDA .... Retail Paint and Wallpaper Distributors of America [*Later, NDPA*]

RPWE........ Butuan, Agusan [*Philippines*] [*ICAO location identifier*]   (ICLI)

RPWG .... Dipolog, Zamboanga Del Norte [*Philippines*] [*ICAO location identifier*]   (ICLI)

RPWI........ Ozamis, Misamis Oriental [*Philippines*] [*ICAO location identifier*]   (ICLI)

RPWJ .... Jolo, Sulu [*Philippines*] [*ICAO location identifier*]   (ICLI)

RPWK........ Tacurong/Kenram, Cotabato [*Philippines*] [*ICAO location identifier*]   (ICLI)

RPWL........ Cagayan De Oro, Misamis Oriental [*Philippines*] [*ICAO location identifier*]   (ICLI)

RPWM ...... Malabang, Lanao Del Sur [*Philippines*] [*ICAO location identifier*]   (ICLI)

RPWN .... Bongao/Sanga-Sanga, Sulu [*Philippines*] [*ICAO location identifier*]   (ICLI)

RPWP........ Pagadian, Zamboanga Del Sur [*Philippines*] [*ICAO location identifier*]   (ICLI)

RPWS........ Surigao, Surigao Del Norte [*Philippines*] [*ICAO location identifier*]   (ICLI)

RPWT........ Del Monte, Bukidnon [*Philippines*] [*ICAO location identifier*]   (ICLI)

RPWV........ Buenavista, Agusan [*Philippines*] [*ICAO location identifier*]   (ICLI)

RPWW ...... Tandag, Surigao Del Sur [*Philippines*] [*ICAO location identifier*]   (ICLI)

RPWX........ Iligan, Lanao Del Norte [*Philippines*] [*ICAO location identifier*]   (ICLI)

RPWY........ Malaybalay, Bukidon [*Philippines*] [*ICAO location identifier*]   (ICLI)

RPWZ........ Bislig, Surigao Del Sur [*Philippines*] [*ICAO location identifier*]   (ICLI)

RPX .... Roundup, MT [*Location identifier*] [*FAA*]   (FAAL)

RPXC......... Tarlac (Crow Valley) [*Philippines*] [*ICAO location identifier*]   (ICLI)

RPXG......... Lubang, Occidental Mindoro [*Philippines*] [*ICAO location identifier*]   (ICLI)

RPXI.......... Itbayat, Batanes [*Philippines*] [*ICAO location identifier*]   (ICLI)

RPXJ .... Jomalig, Quezon [*Philippines*] [*ICAO location identifier*]   (ICLI)

RPXM........ Fort Magsaysay, Nueva Ecija [*Philippines*] [*ICAO location identifier*]   (ICLI)

RPXP......... Poro Point, La Union [*Philippines*] [*ICAO location identifier*]   (ICLI)

RPXR......... Corregidor, Cavite [*Philippines*] [*ICAO location identifier*]   (ICLI)

RPXT......... Alabat, Quezon [*Philippines*] [*ICAO location identifier*]   (ICLI)

RPXU .... Sorsogon, Sorsogon [*Philippines*] [*ICAO location identifier*]   (ICLI)

RPY .... Blythe, CA [*Location identifier*] [*FAA*]   (FAAL)

RPY .... Roll, Pitch, and Yaw

RPZ............ Rada Pomocy Zydom [*A publication*]

RPZDA...... Regelungstechnik und Prozess-Datenverarbeitung [*A publication*]

RQ.............. Arab Wing Nigeria Ltd. [*Nigeria*] [*ICAO designator*]   (FAAC)

RQ.............. RASD Quarterly [*American Library Association*] [*A publication*]

RQ.............. Recovery Quotient

RQ.............. Reference Quarterly [*A publication*]

RQ.............. Renaissance Quarterly [*A publication*]

RQ............. Reportable Quantity [*Hazardous substance emergency response*]
RQ............. Request (FAAC)
R/Q........... Request for Quotation (AAG)
R/Q........... Resolver/Quantizer (IEEE)
RQ............. Respiratory Quotient [*Also, Q*] [*Physiology*]
RQ............. Restoration Quarterly [*A publication*]
RQ............. Riverside Quarterly [*A publication*]
RQ............. Roemische Quartalschrift fuer Christliche Altertumskunde und fuer Kirchengeschichte [*A publication*]
RQ............. RQ. Reference Quarterly [*American Library Association. Reference Services Division*] [*A publication*]
RQA........... Recursive Queue Analyzer (IEEE)
R & QA ...... Reliability and Quality Assurance
RQA........... Roemische Quartalschrift fuer Christliche Altertumskunde und fuer Kirchengeschichte [*A publication*]
RQAHA..... Research Quarterly. American Association for Health, Physical Education, and Recreation [*A publication*]
RQAK....... Roemische Quartalschrift fuer Christliche Altertumskunde und fuer Kirchengeschichte [*A publication*]
RQAO....... Reliability and Quality Assurance Office [*NASA*]
RQBE .... Relational Query-by-Example [*Computer interface*] [*FoxPro*] (PCM)
RQC........... RADAR Quality Control
RQC........... Reliability and Quality Control (MCD)
RQCAK ..... Roemische Quartalschrift fuer Christliche Altertumskunde und fuer Kirchengeschichte [*A publication*]
RQCAKG .. Roemische Quartalschrift fuer Christliche Altertumskunde und fuer Kirchengeschichte [*A publication*]
R Q Ch A K ... Roemische Quartalschrift fuer Christliche Altertumskunde und fuer Kirchengeschichte [*A publication*]
RQCL .... Request Clearance [*Aviation*] (FAAC)
RQD........... Raised Quarter Deck [*of a ship*] (DS)
RQD........... Rock Quality Designation [*Nuclear energy*] [*Mining technology*] (NRCH)
RQDCZ ..... Request Clearance to Depart Control Zone [*Aviation*] (FAAC)
RQDP .... Request, Quandary and Deferment Plan
RQE........... Relative Quantum Efficiency (OA)
RQE........... Responsive Quantum Efficiency
RQECZ...... Request Clearance to Enter Control Zone [*Aviation*] (FAAC)
RQI........... Rayleigh Quotient Iteration
RQIAC...... Requires Immediate Action (NOAA)
RQK........... Roemische Quartalschrift fuer Kirchengeschichte [*A publication*]
RQL........... Reference Quality Level (IEEE)
RQL........... Rejectable Quality Level
RQMC....... Regimental Quartermaster-Corporal [*British*]
RQMD....... Richmond Quartermaster Depot [*Virginia*] [*Merged with Defense General Supply Center*]
RQMS .... Regimental Quartermaster-Sergeant [*British*]
RQMT....... Requirement (AFM)
RQN........... Radial Quantum Number
RQN........... Requisition (AFM)
RQO........... River Quality Objective [*British*] (DCTA)
RQP........... Request Permission (FAAC)
RQP........... Resistor Qualification Program
RQQPRI.... Recommended Qualitative and Quantitative Personnel Requirements Information [*Military*] (MCD)
RQR........... Require (AAG)
RQRD........ Required
RQRP .... Request Reply (FAAC)
RQS........... Rate Quoting System
RQS........... Ready Qualified for Standby [*Military*]
RQS........... Request Supplementary Flight Plan Message [*Aviation code*]
RQS........... River Quality Standard [*British*] (DCTA)
RQS........... Roemische Quartalschrift fuer Christliche Altertumskunde und fuer Kirchengeschichte [*A publication*]
RQT........... Reenlistment Qualification Test [*Military*] (MCD)
RQT........... Reliability Qualification Test (CAAL)
RQT........... Resistor Qualification Test
RQTAO..... Request Time and Altitude Over [*Aviation*] (FAAC)
RQTO........ Request Travel Order (NOAA)
RQTP........ Resistor Qualification Test Program
R/QTR....... Rear Quarter [*Automotive engineering*]
RQTS........ Requirements (KSC)
RQTV .... Requirements Volatility
RQUS........ Remote Query Update System [*Data processing*]
RQY........... Elkins, WV [*Location identifier*] [*FAA*] (FAAL)
RQY........... Relative Quantum Yield
RQZ........... Huntsville, AL [*Location identifier*] [*FAA*] (FAAL)
RR............. Naval Research Reviews [*A publication*]
RR............. Pike and Fischer's Radio Regulations [*A publication*] (DLA)
RR............. RADAR Range Station (FAAC)
RR............. Radiation Reaction [*Cells*] [*Medicine*]
RR............. Radiation-Resistant
RR............. Radiation Response
RR............. Radiation Retinopathy [*Ophthalmology*]
R/R........... Radio and RADAR
RR............. Radio Range
RR............. Radio Recognition
RR............. Radio Regulations

RR............. Radio Relay (CINC)
RR............. Radio Research
RR............. Radioreceptor [*Assay method*] [*Clinical chemistry*]
RR............. RAF-1 Group [*Air Transport*] [*Great Britain*] [*ICAO designator*] (FAAC)
RR............. Railroad
RR............. Rand Rifles [*British military*] (DMA)
RR............. Range Rate (NASA)
RR............. Rapid Rectilinear
RR............. Rarely Reversed [*Decisions in law*]
RR............. Raritan River Rail Road Co. [*AAR code*]
RR............. Rate Ratio
RR............. Rate Rebate [*British*]
R & R........ Rate and Rhythm [*of pulse*]
RR............. Rated Radius [*Automotive engineering*]
RR............. Rattus Rattus [*The ship or black rat*]
RR............. Readiness Region [*Military*]
RR............. Readiness Review (KSC)
RR............. Readout and Relay
RR............. Ready Reference
RR............. Rear (AABC)
RR............. Receive Ready [*Data processing*] (IEEE)
RR............. Receiver Room [*Navy*] (CAAL)
RR............. Receiving Report (AAG)
RR............. Recipient Rights
RR............. Recoilless Rifle
RR............. Recommended for Re-Engagement [*British*]
RR............. Record Rarities [*Record label*]
RR............. Record Research [*A publication*]
R/R........... Record/Retirement
R/R........... Record/Retransmit (IEEE)
RR............. Record Review [*A publication*]
RR............. Records and Recording [*A publication*]
R & R........ Records and Reports
RR............. Recovery Reliability (MCD)
RR............. Recovery Room
RR............. Recruit Roll [*Navy*]
RR............. Recurrence Rate
RR............. Rediscount Rate
RR............. Redstone Resources, Inc. [*Toronto Stock Exchange symbol*]
RR............. Reduced Range
RR............. Redundancy Reduction (AAG)
RR............. Reentry Range
RR............. Reference Register [*Data processing*]
RR............. Reflectors [*JETDS nomenclature*] [*Military*] (CET)
RR............. Reformed Review [*A publication*]
R & R........ Refueling and Rearming [*Air Force*]
RR............. Regional Railroad
RR............. Register to Register (MCD)
RR............. Registered Representative [*Wall Street stock salesman*]
R & R........ Regurgitate and Reingest [*Animal behavior*]
RR............. Rehabilitation Record
R & R........ Reinstatement and Replacement (ADA)
RR............. Relative Rank
RR............. Relative Response
RR............. Relative Risk [*Medicine*]
RR............. Relay Rack [*Telecommunications*] (TEL)
RR............. Relief Radii (MSA)
RR............. Religious Roundtable (EA)
RR............. Removal-Replacement
R & R........ Remove and Replace (KSC)
RR............. Rendezvous RADAR [*NASA*]
R & R........ Rendezvous and Recovery (NASA)
RR............. Renegotiation Regulations
RR............. Renin Release [*Endocrinology*] (MAE)
RR............. Rent Regulation (Office of Rent Stabilization) [*Economic Stabilization Agency*] [*A publication*] (DLA)
R/R........... Repair/Rebuild (MCD)
R/R........... Repair or Replacement
R & R........ Repair and Return
RR............. Repeatedly Reactive
RR............. Repetition Rate
RR............. Report Immediately upon Reaching [*Aviation*] (FAAC)
R & R........ Reporting and Requisitioning [*Air Force*]
RR............. Required Reserves
RR............. Requirements Review [*NASA*] (NASA)
RR............. Requisition Restriction Code (DNAB)
RR............. Reroute [*Telecommunications*] (TEL)
RR............. Research Report
R & R........ Research and Reporting Committee [*Interstate Conference of Employment Security Agencies*] (OICC)
RR............. Reservatis Reservandis [*With All Reserve*] [*Latin*]
RR............. Reserve Regiment [*British military*] (DMA)
RR............. Resonance Raman
RR............. Resource Report
RR............. Respiratory Rate [*Medicine*]
RR............. Response Regulator [*Biochemistry*]
RR............. Responsible Receiver
R & R........ Rest and Recreation
R & R........ Rest and Recuperation [*Military*]
R & R......... Rest and Rehabilitation [*Marine Corps*]

RR .... Retired Reserve [*Military*]
RR .... Retro-Rocket [*Army*]   (AABC)
RR .... Return Rate   (IEEE)
RR .... Return Register
RR .... Revenue Release [*A publication*]   (DLA)
RR .... Reverse Recovery [*Electronics*]
RR .... Reverse Reduction   (DS)
RR .... Review of Religion [*A publication*]
RR .... Review for Religious [*A publication*]
RR .... Review of Reviews [*London*] [*A publication*]
RR .... Revised Reports [*Legal*] [*British*]
RR .... Revision Record   (MSA)
RR .... Rhodesia Regiment [*British military*]   (DMA)
RR .... Rhymney Railway [*Wales*]
RR .... Ricerche Religiose [*A publication*]
R & R .... Rich & Rare Canadian Whisky [*Gooderham's*]
RR .... Ridge Regression [*Statistics*]
RR .... Rifle Range
RR .... Right Rear
RR .... Right Reverend [*Of an abbot, bishop, or monsignor*]
RR .... Rights Reserved
RR .... Rigid-Rotor [*Calculations*]
RR .... Risk Ratio
R & R .... Rock and Roll [*Music*]
R & R .... Rock and Rye
RR .... Rodman & Renshaw Capital Group [*NYSE symbol*]   (SPSG)
RR .... Roemische Religions-Geschichte [*A publication*]   (OCD)
RR .... Roll Radius   (MCD)
RR .... Roll Roofing   (AAG)
RR .... Rolls-Royce [*Automobile*]
RR .... Roman Revolution [*A publication*]
RR .... Romanic Review [*A publication*]
RR .... Ronald Reagan [*US president, 1911-*]
RR .... Root Rot [*Plant pathology*]
RR .... Rough Riders [*The City of London Yeomanry*] [*Military unit*] [*British*]
RR .... Round Robin   (IEEE)
RR .... Routine Relay   (KSC)
R & R .... Routing and Record Sheet [*Air Force*]
RR .... Running Reverse
RR .... Rural Resident   (OICC)
RR .... Rural Route
RR .... Rush Release
R & R .... Russell and Ryan's English Crown Cases [*A publication*]   (DLA)
RR .... Russian Review [*A publication*]
RR .... Ruthenium Red [*Inorganic chemistry*]   (OA)
RR .... Very Rare [*Numismatics*]
R of R's ...... Review of Reviews [*A publication*]
RRA .... Dallas-Fort Worth, TX [*Location identifier*] [*FAA*]   (FAAL)
RRA .... Race Relations Act [*1976*] [*British*]   (DCTA)
RRA .... Radiation Research Associates, Inc.   (NRCH)
RRA .... Radio Relay Aircraft   (CET)
RRA .... Radioreceptor Assay [*Clinical chemistry*]
RRA .... Railroad Retirement Act   (GFGA)
RRA .... RAM [*Reliability, Availability, and Maintainablity*] Rationale Annex [*Army*]
RRA .... Ranger Regimental Association   (EA)
RRA .... Reclamation Reform Act [*1982*]
RRA .... Record Retention Agreement [*IRS*]
RRA .... Redmond, R. A., Los Angeles CA [*STAC*]
RRA .... Registered Record Administrator [*American Medical Record Association*] [*Medicine*]
RRA .... Religious Research Association   (EA)
RRA .... Remote Record Address
RRA .... Reserve Recognition Accounting [*Securities and Exchange Commission*]
RRA .... Resident Research Associate
R & RA .... Retraining and Reemployment Administration [*Terminated, 1947*]
RRA .... Review of Reviews [*United States*] [*A publication*]
RRA .... Rubber Reclaimers Association [*Later, NARI*]   (EA)
RRA .... Rubber Recyclers Association   (EA)
RRAC .... Race Relations Advisory Committee [*Trades Union Congress*] [*British*]   (DCTA)
RRAC .... Reactor Review and Audit Committee [*Oak Ridge National Laboratory*]
RRAC .... Regional Resources Advisory Committee [*Army*]   (AABC)
RR et AC.... Rosea Rubeae et Aureae Crucis [*The Order of the Rose of Ruby and the Cross of Gold*]
RRACD ..... Ciencia e Cultura (Sao Paulo). Suplemento [*A publication*]
RRAD .... Red River Army Depot [*Texas*]   (AABC)
RRAD .... Roll Ratio Adjust Device   (MCD)
R Radical Pol Econ ... Review of Radical Political Economics [*A publication*]
R Radic Polit Econ ... Review of Radical Political Economics [*A publication*]
R Rad Pol Econ ... Review of Radical Political Economics [*A publication*]
RRAEA ...... Rendiconti. Riunione Annuale. Associazione Elettrotecnica Italiana [*A publication*]
RRAF .... Ready Reserve of the Armed Forces
RRAF .... Royal Rhodesian Air Force
RRALA ...... Radiochemical and Radioanalytical Letters [*A publication*]

RRAM .... Roman Rule in Asia Minor to the End of Third Century After Christ [*A publication*]
RRAP........ Residential Rehabilitation Assistance Program [*Canada*]
RRAR .... ROM Return Address Register
RRAS........ Radiofrequency Resonance Absorption   (MCD)
RRB .... R. R. Bowker Co. [*Publisher*]
RRB .... RADAR Reflective Balloon
RRB .... Radio Research Board   (DEN)
RRB .... Railroad Retirement Board
RRB .... Rapid Response Bibliography Service [*Information retrieval*]   (AEBS)
RRB .... Regular Reenlistment Bonus [*Military*]
RRB .... Requirements Review Board   (SSD)
RRB .... Rubber Reserve Board [*of the Reconstruction Finance Corp.*]
RRBC........ Rat Red Blood Cell
RRBFC ...... Red River Boys Fan Club [*Inactive*]   (EA)
RRBLB ..... United States Railroad Retirement Board. Law Bulletin [*A publication*]   (DLA)
RRBN .... Round Robin   (FAAC)
RRBODI.... Brazilian Journal of Botany [*A publication*]
RRB Q Rev ... RRB [*Railroad Retirement Board*] Quarterly Review [*A publication*]
RRB (Railroad Retirement Bd) Q R ... RRB (Railroad Retirement Board) Quarterly Review [*A publication*]
RRB Rept... Radio Research Board. Report. [*Australia*] [*A publication*]
RRC .... Coinage of the Roman Republic [*A publication*]
RRC .... RADAR Return Code
RRC .... Radiation Recorder Controller   (NRCH)
RRC .... Radiation Resistance Cable
RRC .... Radio Receptor Co.
RRC .... Radio Relay Center   (NATG)
RRC .... Radio Research Co.
RRC .... Railroad Record Club [*Commercial firm*]   (EA)
RRC .... Rainy River Community College, International Falls, MN [*OCLC symbol*]   (OCLC)
RRC .... Ravenroc Resources Ltd. [*Vancouver Stock Exchange symbol*]
RRC .... Reactor Recirculation Cooling [*Nuclear energy*]   (NRCH)
R & RC...... Reactors and Reactor Control   (MCD)
RRC .... Readiness Reportable Code   (DNAB)
RRC .... Receiving Report Change   (AAG)
RRC .... Recognized Rescue Center [*Navy*]   (DNAB)
RRC .... Reconstructionist Rabbinical College [*Pennsylvania*]
RR & C...... Records, Reports, and Control   (AFM)
RRC .... Recreation Resources Center [*University of Wisconsin*] [*Research center*]   (RCD)
RRC .... Recruit Reception Center
RRC .... Red River Community College [*UTLAS symbol*]
RRC .... Reentry Rate Command [*NASA*]
RRC .... Refractories Research Center [*Ohio State University*] [*Research center*]   (RCD)
RRC .... Refugee Resource Center [*Defunct*]   (EA)
RRC .... Regional Resource Center
RRC .... Regional Response Center [*Environmental Protection Agency*]   (EG)
RRC .... Regional Review Consultants [*American Occupational Therapy Association*]
RRC .... Regular Route Carrier
R/RC........ Removal/Recertification
RRC .... Report Review Committee [*National Academy of Sciences*]
RRC .... Reporting Requirements Code   (DNAB)
RRC .... Reports of Rating Cases [*Legal*] [*British*]
RRC .... Requirements Review Committee [*Navy*]
RRC .... Research Resources Center [*University of Illinois at Chicago*] [*Research center*]   (RCD)
RRC .... Residency Review Committee [*Medicine*]
RRC .... Resuscitation Research Center [*University of Pittsburgh*] [*Research center*]   (RCD)
RRC .... Retrograde River Crossing   (MCD)
RRC .... Retrovirus Research Center [*Veterans Administration Medical Center*] [*Baltimore, MD*]
RRC .... Rheology Research Center [*University of Wisconsin - Madison*] [*Research center*]   (RCD)
RRC .... Rigid Raiding Craft [*British military*]   (DMA)
RRC .... Road Runners Club of America
RRC .... Rocket Research Corp.   (MCD)
RRC .... Rodale Research Center [*Horticulture*]
RRC .... Roll Ratio Controller   (MCD)
RRC .... Rollin' Rock Club   (EA)
RRC .... Roof Research Center [*Oak Ridge, TN*] [*Oak Ridge National Laboratory*] [*Department of Energy*]   (GRD)
RRC .... Routine Respiratory Care [*Medicine*]
RRC .... Royal Red Cross [*British*]
RRC .... Rubber Reserve Committee [*Navy*]
RRC .... Rubber Reserve Co. [*Dissolved, 1935, functions transferred to Reconstruction Finance Corporation*]
RRC .... Rural Referral Center [*Health care*]
RRC .... Russell Research Center [*Department of Agriculture*]
RRC .... Russian Research Center [*Harvard University*] [*Research center*]   (RCD)
RRC .... Ryde's Rating Cases [*A publication*]   (DLA)
RRCA .... Rhinelander Rabbit Club of America   (EA)

RRCA .... Road Runners Club of America (EA)
RRCAH ..... Roll Rate Command/Attitude Hold (MCD)
RR & Can Cas ... Railway and Canal Cases [*England*] [*A publication*] (DLA)
RRCC........ Reduced Rate Contribution Clause [*Insurance*]
R & RCC.... Russell and Ryan's English Crown Cases Reserved [*A publication*] (DLA)
RRCCC...... Regional Recreation and Conservation Consultative Committee [*Thames Water Authority*] [*British*]
RRCEF ...... Redwood Records Cultural and Educational Fund (EA)
RRCEM..... Residency Review Committee for Emergency Medicine (EA)
RRCGDX... Australia. Commonwealth Scientific and Industrial Research Organisation. Division of Animal Genetics. Research Report [*A publication*]
RRCH .... Roman Republican Coin Hoards [*A publication*]
RRCM ...... Roberts Radio Current Meter (NOAA)
RRCN .... Receiving Report Change Notice (AAG)
RR & Cn Cas ... Railway and Canal Cases [*1835-54*] [*A publication*] (DLA)
RRCO .... Radio Research Coordination Officer [*Air Force*]
RRCO .... Royal Resources Corp. [*NASDAQ symbol*] (NQ)
RRCOD ..... Resource Recovery and Conservation [*A publication*]
RRCOTAAOSOCOTWAOS ... Rollin' Rock Club of Texas and Any Other State or Country of the World and Outer Space
RRCRB...... Recent Results in Cancer Research [*A publication*]
RRC (Rep) React Res Cent Kalpakkam ... RRC (Report). Reactor Research Centre. Kalpakkam [*A publication*]
RR Cr R ..... Revised Reports, Criminal Rulings [*1862-75*] [*India*] [*A publication*] (DLA)
RRCS........ Railroad Communication System
RRCS........ Reentry RADAR Cross Section
RRCS........ Revenue Receipts Control Sheets [*IRS*]
RRCU .... Remote Range Control Unit (MCD)
RRCUS..... Rhodesian Ridgeback Club of the US (EA)
RRCVR...... Remote Receiver (FAAC)
RRD.......... Reactor Radiation Division [*National Institute of Standards and Technology*]
RRD.......... Reactor Research and Development
RRD.......... Receive, Record, Display
RR & D ...... Rehabilitation Research and Development Program [*Veterans Administration*] (GFGA)
RRD.......... Reliability Requirements Directive
RR & D ...... Reparations, Removal, and Demolition [*Section*] [*Industry Branch, US Military Government, Germany*]
RRD.......... Replacement Regulating Detachment [*Army*]
RRD.......... Requisition Received Date [*Bell System*] (TEL)
RRD.......... Resonant Reed Decoder
RRD.......... Retendering Receipt Day (NRCH)
RRD.......... Roosevelt Roads [*Puerto Rico*] [*Seismograph station code, US Geological Survey*] (SEIS)
RRD.......... Route/Route Destination [*Telecommunications*] (TEL)
RRDA .... Rendezvous Retrieval, Docking, and Assembly [*of space vehicle or orbital station*] [*NASA*] (AAG)
RRDA .... Repetitive Report Distribution Audit (AAG)
RRDB .... Research Results Data Base [*Department of Agriculture*] [*Information service or system*] (IID)
RRDE .... Radio Research and Development Establishment (MCD)
RRDE .... Rotating Ring Disk Electrode
RRDECA... Roy Rogers - Dale Evans Collectors Association (EA)
RRDF........ RO/RO [*Roll-On/Roll-Off*] Discharge Facility [*Army*] (RDA)
RRDFCS.... Redundant Reconfigurable Digital Flight Control System (MCD)
RRDO....... Register of Rivers Discharging into the Oceans [*United Nations Environment Programme*] (MSC)
RRDR .... Raw RADAR Data Recorder
RRDS........ Regents Renaissance Drama Series [*A publication*]
RRDS........ Relative Record Data Set
RRDU .... Recreation Research Demonstration Unit (RDA)
RRE .... Marree [*Australia*] [*Airport symbol*] [*Obsolete*] (OAG)
RRE .... Race-Relations Education Program [*Military*] (DNAB)
RRE .... RADAR Research Establishment [*British*]
RRE .... Radiation Related Eosinophilia [*Medicine*] (AAMN)
R & RE...... Radiation and Repair Engineering [*Nuclear energy*] (NRCH)
RRE .... Railroad Enthusiasts (EA)
RRE .... Range Rate Error
RRE .... Ras Responsive Element [*Genetics*]
RRE .... Receive Reference Equivalent [*Telecommunications*] (TEL)
RRE .... Reg Resources Corp. [*Vancouver Stock Exchange symbol*]
RRE .... Review of Regional Economics and Business [*A publication*]
RRE .... Rolls-Royce Enthusiasts (EA)
RRE .... Roster of Required Events
RR & E...... Round, Regular, and Equal [*With reference to pupils of eyes*]
RRE .... Royal RADAR Establishment [*British*] [*Research center*]
RREA........ Rendezvous RADAR Electronics Assembly [*NASA*] (MCD)
RREAS...... Race Relations Employment Advisory Service [*British*]
RREB........ Race-Relations Education Board [*Military*] (DNAB)
RREC........ Reading Research and Education Center [*Champaign, IL*] [*Department of Education*] (GRD)
RREC........ Rehabilitation Record
RREC........ Rice Research and Extension Center [*University of Arkansas*] [*Research center*] (RCD)
R Regional Econ and Bus ... Review of Regional Economics and Business [*A publication*]

RRel .... Review of Religion [*A publication*]
R Rel .... Review for Religious [*A publication*]
R of Religion ... Review of Religion [*A publication*]
R Relig Res ... Review of Religious Research [*A publication*]
R Rel Res ... Review of Religious Research [*A publication*]
RR/EO....... Race Relations/Equal Opportunity [*Military*] (AABC)
RRep .... Records Repository [*Air Force*] (AFM)
RREP........ Reed Reference Electronic Publishing
RRERD...... Resource Recovery and Energy Review [*A publication*]
RRESA...... Rastitel'nye Resursy [*A publication*]
R Rest DS ... Regents Restoration Drama Series [*A publication*]
RRET........ Rainier Realty Investors [*Seattle, WA*] [*NASDAQ symbol*] (NQ)
RRETA...... Reports. Research Institute of Electrical Communication. Tohoku University [*A publication*]
RREU .... Rendezvous RADAR Electronics Unit [*NASA*] (MCD)
RRev .... Records Review [*Air Force*] (AFM)
RRev .... Rijecka Revija [*A publication*]
RREVA...... Residue Reviews [*A publication*]
RRF........... Racing Research Fund [*Defunct*] (EA)
RRF........... Ragged Red Fibers [*Muscle pathology*]
RRF........... Rapid Reaction Forces [*Army*] (AABC)
RRF........... Raptor Research Foundation (EA)
RRF........... Reading Reform Foundation (EA)
RRF........... Ready Reserve Fleet
RRF........... Ready Reserve Force [*Military*]
RRF........... Realty Refund Trust SBI [*NYSE symbol*] (SPSG)
RRF........... Reconnaissance Reporting Facility
RRF........... Red Resistance Front [*Netherlands*] [*Political party*]
RRF........... Reed Reactor Facility [*Reed College*] [*Research center*] (RCD)
RRF........... Regional Relay Facility (DNAB)
RRF........... Rehabilitation Research Foundation (EA)
RRF........... Resonant Reed Filter
RRF........... Revised Recommended Findings
RRF........... Rift-Rift-Fracture [*Geology*]
RRF........... Riot Relief Fund (EA)
RRF........... Royal Regiment of Fusiliers [*Military unit*] [*British*]
RRFC........ Robert Redford Fan Club (EA)
RRFC........ Robin Right Fan Club (EA)
RRFIA .... Radiobiologia, Radioterapia, e Fisica Medica [*A publication*]
RRFO........ Rhine River Field Organization [*Post-World War II*]
RRFS .... Range Rate Frequency Synthesizer
RRFT........ Right Rear Fluid Temperature [*Automotive engineering*]
RRG .... Point Mugu, CA [*Location identifier*] [*FAA*] (FAAL)
RRG .... RADAR Range Gate
RRG .... Rental Rehabilitation Grant [*Department of Housing and Urban Development*] (GFGA)
RRG .... Requirements Review Group [*Air Staff*] [*Air Force*] (MCD)
RRG .... Research Review Group (NRCH)
RRG .... Resource Request Generator
RRG .... Restabilization Reset Generator (SAA)
RRG .... Rodrigues Island [*Mauritius*] [*Airport symbol*] (OAG)
RRG .... Roll Reference Gyro (AAG)
RRH.......... Rural Rental Housing [*Loans*] [*Farmers Home Administration*]
RRHDAC.. Reports on Rheumatic Diseases [*A publication*]
RRHFF...... Rock and Roll Hall of Fame Foundation (EA)
RRHPF...... Ronald Reagan Home Preservation Foundation (EA)
RR-HPO..... Rapid Recompression-High Pressure Oxygen [*Medicine*] (MAE)
RRI .... Barora [*Solomon Islands*] [*Airport symbol*] (OAG)
RRI .... Radio Republik Indonesia [*Radio network*]
RRI .... Range Rate Indicator
RRI .... Refugee Relief International (EA)
RRI .... Reimbursement Refund Indicator [*Military*] (AFIT)
RRI .... Rendezvous RADAR Indicator [*NASA*] (NASA)
RRI .... Reroute Inhibit [*Telecommunications*] (TEL)
RRI .... Resident Reactor Inspector [*Nuclear energy*] (NRCH)
RRI .... Revised Ring Index [*A publication*]
RRI .... Revista/Review Interamericana [*A publication*]
RRI .... Riverside Research Institute (MCD)
RRI .... Rocket Research Institute
RRI .... Romex Resources, Inc. [*Vancouver Stock Exchange symbol*]
RRIC........ Race Relations Information Center [*Defunct*]
RRIC........ RADAR Repeater Indicator Console
RRIC (Rubber Res Inst Ceylon) Bull ... RRIC (Rubber Research Institute of Ceylon) Bulletin [*A publication*]
RRIF......... Registered Retirement Investment Fund [*Canada*]
RRIHS....... Regional Research Institute for Human Services [*Portland State University*] [*Research center*] (RCD)
RRIL......... Rendiconti. Reale Istituto Lombardo di Scienze e Lettere [*Milan*] [*A publication*]
RR-IM .... Office of Research and Reports, Intelligence Memoranda [*CIA*]
RRIM .... Reinforced Reaction Injection Molding [*Plastics technology*]
RRIM Technol Ser Rep ... RRIM [*Rubber Research Institute of Malaysia*] Technology Series Report [*A publication*]
RRIM Train Man Soils Manage Soils Nutr Hevea ... RRIM [*Rubber Research Institute of Malaysia*] Training Manual on Soils, Management of Soils, and Nutrition of Hevea [*A publication*]
RRIN .... Readiness Risk Index Number (NG)
RRIPM....... Rapid Response Interference Prediction Model (MCD)

RRIS .... Radiological Release Information System (MCD)
RRIS .... Railroad Research Information Service [*National Academy of Sciences*] [*Information service or system*]
RRIS .... Remote RADAR Integration Station [*Military*]
RRISL Bull ... RRISL [*Rubber Research Institute of Sri Lanka*] Bulletin [*A publication*]
RRI Sri Lanka Bull ... RRISL (Rubber Research Institute of Sri Lanka) Bulletin [*A publication*]
RRI & StL ... Rockford, Rock Island & St. Louis Railroad
RRITA .... Report. Research Institute of Science and Technology. Nihon University [*A publication*]
R River Plate ... Review of the River Plate [*A publication*]
RRJaNS .... Rodnoj i Russkij Jazyki v Nacional'noj Skole [*A publication*]
RRK .... Redaurum Red Lake Mines Ltd. [*Toronto Stock Exchange symbol*]
RRK .... Retaining Ring Kit
RRKM .... Rice, Ramsperger, Kassel, Marcus [*Developers of a theorem in chemical kinetics, designated by the initial letters of their last names*]
RRL .... Merrill, WI [*Location identifier*] [*FAA*] (FAAL)
RRL .... Rabbit Reticulocyte Lysate [*Biochemistry*]
RRL .... Radio Relay Link (NATG)
RRL .... Radio Research Laboratory
RRL .... Ralston Purina Co., Corporate Library, St. Louis, MO [*OCLC symbol*] (OCLC)
RRL .... Ranchmen's Resources Ltd. [*Toronto Stock Exchange symbol*]
RRL .... Rayleigh Radiation Law [*Physics*]
RRL .... Regimental Reserve Line
RRL .... Registered Record Librarian [*Medicine*]
RRL .... Reserve Retired List [*Military*]
RRL .... Road Research Laboratory [*British*]
RRL .... Rocket Research Laboratories (KSC)
RRL .... Ruby Rod LASER
RRL .... Rudder Reference Line [*NASA*] (NASA)
RRL .... Runway Remaining Lights [*Aviation*]
RRL .... Ruthenium Red Staining Layer [*Biology*]
RRLC .... Radiation-Resistant Linear Circuit
RRLC .... Redwood Region Logging Conference (EA)
RRLC .... Rochester Regional Library Council [*Information service or system*] (IID)
RRLR .... Road Race Lincoln Register (EA)
RRL Rep (UK) ... RRL [*Road Research Laboratory*] Report (UK) [*A publication*]
RRLT .... Right Rear Lining Temperature [*Automotive engineering*]
RRLTD ...... Report. Research Laboratory of Engineering Materials. Tokyo Institute of Technology [*A publication*]
RRLTU ...... Recruit Remedial Literacy Training Unit (DNAB)
RRM .... Rate of Return Method [*Insurance*]
RRM .... Rayleigh-Ritz Method [*Physics*]
RRM .... Red Resource Monitoring (MCD)
RRM .... Reliant Resources Ltd. [*Vancouver Stock Exchange symbol*]
RRM .... Renegotiated-Rate Mortgage
RRM .... Reports, Reviews, Meetings
RRM .... RNA [*Ribonucleic Acid*] Recognition Motif [*Genetics*]
RRM .... Runaway Rotating Machine
RRMC .... Royal Roads Military College [*Royal Roads, BC*]
RRMF .... RADAR Reflectivity Measuring Facility
RRMG .... Reactor Recirculation Motor Generator (IEEE)
RRMN .... Railroadmen's Federal Savings & Loan Association [*NASDAQ symbol*] (NQ)
RRMRP ..... Ready Reserve Mobilization Reinforcement Pool [*Army*]
RRMRS ..... Ready Reserve Mobilization Reinforcement System [*Army*]
RRMS .... Reserve Readiness and Mobility Squadron
RRMS .... Revenue Requirements Modeling System [*Department of Energy*] (GFGA)
RRMTA ..... Reactor Materials [*A publication*]
RRN .... Rapid Reinforcement of NATO (MCD)
RRN .... Relative Record Number [*Data processing*]
RRN .... Running Research News [*A publication*]
RRN .... Serra Norte [*Brazil*] [*Airport symbol*] (OAG)
rRNA .... Ribonucleic Acid, Ribosomal [*Biochemistry, genetics*]
RRNC .... Ranger Rick's Nature Club (EA)
RRNGA ..... Razvedka i Razrabotka Neftyanykh i Gazovykh Mestorozhdenii [*A publication*]
RRNN .... Reproductive Rights National Network (EA)
RRNS .... Redundant Residue Number System (IEEE)
RRNS .... Related Returns Notification System [*IRS*]
RRO .... Recipient Rights Officer
RRO .... Regimental Reserve Officer (ADA)
RRO .... Renegotiation Regional Office
RRO .... Responsible Reporting Office [*Telecommunications*] (TEL)
RRO .... Richport Resources Ltd. [*Vancouver Stock Exchange symbol*]
RROA .... Railroadians of America (EA)
RROC .... Rolls-Royce Owners' Club (EA)
RROO .... Richport Resources Ltd. [*Vancouver, BC*] [*NASDAQ symbol*] (NQ)
RROS .... Resistive Read-Only Storage
R & ROTC ... Reserve and Reserve Officers' Training Corps [*Army*]
RROU .... Remote Readout Unit
RRP .... Radio Relay Pod
RRP .... Range Ring Profile (MCD)

RRP .... Reactor Refueling Plug (NRCH)
RRP .... Ready Replacement Pilot
RRP .... Recommended Retail Price
RRP .... Recoverable Repair Parts
RRP .... Regional Project Research Program (EA)
RRP .... Regular Retail Price
RRP .... Relative Refractory Period [*Medicine*]
RRP .... Relay Rack Panel
RRP .... Religious Requirements and Practices [*A publication*]
RRP .... Rental Rehabilitation Program [*Department of Housing and Urban Development*] (GFGA)
RRP .... Republican Reliance Party [*Cumhuriyetci Guven Partisi - CGP*] [*Turkey*] [*Political party*] (PPW)
RRP .... Reverse Repurchase Agreement [*Investment term*]
RRP .... Reviews of Research and Practice. Institute for Research into Mental and Multiple Handicap [*Elsevier Book Series*] [*A publication*]
RRP .... Rock Hill, SC [*Location identifier*] [*FAA*] (FAAL)
RRP .... Roosevelt Roads [*Puerto Rico*] [*Seismograph station code, US Geological Survey*] [*Closed*] (SEIS)
RRP .... Rotterdam-Rhine Pipeline [*Oil*]
RRP .... Rough River Petroleum Corp. [*Vancouver Stock Exchange symbol*]
RRP .... Rudder Reference Plane [*NASA*] (NASA)
RRP .... Runway Reference Point [*Aviation*] (FAAC)
RRPA .... Relativistic Random-Phase Approximation [*Electrodynamics*]
RRPA .... Ruhr Regional Planning Authority [*Post-World War II*]
RRPB .... Retraining and Reemployment Policy Board
RRPC .... Reserve Reinforcement Processing Center [*Army*] (AABC)
RRPD .... Runway Reference Point Downwind [*Aviation*] (FAAC)
RRPE .... Union for Radical Review of Radical Political Economics [*A publication*] (EAAP)
RRPI .... Relative Rod Position Indication [*Nuclear energy*] (NRCH)
RRPI .... Rotary Relative Position Indicator [*Nuclear energy*] (NRCH)
RRPL .... Recommend Repair Parts List
RRPP .... Reverends Peres [*Reverend Fathers*] [*French*]
RRPR .... Reduced Range Practice Rocket [*Army*]
RRPRD ..... RTP. Regelungstechnische Praxis [*A publication*]
RRPS .... Ready Reinforcement Personnel Section [*Air Force*] (AFM)
RRPS .... Ronald Reagan Philatelic Society (EA)
RRPSDW .. Reading Psychology [*A publication*]
RRPU .... Runway Reference Point Upwind [*Aviation*] (FAAC)
RRQ .... Rock Rapids, IA [*Location identifier*] [*FAA*] (FAAL)
RRQ .... Romanic Review Quarterly [*A publication*]
RRR .... Exceedingly Rare [*Numismatics*]
RRR .... RADAR Radiation Receiver
RRR .... Railroad Reports [*United States*] [*A publication*] (DLA)
RRR .... Raleigh Research Reactor
RRR .... RAM [*Reliability, Availability, and Maintainability*] Rationale Report [*Army*]
RRR .... Range and Range Rate
RRR .... Range Rover Register [*An association*] (EAIO)
RRR .... Rapid Runway Repair
RRR .... Reader Railroad [*AAR code*]
RRR .... Readin', Ritin', and Rithmetic [*Also, 3R's*]
RRR .... Readiness Removal Rate (DNAB)
RRR .... Records, Racing, and Rallying [*Sporting aviation*]
RRR .... Red Red Rose (EA)
RRR .... Reduced Residual Radiation
RRR .... Regular Rate and Rhythm [*Cardiology*] (AAMN)
RRR .... Relay, Reporter, Responder (DWSG)
RRR .... Relief, Recovery, Reform [*Elements of the New Deal*]
RRR .... Renin-Release Rate [*Endocrinology*] (MAE)
RRR .... Repairable Return Rate (DNAB)
RRR .... Required Rate of Return [*Finance*]
RRR .... Residential Resources Mortgage Investment [*AMEX symbol*] (SPSG)
RRR .... Residual Resistance Ratio [*Metal purity*]
RRR .... Resistor-Reactor Rectifier
RRR .... Resource Requirements Request [*Military*] (MCD)
RRR .... Resurfacing, Restoration, and Rehabilitation [*US Federal Highway Administration*]
RRR .... Review of Religious Research [*A publication*]
RRR .... Rework Removal Rate
RRR .... Riverton Resources Corp. [*Vancouver Stock Exchange symbol*]
RRR .... Royal Rhodesia Regiment [*British military*] (DMA)
RRR .... Rum, Romanism, and Rebellion [*Phrase coined during the Presidential campaign of 1884 to describe the Democratic party*]
RRR .... University of Rochester, Rochester, NY [*OCLC symbol*] (OCLC)
RRRC .... Regulatory Requirements Review Committee [*Nuclear energy*] (NRCH)
RRRC .... TRI-R Systems Corp. [*NASDAQ symbol*] (NQ)
RRRE .... RADAR Range-Rate Error
RRREA ...... Radiation Research Reviews [*A publication*]
RRRED ...... Reclamation and Revegetation Research [*A publication*]
RR Rep ...... Railroad Reports [*A publication*] (DLA)
RRRLC ...... Rochester Regional Research Library Council [*Rochester, NY*] [*Library network*]

RRRPD...... Reseau de Radio Rurale des Pays en Developpement [*Developing Countries Farm Radio Network*] (EAIO)
RRRR........ Railroad Revitalization and Regulatory Reform Act [*1976*]
RRRRR...... Receipt [*British naval signaling*]
RRRRRR... Remedial Readin', Remedial Ritin', and Remedial Rithmetic [*Also, 6R's*] [*Humorous interpretation of the three R's*]
RRRS........ Route Relief Requirements System [*Telecommunications*] (TEL)
RRRV .... Rate of Rise of Restriking Voltage (IEEE)
RRS........... Dothan, AL [*Location identifier*] [*FAA*] (FAAL)
RRS........... RADAR Ranging System
RRS........... Radiation Research Society (EA)
RRS........... Radio Receiver Set
RRS........... Radio Recording Spectrophotometer
RRS........... Radio Relay Squadron
RRS........... Radio Relay Station
RRS........... Radio Relay System
RRS........... Radio Remote Set (CAAL)
RRS........... Radio Research Station [*British*]
RRS........... Range Rate Search (MCD)
RRS........... Rational Recovery Systems (EA)
RRS........... Reaction Research Society (EA)
RRS........... Reactor Recirculating System (NRCH)
RRS........... Reactor Refueling System (NRCH)
RRS........... Reactor Regulating System (NRCH)
RRS........... Readiness Reportable Status (NVT)
RRS........... Ready Reportable Status (MCD)
RRS........... Reconnaissance Reporting System
RRS........... Red River Settlement [*Canada*]
RRS........... Reed Relay Scanner
RRS........... Regulatory Reform Staff [*Environmental Protection Agency*] (EPA)
RRS........... Relay Radio Subsystem [*NASA*]
RRS........... Remaining Radiation Service (NATG)
RRS........... Reminder of Route Same (SAA)
RRS........... Remington's Revised Statutes [*A publication*] (DLA)
RRS........... Rendezvous RADAR System [*NASA*] (MCD)
RRS........... Required Response Spectrum (IEEE)
RRS........... Research Referral Service [*International Federation for Documentation*] [*Information service or system*] (IID)
RRS........... Resin Regeneration Subsystem [*Nuclear energy*] (NRCH)
RRS........... Resonance Raman Scattering [*Spectroscopy*]
RRS........... Resonance Raman Spectroscopy
RRS........... Resources and Referral Services (OICC)
RRS........... Restraint Release System (KSC)
RRS........... Retired Reserve Section
RRS........... Retransmission Request Signal [*Telecommunications*] (TEL)
RRS........... Retrograde Rocket System
RRS........... Revised Statutes of Nebraska, Reissue
RRS........... River and Rainfall Station [*National Weather Service*] (NOAA)
RRS........... Roll Rate Sensor
RRS........... Roo Rat Society (EA)
RRS........... Roros [*Norway*] [*Airport symbol*] (OAG)
RRS........... Royal Research Ship [*British*]
RRSCS...... Rate Stabilization and Control System (MCD)
RRSM........ Rough Riding Sergeant-Major [*British military*] (DMA)
RRSP........ Registered Retirement Savings Plan [*Canada*]
RRSSM ..... Rough Riding Staff Sergeant-Major [*British military*] (DMA)
RRSTRAF ... Ready Reserve Strategic Army Forces
RRSV......... Red Ringspot Virus [*of blueberry*]
RRSV......... Rice Ragged Stunt Virus [*Plant pathology*]
RRT .... Railroad Retirement Tax [*IRS*]
RRT .... Railroad Transport (NATG)
RRT .... Randomized Response Technique [*Statistics*]
RRT .... Ready Round Transporter (NATG)
RRT .... Reentry Reference Time [*NASA*]
RRT .... Regional Response Team [*Environmental Protection Agency*] (EG)
RRT .... Registered Recreation Therapist
RRT .... Registered Respiratory Therapist
RRT .... Relative Retention Time
RRT .... Rendezvous RADAR Transducer [*NASA*] (NASA)
RR/T......... Rendezvous RADAR/Transponder [*NASA*] (KSC)
RRT .... Request for Review of Tooling
RRT .... Requirements Review Team
RRT .... Requisite Remedial Technology (EPA)
RRT .... Resazurin Reduction Time [*Medicine*] (MAE)
RRT .... Resource Recycling Technologies, Inc. [*AMEX symbol*] (SPSG)
RRT .... Ring-Ring Trip [*Telecommunications*] (TEL)
RRT .... Robert Mines Ltd. [*Vancouver Stock Exchange symbol*]
RRTA......... Railroad Retirement Tax [*IRS*]
RRTCD...... Tokyo Denki Daigaku Kenkyu Hokoku [*A publication*]
RRTD .... Rural Rehabilitation Technologies Database [*University of North Dakota*] [*Information service or system*] (IID)
RRTE......... Reroute (FAAC)
RRTIS .... Renewable Resources Technical Information System [*Forest Service*]
RRTS......... Radiometer Recording Titration System [*Experimentation*]
RRTS......... Range-Rate Tracking System
RRU.......... Cedar Rapids, IA [*Location identifier*] [*FAA*] (FAAL)

RRU.......... Radio Research Unit [*Army*] (AABC)
RRU.......... Radiobiological Research Unit (IEEE)
RRU.......... Remington-Rand UNIVAC
RRU.......... Remote Readout Unit
RRU.......... Remote Request Unit (CAAL)
RRU.......... Resource Recycling Unit
RRU.......... Retro-Rocket UNIVAC (MUGU)
R RUL........ Renegotiation Rulings (DLA)
RRUSEO... University of Miami. Rosenstiel School of Marine and Atmospheric Science. Research Review [*A publication*]
RRV .... Denver, CO [*Location identifier*] [*FAA*] (FAAL)
RRV .... Raspberry Ringspot Virus [*Plant pathology*]
RRV .... Rotor Reentry Vehicle
RRVSGA... Red River Valley Sugarbeet Growers Association (EA)
RRV & W... Red River Valley & Western Railroad [*North Dakota*]
RRW .... Jacksonville, FL [*Location identifier*] [*FAA*] (FAAL)
RRW .... Radiation-Resistant Wire
RRW .... Royal Regiment of Wales [*Military unit*] [*British*]
RRWBDG ... Report of Research. Worcester Foundation for Experimental Biology [*A publication*]
RRWL........ Renaissance and Renascences in Western Literature [*A publication*]
RRWU .... Rhodesia Railway Workers' Union
RRX .... Railroad Crossing [*Telecommunications*] (TEL)
RRX .... Ronrico Explorations Ltd. [*Vancouver Stock Exchange symbol*]
R & Ry CC ... Russell and Ryan's English Crown Cases [*A publication*] (DLA)
RS .... Aerotransportes [*Argentina*] [*ICAO designator*] (FAAC)
RS .... IEEE Reliability Society (EA)
RS .... Rabbinic Supervisor (BJA)
RS .... Rabbinical School (BJA)
RS .... Rabbinical Seminary (BJA)
R & S......... Raben & Sjogren [*Publisher*] [*Sweden*]
RS .... Raccolta Sistematica del Diritto Federale [*Switzerland*] [*A publication*]
RS .... Rachmaninoff Society [*Record label*]
RS .... RADAR Scanner
RS .... RADAR Scattering
RS .... RADAR Selector (MCD)
RS .... RADAR Set
RS .... RADAR Simulator (CET)
RS .... RADAR Start (CET)
RS .... Radiated Susceptibility (IEEE)
RS .... Radiation Sensitive [*Physiology*]
RS .... Radiation Source (NRCH)
RS .... Radio Duties - Special
RS .... Radio Simulator
RS .... Radio Station [*Maps and charts*]
RS .... Radio Supervisor [*British*]
RS .... Radio Switchboard (CAAL)
RS .... Radius of Safety (MCD)
RS .... Radular Sac
RS .... Ragtime Society (EA)
RS .... Railway Station (ROG)
RS .... Rain and Snow [*Sleet*] [*Meteorology*]
RS .... Raman Scattering [*Spectroscopy*]
RS .... Raman Spectroscopy
RS .... Random Saccades [*Ophthalmology*]
RS .... Random Splice [*Telecommunications*] (TEL)
RS .... Range Safety [*NASA*] (KSC)
R & S......... Range and Safety (AAG)
RS .... Range Selector
R/S............ Range Surveillance
RS .... Rapid Setting [*Asphalt grade*]
RS .... Ras Shamra (BJA)
RS .... Raster Suppression [*of color images*]
RS .... Rating Schedule [*Medicine*] (MAE)
RS .... Rating Sheet [*Psychometrics*]
RS .... Rauwolfia Serpentina [*A plant, the root extract of which is used medicinally*]
RS .... Raw Stock
RS .... RAWINSONDE [*Radiosonde and RADAR Wind Sounding*] [*Upper air observation*] (NASA)
RS .... Ray Society (EA)
RS .... Re-Solv, the Society for the Prevention of Solvent and Volatile Substance Abuse [*British*] (EAIO)
RS .... Reactor Safeguards (NRCH)
RS .... Reader Stop [*Data processing*] (BUR)
RS .... Readiness Squadron (DNAB)
RS .... Reading of Standard
RS .... Ready Service (AAG)
RS .... Real Storage
RS .... Realites Secretes [*A publication*]
RS .... Rearranging Sequence [*Genetics*]
RS .... Rebuild Standard [*Marine Corps*]
RS .... Receiver Station
RS .... Receiving Ship [*or Station*]
RS .... Reception Station
RS .... Recipient's Serum [*In blood matching*]
RS .... Reciprocating Steam (MCD)
RS .... Reclaimed Wheat Grass/Shrub Cover [*Agriculture*]

RS	....	Recognition Structure [*Immunochemistry*]
RS	....	Recommended Standard [*Telecommunications*] (TEL)
RS	....	Reconfiguration System (MCD)
RS	....	Reconnaissance Satellite
R & S	....	Reconnaissance and Security [*Military*] (INF)
RS	....	Reconnaissance Squadron [*Military*]
RS	....	Reconnaissance-Strike [*Military*]
RS	....	Reconnaissance Strip [*Military*] (AFM)
R & S	....	Reconnaissance and Surveillance (MCD)
RS	....	Reconstitution Site (NVT)
RS	....	Record Separator [*Control character*] [*Data processing*]
RS	....	Recording Secretary
RS	....	Recreation Supervisor [*Red Cross*]
RS	....	Recruiting Service
RS	....	Recruiting Station
RS	....	Recruitment Surveys [*Army*] [*British*]
RS	....	Rectal Sinus
RS	....	Rectal Suppository [*Medicine*]
RS	....	Rectified Spirits (ROG)
RS	....	Rectus-Sinister [*Nomenclature system*] [*Biochemistry*]
RS	....	Recueil Systematique du Droit Federal [*Switzerland*] [*A publication*]
RS	....	Redeemable Stock
RS	....	Reduced Smoke (MCD)
RS	....	Reduced Strength (MCD)
RS	....	Reducing Sugar
RS	....	Redundancy Status [*NASA*] (MCD)
RS	....	Redundant Set [*NASA*] (MCD)
RS	....	Reed-Sternberg Cell [*Medicine*] (MAE)
RS	....	Reel Sequence [*Data processing*]
R & S	....	Reenlistment and Separation [*Military*] (AFM)
RS	....	Reentry System (AFM)
RS	....	Reference Serum [*Clinical chemistry*]
RS	....	Reference Standard
RS	....	Reformed Spelling
RS	....	Refrigeration System (MCD)
RS	....	Refurbishment Spare (NASA)
RS	....	Regional Authorities (Scotland)
RS	....	Register Select
RS	....	Register of Shipping of the USSR [*Ship classification society*] (DS)
RS	....	Register and Storage (MCD)
RS	....	Registered Sanitarian
RS	....	Regular Savings
RS	....	Regular Station [*Military*]
RS	....	Regularly Scheduled [*Red Cross Volunteer*]
RS	....	Regulating Station [*Military*]
RS	....	Regulation Station [*Air Force*]
RS	....	Reinforcing Stimulus
RS	....	Reiter's Syndrome [*Medicine*]
R/S	....	Rejection Slip (ADA)
RS	....	Relative Sweetness
R/S	....	Relay Set [*Telecommunications*] (TEL)
RS	....	Reliability Summary (KSC)
RS	....	Religious Studies [*A publication*]
RS	....	Religious Studies [*Secondary school course*] [*British*]
RS	....	Relocation Site (NVT)
RS	....	Reminder Shock
R/S	....	Remote Site [*NASA*] (KSC)
RS	....	Remote Station
RS	....	Remotely Settable Fuze (MCD)
R & S	....	Ren and Stimpy [*Cartoon characters*]
RS	....	Renal Specialist [*Medicine*]
RS	....	Renin Substrate [*Biochemistry*]
R & S	....	Renovation and Storage [*Military*] (AFIT)
RS	....	Rephael Society (EA)
RS	....	Report of Survey [*Military*]
R & S	....	Reports and Statistics Branch [*US Military Government, Germany*]
RS	....	Reprint of the Statutes of New Zealand [*A publication*]
RS	....	Reproductive Success [*Genetics*]
RS	....	Republicains Sociaux [*Social Republicans*] [*France*] [*Political party*] (PPE)
RS	....	Request to Send
RS	....	Request for Services [*Social Security Administration*]
RS	....	Request for Support (MCD)
RS	....	Research Scientist (ADA)
R & S	....	Research and Statistics (IEEE)
RS	....	Research on Steroids [*Elsevier Book Series*] [*A publication*]
RS	....	Research Studies [*Pullman*] [*A publication*]
R & S	....	Research and Study
RS	....	Research Summary
RS	....	Research Systems (MCD)
RS	....	Reserve Section [*Military*]
RS	....	Reserve Stock (SAA)
RS	....	Reset
RS	....	Reset-Set [*Data processing*]
RS	....	Reset Steering
RS	....	Resident School (MUGU)
RS	....	Resistance Soldering
RS	....	Resistant Sporangia [*Botany*]

RS	....	Resorcinol-Sulfur [*Organic chemistry*] (MAE)
RS	....	Resources Section [*Resources and Technical Services Division*] [*American Library Association*]
RS	....	Respiratory Syncytial [*Virus*]
RS	....	Respiratory System [*Medicine*]
RS	....	Response-Stimulus
RS	....	Responsus [*To Answer*] [*Latin*]
RS	....	Resume Sheet
RS	....	Retail Shops and Stores [*Public-performance tariff class*] [*British*]
R-S	....	Reticulated Siderocyte [*Cytology*] (AAMN)
RS	....	Return to Saturation
RS	....	Return to Situation (SAA)
RS	....	Revenue Sharing
RS	....	Reverberation Strength
RS	....	Reversal Shift [*Psychometrics*]
RS	....	Review of Symptoms [*Medicine*]
RS	....	Revised Statutes
R/S	....	Revolutions per Second
RS	....	Reye's Syndrome [*Medicine*]
RS	....	Rheinflugzeugbau [*Germany*] [*ICAO aircraft manufacturer identifier*] (ICAO)
R de S	....	Ricardus Petronius de Senis [*Deceased, 1314*] [*Authority cited in pre-1607 legal work*] (DSA)
RS	....	Ricerche Slavistiche [*A publication*]
RS	....	Right Sacrum [*Medicine*] (KSC)
RS	....	Right Safety [*Sports*]
RS	....	Right Side
RS	....	Ringer's Solution [*Physiology*]
RS	....	Ripon Society (EA)
R/S	....	Road Service
RS	....	Road Space [*Military*]
RS	....	[*The*] Roberval & Saguenay Railway Co. [*AAR code*]
RS	....	Rochelle Salt [*Potassium Sodium Tartrate*] [*Organic chemistry*]
RS	....	Rocket System (MCD)
RS	....	Rocznik Slawistyczny [*A publication*]
RS	....	Roll Stabilization
RS	....	Roller Shutter
RS	....	Rolling Stone [*A publication*]
RS	....	Rolls Series [*A publication*] (DLA)
RS	....	Romanische Studien [*A publication*]
RS	....	Root Stock [*Botany*]
RS	....	Route Selector
RS	....	Route Switching [*Telecommunications*] (TEL)
RS	....	Routing Slip [*Military*]
RS	....	Royal Scots [*Military unit*]
RS	....	Royal Society [*British*]
RS	....	Rubble Stone (AAG)
RS	....	Rudder Station (MCD)
RS	....	Rural Sociology [*A publication*]
Rs	....	Sri Lanka Rupee [*Monetary unit*] (IMH)
RS	....	Syntex Laboratories, Inc. [*Research code symbol*]
RSA	....	American Railway and Airline Supervisors Association (EA)
RSA	....	Rabbit Serum Albumin [*Immunology*]
RSA	....	Rack Service Association (EA)
RSA	....	RADAR Service Area
RSA	....	RADAR Signature Analysis [*Air Force*]
RSA	....	Railway Supply Association (EA)
RSA	....	Range Safety Approval (MUGU)
RSA	....	Rat Serum Albumin [*Immunology*]
RSA	....	Rate Sensor Assembly (MCD)
RSA	....	Rate Subsystem Analyst (MUGU)
RSA	....	Rational Self-Analysis [*Psychology*] (DHSM)
RSA	....	Redstone Arsenal [*Huntsville, AL*] [*Army*]
RSA	....	Reference Satellite A (NASA)
RSA	....	Regional Office Systems [*Data processing*]
RSA	....	Regional Science Association (EA)
RSA	....	Regional Studies Association [*British*] (EAIO)
RSA	....	Regular Spiking Activity [*Electrophysiology*]
RSA	....	Rehabilitation Services Administration [*Office of Special Education and Rehabilitive Services, Department of Education*]
RSA	....	Relative Specific Activity
RSA	....	Relative Standard Accuracy [*Testing methodology*]
RSA	....	Remote Station Alarm
RSA	....	Remote Storage Activities
RSA	....	Renaissance Society of America (EA)
RSA	....	Rental Service Association (EA)
RSA	....	Repair Sevice Attendant [*Telecommunications*] (TEL)
RSA	....	Report from South Africa [*A publication*]
RSA	....	Republiek van Suid-Afrika [*Republic of South Africa*] [*Afrikaans*]
RSA	....	Requirements Statement Analyzer
RSA	....	Research Security Administrators
RSA	....	Research Society on Alcoholism (EA)
RSA	....	Resource Sharing Alliance [*Library consortium*] (IT)
RSA	....	Respiratory Sinus Arrhythmia [*Medicine*]
RSA	....	Retire to Staging Area [*Military*]
RSA	....	Revest-Shamir-Adelman [*Encryption Algorithm*] [*Theoretical mathematics*] (PCM)
RSA	....	Revised Shapley Ames [*Catalogue of Bright Galaxies*]

RSA............ Revised Statutes of Alberta [*Canada*] [*A publication*]   (DLA)
RSA............ Revised Statutes Annotated [*A publication*]   (DLA)
RSA............ Rheometrics Sound Analyzer
RSA............ Rhetoric Society of America   (EA)
RSA............ Rhythmic Slow Activity [*Electroencephalography*]
RSA............ Ridden Standardbred Association   (EA)
RSA............ Right Sacroanterior [*A fetal position*] [*Obstetrics*]
RSA............ Rivest-Shamir-Adelman [*Cryptography*]
RSA............ Rotary Servo Actuator
RSA............ Royal Scottish Academician
RSA............ [*The*] Royal Scottish Academy
RSA............ Royal Society of Antiquaries
RSA............ Royal Society of the Arts [*British*]
RSA............ Rubber Shippers Association [*Defunct*]
RSA............ Rural Sanitary Authority [*British*]
RSA............ Santa Rosa [*Argentina*] [*Airport symbol*]   (OAG)
RSAA........ Romanian Studies Association of America   (EA)
RSAA........ Royal Society for Asian Affairs [*British*]   (DI)
RSAAF...... Royal South African Air Force
RSABA........ Revista. Sociedad Argentina de Biologia [*A publication*]
RSAC........ RADAR Significance Analysis Code
RSAC........ Radiological Safety Analysis Computer   (MCD)
RSAC........ Region, State, Area, County [*Code*] [*DoD*]
RSAC........ Remote Slave Aircraft   (MCD)
RSAD........ Remote Safe-and-Arm Device
RSAF........ Republic of Singapore Air Force   (PDAA)
RSAF........ Royal Saudi Air Force
RSAF........ Royal Small Arms Factory [*British*]
RSAF........ Royal Swedish Air Force
RSAG........ Reserve Storage Activity, Germersheim, West Germany [*Military*]
RSAI........ Royal Society of Antiquaries of Ireland
RSAI........ Rutgers Social Attribute Inventory [*Psychology*]
RSAK........ Reserve Storage Activity, Kaiserslautern, West Germany [*Military*]
RSAL........ Reports. Research Committee. Society of Antiquaries of London [*A publication*]
RSAL........ Reserve Storage Activity, Luxembourg [*Military*]
RSALT...... Running, Signal, and Anchor Lights
RSAM....... Real-Time Seismic Amplitude Measurement
RSAMC...... Royal Society of Arts, Manufacturing and Commerce [*London*]
RSAND..... Reserve Systems Analysis Division [*Military*]   (DNAB)
R San I....... Royal Sanitary Institute [*Later, RSH*] [*British*]
R San Inst Jnl ... Royal Sanitary Institute. Journal [*A publication*]
R Sanit Inst J ... Royal Sanitary Institute. Journal [*A publication*]
RSAP........ Regional Science Association. Papers and Proceedings [*A publication*]
RSAP........ Revolutionaire Socialistische Arbeiders Partij [*Revolutionary Socialist Workers' Party*] [*Netherlands*] [*Political party*]   (PPE)
RSARR...... Republic of South Africa Research Reactor
RSAS........ Revenue Sharing Advisory Service   (EA)
RSAS........ Royal Sanitary Association of Scotland
RSB........... Radiation Safety Booklet   (DNAB)
RSB........... Range Safety Beacon [*NASA*]   (AAG)
RSB........... Ravensbos [*Netherlands*] [*Seismograph station code, US Geological Survey*]   (SEIS)
RSB........... Reactor Service Building   (NRCH)
RSB........... Reconnaissance Strike Bomber
RSB........... Recycling Sourcebook [*A publication*]
RSB........... Reduced-Size Blueprint   (NG)
RSB........... Reference Standards Book [*Military*]
RSB........... Regimental Stretcher-Bearer
RSB........... Regional Shipping Boards [*NATO*]   (NATG)
RSB........... Repair Service Bureau [*Telecommunications*]   (TEL)
RSB........... Retail Sales Battery [*Employment test*]
RSB........... Reticulocyte Standard Buffer
RSB........... Revista. Sociedad Bolivariana [*A publication*]
RSB........... Rhondda & Swansea Bay Railway [*Wales*]
RSB........... Right Sternal Border [*Medicine*]
RSB........... Rochester Subway Co. [*AAR code*]
RSB........... Roller Skating Business Magazine [*A publication*]   (EAAP)
RSB........... Roseberth [*Australia*] [*Airport symbol*] [*Obsolete*]   (OAG)
RSB........... Rudder Speed Brake   (MCD)
RSBA........ Rail Steel Bar Association [*Later, SMA*]   (EA)
RSBC....... Revised Statutes of British Columbia [*A publication*]   (ILCA)
RSB(E)...... Regional Shipping Board (East) [*NATO*]
RSBEI....... Registered Student of the Institution of Body Engineers [*British*]   (DBQ)
R Sb Ekonom Promysl D ... Referativnyi Sbornik. Ekonomika Promyslennosti. D. Primenenie Matematiceskih Metodov v Ekonomiceskih Issledovanijah i Planirovanii [*A publication*]
RSBKDD... Reports. State Biological Survey of Kansas [*A publication*]
RSBO........ Refined Soybean Oil
RSBRC...... Reference and Subscription Books Review Committee [*American Library Association*]
RSBS .... RADAR Safety Beacon System   (MCD)
RSBTA3 .... Rio Grande Do Sul. Departamento Producao Animal. Divisao de Zootecnia. Servico de Experimentacao Zootecnia. Boletim Tecnico [*A publication*]

RSB(W)..... Regional Shipping Board (West) [*NATO*]
RSC........... Racing Service Center [*Motorcycle racing*]
RSC........... RADAR Scan Converter [*Military*]   (CAAL)
RSC........... RADAR Sea Clutter
RSC........... RADAR Set Control
RSC........... RADAR System Console [*Military*]   (CAAL)
RSC........... RADAR System Controller [*Military*]   (CAAL)
RSC........... Radiation Shielding Computer Codes [*Database*] [*Oak Ridge National Laboratory*] [*Department of Energy*] [*Information service or system*]   (CRD)
RSC........... Railway Systems Control [*A publication*]
RSC........... Range Safety Command [*or Control*] [*NASA*]
RSC........... Rat Skin Collagen
RSC........... Rational Self-Counseling [*Psychology*]   (DHSM)
RSC........... Reactor Safety Commission [*Germany*]
RSC........... Reactor Safety Coordinator [*Nuclear energy*]   (NRCH)
RSC........... Reactor Steam Cycle
RSC........... Reader Service Card
RSC........... Record Status Code [*Military*]   (AABC)
RSC........... Referee Stops Contest [*Amateur boxing*]
RSC........... Regional Service Center [*Military*]   (CINC)
RSC........... Regular, Slotted, Corrugated [*Container*]
RSC........... Reinforcement Support Category [*DoD*]
RSC........... Relative System Capability
RSC........... Release Schedule Code   (SAA)
RS & C ...... Reliability, Surveillance, and Control   (SAA)
RSC........... Religious Sisters of Charity [*Roman Catholic religious order*]
RSC........... Remote Sensing Center [*Texas A & M University*] [*Research center*]   (RCD)
RSC........... Remote Store Controller
RSC........... Replacement and School Command [*Military*]
R & SC .... Replacement and School Command [*Military*]
RSC........... Rescue Subcenter [*Aviation*]   (FAAC)
RSC........... Reserve Service Control [*Navy*]
RSC........... Resident Shop Control   (SAA)
RSC........... Residential Sales Council   (EA)
RSC........... Residential Support Center   (OICC)
RSC........... Resort Air Service, Inc. [*Southern Pines, NC*] [*FAA designator*]   (FAAC)
RSC........... Restart Capability   (AAG)
RSC........... Rested-State Contraction [*Obstetrics*]   (MAE)
RSC........... Reversible Sickled Cell [*Hematology*]
RSC........... Revised Statutes of Canada [*Canada Department of Justice*] [*Information service or system*]   (CRD)
RSC........... Rework Support Conference [*Military*]   (DNAB)
RSC........... Riga [*Former USSR*] Skulte Airport [*Airport symbol*] [*Obsolete*]   (OAG)
RSC........... Right-Sided Colon Cancer [*Medicine*]
RSC........... Right Stage Center [*A stage direction*]
RSC........... Road Safety Committee [*British police*]
RSC........... Royal Shakespeare Company [*British*]
RSC........... Royal Society of Canada
RSC........... Royal Society of Chemistry [*Formed by a merger of Chemical Society and Royal Institute of Chemistry*]   (EAIO)
RSC........... Rules of the Supreme Court [*A publication*]   (DLA)
RSC........... Runway Surface Condition [*Aviation*]   (MCD)
RSC........... Rural Service Center [*Agency for International Development*]
RSC........... Russell Sage College [*New York*]
RSC........... Saint Charles Borromeo Seminary, Overbrook, PA [*OCLC symbol*]   (OCLC)
RSCA........ Religious Speech Communication Association   (EA)
RScA......... Right Scapulo-Anterior [*A fetal position*] [*Obstetrics*]
RSCAA...... Radio Shack Computer Alumni Association   (EA)
RSCAAL ... Remote Sensing Chemical Agent Alarm [*Army*]   (INF)
RSCC........ Remote-Site Command Computer [*NASA*]
RSCC........ Remote-Site Computer Complex [*NASA*]
RSCC........ Republican Senatorial Campaign Committee
RSCCDS.... Reactivity and Structure Concepts in Organic Chemistry [*A publication*]
RSCD........ Report Series Codes Dictionary [*A publication*]
RSCD........ Request to Start Contract Definition
RSCDSA ... Religion and Socialism Commission of the Democratic Socialists of America   (EA)
RSCF .... Rotating Spherical Convection Facility   (SSD)
RSCG......... Radio Set Control Group
RSCG......... Roux Seguela Cayzac & Goudard [*Advertising agency*]   (ECON)
RSCH .... Range Scheduling   (MUGU)
RSCH .... Ready Spares Chassis
RSCH .... Research   (AFM)
RSCH .... Rowley-Scher Reprographics, Inc. [*Beltsville, MD*] [*NASDAQ symbol*]   (NQ)
RSCHM .... Royal School of Church Music [*British*]
R Sch Mines J ... Royal School of Mines. Journal [*England*] [*A publication*]
RSCHOPSDET ... Research Operations Detachment   (DNAB)
RSCIE .... Remote Station Communication Interface Equipment
R Sci Instr ... Review of Scientific Instruments [*A publication*]
RSCJ .... Society of the Sacred Heart [*Roman Catholic women's religious order*]
RSCL .... Radioactive Sodium Chemistry Loop
RSCM........ Recoiling Structural Contour Map [*Surface analysis*]
RSCM........ Royal School of Church Music [*British*]

RscMtge..... Resource Mortgage Capital, Inc. [*Associated Press abbreviation*]   (APAG)
RSCN........ Registered Sick Children's Nurse [*British*]
RSCO........ Rules of the Supreme Court, Order [*Number*]   (ILCA)
RS Comp.... Statutes of Connecticut, Compilation of 1854 [*A publication*]   (DLA)
R Scott Mus Inf Ser Geol ... Royal Scottish Museum. Information Series. Geology [*A publication*]
RScP .... Right Scapuloposterior [*A fetal position*] [*Obstetrics*]
RSCQAX... Riviera Scientifique [*A publication*]
RSCR......... Range Safety Command Receiver [*NASA*]   (KSC)
RSCR........ Reserve Special Commendation Ribbon
RSCS .... Range Safety Command System [*NASA*]   (AAG)
RSCS .... Rate Stabilization and Control System
RSCS .... Remote Spooling Communications Subsystem [*IBM Corp.*] [*Data processing*]   (IBMDP)
RSCS .... Rod Sequence Control System [*Nuclear energy*]   (NRCH)
RSCSA ...... Railway Signal and Communications Suppliers Association [*Later, RSS*]   (EA)
RSCT........ Rohde Sentence Completions Test [*Psychology*]
RSCT........ Royal Society of Canada. Transactions [*A publication*]
RSCU........ Rescue   (FAAC)
RSCW....... Research Reactor, State College of Washington   (NRCH)
RSD .... Radiance Spectral Distribution
RSD .... Raised   (MSA)
RSD .... Raised Shelter Deck   (DS)
RSD .... Range Support Directive   (SAA)
RSD .... Rassemblement des Socialistes et des Democrates [*Rally of Socialists and Democrats*] [*Reunion*] [*Political party*]   (PPW)
RSD .... Ratoon Stunting Disease [*of sugarcane*]
RS & D...... Receipt, Storage, and Delivery [*Business term*]
RSD .... Reentry Systems Department
RSD .... Reference Services Division [*of ALA*] [*Later, RASD*]   (EA)
RSD .... Reflex Sympathetic Dystrophy [*Medicine*]
RSD .... Refueling Shutdown   (IEEE)
RSD .... Relative Standard Deviation [*Statistics*]
RSD .... Relative Stock Density [*Pisciculture*]
RSD .... Requirements and Specifications Document [*NASA*]   (NASA)
RSD .... Research Services Department [*United Way of Greater Indianapolis*] [*Indiana*] [*Information service or system*]   (IID)
RSD .... Research Services Directory [*A publication*]
RSD .... Resigned
RSD .... Responsible System Designer   (NRCH)
RSD .... Roadside Delivery   (ADA)
RSD .... Rock Sound [*Bahamas*] [*Airport symbol*]   (OAG)
RSD .... Rolling Steel Door [*Technical drawings*]
RSD .... Rosehaugh Stanhope Developments [*Commercial firm*] [*British*]
RSD .... Royal Society, Dublin
RSDA........ Reflex Sympathetic Dystrophy Association   (EA)
RSDB......... SCB [*Statistika Centralbyran*] Regional Statistical Data Base [*Sweden*] [*Information service or system*]   (CRD)
RSDC........ Radiation Subprogramme Data Center [*Marine science*]   (MSC)
RSDC........ Range Safety Data Coordinator   (SAA)
RSDC........ Remote Secure Data Change   (DNAB)
RSDG .... Raster Scan Display Generator   (MCD)
RSDG .... Royal Scots Dragoon Guards [*British military*]   (DMA)
RSDI......... Retirement, Survivors, or Disability Insurance [*Social Security Administration*]   (GFGA)
RSDL........ Resdel Industries [*NASDAQ symbol*]   (NQ)
RSDLP ...... Russian Social-Democratic Labor Party [*Political party*]
RSDLP(B) ... Russian Social-Democratic Labor Party (Bolsheviks) [*Political party*]
RSDNT...... Resident
RSDP........ Remote Shutdown Panel   (IEEE)
RSDP........ Remote-Site Data Processor [*NASA*]
RSDr......... Doctor of Social Sciences
RSDRP ...... Rossiiskaia Sotsial-Demokraticheskaia Rabochaya Partiia [*Russian Social Democratic Workers' Party*] [*Political party*]   (PPE)
RSDS........ RADAR Systems Design Section
RSDS........ Range Safety Destruct System
RSDT........ Regulations of Office of the Secretary, Department of Transportation
RSDT........ Remote Station Data Terminal
RSDU .... RADAR Storm Detection Unit
RSDW .... Ross Sea Deep Water [*Marine science*]   (MSC)
RSDWP...... Russian Social-Democratic Workers Party
RSE........... RADAR Search Equipment
RSE........... Raid Size Estimate
RSE........... Receiving Site Equipment [*NASA*]
RSE........... Reference Sensing Element   (DNAB)
RSE........... Reference Standards Equipment [*Deep Space Instrumentation Facility, NASA*]
RSE........... Remote Sensing of Environment [*A publication*]   (DNAB)
RSE........... Renewable Sources of Energy [*A publication*]
RSE........... Request Select Entry [*Data processing*]
RSE........... Resistance Soldering Equipment
RSE........... Resource Engineering, Inc. [*AMEX symbol*]   (SPSG)

RSE........... Review of Social Economy [*A publication*]
RSE........... Richmond Stock Exchange   (IIA)
RSE........... Royal Society of Edinburgh
RSE........... Rutgers Studies in English [*A publication*]
RSE........... Sydney-Rose Bay [*Australia*] [*Airport symbol*]   (OAG)
RSEA......... Reference Sensing Element Amplifier
R Se As Stud ... Review of Southeast Asian Studies [*Singapore*] [*A publication*]
RSEC......... Regional Science Experience Center
RSEC......... Regional Solar Energy Center
RSEC......... Representative Shuttle Environmental Control [*System*] [*NASA*]
RSECS...... Representative Shuttle Environmental Control System [*NASA*]   (MCD)
RSED........ Refund Statute Expiration Date [*IRS*]
RSEEA ...... Remote Sensing of Environment [*A publication*]
RSEP .... Restraint System Evaluation Program [*Department of Transportation*]
RSEP .... [*H. B.*] Robinson Steam Electric Plant   (NRCH)
RSER........ Remote Sensing of Earth Resources
RSER........ Rotary Stylus Electronics Recorder
RSES .... Refrigeration Service Engineers Society   (EA)
RSES .... Rosenberg Self-Esteem Scale
RSEU........ Remote Scanner-Encoder Unit [*Bell Laboratories*]
RSEW....... Resistance Seam Welding
RSEW-HF ... Resistance Seam Welding - High Frequency
RSEW-I..... Resistance Seam Welding - Induction
RSF........... Radial Structure Function [*of solid catalysts*]
RSF........... Receiving-Safing Facility [*NASA*]   (MCD)
RSF........... Reciprocal Cross Sterile Females [*Genetics*]
RSF........... Refurbish and Subassemblies Facilities [*NASA*]   (NASA)
RSF........... Reject Suspense File [*Army*]
RSF........... Relative Sensitivity Factor [*Analytical chemistry*]
RSF........... Relative Substitution Frequency [*of amino acids in proteins*]
RSF........... Remote Support Facility
RSF........... Requisition Status File   (DNAB)
RSF........... Research Systems Facility
RSF........... Residual Support Force [*After main force redeployment*] [*Military*]
RSF........... Retail Stores Forum   (EA)
RSF........... Rhododendron Species Foundation   (EA)
RSF........... Risk Studies Foundation   (EA)
RSF........... Roll Sheet Feeder
RSF........... Rough Sunk Face [*Construction*]
RSF........... Royal Scots Fusiliers [*Military unit*]
RSF........... Russian Student Fund [*Defunct*]   (EA)
RSFA......... Roller Skating Foundation of America   (EA)
RSFC........ Republic Savings Financial Corp. [*NASDAQ symbol*]   (NQ)
RSFC........ Ricky Skaggs International Fan Club   (EA)
RSFC........ Rolling Stones Fan Club   (EA)
RSFC........ Ronnie Smith Fan Club   (EA)
RSFFA...... Rendiconti. Scuola Internazionale di Fisica "Enrico Fermi" [*A publication*]
RSFPP...... Retired Servicemen's Family Protection Plan [*Military*]
RSFQ........ Rapid Single-Flux Quantum Circuit [*Physics*]
RSFSA...... Rendiconti. Seminario della Facolta di Scienze. Universita di Cagliari [*A publication*]
RSFSR...... Russian Soviet Federated Socialist Republic
RSG .... Rabbi Saadia Gaon [*Jewish scholar, 882-942*]   (BJA)
RSG .... RADAR Set Group [*HAWK missile*]   (MCD)
RSG .... RADAR Signal Generator   (MCD)
RSG .... RADAR Systems Group [*of General Motors Corp.*]
RSG .... Range Safety Group [*Range Commanders Council*] [*White Sands Missile Range, NM*]
RSG .... Rate Signal Generator   (AAG)
RSG .... Rate Support Grant [*British*]
RSG .... Rate Switching Gyro   (MCD)
RSG .... Reassign   (AABC)
RSG .... Receiving Stolen Goods
RSG .... Red Supergiant [*Astronomy*]
RSG .... Reenlistment Steering Group [*Military*]   (MCD)
RSG .... Reference Signal Generator
RSG .... Regional Seat of Government
RSG .... Relay Switch Group
RSG .... Research Study Group   (NATG)
RSG .... Resident Study Group [*Army*]   (MCD)
RSG .... Resource Service Group Ltd. [*Toronto Stock Exchange symbol*]
RSG .... Rising   (FAAC)
RSG .... Rocksprings, TX [*Location identifier*] [*FAA*]   (FAAL)
RSG .... Royal Scots Greys [*Military unit*]
RSGB........ Radio Society of Great Britain [*Potters Bar, Hertfordshire, England*]   (EAIO)
RSGI........ Riverside Group, Inc. [*Jacksonville, FL*] [*NASDAQ symbol*]   (NQ)
RSGMT..... Reassignment
RSGN .... Reassign
RSGPB...... Rinsan Shikenjo Geppo [*A publication*]
RSGS .... Ranges and Space Ground Support   (AAG)
RSGS........ Royal Scottish Geographical Society
RSH .... RADAR Status History
RSH .... Resin Sluice Header   (NRCH)

RSH........... Ring Systems Handbook [*American Chemical Society*] [*A publication*]
RSH........... Royal Society of Health [*Formerly, R San I*] [*British*]
RSH........... Russian Mission [*Alaska*] [*Airport symbol*]   (OAG)
RSHA....... Reichssicherheitshauptampt [*Central Security Office of the Reich*] [*NAZI Germany*]
RSHC....... Research in the Sociology of Health Care [*A publication*]
RSHEA...... Royal Society of Health. Journal [*A publication*]
RSHF........ Room Sensible Heat Factor
RSHI......... Rough Service, High Impact   (DNAB)
RSHKA6 ... Bulletin. Forestry and Forest Products Research Institute [*A publication*]
RSHM....... Religious of the Sacred Heart of Mary [*Roman Catholic women's religious order*]
RSHNDI ... Annual Report. Hokkaido Branch. Forestry and Forest Products Research Institute [*A publication*]
RSHS........ Railroad Station Historical Society   (EA)
RSHX........ Recirculation Spray Heat Exchanger [*Nuclear energy*]   (NRCH)
RSI........... Air Sunshine, Inc. [*Ft. Lauderdale, FL*] [*FAA designator*]   (FAAC)
RSI........... East-West Resource Systems Institute [*Research center*]   (RCD)
rsi............. Race Specific Incompatibility
RSI........... RADAR Scope Interpretation   (AAG)
RSI........... Radiation Shielding Information Data Base [*Oak Ridge National Laboratory*] [*Department of Energy*] [*Information service or system*]   (CRD)
RSI........... Rationalization, Standardization, and Integration [*or Interoperability*] [*Program*] [*Army*]   (INF)
RSI........... Reactor Siting Index   (NRCH)
RSI........... Realty South Investors, Inc. [*AMEX symbol*]   (SPSG)
RSI........... Receipt, Storage, and Issue [*Army*]   (AABC)
R(SI)......... Reconstruction, Social Insurance [*British*] [*World War II*]
RSI........... Record Status Indicator [*Military*]   (AABC)
RSI........... Reflected Signal Indication [*Air Force*]
RSI........... Regional Safety Inspector [*Ministry of Agriculture, Fisheries, and Food*] [*British*]
RSI........... Register Sender Inward [*Telecommunications*]   (TEL)
RSI........... Religious Science International   (EA)
RSI........... Remote Sensing Institute [*South Dakota State University*] [*Research center*]   (RCD)
RSI........... Repetitive Strain Injury   (PCM)
RSI........... Replacement Stream Input [*Military*]
RSI........... Repressor-Sensitizer Index [*Psychology*]
RSI........... Repubblica Sociale Italiana [*Italian Socialist Republic*] [*Founded by Mussolini*] [*1943-1945*]
RSI........... Research Studies Institute
R-SI.......... Restricted-Security Information   (DNAB)
RSI........... Reusable Surface Insulation [*NASA*]
RSI........... Rio Sidra [*Panama*] [*Airport symbol*]   (OAG)
RSI........... Roll Stability Indicator [*NASA*]   (KSC)
RSI........... Roofing/Siding/Insulation [*A publication*]
RSI........... Rotary Shaft Indicator
RSI........... Royal Sanitary Institute   (ROG)
RSI........... Royal Signals Institution [*British*]   (DEN)
RS & I....... Rules, Standards, and Instructions
RSIC......... Radiation Shielding Information Center [*Department of Energy*] [*Oak Ridge, TN*]
RSIC......... Redstone Scientific Information Center [*Army*]
RSIC......... Responding Superior in Command   (MCD)
RSIC......... RSI [*Resource Services, Inc.*] Corp. [*NASDAQ symbol*]   (NQ)
R-SICU...... Respiratory-Surgical Intensive Care Unit [*of a hospital*]   (AAMN)
RSID........ Resource Identification Table [*Data processing*]
RSIDA....... Research and Industry [*A publication*]
R Signals Radar Establ Newsl Res Rev ... Royal Signals and Radar Establishment. Newsletter and Research Review [*A publication*]
R SIGS....... Royal Corps of Signals [*British*]   (DMA)
RSIH........ RSI Holdings, Inc. [*NASDAQ symbol*]   (NQ)
RSIHM...... Reparation Society of the Immaculate Heart of Mary   (EA)
RSIJA....... Journal. Royal College of Surgeons in Ireland [*A publication*]
RSIM........ RADAR Simulator   (MSA)
RSIM........ Retrospective Single Ion Monitoring [*Analytical chemistry*]
RSIP........ RADAR Systems Improvement Program   (DWSG)
RSIP........ Reusable Software Implementation Program   (SSD)
RSIPR....... Reactor System with Interstage Product Removal [*Chemical engineering*]
RSIR......... International Statistical Institute. Review [*A publication*]
RSIS......... Radical Science Information Service [*News service attempting to interrelate radical politics and scientific issues*]
RSIS......... Reed Stenhouse Investment Services [*British*]
RSIS......... Rotorcraft Systems Integration Simulator [*Joint Army-NASA program*]   (RDA)
RSITA ...... Reglement du Service International des Telecommunications de l'Aeronautique
R/SITU ..... Respiratory/Surgical Intensive Therapy Unit [*of a hospital*]
RSIUFL..... Release Suspension for Issue and Use of Following Lots [*Military*]
RSIVP....... Rapid Sequence Intravenous Pyelogram [*Medicine*]
RSJ........... Resistively-Shunted Junction [*Physics*]
RSJ........... Rolled-Steel Joist

RSJ........... Rolling-Stock Jigsaws [*British*]
RSKERL.... Robert S. Kerr Environmental Research Laboratory [*Ada, OK*] [*Environmental Protection Agency*]   (GRD)
RSKU........ Reza Shah Kibur University [*Iran*]
RS KY Agric Exp Stn ... RS. Kentucky Agricultural Experiment Station [*A publication*]
RSL........... Radio Standards Laboratory [*National Institute of Standards and Technology*]
RS or L....... Rated Same or Lower
RSL........... Reading on Statute Law [*A publication*]   (DLA)
RSL........... Received Signal Level [*Telecommunications*]   (TEL)
RSL........... Reconnaissance and Security Line
RSL........... Red Suspender League   (EA)
RSL........... Reference Standards Laboratory [*Deep Space Instrumentation Facility, NASA*]
RSL........... Relative Sea Level
RSL........... Remote Sensing Laboratory [*University of Kansas, University of Minnesota*] [*Research center*]   (MCD)
RSL........... Remote Sprint Launching [*Military*]
RSL........... Requirements Statement Language
RSL........... Research Services Ltd. [*Database producer*] [*Wembley, Middlesex, England*]
RSL........... Resource Support List [*NASA*]   (MCD)
RSL........... Returned Servicemen's League [*British military*]   (DMA)
RSL........... Revolutionary Socialist League   (EA)
RSL........... Ricerche Slavistiche [*A publication*]
RSL........... Ripe Skin Liquid [*A banana substrate*]
RSL........... Road Service Licence [*British*]   (DCTA)
RSI........... Rocznik Slawistyczny [*A publication*]
RSL........... Roselend [*France*] [*Seismograph station code, US Geological Survey*]   (SEIS)
RSL........... Royal Society of Literature [*British*]
RSL........... Royal Society, London [*British*]
RSL........... RSI Retail Solutions, Inc. [*Vancouver Stock Exchange symbol*]
RSL........... Rumsford Sandy Loam [*Type of soil*]
RSL........... Russell, KS [*Location identifier*] [*FAA*]   (FAAL)
RSLA........ Range Safety Launch Approval   (AFM)
RSLA........ Republic Capital Group, Inc. [*NASDAQ symbol*]   (NQ)
RSlav........ Ricerche Slavistiche [*A publication*]
RSlav........ Romanoslavica [*A publication*]
RSLB........ Right Short Leg Brace [*Medicine*]
RSII.......... Radovi Slavenskog Instituta [*A publication*]
RSLit .... Riverside Studies in Literature [*A publication*]
RSLMDZ.. Swedish University of Agricultural Sciences. Department of Microbiology. Report [*A publication*]
RSLPI....... Recombinant Secretory Leukoprotease Inhibitor [*Biochemistry*]
RSLS .... Receiver Side Lobe Suppression   (MCD)
RSLS .... Redundant Set Launch Sequencer   (MCD)
RSLTDM .. Swedish University of Agricultural Sciences. Department of Horticultural Science. Report [*A publication*]
RSLTS....... Results
RSIU .... Rocenka Slovanskeho Ustavu v Praze [*A publication*]
RSLV .... Resolve   (NASA)
RSLVDS.... Swedish University of Agricultural Sciences. Department of Plant Husbandry. Report [*A publication*]
RSLVR ...... Resolver   (MSA)
RSM .... Radiation Signature Measurement
RSM .... Radiation Survey Meter [*NASA*]
RSM .... Radio Squadron Mobile   (MUGU)
RSM .... Rapeseed Meal
RSM .... Rapidly Solidified Materials
RSM .... Ready Service Magazine [*Military*]   (DNAB)
RSM .... Real Storage Management [*Data processing*]   (IBMDP)
RSM .... Reconnaissance Strategic Missile
RSM .... Reed Switching Matrix
RSM .... Regimental Sergeant Major [*Army*]
RSM .... Remote Monitoring Services Manager [*Telecommunications*]
RSM .... Resource Status Monitor [*Systems Center, Inc.*]
RSM .... Response Surface Methodology
RSM .... Resume   (NASA)
RSM .... Revised Statutes of Manitoba [*Canada*] [*A publication*]   (DLA)
RSM .... Rivet Setting Machine
RSM .... Robert Strange McNamara [*US Secretary of Defense, 1961-68*]
RS & M...... Royal Sappers and Miners [*British military*]   (DMA)
RSM .... Royal School of Mines [*British*]
RSM .... Royal School of Musketry [*Hythe*] [*Military*] [*British*]   (ROG)
RSM .... Royal Society of Medicine [*British*]
RSM .... Royal Society of Musicians of Great Britain
RSM .... Royal Surrey Militia [*British military*]   (DMA)
RSM .... Sisters of Mercy [*Roman Catholic religious order*]
RSMA....... Radiological Systems Microfilm Associates   (EA)
RSMA....... Railway Supply Manufacturers Association   (EA)
RSMA....... Railway Systems and Management Association   (EA)
RSMA....... Royal Society of Marine Artists [*Formerly, SMA*] [*British*]
RSMAS ..... Rosenstiel School of Marine and Atmospheric Science [*University of Miami*] [*Research center*]   (RCD)
RSmB........ Bryant College, Smithfield, RI [*Library symbol*] [*Library of Congress*]   (LCLS)
RSMD .... Resource Systems Management Division [*Environmental Protection Agency*]   (GFGA)
RS & MD... Riots, Strikes, and Malicious Damage [*Insurance*]   (ADA)

RSME........ Royal School of Military Engineering [*British military*]   (DMA)
RSMF........ Royal Society of Medicine Foundation   (EA)
RSMFA ..... Rendiconti. Seminario Matematico e Fisico di Milano [*A publication*]
RSMG .... Rotorcraft Simulator Motion Generator [*Army*]   (RDA)
RSMGB...... Royal Society of Musicians of Great Britain   (EAIO)
RSMJA ..... Royal School of Mines. Journal [*A publication*]
RSMLC ..... Red de Salud de las Mujeres Latinoamericanas y del Caribe [*Latin American and Caribbean Women's Health Network*]   (EAIO)
RSMM ...... Redundant System Monitor Model [*NASA*]   (MCD)
Rs Mod Physics ... Reviews of Modern Physics [*A publication*]
RSMR........ Raw Stock Material Requirements
RSMR........ Rayleigh Scattering of Moessbauer Resonance [*Physics*]
RSMS .... Radio Spectrum Measurement System [*National Telecommunications and Information Administration*]
RSMT........ Ras Shamra Mythological Texts   (BJA)
RSMT........ Red Sea Mission Team   (EA)
RSMT........ Reliability Safety Margin Test
RSN .... Radiation Surveillance Network [*Public Health Service*]
RSN .... Radio Supernovae [*Astrophysics*]
RSN .... Random Sequence Number   (DNAB)
RSN .... Rassemblement pour le Salut National [*Rally for National Salvation*] [*Senegal*]   (PD)
RSN .... Ready, Soon, Now (Approach) [*Marketing*]
RSN .... Reason   (AFM)
RSN .... Reference Sequence Number [*Online bibliographies*]
RSN .... Reject Sequence Number [*Data processing*]
RSN .... Report Serial Number [*Army*]
RSN .... Research Surveillance Network
RSN .... Resonate   (KSC)
RSN .... Revised Statutes of Newfoundland [*Canada*] [*A publication*]   (DLA)
RSN .... Royal School of Needlework [*British*]
RSN .... Ruston, LA [*Location identifier*] [*FAA*]   (FAAL)
RSNA .... Radiological Society of North America   (EA)
RSNA .... Royal Society of Northern Antiquaries   (ROG)
RSNB........ Revised Statutes of New Brunswick [*Canada*] [*A publication*]   (DLA)
RSNC........ Royal Society for Nature Conservation   (EAIO)
RSNF........ Royal Saudi Arabian Navy Forces   (MCD)
RSNGS...... Rancho Seco Nuclear Generating Station   (NRCH)
RSNO .... Referral Service Network Office
RSNP........ Registered Student Nurse Program [*Military*]   (AABC)
RSNS .... Revised Statutes of Nova Scotia [*Canada*] [*A publication*]   (DLA)
RSNT........ Revised Single Negotiating Text [*UN Law of the Sea Conference*]
RSO .... Radiation Safety Officer [*Nuclear energy*]   (NRCH)
RSO .... Radio Symphony Orchestra
RSO .... Radiological Safety Office [*or Officer*]   (NASA)
RSO .... Radiosonde Observation   (MUGU)
RSO .... Railway Sorting Office
RSO .... Railway Suboffice
RSO .... Ramus Supraorbitalis [*Anatomy*]
RSO .... Range Safety Officer [*Military*]
RSO .... Range Support Operation
RSO .... Reactor Standards Office [*Oak Ridge National Laboratory*]
RSO .... Reactor System Outline [*Nuclear energy*]   (NRCH)
RSO .... Reconnaissance and Survey Officer [*Military*]   (AABC)
RSO .... Reconnaissance System Officer   (MCD)
RSO .... Regimental Supply Officer [*Army*]
RSO .... Regional Safety Officer [*British*]   (DCTA)
RSO .... Regional Security Officer [*Foreign Service*]
RSO .... Register Sender Outward [*Telecommunications*]   (TEL)
RSO .... Reproduction Service Order   (SAA)
RSO .... Research Ship of Opportunity
RSO .... Resident Surgical Officer [*British*]
RSO .... Resonans [*A publication*]
RSO .... Revenue Sharing Office [*Treasury*]   (OICC)
RSO .... Revised Statutes of Ontario [*Canada*] [*A publication*]   (DLA)
RSO .... Revolutionaere Sozialisten (Oesterreichs) [*Revolutionary Socialists (Austria)*] [*Political party*]   (PPE)
RSO .... Right Salpingo-Oophorectomy [*Medicine*]
RSO .... Runway Supervisory Officer [*Aviation*]   (MCD)
RSO .... Rural Suboffice [*British*]
RSOB........ Russell Senate Office Building [*Also, OSOB*] [*Washington, DC*]   (DLA)
RSOC........ Remote Sensing Oceanography [*Navy*]
R Soc Can .. Royal Society of Canada. Transactions [*A publication*]
R Soc Can Proc ... Royal Society of Canada. Proceedings [*A publication*]
R Soc Can Proc Trans ... Royal Society of Canada. Proceedings and Transactions [*A publication*]
R Soc Can Symp ... Royal Society of Canada. Symposium [*A publication*]
R Soc Chem Annu Rep Sect A Inorg Chem ... Royal Society of Chemistry. Annual Reports. Section A. Inorganic Chemistry [*A publication*]
R Soc Chem Annu Rep Sect B ... Royal Society of Chemistry. Annual Reports. Section B. Organic Chemistry [*A publication*]
R Soc Chem Annu Rep Sect C ... Royal Society of Chemistry. Annual Reports. Section C. Physical Chemistry [*A publication*]

R Soc Chem Faraday Discuss ... Royal Society of Chemistry. Faraday Discussions [*A publication*]
R Soc Chem Faraday Symp ... Royal Society of Chemistry. Faraday Symposia [*A publication*]
R Soc Chem Spec Publ ... Royal Society of Chemistry. Special Publication [*A publication*]
R Soc Econ ... Review of Social Economy [*A publication*]
R Soc Edinb Proc Sect B ... Royal Society of Edinburgh. Proceedings. Section B. Biology [*A publication*]
R Soc Edinburgh Commun Phys Sci ... Royal Society of Edinburgh. Communications. Physical Sciences [*A publication*]
R Soc Edinburgh Proc Sect A Math ... Royal Society of Edinburgh. Proceedings. Section A. Mathematics [*A publication*]
R Soc Edinburgh Proc Sect A Math Phys Sci ... Royal Society of Edinburgh. Proceedings. Section A. Mathematical and Physical Sciences [*A publication*]
R Soc Edinburgh Proc Sect B Nat Environ ... Royal Society of Edinburgh. Proceedings. Section B. Natural Environment [*A publication*]
R Soc Edinburgh Trans ... Royal Society of Edinburgh. Transactions [*A publication*]
R Soc Edinburgh Trans Earth Sci ... Royal Society of Edinburgh. Transactions. Earth Sciences [*A publication*]
R Soc Esp Fis Quim Reun Bienal ... Real Sociedad Espanola de Fisica y Quimica. Reunion Bienal [*A publication*]
R Soc Health Health Congr Pap ... Royal Society for the Promotion of Health. Health Congress. Papers [*A publication*]
R Soc Health Health Congr Pap Discuss ... Royal Society of Health. Health Congress. Papers for Discussion [*A publication*]
R Soc Health J ... Royal Society of Health. Journal [*A publication*]
R Social Economy ... Review of Social Economy [*A publication*]
R Sociol ...... Revija za Sociologiju [*A publication*]
R Soc London Proc ... Royal Society of London. Proceedings [*A publication*]
R Soc London Proc A ... Royal Society of London. Proceedings. Series A. Mathematical and Physical Sciences [*A publication*]
R Soc London Proc Ser B ... Royal Society of London. Proceedings. Series B. Biological Sciences [*A publication*]
R Soc Lond Philos Trans ... Royal Society of London. Philosophical Transactions [*A publication*]
R Soc Lond Philos Trans Ser A ... Royal Society of London. Philosophical Transactions. Series A [*A publication*]
R Soc Lond Philos Trans Ser B ... Royal Society of London. Philosophical Transactions. Series B [*A publication*]
R Soc Lond Proc Ser B ... Royal Society of London. Proceedings. Series B. Biological Sciences [*A publication*]
R Soc Med J ... Royal Society of Medicine. Journal [*A publication*]
R Soc Med Serv Ltd Int Congr Symp Ser ... Royal Society of Medicine Services Ltd. International Congress and Symposium Series [*A publication*]
R Soc NSW Monogr ... Royal Society of New South Wales. Monograph [*A publication*]
R Soc NZ Bull ... Royal Society of New Zealand. Bulletin [*A publication*]
R Soc NZJ ... Royal Society of New Zealand. Journal [*A publication*]
R Soc NZ Proc ... Royal Society of New Zealand. Proceedings [*A publication*]
R Soc NZ Trans Proc ... Royal Society of New Zealand. Transactions and Proceedings [*A publication*]
R Soc Promot Health J ... Royal Society for the Promotion of Health. Journal [*A publication*]
R Soc Queensl Proc ... Royal Society of Queensland. Proceedings [*A publication*]
R Soc S Afr Trans ... Royal Society of South Africa. Transactions [*A publication*]
R Soc S Aust Trans ... Royal Society of South Australia. Transactions [*A publication*]
R Soc Tasmania Pap Proc ... Royal Society of Tasmania. Papers and Proceedings [*A publication*]
R Soc Theory ... Review of Social Theory [*A publication*]
R Soc Victoria Proc ... Royal Society of Victoria. Proceedings [*A publication*]
R Soc West Aust J ... Royal Society of Western Australia. Journal [*A publication*]
RSOG .... Reserve Special Operations Group [*Army*]
RSOHJ...... Royal Society of Health. Journal [*A publication*]
RSOLB ..... Research Outlook [*A publication*]
RSO/MFSO ... Range Safety Officer / Missile Flight Safety Officer [*Military*]   (SAA)
RSOP........ Range Safety Operational Plan   (MUGU)
RSOP........ Readiness Standing Operating Procedures [*Military*]   (INF)
RSOP........ Reconnaissance, Selection, and Occupation of Position [*Military*]
RSOPN...... Resumed Operation   (FAAC)
RSOR .... Range Safety Operations Requirement
RSOS........ Resident Supervisor of Shipping [*Navy*]   (DNAB)
RSP........... RADAR Signal Processor
RSP........... Radii of Standard Parallels
RSP........... Radio Switch Panel
RSP........... Random Smooth Pursuit [*Ophthalmology*]
RSP........... Range Solar Panel
RSP........ Range Sorting Program
RSP........... Range Support Plan   (MUGU)
RSP........... Rapid Site Preparation
RSP........... Rapid Solidification Process   (MCD)

RSP............ Rassemblement Socialiste Progressiste [*Tunisia*] [*Political party*]   (EY)
RSP............ Rate Sensing Package   (AAG)
RSP............ Reactive Soil Pool [*Agriculture*]
RSP............ Reactivity Surveillance Procedures [*Nuclear energy*]   (NRCH)
RSP............ Reader/Sorter Processor
RSP............ Real-Time Signal Processor   (MCD)
RSP............ Receiving Stolen Property
RSP............ Reconnaissance and Security Positions [*Military*]
RSP............ Record Select Program [*Data processing*]
RSP............ Recoverable Sparoair Probe   (MUGU)
RSP............ Reinforced Structural Plastic
RSP............ Remote Sensor Platoon
RSP............ Remote Shutdown Panel [*Nuclear energy*]   (NRCH)
RSP............ Remote Switching Partition   (HGAA)
RSP............ Render Safe Procedure [*Military*]
RSP............ Rendezvous Station Panel [*NASA*]   (MCD)
RSP............ Replenishment Spare Part
RSP............ Replication Synchronization Process [*Telecommunications*]   (TEL)
RSP............ Required Space Character [*Data processing*]
RSP............ Reserve Stock Point
RSP............ Respirable Suspended Particulates
RSP............ Responder Beacon
RSP............ Restoration Priority [*Telecommunications*]   (TEL)
RSP............ Retail Stockage Policy
RSP............ Revolutionaire Socialistische Partij [*Revolutionary Socialist Party*] [*Netherlands*] [*Political party*]   (PPE)
RSP............ Revolutionary Socialist Party [*India*] [*Political party*]   (PPW)
RSP............ Right Sacroposterior [*A fetal position*] [*Obstetrics*]
RSP............ Robotic Sample Processor [*Automation*]
RSP............ Rocky Slope Pipeline
RSP............ Roll Stabilization Platform
RSP............ Roscoe, Snyder & Pacific Railway Co. [*AAR code*]
RSP............ Rotating Shield Plug [*Nuclear energy*]   (NRCH)
RSP............ Rotation in a Selected Plane
RSP............ Route Selection Program   (SAA)
RSP............ Rural Satellite Program [*US Agency for International Development*] [*Washington, DC*] [*Telecommunications*]   (TSSD)
RSPA......... Railway Systems and Procedures Association [*Later, RSMA*]
RSPA......... Research and Special Programs Administration [*Department of Transportation*] [*Washington, DC*]   (GRD)
RSPA......... Royal Society for the Prevention of Accidents [*British*]
RSPB......... Retail Stockage Policy, Bulk Supplies   (MCD)
RSPB......... Royal Society for the Protection of Birds [*British*]
RSPCA...... Royal Society for the Prevention of Cruelty to Animals [*British*]
RSPD......... Rapid Solidification Plasma Deposition [*Metallurgy*]
RSPD......... Research and Special Project Division [*Bureau of National Affairs*] [*Information service or system*]   (IID)
RSPD......... Respond   (MSA)
RSPE......... RADAR Signalling Processing Equipment
RSPE......... Retail Stockage Policy, Evaluation   (MCD)
RSPEI....... Revised Statutes of Prince Edward Island [*Canada*]
RSPI......... Resident-Shared Page Index [*Data processing*]   (OA)
RSPI......... Residential Space Planners International   (EA)
RSPK........ Recurrent Spontaneous Psychokinesis [*Poltergeist*] [*Parapsychology*]
RSPL........ RADAR Significant Power Line
RSPL........ Recommended Spare Parts List [*NASA*]
RSPM....... Random Spatial Phase Modulator
RS/PM...... Rapid Solidification/Powder Metallurgy
RSPMB.... Research in the Psychology of Music [*A publication*]
RSPMP..... Ready Store Positive Maintenance Program   (MCD)
RSPO........ Rail Services Planning Office [*Interstate Commerce Commission*]
RSPO........ Railway Station Police Officer [*British*]
RSPP........ Radio Simulation Patch Panel   (CET)
RSPP........ Royal Society of Portrait Painters [*British*]
Rspr........... Rechtspraak [*Case Law, Judicial Decisions*] [*Netherlands*]   (ILCA)
Rspr........... Rechtsprechung [*Court Practice*] [*German*]   (ILCA)
Rspr Arb.... Rechtsprechung in Arbeitssachen [*Labor Court Reports*] [*German*]   (ILCA)
RSPRT...... Robust Sequential Probability Ratio Test [*Navy*]
RSPS........ Range Solar Panel Substrate
RSPS........ Response   (MSA)
RSPT........ Rayleigh-Schrodinger Perturbation Theory [*Physical chemistry*]
RSPT........ Real Storage Page Table [*Data processing*]   (BUR)
RSPTA...... Recherche Spatiale [*A publication*]
RSPTCH... Response Technologies, Inc. [*Associated Press abbreviation*]   (APAG)
RSPTR...... Respirator   (MSA)
RSPUB9.... Journal of Public Health [*A publication*]
RSPV........ Respective   (AABC)
RSPWC..... Royal Society of Painters in Water-Colours [*British*]
RSQ........... Rescue   (AAG)
RSQ........... Revised Statutes of Quebec [*Canada*] [*A publication*]   (DLA)
RSQ........... Rhetoric Society. Quarterly [*A publication*]
RSQBT...... Rescue Boat
RSQC......... Reliability, Safety, and Quality Control

RSR............ Congregation of Our Lady of the Holy Rosary [*Roman Catholic women's religious order*]
RSR............ En Route Surveillance RADAR
RSR............ Radiological Safety Review [*Nuclear energy*]   (NRCH)
RSR............ Raiding Support Regiment [*British Royal Marines*] [*World War II*]
RSR............ Range Safety Report [*NASA*]   (AAG)
RSR............ Rapid Solidification Rate   (IEEE)
RSR............ Reactor Safety Research [*Nuclear energy*]
RSR............ Ready Service Ring   (NG)
RSR............ Recherches de Science Religieuse [*A publication*]
RSR............ Red Sulfhydryl Reagent
RSR............ Reference Services Review [*A publication*]
RSR............ Refracted Surface-Reflected Ray
RSR............ Regular Sinus Rhythm [*Physiology*]
RSR............ Republica Socialista Romania [*Socialist Republic of Romania*]   (EY)
RSR............ Request for Scientific Research   (AAG)
RSR............ Required Supply Rate [*Military*]   (AABC)
RSR............ Research Study Requests
RSR............ Residue Solvent Refining [*Lummus Crest, Inc. process*]
RSR............ Resorufin [*Organic chemistry*]
RSR............ Resources Status Report
RS & R...... Retail, Service, and Repair
RSR............ Revised Supplementary Regulation
RSR............ Right Element Shift Right   (SAA)
RSR............ Riser Foods, Inc. [*AMEX symbol*]   (SPSG)
RSR............ Rocket Scoring Reliability   (MCD)
RSR............ Rocket Stabilized Rod
RSR............ Rod Select Relay   (IEEE)
RSR............ Rotary Seal Ring
RSR............ Route Surveillance RADAR
RSR............ Rover Sports Register [*An association*]   (EAIO)
RSR............ Royal Sussex Regiment [*Military unit*] [*British*]
RSR............ Worcester, MA [*Location identifier*] [*FAA*]   (FAAL)
RSRA........ Rotor Systems Research Aircraft [*Army/NASA*]
RSRB........ Redesigned Solid Rocket Booster
RSRC......... RSR Corp. [*NASDAQ symbol*]   (NQ)
RSRE........ Royal Signals and RADAR Establishment [*Computer chip designer*] [*England*]
RSRE........ Royal Signals Research Establishment [*British*]
RSRE Newsl Res Rev ... RSRE [*Royal Signals and RADAR Establishment*] Newsletter and Research Review [*A publication*]
RSRF........ Riser Foods, Inc. [*NASDAQ symbol*]   (NQ)
RSRM....... Raiding Squadron Royal Marines [*British military*]   (DMA)
RSRM....... Redesigned Solid Rocket Motor
RSRM....... Reduced Smoke Rocket Motor   (MCD)
RSROA..... Roller Skating Rink Operators Association   (EA)
RSRP........ Remote Sensing Research Program [*University of California*]
RSRP........ Rossica Society of Russian Philately   (EA)
RSRPB...... Research and the Retarded [*A publication*]
RSRS .... Radio and Space Research Station [*Later, Appleton Laboratory*] [*British*]   (MCD)
RSRS........ Range Safety Receiving Station
RSRS........ Reser's Fine Foods, Inc. [*NASDAQ symbol*]   (NQ)
Rsrt........... Resort
RSRTIN.... Resort Income Investors, Inc. [*Associated Press abbreviation*]   (APAG)
RSRV........ Rotor Systems Research Vehicle
RSRW....... Remote Short Range Wind Sensor   (MCD)
RSS........... RADAR Seeker Simulator [*Military*]   (CAAL)
RSS........... RADAR Sensing System [*Military*]   (CAAL)
RSS........... RADAR Signal Simulator
RSS........... Radiated Simulation System   (MCD)
RSS........... Radio Security Service [*British*]
RSS........... Radio Subsystem
RS(S)........ Radio Supervisor (Special) [*British military*]   (DMA)
RSS........... Rail Surveillance Service [*Military Traffic Management Command*]
RSS........... Railway Systems Suppliers   (EA)
RSS........... Range Safety Switch [*NASA*]   (MCD)
RSS........... Range Safety System [*NASA*]
RSS........... Range Slaving System
RSS........... Rapid Scanning of Spectra [*Instrumentation*]
RSS........... Rashtriya Swayamsevak Sangh [*National Union of Selfless Servers*] [*Militant Hindu organization*] [*India*]
RSS........... Reactant Service System
RSS........... Reactants Supply System [*NASA*]   (KSC)
RSS........... Reactive Stream Separation   (MCD)
RSS........... Reactor Safety Study [*Nuclear energy*]
RSS........... Reactor Shutdown System [*Nuclear energy*]   (NRCH)
RSS........... Ready Service Spares
RSS........... Real-Time Switching System
RS & S...... Receiving, Shipping, and Storage   (NASA)
RSS........... Recombination Signal Sequence [*Immunology*]
RSS........... Reed Stenhouse Companies Ltd. [*Toronto Stock Exchange symbol*]
RSS........... Reference Sound Source
RSS........... Refrigeration System [*or Subsystem*] [*Skylab*] [*NASA*]
RSS........... Refrigeration System Shield   (MCD)
RSS........... Regiae Societatis Sodalis [*Fellow of the Royal Society*]

RSS .... Registered Shoeing Smith [*Blacksmith*] [*Scotland*]
RSS .... Rehabilitation Service Series
RSS .... Rehabilitation Support Schedule   (AFM)
RSS .... Relative System Sensitivity
RSS .... Relaxed Static Stability [*Aviation*]
RSS .... Remote Safing Switch
RSS .... Remote Sensing Society [*Nottingham, England*]   (EAIO)
RSS .... Remote Shutdown System   (IEEE)
RSS .... Remote Slave Station   (MCD)
RSS .... Remote Switching System [*Telecommunications*]
RSS .... Repair and Storage Shelter   (SAA)
RSS .... Repeat Squawk Sheet   (MCD)
RSS .... Requirements Status System [*NASA*]
RSS .... Residual Sum of Squares [*Statistics*]
RSS .... Resource Survey Satellite
RSS .... Restricted Stepsize [*Statistics*]
RSS .... Retention Spermatemia Syndrome [*Medicine*]
RSS .... Retentive Substrate Shield [*i.e., saucer*] [*Slang*]
RSS .... Revised Statutes of Saskatchewan [*Canada*] [*A publication*]   (DLA)
RSS .... Reye's Syndrome Society [*Later, NRSF*]   (EA)
RSS .... Rib Structure Station [*NASA*]   (MCD)
RSS .... Ribbed Smoke Sheet [*Natural rubber*]
RSS .... Ride Smoothing System [*Aviation*]
RSS .... Rifle Sharpshooter
RSS .... Rigid Space Structure
RSS .... Ripe Skin Solid [*A banana substrate*]
RSS .... Rockdale, Sandow & Southern Railroad Co. [*AAR code*]
RSS .... Roger Sessions Society   (EA)
RSS .... Roland International Corp. Sound Space [*Electronic music*]
RSS .... Romance of Science Series [*A publication*]
RSS .... Rome and the Study of Scripture [*A publication*]   (BJA)
RSS .... Root-Sum-Square
RSS .... Roseires [*Sudan*] [*Airport symbol*]   (OAG)
RSS .... Rotary Shaft Seal
RSS .... Rotary Stepping Switch
RSS .... Rotary Symbol Switch   (MCD)
RSS .... Rotating Service Structure [*Kennedy Space Center*]   (MCD)
RSS .... Routing and Switching System
RSS .... Royal Shakespeare Society [*British*]   (DI)
RSS .... Royal Statistical Society [*British*]   (DI)
RSS .... Rural Sociological Society   (EA)
RSSAILA .. Returned Sailors', Soldiers', Airmen's Imperial League of Australia [*British military*]   (DMA)
RSSC .... Remote-Site Simulator Console [*NASA*]
RSSCW ..... Research Studies. State College of Washington [*Pullman*] [*A publication*]
RSSE .... Russian Spring-Summer Encephalitis [*Medicine*]
RSSEL....... Recommended Special Support Equipment List
RSSF......... Retrievable Surface Storage Facility [*Nuclear energy*]
RSSF......... Roller Speed Skating Federation   (EA)
RSSI .... Railway Systems Suppliers   (EA)
RSSJ.......... Researches in the Social Sciences on Japan. East Asian Institute. Columbia University [*A publication*]
RSSJA .... Journal. Royal Statistical Society. Series C. Applied Statistics [*A publication*]
RSSK .... Rigid Seat Survival Kit   (NG)
RSSLI........ Radovi Staroslavenskog Instituta [*A publication*]
RSSMAP... Reactor Safety Study Methodology Application Program [*Nuclear energy*]   (NRCH)
RSSME3 ... Swedish University of Agricultural Sciences. Reports in Forest Ecology and Forest Soils [*A publication*]
RSSN........ Reaction-Sintered Silicon Nitrate
RSSN........ Research Space Surveillance Network
RSSND....... Roessing [*A publication*]
RSSP .... Range Single Shot Probability [*Military*]
RSSPCC .... Royal Scottish Society for Prevention of Cruelty to Children
RSSPL....... Recommended Spares and Spare Parts List
RSSPO ...... Resident Space Shuttle Project Office [*NASA*]   (NASA)
R & S SQ .. Repair and Salvage Squadron [*Military*]
RSSRT....... Russell Sage Social Relations Test [*Psychology*]
RSSSS.......... Rashtriya Swayamseyak Sangh [*National Union of Selfless Servers*] [*Militant Hindu organization*] [*India*]   (PD)
RSSSS.......... Reusable Space Shuttle System [*Aerospace*]   (KSC)
RSSSS.......... Robotic Substrate Servicing System [*Space Automation and Robotics Center*] [*NASA*]
RSST .... Reserve Station Service Transformer [*Nuclear energy*]   (NRCH)
RSSU........ Remote-Site Simulation Unit [*Navy*]   (NVT)
RSSU........ Remote System Support Utility [*Telematics International, Inc.*]
RS Supp..... Supplement to the Revised Statutes [*A publication*]   (DLA)
RSSW .... Ross Sea Shelf Water [*Ross Ice Shelf Project*]
RSSZ .... Rung Sat Special Zone [*Vietnam*]
RST........... RADAR Start   (MSA)
RST........... RADAR Systems Technician   (MCD)
RST........... Radiometric Sun Tracer
RST........... Radiosensitivity Test   (AAMN)
RST........... Range Search and Track   (MCD)
RST........... Rapid Solidification Technology [*Metallurgy*]
RST........... Read Symbol Table
RST........... Readability, Strength, Tone
RST........... Recessed Selectromatic Terminal   (NASA)

RST........... Recognition Suppression Technique
RST........... Recovery Sequence Tester
RST........... Reentry System Technology [*Aerospace*]
RST........... Reflector Support Truss
RST........... Register and Self-Test
RST........... Reinforcing Steel [*Technical drawings*]
RST........... Religious of St. Andrew [*Roman Catholic religious order*]
RST........... Remote Station [*Data processing*]
RST........... Requirements for Scheduled Test   (MUGU)
RSt .... Research Studies [*A publication*]
RST........... Research Study Team
RST........... Reset [*Telecommunications*]   (TEL)
RST........... Reset-Set Trigger
RST........... Resin Skived Tape
RST........... Resistance   (AABC)
RST........... Resort Airlines [*Baltimore, MD*] [*FAA designator*]   (FAAC)
RST........... Rest
RST........... Restore   (MSA)
RST........... Review of Economic Studies [*A publication*]
RST........... Rework/Scrap Tag   (MCD)
RST........... Right Sacrotransverse [*A fetal position*] [*Obstetrics*]
RST........... Right Store   (SAA)
RST........... Rochester [*Minnesota*] [*Airport symbol*]   (OAG)
RST........... Rolling Stock   (CINC)
RST........... Rough Saw Template   (MCD)
RST........... Routine Sequence Table
RST........... Royal Scot Resources [*Vancouver Stock Exchange symbol*]
RST........... Royal Society of Teachers [*British*]
R Sta .... Radio Telegraph Station
RSTA .... Reconnaissance, Surveillance, and Target Acquisition Center [*Army*] [*Fort Monmouth, NJ*]   (MCD)
RSta .... Regulating Station [*Army*]
RSTAA ...... Reconnaissance, Surveillance, and Target Acquisition Aircraft   (MCD)
RSTA/BMC3 ... Reconnaissance, Surveillance, and Target Acquisition/Battle Management Command, Control, and Communications   (MCD)
RSTA & E ... Reconnaissance, Surveillance, Target Acquisition, and Engagement   (MCD)
RSTC .... RADAR Ship Target Classification [*Military*]   (CAAL)
RSTC .... Recreational Scuba Training Council   (EA)
RSTC .... Remote-Site Telemetry Computer [*NASA*]
RSTD........ Restricted
RSTG........ Roasting   (MSA)
RSTINT .... Resorts International, Inc. [*Associated Press abbreviation*]   (APAG)
RSTK .... Relay Servicing Tool Kit
RSTL .... Red Status Timeline
RSTL .... Relaxed Skin Tension Line [*Dermatology*]
RSTMH .... Royal Society of Tropical Medicine and Hygiene [*British*]   (EAIO)
RSTN........ Radio Solar Telescope Network   (MCD)
RSTN........ Regional Seismic Test Network [*Nuclear explosion detection*]
RSTN........ Resource Technology [*A publication*]
RSTO........ Rose's Stores, Inc. [*NASDAQ symbol*]   (NQ)
R/STOL .... Reduced/Short Takeoff and Landing [*Aircraft*]
RStorLettRel ... Rivista di Storia e Letteratura Religiosa [*Florence*] [*A publication*]   (BJA)
RSTP .... Real-Time Statistical and Terminal Profile [*IRS*]
RSTP .... Remote-Site Telemetry Processor [*NASA*]   (KSC)
RSTPF....... Rustproof   (MSA)
RSTR .... Resistor
RSTR .... Restrict   (MSA)
RSTRD...... Restricted
RSTRT ...... Restart   (NASA)
RSTS .... RADAR System Test Station   (MCD)
RSTS .... Resource-Sharing Time-Sharing System
RSTS .... Retirement Systems Testing Section [*Social Security Administration*]
RSTS .... Sunresorts Ltd. NV [*New York, NY*] [*NASDAQ symbol*]   (NQ)
R Stuart Pap ... Royal Stuart Papers [*A publication*]
R Stud .... Romanische Studien [*A publication*]
RSTV......... Rice Stripe Virus [*Plant pathology*]
R St Wi ...... Recht, Staat, Wirtschaft [*A publication*]
RSTY......... Rusty Pelican Restaurants, Inc. [*NASDAQ symbol*]   (NQ)
RSU .... Rating Scale Unit [*Acoustics*]
RSU .... Recorder Switch Unit
RSU .... Regional Science and Urban Economics [*Netherlands*] [*A publication*]
RSU .... Register Storage Unit
RSU .... Relay Storage Unit
RSU .... Remote Service Unit   (NASA)
RSU .... Remote Subscriber Unit [*Telecommunications*]
RSU .... Remote Switching Unit [*Telecommunications*]
RSU .... Repair and Salvage Unit [*British military*]   (DMA)
RSU .... Rescue Support Umbilical   (MCD)
RSU .... Rocenka Slovanskeho Ustavu [*A publication*]
RSU .... Runway Supervisory Unit [*Aviation*]   (FAAC)
RSUED..... Regional Science and Urban Economics [*A publication*]
RSUP........ REGIS [*Relational General Information System*] System Users' Group   (EA)

RSUSEV.... Arkansas. Agricultural Experiment Station. Research Series [*A publication*]
RSUT........ Remote Start Unit Trainer (DWSG)
RSUTA...... Reconstruction Surgery and Traumatology [*A publication*]
RSV........... Armored Reconnaissance Scout Vehicle [*Army*] (RDA)
RSV........... Diesel Run Control Solenoid Valve (IEEE)
RSV........... Random Sine Vibration
RSV........... Rat Sarcoma Virus
RSV........... Rat Seminal Vesicle
RSV........... Recently Separated Veteran
RSV........... Reconnaissance Scout Vehicle (MCD)
RSV........... Red Lake & Sun Valley [*Vancouver Stock Exchange symbol*]
RSV........... Remove Shutoff Valve (KSC)
RSV........... Research Safety Vehicle [*Department of Transportation*]
RSV........... Reserve (MSA)
RSV........... Reservoir [*Board on Geographic Names*]
RSV........... Respiratory Syncytial Virus
RSV........... Revised Standard Version [*of the Bible, 1952*]
RSV........... Right Subclavian Vein [*Anatomy*]
RSV........... Robinson, IL [*Location identifier*] [*FAA*] (FAAL)
RSV........... Rous Sarcoma Virus [*Same as ASV*]
RSVA...... Randolph-Sheppard Vendors of America (EA)
RSV-Br ...... Rous Sarcoma Virus, Bryan [*Strain*]
RSVC........ Resident Supervisor Call (BUR)
RSVE........ Reconstituted Sendai Virus Envelope [*Immunology*]
RSVN .... Reservation (FAAC)
RSVP........ Radiation Spectral Visual Photometer
RSVP........ Rapid Sampling Vertical Profiler [*Oceanography*]
RSVP........ Rapid Serial Visual Presentation [*Data processing*]
RSVP........ Remote System Verification Program
RSVP........ Repondez, s'll Vous Plait [*The Favor of an Answer is Requested*] [*French*]
RSVP........ Research Selected Vote Profile [*Election poll*]
RSVP........ Research Society for Victorian Periodicals (EA)
RSVP........ Response Segmentation and Validation Program [*Donnelley Marketing Information Services*] [*Information service or system*] (IID)
RSVP........ Restartable Solid Variable Pulse [*Motor*] (MCD)
RSVP........ Retired Senior Volunteer Program (EA)
RSVP........ Ride Shared Vehicle Paratransit [*Transportation system*]
RSVP........ Rotating Surveillance Vehicle Platform [*Military*] (MCD)
RSVP........ Rural Southern Voice for Peace [*An association*] (EA)
RSVPI....... Retired Senior Volunteer Program International (EA)
RSVR........ Reservoir (AAG)
RSVR........ Resolver (AAG)
RSV(RV) ... Revised Standard Version of the Bible [*A publication*] (BJA)
RSV-SR .... Rous Sarcoma Virus, Schmidt-Ruppin [*Strain*]
RSVT........ Stetson Reading-Spelling Vocabulary Test [*Educational test*]
RSVTN...... Reservation
RSW .... Fort Myers [*Florida*] [*Airport symbol*] (OAG)
RSW .... Fort Myers, FL [*Location identifier*] [*FAA*] (FAAL)
RS(W)....... Radio Supervisor (Warfare) [*British military*] (DMA)
RSW .... Rattlesnake Hills [*Washington*] [*Seismograph station code, US Geological Survey*] (SEIS)
RSW .... Raw Service Water [*Nuclear energy*] (NRCH)
RSW .... Refrigerated Seawater
RSW .... Repeating Slide Wire
RSW .... Resistance Spot Welding
RSW .... Retarded Surface Wave
RSW .... Royal Scottish Society of Painters in Water Colours
R Swaziland Soc Sci Technol J ... Royal Swaziland Society of Science and Technology. Journal [*A publication*]
RSWB........ Raumordnung, Stadtebau, Wohnungswesen, Bauwesen [*Fraunhofer Society*] [*Germany*] (IID)
RSWC........ Right Side Up with Care
RSWC........ Royal Society of Painters in Water-Colours [*British*] (ROG)
RSWD .... Regiment South Western District [*British military*] (DMA)
R Swed Acad Eng Sci Proc ... Royal Swedish Academy of Engineering Sciences. Proceedings [*A publication*]
R Swed Inst Eng Res Proc ... Royal Swedish Institute for Engineering Research. Proceedings [*A publication*]
RSWPS...... Repetitive Square Wave Potential Signal [*Electrochemistry*]
RSWS .... Royal Scottish Water-Colour Society (ROG)
RSWSU ..... Research Studies. Washington State University [*Pullman*] [*A publication*]
RSWW....... Ross Sea Winter Water [*Marine science*] (MSC)
RSY........... Lumberton, NC [*Location identifier*] [*FAA*] (FAAL)
RSY........... Rigelyn Security [*Vancouver Stock Exchange symbol*]
RSYCA...... Railway Systems Control [*A publication*]
RSYCS....... Rosy Cross [*Freemasonry*]
RSYN .... Reactor Synthesis
RSYS .... Responsible System (NASA)
RSYS .... Restaurant Systems, Inc. [*NASDAQ symbol*] (NQ)
RSZ........... Phoenix, AZ [*Location identifier*] [*FAA*] (FAAL)
RT .... Air Tungaru (Gilbert Islands) [*British*] [*ICAO designator*] (ICDA)
RT .... Electric Current Relay
RT .... Rachidian Tooth
RT............. RADAR Transparency (MCD)
R/T .... RADAR Trigger (CET)
RT............. Radiation Therapy [*Medicine*]

RT .... Radio Technician
RT .... Radio Telegraphy (ADA)
RT .... Radio Telephone (MSA)
RT .... Radio/Television Repair Program [*Association of Independent Colleges and Schools specialization code*]
RT .... Radio Times [*A publication*]
RT .... Radio Tracking (KSC)
RT .... Radio Transmitter
RT .... Radiographic Test [*Nuclear energy*] (NRCH)
RT .... Radiologic Technologist
RT .... Radiotelegraphy
RT .... Radiotelephone
R/T .... Radiotelephony
RT .... Radiotherapy (AAMN)
RT .... Radium Therapy [*Clinical chemistry*] (MAE)
RT .... Radular Teeth
RT .... Rail Tractor [*British*]
RT .... Rail Transport
RT .... Raintight (MSA)
RT .... Raise Top (OA)
RT .... Randomized Trial [*Statistics*]
RT .... Range-to-Target (NASA)
RT .... Range Timing (AAG)
RT .... Range Tracking
RT .... Ranger Tab [*Military decoration*]
RT .... Rangetaker [*British military*] (DMA)
RT .... Rate (AAG)
RT .... Rate Transmitter
RT .... Rated Time (IEEE)
RT .... Ratio Transformer [*Unit*]
RT .... Rational Therapy [*Short form for rational-emotive therapy*]
RT .... Reaction Time
RT .... Reactor Trip [*Nuclear energy*] (NRCH)
RT .... Read Tape [*Data processing*]
RT .... Reader Tape [*Contact*] (MCD)
RT .... Reading Teacher [*A publication*]
RT .... Reading Test
RT .... Readout Technique
RT .... Real Time [*Computer*] [*Data processing*]
RT .... Receive-Transmit [*Radio*]
RT .... Received Text (ROG)
R/T .... Receiver/Transmitter [*Radio*] (KSC)
RT .... Receiving Test (DNAB)
RT .... Receiving Tube
RT .... Recherches Theatrales [*A publication*]
RT .... Record Transfer
R/T .... Record of Trial [*Army*] (AABC)
RT .... Recovery Time [*Military*] (AFIT)
RT .... Recreational Therapist [*or Therapy*]
RT .... Recueillis Temporaires [*Temporarily Taken In*] [*Of unadoptable children*] [*French*]
RT .... Red Tetrazolium [*Also, TPTZ, TTC*] [*Chemical indicator*]
RT .... Reduced Tillage System [*Agriculture*]
RT .... Reduction Tables
RT .... Reference Trajectory [*NASA*] (KSC)
RT .... Refrigerated Trap [*Biotechnology*]
Rt .... Regelungstechnik [*A publication*]
RT .... Regional Treasurer [*British*]
RT .... Register Ton
RT .... Register Traffic [*Telecommunications*] (TEL)
RT .... Register Transfer [*Data processing*]
R/T .... Register Translator [*Telecommunications*] (TEL)
RT .... Registered Technician [*American Registry of X-ray Technicians*]
RT .... Registered Trademark (CDAI)
RT .... Regression Testing [*Data processing*] (IEEE)
RT .... Rehabilitation Therapist [*or Therapy*]
RT .... Rejection Tag (AAG)
RT .... Related Term [*Indexing*]
RT .... Relaxation Time
RT .... Relaxation Training [*Psychology*]
RT .... Relay Tester
RT .... Relay Transmitter
RT .... Release Transmittal (MCD)
RT .... Released Time
RT .... Religious Theatre [*A publication*]
RT .... Relocation Time
RT .... Remote Terminal [*Data processing*]
RT .... Renal Transplant [*Nephrology*]
RT............. Repair Time
R/T .... Reperforator/Transmitter [*Teletypewriter*] [*Data processing*]
RT .... Request Translator (SAA)
RT .... Research and Technology
R & T......... Research and Technology
RT .... Reserve Training
RT .... Reset Trigger
RT .... Residence Time [*Chemistry*]
R-T............. Resistance Test (NASA)
RT .... Resistor Tolerance
RT .... Resistor Transistor
RT .... Resorts International, Inc. [*AMEX symbol*] (SPSG)

RT .... Respiratory Therapy [*Medicine*]
RT .... Response Time [*Data processing*]
RT .... Resting Tension [*Biology*]
RT .... Resuscitation Team
RT .... Resuscitation Therapy
RT .... Retention Time [*Data processing*]
RT .... Retraining   (OICC)
RT .... Retro Table [*NASA*]
RT .... Retroviral Transcript [*Genetics*]
RT .... Return Ticket
RT .... Reverse Transcriptase [*An enzyme*]
R/T .... Revolving Radio Beacon [*ITU designation*]   (CET)
R/T .... Rho/Theta
RT .... Rigging Tool   (MCD)
RT .... Right   (EY)
RT .... Right Tackle [*Football*]
RT .... Right Thigh [*Medicine*]   (MAE)
RT .... Right Time of Departure/Arrival   (DS)
RT .... Right Turn after Takeoff [*Aviation*]   (FAAC)
RT .... Ring Trip [*Telecommunications*]   (TEL)
RT .... Ringing Tone [*Telecommunications*]   (TEL)
RT .... RISC [*Reduced-Instruction Set Computer*] Technology [*IBM Corp.*]
RT .... Rise Time   (DEN)
RT .... [*The*] River Terminal Railway Co. [*AAR code*]
R & T .... Road and Track [*A publication*]
RT .... Road Traffic
RT .... Road Transport   (NATG)
RT .... Road Truck [*Shipping*]   (DCTA)
RT .... Robotic Telepresence
RT .... Rocket Target
RT .... Romain de Tirtoff [*Also known as ERTE*] [*Couturier*]
RT .... Room Temperature
RT .... Root [*Mathematics*]   (ROG)
RT .... Rotation Discrete Rate
rt............... Rotten [*Quality of the bottom*] [*Nautical charts*]
RT .... Rough Terrain [*Military*]   (AABC)
RT .... Rough Times [*Formerly, Radical Therapist*] [*A publication*]
R & T .... Rough and Tumble Engineers' Historical Association   (EA)
RT .... Round Table [*Australia*] [*A publication*]
RT .... Round Trip
RT .... Route   (AABC)
RT .... Route Treatment [*Telecommunications*]   (TEL)
RT .... Router Template
RT .... Routine Tag   (SAA)
RT .... Royal Tombs of the First Dynasty [*A publication*]
RT .... Royalty Trust
RT .... Rubber-Tired   (SAA)
RT .... Rufous-Sided Towhee [*Ornithology*]
RT .... Running Time [*Movies*]   (CDAI)
RT .... Running Title
RT .... Runnymead Trust [*An association*]   (EAIO)
RT .... Runup and Taxi [*Air Force*]
R & T .... Rush & Tomkins [*Commercial firm*] [*British*]
RT .... Ruth [*Old Testament book*]
RT .... Rye Terms
Rt .... Tetrachoric Correlation [*Psychology*]
RT .... Total Reserves
RT .... Transportes Aereos de Timor [*Portugal*] [*ICAO designator*] [*Obsolete*]   (FAAC)
rT₃.............. Reverse Triiodothyronine [*Endocrinology*]
RTA .... RADAR Terrain Analysis
RTA .... Radically Tapered Antenna
RTA .... Radix Teachers Association   (EA)
RTA .... Rail Travel Authorization [*Military*]
RTA .... Railway Tie Association   (EA)
RTA .... Rapid Thermal Annealing [*Physics*]
RTA .... Rattler Resources [*Vancouver Stock Exchange symbol*]
RTA .... Reactivity Test Assembly [*Nuclear energy*]
RTA .... Ready-to-Assemble
RTA .... Real-Time Accumulator
RTA .... Real-Time Analyzer [*Electronics*]
RTA .... Reciprocal Trade Agreement
RTA .... Refrigeration Trade Association of America
RTA .... Reliability Test Assembly
RTA .... Reliable Test Analyzer [*Data processing*]
RTA .... Religious and Theological Abstracts [*A publication*]
RTA .... Remote Test Access [*Telecommunications*]   (TEL)
RTA .... Remote Trunk Arrangement [*Telecommunications*]   (TEL)
RTA .... Renal Tubule Acidosis [*Medicine*]
RTA .... Request for Technical Action   (MCD)
RTA .... Riberalta [*Bolivia*] [*Seismograph station code, US Geological Survey*] [*Closed*]   (SEIS)
RTA .... Rise-Time Analyzer
RTA .... Road Traffic Accident [*British*]
RTA .... Road Traffic Act [*1962*] [*British*] [*A publication*]   (DLA)
RTA .... Rotor Test Apparatus   (MCD)
RTA .... Rotuma [*Fiji*] [*Airport symbol*]   (OAG)
RTA .... Royal Thai Army
RTA .... Rubber Trade Association of New York   (EA)
RTAC......... Real-Time Adaptive Control

RTAC......... Regional Technical Aid Center [*Agency for International Development*]
RTAC......... Research and Technology Advisory Council [*Terminated, 1977*] [*NASA*]   (EGAO)
RTAC......... Roads and Transportation Association of Canada [*Ottawa, ON*] [*Formerly, Canadian Good Roads Association*] [*Research center*]
RTACF...... Real-Time Auxiliary Computing Facility [*Apollo*] [*NASA*]
RTACS ..... Real-Time Adaptive Control System [*Military*]   (CAAL)
RTAD .... Router Adapter
RTAF........ Report to Armed Forces
RTAF........ Royal Thai Air Force
RTAFB ..... Royal Thai Air Force Base   (CINC)
RTAFCONV ... Royal Thai Air Force Contingent, Vietnam
RTAG .... Range Technical Advisory Group
RTAM .... Recherches de Theologie Ancienne et Medievale [*A publication*]
RTAM .... Remote Telecommunications Access Method [*Data processing*]
RTAM .... Remote Terminal Access Method [*Data processing*]   (BUR)
RTAM .... Resident Terminal Access Method [*Data processing*]
RTANG ..... Right Angle
RTAP .... Rural Technical Assistance Program [*Department of Transportation*]
RTAPS ...... Real-Time Terminal Application Program System [*Data processing*]
RTARF ...... Royal Thai Armed Forces   (CINC)
RTARP ..... Royal Thai Army Rebuild Plant   (MCD)
RTATD8... Annual Report. Tokyo University of Agriculture and Technology [*A publication*]
R Taxation Individuals ... Review of Taxation of Individuals [*A publication*]
RTB .... Radial Time Base
RTB .... Radiodiffusion-Television Belge [*Belgian Radio Broadcasting and Television System*]
RTB .... Ranger Training Brigade [*Fort Benning, GA*] [*Army*]   (INF)
RTB .... Read Tape Binary [*Data processing*]   (IEEE)
RTB .... Reason to Believe   (ECON)
RTB .... Resistance Temperature Bridge   (SAA)
RTB .... Resistance Temperature Bulb [*NASA*]
RTB .... Resolver Tracking Bridge
RTB .... Response/Throughput Bias [*Data processing*]   (BUR)
RTB .... Return to Base [*Military*]
RTB .... Roatan [*Honduras*] [*Airport symbol*]   (OAG)
RTB .... Rocket Test Base
RTB .... Rural Telephone Bank [*Department of Agriculture*]
RTBA........ Rate to Be Agreed [*Business term*]   (DCTA)
RTBF .... Radio-Television Belge de la Communaute Culturelle Francaise [*Broadcasting organization*] [*Belgium*]   (EY)
RTBG........ Record and Tape Buyer's Guide [*A publication*]
RTBISC..... Radiodiffusion-Television Belge - Institut des Services Comuns [*Belgian Radio Broadcasting and Television - Common Services Institute*]
RTBM....... Real-Time BIT [*Binary Digit*] Mapping
RTBM....... Recoverable Test Bed Missile
RTBT....... Resonant Tunneling Bipolar Transistor [*Electronics*]
RTBV....... Rice Tungro Bacilliform Virus [*Plant pathology*]
RTC .... RADAR Tracking Center [*or Control*]
RTC .... Radio Tecnica Colombiana
RTC .... Radio Transmission Control   (NATG)
RTC .... Radio Tuned Circuit   (DEN)
RTC .... Radiodiffusion-Television Congolaise [*Congolese Radio and Television*]   (AF)
RTC .... Rails-to-Trails Conservancy   (EA)
RTC .... Range Telemetry Central [*Aerospace*]
RTC .... Ratchet   (AAG)
RTC .... Reader Tape Contact
RTC .... Real-Time Captioning [*for the deaf*]
RTC .... Real-Time Clock [*Data processing*]   (MCD)
RTC .... Real-Time Command [*Data processing*]
RTC .... Real-Time Computer
RTC .... Real-Time Conference [*GEnie*] [*Telecommunications*]
RTC .... Real-Time Control [*Data processing*]   (MCD)
RTC .... Real-Time Counter [*Data processing*]
RTC .... Reconstruction of Town and Country [*British*] [*World War II*]
RTC .... Recruit Training Center
RTC .... Recueil Tablettes Chaldeennes [*A publication*]
RTC .... Reference Test Chart
RTC .... Reference Transfer Calibrator   (OA)
RTC .... Regional Term Contract
RTC .... Regional Transport Commissioner
RTC .... Rehabilitation Research and Training Centers [*Department of Health and Human Services*]
RTC .... Relative Time Clock [*Data processing*]   (MDG)
RTC .... Remote Terminal Controller
RTC .... Removable Top Closure [*Nuclear energy*]   (NRCH)
RTC .... Replacement Training Center [*Military*]
RTC .... Reproductive Toxicology Center [*Database*]   (IID)
RTC .... Required Technical Characteristic [*Military*]   (CAAL)
RTC .... Requirements Type Contract [*Military*]   (AABC)
RTC .... Reserve Training Corps
RTC .... Residential Training College [*for disabled people*] [*British*]

RTC .... Residential Treatment Center [*Department of Health and Human Services*] (GFGA)
RTC .... Resolution Trust Corp. [*Federal government instrumentality, established in 1989*]
RTC .... Resort Timesharing Council (EA)
RTC .... Responsible Training Center [*Air Training Command*] (MCD)
RTC .... Return to Clinic [*Nursing*]
RTC .... Return to Control
RTC .... Reverse Transfer Capacitance
RTC .... Ridiculous Theatrical Company
RTC .... Rochester Telephone Corp. [*NYSE symbol*] (SPSG)
RTC .... Rocket Technique Committee
RTC .... Room Temperature Cure (NASA)
RTC .... Royal Tank Corps [*Military unit*] [*British*]
RTC-30 ...... Rehabilitation Research and Training Center in Blindness and Low Vision [*Mississippi State University*] [*Research center*] (RCD)
RTCA........ Race Track Chaplaincy of America (EA)
RTCA........ Radio Technical Commission for Aeronautics (EA)
RTCA........ Radio-Television Correspondents Association (EA)
RTCA........ Real-Time Casualty Assessment (MCD)
RTCA........ Ribofuranosyltriazolecarboxamide [*Ribavirin*] [*Antiviral compound*]
RTCANI.... Rav Tov Committee to Aid New Immigrants [*Later, RTIJRO*] (EA)
RTCB........ ROTI [*Recording Optical Tracking Instrument*] Tracker - Cocoa Beach [*NASA*] (KSC)
RTCB........ Run to Cladding Breach [*Nuclear energy*] (NRCH)
RTCC........ Radiant Technology Corp. [*NASDAQ symbol*] (NQ)
RTCC........ Real-Time Command Controller [*Data processing*] (NASA)
RTCC........ Real-Time Computer Center [*NASA*] (NASA)
RTCC........ Real-Time Computer Command [*NASA*] (NASA)
RTCC........ Real-Time Computer Complex [*NASA*]
RTCDS...... Real-Time Cinetheodolite Data System
RtCE .... Right to a Comprehensive Education [*British*]
RTCE......... Rotation/Translation Control Electronics (NASA)
RTCF .... Real-Time Combined File [*IRS*]
RTCF .... Real-Time Computer Facility
RTCH........ Radiation Technology, Inc. [*NASDAQ symbol*] (NQ)
RTCH........ Rough Terrain Container Handler (MCD)
RTCIL .... Research and Training Center on Independent Living (EA)
RTCL........ Reticle [*Optics*]
RTCM .... Radio Technical Commission for Maritime Services (TSSD)
RTC Met Cl J ... RTC [*Royal Technical College*] Metallurgical Club. Journal [*A publication*]
RTCO .... Record Time Compliance Order
RTCOD ..... [*The*] Research and Technology Coordinating Document [*Army*] (RDA)
RTCP........ Radio Transmission Control Panel (NATG)
RTCP........ Real-Time Communications Processor (NASA)
RTCP........ Resident Training and Counseling Programs (OICC)
RTCS........ Real-Time Calling Standards [*Chromatography*]
RTCS........ Real-Time Communication System
RTCS........ Real-Time Computer System
RTCTO ...... Record Time Compliance Technical Order (AAG)
RTCU .... Real-Time Control Unit
RTCU .... Router Cutter [*Tool*] (AAG)
RTCVD...... Rapid Thermal Chemical Vapor Deposition [*Coating technology*] [*Semiconductor technology*]
RTC(W)..... Recruit Training Command (Women) (DNAB)
RTD .... Delayed [*Indicates delayed meteorological message*] (FAAC)
RTD .... Radiodiffusion-Television de Djibouti
RTD .... Range Time Decoder
RTD .... Rate Damping (NASA)
RTD .... Rate Dumping (MCD)
RTD .... Read Tape Decimal
RTD .... Real-Time Decoder
RTD .... Real Time Developments [*Commercial firm*] [*British*]
RTD .... Real-Time Display
RTD .... Reliability Technical Directive (AAG)
RTD .... Remote Temperature Detector
RTD .... Replacement Task Distribution
RTD .... Replacement Training Detachment (MCD)
RTD .... Research and Technology Division [*Air Force*]
RTD .... Research Thrust Division [*Washington, DC*] [*DoD*] (GRD)
RTD .... Residence Time Distribution [*Chemical engineering*]
RTD .... Resistance Temperature Detector [*Nuclear energy*]
RTD .... Resistance Temperature Device [*Nuclear energy*] (NRCH)
RTD .... Retard (MSA)
rtd .... Retarded (MAE)
RTD .... Retired
RTD .... Return to Duty [*Military*]
RTD .... Returned [*Medicine*] (DHSM)
RTD .... Road Traffic Division [*British police*]
RTD .... Routine Test Dilution [*Analysis*]
RTD .... Royal Tombs of the First Dynasty [*A publication*]
RTD .... Run-Time Debugger [*Data processing*] (PCM)
RTDA .... Radio and Television Dealers' Association
RTDA .... Retail Tobacco Dealers of America (EA)
RTDA .... Returned Absentees
RTDAP...... RADAR Target Data Analog Processor (MCD)

RTDB .... Research Training and Development Branch [*Bethesda, MD*] [*National Heart, Lung, and Blood Institute*] (GRD)
RTDC .... Real-Time Data Channel (IEEE)
RTDC .... Retardation Coil (MSA)
RTDC .... Rocket-Thrown Depth Charge (NG)
RTDD .... Real-Time Data Distribution
RTDD .... Remote Timing and Data Distribution
RTDDC .... Real-Time Digital Data Correction (MUGU)
RTDE .... Range Time Data Editor [*NASA*] (KSC)
RTD & E.... Research, Test, Development, and Evaluation (SSD)
RTDF....... Real-Time Data File (NOAA)
RTDG........ Radio and Television Directors Guild [*Later, DGA*]
RTDHS ..... Real-Time Data Handling System
RTDP......... RADAR Target Data Processor (MCD)
RTDR .... Reliability Test Data Report
RTDS........ Real-Time Data System
RTDT .... Real-Time Data Translator
RTDVA ..... Rechentechnik-Datenverarbeitung [*A publication*]
RTE .... Radiative Transfer Equation
RTE .... Radio Telefis Eireann [*Radio and television network*] [*Ireland*]
RTE .... Radio Trans-Europe
RTE .... Radio Trunk Extension (NATG)
RTE .... RADOME [*RADAR Dome*] Test Equipment
RTE .... Railway Transport Establishment [*British military*] (DMA)
RTE .... Ready to Eat [*Cereals*]
RTE .... Real-Time Engine (MCD)
RTE .... Real-Time Executive [*Data processing*]
RTE .... Receiver Test Equipment
RTE .... Recovery Techniques Evaluation [*NASA*] (KSC)
RTE .... Regenerative Turboprop Engines
RTE .... Reliability Test Evaluation (AAG)
RTE .... Remote Terminal Emulator [*For teleprocessing validation*]
RTE .... Repair Test Equipment [*Aviation*]
RTE .... Request to Expedite
RTE .... Research Training and Evaluation (OICC)
RTE .... Resident Training Equipment (MCD)
RTE .... Residual Total Elongation [*Nuclear energy*] (NRCH)
RTE .... Responsible Test Engineer [*NASA*] (NASA)
RTE .... Return to Earth [*NASA*]
RTE .... Return from Exception [*Data processing*]
RTE .... Route (AFM)
RTE .... Royal Trust Energy Income Fund Trust Units [*Toronto Stock Exchange symbol*]
RTE .... RTE Corp. [*NYSE symbol*] (SPSG)
RTE .... RTE. Radio-TV-Electronics [*A publication*]
RTE-B....... Real-Time Basic [*Data processing*] (MDG)
RTEC........ Restec Systems, Inc. [*NASDAQ symbol*] (NQ)
RTech....... Radiology Technician [*or Technologist*] (AAMN)
R Tech Coll Metall Club J ... Royal Technical College. Metallurgical Club. Journal [*A publication*]
RTECS ...... Registry of Toxic Effects of Chemical Substances [*Department of Health and Human Services*] [*Information service or system*] [*A publication*]
RTECS ...... Residential Transportation Energy Consumption Survey [*Department of Energy*] (GFGA)
RTED .... Return-to-Earth Digital [*NASA*]
RTEG........ River Transport Escort Group (CINC)
RTEK........ Rise Technology, Inc. [*NASDAQ symbol*] (NQ)
RTel .... Radio Telemetry
RTEL........ Radio Telephony (MSA)
R Telev Soc J ... Royal Television Society. Journal [*A publication*]
RTEM....... RADAR Tracking Error Measurement
RT & EPS ... Rapid Transit and Electrical Power Systems
RTES .... Radio and Television Executives' Society [*Later, IRTS*]
RTES .... Real-Time Engine Simulation (MCD)
RTES .... Real-Time Executive System [*SEMIS*]
RTESB ...... Radio-TV-Electronic Service [*Later, RTE. Radio-TV-Electronic*] [*A publication*]
RTF........... Radio Transmission Facility
RTF........... Radiodiffusion-Television Francaise [*French Radio Broadcasting and Television System*]
RTF........... Radiotelephone
RTF........... Razor Trade Federation [*A union*] [*British*]
RTF........... Ready to Fire (MCD)
RTF........... Real-Time FORTRAN [*Data processing*]
RTF........... Reconnaissance Task Force (AFM)
RTF........... Reconnaissance Technical Flight [*Air Force*]
RTF........... Refilled, Tapped, and Fractionated [*Rock formation*] [*Geology*]
RTF........... Reliability Task Force (MCD)
RTF........... Religious Task Force (EA)
RTF........... Replication and Transfer [*Medicine*] (MAE)
RTF........... Reports Tempore Finch, English Chancery [*A publication*] (DLA)
RTF........... Resistance Task Force (EA)
RTF........... Resistance Transfer Factor [*of microorganisms to drugs*]
RTF........... Respiratory Tract Fluid [*Medicine*]
RTF........... Rich Text Format [*Data processing*] (BYTE)
RTF........... Rocket Test Facility
RTF........... Room Temperature Fluorescence [*Physics*]
RTF........... Rotational Test Facility [*NASA*]
RTF........... Rubber-Tile Floor [*Technical drawings*]

RTFC	Randy Travis Fan Club (EA)
RTFC	Retired Teamsters Fellowship Club (EA)
RTFCA	Religious Task Force on Central America (EA)
RTFES	Religious Task Force on El Salvador (EA)
RTFFRJ	Research Task Force for the Future of Reform Judaism (EA)
RTFL	Rough Terrain Fork Lift
RTFL	Rough Terrain Front Loader (MCD)
RTFLFT	Rough Terrain Forklift [Military]
RTFLT	Rough Terrain Forklift Truck (MCD)
RTFM	Router Form
RTFMS	Radio Transmission Frequency Measuring System
RTFR	Reliability Trouble and Failure Report
RTFS	Razor Trade Forgers' Society [A union] [British]
RTFT	Rough Terrain Forklift Truck
RTFV	RADAR Target Folder Viewer
RTG	Radioactive Thermoelectric Generator [Nuclear energy] (NRCH)
RTG	Radiodiffusion-Television Gabonaise [Gabonese radio and television network]
RTG	Radiodiffusion-Television Guineenne [Guinean radio and television network]
RTG	Radioisotope Thermoelectric Generator
RTG	Radiotelegraph
RTG	Range to Go
RTG	Range to Ground (MCD)
RTG	Rare Tube Gas
RTG	Rating (MUGU)
RTG	Reconnaissance Technical Group [Air Force]
RTG	Reglement Telegraphique [Telegraph Regulations] [French]
RTG	Requirements Tape Generator [NASA]
RTG	Reusable Training Grenade
RTG	Routing
RTG	Royal Thai Government
RTG	Ruteng [Indonesia] [Airport symbol] (OAG)
RTGB	Reactor Turbine Generator Board [Nuclear energy] (NRCH)
RTGD	Real-Time Graphic Display
RTGD	Room Temperature Gamma Detector
RTGF	Rat Transforming Growth Factor [Biochemistry]
RTGp	Reconnaissance Technical Group [Air Force] (AFM)
RTGp	Reconnaissance Training Group [Air Force] (AFM)
RTGp	Retraining Group [Air Force] (AFM)
RTGS	Real-Time Gross Settlement [Banking] (ECON)
RTGS	Return to Government Stores (SAA)
RTGU	Router Guide
RTGV	Real-Time Generation of Video
RTH	Houston Oil Royalty Trust UBI [NYSE symbol] (SPSG)
RTH	New York, NY [Location identifier] [FAA] (FAAL)
RTh	Radio-Telephone (High Frequency) [Telecommunications] (DS)
RTH	Radio Thailand (FEA)
RTH	Regional Telecommunications Hub [Telecommunications] (TEL)
RTH	Relay Transformer Header
RTH	Reports of Cases Concerning Settlements Tempore Holt [England] [A publication] (DLA)
RTH	Reports Tempore Hardwicke [England] [A publication] (DLA)
RTH	Retail Business. A Monthly Journal Concerned with Consumer Goods Markets, Marketing and Management, and Distribution in the United Kingdom [A publication]
RTH	Ridgeway's Reports Tempore Hardwicke, Chancery and English King's Bench [A publication] (DLA)
RThAbstr	Religious and Theological Abstracts [A publication]
RThAM	Recherches de Theologie Ancienne et Medievale [A publication]
R T Hardw	Reports Tempore Hardwicke, English King's Bench [A publication] (DLA)
RTHC	Rotation Translation Hand Controller (NASA)
RTHK	Radio Television Hong Kong
R T Holt	Reports Tempore Holt, English King's Bench [A publication] (DLA)
RtHon	Right Honourable (EY)
RThQr	Revue de Theologie et des Questions Religieuses [A publication] (BJA)
R Th R	Reformed Theological Review [A publication]
RTHS	Real-Time Hybrid System (NASA)
RTI	RADAR Target Identification
RTI	Radiation Transfer Index
RTI	Radiodiffusion-Television Ivoirienne [Ivory Coast Radio and Television] (AF)
RTI	Railroad Transportation Insurers [Defunct] (EA)
RTI	Real-Time Interface [Data processing]
RTI	Referred-to-Input
RTI	Related Technical Instruction [Bureau of Apprenticeship and Training] [Department of Labor]
RTI	Relaxation Time Index [Cardiology]
RTI	Renault Truck Industries [British subsidiary of Renault Vehicules Industriels]
RTI	Request for Technical Information [Military]
RTI	Research Triangle Institutes [Duke University, University of North Carolina at Chapel Hill, and North Carolina State University at Raleigh] [Research center]
RTI	Resilient Tile Institute [Later, RFCI] (EA)
RTI	Respiratory Tract Infection [Medicine]
RTI	Review of Taxation of Individuals [A publication]
RTI	Right Turn, International (EA)
RTI	Rise-Time Indicator
RTI	RMI Titanium [NYSE symbol] (SPSG)
RTI	Role Taking Inventory
RTI	Room, Tax, and Incidentals
RTI	Root Tolerance Index [Botany]
RTI	Roti [Indonesia] [Airport symbol] (OAG)
RTI	Round Table International (EA)
RTIC	Rotor Temperature Indicator and Control [Instrumentation]
RTICBT	Communication. Department of Agricultural Research. Royal Tropical Institute [Amsterdam] [A publication]
RTIF	Real-Time Interface [Data processing] (NASA)
RTII	RTI, Inc. [NASDAQ symbol] (NQ)
RTIJRO	Rav Tov International Jewish Rescue Organization (EA)
RTIO	Real-Time Input/Output Interface Subsystem [Space Flight Operations Facility, NASA]
RTIO	Remote Terminal Input/Output
RTI/OC	Real-Time Input/Output Controller [Data processing] (IEEE)
RTIP	RADAR Target Identification Point (AFM)
RTIP	Real-Time Interactive Processor (MCD)
RTIP	Remote Terminal Interactive Processor (MCD)
RTIP	Remote Terminal Interface Package
RTIR	Reliability and Trend Indicator Reports (AAG)
RTIRS	Real-Time Information Retrieval System
RTIS	Real-Time Information Retrieval System [Data processing] (HGAA)
RTIS	Rockwell Technical Information System [Rockwell International Corp.] [Information service or system] (IID)
RTITB	Road Transport Industry Training Board [British] (DCTA)
RTIV	Rice Tungro Isometric Virus [Plant pathology]
RTK	Range Tracker (KSC)
RTK	Receptor Tyrosine Kinase [Biochemistry]
RTK	Record Test Kit
RTK	Response Technologies [AMEX symbol] (SPSG)
RTK	Right to Know [Laws]
RTK	Roanoke Rapids, NC [Location identifier] [FAA] (FAAL)
RTKHA	Radiotekhnika (Kharkov) [A publication]
RTL	RADAR Threshold Lobe Limit (CET)
RTL	Radial Transmission Line
RTL	Radio Television Luxembourgeoise [Radio Television Luxembourg] [French]
RTL	Radioisotope Transport Loop [Nuclear energy] (NRCH)
RTL	Radiomaritime Telex Letter
RTL	Real-Time Language [Data processing] (IEEE)
RTL	Refrigerated Transmission Line
RTL	Regeneration Thermoluminescence
RTL	Regimental Training Line [Army]
RTL	Register Transfer Language [Data processing] (CSR)
RTL	Register Transfer Level
RTL	Register-Transistor Logic [Data processing]
RTL	Reinforced Tile Lintel [Technical drawings]
RTL	Relative Transcription Level [Genetics]
RTL	Research and Technology Laboratories [Army] (RDA)
RTL	Resin-Treated Liner
RTL	Resistor-Transistor Logic [Data processing] (BUR)
RTL	Resource Tie Line [An association]
RTL	Responsible Task Leader (SSD)
RTL	Run-Time Library [Interdata]
rt lat	Right Lateral [Medicine] (MAE)
Rt Law Rep	Rent Law Reports [India] [A publication] (DLA)
RTLF	Association of Railway Trainmen and Locomotive Firemen
RTLG	Radio Telegraph (MSA)
RTLO	Regional Training Liaison Officer [Ministry of Agriculture, Fisheries, and Food] [British]
RTLP	Reference Transmission Level Point [Telecommunications]
RTLS	Return to Launch Site [NASA]
RTLT	Round-Trip Light Time
RTM	RADAR Target Materiel (AFM)
RTM	Radiation Test Model
RTm	Radio-Telephone (Medium Frequency) [Telecommunications] (DS)
RTM	Radio Television Malaysia
RTM	Radio-Television Malgache [Malagasy Radio and Television] (AF)
RTM	Radio-Television Marocaine [Moroccan Radio and Television] (AF)
RTM	Radio Thrust Misalignment
RTM	[The] Railway Transfer Co. of the City of Minneapolis [AAR code]
RTM	Rapid Tuning Magnetron
RTM	Rassemblement des Travaillistes Mauriciens [Mauritius] [Political party] (EY)
RTM	Real-Time Metric
RTM	Real-Time Monitor [Systems Engineering Labs]
RTM	Receiver-Transmitter-Modulator
RTM	Reconnaissance Tactical Missile
RTM	Recording Tachometer (IEEE)

RTM .... Recovery Termination Management [*Data processing*]
RTM .... Refrigerant Transport Module [*Air-conditioning*] (PS)
RTM .... Regional Transport Model [*Environmental Protection Agency*] (GFGA)
RTM .... Register Transfer Module [*Data processing*] (MDG)
RTM .... Registered Trademark (DEN)
RTM .... Regulatory Technical Memorandum [*Nuclear energy*] (NRCH)
RTM .... Representative Town Meeting
RTM .... Requirements Traceability Matrix
RTM .... Research Technical Memorandum
RTM .... Resin Transfer Molding [*Plastics technology*]
RTM .... Response Time Module
RTM .... Revenue Ton-Miles
RTM .... Room-Temperature Metallizing (SAA)
RTM .... Rotterdam [*Netherlands*] [*Airport symbol*] (OAG)
RTM .... Royal Trust Co. Mortgage Corp. [*Toronto Stock Exchange symbol*]
RTM .... Running Time Meter (AAG)
RTMA ...... Radio and Television Manufacturers Association
RTMAGV ... Royal Thai Military Assistance Group, Vietnam
RTMC ...... Royal Thai Marine Corps (CINC)
RTMD ...... Real-Time Multiplexer Display
RTMOS ..... Real-Time Multiprogramming Operating System [*Data processing*] (IEEE)
RTMP .... Rapid Thermal Melt Processed [*Inorganic chemistry*]
RTMP .... Routing Maintenance Protocol (BYTE)
RTMS .... RADAR Target Measuring System (MCD)
RTMS .... Real-Time Memory System
RTMS .... Real-Time Multiprogramming System
RTMS .... Rocket Thrust Measuring System
RTMSW .... Real-Time DSN [*Deep Space Network*] Monitor Software Assembly [*NASA*]
RTMTR ..... Remote Transmitter (FAAC)
RTN .... North Country Library System, Watertown, NY [*OCLC symbol*] (OCLC)
RTN .... Radial, Tangential, Normal
RTN .... Radio Telescope Network
RTN .... Raton, NM [*Location identifier*] [*FAA*] (FAAL)
RTN .... Raytheon Co. [*NYSE symbol*] (SPSG)
RTN .... Recompression Thermonuclear
RTN .... Recursive Transition Network [*Language analysis*] (BYTE)
RTN .... Registered Trade Name
RTN .... Relative Threat Number [*Military*] (CAAL)
RTN .... Remote Terminal Network
RTN .... Remote Tracking Network
RTN .... Renal Tubule Necrosis [*Medicine*]
RTN .... Report Test Number [*NASA*]
RTN .... Resistor Terminating Network
RTN .... Retain (KSC)
RTN .... Return (AAG)
RTN .... Return to Neuter
RTN .... Rota [*Nicaragua*] [*Seismograph station code, US Geological Survey*] (SEIS)
RTN .... Routine
RTN .... Royal Thai Navy (CINC)
RTN .... RTN: Radio Television News [*A publication*] (APTA)
RTNA ...... Regional Television News Australia
RTN(ARRT) ... Registered Technologist in Nuclear Medicine Technology (American Registry of Radiologic Technologists) (MAE)
RTNB ...... Radio-Television Nationale du Burundi (EY)
RTNC ...... Radio-Television Nationale Congolaise
RTND ...... Retained (FAAC)
RTND ...... Returned
RTNDA ..... Radio-Television News Directors Association (EA)
RTNE ...... Radio Technical New Entrant [*Telecommunications*] (OA)
RTNE ...... Routine (FAAC)
RTNEE ...... Returnee [*Military*]
R/T Net ..... Radio/Telephone Network [*Nuclear energy*] (GFGA)
RTNF ...... Recombinant Tumor Necrosis Factor [*Biochemistry*]
RTNG .... Retaining (MSA)
RTNLB ...... Rationalisierung [*Munich*] [*A publication*]
RTNOBE... Round Table of National Organizations for Better Education (EA)
RTNP .... Red Tag News Publications [*Later, RTNPA*] (EA)
RTNPA ..... Red Tag News Publications Association (EA)
RTNR .... Retainer (MSA)
RTNR .... Ringtone No Reply [*Telecommunications*] (TEL)
RTNS .... Rotating Target Neutron Source [*Nuclear physics*]
RTO .... Radiotelephone Operator
RTO .... Rail Transportation Officer [*Military*]
RTO .... Railway Traffic Officer [*Military*]
RTO .... Range Training Officer (MCD)
RTO .... Reactor Trip Override [*Nuclear energy*] (NRCH)
RTO .... Real-Time Operation
rto .... Recto (BJA)
RTO .... Referred-to-Output
RTO .... Regional Team of Officers [*British*]
RTO .... Regional Telecommunications Office [*DoD*]
RTO .... Regional Training Officer (OICC)
RTO .... Rejected Takeoff [*Aviation*] (MCD)
RTO .... Reliability Test Outline (AAG)

RTO .... Report Time Over [*Aviation*] (FAAC)
RTO .... Request to Off-Load [*Shipping*] (DS)
RTO .... Responsible Test Organization [*NASA*] (MCD)
RTO .... Road Traffic Officer [*British police*]
RTOG .... Radiation Therapy Oncology Group (EA)
RTOK .... Retest OK (MCD)
RTOL .... Reduced Takeoff and Landing [*Aviation*]
RTOL .... Rotary Takeoff and Landing [*Aviation*] (AIA)
RTOP .... Research and Technology Objectives and Plans [*NASA*] (NASA)
RTOP .... Research and Technology Operating [*or Operations*] Plan [*NASA*]
RTOPS ..... Research and Technology Objectives and Plans Summary [*NASA*] [*Information service or system*] (CRD)
RTOR .... Right Turn on Red [*i.e., on red traffic signal*]
RTor.......... Rocznik Torunski [*A publication*]
RTOS........ Real-Time Operating System [*Control Data Corp.*]
RTOS........ Real-Time Optical System (MCD)
RTOT .... Range Track on Target [*Air Force*]
RTOW .... Regulated [*or Restricted*] Takeoff Weight (MCD)
RTP........... Radio Televisao Portuguesa [*Portuguese Radio-Television System*]
RTP........... Rapid Thermal Processing [*Semiconductor technology*]
RTP........... Reactor Thermal Power (IEEE)
RTP........... Real-Time Peripheral (IEEE)
RTP........... Real-Time Position (AAG)
RTP........... Real-Time Profiler [*Instrumentation*]
RTP........... Recruitment and Training Program
RTP........... Reebok Tennis Professional [*Shoes*]
RTP........... Reference Telephonic Power (DEN)
RTP........... Reich & Tang LP [*NYSE symbol*] (SPSG)
RTP........... Reinforced Theatre Plan [*Military*] [*British*]
RTP........... Reinforced Thermoplastics
RTP........... Relative Threat Priority [*Military*] (CAAL)
RTP........... Reliability Test Plan (MCD)
RTP........... Remote Transfer Point
RTP........... Republican Turkish Party [*Cyprus*] [*Political party*]
RTP........... Request to Purchase
RTP........... Request for Technical Proposal [*Military*]
RTP........... Requirement and Test Procedures
RTP........... Research Triangle Park [*North Carolina*]
RTP........... Resistor Test Program
RTP........... Resource Teaching Program (OICC)
RTP........... Reverse Tie Point (KSC)
RTP........... Room-Temperature Phosphorimetry [*Spectrometry*]
RTP........... Rotex Turret Punch
RTP........... Rutland Plains [*Australia*] [*Airport symbol*] [*Obsolete*] (OAG)
RTPA .... Rail Travel Promotion Agency [*Defunct*] (EA)
RTPC........ Real-Time Process Control
RTPC........ Restrictive Trade Practices Commission
RT-PCR .... Reverse Transcription-Polymerase Chain Reaction
RTPCVD ... Rapid Thermal Processing Chemical Vapor Deposition [*Coating technology*] [*Semiconductor technology*]
RTPG........ Rubinstein-Taybi Parent Group (EA)
RTPH .... Round Trips per Hour (MSA)
RTPI .... Royal Town Planning Institute [*British*]
RTPI J ...... Royal Town Planning Institute. Journal [*A publication*]
RTPL .... Real-Time Procedural Language [*Data processing*] (MDG)
RTPLRS ... Real-Time Position Location Reporting System (MCD)
RTPM........ Real-Time Program Management
RTPR........ Reference Theta Pinch Reactor
RTPU........ Rigid Thermoplastic Polyurethane [*Organic chemistry*]
RTQ .... Real-Time Quotes [*Information retrieval*]
RTQ .... Rutter Teacher Questionnaire
RTQA .... Reports Tempore Queen Anne [*11 Modern*] [*England*] [*A publication*] (DLA)
RTQC .... Real-Time Quality Control
RTR .... Le Regiment de Trois-Rivieres [*British military*] (DMA)
R TR.......... Radio Tower
RTR .... Reading Test and Reviews [*A publication*]
RTR .... Real-Time Readout
RTR .... Recovery Temperature Ratio
RTR .... Recreational Therapist Registered
RTR .... Red Blood Cell Turnover Rate [*Hematology*]
RTR .... Reformed Theological Review [*A publication*]
RTR .... Reliability Test Requirements (AAG)
RTR .... Remote Transmitter
RTR .... Repair Time Ratio
RTR .... Repeater Test Rack (DEN)
RTR .... Resonance Test Reactor
RTR .... Response Time Reporting
RTR .... Restoration and Eighteenth Century Theatre Research [*A publication*]
RTR .... Return and Restore Status Register [*Data processing*]
RTR .... Returning to Ramp [*Aviation*] (FAAC)
RTR .... Ribbon-to-Ribbon Regrowth [*of silicon for photovoltaic cells*]
RTR .... Road Traffic Reports [*A publication*] (DLA)
RTR .... Rotor (MSA)
RTR .... Royal Tank Regiment [*Military unit*] [*British*]
Rtr .... Ruth Rabbah (BJA)
RTR .... Ryder Truck Rental

RTRA......... Road Traffic Regulation Act [*Town planning*] [*British*]
RTR(ARRT) ... Registered Technologist in Radiography (American Registry of Radiologic Technologists) (MAE)
RTRC......... Radio and Television Research Council (EA)
RTRC......... Radiotelemetry and Remote Control (MCD)
RTRC......... Regional Teacher Resource Center [*NASA*]
RTRC......... Regional Technical Report Centers [*Department of Commerce*]
RTRCDS ... Real-Time Reconnaissance Cockpit Display System [*or Subsystem*]
RTRD .... Retard (FAAC)
RT Regelungstech ... RT. Regelungstechnik [*West Germany*] [*A publication*]
RTREV...... Right Reverend [*Of an abbot, bishop, or monsignor*]
RTRN .... Return (FAAC)
RTRO .... Real-Time Readout
RTRS .... Real-Time Rescheduling Subsystem
RTRS......... Reuters Holdings Ltd. [*New York, NY*] [*NASDAQ symbol*] (NQ)
RTRSOC ... Real-Time Reporting System on Oceanic Conditions (SSD)
RTRSW ..... Rotary Switch (MSA)
RTRV........ Retrieve (MSA)
RT RV .... Right Reverend [*Of an abbot, bishop, or monsignor*]
RTRY........ Rotary
RTS........... RADAR Target Simulator
RTS........... RADAR Test Set
RTS........... RADAR Test Station (MCD)
RTS........... RADAR Test System
RTS........... RADAR Tracking Station [*Military*]
RTS........... RADAR Tracking System
RTS........... Radial Tuned Suspension (ADA)
RTS........... Radio-Television Scolaire [*French*]
RTS........... Radio Television Seychelles
RTS........... Radio-Television Singapore
RTS........... Radio Wire Broadcasting Network
RTS........... Radiodiffusion-Television du Senegal [*Radio and television network*] [*Senegal*]
RTS........... Radiotelemetry Subsystem
RTS........... Radioteletypewriter Set
RTS........... Rail Transfer System (KSC)
RTS........... Range Time Signal
RTS........... Range Timing System
RTS........... Rapid Transit System (DCTA)
RTS........... Rapid Transmission and Storage [*Goldmark Corp.*] [*TV system*]
RTS........... Ratio Test Set
RTS........... Reactive Terminal Service [*International Telephone & Telegraph computer*]
RTS........... Reactor Trip System [*Nuclear energy*] (NRCH)
RTS........... Readiness Training Squadron [*Military*] (NVT)
RTS........... Ready to Send [*Computer command*] (PCM)
RTS........... Real-Time Simulation
RTS........... Real-Time Subroutines
RTS........... Real-Time Supply [*NASA*] (MCD)
RTS........... Real-Time System
RTS........... Reconnaissance Technical Squadron [*Air Force*] (CINC)
RTS........... Recorded Time Signal
RT/S.......... Refrigeration Technician/Specialist (AAG)
RTS........... Refueling Water Transfer and Storage [*Nuclear energy*] (NRCH)
RTS........... Regional Technical Support [*Military*]
RTS........... Relay Telemetry Subsystem [*NASA*]
RTS........... Relay Test System
RTS........... Religious Tract Society [*British*]
RTS........... Remember That Song (EA)
RTS........... Remote Targeting System
RTS........... Remote Terminal Supervisor (CMD)
RTS........... Remote Test System [*Bell System*]
RTS........... Remote Tracking Site [*Military*]
RTS........... Remote Tracking Station [*NASA*]
RTS........... Renaissance Text Series [*A publication*]
RTS........... Repaired This Station (AFM)
RTS........... Reparatur-Technische Station [*Repair and Technical Station*] [*German*]
RTS........... Request to Send
RTS........... Research and Technical Services [*Military*]
RTS........... Research Test Site (AAG)
RTS........... Resolute Resources [*Vancouver Stock Exchange symbol*]
RTS........... Resolve through Sharing (EA)
RTS........... Return to Search
RTS........... Return to Sender
RTS........... Return to Service [*Aviation*]
RTS........... Return to Stores
RTS........... Return from Subroutine [*Data processing*]
RTS........... Return to Supplier (MCD)
RTS........... Rights [*Stock market term*]
RTS........... River Thames Society [*British*]
RTS........... Rosner Television Systems, Inc. [*New York, NY*] [*Telecommunications*] (TSSD)
RTS........... Rotary Thumbwheel Switch
RTS........... Rottnest Island [*Australia*] [*Airport symbol*] (OAG)
RTS........... Royal Television Society [*British*]
RTS........... Royal Toxophilite Society [*British*]

RTS........... Rural Telephone System [*Telecommunications*] (OA)
RTS........... Russ Togs, Inc. [*NYSE symbol*] (SPSG)
RTSA........ RADAR Target Signature Analysis
RTSA........ Radio Tracking System Analyst (MUGU)
RTSC........ Recommended Test Sequence Chart (MCD)
RTSC........ Replacement and Training School Command [*Military*]
RTSD........ Resources and Technical Services Division [*American Library Association*] [*Later, ALCTS*] (EA)
RTSD........ Royal Thai Survey Department (CINC)
RTSD CCS ... RTSD [*Resources and Technical Services Division*] Cataloging and Classification Section
RTSD LRTS ... RTSD [*Resources and Technical Services Division*] Library Resources and Technical Services [*A publication*]
RTSD PLMS ... RTSD [*Resources and Technical Services Division*] Preservation of Library Materials Section
RTSD RLMS ... RTSD [*Resources and Technical Services Division*] Reproduction of Library Materials Section
RTSD RS... RTSD [*Resources and Technical Services Division*] Resources Section
RTSDS ...... Real-Time Scheduling Display System
RTSD SS ... RTSD [*Resources and Technical Services Division*] Serials Section
RTSF .... Real-Time Simulation Facility [*NASA*] (MCD)
RTSM....... Return to Stock Memo
RTSP .... Real-Time Signal Processor (NVT)
RTSq......... Reconnaissance Technical Squadron [*Air Force*] (AFM)
RTSS .... Real-Time Scientific System
RTSS .... Returning to School Syndrome
RTST .... Radio Technician Selection Test [*Military*]
RTST .... Right Start [*NASDAQ symbol*] (SPSG)
RTSTA ...... Railway Track and Structures [*A publication*]
RTT .... Radet for Teknisk Terminologi [*Norwegian Council for Technical Terminology*] [*Oslo*] [*Information service or system*] (IID)
RTT .... Radiation Therapy Technician
RTT .... Radiation Tracking Transducer
RTT .... Radio Television Tunisien [*Tunisian Radio and Television*] (AF)
RTT .... Radiotelemetric Theodolite
RTT .... Radioteletypewriter
RTT .... Rate of Turntable
RTT .... Receiver Threshold Test (CET)
RTT .... Rectangular Tongue Terminal
RTT .... Regie des Telegraphes et des Telephones [*Belgium*] [*Telecommunications service*] (TSSD)
RTT .... Remote Tuning Technique
RTT .... Requirements Traceability Tool [*Data processing*]
RTT .... Research in Text Theory/Untersuchungen zur Text-Theorie [*A publication*]
RTT .... Resonant Tunneling Transistor [*Electronics*]
RTT .... Return Trip Time
RTT .... Ring Tongue Terminal
RTT .... Rocket-Thrown Torpedo
RTT .... Role-Taking Task
RTTA........ Range Tower Transfer Assembly (KSC)
RTTA........ Ranging Tone Transfer Assembly
RTTAA...... Railway Telegraph and Telephone Appliance Association
RTT(ARRT) ... Registered Technologist in Radiation Therapy Technology (American Registry of Radiologic Technologists) (MAE)
RTTC........ Road Time Trials Council [*Bicycle racing competition*] [*British*]
RTTD .... Real-Time Telemetry Data (MCD)
RTTDS...... Real-Time Telemetry Data System
RTTL........ Rattail [*Metallurgy*]
RTTL........ Real-Time Temporal Logic [*Data processing*]
RTTL........ Running Telltale Light (MSA)
RTTM....... Real-Time Transient Model [*Data processing*]
RTTOS..... Real-Time Tactical Operating System (MCD)
RTTP........ Router Template (AAG)
RTTS........ RADAR Telephone Transmission System
RTTS .... Reaction Torque Temperature Sensitivity
RTTS .... Real-Time Telemetry System
RTTS .... Rover Tester Test Set
RTTV........ Real-Time Television
RTTV........ Research Target and Test Vehicle
RTTY........ Radioteletypewriter
RTU .... RADAR Timing Unit
RTU .... Railroad Telegraphers Union
RTU .... Range Transfer Unit (MCD)
RTU .... Ready to Use
RTU .... Receiver/Transmitter Unit
RTU .... Recovery Task Unit
RTU .... Reinforcement Training Unit [*Army*] (AABC)
RTU .... Remote Terminal Unit
RTU .... Renal Transplant Unit [*National Health Service*] [*British*] (DI)
RTU .... Replacement Training Unit [*Military*]
RTU .... Reserve Training Unit (MCD)
RTU .... Response Test Unit
RTU .... Return to Unit [*Military*] [*British*]
RTU .... Right to Use [*Telecommunications*] (TEL)

RT₃U .... Resin T₃ Uptake [*Endocrinology*]
RT₄U .... Resin T₄ Uptake [*Endocrinology*]
RTUA .... Recognition Technologies Users Association (EA)
RTUM ...... Revolutionary Trade Union Movement [*Czechoslovakia*]
RTv .... Radio-Telephone (Very-High Frequency)
          [*Telecommunications*] (DS)
RTV .... Radiodiffusion-Television (Upper Volta) [*Radio and television*
          network]
RTV .... Real-Time Video
RTV .... Recovery Test Vehicle
RTV .... Reentry Test Vehicle [*Air Force*]
RTV .... Research Test Vehicle
RTV .... Retrieve Resources Ltd. [*Vancouver Stock Exchange symbol*]
RTV .... Returned to Vendor (AAG)
RTV .... Rhodesian Television (AF)
RTV .... Rice Tungro Virus
RTV .... Rocket Test Vehicle (MCD)
RTV .... Room Temperature Vulcanizing (MCD)
RTV .... Rough Terrain Vehicle
RTVA .... Radio Television de Andalucia [*Spain*] (EY)
RTVB....... Rumbo Tools for Visual Bask [*Data processing*]
RTVD .... Radiotelevision Dominicana [*Dominican Radio and*
          Television] [*Dominican Republic*]
RTVE........ Radiotelevision Espanola [*Spanish*]
RTVM ...... Radio Television Madrid [*Spain*] (EY)
RTVMU .... Radiotelevision Murciana [*Spain*] (EY)
RTVP........ Real-Time Video Processing
RTVS........ Radio/Television Services [*Washington State University*]
          [*Pullman*] [*Telecommunications service*] (TSSD)
RTVS .... Real Time Velocimeter System [*Army*] (RDA)
RTVS........ Relay Test and Verification System (MCD)
RTVV........ Radiotelevision Valencia [*Spain*] (EY)
RTW .... Manitoba Reports Tempore Wood [*Canada*] [*A*
          publication] (DLA)
RTW .... Railway Tank Wagon [*British military*] (DMA)
RTW .... Ready-to-Wear [*Clothing*]
RTW .... Right to Work
RTW .... Right Worshipful
RTW .... Round the World
RTWB....... Richardson's Theological Word Book [*A publication*] (BJA)
RTWO....... R-2000 Corp. [*Neptune, NJ*] [*NASDAQ symbol*] (NQ)
RTWS....... Raw Type Write Submodule
R & T WUIS ... Research and Technology Work Unit Information System
          [*Database*] [*Defense Technical Information*
          Center] (CRD)
RTWUS..... Research and Technology Work Unit Summary
RTX .... Rapid Transit Experimental [*Gas-turbine bus*]
RTX .... Real-Time Executive
RTX .... Report Time Crossing [*Aviation*] (FAAC)
RTX .... Revenue Canada Taxation Library [*UTLAS symbol*]
RTY .... Merty [*Australia*] [*Airport symbol*] [*Obsolete*] (OAG)
RTY .... Muscatine, IA [*Location identifier*] [*FAA*] (FAAL)
RTY .... Rarity (WGA)
RTYC........ Royal Thames Yachting Club [*British*]
RTYV........ Rice Transitory Yellowing Virus [*Plant pathology*]
RTZ .... Radio Tanzania Zanzibar
RTZ .... Return-to-Zero [*Recording scheme*]
RTZ .... Ritz Resources Ltd. [*Vancouver Stock Exchange symbol*]
RTZ .... RTZ Corp. [*NYSE symbol*] (SPSG)
RTZ .... RTZ Corp. [*Associated Press abbreviation*] (APAG)
RU............. Are You? [*Communication*]
RU............. Compagnie de Transports Aeriens [*Switzerland*] [*ICAO*
          designator] (FAAC)
Ru.............. Gosudarstvennaia Biblioteka SSR Imeni V. I. Lenina [*Lenin*
          State Library of the USSR], Moscow, Soviet Union
          [*Library symbol*] [*Library of Congress*] (LCLS)
RU............. RADAR Unit (MCD)
RU............. Railway Underwriter
RU............. Rain Umbrella [*An association*] (EA)
RU............. Range Unit
RU............. Range User
RU............. Rat Unit
RU............. Reading of Unknown
RU............. Ready Use [*British*]
RU............. Refrigeration Unit (KSC)
RU............. Regular Unleaded [*Shell Oil Co.*]
RU............. Reinforcement Unit [*British military*] (DMA)
RU............. Relative Unit [*Typography*]
RU............. Release Unit [*Army*] (AABC)
RU............. Remote Unit (NASA)
RU............. Renaissance Universal (EA)
R & U .... Repairs and Upkeep [*Military*]
R & U .... Repairs and Utilities [*Military*]
RU............. Repeat Unit [*Genetics*]
RU............. Replaceable Unit
RU............. Replacement Unit
RU............. Reproducing Unit
RU............. Request/Response Unit [*Data processing*]
RU............. Reserve Unit [*Equal to one US dollar*] [*International finance*]
          [*Former USSR*]
RU............. Resin Uptake [*Endocrinology*]

RU............. Resistance Unit (MAE)
RU............. Respiratory Unit [*Medicine*]
RU............. Retransmission Unit [*RADA*] [*Army*] (RDA)
RU............. Retrograde Urogram [*Medicine*] (MAE)
RU............. Right Upper [*Medicine*]
RU............. Roentgen Unit [*Also, r*] [*Measuring X and gamma radiations*]
RU............. Roussel [*France*] [*Research code symbol*]
Ru............. Rufinus [*Flourished, 1150-86*] [*Authority cited in pre-1607 legal*
          work] (DSA)
RU............. Rugby Union [*Controlling body of British rugby football*]
Ru............. Ruins
RU............. Runic [*Language, etc.*] (ROG)
Ru............. Rural
Ru............. Ruth [*Old Testament book*]
Ru............. Ruthenium [*Chemical element*]
ru............. Rutile [*CIPW classification*] [*Geology*]
RU............. Rutin [*Organic chemistry*]
RU............. Unborrowed Reserves
RU............. University of Rhode Island, Kingston, RI [*Library symbol*]
          [*Library of Congress*] (LCLS)
RU............. Ursuline Nuns of the Congregation of Tildonk, Belgium
          [*Roman Catholic religious order*]
RU-486 ..... Roussel Uclaf "Once-a-Month" Pill [*Contraceptive*]
RUA........... Arua [*Uganda*] [*Airport symbol*] (OAG)
RUA........... Retailer's Uniform Agency
RUA........... Right Upper Arm [*Medicine*]
RUA........... Royal Ulster Academy of Painting, Sculpture, and Architecture
          [*Ireland*]
RUAC .... Remote User Access System [*Telecommunications*]
RUAGA ..... Rubber Age [*A publication*]
Ruakura Farm Conf Proc ... Ruakura Farmers' Conference. Proceedings [*New*
          Zealand] [*A publication*]
Ruakura Farmers Conf Proc ... Ruakura Farmers' Conference. Proceedings [*A*
          publication]
RUAT .... Report upon Arrival Threat [*Army*] (AABC)
RUB .... Revue. Universite de Bruxelles [*A publication*]
RUB .... Rich Urban Biker [*Lifestyle classification*]
RUB .... Rubber (AAG)
RUB .... Rubefacient [*Producing Heat and Redness of the Skin*]
          [*Medicine*] (ROG)
RUB .... Ruber [*Red*] [*Pharmacy*]
RUB .... Ruble [*Monetary unit*] [*Former USSR*]
RUB .... Rubric (DLA)
RUB .... Ruby Mountain Mines [*Vancouver Stock Exchange symbol*]
RuB .... Russkoe Bogatstvo [*A publication*]
RUBAC ..... Relative Universal Business Automation Code
Rubb Board Bull ... Rubber Board. Bulletin [*India*] [*A publication*]
Rubb Chem ... Rubber Chemistry and Technology [*A publication*]
Rubb Dev ... Rubber Developments [*A publication*]
Rubber Age (NY) ... Rubber Age (New York) [*A publication*]
Rubber Age Synth ... Rubber Age and Synthetics [*A publication*]
Rubber Board Bull (India) ... Rubber Board Bulletin (India) [*A publication*]
Rubber Bul ... Rubber Statistical Bulletin [*A publication*]
Rubber Chem & Tech ... Rubber Chemistry and Technology [*A publication*]
Rubber Chem Technol ... Rubber Chemistry and Technology [*A publication*]
Rubber Dev ... Rubber Developments [*A publication*]
Rubber Devs ... Rubber Developments [*A publication*]
Rubber Dev Suppl ... Rubber Developments. Supplement [*A publication*]
Rubber Devts ... Rubber Developments [*A publication*]
Rubber Dig (Tokyo) ... Rubber Digest (Tokyo) [*A publication*]
Rubber Div Symp ... Rubber Division Symposia [*A publication*]
Rubber Ind ... Rubber Industry [*A publication*]
Rubber Ind (London) ... Rubber Industry (London) [*A publication*]
Rubber Ind (NY) ... Rubber Industry (New York) [*A publication*]
Rubber J .... Rubber Journal [*A publication*]
Rubber J Int Plast ... Rubber Journal and International Plastics [*A*
          publication]
Rubber Plant Conf Souvenir ... Rubber Planters' Conference. Souvenir [*A*
          publication]
Rubber Plast ... Rubber and Plastics [*A publication*]
Rubber Plast Age ... Rubber and Plastics Age [*A publication*]
Rubber Plast Wkly ... Rubber and Plastics Weekly [*A publication*]
Rubber Res Inst Ceylon Advis Circ ... Rubber Research Institute of Ceylon.
          Advisory Circular [*A publication*]
Rubber Res Inst Ceylon Annu Rep ... Rubber Research Institute of Ceylon.
          Annual Report [*A publication*]
Rubber Res Inst Ceylon Annu Rev ... Rubber Research Institute of Ceylon.
          Annual Review [*A publication*]
Rubber Res Inst Ceylon Bull ... Rubber Research Institute of Ceylon. Bulletin
          [*A publication*]
Rubber Res Inst Ceylon Q Circ ... Rubber Research Institute of Ceylon.
          Quarterly Circular [*A publication*]
Rubber Res Inst Ceylon Q J ... Rubber Research Institute of Ceylon. Quarterly
          Journal [*A publication*]
Rubber Res Inst Malaya Annu Rep ... Rubber Research Institute of Malaya.
          Annual Report [*A publication*]
Rubber Res Inst Malaya Bull ... Rubber Research Institute of Malaya. Bulletin
          [*A publication*]
Rubber Res Inst Malaya Circ ... Rubber Research Institute of Malaya.
          Circular [*A publication*]

Rubber Res Inst Malaya Plant Bull ... Rubber Research Institute of Malaya. Planters' Bulletin [*A publication*]
Rubber Res Inst Malaya Plant Man ... Rubber Research Institute of Malaya. Planting Manual [*A publication*]
Rubber Res Inst Malaya Q J ... Rubber Research Institute of Malaya. Quarterly Journal [*A publication*]
Rubber Res Inst Malaya Rep ... Rubber Research Institute of Malaya. Report [*A publication*]
Rubber Res Inst Malays Annu Rep ... Rubber Research Institute of Malaysia. Annual Report [*A publication*]
Rubber Res Inst Malays J ... Rubber Research Institute of Malaysia. Journal [*A publication*]
Rubber Res Inst Malays Plant Bull ... Rubber Research Institute of Malaysia. Planters' Bulletin [*A publication*]
Rubber Res Inst Malays Plant Conf Proc ... Rubber Research Institute of Malaysia. Planters' Conference. Proceedings [*A publication*]
Rubber Res Inst Malays Technol Ser Rep ... Rubber Research Institute of Malaysia. Technology Series Report [*A publication*]
Rubber Res Inst (Sri Lanka) Advis Circ ... Rubber Research Institute (Sri Lanka). Advisory Circular [*A publication*]
Rubber Res Inst (Sri Lanka) Annu Rev ... Rubber Research Institute (Sri Lanka). Annual Review [*A publication*]
Rubber Res Inst Sri Lanka Bull ... Rubber Research Institute of Sri Lanka. Bulletin [*A publication*]
Rubber Res Inst Sri Lanka J ... Rubber Research Institute of Sri Lanka. Journal [*A publication*]
Rubber Res Inst (Sri Lanka) Q J ... Rubber Research Institute (Sri Lanka). Quarterly Journal [*A publication*]
Rubber Technol ... Rubber Technology [*A publication*]
Rubber Wld ... Rubber World [*A publication*]
Rubb (India) ... Rubber (India) [*A publication*]
Rubb J .... Rubber Journal and International Plastics [*A publication*]
Rubb News ... Rubber News [*A publication*]
Rubb Plast Age ... Rubber and Plastics Age [*A publication*]
Rubb Plast Fire Flamm Bull ... Rubber and Plastics Fire and Flammability Bulletin [*A publication*]
Rubb Plast News ... Rubber and Plastics News [*A publication*]
Rubb Plast News 2 ... Rubber and Plastics News. 2 [*A publication*]
Rubb Statist Bull ... Rubber Statistical Bulletin [*A publication*]
Rubb World ... Rubber World [*A publication*]
Rub Conv ... Rubinstein on Conveyancing [*5th ed.*] [*1884*] [*A publication*]   (DLA)
RUBD .... Rubberized   (AAG)
RuBeMiA .. Akademiia Nauk Belorusskaia SSR, Fundamemtalnaia Biblioteka Imeni Ia. Kolasa [*Academy of Sciences of the Belorussian SSR, J. Kolasa Fundamental Library*], Minsk, Belorussian SSR, Soviet Union [*Library symbol*] [*Library of Congress*]   (LCLS)
Rubey Vol .. Rubey Volume [*A publication*]
RuBi .... Ruch Biblijny i Liturgiczny [*Cracow*] [*A publication*]
RUBIDIC .. Rubidazone [*Zorubicin*]/DIC [*Dacarbazine*] [*Antineoplastic drug regimen*]
RUBISCO ... Ribulosebisphosphate Carboxylase/Oxygenase [*An enzyme*]
Rubmd .... Rubbermaid, Inc. [*Associated Press abbreviation*]   (APAG)
RUBN .... Russian, Ukrainian, and Belorussian Newspapers [*A bibliographic publication*]
RuBP .... Ribulosebisphosphate [*Also, RDP*] [*Biochemistry*]
RuBPCase ... Ribulosebisphosphate Carboxylase [*An enzyme*]
RuBPC/O .. Ribulosebisphosphate Carboxylase/Oxygenase [*Also, RUBISCO*] [*An enzyme*]
RUBR .... Rubber Research Elastomerics, Inc. [*NASDAQ symbol*]   (NQ)
RU Brux ..... Revue. Universite de Bruxelles [*A publication*]
RUBruxelles ... Revue. Universite de Bruxelles [*Brussels*] [*A publication*]
RUBSG .... Recovery Unit and Base Support Group [*Air Force*]
RUBSH ...... Rubbish
RUBSSO ... Rossendale Union of Boot, Shoe, and Slipper Operatives [*British*]   (DCTA)
Rub Trends ... Rubber Trends [*A publication*]
RUBWA .... Rubber World [*A publication*]
RUC .... Reporting Unit Code [*Data processing*]
RUC .... Riverine Utility Craft [*Vehicle for transporting through shallow water and snow*] [*Navy symbol*]
RUC .... Royal Ulster Constabulary [*British*]
RuC .... Ruperto-Carola [*A publication*]
RUCA .... Russell Cave National Monument
RUCAG ..... Residential Utility Consumer Action Group
RuchBL ...... Ruch Biblijny i Liturgiczny [*Cracow*] [*A publication*]
Ruch L .... Ruch Literacki [*A publication*]
RuchM .... Ruch Muzyczny [*A publication*]
Ruch Muz .. Ruch Muzyczny [*A publication*]
Ruch Prawn Ekon Socjol ... Ruch Prawniczy Ekonomiczny i Socjologiczny [*A publication*]
Rucker .... Rucker's Reports [*43-46 West Virginia*] [*A publication*]   (DLA)
RUCS .... Racial Unconscious [*Psychiatry*]
RUD .... Rudder   (AAG)
RUDAEE ... Report of Unsatisfactory or Defective Airborne Electronic Equipment [*Navy*]
RUDAOE .. Report of Unsatisfactory or Defective Aviation Ordnance Equipment [*Navy*]

RUDD .... Remote Underwater Detection Device [*Navy*]
Rud Glas ... Rudarski Glasnik [*A publication*]
RUDH .... Reserve Shutdown Unplanned Derated Hours [*Electronics*]   (IEEE)
RUDI .... Regional Urban Defense Intercept
RUDI .... Report of Unsatisfactory or Defective Instrumentation [*Navy*]
RUDI .... Restricted Use Digital Instrument   (OA)
RUDICK ... Ruddick Corp. [*Associated Press abbreviation*]   (APAG)
RUDIM ..... Rudimentary   (ROG)
RUDIS .... Reference Your Dispatch   (NOAA)
RUDM .... Report of Unsatisfactory or Defective Material [*Aircraft*] [*Navy*]
RUDMIN .. Report of Unsatisfactory or Defective Mine [*Navy*]   (NG)
RUDMINDE ... Report of Unsatisfactory or Defective Mine, Depth Charge, or Associated Equipment [*Navy*]   (NG)
Rudodobiv Metal ... Rudodobiv i Metalurgiya [*A publication*]
Rudodobiv Metal (Sofia) ... Rudodobiv i Metalurgiya (Sofia) [*Bulgaria*] [*A publication*]
Rudodob Metal ... Rudodobiv i Metalurgiya [*Bulgaria*] [*A publication*]
Rudolstaedter Heimath ... Rudolstaedter Heimathefte Beitraege zur Heimatkunde des Kreises Rudolstaedt [*A publication*]
Rudoobraz Procesi Miner Nakhodisha ... Rudoobrazuvatelni Procesi i Mineralni Nakhodisha [*Sofia*] [*A publication*]
RUDTORPE ... Report of Unsatisfactory or Defective Torpedo Equipment [*Navy*]   (NG)
RUDVA ..... Rubber Developments [*A publication*]
RUDY .... Rudy's Restaurant Group, Inc. [*NASDAQ symbol*]   (NQ)
Rudy Met Niezelaz ... Rudy i Metale Niezelazne [*A publication*]
RUE .... Right Upper Entrance [*A stage direction*]
RUE .... Right Upper Extremity [*Medicine*]
RUE .... Russellville, AR [*Location identifier*] [*FAA*]   (FAAL)
Ruegg Emp L ... Ruegg on Employer's Liability [*9th ed.*] [*1922*] [*A publication*]   (DLA)
RUER .... SSRC [*Social Science Research Council*] Research Unit on Ethnic Relations [*Research center*] [*British*]   (IRC)
RUF .... Minocqua-Woodruff, WI [*Location identifier*] [*FAA*]   (FAAL)
RUF .... Radiation Usage Factor   (MCD)
RUF .... Resource Utilization Factor
RUF .... Revolutionary United Front [*Sierra Leone*] [*Political party*]   (EY)
RUF .... Revolving Underwriting Facility [*Finance*]
RUF .... Rigid Urethane Foam
RUF .... Rough   (FAAC)
Ruf .... Rufinus [*Flourished, 1150-86*] [*Authority cited in pre-1607 legal work*]   (DSA)
RUFAS ..... Remote Underwater Fisheries Assessment System [*National Oceanic and Atmospheric Administration*]
RUFC .... Rugby Union Football Club [*British*]   (DAS)
RUFE .... Zeitschrift fuer Rundfunk und Fernsehen [*Journal for Radio and Television*] [*NOMOS Datapool*] [*Information service or system*]
Ruff .... Ruffhead's Edition of the Statutes, by Serjeant Runnington [*1235-1785*] [*A publication*]   (DLA)
Ruff .... Ruffin and Hawks' Reports [*8 North Carolina*] [*A publication*]   (DLA)
Ruff .... Statutes at Large, Ruffhead's Edition [*England*] [*A publication*]   (DLA)
Ruff Fin Suc Rep ... Howard Ruff's Financial Success Report [*A publication*]
Ruff & H .... Ruffin and Hawks' Reports [*8 North Carolina*] [*A publication*]   (DLA)
Ruffh St ...... Ruffhead's English Statutes [*A publication*]   (DLA)
Ruff St .... Ruffhead's English Statutes [*A publication*]   (DLA)
RUFORM ... Reference Your Form   (FAAC)
RUFP .... Regulations under the Federal Power Act
RUG .... Coronet Carpets, Inc. [*Toronto Stock Exchange symbol*]
RUG .... Recomp Users Group [*Data processing*]
RUG .... Regional User Group [*Data processing*]
RUG .... Resource Utilization Group   (DHSM)
RUG .... Retrograde Ureterogram [*Medicine*]
RUG .... ROSCOE User Group [*Princeton, NJ*]   (CSR)
RUG .... Rugby, ND [*Location identifier*] [*FAA*]   (FAAL)
RUG .... Rutgers-[*The*] State University, Graduate School of Library and Information Science, New Brunswick, NJ [*OCLC symbol*]   (OCLC)
RUGED ..... Rural Georgia [*A publication*]
RUGLA ..... Rudarski Glasnik [*A publication*]
RUH .... Range Users Handbook
RUH .... Riyadh [*Saudi Arabia*] [*Airport symbol*]   (OAG)
RUHP .... Rescue Unit Home Port [*Navy*]   (NVT)
RUI .... Research in Undergraduate Institutions [*A National Science Foundation program*]
RUI .... Royal University of Ireland
RUI .... Ruidoso [*New Mexico*] [*Airport symbol*]   (OAG)
RUI .... Ruidoso, NM [*Location identifier*] [*FAA*]   (FAAL)
RUIA .... Railroad Unemployment Insurance Act   (GFGA)
RUIMB ...... Ruimtevaart [*A publication*]
RUIN .... Regional and Urban Information Network [*Washington, DC*]
Ruin .... [*Carolus*] Ruinus [*Deceased, 1530*] [*Authority cited in pre-1607 legal work*]   (DSA)
RuJ .... Rusky Jazyk [*A publication*]
RUKBA ..... Royal United Kingdom Benevolent Institution

RuKiFrA .... Akademiia Nauk Kirgizskoi SSR, Tsentralnaia Nauchaia Biblioteka [*Academy of Sciences of the Kirghiz SSR, Central Scientific Library*], Frunze, Kirghiz SSR, Soviet Union [*Library symbol*] [*Library of Congress*]   (LCLS)
RuL .... Gosudarstvennaia Publichnaia Biblioteka Imeni Saltykova-Shchedrina [*State Saltikov-Shchedrin Public Library*], Leningrad, Soviet Union [*Library symbol*] [*Library of Congress*]   (LCLS)
RUL .... Representative of the Senate of the University of London   (ROG)
RUL .... Revue. Universite Laval [*Quebec*] [*A publication*]
RUL .... Revue. Universite de Lyon [*A publication*]
RUL .... Right Upper Eyelid [*Medicine*]
RUL .... Right Upper Limb [*Medicine*]
RUL .... Right Upper Lobe [*of lung*] [*Medicine*]
RUL .... Right Upper Lung [*Medicine*]   (MAE)
RUL .... Rikkyo University Library [*UTLAS symbol*]
RUL .... Rule Resources Ltd. [*Vancouver Stock Exchange symbol*]
RUL .... Ruled
RuLA .... Akademiia Nauk SSSR [*Academy of Sciences of the USSR*], Leningrad, Soviet Union [*Library symbol*] [*Library of Congress*]   (LCLS)
Rul Cas ...... Campbell's Ruling Cases [*England*] [*A publication*]   (DLA)
RULE .... Restructuring the Undergraduate Learning Environment [*National Science Foundation*]
RULE .... Rule Industries, Inc. [*NASDAQ symbol*]   (NQ)
Rules Sup Ct ... Rules of the Supreme Court [*A publication*]   (DLA)
RULET ...... Reference Your Letter   (NOAA)
RuLit .... Ruch Literacki [*Krakow*] [*A publication*]
Ru L T ...... Russian Literature Triquarterly [*A publication*]
RuLU-N ..... Leningradskii Universitet, Nauchnaia Biblioteka Imeni Gor'kogo [*Leningrad State University, Gor'kii Scientific Library*], Leningrad, Soviet Union [*Library symbol*] [*Library of Congress*]   (LCLS)
RUM .... Railwaymen's Union of Malaya
RUM .... Remote Underwater Manipulator [*Oceanography*]
RUM .... Remote Unit Monitor   (MCD)
RUM .... Resource Unit Management
RUM .... Resource Utilization Monitor
rum .... Romanian [*MARC language code*] [*Library of Congress*]   (LCCP)
RUM .... Rotary Ultrasonic Machining [*Manufacturing term*]
RUM .... Rumangabo [*Zaire*] [*Seismograph station code, US Geological Survey*]   (SEIS)
RUM .... Rumania
RUM .... Rumjartar [*Nepal*] [*Airport symbol*] [*Obsolete*]   (OAG)
RUM .... San Marcos, TX [*Location identifier*] [*FAA*]   (FAAL)
RUMAS ..... Reserve Unit Manpower Authorization System   (MCD)
RUMC .... Ruby Mining Co. [*NASDAQ symbol*]   (NQ)
RUMEA .... Rudodobiv i Metalurgiya [*A publication*]
RUMEM .... Reference Your Memorandum   (NOAA)
RUMEMO ... Reference Your Memorandum   (FAAC)
RUMES ..... Reference Your Message   (FAAC)
RuMG .... Gosudarstvennaia Publichnaia Nauchno-Tekhnicheskaia Biblioteka SSSR [*State Public Scientific and Technical Library*], Moscow, Soviet Union [*Library symbol*] [*Library of Congress*]   (LCLS)
RUMG .... Revista. Universidade de Minas Gerais [*A publication*]
RuMHi ...... State Public Historical Library, Moscow, Soviet Union [*Library symbol*] [*Library of Congress*]   (LCLS)
RUMIA ..... Rundfunktechnische Mitteilungen [*A publication*]
RuMIN ..... Institut Nauchnoi Informatsii po Obshchestvennym Naukam, Akademiia Nauk SSSR [*Institute of Scientific Information on Social Sciences, Academy of Sciences of the USSR*], Moscow, Soviet Union [*Library symbol*] [*Library of Congress*]   (LCLS)
RUMIN ..... Ruminant
RuMLit ...... Vsesoiuznaia Gosudarstvennaia Biblioteka Inostrannoi Literatury [*All-Union State Library of Foreign Literature*], Moscow, Soviet Union [*Library symbol*] [*Library of Congress*]   (LCLS)
RUMMA ... Russian Metallurgy [*English Translation*] [*A publication*]
Rum Med Rev ... Rumanian Medical Review [*A publication*]
RUMOD .... Regional Underground Monolith Disposal [*Hazardous wastes*]
RuMoKisA ... Akademiia Nauk Moldavskoi SSR, Tsentralnaia Nauchnaia Biblioteka [*Academy of Sciences of the Moldavian SSR, Central Scientific Library*], Kishivev, Moldavian SSR, Soviet Union [*Library symbol*] [*Library of Congress*]   (LCLS)
RUMP .... Radio-Controlled Ultraviolet Measurement Program   (MUGU)
RUMP .... Remote Underwater Marine Probe   (SAA)
RUMPS ..... Raw Umber and Maize Preservation Society [*An association*]
RUMR .... Routine Unsatisfactory Material Report   (MCD)
Rum Sci Abstr ... Rumanian Scientific Abstracts [*A publication*]
RUMUDA ... Reports. USA Marine Biological Institute. Kochi University [*A publication*]
RUN .... Rassemblement pout l'Unite Nationale [*Cameroon*] [*Political party*]   (EY)
RUN .... Reduction Unlimited
RUN .... Reunion Island [*Airport symbol*]   (OAG)
RUN .... Rewind and Unload

RUN .... Rockmaster Resources [*Vancouver Stock Exchange symbol*]
run .... Rundi [*MARC language code*] [*Library of Congress*]   (LCCP)
RUN .... Runstream [*Data processing*]
RUN .... Ruthven [*California*] [*Seismograph station code, US Geological Survey*]   (SEIS)
RUnBrux ... Revue. Universite de Bruxelles [*A publication*]
RUNCIBLE ... Revised Unified New Compiler with Its Basic Language Extended [*Data processing*]
Rundfunk & F ... Rundfunk und Fernsehen [*A publication*]
Rundfunktech Mitt ... Rundfunktechnische Mitteilungen [*A publication*]
RUNDH ..... Reserve Shutdown Unit Derated Hours [*Electronics*]   (IEEE)
RUNEL ..... Runway-End Lighting [*Aviation*]
RUNID ...... Run Identification [*Data processing*]
R Univ Bruxelles ... Revue. Universite de Bruxelles [*A publication*]
R de l'Univ Laval ... Revue. Universite Laval [*A publication*]
R de l'Univ d'Ott ... Revue. Universite d'Ottawa [*A publication*]
R Univ Ottawa ... Revue. Universite d'Ottawa [*A publication*]
R de l'Univ de Sherbrooke ... Revue. Universite de Sherbrooke [*A publication*]
RUnLav ..... Revue. Universite Laval [*A publication*]
Runn .... Runnell's Reports [*38-56 Iowa*] [*A publication*]   (DLA)
Runn .... Statutes at Large, Runnington's Edition [*England*] [*A publication*]   (DLA)
Runn Eject ... Runnington on Ejectment [*2nd ed.*] [*1820*] [*A publication*]   (DLA)
Runnell ...... Runnell's Reports [*38-56 Iowa*] [*A publication*]   (DLA)
Runn Stat ... Runnington on Statutes [*A publication*]   (DLA)
Runn Times ... Running Times [*A publication*]
Runn World ... Runner's World [*A publication*]
RUnOtt ...... Revue. Universite d'Ottawa [*A publication*]
RUNT .... Russian Underground Nuclear Test   (MCD)
RUO .... Revue. Universite d'Ottawa [*A publication*]
RUO .... Right Ureteral Orifice [*Medicine*]
RUOQ ...... Right Upper Outer Quadrant [*Site of injection*] [*Medicine*]
RUOt .... Revue. Universite d'Ottawa [*A publication*]
RU Ottawa ... Revue. Universite d'Ottawa [*A publication*]
RUP .... Raza Unida Party   (EA)
RUP .... Restricted Use Pesticide [*Environmental Protection Agency*]   (GFGA)
RUP .... Rupertsland Resources Co. Ltd. [*Toronto Stock Exchange symbol*]
RUPAA ..... Rubber and Plastics Age [*A publication*]
RUPBX ...... Reference Your Public Branch Exchange Message   (SAA)
Rupert J ...... Rupert Journal [*A publication*]
Rupert Newsl ... Rupert Newsletter [*A publication*]
RUPHO ..... Reference Your Telephone Call   (NOAA)
RUPPERT ... Reserve Unit Personnel Performance Report
Ruppie .... Republican Urban Professional [*Lifestyle classification*]
RUPT .... Interrupt   (NASA)
RUPT .... Rupture   (NASA)
RUQ .... Rifle Unqualified [*Military*]
RUQ .... Right Upper Quadrant [*of abdomen*] [*Medicine*]
RUQ .... Salisbury, NC [*Location identifier*] [*FAA*]   (FAAL)
RUR .... Reference Update Review   (SSD)
RUR .... Resin Uptake Ratio [*Endocrinology*]
RUR .... Rossum's Universal Robots [*Acronym is title of play by Karel Capek*]
RUR .... Royal Ulster Rifles [*Military unit*] [*British*]
RUR .... Rurutu Island [*French Polynesia*] [*Airport symbol*]   (OAG)
rur .... Russian SFSR [*MARC country of publication code*] [*Library of Congress*]   (LCCP)
RUR .... Russkaja Rech' [*A publication*]
Rur Advis Leafl Edinb Sch Agric ... Rural Advisory Leaflet. Edinburgh School of Agriculture [*A publication*]
Rur Afr .... Rural Africana [*A publication*]
Rural Am ... Rural America [*A publication*]
Rural Develop ... Rural Development [*A publication*]
Rural Dev Res Educ ... Rural Development. Research and Education [*A publication*]
Rural Dev Res Rep US Dep Agric Econ Stat Coop Serv ... Rural Development Research Report. United States Department of Agriculture. Economics, Statistics, and Cooperatives Service [*A publication*]
Rural Elec N ... Rural Electrification News [*A publication*]
Rural GA ... Rural Georgia [*United States*] [*A publication*]
Rural Life Res ... Rural Life Research [*A publication*]
Rural Newsl ... Rural Newsletter. Central Coast Agricultural Research and Extension Committee [*A publication*]   (APTA)
Rural N Y ... Rural New Yorker [*A publication*]
Rural Recreat Tour Abstr ... Rural Recreation and Tourism Abstracts [*A publication*]
Rural Res ... Rural Research. Commonwealth Scientific and Industrial Research Organisation [*A publication*]   (APTA)
Rural Res CSIRO ... Rural Research. Commonwealth Scientific and Industrial Research Organisation [*A publication*]
RURALS ... Range Utilization Resources and Allocation Listings   (SAA)
Rural Socio ... Rural Sociology [*A publication*]
Rural Sociol ... Rural Sociology [*A publication*]
RURAX ..... Rural Automatic Exchange [*Telecommunications*]   (TEL)
RURCA ..... Rural Research [*A publication*]
RUREQ ..... Reference Your Requisition   (NOAA)

Rur Ind....... Rural India [*A publication*]
RURLAM ... Replacement Unit Repair Level Analysis Model
Rur Newsl.. Rural Newsletter [*A publication*]   (APTA)
RURP .... Realised Ultimate Reality Piton [*Mountain climbing*]
RURPOP... Rural Population File   (MCD)
Rur Prod ...... Rural Production [*A publication*]
RURQN..... Reference Your Requisition   (FAAC)
Rur Res ...... Rural Research [*A publication*]   (APTA)
Rur Res CSIRO ... Rural Research. Commonwealth Scientific and Industrial
        Research Organisation [*A publication*]   (APTA)
Rur Res CSIRO (Aust) ... Rural Research. Commonwealth Scientific and
        Industrial Research Organisation (Australia) [*A
        publication*]
Rur Sociol .. Rural Sociology [*A publication*]
RURTI....... Recurrent Upper Respiratory Tract Infection
        [*Medicine*]   (ADA)
RUS .... Marau [*Solomon Islands*] [*Airport symbol*]   (OAG)
RUS .... Rapid City, SD [*Location identifier*] [*FAA*]   (FAAL)
RUS .... Rice University. Studies [*A publication*]
RUS .... Rural Uplook Service [*Ithaca, NY*]
RUS .... Russ Berrie & Co. [*NYSE symbol*]   (SPSG)
Rus .... Russell's Election Cases [*1874*] [*Nova Scotia*] [*A
        publication*]   (DLA)
Rus .... Russell's English Chancery Reports [*A publication*]   (DLA)
RUS .... Russia
rus .... Russian [*MARC language code*] [*Library of Congress*]   (LCCP)
RUS .... Rust College, Holly Springs, MS [*OCLC symbol*]   (OCLC)
RUSC........ Rusco Industries, Inc. [*NASDAQ symbol*]   (NQ)
RUSCA....... Rural Sociology [*A publication*]
Rus & C Eq Cas ... Russell and Chesley's Nova Scotia Equity Cases [*A
        publication*]   (DLA)
RUSDIC.... Russian Dictionary [*A publication*]
RUSE........ Rutgers University. Studies in English [*A publication*]
RUSEC....... Romanian-US Economic Council   (EA)
Rus EC....... Russell's Contested Election Cases [*Massachusetts*] [*A
        publication*]   (DLA)
Rus EC....... Russell's Irish Election Reports [*A publication*]   (DLA)
RUSEF ...... Rational Use of the Sea Floor Program [*National Oceanic and
        Atmospheric Administration*]   (MSC)
Rus Elec Rep ... Russell's Election Cases [*1874*] [*Nova Scotia*] [*A
        publication*]   (DLA)
RUSEng..... Rajasthan University. Studies in English [*A publication*]
Rus Eq Rep ... Russell's Nova Scotia Equity Decisions [*A publication*]   (DLA)
Rus ER....... Russell's Election Cases [*1874*] [*Nova Scotia*] [*A
        publication*]   (DLA)
RusF........... Russkij Fol'klor [*A publication*]
RUSH .... Remote User Shared Hardware [*Data processing*]
Rush-Presbyt-St Luke's Med Bull ... Rush-Presbyterian-St. Luke's Medical
        Center. Bulletin [*A publication*]
Rush-Presbyt-St Luke's Med Cent Res Rep ... Rush-Presbyterian-St. Luke's
        Medical Center. Research Report [*A publication*]
Rushw .... Rushworth's Historical Collections [*A publication*]   (DLA)
RUSI......... Journal. Royal United Services Institute for Defence Studies [*A
        publication*]
RUSI......... Royal United Services Institute for Defence Studies [*British*]
Rusk N....... Ruskin Newsletter [*A publication*]
RusL........... Russkaja Literatura [*A publication*]
Rus Ling..... Russian Linguistics [*A publication*]
Rus LT .... Russian Literature Triquarterly [*A publication*]
RUSM .... Royal United Service Museum [*British military*]   (DMA)
RUSNO ..... Resident United States Naval Officer
Rus P......... Russian Pharmacopoeia [*A publication*]
RUSPAND ... Russian-Spanish Dictionary [*A publication*]   (SAA)
RusR .... Russian Review [*A publication*]
RusR .... Russkaja Rech' [*A publication*]
Rus Re....... Russkaja Rech' [*A publication*]
RUSS .... Remote User Service Station   (MCD)
Russ .... Russell's Contested Election Cases [*Massachusetts*] [*A
        publication*]   (DLA)
Russ .... Russell's Election Cases [*1874*] [*Nova Scotia*] [*A
        publication*]   (DLA)
Russ .... Russell's English Chancery Reports [*A publication*]   (DLA)
RUSS........ Russet
RUSS........ Russia
Russ Annu Geol Mineral ... Russian Annual of Geology and Mineralogy [*A
        publication*]
Russ Arb ... Russell on Arbitrators [*A publication*]   (DLA)
RussBr .... Russ Berrie & Co., Inc. [*Associated Press
        abbreviation*]   (APAG)
Russ & C .... Russell and Chesley's Nova Scotia Reports [*10-12 Nova Scotia
        Reports*] [*1875-79*] [*A publication*]   (DLA)
Russ Cast Prod ... Russian Castings Production [*A publication*]
Russ Cast Prod Engl Transl ... Russian Castings Production (English
        Translation) [*A publication*]
Russ & C Eq Cas ... Russell and Chesley's Nova Scotia Equity Cases [*A
        publication*]   (DLA)
Russ Ch...... Russell's English Chancery Reports [*A publication*]   (DLA)
Russ Chem Pharm J ... Russian Chemico-Pharmaceutical Journal [*A
        publication*]
Russ Chem Rev ... Russian Chemical Reviews [*A publication*]

Russ Chem Rev (Engl Transl) ... Russian Chemical Reviews (English
        Translation) [*A publication*]
Russ & Ches ... Russell and Chesley's Nova Scotia Reports [*A
        publication*]   (DLA)
Russ & Ches Eq ... Russell and Chesley's Nova Scotia Equity Reports [*A
        publication*]   (DLA)
Russ Con El (Mass) ... Russell's Contested Election Cases [*Massachusetts*] [*A
        publication*]   (DLA)
Russ Cr ...... Russell on Crimes and Misdemeanors [*A publication*]   (DLA)
Russ Crim .. Russell on Crime [*12th ed.*] [*1964*] [*A publication*]   (DLA)
Russ Crimes ... Russell on Crimes and Misdemeanors [*A publication*]   (DLA)
Russ El Cas ... Russell's Election Cases [*1874*] [*Nova Scotia*] [*A
        publication*]   (DLA)
Russ Elect Cas ... Russell's Contested Election Cases [*Massachusetts*] [*A
        publication*]   (DLA)
Russ Elect Cas ... Russell's Election Cases [*Nova Scotia*] [*A
        publication*]   (DLA)
Russell .... Russell Corp. [*Associated Press abbreviation*]   (APAG)
Russell .... Russell's Nova Scotia Equity Decisions [*A publication*]   (DLA)
Russell-Cotes Mus Bul ... Russell-Cotes Art Gallery and Museum. Bulletin [*A
        publication*]
Russell NS ... Russell's Nova Scotia Equity Decisions [*A publication*]   (DLA)
Russ Eng J ... Russian Engineering Journal [*A publication*]
Russ Eng J (Engl Transl) ... Russian Engineering Journal (English
        Translation) [*A publication*]
Russ En J... Russian Engineering Journal [*A publication*]
Russ & Eq .. Russell and Chesley's Nova Scotia Equity Reports [*A
        publication*]   (DLA)
Russ Eq ...... Russell's Nova Scotia Equity Cases [*A publication*]   (DLA)
Russ Eq Cas ... Russell's Nova Scotia Equity Cases [*A publication*]   (DLA)
Russ Eq Rep ... Russell's Nova Scotia Equity Decisions [*A
        publication*]   (DLA)
Russ Fact ... Russell on Factors and Brokers [*A publication*]   (DLA)
Russ & G.... Russell and Geldert's Nova Scotia Reports [*13-27 Nova Scotia
        Reports*] [*1879-95*] [*Canada*] [*A publication*]   (DLA)
Russ & Geld ... Russell and Geldert's Nova Scotia Reports [*A
        publication*]   (DLA)
Russ Ger Her Sci Technol ... Russian-German Herald of Science and
        Technology [*A publication*]
Russ Hist ... Russian History [*A publication*]
Russian J Physical Chem ... Russian Journal of Physical Chemistry [*A
        publication*]
Russian Math Surveys ... Russian Mathematical Surveys [*A publication*]
Russian R... Russian Review [*A publication*]
Russian Rev ... Russian Review [*A publication*]
Russ & Jap PC ... Russian and Japanese Prize Cases [*London*] [*A
        publication*]   (DLA)
Russ J Inorg Chem ... Russian Journal of Inorganic Chemistry [*A publication*]
Russ J Inorg Chem (Engl Transl) ... Russian Journal of Inorganic Chemistry
        (English Translation) [*A publication*]
Russ J Phys Chem ... Russian Journal of Physical Chemistry [*A publication*]
Russ J Phys Chem (Engl Transl) ... Russian Journal of Physical Chemistry
        (English Translation) [*A publication*]
Russkaia L ... Russkaia Literatura [*A publication*]
Russk Arkh Protist ... Russkii Arkhiv Protistologii [*A publication*]
Russk Med ... Russkaia Meditsina [*A publication*]
Russ-K Min Ges St Petersburg Verh ... Russisch-Kaiserliche Mineralogische
        Gesellschaft zu St. Petersburg. Verhandlungen [*A
        publication*]
Russ Lit...... Russkaja Literatura [*A publication*]
Russ Lit Tr ... Russian Literature Triquarterly [*A publication*]
Russ & M... Russell and Mylne's English Chancery Reports [*1829-33*] [*A
        publication*]   (DLA)
Russ Math Surv ... Russian Mathematical Surveys [*A publication*]
Russ Merc Ag ... Russell on Mercantile Agency [*A publication*]   (DLA)
Russ Met..... Russkaja Meditsina [*A publication*]
Russ Metall ... Russian Metallurgy [*A publication*]
Russ Metall (Engl Transl) ... Russian Metallurgy (English Translation) [*A
        publication*]
Russ Metall Fuels ... Russian Metallurgy and Fuels [*A publication*]
Russ Metall Min ... Russian Metallurgy and Mining [*A publication*]
Russ & My ... Russell and Mylne's English Chancery Reports [*1829-33*] [*A
        publication*]   (DLA)
Russ N Sc... Russell's Nova Scotia Equity Cases [*A publication*]   (DLA)
Russ Pharmacol Toxicol ... Russian Pharmacology and Toxicology [*A
        publication*]
Russ Pharmacol Toxicol (Engl Transl) ... Russian Pharmacology and
        Toxicology (English Translation) [*A publication*]
Russ Physiol J ... Russian Physiological Journal [*A publication*]
Russ & R.... Russell and Ryan's English Crown Cases Reserved [*1799-1823*]
        [*A publication*]   (DLA)
Russ R........ Russian Review [*A publication*]
Russ & RCC ... Russell and Ryan's English Crown Cases Reserved [*168
        English Reprint*] [*1799-1823*] [*A publication*]   (DLA)
Russ & RCC (Eng) ... Russell and Ryan's English Crown Cases Reserved
        [*1799-1823*] [*A publication*]   (DLA)
Russ & R Cr Cas ... Russell and Ryan's English Crown Cases Reserved [*A
        publication*]   (DLA)
Russ Rev .... Russian Review [*A publication*]
Russ Rev Biol ... Russian Review of Biology [*A publication*]

Russ & Ry .. Russell and Ryan's English Crown Cases Reserved [*A publication*]   (DLA)
Russ T Eld ... Russell's English Chancery Reports Tempore Elden [*A publication*]   (DLA)
RUSSWO ... Revised Uniform Summary of Surveyed Weather Observations   (MCD)
Rust .... De Re Rustica [*of Varro*] [*Classical studies*]   (OCD)
RUSTA ...... Rustica [*A publication*]
RUSTAN ... Russian Text Analyzer
RUSTIC .... Regional and Urban Studies Information Center [*Department of Energy*]   (IID)
Rust Prev Control ... Rust Prevention and Control [*A publication*]
RUT .... Remote User Terminal [*Data processing*]   (CAAL)
RUT .... Resource Utilization Time   (NASA)
RUT .... Room Usage Time
RUT .... Rooms Using Television [*Television ratings*]
RUT .... Rubber Trends [*A publication*]
RUT .... Ruta [*Rue*] [*Pharmacy*]   (ROG)
RUT .... Ruth [*Nevada*] [*Seismograph station code, US Geological Survey*] [*Closed*]   (SEIS)
RUT .... Rutland [*Vermont*] [*Airport symbol*]   (OAG)
RUT .... Rutland Railway Corp. [*AAR code*] [*Terminated*]
RUT .... Standard Regional Route Transmitting Frequencies [*Communications*]   (FAAC)
Rut-Cam LJ ... Rutgers-Camden Law Journal [*A publication*]
RUTD .... Rutlandshire [*County in England*]   (ROG)
RUTEL ...... Reference Your Telegram   (FAAC)
Rutg Cas .... Rutger-Waddington Case [*1784*] [*New York City*] [*A publication*]   (DLA)
Rutgers Camden L J ... Rutgers-Camden Law Journal [*A publication*]
Rutgers Comput and Technol Law J ... Rutgers Computer and Technology Law Journal [*A publication*]
Rutgers J Comp & L ... Rutgers Journal of Computers and the Law [*A publication*]
Rutgers J Computers & Law ... Rutgers Journal of Computers and the Law [*A publication*]
Rutgers J Computer Tech and L ... Rutgers Journal of Computers, Technology, and the Law [*A publication*]
Rutgers J Comput & Law ... Rutgers Journal of Computers and the Law [*A publication*]
Rutgers J Comput Technol and Law ... Rutgers Journal of Computers, Technology, and the Law [*A publication*]
Rutgers Jrnl ... Rutgers Computer and Technology Law Journal [*A publication*]
Rutgers LJ ... Rutgers Law Journal [*A publication*]
Rutgers L Rev ... Rutgers Law Review [*A publication*]
Rutgers State Univ Coll Eng Eng Res Bull ... Rutgers State University. College of Engineering. Engineering Research Bulletin [*A publication*]
Rutgers State Univ Coll Eng Eng Res Publ ... Rutgers State University. College of Engineering. Engineering Research Publication [*A publication*]
Rutgers UL Rev ... Rutgers University. Law Review [*A publication*]   (DLA)
Rutgers Univ Annu Res Conf Bur Biol Res ... Rutgers University. Annual Research Conference of the Bureau of Biological Research [*A publication*]
Rutgers Univ Bur Biol Res Annu Conf Protein Metab Proc ... Rutgers University. Bureau of Biological Research. Annual Conference on Protein Metabolism. Proceedings [*A publication*]
Rutgers Univ Bur Biol Res Serol Mus Bull ... Rutgers University. Bureau of Biological Research. Serological Museum. Bulletin [*A publication*]
Rutgers Univ Bur Eng Res Eng Res Publ ... Rutgers University. Bureau of Engineering Research. Engineering Research Publication [*A publication*]
Rutgers Univ Bur Miner Res Bull ... Rutgers University. Bureau of Mineral Research. Bulletin [*A publication*]
Rutgers Univ Coll Eng Eng Res Bull ... Rutgers University. College of Engineering. Engineering Research Bulletin [*A publication*]
Rutg L Rev ... Rutgers Law Review [*A publication*]
Rutherford Appleton Lab Rep RAL ... Rutherford Appleton Laboratory. Report RAL [*A publication*]
Rutherford Appleton Lab Rep RL ... Rutherford Appleton Laboratory. Report RL [*A publication*]
Rutherford Lab Rep ... Rutherford Laboratory. Report [*A publication*]
Rutherford Lab Tech Rep RL ... Rutherford Laboratory. Technical Report RL [*A publication*]
Ruth Inst .... Rutherford's Institutes of Natural Law [*A publication*]   (DLA)
RuthR .... Ruth Rabbah   (BJA)
Rut J Comp L ... Rutgers Journal of Computers, Technology, and the Law [*A publication*]
RUTLDS ... Rutlandshire [*County in England*]
Rut LJ .... Rutgers Law Journal [*A publication*]
Rut LR .... Rutgers Law Review [*A publication*]
RUTOP ..... Rutowski Optimization [*Computer program*]
RuTuAsA ... Akademiia Nauk Turkmenskoi SSR, Tsentralnaia Nauchnaia Biblioteka [*Academy of Sciences of Turkmen SSR, Central Scientific Library*], Ashkhabad, Turkmen, SSR, Soviet Union [*Library symbol*] [*Library of Congress*]   (LCLS)

RUTWX .... Reference Your TWX [*Teletypewriter Communications*]   (FAAC)
RuUk .... Gosudartsvennaia Publichnaia Biblioteka Ukrainskoi SSR [*State Public Library of the Ukrainian SSR*], Kiev, Soviet Union [*Library symbol*] [*Library of Congress*]   (LCLS)
RUUR .... Regrade Unclassified Upon Receipt [*Air Force*]
RUUWS .... Research Underwater-Unmanned Weapons Sensor   (DNAB)
RUV .... Bellefontaine, OH [*Location identifier*] [*FAA*]   (FAAL)
RUV .... Rauvai [*Tuamotu Archipelago*] [*Seismograph station code, US Geological Survey*]   (SEIS)
RUWS .... Remote Unmanned Work System [*Navy*]
RUX .... Baltimore, MD [*Location identifier*] [*FAA*]   (FAAL)
RV .... Israel Aircraft Industries Ltd. [*ICAO aircraft manufacturer identifier*]   (ICAO)
RV .... Rabies Virus
RV .... RADAR Vector   (SAA)
RV .... Radikale Venstre [*Radical Liberals*] [*Denmark*] [*Political party*]   (PPE)
RV .... Radio Vatican [*Vatican State*]   (PDAA)
RV .... Radio Vehicle   (DEN)
RV .... Rahway Valley R. R. [*AAR code*]
RV .... Random Variable [*Statistics*]
R/V .... Range to Velocity [*Ratio of the RADAR platform*]
RV .... Raphanus Virus [*Plant pathology*]
RV .... Rat Virus [*Immunology*]   (MAE)
RV .... Rateable Value [*Property value*] [*British*]
RV .... Rated Voltage
RV .... Raven [*A publication*]
RV .... Reaction Voltage
RV .... Reactor Vessel [*Nuclear energy*]
RV .... Reading and Vocabulary Test [*Also, RVT*] [*Military*]
RV .... Realizable Value   (ADA)
RV .... Rear View [*Technical drawings*]
R/V .... Rear View   (AAG)
RV .... Recipient Value   (GFGA)
RV .... Recirculation Valve   (MCD)
RV .... Recovery Vehicle [*NASA*]   (NASA)
RV .... Recovery Vessel [*NASA*]   (NASA)
RV .... Recreational Vehicle
RV .... Recycling Valve
RV .... Reed Valve [*Automotive engineering*]
RV .... Reentry Vehicle [*Aerospace*]
RV .... Reeve Aleutian Airways, Inc. [*ICAO designator*]   (OAG)
RV .... Reeves MacDonald Mines [*Vancouver Stock Exchange symbol*]
RV .... Reference Voltage
RV .... Refugee Voices, a Ministry with Uprooted Peoples   (EA)
RV .... Reinforcement Value [*Psychology*]
RV .... Relaxation Volume   (MAE)
RV .... Release Valve [*Nuclear energy*]   (NRCH)
RV .... Released Value [*Freight*]
RV .... Relief Valve
RV .... Remaining Velocity [*Ballistics*]
RV .... Renal Vessel [*Medicine*]
RV .... Rendezvous
RV .... Rendezvous Vehicle [*NASA*]   (KSC)
RV .... Rescue Vessel
RV .... Research Vehicle
RV .... Research Vessel
RV .... Residual Variance
RV .... Residual Volume [*Physiology*]
RV .... Respiratory Volume [*Medicine*]   (MAE)
RV .... Retrieval Vessel   (NASA)
RV .... Retroversion
RV .... Retrovirus
Rv .... Revelation [*New Testament book*]
RV .... Reverberation Time
Rv .... Revised [*Regulation or order revised*] [*Used in Shepard's Citations*] [*Legal term*]   (DLA)
RV .... Revised Version [*of the Bible, 1881*]
RV .... Rheinische Vierteljahresblaetter [*A publication*]
RV .... Rifle Volunteers
RV .... Right Ventricle [*of heart*] [*Cardiology*]
RV .... Robotic Vehicle   (RDA)
RV .... Rod Valgallianse [*Red Electoral Alliance*] [*Norway*]   (PPE)
RV .... Routine Verification   (SSD)
RV .... Roving Vehicle [*NASA*]
RV .... Rubella Virus
RV .... Runway Visibility [*Aviation*]   (AFM)
RV .... Russell Viper [*Time*]   (MAE)
RV .... RV: Recreational Vehicles [*A publication*]   (APTA)
RVA .... Farafangana [*Madagascar*] [*Airport symbol*]   (OAG)
RVA .... Raven Air [*Anchorage, AK*] [*FAA designator*]   (FAAC)
RVA .... Reactive Volt-Ampere Meter
RVA .... Recorded Voice Announcement [*Telecommunications*]   (IBMDP)
RVA .... Red-Figured Vases of Apulia [*A publication*]
RVA .... Regular Veterans Association of the United States   (EA)
RVA .... Relative Virtual Address
RVA .... Relative Volt-Ampere
RVA .... Reliability Variation Analysis
RVA .... Remote Voltage Adjustment

RVA .... Rib-Vertebra Angle [*Anatomy*]
RVA .... Right Ventricular Assistance [*Cardiology*]
RVA .... Right Visual Acuity [*Medicine*]
RVA .... Roberts Wesleyan College, K. B. Keating Library, Rochester, NY [*OCLC symbol*] (OCLC)
RVAAP ...... Ravenna Army Ammunition Plant (AABC)
RVACS ...... Reactor Vessel Auxiliary Cooling System
RVAD .... Rib-Vertebra Angle Difference [*Anatomy*]
RVAH .... Reconnaissance Attack Squadron [*Navy*] (NVT)
RVANCS ... Remote View Airborne Night Classification System
RVARM .... Recording Varmeter (MSA)
RVAS .... Records. Victorian Archaeological Survey [*A publication*] (APTA)
RVAT .... Retinal Visual Acuity Tester [*Ophthalmology*]
RVAV .... Regulating Valve Actuating Valve (KSC)
RVAW ...... Readiness Patrol Squadron [*Navy*] (NVT)
RVB .... RADAR Video Buffer
RVB .... Rear Vacuum Break [*Automotive engineering*]
RVB .... Red Venous Blood [*Hematology*] (MAE)
RVB .... Resonating Valence Bond [*Physical chemistry*]
RVB .... Rheinische Vierteljahresblaetter [*A publication*]
RVB .... Rochester Gas & Electric Corp., TIC Library, Rochester, NY [*OCLC symbol*] (OCLC)
RVB .... Royal Veteran Battalion [*British military*] (DMA)
RVBR .... Riveting Bar [*Tool*] (AAG)
RV Bsns ..... Recreational Vehicle Business [*A publication*]
RVC .... RADAR Video Controller [*Military*] (CAAL)
RVC .... Ramakrishna - Vivekananda Center (EA)
RVC .... Random Vibration Control
RVC .... Relative Velocity Computer
RVC .... Remote-Voice Control
RVC .... Reticulated Vitreous Carbon
RVC .... Retired Volunteer Coordinator
RVC .... Review of Economic Studies [*Edinburgh*] [*A publication*]
RVC .... Rifle Volunteer Corps [*Military unit*] [*British*]
RVC .... RNA [*Ribonucleic Acid*] Virus Capsid
RVC .... Rochester General Hospital Library, Rochester, NY [*OCLC symbol*] (OCLC)
RVC .... Rotary Voice Coil [*Computer technology*]
RVC .... Royal Veterinary College [*British*]
RVC .... Royal Victorian Chain
RVCC .... Reeves Communication Corp. [*NASDAQ symbol*] (NQ)
RVCCB ...... Reviews on Coatings and Corrosion [*A publication*]
RVCDA ..... Recreational Vehicle Club Directors of America (EA)
RVCF .... Remote Vehicle Checkout Facility [*NASA*] (NASA)
RVCI .... Royal Veterinary College of Ireland
RVCM ...... Recent Vertical Crustal Movement [*Geology*]
RVCM ...... Republic of Vietnam Campaign Medal [*Military decoration*]
RVCV .... Raspberry Vein Chlorosis Virus [*Plant pathology*]
RVD .... Dutchess County Mental Health Center, Poughkeepsie, NY [*OCLC symbol*] [*Inactive*] (OCLC)
RVD .... RADAR Video Digitizer
RVD .... Relative Vertebral Density
RVD .... Remote Virtual Disk [*Data processing*]
RVD .... Residual Vapor Detector (NATG)
RVD .... Right Ventricular Dimension [*Cardiology*]
RVD .... Right Ventricular Dysfunction [*Medicine*]
RVD .... Royal Victoria Dock [*British*] (ROG)
RVDA .... Recreation Vehicle Dealers Association of North America (EA)
RV Dealer .. Recreational Vehicle Dealer [*A publication*]
RVDO .... Right Ventricular Diastolic Overload [*Cardiology*] (AAMN)
RVDP .... RADAR Video Data Processor
RVDP .... Relief Valve Discharge Piping [*Nuclear energy*] (NRCH)
RVDT .... Rotary Variable Differential Transducer [*or Transformer*]
RVDT .... Rotational Voltage Displacement Transmitter
RVE .... RADAR Video Extractor
RVE .... Representative Volume Element
RVE .... Right Ventricular Enlargement [*Cardiology*]
RVE .... Rochester Institute of Technology, Wallace Memorial Library, Rochester, NY [*OCLC symbol*] (OCLC)
RVE .... Royce Ventures Ltd. [*Vancouver Stock Exchange symbol*]
RVE .... Saravena [*Colombia*] [*Airport symbol*] (OAG)
RVED-CMP ... Right Ventricular End-Diastolic Compliance [*Cardiology*]
RVEDP ...... Right Ventricular End-Diastolic Pressure [*Cardiology*]
RVEDPI ..... Right Ventricular End-Diastolic Pressure Index [*Cardiology*]
RVEDV ..... Right Ventricle End-Diastolic Volume [*Cardiology*]
RVEE .... Holiday RV Superstores, Inc. [*NASDAQ symbol*] (NQ)
RVER .... Regional Veterans Employment Representative [*Department of Labor*]
RVESV ...... Right Ventricular End-Systolic Volume [*Cardiology*]
RVETA5 .... Refuah Veterinarith [*A publication*]
R Vet Agric Univ Steril Res Inst Annu Rep ... Royal Veterinary and Agricultural University. Sterility Research Institute. Annual Report [*A publication*]
R Vet Agric Univ Yearb (Copenhagen) ... Royal Veterinary and Agricultural University. Yearbook (Copenhagen) [*A publication*]
RvEx .... Review and Expositor [*A publication*]
RVF .... Rate Variance Formula [*Air Force*]
RVF .... Rift Valley Fever
RVF .... Right Visual Field [*Psychometrics*]

RVF .... Rochester Psychiatric Center Library, Rochester, NY [*OCLC symbol*] (OCLC)
RVFN .... Report of Visit of Foreign Nationals (AAG)
RVFV .... Rift Valley Fever Virus [*Medicine*]
RVFX .... Rivet Fixture (AAG)
RVG .... Chicago, IL [*Location identifier*] [*FAA*] (FAAL)
RVG .... Reference-Voltage Generator
RVG .... Right Ventral Gluteal [*Injection site*]
RVG .... Right Visceral Ganglion [*Medicine*]
RVG .... Rotating Vertical Gradiometer
RVG .... Rumrill-Hoyt Corp., Library, Rochester, NY [*OCLC symbol*] (OCLC)
RV/GC .... Reentry Vehicle and Ground Control [*NASA*] (KSC)
RVGG .... Rotating Vertical Gravity Gradiometer
RVGPA ...... Reviews of Geophysics [*Later, Reviews of Geophysics and Space Physics*] [*A publication*]
RVH .... Renovascular Hypertension [*Medicine*]
RVH .... Reserve Veterinary Hospital [*British military*] (DMA)
RVH .... Right Ventricular Hypertrophy [*Cardiology*]
RVH .... St. Bernard's Seminary and College Library, Rochester, NY [*OCLC symbol*] (OCLC)
RVI .... Recorded Video Imaging (MCD)
RVI .... Recreational Vehicle Institute
RVI .... Relative Value Index [*Medicine*] (MAE)
RVI .... Renault Vehicules Industriels
RVI .... Reverse Interrupt Character [*Keyboard*]
RVI .... Saint Mary's Hospital, Medical Library, Rochester, NY [*OCLC symbol*] (OCLC)
RVIA .... Recreation Vehicle Industry Association (EA)
RVIAJ .... Royal Victorian Institute of Architects. Journal [*A publication*]
RVIMI .... Rubella Virus-Induced Mitotic Inhibitor
RVIS .... Reactor and Vessel Instrumentation System [*Nuclear energy*] (NRCH)
RVJ .... Reidsville, GA [*Location identifier*] [*FAA*] (FAAL)
RVJ .... Sear-Brown Associates Information Center Library, Rochester, NY [*OCLC symbol*] (OCLC)
RVJS .... Reentry Vehicle Jamming Simulator [*Army*]
RVK .... Sybron Corp., Medical Products Division Library, Rochester, NY [*OCLC symbol*] (OCLC)
RVL .... Reedsville, PA [*Location identifier*] [*FAA*] (FAAL)
RVL .... Revell-Monogram Inc. [*AMEX symbol*] (SPSG)
RVL .... Revere Resources [*Vancouver Stock Exchange symbol*]
RVL .... Rolling Vertical Landing (MCD)
RVL .... Royal Viking Line [*Kloster Cruises of Norway*]
RVL .... Sybron Corp., Pfaudler Division Technical Library, Henrietta, NY [*OCLC symbol*] (OCLC)
RVLA .... Roanoke Valley Library Association [*Library network*]
RVLG .... Revolving
RVLG .... Right Ventrolateral Gluteal [*Site of injection*] [*Medicine*]
RVLI .... Raksti. Latvijas PSR Zinatnu Akademija. Valodas und Literatura Instituta [*A publication*]
RVLIS .... Reactor Vessel Water Level Indication System (IEEE)
RVLR .... Revolver [*Military*] (AABC)
RVLV .... Revolve (MSA)
RVM .... Reactive Voltmeter
RVM .... Reentry Vehicle Module [*NASA*] (KSC)
RVM .... Repertoire de Vedettes-Matiere [*Laval Subject Authority Records*] [*UTLAS symbol*]
RVM .... Residual Volatile Matter [*Chemistry*]
RVm .... Revised Version [*of the Bible*], Margin
RVM .... Rio Vista Mine [*California*] [*Seismograph station code, US Geological Survey*] (SEIS)
RVM .... Sybron Corp., Taylor Division Research Library, Rochester, NY [*OCLC symbol*] (OCLC)
RVMR .... Routine Unsatisfactory Material Report
RVN .... Republic of Vietnam
RVN .... Requirements Verification Network [*NASA*] (NASA)
RVN .... Retrolabyrinthine Vestibular Neurectomy [*Medicine*]
RVN .... Rogersville, TN [*Location identifier*] [*FAA*] (FAAL)
RVN .... Rovaniemi [*Finland*] [*Airport symbol*] (OAG)
RVN .... Women's Career Center Library, Rochester, NY [*OCLC symbol*] (OCLC)
RVNAF ...... Republic of Vietnam Air Force
RVNAF ...... Republic of Vietnam Armed Forces
RVNAFHMFC ... Republic of Vietnam Armed Forces Honor Medal, First Class [*Military decoration*]
RVNAFHMSC ... Republic of Vietnam Armed Forces Honor Medal, Second Class [*Military decoration*]
RVNCAMFC ... Republic of Vietnam Civil Actions Medal, First Class [*Military decoration*]
RVNCAMSC ... Republic of Vietnam Civil Actions Medal, Second Class [*Military decoration*]
RVNCAMUC ... Republic of Vietnam Civil Actions Medal, Unit Citation [*Military decoration*] (GFGA)
RVNCM ... Republic of Vietnam Campaign Medal [*Military decoration*]
RVNF .... Republic of Vietnam Forces
RVNGCUC ... Republic of Vietnam Gallantry Cross, Unit Citation [*Military decoration*] (GFGA)
RVNGCUCW/P ... Republic of Vietnam Gallantry Cross Unit Citation with Palm [*Military decoration*]
RVNMC .... Republic of Vietnam Marine Corps

RVNN........ Republic of Vietnam Navy
RVNT .... Reentry Vehicle Nosetip [*Aerospace*]   (MCD)
RVO........... Aquinas Institute Library, Rochester, NY [*OCLC symbol*]   (OCLC)
RVO........... Lubbock, TX [*Location identifier*] [*FAA*]   (FAAL)
RVO........... Regional Veterinary Officer [*British*]
RVO........... Relaxed Vaginal Outlet [*Medicine*]
RVO........... Royal Victorian Order
RVO........... Runway Visibility Observer [*Aviation*]   (FAAC)
RVOT .... Right Ventricular Outflow Tract [*Cardiology*]
RVP .... Avon Junior/Senior High School Library, Avon, NY [*OCLC symbol*]   (OCLC)
RVP .... RADAR Video Processor [*Military*]   (CAAL)
RVP .... Raster-to-Vector Processor [*Computer graphics technology*]
RVP .... RCA Video Productions
RVP .... Red Veterinary Petrolatum   (MAE)
RVP .... Reid Vapor Pressure
RVP .... Renal Venous Pressure   (OA)
RVP .... Reutilization Value Percentage [*DoD*]
RVP .... Roll Vertical Pendulum   (SAA)
RVP .... Rotary Vacuum Pump
RVPA........ Rivet Pattern   (AAG)
RVPMB.... Review of Psychology of Music [*A publication*]
RVQ........... Benjamin Franklin High School Library, Rochester, NY [*OCLC symbol*]   (OCLC)
RVR .... Bishop Kearney High School Library, Rochester, NY [*OCLC symbol*]   (OCLC)
RVR .... Cruise America [*AMEX symbol*]   (SPSG)
RVR .... RADAR Video Recorder
R & VR....... Rating and Valuation Reporter [*A publication*]
RVR .... Reactor Visual Range   (HGAA)
RVR .... Renal Vascular Resistance [*Medicine*]
RVR .... Resistance to Venous Return [*Medicine*]   (MAE)
RVR .... Response Vacuum Reducer [*Mechanical engineering*]
RVR .... Reverse Velocity Rotor
RVR .... Rim Vent Release [*Safety device for aerosol containers*]
RVR .... River   (FAAC)
RVR .... Riverside [*California*] [*Seismograph station code, US Geological Survey*]   (SEIS)
RVR .... Runway Visual Range [*Aviation*]
RVRA .... Recreation Vehicle Rental Association   (EA)
RV/RA....... Renal Vein/Renal Activity [*Ratio*] [*Medicine*]
RVRA .... Renal Venous Renin Assay [*Medicine*]   (MAE)
RVRA .... Runway Visual Range Average [*Aviation*]   (FAAC)
RVRANO .. Runway Visual Range Average Not Available [*Aviation*]   (FAAC)
RVRC........ Renal Vein Renin Concentration [*Medicine*]
RVRM .... Runway Visual Range Midpoint [*Aviation*]
RVRNO ..... Runway Visual Range Not Available [*Aviation*]   (FAAC)
RVRR .... Runway Visual Range Rollout [*Aviation*]   (FAAC)
RVRRNO .. Runway Visual Range Rollout Not Available [*Aviation*]   (FAAC)
RVRS........ Runway Vision Range System [*Aviation*]   (DWSG)
RVRT........ Runway Visual Range Touchdown [*Aviation*]   (FAAC)
RVRTNO .. Runway Visual Range Touchdown Not Available [*Aviation*]   (FAAC)
RVRU .... RADAR Video Recorder Unit
RVS........... Brighton High School Library, Rochester, NY [*OCLC symbol*]   (OCLC)
RVS........... Radius Vector Subroutine
RVS........... Reentry Vehicle Separation [*Aerospace*]   (MUGU)
RVS........... Reentry Vehicle Simulator [*Aerospace*]   (AAG)
RVS........... Relative Value Scale [*or Schedule or Study*] [*Medicine*]
RVS........... Remote Viewing System
RVS........... Reported Visual Sensation [*Medicine*]   (MAE)
RVS........... Requirements Validation Study   (MCD)
RVS........... Research Vessel Service [*British*]   (IRUK)
RVS........... Reverse   (MSA)
RVS........... Revise   (FAAC)
RVS........... Riverside Mountains [*California*] [*Seismograph station code, US Geological Survey*]   (SEIS)
RVS........... Rocketborne Vacuum System
RVS........... Tulsa, OK [*Location identifier*] [*FAA*]   (FAAL)
RVSBL .... Reversible   (MSA)
RVSE....... Reverse   (AABC)
RVSFC ...... Ricky and Vince Smith Fan Club   (EA)
RVSS .... Reactor Vessel Support System   (IEEE)
RVSSC..... Reverse Self Check   (AAG)
RVST....... Russel Viper Serum Time [*Clinical chemistry*]
RVSVP ..... Repondez Vite, s'Il Vous Plait [*Please Reply at Once*] [*French*]
RVSW..... Right Ventricular Stroke Work [*Cardiology*]
RVSWI..... Right Ventricular Stroke Work Index [*Cardiology*]
RVSZ....... Riveting Squeezer [*Tool*]   (AAG)
RVT .... Brockport High School Library, Brockport, NY [*OCLC symbol*]   (OCLC)
RVT .... Reading and Vocabulary Test [*Also, RV*] [*Military*]
RVT .... Reliability Verification Tests
RVT .... Renal Vein Thrombosis [*Medicine*]
RVT .... Resource Vector Table [*Data processing*]   (IBMDP)
RVT .... Rivet   (MSA)
RVT .... Royce Value Trust, Inc. [*NYSE symbol*]   (SPSG)

RVTC........ Rochester Volunteer Training Corps [*British military*]   (DMA)
RVTD .... Riveted   (MSA)
RVTK....... Revotek, Inc. [*NASDAQ symbol*]   (NQ)
RV/TLC .... Residual Volume/Total Lung Capacity Ratio [*Physiology*]   (MAE)
RVTO .... Reentry Vehicle Test and Observables [*Air Force*]
RVTOL...... Rolling Vertical Takeoff and Landing [*Aviation*]   (MCD)
RVTSA ..... Research in Veterinary Science [*A publication*]
RVU.......... Caledonia-Mumford Junior/Senior High School Library, Caledonia, NY [*OCLC symbol*]   (OCLC)
RVU.......... Relative Value Unit
RVU.......... Relief Valve Unit
RVV .... Cardinal Mooney High School Library, Rochester, NY [*OCLC symbol*]   (OCLC)
RVV .... Regional Vascular Volume [*Hematology*]
RVV .... Religionsgeschichtliche Versuche und Vorarbeiten [*A publication*]
RVV .... Romanistische Versuche und Vorarbeiten [*A publication*]
RVV .... Rubella Vaccine-Like Virus   (AAMN)
RVV .... Runway Visibility Values [*Aviation*]
RVVNO...... Runway Visibility Not Available [*Aviation*]   (FAAC)
RVW .... Charles H. Roth High School Library, Henrietta, NY [*OCLC symbol*]   (OCLC)
RVW .... Ralph Vaughan Williams [*British composer, 1872-1958*]
RVW .... Right Ventricular Weight [*Cardiology*]
RVW .... Riverwood International Corp. [*NYSE symbol*]   (SPSG)
RVX .... Charlotte Junior/Senior High School Library, Rochester, NY [*OCLC symbol*]   (OCLC)
RVX .... Reentry Vehicle, Experimental [*Aerospace*]
RVX .... Robot Vehicle Expressway
RVY .... Churchville-Chili Senior High School Library, Rochester, NY [*OCLC symbol*]   (OCLC)
RVY .... Clarksville Flying Service, Inc. [*Clarksville, AR*] [*FAA designator*]   (FAAC)
RVY .... Rivera [*Uruguay*] [*Airport symbol*]   (OAG)
RVZ .... Dansville Senior High School Library, Dansville, NY [*OCLC symbol*]   (OCLC)
RW............. Hughes Air Corp. [*ICAO designator*]   (ICDA)
RW............. R. Warren [*Pseudonym used by Charles Ashton*]
RW............. Race Weight [*of a horse*]
RW............. Radiation Weapon   (AAG)
RW............. Radical Women   (EA)
RW............. Radiological Warfare
RW............. Radiological Warhead
RW............. Radiological Weapons
RW............. Ragweed [*Immunology*]
R & W .... Rail and Water [*Shipping*]
RW............. Rail and Water [*Shipping*]
RW............. Railway
RW............. Rain Showers [*Meteorology*]   (FAAC)
RW............. Ramo Wooldridge [*Later, TRW, Inc.*]
R/W .... Ramo-Wooldridge-Thompson Corp. [*Later, TRW, Inc.*]   (AAG)
RW............. Random Walk
RW............. Random Widths [*Lumber*]
RW............. Raw Water [*Nuclear energy*]
RW............. RAWINSONDE [*Radiosonde and RADAR Wind Sounding*] [*Upper air observation*]
R-W........... Read-Write [*Data processing*]   (MSA)
RW............. Real Wages [*Economics*]
R d W .... Rechtsarchiv der Wirtschaft [*A publication*]
RW............. Rechtswissenschaft [*Jurisprudence*] [*German*]   (ILCA)
RW............. Reclaimed Wheat Grass Cover [*Agriculture*]
RW............. Reconnaissance Wing [*Military*]
R(W)........... Reconstruction, Workmen's Compensation [*British*] [*World War II*]
RW............. Recreation and Welfare [*Navy*]
RW............. Recruiting Warrant
RW............. Red-Bellied Woodpecker [*Ornithology*]
RW............. Reduced Weight   (DCTA)
RW............. Reel and Wheel [*Freight*]
RW............. Reformed World [*A publication*]
RW............. Region Wide [*Forestry*]
RW............. Regions of the World [*A publication*]
RW............. Relative Worth   (MCD)
R/W .... Report Writer [*Data processing*]
RW............. Republic Airlines West, Inc. [*ICAO designator*]   (FAAC)
RW............. Resistance Welding   (IEEE)
RW............. Response Word   (NASA)
RW............. Restaurant Wine [*License*]
RW............. Retail World [*A publication*]
R/W .... Returned to Work
RW............. Reverse Work   (WGA)
RW............. Reverse Wound   (MCD)
RW............. Review
RW............. Rewind
RW............. Richardsons Westgarth [*Commercial firm*] [*British*]
RW............. Rideal-Walter Coefficient [*Pharmacy*]
R of W .... Right of Way
RW............. Right of Way
RW............. Right Wing

RW............ Right Worshipful
RW.............. Right Worthy
RW.............. River Water [*Nuclear energy*]   (NRCH)
RW.............. Riveted and Welded [*Shipping*]   (DS)
RW.............. Rotary Wing [*Aircraft designation*]
RW.............. Rough Weather [*A publication*]
R & W........ Routing and Work [*Military*]
RW.............. Rowa-Wagner KG [*Germany*] [*Research code symbol*]
RW.............. Royal Warrant [*British*]   (ADA)
RW.............. Royal Warwickshire Regiment [*Military unit*] [*British*]
RW.............. Runner's World [*A publication*]
RW.............. Runway [*Aviation*]
rw .... Rwanda [*MARC country of publication code*] [*Library of Congress*]   (LCCP)
RW.............. Rwanda [*ANSI two-letter standard code*]   (CNC)
RWA.......... E. J. Wilson High School Library, Spencerport, NY [*OCLC symbol*]   (OCLC)
RWa........... George Hail Free Library, Warren, RI [*Library symbol*] [*Library of Congress*]   (LCLS)
RWA.......... RADWASTE [*Radioactive Waste*] Area [*Nuclear energy*]   (NRCH)
RWA.......... Railway Wheel Association [*Defunct*]   (EA)
RWA.......... Raoul Wallenberg Association [*See also RWF*]   (EA)
RWA.......... Reaction Wheel Assembly   (MCD)
RWA.......... Rectangular Wave-Guide Assembly
RWA.......... Regional Water Authority [*British*]
RWA.......... Rippled Wall Amplifier
RWA.......... Romance Writers of America   (EA)
RWA.......... Rotary Wing Aircraft
RWA.......... Royal West of England Academy
RWA.......... Rwanda [*ANSI three-letter standard code*]   (CNC)
RWAFF.... Royal West African Frontier Force [*Military unit*] [*British*]
RWAGE.... Ragweed Antigen E [*Immunology*]
RWAH...... Rotor Wing Agricultural Hours [*Aviation*]   (AIA)
RWAHSJ.. Royal Western Australian Historical Society. Journal [*A publication*]   (ADA)
RWAMD... Radioactive Waste Management [*A publication*]
RWar .... Warwick Public Library, Warwick, RI [*Library symbol*] [*Library of Congress*]   (LCLS)
RWARF.... Royal Warwickshire Fusiliers [*British military*]   (DMA)
RWarR....... Rhode Island Junior College, Knight Campus, Warwick, RI [*Library symbol*] [*Library of Congress*]   (LCLS)
R War R..... Royal Warwickshire Regiment [*Military unit*] [*British*]   (DMA)
RWASG..... Radiation Weapons Analysis Systems Group   (SAA)
RWAVA ... Rheinisch-Westfaelische Akademie der Wissenschaften Natur-, Ingenieur-, und Wirtschaftswissenschaften. Vortraege [*A publication*]
RWAW...... United Union of Roofers, Waterproofers, and Allied Workers
RWB......... Rear Wheel Brake
RWB......... Rod Withdrawal Block [*Nuclear energy*]   (NRCH)
RWB......... Roger Williams College, Bristol, RI [*OCLC symbol*]   (OCLC)
RWB......... Royal Winnipeg Ballet
RWBH....... Records Will Be Handcarried [*Army*]   (AABC)
RWBN...... Red and White Beacon [*Nautical charts*]
RWC......... East Junior/Senior High School Library, Rochester, NY [*OCLC symbol*]   (OCLC)
RWC......... Radioactive Waste Campaign   (EA)
RWC......... Rainwater Conductor   (AAG)
RWC......... Raw Water Cooling
RWC......... Reactor Water Cleanup [*Nuclear energy*]   (NRCH)
RWC......... Read, Write, and Compute
RWC......... Read-Write-Continue [*Data processing*]
RWC......... Relative Water Content
RWC......... Remote Workcenter
RWC......... Residential Wood Combustion
RWC......... Roberts Wesleyan College [*Rochester, NY*]
RWCH...... Republican Women of Capitol Hill   (EA)
RWCNEC ... Reports of the Working Committees. Northeast Conference [*A publication*]
RWCS....... Reactor Water Cleanup System [*Nuclear energy*]   (NRCH)
RWCS....... Red Wing Collectors Society   (EA)
RWCS....... Report Writer Control System [*COBOL*] [*Data processing*]
RWCU....... Reactor Water Cleanup [*Nuclear energy*]   (NRCH)
RWCUS..... Raoul Wallenberg Committee of the United States   (EA)
RWD......... Eastridge High School Library, Rochester, NY [*OCLC symbol*]   (OCLC)
RWD......... Reaction with Distillation [*Koch Engineering Co.*] [*Chemical engineering*]
RWD......... Rear Wheel Drive
RWD......... Regional WIN [*Work Incentive*] Director [*Department of Health and Human Services*]   (GFGA)
RWD......... Regular Way Delivery
RWD......... Regular World Day
RWD......... Rewind
RWD......... Right Wing Down [*Aviation*]
RWDCA .... Red and White Dairy Cattle Association   (EA)
RWDGM... Right Worshipful Deputy Grand Master [*Freemasonry*]
R/WDO..... Rear Window [*Automotive engineering*]
RWDS .... RADWASTE [*Radioactive Waste*] Disposal System [*Nuclear energy*]   (NRCH)
RWDSU .... Retail, Wholesale, and Department Store Union   (EA)

RWE......... Edison Technical and Occupational Educational Center Library, Rochester, NY [*OCLC symbol*]   (OCLC)
RWE......... Radio Warfare Establishment [*British military*]   (DMA)
RWE......... Ralph Waldo Emerson [*Initials used as pseudonym*]
RWE......... Review of World Economics [*A publication*]
RWE......... REWE Echo. Fachzeitschrift fuer Modernen Handel [*A publication*]
RWE......... Rheinisch-Westfaelisches Electrizitaetswerk AG [*Rheine-Westphalian Electricity Co.*] [*Germany*]
RWe.......... Westerly Public Library, Westerly, RI [*Library symbol*] [*Library of Congress*]   (LCLS)
RWEA .... Royal West of England Academy
RWED ...... Read/Write Extend Delete
R Week ..... Rechtskundig Weekblad [*A publication*]
RWEL....... Rockwell Oil Co. [*NASDAQ symbol*]   (NQ)
RWEMA ... Ralph Waldo Emerson Memorial Association   (EA)
RWES....... Ralph Waldo Emerson Society   (EA)
RWES....... Resources West, Inc. [*NASDAQ symbol*]   (NQ)
RWF .... Fairport High School Library, Fairport, NY [*OCLC symbol*]   (OCLC)
RWF .... Raoul Wallenberg Foreningen [*Raoul Wallenberg Association - RWA*]   (EAIO)
RWF .... Redwood Falls, MN [*Location identifier*] [*FAA*]   (FAAL)
RWF .... Roundtable for Women in Foodservice [*Later, RWFBH*]   (EA)
RWF .... Roush, W. F., Miami FL [*STAC*]
RWF .... Royal Welch [*or Welsh*] Fusiliers [*Military unit*] [*British*]
RWF .... Rozprawy Wydzialu Filologicznego Polskiej Akademyi Umiejetnosci [*A publication*]
RwF............ Rwandan Franc [*Monetary unit*]   (IMH)
RWFBH ... Roundtable for Women Food-Beverage-Hospitality   (EA)
RWFC........ Randy Wade Fan Club   (EA)
RWFC........ Red Wings For'Em Club   (EA)
RWFSDH ... Reports on the World Fertility Survey [*A publication*]
RWG......... Bakersfield Aviation Services [*Bakersfield, CA*] [*FAA designator*]   (FAAC)
RWG......... Gates-Chili Senior High School Library, Rochester, NY [*OCLC symbol*]   (OCLC)
RWG......... Radio Writers' Guild [*Later, WGA*]
RWG......... Redwing Resources, Inc. [*Vancouver Stock Exchange symbol*]
RWG......... Reliability Working Group   (AAG)
RWG......... Rigid Waveguide
RWG......... Roebling Wire Gauge
RWGM..... Right Worshipful Grand Master [*Freemasonry*]
RWGR ...... Right Worthy Grand Representative [*Freemasonry*]
RWGS ...... Right Worthy Grand Secretary [*Freemasonry*]   (ADA)
RWGT ...... Right Worthy Grand Templar [*Freemasonry*]
RWGT ...... Right Worthy Grand Treasurer [*Freemasonry*]
RWGW..... Right Worthy Grand Warden [*Freemasonry*]
RWGW..... Right Worthy Grand Worshipful [*Freemasonry*]   (ROG)
RWH......... Geneseo Junior/Senior High School Library, Geneseo, NY [*OCLC symbol*]   (OCLC)
RWH......... RADAR Warning and Homing
RWH......... Rainwater Head
RWH......... Rotor Wing Hours [*Aviation*]   (AIA)
RWHD....... Rawhide   (MSA)
RWI .... Greece-Arcadia Junior/Senior High School Library, Rochester, NY [*OCLC symbol*]   (OCLC)
RWI .... RADAR Warning Installation   (NATG)
RWI .... Radio Wire Integration [*Military*]
RWI .... Read-Write-Initialize [*Data processing*]
RWI .... Regular World Interval
RWI .... Remote Weight Indicator
RWI .... Rocky Mount [*North Carolina*] [*Airport symbol*]   (OAG)
RWIB........ Rioja Wine Information Bureau   (EA)
RWIY....... Royal Wiltshire Imperial Yeomanry [*British military*]   (DMA)
RWJ.......... Greece-Athena Junior/Senior High School Library, Rochester, NY [*OCLC symbol*]   (OCLC)
RWJ.......... Robert Wood Johnson Medical School [*New Jersey*]
RWJGW.... Right Worthy Junior Grand Warden [*Freemasonry*]
RWK......... Greece-Olympia High School Library, Rochester, NY [*OCLC symbol*]   (OCLC)
RWK......... Queen's Own Royal West Kent Regiment [*Military unit*] [*British*]
RWK......... Remaining Work
RWK......... Renwick Explorations Ltd. [*Vancouver Stock Exchange symbol*]
RWK......... Rework   (AAG)
RWkEPA... United States Environmental Protection Agency, National Marine Water Quality Laboratory, West Kingston, RI [*Library symbol*] [*Library of Congress*]   (LCLS)
RWL .... H. W. Schroeder Junior/Senior High School Library, Webster, NY [*OCLC symbol*]   (OCLC)
RWL .... Raised White Letters [*Tire design*] [*Automotive engineering*]
RWL .... Rawlins, WY [*Location identifier*] [*FAA*]   (FAAL)
RWL .... Relative Water Level
RWL .... Revolutionary Workers League [*Canada*]
RWL .... Richwell Resources Ltd. [*Vancouver Stock Exchange symbol*]
RWLB....... Regional War Labor Board
RWLR....... Relative Water-Level Recorder
RWM......... Hilton High School Library, Hilton, NY [*OCLC symbol*]   (OCLC)

RWM......... Radioactive Waste Management
RWM......... Read-Write Memory [*Data processing*] (MCD)
RWM......... Rectangular Wave Modulation (IEEE)
RWM......... Resistance Welding Machine
RWM......... Right Worshipful Master [*Freemasonry*] (ROG)
RWM......... Rod Worth Minimizer [*Nuclear energy*] (NRCH)
RWM...... Roll Wrapping Machine
RWMA...... Resistance Welder Manufacturers Association (EA)
RWMAC... Radioactive Waste Management Advisory Committee
RWMEB.... Railway Mechanical Engineer [*A publication*]
RWN.......... Holly Junior/Senior High School Library, Holly, NY [*OCLC symbol*] (OCLC)
RWN.......... Rawdon Resources Ltd. [*Vancouver Stock Exchange symbol*]
RWN.......... Winamac, IN [*Location identifier*] [*FAA*] (FAAL)
RWNBH.... Records Will Not Be Handcarried [*Army*] (AABC)
RWND....... Rewind (MSA)
RWNF .... Ryan White National Fund (EA)
RWO.......... Honeoye Falls-Lima Senior High School Library, Honeoye Falls, NY [*OCLC symbol*] (OCLC)
RWO.......... Kodiak, AK [*Location identifier*] [*FAA*] (FAAL)
RWO.......... Reconnaissance Watch Officer (MCD)
RWO.......... Regional Works Officer [*British*]
RWO.......... Reimbursable Work Order [*Navy*] (NG)
RWO.......... Riddare af Wasa Order [*Knight of the Order of Vasa*] [*Sweden*]
RWO.......... Routine Work Order (KSC)
RWoH....... Harris Institute, Woonsocket, RI [*Library symbol*] [*Library of Congress*] (LCLS)
RWoU....... Union Saint-Jean-Baptiste d'Amerique, Woonsocket, RI [*Library symbol*] [*Library of Congress*] (LCLS)
RWP .... James Madison High School Library, Rochester, NY [*OCLC symbol*] (OCLC)
RWP .... Radiation Work Permit [*Nuclear energy*] (NRCH)
RWP .... Radio Wave Propagation
RWP .... Radio Working Party
RWP .... RADWASTE [*Radioactive Waste*] Work Permit [*Nuclear energy*] (NRCH)
RWP .... Rainwater Pipe [*Construction*]
RWP .... Rawalpindi/Islamabad [*Pakistan*] [*Airport symbol*] [*Obsolete*] (OAG)
RWP .... Reactor Work Permit (IEEE)
RWP .... Reformacja w Polsce [*A publication*]
RWP .... Regiment Western Province [*British military*] (DMA)
RWP .... Rifle and Weapons Platoon [*Army*] [*Obsolete*] (AABC)
RWP .... Romanian Workers' Party [*Political party*]
RWPC....... RADWASTE [*Radioactive Waste*] Process Cell [*Nuclear energy*] (NRCH)
RWPG ...... Real World Problem Generation
RWPH....... River Water Pumphouse [*Nuclear energy*] (NRCH)
RWPI........ Ridgewood Properties, Inc. [*Atlanta, GA*] [*NASDAQ symbol*] (NQ)
RWQ......... James Monroe High School Library, Rochester, NY [*OCLC symbol*] (OCLC)
RWR .... James Sperry High School Library, Henrietta, NY [*OCLC symbol*] (OCLC)
RWR .... RADAR Warning Receiver (MCD)
RWR .... Radioactive Waste Reduction [*Nuclear energy*] (NRCH)
R-W-R ...... Rail-Water-Rail [*Shipping*]
RWR .... Read/Write Register
RWR .... Relative Weight Response
RWR .... Reward Resources Ltd. [*Vancouver Stock Exchange symbol*]
RWR .... Romance Writers Report [*A publication*] (EAAP)
RWR .... Ronald Wilson Reagan [*US president, 1911-*]
RWRAT..... Replacement Weather Reconnaissance Aircraft (DNAB)
RWRC ...... Remain Well to Right of Course [*Aviation*] (FAAC)
RWRSq..... Rescue and Weather Reconnaissance Squadron [*Air Force*]
RWRW ..... Rescue and Weather Reconnaissance Wing [*Air Force*]
RWS .... Camp Springs, MD [*Location identifier*] [*FAA*] (FAAL)
RWS .... John Marshall High School Library, Rochester, NY [*OCLC symbol*] (OCLC)
RWS .... RADAR Warning System (MCD)
RWS .... Radioactive Waste System [*Nuclear energy*] (NRCH)
RWS .... Range While Search
RWS .... Reaction Wheel Scanner
RWS .... Reaction Wheel Systems (AAG)
RWS .... Receiver Waveform Simulation [*Telecommunications*] (OA)
RWS .... Regional Warning System
RWS .... Regional Weather Service (NOAA)
RWS .... Release with Service (OICC)
RWS .... Religionswissenschaftliche Studien [*A publication*]
RWS .... Royal Society of Painters in Water-Colours [*British*]
RWS .... Royal West Surrey [*Regiment*] [*Military unit*] [*British*]
RWS .... Royal West Sussex [*Regiment*] [*Military unit*] [*British*]
RWSF....... RADWASTE [*Radioactive Waste*] Solidification Facility [*Nuclear energy*] (NRCH)
RWSF....... Revolutionary War Studies Forum (EA)
RWSF....... Roosevelt Warm Springs Foundation (EA)
RWSGW.... Right Worshipful Senior Grand Warden [*Freemasonry*]
RWSS....... RADWASTE [*Radioactive Waste*] Sample Station [*Nuclear energy*] (NRCH)
RWSS....... River Water Supply System (IEEE)
RWST....... Refueling Water Storage Tank [*Nuclear energy*] (NRCH)

RWT.......... Kendall High School Library, Kendall, NY [*OCLC symbol*] (OCLC)
RWT .... RADAR Warning Trainer (MCD)
RWT .... Read-Write Tape [*Data processing*]
RWT .... Refueling Water Tank [*Nuclear energy*] (NRCH)
RWTA ...... River Water Treatment Area [*Nuclear energy*] (NRCH)
RWTH...... Rotary Wing Turbine Hours [*Aviation*] (AIA)
RWTI....... RW Technology, Inc. [*NASDAQ symbol*] (NQ)
RWTS....... Regenerant Waste Treatment Subsystem [*Nuclear energy*] (NRCH)
RWU.......... Keshequa Junior/Senior High School Library, Nunda, NY [*OCLC symbol*] (OCLC)
RWV .... L. C. Obourn High School Library, East Rochester, NY [*OCLC symbol*] (OCLC)
RWV .... Radial Wall Variation [*Tire design*] [*Automotive engineering*]
RWV .... Radioactive Waste Vent [*Nuclear energy*] (NRCH)
RWV .... Read-Write-Verify [*Data processing*]
RWV .... Rubbery Wood Virus
RWV .... Rustad/Wickhem/Video, Inc. [*Madison, WI*] (TSSD)
RWVD ...... Real World Visual Display
RWVR ...... Real World Vehicular Rate
RWW .... Lester B. Forman Central Library, Fairport, NY [*OCLC symbol*] (OCLC)
RWX .... Letchworth Junior/Senior High School Library, Gainesville, NY [*OCLC symbol*] (OCLC)
RWY .... Livonia High School Library, Livonia, NY [*OCLC symbol*] (OCLC)
RWY .... Railway
RWY .... Royal Wiltshire Yeomanry [*Military unit*] [*British*]
RWY .... Runway (AAG)
Rwy Age.... Railway Age [*A publication*]
RWZ.......... McQuaid Jesuit High School Library, Rochester, NY [*OCLC symbol*] (OCLC)
RX.............. Comite International de la Croix-Rouge [*International Committee of the Red Cross*] [*ICAO designator*] (FAAC)
RX.............. Excess Reserves
RX.............. Rank Xerox
RX.............. Receiver [*or Reception*] [*Radio*] (NATG)
Rx.............. Recipe [*Used as a symbol for medical prescriptions*]
RX.............. Reconnaissance-Experimental Aircraft
RX.............. Register and Indexed Storage (MCD)
RX.............. Remote Exchange [*Telecommunications*] (TEL)
RX.............. Repairable Exchange
RX.............. Report Crossing [*Aviation*] (FAAC)
RX.............. Resolver-Transmitter
RX.............. Rix-Dollar [*British*] (ROG)
RX.............. Rupees [*Monetary unit*] [*Ceylon, India, and Pakistan*] (ROG)
RX.............. Rush [*on teletype messages*]
RXA.......... Mount Morris Junior/Senior High School Library, Mount Morris, NY [*OCLC symbol*] (OCLC)
RXA.......... Roxana Resources Ltd. [*Vancouver Stock Exchange symbol*]
RXB .... Nazareth Academy Library, Rochester, NY [*OCLC symbol*] (OCLC)
RXC .... Our Lady of Mercy High School Library, Rochester, NY [*OCLC symbol*] (OCLC)
RXCH........ Rexco Industries, Inc. [*NASDAQ symbol*] (NQ)
RXD.......... Penfield High School Library, Penfield, NY [*OCLC symbol*] (OCLC)
RXE .... Perry Junior/Senior High School Library, Perry, NY [*OCLC symbol*] (OCLC)
RXF........... Pittsford-Medon High School Library, Pittsford, NY [*OCLC symbol*] (OCLC)
RXF........... Rexford [*Montana*] [*Seismograph station code, US Geological Survey*] (SEIS)
RXG .... Pittsford-Sutherland High School Library, Pittsford, NY [*OCLC symbol*] (OCLC)
RXH.......... R. L. Thomas High School Library, Webster, NY [*OCLC symbol*] (OCLC)
RXH.......... Rexham Corp. [*NYSE symbol*] (SPSG)
RXI .... Rexplore Resources International Ltd. [*Vancouver Stock Exchange symbol*]
RXI .... St. Agnes High School Library, Rochester, NY [*OCLC symbol*] (OCLC)
RXJ .... Thomas Jefferson Junior/Senior High School Library, Rochester, NY [*OCLC symbol*] (OCLC)
RXK .... Newark, OH [*Location identifier*] [*FAA*] (FAAL)
RXK .... Warsaw High School Library, Warsaw, NY [*OCLC symbol*] (OCLC)
RXL .... Rank Xerox Ltd. [*Xerox subsidiary*]
RXL .... Wayland Senior High School Library, Wayland, NY [*OCLC symbol*] (OCLC)
RXLI .... Recessive X-Linked Ichthyosis [*Medicine*]
RXM .... Rexford Minerals Ltd. [*Vancouver Stock Exchange symbol*]
RXM .... RX Medical Services [*AMEX symbol*] (SPSG)
RXM .... West Irondequoit High School Library, Rochester, NY [*OCLC symbol*] (OCLC)
RX Med ..... RX Medical Services Corp. [*Associated Press abbreviation*] (APAG)
RXN.......... Islip, NY [*Location identifier*] [*FAA*] (FAAL)
RXN.......... Reaction [*Medicine*]
RXN.......... Rexene Corp. [*NYSE symbol*] (SPSG)

RXN .... Wheatland-Chili Junior/Senior High School Library, Scottsville, NY [*OCLC symbol*] (OCLC)
RXO .... York High School Library, Retsof, NY [*OCLC symbol*] (OCLC)
RXP .... American Baptist Historical Society Library, Rochester, NY [*OCLC symbol*] (OCLC)
RXP .... Radix Point
RXQ .... Lincoln First Bank of Rochester Library Service, Rochester, NY [*OCLC symbol*] (OCLC)
RXQ .... Washington, DC [*Location identifier*] [*FAA*] (FAAL)
RXR .... Rainex Industries [*Formerly, Rainex Resources Ltd.*] [*Vancouver Stock Exchange symbol*]
RXR .... Revco D.S., Inc. [*NYSE symbol*] (SPSG)
RXS .... RADAR Cross Section
RXS .... Roxas City [*Philippines*] [*Airport symbol*] (OAG)
RXSC .... Rexcom Systems Corp. [*Houston, TX*] [*NASDAQ symbol*] (NQ)
RXT .... Right Exotropia [*Ophthalmology*]
RxTV .... Prescription Television
RXW .... Roxwell Gold Mines [*Vancouver Stock Exchange symbol*]
RXW .... Watersmeet, MI [*Location identifier*] [*FAA*] (FAAL)
RXX .... Reako Exploration [*Vancouver Stock Exchange symbol*]
RXY .... Roxy Petroleum Ltd. [*Toronto Stock Exchange symbol*]
RXZ .... Chicago, IL [*Location identifier*] [*FAA*] (FAAL)
RY .... Railway (AFIT)
RY .... Redcoat Air Cargo Ltd. [*British*] [*ICAO designator*] (ICDA)
RY .... Relative Yield [*Agriculture*]
RY .... Relay (DEN)
RY .... Residual Yield [*Agriculture*] (OA)
RY .... Riley Aeronautics Corp. [*ICAO aircraft manufacturer identifier*] (ICAO)
RY .... Roll Yoke
RY .... Rotterdam Airlines [*Netherlands*] [*ICAO designator*] (FAAC)
RY .... Royal (ROG)
RY .... Royal Bank of Canada [*Toronto Stock Exchange symbol*] [*Vancouver Stock Exchange symbol*]
RY .... Royal Yeomanry [*Military unit*] [*British*]
RY .... Runway (FAAC)
ry .... Rydberg [*Unit of energy*] [*Atomic physics*] [*Symbol*]
ry .... Ryukyu Islands, Southern [*ja (Japan) used in records cataloged after January 1978*] [*MARC country of publication code*] [*Library of Congress*] (LCCP)
RYA .... Railroad Yardmasters of America (EA)
RYA .... Royal Yachting Association [*British*]
RYa .... Russkii Yazyk v Shkole [*Moscow*] [*A publication*]
Ry Age .... Railway Age [*A publication*]
RYAL .... Royale Airlines, Inc. [*NASDAQ symbol*] (NQ)
RYALM ...... Relay Alarm (AAG)
RYAN .... Ryan's Family Steak Houses, Inc. [*NASDAQ symbol*] (NQ)
Ryan Advis Health Serv Gov Boards ... Ryan Advisory for Health Services Governing Boards [*A publication*]
Ryan & M .. Ryan and Moody's English Nisi Prius Reports [*171 English Reprint*] [*A publication*] (DLA)
Ryan & M (Eng) ... Ryan and Moody's English Nisi Prius Reports [*171 English Reprint*] [*A publication*] (DLA)
RYB .... Raymond, MS [*Location identifier*] [*FAA*] (FAAL)
RYB .... Rybachye [*Former USSR*] [*Seismograph station code, US Geological Survey*] (SEIS)
RYBF .... Royal Business Group, Inc. [*NASDAQ symbol*] (NQ)
Ryb Khoz ... Rybnoe Khozyaistvo [*A publication*]
Rybn Khoz ... Rybnoe Khozyaistvo [*A publication*]
Rybn Khoz (Kiev) ... Rybnoe Khozyaistvo (Kiev) [*A publication*]
Rybn Khoz Resp Mezhved Temat Nauchn Sb ... Rybnoe Khozyaistvo Respublikanskii Mezhvedomstvennyi Tematicheskii Nauchnyi Sbornik [*A publication*]
Rybn Prom-St Dal'n Vost ... Rybnaya Promyshlennost' Dal'nego Vostoka [*A publication*]
Rybokhoz Issled Basseine Balt Morya ... Rybokhozyaistvennye Issledovaniya v Basseine Baltiiskogo Morya [*A publication*]
RYC .... Raychem Corp. [*NYSE symbol*] (SPSG)
RYC .... Raymac Oil Corp. [*Vancouver Stock Exchange symbol*]
RyC .... Religion y Cultura [*A publication*]
RYC .... Rural Youth Corps [*Defunct*] (EA)
Ry & Can .... Reports of Railway and Canal Traffic Cases [*1855-1950*] [*A publication*]
Ry & Can Cas ... Railway and Canal Cases [*England*] [*A publication*] (DLA)
Ry & Can Traf Ca ... Railway and Canal Traffic Cases [*A publication*] (DLA)
Ry & Can Traf Cas ... Reports of Railway and Canal Traffic Cases [*1855-1950*] [*A publication*] (ILCA)
Ry & Can Traffic Cas ... Railway and Canal Traffic Cases [*England*] [*A publication*] (DLA)
Ry & Can Tr Cas ... Reports of Railway and Canal Traffic Cases [*1855-1950*] [*A publication*] (DLA)
Ry Cas .... Reports of English Railway Cases [*A publication*] (DLA)
Ry Cas .... Reports of Railway and Canal Traffic Cases [*1855-1950*] [*A publication*]
Ry & C Cas (Eng) ... Railway and Canal Cases [*England*] [*A publication*] (DLA)
RYCO .... Rynco Scientific Corp. [*NASDAQ symbol*] (NQ)
Ry & Corp Law J ... Railway and Corporation Law Journal [*A publication*] (DLA)

Ry Corp Law Jour ... Railway and Corporation Law Journal [*A publication*] (DLA)
Ry & Corp Law Jour ... Railway and Corporation Law Journal [*A publication*] (DLA)
Ry & C Traffic Cas (Eng) ... Railway and Canal Traffic Cases [*England*] [*A publication*] (DLA)
RYD .... Real Year Dollars (NASA)
Ryde .... Ryde's Rating Appeals [*1871-1904*] [*A publication*] (DLA)
Ryde & K .... Ryde and Konstam's Reports of Rating Appeals [*1894-1904*] [*A publication*] (DLA)
Ryde & K Rat App ... Ryde and Konstam's Reports of Rating Appeals [*1894-1904*] [*A publication*] (DLA)
Ryder .... Ryder Systems, Inc. [*Associated Press abbreviation*] (APAG)
Ryde Rat App ... Ryde's Rating Appeals [*1871-1904*] [*A publication*] (DLA)
Rydge's ...... Rydge's Business Journal [*A publication*] (APTA)
Rydge's Constr Civ Eng & Min Rev ... Rydge's Construction, Civil Engineering, and Mining Review [*A publication*] (APTA)
Rydges Mgmt Serv ... Rydge's Management Service [*A publication*]
RYDMAR ... Reaction-Yield-Detected Magnetic Resonance [*Also, RYDMR*] [*Spectroscopy*]
RYDMR .... Reaction-Yield-Detected Magnetic Resonance [*Also, RYDMAR*] [*Spectroscopy*]
RYE .... Retirement Year Ending [*Army*] (AABC)
RYE .... Royalon Petroleum [*Vancouver Stock Exchange symbol*]
RYEJA .... Royal Engineers Journal [*A publication*]
RYEV........ Radish Yellow Edge Virus [*Plant pathology*]
RyF .... Razon y Fe [*A publication*]
Ry F .... Rymer's Foedera [*20 vols.*] [*1704-35*] [*A publication*] (DLA)
RyFab .... Razon y Fabula [*A publication*]
RYFL .... Family Steak Houses of Florida, Inc. [*Neptune Beach, FL*] [*NASDAQ symbol*] (NQ)
RYFO .... Ryan Foundation International [*India*] (EAIO)
Ry Gaz Int ... Railway Gazette International [*A publication*]
RYHY........ Ryerson & Haynes, Inc. [*Jackson, MI*] [*NASDAQ symbol*] (NQ)
RYK .... Relay Creek Resources Ltd. [*Vancouver Stock Exchange symbol*]
RYK .... Romulus, NY [*Location identifier*] [*FAA*] (FAAL)
RYK .... Rykoff-Sexton, Inc. [*NYSE symbol*] (SPSG)
RYKA .... Ryka, Inc. [*NASDAQ symbol*] (NQ)
RYKHA ..... Rybnoe Khozyaistvo [*A publication*]
RYKOD ..... Ryutai Kogaku [*A publication*]
Rykoff .... Rykoff-Sexton, Inc. [*Associated Press abbreviation*] (APAG)
ryl............... Royal [*Philately*]
RYL .... Royal Trustco Ltd. [*Toronto Stock Exchange symbol*] [*Vancouver Stock Exchange symbol*]
RYL .... Ryland Group, Inc. [*NYSE symbol*] (SPSG)
Ryland........ Ryland Group, Inc. [*Associated Press abbreviation*] (APAG)
Ry Loco & Cars ... Railway Locomotives and Cars [*A publication*]
Ryl Plac Parl ... Ryley's Placita Parliamentaria [*1290-1307*] [*England*] [*A publication*]
RYM .... Reference Your Message [*Military*] (AABC)
RYM .... Revolutionary Youth Movement [*Factions of Students for a Democratic Society. See RYM-I and RYM-II*]
Ry & M ...... Ryan and Moody's English Nisi Prius Reports [*A publication*] (DLA)
RYMAC .... RYMAC Mortgage Investment Corp. [*Associated Press abbreviation*] (APAG)
Ry MCC..... Ryan and Moody's English Crown Cases [*A publication*] (DLA)
Ry & MCC ... Ryan and Moody's English Crown Cases Reserved [*A publication*] (DLA)
Ry Mech & Elec Eng ... Railway Mechanical and Electrical Engineer [*A publication*]
Ry Mech Eng ... Railway Mechanical Engineer [*A publication*]
Ry Med Jur ... Ryan's Medical Jurisprudence [*A publication*] (DLA)
Rymer .... Rymer Foods, Inc. [*Associated Press abbreviation*] (APAG)
Rym F .... Rymer's Foedera [*20 vols.*] [*1704-35*] [*A publication*] (DLA)
RYM-I .... Revolutionary Youth Movement I [*Also known as "Weatherman"*] [*A faction of Students for a Democratic Society*]
RYM-II...... Revolutionary Youth Movement II [*A faction of Students for a Democratic Society*]
Ry & MNP ... Ryan and Moody's English Nisi Prius Reports [*A publication*] (DLA)
Ry Mo .... Rythmes du Monde [*A publication*]
Ry & Moo .. Ryan and Moody [*1823-26*] [*A publication*] (DLA)
Rymr .... Rymer Foods, Inc. [*Associated Press abbreviation*] (APAG)
RYMV .... Rice Yellow Mottle Virus [*Plant pathology*]
RYN.......... Rayon
RYN.......... Ryan Aviation Corp. [*Wichita, KS*] [*FAA designator*] (FAAC)
RYN.......... Ryan Homes, Inc. [*NYSE symbol*] (SPSG)
RYN.......... Tucson, AZ [*Location identifier*] [*FAA*] (FAAL)
RYNA .... Railroad Yardmasters of North America [*Absorbed by RYA*] (EA)
RYNM....... Arlington Realty Investors [*Formerly, Ryan Marketing Investors*] [*NASDAQ symbol*] (NQ)
RYNV .... Robust Yellow Net Virus [*Plant pathology*]
RYO.......... Rio Turbio [*Argentina*] [*Airport symbol*] (OAG)
RYO.......... Royal Oak Mines [*AMEX symbol*] (SPSG)

Ryojun Coll Eng Mem ... Ryojun College of Engineering. Memoirs [*A publication*]
Ryojun Coll Eng Publ ... Ryojun College of Engineering. Publications [*A publication*]
RYP .... Cumberland, MD [*Location identifier*] [*FAA*] (FAAL)
R-Y-P .... Roll, Yaw, Pitch (MCD)
RYPAAO... Annals. Royal College of Physicians and Surgeons of Canada [*A publication*]
RYQ .... Royalstar Resources [*Vancouver Stock Exchange symbol*]
RYR .... Radyr Junction [*Cardiff*] [*Welsh depot code*]
Ry R .... Railway Review [*A publication*]
RYR .... Royal Yeomanry Regiment [*British military*] (DMA)
RYR .... Ryanodine Receptor [*Genetics*]
RYR .... Rymer Foods, Inc. [*NYSE symbol*] (SPSG)
RYRKF ...... Rayrock Resources [*NASDAQ symbol*] (NQ)
RYRQD ..... Reply Requested (NOAA)
RYS .... Railway Stations [*Public-performance tariff class*] [*British*]
RYS .... Royal Yacht Squadron [*British*]
RYS .... Ryan Resources Ltd. [*Vancouver Stock Exchange symbol*]
RYT .... Ray-Net Communications Systems, Inc. [*Vancouver Stock Exchange symbol*]
RYT .... Relative Yield Total [*Agriculture*]
Ryt .... Rytmi [*Record label*] [*Finland*]
RYTC .... Raytech Corp. [*NASDAQ symbol*] (NQ)
Ry Track Struct ... Railway Track and Structures [*A publication*]
RYU .... Rosanky, TX [*Location identifier*] [*FAA*] (FAAL)
RYU .... Ryukoku University [*UTLAS symbol*]
Ryukoku J Humanit Sci ... Ryukoku Journal of Humanities and Sciences [*A publication*]
Ryukyu Med J ... Ryukyu Medical Journal [*A publication*]
RYUSA...... Ryusan To Kogyo [*A publication*]
RYV .... Watertown, WI [*Location identifier*] [*FAA*] (FAAL)
RYY .... Marietta, GA [*Location identifier*] [*FAA*] (FAAL)
RZ .... Air Anjou Transports [*France*] [*ICAO designator*] (FAAC)
RZ .... Rada Zydowska [*A publication*]
RZ .... Radostna Zeme [*A publication*]
RZ .... Radovi (Filozofski Fakultet-Zadar) [*A publication*]
R & Z .... Range and Zero [*NASA*] (KSC)
RZ .... Reaction Zone
RZ .... Reconnaissance Zone
RZ .... Recovery Zone (MCD)
RZ .... Referativnyi Zhurnal. Informatika [*A publication*]
RZ .... Regal-Zonophone [*Record label*] [*Great Britain*]
RZ .... Regiment de Zouaves
RZ .... Resistance Zone
RZ .... Return-to-Zero Recording [*Data processing*]
Rz .... Retzius [*Neuron*]
RZ .... Revolutionary Cells [*Revolutionary group*] [*West Germany*]
Rz .... Rhizome [*Botany*]
RZ .... Rueckenfallschirm mit Zwangsausloesung [*Static-line, backpack parachute*] [*German military - World War II*]
RZA .... Religious Zionists of America (EA)
RZA .... Santa Cruz [*Argentina*] [*Airport symbol*] (OAG)
R Z Avtomat Telemeh i Vycisl Tehn ... Referativnyi Zhurnal. Avtomatika. Telemehanika i Vycislitelnaja Tehnika [*A publication*]
RZBLA ...... Referativnyi Zhurnal. Biologiya [*A publication*]
RZC .... Fayetteville, AR [*Location identifier*] [*FAA*] (FAAL)
RZE .... Rzeszow [*Poland*] [*Airport symbol*] (OAG)
RZETA...... Rozprawy Elektrotechniczne [*A publication*]
RZF........... Riemann Zeta Function [*Mathematics*]
R Z Fiz .... Referativnyi Zhurnal. Fizika [*A publication*]
RZFZA ...... Referativnyi Zhurnal. Fizika [*A publication*]
RZh Avtomat Telemekh i Vychisl Tekhn ... Akademiya Nauk SSSR. Institut Nauchnoi Informatsii. Referativnyi Zhurnal. Avtomatika. Telemekhanika i Vychislitel'naya Tekhnika [*A publication*]
RZh Mat .... Akademiya Nauk SSSR. Institut Nauchnoi Informatsii. Referativnyi Zhurnal. Matematika [*A publication*]
RZh Tekhn Kibernet ... Akademiya Nauk SSSR. Institut Nauchnoi i Tekhnicheskoi Informatsii. Referativnyi Zhurnal. Tekhnicheskaya Kibernetika [*A publication*]
RZINA....... Rozprawy Inzynierskie [*A publication*]
RZInformat ... Referativnyi Zhurnal. Informatika [*A publication*]
RZKibernet ... Referativnyi Zhurnal. Kibernetika [*A publication*]
RZL........... Rensselaer, IN [*Location identifier*] [*FAA*] (FAAL)
RZL........... Return-to-Zero Level
RZM .... Return-to-Zero Mark
RZMA .... Rolled Zinc Manufacturers Association [*Defunct*] (EA)
RZMat....... Referativnyi Zhurnal. Matematika [*A publication*]
RZMeh ...... Referativnyi Zhurnal. Mehanika [*A publication*]
RZMTA..... Referativnyi Zhurnal. Metallurgiya [*A publication*]
RZNDA ..... Razvedka Nedr [*A publication*]
RZ(NP)...... Nonpolarized Return-to-Zero Recording [*Data processing*] (IBMDP)
RZO .... Demopolis, AL [*Location identifier*] [*FAA*] (FAAL)
RZONA..... Razvedka i Okhrana Nedr [*A publication*]
RZ(P)......... Polarized Return-to-Zero Recording [*Data processing*] (IBMDP)
RZP........... Provincetown, MA [*Location identifier*] [*FAA*] (FAAL)
RZS........... Rolled Zinc Sheet
RZS........... Royal Zoological Society [*British*]
RZSF .... Radovi Zavoda za Slavensku Filologiju [*A publication*]

RZSI .... [*The*] Royal Zoological Society of Ireland (DI)
RZSS .... Royal Zoological Society of Scotland (EAIO)
RZT .... Chillicothe, OH [*Location identifier*] [*FAA*] (FAAL)
RZZ .... Roanoke Rapids, NC [*Location identifier*] [*FAA*] (FAAL)

S

S .... Aerospatiale [*Societe Nationale Industrielle Aerospatiale*] (Sud Aviation) [*France*] [*ICAO aircraft manufacturer identifier*]   (ICAO)
S .... Antisubmarine [*Designation for all US military aircraft*]
S .... Apparent Power [*Symbol*]   (DEN)
S .... Boltzmann Constant [*Statistical mechanics*]
S .... Codex Sinaiticus   (BJA)
S .... Detecting [*JETDS nomenclature*]
S .... Entropy [*Symbol*] [*IUPAC*]
S .... Esses [*Phonetic alphabet*] [*Pre-World War II*]   (DSUE)
S .... Expenditure Saved [*Economics*]
S .... Fun Fairs [*Public-performance tariff class*] [*British*]
S .... Isis-Chemie KG [*Germany*] [*Research code symbol*]
S .... Magnetic Solar Daily Variation
S .... New York Supplement [*A publication*]   (DLA)
s .... Path, Length of Arc [*Symbol*] [*IUPAC*]
(S) .... Paymaster [*Navy*] [*British*]
S .... Permissible Working Stress
S .... Pitman-Moore Co. [*Research code symbol*]
S .... Pounds per Square Inch   (AAG)
S .... Poynting Vector [*Symbol*] [*Electromagnetism*]   (DEN)
S .... Range Bearing [*JETDS nomenclature*]
S .... Reluctance [*Symbol*]   (DEN)
S .... Sabbath
S .... Sabin [*Unit of acoustic measurement*]   (DEN)
S .... Sable [*Heraldry*]
S .... Sacral
S .... Sacred
S .... Sacrifice [*Baseball*]
S .... Sacrum
S .... Sadism [*or Sadist*]   (CDAI)
S .... Saduccus [*Flourished, 13th century*] [*Authority cited in pre-1607 legal work*]   (DSA)
S .... Saeculum
(S) .... Safe [*Task classification*] [*NASA*]   (NASA)
S .... Safety [*Football*]
S .... Sailing Ship
S .... Saint
S .... [*Bartholomaeus de*] Saliceto [*Deceased, 1411*] [*Authority cited in pre-1607 legal work*]   (DSA)
S .... Saline
S .... Salmonella [*Bacteriology*]   (MAE)
S .... Salvageable   (AAG)
S .... Same Case [*Same case as case cited*] [*Used in Shepard's Citations*] [*Legal term*]   (DLA)
S .... Sample
S .... Samuel [*Old Testament book*]   (BJA)
S .... San Francisco [*California*] [*Mint mark, when appearing on US coins*]
S .... Sand [*Quality of the bottom*] [*Nautical charts*]
S .... Sandra [*Genotype of Phlox paniculata*]
S .... Sapwood [*Forestry*]
S .... Satang [*Monetary unit in Thailand*]
s .... Satellite [*Chromosomal*] [*Medicine*]   (MAE)
S .... Saturation   (MAE)
S .... Saturday
S .... Saturn
S .... Savanna Zone Soil [*Agriculture*]
S .... Savings [*Economics*]
S .... Saxon
S .... Scalar [*Mathematics*]   (ROG)
S .... Scanning
S .... Scarce [*Numismatics*]
S .... Scattering Coefficient [*Photometry*]
S .... Schedule
S .... Schilling [*Monetary unit*] [*Austria*]
S .... Schistosoma [*A parasitic fluke*]   (MAE)
S .... [*Wolfgang*] Schmieder [*When used in identifying J. S. Bach's compositions, refers to cataloging of his works by musicologist Schmieder*]
S .... School

S .... Science   (WGA)
S .... Scilicet [*Namely*] [*Latin*]   (DLA)
S .... Scot
S .... Scouting [*Naval aircraft designation*]
S .... Scribe
S .... Scuttle
S .... Scythian [*Geology*]
S .... Sea   (ADA)
S .... Sea-Air Temperature Difference Correction
S .... Seaman [*Navy*]
S .... Seaplane [*Navy*]
S .... Search
S .... Searle's Cape Of Good Hope Reports [*South Africa*] [*A publication*]   (DLA)
S .... Searle's Cases in the Supreme Court [*1850-67*] [*South Africa*] [*A publication*]   (DLA)
S .... Sears, Roebuck & Co. [*NYSE symbol*]   (SPSG)
S .... Seasonal [*Business term*]   (OICC)
S .... Seat   (WGA)
S .... Second [*or Secondary*]
s .... Second [*Symbol*] [*SI unit of time*]
s .... Secondary [*Preferred form is sec*] [*Chemistry*]
S .... Secondary Modern School [*British*]
S .... Secondary [*or Shake*] Wave [*Earthquakes*]
S .... Secret [*Security classification*]
S .... Secretary
S .... Secretin [*Endocrinology*]
S .... Secretory Substance [*Botany*]
S .... Section
S .... Sedentary [*Biology*]
S .... Seder of Triennial Cycle   (BJA)
s .... Sedimentation Coefficient [*Physical chemistry*]
S .... See
S .... Seelenlaenge [*Barrel length*] [*German military - World War II*]
S .... Seguente [*And Following*] [*Italian*]   (ILCA)
S .... Seite [*Page*] [*German*]
S .... Self-Pollinated [*Botany*]
S .... Selvi [*Italy*] [*Research code symbol*]
S .... Semi
S .... Semi-Registered Tank [*Liquid gas carriers*]
S .... Semiannually
S .... Semis [*One-Half*] [*Pharmacy*]
S .... Sen [*Monetary unit in Japan*]
S .... Senate
S .... Senate Bill [*with number*]   (GPO)
S .... Senor [*Mister*] [*Spanish*]
S .... Sensation [*Psychology*]
S .... Sensitivity   (DEN)
S .... Sent [*Communications*]   (FAAC)
S .... Sentence [*Linguistics*]
S .... Senza [*Without*] [*Music*]
S .... Separation
S .... September [*A publication*]
S .... September
S .... Sepulchrum [*Sepulchre*] [*Latin*]
S .... Sepultus [*Buried*] [*Latin*]
S .... Serial
S .... Series
S .... Serine [*One-letter symbol; see Ser*]
S .... Sermon
S .... Serum
S .... Service [*Military document classification*]   (INF)
S .... Servicing
S .... Servier [*France*] [*Research code symbol*]
S .... Sesquiplane [*Navy*]
S .... Set
S .... Set Meals [*School meals*] [*British*]
S .... Seven   (ROG)
S .... Seventy   (ROG)
S .... Severity
S .... Sewage Disposal [*British Waterways Board sign*]

S................	Shaft Horsepower
S................	Shaft Main Engine
S................	Shape Descriptor [*S-curve, for example. The shape resembles the letter for which it is named*]
S................	Shape Factor of a Structure [*Heat transmission symbol*]
S................	Shares [*Following a figure, indicates number of 100-share lots in a transaction; e.g., 4s indicates 400 shares*] [*NYSE symbol*] (SPSG)
S................	Sharp
s................	Sharpshooter [*Army*]
S................	Shaw, Dunlop, and Bell's Scotch Court of Session Reports, First Series [*A publication*] (DLA)
S................	Shaw's Scotch Appeal Cases, House of Lords [*A publication*] (DLA)
S................	Shaw's Scotch Court of Session Cases [*A publication*] (DLA)
S................	Shear [*Type of seismic wave*]
S................	Sheep (ROG)
S................	Sheet [*Genetics*]
S................	Shell
S................	Shelter [*Bureau of the Census*]
S................	Sheltered [*Takeoff area for seaplanes*] [*For chart use only*]
S................	Shelters [*JETDS nomenclature*] [*Military*] (CET)
S................	Shilling [*Monetary unit in Britain*] [*Obsolete*]
S................	Ship
S................	Shire (ADA)
S................	Short Circuit
S................	Shrub [*Botany*]
S................	Shunt Ahead [*Railroad signal arm*] [*British*]
S................	Sick
S................	Side
S................	Siderocyte [*Hematology*] (AAMN)
S................	Sidrah (BJA)
S................	Siecle [*Century*] [*French*]
S................	Siemens [*Symbol*] [*SI unit of electric conductance*]
S................	Sierra [*Phonetic alphabet*] [*International*] (DSUE)
S................	Sigma Mines (Quebec) Ltd. [*Toronto Stock Exchange symbol*]
S................	Sign [*or Signed*]
S................	Signa [*Write*] [*Pharmacy*]
S................	Signal [*Telecommunications*] (TEL)
S................	Signal Strength [*Broadcasting*]
S................	Signaller [*British military*] (DMA)
S................	Signature
/S/............	Signed [*Before signature on typed copy of a document, original of which was signed*]
S................	Signetur [*Let It Be Entitled*] [*Pharmacy*] (ROG)
S................	Signor [*Mister*] [*Italian*]
S................	Silent [*Dance terminology*]
S................	Silicate
S................	Silk (AAG)
S................	Silver
S................	Silversmith
S................	Simes [*Italy*] [*Research code symbol*]
S................	Similarity Index
S................	Simon de Bisignano [*Flourished, 1174-79*] [*Authority cited in pre-1607 legal work*] (DSA)
S................	Simon de Paris [*Deceased, 1273*] [*Authority cited in pre-1607 legal work*] (DSA)
S................	Simplex
S................	Simultaneous Transmission of Range Signals and Voice
S................	Sine [*Without*] [*Latin*]
S................	Single [*One way fare*] [*British*]
S................	Single
S................	Single Silk [*Wire insulation*]
S................	Singular
(S)............	Sinister [*Counterclockwise configuration*] [*Biochemistry*]
S................	Sinister [*Left*] [*Latin*]
S................	Sinistra [*Left Hand*] [*Music*]
S................	Sink
S................	Sire
S................	Sister
S................	Site [*Archaeology*]
S................	Situs [*Placed*] [*Latin*]
S................	Sixteenmo [*Book from 15 to 17-1/2 centimeters in height*]
S................	Sixth Word Designator [*Data processing*]
S................	Skid (AAG)
S................	Slate (KSC)
S................	Slave [*LORAN stations*]
S................	Slavia [*A publication*]
S................	Sleeping [*Medicine*]
S................	Slewed [*Antenna*]
S................	Slip
S................	Slipped Up [*Horse racing*]
S................	Slope [*Technical drawings*]
S................	Slow
S................	Slow Muscle [*Skeletal muscle pharmacology*]
S................	Small [*Size designation for clothing, etc.*]
S................	Smooth [*Appearance of bacterial colony*]
S................	Smooth Sea [*Navigation*]
S................	Snack (CDAI)
S................	Sniper [*British military*] (DMA)
S................	Snow [*Meteorology*]
S................	Socialist
S................	Socialist Group [*EC*] (ECED)
S................	Society
S................	Socius [*or Sodalis*] [*Fellow*]
S................	Soft
S................	Software [*Data processing*]
S................	Soiled [*Deltiology*]
S................	Sol [*Monetary unit in Peru*]
S................	Solar (ADA)
S................	Solco Basel AG [*Switzerland*] [*Research code symbol*]
S................	Soldering
S................	Solicitor's Opinion [*A publication*] (DLA)
(s)............	Solid [*Chemistry*]
S................	Solid
S................	Solidus [*Shilling*] [*Latin*]
S................	Solitary [*Biology*]
S................	Solo [*Music*]
S................	Solubility
S................	Somaliland Scouts [*Military unit*] [*British*]
S................	Son
S................	SONAR [*Sonic Azimuth and Ranging*] [*British military*] (DMA)
S................	Song (ROG)
S................	Soprano
S................	Sou [*Monetary unit in France*]
S................	Sough (AAG)
S................	Sound [*Audiology*]
S................	Sound Tape [*Films, television, etc.*]
S................	Source
S................	South [*or Southern*]
s------..........	South America [*MARC geographic area code*] [*Library of Congress*] (LCCP)
S................	Southern Reporter [*A publication*] (DLA)
S................	Spacer
S................	Spade (ADA)
S................	Spar [*Buoy*]
S................	Spares
S................	Spatial Ability [*Psychology*]
S................	Speak
S................	Special
s................	Special Abilities of an Individual [*Symbol*] [*Psychology*]
S................	Special Air Mission [*Military aircraft identification prefix*] (FAAC)
S................	Special Types [*JETDS nomenclature*]
S................	Specialist [*Ecology*]
S................	Species
S................	Specific Factor
S................	Specific Surface
S................	Specification
S................	Spectator [*A publication*]
S................	Speculum [*A publication*]
S................	Speech
S................	Speed
S................	Sphere [*or Spherical*]
s................	Spin Quantum Number [*Atomic physics*] (DEN)
S................	Spinster
S................	Spirillum [*Bacteriology*] (MAE)
S................	Split [*In stock listings of newspapers*]
S................	Spoilers in Nozzle
S................	Sponsored
S................	Spontaneous
S................	Spool
S................	Sport [*In automobile model name "Honda Civic S"*]
S................	Spring-Burned [*Ecology*]
S................	Spurs [*Horse racing*]
S................	Squadron
S................	Staatsblad van het Koninkrijk der Nederlanden [*A publication*]
S................	Stack
S................	Stackable Container (DCTA)
S................	Staff [*License plate code assigned to foreign diplomats in the US*]
S................	Staff
S................	Stand
S................	Standard
s................	Standard Deviation [*Also, SD*] [*Statistics*]
S................	Staphylococcus [*Medicine*] (MAE)
S................	Star (NASA)
S................	Starboard
S................	Start (KSC)
s................	Stat [*Unit of radioactive disintegration rate*]
S................	State [*Telecommunications*]
S................	Static
S................	Station
S................	Stationary
S................	Statue (ADA)
S................	Status Required [*Civil Service*]
S................	Statute
S................	Steamer
S................	Steamship (DS)
S................	Steel
S................	Stem

S	Stephanus Provincialis [*Flourished, 1290-97*] [*Authority cited in pre-1607 legal work*] (DSA)
S	Stere [*Metric measure of volume*]
S	Stereo (CDAI)
S	Stereo Broadcast [*British*]
S	Stimulus
S	Stock
S	Stockbroker
S	Stolen Base [*Baseball*]
S	Stopping Power
S	Storage
S	Stores [*British military*] (DMA)
S	Straight
S	Straight-In [*Aviation*] (FAAC)
s	Strange [*Quark*] [*Atomic physics*]
S	Stratum (BJA)
S	Stratus [*Meteorology*]
S	Street [*Bureau of the Census*]
S	Strength (DS)
S	Streptococcus [*Medicine*] (MAE)
S	Streptomycin [*An antibiotic*]
S	Streptozocin [*Antineoplastic drug*]
S	Stroke of Piston in Inches [*Railroad term*]
S	Studio [*A publication*]
S	Stung [*by bees*] [*Medicine*]
S	Subcompact [*Car size*]
S	Subito [*Immediately; Suddenly*] [*Music*]
S	Subject [*Psychology*]
S	Subject [*of a proposition in logic*]
S	Subluxation [*Chiropractic*]
S	Submarine
s	Submerged Pump [*Liquid gas carriers*]
S	Substantive
S	Substrate, Free [*Enzyme kinetics*]
S	Succeeded
S	Successor
S	Sucre [*Monetary unit*] [*Ecuador*]
S	Sud [*South*] [*French*] (ROG)
S	Sugar [*Phonetic alphabet*] [*Royal Navy*] [*World War I*] [*Pre-World War II*] [*World War II*] (DSUE)
S	Suit
S	Suitability (CAAL)
S	Sulfamethoxazole [*Also, SMX, SMZ*] [*Antibacterial compound*]
S	Sulfate
S	Sulfur [*Chemical element*]
S	Sum (MAE)
S	Sumendus [*To Be Taken*] [*Pharmacy*]
S	Summary
S	Summer [*Vessel load line mark*]
S	Summit Books [*Publisher's imprint*]
S	Sun
S	Sunday
S	Sunny [*Meteorology*] (ADA)
S	Super
S	Superb
S	Superficial
S	Superior
S	Supernatant [*Protein*] [*Cytology*]
S	Superseded [*New regulation or order substituted for an existing one*] [*Used in Shepard's Citations*] [*Legal term*] (DLA)
S	Supply [*Economics*]
S	Supply [*Department aboard a carrier*] [*Navy*]
S	Supravergence (AAMN)
S	Supreme Court Reporter [*A publication*] (DLA)
S	Sur [*On*] [*French*]
S	Surface Area
S	Surfaced
S	Surgeon [*Navy*] [*British*] (ROG)
S	Surgery [*Medical Officer designation*] [*British*]
S	Surplus
S	Surrogate
S	Survey
S	Survival
S	Susceptible
S	Suus [*His*] [*Latin*]
S	Svedberg Unit [*Physical chemistry*]
S	Sweden [*IYRU nationality code*]
S	Switch
S	Switchboard [*Telecommunications*] (TEL)
s	Symmetrical [*Also, sym*] [*Chemistry*]
s	Symmetry Number [*Symbol*] [*IUPAC*]
S	Symposium [*A publication*]
S	Synchronized Sleep
S	Synchronous
S	Synoptic [*Meteorology*]
S	Synthesis [*Phase in mitosis*] [*Cytology*]
S	System
s	Thio [*or Mercapto*] [*As substituent on nucleoside*] [*Biochemistry*]
S	Thiouridine [*One-letter symbol; see Srd*]
S	Water Surface Craft [*JETDS nomenclature*]
S	Wyeth Laboratories [*Research code symbol*]
S-1	Personnel Section [*in Army brigades or smaller units, and in Marine Corps units smaller than a brigade; also, the officer in charge of this section. Also refers to adjutant - 1st staff section, brigades, and lower units*]
S-2	Intelligence Section [*in Army brigades or smaller units, and in Marine Corps units smaller than a brigade; also, the officer in charge of this section*]
2-S	Selective Service Class [*for Registrant Deferred Because of Activity in Study*]
S-3	Operations and Training Section [*in Army brigades or smaller units, and in Marine Corps units smaller than a brigade; also, the officer in charge of this section*]
S3	Signal Selection Switchboard (CAAL)
3S	Simplification, Standardization, Specialization [*Economics*]
S3	Simulation in the Service of Society
S³	Small Scientific Satellite [*NASA*]
3S	Standard Supply System [*Army*] (RDA)
S3	Synergistic Strike System
S3	Systems and Software Simulator
S-4	Logistics Section [*in Army brigades or smaller units, and in Marine Corps units smaller than a brigade; also, the officer in charge of this section*]
4S	Society for Social Studies of Science (EA)
S4	Stanford School Scheduling System
S4	Supply Officer [*Army*]
S5	Civil Affairs Officer [*Army*] (AABC)
S7	Seller's Delivery in Seven Days [*Stock exchange term*]
S/40	Sex Over Forty [*A publication*]
4S's	Sex, Silk, Swords, and Swash [*Elements of historical romances*]
4S's	Stealth Aircraft, Sea-Launched Cruise Missiles, SDI [*Strategic Defense Initiative*]-Like Devices, Space Systems [*High-tech weaponry*]
4S's	Sun, Sand, Sea, Sex [*Used in advertising by travel agencies*]
S (Day)	Day on which deployment to war stations of submarines is ordered [*NATO exercises*] (NATG)
S (Test)	Suitability Test [*Military*] (CAAL)
SA	Air-Cushion Vehicle built by Societe National Industrielle Aerospatiale [*France*] [*Usually used in combination with numerals*]
sa-----	Amazon River and Basin [*MARC geographic area code*] [*Library of Congress*] (LCCP)
S & A	Bureau of Supplies and Accounts [*Later, NSUPSC*] [*Navy*]
SA	Le Syllabaire Accadien [*A publication*] (BJA)
SA	Missionary Sisters of Our Lady of Africa [*White Sisters*] [*Roman Catholic religious order*]
SA	Sable [*Heraldry*]
S & A	Safe-and-Arm (KSC)
S/A	Safe Arm
S/A	Safe Arrival
SA	Safety Analysis [*Nuclear energy*] (NRCH)
S & A	Safety and Arming Device
SA	Safety Assessment
SA	Safing Area [*NASA*] (NASA)
SA	Sail Area
SA	Salicylic Acid [*Organic chemistry*]
SA	Salt Acid
SA	Salt Added
SA	Salvation Army (EA)
Sa	Samarium [*Obsolete form; see Sm*] [*Chemical element*]
SA	Sample Array
SA	Sample Assembly (MCD)
Sa	Samtiden [*A publication*]
SA	Sandstorm
Sa	Sanguinarine [*Biochemistry*]
SA	Sanitary Authority [*British*] (ROG)
SA	Sarcastics Anonymous (EA)
SA	Sarcoma [*Medicine*]
SA	Saturday
SA	Saturn Apollo [*NASA*] (KSC)
SA	Saudi Arabia [*ANSI two-letter standard code*] (CNC)
SA	Saunders Aircraft Corp. Ltd. [*Canada*] [*ICAO aircraft manufacturer identifier*] (ICAO)
S & A	Saunders and Austin's Locus Standi Reports [*1895-1904*] [*A publication*] (DLA)
SA	Sausage Aerial [*Radio*]
SA	Savannah & Atlanta Railway Co. [*AAR code*]
SA	Savings Account
SA	Sawmakers' Association [*A union*] [*British*]
SA	Scaling Amplifier
SA	Scenic America (EA)
S/A	Scheduled/Actual (NASA)
SA	Schizophrenics Anonymous (EA)
S of A	School of Artillery [*British military*] (DMA)
SA	Science Abstracts [*A publication*]
SA	Science Advisors [*Army*] (RDA)
S & A	Science and Application (NASA)
SA	Scientific American [*A publication*]
SA	Scientific Assistant [*Ministry of Agriculture, Fisheries, and Food*] [*British*]

SA .... Scleroderma Association   (EA)
SA .... Scoliosis Association   (EA)
SA .... Scout Association   (EAIO)
SA .... Seaman Apprentice [Navy rating]
SA .... Seasonally Adjusted   (WGA)
SA .... Second Attack [Men's lacrosse position]
SA .... Secondary Amenorrhea [Medicine]   (MAE)
SA .... Secondary Anemia [Medicine]   (MAE)
SA .... Secretary of the Army
SA .... Secundum Artem [According to the Art] [Latin]
SA .... Security Alarm Technician Program [Association of
                    Independent Colleges and Schools specialization code]
SA .... Security Assistance   (MCD)
SA .... See Also [Indexing code]
SA .... Seiners Association [Later, PSVOA]
SA .... Select Address
SA .... Selected Ammunition   (RDA)
SA .... Selective Availability
SA .... Self-Administered [Drugs]
SA .... Semen Analysis
SA .... Semiannual
SA .... Semiautomatic
SA .... Senior Advisor [Military]
SA .... Sense Amplifier
SA .... Sensible Atmosphere   (SAA)
SA .... Sensitized Activated
SA .... Separat-Abdruck   (BJA)
SA .... Separated Atom [Atomic physics]
SA .... Sequential Automated
SA .... Serendipity Association   (EA)
SA .... Serra
SA .... Serum Albumin [Serology]
SA .... Servant Allowance [British military]   (DMA)
S/A.............. Service Action   (AAG)
SA .... Service Adviser [or Attache] [British]
SA .... Service Agreement   (MCD)
SA .... Service Air [Nuclear energy]   (NRCH)
S/A.............. Service Application [Military]   (AFIT)
SA .... Service Arm   (KSC)
SA .... Service Assistant [Telecommunications]   (TEL)
SA .... Serviced Apartment
SA .... Servo Amplifier
SA .... Seventh Avenue [New York City]
SA .... Sex Appeal [Slang]
SA .... Sexaholics Anonymous   (EA)
SA .... Sexual Abuse
SA .... Shaft Angle [Technical drawings]
SA .... Shell Analysis
SA .... Shift Advance Driver
SA .... Ship Abstracts [Helsinki University of Technology]
                    [Bibliographic database]
SA .... Ship to Aircraft   (DEN)
S/A.............. Ship Alteration   (MCD)
S/A.............. Shipped Assembled
SA .... Shipping Annual Data [Department of Commerce]   (GFGA)
SA .... Shipping Authority
SA .... Shock Attenuation   (AAG)
SA .... Shop Accessory [Drawing]   (NG)
SA .... Shops Act [1950] [British]   (ILCA)
SA .... Shortening Allowance [Carpentry]
SA .... Sicanna Industries Ltd. [Vancouver Stock Exchange symbol]
S & A.......... Sickness and Accident [Insurance]
SA .... Sideroblastic Anemia [Hematology]
SA .... Siegfried AG [Switzerland] [Research code symbol]
SA .... Sierra
SA .... Signal Access
SA .... Signal Analysis
SA .... Signal Analyzer
SA .... Signal Attenuation   (AAG)
SA .... Signature Analysis
SA .... Simple Alert   (NATG)
SA .... Simulated Annealing [Physics]
sa.............. Sin Ano [Without Year] [Publishing] [Spanish]
SA .... Sine Anno [Without Date of Publication] [Latin]
SA .... Single Access   (MCD)
SA .... Single Action [Firearm]
SA .... Single Armor [Telecommunications]   (TEL)
SA .... Sinoatrial [Medicine]
SA .... Sinoauricular [Medicine]
SA .... Sinus Aestuum [Bay of Billows] [Lunar area]
SA .... Sinus Arrhythmia [Cardiology]   (MAE)
SA .... Sister of Arts
SA .... Site Activation [NASA]   (MCD)
SA .... Situation Audit   (MCD)
SA .... Slightly Active   (MAE)
SA .... Slow-Acting [Pharmacy]
SA .... Slugging Average [Baseball]
SA .... Small Arms [All firearms other than cannon]
SA .... Smithsonian Associates [Later, Smithsonian Resident Associate
                    Program]
SA .... Snap Action

SA .... Socialist Action [An association]   (EA)
S/A.............. Societa Anonima [Stock company] [Italian]
SA .... Societas Adunationis [Franciscan Friars or Sisters of the
                    Atonement] [Roman Catholic religious order]
SA .... Society of Actuaries
SA .... Society of Alexandria [Defunct]   (EA)
SA .... Society of Antiquaries [British]
SA .... Society of Archivists [British]
SA .... Society of Arts [British]
SA .... Sociological Abstracts [Sociological Abstracts, Inc.]
                    [Information service or system] [A publication]
SA .... Sociological Analysis [A publication]
SA .... Software Applications
SA .... Soil Association [Bristol, England]   (EAIO)
SA .... Solar Array   (KSC)
SA .... Soluble in Alkaline Solution
SA .... Solution Annealed   (MCD)
SA .... Son Altesse [His or Her Highness] [French]
SA .... Sonderabdruck   (BJA)
SA .... Soprano, Alto
SA .... Soul Asylum [Rock-music group]
SA .... Source Address
SA .... South Africa [IYRU nationality code]
sa.............. South Africa [MARC country of publication code] [Library of
                    Congress]   (LCCP)
SA .... South African Airways [ICAO designator]
SA .... South African Law Reports [A publication]
SA .... South America
SA .... South Arabian   (BJA)
SA .... South Atlantic
SA .... South Australiana [A publication]   (APTA)
SA .... Southbank Aviation [Australia]
SA .... Southern Association [Baseball league]
SA .... Sovietskaia Archeologiia [A publication]
SA .... Space Aeronautics [A publication]
S/A.............. Space Available   (ADA)
SA .... Spacecraft Adapter [NASA]
SA .... Speaker Amplifier
SA .... Special Access
SA .... Special Action [Military]   (AFM)
S/A.............. Special Activities [Air Force]
SA .... Special Agent   (AFM)
SA .... Special Application [Lift truck]
SA .... Special Area [RADAR]
SA .... Special Artificer [Navy]
SA .... Special Assignment [Navy]
SA .... Special Assistant   (GFGA)
SA .... Specialty Advertising Business [A publication]   (EAAP)
SA .... Specific Activity
SA .... Specific Antigen [Immunology]
SA .... Spectrograph Assembly   (KSC)
SA .... Spectrum Analysis
SA .... Speech Activities [A publication]
SA .... Sperm Aster [Cytology]
SA .... Speronara [Ship's rigging]   (ROG)
SA .... Spin Axis   (AAG)
SA .... Splice Acceptor [Genetics]
SA .... Splitting Amplifier   (AFM)
SA .... Sponsored [or Sponsoring] Agency   (MCD)
SA .... Sports Ambassadors   (EA)
SA .... Spouse's Allowance [Canada]
SA .... Springfield Armory [Army]
SA .... Stage II Apparel Corp. [AMEX symbol]   (SPSG)
SA .... Standard Accuracy [Analytical chemistry]
SA .... Standard Addition
SA .... Standard Agena [NASA]   (KSC)
SA .... Staphylococcus Aureus [Microbiology]
sA.............. Statampere [Also, statA] [Unit of electric current]
SA .... State Agency [Formerly, the Disability Determination Services]
                    [Social Security Administration]   (OICC)
S/A.............. State Agent [Insurance]
SA .... State's Attorney
SA .... Station Address [Data processing]   (BUR)
SA .... Statocyst Anlage
S/A.............. Status and Alert   (AAG)
SA .... Statutes of Alberta [Canada] [Information service or
                    system]   (IID)
SA .... Stokes-Adams [Syndrome] [Medicine]
SA .... Stone Arch [Bridges]
SA .... Storage Activity
SA .... Storage Allocator [Telecommunications]   (TEL)
S/A.............. Storage Area   (KSC)
SA .... Store Address
SA .... Store Automation
SA .... Stores Accountant [British military]   (DMA)
SA .... Stores Assistant [British military]   (DMA)
S on A.......... Stratford-On-Avon, England
SA .... Stress Anneal   (KSC)
SA .... Stretch-Activated Ion Channel
SA .... Structured Analysis [Programming language] [1977]   (CSR)
SA .... Students for America   (EA)

SA	Studies in Astronautics [*Elsevier Book Series*] [*A publication*]
SA	Studio Address (WDMC)
SA	Sturmabteilung [*German*] [*Political party*] (PPE)
SA	Styrene-Acrylonitrile [*Also, SAN*] [*Organic chemistry*]
SA	Sub Anno [*Under the Year*] [*Latin*]
SA	Subaccount (NASA)
SA	Subarachnoid [*Medicine*]
SA	Subassembly
SA	Subcontract Agreement (MCD)
SA	Subject to Approval
SA	Submerged Arc (OA)
SA	Subsequent Access (BYTE)
SA	Subsistence Allowance
SA	Substitution Authorization (AAG)
SA	Successive Approximation (IEEE)
S/A............	Such As
S & A..........	Sugar and Acetone [*Medicine*]
SA	Sugar Association
SA	Sulfonamide
SA	Summing Amplifier
SA	Supervisory Authority
SA	Superwomen Anonymous [*Later, Overachievers Anonymous*] (EA)
SA	Supplemental Agreement (NG)
S & A..........	Supplies and Accounts
SA	Supply Accountant [*Navy*] [*British*]
SA	Supply Activity
SA	Support Activity (MCD)
SA	Support Agency [*NASA*] (KSC)
SA	Support Area [*NASA*] (MCD)
SA	Supporting Arms [*Navy*] [*A publication*]
SA	Surface/Air (NATG)
SA	Surface Area
SA	Surgeon's Assistant [*Medicine*]
SA	Surgical Anastomosis [*Medicine*]
S & A..........	Surveillance and Accountability (NRCH)
S & A..........	Surveillance and Analysis [*Environmental Protection Agency*] (GFGA)
SA	Surveillance Approach (FAAC)
S/A............	Survivorship Agreement [*Legal term*] (DLA)
SA	Sustained Action [*Pharmacy*]
SA	Sweep, Acoustic [*British military*] (DMA)
SA	Sweet Adelines (EA)
SA	Swept Area [*Automotive engineering*]
SA	Swing Arm (KSC)
SA	Switching Devices [*JETDS nomenclature*] [*Military*] (CET)
SA	Symbolae Arctoae [*A publication*]
SA	Symbolic Assembler (IEEE)
SA	Sympathetic Activity [*Physiology*]
SA	Synchro Amplifier
SA	System Administrator [*Data processing*]
SA	System Assessment
SA	Systemic Antibiotic [*Medicine*]
SA	Systems Address
SA	Systems Analysis
SA	Systems Analyst
SA	Systems Architecture [*British*]
SA	VEB Farbenfabrik Wolfen [*East Germany*] [*Research code symbol*]
SAA	S-Band Acquisition Antenna [*Deep Space Instrumentation Facility, NASA*]
SAA	Saatchi & Saatchi Co. Ltd. [*NYSE symbol*] (SPSG)
SAA	Safety Assurance Analysis (NASA)
SAA	Sakai [*Japan*] [*Seismograph station code, US Geological Survey*] [*Closed*] (SEIS)
SAA	Sales Automation Association (EA)
SAA	Santiago Capital [*Vancouver Stock Exchange symbol*]
SAA	Saratoga, WY [*Location identifier*] [*FAA*] (FAAL)
SAA	Satellite Attitude Acquisition
SAA	Saturn Apollo Application [*NASA*] (KSC)
SAA	Saudia Arabia Airlines
SAA	Schweizer Anglistische Arbeiten [*A publication*]
SAA	Science and Applications [*NASA*] (SSD)
SAA	Senior Army Advisor
SAA	Serum Amyloid A [*Clinical chemistry*]
SAA	Service Action Analysis (AAG)
SAA	Servo-Actuated Assembly
SAA	Severe Aplastic Anemia [*Hematology*]
SAA	Sex Addicts Anonymous (EA)
SAA	Sexual Abuse Anonymous (EA)
SAA	Shakespeare Association of America (EA)
SAA	Shelter Advertising Association [*Minneapolis, MN*] (EA)
SAA	Signal Appliance Association [*Later, RSS*]
SAA	Simulated Accelerometer Assembly
SAA	Single Article Announcement [*American Chemical Society publication*]
SAA	Slot Array Antenna
SAA	Small Arms Ammunition
SAA	Social Administration Association [*British*]
SAA	Society for Academic Achievement (EA)
SAA	Society for American Archaeology (EA)

SAA	Society of American Archivists (EA)
SAA	Society of Animal Artists (EA)
SAA	Society for Applied Anthropology (AEBS)
SAA	Society of Archer-Antiquaries (EA)
SAA	Society of Architectural Administrators (EA)
SAA	Society for Asian Art (EA)
SAA	Society of Automotive Analysts (EA)
SAA	Some American Artists [*An association*] (EA)
SAA	South African Airways (AF)
SAA	South African Alliance (PPW)
SAA	South Atlantic Anomaly [*NASA*] (KSC)
SAA	South Australian Artillery [*British military*] (DMA)
SAA	Southern Africa Association [*British*] (EAIO)
SAA	Southern Ash Association [*Defunct*] (EA)
SAA	Special Arbitrage Account
SAA	Special Assignment Airlift [*Air Force*] (AFM)
SAA	Specialty Advertising Association [*Later, SAAI*]
SAA	Speech Association of America [*Later, SCA*] (EA)
SAA	Sri Aurobindo Association (EA)
SAA	Staff Administrative Assistant [*Army*] (AABC)
SAA	State Administrative Agency (GFGA)
SAA	State Applicant Agency (GFGA)
SAA	State Approving Agency [*Bureau of Apprenticeship and Training*] [*Department of Labor*]
SAA	Static Allegation Analyzer [*Data processing*]
SAA	Step Adjustable Antenna
SAA	Stepfamily Association of America (EA)
SAA	Stokes-Adams Attack [*Medicine*] (MAE)
SAA	Summary Activity Account [*Army*] (AABC)
SAA	Sunflower Association of America [*Later, NSA*] (EA)
SAA	Sunglass Association of America (EA)
SAA	Supima Association of America (EA)
SAA	Surety Association of America [*Iselin, NJ*] (EA)
SAA	Surface Active Agents (ADA)
SAA	Survival Air-to-Air (MCD)
SAA	Suzuki Association of the Americas (EA)
SAA	Syrian Arab Airlines
SAA	System Application Architecture [*IBM Corp.*]
SAAA........	San Antonio De Areco [*Argentina*] [*ICAO location identifier*] (ICLI)
SAAA........	Scottish Amateur Athletic Association
SAA/AA	American Antiquity. Society for American Archaeology [*A publication*]
SAAARNG ...	Senior Army Advisor, Army National Guard (AABC)
SAAB........	Selected and Amplified Binding [*Sequence or site*] [*Genetics*]
SAAB........	South African Archaeological Bulletin [*A publication*]
SAAB........	Svenska Aeroplan Aktiebolaget [*Swedish automobile manufacturer; acronym used as name of its cars*]
SAAC........	Concordia/Commodoro Pierrest Egui [*Argentina*] [*ICAO location identifier*] (ICLI)
SAAC........	Schedule Allocation and Control (NASA)
SA/AC......	Scientific Adviser to the Army Council [*World War II*]
SAAC........	Security Assistance Accounting Center [*Military*] (AFIT)
SAAC........	Seismic Array Analysis Center [*IBM Corp.*]
SAAC........	Shelby American Automobile Club (EA)
SAAC........	Simulator for Air-to-Air Combat [*Air Force*]
SAAC........	Society for the Advancement of Ambulatory Care (EA)
SAAC........	South American Athletic Confederation (EAIO)
SAAC........	Space Applications Advisory Committee
SAAC........	Special Assistant for Arms Control [*Military*]
SAACI	Salesmen's Association of the American Chemical Industry [*Later, SACI*] (EA)
SAACONS ...	Standard Army Automated Contracting System (RDA)
SAACT	Surveillance and Accountability Control Team (MCD)
SAAD	Sacramento Army Depot [*California*] (AABC)
SAAD	San Antonio Air Depot [*Air Force*]
SAAD	Small Arms Ammunition Depot
SAAD	Societe des Amis d'Alexandre Dumas (EA)
SAAD	Society for the Advancement of Anaesthesia in Dentistry (EAIO)
SAAD	Sperry Air Arm Division
SAAD Dig ...	SAAD [*Society for the Advancement of Anaesthesia in Dentistry*] Digest [*A publication*]
SA Advertiser (Newspr) ...	South Australian Advertiser Reports (Newspaper) [*A publication*] (APTA)
SAAEB	South African Atomic Energy Board
SAAF	Saudi Arabian Air Force
SAAF	Sherman Army Airfield [*Fort Leavenworth, KS*]
SAAF	Sino-American Amity Fund (EA)
SAAF	Small Arms Alignment Fixture [*Weaponry*] (INF)
SAAF	Small Austere Air Field (MCD)
SAAF	South African Air Force
SAAFA	Astrometriya i Astrofizika [*A publication*]
SAAG	Gualeguaychu [*Argentina*] [*ICAO location identifier*] (ICLI)
SAAG	Science and Applications Advocacy Group
SAA/HO ...	Human Organization. Society for Applied Anthropology [*A publication*]
SAAHS......	Stability Augmentation Attitude Hold System [*Aviation*]
SAAI.........	Punta Indio [*Argentina*] [*ICAO location identifier*] (ICLI)
SAAI.........	Specialty Advertising Association International [*Irving, TX*] (EA)

SAAJ .... Junin [*Argentina*] [*ICAO location identifier*]   (ICLI)
SAAJA ...... Soviet Astronomy [*English Translation*] [*A publication*]
SAAL......... Single Address Assembly Machine Language [*Data processing*]   (MCD)
SAAL........ Single-Axis Acoustic Levitator
Saalb Jb ..... Saalburg-Jahrbuch. Bericht des Saalburg-Museums [*A publication*]
SA-ALC..... San Antonio Air Logistics Center [*Formerly, SAAMA*] [*Air Force*]   (NASA)
SAALCK ... State Assisted Academic Library Council of Kentucky [*Library network*]
SAALC/MM ... San Antonio Air Logistics Center, Directorate of Materiel Management [*Kelly Air Force Base, TX*]
SAAM .... Mazaruca [*Argentina*] [*ICAO location identifier*]   (ICLI)
SAAM .... Simulation Analysis and Modeling
SAAM .... Small-Animal Anesthesia Machine [*Instrumentation*]
SAAM ...... Special Air Force Airlift Mission   (NASA)
SAAM .... Special Assignment Air Mission [*Navy*]   (NVT)
SAAM .... Special Assignment Airlift Movement [*Army*]   (AABC)
SAAMA..... San Antonio Air Materiel Area [*Later, SA-ALC*] [*Air Force*]
SAAMI...... Sporting Arms and Ammunition Manufacturers Institute   (EA)
SAAMS .... Special Airlift Assignment Missions [*Military*]
SAAMS .... Special Application Alarm Monitoring System
SAAN .... Pergamino [*Argentina*] [*ICAO location identifier*]   (ICLI)
SAAN .... South African Associated Newspapers
SAAO .... South African Astronomical Observatory
SAAP........ Parana/Gral Urquiza [*Argentina*] [*ICAO location identifier*]   (ICLI)
SAAP........ Saranton Army Ammunition Plant   (AABC)
SAAP........ Saturn Apollo Applications Program [*NASA*]
SAAP........ Society for the Advancement of American Philosophy   (EA)
SAAP........ South Atlantic Anomaly Probe [*NASA-CNAE*]
SAAPCC ... South African Administrative Pay and Clerical Corps [*British military*]   (DMA)
SAA/R .... Relaciones. Sociedad Argentina de Antropologia [*A publication*]
SAAR........ Rosario [*Argentina*] [*ICAO location identifier*]   (ICLI)
SAAR........ Saw Arbor [*Tool*]
SAARC...... South Asian Association for Regional Cooperation
SA Arch J .. SA [*South African*] Archives Journal [*A publication*]
SAARD..... Slow-Acting Antirheumatic Drug [*Pharmacy*]
SAARF ...... Special Allied Airborne Reconnaissance Force [*Teams parachuted into POW areas to take supplies to prisoners or to help them get out*] [*World War II*]
SAAS .... School of Applied Aerospace Sciences [*Air Force*]
SAAS .... Science Achievement Awards for Students
SAAS .... Shuttle Aerosurface Actuator Simulator [*NASA*]   (MCD)
SAAS .... Society for the Advancement of Agricultural Studies [*British*]
SAAS .... Society of African and Afro-American Students
SAAS .... Soldier as a System [*Symposium*]   (RDA)
SAAS .... Something about the Author Autobiography Series [*A publication*]
SAAS .... Southern Association of Agricultural Scientists   (EA)
SAAS .... Special Ammunition and Analysis Section [*Picatinny Arsenal*] [*Dover, NJ*]
SAAS .... Standard Army Ammunition System   (AABC)
SAAS .... Stress Analysis of Axisymmetric Solids   (MCD)
SAAS Bull Biochem Biotechnol ... SAAS [*Southern Association of Agricultural Scientists*] Bulletin. Biochemistry and Biotechnology [*A publication*]
SAASC ...... San Antonio Air Service Command [*Air Force*]
SAAST ...... Self-Administered Alcoholism Screening Test
SAASW ..... Sub-Antarctic Surface Water [*Marine science*]   (MSC)
SAAT........ Satellite Attitude Acquisition Technique
SAAT........ Systems Analyst Aptitude Test
SAATAS.... South Australia & Territory Air Services   (FAAC)
Saatchi .... Saatchi & Saatchi Co. Ltd. [*Associated Press abbreviation*]   (APAG)
Saatgut-Wirt ... Saatgut-Wirtschaft [*A publication*]
Saatgut-Wirtsch ... Saatgut-Wirtschaft [*A publication*]
SAATMS .. Satellite-Based Advanced Air Traffic Management System [*Department of Transportation*]
SAATSC.... San Antonio Air Technical Service Command [*Air Force*]
SAAU .... Selfreliance Association of American Ukrainians   (EA)
SAAU .... Swiss Association of Autonomous Unions
SAAU .... Villaguay [*Argentina*] [*ICAO location identifier*]   (ICLI)
SAAUSAR ... Senior Army Advisor, United States Army Reserve   (AABC)
SAAV........ Santa Fe/Sauce Viejo [*Argentina*] [*ICAO location identifier*]   (ICLI)
SAAVS ...... Submarine Acceleration and Velocity System
SAAWA..... Schweizer Archiv fuer Angewandte Wissenschaft und Technik [*A publication*]
SAAWC..... Sector Antiair Warfare Coordinator [*Center*]   (NVT)
SAAX........ Saturn Airways, Inc. [*Air carrier designation symbol*]
SAB........... Saba [*Netherlands Antilles*] [*Airport symbol*]   (OAG)
SAB........... Sabbath
SAB........... Sabhawala [*India*] [*Geomagnetic observatory code*]
SAB........... Sabine Corp. [*NYSE symbol*]   (SPSG)
Sab .... Sabinus [*Flourished, 5th or 6th century*] [*Authority cited in pre-1607 legal work*]   (DSA)
SAB........... Sabotage [*FBI standardized term*]

SAB........... Sabouraud Dextrose Agar [*Microbiology*]
SAB........... Same as Above
SAB........... Same as Basic   (KSC)
SAB........... Satellite Assembly Building   (MCD)
SAB........... School of American Ballet [*New York*]
SAB........... Science Advisory Board [*Environmental Protection Agency*]
SAB........... Scientific Advisory Board [*Air Force*]
SAB........... Sealed Argon Bubbling [*Steelmaking*]
SAB........... Shakespeare Association. Bulletin [*A publication*]
SAB........... Shuttle Avionics Breadboard [*NASA*]   (NASA)
SAB........... Signal Aviation Branch
SAB........... Significant Asymptomatic Bacteriuria [*Medicine*]   (MAE)
SAB........... Silk Association of Great Britain   (EAIO)
SAB........... Site Activation Board [*NASA*]   (KSC)
SAB........... Sitzungsberichte. Deutsche (Preussische) Akademie der Wissenschaften zu Berlin. Philosophisch-Historische Klasse [*Berlin*] [*A publication*]
SAB........... Snap Action Bimetal [*Automotive engineering*]
SAB........... Societe Anonyme Belge d'Exploitation de la Navigation Aerienne [*Sabena Belgian World Airlines*]
SAB........... Society of American Bacteriologists [*Later, ASM*]
SAB........... Society for Applied Bacteriology   (EA)
SAB........... Solar Alignment Bay   (OA)
SAB........... Solar Array Batteries
SAB........... Solid Assembly Building
SAB........... Soprano, Alto, Bass
SAB........... South Atlantic Bulletin [*A publication*]
SAB........... Space Applications Board [*National Academy of Engineering*]
SAB........... Spacecraft Assembly Building [*NASA*]   (MCD)
SAB........... Special Antarctic Blend [*Fuel*]
SAB........... Special Assessment Bond
SAB........... Stack Access Block
SAB........... Statistics and Analysis Branch [*Public Health Service*] [*Information service or system*]   (IID)
SAB........... Storage and Assembly Building [*NASA*]   (NASA)
SAB........... Strategic Assessment Branch [*Office of Oceanography and Marine Assessment*] [*National Oceanic and Atmospheric Administration*]
SAB........... Structural Adhesive Bond
SAB........... Subarachnoid Block [*Medicine*]   (MAE)
SAB........... Subject as Above [*Military*]   (AABC)
SAB........... Support Activities Building [*National Security Agency*]
SAB........... Supporting Assistance Bureau [*Agency for International Development*]
SAB........... System Advisory Board
SABA........ Buenos Aires [*Argentina*] [*ICAO location identifier*]   (ICLI)
SABA........ Serbian-American Bar Association   (EA)
SABA........ Small, Able Battlefield Aircraft [*Military*] [*British*]
SABA........ Small Agile Battlefield Aircraft [*British Aerospace Ltd.*]
SABA........ Society for the Advancement of Behavior Analysis   (EA)
SABA........ South African Black Alliance [*Political party*]   (PPW)
SABA........ Swimmer's Air Breathing Apparatus [*Deep-sea diving*]
Sabah For Rec ... Sabah Forest Record [*A publication*]
Sabah Soc J ... Sabah Society. Journal [*A publication*]
SA Bank Officials J ... South Australian Bank Officials' Journal [*A publication*]   (APTA)
SABAR...... Satellites, Balloons, and Rockets [*Air Force program*]
SABBA ...... System Analysis - Building Block Approach [*Ge Cae International and Gen-Red Ltd.*] [*Software package*]   (NCC)
SABC........ Buenos Aires (Edificio Condor) [*Argentina*] [*ICAO location identifier*]   (ICLI)
SABC........ South African Broadcasting Corp.
Sabchota Med ... Sabchota Meditsina [*A publication*]
SABCO...... Society for the Area of Biological and Chemical Overlap
SABCO J... SABCO [*Society for the Areas of Biological and Chemical Overlap*] Journal [*A publication*]
SABE........ Buenos Aires/Aeroparque, Jorge Newbery [*Argentina*] [*ICAO location identifier*]   (ICLI)
SABE........ Society for Automation in Business Education [*Later, SDE*]   (EA)
SABENA ... Societe Anonyme Belge d'Exploitation de la Navigation Aerienne [*Belgian World Airlines*] [*Facetious translation: Such a Bad Experience, Never Again*]
SABER ...... SECNAV [*Secretary of the Navy*] Advisory Board on Educational Requirements   (NG)
SABER ...... Simplified Acquisition of Base Engineering Requirements [*Air Force*]
SABER ...... Surface-to-Air Beam Rider   (MCD)
SABER ...... Swing-Arm Beam Erector   (MCD)
SABET ...... SECNAV [*Secretary of the Navy*] Advisory Board on Education and Training [*Pensacola, FL*]   (EGAO)
SABEW .... Society of American Business Editors and Writers [*Columbia, MO*]   (EA)
SABH .... Simultaneous Automatic Broadcast Homer   (FAAC)
SABHI...... Sabouraud Dextrose Agar and Brain-Heart Infusion [*Microbiology*]
SaBi .... La Sacra Bibbia [*Turin*] [*A publication*]   (BJA)
SABINE .... Systeme d'Acces a la Banque Informatique des Nomenclatures Europeennes [*Database*] [*EC*]   (ECED)
SABIR .... Semiautomatic Bibliographic Information Retrieval

SABIRS..... Semiautomatic Bibliographic Information Retrieval System (DIT)
SABL........ Serialized Assembly Breakdown List (SAA)
SABLE...... Semiautomatic BOMARC Local Environment (MCD)
SABM........ Buenos Aires (Servicio Meteorologico Nacional) [*Argentina*] [*ICAO location identifier*] (ICLI)
SABM........ Set Asynchronous Balanced Mode
SA/BM...... Systems Analysis and Battle Management [*Military*] (RDA)
SABMAR.. Service-Craft and Boats Machine Accounting Report [*Navy*] (NG)
SABMIS.... Seaborne [*or Ship-Launched*] Antiballistic Missile Intercept System [*Navy*]
SabnR........ Sabine Royalty Trust [*Associated Press abbreviation*] (APAG)
SABNWTR ... Science Advisory Board of the Northwest Territories. Report [*Canada*] [*A publication*]
SABNWTRP ... Science Advisory Board of the Northwest Territories. Research Paper [*Canada*] [*A publication*]
SABNWTWP ... Science Advisory Board of the Northwest Territories. Working Paper [*A publication*]
SABO........ Sense Amplifier Blocking Oscillator
SABOA..... Sabouraudia [*A publication*]
SABOD..... Same as Basic Operations Directive (KSC)
SABOJ...... South Australian Bank Officials' Journal [*A publication*] (APTA)
SABOR..... Same as Basic Or (MUGU)
SABOSE ... SECNAV [*Secretary of the Navy*] Advisory Board on Scientific Education (DNAB)
SABP........ Skeletal Axis of Basal Piece
SABP........ Spontaneous Acute Bacterial Peritonitis [*Medicine*]
SABR........ Society for American Baseball Research (EA)
SABR........ Symbolic Assembler for Binary Relocatable Programs
SABRAC ... Sabra Computer (DNAB)
Sabrao Newslett ... Sabrao Newsletter [*A publication*]
SABRB...... Siemens-Albis Berichte [*A publication*]
SABRE...... SAGE [*Semiautomatic Ground Environment*] Battery Routing Equipment
SABRE...... Sales and Business Reservations Done Electronically
SABRE...... Secure Airborne RADAR Equipment
SABRE...... Self-Aligning Boost and Reentry [*Air Force*]
SABRE...... Semiautomated Business Research Environment [*Computerized reservation network*] [*American Airlines*]
SABRE...... Store Access Bus Recording Equipment [*Telecommunications*] (TEL)
SABRE...... Sweden and Britain RADAR Auroral Experiment [*Ionospheric physics*]
SABRE...... System for Autonomous Bodies Reporting and Evaluation [*Joint project of the Government of Bangladesh and United Nations Department of Technical Co-operation for Development*] [*Information service or system*]
SABRF...... Skeletal Axis of Branchial Filament
SABRI....... Serikat Buruh Rokok Indonesia [*Cigarette Workers' Union of Indonesia*]
SABRS...... Standard Accounting, Budgeting, and Reporting System [*Military*] (GFGA)
SABS........ Congregation of the Sisters of the Adoration of the Blessed Sacrament [*Kerala, India*] (EAIO)
S/ABS...... Shock Absorber [*Automotive engineering*]
SABS........ South African Bureau of Standards [*National standards organization*]
SABS........ Stabilizing Automatic Bomb Sight
SABS Bull ... SABS [*South African Bureau of Standards*] Bulletin [*A publication*]
SABU........ Self-Adjusting Ball-Up [*A state of confusion which may, or may not, clear up of itself*] [*Military slang*]
SABW........ Society of American Business Writers [*Later, SABEW*]
Sac.............. De Sacrificiis Abelis et Caini [*Philo*] (BJA)
SAC............ Saccharin [*Sweetening agent*]
SAC............ Sacramento, CA [*Location identifier*] [*FAA*] (FAAL)
SAC............ Sacrifice [*Baseball*]
Sac.............. Sacris Eruditi. Jaarboek voor Godsdienstwetenschappen [*A publication*]
SAC............ Sacristan
SAC............ Safety Advisory Committee (MCD)
SAC............ Sahali Resources, Inc. [*Vancouver Stock Exchange symbol*]
SAC............ Saint Ambrose College [*Davenport, IA*]
SAC............ Saint Anselm's College [*Manchester, NH*]
SAC............ Saint Anselm's College, Manchester, NH [*OCLC symbol*] (OCLC)
SAC............ Saint Augustine's College [*Raleigh, NC*]
SAC............ Salute America Committee (EA)
SAC............ San Andreas Lake [*California*] [*Seismograph station code, US Geological Survey*] (SEIS)
SAC............ San Antonio College [*Texas*]
SAC............ Santa Ana College [*California*]
SAC............ Scene-of-Action Commander [*Navy*] (NVT)
SAC............ School of Army Co-Operation [*Air Force*] [*British*]
SAC............ Scientific Advisory Committee [*Presidential*] [*Terminated*]
SAC............ Scientific Advisory Council [*Ministry of Supply*] [*British*] [*World War II*]
SAC............ Scottish Arts Council (EAIO)
SAC............ Scottish Automobile Club (DI)

SAC............ Scriptomatic Addressing Computer (HGAA)
SAC............ Secondary Accountability Center (AAG)
SAC............ Secondary Address Code
SAC............ Sectional Aeronautical Chart (NOAA)
SAC............ Security Access Control [*Data processing*]
SAC............ Self-Adjusting Clutch
SAC............ Semiautomatic Coding
SAC............ Semiautomatic Controller (CAAL)
SAC............ Senate Appropriations Committee (NVT)
SAC............ Senior Aircraftman [*British military*] (DMA)
SAC............ Service Application Code [*Navy*]
SAC............ Serving Area Concept [*Bell System*]
SAC............ Servo Adapter Coupler
SAC............ Shipbuilding Advisory Council [*British*]
SAC............ Ships Air Coordinator (MCD)
SAC............ Side-Arm Controller [*Aviation*]
SAC............ Signal Analysis Course [*Navy*] (DNAB)
SAC............ Signature Authorization Card [*or Chart*] (AAG)
SAC............ Single Acting Cylinder
SAC............ Single Address Code (AAG)
SAC............ Sisters of the Holy Guardian Angels [*Roman Catholic religious order*]
SAC............ Soaring Association of Canada
SAC............ Social and Athletic Club
SAC............ Sociedad Anglo-Chilena [*Anglo-Chilean Society*] (EAIO)
SAC............ Societe Africaine de Culture [*Society of African Culture*]
SAC............ Society of African Culture [*France*] (EAIO)
SAC............ Society for American Cuisine [*Later, SCA*] (EA)
SAC............ Society for Analytical Chemistry [*British*]
SAC............ Society for Analytical Cytology (EA)
SAC............ Society of the Catholic Apostolate [*Pallottines*] [*Roman Catholic men's religious order*]
SAC............ South-African Constabulary [*Military*] [*British*] [*Defunct*] (ROG)
SAC............ South Atlantic Coast
SAC............ South Carolina Electric & Gas Co. [*NYSE symbol*] (SPSG)
SAC............ Southern Africa Committee (EA)
SAC............ Southwest Athletic Conference (EA)
SAC............ Special Accounting Class [*Navy*] (DNAB)
SAC............ Special Advisory Committee [*Navy*] (DNAB)
SAC............ Special Agent in Charge [*FBI*]
SAC............ Special Area Code [*Bell System*]
SAC............ Specific Acoustic Capacitance
SAC............ Spectrum Analyzer Component (MCD)
SAC............ Spiritual Advisory Council (EA)
SAC............ Sport for All Clearinghouse [*Belgium*] (EAIO)
SAC............ Sprayed Acoustical Ceiling [*Technical drawings*]
S/AC......... Stabilization/Attitude Control [*NASA*] (NASA)
SAC............ Standard Agena Clamshell [*NASA*] (KSC)
SAC............ Standard Aircraft Characteristics
SAC............ Standing Armaments Committee [*NATO*] (NATG)
SAC............ Staphylococcus Aureus Cervan [*Microbiology*]
SAC............ Starptautiskas Apmainas Centrs [*International Exchange Center*] [*Latvia*] (EAIO)
SAC............ Starting Air Compressor (CAAL)
SAC............ State Advisory Committee [*Department of Education*]
SAC............ State Apprenticeship Council [*Bureau of Apprenticeship and Training*] [*Department of Labor*]
SAC............ Statistical Advisory Committee [*UN Food and Agriculture Organization*]
SAC............ Statistical Analysis Center (OICC)
SAC............ Storage Access Channel (CMD)
SAC............ Storage Access Control [*Data processing*]
SAC............ Store and Clear
SAC............ Store and Clear Accumulator [*Data processing*]
SAC............ Storeman's Action Copy (DNAB)
SAC............ Strategic Air Command [*Air Force*]
SAC............ Strategic Alert Cadre (NVT)
SAC............ Studies in the Age of Chaucer [*A publication*]
SAC............ Studies in Ancient Civilization [*Elsevier Book Series*] [*A publication*]
SAC............ Subarea Advisory Council [*Generic term*] (DHSM)
SAC............ Submitting Activity Code
SAC............ Substance Abuse Coordinator [*Navy*] (DNAB)
SAC............ Sudanese African Congress [*Political party*] (MENA)
SAC............ Sugar Association of the Caribbean [*Port Of Spain, Trinidad*] (EAIO)
SAC............ Sulfuric Acid Concentrate (MCD)
SAC............ Sunbeam Alpine Club (EA)
SAC............ Suore Missionarie dell'Apostolato Cattolico [*Missionary Sisters of the Catholic Apostolate*] [*Rome, Italy*] (EAIO)
SAC............ Supplemental Air Carrier (MCD)
SAC............ Supply Administration Center [*DoD*] (MCD)
SAC............ Supply Availability Card (MCD)
SAC............ Support Action Center [*NASA*] (MCD)
SAC............ Support Assessment Capability
SAC............ Supporting Arms Coordinator [*Air Force*] (NVT)
SAC............ Supreme Allied Command [*or Commander*] [*Headquarters in London*] [*World War II*]
SAC............ Surveyors Appointments Consultancy [*Royal Institute of Chartered Surveyors*] [*British*]

SAC............ Suspended and Canceled Pesticides [*Environmental Protection Agency*] (GFGA)
SAC............ Sussex Archaeological Collections [*A publication*]
SAC............ Sustained Abdominal Compression [*Gastroenterology*]
SAC............ Sveriges Arbetares Centralorganisation [*Central Organization of Swedish Workers*]
SAC............ Synchro Azimuth Converter
SAC............ Synchronous Astro Compass (SAA)
SAC............ System Assessment Capability
SAC............ System Automation Corp. [*Information service or system*] (IID)
SAC............ Systems Acquisition Career
SAC............ Systems Auditability and Control [*Data processing*]
SACA......... Cordoba/Area de Material [*Argentina*] [*ICAO location identifier*] (ICLI)
SACA......... Service Action Change Analysis (AAG)
SACA......... Special Assistant for Consumer Affairs [*White House*] [*Obsolete*]
SACA......... Steam Automobile Club of America (EA)
SACA......... Studebaker Automobile Club of America (EA)
SACA......... Student Action Corps for Animals (EA)
SACA......... Study Advisory Committee on Aeronautics [*National Academy of Engineering*]
SACA......... Subversive Activities Control Act of 1950
SACACCS ... Strategic Air Command Automated Command Control System (AFM)
SACAM..... Ship Acquisition Contract Administration Manual (MCD)
SACAY...... SECNAV [*Secretary of the Navy*] Advisory Commission on Youth (NG)
SACB......... Subversive Activities Control Board [*Later, Federal Internal Security Board*]
SACBC...... Southern African Catholic Bishops' Conference (EAIO)
SACBC-JPC ... Southern African Catholic Bishops' Conference - Justice and Peace Commission (EAIO)
SACC......... La Cumbre [*Argentina*] [*ICAO location identifier*] (ICLI)
SACC......... San Antonio Contracting Center [*Air Force*]
S/ACC .... Scientific/Academic Computing Center [*State University of New York Health Science Center at Brooklyn*] [*Research center*] (RCD)
SACC......... Slovak-American Cultural Center (EA)
SACC......... Society for Anthropology in Community Colleges (EA)
SACC......... State Auditors Coordinating Committee (EA)
SACC......... Supplemental Air Carrier Conference [*Defunct*] (EA)
SACC......... Supporting Arms Coordination Center [*Air Force*]
SACCAR ... Southern African Centre for Co-Operation in Agricultural Research (EY)
SACCD...... Saccharum [*A publication*]
SACCEI..... Strategic Air Command Communications-Electronics Instruction
SACCH...... Saccharatae [*Sugar-Coated*] [*Pharmacy*]
SACCHS ... Scottish Advisory Committee on Computers in the Health Service
SACCOM ... Strategic Air Command Communications (MCD)
SACCOMNET ... Strategic Air Command Communications Network
SACCON... Strategic Air Command Command Control Network
SACCP ...... Strategic Air Command Command Post
SACCS ...... Strategic Air Command Communications [*or Control*] System [*Military*]
SACCS-DPS ... SAC [*Strategic Air Command*] Automated Command Control System - Data Processing System (MCD)
SACD......... Coronel Olmedo [*Argentina*] [*ICAO location identifier*] (ICLI)
Sac D......... Sacra Doctrina. Quaderni Periodici di Teologia e di Filosofia [*A publication*]
SACD......... Societe des Auteurs et Compositeurs Dramatiques [*Society of Dramatic Authors and Composers*] [*Paris, France*] (EAIO)
SACD......... Society of Americans of Colonial Descent (EA)
SACD......... Subacute Combined Degeneration [*of spinal cord*] [*Medicine*] (AAMN)
SACDA...... Surplus Agricultural Commodities Disposal Act of 1982
SACDEF.... Strategic Avionics Crewstation Design Evaluation Facility
SACDIN.... Strategic Air Command Digital Information Network (MCD)
SACDM..... Study and Action Course in District Management [*LIMRA*]
SACDNU .. Sudan African Closed Districts National Union
SAC(DP) ... Scientific Advisory Committee, Defence Services Panel [*British*] [*World War II*]
SACDRS ... Standard Air Carrier Delay Reporting System
SACE......... Cordoba [*Argentina*] [*ICAO location identifier*] (ICLI)
SacE.......... Sacris Erudiri. Jaarboek voor Godsdienstwetenschappen [*A publication*]
SACE......... Semiautomatic Checkout Equipment [*DoD*]
SACE......... Serum Angiotensin Converting Enzyme [*Activity*] [*Serology*]
SACE......... Shore-Based Acceptance Checkout Equipment
SACEA...... Sino-American Cultural and Economic Association
SACED...... South African Journal of Continuing Medical Education [*A publication*]
SACEM..... Society for the Advancement of Continuing Education for Ministry (EA)
SA Census & Statistics Bul ... Australia. Commonwealth Bureau of Census and Statistics. South Australian Office. Bulletin [*A publication*] (APTA)

SA Cereb Palsy J ... SA [*South African*] Cerebral Palsy Journal [*A publication*]
SACEUR ... Supreme Allied Commander, Europe [*NATO*]
SACEUREP ... Supreme Allied Commander, Europe Representative [*NATO*] (NATG)
SACF......... Cordoba [*Argentina*] [*ICAO location identifier*] (ICLI)
SACFI....... Scholars and Citizens for Freedom of Information (EA)
SACG........ Cordoba [*Argentina*] [*ICAO location identifier*] (ICLI)
SACG........ Senior Arms Control Group [*National Security Council*]
SACH .... Solid Ankle Cushion Heel [*Foot prosthesis*]
SACh .... Studies in Analytical Chemistry [*Elsevier Book Series*] [*A publication*]
SACHC...... Soviet-American Committee on Health Cooperation
SACHQ ..... Strategic Air Command Headquarters (AAG)
Sachse NM ... Sachse's Minutes, Norwich Mayoralty Court [*A publication*] (DLA)
SACI......... Pilar [*Argentina*] [*ICAO location identifier*] (ICLI)
SACI......... Sales Association of the Chemical Industry (EA)
SACI......... Secondary Address Code Indicator
SACI......... South Atlantic Cooperative Investigations [*Military*]
SACIM..... Southern African Center for Ivory Marketing
SACL........ Laguna Larga [*Argentina*] [*ICAO location identifier*] (ICLI)
SACL........ South African Confederation of Labour
SACL........ Space and Component Log
SACL........ Standards and Calibration Laboratory (KSC)
SACLA ...... Srpski Arhiv za Celokupno Lekarstvo [*A publication*]
SACLAMP ... Strategic Air Command Low-Altitude Missile Program [*Air Force*]
SACLANT ... Supreme Allied Commander, Atlantic [*NATO*]
SACLANTCEN ... Supreme Allied Atlantic Command Anti-Submarine Warfare Research Centre [*NATO*] [*Italy*]
SACLANTCEN ... Supreme Allied Commander, Atlantic, Antisubmarine Warfare Research Center [*NATO*]
SACLANTREPEUR ... Supreme Allied Commander, Atlantic, Representative in Europe [*NATO*]
SACLAU ... SACLANT [*Supreme Allied Commander, Atlantic*] Authentification System [*NATO*] (NATG)
SACLEX... SACLANT [*Supreme Allied Commander, Atlantic*] Standing Exercise Orders [*NATO*] (NATG)
Sac Lit D.... Doctor of Sacred Literature
SACLO...... Strategic Air Command Liaison Officer
SACLOS... Semiautomatic Command to Line of Sight [*Military*]
Sac M........ Sacred Music [*A publication*]
SACM........ School of Acquisition Management [*Army*]
SACM........ Simulated Aerial Combat Maneuver
SACM....... Statistical Adiabatic Channel Model [*Physical chemistry*]
SACM....... Villa Gral, Mitre [*Argentina*] [*ICAO location identifier*] (ICLI)
SACMA..... Suppliers of Advanced Composite Materials Association [*Arlington, VA*] (EA)
SACMAP .. Selective Automatic Computational Matching and Positioning (MCD)
SACMAPS ... Selective Automatic Computational Matching and Positioning System
SACMDR ... Site Activation Commander [*Army*] (AABC)
SACMED ... Supreme Allied Commander, Mediterranean [*World War II*]
SAC/MEP ... Strategic Air Command/Minuteman Education Program (AFM)
SACMP ..... South African Corps of Military Police [*British military*] (DMA)
SACMPC .. Systems Acquisition Career Management Personnel Center [*DoD*]
SACN........ Ascochinga [*Argentina*] [*ICAO location identifier*] (ICLI)
SACNA..... South Africa Club of North America [*Defunct*] (EA)
SACNAS ... Society for Advancement of Chicanos and Native Americans in Science (EA)
SACNET ... Secure Automatic Communications Network
SACO .... Cordoba [*Argentina*] [*ICAO location identifier*] (ICLI)
SACO .... Select Address and Contract Operate
SACO .... Service Administratif Canadien Outre-Mer [*Canadian Executive Service Overseas - CESO*]
SACO .... Sino American Cooperative Organization (EA)
SACO .... Supporting Administrative Contracting Officer (AFIT)
SACO .... Sveriges Akademikers Centralorganisation [*Swedish Confederation of Professional Associations*]
SACOA..... Southern Appalachian Coal Operators Association (EA)
SAC-OA .... Strategic Air Command Office of Operations Analysis
SACOD ..... South African Congress of Democrats
SACOM .... SECNAV [*Secretary of the Navy*] Advisory Commission on Manpower (NG)
SACOM .... Ship's Advanced Communications (SAA)
SACOM .... Southern Area Command [*Military*] (AABC)
SACON .... Shock-Absorbing Concretes (RDA)
SACON ..... Shock Attenuating Cellular Concrete [*Army*]
SACON ..... Structural Analysis Consultant (MCD)
SACOPD... Smoking-Attributable Chronic Obstructive Pulmonary Disease
SACOPS... Strategic Air Command Operational Planning System (MCD)
SACP........ Chepes [*Argentina*] [*ICAO location identifier*] (ICLI)
SACP........ Sacrificial Anode Cathodic Protection (MCD)
SACP........ Selected Area Channelling Pattern (MCD)
SACP........ Society for Asian and Comparative Philosophy (EA)
SACP........ South African Communist Party

SACP......... Special Assistant for Civilian Personnel [*Navy*] (DNAB)
SACP........ Strategic Air Command Project Office (AAG)
SACPAN... Stemming and Closure Panel [*Terminated, 1975*] [*DoD*] (EGAO)
SACPB...... South African Chemical Processing [*A publication*]
SACP/EEO ... Special Assistant for Civilian Personnel / Equal Employment Opportunity [*Navy*] (DNAB)
SACPG...... Senior Arms Control Planning Group [*Pronounced "sack pig"*] [*DoD*]
SACPO...... Saigon Area Civilian Personnel Office [*Vietnam*]
SACPO...... South African Colored People's Organization
SACPPL.... Standing Advisory Committee on Private Pilot Licensing [*British*] (AIA)
SACQ........ Monte Quemado [*Argentina*] [*ICAO location identifier*] (ICLI)
SACR........ Sacrament (ROG)
SACR........ Sacred (ROG)
SACR........ Sacrifice (ROG)
SACR........ Sacrist
SACR........ Semiautomatic Coordinate Reader (DNAB)
SACR........ Strategic Air Command Regulations (AAG)
SACRA...... Student Alliance for Christian Renewal in America
Sacramnt B ... Sacramento Bee [*A publication*]
Sacred Mus ... Sacred Music [*A publication*]
SACROC.... Scurry Area Canyon Reef Operators Committee
SACS........ Satellite Attitude-Control Simulator [*NASA*]
SACS........ Satellite Control Squadron
SACS......... Scheduling Activity Control System [*PA Computers & Telecommunications Ltd.*] [*Software package*] (NCC)
SACS........ Selective High-Frequency Antenna Coupler System [*Military*] (CAAL)
SACS........ Sensor Accuracy Check Site (MCD)
SACS........ Services After-Care Scheme [*British*]
SACS........ Ship Alteration Completion System
SACS........ Shipyard Accuracy Checksite (MCD)
SACS........ Sino-American Cultural Society (EA)
SACS........ Software Avionics Command Support (NASA)
SACS........ Solar Altitude Control System
SACS........ SONAR Accuracy Check Site (NVT)
SACS........ Southern Association of Colleges and Schools (EA)
SACS........ Structure and Composition System [*Military*] (AABC)
SACS........ Synchronous Altitude Communications Satellite
SACS........ Systems Software Avionics Command Support (MCD)
SACS........ Villa De Soto [*Argentina*] [*ICAO location identifier*] (ICLI)
SACSA...... Special Assistant for Counterinsurgency and Special Activities [*Military*] (AFM)
SACSA...... Standing Advisory Committee for Scientific Advice [*Oslo Commission*] (DCTA)
SACSEA.... Supreme Allied Command [*or Commander*], Southeast Asia
SACSIR.... South African Council for Scientific and Industrial Research
SAC/SSW ... Special Assistant to the Chief of Staff for Special Warfare [*Army*]
SACT......... Gobernador Gordillo [*Argentina*] [*ICAO location identifier*] (ICLI)
SACT........ Sinoatrial Conduction Time [*Cardiology*]
SACT......... System Availability Calculation Tool [*Science Applications International Corp.*] (MCD)
SACTO...... Sacramento Test Operations (MCD)
SACTTYNET ... Strategic Air Command Teletype Network
SACTU...... South African Congress of Trade Unions
SACTW...... South African Council of Transport Workers
SACU........ Cordoba [*Argentina*] [*ICAO location identifier*] (ICLI)
SACU........ Service for Admission to College and University [*Canada*] (AEBS)
SACU........ Society for Anglo-Chinese Understanding [*British*] (EAIO)
SACU........ South African Customs Union
SACU........ Stand-Alone Digital Communications Unit (MCD)
SACUBO... Southern Association of College and University Business Officers (AEBS)
SACUS...... Southern Association on Children under Six (EA)
SACV......... Villa Maria Del Rio Seco [*Argentina*] [*ICAO location identifier*] (ICLI)
SACVAR ... Ship Alteration Cost Variance Account Report
SACW........ Senior Aircraftwoman [*British military*] (DMA)
SAD.......... Saddle (AAG)
SAD.......... Saddleback Community College District, Mission Viejo Campus, Mission Viejo, CA [*OCLC symbol*] (OCLC)
Sad .... Sadler's Pennsylvania Cases [*A publication*] (DLA)
SAD.......... Safe-and-Arm Device
SAD........... Safety Analysis [*or Assurance*] Diagram [*Nuclear energy*] (NRCH)
SAD.......... Safety, Arming, and Destruct (MCD)
SAD.......... Safety and Arming Device [*Military*] (AABC)
SAD.......... Safford, AZ [*Location identifier*] [*FAA*] (FAAL)
sad............. Sandawe [*MARC language code*] [*Library of Congress*] (LCCP)
S & AD...... Science and Applications Directorate [*NASA*]
SAD.......... Search and Destroy (MCD)
SAD........... Seasonal Affective Disorder [*Type of depression caused by long nights, short days*]
SAD........... Selected Area [*Electron*] Diffraction [*Also, SAED*] [*Analysis of solids*]
SAD........... Self-Assessment Depression Scale (AAMN)

SAD........... Semiconductor Anticoincidence Detector
SAD........... Sentence Appraiser and Diagrammer
SAD.......... Service Action Drawing (AAG)
SAD........... Ship Acoustics Department [*David W. Taylor Naval Ship Research and Development Center*]
SAD........... Shuttle Authorized Document [*NASA*] (NASA)
SAD........... Silverado Mines Ltd. [*Vancouver Stock Exchange symbol*]
SAD........... Simple, Average, or Difficult (AAG)
SAD........... Single Administrative Document [*European trade contract*] [*1986*] (DCTA)
SAD........... Sinoaortic Deafferentation [*Medicine*]
SAD........... Sinoaortic Denervation [*Physiology*]
SAD........... Situation Attention Display
S-A-D........ Sleep Disturbance with Anxiety and Depression [*Combat behavior disorder*] [*Military*] (INF)
SAD........... Social Avoidance Distress [*Scale*]
SAD........... Society of the Ark and the Dove (EA)
SAD........... Source-to-Axis Distance (MAE)
SAD........... South American Datum
SAD........... South Atlantic Division [*Army Corps of Engineers*]
SAD........... Soviet Air Defense
SAD........... Soviet Air Demonstration
SAD........... Space Antennae Diversity [*Telecommunications*] (TEL)
SAD........... Spacecraft Attitude Display (MCD)
SAD........... Special Artificer, Special Synthetic Training Devices [*Navy*]
SAD........... Station Address Directory [*Army*]
SAD........... Status Advisory Display (MCD)
SAD........... Store Address Director
SAD........... Submarine Anomaly Detection [*Navy*] (NVT)
SAD........... Sugar, Acetone, Diacetic Acid [*Test*] [*Medicine*]
SAD........... Supervisory Aptitude Development [*In George Lee Walker novel "The Chronicles of Doodah"*]
SAD........... Support Air Direction [*Navy*]
SAD........... Supporting Arms Department [*Navy*] (DNAB)
SAD........... Surface Area Decay [*Plant pathology*]
SAD........... Survival Assistance Director [*Federal disaster planning*]
SAD........... Sympathetic Aerial Detonation [*Air Force*]
SAD........... System Allocation Document [*NASA*] (NASA)
SAD........... System Analysis Drawing
SAD........... Systems Analysis Document (MCD)
SAD........... Systems Automation Division [*Navy*] (DNAB)
SADA........ Seismic Array Data Analyzer (IEEE)
SADA .... Southern Appalachian Dulcimer Association (EA)
SADAP...... Simplified Automatic Data Plotter
SADAP...... State Alcoholism and Drug Abuse Profile [*Public Health Service*] [*Information service or system*] (IID)
SADAR...... Satellite Data Reduction [*Processor system*]
SADARM ... Search and Destroy Armor Munition (MCD)
SADARM ... Selected Armor Defeating Artillery Munition
SADARM ... Selected Armor Defeating Artillery Munitions (MCD)
SADARM ... Sense [*or Search*] and Destroy Armor Munition
SAD Beng.. Select Cases, Sadr Diwani [*Bengal*] [*A publication*] (DLA)
SAD Bom... Sadr Diwani Adalat Reports [*Bombay, India*] [*A publication*] (DLA)
SADBU...... Small and Disadvantaged Business Utilization [*Department of Commerce*]
SADBUS ... Small and Disadvantaged Business Utilization Specialist [*Federal government*] (GFGA)
SADC........ Sector Aid Defense Commander (NATG)
SADC........ Sequential Analog-Digital Computer (DIT)
SADC........ Sneak Attack Defense Coordinator [*Military*] (CAAL)
SADD........ Buenos Aires/Don Torcuato [*Argentina*] [*ICAO location identifier*] (ICLI)
SADD........ Semiautomatic Detection Device
SADD........ Students Against Driving Drunk (EA)
SaDDC ...... Durban City Council, Durban, South Africa [*Library symbol*] [*Library of Congress*] (LCLS)
SADE......... Specialized Armoured Development Establishment [*British military*] (DMA)
SADE........ Structural Assembly Demonstration Experiment (MCD)
SADE........ Superheat Advanced Demonstration Experiment [*Nuclear energy*]
SADE......... Symbolic Application Debugging Environment
SADEC...... Spin Axis Declination [*Aerospace*] (MCD)
SADELCA ... Sociedad Aerea del Caqueta [*Airline*] [*Colombia*]
SADEMS .. Salt Dome Experimental Monitoring System (GFGA)
SA Dep Agric Tech Bull ... South Australia. Department of Agriculture. Technical Bulletin [*A publication*] (APTA)
SADEYA ... Sociedad Astronomica de Espana y America [*Hispano-American Astronomical Society*] (EAIO)
SADF......... San Fernando [*Argentina*] [*ICAO location identifier*] (ICLI)
SADF........ Semi-Automatic Document Feeder (HGAA)
SADF........ South African Defence Forces
SADG .... Monte Grande [*Argentina*] [*ICAO location identifier*] (ICLI)
SADGE..... SAGE [*Semi-Automatic Ground Equipment*] Data Generator (SAA)
SADH .... Succinic Acid - Dimethylhydrazide [*Plant growth retardant*]
SADI.......... Secretarial Automated Data Index
SADI......... Selling-Areas Distribution Index (WDMC)
SADIC....... Solid-State Analog-to-Digital Computer

SADID4.....	Annual Research Reviews. Sphingolipidoses and Allied Disorders [*A publication*]
SADIE.......	Scanning Analog-to-Digital Input Equipment [*National Institute of Standards and Technology*]
SADIE.......	Secure Automatic Data Information Exchange [*System*]
SADIE.......	Semiautomatic Decentralized Intercept Environment [*Air Force*]
SADIE.......	Sterling and Decimal Invoicing Electronically (IEEE)
SADIS	Shipboard Automated Decoy Integration System [*Navy*]
Sadivn Resp Mizhvid Nauk-Temat Zb ... Sadivnytstvo Respublikanskyi Mizhvidomchyi Naukovo-Tematychnyi Zbirnik [*A publication*]	
SADJ	Jose C. Paz/Dr. Mariano More [*Argentina*] [*ICAO location identifier*] (ICLI)
SADL........	La Plata [*Argentina*] [*ICAO location identifier*] (ICLI)
SADL........	Sadlier [*William H.*], Inc. [*NASDAQ symbol*] (NQ)
SADL........	Ships Authorized Data List
SADL........	Significant Activity of Daily Living [*Insurance*]
SADL........	Spares Application Data List
SADL........	Special Automated Distribution List (AFIT)
SADL........	Sterilization Assembly Development Laboratory [*NASA*]
SADL........	Synchronous Automatic Dial Language
Sadler	Sadler's Pennsylvania Cases [*A publication*] (DLA)
Sadler (PA) ...	Sadler's Pennsylvania Cases [*A publication*] (DLA)
SADM	Moron [*Argentina*] [*ICAO location identifier*] (ICLI)
SADM	Secretary of the Army Decision Memorandum [*Army*] (RDA)
SADM	Solar Array Drive Motor
SADM	Special Atomic Demolition Munitions [*Military*] (AABC)
SADM	System Acquisition Decision Memorandum (MCD)
SADMG	Special Artificer, Special Devices, Machine Gun Trainer [*Navy*]
SADNWF ...	Sadr Diwani Adalat Cases, Northwest Frontier [*Pakistan*] [*A publication*] (DLA)
SaDo	Sacra Doctrina [*A publication*]
SADOAJ ...	Sadovodstvo [*Moscow*] [*A publication*]
Sado Mar Biol Stn Niigata Univ Spec Publ ... Sado Marine Biological Station. Niigata University. Special Publication [*A publication*]	
SADOPS ...	Ships Angle-Tracking and Doppler System (SAA)
SADOT	Structures Assembly Deployment and Operations Technology (SSD)
Sadovod......	Sadovodstvo [*A publication*]
Sadovod Vinograd Vinodel Mold ... Sadovodstvo Vinogradarstvo i Vinodelia Moldavii [*A publication*]	
SADP........	El Palomar [*Argentina*] [*ICAO location identifier*] (ICLI)
SADP........	Scales of Attitudes toward Disabled Persons [*Occupational therapy*]
SADP........	Scandinavian Association of Directory Publishers (EAIO)
SADP........	Selected Area Electron Diffraction Pattern [*Analysis of solids*]
SADP........	Small Area Direct Path [*Military*] (CAAL)
SADP........	Structured Analysis, Design, and Programming [*Data processing*]
SADP........	Synthetic Array Data Processor
SADP........	System Architecture Design Package
Sad PA Cas ...	Sadler's Pennsylvania Cases [*1885-88*] [*A publication*] (DLA)
Sad PA Cs ...	Sadler's Pennsylvania Cases [*1885-88*] [*A publication*] (DLA)
SADPO......	Systems Analysis and Data Processing Office
SADQ	Quilmes [*Argentina*] [*ICAO location identifier*] (ICLI)
SADQ	Severity of Alcohol Dependence Questionnaire
SADR........	Merlo [*Argentina*] [*ICAO location identifier*] (ICLI)
SADR........	Saharan Arab Democratic Republic [*Morocco*] (PD)
SADR........	Secure Acoustic Data Relay (NVT)
SADR........	Severity Adjusted Death Rate [*Medicine*] (DHSM)
SADR........	Six Hundred Megacycle Air Defense RADAR
SADRAM ...	Seek and Destroy RADAR-Assisted Mission (MCD)
SADRI	Social and Demographic Research Institute [*University of Massachusetts*] [*Research center*] (RCD)
SADRT......	Secure Acoustic Data Relay Terminal (MCD)
SADS........	San Justo/Aeroclub Argentino [*Argentina*] [*ICAO location identifier*] (ICLI)
SADS........	Schedule for Affective Disorders and Schizophrenia [*Psychological interview*]
SADS........	Semiautomatic Defense System (NG)
SADS........	Semiconductor Anticoincidence Detection System
SADS........	Senate Appropriations Defense Subcommittee
SADS........	Simulated Air Defense System [*RADAR*]
SADS........	Single Application Data Sheet
SADS........	Social Avoidance and Distress Scale [*Psychology*]
SADS........	Solar Array Drive System
SADS........	Submarine Active Detection System
SADS........	Swiss Air Defense System
SADS........	System Architecture Development Study [*NATO Integrated Communications System*] (NATG)
SADSAC ...	Sampled Data Simulator and Computer
SADSAC ...	Seiler ALGOL Digitally Simulated Analog Computer
SADSAC ...	Small Acoustic Device Simulating Aircraft Carrier (NVT)
SADSACT ...	Self-Assigned Descriptors from Self and Cited Titles [*Automatic indexing*]
SADSC	San Antonio Data Services Center [*Military*]
SADS-C.....	Schedule for Affective Disorders and Schizophrenia - Change Version [*Personality development test*] [*Psychology*]
SADS-L.....	Schedule for Affective Disorders and Schizophrenia - Lifetime Version [*Personality development test*] [*Psychology*]
SADS-TG ..	Submarine Active Detection System - Transmit Group [*Navy*]
SADT........	Self-Accelerating Decomposition Temperature
SADT........	Special Active Duty for Training [*Military*] (AABC)
SADT........	Structured Analysis and Design Technique [*Programming language*] [*1978*]
SADT........	Surface Alloy Diffused-Base Transistor
SADTC......	SHAPE [*Supreme Headquarters Allied Powers Europe*] Air Defense Technology Center [*Later, STC*] [*NATO*]
Sadtler Commer Spectra ... Sadtler Commercial Spectra [*United States*] [*A publication*]	
SADTS	Safety and Arming Detection Test Set (DWSG)
SADU	Sea Search Attack Development Unit
SADV	Semiannual Density Variation [*Geophysics*]
SADZ........	Matanza/Aeroclub Universita Rio [*Argentina*] [*ICAO location identifier*] (ICLI)
SAE...........	Ogallala, NE [*Location identifier*] [*FAA*] (FAAL)
SAE...........	Sable Resources Ltd. [*Vancouver Stock Exchange symbol*]
SaE...........	Sanguinarine Extract [*Biochemistry*]
SAE...........	Self-Addressed Envelope
SAE...........	Semi-Actuator Ejector (MCD)
SAE...........	Senior Assistant Editor [*Publishing*]
SAE...........	Service Acquisition Executive [*DoD*]
SAE...........	Shaft Angle Encoder (KSC)
SAE...........	Simple Arithmetic Expression
SAE...........	Site Acceptance Evaluation [*Army*] (AABC)
SAE...........	Society for the Advancement of Education (EA)
SAE...........	Society for the Anthropology of Europe (EA)
SAE...........	Society of Automotive Engineers [*Acronym is now organization's official name*] (EA)
SAE...........	Solar Array Experiment (SSD)
SAE...........	Son Altesse Electorale [*His Highness the Elector*] [*French*] (ROG)
SAE...........	Soviet Antarctic Expedition
SAE...........	Specialized Armoured Establishment [*British military*] (DMA)
SAE...........	Spiral Aftereffect [*Aerospace*]
SAE...........	Stamped Addressed Envelope
SAE...........	Standard Average European
SAE...........	Steering Angle Error
SAE...........	Stop at Expiration [*Magazine subscriptions*]
SAE...........	Student Action for Education [*Defunct*] (EA)
SAE...........	Subcortical Arteriosclerotic Encephalopathy [*Medicine*]
SAE...........	Supersonic Aircraft Engine
SAEA........	Southeastern Adult Education Association (AEBS)
SAEA........	Southwest Atomic Energy Associates
SAE Australas ... SAE [*Society of Automotive Engineers*] Australasia [*A publication*]	
SAEB	Self-Adjusting Electric Brake
SAEB	Special Army Evaluation Board (AABC)
SAEBA	Soviet Antarctic Expedition. Information Bulletin [*English Translation*] [*A publication*]
SAEC........	Saeculum [*Age, Century, Generation, Lifetime*] [*Latin*] (ROG)
SAEC........	South American Explorers Club (EA)
SAEC........	Southern Agricultural Energy Center
SAEC........	State Administration of Exchange Control [*China*]
SAEC........	Sumitomo Atomic Energy Commission [*Japan*]
Saechs Heimatbl ... Saechsische Heimatblaetter [*A publication*]	
Saeculum....	Saeculum. Jahrbuch fuer Universalgeschichte [*A publication*]
SAED........	Selected Area Electron Diffraction [*Also, SAD*] [*Surface analysis*]
SAED........	Societe des Amis d'Eugene Delacroix (EAIO)
SA Ed........	South Australian Education [*A publication*] (APTA)
SAED........	Systems Analysis and Engineering Development [*Naval Air Development Center*] (MCD)
SAEDA......	Subversion and Espionage Directed Against US Army and Deliberate Security Violations (AABC)
SAEDE......	Sensory Aids Evaluation and Development Center [*MIT*]
SAEDFR ...	Scholars Against the Escalating Danger of the Far Right (EA)
SA Ed Gaz ...	Education Gazette. South Australia Department of Education [*A publication*] (APTA)
SAEF	Ezeiza [*Argentina*] [*ICAO location identifier*] (ICLI)
SAEF	SEAQ Automated Execution Facility [*Software package*]
SAEF	Small-Order Automatic Execution Facility [*London Stock Exchange*] [*British*]
SAEF	Spacecraft Assembly and Encapsulation Facility [*NASA*] (NASA)
SAEF	State Administrative Expense Funds
SAEH	Society for Automation in English and the Humanities [*Later, SDE*]
SAE Handb ...	SAE [*Society of Automotive Engineers*] Handbook [*A publication*]
SAEI	Sumitomo Atomic Energy Industries Ltd. [*Japan*]
SAE J........	SAE [*Society of Automotive Engineers*] Journal [*A publication*]
SAEJA......	SAE [*Society of Automotive Engineers*] Journal [*A publication*]
SAE J Automot Eng ... SAE [*Society of Automotive Engineers*] Journal of Automotive Engineering [*A publication*]	
SAE Journ ...	SAE [*Society of Automotive Engineers*] Journal [*A publication*]
SAE Meet Pap ...	Society of Automotive Engineers. Meeting. Papers [*A publication*]
SAEMR.....	Small Arms Expert Marksmanship Ribbon [*Military decoration*] (AFM)
SAEND......	Save Energy [*A publication*]

Saenger Musikanten Z ... Saenger- und Musikantenzeitung [*A publication*]
SAEP .... South African Education Program [*New York, NY*]
SAE Prepr ... SAE [*Society of Automotive Engineers*] Preprints [*A publication*]
SAE Proc ... Society of Automotive Engineers. Proceedings [*A publication*]
SAE Prog Technol ... SAE [*Society of Automotive Engineers*] Progress in Technology [*United States*] [*A publication*]
SAE Q Trans ... SAE [*Society of Automotive Engineers*] Quarterly Transactions [*A publication*]
SAE Quart Trans ... SAE [*Society of Automotive Engineers*] Quarterly Transactions [*A publication*]
SAERB ...... South African Electrical Review [*A publication*]
SAES .... Scanning Auger Electron Spectroscopy
SAES .... Special Assistant for Environmental Services [*Military*]
SAES .... Stand-Alone Engine Simulator   (NASA)
SAES .... State Agricultural Experiment Station
SAESA ...... SAE [*Society of Automotive Engineers*] Special Publications [*A publication*]
SAE (Soc Automot Eng) Tech Pap ... SAE (Society of Automotive Engineers) Technical Papers [*A publication*]
SAE Spec Publ ... SAE [*Society of Automotive Engineers*] Special Publications [*A publication*]
SAET .... Society for the Advancement of Economic Theory   (EA)
SAET .... Spiral Aftereffect Test [*Psychology*]   (AEBS)
SAETA ...... SA Ecuatoriana de Transportes Aereos [*Airline*] [*Ecuador*]
SAETB ...... SAE [*Society of Automotive Engineers*] Technical Progress Series [*A publication*]
SAE Tech Lit Abstr ... SAE [*Society of Automotive Engineers*] Technical Literature Abstracts [*A publication*]
SAE Tech Pap ... SAE [*Society of Automotive Engineers*]. Technical Papers [*A publication*]
SAE Tech Pap Ser ... SAE [*Society of Automotive Engineers*]. Technical Paper Series [*A publication*]
SAE Tech Prog Ser ... SAE [*Society of Automotive Engineers*] Technical Progress Series [*A publication*]
SAE Trans ... SAE [*Society of Automotive Engineers*] Transactions [*A publication*]
Saeugetierkd Mitt ... Saeugetierkundliche Mitteilungen [*A publication*]
SAEV .... Ezeiza [*Argentina*] [*ICAO location identifier*]   (ICLI)
SAEW .... Ship's Advanced Electronic Warfare   (MCD)
SAEWG ...... Standing Air Emissions Work Group [*Environmental Protection Agency*]   (GFGA)
SAEWS ..... Ship's Advanced Electronic Warfare System   (NVT)
SAEZ .... Buenos Aires [*Argentina*]/Ezeiza [*Argentina*] [*ICAO location identifier*]   (ICLI)
SAF .... SAF [*Society of American Florists*]- The Center for Commercial Floriculture   (EA)
SAF .... Safe, Arm, and Fuze
SAF .... Safed [*Israel*] [*Seismograph station code, US Geological Survey*] [*Closed*]   (SEIS)
SAF .... Safety   (KSC)
SAF .... Sample Air Filter
SAF .... San Andreas Fault
SAF .... Santa Fe [*New Mexico*] [*Airport symbol*]   (OAG)
SAF .... Save America's Forests [*An association*]   (EA)
SAF .... Scandinavian American Fraternity   (EA)
SAF .... School of Aerial Fighting [*British military*]   (DMA)
SAF .... Scrapie-Associated Fibrils [*Neuroanatomy*]
SAF .... Scudder New Asia Fund [*NYSE symbol*]   (SPSG)
SAF .... Second Amendment Foundation   (EA)
SAF .... Secretary of the Air Force
SAF .... Secure Automated Fabrication [*Line*] [*Nuclear energy*]
SAF .... Segment Address Field
SAF .... Self-Articulating Femoral [*Medicine*]
SAF .... Service to the Armed Forces
SAF .... Shark Attack File   (DNAB)
SAF .... Shielding Analysis Form [*Civil Defense*]
SAF .... Single Action [*Maintenance*] Form   (NVT)
SAF .... Society of American Florists   (EA)
SAF .... Society of American Foresters   (EA)
SAF .... Source Acquisitions File   (MCD)
SAF .... South Africa   (EY)
SAF .... South Africa Foundation   (EA)
SA & F ...... Southern Airlines and Freighters [*Australia*]
SAF .... Southern Attack Force [*Navy*]
SAF .... Spacecraft Assembly Facility [*NASA*]
SAF .... Spanish Air Force
SAF .... Special Action Force [*Military*]
SAF .... Specification Approval Form   (MCD)
SAF .... Spin Armed Fuze
SAF .... Star Alliance Foundation   (EA)
SAF .... Stem Cell Activating Factor [*Biochemistry*]
SAF .... Sterilization Assembly Facility
SAF .... Strategic Air Force
SAF .... Structural Adjustment Facility [*Finance*]
SAF .... Students Against Fires [*International student engineering project for 1972-73 sponsored by Student Competitions on Relevant Engineering - SCORE*]
SAF .... Studies in American Fiction [*A publication*]
SAF .... Subject Authority File, Washington, DC [*UTLAS symbol*]
SAF .... Subject to the Availability of Funds   (MCD)

SAF .... Super Abrasion Furnace [*Carbon black manufacture*]
SAF .... Support Action Form   (MCD)
SAF .... Suppressor Activating Factor [*Immunology*]
SAF .... Svenska Arbetsgivareforeningen [*An employers' confederation*] [*Sweden*]
SAF .... Swedish Air Force
SAF .... Switchable Acoustic Filter
SAF .... Symmetry-Adapted Function
SAF .... Symposium on Applications of Ferroelectrics [*IEEE*]
SAF .... Syrian Air Force   (BJA)
SAFA .... School Assistance in Federally Affected Areas
SAFA .... Service d'Aide aux Forces Alliees [*World War II*]
SAFA .... Society of Air Force Anesthesiologists [*Later, DMEF*]   (EA)
SAFA .... Society for Automation in the Fine Arts [*Later, SDE*]
SAFA .... Solar Array Failure Analysis
SAFA .... Soluble Antigen Fluorescent-Antibody [*Immunology*]
SAFAA ...... Secretary of the Air Force, Administrative Assistant
SAFAD ..... Small Arms for Air Defense   (MCD)
SAFAH ...... Supplemental Assistance for Facilities to Assist the Homeless [*Department of Housing and Urban Development*]   (GFGA)
Saf Air Ammonia Plants ... Safety in Air and Ammonia Plants [*A publication*]
SAF/AL ..... Assistant Secretary of the Air Force (Research, Development, and Logistics)
SAFARI .... Semiautomatic Failure Anticipation Recording Instrumentation
SAFARI .... South African Fundamental Atomic Reactor Installation
SAFARI .... Spiro Agnew Fans and Rooters, Inc.
Saf Asp Fuel Behav Off Norm Accid Cond Proc CSNI Spec Meet ... Safety Aspects of Fuel Behaviour in Off-Normal and Accident Conditions. Proceedings of a CSNI Specialist Meeting [*A publication*]
SAFB .... Scott Air Force Base [*Illinois*]
SAFB .... Shaw Air Force Base [*South Carolina*]
SAFB .... Sheppard Air Force Base [*Texas*]   (AAG)
SAFC .... SAFECO Corp. [*NASDAQ symbol*]   (NQ)
SAFC .... Swiss Association for Friendship with China   (EAIO)
SAFCA ...... Safeguard Communications Agency [*Army*]
SAFCB ...... Secretary of the Air Force Correction Board
SAFCMD .. Safeguard Command [*Army*]   (AABC)
SAFCO ...... Standing Advisory Committee on Fisheries of the Caribbean Organization
SAFCOM .. Safeguard System Command [*Obsolete*] [*Army*]
SAFCPM ... Safeguard Communications Program Manager [*Army*]   (AABC)
SAFCPMO ... Safeguard Communications Program Management Office [*Army*]   (AABC)
SAFCTF .... Safeguard Central Training Facility [*Army*]   (AABC)
SAFD .... Plastics (Southern Africa) [*A publication*]
SAFD .... Society of American Fight Directors   (EA)
Saf Dig ...... Safety Digest [*Japan*] [*A publication*]
SAFDL ...... Specified Acceptable Fuel Design Limit [*Nuclear energy*]   (NRCH)
SAFE .... Safe Access to Files of Estate [*Howrex Corp.*] [*Information service or system*]   (IID)
SAFE .... Safeguards Analysis for Effluents
SAFE .... Safeguards Automated Facility Evaluation [*Nuclear energy*]   (NRCH)
SAFE .... Safety and Functional Evaluation [*Occupational therapy*]
SAFE .... SafetyTek Corp. [*NASDAQ symbol*]   (SPSG)
SAFE .... San Andreas Fault Experiment
SAFE .... Santa Fe [*Argentina*] [*ICAO location identifier*]   (ICLI)
SAFE .... Satellite Alert Force Employment
SAFE .... Save Animals from Extinction [*An association*] [*Later, WPTI*]
SAFE .... Security American Finance Enterprises, Inc. [*NASDAQ symbol*]   (NQ)
SAFE .... Security, Aptitude, Fitness Evaluation [*Test*]
S/AFE .... Seismic/Acoustic Feature Extraction   (MCD)
SAFE .... Selected Areas for Evasion [*Military*]   (MCD)
SAFE .... Self-Acceptance, Faulty Information, Effectiveness Counselling or Training [*Sex therapy*]
SAFE .... Sequential Analysis for Force Development   (MCD)
SAFE .... Settlement and Accelerated Funds Exchange [*Chicago, IL*]
SAFE .... Shelter Available for Emergency
SAFE .... Simulation-Aided Fault Evaluation   (MCD)
SAFE .... Society to Advance Foreclosure Education   (EA)
SAFE .... Society for the Advancement of Fission Energy   (EA)
SAFE .... Society for the Application of Free Energy   (EA)
SAFE .... Society of Associated Financial Executives
SAFE .... Software Abstracts for Engineers [*CITIS Ltd.*] [*Ireland*] [*Information service or system*]   (CRD)
SAFE .... Solar Array Flight Experiment   (MCD)
SAFE .... Solvent Abuse Foundation for Education   (EA)
SAFE .... South America and Far East
SAFE .... Spectronix Automatic Fire Extinguishing [*System*] [*For armored vehicles*]
SAFE .... Stationary Attachment and Flexible Endoskeleton
SAFE .... Stock Assessment and Fishery Investigations [*National Marine Fisheries Service*]   (NOAA)
SAFE .... Store and Forward Element [*Telecommunications*]   (TEL)
SAFE .... Straits Air Freight Express [*Australia*]
SAFE .... Strategy and Force Evaluation   (MCD)
SAFE .... Students Against Famine Everywhere   (EA)

SAFE......... Suntanning Association for Education (EA)
SAFE......... Support for the Analysts' File Environment (MCD)
SAFE......... Survival [*formerly, Space*] and Flight Equipment Association [*Later, SAFE Association*]
SAFE......... System, Area, Function, Equipment
SAFEA...... Safety [*A publication*]
SAFEA...... Survival and Flight Equipment Association [*Later, SAFE Association*] (EA)
SAFE-BAR ... Safeland Barrier (DNAB)
SAFECEN ... Safety Center (DNAB)
Safecrd....... SafeCard Services, Inc. [*Associated Press abbreviation*] (APAG)
Safe Manag ... Safety Management [*A publication*]
Saf Eng ...... Safety Engineering [*A publication*]
SAFEPLAN ... Submarine Air Frequency Plan (DNAB)
SAFER ...... Sequential Action Flow Routine [*Military*] [*British*]
SAFER ...... Special Aviation Fire and Explosion Reduction (EGAO)
SAFER ...... Systematic Aid to Flow on Existing Roads [*Traffic-control system*]
SAFE TRIP ... Students Against Faulty Tires Ripping in Pieces [*Student legal action organization*]
SAFETY.... Safety Always Follows Everything You Do [*Sign*]
Safety Ed ... Safety Education [*A publication*]
Safety Educ ... Safety Education [*A publication*]
Safety Eng ... Safety Engineering [*A publication*]
Safety Maint ... Safety Maintenance [*A publication*]
Safety Maint & Prod ... Safety Maintenance and Production [*A publication*]
Safety Surv ... Safety Surveyor [*A publication*]
Safeway...... Safeway, Inc. [*Associated Press abbreviation*] (APAG)
SAFF .... Safing, Arming, Fusing, and Firing [*Military*] (MCD)
SAFF .... Store and Forward Facsimile
SAFFE....... Society of Americans for Firearms Elimination (EA)
SAFFI....... Special Assembly for Fast Installations [*Telecommunications*] (TEL)
SAFFM ..... Secretary of the Air Force, Financial Management
SAFFUC.... Sudan African Freedom Fighters' Union of Conservatives
SAFFWALD ... Saffron Walden [*Municipal borough in England*]
SAFGC...... Secretary of the Air Force General Counsel
Saf Health Welfare ... Safety, Health, and Welfare [*A publication*]
Saf Hlth Bull ... Safety and Health Bulletin [*A publication*]
Saf Hyg (Osaka) ... Safety and Hygiene (Osaka) [*Japan*] [*A publication*]
SAFI .... Semiautomatic Flight Inspection [*FAA*]
SAFI .... Senior Air Force Instructor
SAFI .... Sholem Aleichem Folk Institute (EA)
SAFI .... Stock Assessment and Fishery Investigations Program [*National Oceanic and Atmospheric Administration*] (GFGA)
SAFIE....... Secretary of the Air Force, Special Assistant for Installations
SAFIL....... Secretary of the Air Force (Installations and Logistics)
SAFIM ...... Separated Associated Fluid Interaction Model [*Chemical engineering*]
SAFIMDA ... School Aid to Federally Impacted and Major Disaster Areas (OICC)
SAFIN .... Secretary of the Air Force, Special Assistant for Intelligence
SAFIRE..... Systems Analysis for Integrated Relief Variation [*Engineering*]
SAFIS....... Secretary of the Air Force, Office of Information Services
SAFIS........ Substance Abuse Facility Information System [*Department of Health and Human Services*] (GFGA)
SAFISY ..... Space Agency Forum on International Space Year
SAFITP ...... Safeguard Integrated Training Plan [*Army*] (AABC)
SAFJB....... South African Forestry Journal [*A publication*]
S Af J Econ ... South African Journal of Economics [*Suid-Afrikaanse Tydskrif vir Ekonomie*] [*A publication*]
SAFLL....... Secretary of the Air Force, Office of Legislative Liaison
SAFLOG ... Safeguard Logistics Command [*Army*] (AABC)
SAFM........ Sanderson Farms, Inc. [*NASDAQ symbol*] (NQ)
Saf Maint ... Safety Maintenance [*A publication*]
Saf Maint Proc ... Safety Maintenance and Production [*A publication*]
Saf Manage ... Safety Management [*A publication*]
Saf Mines... Safety in Mines [*A publication*]
Saf Mines Res Establ GB Rep ... Safety in Mines Research Establishment. Great Britain. Report [*A publication*]
Saf Mines Res Establ (GB) Res Rep ... Safety in Mines Research Establishment (Great Britain). Research Report [*A publication*]
Saf Mines Res Test Branch GB Res Rep ... Safety in Mines Research and Testing Branch. Great Britain. Research Report [*A publication*]
SAFMP ..... Assistant Secretary of the Air Force (Manpower and Personnel)
SAFMR ..... Secretary of the Air Force, Manpower and Reserve Affairs
SAFMS...... Secretary of the Air Force, Missile and Satellite Systems (SAA)
SAFMSC... Safeguard Materiel Support Command [*Army*] (AABC)
Saf News Bull ... Safety News Bulletin [*A publication*] (APTA)
Saf Newsl... Safety Newsletter [*A publication*]
SAFNGS ... Small Arms Flash, Noise Gunfire Simulator [*Army*]
SAFO......... Safe Altitude Fuzing Option (SAA)
SAFO......... Secretary of the Air Force Order (AFM)
SAFO......... Senior Acting Field Officer [*Military*] [*British*] (ROG)
SAFO........ Senior Air Force Officer [*Present*] (AFM)
SAFOAT ... South African Avifauna Series. Percy Fitzpatrick Institute of African Ornithology. University of Cape Town [*A publication*]

SAFOC...... Semiautomatic Flight Operations Center
SAFOC...... Syndicat Autonome des Fonctionnaires d'Oubangi-Chari [*Autonomous Union of the Workers of Ubangi-Shari*]
SAFOH ..... Society of American Florists and Ornamental Horticulturists [*Later, SAF*]
SAFOI .... Secretary of the Air Force, Office of Information
SAFOR....... Semi-Automated Forces [*Army*] (RDA)
SAFP .... Society of Air Force Physicians (EA)
SAFPACC ... Safeguard Public Affairs Coordinating Committee [*Army*] (AABC)
SAFPC...... Secretary of the Air Force Personnel Council
SAFPD ...... Safety Practitioner [*A publication*]
SAFPLAN ... Submarine Area Frequency Plan [*Navy*]
SAFPO ...... Safeguard Project Office (MCD)
Saf Pract ... Safety Practitioner [*A publication*]
SAFR .... Senior Air Force Representative (AFM)
SAFR .... Social Assessment of Fisheries Resources
SAFR .... Sodium Advanced Fast Reactor
SAFR .... Source Application of Funds Report (MCD)
S Afr.......... South Africa
SAFR .... Supplementary Application Forms Required [*Civil Service*]
S Afr Annu Insur Rev ... South African Annual Insurance Review [*A publication*]
S Afr AR .... Annual Economic Report. South African Reserve Bank [*A publication*]
S Afr Archaeol Bull ... South African Archaeological Bulletin [*A publication*]
S Afr Archaeol Soc Goodwin Ser ... South African Archaeological Society. Goodwin Series [*A publication*]
S Afr Archit J ... South African Architectural Journal [*A publication*]
S Afr Archit Rec ... South African Architectural Record [*A publication*]
S Afr Arch Ophthalmol ... South African Archives of Ophthalmology [*A publication*]
S-Afr Argief Oftalmol ... Suid-Afrikaanse Argief vir Oftalmologie [*A publication*]
SAFRAS.... Self-Adaptive Flexible Format Retrieval and Storage System [*Data processing*] (IID)
S Afr Assoc Adv Sci Spec Publ ... South African Association for the Advancement of Science. Special Publication [*A publication*]
S Afr Assoc Mar Biol Res Bull ... South African Association for Marine Biological Research. Bulletin [*A publication*]
S Afr At Energy Board Rep PEL ... South Africa. Atomic Energy Board. Report PEL [*A publication*]
S Afr At Energy Board Rep PER ... South Africa. Atomic Energy Board. Report PER [*A publication*]
S Afr Bakery Confect Rev ... South African Bakery and Confectionery Review [*A publication*]
S Afr Bank ... South African Reserve Bank. Quarterly Bulletin [*A publication*]
S Afr Bankers J ... South African Bankers' Journal [*Cape Town, South Africa*] [*A publication*] (DLA)
S Afr Bee J ... South African Bee Journal [*A publication*]
S-Afr Bosbou Tydskr ... Suid-Afrikaanse Bosbou Tydskrif [*A publication*]
S Afr Build ... South African Builder [*A publication*]
S Afr Bur Stand Bull ... South African Bureau of Standards. Bulletin [*A publication*]
S Afr Cancer Bull ... South African Cancer Bulletin [*A publication*]
S Afr (Cape Good Hope) Dep Nat Conserv Rep ... South Africa (Cape Of Good Hope) Department of Nature. Conservation Report [*A publication*]
S Afr Chart Account ... South African Chartered Accountant [*A publication*]
S Afr Chem Process ... South African Chemical Processing [*A publication*]
S Afr Citrus J ... South African Citrus Journal [*A publication*]
S Afr Constr World ... South African Construction World [*A publication*]
S Afr Corros Conf ... South African Corrosion Conference [*A publication*]
S Afr Corros J ... South African Corrosion Journal [*A publication*]
S Afr Counc Sci Ind Res Nat Bldg Res Inst Bull ... South Africa. Council for Scientific and Industrial Research. National Building Research Institute. Bulletin [*A publication*]
S Afr CSIR Air Pollut Group Annu Rep ... South Africa CSIR [*Council for Scientific and Industrial Research*] Air Pollution Group. Annual Report [*A publication*]
S Afr CSIR Air Pollut Res Group Annu Rep ... South Africa CSIR [*Council for Scientific and Industrial Research*] Air Pollution Research Group. Annual Report [*A publication*]
S Afr CSIR Air Pollut Res Group Rep APRG ... South African Council for Scientific and Industrial Research. Air Pollution Research Group. Report APRG [*A publication*]
S Afr CSIR Annu Rep ... South Africa CSIR [*Council for Scientific and Industrial Research*] Annual Report [*A publication*]
S Afr CSIR Rep BOU ... South African Council for Scientific and Industrial Research. Report Series BOU [*A publication*]
S Afr CSIR Res Rep ... South Africa CSIR [*Council for Scientific and Industrial Research*] Research Report [*A publication*]
S Afr CSIR Spec Rep ... South Africa CSIR [*Council for Scientific and Industrial Research*] Special Report [*A publication*]
S Afr CSIR Spec Rep WISK ... South African Council for Scientific and Industrial Research. Special Report. Series WISK [*A publication*]
SAFRD ...... Assistant Secretary of the Air Force (Research and Development)
SAFRD ...... South African Food Review [*A publication*]

S Afr Dent J ... South African Dental Journal [*A publication*]
S Afr Dep Agric Entomol Mem ... South Africa. Department of Agriculture. Entomology Memoir [*A publication*]
S Afr Dep Agric Fish Entomol Mem ... South Africa. Department of Agriculture and Fisheries. Entomology Memoir [*A publication*]
S Afr Dep Agric Fish Tech Commun ... South Africa. Department of Agriculture and Fisheries. Technical Communication [*A publication*]
S Afr Dep Agric Tech Serv Bot Surv Mem ... South Africa. Department of Agricultural Technical Services. Botanical Survey Memoir [*A publication*]
S Afr Dep Agric Tech Serv Bull ... South Africa. Department of Agricultural Technical Services. Bulletin [*A publication*]
S Afr Dep Agric Tech Serv Entomol Mem ... South Africa. Department of Agricultural Technical Services. Entomology Memoirs [*A publication*]
S Afr Dep Agric Tech Serv Pam ... South Africa. Department of Agricultural Technical Services. Pamphlet [*A publication*]
S Afr Dep Agric Tech Serv Sci Bull ... South Africa. Department of Agricultural Technical Services. Scientific Bulletin [*A publication*]
S Afr Dep Agric Tech Serv Tech Commun ... South Africa. Department of Agricultural Technical Services. Technical Communication [*A publication*]
S Afr Dep Agric Water Supply Entomol Mem ... South Africa. Department of Agriculture and Water Supply. Entomology Memoir [*A publication*]
S Afr Dep Agric Water Supply Tech Commun ... South Africa. Department of Agriculture and Water Supply. Technical Communication [*A publication*]
S-Afr Dep Bosbou Jaarversl ... Suid-Afrika. Departement van Bosbou Jaarverslag [*A publication*]
S Afr Dep For Annu Rep ... South Africa. Department of Forestry. Annual Report [*A publication*]
S Afr Dep For Bull ... South Africa. Department of Forestry. Bulletin [*A publication*]
S-Afr Dep Landbou-Teg Dienste Teg Meded ... Suid-Afrika. Departement van Landbou-Tegniese Dienste Tegniese Mededeling [*A publication*]
S Afr Dep Landbou Visserye Teg Meded ... Suid-Afrika. Departement van Landbou Visserye Tegniese Mededeling [*A publication*]
S Afr Dep Landbou Viss Teg Meded ... Suid-Afrika. Departement van Landbou en Visserye. Tegniese Mededeling [*A publication*]
S Afr Dep Mines Coal Surv Mem ... South Africa. Department of Mines. Coal Survey Memoir [*A publication*]
S Afr Dep Mines Geol Surv Ann Geol Surv ... South Africa. Department of Mines. Geological Survey. Annals of the Geological Survey [*A publication*]
S Afr Dep Mines Geol Surv Div Geol Surv Mem ... South Africa. Department of Mines. Geological Survey Division. Geological Survey Memoirs [*A publication*]
S Afr Dep Mines Quart Inform Circ Miner ... South Africa. Department of Mines. Quarterly Information Circular. Minerals [*A publication*]
S Afr Div Sea Fish Annu Rep ... South Africa. Division of Sea Fisheries. Annual Report [*A publication*]
S Afr Div Sea Fish Fish Bull ... South Africa. Division of Sea Fisheries. Fisheries Bulletin [*A publication*]
S Afr Div Sea Fish Invest Rep ... South Africa. Division of Sea Fisheries. Investigational Report [*A publication*]
S Afr Electr Rev ... South African Electrical Review [*A publication*]
S Afr Electr Rev Eng ... South African Electrical Review and Engineer [*A publication*]
S Afr Eng ... South African Engineer [*A publication*]
S Afr Eng Electr Rev ... South African Engineer and Electrical Review [*A publication*]
S Afr Eng Met Ind Rev ... South African Engineer and Metal Industries Review [*A publication*]
S Afr Food Rev ... South African Food Review [*A publication*]
S Afr For J ... South African Forestry Journal [*A publication*]
S Afr Friesland J ... South African Friesland Journal [*A publication*]
S Afr Geogr ... South African Geographer [*A publication*]
S Afr Geogr J ... South African Geographical Journal [*A publication*]
S Afr Geol Surv Bibliogr Subj Index S Afr Geol ... South Africa. Geological Survey. Bibliography and Subject Index of South African Geology [*A publication*]
S Afr Geol Surv Bull ... South Africa. Department of Mines. Geological Survey. Bulletin [*A publication*]
S Afr Geol Surv Explan Sheets ... South Africa. Geological Survey. Explanation of Sheets [*A publication*]
S Afr Geol Surv Handb ... South Africa. Geological Survey. Handbook [*A publication*]
S Afr Geol Surv Mem ... South Africa. Department of Mines. Geological Survey. Memoir [*A publication*]
S Afr Geol Surv Seismol Ser ... South Africa. Geological Survey. Seismologic Series [*A publication*]
S Afr Geol Surv South-West Afr Ser ... South Africa. Geological Survey. South-West Africa Series [*A publication*]
S Afr Hist J ... South African Historical Journal [*A publication*]
S African .... South African Patent Document [*A publication*]

S African J Commun Disorders ... South African Journal of Communication Disorders [*A publication*]
S African J Psychol ... South African Journal of Psychology [*A publication*]
S African Lib ... South African Libraries [*A publication*]
S African Lib Q Bull ... South African Library Quarterly Bulletin [*A publication*]
S Afr Ind Chem ... South African Industrial Chemist [*A publication*]
S Afr Inst Assayers Anal Bull ... South African Institute of Assayers and Analysts. Bulletin [*A publication*]
S Afr Inst Chem Eng Natl Meet ... South African Institution of Chemical Engineers. National Meeting [*A publication*]
S Afr Inst Mech Eng J ... South African Institution of Mechanical Engineers. Journal [*A publication*]
S Afr Inst Med Res Annu Rep ... South African Institute for Medical Research. Annual Report [*A publication*]
S Afr Inst Med Res Publ ... South African Institute for Medical Research. Publications
S Afr Inst Min Metall J ... South African Institute of Mining and Metallurgy. Journal [*A publication*]
S Afr Insur Mag ... South African Insurance Magazine [*A publication*]
S Afr Int ..... South Africa International [*A publication*]
S Afr J Agric Ext ... South African Journal of Agricultural Extension [*A publication*]
S Afr J Agric Sci ... South African Journal of Agricultural Science [*A publication*]
S Afr J Agr Sci ... South African Journal of Agricultural Science [*A publication*]
S Afr J Anim Sci ... South African Journal of Animal Science [*A publication*]
S Afr J Antarct Res ... South African Journal of Antarctic Research [*A publication*]
S Afr J Antarct Res Suppl ... South African Journal of Antarctic Research. Supplement [*A publication*]
S Afr J Bot ... South African Journal of Botany [*A publication*]
S Afr J Bus Manage ... South African Journal of Business Management [*A publication*]
S Afr J Chem ... South African Journal of Chemistry [*A publication*]
S Afr J Chem/S Afr Tydskr Chem ... South African Journal of Chemistry/ Suid-Afrikaanse Tydskrif vir Chemie [*A publication*]
S Afr J Clin Sci ... South African Journal of Clinical Science [*A publication*]
S Afr J Comm Disorders ... South African Journal of Communication Disorders [*A publication*]
S Afr J Commun Disord ... South African Journal of Communication Disorders [*A publication*]
S Afr J Contin Med Educ ... South African Journal of Continuing Medical Education [*A publication*]
S Afr J Crim L ... South African Journal of Criminal Law and Criminology [*A publication*]
S Afr J Crim Law Criminol ... South African Journal of Criminal Law and Criminology [*A publication*]
S Afr J Dairy Sci ... South African Journal of Dairy Science [*A publication*]
S Afr J Dairy Technol ... South African Journal of Dairy Technology [*A publication*]
S Afr J Ec .. South African Journal of Economics [*Suid-Afrikaanse Tydskrif vir Ekonomie*] [*A publication*]
S Afr J Econ ... South African Journal of Economics [*Suid-Afrikaanse Tydskrif vir Ekonomie*] [*A publication*]
S Afr J Educ ... South African Journal of Education [*A publication*]
S Afr J Enol Vitic ... South African Journal for Enology and Viticulture [*A publication*]
S Afr Jersey ... South African Jersey [*A publication*]
S Afr J Ethnol ... South African Journal of Ethnology [*A publication*]
S Afr J Geol ... South African Journal of Geology [*A publication*]
S Afr J Hosp Med ... South African Journal of Hospital Medicine [*A publication*]
S Afr J Ind ... South African Journal of Industries [*A publication*]
S Afr J Ind Labour Gaz ... South African Journal of Industries and Labour Gazette [*A publication*]
S Afr J Lab Clin Med ... South African Journal of Laboratory and Clinical Medicine [*A publication*]
S Afr J Labour Relat ... South African Journal of Labour Relations [*A publication*]
S Afr J Libr Inf Sci ... South African Journal for Librarianship and Information Science [*A publication*]
S Afr J Mar Sci ... South African Journal of Marine Science [*A publication*]
S Afr J Med Lab Technol ... South African Journal of Medical Laboratory Technology [*A publication*]
S Afr J Med Sci ... South African Journal of Medical Sciences [*A publication*]
S Afr J Musicology ... South African Journal of Musicology [*A publication*]
S Afr J Music Therap ... South African Journal of Music Therapy [*A publication*]
S Afr J Nutr ... South African Journal of Nutrition [*A publication*]
S Afr J Nutr/S Afr Tydskr Voeding ... South African Journal of Nutrition/ Suid-Afrikaanse Tydskrif vir Voeding [*A publication*]
S Afr J Obstet Gynaecol ... South African Journal of Obstetrics and Gynaecology [*A publication*]
S Afr J Occup Ther ... South African Journal of Occupational Therapy [*A publication*]
S Afr J Philos ... South African Journal of Philosophy [*A publication*]
S Afr J Photogramm Remote Sensing Cartogr ... South African Journal of Photogrammetry. Remote Sensing and Cartography [*A publication*]

S Afr J Phys ... South African Journal of Physics [*A publication*]
S Afr J Physiother ... South African Journal of Physiotherapy [*A publication*]
S Afr J Plant Soil ... South African Journal of Plant and Soil [*A publication*]
S Afr J Psychol ... South African Journal of Psychology [*A publication*]
S Afr J Radiol ... South African Journal of Radiology [*A publication*]
S Afr J Sci ... South African Journal of Science [*A publication*]
S Afr J Sci Suppl ... South African Journal of Science. Supplement [*A publication*]
S Afr J Sports Med ... South African Journal of Sports Medicine [*A publication*]
S Afr J Surg ... South African Journal of Surgery [*A publication*]
S Afr J Surg/S Afr Tydskr Chir ... South African Journal of Surgery/Suid-Afrikaanse Tydskrif vir Chirurgie [*A publication*]
S Afr J Wildl Res ... South African Journal of Wildlife Research [*A publication*]
S Afr J Wild Res ... South African Journal of Wildlife Research [*A publication*]
S Afr J Zool ... South African Journal of Zoology [*A publication*]
S Afr Kankerbull ... Suid-Afrikaanse Kankerbulletin [*A publication*]
SAfrL......... Studies in African Literature [*A publication*]
S Afr Labour Bull ... South African Labour Bulletin [*A publication*]
S Afr Lapid Mag ... South African Lapidary Magazine [*A publication*]
S Afr Law J ... South African Law Journal [*A publication*]
S Afr Libr... South African Libraries [*A publication*]
S Afr LJ..... South African Law Journal [*A publication*]
S Afr LR .... South African Law Reports [*A publication*]
S Afr LR App ... South African Law Reports, Appellate [*A publication*] (DLA)
S Afr L Rev ... South African Law Review [*A publication*] (DLA)
S Afr LT..... South African Law Times [*A publication*] (DLA)
S Afr Mach Tool Rev ... South African Machine Tool Review [*A publication*]
S Afr Mater Handl News ... South African Materials Handling News [*A publication*]
S Afr Mech Eng ... South African Mechanical Engineer [*A publication*]
S Afr Mech Engr ... South African Mechanical Engineer [*A publication*]
S Afr Med Equip News ... South African Medical Equipment News [*A publication*]
S Afr Med J ... South African Medical Journal [*A publication*]
S Afr Med Tim ... South African Medical Times [*A publication*]
S-Afr Med Tydskr ... Suid-Afrikaanse Mediese Tydskrif [*A publication*]
S Afr Min Eng J ... South African Mining and Engineering Journal [*A publication*]
S Afr Min J ... South African Mining Journal [*A publication*]
S Afr Min Rev ... South African Mining Review [*A publication*]
S Afr Min World ... South African Mining World [*A publication*]
S Afr Mus Ann ... South African Museum. Annals [*A publication*]
S Afr Music Teach ... South African Music Teacher [*A publication*]
S Afr Mus Rep ... South African Museum Report [*A publication*]
S Afr Nucl Dev Corp Rep ... South Africa. Nuclear Development Corporation. Report PER [*A publication*]
S Afr Numis J ... South African Numismatic Journal [*A publication*]
S Afr Nurs J ... South African Nursing Journal [*A publication*]
S Afr Optom ... South African Optometrist [*A publication*]
S Afr Outl .. South African Outlook [*A publication*]
S Afr Outlook ... South African Outlook [*A publication*]
S Afr Panorama ... South African Panorama [*A publication*]
S Afr Pat Doc ... South Africa. Patent Document [*A publication*]
S Afr Pat Trade Marks Off Pat J Incl Trade Marks Des ... South Africa. Patent and Trade Marks Office. Patent Journal, Including Trade Marks and Designs [*A publication*]
S Afr Pharm J ... South African Pharmaceutical Journal [*A publication*]
S Afr Pneumoconiosis Rev ... South African Pneumoconiosis Review [*A publication*]
S Afr Poult Bull ... South African Poultry Bulletin [*A publication*]
S Afr Pract ... South African Practitioner [*A publication*]
SAFRR ...... Secretary of the Air Force, Requirements Review
S Afr Radiogr ... South African Radiographer [*A publication*]
S Afr Railw ... South African Railways [*A publication*]
S Afr Rep Secr Water Affairs ... South Africa. Report of the Secretary for Water Affairs [*A publication*]
S Afr Sci..... South African Science [*A publication*]
S Afr Sea Fish Branch Invest Rep ... South Africa. Sea Fisheries Branch. Investigational Report [*A publication*]
S Afr Sea Fish Inst Invest Rep ... South Africa. Sea Fisheries Institute. Investigational Report [*A publication*]
S Afr Sea Fish Res Inst Invest Rep ... South Africa. Sea Fisheries Research Institute. Investigational Report [*A publication*]
S Afr Shipp News Fish Ind Rev ... South African Shipping News and Fishing Industry Review [*A publication*]
S Afr Spectrosc Conf Proc ... South African Spectroscopy Conference. Proceedings [*A publication*]
S-Afr Spoorwee ... Suid-Afrikaanse Spoorwee [*South Africa*] [*A publication*]
S Afr Stat... South African Statistical Journal [*A publication*]
S Afr Stat J ... South African Statistical Journal [*A publication*]
S Afr Sugar Assoc Exp Stn Annu Rep ... South African Sugar Association Experiment Station. Annual Report [*A publication*]
S Afr Sugar Assoc Exp Stn Bull ... South African Sugar Association Experiment Station. Bulletin [*A publication*]
S Afr Sugar J ... South African Sugar Journal [*A publication*]

S Afr Sugar Tehnol Assoc Proc Annu Congr ... South African Sugar Technologists' Association. Proceedings. Annual Congress [*A publication*]
S Afr Sugar Year Book ... South African Sugar Year Book [*A publication*]
S Afr Sug J ... South African Sugar Journal [*A publication*]
S Afr Surv J ... South African Survey Journal [*A publication*]
S Afr Tax ... South African Tax Cases [*A publication*] (DLA)
S Afr Tax Cas ... South African Tax Cases [*A publication*] (DLA)
S Afr Text.. South African Textiles [*A publication*]
S Afr Transp ... South African Transport [*A publication*]
S Afr Treas ... South African Treasurer [*A publication*]
S Afr Tunnel ... South African Tunnelling [*A publication*]
S Afr Tunnelling ... South African Tunnelling [*A publication*]
S-Afr Tydsk Natuurwet Tegnol ... Suid-Afrikaanse Tydskrif vir Natuurwetenskap en Tegnologie [*A publication*]
S-Afr Tydskr Antarkt Navors ... Suid-Afrikaanse Tydskrif vir Antarktiese Navorsing [*A publication*]
S Afr Tydskr Chem ... Suid-Afrikaanse Tydskrif vir Chemie [*A publication*]
S-Afr Tydskr Chir ... Suid-Afrikaanse Tydskrif vir Chirurgie [*A publication*]
S-Afr Tydskr Dierkd ... Suid-Afrikaanse Tydskrif vir Dierkunde [*A publication*]
S-Afr Tydskr Geneeskd ... Suid-Afrikaanse Tydskrif vir Geneeskunde [*A publication*]
S-Afr Tydskr Lab Kliniekwerk ... Suid-Afrikaanse Tydskrif vir Laboratorium en Kliniekwerk [*A publication*]
S-Afr Tydskr Landbouwet ... Suid-Afrikaanse Tydskrif vir Landbouwetenskap [*A publication*]
S Afr Tydskr Med Lab Tegnol ... Suid-Afrikaanse Tydskrif vir Mediese Laboratorium-Tegnologie [*A publication*]
S Afr Tydskr Natuurwet Tegnol ... Suid-Afrikaanse Tydskrif vir Natuurwetenskap en Tegnologie [*A publication*]
S-Afr Tydskr Obstet Ginekol ... Suid-Afrikaanse Tydskrif vir Obstetrie en Ginekologie [*A publication*]
S Afr Tydskr Plant Grond ... Suid-Afrikaanse Tydskrif vir Plant en Grond [*A publication*]
S-Afr Tydskr Radiol ... Suid-Afrikaanse Tydskrif vir Radiologie [*A publication*]
S Afr Tydskr Seewetenskap ... Suid-Afrikaanse Tydskrif vir Seewetenskap [*A publication*]
S-Afr Tydskr Suiweltegnol ... Suid-Afrikaanse Tydskrif vir Suiweltegnologie [*A publication*]
S-Afr Tydskr Veekd ... Suid-Afrikaanse Tydskrif vir Veekunde [*A publication*]
S-Afr Tydskr Voeding ... Suid-Afrikaanse Tydskrif vir Voeding [*A publication*]
S-Afr Tydskr Wet ... Suid-Afrikaanse Tydskrif vir Wetenskap [*A publication*]
S Afr Tydskr Wysbegeerte ... Suid-Afrikaanse Tydskrif vir Wysbegeerte [*A publication*]
S-Afr Wet Nywerheid-Navorsingsraad Navorsingsversl ... Suid-Afrikaanse Wetenskaplike en Nywerheidnavorsingsraad. Navorsingsverslag [*A publication*]
S-Afr Wet Nywerheid-Navorsingsraad Spes Versl ... Suid-Afrikaanse Wetenskaplike en Nywerheidnavorsingsraad. Spesiale Verslag [*A publication*]
S Afr Wool Text Res Inst Annu Rep ... South African Wool Textile Research Institute. Annual Report [*A publication*]
S Afr Wool Text Res Inst Bull ... South African Wool and Textile Research Institute. Bulletin [*A publication*]
S Afr Wool Text Res Inst Dig ... South African Wool Textile Research Institute. Digest [*A publication*]
S Afr Wool Text Res Inst SAWTRI Spec Publ ... South African Wool and Textile Research Institute. SAWTRI Special Publication [*A publication*]
S Afr Wool Text Res Inst Tech Rep ... South African Wool Textile Research Institute. Technical Report [*A publication*]
S Afr Yearb Int Law ... South African Yearbook of International Law [*A publication*]
S Afr YIL... South African Yearbook of International Law [*A publication*]
SAFS .... Safing, Arming, and Fusing System [*Military*] (MCD)
SAFS .... Secondary Air Force Specialty
SAFSC-D .. Safeguard System Command-RDT & E [*Research, Development, Test, and Evaluation*] Directorate [*Obsolete*] [*Army*] (MCD)
Saf Sci Abstr ... Safety Science Abstracts Journal [*A publication*]
Saf Sci Abstr J ... Safety Science Abstracts Journal [*A publication*]
SAFSCOM ... Safeguard System Command [*Obsolete*] [*Army*] (AABC)
SAFSEA.... Safeguard System Evaluation Agency [*Army*] (AABC)
Saf Ser IAEA ... Safety Series. IAEA [*International Atomic Energy Agency*] [*A publication*]
SAFSIM .... Safeguard System Simulation [*Missile system evaluation*] [*Army*] (RDA)
SAFSL....... Secretary of the Air Force Space Liaison (MCD)
SAFSM...... Safeguard System Manager [*Army*]
SAFSO ...... Safeguard System Office [*Army*] (AABC)
SAFSP...... Secretary of the Air Force, Special Projects
SAFSR...... Society for the Advancement of Food Service Research (EA)
Saf Surv ... Safety Surveyor [*United Kingdom*] [*A publication*]
SAFT .... Safety
SAFT .... Society for the Advancement of the Field Theory (EA)
SAFTAC.... Semiautomatic Facility for Terminal Area Control
SAFTCP.... Safeguard Tactical Communications Plan [*Army*] (AABC)

SAFTCS .... Safeguard Tactical Communications System [*Army*]   (AABC)
SaftKl......... Safety-Kleen Corp. [*Associated Press abbreviation*]   (APAG)
SAFTO ...... South African Foreign Trade Organisation
SAFTRANS ... Safeguard Transportation System [*Army*]   (AABC)
SAFTU ...... South African Federation of Trade Unions
Safugetierkd Mitt ... Safugetierkundliche Mitteilungen [*A publication*]
SAFUS ...... Under Secretary of the Air Force
SAFV .... Separator Assembly Fuel-Vacuum [*Automotive engineering*]
SAFWA ...... Southeastern Association of Fish and Wildlife Agencies   (EA)
Safwy .... Safeway, Inc. [*Associated Press abbreviation*]   (APAG)
SAFX .... Saw Fixture [*Tool*]   (AAG)
s-ag--- .... Argentina [*MARC geographic area code*] [*Library of Congress*]   (LCCP)
SAG .... Saga [*Japan*] [*Seismograph station code, US Geological Survey*]   (SEIS)
SAG .... Sage Energy Co. [*AMEX symbol*]   (SPSG)
Sag .... Saggiatore [*A publication*]
SAG .... Sagitta [*Mathematics*]
SAG .... Sagwon, AK [*Location identifier*] [*FAA*]   (FAAL)
SAG .... Saint Anthony's Guild
SAG .... St. Apollonia Guild   (EA)
SAG .... Salicyl Acyl Glucuronide [*Organic chemistry*]
sag .... Sango [*MARC language code*] [*Library of Congress*]   (LCCP)
SAG .... Schweizerische Afrika-Gesellschaft [*Swiss Society of African Studies*]   (EAIO)
SAG .... Screen Actors Guild   (EA)
SAG .... Secretaria de Agricultura y Ganaderia [*Mexico*]
SAG .... Seismic Air Gun
SAG .... Semiactive Guidance [*Military*]   (IIA)
SAG .... Semiautogenous Grinding System [*Ore-crushing process*]
SAG .... Senior Advisory Group [*Nuclear Regulatory Commission*]   (GFGA)
SAG .... Service Advisory Group   (NATG)
SAG .... Signal Actuated Gate
SAG .... Significant Air Gap
SAG .... Society of Arthritic Gardeners
SAg .... Soluble Antigen [*Immunochemistry*]
SAG .... Sowjetische Aktiengesellschaften [*Soviet Corporations*] [*Germany*]
SAG .... Special Activities Group [*Air Force*]
SAG .... Standard Address Generator   (IEEE)
SAG .... Strategic Communications Ltd. [*Vancouver Stock Exchange symbol*]
SAG .... Study Advisory Group [*Army*]
SAG .... Stuttgarter Arbeiten zur Germanistik [*A publication*]
SAG .... Submarine Analysis Group [*Navy*]   (CAAL)
S/Ag .... Supervised Agency [*DLA*]
SAG .... Surface Action Group [*Military*]   (NVT)
SAG .... Surface Attack Group [*Navy*]   (CAAL)
SAG .... Swiss Agammaglobulinemia [*Medicine*]   (MAE)
SAG .... System Application Group   (SAA)
SAG .... Systems Analysis Group
Saga .... Saga Communications, Inc. [*Associated Press abbreviation*]   (APAG)
SAGA .... Saint-Gaudens National Historic Site
SAGA .... Sand and Gravel Association of Great Britain
SAGA .... Short-Arc Geodetic Adjustment [*Geophysics*]
SAGA .... Smocking Arts Guild of America   (EA)
SAGA .... Society of American Graphic Artists   (EA)
SAGA .... Software AG Systems, Inc. [*NASDAQ symbol*]   (NQ)
SAGA .... Stage and Arena Guild of America
SAGA .... Studies, Analysis, and Gaming Agency [*Military*]
SAGA .... System for Automatic Generation and Analysis
Saga-Book ... Saga-Book. Viking Society for Northern Research [*A publication*]
SAGA Bull ... SAGA [*Sand and Gravel Association Ltd.*] Bulletin [*A publication*]
Saga S .... Saga och Sed [*A publication*]
SAGB......... Sage Broadcasting Corp. [*NASDAQ symbol*]   (NQ)
SAGB........ Schizophrenia Association of Great Britain
SAGB........ Senior Advisory Group on Biotechnology [*British*]
SAGB........ Spiritualist Association of Great Britain
SAGCI....... Semiautomatic Ground Control of Interceptors   (SAA)
SAGE........ Sage Drilling Co., Inc. [*NASDAQ symbol*]   (NQ)
SAGE........ Science and Geography Education [*Database*]
SAGE........ Scientific Advisory Group on Effects [*DoD*] [*Washington, DC*]   (EGAO)
SAGE........ Semiautomatic Ground Environment [*Military*]
SAGE........ Senior Action in a Gay Environment   (EA)
SAGE........ Skylab Advisory Group for Experiments [*NASA*]
SAGE........ Society for the Advancement of the George Economy [*Defunct*]   (EA)
SAGE........ Society for the Advancement of Good English   (EA)
SAGE........ Solar-Assisted Gas Energy [*Water heating*] [*NASA*]
SAGE........ South African General Electric Co.
SAGE........ Soviet-American Gallium Experiment [*Particle physics*]
SAGE........ Special Assistant for Growing Enterprises [*Division of National American Wholesale Grocer's Association*]
SAGE........ Spoiler Assisted Ground Effect   (MCD)
SAGE........ Sterilization Aerospace Ground Equipment   (KSC)
SAGE........ Strategic Analysis Guidance and Estimate   (MCD)

SAGE......... Stratospheric Aerosol Gas Experiment
Sage Annu R Communic Res ... Sage Annual Reviews of Communication Research [*A publication*]
SAGEE...... Surface-Air-Generated Electronic Environment   (SAA)
Sage Elect Stud Yb ... Sage Electoral Studies Yearbook [*A publication*]
Sage Fam Stud Abstr ... Sage Family Studies Abstracts [*A publication*]
Sage Int Yb For Pol Stud ... Sage International Yearbook of Foreign Policy Studies [*A publication*]
Sage/JIAS ... Journal of Inter-American Studies and World Affairs. Sage Publication for the Center for Advanced International Studies. University of Miami [*A publication*]
SAGEM..... Societe d'Applications Generals d'Electricite et de Mecanique [*France*]
SA Geol Atlas Ser ... South Australia. Geological Survey. Atlas Series [*A publication*]   (APTA)
SA Geol Surv Bull ... South Australia. Geological Survey. Bulletin [*A publication*]   (APTA)
SA Geol Surv Geol Atlas 1 Mile Ser ... South Australia. Geological Survey. Geological Atlas. 1 Mile Series [*A publication*]   (APTA)
SA Geol Surv Rep Invest ... South Australia. Geological Survey. Report of Investigations [*A publication*]   (APTA)
Sage Pap CP ... Sage Professional Papers in Comparative Politics [*A publication*]
Sage Pub Admin Abstr ... Sage Public Administration Abstracts [*A publication*]
Sage Public Adm Abstr ... Sage Public Administration Abstracts [*A publication*]
SAGES ...... Society American Gastrointestinal Endoscopic Surgeons   (EA)
Sage Urban Abs ... Sage Urban Abstracts [*A publication*]
Sage Urban Stud Abstr ... Sage Urban Studies Abstracts [*A publication*]
Sage Urb Stud Abstr ... Sage Urban Studies Abstracts [*A publication*]
Sage Yb Polit Publ Pol ... Sage Yearbooks in Politics and Public Policy [*A publication*]
Sage Yb Women's Pol ... Sage Yearbook in Women's Policy Studies [*A publication*]
SAGFC ...... Southeastern Association of Game and Fish Commissioners [*Later, SAFWA*]   (EA)
SAGG .... South Australian Government Gazette [*A publication*]
SAGGBS ... Salvation Army Guides and Guards, Brownies, and Sunbeams   (EAIO)
SAGGE...... Synchronous Altitude Gravity Gradient Experiment
Sagg Fen .... Saggi Fenici [*A publication*]
Saggi .... Saggi e Ricerche di Letteratura Francese [*A publication*]
SAGI......... South-African Garrisons Institutes [*Military*] [*British*]   (ROG)
SAGI......... Specialty Advertising Guild International [*Later, SAA*]   (EA)
SAGJ......... South African Geographical Journal [*A publication*]
SAGLBQ ... Acta Geographica Lodziensia [*A publication*]
SAGM .... Separate Absorption, Grading, and Multiplication Layers [*Semiconductor technology*]
SAGMI...... Surface Attack Guided Missile   (MCD)
SAGMN .... Sudhoffs Archiv fuer Geschichte der Medizin und der Naturwissenschaften [*A publication*]
SAGMOS ... Self-Aligning Gate Metal Oxide Semiconductor   (IEEE)
SAGN .... Sagkeeng News [*Fort Alexander, MB*] [*A publication*]
SAGO .... Latin America Center [*Acronym is based on foreign phrase*] [*Belgium*]
SA-GOR .... Security Assistance - General Operational Requirement [*Military*]   (AFIT)
SAGP........ Society for Ancient Greek Philosophy   (EA)
SAGP........ Streptococcal Acidic Glycoprotein [*Antineoplastic drug*]
SAGPGG... Sheep Anti-Guinea Pig Gamma Globulin   (OA)
SAGS........ Scandinavian-American Genealogical Society   (EA)
SAGS........ Semiactive Gravity-Gradient System [*NASA*]
SAGSET.... Society for Academic Gaming and Simulation in Education and Training
SAGT........ Scottish Association of Geography Teachers [*British*]
SAGT........ Solarized Advanced Gas Turbine   (MCD)
SAGTA...... School and Group Travel Association   (EAIO)
SAGU .... Saguaro National Monument
Sague Med ... Saguenay Medical [*A publication*]
SAGW .... Surface-to-Air Guided Weapon [*British*]
SAH .... S-Adenosylhomocysteine [*Biochemistry*]
SaH........... Saat auf Hoffnung   (BJA)
SAH .... Sachem Exploration [*Vancouver Stock Exchange symbol*]
Sah .... Sahara
SAH .... Sahara Casino Partnership [*NYSE symbol*]   (SPSG)
SAH .... Sanaa [*Yemen Arab Republic*] [*Airport symbol*]   (OAG)
SaH........... Sandoz Pharmaceuticals [*Research code symbol*]
SAH .... School of Applied Health [*University of Texas*]
SAH .... Security Archives Holdings [*Data storage company*] [*British*]
SAH .... Semiactive Homer [*Missiles*]
SAH .... Sitzungsberichte. Heidelberg Akademie der Wissenschaften. Philosophisch-Historische Klasse [*A publication*]
SAH .... Society of Aeronautical Historians [*Netherlands*]   (EAIO)
SAH .... Society of American Historians   (EA)
SAH .... Society of Architectural Historians   (EA)
SAH .... Society of Automotive Historians   (EA)
SAH .... Standard Allowed Hours
SAH .... Standard Average Hour   (HGAA)
SAH .... Stratford-On-Avon Herald [*A publication*]
SAH .... Subarachnoid Hemorrhage [*Medicine*]

SAH.......... Supreme Allied Headquarters [*World War II*]
SAH.......... Svenska Akademiens Handlingar [*A publication*]
SAHA....... Society of American Historical Artists   (EA)
SAHARA... Synthetic Aperture High Altitude RADAR   (AAG)
SAHC....... Chosmadal [*Argentina*] [*ICAO location identifier*]   (ICLI)
SAHC....... S-Adenosylhomocysteine [*Biochemistry*]
SAHC....... Self-Aligning Hydraulic Cylinder
SahCas...... Sahara Casino Partners Ltd. [*Associated Press abbreviation*]   (APAG)
Sah de Dem ... Sahara de Demain [*A publication*]
SAHEA ..... Sanitaer- und Heizungstechnik [*A publication*]
SAHF........ Semiautomatic Height Finder
SAHG....... Die Sumerischen und Akkadischen Hymnen und Gebete [*Zurich/Stuttgart*] [*A publication*]
SAH(GB)... Society of Architectural Historians (of Great Britain)
SAHH....... Society for Austrian and Habsburg History   (EA)
SAHI .... Sagamore Hill National Historic Site
SAHJ........ Society of Automotive Historians. Journal [*A publication*]
SAHL .... Salvation Army Home League [*See also LF*]   (EAIO)
SaHMI ...... Sachs, "History of Musical Instruments" [*A publication*]
SAHOA ..... Saiko To Hoan [*A publication*]
SA Homes & Gardens ... South Australian Homes and Gardens [*A publication*]   (APTA)
SAHPS...... Solar Energy Assisted Heat Pump System
SAHR .... Fuerte Gral Roca [*Argentina*] [*ICAO location identifier*]   (ICLI)
SAHR .... Semi-Active Homing RADAR [*Military*]   (RDA)
SAHRS...... Standard Attitude Heading Reference System   (MCD)
SAHS........ Swedish-American Historical Society   (EA)
SAHS........ Swiss-American Historical Society   (EA)
SAHS........ Swiss American Historical Society. Newsletter [*A publication*]
SAHSA...... Servicio Aereo de Honduras Sociedad Anonima
SAHYB..... Simulation of Analog and Hybrid Computers
SAI............ Allstar Inns Ltd. [*AMEX symbol*]   (SPSG)
SAI............ Saigo [*Japan*] [*Seismograph station code, US Geological Survey*]   (SEIS)
SAI............ Sales Activity Index   (WDMC)
SAI............ Schizophrenics Anonymous International [*Later, Canadian Schizophrenia Foundation*]   (EA)
SAI............ Science Applications, Inc.   (NRCH)
SAI............ Science Associates/International [*Publisher*]   (EA)
SAI............ Scientific Aid to Indochina [*Task force established 1973 by Scientists' Institute for Public Information*]
SAI............ Scientific Associates, Inc.   (AAG)
SAI............ Scottish Agricultural Industries [*Commercial firm*]
SAI............ Scriptwriters' Association International [*Defunct*]   (EA)
SAI............ Secondary Air Injection [*Automotive engineering*]
SAI............ Self-Actualization Inventory [*Test*]
SAI............ Self-Analysis Inventory [*Psychology*]
SAI............ Seltene Assyrische Ideogramme [*A publication*]
SAI............ Senior Advocates International [*Defunct*]   (EA)
SAI............ Senior Army Instructor
SAI............ Shoplifters Anonymous International   (EA)
SAI............ Sigma Alpha Iota [*International professional music fraternity for women*]   (EA)
SAI............ Social Adequacy Index
SAI............ Societa Anonima Italiana [*Stock company*] [*Italian*]
SAI............ Society of American Inventors   (EA)
SAI............ Software Access International, Inc. [*Information service or system*]   (IID)
SAI............ Sold as Is [*Philately*]
SAI........ Son Altesse Imperiale [*His or Her Imperial Highness*] [*French*]
sai............. South American Indian [*MARC language code*] [*Library of Congress*]   (LCCP)
SAI............ Southern Alberta Institute of Technology [*UTLAS symbol*]
SAI............ Special Accident Insurance   (MCD)
SAI............ Specific Acoustic Impedance
SAI............ Spherical Attitude Indicator   (MCD)
SAI........... Standby Airspeed [*or Attitude*] Indicator   (MCD)
SAI............ State Agency Issuance [*Employment and Training Administration*]   (OICC)
SAI............ Statistical Abstracts of Israel [*A publication*]
SAI............ Steering Axis Inclination [*Automotive engineering*]
SAI............ Stern Activities Index [*Psychology*]
SAI............ Student Aid Index [*Department of Education*]   (GFGA)
SAI............ Subarchitectural Interface
SAI............ Suburban Action Institute [*Later, MAI*]   (EA)
SAI............ Sudden Auroral Intensity
SAI............ Sugar Association, Inc.   (EA)
SAI............ Sun Air International [*Ft. Lauderdale, FL*] [*FAA designator*]   (FAAC)
SAI............ Surveillance Aided Intercept   (NVT)
SAI............ System Analysis Indicator   (MCD)
SAIA .... Survival of American Indians Association   (EA)
SAIAN....... Survey of American Indians and Alaska Natives [*Department of Health and Human Services*]   (GFGA)
SAIAS .... Ship Aircraft Inertial Alignment System   (NG)
SAIB .... Safe Area Intelligence Brief   (MCD)
SAIB .... Sucrose Acetate Isobutyrate [*Organic chemistry*]
Saibanshu .. Saiko Saibansho Saibanshu [*A publication*]
SAIBB .... Soil Association. Information Bulletin and Advisory Service [*A publication*]

SAIC .... School of the Art Institute of Chicago
SAIC .... Science Applications International Corp.
SAIC .... Small Arms Interpost Competition [*Military*]
SAIC .... South African Indian Congress   (PD)
SAIC .... Special Agent in Charge [*Department of the Treasury*]
SAIC .... Switch Action Interrupt Count
SAICAR .... Succinoaminoimidazolecarboxamide Ribonucleotide [*Biochemistry*]
SAICDB .... Israel. Institute of Field and Garden Crops. Scientific Activities [*A publication*]
SAICETT .. South African Institute of Civil Engineering Technicians and Technologists   (EAIO)
SAID......... Safe Area Intelligence Description   (MCD)
SAID.......... Safety Analysis Input Data [*Nuclear energy*]   (NRCH)
SAID......... Semiautomatic Integrated Documentation
SAID......... Shuttle Avionics Integration Division [*NASA*]   (SSD)
SAID......... Specific Adaptation to Improved Demands [*Sports medicine*]
SAID......... Speech Auto-Instructional Device
SAID......... Supplementary Aviation Information Display
SAIDET .... Single-Axis Inertial Drift Erection Test
Said Med J ... Said Medical Journal [*A publication*]
SAIDS .... Simian Acquired Immunodeficiency Syndrome [*Animal pathology*]
SAIDS .... Space Analyst Intervention Display System   (MCD)
SAIE .... Source and Application Inspection Equipment
SAIE .... Special Acceptance Inspection Equipment
SAIEDH .... Israel. Institute of Agricultural Engineering. Scientific Activities [*A publication*]
SAIF .... Savings Association Insurance Fund [*Functions transferred from FSLIC, 1989*] [*Pronounced "safe"*]
SAIF .... Standard Avionics Integrated Fuzing [*Air Force*]
SAIFER..... Safe Arm Initiation from Electromagnetic Radiation
SAIG......... SAI Group, Inc. [*NASDAQ symbol*]   (NQ)
SAIG......... South Australian Industrial Gazette [*A publication*]   (APTA)
SAIGA...... Saishin Igaku [*A publication*]
SAIGB....... Sangyo Igaku [*A publication*]
SAIH .... Studentenes og Akademikernes Internasjonale Hjelpefond [*Norway*]
SAIHDO ... Israel. Institute of Horticulture. Scientific Activities [*A publication*]
SAII .... Sage Analytics International, Inc. [*Provo, UT*] [*NASDAQ symbol*]   (NQ)
SAIIC .... South and Central American Indian Information Center   (EA)
SA III VC .. 3rd Sussex Artillery Volunteer Corps [*British military*]   (DMA)
SAIL .... Charter Bancshares [*NASDAQ symbol*]   (SPSG)
SAIL .... Sea-Air Interaction Laboratory [*Oceanography*]
SAIL .... Ship Active Item Listing   (DNAB)
SAIL .... Ship's Armament Inventory List [*Navy*]
SAIL .... Shuttle Avionics Integration Laboratory [*NASA*]
SAIL .... Simple Analytical Interactive Language [*Data processing*]
SAIL .... Stanford Artificial Intelligence Laboratory [*Stanford University*]
SAILA .... Sail Assist International Liaison Associates   (EA)
SAILA .... Sault Area International Library Association [*Library network*]
SAILEDREP ... Sailing Report [*Navy*]   (NVT)
SAILER..... Staffing of African Institutions for Legal Education and Research [*An association*] [*Later, International Legal Center*]
SAILORD ... Sailing Order [*Navy*]   (NVT)
SAILREP .. Sailing Report [*Navy*]
SAILS........ Seagoing Assembly-Integration-Launch System
SAILS........ Simplified Aircraft Instrument Landing System
SAILS........ Standard Army Intermediate Level Supply System [*or Subsystem*]
SAIM........ Scottish Amicable Investment Managers [*Finance*]
SAIM........ Semiautomatic Inserting Machine   (SAA)
SAIM........ South America Indian Mission [*Later, SAM*]   (EA)
SAIM........ Systems Analysis and Integration Model   (MCD)
SAIME J ... South African Institution of Mechanical Engineers. Journal [*A publication*]
SAIMI .... Societe des Amis de l'Institut Metapsychique International [*Society of Friends of the International Metaphysical Institute*]   (EAIO)
SAIMR...... South African Institute for Medical Research
SAIMS ...... Selected Acquisitions, Information, and Management System
SAIMS ...... Supersonic Airborne Infrared Measurement System   (MCD)
SAIN......... Society for Advancement in Nursing   (EA)
SAIN......... Systems Associates, Inc. [*NASDAQ symbol*]   (NQ)
Sainan-G-D ... Sainan-Gakuin-Daigaku   (BJA)
SAINET ..... Science Applications, Inc. Global Computer Network   (MCD)
Sains Malays ... Sains Malaysiana [*Malaysia*] [*A publication*]
SA Inst J.... South Australian Institutes. Journal [*A publication*]   (APTA)
Saint.......... Saint's Digest of Registration Cases [*England*] [*A publication*]   (DLA)
SAINT .... Salzburg Assembly: Impact of the New Technology
SAINT .... Satellite Array for International and National Telecommunications   (MCD)
SAINT .... Satellite Inspection Technique   (MCD)
SAINT .... Satellite Inspector and Satellite Interceptor [*Air Force spacecraft program*]
SAINT .... Satellite Interceptor   (KSC)

SAINT ...... Self-Aligning Implantation of N-Layer Technology (MCD)
SAINT ...... Strategic Artificially Intelligent Nuclear Transport [*Robot series designation in 1986 movie "Short Circuit"*]
SAINT ...... Symbolic Automatic Integrator
SAINT ...... Systems Analysis of an Integrated Network of Tasks [*Air Force*]
Saint Lawrence Univ Geol Inf and Referral Service Bull ... Saint Lawrence University. Geological Information and Referral Service. Bulletin [*A publication*]
Saint Louis Univ LJ ... St. Louis University. Law Journal [*A publication*]
SAINTS.... Single Attack Integrated System
SAIORG.... Supreme Assembly, International Order of Rainbow for Girls [*Freemasonry*] (EA)
SAIP .... Service Aircraft Instrumentation Package (MCD)
SAIP .... Ship Acquisition and Improvement Panel [*Navy*] (CAAL)
SAIP .... Societe d'Applications Industrielle de la Physique
SAIP .... Spares Acquisition Integrated with Production
SAIP .... Submarine Antenna Improvement Program [*Military*]
SAIP .... Systems Acquisition and Implementation Program [*Environmental Protection Agency*] (GFGA)
SAIPL....... Spares Acquisition Incorporated with Production List (MCD)
SAIPMS... Science Applications Incorporated Plan Monitoring System
SAIR .... Saugus Ironworks National Historic Site
SAIR .... Semiannual Inventory Report [*Military*] (AFM)
SAIR .... South Australian Industrial Reports [*A publication*] (APTA)
Sairaanh Vuosik ... Sairaanhoidon Vuosikirja [*A publication*]
SAIRI ...... Supreme Assembly for the Islamic Revolution in Iraq [*Political party*] (ECON)
SAIRR ...... South African Institute of Racial Relations
SAIRS..... Standardized Advanced Infrared System [*Army*]
SAIS .... School of Advanced International Studies
SAIS .... Science and Applications Information System (SSD)
SAIS .... Societa Agricola Italo-Somala [*Italo-Somali Agricultural Society*]
SAIS .... Society for American Indian Studies (EA)
SAIS .... Southwestern American Indian Society [*Later, SAISR*] (EA)
SAISA ..... South Atlantic Intercollegiate Sailing Association
SAISAC..... Ship's Aircraft Inertial System Alignment Console
SAISB....... South African Individual Scale for the Blind [*Intelligence test*]
SAI-SDDL ... Science Applications, Inc. - Software Design and Documentation Language (MCD)
SAISDP..... Israel. Institute of Animal Science. Scientific Activities [*A publication*]
SAISR........ Society for American Indian Studies and Research [*Formerly, SAIS*] (EA)
SAIS Rev ... SAIS [*School of Advanced International Studies*] Review [*A publication*]
SAIT .... Southern Alberta Institute of Technology [*Calgary, AB*]
SAIT News ... SAIT [*South Australian Institute of Teachers*] Newsletter [*A publication*] (APTA)
Sait Not...... Saitabi. Noticiario de Historia, Arte, y Arqueologia de Levante [*A publication*]
Saito Ho-On Kai Mus Nat Hist Res Bull ... Saito Ho-On Kai Museum of Natural History. Research Bulletin [*A publication*]
Saito Ho-On Kai Mus Res Bull ... Saito Ho-On Kai Museum Research Bulletin [*A publication*]
SAITR ...... Special Artificer, Instruments, Typewriter, and Office Equipment Repairman [*Navy*]
SAIW......... Sun Artificial Intelligence Workstation
SAIWR...... Special Artificer, Instruments, Watch Repairman [*Navy*]
SAJ .... Golden Eagle Aviation [*Bedford, MA*] [*FAA designator*] (FAAC)
SAJ .... St. Joseph Light & Power Co. [*NYSE symbol*] (SPSG)
SAJ .... Saints Alive in Jesus (EA)
SAJ .... Salon Resources Corp. [*Vancouver Stock Exchange symbol*]
SAJ .... Society for the Advancement of Judaism (EA)
SAJ .... South African Journal of Economics [*Suid-Afrikaanse Tydskrif vir Ekonomie*] [*A publication*]
SAJA .... Special Approaches to Juvenile Assistance [*Defunct*] (EA)
SAJAA ..... South African Journal of African Affairs [*A publication*]
SAJAC...... South African Journal of Animal Science [*A publication*]
SAJAR ...... South African Journal of Antarctic Research [*A publication*]
SAJBDD ... Suid-Afrikaanse Tydskrif vir Plantkunde [*A publication*]
SAJC......... Southern Association of Junior Colleges (AEBS)
SAJCD ...... South African Journal of Chemistry [*A publication*]
SAJE .... South African Journal of Economics [*Suid-Afrikaanse Tydskrif vir Ekonomie*] [*A publication*]
SA J Educ Res ... South Australian Journal of Education Research [*A publication*] (APTA)
SAJER....... South Australian Journal of Education Research [*A publication*] (APTA)
SAJH......... San Juan Island National Historic Park
SAJI.......... Saw Jig [*Tool*]
SAJIB........ Societe d'Animation du Jardin et de l'Institut Botaniques [*Canada*]
SAJL......... Studies in American Jewish Literature [*A publication*]
SAJMA ..... South African Journal of Medical Sciences [*A publication*]
SAJMMC ... San Antonio Joint Military Medical Command
SAJPA...... South African Journal of Physiotherapy [*A publication*]
SAJPEM... Suid-Afrikaanse Tydskrif vir Wysbegeerte [*A publication*]
SAJRA ...... South African Journal of Radiology [*A publication*]

SAJ Res Sport Phys Educ Recreat ... SA [*South African*] Journal for Research in Sport. Physical Education and Recreation [*A publication*]
SAJS......... School for Advanced Jewish Studies (BJA)
SAJS......... South African Journal of Science [*A publication*]
SAJSA ...... South African Journal of Science [*A publication*]
SAJSB ...... South African Journal of Surgery [*A publication*]
SAJSEV .... Suid-Afrikaanse Tydskrif vir Plant en Grond [*A publication*]
SA J Sports Med ... SA [*South African*] Journal of Sports Medicine [*A publication*]
SAJTA...... South African Journal of Medical Laboratory Technology [*A publication*]
SAJZD ...... South African Journal of Zoology [*A publication*]
SAK .... Die Sumerischen und Akkadischen Koeningsinschriften [*A publication*] (BJA)
SAK .... Kalispell, MT [*Location identifier*] [*FAA*] (FAAL)
SAK .... Sakata [*Japan*] [*Seismograph station code, US Geological Survey*] (SEIS)
SAK .... Saudarkrokur [*Iceland*] [*Airport symbol*] (OAG)
SAK .... Stall Lake Mines [*Vancouver Stock Exchange symbol*]
SAK .... Stop Acknowledge (CMD)
SAK .... Sveriges Arbetarepartiet Kommunisterna [*Swedish Workers' Communist Party*] [*Political party*] (PPW)
SAK .... University of Saskatchewan Libraries [*UTLAS symbol*]
SAKAD..... Sangyo To Kankyo [*A publication*]
SAKB........ Suider Afrikaanse Katolieke Biskopsraad [*Southern African Catholic Bishops' Conference - SACBC*] (EAIO)
Sakharth SSR Mecn Akad Gamothvl Centr Srom ... Sakharthvelos SSR Mecnierebatha Akademia Gamothvlithi Centris Sromebi [*A publication*]
Sakharth SSR Mecn Akad Marthw Sistem Inst Srom ... Sakharthvelos SSR Mecnierebatha Akademia Marthwis Sistemebis Instituti Sromebi [*A publication*]
Sakharth SSR Mecn Akad Math Inst Srom ... Sakharthvelos SSR Mecnierebatha Akademia A. Razmadzis Sahelobis Thbilsis Mathematikis Institutis Sromebi [*A publication*]
Sakharth SSR Mecn Akad Moambe ... Sakharthvelos SSR Mecnierebatha Akademia Moambe [*A publication*]
SAKHB...... Sangyo Anzen Kenkyusho Hokoku [*A publication*]
Sakh Prom ... Sakharnaya Promyshlennost [*A publication*]
Sakh Promst ... Sakharnaya Promyshlennost [*A publication*]
Sakh Svekla ... Sakharnaya Svekla [*A publication*]
SAKI .... Solatron Automatic Keyboard Instructor
SAKOD ..... Sangyo Kogai [*A publication*]
SAKSO...... Collective name of Soren Frandsen, Asbjorn Jensen, Kurt Frederiksen, Soren Lundh, and Ole Rud Nielsen when writing in collaboration
Sakura X-Ray Photogr Rev ... Sakura X-Ray Photographic Review [*Japan*] [*A publication*]
SAL............ Anderson County Library, Anderson, SC [*OCLC symbol*] (OCLC)
SAL............ Saharan Air Layer [*Meteorology*]
SAL............ Salad (WGA)
SAL............ Salary (ADA)
SAL............ Sales and Marketing Management [*A publication*]
Sal............. Salesianum [*A publication*]
Sal............. [*Bartholomaeus de*] Saliceto [*Deceased, 1411*] [*Authority cited in pre-1607 legal work*] (DSA)
sal............. Salicylate [*Medicine*]
SAL............ Saline
Sal............. Salinger's Reports [*88-117 Iowa*] [*A publication*] (DLA)
SAL............ Salinometer (KSC)
sal............. Salishan [*MARC language code*] [*Library of Congress*] (LCCP)
sal............. Saliva (MAE)
SAL............ Salivation [*Treatment for syphilis*] [*Slang*] [*British*] (DSUE)
sal............. Salmon [*Philately*]
Sal............. Salmonella [*Bacteriology*]
SAL............ Salo [*Italy*] [*Seismograph station code, US Geological Survey*] (SEIS)
sal............. Salt (MAE)
SAL............ Saluting (MSA)
SAL............ Salvation Army Shelter (DSUE)
SAL............ Salvex Resources Ltd. [*Vancouver Stock Exchange symbol*]
SAL............ San Salvador [*El Salvador*] [*Airport symbol*] (OAG)
SAL............ Sandhills Agriculture Laboratory [*University of Nebraska - Lincoln*] [*Research center*] (RCD)
SAL............ Saperstein & Associates Ltd. [*Vancouver, BC*] [*Telecommunications*] (TSSD)
SAL............ Scientific Airlock (MCD)
SAL............ Sea-Animal Locomotion (SAA)
SAL............ Seaboard Air Line R. R. [*Later, SCL*] [*AAR code*]
SAL............ Secundum Artis Leges [*According to the Rules of the Art*] [*Latin*] (ADA)
SAL............ Selected Altitude Layer [*Decoder*]
SAL............ Semiactive LASER [*Military*] (CAAL)
SAL............ Sensorineural Acuity Level [*Medicine*]
SAL............ Service Action Log (AAG)
SAL............ Ship Authorized Leave (NG)
SAL............ Ship Authorized Level (MCD)
SAL............ Shipboard Allowance List (MSA)
SAL............ Short Approach Light [*Aviation*]

SAL........... Shuttle Avionics Laboratory [*NASA*] (NASA)
SAL........... Solar Age. A Magazine of the Sun [*A publication*]
SAL........... Solar Arc Lamp
SAL........... Solar Array Leaf
SAL........... Sons of the American Legion (EA)
SAL........... South Atlantic League [*Nickname: Sally*] [*Baseball*]
SAL........... Southern Airlines [*Australia*]
SAL........... Southwestern American Literature [*A publication*]
SAL........... Space Astronomy Laboratory [*University of Florida*] [*Research center*] (RCD)
SAL........... Special Ammunition Load [*Army*] (AABC)
SAL........... SQL [*Structured Query Language*] Windows Application Language [*Data processing*]
SAL........... Standard Acceptance Limits
SAL........... Station Allowance Unit (NATG)
SAL........... Strategic Arms Limitation
SAL........... Structural Adjustment Loan [*World Bank*]
SAL........... Structured Assembly Language
Sal............. Student Loan Marketing Association [*Associated Press abbreviation*] (APAG)
SAL........... Studies in African Linguistics [*A publication*]
SAL........... Subject Authority List [*NASA*]
SAL........... Submarine Alerting and Loading System
SAL........... Submarine Alerting and Locating [*Navy*]
SAL........... Suid-Afrikaanse Lugmag [*South African Air Force*] [*See also SALM, SAAF*]
SAL........... Supersonic Aerophysics Laboratory (MCD)
SAL........... Surface Mail Air Lifted (ADA)
SAL........... Symbolic Assembly Language [*Data processing*] (DIT)
SAL........... System Access Layer [*Data processing*]
SAL........... Systems Assembly Language [*Data processing*] (IEEE)
SALA........ Scientific Assistant Land Agent [*Ministry of Agriculture, Fisheries, and Food*] [*British*]
SALA........ Secret Army for the Liberation of Armenia
SALA........ Servicios Aeronauticos Latina America
SALA........ Solar Arc Lamp Assembly
SALA........ Southwest Alliance for Latin America (EA)
SALA........ Statistical Abstract of Latin America [*A publication*]
SALALM .. Seminar on the Acquisition of Latin American Library Materials (EA)
SA Law Reports CP ... South African Law Reports, Cape Provincial Division [*1910-46*] [*A publication*] (DLA)
SA Law Reports CPD ... South African Law Reports, Cape Provincial Division [*1910-46*] [*A publication*] (DLA)
SA Law Reports NPD ... South African Law Reports, Natal Province Division [*1910-46*] [*A publication*] (DLA)
SA Law Reports SWA ... Reports of the High Court of South-West Africa [*A publication*] (DLA)
SA Law Soc Bull ... South Australian Law Society. Bulletin [*A publication*] (APTA)
SalBrHI..... Salomon Brothers High Income Fund [*Associated Press abbreviation*] (APAG)
SALC........ Sacramento Air Logistics Center (NASA)
SALC........ SAL Cable Communications [*NASDAQ symbol*] (NQ)
SALC........ Secret Army for the Liberation of Corsica
SALC........ Special Associated Logistics Course (MCD)
Sal Comp Cr ... Salaman's Liquidation and Composition with Creditors [*2nd ed.*] [*1882*] [*A publication*] (DLA)
SALCR...... South Australian Licensing Court. Reports [*A publication*] (APTA)
SALCV...... Solanum Apical Leaf-Curling Virus
Saldat Auto ... Saldatura Autogena [*A publication*]
SALDRI .... Semiautomatic Low-Data-Rate Input (SAA)
SALDV ..... Salvage Dive [*Military*] (MUGU)
SALE........ Safeguards Analytical Laboratory Evaluation [*Nuclear energy*]
SALE........ Silicon Avalanche Light Emitter
SALE........ Simple Algebraic Language for Engineers [*Data processing*]
SALE........ Simulated Air Launch Environment (MCD)
SALE........ Special Ammunition Logistical Element
SALEA ...... Sanshi Kenkyu [*A publication*]
SALEM ..... Salem Corp. [*Associated Press abbreviation*] (APAG)
SALES....... Ship Aircraft Locating Equipment
Sales Mgt... Sales Management [*Later, Sales and Marketing Management*] [*A publication*]
Sales & Mkt Mgt ... Sales and Marketing Management [*A publication*]
Sales TC .... Sales Tax Cases [*A publication*] (APTA)
SALF .... Society of American Legion Founders (EA)
SALF .... Somali Abo Liberation Front [*Ethiopia*] [*Political party*] (PD)
SALF .... Sudan African Liberation Front
SALG .... South American Liaison Group (CINC)
SALGEP.... Scottish Association of Local Government to Educational Psychologists [*British*]
SAL-GP..... Semiactive LASER-Guided Projectile (MCD)
SALH .... South Alberta Light Horse (DMA)
Sali............ [*Bartholomaeus de*] Saliceto [*Deceased, 1411*] [*Authority cited in pre-1607 legal work*] (DSA)
SALI .... Selected Abstracts: Library, Information [*Australia*] [*A publication*]
SALI .... Suburban Airlines, Inc. [*NASDAQ symbol*] (NQ)
SALI .... Surface Analysis by LASER Ionization
SALIA7 ..... Ernaehrungswissenschaft [*A publication*]

Salic .... [*Bartholomaeus de*] Saliceto [*Deceased, 1411*] [*Authority cited in pre-1607 legal work*] (DSA)
SALIC .... Salicional [*Music*]
Salice......... [*Bartholomaeus de*] Saliceto [*Deceased, 1411*] [*Authority cited in pre-1607 legal work*] (DSA)
SALINET ... Satellite Library Information Network
SAL/IR..... Semiactive LASER/Infrared (DWSG)
SALIS....... Salisbury [*England*]
SALIS....... Substance Abuse Librarians and Information Specialists (EA)
Salisbury Med Bull ... Salisbury Medical Bulletin [*A publication*]
Salisbury Rev ... Salisbury Review [*A publication*]
SALit .... Studies in American Literature [*Chu Shikoku*] [*A publication*]
SA L J........ South African Law Journal [*A publication*]
Salk .... Salkeld's English King's Bench Reports [*91 English Reprint*] [*A publication*] (DLA)
Salk (Eng) .. Salkeld's English King's Bench Reports [*91 English Reprint*] [*A publication*] (DLA)
SALL .... Sallust [*Roman historian, 86-34BC*] [*Classical studies*] (ROG)
SALL .... Shore Activity Load List
SALLB...... South Australian Law Librarians Bulletin [*A publication*]
SALLIEM ... Sallie Mae [*Student Loan Marketing Association*] [*Associated Press abbreviation*] (APAG)
SALLIE MAE ... Student Loan Marketing Association [*See also SLMA*]
SALLM ..... Sallie Mae [*Student Loan Marketing Association*] [*Associated Press abbreviation*] (APAG)
Salm.......... Salmagundi [*A publication*]
Salm .... Salmanassar (BJA)
Salm .... Salmanticensis [*A publication*]
SALM........ Salvation Army League of Mercy [*British*] (EAIO)
SALM....... Single Anchor Leg Mooring [*Oil platform*]
SALM....... Society of Air Line Meteorologists
Salm Abr ... Salmon's Abridgment of State Trials [*A publication*] (DLA)
Salmant..... Salmanticensis [*Salmanca, Spain*] [*A publication*] (BJA)
SalmFd...... Salomon Brothers Fund [*Associated Press abbreviation*] (APAG)
Salmon Trou Mag ... Salmon and Trout Magazine [*A publication*]
Salmon Trout Mag ... Salmon and Trout Magazine [*A publication*]
Salm St R... Salmon's Edition of the State Trials [*A publication*] (DLA)
SALN........ Sahlen & Associates, Inc. [*Deerfield Beach, FL*] [*NASDAQ symbol*] (NQ)
SALO........ State Aviation Liaison Official (NOAA)
SALO........ Stop Authorization and Lift Order (AAG)
SALOA ...... Special Arc Light Operation Area (DNAB)
Salomn...... Salomon, Inc. [*Associated Press abbreviation*] (APAG)
SALOP...... Shrewsbury [*British depot code*]
SALOP...... Shropshire [*County in England*]
SALORS ... Structural Analysis of Layered Orthotropic Ring-Stiffened Shells [*Computer program*] [*NASA*]
SALP .... Sodium Aluminum Phosphate [*Inorganic chemistry*]
SALP .... South African Labour Party
SALP .... Systematic Assessment of Licensee Performance [*Nuclear energy*] (NRCH)
SALPHIB ... Salomon Phibro Oil Trust [*Associated Press abbreviation*] (APAG)
Sal Publ ..... Salud Publica [*A publication*]
SALR .... Saturation Adiabatic Lapse Rate [*Meteorology*] (ADA)
SALR .... South African Law Reports [*A publication*]
SALR .... South Australian Law Reports [*A publication*] (APTA)
SALR .... Synthetic Aperture LASER RADAR
SALRA ...... Schweizer Aluminium Rundschau [*A publication*]
SALRC ...... Society for the Assistance of Ladies in Reduced Circumstances [*British*] (DI)
SALRCP.... South African Law Reports, Cape Provincial Division [*1910-46*] [*A publication*] (DLA)
SAL Reports OPD ... South African Law Reports, Orange Free State Provincial Division [*1910-46*] [*A publication*] (DLA)
SALR SWA ... South African Law Reports, South West African Reports [*A publication*] (DLA)
SALS .... Short Approach Light System [*Aviation*]
SALS .... Small-Angle Light Scattering
SALS .... Solid-State Acoustoelectric Light Scanner
SALS .... Southern Adirondack Library System [*Library network*]
SALS .... Southern African Literature Society [*Botswana*] (EAIO)
SALS .... Standard Army Logistics System
SALSF....... Short Approach Light System with Sequenced Flashers [*Aviation*]
SALS-K ..... Single Ammunition Logistics System - Korea (MCD)
SALSSAH ... Serials in Australian Libraries: Social Sciences and Humanities [*A publication*] (APTA)
SALSSAH/NRT ... Serials in Australian Libraries: Social Sciences and Humanities/Newly Reported Titles [*A publication*] (APTA)
SALSU ...... Singapore Admiralty Local Staff Union
SaLSUA .... Sierra Leone Students Union of the Americas (EA)
Salt............ De Saltatione [*of Lucian*] [*Classical studies*] (OCD)
SALT .... Saltash [*England*]
SALT .... Salton/Maxim Housewares [*NASDAQ symbol*] (SPSG)
SALT .... Salvation and Laughter Together (EA)
SALT .... Self-Contained All-Weather Landing and Taxiing (MCD)
SALT .... Serum Alanine Aminotransferase [*An enzyme*]
SALT .... Sisters All Learning Together [*Feminist group*]

SALT .... Size, Activity, Location, Type Report [*Military*] (INF)
SALT .... Skin-Associated Lymphoid Tissue [*Dermatology*]
SALT .... Society of American Law Teachers (EA)
SALT .... Society for Applied Learning Technology (EA)
SALT .... South African Law Times [*A publication*] (DLA)
SALT .... Speech and Language Technology [*British*]
SALT .... State Agency Libraries of Texas [*Library network*]
SALT .... Strategic Arms Limitation Treaty (MCD)
SALT .... Subscribers' Apparatus Line Tester
　　　　　　[*Telecommunications*] (TEL)
SALT .... Symbolic Algebraic Language Translator [*Data processing*]
Salt C R ...... New Salt Creek Reader [*A publication*]
SALTE ...... Semiautomatic Line Test Equipment (NG)
SalTerz ...... Sal Terrae. Revista Hispanoamericana de Cultura Ecclesiastica
　　　　　　[*Santander, Spain*] [*A publication*] (BJA)
SALTHQ... Strike Command Alternate Headquarters [*Military*] (AABC)
SALTI....... Summary Accounting for Low-Dollar Turnover Items [*Army*]
Salt Lake Min Rev ... Salt Lake Mining Review [*A publication*]
Salt Lake M Rv ... Salt Lake Mining Review [*A publication*]
Salt Lk Tr .. Salt Lake City Tribune [*A publication*]
Salt Mon (Taipei) ... Salt Monthly (Taipei) [*A publication*]
SALT-P ..... Slosson Articulation, Language Test with Phonology [*Child
　　　　　　development test*]
Salt Res Ind ... Salt Research and Industry [*A publication*]
Salt Res Ind J ... Salt Research and Industry Journal [*A publication*]
SALTS...... Systems Alterations Status
Salud Ocup ... Salud Ocupacional [*A publication*]
Salud Publica Mex ... Salud Publica de Mexico [*A publication*]
SALUT ...... Sea, Air, Land, and Underwater Targets [*Navy*]
SALUTE ... Size, Activity, Location, Unit, Time, Equipment (MCD)
Salute Italia Med ... Salute Italia Medica [*A publication*]
SALV .... Duty Salvage Ship [*Navy*] (NVT)
SALV .... Salvador [*Brazil*] (ROG)
SALV .... Salvage [*Military*] (AFM)
Salvav........ Salvavidas [*A publication*]
SALVDIVB ... Salvage Diver Badge [*Military decoration*] (GFGA)
Salv Div Bad ... Salvage Diver Badge [*Military decoration*]
SALVDV ... Salvage Dives [*Army*]
SALVEX.... Salvage Exercise (MCD)
SALVOPS ... Salvage Operations [*Navy*] (NVT)
SALVTNG ... Salvage Training [*Navy*] (NVT)
SALWIS.... Shipboard Air-Launched Weapons Installation System (NG)
SALX .... Shamrock Airlines [*Air carrier designation symbol*]
SALY .... Salary (ROG)
Salzburger Beitr Paracelsusforsch ... Salzburger Beitraege zur
　　　　　　Paracelsusforschung [*A publication*]
Salzburger Jrbh Phil ... Salzburger Jahrbuch fuer Philosophie [*A publication*]
Salzburg Haus Nat Ber Abt B Geol-Mineral Samml ... Salzburg Haus der
　　　　　　Natur. Berichte. Abteilung B. Geologisch-Mineralogische
　　　　　　Sammlungen [*A publication*]
Salz St Ang ... Salzburger Studien zur Anglistik und Amerikanistik [*A
　　　　　　publication*]
SAM .... S-Adenosylmethionine [*Also, AdoMet, SAMe*] [*Biochemistry*]
SAM .... Safety Activation Monitor (IEEE)
SAM .... Salamo [*Papua New Guinea*] [*Airport symbol*] (OAG)
SAM .... Salicylamide [*Analgesic compound*]
SAM .... SAM [*Society for Advancement of Management*] Advanced
　　　　　　Management Journal [*A publication*]
Sam .... Samaria (BJA)
Sam .... Samaritan (BJA)
sam .... Samaritan Aramaic [*MARC language code*] [*Library of
　　　　　　Congress*] (LCCP)
SAM .... Samarkand [*Former USSR*] [*Seismograph station code, US
　　　　　　Geological Survey*] (SEIS)
Sam .... Samisdat [*A publication*]
Sam .... Sammlung [*A publication*]
SAM .... Sample and Analysis Management System [*Data processing*]
SAM .... Sampling and Analytical Method
Sam .... Samson (BJA)
SAM .... Samson Energy Co. Ltd. [*AMEX symbol*] (SPSG)
SAM .... Samsville, IL [*Location identifier*] [*FAA*] (FAAL)
Sam .... Samuel [*Old Testament book*]
SAM .... Scanning Acoustic Microscope
SAM .... Scanning Auger Microscopy
SAM .... School of Aerospace Medicine [*Formerly, School of Aviation
　　　　　　Medicine*]
SAM .... School in Agency Management [*LIMRA*]
SAM .... School Apperception Method [*Psychology*]
SAM .... School of Assets Management [*Army*] [*Later, School of Materiel
　　　　　　Readiness*]
SAM .... School Attitude Measure [*Test*] [*Canadian Comprehensive
　　　　　　Assessment Program*]
S Am .... Scientific American [*A publication*]
SAM .... Screen Activated Machine [*Parimutuel wagering*]
SAM .... Script Applier Mechanism [*Programming language*]
　　　　　　[*1975*] (CSR)
SAM .... Sea Air Mariner
SAM .... Selective Automatic Monitoring
SAM .... Self-Assembled Monolayer [*Physical chemistry*]
SAM .... Self-Propelled Anthropomorphic Manipulator [*Moon machine*]
SAM .... Semantic Analyzing Machine

SAM .... Semiautomatic Active Memory (SAA)
SAM .... Semiautomatic Film Mounter (SAA)
SAM .... Semiautomatic Mathematics (IEEE)
SAM .... Semiautomatic Mounter [*3M Co.*]
SAM .... Send-a-Message (MCD)
SAM .... Sensing with Active Microwave
SAM .... Sequential Access Memory [*Data processing*] (IEEE)
SAM .... Sequential Access Method [*IBM Corp.*] [*Data processing*]
SAM .... Serial Access Memory [*Data processing*]
SAM .... Service Aggregated Module
SAM .... Service Attitude Measurement [*Bell System*]
Sam .... Serving Advertising in the Midwest [*Later, Adweek*] [*A
　　　　　　publication*]
SAM .... Sex Arousal Mechanism [*Medicine*]
SAM .... Shared Appreciation Mortgage [*Banking*]
SAM .... Shuttle Attachment Manipulator [*NASA*]
SAM .... Signal Analyzing Monitor (KSC)
SAM .... Signal [*System*] for Assessment and Modification [*of behavior*]
　　　　　　[*Patented*]
SAM .... Simple Architecture Microprocessor
SAM .... Simulated Assignment Model
SAM .... Simulation of Analog Methods [*Data processing*]
SAM .... Single Application Method [*College admissions*]
SAM .... Sinusoidal Amplitude Modulation [*Physics*]
SAM .... Sitzungsberichte. Bayerische Akademie der Wissenschaften
　　　　　　[*Munich*] [*A publication*]
SAM .... Sociedad Aeronautica de Medellin Consolidada [*Colombia*]
SAM .... Societe des Americanistes
SAM .... Society for Adolescent Medicine (EA)
SAM .... Society for Advancement of Management [*Cincinnati,
　　　　　　OH*] (EA)
SAM .... Society of American Magicians (EA)
SAM .... Society of Americanists [*Paris, France*] (EA)
SAM .... Society of Antique Modelers (EA)
SAM .... Society for Asian Music (EA)
SAM .... Soldier, Sailor, Airman, Marine [*A publication*]
SAM .... Sort and Merge
SAM .... Sound Absorption Material [*Aviation*]
SAM .... Sourcebook in Applied Mathematics [*National Science
　　　　　　Foundation project*]
SAM .... South America Mission (EA)
SAM .... South American
SAM .... Southern Appalachian Migrant [*Cincinnati slang*]
SAM .... Space Assemble and Maintenance (SSD)
SAM .... Space Available Mail [*Military*] (AABC)
SAM .... Special Advisory Message
SAM .... Special Air Mission [*Aircraft*] [*Military*]
SAM .... Spills, Accidents, and Mixtures [*of Exxon Corp.'s "Stop SAM"
　　　　　　safety program*]
SAM .... Spinal Analysis Machine
SAM .... Squarewave Amplitude Modulation
SAM .... Stabilized Assay Meter (NRCH)
SAM .... Stage Assembly and Maintenance [*Building*]
SAM .... Standard Addition Method [*Mathematics*]
SAM .... Standard Assembly Module [*Eastman Kodak Co.*]
SAM .... Standard Avionics Module (MCD)
SAM .... Stationing Analysis Model [*Military*] (GFGA)
SAM .... Stimuli and Measurements (KSC)
SAM .... Strachey and McIlroy [*in SAM/76, a programming language
　　　　　　named after its authors and developed in 1976*] (CSR)
SAM .... Stratospheric Aerosol Measurement [*or Monitor*]
　　　　　　[*Meteorology*]
SAM .... Strela Antiaircraft Missiles
SAM .... Stroboscopic Analyzing Monitor [*Instrumentation*]
SAM .... Strong Absorption Model [*Nuclear physics*] (OA)
SAM .... Structural Acoustic Monitor
SAM .... Structural Assembly Model [*NASA*]
SAM .... Student Achievement Monitoring [*Vocational guidance*]
SAM .... Studies in Applied Mechanics [*Elsevier Book Series*] [*A
　　　　　　publication*]
SAM .... Study of American Markets [*US News and World Report*]
SAM .... Subject Activity Monitor [*Device used in biological research*]
SAM .... Subsequent Address Message [*Telecommunications*] (TEL)
SAM .... Substitute Alloy Material [*Nuclear energy*]
SAM .... Substrate Adhesion Molecule [*Cytology*]
SAM .... Substrate-Attached Material [*Cytology*]
SAM .... Subsynoptic Advection Model
SAM .... Subtraction, Addition, Multiplication
SAM .... Sulfated Acid Mucopolysaccharide [*Medicine*] (MAE)
SAM .... Sulfur-Asphalt Module [*Road-paving technology*]
SAM .... Surface-Active Material
SAM .... Surface-to-Air Missile
SAM .... Symbolic and Algebraic Manipulation (IEEE)
SAM .... Synchronous Amplitude Modulation
SAM .... System Accuracy Model
SAM .... System Activity Monitor [*Data processing*]
SAM .... System for Automatic Message Switching
　　　　　　[*Telecommunications*] (TSSD)
SAM .... Systems Adapter Module
SAM .... Systems Analysis Module (IEEE)
SAM .... Systolic Anterior Motion [*Cardiology*]

SAMA .... Gral Alvear [*Argentina*] [*ICAO location identifier*] (ICLI)
SAMA .... Sacramento Air Materiel Area
SAMA .... Salem Maritime National Historic Site
SAMA .... Saudi Arabian Monetary Agency [*Riyadh*]
SAMA .... Scientific Apparatus Makers Association [*Later, SAMAGA*] (EA)
SAMA .... Serum Agar Measuring Aid
SAMA .... Site Approval and Market Analysis [*FHA*]
SAMA .... Sociedad de Amistad Mexico Albania [*Mexico-Albania Friendship Society*] (EAIO)
SAMA .... Specialty Automotive Manufacturers Association [*Newport Beach, CA*] (EA)
SAMA .... Student American Medical Association [*Later, AMSA*] (EA)
SAMA .... Survey of Adults and Markets of Affluence [*Monroe Mendelsohn Research, Inc.*] [*Information service or system*] (CRD)
SAMAA..... Special Assistant for Military Assistance Affairs [*Army*] (AABC)
SAMAC..... Scientific and Management Advisory Committee [*Terminated, 1973*] [*Army Computer Systems Command*]
SAMAC..... Swedish American Museum Association of Chicago (EA)
SAMADB ... State and Metropolitan Area Data Book [*Bureau of the Census*] (GFGA)
SAM Advanced Mgt J ... SAM [*Society for Advancement of Management*] Advanced Management Journal [*A publication*]
SAM Adv Man ... SAM [*Society for Advancement of Management*] Advanced Management Journal [*A publication*]
SAMAE..... Southern Air Materiel Area, Europe
SAMAGA ... SAMA [*Scientific Apparatus Makers Association*] Group of Associations (EA)
SAMANTHA ... System for the Automated Management of Text from a Hierarchical Arrangement
SAMAP..... Southern Air Materiel Area, Pacific [*Army*] (AFIT)
SAM-APD ... Separate Absorption and Multiplication Region Avalanche Photodiode
SAMAR..... Ship Activation, Maintenance, and Repair
SAMAR..... Surface-to-Air Missile Availability Report (NG)
Samaru Agric Newsl ... Samaru Agricultural Newsletter [*A publication*]
Samaru Agr Newslett ... Samaru Agricultural Newsletter [*A publication*]
Samaru Inst Agric Res Soil Surv Bull ... Samaru Institute for Agricultural Research. Soil Survey Bulletin [*A publication*]
Samaru Misc Pap ... Samaru Miscellaneous Paper [*A publication*]
Samaru Res Bull ... Samaru Research Bulletin [*A publication*]
SAMAS..... Security Assistance Manpower Accounting System (MCD)
SAMAS..... Service-Craft and Boats Machine Accounting System [*Navy*] (DNAB)
SA Mast Build ... South Australian Master Builder [*A publication*]
SAM-B ...... School of Aviation [*later, Aerospace*] Medicine - Brooks
SAMB....... Secondary Aircraft Maintenance Base
SAMBA..... Saudi American Bank
SAMBA..... Special Agents Mutual Benefit Association [*FBI standardized term*]
SAMBA..... Systems Approach to Managing BUSHIPS [*Bureau of Ships; later, NESC or ESC*] Acquisition [*Navy*] (MCD)
Sambalpur Univ J Sci Technol ... Sambalpur University. Journal of Science and Technology [*A publication*]
Sam BN...... Samuel Butler Newsletter [*A publication*]
SAMBO..... Strategic Antimissile Barrage Objects
SAMBUD ... System for Automation of Materiel Plan for Army Materiel/Budget (AABC)
SAMC....... Cristo Redentor [*Argentina*] [*ICAO location identifier*] (ICLI)
SAMC....... Solar Age Industries, Inc. [*Albuquerque, NM*] [*NASDAQ symbol*] (NQ)
SAMC....... South African Medical Corps
SAMC....... Southern Africa Media Center (EA)
SAMC....... Surface Ammunition Malfunction Control (DNAB)
SAMCEP .. Self-Protected Air-to-Air Missile Concept Evaluation Program [*Army*]
SamChron ... Samaritan Chronology (BJA)
SAMCO .... Sales Associates Management Corp. [*Palm Springs, CA*] (EA)
SAMCOS .. Senior Army Materiel Command Orientation Seminar
SAMCTT .. School of Aerospace Medicine Color Threshold Test
SAMCU .... Special Airborne Medical Care Unit (MCD)
SAMD ...... Surface-to-Air Missile Development
SAMDA .... Standard Asset Management and Disposition Agreement [*Resolution Trust Corp.*]
SAM-DC ... S-Adenosylmethionine Decarboxylase [*An enzyme*]
SAM-D/CDP ... Surface-to-Air Missile-Development, Contract Definition (SAA)
SAME........ Mendoza/El Plumerillo [*Argentina*] [*ICAO location identifier*] (ICLI)
SAMe......... S-Adenosylmethionine [*Also, AdoMet, SAM*] [*Biochemistry*]
SAME........ [*The*] S & M Co. [*NASDAQ symbol*] (NQ)
SAME........ Sensory-Afferent/Motor-Efferent [*Neurology*]
SAME....... Society of American Military Engineers (EA)
SAME....... Spanish Association for Medical Education [*British*] (EAIO)
SAME........ Students Against Misleading Enterprises [*Student legal action organization*]
SAMEA..... South African Mechanical Engineer [*A publication*]
SAMEB..... SA [*South African*] Mining and Engineering Journal [*A publication*]

SAMED..... South African Medical Literature [*South African Research Council*] [*Information service or system*] (CRD)
Same Day Surg ... Same-Day Surgery [*A publication*]
SAMEM.... Sustained-Attrition Minefield Evaluation Model (DNAB)
S Amer .... South America
SA Methodist ... South Australian Methodist [*A publication*] (APTA)
SAMEX..... Shuttle Active-Microwave Experiments (MCD)
SAMEX..... Surface-to-Air Missile Exercise (NVT)
SAMF....... Mendoza [*Argentina*] [*ICAO location identifier*] (ICLI)
SAMF....... Salvation Army Medical Fellowship (EAIO)
SAMF....... Seaborne Army Maintenance Facilities
SAMF....... Ship's Air Maintenance Facility [*Navy*] (NVT)
SAmF......... Studies in American Fiction [*A publication*]
SAMF....... Switchable Acoustic Matched Filter
SAMFU..... Self-Adjusting Military Foul-Up [*Slang*]
SA & MGS ... Small Arms and Machine Gun School [*British military*] (DMA)
SAMH....... Scottish Association for Mental Health [*British*]
SAmH........ Studies in American Humor [*A publication*]
SAMH....... Valle Hermoso [*Argentina*] [*ICAO location identifier*] (ICLI)
SAMHSJ .. South Australian Methodist Historical Society. Journal [*A publication*] (ADA)
SAMI........ Sales and Marketing Information Ltd. [*Database producer*] (IID)
SAMI........ San Martin [*Argentina*] [*ICAO location identifier*] (ICLI)
SAMI........ Selling Areas-Marketing, Inc. [*New York, NY*] [*Originator and database*] [*Information service or system*] (IID)
SAMI........ Sequential Assessment of Mathematics Inventory
SAMI........ Single Action Maintenance Instruction (NG)
SAMI........ Socially Acceptable Monitoring Instruments [*Medicine*]
SAMI........ Systems Acquisition Management Inspection
SAMI........ United Satellite/America, Inc. [*NASDAQ symbol*] (NQ)
SAMICS.... Solar Array Manufacturing Industry Costing Standards
SAMICS.... Systems Applications of Millimeter Wave Contact Seeker (MCD)
SAMID...... Ship Antimissile Integrated Defense [*Program*] [*Navy*]
SAMID...... Surface-to-Air Missile Intercept Development
SAMIDF ... Systematic and Applied Microbiology [*A publication*]
SA Min Eng J ... SA [*South African*] Mining and Engineering Journal [*A publication*]
SAMIP ...... Surface-to-Air Missile Improvement Program (MCD)
SAMIPAC ... Societe Auxiliare et Miniere du Pacifique [*France*] (PDAA)
SAMIS ...... Security Assistance Management Information System (MCD)
SAMIS ...... Ship Alteration Management Information System [*Navy*] [*Discontinued*]
SAMIS ...... Solar Array Manufacturing Industry Simulation
SAMIS ...... Standard Army Management Information System (MCD)
SAMIS ...... Structural Analysis and Matrix Inversion System [*Nuclear energy*] (NRCH)
SAMJ .... Jachal [*Argentina*] [*ICAO location identifier*] (ICLI)
SAMJ .... Sami Medica. Journal. Sami Medical Association [*A publication*]
SAMJA ..... South African Medical Journal [*A publication*]
SAML....... Nationella Samlingspartiet [*National Coalition Party*] [*Finland*] [*Political party*] (PPE)
SAML....... Sam & Libby, Inc. [*NASDAQ symbol*] (SPSG)
Saml.......... Samlaren [*A publication*]
Saml.......... Samuel [*Old Testament Book*] (WGA)
SAML....... Sinus Histiocytes with Massive Lymphadenopathy [*Clinical chemistry*]
SAML....... Standard Army Management Language (AABC)
SAML....... Studies in American Literature [*The Hague*] [*A publication*]
SAMLA..... Southern Atlantic Modern Language Association
SAMM ...... Malargue [*Argentina*] [*ICAO location identifier*] (ICLI)
SAMM ...... Standard Automated Materiel Management System [*DoD*]
SAMMA ... Stores Account Material Management Afloat (NG)
SAMMA/SAL ... Stores Account Material Management Afloat / Ship Authorization Level (DNAB)
Sammel Bl Ingolstadt ... Sammelblatt der Historischer Verein Ingolstadt [*A publication*]
SAMMI..... Signature Analysis Methods for Mission Identification
SAMMIE.. Scheduling Analysis Model for Mission Integrated Experiments [*NASA*] (KSC)
SAMMIE.. System for Aiding Man-Machine Interaction [*Prime Computer (UK) Ltd. and Prime Computers CAD/CAM Ltd.*] [*Software package*] (NCC)
Samml Geol Fuehrer ... Sammlung Geologischer Fuehrer [*A publication*]
Samml Goeschen ... Sammlung Goeschen [*A publication*]
Sammlung Wichmann NF ... Sammlung Wichmann. Neue Folge [*A publication*]
Samml Vergiftungsfaellen ... Sammlung von Vergiftungsfaellen [*A publication*]
Samml Zwangl Abh Geb Psychiatr Neurol ... Sammlung Zwangloser Abhandlungen aus dem Gebiete der Psychiatrie und Neurologie [*A publication*]
SAMMS.... Ship Alteration Material Management System
SAMMS.... Standard Automated Materiel Management System [*DoD*]
SAMNAM ... Samradet for Nordisk Amatormusik [*Arhus, Denmark*] (EAIO)
SAM-NIS ... Screen for Aeronautical Material - Not in Stock (DNAB)
SAMO .... Simulated Ab Initio Molecular Orbitals [*Atomic physics*]

SAMOA .... Systematic Approach to Multidimensional Occupational Analysis (MCD)
Samoan Pac LJ ... Samoan Pacific Law Journal [*A publication*]
Samoan PLJ ... Samoan Pacific Law Journal [*A publication*] (DLA)
SAMOD .... Secretary of the Army's Mobility, Opportunity, and Development Program (MCD)
Samoletostr Tekh Vozdushn Flota ... Samoletostroenie i Tekhnika Vozdushnogo Flota [*A publication*]
SAMOS..... Satellite-Missile Observation Satellite [*or System*]
SAMOS..... Silicon and Aluminum Metal-Oxide Semiconductor (ADA)
SA Motor... South Australian Motor [*A publication*] (APTA)
SAMP....... La Paz [*Argentina*] [*ICAO location identifier*] (ICLI)
SAMP....... Sample (AAG)
SAMP....... Shuttle Automated Mass Properties [*NASA*] (MCD)
SAMP....... Small Arms Master Plan [*Military document*] (INF)
SAMP....... Stuntmen's Association of Motion Pictures (EA)
SAMP....... Stuntwomen's Association of Motion Pictures (EA)
SAMPAC .. Society of Advertising Musicians, Producers, Arrangers, and Composers
SAMPAM ... System for Automation of Materiel Plans for Army Material (MCD)
SAMPAP .. Security Assistance Master Planning and Phasing
SAMPD..... Science Analysis and Mission Planning Directorate [*NASA*]
SAMPE..... Society for the Advancement of Material and Process Engineering (EA)
SAMPE..... Society of Aerospace Material and Process Engineers (AEBS)
SAMPE J .. SAMPE [*Society for the Advancement of Material and Process Engineering*] Journal [*A publication*]
SAMPE Q ... SAMPE [*Society for the Advancement of Material and Process Engineering*] Quarterly [*A publication*]
SAMPE Qtly ... SAMPE [*Society for the Advancement of Material and Process Engineering*] Quarterly [*A publication*]
SAM-PEX ... Solar, Anomalous, and Magnetospheric Particle Explorer Satellite
SAMPF ..... Sampford [*England*]
SAMPLE... Single Assignment Mathematical Programming Language [*1971*] [*Data processing*] (CSR)
Sampling Assaying Precious Met Proc Int Semin ... Sampling and Assaying of Precious Metals. Proceedings. International Seminar [*A publication*]
SAMPS ..... Shore Activity Manpower Planning System (DNAB)
SAMPSP... Security Assistance Master Planning and Phasing (MCD)
SAMQ .... Mendoza Aeroparque [*Argentina*] [*ICAO location identifier*] (ICLI)
SAMQA .... SAMPE [*Society for the Advancement of Material and Process Engineering*] Quarterly [*A publication*]
SAMR....... San Rafael [*Argentina*] [*ICAO location identifier*] (ICLI)
SAM & R ... Ship Activation, Maintenance, and Repair
SAMR....... Special Assistant for Material Readiness [*Army*]
SAMRA..... Sino-American Medical Rehabilitation Association
SAMRAF .. South African Military Refugee Aid Fund (EA)
SAMRD..... South African Machine Tool Review [*A publication*]
SAMRT..... Shared Aperture Medium-Range Tracker (MCD)
SAMS....... Sample Method Survey [*for family housing requirements*] [*Military*] (AABC)
SAMS....... Sampling Analog Memory System
SAMS....... San Carlos [*Argentina*] [*ICAO location identifier*] (ICLI)
SAMS....... Sandia Air Force Material Study (MCD)
SAMS....... Satellite Automatic Monitoring System [*Programming language*]
SAMS....... Security Assistance Management Squadron
SAMS....... Semiautomatic Meteorological Station (SAA)
SAMS....... Ship Alteration Material Survey (DNAB)
SAMS....... Ship's Alteration Management System [*Navy*]
SAMS....... Shore Activity Management Support [*Navy*] (NVT)
SAMS....... Shuttle Attachment Manipulator System [*NASA*]
SAMS....... Shuttle Automated Management System (SSD)
SAMS....... Society for Advanced Medical Systems [*Later, AMIA*]
SAMS....... Space Assembly, Maintenance, and Servicing (SSD)
SAMS....... Standard Army Maintenance System (AABC)
SAMS....... Stratospheric and Mesospheric Sounder
SAMS....... Study Attitudes and Methods Survey [*Study skills test*]
SAMS....... Surface-to-Air Missle System [*Military*]
SAMSA ..... Standard Army Management System - Supply Support Arrangement
SAM-SAC ... Specialized Aircraft Maintenance - Strategic Air Command (AAG)
SAM/SAR ... South America/South Atlantic Region [*DoD*]
SAMSARS ... Satellite-Based Maritime Search and Rescue System [*Telecommunications*] (TEL)
SAMSAT .. Solar Activity Monitoring Satellite (MCD)
SAM/SAT ... South America/South Atlantic Region [*Aviation*]
SAMSAT .. Surface-to-Air Missile Servicing, Assembly, and Test
SAMSEM ... Ship Antimissile System Engagement Model [*Navy*] (CAAL)
SAMSI ...... Spacecraft Array for Michelson Spectral Inferometry
SAMSIM ... Surface-to-Air Missile Simulation Model (MCD)
SAMSO ..... Space and Missile Systems Office [*Air Force*]
SAMSO..... Space and Missile Systems Organization [*Merger of Ballistic Systems Division and Space Systems Division*] [*Air Force*]
SAMSO..... Systems Analysis of Manned Space Operations (MCD)
SAMSOM ... Support Availability Multisystem Operational Model

SAMSON ... Samson Energy Co. Ltd. [*Associated Press abbreviation*] (APAG)
SAMSON ... Sources of Ambient MicroSeismic Oceanic Noise Experiment [*Office of Naval Research*]
SAMSON ... Strategic Automatic Message-Switching Operational Network [*Canada*] (MCD)
SAMSON ... System Analysis of Manned Space Operations (MCD)
SAMSOR .. Space and Missile Systems Organization Regulation [*Later, SDR*] [*Air Force*] (NASA)
SAMSOT .. SAMID [*Ship Antimissile Integrated Defense*] System Operational Test [*Navy*] (NVT)
SAMSq...... Special Air Mission Squadron [*Vietnam Air Force*] (AFM)
SAMS-USA ... South American Missionary Society of the Episcopal Church (EA)
SAMT....... Semiautomated Mechanical Transmission [*Automotive engineering*]
SAMT....... Simulated Aircraft Maintenance Trainer (MCD)
SAMT....... State-of-the-Art Medium Terminal
SAMTEC .. Space and Missile Test Center [*Air Force*]
SAMTEC/DET 1 ... Space and Missile Test Center Detachment 1 [*Patrick Air Force Base, FL*]
SAMTECM ... Space and Missile Test Center Manual [*Air Force*] (MCD)
SAMTO..... Space and Missile Test Organization [*Air Force*] [*Vandenberg Air Force Base, CA*]
SAMTS ..... Simulated A/C Maintenance Training System (MCD)
SAMU .... Uspallata [*Argentina*] [*ICAO location identifier*] (ICLI)
SA Museum Rec ... South Australian Museum. Records [*A publication*] (APTA)
SA Mus Tcr ... South Africa Music Teacher [*A publication*]
SAMV....... Mendoza [*Argentina*] [*ICAO location identifier*] (ICLI)
Samv .... Samvirke [*A publication*]
SAMWG ... Standing Air Monitoring Work Group [*Environmental Protection Agency*] (GFGA)
SAN .... Gato, CA [*Location identifier*] [*FAA*] (FAAL)
SAN .... San Carlos Milling Co., Inc. [*AMEX symbol*] (SPSG)
SAN .... San Diego [*California*] [*Airport symbol*] (OAG)
SAN .... San Francisco Helicopter Airlines [*Air carrier designation symbol*]
SAN .... San Francisco Operations Office [*Energy Research and Development Administration*]
SAN .... SAN: Journal of the Society for Ancient Numismatics [*A publication*]
SAN .... Sanatorium
SAN .... Sandersville Railroad Co. [*AAR code*]
SAN .... Sandwich (MSA)
San .... Sanford's Reports [*59 Alabama*] [*A publication*] (DLA)
SAN .... Sanitary (AAG)
SAN .... Sanitation (WGA)
san............ Sanskrit [*MARC language code*] [*Library of Congress*] (LCCP)
SAN .... Santiago [*Chile*] [*Seismograph station code, US Geological Survey*] (SEIS)
SAN .... School of Air Navigation [*British*]
SAN .... Servicios Aereos Nacionales [*Airline*] [*Ecuador*]
SAN .... Severe Acoustic Noise
SAN .... Ship Account Number [*Navy*]
SAN .... Shipping Accumulation Numbers (AAG)
SAN .... Sinoatrial Node [*Medicine*]
SAN .... Society for Ancient Numismatics (EA)
SAN .... Space Age News (AAG)
SAN .... Srpska Akademija Nauka i Umetnosti [*Belgrade, Yugoslavia*]
SAN .... Standard Address Number [*Publishing*]
SAN .... Styrene-Acrylonitrile [*Also, SA*] [*Organic chemistry*]
SAN .... Subsidiary Account Number
SAN .... System Advisory Notice
SANA .... Slavic American National Association (EA)
SANA .... Societa Anonima Navigazione Aerea [*Italy*]
SANA .... Soycrafters Association of North America (EA)
SANA .... Soyfoods Association of North America (EA)
SANA .... Specialty Advertising National Association [*Later, SAA*] (EA)
SANA .... State, Army, Navy, Air (AABC)
SANA .... Syrian Arab News Agency
SANAA ..... Servicio Autonomo Nacional de Acueductos y Alcantarillados [*Honduras*]
SANACC... State-Army-Navy-Air Force Coordinating Committee [*Terminated, 1949*] (EGAO)
SANAE...... South African National Antarctic Expedition
SANAFREQ ... Safety/NATOPS Frequency (MCD)
San Anto E ... San Antonio Executive [*A publication*]
SANAT....... Sanatorium
SA Nat....... South Australian Naturalist [*A publication*] (APTA)
SA Naturalist ... South Australian Naturalist [*A publication*] (APTA)
SANB........ South African National Bibliography
SANBAR... Sanders Barotropic
SANBB...... Sankhya. Series B. Indian Journal of Statistics [*A publication*]
Sanb & B Ann St ... Sanborn and Berryman's Annotated Statutes [*Wisconsin*] [*A publication*] (DLA)
San Bernardino County Med Soc Bull ... San Bernardino County Medical Society. Bulletin [*California*] [*A publication*]
SANC .... Catamarca [*Argentina*] [*ICAO location identifier*] (ICLI)
SANC .... Sanctuary [*Naval cadet's hiding place for smoking*] [*Slang*] [*British*] (DSUE)

SANC .... Slovak-American National Council (EA)
SANCAD... Scottish Association for National Certificates and Diplomas
San Ch ...... Sandford's New York Chancery Reports [*A publication*] (DLA)
SANCIP .... SACLANT [*Supreme Allied Commander, Atlantic*] Approved NATO Common Infrastructure Program (NATG)
San D .... Doctor of Sanitation
SAND .... Sampling Aerospace Nuclear Debris
SAND .... Sandata, Inc. [*NASDAQ symbol*] (NQ)
Sand .... Sandford's New York Superior Court Reports [*3-7 New York*] [*A publication*] (DLA)
SAND .... Shelter Analysis for New Designs (DNAB)
SAND .... Site Activation Need Date [*NASA*] (NASA)
SAND .... Sorting and Assembly of New Data
SANDA ..... Supplies and Accounts
SANDAC... Sandia Airborne Computer
Sandal .... Sandalion. Quaderni di Cultura Classica, Cristiana, e Medievale [*A publication*]
Sandars Just Inst ... Sandars' Edition of Justinian's Institutes [*A publication*] (DLA)
SANDASO ... Bureau of Supplies and Accounts Shipment Order [*Obsolete*] [*Navy*]
Sand Ch ..... Sandford's New York Chancery Reports [*A publication*] (DLA)
Sand Ch R ... Sandford's New York Chancery Reports [*A publication*] (DLA)
Sand Chy ... Sandford's New York Chancery Reports [*A publication*] (DLA)
Sand Dune Res ... Sand Dune Research [*A publication*]
Sand Essays ... Sanders' Essays on Uses and Trusts [*5th ed.*] [*1844*] [*A publication*] (DLA)
Sandf .... Sandford's New York Superior Court Reports [*3-7 New York*] [*A publication*] (DLA)
Sandf Ch .... Sandford's New York Chancery Reports [*A publication*] (DLA)
Sandf Ch (NY) ... Sandford's New York Superior Court Reports [*3-7 New York*] [*A publication*] (DLA)
Sandf Ch Rep ... Sandford's New York Chancery Reports [*A publication*] (DLA)
Sandf (NY) ... Sandford's New York Superior Court Reports [*3-7 New York*] [*A publication*] (ILCA)
Sandf (NY) R ... Sandford's New York Superior Court Reports [*A publication*] (DLA)
Sandford .... Sandford's New York Superior Court Reports [*A publication*] (DLA)
Sandford's SCR ... Sandford's New York Superior Court Reports [*A publication*] (DLA)
Sandford's Sup Ct R ... Sandford's New York Superior Court Reports [*A publication*] (DLA)
Sandf R ...... Sandford's New York Superior Court Reports [*A publication*] (DLA)
Sandf SC.... Sandford's New York Superior Court Reports [*A publication*] (DLA)
Sandf SCR ... Sandford's New York Superior Court Reports [*A publication*] (DLA)
SANDFSO ... Sea and Foreign Service Office (DNAB)
Sandf Suc... Sandford's Heritable Succession in Scotland [*A publication*] (DLA)
Sandf Sup CR ... Sandford's New York Superior Court Reports [*A publication*] (DLA)
Sandf Sup Ct ... Sandford's New York Superior Court Reports [*A publication*] (DLA)
Sandf Superior Court R ... Sandford's New York Superior Court Reports [*A publication*] (DLA)
Sand & H Dig ... Sandels and Hill's Digest of Statutes [*Arkansas*] [*A publication*] (DLA)
Sandia Lab Tech Rep SAND ... Sandia National Laboratories. Technical Report SAND [*A publication*]
Sandia Natl Lab Tech Rep SAND ... Sandia National Laboratories. Technical Report SAND [*A publication*]
Sandia SN ... Sandia Science News [*A publication*]
San Diego B ... San Diego Business Journal [*A publication*]
San Diego Biomed Symp Proc ... San Diego Biomedical Symposium. Proceedings [*A publication*]
San Diego L Rev ... San Diego Law Review [*A publication*]
San Diego Soc Nat Hist Mem ... San Diego Society of Natural History. Memoirs [*A publication*]
San Diego Soc Nat History Occasional Paper Trans ... San Diego Society of Natural History. Occasional Papers. Transactions [*A publication*]
San Diego Soc Nat History Trans ... San Diego Society of Natural History. Transactions [*A publication*]
San Diego Soc N H Tr ... San Diego Society of Natural History. Transactions [*A publication*]
San Diego Symp Biomed Eng Proc ... San Diego Symposium for Biomedical Engineering. Proceedings [*A publication*]
San Diego U ... San Diego Union [*A publication*]
Sand Inst Just Introd ... Sandars' Edition of Justinian's Institutes [*A publication*] (DLA)
Sand I Rep ... Sandwich Islands Reports [*Hawaii*] [*A publication*] (DLA)
Sand Isls .... Sandwich Islands
San DLR .... San Diego Law Review [*A publication*]
Sandl St Pap ... Sandler's State Papers [*A publication*] (DLA)
SANDOCC ... San Diego Oceanic Coordinating Committee
Sandoz Bull ... Sandoz Bulletin [*A publication*]

Sand R .... Sandford's New York Superior Court Reports [*A publication*] (DLA)
SANDRA... Structure and Reference Analyzer [*IBM Corp.*] [*Chemistry*]
SANDS...... Structural Analysis Numerical Design System
SAND (Sandia Natl Lab) ... SAND (Sandia National Laboratories) [*A publication*]
Sand SC ..... Sandford's New York Superior Court Reports [*A publication*] (DLA)
Sands Ch.... Sandford's New York Chancery Reports [*A publication*] (DLA)
Sands Clays Miner ... Sands, Clays, and Minerals [*A publication*]
Sand SCR .. Sandford's New York Superior Court Reports [*A publication*] (DLA)
Sandst .... Sandstone [*Lithology*]
Sand Sup Ct Rep ... Sandford's New York Superior Court Reports [*A publication*] (DLA)
Sand Supr Ct R ... Sandford's New York Superior Court Reports [*A publication*] (DLA)
Sand Uses and Trusts ... Sanders' Essays on Uses and Trusts [*A publication*] (DLA)
SANDY ..... Sandy Corp. [*Associated Press abbreviation*] (APAG)
SANE........ National Committee for a Sane Nuclear Policy [*"SANE" alone now used as organization name*] (EA)
San E......... Sanitary Engineer [*Academic degree*]
SANE........ Santiago Del Estero [*Argentina*] [*ICAO location identifier*] (ICLI)
SANE........ Schizophrenia: a National Emergency [*An association*] [*British*]
SANE........ Scientific Applications of Nuclear Explosions (SAA)
SANE........ Severe Acoustic Noise Environment
SANE........ Sources from the Ancient Near East [*A publication*]
SANE........ Standard Apple Numerics Environment [*Software*] [*Apple Computers, Inc.*]
SANET...... Supplement to Ancient Near Eastern Texts [*A publication*]
SANF......... Salvation Army Nurses' Fellowship (EAIO)
SanF.......... San Francisco Magazine [*A publication*]
SANF......... Sanford Corp. [*Bellwood, IL*] [*NASDAQ symbol*] (NQ)
SANF......... Sanford Recreation Area
Sanf........... Sanford's Reports [*59 Alabama*] [*A publication*] (DLA)
SANF........ South African Naval Forces
San Fernando Val Dent Soc Bull ... San Fernando Valley Dental Society. Bulletin [*US*] [*A publication*]
San Fern Val LR ... San Fernando Valley Law Review [*A publication*]
San Fern VL Rev ... San Fernando Valley Law Review [*A publication*]
San FLJ ..... San Francisco Law Journal [*A publication*] (DLA)
Sanf (NY)... Sandford's New York Superior Court Reports [*3-7 New York*] [*A publication*] (DLA)
Sanford's Ch R ... Sandford's New York Chancery Reports [*A publication*] (DLA)
San Fran B ... San Francisco Business Journal [*A publication*]
San Francisco Bus ... San Francisco Business [*A publication*]
San Francisco Med ... San Francisco Medicine [*A publication*]
San Francisco Micro Soc Tr ... San Francisco Microscopical Society. Transactions [*A publication*]
San Fran Cro ... San Francisco Chronicle [*A publication*]
San Fran Law Bull ... San Francisco Law Bulletin [*A publication*] (DLA)
San Fran LB ... San Francisco Law Bulletin [*A publication*] (ILCA)
San Fran LJ ... San Francisco Law Journal [*A publication*] (DLA)
San Fran Opera ... San Francisco Opera Magazine [*A publication*]
San Fr LB .. San Francisco Law Bulletin [*A publication*] (DLA)
San Fr LJ... San Francisco Law Journal [*A publication*] (DLA)
Sang .... Sangre [*A publication*]
SANG .... Saudi Arabian National Guard (RDA)
SANG .... Standardized Aeronautical Navigation/Guidance [*Program*] [*Air Force*]
San Gabriel Val Dent Soc Bull ... San Gabriel Valley Dental Society. Bulletin [*A publication*]
SANGB...... Selfridge Army/Air National Guard Base (MCD)
SANGFPT ... Spherical Angles from Points (MCD)
Sang Natak ... Sangeet Natak [*New Delhi*] [*A publication*]
SANGruz... Soobscenija Akademji Nauk Gruzinskoj SSR [*A publication*]
SANH........ Rio Hondo/Las Termas [*Argentina*] [*ICAO location identifier*] (ICLI)
Sanh.......... Sanhedrin (BJA)
Sanh.......... Sanherib (BJA)
SANH........ Somerset Archaeology and Natural History [*A publication*]
SANI......... Tinogasta [*Argentina*] [*ICAO location identifier*] (ICLI)
Sanid Aeronaut ... Sanidad Aeronautica [*A publication*]
Sanid Benef Munic ... Sanidad y Beneficiencia Municipal [*A publication*]
Sanifil .... Sanifill, Inc. [*Associated Press abbreviation*] (APAG)
SANINSP ... Sanitation Inspector [*Military*] (AABC)
Sanit .... Sanitarium
Sanit.......... Sanitary
Sanitary & Heat Eng ... Sanitary and Heating Engineering [*A publication*]
Sanit Eng Pap Colo State Univ ... Sanitary Engineering Papers. Colorado State University [*A publication*]
Sanit Heiz Tech ... Sanitaer- und Heizungstechnik [*A publication*]
Sanit Heizungstech (Duesseldorf) ... Sanitaer- und Heizungstechnik (Duesseldorf) [*A publication*]
Sanit Heizungstechnik ... Sanitaer- und Heizungstechnik [*West Germany*] [*A publication*]
Sanit Nytt .. Sanitets Nytt Utgitt av Forsvarets Sanitet [*A publication*]

Sanit Okh Vodoemov Zagryaz Prom Stochnymi Vodami ... Sanitarnaya Okhrana Vodoemov ot Zagryazneniya Promyshlennymi Stochnymi Vodami [*A publication*]
Sanit Rec J Munic Eng ... Sanitary Record and Journal of Municipal Engineering [*A publication*]
Sanit Rec Munic Eng ... Sanitary Record and Municipal Engineering [*A publication*]
SAnitRt...... Santa Anita Realty Enterprises, Inc. [*Associated Press abbreviation*]   (APAG)
Sanit Tekh ... Sanitarnaya Tekhnika [*A publication*]
SANJA...... South African Nursing Journal [*A publication*]
San Jose Bus ... San Jose Business Journal [*A publication*]
San Jose M ... San Jose Mercury News [*A publication*]
San Jose Stud ... San Jose Studies [*A publication*]
San Just ..... Sandars' Edition of Justinian's Institutes [*A publication*]   (DLA)
SANKA...... Sans Caffeine [*Acronym used as brand name*]
Sanken Tech Rep ... Sanken Technical Report [*A publication*]
Sankhya A ... Sankhya. Series A. Indian Journal of Statistics [*A publication*]
Sankhya B ... Sankhya. Series B. Indian Journal of Statistics [*A publication*]
Sankhya C ... Sankhya. Series C. Indian Journal of Statistics [*A publication*]
Sankhya Indian J Stat Ser B ... Sankhya. Series B. Indian Journal of Statistics [*A publication*]
Sankhya Ser A ... Sankhya. Series A [*A publication*]
Sankhya Ser A ... Sankhya. Series A. Indian Journal of Statistics [*A publication*]
Sankhya Ser B ... Sankhya. Series B. Indian Journal of Statistics [*A publication*]
SANL........ La Rioja/Cap. V. Almandos Almonacid [*Argentina*] [*ICAO location identifier*]   (ICLI)
SANLF ...... Saudi Arabian National Liberation Front [*Political party*]   (BJA)
SANM .... Synthetic Algal Nutrient Medium
SAN MIG ... San Miguel Beer   (DSUE)
SANNA ..... Schweizer Archiv fuer Neurologie, Neurochirurgie, und Psychiatrie [*A publication*]
SANNAW ... Archives Suisses de Neurologie, Neurochirurgie, et de Psychiatrie/Archivio Svizzero di Neurologia, Neurochirurgia, e Psichiatria [*A publication*]
SANO .... Chilecito [*Argentina*] [*ICAO location identifier*]   (ICLI)
SANOVA .. Simultaneous Analysis of Variance
SANP........ Secondary Auxiliary Nuclear Power
SANR .... Subject to Approval No Risk
SANROC... South African Non-Racial Olympic Committee   (EAIO)
SANS........ Schedule for the Assessment of Negative Symptoms [*Psychometrics*]
SANS........ Simplified Account - Numbering System
SANS........ Small-Angle Neutron Scattering
SANS........ South African Naval Service
SANS........ Students Against Nuclear Suicide   (EA)
SANS........ Swimmer and Navigation System [*Navy*]   (CAAL)
SANSAN... San Francisco, San Diego [*Proposed name for possible "super-city" formed by growth and mergers of other cities*]
SANSC ...... Sanscrit
SANSET.... Seaman Apprentice, Nuclear Submarine Engineering Technician [*Navy rating*]   (DNAB)
SANSK ...... Sanskrit [*Language, etc.*]
SANSS ...... Structure and Nomenclature Search System [*Formerly, SSS*] [*Chemical Information Systems, Inc.*] [*Information service or system*]
SANT........ Santa Monica Bank [*NASDAQ symbol*]   (NQ)
SANT........ Studien zum Alten und Neuen Testament [*A publication*]
S Ant......... Suomen Antropologi/Antropologi i Finland [*A publication*]
SANT........ Tucuman/Teniente Benjamim Matienzo [*Argentina*] [*ICAO location identifier*]   (ICLI)
SANTA...... Souvenir and Novelty Trade Association   (EA)
Santa Barbara Mus Nat History Dept Geology Bull ... Santa Barbara Museum of Natural History. Department of Geology. Bulletin [*A publication*]
Santa Barbara Soc N H B ... Santa Barbara Society of Natural History. Bulletin [*A publication*]
Santa Clara L ... Santa Clara Law [*A publication*]
Santa Clara Law ... Santa Clara Lawyer [*A publication*]
Santa Clara LR ... Santa Clara Law Review [*A publication*]   (ILCA)
Santa Clara L Rev ... Santa Clara Law Review [*A publication*]
Sant Cl LR ... Santa Clara Law Review [*A publication*]
Sante .... Sante Mentale au Canada [*A publication*]
Sante Secur Soc ... Sante Securite Sociale [*A publication*]
Santo Tomas J Med ... Santo Tomas Journal of Medicine [*A publication*]
SANU .... San Juan [*Argentina*] [*ICAO location identifier*]   (ICLI)
SANU .... Sudan African National Union [*Political party*]
SANUM .... South Africa National Union for Mineworkers
SA Nurs J .. South African Nursing Journal [*A publication*]
SANW .... Ceres [*Argentina*] [*ICAO location identifier*]   (ICLI)
SANWFZ.. South Asia Nuclear Weapons-Free Zone
SANY .... Sanyo Electric Co. Ltd. [*NASDAQ symbol*]   (NQ)
Sanyal .... Sanyal's Criminal Cases between Natives and Europeans [*1796-1895*] [*India*] [*A publication*]   (DLA)
SANYD ..... Sanitets Nytt [*A publication*]
SAO .... Saharan Air Outbreak [*Meteorology*]

SAO.......... San Andreas Geological Observatory [*California*] [*Seismograph station code, US Geological Survey*]   (SEIS)
SAO .... Sandia Area Office [*Energy Research and Development Administration*]
SAO .... Sao Paulo [*Brazil*] [*Airport symbol*]   (OAG)
SAO .... Scottish Association of Opticians   (DAS)
SAO .... Secret Army Organization [*English initialism for OAS, terrorist group in Algeria and metropolitan France*]
SAO .... Secretin-Stimulated Acid Output [*Clinical chemistry*]
SAO .... Security Assistance Office
SAO .... Select Address and Operate
SAO .... Selected Attack Option   (MCD)
SAO .... Semiannual Oscillation [*Astronomy*]
SAO .... Senior Administrative Officer [*British military*]   (DMA)
SAO .... Single Airlift Organization   (CINC)
SAO .... Single Attack Option
SAO .... Smithsonian Astrophysical Observatory [*Cambridge, MA*]
SAO .... Smithsonian Institution. Astrophysical Observatory [*A publication*]
SAO .... Smooth Approach Orifice [*Mechanical engineering*]
SAO .... Social Actions Office [*or Officer*] [*Air Force*]   (AFM)
SAO .... Sonobuoy Acoustic Operator [*Navy*]   (CAAL)
SAO .... Special Access Only   (MCD)
SAO .... Special Action Office [*Phased out, 1975*] [*Department of Justice*]
SAO .... Special Activities Office [*Air Force*]   (AFM)
SAO .... Special Air Operations
SAO .... Special Analysis Office
SAO .... Special Artificer, Optical [*Navy*]
SAO .... Special Astrophysics Observatory
SAO .... Splanchnic Artery Occlusion [*Medicine*]
SAO .... Squadron Accountant Officer [*Navy*] [*British*]
SAO .... Staff Administrative Office [*Military*]
SAO .... Subsidiary/Affiliate Order   (MCD)
SAO .... Support Air Observation [*Navy*]
SAO .... Survey of Agency Opinion [*LIMRA*]
SAO .... Survival Assistance Officer [*Army*]   (AABC)
SAO .... Systems Acquisition Officer [*Military*]   (AFIT)
SAO .... Systems Analysis Office
SAOABX... Archivos. Sociedad Americana de Oftalmologia y Optometria [*A publication*]
SAOAS..... Secretary of the Army, Office of the Assistant Secretary
SAOAS..... Staff Association of the Organization of American States   (EA)
SAOB .... Svenska Akademiens Ordbok [*A publication*]
SAOC .... Rio Cuarto/Area de Material [*Argentina*] [*ICAO location identifier*]   (ICLI)
SAOC .... Scottish Association of Operative Coachmakers [*A union*]
SAOC .... Space and Astronautics Orientation Course   (NG)
SAOC .... Studies in Ancient Oriental Civilization. The Oriental Institute of the University of Chicago [*A publication*]
SAOCS..... Submarine Air Optical Communications System   (MCD)
SAOD .... Villa Dolores [*Argentina*] [*ICAO location identifier*]   (ICLI)
SAODAP... Special Action Office for Drug Abuse Prevention [*Terminated, 1975*] [*FDA*]
SAOE .... Embalse Rio Tercero [*Argentina*] [*ICAO location identifier*]   (ICLI)
SAOG .... Satellite Operations Group [*Military*]
SAOL........ Laboulaye [*Argentina*] [*ICAO location identifier*]   (ICLI)
SAOM .... Marcos Juarez [*Argentina*] [*ICAO location identifier*]   (ICLI)
SAO/MEX ... Special Action Office for Mexico [*Drug Enforcement Administration*]
Sao Paulo Brazil Inst Pesqui Tecnol Bol ... Sao Paulo, Brazil. Instituto de Pesquisas Tecnologicas. Boletin [*A publication*]
Sao Paulo Inst Agron (Campinas) Bol ... Sao Paulo. Instituto Agronomico (Campinas). Boletim [*A publication*]
Sao Paulo Inst Agron (Campinas) Bol Tec ... Sao Paulo. Instituto Agronomico (Campinas). Boletim Tecnico [*A publication*]
Sao Paulo Inst Agron (Campinas) Circ ... Sao Paulo. Instituto Agronomico (Campinas). Circular [*A publication*]
Sao Paulo Inst Geogr Geol Bol ... Sao Paulo. Instituto Geografico e Geologico. Boletim [*A publication*]
Sao Paulo Inst Geogr Geol Relat ... Sao Paulo. Instituto Geografico e Geologico. Relatorio [*A publication*]
Sao Paulo Univ Inst Geocienc Bol ... Sao Paulo. Universidade. Instituto de Geociencias. Boletim [*A publication*]
Sao Paulo Univ Inst Geogr Geogr Planejamento ... Sao Paulo. Universidade. Instituto de Geografia. Geografia e Planejamento [*A publication*]
Sao Paulo Univ Inst Geogr Geomorfol ... Sao Paulo. Universidade. Instituto de Geografia. Geomorfologia [*A publication*]
Sao Paulo Univ Inst Geogr Ser Teses Monogr ... Sao Paulo. Universidade. Instituto de Geografia. Serie Teses e Monografias [*A publication*]
SAOR .... Villa Reynolds [*Argentina*] [*ICAO location identifier*]   (ICLI)
SA Ornithol ... South Australian Ornithologist [*A publication*]   (APTA)
SA Ornithologist ... South Australian Ornithologist [*A publication*]   (APTA)
SAOS......... Select Address [*and Provide*] Output Signal
SAOT .... Semiactive on Target
SAOTA...... Shrimp Association of the Americas   (EA)
SAOU .... San Luis [*Argentina*] [*ICAO location identifier*]   (ICLI)
SAP........... ASAP Air, Inc. [*Fort Worth, TX*] [*FAA designator*]   (FAAC)

SAP........... Sampling and Analysis Plan
SAP........... San Antonio Public Library, San Antonio, TX [*OCLC symbol*]   (OCLC)
SAP........... San Pedro Sula [*Honduras*] [*Airport symbol*]   (OAG)
sap............. Saponification [*or Saponify*] [*Analytical chemistry*]   (AAMN)
SAP........... Sapporo [*Japan*] [*Seismograph station code, US Geological Survey*]   (SEIS)
SAP........... Scientific Advisory Panel [*Arlington, VA*] [*Environmental Protection Agency*]   (EGAO)
SAP........... Scorched Aluminum Powder
SAP........... Scouting and Amphibian Plane [*Coast Guard*]
SAP........... Scruple Apothecaries
SAP........... Seaborne Aircraft Platform   (ADA)
SAP........... Second Audio Program
SAP........... Security Assistance Program   (MCD)
SAP........... Semi-Armor-Piercing [*Projectile*] [*Nickname: Sex-Appeal Pete*] [*Military*]
SAP........... Seminal Acid Phosphatase [*An enzyme*]
SAP........... Separate Audio Program [*Television broadcasting*]
SAP........... Serum Alkaline Phosphatase [*Clinical chemistry*]
SAP........... Serum Amyloid P [*Clinical chemistry*]
SAP........... Service Access Point
SAP........... Service Advertising Protocol [*Data processing*]   (PCM)
SAP........... Seychelles Agence de Presse [*News agency*]   (EY)
SAP........... Share Assembly Program [*Data processing*]
SAP........... Ship Acquisition Plan [*Navy*]
SAP........... Ship Alteration Package [*Navy*]   (DNAB)
SAP........... Shipboard Acoustic Processor [*Navy*]   (CAAL)
SAP........... Shipboard Antenna Pedestal
SAP........... Simple Assembly Plan
SAPE......... Single-Axis Platform
SAP........... Sintered Aluminum Powder
SAP........... Site Activation Phase
SAP........... Skeletal Axis of Pinnule
SAP........... Social Action Party [*Thailand*] [*Political party*]   (FEA)
SAP........... Socialistische Arbeiderspartij [*Socialist Workers' Party*] [*Netherlands*] [*Political party*]   (PPW)
SAP........... Society for Adolescent Psychiatry   (EA)
SAP........... Society for American Philosophy [*Defunct*]   (EA)
SAP........... Sodium Acid Pyrophosphate [*Also, SAPP*] [*Leavening agent, meat additive*]
SAP........... Soon as Possible
SAP........... South African Party [*Political party*]   (PPW)
SAP........... Soysal Adelet Partisi [*Social Justice Party*] [*Turkish Cyprus*] [*Political party*]   (PPE)
SAP........... Special and Administrative Provisions [*of the Tariff Act of 1930*]
SAP........... Sphingolipid Activator Protein [*Biochemistry*]
SAP........... Spot Authorization Plan [*WPB*] [*Obsolete*]
SAP........... Spy Against Pollution [*An association*]
SAP........... Squadron Aid Post   (ADA)
SAP........... Staphylococcus aureus Protease [*An enzyme*]
SAP........... State Association President [*American Occupational Therapy Association*]
SAP........... Steroidogenesis Activator Polypeptide
SAP........... Strain Arrestor Plate [*NASA*]   (NASA)
SAP........... Strategic Advantages Profile
SAP........... Strong Anthropic Principle [*Term coined by authors John Barrow and Frank Tipler in their book, "The Anthropic Cosmological Principle"*]
SAP........... Structural Analysis Program   (MCD)
SAP........... Student Aid Project
SAP........... Subassembly Precision   (MCD)
SAP........... Subject Access Project
SAP........... Sumerian Animal Proverbs   (BJA)
SAP........... Supervisory Airplane Pilot
SAP........... Supportability Assurance Program
SAP........... Surface Aligned Photochemistry [*Physics*]
SAP........... Sveriges Socialdemokratiska Arbetareparti [*Swedish Social Democratic Labor Party*] [*Political party*]   (PPW)
SAP........... Symbolic Address Program
SAP........... Symbolic Assembly Program [*Data processing*]
SAP........... System Alignment Procedure   (NATG)
SAP........... Systemic Arterial Pressure [*Medicine*]
SAP........... Systems Assurance Program [*IBM Corp.*]
SAPA........ Sciences - A Process Approach [*National Science Foundation*]
SapA .... Societa in Accomandita per Azioni [*Limited Partnership with Shares*] [*Italian*]   (IMH)
SAPA........ South African Press Association
SAPAA3.... Escuela Nacional de Agricultura [*Chapingo*]. Serie de Apuntes [*A publication*]
SAPAI ...... Salesmen's Association of Paper and Allied Industries   (EA)
SA Parl Deb ... South Australia. Parliamentary Debates [*A publication*]   (APTA)
SA Parl Parl Deb ... South Australia. Parliament. Parliamentary Debates [*A publication*]   (APTA)
SAPAS...... Semiautomatic Population Analysis System   (MCD)
SAPAT ...... South African Picture Analysis Test [*Psychology*]
SAPC........ Shipowners Association of the Pacific Coast [*Defunct*]   (EA)
SAPC......... Small Arms Post Competition
SAPC......... Substance Abuse Problem Checklist

SAPC........ Supported Aqueous-Phase Catalysis [*Chemistry*]
SAPC........ Suspended Acoustical-Plaster Ceiling [*Technical drawings*]
SAPCHE... Semiautomatic Program Checkout Equipment   (AAG)
SAPCO..... Security Assistance Policy Coordinating Office [*Military*]
SAPCO..... Single-Asset Property Company [*British*]
SAPCO..... Sudanese African People's Congress [*Political party*]   (EY)
SAPD....... Self-Administration of Psychotropic Drugs   (AAMN)
SAPD....... South Australia. Parliamentary Debates [*A publication*]
SAPDF ..... Social Activist Professors Defense Foundation   (EA)
SAPDO..... Special Accounts Property Disposal Officer [*Military*]
SAPE........ Society for Automation in Professional Education [*Later, SDE*]
SAPE........ Solenoid Array Pattern Evaluator
SAPEA ..... Sapere [*A publication*]
SAPEC ..... Savings Associations Political Education Committee
SAPED ..... Salt 'n' Pepper [*A publication*]
SAPENF.... Societe Americaine pour l'Etude de la Numismatique Francaise   (EA)
SAPF .... Suider-Afrika Padfederasie [*Southern Africa Road Federation - SARF*]   (EAIO)
SAPFE...... Seaman Apprentice, Polaris Field Electronics [*Navy rating*]   (DNAB)
SAPFL....... Seaman Apprentice, Polaris Field Launcher [*Navy rating*]   (DNAB)
SAPFT...... Special Adviser to the President on Foreign Trade [*New Deal*]
SAPFU ..... Surpassing All Previous Foul Ups [*Military slang*] [*Bowdlerized version*]
saph........... Sapphire [*Philately*]
SAPhA....... Student American Pharmaceutical Association [*Later, APhA-ASP*]   (EA)
SAPHD ..... South African Journal of Physics [*A publication*]
SAPHE...... Semi-Armor-Piercing High Explosive [*Projectile*]   (MCD)
SAPHYDATA ... Panel on the Acquisition, Transmission, and Processing of Hydrological Data [*Marine science*]   (MSC)
SAPI .... Sales Association of the Paper Industry [*New York, NY*]   (EA)
SAPI .... Semi-Armor-Piercing Incendiary [*Projectile*]   (NATG)
SAPIENS.. Spreading Activation Processor for Information Encoded in Network Structure [*Department of Education*]
SAPIR .... System of Automatic Processing and Indexing of Reports
SAPIS........ State Alcoholism Profile Information System [*Public Health Service*]   (IID)
SAPL........ Seacoast Anti-Pollution League   (EA)
SAPL........ Service Action Parts List   (AAG)
SAPL........ Society for Animal Protective Legislation   (EA)
SAPL........ Spartan-Approved Parts List [*Missiles*]   (MCD)
SAPLIC..... Small Arms Projected Line Charge [*Military*]   (INF)
SAPM........ Scottish Association of Plane Makers [*A union*]
SAPNA...... South African Panorama [*A publication*]
SAPNA...... Succinyl-Alanyl-para-Nitroanilide [*Biochemistry*]
SaPNFB.... National Film Board, Pretoria, South Africa [*Library symbol*] [*Library of Congress*]   (LCLS)
SAPO........ Sarawak People's Organization [*Malaysia*] [*Political party*]   (PPW)
SAPO........ Silicoaluminophosphate [*Inorganic chemistry*]
SAPO........ Special Aircraft Project Office   (AAG)
SAPO........ Subarea Petroleum Office [*Military*]
SAPOA...... Savremena Poljoprivreda [*A publication*]
SAPOAB... Contemporary Agriculture [*A publication*]
SAPON ..... Saponaria [*Soapwort*] [*Pharmacology*]   (ROG)
SAPON ..... Saponification [*Analytical chemistry*]
SAPOV..... Subarea Petroleum Office, Vietnam [*Military*]
SAPP .... Security, Accuracy, Propriety, and Policy
S App .... Shaw's Scotch Appeal Cases, House of Lords [*1821-24*] [*A publication*]   (DLA)
SAPP .... Skeletal Axis of Palp
SAPP .... Sodium Acid Pyrophosphate [*Also, SAP*] [*Leavening agent, meat additive*]
SAPP .... Soul Assurance Prayer Plan   (EA)
SAPP .... South Australian Parliamentary Papers [*A publication*]
SAPP .... Special Airfield Pavement Program   (NATG)
SAPPHIRE ... Synthetic Aperture Precision Processor High Reliability   (MCD)
SAPPMA .. San Antonio Procurement and Production Materiel Area [*Air Force*]
Sapporo Med J ... Sapporo Medical Journal [*A publication*]
SAPR .... Semiannual Progress Report
SAPR .... South Australian Planning Reports [*A publication*]   (APTA)
SAPR .... Summary Area Problem Report   (AAG)
SAPRA...... Sakharnaya Promyshlennost [*A publication*]
SAPRC...... Security Assistance Program Review Commission
SAPS .... Scandinavian Association of Paediatric Surgeons   (EAIO)
SAPS .... Scandinavian Association of Plastic Surgeons [*See also NPF*]   (EAIO)
SAPS .... Selected Alternate Processing Separation   (MCD)
SAPS .... Servico de Alimentacao da Providencia Social [*Brazil*]
SAPS .... Shippingport Atomic Power Station   (NRCH)
SAPS .... Signal Algorithmic Processing System [*Navy*]
SAPS .... Small Area Plotting Sheet
SaPS .... South African Council for Scientific and Industrial Research, Pretoria, South Africa [*Library symbol*] [*Library of Congress*]   (LCLS)
SAPS .... Standalone Prediction System

SAPS	Surety Agents Promotional Society [*Defunct*] (EA)
SaPSL.......	State Library, Pretoria, South Africa [*Library symbol*] [*Library of Congress*] (LCLS)
SA/PSP	Site Activation/Phased Support Plan [*Military*] (MCD)
SAPST	Special Assistant to the President for Science and Technology
SAPT	South Africa Department of Posts and Telecommunications (TSSD)
SAPT	Symmetry-Adapted Perturbation Theory [*Physical chemistry*]
SAPTA	SAE [*Society of Automotive Engineers*] Progress in Technology [*A publication*]
SA Pub Serv R ...	South Australian Public Service Review [*A publication*] (APTA)
SAPUC.....	Sintered Aluminum Powder-Clad Uranium Carbide
SAPV.........	Secondary Air Pulse Valve [*Automotive engineering*]
SAPW........	United Stone and Allied Products Workers of America [*Later, USWA*]
SAQ	Pittsburgh, PA [*Location identifier*] [*FAA*] (FAAL)
SAQ	San Andros [*Bahamas*] [*Airport symbol*] (OAG)
SAQ	Short Arc Quads [*Medicine*]
SAQ	South Atlantic Quarterly [*A publication*]
SAQ	Springbank Aviation Ltd. [*Canada*] [*FAA designator*] (FAAC)
SAQAD	Submarine Antenna Quality Assurance Directory [*Navy*] (DNAB)
SAQAF	Submarine Antenna Quality Assurance Facility [*Navy*] (DNAB)
SAQC	Statistical Analysis and Quality Control
SAQR	Substance Abuse Quarterly Report [*Navy*] (DNAB)
SAQS........	Single Agency Qualification Standards [*Aviation*] (FAAC)
SAQT.........	Sociedad Panamericana de Quimioterapia de la Tuberculosis [*Pan American Society for Chemotherapy of Tuberculosis - PASCT*] (EA)
SAR...........	National Society, Sons of the American Revolution (EA)
SAR...........	Safety Analysis Report [*Nuclear energy*]
SAR...........	Safety Assessment Report (MCD)
SAR...........	Sales Authorization Request
SAR...........	Sample Acceptance Rate [*Statistics*]
SAR...........	Santa Anita Realty Enterprises, Inc. [*NYSE symbol*] (SPSG)
SAR...........	Santa Rosa Junior College, Santa Rosa, CA [*OCLC symbol*] (OCLC)
SAR...........	Sarajevo [*Yugoslavia*] [*Seismograph station code, US Geological Survey*] (SEIS)
SAR...........	Sarcoidosis [*Medicine*]
Sar............	Sarcosine [*Biochemistry*]
Sar............	Sarcosyl [*Biochemistry*]
SAR...........	Sardinia [*Italy*] (ROG)
Sar............	Sarswati's Privy Council Judgments [*India*] [*A publication*] (DLA)
SAR...........	Saudi Arabian Riyal [*Monetary unit*] (DS)
SAR...........	Schedule Allocation Requirements (AAG)
SAR...........	Schedule and Request (MCD)
SAR...........	School of American Research [*Research center*] (RCD)
SAR...........	Sea-Air Rescue
SAR...........	Search and Release (AAG)
SAR...........	Search and Rescue Program [*Coast Guard*]
SAR...........	Segment Address Register [*Telecommunications*]
SAR...........	Selected Acquisition Report [*Military*]
SAR...........	Semiactive RADAR (MCD)
SAR...........	Semiannual Report
SAR...........	Semiautomatic Rifle [*Army*]
SAR...........	Senior Army Representative
SAR...........	Service Analysis Report [*Telecommunications*] (TEL)
SAR...........	Service Analysis Request [*Telecommunications*] (TEL)
SAR...........	Service Aptitude Rating [*Military*] (NVT)
SAR...........	Service Assigned Requests (MCD)
SAR...........	Sexual'Attitude Reassessment [*Medicine*]
SAR...........	Siemens Agronaut Reactor [*Germany*]
SAR...........	Significant Action Report [*Military*] (MCD)
SAR...........	Silver Acorn Developments [*Vancouver Stock Exchange symbol*]
SAR...........	Simulated Acid Rain
SAR...........	Single-Axis Reference
SAR...........	Single-BIT [*Binary Digit*] Alternation Recording
SAR...........	Site Acceptance Review [*Military*]
SAR...........	Society for Animal Rights [*Later, ISAR*] (EA)
SAR...........	Society of Authors' Representatives (EA)
SAR...........	Sodium-Adsorption-Ratio
SAR...........	Software Acceptance Review
SAR...........	Son Altesse Royale [*His or Her Royal Highness*] [*French*]
SAR...........	SONAR Acoustique Remorque [*Acoustic imaging system*] [*French*]
SAR...........	Sons of the American Revolution
SAR...........	Source Address Register [*Telecommunications*]
SAR...........	South African Railways
SAR...........	South African Republic
SAR...........	South African Republic High Court Reports [*A publication*] (DLA)
SAR...........	South Asian Review [*A publication*]
SAR...........	South Australian Government Railways
SAR...........	South Australian Industrial Reports [*A publication*] (APTA)
SAR...........	Spacecraft Acceptance Review (MCD)
SAR...........	Sparta, IL [*Location identifier*] [*FAA*] (FAAL)
SAR...........	Special Access Required
SAR...........	Special Aeronautical Requirement [*Navy*] (NG)
SAR...........	Specific Absorption Rate
SAR...........	Specific Acoustic Resistance
SAR...........	Specific Activity Report
SAR...........	Specifically Authorized Representative [*Air Force*]
SAR...........	Specification Approval Record (MCD)
SAR...........	Stable Auroral Red [*Arc*] [*Geophysics*]
SAR...........	Standardized Admissions Ratios [*Hospital activity analysis*]
SAR...........	Standing Authority Release [*For perishables*] [*Business term*]
SAR...........	Start Action Request [*Environmental Protection Agency*]
SAR...........	Starting Air Receiver (AAG)
SAR...........	Stock Appreciation Relief [*British*]
SAR...........	Stock Appreciation Rights [*Method of compensation for top executives*]
SAR...........	Storage Address Register [*Telecommunications*]
SAR...........	Street Address Record [*Telecommunications*] (TEL)
SAR...........	Structure Activity Relationship
SAR...........	Student Aid Report [*Department of Education*]
SAR...........	Studies in the American Renaissance [*A publication*]
SAR...........	Study and Review [*Reports*] (RDA)
SAR...........	Subauroral Red [*Arc*] [*Geophysics*]
SAR...........	Submarine Advanced Reactor
SAR...........	Subsequent Application Review
SAR...........	Substance Abuse Report [*Navy*] (DNAB)
SAR...........	Substitution Approval Request (MCD)
SAR...........	Successive Accelerated Replacement
SAR...........	Successive Approximation Register [*Data processing*]
SAR...........	Sulfuric Acid Regenerator (MCD)
SAR...........	Sum of Absolute Residuals [*Mathematics*]
SAR...........	Summary Analysis Report (NASA)
SAR...........	Super-Abrasion-Resistant [*Lucite glazing material*]
SAR...........	Support Air Request [*Net*] [*Navy communications*]
SAR...........	Symbol Acquisition Routine
SAR...........	Synthetic Aperture RADAR
SAR...........	Syrian Arab Republic
SAR...........	System Acquisition Report
SAR...........	System Analysis Report
SAR...........	System Array RADAR (KSC)
SAR...........	System Availability Report
SAR...........	Systemic Acquired Resistance [*Medicine*]
SAR...........	Systemic Arterial Resistance [*Medicine*]
SAR...........	Systemic Availability Ratio [*Physiology*]
SAR...........	Systems Assessment Review [*NASA*] (KSC)
SARA.......	Saralasin [*Antihypertensive*]
SARA........	Saratoga Mines, Inc. [*NASDAQ symbol*] (NQ)
SARA........	Saratoga National Historical Park
SARA........	Saratoga Trunk (DSUE)
SARA........	Satellite Angular Radiometer (NOAA)
SARA........	Saturates, Aromatics, Resins, and Asphaltenes [*Crude oil analysis*]
SARA........	Search and Rescue Aid
SARA........	Sequential Automatic Recorder and Annunciator
SARA........	Sexual Assault Research Association (EA)
SARA........	Ship Angle and Range (SAA)
SARA........	Society of American Registered Architects (EA)
SARA........	Still Another Response Averager
SARA........	Superfund Amendment and Reauthorization Act [*1986*]
SARA........	System for Anesthetic and Respiratory Analysis
SARA........	Systems Analysis and Resource Accounting [*Data processing system*]
Sarabhai M Chem Tech News Serv ...	Sarabhai M. Chemicals. Technical News Service [*A publication*]
SARAC......	Steerable Array for RADAR and Communications (CET)
SARAD......	South African Rates and Data [*A publication*] (IMH)
SARAH	Search and Range Homing
SARAH	Search and Rescue and Homing
SARAH	Semiactive RADAR Alternate Head
SARAH	Semiautomatic Range Azimuth and Height [*Subsystem*]
SA Railways ...	South Australian Railways Institute. Magazine [*A publication*] (APTA)
SA Railways Institute Mag ...	South Australian Railways Institute. Magazine [*A publication*] (APTA)
SaraL	Sara Lee Corp. [*Associated Press abbreviation*] (APAG)
SaraLee.......	Sara Lee Corp. [*Associated Press abbreviation*] (APAG)
SARARC ...	Subauroral Red Arc [*Geophysics*]
Sarat Ch Sent ...	Saratoga Chancery Sentinel [*1841-47*] [*New York*] [*A publication*] (DLA)
SARAW.....	Sarawak [*Malaysia*] (ROG)
SarawakMJ ...	Sarawak Museum. Journal [*A publication*]
Sarawak Mus J ...	Sarawak Museum. Journal [*A publication*]
Sarawak Res Branch Dep Agric Annu Rep ...	Sarawak. Research Branch. Department of Agriculture. Annual Report [*A publication*]
SARB........	State Air Resources Board
Sarbah........	Sarbah's Fanti Law Reports [*Gold Coast*] [*A publication*] (DLA)
Sarbah FC ...	Sarbah's Fanti Customary Laws [*Ghana*] [*A publication*] (DLA)
SARBE	Search and Rescue-Beacon Equipment (MCD)
SARBICA ...	Southeast Asian Regional Branch of the International Council on Archives (EAIO)

SARC......... Corrientes [*Argentina*] [*ICAO location identifier*]   (ICLI)
SARC......... Sarcasm   (DSUE)
sarc............ Sarcoma [*Medicine*]   (MAE)
SARC......... Search and Rescue Center   (CINC)
SARC......... Secure Airborne RADAR Control
SAR-C....... Synthetic Aperture RADAR - C-Band   (SSD)
SARC......... System Acquisition Review Council [*Army*]
SARC......... Systems Analysis and Research Corp.
SARCALM ... Synthetic Array RADAR Command Air-Launched Missile
SARCAP ... Search and Rescue - Civil Air Patrol   (MCD)
SARCAR ... Smithsonian Archaeometric Research Collection and Records [*Facility*]
SARCC...... Search and Rescue Coordination Center [*Air Force*]
SARCCUS ... South African Regional Committee for Conservation and Utilization of Soil
SARCEN ... Search and Rescue Central [*Navy*]
Sar Ch Sen ... Saratoga Chancery Sentinel [*New York*] [*A publication*]   (DLA)
Sarcolemma Proc Annu Meet Int Study Group Res Card Metab ... Sarcolemma. Proceedings. Annual Meeting. International Study Group for Research in Cardiac Metabolism [*A publication*]
SARCOM ... Search and Rescue Communicator [*Navy*]
SARCUP ... Search and Rescue Capability Upgrade Project [*Canadian Navy*]
SARD........ Resistencia (Ciudad) [*Argentina*] [*ICAO location identifier*]   (ICLI)
SARD........ Sardinia
SARD........ Simulated Aircraft RADAR Data
SARD........ Solar Array Release and Deployment   (MCD)
SARD........ Special Airlift Requirement Directive [*Air Force*]   (AFM)
SARD........ Special Airlift Requirement Document [*Army*]
SARD........ Statistical Analysis and Reports Division [*Washington, DC*] [*Administrative Office of the US Courts*]   (GRD)
SARD........ Support and Range Development   (MUGU)
SARD........ Synchronized Accumulating Radioisotope Detection
SARDA..... Society for Aid and Rehabilitation of Drug Addicts [*Hong Kong*]
SARDA...... State and Regional Defense Airlift Plan [*FAA, Civil Defense*]
SARDC...... Small Arms Research and Development Center [*Army*]
SARDEC ... Societe des Auteurs, Rechurchistes, Documentalistes, et Compositeurs [*Canada*]
Sardegna Econ ... Sardegna Economica [*A publication*]
SARDET ... Search and Rescue Detachment [*Navy*]   (NG)
SARDIP .... Stricken Aircraft Reclamation and Disposal Program [*Navy*]   (NG)
SARDPO... San Antonio Research and Development Procurement Office [*Air Force*]
SARDS..... Special Air Route Designators   (CINC)
SARDX..... Sardonyx [*Gemstone*]   (ROG)
SARE........ Resistencia [*Argentina*] [*ICAO location identifier*]   (ICLI)
SARE........ Safety Review [*A publication*]
SARE........ Southeast Asian Review of English [*A publication*]
SARE-A.... Saturday Review [*A publication*]
SAREA...... Sinus Area of Leaf [*Botany*]
SARED...... Supporting Applied Research and Exploratory Development [*National Weather Service*]
SAREF ...... Safety Research Experiment Facility [*Nuclear energy*]
SA Regr ..... South Australian Register [*A publication*]   (APTA)
SA Regr (Newspr) ... South Australian Register Reports (Newspaper) [*A publication*]   (APTA)
SAREP ...... Speech and Reading Enrichment Program
SA Res Service Bibliog ... South Australia. Public Library. Research Service. Bibliographies [*A publication*]   (APTA)
SARev...... South Asian Review [*A publication*]
SARev .... South Atlantic Review [*A publication*]
SAREX...... Search and Rescue Exercise   (MCD)
SAREX...... Shuttle Amateur Radio Experiment [*NASA*]
SARF........ Formosa [*Argentina*] [*ICAO location identifier*]   (ICLI)
SARF .... Semiautomated Reconstruction Facility [*Military*]   (CAAL)
SARF .... Southeast Asia Rescue Foundation   (EA)
SARF .... Southern Africa Road Federation [*See also SAPF*]   (EAIO)
Sar FCL ..... Sarbah's Fanti Customary Laws [*Ghana*] [*A publication*]   (DLA)
Sar FLR ..... Sarbah's Fanti Law Cases [*1845-1903*] [*Ghana*] [*A publication*]   (DLA)
Sar FNC..... Sarbah's Fanti National Constitution [*Ghana*] [*A publication*]   (DLA)
SARFS....... Subordinate Army Field Services
Sarg........... Sargonic   (BJA)
SARG........ Synthetic Aperture RADAR Guidance   (MCD)
SARG........ Synthetic Aperture RADAR Retransmission Guidance   (MCD)
Sar Gaz ...... Sarawak Gazette [*Kuching*] [*A publication*]
Sarget........ Sargetia. Acta Musei Devensis [*A publication*]
Sargetia Ser Sci Nat ... Sargetia [*Acta Devensis*]. Series Scientia Naturae [*A publication*]
SARGUN .. Synthetic Aperture RADAR Gun [*NASA*]
SARI......... Iguazu/Cataratas Del Iguazu [*Argentina*] [*ICAO location identifier*]   (ICLI)
SARI......... Share-a-Ride International   (EA)
SARI......... Silicon Architectures Research Initiative [*British*]
SARI......... Standby Altitude Reference Indicator   (MCD)

SARIE .... Semiautomatic RADAR Identification Equipment   (MCD)
SARIHHWP ... Serendipity Association for Research and Implementation of Holistic Health and World Peace   (EA)
SARIPADI ... Serikat Pamong Desa Indonesia [*Village Officials' Union of Indonesia*]
SARIS........ Synthetic Aperture RADAR Interpretation System [*NASA*]   (MCD)
SARISA..... Surface Analysis by Resonance Ionization of Sputtered Atoms
SARK........ Saville Advanced Remote Keying   (MCD)
SARL........ Paso De Los Libres [*Argentina*] [*ICAO location identifier*]   (ICLI)
SARL........ Societe a Responsabilite Limitee [*Private Limited Company*] [*French*]
SARL........ Subtropical Agricultural Research Laboratory [*Weslaco, TX*] [*Department of Agriculture*]   (GRD)
SARLA ..... South African Rock Lobster Association [*Defunct*]
SARLANT ... Search and Rescue, Atlantic [*Coast Guard*]
SARM........ Monte Caseros [*Argentina*] [*ICAO location identifier*]   (ICLI)
SARM........ Set Asynchronous Response Mode
SARM........ Standard Analytical Reference Material   (MCD)
SARM........ Standard Antiradiation Missile   (MCD)
SARM........ System Acquisition Review Memorandum [*Army*]
SARMIT ... Sport and Recreation Association of RMIT [*Royal Melbourne Institute of Technology*] Union
Sar Mus J .. Sarawak Museum. Journal [*Kuching*] [*A publication*]
SARNI....... Serikat Nelajan Indonesia [*Sailors' Union of Indonesia*]
SARO .... Ituzaingo [*Argentina*] [*ICAO location identifier*]   (ICLI)
SAROAD... Storage and Retrieval of Aerometric Data [*Database*] [*Sigma Data Services Corp.*] [*Information service or system*]   (CRD)
SARP .... Posadas [*Argentina*] [*ICAO location identifier*]   (ICLI)
SARP .... Safety Analysis Report for Packaging [*NASA*]   (NASA)
SARP .... Schedule, Analysis, and Review Procedure [*NASA*]   (KSC)
SARP .... Schedule and Resources Procedure [*NASA*]   (KSC)
SARP .... Scheduling and Reporting [*or Review*] Procedure [*NASA*]   (KSC)
SARP .... Scramble and Recovery Procedure   (SAA)
SARP .... Severe Accident Research Plan [*Nuclear energy*]   (NRCH)
SARP .... Ship Alteration and Repair Package [*Navy*]   (CAAL)
SARP .... Shuttle Astronaut Recruitment Program [*NASA*]   (MCD)
SARP .... Signal Automatic RADAR Processing
SARP .... Small Autonomous Research Package
SARP .... Space Allocation Requirement Procedures   (MCD)
SARP .... Space Allocation and Reservation Program   (MCD)
SARP .... Standards and Recommended Practices
SARP .... Storage and Retrieval Processor   (MCD)
SARPAC ... Search and Rescue, Pacific [*Coast Guard*]   (DNAB)
SARPF....... Strategic Air Relocatable Photographic Facility   (CINC)
SARPMA .. San Antonio Real Property Maintenance Agency [*Military*]
SARPS....... Standards and Recommended Practices [*International Civil Aviation Organization*]
SARR........ Resistencia [*Argentina*] [*ICAO location identifier*]   (ICLI)
SARRA ...... Short-Arc Reduction of RADAR Altimetry
SARRP ...... Severe Accident Risk Reduction Program [*Nuclear energy*]   (NRCH)
SARS........ Presidencia R. Saenz Pena [*Argentina*] [*ICAO location identifier*]   (ICLI)
SaRS.......... Safety and Reliability Society [*British*]
SARS........ Secretary of the Army Research and Study [*Fellowship*]
SARS........ Semiautomated Reconstruction System [*Military*]   (CAAL)
SARS........ Sensor Analog Relay System
SARS........ Ship Attitude Record System
SARS........ Simulated Airborne RADAR System   (MCD)
SARS........ Single Allocation and Reservation Study   (MCD)
SARS........ Single-Axis Reference System
SARS........ Solar Array Reorientation System
SARS........ Spares Accounting Replenishment System [*NASA*]   (KSC)
SARS........ Static Automatic Reporting System   (MCD)
SARS........ Stellar Attitude Reference Study
SARS........ Synthetic Array RADAR System
SARSA ...... Social Affairs Recreation and Sports Association
SARSAT.... Search and Rescue Satellite [*Navy*]
SARSAT.... Search and Rescue Satellite-Aided Tracking [*NASA*]
SARSAT.... Synthetic Aperture RADAR Satellite [*NASA*]   (SSD)
SARSEX.... Synthetic Aperture RADAR Signature Experiment [*Oceanography*]
SARSIM.... Search and Rescue Simulation [*Coast Guard*]
SARSS....... Search and Rescue Satellite System [*Navy*]   (MCD)
SARSS....... Standard Army Retail Supply System
SART........ St. Alban's Repertory Theater [*Washington, DC*]
SART........ Seattle Army Terminal
SART........ Society for Assisted Reproductive Technology   (EA)
SART........ Special Army Review Team   (MCD)
SART........ Standard Acid Reflux Test [*Clinical chemistry*]
SART........ Stimuli Analog Refresh Table [*NASA*]   (MCD)
SART........ Stop All Racist Tours [*An association*] [*British*]
SARTACK ... Search AntiRADAR Tactical Aircraft, K-Band
SARTEL.... Search and Rescue, Telephone [*Coast Guard*]
SARTOC... Southern Africa Regional Tourism Council   (EAIO)
SARTS....... Satisfaction of Army Requirements through Space   (MCD)
SARTS....... Small Arms Readiness Training Section [*National Guard*]

SARTS......	Small Arms Remote Target System (MCD)
SARTS......	Switched Access Remote Test System [*Bell System*]
SARU	Resistencia [*Argentina*] [*ICAO location identifier*] (ICLI)
SARU	System Analysis Research Unit
SARUM	Bishop of Salisbury [*British*]
SARUS	Search and Rescue Using Satellites [*Air Force*]
SARV........	Satellite Aeromedical Research Vehicle
SARVIP.....	Survival Army Recovery Vest, Insert, and Pockets
SAS..........	Lithuanian Catholic Students' Association "Ateitis" (EA)
SAS..........	St. Andrew Goldfields Ltd. [*Toronto Stock Exchange symbol*]
SAS..........	St. Andrew Society [*Edinburgh, Scotland*] (EAIO)
SAS..........	Salicylazosulfapyridine [*Antibacterial*]
SAS..........	Salton City, CA [*Location identifier*] [*FAA*] (FAAL)
SAS..........	Sample Array System (KSC)
SAS..........	Sand-Asphalt-Sulfur [*Road paving material*]
SAS..........	Saskatoon [*Saskatchewan*] [*Seismograph station code, US Geological Survey*] [*Closed*] (SEIS)
SAS..........	Satellite Attack Sensor
SAS..........	Scandinavian Airlines System [*Sweden*]
SAS..........	Schiapparelli [*Italy*] [*Research code symbol*]
SAS..........	SEAL [*Subsea Equipment Associates Ltd.*] Atmospheric System
SAS..........	Sealed Authentication System [*Military*]
SAS..........	Seasonal Agricultural Service
SAS..........	Secondary Alarm Station [*Nuclear energy*] (NRCH)
SAS..........	Sections Administratives Specialisees [*French Army*]
SAS..........	Secure Authentication System (IIA)
SAS..........	Security Agency Study [*Nuclear energy*] (NRCH)
SAS..........	Security Assistance and Sales [*DoD*]
SAS..........	Segment Arrival Storage Area (KSC)
SAST........	Self-Adaptive System
SAS..........	Sensor and Source
SAS..........	Service Activity System
SAS..........	Service Air System (NRCH)
SAS..........	Service Annual Survey [*Bureau of the Census*] (GFGA)
SAS..........	Sex Attitudes Survey [*Psychology*]
SAS..........	Shakespearean Authorship Society [*Later, SAT*] (EA)
SAS..........	Sherwood Anderson Society (EA)
SAS..........	Ship Alteration Suite [*Navy*] (CAAL)
SAS..........	Side-Angle-Side (Rule) [*Geometry*]
SAS..........	Signal Airways Service
SAS..........	Signal Analysis System [*Electronics*]
SASCL.......	Silicon Avalanche Suppressor [*Telecommunications*]
SAS..........	Single Angle Scattering
SAS..........	Single Anomalous Scattering [*Crystallography*]
SAS..........	Single Audio System (CAAL)
SAS..........	Sklar Aphasia Scale [*Psychology*]
SAS..........	Sleep Apnea Syndrome [*Medicine*]
SaS...........	Slovo a Slovesnost [*A publication*]
SAS..........	Small-Angle Scattering (OA)
SAS..........	Small Applications Satellite (KSC)
SAS..........	Small Arms School [*British military*] (DMA)
SAS..........	Small Astronomy Satellite
SAS..........	Small-Probe Atmospheric Structure [*NASA*]
SAS..........	Snake Approach Scale [*Psychology*]
SAS..........	Snap Action Switch
SAS..........	Societatis Antiquariorum Socius [*Fellow of the Society of Antiquaries*] [*British*]
SAS..........	Society of American Silversmiths (EA)
SAS..........	Society for Applied Sociology (EA)
SASHA......	Society for Applied Spectroscopy (EA)
SAS..........	Society for Armenian Studies (EA)
SAS..........	Society of Australasian Specialists [*Later, SASO*]
SAS..........	Sodium Alkane Sulfonate [*Detergent intermediate*]
SAS..........	Sodium Aluminum Sulfate [*Organic chemistry*]
SAS..........	Solar Array Structure
SAS..........	Solar Array System (MCD)
SAS..........	Solar Aspect Sensor
SAS..........	Solomons Ano Sagufenua [*Political party*] [*Solomon Islands*] (FEA)
SAS..........	Son Altesse Serenissime [*His or Her Serene Highness*] [*French*]
SAS..........	Sound Amplification System
SAS..........	South American Series [*A publication*]
SAS..........	South Asian Seas
SAS..........	Southern Anthropological Society
SAS..........	Southern Appalachian Studies [*Defunct*] (EA)
SAS..........	Soviet Academy of Sciences
SAS..........	Space Activity Suit
SAS..........	Space Adaptation Syndrome [*NASA*]
SAS..........	Spacecraft Antenna System
SAS..........	Special Access Space (CAAL)
SAS..........	Special Activities Squadron [*Air Force*]
SAS..........	Special Air Service [*British commando unit*]
SAS..........	Special Ammunition Section [*Picatinny Arsenal*] [*Army*]
SAS..........	Special Ammunition Site [*Army*]
SAS..........	Special Ammunition Stockage [*Army*] (AABC)
SAS..........	Special Ammunition Storage (RDA)
SAS..........	Special Army Squadron [*British*] (DI)
SAS..........	Stability Augmentation System [*or Subsystem*] [*FAA*]
SAS..........	Staff Administrative Specialist [*Military*]
SAS..........	Statement of Auditing Standards
SAS..........	Station Air System [*Nuclear energy*] (NRCH)

SAS..........	Statistical Analysis System [*Programming language*] [*1966*]
SAS..........	Sterile Aqueous Suspension
SAS..........	Strategic Aerospace Summary
SAS..........	Strategic Area Study (MCD)
SAS..........	Sum of Adjacent Spans
SAS..........	Superior Atrial Septum [*Anatomy*]
SAS..........	Supersonic Attack Seaplane
SAS..........	Support Amplifier Station [*Telecommunications*] (OA)
SAS..........	Supravalvular Aortic Stenosis [*Cardiology*]
SAS..........	Surface Active Substances (IEEE)
SAS..........	Survival Avionics System [*Military*] (CAAL)
SAS..........	Suspended Aluminosilicate
SAS..........	Suspended Array System [*To detect submarines*]
SAS..........	SverigeAmerika Stiftelsen [*Sweden-American Foundation*] (EAIO)
SAS..........	Switched Access System [*Telecommunications*] (TEL)
SAS..........	System Acquisition School (MCD)
SAS..........	System Analysis Study
SAS..........	System Application Software [*Data processing*] (BUR)
SASA........	Salta [*Argentina*] [*ICAO location identifier*] (ICLI)
SASA........	Severe Accident Sequence Analysis [*Nuclear energy*] (NRCH)
SASA........	Ski Area Suppliers Association (EA)
SASA........	Small Arms Systems Agency [*Army*] (RDA)
SASA........	South Asian Studies Association of Australia and New Zealand
SASA........	Special Ammunition Supply Activity (MCD)
SASAE......	Supplements. Annales. Service des Antiquites de l'Egypt [*Cairo*] [*A publication*]
SASAR......	Segmented Aperture-Synthetic Aperture RADAR
SASAS......	Southern Africa Society of Aquatic Scientists (EAIO)
SASAT	Shipboard Antisubmarine Attack Teacher [*Navy*]
SASB	Structural Analysis of Social Behavior
SASBO......	Southeastern Association of School Business Officials (AEBS)
SASC	Salta [*Argentina*] [*ICAO location identifier*] (ICLI)
SASC	Sasco Cosmetics [*NASDAQ symbol*] (NQ)
SASC	Semiautomatic Stock Control
SASC	Senate Armed Services Committee
SASC	Senior Appointments Selection Committee [*British*]
SASC	Small Arms School Corps [*Military*] [*British*]
SASC	Subject Analysis Systems Collection [*University of Toronto*] [*Information service or system*] (IID)
SA Sch Post ...	South Australian School Post [*A publication*] (APTA)
SASCL.......	St. Ansgar's Scandinavian Catholic League (EA)
SASCOM ..	Southern Atlantic Satellite Communication
SASCOM ..	Special Ammunition Support Command [*Army*] (AABC)
SASCON...	Southern African Solidarity Congress [*Zimbabwe*] [*Political party*] (PPW)
SASD........	Static Adjustable Speed Drive
SASD........	Strategies and Air Standards Division [*Environmental Protection Agency*] (GFGA)
SA/SD	Structured Analysis/Structured Design (MCD)
SASDT	Ships and Aircraft Supplemental Data Tables [*Navy*]
SASE	Self-Addressed Stamped Envelope
SASE	Small Arms Suppression Evaluation (MCD)
SASE	Space Adaptation Syndrome Experiment [*Pronounced "Sassy"*] [*Space shuttle experiment developed in Canada*]
SASF	SIDPERS [*Standard Installation/Division Personnel System*] Authorized Strength File [*Military*] (AABC)
SASG........	Security Assistance Steering Group [*Military*]
SASG........	Smoke/Aerosol Steering Group [*DARCOM*] (RDA)
SASHA......	Sanfujinka No Shimpo [*A publication*]
SASHEP ...	Study of Accreditation of Selected Health Educational Programs
SA Shipp News ...	South African Shipping News and Fishing Industry Review [*A publication*]
SASI	Ships and Air Systems Integration [*Navy*]
SASI	Shugart Associates Systems Interface
SASI	Society of Air Safety Investigators [*Later, ISASI*]
SASI	Southern Association of Science and Industry (EA)
SASI	Surface Air System Integration
SASI	System Automation Software, Inc.
SASI	System on Automotive Safety Information [*General Motors Corp.*] [*Information service or system*]
S Asia R	South Asian Review [*A publication*]
SASIDS.....	Stochastic Adaptive Sequential Information Dissemination System
SASILO.....	Schriftenreihe. A. Stifer-Institut des Landes Oberoesterreich [*A publication*]
SASITS	Submarine Advanced Signal Training System (DNAB)
SASJ.........	Jujuy [*Argentina*] [*ICAO location identifier*] (ICLI)
SASJ.........	Self-Aligning Swivel Joint
SASK	Saskatchewan [*Canadian province*]
Sask	Saskatchewan Law Reports [*Canada*] [*A publication*] (DLA)
Saskatchewan Dept Nat Res Ann Rept Mineral Res Br Misc Paper ...	Saskatchewan. Department of Natural Resources. Annual Report. Mineral Resources Branch. Miscellaneous Paper [*A publication*]
Saskatchewan Geol Survey Rept ...	Saskatchewan Geological Survey. Report [*A publication*]
Saskatchewan L Rev ...	Saskatchewan Law Review [*A publication*]
Saskatch Med Quart ...	Saskatchewan Medical Quarterly [*A publication*]
Sask Bar Rev ...	Saskatchewan Bar Review [*A publication*]
Sask BR	Saskatchewan Bar Review [*A publication*]

Sask B Rev ... Saskatchewan Bar Review [*A publication*]
Sask Bul..... Saskatchewan Bulletin [*A publication*]
Sask Busn .. Saskatchewan Business [*A publication*]
Sask Dep Miner Resour Geol Sci Br Precambrian Geol Div Rep ...
     Saskatchewan. Department of Mineral Resources.
     Geological Sciences Branch. Precambrian Geology
     Division. Report [*A publication*]
Sask Dep Miner Resour Pet Natural Gas Reservoir Ann ... Saskatchewan.
     Department of Mineral Resources. Petroleum and Natural
     Gas Reservoir. Annual [*A publication*]
Sask Dep Miner Resour Rep ... Saskatchewan. Department of Mineral
     Resources. Report [*A publication*]
Sask Dep Nat Resour Fish Branch Fish Rep ... Saskatchewan. Department of
     Natural Resources. Fisheries Branch. Fisheries Report [*A
     publication*]
Sask Dep Nat Resour Fish Wildl Branch Fish Rep ... Saskatchewan.
     Department of Natural Resources. Fisheries and Wildlife
     Branch. Fisheries Report [*A publication*]
Sask Ed Admin ... Saskatchewan Education Administrator [*A publication*]
Sask Gaz.... Saskatchewan Gazette [*A publication*]
Sask Geol Soc Spec Publ ... Saskatchewan Geological Society. Special
     Publication [*A publication*]
Sask Hist ... Saskatchewan History [*A publication*]
Sask L........ Saskatchewan Law [*A publication*]   (DLA)
Sask Law Rev ... Saskatchewan Law Review [*A publication*]
Sask Libr ... Saskatchewan Library [*A publication*]
Sask LR ..... Saskatchewan Law Reports [*Canada*] [*A publication*]   (DLA)
Sask LR ..... Saskatchewan Law Review [*A publication*]
Sask L Rev ... Saskatchewan Law Review [*A publication*]
Sask Power Corp SPC Rep ... Saskatchewan Power Corp. SPC Report [*A
     publication*]
Sask (Prov) Dep Miner Resour Rep ... Saskatchewan (Province). Department
     of Mineral Resources. Report [*A publication*]
Sask R........ Saskatchewan Law Reports [*A publication*]   (DLA)
Sask Res Counc Eng Div Rep ... Saskatchewan Research Council. Engineering
     Division. Report [*A publication*]
Sask Res Counc Eng Div Rep E ... Saskatchewan Research Council.
     Engineering Division. Report E [*A publication*]
Sask Res Counc Geol Div Circ ... Saskatchewan Research Council. Geology
     Division. Circular [*A publication*]
Sask Res Counc Geol Div Rep ... Saskatchewan Research Council. Geology
     Division. Report [*A publication*]
Sask Res Counc Geol Div Rep G ... Saskatchewan Research Council. Geology
     Division. Report G [*A publication*]
Sask Res Counc Phys Div Rep ... Saskatchewan Research Council. Physics
     Division. Report [*A publication*]
Sask Res Counc Publ ... Saskatchewan Research Council. Publication
Sask Res Counc Rep E ... Saskatchewan Research Council. Report E [*A
     publication*]
Sask Res Counc Tech Rep ... Saskatchewan Research Council. Technical
     Report [*A publication*]
Sask Rev Stat ... Saskatchewan Revised Statutes [*Canada*] [*A
     publication*]   (DLA)
Sask Stat.... Saskatchewan Statutes [*Canada*] [*A publication*]   (DLA)
SaskTel...... Saskatchewan Telecommunications [*Regina*] [*Information
     service or system*]   (IID)
SASL .... Service Approved Status List [*Navy*]   (DNAB)
SASM........ Smithsonian Air and Space Museum
SASM........ Society for Automation in the Sciences and Mathematics
SASM........ Special Assistant for Strategic Mobility [*Military*]   (AFM)
SASM........ Supersonic Antiship Missile   (MCD)
Sasmira Tech Dig ... Sasmira Technical Digest [*A publication*]
SASMS...... Special Assistant for Surface Missile System
SASN........ Special Assistant to the Secretary of the Navy
SASNA...... South African Shipping News and Fishing Industry Review [*A
     publication*]
SASO........ Oran [*Algeria*] [*ICAO location identifier*]   (ICLI)
SASO........ Sasol Ltd. [*NASDAQ symbol*]   (NQ)
SASO........ Senior Air Staff Officer [*British*]
SASO........ Society of Australasian Specialists/Oceania   (EA)
SASO........ South African Students' Organization   (PD)
SASO........ Superintending Armament Supply Officer [*British
     military*]   (DMA)
SASOC...... School Administrators and Supervisors Organizing Committee
     [*Later, AFSA*]   (EA)
SASOP...... Sudan. Antiquities Service. Occasional Papers [*A publication*]
SASP .... Science and Application Space Platform   (MCD)
SASP .... Shortest Activity from Shortest Project
SASP .... Single Advanced Signal Processor [*Military*]   (CAAL)
SASP .... Site Activation and Support Plan   (MCD)
SASP .... Society for the Advancement of Social Psychology   (EA)
SASP .... Special Ammunition Supply Point [*Army*]
SASP .... Stand Alone Support Program
SASP .... State Agency for Surplus Property
SASP .... State Airport System Plan [*Department of Transportation*]
SASP .... Submarine Analytic Search Program [*Navy*]   (CAAL)
SA-SPM .... Socialist Alliance - Socialist Party of Macedonia [*Political
     party*]   (EY)
SASPS....... SAMMS [*Standard Automated Materiel Management System*]
     Automated Small Purchase System
SASQ........ La Quiaca [*Argentina*] [*ICAO location identifier*]   (ICLI)

SASq......... Strategic Aerospace Squadron [*Air Force*]
SASQUA... Southern African Society for Quaternary Research   (EAIO)
SASR .... Rivadavia [*Argentina*] [*ICAO location identifier*]   (ICLI)
SASR .... South Australian State Reports [*A publication*]
SASRS...... Satellite-Aided Search and Rescue System
     [*Telecommunications*]
SASS......... Saturn Automatic Software System [*NASA*]
SASS......... Schedules and Status Summary [*NASA*]   (KSC)
SASS......... School and Staffing Survey [*Department of
     Education*]   (GFGA)
SASS......... SEASAT [*Sea Satellite*]- A Scatterometer System [*NASA*]
SASS......... Small Airbreathing System Synthesis   (MCD)
SASS......... Society for the Advancement of Scandinavian Study   (EA)
SASS......... Society for Automation in the Social Sciences [*Later, SDE*]
SASS......... Source Assessment Sampling System [*Environmental
     Protection Agency*]
SASS......... South Australian Secrets Summary [*A publication*]   (APTA)
SASS......... South Australian Social Science [*Information service or system*]
     [*A publication*]   (APTA)
SASS......... Spark Chamber Automatic Scanning System   (DNAB)
SASS......... Special Aircraft Service Shop   (NG)
SASS......... SPEEDEX [*Systemwide Project for Electronic Equipment at
     Depots Extended*] Automatic Scheduling System
     [*Military*]
SASS......... Spreadsheet Anthropometric Scaling System [*Army*]   (RDA)
SASS......... Standard Army Supply System
SASS......... Strategic Airborne Surveillance System [*Military*]
SASS......... Strategic Alerting Sound System   (AAG)
SASS......... Supplement Aviation Spares Report   (MCD)
SASS......... Suspended Array Surveillance System [*To detect submarines*]
SASS......... Systems and Services Section [*Library Administration and
     Management Association*]
SASSAR.... Suid-Afrikaanse Spoorwee/South African Railways [*A
     publication*]
SASSC...... Senate Aeronautical and Space Sciences Committee   (AAG)
SASSE...... Synchronous Altitude Spin-Stabilized Experiment
SASSI .... Synthetic Amorphous Silica and Silicates Industry
     Association   (EA)
SASSIA .... Synthetic Amorphous Silica and Silicates Industry
     Association   (EA)
SASSIF...... Self-Adjusting System of Scientific Information Flow
SASSM...... Surface-to-Air, Surface-to-Surface Missile   (MCD)
SASSTIXS ... Satellite Air, Surface, Subsurface Tactical Information
     Exchange System [*Navy*]   (CAAL)
SASSY....... Small Angle Separator System [*Superheavy element research*]
SASSY....... Supported Activities Supply System [*Marine Corps*]
SAST .... Safety Standards
SAST .... Serum Aspartate Aminotransferase [*An enzyme*]
SAST .... Service Announcements in Science and Technology [*National
     Technical Information Service*]   (EA)
SAST .... Single Asphalt Surface Treatment
SAST .... Society for the Advancement of Space Travel [*Defunct*]   (MCD)
SAST .... Tartagal/Gral Mosconi [*Argentina*] [*ICAO location
     identifier*]   (ICLI)
SASTAJ .... SASTA [*South Australian Science Teachers Association*]
     Journal [*A publication*]   (APTA)
SASTA Jl .. SASTA [*South Australian Science Teachers Association*]
     Journal [*A publication*]
SASTAR.... Support Activities Staffing Review   (MCD)
SASTE....... Semiautomatic Shop Test Equipment   (NG)
SA Storekeepers J ... South Australian Storekeepers and Grocers Journal [*A
     publication*]   (APTA)
SASTP....... Stand-Alone Self-Test Program [*NASA*]   (MCD)
SASTU...... Signal Amplitude Sampler and Totalizing Unit   (IEEE)
SASU........ Saturn Apollo Systems Utilization [*NASA*]
SASUTA ... Southern African Society of University Teachers of
     Accounting   (EAIO)
SASV .... Secondary Air Switching Valve [*Automotive engineering*]
SASV .... Sisters of the Assumption of the Blessed Virgin [*Roman
     Catholic religious order*]
SASV .... Snap Action Spool Valve
SASWREC ... SACLANT [*Supreme Allied Commander, Atlantic*]
     Antisubmarine Warfare Research Center   (NATG)
SAT........... Canadian Satellite Communications, Inc. [*Toronto Stock
     Exchange symbol*]
SAT........... Die Schriften des Alten Testaments in Auswahl Neu Uebersetzt
     und fuer die Gegenwart Erklaert [*Goettingen*] [*A
     publication*]
SAT........... Safe Arming Time
SAT........... Salamaua Aerial Transport [*Australia*]
SAT........... Salt Aggregation Test [*Clinical chemistry*]
SAT........... Sampler Address Translator
SAT........... San Antonio [*Texas*] [*Airport symbol*]
SAT........... Sang-Tuda [*Former USSR*] [*Seismograph station code, US
     Geological Survey*] [*Closed*]   (SEIS)
SAT........... Satellite
Sat............. Satellite Science Fiction [*A publication*]
Sat............. Satirae [*or Sermones*] [*of Horace*] [*Classical studies*]   (OCD)
SAT........... Satisfactory   (AABC)
Sat............. Satura [*of Petronius*] [*Classical studies*]   (OCD)
SAT........... Saturate   (AAG)

SAT...........	Saturatus [*Saturated*] [*Pharmacy*]
SAT...........	Saturday (EY)
SAT...........	Saturn [*Rocket*] (KSC)
SAT...........	Saturn
Sat.............	Saturn [*Record label*] [*France*]
Sat.............	Saturnalia [*of Macrobius*] [*Classical studies*] (OCD)
SAT...........	Schafer Value Trust, Inc. [*NYSE symbol*] (SPSG)
SAT...........	Scholastic Aptitude Test [*Trademark of the College Entrance Examination Board*]
SAT...........	School Ability Test [*Psychology*]
SAT...........	School of Applied Tactics [*AAFSAT*]
SAT...........	Scientific Advisory Team [*Navy*] (MCD)
SAT...........	Scientific and Technical (MCD)
SAT...........	Security Alert Team [*Military*] (AFM)
SAT...........	Security Assistance Team [*Military*] (AABC)
SAT...........	Semiarid Tropics [*Geography*]
SAT...........	Semiautomatic Test Equipment [*NASA*]
SAT...........	Senior Apperception Technique [*Personality development test*] [*Psychology*]
SAT...........	Senior Aptitude Tests [*Educational test*]
SAT...........	Sennacieca Asocio Tutmonda [*Nationless Worldwide Association*] (EAIO)
SAT...........	Serial Accountability Transmittal
SAT...........	Serum Agglutination Test (OA)
SAT...........	Service Acceptance Trials (NVT)
SAT...........	Shakespearean Authorship Trust [*England*] (EAIO)
SAT...........	Ship Acceptance Test [*Navy*] (CAAL)
SAT...........	Ship's Apparent Time [*Navigation*]
SAT...........	Silicon Annular Transistor
SAT...........	Sine Acido Thymonucleico [*Without Thymonucleic Acid*]
SAT...........	Site Acceptance Test [*Military*] (AABC)
SAT...........	Site Alteration Tests
SAT...........	Site Assignment Time
SAT...........	Sitting Atop [*Molecular configuration*]
SAT...........	Small Angle Tagger (MCD)
SAT...........	Small Arms Transmitter [*Army*] (INF)
SAT...........	Snap Action Thermostat
SAT...........	Societa Anonima Transadriatica [*Italy*]
SAT...........	Software Acceptance Test
SAT...........	Sound-Apperception Test [*Psychology*]
SAT...........	South Atlantic
SAT...........	Southern African Territories
SAT...........	Southern Air Transport, Inc.
SAT...........	Space Available Travel
SAT...........	Speaker Authentication Technique
SAT...........	Special Assistance Team [*Navy*] (NG)
SAT...........	Specific Aptitude Test
SAT...........	Specified Actions Table [*Military*]
SAT...........	Spiral Aftereffect Test [*Psychology*]
SAT...........	Stabilization Assurance Test (IEEE)
SAT...........	Standard Area of Tinplate [*100,000 square inches*]
SAT...........	Stanford Achievement Test [*Education*]
SAT...........	Staphylococcus Adherence Test [*Clinical chemistry*]
SAT...........	Static Air Temperature
SAT...........	Stepped Atomic Time [*National Institute of Standards and Technology*]
SAT...........	Strategic American Traveler
SAT...........	Structural Analysis Technologies, Inc.
SAT...........	Study of Appeal Tribunals [*British*]
SAT...........	Subacute Thyroiditis [*Medicine*]
SAT...........	Subassembly Template (MCD)
SAT...........	Subscriber Access Terminal
SAT...........	Subsumed Abilities Test [*Student attitudes test*]
SAT...........	Successive Approximation Technique (NOAA)
SAT...........	Support Analysis Test
SAT...........	Surface Aerospace Technology
SAT...........	Surface Antenna Terminal (MCD)
SAT...........	Surveillance, Acquisition, and Tracking [*Military*] (RDA)
SAT...........	Sustained Airborne Training [*Army*] (INF)
SAT...........	System Access Technique [*Sperry UNIVAC*]
SAT...........	System Alignment Test (NVT)
SAT...........	Systematic Assertiveness Training
SAT...........	Systems Acceptance Tests (KSC)
SAT...........	Systems Approach to Training [*NASA*] (MCD)
SATA.........	Die Schriften des Alten Testaments in Auswahl Neu Uebersetzt und fuer die Gegenwart Erklaert [*Goettingen*] [*A publication*]
SATA.........	Safety and Arming Test Aid (MCD)
SATA.........	Satellite Automatic Tracking Antenna (MCD)
SATA.........	Sociedade Acoriana de Transportes Aereos Ltda. [*Airline*] [*Portugal*]
SATA.........	Something about the Author [*A publication*]
SATA.........	Student Air Travel Association
SATA.........	Subsonic Aerodynamic Testing Association (MCD)
SATA.........	Supervisory, Administrative, and Technical Association [*Union of Ship Distribution and Allied Workers*] [*British*] (DCTA)
SATAF......	Shuttle Activation Task Force [*NASA*] (NASA)
SATAF......	Site Activation Task Force [*Military*]
SATAF......	Site Activity [*or Alternation*] Task Force [*NASA*] (KSC)

SATAM.....	Syndicat Autonome des Travailleurs de la Alimentation de Madagascar [*Autonomous Union of Food Workers of Madagascar*]
SATAN......	Satellite Active Nullifier [*Antisatellite weapon*]
SATAN......	Satellite Automatic Tracking Antenna
SATAN......	Sensor for Airborne Terrain Analysis
SATAN......	Strobes Against Troops at Night (MCD)
SATANAS ...	Semiautomatic Analog Setting (IEEE)
SATANS ...	Static and Transient Analysis, Nonlinear, Shells [*Computer program*] [*Navy*]
SATANT ...	Satellite Antenna (DWSG)
SATAR......	Satellite for Aerospace Research [*NASA*]
SA Tax Cas ...	South African Tax Cases [*A publication*] (DLA)
SATB........	Simulated Air Training Bundle (MCD)
SATB........	Soprano, Alto, Tenor, Bass
SATB........	South African Tourism Board
SATB........	Specific Aptitude Test Battery
SATC........	Clorinda [*Argentina*] [*ICAO location identifier*] (ICLI)
SATC........	Ship Automatic Torpedo Countermeasures (MCD)
SATC........	South African Tax Cases [*A publication*] (DLA)
SATC........	Students Army Training Corps
SATC........	Suspended Acoustical-Tile Ceiling [*Technical drawings*]
SATCA......	Sino-American Technical Cooperation Association
SATCAMS ...	Semiautomatic Tactical Control and Airspace Management System (MCD)
SATCC......	Southern Air Traffic Control Centre [*British*]
SATCH......	Salicylaldehyde Thiocarbohydrazone [*Organic chemistry*]
SATCHMO ...	Satchel Mouth [*Nickname of late trumpeter Louis Armstrong*]
SATCO......	Senior Air Traffic Control Officer (NATG)
SATCO......	Signal Automatic Air Traffic Control System
SATCO......	Supervisory Air Traffic Control Organization [*FAA*]
SATCOM ...	Satellite Command
SATCOM ...	Satellite Communications [*Military*]
SATCOM ...	Scientific and Technical Communication
SATCOMA ...	Satellite Communications Agency [*AEC/DCA*]
SATCOM AGEN ...	Satellite Communications Agency [*Army*]
SATCON ...	Satellite Condition [*Military*] (AABC)
SATCRIS ..	Semi-Arid Tropical Crops Information Service (IID)
SATCS.......	Scandinavian Association for Thoracic and Cardiovascular Surgery (EA)
SATD........	El Dorado [*Argentina*] [*ICAO location identifier*] (ICLI)
SATD........	Saturated
SATD........	Seattle Army Terminal Detachment (AABC)
SATD........	Simulation and Training Device [*Army*]
SATD........	Strike Aircraft Test Directorate [*Military*] (CAAL)
SATDAT ...	Satellite Data (MCD)
SATDB......	Sangyo To Denki [*A publication*]
SATDPI.....	Salesmen's Association of the Textile Dyeing and Printing Industry (EA)
SATE........	Semiautomatic Test Equipment [*NASA*]
SATE........	Special Acceptance Test Equipment (MCD)
SATE........	Study of Army Test and Evaluation (MCD)
SATEA......	Soviet Atomic Energy [*English Translation*] [*A publication*]
SA Teachers J ...	SA [*South Australia*] Teachers' Journal [*A publication*] (APTA)
SA Teach J ...	South Australian Teachers' Journal [*A publication*] (APTA)
SATEC......	Semiautomatic Technical Control
SATEC......	Societe d'Aide Technique et de Cooperation [*An independent French company*]
SATELCO ...	Satellite Telecommunications Co. [*Japanese-American firm*]
SATELDATA ...	Satellite Databank [*European Space Agency*] [*Database*]
Satel Dir.....	Satellite Communications. Satellite Industry Directory [*A publication*]
Satell Commun ...	Satellite Communications [*A publication*]
Satellite......	Satellite Communications [*A publication*]
SATELLITE ...	Scientific and Technological Library Literature [*Conference*]
SATELLORB ...	Satellite Simulation Observation and Research Balloon [*Military*] (DNAB)
Satel News ...	Satellite News [*A publication*]
SATENA...	Servicio de Aeronavegacion a Territorios Nacionales [*Colombian airline*]
Sat E P.......	Saturday Evening Post [*A publication*]
Sat Eve Post ...	Saturday Evening Post [*A publication*]
SATF........	Shortest Access Time First
SATF........	Strategic Area Task Force (SAA)
SATF........	Substituted Anilines Task Force (EA)
SATFAL....	Satellite Data for Fallout (MCD)
SATFOR...	Special Air Task Force [*Navy*]
SATFY......	Satisfactory (AFM)
SATG........	Goya [*Argentina*] [*ICAO location identifier*] (ICLI)
SATG........	Saturating (WGA)
SATGA......	Societe Aerienne de Transport Guyane Antilles [*French Guiana Air Transport*]
SAT GCI....	Satellite Ground Controlled Interception (NATG)
SATH	St. Thomas National Historic Site
SATH	Society for the Advancement of Travel for the Handicapped (EA)
SATHA	Schweizer Archiv fuer Tierheilkunde [*A publication*]
SATI.........	Bernardo De Irigoyen [*Argentina*] [*ICAO location identifier*] (ICLI)
SATI.........	Satellite Information Systems Co. [*NASDAQ symbol*] (NQ)

SATI .... Society for the Advancement of the Tourism Industry
SATIF .... Scientific and Technical Information Facility [*NASA*]
SATIN .... SAC [*Strategic Air Command*] Automated Total Information Network   (MCD)
SATIN .... SAGE [*Semiautomatic Ground Environment*] Air Traffic Integration
SATIN .... Satellite Inspector System   (AAG)
SATIPS ..... Society of Assistants Training in Preparatory Schools [*British*]
SATIR .... System for Evaluation of Tactical Information on Missile Destroyers
SATIRE ..... Scientific and Technical Information Reviewed and Exploited [*A publication*]   (RDA)
SATIRE ..... Semiautomatic Technical Information Retrieval
Satire N. ..... Satire Newsletter [*A publication*]
SatireNL .... Satire Newsletter [*A publication*]
SATIS .... Satisfactory   (AAG)
SATIS .... Southern Africa - The Imprisoned Society [*An association*] [*British*]
SATISFN .. Satisfaction   (ROG)
SATISFY ... Satisfactory   (ROG)
SATIVA .... Society for Agricultural Training through Integrated Voluntary Activities   (EA)
SATK .... Las Lomitas [*Argentina*] [*ICAO location identifier*]   (ICLI)
SATK .... Strike Attack [*Military*]
SATKA ...... Surveillance, Acquisition, Tracking, and Kill Assessment [*Section of SDI - Strategic Defense Initiative*]
SATKB ...... Sanitarnaya Tekhnika [*A publication*]
SATL .... Satellite   (AABC)
SATL .... Satellite Auction Network, Inc. [*Irving, TX*] [*NASDAQ symbol*]   (NQ)
SATL .... Science and Advanced Technology Laboratory [*Army*]   (RDA)
SATL .... South Atlantic
SATL .... Surgical Achilles Tendon Lengthening [*Medicine*]
SATLAB .... Simulation and Training Laboratory   (SSD)
S Atlan Bull ... South Atlantic Bulletin [*A publication*]
S Atlantic Q ... South Atlantic Quarterly [*A publication*]
SATLCONO ... Satellite Control Officer [*Air Force*]
S Atl Q .... South Atlantic Quarterly [*A publication*]
S Atl Quart ... South Atlantic Quarterly [*A publication*]
S Atl Rev ...... South Atlantic Review [*A publication*]
SATM .... Mercedes [*Argentina*] [*ICAO location identifier*]   (ICLI)
SAT-M ...... Scholastic Aptitude Test - Mathematics [*College Entrance Examination Board*]
SATM .... Sodium Aurothiomalate [*Organometallic chemistry*]
SATM .... Supply and Training Mission [*Military*]   (CINC)
Sat Men ..... Saturae Menippeae [*of Varro*] [*Classical studies*]   (OCD)
SATMO ..... Security Assistance Training Management Office [*Army*]
SATN .... Saturation
Sat N .... Saturday Night [*A publication*]
SATN .... Saturn Energy & Resources Ltd. [*Vancouver, BC*] [*NASDAQ symbol*]   (NQ)
SATNAV ... Satellite Navigation   (AABC)
SATNET ... Satellite Data Broadcast Networks, Inc. [*New York, NY*] [*Telecommunications*]   (TSSD)
Sat NL .... Satire Newsletter [*A publication*]
SATO .... Obera [*Argentina*] [*ICAO location identifier*]   (ICLI)
SATO .... Scheduled Airlines Ticket Office
SATO .... Scheduled Airlines Traffic Office [*Military*]
SATO .... Self-Aligning Thick Oxide [*Process*]
SATO .... Shuttle Attached Teleoperator [*NASA*]   (NASA)
SATO .... South American Travel Organization
SATO .... Station Airline Ticket Office   (MCD)
SATO .... Supply and Transportation Operations [*NASA*]   (NASA)
SATO .... Synthetic Aircraft Turbine Oil
SATOBS ... Satellite Observations   (SAA)
SATODP ... Satellite Tracking Orbit Determination Program
Sat Oklahom ... Saturday Oklahoman and Times [*A publication*]
SATON ..... Satisfaction   (ROG)
SATO-OS ... Schedule Airlines Tour Office - Overseas
Sat Orb Int ... Satellite Orbit International [*A publication*]
SATOUR ... South African Tourism Board   (EA)
SATP .... Security Assistance Training Program [*Military*]
SATP .... Small Arms Target Practice [*Navy*]
SATP .... Software Acceptance Test Procedures
SATP .... Stabilization, Acquisition, Tracking, and Pointing
SATP .... Supplier Assurance Test Procedures
SATPATT ... Satellite Paper Tape Transfer
SATR .... Reconquista [*Argentina*] [*ICAO location identifier*]   (ICLI)
Sat R .... Saturday Review [*A publication*]
SATR .... Scheduled Air Transport Rating
SATR .... So as to Reach [*Aviation*]   (FAAC)
SATRA ...... Science and Technology Research Abstracts [*A publication*]
SATRA ...... Shoe and Allied Trades Research Association [*Later, Footwear Technology Centre*] [*British*]   (EA)
SATRA ...... Soviet-American Trade Association
SATRA Bull ... SATRA [*Shoe and Allied Trades Research Association*] Bulletin [*A publication*]
SATRAC ... Satellite Automatic Terminal Rendezvous and Coupling   (MCD)
SATRACK ... Satellite Tracking   (MCD)
SATRAM .. Systeme d'Atterrissage a Trajectoires Multiples [*Aviation*]

SATRAN ... Satellite Reconnaissance Advance Notice   (MCD)
Sat R Arts .. Saturday Review of the Arts [*A publication*]
Sat R Ed .... Saturday Review of Education [*A publication*]
Sat Rev ..... Saturday Review [*A publication*]
Sat R Lit .... Saturday Review of Literature [*A publication*]
SATROS ... Science and Technology Regional Organizations [*British*]
Sat R Sci .... Saturday Review of the Sciences [*A publication*]
Sat R Soc .... Saturday Review of Society [*A publication*]
Sat R/World ... Saturday Review/World [*A publication*]
SATS .... S. Allan Taylor Society   (EA)
SATS .... Satellite Antenna Test System [*NASA*]
SATS .... Short Airfield for Tactical Support [*Marine Corps*]
SATS .... Shuttle Avionics Test System [*NASA*]   (NASA)
SATS .... Simulated Airborne Transpondent System   (MCD)
SATS .... Single Array Test System   (MCD)
SATS .... Small Applications Technology Satellite   (MCD)
SATS .... Small Arms Target System [*British military*]   (DMA)
SATS .... Social and Technical Sciences
SATS .... Station Accommodation Test Set   (SSD)
SATS .... Surrogate Acquilla Training System [*Army*]
SATS .... Synthetic Armed Aircraft Training System   (SAA)
SATSA ...... Signal Aviation Test and Support Activity
SATSERV ... Services by Satellite, Inc. [*Defunct*]
SATSIM .... Satellite Simulation [*Military*]   (CAAL)
SATSIM .... Saturation Countermeasures Simulator
SATSLAM ... Satellite-Tracked Submarine-Launched Antimissile   (MCD)
sat sol .... Saturated Solution [*Pharmacy*]   (WGA)
SATT .... Science, Applications, Technology Transfer, and Training [*System*] [*National Institutes of Health*]
SATT .... Semiautomatic Transistor Tester [*NASA*]
SATT .... Strowger Automatic Toll Ticketing [*Telecommunications*]
SATTDF .... Suid-Afrikaanse Tydskrif vir Natuurwetenskap en Tegnologie [*A publication*]
SAT for TEE ... System Approach to Training for Transfer Effectiveness Evaluation   (DNAB)
SATTR .... Satisfactory to Transfer   (NOAA)
SATU .... Curuzu Cuatia [*Argentina*] [*ICAO location identifier*]   (ICLI)
SATU .... Singapore Association of Trade Unions
SATU .... South African Typographical Union
SATUCC ... Southern African Trade Union Coordination Council [*Gaborone, Botswana*]   (EAIO)
SATUD ..... South African Tunnelling [*A publication*]
SatUK .... Satellite United Kingdom
SATUR ...... Saturate   (AAG)
Saturated Heterocycl Chem ... Saturated Heterocyclic Chemistry [*A publication*]
Saturday Rev ... Saturday Review [*A publication*]
SATURN ... Simulation and Assignment of Traffic to Urban Road Networks [*Kins Developments Ltd.*] [*Software package*]   (NCC)
SAT-V .... Scholastic Aptitude Test - Verbal [*College Entrance Examination Board*]
SATW .... Society of American Travel Writers   (EA)
SATX .... Satellite Express [*Telecommunications*]
Sau .... All India Reporter, Saurashtra [*1950-57*] [*A publication*]   (DLA)
SAU .... Saltair [*Utah*] [*Seismograph station code, US Geological Survey*]   (SEIS)
SAU .... Samarkano Resources [*Vancouver Stock Exchange symbol*]
SAU .... Saudi Arabia [*ANSI three-letter standard code*]   (CNC)
SAU .... Saugeen Ontario Library Service [*UTLAS symbol*]
SAU .... Sausalito, CA [*Location identifier*] [*FAA*]   (FAAL)
SAU .... Sawu [*Indonesia*] [*Airport symbol*]   (OAG)
SAU .... Scandinavian Association of Urology   (EA)
SAU .... Scientific Arithmetic Unit
SAU .... Search Attack Unit
SAU .... Secure Access Unit   (HGAA)
SAU .... Separate Administrative Unit [*Work Incentive Program*]
SAU .... Signal Acquisition Unit   (NASA)
SAU .... Smallest Addressable Unit
SAU .... Social Affairs Unit [*British*]
SAU .... Spectrum Analysis Unit
SAU .... Sprawozdania Akademii Umiejetnosci [*A publication*]
SAU .... Standard Advertising Unit [*System introduced to make national newspaper advertising pages uniform in size and format and to replace the agate line with the inch as a unit of measure*]
SAU .... Statistical Analysis Unit
SAU .... Strap-Around Unit [*NASA*]   (NASA)
SAU .... Surface Attack Unit
SAU .... System [*or Subsystem*] Availability Unit
SAUCB ..... Soviet Automatic Control [*English Translation*] [*A publication*]
SAUCERS ... Space and Unexplained Celestial Events Research Society   (EA)
Saudi Arabia Dir Gen Miner Resour Bull ... Saudi Arabia. Directorate General of Mineral Resources. Bulletin [*A publication*]
Saudi Arabia Dir Gen Miner Resour Geol Map ... Saudi Arabia. Directorate General of Mineral Resources. Geologic Map [*A publication*]
Saudi Arabia Dir Gen Miner Resour Geol Map GM ... Saudi Arabia. Directorate General of Mineral Resources. Geologic Map GM [*A publication*]

Saudi Arabia Dir Gen Miner Resour Miner Resour Rep Invest ... Saudi Arabia. Directorate General of Mineral Resources. Mineral Resources Report of Investigations [*A publication*]

Saudi Arabia Dir Gen Miner Resour Miner Resour Res ... Saudi Arabia. Directorate General of Mineral Resources. Mineral Resources Research [*A publication*]

Saudi Arabia Proj Rep US Geol Surv ... Saudi Arabia Project Report. US Geological Survey [*A publication*]

SAUFI .... Sindacato Autonomo Unificato Ferrovieri Italiani [*Autonomous Union of Italian Railroad Workers*]

SAU & G.... San Antonio, Uvalde & Gulf Railroad Co.

Saugar Univ J Part 2 ... Saugar University. Journal. Part 2. Science [*A publication*]

Saugertierkd Mitt ... Saugetierkundliche Mitteilungen [*A publication*]

Saugetierkundliche Mitt ... Saugetierkundliche Mitteilungen [*A publication*]

SAUK .... Scoliosis Association of the United Kingdom   (EAIO)

Sau LR .... Saurastra Law Reports [*India*] [*A publication*]   (DLA)

Sauls .... Reports Tempore Saulsbury [*5-6 Delaware*] [*A publication*]   (DLA)

Saund .... Saunders' King's Bench Reports [*1666-73*] [*A publication*]   (DLA)

Saund & A ... Saunders and Austin's Locus Standi Reports [*1895-1904*] [*A publication*]   (DLA)

Saund Ass .. Saunders on Assault and Battery [*1842*] [*A publication*]   (DLA)

Saund & Aust ... Saunders and Austin's Locus Standi Reports [*A publication*]   (DLA)

Saund & B ... Saunders and Bidder's Locus Standi Reports [*England*] [*A publication*]   (DLA)

Saund Bast ... Saunders on Affiliation and Bastardy [*11th ed.*] [*1915*] [*A publication*]   (DLA)

Saund & BC ... Saunders and Cole's English Bail Court Reports [*1846-48*] [*A publication*]   (DLA)

Saund BC... Saunders and Cole's English Bail Court Reports [*82 RR*] [*1846-48*] [*A publication*]   (DLA)

Saund & C ... Saunders and Cole's English Bail Court Reports [*1846-48*] [*A publication*]   (DLA)

Saunders Monogr Clin Radiol ... Saunders Monographs in Clinical Radiology [*A publication*]

Saund & M ... Saunders and Macrae's English County Courts and Insolvency Cases [*County Courts Cases and Appeals, II-III*] [*A publication*]   (DLA)

Saund & Mac ... Saunders and Macrae's English County Court Cases [*A publication*]   (DLA)

Saund Mag Pr ... Saunders' Magistrates' Courts Practice [*6th ed.*] [*1902*] [*A publication*]   (DLA)

Saund Mil L ... Saunders' Militia Law [*4th ed.*] [*1855*] [*A publication*]   (DLA)

Saund Mun Reg ... Saunders' Municipal Registration [*2nd ed.*] [*1873*] [*A publication*]   (DLA)

Saund Neg ... Saunders on Negligence [*2nd ed.*] [*1878*] [*A publication*]   (DLA)

Saund Pl & Ev ... Saunders' Pleading and Evidence [*A publication*]   (DLA)

Saund Prec ... Saunders' Precedents of Indictments [*3rd ed.*] [*1904*] [*A publication*]   (DLA)

Saund War ... Saunders on Warranties and Representations [*1874*] [*A publication*]   (DLA)

SAUR .... Small Auxin Up RNA [*Ribonucleic Acid*] [*Botany*]

SAUS......... Sausage   (DSUE)

SAUS......... Soccer Association of the United States   (EA)

Sau & Sc..... Sausse and Scully's Irish Rolls Court Reports [*1837-40*] [*A publication*]   (DLA)

S Aus Nat Gal Bul ... South Australia. National Gallery. Bulletin [*A publication*]

Sausse & Sc ... Sausse and Scully's Irish Rolls Court Reports [*1837-40*] [*A publication*]   (DLA)

S Aust .... South Australia

S Aust .... South Australiana [*A publication*]   (APTA)

S Aust Clinics ... South Australian Clinics [*A publication*]   (APTA)

S Aust Coal Abstr Bull ... South Australian Coal Abstract Bulletin [*A publication*]   (APTA)

S Aust Dir Mines Gov Geol Annu Rep ... South Australia. Director of Mines and Government Geologist. Annual Report [*A publication*]

S Aust Geol Atlas Ser ... South Australia. Geological Survey. Atlas Series [*A publication*]   (APTA)

S Aust Geol Surv Bull ... South Australia. Geological Survey. Bulletin [*A publication*]   (APTA)

S Aust Geol Surv 1:250000 Geol Ser ... South Australia. Geological Survey. 1:250,000 Geological Series [*A publication*]   (APTA)

S Aust Geol Surv Q Geol Notes ... South Australia. Geological Survey. Quarterly Geological Notes [*A publication*]

S Aust Geol Surv Rep Invest ... South Australia. Geological Survey. Report of Investigations [*A publication*]   (APTA)

S Aust Indus R ... South Australia Industrial Reports [*A publication*]   (DLA)

S Austl Acts ... South Australia Acts [*1866-1936*] [*A publication*]   (DLA)

S Austl LR ... South Australian Law Reports [*A publication*]

S Aust LR .. South Australian Law Reports [*A publication*]

S Austl Stat ... South Australian Statutes [*1837-1975*] [*A publication*]   (DLA)

S Aust Miner Resour Rev ... South Australia Mineral Resources Review [*A publication*]

S Aust Nat ... South Australian Naturalist [*A publication*]   (APTA)

S Aust Orn ... South Australian Ornithologist [*A publication*]   (APTA)

S Aust Ornithol ... South Australian Ornithologist [*A publication*]

S Australia Geol Surv Rep Invest ... South Australia. Geological Survey. Report of Investigations [*A publication*]

S Australiana ... South Australiana [*A publication*]   (APTA)

S Aust Rep Mus Board ... South Australia. Report of the Museum Board [*A publication*]

S Austrl LR ... South Australian Law Reports [*A publication*]   (ILCA)

S Aust Teach J ... South Australian Teachers' Journal [*A publication*]

S Aust Wheatgr ... South Australian Wheatgrower [*A publication*]

SAUT........ Scottish Association of University Teachers [*A union*]

SAUZA...... Stroitel'stvo i Arkhitektura Uzbekistana [*A publication*]

SaV .... Saguaro Cactus Virus

SAV .... Savannah [*Tasmania*] [*Seismograph station code, US Geological Survey*]   (SEIS)

SAV .... Savannah [*Georgia*] [*Airport symbol*]   (OAG)

SAV .... Savannah Electric & Power Co. [*NYSE symbol*]   (SPSG)

SAV .... Saveloy   (DSUE)

Sav .... Savile's English Common Pleas Reports [*A publication*]   (DLA)

Sav .... Savings   (DLA)

SAV .... Savior

Sav .... Savremenik [*A publication*]

SAV .... Schweizerisches Archiv fuer Volkskunde [*A publication*]

SAV .... Service Availability [*AT & T*]

SAV .... Slovenska Akademia Vied [*A publication*]

SAV .... Small Affluent Variable [*Moko disease of banana*] [*Plant pathology*]

SAV .... Society Against Vivisection   (EA)

SAV .... Society of American Ventriloquists   (EA)

SAV .... Spectra Ventures Ltd. [*Vancouver Stock Exchange symbol*]

SAV .... Standard Acceptance Value

SAV .... Statens Avtalsverk [*Sweden*]

SAV .... Stock at Valuation

SAV .... Strollad ar Vro [*Country Party*] [*France*] [*Political party*]   (PPW)

SAV .... Student Alternatives to Violence [*Defunct*]   (EA)

SAV .... Submerged Aquatic Vegetation

SAVA........ Piedra Del Aguila [*Argentina*] [*ICAO location identifier*]   (ICLI)

SAVA........ Servicios do Aerotaxisa e Abastecimento do Vale Amazonica [*Airline*] [*Brazil*]

SAVA........ Sexual Abuse Victims Anonymous [*Canada*]

SAVA........ Standard Army Vetronics Architecture   (RDA)

SAVAC...... Simulates, Analyzes, Visualizes, Activated Circuitry   (DNAB)

SAVAK...... Sazemane Attalat Va Anmiyate Keshvar [*Iranian security and intelligence organization*]

SAVAS...... Six-Factor Automated Vocational Assessment System [*Vocational guidance test*]

SAVASI..... Simple [*or Simplified*] Abbreviated Visual Approach Slope Indicator [*FAA*]

SAVB........ El Bolson [*Argentina*] [*ICAO location identifier*]   (ICLI)

Sav Bank J ... Savings Bank Journal [*A publication*]

SAVBOND ... War Savings Bond [*Allotment for purchase*] [*Navy*]

SAVC........ Air-Cushion Vehicle built by Sealand Air Cushion Vehicles [*US*] [*Usually used in combination with numerals*]

SAVC........ Comodoro Rivadavia/Gral Mosconi [*Argentina*] [*ICAO location identifier*]   (ICLI)

SAVC........ Society for the Anthropology of Visual Communication   (EA)

Sav Conf Law ... Savigny's Conflict of Laws [*2nd ed.*] [*1880*] [*A publication*]   (DLA)

SAVD .... El Maiten [*Argentina*] [*ICAO location identifier*]   (ICLI)

SAVDAT ... Save Data   (SAA)

SAVDEP ... Savings Depot [*Military*]   (DNAB)

SAV-DEP-SYS ... Savings Deposit System [*Military*]   (DNAB)

SAVE........ Energy Resources of North Dakota, Inc. [*NASDAQ symbol*]   (NQ)

SAVE........ Esquel [*Argentina*] [*ICAO location identifier*]   (ICLI)

SavE.......... Savannah Electric & Power Co. [*Associated Press abbreviation*]   (APAG)

SAVE........ Self-Learning Audio Visual Education [*National Foundation for the Prevention of Oral Disease*]

SAVE........ Sensitive Activity Vulnerability Estimate

SAVE........ Service Activities of Voluntary Engineers

SAVE........ Shoppers Association for Value Economy   (EA)

SAVE........ Shortages and Valuable Excesses [*Navy*]   (NG)

SAVE........ Situation Analysis and Valuability Estimate   (MCD)

SAVE........ Society of American Value Engineers   (EA)

SAVE........ Society of American Vintage-Radio Enthusiasts

SAVE........ Society of Americans for Vashchenko Emigration   (EA)

SAVE........ Spray Aeration Vacuum Extraction System [*Navy*]

SAVE........ Stop Addiction through Voluntary Effort

SAVE........ Student Action Voters for Ecology

SAVE........ Students Against Volvo Exaggerations [*Student legal action organization*]

SAVE........ System for Automatic Value Exchange [*Data processing*]

SAVE........ System Availability Estimator

SAVE........ System Avionics Value Estimation

SAVE........ Systematic Alien Verification for Entitlements [*Immigration and Naturalization Service*]

SAVED...... State-of-the-Art Vehicle Engineering Documentation   (MCD)

SAVER...... Shuttle Avionics Verification and Evaluation [*NASA*]   (NASA)

SAVER...... Stowable Aircrew Vehicle Escape Rotoseat   (MCD)

SAVER ...... Study to Assess and Validate Essential Reports [*Military*] (AABC)
SAVES ...... Sizing Aerospace Vehicle Structures [*NASA*]
SAVES ...... States Audiovisual Education Study
SAVF .... Comodoro Rivadavia [*Argentina*] [*ICAO location identifier*] (ICLI)
SAVH .... Las Heras [*Argentina*] [*ICAO location identifier*] (ICLI)
SAVICOM ... Society for the Anthropology of Visual Communication
Savigny Hist Rom Law ... Savigny's History of the Roman Law [*A publication*] (DLA)
Savile .... Savile's English Common Pleas Reports [*123 English Reprint*] [*1580-94*] [*A publication*] (DLA)
SAVIM ...... Survivability and Vulnerability Improvement Modification [*Army*] (RDA)
Savings Bank J ... Savings Bank Journal [*A publication*]
Savings Banks Internat ... Savings Banks International [*A publication*]
SAVITAR ... Sanders Associates Video Input/Output Terminal Access Resource [*Data processing*] (IEEE)
SAVL .... Studien zur Allgemeinen und Vergleichenden Literaturwissenschaft [*A publication*]
Sav & Loan N ... Savings and Loan News [*A publication*]
Sav Loan News ... Savings and Loan News [*A publication*]
SAVM .... Lago Musters [*Argentina*] [*ICAO location identifier*] (ICLI)
SAVMO .... Service Audiovisual Management Office [*Army*]
SavnFd .... Savannah Foods & Industries, Inc. [*Associated Press abbreviation*] (APAG)
Savng Inst ... Savings Institutions [*A publication*]
SAVO .... San Antonio Oeste [*Argentina*] [*ICAO location identifier*] (ICLI)
SAVO .... Schultz Sav-O Stores, Inc. [*NASDAQ symbol*] (CTT)
SAVOR ...... Single-Actuated Voice Recorder
SAVP .... Paso De Indios [*Argentina*] [*ICAO location identifier*] (ICLI)
Sav Pos ...... Savigny on Possessions [*6th ed.*] [*1848*] [*A publication*] (DLA)
Sav Priv ..... Trial of the Savannah Privateers [*A publication*] (DLA)
SAVQ .... Maquinchao [*Argentina*] [*ICAO location identifier*] (ICLI)
SAVR .... Alto Rio Senguerr [*Argentina*] [*ICAO location identifier*] (ICLI)
SAVR .... Savers', Inc. [*NASDAQ symbol*] (NQ)
Savremena Poljopr ... Savremena Poljoprivreda [*A publication*]
Savrem Med (Sofia) ... Savremenna Meditsina (Sofia) [*A publication*]
Savrem Poljoprivreda ... Savremena Poljoprivreda [*A publication*]
SAVS .... Safeguards Area Ventilation System [*Nuclear energy*] (NRCH)
SAVS .... Scottish Anti-Vivisection Society (DI)
SAVS .... Sierra Grande [*Argentina*] [*ICAO location identifier*] (ICLI)
SAVS .... Status and Verification System [*NASA*] (KSC)
SAVT .... Save Area Table [*Data processing*] (IBMDP)
SAVT .... Secondary Address Vector Table [*Data processing*] (IBMDP)
SAVT .... Trelew/Almirante Zar [*Argentina*] [*ICAO location identifier*] (ICLI)
SAVU .... Comodoro Rivadavia [*Argentina*] [*ICAO location identifier*] (ICLI)
SAVV .... Viedma/Gobernador Castello [*Argentina*] [*ICAO location identifier*] (ICLI)
Savv Kn ...... Savvina Kniga [*A publication*]
SAVY .... Puerto Madryn [*Argentina*] [*ICAO location identifier*] (ICLI)
Sav Zeitschr ... Zeitschrift der Savigny-Stiftung fuer Rechtsgeschichte. Romanistische Abteilung [*A publication*] (OCD)
SAW .... Gwinn, MI [*Location identifier*] [*FAA*] (FAAL)
SAW .... St. Andrews [*Washington*] [*Seismograph station code, US Geological Survey*] (SEIS)
SAW .... Sample Assignment Word
SAW .... Satellite Attack Warning
Saw .... Sawyer's United States Circuit Court Reports [*A publication*] (DLA)
SAW .... Scottish Association of Writers [*British*]
SAW .... Search-a-Word [*Neuropsychology test*]
SAW .... Seasonal Agricultural Worker
SAW .... Selectively Aimable Warhead (MCD)
SAW .... Semiautomatic Weapons
SAW .... Signal Aircraft Warning
SAW .... Simulate Antiaircraft Weapons (SAA)
SAW .... Sitzungsberichte. Akademie der Wissenschaft in Wien [*A publication*]
SAW .... Small Arms Weapon
SAW .... Society of American Wars (EA)
SAW .... Solar Array Wing (MCD)
SAW .... South Albuquerque Works [*AEC*]
SAW .... Southern Army Worm [*Agronomy*]
SAW .... Sozialistische Arbeitswissenschaft [*A publication*]
SAW .... Special Agricultural Worker
SAW .... Special Air Warfare (AFM)
SAW .... Squad Automatic Weapon [*Army*]
SAW .... Strategic Aerospace Wing [*Air Force*]
SAW .... Strike Anywhere [*Match*]
SAW .... Subantarctic Water
SAW .... Submerged Arc Weld
SAW .... Surface Acoustic Wave [*Microwave system*]
SAWA ...... Lago Argentino [*Argentina*] [*ICAO location identifier*] (ICLI)
SAWA ...... Screen Advertising World Association [*British*] (EAIO)
SAWA ...... Society of Anaesthetists of West Africa [*Nigeria*] (EAIO)

SAWANS .. South African Women's Auxiliary Naval Service [*British military*] (DMA)
SAWAS ..... South African Women's Auxiliary Services
SA Waterabstr ... SA [*South African*] Waterabstracts [*A publication*]
SAWB .... Base Marambio [*Argentina*] [*ICAO location identifier*] (ICLI)
SAWB .... Sitzungsberichte. Akademie der Wissenschaften zu Berlin [*A publication*]
SAWBET .. Supply Action Will Be Taken
SAWC .... Special Air Warfare Center
SAWD ...... Puerto Deseado [*Argentina*] [*ICAO location identifier*] (ICLI)
SAWD ...... Solid Amine Water Desorbed (NASA)
SAWE .... Rio Grande [*Argentina*] [*ICAO location identifier*] (ICLI)
SAWE .... Simulated Area Weapons Effects
SAWE .... Society of Allied Weight Engineers (EA)
SAWE-IF .. Simulated Area Weapons Effects - Indirect Fire
SAWE-NBC-CAS ... Simulated Area Weapons Effects - Nuclear, Biological, Chemical - Casualty Assesment System [*Army*]
SAWF .... Special Air Warfare Forces (AFM)
SAWG ...... Rio Gallegos [*Argentina*] [*ICAO location identifier*] (ICLI)
SAWG ...... Schedule and Allocations Working Group [*NASA*] (KSC)
SAWG ...... Special Advisory Working Group (NATG)
SAWg .... Strategic Aerospace Wing [*Air Force*] (AFM)
SAWGUS ... Standoff/Attack Weapons Guidance Utility Study (MCD)
SAWH .... Ushuaia [*Argentina*] [*ICAO location identifier*] (ICLI)
SAWI .... Society for Animal Welfare in Israel (EAIO)
SAWIC ...... South African Water Information Centre [*Information service or system*] (IID)
SAWID ...... Shipboard Acoustic Warfare Integrated Defense (NVT)
SAWJ .... San Julian/Cap. D. J. D. Vasquez [*Argentina*] [*ICAO location identifier*] (ICLI)
SAWLT ..... South African Written Language Test [*Educational test*]
SAWM ...... Rio Mayo [*Argentina*] [*ICAO location identifier*] (ICLI)
SAWM ...... Sitzungsberichte. Akademie der Wissenschaften zu Muenchen [*A publication*]
SAWMA.... Soil and Water Management Association [*British*]
SAWMA.... Southern African Wildlife Management Association [*See also NVSA*] (EAIO)
SAWMARCS ... Standard Aircraft Weapon Monitor and Release Control System (NG)
SAWO .... Surface Acoustic Wave Oscillator [*Telecommunications*] (TEL)
SAWP .... Perito Moreno [*Argentina*] [*ICAO location identifier*] (ICLI)
SAWP .... Socialist Alliance of the Working People [*Serbia*] [*Political party*]
SAWP .... Society of American Wood Preservers (EA)
SAWPHK ... Saechsische Akademie der Wissenschaften zu Leipzig. Philologisch-Historische Klasse [*A publication*]
SAWPY ..... Socialist Alliance of the Working People of Yugoslavia [*Political party*] (EY)
SAWR .... Gobernador Gregores [*Argentina*] [*ICAO location identifier*] (ICLI)
SAWRS ..... Supplementary Aviation Weather Reporting Station [*National Weather Service*] (FAAC)
SAWS .... Jose De San Martin [*Argentina*] [*ICAO location identifier*] (ICLI)
SAWS .... Satellite Attack Warning System
SAWS .... Seventh-Day Adventist World Service [*Superseded by ADRA*] (EA)
SAWS .... Silent Attack Warning System (MCD)
SAWS .... Small Arms Weapon Study [*Army*]
SAWS .... Small Arms Weapons System (NATG)
SAWS .... Solar Array Wing Simulator (MCD)
SAWS .... Special Airborne Weapon Subsystem (MCD)
SAWS .... Squad Automatic Weapon System [*Army*]
SAWS .... Subacoustic Warfare System
SAWS .... Submarine Acoustic Warfare System [*Navy*] (MCD)
SAWT .... Rio Turbio [*Argentina*] [*ICAO location identifier*] (ICLI)
SAWTRI Annu Rep ... South African Wool and Textile Research Institute. Annual Report [*A publication*]
Sawtri Bull ... Sawtri Bulletin [*A publication*]
SAWTRI Dig ... SAWTRI [*South African Wool and Textile Research Institute*] Digest [*A publication*]
SAWTRI Spec Publ ... SAWTRI [*South African Wool and Textile Research Institute*] Special Publication
SAWTRI Tech Rep ... SAWTRI (South African Wool and Textile Research Institute) Technical Report [*A publication*]
SAWU .... Santa Cruz [*Argentina*] [*ICAO location identifier*] (ICLI)
SAWW ...... Sitzungsberichte. Akademie der Wissenschaften in Wien [*A publication*]
Sawy .... Sawyer's United States Circuit Court Reports [*A publication*] (DLA)
Sawyer Circt ... Sawyer's United States Circuit Court Reports [*A publication*] (DLA)
Sawyer's Gas Turbine Int ... Sawyer's Gas Turbine International [*A publication*]
Sawyer US Ct Rep ... Sawyer's United States Circuit Court Reports [*A publication*] (DLA)
SAX .... Sambu [*Panama*] [*Airport symbol*] (OAG)
SAX .... Saxon
Sax .... Saxony
SAX .... Saxophone [*Music*]

Sax	Saxton's New Jersey Chancery Reports [A publication] (DLA)
SAX...........	Small-Angle X-ray [Instrumentation]
SAX...........	Small Automatic Exchange [Telecommunications] (TEL)
SAX...........	Sparta, NJ [Location identifier] [FAA] (FAAL)
SAX...........	States Exploration Ltd. [Toronto Stock Exchange symbol]
SAX...........	Strong Anion Exchanger [Chemistry]
SAXA........	Slotted Array X-Band Antenna
SAXD........	Small-Angle X-Ray Diffraction
SAXI.........	Saxton Industries Ltd. [NASDAQ symbol] (NQ)
SAXL........	Short-Arc Xenon Lamp
SAXLE	Single Cantilevered Axle
SAXO	Saxon Oil Co. [Dallas, TX] [NASDAQ symbol] (NQ)
SAXS	Small-Angle X-Ray Scattering
Saxt...........	Saxton's New Jersey Chancery Reports [A publication] (DLA)
Saxt Ch	Saxton's New Jersey Chancery Reports [A publication] (DLA)
SAY...........	Salisbury [Zimbabwe] [Airport symbol] [Obsolete] (OAG)
Say	Sayer's English King's Bench Reports [96 English Reprint] [A publication] (DLA)
SAY...........	Science Fiction Adventures Yearbook [A publication]
SAY...........	Severe Aster Yellows [Plant pathology]
SAY...........	Soccer Association for Youth (EA)
SAY...........	Speaking to American Youth (AEBS)
SAY...........	Stanley Resources [Vancouver Stock Exchange symbol]
SAYE........	Save as You Earn [National Savings Plan] [British]
Sayer	Sayer's English King's Bench Reports [96 English Reprint] [1751-56] [A publication] (DLA)
Sayer (Eng) ...	Sayer's English King's Bench Reports [96 English Reprint] [A publication] (DLA)
SAYFC	Scottish Association of Young Farmers' Clubs (EAIO)
SAYKA......	Sovistva Atomnykh Yader [Former USSR] [A publication]
Sayles' Ann Civ St ...	Sayles' Annotated Civil Statutes [Texas] [A publication] (DLA)
Sayles' Civ St ...	Sayles' Revised Civil Statutes [Texas] [A publication] (DLA)
Sayles' Rev Civ St ...	Sayles' Revised Civil Statutes [Texas] [A publication] (DLA)
Sayles' St ...	Sayles' Revised Civil Statutes [Texas] [A publication] (DLA)
Sayles' Supp ...	Supplement to Sayles' Annotated Civil Statutes [Texas] [A publication] (DLA)
SAYP........	SAY Packaging, Inc. [NASDAQ symbol] (NQ)
Sayre Adm Cas ...	Sayre's Cases on Admiralty [A publication] (DLA)
SAZ...........	Sasstown [Liberia] [Airport symbol] (OAG)
SAZ...........	Staples, MN [Location identifier] [FAA] (FAAL)
SAZA........	Azul [Argentina] [ICAO location identifier] (ICLI)
SAZB........	Bahia Blanca/Comdte. Espora [Argentina] [ICAO location identifier] (ICLI)
SAZC........	Cnel. Suarez [Argentina] [ICAO location identifier] (ICLI)
SAZD........	Dolores [Argentina] [ICAO location identifier] (ICLI)
SAZE........	Pigue [Argentina] [ICAO location identifier] (ICLI)
SAZF........	Olavarria [Argentina] [ICAO location identifier] (ICLI)
SAZG........	General Pico [Argentina] [ICAO location identifier] (ICLI)
SAZH	Tres Arroyos [Argentina] [ICAO location identifier] (ICLI)
SAZI.........	Bolivar [Argentina] [ICAO location identifier] (ICLI)
SAZJ	Benito Juarez [Argentina] [ICAO location identifier] (ICLI)
SAZK........	Cerro Catedral [Argentina] [ICAO location identifier] (ICLI)
SAZL........	Santa Teresita [Argentina] [ICAO location identifier] (ICLI)
SAZM.......	Mar Del Plata [Argentina] [ICAO location identifier] (ICLI)
SAZN	Neuquen [Argentina] [ICAO location identifier] (ICLI)
SAZO	Necochea [Argentina] [ICAO location identifier] (ICLI)
SAZO	Seeker Azimuth Orientation [Air Force]
SAZP........	Pehuajo/Comodoro P. Zanni [Argentina] [ICAO location identifier] (ICLI)
SAZQ........	Rio Colorado [Argentina] [ICAO location identifier] (ICLI)
SAZR........	Santa Rosa [Argentina] [ICAO location identifier] (ICLI)
SAZS	San Carlos De Bariloche [Argentina] [ICAO location identifier] (ICLI)
SAZT........	Tandil [Argentina] [ICAO location identifier] (ICLI)
SAZU........	Puelches [Argentina] [ICAO location identifier] (ICLI)
SAZV........	Villa Gesell [Argentina] [ICAO location identifier] (ICLI)
SAZW.......	Cutral-Co [Argentina] [ICAO location identifier] (ICLI)
SAZX........	Nueve De Julio [Argentina] [ICAO location identifier] (ICLI)
SAZY........	San Martin De Los Andes/Chapelco [Argentina] [ICAO location identifier] (ICLI)
SAZZ........	Saztec International, Inc. [NASDAQ symbol] (NQ)
SB	Automotive Engine Rebuilders Association. Service Bulletin [A publication] (EAAP)
SB	Bachelor of Science
SB	Beauval Public Library, Saskatchewan [Library symbol] [National Library of Canada] (NLC)
SB	International Standard Book Number [Online database field identifier]
SB	La Sacra Bibbia [Turin] [A publication] (BJA)
SB	La Sainte Bible [A publication] (BJA)
SB	S-Band (KSC)
SB	SAAB-Scania AB [Sweden] [ICAO aircraft manufacturer identifier] (ICAO)
SB	Salary Band [British] (DCTA)
SB	Sales Book
SB	Salomon, Inc. [NYSE symbol] (SPSG)
SB	Santa Barbara [Television program]
SB	Sarah Bernhardt [French actress, 1844-1923]

S & B	Saunders and Bidder's Locus Standi Reports [1905-19] [A publication] (DLA)
SB	Savannah Bank of Nigeria
SB	Save a Baby [Later, LGM] (EA)
SB	Savings Bank
SB	Savings Bond [Treasury Department security]
SB	Schistosoma Bovis [Parasitic fluke]
SB	Schweizer Buch [A publication]
SB	Science Books [A publication]
SB	Science Books and Films [A publication]
SB	Scissors Bridge (DWSG)
SB	Scoring Booklet (MCD)
SB	Scouting-Bombing Plane [When prefixed to Navy aircraft designation]
SB	Scrieve Board
SB	Sea Base (MCD)
SB	Seaboard World Airlines, Inc. [ICAO designator]
SB	Secondary Battery [Military]
SB	Secondary Buffer [Chemistry]
SB	Section Base [Military]
SB	Securing Bands
SB	Selection Board [Military]
SB	Selective Bibliography (MCD)
SB	Selmer Bandwagon [A publication]
SB	Senate Bill [in state legislatures]
SB	Senior Beadle [Ancient Order of Foresters]
SB	Separately Binned
SB	Serial Binary (CET)
SB	Serial Block (MSA)
SB	Serum Bilirubin [Clinical chemistry]
SB	Service Bulletin
SB	Serving Brother [Church of England]
SB	Shanti Bahini [Peace Force] [Bangladesh] [Political party]
SB	Shaper Block (MCD)
SB	Shipbuilding [Navy]
SB	Shipping Board
SB	Shoot Bud [Botany]
SB	Short Bill
SB	Shortness of Breath [Cardiology]
S/B	Should Be
SB	Shrunk Back-to-Back [Packaging of volumes] [Publishing]
SB	Sick Bay
SB	Sideband [Radio frequency] (AAG)
SB	Sideroblast [Hematology] (AAMN)
SB	Signal to Background
SB	Signal Battalion [Army]
SB	Signal Boatswain
SB	Signature Book (ROG)
SB	Silver Braze (MSA)
SB	Simultaneous Broadcast
SB	Single Blind [Experimental condition]
SB	Single Braid (CET)
SB	Single-Breasted
SB	Single Breath
SB	Single-Ended Boiler (DS)
SB	Sink Beater (ADA)
SB	Sinus Bradycardia [Cardiology]
SB	Sitzungsbericht [Transaction] [German]
SB	Skandinaviska Banken. Quarterly Review [Later, Skandinaviska Enskilda Banken. Quarterly Review] [A publication]
SB	Sleeve Bearing (KSC)
SB	Slow Burning
SB	Small Block [Automotive engineering]
SB	Small Bonds
SB	Small Bore (ADA)
SB	Small Bowel
SB	Small Business
Sb	Small-Mouth Bass [Ichthyology]
S & B	Smith and Batty's Irish King's Bench Reports [1824-25] [A publication] (DLA)
SB	Smooth Bore [Ballistics]
SB	Snow Biz [An association] (EA)
SB	Social Biology Films [National Science Foundation project]
SB	Society for Biomaterials (EA)
SB	Sociologisch Bulletin [A publication]
SB	Sociologists in Business (EA)
SB	Sodium Bicarbonate [Inorganic chemistry]
SB	Sodium Bisulfite [Inorganic chemistry]
SB	Sodium Borate [Inorganic chemistry]
SB	Solid Base Bullet
SB	Solid Body [Technical drawings]
SB	Solomon Islands [ANSI two-letter standard code] (CNC)
SB	Soncino Blaetter [A publication]
SB	Sonobuoy (NVT)
SB	Soot Blower (AAG)
SB	Sources Bibliques [Paris] [A publication]
SB	South Britain [England and Wales]
SB	South Buffalo Railway Co. [AAR code]
SB	Southbound
S B	Sovetskaya Bibliografia [A publication]

SB .... Soviet Biotechnology [*A publication*]
SB .... Space Base [*NASA*] (KSC)
SB .... Space Booster (SAA)
SB .... Special Bibliography
SB .... Special Billing [*Telecommunications*] (TEL)
SB .... Special Branch [*British police*]
SB .... Special Bulletin. New York Department of Labor [*A publication*] (DLA)
SB .... Speed Brake (MCD)
SB .... Spin Block (MSA)
SB .... Spina Bifida [*Medicine*]
SB .... Splash Block
SB .... Sports Bribery [*FBI standardized term*]
SB .... Spring Back (ADA)
SB .... Stabilized Breakdown
SBAM .... Standard Babylonian (BJA)
SB .... Standard Bead
SB .... Standby
SB .... Standby Base [*Air Force*] (AFM)
SBAE .... Stanford-Binet [*Intelligence test*] [*Education*]
SB .... Statement of Billing
SB .... Statistical Bulletin
SB .... Status Board [*Automated*] (MCD)
SB .... Statute Book (ADA)
SB .... Steamboat
S & B .... Sterilization and Bath
SB .... Sternal Border [*Anatomy*]
Sb .... Stibium [*Antimony*] [*Chemical element*]
sb .... Stilb [*Unit of luminance*]
SB .... Stillborn [*Medicine*]
SB .... Stockbroker
SB .... Stolen Base [*Baseball*]
SB .... Stove Bolt
Sb .... Strabismus [*Medicine*]
SB .... Straight Binary
SB .... Stretcher-Bearer
SB .... Studies in Bibliography [*A publication*]
SB .... Stuffing Box
SB .... Styrene Butadiene [*Organic chemistry*]
SB .... Sub Branch [*Banking*]
SB .... Subbituminous
SB .... Submarine Base [*Navy*]
SB .... Submarine Boat [*British*] (ROG)
SB .... Submarine Fog Bell [*Mechanical*] [*Maps and charts*]
SB .... Substantive
SB .... Superbananas
SB .... Supplementary Benefits
SB .... Supply Bulletin [*Military*]
SB .... Support Box
SBAU .... Supreme Bench [*Legal term*] (DLA)
SB .... Surface Binding [*Immunochemistry*]
SB .... Surplus Budget
sb .... Svalbard and Jan Mayen [*MARC country of publication code*] [*Library of Congress*] (LCCP)
SB .... Switchboard
SB .... Switchboard Operator [*Navy*]
SB .... Symbiotic Bacteria [*Ecology*]
SB .... Synchronization Base [*NASA*] (NASA)
SB .... Synchronization Bit (MSA)
SBA .... Saabruecker Beitraege zur Altertumskunde [*Bonn*] [*A publication*] (BJA)
SBA .... Santa Barbara [*California*] [*Airport symbol*] (OAG)
SBA .... Satellite Broadcasters Association (EA)
SBA .... Sbarro, Inc. [*AMEX symbol*] (SPSG)
SBA .... School Band of America (AEBS)
SBA .... School Bookshop Association [*British*] (DI)
SBA .... Scott Base [*Antarctica*] [*Geomagnetic observatory code*]
SBA .... Scott Base [*Antarctica*] [*Seismograph station code, US Geological Survey*] (SEIS)
SBA .... Seat Back Assembly [*Aerospace*] (MCD)
SBA .... Second Bombardment Association (EA)
SBA .... Secondary Butyl Alcohol [*Organic chemistry*]
SBA .... Service Brake Activator [*Automotive engineering*]
SBA .... Setback Axle [*Truck engineering*]
SBA .... Shaped Beam Antenna
SBA .... Shared Batch Area [*Data processing*] (IBMDP)
SBA .... Show Business Association [*New York, NY*] (EA)
SBA .... Siamese Breeders of America [*Later, GSCC*] (EA)
SBA .... Sick Bay Attendant [*Navy*]
SBA .... Sitzungsberichte. Bayerische Akademie der Wissenschaften [*A publication*]
SBA .... Small Business Administration
SBA .... Small Businesses' Association [*British*] (DCTA)
SB of A .... Smaller Business of America [*Defunct*] (EA)
SBA .... Social Behavior Assessment [*Social skills test*]
SBA .... Society of Batik Artists [*Inactive*] (EA)
SBI .... Sovereign Base Area (DNAB)
SBA .... Soybean Agglutinin [*Immunology*]
SBA .... Spirit and Breath Association (EA)
SBA .... Standard Beam Approach [*British aircraft landing method*]
SBA .... Standard Chartered Review [*A publication*]

SBA .... Standing British Army
SBA .... Steroid-Binding Assay [*Clinical chemistry*]
SBA .... Structural Board Association (EA)
SBA .... Structure Borne Acoustics (KSC)
SBA .... Studies in Biblical Archaeology [*A publication*]
SBA .... Sun Basin Airlines [*Moses Lake, CA*] [*FAA designator*] (FAAC)
SBA .... Support Base Activation (AAG)
SBA .... Susan B. Anthony Dollar
SBA .... Sweet Bugger All [*An exclamation*] [*Slang*] [*British*] (DSUE)
SBA .... Systems Builders Association (EA)
SBAA .... Conceicao Do Araguaia [*Brazil*] [*ICAO location identifier*] (ICLI)
SBAA .... Ships-in-Bottles Association of America (EA)
SBAA .... Spina Bifida Association of America (EA)
SBAAM .... Small Business Association of Apparel Manufacturers (EA)
SBAC .... Small Business Assistance Center [*Worcester, MA*] (EA)
SBAC .... Society of British Aerospace Companies (MCD)
SBAC .... Society of British Aircraft Constructors
SBAE .... Stabilized Bombing Approach Equipment [*Navy*]
SBAF .... Rio De Janeiro/Afonsos [*Brazil*] [*ICAO location identifier*] (ICLI)
SBAFWP ... Standby Auxiliary Feed Water Pump (IEEE)
SBAG .... Schweizer Beitraege zur Allgemeinen Geschichte [*A publication*]
SBAH .... Sodium Bis(methoxyethoxy)aluminum Hydride [*Organic chemistry*]
S-Bahn ...... Schnellbahn [*High-Speed Railway*] [*German*]
SBAkWissWien ... Sitzungsberichte der Oesterreichischen Akademie der Wissenschaften in Wien [*A publication*] (BJA)
SBAM .... Amapa [*Brazil*] [*ICAO location identifier*] (ICLI)
SBAM .... Space-Based Antimissile
SBAMA ..... San Bernardino Air Materiel Area
SBAMP .... Sea-Based Air Master Plan (MCD)
SBAN .... Anapolis (Base Aerea) [*Brazil*] [*ICAO location identifier*] (ICLI)
SBANE ...... Smaller Business Association of New England [*Waltham, MA*] (EA)
SBAP .... Simple Bin Assignment Problem
SBAP .... Small Business Assistance Program
SBAP .... Society of Business Advisory Professions (EA)
SBAR .... Aracaju/Santa Maria [*Brazil*] [*ICAO location identifier*] (ICLI)
SBAR .... San/Bar Corp. [*NASDAQ symbol*] (NQ)
S Bar J ...... State Bar Journal of California [*A publication*] (DLA)
SBARMO Bull ... SBARMO [*Scientific Ballooning and Radiations Monitoring Organization*] Bulletin [*A publication*]
SBARRO ...... Sbarro, Inc. [*Associated Press abbreviation*] (APAG)
SBAS .... S-Band Antenna Switch (MCD)
SBASI .... Single Bridgewire Apollo Standard Initiator [*Explosive*]
SBAU .... Aracatuba [*Brazil*] [*ICAO location identifier*] (ICLI)
SBAV .... Teodoro Sampaio/Usina Porto Primavera [*Brazil*] [*ICAO location identifier*] (ICLI)
SBAW .... Sitzungsberichte. Bayerische Akademie der Wissenschaften [*A publication*]
SBAWSEF ... Susan B. Anthony Women's Spirituality Education Forum (EA)
SBAWW .... Sitzungsberichte. Akademie der Wissenschaft in Wien [*A publication*]
SBB .... Sabina Resources Ltd. [*Vancouver Stock Exchange symbol*]
SBB .... Saddle Back Butte [*California*] [*Seismograph station code, US Geological Survey*] (SEIS)
SBB .... Satellite Busy Box (SSD)
SBB .... Saudi-British Bank
SBB .... Schweizerische Bundesbahnen [*Swiss Federal Railways*]
SBB .... Self-Balancing Bridge
SBB .... Serikat Buruh Batik [*Batik Workers' Union*] [*Indonesia*]
SBB .... Silicon-Borne Bonds (SAA)
SBB .... Single-Band Beaconry [*RADAR*]
SBB .... Soncino Books of the Bible [*London*] [*A publication*] (BJA)
SBB .... Studies in Bibliography and Booklore [*A publication*]
SBB .... Subtract with Borrow [*Data processing*] (PCM)
SBB .... System Building Block [*Data processing*]
SBBA .... Boca Do Acre [*Brazil*] [*ICAO location identifier*] (ICLI)
SBBA .... Spanish-Barb Breeders Association (EA)
SBBAW ..... Sitzungsberichte. Bayerische Akademie der Wissenschaften [*A publication*]
SBBE .... Belem/Val-De-Caes [*Brazil*] [*ICAO location identifier*] (ICLI)
SB Berlin ... Sitzungsberichte. Deutsche Akademie der Wissenschaften zu Berlin. Klasse fuer Sprachen, Literatur, und Kunst [*A publication*]
SBBF .... Silicone-Based Brake Fluid [*Automotive engineering*]
SBBG .... Baje/Cmt. Gustavo Kraemer [*Brazil*] [*ICAO location identifier*] (ICLI)
SBBH .... Belo Horizonte/Pampulha [*Brazil*] [*ICAO location identifier*] (ICLI)
SBBI .... Curitiba/Bacacheri [*Brazil*] [*ICAO location identifier*] (ICLI)
SBBI .... Stocks, Bonds, Bills, and Inflation [*Investment term*]
Sb Biokhim Zerna Akad Nauk SSSR Inst Biokhim A N Bakha ... Sbornik. Biokhimiya Zerna. Akademiya Nauk SSSR. Institut Biokhimii Imeni A. N. Bakha [*A publication*]
SBBKA ...... Seibutsu Butsuri Kagaku [*A publication*]

SBBL .... Belem [*Brazil*] [*ICAO location identifier*]   (ICLI)
SBBN .... Standard Big Bang Nucleosynthesis [*Cosmology*]
SBBQ .... Barbacena [*Brazil*] [*ICAO location identifier*]   (ICLI)
SBBR .... Brasilia/Internacional [*Brazil*] [*ICAO location identifier*]   (ICLI)
SBBS .... Brasilia [*Brazil*] [*ICAO location identifier*]   (ICLI)
SBBT .... Barretos [*Brazil*] [*ICAO location identifier*]   (ICLI)
SBBT .... Short Basic Battery Test   (NVT)
SBBU .... Bauru [*Brazil*] [*ICAO location identifier*]   (ICLI)
SBBUD ...... SBARMO [*Scientific Ballooning and Radiations Monitoring Organization*] Bulletin [*A publication*]
SBBV .... Boa Vista/Internacional [*Brazil*] [*ICAO location identifier*]
SBBW .... Barra Do Garcas [*Brazil*] [*ICAO location identifier*]   (ICLI)
SBC .... Baptist College at Charleston, Charleston, SC [*OCLC symbol*]   (OCLC)
SBC .... Ferrocarril Sonora Baja California SA de CV [*AAR code*]
SBC .... Saint Basil's College [*Stamford, CT*]
SBC .... Saint Benedict College [*Indiana*]
SBC .... Saint Bernard College [*Alabama*]
SBC .... Sam Browne's Cavalry [*British military*]   (DMA)
SBC .... Santa Barbara [*California*] [*Seismograph station code, US Geological Survey*]   (SEIS)
SBC .... Save the Battlefield Coalition   (EA)
SBC .... Schmidt-Baker Camera   (IIA)
SBC .... Senate Budget Committee
SBC .... Service Bureau Corp.
SBC .... Sibasa [*South Africa*] [*Airport symbol*]   (OAG)
SBC .... Signal Board Computer   (HGAA)
SBC .... Simpson Bible College [*Later, Simpson College*] [*California*]
SBC .... Single Board Computer
SBC .... Single Burst Correcting
SBC .... Small Bayonet Cap
SBC .... Small Business Centre [*British*]
SBC .... Small Business Computer   (BUR)
SBC .... Soleil-Babinet Compensator [*Optics*]
SBC .... Solid Bowl Centrifuge
SBC .... SONAR Breakout Cable
SBC .... Southeastern Bible College [*Lakeland, FL*]
SBC .... Southern Baptist College [*Walnut Ridge, AR*]
SBC .... Southern Baptist Convention
SBC .... Southwestern Bell Corp. [*NYSE symbol*]   (SPSG)
SBC .... Spaceborne Computer
SBC .... Special Back Care [*Medicine*]
SBC .... Speed Brake Command   (NASA)
SBC .... Standard Boundary Condition
SBC .... Standard Buried Collector [*Circuit*]
SBC .... Standing Balance: Eyes Closed [*Test*] [*Occupational therapy*]
SBC .... Start Breguet Cruise [*SST*]
SBC .... Statutes of British Columbia [*British Columbia Attorney General's Ministry*] [*Information service or system*] [*A publication*]   (CRD)
SBC .... Strict Bed Confinement [*Medicine*]
SBC .... Studies in Browning and His Circle [*A publication*]
SBC .... Styrene Block Copolymer [*Plastics technology*]
SBC .... Sue Bennett College [*London, KY*]
SBC .... Summary Billing Card   (AFM)
SBC .... Supplementary Benefits Commission [*Department of Employment*] [*British*]
SBC .... Surrogates by Choice   (EA)
SBC .... Survey of Basic Competencies [*Achievement test*]
SBC .... Sweet Briar College [*Virginia*]
SBC .... Swiss Bank Corp.
SBC .... Swiss Broadcasting Corp.
SBCA .... Cascavel [*Brazil*] [*ICAO location identifier*]   (ICLI)
SBCA .... Saint Bernard Club of America   (EA)
SBCA .... Satellite Broadcasting and Communications Association   (EA)
SBCA .... SBC [*Swiss Bank Corp.*] Australia
SBCA .... Seat Belt Control Apparatus
SBCA .... Sensor-Based Control Adapter
SBCA .... Small Business Council of America   (EA)
SBCA .... Soybean Council of America [*Defunct*]
SBCABE .... Annual Symposium on Biomathematics and Computer Science in the Life Sciences. Abstracts [*A publication*]
SBCBA ...... Sounding Brass and the Conductor [*A publication*]
SBCC .... Cachimbo [*Brazil*] [*ICAO location identifier*]   (ICLI)
SBCC .... St. Brendan Cup Committee in America [*Defunct*]   (EA)
SBCC .... Senate Bonding and Currency Committee   (OICC)
SBCC .... Separate Bias, Common Control
SBCC .... Southern Building Code Congress, International
SBCCA ...... Still Bank Collectors Club of America   (EA)
SBCCI .... Southern Building Code Congress, International   (EA)
SBCD .... Campo Grande [*Brazil*] [*ICAO location identifier*]   (ICLI)
SBCD .... School-Based Curriculum Development   (ADA)
SB/CD .... Short Bed/Continuous Development [*Chamber for thin-layer chromatography*] [*Analytical biochemistry*]
SBCD .... Special Business and Contract Directories [*A publication*]
SBCD .... Subtract BCD [*Binary Coded Decimal*] Number [*Data processing*]
SBCE .... Bachelor of Science in Civil Engineering
SBCE .... Concordia [*Brazil*] [*ICAO location identifier*]   (ICLI)

SBCED ...... Scientific Bulletin. Canada Centre for Mineral and Energy Technology [*A publication*]
SBCF .... Belo Horizonte/Confins [*Brazil*] [*ICAO location identifier*]   (ICLI)
SBCF .... Seacoast Banking Corp. of Florida [*Stuart, FL*] [*NASDAQ symbol*]   (NQ)
SBCF .... Southern Baptist Convention Flyers [*Defunct*]   (EA)
SBCG .... Campo Grande/Internacional [*Brazil*] [*ICAO location identifier*]   (ICLI)
SBCH .... Chapeco [*Brazil*] [*ICAO location identifier*]   (ICLI)
SBCI .... Carolina [*Brazil*] [*ICAO location identifier*]   (ICLI)
SBCI .... Swiss Bank Corp. International
SBCJ .... Maraba/Carajas [*Brazil*] [*ICAO location identifier*]   (ICLI)
SBCJ .... Store Block Control Journal [*Military*]   (AABC)
SBCL .... Cruz Alta/Carlos Ruhl [*Brazil*] [*ICAO location identifier*]   (ICLI)
SBCLS ...... South Bay Cooperative Library System [*Library network*]
SBCM .... Criciuma [*Brazil*] [*ICAO location identifier*]   (ICLI)
SBCO .... Porto Alegre/Canoas [*Brazil*] [*ICAO location identifier*]   (ICLI)
SBCO .... Shipbuilding Company
SBC/OC .... Swiss Bank Corp./O'Connor & Associates Services   (ECON)
SBCORP ... Shipbuilding Corp.
SBCP .... Campos/Bartolomeu Lisandro [*Brazil*] [*ICAO location identifier*]   (ICLI)
SBCP .... Spanish Base Construction Program
SBCPO ...... Sick Bay Chief Petty Officer [*British military*]   (DMA)
SBCR .... Corumba/Internacional [*Brazil*] [*ICAO location identifier*]   (ICLI)
SB & CR .... Stock Balance and Consumption Report   (AFM)
SBCR .... Stock Balance and Consumption Report   (NASA)
SBCS .... Series Book Collectors' Society   (EA)
SBCS .... Shore-Based Correlation Subsystem [*Navy*]   (CAAL)
SBCS .... Steam Bypass Control System [*Nuclear energy*]   (NRCH)
SBCT .... Curitiba/Afonso Pena [*Brazil*] [*ICAO location identifier*]   (ICLI)
SBCU .... Sensor-Based Control Unit [*Data processing*]
SBCV .... Caravelas [*Brazil*] [*ICAO location identifier*]   (ICLI)
SBCW .... Curitiba [*Brazil*] [*ICAO location identifier*]   (ICLI)
SBCY .... Cuiaba/Marechal Rondon [*Brazil*] [*ICAO location identifier*]   (ICLI)
SBCZ .... Cruzeiro Do Sul/Internacional [*Brazil*] [*ICAO location identifier*]   (ICLI)
SBD .... "Dauntless" Single-Engine Scout-Bomber [*Navy symbol*]
S-BD .... S-Band   (NASA)
SBD .... San Bernardino, CA [*Location identifier*] [*FAA*]   (FAAL)
SBD .... San Bernardino Public Library, San Bernardino, CA [*OCLC symbol*]   (OCLC)
SBD .... Savings Bond Division [*Navy*]
SBD .... Schematic Block Diagram [*NASA*]   (NASA)
SBD .... Schoolbestuur [*A publication*]
SBD .... Schottky Barrier Diode [*Electronics*]
SBD .... Shipboard Decoy   (DWSG)
SBD .... Space Business Daily [*A publication*]
SBD .... Special Business Directories [*A publication*]
SBD .... Standard Bibliographic Description
SBD .... Steel Beam Design [*Modray Ltd.*] [*Software package*]   (NCC)
SBD .... Straight Bag Drainage [*Medicine*]   (MAE)
SBD .... Strawboard [*Shipping*]
SBD .... Subcontractor Bid Document   (MCD)
SBD .... Sunbird Airlines, Inc. [*Maiden, NC*] [*FAA designator*]   (FAAC)
SBD .... Surface Barrier Detector
SBDAW ..... Sitzungsberichte. Deutsche Akademie der Wissenschaften zu Berlin. Klasse fuer Sprachen, Literatur, und Kunst [*A publication*]
SBDAWB .. Sitzungsberichte. Deutsche Akademie der Wissenschaften zu Berlin. Klasse fuer Sprachen, Literatur, und Kunst [*A publication*]
SBDC .... Shipbuilding and Drydock Company
SBDC .... Small Business Development Center [*Lehigh University, University of Alabama in Birmingham*] [*Research center*]
SBDC .... Small Business Development Corp.
SBDCP ...... Seaboard Corp. [*Associated Press abbreviation*]   (APAG)
SBDH .... Sociedade Brasileira de Discos Historicos J. Leon [*Record label*] [*Brazil*]
SBDK .... Sound Bytes Developer's Kit [*Data processing*]
SBDL .... Solid Blank Delay Line
SBDM .... School-Based Decision Making   (ADA)
SBDN .... Presidente Prudente [*Brazil*] [*ICAO location identifier*]   (ICLI)
SBDO .... Space Business Development Operation   (AAG)
SBDP .... Serikat Buruh Djawatan Perindustrian [*Department of Industry Workers' Union*] [*Indonesia*]
SBDPU ...... Serikat Buruh Djawantan Pekerdjaan Umun [*Public Works' Union*] [*Indonesia*]
SBDT .... Surface Barrier Diffused Transistor
SBE .... S-Band Exciter [*System*] [*Also, SBES*]
SBE .... Sacred Books of the East [*A publication*]   (BJA)
SBE .... Selebi-Pikwe [*Botswana*] [*Later, PKW*] [*Airport symbol*]   (OAG)
SBE .... Self Breast Examination [*for cancer*]
SBE .... Semana Biblica Espanola [*A publication*]
SBE .... Shortness of Breath on Exertion [*Cardiology*]

SBE............ Simple Boolean Expression [*Mathematics*]
SBE............ Societe de Biologie Experimentale [*Society for Experimental Biology*] (EAIO)
SBE............ Society of Broadcast Engineers (EA)
SBE............ Society of Business Economists (EAIO)
SBE............ Society for Business Ethics [*Santa Clara, CA*] (EA)
SBE............ Solar Beam Experiment
SbE .... South by East
SBE............ Southwest Journal of Business and Economics [*A publication*]
SBE............ Sporadic Bovine Encephalomyelitis [*Veterinary medicine*]
SBE............ State Board of Education (OICC)
SBE............ Strategic Bomber Enhancement (MCD)
SBEA......... Sub BIT [*Binary Digit*] Encoder (MCD)
SBE............ Subacute Bacterial Endocarditis [*Medicine*]
SBEC......... Single-Board Engine Controller [*Automotive engineering*]
SBED........ Serial BIT [*Binary Digit*] Error Detector
SBEE .... Bachelor of Science in Electrical Engineering
SBEED ...... Storage Battery Electric Energy Demonstration
SBEG......... Manaus/Eduardo Gomes [*Brazil*] [*ICAO location identifier*] (ICLI)
SBEI .... SBE, Inc. [*NASDAQ symbol*] (NQ)
SBEI .... Starch-Branching Enzyme I [*Plant genetics*]
SBEK........ Jacare-Acanga [*Brazil*] [*ICAO location identifier*] (ICLI)
S Bell........ Bell's House of Lords Scotch Appeal Cases [*1842-50*] [*A publication*] (DLA)
SBEN......... Campos/Plataforma SS-17 [*Brazil*] [*ICAO location identifier*] (ICLI)
SBER .... Eirunepe [*Brazil*] [*ICAO location identifier*] (ICLI)
SBER .... Self-Balancing Electronics Recorder
Sber........... Sitzungsbericht [*Transaction*] [*German*] (BJA)
SBER .... Subbit Error Rate
Sber Bayer Akad Wiss ... Sitzungsberichte. Bayerische Akademie der Wissenschaften zu Muenchen [*A publication*]
Sber Dt Akad Landwwiss Berl ... Sitzungsberichte. Deutsche Akademie der Landwirtschaftswissenschaften zu Berlin [*A publication*]
Sber Ges Morph Physiol Muench ... Sitzungsberichte. Gesellschaft fuer Morphologie und Physiologie in Muenchen [*A publication*]
Sber Ges Naturf Freunde Berl ... Sitzungsberichte. Gesellschaft Naturforschender Freunde zu Berlin [*A publication*]
SBES .... S-Band Exciter System [*Also, SBE*]
SBES .... Sao Pedro Da Aldeia [*Brazil*] [*ICAO location identifier*] (ICLI)
SBET .... Pedregulho/Estreito [*Brazil*] [*ICAO location identifier*] (ICLI)
SBET .... Screen-Based Electronic Typewriter (WDMC)
SBET .... Society of Biomedical Equipment Technicians (EA)
SBETC....... Small Business Export Trade Corp.
SBEU........ Singapore Bank Employees' Union
SBEUA...... Small Business and Economic Utilization Advisor [*Army*] (AABC)
SBF .... Salomon Brothers Fund [*NYSE symbol*] (SPSG)
SBF .... Science Books and Films [*A publication*]
SBF .... Scientific Balloon Facility
SBF .... Serologic Blocking Factor [*Cardiology*]
SBF .... Short Backfire [*Antenna*]
SBF .... Silicone Brake Fluid (MCD)
SBF .... Single Barrier Failure (SSD)
SBF .... Single Black Female [*Classified advertising*] (CDAI)
SBF .... Societe Burundaise de Financement [*Development bank*] (EY)
SBF .... Society of Business Folk [*Brown Deer, WI*] (EA)
SBF .... Southern Baptist Foundation (EA)
SBF .... Soy Base Formula [*Nutrition*]
SBF .... Splanchnic Blood Flow [*Physiology*]
SBF .... Standby Flying [*British military*] (DMA)
SBF .... Stonebridge, Inc. [*Toronto Stock Exchange symbol*]
SBF .... Surface Burst Fuze
SBFA .... Set Back Front Axle [*Automotive engineering*]
SBFA .... Small Business Foundation of America [*Boston, MA*] (EA)
SBFAW ..... Sitzungsberichte. Finnische Akademie der Wissenschaften [*A publication*]
SBFC .... Franca [*Brazil*] [*ICAO location identifier*] (ICLI)
SBFC .... Sawyer Brown Fan Club (EA)
SBFC .... Standby for Further Clearance [*Aviation*] (FAAC)
SBFI.......... Foz Do Iguacu/Cataratas [*Brazil*] [*ICAO location identifier*] (ICLI)
SBFI.......... Specialised Banking Furniture International [*Manufacturer*] [*British*]
SBFL......... Florianopolis/Hercilioluz [*Brazil*] [*ICAO location identifier*] (ICLI)
SBFLA....... Studii Biblici Franciscani. Liber Annuus [*A publication*] (BJA)
SBFM .... Silver-Band Frequency Modulation (IEEE)
SBFN .... Fernando De Noronha [*Brazil*] [*ICAO location identifier*] (ICLI)
SBFS......... Southstate Bank for Savings [*NASDAQ symbol*] (NQ)
SBFSDH ... Synopses of the British Fauna. New Series [*A publication*]
SBFT .... Fronteira [*Brazil*] [*ICAO location identifier*] (ICLI)
SBFT .... Small Bowel Follow-Through [*Medicine*] (MAE)
SBFU .... Alpinopolis/Furnas [*Brazil*] [*ICAO location identifier*] (ICLI)
SBFU .... Standby Filter Unit (IEEE)
SBFZ .... Fortaleza/Pinto Martins [*Brazil*] [*ICAO location identifier*] (ICLI)
SBG........... School Board Gazette [*A publication*]
SBG........... Scottish Bus Group Ltd. (DCTA)

SBG........... Selenite Brilliant Green (MAE)
SBG........... Southern Business Group [*Commercial firm*] [*British*]
SBG........... Staatsbibliothek Preuss. Kulturbesitz - Gesamtkat. U. Dok., Berlin, Federal Republic of Germany [*OCLC symbol*] (OCLC)
SBG........... Standard Battery Grade
SBG........... Starburst Galaxy [*Astronomy*]
SBG........... Steinberg, Inc. [*Toronto Stock Exchange symbol*]
SBG........... Strategic Bomber Group
SBG........... Universite de Sherbrooke, Publications Officielles [*UTLAS symbol*]
SBGA........ Brasilia/Gama [*Brazil*] [*ICAO location identifier*] (ICLI)
SBGA........ Serum Beta-Glucuronidase Activity [*Serology*]
SBGDA...... Spisanie na Bulgarskoto Geologichesko Druzhestvo [*A publication*]
SBGGAKOPR ... Sitzungsberichte. Gesellschaft fuer Geschichte und Altertumskunde der Ostseeprovinzen Russlands [*A publication*]
SBGGAKR ... Sitzungsberichte. Gesellschaft fuer Geschichte und Altertumskunde der Ostseeprovinzen Russlands [*A publication*]
SBGI......... Serikat Buruh Gelas Indonesia [*Glass Workers' Union of Indonesia*]
SBGKAT ... Godishnik na Sofiiskiya Universitet. Biologicheski Fakultet. Kniga 2. Botanika, Mikrobiologiya, Fiziologiya, i Biokhimiya Rasteniyata [*A publication*]
SBGL........ Rio De Janeiro/Internacional Galeao [*Brazil*] [*ICAO location identifier*] (ICLI)
SBGM....... Guajara-Mirim [*Brazil*] [*ICAO location identifier*] (ICLI)
SBGMA..... Sitzungsberichte. Gesellschaft zur Befoerderung der Gesamten Naturwissenschaften zu Marburg [*A publication*]
SBGMS ..... Shipbuilders', Boiler, and Gasometer Makers' Society [*A union*] [*British*]
SBGO .... Goiania/Santa Genoveva [*Brazil*] [*ICAO location identifier*] (ICLI)
SBGP .... Campos/Plataforma PNA-1 [*Brazil*] [*ICAO location identifier*] (ICLI)
SBGP .... Serikat Buruh Gula Proklamasi [*Sugar Workers' Union*] [*Indonesia*]
SBGP .... Strategic Bomber Group
SBGR......... Sao Paulo/Internacional Guarulhos [*Brazil*] [*ICAO location identifier*] (ICLI)
SBGS........ Ponta Grossa [*Brazil*] [*ICAO location identifier*] (ICLI)
SBGSN ..... Serikat Buruh Garam dan Soda Negeri [*Salt Workers' Association*] [*Indonesia*]
SBGT........ Standby Gas Treatment [*Nuclear energy*] (GFGA)
SBGTS....... Standby Gas Treatment System [*Nuclear energy*] (NRCH)
SBGW....... Guaratingueta [*Brazil*] [*ICAO location identifier*] (ICLI)
SBH .... St. Barthelemy [*Leeward Islands*] [*Airport symbol*] (OAG)
SBH .... Sea Blue Histiocytosis [*Medicine*]
SBH .... Sequencing by Hybridization [*Genetics*]
SBH .... SmithKline Beecham Ltd. ADS [*NYSE symbol*] (SPSG)
SBH .... Sodium Borohydride [*Inorganic chemistry*]
SBH .... Southern Blot Hybridization [*Biochemistry*]
SBH .... State Board of Health (MAE)
SBH .... State University of New York, Health Sciences Library, Buffalo, NY [*OCLC symbol*] (OCLC)
SBH .... Strip-Buried Heterostructure [*Telecommunications*] (TEL)
SBH .... Sumerisch-Babylonische Hymnen [*A publication*] (BJA)
SBH .... Supermassive Black Hole [*Cosmology*]
SBH .... Switch Busy Hour [*Telecommunications*] (IEEE)
SBHAD7 ... Social Biology and Human Affairs [*A publication*]
SBHAW .... Sitzungsberichte. Heidelberg Akademie der Wissenschaft [*A publication*]
SBHC .... Society of the Bible in the Hands of Its Creators (EA)
SBHC .... Speed Brake Hand Control (NASA)
SBHC .... Studies in Browning and His Circle [*A publication*]
S B Heidelberg ... Sitzungsberichte. Heidelberg Akademie der Wissenschaften. Philosophisch-Historische Klasse [*A publication*]
SBHEU ..... Singapore Business Houses Employees' Union
SBHRAL... Biometrie Humaine [*A publication*]
SBHRG ..... Space-Based Hypervelocity Rail Gun [*Military*] (SDI)
SBHRT...... Serikat Buruh Hotel, Rumah-Makan dan Toko [*Hotel, Restaurant and Shops' Workers' Union*] [*Indonesia*]
SBHT........ Altamira [*Brazil*] [*ICAO location identifier*] (ICLI)
SBHT........ Studies in Burke and His Time [*A publication*]
SBI............ Columbia Bible College, Columbia, SC [*OCLC symbol*] (OCLC)
SBI............ Sabine Pass, TX [*Location identifier*] [*FAA*] (FAAL)
SBI............ Santa Barbara Island (MUGU)
SBI............ Satellite-Borne Instrumentation (SAA)
SBI............ Scientific Bureau of Investigation [*In radio series "Armstrong of the SBI"*]
SBI............ Serikat Buruh Industri [*Industrial Workers' Union*] [*Indonesia*]
SB-I........... Service de Bibliographie sur l'Informatique [*Paris Gestion Informatique*] [*France*] [*Information service or system*] (CRD)
SBI............ Shared Bibliographic Input
SBI............ Shares of Beneficial Interest [*Stock exchange term*]
SBI............ Shriners Burn Institute
SBI............ Significant Business Issue (MCD)

SBI	Single Byte Interleaved
SBI	Small Business Institute [*Small Business Administration*]
SBI	Soil Brightness Index
SBI	Somerville Belkin Industries Ltd. [*Toronto Stock Exchange symbol*]
SBI	Soviet Bureau of Information
SBI	Soybean (Trypsin) Inhibitor [*Biochemistry*]
SBI	Space-Based Interceptor [*Military*] (SDI)
SBI	Special Background Investigation (NVT)
SBI	State Bank of India (PDAA)
SBI	Steel Boiler Institute [*Defunct*]
SBI	Sun Belt Institute (EA)
SBI	Synchronous Bus Interface [*Data processing*] (HGAA)
SBI	Synfuels Bibliography and Index [*A publication*]
SBIA	Small Business Innovation Development Act [*1982*]
SBIBD	Symmetrical Balanced Incomplete Block Designs (MCD)
SBIC	Small Business Investment Company [*Generic term*]
SBICo	Small Business Investment Company [*Generic term*]
SBIE	Shared Bibliographic Input Experiment [*Special Libraries Association*]
SBIG	[*The*] Seibels Bruce Group, Inc. [*NASDAQ symbol*] (NQ)
SBIL	Ilheus [*Brazil*] [*ICAO location identifier*] (ICLI)
SBILS	Scanning Beam Instrument Landing System (KSC)
SBIN	Fort Battleford National Historic Park, Parks Canada [*Parc Historique National Fort Battleford, Parcs Canada*] Battleford, Saskatchewan [*Library symbol*] [*National Library of Canada*] (NLC)
Sb Inst Fiz Akad Nauk Gruz SSR	Sbornik. Ordena Trudovogo Krasnogo Znameni Institut Fiziki. Akademiya Nauk Gruzinskoj SSR [*A publication*]
SBIO	Synbiotics Corp. [*NASDAQ symbol*] (NQ)
SBIP	Ipatinga/Usiminas [*Brazil*] [*ICAO location identifier*] (ICLI)
SBIR	Small Business Innovation Research Program [*Small Business Administration*]
SBIR	Storage Bus in Register
SBIS	Sustaining Base Information Service [*or System*] [*Army*] (RDA)
SBIT	Itumbiara/Hidroelectrica [*Brazil*] [*ICAO location identifier*] (ICLI)
SBIZ	Hawkeye Entertainment, Inc. [*NASDAQ symbol*] (NQ)
SBIZ	Imperatriz [*Brazil*] [*ICAO location identifier*] (ICLI)
SBJ	Journal. State Bar of California [*A publication*] (DLA)
SBJ	Saul Bellow Journal [*A publication*]
SBJ	Savings Bank Journal [*A publication*]
SBJ	Schottky Barrier Junction [*Electronics*]
SBJ	Solberg, NJ [*Location identifier*] [*FAA*] (FAAL)
SBJ	Subjunctive [*Grammar*] (WGA)
SBJC	Belem/Julio Cesar [*Brazil*] [*ICAO location identifier*] (ICLI)
SBJF	Juiz De Fora/Francisco De Assis [*Brazil*] [*ICAO location identifier*] (ICLI)
SBJP	Joao Pessoa/Presidente Castro Pinto [*Brazil*] [*ICAO location identifier*] (ICLI)
SBJR	Rio De Janeiro/Jacarepagua [*Brazil*] [*ICAO location identifier*] (ICLI)
SBJV	Joinville [*Brazil*] [*ICAO location identifier*] (ICLI)
SBK	St. Brieuc [*France*] [*Airport symbol*] (OAG)
SBK	Signet Banking Corp. [*NYSE symbol*] (SPSG)
SBK	Single-Beam Klystron (MSA)
SBK	Society for Behavioral Kinesiology
SBK	Softwood Bleached Kraft [*Pulp and paper technology*]
SBK	South Brooklyn Railway Co. [*AAR code*]
sbk	Subangular Blocky Soil [*Agriculture*]
SBK	System Builder Kit [*Digital Research, Inc.*] [*Data processing*] (PCM)
SBK	Universite de Sherbrooke, Bibliotheque [*UTLAS symbol*]
SBKAW	Sitzungsberichte. Kaiserliche Akademie der Wissenschaften in Wien [*A publication*]
SBKAWW	Sitzungsberichte. Kaiserliche Akademie der Wissenschaften in Wien [*A publication*]
SBKEW	Space-Based Kinetic Energy Weapon [*Military*] (MCD)
SBKG	Campina Grande/Joao Suassuna [*Brazil*] [*ICAO location identifier*] (ICLI)
SBKKV	Space-Based Kinetic Kill Vehicle [*Military*]
SBKP	Sao Paulo (Campinas)/Viracopos [*Brazil*] [*ICAO location identifier*] (ICLI)
SBKS	Suburban Bankshares, Inc. [*Lake Worth, FL*] [*NASDAQ symbol*] (NQ)
SBKU	Cucui [*Brazil*] [*ICAO location identifier*] (ICLI)
s-bl---	Brazil [*MARC geographic area code*] [*Library of Congress*] (LCCP)
SBL	Santa Ana [*Bolivia*] [*Airport symbol*] [*Obsolete*] (OAG)
SBL	Schildersblad. Algemeen Vakblad voor het Schildersbedrijf en Afwerkingsbedrijf [*A publication*]
SBL	Sealed Beam Lamp
SBL	Serrated Black Letters [*Tire design*] [*Automotive engineering*]
SBL	Society of Biblical Literature (EA)
SBL	Soybean Lecithin [*Biochemistry*]
SBL	Space-Based LASER
SBL	Sporadic Burkitt's Lymphoma [*Medicine*]
SBL	Staphylococcal Bacteriophage Lysate

SBL	State University of New York at Buffalo, Law Library, Buffalo, NY [*OCLC symbol*] (OCLC)
SBL	Strong Black Liquor [*Pulp and paper technology*]
SBL	Studies in Black Literature [*A publication*]
SBL	Styrene-Butadiene Latexes [*Organic chemistry*]
SBL	Surface Boundary Layer (MCD)
SBL	Symbol Technologies, Inc. [*NYSE symbol*] (SPSG)
SBLA	Shore-Based Landing Aids (MCD)
SBLA	Small Business Loans Act [*Canada*]
SBLB	Labrea [*Brazil*] [*ICAO location identifier*] (ICLI)
SBLC	Shallow Bed Liquid Chromatography
SBLC	Small Business Legislative Council [*Washington, DC*] (EA)
SBLC	Standby Liquid Control [*Nuclear energy*] (NRCH)
SBLE	Society of Biblical Literature and Exegesis [*Later, SBL*] (EA)
SB (Leipzig)	Sitzungsberichte. Saechsische Akademie der Wissenschaften (Leipzig) [*A publication*]
SBLI	Savings Bank Life Insurance
SBLI	Staff Builders, Inc. [*NASDAQ symbol*] (NQ)
SBLJ	Lajes [*Brazil*] [*ICAO location identifier*] (ICLI)
SBLMC	Styrene Butadiene Latex Manufacturers Council (EA)
SBLN	Lins [*Brazil*] [*ICAO location identifier*] (ICLI)
SBLO	Londrina [*Brazil*] [*ICAO location identifier*] (ICLI)
SBLO	Strong Black Liquor Oxidation [*Pulp and paper technology*]
SBLOCA	Small-Break Loss of Coolant Accident [*Nuclear energy*] (NRCH)
SBLP	Bom Jesus Da Lapa [*Brazil*] [*ICAO location identifier*] (ICLI)
SBLP	Simplified Bank Loan Participation Plan [*Small Business Administration*]
SBLS	Lagoa Santa [*Brazil*] [*ICAO location identifier*] (ICLI)
SBLS	Spaceborne LASER Ranging
SBLSA	Small Business and Labor Surplus Advisor (AABC)
SBL Sem Pap	Society of Biblical Literature. Seminar Papers [*A publication*]
SBM	College of Charleston, Charleston, SC [*OCLC symbol*] (OCLC)
SBM	St. Louis, Brownsville & Mexico [*AAR code*]
SBM	SBM Industries [*Formerly, Speed-O-Print Business Machines Corp.*] [*AMEX symbol*] (SPSG)
SBM	School in Basic Management [*LIMRA*]
SBM	Science-by-Mail (EA)
SBM	Sheboygan [*Wisconsin*] [*Airport symbol*] (OAG)
SBM	Sheboygan, WI [*Location identifier*] [*FAA*] (FAAL)
SBM	Single Black Male [*Classified advertising*]
SBM	Single-Buoy Mooring [*Oil tanker*]
SBM	Single-Point Mooring Buoy [*Navy*]
SBM	Societe des Bains de Mer [*Monte Carlo*]
SBM	Society of Behavioral Medicine (EA)
SBM	Stuttgarter Biblische Monographien [*Stuttgart*] [*A publication*]
SBM	Submerge [*or Submersible*] (KSC)
SBM	Submit (AABC)
SBM	Super Bit Mapping [*Compact-disc technology*] (PS)
SBM	System Balance Measure (BUR)
SBMA	Maraba [*Brazil*] [*ICAO location identifier*] (ICLI)
SBMA	Service Business Marketing Association (EA)
SBMA	SINS [*Ship Inertial Navigational System*] Bedplate Mirror Assembly
SBMA	Spinal and Bulbar Muscular Atrophy [*Medicine*]
SBMA	Steel Bar Mills Association [*Later, SMA*] (EA)
SBMD	Stochastic Boundary Molecular Dynamics [*Force energy simulation method*]
SBMDL	Submodel
SBME	Macae [*Brazil*] [*ICAO location identifier*] (ICLI)
SBME	Society of Business Magazine Editors [*Later, ASBPE*]
SBMEA	Space Biology and Medicine [*English Translation*] [*A publication*]
SBMG	Maringa [*Brazil*] [*ICAO location identifier*] (ICLI)
SBMI	School Bus Manufacturers Institute (EA)
SBM Ind	SBM Industries [*Associated Press abbreviation*] (APAG)
SBMK	Montes Claros [*Brazil*] [*ICAO location identifier*] (ICLI)
SBML	Marilia [*Brazil*] [*ICAO location identifier*] (ICLI)
SBML	Smooth Bore Muzzle Loading [*British military*] (DMA)
SBMN	Manaus/Ponta Pelada [*Brazil*] [*ICAO location identifier*] (ICLI)
SBMO	Maceio/Palmares [*Brazil*] [*ICAO location identifier*] (ICLI)
SBMPL	Simultaneous Binaural Midplane Localization [*Audiometry*]
SBMQ	Macapa/Internacional [*Brazil*] [*ICAO location identifier*] (ICLI)
SBMR	Manoel Ribas [*Brazil*] [*ICAO location identifier*] (ICLI)
SBMS	Mocoro/Dix-Sept Rosado [*Brazil*] [*ICAO location identifier*] (ICLI)
SBMSI	Serikat Buruh Minjak Shell Indonesia [*Union of Oil Workers for Shell of Indonesia*]
SBMSS	Shore-Based Message Service System (DNAB)
SBMSTE	Space and Ballistic Missile System Training Equipment (SAA)
SBMT	Sao Paulo/Marte [*Brazil*] [*ICAO location identifier*] (ICLI)
SBMU	Manaus [*Brazil*] [*ICAO location identifier*] (ICLI)
SBMV	Southern Bean Mosaic Virus
SBMV-B	Southern Bean Mosaic Virus - Strain B
SBMV-C	Southern Bean Mosaic Virus - Cowpea Strain
SBMW	Serikat Buruh Maclaine, Watson [*Maclaine Watson Co. Workers' Union*] [*Indones ia*]
SBMY	Manicore [*Brazil*] [*ICAO location identifier*] (ICLI)
SBMZ	Porto De Moz [*Brazil*] [*ICAO location identifier*] (ICLI)

SBN .... Buffalo Narrows Public Library, Saskatchewan [*Library symbol*] [*National Library of Canada*] (NLC)
SBN .... Scrip. Leader in World Pharmaceutical News [*A publication*]
SBN .... Sheridan Broadcasting Network
SBN .... Sino Business Machine [*Vancouver Stock Exchange symbol*]
SBN .... Small Business Network [*Baltimore, MD*] (EA)
SBN .... South Bend [*Indiana*] [*Airport symbol*] (OAG)
SBN .... Spaceborne (KSC)
SBN .... Standard Book Number
SBN .... Strontium-Barium-Niobidium [*Inorganic chemistry*]
SBN .... Subic Bay News [*A publication*] (DNAB)
SBN .... Suburban Airlines [*Red Bank, NJ*] [*FAA designator*] (FAAC)
SBN .... Sunbelt Nursery Group, Inc. [*AMEX symbol*] (SPSG)
SBN$_2$ .... Single Breath Nitrogen [*Test*] [*Medicine*]
SBND .... Southbound (FAAC)
SBNF .... Navegantes [*Brazil*] [*ICAO location identifier*] (ICLI)
SBNH .... Society for the Bibliography of Natural History (EA)
SBNL .... Submarine Base, New London [*Connecticut*] [*Navy*]
SBNM .... Santo Angelo [*Brazil*] [*ICAO location identifier*] (ICLI)
SBNO .... Senior British Naval Officer
SBNOWA ... Senior British Naval Officer, Western Atlantic
SBNPB .... Space-Based Neutral Particle Beam [*Military*] (SDI)
SBNS .... Society of British Neurological Surgeons
SBNT .... Natal/Augusto Severo [*Brazil*] [*ICAO location identifier*] (ICLI)
SBNT .... Single-Breath Nitrogen Test [*Physiology*]
s-bo--- .... Bolivia [*MARC geographic area code*] [*Library of Congress*] (LCCP)
SBO .... Salina [*Utah*] [*Airport symbol*] (OAG)
SBO .... Showboat, Inc. [*NYSE symbol*] (SPSG)
SBO .... Silver Box Resources [*Vancouver Stock Exchange symbol*]
SBO .... Small Bowel Obstruction [*Medicine*] (MAE)
SBO .... Small Business Office
SBO .... Small Business Ombudsman [*Federal government*] (GFGA)
SBO .... Soybean Oil
SBO .... Specific Behavioral Objectives [*Aviation*]
SBO .... Standing Balance: Eyes Open [*Test*] [*Occupational therapy*]
SBO .... Studia Biblica et Orientalia [*Rome*] [*A publication*] (BJA)
SBO .... Swainsboro, GA [*Location identifier*] [*FAA*] (FAAL)
SBOA .... Specialty Bakery Owners of America (EA)
SBOAA ...... Soobshcheniya Byurakanskoi Observatorii Akademiya Nauk Armyanskoi SSR [*A publication*]
SbOAW ..... Sitzungsberichte. Oesterreichische Akademie der Wissenschaften in Wien. Philosophisch-Historische Klasse [*A publication*]
SBOI .... Oiapoque [*Brazil*] [*ICAO location identifier*] (ICLI)
SBol .... Strenna Bolognese [*A publication*]
SBOLS ..... Shadow Box Optical Landing System
SBOM .... Soybean Oil Meal
SBON .... Siboney Corp. [*NASDAQ symbol*] (NQ)
SBOOM .... Sonic Boom [*Computer program*] [*NASA*]
SBOS .... Boston Bancorp [*Formerly, South Boston Savings Bank*] [*NASDAQ symbol*] (NQ)
SBOS .... Silicon-Borne Oxygen System (SAA)
SBOSI .... Serikat Buruh Obat Seluruh Indonesia [*All Indonesian Medicinal Factory Workers' Union*]
SBOST ...... Slavonic Benevolent Order of the State of Texas [*Temple, TX*] (EA)
SBOT .... Sacred Books of the Old Testament [*The "Rainbow Bible"*] [*A publication*] (BJA)
SBOU .... Ourinhos [*Brazil*] [*ICAO location identifier*] (ICLI)
SBP .... Etudes et Expansion [*A publication*]
SBP .... San Luis Obispo [*California*] [*Airport symbol*] (OAG)
SBP .... Scleral Buckling Procedure [*Medicine*] (MAE)
SBP .... Sec-Butyl Percarbonate [*Organic chemistry*]
SBP .... Serikat Buruh Pegadaian [*Pawnshop Workers' Union*] [*Indonesia*]
SBP .... Serikat Buruh Penerbangan [*Airways' Unions*] [*Indonesia*]
SBP .... Service Benefit Plan [*Military*] (AABC)
SBP .... Shop Procedure Bulletin [*A publication*] (EAAP)
SBP .... Shore-Based Prototype [*Nuclear energy*] (OA)
SBP .... Societe Beneluxienne de Phlebologie [*Benelux Phlebology Society - BPS*]
SBP .... Society for Behaviorial Pediatrics (EA)
SBP .... Society of Biological Psychiatry (EA)
SBP .... Sonic Boom Panel [*Aerospace*] (MCD)
SBP .... Sosyalist Birlik Partisi [*Socialist Unity Party*] [*Turkey*] [*Political party*] (EY)
SBP .... Soziale Buergerpartei [*Social Citizen's Party*] [*Germany*] [*Political party*] (PPW)
SBP .... Spaceborne Programmer
SBP .... Special Block Purchase
SBP .... Special Businessowners Policy [*Insurance*]
SBP .... Spontaneous Bacterial Peritonitis [*Medicine*]
SBP .... Squalene-Binding Protein [*Biochemistry*]
SBP .... Standard Brands Paint Co. [*NYSE symbol*] (SPSG)
SBP .... Standard Businessowners Policy [*Insurance*]
SBP .... Steroid-Binding Plasma Protein
SBP .... Subic Bay [*Philippines*] [*Seismograph station code, US Geological Survey*] [*Closed*] (SEIS)
SBP .... Sulfate-Binding Protein [*Biochemistry*]

SBP .... Sumerian and Babylonian Psalms [*A publication*] (BJA)
SBP .... Survivor Benefit Plan [*For survivors of retired military personnel*]
SBP .... Systemic Blood Pressure [*Medicine*] (MAE)
SBP .... Systolic Blood Pressure [*Medicine*]
SBPA .... Porto Alegre/Salgado Filho [*Brazil*] [*ICAO location identifier*] (ICLI)
SBPA .... Southern Baptist Press Association (EA)
SBPAW .... Sitzungsberichte. Kaiserliche Preussische Akademie der Wissenschaften [*Berlin*] [*A publication*]
SBPAWB... Sitzungsberichte. Kaiserliche Preussische Akademie der Wissenschaften (Berlin) [*A publication*]
SBPB .... Parnaiba [*Brazil*] [*ICAO location identifier*] (ICLI)
SBPB .... Space-Based Particle Beam [*Military*] (SDI)
SBPC .... Pocos De Caldas [*Brazil*] [*ICAO location identifier*] (ICLI)
SBPD .... Society of Business Publication Designers [*Later, SPD*] (EA)
SBPF .... Passo Fundo/Lauro Kurtz [*Brazil*] [*ICAO location identifier*] (ICLI)
SBPG .... Paranagua [*Brazil*] [*ICAO location identifier*] (ICLI)
SBPG .... Serikat Buruh Perusahaan Gula [*Sugar Workers' Union*] [*Indonesia*]
SBPH .... Porto Velho [*Brazil*] [*ICAO location identifier*] (ICLI)
SBPH .... Single Burst Probability of Hit [*Military*] (AABC)
SBPH .... Submarine Base, Pearl Harbor [*Navy*] (DNAB)
SBPI .... Petropolis/Pico do Couto [*Brazil*] [*ICAO location identifier*] (ICLI)
SBPI .... Serikat Buruh Pelabuhan Indonesia [*Dockworkers' Union of Indonesia*]
SBPI .... Serikat Buruh Pendjahit Indonesia [*Tailors' Union of Indonesia*]
SBPI .... Southern Baptist Periodical Index [*A publication*]
SBPK .... Pelotas [*Brazil*] [*ICAO location identifier*] (ICLI)
SBPKB...... Serikat Buruh Persuahaan Kaju and Bangunan [*Building, Road and Irrigation Workers' Union*] [*Indonesia*]
SBPL .... Petrolina [*Brazil*] [*ICAO location identifier*] (ICLI)
SBPN .... Porto Nacional [*Brazil*] [*ICAO location identifier*] (ICLI)
SBPP .... Ponta Pora/Internacional [*ICAO location identifier*] (ICLI)
SBPP .... Serikat Buruh Pelabuhan dan Pelajaran [*Dockworkers' Union*] [*Indonesia*]
SBPPK...... Serikat Buruh Pendidikan, Pengadjaran dan Kebudjaan [*Department of Education Workers' Union*] [*Indonesia*]
SBPR .... Piracaba [*Brazil*] [*ICAO location identifier*] (ICLI)
SBPR .... Society for Back Pain Research [*British*]
SBPR Bol... SBPR Boletin [*A publication*]
SBPS .... Savings Bank of Puget Sound [*NASDAQ symbol*] (NQ)
SBPT .... Serikat Buruh Perhubungan dan Transport [*Communications and Transportation Workers' Union*] [*Indonesia*]
SBPT .... Serikat Buruh Pertambangan Timah [*Tin Mine Labor Union*] [*Indonesia*]
SBPT .... Societe Beninoise pour la Promotion du Tourisme (EY)
SBPU .... Serikat Buruh Pekerdjaan Umum [*Public Workers' Ministry Union*] [*Indonesia*]
SBPV .... Porto Velho [*Brazil*] [*ICAO location identifier*] (ICLI)
SBPW .... Pindamonhangaba/Visaba [*Brazil*] [*ICAO location identifier*] (ICLI)
SBPW .... Special Board for Public Works [*New Deal*]
SBQ .... Grenada, MS [*Location identifier*] [*FAA*] (FAAL)
SBQ .... Serikat Buruh Qantas [*Qantas Labor Union*] [*Indonesia*]
SBQV......... Vitoria Da Conquista [*Brazil*] [*ICAO location identifier*] (ICLI)
SBR .... Saber Aviation, Inc. [*Charlotte, NC*] [*FAA designator*] (FAAC)
SBR .... Sabine Royalty Trust [*NYSE symbol*] (SPSG)
SBR .... Sale by Reference
SBR .... School Book Review [*A publication*]
SBR .... Scripps-Booth Register [*An association*] (EA)
SBR .... Seat Bucket Read (NG)
SBR .... Segment Base Register (BUR)
SBR .... Sequencing Batch Reactor [*Chemical engineering*]
SBR .... Service Billing Record
SBR .... Signal to Background Ratio [*Instrumentation*]
SBR .... Small Box-Respirator [*British military*] (DMA)
SBR .... Small Business Report [*A publication*]
SBR .... Society of Bead Researchers (EA)
SBR .... Society for Biological Rhythm
SBR .... Soviet Breeder Reactor
SBR .... Space-Based RADAR (MCD)
SBR .... Standard Busy Rate (NATG)
SBR .... Starburst Energy [*Vancouver Stock Exchange symbol*]
SBR .... Stimulus-Bound Repetition [*Medicine*]
SBR .... Storage Buffer Register
SBR .... Strand Burning Rate (MCD)
SBR .... Strict Bed Rest [*Medicine*]
SBR .... Styrene-Butadiene Rubber [*Also, GR-S*] [*Synthetic rubber*]
SBR .... Supplemental Budget Request
SBRB .... Rio Branco/Presidente Medici [*Brazil*] [*ICAO location identifier*] (ICLI)
SBRC .... Santa Barbara Research Center [*Hughes Aircraft Co.*]
SBRC .... Southwest Border Regional Commission [*Department of Commerce*]
SBRE .... Recife [*Brazil*] [*ICAO location identifier*] (ICLI)
SBRF .... Recife/Guararapes [*Brazil*] [*ICAO location identifier*] (ICLI)

SBRG......... Seeburg Corp. [*NASDAQ symbol*]   (NQ)
SBRI .... Serikat Buruh Rokok Indonesia [*Cigarette Workers' Union of Indonesia*]
SBRI .... Southwest Biomedical Research Institute [*Arizona State University*] [*Research center*]   (RCD)
SBRI .... Space Biomedical Research Institute [*Houston, TX*] [*NASA*]
SBRIMCD ... Sun Bay Recovery - International Missing Children's Division   (EA)
SBRJ......... Rio De Janeiro/Santos Dumont [*Brazil*] [*ICAO location identifier*]   (ICLI)
SB-RK....... Bomber [*Russian aircraft symbol*]
SBRP .... Ribeirao Preto/Leite Lopes [*Brazil*] [*ICAO location identifier*]   (ICLI)
SBRP .... Sonic Boom Research Program
SBRP .... Submarine Reportback Processor Unit   (DWSG)
SBRQ......... Sao Roque [*Brazil*] [*ICAO location identifier*]   (ICLI)
SBRRI .... Serikat Buruh Radio Republik Indonesia [*Broadcasting Workers' Association of Indonesia*]
SBRS .... Resende [*Brazil*] [*ICAO location identifier*]   (ICLI)
SBRS .... Social Behavior Rating Scale
SBRU......... Subaru of America, Inc. [*NASDAQ symbol*]   (NQ)
SBRV .... Small Ballistic Reentry Vehicle
SBS .... Salem Corp. [*AMEX symbol*]   (SPSG)
SBS .... Samuel Butler Society [*Defunct*]   (EA)
SBS .... Satellite Business Systems [*McLean, VA*] [*Telecommunications*]   (MCD)
SBS .... Scarborough Board of Education [*UTLAS symbol*]
SBS .... Semiconductor Bilateral Switch   (MSA)
SBS .... Sensor Based System   (BUR)
SBS .... Serially Balanced Sequence [*Statistics*]
SBS .... Short Beam Shear
SBS .... Sick Building Syndrome [*Medicine*]
SBS .... Sidi-Bou-Said [*Tunisia*] [*Seismograph station code, US Geological Survey*]   (SEIS)
SBS .... Silicon Bilateral Switch
SBS .... Single-Business Service
SBS .... Sisters of the Blessed Sacrament [*Roman Catholic religious order*]
SBS .... Small Business Sourcebook [*A publication*]
SBS .... Small Business Specialist [*DoD*]
SBS .... Small Business System   (ADA)
SBS .... Social Behavior Standards
SBS .... Social-Breakdown Syndrome   (MAE)
SBS .... Soeurs de Bon Sauveur [*France*]   (EAIO)
SBS .... Solid Bleached Sulphate [*Fiber for paperboard packaging*]
SBS .... Southern Base Section [*England*]
SBS .... Spaniel Breeders Society   (EA)
SBS .... Spanish Benevolent Society "La Nacional"   (EA)
SBS .... Spanish Broadcasting System
SBS .... Special Block Sale
SBS .... Special Boat Section [*British military*]   (DMA)
SBS .... Special Boat Squadron [*British commando unit*]
SBS .... Standby Status   (AAG)
SBS .... Steamboat Springs [*Colorado*] [*Airport symbol*]   (OAG)
SBS .... Steel Building System
SBS .... Stimulated Brillouin Scattering
SBS .... Straight Binary Second
SBS .... Strategic Balkan Services [*World War II*]
SBS .... Strategic Bombing Survey
SBS .... Strategic Business Segment
SBS .... Stuttgarter Bibelstudien [*A publication*]
SBS .... Stuttgarter Bibelstudien. Katholisches Bibelwerk [*Stuttgart*] [*A publication*]   (BJA)
SBS .... Styrene-Butadiene-Styrene [*Copolymer*]
SBS .... Subscript Character [*Data processing*]
SBS .... Superburn Systems Ltd. [*Vancouver Stock Exchange symbol*]
SBS .... Survey of Basic Skills [*Achievement test*]
SBS .... Swedish Behavioural Sciences [*Database*] [*National Library for Psychology and Education*] [*Information service or system*]   (CRD)
SBS .... Sweep Back Station   (MCD)
SBS .... Swiss Benevolent Society of New York   (EA)
SBS .... System Breakdown Structure [*Military*]   (AFIT)
SBSA .... Sao Carlos/Francisco Pereira Lopez [*Brazil*] [*ICAO location identifier*]   (ICLI)
SBSA .... Society of Basque Studies in America   (EA)
SBSA .... State Bank of South Australia
SBSanE ...... Bachelor of Science in Sanitary Engineering
SBSAW ..... Sitzungsberichte. Saechsische Akademie der Wissenschaften (Leipzig). Philologisch-Historische Klasse [*A publication*]
SBSAWL... Sitzungsberichte. Saechsische Akademie der Wissenschaften (Leipzig). Philologisch-Historische Klasse [*A publication*]
SBSB .... Small Business Service Bureau [*Worcester, MA*]   (EA)
SBSBA...... Scottish Blackface Sheep Breeders Association
SBSBDV.... Symposium. British Society for Developmental Biology [*A publication*]
SBSBS ...... Smith Benevolent Sick and Burial Society [*British*]
SBSC .... Rio De Janeiro/Santa Cruz [*Brazil*] [*ICAO location identifier*]   (ICLI)
SBSC .... Saint Bernardine of Siena College [*New York*]
SBSC .... Saint Bernard's Seminary and College [*New York*]

SBSC .... Separate Bias, Single Control
SBSCA...... Small Business Support Center Association [*Houston, TX*]   (EA)
SBSD .... Subside   (FAAC)
SB/SDB ..... Small Business / Small Disadvantaged Business   (SSD)
SBSG .... Small Business Systems Group [*Westford, MA*] [*Telecommunications*]   (TSSD)
SBSI.......... Seabrook Sea Island Cotton
SBSI.......... Serikat Buruh Seluruh Indonesia [*All Indonesian Laborers' Union*]
SBSI.......... Small Business Start-Up Index [*A publication*]
SBSJ .... Sao Jose Dos Campos [*Brazil*] [*ICAO location identifier*]   (ICLI)
SBSK .... Samodzielna Brygada Strzelcow Karpackich [*Poland*]
SBSKK...... Serikat Buruh Sepatu Keradjinan Kulit Karet [*Shoe Workers' Union*] [*Indonesia*]
SBSL .... Sao Luis/Marechal Cunha Machado [*Brazil*] [*ICAO location identifier*]   (ICLI)
SBSM .... Santa Maria [*Brazil*] [*ICAO location identifier*]   (ICLI)
SBSM .... Sisterhood of Black Single Mothers   (EA)
SBSN .... Santarem/Internacional [*Brazil*] [*ICAO location identifier*]   (ICLI)
SBSP.......... Sao Paulo/Congonhas [*Brazil*] [*ICAO location identifier*]   (ICLI)
SBSP.......... Single Base Solid Propellant   (MSA)
SB Sqn ...... Special Boat Squadron [*British commando unit*]   (DMA)
SBSR .... Sao Jose Do Rio Preto [*Brazil*] [*ICAO location identifier*]   (ICLI)
SBSS .... Space-Based Space Surveillance   (MCD)
SBSS.......... Spare Band Surveillance System   (MCD)
SBSS .... Standard Base Supply System [*Military*]   (AFIT)
SBST .... Santos [*Brazil*] [*ICAO location identifier*]   (ICLI)
SBStJ......... Serving Brother, Order of St. John of Jerusalem [*British*]
SBSTR...... Substrate [*Electronics*]
SBSUSA.... Sport Balloon Society of the United States of America   (EA)
SBSV .... Salvador/Dois de Julho [*Brazil*] [*ICAO location identifier*]   (ICLI)
SBSY .... Cristalandia/Santa Isabel do Morro [*Brazil*] [*ICAO location identifier*]   (ICLI)
SBT............ Salina Board of Trade   (EA)
SBT............ San Benito [*California*] [*Seismograph station code, US Geological Survey*]   (SEIS)
SBT............ San Bernardino, CA [*Location identifier*] [*FAA*]   (FAAL)
SBT............ Screening Breath Tester [*Drunken driving*]
SBT............ Seabright Resources, Inc. [*Toronto Stock Exchange symbol*]
SBT............ Segregated Ballast Tank [*Shipping construction*]
SBT............ Serikat Buruh Tambang [*Mine Workers' Union*] [*Indonesia*]
SBT............ Serikat Buruh Teknik [*Technicians' Union*] [*Indonesia*]
SBT............ Serikat Buruh Textil [*Textile Workers' Union*] [*Indonesia*]
SBT............ Serum Bactericidal Titer [*Clinical chemistry*]
SBT............ Shakespeare Birthplace Trust   (EA)
SBT............ Shanghai Book Traders
SBT............ Shipboard Test [*Navy*]   (DNAB)
SBT............ Side Buoyancy Tank
SBT............ Simultaneous Baseband Transmission [*of information*]
SBT............ Single-Breath Test   (MAE)
SBT............ Six BIT [*Binary Digit*] Transcode   (CMD)
SBT............ Small Boat
SBT............ Smith Barney Municipal Fund [*AMEX symbol*]   (SPSG)
SBT............ Sodium Bitartrate [*Inorganic chemistry*]
SBT............ Space-Based Tug [*NASA*]
SBT............ Studies in Biblical Theology [*A publication*]
SBT............ Submarine Bathythermograph
SBT............ Submarine Bubble Target [*British military*]   (DMA)
SBT............ Surface Barrier Transistor
SBT............ Svensk Botanisk Tidskrift [*A publication*]
SBT............ System Burning Time
SBTC......... SBT Corp. [*NASDAQ symbol*]   (NQ)
SBTC......... Sino-British Trade Council   (DS)
SBTC......... Speedbrake Thrust Control [*Aerospace*]   (MCD)
SBTC......... Tapuruquara [*Brazil*] [*ICAO location identifier*]   (ICLI)
SBTE .... Teresina [*Brazil*] [*ICAO location identifier*]   (ICLI)
SBTF......... Tefe [*Brazil*] [*ICAO location identifier*]   (ICLI)
SBTG......... Sabotage   (AABC)
SBTI .... Soybean Trypsin Inhibitor
SBTK........ Tarauaca [*Brazil*] [*ICAO location identifier*]   (ICLI)
SBTM........ S-Band Telemetry Modification Kit   (SAA)
SBTOW.... Standby Towship [*Navy*]   (NVT)
SBTP .... Serikat Buruh Teknik dan Pelabuhan [*Technical and Harbour Workers' Union*] [*Indonesia*]
SBTS .... Shore-Based Tracking System
SBTS .... Strategic Bombardment Training Squadron
SBTS .... Stretch Block Template Set   (MCD)
SBTT .... Serikat Buruh Tambang Timah [*Tin Mine Laborers' Union*] [*Indonesia*]
SBTT .... Southern Bell Telephone & Telegraph Co.   (KSC)
SBTT .... Tabatinga/Internacional [*Brazil*] [*ICAO location identifier*]   (ICLI)
SBTU........ Serikat Buruh Teknik Umum [*Indonesia*]
SBTU........ Tucurui [*Brazil*] [*ICAO location identifier*]   (ICLI)
SBU .... Blue Earth, MN [*Location identifier*] [*FAA*]   (FAAL)

SBU .... Mois Economique et Financier [*A publication*]
SBU .... Saint Bonaventure University [*New York*]
SBU .... Scottish Badminton Union   (EAIO)
SBU .... Secondary Building Unit [*Physical chemistry*]
SBU .... Silver Brazing Union   (MSA)
SBU .... Skirt Buildup   (SAA)
SBU .... Small Base Unit [*Telecommunications*]
SBU .... Small Battle Unit [*Navy*]   (NVT)
SBU .... Small Business United [*Later, NSBU*]   (EA)
SBU .... Software Block Update [*Army*]
SBU .... Special Business Unit
SBU .... Springbok [*South Africa*] [*Airport symbol*]   (OAG)
SBU .... Stansbury Island [*Utah*] [*Seismograph station code, US
                Geological Survey*] [*Closed*]   (SEIS)
SBU .... Station Buffer Unit [*Data processing*]
SBU .... Strategic Business Unit
SBU .... Svensk Biblisk Uppslagverk [*A publication*]   (BJA)
SBU .... Symbolae Biblicae Upsalienses [*A publication*]
SBUA........ Sao Gabriel Da Cachoeira [*Brazil*] [*ICAO location
                identifier*]   (ICLI)
SBUE........ Switch-Backup Entry [*NASA*]   (KSC)
SBUF........ Paulo Afonso [*Brazil*] [*ICAO location identifier*]   (ICLI)
SBUG .... Uruguaiana/Rubem Berta [*Brazil*] [*ICAO location
                identifier*]   (ICLI)
SBUI......... Carauari [*Brazil*] [*ICAO location identifier*]   (ICLI)
SBUL......... Uberlandia [*Brazil*] [*ICAO location identifier*]   (ICLI)
SBUP........ Castillo/Urubupunga [*Brazil*] [*ICAO location
                identifier*]   (ICLI)
SBUPAC ... Symbolae Botanicae Upsalienses [*A publication*]
SBUR........ Uberaba [*Brazil*] [*ICAO location identifier*]   (ICLI)
SBURCS.... Six-BIT [*Binary Digit*] Universal Random Character Set [*Data
                processing*]
SBUV........ Solar Backscatter Ultraviolet [*Ozone measurement*]
SBUV........ Solar and Backscatter Ultraviolet Spectrometer   (MCD)
SBUV/TOMS ... Solar and Backscattered Ultraviolet and Total Ozone
                Mapping System
SBV........... Sabah [*Papua New Guinea*] [*Airport symbol*]   (OAG)
SBV........... Semiautomatic Bleeder Valve
SBV........... Single Binocular Vision
SBV........... South Boston, VA [*Location identifier*] [*FAA*]   (FAAL)
SBV........... Space Biospheres Venture [*Commercial firm*]   (ECON)
SBV........... State Bank of Victoria [*Australia*]
SBVC........ San Bernardino Valley College [*California*]
SBVE........ State Board of Vocational Education [*State Board of
                Education*]   (OICC)
SBVG........ Varginha/Jam Brigadeiro Trompowsky [*Brazil*] [*ICAO location
                identifier*]   (ICLI)
SBVH .... Schwaebische Blaetter fuer Volksbildung und Heimatpflege [*A
                publication*]
SBVH .... Vilhena [*Brazil*] [*ICAO location identifier*]   (ICLI)
SBVM....... Societe de la Bourse de Valeurs Mobilieres de Bruxelles [*Stock
                exchange*] [*Belgium*]   (EY)
SBVS .... Saga-Book. Viking Society for Northern Research [*A
                publication*]
SBVS .... Shield Building Ventilation System [*Nuclear energy*]   (NRCH)
SBVT........ Vitoria/Goiabeira [*Brazil*] [*ICAO location identifier*]   (ICLI)
Sb Vynalezu ... Sbirka Vynalezu [*A publication*]
SBW.......... Shebandowan Resources [*Vancouver Stock Exchange symbol*]
SBW.......... Sibu [*Malaysia*] [*Airport symbol*]   (OAG)
SbW .... South by West
SBW.......... Spectral Bandwidth
SBW.......... Spruce Budworm
SBW.......... Steel Basement Window
SBW.......... Submarine Warfare   (MCD)
SBWA........ 2nd Bomb Wing Association   (EA)
SbWAk...... Sitzungsberichte. Wiener Akademie [*A publication*]
SBWG....... Strategic Bomb Wing [*Military*]
S B Wien.... Sitzungsberichte. Oesterreichische Akademie der
                Wissenschaften in Wien [*A publication*]
SBWM/F... Southern Baptist Women in Ministry/Folio   (EA)
SBWMV.... Soilborne Wheat Mosaic Virus
SBWR....... Simplified Boiling Water Reactor [*Developed by General
                Electric Co.*] [*Nuclear energy*]
SBWU .... Singapore Bus Workers' Union
SBWX....... Seaboard World Airlines, Inc. [*Air carrier designation symbol*]
SBX........... S-Band Transponder
SBX........... Seabright Explorations, Inc. [*Toronto Stock Exchange symbol*]
SBX........... Shelby, MT [*Location identifier*] [*FAA*]   (FAAL)
SBX........... Student Book Exchange
SBX........... Subsea Beacon/Transponder
SBXG........ Barra Do Garcas/Xingu [*Brazil*] [*ICAO location
                identifier*]   (ICLI)
SBXV .... Xavantina [*Brazil*] [*ICAO location identifier*]   (ICLI)
SBY........... Salisbury [*Maryland*] [*Airport symbol*]   (OAG)
SBY........... Salisbury, MD [*Location identifier*] [*FAA*]   (FAAL)
SBY........... Sand Bay [*Alaska*] [*Seismograph station code, US Geological
                Survey*] [*Closed*]   (SEIS)
SBY........... Shapiro, Barney, Newark NJ [*STAC*]
SBY........... Standby [*Airlines*]
SBYA........ Iauarete [*Brazil*] [*ICAO location identifier*]   (ICLI)

SBYS .... Piracununga/Campo Fontenelle [*Brazil*] [*ICAO location
                identifier*]   (ICLI)
SBZ........... Sibiu [*Romania*] [*Airport symbol*]   (OAG)
SBZ........... Sowjetische Besatzungszone [*Soviet Occupation Zone*] [*East
                Germany*]
SBZ Sanit Heiz Klimatech ... SBZ Sanitaer-, Heizungs-, und Klimatechnik
                [*West Germany*] [*A publication*]
SC .... All India Reporter, Supreme Court Reports [*A
                publication*]   (DLA)
SC .... Cape Of Good Hope Reports [*South Africa*] [*A
                publication*]   (DLA)
SC .... Catalan Solidarity [*Political party*]   (PPW)
SC .... Christian Scientist
SC .... Congregation of the Servants of Christ [*Anglican religious
                community*]
SC .... Court of Session Cases [*Scotland*] [*A publication*]   (DLA)
SC .... Cruiser Submarine [*Navy symbol*] [*Obsolete*]
SC .... Juta's Supreme Court Reports [*1880-1910*] [*Cape Of Good
                Hope, South Africa*] [*A publication*]   (DLA)
SC .... Manetti Roberts [*Italy*] [*Research code symbol*]
Sc .... Nederlandse Staatscourant [*A publication*]
SC .... Quebec Official Reports, Superior Court [*A publication*]   (DLA)
SC .... Sabra Connection [*An association*]   (EA)
SC .... Saccharomyces Cerevisiae [*Bacterium*]
SC .... Sacra Congregatio [*Sacred Congregation*] [*Latin*]
SC .... Sacrococcygeal [*Anatomy*]
SC .... Sacrosanctam Concilium [*Constitution on the Sacred Liturgy*]
                [*Vatican II document*]
SC .... Sad Case [*An unpopular person*] [*Teen slang*]
SC .... Safe Custody [*Banking*]
SC .... Saffery Champness International [*British accounting firm*]
S/C............ Sales Code
SC .... Sales Costs
SC .... Salesianorum Congregatio [*Congregation of St. Francis of Sales*]
                [*Salesian Fathers*] [*Roman Catholic religious order*]
SC .... Salmagundi Club   (EA)
SC .... Salvage Charges
SC .... Same Case [*Law*]
SC .... Same Coupling [*Music*]
SC .... Sandia Corp.
SC .... Sanitary Corps
SC .... Sanitation Center [*Food Service*] [*Army*]
SC .... Satellite Communications [*Military*]
SC .... Satellite Computer
SC .... Saturable Core   (MSA)
SC .... Saturn Coupe [*An automobile*]   (ECON)
S & C......... Saunders and Cole's English Bail Court Reports [*A
                publication*]   (DLA)
Sc .... Scaccaria [*Exchequer*] [*Latin*]   (DLA)
SC .... Scale
Sc .... Scammon's Reports [*2-5 Illinois*] [*A publication*]   (DLA)
SC .... Scandinavian
Sc .... Scandium [*Chemical element*]
SC .... Scapula
SC .... Scarce [*Bookselling*]   (ROG)
SC .... Scavenge   (AAG)
SC .... Scene
SC .... Scented Cape [*Tea trade*]   (ROG)
SC .... Schilling [*Monetary unit*]   (ROG)
S/C............ Schmidt-Cassegrain [*Telescope*]
Sc .... Schmidt Number [*IUPAC*]
SC .... School Certificate
SC .... School Construction   (OICC)
SC .... Schools Council [*British*]
SC .... Schooner   (ROG)
SC .... Schwann Cell [*Biology*]
Sc .... Science [*A publication*]
SC .... Science
SC .... Science and Culture [*A publication*]
Sc .... Scientia [*A publication*]
Sc .... Scientia. Organo Internazionale di Sintesi Scientifica [*A
                publication*]
SC .... Scilicet [*Namely*] [*Legal term*] [*Latin*]
SC .... Scintillation Counter [*Instrumentation*]
SC .... Scope Change   (MCD)
SC .... Score   (AABC)
Sc .... Scoriae [*Quality of the bottom*] [*Nautical charts*]
SC .... Scoring Criteria   (MCD)
SC .... Scots
SC .... Scotsman [*A publication*]
SC .... Scottish Aviation Ltd. [*ICAO aircraft manufacturer
                identifier*]   (ICAO)
SC .... Scottish Constitution   (ADA)
Sc .... Scott's English Common Pleas Reports [*A publication*]   (DLA)
SC .... Scrap Carriage [*British military*]   (DMA)
SC .... Screen Coordinator [*Military*]   (CAAL)
SC .... Screen Flag [*Navy*] [*British*]
SC .... Screw
S/C............ Screwed and Coupled
SC .... Script [*Films, television, etc.*]
Sc .... Scriptorium [*A publication*]

SC	Scruple
SC	Sculpsit [*He, or She, Engraved It*] [*Latin*]
SC	Sculptor
SC	Sculpture Center (EA)
SC	Scuola Cattolica [*A publication*]
Sc	Scutum [*of Hesiod*] [*Classical studies*] (OCD)
SC	[*The*] Seal Cylinders of Western Asia [*A publication*] (BJA)
SC	Seamen's Center [*Later, Seamen and International House*] (EA)
S & C	Search and Clear [*Military*]
SC	Search Control (IEEE)
SC	Searchlight Carrier [*British*]
SC	Searle [*G. D.*] & Co. [*Research code symbol*]
SC	Seat Cabs
SC	Seco-Cemp Ltd. [*Toronto Stock Exchange symbol*]
SC	Secondary Code
SC	Secondary Confinement [*or Containment*] [*Nuclear energy*] (IEEE)
S-C	Secret and Confidential Files [*Navy*]
SC	Secretory Component [*Supersedes SP, TP*] [*Immunology*]
SC	Secular College
SC	Security Call [*Economics*]
SC	Security Council of the United Nations
SC	See Comments [*Routing slip*]
SC	See Copy
SC	Seed Coat [*Botany*]
SC	Segment Control (SSD)
SC	Select Cases [*Oudh, India*] [*A publication*] (DLA)
SC	Select Committee
SC	Selector Channel
SC	Self-Care [*Medicine*]
SC	Self-Check (AAG)
SC	Self-Closing
SC	Self Compatible
S/C	Self-Contained [*Housing*] [*British*]
SC	Self-Contained
SC	Semicactus [*Horticulture*]
SC	Semicircular (MAE)
SC	Semiclosed [*Anatomy*]
SC	Semiconductor
SC	Senatus Consulto [*By the Decree of the Senate*] [*Latin*]
SC	Senatus Consultum [*Classical studies*] (OCD)
SC	Sending Complete [*Telecommunications*] (TEL)
SC	Senior Cameraman
SC	Senior Counsel [*Ireland*]
S/C	Sensor Controller (MCD)
SC	Separate Cover
SC	Sequence Charts (AAG)
SC	Sequence Controller
SC	Sequence Counter
SC	Servants of Charity [*Roman Catholic men's religious order*]
S/C	Service Ceiling
SC	Service Center [*IRS*]
SC	Service Certificate [*Military*] [*British*]
SC	Service Change
SC	Service Charge [*Banking*]
SC	Service Club [*Military enlisted men's club*]
SC	Service Code [*Telecommunications*] (TEL)
SC	Service Command [*Marine Corps*]
SC	Service Connected [*Medicine*]
SC	Servicos Aereos Cruzeiro do Sul SA [*Brazil*] [*ICAO designator*] (FAAC)
SC	Session Cases [*Legal term*] [*British*]
SC	Session Control [*Data processing*] (IBMDP)
SC	Set/Clear [*Flip-flop*] [*Data processing*]
SC	Set Clock
S/C	Set Course [*Navigation*]
SC	Severest Critic [*Initialism used by E. B. White to describe his wife*]
SC	Sex Change [*Biology*]
SC	Sex Chromatin (MAE)
SC	Seychelles [*ANSI two-letter standard code*] (CNC)
SC	Shaft Center (MSA)
SC	Shakespearean Criticism [*A publication*]
SC	Shaped Charge [*of explosive*]
SC	Shaping Circuit [*Electronics*] (OA)
SC	Sharp Cash [*Prompt payment*]
SC	Shell Transport & Trading Co. Ltd. [*NYSE symbol*] (SPSG)
SC	Shift Control Counter [*Data processing*] (MDG)
SC	Ship Casualty Library [*Maritime Data Network, Inc.*] [*Information service or system*] (CRD)
S & C	Shipper and Carrier [*Business term*]
SC	Shipping Container
SC	Shipping Contract (MCD)
SC	Ship's Cook [*Navy*]
SC	Shop Call (MCD)
SC	Shop Carpenter
SC	Shopping Concourses [*Public-performance tariff class*] [*British*]
SC	Short Circuit
SC	Short Course [*of instruction*]
SC	Should Cost (MCD)
SC	Sickle Cell [*Medicine*]
SC	Side Cabin
Sc	Side Car [*Army*]
SC	Side Contact [*Valves*] (DEN)
SC	Sierra Club (EA)
S/C	Signal-to-Clutter
SC	Signal Comparator
SC	Signal Conditioner
S & C	Signal and Conditioning (KSC)
SC	Signal Corps [*Later, Communications and Electronics Command*] [*Army*]
SC	Significant Characteristics (MCD)
SC	Silicone Coated
SC	Silver Certificate
SC	Silvered Copper [*Wire*] (IEEE)
SC	Simulation Coordinator
SC	Simulator Control (MCD)
SC	Sine Correction [*Without lenses*] [*Ophthalmology*]
SC	Sine-Cosine
S & C	Singh & Choudry [*Publisher*] [*British*]
SC	Single Carburetor [*Automotive engineering*]
SC	Single Case
SC	Single Cell
SC	Single Chemical (MAE)
SC	Single Circuit [*Electricity*]
SC	Single Column
SC	Single Comb
SC	Single Contact [*Switch*]
SC	Single Counter
SC	Single Crochet
SC	Single Crystal
SC	Sinusoidal Collagen [*Anatomy*]
SC	Sisters of Charity [*Anglican religious community*]
SC	Sisters of Charity [*Roman Catholic religious order*]
SC	Sisters of Charity of Saint Vincent de Paul (EA)
SC	Site Contingency [*Nuclear energy*] (NRCH)
S & C	Sized and Calendered [*Paper*]
SC	Sized and Calendered [*Paper*]
SC	Skill Component
SC	Skin Conductance
SC	Slip Coupling (DS)
SC	Slow Component
SC	Slow Curing [*Asphalt grade*]
SC	Small Capitals [*Typography*]
SC	Small Compact [*Car size*]
SC	Small Craft
SC	Smooth Contour [*Technical drawings*]
SC	Snellen Chart [*Ophthalmology*]
SC	Snow Cover [*Meteorology*]
SC	So-Called
SC	Social Casework [*A publication*]
SC	Social Compass [*A publication*]
SC	Social Credit Party [*British*]
SC	Socialist Commentary [*A publication*]
S en C	Sociedad en Comandita [*Limited partnership company*] [*Spanish*]
SC	Societas Fratrum Sacris Cordis [*Brothers of the Sacred Heart*] [*Roman Catholic religious order*]
SC	Society of the Cincinnati (EA)
SC	Society for Cryobiology (EA)
S/C	Software Contractor [*NASA*] (NASA)
SC	Soil Characteristics
SC	Soil Conservation [*A publication*]
SC	Solar Cell
SC	Soldier Capabilities
SC	Sole Charge [*Ecclesiastical*] [*British*] (ROG)
SC	Solid Core [*Technical drawings*]
SC	Solid-State Circuit (MCD)
S/C	Son Compte [*His, or Her, Account*] [*French*]
SC	SONAR Channel [*Navy*] (CAAL)
SC	Soncino Chumash [*A publication*] (BJA)
SC	Songwriters Club [*Later, SLC*] (EA)
SC	Sons of Charity [*France*] (EAIO)
SC	Sound Channel [*Navy*] (CAAL)
SC	Source Code
SC	Sources Chretiennes [*Paris*] [*A publication*]
SC	South Carolina [*Postal code*]
SC	South Carolina Musician [*A publication*]
SC	South Carolina Reports [*A publication*] (DLA)
Sc	South Carolina State Library, Columbia, SC [*Library symbol*] [*Library of Congress*] (LCLS)
SC	Southern California
SC	Southern Classification
SC	Southern Command [*British military*] (DMA)
SC	Southern Conference (EA)
SC	Southwark College [*London, England*]
SC	Spacecraft (MCD)
S/C	Spacecraft/Capsule
SC	Spark Control [*Automotive engineering*]
SC	Special Access, Compartmented (MCD)
SC	Special Care [*Medicine*]

SC .... Special Circuit
SC .... Special Circular
S/C .... Special Conditions   (MCD)
SC .... Special Constable
SC .... Specialty Code
SC .... Specific Cueing
SC .... Specification Change
SC .... Speed Controller [*Nuclear energy*]   (NRCH)
SC .... Spermatocyte
SC .... Spiroplasmavirus citri [*Bacteriology*]
SC .... Splat Cooled   (OA)
S/C .... Splitter/Combiner   (NASA)
SC .... Sports Council [*British*]   (EAIO)
SC .... Sporulation Capacity [*of fungi*]
SC .... Spot Check   (AAG)
SC .... Spread Correlation
SC .... Spreading Coefficient
SC .... Spring Conditions [*Skiing*]
S & C .... Squamous Cell Carcinoma [*Also, SCC*] [*Medicine*]
S & C .... Stabilization and Control [*Aerospace*]   (KSC)
S/C .... Stabilization and Control [*Aerospace*]   (GFGA)
SC .... Stack (Pipe) Cut [*Sanitation*] [*British*]   (ROG)
SC .... Staff Captain [*Military*] [*British*]
SC .... Staff Car [*British*]
SC .... Staff College [*Military*]
SC .... Staff Corps
SC .... Stage Center [*A stage direction*]
SC .... Standard Candle [*Power*]
SC .... Standard Conditions
S & C .... Standards and Control
SC .... Standing Committee   (ADA)
SC .... Standing Crop
SC .... Star of Courage [*Award*] [*British*]
SC .... Starfleet Command [*An association*]   (EA)
SC .... Start Computer
SC .... Start Conversion [*Data processing*]
sC .... Statcoulomb [*Also, Fr, statC*] [*Unit of electric charge*]
SC .... Statement of Capability [*NASA*]
S/C .... Statement of Charges [*Army*]
SC .... Statement of Compatibility [*NASA*]   (MCD)
SC .... Statistical Control
SC .... Statistics Canada
SC .... Status Statement [*Online database field identifier*]
S of C .... Statutes of Canada [*A publication*]   (DLA)
SC .... Statutes of Canada
SC .... Steel Casting
SC .... Steel Cored [*Conductors*]
SC .... Steering Committee   (NATG)
Sc .... Stellacyanin
SC .... Stellar Camera
SC .... Stendhal Club [*A publication*]
SC .... Stepchild [*or Children*]   (DNAB)
SC .... Stepped Care [*Medicine*]
S1C .... Sternoclavicular [*Joint*] [*Anatomy*]
SC .... Stimulus, Conditioned   (AAMN)
SC .... Stock Certificate [*Investment term*]
Sc .... Stonecat [*Ichthyology*]
SC .... Stop-Continue   (DEN)
SC .... Stopcock
SC .... Storage Capacity   (AAG)
SC .... Stored Command
S/C .... Stowage Container
S & C .... Strategic and Critical Raw Material [*Military*]
SC .... Stratified Charge [*Automotive engineering*]
SC .... Stratocumulus [*Cloud*] [*Meteorology*]
SC .... Stress Cracking [*Metallurgy*]
SC .... Strike Command [*Military*]
S/C .... Strip Chart [*Recorder*] [*NASA*]   (NASA)
SC .... Stronnictwo Chlopskie [*Peasants' Party*] [*Poland*] [*Political party*]   (PPE)
SC .... Su Cuenta [*Your Account*] [*Business term*] [*Spanish*]
S/C .... Subcable   (KSC)
S/C .... Subcarrier   (AAG)
SC .... Subclavian [*Anatomy*]
SC .... Subcommittee
S/C .... Subcontract
SC .... Subcontractor   (NATG)
SC .... Subcorneal [*Ophthalmology*]   (AAMN)
SC .... Subcours
SC .... Subcutaneous [*Beneath the Skin*] [*Medicine*]
SC .... Subject Classification [*Library science*]
SC .... Submarine Chaser [*110 foot*]
S/C .... Submarine Coxswain [*British military*]   (DMA)
SC .... Succinylcholine [*Biochemistry*]   (MAE)
SC .... Sudden Commencement
SC .... Suffolk and Cambridgeshire Regiment [*British military*]   (DMA)
SC .... Sugar-Coated [*Pharmacy*]
SC .... Suisse Contemporaine [*A publication*]
SC .... Summary Court [*Navy*]
SC .... Sumter & Choctaw Railway Co. [*AAR code*]

SC .... Super Coupe [*Model of automobile*]
SC .... Supercalendered [*Paper*]
S/C .... Superconducting Magnetic   (MCD)
SC .... Supercritical Chromatography
SC .... Superimposed Coding [*Data processing*]   (DIT)
SC .... Superimposed Current
SC .... Superintending Cartographer [*Navy*] [*British*]
SC .... Superior Colliculus [*Brain anatomy*]
SC .... Superior Court   (DLA)
SC .... Supervisor's Console
SC .... Supervisory Control
SC .... Supplemental Contract   (AAG)
SC .... Supplementary Information [*Telecommunications*]   (TEL)
SC .... Supply Catalog [*Military*]   (AABC)
SC .... Supply Control [*Military*]
SC .... Supply Corps
SC .... Support Center
SC .... Support Chief
SC .... Support Command [*Army*]
SC .... Support Concept Manual [*Marine Corps*]
SC .... Support Contractor   (MCD)
SC .... Support Controller [*NASA*]   (KSC)
SC .... Support Coordinator   (AAG)
SC .... Supporting Cells [*Zoology*]
SC .... Suppressed Carrier   (IEEE)
SC .... Supreme Council [*Freemasonry*]   (ROG)
SC .... Supreme Court
SC .... Supreme Court Reporter [*National Reporter System*] [*A publication*]   (DLA)
SC .... Surface Combustion [*Reducing gas process*]
SC .... Surface Command [*NASA*]   (MCD)
SC .... Surgeon-Captain [*British military*]
SC .... Surgeon-Commander [*British military*]
SC .... Surgical Capsule [*of prostate gland*]
SC .... Surrogates by Choice   (EA)
SC .... Surveillance Compliance [*Nuclear energy*]   (NRCH)
S & C .... Swan and Critchfield's Revised Statutes [*Ohio*] [*A publication*]   (DLA)
SC .... Swimmer-Canoeist [*British military*]   (DMA)
SC .... Swimming Club
SC .... Switching Cell   (IEEE)
SC .... Sylvania Central Railroad   (IIA)
SC .... Symbolic Code   (AAG)
SC .... Synanon Church   (EA)
SC .... Synaptonemal Complex [*Botanical cytology*]
SC .... Synchro-Cyclotron
SC .... Synchrocyclotron [*Particle physics*]
SC .... Synchronization Coefficient
SC .... Synclinal [*Geology*]
SC .... System Capability
SC .... System Controller [*Military*]   (CAAL)
SC .... Systems Command [*Air Force*]
SC .... Systolic Click [*Cardiology*]
S1C .... Seaman, First Class [*Navy*]
SCA .... Air Weather Service, Technical Library, Scott AFB, IL [*OCLC symbol*]   (OCLC)
SCA .... Archibald Library, Caronport, Saskatchewan [*Library symbol*] [*National Library of Canada*]   (NLC)
SCA .... SAAB Club of North America [*Acronym is based on former name, SAAB Clubs of America*]   (EA)
SCA .... Sag-Control Agent [*Automotive painting and finishing*]
SCA .... Sako Collectors Association   (EA)
SCA .... Saluki Club of America   (EA)
SCA .... Samoyed Club of America   (EA)
SCA .... Santa Cruz [*Argentina*] [*Seismograph station code, US Geological Survey*] [*Closed*]   (SEIS)
SCA .... Satellite Committee Agency [*Army*]   (MCD)
SCA .... Satellite Communications Agency [*Army*]
SCA .... Save the Children Alliance [*Gentofte, Denmark*]   (EAIO)
Sca .... Scala [*Record label*]
Sca .... Scandinavica [*A publication*]
SCA .... Scarborough Public Library [*UTLAS symbol*]
SCA .... Schedule Change Authorization [*NASA*]   (NASA)
SCA .... Schipperke Club of America   (EA)
SCA .... School and College Ability [*Test*] [*of ETS*]
SCA .... Science Clubs of America   (EA)
SCA .... Science Fiction Classics Annual [*A publication*]
SCA .... Scientific Computing and Automation
SCA .... Scottish Courts Administration   (ILCA)
SCA .... Screen Composers of America   (EA)
SCA .... Sea Cadet Association   (EAIO)
SCA .... Sebright Club of America   (EA)
SCA .... Secondary Communications Authorization   (IEEE)
SCA .... Secondary Control Assembly [*Nuclear energy*]   (NRCH)
SCA .... Selectivity Clear Accumulator
SCA .... Senior Citizens of America [*Defunct*]   (EA)
SCA .... Sequence Control Area [*NASA*]   (KSC)
SCA .... Sequencer Control Assembly
SCA .... Service Cinematographique des Armees [*France*]
SCA .... Service and Compliance Administration [*US wage/price controls agency*]

SCA...........	Service Contract Act [*1965*]
SCA...........	Service Cryptologic Agencies [*Military*]
SCA...........	Servo Corp. of America [*AMEX symbol*] (SPSG)
SCA...........	Sex Chromosome Abnormality
SCA...........	Shareholder Credit Accounting
SCA...........	Shelby Can-Am [*Racing car*]
SCA...........	Shields Class Association (EA)
SCA...........	Ship Constructive Association [*A union*] [*British*]
SCA...........	Ship Cost Adjustment [*Navy*]
SCA...........	Shipbuilders Council of America (EA)
SCA...........	Shipping Control Authority (NVT)
SCA...........	Shooters Club of America [*Defunct*]
SCA...........	Should Cost Analysis (MCD)
SCA...........	Shuttle Carrier Aircraft [*NASA*] (NASA)
SCA...........	Sickle Cell Anemia [*Medicine*]
SCA...........	Signal Conditioning Assembly [*NASA*] (KSC)
SCA...........	Simulated Core Assembly [*Nuclear energy*] (NRCH)
SCA...........	Simulation Control Area [*NASA*] (MCD)
SCA...........	Simulation Conversion Assembly [*Deep Space Instrumentation Facility, NASA*]
SCA...........	Single Channel Analyzer
SCA...........	Ski Council of America [*Defunct*] (EA)
SCA...........	Small-Caliber Ammunition (MSA)
SCA...........	Smithsonian Contributions to Anthropology [*A publication*]
SCA...........	Smithsonian Contributions to Astrophysics [*A publication*]
SCA...........	Smoke Control Association (EA)
SCA...........	Sneak Circuit Analysis [*NASA*] (NASA)
SCA...........	Societe Canadienne des Anesthesistes [*Canadian Anaesthetists' Society*] (EAIO)
SCA...........	Societe Canadienne d'Astronomie
SCA...........	Society of Canadian Artists [*Formerly, Society of Co-Operative Artists*]
SCA...........	Society of Cardiovascular Anesthesiologists (EA)
SCA...........	Society for Commercial Archeology (EA)
SCA...........	Society for Coptic Archaeology (EA)
SCA...........	Society for Creative Anachronism (EA)
SCA...........	Society for Cultural Anthropology (EA)
SCA...........	Software Control Authorization [*NASA*] (KSC)
SCA...........	Soldiers Christian Association [*British military*] (DMA)
SCA...........	Sonar Class Association (EA)
S Ca...........	South Carolina Reports [*A publication*] (DLA)
SCA...........	South Central Air, Inc. [*Kenai, AK*] [*FAA designator*] (FAAC)
SCA...........	Southern Communications Area [*Military*]
SCA...........	Southern Cotton Association (EA)
SCA...........	Soybean Council of America [*Defunct*] (EA)
SCA...........	Spacecraft Adapter [*NASA*] (KSC)
SCA...........	SPALTRA [*Special Projects Alterations, Training*] Control Activity
SCA...........	Specific Combining Ability
SCA...........	Specification Compliance Agreement (MCD)
SCA...........	Speech Communication Association (EA)
SCA...........	Speed Coaches Association (EA)
SCA...........	Sperm-Coating Antigen
SCA...........	Spinach Carbonic Anhydrase [*An enzyme*]
SCA...........	Standard Consolidated Area [*Bureau of Census*]
SCA...........	Steel-Cored-Aluminium
SCA...........	Sterba Curtain Antenna
SCA...........	Stevengraph Collectors' Association (EA)
SCA...........	Stock Company Association [*Defunct*] (EA)
SCA...........	Stock Control Activity (AFIT)
SCA...........	Student Conservation Association (EA)
SCA...........	Subcarrier Authorization (MSA)
SCA...........	Subcarrier Channel [*Telecommunications*]
SCA...........	Subchannel Adapter
SCA...........	Subcontract Authorization (AAG)
SCA...........	Subcritical Assembly (DEN)
SCA...........	Subsequent Coupons Attached
SCA...........	Subsidiary Communications Authorization [*Facilities used to transmit background music to subscribing customers*]
SCA...........	Summary Cost Account [*Military*] (AABC)
SCA...........	Superior Cerebellar Artery [*Anatomy*]
SCA...........	Support Centers of America [*An association*] (EA)
SCA...........	Supreme Court Appeals [*India*] [*A publication*] (ILCA)
SCA...........	Supreme and Exchequer Courts Act [*Canada*] (ILCA)
SCA...........	Surface Coatings Abstracts [*Paint Research Association of Great Britain*] [*Bibliographic database*]
SCA...........	Surgical Care Affiliates, Inc. [*NYSE symbol*] (SPSG)
SCA...........	Survey of Current Business [*Washington, DC*] [*A publication*]
SCA...........	Swedish Council of America (EA)
SCA...........	Switch Control Assembly
SCA...........	Switzerland Cheese Association (EA)
SCA...........	Synagogue Council of America (EA)
SCA...........	Synchronous Communications Adapter
SCA...........	System Comparison Analysis [*Bell System*]
SCA...........	System Control Area
SCAA........	Skin Care Association of America (EA)
SCAA.........	Specialty Coffee Association of America (EA)
SCAA.........	Spill Control Association of America (EA)
SCAA........	Superconductor Applications Association (EA)
SCAA.........	Sussex Cattle Association of America (EA)
SCAAN......	System for Computerized Application Analysis [*Automotive engineering*]
SCAAP.....	Special Commonwealth African Assistance Plan
SCAAS......	Strategic Communication and Alerting System
SCAB........	Single Chain Antibody Fragment [*Botany*] (ECON)
SCAB........	Streptozocin, CCNU [*Lomustine*], Adriamycin, Bleomycin [*Antineoplastic drug regimen*]
SCABG......	Single Coronary Artery Bypass Graft [*Cardiology*]
SCAC.........	Ancud/Pupelde [*Chile*] [*ICAO location identifier*] (ICLI)
Scac...........	Scaccaria Curia [*Court of Exchequer*] [*Latin*] (DLA)
SCAC.........	School and College Advisory Center [*Later, EGASCAC*] (EA)
SCAC.........	Self-Cleaning Air Cleaner
SCAC.........	Standard Carriers Alpha Code (MCD)
SCAC.........	Support Careers Advisory Committee [*Environmental Protection Agency*] (EPA)
SC Acad Sci Bull ...	South Carolina Academy of Science. Bulletin [*A publication*]
SC Acts	Acts and Joint Resolutions. South Carolina [*A publication*]
SC Acts	Acts and Joint Resolutions of the State of South Carolina [*A publication*] (DLA)
SCAD........	Savannah College of Art and Design [*Georgia*]
SCAD........	Scan Converter and Display [*Systems*]
SCAD........	Schenectady Army Depot (AABC)
SCAD........	Small Current Amplifying Device
SCAD........	Societe Canadienne pour l'Analyse de Documents [*Indexing and Abstracting Society of Canada*]
SCAD........	State Commission Against Discrimination
SCAD........	Strategic Bomber Penetration Decoy [*Air Force*]
SCAD........	Subsonic Cruise Armed Decoy [*Air Force*]
SCAD........	Systeme Communautaire d'Acces a la Documentation [*Database*] [*EC*] (ECED)
SCADA......	Student Coalition Against Drug Abuse
SCADA......	Supervisory Control and Data Acquisition (IEEE)
SCADAR..	Scatter Detection and Ranging
SCADC......	Standard Central Air Data Computer
SCADE.....	Signal Conditioning and Detection Electronics (MCD)
SCADEU...	Scottish Adult Basic Education Unit
SCADS	SAS Census Access and Display System [*Information service or system*] (IID)
SCADS	Scanning Celestial Attitude Determination System
SCADS	Shipborne Containerized Air Defense System
SCADS	Simulation of Combined Analog Digital Systems [*Data processing*] (IEEE)
SCADS	Sioux City Air Defense Sector [*ADC*]
SCADS	Speech Command Auditory Display System (MCD)
Sc Advocate ...	Science Advocate [*A publication*]
SCAE........	Scottish Center for Agricultural Engineering
SCAE........	Scottish Centre of Agricultural Engineering [*British*] (IRUK)
SCAE........	Society for Computer-Aided Engineering (EA)
SCAEC......	Submarine Contact Analysis and Evaluation Center (NVT)
SCAEF......	Supreme Commander, Allied Expeditionary Force [*World War II*]
Scaen Rom Frag ...	Scaenicorum Romanorum Fragmenta [*A publication*] (OCD)
SCAEPA....	Society for Computer Applications in Engineering, Planning, and Architecture [*Later, CEPA*] (EA)
SCAF	Self-Centered-Altruism Fad
SCAF	Supersonic Cruise Attack Fighter (MCD)
SCAF	Suppressor Cell Activating Factor [*Biochemistry*]
SCAF	Supreme Commander of Allied Forces (ADA)
SCAFB.......	Schilling Air Force Base (AAG)
SCAFEDS ...	Space Construction Automated Fabrication Experiment Definition Study (MCD)
SCAG........	Sandoz Clinical Assessment of Geriatrics [*Psychometrics*]
SCAG........	Southern California Association of Governments
SCAG.........	Special COMSEC Advisory Group [*US Army Communications Command*] (MCD)
SC Ag Dept ...	South Carolina. Department of Agriculture, Commerce, and Industries. Publications [*A publication*]
SC Ag Exp ...	South Carolina. Agricultural Experiment Station. Publications [*A publication*]
SC Agric Exp Stn Bull ...	South Carolina. Agricultural Experiment Station. Bulletin [*A publication*]
SC Agric Exp Stn Circ ...	South Carolina. Agricultural Experiment Station. Circular [*A publication*]
SC Agric Exp Stn Tech Bull ...	South Carolina. Agricultural Experiment Station. Technical Bulletin [*A publication*]
SC Agr Res ...	South Carolina Agricultural Research [*A publication*]
SC/AH.......	System Coordinator / Anomaly Handler (SSD)
SCAHR......	School of Community and Allied Health Resources
ScAi	Aiken-Bamberg-Barnwell-Edgefield Regional Library, Aiken, SC [*Library symbol*] [*Library of Congress*] (LCLS)
SCAI	Societe des Comptables en Administration Industrielle du Canada
SCA & I	Society for Cardiac Angiography and Interventions (EA)
ScAiD	E. I. Du Pont de Nemours & Co., Aiken, SC [*Library symbol*] [*Library of Congress*] (LCLS)
SCAIF........	Sertoli-Cell Androgenic Inhibitory Factor [*Endocrinology*]
SCAJAP....	Shipping Control Administrator Japan
SCAJAP....	Shipping Control Authority, Japan (DNAB)
SCAL........	Silver City Airways Ltd.

SCAL......... Skin Diver Contact Air Lenses
SCAL......... STAR [*Self Testing and Reporting*] Computer Assembly Language
SCALA ...... Society of Chief Architects of Local Authorities [*British*]
S Cal Ac Sc B ... Southern California Academy of Sciences. Bulletin [*A publication*]
SCALD...... Structural Computer-Aided Logic Design
SCALE ...... Scales of Creativity and Learning Environment [*Educational test*]
SCALE ...... Space Checkout and Launch Equipment
SCALE ...... Supreme Court Almanac [*India*] [*A publication*]
SCALER.... Statistical Calculation and Analysis of Engine Removal [*Navy*]
S Calif Law Rev ... Southern California Law Review [*A publication*]
S Cal Law R ... Southern California Law Review [*A publication*]
S Cal L Rev ... Southern California Law Review [*A publication*]
SCALO...... Scanning Local Oscillator (NG)
SCALP....... Students Concerned about Legal Prices [*Student legal action organization*]
SCALP....... Suit, Contamination Avoidance, and Liquid Protection [*Army*]
S CA LR.... Southern California Law Review [*A publication*]
SCALRA ... Scottish Adult Literacy Resource Agency
Scam .... Scammon's Reports [*2-5 Illinois*] [*A publication*] (DLA)
Sc Am......... Scientific American [*A publication*]
SCAM....... Selection Classification Age Maturity Program [*Medical screening procedure for athletes*]
SCAM....... Soil Classification and Mapping Branch [*Department of Agriculture*] (IID)
SCAM....... Soviet Cost Analysis Model [*CIA*]
SCAM....... Spectrum Characteristics Analysis and Measurement [*FAA*]
SCAM....... Standing Conference for Amateur Music [*British*]
SCAM....... Station Control and Monitoring
SCAM....... Strike Camera (MCD)
SCAM....... Study Course in Agency Management [*LIMRA*]
SCAM....... Subsonic Cruise Armed Missile/Decoy [*Air Force*] (MCD)
SCAM....... Synchronous Communications Access Method
SCAMA.... Scientific American [*A publication*]
SCAMA..... Service Central des Approvisionements et Materiels Americains [*Central Office of American Supplies and Equipment*] [*World War II*]
SCAMA..... Skewed Circular Arc Method of Analysis
SCAMA..... Station Conferencing and Monitoring Arrangement [*NASA*]
SCAMA..... Switching, Conferencing, and Monitoring Arrangement [*NASA*]
SCAMC..... Symposium on Computer Applications in Medical Care [*Baltimore, MD*]
SCAM/D... Subsonic Cruise Armed Missile/Decoy [*Air Force*]
SCAMP..... Scholarships for Children of American Military Personnel (DNAB)
SCAMP..... Sectionalized Carrier and Multipurpose Vehicle [*Military*]
SCAMP..... Self-Contained Airborne Multipurpose Pod (MCD)
SCAMP..... Self-Contained Ancillary Modular Platform [*Woods Hole Oceanographic Institution*]
SCAMP..... Self-Propelled Crane for Aircraft Maintenance and Positioning (MCD)
SCAMP..... Sensor Control and Management Platoon [*Marine Corps*]
SCAMP..... Signal Conditioning Amplifier
SCAMP..... Single Channel Amplitude Monopulse Processing
SCAMP..... Small-Caliber Ammunition Modernization Program [*Army*] (RDA)
SCAMP..... Space-Controlled Army Measurements Probe
SCAMP..... Sperry Computer-Aided Message Processor [*British*]
SCAMP..... Standard Configuration and Modification Program [*Military*]
SCAMP..... Succinyl CAMP [*Biochemistry*]
SCAMP..... Summer Campus, Advanced Mathematics Program [*Institute for Defense Analysis*]
SCAMP..... System/Command Accounting/Monitoring of Projects (DNAB)
SCAMPERS ... Standard Corps-Army-MACOM [*Major Army Command*] Personnel System (AABC)
SCAMPS... Small Computer Analytical and Mathematical Programming System (IEEE)
SCAMPTME ... Succinyl CAMP Tyrosine Methyl Ester [*Biochemistry*]
SCAMS..... Scanning Microwave Spectrometer
Sc Am Sup ... Scientific American. Supplement [*A publication*]
SCAN .... Alliance Imaging, Inc. [*NASDAQ symbol*] (SPSG)
ScAn........... Anderson County Library, Anderson, SC [*Library symbol*] [*Library of Congress*] (LCLS)
SCAN .... Satellite Cable Audio Networks [*Cable-television service*]
SCAN .... Savings Comparative Analysis [*Federal Home Loan Bank Board*] [*Database*]
SCAN .... Scandinavian
Scan .... Scandinavian Studies [*A publication*]
Scan .... Scandinavica [*A publication*]
SCAN .... Scanfile [*Database*] [*Australia*]
SCAN .... Scanner Association of North America (EA)
SCAN .... Scintiscan [*Medicine*]
SCAN .... Screening Test for Identifying Central Auditory Disorders
SCAN .... Seismic Computerized Alert Network [*For warning of an earthquake*]
SCAN .... Selected Current Aerospace Notices [*NASA*]
SCAN .... Self-Correcting Automatic Navigator
SCAN .... Seniors Cooperative Alert Network [*An association*] (EA)
SCAN .... Sensor Controller Alert Network

SCAN .... Service Center Advantage Network [*Federal-Mogul Corp.*]
SCAN .... Service Center for Aging Information [*Department of Health and Human Services*] [*Information service or system*] (IID)
SCAN .... Shipboard Communication Area Network (DWSG)
SCAN .... Short Current Abstracts and Notes (DIT)
SCAN .... Signal Corps Administrative Network [*Obsolete*] [*Army*]
SCAN .... Silent Communication Alarm Network [*NASA*]
SCAN .... Simplified Colorimetric Analysis (MCD)
SCAN .... Small Computers in the Arts Network (EA)
SCAN .... Southern California Answering Network [*Los Angeles Public Library*] [*Information service or system*]
SCAN .... Spares Change Advance Notice (MCD)
SCAN .... State of California Answering Network [*Information service or system*] (IID)
SCAN .... Stock Control and Analysis (BUR)
SCAN .... Stock Market Computer Answering Network [*British*]
SCAN .... Student Career Automated Network (IEEE)
SCAN .... Supermarket Computer Answering Service (OA)
SCAN .... Surface Condition Analyzer (MCD)
SCAN .... Suspected Child Abuse and Neglect
SCAN .... Switched Circuit Automatic Network [*Army*]
SCAN .... System for Collection and Analysis of Near-Collision Reports (AAG)
SCANA..... SCANA Corp. [*Associated Press abbreviation*] (APAG)
SCANA..... Self-Contained Adverse-Weather Night Attack
SCANCAP ... System for Comparative Analysis of Community Action Programs [*Information service or system*] (AEBS)
SCAND ..... Scandinavia
Scand .... Scandinavica [*A publication*]
SCAND ..... Single Crystal Automatic Neutron Diffractometer
Scand Actuar J ... Scandinavian Actuarial Journal [*A publication*]
SCANDAL ... Select Committee to Arrange a New Deal to Avoid Litigation [*Toledo, OH, groupformed in 1973 to humorously protest results of the Michigan-Toledo "War of 183 5"*]
Scand Audiol ... Scandinavian Audiology [*A publication*]
Scand Audiol Suppl ... Scandinavian Audiology. Supplement [*A publication*]
SCANDC... Scandinavia Co. [*Associated Press abbreviation*] (APAG)
Scand Ec Hist Rev ... Scandinavian Economic History Review [*A publication*]
Scand Econ Hist Rev ... Scandinavian Economic History Review [*A publication*]
SCANDEFA ... Scandinavian Dental Fair [*Danish Dental Association*]
SCANDI.... Surveillance Control and Driver Information [*Traffic system*]
Scandinavian Econ Hist R ... Scandinavian Economic History Review [*A publication*]
Scandinavian Publ Libr Q ... Scandinavian Public Library Quarterly [*A publication*]
Scandinavian R ... Scandinavian Review [*A publication*]
Scandinav J Clin Lab Invest ... Scandinavian Journal of Clinical and Laboratory Investigation [*A publication*]
Scandinav J Econ ... Scandinavian Journal of Economics [*A publication*]
Scandinav J Gastroent ... Scandinavian Journal of Gastroenterology [*A publication*]
Scandinav J Haemat ... Scandinavian Journal of Haematology [*A publication*]
Scandinav J Resp Dis ... Scandinavian Journal of Respiratory Diseases [*A publication*]
Scand J Behav Ther ... Scandinavian Journal of Behaviour Therapy [*A publication*]
Scand J Clin Lab Inv ... Scandinavian Journal of Clinical and Laboratory Investigation [*A publication*]
Scand J Clin Lab Invest ... Scandinavian Journal of Clinical and Laboratory Investigation [*A publication*]
Scand J Clin Lab Invest Suppl ... Scandinavian Journal of Clinical and Laboratory Investigation. Supplement [*A publication*]
Scand J Dent Res ... Scandinavian Journal of Dental Research [*A publication*]
Scand J Econ ... Scandinavian Journal of Economics [*A publication*]
Scand J For Res ... Scandinavian Journal of Forest Research [*A publication*]
Scand J Gastroenterol ... Scandinavian Journal of Gastroenterology [*A publication*]
Scand J Gastroenterol Suppl ... Scandinavian Journal of Gastroenterology. Supplement [*A publication*]
Scand J Haematol ... Scandinavian Journal of Haematology [*A publication*]
Scand J Haematol Suppl ... Scandinavian Journal of Haematology. Supplement [*A publication*]
Scand J Haematol Suppl Ser Haematol ... Scandinavian Journal of Haematology. Supplement. Series Haematological [*A publication*]
Scand J Immunol ... Scandinavian Journal of Immunology [*A publication*]
Scand J Immunol Suppl ... Scandinavian Journal of Immunology. Supplement [*A publication*]
Scand J Infect Dis ... Scandinavian Journal of Infectious Diseases [*A publication*]
Scand J Infect Dis Suppl ... Scandinavian Journal of Infectious Diseases. Supplement [*A publication*]
Scand J Metall ... Scandinavian Journal of Metallurgy [*A publication*]
Scand J Plast Reconstr Surg ... Scandinavian Journal of Plastic and Reconstructive Surgery [*A publication*]
Scand J Plast Reconstr Surg Suppl ... Scandinavian Journal of Plastic and Reconstructive Surgery. Supplement [*A publication*]
Scand J Plast Recon Surg ... Scandinavian Journal of Plastic and Reconstructive Surgery [*A publication*]

Scand J Prim Health Care ... Scandinavian Journal of Primary Health Care [*A publication*]
Scand J Psychol ... Scandinavian Journal of Psychology [*A publication*]
Scand J Rehabil Med ... Scandinavian Journal of Rehabilitation Medicine [*A publication*]
Scand J Rehabil Med Suppl ... Scandinavian Journal of Rehabilitation Medicine. Supplement [*A publication*]
Scand J Rehab Med ... Scandinavian Journal of Rehabilitation Medicine [*A publication*]
Scand J Respir Dis ... Scandinavian Journal of Respiratory Diseases [*A publication*]
Scand J Respir Dis Suppl ... Scandinavian Journal of Respiratory Diseases. Supplement [*A publication*]
Scand J Rheumatol ... Scandinavian Journal of Rheumatology [*A publication*]
Scand J Rheumatol Suppl ... Scandinavian Journal of Rheumatology. Supplement [*A publication*]
Scand J Soc Med ... Scandinavian Journal of Social Medicine [*A publication*]
Scand J Soc Med Suppl ... Scandinavian Journal of Social Medicine. Supplement [*A publication*]
Scand J St ... Scandinavian Journal of Statistics [*A publication*]
Scand J Statist ... Scandinavian Journal of Statistics. Theory and Applications [*A publication*]
Scand J Stat Theory and Appl ... Scandinavian Journal of Statistics. Theory and Applications [*A publication*]
Scand J Thorac Cardiovasc Surg ... Scandinavian Journal of Thoracic and Cardiovascular Surgery [*A publication*]
Scand J Thorac Cardiovasc Surg Suppl ... Scandinavian Journal of Thoracic and Cardiovascular Surgery. Supplement
Scand J Urol Nephrol ... Scandinavian Journal of Urology and Nephrology [*A publication*]
Scand J Urol Nephrol Suppl ... Scandinavian Journal of Urology and Nephrology. Supplement [*A publication*]
Scand J Work Envir Hlth ... Scandinavian Journal of Work Environment and Health [*A publication*]
Scand J Work Environ Health ... Scandinavian Journal of Work Environment and Health [*A publication*]
SCANDOC ... Scandinavian Documentation Center [*Washington, DC*]
Scand Oil-Gas Mag ... Scandinavian Oil-Gas Magazine [*A publication*]
Scand Paint Printing Ink Res Inst Rept ... Scandinavian Paint and Printing Ink Research Institute. Reports [*A publication*]
Scand Polit St ... Scandinavian Political Studies [*A publication*]
Scand Pol Stud ... Scandinavian Political Studies [*A publication*]
Scand Public Lib Q ... Scandinavian Public Library Quarterly [*A publication*]
Scand Publ Libr Q ... Scandinavian Public Library Quarterly [*A publication*]
Scand R ...... Scandinavian Review [*A publication*]
Scand Refrig ... Scandinavian Refrigeration [*Norway*] [*A publication*]
Scand Stud ... Scandinavian Studies [*A publication*]
Scand Stud Criminol ... Scandinavian Studies in Criminology [*A publication*]   (DLA)
Scand Stud in L ... Scandinavian Studies in Law [*A publication*]
Scand Stud Law ... Scandinavian Studies in Law [*A publication*]
Scand Stud No ... Scandinavian Studies and Notes [*A publication*]
Scand Yb .... Scandinavian Yearbook [*A publication*]
Scan Electron Microsc ... Scanning Electron Microscopy [*A publication*]
SCANIIR ... Surface Composition by Analysis of Neutral and Ion Impact Radiation [*Qualitative analysis*]
Scan J Sports Sci ... Scandinavian Journal of Sports Sciences [*A publication*]
Scan J Stat ... Scandinavian Journal of Statistics. Theory and Applications [*A publication*]
SCanL .... Studies in Canadian Literature [*A publication*]
SCAN MAG ... Scandalum Magnatum [*Defamation of Dignity*] [*Latin*]   (ROG)
Scanning Electron Microsc ... Scanning Electron Microscopy [*A publication*]
SCANO ..... Automatic Scanning Unit Inoperative [*Aviation*]   (FAAC)
SCANP ...... Scandinavian Periodicals Index in Economics and Business [*Helsinki School of Economics Library*] [*Information service or system*]
SCANPED ... System for Comparative Analysis of Programs For Educational Development [*Information service or system*]   (AEBS)
Scan R .... Scandinavian Review [*A publication*]
SCANS ...... Scheduling and Control by Automated Network System
SCANS ...... Secretary's Commission on Achieving Necessary Skills [*Department of Labor*]
SCANS ..... System Checkout Automatic Network Simulator
SCANSAR ... Scanning Synthetic Aperture RADAR
Scan Soc Forensic Odontol Newsl ... Scandinavian Society of Forensic Odontology. Newsletter [*A publication*]
SCAN-Test ... Scandinavian Pulp, Paper and Board Testing Committee [*Sweden*]   (EAIO)
SCAO .... Senior Civil Affairs Officer
SCAO .... Standing Committee on Army Organization [*British*]
SCAO .... Standing Conference of Atlantic Organisations [*British*]   (EAIO)
SCAOK ..... Automatic Scanning Unit Operative [*Aviation*]   (FAAC)
SCAO(P) ... Senior Civil Affairs Office, Police [*British*]
SCAP .... Alto Palena/Alto Palena [*Chile*] [*ICAO location identifier*]   (ICLI)
SCAP .... Service Center Audit Program [*IRS*]
SCAP .... Silent Compact Auxiliary Power
SCAP .... Silicon Capacitance Absolute Pressure Sensor
SCAP .... Slow Component Axonal Particulate [*Neurology*]
SCAP .... Small Communications Augmentation Package   (MCD)

SCAP .... Space Charge Atomizing Precipitaters   (KSC)
SCAP .... Superfund Comprehensive Accomplishment Plan [*Environmental Protection Agency*]   (GFGA)
SCAP .... Supreme Commander, Allied Powers [*World War II*]   (MUGU)
SCAP .... Svenska Cellulosa Aktiebolaget [*Sundsvall, Sweden*] [*NASDAQ symbol*]
SCAP .... Systems Concepts and Procedures
SCAPA ..... Society for Checking the Abuses of Public Advertising [*British*]
SCAPE ...... Self-Contained Atmospheric Personnel [*or Protective*] Ensemble [*Suit*] [*Aerospace*]
SCAPE ...... System Compatibility and Performance Evaluation [*Military*]   (CAAL)
SCAPS ...... Site Characterization and Analysis Penterometer System [*Army*]   (RDA)
SCAPS ...... Small Capitals [*Typography*]
SCAR .... Arica/Internacional Chacalluta [*Chile*] [*ICAO location identifier*]   (ICLI)
SCAR .... Satellite Capture and Retrieval   (AFM)
SCAR .... Scandinavian Council for Applied Research
SCAR .... Scandinavian Review [*A publication*]
scar .... Scarlet [*Philately*]
SCAR .... Schools' Campaign Against Racism [*British*]   (DI)
SCAR .... Scientific Committee on Antarctic Research [*ICSU*] [*Cambridge, England*]   (EAIO)
SCAR .... Signal Conditioner Assembly Request   (MCD)
SCAR .... Signal Conditioner Assembly Review   (MCD)
S Car .... South Carolina Reports [*A publication*]   (DLA)
SCAR .... Spacecraft Assessment Report [*NASA*]   (KSC)
SCAR .... Special Committee on Atlantic Research
SCAR .... Special Committee on Atomic Research [*Pugwash Conference*]
SCAR .... Special International Committee on Antarctic Research
SCAR .... Status Control Alert and Reporting   (MCD)
SCAR .... Strike Control and Reconnaissance [*Aircraft*]
SCAR .... Structure-Carcinogenic Activity Relationship [*Biochemistry*]
SCAR .... Subcaliber Aircraft Rocket
SCAR .... Submarine Celestial Altitude Recorder [*Navy*]
SCAR .... Subsequent Contrast Application Review   (MCD)
SCAR .... Supersonic Cruise Aircraft [*or Airplane*] Research [*NASA*]
SCAR .... Supplier Corrective Action Request
SCARA ..... Selective Compliance Assembly Robot Arm [*IBM Corp.*]
SCARAB ... Submersible Craft Assisting Repair and Burial [*Autonomous underwater vehicle*]
Scarabot ..... [*Arnaldus*] Scaraboti [*Flourished, 1310-35*] [*Authority cited in pre-1607 legal work*]   (DSA)
Scarborough Dist Archaeol Soc Res Rep ... Scarborough District Archaeological Society. Research Reports [*A publication*]
SCARDE ... Study Committee on Analysis of Research, Development, and Engineering
SCARE ...... Structural Ceramic Analysis and Reliability Evaluation [*NASA*]
SCAReU .... Stanford Community Against Reagan University [*Group opposed to proposed Ronald Reagan presidential library at Stanford University*]
SCARF ...... Santa Cruz Acoustic Range Facility [*Navy*]
SCARF ...... Self-Contained Automated Robotic Factory
SCARF ...... Side-Looking Coherent All-Range Focused
SCARF ...... Special Committee on the Adequacy of Range Facilities   (MUGU)
SCARF ...... Survey of Change and Residential Finance [*Census Bureau*]
SCARF ...... System Control Audit Review File [*Data processing*]
SCARLO ... San Carlos Milling Co., Inc. [*Associated Press abbreviation*]   (APAG)
SCARP ...... Society for Comic Art Research and Preservation
S Car R ...... South Carolina Law Reports [*A publication*]   (DLA)
SCARS ...... SACEUR [*Supreme Allied Commander, Europe*] Command Alerting Reporting System [*Army*]
SCARS ...... Serialized Control and Record [*or Reporting*] System   (NASA)
SCARS ...... Sneak Circuit Analysis Report Summary [*NASA*]   (GFGA)
SCARS ...... Software Configuration Accounting and Reporting System
SCARS ...... Southern's Computer-Assisted Retrieval Service [*University of Southern Mississippi*]   (OLDSS)
SCARS ...... Status Control Alert Reporting System   (NATG)
SCARS ...... System Control and Receiving Station [*Air Force*]
SCART ...... Sperry Continuity and Resistance Tester
SCARWAF ... Special Category Army with Air Force
SCAS .... Signal Corps Aviation School [*Obsolete*] [*Army*]
SCAS .... Society for Companion Animal Studies   (EAIO)
SCAS .... Southwest Center for Advanced Studies [*Later, University of Texas at Dallas*]
SCAS .... Stability Control Augmentation System   (NVT)
SCAS .... State Cost Accounting System   (OICC)
SCAS .... Subsystem Computer Application Software   (MCD)
SCASA ..... Straight Chiropractic Academic Standards Association   (EA)
SCASG ...... SONAR Calibration and Alignment Steering Group
SCASH .... Scottish Committee Action on Smoking and Health   (EAIO)
SCASP ...... Sequence of Coverage and Speed   (SAA)
SCASS .... Signal Corps Aircraft Signal Service [*Obsolete*] [*Army*]
Sc As Trinidad Pr ... Scientific Association of Trinidad. Proceedings [*A publication*]
SCAT .... Scat Hovercraft, Inc. [*Miami, FL*] [*NASDAQ symbol*]   (NQ)
SCAT .... Scatterometer
SCAT .... Scatula [*Package*] [*Pharmacy*]

SCAT........ School and College Ability Test [*of ETS*]
SCAT........ Schottky Cell Array Technology
SCAT........ Scout-Attack [*Helicopter*]   (MCD)
SCAT........ Security Control of Air Traffic [*FAA*]
SCAT........ Selected Calibration and Alignment Test   (MCD)
SCAT........ Self-Contained Automatic Transmitter   (MCD)
SCAT........ Sequential Component Automatic Testing   (MSA)
SCAT........ Service Code Automatic Tester [*Automotive engineering*]
SCAT........ Service Command Air Transportation
SCAT........ Share Compiler-Assembler, Translator
SCAT........ Sheep Cell Agglutination Test
SCAT........ Sickle Cell Anemia Test [*Medicine*]   (AAMN)
SCAT........ Small Car Automatic Transit [*System*]
SCAT........ Solid Catalysts   (KSC)
SCAT........ Solution to Customer Aircraft Troubles   (MCD)
SCAT........ South Pacific Combat Air Transport [*World War II*]
SCAT........ Space Communications and Tracking
SCAT........ Special Advisory Committee on Telecommunications
SCAT........ Speed Command Attitude/Target [*FAA*]
SCAT........ Speed Control Approach/Takeoff
SCAT........ Sperry Canada Automatic Tester
SCAT........ State Change Algorithm Translator
SCAT........ Storage, Checkout, and Transportation [*Rack*] [*Aerospace*]
SCAT........ Submarine Classification and Tracking
SCAT........ Supersonic Commercial Air Transport [*NASA*]
SCAT........ Surface-Controlled Avalanche Transistor
SCAT........ System Commonality Analysis Tool   (SSD)
SCAT........ Systems Consolidation of Accessions and Trainees
               [*Military*]   (AABC)
SCATA...... Survival Sited Casualty Treatment Assemblage   (AFM)
SCATANA ... Security Control of Air Traffic and Air Navigation Aids [*FAA*]
SCATE...... Self-Checking Automatic Testing Equipment
SCATE...... Space Chamber Analyzer - Thermal Environment [*NASA*]
SCATE...... Stromberg-Carlson Automatic Test Equipment
SCATER.... Security Control of Air Traffic and Electromagnetic Radiations
               [*During an air defense emergency*] [*FAA*]
Scates' Comp St ... Treat, Scates, and Blackwell's Compiled Illinois Statutes [*A
               publication*]   (DLA)
SCATHA... Satellite Charging at High Altitude   (MCD)
SCATHA... Spacecraft Charging at High Altitudes [*Satellite*]
SCAT ORIG ... Scatula Originalis [*Original Package*] [*Pharmacy*]
SCATS...... Scheduling and Tracking System   (MCD)
SCATS...... Self-Contained Automatic Test System
SCATS...... Sequentially Controlled Automatic Transmitter Start
SCATS...... Simulation, Checkout, and Training System
SCATS...... Simulation Control and Training System   (NASA)
SCATS...... Surface Combatant Airborne Tactical System   (MCD)
SCATT...... Scientific Communication and Technology Transfer [*System*]
               [*University of Pennsylvania*]
SCATT...... Shared Catalog Accessed Through Terminals [*Data processing
               system*]
SCATTOR ... Small Craft Assets, Training, and Turnover of
               Resources   (DNAB)
SCAUA...... Scientific Australian [*A publication*]
SCAUL...... Standing Conference of African University Libraries [*Lagos,
               Nigeria*]
SCAULWA ... Standing Conference of African University Libraries   (EAIO)
SCA(UN)... Department of Security Council Affairs of the United Nations
Scaur......... Pro Scauro [*of Cicero*] [*Classical studies*]   (OCD)
SCAV......... Scavenge   (AAG)
SCAW....... Scientists' Center for Animal Welfare   (EA)
SCAW....... Supreme Camp of the American Woodmen   (EA)
SCAWD..... Scottish Churches Action for World Development   (EAIO)
SCAWH-SAWRH ... Signal Company Aircraft Warning Hawaii - Signal
               Aircraft Warning Regiment Hawaii Association   (EA)
SCAWNA ... Self-Contained Adverse-Weather Night Attack   (MCD)
SCAWU..... Singapore Clerical and Administrative Workers' Union
Sc Azione ... Scuola in Azione [*A publication*]
Sc B........... Bachelor of Science
ScB............. Beaufort County Library, Beaufort, SC [*Library symbol*]
               [*Library of Congress*]   (LCLS)
SCB........... Sample Collection Bag [*NASA*]
SCB........... Scarborough [*Ontario*] [*Seismograph station code, US
               Geological Survey*] [*Closed*]   (SEIS)
SCB........... Schedule Change Board [*NASA*]   (NASA)
SCB........... Scholarly Book Center [*ACCORD*] [*UTLAS symbol*]
SCB........... School of Classical Ballet [*American Ballet Theater Foundation*]
Sc B........... Scientiae Baccalaureus [*Bachelor of Science*] [*Latin*]
SCB........... Scorpion Resources [*Vancouver Stock Exchange symbol*]
SCB........... Scribner, NE [*Location identifier*] [*FAA*]   (FAAL)
SCB........... Secondary Carpet Backing
SCB........... Segment Control BIT [*Binary Digit*]
SCB........... Selection Control Board [*NASA*]   (NASA)
SCB........... Selector Control Box [*Aerospace*]   (MCD)
SCB........... Selenite Cystine Broth   (OA)
SCB........... Semiconductor Bridge
SCB........... Session Control Block [*Data processing*]   (BUR)
SCB........... Ship Characteristics Board
SCB........... Shipowners Claims Bureau [*New York, NY*]   (EA)
SCB........... Ships Characteristics Board
SCB........... Ship's Cook, Butcher [*Navy*]

SCB........... Silicon Cell Bridge
SCB........... Silicon Circuit Board
SCB........... Silver Cadmium Battery
SCB........... Site Control Block [*Data processing*]   (OA)
SCB........... Society for Conservation Biology   (EA)
SCB........... Soeurs de la Charite de Besancon [*Sisters of Charity*]
               [*France*]   (EAIO)
SCB........... Software Control Board [*Apollo*] [*NASA*]
SCB........... South Central Bulletin [*A publication*]
SCB........... Specification Control Board [*NASA*]   (NASA)
SCB........... Stack Control Block
SCB........... Station Control Block [*Data processing*]   (IBMDP)
SCB........... Strictly Confined to Bed [*Medicine*]
SCB........... Student Contact Book [*A publication*]
SCB........... Survey of Current Business [*United States*] [*A publication*]
SCBA........ Balmaceda/Balmaceda [*Chile*] [*ICAO location
               identifier*]   (ICLI)
ScBa........... Lexington County Circulating Library, Batesburg, SC [*Library
               symbol*] [*Library of Congress*]   (LCLS)
SCBA........ Self-Contained Breathing Apparatus
SCBA........ Supreme Circle Brotherhood of America   (EA)
SCBAL...... Standard Chartered Bank Australia Ltd.   (ADA)
Sc BAM .... Bachelor of Science in Applied Mathematics
SC in Banco ... Supreme Court in Banco [*Canada*] [*A publication*]   (DLA)
S & C Bank ... Standard and Chartered Review [*Formerly, Standard Bank
               Review*] [*Later, Standard Chartered Review*] [*A
               publication*]
Sc BC .... Bachelor of Science in Chemistry
SCBCA...... Small Claims Board of Contract Appeals
SCBCL-C... Societe Commerciale de Banque Credit Lyonnais-
               Cameroun   (EY)
SC BCP...... SC Bancorp [*Associated Press abbreviation*]   (APAG)
SCBD........ Scan Conversion and Bright Display
SCBD........ Seller's Approved Configuration Baseline Document
               [*NASA*]   (NASA)
Sc BE .... Bachelor of Science in Engineering
SCBE........ Societe Canadienne des Brevets et d'Exploitation
SCBF .... Sacred Cat of Burma Fanciers   (EA)
SCBF .... Spinal Cord Blood Flow
SCBL .... Quilpue/Mil el Belloto [*Chile*] [*ICAO location
               identifier*]   (ICLI)
SCBL .... Scotts Bluff and Agate Fossil Beds National Monuments
SCBNP...... Society for the Collection of Brand-Name Pencils
               [*Inactive*]   (EA)
Sc BP .... Bachelor of Science in Physics
SCBQ........ Santiago/Mil el Bosque [*Chile*] [*ICAO location
               identifier*]   (ICLI)
SCBR........ Serum Cholesterol-Binding Reserve [*Medicine*]
SCBR........ Stationary Catalytic Basket Reactor [*Chemical engineering*]
SCBR........ Steam-Cooled Breeder Reactor [*Nuclear energy*]
SCBS........ Saint Charles Borromeo Seminary [*Pennsylvania*]
SCBS .... Society for the Conservation of Bighorn Sheep   (EA)
SC/BSE ..... Scientific Co-Operation Bureau for the European and North
               American Region [*United Nations*]   (EA)
SCBT .... Society of Computed Body Tomography   (EA)
SCBU........ Special Care Baby Unit [*Medicine*]
SCBUB ..... Sierra Club. Bulletin [*A publication*]
SCBUB8..... Sierra Club. Bulletin [*A publication*]
SCBW........ Society of Children's Book Writers   (EA)
SCC........... Cameron's Supreme Court Cases [*Canada*] [*A
               publication*]   (DLA)
ScC............. Charleston Library Society, Charleston, SC [*Library symbol*]
               [*Library of Congress*]   (LCLS)
SCC........... Deadhorse [*Alaska*] [*Airport symbol*]   (OAG)
SCC........... Deadhorse, AK [*Location identifier*] [*FAA*]   (FAAL)
SCC........... Sacra Congregatio Concilii [*Sacred Congregation of the
               Council*] [*Latin*]
SCC........... Safety Control Center   (NASA)
SCC........... SAGE [*Semiautomatic Ground Environment*] Control Center
SCC........... Salivary Caffeine Clearance [*Physiology*]
SCC........... Santa Cruz [*California*] [*Seismograph station code, US
               Geological Survey*] [*Closed*]   (SEIS)
SCC........... Satellite Communication Concentrator
SCC........... Satellite Communications Controller
SCC........... Satellite Control Center
SCC........... Satellite-Controlled Clock
SCC........... Scandinavian Collectors Club   (EA)
SCC........... Scarborough Campus, University of Toronto [*UTLAS symbol*]
SCC........... Schools Councils Classics Committee [*British*]
SCC........... Science Council of Canada
SCC........... Science Fiction Chronicle [*A publication*]
SCC........... Sea Cadet Corps [*Navy*] [*British*]
SCC........... Sears Canada, Inc. [*Toronto Stock Exchange symbol*]
SCC........... Secondary Combustion Chamber [*Furnace technology*]
SCC........... Secondary Containment Cooling   (IEEE)
SCC........... Security Capital Corp. [*AMEX symbol*]   (SPSG)
SCC........... Security Commodity Code   (AAG)
SCC........... Security Control Center [*NASA*]   (KSC)
SCC........... Security Coordination Committee   (NATG)
SCC........... Select Cases in Chancery [*Legal*] [*British*]

SCC............ Select Cases in Chancery Tempore King, Edited by Macnaghten [*England*] [*A publication*]   (DLA)
SCC............ Self-Contained Canister   (MCD)
SCC............ Senate Children's Caucus   (EA)
SCC............ Senate Copper Caucus   (EA)
SCC............ Senior Command Course [*British military*]   (DMA)
SCC............ Sequence Control Chart
SCC............ Sequential Control Counter [*Data processing*]   (BUR)
scc .... Serbo-Croatian (Cyrillic) [*MARC language code*] [*Library of Congress*]   (LCCP)
SCC............ Serial Communications Controller
SCC............ Service Change Committee [*Military*]
SCC............ Services for Crippled Children
SCC............ Servo Control Cabinet [*Military*]   (CAAL)
SCC............ Set Conditionally [*Data processing*]
SCC............ Sexual Concerns Checklist [*Premarital and marital relations test*]
SCC............ Ship Control Center
SCC............ Short-Circuit Current
SCC............ Short-Course Chemotherapy [*Medicine*]
SCC............ Signaling Conversion Circuit [*Telecommunications*]   (TEL)
SCC............ Simplified Computer Code
SCC............ Simulation Control Center [*NASA*]   (KSC)
SCC............ Single Conductor Cable   (MSA)
SCC............ Single Copy Complexity [*Genetics*]
SCC............ Single Cotton-Covered [*Wire insulation*]
SCC............ Slice Control Central   (SAA)
SCC............ Slidell Computer Complex [*NASA*] [*Slidell, LA*]
SCC............ Small Cell Cancer [*Oncology*]
SCC............ Small Center Contact
SCC............ Small Compressor Colorimeter   (MCD)
SCC............ Societe Canadienne de Cardiologie [*Canadian Cardiovascular Society*]   (EAIO)
SCC............ Societe Canadienne de Criminologie
SCC............ Societe Chimique des Charbonnages [*France*]
SCC........... Society for Children with Craniosynostosis   (EA)
SCC............ Society for the Christian Commonwealth
SCC............ Society of Cosmetic Chemists   (EA)
SCC............ Soeurs de la Croix de Chavanod [*Sisters of the Cross of Chavanod*] [*France*]   (EAIO)
SCC............ Software Checkout Console [*Army*]
SCC............ Somatic Cell Concentration   (OA)
SCC............ Source Classification Code [*Environmental Protection Agency*]
SCC............ Southern Connecticut State College, Division of Library Science, New Haven, CT [*OCLC symbol*]   (OCLC)
SCC............ Space Chamber Complex   (MCD)
SCC............ Space Control Station
SCC............ Spacecraft Control Center [*NASA*]   (KSC)
SCC............ Spark Control Computer [*Automotive engineering*]
SCC............ Special Coordinating Committee [*National Security Council*] [*Terminated, 1981*]
SCC............ Specialized Common Carrier [*Telecommunications*]   (NRCH)
SCC............ Specific Clauses and Conditions   (NATG)
SCC............ Specification for Contract Change   (DNAB)
SCC............ Speed Control Circuit   (DNAB)
SCC............ Splenium of the Corpus Callosum [*Anatomy*]
SCC............ Squadron Control Center   (AAG)
SCC............ Squamous Cell Carcinoma [*Also, SC*] [*Medicine*]
SCC............ Stabilized Core Composite [*Materials science*]
SCC............ Standard Commodity Classification [*Military*]
SCC............ Standard Commodity Codes   (MCD)
SCC............ Standard Consultative Commission [*for resolving compliance disputes arising from SALT 1 accord*]
SCC............ Standard Cubic Centimeter   (KSC)
SCC............ Standardized Cost Categories
scc............. Standards Council of Canada [*See also CCNO*]
SCC............ Standing Consultative Commission [*SALT agreements*] [*US/USSR*]
SCC............ Standing Interdepartmental Committee on Censorship [*War Cabinet*] [*British*]
SCC............ Starcraft Campers Club   (EA)
SCC............ State Coordination Committee [*Responsible for administering the Work Incentive Program at the state level*]
SCC............ State Corporation Commission
SCC............ Steel Carriers Conference [*Later, RDCC*] [*An association*]   (EA)
SCC............ Steering Control Console   (DNAB)
SCC............ Stock Clearing Corp. [*NYSE*]
SCC............ Stock Control Center [*Army*]
SCC............ Storage Connecting Circuit [*Teletype*]
SCC............ Strategic Communications Command [*Army*]   (MCD)
SCC............ Stress Corrosion Cracking [*Metals*]
SCC............ Student of Codrington College [*Barbados*]
SCC............ Studies in Comparative Communism [*A publication*]
SCC............ Studio Collector's Club   (EA)
SC(C)........ Submarine Chaser (Control) [*110 foot*] [*Obsolete*]
SCC............ Submission Control Code   (MCD)
SCC............ Sunbeam Car Club   (EA)
SCC............ Suore della Carita Cristiana [*Sisters of Christian Charity*] [*Italy*]   (EAIO)
SCC............ Super-Critical Cryogenics   (SAA)

SCC............ Supervisor Control Console
SCC............ Supervisory Control Conference   (KSC)
SCC............ Supply Control Center [*Military*]
SCC............ Supreme Court of Canada
SCC............ Supreme Court Cases [*India*] [*A publication*]   (DLA)
SCC............ Supreme Court Circular [*Ceylon*] [*A publication*]   (ILCA)
SCC............ Surface Combat Condition   (DNAB)
SCC............ Surveillance Coordination Center   (NATG)
SCC............ Switching Control Center [*Bell System*]
SCC............ Synchronous Communications Controller
SCC............ Syndicat des Communications Canada
SCC............ System Command Center   (FAAC)
SCC............ System Communication Controller
SCC............ System Control Code   (MCD)
SCC............ System Control Console   (MCD)
SCC............ System Coordinate Center [*Military*]   (CAAL)
SCC............ Systems Control Center
SCCA......... Single Cell Cytotoxicity Assay [*Clinical chemistry*]
SCCA......... Society of Canadian Cine Amateurs
SCCA......... Society of Company and Commercial Accountants [*Edgbaston, Birmingham, England*]   (EAIO)
SCCA......... Southeastern Cottonseed Crushers Association   (EA)
SCCA......... Specification Compliance Concept Agreements   (MCD)
SCCA......... Sports Car Club of America   (EA)
SCCA......... Subcontract Change Authorization   (AAG)
SCCAC...... Society for Conceptual and Content Analysis by Computer   (EA)
SCC-ACO ... Strategic Communications Command Advanced Concepts Office [*Army*]
SC Cas .... Supreme Court Cases [*A publication*]   (DLA)
ScCatt .... Scuola Cattolica [*A publication*]
ScCB .... Baptist College at Charleston, Charleston, SC [*Library symbol*] [*Library of Congress*]   (LCLS)
SCCB......... Safety Change Control Board   (MCD)
SCCB .... Site Configuration Control Board [*NASA*]   (NASA)
SCCB .... Software Configuration Control Board   (KSC)
SCCBS...... Science Council of Canada. Background Study [*A publication*]
SCCC......... Chile Chico/Chile Chico [*Chile*] [*ICAO location identifier*]   (ICLI)
ScCC......... College of Charleston, Charleston, SC [*Library symbol*] [*Library of Congress*]   (LCLS)
SCCC......... Satellite Communications Control Centre [*British*]
SCCC......... System Casualty Control Console [*Military*]   (CAAL)
SCCCE ...... Society of Certified Consumer Credit Executives   (EA)
ScCCit........ Citadel, Charleston, SC [*Library symbol*] [*Library of Congress*]   (LCLS)
SCCD........ Iquique/Los Condores [*Chile*] [*ICAO location identifier*]   (ICLI)
ScCDHHi.. Dalcho Historical Society of the Episcopal Diocese of South Carolina, Charleston, SC [*Library symbol*] [*Library of Congress*]   (LCLS)
SCCE .... Satellite Configuration Control Element   (MCD)
SCCE .... School and College Conference on English
SCCE .... Scottish Council for Community Education
SCCE .... Society of Certified Credit Executives [*St. Louis, MO*]   (EA)
SCCEA ...... Strategic Communications Command Equipment Applications Directorate [*Army*]
SCCF .... Calama/El Loa [*Chile*] [*ICAO location identifier*]   (ICLI)
ScCF .... Charleston County Library, Charleston, SC [*Library symbol*] [*Library of Congress*]   (LCLS)
SCCF .... Satellite Communication Control Facility
SCCF .... Security Clearance Case Files [*Military*]   (AABC)
SCCF .... Service Center Control File [*IRS*]
SCCG........ Station Communications Control Group [*Ground Communications Facility, NASA*]
SCCH .... Chillan/Gral, Bernardo O'Higgins [*Chile*] [*ICAO location identifier*]   (ICLI)
SCCH .... Society of Cinema Collectors and Historians   (EA)
SCCH .... Standard Cubic Centimeters per Hour   (MCD)
ScChwC .... Chesterfield-Marlboro Technical College, Cheraw, SC [*Library symbol*] [*Library of Congress*]   (LCLS)
SCCI .... Punta Arenas/Internacional Carlos Ibanez Del Campo [*Chile*] [*ICAO location identifier*]   (ICLI)
SCCI .... Smurf Collectors' Club International   (EA)
SCC(I)........ Special Coordination Committee (Intelligence)   (MCD)
SCCJ......... Supreme Court of Canada Judgements [*Canada Department of Justice*] [*Information service or system*]   (CRD)
SCCL .... Safety Compliance Certification Label [*Automotive engineering*]
SCCL .... Scottish Council for Civil Liberties   (DI)
SCCL .... Small Cell (Anaplastic) Carcinoma of the Lung [*Oncology*]
SCCL .... Supply Catalog Components List [*Military*]
ScCleU....... Clemson University, Clemson, SC [*Library symbol*] [*Library of Congress*]   (LCLS)
ScCliJ .... Jacobs Library, Clinton, SC [*Library symbol*] [*Library of Congress*] [*Obsolete*]   (LCLS)
ScClP .... Presbyterian College, Clinton, SC [*Library symbol*] [*Library of Congress*]   (LCLS)
ScClTO...... Thornwell Orphanage, Clinton, SC [*Library symbol*] [*Library of Congress*]   (LCLS)

ScCM......... Medical University of South Carolina, Charleston, SC [*Library symbol*] [*Library of Congress*] (LCLS)
SCCM........ Sertoli-Cell Culture Medium [*Clinical chemistry*]
SCCM........ Single Chamber Controllable Motor (MCD)
SCCM........ Society of Critical Care Medicine (EA)
SCCM........ Standard Cubic Centimeters per Minute (NASA)
SCCM........ Standing Commission on Church Music (EA)
ScCMP...... Middleton Place, Charleston, SC [*Library symbol*] [*Library of Congress*] (LCLS)
ScCMu....... Charleston Museum Library, Charleston, SC [*Library symbol*] [*Library of Congress*] (LCLS)
SCCN........ Subcontract [*or Subcontractor*] Change Notice (KSC)
SCCNC....... Society of Critical Care Nurses of Canada
SCC NR..... Special Cryptologic Control Number (DNAB)
SCCO........ Security Classification Control Officer [*Military*]
ScCoAH..... South Carolina Department of Archives and History, Columbia, SC [*Library symbol*] [*Library of Congress*] (LCLS)
ScCoB .... Benedict College, Columbia, SC [*Library symbol*] [*Library of Congress*] (LCLS)
ScCoB .... Columbia Bible College, Columbia, SC [*Library symbol*] [*Library of Congress*] (LCLS)
ScCoC .... Columbia College, Columbia, SC [*Library symbol*] [*Library of Congress*] (LCLS)
SC Code ..... Code of Laws of South Carolina [*A publication*] (DLA)
SC Code Ann ... Code of Laws of South Carolina, Annotated [*A publication*] (DLA)
Sc Code Ann (Law Co-Op) ... Code of Laws of South Carolina Annotated (Lawyers Co-Op) [*A publication*]
SC Code Regs ... Code of Laws of South Carolina Annotated. Code of Regulations [*A publication*]
ScCoGS...... Church of Jesus Christ of Latter-Day Saints, Genealogical Society Library, Columbia Branch, Columbia, SC [*Library symbol*] [*Library of Congress*] (LCLS)
ScCon........ Horry County Memorial Library, Conway, SC [*Library symbol*] [*Library of Congress*] (LCLS)
Sc Conspectus ... Science Conspectus [*A publication*]
ScCoR .... Richland County Library, Columbia, SC [*Library symbol*] [*Library of Congress*] (LCLS)
Sc Costs ..... Scott's ABC Guide to Costs [*2nd ed.*] [*1910*] [*A publication*] (DLA)
ScCoT .... Lutheran Theological Southern Seminary, Columbia, SC [*Library symbol*] [*Library of Congress*] (LCLS)
ScCoV .... United States Veterans Administration Hospital, Columbia, SC [*Library symbol*] [*Library of Congress*] (LCLS)
SCCP .... Sabah Chinese Consolidated Party [*Political party*] [*Malaysia*] (FEA)
SCCP .... Signaling Connection Control Part [*Telecommunications*]
SCCP .... Systems Change Control Procedure [*Social Security Administration*]
SCCPG ...... Satellite Communications Contingency Planning Group (NATG)
SCCR........ Science Council of Canada. Report [*A publication*]
SCCR........ Society for Cross-Cultural Research (EA)
SCCR........ Stanford Center for Chicano Research [*Stanford University*] [*Research center*] (RCD)
SCCR........ Subcontractor Change Request (MCD)
ScCRC .... Charleston Diocesan Archives, Roman Catholic Church, Charleston, SC [*Library symbol*] [*Library of Congress*] (LCLS)
SCCRI .... Swedish Cement and Concrete Research Institute (MCD)
SCCS .... Satellite Communications Control System (MCD)
SCCS .... Secondary Chemical Control System [*Nuclear energy*] (NRCH)
SCCS .... Sodium Chemistry Control System [*Westinghouse Corp.*] (IEEE)
SCCS .... Software Controlled Communication Services (MCD)
SCCS .... Source Code Control System [*Data processing*]
SCCS .... Souvenir Card Collectors Society (EA)
SCCS .... Souvenir China Collectors Society (EA)
SCCS .... Special Consultative Committee on Security [*OAS*]
SCCS .... Standard Commodity Classification System (NG)
SCCS .... Standard Cross-Cultural Sample [*Human Relations Area Files*] [*Information retrieval*]
SCCS .... Standard Cubic Centimeters per Second (NASA)
SCCS .... Standby Core Cooling System [*Nuclear energy*] (NRCH)
SCCS .... STRICOM [*Strike Command*] Command and Control System [*Army*] (AABC)
SCCS .... Switching Control Center System [*Telecommunications*] (TEL)
SCCSA ...... Sports Car Collectors Society of America (EA)
ScCSM ...... Old Slave Mart Museum, Charleston, SC [*Library symbol*] [*Library of Congress*] (LCLS)
SCC Spec... Soap/Cosmetics/Chemical Specialties [*A publication*]
SCCSS........ Science Council of Canada. Special Study [*A publication*]
ScCT .... Trident Technical College, Palmer Campus, Charleston, SC [*Library symbol*] [*Library of Congress*] (LCLS)
SCC-TED .. Strategic Communications Command - Test and Evaluation Directorate [*Army*]
SCCTR ...... Standing Committee for Controlled Thermonuclear Research [*Terminated, 1973*] [*AEC*] (EGAO)
SCCTSD.... Society of Catholic College Teachers of Sacred Doctrine [*Later, CTS*] (EA)

SCCU........ Single Channel Control Unit
SCCU........ Spacecraft Command Control Unit (KSC)
SCCU........ Specialist Claims Control Unit [*British*]
SCCUK..... Swedish Chamber of Commerce for the United Kingdom (DS)
SCCUS ...... Swedish Chamber of Commerce of the United States [*Later, Swedish-American Chamber of Commerce*]
ScCV .... United States Veterans Administration Hospital, Charleston, SC [*Library symbol*] [*Library of Congress*] (LCLS)
SCCW....... Scarritt College for Christian Workers [*Tennessee*]
SCCWRP... Southern California Coastal Water Research Project (NOAA)
SCCWRP TR ... SCCWRP (Southern California Coastal Water Research Project). TR [*A publication*]
SCCY .... Coyhaique/Teniente Vidal [*Chile*] [*ICAO location identifier*] (ICLI)
SCCZ......... Punta Arenas [*Chile*] [*ICAO location identifier*] (ICLI)
SCD .... Darlington County Library, Darlington, SC [*OCLC symbol*] (OCLC)
SCD .... Doctor of Commercial Science
Sc D........... Doctor of Science
SCD .... S-Band Cassegrain Diplexer
SCD .... Satellite Control Department
SCD .... Schedule (AABC)
SCD .... Schneider Corp. [*Toronto Stock Exchange symbol*]
SCD .... Science Communication Division [*George Washington University Medical Center*] [*Information service or system*] (IID)
Sc D........... Scientiae Doctor [*Doctor of Science*] [*Latin*]
SCD .... Scientific Computer Division [*Army Tank-Automotive Command*]
ScD .... Scintillation Detector (IEEE)
SCD .... Screen Door
SCD .... Screwed (MDG)
SCD .... Secondary Current Distribution [*Electroplating*]
SCD .... Security Coding Device (NATG)
SCD .... Senile Cognitive Decline [*Medicine*]
SCD .... Senior Citizen Discount
SCD .... Service Computation Date [*Military*] (AFM)
SCD .... Service Connected Disability [*Medicine*] (AAMN)
SCD .... Service Control Drawing
SCD .... Servo Chart Drive
SCD .... Ship's Center Display [*Navy*] (NVT)
SCD .... Sickle Cell Disease [*Medicine*]
SCD .... Signal Canceling Device
SCD .... Significant Construction Deficiency [*Nuclear energy*] (NRCH)
SCD .... Simulated Communications Deception [*Army*] (INF)
SCD .... Slovenian Christian Democrats [*Political party*]
SCD .... Society of Craft Designers (EA)
SCD .... Software Conceptual Design [*Data processing*]
SCD .... Soil Conservation District [*Agriculture*]
SCD .... Source Control Document (NASA)
SCD .... Source Control Drawing
SCD .... Space Control Document [*NASA*] (KSC)
SCD .... Specification Control Document [*or Drawing*] [*NASA*] (NASA)
SCD .... Spreading Cortical Depression
SCD .... State Civil Defense
SCD .... Static Column Decode [*Data processing*]
SCD .... Sterile Connection Device [*Medicine*]
SC & D....... Stock Control and Distribution (AFM)
SCD .... Strategic Communications Division [*Military*]
SCD .... Streaming Current Detector
SCD .... Structure-Chart Diagramer [*Data processing*]
SCD .... Subacute Combined Degeneration [*of spinal cord*] [*Medicine*]
SCD .... Subcarrier Discriminator
SCD .... Subcontract Deviation
SCD .... Subject Captain's Discretion [*Aviation*] (FAAC)
SCD .... Sudden Cardiac Death [*Medicine*]
SCD .... Sudden Coronary Death (MAE)
SCD .... Sulfur Chemiluminescence Detector
SCD .... Supply, Commissary, and Disbursing [*Navy*]
SCD .... Surrey Commercial Dock [*British*]
SCD .... Surveillance Criticality Designator [*DoD*]
SCD .... Sylacauga, AL [*Location identifier*] [*FAA*] (FAAL)
SCD .... System Coordination Document
SCD .... Systems, Components, and Displays
ScDa......... Darlington County Library, Darlington, SC [*Library symbol*] [*Library of Congress*] (LCLS)
SCDA......... Iquique/Gral Diego Aracena [*Chile*] [*ICAO location identifier*] (ICLI)
SCDA......... Safing, Cool Down, and Decontamination Area [*NASA*] (NASA)
ScDA......... Scapulodextra Anterior [*A fetal position*] (AAMN)
SCDA......... SEATO [*Southeast Asia Treaty Organization*] Central Distribution Agency (NATG)
SCDA......... Situational Control of Daily Activities
SCDAP...... Severe Core Damage Analysis Package [*Nuclear energy*] (NRCH)
SCDC........ Scottish Cooperative Development Committee
SCDC........ Service Coding and Data Collection (AAG)
SCDC........ Societe des Comptables de Direction au Canada [*Society of Management Accountants of Canada - SMAC*]

SCDC......... Source Coding and Data Collection
SCDC......... Strategic Concepts Development Center [*National Defense University*]
SCDC......... Supreme Court Reports, District of Columbia [*A publication*]   (DLA)
SCDCNS ... Supreme Court Reports, District of Columbia, New Series [*A publication*]   (DLA)
SCDCU...... Section Chief, Display Control Unit [*Army*]
SC/DDS .... Sensor Control/Data Display Set   (MCD)
Sc D in Ed ... Doctor of Science in Education
SC Dent J .. South Carolina Dental Journal [*A publication*]
ScDeV........ Voorhees College, Denmark, SC [*Library symbol*] [*Library of Congress*]   (LCLS)
SCDFGNY ... Sickle Cell Disease Foundation of Greater New York   (EA)
Sc D Govt... Doctor of Science in Government
Sc D in Hyg ... Doctor of Science in Hygiene
SCDI......... Science Dimension [*A publication*]
SCDI......... Scottish Council of Development and Industry   (DI)
SCDI......... Serious Chemical Distribution Incident
SCDI......... Short Children's Depression Inventory [*Psychology*]
SCDIA ...... Science Digest [*Chicago*] [*A publication*]
SC Dig....... Cassel's Supreme Court Digest [*Canada*] [*A publication*]   (DLA)
Sc Dimension ... Science Dimension [*A publication*]
Sc & Div..... Law Reports, Scotch and Divorce Appeals [*A publication*]   (DLA)
Sc & Div App ... Scotch and Divorce Appeals [*English Law Reports*] [*A publication*]   (DLA)
SC Div Bad ... Second Class Diver Badge [*Military decoration*]
SC Div Geol Geol Notes ... South Carolina. Division of Geology. Geologic Notes [*A publication*]
SC Div Geol Miner Resour Ser ... South Carolina. Division of Geology. Mineral Resources Series [*A publication*]
SC Div Geol Misc Rep ... South Carolina. Division of Geology. Miscellaneous Report [*A publication*]
SC Div Geology Mineral Industries Lab Monthly Bull ... South Carolina. Division of Geology. Mineral Industries Laboratory. Monthly Bulletin [*A publication*]
SCDL......... Saturated Current Demand Logic
SCDL......... Ship Configuration Detail List [*Navy*]
SCDL......... Stabilized Carbon Dioxide LASER
SCDL......... Surveillance and Control Data Link [*Military*]
SCDM .... Solar Corona Diagnostic Mission [*NASA*]   (SSD)
Sc D (Med) ... Doctor of Medical Science
SCDMR..... Steam-Cooled Deuteriated Water-Moderated Reactor [*Nuclear energy*]
ScdNE........ Scudder New Europe Fund [*Associated Press abbreviation*]   (APAG)
SCD OCSA ... Staff Communications Division, Office, Chief of Staff, Army   (AABC)
SCD OC of SA ... Staff Communications Division, Office, Chief of Staff, Army   (AABC)
Sc DP .... Right Scapuloposterior Position [*of the fetus*] [*Obstetrics*]
ScDP......... Scapulodextra Posterior [*A fetal position*]   (AAMN)
SCDP......... Sedimentary Chlorophyll Degradation Product [*Paleontology*]
SCDP......... Simulation Control Data Package [*NASA*]   (NASA)
SCDP......... Society of Certified Data Processors [*Superseded by AICCP*]   (EA)
SCDP......... Southern Cooperative Development Program [*Sponsored by Southern Consumers Education Foundation*]
SCDP......... Steel Cadmium Plated
SCDR........ Screwdriver   (MSA)
SCDR........ Seller Critical Design Review [*NASA*]   (NASA)
SCDR........ Shuttle Critical Design Review [*NASA*]   (NASA)
SCDR........ Software Critical Design Review [*NASA*]   (NASA)
SCDR........ Subcontractor Critical Design Review [*NASA*]
SCDR........ Subsystem Controller Definition Record [*Data processing*]   (IBMDP)
SCDRL...... Subcontractor Data Requirements List   (DNAB)
SCDS......... Scan Converter Display System   (MCD)
SCDS......... Sensor Communication and Display System   (MCD)
SCDS........ Shipboard Chaff Decoy System [*Navy*]
SCDS......... Signal Circuits Design Section
SCDS......... Staff of Chief of Defence Staff [*British*]
SCDSB ...... Suppressed-Carrier Double Sideband
SCDSD..... Scientific Clearinghouse and Documentation Services Division [*National Science and Technology Authority*] [*Information service or system*]   (IID)
SCD (St V) ... Supreme Court Decisions (St. Vincent) [*1928-36*] [*A publication*]   (DLA)
SCDU .... Signal Conditioning and Display Unit [*NASA*]   (NASA)
S & CDU.... Switch and Cable Distribution Unit   (AAG)
ScDwE .... Erskine College, Due West, SC [*Library symbol*] [*Library of Congress*]   (LCLS)
ScDwE-T ... Erskine College, Erskine Theological Seminary, Due West, SC [*Library symbol*] [*Library of Congress*]   (LCLS)
ScE............ Edgefield County Library, Edgefield, SC [*Library symbol*] [*Library of Congress*]   (LCLS)
SCE........... St. Petersburg Commodity Exchange [*Russian Federation*]   (EY)
SCE........... Saturated Calomel Electrode [*Electrochemistry*]

Sce............. [*Quintus Mucius*] Scaevola [*Flourished, 1st century*] [*Authority cited in pre-1607 legal work*]   (DSA)
SCE........... Scan Conversion Equipment [*Television*]
SCE........... SCEcorp. [*Formerly, Southern California Edison Co.*] [*NYSE symbol*]   (SPSG)
SCE........... Schedule Compliance-Evaluation [*Polaris*]
SCE........... Schellex Gold [*Vancouver Stock Exchange symbol*]
SCE........... Schlegeis [*Austria*] [*Seismograph station code, US Geological Survey*]   (SEIS)
ScE............ Sciences Ecclesiastiques [*Montreal-Brussels*] [*A publication*]
SCE........... Scottish Certificate of Education
SCE........... Scribe Ezra [*Freemasonry*]
SCE........... Secretory Carcinoma of Endometrium
SCE........... Select Cases Relating to Evidence (Strange) [*A publication*]   (DLA)
SCE........... Selection Control Element
SCE........... Separated Career Employee
SCE........... Service Cryptologic Elements [*Army*]
SCE........... Siberia Commodity Exchange [*Russian Federation*]   (EY)
SCE........... Signal Conditioning Equipment
SCE........... Signal Conversion Equipment [*Telecommunications*]
SCE........... Significant Combat Equipment [*Army*]
SCE........... Single-Charge Exchange [*Physics*]   (OA)
SCE........... Single Cotton-Covered Enameled [*Wire insulation*]   (DEN)
SCE........... Single Cycle Execute
SCE........... Sister Chromatid Exchange [*Cytology*]
SCE........... Situationally Caused Error
SCE........... Small Current Element
SCE........... Societe Canadienne d'Esthetique [*Canadian Society for Aesthetics - CSAC*]
SCE........... Society of Carbide Engineers [*Later, SCTE*]   (EA)
SCE........... Society of Christian Engineers   (EA)
SCE........... Society of Christian Ethics   (EA)
SCE........... Society for Clinical Ecology [*Later, AAEM*]   (EA)
SCE........... Society for Creative Ethics [*Later, SPC*]   (EA)
SCE........... Solar Corona Explorer [*Project*] [*NASA*]
SCE........... Solder Circuit Etch
SCE........... Source   (MSA)
SCE........... Space Cabin Environment [*Skylab*] [*NASA*]
SCE........... Spacecraft Command Encoder   (MCD)
SCE........... Special Conditioning Equipment
SCE........... Spectrum Communications & Electronics Corp. [*Telecommunications service*]   (TSSD)
SCE........... Stabilization Control Electronics
SCE........... Staff Civil Engineer [*Military*]   (DNAB)
SCE........... Stage Calibration Equipment   (SAA)
SCE........... Standard Calomel Electrode
SCE........... State College [*Pennsylvania*] [*Airport symbol*]   (OAG)
SCE........... State College, PA [*Location identifier*] [*FAA*]   (FAAL)
SCE........... Stored Controlled Energy
SCE........... Stratified-Charge Engine [*Auto engine*]
SCE........... Strukturen Christlicher Existenz [*A publication*]
SCE........... Supercritical Extract [*Separation technology*]
SCE........... Superintending Civil Engineer [*British*]
SCE........... Swedish Cypress Expedition [*A publication*]
SCE........... United States Air Force, Armament Laboratory, Technical Library, Eglin AFB, FL [*OCLC symbol*]   (OCLC)
ScEA.......... John R. Abney Collection, Edgefield County Library, Edgefield, SC [*Library symbol*] [*Library of Congress*]   (LCLS)
ScEa.......... Pickens County Library, Easley, SC [*Library symbol*] [*Library of Congress*]   (LCLS)
SCEA........ Service Children's Education Authority [*Ministry of Defence*] [*British*]
SCEA........ Signal Conditioning Electronics Assembly
SCEA........ Society of Communications Engineers and Analysts
SCEA........ Society of Cost Estimating and Analysis   (EA)
SCEAR...... Scientific Committee on the Effects of Atomic Radiation
SCEB........ SHAPE [*Supreme Headquarters Allied Powers Europe*] Communications Electronics Board [*NATO*]   (NATG)
SCEB .... Societe Canadienne des Etudes Bibliques [*Canadian Society of Biblical Studies - CSBS*]
SCEB .... Syndicat Canadien des Employes de Bureau [*Canadian Office Employees Union - COEU*]
SCEC........ Societe Canadienne des Eleveurs de Chevres
SCEC........ Societe Canadienne des Etudes Classiques [*Classical Association of Canada - CAC*]
SCEC........ Spaceborne Computer Engineering Conference   (MCD)
SCEC........ Student Council for Exceptional Children   (AEBS)
SCECC ...... Societe Canadienne pour l'Etude Comparee des Civilisations [*Canadian Society for the Comparative Study of Civilizations - CSCSC*]
ScEccl .... Sciences Ecclesiastiques [*A publication*]
SCECI....... Societe Canadienne d'Education Comparee et Internationale
SCEcp........ SCEcorp [*Formerly, Southern California Edison Co.*] [*Associated Press abbreviation*]   (APAG)
SCEd.......... Southern California Edison Co. [*Associated Press abbreviation*]   (APAG)
Sc Ed D .... Doctor of Science in Education
SCEDSIP Bull ... SCEDSIP [*Standing Conference on Educational Development Services in Polytechnics*] Bulletin [*A publication*]

SCEE......... Societe Canadienne pour l'Etude de l'Education [*Canadian Society for the Study of Education - CSSE*]
SCEE......... Southern Coalition for Educational Equity   (EA)
SCEE......... Student Committee for Economic Education   (EA)
SCEEB...... Scottish Certificate of Education Examination Board
SCEEE....... Southeastern Center for Electrical Engineering Education [*Air Force*]
SCEERR.... Sacra Congregatio Episcoporum et Regularium [*Sacred Congregation of Bishops and Regulars*] [*Latin*]
SCEES...... Service Central des Enquetes et Etudes Statistiques [*Central Service for Statistical Inquiries and Studies*] [*Ministry of Agriculture*] [*Paris, France*]
SCEES...... Societe Canadienne pour l'Etude de l'Enseignement Superieur [*Canadian Society for the Study of Higher Education - CSSHE*]
SCEET....... Support Concept Economic Evaluation Technique   (MCD)
SCEF......... Isla Rey Jorge/Centro Meteorologico Antartico Presidente Frei [*Chile*] [*ICAO location identifier*]   (ICLI)
SCEF......... Southern Conference Educational Fund   (EA)
SC/EFC..... Spoiler Control/Elevator Feel Computer   (MCD)
SC/EFC CP ... SC/EFC [*Spoiler Control/Elevator Feel Computer*] Control Panel   (MCD)
SCEFS....... Spoiler Control Elevator Feel System   (MCD)
SCEH........ Society for Clinical and Experimental Hypnosis   (EA)
SCEI......... Safe Car Educational Institute
SCEI......... Societe Canadienne pour les Etudes Italiennes [*Canadian Society for Italian Studies - CSIS*]
SCEI......... Special Committee on Environmental Information [*Special Libraries Association*]
SCEIBF..... Standing Conference for Europe of the International Basketball Federation   (EAIO)
SCEIL....... Service Ceiling
SCEIO....... Societe Canadienne pour Etudes d'Intelligence par Ordinateur
SCEKS...... Spectrum Clear Except Known Signals   (MUGU)
SCEL......... Santiago/Internacional Arturo Merino Benitez [*Chile*] [*ICAO location identifier*]   (ICLI)
scel............ Scellino [*Shilling*] [*Monetary unit*] [*Italian*]
SCEL........ Signal Corps Engineering Laboratories [*Obsolete*] [*Army*]
SCEL........ Small Components Evaluation Loop [*Nuclear energy*]   (NRCH)
SCEL........ Standing Committee on Education in Librarianship
SCELBAL ... Scientific Elementary Basic Language [*1963*] [*Data processing*]   (CSR)
SCEM........ Santiago/Arturo Merino Benitez (Edificio Direccion Meteorologica) [*Chile*] [*ICAO location identifier*]   (ICLI)
SCEN........ Santiago/Edificio Navegacion Aerea Arturo Merino Benitez [*Chile*] [*ICAO location identifier*]   (ICLI)
Scen............ Scenario [*A publication*]
SCEN........ Societe Canadienne pour l'Etude des Noms [*Canadian Society for the Study of Names - CSSN*]
SCEN........ South Central
SCENA...... Science and Engineering [*A publication*]
SCENE..... Studies of Coastal and Estuarine Environments [*National Oceanic and Atmospheric Administration*]   (MSC)
SCENIC .... Scientific Engineering Information Center   (KSC)
Scenic Trips Geol Past ... Scenic Trips to the Geologic Past [*A publication*]
SCEO........ Senior Chief Executive Officer [*Civil Service*] [*British*]
SCEO........ Station Construction Engineering Officer
SCEP......... Secure Communications Equipment Program [*Air Force*]   (CET)
SCEP......... Significant Criminal Enforcement Project [*Bureau of Alcohol, Tobacco, and Firearms*]
SCEP......... Societe Canadienne d'Enseignement Postscolaire
SCEP......... Study of Critical Environmental Problems [*MIT*]
SCEPC....... Senior Civil Emergency Planning Committee [*NATO*]   (NATG)
SCEPS...... Solar Cell Electric Power System   (RDA)
SCEPS...... Stored Chemical Energy Propulsion System
SCEPTR.... Suitcase Emergency Procedures Trainer   (MCD)
SCEPTRE ... Sceptre Resources Ltd. [*Associated Press abbreviation*]   (APAG)
SCEPTRE ... System for Circuit Evaluation and Prediction of Transient Radiation Effect   (MCD)
SCEPTRE ... System Computerized for Economical Performance, Tracking, Recording and Evaluation [*North Central Airlines*]
SCEPTRE ... System for Constant Elevation Precipitation Transmission and Recording
SCEPTRON ... Spectral Comparative Pattern Recognizer
SCE & PWD ... Staff Civil Engineer and Public Works Department   (DNAB)
SC Eq........ South Carolina Equity Reports [*A publication*]   (DLA)
SCER......... Quintero [*Chile*] [*ICAO location identifier*]   (ICLI)
SCER........ Sheffield Centre for Environmental Research [*British*]   (CB)
SCER......... Societe Canadienne pour l'Etude de la Religion [*Canadian Society for the Study of Religion - CSSR*]
SCER........ Societe Canadienne d'Etudes de la Renaissance [*Canadian Society for Renaissance Studies - CSRS*]
SCER........ Standing Commission on Ecumenical Relations of the Episcopal Church   (EA)
SCERGA ... Societe Canadienne d'Economie Rurale et Gestion Agricole [*Canadian Agricultural Economics and Farm Management Society - CAEFMS*]
SCERT ...... System and Computer Evaluation Revision Technique

SCERT ...... Systems and Computers Evaluation and Review Technique [*Data processing*]
ScEs........... Science et Esprit [*A publication*]
SCES .... State Cooperative Extension Service
SCESBH ... Smithsonian Contributions to the Earth Sciences [*A publication*]
SCESOM .. Service Canadien pour les Etudiants et les Stagiaires d'Outre-Mer
SCESWUN ... Standing Committee on the Economic and Social Work of the United Nations
SCET .... Scottish Council for Educational Technology   (IID)
SCET .... Spacecraft Event Time
SCETA ...... Societe de Controle et d'Exploitation de Transports Auxiliaires [*France*]
SCETV ...... South Carolina Educational Television [*Columbia*] [*Telecommunications*]   (TSSD)
SCEU........ Selector Channel Emulation Unit
SCEWA..... Society for Citizen Education in World Affairs [*Later, CEA*]
SCEZ......... Santiago [*Chile*] [*ICAO location identifier*]   (ICLI)
SCF........... Florence County Library, Florence, SC [*OCLC symbol*]   (OCLC)
SCF........... Phoenix [*Arizona*] Scottsdale [*Airport symbol*]   (OAG)
SCF........... S-Band Composite Feed
SCF........... Samoth Capital Corp. [*Toronto Stock Exchange symbol*]
SCF........... Sampled Channel Filter
SCF........... Satellite Control Facility [*Sunnyvale, CA*] [*NASA*]
SCF........... Save the Children Federation   (EA)
SCF........... Save the Children Fund [*British*]   (EAIO)
SCF........... Scandinavia Co. [*Formerly, Scandinavia Fund, Inc.*] [*AMEX symbol*]   (SPSG)
SCF........... Schedule Control File
SCF........... Schematic Concept Formation
SCF........... Science Fantasy [*A publication*]
SCF........... Scientific Computing Facility
SCF........... Secondary Checkpoint File
SCF........... Sectional Center Facility [*First three digits of the ZIP code*] [*US Postal Service*]
SCF........... Sectional Center Facility [*Air Force*]   (AFM)
SCF........... Self-Consistent Field [*Quantum mechanics*]
SCF........... Senior Chaplain to the Forces [*British*]
SCF........... Sequential Compatibility Firing [*Aerospace*]
SCF........... Signature Characterization Facility   (MCD)
SCF........... Single Catastrophic Failure   (AAG)
SCF........... Single Cost Factor
SCF........... Single Crystal Filament
SCF........... Skin Cancer Foundation   (EA)
SCF........... Slovak Catholic Federation   (EA)
SCF........... Small Company Fund [*Phillips and Drew Fund Management*] [*British*]
SCF........... SNAP [*Systems for Nuclear Auxiliary Power*] Critical Facility   (NRCH)
SCF........... Sociedad Centroamericana de Farmacologia [*Central American Society of Pharmacology - CASP*]   (EAIO)
SCF........... Society of the Compassionate Friends [*Later, TCF*]   (EA)
SCF........... Sodium Cleaning Facility [*Nuclear energy*]   (NRCH)
SCF........... Solution Crystal Facility   (SSD)
SCF........... Spacecraft Checkout Facility
SCF........... Spacecraft Control Facility [*NASA*]   (MCD)
SCF........... Spherical Cavity Flow
SCF........... Spinning Continuous Filament
SCF........... Spinning Crucible Furnace
SCF........... Standard Charge Factor   (NASA)
SCF........... Standard Cubic Foot
SCF........... Station Code File
SCF........... Statistical Collection File   (NASA)
SCF........... Steinbeck Center Foundation   (EA)
SCF........... Stem Cell Factor [*Genetics*]
SCF........... Stress Concentration Factor   (MCD)
SCF........... Subchorionic Fibrin [*Obstetrics*]
SCF........... Sunnyvale Control Facility [*California*] [*NASA*]   (NASA)
SCF........... Supercritical Fluid
SCF........... Support Carrier Force
SCF........... System Change Failure   (SAA)
SCFA .... Antofagasta/Internacional Cerro Moreno [*Chile*] [*ICAO location identifier*]   (ICLI)
SCFA .... Segmented Continuous Flow Analysis [*Analytical chemistry*]
SCFA .... Short-Chain Fatty Acids [*Biochemistry*]
SCFA .... Slovak Catholic Federation of America [*Later, SCF*]   (EA)
SCFB .... South Carolina Federal Corp. [*NASDAQ symbol*]   (NQ)
SCFB .... Swirling Circulating Fluidized Bed
SCFBC....... Staged-Cascade Fluidized Bed Combustion
SCFBR....... Steam-Cooled Fast Breeder Reactor [*Nuclear energy*]
SCFC .... Scientific Communications, Inc. [*Garland, TX*] [*NASDAQ symbol*]   (NQ)
SCFC .... Southern California Film Circuit [*Library network*]
SCFC .... Steve Cochran Fan Club   (EA)
SCFCS....... Standing Committee on the Free Circulation of Scientists [*International Council of Scientific Unions*]
SCFD........ Standard Cubic Feet per Day
S/CFDR..... Survivability/Crash Flight Data Recorder   (MCD)
SC & FE..... Sierra Club and Friends of the Earth [*Marine science*]   (MSC)

SCFE .... Supercritical Fluid Extraction [*Also, SFE*] [*Chemical engineering*]
SCFEL .... Standard COMSEC [*Communications Security*] Facility Equipment List
SCFF .... Scotopic Critical Flicker Frequency [*Magnetic environment*]
SCFGVPT ... Southern California Figure-Ground Visual Perception Test
SCFH .... Standard Cubic Feet per Hour   (AAG)
SCFI .... Streptococcal Chemotactic Factor Inhibitor [*Immunochemistry*]
ScFl .... Florence County Library, Florence, SC [*Library symbol*] [*Library of Congress*]   (LCLS)
ScFlM .... Francis Marion College, Florence, SC [*Library symbol*] [*Library of Congress*]   (LCLS)
ScFlT .... Florence-Darlington Technical College Library, Florence, SC [*Library symbol*] [*Library of Congress*]   (LCLS)
SCFM .... Porvenir/Capitan Fuentes Martinez [*Chile*] [*ICAO location identifier*]   (ICLI)
SCFM .... Scanforms, Inc. [*NASDAQ symbol*]   (NQ)
SCFM .... Standard Cubic Feet per Minute
SCFM .... Subcarrier Frequency Modulation [*Telecommunications*]   (TEL)
SCFMA .... Summer and Casual Furniture Manufacturers Association   (EA)
SCFMO ..... Self-Consistent Field Molecular Orbital   (OA)
SCFO .... Science Forum [*A publication*]
SCFOA ..... Schiffbauforschung [*A publication*]
SCFOB ...... Science Forum [*A publication*]
SCFP .... Science Career Facilitation Project [*National Science Foundation*]
SCFP .... Syndicat Canadien de la Fonction Publique [*Canadian Union of Public Employees - CUPE*]
SCFPA ...... Structural Cement-Fiber Products Association   (EA)
SCFS .... S-Band Composite Feed System
SCFS .... Slip-Cast-Fused Silica   (RDA)
SCFS .... Standard Cubic Feet per Second   (AAG)
SCFSEC .... Standing Committee of French-Speaking Ethnical Communities   (EA)
SCFT .... Futaleufu/Futaleufu [*Chile*] [*ICAO location identifier*]   (ICLI)
SCFTS ...... Small Card Final Test System   (SAA)
SCFZ .... Antofagasta [*Chile*] [*ICAO location identifier*]   (ICLI)
SCG .... Air Force Geophysics Laboratory Research Library, Hanscom AFB, MA [*OCLC symbol*]   (OCLC)
ScG .... Greenville County Library, Greenville, SC [*Library symbol*] [*Library of Congress*]   (LCLS)
SCG .... St. Claude [*Guadeloupe*] [*Seismograph station code, US Geological Survey*]   (SEIS)
SCG .... SCANA Corp. [*NYSE symbol*]   (SPSG)
Sc G .... Science Gossip [*A publication*]
SCG .... Scientific Computing Group [*University of Toronto*] [*Research center*]   (RCD)
SCG .... Scoring   (ADA)
SCG .... Screen Cartoonists Guild [*Defunct*]   (EA)
SCG .... Search for Common Ground   (EA)
SCG .... Security Classification Guide   (AFM)
SCG .... Seismocardiography [*Medicine*]
SCG .... Self Changing Gear   (DCTA)
SCG .... SEMMS [*Solar Electric Multiple-Mission Spacecraft*] Coordinating Group [*NASA*]
SCG .... Sequential Control Guidance   (KSC)
SCG .... Serum Chemistry Graft   (MAE)
SCG .... Shipcraft Guild   (EA)
SCG .... Sight Current Generator
SCG .... Sigma Science [*Vancouver Stock Exchange symbol*]
SCG .... Sliding-Coil Gauge   (RDA)
SCG .... Social Credit Group [*British*]   (DAS)
SCG .... Societe Canadienne de Geotechnique [*Canadian Geotechnical Society*]   (EAIO)
SCG .... Society of the Classic Guitar   (EA)
SCG .... Sodium Cromoglycate [*Pharmacology*]
SCG .... Solution Crystal Growth
SCG .... Space Charge Grid
SCG .... Space and Communications Group [*of General Motors Corp.*]
SCG .... Special Consultative Group [*NATO*]
SCG .... Steel Carriers Group [*Later, RDCC*]   (EA)
SCG .... Stored Cold Gas
SCG .... Supercritical Gas Extraction
SCG .... Superior Cervical Ganglion [*Anatomy*]
ScGa .... Cherokee County Public Library, Gaffney, SC [*Library symbol*] [*Library of Congress*]   (LCLS)
SCGA .... Sodium-Cooled Graphite Assembly [*Nuclear energy*]
SCGA .... Southern Cotton Ginners Association   (EA)
SCGA .... Synergistic Communications Group, Inc. [*NASDAQ symbol*]   (NQ)
ScGaL .... Limestone College, Gaffney, SC [*Library symbol*] [*Library of Congress*]   (LCLS)
SCGB .... Ski Club of Great Britain   (DI)
ScGBJ .... Bob Jones University, Greenville, SC [*Library symbol*] [*Library of Congress*]   (LCLS)
SCGC .... Societe Canadienne de Genie Civil
SCGC .... Society of Carnival Glass Collectors
SCGCh .... Societe Canadienne du Genie Chimique
SCGD .... Specification Control Group Directive   (KSC)

SCGDL ...... Signal Corps General Development Laboratory [*Obsolete*] [*Army*]
SCGE .... Sioux City Grain Exchange   (EA)
SCGE .... Societe Canadienne de Genie Electrique
ScGeo .... Georgetown County Memorial Library, Georgetown SC [*Library symbol*] [*Library of Congress*]   (LCLS)
ScGF .... Furman University, Greenville, SC [*Library symbol*] [*Library of Congress*]   (LCLS)
SCGGA ...... Sonoma County Grape Growers Association   (EA)
SCGI .... Small College Goals Inventory [*Test*]
SCGI .... Starstream Communications Group, Inc. [*NASDAQ symbol*]   (NQ)
SCGM .... Senior Cook General Mess [*British military*]   (DMA)
SCGM .... Societe Canadienne de Genie Mecanique
SCGMB .... Societe Canadienne de Genie Medical et Biologique
SCGP .... Scrabble Crossword Game Players [*Later, NSA*]   (EA)
SCGP .... Self-Contained Guidance Package   (AAG)
SCGR .... Societe Canadienne du Genie Rural
ScGrw .... Abbeville-Greenwood Regional Library, Greenwood, SC [*Library symbol*] [*Library of Congress*]   (LCLS)
ScGrwL ...... Lander College, Greenwood, SC [*Library symbol*] [*Library of Congress*]   (LCLS)
ScGrwP ..... Piedmont Technical College, Greenwood, SC [*Library symbol*] [*Library of Congress*]   (LCLS)
SCGSS ...... Signal Corps Ground Signal Service [*Obsolete*] [*Army*]
SCGSS ...... Super-Critical Gas Storage System [*NASA*]   (KSC)
SCGT .... Stanford's Compendium of Geography and Travel [*A publication*]
SCGZ .... Puerto Williams/Guardia-Marina Zanartu [*Chile*] [*ICAO location identifier*]   (ICLI)
SCH .... AFSC Technical Information Center, Washington, DC [*OCLC symbol*]   (OCLC)
SCH .... Schedule   (AAG)
SCH .... Schefferville [*Quebec*] [*Seismograph station code, US Geological Survey*]   (SEIS)
SCH .... Scheme   (ADA)
SCH .... Schenectady, NY [*Location identifier*] [*FAA*]   (FAAL)
SCH .... Schering [*Italy*] [*Research code symbol*]
SCH .... Schering-Plough Corp. [*Research code symbol*]
SCH .... Scherl and Roth Orchestra News [*A publication*]
SCH .... Schiller [*German poet, 1759-1805*]   (ROG)
SCH .... Schilling [*Monetary unit*] [*Austria*]
Sch .... Schist [*Quality of the bottom*] [*Nautical charts*]
SCH .... Schoenaur Rifle
SCH .... Scholar
SCH .... Scholarship
Sch .... Scholastik [*A publication*]
SCH .... Scholium [*Note*] [*Latin*]
SCH .... School   (AFM)
Sch .... School [*Toronto*] [*A publication*]
SCH .... Schooner
SCH .... Schreiber Resources Ltd. [*Vancouver Stock Exchange symbol*]
Sch .... Schultz Number
SCH .... Schwab [*Charles*] Corp. [*NYSE symbol*]   (SPSG)
SCH .... Search   (MCD)
SCH .... Sector Command Headquarters   (SAA)
SCH .... Seizures per Circuit per Hour [*Telecommunications*]   (TEL)
SCH .... Sequencer Chassis
SCH .... Shelter Complex Headquarters [*Civil Defense*]
SCH .... Sisters of Charity of St. Vincent de Paul, Halifax [*Roman Catholic religious order*]
SCH .... Societe Canadienne d'Hermeneutique [*Canadian Society for Hermeneutics - CSH*]
SCH .... Society for Calligraphy and Handwriting   (EA)
SCh .... Society of Christ [*Roman Catholic men's religious order*]
SCH .... Society for Colonial History [*Defunct*]   (EA)
SCH .... Socket Head   (AAG)
SCH .... Sole Community Hospital
SCh .... Sources Chretiennes [*A publication*]
SCH .... Square Cartridge Heater
SCH .... Store Channel   (SAA)
SCH .... Student Credit Hours
SCH .... Studia ad Corpus Hellenisticum Novi Testamenti   (BJA)
SCH .... Studies in Church History [*A publication*]
SCh .... Succinylcholine [*Biochemistry*]
SCH .... Supporting Checkout
SCHA .... Copiapo/Chamonate [*Chile*] [*ICAO location identifier*]   (ICLI)
Scha .... [*Simon*] Schardius [*Deceased, 1573*] [*Authority cited in pre-1607 legal work*]   (DSA)
ScHaC .... Coker College, Hartsville, SC [*Library symbol*] [*Library of Congress*]   (LCLS)
Sch Activities ... School Activities [*A publication*]
Schalk .... Schalk's Jamaica Reports [*A publication*]   (DLA)
Sch Aq R .... Schultes' Aquatic Rights [*1811*] [*A publication*]   (DLA)
Sch Arts ..... School Arts Magazine [*A publication*]
Sch Arts M ... School Arts Magazine [*A publication*]
SCHASE ... Steeplechase
Schatzkammer ... Schatzkammer der Deutschen Sprachlehre. Dichtung und Geschichte [*A publication*]
SCHAVMED ... School of Aviation Medicine [*Later, School of Aerospace Medicine*]   (MCD)

SChB......... Small Chemical Businesses [*American Chemical Society*]
Sch Bailm... Schouler on Bailments [*A publication*]   (DLA)
Sch Bell...... School Bell [*A publication*]   (APTA)
SC-HC....... Scattered-to-Heavy Clouds [*Meteorology*]   (DNAB)
SCHC .... Society of the Companions of the Holy Cross   (EA)
Sch Coach.. Scholastic Coach [*A publication*]
Sch & Com ... School and Community [*A publication*]
Sch Community News ... School and Community News [*A publication*]   (APTA)
Sch Counsel ... School Counselor [*A publication*]
SCHCR...... Stanford Center for Health Care Research [*Closed, 1978*]
SCHD .... Scheduling
Sch Days... School Days [*A publication*]   (APTA)
Sch Dent Serv Gaz (NZ) ... School Dental Services Gazette (Wellington, New Zealand) [*A publication*]
Sch Dom Rel ... Schouler on Domestic Relations [*A publication*]   (DLA)
SCHE .... Scheme   (ROG)
SChE........ Serum Cholinesterase [*An enzyme*]
SCHE .... Societe Canadienne de l'Histoire de l'Eglise [*Canadian Society of Church History - CSCH*]
SCHEC...... Societe Canadienne de l'Histoire de l'Eglise Catholique [*Canadian Catholic History Association - CCHA*]
SCHED ..... Schedule   (KSC)
Sch Ed........ School and Home Education [*Illinois*] [*A publication*]
Sched Discounts Differentials Serv Charges Applying Wheat ... Schedule of Discounts, Differentials, and Service Charges Applying to Wheat [*A publication*]
SCHEDE... Schedule   (ROG)
SCHEIB .... Scheib [*Earl*], Inc. [*Associated Press abbreviation*]   (APAG)
Scheif Pr .... Scheiffer's Practice [*A publication*]   (DLA)
Sch (El Ed) ... School (Toronto) (Elementary Edition) [*A publication*]
SCHEM...... Schematic
Sch Eng Bull NC State Univ ... School of Engineering. Bulletin. North Carolina State University [*A publication*]
Scher.......... Scherer's New York Miscellaneous Reports [*22-47*] [*A publication*]   (DLA)
Scherer....... Scherer [*R.P.*] Corp. [*Associated Press abbreviation*]   (APAG)
SCHERZ ... Scherzando [*Playful*] [*Music*]
Sch Exec .... School Executive [*A publication*]
Sch Executives M ... School Executives Magazine [*A publication*]
SchF.......... Schultexte aus Fara [*A publication*]
Sch Foodserv Res Rev ... School Foodservice Research Review [*A publication*]
SchG .... Schiedsgericht [*Arbitration Court*] [*German*]   (ILCA)
SCHG .... Supercharge
SCHGM .... South Carolina Historical and Genealogical Magazine [*A publication*]
Sch Guidance W ... School Guidance Worker [*A publication*]
SChH........ Studies in Church History [*A publication*]
SCHHA..... Schiff und Hafen [*A publication*]
Sch Health Rev ... School Health Review [*A publication*]
Sch and Home ... School and Home [*A publication*]
Sch H & W ... Schouler on Husband and Wife [*A publication*]   (DLA)
ScHi .... South Carolina Historical Society, Charleston, SC [*Library symbol*] [*Library of Congress*]   (LCLS)
Schiffstechnik ... Schiffstechnik. Forschungshefte fuer Schiffbau und Schiffsmaschinenbau [*A publication*]
Schild Steier ... Schild von Steier. Beitraege zur Steierischen Vor- und Fruehgeschichte und Muenzkunde [*A publication*]
SC His M... South Carolina Historical and Genealogical Magazine [*A publication*]
SC Hist Assn Proc ... South Carolina Historical Association. Proceedings [*A publication*]
SC Hist Mag ... South Carolina Historical Magazine [*A publication*]
SCHIZ....... Schizophrenia [*Medicine*]
schizo .... Schizophrenia [*Psychology*]
Schizophr Bull ... Schizophrenia Bulletin [*A publication*]
Schizophr Syndr ... Schizophrenic Syndrome [*A publication*]
Schizophr Syndr Annu Rev ... Schizophrenic Syndrome: An Annual Review [*A publication*]
SCHJ .... Societe Canadienne de l'Histoire Juive [*Canadian Jewish Historical Association - CJHS*]
SCHL........ Court of Session Cases, House of Lords [*Scotland*] [*A publication*]   (DLA)
SCHL........ School   (WGA)
SC(HL)...... Sessions Cases (House of Lords) [*Legal*] [*British*]
SCHL........ Societe Canadienne d'Hypotheques et de Logement [*Central Mortgage and Housing Corp. - CMHC*]
SCHLA...... School for Latin America [*Military*]   (AFM)
Schlachtofwes Lebensmittelueberwach ... Schlachtofwesen Lebensmittelueberwachung [*A publication*]
Sch L Bull .. School Law Bulletin [*A publication*]
Sch & Lef ... Schoales and Lefroy's Irish Chancery Reports [*A publication*]   (DLA)
Sch Leg Rec ... Schuylkill's Pennsylvania Legal Record [*A publication*]   (DLA)
Schleif Polier Oberflaechentech ... Schleif-, Polier-, und Oberflaechentechnik [*A publication*]
Schleif Poliertech (Hoya Weser Ger) ... Schleif- und Poliertechnik (Hoya-Weser, Germany) [*A publication*]
Schles Ges Jber ... Schlesische Gesellschaft fuer Vaterlaendische Kultur. Jahres-Bericht [*A publication*]

Schlesw-Holst Bienenztg ... Schleswig-Holsteinisches Bienenzeitung [*A publication*]
Schleswig Holsteinisches Aerztebl ... Schleswig-Holsteinisches Aerzteblatt [*A publication*]
Sch Lib...... School Librarian [*A publication*]
Sch Lib...... School Libraries [*A publication*]
Sch Lib Assn Calif Bul ... School Library Association of California. Bulletin [*A publication*]
Sch Lib Can ... School Libraries in Canada [*A publication*]
Sch Lib J.... School Library Journal [*A publication*]
Sch Lib Med N ... School Library-Media News [*A publication*]
Sch Libn..... School Librarian [*A publication*]
Sch Libr ..... School Libraries [*A publication*]
Sch Lib R ... School Library Review and Educational Record [*A publication*]
Sch Libr Bull ... School Library Bulletin [*A publication*]   (APTA)
Sch Librn ... School Librarian and School Library Review [*Later, School Librarian*] [*A publication*]
Schlief-Poliertech ... Schlief- und Poliertechnik [*West Germany*] [*A publication*]
Sch Life...... School Life [*A publication*]
Schlmb....... Schlumberger Ltd. [*Associated Press abbreviation*]   (APAG)
Sch LR....... Schuylkill's Pennsylvania Legal Record [*A publication*]   (DLA)
SCHLS ...... Schluszsatz [*Finale*] [*Music*]
SCHLSHIP ... Schoolship [*Navy*]   (NVT)
SCHLSHP ... Scholarship
SCHLT...... Searchlight   (MSA)
SCHM .... Schematic   (AAG)
Schm......... Schoolmaster [*Navy*] [*British*]
Sch M .... Schweizer Monatshefte [*A publication*]
SCHM .... Societe Canadienne d'Histoire de la Medecine [*Canadian Society for the History of Medicine - CSHM*]
SCHM .... South Carolina Historical and Genealogical Magazine [*A publication*]
Sch Manag ... School Management [*A publication*]
Sch Manage ... School Management Bulletin [*A publication*]   (APTA)
Sch Management ... School Management [*A publication*]   (APTA)
Sch Management Bul ... School Management Bulletin [*A publication*]   (APTA)
Schm Civil Law ... Schmidt's Civil Law of Spain and Mexico [*A publication*]   (DLA)
Sch Media Q ... School Media Quarterly [*A publication*]
Schmerz Narkose Anaesth ... Schmerz. Narkose-Anaesthesie [*A publication*]
Schm Exp... Schmitthoff. Export Trade [*A publication*]   (ILCA)
Sch Mgt..... School Management [*A publication*]
Schmidt Civ Law ... Schmidt's Civil Law of Spain and Mexico [*A publication*]   (DLA)
Schmierstoffe Schmierungstech ... Schmierstoffe und Schmierungstechnik [*East Germany*] [*A publication*]
Schmierst Schmierungstech ... Schmierstoffe und Schmierungstechnik [*A publication*]
Schmiertech Tribol ... Schmiertechnik und Tribologie [*A publication*]
SCHMILSCIO ... School of Military Sciences Officer [*Air Force*]
Sch Mines Q ... School of Mines Quarterly [*A publication*]
Schm LJ..... Schmidt's Law Journal [*New Orleans*] [*A publication*]   (DLA)
Schmollers Jahrb ... Schmollers Jahrbuch fuer Gesetzgebung, Verwaltung und Volkswirtschaft im Deutschen Reiche [*A publication*]
SCHMOO ... Space Cargo Handler and Manipulator for Orbital Operations
SCHMR .... Schoolmaster   (ROG)
Sch Mus .... School Music [*A publication*]
Sch Mus B ... Bachelor of School Music
Schn .... [*Johannes*] Schneidewein [*Deceased, 1568*] [*Authority cited in pre-1607 legal work*]   (DSA)
SCHND..... Soon Chun Hyang Taehak Nonmunjip [*A publication*]
Schneeberger Hb ... Schneeberger Heimatbuechlein [*A publication*]
Schneid ...... [*Johannes*] Schneidewein [*Deceased, 1568*] [*Authority cited in pre-1607 legal work*]   (DSA)
Schnell Inf Hydraul & Pneum ... Schnell Informationen Hydraulik und Pneumatik [*A publication*]
Schnurpfeils Rev Glass Works ... Schnurpfeil's Review for Glass Works [*A publication*]
SCHO .... Scholar [*or Scholarship*]   (ROG)
SCHO .... Societe Canadienne d'Histoire Orale [*Canadian Oral History Association - COHA*]
SCHO .... Standard Controlled Heterodyne Oscillator
Schoales & L ... Schoales and Lefroy's Irish Chancery Reports [*A publication*]   (DLA)
Schoenberg Inst ... Arnold Schoenberg Institute. Journal [*A publication*]
Schol .... Scholar
SCHOL ..... Scholarship
Schol .... Scholastik. Vierteljahresschrift fuer Theologie und Philosophie [*A publication*]
Schol .... Scholia [*Classical studies*]   (OCD)
Schol .... Scholiast [*Classical studies*]   (OCD)
SCHOL ..... Scholium [*Note*] [*Latin*]   (ROG)
SCHOLAR ... Schering-Oriented Literature Analysis and Retrieval System [*Schering-Plough Corp.*] [*Information service or system*]   (IID)
Scholarly Pub ... Scholarly Publishing [*A publication*]
Scholar Pub ... Scholarly Publishing [*A publication*]
Scholastic... Senior Scholastic [*Teacher Edition*] [*A publication*]
Scholastic D ... Scholastic Debater [*A publication*]

Schol Bern ... Scholia Bernensia ad Vergilii Bucolica et Georgica [*A publication*]   (OCD)
Schol Bob ... Scholia Bobiensia [*Classical studies*]   (OCD)
Schol Coach ... Scholastic Coach [*A publication*]
Schol Cruq ... Scholia Cruquiana [*Classical studies*]   (OCD)
Schol Flor Callim ... Scholia Florentina in Callimachum [*Classical studies*]   (OCD)
Schol S .... Scholia Satyrica [*A publication*]
Schol Teach ... Scholastic Teacher [*A publication*]
Schol Teach JH/SH Ed ... Scholastic Teacher. Junior/Senior High Teacher's Edition [*A publication*]
Schomberg Mar Laws Rhodes ... Schomberg's Treatise on the Maritime Laws of Rhodes [*A publication*]   (DLA)
School of Advanced Studies Rev ... School of Advanced International Studies. Review [*A publication*]   (DLA)
School Arts M ... School Arts Magazine [*A publication*]
School & Col ... School and College [*A publication*]
School Fam ... School Family [*A publication*]   (APTA)
School Law Bul (Univ NC) ... School Law Bulletin (University of North Carolina) [*A publication*]
School Lib ... School Libraries [*A publication*]
School Libs Aust ... School Libraries in Australia [*A publication*]
School of LR ... School of Law. Review. Toronto University [*Canada*] [*A publication*]   (DLA)
School L Rep (Nat'l Org on Legal Probs in Educ) ... School Law Reporter. National Organization on Legal Problems in Education [*A publication*]   (DLA)
Schoolmens W Univ PA Proc ... Schoolmen's Week. University of Pennsylvania. Proceedings [*A publication*]
School Mus ... School Musician [*A publication*]
School Organ Manage Abstr ... School Organisation and Management Abstracts [*A publication*]
School Psych Rev ... School Psychology Review [*A publication*]
School Rev ... School Review. A Journal of Secondary Education [*A publication*]
School and Soc ... School and Society [*A publication*]
Schopenhauer-Jahr ... Schopenhauer-Jahrbuch [*A publication*]
Schopenhauer-Jahrb ... Schopenhauer-Jahrbuch [*A publication*]
Schott Inf ... Schott Information [*A publication*]
Schouler Bailm ... Schouler on Bailments [*A publication*]   (DLA)
Schouler Dom Rel ... Schouler on Domestic Relations [*A publication*]   (DLA)
Schouler Pers Prop ... Schouler on the Law of Personal Property [*A publication*]   (DLA)
Schouler US Hist ... Schouler's History of the United States under the Constitution [*A publication*]   (DLA)
SchP .... Ordo Clericorum Regularium Pauperum Matris Dei Scholarum Piarum [*Roman Catholic men's religious order*]
SchP .... Scholarly Publishing [*A publication*]
Sch & Parent ... School and Parent [*A publication*]   (APTA)
Sch Per Prop ... Schouler on the Law of Personal Property [*A publication*]   (DLA)
Sch Pharm Bull Univ Wis Ext Div ... School of Pharmacy. Bulletin. University of Wisconsin. Extension Division [*A publication*]
SCHPM ..... Societe Canadienne d'Histoire et de Philosophie des Mathematiques [*Canadian Society for the History and Philosophy of Mathematics - CSHPM*]
SCHPS ...... Societe Canadienne d'Histoire et de Philosophie des Sciences [*Canadian Society for the History and Philosophy of Science - CSHPS*]
Sch Psychol R ... School Psychology Review [*A publication*]
SCHR .... Cochrane/Cochrane [*Chile*] [*ICAO location identifier*]   (ICLI)
SCHR .... Scherer Healthcare, Inc. [*NASDAQ symbol*]   (CTT)
Sch R .... School Review [*A publication*]
SCHR .... Schooner
SCHR .... Societe Canadienne d'Histoire de la Rhetorique [*See also CSHR*] [*Canada*]
SCHR .... Supervisory Change Relations Test
Schrad .... [*Ludolphus*] Schrader [*Deceased, 1589*] [*Authority cited in pre-1607 legal work*]   (DSA)
Sch Reg ...... Schuylkill's Pennsylvania Register [*A publication*]   (DLA)
Sch Rev ...... School Review [*A publication*]
Schr Geb Brennst Geol ... Schriften aus dem Gebiet der Brennstoff-Geologie [*A publication*]
Schriftenr Aerztl Fortbild ... Schriftenreihe der Aerztlichen Fortbildung [*A publication*]
Schriftenr Agrarwiss Fak Univ Kiel ... Schriftenreihe. Agrarwissenschaftliche Fakultaet. Universitaet Kiel [*A publication*]
Schriftenr Bauforsch Reihe Tech Organ ... Schriftenreihen der Bauforschung. Reihe Technik und Organisation [*A publication*]
Schriftenr Bayer Landesamt Wasserwirt ... Schriftenreihe. Bayerisches Landesamt fuer Wasserwirtschaft [*A publication*]
Schriftenr Bundesverb Dtsch Kalkind ... Schriftenreihe. Bundesverband der Deutschen Kalkindustrie [*A publication*]
Schriften Dtsch Atomforums ... Schriftenreihe des Deutschen Atomforums [*A publication*]
Schriftenreihe Didaktik Math ... Schriftenreihe Didaktik der Mathematik [*A publication*]
Schriftenreihe Landwirt Fak Univ Kiel ... Schriftenreihe der Landwirtschaftlichen Fakultaet der Universitaet Kiel [*A publication*]
Schriftenreihe Math ... Schriftenreihe fuer Mathematik [*A publication*]

Schriftenreihe Math Inst Univ Muenster ... Schriftenreihe. Mathematisches Institut. Universitaet Muenster [*A publication*]
Schriftenreihe Rechenzentrum Univ Koeln ... Schriftenreihe des Rechenzentrums. Universitaet zu Koeln [*A publication*]
Schriftenreihe Zentralinst Math Mech ... Schriftenreihe. Zentralinstitut fuer Mathematik und Mechanik [*A publication*]
Schriftenr Forschungsgem Schweiz Lackfabr ... Schriftenreihe. Forschungsgemeinschaft Schweizerischer Lackfabrikanten [*A publication*]
Schriftenr Forstl Fak Univ Goettingen ... Schriftenreihe. Forstliche Fakultaet. Universitaet Goettingen und Mitteilungen. Niedersaechsische Forstliche Versuchsanstalt [*A publication*]
Schriftenr Geb Off Gesundheitswes ... Schriftenreihe aus dem Gebiete des Oeffentlichen Gesundheitswesens [*A publication*]
Schriftenr Intensivmed Notfallmed Anaesthesiol ... Schriftenreihe Intensivmedizin, Notfallmedizin, Anaesthesiologie [*A publication*]
Schriftenr Int Ges Nahr Vitalst Forsch eV ... Schriftenreihe. Internationale Gesellschaft fuer Nahrungs- und Vitalstoff-Forschung eV [*A publication*]
Schriftenr Landesanst Immissionsschutz ... Schriftenreihe. Landesanstalt fuer Immissionsschutz [*West Germany*] [*A publication*]
Schriftenr Landschaftspflege Naturschutz ... Schriftenreihe fuer Landschaftspflege und Naturschutz [*A publication*]
Schriftenr Lebensmittelchem Lebensmittelqual ... Schriftenreihe. Lebensmittelchemie, Lebensmittelqualitaet [*A publication*]
Schriften Neurol ... Schriftenreihe Neurologie [*A publication*]
Schriften Neurol-Neurol Ser ... Schriftenreihe Neurologie-Neurology Series [*A publication*]
Schriftenr Oesterr Wasserwirtschaftsverb ... Schriftenreihe. Oesterreichischer Wasserwirtschaftsverband [*A publication*]
Schriftenr Otto Graf Inst Univ Stuttgart ... Schriftenreihe. Otto-Graf-Institut. Universitaet Stuttgart [*A publication*]
Schriftenr Schweissen Schneiden Ber ... Schriftenreihe Schweissen Schneiden. Bericht [*A publication*]
Schriftenr Theor Prax Med Psychol ... Schriftenreihe zur Theorie und Praxis der Medizinischen Psychologie [*A publication*]
Schriftenr Vegetationskd ... Schriftenreihe fuer Vegetationskunde [*A publication*]
Schriftenr Versuchstierkd ... Schriftenreihe Versuchstierkunde [*A publication*]
Schriftenr Ver Wasser Boden Lufthyg ... Schriftenreihe. Verein fuer Wasser, Boden, und Lufthygiene [*A publication*]
Schriftenr Zementind ... Schriftenreihe der Zementindustrie [*A publication*]
Schriften Wirtschaftwiss Forsch ... Schriften zur Wirtschaftwissenschaftlichen Forschung [*A publication*]
Schrift Naturf Gesellsch Kopenhagen ... Schriften. Naturforschende Gesellschaft zu Kopenhagen [*A publication*]
Schrifttum Agrarwirt ... Schrifttum der Agrarwirtschaft [*A publication*]
Schr Math Inst Univ Muenster 2 ... Schriftenreihe. Mathematisches Institut. Universitaet Muenster. 2 Serie [*A publication*]
Schr Math Inst Univ Munster ... Schriftenreihe. Mathematisches Institut. Universitaet Muenster [*A publication*]
Schr Naturwiss Ver Schleswig-Holstein ... Schriften. Naturwissenschaftlicher Verein fuer Schleswig-Holstein [*A publication*]
SchrPl .... Schering-Plough Corp. [*Associated Press abbreviation*]   (APAG)
Schrreihe Forstl Fak Univ Goettingen ... Schriftenreihe. Forstliche Fakultaet. Universitaet Goettingen [*A publication*]
SCHRUB ... Schmidt Rubin Rifle
Schr Ver Verbr Naturwiss Kennt Wien ... Schriften. Verein zur Verbreitung Naturwissenschaftlicher Kenntnisse in Wien [*A publication*]
SCHS .... School Squadron [*Air Force*]
SCHS .... Scottish Church History Society   (EAIO)
SCHS .... Small Component Handling System [*Nuclear energy*]   (NRCH)
SCHS .... Supreme Court Historical Society   (EA)
SCHSA ...... Soap and Chemical Specialties [*Later, Soap/Cosmetics/Chemical Specialties*] [*A publication*]
Sch Sci & Math ... School Science and Mathematics [*A publication*]
Sch Sci Rev ... School Science Review [*England*] [*A publication*]
Sch (Sec Ed) ... School (Toronto) (Secondary Edition) [*A publication*]
Sch Shop ... School Shop [*A publication*]
Sch & Soc ... School and Society [*A publication*]
Sch Trust ... School Trustee [*A publication*]
SCHULT ... Schult Homes Corp. [*Associated Press abbreviation*]   (APAG)
Schupo .... Schutzpolizist [*Policeman*] [*German*]
Schuy Leg Rec (PA) ... Schuylkill's Pennsylvania Legal Record [*A publication*]   (DLA)
Schuyl Legal Rec ... Schuylkill's Pennsylvania Legal Record [*A publication*]   (DLA)
Schuyl Leg Rec ... Schuylkill's Pennsylvania Legal Record [*A publication*]   (DLA)
Schuyl Leg Reg ... Schuylkill's Legal Register [*Pennsylvania*] [*A publication*]   (ILCA)
Schuy Reg (PA) ... Schuylkill's Pennsylvania Register [*A publication*]   (DLA)
SCHVD ..... Sachverhalte [*A publication*]
SCHWA ...... Schweisstechnik Soudure [*A publication*]
Schwab .... Schwab [*Charles*] Corp. [*Associated Press abbreviation*]   (APAG)
Schwaeb Imkerkal ... Schwaebischer Imkerkalender [*A publication*]

Schw A Neur ... Schweizer Archiv fuer Neurologie, Neurochirurgie, und Psychiatrie [*A publication*]
SchwArchV ... Schweizerisches Archiv fuer Volkskunde [*A publication*]
Schwarz Int L ... Schwarzenberger's Manual of International Law [*A publication*]   (DLA)
Schwarz Man Int L ... Schwarzenberger's Manual of International Law [*A publication*]   (ILCA)
Schweisstech Soudure (Zurich) ... Schweisstechnik Soudure (Zurich) [*A publication*]
Schweiz Alum Rundsch ... Schweizer Aluminium Rundschau [*A publication*]
Schweiz Arch ... Schweizer Archiv [*A publication*]
Schweiz Arch Angew Wiss Tech ... Schweizer Archiv fuer Angewandte Wissenschaft und Technik [*A publication*]
Schweiz Archiv f Volksk ... Schweizerisches Archiv fuer Volkskunde [*A publication*]
Schweiz Arch Neurol Neurochir Psychiatr ... Schweizer Archiv fuer Neurologie, Neurochirurgie, und Psychiatrie [*A publication*]
Schweiz Arch Neurol Psychiatr ... Schweizer Archiv fuer Neurologie und Psychiatrie [*A publication*]
Schweiz Arch Tierh ... Schweizer Archiv fuer Tierheilkunde [*A publication*]
Schweiz Arch Tierh (Bern) ... Schweizerisches Archiv fuer Tierheilkunde und Tierzucht (Bern) [*A publication*]
Schweiz Arch Tierheilkd ... Schweizer Archiv fuer Tierheilkunde [*A publication*]
Schweiz Arch Verkehrswiss und Verkehrspol ... Schweizerisches Archiv fuer Verkehrswissenschaft und Verkehrspolitik [*A publication*]
Schweiz Chem Ztg Tech Ind ... Schweizer Chemiker-Zeitung Technik-Industrie [*A publication*]
Schweizer Archiv Verkehrswiss u -Polit ... Schweizerisches Archiv fuer Verkehrswissenschaft und Verkehrspolitik [*A publication*]
Schweizer Arch Tierheilk ... Schweizer Archiv fuer Tierheilkunde [*A publication*]
Schweizer Arch Volksk ... Schweizer Archiv fuer Volkskunde [*A publication*]
Schweizer Natschutz ... Schweizer Naturschutz [*A publication*]
Schweiz Ing & Archit ... Schweizer Ingenieur und Architekt [*A publication*]
Schweiz Jb f Internat Recht ... Schweizerisches Jahrbuch fuer Internationales Recht/Annuaire Suisse de Droit International [*Zurich, Switzerland*] [*A publication*]   (DLA)
Schweiz Landtech ... Schweizer Landtechnik [*A publication*]
Schweiz Mh ... Schweizer Monatshefte [*A publication*]
Schweiz Muenzbl ... Schweizer Muenzblaetter [*Switzerland*] [*A publication*]
Schweiz Naturschutz Prot Nat ... Schweizer Naturschutz. Protection de la Nature [*A publication*]
Schweiz Volkskd ... Schweizer Volkskunde [*A publication*]
Schweiz Z f Strafrecht ... Schweizerische Zeitschrift fuer Strafrecht/Revue Penale Suisse [*Berne, Switzerland*] [*A publication*]   (DLA)
Schwenk ..... Schwenckfeldiana [*A publication*]
SchwM .... Schweizer Monatshefte [*A publication*]
Schw Mbl ... Schweizer Muenzblaetter [*A publication*]
SchwMH ... Schweizer Monatshefte [*Zurich*] [*A publication*]
SCHWR .... Steam-Cooled Heavy-Water Reactor
Schwtz .... Schwitzer, Inc. [*Associated Press abbreviation*]   (APAG)
SchwV .... Schweizer Volkskunde [*A publication*]
SCI .... Council for the Securities Industry [*Levy*] [*British*]
SCI .... Sacra Congregatio Indicis [*Sacred Congregation of the Index*] [*Latin*]
SCI .... Safari Club International   (EA)
SCI .... San Clemente Island [*California*] [*Seismograph station code, US Geological Survey*]   (SEIS)
SCI .... San Clemente Island
SCI .... Sand Collectors International   (EAIO)
SCI .... Santa Cruz Island   (MUGU)
SCI .... Savio Club International   (EA)
SCI .... Scaleable Coherent Interface [*Data processing*]
SCI .... Schedule-Cost Index   (MCD)
SCI .... SCI Satellite Conferencing International Corp. [*Formerly, Valclair Resources, Ltd.*] [*Vancouver Stock Exchange symbol*]
SCI .... Science [*A publication*]
SCI .... Science   (AFM)
SCI .... Science Citation Index [*A publication*]
SCI .... Science of Creative Intelligence [*Transcendental meditation*]
SCI .... Science Curriculum Improvement [*Study*] [*Education*]
SCI .... Scientific Computers, Inc.   (MCD)
SCI .... Scripta Classica Israelica [*A publication*]
ScI .... Scripta Islandica [*A publication*]
SCI .... Seabee Club International   (EA)
SCI .... Sealable Coherent Interface [*Data processing*]
SCI .... Seamen's Church Institute of New York/New Jersey   (EA)
SCI .... Security Container Institute [*Inactive*]   (EA)
SCI .... Selected Configured Item   (MCD)
SCI .... Seminar Clearinghouse International, Inc. [*Information service or system*]   (IID)
SCI .... Sensitive Compartmented Information [*Military*]
SCI .... Sequential Comparison Index [*Measures effect of chemical pollution in lakes and streams*]
SCI .... Serial Communication Interface [*Data processing*]
SCI .... Service Change Information   (MCD)
SCI .... Service Civil International [*Australia*]

SCI .... Service Civil International [*International Voluntary Service*] [*India*]
SCI .... SES [*Shuttle Engineering System*] Cockpit Interface [*NASA*]   (SSD)
SCI .... Sexual Communications Inventory [*Marital relations test*] [*Psychology*]
SCI .... Ship Controlled Intercept [*RADAR*] [*Navy*]
SCI .... Shipping Container Institute
SCI .... Shipping Corp. of India Ltd.
SCI .... Ship's Capability Impaired [*Navy*]
SCI .... Short Circuit
SCI .... Signal Corps Item [*Obsolete*] [*Army*]   (NATG)
SCI .... Simulation Councils, Inc.
SCI .... Single-Channel Interface [*Data processing*]
SCI .... Single Column Inch   (ADA)
SCI .... Sister Cities International   (EA)
SCI .... Slot Cell Inserter
SCI .... Small Craft Instructor [*Red Cross*]
SCI .... Smoke Curtain Installation [*British military*]   (DMA)
SCI .... Societe de Chimie Industrielle   (EA)
SCI .... Society of Chemical Industry   (EA)
SCI .... Society of Composers   (EA)
SCI .... Soft Cast Iron
SCI .... Software Configuration Item [*Data processing*]
SCI .... Source Code Indicator   (MCD)
SCI .... Special Compartment Intelligence [*DoD*]   (MCD)
SCI .... Special Control Item [*Code*]
SCI .... Special Customs Invoice
SCI .... Spinal Cord Injury [*Medicine*]
SCI .... Spinal Cord-Insured   (MCD)
SCI .... Sponge and Chamois Institute   (EA)
SCI .... Staging Connections, Inc. [*Telecommunications service*]   (TSSD)
SCI .... Stampe Club International   (EA)
SCI .... Steel Construction Institute [*British*]   (IRUK)
SCI .... Stein Collectors International   (EA)
SCI .... Stem Cell Inhibitor [*Cytology*]
SCI .... Stratospheric Circulation Index [*Geophysics*]
SCI .... Stroke Club International   (EA)
SCI .... Structured Clinical Interview
SCI .... Supervisory Cost Inspector [*Navy*]
SCI .... Switch Closure In   (MCD)
SCI .... Switched Collector Impedance [*Electronics*]   (OA)
SCI .... System Control Interface
SciA .... Scientific American [*A publication*]
SCIA .... Signal Corps Intelligence Agency [*Obsolete*] [*Army*]
SCIA .... Smart Card Industry Association   (EA)
SCIA .... Social Competence Inventory for Adults [*Psychology*]
SCIA .... Systems Change Impact Analysis [*Social Security Administration*]
SciAb .... Science Abstracts [*A publication*]
Sci Abstr .... Science Abstracts [*A publication*]
Sci Abstr Ch ... Science Abstracts of China [*A publication*]
Sci Abstr China Biol Sci ... Science Abstracts of China. Biological Sciences [*A publication*]
Sci Abstr China Chem Chem Technol ... Science Abstracts of China. Chemistry and Chemical Technology [*A publication*]
Sci Abstr China Math Phys Sci ... Science Abstracts of China. Mathematical and Physical Sciences [*A publication*]
Sci Abstr China Med ... Science Abstracts of China. Medicine [*A publication*]
Sci Abstr China Tech Sci ... Science Abstracts of China. Technical Sciences [*A publication*]
Sci Abstr Sect A Phys Abstr ... Science Abstracts. Section A. Physics Abstracts [*A publication*]
SCIADJ ..... Centro Internacional de Agricultura Tropical [*CIAT*]. Series Seminars [*A publication*]
Sci Adv Mater Process Eng Proc ... Science of Advanced Materials and Process Engineering. Proceedings [*A publication*]
Sci Adv Mater Process Eng Q ... Science of Advanced Materials and Process Engineering. Quarterly [*United States*] [*A publication*]
Sci Aer Aerotech ... Science Aerienne et l'Aerotechnique [*A publication*]
Sci Ag .... Scientific Agriculture [*A publication*]
Sci Agr .... Scientific Agriculture [*A publication*]
Sci Agric .... Science in Agriculture [*A publication*]
Sci Agric Bohemoslov ... Scientia Agriculturae Bohemoslovaca [*A publication*]
Sci Agric PA State Univ Agric Exp Stn ... Science in Agriculture. Pennsylvania State University. Agricultural Experiment Station [*A publication*]
Sci Agric (Taipei) ... Scientific Agriculture (Taipei) [*A publication*]
Sci Agron Rennes ... Sciences Agronomiques Rennes [*A publication*]
Sci Alaska Proc Alaskan Sci Conf ... Science in Alaska. Proceedings. Alaskan Science Conference [*A publication*]
Sci Aliment ... Scienza dell'Alimentazione [*A publication*]
Sci Aliments ... Sciences des Aliments [*A publication*]
Sci Am .... Scientific American [*A publication*]
Sci Amer .... Scientific American [*A publication*]
Sci Am Monthly ... Scientific American Monthly [*A publication*]
Sci Am S ... Scientific American. Supplement [*A publication*]
Sci Ann Fac Phys Math Aristotelian Univ Thessaloniki ... Scientific Annals. Faculty of Physics and Mathematics. Aristotelian University of Thessaloniki [*A publication*]

Sci Appliance ... Science and Appliance [*A publication*]
SCIAPS..... Senate Comprehensive Integrated Automated Printing System
SciArch ...... Science and Archaeology [*A publication*]
Sci & Archaeol ... Science and Archaeology [*A publication*]
Sci Art Min ... Science and Art of Mining [*A publication*]
SCIAS .... Society of Chemical Industry, American Section   (EA)
SCIAS .... Supreme Council of the Independent Associated
          Spiritualists   (EA)
SciAtl .... Scientific-Atlanta, Inc. [*Associated Press abbreviation*]   (APAG)
Sci Atmos Sin ... Scientia Atmospherica Sinica [*A publication*]
SCIATS ...... Small Craft Instruction and Training School [*Navy*]
Sci Aust...... Scientific Australian [*A publication*]   (APTA)
Sci Aust Technol ... Science and Australian Technology [*A
          publication*]   (APTA)
Sci Av......... Sciences et Avenir [*A publication*]
Sci Avenir .. Sciences et Avenir [*France*] [*A publication*]
SCIB .... Significant Counterintelligence Briefs   (AFM)
Sci Basis Med ... Scientific Basis of Medicine [*A publication*]
Sci Basis Nucl Waste Manage Proc Mater Res Soc Annu Meet ... Scientific
          Basis for Nuclear Waste Management. Proceedings.
          Materials Research Society Annual Meeting [*A publication*]
Sci Basis Psychiatr ... Scientific Basis of Psychiatry [*A publication*]
Sci Bas Med Ann Rev ... Scientific Basis of Medicine. Annual Review [*A
          publication*]
Sci Biol J.... Science of Biology Journal [*A publication*]
Sci Biol Ser ... Science of Biology Series [*A publication*]
Sci Bk......... Science Books and Films [*A publication*]
Sci Bks .... Science Books [*A publication*]
Sci Bks & Films ... Science Books and Films [*A publication*]
SCIBP .... Special Committee for the International Biological Program
          [*National Research Council*]
Sci Bul .... Science Bulletin for Teachers in Secondary Schools [*A
          publication*]   (APTA)
Sci Bull Academ Min Metall (Krakow) Geol ... Scientific Bulletins. Academy
          of Mining and Metallurgy (Krakow). Geology [*A
          publication*]
Sci Bull Acad Min Metall (Krakow) Ceram ... Scientific Bulletins. Academy of
          Mining and Metallurgy (Krakow). Ceramics [*A
          publication*]
Sci Bull Acad Min Metall (Krakow) Electrif Mech Min Metall ... Scientific
          Bulletins. Academy of Mining and Metallurgy (Krakow).
          Electrification and Mechanization in Mining and
          Metallurgy [*A publication*]
Sci Bull Acad Min Metall (Krakow) Math Phys Chem ... Scientific Bulletins.
          Academy of Mining and Metallurgy (Krakow).
          Mathematics, Physics, Chemistry [*A publication*]
Sci Bull Acad Min Metall (Krakow) Metall Foundry Pract ... Scientific
          Bulletins. Academy of Mining and Metallurgy (Krakow).
          Metallurgy and Foundry Practice [*A publication*]
Sci Bull Acad Min Metall (Krakow) Min ... Scientific Bulletins. Academy of
          Mining and Metallurgy (Krakow). Mining [*A publication*]
Sci Bull Acad Min Metall (Krakow) Spec Ser ... Scientific Bulletins. Academy
          of Mining and Metallurgy (Krakow). Special Series [*A
          publication*]
Sci Bull At Energy New Energ Organ ... Scientific Bulletin. Atomic Energy
          and New Energies Organization [*A publication*]
Sci Bull Can Cent Miner Energy Technol ... Scientific Bulletin. Canada Centre
          for Mineral and Energy Technology [*A publication*]
Sci Bull Coll Agric Univ Ryukyus Okinawa ... Science Bulletin. College of
          Agriculture. University of Ryukyus. Okinawa [*A
          publication*]
Sci Bull Cotton Res Inst Sindos ... Science Bulletin. Cotton Research Institute.
          Sindos [*A publication*]
Sci Bull Dep Agric For Un S Afr ... Science Bulletin. Department of
          Agriculture and Forestry. Union of South Africa [*A
          publication*]
Sci Bull Dep Agric NSW ... Science Bulletin. Department of Agriculture. New
          South Wales [*A publication*]   (APTA)
Sci Bull Dept Agr NSW ... Science Bulletin. Department of Agriculture. New
          South Wales [*A publication*]
Sci Bull Dept Agr S Afr ... Science Bulletin. Department of Agriculture. South
          Africa [*A publication*]
Sci Bull Des Bot Gard Ariz ... Science Bulletin. Desert Botanical Garden of
          Arizona [*A publication*]
Sci Bull Fac Agric Kyushu Univ ... Science Bulletin. Faculty of Agriculture.
          Kyushu University [*A publication*]
Sci Bull Fac Agr Kyushu Univ ... Science Bulletin. Faculty of Agriculture.
          Kyushu University [*A publication*]
Sci Bull Fac Ed Nagasaki Univ ... Science Bulletin. Faculty of Education.
          Nagasaki University [*A publication*]
Sci Bull Fac Educ Nagasaki Univ ... Science Bulletin. Faculty of Education.
          Nagasaki University [*A publication*]
Sci Bull Fac Lib Arts Educ Nagasaki Univ ... Science Bulletin. Faculty of
          Liberal Arts and Education. Nagasaki University [*A
          publication*]
Sci Bull Repub S Afr Dept Agr Tech Serv ... Science Bulletin. Republic of
          South Africa. Department of Agricultural Technical
          Services [*A publication*]
Sci Bull Sci Found Philipp ... Science Bulletin. Science Foundation of the
          Philippines [*A publication*]

Sci Bull Stanislaw Staszic Univ Min Metall Ceram ... Scientific Bulletins.
          Stanislaw Staszic University of Mining and Metallurgy.
          Ceramics [*A publication*]
Sci Bull Stanislaw Staszic Univ Min Metall Geol ... Scientific Bulletins.
          Stanislaw Staszic University of Mining and Metallurgy.
          Geology [*A publication*]
Sci Bull Stanislaw Staszic Univ Min Metall Math Phys Chem ... Scientific
          Bulletins. Stanislaw Staszic University of Mining and
          Metallurgy. Mathematics, Physics, Chemistry [*A
          publication*]
Sci Bull Stanislaw Staszic Univ Min Metall Min ... Scientific Bulletins.
          Stanislaw Staszic University of Mining and Metallurgy.
          Mining [*A publication*]
Sci Bull Stanislaw Staszic Univ Min Metall Sozol Sozotech ... Scientific
          Bulletins. Stanislaw Staszic University of Mining and
          Metallurgy. Sozology and Sozotechnics [*A publication*]
Sci Bull Stanislaw Staszic Univ Min Metall Spec Ser ... Scientific Bulletins.
          Stanislaw Staszic University of Mining and Metallurgy.
          Special Series [*A publication*]
Sci Bull Univ Agric Sci ... Scientific Bulletin. University of Agricultural
          Sciences [*A publication*]
Sci Bull Univ Kans ... Science Bulletin. University of Kansas [*A publication*]
Sci Bull Univ Kansas ... Science Bulletin. Kansas University [*A publication*]
SCIC .... Curico/General Freire [*Chile*] [*ICAO location
          identifier*]   (ICLI)
SCIC .... Secretariat des Conferences Intergouvernementales
          Canadiennes
SCIC .... Semiconductor Integrated Circuit
SCIC .... Single-Column Ion Chromatography
SCIC .... Special Control Item Code
SCICC .... Service Center Internal Computer Code [*Data processing*]
Sci Ceram... Science of Ceramics [*England*] [*A publication*]
SCICF .... Safari Club International Conservation Fund   (EA)
SCICFNDT ... Standing Committee for International Cooperation within the
          Field of Non-Destructive Testing   (EA)
Sci & Child ... Science and Children [*A publication*]
Sci China A ... Science in China. Series A. Mathematics, Physics, Astronomy,
          and Technological Sciences [*A publication*]
Sci China B ... Science in China. Series B. Chemistry, Life Sciences, and Earth
          Sciences [*A publication*]
Sci China Ser A ... Science in China. Series A. Mathematics, Physics,
          Astronomy, and Technological Sciences [*A publication*]
Sci Chron (Karachi) ... Science Chronicle (Karachi) [*A publication*]
Sci Cit Ind ... Science Citation Index [*A publication*]
Sci Cit Index ... Science Citation Index [*A publication*]
SCICLOPS ... Systems Control, Incorporated Computerized Library
          Operations [*Information service or system*]   (IID)
Sci Comput Program ... Science of Computer Programming [*A publication*]
Sci Comput Programming ... Science of Computer Programming [*A
          publication*]
Sci Conf Ges Dtsch Naturforsch Aerzte ... Scientific Conference. Gesellschaft
          Deutscher Naturforscher und Aerzte [*A publication*]
Sci Counc Afr South Sahara Publ ... Scientific Council for Africa South of the
          Sahara. Publication [*A publication*]
Sci Counc Jap Annu Rep ... Science Council of Japan. Annual Report [*A
          publication*]
Sci Couns ... Science Counselor [*A publication*]
SCICS .... Spinal Cord Injury Care System [*University of Alabama in
          Birmingham*] [*Research center*]   (RCD)
Sci Cult ...... Science and Culture [*A publication*]
Sci Cult (New Delhi) ... Science and Culture (New Delhi) [*A publication*]
Sci D .... Doctor of Science
SCID.......... Scios, Inc. [*Formerly, California Biotechnology, Inc.*]
          [*NASDAQ symbol*]   (SPSG)
SCID .... Severe Combined Immune Deficiency [*Immunology*]
SCID .... Small Column Insulated Delays   (MCD)
SCID .... Subcommutator Identification [*NASA*]
SCID-A ...... Studies in Comparative International Development [*A
          publication*]
SCIDE .... Servicio Cooperativo Interamericano de Educacion
Sci Dep Bull United Plant Assoc South India ... Scientific Department
          Bulletin. United Planters' Association of Southern India [*A
          publication*]
Sci Dig .... Science Digest [*A publication*]
Sci Digest... Science Digest [*A publication*]
Sci Diliman ... Science Diliman [*A publication*]
Sci Dimens ... Science Dimension [*A publication*]
Sci Dimension ... Science Dimension [*A publication*]
SCIDNT .... System Control Incorporated Identification Program [*Navy*]
Sci Drugs (Tokyo) ... Science of Drugs (Tokyo) [*A publication*]
SCIE .... Concepcion/Carriel Sur [*Chile*] [*ICAO location
          identifier*]   (ICLI)
SCIE .... Scicom Data Services Ltd. [*Formerly, Scientific Computers*]
          [*NASDAQ symbol*]   (NQ)
SCIE .... Stolen Children Information Exchange   (EA)
SCIEA .... Science [*A publication*]
SCIEC........ Southern California Industry-Education Council   (SAA)
Sci Ed .... Science Education [*A publication*]
Sci Ed News ... Science Education Newsletter [*A publication*]   (APTA)
Sci Educ ..... Science Education [*A publication*]

Sci Educ Adm Agric Rev Man ARM-NE ... Science and Education Administration. Agricultural Reviews and Manuals. ARM-NE [*A publication*]
Sci Educ Adm Agric Rev Man ARM-W ... Science and Education Administration. Agricultural Reviews and Manuals. ARM-W [*A publication*]
Sci Educ Adm North Cent Reg Publ ... Science and Education Administration. North Central Region Publication [*A publication*]
Sci 80 (Eighty) ... Science 80 (Eighty) [*A publication*]
Sci Elec ...... Scientia Electrica [*A publication*]
Sci Electr.... Scientia Electrica [*A publication*]
Science ...... Science for People [*A publication*]
SCIENCE ... Stimulation des Cooperations Internationaux et des Echanges Necessaires aux Chercheurs Europeennes [*Stimulation of International Cooperation and the Necessary Exchanges of European Scientists*] [*EEC*]
Science Ed ... Science Education [*A publication*]
Science et Industrie Phot ... Science et Industries Photographiques [*A publication*]
Science N L ... Science News Letter [*A publication*]
Science Prog ... Science Progress [*A publication*]
Sciences Assoc Fr Av Sci ... Sciences. Association Francaise pour l'Avancement des Sciences [*A publication*]
Sciences (NY) ... Sciences (New York) [*A publication*]
Sciences NY Acad Sci ... Sciences. New York Academy of Sciences [*A publication*]
Sciences Pol ... Sciences Politiques [*A publication*]
Science and Tech Libs ... Science and Technology Libraries [*A publication*]
Sciencia Med ... Sciencia Medica [*A publication*]
Sci Eng ...... Science and Engineering [*A publication*]
Sci and Eng Rep Def Acad ... Scientific and Engineering Reports. Defense Academy [*A publication*]
Sci and Eng Rep Natl Def Acad (Jpn) ... Scientific and Engineering Reports. National Defense Academy (Japanese) [*A publication*]
Sci & Eng Rep Saitama Univ C ... Science and Engineering Reports. Saitama University. Series C [*A publication*]
Sci and Eng Rep Saitama Univ Ser C ... Science and Engineering Reports. Saitama University. Series C [*A publication*]
Sci Eng Rev Doshisha Univ ... Science and Engineering Review. Doshisha University [*A publication*]
Sci Enseign Sci ... Sciences et l'Enseignement des Sciences [*A publication*]
SCIENT .... Scientific
Scient Agric ... Scientific Agriculture [*A publication*]
Scient Am .. Scientific American [*A publication*]
Scient Amer ... Scientific American [*A publication*]
Scient Am Suppl ... Scientific American. Supplement [*A publication*]
Scient Film Rev ... Scientific Film Review [*A publication*]
Scient Hort ... Scientific Horticulture [*A publication*]
Scientia Genet ... Scientia Genetica [*A publication*]
Scientiarum Hist ... Scientiarum Historia [*A publication*]
Scient Instrum ... Scientific Instruments [*A publication*]
Scient Mon ... Scientific Monthly [*A publication*]
Scient Month ... Scientific Monthly [*A publication*]
Scient Pap Coll Gen Educ Tokyo ... Scientific Papers. College of General Education. University of Tokyo [*A publication*]
Scient Papers Civil Vet Dept (Madras) ... Scientific Papers. Civil Veterinary Department (Madras) [*A publication*]
Scient Proc R Dubl Soc ... Scientific Proceedings. Royal Dublin Society [*A publication*]
Scient Rep Fac Agric Okayama Univ ... Scientific Reports. Faculty of Agriculture. Okayama University [*A publication*]
Scient Rep Govt Inst Infect Dis Tokyo Imp Univ ... Scientific Reports. Government Institute for Infectious Diseases. Tokyo Imperial University [*A publication*]
Scient Rep Kyoto Prefect Univ Agric ... Scientific Reports. Kyoto Prefectural University. Agriculture [*A publication*]
Scient Res (Bangladesh) ... Scientific Researches (Bangladesh) [*A publication*]
Scient Trans Dubl Soc ... Scientific Transactions. Royal Dublin Society [*A publication*]
Scient Work ... Scientific Worker [*A publication*]
Sci Environ ... Science and Environment [*A publication*]
Scienza Aliment ... Scienza dell'Alimentazione [*A publication*]
Scienza Tecnol Aliment ... Scienza e Tecnologia degli Alimenti [*A publication*]
Sci Espr ...... Science et Esprit [*A publication*]
Sci Esprit ... Science et Esprit [*A publication*]
Sci Exploration ... Science Exploration [*Changsha*] [*A publication*]
SCIF .... Daughters of the Sacred Heart of Jesus [*Bethlehemite Sisters*] [*Roman Catholic religious order*]
SCIF .... Science Forum [*A publication*]
SCIF .... Special Compartmented Intelligence Facility [*DoD*]
SCIF .... Static Column Isoelectric Focusing [*Materials processing*]
SCIF .... Systems Certification and Integration Facility
SCI FA .... Scire Facias [*Please make known*] [*A writ to enforce, annul, or vacate a judgment, patent, charter or other matter of record*] [*Legal term*] [*Latin*]
Sci Fa ad Dis Deb ... Scire Facias ad Disprobandum Debitum [*Latin*] (DLA)
Sci Farm..... Science for the Farmer [*A publication*]
Sci Farm..... Scienza del Farmaco [*A publication*]
Sci Farmer ... Science for the Farmer [*A publication*]
SCIFC........ Sandy Croft International Fan Club (EA)
SCI-FI........ Science Fiction [*Also, SF*]

Sci Fict Book Rev Index ... Science Fiction Book Review Index [*SFBRI*] [*A publication*]
Sci Fiction Bk Rev Ind ... Science Fiction Book Review Index [*A publication*]
Sci Fict St... Science Fiction Studies [*A publication*]
Sci For....... Science Forum [*A publication*]
Sci For Prod ... Science of Forest Products [*A publication*]
Sci Forum... Science Forum [*A publication*]
Sci Freedom ... Science and Freedom [*A publication*]
SCIGA .... Society of Chemical Industry (London). Monograph [*A publication*]
SCIGB .... Sicherheitsingenieur [*A publication*]
Sci Genet.... Scientia Genetica [*A publication*]
Sci Geol Bull ... Sciences Geologiques. Bulletin [*A publication*]
Sci Geol Bull Inst Geol Univ Louis Pasteur Strasbourg ... Sciences Geologiques. Bulletin. Institut de Geologie. Universite Louis Pasteur de Strasbourg [*France*] [*A publication*]
Sci Geol Mem ... Sciences Geologiques. Memoires [*A publication*]
Sci Geol S .. Scientia Geologica Sinica [*A publication*]
Sci Geol Sin ... Scientia Geologica Sinica [*A publication*]
Sci Gov Rep ... Science and Government Report [*United States*] [*A publication*]
Sci Govt Rep ... Science and Government Report [*A publication*]
SCIGY .... Special Committee for the International Geophysical Year
SCIH.......... Societe Canadienne d'Ingenierie Hospitaliere
Sci Hist .... Scientiarum Historia [*A publication*]
Sci Hort...... Scientific Horticulture [*A publication*]
Sci Hortic... Scientia Horticulturae [*A publication*]
Sci Hortic (Amst) ... Scientia Horticulturae (Amsterdam) [*A publication*]
Sci Hortic (Canterbury) ... Scientific Horticulture (Canterbury) [*A publication*]
Sci Hum Life ... Science of Human Life [*A publication*]
SCII .... Science in Iceland [*A publication*]
SCII .... Southland Communication, Inc. [*NASDAQ symbol*] (NQ)
SCII .... Strong-Campbell Interest Inventory [*Vocational guidance*]
Sci Icel .... Science in Iceland [*A publication*]
Sci Ilus ...... Science Illustrated [*A publication*]
Sci Ind....... Science et Industrie [*A publication*]
Sci Ind....... Science and Industry [*A publication*]
Sci Ind Ed Metall Constr Mec Energ ... Science et Industrie. Edition Metallurgie. Construction, Mecaniques, Energie [*A publication*]
Sci Ind Equip Bull ... Scientific and Industrial Equipment Bulletin [*A publication*] (APTA)
Sci Ind (Karachi) ... Science and Industry (Karachi) [*A publication*]
Sci in Ind (Lond) ... Science in Industry (London) [*A publication*]
Sci Ind (Melbourne) ... Science and Industry (Melbourne) [*A publication*]
Sci Ind (Philips) ... Science and Industry (Philips) [*The Netherlands*] [*A publication*]
Sci Ind Phot ... Science et Industries Photographiques [*A publication*]
Sci Ind Photogr ... Science et Industries Photographiques [*A publication*]
Sci Ind Spat ... Sciences et Industries Spatiales [*Switzerland*] [*A publication*]
Sci Ind Spatiales Space Res Eng Weltraumforsch Ind ... Sciences et Industries Spatiales, Space Research and Engineering, Weltraumforschung und Industrie [*A publication*]
Sci Inf News ... Science Informations News. National Science Foundation [*A publication*]
Sci Inf Notes ... Scientific Information Notes [*A publication*]
Sci Info N... Scientific Information Notes [*A publication*]
Sci Ins Contr ... Scientific Insect Control [*A publication*]
Sci Insect Control (Kyoto) ... Scientific Insect Control (Kyoto) [*A publication*]
Sci Instr ..... Scientific Instruments [*A publication*]
Sci Instr J Phys E ... Scientific Instruments. Journal of Physics. E [*A publication*]
Sci Instrum ... Journal of Physics. E: Scientific Instruments [*A publication*]
Sci Int (Lahore) ... Science International (Lahore) [*A publication*]
Sci Invest Freshwater Salmon Fish Res Scott Home Dep ... Scientific Investigations. Freshwater and Salmon Fisheries Research. Scottish Home Department [*A publication*]
Sci Invest Freshw Salmon Fish Res Scott Home Dep ... Scientific Investigations. Freshwater and Salmon Fisheries Research. Scottish Home Department [*A publication*]
Sci Island ... Scientia Islandica [*A publication*]
SCI-IVS..... SCI-International Voluntary Service (EA)
Sci J .... Science Journal [*A publication*]
Sci J (Lond) ... Science Journal (London) [*A publication*]
Sci Jour...... Science Journal [*A publication*]
Sci J R Coll Sci ... Scientific Journal. Royal College of Science [*A publication*]
Sci J Shivaji Univ ... Science Journal. Shivaji University [*A publication*]
SCIL .... Scilicet [*Namely*] [*Legal term*] [*Latin*]
SCIL .... Selected Configuration Item List (MCD)
SCIL .... Ship's Construction Item List (MCD)
SCIL .... Small Computers in Libraries [*A publication*]
SCIL .... Soft Consumable Item List
SCIL .... Support Center International Logistics [*Army*]
Sciland....... Scienceland [*A publication*]
Sci Leafl..... Science Leaflet [*A publication*]
Sci Life....... Science and Life [*A publication*]
Sci Light .... Science of Light [*A publication*]
SCILL......... Southern California Interlibrary Loan Project [*Library network*]
Sci Lubr ..... Scientific Lubrication [*A publication*]
Sci Lubr Liq Fuel ... Scientific Lubrication and Liquid Fuel [*A publication*]

SCIM......... Congregation des Soeurs Servantes du Coeur Immaculae de Marie [*Servants of the Immaculate Heart of Mary*] [*Good Shepherd Sisters*] [*Roman Catholic religious order*]
SCIM......... Savage's Cognitive Impairment Model
SCIM......... Selected Categories in Microfiche [*National Technical Information Service*]
SCIM......... Speech Communications Index Meter
SCIM......... Standard Cubic Inches per Minute (AAG)
SCIM......... Subject Codes for Intelligence Management (MCD)
Sci Mac...... Science of Machine [*Japan*] [*A publication*]
Sci Man...... Science of Man and Australasian Anthropological Journal [*A publication*]
Sci March.. Science on the March [*A publication*]
Sci Mat...... Scienze Matematiche [*A publication*]
Sci Mech.... Science and Mechanics [*A publication*]
Sci Med...... Sciences Medicales [*A publication*]
Sci Med Ital ... Scientia Medica Italica [*A publication*]
Sci Med Ital (Engl Ed) ... Scientia Medica Italica (English Edition) [*A publication*]
Sci Med Man ... Science, Medicine, and Man [*A publication*]
Sci Meet..... Scientific Meetings [*A publication*]
Sci Mem Kazan State Univ ... Scientific Memoirs. Kazan State University [*A publication*]
SCIMGT ... Science Management Corp. [*Associated Press abbreviation*] (APAG)
SCIMITAR ... System for Countering Interdiction Missiles and Targets RADARs (MCD)
Sci Mo........ Scientific Monthly [*A publication*]
Sci Monogr Univ Wyo Agric Exp Stn ... Science Monograph. University of Wyoming. Agricultural Experiment Station [*A publication*]
Sci Monogr Wyo Expl Stn ... Science Monograph. Wyoming Experimental Station [*A publication*]
SCIMP ...... Selective Cooperative Indexing of Management Periodicals [*Database*] [*European Business School Librarians Group*] [*Information service or system*] (CRD)
SCIMP ...... Self-Contained Imaging Micro-Profiler [*Instrumentation*]
SCIMPEX ... Syndicat des Commercants Importateurs et Exportateurs de l'Ouest African [*Union of Commercial Importers and Exporters of West Africa*]
Sci Mus Minn Monogr ... Science Museum of Minnesota. Monograph [*A publication*]
Sci N .... Science News [*A publication*]
SCIN.......... Self-Canceling Installment Note
SCINA....... Science and Culture [*A publication*]
Sci Nat....... Science et Nature [*A publication*]
Sci New Guinea ... Science in New Guinea [*A publication*]
Sci News .... Science News [*A publication*]
Sci News (Harmondsworth) ... Science News (Harmondsworth) [*A publication*]
Sci News Lett ... Science News Letter [*United States*] [*A publication*]
Sci News (Washington DC) ... Science News (Washington, D.C.) [*A publication*]
Sci NL........ Science News Letter [*A publication*]
Sci Nourishment ... Science of Nourishment [*A publication*]
SCINT .... Scintillator [*Nucleonics*]
Sci Nuncius Radiophonicus ... Scientiarum Nuncius Radiophonicus [*A publication*]
SCIO.......... Scios Nova [*NASDAQ symbol*] (SPSG)
SCIO.......... Staff Counterintelligence Officer [*Military*] (NVT)
SCIOP........ Social Competence Inventory for Older Persons [*Psychology*]
Sci Opin ..... Scientific Opinion [*A publication*]
Sci Orient... Scientia Orientalis [*A publication*]
SCIP .... Isla De Pascua/Mataveri [*Easter Island*] [*Chile*] [*ICAO location identifier*] (ICLI)
SCIP .... Scanning for Information Parameters
SCIP .... School Curriculum Industry Partnership [*British*] (ECON)
SCIP .... Sea Counterinfiltration Patrol (CINC)
SCIP .... Self-Contained Instrument Package (KSC)
SCIP .... Ship's Capability Impaired for Lack of Parts [*Navy*]
SCIP .... Society of Competitor Intelligence Professionals (EA)
SCIP .... Solid Cast Iron Propeller (DS)
SCIP .... Special Crisis Intervention Program (OICC)
SCIP .... Stanford Center for Information Processing [*Stanford University*] [*Later, CIT*]
Sci Paed Ex ... Scientia Paedagogica Experimentalis [*A publication*]
Sci Paed Exp ... Scientia Paedagogica Experimentalis [*A publication*]
Sci Pap Coll Ed ... Scientific Papers. College of General Education [*A publication*]
Sci Pap Coll Gen Educ Univ Tokyo ... Scientific Papers. College of General Education. University of Tokyo [*A publication*]
Sci Pap Coll Gen Educ Univ Tokyo (Biol Part) ... Scientific Papers. College of General Education. University of Tokyo (Biological Part) [*A publication*]
Sci Paperbacks ... Science Paperbacks [*A publication*]
Sci Papers College Gen Ed Univ Tokyo ... Scientific Papers. College of General Education. University of Tokyo [*A publication*]
Sci Papers Prague ICT C ... Scientific Papers. Prague Institute of Chemical Technology. Part C. Organic Chemistry and Technology [*A publication*]
Sci Pap Fac Eng Tokushima Univ ... Scientific Papers. Faculty of Engineering. Tokushima University [*A publication*]

Sci Pap Imp Fuel Res Inst (Jpn) ... Scientific Papers. Imperial Fuel Research Institute (Japan) [*A publication*]
Sci Pap Inst Algol Res Fac Sci Hokkaido Univ ... Scientific Papers. Institute of Algological Research. Faculty of Science. Hokkaido University [*A publication*]
Sci Pap Inst Chem Technol Pardubice ... Scientific Papers. Institute of Chemical Technology. Pardubice [*A publication*]
Sci Pap Inst Chem Technol (Prague) Chem Eng Autom ... Scientific Papers. Institute of Chemical Technology (Prague). Chemical Engineering and Automation [*A publication*]
Sci Pap Inst Electr Power Eng Wroclaw Tech Univ ... Scientific Papers. Institute of Electric Power Engineering. Wroclaw Technical University [*A publication*]
Sci Pap Inst Phys and Chem Res ... Scientific Papers. Institute of Physical and Chemical Research [*A publication*]
Sci Pap Inst Phys Chem Res (Jpn) ... Scientific Papers. Institute of Physical and Chemical Research (Japan) [*A publication*]
Sci Pap Inst Phys Chem Res (Tokyo) ... Scientific Papers. Institute of Physical and Chemical Research (Tokyo) [*A publication*]
Sci Pap Osaka Univ ... Scientific Papers. Osaka University [*A publication*]
Sci Pap Prague Inst Chem Technol G Mineral ... Scientific Papers. Prague Institute of Chemical Technology. G. Mineralogy [*A publication*]
Sci Pap Prague Inst Chem Technol Sect Chem Eng ... Scientific Papers. Prague Institute of Chemical Technology. Section: Chemical Engineering [*A publication*]
Sci Peche.... Science et Peche [*A publication*]
Sci Peo ...... Science for People [*A publication*]
Sci Peopl ... Science for People [*A publication*]
Sci Pest Contr ... Scientific Pest Control [*A publication*]
Sci Pest Control ... Scientific Pest Control [*A publication*]
Sci Pest Control (Kyoto) ... Scientific Pest Control (Kyoto) [*A publication*]
Sci Pharm ... Scientia Pharmaceutica [*A publication*]
Sci Pharm Biol Lorraine ... Sciences Pharmaceutiques et Biologiques de Lorraine [*A publication*]
Sci Pict ...... Science Pictorial [*People's Republic of China*] [*A publication*]
SCIPIO...... Sales Catalog Index Project Input On-Line [*Cleveland Museum of Art*] [*Information service or system*] (IID)
SCIPMIS .. Standard Civilian Personnel Management Information System [*Army*]
SCIPP........ Sacrococcygeal to Inferior Pubic Point [*Anatomy*] (MAE)
SCIPP........ Santa Cruz Institute for Particle Physics [*University of California, Santa Cruz*] [*Research center*] (RCD)
SCIPP........ Silcon-Computing Instrument Patch-Programmed (SAA)
Sci Pro........ Science Progress [*A publication*]
Sci Pro........ Scientific Progress [*London*] [*A publication*]
Sci Proc Cardiff Med Soc ... Scientific Proceedings. Cardiff Medical Society [*A publication*]
Sci Proc Dublin Soc ... Scientific Proceedings. Royal Dublin Society [*A publication*]
Sci Proc R Dublin Soc ... Scientific Proceedings. Royal Dublin Society [*A publication*]
Sci Proc R Dublin Soc A ... Scientific Proceedings. Royal Dublin Society. Series A [*A publication*]
Sci Proc R Dublin Soc New Ser ... Scientific Proceedings. Royal Dublin Society. New Series [*A publication*]
Sci Proc R Dublin Soc Ser A ... Scientific Proceedings. Royal Dublin Society. Series A [*A publication*]
Sci Proc R Dublin Soc Ser B ... Scientific Proceedings. Royal Dublin Society. Series B [*A publication*]
Sci Proc Roy Dublin Soc Ser B ... Scientific Proceedings. Royal Dublin Society. Series B [*A publication*]
Sci Prog...... Science Progress [*A publication*]
Sci Prog Decouverte ... Science Progres Decouverte [*A publication*]
Sci Prog (Lond) ... Science Progress (London) [*A publication*]
Sci Prog (London) ... Science Progress (London) [*A publication*]
Sci Prog Nat ... Science, Progres, la Nature [*A publication*]
Sci Prog Nat (Paris) ... Science, Progres, la Natur (Paris) [*A publication*]
Sci Prog (New Haven) ... Science in Progress (New Haven) [*A publication*]
Sci Prog (Oxf) ... Science Progress (Oxford) [*A publication*]
Sci Progr .... Science Progress [*A publication*]
Sci Progr Decouverte ... Science Progres Decouverte [*A publication*]
Sci Psychoanal ... Science and Psychoanalysis [*A publication*]
Sci Publ Af ... Science and Public Affairs. Bulletin of the Atomic Scientists [*A publication*]
Sci Publ For Timber Ind ... Scientific Publications of Forestry and Timber Industry [*A publication*]
Sci Publ Fuji Photo Film C ... Scientific Publications. Fuji Photo Film Co. Ltd. [*A publication*]
Sci Publ Fuji Photo Film Co Ltd ... Scientific Publications. Fuji Photo Film Co. Ltd. [*Japan*] [*A publication*]
Sci Public Aff Bull At Sci ... Science and Public Affairs. Bulletin of the Atomic Scientists [*A publication*]
Sci Public Policy ... Science and Public Policy [*A publication*]
Sci Publ Pan Am Health Organ ... Scientific Publication. Pan American Health Organization [*A publication*]
Sci Publ Pol ... Science and Public Policy [*A publication*]
Sci Publ Res Inst Radiol Radiat Hyg ... Scientific Publications. Research Institute of Radiology and Radiation Hygiene [*Bulgaria*] [*A publication*]

Sci Publ Sci Mus Minn ... Scientific Publications. Science Museum of Minnesota [*A publication*]
Sci Publ Sci Mus (St Paul) ... Scientific Publications. Science Museum of Minnesota (St. Paul) [*A publication*]
Sci Pub Pol ... Science and Public Policy [*A publication*]
Sci Q Natl Univ Peking ... Science Quarterly. National University of Peking [*A publication*]
Sci R.......... Science Review [*Manila*] [*A publication*]
SCIR .... Society of Cardiovascular and Interventional Radiology (EA)
SCIR .... Subsystem Capability Impact Reporting [*Military*] (NVT)
SCIRA ...... Science Review [*Manila*] [*A publication*]
SCIRA ...... Snipe Class International Racing Association (EA)
SCIRA .... Stable Carbon Isotope Ratio Analysis [*For determining material source*]
SCIRA .... State Central Information Reception Agency
SCIRC .... Spinal Cord Injury Research Center [*Ohio State University*] [*Research center*] (RCD)
S Circular... South Circular [*A publication*]
Sci Rec ...... Science Record [*A publication*]
Sci Rec (Chin Ed) ... Science Record (Chinese Edition) [*People's Republic of China*] [*A publication*]
Sci Rec (Peking) ... Science Record (Peking) [*A publication*]
Sci Rec S M Kirov Kaz State Univ ... Scientific Records. S. M. Kirov Kazakh State University [*A publication*]
Sci Rep Agric Coll Norway ... Scientific Reports. Agricultural College of Norway [*A publication*]
Sci Rep Agric Col Norw ... Scientific Reports. Agricultural College of Norway [*A publication*]
Sci Rep Agric Exped Cambodia ... Scientific Reports. Agricultural Expedition to Cambodia [*A publication*]
Sci Rep Br Antarct Surv ... Scientific Reports. British Antarctic Survey [*A publication*]
Sci Rep Cent Res Inst Kasauli ... Scientific Report. Central Research Institute. Kasauli [*A publication*]
Sci Rep College Gen Ed Osaka Univ ... Science Reports. College of General Education. Osaka University [*A publication*]
Sci Rep Coll Gen Educ Osaka Univ ... Science Reports. College of General Education. Osaka University [*Japan*] [*A publication*]
Sci Rep Ehime Agric Coll ... Scientific Reports. Ehime Agricultural College [*A publication*]
Sci Rep Fac Agr Ibaraki Univ ... Scientific Report. Faculty of Agriculture. Ibaraki University [*A publication*]
Sci Rep Fac Agric Ibaraki Univ ... Scientific Reports. Faculty of Agriculture. Ibaraki University [*A publication*]
Sci Rep Fac Agric Kobe Univ ... Science Reports. Faculty of Agriculture. Kobe University [*A publication*]
Sci Rep Fac Agric Meijo Univ ... Scientific Reports. Faculty of Agriculture. Meijo University [*A publication*]
Sci Rep Fac Agr Okayama Univ ... Scientific Report. Faculty of Agriculture. Okayama University [*A publication*]
Sci Rep Fac Ed Gifu Univ Natur Sci ... Science Reports. Faculty of Education. Gifu University. Natural Science [*A publication*]
Sci Rep Fac Educ Fukushima Univ ... Science Reports. Faculty of Education. Fukushima University [*Japan*] [*A publication*]
Sci Rep Fac Educ Gunma Univ ... Science Reports. Faculty of Education. Gunma University [*A publication*]
Sci Rep Fac Liberal Art Educ Gifu Univ Natur Sci ... Science Report. Faculty of Liberal Arts and Education. Gifu University. Natural Science [*A publication*]
Sci Rep Fac Sci Ege Univ ... Scientific Reports. Faculty of Science. Ege University [*A publication*]
Sci Rep Fac Sci Kyushu Univ Geol ... Science Reports. Faculty of Science. Kyushu University. Geology [*Japan*] [*A publication*]
Sci Rep Gov Inst Infect Dis Tokyo Imp Univ ... Scientific Reports. Government Institute for Infectious Diseases. Tokyo Imperial University [*A publication*]
Sci Rep Gunma Univ ... Science Reports. Gunma Universtiy [*A publication*]
Sci Rep Hirosaki Univ ... Science Reports. Hirosaki University [*A publication*]
Sci Rep Hokkaido Fish Exp Stn ... Scientific Reports. Hokkaido Fisheries Experimental Station [*A publication*]
Sci Rep Hokkaido Salmon Hatchery ... Scientific Reports. Hokkaido Salmon Hatchery [*A publication*]
Sci Rep Hoyo Univ Agr ... Scientific Report. Hoyo University of Agriculture [*A publication*]
Sci Rep Hyogo Univ Agr Fac Agr Kobe Univ ... Science Reports. Hyogo University of Agriculture and Faculty of Agriculture. Kobe University [*A publication*]
Sci Rep Hyogo Univ Agric ... Science Reports. Hyogo University of Agriculture [*A publication*]
Sci Rep Hyogo Univ Agric Ser Agric ... Science Reports. Hyogo University of Agriculture. Series Agriculture [*A publication*]
Sci Rep Hyogo Univ Agric Ser Agric Chem ... Science Reports. Hyogo University of Agriculture. Series Agricultural Chemistry [*A publication*]
Sci Rep Hyogo Univ Agric Ser Agric Hortic ... Science Reports. Hyogo University of Agriculture. Series Agriculture and Horticulture [*A publication*]
Sci Rep Hyogo Univ Agric Ser Agric Technol ... Science Reports. Hyogo University of Agriculture. Series Agriculture Technology [*A publication*]

Sci Rep Hyogo Univ Agric Ser Nat Sci ... Science Reports. Hyogo University of Agriculture. Series Natural Science [*A publication*]
Sci Rep Hyogo Univ Agric Ser Plant Prot ... Science Reports. Hyogo University of Agriculture. Series Plant Protection [*A publication*]
Sci Rep Hyogo Univ Agric Ser Zootech Sci ... Science Reports. Hyogo University of Agriculture. Series Zootechnical Science [*A publication*]
Sci Rep (India) ... Science Reporter (India) [*A publication*]
Sci Rep Indian Agric Res Inst ... Scientific Reports. Indian Agricultural Research Institute [*A publication*]
Sci Rep Inter-Union Comm Geodyn ... Scientific Report. Inter-Union Commission on Geodynamics [*A publication*]
Sci Rep Ist Super Sanita ... Scientific Reports. Istituto Superiore di Sanita [*A publication*]
Sci Rep Kagawa Prefect Fish Exp Stn ... Scientific Reports. Kagawa Prefectural Fisheries Experimental Station [*A publication*]
Sci Rep Kagoshima Univ ... Science Reports. Kagoshima University [*A publication*]
Sci Rep Kanazawa Univ ... Science Reports. Kanazawa University [*A publication*]
Sci Rep Kanazawa Univ Part II Biol Geol ... Science Reports. Kanazawa University. Part II. Biology and Geology [*A publication*]
Sci Rep Kyoto Prefect Univ Agric ... Scientific Reports. Kyoto Prefectural University. Agriculture [*A publication*]
Sci Rep Kyoto Prefect Univ Nat Sci Life Sci ... Scientific Reports. Kyoto Prefectural University. Natural Science and Life Science [*Japan*] [*A publication*]
Sci Rep Kyoto Prefect Univ Nat Sci Living Sci Welfare Sci ... Scientific Reports. Kyoto Prefectural University. Natural Science, Living Science, and Welfare Science [*Japan*] [*A publication*]
Sci Rep Kyoto Prefect Univ Natur Sci Living Sci ... Kyoto Prefectural University. Scientific Reports. Natural Science and Living Science [*A publication*]
Sci Rep Kyoto Pref Univ ... Scientific Report. Kyoto Prefectural University [*A publication*]
Sci Rep Kyoto Pref Univ Natur Sci Living Sci ... Kyoto Prefectural University. Scientific Reports. Natural Science and Living Science [*A publication*]
Sci Rep Lab Amphib Biol Hiroshima Univ ... Scientific Report. Laboratory for Amphibian Biology. Hiroshima University [*A publication*]
Sci Rep Matsuyama Agric Coll ... Scientific Reports. Matsuyama Agricultural College [*A publication*]
Sci Rep Meiji Seika Kaisha ... Scientific Reports. Meiji Seika Kaisha [*A publication*]
Sci Rep Miyagi Agr Coll ... Scientific Report. Miyagi Agricultural College [*A publication*]
Sci Rep Natl Tsing Hua Univ Ser A ... Science Reports. National Tsing Hua University. Series A. Mathematical, Physical, and Engineering Sciences [*A publication*]
Sci Rep Natl Tsing Hua Univ Ser C ... Science Reports. National Tsing Hua University. Series C. Geological, Geographical, and Meteorological Sciences [*A publication*]
Sci Rep Natl Univ Peking ... Science Reports. National University of Peking [*A publication*]
Sci Rep Niigata Univ Ser A ... Science Reports. Niigata University. Series A. Mathematics [*A publication*]
Sci Rep Niigata Univ Ser B ... Science Reports. Niigata University. Series B. Physics [*A publication*]
Sci Rep Niigata Univ Ser C ... Science Reports. Niigata University. Series C. Chemistry [*A publication*]
Sci Rep Niigata Univ Ser D Biol ... Science Reports. Niigata University. Series D. Biology [*A publication*]
Sci Rep Niigata Univ Ser E ... Science Reports. Niigata University. Series E. Geology and Mineralogy [*A publication*]
Sci Rep Niigata Univ Ser F Geol Mineral ... Science Reports. Niigata University. Series F. Geology and Mineralogy [*A publication*]
Sci Rep Osaka Univ ... Science Reports. Osaka University [*A publication*]
Sci Rep Res Inst Engrg Kanagawa Univ ... Science Reports. Kanagawa University. Research Institute for Engineering [*A publication*]
Sci Rep Res Inst Theor Phys Hiroshima Univ ... Scientific Reports. Research Institute for Theoretical Physics. Hiroshima University [*Japan*] [*A publication*]
Sci Rep Res Inst Tohoku Univ ... Science Reports. Research Institutes. Tohoku University [*A publication*]
Sci Rep Res Inst Tohoku Univ A ... Science Reports. Research Institutes. Tohoku University. Series A. Physics, Chemistry, and Metallurgy [*A publication*]
Sci Rep Res Inst Tohoku Univ Med ... Science Reports. Research Institutes. Tohoku University. Series C. Medicine [*A publication*]
Sci Rep Res Inst Tohoku Univ Ser A ... Science Reports. Research Institutes. Tohoku University. Series A. Physics, Chemistry, and Metallurgy [*A publication*]
Sci Rep Res Inst Tohoku Univ Ser B ... Science Reports. Research Institutes. Tohoku University. Series B. Technology [*A publication*]
Sci Rep Res Inst Tohoku Univ Ser C ... Science Reports. Research Institutes. Tohoku University. Series C. Medicine [*A publication*]

Sci Rep Res Inst Tohoku Univ Ser C Med ... Science Reports. Research Institutes. Tohoku University. Series C. Medicine [*A publication*]

Sci Rep Res Inst Tohoku Univ Ser D ... Science Reports. Research Institutes. Tohoku University. Series D [*A publication*]

Sci Rep Res Inst Tohoku Univ Ser D Agric ... Science Reports. Research Institutes. Tohoku University. Series D. Agriculture [*A publication*]

Sci Rep Saikyo Univ Agric ... Scientific Reports. Saikyo University. Agriculture [*A publication*]

Sci Rep Saitama Univ Ser A ... Science Reports. Saitama University. Series A. Mathematics, Physics, and Chemistry [*A publication*]

Sci Rep Saitama Univ Ser B Biol Earth Sci ... Science Reports. Saitama University. Series B. Biology and Earth Sciences [*A publication*]

Sci Rep Shiga Pref Jr Coll ... Scientific Report. Shiga Prefectural Junior College [*A publication*]

Sci Rep Shima Marinel ... Science Report. Shima Marineland [*A publication*]

Sci Rep Soc Res Phys Chem ... Science Reports. Society for the Research of Physics Chemistry [*A publication*]

Sci Rep Tohoku Imp Univ Ser 1 ... Science Reports. Tohoku Imperial University. Series 1. Mathematics, Physics, Chemistry [*A publication*]

Sci Rep Tohoku Imp Univ Ser 3 ... Science Reports. Tohoku Imperial University. Series 3. Mineralogy, Petrology, Economic Geology [*A publication*]

Sci Rep Tohoku Imp Univ Ser 4 ... Science Reports. Tohoku Imperial University. Series 4. Biology [*A publication*]

Sci Rep Tohoku Univ ... Science Reports. Tohoku University [*A publication*]

Sci Rep Tohoku Univ A ... Science Reports. Tohoku University. Series A [*A publication*]

Sci Rep Tohoku Univ Eighth Ser Phys and Astron ... Science Reports. Tohoku University. Eighth Series. Physics and Astronomy [*A publication*]

Sci Rep Tohoku Univ Fifth Ser ... Science Reports. Tohoku University. Fifth Series [*A publication*]

Sci Rep Tohoku Univ Fifth Ser Geophys ... Science Reports. Tohoku University. Fifth Series. Geophysics [*A publication*]

Sci Rep Tohoku Univ First Ser ... Science Reports. Tohoku University. First Series [*Japan*] [*A publication*]

Sci Rep Tohoku Univ Fourth Ser (Biol) ... Science Reports. Tohoku University. Fourth Series. Biology [*A publication*]

Sci Rep Tohoku Univ I ... Science Reports. Tohoku University. First Series [*A publication*]

Sci Rep Tohoku Univ Second Ser (Geol) ... Science Reports. Tohoku University. Second Series. Geology [*A publication*]

Sci Rep Tohoku Univ Ser 5 ... Science Reports. Tohoku University. Fifth Series. Geophysics [*Japan*] [*A publication*]

Sci Rep Tohoku Univ Ser IV ... Scientific Report. Tohoku University. Series IV. Biology [*A publication*]

Sci Rep Tohoku Univ Seventh Ser ... Science Reports. Tohoku University. Seventh Series [*Japan*] [*A publication*]

Sci Rep Tohoku Univ Third Ser ... Science Reports. Tohoku University. Third Series. Mineralogy, Petrology, and Economic Geology [*Japan*] [*A publication*]

Sci Rep Tohoku Univ 8th Series ... Science Reports. Tohoku University. Eighth Series [*A publication*]

Sci Rep Tokyo Bunrika Daigaku Sect A ... Science Reports. Tokyo Bunrika Daigaku. Section A. Mathematics, Physics, Chemistry [*A publication*]

Sci Rep Tokyo Bunrika Daigaku Sect B ... Science Reports. Tokyo Bunrika Daigaku. Section B [*A publication*]

Sci Rep Tokyo Bunrika Daigaku Sect C ... Science Reports. Tokyo Bunrika Daigaku. Section C [*A publication*]

Sci Rep Tokyo Kyoiku Daigaku Sect A ... Science Reports. Tokyo Kyoiku Daigaku. Section A [*A publication*]

Sci Rep Tokyo Kyoiku Daigaku Sect B ... Science Reports. Tokyo Kyoiku Daigaku. Section B [*A publication*]

Sci Rep Tokyo Kyoiku Daigaku Sect C ... Science Reports. Tokyo Kyoiku Daigaku. Section C [*A publication*]

Sci Rep Tokyo Univ Educ Sect A ... Science Reports. Tokyo University of Education. Section A [*A publication*]

Sci Rep Tokyo Woman's Christian College ... Science Reports. Tokyo Woman's Christian College [*A publication*]

Sci Rep Tokyo Woman's Christian Univ ... Tokyo Woman's Christian University. Science Reports [*A publication*]

Sci Rep Univ Chekiang ... Science Reports. University of Chekiang [*A publication*]

Sci Rep Whales Res Inst (Tokyo) ... Scientific Reports. Whales Research Institute (Tokyo) [*A publication*]

Sci Rep Yamaguchi Univ ... Science Reports. Yamaguchi University [*A publication*]

Sci Rep Yokohama Natl Univ I ... Science Reports. Yokohama National University. Section I. Mathematics, Physics, and Chemistry [*A publication*]

Sci Rep Yokohama Natl Univ Sect I ... Science Reports. Yokohama National University. Section I. Mathematics, Physics, and Chemistry [*A publication*]

Sci Rep Yokohama Natl Univ Sect II Biol Geol ... Science Reports. Yokohama National University. Section II. Biology and Geology [*A publication*]

Sci Rep Yokohama Natl Univ Sect II Biol Geol Sci ... Science Reports. Yokohama National University. Section II. Biological and Geological Sciences [*A publication*]

Sci Rep Yokohama Nat Univ Sect 2 ... Science Reports. Yokohama National University. Section 2. Biological and Geological Sciences [*A publication*]

Sci Rep Yokohama Nat Univ Sect I ... Science Reports. Yokohama National University. Section I. Mathematics and Physics [*A publication*]

Sci Rep Yokosuka City Mus ... Science Report. Yokosuka City Museum [*A publication*]

Sci Rep Yokosuka Cy Mus ... Science Report. Yokosuka City Museum [*A publication*]

Sci Res ...... Scientific Researches [*A publication*]

Sci Res Abstr ... Science Research Abstracts [*A publication*]

Sci Res Abstr A ... Science Research Abstracts. Part A. Superconductivity, Magnetohydrodynamics, and Plasmas. Theoretical Physics [*A publication*]

Sci Res Abstr J ... Science Research Abstracts Journal [*A publication*]

Sci Res Abstr J B ... Science Research Abstracts Journal. Part B. Laser and Electro-Optic Reviews, Quantum Electronics, and Unconventional Energy Sources [*A publication*]

Sci Res Abstr J Part A ... Science Research Abstracts Journal. Part A. Super Conductivity, Magnetohydrodynamics and Plasmas, Theoretical Physics [*A publication*]

Sci Res Abstr J Part B ... Science Research Abstracts Journal. Part B. Laser and Electro-Optic Reviews, Quantam Electronics, and Unconventional Energy [*A publication*]

Sci Res Br Univ Coll ... Scientific Research in British Universities and Colleges [*A publication*]

Sci Res Counc Jam J ... Scientific Research Council of Jamaica. Journal [*A publication*]

Sci Res (Dacca) ... Scientific Research (Dacca) [*Pakistan*] [*A publication*]

Sci Res (Dacca, Bangladesh) ... Scientific Researches (Dacca, Bangladesh) [*A publication*]

Sci Res Natl Sci Ed ... Scientific Research. Natural Science Edition [*People's Republic of China*] [*A publication*]

Sci Res News ... Science Research News [*A publication*]

Sci Res News (Kanpur) ... Science Research News (Kanpur) [*A publication*]

Sci Res (NY) ... Scientific Research (New York) [*A publication*]

Sci Resour Lett ... Science Resource Letter [*A publication*]

Sci Rev ...... Scienca Revuo [*A publication*]

Sci Rev ...... Science Review [*A publication*]

Sci Rev (Belgrade) ... Scienca Revuo (Belgrade) [*A publication*]

Sci Rev Int Sci Asoc Esperantista ... Scienca Revuo. Internacia Scienca Asocio Esperantista [*A publication*]

Sci Rev (Manila) ... Science Review (Manila) [*A publication*]

Sci Rev (Neth) ... Scienca Revuo (Netherlands) [*A publication*]

Sci Rondo... Scienca Rondo [*A publication*]

Sci R Toh A ... Science Reports. Research Institutes. Tohoku University. Series A. Physics, Chemistry, and Metallurgy [*A publication*]

SCIS .... Safety Containment Isolation System　(IEEE)

SCIS .... SCI Systems, Inc. [*NASDAQ symbol*]　(NQ)

SCIS .... Science Curriculum Improvement Study [*Education*]

SC Is .... Selected Judgments of the Supreme Court of Israel [*A publication*]　(DLA)

SCIS .... Social Change in Sweden [*A publication*]

SCIS .... Spacecraft Interface Specification　(MCD)

SCIS .... Spinal Cord Injury Service [*Medicine*]

SCIS .... Standard Cubic Inches per Second　(NASA)

SCIS .... Survivable Communications Integration System

Sci S Afr..... Scientific South Africa [*A publication*]

SCISCM.... Single Carrier Initiated Single Carrier Multiplication　(MCD)

Sci & Scty... Science and Society [*A publication*]

SCISEARCH ... Science Citation Index Search [*Institute for Scientific Information*] [*Philadelphia, PA*] [*Bibliographic database*]

Sci Ser Inland Waters Branch Can ... Scientific Series. Inland Waters Branch. Canada [*A publication*]

Sci Ser Inland Waters Dir (Can) ... Scientific Series. Inland Waters Directorate (Canada) [*A publication*]

Sci Ser Inland Waters Lands Dir (Can) ... Scientific Series. Inland Waters/Lands Directorate (Canada) [*A publication*]

Sci Serves Farm ... Science Serves Your Farm [*A publication*]

Sci Silvae ... Scientia Silvae [*A publication*]

Sci Sin........ Scientia Sinica [*A publication*]

Sci Sin B .... Scientia Sinica. Series B. Chemical, Biological, Agricultural, Medical, and Earth Sciences [*A publication*]

Sci Sinica ... Scientia Sinica [*A publication*]

Sci Sinica Ser A ... Scientia Sinica. Series A. Mathematical, Physical, Astronomical, and Technical Sciences [*A publication*]

Sci Sinica Ser B ... Scientia Sinica. Series B. Chemical, Biological, Agricultural, Medical, and Earth Sciences [*A publication*]

Sci Sinica Suppl ... Scientia Sinica. Supplement [*A publication*]

Sci Sin Ser B (Engl Ed) ... Scientia Sinica. Series B. Chemical, Biological, Agricultural, Medical, and Earth Sciences (English Edition) [*A publication*]

Sci Sinter ... Science of Sintering [*A publication*]

Sci Sintering ... Science of Sintering [*A publication*]

SCISO .... Supreme Court, Individual Slip Opinions

Sci Soc........ Science and Society [*A publication*]

Sci Soc....... Sciences Sociales [*A publication*]
Sci Sol .... Science du Sol [*A publication*]
SCISOR..... System for Conceptual Information Summarization, Organization, and Retrieval [*Software package*] (IT)
SCI/SR ...... Shakaichosa-Kenkyusho Consumer Index Summary Report [*Marketing Intelligence Corp.*] [*Japan*] [*Information service or system*] (CRD)
SCISRS ..... Sigma Center Information Storage and Retrieval System
Sci Stud ...... Science Studies [*A publication*]
Sci Stud St Bonaventure Univ ... Science Studies. St. Bonaventure University [*A publication*]
SCIT .... Science Teacher [*A publication*]
SCIT .... Scientific, Inc. [*NASDAQ symbol*] (NQ)
SCIT .... Small Craft Instructor Trainer [*Red Cross*]
SCIT .... Smaller Companies International Trust [*British*]
SCIT .... Special Commissions of Income Tax [*British*]
SCIT .... Standard Change Integration and Tracking (NASA)
SCIT .... Standardization Control of Industry Quality Tools [*Military*] (INF)
SCIT .... Subcommittee on Interzonal Trade [*Allied German Occupation Forces*]
Sci Teach ... Science Teacher [*A publication*]
Sci Teach (New Delhi) ... Science Teacher (New Delhi) [*A publication*]
Sci Teach News ... Science Teachers News [*A publication*] (APTA)
SCITEC..... [*The*] Association of the Scientific, Engineering, and Technological Community of Canada
Sci Tec ...... Scienza e Tecnica [*A publication*]
Sci Tech ..... Science and Australian Technology [*A publication*] (APTA)
Sci Tech ..... Science and Technology [*A publication*]
Sci Tech Aerosp Rep ... Scientific and Technical Aerospace Reports [*NASA*] [*A publication*]
Sci & Tech Aerosp Reports ... Scientific and Technical Aerospace Reports [*NASA*] [*A publication*]
Sci Tech Armement ... Sciences et Techniques de l'Armement [*A publication*]
Sci Tech Eau ... Sciences et Techniques de l'Eau [*A publication*]
Sci Tech Human Values ... Science, Technology, and Human Values [*A publication*]
Sci Tech Inf Process ... Scientific and Technical Information Processing [*A publication*]
Sci Tech Inf Process (Engl Transl) ... Scientific and Technical Information Processing (English Translation) [*A publication*]
Sci Tech Inf Process (Eng Transl Nauchno-Tekh Inf Ser I) ... Scientific and Technical Information Processing (English Translation of Nauchno-Tekhnicheskaya Informatsiya Seriya I) [*A publication*]
Sci Techn Aerospace Rep ... Scientific and Technical Aerospace Reports [*NASA*] [*A publication*]
Sci Tech News ... Science and Technology News [*A publication*]
Sci Technol ... Science and Technology [*A publication*]
Sci Technol ... Sciences and Technologies. Korea University [*Republic of Korea*] [*A publication*]
Sci Technol Aliment ... Science et Technologie Alimentaire [*People's Republic of China*] [*A publication*]
Sci Technol China ... Science and Technology in China [*A publication*]
Sci Technol Jpn ... Science and Technology of Japan [*A publication*]
Sci Technol Korea Univ ... Sciences and Technologies. Korea University [*A publication*]
Sci Technol Libr ... Science and Technology Libraries [*A publication*]
Sci Technol (San Diego) ... Science and Technology (San Diego) [*A publication*]
Sci Technol Ser ... Science Technology Series [*United States*] [*A publication*]
Sci Technol (Surrey Hills Aust) ... Science and Technology (Surrey Hills, Australia) [*A publication*]
Sci Tech (Paris) ... Sciences et Techniques (Paris) [*A publication*]
Sci Tech Pharm ... Sciences et Techniques Pharmaceutiques [*A publication*]
Sci Tech Rep Soap Deterg Assoc ... Scientific and Technical Report. Soap and Detergent Association [*A publication*]
Sci Tec Latt-Casearia ... Scienza e Tecnica Lattiero-Casearia [*A publication*]
Sci Tecnol Alimenti ... Scienza e Tecnologia degli Alimenti [*A publication*]
SCITEC-PAC ... Science and Technology Political Action Committee (EA)
SCITEF ..... Software and Interoperability Test Facility [*Fort Huachuca, AZ*] [*United States Army Electronic Proving Ground*] (GRD)
Sci Terre .... Sciences de la Terre [*A publication*]
Sci Terre Inf Geol ... Sciences de la Terre. Informatique Geologique [*A publication*]
Sci Terre Mem ... Sciences de la Terre. Memoires [*A publication*]
Sci Today (Bombay) ... Science Today (Bombay) [*A publication*]
Sci Tools .... Science Tools [*A publication*]
Sci Total Environ ... Science of the Total Environment [*A publication*]
Sci Tree Top ... Scientific Tree Topics [*A publication*]
SCIU......... Selector Control Interface Unit (MCD)
SCIU......... Spacecraft Interface Unit (NASA)
SCI-USA ... Service Civil International - United States of America (EA)
Sci USSR... Science in USSR [*A publication*]
SCIV......... Subclavian Intravenous Injection [*Medicine*]
Sci Vie........ Science et Vie [*A publication*]
SCIWE ...... Synthesis Center of the Institute for Wholistic Education (EA)
Sci Works For Res Inst (Zvolen) ... Scientific Works. Forest Research Institute (Zvolen) [*A publication*]

Sci Works Higher Inst Agric Sofia Agric Fac Ser Plant Grow ... Scientific Works. Higher Institute of Agriculture. Sofia. Agricultural Faculty. Series. Plant Growing [*A publication*]
Sci Works High Med Inst Pleven ... Scientific Works. Higher Medical Institute of Pleven [*A publication*]
Sci Works Poult Sci Poult Res Inst ... Scientific Works. Poultry Science. Poultry Research Institute [*A publication*]
Sci Works Res Inst Anim Prod Nitra ... Scientific Works. Research Institute of Animal Production at Nitra [*A publication*]
Sci Works Res Inst Epidemiol Microbiol (Sofia) ... Scientific Works. Research Institute of Epidemiology and Microbiology (Sofia) [*A publication*]
Sci World... Scholastic Science World [*A publication*]
Sci World... Scientific World [*England*] [*A publication*]
SCIX .... Scitex Corp. Ltd. [*NASDAQ symbol*] (NQ)
Sci Yearb Vet Fac (Thessalonica) ... Scientific Yearbook. Veterinary Faculty (Thessalonica) [*A publication*]
SCIZ .... Isla De Pascua [*Easter Island*] [*Chile*] [*ICAO location identifier*] (ICLI)
SCJ .... Congregatio Sacerdotum a Corde Jesu [*Congregation of the Priests of the Sacred Heart of Jesus*] [*Roman Catholic religious order*]
SC J .... Nebraska Supreme Court Journal [*A publication*] (DLA)
SCJ .... Science Council of Japan (MCD)
SCJ .... Section of Criminal Justice [*American Bar Association*] (EA)
SC(J)......... Sessions Cases (Judiciary Reports) [*Legal*] [*British*]
SCJ .... Shaped Charge Jet (MCD)
SCJ .... Siberian Chemistry Journal [*A publication*]
SC & J ...... Signal Collection and Jamming
SCJ .... Sisters of the Child Jesus [*Roman Catholic religious order*]
SCJ .... Sixteenth Century Journal [*A publication*]
SCJ .... Society for Collegiate Journalists (EA)
SCJ .... Spertus College of Judaica [*Chicago, IL*] (BJA)
SCJ .... Squamocolumnar Junction [*Medicine*] (MAE)
SCJ .... Stretch Chuck Jaws (MCD)
SCJ .... Super Cobra Jet [*Automotive engineering*]
SC J .... Supreme Court Journal [*India*] [*A publication*] (DLA)
SCJ .... Supreme Court of Justice [*British*] (ROG)
SCJ .... Sydney Cinema Journal [*A publication*] (APTA)
SCJA .... Senior Conformation Judges Association (EA)
SCJAEF ... Senior Conformation Judges Association Education Fund (EA)
SCJB......... Jamaica Supreme Court Judgment Books [*A publication*] (DLA)
SCJC......... Saint Catharine Junior College [*Kentucky*]
Sc J Cl Inv ... Scandinavian Journal of Clinical and Laboratory Investigation [*A publication*]
Sc J Dent R ... Scandinavian Journal of Dental Research [*A publication*]
Sc J Gastr .. Scandinavian Journal of Gastroenterology [*A publication*]
Sc J Haemat ... Scandinavian Journal of Haematology [*A publication*]
Sc J Hist .... Scandinavian Journal of History [*A publication*]
Sc J Immun ... Scandinavian Journal of Immunology [*A publication*]
Sc J In Dis ... Scandinavian Journal of Infectious Diseases [*A publication*]
SCJM .... Sisters of Charity of Jesus and Mary [*See also ZLJM*] [*Belgium*] (EAIO)
SCJO .... Osborno/Canal Bajo [*Chile*] [*ICAO location identifier*] (ICLI)
Sc J Plast ... Scandinavian Journal of Plastic and Reconstructive Surgery [*A publication*]
Sc J Psycho ... Scandinavian Journal of Psychology [*A publication*]
Sc J Re Med ... Scandinavian Journal of Rehabilitation Medicine [*A publication*]
Sc J Resp D ... Scandinavian Journal of Respiratory Diseases [*A publication*]
Sc J Rheum ... Scandinavian Journal of Rheumatology [*A publication*]
SCJS......... Seminary College of Jewish Studies (BJA)
Sc J S Med ... Scandinavian Journal of Social Medicine [*A publication*]
ScJTh........ Scottish Journal of Theology [*Edinburgh*] [*A publication*]
Sc J Thor C ... Scandinavian Journal of Thoracic and Cardiovascular Surgery [*A publication*]
SCJUA ...... Science Journal Incorporating Discovery [*A publication*]
Sc Jur........ Scottish Jurist [*A publication*] (DLA)
Sc J Urol N ... Scandinavian Journal of Urology and Nephrology [*A publication*]
SCK........... Air Force Weapons Laboratory, Kirtland AFB, NM [*OCLC symbol*] (OCLC)
s-ck---........ Colombia [*MARC geographic area code*] [*Library of Congress*] (LCCP)
SCK........... SC Bancorp [*AMEX symbol*] (SPSG)
SCK........... Serum Creatine Kinase [*An enzyme*]
SCK........... Sisters of Christ the King [*Roman Catholic religious order*]
SCK........... SS Airways, Inc. [*Mission, KS*] [*FAA designator*] (FAAC)
SCK........... Stockton [*California*] [*Airport symbol*] (OAG)
SCK........... Stockton, CA [*Location identifier*] [*FAA*] (FAAL)
SCK........... Studiecentrum voor Kernenergie [*Also, CEEN, NERC*] [*Center for Nuclear Energy Studies*] [*Belgium*] (NRCH)
SCKD........ Society of Certified Kitchen Designers (EA)
SCKLS...... South Central Kansas Library System [*Library network*]
SCKSJ ...... Supreme Commandery Knights of St. John (EA)
SCKTPT.... Southern California Kinesthesia and Tactile Perception Tests
ScKW........ Williamsburg Technical College, Kingstree, SC [*Library symbol*] [*Library of Congress*] (LCLS)
s-cl---.......... Chile [*MARC geographic area code*] [*Library of Congress*] (LCCP)

SCL............ Great Falls, MT [*Location identifier*] [*FAA*] (FAAL)
SCL............ Santa Clara Lawyer [*A publication*]
SCL............ Santa Clara - Ricard [*California*] [*Seismograph station code, US Geological Survey*] [*Closed*] (SEIS)
SCL............ Santiago [*Chile*] [*Airport symbol*] (OAG)
SCL............ Save a Cat League (EA)
SCL............ Scale
SCL............ Scarlet (ROG)
SCL............ Scrap Classification List [*DoD*]
Scl .... Sculptor [*Constellation*]
SCL............ Seaboard Coast Line Railroad Co. [*Subsidiary of Seaboard Coast Line Industries*] [*Later, CSX Corp.*] [*AAR code*]
SCL............ Secondary Coolant Line [*or Loop*] [*NASA*] (NASA)
SCL............ Select Cases in Chancery Tempore King [*25 English Reprint*] [*1724-33*] [*A publication*] (DLA)
SCL............ Selectively Cross Linked
SCL............ Senior Citizens League [*Defunct*] (EA)
SCL............ Sequential Control Logic
SCL............ Serum Cholesterol Level [*Clinical chemistry*] (OA)
SCL............ Serum Copper Level [*Clinical chemistry*] (AAMN)
SCL............ Service Control Layer [*Data processing*]
SCL............ Shaped Charge Liner
SCL............ Shaw Cablesystems Ltd. [*Toronto Stock Exchange symbol*]
SCL............ Ship Configuration List [*Navy*] (CAAL)
SCL............ Signal Corps Laboratory [*Obsolete*] [*Army*]
SCL............ Signal Corps Letter (MCD)
SCL............ Simmons College, Boston, MA [*OCLC symbol*] (OCLC)
SCL............ Single Composition Lathe-Cut [*Dental alloy*]
SCL............ Sinus Cycle Length [*Cardiology*]
SCL............ Sisters of Charity (of Leavenworth) [*Roman Catholic religious order*]
SCL............ Site Concurrence Letter (AFM)
SCL............ Skin Conductance Level [*Physiology*]
SCL............ Society for Caribbean Linguistics [*St. Augustine, Trinidad*] (EAIO)
SCL............ Society for Computers and Law [*Abingdon, Oxfordshire, England*] (EAIO)
SCL............ Society of County Librarians [*British*]
SCL............ Sofati Container Line [*Shipping line*]
SCL............ Soft Contact Lens
SCL............ Software Career Link [*Database producer*] [*Burlington, MA*]
SCL............ South Carolina Law Reports [*Pre-1868*] [*A publication*] (DLA)
SCL............ South Central Regional Library System [*UTLAS symbol*]
SCL............ Southeastern Composers' League (EA)
SCL............ Southern California Law Review [*A publication*]
SCL............ Space Charge Limited
SCL............ Space Component Lifetime (SSD)
SCL............ Specification Change Log [*NASA*] (NASA)
SCL............ Spontaneous Cycle Length
SCL............ Standard Classification List [*Military*]
SCL............ Standard Conventional Load
SCL............ Stendhal Club [*A publication*]
SCL............ Stepan Chemical Co. [*AMEX symbol*] (SPSG)
SCL............ Stock Corporation Law [*A publication*] (DLA)
SCL............ String Control Language [*Data processing*]
SCL............ Student of the Civil Law
SCL............ Studies in Canadian Literature [*A publication*]
SCL............ Super Chevys Limited (EA)
SCL............ Symbolic Correction Loader
SCL............ Symmetric Clipper
SCL............ Symphony Command Language [*Data processing*]
SCL............ System Command Language [*Data processing*]
SCL............ Systems Component List (KSC)
SCL............ Systems Control Language [*Data processing*]
Sc LA .... Left Scapuloanterior Position [*of the fetus*] [*Obstetrics*]
ScLangU..... United Merchants Research Center, Langley, SC [*Library symbol*] [*Library of Congress*] (LCLS)
Sc La R....... Scottish Land Court Reports [*Supplement to Scottish Law Review*] [*A publication*] (DLA)
Sc La Rep... Report by the Scottish Land Court [*A publication*] (DLA)
Sc La Rep Ap ... Appendices to the Report of the Scottish Land Court [*A publication*] (DLA)
Sc La Rep App ... Appendices to the Report of the Scottish Land Court [*A publication*] (DLA)
SCLAT ...... Service Central de la Lutte Anti-terroriste [*Central Anti-Terrorist Service*] [*France*] (ECON)
ScLau .... Laurens County Library, Laurens, SC [*Library symbol*] [*Library of Congress*] (LCLS)
SCLAV ...... Sclavonic [*Language, etc.*] (ROG)
SCLB .... Southern Corn Leaf Blight (OA)
SCLC .... Small-Cell Lung Cancer [*Oncology*]
SCLC .... Southern Christian Leadership Conference (EA)
SCLC .... Space-Charge-Limited Current
SCLCS....... Ship Command-Launch Control Subsystem [*Navy*] (CAAL)
SCLDF ...... Sierra Club Legal Defense Fund (EA)
SCLE .... Santiago/Los Leones [*Chile*] [*ICAO location identifier*] (ICLI)
SCLE .... Society and Leisure [*Czechoslovakia*] [*A publication*]
SCLE .... Subacute Cutaneous Lupus Erythematosus [*Medicine*]
SCLEC....... Signal Corps Logistics Evaluation Committee [*Obsolete*] [*Army*] (KSC)
SCLER....... Scleroscope

SCLER...... Sclerosis [*Medicine*]
SCLERA.... Santa Catalina Laboratory for Experimental Relativity by Astrometry [*University of Arizona*] [*Research center*] (RCD)
SCLERO ... Scleroderma [*Medicine*]
SCLF .... Single Crystal LASER Fusion [*For dating of geological material*]
SCLI .... Somerset and Cornwall Light Infantry [*British military*] (DMA)
SC Libn...... South Carolina Librarian [*A publication*]
SCLing....... Siouan and Caddoan Linguistics [*A publication*]
S Clin North America ... Surgical Clinics of North America [*A publication*]
Sc LJ .... Scottish Law Journal and Sheriff Court Record [*A publication*] (DLA)
Sc L J .... Scottish Literary Journal [*A publication*]
SCLJ......... South Carolina Law Journal [*A publication*] (DLA)
SCLK .... Ship's Clerk
SCLL .... Sandia Corporation, Livermore Laboratory
SCLL .... Supreme Committee for the Liberation of Lithuania (EA)
SCLL .... Vallenar/Vallenar [*Chile*] [*ICAO location identifier*] (ICLI)
Scl & Lbr Bul ... Social and Labour Bulletin [*A publication*]
SC LM .... Scottish Law Magazine and Sheriff Court Reporter [*A publication*] (DLA)
SCLM........ Stability, Control, and Load Maneuvers [*Aerospace*] (MCD)
SCLN........ Semicolon (FAAC)
SCLO......... Self-Consistent Local Orbital [*Method*] [*Mathematics*]
SCLO......... Statistical Clearance Liaison Officer [*Army*] (AABC)
SCLOG...... Security Log [*Telecommunications*] (TEL)
Sc LP........ Left Scapuloposterior Position [*of the fetus*] [*Obstetrics*]
SCLP .... Santiago/Lo Prado [*Chile*] [*ICAO location identifier*] (ICLI)
Scl Problems ... Social Problems [*A publication*]
SC L Q ...... South Carolina Law Quarterly [*A publication*]
SCLR .... Santa Clara Law Review [*A publication*] (ILCA)
Sc LR .... Scottish Law Reporter [*A publication*] (DLA)
Sc LR .... Scottish Law Review and Sheriff Court Reports [*A publication*] (DLA)
SC LR .... South Carolina Law Review [*A publication*]
SCLRA ..... School Review [*A publication*]
Sc L Rep..... Scottish Law Reporter [*Edinburgh*] [*A publication*] (DLA)
SC L Rev.... South Carolina Law Review [*A publication*]
SCLS......... Serra Cooperative Library System [*Library network*]
SCLS......... Shipboard Command and Launch Subsystem (MCD)
SCLS......... South Central Library System [*Library network*]
SCLS......... Star Classics, Inc. [*NASDAQ symbol*] (NQ)
SCLSA....... Scandinavian Journal of Clinical and Laboratory Investigation. Supplement [*A publication*]
Scl Sci Q .... Social Science Quarterly [*A publication*]
Scl Sec Bul ... Social Security Bulletin [*A publication*]
Sc LT .... Scots Law Times [*A publication*] (DLA)
SCLV .... Subclavian Vein [*Anatomy*]
SCLY .... Scullery (MSA)
Sc M.......... Master of Science
SCM .... S-Band Cassegrain Monopulse
SCM .... Sacra Caesarea Majestas [*Sacred Imperial Majesty*] [*Latin*]
SCM .... Samarium Cobalt Magnet
SCM .... Sanctae Memoriae [*Of Holy Memory*] [*Latin*]
SCM .... Scammon Bay [*Alaska*] [*Airport symbol*] (OAG)
SCM .... Scammon Bay, AK [*Location identifier*] [*FAA*] (FAAL)
SCM .... School Musician. Director and Teacher [*A publication*]
SCM .... SCM Corp. [*Formerly, Smith-Corona Marchant, Inc.*] [*NYSE symbol*] (SPSG)
SCM .... Selective Complement Accumulator
SCM .... Self-Contained Munitions
SCM .... Sender's Composition Message [*Cable*]
SCM .... Service Command Module [*Aerospace*] (MCD)
SCM .... Sheep Creek Mountain [*Alaska*] [*Seismograph station code, US Geological Survey*] (SEIS)
SCM .... Signal Conditioning Module
SCM .... Simulated Core Mock-Up [*or Model*] [*Nuclear energy*] (NRCH)
SCM .... Single-Channel MODEM [*Telecommunications*] (TEL)
SCM .... Single Crystal Meteorite
SCM .... Siscoe Callahan [*Vancouver Stock Exchange symbol*]
SCM .... Site Configuration Message [*NASA*]
SCM .... Small-Core Memory [*Data processing*]
SCM .... Society of Community Medicine [*Later, SPH*] (EAIO)
SCM .... Society for Computer Medicine [*Later, AMIA*] (EA)
SCM .... Software Configuration Management (IEEE)
SCM .... Solar Cell Module
SCM .... Soluble Cytotoxic Mediator [*Immunology*]
SCM .... Spacecraft Material [*NASA*] (SSD)
SCM .... Spares Calculation Model
SCM .... Special Court-Martial
SCM .... Specification Change Memorandum
SCM .... Spleen Concanavalin A Medium [*Immunoassay*]
SCM .... Squadron Corporal-Major [*British military*] (DMA)
SCM .... Stamp Cancelling Machine (DCTA)
SCM .... Standard Cubic Meter
SCM .... STARAN [*Stellar Attitude Reference and Navigation*] Control Module (OA)
SCM .... State-Certified Midwife [*British*]
SCM .... Steam Condensing Mode [*Nuclear energy*] (NRCH)

SCM .... Sternocleidomastoid [*Anatomy*]
SCM .... Stillman College, Tuscaloosa, AL [*OCLC symbol*]   (OCLC)
S & CM ...... Strategic and Critical Materials [*Military*]
SCM .... Strategic Cruise Missile   (MCD)
SCM .... Streamline Curvature Method [*Computer program*]
SCM .... Streptococcal Cell Membrane [*Microbiology*]
SCM .... Strouds Creek & Muddtley Railroad [*AAR code*]
SCM .... Student Christian Movement [*British*]
SCM .... Subscribers' Concentration Module
                [*Telecommunications*]   (TEL)
SCM .... Subsystem Configuration Management [*or Monitoring*]
                [*NASA*]   (NASA)
SCM .... Summary Court-Martial [*Army*]
SCM .... Superconducting Magnet   (IEEE)
SCM .... Supervision Control Module [*Telecommunications*]   (TEL)
SCM .... Supply Categories of Material   (MCD)
SCM .... Suppressed-Carrier Modulation
SCM .... Surface Contamination Module   (DWSG)
SCM .... Sussex County Magazine [*A publication*]
SCM .... Sustained Competitive Motivation
SCM .... System Control Module [*NASA*]   (GFGA)
SCM .... System Control and Monitor [*Telecommunications*]   (TSSD)
SCM .... Systems Control Microprocessor
SCMA .... Silk Commission Manufacturers Association [*Defunct*]   (EA)
SCMA .... Southern Cypress Manufacturers Association   (EA)
SCMAI ...... Staff Committee on Mediation, Arbitration, and Inquiry
                [*American Library Association*]
SC Mar Resour Cent Tech Rep ... South Carolina. Marine Resources Center.
                Technical Report [*A publication*]
SCMAT ..... Southern California Motor Accuracy Test
SCMB .... Seaby's Coin and Medal Bulletin [*A publication*]
SCMB .... Standard Chartered Merchant Bank [*Singapore*]
SCMB .... Subsystem Configuration Management Board [*NASA*]   (GFGA)
SCMB .... System Configuration Management Board   (SSD)
SCMC .... S-Carboxymethylcysteine [*An amino acid*]
SCMC .... Sisters of Charity of Our Lady, Mother of the Church [*Roman
                Catholic religious order*]
SCMC .... Societe de Construction des Musees du Canada
SCMC .... Sodium(carboxymethyl)cellulose [*Organic chemistry*]
SCMC .... Strategic Cruise Missile Carrier
SCMC .... Supply Category of Material Code
SCMD .... Santiago/Ministerio de Defensa Nacional [*Chile*] [*ICAO
                location identifier*]   (ICLI)
SCMD .... Selectively Conductive Molding Device
SCME .... American Federation of State, County, and Municipal
                Employees
SCME .... Service Center Math Error [*IRS*]
SCME .... Society of Clinical and Medical Electrologists   (EA)
SCME .... Surgut Commodity and Raw Materials Exchange [*Russian
                Federation*]   (EY)
SCMF .... Single Contact Midge Flange
SCMF .... Societe Canadienne de Musique Folklorique
SCMG .... Sierra Carriers and Mountaineering Group   (EA)
Sc M in Hyg ... Master of Science in Hygiene
SCMI .... Society to Conquer Mental Illness [*Defunct*]   (EA)
SCMM ...... Selections from China Mainland Magazines [*US Consulate,
                Hongkong*] [*A publication*]
SCMM ...... Sisters of Charity of Our Lady, Mother of Mercy [*Roman
                Catholic religious order*]
SCMM ...... Society of Catholic Medical Missionaries, Inc. [*Medical Mission
                Sisters*] [*Roman Catholic religious order*]
SCMO .... Senior Clinical Medical Officer [*British*]
SCMO .... Societe Canadienne de Meteorologie et d'Oceanographie
                [*Canadian Meteorological and Oceanographic Society -
                CMOS*]
SCMO .... Societe pour une Confederation au Moyen-Orient [*Society for
                Middle East Confederation - SMEC*] [*Israel*]   (EAIO)
SCMO .... Studie- en Informatiecentrum TNO voor Milieu-Onderzoek
                [*TNO Study and Information Center on Environmental
                Research*] [*Information service or system*]   (IID)
SCMO .... Subsidiary Communications Multiplex Operation [*FM radio
                frequency unused portion*]
SCMO .... Summary Court-Martial Order [*Army*]
SCMOD .... Scale Model
SCMOV..... Subterranean Clover Mottle Virus [*Plant pathology*]
SCMP .... Second-Class Mail Publications [*Later, ASCMP*]   (EA)
SCMP .... Service Craft Modernization Program [*Navy*]   (CAAL)
SCMP .... Society of Company Meeting Planners   (EA)
SCMP .... South China Morning Post [*A publication*]
SCMP .... Sulfonated Chemimechanical Pulp [*Pulp and paper technology*]
SCMP .... Support Center Management Plan   (AAG)
SCMP .... System Contractor Management Plan [*NASA*]   (NASA)
SCMPBN .. South China Morning Post (Business News) [*A publication*]
SCMPT ..... Sperm Cervical Mucus Penetration Test [*Clinical chemistry*]
SCMR....... Secretary's Committee on Mental Retardation [*Department of
                Health and Human Services*]
SCMR....... South Canterbury Mounted Rifles [*British military*]   (DMA)
SCMR....... Special Committee on Migration and Resettlement
                [*Department of State*] [*World War II*]
SCMR........ Surface Composition Mapping Radiometer [*NASA*]

SCMS .... Scientific Measurement Systems, Inc. [*Austin, TX*] [*NASDAQ
                symbol*]   (NQ)
SCMS .... Serial Copy Management System [*for digital audio tape
                recording machines*]
SCMS .... Signal Command Management System [*Military*]   (AABC)
SCMS .... Somali Current Monitoring System [*Marine science*]   (MSC)
SCMS .... Standard Configuration Management Systems
                [*Military*]   (AFIT)
SCMT .... Single-Cause Mortality Tape [*National Center for Health
                Statistics databank*]
SCMT .... Subcontract Management Team [*NASA*]   (SSD)
Sc Mun App Rep ... Scotch Munitions Appeals Reports [*Edinburgh and
                Glasgow*] [*A publication*]   (DLA)
SCMV....... Santa Cruz Mountain Vintners   (EA)
SCMV........ Sugar Cane Mosaic Virus
SCN .... Citadel, Daniel Library, Charleston, SC [*OCLC
                symbol*]   (OCLC)
SCN .... Saarbrucken [*Germany*] [*Airport symbol*]   (OAG)
SCN .... Satellite Communications Network, Inc. [*Edison, NJ*]
                [*Telecommunications*]   (TSSD)
SCN .... Satellite Conference Network, Inc. [*New York, NY*] [*NYSE
                symbol*] [*Telecommunications service*]   (TSSD)
SCN .... Satellite Control Network
SCN .... Scanner [*Data processing*]
SCN .... Schematic Change Notice
SCN .... Screen [*Technical drawings*]
SCN .... Scribe Nehemiah [*Freemasonry*]
SCN .... Search Control Number   (MCD)
SCN .... Secretary's Commission on Nursing [*Department of Health and
                Human Services*]
SCN .... Securities Communications Network, Inc. [*Englewood,
                CO*]   (TSSD)
SCN .... Self-Checking Number
SCN .... Self-Compensating Network [*Telecommunications*]   (TEL)
SCN .... Self-Contained Navigation [*NASA*]
SCN .... Sensitive Command Network
SCN .... Seventeenth-Century News [*A publication*]
SCN .... Shipbuilding and Conversion, Navy
SCN .... Ships Construction, Navy [*Funding*]
SCN .... Shop Control Number   (DNAB)
SCN .... Shortest Connected Network
SCN .... Show Cause Notice
SCN .... Silent Canyon Resources Ltd. [*Vancouver Stock Exchange
                symbol*]
SCN .... Single Crystal Needle
SCN .... Sisters of Charity (of Nazareth) [*Roman Catholic religious
                order*]
SCN .... Sorting Code Number   (DCTA)
SCN .... Southern Command Network [*Military*]   (GFGA)
SCN .... Soybean Cyst Nematode [*Botany*]
SCN .... Special Care Nursery
SCN .... Special Change Notice   (KSC)
SCN .... Specific Control Number
SCN .... Specification Change Notice [*NASA*]
SCN .... Stock Control Number
SCN .... Summary and Charge Number
SCN .... Sunset Crater National Monument [*Arizona*] [*Seismograph
                station code, US Geological Survey*]   (SEIS)
SCN .... Supply Corps, Navy
SCN .... Suprachiasmatic Nucleus [*or Nuclei*] [*of the hypothalamus*]
                [*Anatomy*]
SCN .... Sylvania-Corning Nuclear Corp.
SCN .... System Change Notice
SCN .... System Control Number
SCNA .... Self-Contained Night Attack   (MCD)
SCNA .... Sikh Council of North America   (EA)
SCNA .... Sudden Cosmic-Noise Absorption
SCNAWAF ... Special Category Navy with Air Force
SCNB......... Societe Nationale des Chemins de Fer Belges [*Belgian National
                Railways*]
ScNC.......... Newberry College, Newberry, SC [*Library symbol*] [*Library of
                Congress*]   (LCLS)
SCNC........ South Carolina National Corp. [*NASDAQ symbol*]   (NQ)
SCNCA..... Sciences [*New York*] [*A publication*]
SCND .... Scientific Industries, Inc. [*NASDAQ symbol*]   (NQ)
SCND .... Second   (FAAC)
scnDNA ..... Deoxyribonucleic Acid, Single Copy Nuclear [*Biochemistry,
                genetics*]
SCNDVA... Standing Committee on National Defence and Veterans Affairs
                [*Canada*]
SCNEB ...... Science News [*Washington, DC*] [*A publication*]
SCNG .... Scan-Graphics, Inc. [*NASDAQ symbol*]   (NQ)
SCNG .... Scanning   (MSA)
SCNI .... Select Committee on Nationalised Industries [*British*]
SC (Nig) ..... Judgments of the Supreme Court of Nigeria [*A
                publication*]   (DLA)
SCNMV..... Sweet Clover Necrotic Mosaic Virus [*Plant pathology*]
SCNN .... Scan-Tron Corp. [*NASDAQ symbol*]   (NQ)
SCNO .... Savio Club National Office   (EA)
SCNO .... Senior Canadian Naval Officer [*British military*]   (DMA)

ScNoaSH... North Augusta Senior High School, North Augusta, SC [*Library symbol*] [*Library of Congress*] (LCLS)

SCNPWC .. Standing Committee for Nobel Prize Winners' Congresses (EA)

SCNR........ Scanner (MSA)

SCNR........ Scientific Committee of National Representatives [*NATO*]

Sc NR......... Scott's New English Common Pleas Reports [*A publication*] (DLA)

SCNR........ Sequence Control Number Register [*Data processing*]

SCNR........ Solid-Core Nuclear Rocket [*NASA*]

SCNR........ Supreme Council for National Reconstruction [*South Korea*]

SCNS........ Self-Contained Navigation System [*NASA*]

SCNS........ Subcutaneous Nerve Stimulation [*For treatment of pain*]

SCN/SIN... Sensitive Command Network/Sensitive Information Network (CET)

SCNTN...... Self-Contained

SCNUL...... Standing Conference on National and University Libraries [*British*]

SC Nurs .... South Carolina Nursing [*A publication*]

SCO .... Converse College, Spartanburg, SC [*OCLC symbol*] (OCLC)

SCO .... Manetti Roberts [*Italy*] [*Research code symbol*]

SCO .... Sales Contracting Officer [*Army*]

SCO .... Santa Cruz Operation [*Computer manufacturer*] (PCM)

SCO .... Sarawak Communist Organization [*Malaya*]

ScO .... Scientific Officer [*Also, SO*] [*Ministry of Agriculture, Fisheries, and Food*] [*British*]

SCO .... Scobey, MT [*Location identifier*] [*FAA*] (FAAL)

SCO .... Score Resources [*Vancouver Stock Exchange symbol*]

SCO .... Scoresbysund [*Greenland*] [*Seismograph station code, US Geological Survey*] [*Closed*] (SEIS)

Sco.............. Scorpius [*Constellation*]

SCO .... Scottish (ROG)

Sco.............. Scott's English Common Pleas Reports [*A publication*] (DLA)

SCO .... Scout [*or Scouting*] (DNAB)

SCO .... Selective Conscientious Objection

SCO .... Senior Chief Officer [*British military*] (DMA)

SCO .... Service Cryptologic Organizations (MCD)

SCO .... Single Crystal Orthoferrites

SCO .... Sisters of Charity of Ottawa [*Grey Nuns of the Cross*] [*Roman Catholic religious order*]

SCO .... Smith Corona Corp. [*NYSE symbol*] (SPSG)

SCO .... Society of Commissioned Officers (EA)

SCO .... Software Change Order (MCD)

SCO .... Southern College of Optometry [*Tennessee*]

S/CO.......... Spacecraft Observer (KSC)

SCO .... Spacecraft Operations [*NASA*] (KSC)

SCO .... Squadron Command Officer (AAG)

SCO .... Squadron Constructor Officer [*Navy*] [*British*]

SCO .... Staff Communications Office [*Army*]

SCO .... Start Checkout [*NASA*] (NASA)

SCO .... State Coordinating Officer [*Federal disaster planning*]

SCO .... Statistical Control Office [*or Officer*] [*Military*]

SCO .... Subcarrier Oscillator

SCO .... Subcommissural Organ [*Neuroanatomy*]

SCO .... Subcontract Consignment Order

SCO .... Successor Contracting Officer (MCD)

SCO .... Supercritical Oxygen (MCD)

SCO .... Switch Closure Out (MCD)

SCO .... Synthetic Crude Oil [*Fuel technology*]

SCO .... System Counterpart Officer [*Military*] (AFIT)

SCOA .... Saluki Club of America (EA)

SCOA .... Sample Cave Operating Area [*Nuclear energy*] (NRCH)

SCOA .... SCOA Industries, Inc. [*Canton, MA*] [*NASDAQ symbol*] (NQ)

SCOA .... Supreme Council Order of the Amaranth (EA)

SCOAL...... Short-Term Coal Analysis System [*Department of Energy*] (GFGA)

SCOB........ Scattered Clouds or Better (SAA)

SCOBA...... Standing Conference of the Canonical Orthodox Bishops in the Americas (EA)

SCOBBS.... School of Combined Operations, Beach and Boat Section [*Military*] [*British*]

SCOBO ..... Satellite Collection Buoy Observations

SCOBOL... Structured COBOL

SCOC........ Sediment Community Oxygen Consumption [*Marine biology*]

SCOC........ Senior Commanders Orientation Course (MCD)

SCOC........ Short-Circuit Output Current

SCOC........ Societe Canadienne d'Orientation et de Consultation

SCOC........ Spanish Chamber of Commerce [*Taiwan*] (EAIO)

SCOC........ Support Command Operations Center [*Military*]

SCOCE...... Special Committee on Compromising Emanations [*Military*] (AABC)

SCOCLIS.. Standing Conference of Co-Operative Library and Information Services [*British*]

Sco Costs.... Scott's Costs in the High Court [*4th ed.*] [*1880*] [*A publication*] (DLA)

SCOD .... Societe Cooperative Oecumenique de Developpement [*Ecumenical Development Cooperative Society - EDCS*] [*Netherlands*] (EAIO)

SCOD .... South Coast One Design [*Cruising boat*]

SCOD .... Specific Chemical Oxygen Demand Value [*for Complete Oxidation*]

SCODA ..... Scan Coherent Doppler Attachment

SCODL...... Scan Conversion Object Description Language [*Data processing*] (PCM)

SCODS ...... Study Commission on Ocean Data Stations [*Marine science*] (MSC)

SCOE......... Special Checkout Equipment [*NASA*] (NASA)

SCOEG...... Standing Conference of Employers of Graduates [*British*]

SCOFA ...... Shipping Control Office, Forward Area [*Navy*]

SCOFF ...... Simplified Combustion Form Function (MCD)

SCOFOR... Scottish Forces [*World War II*]

SCOFOR... Scouting Force [*Navy*]

ScoGaelS ... Scottish Gaelic Studies [*A publication*]

ScoGS .... Scottish Gaelic Studies [*A publication*]

S and COH ... Son and Coheir [*Genealogy*]

SCOH .... Staff Corporal of Horse [*British military*] (DMA)

SCOHR ...... Students Committee on Human Rights

Sco Int........ Scott's Intestate Laws [*A publication*] (DLA)

Sco & J Tel ... Scott and Jarnigan on the Law of Telegraphs [*A publication*] (DLA)

SCOL......... School (NVT)

SCOLA ...... Second Consortium of Local Authorities

SCOLAG Bull ... Scottish Legal Action Group. Bulletin [*A publication*] (DLA)

Scol Anon... Scolia Anonyma [*Classical studies*] (OCD)

SCOLAR ... Standard Costing of Laboratory Resources

Scol Att ...... Scolia Attica [*Classical studies*] (OCD)

SCOLAVNMED ... School of Aviation Medicine [*Later, School of Aerospace Medicine*]

SCOLCAP ... Scottish Libraries Cooperative Automation Project

SCOLE ...... Spacecraft Control Laboratory Experiment (MCD)

SCOLE ...... Standing Committee on Library Education [*American Library Association*]

SCOLMA ... Standing Conference on Library Materials on Africa [*British*]

SCOLSHIP ... Schoolship [*Navy*] (NVT)

SCOM .... Scientific Committee [*NATO*] (NATG)

SCOM .... SCS/Compute, Inc. [*St. Louis, MO*] [*NASDAQ symbol*] (NQ)

SCOM .... Site Cutover Manager [*Telecommunications*] (TEL)

SCOM .... Spacecraft Communicator

SCOM .... Supervisory Communication Relations Test

SCOMA .... Shipping Control Office, Marianas [*Navy*]

SCOMO .... Satellite Collection of Meteorological Observations

S/COMPT ... Side Compartment [*Automotive engineering*]

SCON .... Quellon/Ad Quellon [*Chile*] [*ICAO location identifier*] (ICLI)

SCON .... Santiago/Quinta Normal [*Chile*] [*ICAO location identifier*] (ICLI)

SCON .... Syscon Corp. [*NASDAQ symbol*] (NQ)

Scone & Upper Hunter Hist Soc J ... Scone and Upper Hunter Historical Society. Journal [*A publication*] (APTA)

Sco NR....... Scott's New English Common Pleas Reports [*A publication*] (DLA)

SCONRES ... Senate Concurrent Resolution (AFIT)

SCONS...... Shipment Control System [*Military*]

SCONT...... Ship Control

SCONUL... Standing Conference on National and University Libraries [*British*]

SCOOP...... Scientific Computation of Optimal Programs (IEEE)

SCOOP...... Scientific Computation of Optimum Procurement [*Air Force*]

SCOOP...... Strategic Confirmation of Optical Phenomenology

SCOOP...... Support Plan to Continuity of Operations Plan [*Military*]

SCOP......... Ferrocarril del Sureste [*AAR code*]

SCOP......... Scopolamine [*Anticholinergic compound*]

SCOP......... Single Copy Order Plan [*Later, STOP*] [*Bookselling*]

SCOP......... Steering Committee on Pilotage (DS)

SCOPE ...... Schedule-Cost-Performance (IEEE)

SCOPE ...... Scientific Committee on Problems of the Environment [*ICSU*] (EA)

SCOPE ...... Scope Industries [*Associated Press abbreviation*] (APAG)

SCOPE ...... Scripps Cooperative Oceanic Productivity Expedition [*1956*]

SCOPE ...... Selected Contents of Periodicals for Educators (AEBS)

SCOPE ...... Senior Citizens' Opportunities for Personal Enrichment [*Federal antipoverty program*]

SCOPE ...... Sequential Customer Order Processing Electronically

SCOPE ...... Service Center of Private Enterprise

SCOPE ...... Simple Checkout-Oriented Program Language

SCOPE ...... Simple Communications Programming Environment [*Data processing*]

SCOPE ...... Southern Coastal Plains Expedition [*National Oceanic and Atmospheric Administration*] (MSC)

SCOPE ...... Special Committee on Paperless Entries [*California interbank group*]

SCOPE ...... Special Committee on Problems of the Environment [*of International Council of Scientific Unions*]

SCOPE ...... Stromberg Central Operations Panel - Electric

SCOPE ...... Student Council on Pollution and the Environment [*Association conceived in late 1969 by then Secretary of the Interior Walter J. Hickel*]

SCOPE ...... Subsystem for the Control of Operations and Plan Evaluation

SCOPE ...... Summer Community Organization and Political Education Program

SCOPE ...... Supervisory Control of Program Execution (MCD)

SCOPE ...... Supportive Council on Preventive Effort [*Ohio*]

SCOPE ...... System to Coordinate the Operation of Peripheral Equipment

SCOPES.... Squad Combat Operations Exercise, Simulation [*Military*]
SCOPP...... School-College Orientation Program of Pittsburgh
SCOPS ...... Select Committee on Ocean Policy Study [*Federal Council for Science and Technology*]
SCOR........ Scientific Committee on Oceanic Research [*ICSU*] [*Halifax, NS*]   (EAIO)
Scor............ Scorpius [*Constellation*]
SCOR........ Self-Calibrating Omnirange
SCOR........ Small Cycle Observation Recording
SCOR........ Special Center of Research [*HEW*]
SCOR........ Special Committee on Oceanographic Research
SCOR........ Specialized Center of Research in Atherosclerosis [*University of Chicago*] [*Research center*]   (RCD)
SCOR........ Specialized Center of Research in Ischemic Heart Disease [*University of Alabama at Birmingham*] [*Research center*]   (RCD)
SCOR........ Standing Conference on Refugees [*British*]
SCOR........ Status Control of Rejections   (MCD)
SCOR........ Syncor International Corp. [*NASDAQ symbol*]   (NQ)
SCORAN... Scorer and Analyzer [*Computerized educational testing*]
ScOrC........ Claflin College, Orangeburg, SC [*Library symbol*] [*Library of Congress*]   (LCLS)
SCORDES ... Sferics Correlation Detection System
SCORE...... Satellite Computer-Operated Readiness Equipment [*SSD*]
SCORE...... Scientific Cooperative Operational Research Expedition [*National Oceanic and Atmospheric Administration*]   (MSC)
SCORE...... Selection Copy and Reporting   (IEEE)
SCORE...... Selective Conversion and Retention [*Navy*]
SCORE...... Service Corps of Retired Executives Association [*Washington, DC*]   (EA)
SCORE...... Short Course Off-Road Event [*Off-road vehicle racing*]
SCORE...... Signal Communication by Orbiting Relay Equipment [*Radio*]
Score......... Simulated Combat Operations Range Equipment   (MCD)
SCORE...... Solving Community Obstacles and Restoring Employment [*Occupational therapy*]
SCORE...... Southern California Off-Road Event [*An association*]
SCORE...... Space Communications for Orbiting Relay Equipment   (MCD)
SCORE...... Special Claim on Residual Equity
SCORE...... Spectral Combinations for Reconnaissance Exploitation [*Photography*]
SCORE...... Standing Committee on Regulatory Effectiveness [*Nuclear Regulatory Commission*]   (NRCH)
SCORE...... Stratified Charge, Omnivorous Rotary Engine [*Automotive engineering*]
SCORE...... Street Corner Offense Reduction Experiment
SCORE...... Student Competitions on Relevant Engineering
SCORE...... Subsystem Control of Required Equipment   (MCD)
SCORE...... Supervisory Coaching Relations Test
SCORE...... System for Computerized Olympic Results and Events [*Texas Instruments, Inc.*]
SCORE...... System Cost and Operational Resource Evaluation   (MCD)
SCORE...... Systematic Communications of Range Effectiveness   (MUGU)
SCORE...... Systems Coordinative Reporting   (MCD)
SCORES.... Scenario-Oriented Recurring Evaluation System [*Military*]
SCORES.... Standard Combat Oriented Recurring Evaluation System [*Military*]
SCORN ..... Special Committee Opposing Resurgent Nazism
SCORON .. Scouting Squadron
SCOROR.... Secretary's Committee on Research on Reorganization [*Navy*]
S/Corp ...... Staff Corporal [*British military*]   (DMA)
SCORP...... Statewide Comprehensive Outdoor Recreation Plan
SCORPI .... Subcritical Carbon-Moderated Reactor Assembly for Plutonium Investigations   (MCD)
SCORPIO ... Subject-Content-Oriented Retriever for Processing Information On-Line [*Congressional Research Service*]
ScOrS .... South Carolina State College, Orangeburg, SC [*Library symbol*] [*Library of Congress*]   (LCLS)
SCOR U..... SCOR US Corp. [*Associated Press abbreviation*]   (APAG)
SCORU ...... Statistical Control and Operations Records Unit [*Air Force*]
SCOS .... Scottish Certificate in Office Studies
ScoS .... Scottish Studies [*A publication*]
SCOS .... Small Computer and Office Systems [*Honeywell, Inc.*]
SCOS .... Subsystem Computer Operating System [*NASA*]   (NASA)
SCOSA ...... Sadtler Commercial Spectra [*A publication*]
SCOSE ...... Standing Committee on Submarine Escape [*British military*]   (DMA)
SCOST ...... Special Committee on Space Technology   (KSC)
SCOSTEP ... Scientific Committee on Solar Terrestrial Physics   (EA)
SCOT........ Satellite Communication Terminal [*Navy*] [*British*]   (MCD)
SCOT........ Satellite Communications Overseas Transmission
SCOT........ Scotland [*or Scottish*]   (EY)
SCOT........ Scott & Stringfellow Financial, Inc. [*Richmond, VA*] [*NASDAQ symbol*]   (NQ)
SCOT........ Scottish [*or Scotsman*]   (ROG)
SCOT........ Shell Claus Offgas Treating [*Chemical engineering*]
SCOT........ Shipborne SATCOM Terminal [*British*]
SCOT........ Shippers for Competitive Ocean Transportation [*Washington, DC*]   (EA)
SCOT........ Standby Compatible One-Tape [*System*]
SCOT........ Steel Car of Tomorrow

SCOT........ Supplementary Checkout Trailer
SCOT........ Support-Coated Open-Tubular [*Column*] [*Chromatography*]
SCOTAC... Speech-Compatible Tactile Communicant   (MCD)
Scot A Forum ... Scottish Archaeological Forum [*A publication*]
Scot Agr ..... Scottish Agriculture [*A publication*]
Scot AL...... Scottish Art and Letters [*A publication*]
SCOTAPLL ... Standing Conference on Theological and Philosophical Libraries in London
Scot App Rep ... Scottish Appeal Reports [*A publication*]   (DLA)
Scot Archaeol Forum ... Scottish Archaeological Forum [*A publication*]
Scot Art R .. Scottish Art Review [*A publication*]
Scot Art Rev ... Scottish Art Review [*A publication*]
SCOTBEC ... Scottish Business Education Council   (DCTA)
SCOTBUILD ... Scottish Building and Public Works Exhibition [*Scottish Exhibitions Ltd.*]   (TSPED)
SCOTCH... Summer Cultural Opportunities for Teams and Children [*National music program*]
SCOTEC ... Scottish Technical Education Council [*British*]
Scot Edu St ... Scottish Educational Studies [*A publication*]
SCOTENG ... Scottish Engineering Exhibition for Design, Production, and Automation [*Scottish Exhibitions Ltd.*]   (TSPED)
Scot Geog M ... Scottish Geographical Magazine [*A publication*]
Scot Geogr Mag ... Scottish Geographical Magazine [*A publication*]
Scot GM..... Scottish Geographical Magazine [*A publication*]
Scot His R ... Scottish Historical Review [*A publication*]
Scot Hist R ... Scottish Historical Review [*A publication*]
Scot Hist Riv ... Scottish Historical Review [*A publication*]
SCOTHOT ... Scottish Hotel, Catering, and Licensed Trade Exhibition [*Scottish Exhibitions Ltd.*]   (TSPED)
SCOTICE ... Scotland to Iceland Submarine Cable System [*Telecommunications*]   (TEL)
Scot J Geol ... Scottish Journal of Geology [*A publication*]
Scot J PE ... Scottish Journal of Physical Education [*A publication*]
Scot J Pol Econ ... Scottish Journal of Political Economy [*A publication*]
Scot J Poli ... Scottish Journal of Political Economy [*A publication*]
Scot J Rel... Scottish Journal of Religious Studies [*A publication*]
Scot J Rel St ... Scottish Journal of Religious Studies [*A publication*]
ScotJt......... Scottish Journal of Theology [*A publication*]
Scot J Th.... Scottish Journal of Theology [*A publication*]
Scot J Theo ... Scottish Journal of Theology [*A publication*]
Scot Jur .... Scottish Jurist [*A publication*]   (DLA)
SCOTL ...... Scotland   (ROG)
ScotL.......... Scottish Language [*A publication*]
Scot Law J ... Scottish Law Journal [*Glasgow*] [*A publication*]   (DLA)
Scotl Dep Agric Fish Mar Res ... Scotland Department of Agriculture and Fisheries. Marine Research [*A publication*]
Scotl Dep Agric Fish Tech Bull ... Scotland Department of Agriculture and Fisheries. Technical Bulletin [*A publication*]
Scot Lit J ... Scottish Literary Journal [*A publication*]
Scot LJ....... Scottish Law Journal and Sheriff Court Record [*A publication*]   (DLA)
Scot LM ..... Scottish Law Magazine and Sheriff Court Reporter [*A publication*]   (DLA)
Scot L Mag ... Scottish Law Magazine [*Edinburgh, Scotland*] [*A publication*]   (DLA)
Scot LR ...... Scottish Law Reporter [*A publication*]   (DLA)
Scot LR ...... Scottish Law Review [*A publication*]
Scot L Rep ... Scottish Law Reporter [*A publication*]   (DLA)
Scot L Rev ... Scottish Law Review [*A publication*]
Scot LT ...... Scots Law Times [*A publication*]   (DLA)
Scot Med J ... Scottish Medical Journal [*A publication*]
SCOTMET ... Scottish Metropolitan [*Property developer*]
Scotmn .... Scotsman Industries, Inc. [*Associated Press abbreviation*]   (APAG)
ScotNAE.... Scottish National Antarctic Expedition [*1902-04*]
SCOTNATS ... Scottish Nationalists
Scot Parl Acts ... Acts of the Parliaments of Scotland   (DLA)
Scot R........ Scottish Review [*A publication*]
SCOTRACEN ... Scouting Training Center [*Navy*]
SCOTS ...... Surveillance and Control of Transmission Systems [*Bell Laboratories*]
SCOTS ...... System Checkout Test Set   (MCD)
Scots LTR ... Scots Law Times Reports [*A publication*]   (DLA)
Scots Mag ... Scots Magazine [*A publication*]
Scotsman Mag ... Scotsman Magazine [*A publication*]
Scots RR .... Scots Revised Reports [*1707-1873*] [*A publication*]   (DLA)
Scot Stud.... Scottish Studies [*A publication*]
Scott.......... Scott's English Common Pleas Reports [*A publication*]   (DLA)
Scott.......... Scott's Reports [*25, 26 New York Civil Procedure*] [*A publication*]   (DLA)
SCOTT...... Single Channel Objective Tactical Terminal [*Army*]   (RDA)
SCOTT...... Synchronous Continuous Orbital Three-Dimensional Tracking
Scott Agric ... Scottish Agriculture [*A publication*]
Scott Art Rev ... Scottish Art Review [*A publication*]
Scott Australas ... Scottish Australasian [*A publication*]   (APTA)
Scott Bankers Mag ... Scottish Bankers Magazine [*A publication*]
Scott Bee J ... Scottish Bee Journal [*A publication*]
Scott Beekeep ... Scottish Beekeeper [*A publication*]
Scott Beekpr ... Scottish Beekeeper [*A publication*]
Scott Birds ... Scottish Birds [*A publication*]

Scott Birds J Scott Ornithol Club ... Scottish Birds. Journal. Scottish Ornithologists' Club [*A publication*]
Scott Econ Bull ... Scottish Economic Bulletin [*A publication*]
Scott Econ Soc Hist ... Scottish Economic and Social History [*A publication*]
Scott Educ Rev ... Scottish Educational Review [*A publication*]
Scott Elect Engr ... Scottish Electrical Engineer [*A publication*]
Scott (Eng) ... Scott's English Common Pleas Reports [*A publication*]   (DLA)
Scott Field ... Scottish Field [*A publication*]
Scott Fish Bull ... Scottish Fisheries Bulletin [*A publication*]
Scott Fish Res Rep ... Scottish Fisheries Research Report [*A publication*]
Scott Fmr ... Scottish Farmer and Farming World [*A publication*]
Scott For .... Scottish Forestry [*A publication*]
Scott For J ... Scottish Forestry Journal [*A publication*]
Scott Genealog ... Scottish Genealogist [*A publication*]
Scott Geogr Mag ... Scottish Geographical Magazine [*A publication*]
Scott Hist Rev ... Scottish Historical Review [*A publication*]
Scott Ind Hist ... Scottish Industrial History [*A publication*]
ScottInst .... Scott Instruments Corp. [*Associated Press abbreviation*]   (APAG)
Scottish Art R ... Scottish Art Review [*A publication*]
Scottish Bankers M ... Scottish Bankers Magazine [*A publication*]
Scottish Econ Bul ... Scottish Economic Bulletin [*A publication*]
Scottish Ednl J ... Scottish Educational Journal [*A publication*]
Scottish Ednl Studies ... Scottish Educational Studies [*A publication*]
Scottish Geog Mag ... Scottish Geographical Magazine [*A publication*]
Scottish Georgian Soc Bull ... Scottish Georgian Society. Bulletin [*A publication*]
Scottish J Pol Economy ... Scottish Journal of Political Economy [*A publication*]
Scottish Mus ... Scottish Music and Drama [*A publication*]
Scott J .... Reporter, English Common Bench Reports [*A publication*]   (DLA)
Scott J Adult Educ ... Scottish Journal of Adult Education [*A publication*]
Scott J Agric ... Scottish Journal of Agriculture [*A publication*]
Scott J Geol ... Scottish Journal of Geology [*A publication*]
Scott J Polit Econ ... Scottish Journal of Political Economy [*A publication*]
Scott J Theology ... Scottish Journal of Theology [*A publication*]
Scott Jur .... Scottish Jurist [*A publication*]
Scott Labour Hist Soc J ... Scottish Labour History Society Journal [*A publication*]
Scott Lang ... Scottish Language [*A publication*]
Scott Life-Boat ... Scottish Life-Boat [*A publication*]
Scott Lit J .. Scottish Literary Journal [*A publication*]
Scott Mar Biol Assoc Annu Rep ... Scottish Marine Biological Association. Annual Report [*A publication*]
Scott Marxist ... Scottish Marxist [*A publication*]
Scott Med J ... Scottish Medical Journal [*A publication*]
Scott Mountaineering Club J ... Scottish Mountaineering Club Journal [*A publication*]
Scott Nat .... Scottish Naturalist [*A publication*]
Scott NR .... Scott's New English Common Pleas Reports [*A publication*]   (DLA)
ScottP .... Scott Paper Ltd. [*Associated Press abbreviation*]   (APAG)
Scott R .... Scottish Review [*A publication*]
SCOTT-R ... Super-Critical, Once-Thru Tube Reactor [*Experiment*] [*General Electric Co.*]
Scott Rep .... Scott Report [*A publication*]
Scott Rev .... Scottish Review [*A publication*]
Scott S .... Scottish Studies [*A publication*]
Scott Stud ... Scottish Studies [*A publication*]
Scotts Turfgrass Res Conf Proc ... Scotts Turfgrass Research Conference. Proceedings [*A publication*]
Scott Trade Union Rev ... Scottish Trade Union Review [*A publication*]
Scott Tradit ... Scottish Tradition [*A publication*]
Scott Wildl ... Scottish Wildlife [*A publication*]
SCOU .... Ship Course
SC Oudh .... Oudh Select Cases [*India*] [*A publication*]   (DLA)
SCOUS ...... Spectrum Clear of Unknown Signals   (MUGU)
SCOUT ...... Surface-Controlled Oxide Unipolar Transistor
Scouting in NSW ... Scouting in New South Wales [*A publication*]   (APTA)
SCOW .... Scottish Convention of Women   (DI)
SCOWAH ... Schmulowitz Collection of Wit and Humor [*San Francisco Public Library*]
SCOWR ..... Special Committee on Water Research [*International Council of Scientific Unions*]
SCP .... Brotherhood of Sleeping Car Porters [*Later, BRAC*]   (EA)
SCP .... SAGE [*Semiautomatic Ground Environment*] Computer Program
SCP .... St. Catharines Public Library [*UTLAS symbol*]
SCP .... Satellite Cloud Photograph
SCP .... Satin Chrome Plated
SCP .... Scanner Control Power   (MCD)
SCP .... Scanning Phased Array
SCP .... Schematic Change Proposal
SCP .... Scoops [*A publication*]
SCP .... Scope Industries [*AMEX symbol*]   (SPSG)
SCP .... Scottish Conservative Party [*Political party*]
SCP .... Scrip   (ROG)
SCP .... Script [*Films, television, etc.*]
SCP .... Secondary Control Point
SCP .... Sector Command Post [*Military*]

SCP .... Secure Conferencing Project
SCP .... Security Classification Procedure [*Military*]
SCP .... Self-Consistent Phonon
SCP .... Senior Companion Program   (EA)
SCP .... Serial Character Printer   (OA)
SCP .... Sertoli-Cell Protein [*Immunology*]
SCP .... Service Control Point [*DoD*]   (AFIT)
SCP .... Servo-Controlled Positioner
SCP .... Sheep Choroid Plexus
SCP .... Short-Circuit Protection
SCP .... Silver Cup Resources Ltd. [*Vancouver Stock Exchange symbol*]
SCP .... Simplified Clearance Procedure [*Customs*]   (DS)
SCP .... Simulation Control Program [*Military*]   (CAAL)
SCP .... Simulator Control Panel [*NASA*]
SCP .... Sindbis Core Protein [*Virology*]
SCP .... Single-Cell Protein
SCP .... Single Component Peak [*Spectra*]
SCP .... Small Cardioactive Peptide [*Biochemistry*]
SCP .... Smaller Communities Program [*Department of Labor*]
SCP .... Social Credit Party of Canada [*Parti Credit Social du Canada*]   (PPW)
SCP .... Societe Canadienne de Pedatrie [*Canadian Paediatric Society*]   (EAIO)
SCP .... Societe Canadienne de la Population [*Canadian Population Society - CPS*]
SCP .... Societe Culinaire Philanthropique [*New York, NY*]   (EA)
SCP .... Society of California Pioneers   (EA)
SCP .... Society of Christian Philosophers   (EA)
SCP .... Society for Czechoslovak Philately   (EA)
SCP .... Sodium Cellulose Phosphate [*Kidney-stone drug*]
SCP .... Software Change Proposal   (MCD)
SCP .... Solar Cell Panel
SCP .... Sonobuoy Control Panel
SCP .... Spacecraft Platform [*NASA*]
SCP .... Spanish Communist Party
SCP .... Special Category Patient [*Aeromedical evacuation*]
SCP .... Specific Candlepower   (NASA)
SCP .... Specific Cleavage Product [*Biochemistry*]
SCP .... Spherical Candlepower
SCP .... Spiritual Counterfeits Project   (EA)
SCP .... Standardized Care Plans [*for hospitals*]
SCP .... State College [*Pennsylvania*] [*Seismograph station code, US Geological Survey*]   (SEIS)
SCP .... Station Communications Processor
SCP .... Sterol Carrier Protein
SCP .... Storage Control Processor   (NOAA)
SCP .... Stromberg-Carlson Practices [*Telecommunications*]   (TEL)
SCP .... Structural Ceramic Panel
SCP .... Studies in Classical Philology [*A publication*]
SCP .... Subcontract Proposal   (AAG)
SCP .... Sudanese Communist Party [*Political party*]   (PD)
SCP .... Sulfachloropyridazine [*Antibacterial*]
SCP .... Supervisor's Control Panel
SCP .... Supervisory Control Program [*Burroughs Corp.*]
SCP .... Supplier Change Proposal   (MCD)
SCP .... Supplier's Contract Property   (MCD)
SCP .... Supply Cataloging Program
SCP .... Supply Control Plan [*World War II*]
SCP .... Surveillance Communication Processor [*Aviation*]   (OA)
SCP .... Survey Control Point [*Military*]
SCP .... Symbolic Conversion Program   (BUR)
SCP .... Synthetic Fuels Commercialization Program [*Also, SFCP*] [*Energy Resources Council*]
SCP .... Syrian Communist Party [*Political party*]   (PPW)
SCP .... System Change Package
SCP .... System Communication Pamphlet   (IEEE)
SCP .... System Concept Paper [*Army*]   (RDA)
SCP .... System Control Processor [*Honeywell, Inc.*]
SCP .... System Control Programming [*Data processing*]
SCP .... Systems Change Proposal   (AFM)
SCP .... Without Chest Pain [*Medicine*]
SCPA .... Semiconductor Chip Protection Act of 1984
SCPA .... Solar Cell Panel Assembly
SCPA .... Southern Coal Producers Association [*Defunct*]   (EA)
SCPA .... Southern College Personnel Association   (AEBS)
SCPA .... Spacecraft Payload Adapter   (MCD)
Sc Paed ...... Scientia Paedagogica [*A publication*]
Sc Parliament ... Science in Parliament [*A publication*]
SCPC .... Signal Corps Pictorial Center [*Obsolete*] [*Army*]
SCPC .... Single-Channel-per-Carrier [*Telecommunications*]
SCPCE ...... Societe Canadienne pour la Prevention de Cruaute aux Enfants
SCPCU ...... Society of Chartered Property and Casualty Underwriters   (EA)
SCPD .... Scratch Pad [*Data processing*]
Sc-PD .... Silicon Photodiode
SCPD .... Staff Civilian Personnel Division [*Army*]
S & CP Dec ... Ohio Decisions [*A publication*]   (DLA)
SCPD OCSA ... Staff Civilian Personnel Division, Office, Chief of Staff, Army   (AABC)
SCPD OC of SA ... Staff Civilian Personnel Division, Office, Chief of Staff, Army   (AABC)
SCPE .... Scope, Inc. [*NASDAQ symbol*]   (NQ)

SCPE .... Simplified Collective Protection Equipment [*Military*] (RDA)
SCPE .... Specialized Customer Premises Equipment [*for the handicapped*]
Sc for People ... Science for People [*A publication*]
SCPF .... Sacra Congregatio de Propaganda Fide [*Sacred Congregation for the Propagation of the Faith*] [*Latin*]
SCPGB ...... Revista. Sociedad Cientifica del Paraguay [*A publication*]
SCPH........ Societe Canadienne des Pharmaciens d'Hopitaux [*Canadian Society of Hospital Pharmacists*] (EAIO)
SCPI .... Scientists' Committee for Public Information [*Defunct*]
SCPI .... Small Computer Program Index [*No longer published*] [*ALLM Books*] (IID)
SCPI .... Structural Clay Products Institute [*Later, BIA*] (EA)
SCPK .... Serum Creatine Phosphokinase [*An enzyme*] (AAMN)
SCPL .... Senior Commercial Pilot's Licence [*British*] (DBQ)
SCPL .... Signal Corps Photographic Laboratory [*Obsolete*] [*Army*]
SCPL .... Staff of Chief of Personnel and Logistics [*British military*] (DMA)
S/Cpl. .... Staff Corporal [*British military*] (DMA)
SCPL/H ... Senior Commercial Pilot's Licence/Helicopters [*British*] (AIA)
SCPM .... Sample Collection and Preparation Module [*X-ray spectrometry*]
SCPM........ Scanning Chemical Potential Microscope
SCPM........ Semiautomatic Circuit Performance Monitor [*Navy*] (MCD)
SCPM........ Silwood Centre for Pest Management [*Imperial College*] [*British*] (CB)
SCPMT ..... Southern California Perceptual Motor Tests
SCPN .... Scorpion Technologies, Inc. [*NASDAQ symbol*] (NQ)
SCPNT ..... Southern California Postrotary Nystagmus Test
SCPO........ Second-Class Post Office
SCPO........ Senior Chief Petty Officer [*Navy rating*]
SCPP .... Sierra Cooperative Pilot Project [*Department of the Interior*]
SCPP .... Sovereign Chemical & Petroleum Products, Inc. [*Chicago, IL*] [*NASDAQ symbol*] (NQ)
SCPP .... Supreme Court, Preliminary Prints
SCPP .... Surveyor Command Preparation Program [*Aerospace*]
SCPPS....... Secondary Containment Purge and Pressure Control System [*Nuclear energy*] (NRCH)
SCPR .... Semiconductor Parameter Retrieval [*Information Handling Services*] [*Database*]
SCPR .... Sri Chinmoy Oneness-Home Peace Run [*An association*] (EA)
SCPR .... Standard Cardiopulmonary Resuscitation
SCPRA ..... Science Progress [*Oxford*] [*A publication*]
SCPRF...... Structural Clay Products Research Foundation [*Absorbed by BIA*] (EA)
SCPS......... [*The*] Scopas Technology Co., Inc. [*NASDAQ symbol*] (NQ)
SCPS......... Servo-Controlled Positioning System
SCPS......... Society of Civil and Public Servants [*A union*] [*British*] (DCTA)
SCP(S)...... Subscribers' Call Processing (Subsystem) [*Telecommunications*] (TEL)
SCPS......... Survivable Collective Projected System
SCPS......... Survivable Collision Protection System (DWSG)
SCPSC....... South Carolina Public Service Commission Reports [*A publication*] (DLA)
SCPT .... SAGE [*Semiautomatic Ground Environment*] Computer Programming Training
SCPT .... Script Systems, Inc. [*Hackensack, NJ*] [*NASDAQ symbol*] (NQ)
SCPT .... Security Control Point [*Military*] (MUGU)
SCPT .... Self-Consistent Perturbation Theory [*Physics*]
SCPTR....... Standing Committee on Personnel Training and Readiness [*Navy*]
SCPYB....... Social Policy [*A publication*]
SCQ .... Hanscom Air Force Base, Base Library, Hanscom AFB, MA [*OCLC symbol*] (OCLC)
SCQ .... Saco Resources [*Vancouver Stock Exchange symbol*]
SCQ .... Santiago De Compostela [*Spain*] [*Airport symbol*] (OAG)
SCQ .... Sisters of Charity of Quebec [*Grey Nuns*] [*Roman Catholic religious order*]
SCQC........ Scout Crew Qualification Course [*Army*]
SCQE........ Squad Combat Qualification Exercise [*Army*] (INF)
SCR........... Canada. Supreme Court Reports [*A publication*]
SCR........... Cape Colony Supreme Court Reports [*A publication*] (DLA)
SCR........... Chinook Regional Library, Swift Current, Saskatchewan [*Library symbol*] [*National Library of Canada*] (NLC)
SCR........... Juta's Supreme Court Cases [*1880-1910*] [*Cape Of Good Hope, South Africa*] [*A publication*] (DLA)
SCR........... Law Reports of Supreme Court of Sarawak, North Borneo, and Brunei [*A publication*] (DLA)
SCR........... San Cristobal [*Chile*] [*Seismograph station code, US Geological Survey*] [*Closed*] (SEIS)
SCR........... Scanning Control Register
SCR........... Schedule Change Report
SCR........... Schedule Change Request [*NASA*] (NASA)
SCR........... Score (ROG)
SCR........... Scourer[s] [*or Scouring*] [*Freight*]
SCR........... Scranton Public Library, Scranton, PA [*OCLC symbol*] (OCLC)
Scr .... Scrapie [*Animal pathology*]
SCR........... Scratch

SCR........... Screen (WGA)
SCR........... Screw (AAG)
scr............. Scribe [*MARC relator code*] [*Library of Congress*] (LCCP)
Scr .... Scrinium [*A publication*]
SCR........... Scrip (ADA)
Scr .... Scripture (BJA)
SCR........... Scruple
SCR........... Scrutiny [*A publication*]
SCR........... Scurry-Rainbow Oil Ltd. [*Toronto Stock Exchange symbol*]
SCR........... Sea Containers Ltd. [*NYSE symbol*] (SPSG)
SCR........... Section Cross Reference (MCD)
SCR........... Security Airways & Freight Express, Inc. [*Glen Burnie, MD*] [*FAA designator*] (FAAC)
SCR........... Security Change Request [*Military*] (GFGA)
SCR........... Selective Catalytic Reduction
SCR........... Selective Chopper Radiometer
SCR........... Selenium Control Rectifier [*Nuclear energy*] (NRCH)
SCR........... Self-Consistent Renormalization Theory [*Quantum mechanics*]
SCR........... Semiconductor
SCR........... Semiconductor-Controlled Rectifier
SCR........... Senate Concurrent Resolution (CDAI)
SCR........... Senior Common Room [*in British colleges and public schools*]
SCR........... Senior Contractor Representative
SCR........... Sequence Checking Routine
scr............. Serbo-Croatian (Roman) [*MARC language code*] [*Library of Congress*] (LCCP)
SCR........... Series Control Relay
SCr .... Serum Creatinine [*Hematology*]
SCR........... Set Complete Radio
SCR........... Shift Count Register
SCR........... Ship to Component Record [*Navy*]
SCR........... Short-Circuit Ratio
SCR........... Short Consensus Repeat [*Biochemistry*]
SCR........... Signal Conditioning Rack
SCR........... Signal Conversion Relay [*Telecommunications*] (TEL)
SCR........... Signal Corps Radio [*Followed by model number*] [*Obsolete*] [*Army*]
SCR........... Silicon-Controlled Rectifier [*Electronics*]
SCR........... Simulation and Control Rack
SCR........... Single-Channel Reception (DEN)
SCR........... Single Character Recognition
SCR........... Skin Conductance Response
SCR........... Sneak Circuit Report [*NASA*] (NASA)
SCR........... Society of Cardiovascular Radiology [*Later, SCVIR*] (EA)
SCR........... Society for Cultural Relations between the Peoples of the British Commonwealth and the USSR
SCR........... Sodium-Cooled Reactor [*Nuclear energy*]
SCR........... Software Change Request [*NASA*]
SCR........... Software Correction Report (CAAL)
SCR........... Software Cost Reduction [*Data processing*]
SCR........... Solar Cosmic Radiation [*or Ray*]
SCR........... [*Department of*] Soldiers' Civil Reestablishment [*Canada*]
SCR........... SONAR Control Room
SCR........... South Carolina Reports [*A publication*] (DLA)
SCR........... South Carolina Review [*A publication*]
SCR........... Soviet Cybernetics Review [*A publication*]
SCR........... Spacecraft Received Time
SCR........... Spanish Communication Region [*Air Force*] (MCD)
SCR........... Spares Coordination Record (SAA)
SCR........... Special Certification Roster
SCR........... Specific Commodity Rates (DS)
SCR........... Specification Clarification Request (MCD)
SCR........... Speed Change Rate
SCR........... Stable Continental Region [*Geology*]
SCR........... Standard Chartered Review [*A publication*]
SCR........... Static Card Reader
SCR........... Strip Chart Recorder [*NASA*]
SCR........... Structurally Conserved Region [*Biochemistry*]
SCr .... Strumenti Critica [*A publication*]
S Cr .... Strumenti Critici [*A publication*]
SCR........... Studies in Comparative Religion [*A publication*]
SCR........... Sub-Chief Ranger [*Ancient Order of Foresters*]
SCR........... Subcontractor (SAA)
SCR........... Summary Control Report [*Planning and Production*] [*Navy*]
SCR........... Supersonic Combustion Ramjet
SCR........... Support Control Room [*NASA*] (KSC)
SCR........... Supreme Court Reports [*India*] [*A publication*] (DLA)
SCR........... Supreme Court Reports [*New South Wales, Australia*] [*A publication*] (DLA)
SCR........... Supreme Court Reports [*1928-41, 1946-51*] [*Sarawak*] [*A publication*] (DLA)
SCR........... Supreme Court Reports [*Canada Department of Justice*] [*Information service or system*] (CRD)
SCR........... Surface-Contour RADAR
SCR........... Syrene-Chloroprene Rubber
SCR........... System Change Request
SCR........... System Conceptual Requirement (SSD)
SCR........... System Control Registers [*Data processing*]
SCR........... System Control Routine
SCRA........ Single Channel Radio Access Subsystem (MCD)
SC & RA .... Specialized Carriers and Rigging Association (EA)

SCRA......... Stanford Center for RADAR Astronomy
SCRA......... Steel Can Recycling Association (EA)
SCRA......... Supreme Council of the Royal Arcanum [*Boston, MA*] (EA)
SCRAA...... Standing Conference of Regional Arts Associations [*British*] (DI)
SCRAC...... Standing Conference of Regional Advisory Councils for Further Education
SCRAG...... Senior Civilian Representative, Attorney General [*Department of Justice civil disturbance unit*]
SCRAM..... Safety Control Rod Axe Man [*Nuclear energy*] (IEEE)
SCRAM..... Scottish Campaign to Resist the Atomic Menace
SCRAM..... Selective Combat Range Artillery Missile
SCRAM..... Self-Corrected Remedial Aid and Media [*Teaching method*]
SCRAM..... Service Change Release and Manufacture (MCD)
SCRAM..... Several Compilers Reworked and Modified
SCRAM..... Short-Range Attack Missile
SCRAM..... Signal Corps Random-Access Memory (DNAB)
SCRAM..... Space Capsule Regulator and Monitor
SCRAM..... Spares Components Reidentification and Modification [*Program*] [*DoD*]
SCRAM..... Spares Control, Release, and Monitoring
SCRAM..... Special Criteria for Retrograde of Army Materiel (AABC)
SCRAM..... Supersonic Combustion Ramjet Missile
SCRAM..... Synanon Committee for Responsible American Media [*Later, SCRAP*]
SCRAM Energy Bull ... SCRAM [*Scottish Campaign to Resist the Atomic Menace*] Energy Bulletin [*A publication*]
SCRAMJET ... Supersonic Combustion Ramjet
SCRAMM ... System Calibration, Repair, and Maintenance Model [*Military*] (CAAL)
SCraneN .... Stephen Crane Newsletter [*A publication*]
SCRAP ...... Selective Curtailment of Reports and Paperwork [*Navy*]
SCRAP ...... Series Computation of Reliability and Probability [*Data processing*]
SCRAP ...... Simple Complex Reaction-Time Apparatus
SCRAP ...... Society for Completely Removing All Parking Meters
SCRAP ...... Students Challenging Regulatory Agency Proceedings [*Student legal action organization*]
SCRAP ...... Super-Caliber Rocket-Assisted Projectile (IEEE)
SCRAP ...... Synanon Committee for a Responsible American Press (EA)
SCRAPE.... Screening Country Requirements Against Plus Excess [*DoD*]
SCRATA ... Steel Castings Research and Trade Association [*Sheffield, England*] (EAIO)
Scrat Bdg Soc ... Scratchley's Building Societies [*5th ed.*] [*1883*] [*A publication*] (DLA)
Scrat & Bra ... Scratchley and Brabook's Building Societies [*2nd ed.*] [*1882*] [*A publication*] (DLA)
SCRATCHPAD ... [*A*] Programming Language (CSR)
Scrat Life Ass ... Scratchley's Life Assurance [*13th ed.*] [*1887*] [*A publication*] (DLA)
SCRB......... Software Configuration Review Board (CAAL)
SCRB......... Structured Case Review Blank
SCRBA ...... Student Committee for the Right to Bear Arms [*Defunct*] (EA)
Scr Bull ...... Scripture Bulletin [*A publication*]
SCRC......... Superfund Community Relations Coordinator [*Environmental Protection Agency*] (GFGA)
SCRD......... Scientific Radio Systems, Inc. [*NASDAQ symbol*] (NQ)
SCRD......... Secondary Control Rod Driveline [*Nuclear energy*] (NRCH)
SCRD......... Student Coalition for the Right to Drink [*Defunct*] (EA)
SCRD......... Vina Del Mar/Rodelillo [*Chile*] [*ICAO location identifier*] (ICLI)
SCRDB...... Screwed Bonnet
SCRDE...... Stores and Clothing Research and Development Establishment [*British*]
Scr Demolinguist ... Scritti Demolinguistici [*A publication*]
SCRDM...... Secondary Control Rod Drive Mechanism [*Nuclear energy*] (NRCH)
SCRDN...... Screw Down
SCRE......... Scandinavian Review [*A publication*]
SCRE......... Scottish Council for Research in Education
SCrE .... South Carolina Electric & Gas Co. [*Associated Press abbreviation*] (APAG)
SCRE......... Stratified Charge Rotary Engine (DWSG)
SCRE......... Supreme Cossack Representation in Exile (EA)
SCREB ...... Scientific Research [*A publication*]
Screen Ed... Screen Education [*A publication*]
Screen Ed Notes ... Screen Education Notes [*A publication*]
SCREENEX ... Screening Exercise [*Military*] (NVT)
SC Reg .... South Carolina State Register [*A publication*]
SC Rep....... Juta's Supreme Court Cases [*1880-1910*] [*Cape Of Good Hope, South Africa*] [*A publication*] (DLA)
SC Res ...... Senate Concurrent Resolution (DLA)
SC Research Plan Devel Board Bull ... South Carolina Research Planning and Development Board. Bulletin [*A publication*]
SC Resour Cent Tech Rep ... South Carolina. Marine Resources Center. Technical Report [*A publication*]
Sc Rev Rept ... Scots Revised Reports [*A publication*] (DLA)
S & C Rev St ... Swan and Critchfield's Revised Statutes [*Ohio*] [*A publication*] (DLA)
SCREWS... Solar Cosmic Ray Early Warning System (MUGU)
SCRF .... Small Craft Repair Facility [*Navy*] (NVT)

Scr Fac Sci Nat Univ Purkynianae Bru Biol ... Scripta Facultatis Scientiarum Naturalium Universita J. E. Purkyne Brunensis. Biiologia [*A publication*]
Scr Fac Sci Nat Univ Purkynianae Brun ... Scripta Facultatis Scientiarum Naturalium Universitatis Purkynianae Brunensis [*A publication*]
Scr Fac Sci Nat Univ Purkynianae Brunensis Geol ... Scripta Facultatis Scientiarum Naturalium Universitatis Purkynianae Brunensis. Geologia [*A publication*]
Scr Fac Sci Nat Univ Purkynianae Brunensis Phys ... Scripta Facultatis Scientiarum Naturalium Universitatis Purkynianae Brunensis. Physica [*A publication*]
SCRG......... Rancagua/De La Independencia [*Chile*] [*ICAO location identifier*] (ICLI)
SCRG......... Societe Canadienne de Recherche en Geriatrie
SCRG......... Stationary Cosmic Ray Gas
SCRG......... System Change Review Group [*George C. Marshall Space Flight Center*] (NASA)
Scr Geobot ... Scripta Geobotanica [*A publication*]
Scr Geogr ... Scripta Geographica [*A publication*]
Scr Geol (Leiden) ... Scripta Geologica (Leiden) [*A publication*]
ScrH........... Scripta Hierosolymitana [*A publication*]
ScrHier ...... Scripta Hierosolymitana [*Jerusalem*] [*A publication*]
Scr Hieros ... Scripta Hierosolymitana. Publications of the Hebrew University. Jerusalem [*A publication*]
ScrHierosol ... Scripta Hierosolymitana [*Jerusalem*] [*A publication*]
Scr Hierosolymitana ... Scripta Hierosolymitana [*A publication*]
Scr Hierosolymitana Publ Heb Univ (Jerus) ... Scripta Hierosolymitana. Publications of the Hebrew University (Jerusalem) [*A publication*]
ScRhW....... Winthrop College, Rock Hill, SC [*Library symbol*] [*Library of Congress*] (LCLS)
SCRI .... Science Court and Research Institute (EA)
SCRI .... Scientists' Committee for Radiation Information (EA)
SCRI .... Scottish Crop Research Institute [*Research center*] (IRC)
SCRI .... South Central Reservoir Investigation [*Department of the Interior*] (GRD)
SCRI .... Southern Center for Research and Innovation, Inc. [*University of Southern Mississippi*] [*Research center*] (RCD)
SCRI .... Supercomputer Computations Research Institute [*Florida State University*] [*Research center*] (RCD)
Scrib.......... Scribner's Monthly [*A publication*]
Scrib Com .. Scribner's Commentator [*A publication*]
Scrib Dow .. Scribner on the Law of Dower [*A publication*] (DLA)
SCRIBE..... System for Correspondence Recording and Interrogation by EDP [*Electronic Data Processing*]
Scrib M ...... Scribner's Magazine [*A publication*]
Scribn Mag ... Scribner's Magazine [*A publication*]
Scr I Donn ... Scripta Instituti Donneriana Aboensis [*A publication*]
Scri Geol .... Scripta Geologica [*A publication*]
SCRIM ...... Sideway Force Coefficient Routine Investigating Machine [*Department of Transport*] [*British*]
SCRIM ...... Supersonic Cruise Intermediate Range Missile (MCD)
SCRIMP.... Save Cash, Reduce Immediately Meat Prices [*Boston, MA, group protesting high cost of food, 1973*]
Scrinia Flor Sel ... Scrinia Florae Selectae [*A publication*]
Scrin Theol ... Scrinium Theologicum. Contributi di Scienze Religiose [*A publication*]
Scrip........... Scriptorium [*A publication*]
SCRIP........ Scriptum [*Something Written*] [*Latin*] (ROG)
SCRIP........ Scripture
SCRIP........ Single-Chain Ribosome-Inactivating Protein [*Biochemistry*]
SCRIP........ Statine Congener of Renin Inhibitory Peptide [*Biochemistry*]
SCRIP........ System for Controlling Returns in Inventory and Production Data [*IRS*]
Scrip Metal ... Scripta Metallurgica [*A publication*]
Scripps....... Scrippts [*E.W.*] Co. [*Associated Press abbreviation*] (APAG)
Scripps Inst Oceanogr Bull ... Scripps Institution of Oceanography. Bulletin [*A publication*]
Scripps Inst Oceanogr Contrib ... Scripps Institution of Oceanography. Contributions [*A publication*]
SCRIPT ..... Scientific and Commercial Subroutine Interpreter and Program Translator
Script .... Scriptorium [*A publication*]
SCRIPT..... Scripture
Script .... Scripture [*A publication*]
SCRIPT..... Support for Creative Independent Production Talent [*EC*] (ECED)
SCRIPT ..... System Controlling Research Image Processing Tasks (MCD)
Scripta Fac Sci Natur UJEP Brunensis Biol ... Scripta Facultatis Scientiarum Naturalium Universita J. E. Purkyne Brunensis. Biologia [*A publication*]
Scripta Fac Sci Natur UJEP Brunensis Chem ... Scripta Facultatis Scientiarum Naturalium Universita J. E. Purkyne Brunensis. Chemia [*A publication*]
Scripta Fac Sci Natur UJEP Brunensis Geol ... Scripta Facultatis Scientiarum Naturalium Universita J. E. Purkyne Brunensis. Geologia [*A publication*]
Scripta Fac Sci Natur UJEP Brunensis Math ... Scripta Facultatis Scientiarum Naturalium Universita J. E. Purkyne Brunensis. Mathematica [*A publication*]

Scripta Fac Sci Natur UJEP Brunensis Phys ... Scripta Facultatis Scientiarum Naturalium Universita J. E. Purkyne Brunensis. Physica [*A publication*]
Scripta Math ... Scripta Mathematica [*A publication*]
Script B ...... Scripture Bulletin [*A publication*]
Script Eccl Hisp Lat ... Scriptores Ecclesiastici Hispano-Latini Veteris et Medii Aevi [*A publication*]
Script Lat Hib ... Scriptores Latini Hiberniae [*A publication*]
SCRIS .... Southern California Regional Information Study [*Bureau of Census*]
Scriv Cop .... Scriven on the Law of Copyholds [*7th ed.*] [*1896*] [*A publication*] (DLA)
Scriven .... Scriven on the Law of Copyholds [*A publication*] (DLA)
SCRJ .... Supersonic Combustion Ramjet
ScrJud .... Scripta Judaica [*Oxford*] [*A publication*]
SCRL .... Sensory Communication Research Laboratory [*Gallaudet College*] [*Research center*] (RCD)
SCRL .... Signal Corps RADAR Laboratory [*Obsolete*] [*Army*]
SCRL .... Skill Components Research Laboratory [*Air Force*] (MCD)
SCRL .... Station Configuration Requirement List [*NASA*] (MCD)
SCR (L) ...... Supreme Court Reports (Law) [*New South Wales*] [*A publication*] (APTA)
SCRLC ...... South Central Research Library Council [*Library network*] (IID)
Scr LT .... Scranton Law Times [*Pennsylvania*] [*A publication*] (DLA)
SCRLV ...... Subterranean Clover Red Leaf Virus
SCRM .... Isla Rey Jorge/Base Aerea Teniente R. Marsh Martin [*Chile*] [*ICAO location identifier*] (ICLI)
SCRM .... Secondary Certified Reference Material [*Nuclear energy*] (NRCH)
Scr Med (Brno) ... Scripta Medica (Brno) [*A publication*]
Scr Med Fac Med Univ Brun Olomuc ... Scripta Medica. Facultatum Medicinae. Universitatum Brunensis et Olomucencis [*Czechoslovakia*] [*A publication*]
Scr Met ...... Scripta Metallurgica [*A publication*]
Scr Metall ... Scripta Metallurgica [*A publication*]
Scr Minora ... Scripta Minora-Regiae Societatis Humaniorum Litterarum Lundensis [*A publication*]
SCRMV ..... Scrophularia Mottle Virus [*Plant pathology*]
SCRN .... Screen[s] [*or Screening*] [*Freight*]
scRNP .... Ribonucleoprotein, Small Cytoplasmic
SCR (NS) (NSW) ... Supreme Court Reports (New Series) (New South Wales) [*A publication*] (APTA)
SCRNSW .. New South Wales Supreme Court Reports [*A publication*] (DLA)
SCR (NSW) ... Supreme Court Reports (New South Wales) [*A publication*] (APTA)
SCR (NSW) Eq ... Supreme Court Reports (Equity) (New South Wales) [*A publication*] (APTA)
SCRO .... Scottish Criminal Records Office [*Office of Population Census and Surveys*] [*British*]
SCRO .... Societe Canadienne de la Recherche Operationnelle
SCROLL ... String and Character Recording Oriented Logogrammatic Language [*1970*] [*Data processing*] (CSR)
SCROOGE ... Society to Curtail Ridiculous, Outrageous, and Ostentatious Gift Exchange (EA)
SC/ROSTENA ... Bureau Regional de Science et de Technologie pour l'Europe et l'Amerique du Nord [*Regional Office for Science and Technology for Europe and North America*] (EAIO)
SCRP .... Scripps-Howard Broadcasting Co. [*NASDAQ symbol*] (NQ)
SCRP .... Societe Canadienne des Relations Publiques
SCRP .... Superfund Community Relations Program [*Environmental Protection Agency*] (GFGA)
SCRP .... Supplemental Conventional Reading Program [*Education*]
SCRPA ...... Science Reporter [*New Delhi*] [*A publication*]
SCR (Q) ..... Queensland. Supreme Court. Reports [*A publication*] (APTA)
Sc RR .... Scotch Revised Reports [*A publication*] (DLA)
SCRS .... Secondary Control Rod System [*Nuclear energy*] (NRCH)
SCRS .... Self-Control Rating Scale
SCRS .... Service Center Replacement System [*Data processing*]
SCRS .... Society of Collision Repair Specialists (EA)
SCRS .... Strip Chart Recorder System [*NASA*]
Scr Sci Med Annu Sci Pap ... Scripta Scientifica Medica. Annual Scientific Papers [*A publication*]
SCRT .... Sealed Cathode Ray Tube
SCRT .... Subscribers' Circuit Routine Tester [*Telecommunications*] (TEL)
SCRTA ...... Steel Castings Research and Trade Association [*British*]
SCRTC ...... Signal Corps Replacement Training Center [*Obsolete*] [*Army*]
SCRTERM ... Screw Terminal
ScrTheol .... Scripta Theologica [*Pamplona*] [*A publication*]
SCRTY ...... Security
SCRUMPie ... Socially Concerned Upwardly Mobile Professional [*Lifestyle classification*]
Scrut Charter ... Scrutton on Charter-Parties [*18th ed.*] [*1974*] [*A publication*] (DLA)
Scrutton ..... Scrutton on Charter-Parties [*16 eds.*] [*1886-1955*] [*A publication*] (DLA)
SCRWC ..... Sierra Club Radioactive Waste Campaign [*Later, RWC*] (EA)
ScS .... Reflected S Wave [*Earthquakes*]

SCS .... Safety Control Switch
SCS .... Safety-Critical Systems/Software [*British*]
SCS .... Saint Charles Seminary [*Later, SCBS*] [*Pennsylvania*]
SCS .... Santa Clara Systems, Inc. [*San Jose, CA*] [*Telecommunications service*] (TSSD)
SCS .... Satellite Communications Subsystem
SCS .... Satellite Control Satellite [*Telecommunications*] (TEL)
SCS .... Satellite Control Section (SSD)
SCS .... Satellite Control Squadron
SCS .... Satellite Test Center Communications Subsystem (MCD)
SCS .... Scan Converter [*or Counter*] System
ScS .... Scandinavian Studies and Notes [*A publication*]
SCS .... Scheduled Cargo Service (IIA)
SCS .... Scientific Civil Service [*British*]
SCS .... Scientific Control Systems (DIT)
ScS .... Scottish Studies [*A publication*]
SCS .... Screening and Costing Staff [*NATO*] (NATG)
SCS .... Sea Control Ship [*Navy*] (NVT)
SCS .... Secondary Control Ship [*Navy*] (NVT)
SCS .... Secondary Control System (MCD)
SCS .... Secondary Coolant System [*Nuclear energy*] (NRCH)
SCS .... Secret Control Station [*NASA*] (KSC)
SCS .... Secret Cover Sheet (AAG)
SCS .... Section Control Station [*RADAR*]
SCS .... Secure Communications System [*Military*] (CAAL)
SCS .... Security Container System [*Army*] (AABC)
SCS .... Selected Cancers Study [*Centers for Disease Control*]
SCS .... Semiconductor Controlled Switch (MSA)
SCS .... Senior Citizen's Services [*A publication*]
SCS .... Septuagint and Cognate Studies (BJA)
SCS .... Sequence Control System (KSC)
SCS .... Sequencing and Command Systems Specialist [*NASA*]
SCS .... Ship Control Station [*Navy*] (CAAL)
SCS .... Short-Circuit-Stable
SCS .... Shutdown Cooling System [*Nuclear energy*] (NRCH)
SCS .... Sicasica [*Bolivia*] [*Seismograph station code, US Geological Survey*] [*Closed*] (SEIS)
SCS .... Sidewinder Control System (DWSG)
SCS .... Sigmacom Systems [*Vancouver Stock Exchange symbol*]
SCS .... Signal Center and School [*Army*] (MCD)
SCS .... Signal Communications System [*Air Force*]
SCS .... Signal Conditioning System (KSC)
SCS .... Silicon-Controlled Switch
SCS .... Simulation Control Subsystem (KSC)
SCS .... Single Channel Simplex
SCS .... Single Composition Spherical [*Dental alloy*]
SCS .... Single Control Support (BUR)
SCS .... Slovak Catholic Sokol (EA)
SCS .... Slow Code Scanner
SCS .... Small Components Structural
SCS .... Small Computer System
SCS .... Social Competence Scale
SCS .... Societe en Commandite Simple [*Simple Partnership*] [*Belgium*]
SCS .... Society for Carribean Studies (EAIO)
SCS .... Society for Ch'ing Studies (EA)
SCS .... Society for Cinema Studies (EA)
SCS .... Society of Civil Servants [*British*]
SCS .... Society of Clinical Surgery [*Defunct*] (EA)
SCS .... Society for Computer Simulation [*Later, SCSI*] (EA)
SCS .... Society for Conservative Studies [*Later, YAF*] (EA)
SCS .... Society of Construction Superintendents (EA)
SCS .... Society of Cosmetic Scientists (EAIO)
SCS .... Society of County Secretaries [*British*]
SCS .... Sodium Cellulose Sulfate [*Organic chemistry*]
SCS .... Sodium Characterization System [*Nuclear energy*] (NRCH)
SCS .... Software Communications Service
SCS .... Soil Conservation Service [*Department of Agriculture*]
SCS .... Solar Collector Subassembly (MCD)
SCS .... Solent Container Service [*British*] (DS)
SCS .... Solid Combustion Synthesis [*Physics*]
SCS .... SONAR Calibration Set
SCS .... SONAR Communications Set
SCS .... Soybean Corn Silage (OA)
SCS .... Space Cabin Simulator (IEEE)
SCS .... Space Command Station (AAG)
SCS .... Spacecraft Control System (NASA)
SCS .... Spacecraft System [*NASA*] (KSC)
SCS .... Spanish Colonial Style [*Cigars*]
SCS .... Special Communications System (MCD)
SCS .... Special Contingency Stockpile [*Military*] (AABC)
SCS .... Speed Class Sequencing
SCS .... Spinal Cord Society (EA)
SCS .... Stabilization and Control System [*or Subsystem*] [*NASA*]
SCS .... Standard Coordinate System (KSC)
SCS .... Stationing Capability System [*Army*] (AABC)
SCS .... Statistical Control System
SCS .... Stiffened Cylindrical Shell
SCS .... Stimulated Compton Scattering [*Spectroscopy*]
SCS .... Stop Control Braking System [*Lucas Girling*]
SC & S ...... Strapped, Corded, and Sealed [*As, of a package or bale*]
SCS .... Student's Confidential Statement [*Education*]

SCS............	Suit Communication System [*for spacesuits*] [*NASA*]
SCS............	Superintendent of Car Service
SCS............	Supervisory Control System (MCD)
SCS............	Supply Control Study
SCS............	Surface Composition Strengthened
SCS............	Suspect Chemicals Sourcebook [*Roytech Publications*] [*Information service or system*] (CRD)
SCS............	Sussex Cattle Society (EAIO)
SCS............	Swedish Colonial Society (EA)
SCS............	Sweeping Current Supply
SCS............	Sweetens Computer Services [*British*]
SCS............	University of South California, School of Library Science, Los Angeles, CA [*OCLC symbol*] (OCLC)
SCSA.........	Ship Constructive and Shipwrights' Association [*A union*] [*British*]
SCSA.........	Siamese Cat Society of America (EA)
SCSA.........	Soil Conservation Society of America (EA)
SCSA.........	Sports Car Collectors Society of America [*Later, SCCSA*] (EA)
SCSA.........	Standard Consolidated Statistical Area [*Census Bureau*]
SCSA.........	Steering Committee for Sustainable Agriculture [*Later, CSA*] (EA)
SCSA.........	Supreme Council for Sport in Africa [*See also CSSA*] [*Yaounde, Cameroon*] (EAIO)
SCSB.........	Standard Capital Superannuation Benefit [*British*]
SCSBCVG ...	Suore di Carita delle Sante Bartolomea Capitanio e Vincenza Gerosa [*Sisters of Charity of Saints Bartholomew Capitanio And Vincent Gerosa*] [*Italy*] (EAIO)
SCSBM	Society for Computer Science in Biology and Medicine
SCSC.........	Santiago/Ciudad [*Chile*] [*ICAO location identifier*] (ICLI)
SCSC.........	Secondary Curriculum Study Center [*of NASSP*]
SCSC.........	Sorores a Caritate Sanctae Crucis [*Sisters of Mercy of the Holy Cross*] [*Roman Catholic religious order*]
SCSC.........	South Carolina State College
Sc-SC.........	South Carolina Supreme Court, Columbia, SC [*Library symbol*] [*Library of Congress*] (LCLS)
SCSC.........	Southern Connecticut State College [*New Haven*]
SCSC.........	Strategic Conventional Standoff Capability (MCD)
SCSC.........	Summer Computer Simulation Conference
SCSCA......	Schweissen und Schneiden [*A publication*]
SCSCB......	Sisters of Charity of St. Charles Borromeo [*See also LCB*] (EAIO)
SCSCCL....	Sellin Center for Studies in Criminology and Criminal Law (EA)
SCSCD7	Smithsonian Contributions to the Marine Sciences [*A publication*]
SCSCLC....	Single-Carrier Space-Charge-Limited Current
SCSCO......	Secure Submarine Communications (KSC)
SC (Scot)....	Scottish Court of Session Cases, New Series [*A publication*] (DLA)
Sc SD.........	Doctor of Social Sciences
SCSD........	School Construction Systems Development [*Project*] [*of Educational Facilities Laboratories*]
SCSD.........	Simulation and Control Systems Division [*General Electric Co.*] (MCD)
SCSE.........	La Serena/La Florida [*Chile*] [*ICAO location identifier*] (ICLI)
SCSE.........	Smooth Curve - Smooth Earth
SCSE.........	State Commission for Space Exploration [*Former USSR*]
SCSEP......	Senior Community Service Employment Program (EA)
Sc Sess Cas ...	Scotch Court of Session Cases [*A publication*] (DLA)
SCSG........	Signal Conditioning Subsystem Group (MCD)
SCSG.........	Superior Cervical Sympathetic Ganglia [*Anatomy*]
SCSGIG.....	Supreme Council Sovereign Grand Inspectors General [*Freemasonry*]
SCSH........	Sisters of Charity of St. Hyacinthe [*Grey Nuns*] [*Roman Catholic religious order*]
SCSH........	Structural Carbon Steel Hard
SCSH........	Survey of the Chronic Sick and Handicapped [*British*]
SCSHX......	Shutdown Cooling System Heat Exchange [*Nuclear energy*] (NRCH)
SCSI.........	Sensors and Control Systems Institute [*Beltsville, MD*] [*Department of Agriculture*] (GRD)
SCSI.........	Small Computer System Interface [*Pronounced "scuzzy"*]
SCSI.........	Societe Canadienne de la Surete Industrielle
SCSI.........	Society for Computer Simulation International (EA)
SCSIT.......	Southern California Sensory Integration Test [*Ayres*] [*Education*]
SCSJAT	Sisters of Charity of St. Jeanne Antide Thouret [*Italy*] (EAIO)
SCSL........	Sandia Corporation, Sandia Laboratory (AABC)
ScSl...........	Scandoslavica [*A publication*]
SCSL.........	Sisters of Charity of St. Louis [*Roman Catholic religious order*]
SCSL.........	Standing Lenticular Stratocumulus [*Meteorology*] (FAAC)
SCSL.........	Suncoast Savings & Loan Association [*Hollywood, FL*] [*NASDAQ symbol*] (NQ)
SCSLA......	Science du Sol [*A publication*]
SCSLP......	Smithsonian Center for Short-Lived Phenomena
SCS(LS).....	Sea Control Ship (Lead Ship) [*Navy*] (MCD)
SCSM	Structural Carbon Steel Medium
SCSMHPS ...	Special Constituency Section for Mental Health and Psychiatric Services (EA)
SCSN.........	Santo Domingo/Santo Domingo [*Chile*] [*ICAO location identifier*] (ICLI)

SCSN.........	Standard Computer Software Number
ScSo...........	Science and Society [*A publication*]
SCSO.........	Space Communications Station Operation
SCSO.........	Superconducting Cavity Stabilized Oscillator [*For clocks*]
ScSocD......	Doctor of Social Science
ScSocL.......	Licence in Social Science [*British*]
Sc Soc San Antonio B ...	Scientific Society of San Antonio. Bulletin [*A publication*]
SCSP.........	Secretariat of the Council for Scientific Policy [*British*]
SCSP.........	Serum Cancer-Suppressive Peptide [*Oncology*]
SCSP.........	Smaller Communities Services Program [*Department of Labor*]
SCSP.........	Solid Cast Steel Propeller (DS)
ScSp...........	Spartanburg County Public Library, Spartanburg, SC [*Library symbol*] [*Library of Congress*] (LCLS)
SC/SP.......	Supracondylar/Suprapatellar [*Prosthesis*]
SCSP.........	System Calibration Support Plan [*Air Force*] (CET)
ScSpC	Converse College, Spartanburg, SC [*Library symbol*] [*Library of Congress*] (LCLS)
S & C Spec ...	Soap/Cosmetics/Chemical Specialties [*A publication*]
ScSpM	Milliken Research Corp., Research Library, Spartanburg, SC [*Library symbol*] [*Library of Congress*] (LCLS)
SCSPS	Standing Committee on the Safeguard of the Pursuit of Science [*International Council of Scientific Unions*]
ScSpW	Wofford College, Spartanburg, SC [*Library symbol*] [*Library of Congress*] (LCLS)
ScSpW-MHi ...	Methodist Historical Society, South Carolina Conference of the Methodist Church, Wofford College, Spartanburg, SC [*Library symbol*] [*Library of Congress*] (LCLS)
SCSR	Segundo Corral/Segundo Corral Alto [*Chile*] [*ICAO location identifier*] (ICLI)
SCSR	Self-Contained Self-Rescuer [*Breathing device*]
SCSR	Ship Construction Subsidy Regulations [*Canada*]
SCSRS	Shoe Cove Satellite Receiving Station [*Canada*]
SCSRS-S ...	Standard Command Supply Review System - SAILS
SCSS.........	Satellite Communications System Control (NATG)
SCSS.........	School Child Stress Scale [*Child development test*] [*Psychology*]
SCSS.........	Scottish Council of Social Service (DI)
SCSS.........	Self-Contained Starting System [*NASA*]
SCSS.........	Sequence Coding and Search System
SCSS.........	State Controller and System Services [*NASA*]
SCSS.........	Structural Carbon Steel Soft
SCSST.......	Standing Conference on School Science and Technology [*British*]
SCST	Castro/Gamboa [*Chile*] [*ICAO location identifier*] (ICLI)
SCST	Scan Converter Storage Tube
ScSt...........	Scandinavian Studies [*A publication*]
SCST	Society of Commercial Seed Technologists (EA)
SC State Devel Board Div Geology Bull Geol Notes ...	South Carolina State Development Board. Division of Geology. Bulletin. Geologic Notes [*A publication*]
SCSTC......	Senior Citizen Ski Touring Committee (EA)
Sc St Crim ...	Scandinavian Studies in Criminology [*1965*] [*A publication*] (DLA)
Sc St L........	Scandinavian Studies in Law [*A publication*] (DLA)
Sc St N	Scandinavian Studies and Notes [*A publication*]
Sc Stud	Scandinavian Studies [*A publication*]
Sc Stud Criminol ...	Scandinavian Studies in Criminology [*1965*] [*A publication*] (DLA)
Sc Stud L......	Scandinavian Studies in Law [*A publication*]
Sc Stud Law ...	Scandinavian Studies in Law [*A publication*]
SCSU.........	St. Cloud State University
ScSu...........	Sumter County Library, Sumter, SC [*Library symbol*] [*Library of Congress*] (LCLS)
ScSuM	Morris College, Sumter, SC [*Library symbol*] [*Library of Congress*] (LCLS)
ScSum	Timrod Library, Summerville, SC [*Library symbol*] [*Library of Congress*] (LCLS)
SCSW	Super-Chilled Seawater
SCT...........	Air Force Institute of Technology, Wright-Patterson AFB, OH [*OCLC symbol*] (OCLC)
SCT...........	S-Band Cassegrain Transmit
SCT...........	Sacrococcygeal Teratoma [*Oncology*]
S-C-T	Salinity-Conductivity-Temperature
SCT...........	Salmon Calcitonin [*Endocrinology*]
SCT...........	Sample Control Tape [*Data processing*]
SCT...........	Satellite Communication Terminal (MCD)
SCT...........	Scan Conversion Tube
SCT...........	Scanning Telescope (KSC)
SCT...........	Scattered
SCT...........	Schottky Clamped Transistor
SCT...........	Scintrex Ltd. [*Toronto Stock Exchange symbol*]
SCT...........	Scorpion Toxin [*Immunology*]
SCT...........	Scotsman Industries, Inc. [*NYSE symbol*] (SPSG)
SCT...........	Scotty Lake [*Alaska*] [*Seismograph station code, US Geological Survey*] (SEIS)
SCT...........	Scout (AABC)
SCT...........	Screen Capture Test [*Data processing*]
Sct	Scutum [*Constellation*]
SCT...........	Semiconductor Curve Tracer
SCT...........	Sentence Completion Technique [*or Test*]
SCT...........	Sequence Checking Tape

SCT............	Service Counter Terminal [*Banking*]
SCT............	Sex Chromatin Test (MAE)
SCT............	Sickle Cell Trait (AAMN)
SCT............	Single-Cell Test (MCD)
SCT............	Single Channel Transponder (MCD)
SCT............	Sioux City Terminal Railway [*AAR code*]
SCT............	Skylab Communication Terminal [*NASA*] (KSC)
SCT............	Societe Canadienne de Theologie [*Canadian Theological Society - CTS*]
SCT............	Society of Cardiological Technicians [*British*]
SCT............	Society of Cleaning Technicians (EA)
SCT............	Society for Clinical Trials (EA)
SCT............	Society of Commercial Teachers (EAIO)
SCT............	Society of County Treasurers [*British*]
SCT............	SONAR Certification Test
SCT............	Source Coding Team (SAA)
SCT............	Sous-Commission des Cartes Tectoniques [*Subcommittee for Tectonic Maps of the Commission for the Geological Map of the World - STMCGMW*] (EAIO)
SCT............	South Central Air Transport, Inc. [*Natchez, MS*] [*FAA designator*] (FAAC)
SCT............	Space Combat Tactics (SAA)
SCT............	Special Characters Table [*Data processing*] (IBMDP)
SCT............	Special Crew Time (DNAB)
SCT............	Spectral Control Technique
SCT............	Spectrographic Telescope
SCTB.........	Staphylococcal Clumping Test [*Medicine*] (AAMN)
SCT............	Step Control Table (CMD)
SCT............	Structural Clay Tile [*Technical drawings*]
SCT............	Student Coalition for Truth (EA)
SCT............	Subroutine Call Table [*Data processing*]
SCT............	Subscriber Carrier Terminal [*Telecommunications*] (TEL)
SCT............	Sugar-Coated Tablet
S Ct...........	Supreme Court Reporter [*A publication*] (DLA)
SCt............	Supreme Court Reports
SCT............	Surface Charge Transistor [*Electronics*] (OA)
SCT............	Swap Control Table [*Data processing*] (BYTE)
SCT............	System Circuit Test
SCTA.........	System Compatibility Tests
SCTA.........	Secondary Container Transfer Area [*Nuclear energy*] (NRCH)
SCTA.........	Ships' Clerk Trade Association [*A union*] [*British*]
SCTA.........	Southern California Timing Association (EA)
SCTA.........	Steel Carriers Tariff Association, Inc. [*Riverdale, MD*]
SCTA.........	Stone Carvers Trade Association [*A union*] [*British*]
SCTB.........	Santa Cruz Test Base (MCD)
SCTB.........	Santiago/Eulogio Sanchez [*Chile*] [*ICAO location identifier*] (ICLI)
ScTB.........	Scottish Tourist Board (DCTA)
S Ct Bull (CCH) ...	United States Supreme Court Bulletin (Commerce Clearing House) [*A publication*] (DLA)
SCTC.........	Self-Contained Training Capability (DNAB)
SCTC.........	Small Craft Training Center
SC/TC.......	Spacecraft Test Conductor (SAA)
SCTC.........	Submarine Chaser Training Center [*Navy*]
SCTC.........	Systems & Computer Technology Corp. [*NASDAQ symbol*] (NQ)
SCTC.........	Temuco/Maquehue [*Chile*] [*ICAO location identifier*] (ICLI)
SC (T & C) ...	Thompson and Cook's New York Supreme Court Reports [*A publication*] (DLA)
SCTCA......	SAC [*Strategic Air Command*] Channel and Traffic Control Agency (SAA)
SCTCA......	Schweisstechnik [*Berlin*] [*A publication*]
SctCHt.......	Scout Car, Half Track [*Army*]
SCTD........	Scattered
SCTD........	Scottish Centre for the Tuition of the Disabled [*Queen Margaret College*] (CB)
SCTD........	Subcaliber Training Device [*Military*] (AABC)
SCTE.........	Puerto Montt/Internacional El Tepual [*Chile*] [*ICAO location identifier*] (ICLI)
SCTE.........	Science of the Total Environment [*A publication*]
SCTE.........	Society of Cable Television Engineers (EA)
SCTE.........	Society of Carbide and Tool Engineers (EA)
SCTE.........	Spacecraft Central Timing Equipment [*NASA*]
SCTF.........	Santa Cruz Test Facility (SAA)
SCTF.........	SHAPE [*Supreme Headquarters Allied Powers Europe*] Centralized Training Facility [*NATO*] (NATG)
SCTF.........	Sodium Chemical Technology Facility [*Nuclear energy*] (NRCH)
SCTH	Service Center for Teachers of History (EA)
SCTHA......	Ssu Ch'uan Ta Hsueh Hsueh Pao - Tzu Jan K'o Hsueh [*A publication*]
SCTI.........	Santiago/Internacional Los Cerillos [*Chile*] [*ICAO location identifier*] (ICLI)
SCTI.........	Scott Instruments Corp. [*NASDAQ symbol*] (NQ)
SCTI.........	Sodium Components Test Installation [*Nuclear energy*]
SCTI.........	Solid Carbide Tool Institute (EA)
SCTI.........	University of Southern California Tax Institute (DLA)
SCTL........	Short-Circuited Transmission Line
SCTL........	Small Components Test Loop [*Nuclear energy*]
SCTL........	Societe Canadienne des Technologistes de Laboratoire [*Canadian Society of Laboratory Technologists*] (EAIO)

SCTN.........	Chaiten/Chaiten [*Chile*] [*ICAO location identifier*] (ICLI)
SCTN.........	Service Center Taxpayer Notice [*IRS*]
SCTO.........	Societe Canadienne des Technologistes en Orthopedie [*Canadian Society of Orthopaedic Technologists*] (EAIO)
SCTO.........	Soft Carrier Turn Off (HGAA)
SCTOA.....	Science Tools [*A publication*]
SCTOC......	Satellite Communications Test Operations Center
Sc Total Env ...	Science of the Total Environment [*A publication*]
SCTP	Ship Construction Test Plan [*Navy*] (CAAL)
SCTP	Straight Channel Tape Print [*Data processing*] (KSC)
SCTP	Syndicat Canadien des Travailleurs du Papier [*Canadian Paperworkers Union - CPU*]
SCTPP.......	Straight Channel Tape Print Program [*Data processing*] (KSC)
SCTR.........	Scooter (AAG)
SCTR.........	Sector (MSA)
SCTR.........	Signal Corps Technical Requirements (MCD)
SCTR.........	Single Channel Transponder (DWSG)
SCTRACEN ...	Submarine Chaser Training Center [*Navy*]
S Ct Rev ...	Supreme Court Review [*A publication*]
SCTS	SFOF [*Space Flight Operations Facility*] Communications Terminal Subsystem [*NASA*]
SCTS	System Components Test Station (MCD)
SCTTB......	Schmiertechnik und Tribologie [*A publication*]
SCTTU	Scottish Council of Textile Trade Unions (DCTA)
SCTV	Second City Television [*Television program, the title of which was later changed to its initialism*]
SCTV	Standing Conference on Television Viewing [*British*]
SCTV-GDHS ...	Spacecraft Television - Ground Data Handling System [*NASA*]
SCTY	Security (AFM)
SCTYB	Science Today (Bombay) [*A publication*]
SCTYG	Security Group [*Military*]
SCTYPOLICESq ...	Security Police Squadron [*Air Force*]
SCTYSERSCH ...	Security Service School [*Air Force*]
SCTYSq......	Security Squadron [*Air Force*]
SCTZ	Puerto Montt [*Chile*] [*ICAO location identifier*] (ICLI)
SCU	6585th Test Group Technical Information Center, Holloman AFB, NM [*OCLC symbol*] (OCLC)
SCU	S-Band Cassegrain Ultra
SCU	Santiago [*Cuba*] [*Airport symbol*] (OAG)
SCU	Scanner Control Unit
SCU	Schweizer Buchhandel [*A publication*]
SCU	Scottish Church Union
SCU	Secondary Control Unit [*Aerospace*] (AAG)
SCU	Selector Checkout Unit
SCU	Sensor Control Unit (MCD)
SCU	Sequence Control Unit [*Aerospace*] (KSC)
SCU	Service Command Unit
SCU	Service and Cooling Umbilical [*Aerospace*] (MCD)
SCU	Servicing Control Unit [*Telecommunications*] (TEL)
SCU	Sheep Canyon [*Utah*] [*Seismograph station code, US Geological Survey*] [*Closed*] (SEIS)
SCU	Signal Conditioning Unit (NASA)
SCU	Signal Control Unit (NASA)
SCU	Single Conditioning Unit
scu	South Carolina [*MARC country of publication code*] [*Library of Congress*] (LCCP)
SCU	Special Care Unit
SCU	Stable Control Unit
SCU	Stand-Alone Computer Unit
SCU	Static Checkout Unit (KSC)
SCU	Station Control Unit
SCU	Statistical Control Unit [*Military*]
SCU	Storage Control Unit
SCU	Subscribers' Concentrator Unit [*Telecommunications*] (TEL)
SCU	Sulfur-Coated Urea [*Chemical technology*]
SCU	Surface Control Unit
SCU	Switch Control Unit (MCD)
SCU	Synchronous Controller Unit
SCU	System Configuration Unit (MCD)
SCU	System Control Unit
ScU	University of South Carolina, Columbia, SC [*Library symbol*] [*Library of Congress*] (LCLS)
SCUA	Suez Canal Users Association (NATG)
SCUAE......	State Committee on the Utilization of Atomic Energy [*Former USSR*]
SCUAS	Standing Conference of University Appointments Services [*British*]
ScUB.........	Scandinavian University Books [*A publication*]
SCUBA......	Self-Contained Underwater Breathing Apparatus
SCUBADIV ...	Scuba Diver Badge [*Military decoration*] (GFGA)
SCUC........	Satellite Communications Users Conference [*Convention*] (TSSD)
SCUCC Dec ...	South Carolina Unemployment Compensation Commission Decisions [*A publication*] (DLA)
SCUCCR ...	South Carolina Unemployment Compensation Commission Reports of Hearings [*A publication*] (DLA)
Scu Citta	Scuola e Citta [*A publication*]
SCUD	Scunner [*Missile*]
SCUD	Subsonic Cruise Unarmed Decoy [*Air Force*] (MCD)

ScudNA ..... Scudder New Asia Fund [*Associated Press abbreviation*] (APAG)
SCUDS ...... Simplification, Clarification, Unification, Decimalization, Standardization
SCUE .... Standing Conference on University Entrance [*British*] (DI)
SCUIO ...... Standing Conference of University Information Officers [*British*]
Scul .... Sculptor [*Constellation*]
SCUL .... Simulation of the Columbia University Libraries [*Data processing research*]
SCUL .... Soundings. University of California. Library [*Santa Barbara*] [*A publication*]
ScU-L .... University of South Carolina, Law School, Columbia, SC [*Library symbol*] [*Library of Congress*] (LCLS)
SCULL ...... Serial Communication Unit for Long Links
SCULP ...... Sculpsit [*He, or She, Engraved It*] [*Latin*]
SCULP ...... Sculptor
SCULP ...... Sculpture (ROG)
Sculp Int .... Sculpture International [*A publication*]
SCULPS ... Sculpsit [*He, or She, Engraved It*] [*Latin*]
SCULPT .... Sculptor [*or Sculpture*]
Sculpt Hellenist Age ... Sculpture of the Hellenistic Age [*A publication*] (OCD)
Sculpt R ..... Sculpture Review [*A publication*]
SCUM ...... Society for Cutting Up Men
ScU-M .... University of South Carolina, School of Medicine, Columbia, SC [*Library symbol*] [*Library of Congress*] (LCLS)
SCUMRA ... Societe Central de l'Uranium et des Minerals et Metaux Radioactifs [*France*]
SC(UN) ...... Security Council of the United Nations
SC Univ Pubs Phys Sci Bull ... South Carolina University. Publications. Physical Sciences Bulletin [*A publication*]
Scuola Dir ... Scuola e Diritto [*A publication*]
SCUP .... School, College, and University Partnerships Program [*Department of Education*] (GFGA)
SCUP .... School Computer Use Plan (IEEE)
SCUP .... Scupper
SCUP .... Service Center Unpostable [*IRS*]
SCUP .... Society for College and University Planning (EA)
SCUPA ...... Single-Chain Urokinase-Like Plasminogen Activator [*Anticlotting agent*]
SCUPU ...... Self-Contained Underwater Pinger Unit [*SONAR*]
SCUR .... Selected Command Unit Review (MCD)
SCURRN .. Scurry-Rainbow Oil Ltd. [*Associated Press abbreviation*] (APAG)
SCUS .... Supreme Court of the United States
ScU-S .... University of South Carolina, Science Library, Columbia, SC [*Library symbol*] [*Library of Congress*] (LCLS)
SCUSA ..... Student Conference on United States Affairs
Scu Salern ... Scuola Salernitana [*A publication*]
SCUSE ...... Special Committee for United States Exports [*Washington, DC*] (EA)
ScU-Su .... University of South Carolina at Sumter, Sumter, SC [*Library symbol*] [*Library of Congress*] (LCLS)
Scut .... Scutum [*Constellation*]
Scut .... Scutum [*of Hesiod*] [*Classical studies*] (OCD)
SCUTREA ... Standing Conference on University Teaching and Research in the Education of Adults [*British*] (DI)
SCUU .... Southern College University Union
SCV .... Eglin Regional Hospital Library, Eglin AFB, FL [*OCLC symbol*] (OCLC)
SCV .... Saguaro Cactus Virus [*Plant pathology*]
SCV .... St. Croix [*Virgin Islands*] [*Seismograph station code, US Geological Survey*] (SEIS)
SCV .... Seaclutter Visibility [*Navy*] (CAAL)
SCV .... Side Control Valves
SCV .... Simultaneous Chest Compression and Ventilation [*Medicine*]
SCV .... Smooth, Capsulated, Virulent [*Bacteriology*]
SCV .... Solar Constant Variations
SCV .... Sons of Confederate Veterans (EA)
SCV .... South Atlantic Ltd. [*Vancouver Stock Exchange symbol*]
SCV .... Speed Control Valve
SCV .... Steam-Conditioning Valve
SCV .... Steel Containment Vessel [*Nuclear energy*] (NRCH)
SCV .... Stock Change Voucher [*Military*] (AFIT)
SCV .... Strip Chart Viewer
SCV .... Sub Center Visibility (MCD)
SCV .... Sub Clutter Visibility
SCV .... Suceava [*Romania*] [*Airport symbol*] (OAG)
SCV .... Supersonic Cruise Missile
SCV .... System Compatibility Vehicle
SCV .... System Component Verification
SCVD .... Valdivia/Pichoy [*Chile*] [*ICAO location identifier*] (ICLI)
SCVIA ...... Science et Vie [*A publication*]
SCVIR ...... Society of Cardiovascular and Interventional Radiology (EA)
SCVM .... Shuttle Command and Voice Multiplexer (MCD)
SCVTR ...... Scan Converting Video Tape Recorder (MCD)
SCW .... AFWAL [*Air Force Wright Aeronautical Laboratories*] Technical Information Center, Wright-Patterson AFB, OH [*OCLC symbol*] (OCLC)

SCW .... St. Clair Paint & Wallpaper Corp. [*Toronto Stock Exchange symbol*]
SCW .... Schoenwereld. Vakblad voor de Schoenlederbranche [*A publication*]
SCW .... Sherman Crater - Mount Baker [*Washington*] [*Seismograph station code, US Geological Survey*] [*Closed*] (SEIS)
SCW .... Silicone Carbide Whisker
SCW .... Society of Colonial Wars
SCW .... State College of Washington
SCW .... Super-Critical Wing
SCW .... Supercritical Water
SCW .... Superintendent of Contract Work [*Navy*]
ScWal .... Oconee County Library, Walhalla, SC [*Library symbol*] [*Library of Congress*] (LCLS)
SC Water Resour Comm Rep ... South Carolina. Water Resources Commission. Report [*A publication*]
SCWC .... Special Commission on Weather Modification
SC/WCA ... Sneak Circuit/Worst Case Analysis (MCD)
SCWCU ..... Supreme Council of the Western Catholic Union [*Later, Western Catholic Union*] (EA)
SCWDS ..... Southeastern Cooperative Wildlife Disease Study [*University of Georgia*] [*Research center*] (RCD)
SCWEP ..... Spinnable Cotton Waste Equalization Program
SCWFA ..... Schip en Werf [*A publication*]
SCWG .... Satellite Communications Working Group [*NATO*] (NATG)
SCWGA ..... Sonoma County Wineries Association [*Acronym is based on former name, Sonoma County Wine Growers Association*] (EA)
SCWIA ...... South Carolina Wildlife [*A publication*]
SC Wildl ..... South Carolina Wildlife [*A publication*]
ScWL .... Single-Comb White Leghorn [*Poultry*]
SCWO ...... Supercritical Water Oxidation [*Waste disposal technology*]
SCWPH ..... Students Concerned with Public Health [*Defunct*] (EA)
SCWPLR ... Special Committee for Workplace Product Liability Reform (EA)
SCWR .... Supercritical Water Reactor
SCWS .... Scottish Co-Operative Wholesale Society
SCWSL ..... Small Caliber Weapon Systems Laboratory (MCD)
SCWT .... System Cold Wire Tests
SCX .... Oneida, TN [*Location identifier*] [*FAA*] (FAAL)
SCX .... Single-Charge Exchange
SCX .... Solar Coronal X-Ray
SCX .... Starrett [*L. S.*] Co. [*NYSE symbol*] (SPSG)
SCX .... Strong Cation Exchanger [*Chemistry*]
SCY .... Scan Converter Yoke
SCY .... Scurry, TX [*Location identifier*] [*FAA*] (FAAL)
SCY .... Society Corp. [*NYSE symbol*] (SPSG)
SCYL .... Single-Cylinder
SCZ .... Santa Cruz [*Solomon Islands*] [*Airport symbol*] (OAG)
SCZ .... Schwitzer, Inc. [*NYSE symbol*] (SPSG)
SCZ .... State Coastal Zone (NOAA)
SD .... Decisions of the Sadr Court [*1845-62*] [*Bengal, India*] [*A publication*] (DLA)
SD .... Diamant [*France*] [*Research code symbol*]
SD .... Safe Deposit [*Business term*]
SD .... Safety Destructor (NG)
SD .... Said (ROG)
SD .... Sailed
S/D .... Sailing Date (DS)
SD .... Sailing Directions [*British*]
S/D .... Salaried Direct [*Ratio*]
SD .... Salt Depletion
SD .... Salutem Dicit [*Sends Greetings*] [*Latin*]
SD .... Same Day
SD .... Sammlung Dieterich [*A publication*]
SD .... Sample Data (NG)
SD .... Sample Delay
SD .... Sand (WGA)
SD .... Sash Door
SD .... Saturation Deficit
SD .... Scaling and Display (NASA)
SD .... Scandinavian Delegation [*British*]
SD .... Scanning Densitometer [*Instrumentation*]
SD .... Schematic Diagram
SD .... Scientiae Doctor [*Doctor of Science*] (ADA)
SD .... Scientific Design [*Group*]
SD .... Scientific Detective Monthly [*A publication*]
SD .... Scottish District [*Council*]
SD .... Scram Discharge [*Nuclear energy*] (NRCH)
SD .... Sea Damaged
S/D .... Seadrome
SD .... Search Depth [*Navy*] (NVT)
S & D .... Search and Destroy [*Army*] (AABC)
SD .... Seasonal Derating (IEEE)
SD .... Seasoned (WGA)
SD .... Secchi Disk
SD .... Second Defense [*Men's lacrosse position*]
SD .... Second Difference [*Statistics*] (OA)
SD .... Secondary Distribution [*Investment term*]
SD .... Secretary of Defense
SD .... Sedan

SD	Seed (WGA)
SD	Segregation Distorter [*Genetics*]
SD	Seismic Detector (MCD)
SD	Seize Detector
SD	Selenium Diode
SD	Self-Destroying [*Projectile*]
SD	Self-Destruct
SD	Semantic Differential
SD	Semi-Darkness (DNAB)
SD	Semidetached (ADA)
SD	Semidiameter
SD	Seminars Directory [*A publication*]
SD	Senate Document
SD	Senatus Decreto [*By Decree of the Senate*] [*Latin*]
SD	Send Data [*Data processing*]
SD	Send Digits [*Telecommunications*] (TEL)
SD	Senile Dementia [*Medicine*]
SD	Senior Deacon [*Freemasonry*]
SD	Senior Director [*FAA*] (FAAC)
SD	Septal Defect [*Medicine*]
SD	Serializer/Deserializer
SD	Serine Dehydratase [*An enzyme*]
SD	Serologically Defined [*Immunology*]
SD	Serologically Determined [*Medicine*]
SD	Serum Defect [*Medicine*] (MAE)
SD	Service Dated (ROG)
SD	Service Dress
SD	Servicing Diagram
SD	Servus Dei [*Servant of God*] [*Latin*]
SD	Several Dates
SD	Severe Duty [*Truck*]
SD	Severely Diabetic
SD	Sewed
SD	Sewer Drain
SD	Shakedown [*Nuclear energy*] (NRCH)
S & D	Shaw, Dunlop, and Bell's Scotch Court of Session Reports, First Series [*1821-38*] [*A publication*] (DLA)
SD	Shell-Destroying [*Device*]
SD	Shelter Deck (DNAB)
SD	Shield of David (BJA)
SD	Ship Destination Test [*Intelligence test*]
SD	Shop Drawing (AAG)
SD	Short Day [*Botany*]
SD	Short Delay
SD	Short Delivery
SD	Short Duration
SD	Shoulder Disarticulation [*Medicine*] (MAE)
SD	Shoulder Dislocation
SD	Shower Drain (AAG)
S/D	Shut Down
SD	Sicherheitsdienst [*Police Duty*] [*NAZI Germany*]
S-D	Sickle Cell Hemoglobin D [*Disease*] [*Medicine*]
SD	Side Deck
SD	Side Door
SD	Side Drum
SD	Siegfried AG [*Switzerland*] [*Research code symbol*]
SD	Sight Draft [*Business term*]
SD	Signals Division [*British military*] (DMA)
SD	Signed (WGA)
SD	Significant Digit [*Mathematics*]
SD	Simple Design
SD	Sine Dato [*Undated book*] [*Latin*]
SD	Sine Die [*Without Day*] [*Latin*]
SD	Single Deck [*Navigation*]
SD	Single Determination
SD	Single Diaphragm [*Automotive engineering*]
SD	Single Distilled
SD	Single Domain [*Grains in rocks*] [*Geophysics*]
S & D	Single and Double [*Reduction gears*]
SD	Site Defense [*Military*] (AABC)
SD	Situation Display
SD	Skid
SD	Skin Destruction [*Medicine*]
SD	Skin Dose
SD	Sliding Door
SD	Slope Difference [*Statistics*]
SD	Slowdown
s/d	Small Damage (DS)
SD	Small-Scale Disturbance Field
SD	Smoke Detector (NASA)
SD	Social Democratic Party [*Germany*]
SD	Socialdemokratiet i Danmark [*Social Democratic Party of Denmark*] [*Political party*] (PPE)
SD	Societas Docta (EA)
SD	Soft Drawn
SD	Software Dynamics [*Buena Park, CA*] (TSSD)
SD	Solar Dynamic (SSD)
SD	Solicitation Document
SD	Solid Drawn
S & D	Song and Dance Act [*Slang*]
SD	Sort File Description [*Data processing*]
SD	Sorties per Day [*Air Force*] (AFIT)
SD	Sound [*Films, television, etc.*]
SD	Sound [*Board on Geographic Names*]
SD	Sounding Doubtful [*Nautical charts*]
SD	Source/Destination [*Inspection/Acceptance Point*] (MCD)
SD	Source Document [*Data processing*]
SD	South Dakota [*Postal code*]
SD	South Dakota Compiled Laws, Annotated [*A publication*] (DLA)
SD	South Dakota Musician [*A publication*]
SD	South Dakota Reports [*A publication*] (DLA)
Sd	South Dakota State Library Commission, Pierre, SD [*Library symbol*] [*Library of Congress*] (LCLS)
SD	South Division (ROG)
SD	Southern District (DLA)
SD	Space Digest [*A publication*]
SD	Space Division [*Air Force*] [*Los Angeles, CA*]
SD	Spare Disposition (MCD)
SD	Special Delivery
SD	Special Document
SD	Special Duty [*Military*]
SD	Specially Denatured
SD	Specification for Design
SD	Specification Document [*NASA*] (NASA)
SD	Spectacle Dispenser [*Navy technician*]
SD	Spectral Distribution
SD	Speed Density
SD	Speed Disk [*Computer program*] (PCM)
SD	Spin Device
SD	Spin-Dipolar [*Physics*]
SD	Splice Donor [*Genetics*]
SD	Splitter Damper (OA)
SD	Spontaneous Delivery [*Obstetrics*]
Sd	Sprachdienst [*A publication*]
SD	Sprache und Dichtung [*A publication*]
SD	Square Law Detector [*Telecommunications*] (OA)
SD	Staff Development (ADA)
SD	Staff Duties [*Military*] [*British*]
SD	Stage Direction
SD	Stage Door [*Theatrical slang*]
SD	Stamp Duty
SD	Standard Decision (MCD)
SD	Standard Deduction
SD	Standard Design [*of a vessel*] (DS)
SD	Standard Deviation [*Also, s*]
SD	Standard Dress [*Military*] [*British*]
SD	Standard Oil Co. of California [*NYSE symbol*] [*Delisted*] [*Vancouver Stock Exchange symbol*] (SPSG)
SD	Standardization Data
SD	Standardization Directory
SD	Standards Development (IEEE)
SD	Stands Detached [*Freight*]
SD	Stars of David (EA)
SD	State Department
SD	State Director
S/D	Statement of Differences
SD	Station Director [*Deep Space Instrumentation Facility, NASA*]
SD	Statutory Declaration
SD	Steel Deck (ADA)
SD	Stein & Day [*Publishers*]
SD	Stereo Directional
SD	Stern Discharge
SD	Steward [*Navy rating*]
Sd	Stimulus, Discriminative (MAE)
Sd	Stimulus Drive (MAE)
SD	Stock Dividend [*Investment term*]
SD	Stone Disintegration [*Urology*]
S & D	Storage and Distribution
S/D	Storage or Distribution
SD	Stores Depot [*British military*] (DMA)
SD	Storm Data [*A publication*]
SD	Storm Deck [*Naval engineering*]
SD	Storm Detection [*RADAR*]
SD	Storm Drain [*Technical drawings*]
SD	Stowage Drawer
SD	Straight Duty
SD	Strength Differential [*Steel*]
SD	Strength-Duration (Curve) [*Prosthesis*]
SD	Streptodornase [*An enzyme*]
SD	Stronnictwo Demokratyczne [*Democratic Party*] [*Poland*] [*Political party*] (PPE)
SD	Structural Detail (AAG)
SD	Structural Dynamics (KSC)
SD	Studia et Documenta ad Iura Orientis Antiqui Pertinenta [*Leiden*] [*A publication*] (BJA)
SD	Study Director (MCD)
SD	Subcontractor Data
SD	Subdural [*Anatomy*]
SD	Submarine Detector (ADA)
SD	Subtotal Discectomy [*Medicine*]
SD	Sudan [*ANSI two-letter standard code*] (CNC)

SD	Sudan Airways [*ICAO designator*] (FAAC)
SD	Sudden Death [*Medicine*]
S-D.............	Sudden Death [*Tiebreaking in sports*]
SD	Sugar Determination
SD	Sum of Digits (SAA)
SD	Sun's Declensions [*Astronomy*] (ROG)
SD	Super Diesel [*Automotive engineering*]
SD	Super Duty [*Automotive engineering*]
SD	Superintendent of Documents [*US Government Printing Office*]
SD	Supplier Documentation (NASA)
SD	Supply Department [*Navy*]
SD	Supply Depot
SD	Supply Detachment [*British military*] (DMA)
SD	Supply Duct [*Nuclear energy*] (NRCH)
SD	Support Directive (KSC)
SD	Support [*or Supporting*] Document (KSC)
SD	Surface Duct [*Navy*] (CAAL)
SD	Surridge Dawson [*Commercial firm*] [*British*]
SD	Surveillance Drone [*Air Force*]
SD	Survival Dose
Sd	Suspended [*Regulation or order suspended*] [*Used in Shepard's Citations*] [*Legal term*] (DLA)
SD	Swaziland
SD	Sweep Driver
SD	Switch Driver
SD	Syllable Duration [*Entomology*]
SD	Synchronous Detector [*Electronics*] (OA)
SD	Synthetic Dextrose [*Biochemistry*]
SD	System Demonstration [*Military*]
SD	System Description
SD	System Designator (AFIT)
SD	System Drawer
SD	Systems Designers [*Software manufacturer*] [*British*]
SD	Systems Development (MCD)
SD	Systems Directorate [*Army*] (RDA)
SD	Systems Division [*Department of Commerce*] [*Information service or system*] (IID)
S/D	Systolic to Diastolic [*Cardiology*] (MAE)
SD	Systolic Discharge [*Cardiology*]
SD1	Steward, First Class [*Navy rating*]
S 2d	New York Supplement, Second Series [*A publication*] (DLA)
SD2	Steward, Second Class [*Navy rating*]
SD3	Steward, Third Class [*Navy rating*]
SDA	Augustana College, Sioux Falls, SD [*OCLC symbol*] (OCLC)
SDA	Baghdad-Saddam [*Iraq*] [*Airport symbol*] (OAG)
SDA	Sacrodextra Anterior [*A fetal position*] [*Obstetrics*]
SDA	Sadr Diwani Adalat Reports [*India*] [*A publication*] (DLA)
SD & A.......	San Diego & Arizona Railway
SDA	Schweizerische Depeschenagentur AG [*Swiss News Agency*] (EY)
SDA	Scottish Development Agency (DS)
SDA	Scottish Diploma in Agriculture
SDA	Screen Design Aid [*Data processing*] (HGAA)
SDA	Screw Displacement Axis
SDA	Section Department Authority
SDA	Seismic Data Analysis
SDA	Self-Defence Agency [*Japan*] (ECON)
SDA	Semidehydroascorbate [*Biochemistry*]
SDA	Sequential Degradation Analysis
SDA	Service Delivery Area [*Job Training and Partnership Act*] (OICC)
SDA	Seventh-Day Adventist
SDA	Sex Discrimination Act [*1975*] [*British*] (DCTA)
SDA	Shaft Drive Axis [*Aerospace*] (KSC)
SDA	Shenandoah, IA [*Location identifier*] [*FAA*] (FAAL)
SDA	Ship's Destination Authority (NVT)
SDA	Shoulder Disarticulation [*Medicine*]
SDA	Significant Digit Arithmetic
SDA	Simple Doublet Antenna
SDA	Sleeve Dipole Antenna
SDA	Slowdown Area
SDA	Soap and Detergent Association (EA)
SDA	Social Democratic Alliance [*British*]
SDA	Social-Democratic Association [*Political party*] (EAIO)
SDA	Solvent Deasphalting
SDA	Somali Democratic Alliance [*Political party*] (EY)
SDA	Source Data Acquisition (BUR)
SDA	Source Data Automation [*Military*]
SDA	Special Disbursing Agent, Bureau of Indian Affairs [*United States*] (DLA)
SDA	Special Duty Assignment (AFM)
SDA	Specially Denatured Alcohol
SDA	Specific Dynamic Action [*of foods*] [*Physiology*]
SDA	Spectral Distribution Analyzer
SDA	Spontaneous Divergent Academic [*Test*] [*Education*]
SDA	Stacked Dipole Array
SDA	Standard Gold Mines Ltd. [*Vancouver Stock Exchange symbol*]
SDA	Statistical Distribution Analyzer
SDA	Step Down Amplifier
SDA	Stepwise Discriminant Analysis

SDA	Stereo Dimensional Array
SDA	Steroid-Dependent Asthmatic [*Medicine*]
SDA	Stevens-Duryea Associates (EA)
SDA	Stirrer Drive Assembly
SDA	Stranka Demokratske Akcije [*Party of Democratic Action*] [*Bosnia-Herzegovina*] [*Political party*] (EY)
SDA	Students for Democratic Action
SDA	Subcarrier Demodulator Assembly [*Deep Space Instrumentation Facility, NASA*]
SDA	Succinic Dehydrogenase Activity
SDA	Sulfadiazine [*Antibiotic*]
SDA	Superficial Distal Axillary [*Lymph node*]
SDA	Supplier Data Approval [*Nuclear energy*] (NRCH)
SDA	Supporting Data Analysis
SDA	Surface Design Association (EA)
SDA	Sweet Damn All [*Nothing At All*] [*Slang*]
SDA	Symbolic Device Address
SDA	Symbolic Disk Address (AFM)
SDA	Symbols-Digits-Alphabetics
SDA	System Design Agency [*Bell Telephone Laboratory*] (MCD)
SDA	Systems Data Analysis
SDA	Systems Dynamic Analyzer
SDAA	Salt Distributors Association of America (EA)
SDAA	Servicemen's Dependents Allowance Act
SDAA	Skein Dyers Association of America [*Later, SRPDAA*] (EA)
SDAA	Stacked Dipole Aerial Array
SdAbA	Alexander Mitchell Library, Aberdeen, SD [*Library symbol*] [*Library of Congress*] (LCLS)
SdAbN	Northern State College, Aberdeen, SD [*Library symbol*] [*Library of Congress*] (LCLS)
SdAbP........	Presentation College, Aberdeen, SD [*Library symbol*] [*Library of Congress*] (LCLS)
SDAC........	Seismic Data Analysis Center
SDAC........	Shelby Dodge Automobile Club [*Inactive*] (EA)
SDAC........	Shipping Defence Advisory Committee [*General Council of British Shipping*] (DS)
SDACMG ...	Seventh-Day Adventist Church Musicians Guild (EA)
SDAD	Satellite Digital and Analog Display
SDAD	Special Domestically Available Documents [*NASA*] (KSC)
SDADA	Seventh-Day Adventist Dietetic Association (EA)
SD Admin R ...	Administrative Rules of South Dakota [*A publication*] (DLA)
SD Admin Reg ...	South Dakota Register [*A publication*] (DLA)
SDADS......	Satellite Digital and Display System
SDAE........	San Diego & Arizona Eastern Railway Co. [*AAR code*]
SDAE........	Source Data Automation Equipment
SDAF........	Solid-Rocket Booster Disassembly Facility [*NASA*] (NASA)
SDAF........	Special Defense Acquisition Fund [*Military*]
SDAFRS....	Source Data Automated Fitness Report System [*Military*] (DNAB)
SD Ag Exp ...	South Dakota. Agricultural Experiment Station. Publications [*A publication*]
SD Agric Exp Stn Bull ...	South Dakota. Agricultural Experiment Station. Bulletin [*A publication*]
SD Agric Exp Stn Circ ...	South Dakota. Agricultural Experiment Station. Circular [*A publication*]
SD Agric Exp Stn Tech Bull ...	South Dakota. Agricultural Experiment Station. Technical Bulletin [*A publication*]
SDAHS......	Studies. Dutch Archaeological and Historical Society [*A publication*]
S DAK........	South Dakota
S Dak	South Dakota Reports [*A publication*] (DLA)
S Dak Acad Sci Proc ...	South Dakota Academy of Science. Proceedings [*A publication*]
S Dak Agr Expt Sta Tech Bull ...	South Dakota. Agricultural Experiment Station. Technical Bulletin [*A publication*]
S Dak Bus R ...	South Dakota Business Review [*A publication*]
SDAKC......	Seventh-Day Adventist Kinship Canada (EAIO)
S Dak Farm Home Res ...	South Dakota Farm and Home Research [*A publication*]
S Dak Geol Surv Bull ...	South Dakota. Geological Survey. Bulletin [*A publication*]
S Dak Geol Surv Circ ...	South Dakota. Geological Survey. Circular [*A publication*]
S Dak Geol Survey Oil and Gas Inv Map Rept Inv ...	South Dakota. Geological Survey. Oil and Gas Investigations Map. Report of Investigation [*A publication*]
S Dak His R ...	South Dakota Historical Review [*A publication*]
S Dak His S ...	South Dakota State Historical Society. Collections [*A publication*]
S Dak HR ..	South Dakota Historical Review [*A publication*]
SDAKI......	Seventh Day Adventist Kinship International (EA)
S Dak J Med ...	South Dakota Journal of Medicine [*A publication*]
S Dak J Med Pharm ...	South Dakota Journal of Medicine and Pharmacy [*A publication*]
S Dak Lib Bull ...	South Dakota Library Bulletin [*A publication*]
S Dak Libr Bull ...	South Dakota Library Bulletin [*A publication*]
S Dak Rev ...	South Dakota Review [*A publication*]
S Dak Sch Mines B ...	South Dakota. School of Mines. Bulletin [*A publication*]
S Dak State Geologist Bienn Rept ...	South Dakota State Geologist. Biennial Report [*A publication*]

S Dak State Univ Coop Ext Serv ... South Dakota State University. Cooperative Extension Service [*A publication*]
SdAl .... Alcester Public Library, Alcester, SD [*Library symbol*] [*Library of Congress*] (LCLS)
SDAL .... Switched Data Access Line
SD Ala .... United States District Court for the Southern District of Alabama (DLA)
SdAle .... Alexandria Public Library, Alexandria, SD [*Library symbol*] [*Library of Congress*] (LCLS)
SDAM .... Social Democratic Alliance of Macedonia [*Political party*] (EY)
SDAM .... Standard Deviation above the Mean [*Statistics*]
SDA Mad .. Madras Sadr Diwani Adalat Reports [*India*] [*A publication*] (DLA)
SDAML ..... Send by Airmail (NOAA)
SDANA ..... Shrine Directors Association of North America (EA)
SDAP .... Sociaal-Democratische Arbeiders Partij [*Social Democratic Workers' Party*] [*Netherlands*] [*Political party*] (PPE)
SDAP .... Special Duty Assignment Pay [*Army*] (INF)
SDAP .... System Development and Performance
SDAP .... Systems Development and Acquisition Plan (MCD)
SDAP .... Systems Development Analysis Program
SDAPP ...... Special Duty Assignment Proficiency Pay [*Air Force*]
SdAr .... Arlington Public Library, Arlington, SD [*Library symbol*] [*Library of Congress*] (LCLS)
SDAR .... Submarine Departure Approval Request (DNAB)
SdArm .... Armour Public Library, Armour, SD [*Library symbol*] [*Library of Congress*] (LCLS)
SDAS .... Scientific Data Automation System (IEEE)
SDAS .... Shared Demand Assignment Signaling (MCD)
SDAS .... Simplified Directional Approach System [*Aviation*]
SDAS .... Sound Data Acquisition System [*Automotive engineering*]
SDAS .... Source Data Automation System [*Military*] (AABC)
SDA-S .... System Design Agency-Subcontractor Design Direction (MCD)
SDAS .... Systems Data Analysis Section
SDAT .... Safe Driver Attitude Test [*Educational test*]
SDAT .... Senile Dementia of the Alzheimer Type [*Medicine*]
SDAT .... Spacecraft Data Analysis Team [*NASA*]
SDAT .... Stanford Diagnostic Arithmetic Test
SDAT .... Stationary Digital Audio Tape
SDAU .... Subscriber Digital Access Unit [*Telecommunications*]
SDAUG ..... SDA [*Software Design Associates*] Users' Groups [*Later, IUG*] (EA)
SDAV .... Sialodacryoadenitis [*Virology*]
SDAW .... Sitzungsberichte. Deutsche Akademie der Wissenschaften zu Berlin [*A publication*]
SDAWB ..... Sitzungsberichte. Deutsche Akademie der Wissenschaften zu Berlin [*A publication*]
SDB .... Sa Da Bandeira [*Angola*] [*Seismograph station code, US Geological Survey*] (SEIS)
SDB .... Salesians of Don Bosco [*Roman Catholic men's religious order*]
SDB .... Sandberg, CA [*Location identifier*] [*FAA*] (FAAL)
SDB .... Seaward Defence Boat [*British military*] (DMA)
SDB .... Securities Data Base System [*Information service or system*] (IID)
SDB .... Segment Descriptor Block
SDB .... Shakespeare Data Bank, Inc. [*Information service or system*] (IID)
SDB .... Shallow Draft Barge (MCD)
SDB .... Shallow Draft Board (NASA)
SD & B .... Shaw, Dunlop, and Bell's Scotch Court of Session Reports, First Series [*1821-38*] [*A publication*] (DLA)
SDB .... Skill Development Base [*Army*] (AABC)
SDB .... Small Disadvantaged Business [*Department of Commerce*]
SDB .... Sociaal-Democratische Bond [*Social Democratic League*] [*Netherlands*] [*Political party*] (PPE)
SDB .... Society for Developmental Biology (EA)
SDB .... South Dakota Business Review [*A publication*]
SdB .... South Dakota State University, Brookings, SD [*Library symbol*] [*Library of Congress*] (LCLS)
SDB .... South Dakota State University, Brookings, SD [*OCLC symbol*] (OCLC)
SDB .... Spacecraft Design Book
SDB .... Special District Bond
SDB .... Square Die Bushing
SDB .... State Development Bank [*Hungary*]
SDB .... Storage Data Bus
SDB .... Strength and Dynamics Branch [*Air Force*]
SDB .... Supplement au Dictionnaire de la Bible [*A publication*]
sdb .... Symbolic Debugger [*Also, SOLD, SYMDEB*] [*Data processing*] (BYTE)
SDB .... System Data Buffer (MCD)
SDB .... System Database
SDBC .... Small Disadvantaged Business Concerns
SDBCS .... Steam Dump Bypass Control System [*Nuclear energy*] (NRCH)
SdBer .... Beresford Public Library, Beresford, SD [*Library symbol*] [*Library of Congress*] (LCLS)
SdBf .... Belle Fourche Public Library, Belle Fourche, SD [*Library symbol*] [*Library of Congress*] (LCLS)
SDBF .... System Development Breadboard Facility
SDBGC ...... Seventh Day Baptist General Conference (EA)

SDBHS ...... Seventh Day Baptist Historical Society (EA)
SDBI .... Specifications Drawing Baseline Index (DNAB)
SD Bird Notes ... South Dakota Bird Notes [*A publication*]
SDB Jo .... South Dakota Bar Journal [*A publication*] (DLA)
SDBL .... Sight Draft Bill of Lading Attached [*Business term*]
SdB-M .... South Dakota State University, Minuteman Graduate Center Library, Ellsworth AFB, Rapid City, SD [*Library symbol*] [*Library of Congress*] (LCLS)
SDBMS ..... Seventh Day Baptist Missionary Society (EA)
SdBo .... Bonesteel Public Library, Bonesteel, SD [*Library symbol*] [*Library of Congress*] (LCLS)
SDBO .... Societe de Banque Occidentale [*France*] (EY)
SDBP .... Supine Diastolic Blood Pressure [*Medicine*]
Sd-BPH ..... South Dakota State Library for the Handicapped, Pierre, SD [*Library symbol*] [*Library of Congress*] (LCLS)
SdBro .... Brookings Public Library, Brookings, SD [*Library symbol*] [*Library of Congress*] (LCLS)
SdBrS .... Bristol Independent School District Library, Bristol, SD [*Library symbol*] [*Library of Congress*] (LCLS)
SDBS .... Sodium Dodecylbenzene Sulfonate [*Organic chemistry*]
SD & B Sup ... Shaw, Dunlop, and Bell's Supplement, Containing House of Lords Decisions [*A publication*] (DLA)
SD & B Supp ... Shaw, Dunlop, and Bell's Supplement, Containing House of Lords Decisions [*Scotland*] [*A publication*] (DLA)
SdBu .... Burke Public Library, Burke, SD [*Library symbol*] [*Library of Congress*] (LCLS)
SDBU/CR ... [*Office of*] Small and Disadvantaged Business Utilization and Civil Rights [*See also OSDBU*] [*Federal government*] (NRCH)
SDBWF ..... Seventh Day Baptist World Federation (EA)
SDBY .... Standby
SDC .... Chief Steward [*Later, MSC*] [*Navy rating*]
SDC .... Salivary Duct Carcinoma [*Oncology*]
SDC .... Salt Data Centre [*British*]
SDC .... Same Distribution Center Service Area [*US Postal Service*]
SDC .... Sample Data Collection
SDC .... San Diego - Robinson [*California*] [*Seismograph station code, US Geological Survey*] [*Closed*] (SEIS)
SDC .... Sands Minerals [*Vancouver Stock Exchange symbol*]
SDC .... Scientific Data Center (MCD)
SDC .... Scientific Documentation Center Ltd. [*Dunfermline, Fife, Scotland*]
SDC .... Seaward Defense Craft (NATG)
SDC .... Secondary Distribution Center (AAG)
SDC .... Secure Data Cartridge (BYTE)
SDC .... Seismological Data Center [*Environmental Science Services Administration*]
SDC .... Seize Detector Control
SDC .... Self-Defense Corps [*Vietnam*]
SDC .... Self-Destruct Circuit (SAA)
SDC .... Semiconductor Devices Council [*Joint Electronic Device Engineering Council*] (MCD)
SDC .... September Days Club (EA)
SDC .... Serum Digoxin Concentration [*Clinical chemistry*]
SDC .... Several Dancers Core [*Houston, TX and Atlanta, GA*]
SDC .... Shaft-Driven Counter
SDC .... Shield Design Code [*Nuclear energy*] (NRCH)
SDC .... Shipment Detail Card [*Military*]
SDC .... Shutdown Cooling [*Nuclear energy*] (NRCH)
SDC .... Signal Data Converter
SDC .... Single Drift Correction
SDC .... Situation Display Converter
SDC .... Society of Daily Communicants [*Defunct*] (EA)
SD-C .... Society of Designer-Craftsmen [*British*] (EAIO)
SDC .... Society of the Divine Compassion [*Anglican religious community*]
SDC .... Society of Dyers and Colourists (EAIO)
SDC .... Sodium Deoxycholate [*Organic chemistry*]
SDC .... Software Development Computer [*NASA*] (NASA)
SDC .... Solid Dielectric Cable
SDC .... SONAR Data Computer [*Navy*] (CAAL)
SDC .... Southern Defense Command [*Army*]
SDC .... Space Data Corp.
SDC .... Space Defense Center [*Military*] (MCD)
SDC .... Space Defense Corp. (MCD)
SDC .... Space Development Corp.
SDC .... Spacecraft Data Simulator [*NASA*] (KSC)
SDC .... Spares Disposition Code [*NASA*] (NASA)
SDC .... Special Day Class [*Education*]
SDC .... Special Devices Center [*Navy*]
SDC .... Specific Damping Capacity [*Metals*]
SDC .... Stabilization Data Computer
SDC .... Standard Data Chain
SDC .... State Data Center [*Bureau of the Census*] (GFGA)
SDC .... State Defense Council
SDC .... Static Dielectric Constant
SDC .... Station Directory Control (SAA)
SDC .... Strategic Defense Command [*Military*] (SDI)
SDC .... Strategic Direction Center (MCD)
SDC .... Structural Design Criteria [*Nuclear energy*]
SDC .... Studebaker Driver's Club (EA)

SDC	Subcontractor's Data Catalog (MCD)
SDC	Submersible Decompression Chamber [*Underwater tank*]
SDC	Submersible Diving Capsule [*Oceanography*]
SDC	Succinyldicholine [*Biochemistry*] (MAE)
SDC	Sundance Airways, Inc. [*San Antonio, TX*] [*FAA designator*] (FAAC)
SDC	Supply Distribution Center [*Military*] (AFIT)
SDC	Support Design Change
SDC	System for Data Calculation [*Information retrieval*]
SDC	System Design Confirmation
SDC	System Designator Code (AFM)
SDC	System Development Corp. [*Information service or system*] (IID)
SDC	Systems Development District (AAG)
SDC	Yankton College, Yankton, SD [*OCLC symbol*] (OCLC)
SdCa	Canton Carnegie Public Library, Canton, SD [*Library symbol*] [*Library of Congress*] (LCLS)
SDCA	Scottish Deerhound Club of America (EA)
SD Cal	United States District Court for the Southern District of California (DLA)
SdCan	Canova Public Library, Canova, SD [*Library symbol*] [*Library of Congress*] (LCLS)
SdCar	Carthage Public Library, Carthage, SD [*Library symbol*] [*Library of Congress*] (LCLS)
SDCC	Simulation Data Conversion Center [*Space Flight Operations Facility, NASA*]
SDCC	Small-Diameter Component Cask [*Nuclear energy*] (NRCH)
SDCC	Society of the Descendants of the Colonial Clergy (EA)
SDCD	[*Adjusted*] Sea Duty Commencement Date
SDCE	Scientific Data Collection Exercise
SDCE	Society of Die Casting Engineers (EA)
SDCF	Sampled Data Channel Filter
SdCh	Chamberlain Public Library, Chamberlain, SD [*Library symbol*] [*Library of Congress*] (LCLS)
SDCH	Society of Descendants of Colonial Hispanics (EA)
SDCI	Singles and Doubles Configuration Interaction [*Quantum chemistry*] (MCD)
SDCIS	Supplier Data Control Information System (MCD)
SdCl	Clark Public Library, Clark, SD [*Library symbol*] [*Library of Congress*] (LCLS)
SDCL	South Dakota Codified Laws [*A publication*]
SDCL	Supplier Documentation Checklist (NASA)
SDCL	Symptom Distress Check List [*Medicine*] (MAE)
SdCla	Claremont Public Library, Claremont, SD [*Library symbol*] [*Library of Congress*] (LCLS)
SDCM	Master Chief Steward [*Later, MSCM*] [*Navy rating*]
SDC Mag...	Systems Development Corp. Magazine [*A publication*]
SdCo	Colome Public Library, Colome, SD [*Library symbol*] [*Library of Congress*] (LCLS)
SD Codified Laws ... South Dakota Codified Laws [*A publication*] (DLA)
SD Codified Laws Ann ... South Dakota Codified Laws, Annotated [*A publication*] (DLA)
SDCOI	Sector Direction Center Operating Instruction (SAA)
SD Comm...	Doctor of Science in Commerce
SD Compiled Laws Ann ... South Dakota Compiled Laws, Annotated [*A publication*] (DLA)
SD Comp Laws Ann ... South Dakota Compiled Laws, Annotated [*A publication*] (DLA)
SDCP	Sample Data Collection Plan (MCD)
SDCP	Summary Development Cost Plan [*NASA*] (NASA)
SDCP	Supply Demand Control Point [*Military*]
SDCR	Source Data Communication Retrieval
SDCS	SAIL [*Shuttle Avionics Integration Laboratory*] Data Communications System [*NASA*] (NASA)
SDCS	Sample Data Control System (MCD)
SDCS	Science Data Conditioning System
SDCS	Senior Chief Steward [*Navy rating*] [*Later, MSCS*]
SDCS	Shutdown Cooling System [*Nuclear energy*] (NRCH)
SDCS	Simulation Data Conversion System [*Space Flight Operations Facility, NASA*]
SDCS	Single Differential Cross Section
SDCT	Slosson Drawing Coordination Test
SdCu	Custer County Library, Custer, SD [*Library symbol*] [*Library of Congress*] (LCLS)
SDCW	San Diego College for Women [*California*]
SDD	Lubango [*Angola*] [*Airport symbol*] (OAG)
SDD	Santo Domingo [*Ciudad Trujillo*] [*Dominican Republic*] [*Seismograph station code, US Geological Survey*] (SEIS)
SDD	Scientific Discoveries and Discoverers [*A publication*]
SDD	Scottish Development Department (DCTA)
SDD	Scottish Diploma in Dairying
SDD	Second Development Decade [*United Nations*]
SDD	Selected Dissemination of Documents
SD/D	Service Deputy/Director (MUGU)
SDD	Shuttle Design Directive [*NASA*] (NASA)
SDD	Sierra Nevada Gold [*Vancouver Stock Exchange symbol*]
SDD	Signal Data Demodulator
SDD	Silicon Disk Drive [*Data processing*]
SDD	Single Diaphragm Distributor [*Automotive engineering*]
SDD	Sioux Falls Public Library, Sioux Falls, SD [*OCLC symbol*] (OCLC)

SDD	Slowdown Density
SDD	Sodium Dimethyldithiocarbamate [*Also, SDDC*] [*Organic chemistry*]
SDD	Software Description Document [*NASA*] (NASA)
SDD	Software Design Description [*Data processing*] (IEEE)
SDD	Software Design Document [*NASA*] (NASA)
SDD	Spark Delay Device [*Automotive engineering*]
SDD	Specially Designated Distributor [*Liquor*]
SDD	Stacy Design and Development, Inc. [*Telecommunications service*] (TSSD)
SDD	Standard Delivery Date [*Military*]
SDD	Store Door Delivery
SDD	Stored Data Description
SDD	Stress Degree Day [*Crop inventory*]
SDD	Subchannel Data Distributor (KSC)
SDD	Subsystem Design Description (MCD)
SDD	Synthetic Dynamic Display [*Aviation*] (OA)
SDD	System Design Description [*Nuclear energy*] (NRCH)
SDD	System Design Document [*NASA*] (MCD)
SDD	Systems Definition Directive [*Military*] (AFM)
SDD	Systems Development Department [*David W. Taylor Naval Ship Research and Development Center*]
SDDAA	School Dropout Demonstration Assistance Act
SDDC	Self Determination for DC [*District of Columbia*] (EA)
SDDC	Silver Diethyldithiocarbamate [*Organic chemistry*]
SDDC	Sodium Dimethyldithiocarbamate [*Organic chemistry*] [*Also, SDD*]
SDDC	Sterile Disposable Device Committee [*Defunct*]
SDDD	Software Detailed Design Document [*Army*]
SDDE	Surface Demand Diving Equipment
SDDE	System Design and Development Environment
SdDel	Dell Rapids Carnegie Public Library, Dell Rapids, SD [*Library symbol*] [*Library of Congress*] (LCLS)
SDDIDP ...	Survey of Digestive Diseases [*A publication*]
SDDL	Stored Data Definition Language
SDDM	Secretary of Defense Decision Memorandum
SDD-NU	Summaries of Doctoral Dissertations. Northwestern University [*A publication*]
SDDP	Sight Draft Documents Against Payment [*Business term*]
SdDr	Draper Public Library, Draper, SD [*Library symbol*] [*Library of Congress*] (LCLS)
SDDR	Standard Digital Data Recorder (DWSG)
SDDRA	Showa Densen Denran Rebyu [*A publication*]
SdDs	De Smet Public Library, De Smet, SD [*Library symbol*] [*Library of Congress*] (LCLS)
SDDS	Satellite Data Distribution System
SDDS	Scientific Document Delivery System
SDDS	Secondary Data Display System (MCD)
SDDS	Signal Data Demodulator Set [*or System*]
SDDS	Solid Discharge Data System [*Environmental Protection Agency*] (GFGA)
SDDS	Switched Digital Data Service [*Southern New England Telephone*]
SD/DS	Synchro-Digital/Digital-Synchro (CAAL)
SDDTTG...	Stored Data Definition and Translation Task Group
SDDU	Simplex Data Distribution Unit
SDDUW	Summaries of Doctoral Dissertations. University of Wisconsin [*A publication*]
SDE	Santiago Del Estero [*Argentina*] [*Airport symbol*] (OAG)
SDE	Self-Disinfecting Elastomer
SDE	Simple Designational Expression
SDE	Simultaneous Distillation-Extraction [*Chemical engineering*]
SDE	Societe de Droits d'Execution du Canada [*Performing Rights Organization of Canada - PROC*]
SDE	Society of Data Educators (EA)
SDE	Software Development Environment [*NCR Corp.*]
SDE	Source Data Entry
SDE	Space Division Evaluator [*NASA*] (NASA)
SDE	Specific Dynamic Effect [*Medicine*]
SDE	Standard Data Element [*Army*] (AABC)
SDE	Standard-Dose Epinephrine [*Medicine*]
SDE	Standard Etac Corp. [*Toronto Stock Exchange symbol*]
SDE	Steam Distillation Extraction
SDE	Students for Data Education (IEEE)
SDE	Support Data Engineering (MCD)
SDEC	Sequential Detection of Emerging Competitive Target
SDE & C ...	Standard Data Element and Codes [*Air Force*]
SDECE	Service de Documentation Exterieure et de Contre-Espionnage [*Pronounced "suh-deck"*] [*Intelligence organization*] [*France*] [*Later, DGSE*]
SdEd	Edgemont Public Library, Edgemont, SD [*Library symbol*] [*Library of Congress*] (LCLS)
SdEdH	Edgemont High School, Edgemont, SD [*Library symbol*] [*Library of Congress*] (LCLS)
S/DEFL	Stone Deflector [*Automotive engineering*]
SDEG	Special Doctrine Equipment Group [*Army*]
SDE/GWIS ... Sigma Delta Epsilon, Graduate Women in Science (EA)
SdEl	Elkton Public Library, Elkton, SD [*Library symbol*] [*Library of Congress*] (LCLS)
Sdelovaci Tech ... Sdelovaci Technika [*A publication*]
SDEO	Second Division of Executive Officers [*A union*] [*British*]

SDER........ Standardized Distributed Energy Release (MCD)
SDERDN... Seminars in Dermatology [A publication]
SdEs........... Estelline Public Library, Estelline, SD [Library symbol] [Library of Congress] (LCLS)
SDES........ Submarine Data Extraction System [Navy] (CAAL)
SDESG ...... Strapdown Electrically Suspended Gyro (KSC)
SdEu .... Eureka Public Library, Eureka, SD [Library symbol] [Library of Congress] (LCLS)
SDEV........ [The] Software Developer's Co., Inc. [NASDAQ symbol] (NQ)
SDF........... Louisville [Kentucky] [Airport symbol] (OAG)
SDF........... Safing and Deservicing Facility [NASA] (NASA)
SDF........... Sanatana Dharma Foundation (EA)
SDF........... Satellite Distribution Frame [Telecommunications] (TEL)
SDF........... Screen Definition Facility [Data processing]
SDF........... Seasonal Derating Factor (IEEE)
SDF........... Self-Defense Force [Japan]
SDF........... Ship Description File (DNAB)
SDF........... Ship Design File (OA)
SDF........... Simplified Directional Facility [Aviation]
SDF........... Simultaneous Double Fire [Automotive engineering]
SDF........... Single Defruit [Aviation] (FAAC)
SDF........... Single Degree of Freedom [Also, SDOF] [Acoustics]
SDF........... Sioux Falls College, Sioux Falls, SD [OCLC symbol] (OCLC)
SDF........... Slow Death Factor [Medicine]
SDF........... Social Democratic Federation [Later, SDP] [Early British political party, members of which were sometimes referred to as "Silly Damn Fools"]
SDF........... Social Democratic Federation [Iceland] [Political party] (PPW)
SDF........... Social Democratic Federation [Japan] [Political party] (PPW)
SDF........... Social Democratic Front [Ghana] [Political party] (PPW)
SDF........... Social Democratic Front [Cameroon] [Political party] (EY)
SDF........... Software Development Facility [Military] (CAAL)
SDF........... Software Development File
SDF........... Software Development Folder (MCD)
SDF........... Sonic Depth Finder
SDF........... Source Development Fund [Supply and Services Canada]
SDF........... Source Document Folders [IRS]
SDF........... Southern Development Foundation (EA)
SDF........... Special Denatured Formula [Applied to alcohol]
SDF........... Spectral Density Function
SDF........... Standard Distribution Format [Data processing]
SDF........... Standard Drug File [Derwent Publications Ltd.] [Database]
SDF........... Static Direction Finder
SDF........... Stopping Distance Factor (MCD)
SDF........... Stowe-Day Foundation (EA)
SDF........... Strategic Defensive Forces [Army] (AABC)
SDF........... Structural Dynamics Malfunction
SDF........... Student Description Form [Psychology]
SDF........... Sudan Defence Force [British]
SDF........... Sundorph Aeronautical Corp. [Cleveland, OH] [FAA designator] (FAAC)
SDF........... Supergroup Distribution Frame [Telecommunications] (TEL)
SDF........... Surface Direct Fire [Navy] (CAAL)
SDF........... Swedish Defense Forces
SDF........... System Data Format [Data processing]
SDF........... System Development Facility [NASA] (KSC)
SD Farm Home Res ... South Dakota Farm and Home Research [A publication]
SD Farm Home Res SD Agric Exp Stn ... South Dakota Farm and Home Research. South Dakota Agricultural Experiment Station [A publication]
SDFAUS ... State Defense Force Association of the United States (EA)
SDFC......... Space Disturbance Forecast Center [Environmental Science Services Administration] (IEEE)
SDFC......... Standardized Discriminant Function Coefficient
SDFG......... Single-Degree-of-Freedom Gyroscope (SAA)
SDFL......... Schottky Diode FET [Field Effect Transistor] Logic
SD Fla........ United States District Court for the Southern District of Florida (DLA)
SDFN........ SONAR Dome Flow Noise
SDFOV...... Simultaneous Dual Field of View
SdFr .... Freeman Public Library, Freeman, SD [Library symbol] [Library of Congress] (LCLS)
SDFRA ...... Reports. Faculty of Science. Shizuoka University [A publication]
SDFS .... Same-Day Funds Settlement [Securities and Exchange Commission]
SD/FS........ Smoke Detector/Fire Suppression (GFGA)
SDFS .... Standard Disk Filing System
SDFSNM .. Sons and Daughters of the First Settlers of Newbury, Massachusetts (EA)
SDFTN ...... Soda Fountain
SDG .... Sacred Dance Guild (EA)
SDG .... Scan Display Generator
SDG .... Schriften. Droste-Gesellschaft [A publication]
SDG .... Screen Directors' Guild of America [Later, DGA]
SDG .... Siding (AAG)
SDG .... Signed, Directed Graph [Mathematics]
SDG .... Simulated Data Generator
SDG .... Situation Display Generator
SDG .... Soli Deo Gloria [Glory to God Alone] [Latin]

SDG .... Special Development Groups [Navy]
SDG .... Stormont, Dundas and Glengarry Highlanders [British military] (DMA)
SDG .... Strapdown Gyroscope (SAA)
SDG .... Subminiature Displacement Gyroscope
SDG .... Sucrose Density Gradients
SDG .... Sundance Gold Mining Ltd. [Vancouver Stock Exchange symbol]
SDG .... Supplier Documentation Group [NASA] (NASA)
SDG .... System Design Group (MCD)
SDGA .... Single Degaussing Cable
SDGA .... Sucrose Density Gradient Analysis [Clinical chemistry]
SD GA .... United States District Court for the Southern District of Georgia (DLA)
SDGC .... Simulated Distillation Gas Chromatography
SDGC .... Sun-Diamond Growers of California (EA)
SDGE........ Situation Display Generator Element
SdGe .... Sully-Potter County Library, Gettysburg, SD [Library symbol] [Library of Congress] (LCLS)
SD Geol Surv Bull ... South Dakota. Geological Survey. Bulletin [A publication]
SD Geol Surv Misc Invest ... South Dakota. Geological Survey. Miscellaneous Investigations [A publication]
SD Geol Surv Rep Invest ... South Dakota. Geological Survey. Report of Investigations [A publication]
SD Geol Surv Spec Rep ... South Dakota. Geological Survey. Special Report [A publication]
SDGF......... Schwannoma-Derived Growth Factor [Biochemistry]
SDGH........ Sweet Dough
SDgo .... San Diego Gas & Electric Co. [Associated Press abbreviation] (APAG)
SDGRA...... Report of Investigations. South Dakota Geological Survey [A publication]
SDGW .... Structural Design Gross Weight
SDH .... Scottish Diploma in Horticulture
SDH .... Seasonal Derated Hours (IEEE)
SDH .... Serine Dehydrase [An enzyme] (MAE)
SDH .... Single Dad's Hotline (EA)
SDH .... Slavistische Drukken en Herdrukken [A publication]
SDH .... Software Development Handbook [NASA] (NASA)
SDH .... Sorbitol Dehydrogenase [Also, Sorb D] [An enzyme]
SDH .... South Dakota Historical Resource Center, Pierre, SD [OCLC symbol] (OCLC)
SDH .... Spinal Dorsal Horn [Anatomy]
SDH .... Structured Document Handbook [Data processing]
SDH .... Styling Data Handling
SDH .... Subdural Hematoma [Medicine]
SDH .... Succinic Dehydrogenase [An enzyme]
SDH .... Support Dogs for the Handicapped (EA)
SDH .... Synchronous Digital Hierarchy [Data processing]
SDH .... System Development Handbook [NASA] (NASA)
SDHD .... Society of Daughters of Holland Dames (EA)
SDHD........ Sudden-Death Heart Disease [Medicine]
SDHE .... Spacecraft Data Handling Equipment
SdHi........... South Dakota Department of Cultural Affairs, Historical Resources Center, Pierre, SD [Library symbol] [Library of Congress] (LCLS)
SdHig......... Hyde County Library, Highmore, SD [Library symbol] [Library of Congress] (LCLS)
SDHIRS .... Subdistrict Headquarters Induction and Recruiting Station [Navy]
SdHM....... Minnehaha County Rural Library, Hartford, SD [Library symbol] [Library of Congress] (LCLS)
SdHow ...... Howard Public Library, Howard, SD [Library symbol] [Library of Congress] (LCLS)
SDHP .... Sosyal Demokrasi Halkci Partisi [Social Democratic Populist Party] [Turkey] [Political party] (MENA)
SDHR .... South Dakota Historical Review [A publication]
SDHS .... Satellite Data Handling System
SDHS .... Society of Dance History Scholars (EA)
SdHsV .... United States Veterans Administration Center, Hot Springs, SD [Library symbol] [Library of Congress] (LCLS)
SDHT .... Selectively Doped Heterostructure Transistor
SdHuro ...... Huron Public Library, Huron, SD [Library symbol] [Library of Congress] (LCLS)
SdHuroC... Huron College, Huron, SD [Library symbol] [Library of Congress] (LCLS)
SDI............ Saab Direct Ignition [Automotive engineering]
SDI............ Saidor [Papua New Guinea] [Airport symbol] (OAG)
SDI............ Saudi Arabian
SDI............ Saudi Arabian Airlines
SDI............ Selected Descriptive Item
SDI............ Selective Dissemination of Information [System] [Data processing]
SDI............ Self-Description Inventory [Vocational guidance test]
SDI............ Serial Dilution Indicator [Clinical chemistry]
SDI............ [Family Planning Program] Service Delivery Improvement Research [Department of Health and Human Services] [Washington, DC]

SDI............	Service de Documentation Interministerielle [*Interministerial Documentation Service*] [*National Telecommunications Research Center*] [*Information service or system*] (IID)
SDI............	Ship's Drawing Index (DNAB)
SDI............	Situation Display Indicator [*Aviation*] (OA)
SDI............	Society of Designers in Ireland (EAIO)
SDI............	Source Data Information
SDI............	Specifications Drawing Index (DNAB)
SDI............	Standard Data Interface [*Data processing*]
SDI............	Standard Deviation Interval [*Medicine*]
SDI............	Standardized Discharge Instructions [*for hospital patients*]
SDI............	Stars of David International (EAIO)
SDI............	State Disability Insurance
SDI............	Steel Deck Institute (EA)
SDI............	Steel Door Institute (EA)
SDI............	Strategic Defense Initiative [*Commonly known as "Starwars"*] [*Facetiously translated as "Silly Damn Idea"*]
SDI............	Subcontractor Data Item
SDI............	Submarine Detector Instructor [*British military*] (DMA)
SDI............	Super Data Interchange [*Data processing*] (HGAA)
SDI............	Supplier Data Item (MCD)
SDI............	Support Directive Instruction (KSC)
SDI............	Symbolic Displays, Inc. (MCD)
SD & I.......	System Development and Integration (MCD)
SDI............	Systems Designers International Ltd. [*British*] (IRUK)
SDIA..........	Small Defense Industries Association [*Later, Strategic Industries Association*]
SDIAC........	Strategic Defense Initiative Advisory Council [*Military*] (SDI)
SDIC..........	STC Communications Subsystem Distribution Interface Cabinet (MCD)
SDICC.......	Societe de Developpement de l'Industrie Cinematographique Canadienne [*Canadian Film Development Corp. - CFDC*]
SDID..........	Supplier Data Item Description (MCD)
SDIE..........	Special Defense Intelligence Estimate (MCD)
SDieGs.......	San Diego Gas & Electric Co. [*Associated Press abbreviation*] (APAG)
SDIF..........	Schistosome-Derived Immunosuppressive Factor [*Immunology*]
SDIF..........	Software Development and Integration Facility [*NASA*] (NASA)
SDIG..........	Screen Directors International Guild [*Absorbed by Directors Guild of America*] (EA)
SDIHD.......	Sudden-Death Ischemic Heart Disease [*Medicine*]
SDII..........	Special Devices, Inc. [*NASDAQ symbol*] (SPSG)
SDII..........	Strategic Defense Initiative Institute [*Military*] (SDI)
SDI-KWOC ...	Selected Dissemination of Information - Key Word Out of Context (DNAB)
SDILINE...	Selective Dissemination of Information Online [*National Library of Medicine*] [*Bethesda, MD*] [*Bibliographic database*]
SD Ill	United States District Court for the Southern District of Illinois (DLA)
SDIM........	System for Documentation and Information in Metallurgy [*Fachinformationszentrum Werkstoffe eV*] [*Information service or system*] (IID)
SDIMU......	Strapdown Inertial Measuring Unit (MCD)
SDIN	Special Defence Intelligence Notice (MCD)
SD Ind.......	United States District Court for the Southern District of Indiana (DLA)
SDIO	Serial Digit Input/Output [*Data processing*]
SDIO	Strategic Defense Initiative Organization [*Washington, DC*] [*DoD*] (GRD)
SD Iowa	United States District Court for the Southern District of Iowa (DLA)
SDIP..........	Specifically Designated Intelligence Position (AFM)
SDIP..........	Strengthening Developing Institutions Program [*HEW*]
SDIP..........	System Description and Implementation Plan [*Navy*]
SDIS..........	Ship Distance
SDIS..........	Ship Draft Indicating System (MSA)
SDISDC	Sexuality and Disability [*A publication*]
SDISM	Strategic Defense Initiative System Effectiveness Model [*Military*]
SDIT..........	Service de Documentation et d'Information Techniques de l'Aeronautique
SDIT..........	Ship Draft Indicator Transmitter (MSA)
SDI/UC.....	State Disability Insurance - Unemployment Compensation
SDIZ..........	Submarine Defense Identification Zone
SDJ............	Greensboro, NC [*Location identifier*] [*FAA*] (FAAL)
SDJ............	Sanada [*Japan*] [*Seismograph station code, US Geological Survey*] (SEIS)
SDJ............	Sendai [*Japan*] [*Airport symbol*] (OAG)
SDJ............	Senn d'Or [*Vancouver Stock Exchange symbol*]
SDJ............	Society of the Devotees of Jerusalem (EA)
SD J Med ..	South Dakota Journal of Medicine [*A publication*]
SD J Med Pharm ...	South Dakota Journal of Medicine and Pharmacy [*A publication*]
S & DJR.....	Somerset & Dorset Joint Railway [*British*]
SDK	Sandakan [*Malaysia*] [*Airport symbol*] (OAG)
SDK	Seljacko-Demokratska Koalicija [*Peasant-Democratic Coalition*] [*Former Yugoslavia*] [*Political party*] (PPE)
SDK	Shelter Deck

SDK	Si De Ka Quarterly [*Ann Arbor, MI*] [*A publication*] (DLA)
SDK	Sigma Delta Kappa [*Fraternity*]
SDK	Software Developer's Kit [*Data processing*] (BYTE)
SDK	Studebaker's Resource Development Ltd. [*Formerly, Rio Blanco Resources Ltd.*] [*Vancouver Stock Exchange symbol*]
SDK	System Design Kit
SDK	System Developers' Kit [*Computer hardware*] [*Microsoft, Inc.*] (PCM)
SdKJ........	Jackson-Washabaugh County Library, Kadoka, SD [*Library symbol*] [*Library of Congress*] (LCLS)
SDKOD	Saitama Daigaku Kiyo. Kogakubu [*A publication*]
SDKSB	Saitama Daigaku Kiyo. Shizenkagaku-Hen [*A publication*]
SdL...........	Hearst Free Library, Lead, SD [*Library symbol*] [*Library of Congress*] (LCLS)
SDL...........	National Council, Sons and Daughters of Liberty (EA)
SDL...........	Saddle (MSA)
SDL...........	Scenario Development Language [*Military*] (CAAL)
SDL...........	Scientific DataLink [*Comtex Scientific Corp.*] [*Information service or system*] (IID)
SDL...........	Scottie Gold Mines Ltd. [*Vancouver Stock Exchange symbol*]
SDL...........	Scottsdale, AZ [*Location identifier*] [*FAA*] (FAAL)
SDL...........	Security Devices Laboratory (SAA)
SDL...........	Seedling (WGA)
SDL...........	Seismic Data Laboratory [*Teledyne Geotech*]
SDL...........	Self-Directed Learning (ADA)
SDL...........	Semiconductor Diode LASER [*Also, TDL*]
SDL...........	Sensory Distal Latency [*Medicine*]
SDL...........	Shaft Driver, Left
SDL...........	SHORAD [*Short Range Air Defense*] Data Link [*Army*]
SDL...........	Simulation Data Language
SDL...........	Single Driver's License [*Law*]
SDL...........	Slowdown Length
SDL...........	Software Design Language
SDL...........	Software Development Laboratory [*NASA*] (NASA)
SDL...........	Software Development Language [*Burroughs Corp.*]
SDL...........	Software Development Library
SDL...........	Sonic Delay Line
SDL...........	Space Disturbances Laboratory [*Boulder, CO*]
SDL...........	Space Dynamics Laboratories [*Utah State University*] [*Research center*] (RCD)
SDL...........	Specification and Description Language [*Telecommunications*] (TEL)
SDL...........	Standard Deviation of the Logarithm [*Statistics*]
SDL...........	Standard Distribution List [*NASA*]
SDL...........	Stark County District Library, Canton, OH [*OCLC symbol*] (OCLC)
SDL...........	State-Dependent Learning [*Psychology*]
SDL...........	Strip Delay Line
SDL...........	Sundsvall [*Sweden*] [*Airport symbol*] (OAG)
SDL...........	Supporting Document List
SDL...........	Surplus Distribution List (AAG)
SDL...........	System Descriptive Language [*Data processing*] (IEEE)
SDL...........	System Design Language
SDL...........	System Development Language [*1971*] [*Data processing*] (CSR)
SDL...........	System Directory List [*Data processing*] (BUR)
SDL...........	Systematic Design Language [*Data processing*]
SDL...........	Systems Development Laboratories (MCD)
SD Laws....	Laws of South Dakota [*A publication*]
SDLC........	Synchronous Data-Link Control [*Telecommunications*]
SDLC........	System Data Link Control [*Telecommunications*]
SDLC........	System Development Life Cycle
SdLeH.......	Lennox High School Library, Lennox, SD [*Library symbol*] [*Library of Congress*] (LCLS)
SdLem........	Lemmon Public Library, Lemmon, SD [*Library symbol*] [*Library of Congress*] (LCLS)
SdLemH	Lemmon High School Library, Lemmon, SD [*Library symbol*] [*Library of Congress*] (LCLS)
SDLM........	Scheduled Depot Level Maintenance [*Navy*]
SDLM.......	Special Depot Level Maintenance
SDLM.......	Standard Depot Level Maintenance (MCD)
SDLO........	State, Defense Liaison Office [*Federal government*] (AABC)
SDLP.........	Social Democratic and Labour Party [*Northern Ireland*] [*Political party*] (PPW)
SDLP.........	Social Democratic and Liberal Party [*British*] [*Political party*]
SDLP.........	Societe de Developpement du Livre et du Periodique [*Society for the Development of Books and Periodicals*] [*Canada*]
SD LR	South Dakota Law Review [*A publication*]
SD L Rev....	South Dakota Law Review [*A publication*]
SDLT.........	Static/Dynamic Load Technology (SSD)
SDLV........	Shuttle-Derived Launch Vehicle [*NASA*] (SSD)
SdM	Mitchell Public Library, Mitchell, SD [*Library symbol*] [*Library of Congress*] (LCLS)
SDM	National Association of Special Delivery Messengers [*Later, APWU*] [*AFL-CIO*]
SDM	Samsonov Density Meter [*Gravimetrics*]
SDM	San Diego, CA [*Location identifier*] [*FAA*] (FAAL)
SDM	Santiago De Maria [*El Salvador*] [*Seismograph station code, US Geological Survey*] (SEIS)
SDM	School in District Management [*LIMRA*]

SDM .... Schwarz Differential Medium (OA)
SDM .... Selective Dissemination of Microfiche
SDM .... Semiconductor Disk Memory
SDM .... Sensory Detection Method [*for measuring blood pressure*]
SDM .... Sequency-Division Multiplexing (IEEE)
SDM .... Ship Design Manager
SDM .... Short-Delay Monostable [*Circuitry*]
SDM .... Shutdown Margin [*Nuclear energy*] (NRCH)
SDM .... Shutdown Mode (IEEE)
SDM .... Shuttle Data Management [*NASA*] (MCD)
SdM .... Siglo de las Misiones [*A publication*]
SDM .... Signal Density Model (MCD)
SDM .... Simulated Dynamic Missile [*Military*] (CAAL)
SDM .... Site Defense of Minuteman [*Missiles*] (MCD)
SDM .... Site-Directed Mutagenesis [*Biochemistry*]
SDM .... Slowdown Model
SDM .... Soma Dendrite Membrane
SDM .... Somali Democratic Movement [*Political party*] (EY)
SDMa .... Sons and Daughters of Malta (EA)
SDM .... Space Division Multiplexing [*Physics*]
SDM .... Spares Determination Method [*Bell System*]
SDM .... Sparse Distributed Memory [*Data processing*]
SDM .... Specially Designated Merchant [*Liquor sales*]
SDM .... Standard Deviation of the Mean (AAMN)
SDM .... Standardization Design Memoranda (IEEE)
SDM .... STARAN Debug Module
SDM .... Statistical Delta Modulation
SDM .... Statistical-Dynamical Model
SDM .... Structural Development Model
SDM .... Structural Dynamics Modification
SDM .... Structures, Structural Dynamics, and Materials (MCD)
SDM .... Subdivision Manager
SDM .... Subsystem Design Manual [*NASA*] (MCD)
SDM .... Sugar Cane Downy Mildew [*Plant pathology*]
SDM .... Synchronous Digital Machine
SDM .... System Definition Manual [*NASA*] (NASA)
SDM .... Systems Design Methodology [*Data processing*] (HGAA)
SDM .... Systems Development Methodology [*Data processing*] (HGAA)
SdMa .... Bennett County Library, Martin, SD [*Library symbol*] [*Library of Congress*] (LCLS)
SDMA ...... Sam Davis Memorial Association (EA)
SDMA ...... Shared Direct Memory Access [*Sperry UNIVAC*]
SDMA ...... Sodium Dihydrobis(methoxyethoxy)aluminate [*Organic chemistry*]
SDMA ...... Space Division Multiple Access
SDMAA .... Stroitel'nye i Dorozhnye Mashiny [*A publication*]
SdMadT..... Dakota State College, Madison, SD [*Library symbol*] [*Library of Congress*] (LCLS)
SdMar....... Dakota Wowapipahi Library, Marty, SD [*Library symbol*] [*Library of Congress*] (LCLS)
SDME........ Synchronous Data Modern Equipment
SDMEA..... South Dakota Journal of Medicine [*A publication*]
SdMeS .... Menno Public School Library, Menno, SD [*Library symbol*] [*Library of Congress*] (LCLS)
SD (Met).... Doctor of Science in Metallurgy
SDMH....... Symmetrical-Dimethylhydrazine [*Organic chemistry*]
SdMi .... Hand County Library, Miller, SD [*Library symbol*] [*Library of Congress*] (LCLS)
S-DMICC ... State-Defense Military Information Control Committee (AFM)
SdMil......... Milbank Carnegie Library, Milbank, SD [*Library symbol*] [*Library of Congress*] (LCLS)
SDMIS ...... Standard Depot Management Information System [*Army*]
SDMIS ...... Standardization Data Management Information System
SD Miss..... United States District Court for the Southern District of Mississippi (DLA)
SDMIX...... South Dakota Medical Information Exchange [*University of South Dakota*] [*Sioux Falls*] [*Telecommunications*] (TSSD)
SDMJ........ September, December, March, and June [*Denotes quarterly payments of interest or dividends in these months*] [*Business term*]
SdMo .... A. H. Brown Public Library, Mobridge, SD [*Library symbol*] [*Library of Congress*] (LCLS)
SDMO ...... Specifications and Data Management Office [*Military*]
SDMO ...... Subcommand Data Management Office [*Military*] (AFIT)
SDMS....... Shipboard Data Multiplex System (MCD)
SDMS....... Society of Diagnostic Medical Sonographers (EA)
SDMS....... Spatial Data Management System (MCD)
SDMS....... Supplier Data Management System (MCD)
SDMT....... Stanford Diagnostic Mathematics Test [*Education*]
SDMT....... Stress and Degraded Mode Test (CAAL)
SdMW ...... Dakota Wesleyan University, Mitchell, SD [*Library symbol*] [*Library of Congress*] (LCLS)
SDN .... North American Baptist Seminary, Sioux Falls, SD [*OCLC symbol*] (OCLC)
SDN .... Sandane [*Norway*] [*Airport symbol*] (OAG)
SDN .... Satellite Data Network [*AgriData Resources, Inc.*] [*Telecommunications service*] [*Defunct*] (TSSD)
SDN .... Secret Document Number
SDN .... Separation Designation Number

SDN .... Service Dealer's Newsletter [*Lynott Associates*] [*A publication*] (IID)
SDN .... Sexually Dimorphic Nucleus [*Brain anatomy*]
SDN .... Societe Demographique Nordique [*Nordic Demographic Society - NDS*] (EAIO)
SDN .... Societe des Nations [*League of Nations*]
SDN .... Sodisco, Inc. [*Toronto Stock Exchange symbol*]
SDN .... Software Defined Network [*Telecommunications*]
SDN .... Software Development Note [*NASA*] (NASA)
SDN .... Solution-Dyed Nylon
SDN .... Strapdown Navigator
SDN .... Subdeacon
SDN .... Subscriber's Directory Number [*Telecommunications*] (TEL)
SDN .... Sudan [*ANSI three-letter standard code*] (CNC)
SDN .... Swindon [*British depot code*]
SDN .... Synchronized Digital Network [*Telecommunications*] (TEL)
SDN .... System Development Notification
SDNB .... SDNB Financial Corp. [*NASDAQ symbol*] (NQ)
SDNCO ..... Staff Duty Noncommissioned Officer [*Army*]
SdNe .... Newell Public Library, Newell, SD [*Library symbol*] [*Library of Congress*] (LCLS)
SdNeu .... New Underwood Public Library, New Underwood, SD [*Library symbol*] [*Library of Congress*] (LCLS)
SDNIA...... Saga Daigaku Nogaku Iho [*A publication*]
SDNID7 .... Bulletin. Faculty of Agriculture. Saga University [*A publication*]
SDNR .... Screw Down Non-Return Valve (DS)
SDNRIU.... Secure Digital Net Radio Interface Unit [*Army*] (RDA)
SDNS........ Secure Data Network System [*Data processing*]
SDN & SU ... Step-Down and Step-Up (MSA)
SDNT .... Student
SD Nurse ... South Dakota Nurse [*A publication*]
SDNY .... United States District Court for the Southern District of New York (DLA)
SDO .... Oglala Sioux Community College, Learning Resources Center, Pine Ridge, SD [*OCLC symbol*] (OCLC)
SdO .... Onida Public Library, Onida, SD [*Library symbol*] [*Library of Congress*] (LCLS)
SDO .... Salado [*Chile*] [*Seismograph station code, US Geological Survey*] [*Closed*] (SEIS)
SDO .... San Diego Gas & Electric Co. [*NYSE symbol*] (SPSG)
SDO .... Schedules Duty Officer (KSC)
SDO .... Senior Duty Officer [*Air Force*] [*British*]
SDO .... Serra Dor [*A publication*]
SDO .... Shielded Diatomic Orbitals [*Atomic physics*]
SDO .... Ship Development Objective [*Navy*]
SDO .... Shipboard Distribution Only [*Navy*] (CAAL)
SDO .... Signal Distribution Officer [*British military*] (DMA)
SDO .... Sod House, NV [*Location identifier*] [*FAA*] (FAAL)
SDO .... SONAR Detection Opportunity [*Navy*] (CAAL)
SDO .... Source Data Operation (MDG)
SDO .... Special Duty Officer (MCD)
SDO .... Special Duty Only [*Military*]
SDO .... Specialist Duty Only [*Navy personnel designation*]
SDO .... Squadron Duty Officer [*Navy*] (NVT)
SDO .... Staff Duty Officer [*Army*]
SDO .... Station Duty Officer [*Navy*]
SDO .... Synthetic Drying Oil
SDO .... Systems Development Office [*National Weather Service*]
SDOB .... Scaled Depth of Burst (MCD)
S Doc.......... Senate Document (DLA)
SDOC .... Specific Direct Operating Costs
SDOE .... State Department of Education (OICC)
SDOF........ Single Degree of Freedom [*Also, SDF*] [*Acoustics*]
SDOG........ Sendschrift. Deutsche Orient-Gesellschaft [*Leipzig*] [*A publication*]
SD Ohio..... United States District Court for the Southern District of Ohio (DLA)
SDOM ...... Society of Dirty Old Men (EA)
SDOM ...... Standard Deviation of Means [*Statistics*]
SDOP .... Sons and Daughters of Oregon Pioneers (EA)
SDOPR..... Sound Operator [*Navy*]
SDOSD..... Standard Deviation of Standard Deviation [*Statistics*]
SDP........... National Society of Sons and Daughters of the Pilgrims (EA)
SDP........... Sacrodextra Posterior [*A fetal position*] [*Obstetrics*]
SDP........... Sand Point [*Alaska*] [*Airport symbol*] (OAG)
SDP........... Sand Point, AK [*Location identifier*] [*FAA*] (FAAL)
SDP........... Scottish Diploma in Poultry Husbandry
SDP........... Sea Duty Pay [*Navy*]
SDP........... Sentry Dog Patrol (AFM)
SDP........... Serb Democratic Party [*Croatia*] [*Political party*] (EY)
SDP........... Serbian Democratic Party [*Bosnia-Herzegovina*] [*Political party*] (EY)
SDP........... Set-Down Pool [*Nuclear energy*] (NRCH)
SDP........... Seychelles Democratic Party
SDP........... Shelf Dynamics Program [*CUE*] (MSC)
SDP........... Ship Development Plan [*Navy*]
SDP........... Short-Day Plant [*Botany*]
SDP........... Shuttle Data Processor [*NASA*] (MCD)
SDP........... Signal Data Processor
SDP........... Signal Dispatch Point [*Telecommunications*] (TEL)
SDP........... Silicon Diode Pellet

SDP........... Singapore Democratic Party [*Political party*] (PPW)
SDP........... Single Department Purchasing [*Agency*] [*Military*]
SDP........... Sirotherm Demineralization Process
SDP........... Sisters of Divine Providence [*Munster, Federal Republic of Germany*] (EAIO)
SDP........... Site Data Processor
SDP........... Site Development and Facilities Utilization Plan [*Oak Ridge National Laboratory*]
SDP........... Slowdown Power
SDP........... Small Distribution Phenomena
SDP........... Smoke Dispersion Pod
SDP........... Social-Democrat Party [*Zambia*] [*Political party*] (EY)
SDP........... Social Democratic Party [*Albania*] [*Political party*] (EY)
SDP........... Social Democratic Party [*Hungary*] [*Political party*]
SDP........... Social Democratic Party [*Philippines*] [*Political party*] (PPW)
SDP........... Social Democratic Party [*Nigeria*] [*Political party*]
SDP........... Social Democratic Party [*Thailand*] [*Political party*] (PPW)
SDP........... Social Democratic Party [*Germany*] [*Political party*]
SDP........... Social Democratic Party [*Australia*] [*Political party*]
SDP........... Social Democratic Party [*Trinidad and Tobago*] [*Political party*] (PPW)
SDP........... Social Democratic Party [*Iceland*] [*Political party*] (PPW)
SDP........... Social Democratic Party [*British*] [*Political party*]
SDP........... Socialist Democratic Party [*South Korea*] [*Political party*] (EY)
SDP........... Software Development Plan [*NASA*] (NASA)
SDP........... Solar Desalination Plant
SDP........... Sosyal Demokrat Partisi [*Social Democratic Party*] [*Turkish Cyprus*] [*Political party*] (EY)
SDP........... Source Data Processing
SDP........... Sozial Demokratesch Partei [*Social Democratic Party*] [*Luxembourg*] [*Political party*] (PPE)
SDP........... Spectral Dependence Photocurrent
SDP........... Standard Data Processor (SSD)
SDP........... State Data Program [*Information service or system*] (IID)
SDP........... Station Data Processing
SDP........... Steyr-Daimler-Puch [*Manufacturing firm*] [*Automotive engineering*]
SDP........... Storage and Distribution Point [*Military*] (AFM)
SDP........... Stornaway Central Development [*Vancouver Stock Exchange symbol*]
SDP........... Stranka Demokratskih Reformi [*Party of Democratic Reform*] [*Slovenia*] [*Political party*] (EY)
SDP........... Stratospheric Dust Particle
SdP........... Sudetendeutsche Partei [*Sudeten German Party*] [*Former Czechoslovakia*] [*Political party*] (PPE)
SDP........... Sulfonyldiphenol [*Organic chemistry*]
SDP........... Sun Distributors LP Class A [*NYSE symbol*] (SPSG)
SDP........... Suomen Sosialidemokraattinen Puolue [*Finnish Social Democratic Party*] [*Political party*] (EAIO)
SDP........... Supplier Data Package (NASA)
SDP........... Supply Distribution Point
SDP........... Surface Deformation Pattern
SDP........... Survey Data Processing
Sdp........... Suspended in Part [*Regulation or order suspended in part*] [*Legal term*] (DLA)
SDP........... Swaziland Democratic Party
SDP........... System Decision Paper
SDP........... System Design Proposal [*Navy*]
SDP........... Systems Development Package [*or Plan*] [*Military*] (NG)
SdPa........... Parker Public Library, Parker, SD [*Library symbol*] [*Library of Congress*] (LCLS)
SDPA........ Small Defense Plants Administration [*Terminated, 1953*]
SDPC........ Shuttle Data Processing Complex [*NASA*] (MCD)
SDPC........ Social Democratic Party of Canada
SDPC........ Social Democratic Party of Croatia [*Political party*]
SDPD........ Special Defense Projects Department
SDPDA...... Special Defense Property Disposal Account [*DoD*]
SdPEC....... South Dakota Department of Education and Cultural Affairs, Historical Resources Center, Pierre, SD [*Library symbol*] [*Library of Congress*] (LCLS)
SDPF........ Science Data Processing Facility (SSD)
SDPF........ Sensor Data Processing Facility (MCD)
SDPF........ Social-Democratic Party of Finland
SDPFE....... Select Documents of the Principates of the Flavian Emperors [*A publication*]
SDPH........ Social Democratic Party of Hungary [*Political party*] (EAIO)
SdPiO........ Oglala Sioux Community College, Pine Ridge, SD [*Library symbol*] [*Library of Congress*] (LCLS)
SDPJ........ Social Democratic Party of Japan [*Political party*] (EAIO)
SdPl........... Plankinton City Library, Plankinton, SD [*Library symbol*] [*Library of Congress*] (LCLS)
SDPL........ Safeguard Data Processing Laboratory [*Army*] (AABC)
SDPL........ Sensor Data Processing Laboratory (MCD)
SDPL........ Servomechanisms and Data Processing Laboratory [*Massachusetts Institute of Technology*] (MCD)
SDPO........ Site Defense Project Office [*Military*] (AABC)
SDPO........ Space Defense Project Office [*AMC*]
SDPP........ Social Democracy Popularist Party [*Turkey*] [*Political party*]
SDPP........ Succinimidyl Diphenyl Phosphate [*Organic chemistry*]

SDP-PDR.. Social Democratic Party - Party of Democratic Reform [*Croatia*] [*Political party*]
SdPr........... Presho Public Library, Presho, SD [*Library symbol*] [*Library of Congress*] (LCLS)
SDPR........ Sons and Daughters of Pioneer Rivermen (EA)
SDPR........ System Design and Performance Requirements
SDPS........ Signal Data Processing System
SDPS........ Social Democratic Party of Slovenia [*Political party*] (EY)
SDPT........ Structured Doll Play Test [*Psychology*]
SDPU........ Socialist and Democratic People's Union [*Mauritania*] [*Political party*] (EY)
SDQ........... Santo Domingo [*Dominican Republic*] [*Airport symbol*] (OAG)
SDQ........... Self-Description Questionnaire
SDQ........... Student Description Questionnaire
SDQA........ SAFSCOM [*Safeguard System Command*] Document Quality Audit (MCD)
SDQFC...... Sir Douglas Quintet Fan Club (EA)
SDR .... New York State Department Reports [*A publication*] (DLA)
SdR .... Rapid City Public Library, Rapid City, SD [*Library symbol*] [*Library of Congress*] (LCLS)
SDR .... Santander [*Spain*] [*Airport symbol*] (OAG)
SDR .... Schlumberger-Doll Research Center, Ridgefield, CT [*OCLC symbol*] (OCLC)
SDR .... Scientific Data Recorder
SDR .... Search Decision Rule [*Data processing*]
SDR .... Seismic Detection and Ranging
SDR .... Self-Decoding Readout
SDR .... Sender (KSC)
SDR .... Sensor Data Record [*For spacecraft*]
SDR .... Service Difficulty Report (MCD)
SDR .... Sezione Demografia e Razza [*A publication*]
SDR .... Shaft Driver, Right
SDR .... Sheffield District Railway (ROG)
SDR .... Ship Destination Room (NATG)
SDR .... Ship Diversion Room (NATG)
SDR .... Shipment Document Release [*Military*] (AFIT)
SDR .... Signal Data Recorder [*or Reproducer*] (MCD)
SDR .... Signal Distribution Room [*NASA*] (KSC)
SDR .... Significant Deficiency Report [*Nuclear energy*] (IEEE)
SDR .... Simple Detection Response
SDR .... Single-Drift Region (IEEE)
SDR .... Sisters of the Divine Redeemer [*Roman Catholic religious order*]
SDR .... Site Defense RADAR
SDR .... Sloane, Donald R., New York NY [*STAC*]
SDR .... Small Development Requirement [*Military*]
SDR .... SNAP [*Systems for Nuclear Auxiliary Power*] Development Reactor
SDR .... Snyder, TX [*Location identifier*] [*FAA*] (FAAL)
SDR .... Society for Drug Research (EAIO)
SDR .... Sodium Deuterium Reactor
SDR .... Software Design Requirement [*NASA*] (NASA)
SDR .... Software Design Review [*NASA*] (MCD)
SDR .... Solid Ducted Rocket (MCD)
SDR .... Solution Development Record
S & DR...... Somerset & Dorset Joint Railway [*British*] (ROG)
SDR .... SONAR Data Recorder
SDR .... Sophisticated Data Research, Inc. [*Information service or system*] (IID)
SDR .... Sounder (MSA)
SDR .... South Dakota Review [*A publication*]
SDR .... South Devon Railway (ROG)
SDR .... Space Division Regulation [*NASA*] (NASA)
SDR .... Spacelab Disposition Record [*NASA*] (NASA)
SDR .... Special Dispatch Rider
SDR .... Special Drawing Rights [*International Monetary Fund*]
SDR .... Spin Dependent Resonance [*Physics*]
SDR .... Splash Detection RADAR [*Military*]
SDR .... Standard Deviation of the Regression [*Statistics*]
SDR .... State-Dependent Retrieval [*Psychology*]
SDR .... Statistical Data Recorder [*Data processing*] (MDG)
SDR .... Storage Data Register (MCD)
SDR .... Strip Domain Resonance
SDR .... Stroud Resources Ltd. [*Toronto Stock Exchange symbol*]
SDR .... Subcontract Data Requirement
SDR .... Succession Duties Reports [*A publication*] (ILCA)
SDR .... Successive Discrimination Reversal
SDR .... Sueddeutscher Rundfunk [*South German Radio Network*]
SDR .... Survey of Doctorate Recipients [*National Research Council*] [*Database*]
SDR .... System Data Record
SDR .... System for Data Retrieval [*Information retrieval*]
SDR .... System Definition Record [*Data processing*] (IBMDP)
SDR .... System Definition Requirements
SDR .... System Design Report [*NATO*] (NATG)
SDR .... System Design Review [*NASA*] (NASA)
SDR .... System Development Requirement [*Air Force*]
SDR .... System Discrepancy Report
S DRAKE .. Second Dynamic Response and Kinematics Experiment [*Marine science*] (MSC)

SDRB.........	Software Design Review Board [*NASA*] (NASA)
SDRB.........	Supplier Documentation Review Board [*NASA*] (NASA)
SDR & C....	Shipment Document Release and Control [*Military*] (AFIT)
SDRC..........	Structural Dynamics Research Corp. [*NASDAQ symbol*] (NQ)
SDRC Ops ...	South Dakota Board of Railroad Commissioners Opinions [*A publication*] (DLA)
SDRD	Supplier Data Requirements Description (NASA)
SDRD	Supplier Documentation Review Data (NASA)
SDRDDC...	Survey of Drug Research in Immunologic Disease [*A publication*]
SdRe...........	Redfield Carnegie Library, Redfield, SD [*Library symbol*] [*Library of Congress*] (LCLS)
SD Reg.......	South Dakota Register [*A publication*]
SDRL.........	Seller Data Requirements List (MCD)
SDRL.........	Subcontractor Data Requirements List
SDRL.........	Supplier Data Requirements List (NASA)
SDRM	San Diego Railroad Museum (EA)
SdRM	South Dakota School of Mines and Technology, Rapid City, SD [*Library symbol*] [*Library of Congress*] (LCLS)
SdRN	National College of Business, Rapid City, SD [*Library symbol*] [*Library of Congress*] (LCLS)
SDRN	Supplier Data Review Notice (DNAB)
SDRNG	Sound Ranging (MUGU)
SDRP..........	Simulated Data Reduction Program
SDRP.........	Socjaldemokracja Rzeczypospolitej Polskiej [*Social Democracy of the Republic of Poland*] [*Political party*] (EY)
SdRS..........	Saint Martins Academy, Rapid City, SD [*Library symbol*] [*Library of Congress*] (LCLS)
SDRS.........	Signal Data Recording Set (MCD)
SDRS.........	Splash Detection RADAR System (MCD)
SDRSA.......	Shimane Daigaku Ronshu: Shizen Kagaku [*A publication*]
SDRT........	Slot Dipole Ranging Test (OA)
SDRT.........	Spadafore Diagnostic Reading Test [*Educational test*]
SDRT.........	Stanford Diagnostic Reading Test [*Education*]
SDRT.........	Technical Research Sub-Department [*French*] [*Acronym is based on foreign phrase*]
SD Rulings ...	Stamp Duties Rulings [*Australia*] [*A publication*]
SDRW	SONAR Dome Rubber Window (NVT)
S-DRY	Surfaced Dry [*Lumber*]
SDS.............	Safety Data Sheet (KSC)
SDS.............	St. David's Society of the State of New York (EA)
SDS.............	Same Day Surgery [*Medicine*]
SDS.............	Samostalna Demokratska Stranka [*Independent Democratic Party*] [*Former Yugoslavia*] [*Political party*] (PPE)
SDS.............	Sample Display Service [*Department of Commerce*]
SDS.............	Sanatorio Duran [*Costa Rica*] [*Seismograph station code, US Geological Survey*] (SEIS)
SDS.............	Satellite Data System [*Air Force*]
SDS.............	School Dental Service
SDS.............	Scientific Data System [*Later, XDS*]
SDS.............	Secret Delivery Station (SAA)
SDS.............	Self-Directed Search
SDS.............	Self-Rating Depression Scale [*Psychology*]
SDS.............	Senior Direction Station (SAA)
SDS.............	Sensory Deprivation Syndrome [*Medicine*]
SDS.............	Servo Drive System
SDS.............	Sexual Differentiation Scale [*Psychometrics*]
SDS.............	Shared Data Set (OA)
SDS.............	Ship Defense System
SDS.............	Shop Distribution Standards (KSC)
SDS.............	Short Distance Swimmer
SDS.............	Shuttle Dynamic Simulation [*NASA*] (NASA)
SDS.............	Sign-Digit Subtractor
SDS.............	Signal Distribution System
SDS.............	Simulating Digital Systems
SDS.............	Simulation Data Subsystem (KSC)
SDS.............	Sisters of the Divine Saviour [*Roman Catholic religious order*]
SDS.............	Smoke Destruction System
SDS.........	Sodium Dodecyl Sulfate [*Also, SLS*] [*Organic chemistry*]
SDS.............	Software Design Specification [*NASA*] (NASA)
SDS.............	Software Development System
SDS.............	Solar Disk Simulator
SDS.............	Sons and Daughters of the Soddies (EA)
SDS.............	South Dakota State Library Commission, Pierre, SD [*OCLC symbol*] (OCLC)
SDS.............	Sozialistischer Deutscher Studentenbund [*Student political organization*] [*Germany*]
SDS.............	Space Defense System (AAG)
SDS.............	Space Division Switching [*Telecommunications*]
SDS.............	Space Documentation Service [*NASA/ESRO*] (DIT)
SDS.............	Spacecraft Design Specification
SDS.............	Special Distress Signal (DEN)
SDS.............	Special Docking Simulator [*NASA*] (KSC)
SDS.............	Spectrometer Digital System
SDS.............	Splash Detection System
SDS.............	Srpska Demokratska Stranka [*Serb Democratic Party*] [*Political party*]
SDS.............	Standard Depot System [*Army*]
SDS.............	Status Display Support (MCD)
SDS.............	Steam Dump System [*Nuclear energy*] (NRCH)
SDS.............	Steering Damping System [*Aerospace*] (MCD)

SDS............	Stimulator of DNA Synthesis [*Immunochemistry*]
SDS............	Strategic Defense System [*DoD*]
SDS............	Students for a Democratic Society (EA)
SDS............	Submerged Demineralizer System [*Water purification*]
SDS............	Subvent Datenbank Systeme [*Innovationstechnik GmbH & Co.*] [*Hamburg, Federal Republic of Germany*] [*Information service or system*] (IID)
SDS............	Sudden Death Syndrome [*in children*] [*Medicine*]
SDS............	Sudden Drowning Syndrome
SDS............	Supplemental Data Sheet
SDS............	Supplier Data Sheet
SDS............	Supplier Delivery Schedules [*Chrysler Corp.*]
SDS............	Sweet Dough Stabilizer [*Brand of bakery product from H. C. Brill Co., Inc.*]
SDS............	Swimmer Distress Signal [*Navy*] (CAAL)
SDS............	Sydsvenska Dagbladet Snaellposten [*A publication*]
SDS............	Synchronous Data Set (NOAA)
SDS............	System Data Synthesizer (KSC)
SDS............	System Design Specification
SDS............	Systematic Design Language [*Data processing*]
SDSAM.....	Specifically Designated Special Air Mission [*Aircraft*] [*Air Force*]
SDSB	[*The*] Southold Savings Bank [*NASDAQ symbol*] (NQ)
SDSBE	San Diego Symposium for Biomedical Engineering
SDSC.........	San Diego State College [*California*]
SDSC.........	San Diego Supercomputer Center [*California*] [*National Science Foundation*]
Sd-SC........	South Dakota Supreme Court Library, Pierre, SD [*Library symbol*] [*Library of Congress*] (LCLS)
SD Sch Mines Bull ...	South Dakota. School of Mines. Bulletin [*A publication*]
SDSD........	Saco Defense Systems Division [*Maremont Corp.*] (RDA)
SDSD........	Satellite Data Services Division [*National Oceanic and Atmospheric Administration*] [*Information service or system*] (IID)
SDSD........	Single Disk Storage Device [*Data processing*] (BUR)
SDSE	Society of the Descendants of the Schwenkfeldian Exiles (EA)
SD Sess Laws ...	South Dakota Session Laws [*A publication*] (DLA)
SDSH	Society Devoted to the Sacred Heart [*Roman Catholic women's religious order*]
SDSI	Shared Data Set Integrity
SdSi...........	Sisseton Library, Sisseton, SD [*Library symbol*] [*Library of Congress*] (LCLS)
SdSif	Sioux Falls Carnegie Free Public Library, Sioux Falls, SD [*Library symbol*] [*Library of Congress*] (LCLS)
SdSifA	Augustana College, Sioux Falls, SD [*Library symbol*] [*Library of Congress*] (LCLS)
SdSifB.......	North American Baptist Seminary, Sioux Falls, SD [*Library symbol*] [*Library of Congress*] (LCLS)
SdSifC.......	Sioux Falls College, Sioux Falls, SD [*Library symbol*] [*Library of Congress*] (LCLS)
SdSifH	Coolidge High School Library, Sioux Falls, SD [*Library symbol*] [*Library of Congress*] (LCLS)
SdSifV.......	United States Veterans Administration Center, Sioux Falls, SD [*Library symbol*] [*Library of Congress*] (LCLS)
SDSL.........	Sail Dynamics Simulation Laboratory (MCD)
SDSL.........	Subject Directory of Special Libraries and Information Centers [*A publication*]
SDSM........	Socijaldemokratski Savez Makedonije [*Social Democratic Alliance of Macedonia*] [*Political party*] (EY)
SD SMS CLSD ...	Side Seams Closed [*Freight*]
SDSP	Space Defense Systems Program (DNAB)
SdSpe.........	Grace Balloch Memorial Library, Spearfish, SD [*Library symbol*] [*Library of Congress*] (LCLS)
SdSpen.......	Hanson-McCook County Regional Library, Spencer, SD [*Library symbol*] [*Library of Congress*] (LCLS)
SdSpeT	Black Hills State College, Spearfish, SD [*Library symbol*] [*Library of Congress*] (LCLS)
SdSpU........	University of South Dakota at Springfield, Springfield, SD [*Library symbol*] [*Library of Congress*] (LCLS)
SDSRS......	Subcontractor Data Status Reporting System (MCD)
SDS & RU ...	Soil Data Storage and Retrieval Unit [*Department of Agriculture*] (IID)
SDSS	San Diego Shrinkers Society (EA)
SDSS	Satellite Data System Spacecraft [*Air Force*]
SDSS	Satellite Data System Study [*Air Force*] (SSD)
SDSS	Self-Deploying Space Station
SDSS	Single and Double Simultaneous Stimulation [*Neuropsychology test*]
SDSS	Space Division Shuttle Simulator [*NASA*] (NASA)
SDSS	STS [*Space Transportation System*] Data Select Switch (MCD)
SDSSE.......	Science Data System Support Equipment
SDSST.......	Single and Double Simultaneous Stimulation Test [*Neuropsychology test*]
SdSt	Sturgis Public Library, Sturgis, SD [*Library symbol*] [*Library of Congress*] (LCLS)
SD State Geol Surv Spec Rep ...	South Dakota. State Geological Survey. Special Report [*A publication*]
SD St BJ	South Dakota State Bar Journal [*A publication*] (DLA)
SDSU.........	San Diego State University [*California*]
SDSU.........	South Dakota State University [*Brookings, SD*]

SDSVF...... State Dependent State Variable Feedback [*Rocket engine*] [*NASA*]
SDSW........ Sense Device Status Word
SDT .... National College Library, Rapid City, SD [*OCLC symbol*]   (OCLC)
SDT .... Sacrodextra Transversa [*A fetal position*] [*Obstetrics*]
SDT .... Saidu Sharif [*Pakistan*] [*Airport symbol*]   (OAG)
SDT .... Sanderson Tech, Inc. [*Vancouver Stock Exchange symbol*]
SDT .... Saturated Discharge Temperature [*Refrigeration*]
SDT .... Scaling and Display Task   (NASA)
SDT .... Science Data Team
SDT .... Scientific Distribution Technique
SDT .... Sea Depth Transducer
SDT .... Second Destination Transportation   (MCD)
SDT .... Self-Development Test [*Military*]   (INF)
SDT .... Senior Director Technician   (SAA)
SDT .... Serial Data Transmission
SDT .... Serum Dilution Test [*Clinical chemistry*]
SDT .... Shell-Destroying Tracer [*Ammunition*]
SDT .... Shipboard Data Terminal   (MCD)
SDT .... Shock-to-Detonation Transition   (MCD)
SDT .... Shoot Down Test   (SAA)
SDT .... Shuttle Data Tape   (NASA)
SDt.......... Side Tank [*on a ship*]   (DS)
SDt............ Sifre on Deuteronomy [*A publication*]   (BJA)
SDT .... Signal Detection Theory
SDT .... Simplified Drive Train [*Navistar International Corp.*] [*Truck engineering*]
SDT .... Simulated Data Tape
SDT .... Simulated Dynamic Target [*Military*]   (CAAL)
SDT .... Skylab Data Task [*NASA*]
SDT .... Society of Dairy Technology [*British*]
SDT .... Soldier Data Tag
SDT .... Source Distribution Technique
SDT .... Speedy Drill Template   (MCD)
SD & T....... Staff Duties and Training [*British military*]   (DMA)
SDT .... Standard Data Terminal
SDT .... Start-Data-Traffic [*Data processing*]   (IBMDP)
SDT .... Steered Directional Transmission   (MCD)
SDT .... Step-Down Transformer
SDT .... Stromberg Dexterity Test [*Education*]
SDT .... Structural Dynamic Test [*NASA*]   (NASA)
SDT .... Subpoena Duces Tecum [*Legal term*] [*Latin*]   (HGAA)
SDT .... Supplier Data Transmittal   (MCD)
SD/T......... Surface Detector/Tracker [*Navy*]   (CAAL)
SDT .... Surveillance Data Transmission
SDT .... System Dynamic Tester
SDTA........ Scottish Dance Teacher's Alliance [*Glasgow, Scotland*]   (EAIO)
SDTA........ Stewardsman Apprentice, Steward, Striker [*Navy rating*]
SDTA........ Structural Dynamic Test Article [*NASA*]   (NASA)
SD Tex....... United States District Court for the Southern District of Texas   (DLA)
SDTGA...... Staedtetag [*A publication*]
SDTI........ Selective Dissemination of Technical Information [*Data processing*]
SDTI......... Student Developmental Task Inventory [*Educational test*]
SDTIM...... Society for the Development of Techniques in Industrial Marketing [*British*]
SDTK........ Supported Drift Tube Klystron
SDTN .... Space and Data Tracking Network   (SSD)
SDTN .... Stewardsman, Steward, Striker [*Navy rating*]
SDTP........ Startover Data Transfer and Processing [*Program*]
SDTP PROGRM ... Startover Data Transfer and Processing Program
SDTR......... Serial Data Transmitter/Receiver [*Telecommunications*]   (TEL)
SDTS......... Satellite Data Transmission System   (DIT)
SDTT......... Silicon Diode Target Tube
SDU.......... Huron College, Huron, SD [*OCLC symbol*]   (OCLC)
SDU.......... Memphis, TN [*Location identifier*] [*FAA*]   (FAAL)
SDU.......... Rio De Janeiro-Dumont [*Brazil*] [*Airport symbol*]   (OAG)
SDU.......... Self-Destruct Unit
SDU.......... Shelter Decontamination Unit
SDU.......... Signal Distribution Unit   (AAG)
SDU.......... Source Data Utility
sdu............ South Dakota [*MARC country of publication code*] [*Library of Congress*]   (LCCP)
SDU.......... Soziale Demokratische Union [*Social Democratic Union*] [*Germany*] [*Political party*]   (PPW)
SDU.......... Spectrum Display Unit
SDU.......... Stand-Alone Diplay Unit
SDU.......... Standard Deviation Unit [*Statistics*]   (MAE)
SDU.......... Station Display Unit
SDU.......... Students for a Democratic University [*Canada*]
SDU.......... Subcarrier Delay Unit
SDU.......... Surface Drone Unit [*Navy*]   (CAAL)
SdU........... University of South Dakota, Vermillion, SD [*Library symbol*] [*Library of Congress*]   (LCLS)
SDUK .... Society for the Diffusion of Useful Knowledge
SdU-L........ University of South Dakota, Law Library, Vermillion, SD [*Library symbol*] [*Library of Congress*]   (LCLS)

SdU-M....... University of South Dakota, Medical School, Vermillion, SD [*Library symbol*] [*Library of Congress*]   (LCLS)
SDUN....... Standun, Inc. [*NASDAQ symbol*]   (NQ)
SDU-NDP ... Slovenian Democratic Union - National Democratic Party [*Political party*]   (EY)
SD Uniform Prob Code ... South Dakota Uniform Probate Code [*A publication*]   (DLA)
SDUSA...... Social Democrats, USA   (EA)
SDV .... Santo Domingo [*Venezuela*] [*Seismograph station code, US Geological Survey*]   (SEIS)
SDV .... Satsuma Dwarf Virus [*Plant pathology*]
SDV .... Scram Discharge Volume [*Nuclear energy*]   (NRCH)
SDV .... Shuttle Derived Vehicle   (MCD)
SDV .... Slowed-Down Video [*RADAR*]
SDV .... Society of Divine Vocations [*Vocationist Fathers*] [*Roman Catholic religious order*]
SDV .... Solar Daily Variation
SDV .... Soybean Dwarf Virus [*Plant pathology*]
SDV .... Spark Delay Valve [*Automotive engineering*]
SDV .... Specific Desensitizing Vaccine [*Medicine*]   (ADA)
S Dv .... Sprache und Datenverarbeitung [*A publication*]
SDV .... Swimmer Delivery Vehicle [*Navy symbol*] [*Obsolete*]   (MCD)
SDV .... Tel Aviv/Yafo [*Israel*] [*Airport symbol*]   (OAG)
SdV .... Vermillion Public Library, Vermillion, SD [*Library symbol*] [*Library of Congress*]   (LCLS)
S-DVB....... Styrene-Divinylbenzene [*Organic chemistry*]
SDVF........ Software Development and Verification Facilities [*NASA*]   (NASA)
SDVI........ Service Disabled Veterans Insurance
SDW .... Dakota Wesleyan University, Layne Library, Mitchell, SD [*OCLC symbol*]   (OCLC)
SDW .... S. D. Warren [*Paper manufacturer*]
SDW .... Segment Descriptor Word
SDW .... Side Wheel   (DS)
SDW .... Six-Day War [*Arab-Israeli War, 1967*]   (BJA)
SDW .... Southdown, Inc. [*NYSE symbol*]   (SPSG)
SDW .... Spin-Density Wave [*Physics*]
SDW .... Standing Detonation Wave
SDW .... Sterile Distilled Water
SDW .... Swept Delta Wing
SdW .... Watertown Regional Library, Watertown, SD [*Library symbol*] [*Library of Congress*]   (LCLS)
SDWA ...... Safe Drinking Water Act [*1974*]
SdWa .... Wagner Public Library, Wagner, SD [*Library symbol*] [*Library of Congress*]   (LCLS)
SD Water Resour Comm Rep Invest ... South Dakota. Water Resources Commission. Report of Investigations [*A publication*]
SdWau .... Waubay Public Library, Waubay, SD [*Library symbol*] [*Library of Congress*]   (LCLS)
SdWe .... Webster Public Library, Webster, SD [*Library symbol*] [*Library of Congress*]   (LCLS)
SdWes........ Wessington Springs Carnegie Public Library, Wessington Springs, SD [*Library symbol*] [*Library of Congress*]   (LCLS)
SdWinT ..... Tripp County Library, Winner, SD [*Library symbol*] [*Library of Congress*]   (LCLS)
SDWRF..... Stochastic Dominance with Respect to Function [*Statistics*]
SD W Va.... United States District Court for the Southern District of West Virginia   (DLA)
SDX .... Satellite Data Exchange
SDX .... Sedona [*Arizona*] [*Airport symbol*]   (OAG)
S + DX...... Speech with Duplex Telegraph
SDXKDT... Shanxi University Journal. Natural Science Edition [*A publication*]
SDY .... Mount Marty College, Yankton, SD [*OCLC symbol*]   (OCLC)
SDY .... Sandy Corp. [*AMEX symbol*]   (SPSG)
SDY .... Sidney [*Montana*] [*Airport symbol*]   (OAG)
SDY .... Sidney, MT [*Location identifier*] [*FAA*]   (FAAL)
SdY .... Yankton Community Library, Yankton, SD [*Library symbol*] [*Library of Congress*]   (LCLS)
SdYC......... Yankton College, Yankton, SD [*Library symbol*] [*Library of Congress*]   (LCLS)
SdYM .... Mount Marty College, Yankton, SD [*Library symbol*] [*Library of Congress*]   (LCLS)
SDYN .... Staodyn, Inc. [*NASDAQ symbol*]   (NQ)
SDZ .... Southern Pines, NC [*Location identifier*] [*FAA*]   (FAAL)
SDZ .... Stardust Ventures [*Vancouver Stock Exchange symbol*]
SDZ .... Stimmen der Zeit   (BJA)
SDZ .... Surface Danger Zone [*Military*]   (INF)
SE .... British Charter [*British*] [*ICAO designator*]   (ICDA)
SE .... Ferrocarriles Unidos del Sureste, SA de CV [*AAR code*]
SE .... Sacris Eruditi. Jaarboek voor Godsdienstwetenschappen [*A publication*]
SE .... Safety Equipment [*British military*]   (DMA)
SE .... Safety Evaluation   (NRCH)
S & E......... Salaries and Expenses
SE .... Sales Engineer
SE .... Saline Enema [*Medicine*]
SE .... Sanford & Eastern Railroad [*AAR code*] [*Terminated*]
SE .... Sanitary Engineer [*Academic degree*]
SE .... Santos Dumont Experimental [*British military*]   (DMA)

SE	Saorstat Eireann [*Irish Free State*]
SE	Saponification Equivalent [*Analytical chemistry*]
SE	Schleicher-Bruns [*Germany*] [*ICAO aircraft manufacturer identifier*] (ICAO)
SE	School of Engineering (MCD)
SE	Sciences Ecclesiastiques [*A publication*]
S & E	Scientific and Engineering
S & E	Scientists and Engineers (RDA)
SE	Scouting Experimental [*British*] (DMA)
SE	Sea [*Maps and charts*]
SE	Second Entrance [*Theatrical slang*]
SE	Secondary Electron (MCD)
SE	Secretarial, Word Processing, and/or Medical Office Assistant Programs [*Association of Independent Colleges and Schools specialization code*]
SE	Securities Transaction [*Banking*]
SE	Seeing Eye [*An association*] (EA)
SE	Selenium [*Chemical element*]
SE	Seleucid Era (BJA)
SE	Self Employment [*Social Security Administration*] (OICC)
SE	Self-Evident Statement [*Used in correcting manuscripts, etc.*]
Se	Semeia [*A publication*]
Se	Semiotica [*A publication*]
SE	Senegal [*IYRU nationality code*] (IYR)
SE	Senior Editor [*Publishing*]
S & E	Sensor and Effector (SSD)
SE	September (ADA)
SE	Sequence of Events
SE	Series
SE	Series Statement [*Online database field identifier*]
SE	Service Engineer
SE	Service Equipment (AAG)
S & E	Services and Equipment
SE	Set
se	Seychelles [*bi (British Indian Ocean Territory) used in records cataloged before January 1978*] [*MARC country of publication code*] [*Library of Congress*] (LCCP)
SE	Shareholders' Equity [*Business term*]
SE	Shelter Equipment
SE	Sherritt Gordon Mines Ltd. [*Toronto Stock Exchange symbol*]
SE	Shielding Effectiveness (IEEE)
SE	Shift Engineer (NRCH)
SE	Shoot Emergence [*Botany*]
SE	Side Effect [*Medicine*]
SE	Signal Excess (NVT)
SE	Single End
SE	Single-Ended, Cylindrical Boiler [*Navy*]
SE	Single Engine
SE	Single Entry [*Bookkeeping*]
S-E	Skandinaviska Enskilda Banken [*Scandinavian Private Bank*] [*Sweden*]
SE	Slip End (OA)
SE	Slovenski Etnograf [*A publication*]
SE	Small End (OA)
SE	Smoke Extract
SE	Social Education [*A publication*]
SE	Social Emotional
SE	Society of Engineers
SE	Society of Ethnobiology (EA)
SE	Socioeconomic
SE	Software Engineering (MCD)
SE	Soil Extract
SE	Solanaceae Enthusiasts (EA)
SE	Solar Ecliptic
SE	Solar Explorer [*NASA*]
SE	Solid Extract [*Pharmacy*]
SE	Solidaridad Espanola [*Spanish Solidarity*] [*Political party*] (PPW)
SE	Sonic Extract [*Cytology*]
SE	Southeast
SE	Southeastern Reporter [*National Reporter System*] [*A publication*] (DLA)
SE	Southern Europe (NATG)
SE	Sovetskaja Estonija [*A publication*]
SE	Sovetskaja Etnografija [*A publication*]
SE	Space Exploration (AAG)
SE	Spatial Emotional (Stimuli)
SE	Special Edition [*Car model designation*]
SE	Special Equipment
SE	Specialized Exhibition (IMH)
SE	Spectral Edge [*Cardiology*]
SE	Sphenoethmoidal [*Suture*] [*Medicine*]
SE	Spherical Equivalent
SE	Spherical Eyeball [*Aviation*] (OA)
SE	Spin-Echo Scan [*Roentgenology*]
SE	Split End [*Football*]
SE	Stable Element
SE	Staff Engineer [*Navy*] [*British*] (ROG)
SE	Stage of Exhaustion [*of gas*] [*Medicine*]
SE	Stamped Envelope
SE	Standard English
SE	Standard Error
S/E	Standardization/Evaluation (AFM)
SE	Starch Equivalent
S-E	Starr-Edwards [*Prosthesis*] (AAMN)
SE	Starter Electrode
SE	Stationary Eddy
SE	Status Enquiry [*British*]
SE	Status Epilepticus [*Medicine*]
SE	Steam Emulsion
SE	Stock Exchange
SE	Storage Element (MCD)
SE	Straight Edge [*Philately*]
SE	Studies in English [*A publication*]
SE	Subcontract Engineers (MCD)
SE	Subcritical Experiment [*Nuclear energy*]
se	Sugary Enhancer [*A gene in sweet corn*]
SE	Summer Emergency [*Vessel load line mark*]
SE	Sun Electric Corp. [*NYSE symbol*] (SPSG)
SE	Sunday Express [*United Kingdom*] [*A publication*]
SE	Superintending Engineer (ADA)
S & E	Supplies and Equipage [*Military*] (CINC)
SE	Support Equipment (AFM)
S & E	Surveillance and Entry
SE	Sustainer Engine (AAG)
SE	Sustaining Engineering
SE	Sweden [*Aircraft nationality and registration mark*] (FAAC)
SE	Sweden [*ANSI two-letter standard code*] (CNC)
SE	System Effectiveness [*Army*] (AABC)
SE	System Element (NASA)
SE	System Expansion [*In "Macintosh SE"*] [*Apple Computer, Inc.*]
SE	Systems Engineer [*or Engineering*] [*Data processing*]
S1E	Surfaced One Edge [*Technical drawings*]
SE2	Scientists and Engineers for Secure Energy (EA)
SEA	Clemson University, Clemson, SC [*OCLC symbol*] (OCLC)
SEA	Marine Manufacturers Safety Equipment Association (EA)
SEA	Safety Engineering Analysis (AFM)
SEA	Sailing Education Association
Sea	Sankt Eriks Arsbok [*A publication*]
SEA	Scandinavian Endodontic Association [*Sweden*] (EAIO)
SEA	Scanning Electrostatic Analysis (NASA)
SEA	Science and Education Administration [*Department of Agriculture*]
SEA	Scientific Exchange Agreement
SEA	Sea Echelon Area [*Navy*] (NVT)
SEA	Sea Education Association (EA)
SEA	Seaboard World Airlines, Inc. (MCD)
SEA	Seashore Environmental Alliance
SEA	Seasonal Employees in Agriculture
SEA	Seattle [*Washington*] [*Seismograph station code, US Geological Survey*] [*Closed*] (SEIS)
SEA	Seattle/Tacoma [*Washington*] [*Airport symbol*] (OAG)
SEA	Securities Exchange Act [*1934*]
SEA	Selective Early Annuity [*Army*]
SEA	Senior Enlisted Academy [*Navy*]
SEA	Senior Enlisted Advisor [*Navy*]
SEA	Senior Executives Association (EA)
SEA	Service Educational Activities [*Military*] (AABC)
SEA	Service Employers Association (EA)
SEA	Sheep Erythrocyte Agglutination [*Test*]
SEA	Ship/Equipment/Alterations [*Navy*] (NG)
SEA	Ships Editorial Association [*Navy*]
SEA	Silicon Elastimeter Ablator (NASA)
SEA	Sindicato de Escritores y Artistas [*Ecuador*]
SEA	Single European Act [*EEC*]
SEA	Socialist Educational Association [*British*]
SEA	Societe d'Electronique et d'Automatique [*Became part of Compagnie Internationale d'Informatique*]
SEA	Society for Education through Art [*British*]
SEA	Society for the Elimination of Acronyms
SEA	Society of Evangelical Agnostics (EA)
SEA	Sociology of Education Association (EA)
SEA	SONAR Evaluation and Assistance [*Teams*]
SEA	Sound Effects Amplifier (IIA)
SEA	Southeast Air, Inc. [*New Bedford, MA*] [*FAA designator*] (FAAC)
SEA	Southeast Asia
SEA	Southern Economic Association (EA)
SEA	SPALT [*Special Projects Alterations*] Evaluation Area
SEA	Special Equipment Authorization (AAG)
SEA	Specific Energy Absorption
SEA	Spherical Electrostatic Analyzer
SEA	Spontaneous Electrical Activity [*Physiology*] (AAMN)
SEA	Standard Electronic Assembly
SEA	Staphylococcal Enterotoxin A [*Medicine*]
SEA	State Economic Area [*Bureau of Economic Analysis*] [*Department of Commerce*]
SEA	State Education Agency [*Department of Education*]
SEA	State Enforcement Agreement [*Environmental Protection Agency*] (GFGA)
SEA	State-EPA [*Environmental Protection Agency*] Agreements (EG)

SEA............ Static Error Analysis
SEA............ Statistical Energy Analysis [*or Approach*] [*Vibration analysis*]
SEA............ Students for Ecological Action
SEA............ Studies in Economic Analysis [*A publication*]
SEA............ Studies in Educational Administration [*A publication*] (APTA)
SEAG............ Studies in English and American [*A publication*]
SEA............ Styrene and Ethylbenzene Association (EA)
SEA............ Subterranean Exploration Agency
SEA............ Sudden Enhancement of Atmospherics [*NASA*]
SEA............ Sulphur Extended Asphalt [*Paving material*]
SEA............ Survival Education Association (EA)
SEA............ Susquehanna Environmental Advocates (NRCH)
SEA............ Svensk Exegetisk Arsbok [*A publication*]
SEA............ System Engineering Analysis
SEA............ System Error Analysis
SEA............ Systems Effectiveness Analyzer (IEEE)
SEAAC...... Southeast Asian Art and Culture [*Foundation*]
SEAADSA ... Sea Automated Data Systems Activity [*Navy*]
SEA/B....... Sea Energy Absorber/Bumper Barge (SAA)
SEAB......... Seaboard Savings & Loan Association [*Virginia Beach, VA*] [*NASDAQ symbol*] (NQ)
SEABASS ... Ships Emergency Automatic Buoyancy and Stability System [*Seabass Ltd.*]
SEABEE.... Construction Battalion [*CB*] [*Acronym is a phonetic reference to a member of this Naval unit*]
SEABT...... SEABEE Team [*Navy*] (NVT)
SEABU...... Southeast Asia Buildup (CINC)
Seab Vend ... Seaborne on Vendors and Purchasers [*9th ed.*] [*1926*] [*A publication*] (DLA)
Seabys Coin Bull ... Seaby's Coin and Medal Bulletin [*A publication*]
SeaC........... Sea Containers Ltd. [*Associated Press abbreviation*] (APAG)
SEAC........ Seacoast
SEAC........ Social and Economic Archive Centre [*British*]
SEAC........ Society for Economic, Social, Cultural Study and Expansion in Central Africa
SEAC........ Society for Electroanalytical Chemistry
SEAC........ Southeast Archeological Center [*US Department of the Interior*] [*Research center*] (RCD)
SEAC........ Southeast Asia Center (EA)
SEAC........ Southeast Asia Command
SEAC........ Specialized Employability Assistance to Claimants (OICC)
SEAC........ Standards Eastern [*or Electronic*] Automatic Computer [*National Institute of Standards and Technology*]
SEAC........ Submarine Exercise Area Coordinator [*Navy*] (NVT)
SEACAD... Sea Cadet Cruise [*Navy*] (NVT)
SEACALMIS ... Sea Systems Calibration Management Information System (DNAB)
SEACDT ... Southeast Asia Collective Defense Treaty (AABC)
SEACF....... Support Equipment Assembly and Checkout Facility [*NASA*] (NASA)
SEACO...... Senior Enlisted Advisor, Communications/Operations [*Navy*] (DNAB)
SEACOM ... Southeast Asia Commonwealth
SEACOM ... Southeast Asia Communications (MCD)
SEACON... Seafloor Construction Experiment [*Navy*]
SeaCont...... Sea Containers Ltd. [*Associated Press abbreviation*] (APAG)
SEACOORD ... Southeast Asia Coordination Council [*Military*]
SEACOP ... Strategic Sealift Contingency Planning System [*Army*] (AABC)
SEACORE ... Southeast Asia Communications Research (MCD)
SEACS...... Search of Enemy Air Defense (MCD)
SEACS....... Ship Equipment Accounting System (MCD)
SeaCt .... Sea Containers Ltd. [*Associated Press abbreviation*] (APAG)
SE/ACT..... Southern Europe - ACTISUD [*Authority for the Coordination of Inland Transport in Southern Europe*] [*NATO*] (NATG)
SEAD......... Scottish Education and Action for Development (EAIO)
SEAD......... Seneca Army Depot [*New York*] (AABC)
SEAD........ Suppression of Enemy Air Defenses (AABC)
SEAD........ Survivable Electronic Air Defense
SEADAB... Southeast Asia DataBase (MCD)
SEADAC... Seakeeping Data Analysis Center [*Navy*]
SEADAG... Southeast Asia Development Advisory Group [*Department of State*]
SEADCUG ... NAVSEA Data Communications Users Group [*Navy*]
SEADD...... South-East Asia Development Division [*Overseas Development Administration*] [*British*] (DS)
SEADEX ... Seaward Defense Exercise [*NATO*] (NATG)
SEADROP ... Small Expendable Air-Dropped Remote Ocean Platform [*Marine science*] (MSC)
SEADS ...... Shuttle Entry Air Data Sensor [*NASA*] (MCD)
SEADS ...... Shuttle Entry Air Data System [*or Subsystem*] (NASA)
SEADS ...... Survivable and Effective Airbreathing Defense [*Study*] (MCD)
SEADU...... Sea Duty
SEA-EX..... Sealift Express [*Military*]
SEAF......... Seafoods from Alaska, Inc. [*NASDAQ symbol*] (NQ)
SEAFAC.... System Engineering Analysis Facility (MCD)
SEAFAR.... Search and Automatic Track Fixed Array RADAR
SEAFDC.... South East Asian Fisheries Development Centre (EAIO)
SEAFDEC ... South East Asian Fisheries Development Centre
Sea Fish Res Stn (Haifa) Bull ... Sea Fisheries Research Station (Haifa). Bulletin [*A publication*]

Seafood Bus ... Seafood Business [*A publication*]
Seafood Export J ... Seafood Export Journal [*A publication*]
Seafood Merch ... Seafood Merchandising [*A publication*]
SEAFRON ... Sea Frontier
Sea Front ... Sea Frontiers [*A publication*]
SEAG......... Sea Galley Stores, Inc. [*NASDAQ symbol*] (NQ)
SEAgel....... Safe Emulsion Agar Gel [*Organic chemistry*]
Seag Parl Reg ... Seager on Parliamentary Registration [*A publication*] (DLA)
Sea Grant Coll Tech Rep Univ Wis ... Sea Grant College Technical Report. University of Wisconsin [*A publication*]
Sea Grant LJ ... Sea Grant Law Journal [*A publication*] (DLA)
Sea Grant L & Pol'y J ... Sea Grant Law and Policy Journal [*A publication*] (DLA)
Sea Grant Pub Ind ... Sea Grant Publications Index [*A publication*]
Seagrm....... [*The*] Seagram Co. Ltd. [*Associated Press abbreviation*] (APAG)
SEAGS ...... Southeast Asian Geotechnical Society (EAIO)
Seagul .... Seagull Energy Corp. [*Associated Press abbreviation*] (APAG)
SEAIC .... Southeast Asia Information Center (NG)
SEAID .... Support Equipment Abbreviated Items Description [*NASA*] (NASA)
SEAIG .... Southeast Asia Information Group (AFM)
SEAIMP..... Solar Eclipse Atmospheric and Ionospheric Measurements Project (IEEE)
SEAISI...... South East Asia Iron and Steel Institute (EA)
SEAITACS ... Southeast Asia Integrated Tactical Air Control System (CINC)
SEAJS....... Southeast Asian Journal of Sociology [*Singapore*] [*A publication*]
SEAJT....... South East Asia Journal of Theology [*A publication*]
SEAK........ Seahawk Oil International, Inc. [*NASDAQ symbol*] (NQ)
SEAL......... Los Alamos [*Ecuador*] [*ICAO location identifier*] (ICLI)
SEAL......... Sea, Air, and Land
SEAL......... Sea, Air, and Land Team [*Refers to Navy personnel trained in unconventional warfare*]
SEAL........ Seal Fleet, Inc. [*NASDAQ symbol*] (NQ)
SEAL........ Ship's Electronics Allowance List [*Navy*]
SEAL........ Signal Evaluation Airborne Laboratory [*FAA*]
SEAL......... Solar Energy Applications Laboratory [*Colorado State University*] [*Research center*] (RCD)
SEAL......... Standard Electronic Accounting Language [*Data processing*] (BUR)
SEAL........ Subsea Equipment Associates Ltd. [*Bermuda*]
SEALAB.... Sea Laboratory
SealAr....... Sealed Air Corp. [*Associated Press abbreviation*] (APAG)
SEALF....... Semiempirical Absorption Loss Formula [*Radio*]
SEALF...... Southeast Asia Land Forces [*British*]
SEALITE .. Systematic Evaluation and Analysis of a LASER in a Test Environment (MCD)
SEALLINC ... Southeast Louisiana Library Network Cooperative [*Library network*]
SEALOB ... Sealift Obligation Report [*Army*]
SEALOCK ... Search, Locate, Communications, or Kill (MCD)
SEALR ...... Southeast Asia Logistic Requirement (AFM)
SEALS...... Severe Environmental Air Launch Study (KSC)
SEALS....... Stored Energy Actuated Lift System
SEAM....... Ambato [*Ecuador*] [*ICAO location identifier*] (ICLI)
SEAM....... Scanning Electro-Acoustic Microscopy (MCD)
SEAM....... Seaman Furniture Co., Inc. [*Uniondale, NY*] [*NASDAQ symbol*] (NQ)
SEAM....... Sidewinder Expanded Acquisition Mode (MCD)
SEAM....... Society for the Emancipation of the American Male
SEAM....... Sociology and Economic Aspects of Medicine [*American Medical Association*] [*Information service or system*] (CRD)
SEAM....... Software Engineering and Management
SEAM....... Software Enhancement and Maintenance [*Contract*]
SEAM....... Southeast Asia Microfilm Project [*Library network*]
SEAM....... Subset Extraction and Association Measurement
SEAM....... Surface Environment and Mining Program
SEAMAP .. Systematic Exploration and Mapping Program [*National Oceanic and Atmospheric Administration*] (MSC)
SeaMARCI ... Sea Mapping and Remote Characterization I [*Oceanography*]
SEAMARF ... Southeast Asia Military Air Reservation Facility (CINC)
Seamens J ... Seamen's Journal [*A publication*] (APTA)
SEAMEX .. Seamanship Exercise (NVT)
SEAMIC ... Southeast Asia Management Information Center [*Navy*]
SEAMINFO ... Surface Mining and Environment Information System [*University of Arizona*] (IID)
SEAMIST ... Seavan Management Information System
SEAMO...... Southeast Asian Ministers of Education Organization
SEAMOD ... Sea Systems Modification and Modernization by Modularity [*Program*] (DNAB)
SEAMORE ... Southeast Asia Mohawk Revision Program [*Army aviation*]
SEAMS ...... Southeast Asian Mathematical Society [*Singapore, Singapore*]
SEAMS ..... Special Electronics Air Mobility System [*Army*]
SEAMS ..... Support Equipment Asset Management Subsystem (MCD)
SEAMS ..... System Effectiveness Assurance Management System (MCD)
SEAMUS... Society for Electro-Acoustic Music in the United States (EA)
SEAN........ Ana Maria [*Ecuador*] [*ICAO location identifier*] (ICLI)
SEAN........ Scientific Event Alert Network [*Smithsonian Institution*] [*Washington, DC*] (MCD)

SEAN........ Senior Enlisted Advisor, Navy (DNAB)
SEAN........ Strapdown Electrically Suspended Gyro Aerospace Navigation [*System*]
SEAN........ Syndicat des Enseignants Africains du Niger [*African Union of Teachers of Niger*]
Seanad Deb ... Seanad Debates [*Ireland*] [*A publication*]
SEAN Bull ... SEAN [*Scientific Event Alert Network*] Bulletin [*Washington, DC*] [*A publication*]
SEANC...... Southeast Asia NOTAM [*Notice to Airmen*] Center [*Military*]
Seance Pub Ann Acad Pharm ... Seance Publique Annuelle. Academie de Pharmacie [*A publication*]
SEANITEOPS ... Southeast Asia Night Operations [*Army*]
Sean O Cas ... Sean O'Casey Review [*A publication*]
SEAOC...... Structural Engineers Association of California (EA)
SEAOPSS ... Southeast Asia Operational Sensor System (MCD)
SEAOR...... Southeast Asia Operational Requirements (MCD)
SEAP........ Arapicos [*Ecuador*] [*ICAO location identifier*] (ICLI)
SEAP........ SEATO [*Southeast Asia Treaty Organization*] Administrative Publication
SEAP........ Southeast Asia Program [*Cornell University*] [*Research center*] (RCD)
SEAP........ Special Economic Acquisition Provision [*Procurement*]
SEAPA...... Society of Petroleum Engineers. American Institute of Mining, Metallurgical, and Petroleum Engineers. Papers [*A publication*]
SEAPA...... Spectrothermal Emission Aerosol Particle Analyzer
SEAPAC.... Sea Activated Parachute Automatic Crew Release (MCD)
SEAPADS ... Sea Planning Automated Data System
SEAPEX.... Southeast Asia Petroleum Exploration Society
SEAPG...... Support Equipment Acquisition Planning Group [*NASA*] (NASA)
SEAPRO ... Southeast Asia Programs Directorate
SEAPT ...... Seaport
Sea Pwr A .. Almanac of Seapower [*A publication*]
SeAQ........ Southeast Asia Quarterly [*A publication*]
SEAQ........ Stock Exchange Automated Quotation System [*British*]
SEAR........ Arajuno [*Ecuador*] [*ICAO location identifier*] (ICLI)
SEAR........ Safeguard Emergency Action Report [*Army*] (AABC)
SEAR........ Safety Evaluation Audit Report [*Nuclear energy*] (NRCH)
SEAR........ Summary Engineering Assessment Report (MCD)
SEAR........ System Engineering Analysis Report
SEAR........ Systematic Effort to Analyze Results
SEARA...... Stockpile Evaluation and Reliability Assessment Program
SEARAM .. Semiactive RADAR Missile
Seara Med ... Seara Medica [*A publication*]
Seara Med Neurocir ... Seara Medica Neurocirurgica [*A publication*]
SEA RARE ... Sea Reinforcement and Resupply of Europe (MCD)
SEARC...... Southeast Asia Regional Council
SEARCA ... SEAMEO [*Southeast Asia Ministers of Education Organization*] Regional Center for Graduate Study and Research in Agriculture [*Research center*] [*Philippines*] (IRC)
SEARCC ... Southeast Asia Regional Computer Confederation (EA)
SEARCH... Science, Engineering, and Related Career Hints [*A publication*] [*Scientific Manpower Commission*]
SEARCH... Scientific Evaluation and Research of Charismatic Healing [*An association*] (EA)
SearcH....... Siberian Husky Eye Anomaly Research Committee (EA)
SEARCH... System for Electronic Analysis and Retrieval of Criminal Histories [*Project succeeded by National Crime Information Center*] [*Department of Justice*]
SEARCH... System Evaluation and Reliability Checker
SEARCH... System for Exploring Alternative Resource Commitments in Higher Education [*Data processing*]
Search Agric Ent (Ithaca NY) ... Search Agriculture. Entomology (Ithaca, New York) [*A publication*]
Search Agric (Geneva NY) ... Search Agriculture (Geneva, New York) [*A publication*]
Search Agric NY State Agric Exp Stn (Ithaca) ... Search Agriculture. New York State Agricultural Experiment Station (Ithaca) [*A publication*]
SEARCHEX ... Sea/Air Search Exercise [*NATO*] (NATG)
SEARCHS ... Shuttle Engineering Approach/Rollout Control Hybrid Simulation (NASA)
Search & Seizure Bull ... Search and Seizure Bulletin [*A publication*] (DLA)
Search and Seizure L Rep ... Search and Seizure Law Report [*A publication*]
Search Together ... Searching Together [*A publication*]
SEAREQ ... Sea Requirement [*Canadian Navy*]
SEAREX.... Sea/Air Chemical Exchange [*Marine science*] (MSC)
Searle........ Searle's Supreme Court Reports [*1850-67*] [*Cape Colony*] [*A publication*] (DLA)
Searle Dig .. Searle's Minnesota Digest [*A publication*] (DLA)
Searle & Sm ... Searle and Smith's English Probate and Divorce Reports [*1859-60*] [*A publication*] (DLA)
Searle Sm... Searle and Smith's English Probate and Divorce Reports [*A publication*] (DLA)
SEARNG... South East Asian Region Network for Geosciences [*International Council of Scientific Unions*]
Sears .... Sears, Roebuck & Co. [*Associated Press abbreviation*] (APAG)
Sears Found Marine Research Mem ... Sears Foundation for Marine Research. Memoir [*A publication*]
SEAS .... Ascazubi [*Ecuador*] [*ICAO location identifier*] (ICLI)

SEAS .... Centre of South-East Asian Studies [*University of Hull*] [*British*] (CB)
SEAS .... Science Accessories Corp. [*NASDAQ symbol*] (NQ)
SEAS .... Sea School [*Marine Corps*]
SEAS .... Seasons. Federation of Ontario Naturalists [*A publication*]
SEAS .... Selected Effects Armament Subsystem [*Army*] (RDA)
SEAS .... Share European Association (HGAA)
SEAS .... Ship/Equipment/Alterations Summary [*Navy*] (NG)
SEAS .... Shipboard Environmental Data Acquisition System [*National Oceanic and Atmospheric Administration*] (MSC)
SEAS .... Shoreline Erosion Advisory Service [*Bureau of Flood Protection*]
SEAS .... Strategic Environmental Assessment System [*Environmental Protection Agency*]
SEAS .... Support Equipment Avionics System
SEAS .... Surveillance Environmental Acoustic Support [*Military*] (CAAL)
SEAS .... Surveillance Environmental Acoustic Support Project [*Naval Ocean Research and Development Activity*] [*Mississippi*]
SEAS .... System Enhancement and Support [*Military*] (CAAL)
Se As Aff... Southeast Asian Affairs [*Singapore*] [*A publication*]
SEASAME ... Southeast Asian Science and Mathematics Experiment [*RECSAM*]
SEASAR... Sea Synthetic Aperture RADAR
SEASAT.... Sea Satellite [*NASA*]
SEASC...... Scientific Exploration of the Atlantic Shelf Committee
Se As Chron ... Southeast Asia Chronicle [*A publication*]
SEASCO ... Southeast Asia Science Cooperation Office
SEASET.... Separate Effects and Systems Effects Tests [*Nuclear energy*] (NRCH)
SEASIA..... Southeast Asia (NG)
SE Asia ..... Southeast Asia Chronicle [*A publication*]
SE Asia J Th ... Southeast Asia Journal of Theology [*A publication*]
Se As Iron Steel Inst Q ... Southeast Asia Iron and Steel Institute Quarterly [*Singapore*] [*A publication*]
Se As J Soc Sci ... Southeast Asian Journal of Social Science [*Singapore*] [*A publication*]
Se As J Theo ... South East Asia Journal of Theology [*Singapore*] [*A publication*]
Sea & Sm ... Searle and Smith's English Probate and Divorce Reports [*A publication*] (DLA)
S E As R..... South East Asian Review [*India*] [*A publication*]
S E As Stud ... South East Asian Studies [*Kyoto*] [*A publication*]
SEASTAG ... Southeast Asia Treaty Organization Standardization Agreement
SEAT........ Atacames [*Ecuador*] [*ICAO location identifier*] (ICLI)
SEAT........ Sociedad Espanol de Automoviles de Turismo [*Spanish automobile manufacturer; acronym used as name of its cars*]
SEAT........ Standardization and Evaluation Assistance Team [*Military*]
SEAT........ Stock Exchange Automated Trading
SEATA ...... Sea Technology [*A publication*]
SEATAC.... Southeast Asian Agency for Regional Transport and Communications Development (EAIO)
SEATAF.... Southern European Atomic Task Force [*Military*]
SEATAR ... Search and Automatic Track Array RADAR
SEATAR ... Studies on East Asia Tectonics and Resources [*Marine science*] (MSC)
SEATEC.... Sea Test and Evaluation Capability [*Navy*] (CAAL)
Sea Technol ... Sea Technology [*A publication*]
SEATELCOM ... Southeast Asia Telecommunications System [*Military*] (AABC)
Seat F Ch ... Seaton's Forms in Chancery [*A publication*] (DLA)
SEATIC..... Southeast Asia Translation and Interrogation Center [*Navy*]
SEATICC.. Southeast Asia Tactical Information Communications Center (DNAB)
SEATO Med Res Monogr ... Southeast Asia Treaty Organization. Medical Research Monograph [*A publication*]
SEATRAD ... Southeast Asia Tin Research and Development Center [*Malaysia*] (IRC)
Seatrade BR ... Seatrade Business Review [*A publication*]
Seatrade S ... Fuel Economy. A Seatrade Study [*A publication*]
Seatrade We ... Seatrade Week [*A publication*]
SEATS....... Shubert Entertainment and Arts Ticketing System [*National computerized theatre-ticket selling system*]
SEATS....... Special Education Administration Task Simulation Game
Seattl Bsn... Seattle Business [*A publication*]
(Seattle) Q ... Quarterly Review (Seattle) [*A publication*]
Seattle Sym ... Seattle Symphony Orchestra. Program Notes [*A publication*]
Seattle T..... Seattle Times [*A publication*]
SEA-URICA ... South East Asia Universal Realtime Information Cataloging and Administration System
Sea Vend .... Seaborne on Vendors and Purchasers [*9th ed.*] [*1926*] [*A publication*] (DLA)
SEAVEY ... Sea-to-Shore Rotation Survey (DNAB)
Sea View Hosp Bull ... Sea View Hospital. Bulletin [*A publication*]
SEAWARS ... Seawater Activated Release System [*Navy*] (CAAL)
Seaway Rev ... Seaway Review [*A publication*]
SEAWBS... Southeast Asia Wideband System [*Military*]
SEAWEA.. Sea and Weather Observations [*Navy*] (NVT)
SEA/W/O MEPS ... South Eastern Alaska/Washington/Oregon Minimum Earned Premium Scale [*Aviation*] (AIA)

SEAX......... Seaxe Energy Corp. [*Jackson, MS*] [*NASDAQ symbol*]   (NQ)
SEAX......... Span East Airlines, Inc. [*Air carrier designation symbol*]
Sea Yrbk .... Seatrade North American Yearbook [*A publication*]
SEB............ Scientific Equipment Bay [*NASA*]   (KSC)
SEB............ Scottish Examining Board   (DCTA)
SEB............ Seaboard Corp. [*AMEX symbol*]   (SPSG)
SEB............ Sebenico [*Yugoslavia*] [*Seismograph station code, US Geological Survey*] [*Closed*]   (SEIS)
SEB............ Sebha [*Libya*] [*Airport symbol*]   (OAG)
Seb .... Sebir [*or Sebirin*]   (BJA)
SEB............ Secondary Education Board
SEB............ Selective Enlistment Bonus [*Navy*]   (NVT)
SEB............ Single-Ended Boiler   (DS)
SEB............ Skandinaviska Enskilda Banken [*Sweden*]
SEB............ Social and Emotional Behavior
SEB............ Societe des Etudes Bloyennes [*France*]   (EAIO)
SEB............ Society for Economic Botany   (EA)
SEB............ Society for Experimental Biology   (EAIO)
SEB............ Socio-Economic Benefit
SEB............ Software Engineering Bibliographic Database [*Air Force Systems Command*] [*Information service or system*]   (CRD)
SEB............ Source Evaluation Board [*NASA*]
SEB............ South Equatorial Belt [*Planet Jupiter*]
SEB............ Southern European Broadcasting Service [*DoD*]   (GFGA)
SEB............ Special Enlistment Bonus   (MCD)
SEB............ Staphylococcal Enterotoxin B [*Medicine*]
SEB............ Statistische Studien (Brussels) [*A publication*]
SEB............ Strip Electron Beam
SEB............ Structural Engineering Bulletin [*Department of Housing and Urban Development*] [*A publication*]   (GFGA)
SEB............ Support Equipment Building [*NASA*]   (NASA)
SEB............ Support Equipment Bulletin   (MCD)
SEB............ System Error Bridge
SEB............ Systems Engineering Branch [*NASA*]   (NASA)
SEBA........ Babahoyo [*Ecuador*] [*ICAO location identifier*]   (ICLI)
SEBA........ Staphylococcal Enterotoxin B Antisera [*Medicine*]
Sebast Med ... Sebastianus Medices [*Flourished, 16th century*] [*Authority cited in pre-1607 legal work*]   (DSA)
Sebast Sap ... Sebastianus Sapia [*Deceased, 1523*] [*Authority cited in pre-1607 legal work*]   (DSA)
Sebast Vant ... Sebastianus Vantius [*Flourished, 16th century*] [*Authority cited in pre-1607 legal work*]   (DSA)
SEBBETSI ... Serikat Buruh Beras dan Seluruh Indonesia [*Rice and Tapioca Workers' Union of Indonesia*]
SEBC .... Bahia De Caraquez [*Ecuador*] [*ICAO location identifier*]   (ICLI)
SEBC .... South-Eastern Bible College [*Florida*]
SEBD........ Bola De Oro [*Ecuador*] [*ICAO location identifier*]   (ICLI)
SEBD........ Software Engineering Bibliographic Data Base [*Data and Analysis Center for Software*] [*Information service or system*]
SEBDA...... Serikat Buruh Daehrah Autonoom [*Civil Servants' Union*] [*Indonesia*]
SEBE .... La Beata [*Ecuador*] [*ICAO location identifier*]   (ICLI)
SEbE......... Southeast by East
SEB/EB..... Economic Botany. New York Botanical Garden for the Society for Economic Botany [*A publication*]
SEBH........ Balao Chico [*Ecuador*] [*ICAO location identifier*]   (ICLI)
SEBI .... Boliche [*Ecuador*] [*ICAO location identifier*]   (ICLI)
SEBI .... Securities and Exchange Board of India   (ECON)
SEBIC....... Sustained Electron Bombardment-Induced Conductivity
SEBL........ Self-Emptying Blind Loop [*Gastroenterology*]
SEBL........ Single European Banking Licence
SEBM....... Society for Experimental Biology and Medicine   (EA)
SEBQ........ Senior Enlisted Bachelor Quarters [*Army*]   (AABC)
SEBS .... Single-Ended Boiler Survey   (DS)
SEbS......... Southeast by South
SEBS .... Submarine Emergency Buoyancy System
Seb Sapi..... Sebastianus Sapia [*Deceased, 1523*] [*Authority cited in pre-1607 legal work*]   (DSA)
SEB Symp ... Symposia. Society for Experimental Biology [*A publication*]
SEBT .... El Batan [*Ecuador*] [*ICAO location identifier*]   (ICLI)
Seb Trade-Marks ... Sebastian on Trade-Marks [*A publication*]   (DLA)
Seb Tr M ... Sebastian on Trade-Marks [*5th ed.*] [*1911*] [*A publication*]   (DLA)
SEBUA...... Seibutsu Butsuri [*A publication*]
SEBUMI ... Serikat Buruh Minjak, Stanvac [*Oil Workers' Union, Stanvac*] [*Indonesia*]
SEBV .... Solder End Ball Valve
Seb Vant .... Sebastianus Vantius [*Flourished, 16th century*] [*Authority cited in pre-1607 legal work*]   (DSA)
s-ec--- .... Ecuador [*MARC geographic area code*] [*Library of Congress*]   (LCCP)
SEC............ Safeguards Equipment Cabinet   (IEEE)
SEC............ Sanitary Engineering Center
S & EC ...... Science & Engineering Consultants [*Reston, VA*]   (TSSD)
SEC............ Scientific and Engineering Computation
SEC............ Scientific Estimates Committee [*Military*]   (AABC)
SeC............ Scuola e Cultura del Mondo [*A publication*]

SEC............ SEC: Bi-Monthly Magazine for Employees of the State Electricity Commission of Victoria [*A publication*]   (APTA)
SEC............ Secant
SEC............ Second   (AFM)
Se C .... Second Coming [*A publication*]
Sec............. Secondary [*Chemistry*]
SEC............ Secondary
SEC............ Secondary Electron Conduction [*Television camera system*]
SEC............ Secondary Emission Conductivity
SEC............ Secret   (AFM)
SEC............ Secretariat
SEC............ Secretary [*A publication*]
SEC............ Secretary   (EY)
SEC............ Section
SEC............ Sector
SEC............ Secular
SEC............ Secundum [*According To*] [*Latin*]
SEC............ Secure   (KSC)
SEC............ Securities [*or Security*]   (AAG)
SEC............ Securities and Exchange Commission
S & EC ...... Securities and Exchange Commission
SEC............ Securities and Exchange Commission Decisions and Reports [*A publication*]   (DLA)
SEC............ Securities and Exchange Commission, Washington, DC [*OCLC symbol*]   (OCLC)
Sec............. Secus [*Otherwise*] [*Latin*]   (ILCA)
SEC............ Sensor and Engagement Controller [*Army*]
SEC............ Sensormatic Canada Ltd. [*Toronto Stock Exchange symbol*]
SEC............ Sequential Events Controller [*NASA*]   (NASA)
SEC............ Shaftless Expander-Compressor
SEC............ Simple Electronic Computer [*Birkbeck College*] [*London, England*]   (DEN)
SEC............ Single Error Correcting
SEC............ Size Exclusion Chromatography
SEC............ Social and Economic Commentaries on Classical Texts [*A publication*]
SEC............ Social Economic Council [*Sociaal Economische Raad*] [*Netherlands*]
SEC............ Societe des Ecrivains Canadiens [*Society of Canadian Writers*]
SEC............ Societe Europeenne de Culture [*European Society of Culture - ESC*]   (EAIO)
SEC............ Society for Educative Communication   (EA)
SEC............ Society of Exchange Counselors   (EA)
SEC............ Soft Elastic Capsule [*Pharmacy*]
SEC............ Solar Energy Collector
SEC............ Solar Energy Concentrator
SEC............ Solid Electrolyte Capacitor
SEC............ Source Evaluation Committee [*NASA*]   (NASA)
SEC............ South Equatorial Current [*Oceanography*]   (MSC)
SEC............ Southeastern Command
SEC............ Southeastern Commuter Airlines [*Auburn, AL*] [*FAA designator*]   (FAAC)
SEC............ Southeastern Conference   (EA)
SEC............ Space Environmental Chamber   (AAG)
SEC............ Special Emergency Campaign [*Red Cross fund-raising*]
SEC............ Specific Energy Consumption [*Automotive engineering*]
SEC............ Spectroelectrochemistry
SEC............ Staff Evaluation Coordinators   (MCD)
SEC............ Standard Error of Calibration
SEC............ Standard Evaluation Cylinder   (MCD)
SEC............ Standards and Ethics Commission [*American Occupational Therapy Association*]
SEC............ Standing with Eyes Closed [*Equilibrium test*]
SEC............ Sterling Electronics Corp. [*AMEX symbol*]   (SPSG)
SEC............ Stevens Creek [*California*] [*Seismograph station code, US Geological Survey*]   (SEIS)
SEC............ Stock Exchange Council [*British*]
SEC............ Structural Engineers Councils   (KSC)
SEC............ Submarine Element Coordinator   (NVT)
SEC............ Sulphur Export Corp. [*An association*]   (EA)
SEC............ Supply Executive Committee [*NATO*]   (NATG)
SEC............ Support Equipment Change   (MCD)
SEC............ Switch Element Controller [*Telecommunications*]
SEC............ Switching Equipment Congestion [*Telecommunications*]   (TEL)
SECA........ Catarama [*Ecuador*] [*ICAO location identifier*]   (ICLI)
SECA........ Self-Employment Contributions Act of 1954 [*under which self-employed persons contribute to OASDI coverage for themselves*]
SECA........ Shiatsu Education Center of America [*Later, Ohashi Institute - OI*]   (EA)
SECA........ Solar Energy Construction Association   (EA)
SECA........ Southern Educational Communications Authority [*Television network*] [*Obsolete*]
SECA........ Sportbike Enthusiast Club of America   (EA)
SECAB ...... Secretaria Ejecutiva Permanente del Convenio Andres Bello [*Permanent Executive Secretariat of the Andres Bello Convention*]   (EAIO)
SECAC ...... Sectional Aeronautical Chart

SEC Accounting R CCH ... SEC [*Securities and Exchange Commission*] Accounting Rules. Commerce Clearing House [*A publication*]
SECAD...... Services Engineering Computer-Aided Design [*Pierce Management Services*] [*Software package*]   (NCC)
SECAD...... Support Equipment Concept Approval Data
SECAL ...... Sectoral Adjustment Loan [*World Bank*]
SECAL ...... Selected Calling System [*Military*]   (AFM)
SECAM..... Sequence Electronique Couleur avec Memoire [*Color Sequence with Memory*] [*French color television system*]
SECAM..... Systeme Electronique Couleur avec Memoire [*French broadcast color standard*]
SECAN...... Standing Group Communication Security and Evaluation Agency Washington
SECANT ... Separation and Control of Aircraft Using Nonsynchronous Techniques [*Collision avoidance*] [*RCA*]
SECAP ...... Systems Experiment Correlation and Analysis Program   (MCD)
SECAR ...... Secondary RADAR   (IEEE)
SECARMY ... Secretary of the Army
SEC ART... Secundum Artem [*According to the Art*] [*Latin*]
SECAS...... Ship Equipment Configuration Accounting System   (NVT)
SECB........ Security Bancorp, Inc. [*NASDAQ symbol*]   (NQ)
SECBASE ... Section Base [*Navy*]   (DNAB)
Sec Bk Judg ... Second Book of Judgments (Huxley) [*England*] [*A publication*]   (DLA)
SECC........ Condorcocha [*Ecuador*] [*ICAO location identifier*]   (ICLI)
SECC........ Safe Energy Communication Council   (EA)
SECC........ Scientific and Engineering Computing Council   (MCD)
SECC........ South Equatorial Countercurrent [*Oceanography*]   (MSC)
SECC........ State Emergency Communications Committee [*National Oceanic and Atmospheric Administration*]   (GFGA)
SECC........ Studies in Eighteenth-Century Culture [*A publication*]
SECC........ Sun Equities Corp. [*NASDAQ symbol*]   (NQ)
SECC........ Survivable Enduring Command and Control
SECCA ...... Southeastern Center for Contemporary Art [*North Carolina*]
Sec City...... Second City [*A publication*]
SEC Compl (P-H) ... Securities and Exchange Commission Compliance (Prentice-Hall, Inc.) [*A publication*]   (DLA)
SECD........ Second Bancorp [*NASDAQ symbol*]   (SPSG)
SECD........ Secondary   (AABC)
SECD........ Secured   (ROG)
SECDA ...... Southeastern Community Development Association   (EA)
SECDED ... Single-BIT [*Binary Digit*] Error Correction and Double-BIT [*Binary Digit*] Error Detection
SECDEF.... Secretary of Defense
Sec D & M ... Security Distributing and Marketing [*A publication*]
SEC Docket ... Securities and Exchange Commission Docket [*A publication*]   (DLA)
Secd Pt Edw III ... Year Books, Part III [*England*] [*A publication*]   (DLA)
Secd Pt H VI ... Year Books, Part VIII [*England*] [*A publication*]   (DLA)
SECDY...... Secondary
SECE........ Santa Cecilia [*Ecuador*] [*ICAO location identifier*]   (ICLI)
SECE........ Selfhelp of Emigres from Central Europe   (EA)
Sec Ed .... Secondary Education [*A publication*]
SECED...... Society for Earthquake and Civil Engineering Dynamics [*British*]
SECEM ..... Support Equipment Cost Effectiveness Model   (MCD)
Sec & Ex C ... Securities and Exchange Commission   (DLA)
SECF .... Somali Eastern and Central Front [*Political party*]   (EY)
SECF .... Surface Effect Cruiser Escort   (DNAB)
Sec & Fed Corp L Rep ... Securities and Federal Corporate Law Report [*A publication*]
SECFLT .... Second Fleet [*Atlantic*] [*Navy*]
SEC-FT ...... Second-Foot   (DNAB)
SECG......... Silver Eureka Corp. [*NASDAQ symbol*]   (NQ)
SECGRUHQ ... Security Group Headquarters
SECH .... Chone [*Ecuador*] [*ICAO location identifier*]   (ICLI)
SECH .... Secant, Hyperbolic
Sechenov J Physiol USSR ... Sechenov Journal of Physiology of the USSR [*A publication*]
Sechenov Physiol J USSR ... Sechenov. Physiological Journal of the USSR [*A publication*]
SECHT...... Scoping Emergency Cooling Heat Transfer [*Nuclear energy*]   (KSC)
SECI .... Support Equipment Critical Item   (MCD)
Sec Ind Digest ... Secondary Industries Digest [*A publication*]   (APTA)
Sec Ind R.... Securities Industry Review [*Singapore*] [*A publication*]
SECINSP .. Security Inspection [*Military*]   (NVT)
Sec Int .... Secretary of the Interior   (DLA)
SECIR .... Semiautomatic Encoding of Chemistry for Information Retrieval   (DIT)
SECIT........ Syndicat des Employes Indigenes du Commerce du Togo [*Union of Indigenous Employees of Commerce of Togo*]
SECJA....... Southern Economic Journal [*United States*] [*A publication*]
SEC Jud Dec ... Securities and Exchange Commission Judicial Decisions [*A publication*]   (DLA)
SECL .... Chiles [*Ecuador*] [*ICAO location identifier*]   (ICLI)
secl .... Secretarial   (WGA)
SECL .... Ship Equipment Configuration List   (MCD)
SECLA ...... Southeastern Connecticut Library Association [*Library network*]

SEC LEG... Secundum Legem [*According to Law*] [*Latin*]
Sec L Rev ... Securities Law Review [*A publication*]
SECLT....... Second Lieutenant [*Army*]
SECM....... Clementina [*Ecuador*] [*ICAO location identifier*]   (ICLI)
SECM....... Scanning Electrochemical Microscope
SECM....... School of English Church Music [*Later, RSCM*]
SECM........ Secom General Corp. [*NASDAQ symbol*]   (NQ)
SEC Mag ... SEC Magazine: Journal of the State Electricity Commission of Victoria [*A publication*]   (APTA)
Sec Mgmt... Security Management [*A publication*]
Sec Mgt...... Security Management [*A publication*]
SECMID ... Scanning Electrochemical Microscope-Induced Desorption
SECMR ..... Sector Manager [*Aviation*]   (FAAC)
SECN........ Section   (ROG)
SECN........ Sex Education Coalition News [*A publication*]
SECN........ Supplements to Electroencephalography and Clinical Neurophysiology [*Elsevier Book Series*] [*A publication*]
SECNA ...... Secretary of the Navy   (NOAA)
SEC NAT ... Secundum Naturam [*According to Nature*] [*Latin*]
SECNAV ... Secretary of the Navy
SECNAVINST ... Secretary of the Navy Instruction
SEC News ... SEC [*US Securities and Exchange Commission*] News Digest [*A publication*]
SECNY...... Sales Executives Club of New York   (EA)
SECO......... Coca [*Ecuador*] [*ICAO location identifier*]   (ICLI)
SECO........ Securities and Exchange Commission
SECO........ Securities and Exchange Commission Organization
SECO........ Self-Regulating Error-Correct Coder-Decoder
SECO........ Sequential Coding
SECO........ Sequential Control [*Teletype*] [*Data processing*]
SECO........ Station Engineering Control Office [*Telecommunications*]   (TEL)
SECO........ Steam and Electric Cogeneration [*Power source*]
SECO........ Sustainer-Engine Cutoff [*Aerospace*]
SECOBI .... Servicio de Consulta a Bancos de Informacion [*Database Consultation Service*] [*Information service or system*] [*Mexico*]   (IID)
SECOF ...... Shipboard Environmental Checkout Facility   (DNAB)
SECOFF.... Section Office
SECOIN.... Security Consultants International
SECOL ...... Southeastern Conference on Linguistics
SECOLAS ... Southeastern Conference on Latin American Studies [*United States*]
SECOLAS A ... SECOLAS [*Southeastern Conference on Latin American Studies*] Annals [*A publication*]
SECOLR ... SECOL [*Southeastern Conference on Linguistics*] Review [*A publication*]
SECOM..... School Emergency Communication
SECOMO ... Software Engineering Cost Model
SECON...... Secondary Electron Conduction [*Television camera system*]
Secondary Teach ... Secondary Teacher [*A publication*]   (APTA)
Second Cent ... Second Century [*A publication*]
Second Ed .. Secondary Education [*A publication*]
Second Opin Health Care Issues ... Second Opinions of Health Care Issues [*A publication*]
Second Teach ... Secondary Teacher [*A publication*]
S Econ J ..... Southern Economic Journal [*A publication*]
SECONNS ... Satellite ECCM [*Electronics Counter Countermeasure*] Communications Neural Network Syster
SECOR...... Sequential Collation [*or Collection*] of Ranges [*Army*]
SECOR...... Sequential Correlation
SECOR...... Sequential Cosine Ranging [*System*]   (MUGU)
SECORD... Secure Voice Cord Board [*Telecommunications*]   (TEL)
SECP .... [*Division of*] Shore Establishment and Civilian Personnel [*Navy*]
SECP .... Software Engineering Change Proposal   (MCD)
SECP .... Solar Energy Conservation Program [*Department of Energy*]
SECP .... State Energy Conservation Program
SECP .... Subcontractor Engineering Change Proposal   (MCD)
SecPac........ Security Pacific [*Bank*]   (ECON)
SecPac....... Security Pacific Bank [*Hong Kong*]
SECPR...... Standard External Cardiopulmonary Resuscitation
SECPS...... Secondary Propulsion System [*NASA*]   (KSC)
SECR........ Curaray [*Ecuador*] [*ICAO location identifier*]   (ICLI)
SECR........ Secor Bank, Federal Savings Bank [*NASDAQ symbol*]   (NQ)
SECR........ Secretariat
SE & CR .... Southeastern & Chatham Railway [*Nickname: Seldom Ever Caught Running*]
SECRA ...... Secondary RADAR [*RADAR beacon*]
SEC REG... Secundum Regulam [*According to Rule*] [*Latin*]
Sec Reg Guide ... Securities Regulation Guide [*Prentice-Hall, Inc.*] [*A publication*]   (DLA)
Sec Reg Guide P-H ... Securities Regulation Guide. Prentice-Hall [*A publication*]
Sec Reg LJ ... Securities Regulation Law Journal [*A publication*]
Sec Reg & L Rep ... Securities Regulation and Law Reports [*Bureau of National Affairs*] [*A publication*]
Sec Reg & L Rep BNA ... Securities Regulation and Law Report. Bureau of National Affairs [*A publication*]
Sec Reg & Trans ... Securities Regulations and Transfer Report [*A publication*]

SECREP.... Regional Representative of the Secretary of Transportation
SECRG...... Securing
SECRL...... Secretarial
Secr Pap Int Wheat Counc ... Secretariat Papers. International Wheat Council [*A publication*]
SECS .... Seagrass Ecosystems Component Study [*Marine science*]   (MSC)
SECS .... Selective Electron-Capture Sensitization [*Analytical chemistry*]
SECS .... Sequential Events Control System [*NASA*]   (KSC)
SECS .... Shuttle Events Control Subsystem [*NASA*]   (NASA)
SECS .... Simulation and Evaluation of Chemical Synthesis [*Data processing*]
SECS .... Single-Engine Control Speed   (DNAB)
SECS .... Solar Electric Communication Satellite
SECS .... Space Environmental Control System   (AAG)
SECS .... Stem Elevated Camera System
SECSA .... Single Engine Control System Application   (MCD)
SECSTA ... Naval Security Station
SECSW ..... Science and Engineering Committee for a Secure World   (EA)
SECSY...... Spin-Echo Correlated Spectroscopy
SECT .... Firing Field Equipment Service [*French*] [*Acronym is based on foreign phrase*]
SECT .... Secretariat
SECT .... Section   (KSC)
SECT .... Submarine Emergency Communications Transmitter
SECTAM ... Sterile Environmental Control Technology Applications to Medicine
SECTASKFLT ... Second Task Fleet
SECTBASE ... Section Base [*Navy*]
SECTDQ ... Centro Internacional de Agricultura Tropical [*CIAT*]. Series EE [*A publication*]
Sec Teach... Secondary Teacher [*A publication*]   (APTA)
Sec Teacher ... Secondary Teacher [*A publication*]   (APTA)
SECTL...... Secretarial
SECTLZD ... Sectionalized
SEC-TREAS ... Secretary-Treasurer   (DNAB)
SECTY ...... Secretary
SECU......... Cuenca [*Ecuador*] [*ICAO location identifier*]   (ICLI)
SECU......... Slave Emulator Control Unit
SEC(UN)... Secretariat of the United Nations
SECURE ... Systems Evaluation Code Under Radiation Environment
Security Surv ... Security Surveyor [*A publication*]
Secur Manage ... Security Management [*A publication*]
Secur Med Trav ... Securite et Medecine du Travail [*A publication*]
Secur R Law ... Securities Regulation Law Journal [*A publication*]
SECUS ...... Supreme Emblem Club of the United States   (EA)
SECWAR .. Secretary of War [*Obsolete*]
Sec Wave ... Second Wave [*A publication*]
Sec World .. Security World [*A publication*]
SECX......... Southern Electronics Corp. [*Tucker, GA*] [*NASDAQ symbol*]   (NQ)
SECY........ Secretary
SECY........ Security
SED .... Sale/Engineering/Development [*Honda*] [*Automotive engineering*]
SED .... Sanitary Engineering Division [*MIT*]   (MCD)
SED .... Saturn Electrostatic Discharges [*Planetary science*]
SED .... Scarborough Board of Education [*Professional Education Library*] [*UTLAS symbol*]
SED .... Scottish Education Department
SED .... Sedan   (AAG)
SED .... Sedative [*Medicine*]   (ROG)
SED .... Seddin [*German Democratic Republic*] [*Later, NGK*] [*Geomagnetic observatory code*]
Sed .... Sedes [*A Stool*] [*Medicine*]
SED .... Sediment [*or Sedimentation*]
SED .... Sedition [*FBI standardized term*]
SED .... Sedona Air Center [*West Sedona, AZ*] [*FAA designator*]   (FAAC)
SED .... Segmented Expanding Die   (MCD)
SED .... Semiequilibrium Dialysis [*Physical chemistry*]
SED .... Sensor Evolutionary Development   (MCD)
SED .... Sequence Event Diagram   (DNAB)
SED .... Seriously [*or Severely*] Emotionally Disturbed
SED .... Shipper's Export Declaration [*Customs Service*]
SED .... Shore Establishments Division [*Navy*]
SED .... Skin Erythema Dose [*Medicine*]
SED .... Software Engineering Data [*Data and Analysis Center for Software*] [*Information service or system*]
SED .... Software Engineering Design [*Army*]
SED .... Solar Energy Density
SED .... Sound Energy Density
SED .... Sozialistische Einheitspartei Deutschlands [*Socialist Unity Party of Germany*] [*Political party*]   (PPW)
SED .... Space Environment Division [*NASA*]
SED .... Special Electrical Devices   (AABC)
SED .... Spectral Energy Distribution
SED .... Spondyloepiphysial Dysplasia [*Medicine*]
SED .... Staphylococcal Enterotoxin D [*Medicine*]
SED .... State Executive Director
SED .... Status Entry Device [*Telecommunications*]   (TEL)

SED .... Stray Energy Detector
SED .... Strong Exchange Degeneracy [*Physics*]   (OA)
SED .... Students for Economic Democracy   (EA)
SED .... Sun Entertainment [*Vancouver Stock Exchange symbol*]
SED .... Survey of English Dialects [*A publication*]
SED .... Swansea East Dock [*Welsh depot code*]
SED .... System Engineering Division [*Apollo Spacecraft Program Office*]
SED .... System Entry Date [*Military*]   (AFIT)
SED .... Systems Effectiveness Demonstration   (NG)
SE 2d......... Southeastern Reporter, Second Series [*A publication*]   (DLA)
SEDA......... Safety Equipment Distributors Association   (EA)
SEDA......... Side Effects of Drugs. Annual [*Elsevier Book Series*] [*A publication*]
SEDA......... State Emergency Defense Airlift
SEDA......... Structured Exploratory Data Analysis
SEDACS.... Support Equipment Data Acquisition and Control System   (MCD)
Sedalia N H Soc B ... Sedalia Natural History Society. Bulletin [*A publication*]
SEDAR...... Shipborne Electronic Deflection Array RADAR   (MCD)
SEDAS ...... Spurious Emission Detection Acquisition System   (MCD)
SEDC......... Society for Emotional Development in Children [*Canada*]
SEDC......... Steam Engine Direct Connected   (MSA)
SEDCOR... Specialty Electronics Development Corp.
SEDD .... Special Extra Deep Drawing   (MCD)
SEDD .... Systems Evaluation and Development Division [*NASA*]
SEDES ...... Societe d'Etudes pour le Developpement Economique et Social [*Society for the Study of Economic and Social Development*] [*Information service or system*] [*France*]   (IID)
SEDFC ...... Steve Earle and Dukes Fan Organization   (EA)
SEDFRE.... Scholarship, Education, and Defense Fund for Racial Equality
Sedg Dam ... Sedgwick on the Measure of Damage [*A publication*]   (DLA)
SEDGE...... Special Experimental Display Generation Program   (SAA)
Sed Geol.... Sedimentary Geology [*A publication*]
Sedg L Cas ... Sedgwick's Leading Cases on Damages [*A publication*]   (DLA)
Sedg L Cas ... Sedgwick's Leading Cases on Real Property [*A publication*]   (DLA)
Sedg Stat Law ... Sedgwick on Statutory and Constitutional Law [*A publication*]   (DLA)
Sedg St & Const Law ... Sedgwick on Statutory and Constitutional Law [*A publication*]   (DLA)
Sedg & W Tit ... Sedgwick and Wait on the Trial of Title to Land [*A publication*]   (DLA)
Sedg & W Tr Title Land ... Sedgwick and Wait on the Trial of Title to Land [*A publication*]   (DLA)
SEDI......... Software Engineering Demonstrator Initiative [*British*]
SEDIC .... Sociedad Espanola de Documentacion e Informacion Cientifica [*Spanish Society for Documentation and Information Sciences*] [*Information service or system*]   (IID)
Sediment Ge ... Sedimentary Geology [*A publication*]
Sediment Geol ... Sedimentary Geology [*A publication*]
Sedimentol ... Sedimentology [*A publication*]
SEDIS........ Service Information-Diffusion [*Information Dissemination Office*] [*National Institute for Research in Informatics and Automation*] [*Information service or system*]   (IID)
SEDIS........ Surface Emitter Detection, Identification System [*Navy*]
SEDIT .... Sophisticated String Editor   (IEEE)
SEDL .... Southwest Educational Development Laboratory   (EA)
SEDM....... Society for Experimental and Descriptive Malacology   (EA)
SEDM....... Status Entry Device Multiplexer [*Telecommunications*]   (TEL)
SEDME..... Survey Electronics Distance Measuring Equipment   (MCD)
SEDME..... Surveying Equipment Distance Measuring Electronic   (MCD)
SEDOC...... European System for the International Clearing of Vacancies and Applications for Employment [*EC*]   (ECED)
SEDOR...... Spin Echo Double Resonance [*Physics*]
SEDP......... Support for Engineer Development Priorities   (MCD)
SEDPC ...... Scientific and Engineering Data Processing Center
SEDR......... Science Education Development and Research Division [*National Science Foundation*]   (GRD)
SEDR......... Service Engineering Department Report
SEDR......... Supplementary Experiment Data Record [*Aerospace*]
SEDR......... System Effective Data Rate   (BUR)
SEDR......... Systems Engineering Department Report   (IEEE)
SEDS .... Social and Economic Development Strategy
SEDS .... Social-Emotional Dimension Scale [*Behavior problems test*]
SEDS .... Society for Educational Data Systems [*Later, SDE*]
SEDS .... Space Electronics Detection System   (KSC)
SEDS .... State Energy Data System [*Department of Energy*] [*Database*]
SEDS .... Students for the Exploration and Development of Space   (EA)
SEDS .... Support Equipment Data System
SEDS .... System Effectiveness Data System [*Air Force*]
SEDSCAF ... Standard ELINT Data System Codes and Format   (NVT)
SEDSDR ... Support Equipment Delivery Schedule Delinquency Report   (MCD)
SEE............ San Diego/Santee, CA [*Location identifier*] [*FAA*]   (FAAL)
SEE............ Sealed Air Corp. [*NYSE symbol*]   (SPSG)
SEE............ Secondary Electron Emission
SEE............ Seeing Essential English [*Sign language system for the hearing impaired*]

SEE............ Senior Environmental Employment Program [*Environmental Protection Agency*]
SEE............ Signals Experimental Establishment [*British military*]   (DMA)
SEE............ Signing Exact English [*Sign language system for the hearing impaired*]
SEE............ Small Emplacement Excavations [*or Excavator*] [*Army*]
SEE............ Societe d'Etudes et d'Expansion [*Studies and Expansion Society - SES*] [*Later, Et Ex*]   (EAIO)
SEE............ Societie pour l'Expansion des Exportations [*Export Development Corp.*] [*Canada*]
SEE............ Society of Earthbound Extraterrestrials   (EA)
SEE............ Society of Electronics Engineers
SEE............ Society of Environmental Engineers [*Later, Institute of Environmental Sciences*]
SEE............ Society of Explosives Engineers   (EA)
SEE............ Southeastern Electric Exchange
SEE............ Special Purpose End Effector   (MCD)
SEE............ Standard End Effector   (NASA)
SEE............ Standard Error of Estimate
SEE............ Staphylococcal Enterotoxin E [*Medicine*]
SEE............ Studies in Educational Evaluation [*A publication*]
SEE............ Summer Educational Enrichment
SEE............ Sun Earth Explorer [*Satellite*] [*NASA*]
SEE............ Support Equipment Exhibit   (MCD)
SEE............ Surgical Eye Expeditions International   (EAIO)
SEE............ Survival, Evasion, and Escape [*Military*]
SE & E...... Survival, Evasion, and Escape [*Military*]   (AABC)
SEE............ Systems Effectiveness Engineering   (MCD)
SEE............ Systems Effectiveness Evaluation   (NG)
SEE............ Systems Efficiency Expert
SEE............ Systems Equipment Engineer [*Telecommunications*]   (TEL)
SEEA......... Societe Europeenne d'Energie Atomique
SEEA......... Software Error Effects Analysis
SEE/AN.... Systems Effectiveness Evaluation/Analyzer   (DNAB)
SEEAPAC... Shore Electronic Engineering Activity, Pacific
SEEB......... Seeburg Industries, Inc. [*NASDAQ symbol*]
SEECA...... Solar Energy and Energy Conservation Act of 1980
SEECA...... State Environmental Education Coordinators Association   (EA)
SEECCIASDI... Standing EEC [*European Economic Community*] Committee of the International Association of the Soap and Detergent Industry [*See also CPCEAISD*] [*Brussels, Belgium*]   (EAIO)
SEECL....... Solar Energy and Energy Conversion Laboratory [*University of Florida*] [*Research center*]   (RCD)
SEED......... DEKALB Genetics Corp. [*NASDAQ symbol*]   (NQ)
SEED......... Safe Eye Exposure Distance [*Air Force*]
SEED......... Scientists and Engineers in Economic Development [*National Science Foundation*]
SEED......... Self Electrooptic Effect Device [*Optical analog of a transistor*]
SEED......... Sewall Early Education Developmental Profiles
SEED......... Skill Escalation Employment Development   (EA)
SEED......... Special Elementary Education for the Disadvantaged
SEED......... Supply of Essential Engineering Data
SEED......... Support for East European Democracies Act [*1989*]
Seed Bull.... Seed Bulletin [*A publication*]
Seed Gard Merch... Seed and Garden Merchandising [*A publication*]
SEEDIS..... Socio-Economic Demographic Information System [*Lawrence Berkeley Laboratory*] [*Database*]
Seed and Nursery Tr... Seed and Nursery Trader [*A publication*]   (APTA)
Seed Res..... Seed Research [*A publication*]
Seed Res (New Delhi)... Seed Research (New Delhi) [*A publication*]
SEEDS...... Ship's Electrical and Electronic Data System   (DNAB)
SEEDS...... Space Exposed Experiment Developed for Students
Seed Sci Techn... Seed Science and Technology [*A publication*]
Seed Sci Technol... Seed Science and Technology [*A publication*]
Seed Trade Rev... Seed Trade Review [*A publication*]
SEEE......... Studies in Electrical and Electronic Engineering [*Elsevier Book Series*] [*A publication*]
SEEEE....... Societe Europeenne d'Etudes et d'Essais d'Environnment [*France*]   (PDAA)
SEEF......... Scientists and Engineers Emigrant Fund
SEEHRL... Sanitary Engineering and Environmental Health Research Laboratory [*Research center*]   (RCD)
SEEI......... Selected Essays. English Institute [*A publication*]
SEEI......... Special Essential Elements of Information   (MCD)
SEEI......... Support Equipment End Item   (MCD)
SEE-IN... Significant Events Evaluation and Information Network
SEEJ......... Slavic and East European Journal [*A publication*]
SEEK........ Search for Education, Elevation, and Knowledge [*Program*]
SEEK........ Survival, Escape, and Evasion Kit [*Navy*]   (NG)
SEEK........ Systems Evaluation and Exchange of Knowledge [*Data processing*]
SEEN........ Syndicat d'Etudes de l'Energie Nucleaire [*Belgium*]
SEEO........ Salvis Erroribus et Omissis [*Errors and Omissions Excepted*] [*Latin*]
SEEO........ Shore Electronic Engineering Office [*Navy*]
SEEP........ Sex Equity in Education Program   (EA)
SEEP........ Shelf Edge Exchange Processes [*Oceanography*]   (NOAA)
SEEP........ Sixth Fleet Escort Evaluation Program [*Navy*]
SEEP......... Stimulated Emission of Energetic Particles [*Experiment for study of radio waves*]

SEEQ........ SEEQ Technology, Inc. [*NASDAQ symbol*]   (NQ)
SEEQ........ Side-Effects Expectancy Questionnaire [*Psychology*]
SEER........ Seasonal Energy-Efficiency Ratio [*of heat pumps, air conditioners, etc.*]
SEER........ Sensor Experimental Evaluation and Review [*Strategic Defense Initiative*]
SEER........ Service des Etudes Ecologiques Regionales [*Canada*]
SEER........ Slavonic and East European Review [*A publication*]
SEER........ Student Exposition on Energy Resources [*Project*]
SEER........ Submarine Explosive Echo Ranging
SEER........ Supervisory Electronic Engineer [*Radio*]
SEER........ Surveillance, Epidemiology, and End-Results [*Program*] [*National Cancer Institute*]
SEER........ Sustainable Equilibrium Exchange Rate [*Economics*]
SEER........ System for Electronic Evaluation and Retrieval [*Data processing*]
SEER........ Systems Engineering, Evaluation, and Research   (MCD)
SEERB..... South African Engineer and Electrical Review [*A publication*]
SEEREP.... Ships' Essential Equipment Requisition Expediting Program [*Navy*]   (NVT)
SEERS...... Senior Enlisted Evaluation Reports [*Military*]   (INF)
SEES......... Esmeraldas/General Rivadeneira [*Ecuador*] [*ICAO location identifier*]   (ICLI)
SEES......... Slavic and East European Section [*Association of College and Research Libraries*]
SEES......... Slavic and East European Studies [*A publication*]
SEES........ Standard Entry/Exit System [*Army*]
SEES........ System Effectiveness Engineering Section
SEET........ Science End-to-End Test [*Space*]
SEETB...... Scottish, English, and European Textiles [*Commercial firm*]
SEETB...... South East England Tourist Board   (DCTA)
SEETEC.... Sight Enhancement, Education, and Technology
SE Eur..... Southeastern Europe [*A publication*]
SEEX........ Systems Evaluation Experiment   (MCD)
SEF.......... SALT Education Fund [*Defunct*]   (EA)
SEF.......... Sebring, FL [*Location identifier*] [*FAA*]   (FAAL)
Sef............ Sefarad [*A publication*]
SEF.......... Self-Extinguishing Fiber [*Monsanto Co. trademark*]
SEF.......... Sequential Excitation Fluorescence [*Aviation*] [*Navy*]
SEF.......... Shielding Effectiveness Factor
SEF.......... Simple Environment Factor
SEF.......... Simulated Engine Failure   (ADA)
SEF.......... Small-End Forward [*of command module*]
SEF.......... Software Engineering Facility
SEF.......... Solar Energy Flux
SEF.......... Somatically Evoked Field [*Neurophysiology*]
SEF.......... Sound Energy Flux
SEF.......... Southern Education Foundation   (EA)
SEF.......... Space Education Foundation [*Later, AEF*]
SEF.......... Space Environmental Facility   (SAA)
SEF.......... Special Entry Flying List [*Navy*] [*British*]
SEF.......... Stability Enhancement Function [*Aviation*]   (GFGA)
SEF.......... Standard External File
SEF.......... Staphylococcus Aureus Enterotoxin F [*Toxic shock toxin*]
SEF.......... Supermarketing [*A publication*]
SEF.......... Surface Effect Ship
SEF.......... Systems Engineering Facility [*Defense Communications Agency*]   (RDA)
SE/FAC..... Support Equipment/Facility [*NASA*]   (NASA)
SEFACAN... Segregator, Facer, Canceller Machine
SEFAR...... Sonic End Fire for Azimuth and Range
SE & FBR.. Science Fiction and Fantasy Book Review [*A publication*]
SEFC........ Southeast Fisheries Center [*Miami, FL*] [*National Marine Fisheries Service*]   (MSC)
SEFCL....... Southeastern Fish Control Station [*Department of the Interior*]   (GRD)
SEFD........ Seafood, Inc. [*NASDAQ symbol*]   (NQ)
SEFD........ Solar Energy Flux Density
SEFDAO... Side Effects of Drugs [*A publication*]
SEFE........ Standardization Evaluation Flight Examiner
SEFEL....... Secretariat Europeen des Fabricants d'Emballages Metalliques Legers [*European Secretariat of Manufacturers of Light Metal Packages*]   (EA)
SEFES...... Southeastern Forest Experiment Station [*Department of Agriculture*] [*Asheville, NC*]   (GRD)
SEFEWS... Scientists and Engineers Field Experience with Soldiers   (RDA)
SEFF........ Snakeye Free-Fall [*Navy*]   (DNAB)
SEFI.......... Sequential Electric Fuel Injection [*Automotive engineering*]
SEFI.......... Societe Europeenne pour la Formation des Ingenieurs [*European Society for Engineering Education*]   (EA)
SEFIC....... Seventh Fleet Intelligence Center [*Navy*]
SEFIP....... Statistical Estimation Fault Isolation Procedure   (MCD)
SEFLO..... Sequence Flow [*Tracing technique*]
SEFM...... Support Equipment Field Modification   (AAG)
SEFOR..... Southwest Experimental Fast Oxide Reactor [*Nuclear energy*]
SEFR........ Shielding Experiment Facility Reactor [*Nuclear energy*]
SEFR........ Support Equipment for Robot   (DWSG)
SEFR........ System Effectiveness Forecast Report
SEFRL....... Southeastern Field Research Laboratory [*Pennsylvania State University*]
SEFS.......... Special Elite Forces Society   (EA)

SefT	Sefer Torah. Post-Talmudic Tractate (BJA)
SEFT	Single Engine Flight Training
SEFT	Society for Education in Film and Television [*British*]
SEFT	Spin-Echo Fourier Transform [*Physics*]
SEG...........	Saturday Evening Girls [*Decorators of Arts and Crafts pottery*]
SEG...........	Screen Extras Guild (EA)
SEG...........	Sealing
Seg	Segismundo [*A publication*]
SEG...........	Segment (AAG)
SEG...........	Segno [*Sign*] [*Music*]
SEG...........	Segue [*Follows*] [*Music*]
SEG...........	Selective Epitaxial Growth [*Semiconductor technology*]
SEG...........	Selinsgrove, PA [*Location identifier*] [*FAA*] (FAAL)
SEG...........	Sequence of Events Generator
SEG...........	Side Entry Goniometer
SEG...........	Sliding Electron Gun
SEG...........	Society of Economic Geologists (EA)
SEG...........	Society of Exploration Geophysicists (EA)
SEG...........	Sonoencephalogram (AAMN)
SEG...........	Special Effect Generator [*Video technology*]
SEG...........	Standardization Evaluation Group (AFM)
SEG...........	Subesophageal Ganglion [*Anatomy*]
SEG...........	Supplementum Epigraphicum Graecum [*A publication*]
SEG...........	System Engineering Groundrule [*NASA*] (NASA)
SEG...........	Systems Engineering Group [*Air Force*]
SEG...........	Systems Evaluation Group
SEGBA......	Servicios Electricos del Gran Buenos Aires, SA [*Electrical utility*] [*Argentina*]
SEGD........	Society of Environmental Graphics Designers (EA)
SEGE........	Guale [*Ecuador*] [*ICAO location identifier*] (ICLI)
SEGEA......	Orthopaedic Surgery [*A publication*]
SEGH........	Society for Environmental Geochemistry and Health (EA)
SEGI........	Sports/Entertainment Group, Inc. [*NASDAQ symbol*] (NQ)
SEGL........	Gul [*Ecuador*] [*ICAO location identifier*] (ICLI)
SEGM.......	Segment
SEGR........	Guarumal [*Ecuador*] [*ICAO location identifier*] (ICLI)
SEG/R & T ...	Systems Engineering Group/Research and Technology [*Air Force*]
SEGS	Galapagos (Baltra) [*Ecuador*] [*ICAO location identifier*] (ICLI)
SEGS	Solar Electric Generating System
SEGU	Guayaquil/Simon Bolivar [*Ecuador*] [*ICAO location identifier*] (ICLI)
Segu	[*Didacus de*] Segura [*Flourished, 16th century*] [*Authority cited in pre-1607 legal work*] (DSA)
SEGZ........	Gualaquiza [*Ecuador*] [*ICAO location identifier*] (ICLI)
SEH	Sehore [*India*] [*Seismograph station code, US Geological Survey*] (SEIS)
SEH	Shuttle Electronic Hardware [*NASA*]
SEH	Single-Engined Helicopter (MCD)
SEH	Societe Europeenne d'Hematologie
SEH	Solar Equivalent Hours
SEH	Southern Economic Journal [*A publication*]
SEH	Spartech Corp. [*AMEX symbol*] (SPSG)
SEH	Star/Earth Horizon Sightings
SEH	Strobel, E. H., Saint Louis MO [*STAC*]
SEH	Subependymal Hemorrhage [*Medicine*]
SEHAB.....	Sea Rehabilitation [*Navy*] (NVT)
SEHHW	Social and Economic History of the Hellenistic World [*A publication*]
SEHI.........	Cotacachi [*Ecuador*] [*ICAO location identifier*] (ICLI)
SE-HPLC ..	Size Exclusion-High Performance Liquid Chromatography
SEHR	Scandinavian Economic History Review [*A publication*]
SEHT	Hacienda Taura [*Ecuador*] [*ICAO location identifier*] (ICLI)
SEI	Safety Equipment Institute (EA)
SEI	Seitel, Inc. [*NYSE symbol*] (SPSG)
SEI	Self Employment Income [*Social Security Administration*] (OICC)
SEI	Senhor Do Bonfim [*Brazil*] [*Airport symbol*] (OAG)
SEI	Shane Resources [*Vancouver Stock Exchange symbol*]
SEI	Societa Editrice Internazionale [*Italy*] [*Publisher*]
SEI	Societas Ergophthalmologica Internationalis [*International Ergophthalmological Society*] [*Stockholm, Sweden*] (EAIO)
SEI	Society of Engineering Illustrators (EA)
SEI	Software Engineering Institute [*DoD*]
SEI	Solid Electrolyte Interphase [*Battery technology*]
SEI	Special Engineering Investigation (MCD)
SEI	Special Equipment Item (MCD)
SEI	Special Experience Identifier [*Military*]
SEI	Statistical Engineering Institute (MCD)
SEI	Stern Environment Indexes [*Psychology*]
SEI	Stockpile Entry Inspection [*Navy*] (NG)
SEI	Stray Energy Indicator
SEI	Stress Evaluation Inventory [*Test*]
SEI	Support Equipment Illustration (MCD)
SEI	Support Equipment Installation [*NASA*] (NASA)
SEI	System Engineering Instrumentation (NASA)
SEI	System/Equipment Inventory
SE & I	Systems Engineering and Integration
SEIA	Security Equipment Industry Association (EA)
SEIA	Solar Energy Industries Association (EA)

SEIA	Solar Energy Institute of America [*Later, SEINAM*] (MCD)
SEIAC	Science Education Information Analysis Center [*ERIC*]
SEIB	Ibarra [*Ecuador*] [*ICAO location identifier*] (ICLI)
SEIB	Service des Etudes et Inventaires Bio-Physiques [*Quebec*]
SEIB	Statistical and Economic Information Bulletin for Africa [*A publication*]
SEIC	SEI Corp. [*NASDAQ symbol*] (NQ)
SEIC	Solar Energy Information Center
SEIC	Syndicat de l'Emploi et de l'Immigration du Canada
SEIC	System Effectiveness Information Central
SEICO	Science and Engineering Information Center Co. (IID)
SEICO	Support Equipment Installation and Checkout [*NASA*] (NASA)
SEID	Support Equipment Illustration Data (MCD)
SEIDB	Solar Energy Information Data Bank [*Department of Energy*]
SEIE	Solvent Extraction and Ion Exchange [*A publication*]
SEIE	Submarine Escape Immersion Equipment
SEIF..........	Speak Easy International Foundation (EA)
Seifen Fachbl ...	Seifen Fachblatt [*A publication*]
Seifen Ole ..	Seifen, Oele, Fette, Waechse [*A publication*]
Seifensieder Ztg ...	Seifensieder-Zeitung [*A publication*]
Seifensieder Ztg Allg Oel Fett Ztg ...	Seifensieder-Zeitung in Gemeinschaft auf Kriegsdauer mit Allgemeine Oel- und Fett-Zeitung [*A publication*]
Seifens Zt...	Seifensieder-Zeitung [*A publication*]
SEIFR........	Support Equipment End Item Funding Report (MCD)
SEIG	Intag [*Ecuador*] [*ICAO location identifier*] (ICLI)
SEIGA	Seishin Igaku [*A publication*]
Seign Rep...	Lower Canada Seignorial Questions Reports [*A publication*] (DLA)
SEIJAN.....	Congenital Anomalies [*A publication*]
SEIJD........	Seijinbyo [*A publication*]
Seikag	Seikagaku [*Journal of the Japanese Biochemical Society*] [*A publication*]
Sei-i-Kai Med J ...	Sei-i-Kwai Medical Journal [*A publication*]
Seik Ziho ...	Seiken Ziho. Report of the Kihara Institute for Biological Research [*A publication*]
SEIL	Science Experiments Integration Laboratories
SEIL	Southeastern Educational Improvement Laboratory [*Research Triangle Park, NC*] [*Department of Education*] (GRD)
SEIM	Isla San Miguel [*Ecuador*] [*ICAO location identifier*] (ICLI)
SEIMC	Special Education Instructional Materials Centers [*Office of Education*] [*Database producer*] (IID)
SEIMS.......	State Economic Information Management System [*State Department*] [*Database*]
SEINAM ...	Solar Energy Institute of North America (EA)
SEIOD.......	Spogli Elettronici dell'Italiano delle Origini e del Duecento [*A lexical, morphological, and syntactical inventory of Old Italian texts*]
SEIP	System Engineering Implementation Plan
SEIR	Solar Energy Intelligence Report [*Business Publishers Inc.*] [*No longer available online*] [*Information service or system*] (CRD)
SEIR	Southeast Indian Ridge [*Antarctica*] [*Geology*]
SEIR	Susceptible, Exposed, Infected or Immune, Recovered [*Epidemiological model*]
SEIRS........	Suppliers and Equipment Information Retrieval System [*International Civil Aviation Organization*] [*Databank*] [*Information service or system*] (IID)
SEIS..........	Solar Energy Information Services (IID)
SEIS..........	Submarine Emergency Identification Signal (NG)
SEIS..........	Supplemental Environmental Impact Statement [*Department of Agriculture*]
SEISA........	South Eastern Intercollegiate Sailing Association
Seish Iga	Seishin Igaku [*A publication*]
Seish Shink Zass ...	Seishin Shinkeigaku Zasshi [*A publication*]
Seism Instrum ...	Seismic Instruments [*A publication*]
SEISMOG ...	Seismographic
SEISMOL ...	Seismologic
Seismol Bull ...	Seismological Bulletin [*A publication*]
Seismol and Geol ...	Seismology and Geology [*A publication*]
Seismol Invest ...	Seismological Investigations. British Association for the Advancement of Science [*A publication*]
Seismolog Soc Am Bull ...	Seismology Society of America. Bulletin [*A publication*]
Seismol Ser Earth Phys Branch ...	Seismological Series of the Earth Physics Branch [*A publication*]
Seismol Ser Geol Surv (S Afr) ...	Seismologic Series. Geological Survey (South Africa) [*A publication*]
Seismol Serv Can Seismol Ser ...	Seismological Service of Canada. Seismological Series [*A publication*]
Seismol Soc Am Bul ...	Seismological Society of America. Bulletin [*A publication*]
Seismostoikost Sooruzh ...	Seismostoikost Sooruzhenii [*Former USSR*] [*A publication*]
Seism Prib Instrum Sredstva Seism Nabl ...	Seismichiskie Pribory. Instrumental'naye Sredstva Seismicheskikh Nablyudenii [*A publication*]
SEIT	Satellite Educational and Informational Television
SEIT	Supervisory Electronic Installation Technician
SEIT	System Engineering Integration and Test (MCD)

SEIT .... System Evaluation, Integration, and Test (MCD)
SEITA Ann Dir Etud Equip Sect 2 ... SEITA [*Service d'Exploitation
     Industrielle des Tabacs et des Allumettes*] Annales de la
     Direction des Etudes de l'Equipement. Section 2 [*A
     publication*]
SEITA Annls ... Service d'Exploitation Industrielle des Tabacs et des
     Allumettes. Annales de la Direction des Etudes et de
     l'Equipement [*A publication*]
Seitel .... Seitel, Inc. [*Associated Press abbreviation*] (APAG)
SEIU......... Service Employees International Union (EA)
SEIWG...... Security Equipment Integration Working Group
SE/IWT..... Southern Europe - Inland Waterways Transport
     [*NATO*] (NATG)
SEJ .... Australian Stock Exchange Journal [*A publication*] (APTA)
SEJ .... Security Pacific National Bank. Quarterly Economic Report [*A
     publication*]
SEJ .... Sliding Expansion Joint [*Technical drawings*]
SEJ .... Southern Economic Journal [*A publication*]
SEJA .... Jaramillo [*Ecuador*] [*ICAO location identifier*] (ICLI)
SEJCR...... Societe Europeenne des Jeunes de la Croix-Bleue [*European
     Society for Blue Cross Youth - ESBCY*] (EAIO)
SEJG .... Sacris Erudiri. Jaarboek voor Godsdienstwetenschappen [*A
     publication*]
SEJI.......... Jipijapa [*Ecuador*] [*ICAO location identifier*] (ICLI)
SEJI.......... State Education Journal Index [*A publication*]
SEK........... Synomospondia Ergaton Kyprou [*Cyprus Workers'
     Confederation*] ["*Free Labour Syndicats*"]
SEKE .... Sosialistikon Ergatikon Komma tis Elladas [*Socialist Labor
     Party of Greece*] [*Forerunner of Greek Communist Party
     (KKE)*] (PPE)
SEKF .... Sister Elizabeth Kenny Foundation [*Later, SKI*]
SEKLS....... Southeast Kansas Library System [*Library network*]
SEKRLC.... Southeastern Kentucky Regional Library Cooperative [*Library
     network*]
Sek San Fuji Sor ... Sekai San Fujinka Soran. Survey of World Obstetrics and
     Gynaecology [*A publication*]
Sel .... Ducretet-Thomson [*Formerly, Ducretet Selmer*] [*Record label*]
     [*France*]
SEL........... Safety Engineering Laboratory [*British*] (IRUK)
SEL........... Satellite Experiment Laboratory [*National Oceanic and
     Atmospheric Administration*] (GRD)
SEL........... School of Electric Light [*British military*] (DMA)
SEL........... Scouts' Esperanto League (EA)
SEL........... Select [*or Selection*] (AAG)
SEL........... Selected Equipment List (NVT)
sel.............. Selection [*Literature*]
Sel .... Seleucid Era (BJA)
SEL........... Seligman Select Municipal Fund [*NYSE symbol*] (SPSG)
SEL........... Selkirk College Library [*UTLAS symbol*]
sel.............. Selkup [*MARC language code*] [*Library of Congress*] (LCCP)
SEL........... Semi-Effective List [*British military*] (DMA)
SEL........... Semlyachik [*Former USSR*] [*Seismograph station code, US
     Geological Survey*] (SEIS)
SEL........... Seoul [*South Korea*] [*Airport symbol*] (OAG)
SEL........... Seton Co. [*AMEX symbol*] (SPSG)
SEL........... Signal Engineering Laboratories (AAG)
SEL........... Single Engine Land [*Pilot rating*] (AIA)
SEL........... Skolta Esperanto-Ligo [*Scouts' Esperanto League*] (EAIO)
SEL........... Socialist Electoral League [*Norway*] (PPW)
SEL........... Software Engineering Laboratory [*NASA*] (MCD)
SEL........... Solar Environmental Laboratory [*National Oceanic and
     Atmospheric Administration*]
SEL........... Southeastern Educational Laboratory
SEL........... Space Environment Laboratory [*Department of Commerce*]
     [*National Oceanic and Atmospheric Administration*]
     [*Boulder, CO*]
SEL........... Spontaneously Emitted Light
SEL........... Standard Elektrik Lorenz AG [*Germany*]
SEL........... Stanford Electronics Laboratory [*Stanford University*]
     [*Research center*] (MCD)
SEL........... Star/Earth Landmark Sightings
SEL........... Studies in English Literature [*A publication*]
SEL........... Super Einspritz Lang [*Fuel-injection, long wheelbase*] [*As in 450
     SEL, the model number of a Mercedes-Benz automobile*]
SEL........... Support Equipment List [*Navy*]
SELE......... Surface Emitting LASER
SEL........... System Electronics Laboratory (MCD)
SEL........... System Engineering Laboratories (MCD)
SELA .... Lago Agrio [*Ecuador*] [*ICAO location identifier*] (ICLI)
SELA .... Southeastern Library Association (AEBS)
SELA .... Systeme Economique Latino-Americain [*Latin American
     Economic System - LAES*] [*French*]
SELACJ .... Secretariado Latinoamericano de la Compania de Jesus [*Latin
     American Bureau of Society of Jesus*] (EAIO)
Sel Annu Rev Anal Sci ... Selected Annual Reviews of the Analytical Sciences
     [*A publication*]
Sel App Beng ... Selected Appeals, Sadr Diwani Adalat [*Bengal, India*] [*A
     publication*] (DLA)
SELAS....... Selas Corp. of America [*Associated Press
     abbreviation*] (APAG)

SELAVIP .. Servicio Latinoamericano y Asiatico de Vivienda Popular
     [*Latin American and Asian low Income Housing Service*]
     [*Chile*] (EAIO)
SelBab........ Babylonian Seleucid Era (BJA)
Sel Bibliogr Algae ... Selected Bibliography on Algae [*A publication*]
Sel Bibliogr Middle East Geol ... Selected Bibliography of Middle East
     Geology [*A publication*]
SELC .... La Cecilia [*Ecuador*] [*ICAO location identifier*] (ICLI)
SELC .... South East London College [*London, England*]
SELC .... Synod of Evangelical Lutheran Churches (IIA)
SELCAL.... Selective Calling [*Radio*]
Sel Cancer Ther ... Selective Cancer Therapeutics [*A publication*]
Sel Cas .... Select Cases, Central Provinces [*India*] [*A publication*] (DLA)
Sel Cas Ch ... Select Cases in Chancery [*England*] [*A publication*] (DLA)
Sel Cas Ch (T King) ... Select Cases in Chancery Tempore King [*25 English
     Reprint*] [*1724-33*] [*A publication*] (DLA)
Sel Cas DA ... Select Cases, Sadr Diwani Adalat [*India*] [*A
     publication*] (DLA)
Sel Cas Ev ... Select Cases in Evidence (Strange) [*England*] [*A
     publication*] (DLA)
Sel Cas KB Edw I ... Select Cases in King's Bench under Edward I (Sayles)
     [*England*] [*A publication*] (DLA)
Sel Cas NF ... Select Cases, Newfoundland [*A publication*] (DLA)
Sel Cas NWP ... Select Cases, Northwest Provinces [*India*] [*A
     publication*] (DLA)
Sel Cas NY ... Yate's Select Cases [*1809*] [*New York*] [*A publication*] (DLA)
Sel Cas with Opin ... Select Cases with Opinions by a Solicitor [*A
     publication*] (DLA)
Sel Cas SDA ... Select Cases, Sadr Diwani Adalat [*Bengal, Bombay, India*] [*A
     publication*] (DLA)
Sel Cas T Br ... [*Charles Purton*] Cooper's Select Cases Tempore Brougham
     [*A publication*] (DLA)
Sel Cas T King ... Select Cases in Chancery Tempore King [*England*] [*A
     publication*] (DLA)
Sel Cas T Nap ... Select Cases Tempore Napier [*Ireland*] [*A
     publication*] (DLA)
Sel Ca T King ... Select Cases in Chancery Tempore King [*25 English Reprint*]
     [*1724-33*] [*A publication*] (DLA)
SELCH ...... Selector Channel
Sel Ch Cas ... Select Cases in Chancery Tempore King, Edited by Macnaghten
     [*England*] [*A publication*] (DLA)
Sel Col Cas ... Select Collection of Cases [*England*] [*A publication*] (DLA)
SELCOM .. Select Committee [*Army Materiel Command*]
SELCTV.... Selected Television [*Commercial firm*] [*British*]
Seld .... Selden's New York Reports [*5-10 New York*] [*A
     publication*] (DLA)
SELD......... Snakeye Low-Drag [*Navy*] (DNAB)
SELDADS ... Space Environment Laboratory Data Acquisition and Display
     System [*National Oceanic and Atmospheric
     Administration*]
Sel Dec Bomb ... Select Cases, Sadr Diwani Adalat [*Bombay, India*] [*A
     publication*] (DLA)
SEL DECK ... Select Decking [*Lumber*]
Sel Dec Madr ... Select Decrees, Sadr Adalat [*Madras, India*] [*A
     publication*] (DLA)
Selden .... Selden's New York Court of Appeals Reports [*A
     publication*] (DLA)
Selden Notes ... Selden's New York Court of Appeals Notes of Cases [*1st ed.*]
     [*1853*] [*A publication*] (DLA)
Seld Fl........ Selden's Dissertatio ad Fletam [*A publication*] (ILCA)
Seld J .... Selden's Jani Anglorum [*A publication*] (ILCA)
Seld JP....... Selden's Judicature in Parliaments [*1681*] [*A
     publication*] (DLA)
Seld Mar Cl ... Selden's Mare Clausum [*A publication*] (ILCA)
Seld Mare Claus ... Selden's Mare Clausum [*A publication*] (DLA)
Seld Notes ... Selden's New York Court of Appeals Notes [*A
     publication*] (DLA)
Seld Off Ch ... Selden's Office of Lord Chancellor [*1671*] [*A
     publication*] (DLA)
Seld R........ Selden's New York Court of Appeals Reports [*A
     publication*] (DLA)
Seld Soc ..... Selden Society (DLA)
Seld Soc Yrbk ... Selden Society Yearbook [*United States*] [*A
     publication*] (DLA)
Seld Tit Hon ... Selden's Titles of Honor [*A publication*] (DLA)
SELE .... SelecTronics, Inc. [*NASDAQ symbol*] (NQ)
SELEC....... Select (ROG)
SELEC....... Superelastic LASER Energy Conversion (MCD)
Selec Ed R ... Selections from the Edinburgh Review [*A publication*]
Selecta Math Soviet ... Selecta Mathematica Sovietica [*A publication*]
Selecta Statist Canadiana ... Selecta Statistica Canadiana [*A publication*]
Select Canc ... Selective Cancer Therapeutics [*A publication*]
Selected Reports ... Selected Reports in Ethnomusicology [*A publication*]
Selected Water Resources Abstr ... Selected Water Resources Abstracts [*A
     publication*]
Select J....... Select Journal [*A publication*]
Selec Water Resources Abstr ... Selected Water Resources Abstracts [*A
     publication*]
Selek Semenovod ... Selektsiya i Semenovodstvo [*A publication*]
Selekts Semenov ... Selektsiya i Semenovodstvo [*A publication*]
Sel Electrode Rev ... Selective Electrode Reviews [*A publication*]

Selenium Tellurium Abstr ... Selenium and Tellurium Abstracts [*A publication*]
SelEnv .... Selected References on Environmental Quality [*A publication*]
SELEX ...... Systematic Evolution of Ligands by Exponential Enrichment [*Genetics*]
Selez Tec Molit ... Selezione di Tecnica Molitoria [*A publication*]
SELF .... National Citizens Committee to Save Education and Library Funds
SELF .... Self-Eject Launch Facility [*NASA*]   (MCD)
SELF .... Short Expeditious Landing Field   (CINC)
SELF .... Simplicity, Efficiency, Lower Rates, and Fairness Tax Plan
SELF .... Societe des Ecrivains Luxembourgeois de Langue Francaise
SELF .... Student Education Loan Fund [*Minnesota*]
Self Rel ...... Self-Reliance [*A publication*]
SELFTAV ... Self-Conducted Tender Availability [*Navy*]   (NVT)
Self Tr .... Selfridge's Trial [*A publication*]   (DLA)
SELGEM .. Self-Generating Master [*Information management system*] [*Data processing*]
SELI .... Limoncocha [*Ecuador*] [*ICAO location identifier*]   (ICLI)
SE Libn ...... Southeastern Librarian [*A publication*]
SELID .... Serials Librarian [*A publication*]
SeligQual ... Seligman Quality Municipal Fund [*Associated Press abbreviation*]   (APAG)
SeligSel ...... Seligman Select Municipal Fund [*Associated Press abbreviation*]   (APAG)
SELit .... Studies in English Literature [*Japan*] [*A publication*]
SELJ .... La Julia [*Ecuador*] [*ICAO location identifier*]   (ICLI)
SELJ .... Studies in English Literature (Japan) [*A publication*]
SELK .... Selkirkshire [*County in Scotland*]
Sel'Khoz Beloruss ... Sel'skoe Khozyaistvo Belorussii [*A publication*]
Sel'-Khoz Biol ... Sel'skokhozyaistvennaya Biologiya [*A publication*]
Sel Khoz Kazakh ... Sel'skoe Khozyaistvo Kazakstana [*A publication*]
Sel'Khoz Kirgizii ... Sel'skoe Khozyaistvo Kirgizii [*A publication*]
Sel'Khoz Povol ... Sel'skoe Khozyaistvo Povolzh'ya [*A publication*]
Sel'Khoz Sev Kavkaz ... Sel'skoe Khozyaistvo Severnogo Kavkaza [*A publication*]
Sel'Khoz Sev-Zapad Zony ... Sel'skoe Khozyaistvo Severo-Zapadnoi Zony [*A publication*]
Sel Khoz Sev Zap Zony ... Sel'skoe Khozyaistvo Severo-Zapadnoi Zony [*A publication*]
Sel'Khoz Sib ... Sel'skoe Khozyaistvo Sibiri [*A publication*]
Sel Khoz Tadzhik ... Sel'skoe Khozyaistvo Tadzhikistana [*A publication*]
Sel'Khoz Tadzhikistana ... Sel'skoe Khozyaistvo Tadzhikistana [*A publication*]
Sel Khoz Tatarii ... Sel'skoe Khozyaistvo Tatarii [*A publication*]
Sel Khoz Turkmen ... Sel'skoe Khozyaistvo Turkmenistana [*A publication*]
SELL .... Llurimaguas [*Ecuador*] [*ICAO location identifier*]   (ICLI)
SELL .... Sales Environment Learning Laboratory [*Computer-based marketing game*]
SELL .... Studies in English Literature and Language [*Japan*] [*A publication*]
SELL .... Suomi, Eesti, Latvija, Lietuva [*Finland, Estonia, Latvia, Lithuania*]
Sel L Cas.... Select Law Cases [*England*] [*A publication*]   (DLA)
Sell Pr .... Sellon's Practice in the King's Bench [*A publication*]   (DLA)
Sell Prac..... Sellon's Practice in the King's Bench [*A publication*]   (DLA)
SELM .... Loma Larga [*Ecuador*] [*ICAO location identifier*]   (ICLI)
SE/LM .... Systems Engineering/Logistics Management   (MCD)
SelMac....... Macedonian Seleucid Era   (BJA)
Sel Math Sov ... Selecta Mathematica Sovietica [*A publication*]
Sel Med....... Selecciones Medicas [*A publication*]
SEL MERC ... Select Merchantable [*Lumber*]
SELMOUS ... Special English Language Materials for Overseas University Students
SELN .... Limon [*Ecuador*] [*ICAO location identifier*]   (ICLI)
SELN .... Selection   (AAG)
Sel NP....... Selwyn's Law of Nisi Prius [*A publication*]   (DLA)
SELO .... Loja (La Toma) [*Ecuador*] [*ICAO location identifier*]   (ICLI)
Sel Odontol (Sao Paulo) ... Selecoes Odontologicas (Sao Paulo) [*A publication*]
Sel Off Ch ... Selden's Office of Lord Chancellor [*1671*] [*A publication*]   (DLA)
SELOR ...... Ship Emitter Location Report [*Navy*]   (CAAL)
Sel Org Transform ... Selective Organic Transformations [*A publication*]
Sel Pap Am Chem Soc Symp Plast Deform Plym ... Selected Papers Presented. American Chemical Society Symposium on Plastic Deformation of Polymers [*A publication*]
Sel Pap Annu Gas Meas Inst ... Selected Papers. Heart of America Annual Gas Measurement Institute [*A publication*]
Sel Pap Annu Pipeline Oper Maint Inst ... Selected Papers. Heart of America Annual Pipeline Operation and Maintenance Institute [*A publication*]
Sel Pap Carle Clin Carle Found ... Selected Papers. Carle Clinic and Carle Foundation [*A publication*]
Sel Pap Conf Exp Med Surg Primates ... Selected Papers. Conference on Experimental Medicine and Surgery in Primates [*A publication*]
Sel Pap Environ Isr ... Selected Papers on the Environment in Israel [*A publication*]
Sel Pap Heart Am Annu Gas Compressor Inst ... Selected Papers. Heart of America Annual Gas Compressor Institute [*A publication*]

Sel Pap Heart Am Annu Gas Meas Inst ... Selected Papers. Heart of America Annual Gas Measurement Institute [*A publication*]
Sel Pap Inst Human Nutr Prague ... Selected Papers. Institute of Human Nutrition in Prague [*A publication*]
Sel Pap Int Astronaut Congr ... Selected Papers. International Astronautical Congress [*A publication*]
Sel Pap Isr Environ Prot Service ... Selected Papers. Israel. Environmental Protection Service [*A publication*]
Sel Pap Nucl Eng Sci Congr ... Selected Papers. Nuclear Engineering and Science Congress [*A publication*]
Sel Philip Period Index ... Selected Philippine Periodical Index [*A publication*]
Sel Pr .... Sellon's Practice [*A publication*]   (DLA)
Sel PRC Mag ... Selections from People's Republic of China Magazines [*Hong Kong*] [*A publication*]
SELR .... Saturn Engineering Liaison Request [*NASA*]   (KSC)
SELR .... Selector   (AAG)
SELR .... Support Equipment List Requirement   (MCD)
Sel Rand Abstr ... Selected Rand Abstracts [*A publication*]
SELREC.... Shore Electronics Reconnaissance System
SELREFTRA ... Selected Refresher Training [*Navy*]   (NVT)
SELRES ..... Selected Reserve [*Military*]
SELRFT .... Selected Refresher Training [*Navy*]   (NVT)
SELS .... Selective Service
SELS .... Severe Local Storm [*National Weather Service*]
SELS .... Space Environment Laboratory Simulation [*NASA*]
SELSA ...... Southeast Library Service Area [*Library network*]
Sel Sci Pap Ist Super Sanita ... Selected Scientific Papers. Istituto Superiore di Sanita [*A publication*]
Sel Sci Pap Shanghai Chiao Tung Univ ... Selected Scientific Papers. Shanghai Chiao Tung University [*A publication*]
Sel Sci Pap Shanghai Jiao Tong Univ ... Selected Scientific Papers. Shanghai Jiao Tong University [*A publication*]
Sel Semenovod (Kiev) ... Selektsiya i Semenovodstvo (Kiev) [*A publication*]
Sel Semenovod (Mosc) ... Selektsiya i Semenovodstvo (Moscow) [*A publication*]
Sel Semenovod Resp Mezhved Temat Sb ... Selektsiya i Semenovodstvo Respublikanskii Mezhvedomstvennyi Tematicheskii Sbornrik [*A publication*]
Sel Serv L Rep ... Selective Service Law Reporter [*A publication*]   (DLA)
Sel Serv L Rptr ... Selective Service Law Reporter [*A publication*]   (DLA)
Sel'sk Khoz ... Sel'skoe Khozyaistvo [*A publication*]
Sel'sk Khoz Kaz ... Sel'skoe Khozyaistvo Kazakhstana [*A publication*]
Sel'sk Khoz Kirg ... Sel'skoe Khozyaistvo Kirgizii [*A publication*]
Sel'sk Khoz Mold ... Sel'skoe Khozyaistvo Moldavii [*A publication*]
Sel'sk Khoz Podmoskov'ya ... Sel'skoe Khozyaistvo Podmoskov'ya [*A publication*]
Sel'sk Khoz Povolzh'ya ... Sel'skoe Khozyaistvo Povolzh'ya [*A publication*]
Sel'sk Khoz Rubezhom Rastenievod ... Sel'skoe Khozyaistvo za Rubezhom. Rastenievodstvo [*A publication*]
Sel'sk Khoz Sev Zapadn Zony ... Sel'skoe Khozyaistvo Severo-Zapadnoi Zony [*A publication*]
Sel'sk Khoz Tadzh ... Sel'skoe Khozyaistvo Tadzhikistana [*A publication*]
Sel'sk Khoz Tatar ... Sel'skoe Khozyaistvo Tatarii [*A publication*]
Sel'sk Khoz Tatarii ... Sel'skoe Khozyaistvo Tatarii [*A publication*]
Sel'sk Khoz Turkm ... Sel'skoe Khozyaistvo Turkmenistana [*A publication*]
Sel'skokhoz Biol ... Sel'skokhozyaistvennaya Biologiya [*A publication*]
Sel'skokhoz Proizv Nechernozem Zony ... Sel'skokhozyaistvennoe Proizvodstvo Nechernozemnoi Zony [*A publication*]
Sel'skokhoz Proizv Povol ... Sel'skokhozyaistvennoe Proizvodstvo Povolzh'ya [*A publication*]
Sel'skokhoz Proizv Sev Kavkaza TSCHO ... Sel'skokhozyaistvennoe Proizvodstvo Severnogo Kavkaza i TSCHO [*A publication*]
Sel'skokhoz Proizv Sib Dal'nego Vostoka ... Sel'skokhozyaistvennoe Proizvodstvo Sibiri i Dal'nego Vostoka [*A publication*]
Sel'skokhoz Proizv Urala ... Sel'skokhozyaistvennoe Proizvodstvo Urala [*A publication*]
Selskostop Misul ... Selskostopanska Misul [*A publication*]
Selskostop Nauka ... Selskostopanska Nauka [*A publication*]
Selskostop Tekh ... Selskostopanska Tekhnika [*A publication*]
Sel Sortoizuch Agrotekh Plodovykh Yagodnykh Kul't ... Selektsiya, Sortoizuchenie, Agrotekhnika Plodovykh i Yagodnykh Kul'tur [*A publication*]
SEL STR ... Select Structural [*Lumber*]
SELSW...... Selector Switch   (MCD)
SELSYN.... Self-Synchronous [*Trade name*] [*Motor*]
SELT .... Latacunga [*Ecuador*] [*ICAO location identifier*]   (ICLI)
SELT .... SAGE [*Semiautomatic Ground Environment*] Evaluation Library Tape
SELT .... Select Information Systems [*NASDAQ symbol*]   (NQ)
SELT .... Self-Eject Launch Technique [*NASA*]   (KSC)
SELT .... Sheet Explosive Loading Technique
SELTEC ... South East London Technical College [*British*]   (DI)
Sel Teol...... Selecciones de Teologia [*A publication*]
Sel Top Mod Phys ... Selected Topics in Modern Physics [*A publication*]
Sel Top Solid State Phys ... Selected Topics in Solid State Physics [*A publication*]
Sel Top Solid State Theor Phys Proc Lat Am Sch Phys ... Selected Topics in Solid State and Theoretical Physics. Proceedings. Latin American School of Physics [*A publication*]

Sel Vet Ist Zooprofil Sper Lomb Emilia ... Selezione Veterinaria-Istituto Zooprofilattico Sperimentale della Lombardia e dell'Emilia [*A publication*]
SELW .... Selwyn College [*Cambridge*] [*British*] (ROG)
Selw .... Selwyn's Law of Nisi Prius [*England*] [*A publication*] (DLA)
Sel Water Res Abstr ... Selected Water Resources Abstracts [*A publication*]
Sel Water Resour Abstr ... Selected Water Resources Abstracts [*A publication*]
Selw & Barn ... Barnewall and Alderson's English King's Bench Reports [*1st part*] [*A publication*] (DLA)
Selw NP .... Selwyn's Law of Nisi Prius [*England*] [*A publication*] (DLA)
SELY .... Southeasterly [*Meteorology*] (FAAC)
SEM .... Scanning Electron Microscope [*or Microscopy*]
SEM .... Scanning Electron Microscopy [*An association*] [*Later, SMI*] (EA)
SEM .... Schedule Evaluation Model
SEM .... Secondary Electron Multiplier [*Detector*]
SEM .... Secondary Emission Microscope
SEM .... Secondary Emission Monitor
SEM .... Secondary Enrichment Medium [*Microbiology*]
SEM .... Security Environmental Systems, Inc. [*Vancouver Stock Exchange symbol*]
SEM .... Security Management [*A publication*]
SEM .... Seller's Engineering Memo [*NASA*] (NASA)
SEM .... Selma, AL [*Location identifier*] [*FAA*] (FAAL)
Sem .... Semahoth (BJA)
Sem .... Semana [*A publication*]
SEM .... Semaphore
SEM .... Semble [*It Seems*]
SEM .... Semel [*Once*]
SEM .... Semen (WGA)
SEM .... Semi [*One-Half*] [*Pharmacy*]
SEM .... Semicolon
SEM .... Semiconductor Packaging Materials [*AMEX symbol*] (SPSG)
SEM .... Semienriched Minimal [*Agar*]
SEM .... Semimobile (WGA)
SEM .... Seminal (WGA)
Sem .... Seminar [*A publication*]
Sem .... Seminario Conciliar [*A publication*]
SEM .... Seminary
SEM .... Semipalatinsk [*Former USSR*] [*Seismograph station code, US Geological Survey*] (SEIS)
SEM .... Semitic [*Language, etc.*]
sem .... Semitic [*MARC language code*] [*Library of Congress*] (LCCP)
Sem .... Semitica [*Paris*] [*A publication*]
SEM .... Semo Aviation, Inc. [*Malden, MO*] [*FAA designator*] (FAAC)
Sem .... Sempre [*Throughout*] [*Music*]
SEM .... Shared Equity Mortgage
SEM .... Single European Market
SEM .... Singularity Expansion Method (IEEE)
SEM .... Society of Engineers and Machinists [*A union*] [*British*]
SEM .... Society for Ethnomusicology (EA)
SEM .... Society for Experimental Mechanics (EA)
SEM .... Solar Environment Monitor
SEM .... Sortie Effectiveness Model [*NASA*] (MCD)
SEM .... Southeast Missouri State University, Cape Girardeau, MO [*OCLC symbol*] (OCLC)
SEM .... Southern Illinois University at Carbondale Center for Electron Microscopy [*Research center*] (RCD)
SEM .... Space Environment Monitor [*NASA*]
SEM .... Special Electric Motors [*Manufacturing company*] [*British*]
SEM .... Standard Electronic Module (CAAL)
SEM .... Standard Error of the Mean
SEM .... Standard Error of Measurement [*Testing*]
SEM .... Standard Estimating Module (IEEE)
SEM .... State-Event Matrix [*Data processing*]
SEM .... Station Engineering Manual [*Telecommunications*] (TEL)
SEM .... Stereoscan Electron Microscope
SEM .... Stray Energy Monitor
SEM .... Structural Econometric Model [*Statistics*]
SEM .... Stupid Error Message [*Data processing*]
SEM .... Subarray Electronics Module [*Data processing*]
SEM .... Subcontractor Engineering Memorandum (MCD)
S-EM .... Suck-Egg Mule [*A publication*]
SEM .... System Effectiveness Model (CAAL)
SEM .... System Engineering Management [*NASA*]
SEM .... Systems Engineering & Manufacturing Corp. [*AMEX symbol*] (SPSG)
S-E-M .... Systems/Equipment/Munitions [*Army*] (AFIT)
SEM .... Systolic Ejection Murmur [*Cardiology*]
SEMA .... Macara [*Ecuador*] [*ICAO location identifier*] (ICLI)
SEMA .... Semiotic Abstracts [*A publication*]
SEMA .... Societe d'Etudes de Mathematiques Appliquees [*France*]
SEMA .... Special Electronic Mission Aircraft (RDA)
SEMA .... Specialty Equipment Manufacturers Association
SEMA .... Specialty Equipment Market Association [*Later, SFI*] (EA)
SEMAA ..... Safety Equipment Manufacturers Agents Association (EA)
Semaine Med ... Semaine Medicale [*A publication*]
Semaine Vet ... Semaine Veterinaire [*A publication*]
Sem Anal ... Seminaire d'Analyse [*A publication*]
Sem Anal Moderne ... Seminaire d'Analyse Moderne [*A publication*]
Semana Med ... Semana Medica [*A publication*]

Semanario ... Semanario Judicial de la Federacion [*Mexico*] [*A publication*]
Sem Arth Rh ... Seminars in Arthritis and Rheumatism [*A publication*]
SEMAT ...... Ship Electronic Module Assembly Test (DNAB)
SEMATECH ... Semiconductor Manufacturing Technology Consortium
SemBEsp .... Semana Biblica Espanola [*Madrid*] [*A publication*]
Sem Bibl Esp ... Semana Biblica Espanola [*A publication*]
SEMC .... Macas [*Ecuador*] [*ICAO location identifier*] (ICLI)
SEMCA ..... Shipboard Electromagnetic Computability Analysis (DNAB)
SEMCC ..... Southeastern Massachusetts Health Sciences Libraries Consortium [*Library network*]
SEMCIP .... Shipboard Electromagnetic Capability Improvement Program [*Navy*] (NVT)
SEMCOG ... Southeast Michigan Council of Governments [*Detroit, MI*]
SEMCOR ... Semantic Correlation [*Machine-aided indexing*]
SEMD .... Stray Energy Monitor Device
SEMDP ..... Senior Executive/Management Development Plan (DNAB)
SEM/E ...... Ethnos. Statens Etnografiska Museum [*A publication*]
SEME .... Semicon, Inc. [*NASDAQ symbol*] (NQ)
SEM-E ...... Standard Electronic Module-E Format (MCD)
SEMEL in D ... Semel in Die [*Once a Day*] [*Pharmacy*]
Semen Elette ... Sementi Elette [*A publication*]
SEMET ...... Self-Evident Meteorological Code (NATG)
SEMG .... Scanning Electron Micrograph
SEMH ...... Machala [*Ecuador*] [*ICAO location identifier*] (ICLI)
SEMH ...... Service Engineering Man-Hours
Sem Hematol ... Seminars in Hematology [*A publication*]
SEMHI ...... Southeastern Manufactured Housing Institute [*Later, Manufactured Housing Institute*] (EA)
Sem Hop .... Semaine des Hopitaux [*A publication*]
Sem Hop Inf ... Semaine des Hopitaux. Informations [*A publication*]
Sem Hop Paris ... Semaine des Hopitaux de Paris [*A publication*]
Sem Hop Paris Suppl Sem Med Prof Med Soc ... Semaine des Hopitaux de Paris. Supplement: Semaine Medicale Professionnelle et Medico-Sociale [*A publication*]
Sem Hop-The ... Semaine des Hopitaux-Therapeutique [*A publication*]
SEMI .... All American Semiconductor, Inc. [*NASDAQ symbol*] (NQ)
SEMI .... Self-Evacuating Multilayer Insulation [*System*]
SEMI .... Semiconductor Equipment and Materials Institute (EA)
semi .... Semis [*One-Half*] [*Latin*] [*Pharmacy*] (MAE)
SEMI .... Shipboard Electromagnetic Interference [*Navy*] (CAAL)
SEMI .... Societe d'Etudes de Marche et d'Informatique [*Society for the Study of Marketing and Informatics*] [*Information service or system*] [*Defunct*] (IID)
SEMI .... Special Electromagnetic Interference (MCD)
SEMI .... Subendocardial Myocardial Infarction [*Cardiology*] (MAE)
SEMI .... Subendocardial Myocardial Injury [*Cardiology*] (MAE)
Semi-Annu Prog Rep Tokai Works ... Semi-Annual Progress Report. Tokai Works [*A publication*]
SEMICOND ... Semiconductor
Semicond Insul ... Semiconductors and Insulators [*A publication*]
Semicond Int ... Semiconductor International [*A publication*]
Semicond Prod ... Semiconductor Production [*A publication*]
Semicond Prod ... Semiconductor Products [*A publication*]
Semicond Prod and Solid State Technol ... Semiconductor Products and Solid State Technology [*Later, Solid State Technology*] [*A publication*]
Semicond Sci Technol ... Semiconductor Science and Technology [*A publication*]
Semicond Semimet ... Semiconductors and Semimetals [*A publication*]
Semicond Silicon Int Symp Mat Pap ... Semiconductor Silicon. International Symposium on Silicon Materials Science and Technology. Papers [*A publication*]
Semicond Silicon Pap Int Symp Silicon Mater Sci Technol ... Semiconductor Silicon. Papers Presented. International Symposium on Silicon Materials Science and Technology [*A publication*]
semid .... Semidrachma [*Half a Drachm*] [*Latin*] [*Pharmacy*] (MAE)
SEMIDR ... Semidrachma [*Half a Drachma*] [*Pharmacy*]
SEMIH ...... Semihora [*Half an Hour*] [*Pharmacy*]
SEMIKON ... Seminare/Konferenzen [*Seminars/Conferences*] [*Society for Business Information*] [*Information service or system*] [*Defunct*] (IID)
Semin Anesth ... Seminars in Anesthesia [*A publication*]
Semin Arthritis Rheum ... Seminars in Arthritis and Rheumatism [*A publication*]
Seminary Q ... Seminary Quarterly [*A publication*]
Semin Biomass Energy City Farm Ind ... Seminar on Biomass Energy for City, Farm, and Industry [*A publication*]
Semin Chim Etat Solide ... Seminaires de Chimie de l'Etat Solide [*A publication*]
Semin Dermatol ... Seminars in Dermatology [*A publication*]
Semin Drug Treat ... Seminars in Drug Treatment [*A publication*]
Semin Electrochem ... Seminar on Electrochemistry [*A publication*]
Semin Estratigrafia ... Seminarios de Estratigrafia [*Madrid*] [*A publication*]
SEMINEX ... Seminary in Exile [*Liberal-oriented Lutheran seminary*]
Semin Fam Med ... Seminars in Family Medicine [*A publication*]
Sem Infect Dis ... Seminars in Infectious Disease [*A publication*]
Semin Hear ... Seminars in Hearing [*A publication*]
Semin Hematol ... Seminars in Hematology [*A publication*]
Semin Infect Dis ... Seminars in Infectious Disease [*A publication*]
Semin Interventional Radiol ... Seminars in Interventional Radiology [*A publication*]

Semin Liver Dis ... Seminars in Liver Diseases [*A publication*]
Semin Mar Radioecol ... Seminar on Marine Radioecology [*A publication*]
Semin Med ... Seminario Medico [*A publication*]
Semin Migr Relat Soc Health Probl Pap ... Seminar on Migration and Related Social and Health Problems in New Zealand and the Pacific. Papers [*A publication*]
Semin Nephrol ... Seminars in Nephrology [*A publication*]
Semin Neurol ... Seminars in Neurology [*A publication*]
Semin Nucl Med ... Seminars in Nuclear Medicine [*A publication*]
Semin Oncol ... Seminars in Oncology [*A publication*]
Semin Oncol Nurs ... Seminars in Oncology Nursing [*A publication*]
Semin Pap La Trobe Univ Sch Agri ... Seminar Paper. La Trobe University. School of Agriculture [*A publication*]
Semin Perinatol ... Seminars in Perinatology [*A publication*]
Semin Perinatol (NY) ... Seminars in Perinatology (New York) [*A publication*]
Semin Psychiatry ... Seminars in Psychiatry [*A publication*]
Semin Reprod Endocrinol ... Seminars in Reproductive Endocrinology [*A publication*]
Semin Respir Med ... Seminars in Respiratory Medicine [*A publication*]
Semin Roentgenol ... Seminars in Roentgenology [*A publication*]
Semin Ser Soc Exp Biol ... Seminar Series. Society for Experimental Biology [*A publication*]
Semin Speech Lang ... Seminars in Speech and Language [*A publication*]
Semin Sp Lang Hear ... Seminars Speech, Language, Hearing [*A publication*]
Sem Inst Prikl Mat Annotac Dokladov ... Seminar Instituta Prikladnoi Matematiki. Annotacii Dokladov [*A publication*]
Semin Surg Oncol ... Seminars in Surgical Oncology [*A publication*]
Semin Technol INSERM ... Seminaire Technologique. INSERM [*Institut National de la Sante et de la Recherche Medicale*] [*A publication*]
Semin Theor Phys ... Seminar on Theoretical Physics [*A publication*]
Semin Thromb Hemostas ... Seminars in Thrombosis and Hemostasis [*A publication*]
Semin Thromb Hemostasis ... Seminars in Thrombosis and Hemostasis [*A publication*]
Semin Ultrasound ... Seminars in Ultrasound [*Later, Seminars in Ultrasound, CT, and MR*] [*A publication*]
Semin Ultrasound CT MR ... Seminars in Ultrasound, CT, and MR [*A publication*]
Semin Univ Singapore Chem Dep ... Seminar. University of Singapore. Chemistry Department [*A publication*]
Semin Urol ... Seminars in Urology [*A publication*]
SEMIRA ... System of Electronic Marks' Interrogation, Registration, and Administration [*Database*] [*WIPO*] [*United Nations*] (DUND)
SEMIRAD ... Secondary Electron-Mixed Radiation Dosimeter (IEEE)
SEMIS ... Solar Energy Monitor in Space [*NASA*] (MCD)
SEMIS ... State Extension Management Information System [*Department of Agriculture*]
Sem'ja Sk ... Sem'ja Skola [*A publication*]
Sem Jur ... Semaine Juridique [*A publication*]
SEMKA ... Semento Kogyo [*A publication*]
Sem Kond ... Seminarium Kondakovianum [*A publication*]
SEML ... Manglaralto [*Ecuador*] [*ICAO location identifier*] (ICLI)
SEMLAM ... Semiconductor LASER Amplifier
SEMLAT ... Semiconductor LASER Array Techniques
SEMM ... Smoke Effectiveness Manual Model (MCD)
SEMM ... Societe Europeenne de Materials Mobiles [*France*] (PDAA)
SEMM ... Solar Electric Multiple-Mission (MCD)
Sem Math ... Seminars in Mathematics [*A publication*]
Sem Math Sci ... Seminar on Mathematical Sciences [*Yokohama*] [*A publication*]
Sem Math Sup ... Seminaire de Mathematiques Superieures [*A publication*]
Sem Math Superieures ... Seminaire de Mathematiques Superieures [*Montreal*] [*A publication*]
Sem Math V A Steklov ... Seminars in Mathematics. V. A. Steklov Mathematical Institute [*Leningrad*] [*A publication*]
Sem Med ... Semaine Medicale [*A publication*]
Sem Med ... Semana Medica [*A publication*]
Sem Med Esp ... Semana Medica Espanola [*A publication*]
Sem Med Mex ... Semana Medica de Mexico [*A publication*]
Sem Med Prof Med Soc ... Semaine Medicale Professionnelle et Medico-Sociale [*A publication*]
SEMMS ... Solar Electric Multiple-Mission Spacecraft
SEMN ... Slow Extension Motoneuron [*Neurology*]
SEMN ... Superficial Extensor Motoneuron [*Neurology*]
Sem Nephrol ... Seminars in Nephrology [*A publication*]
Sem Nota ... Seminario Nota [*A publication*]
SEMO ... Montalvo [*Ecuador*] [*ICAO location identifier*] (ICLI)
SEMO ... Systems Engineering and Management Operations [*Military*]
Semon ... Semonides [*Seventh century BC*] [*Classical studies*] (OCD)
SEMOPS ... Sequential Multiobjective Problem Solving
SEMP ... Mopa [*Ecuador*] [*ICAO location identifier*] (ICLI)
SEMP ... Sempre [*Throughout*] [*Music*]
SEMP ... Simplified Early Maturities Participation Plan [*Small Business Administration*]
SEMP ... Societe d'Editions Medico-Pharmaceutiques [*Medical-Pharmaceutical Publishing Co.*] [*Information service or system*] [*France*] (IID)
SEMP ... Socioeconomic Military Program (CINC)
SEMP ... Standard Electronics Module Program (MCD)

SEMP ... Superconducting Electromagnetic Propulsion (ECON)
SEMP ... System Engineering Management Plan
SEMPA ... Scanning Electron Microscope and Particle Analyzer
SEMPA ... Scanning Electron Microscopy with Polarization Analysis
SEMPB ... Schiffli Embroidery Manufacturers Promotion Board (EA)
SEMPCK ... Semiconductor Packaging Materials [*Associated Press abbreviation*] (APAG)
Semper Symp ... Semper Symposium [*A publication*]
SEMR ... Support Equipment Management Report (MCD)
SEMRE ... SPRINT Electromagnetic Radiation Evaluation [*Army*] (AABC)
SEMRFL ... Michigan Regional Libraries Film Program at Monroe [*Library network*]
Sem Roentg ... Seminars in Roentgenology [*A publication*]
SEMS ... Monjas Sur [*Ecuador*] [*ICAO location identifier*] (ICLI)
SEMS ... Science and Education Management Staff [*Department of Agriculture*] (GFGA)
Sem S ... Semiotic Scene [*A publication*]
SEMS ... Severe Environment Memory Series [*or System*] [*Data processing*]
SEMS ... Space Environment Monitor System [*NASA*] (NASA)
SEMS ... Steam Engine Makers' Society [*A union*] [*British*]
SEMS ... Stray Energy Monitor System
SEMS ... Support Engineering Manhour Summary (MCD)
SEMS ... System Engineering Management Standard
SEMS ... Systems Engineering and Management Support [*Air Force*]
SEMT ... Manta [*Ecuador*] [*ICAO location identifier*] (ICLI)
SEMT ... Science, Engineering, Medicine, and Technology [*A publication*]
SEMT ... SIGINT/EW [*Signal Intelligence/Electronic Warfare*] Maintenance Trainer [*Army*]
SEMTCH ... Semtech Corp. [*Associated Press abbreviation*] (APAG)
SEMTD8 ... Special Topics in Endocrinology and Metabolism [*A publication*]
SEMTEC ... Southeastern Marine Trades Exhibit and Conference [*National Marine Manufacturers Association*] (TSPED)
Sem Ther ... Semaine Therapeutique [*France*] [*A publication*]
SEMTR ... SPRINT Early Missile Test RADAR [*Army*] (AABC)
SEMTR ... Supervisory Electronic Maintenance Technician [*Relief*]
SEMTSA ... Structural Econometric Modeling Time Series Analysis [*Statistics*]
Se Mulli (New Phys) ... Se Mulli (New Physics) [*A publication*]
Sem Ultrasound ... Seminars in Ultrasound [*A publication*]
sem ves ... Seminal Vesicle [*Anatomy*] (WGA)
Sem Vitivinic ... Semana Vitivinicola [*Spain*] [*A publication*]
SEMY ... Seminary
Sen ... De Senectute [*of Cicero*] [*Classical studies*] (OCD)
SEN ... Lexington, KY [*Location identifier*] [*FAA*] (FAAL)
SEN ... Science Engineering News [*National Oceanic and Atmospheric Administration*]
SeN ... Seara Nova [*A publication*]
SEN ... Semienclosed
SEN ... Senate
SEN ... Senator
SEN ... Sendai [*Mukaiyama*] [*Japan*] [*Seismograph station code, US Geological Survey*] (SEIS)
Sen ... Seneca [*the Elder*] [*First century BC*] [*Classical studies*] (OCD)
Sen ... Seneca [*the Younger*] [*First century AD*] [*Classical studies*] (OCD)
SEN ... Senegal [*ANSI three-letter standard code*] (CNC)
SEN ... Senior (EY)
SEN ... Senlac Resources, Inc. [*Toronto Stock Exchange symbol*]
SEN ... Sennae [*Of Senna*] [*Pharmacy*] (ROG)
SEN ... Sensitive
SEN ... Sensor (AAG)
SEN ... Senza [*Without*] [*Music*]
SEN ... Single Edge Notched
SEN ... Societe Europeenne de Neuro+radiologie [*European Neuroradiological Association*] [*France*] (EAIO)
SEN ... Societe Europeenne de Neuroscience [*European Neuroscience Association - ENA*] (EA)
SEN ... Software Error Notification [*Data processing*]
SEN ... Southern European Network (DNAB)
SEN ... Space Engagement Node
SEN ... Sports Exchange Network [*Cable TV programming service*]
SEN ... State Enrolled Nurse [*British*]
SEN ... Steam Emulsion Number
SEN ... Strike Energy, Inc. [*Vancouver Stock Exchange symbol*]
SEN ... Successor Event Number (DNAB)
SEN ... System Error Notification [*Data processing*]
SEN ... Systems Engineering Notice
SENA ... Nor Antizana [*Ecuador*] [*ICAO location identifier*] (ICLI)
SENA ... Seaport Navigation Co. [*AAR code*] [*Later, SNCO*]
SENA ... Societe d'Energie Nucleaire Franco-Belge des Ardennes [*Belgian-French power consortium*]
SENA ... Sympathetic Efferent Nerve Activity
SENAAL ... Agricultural Science [*Sofia*] [*A publication*]
SENAV ... Senior Naval Aviator (NVT)
SENAVAV ... Senior Naval Aviator
SENAVOMAC ... Senior Naval Officer, Military Airlift Command (MCD)
SENB ... Single Edge Notched Beam [*Materials science and technology*]

SENC......... Nor Cayambe [*Ecuador*] [*ICAO location identifier*] (ICLI)
SenCh .... Senior Chaplain [*Navy*] [*British*]
Senckenb Biol ... Senckenbergiana Biologica [*A publication*]
Senckenberg Biol ... Senckenbergiana Biologica [*A publication*]
Senckenbergische Nat Ges Frankfurt Ber ... Senckenbergische
     Naturforschende Gesellschaft in Frankfurt Am Main.
     Bericht [*A publication*]
Senckenbergischen Naturf Gesell Senckenberg-Buch ... Senckenbergischen
     Naturforschenden Gesellschaft Senckenberg-Buch [*A
     publication*]
Senckenberg Marit ... Senckenbergiana Maritima [*A publication*]
Senckenb Lethaea ... Senckenbergiana Lethaea [*A publication*]
Senckenb Marit ... Senckenbergiana Maritima [*A publication*]
Senckenb Naturforsch Ges Abh ... Senckenbergische Naturforschende
     Gesellschaft. Abhandlungen [*A publication*]
SEND .... Scientists and Engineers for National Development [*Scholarship
     program*]
SEND .... Securities and Exchange Commission News Digest [*A
     publication*]
SEND .... Sentry Data, Inc. [*NASDAQ symbol*] (NQ)
SEND .... Shared Equipment Need Date (NASA)
SEND .... Southend [*County borough in England*]
Sendai Astron Rap ... Sendai Astronomiaj Raportoj [*A publication*]
Sendai Symp Acoustoelectron ... Sendai Symposium on Acoustoelectronics [*A
     publication*]
SENDENTALO ... Senior Dental Officer [*Navy*] (DNAB)
Sen Doc...... Senate Document (DLA)
SENE......... Seneca Foods Corp. [*NASDAQ symbol*] (NQ)
Seneg.......... Senegal
Senegal Cent Rech Oceanogr Dakar-Thiaroye Arch ... Senegal. Centre de
     Recherches Oceanographiques de Dakar-Thiaroye. Archive
     [*A publication*]
Senegal Cent Rech Oceanogr Dakar-Thiaroye Doc Sci ... Senegal. Centre de
     Recherches Oceanographiques de Dakar-Thiaroye.
     Document Scientifique [*A publication*]
Senegal Dir Mines Geol Bull ... Senegal. Direction des Mines et de la
     Geologie. Bulletin [*A publication*]
SENEGAMBIA ... Senegal and Gambia
SENEL ...... Single Noise Exposure Level
SENET ...... Scientific and Engineering Computer Network (MCD)
SENG ...... Single Engine
S in Eng...... Studies in English [*A publication*]
SEngFInstSMM ... Qualified Sales Engineer of the Institute of Sales and
     Marketing Management [*British*] (DBQ)
SEngL........ Studies in English Literature [*The Hague*] [*A publication*]
SENI.......... Nor Iliniza [*Ecuador*] [*ICAO location identifier*] (ICLI)
Sen J .... Senate Journal [*A publication*] (DLA)
Sen Jo .... Senate Journal [*A publication*] (DLA)
SENL........ Standard Equipment Nomenclature List [*Military*]
SENLOG... Sentinel Logistics Command
SEN(M)..... State Enrolled Nurse (Mental Nursing) [*British*] (DBQ)
SENMEDO... Senior Medical Officer [*Military*] (DNAB)
SENMEM ... Senior Member (DNAB)
SEN(MS) .. State Enrolled Nurse (Mental Subnormal Nursing)
     [*British*] (DBQ)
Senn .... Sennaherib (BJA)
SE'NNIGHT ... Seven Nights [*A week*] (ROG)
SENO .... Steam Emulsion Number
SENPD...... Senpaku [*A publication*]
SENPO...... Sentinel Project Office [*Army*] (MCD)
Sen R.......... Seneca Review [*A publication*]
SENR........ Senior
Sen Rep...... Senate Report [*A publication*] (DLA)
Sen Rep...... United States Senate Committee Report [*A publication*] (DLA)
Sens........... De Sensu [*of Aristotle*] [*Classical studies*] (OCD)
SENS........ Sensitive (MSA)
SENS........ Sensor [*Automotive engineering*]
SENS........ Sensory
SENS......... Sentex Sensing Technology, Inc. [*Ridgefield, NJ*] [*NASDAQ
     symbol*] (NQ)
SENS......... Social England Series [*A publication*]
Sens and Actuators ... Sensors and Actuators [*A publication*]
SENSB ...... Sense Processes [*A publication*]
Sen Schol .. Senior Scholastic [*A publication*]
SENSCOM ... Sentinel Systems Command [*Army*] (MCD)
SENSD...... Studies in Environmental Science [*A publication*]
SENSE ...... Society for Ending Needless and Silly Expenditure
     [*British*] (DI)
SENSE ...... Sommers' Equivocation Network for Significant
     Expressions (SAA)
SENSEA.... Sentinel System Evaluation Agency [*DoD*]
Sensibilizirovannaya Fluorests Smesej Parov Met ... Sensibilizirovannaya
     Fluorestsentsiya Smesej Parov Metallov [*A publication*]
SENSIM ... Sensor System Simulation
Sensing........ Remote Sensing [*A publication*]
SENSO...... Sensor Operator (MCD)
SENSO...... Sentinel Systems Office [*Military*]
Sensor .... Sensormatic Electronics Corp. [*Associated Press
     abbreviation*] (APAG)
SENSOR ... Sentinel Event Notification System for Occupational Risks
     [*Medicine*]

Sensor Rev ... Sensor Review [*A publication*]
Sens Process ... Sensory Processes [*A publication*]
Sens Rev..... Sensor Review [*A publication*]
SENT......... Sentence (AABC)
Sent........... Sentenza [*Decision, Judgment*] [*Italian*] (ILCA)
SENTA...... Societe d'Etudes Nucleaires et de Techniques Avancees
     [*France*]
SENTAC ... Society for Ear, Nose, and Throat Advances in Children (EA)
SENT CONF ... Sentence to be Confined [*Navy*] (DNAB)
SENTD...... Sentenced (WGA)
SenTechWeldI ... Senior Technician of the Welding Institute [*British*] (DBQ)
SENT LP... Sentence to Lose Pay [*Navy*] (DNAB)
SENTOS ... Sentinel Operating System (IEEE)
SENTRAB ... Syndicat des Travailleurs des Entreprises, Privees, Travaux
     Publics et Batiments [*Union of Workers of Private
     Enterprises, Public Works and Buildings*] [*Togo*]
SENTRE ... Sensor of Tail Region Emitters (MCD)
SENTRY ... Survey Entry
SENU .... Neuvo Rocafuerte [*Ecuador*] [*ICAO location identifier*] (ICLI)
SENU .... Spectrum Efficient Network Unit (MCD)
SENUSNAVOFFNAVBALTAP ... Senior United States Naval Officer,
     Commander Allied Naval Forces, Baltic
     Approaches (DNAB)
SENV......... Security Environmental Systems, Inc. [*NASDAQ
     symbol*] (NQ)
SenWO ...... Senior Warrant Officer [*British*] (DI)
SENYLRC ... Southeastern New York Library Resources Council [*Highland,
     NY*] [*Library network*]
SEO .... Salvage Engineering Order (MCD)
SEO .... Satellite for Earth Observation
SEO .... Seaport Corp. [*AMEX symbol*] (SPSG)
SEO .... Seguela [*Ivory Coast*] [*Airport symbol*] (OAG)
SEO .... Senior Engineer Officer [*Navy*]
SEO .... Senior Executive Officer [*Civil Service*] [*British*]
SEO .... Senior Experimental Officer [*Also, SExO, SXO*] [*Ministry of
     Agriculture, Fisheries, and Food*] [*British*]
SEO .... Seoul [*Keizyo*] [*South Korea*] [*Seismograph station code, US
     Geological Survey*] (SEIS)
SEO .... Serial Engineering Order (MCD)
SEO .... Shoulder-Elbow Orthosis [*Medicine*]
SEO .... Sin Errores y Omisiones [*Errors and Omissions Excepted*]
     [*Business term*] [*Spanish*]
SEO .... Society of Education Officers [*British*]
SEO .... Special Engineering Order [*NASA*] (NASA)
SEO .... State Energy Office
SEO .... Synchronous Equatorial Orbit [*or Orbiter*] [*NASA*] (KSC)
SEOA .... Pasochoa [*Ecuador*] [*ICAO location identifier*] (ICLI)
SEOC........ Submarine Extended Operating Cycle (NVT)
SEOCS ...... Sun-Earth Observatory and Climatology Satellite
SEODSE ... Special Explosive Ordnance Disposal Supplies and Equipment
     [*Army*] (AABC)
SEOG .... Supplemental Educational Opportunity Grant [*Department of
     Education*]
SEOL......... Olmedo [*Ecuador*] [*ICAO location identifier*] (ICLI)
SEON .... Solar Electro-Optical Network (MCD)
SEOO .... Sauf Erreur ou Omission [*Errors and Omissions Excepted*]
     [*French*]
SEOO .... State Economic Opportunity Office
SEOP........ SHAPE [*Supreme Headquarters Allied Powers Europe*]
     Emergency Operating Procedures [*NATO*] (NATG)
SEOP........ Siecor Electro-Optic Products [*Research Triangle Park,
     NC*] (TSSD)
SEOP........ System Employment and Organizational Plan [*Army*]
SEOPSN ... Select-Operate-Sense
SEOR........ Oro [*Ecuador*] [*ICAO location identifier*] (ICLI)
SEOS........ SIGINT Equipment Operator Simulator [*Military*]
S/EOS .... Standard Earth Observation Satellite (MCD)
SEOS........ Symmetric Exchange of Symmetry [*Spectrometry*]
SEOS........ Synchronous Earth Observatory Satellite [*NASA*]
SEOSS....... Slewable Electro-Optical Sensor System
Seoul J Med ... Seoul Journal of Medicine [*A publication*]
Seoul LJ..... Seoul Law Journal [*A publication*] (DLA)
Seoul Natl Univ Coll Agric Bull ... Seoul National University. College of
     Agriculture. Bulletin [*A publication*]
Seoul Natl Univ Eng Rep ... Seoul National University. Engineering Reports
     [*A publication*]
Seoul Nat Univ Econ R ... Seoul National University. Economic Review [*A
     publication*]
Seoul Nat Univ Eng Rep ... Seoul National University Engineering Report [*A
     publication*]
Seoul Nat Univ Fac Pap Bio Agric Ser ... Seoul National University. Faculty
     Papers. Biology and Agriculture Series [*A publication*]
Seoul Nat Univ Fac Pap Biol Agric Ser E ... Seoul National University Faculty
     Papers. Biology and Agriculture. Series E [*A publication*]
Seoul Nat Univ Fac Pap Med Pharm Ser ... Seoul National University.
     Faculty Papers. Medicine and Pharmacy Series [*A
     publication*]
Seoul Nat Univ Fac Pap Sci Technol Ser ... Seoul National University. Faculty
     Papers. Science and Technology Series [*A publication*]
Seoul Nat Univ J Agric Sci ... Seoul National University. Journal of
     Agricultural Sciences [*A publication*]

Seoul University J Pharm Sci ... Seoul University. Journal of Pharmaceutical Sciences [*A publication*]
Seoul Univ Fac Pap Ser C ... Seoul University. Faculty Papers. Series C. Science and Technology [*A publication*]
Seoul Univ Fac Pap Ser D ... Seoul University. Faculty Papers. Series D. Medicine and Pharmacy [*A publication*]
Seoul Univ Fac Pap Ser E ... Seoul University. Faculty Papers. Series E. Biology and Agriculture [*A publication*]
Seoul Univ J Biol Agric Ser B ... Seoul University. Journal. Series B. Biology and Agriculture [*A publication*]
Seoul Univ J Biol Agr Ser B ... Seoul University. Journal. Series B. Biology and Agriculture [*A publication*]
Seoul Univ J Med Pharm Ser C ... Seoul University. Journal. Series C. Medicine and Pharmacy [*A publication*]
Seoul Univ J Nat Sci ... Seoul University. Journal. Series A. Natural Science [*A publication*]
Seoul Univ J Nat Sci Ser A ... Seoul University. Journal. Series A. Natural Science [*A publication*]
Seoul Univ J Nat Sci Ser B ... Seoul University. Journal. Series B. Natural Science [*A publication*]
Seoul Univ J Nat Sci Ser C ... Seoul University. Journal. Series C. Natural Science [*A publication*]
Seoul Univ J Pharm Sci ... Seoul University. Journal of Pharmaceutical Sciences [*A publication*]
Seoul Univ J Sci Technol Ser A ... Seoul University. Journal. Series A. Science and Technology [*A publication*]
SEOW .... Society of Engineering Office Workers   (EA)
SEP .... Salmonid Enhancement Program [*Canada*]
SEP .... Samenwerkende Elektriciteit Produktie Bedrijven [*Electric utility*] [*Netherlands*]
SEP .... Saturday Evening Post [*A publication*]
SEP .... Scientific and Engineering Personnel [*Military*]
SEP .... Secretaria de Educacon Publica [*Mexico*] [*A publication*]
SE(P) .... Security Executive, Control at Ports [*British*] [*World War II*]
SEP .... Selective Employment Payments [*British*]
SEP .... Selective Employment Plan
SEP .... Self-Elevating Platform
SEP .... Self-Employed Pension [*British*]
SEP .... Sensory Evoked Potential [*Neurophysiology*]
SEP .... Sepal [*Botany*]   (WGA)
SEP .... Separate   (AFM)
SEP .... Separation Parameter
SEP .... Sepia [*Stamp collecting*]   (ROG)
SEP .... September   (AFM)
SEP .... Septuagint [*Version of the Bible*]
SEP .... Sepultus [*Buried*] [*Latin*]
SEP .... Serial Entry Printer
SEP .... Shepherd Products Ltd. [*Toronto Stock Exchange symbol*]
SEP .... Simplified Employee Pension
SEP .... Site Emergency Plan [*Nuclear energy*]   (NRCH)
SEP .... Slow Electrical Process [*Human brain*]
SEPA .... Slug Ejector Punch
SEP .... Society of Engineering Psychologists [*Later, DAEEP*]   (EA)
SEP .... Society for Exact Philosophy   (EA)
SEP .... Society of Experimental Psychologists   (EA)
SEP .... Software End Product [*Army*]
SEP .... Software Engineering Practice
SEP .... Software Enhancement Proposal
SEP .... Solar Electric Power [*or Propulsion*]
SEP .... Solar Energetic Particle
SEP .... Soldier Enhancement Program [*Army*]   (INF)
SEP .... Solid Electrolyte Potentiometry
SEP .... Somatically Evoked Potential [*Neurophysiology*]
SEP .... SOSUS Estimated Position   (NVT)
SEP .... Source Evaluation Panel [*NASA*]   (NASA)
SEP .... Southern Education Program [*Defunct*]   (EA)
SEP .... Space Electronic Package
SEP .... Special Education Programs [*Department of Education*] [*Formerly, BEH*]
SEP .... Special Emphasis Program [*DoD*]
SEP .... Special Enrollment Period [*Department of Health and Human Services*]   (GFGA)
SEP .... Specific Excess Power   (MCD)
SEP .... Sperm Entry Point [*into egg*]
SEP .... Spherical Error Precision [*or Probability*]
SEP .... Stable Element Panel
SEP .... Standard Electronic Package
SEP .... Standard Engineering Practice   (AAG)
SEP .... Standard Error of Prediction
SEP .... Star Epitaxial Planar   (MSA)
SEP .... Stephenville, TX [*Location identifier*] [*FAA*]   (FAAL)
SEP .... Strong Equivalence Principle [*Thermodynamics*]
SEP .... Student Enhancement Program [*Army*]
SEP .... Student Expense Program [*Civil Defense*]
SEP .... Studiegroup voor Europese Politiek   (EA)
SEP .... Supervisor Executive Program [*NASA*]   (KSC)
SEP .... Support Equipment Package [*NASA*]   (NASA)
SEP .... Surface Electrical Property [*Apollo*] [*NASA*]
SEP .... Surface Experiments [*NASA*]
SE(P) .... Surrendered Enemy Personnel
SEP .... Survey of Eastern Palestine [*A publication*]   (BJA)

SEP .... Systematic Evaluation Program [*Nuclear Regulatory Commission*]
SEP .... Systems Effectiveness Plan
SEP .... Systems Engineering Process
SEP .... Systems Extension Plan
SEP .... Systolic Ejection Period [*Cardiology*]
SEPA .... Pastaza [*Ecuador*] [*ICAO location identifier*]   (ICLI)
SEPA .... Soft Enhancement of Percutaneous Absorption [*Pharmacy*]
SEPA .... Southeast Pacific Area
SEPA .... Southeastern Power Administration [*Department of Energy*]
SEPA .... Southeastern Psychological Association   (MCD)
SEPA .... Soviet Extended Planning Annex   (MCD)
SEPA .... Spanish Evangelical Publishers Association   (EA)
SEP & A ..... Special Equipment Parts and Assemblies Section   (AAG)
SEPA .... System Evaluation Planning and Assessment Model   (MCD)
SEPAC .... Space Experiments with Particle Accelerators [*Spacelab mission*]
SEPACFOR ... Southeast Pacific Force [*later, Command*] [*Navy*]
SEPAK ...... Suspension of Expendable Penetration Aids by Kite [*Military*]
SEPAP .... Shuttle Electrical Power Analysis Program [*NASA*]
separ .... Separatum [*Separately*] [*Latin*]   (MAE)
SEPAR .... Shuttle Electrical Power Analysis Report [*NASA*]   (NASA)
Separation Sci Tech ... Separation Science and Technology [*A publication*]
SEPARON ... Separation   (ROG)
Separ Sci .... Separation Science [*Later, Separation Science and Technology*] [*A publication*]
SEPAWG .. Save EPA [*Environmental Protection Agency*] Working Group   (EA)
SE/PB .... Southern Europe - Ports and Beaches [*NATO*]   (NATG)
SEP Btry .... Separate Battery [*Army*]
SEPC .... Space Exploration Program Council [*NASA*]
SEPCEN .... Separation Center [*Navy*]
SEPCOR .... Separate Correspondence   (MCD)
SEPD .... Scottish Economic Planning Department [*British*]
SEPD .... Separated
SEPD .... Special-Environment Powder Diffractometer [*Crystallography*]
SEPD .... State Emergency Planning Director [*Civil Defense*]
SEPE .... Pechichal [*Ecuador*] [*ICAO location identifier*]   (ICLI)
SEPE .... Seattle Port of Embarkation
SEPE .... Separate   (ROG)
SEPE .... Single Escape Peak Efficiency [*Nuclear science*]   (OA)
SEPE .... Societe d'Edition et de Publications en Exlusivite
SEPEA ...... Societe Europeene de Psychiatrie de l'Enfant et de l'Adolescent [*European Society of Child and Adolescent Psychiatry - ESCAP*]   (EAIO)
SEPEL .... Southeastern Plant Environment Laboratories [*Duke University and North Carolina State University*]
SEPEMIAG ... Societe d'Etudes pour l'Equipement Miniere, Agricole, et Industrial du Gabon [*Gabon Society for Study of Mining, Agricultural, and Industrial Equipment*]
SEPG .... Separating
SEPGA ...... Southeastern Pecan Growers Association   (EA)
Seph .... Sephardic [*Jews from Spain, Portugal, North Africa, and the Mediterranean*]   (BJA)
Sep Hydrogen Isot Symp Jt Conf ... Separation of Hydrogen Isotopes. Symposium. Joint Conference. Chemical Institute of Canada and the American Chemical Society [*A publication*]
SEPI .... Pichincha [*Ecuador*] [*ICAO location identifier*]   (ICLI)
SEPI .... Silicon Electro-Physics, Inc. [*NASDAQ symbol*]   (NQ)
SEPI .... Society for the Exploration of Psychotherapy Integration   (EA)
SEPI .... Sylvania Electric Products, Inc.   (KSC)
SEPIL .... Selective Excitation of Probe Ion Luminescence [*Analytical chemistry*]
SEPL .... Playas [*Ecuador*] [*ICAO location identifier*]   (ICLI)
SEPL .... South European Pipeline [*Oil*]
SEPLIS ...... Secretariat Europeen des Professions Liberales, Independantes et Sociales [*European Secretariat of the Liberal, Independant and Social Professions*] [*EC*]   (ECED)
SEPM .... Society for Sedimentary Geology [*Formerly, Society of Economic Paleontologists and Mineralogists*]   (EA)
SEPM Core Workshop ... Society of Economic Paleontologists and Mineralogists. Core Workshop [*A publication*]
SEPM (Soc Econ Paleontol Miner) Field Trip Guideb ... SEPM (Society of Economic Paleontologists and Mineralogists) Field Trip Guidebook [*A publication*]
SEPN .... Separation   (AAG)
SEPO .... Posorja [*Ecuador*] [*ICAO location identifier*]   (ICLI)
SEPO .... Space Electric Power Office [*AEC*]
SEPOL ...... Settlement Problem-Oriented Language [*Data processing*]   (IEEE)
SEPOL ...... Soil Engineering Problem-Oriented Language [*Data processing*]
SEPORT ... Supply and Equipment Report [*Army*]   (AABC)
SEPOS ...... Selected Enlisted Personnel for Overseas Service [*Military*]   (AABC)
SEPP .... Safety Engineering Program Plan [*Military*]   (DNAB)
SEPP .... Seppyo. Journal. Japanese Society of Snow and Ice [*A publication*]
SEPP .... Simplified Employee Pension Plan
SEPPAA .... Single-Employer Pension Plan Amendments Act [*1986*]   (GFGA)

Sep Purif.... Separation and Purification [*A publication*]
Sep Purif M ... Separation and Purification Methods [*A publication*]
Sep Purif Methods ... Separation and Purification Methods [*A publication*]
SEPQUES ... Separation Questionnaire [*Military*] (DNAB)
SEPR .... Sepracor, Inc. [*NASDAQ symbol*] (SPSG)
SEPRD ...... Sensory Processes [*A publication*]
SEPRL....... Southeast Poultry Research Laboratory [*University of Georgia*] [*Research center*] (RCD)
SEPROS.... Separation Processing [*Military*]
SEPS......... Pasaje [*Ecuador*] [*ICAO location identifier*] (ICLI)
SEPS......... Service Module Electrical Power System [*NASA*] (KSC)
SEPS......... Severe Environment Power System (IEEE)
SEPS......... Smithsonian Earth Physics Satellite
SEPS......... Socio-Economic Planning Sciences [*A publication*]
SEPS......... Solar Electric Propulsion System [*NASA*]
SEPS......... System/Equipment Population Summary
SEPSA....... Society of Educational Programmers and Systems Analysts [*Later, SDE*]
SEPS-B..... Socio-Economic Planning Sciences [*A publication*]
Sep Sci .... Separation Science [*Later, Separation Science and Technology*] [*A publication*]
Sep Sci Suppl ... Separation Science. Supplement [*A publication*]
Sep Sci Technol ... Separation Science and Technology [*A publication*]
SEPSME... Social Economic and Political Studies of the Middle East [*A publication*] (BJA)
SEPST ...... Solar Electric Propulsion System Technology
SEPT .... Putumayo [*Ecuador*] [*ICAO location identifier*] (ICLI)
SEPT .... Separate
sept............ Septem [*Seven*] [*Latin*] (MAE)
Sept .... Septem Contra Thebas [*of Aeschylus*] [*Classical studies*] (OCD)
SEPT .... September (EY)
Sept .... Septuagint [*Version of the Bible*] (BJA)
SEPTA .... Southeastern Pennsylvania Transportation Authority
SEPTAR.... Seaborne Powered Target [*Navy*] (NVT)
SEPTD ...... Separated
Sep Technol Pro Eng Found Conf ... Separation Technology. Proceedings. Engineering Foundation Conference [*A publication*]
SEPTEL .... Separate Telegram
SEPTG ...... Separating
SEPTLA .... Southeastern Pennsylvania Theological Library Association [*Library network*]
SEPTR...... Separator
SEPTR...... September (ROG)
SEPU......... Puna [*Ecuador*] [*ICAO location identifier*] (ICLI)
SEPULT.... Sepultus [*Buried*] [*Latin*] (ROG)
SEPV .... Portoviejo [*Ecuador*] [*ICAO location identifier*] (ICLI)
SEPY .... Puyo [*Ecuador*] [*ICAO location identifier*] (ICLI)
SEQ .... Scientific Equipment (KSC)
SEQ .... Seguin, TX [*Location identifier*] [*FAA*] (FAAL)
SEQ .... Self-Esteem Questionnaire [*Personality development test*] [*Psychology*]
SEQ .... Sequel
SEQ .... Sequence (AABC)
SEQ .... Sequente [*And in What Follows*] [*Latin*]
SEQ .... Sequential Pulse Counting [*Spectrometry*]
SEQ .... Sequestrum [*Medicine*]
SEQ .... Sequitur [*It Follows*] [*Latin*]
SEQ .... Storage Equities, Inc. [*NYSE symbol*] (SPSG)
SEQ .... String Education Quarterly [*A publication*]
SEQE......... Quevedo [*Ecuador*] [*ICAO location identifier*] (ICLI)
SEQI......... Storage Equities, Inc. [*NASDAQ symbol*] (NQ)
SEQL......... Sequel Corp. [*Englewood, CO*] [*NASDAQ symbol*] (NQ)
SEQ LUCE ... Sequenti Luce [*The Following Day*] [*Latin*] (ADA)
SEQN .... Quininde [*Ecuador*] [*ICAO location identifier*] (ICLI)
SEQOPT ... Sequential Optimization (MCD)
SEQP......... Supreme Equipment & Systems Corp. [*NASDAQ symbol*] (NQ)
SEQQ .... Sequentes [*or Sequentia*] [*The Following*] [*Plural form*] [*Latin*]
SEQQ .... Sequentibus [*In the Following Places*] [*Latin*] (ADA)
SEQR .... Sequencer (AAG)
SEQREC ... Sequence Recall [*Neuropsychology test*]
SEQS .... Simultaneous Equation Solver [*Computer program*]
SEQU .... Quito/Mariscal Sucre [*Ecudaor*] [*ICAO location identifier*] (ICLI)
sequ .... Sequitur [*It Follows*] [*Latin*] (WGA)
SEQU .... Sequoia and Kings Canyon National Parks
Sequa .... Sequa Corp. [*Associated Press abbreviation*] (APAG)
SEQUAL... Seasonal Equatorial Atlantic Experiment
SEQUEL... Structured English Query Language [*1974*] [*Data processing*] (CSR)
SEQUIN.... Sequential Quadrature Inband [*Television system*] (DEN)
SEQUIP .... Study of Environmental Quality Information Programs (KSC)
SEQUR...... Safety Equipment Requirements
SER........... Cataloging Services Department, OCLC [*Online Computer Library Center*], Inc., Columbus, OH [*OCLC symbol*] (OCLC)
SER........... Safety Evaluation Report [*Nuclear energy*] (NRCH)
SER........... Sandia Engineering Reactor [*Nuclear energy*]
SER........... Sebum Excretion Rate (OA)
SER........... Seder Eliyahu Rabbah (BJA)

SER.......... Selective Early Retirement [*Army*]
SER.......... Sequential Events Recorder
SER.......... Serial (AFM)
SER.......... Series (AAG)
Ser............ Serine [*Also, S*] [*An amino acid*]
SER.......... Sermon
Ser............ Serpens [*Constellation*]
SER.......... Servant
Ser............ Service [*A publication*]
SER.......... Service (NATG)
SER.......... Service, Employment, Redevelopment [*Operation for Mexican-Americans*] [*Later, SER - Jobs for Progress*]
SER.......... Servico, Inc. [*AMEX symbol*] (SPSG)
SeR.......... Sewanee Review [*A publication*]
SER.......... Seymour, IN [*Location identifier*] [*FAA*] (FAAL)
SER.......... Shore Establishment Realignment [*Navy*] (NVT)
SER.......... Sierracin Corp. [*AMEX symbol*] (SPSG)
SER.......... Significant Event Report (IEEE)
SER.......... Sikorsky Engineering Report
SER.......... Silver Eagle Resources [*Vancouver Stock Exchange symbol*]
SER.......... Simultaneous Evoked [*Cortical*] Response [*Neurophysiology*]
SER.......... Single Electron Response [*Electronics*] (OA)
SER.......... Site Evaluation Report (MCD)
SER.......... Smooth [*Surfaced*] Endoplasmic Reticulum [*Cytology*]
SER.......... SNAP [*Systems for Nuclear Auxiliary Power*] Experimental Reactor
SER.......... Sociedad Espanola de Radiodifusion [*Broadcasting organization*]
SER.......... Society for Ecological Restoration (EA)
SER.......... Society for Educational Reconstruction (EA)
SER.......... Society for Epidemiologic Research (EA)
SER.......... Software Engineering Requirement [*Army*]
SER.......... Somatosensory Evoked Response [*Neurophysiology*]
SER.......... South-Eastern Railway [*British*]
SER.......... Space Electric [*or Electronic*] Rocket (DNAB)
SER.......... Stem End Rot [*Plant pathology*]
SER.......... Sua Eccellenza Reverendissima [*His Eminence*] (EY)
SER.......... Summary Earnings Record [*Social Security Administration*] (GFGA)
SER.......... Support Equipment Requirement
SER.......... Surface Electrical Resistivity
SER.......... System Environment Recording (BUR)
SER.......... Systolic Ejection Rate [*Cardiology*] (MAE)
SERA........ Sierra Railroad Co. [*AAR code*]
SERA........ Sierra Semiconductor [*NASDAQ symbol*] (SPSG)
SERA........ Society for Entrepreneurship Research and Application [*Defunct*] (EA)
SERA........ Solar and Electric Racing Association
SERA........ Special Emphasis Reliability Area (MCD)
SERA........ Stop Equal Rights Amendment [*An association*] [*Inactive*] (EA)
SERAA...... Seramikkusu [*A publication*]
SERAC...... Southeastern Regional Arts Council
SERANAK ... Serge and Natalie Koussevitzky [*Acronym was name of summer home of Boston Symphony Orchestra conductor and his first wife*]
SERANDA ... Service Record, Health Record, Pay Account, and Personal Effects [*Military*]
SERAPE.... Simulator Equipment Requirements for Accelerating Procedural Evolution
SERAPHIM ... Systems Engineering Respecting Acquisition and Propagation of Heuristic Instructional Materials [*Chemistry*]
Ser Astron Uniw Adama Mickiewicza Poznaniu ... Seria Astronomia. Uniwersytet Imeni Adama Mickiewicza w Poznaniu [*A publication*]
SERB .... Riobamba [*Ecuador*] [*ICAO location identifier*] (ICLI)
SERB .... Selective Early Retirement Board [*Army*] (INF)
SERB .... Serbia
SERB .... Shuttle Engineering Review Board [*NASA*] (NASA)
SERB .... Societe Europeene de Radiobiologie [*European Society for Radiation Biology - ESRB*] (EAIO)
SERB .... Study of the Enhanced Radiation Belt [*NASA*]
SERB .... Systems Engineering Review Board [*NASA*] (NASA)
Serb Acad Sci Arts Bull ... Serbian Academy of Sciences and Arts. Bulletin [*A publication*]
Serb Acad Sci Arts Glas ... Serbian Academy of Sciences and Arts. Glas [*A publication*]
Serb Acad Sci Arts Monogr Dep Sci ... Serbian Academy of Sciences and Arts. Monographs. Department of Sciences [*A publication*]
Serb Acad Sci Arts Sep Ed Dep Nat Math Sci ... Serbian Academy of Sciences and Arts. Separate Editions. Department of Natural and Mathematical Sciences [*A publication*]
Serb Arch Gen Med ... Serbian Archives of General Medicine [*A publication*]
Serb Arch Med ... Serbian Archives of Medicine [*A publication*]
SERBAUD ... Serikat Buruh Angkutan Udara [*Airways' Union*] [*Indonesia*]
Serb Chem Soc J ... Serbian Chemical Society. Journal [*A publication*]
Serbian Acad Sci and Arts Monogr Dep Tech Sci ... Serbian Academy of Sciences and Arts. Monographs. Department of Technical Sciences [*A publication*]

Ser Bibliogr INTA (Pergamino) ... Serie Bibliografica. Instituto Nacional de Tecnologia Agropecuaria (Pergamino, Argentina) [*A publication*]
Ser Biol Uniw Adama Mickiewicza Poznaniu ... Seria Biologia. Uniwersytet Imeni Adama Mickiewicza w Poznaniu [*A publication*]
SERBIS ..... Southeastern Regional Biomedical Information System   (AEBS)
SERBIUM ... Serikat Buruh Industri dan Umum [*Industrial and General Workers' Union*] [*Indonesia*]
SERBU ...... Serikat Buruh Umum [*General Workers' Union*] [*Indonesia*]
SERBUHI ... Serikat Buruh Harian Indonesia [*Newspaper Employees' Union of Indonesia*]
SERBUMAMI ... Serikat Buruh Makanan dan Minuman [*Food Workers' Union*] [*Indonesia*]
SERBUMIKSI ... Serikat Buruh Minjak Kelapa Seluruh [*Coconut Oil Workers' Union*] [*Indonesia*]
SERBUMIT ... Serikat Buruh Minjak dan Tambang [*Oil and Minerals Workers' Union*] [*Indonesia*]
SERBUMUSI ... Serikat Buruh Muslimin Indonesia [*Moslem Workers' Union of Indonesia*]
SERBUNI ... Serikat Buruh Unilever Indonesia [*Unilever Employees' Union of Indonesia*]
SERBUPI ... Serikat Buruh Perkebunan Indonesia [*Plantation Workers' Union of Indonesia*]
SERBUPRI ... Serikat Buruh Pertambangan Indonesia [*Mining Workers' Union of Indonesia*]
SERC .... Industry/University Cooperative Research Center for Software Engineering [*University of Florida, Purdue University*] [*Research center*]   (RCD)
SERC .... Science and Engineering Research Council [*British*]
SERC .... Smithsonian Environmental Research Center
SERC .... Southeastern Electric Reliability Council [*Regional power council*]
SERC .... Sussex European Research Centre [*Research center*] [*British*]   (IRC)
SERCA ...... Servicios de Carga Aerea [*National Airlines*] [*Costa Rica*]   (EY)
Ser Cana Azucar ... Serie Cana de Azucar [*A publication*]
Ser Chem Uniw Adama Mickiewicza Poznaniu ... Seria Chemia. Uniwersytet Imeni Adama Mickiewicza w Poznaniu [*A publication*]
Ser Conf Union Math Internat ... Serie des Conferences. Union Mathematique Internationale [*A publication*]
SERD .... Stored Energy Rotary Drive
SERD .... Support Equipment Recommendation Data [*NASA*]   (KSC)
SERD .... Support Equipment Requirements Data
SERDA ...... Signals and Electronic Warfare Research and Development Act
Ser Defects Cryst Solids ... Series Defects in Crystalline Solids [*A publication*]
SERDES .... Serializer/Deserializer
Ser Div Ind Chem CSIRO ... Serial. Division of Industrial Chemistry. Commonwealth Scientific and Industrial Research Organisation [*A publication*]   (APTA) ِ
Ser Divulg Agron Angolana ... Serie Divulgacao. Agronomia Angolana [*A publication*]
Ser Divulg Projeto Desenvolvimento Pesqui Florestal ... Serie Divulgacao. Projeto de Desenvolvimento e Pesquisa Florestal [*A publication*]
SERDP ...... Strategic Environmental Research and Development Program [*National Center for Atmospheric Research*]
SERE .... Services Electronic Research Establishment [*British*]   (DEN)
SERE .... Survival, Evasion, Resistance, and Escape [*Military*]   (AFM)
Ser Emp ...... Service Employee [*A publication*]
SERENDIP ... Search for Extraterrestrial Radio Emission from Nearby Developed Intelligent Populations
Serengeti Res Inst Annu Rep ... Serengeti Research Institute. Annual Report [*A publication*]
Ser Entomol (The Hague) ... Series Entomologica (The Hague) [*A publication*]
SEREP .... System Environment Recording, Editing, and Printing [*Data processing*]
SEREP .... System Error Record Editing Program [*Data processing*]
SERET ...... Snakeye Retarded [*Navy*]   (DNAB)
SERF .... Sandia Engineering Reactor Facility [*Nuclear energy*]
SERF .... Service Fracturing Co. [*NASDAQ symbol*]   (NQ)
SERF .... Solar and Energy Research Facility [*University of Arizona*] [*Research center*]   (RCD)
SERF .... Space Environmental Research Facility
SERF .... Special Emergency Reaction Team Facility
SERF .... Special Environmental Radiometallurgy Facility [*Nuclear energy*]   (NRCH)
SERF .... Study of Energy Release in Flares [*International Council of Scientific Unions*]
SERFACE ... South East Regional Forum for Adult and Continuing Education [*British*]   (DI)
SERFE ...... Selection of Exempt Organization Returns for Examination [*IRS*]
Ser Food Mater Sci ... Series in Food Material Science [*A publication*]
SERFORSOPACSUBCOM ... Service Force, South Pacific, Subordinate Command
SERG .... Sergeant
SERG .... Serving   (MSA)
Serg Att ...... Sergeant on Attachment [*A publication*]   (DLA)
Serg Const L ... Sergeant's Constitutional Law [*A publication*]   (DLA)
SERGE ...... Socially and Ecologically Responsible Geographers [*Defunct*]   (EA)

Ser Geol Econ (Braz) Sup Desenvolvimento Nordeste Div Geol ... Serie Geologia Economica (Braz). Superintendencia do Desenvolvimento do Nordeste. Divisao de Geologia [*A publication*]
Serg Land Laws PA ... Sergeant on the Land Laws of Pennsylvania [*A publication*]   (DLA)
Serg LL ...... Sergeant's Land Laws of Pennsylvania [*A publication*]   (DLA)
Serg & Lowb ... English Common Law Reports, Edited by Sergeant and Lowber [*A publication*]   (DLA)
Serg & Lowb Rep ... English Common Law Reports, Edited by Sergeant and Lowber [*A publication*]   (DLA)
Serg Mech L ... Sergeant on Mechanics' Lien Law [*A publication*]   (DLA)
Serg & R ..... Sergeant and Rawle's Pennsylvania Reports [*A publication*]   (DLA)
SERGRAD ... Selected and Retained Graduate   (DNAB)
Serg & Raw ... Sergeant and Rawle's Pennsylvania Reports [*A publication*]   (DLA)
Serg & Rawl ... Sergeant and Rawle's Pennsylvania Supreme Court Reports [*1814-28*] [*A publication*]   (DLA)
SERGT ...... Sergeant
SERH ...... Secretaria de Estado de Recursos Hidricos [*Argentina*]
Ser Haematol ... Series Haematologica [*A publication*]
Ser Handb Mod Psych ... Serial Handbook of Modern Psychiatry [*A publication*]
SERHL ...... Southeastern Radiological Health Laboratory   (SAA)
Ser Hum ..... Series in the Humanities [*A publication*]
SERI .... Aguarico [*Ecuador*] [*ICAO location identifier*]   (ICLI)
SERI .... Society for the Encouragement of Research and Invention   (EA)
SERI .... Solar Energy Research Institute [*Department of Energy*] [*Golden, CO*]
Serials BLL ... Serials in the British Lending Library [*A publication*]
Serials Libn ... Serials Librarian [*A publication*]
Serials Libr ... Serials Librarian [*A publication*]
Serials R .... Serials Review [*A publication*]
Sericult Res ... Sericultural Research [*Japan*] [*A publication*]
Serie Bibliogr Temat ... Serie Bibliografia Tematica [*A publication*]
Ser Inf Conf Cursos Reun Interam Inst Agric Sci ... Serie Informes de Conferencias. Cursos y Reuniones-Inter-American Institute of Agricultural Sciences [*A publication*]
SER-IV ...... Supination, External Rotation - Type IV Fracture
SERIX .... Swedish Environmental Research Index [*Swedish National Environmental Protection Board*] [*Database*]   (IID)
SERJ .... Serjeant [*Military*] [*British*]   (ROG)
SERJ .... Space Electric Ramjet [*Air Force*]
SERJ .... Supercharged Ejector Ramjet [*Aircraft engine*]
Serjt .... Serjeant [*Military*] [*British*]   (DMA)
SERJT-MAJ ... Serjeant-Major [*Military*] [*British*]   (ROG)
SERL .... Sanitary Engineering Research Laboratory [*University of California*]   (MCD)
Ser L .... Serie Linguistica [*A publication*]
SERL .... Services Electronic Research Laboratory [*British*]
SERLANT ... Service Forces, Atlantic [*Navy*]
Ser Lib .... Serials Librarian [*A publication*]
Ser Libr ...... Serials Librarian [*A publication*]
SERLINE ... Serials On-Line [*National Library of Medicine*] [*Bethesda, MD*] [*Database*]
SERL Rep ... SERL [*Sanitary Engineering Research Laboratory*] Report [*A publication*]
SERM .... Sermon   (ROG)
SERM .... Society of Early Recorded Music   (EA)
SERM .... Solar and Earth Radiation Monitor   (NOAA)
SERM .... Syncrude Environmental Research Monograph [*A publication*]
Ser Mat Fis ... Serie di Matematica e Fisica [*A publication*]
SERMCE .. Amalgamated Association of Street, Electric Railway, and Motor Coach Employees of America [*Later, ATU*]
SERME ...... Sign Error Root Modulus Error
SERMIS .... Support Equipment Rework Management Information System [*Navy*]   (GFGA)
SERMLP ... Southeastern Regional Medical Library Program [*Emory University*] [*Library network*]   (IID)
Ser Monogr Inst Zootec ... Serie Monografias. Instituto de Zootecnia [*A publication*]
Ser Mycol .. Series on Mycology [*A publication*]
SERN .... Southeastern [*Meteorology*]   (FAAC)
SERNO ..... Serial Number
SERNO ..... Service Number [*Military*]
SERO .... Santa Rosa [*Ecuador*] [*ICAO location identifier*]   (ICLI)
SERO .... Service Employment Redevelopment Operation   (OICC)
SERO .... System Engineering Release Order   (MCD)
SERODS ... Surface-Enhanced Raman Optical Data Storage Technology [*Developed at Oak Ridge National Laboratory*]
Serol Mus Bull ... Serological Museum Bulletin [*A publication*]
SERON ..... Service Squadron [*Navy*]
Serono Symp Proc ... Serono Symposia. Proceedings [*A publication*]
Serono Symp Publ Raven Press ... Serono Symposia Publications from Raven Press [*A publication*]
SERP .... Self-Employed Retirement Plan [*Keogh plan*]
Serp .... Serpens [*Constellation*]
SERP .... Simulated Ejector Ready Panel
SERP .... Software Engineering Research Projects [*Data and Analysis Center for Software*] [*Database*]

SERP .... Standardization/Evaluation Review Panel   (AFIT)
SERP .... Strategic Environmental Research Program [*DoD*] [*Department of Energy*]
SERP .... Studies in the History and Art of the Eastern Provinces of the Roman Empire [*A publication*]
SERP .... Supervisor's Evaluation of Research Personnel   (AEBS)
SERPA ...... Southeastern Resource Policy Association   (EA)
SERPAC.... Service Forces, Pacific [*Navy*]
Ser Paedopsychiatr ... Series Paedopsychiatrica [*A publication*]
SERPIN..... Serine Proteinase Inhibitor [*Biochemistry*]
Ser Piper .... Serie Piper [*A publication*]
Ser Poeyana Inst Biol Acad Cienc Cuba ... Serie Poeyana. Instituto de Biologia. Academia de Ciencias de Cuba [*A publication*]
Ser Poeyana Inst Zool Acad Cienc Cuba ... Serie Poeyana. Instituto de Zoologia. Academia de Ciencias de Cuba [*A publication*]
SERPS ...... Service Propulsion System [*or Subsystem*] [*NASA*]   (KSC)
SERPS ...... State Earnings-Related Pension Scheme [*British*]
Ser Publ Geogr ... Serial Publications in Geography [*A publication*]
Ser Publ US Northeast Reg Plant Introd Stn ... Serial Publication. United States Northeast Regional Plant Introduction Station [*A publication*]
SERR .... Semiannual RADWASTE [*Radioactive Waste*] Effluent Release   (GFGA)
Ser R .... Serials Review [*A publication*]
SERR .... Serrate   (MSA)
SerrC.......... Serraika Chronika [*A publication*]
Ser Res Publ Assoc Res Nerv Ment Dis ... Series of Research Publications. Association for Research in Nervous and Mental Disease [*A publication*]
SERRON... Service Squadron [*Navy*]
SERRS....... Surface-Enhanced Resonance Raman Scattering [*Spectroscopy*]
SE/RRT...... Southern Europe - Railroad Transport [*NATO*]   (NATG)
SERS .... Rio Saloya [*Ecuador*] [*ICAO location identifier*]   (ICLI)
SERS .... Seaborne Environmental Reporting System
SERS .... Shuttle Equipment Record System [*NASA*]   (NASA)
SERS .... Southern Education Reporting Service
SERS .... State Employees Retirement System
SERS .... Support Equipment Requirements Sheet
SERS .... Surface-Enhanced Raman Scattering [*Spectroscopy*]
Ser Sl .... Serial Slants [*A publication*]
Sert............. Sertorius [*of Plutarch*] [*Classical studies*]   (OCD)
SERT .... Shipboard Electronic Readiness Team [*Navy*]   (CAAL)
SERT .... Single-Electron Rise Time [*Scintillation counting*]   (IEEE)
SE/RT .... Southern Europe - Road Transport [*NATO*]   (NATG)
SERT .... Space Electric [*or Electronic*] Rocket Test
SERT .... Special Education Resource Teacher
SERT .... Special Education Review Team
SERT .... Special Emergency Reaction Team
SERT .... Spinning Satellite for Electric Rocket Test
SERT .... Sustained Ethanol Release Tube [*Pharmacology*]
SERTH ..... Satisfactory Evidence Received This Headquarters
SERT J ...... SERT [*Society of Electronic and Radio Technicians*] Journal [*A publication*]
SERTOMA ... Service to Mankind [*Meaning of name of Sertoma International Organization*]
SERTS....... Solar Extreme Ultraviolet Telescope and Spectrograph   (MCD)
SERUG...... SII [*Systems Integrators, Incorporated*] Eastern Regional Users Group   (EA)
Ser Universitaria ... Serie Universitaria [*A publication*]
SERV .... Serva [*Preserve*] [*Latin*]   (WGA)
SERV .... Servant
SERV .... Servian   (ROG)
SERV .... Service   (AAG)
Serv .... Service: A Review of Agricultural and Chemical Progress [*A publication*]
SERV .... Single-Stage Earth-Orbital Reusable Vehicle   (MCD)
SERV .... Space Emergency Reentry Vehicle [*NASA*]
SERV .... Surface Effect Rescue Vessel [*Coast Guard*]
ServC .... Service Command [*Army*]
Serv Can Faune Cah Biol ... Service Canadien de la Faune. Cahiers de Biologie [*A publication*]
Serv Cent Prot Rayonnem Ionis (Fr) Rapp Act ... Service Central de Protection Contre les Rayonnements Ionisants (France). Rapport d'Activite [*A publication*]
SERVCOMFMFPAC ... Service Command, Fleet Marine Force, Pacific
SERVDIV ... Service Division [*Navy*]
SERVE ...... Serve and Enrich Retirement by Volunteer Experience [*Staten Island, NY, project*]
SERVE ...... Service   (ROG)
Serv Farm Ranch Home ... Serving Farm, Ranch, and Home. Quarterly. University of Nebraska. College of Agriculture and Home Economics. Agricultural Experiment Station [*A publication*]
SERVFOR ... Service Force [*Navy*]
Serv Geol Bolivia Bol ... Servicio Geologico de Bolivia. Boletin [*A publication*]
Serv Geol Ital Mem Descr Carta Geol Ital ... Servizio Geologico d'Italia Memorie Descrittive della Carta Geologica d'Italia [*A publication*]
Serv Geol Port Mem ... Servicos Geologics de Portugal. Memoria [*A publication*]

SERVHEL ... Service Record and Health Record [*Military*]
Service Soc ... Service Social [*A publication*]
Servico .... Servico, Inc. [*Associated Press abbreviation*]   (APAG)
Servico Soc de Comer Bol Bibl ... Servico Social de Comercio. Boletim Bibliografico [*A publication*]
Servico Soc e Soc ... Servico Social e Sociedade [*A publication*]
SERVLANT ... Service Force, Atlantic Fleet
SERVLANTSUBORDCOMD ... Service Force, Atlantic Fleet, Subordinate Command
SERVMART ... Service Mart
SERVNO... Service Number [*Navy*]
SERVO...... Service Office
SERVO...... Servomechanism
SERVON.... Service Squadron [*Navy*]
SERVOTR ... Servotronics, Inc. [*Associated Press abbreviation*]   (APAG)
SERVPA.... Service Record and Pay Record [*Military*]
SERVPAC ... Service Force, Pacific Fleet
SERVPAHEL ... Service Record, Pay Record, and Health Record [*Military*]
SERVREC ... Service Record
SERVS....... Spanish/English Reading and Vocabulary Screening Test
SERVSCOLCOM ... Service School Command [*Navy*]
SERVSCOLCOMDET ... Service Schools Command Detachment [*Navy*]   (DNAB)
Serv Shell Agric Ser A ... Servicio Shell para el Agricultor. Serie A [*A publication*]
Serv Shell Agr Ser A ... Servicio Shell para el Agricultor. Serie A. Informe [*A publication*]
Serv Soc (Bruxelles) ... Service Social (Bruxelles) [*A publication*]
Serv Soc Monde ... Service Social dans le Monde [*A publication*]
Serv Soc (Quebec) ... Service Social (Quebec) [*A publication*]
SERVSOWESPAC ... Service Force, Southwest Pacific Fleet
Serv Stn Merch ... Service Station Merchandising [*A publication*]
SERVT ...... Servant
Serv World ... Service World International [*A publication*]
SERY .... Sarayacu [*Ecuador*] [*ICAO location identifier*]   (ICLI)
SES .... Group Psychotherapy Suitability Evaluation Scale [*Psychology*]
SES .... Samarbetsorganisationen for Emballagefragor i Skandinavien [*Scandinavian Packaging Association*] [*Sweden*]   (EA)
SES .... Satellite Earth Station
SES .... Schriften far Ekonomik un Statistik [*A publication*]
SES .... Science Ethic Society   (EA)
SES .... Scientific Exploration Society   (EA)
SES .... Scottish Economic Society [*British*]
SES .... Seafarers Education Service [*British*]
SES .... Seagrass Ecosystem Study [*Marine science*]   (MSC)
SES .... Seaward Extension Simulator   (SAA)
SES .... Secondary Electron Scattering
SES .... Section d'Eclaireurs-Skieurs [*of Chasseurs Alpins, French Army*]
SES .... Seismic Electric Signal
SES .... Senior Executive Service [*Civil Service*]
SES .... Sequential Environmental Stress
SES .... Service Engine Soon [*Automotive engineering*]
SES .... Service Evaluation System [*Telecommunications*]   (TEL)
SES .... Sesone [*Herbicide*] [*Trademark of Union Carbide Corp.*]
SES .... Shared Energy Savings
SES .... Ship Earth Station [*INMARSAT*]
SES .... Shuttle Engineering Simulation [*NASA*]   (NASA)
SES .... Shuttle Engineering System [*NASA*]   (SSD)
SES .... Sight Erection Support
SES .... Signal Enhancement Seismograph
SES .... Signals Exploitation Space   (MCD)
SES .... Single Engine Sea [*Pilot rating*]   (AIA)
SES .... Small Edison Screw
SES .... Social and Economic Studies [*A publication*]
SES .... Societe des Etudes Socialistes [*Society for Socialist Studies - SSS*]
SES .... Society of Educators and Scholars   (EA)
SES .... Society of Engineering Science   (EA)
SES .... Society for Environmental Stabilization [*Defunct*]   (EA)
SES .... Society of Eye Surgeons   (EA)
SES .... Socioeconomic Status [*or Strata*]
SES .... Soil Erosion Service [*Became Soil Conservation Service, 1935*]
SES .... Solar Eclipse Sensor   (MCD)
SES .... Solar Energy Society [*Later, International Solar Energy Society*]   (EA)
SES .... Solar Environment Simulator
SES .... SONAR Echo Simulator
SES .... Sophia English Studies [*A publication*]
SES .... Space Environment Simulator [*NASA*]
SES .... Space Erectable Structure
SES .... Special Emphasis Study   (NASA)
SES .... Special Exchange Service [*Telecommunications*]   (TEL)
SES .... SPRINT Engagement Simulation [*Missile system evaluation*] [*Army*]   (RDA)
SES .... Standards Engineering Society   (EA)
SES .... State Experiment Stations Division [*of ARS, Department of Agriculture*]
SES .... Stationary Engine Society   (EA)
SES .... Steam Electric Station [*Nuclear energy*]   (NRCH)
SES .... Steam Engine Systems Corp.

SES .... Story of Exploration Series [*A publication*]
SES .... Strategic Engineering Survey [*Navy*]
SES .... Student Evaluation Scale [*Student attitudes test*]
SES .... Studies in Environmental Science [*Elsevier Book Series*] [*A publication*]
SES .... Studies and Expansion Society [*See also SEE*]   (EAIO)
SES .... Study of Education at Stanford [*Stanford University*]
SES .... Suffield [*Alberta*] [*Seismograph station code, US Geological Survey*]   (SEIS)
SES .... Suffield Experimental Station [*Canada*]
SES .... Sunrise Energy Services [*AMEX symbol*]   (SPSG)
SES .... Superexcited Electronic State [*Chemistry*]   (OA)
SES .... Supervisory Electronics Specialist
SES .... Support Equipment Subsystem
SES .... Surface Effects Ship [*Navy symbol*]
SES .... Sustaining Engineering Services
SES .... Sylvania Electronic Systems   (SAA)
SES .... Synergist Erection System [*Medicine*]
SES .... System Evaluation System   (MCD)
SES .... System External Storage
SES .... Systems Engineering Study
SES .... Systems Evaluation Squadron [*Air Force*]
SESA .... Salinas [*Ecuador*] [*ICAO location identifier*]   (ICLI)
SESA .... Seasons Savings Bank [*NASDAQ symbol*]   (NQ)
SESA .... Signal Equipment Support Agency
SESA .... Social and Economic Statistics Administration [*Terminated, 1975*] [*Department of Commerce*]
SESA .... Society for Experimental Stress Analysis [*Later, SEM*]   (EA)
SESA .... Solar Energy Society of America   (EA)
SESA .... Standard Electrica, Sociedad Anonima [*Brazilian affiliate of ITT*]
SESA .... State Employment Security Agency
SESA .... Story of the Empire Series [*A publication*]
SESAC ...... Society of European Stage Authors and Composers
SESAC ...... Space and Earth Science Advisory Committee [*NASA*]
SESAM ..... System for Emission Sampling and Measurement [*Automotive engineering*]
SESAME... Search for Excellence in Science and Mathematics Education [*Graduate program at University of California at Berkeley*]
SESAME... Selected Essential Stockage Availability Method
SESAME... Service, Sort and Merge [*Data processing*]
SESAME... Severe Environmental Storms and Mesoscale Experiment [*National Science Foundation/National Oceanic and Atmospheric Administration*]
SESAME... Systems Engineering Study on Atmospheric Measurements and Equipment   (NOAA)
SESA Pap ... SESA [*Society for Experimental Stress Analysis*] Papers [*A publication*]
SESAT....... Stanford Early School Achievement Test [*Educational test*]
SESB .... Sibambe [*Ecuador*] [*ICAO location identifier*]   (ICLI)
SESC .... Selective Elution Solvent Chromatography
SESC .... Sequential Elution Solvent Chromatography
SESC .... Shuttle Events Sequential Control [*NASA*]   (MCD)
SESC .... South Eastern State College [*Oklahoma*]
SESC .... Space Environment Services Center [*National Oceanic and Atmospheric Administration*] [*Boulder, CO*]   (KSC)
SESC .... Sucua [*Ecuador*] [*ICAO location identifier*]   (ICLI)
SESC .... Surface Environmental Sample Container [*Apollo*] [*NASA*]
SESCI....... Solar Energy Society of Canada, Inc. [*Societe d'Energie Solaire du Cana da*]
SESCO ...... Secure Submarine Communications
SESD .... Santo Domingo De Los Colorados [*Ecuador*] [*ICAO location identifier*]   (ICLI)
SESD .... Space Electronic Security Division [*Military*]
SESDA ...... Serikat Sekerdja Departemen Agama [*Brotherhood of Employees of Department of Religious Affairs*] [*Indonesia*]
SESDA ...... Small Engine Servicing Dealers Association   (EA)
SESDAQ ... Stock Exchange of Singapore Dealing and Automated Quotation System
SESE .... Secadal [*Educador*] [*ICAO location identifier*]   (ICLI)
SESE .... Secure Echo-Sounding Equipment [*SONAR*] [*Navy*]
SESE .... Shuttle Experiment Support Equipment
SE/SE........ Single Entry/Single Exit
SESE .... Space Electronics Support Equipment   (MCD)
SESEF....... Ship Electronics System Evaluation Facility [*Navy*]   (CAAL)
SESG .... Sangay [*Ecuador*] [*ICAO location identifier*]   (ICLI)
SESG .... Southern Europe Shipping Group [*NATO*]   (NATG)
SESH........ San Honorato [*Ecuador*] [*ICAO location identifier*]   (ICLI)
SESI.......... Solar Energy Society of Ireland [*International Solar Energy Society*]
SESI.......... Sur Iliniza [*Ecuador*] [*ICAO location identifier*]   (ICLI)
SE/SI........ Systems Engineering/Systems Integration   (SDI)
SESJ......... San Jose [*Ecuador*] [*ICAO location identifier*]   (ICLI)
SESK .... Silok [*Ecuador*] [*ICAO location identifier*]   (ICLI)
SESL .... San Lorenzo [*Ecuador*] [*ICAO location identifier*]   (ICLI)
SESL.......... Self-Erecting Space Laboratory   (AAG)
SESL.......... Southeastern Savings Bank, Inc. [*NASDAQ symbol*]   (NQ)
SESL.......... Space Environment Simulation Laboratory [*NASA*]
SESLP .... Sequential Explicit Stochastic Linear Programming [*Data processing*]

SESM .... Samborondon [*Ecuador*] [*ICAO location identifier*]   (ICLI)
SESMI....... Systems Engineering Support and Management Integration   (MCD)
SESN .... San Carlos [*Ecuador*] [*ICAO location identifier*]   (ICLI)
SESO .... La Estrella [*Ecuador*] [*ICAO location identifier*]   (ICLI)
SESO .... Senior Equipment Staff Officer [*Air Force*] [*British*]
SESOC ...... Surface Effect Ship for Ocean Commerce
SESOME .. Service, Sort, and Merge [*Data processing*]   (IEEE)
SESP......... Society of Experimental Social Psychology   (EA)
SESP......... Space Experiment Support Program   (MCD)
SESP......... Space Experimental Satellite Program [*NASA*]   (SSD)
SESPA ...... Scientists and Engineers for Social and Political Action [*Later, SFTP*]   (EA)
SESPENDO ... Serikat Buruh Pegawai Negeri dan Daeran Otonom [*Civil Servants Workers' Union*] [*Indonesia*]
SESPO ...... Surface Effect Ships Project Office [*Navy*]
SESPROJ ... Surface Effect Ship Project [*Navy*]   (DNAB)
SESQUIH ... Sesquihora [*An Hour and a Half*] [*Pharmacy*]   (ROG)
SESQUIHOR ... Sesquihora [*An Hour and a Half*] [*Pharmacy*]
SESR .... San Rafael [*Ecuador*] [*ICAO location identifier*]   (ICLI)
SESR .... Selected Equipment Status Report [*Navy*]   (NG)
SESR .... Societe Europeenne de Sociologie Rurale [*European Society for Rural Sociology*]
SESR .... Special Environmental Storage Requirements   (MCD)
SES Rep CSIRO Sol Energy Stud ... SES Report. Solar Energy Studies Unit. Commonwealth Scientific and Industrial Research Organisation [*A publication*]   (APTA)
SESRTCIC ... Statistical, Economic, and Social Research and Training Center for Islamic Countries [*Research center*] [*Turkey*]   (IRC)
SESS .... Session
SESS .... Society of Ethnic and Special Studies   (EA)
SESS .... Space Environmental Support System
SESS .... Summer Employment for Science Students
Sess Ca ...... Scotch Court of Session Cases [*A publication*]   (DLA)
Sess Ca .... Sessions Cases, King's Bench [*1710-48*] [*England*] [*A publication*]   (DLA)
Sess Cas .... Scotch Court of Session Cases [*A publication*]   (DLA)
Sess Cas .... Session Cases. Court of Session [*Scotland*] [*A publication*]
Sess Cas .... Session Cases, High Court of Justiciary Section [*1906-16*] [*Scotland*] [*A publication*]   (DLA)
Sess Cas .... Sessions Cases, King's Bench [*England*] [*A publication*]   (DLA)
Sess Cas J ... Session Cases. High Court of Justiciary [*Scotland*] [*A publication*]
Sess Cas KB ... Sessions Settlement Cases, King's Bench [*England*] [*A publication*]   (DLA)
Sess Cas Sc ... Scotch Court of Session Cases [*A publication*]   (DLA)
Sess N .... Session Notes [*Scotland*] [*A publication*]   (DLA)
Sess Pap CC ... Central Criminal Court Cases, Sessions Papers [*1834-1913*] [*England*] [*A publication*]   (ILCA)
Sess Pap CCC ... Central Criminal Court Cases, Sessions Papers [*1834-1913*] [*England*] [*A publication*]   (DLA)
Sess Pap OB ... Old Bailey's Sessions Papers [*A publication*]   (DLA)
Sest .... Pro Sestio [*of Cicero*] [*Classical studies*]   (OCD)
SEST .... San Cristobal (Galapagos) [*ICAO location identifier*]   (ICLI)
SESTF .... Surface Effect Ship Test Facility [*Navy*]   (DNAB)
SESTM...... Societe Europeenne de la Science et de la Technologie des Membranes [*European Society of Membrane Science and Technology - ESMST*]   (EA)
SESUNC ... Sesuncia [*An Ounce and a Half*] [*Pharmacy*]   (ROG)
SESY .... Sur Cayambe [*Ecuador*] [*ICAO location identifier*]   (ICLI)
SESZ .... Sur Antizana [*Ecuador*] [*ICAO location identifier*]   (ICLI)
Set .... English Settlement and Removal Cases [*Burrow's Settlement Cases*] [*A publication*]   (DLA)
SET........... Safety Education and Training
SET........... Satellite Experimental Terminal   (NATG)
SET........... Scientists, Engineers, Technicians
SET........... Securities Exchange of Thailand
SET........... Security Escort Team [*Military*]
SET........... Selective Electronic Training [*Navy*]   (NG)
SET........... Selective Employment Tax [*British*]
SET........... Self-Employment Tax [*IRS*]
SET........... Self-Extending Translator   (IEEE)
SET........... Senior Electronic Technician [*National Weather Service*]
SET........... Sensory Evaluation Test [*Army*]
SET........... Service Evaluation Telemetry   (AAG)
SET........... Setif [*Algeria*] [*Seismograph station code, US Geological Survey*]   (SEIS)
SET........... Setting   (MSA)
SET........... Settlement   (ROG)
SET........... Settling
SET........... Sheraton Executive Traveler [*Sheraton Corp.*]
SET........... Siemont Resources, Inc. [*Vancouver Stock Exchange symbol*]
SET........... Simplified Engineering Technique
SET........... Simulated Emergency Test
SET........... Single-Electron-Transfer [*Organic chemistry*]
SET........... Single-Electron Tunneling [*Physics*]
SET........... Single Escape Tower
SET........... Society for Environmental Therapy [*British*]
SET........... Society for the Eradication of Television   (EA)
SET........... Software Engineering Technology
SET........... Software Engineering Terminology [*Data processing*]   (IEEE)

SET............ Solar Energy Thermionic [*Program*] [*NASA*]
SET............ Source Evaluation Team [*Army*]
SET............ Space Electronics and Telemetry (MCD)
SET............ Spacecraft Elapsed Time
SET............ Sports Emotion Test [*Research test*] [*Psychology*]
SET............ Stack Entry Time [*Aviation*] (FAAC)
SET............ Standard d'Exchange et de Transfert [*Computer graphics*] [*French*]
SET............ Stepped Electrode Transistor
SET............ Student Empowerment Training Project (EA)
SET............ Studies in English (University of Texas) [*A publication*]
SET............ Submarine Engineering Technical
SET............ Suitability Evaluation Team (MCD)
SE & T .... Supplies, Equipment, and Training [*Civil Defense*]
SET............ Symbol Elaboration Test [*Psychology*]
SET............ Synchro Error Tester
SET............ Syndicat des Enseignants du Togo [*Union of Togolese Teachers*]
SET............ System Extension Test
SET............ Systems Effects Test [*Nuclear energy*] (GFGA)
SET............ Systems Engineering Test (CET)
SET............ Systolic Ejection Time [*Cardiology*] (MAE)
SETA......... Satellite Electrostatic Triaxial Accelerometer
SETA......... Simplified Electronic Tracking Apparatus [*Air Force*]
SETA......... Systems Engineering and Technical Assistance (MCD)
SETA .... Taura [*Ecuador*] [*ICAO location identifier*] (ICLI)
Seta Artif ... Seta Artificiale [*A publication*]
SETAB ...... Sets Tabular Material [*Phototypesetting computer*]
SETAC ...... Sector TACAN [*Tactical Air Navigation*] System
SETAC ...... Society of Environmental Toxicology and Chemistry (EA)
SETAC ...... Specially Equipped Traffic Accident Car [*British police*]
SETAC ...... Systems Engineering and Technical Assistance Contract
SETAD ...... Secure Encryption of Tactical Analog Data
SETAD ...... Secure Transmission of Acoustic Data (NVT)
SETAF...... Southern European Task Force [*NATO*]
SETAR ..... Serial Event Timer and Recorder
SETA-UITA ... Syndicat Europeen des Travailleurs de l'Alimentation, de l'Hotellerie, et des Branches Connexes dans l'UITA [*European Committee of Food, Catering, and Allied Workers' Unions within the IUF - ECF-IUF*] (EAIO)
SETB .... Secondary Education Text-Books [*A publication*]
SETB .... Set Theoretic Language - BALM [*1973*] [*Data processing*] (CSR)
SETB .... Sierra Real Estate Equity Trust '83 [*San Francisco, CA*] [*NASDAQ symbol*] (NQ)
SETB .... Timbre [*Ecuador*] [*ICAO location identifier*] (ICLI)
SETBGT.... Set Ballistic Gain Table
SETC .... Sierra Real Estate Equity Trust '84 Co. [*NASDAQ symbol*] (NQ)
SETC .... Solid Electrolyte Tantalum Capacitor
SETC .... Southeastern Theatre Conference (EA)
SETC .... Submarine Escape Training Centre [*British military*] (DMA)
SETD......... Sledborne Event Time Digitizer
SETD......... Space Environment Test Division [*NASA*]
SE & TD .... Systems Engineering and Technical Direction (AAG)
SETE .... Secretariat for Electronic Test Equipment [*DoD*]
SETE .... Status of Electronic Test Equipment (MCD)
SETE .... Supersonic Expendable Turbojet Engine (MCD)
SETE .... Support and Electronic Test Equipment
SETE .... System Evaluation Test Equipment [*Military*] (CAAL)
SETE .... Tena [*Ecuador*] [*ICAO location identifier*] (ICLI)
SETEL....... Societe Europeenne de Teleguidage [*Five European firms organized in 1958 under French law to act as European prime contractor for production of HAWK missiles*] [*NATO*]
SETEP...... Science and Engineering Technician Education Program [*National Science Foundation*]
SETF .... SNAP [*Systems for Nuclear Auxiliary Power*] Experimental Test Facility
SETF .... STARAN Evaluation and Training Facility
SETG......... Tenguel [*Ecuador*] [*ICAO location identifier*] (ICLI)
SET-GO .... Support and Encouragement for Talent - Gateway to Opportunity [*Project*] (EA)
SETH......... Taisha [*Ecuadaor*] [*ICAO location identifier*] (ICLI)
Set Hall Leg J ... Seton Hall Legislative Journal [*A publication*]
Set H LR.... Seton Hall Law Review [*A publication*]
SETI .... Search for Extraterrestrial Intelligence
SETI .... Societe Europeenne pour le Traitement de l'Information [*European Society for the Processing of Information*]
SETI .... Tiputini [*Ecuador*] [*ICAO location identifier*] (ICLI)
SETID .... Set Identification
SETINA .... Southeast Texas Information Network Association
SETIS........ Societe Europeenne pour l'Etude et l'Integration des Systemes Spatiaux
SETL .... Science Experiment Test Laboratory [*NASA*]
SETL .... Set Theoretic Language [*1971*] [*Data processing*] (CSR)
SETLG ...... Settling (MSA)
SET Manpower Comments ... Scientific Engineering. Technical Manpower Comments [*A publication*]
SETO......... Pacto [*Ecuador*] [*ICAO location identifier*] (ICLI)
SETOLS.... Surface Effect Takeoff and Land System [*Naval aviation*]

Seto Mar Biol Lab Publ ... Seto Marine Biological Laboratory. Publications [*A publication*]
Seton .... Seton's Forms of Decrees, Judgments, and Orders in Equity [*7 eds.*] [*1830-1912*] [*A publication*] (DLA)
Seton Dec... Seton's Forms of Decrees, Judgments, and Orders in Equity [*7th ed.*] [*1912*] [*A publication*] (DLA)
Seton Hall Leg J ... Seton Hall Legislative Journal [*A publication*]
Seton Hall L Rev ... Seton Hall Law Review [*A publication*]
SETP .... Society of Experimental Test Pilots (EA)
SETP .... Tandapi [*Ecuador*] [*ICAO location identifier*] (ICLI)
SETR .... Setter (MSA)
SETR .... Tarapoa [*Ecuador*] [*ICAO location identifier*] (ICLI)
SETS .... Scottish Electrical Training Scheme Ltd. [*British*]
SETS .... Seeker Evaluation Test System [*Military*]
SETS .... Set Equation Transformation System [*1970*] [*Data processing*] (CSR)
SETS .... Site Enforcement Tracking System [*Environmental Protection Agency*] (GFGA)
SETS .... Skylab End-to-End Test System [*NASA*]
SETS .... Solar Electric Test Satellite
SETS .... Solar Energy Thermionic Conversion System [*NASA*]
SETS .... Special Electron Tube Section
SETS .... Standardized Environmental Technical Specifications [*Nuclear energy*] (NRCH)
SETS .... Stereo Electro-Optical Tracking System (MCD)
Sett............ Settlement Cases [*A publication*] (DLA)
SETT .... Submarine Escape Training Tank
SETT .... Teniente Ortiz [*Ecuador*] [*ICAO location identifier*] (ICLI)
SETTA ...... Southeastern Test and Training Area [*Military*] (MCD)
Sett Cas...... Burrow's English Settlement Cases [*A publication*] (DLA)
Sett Cas...... Settlement and Removal Cases in English King's Bench [*A publication*] (DLA)
Settim Med ... Settimana Medica [*Italy*] [*A publication*]
Settim Osp ... Settimana Ospitaliera [*A publication*]
SETTL....... Settler [*Genealogy*]
SETTLET ... Settlement (ROG)
Sett & Rem ... Settlement and Removal Cases in English King's Bench [*A publication*] (DLA)
SETTT....... Settlement (ROG)
SETU......... Sumerian Economic Texts from the Third Ur Dynasty [*A publication*]
SETU......... Tulcan [*Ecuador*] [*ICAO location identifier*] (ICLI)
SEU .... Dynamik im Handel [*A publication*]
SEU .... Saint Edward's University [*Texas*]
SEU .... Sales Education Units
SEU .... Single Event Upset (SSD)
SEU .... Solar Energy Update [*A publication*]
SEU .... Source Entry Utility
SEU .... Southeastern University [*Washington, DC*]
SEU .... Spiral Optics [*Vancouver Stock Exchange symbol*]
SEU .... Subjective Expected Utility [*Concept*] [*Theory used for decision making*]
SEU .... Surgery Expandable Unit (SAA)
SEUG .... Screaming Eagles Users Group (EA)
SEUL......... Servicio Europeo de Universitarios Latinoamericanos [*Belgium*]
SEUL......... Support Equipment Utilization List (NASA)
SEURE...... Systems Evaluation Code Under Radiation Environment (IEEE)
SEUS........ Southeastern United States
SEUSSN... Southeastern United States Seismic Network (NRCH)
SEUY........ Chanduy [*Ecuador*] [*ICAO location identifier*] (ICLI)
S & EV ...... Saratoga & Encampment Valley Railroad (IIA)
SEV........... Scout Evaluation Vehicle
SEV........... Sensor Equivalent Visibility
SEV........... Service City, AK [*Location identifier*] [*FAA*] (FAAL)
SEV........... Sevastopol [*Former USSR*] [*Seismograph station code, US Geological Survey*] [*Closed*] (SEIS)
SEV........... Seven
SEV........... Several
SEV........... Severe [*Used to qualify weather phenomena*]
SEV........... Severed
Sev............. Severus [*of Scriptores Historiae Augustae*] [*Classical studies*] (OCD)
SEV........... Sevres [*China*] (ROG)
SEV........... Shelter Equipment Vault
SEV........... Ship Exercise Vehicle
SEV........... Simcoe Erie Investors Ltd. [*Toronto Stock Exchange symbol*]
SEV........... Small Earlywood Vessel [*Tree-ring property*]
SEV........... Societe d'Ethologie Veterinaire [*Society for Veterinary Ethology - SVE*] [*Edinburgh, Scotland*] (EAIO)
SEV........... Special Equipment Vehicle [*Military*]
SEV........... Split End Vector [*System for plant cell transformation*]
SEV........... SRAM Equivalent Volume (MCD)
SEV........... State Equalized Value [*Real estate*]
SEV........... Stockpile Emergency Verification [*DoD*]
SEV........... Surface Effects Vehicle [*Military*]
SEVA........ Skylab Extravehicular Visor Assembly [*NASA*]
SEVA........ Standup Extravehicular Activity [*Aerospace*]
SEVA........ Surface Extravehicular Activity [*Lunar exploration*]
SEVA........ Valdez [*Ecuador*] [*ICAO location identifier*] (ICLI)

SEVAC ...... Secure Voice Access Console [*Army*] (AABC)
SEVAL ...... Senior Evaluator (MCD)
Sev App Cas ... Sevestre's Bengal High Court Appeal Cases [*1864-68*] [*India*] [*A publication*] (DLA)
SEVAS ...... Secure Voice Access Systems [*Army*] (AABC)
Sev Cent N ... Seventeenth-Century News [*A publication*]
SEVEC ...... Society for Educational Visits and Exchanges in Canada [*Societe Educative de Visites et d'Echanges au Canada*]
Seven Ct N ... Seventeenth-Century News [*A publication*]
SEVENTHFLT ... Seventh Fleet [*Navy*]
Sevestre...... Calcutta Reports of Cases in Appeal [*A publication*] (DLA)
SEVFLT .... Seventh Fleet [*Pacific*] [*Navy*]
Sev HC....... Sevestre's Bengal High Court Reports [*India*] [*A publication*] (DLA)
SEVI .... Villano [*Ecuador*] [*ICAO location identifier*] (ICLI)
SEVL .... Several (ROG)
SEVN........ Sevenson Environmental Services, Inc. [*NASDAQ symbol*] (NQ)
SEVN........ Vinces [*Ecuador*] [*ICAO location identifier*] (ICLI)
SEVOCOM ... Secure Voice Communications (AFM)
SEVP .... Severance Pay [*Military*]
SEVPEN ... Service d'Edition et de Vente des Publications de l'Education Nationale [*A publication*]
Sev SDA..... Sevestre's Sadr Diwani Adalat Reports [*Bengal, India*] [*A publication*] (DLA)
SEVT .... Ventanas [*Ecuador*] [*ICAO location identifier*] (ICLI)
Sev-Vost Kompleks Nauch-Issled Inst Akad Nauk SSSR Sib Otd ... Severo-Vostochnyy Kompleksnyy Nauchno-Issledovatel'skiy Institut Akademiya Nauk SSSR Sibirskoye Otdeleniye [*A publication*]
Sev Zapad Evr Chasti SSSR ... Severo-Zapad Evropeiskoi Chasti SSSR [*A publication*]
SEW.......... Sewage [*or Sewer*] (AAG)
Sew........... Sewanee Review [*A publication*]
SEW.......... Seward [*Alaska*] [*Seismograph station code, US Geological Survey*] (SEIS)
SEW.......... Shipboard Electronics Warfare [*Navy*]
SEW.......... Silicon Epitaxial Wafer
SEW.......... Singer Co. NV [*NYSE symbol*] (SPSG)
SEW.......... SONAR Early Warning
SEW.......... Sozialistische Einheitspartei Westberlins [*Socialist Unity Party of West Berlin*] [*Germany*] [*Political party*] (PPW)
SEW.......... Special Effects Warhead (MCD)
SE & W ...... Start Early and Walk [*Fictitious railroad initialism used to indicate one of the most reliable modes of rural transportation*]
SEW.......... Surface Electromagnetic Wave
SEWACO ... Sensor Weapons Control and Command
Sewage Effluent Water Resour Symp Rep Proc ... Sewage Effluent as a Water Resource. Symposium. Report of Proceedings [*A publication*]
Sewage Ind Waste Eng ... Sewage and Industrial Waste Engineering [*A publication*]
Sewage Ind Wastes ... Sewage and Industrial Wastes [*A publication*]
Sewage Purif Land Drain Water River Eng ... Sewage Purification. Land Drainage. Water and River Engineering [*A publication*]
Sewage Works Eng Munic Sanit ... Sewage Works Engineering and Municipal Sanitation [*A publication*]
Sewage Works J ... Sewage Works Journal [*A publication*]
Sewanee R ... Sewanee Review [*A publication*]
Sewanee Rev ... Sewanee Review [*A publication*]
Sewan R ..... Sewanee Review [*A publication*]
SEWC........ SIGINT/Electronic Warfare Coordination Element (MCD)
S/EWCC ... Signal Intelligence/Electronic Warfare Coordination Center (NVT)
Sew Cor...... Sewell on Coroners [*1843*] [*A publication*] (DLA)
Sewell Sheriffs ... Sewell on the Law of Sheriffs [*A publication*] (DLA)
SEWG....... Sewing (WGA)
SEWHO ...... Shoulder-Elbow-Wrist-Hand Orthosis [*Medicine*]
SEWL........ Southeast Water Laboratory [*Environmental Protection Agency*]
SEWMRPG ... Southern European Western Mediterranean Regional Planning Group [*NATO*] (NATG)
SEWO ...... Shoulder-Elbow-Wrist Orthosis [*Medicine*]
SEWPS...... Safety Weather Probability Study (MCD)
Sew R .... Sewanee Review [*A publication*]
Sew Rev...... Sewanee Review [*A publication*]
SEWS .... Satellite Early Warning System
SEWS .... Sun-End Work Station [*NASA*] (KSC)
SEWS .... Surface Electromagnetic Wave Spectroscopy
Sew Sh ...... Sewell on the Law of Sheriffs [*1842*] [*A publication*] (DLA)
SEWT .... Simulated Electronic Warfare Training [*Army*]
SEWT....... Simulator for Electronic Warfare Training
SEWY....... Seaway Food Town, Inc. [*NASDAQ symbol*] (NQ)
Sex.......... Sextans [*Constellation*]
SEX......... Shipment Exception Code [*Military*] (AFIT)
SEX......... Sodium Ethyl Xanthate [*Organic chemistry*]
SEX......... Summer Experiment Group [*Summer work for engineering undergraduates*]
SEXAFS .... Surface-Extended X-Ray Absorption Fine Structure
SEXC........ Sierra Exploration Co. [*NASDAQ symbol*] (NQ)

Sex Disabil ... Sexuality and Disability [*A publication*]
S Exec Doc ... Senate Executive Document [*A publication*] (DLA)
S Exec Rep ... Senate Executive Report [*A publication*] (DLA)
S/EXH....... Single Exhaust [*Automotive engineering*]
SEXLF....... States Exploration Ltd. [*NASDAQ symbol*] (NQ)
Sex LR ...... Sexual Law Reporter [*A publication*] (DLA)
Sex L Rep .. Sexual Law Reporter [*A publication*] (DLA)
SExO .... Senior Experimental Officer [*Also, SEO, SXO*] [*Ministry of Agriculture, Fisheries, and Food*] [*British*]
SeXO .... Serum Xanthine Oxidase [*Clinical chemistry*] (AAMN)
Sex Plant R ... Sexual Plant Reproduction [*A publication*]
Sex Pomp... Sextus Pomponius [*Flourished, 2nd century*] [*Authority cited in pre-1607 legal work*] (DSA)
SEXPOT ... SPRINT [*Solid-Propellant Rocket Intercept*] Extra Pulse Out of Tail [*Army*]
s expr.......... Sine Expressione [*Without Expressing*] [*Latin*] (MAE)
Sex Prob Ct Dig ... Sex Problems Court Digest [*A publication*] (DLA)
SEXR .... Shoulder External Rotation [*Sports medicine*]
SEXRAT.... Sex Ratio [*Biology*]
Sex Scien ... Working Papers on Sex, Science, and Culture [*A publication*]
Sext .... Liber Sextus Decretalium [*A publication*] (DSA)
Sext .... Sextans [*Constellation*]
SEXT .... Shoulder Extension [*Sports medicine*]
Sext Emp ... Sextus Empiricus [*Third century AD*] [*Classical studies*] (OCD)
Sex Transm Dis ... Sexually-Transmitted Diseases [*A publication*]
SEY........... Block Island, RI [*Location identifier*] [*FAA*] (FAAL)
SEY........... Secondary Electron Yield
SEY........... Selibaby [*Mauritania*] [*Airport symbol*] (OAG)
SEY........... Seymchan [*Former USSR*] [*Seismograph station code, US Geological Survey*] (SEIS)
SEY........... Southeastern Yiddish [*BJA*]
SEY........... Starlight Energy [*Vancouver Stock Exchange symbol*]
SEY........... Summer Employment Youth [*DoD*]
SEYA........ Yaupi [*Ecuador*] [*ICAO location identifier*] (ICLI)
Seybold Rep Off Systems ... Seybold Report on Office Systems [*A publication*]
Seybold Rep Prof Comp ... Seybold Report on Professional Computing [*A publication*]
Seychelles Dep Agric Annu Rep ... Seychelles Department of Agriculture. Annual Report [*A publication*]
Seych LR ... Seychelles Law Reports [*A publication*] (DLA)
SEYF .... Scottish Episcopal Youth Fellowship
SEYM....... Secondary Electron Yield Measurement
Sey Merch Sh ... Seymour's Merchant Shipping Acts [*2nd ed.*] [*1857*] [*A publication*] (DLA)
SEYMS ..... Secondary Electron Yield Measurement System
SEYS .... Secondary Electron Yield System
Seysell........ [*Claudius de*] Seysellis [*Deceased, 1520*] [*Authority cited in pre-1607 legal work*] (DSA)
SEZ........... Mahe Island [*Seychelles Islands*] [*Airport symbol*] (OAG)
SEZ........... Sedona, AZ [*Location identifier*] [*FAA*] (FAAL)
SEZ........... Seifen, Oele, Fette, Waechse. Die Internationale Fachzeitschrift [*A publication*]
Sez............ Sezione [*Division*] [*Italian*] (ILCA)
SEZ........... Special Economic Zone
SEZA .... Zamora [*Ecuador*] [*ICAO location identifier*] (ICLI)
SEzik........ Sapostavitelno Ezikoznanie [*A publication*]
SEZP .... Zumba-Pucupamba [*Ecuador*] [*ICAO location identifier*] (ICLI)
SF............. E. R. Squibb & Sons [*Research code symbol*]
SF............. Fleet Submarine [*Navy symbol*] [*Obsolete*]
SF............. Meiji Seika Kaisha Ltd. [*Japan*] [*Research code symbol*]
SF............. Provisional Sinn Fein [*Northern Ireland*] [*Political party*] (PPW)
SF.............. Royal Scots Fusiliers [*Military unit*] (DMA)
SF............. Sabre Foundation (EA)
SF............. Sacrifice Fly [*Baseball*]
SF............. Safe (NASA)
SF............. Safety Factor
SF............. Safety, Reliability, and Quality Assurance, and Protective Services [*Kennedy Space Center*] [*NASA*] (NASA)
SF.............. Salt Free [*Diet*]
SF............. Sampled Filter (IEEE)
SF............. San Francisco [*California*]
sf................. Sao Tome and Principe [*MARC country of publication code*] [*Library of Congress*] (LCCP)
SF.............. Satiety Factor [*Physiology*]
SF............. Saw Fixture (MCD)
SF............. Scale Factor
SF............. Scarlet Fever [*Medicine*]
SF............. Scheduling Forecast
SF.............. Scheibe-Flugzeugbau GmbH [*Germany*] [*ICAO aircraft manufacturer identifier*] (ICAO)
SF............. School of Chiropody Full Time [*British*]
SF............. Science Fiction [*Also, SCI-FI*]
SF............. Science Fiction [*A publication*]
SF............. Science Frontiers [*An association*] (EA)
SF............. Scleroderma Federation (EA)
SF............. Scouting Force [*Navy*]
SF.............. Sea Flood
SF............. Seasonal Food [*Department of Employment*] [*British*]

SF.............. Secondary Failure [*NASA*] (KSC)
SF.............. Secure Facility (MCD)
S & F .... Security and Facilities [*DoD*]
SF.............. Security Forces [*Japanese army*]
SF.............. Security Forecast [*Control Risks Information Services - CRIS*] [*British*] [*Information service or system*] (IID)
Sf.............. Sefire Inscriptions (BJA)
SF.............. Select Frequency
SF.............. Selection Filter (MCD)
SF.............. Selous Foundation (EA)
SF.............. Semi-Floating [*Automotive engineering*]
SF.............. Semifinished [*Steel or other material*]
SF.............. Semifixed [*Ammunition*] (NATG)
SF.............. Seminal Fluid [*Medicine*]
SF.............. Senate File (OICC)
SF.............. Senior Fellow
SF.............. Separation Factor [*Chemical analysis*]
SF.............. Serum Fibrinogen [*Medicine*] (MAE)
SF.............. Service Factor (MSA)
SF.............. Servicing Flight [*British military*] (DMA)
SF.............. Seva Foundation (EA)
SF.............. Sexagesimo-quarto [*Book up to 7-1/2 centimeters in height*] [*Bibliography*]
Sf.............. Sforzando [*With Additional Accent*] [*Music*]
SF.............. Shell Fragment (MAE)
SF.............. Sherwood Foresters [*Military unit*] [*British*]
SF.............. Shift Forward
SF.............. Shipfitter [*Navy*]
SF.............. Shock Front (SAA)
SF.............. Short Format
SF.............. Shortening Fraction [*Cardiology*]
SF.............. Shrapnel Fragment (MAE)
SF.............. Side Frequency (DEN)
SF.............. Signal Frequency
SF.............. Silicia Fume [*Inorganic chemistry*]
S/F.............. Single Face
SF.............. Single Feeder
S/F.............. Single Flow (NASA)
SF.............. Single Frequency [*Telecommunications*]
SF.............. Single-Fronted (ADA)
SF.............. Sinking Fund [*Finance*]
SF.............. Sinn Fein [*Political front of the Irish Republican Army*]
SF.............. Skin Fibroblast [*Clinical chemistry*]
SF.............. Skip Flag [*Data processing*] (MDG)
SF.............. Sliding Filter (NASA)
SF.............. Slip Factor
SF.............. Slip Fit (MSA)
SF.............. Slot Format [*Microfiltration*]
SF.............. Slow Fire [*Military*]
SF.............. Slow Initial Function (AAMN)
SF.............. Social Forces [*A publication*]
SF.............. Socialisticki Front [*A publication*]
SF.............. Societe Aerienne Francaise d'Affretements [*France*] [*ICAO designator*] (FAAC)
SF.............. Society Farsarotul (EA)
SF.............. Soft [*Horse racing*]
SF.............. Soils and Fertilizers [*A publication*]
SF.............. Solar Flare [*Astronomy*]
SF.............. Soldiers of Freedom (EA)
SF.............. Solid Fuel (ADA)
SF.............. SONAR Frequency [*Military*] (CAAL)
SF.............. Sons of the Holy Family [*Roman Catholic men's religious order*]
SF.............. Sosialistisk Folkepartiet [*Socialist People's Party*] [*Norway*] [*Political party*] (PPE)
S & F .... Sound and Flash [*Military*]
SF.............. Sound and Flash [*Military*]
SF.............. Source Factor [*Nuclear energy*] (NRCH)
SF.............. Source and Fissionable [*Material*] [*Obsolete; see SS*] [*Nuclear energy*]
SF.............. South Following [*Astronomy*]
SF.............. Southern Forest Products Association
SF.............. Space Filler [*Philately*]
SF.............. Space Flight [*A publication*]
SF.............. Spacial Factor
SF.............. Sparing Fitting [*Cargo battens*] [*Shipping*] (DS)
SF.............. Special Facilities
SF.............. Special Fixtures (MCD)
SF.............. Special Forces [*Military*]
SF.............. Special Fraction [*Typography*] (WDMC)
SF.............. Spent Fuel [*Nuclear energy*] (NRCH)
SF.............. Spinal Fluid [*Medicine*]
SF.............. Spiritus Frumenti [*Whisky*] [*Pharmacy*] (ROG)
SF.............. Splicing Factor [*Genetics*]
SF.............. Spontaneous Fission [*Radioactivity*]
SF.............. Sports Foundation (EA)
SF.............. Spot Face
Sf.............. Sprachforum [*A publication*]
SF.............. Spruce-Fast [*Forestry*]
SF.............. Squadron or Flotilla Flag [*Navy*] [*British*]
SF.............. Square Foot

S & F .... Staff and Faculty
SF.............. Stainless Steel Fastenings
SF.............. Standard Form
SF.............. Standard Frequency
SF.............. Stanton Foundation [*Later, KCSF*] (EA)
SF.............. Star Field (MCD)
SF.............. Starlight Foundation (EA)
SF.............. Startled Falcon [*Book written by Thomas Dunn English (1844)*]
SF.............. State Forces [*Army*] [*India*]
SF.............. Statement of Functions (NATG)
sF.............. Statfarad [*Also, statF*] [*Unit of capacitance*]
SF.............. Static Firing [*NASA*] (NASA)
S/F.............. Statute of Frauds [*Business term*]
SF.............. Sterile Females [*Genetics*]
SF.............. Stifel Financial Corp. [*NYSE symbol*] (SPSG)
S & F .... Stock and Fixtures
SF.............. Stock Fund (AFM)
SF.............. Stopped-Flow [*Spectroscopy*]
S/F.............. Store-and-Forward [*Data communications*]
SF.............. Stowage Factor [*Shipping*]
SF.............. Streptococcus faecilis [*Microbiology*]
SF.............. Stress Formula
SF.............. Structure Function
SF.............. Su Favor [*Your Favor*] [*Spanish*]
SF.............. Sub Finem [*Near the End*] [*Latin*]
SF.............. Subcontractor Furnished [*NASA*] (NASA)
SF.............. Subframe
SF.............. Success Factor
SF.............. Successful Flight (MCD)
SF.............. Sufficient Funding (MCD)
SF.............. Sugar Flotation [*Soil testing*]
SF.............. Sugar-Free [*Pharmacy*]
SF.............. Sulfation Factor [*of blood serum*]
SF.............. Sun Factor (ADA)
SF.............. Sunk Face [*Construction*]
SF.............. Sunshine Foundation (EA)
SF.............. Superfund [*Environmental Protection Agency*] (GFGA)
SF.............. Supply Fan (AAG)
SF.............. Surface Foot
SF.............. Surfrider Foundation (EA)
SF.............. Sustaining Fiber
Sf.............. Svedberg Flotation Unit (AAMN)
SF.............. Swedenborg Foundation (EA)
SF.............. Swiss Franc [*Monetary unit*]
SF.............. Symbral Foundation (EA)
SF.............. Syndicat des Fonctionnaires [*Lao Civil Servants' Union*]
SF.............. Synovial Fluid [*Medicine*]
SF1............ Shipfitter, First Class [*Navy*]
SF2............ Shipfitter, Second Class [*Navy*]
SF3............ Shipfitter, Third Class [*Navy*]
SF3............ Society for the Furtherance and Study of Fantasy and Science Fiction (EA)
SF-4 .... Shipping Fever [*An influenza serotype*]
SFA............ Sachs/Freeman Associates, Inc. [*Telecommunications service*] (TSSD)
SFA............ Sadr Foujdaree Adalat Reports [*India*] [*A publication*] (DLA)
SFA............ Saks Fifth Avenue [*Retail department store*]
SFA............ Scandinavian Fraternity of America (EA)
SFA............ Science Fiction Adventures [*1952-1954*] [*A publication*]
SFA............ Scientific-Atlanta, Inc. [*NYSE symbol*] (SPSG)
SFA............ Scottish Football Association (DI)
SFA............ Screw Focusing Adjustment [*Optical*] (ROG)
SFA............ Segment Frequency Algorithm
SFA............ Segmented Flow Analysis
SFA............ Selected Financial Assistance [*British*] (DCTA)
SFA............ Sempervivum Fanciers Association (EA)
SFA............ Service-Factor Amperes (MSA)
SFA............ Seven Falls [*Quebec*] [*Seismograph station code, US Geological Survey*] [*Closed*] (SEIS)
SFA............ Sfax [*Tunisia*] [*Airport symbol*] (OAG)
S & FA .... Shipping and Forwarding Agent
SFA............ Short Field Aircraft
SFA............ Show Folks of America (EA)
SFA............ Sigmund Freud Archives (EA)
SFA............ Simulated Flight - Automatic
SFA............ Single Failure Analysis [*Nuclear energy*] (NRCH)
SFA............ Single-Frequency Approach [*Aviation*] (FAAC)
SFA............ Slide Fastener Association (EA)
SFA............ Slow Flying Aircraft
SFA............ Snack Food Association (EA)
SFA............ Societe Francaise d'Acoustique [*French Society of Acoustics - FSA*] (EAIO)
SFA............ Society of Filipino Accountants (EA)
SFA............ Soil-Derived Fulvic Acid
SFA............ Solid Fuels Administration [*Terminated, 1954*]
SFA............ Soroptimist Federation of the Americas [*Later, Soroptimist International of the Americas*] (EA)
SFA............ Southeastern Fabric Association (EA)
SFA............ Southeastern Fisheries Association (EA)
SFA............ Southern Freight Association
SFA............ Spatial Frequency Analyzer

SFA............ Special Forces Association (EA)
SFA............ Special Forces Auxiliary [*Military*]
SFA............ Special Foreign Activities [*Military*] (AABC)
SFA............ Speech Foundation of America (EA)
SFA............ Standard Fuel Assembly [*Nuclear energy*] (NRCH)
SFA............ Stopped-Flow Analyzer [*Chemical analysis*]
SFA............ Students for America (EA)
SFA............ Subcommittee on Frequency Allocations
SFA............ Sun Finder Assembly [*NASA*]
SFA............ Superficial Femoral Artery [*Anatomy*]
SFA............ Supplementary Failure Analysis [*NASA*] (KSC)
SFA............ Support Facility Annex [*Army*]
SFA............ Surface Fibroblast Antigen [*Cytochemistry*]
SFA............ Surface Force Apparatus [*Physical chemistry*]
SFA............ Surface Forces Apparatus [*For study of bilayers*] [*Physical chemistry*]
SFA............ Symphony Foundation of America (EA)
SFAA......... Society for Applied Anthropology (EA)
SFAA......... Society for French-American Affairs (EA)
SFAAP...... Sunflower Army Ammunition Plant (AABC)
SFAAW..... Stove, Furnace, and Allied Appliance Workers International Union of North America [*AFL-CIO*]
SFAB........ Science Fiction Adventures [*1958-1963*] [*A publication*]
SFAC......... Science Fiction Adventure Classics [*A publication*]
SFAC........ Solid Fuel Advisory Council [*British*] (DI)
SFAC........ Statement of Financial Accounting Concepts
SFACA...... Solid Fuel Advisory Council of America (EA)
SFACI........ Software Flight Article Configuration Inspection [*NASA*] (NASA)
SFAD........ Science Fiction Adventures [*1956-1958*] [*A publication*]
SFAD........ Society of Federal Artists and Designers [*Later, FDC*] (EA)
SFADS...... San Francisco Air Defense Sector [*ADC*]
SFAF .... San Francisco AIDS Foundation (EA)
SFAHD...... Society of the Friends of Ancient and Historical Dubrovnik [*Croatia*] (EAIO)
SFAL .... Samuel Feltman Ammunition Laboratory [*Army*]
SFAL .... Stanley Airport [*Falkland Islands*] [*ICAO location identifier*] (ICLI)
SFANA2.... Sheepfarming Annual [*A publication*]
SFAOD...... Superficial-Femoral Artery Occlusive Disease [*Medicine*]
SFAP .... Society for Folk Arts Preservation (EA)
SFA-PP..... Slovenian Farmers' Association - People's Party (EY)
SFAPS....... Space Flight Acceleration Profile Simulator [*NASA*]
SFAR .... Sound Fixing and Ranging
SFAR .... Special Federal Aviation Regulation [*FAA*]
SFAR .... Special Flight Area Rule [*Aviation*]
SFAR .... System Failure Analysis Report (IEEE)
SFARG ...... SIOP [*Single Integrated Operations Plan*] Force Application Review Group (CINC)
SFAS .... Safety Features Actuation Signal [*Nuclear energy*] (NRCH)
SFAS .... Special Forces Assessment and Selection [*Military*] (INF)
SFAS .... Statement of Financial Accounting Standards
SFAV .... Surrogate Fast Attack Vehicle [*Two-passenger wheeled vehicle*] (INF)
SFAW .... Solid Fuel Administration for War [*World War II*] [*Terminated, 1947*]
SFAW .... Stove, Furnace, and Allied Appliance Workers International Union of North America [*AFL-CIO*]
SFB .... San Francisco [*California*] [*Seismograph station code, US Geological Survey*] [*Closed*] (SEIS)
SFB .... San Francisco Ballet
SFB .... Sanford, FL [*Location identifier*] [*FAA*] (FAAL)
SFB .... Science Fantasy [*A publication*]
SFB .... Semiconductor Functional Block (IEEE)
SFB .... Sender Freies Berlin [*Radio network*] [*West Germany*]
SFB .... Sir Francis Bacon
SFB .... Society of Friendly Boilermakers [*A union*] [*British*]
SFB .... Solid Fiberboard
SFB .... Southwestern Freight Bureau, St. Louis MO [*STAC*]
SFB .... Spinning Form Block (MCD)
SFB .... Standard Federal Bank [*NYSE symbol*] (SPSG)
SFB .... Structural Feedback
SFB .... Sugarcane Farmers Bulletin [*Quezon City*] [*A publication*]
SFBA .... Steamship Freight Brokers Association
SFBARTD ... San Francisco Bay Area Rapid Transit District
SF Bay .... San Francisco Bay Guardian [*A publication*]
SF Bay Gdn ... San Francisco Bay Guardian [*A publication*]
SFBC........ San Francisco Bancorp [*NASDAQ symbol*] (NQ)
SFBCS....... Special Forces Burst Communications Systems [*Army*] (RDA)
SFBF......... Standard Forms Bureau Form [*Insurance*] (IIA)
SFBI......... Spent Fuel Building Isolation [*Nuclear energy*] (NRCH)
SFBL......... Self-Filling Blind Loop [*Gastroenterology*]
SFBM .... Security Federal Savings Bank [*Billings, MT*] [*NASDAQ symbol*] (NQ)
SFBNS...... San Francisco Bay Naval Shipyard
SFBNSY.... San Francisco Bay Naval Shipyard (DNAB)
SFBRI....... Science Fiction Book Review Index 1923-1973 [*A publication*]
SFC........... Chief Shipfitter [*Navy rating*]
SFC........... Colorado Springs, CO [*Location identifier*] [*FAA*] (FAAL)
SFC........... S-Band Frequency Converter
SFC........... St. Francis Center (EA)

SFC........... Saint Francis College [*Indiana; Maine; New York; Pennsylvania; Wisconsin*]
SFC........... San Francisco [*California*] [*Seismograph station code, US Geological Survey*] (SEIS)
SFC........... San Francisco Examiner and Chronicle [*This World Section*] [*A publication*]
SFC........... School Facilities Council of Architecture, Education, and Industry [*Later, ASBO*] (EA)
SFC........... Science Fiction Adventure Classics [*A publication*]
SFC........... Scottish Film Council
SFC........... Sculptured Flexible Circuit [*Electronics*]
SFC........... Sectored File Controller
SFC........... Securities and Futures Commission [*Hong Kong*]
SFC........... Selection Filter Control (MCD)
SFC........... Selector File Channel
SFC........... Sergeant First Class
SFC........... Serial Frame Camera (CAAL)
SFC........... SF Commentary [*A publication*]
SFC........... Ship Fire Control (AAG)
SFC........... Shipborne Fighter Control [*Navy*] (CAAL)
SFC........... Shoes Fan Club (EA)
SFC........... Sight Fire Control
SFC........... Sioux Falls College [*South Dakota*]
SFC........... Sis Fan Club [*Later, RFC*] (EA)
SFC........... Societe Francaise de Chimie [*French Chemical Society - FCS*] (EAIO)
SFC........... Societe Frederic Chopin [*International Frederic Chopin Foundation*] (EAIO)
SfC........... Society for Calligraphy (EA)
SFC........... Society of Flavor Chemists (EA)
SFC........... Solar Forecast Center [*Air Force*] (IEEE)
SFC........... Solid Fat Content [*Food analysis*]
SFC........... Soluble Fibrin-Fibrinogen Complex [*Hematology*]
SFC........... Space Flight Center [*NASA*]
SFC........... Space Forecast Center [*Air Force*] (GFGA)
SFC........... Special Flight Charts [*Air Force*]
SFC........... Special Foreign Currency [*US counterpart funds*]
SFC........... Specific Fuel Consumption
SFC........... Spinal Fluid Count [*Medicine*]
SFC........... Sports Fans Connection [*A publication*]
SFC........... Sports Federation of Canada (EAIO)
SFC........... Star Field Camera [*NASA*]
SFC........... Starfleet Command (EA)
SFC........... State Fund Chairmen [*Red Cross*]
SFC........... Sub-Functional Code (DNAB)
SFC........... Subcritical Fluid Chromatography
SFC........... Supercritical Fluid Chromatography
SFC........... Superior Fine Cognac
SFC........... Surefire Fan Club [*Inactive*] (EA)
SFC........... Surface (AFM)
SFC........... Sweden Now [*A publication*]
SFC........... Switching Filter Connector
SFC........... Sylvia Fan Club (EA)
SFC........... Synchronized Framing Camera
SFC........... Synthetic Fuels Corp. [*Sponsored by the federal government*]
SFCB .... Services de Formation et de Consultation aux Bandes [*Department of Indian and Inuit Affairs*] [*Canada*]
SFCB .... Shipfitter, Construction Battalion [*Navy*]
SFCBB...... Shipfitter, Construction Battalion, Blacksmith [*Navy*]
SFCBM ..... Shipfitter, Construction Battalion, Mechanical Draftsman [*Navy*]
SFCBP...... Shipfitter, Construction Battalion, Pipe Fitter and Plumber [*Navy*]
SFCBR...... Shipfitter, Construction Battalion, Rigger [*Navy*]
SFCBS...... Shipfitter, Construction Battalion, Steelworker [*Navy*]
SFCBW..... Shipfitter, Construction Battalion, Welder [*Navy*]
SFCC .... Sisters for a Christian Community
SFCD......... Stopped-Flow Circular Dichroism [*Spectroscopy*]
SFCE .... Surface
SFCH........ Society of Freight Car Historians (EA)
SFCHD...... Solid Fuel Chemistry [*English Translation*] [*A publication*]
SFCI .... Spirit of the Future Creative Institute [*Commercial firm*] (EA)
SFCM .... Master Chief Shipfitter [*Later, HTCM*] [*Navy rating*]
SFCMP...... Self-Rising Flour and Corn Meal Program [*Later, HBA*] (EA)
SFCO........ Special Forces Co. [*Military*] (CINC)
SFCP .... Shore Fire Control Party [*Military*]
SFCP .... Special Foreign Currency Program [*National Institute of Standards and Technology*]
SFCP .... Suffield Financial Corp. [*NASDAQ symbol*] (NQ)
SFCP .... Synthetic Fuels Commercialization Program [*Also, SCP*] [*Energy Resources Council*]
SFCPTNG ... Shore Fire Control Party Training [*Navy*] (NVT)
SFCR .... Storage Facility Control Room [*Nuclear energy*] (NRCH)
SFCRAO ... Collection of Papers Presented at the Annual Symposium on Fundamental Cancer Research [*A publication*]
SFCRS...... State-Federal Crop Reporting Service
SFCS......... Saint Fidelis College and Seminary [*Pennsylvania*]
SFCS......... Secondary Flow Control System [*Nuclear energy*] (NRCH)
SFCS......... Senior Chief Shipfitter [*Later, HTCS*] [*Navy rating*]
SFCS......... Spent Fuel Cooling System [*Nuclear energy*] (NRCH)
SFCS.......... Surveyor Flight Control Section

SFCS......... Survivable Flight Control System [*Military*]
SFCSI........ Special Foreign Currency Science Information [*Program*] [*National Science Foundation*]
SFCSIP...... Special Foreign Currency Science Information Program [*National Science Foundation*]
SFCSR....... Storage Facility Cable Spreading Room [*Nuclear energy*] (NRCH)
SFCTDX.... Centro Internacional de Agricultura Tropical [*CIAT*]. Series FE [*A publication*]
SFCW........ San Francisco College for Women [*California*]
SFCW........ Search for Critical Weakness [*Aerospace*] (AAG)
SFCW........ Sweep Frequency, Continuous Wave
SFCW(I).... Swept Frequency Continuous Wave Illumination (MCD)
SFD........... Florence-Darlington Technical College Library, Florence, SC [*OCLC symbol*] (OCLC)
SFD........... San Fernando [*Venezuela*] [*Airport symbol*] (OAG)
SFD........... Science Fiction Digest [*A publication*]
SFD........... Signal Flow Diagram (MCD)
SFD........... Single Family Dwelling [*Economics*]
SFD........... Skin-Film Distance [*Medicine*] (MAE)
SFD........... Smith's Food & Drug Class B [*NYSE symbol*] (SPSG)
SFD........... Society of Film Distributors [*British*]
SFD........... Solar Flux Density
SFD........... Sound and Vibration [*A publication*]
SFD........... Source-to-Film Distance [*Radiology*]
SFD........... Sudden Frequency Deviation
SFD........... Suore Francescane di Dillingen [*Sisters of St. Francis of Dillingen - SSFD*] [*Italy*] (EAIO)
SFD........... Supercritical Fluid Desorption [*Chemical engineering*]
SFD........... Symbolic File Directory [*Data processing*] (HGAA)
SFD........... Sympathetic Firing Device [*Military*] (CAAL)
SFD........... System Function Description (IEEE)
SFD........... System Functional Diagram [*or Drawing*] (KSC)
SFD........... Systems Flexowriter Double Case
SFDA........ Sale of Food and Drugs Act [*British*]
SFDA........ Shakey's Franchised Dealers Association (EA)
SFDA........ Special Forces Direct Action [*Army*]
SFDA........ Sulfofluorescein Diacetate [*Biological stain*]
SFDE........ Staff and Faculty Development Elements
SFDH........ Schriften des Freien Deutschen Hochstifts [*A publication*]
SFDI......... Solar Facility Design Integration (MCD)
SFDip........ Society of Floristry Diploma [*British*] (DI)
SFDP........ Societe Francophone de Primatologie [*Francophone Primatological Society - FPS*] [*France*] (EAIO)
SFDP........ Software/Firmware Development Plan
SFDR........ Single-Feeder
SFDR........ Standard Flight Data Recorder
SFDS......... Shipboard Fire Detection System (DWSG)
SFDS........ Smithfield Foods, Inc. [*NASDAQ symbol*] (NQ)
SFDS........ Standby Fighter Director Ship [*Navy*]
SFDS........ Strike Force Data System (NVT)
SFDS........ System Functional Design Specification (MCD)
SFDT........ Signal Format Development Team [*France*]
SFDT........ Site Format Dump Tape (MCD)
SFDW........ Special Friends of Dottie West (EA)
SFE........... Safeguard Scientifics, Inc. [*NYSE symbol*] (SPSG)
SFE........... Scale Factor Error (KSC)
SFE........... Seismic Feature Extraction (MCD)
SFE........... Seller-Furnished Equipment (MCD)
SFE........... Smart Front End
SFE........... Societe Financiere Europeenne
SFE........... Society of Financial Examiners (EA)
SFE........... Society of Fire Engineers
SFE........... Solar Flare Effect [*Physics*]
SFE........... Solid Fuel Engine
SFE........... Solution [*or Solvent*] Free Energy [*Physical chemistry*]
SFE........... Soviet Far East (FEA)
SFE........... Space Frequency Equivalence (MCD)
SFE........... Special Furnished Equipment (MCD)
SFE........... Stacking Fault Energy [*Alloy*]
SFE........... Staged Field Experiment [*Gas production*]
SFE........... Student-Faculty Evaluation
SFE........... Students in Free Enterprise (EA)
SFE........... Studies in Financial Economics [*Elsevier Book Series*] [*A publication*]
SFE........... Supercritical Fluid Extraction [*Also, SCFE*] [*Chemical engineering*]
SFE........... Surf Inlet Mines [*Vancouver Stock Exchange symbol*]
SFE........... Surface-Free Energy
SFE........... Synthetic Fermented Egg [*Animal repellent*]
SFEA........ Scottish Further Education Association [*British*]
SFEA .... Squib Fuse Electrical Assembly (KSC)
SFEA .... Survival [*formerly, Space*] and Flight Equipment Association [*Later, SAFE Association*]
SFEC .... Standard Facility Equipment Card [*Electronics*]
SFeEP........ Santa Fe Energy Partners Ltd. [*Associated Press abbreviation*] (APAG)
SFeET........ Santa Fe Energy Trust [*Associated Press abbreviation*] (APAG)
SFEL......... Standard Facility Equipment List [*Electronics*]
SFEM .... Segner's Fortified Edd Meat [*Growth medium for phage*]
SFEM .... SFE Technologies [*NASDAQ symbol*] (NQ)

SFEM .... Southern Farm Equipment Manufacturers (EA)
SFEMG ...... Single Fiber Electromyography [*Neurophysiology*]
SFENA ...... Societe Francaise d'Equipements pour la Navigation Aerienne (MCD)
SFePC........ Santa Fe Pacific Corp. [*Associated Press abbreviation*] (APAG)
SFePP........ Santa Fe Pacific Pipeline Partners Ltd. [*Associated Press abbreviation*] (APAG)
SFER .... Santa Fe Energy Resources [*Associated Press abbreviation*] (APAG)
SFER .... Siata/Fiat 8V Register (EA)
SFERC....... San Francisco Energy Research Center [*Energy Research and Development Administration*]
SFERICS... Atmospherics (FAAC)
SFERT....... Systeme Fundamental Europeen de Reference pour la Transmission Telephonique [*European master telephone reference system*]
SFEX .... Solar Flare X-Ray Polarimeter (NASA)
SF Examiner ... San Francisco Examiner [*A publication*]
SF/F.......... Science Fiction and Fantasy [*Literary genre*]
SFF .... Science Fiction Foundation (EA)
SFF .... Sea Frontier Force [*Navy*]
SFF .... Self-Forging Fragment [*Warhead*] (MCD)
SFF .... Sheffield [*Tasmania*] [*Seismograph station code, US Geological Survey*] (SEIS)
SFF .... Site Field Force [*Army*] (AABC)
SFF .... Slocan Forest Products Ltd. [*Toronto Stock Exchange symbol*] [*Vancouver Stock Exchange symbol*]
SFF .... Slovene Franciscan Fathers (EA)
SFF .... Small Formation Flyer (SSD)
SFF .... Solar Forecast Facility [*Air Force*] (MCD)
SFF .... Spiritual Frontiers Fellowship [*Later, SFFI*] (EA)
SFF .... Spokane, WA [*Location identifier*] [*FAA*] (FAAL)
SFF .... Standard File Format
SFF .... Step Family Foundation (EA)
SFF .... Supplementary Financing Facility [*International Monetary Fund*]
SFFA .... Fireman Apprentice, Shipfitter [*Navy rating*]
SFFAAM... Fauna Fennica [*A publication*]
SFFAS ...... Superfund Financial Assessment System [*Environmental Protection Agency*] (GFGA)
SFFD .... SFFed Corp. [*Formerly, San Francisco Federal Savings & Loan Association*] [*NASDAQ symbol*] (SPSG)
SFFF.......... Scandinavian Association of Zone-Therapeutists [*Denmark*] (EAIO)
SFFF.......... Sedimentation Field Flow Fractionation [*For separation of colloids*]
SFFF.......... Societas pro Fauna et Flora Fennica [*A publication*]
SFFF.......... Summary Format of Family Functioning
SFFFM...... Societas pro Fauna et Flora Fennica. Memoranda [*A publication*]
SFFI.......... Spiritual Frontiers Fellowship International (EA)
SF/FIA ...... Stock Fund/Financial Inventory Accounting
SFFMP..... State/Federal Fisheries Management Program [*National Marine Fisheries Service*]
SFFN .... Fireman, Shipfitter, Striker [*Navy rating*]
SFFNC ...... Society of the Founders and Friends of Norwich, Connecticut (EA)
SFFS.......... Satellite Frost Forecast System [*Department of Agriculture*]
SFFS.......... Save the Flags of Fort Sumter (EA)
SFFT.......... Superconducting Flux-Flow Transistor [*Physics*]
SFFUR ...... Safety and Flight Failure/Unsatisfactory Report
SFFV.......... Spleen Focus Formation Virus
SF & FW ... Science Fiction and Fantasy Workshop (EA)
s-fg--- .... French Guiana [*MARC geographic area code*] [*Library of Congress*] (LCCP)
SFG........... St. Maarten [*Netherlands Antilles*] [*Airport symbol*] (OAG)
SFG........... Serial Publications of Foreign Governments [*A bibliographic publication*]
SFG........... SF Greats [*A publication*]
SFG........... Signal Flow Graph
SFG........... Signal Frequency Generator [*Telecommunications*] (OA)
SFG........... South Pacific Gold [*Vancouver Stock Exchange symbol*]
SFG........... Spanische Forschungen. Gorresgesellschaft [*A publication*]
SFG........... Special Forces Group [*Military*]
SFG........... Staircase Function Generator
SFG........... Sum Frequency Generation
SFGA .... Steel Fork Grinders' Association [*A union*] [*British*]
SFGD......... Safeguard (AABC)
SFGD......... Safeguard Health Enterprises, Inc. [*NASDAQ symbol*] (NQ)
SFGD......... Shell Flue Gas Desulfurization [*Air pollution control*]
SfgdSc........ Safeguard Scientifics, Inc. [*Associated Press abbreviation*] (APAG)
SFGE .... San Francisco Grain Exchange [*Defunct*] (EA)
SFGEP....... Space Flight Ground Environment Panel [*NASA*] (KSC)
SFGF .... Shope Fibroma Growth Factor [*Biochemistry*]
SFGI......... Security Financial Group, Inc. [*NASDAQ symbol*] (NQ)
SFGL......... Safety Glass [*Technical drawings*]
SFGS......... Southwestern Federation of Geological Societies
SFH .... SF Horizons [*A publication*]
SFH .... Simulated Flight Hour (MCD)
SFH .... Slow Frequency Hopping (MCD)

SFH .... Standard Fading Hour [*National Institute of Standards and Technology*]
SFH .... Super Flux Harness
SFHb .... Stroma-Free Hemoglobin [*Hematology*]
SFHC .... Society of Folk Harpers and Craftsmen   (EA)
SFHF .... Society of the Friends of the Holy Father
SFH-P .... Stroma-Free Hemoglobin Pyridoxylated [*Clinical chemistry*]
SFHS .... Society for French Historical Studies   (EA)
SFI .... Savannah Foods & Industries, Inc. [*NYSE symbol*]   (SPSG)
SFI .... Sequential Fuel Injection [*Automotive engineering*]
SFI .... SF Impulse [*A publication*]
SFI .... SFI Foundation   (EA)
SFI .... Shop-Fixed Interface   (DNAB)
SFI .... Sindacato Ferrovieri Italiani [*Union of Italian Railroad Workers*]
SFI .... Small Flow Indicator
SFI .... Societe Financiere Internationale [*International Finance Society*]
SFI .... Society of Friends of Icons [*Germany*]   (EAIO)
SFI .... Solid Fat Index [*Food analysis*]
SFI .... Southern Forest Institute [*Defunct*]   (EA)
SFI .... Space Flight Instrumentation   (AAG)
SFI .... Spendthrift Farm, Inc. [*AMEX symbol*]   (SPSG)
SFI .... Sport Fishing Institute   (EA)
SFI .... Starfire Resources Ltd. [*Vancouver Stock Exchange symbol*]
SFI .... Statistiques Financieres Internationales [*A publication*]
SFI .... Step Function Input
SFI .... Strategic Facilities Initiative [*Oak Ridge National Laboratory*]
SFIA .... School Fees Insurance Agency Ltd. [*British*]
SFIA .... Sea Fish Industry Authority [*British*]
SFIB .... SFI [*Sport Fishing Institute*] Bulletin [*A publication*]
SFIB .... Southern Freight Inspection Bureau
SFIC .... San Francisco Information Center [*Army Air Warning Service*]
SFic .... Science Fiction [*A publication*]
SFIC .... Societe et Federation Internationale de Cardiologie [*International Society and Federation of Cardiology*] [*Switzerland*]   (EAIO)
SFICEC ..... State-Federal Information Clearinghouse for Exceptional Children
S Fict R ...... Science Fiction Review [*A publication*]
SFID .... Section Francaise de l'Internationale Ouvriere [*French Section of the Workers International*]
SFID .... Set Format Identifier
SFil .... Studime Filologjike [*A publication*]
SFIMR ...... Stock Fund Inventory Management Record [*Military*]   (AFIT)
S-FIN .... Semi-Finished [*Automotive engineering*]
SFIN .... Southland Financial Corp. [*NASDAQ symbol*]   (NQ)
SFInstE ...... Senior Fellow of the Institute of Energy [*British*]   (DBQ)
SFInstF ...... Senior Fellow of the Institute of Fuel [*British*]   (DI)
SFIO .... Section Francaise de l'Internationale Ouvriere [*French Socialist Party*]
SFIQ .... Science Fiction Quarterly [*1951-1958*] [*A publication*]
SFIR .... Specific Force Integrating Receiver [*Air Force*]
SFIREG ..... State FIFRA [*Federal Insecticide, Fungicide, and Rodenticide Act*] Issues Research and Evaluation Group [*Environmental Protection Agency*]   (EGAO)
SFIS .... Selective Fisheries Information Service   (IID)
SFIS .... Stanford French and Italian Studies [*A publication*]
SFIT .... Simplified Fault Isolation Test   (MCD)
SFIT .... Standard Family Interaction Test [*Psychology*]
SFJ .... Sondre Stromfjord [*Greenland*] [*Airport symbol*]   (OAG)
SFJ .... Swept Frequency Jamming
SFK .... Periodiekenparade [*A publication*]
SFK .... Special Function Key [*Calculators*]
SFK .... Stonyfork, PA [*Location identifier*] [*FAA*]   (FAAL)
SFKGA ...... Sprechsaal fuer Keramik, Glas, Email, Silikate [*A publication*]
SFL .... Salt Flat, TX [*Location identifier*] [*FAA*]   (FAAL)
SFL .... San Felipe [*California*] [*Seismograph station code, US Geological Survey*]   (SEIS)
SFL .... Santa Fe Pacific Pipeline LP [*NYSE symbol*]   (SPSG)
SFL .... Sao Filipe [*Cape Verde Islands*] [*Airport symbol*]   (OAG)
SFL .... Scholarships, Fellowships, and Loans [*A publication*]
SFL .... Secondary Freon Loop   (NASA)
SFL .... Sequence Flash Lights [*FAA*]
SFL .... Sexual Freedom League   (EA)
SFL .... Short Flashing Light [*Navigation signal*]
SFL .... Silver Falls Resources [*Vancouver Stock Exchange symbol*]
SFL .... Sizing Float Level
SFL .... Society of Federal Linguists   (EA)
SFL .... Studies in French Literature [*A publication*]
SFL .... Substrate Fed Logic
SFL .... Surinam Florin [*Monetary unit in Surinam*]
SFLC .... San Francisco Laser Center [*Research center*]   (RCD)
SFLD .... Seafield Capital Corp. [*NASDAQ symbol*]   (SPSG)
SFLIS .... Sloga Fraternal Life Insurance Society [*Milwaukee, WI*]   (EA)
SFLJ .... San Francisco Law Journal [*A publication*]   (DLA)
SFLM .... Southern Film Extruders, Inc. [*NASDAQ symbol*]   (NQ)
SFLR .... University of San Francisco. Law Review [*A publication*]
SFLRP .... Society of Federal Labor Relations Professionals   (EA)
SFLS .... Semiflush
SFLS .... Stress Fiber-Like Structure [*Biology*]

SFLX .... Shoulder Flexion [*Sports medicine*]
SFM .... Francis Marion College, Florence, SC [*OCLC symbol*]   (OCLC)
SFM .... San Francisco - Josephine D. Randall Junior Museum [*California*] [*Seismograph station code, US Geological Survey*]   (SEIS)
SFM .... San Francisco Movers Tariff Bureau, San Francisco CA [*STAC*]
SFM .... Sanford, ME [*Location identifier*] [*FAA*]   (FAAL)
SFM .... Scanning Force Microscope
SFM .... Scanning Force Mode [*Microscopy*]
SFM .... Science Fiction Monthly [*A publication*]
SFM .... Serum Free Medium
SFM .... SFM Corp. [*AMEX symbol*]   (SPSG)
SFM .... SFM Corp. [*Associated Press abbreviation*]   (APAG)
SFM .... Shepherds Fold Ministries   (EA)
SFM .... Shipfitter, Metalsmith [*Navy*]
SFM .... Simulated Flight - Manual
SFM .... Simulated Flow Method
SFM .... Sinai Field Mission [*US government*]
SFM .... Sinusoidal Frequency Modulation [*Physics*]
SFM .... Ski-Free Marine [*Vancouver Stock Exchange symbol*]
SFM .... Society for the Family of Man   (EA)
SFM .... Society for Foodservice Management   (EA)
SFM .... Spectrophotofluorometer
SFM .... Storage Facility Manual   (MCD)
SFM .... Surface Feet per Minute
SFM .... Swept Frequency Modulation
SFM .... Switching Mode Frequency Multipliers
SFM .... Symposia. Fondation Merieux [*Elsevier Book Series*] [*A publication*]
SFMA .... Soda Fountain Manufacturers Association
SFMA .... Southern Furniture Manufacturers Association [*Later, AFMA*]   (EA)
SFMA .... Steel Fork Makers' Association [*A union*] [*British*]
SFMA .... Subscription Fulfillment Managers Association [*Later, FMA*]   (EA)
SFME .... Storable Fluid Management Experiment   (NASA)
SFMF .... Student Foreign Missions Fellowship [*Later, IVMF*]   (EA)
SFMG .... Franciscan Missionary Sisters of Assisi [*Roman Catholic religious order*]
SFMI .... Soft Fibre Manufacturers' Institute [*Defunct*]   (EA)
SFMJF .... Satoko and Franz M. Joseph Foundation   (EA)
S 8 Fmkr ..... Super 8 Filmaker [*A publication*]
SFML .... Standard Facility Material List [*Electronics*]
SFMN .... Slow Flexor Motoneuron [*Neurology*]
SFMN .... Superficial Flexor Motoneuron [*Neurology*]
SFMP .... Surplus Facilities Management Program [*Department of Energy*]
SFMR .... Stepped-Frequency Microwave Radiometer [*For measuring rain rate and wind speed*]
SF-MX .... Stopped-Flow Multimixing Spectroflourimeter
SFN .... San Francisco Naval Shipyard
SFN .... Santa Fe [*Argentina*] [*Airport symbol*]   (OAG)
SFN .... Seattle First National Bank, Seattle, WA [*OCLC symbol*]   (OCLC)
SFN .... See Footnote   (ROG)
SFN .... SFRA Newsletter [*A publication*]
SFN .... Ships and Facilities, Navy   (NG)
SFN .... Stefan Resources, Inc. [*Vancouver Stock Exchange symbol*]
SFNA .... Stabilized Fuming Nitric Acid
SFNC .... Simmons First National Corp. [*Pine Bluff, AK*] [*NASDAQ symbol*]   (NQ)
SFNC .... Society of the Founders of Norwich, Connecticut   (EA)
SFNCTU ... Swiss Federation of National-Christian Trade Unions
SFNFC ...... Sally Field National Fan Club   (EA)
SFNL .... Shakespeare on Film Newsletter [*A publication*]
SFNS .... San Francisco Naval Shipyard   (DNAB)
SFNS .... Spear Financial Services, Inc. [*NASDAQ symbol*]   (NQ)
SFNSY ...... San Francisco Naval Shipyard
SFNYA ...... Southern Florist and Nurseryman [*United States*] [*A publication*]
SFO .... Defense Solid Fuels Order [*United States*] [*A publication*]   (DLA)
SFO .... San Fernando Observatory [*Research center*]   (RCD)
SFO .... San Francisco/Oakland [*California*] [*Airport symbol*]   (OAG)
SFO .... Santa Fe Opera [*New Mexico*]
SFO .... Sector Field Office [*Aviation*]   (FAAC)
SFO .... Sector Frequency Only [*Military*]   (CAAL)
SFO .... Secular Franciscan Order [*Roman Catholic religious order*] [*Formerly, TOSF*]
SFO .... Senior Flag Officer [*British military*]   (DMA)
SFO .... Serious Fraud Office [*Proposed*] [*British government*]
SFO .... Service Fuel Oil
SFO .... SFO [*San Francisco and Oakland*] Helicopter Airlines, Inc. [*Air carrier designation symbol*]
SFO .... Simulated Flame Out [*Aviation*]
SFO .... Single-Frequency Outlet
SFO .... Space Flight Operations [*NASA*]
SFO .... Spot Face Other Side [*Technical drawings*]   (MSA)
SFO .... Sterling Forest [*New York*] [*Seismograph station code, US Geological Survey*]   (SEIS)
SFO .... Strathfield Oil & Gas Ltd. [*Toronto Stock Exchange symbol*]

SFO............	Subfornical Organ [*Brain anatomy*]
SFO............	Submarine Fog Oscillator [*Maps and charts*]
SFO............	Superannuation Funds Office [*Inland Revenue*] [*British*]
S & FO	Supply and Fiscal Officer
SFOB........	Special Forces Operational Base [*Army*]
SFOBB	San Francisco-Oakland Bay Bridge
SFOC........	Space Flight Operations Complex [*NASA*]
SFOD........	San Francisco Ordnance District [*Military*]
SFOD........	Space Flight Operations Director [*NASA*]
SFOD........	Special Forces Operational Detachment [*Army*] (AABC)
SFOD-D	[*First*] Special Forces Operational Detachment - Delta [*Military*] (INF)
SFOF	Space Flight Operations Facility [*NASA*]
SFOG........	South Fork Oil & Gas [*NASDAQ symbol*] (NQ)
SFOK........	Sooner Federal Savings & Loan Association [*NASDAQ symbol*] (NQ)
SFOLDS....	Ship Form Online Design System [*British Ship Research Association*] [*Software package*] (NCC)
SFOM.......	Shuttle Flight Operations Manual [*NASA*] (MCD)
SFOM.......	Space Flight Operations Memorandum [*NASA*]
SFOM.......	Stabilized Flight Operations Manual
SFOMS	Ships Force Overhaul Management Systems [*Navy*]
SFOO	San Francisco Operations Office [*Energy Research and Development Administration*]
SFOP	Safety Operating Procedure [*Kennedy Space Center*] [*NASA*] (NASA)
SFOP	Space Flight Operations Plan [*NASA*]
SFORD.....	Sozialistische Forstwirtschaft [*A publication*]
Sforz...........	Sforzando [*With Additional Accent*] [*Music*]
SFP	Franciscan Sisters of the Poor [*Roman Catholic religious order*]
SFP	San Felipe [*Mexico*] [*Seismograph station code, US Geological Survey*] (SEIS)
SFP	Santa Fe Energy Partnership LP [*NYSE symbol*] (SPSG)
SFP	Santa Fe Public Library, Santa Fe, NM [*OCLC symbol*] (OCLC)
SFP	Science Fiction Plus [*A publication*]
SfP	Science for People [*A publication*]
SFP	Screen Filtration Pressure [*Clinical chemistry*] (AAMN)
SFP	Security Filter Processor
SFP	Sforzato Piano [*Sudden change from forte to piano*] [*Music*] (ROG)
SFP	Shipfitter, Pipefitter [*Navy*]
SFP	Shungwayah Freedom Party [*Kenya*]
SFP	Simultaneous Foveal Perception [*Ophthalmology*]
SFP	Single Failure Point [*NASA*] (MCD)
SFP	Sintered Ferrous Part
SFP	Skeleton Flight Plan
SFP	Slack Frame Program
SFP	Slow Filling Period [*Cardiology*]
SFP	Solar Flare Proton
SFP	Spartan-Furnished Property [*Missiles*] (MCD)
SFP	Special Film Project
SFP	Special Furnished Property (MCD)
SFP	Spent Fuel Pit [*Nuclear energy*] (NRCH)
SFP	Spent Fuel Pool [*Nuclear energy*] (NRCH)
SFP	Spinal Fluid Pressure [*Medicine*]
SFP	Stopped Flow Pressure
SFP	Straight Fixed Price
SFP	Strike for Peace [*Later, WDFP*] (EA)
SFP	Students for Peace (EA)
SFP	Summary Financial Program
SFP	Summary Flight Plan (MCD)
SFP	Super Flat Pack
SFP	Surface Fixed Priority
SFP	Sustainer Firing Package
SFP	Svenska Folkpartiet [*Swedish People's Party*] [*Finland*] [*Political party*] (PPE)
SFPA	Science Fiction Poetry Association (EA)
SFPA	Single Failure Point Analysis [*NASA*] (KSC)
SFPA	Southern Forest Products Association (EA)
SFPA	Structural Fire Protection Association [*British*]
SFP-ANGS ...	Standardization Field Panel for Artillery and Naval Gunfire Support [*Army*] (AABC)
SFPAVS	Spent Fuel Pool Area Ventilation System [*Nuclear energy*] (NRCH)
SFPCCS	Spent Fuel Pool Cooling and Cleanup System [*Nuclear energy*] (NRCH)
SFPCS	Spent Fuel Pool Cooling System [*Nuclear energy*] (NRCH)
SFPE.........	San Francisco Port of Embarkation [*Military*]
SFPE.........	Society of Fire Protection Engineers (EA)
SFPE Technol Rep ...	SFPE [*Society of Fire Protection Engineers*] Technology Report [*A publication*]
SFPF.........	Special Federal Project Funds [*Medicaid Program*] (GFGA)
SFPL.........	San Francisco Public Library [*California*]
SFPM	Surface Feet per Minute
SFPOE	San Francisco Port of Embarkation [*Military*]
SFPOMMPAB ...	Society for the Prevention of Married Men Posing as Bachelors
SFPP.........	Spruce Fall Power & Paper [*AAR code*]
SFPPC.......	Science Fiction Pen Pal Club (EA)
SFPPL.......	Short Form Provisioning Parts List [*NASA*] (NASA)

SFPPS	Shore Facilities Planning and Programming System [*Navy*]
SFPRF.......	Semifireproof (MSA)
SFPRL.......	Spartan-Furnished Property Request List [*Missiles*] (MCD)
SFPS.........	Single Failure Point Summary [*NASA*] (NASA)
SFPT.........	Society of Fire Protection Technicians (EA)
SFPTU	Swiss Federation of Protestant Trade Unions
SFQ...........	Science Fiction Quarterly [*1940-1943*] [*A publication*]
SFQ...........	Southern Folklore Quarterly [*A publication*]
SFQ...........	Suffolk, VA [*Location identifier*] [*FAA*] (FAAL)
SFQC........	Special Forces Qualification Course [*Military*] (INF)
SFR...........	Safety of Flight Requirements (AFM)
SFR...........	San Fernando, CA [*Location identifier*] [*FAA*] (FAAL)
SFR...........	San Francisco Review [*A publication*]
SFR...........	San Francisco - Rincon [*California*] [*Seismograph station code, US Geological Survey*] (SEIS)
SFR...........	Santa Fe Energy Resources [*NYSE symbol*] (SPSG)
SFR...........	Santa Fe Regional Library [*Gainsville Public Library*] [*UTLAS symbol*]
SF & R	Scholars' Facsimiles and Reprints [*A publication*]
SfR...........	Scholars' Facsimiles & Reprints, Inc., Delmar, NY [*Library symbol*] [*Library of Congress*] (LCLS)
SFR...........	Science Fiction Review [*A publication*]
SFR...........	Screen Filtration Resistance [*Clinical chemistry*] (AAMN)
SFR...........	Selective File Retrieval
SFR...........	Semi-Fire-Resistive Construction
SFR...........	Sequenced Flashing Lights
SFR...........	Sequential Filter Regeneration [*Automotive engineering*]
SFR...........	Signal Frequency Receiver [*Telecommunications*] (OA)
SFR...........	Simon Fraser Resources [*Vancouver Stock Exchange symbol*]
SFR...........	Small Fluidal Round Colonies [*Moko disease of Banana*] [*Plant pathology*]
SFR...........	Solar Flare Radiation
SFR...........	Space Frame RADOME
SFR...........	Special Federal Responsibilities (OICC)
SFR...........	Special Forces Reconnaissance [*Army*]
SFR...........	Spin Flip Raman [*LASER*]
S & FR	Stability and Frequency Response
SFR...........	Stanford French Review [*A publication*]
SFR...........	Star Formation Rate [*Astronomy*]
SFR...........	Submarine Fleet Reactor
SFR...........	Supervisory Field Representative [*Department of Commerce*] (GFGA)
S FR	Swiss Franc [*Monetary unit*]
SFRA	Science Fiction Research Association (EA)
SFRA	System Fielding Readiness Analysis [*Army*]
SFRA	System Fielding Readiness Assessment [*Army*]
S and FRAN ...	San Francisco [*California*] [*Navy*]
SFRB	[*The*] Atchison, Topeka & Santa Fe Railway Co. - DF Loaders [*AAR code*]
SFRB	San Francisco Review of Books [*A publication*]
SFRC	Soya Food Research Council
SFRCS.......	Steam and Feedwater Line Rupture Control System [*Nuclear energy*] (NRCH)
SFRD........	[*The*] Atchison, Topeka & Santa Fe Railway Co. - Refrigerator Cars [*AAR code*]
SFRD........	Safe Functional Requirements Document (MCD)
SFRD........	Secret Formerly Restricted
SF Rev Bks ...	San Francisco Review of Books [*A publication*]
SFRF........	Sport Fishery Research Foundation [*Later, SFRP*] (EA)
SFRJ........	Solid Fuel Ramjet
SFrL..........	Studies in French Literature [*A publication*]
SFRM	Science Fiction Review. Monthly [*A publication*]
SFRP	Sport Fishery Research Program (EA)
SFrQ	San Francisco Quarterly [*A publication*]
SFRS.........	Search for Random Success [*Aerospace*] (AAG)
SFRS.........	Swept Frequency Radiometer System
SFRSAY	Food Research Institute. Studies [*Stanford*] [*A publication*]
SFRT	Science Fiction and Fantasy RoundTable [*GE Information Services*] [*Information service or system*] (CRD)
SFRY	Socialist Federal Republic of Yugoslavia
SFS	S-Band Feed System
SFS	Saint Francis Seminary [*Wisconsin*]
SFS	San Fernando [*Spain*] [*Geomagnetic observatory code*]
SFS	San Fernando [*Spain*] [*Seismograph station code, US Geological Survey*] (SEIS)
SFs	Saybolt Furol Seconds [*Oil viscosity*]
SFS	School of Field Studies [*Beverly, MA*]
SFS	Science Fiction Stories [*A publication*]
SFS	Science Fiction Studies [*A publication*]
SFS	Science for Schools [*Manila*] [*A publication*]
SFS	Seamen's and Firemen's Society [*A union*] [*British*]
SFS	Sektion fuer Systementwicklung [*GID*] [*Information retrieval*]
SFS	Senior Flight Surgeon [*Army*] (AABC)
SFS	Serial Focal Seizures [*Medicine*]
SFS	Shakespeare for Students [*A publication*]
SFS	Shoot-Fail-Shoot [*Military*]
SFS	Shuttle Flight Status [*NASA*] (MCD)
SFS	Simplified Firing System
SFS	Sine Fraude Sua [*Without Fraud on His Part*] [*Latin*] (DLA)
SFS	Small Firms Service [*British*]
SFS	Smith's Flight System [*Aviation*] (AIA)

SFS .... Society for Foodservice Systems   (EA)
SFS .... Society for Freedom in Science
SFS .... Society for French Studies [*British*]
SFS .... Sodium Formaldehyde Sulfoxylate [*Organic chemistry*]
SFS .... Software Facilities and Standards [*Data processing*]   (TEL)
SFS .... Solicitors' Financial Services [*British*]
SFS .... Sonic Frequency System
SFS .... South San Francisco, CA [*Location identifier*] [*FAA*]   (FAAL)
SFS .... Space Flight Systems   (SAA)
SFS .... Space Futures Society   (EA)
SFS .... Split Function Study   (MAE)
SFS .... Star Field Sensor
SFS .... Steam and Feedwater System [*Nuclear energy*]   (NRCH)
SFS .... Suomen Standardisomisliitto [*Finnish Standards Association*] [*Information service or system*]   (IID)
SFS .... Super Food Services, Inc. [*NYSE symbol*]   (SPSG)
SF & S ...... Supporting Facilities and Services
SFS .... Surfaced Four Sides [*Technical drawings*]
SFS .... Symbolic File Support
SFS .... System Failure Summaries [*NASA*]   (KSC)
SFSA .... Scottish Field Studies Association [*British*]
SFSA .... Steel Founders' Society of America   (EA)
SFSAFBI... Society of Former Special Agents of the Federal Bureau of Investigation   (EA)
SFSAS ...... Standard Fuel Savings Advisor System
SFSC .... San Francisco State College [*Later, California State University*]
SFSCL .... Shunt Feedback Schottky Clamped [*Electronics*]
SFSCPD ... San Francisco Signal Corps Procurement District
SFSCT .... Smooth-Face Structural Clay Tile [*Technical drawings*]
S & FSD ..... Sea and Foreign Service Duty [*A Navy pay status*]
SFSD .... Star Field Scanning Device
S & FSD(A) ... Sea and Foreign Service Duty (Aviation) [*A Navy pay status*]
S & FSD(S) ... Sea and Foreign Service Duty (Submarine) [*A Navy pay status*]
SFSE.......... San Francisco Stock Exchange
SFSI.......... Sunwest Financial Services, Inc. [*NASDAQ symbol*]   (NQ)
SFSL.......... Science Fiction. Review of Speculative Literature [*A publication*]
SFSL.......... Security Federal Savings & Loan Association of Cleveland [*NASDAQ symbol*]   (NQ)
SFSMD ..... Studia Fransisci Scholten Memorial Dicata   (BJA)
SFSN .... Society of French-Speaking Neurosurgeons   (EA)
SFSO .... San Francisco Symphony Orchestra
SFSP.......... Spent Fuel Storage Pool [*Nuclear energy*]   (NRCH)
SFSP.......... Summer Food Service Program [*Department of Agriculture*]   (GFGA)
SFSR.......... Senior Field Service Representative [*DoD*]
SFSR.......... Shipfitter, Ship Repair [*Navy*]
SFSRC....... Shipfitter, Ship Repair, Chipper-Caulker [*Navy*]
SFSRD....... Shipfitter, Ship Repair, Diver [*Navy*]
SFSRF ...... Shipfitter, Ship Repair, Steelworker-Anglesmith [*Navy*]
SFSRL....... Shipfitter, Ship Repair, Driller-Reamer [*Navy*]
SFSRP ...... Shipfitter, Ship Repair, Pipe Fitter-Plumber [*Navy*]
SFSRR....... Shipfitter, Ship Repair, Riveter [*Navy*]
SFSRS ...... Shipfitter, Ship Repair, Shipfitter [*Navy*]
SFSRW..... Shipfitter, Ship Repair, Welder [*Navy*]
SFSS......... Satellite Field Services Stations [*National Weather Service*]
SFSS......... Svenska Fornskriftssaellskapets Skrifter [*A publication*]
SFST......... Scherenfernrohrstand [*Emplacement of battery commander's telescope*] [*German military - World War II*]
SFST.......... Science Fiction Studies [*A publication*]
SFSt .... Swiss-French Studies [*Etudes Romandes*] [*A publication*]
SFSU .... San Francisco State University
SFSU .... Singapore Federation of Services' Unions
SFSU .... Single Frequency Signaling Unit
SFSU-35 .... San Francisco State University Videotex Cable Service [*Telecommunications service*]   (TSSD)
SFSV.......... Svenska Forfattare Utgivna av Svenska Vitterhetssamfundet [*A publication*]
SF Sym ...... San Francisco Symphony. Program Notes [*A publication*]
SF & T ...... Sawyer, Finn & Thatcher [*Advertising agency*]
SFT .... Shaft   (MSA)
SFT .... Sheffield Morning Telegraph [*A publication*]
SFT .... Shift
SFT .... Simulated Flight Tests
SFT .... Skelleftea [*Sweden*] [*Airport symbol*]   (OAG)
SFT .... Skinfold Thickness [*Medicine*]
SFT .... Skyfreight, Inc. [*Seattle, WA*] [*FAA designator*]   (FAAC)
sft .... Soft [*Quality of the bottom*] [*Nautical charts*]
SFT .... Soviet and Eastern European Foreign Trade [*A publication*]
SFT .... Special Flight Test
SFT .... Specific Financial Transactions
SFT .... Spiral Fin Tubing
SFT .... Squeeze Film Test
SFT .... Stacking Fault Tetrahedra [*Metals*]
SFT .... Stanford [*California*] [*Seismograph station code, US Geological Survey*]   (SEIS)
SFT .... Static Firing Test [*NASA*]   (NASA)
SFT .... Stockpile Flight Tests
SFT .... Stop for Tea [*British*]
SFT .... Structural Firing Test [*Military*]   (CAAL)
SFT .... Sufficient Feasibility Test

SFT .... Superfast Train
SFT .... Supplemental Flight Test
SFT .... Swift Independent Corp. [*AMEX symbol*]   (SPSG)
SFT .... System Fault Tolerant [*Novell, Inc.*] [*Orem, UT*] [*Telecommunications*]
SFTA .... Spent Fuel Transportation Accident [*Nuclear energy*]   (NRCH)
SFTA .... Structural Fatigue Test Article [*NASA*]   (NASA)
SFTab .... Special Forces Tab [*Military*]   (GFGA)
SFTAR ..... Subsystem Fault Tree Analysis Report
SFTB .... Science Fiction Times [*A publication*]
SFTB .... Southern Freight Tariff Bureau
SFTC .... Sherman Fairchild Technology Center   (MCD)
SFTC .... Standard Freight Trade Classification [*Council for Mutual Economic Assistance*]   (DS)
SFTCD ...... Senior Fellow, Trinity College, Dublin   (ROG)
SFTE .... Society of Flight Test Engineers   (EA)
SFTF......... Static Firing Test Facility [*NASA*]   (NASA)
SFTFC ...... Search for Tomorrow Fan Club   (EA)
SFTG .... Softguard Systems, Inc. [*Santa Clara, CA*] [*NASDAQ symbol*]   (NQ)
SFTI.......... Special Flight Test Instrumentation   (MCD)
SFTIP....... Special Flight Test Instrumentation Pool   (NG)
SFTL......... Sonic Fatigue Test Laboratory   (AAG)
SFTO........ San Diego Field Test Operations [*Aerospace*]   (AAG)
SFTP........ Science for the People   (EA)
SFTR .... Shipfitter   (AAG)
SFTR .... Summary Flight Test Report   (MCD)
SFTS........ San Francisco Theological Seminary [*San Anselmo, CA*]
SFTS........ Scale Factor Temperature Sensitivity
SFTS........ Service Flying Training School [*British*]
SFTS........ Sickle Forgers' Trade Society [*A union*] [*British*]
SFTS........ Society of Friends of the Touro Synagogue   (EA)
SFTS.......... Space Flight Test System   (MCD)
SFTS.......... Standard Frequency and Time Signals   (IEEE)
SFTS.......... Swept Frequency Topside Sounder   (SAA)
SFTS......... Synthetic Flight Training Simulator
SFTS......... Synthetic Flight Training System [*Army*]
SFTT .... Spent Fuel Transfer Tubes [*Nuclear energy*]   (NRCH)
SFTW .... Stamps for the Wounded   (EA)
SFTWD .... Softwood   (WGA)
SFTWE...... Software   (NASA)
SFTWR .... Software [*Data processing*]   (MCD)
SFTY .... Safety
SFU........... Furman University, Greenville, SC [*OCLC symbol*]   (OCLC)
SFU........... Safia [*Papua New Guinea*] [*Airport symbol*]   (OAG)
SFU........... Sector Field Unit [*Aviation*]   (FAAC)
SFU........... Signals Flying Unit [*British*]
SFU........... Simon Fraser University [*Canada*]
SFU........... Simon Fraser University Library [*UTLAS symbol*]
SFU........... Societe de Fluoration de l'Uranium [*An international nuclear fuel company*]
SFU........... Space Flyer Unit   (SSD)
SFU........... Special Function Unit
SFU........... Standard Firing Unit [*NASA*]   (NASA)
SFU........... Status Fill-In Unit [*Telecommunications*]   (TEL)
SFU........... Suriname Freedom Union   (EA)
SFU........... Synthetic Fuels Update [*A publication*]
SFUGE ..... Singapore Federation of Unions of Government Employees
SF/UIS ..... Space Frame and Unit Integrating System
SFUJA...... Steam and Fuel Users' Journal [*A publication*]
SFUPD ..... Synthetic Fuels Update [*A publication*]
SFUS .... Sovetskoe Finno-Ugrovedenie/Soviet Fenno-Ugric Studies [*A publication*]
SF/USA..... Stopped-Flow/Unsegmented Storage Analyzer [*Chemical analysis*]
SFV .... Semliki Forest Virus
SFV .... Sight Feed Valve
SFV .... Simian Foamy Virus
SFVC .... State Fund Vice Chairmen [*Red Cross*]
SFVCS...... San Francisco Vocational Competency Scale
SFVK .... Svenska Folkskolans Vaenner. Kalender [*A publication*]
SFW.......... Sante Fe [*Panama*] [*Airport symbol*]   (OAG)
SFW.......... Sensor Fuzed Weapon
SFW.......... Shell Fragment Wound [*Medicine*]
SFW.......... Shrapnel Fragment Wound   (MAE)
SFW.......... Software   (NASA)
SFW.......... Special Filter Wheel [*Military*]   (CAAL)
SFW.......... Williston, ND [*Location identifier*] [*FAA*]   (FAAL)
SFWA .... Science Fiction Writers of America   (EA)
SFWA .... Sierra Foothill Winery Association   (EA)
SFWB .... Single Fronted Weatherboard   (ADA)
SFWC .... Supreme Forest Woodmen Circle [*Later, Woodmen of the World Life Insurance Society*]   (EA)
SFWEM ..... Static Feed Water Electrolysis Module [*NASA*]
SFWI .... Ship's Force Work Item   (DNAB)
SFWLI....... Ship's Force Worklist Instruction
SFWM....... Swiss Federation of Watch Manufacturers   (EA)
SFWR .... Stewardesses for Women's Rights
SFWS .... Stopped-Flow Wavelength Scanning [*Spectrometry*]
SFX .... St. Francis Xavier University Library [*UTLAS symbol*]
SFX .... Santa Fe Pacific Corp. [*NYSE symbol*]   (SPSG)

SFX............ Sound Effects [*Script code*]
SFXD........ Semifixed
SFXR........ Super Flash X-Ray   (MCD)
SFY........... Savanna, IL [*Location identifier*] [*FAA*]   (FAAL)
SFY........... Science Fiction Yearbook [*A publication*]
SFY........... Special Fund for Youth [*UNESCO*]   (EAIO)
SFY........... Standard Facility Years [*FAA*]
SFY........... Swift Energy Co. [*NYSE symbol*]   (SPSG)
SFZ........... Pawtucket, RI [*Location identifier*] [*FAA*]   (FAAL)
Sfz........... Sforzando [*With Additional Accent*] [*Music*]
SG............. Command Surgeon [*AFSC*]
SG............. Goldwyn (Samuel) Co. [*AMEX symbol*]   (SPSG)
SG............. Royal South Gloucestershire Light Infantry Militia [*British military*]   (DMA)
SG............. Sa Grace [*His or Her Grace*] [*French*]
SG............. Sa Grandeur [*His or Her Highness*] [*French*]
SG............. Sabah Air [*Malaysia*] [*ICAO designator*]   (FAAC)
SG............. Sachs-Georgi [*Test for syphilis*] [*Also, S-GT*] [*Obsolete*]
SG............. Safety Guide   (NRCH)
SG............. Salisbury Group   (EAIO)
SG............. Salutis Gratia [*For the Sake of Safety*] [*Latin*]
SG............. Sample Gas
SG............. Sawtooth Generator
SG............. Scanning Gate
SG............. Schedule Generator
SG............. School for Girls   (ADA)
S of G........ School of Gunnery [*British military*]   (DMA)
SG............. Schutzgemeinschaft Gegen Meinungsterror [*Guard Society Against Opinion Terror*] [*Germany*]
SG............. Scots Guards [*Military unit*] [*British*]
SG............. Screen Grid [*Electrode or vacuum tube*]
SG............. Sculptors Guild   (EA)
SG............. Sea Grant
SG............. Seabird Group   (EAIO)
SG............. Seaman Gunner [*British*] [*Obsolete*]
SG............. Secretary-General [*United Nations*]
SG............. Security Group [*Military*]   (DNAB)
SG............. Security Guard   (SAA)
SG............. Selling [*Exchange rate marking*] [*British*]
sg.............. Senegal [*MARC country of publication code*] [*Library of Congress*]   (LCCP)
SG............. Senior Gleaners   (EA)
SG............. Senior Grade
SG............. Sergeant   (WGA)
SG............. Serum Globulin [*Medicine*]   (MAE)
SG............. Service Group   (MUGU)
SG............. Set Gate
SG............. Shell Gland
SG............. Shell Gun
SG............. Sheller-Globe Corp.
SG............. Sherrgold, Inc. [*Toronto Stock Exchange symbol*]
SG............. Ship and Goods [*British*]   (ROG)
SG............. Shipcraft Guild   (EA)
SG............. Siculorum Gymnasium [*A publication*]
SG............. Siebelwerke ATG GmbH [*Germany*] [*ICAO aircraft manufacturer identifier*]   (ICAO)
SG............. Sign   (MAE)
SG............. Signal Generator
SG............. Signal Ground   (BUR)
SG............. Signed   (WGA)
SG............. Silica Gel [*Analytical chemistry*]
SG............. Singapore [*ANSI two-letter standard code*]   (CNC)
SG............. Singing
SG............. Single Gourmet   (EA)
SG............. Single Groove [*Insulators*]
Sg.............. Singular   (BJA)
SG............. Sinte Geertruydtsbronne [*A publication*]
SG............. Skin Graft [*Medicine*]
S/G........... Slaved Gyro   (MCD)
S & G........ Smale and Giffard's English Vice-Chancery Reports [*A publication*]   (DLA)
S/G........... Smith/Greenland [*Advertising agency*]
SG............. Smoke Generator
SG............. Snow Grains [*Meteorology*]   (FAAC)
SG............. Socialistische Gids [*A publication*]
SG............. Society of Genealogists   (EA)
SG............. Society of Gilders   (EA)
SG............. Soft Gelatin [*Pharmacy*]
SG............. Sol-Gel [*Materials science*]
SG............. Solicitor General
SG............. Soluble Gelatin
SG............. Solution of Glucose   (OA)
Sg.............. Song of Songs [*Old Testament book*] [*Roman Catholic canon*]   (BJA)
SG............. Sort Generator   (BUR)
SG............. Sound Generation   (MCD)
SG............. South Georgia Railway Co. [*AAR code*] [*Terminated*]
SG............. Sozialgericht [*Social Security Court*] [*German*]   (ILCA)
SG............. Spark Gap   (DEN)
SG............. Special Grade   (DNAB)
SG............. Special Group [*NATO*]

SG............. Specific Gravity [*Also, SPG, SPGR*]
SG............. Spheroidal Graphite [*Ductile iron*]
SG............. Sprach der Gegenwart [*A publication*]
SG............. Stacking Gel [*Biochemistry*]
SG............. Stained Glass
SG............. Standardization Group [*Air Force*]   (AFM)
SG............. Standing Group
SG............. Steam Generator   (NRCH)
SG............. Steel Girder [*Bridges*]
SG............. Steering Group   (MCD)
SG............. Stellate Ganglion [*Neuroanatomy*]
S & G........ Stone and Graham's Court of Referees Reports [*England*] [*A publication*]   (DLA)
S & G........ Stone and Graham's Private Bills Reports [*England*] [*A publication*]   (DLA)
SG............. Stotler Group, Inc. [*AMEX symbol*]   (SPSG)
SG............. Strain Gauge   (KSC)
SG............. Strategic Group [*Military*]
SG............. Structural Gene
SG............. Structural Glass
SG............. Student Guide
SG............. Studium Generale [*A publication*]
S/G........... Su Giro [*Your Draft*] [*Spanish*] [*Business term*]
SG............. Substantia Gelatinosa [*Anatomy*]
SG............. Summation Gallop [*Cardiology*]
SG............. Sun Gate
SG............. Sunkist Growers   (EA)
SG............. Sunset Gun [*Military ceremonial*]
SG............. Sunsweet Growers   (EA)
SG............. Super Group   (NATG)
SG............. Super Guppy   (KSC)
Sg.............. Supplementing [*New matter added to an existing regulation or order*] [*Used in Shepard's Citations*] [*Legal term*]   (DLA)
SG............. Surgeon
SG............. [*The*] Surgeon General [*Army, Air Force*]
SG............. Swamp Glider
SG............. Sweep Generator
SG............. Sydney Gazette [*A publication*]   (APTA)
SG............. Sydney Greens [*Political party*] [*Australia*]
SG............. Symbol Generator
SG............. Syringe   (DNAB)
SG............. System Gain
1SG........... First Sergeant [*Army*]
SGA........... Saga Communications [*AMEX symbol*]   (SPSG)
SGA........... Saga Resources [*Vancouver Stock Exchange symbol*]
SGA........... Savoonga, AK [*Location identifier*] [*FAA*]   (FAAL)
SGA........... Scientific Glass Apparatus Co., Inc.
SGA........... Scottish Games Association   (EAIO)
SGA........... Screened Granulated Aluminate [*Inorganic chemistry*]
SGA........... Sea Grant Association   (EA)
SG & A....... Selling, General, and Administrative Expenses
SGA........... Shirtsleeve Garment Assembly [*NASA*]
SGA........... Sickle Grinders' Association [*A union*] [*British*]
SGA........... Sigma Security, Inc. [*Vancouver Stock Exchange symbol*]
SGA........... Single-Monitor Graphic Adaptor [*Computer graphics*]
SGA........... Slave Gyro Assembly
SGA........... Slavic Gospel Association   (EA)
SGA........... Small for Gestational Age [*Pediatrics*]
SGA........... Societe de Geologie Appliquee aux Gites Mineraux [*Society for Geology Applied to Mineral Deposits*] [*ICSU*]   (EAIO)
SGA........... Society of Gastrointestinal Assistants [*Later, SGNA*]   (EA)
SGA........... Society of Governmental Appraisers [*Later, Association of Governmental Appraisers*]   (EA)
SGA........... Society of Graphic Art [*British*]
SGA........... Solar Greenhouse Association   (EA)
SGA........... Songwriters Guild of America   (EA)
SGA........... Soybean Growers of America   (EA)
SGA........... Spectrometric Gas Analysis
SGA........... Split Group Aperture
SGA........... Spouses of Gays Association   (EA)
SGA........... Standards of Grade Authorization [*Military*]
SGA........... State Guaranteed Agency   (GFGA)
SGA........... Stephens Glacier [*Alaska*] [*Seismograph station code, US Geological Survey*] [*Closed*]   (SEIS)
SGA........... Substantial Gainful Activity [*Social Security Administration*]   (OICC)
SGA........... Superior Geniculate Artery [*Anatomy*]
SGA........... Switch Group Assembly
SGAA......... Sporting Goods Agents Association   (EA)
SGAA......... Stained Glass Association of America   (EA)
SGAC........ Secretariat General for Civil Aviation [*French*]
SGAC........ Silvermine Guild Arts Center   (EA)
SGAC........ State Governmental Affairs Council   (EA)
SGACC...... Secretariat General de l'Aviation Civile et Commerciale [*France*]
SGAD........ Safeguard Army Depot   (AABC)
SGAE........ Studiengesellschaft fuer Atomenergie [*Implements Austria's nuclear program*]   (NRCH)
SGAHRS... Steam Generator Auxiliary Heat Removal System [*Nuclear energy*]   (NRCH)
SGAIG....... Scholars Group Against the Invasion of Grenada   (EA)

SGA J .... SGA [*Society of Gastrointestinal Assistants*] Journal [*A publication*]
SGAK .... Studien zur Germanistik, Anglistik und Komparatistik [*A publication*]
SGAL .... Sage-Allen & Co., Inc. [*NASDAQ symbol*]   (NQ)
SGA of M-A ... Sod Growers Association of Mid-America   (EA)
SGAOR ..... Sitzungsberichte. Gesellschaft fuer Geschichte und Altertumskunde der Ostseeprovinzen Russlands [*A publication*]
SGAS .... Asuncion/Presidente General Stroessner [*Paraguay*] [*ICAO location identifier*]   (ICLI)
SGAS .... Society for German-American Studies   (EA)
SGAS .... Space Geodesy Altimetry Study [*Raytheon Co.*]
SGAS .... Steam Generator Available Signal [*Nuclear energy*]   (NRCH)
SGAT .... Seagate Technology, Inc. [*NASDAQ symbol*]   (NQ)
SGAUA ..... Scitex Graphic Arts Users Association   (EA)
SGAUG ..... Scitex Graphic Arts Users Group [*Later, SGAUA*]   (EA)
SGAUSA ... St. George Association of the USA   (EA)
sGAW .... Specific Airway Conductance
SGAW .... Subgroup on Assessment of Weapons [*NATO*]   (NATG)
SGAY .... Ayolas [*Paraguay*] [*ICAO location identifier*]   (ICLI)
SGB .... Santa Fe, NM [*Location identifier*] [*FAA*]   (FAAL)
SGB .... Schlesische Geschichtsblaetter (Breslau) [*A publication*]
SGB .... Schweizerischer Gewerkschaftsbund [*Swiss Federation of Trade Unions*]
SGB .... Societe Generale de Banque [*Bank Society*] [*Information service or system*]   (IID)
SGB .... Southern Gas Basin [*British*]
SGB .... Steam Generator Blowdown [*Nuclear energy*]   (NRCH)
SGB .... Steam Generator Building [*Nuclear energy*]   (NRCH)
SGB .... Steam Gunboat [*British military*]   (DMA)
SGB .... Stellate Ganglion Blockade [*Anesthesiology*]
SGB .... Strain Gauge Bridge
SGB .... Studien und Mitteilungen zur Geschichte des Benediktiner-Ordens [*A publication*]
SGB .... Switchgear Block   (MSA)
SGBA .... Societe Generale de Banque aux Antilles [*Guadeloupe*]   (EY)
SGBD .... Steam Generator Blowdown [*Nuclear energy*]   (NRCH)
SGBI .... Santa Gertrudis Breeders International   (EA)
SGBIA .... Symposia Genetica et Biologica Italica [*A publication*]
SGBIP .... Subject Guide to Books in Print [*A publication*]
SGBPS .... Steam Generator Blowdown Processing System [*Nuclear energy*]   (NRCH)
SGBS .... Steam Generator Blowdown System [*Nuclear energy*]   (NRCH)
SGBV .... Bella Vista [*Paraguay*] [*ICAO location identifier*]   (ICLI)
SGC .... Saint Gregory College [*Oklahoma*]
SGC .... Salivary Gland Choristoma [*Medicine*]
SGC .... Screen Grid Current
SGC .... Simulated Generation Control
SGC .... Software Generation Center   (MCD)
SGC .... Solicitor General Canada
SGC .... South Georgia College [*Douglas*]
SGC .... Southern Governors Conference
SGC .... Space General Corp.   (MCD)
SGC .... Spartan Guidance Computer [*Missiles*]   (AABC)
SGC .... Spherical Gear Coupling
SGC .... Stabilized Ground Cloud [*NASA*]   (MCD)
SGC .... Stabilizer Gyro Circuit
SGC .... Standard Geographical Classification [*Canada*]
SGC .... Strata Energy Corp. [*Vancouver Stock Exchange symbol*]
SGC .... Students Guide to Childcare [*British*]
SGC .... Supergroup Connector [*Telecommunications*]   (TEL)
SGC .... Superior Geocentric Conjunction
SGC .... Superior Surgical Manufacturing Co., Inc. [*AMEX symbol*]   (SPSG)
Sg C .... Surgeon-Captain [*British military*]   (DMA)
SGC .... Washington, DC [*Location identifier*] [*FAA*]   (FAAL)
SGCA .... Silvermine Guild Center for the Arts [*Later, SGAC*]   (EA)
SGCC .... Safety Glazing Certification Council   (EA)
SGCD .... Society of Glass and Ceramic Decorators   (EA)
SGCE .... Ship Gyrocompass Equipment [*Navy*]   (CAAL)
SGCEC ...... Standing Group Communications-Electronics Committee [*Later, MCEWG*] [*NATO*]   (NATG)
SGCF .... SNAP [*Systems for Nuclear Auxiliary Power*] Generalized Critical Facility
SGCL .... Studies in General and Comparative Literature [*A publication*]
SGCMG ..... Single Gimbal Control Moment Gyro [*Navigation*]
SGCO .... Concepcion [*Paraguay*] [*ICAO location identifier*]   (ICLI)
SGCO .... Schacher, Greentree & Co., Inc. [*New York, NY*] [*NASDAQ symbol*]   (NQ)
SGCP .... Shipboard Gauge Calibration Program   (DNAB)
Sg Cr .... Surgeon-Commander [*British military*]   (DMA)
SGCS .... Silicon Gate-Controlled Switch
SGCS .... Slave Gyro Control System
SGD .... Napa, CA [*Location identifier*] [*FAA*]   (FAAL)
SGD .... Seafloor Geosciences Division   (EA)
SGD .... Self-Generating Dictionary
SGD .... Senior Grand Deacon [*Freemasonry*]
SGD .... Shogun Developments Corp. [*Vancouver Stock Exchange symbol*]
SGD .... Signaling Ground [*Telecommunications*]   (TEL)

SGD .... Signed
SGD .... Sliding Glass Door   (ADA)
SGD .... Society of Geniuses of Distinction   (EA)
SGD .... Society of Glass Decorators [*Later, SGCD*]   (EA)
SGD .... Solar-Geophysical Data [*A publication*]
SGD .... Sonderborg [*Denmark*] [*Airport symbol*]   (OAG)
SGD .... Special Government Design   (DNAB)
SGD .... Specific Granule Deficiency [*Physiology*]
SGD .... Sperry Gyroscope Division [*Sperry Rand Corp.*]   (MCD)
SGD .... Sui Generis Degree
SGDCTO .... Sangre de Cristo [*FAA*]   (FAAC)
SGDE .... Steering Gear Dual Emergency   (MSA)
SGDE .... System Ground Data Equipment [*RADAR*]
SGDF .... Supergroup Distribution Frame [*Telecommunications*]   (TEL)
SGDHF ..... Sodium Glycodihydrofusidate [*Hemolytic*]
SGDI .... Swaging Die [*Tool*]
SGDI .... Switched Ground Discrete Input   (MCD)
SGDN ...... Surgidyne, Inc. [*NASDAQ symbol*]   (NQ)
SGDO .... Switched Ground Discrete Output   (MCD)
SGDPS ..... Second Generation Data Processing System   (MCD)
Sge .... Sagitta [*Constellation*]
SGE .... Secondary Grid Emission
SGE .... Severable Government Equipment
SGE .... Sigma Gamma Epsilon [*Society*]
SGE .... Society of Government Economists   (EA)
SGE .... Starch Gel Electrophoresis   (OA)
SGE .... Subscriber Group Equipment [*Telecommunications*]
SGE .... Super-Critical Gas Extraction [*Chemical engineering*]
SGE .... Support Group Europe [*Military*]
SGEM .... Study Group on Environmental Monitoring [*National Research Council*]
SGEMP ..... System-Generated Electromagnetic Pulse [*Army*]
SGEN .... Encarnacion [*Paraguay*] [*ICAO location identifier*]   (ICLI)
SGen .... Studium Generale [*A publication*]
SGEP .... Socialist Group in the European Parliament [*See also GSPE*]   (EAIO)
S Ger S ...... Stanford German Studies [*A publication*]
SGES .... Society of Grain Elevator Superintendents [*Later, GEAPS*]
SGET .... Spacecraft Ground Elapsed Time
SGEU .... Singapore General Employees' Union
SGF .... Sample Gas Flow
SGF .... Sarcoma Growth Factor
SGF .... Singapore Fund [*NYSE symbol*]   (SPSG)
SGF .... Skeletal Growth Factor [*Genetics*]
SGF .... Small Gene Fragment [*Genetics*]
SGF .... Southern Group of Forces [*Former USSR*]   (NATG)
SGF .... Spermiogenesis Growth Factor [*Biochemistry*]
SGF .... Springfield [*Missouri*] [*Airport symbol*]   (OAG)
SGF .... Springfield, MO [*Location identifier*] [*FAA*]   (FAAL)
SGF .... Steam Generator Feedwater   (DNAB)
SGF .... Stockholmer Germanistische Forschungen [*A publication*]
SGFA .... Asuncion [*Paraguay*] [*ICAO location identifier*]   (ICLI)
SGFC .... Sharon Gless Fan Club   (EA)
SGFI .... Filadelfia [*Paraguay*] [*ICAO location identifier*]   (ICLI)
SGFID .... Seventh Generation Fund for Indian Development   (EA)
SGFMV ..... Sammendrag af Groenlands Fangstilister MV [*A publication*]
SGFNT ...... Significant   (FAAC)
SGFP .... Steam Generator Feed Pump   (IEEE)
SGF Publ ... SGF [*Sveriges Gummitekniska Foerening*] Publicerande [*A publication*]
SGFR .... Single-Nephron Glomerular Filtration Rate [*Medicine*]   (MAE)
SGG .... Saint George Island, AK [*Location identifier*] [*FAA*]   (FAAL)
SGG .... St. George Minerals [*Vancouver Stock Exchange symbol*]
SGG .... Signatures   (WGA)
SGG .... South Georgia [*United Kingdom*] [*Geomagnetic observatory code*]
SGG .... Sustainer Gas Generator
SGGAOPR ... Sitzungsberichte. Gesellschaft fuer Geschichte und Altertumskunde der Ostseeprovinzen Russlands [*A publication*]
SGGP .... Seller's Guide to Government Purchasing [*A publication*]
SGGR .... Guaira [*Paraguay*] [*ICAO location identifier*]   (ICLI)
SGH .... Generale Maatschappij van Belgie. Informatieblad [*A publication*]
SGH .... Serum Growth Hormone [*Endocrinology*]
SGH .... Seth G. Huntington [*Designer's mark on US bicentennial half dollar*]
SGH .... Signal Hill Energy Corp. [*Vancouver Stock Exchange symbol*]
SGH .... Springfield, OH [*Location identifier*] [*FAA*]   (FAAL)
SGH .... Sud-Ghoubbet [*Djibouti*] [*Seismograph station code, US Geological Survey*]   (SEIS)
SGH .... Surgical Hospital [*Medicine*]
SGHB .... Sag Harbor Savings Bank [*NASDAQ symbol*]   (NQ)
SGHI .... Silk Greenhouse, Inc. [*NASDAQ symbol*]   (NQ)
SGHLA ..... Stadt- und Gebaeudetechnik [*A publication*]
SGHW .... Steam-Generating, Heavy-Water [*Reactor*] [*British*] [*Nuclear energy*]   (NRCH)
SGHWR .... Steam-Generating, Heavy-Water Reactor [*British*] [*Nuclear energy*]   (NRCH)
SGI .... Sea Grant Institute [*University of Wisconsin*] [*Research center*]   (RCD)

SGI............	Search Group, Inc. [*An association*] (EA)
SGI............	Servicio Geodesico Interamericano [*Inter-American Geodetic Survey - IAGS*] [*United States*]
SGI............	Sheriff Guards International [*Nigeria*] (EAIO)
SGI............	Silicon Graphics [*NYSE symbol*] (SPSG)
SGI............	Small Group Instructor [*or Instruction*] [*Army*] (INF)
SGI............	Society for Gynecologic Investigation (EA)
SGI............	Specific Gravity Indicator
SGI............	Spring Garden Institute
SGI............	Standard Graphic Interface [*XOR Systems*]
SGI............	Systems Group, Inc. [*Telecommunications service*] (TSSD)
SGIA.........	Sun Glass Institute of America [*Defunct*] (EA)
SGIB.........	Itaipu [*Paraguay*] [*ICAO location identifier*] (ICLI)
SGIB.........	Slattery Group, Inc. [*NASDAQ symbol*] (NQ)
SGIG.........	Sovereign Grand Inspector-General [*Freemasonry*] (ROG)
SGII..........	SGI International [*NASDAQ symbol*] (NQ)
SGIM........	Society of General Internal Medicine (EA)
SGINDEX ...	System Generation Cross-Reference Index [*NASA*]
SGIS	Safeguards Initiation Signal [*Nuclear energy*] (NRCH)
SGIS	Steam Generator Isolation Signal (IEEE)
SGIS	Student Government Information Service (EA)
SGIT	Special Group Inclusive Tour [*Airline fare*]
SGJ...........	Sagarai [*Papua New Guinea*] [*Airport symbol*] (OAG)
SGJ...........	St. Augustine, FL [*Location identifier*] [*FAA*] (FAAL)
SGJ...........	Supersonic Gas Jet
SGJA	Sporting Goods Jobbers Association [*Later, NASGW*]
SGJKT......	Society of Goldsmiths, Jewellers, and Kindred Trades [*A union*] [*British*]
SGJN........	San Juan Nepomuceno [*Paraguay*] [*ICAO location identifier*] (ICLI)
SGJP	Satellite Graphic Job Processor [*Data processing*]
SGK	Hsinkong [*Republic of China*] [*Also, HSI*] [*Seismograph station code, US Geological Survey*] (SEIS)
SGK	Knoxville, TN [*Location identifier*] [*FAA*] (FAAL)
SGKA........	Studien zur Geschichte und Kultur des Alterums [*A publication*] (BJA)
SGKB........	Societe Generale-Komercni Banka [*Former Czechoslovakia*] (EY)
SGKF........	Susan G. Komen Foundation (EA)
SGL...........	Mount Signal [*California*] [*Seismograph station code, US Geological Survey*] (SEIS)
SGL...........	Signal
SGL...........	Single (MSA)
SGL...........	Sleeping Gold Ltd. [*Vancouver Stock Exchange symbol*]
SGL...........	Society of Gas Lighting (EA)
SGL...........	South State Cooperative Library System, Los Angeles, CA [*OCLC symbol*] (OCLC)
SGL...........	Space-Ground Link (MCD)
SGL...........	Spiegel [*Hamburg*] [*A publication*]
SGL...........	Strategic Global Income Fund [*NYSE symbol*] (SPSG)
SGL...........	Studies in German Literature [*A publication*]
SGl............	Sumerisches Glossar [*A publication*] (BJA)
SGL...........	Sunglasses
SGL...........	Superannuation Guarantee Levy
SGL...........	Supermarkets General Corp. [*NYSE symbol*] (SPSG)
S GLAM	South Glamorgan [*County in Wales*]
SGL/B	Boletin. Sociedad Geografica de Lima [*A publication*]
SGLC	Strain Gauge Load Cell
Sg L Cr.......	Surgeon Lieutenant-Commander [*British military*] (DMA)
SGLE	Single (AAG)
SGLF	Scottish Grand Lodge of Freemasons
SGLF	Symposia. Giovanni Lorenzini Foundation [*Elsevier Book Series*] [*A publication*]
SGLI	Servicemen's Group Life Insurance [*Military*]
SGLI	Slave Gyro Leveling Integrator
SGLIC	Steam Generator Level Instrumentation Cabinet [*Nuclear energy*] (NRCH)
SGLL	Studies in the Germanic Languages and Literatures [*A publication*]
SGLLI.......	Section on Gay and Lesbian Legal Issues [*Association of American Law Schools*] (EA)
SGLO	Lobrego, Fortin [*Paraguay*] [*ICAO location identifier*] (ICLI)
SGLO	Standing Group Liaison Officer to the North Atlantic Council
SGLP	Standing Group Representative Liaison Paper to the International Staff [*Obsolete*] [*NATO*] (NATG)
SGLS	Satellite Grand Link System (NATG)
SGLS	Space-Ground Link Station [*NASA*] (NASA)
SGLS	Space-to-Ground Link Subsystem [*NASA*]
SGLSA	Stomatoloski Glasnik Srbije [*A publication*]
SGLV.........	La Victoria (Ex Casado) [*Paraguay*] [*ICAO location identifier*] (ICLI)
SGLWCH ...	Study Group on Labor and Working Class History (EA)
SGM	College Mathieu, Gravelbourg, Saskatchewan [*Library symbol*] [*National Library of Canada*] (NLC)
SGM	Scottish Geographical Magazine [*A publication*]
SGM	Screen Grid Modulation
SGM	Sea Gallantry Medal [*Navy*] [*British*]
SGM	Sergeant Major (AABC)
SGM	Silver Gate [*Montana*] [*Seismograph station code, US Geological Survey*] (SEIS)
SGM	Society for General Microbiology [*British*]
SGM	Society for General Music (EA)
SGM	Soeurs Grises de Montreal [*Sisters of Charity, Grey Nuns of Montreal*] [*Roman Catholic religious order*]
SGM	Spark Gap Modulation
SGM	Standing Group Memorandum [*Obsolete*] [*NATO*] (NATG)
SGM	Strategic Guidance Memo [*Navy*]
SGMA	Sigmaform Corp. [*NASDAQ symbol*] (NQ)
SGMA	Sporting Goods Manufacturers Association [*North Palm Beach, FL*] (EA)
SGMAA	Sporting Goods Manufacturers Agents Association [*Later, SGRA*]
SGMC	Standing Group Meteorological Committee [*Obsolete*] [*NATO*] (NATG)
SGMCI	Sporting Goods Manufacturers' Credit Interchange [*Buffalo, NY*] (EA)
SGMD	Swaging Mandel
SGME........	Mariscal Estigarribia [*Paraguay*] [*ICAO location identifier*] (ICLI)
SGME........	Service Generale des Moyens de l'Enseignement [*Canada*]
SGMH.......	Study Group. Institute for Research into Mental and Multiple Handicap [*Elsevier Book Series*] [*A publication*]
SGMI.........	S-G Metals Industries, Inc. [*NASDAQ symbol*] (NQ)
SGML.......	Standard Generalized Markup Language [*Also, GSML*] [*International Standards Organization*]
SGML.......	Study Group for Mathematical Learning (EA)
SGMN.......	Signalman [*Military*] [*British*]
SGMP.......	Society of Government Meeting Planners (EA)
SGMS	Shipboard Gravity Measuring System
SGMSR	Steam Generator Maximum Steam Rate [*Nuclear energy*] (NRCH)
SGMT	Simulated Greenwich Mean Time (MCD)
SGMT.......	Subgroup Modern Terminal
SGM/USA ...	Scripture Gift Mission/USA (EA)
SGN	Ho Chi Minh [*Vietnam*] [*Airport symbol*] (OAG)
SGN	Saigon [*Vietnam*]
SGN	Sartigan Granite [*Vancouver Stock Exchange symbol*]
SGN	Scan Gate Number
SGN	Seamless Garment Network (EA)
SGN	Self-Generated Noise [*Oceanography*]
SGN	Service Geologique National [*National Geological Survey*] [*Bureau of Geological and Mining Research*] [*Information service or system*] (IID)
sgn.............	Signer [*MARC relator code*] [*Library of Congress*] (LCCP)
SGN	Simulation Gaming News [*A publication*]
SGN	Standing Group, North Atlantic Treaty Organization
SGN	Surgeon [*Military*] [*British*]
SGN	Surgeon General of the Navy
SGNA	Nueva Asuncion [*Paraguay*] [*ICAO location identifier*] (ICLI)
SGNA	Society of Gastroenterology Nurses and Associates (EA)
SGNAD	Shoni Geka Naika [*A publication*]
SGNET	Sea Grant Network [*National Oceanic and Atmospheric Administration*] [*Information service or system*] (IID)
SgnlApl......	Signal Apparel Co., Inc. [*Associated Press abbreviation*] (APAG)
SGNLD......	Signalled (ROG)
SGNLS	Sequential Generalized Nonlinear Least Squares [*Statistics*]
SGNMOS ...	Screen-Grid N-Channel Metal Oxide Semiconductor
SGNR	Signature (AABC)
SGNRA	Surgical Neurology [*Tryon, NC*] [*A publication*]
SGO	Saint George [*Australia*] [*Airport symbol*] (OAG)
SGO	Sea Gold Oil Corp. [*Vancouver Stock Exchange symbol*]
SGO	Seagull Energy Corp. [*NYSE symbol*] (SPSG)
SGO	Society of Geriatric Ophthalmology (EA)
SGO	Society of Gynecologic Oncologists (EA)
SGO	Squadron Gunnery Officer
SGO	Stained Glass Overlay [*Commercial firm*] [*British*]
SGO	Subgenual Organ [*Entomology*]
SGO	Surgeon General's Office
SGO	Surgery, Gynecology, and Obstetrics (MAE)
SGO	Sydney Godolphin Osborne [*Literary signature of 19th-century British writer*]
SGOBA.....	Surgery, Gynecology, and Obstetrics [*A publication*]
SGOG	Steam Generators Owners Group [*Nuclear energy*] (NRCH)
SGOG	Suppressor Grid Orbitron Gauge
SGOL	Olimpo [*Paraguay*] [*ICAO location identifier*] (ICLI)
SGOL	St. Helena Gold Mines Ltd. [*NASDAQ symbol*] (NQ)
SGOMSEC ...	Scientific Group on Methodologies for the Safety Evaluation of Chemicals [*International Council of Scientific Unions*]
SGOP	Seagull Energy Corp. [*NASDAQ symbol*] (NQ)
SGOR	Solution Gas-Oil Ratio
SGOS........	Shuttle Ground Operations Simulator [*NASA*] (NASA)
SGOT	Serum Glutamic Oxaloacetic Transaminase [*An enzyme*]
SGP...........	San Gregorio [*Peru*] [*Seismograph station code, US Geological Survey*] [*Closed*] (SEIS)
SGP...........	Schering-Plough Corp. [*NYSE symbol*] (SPSG)
SGP...........	School Guarantee Program (DNAB)
SGP...........	Secondary Gun Pointer [*Navy*]
SGP...........	Seminiferous Growth Factor [*Biochemistry*]
SGP...........	Serine Glycerophosphatide [*Biochemistry*] (MAE)
SGP...........	Simulated Ground Plane [*Automotive engineering*]
SGP...........	Singapore [*ANSI three-letter standard code*] (CNC)

SGP............ Single Ground Point [*NASA*]   (MCD)
SGP............ Society of General Physiologists   (EA)
SGP............ Society of Ghana Philatelists [*Defunct*]   (EA)
SGP............ Solicitor General, Prairies [*UTLAS symbol*]
SGP............ Soluble Glycoprotein [*Medicine*]   (MAE)
SGP......... South Galactic Pole
SGP......... Southern Galactic Pole
SGP............ Specialty Glass Products, Inc.
SGP............ Staatkundig Gereformeerde Partij [*Netherlands*] [*Political party*] [*BENELUX*]
SGP............ Stabilized Gyro Platform
SGP............ Standard Guidance Package
SGP............ Stephen Greene Press
SGP............ Sudeten German Party
SGP............ Sulfated Glycoprotein [*Biochemistry*]
SGPA......... Stained Glass Professionals Association [*Inactive*]   (EA)
SGPB........ Southern Growth Policies Board
SGPC......... Soviet Government Purchasing Commission [*World War II*]
SGPI......... Pilar [*Paraguay*] [*ICAO location identifier*]   (ICLI)
SGPI......... Superintendent of Government Printing, India   (ROG)
SGPM........ Saint-Gobain-Pont-A-Mousson [*French industrial giant*]
SgpNL .... National Library, Singapore, Singapore [*Library symbol*] [*Library of Congress*]   (LCLS)
SgpNU....... Nangang University, Singapore, Singapore [*Library symbol*] [*Library of Congress*]   (LCLS)
SGPO .... Puerto Pinasco [*Paraguay*] [*ICAO location identifier*]   (ICLI)
SGPO .... Standing Group Representative Communication to the Private Office of the NATO Secretary General [*Obsolete*]   (NATG)
SGPS .... Ciudad Presidente Stroessner [*Paraguay*] [*ICAO location identifier*]   (ICLI)
SGPT......... Serum Glutamic-Pyruvic Transaminase [*An enzyme*]
SgpU .... University of Singapore, Singapore, Singapore [*Library symbol*] [*Library of Congress*]   (LCLS)
SGR .... Greenville County Library, Greenville, SC [*OCLC symbol*]   (OCLC)
SGR .... Houston, TX [*Location identifier*] [*FAA*]   (FAAL)
Sgr............. Sagittarius [*Constellation*]
SGR .... Saturn Energy & Resources Ltd. [*Vancouver Stock Exchange symbol*]
SGR .... School of General Reconnaissance [*Air Force*] [*British*]
SGR .... Science and Government Report [*A publication*]
SGR .... Seismic Group Recorder [*Geophysics*]
SGR .... Self-Generation Reactor [*Nuclear energy*]   (NRCH)
SGR .... Seminal Groove
SGR .... Set Graphics Rendition [*Data processing*]   (PCM)
SGR .... Short Growth Rate   (OA)
SGR .... Singer [*Music*]
SGR .... Sodium Graphite Reactor [*Nuclear energy*]
SGR .... Soft Gamma-Ray Repeater [*Astrophysics*]
SGR .... Stack Gas Reheat [*Air pollution control*]
SGR .... Steam Gas Recycle [*Shale oil process*]
S/GR.......... Steering Gear [*Automotive engineering*]
SGR .... Submandibular Gland Renin [*Endocrinology*]
SGR .... Sugar Land [*Texas*] [*Airport symbol*]   (OAG)
SGRA......... Sporting Goods Representatives Association [*of SIRA*] [*Later, SGAA*]   (EA)
Sg RA .... Surgeon Rear-Admiral [*British military*]   (DMA)
SGRAC....... Supreme Grand Royal Arch Chapter [*Freemasonry*]   (ROG)
SGRAE....... Scientists' Group for Reform of Animal Experimentation   (EA)
SGRCA...... Sodium Graphite Reactor Critical Assembly   (IEEE)
SGRD .... Signal Ground   (AAG)
SGRD .... State Government Research Directory [*A publication*]
SGREP ...... Standing Group Representative [*NASA*]
S-GRN .... Surfaced Green [*Lumber*]
SGRO .... Rosario [*Paraguay*] [*ICAO location identifier*]   (ICLI)
SGRS .... Stockton Geriatric Rating Scale [*Psychology*]
SGRT........ Soviet Geography. Review and Translations [*A publication*]
SGRU .... Sawyers' General Representative Union [*British*]
SGS............ Sage Resources Ltd. [*Vancouver Stock Exchange symbol*]
SGS............ St. George [*South Carolina*] [*Seismograph station code, US Geological Survey*]   (SEIS)
SGS............ Salem Generating Station [*Nuclear energy*]   (GFGA)
SGS............ Scottish Gaelic Studies [*A publication*]
SGS............ Scottish Guild of Servers [*Episcopalian*]
SGS............ Secondary Grammar School   (ADA)
SGS............ Secretary of the General Staff [*Army*]
SGS............ Segmented Gamma Scanner [*Nuclear energy*]   (NRCH)
SGS............ Signal Generating Station   (CET)
SGS............ Single Green Silk-Covered [*Wire insulation*]
SGS............ Sisters of the Good Samaritan   (ADA)
SGS............ Society of the Golden Section [*Inactive*]   (EA)
SGS............ Society of the Good Shepherd [*Anglican religious community*]
SGS............ Software Generation System
SGS............ Solution Gas Drive [*Petroleum engineering*]
SGS............ Song of Songs [*Old Testament book*] [*Roman Catholic canon*]
SGS............ Statistics Gathering System [*NASA*]
SGS............ Steam Generator System [*Nuclear energy*]   (NRCH)
SGS............ Steep Glide Slope   (NASA)
SGS............ Strategy Gaming Society   (EA)
SGS............ Stream Generation Statement [*Data processing*]
SGS............ Stretch Glass Society   (EA)

SGS............ Swiveling Gunner's Station
SGS............ Symbol Generation and Storage [*Data processing*]
SGSC .... Samuel Gompers Stamp Club   (EA)
SGSC .... Standing Group Security Committee [*Obsolete*] [*NATO*]   (NATG)
SGSC .... Strain Gauge Signal Conditioner [*NASA*]   (MCD)
SGSE .... Standard Ground Support Equipment
SGSFU ...... Salt-Glazed Structural Facing Units [*Technical drawings*]
SGSHA...... Shigen Gijutsu Shikenjo Hokoku [*A publication*]
SGSI .... Sage Software, Inc. [*Rockville, MD*] [*NASDAQ symbol*]   (NQ)
SGSI .... Stabilized Glide Slope Indicator   (NVT)
SGSN......... Skylab Ground Support Network [*NASA*]
SGSNY...... St. George's Society of New York   (EA)
SGSO......... Space Ground Support Operations [*NASA*]   (KSC)
SGSP .... Salt Gradient Solar Ponds [*Energy source*]
SGSP .... Single Groove, Single Petticoat [*Insulators*]
SGSP .... Society for Glass Science and Practices   (EA)
SGSR .... Society for General Systems Research   (EA)
SGSRDC .... Selye's Guide to Stress Research [*A publication*]
SGSS .... Study Group on Social Security [*Defunct*]   (EA)
SGSUB...... Salt-Glazed Structural Unit Base [*Technical drawings*]
SGSVDV .... Steam Generator Stop Valve Dump Valve   (IEEE)
SGSYB ...... Stadler Genetics Symposia [*A publication*]
S-GT .... Sachs-Georgi Test [*for syphilis*] [*Also, SG*] [*Obsolete*]
SGT............ Satellite Ground Terminal
SGT............ Schriften. Gesellschaft fuer Theatergeschichte [*A publication*]
SGT............ Seagram's Gin and Tonic
SGT............ Section Gunnery Trainer [*Army*]
SGT............ Segment Table [*Data processing*]   (IBMDP)
SGT............ Sergeant   (AABC)
SGT............ Small Gas Turbine
SGT............ Small Group Therapy
SGT............ Society of Glass Technology   (EAIO)
SGT............ Special Gas Taper [*Thread*]
SGT............ Speculative Gains Tax
SGT............ Starter or Ground, Thermoplastic [*Automotive engineering*]
SGT............ Stuttgart, AR [*Location identifier*] [*FAA*]   (FAAL)
SGT............ Subsystem Ground Test   (MCD)
SGTA........ Servo Gear Train Assembly
SGTADY ... University of Southern California. Institute for Marine and Coastal Studies. Sea Grant Technical Report Series [*A publication*]
Sgte .... Sagitta [*Constellation*]
SGTF .... Steam Generator Test Facility [*Nuclear energy*]   (NRCH)
SGTI .... SATCOM [*Satellite Communications*] Ground Terminal Interoperability
SGTIA .... Standing Group Technical Intelligence Agency [*NATO*]   (NATG)
SGTID ...... Sawyer's Gas Turbine International [*A publication*]
Sgtl............ Sightlines [*A publication*]
SGTM........ Strain Gauge Thrust Meter
SGTM........ Titanium Dioxide Manufacturers Sector Group   (EAIO)
SGTMAJ... Sergeant Major
SGTPS...... Saw Grinders' Trade Protective Society [*A union*] [*British*]
Sgtr .... Sagittarius [*Constellation*]
SGTR........ Standard Government Travel Request
SGTR........ Standardized Government Travel Regulations
SGTR........ Steam Generator Test Rig [*Nuclear energy*]   (NRCH)
SGTR........ Steam Generator Tube Rupture [*Nuclear energy*]   (NRCH)
SGTS .... Satellite Ground Terminal System
SGTS .... Standby Gas Treatment System [*Nuclear energy*]   (NRCH)
SGTS .... Swing Grip Thermal Stripper
SGU .... Saint George [*Utah*] [*Airport symbol*]   (OAG)
SGU .... Saint George, UT [*Location identifier*] [*FAA*]   (FAAL)
SGU .... Sammelbuch Griechischer Urkunden aus Aegypten [*A publication*]   (BJA)
SGU .... Sidewinder Generator Unit   (NG)
SGU .... Single Gun Unit [*British military*]   (DMA)
SGU .... Standard Geographical Unit   (WDMC)
SGU .... Sveriges Geologiska Undersokning [*Geological Survey of Sweden*] [*Uppsala*] [*Information service or system*]   (IID)
SGULF ...... Seagull Resources [*NASDAQ symbol*]   (NQ)
S-G(UN).... Secretary-General of the United Nations
SGUS........ Slovak Gymnastic Union Sokol of the USA   (EA)
SGV .... Saint Genevieve Resources Ltd. [*Toronto Stock Exchange symbol*]
SGV .... Salivary Gland Virus
SGV .... Self-Guided Vehicle
SGV .... Sierra Grande [*Argentina*] [*Airport symbol*]   (OAG)
SGV .... Small Granular Vesicle [*Cytology*]
SGV .... Summlung Gemeinverstaendlicher Vortraege und Schriften aus dem Gebiet der Theologie und Religionsgeschichte [*Tuebingen*] [*A publication*]
Sg VA .... Surgeon Vice-Admiral [*British military*]   (DMA)
SGVS........ Summlung Gemeinverstaendlicher Vortraege und Schriften aus dem Gebiet der Theologie und Religionsgeschichte [*Tuebingen*] [*A publication*]
SGW .... Salt-Glazed Ware
SGW .... Security Guard Window   (AAG)
SGW .... Senior Grand Warden [*Freemasonry*]

SGW .... South Carolina State College, Orangeburg, SC [*OCLC symbol*]　(OCLC)
SGW .... Stone Groundwood [*Pulp and paper technology*]
SGWLC ..... Steam Generator Water Level Control [*Nuclear energy*]　(NRCH)
SGWM ...... Standing Group Working Memorandum [*NATO*]　(NATG)
SGWS .... Shared Graphics Work Space
SGWS .... Stove Grate Workers' Society [*A union*] [*British*]
SGX .... Selector Group Matrix [*Telecommunications*]　(TEL)
SGX .... Songea [*Tanzania*] [*Airport symbol*]　(OAG)
SGX .... Synergistics Industries Ltd. [*Toronto Stock Exchange symbol*]
s-gy--- ...... Guyana [*MARC geographic area code*] [*Library of Congress*]　(LCCP)
SGY .... Skagway [*Alaska*] [*Airport symbol*]　(OAG)
SGY .... Skagway, AK [*Location identifier*] [*FAA*]　(FAAL)
SGY .... Sooner Energy Corp. [*Vancouver Stock Exchange symbol*]
SGym .... Siculorum Gymnasium [*A publication*]
SGYR .... Yasyreta [*Paraguay*] [*ICAO location identifier*]　(ICLI)
SGZ .... Green Bay, WI [*Location identifier*] [*FAA*]　(FAAL)
SGZ .... Signet Resources, Inc. [*Vancouver Stock Exchange symbol*]
SGZ .... Surface Ground Zero
SGZAB ...... Sanyo Gijutsu Zasshi [*A publication*]
SH .... Air-Cushion Vehicle built by Sealand Hovercraft [*England*] [*Usually used in combination with numerals*]
SH .... Sa Hautesse [*His, or Her, Highness*] [*French*]
SH .... Sacred Heart　(ROG)
SH .... Sacrifice Hit [*Baseball*]
Sh .... Safe Hit [*Baseball*]
SH .... St. Helena [*ANSI two-letter standard code*]　(CNC)
SH .... Samaritan Free Hospital [*British*]　(ROG)
S/H .... Sample and Hold　(IEEE)
SH .... Sash　(WGA)
SH .... Schering AG [*Germany*] [*Research code symbol*]
SH .... Schistosoma Hematobium [*A parasitic fluke*]
SH .... Schoolhouse
SH .... Scinde Horse [*British military*]　(DMA)
SH .... Scleroscope Hardness
SH .... Scottish Horse [*British military*]　(DMA)
SH .... Scratch Hardness [*Aerospace*]
SH .... Scripophila Helvetica　(EA)
SH .... Scripta Hierosolymitana　(BJA)
SH .... Scrum Half [*Rugby*]　(WGA)
SH .... Second Harvest, the National Food Bank Network　(EA)
SH .... Secondhand　(ADA)
SH .... Section Heading Code [*Online database field identifier*]
SH .... Sefer ha-Shanah　(BJA)
SH .... Sekira Hodshit [*Tel Aviv*]　(BJA)
SH .... Semester Hour
SH .... Send Hub [*Telegraphy*]　(TEL)
SH .... Sephardic House [*An association*]　(EA)
SH .... Sequence History
SH .... Serum Hepatitis [*Medicine*]
SH .... Service Hours [*Electronics*]　(IEEE)
SH .... Servicio Aereo de Honduras, Sociedad Anonima [*ICAO designator*]　(FAAC)
SH .... Session Handler
SH .... Severely Handicapped
SH .... Severn House [*Publisher*] [*British*]
SH .... Sex Hormone　(MAE)
SH .... Sexual Harassment
SH .... Shackle　(AAG)
Sh .... Shadforth's Reserved Judgements [*A publication*]　(APTA)
SH .... Shale [*Lithology*]
SH .... Shall
Sh .... Shallow
Sh .... Shand's Reports [*11-41 South Carolina*] [*A publication*]　(DLA)
SH .... Shanghai
SH .... Share
Sh .... Shauri　(BJA)
Sh .... [*W. G.*] Shaw's Reports [*30-35 Vermont*] [*A publication*]　(DLA)
Sh .... [*G. B.*] Shaw's Reports [*10, 11 Vermont*] [*A publication*]　(DLA)
Sh .... Shaw's Scotch Appeal Cases [*A publication*]　(DLA)
Sh .... Shaw's Scotch Justiciary Cases [*A publication*]　(DLA)
Sh .... Shaw's Scotch Session Cases [*A publication*]　(DLA)
Sh .... Shaw's Scotch Teind [*Tithe*] Court Reports [*A publication*]　(DLA)
SH .... Sheathing [*Technical drawings*]
SH .... Sheep　(ROG)
SH .... Sheep Skin [*Bookbinding*]　(ROG)
SH .... Sheet　(AAG)
Sh .... Sheldon's Superior Court Reports [*Buffalo, New York*] [*A publication*]　(DLA)
SH .... Shelf [*Technical drawings*]
SH .... Shell Development Co. [*Research code symbol*]
sh............. Shells [*Quality of the bottom*] [*Nautical charts*]
Sh .... Shepherd's Alabama Reports [*A publication*]　(DLA)
Sh .... Shepley's Reports [*13-18, 21-30 Maine*] [*A publication*]　(DLA)
Sh .... Sheriff　(DLA)
S & H .... Sherratt & Hughes [*Commercial firm*] [*British*]

Sh .... Sherwood Number
SH............. Shield　(MSA)
Sh............. Shiel's Cape Times Law Reports [*South Africa*] [*A publication*]　(DLA)
Sh............. Shigella [*Bacteriology*]　(AAMN)
SH............. Shilling [*Obsolete*] [*Monetary unit in Britain*]
SH............. Ship
S & H .... Shipping and Handling
S/H .... Shipping/Handling　(WGA)
Sh............. Shipp's Reports [*66-67 North Carolina*] [*A publication*]　(DLA)
SH............. Ship's Head [*Heading*] [*Navigation*]
SH............. Ship's Serviceman [*Navy rating*]
SH............. Shipwright
Sh............. Shire
Sh............. Shirley's Reports [*49-55 New Hampshire*] [*A publication*]　(DLA)
SH............. Shoal　(ROG)
SH............. Shock　(WGA)
SH............. Shooting [*FBI standardized term*]
SH............. Shop　(WGA)
SH............. Short　(ROG)
SH............. Short Brothers & Harland Ltd. [*ICAO aircraft manufacturer identifier*]　(ICAO)
S/H .... Shorthand
sh............. Shoulder
SH............. Show　(WGA)
SH............. Showers　(AAG)
Sh............. Shower's English King's Bench Reports [*A publication*]　(DLA)
Sh............. Shower's English Parliamentary Cases [*A publication*]　(DLA)
SH............. Shunt [*Electricity*]
SH............. Shuttle　(MCD)
SH............. Sick in Hospital
SH............. Single Heterostructure　(MCD)
SH............. Sinus Histiocytosis [*Medicine*]
S H............. Slovenska Hudba [*A publication*]
SH............. Small Heavy Seeds [*Botany*]
SH............. Social History
SH............. Socially Housed [*Experimental animals*]
SH............. Society for HematoPathology　(EA)
SH............. Society for the Humanities　(EA)
S/H .... Software/Hardware [*Cost*]
SH............. Soldiers' Home [*Later, US Soldiers' and Airmen's Home*] [*Government agency*]
SH............. Somatotrophic [*Growth*] Hormone [*Also, GH, STH*] [*Endocrinology*]
S and H ...... Son and Heir [*Genealogy*]
SH............. Source Handshake
SH............. Southern Hemisphere
SH............. Southland Hussars [*British military*]　(DMA)
SH............. Southlife Holding Co. [*AMEX symbol*]　(SPSG)
SH............. Spanish Heritage　(EA)
sh............. Spanish Territories in Northern Morocco [*Spanish North Africa*] [*MARC country of publication code*] [*Library of Congress*]　(LCCP)
SH............. Special Hazards
SH............. Special Honor
SH............. Specified Hours
S & H .... Speech and Hearing [*Medicine*]
SH............. Speighel Historiael van de Bond van Gentse Germanisten [*A publication*]
S & H .... Sperry & Hutchinson Co.
SH............. Spontaneously Hypertensive [*Medicine*]
SH............. State Hospital　(MAE)
sH............. Stathenry [*Also, statH*] [*Unit of inductance*]
SH............. Station Hospital [*Military*]
SH............. Station House
SH............. Stationary High-Power [*Reactor*]　(NRCH)
SH............. Steel Heads
SH............. Steelton & Highspire Railroad Co. [*AAR code*]
S & H .... Steering and Hydroplane [*British*]
SH............. Stockholder
SH............. Stored Heading　(MCD)
SH............. Stoy Hayward [*Venture capital group*] [*British*]
SH............. Student Handout [*Military training document*]　(INF)
SH............. Student Health　(MAE)
SH............. Sulfhydryl [*Chemistry*]
SH............. Sun-Herald [*A publication*]　(APTA)
S & H .... Sundays and Holidays
SH............. Super-High-Frequency [*Radio wave*]　(NG)
SH............. Superstructure Heater　(DS)
SH............. Surgical History [*Medicine*]
S & H .... Survivability and Hardening　(MCD)
SH............. Switch Handler [*Telecommunications*]　(TEL)
SH............. Switch Hook　(HGAA)
SH............. Sydney Herald [*A publication*]　(APTA)
SH1............ Ship's Serviceman, First Class [*Navy rating*]
SH2............ Ship's Serviceman, Second Class [*Navy rating*]
sh$_2$ .... Shrunken-2 Gene [*In sweet corn*]
SH$_2$ .... Supercritical Hydrogen [*NASA*]　(NASA)
SH3............ Ship's Serviceman, Third Class [*Navy rating*]
S2H2............ Short, Straight Hollow Hosel [*Golf clubs*]

SHA .... Ozark, AL [*Location identifier*] [*FAA*]   (FAAL)
SHA .... Safety Hazard Analysis   (MCD)
SHA .... Sailplane Homebuilders Association   (EA)
SHA .... Sample and Hold Amplifier
SHA .... Scriptores Historiae Augustae [*Classical studies*]   (OCD)
SHA .... Secretariat for Hispanic Affairs (National Conference of
                  Catholic Bishops)   (EA)
SHA .... Shakwak Exploration Co. [*Vancouver Stock Exchange symbol*]
SHA .... Shanghai [*China*] [*Airport symbol*]   (OAG)
ShA .... Shulhan 'Arukh   (BJA)
SHA .... Sidereal Hour Angle
SHA .... Sitzungsberichte. Heidelberg Akademie der Wissenschaft [*A
                  publication*]
SHA .... Smith-Hurd's Illinois Annotated Statutes [*A
                  publication*]   (DLA)
SHA .... Societe Historique Acadienne [*Acadian Historical
                  Society*]   (EA)
SHA .... Society for Historical Archaeology   (EA)
SHA .... Society for Humane Abortion   (EA)
SHA .... Society for Humanistic Anthropology   (EA)
SHA .... Sodium Hydroxide Addition [*Nuclear energy*]   (NRCH)
SHA .... Solid Homogeneous Assembly [*Nuclear energy*]
SHA .... Southern Historical Association   (EA)
SHA .... Special Health Authority [*Government body*] [*British*]
SHA .... Spherical Harmonic Analysis [*Geophysics*]
SHA .... Spring Hill [*Alabama*] [*Seismograph station code, US
                  Geological Survey*]   (SEIS)
SHA .... Station Housing Allowance [*Military*]   (MCD)
SHa .... Sulgi Hymn A   (BJA)
SHA .... Sun-Herald (Australia) [*A publication*]
SHA .... Support Harness Assembly
SHA .... System Hazard Analyses [*NASA*]   (NASA)
SHAA .... Schaak Electronics, Inc. [*NASDAQ symbol*]   (NQ)
SHAA .... Sealed Head Access Area [*Nuclear energy*]   (NRCH)
SHAA .... Serum Hepatitis Associated Antigen [*Hematology*]
SHAA .... Society of Hearing Aid Audiologists [*Later, NHAS*]   (EA)
SHAA-Ab ... Serum Hepatitis Associated Antigen-Antibody [*Hematology*]
SHA-Ab ..... Serum Hepatitis Associated Antibody [*Hematology*]
Shaanxi Med J ... Shaanxi Medical Journal [*A publication*]
Shab .... Shabbath   (BJA)
SHABS ...... Shock Absorber
SHAC .... Small Hydrofoil Aircraft Carrier   (DNAB)
SHAC .... Society for the History of Alchemy and Chemistry   (EA)
SHAC .... Solar Heating and Air Conditioning
Sh Acc .... Hale's Sheriff's Account [*A publication*]   (DLA)
SHACC ..... Servicing Hotels and the Caribbean Community
SHACO ..... Shorthand Coding
SHACOB .. Solar Heating and Cooling of Buildings [*Energy Research and
                  Development Administration*]
SHACV ..... Second Harmonic AC [*Alternating Current*] Voltammetry
                  [*Instrumentation*]
SHAD .... Shallow Habitat Air Dive [*Navy*]
SHAD .... Sharpe Army Depot [*California*]
SHAD .... Shipboard Hazards Appraisal and Defense   (CINC)
SHADCOM ... Shipping Advisory Committee [*NATO*]
SHADE ..... Shielded Hot-Air-Drum Evaporator [*Concentrator for
                  hazardous wastes*]
SHADO ..... Supreme Headquarters, Alien Defense Organization [*in
                  television program "UFO"*]
SHADRAC ... Shelter Housed Automatic Digital Random Access [*Data
                  processing*]
SHAEF ...... Supreme Headquarters, Allied Expeditionary Force [*Europe*]
                  [*World War II*]
SH-AF .... Shelter-Afrique   (EAIO)
SHAF .... Staying Healthy after Fifty [*Project*] [*AARP*]
SHAFB ...... Sheppard Air Force Base [*Texas*]   (AAG)
SHAFR ...... Society for Historians of American Foreign Relations   (EA)
SHAFT ...... Second Home All-Inclusive First Trust [*Real estate*]
SHAFT ...... Shaftsbury [*England*]
SHAG .... Simplified High-Accuracy Guidance [*NASA*]   (NASA)
SHAH .... Shire National Corp. [*NASDAQ symbol*]   (NQ)
SHAK .... Shakespeare
Shakes Jah ... Shakespeare-Jahrbuch [*A publication*]
Shakespeare-Jahrb ... Shakespeare-Jahrbuch [*A publication*]
Shakespeare Q ... Shakespeare Quarterly [*A publication*]
Shakespeare S ... Shakespeare Survey [*A publication*]
Shakes Q ... Shakespeare Quarterly [*A publication*]
Shakes Surv ... Shakespeare Survey [*A publication*]
Shakhtnoe Stroit ... Shakhtnoe Stroitel'stvo [*Former USSR*] [*A publication*]
Shak-Jahrb ... Shakespeare-Jahrbuch [*A publication*]
ShakS .... Shakespeare Studies [*A publication*]
SHAL .... Subject Heading Authority List [*Data processing*]
Shale .... Decrees and Judgments in Federal Anti-Trust Cases [*United
                  States*] [*A publication*]   (DLA)
Shale Ctry ... Shale Country [*A publication*]
Shale Rev ... Shale Review [*A publication*]
Shalm......... Shalmaneser   (BJA)
SHALOM ... Synchronous Halo Monitor [*NASA*]
SHAM .... Salicylhydroxamic Acid [*Chelating agent*]
SHAME .... Save, Help Animals Man Exploits [*Connecticut organization*]

SHAME .... Society to Humiliate, Aggravate, Mortify, and Embarrass
                  Smokers
SHAME .... Stop Hospital and Medical Errors
SHAMS..... Smart Howitzer Automated Management System [*US Army
                  Human Engineering Laboratory*]   (RDA)
SHAMYR ... Shomrei Mitzvot Yotzei Russia   (BJA)
SHAN........ Shannon Oil & Gas [*NASDAQ symbol*]   (NQ)
Shan.......... Shannon's Unreported Tennessee Cases [*A publication*]   (DLA)
Shan Cas.... Shannon's Tennessee Cases [*A publication*]   (DLA)
Shand......... Shand's Reports [*11-41 South Carolina*] [*A publication*]   (DLA)
Shand Pr .... Shand's Practice, Scotch Court of Sessions [*A
                  publication*]   (DLA)
SHANE ..... Steerable Hydrophone Array, Nonlinear Element
Shanghai Environ Sci ... Shanghai Environmental Sciences [*A publication*]
Shanghai Iron Steel Res Inst Tech Rep ... Shanghai Iron and Steel Research
                  Institute. Technical Report [*China*] [*A publication*]
SHANICLE ... Short-Range Navigation Vehicle [*System*] [*Air Force*]
Shankland's St ... Shankland's Tennessee Public Statutes [*A
                  publication*]   (DLA)
Shannon Cas (Tenn) ... Shannon's Unreported Tennessee Cases [*A
                  publication*]   (DLA)
Shannon's Code ... Shannon's Tennessee Annotated Code [*A
                  publication*]   (DLA)
SHANT ..... Shantung [*Province in China*]   (ROG)
Shantung Med J ... Shantung Medical Journal [*People's Republic of China*]
                  [*A publication*]
Shanxi Med J ... Shanxi Medical Journal [*A publication*]
Shanxi Med Pharm J ... Shanxi Medical and Pharmaceutical Journal [*A
                  publication*]
Shanxi Univ J Nat Sci Ed ... Shanxi University. Journal. Natural Science
                  Edition [*A publication*]
SHAP .... Ship Acquisition Plan [*Navy*]   (CAAL)
SHAPA...... Solids Handling and Processing Association   (EAIO)
SHAPE...... Simulated Hospital Administration and Planning Exercise
SHAPE...... Supersonic High-Altitude Parachute Experiment [*NASA*]
SHAPE...... Supreme Headquarters, Allied Powers Europe [*NATO*]
SHAPES ... Spatial, High-Accuracy Position Encoding Sensor   (SSD)
SHAPEX ... SHAPE [*Supreme Headquarters Allied Powers Europe*] Annual
                  Command Exercise [*NATO*]   (NATG)
SHAPM .... Shear Horizontal Acoustic Plate Model [*Instrumentation*]
SHAPM .... Ship Acquisition Project Manager [*Navy*]
Sh App .... Shaw's Scotch Appeal Cases, House of Lords [*A
                  publication*]   (DLA)
ShAr.......... Shulhan 'Arukh   (BJA)
SHAR .... Simplified Hourly Absence Reporting   (MCD)
SHAR .... Sriharikota Island Launch Complex [*India*]
SHARE...... SHARE Foundation   (EA)
SHARE...... Share Happily and Reap Endlessly [*Hollywood women's charity
                  organization*]
SHARE...... Shared Area Resources Exchange [*Library network*]
SHaRE....... Shared Research Equipment Collaborative Research Program
                  [*Oak Ridge, TN*] [*Oak Ridge National Laboratory*]
                  [*Department of Energy*]   (GRD)
SHARE...... So Handicapped All Read Easily
SHARE...... Society to Help Avoid Redundant Effort [*in data processing*]
SHARE...... Soldier Housing and Retirement Equity
SHARE...... Systems for Heat and Radiation Energy [*Nuclear energy*]
SHAREM ... Ship ASW [*Antisubmarine Warfare*] Readiness Effectiveness
                  Measuring Program
SHARES ... Shared Acquisitions and Retention System
Shark Elec ... Sharkey's Practice of Election Committees [*2nd ed.*] [*1866*] [*A
                  publication*]   (DLA)
SHARNB .. Sharnbrook [*England*]
SHARP...... School Health Additional Referral Program [*Public Health
                  Service*]
SHARP...... Senior High Assessment of Reading Performance [*Educational
                  test*]
SHARP...... Ships Analysis and Retrieval Program [*Navy*]
SHARP...... Sperry Heading and Attitude Reference Platform   (SAA)
SHARP...... Stationary [*or Strategic*] High-Altitude Relay Platform
                  [*Microwave airplane*] [*Canada*]
SHARP...... Strategic High Altitude Relay Platform [*Aviation*]
Sharp Cong Ct ... Sharp on Congregational Courts [*A publication*]   (DLA)
Sharpe........ Calendar of Coroners Rolls of the City of London [*A
                  publication*]   (DLA)
Sharpe........ Sharpe's London Magazine [*A publication*]
SHARPE..... Symbolic Hierarchical Automated Reliability and Performance
                  Evaluator
Sharp Ins Dig ... Sharpstein's Insurance Digest [*A publication*]   (DLA)
SHARPS ... Ship/Helicopter Acoustic Range-Prediction System
                  [*Navy*]   (NVT)
SHARPS ... Sonic High-Accuracy Ranging and Positioning System
Sharp Tech J ... Sharp Technical Journal [*A publication*]
Shars Black ... Sharswood's Edition of Blackstone's Commentaries [*A
                  publication*]   (DLA)
Shars Bl Comm ... Sharswood's Edition of Blackstone's Commentaries [*A
                  publication*]   (DLA)
Shars & B Lead Cas Real Prop ... Sharswood and Budd's Leading Cases on
                  Real Property [*A publication*]   (DLA)
Shars Comm L ... Sharswood's Commercial Law [*A publication*]   (DLA)

Shars Law Lec ... Sharswood's Lectures on the Profession of the Law [*A publication*]   (DLA)
Shars Leg Eth ... Sharswood's Legal Ethics [*A publication*]   (DLA)
Shars Tab Ca ... Sharswood's Table of Cases, Connecticut [*A publication*]   (DLA)
SHAS........ Self Help Association for Stammerers [*British*]   (DI)
SHAS........ Shared Hospital Accounting System [*Data processing*]
SHaS........ Shishah Sedarim   (BJA)
SHAT .... Shatterproof Glass Corp. [*NASDAQ symbol*]   (NQ)
SHATC...... SHAPE [*Supreme Headquarters Allied Powers Europe*] Technical Center [*Formerly, SADTC*] [*NATO*]   (NATG)
SHATCPS ... St. Helena, Ascension, and Tristan da Cunha Philatelic Society   (EA)
SHAVE...... Sugar Hotel Alpha Victor Echo [*Apollo 10 astronauts' code for shaving operation*]
SHAVIB.... Shaft Alignment and Vibration   (DNAB)
Shaw .... Shaw Industries, Inc. [*Associated Press abbreviation*]   (APAG)
Shaw .... [*G. B.*] Shaw's Reports [*10, 11 Vermont*] [*A publication*]   (DLA)
Shaw .... [*W. G.*] Shaw's Reports [*30-35 Vermont*] [*A publication*]   (DLA)
Shaw .... Shaw's Scotch Appeal Cases [*A publication*]   (DLA)
Shaw .... Shaw's Scotch Court of Session Cases, First Series [*A publication*]   (DLA)
Shaw .... Shaw's Scotch Justiciary Cases [*A publication*]   (DLA)
Shaw .... Shaw's Scotch Teind [*Tithe*] Court Reports [*A publication*]   (DLA)
SHAW....... Shaw's Supermarkets, Inc. [*East Bridgewater, MA*] [*NASDAQ symbol*]   (NQ)
SHAW....... Sitzungsberichte. Heidelberg Akademie der Wissenschaft [*A publication*]
Shaw App.... Shaw's Scotch Appeal Cases, English House of Lords [*A publication*]   (DLA)
ShawB........ Shaw Bulletin [*A publication*]
SHAWCO ... Students' Health and Welfare Centers Organization
Shaw Crim Cas ... Shaw's Criminal Cases, Scotch Justiciary Court [*A publication*]   (DLA)
Shaw & D... Shaw and Dunlop's Scotch Court of Session Reports, First Series [*A publication*]   (DLA)
Shaw D & B ... Shaw, Dunlop, and Bell's Scotch Court of Session Reports, First Series [*A publication*]   (DLA)
Shaw D & B Supp ... Shaw, Dunlop, and Bell's Supplement, Containing House of Lords Decisions [*Scotland*] [*A publication*]   (DLA)
Shaw Dec ... Shaw's Decisions in Scotch Court of Sessions, First Series [*A publication*]   (DLA)
Shaw Dig.... Shaw's Digest of Decisions [*Scotland*] [*A publication*]   (DLA)
Shaw & Dunl ... Shaw and Dunlop's Scotch Court of Session Reports, First Series [*A publication*]   (DLA)
Shaw Dunl & B ... Shaw, Dunlop, and Bell's Scotch Court of Session Cases, First Series [*1821-38*] [*A publication*]   (DLA)
Shaw (G B) ... [*G. B.*] Shaw's Reports [*10, 11 Vermont*] [*A publication*]   (DLA)
Shaw HL.... Shaw's Scotch Appeal Cases, House of Lords [*1821-24*] [*A publication*]   (DLA)
Shaw J .... John Shaw's Justiciary Cases [*1848-52*] [*Scotland*] [*A publication*]   (DLA)
Shaw Jus.... [*John*] Shaw's Justiciary Cases [*1848-52*] [*Scotland*] [*A publication*]   (DLA)
SHAWL..... Special Hard-Target Assault Weapon LAW   (RDA)
Shaw & M ... Shaw and Maclean's Scotch Appeal Cases [*A publication*]   (DLA)
Shaw & Macl ... Shaw and Maclean's Scotch Appeal Cases [*A publication*]   (DLA)
Shaw & M Sc App Cas ... Shaw and Maclean's Scotch Appeal Cases [*1835-38*] [*A publication*]   (DLA)
ShawN .... Shawmut National Corp. [*Associated Press abbreviation*]   (APAG)
ShawNt ...... Shawmut National Corp. [*Associated Press abbreviation*]   (APAG)
Shaw P .... Patrick Shaw's Justiciary Cases [*1819-31*] [*Scotland*] [*A publication*]   (DLA)
Shaw PL..... Shaw's Parish Law [*A publication*]   (DLA)
Shaw R....... Shaw Review [*A publication*]
Shaw Rev ... Shaw Review [*A publication*]
Shaw Sc App Cas ... Shaw's Scotch Appeal Cases, House of Lords [*1821-24*] [*A publication*]   (DLA)
Shaw TC .... Shaw's Scotch Teind [*Tithe*] Cases [*1821-31*] [*A publication*]   (DLA)
Shaw T Cas ... Shaw's Scotch Teind [*Tithe*] Court Reports [*A publication*]   (DLA)
Shaw Teind ... Shaw's Scotch Teind [*Tithe*] Court Decisions [*1821-31*] [*A publication*]   (DLA)
Shaw (VT) ... [*W. G.*] Shaw's Reports [*30, 35 Vermont*] [*A publication*]   (DLA)
Shaw (VT) ... [*G. B.*] Shaw's Reports [*10, 11 Vermont*] [*A publication*]   (DLA)
Shaw W & C ... Shaw, Wilson, and Courtenay's Scotch Appeals Reports, House of Lords [*A publication*]   (DLA)
Shaw (W G) ... [*W. G.*] Shaw's Reports [*30-35 Vermont*] [*A publication*]   (DLA)
SHAZ .... Spirohydantoin Aziridine [*Biochemistry*]

SHAZAM ... [*Grace of*] Selena, [*Strength of*] Hippolyta, [*Skill of*] Ariadne, [*Fleetness of*] Zephyrus, [*Beauty of*] Aurora, [*Wisdom of*] Minerva [*Word used to change Mary Batson into Mary Marvel in the comic book series*]
SHAZAM ... [*Wisdom of*] Solomon, [*Strength of*] Hercules, [*Stamina of*] Atlas, [*Power of*] Zeus, [*Courage of*] Achilles, [*Speed of*] Mercury [*Word used to change Billy Batson into Captain Marvel in the comic book series*]
SHB .... Nakashibetsu [*Japan*] [*Airport symbol*]   (OAG)
SHB .... Scotty's, Inc. [*NYSE symbol*]   (SPSG)
SHB .... Second-Harmonic Band
SHB .... Shelbyville, IN [*Location identifier*] [*FAA*]   (FAAL)
SHB .... Silhouette Harness Board   (MCD)
SHB .... Sodium Hydroxybutyrate [*Organic chemistry*]
SHB .... Subacute Hepatitis with Bridging [*Medicine*]
S Hb .... Sulfhemoglobin [*Medicine*]   (MAE)
SHBD .... Serum Hydroxybutyrate Dehydrogenase [*An enzyme*]
SHBE........ Southern Hemisphere Balloon Experiment   (SAA)
SHBG .... Sex-Hormone-Binding Globulin [*Endocrinology*]
SHBLDR.... Shipbuilder   (MSA)
SHBS......... ShareBase Corp. [*NASDAQ symbol*]   (NQ)
S and H Bull ... Smoking and Health Bulletin [*A publication*]
SHBZ........ ShowBiz Pizza Time, Inc. [*NASDAQ symbol*]   (CTT)
SHC .... Chief Ship's Serviceman [*Navy rating*]
SHC .... Mount St. Helena [*California*] [*Seismograph station code, US Geological Survey*]   (SEIS)
SHC .... Sacred Heart College [*Cullman, AL*]
SHC .... Schult Homes Corp. [*AMEX symbol*]   (SPSG)
SHC .... Self-Help Crafts [*An association*]   (EA)
SHC .... SENTRY [*Survey Entry*] Hazard Control
SHC .... Seton Hill College [*Greensburg, PA*]
SHC .... Shaklee Corp. [*NYSE symbol*]   (SPSG)
SHC .... Shape and Hamiltonian Consistent [*Physics*]
SHC .... Shell Canada Ltd. [*Toronto Stock Exchange symbol*] [*Vancouver Stock Exchange symbol*]
SHC .... Shipping Coordinating Committee [*Coast Guard*]
SHC .... Shire Indaselassie [*Ethiopia*] [*Airport symbol*]   (OAG)
SHC .... Siena Heights College [*Adrian, MI*]
SHC .... Silicones Health Council   (EA)
SHC .... Sky Harbor Air Service, Inc. [*Cheyenne, WY*] [*FAA designator*]   (FAAC)
SHC .... Societe Historique du Canada [*Canadian Historical Association - CHA*]
SHC .... Sodium Hypochlorite [*Inorganic chemistry*]
SHC .... Southern Hemisphere Cap [*on Triton*]
SHC .... Southern Humanities Conference   (EA)
SHC .... Special Handling Code
SHC .... Spherical Harmonic Coefficient [*Geophysics*]
SHC .... Spring Hill College [*Mobile, AL*]
SHC .... Stanford Humanities Center [*Stanford University*] [*Research center*]   (RCD)
SHC .... Superheat Control [*Boilers*]
SHC .... Superhybrid Composite [*Laminate*]
SHC .... Superior Heliocentric Conjunction
SHC .... Surveillance Helicopter Co. [*Army*]   (AABC)
SHCA .... Safety Helmet Council of America   (EA)
SHCA .... Siberian Husky Club of America   (EA)
SHCA .... Solid Homogeneous Critical Assembly [*Nuclear reactor*] [*Japan*]
SHC-BRC ... Small Homes Council-Building Research Council [*University of Illinois*] [*Research center*]   (RCD)
SHCC .... Statewide Health Coordinating Council
SHCC .... Susan Hayward Collectors Club   (EA)
SHCGSAS ... Shrimp Harvesters Coalition of the Gulf and South Atlantic States   (EA)
Shchorichnyk Ukrayins'ke Bot Tov ... Shchorichnyk Ukrayins'ke Botanichne Tovarystvo [*A publication*]
SHCI......... Salick Health Care, Inc. [*Beverly Hills, CA*] [*NASDAQ symbol*]   (NQ)
SHCJ .... Society for the History of Czechoslovak Jews   (EA)
SHCJ .... Society of the Holy Child Jesus [*Roman Catholic women's religious order*]
SHCM ...... Master Chief Ship's Serviceman [*Navy rating*]
SHCO........ Sulfated Hydrogenated Castor Oil   (MAE)
SHCOS..... Supreme Headquarters, Chief of Staff [*World War II*]
SHCPP ...... Sanitation Handbook of Consumer Protection Programs
SHCR .... Shipping Container
SHCR .... Skyline Hikers of the Canadian Rockies   (EA)
Sh Crim Cas ... Shaw's Justiciary Court, Criminal Cases [*Scotland*] [*A publication*]   (DLA)
SHCRT...... Short Circuit   (AAG)
SHCS .... Senior Chief Ship's Serviceman [*Navy rating*]
SHCS .... Springer Series on Health Care and Society [*A publication*]
SHCSR ...... Spicilegium Historicum Congregationis Smi Redemptoris [*A publication*]
SHCS USAF ... School of Health Care Sciences, United States Air Force   (AFM)
SHCT .... Sheriff Court [*Legal*] [*British*]
SHCT .... Studies in the History of Christian Thought [*A publication*]   (BJA)
Sh Ct Rep... Sheriff Court Reports [*Scotland*] [*A publication*]   (DLA)

Sh Ct of Sess ... Shaw's Scotch Court of Session Cases [*A publication*] (DLA)
SHCW .... Scottish History from Contemporary Writers [*A publication*]
SHD .... Sandhill Decline [*Citrus blight*]
SHD .... Scottish Home Department (ILCA)
SHD .... Shade
SHD .... Shahrud [*Iran*] [*Seismograph station code, US Geological Survey*] (SEIS)
SHD .... Sherwood Group, Inc. [*AMEX symbol*] (SPSG)
SHD .... Shield Development [*Vancouver Stock Exchange symbol*]
SHD .... Ship's Diver [*Navy*] [*British*]
SHD .... Shode
SHD .... Should (ROG)
SHD .... Shroud (AAG)
SHD .... Silo Hardsite Defense
SHD .... Slant Hole Distance [*Nuclear energy*] (OA)
SHD .... Society for the History of Discoveries (EA)
SHD .... Special Handling Designator (MCD)
SHD .... Staunton [*Virginia*] [*Airport symbol*] (OAG)
SHD .... Staunton/Waynesboro/Harrisonburg, VA [*Location identifier*] [*FAA*] (FAAL)
SHd .... Sulgi Hymn D (BJA)
SHDA .... Selenaheptadecanoic Acid [*Organic chemistry*]
SHDC .... Sacred Heart Dominican College [*Texas*]
SHDC .... Subject Headings Used in the Dictionary Catalog [*Later, LCSH*] [*A publication*]
SHDCD ..... Shore Duty Commencemnt Date [*Navy*] (DNAB)
SHDI .... Supraoptic-Hypophyseal Diabetes Insipidus [*Endocrinology*]
Sh Dig .... Shaw's Digest of Decisions [*Scotland*] [*A publication*] (DLA)
SHDN .... Shutdown (NASA)
SHDP .... Supportive Housing Demonstration Program [*Department of Housing and Urban Development*] (GFGA)
SHDPS ..... St. Helena and Dependencies Philatelic Society (EA)
SHDR .... Service and Hardware Difficulty Reports (MCD)
SHDS .... Safety and Health Data Sheet [*Army*]
SHDS .... Second-Harmonic Discrimination System (MCD)
Sh & Dunl .. Shaw and Dunlop's Scotch Court of Session Reports, First Series [*A publication*] (DLA)
SHE .... Securities Hazards Expert [*In film title*]
SHE .... Self-Help Enterprises (EA)
SHE .... Semihomogeneous Experiment [*Nuclear energy*]
SHE .... Sheba Copper Mines [*Vancouver Stock Exchange symbol*]
SHE .... Shemkha [*Former USSR*] [*Seismograph station code, US Geological Survey*] (SEIS)
SHE .... Shenyang [*China*] [*Airport symbol*] (OAG)
SHE .... Siderphile Superheavy Element [*Physics*]
SHE .... Signal Handling Equipment (AAG)
SHE .... Society for the Health Education [*British*]
SHE .... Society for History Education (EA)
SHE .... Society for Human Ecology (EA)
SHE .... Sodium Heat Engine
SHE .... Spares Handling Expense
SHE .... Special Handling Equipment
SHE .... Standard Hydrogen Electrode [*Electrochemistry*]
SHE .... Subject Headings for Engineering [*A publication*]
S/HE .... Sundays and Holidays Excepted
SHE .... Supercritical Helium (KSC)
SHE .... Superheavy Element [*Nuclear physics*]
SHE .... Syrian Hamster Embryonic [*Cells*]
SHEAL ...... Shuttle High-Energy Astrophysics Laboratory [*NASA*] (SSD)
SHEAR ...... Society for Historians of the Early American Republic (EA)
Shear Bar Ex ... Shearwood's Bar Examinations [*A publication*] (DLA)
Shear Cont ... Shearwood on Contract [*1897*] [*A publication*] (DLA)
Shearm & Red Neg ... Shearman and Redfield on the Law of Negligence [*A publication*] (DLA)
Shear Pers Pr ... Shearwood on Personal Property [*1882*] [*A publication*] (DLA)
Shear & R Neg ... Shearman and Redfield on the Law of Negligence [*A publication*] (DLA)
Shear R Pr ... Shearwood on Real Property [*3rd ed.*] [*1885*] [*A publication*] (DLA)
SHEB .... Shebear [*England*]
Sheb .... Shebi'it (BJA)
Shebi .... Shebi'it (BJA)
Shebu .... Shebu'oth (BJA)
SHECD ..... Solar Heating and Cooling [*A publication*]
SHED .... Sealed Housing for Evaporative Determinations [*EPA engine test*]
SHED .... Settlement Houses Employment Development [*Large group of settlement houses*]
SHEDS ...... Ship Helicopter Extended Delivery System [*Navy*] (NVT)
SHEE .... Safe High-Energy Explosive
SHEEO ..... State Higher Education Executive Officers Association (EA)
Sheep Beef Farm Surv ... Sheep and Beef Farm Survey [*A publication*]
Sheepfarm Annu ... Sheepfarming Annual [*A publication*]
Sheepfarming Annu ... Sheepfarming Annual [*A publication*]
Sheepfarming Annu Massey Agr Coll ... Sheepfarming Annual. Massey Agricultural College [*A publication*]
Sheep Goat Handb ... Sheep and Goat Handbook [*A publication*]
Sheet Met Ind ... Sheet Metal Industries [*A publication*]
Sheet Met Platework News ... Sheet Metal and Plateworking News [*A publication*]

SHEFD ...... Sheffield [*England*]
SHEFF ...... Shefford [*England*]
Sheffield Univ Fuel Soc J ... Sheffield University. Fuel Society. Journal [*A publication*]
Sheffield Univ Geol Soc J ... Sheffield University. Geological Society. Journal [*A publication*]
SHEG .... Scottish Health Education Group (DI)
SHEH .... Stanford Honors Essays in the Humanities [*A publication*]
SHEIA .... Steric Hindrance Enzyme Immunoassay [*Clinical chemistry*]
Sheil Ir Bar ... Sheil's Sketches of the Irish Bar [*A publication*] (DLA)
SHEK .... Schweizer Hilfswerk fuer Emigrationskinder (BJA)
Shek .... Shekalim (BJA)
SHEL .... Sheldahl, Inc. [*NASDAQ symbol*] (NQ)
SHEL .... Shore ELINT [*Electromagnetic Intelligence*] System [*Navy*] (NG)
Shel Bank .. Shelford's Bankrupt and Insolvency Law [*3rd ed.*] [*1862*] [*A publication*] (DLA)
Shelby .... Shelby Williams Industries, Inc. [*Associated Press abbreviation*] (APAG)
Shel Ca .... Shelley's Cases in Vol. 1 of Coke's Reports [*A publication*] (DLA)
Sheld .... Sheldon's Superior Court Reports [*Buffalo, New York*] [*A publication*] (DLA)
Sheldon ...... Sheldon's Superior Court Reports [*Buffalo, New York*] [*A publication*] (DLA)
Sheld Subr ... Sheldon on Subrogation [*A publication*] (DLA)
SHELF .... Super-Hard Extremely-Low Frequency (MCD)
Shelf J St Cos ... Shelford on Joint-Stock Companies [*A publication*] (DLA)
Shelf Life Foods Beverages Proc Int Flavor Conf ... Shelf Life of Foods and Beverages. Proceedings. International Flavor Conference [*A publication*]
Shelf Lun ... Shelford on Lunacy [*A publication*] (DLA)
Shelf Mar & Div ... Shelford on Marriage and Divorce [*A publication*] (DLA)
Shel High ... Shelford on Highways [*4th ed.*] [*1869*] [*A publication*] (DLA)
Shel J St Com ... Shelford on Joint Stock Companies [*2nd ed.*] [*1870*] [*A publication*] (DLA)
Shell Agric ... Shell in Agriculture [*A publication*]
Shell Aviat News ... Shell Aviation News [*A publication*]
Shell Bitum Rev ... Shell Bitumin Review [*A publication*]
Shell Devel Co Explor and Production Research Div Pub ... Shell Development Co.. Exploration and Production Research Division. Publi cation [*A publication*]
Shellfish ..... Shellfish. Market Review and Outlook [*A publication*]
Shell House J ... Shell House Journal [*A publication*] (APTA)
Shell J .... Shell Journal [*A publication*] (APTA)
Shell Mag .. Shell Magazine [*England*] [*A publication*]
Shell Polym ... Shell Polymers [*A publication*]
SHELLREP ... Shelling Report [*Military*] (NATG)
ShellTr .... Shell Transport & Trading Co. Ltd. [*Associated Press abbreviation*] (APAG)
Shel Lun ..... Shelford on Lunacy [*2nd ed.*] [*1847*] [*A publication*] (DLA)
Shel M & D ... Shelford on Marriage and Divorce [*1841*] [*A publication*] (DLA)
Shel Mort ... Shelford on Mortmain and Charitable Uses [*1836*] [*A publication*] (DLA)
Shel Prob ... Shelford on Probate, Legacy, Etc. [*2nd ed.*] [*1861*] [*A publication*] (DLA)
SHELREP ... Shelling Report [*Military*]
SHELREPT ... Shelling Report [*Military*] (MUGU)
Shel R Pr St ... Sheldon's Real Property Statutes [*9th ed.*] [*1893*] [*A publication*] (DLA)
Shel Ry .... Shelford on Railways [*4th ed.*] [*1869*] [*A publication*] (DLA)
Shelter .... Shelterforce [*A publication*]
Shel Will ..... Shelford on Wills [*1838*] [*A publication*] (DLA)
Shel Wills .. Shelford on Wills [*A publication*] (DLA)
SHEMA ..... Steam Heating Equipment Manufacturers Association [*Defunct*] (EA)
S-HEMP ..... System - Hydraulic, Electrical, Mechanical, Pneumatic
Shen .... Shenandoah [*A publication*]
SHEN .... Shenandoah National Park
Shep .... Select Cases [*37-39 Alabama*] [*A publication*] (DLA)
Shep .... Shepherd's Alabama Reports [*A publication*] (DLA)
Shep .... Shepley's Reports [*13-18, 21-30 Maine*] [*A publication*] (DLA)
SHEP .... Shock Hydrodynamic Elastic Plastic (MCD)
SHEP .... Solar High-Energy Particles
SHEP .... Systolic Hypertension in the Elderly Program [*Medicine*]
Shep Abr .... Sheppard's Abridgment [*A publication*] (DLA)
Shep Act .... Sheppard's Action on the Case [*A publication*] (DLA)
Shepard Commem Vol Pap Mar Geol ... Shepard Commemorative Volume. Papers on Marine Geology [*A publication*]
Shep Cas .... Sheppard's Cases of Slander, Etc. [*A publication*] (DLA)
Shepherd .... Shepherd's Reports [*19-21, 24-41, 60, 63, 64 Alabama*] [*A publication*] (DLA)
Sheph Sel Cas ... Shepherd's Select Cases [*Alabama*] [*A publication*] (DLA)
Shepley ...... Shepley's Reports [*13-18, 21-30 Maine*] [*A publication*] (DLA)
Shep Prec .... Sheppard's Precedent of Precedents [*9th ed.*] [*1825*] [*A publication*] (DLA)
Shep Sel Cas ... Shepherd's Select Cases [*Alabama*] [*A publication*] (DLA)
SHER .... Scottish Heritable, Inc. [*NASDAQ symbol*] (SPSG)
SHERB ...... Sandia Human Error Rate Bank [*NASA*] (NASA)
SHERB ...... Sherborne [*Urban district in England*]

Sher Ct Rep ... Sheriff Court Reports [*Scotland*] [*A publication*]   (DLA)
SHERK...... [*The*] New Schaff-Herzog Encyclopaedia of Religious Knowledge [*A publication*]   (BJA)
SHERLOC ... Something to Help Everyone Reduce Load on Computers [*Army*]
Sher Mar Ins ... Sherman's Marine Insurance [*A publication*]   (DLA)
Sher Pr....... Sheridan's Practice, King's Bench [*A publication*]   (DLA)
Sherst Delo ... Sherstyanoe Delo [*A publication*]
SHERVICK ... Sherman Tanks Converted into Tractors by Vickers Armstrong
Sherwin...... Sherwin-Williams Co. [*Associated Press abbreviation*]   (APAG)
Shet........... Shetland   (WGA)
Shev .... Shevi'it   (BJA)
Shevu .... Shevu'ot   (BJA)
SHEX .... Sundays and Holidays Excepted [*Business term*]
S & H/exct ... Sundays and Holidays Excepted in Lay Days   (DS)
SHF .... Schiffner Oilfield & Technology Corp. [*Vancouver Stock Exchange symbol*]
SHF .... Sea Heritage Foundation   (EA)
SHF .... Self Help Foundation   (EA)
SHF .... Shawinigan Falls [*Quebec*] [*Seismograph station code, US Geological Survey*] [*Closed*]   (SEIS)
SHF .... Shift   (MSA)
SHF .... Sisters of the Holy Faith [*Roman Catholic religious order*]
SHF .... Sisters of the Holy Family [*Roman Catholic religious order*]
SHF .... Soil and Health Foundation [*Later, RI*]   (EA)
SHF .... Storage-Handling Facility [*Nuclear energy*]   (NRCH)
SHF .... Structures Heating Facility
SHF .... Super-High-Frequency [*Radio wave*]
SHF .... Synthesized Hydrocarbon Fluid [*Petroleum engineering*]
SHF .... University of Sheffield, Postgraduate School of Librarianship, Sheffield, England [*OCLC symbol*]   (OCLC)
SHFA......... Single Conductor, Heat and Flame Resistant, Armor [*Cable*]
SHFCC ...... Shriners Hospitals for Crippled Children   (EA)
SHF/EHF ... Super-High Frequency/Extremely-High Frequency   (MCD)
SHFF .... Societe Historique et Folklorique Francaise   (EA)
SHFG .... Society for History in the Federal Government   (EA)
SHF-GMFSC ... Super-High-Frequency - Ground Mobile Forces Satellite Communications   (MCD)
SHFL......... Shoulder Horizontal Flexion [*Sports medicine*]
SHFS .... Superhyperfine Structure
SHFT......... Shift   (FAAC)
SHF-TDMA-MODEM ... Super-High-Frequency - Time Division Multiple Access - MODEM   (MCD)
SHFTG...... Shafting [*Freight*]
SHFTGR ... Shaft Gear
SHFX......... Shadowfax Resources Ltd. [*NASDAQ symbol*]   (NQ)
SHG........... Second-Harmonic Generation [*LASER*]
SHG........... Selected Honor Guards   (MCD)
SHG........... Sharpe Energy and Resources Ltd. [*Vancouver Stock Exchange symbol*]
SHG........... Shipping   (WGA)
SHG........... Shirttail Gulch [*California*] [*Seismograph station code, US Geological Survey*]   (SEIS)
SHG........... Short-Handed Goal [*Hockey*]
SHG........... Shorthand Typist (Higher Grade) [*British military*]   (DMA)
SHG........... Shungnak [*Alaska*] [*Airport symbol*]   (OAG)
SHG........... Shungnak, AK [*Location identifier*] [*FAA*]   (FAAL)
SHG........... Sister Servants of the Holy Ghost and Mary Immaculate [*Roman Catholic religious order*]
SHG........... Special High Grade [*Zinc metal*]
SHG........... Synthetic Human Gastrin [*Medicine*]   (MAE)
SHGAB8 ... Siriraj Hospital Gazette [*A publication*]
SHGED ..... Shoni Geka [*A publication*]
SHGM....... Shongum Corp. [*Livingston, NJ*] [*NASDAQ symbol*]   (NQ)
SHGM....... Society for the History of the Germans in Maryland   (EA)
SHGNA..... Shigen [*A publication*]
SHGO........ Shop & Go, Inc. [*NASDAQ symbol*]   (NQ)
SHH........... Shenandoah Resources Ltd. [*Vancouver Stock Exchange symbol*]
SHH........... Shishmaref [*Alaska*] [*Airport symbol*]   (OAG)
SHH........... Shishmaref, AK [*Location identifier*] [*FAA*]   (FAAL)
SHH........... Sociedad Honoraria Hispanica   (EA)
SHHD........ Scottish Home and Health Department   (ILCA)
SHHH .... Self-Help for Hard of Hearing People   (EA)
SHHP .... Semihorizontal Heart Position   (MAE)
SHHPB ...... Shu-Hsueh Hsueh-Pao [*A publication*]
SHHV....... Society for Health and Human Values   (EA)
SHI .... Scenic Hudson   (EA)
SHI .... Sheet Iron
SHI .... Shimojishima [*Japan*] [*Airport symbol*]   (OAG)
SHI .... Shiraz [*Iran*] [*Seismograph station code, US Geological Survey*]   (SEIS)
S-HI........... System-Human Interaction
SHID .... Spartan Hardware Inspection Discrepancy [*Missiles*]   (MCD)
SHIEF .... Shared Information Elicitation Facility [*Data processing*]
Shiel........... Cape Times Law Reports, Edited by Shiel [*A publication*]   (DLA)
Shiel .... Shiel's Cape Colony Reports [*A publication*]   (DLA)
Shield .... Shield Civil Service News [*A publication*]

SHIELD .... Supreme Headquarters, International Espionage Law-Enforcement Division [*Organization in comic book "Nick Fury, Agent of SHIELD"*]
SHIELD .... Sylvania High-Intelligence Electronic Defense   (MCD)
Shig............ Shigella [*Bacteriology*]
SHIGD4 .... Japanese Journal of Psychosomatic Medicine [*A publication*]
Shikoku Acta Med ... Shikoku Acta Medica [*A publication*]
Shikoku Agric Res ... Shikoku Agricultural Research [*A publication*]
Shikoku Agr Res ... Shikoku Agricultural Research [*A publication*]
Shikoku Dent Res ... Shikoku Dental Research [*A publication*]
Shikoku J Clin Chem ... Shikoku Journal of Clinical Chemistry [*A publication*]
Shikoku Med J ... Shikoku Medical Journal [*A publication*]
SHIL.......... Shillelagh [*Army surface-to-surface missile*]   (AABC)
SHIL.......... Shiloh National Military Park
Shill WC .... Shillman's Workmen's Compensation Cases [*Ireland*] [*A publication*]   (DLA)
Shimadzu Rev ... Shimadzu Review [*A publication*]
Shimane J Med Sci ... Shimane Journal of Medical Science [*A publication*]
SHIMMS ... Shipboard Integrated Man-Machine System   (SAA)
Shinagawa Refract Tech Rep ... Shinagawa Refractories Technical Report [*A publication*]
Shinagawa Tech Rep ... Shinagawa Technical Report [*A publication*]
SHIN BET ... Israel General Security Service [*Acronym represents Hebrew phrase*]
SHINC ...... Sundays and Holidays Included [*Business term*]
SHINCOM ... Ship Integrated Communications System [*Canadian Navy*]
SHINE....... Self-Help is Necessary Everywhere [*Navy*]   (DNAB)
Shingle....... [*The*] Shingle. Philadelphia Bar Association [*A publication*]   (DLA)
Shinko Electr J ... Shinko Electric Journal [*A publication*]
SHINMACS ... Shipborne Integrated Machinery Control System [*Canadian Navy*]
Shinn Repl ... Shinn's Treatise on American Law of Replevin [*A publication*]   (DLA)
Shinshu Med J ... Shinshu Medical Journal [*Japan*] [*A publication*]
Shinshu Univ Fac Sci J ... Shinshu University. Faculty of Science. Journal [*A publication*]
SHIOER.... Statistical Historical Input/Output Error Rate Utility [*Sperry UNIVAC*]
SHIP.......... Regency Cruises, Inc. [*New York, NY*] [*NASDAQ symbol*]   (NQ)
SHIP.......... Search-Height Integration Program   (SAA)
SHIP.......... Self-Help Improvement Program
SHIP.......... Self-Help Issue Point [*Army*]
SHIP.......... Separator for Heavy Ion Reaction Products
SHIP.......... Shipment
SHIP.......... Slater Hall Information Products [*Database producer*]   (IID)
SHIP.......... Special Handling Inventory Procedure   (MCD)
SHIP.......... Standard Hardware Interface Program
Ship Abstr ... Ship Abstracts [*A publication*]
SHIPACS ... Ship Acquisition Study [*Navy*]
SHIPALT ... Ship Alteration [*Navy*]
Shipbldg Mar Engng Int ... Shipbuilding and Marine Engineering International [*A publication*]
Shipbldg Shipp Rec ... Shipbuilding and Shipping Record [*A publication*]
Ship Boat ... Ship and Boat [*A publication*]
Ship and Boat ... Ship and Boat International [*A publication*]
Ship & Boat Int ... Ship and Boat International [*A publication*]
Shipbuild Mar Engine Build ... Shipbuilder and Marine Engine Builder [*England*] [*A publication*]
Shipbuild Mar Eng Int ... Shipbuilding and Marine Engineering International [*A publication*]
Shipbuild & Mar Engng Int ... Shipbuilding and Marine Engineering International [*A publication*]
Shipbuild Rep ... Shipbuilding and Repair [*A publication*]
Shipcare Marit Manage ... Shipcare and Maritime Management [*A publication*]
Ship Com Aviation ... Shipping, Commerce, and Aviation of Australia [*A publication*]   (APTA)
SHIPCON ... Shipping Control [*NATO*]   (NATG)
SHIPDA ... Shipping Data [*Military*]
SHIPDAFOL ... Shipping Data Follows
SHIPDAT ... Shipping Date
SHIPDTO ... Ship on Depot Transfer Order [*Military*]
Ship Gaz .... Shipping Gazette [*London*] [*A publication*]   (DLA)
SHIPGO .... Shipping Order [*Military*]
SHIPIM .... Ship Immediately [*Military*]
SHIPMT ... Shipment   (DNAB)
SHIPOPS ... Ship(board) Operations [*Navy*]   (DNAB)
SHIPOSI... Ship Operational Support Inventory [*Navy*]   (DNAB)
Shipp.......... Shipp's Reports [*66-67 North Carolina*] [*A publication*]   (DLA)
Shipping Reg P & F ... Shipping Regulation. Pike and Fischer [*A publication*]
Shipping Statis ... Shipping Statistics [*A publication*]
Shipping Statis and Econ ... Shipping Statistics and Economics [*A publication*]
Shipp Weekly ... Shipping Weekly [*A publication*]
Shipp Wld Shipbldr ... Shipping World and Shipbuilder [*A publication*]
Shipp World & Shipb ... Shipping World and Shipbuilder [*A publication*]
Shipp World & Shipbuild ... Shipping World and Shipbuilder [*A publication*]
SHIPREPTECH ... Ship Repair Technician [*Navy*]   (DNAB)

SHIPREQ ... Ship to Apply on Requisition [*Military*]
Ship Res Inst (Tokyo) Pap ... Ship Research Institute (Tokyo). Papers [*A publication*]
SHIPS .... Shipment Planning System [*Military*]
SHIPSTO ... Ship Store Office [*Navy*] (DNAB)
SHIPSUM ... Shipping Summary
SHIPSYSCOM ... Ship Systems Command [*Navy*]
SHIPT .... Shipment
SHIR.......... Ship History and Inventory Record [*Navy*] (NG)
SHIRAN..... S-Band High-Accuracy Ranging and Navigation
Shir Cr L.... Shirley's Sketch of the Criminal Law [*2nd ed.*] [*1889*] [*A publication*] (DLA)
Shir DC Ca ... Shirley's Dartmouth College Case [*A publication*] (DLA)
Shire & Munic R ... Shire and Municipal Record [*A publication*] (APTA)
Shire Munic Rec ... Shire and Municipal Record [*A publication*]
Shirl .... Shirley's Reports [*49-55 New Hampshire*] [*A publication*] (DLA)
Shirley .... Shirley's Reports [*49-55 New Hampshire*] [*A publication*] (DLA)
Shirley Inst Bull ... Shirley Institute. Bulletin [*A publication*]
Shirley Inst Mem ... Shirley Institute. Memoirs [*A publication*]
Shirley Inst Publ ... Shirley Institute Publication
Shirl LC ..... Shirley's Leading Crown Cases [*England*] [*A publication*] (DLA)
Shir Mag L ... Shirley on Magisterial Law [*2nd ed.*] [*1896*] [*A publication*] (DLA)
SHIRTDIF ... Storage, Handling, and Retrieval of Technical Data in Image Formation [*Data processing*] (IEEE)
SHIRTS...... Smith-Houghton Infrared Temperature Sounder (NOAA)
SHIRW...... Shirwell [*England*]
SHIU .... Steering Hover Indicator Unit (MCD)
SHIVA...... Super-High-Intensity Vulnerability Assessor
Shivaji Univ J ... Shivaji University. Journal [*A publication*]
Shivaji Univ Sci J ... Shivaji University. Science Journal [*A publication*]
Shizenshi-Kenkyu Occas Pap Osaka Mus Nat Hist ... Shizenshi-Kenkyu Occasional Papers. Osaka Museum of Natural History [*A publication*]
Shizuoka Univ Fac Sci Rep ... Skizuoka University Faculty of Science. Reports [*A publication*]
Sh-J .... Shakespeare-Jahrbuch [*A publication*]
SHJ........... Shamrock Resources, Inc. [*Vancouver Stock Exchange symbol*]
SHJ........... Sharjah [*United Arab Emirates*] [*Airport symbol*] (OAG)
SHJ........... Shionomisaki [*Japan*] [*Seismograph station code, US Geological Survey*] (SEIS)
SHJ........... Society for Humanistic Judaism (EA)
Sh-Jb .... Shakespeare-Jahrbuch [*A publication*]
SHJC........ Sacred Heart Junior College [*North Carolina; Pennsylvania*]
SHJM....... Sisters of the Sacred Hearts of Jesus and Mary [*Roman Catholic religious order*]
SHJMD..... Soon Chun Hyang Journal of Medicine [*A publication*]
SHJP .... [*A*] History of the Jewish People in the Time of Jesus Christ [*Emil Schurer*] [*A publication*] (BJA)
SHJR........ Senate-House Joint Reports [*A publication*] (DLA)
Sh Jus .... Shaw's Scotch Justiciary Cases [*A publication*] (DLA)
Sh Just...... [*P.*] Shaw's Justiciary Decisions [*Scotland*] [*A publication*] (DLA)
SHK.......... Sehonghong [*Lesotho*] [*Airport symbol*] (OAG)
SHK.......... Shank (AAG)
Shk............ Shikimic Acid [*Biochemistry*]
SHK.......... Shiraki [*Japan*] [*Seismograph station code, US Geological Survey*] (SEIS)
SHK.......... SHL Systemhouse, Inc. [*Toronto Stock Exchange symbol*]
SHK.......... Shock [*A publication*]
SHK.......... Shock (MSA)
SHK.......... Speaker of the House of Keys [*British*] (ROG)
SHK.......... Systems Housekeeping
SHKBDX... Saito Ho-On Kai Museum of Natural History. Research Bulletin [*A publication*]
SHKDN..... Shakedown (AABC)
SHKEA5.... Japanese Journal of Psychology [*A publication*]
SHKI .... SHL Systemhouse, Inc. [*Ottawa, ON*] [*NASDAQ symbol*] (NQ)
SHKKA ..... Shika Kiso Igakkai Zasshi [*A publication*]
SHL .... Amsterdam Studies in the Theory and History of Linguistic Science [*A publication*]
SHL .... Sacred Heart League (EA)
SHL .... Sensorineural Hearing Loss [*Medicine*]
SHL .... Shaw Industries Ltd. [*Toronto Stock Exchange symbol*]
SHL .... Sheldon, IA [*Location identifier*] [*FAA*] (FAAL)
SHL .... Shell (AAG)
SHL .... Shell Canada Ltd. [*UTLAS symbol*]
SHL .... Shellac (MSA)
SHL .... Shillong [*India*] [*Seismograph station code, US Geological Survey*] (SEIS)
SHL .... Shillong [*India*] [*Geomagnetic observatory code*]
Sh L........... Shipwright Lieutenant [*British military*] (DMA)
SHL .... Shoal
SHL .... Southall [*British depot code*]
SHL .... Southern Hockey League
SHL .... Student Homophile League [*Superseded by Gay People at Columbia*] (EA)

SHL-3........ Amsterdam Studies in the Theory and History of Linguistic Science. Series III. Studies in the History of Linguistics [*A publication*]
SHLB........ Shelby Federal Savings Bank [*Indianapolis, IN*] [*NASDAQ symbol*] (NQ)
SHLB........ Simulation Hardware Load Boxes (NASA)
SHLD .... Shield (AAG)
SHLD .... Shift Left Double [*Data processing*] (PCM)
SHLD .... Shoulder (AAG)
SHLDR...... Shoulder (MSA)
ShLH .... Shne Luhot Ha-Berit (BJA)
Sh Lit .... Shortt on Works of Literature [*2nd ed.*] [*1884*] [*A publication*] (DLA)
Sh Litt....... Shortt on Works of Literature [*2nd ed.*] [*1884*] [*A publication*] (DLA)
SHLM .... Schulman [*A.*], Inc. [*NASDAQ symbol*] (NQ)
SHLMA .... Southern Hardwood Lumber Manufacturers Association [*Later, HMA*] (EA)
SHLN .... Shoreline (MSA)
SHLP........ Shiplap (WGA)
SHLS .... Shawnee Library System [*Library network*]
SHLS .... Shoals (MCD)
SHLTCM .. Shelter Components Corp. [*Associated Press abbreviation*] (APAG)
SHLTR ...... Shelter (WGA)
SHLW ...... Shallow (FAAC)
SHLW ...... Simulated High-Level Waste [*Nuclear engineering*]
SHLY........ Shelly Associates, Inc. [*Tustin, CA*] [*NASDAQ symbol*] (NQ)
SHM......... Nanki Shirahama [*Japan*] [*Airport symbol*] (OAG)
SHM......... Security Home Mortgage Investment Corp. [*Toronto Stock Exchange symbol*]
SHM......... Shimizu [*Japan*] [*Seismograph station code, US Geological Survey*] (SEIS)
SHM......... Ship Heading Marker [*Navigation*]
SHM......... Simple Harmonic Motion
SHM......... Sinusoidal Hydrodynamic Modulation [*Electrochemistry*]
SHM......... Stage Handling Manual [*NASA*] (KSC)
Sh & Macl ... Shaw and Maclean's Scotch Appeal Cases [*A publication*] (DLA)
SHMD....... Safety and Health Management Division [*Department of Agriculture*] (GFGA)
SHMD....... Shore Manning Document [*Navy*] (NVT)
SHMED .... State Hazardous Materials Enforcement Development [*Nuclear energy*] (NRCH)
Sh Metal Inds ... Sheet Metal Industries [*A publication*]
SHMI .... Saddlery Hardware Manufacturers Institute [*Defunct*] (EA)
SHMIS..... Society of Headmasters of Independent Schools [*British*]
SHMKR .... Shoemaker (MSA)
SHMN...... Subacute Hepatitis with Multilobular Necrosis [*Medicine*]
SHMO...... Senior Hospital Medical Officer [*British*]
SHMO...... Shadow Mountain National Recreation Area
SHMO....... Social/Health Maintenance Organization [*Department of Health and Human Services*]
SHMP .... Sodium Hexametaphosphate [*Inorganic chemistry*]
SHMRD..... Shire and Municipal Record [*A publication*]
SHMV....... Sunn-Hemp Mosaic Virus [*Plant pathology*]
SHN.......... St. Helena [*ANSI three-letter standard code*] (CNC)
SHN.......... Sclerosing Hyaline Necrosis [*Medicine*]
ShN.......... Shakespeare Newsletter [*A publication*]
shn............ Shan [*MARC language code*] [*Library of Congress*] (LCCP)
SHN.......... Shandon Resources, Inc. [*Vancouver Stock Exchange symbol*]
SHN.......... Shelton, WA [*Location identifier*] [*FAA*] (FAAL)
SHN.......... Shimonoseki [*Japan*] [*Seismograph station code, US Geological Survey*] (SEIS)
SHN.......... Shoney's, Inc. [*NYSE symbol*] (SPSG)
SHN.......... Shorthand Note
SHN.......... Shown (AAG)
SHN.......... Sisterhood of the Holy Nativity [*Episcopalian religious order*]
SHN.......... Spontaneous Hemorrhagic Necrosis [*Medicine*]
SHNA .... SHARAF Name Authority [*UTLAS symbol*]
SHNA .... Shawmut Corp. [*NASDAQ symbol*] (NQ)
SHNAD.... Shoni Naika [*A publication*]
SHNC....... Scottish Higher National Certificate
SHND....... Scottish Higher National Diploma
SHNG....... Shingle
S/HNP....... Skagit/Hanford Nuclear Project (NRCH)
SHNPP..... Shearon Harris Nuclear Power Plant (GFGA)
SHNS .... Shoney's South, Inc. [*NASDAQ symbol*] (NQ)
SHNS .... Society of Head and Neck Surgeons (EA)
SHO.......... Schedule Order (MCD)
SHO.......... Secondary Hypertrophic Osteoarthropathy [*Medicine*]
SHO.......... Senate Historical Office
SHO.......... Senior House Officer [*British*]
SHO.......... Shikotan [*Former USSR*] [*Seismograph station code, US Geological Survey*] (SEIS)
sho............ Shona [*MARC language code*] [*Library of Congress*] (LCCP)
SHO.......... Shore
SHO.......... Showing [*Technical drawings*]
SHO.......... Shutout [*Sports*]
SHO.......... Starrett Housing Corp. [*AMEX symbol*] (SPSG)
SHO.......... Student Health Organizations [*Defunct*]

SHO........... Super High Output [*Model of Ford automobile*]
SHOA........ Superannuation, Home, and Overseas Allowances [*Civil Service*] [*British*]
SHOB....... Shore-Based (CINC)
SHOBOM ... Shore Bombardment [*Navy*] (NVT)
SHOBOMTNG ... Shore Bombardment Training [*Navy*] (NVT)
SHOC........ Self-Help Opportunity Center [*Department of Labor*] [*Washington, DC*] (AEBS)
SHOC........ SHAPE [*Supreme Headquarters Allied Powers Europe*] Operations Center [*NATO*] (NATG)
SHOC........ Software/Hardware Operational Control
SHOCK ..... Students Hot on Conserving Kilowatts [*Student legal action organization*]
Shock Cir Homeostasis Trans Conf ... Shock and Circulatory Homeostasis. Transactions of the Conference [*A publication*]
Shock Vib Bull ... Shock and Vibration Bulletin [*A publication*]
Shock Vib Dig ... Shock and Vibration Digest [*A publication*]
Shock Waves Condens Matter Proc Am Phys Soc Top Conf ... Shock Waves in Condensed Matter. Proceedings. American Physical Society Topical Conference on Shock Waves in Condensed Matter [*A publication*]
SHODOP .. Short-Range Doppler
SHOE........ Shoe City Corp. [*Montgomery, AL*] [*NASDAQ symbol*] (NQ)
Shoe Leather Rep ... Shoe and Leather Reporter [*A publication*]
Shokubai Suppl ... Shokubai. Supplement [*Japan*] [*A publication*]
Shokubutsu Boeki Plant Prot ... Shokubutsu Boeki/Plant Protection [*A publication*]
SHOLS...... Single-Hoist Ordnance Loading System [*Navy*] (DNAB)
SHOMADS ... Short-to-Medium-Range Air Defense System [*Army*] (RDA)
Shome LR .. Shome's Law Reporter [*India*] [*A publication*] (DLA)
SHOND..... Shoni No Noshinkei [*A publication*]
Shoney ...... Shoney's, Inc. [*Associated Press abbreviation*] (APAG)
S'HONG ..... Souchong [*Tea trade*] (ROG)
SHOP........ Shell Higher Olefin Process [*Petrochemistry*]
SHOP........ Shopsmith, Inc. [*NASDAQ symbol*] (NQ)
SHOPAIR ... Short Path Infrared (MCD)
SHOPAT... Shore Patrol [*Navy*] (NVT)
SHOPCO .. Shopco Laurel Centre Ltd. [*Associated Press abbreviation*] (APAG)
Shopko....... Shopko Stores [*Associated Press abbreviation*] (APAG)
ShopTV...... Shopping by Television [*British Telecom*]
SHOR........ Shorewood Packaging Corp. [*NASDAQ symbol*] (NQ)
SHORAD .. Short-Range Air Defense [*Army*] (NATG)
SHORAD C² ... Short-Range Air Defense Command and Control
SHORADS ... Short-Range Air Defense System [*Army*] (RDA)
SHORAN ... Short-Range Navigation
SHORDU ... Shore Duty [*Navy*]
SHOREALT ... Shore Alteration
SHOROC .. Shore-Required Operational Capability [*Navy*]
SHOROUTPUBINST ... Shore Duty Beyond the Seas Is Required by the Public Interest [*Navy*]
SHORPUBINT ... Shore Duty Is Required by the Public Interest [*Navy*]
SHORSTAMPS ... Shore Requirements, Standards, and Manpower Planning System [*Navy*]
Short Course Handb Mineral Assoc Can ... Short Course Handbook. Mineralogical Association of Canada [*A publication*]
Short Course Notes Mineral Soc Am ... Short Course Notes. Mineralogical Society of America [*A publication*]
SHORTD .. Shortened (ROG)
Short Rep Rhod Geol Surv ... Short Report. Rhodesia Geological Survey [*A publication*]
Short Rep South Rhod Geol Surv ... Short Report. Southern Rhodesia Geological Survey [*A publication*]
Shortt Inf ... Shortt on Informations, Criminal, Quo Warranto, Mandamus, and Prohibition [*1887*] [*A publication*] (DLA)
Shortt Inform ... Shortt on Informations, Criminal, Quo Warranto, Mandamus, and Prohibition [*A publication*] (DLA)
Shortt Lit ... Shortt on Literature and Art [*2nd ed.*] [*1884*] [*A publication*] (DLA)
Short Wave Mag ... Short Wave Magazine [*A publication*]
SHORVEY ... Shore Duty Survey
SHOS .... Southern Hospitality Corp. [*NASDAQ symbol*] (NQ)
SHOSJ .... Sovereign Hospitaller Order of St. John (EA)
SHOT .... Shooting, Hunting, Outdoor Trade Show
SHOT .... Society for the History of Technology (EA)
Show .... Shower's English King's Bench Reports [*A publication*] (DLA)
Show .... Shower's English Parliamentary Cases [*A publication*] (DLA)
SHOW....... Showscan Corp. [*NASDAQ symbol*] (NQ)
SHOW....... Showtime [*Cable television channel*]
Showa Wire Cable Rev ... Showa Wire and Cable Review [*Japan*] [*A publication*]
Showbt .... Showboat, Inc. [*Associated Press abbreviation*] (APAG)
Shower KB ... Shower's English King's Bench Reports [*89 English Reprint*] [*1678-95*] [*A publication*] (DLA)
Shower KB (Eng) ... Shower's English King's Bench Reports [*89 English Reprint*] [*A publication*] (DLA)
Shower PC (Eng) ... Shower's English Parliamentary Cases [*1 English Reprint*] [*A publication*] (DLA)
Show KB .... Shower's English King's Bench Reports [*A publication*] (DLA)
Show-Me ... Show-Me News and Views [*Missouri*] [*A publication*]
Show Me Lib ... Show-Me Libraries [*A publication*]

Show Parl Cas ... Shower's English Parliamentary Cases [*1 English Reprint*] [*A publication*] (DLA)
Show PC .... Shower's English Parliamentary Cases [*1 English Reprint*] [*A publication*] (DLA)
SHP .... Santa Helena [*Peru*] [*Seismograph station code, US Geological Survey*] [*Closed*] (SEIS)
SHP .... Securities Shipped as Instructed
SHP .... Seeker Head Position
SHP .... Shaft Horsepower
SHP .... Shaker Heights Public Library, Shaker Heights, OH [*OCLC symbol*] (OCLC)
ShP .... Shakespeare Pictorial [*A publication*]
SHP .... Shape (MSA)
SHP .... Shearon Harris Plant [*Nuclear energy*] (NRCH)
SHP .... Shoal Petroleum [*Vancouver Stock Exchange symbol*]
SHP .... Single Highest Peak [*Aerospace*]
SHP .... Society for Hospital Planning of the American Hospital Association [*Later, SHPM*] (EA)
SHP .... Society for Hungarian Philately (EA)
SHP .... Sosyal Demokrasi Halkci Partisi [*Social Democratic Populist Party*] [*Turkey*] [*Political party*] (EAIO)
SHP .... Southern Hardwood Producers [*Later, HMA*]
ShP .... Southern Historical Press, Easley, SC [*Library symbol*] [*Library of Congress*] (LCLS)
SHP .... Standard Hardware Program [*Military*]
SHP .... Standard Holding Pattern [*Aviation*]
SHP .... Standard Holding Procedure [*Aviation*]
Shp........... Starship. The Magazine about Science Fiction [*A publication*]
SHP .... State Health Plan [*Generic term*] (DHSM)
SHP .... [*The*] Stop & Shop Companies, Inc. [*NYSE symbol*] (SPSG)
SHP .... Surgical Hypoparathyroidism [*Medicine*] (MAE)
SHP .... Wichita Falls, TX [*Location identifier*] [*FAA*] (FAAL)
SHPA .... Prairie Agricultural Machinery Institute, Humboldt, Saskatchewan [*Library symbol*] [*National Library of Canada*] (NLC)
SHPA .... Shelf Paper. Alaska Outer Continental Shelf Office [*A publication*]
SHPBD...... Shipboard (MSA)
SHPC........ Scenic Hudson Preservation Conference [*Later, SHI*] (EA)
SHPCL...... Ship Class
SHPD .... Seeker Head Position Display [*Military*] (CAAL)
SHPD .... Super High-Performance Diesel [*Fuel*]
SHPDA ..... State Health Planning and Development Agency
SHPE .... Society of Hispanic Professional Engineers (EA)
SHPG .... Shipping
SHPHG ..... Shipment of Household Goods (NOAA)
SHPHUJ... Scripta Hierosolymitana. Publications of the Hebrew University (Jerusalem) [*A publication*]
SHPM .... Society for Hospital Planning and Marketing of the American Hospital Association (EA)
SHPMT..... Shipment (AABC)
SHPNG ..... Shipping
SHPO .... State Historic Preservation Office
SHPOL...... Supplemental Health Manpower Shortage Area Placement Opportunity List [*Department of Health and Human Services*] (GFGA)
SHPR........ Shipper
SHPRF ...... Shakeproof (MSA)
SHPS........ Seahead Pressure Simulator
SHPS........ Sodium Hydroxide Purge System (IEEE)
SHPSD...... Shipside (AABC)
SHPT........ Shipment (AAG)
SHPTARBY ... Ship to Arrive By _____ [*Military*]
Sh Q .... Shakespeare Quarterly [*A publication*]
SHQ.......... Shasper Industries Ltd. [*Toronto Stock Exchange symbol*]
SHQ.......... Southwestern Historical Quarterly [*A publication*]
SHQ.......... Squadron Headquarters [*British military*] (DMA)
SHQ.......... Station Headquarters
SHQ.......... Supreme Headquarters
SHR .... Hotel Revue. Wochenzeitung fuer Hotellerie und Tourismus [*A publication*]
SHR .... Scherer [*R.P.*] Corp. [*NYSE symbol*] (SPSG)
SHR .... Scottish Historical Review [*A publication*]
ShR .... Shakespeare Review [*A publication*]
SHR .... Share [*Stock exchange term*]
SHR .... Shepard Insurance Group [*Vancouver Stock Exchange symbol*]
SHR .... Sheridan [*Wyoming*] [*Airport symbol*] (OAG)
SHR .... Sheridan, WY [*Location identifier*] [*FAA*] (FAAL)
SHR .... Shirakawa [*Japan*] [*Seismograph station code, US Geological Survey*] (SEIS)
SHR .... Shore (MCD)
SHR .... Shower
SHR .... Single High-Resolution File [*Data processing*]
SHR .... Sisters of the Holy Redeemer [*Roman Catholic religious order*]
SHR .... Society for Historical Research (EA)
SHR .... Solar Heat Reflecting (KSC)
SHR .... Southern Humanities Review [*A publication*]
SHR .... Spontaneous Hypertensive Rats
SHR .... Standard Hourly Rate
SHR .... Step-Height Ratio [*Crystallography*]
SHR .... Supervisory Human Relations Test

Shr .... [*The*] Taming of the Shrew [*Shakespearean work*]
SHRAM .... Short-Range Air-to-Surface Missile
SHRAP...... Shrapnel
SHRC .... Safety and Health Regulations for Construction [*Bureau of Reclamation*]
SHRC .... Shared Housing Resource Center [*Later, NSHRC*]   (EA)
SHRD .... ShareData, Inc. [*NASDAQ symbol*]   (NQ)
SHRD .... Shift Right Double [*Data processing*]   (PCM)
SHRD .... Shredded [*Freight*]
SHRD .... Shroud [*Engineering*]
SHRD .... Supplemental Heat Rejection Devices   (NASA)
SHRDF...... Shroud Fin [*Engineering*]
SHRDR ..... Shredder   (MSA)
SHRE .... Sahara Resorts [*Las Vegas, NV*] [*NASDAQ symbol*]   (NQ)
SHRF........ Ship Regular Freight [*Military*]   (AABC)
SHRI.......... Sciences and Humanities Research Institute [*Iowa State University*] [*Research center*]   (RCD)
SHRIMP ... Sensitive High Mass Resolution Ion Microprobe
SHRIMP ... Super-High Resolution Ion Microprobe [*Analytical chemistry*]
SHRIV....... Shrivenham [*England*]
SHRM .... SAB Harmon Industries, Inc. [*NASDAQ symbol*]   (NQ)
SHRM .... Society for Human Resource Management   (EA)
Sh & R Neg ... Shearman and Redfield on the Law of Negligence [*A publication*]   (DLA)
SHRNG ..... Shearing   (MSA)
SHROC ..... Shore-Required Operational Capability [*Navy*]   (DNAB)
SHROPS... Shropshire [*County in England*]
SHRP........ Sharpener   (MSA)
SHRP........ Sharper Image Corp. [*NASDAQ symbol*]   (NQ)
SHRP........ Society for History, Research, and Preservation   (EA)
SHRP........ Strategic Highway Research Program [*National Research Council*]
SHRS........ Shores   (MCD)
SHRS........ Shutdown Heat Removal System [*Nuclear energy*]   (NRCH)
SHRS........ Supplementary Heat Removal System   (IEEE)
SHRSDV ... Scottish Historic and Research Society of Delaware Valley   (EA)
Shr Sui .... Shrady on Suicide and Intemperance in Life Insurance [*A publication*]   (DLA)
SHRT .... [*The*] Shirt Shed, Inc. [*NASDAQ symbol*]   (NQ)
SHRT .... Short   (FAAC)
SHRTA...... Scientia Horticulturae (Amsterdam) [*A publication*]
SHRTG ..... Shortage   (AABC)
SHRTWV ... Short Wave   (FAAC)
SHRW .... Sherwood Corp. [*NASDAQ symbol*]   (NQ)
SHS .... Galveston, TX [*Location identifier*] [*FAA*]   (FAAL)
SHS .... Sacred Heart Seminary [*Detroit, MI*]
SHS .... Sample Handling System [*Chemistry*]
SHS .... Sayer Head Sling [*Medicine*]
SHS .... Scandinavian Herpetological Society [*Denmark*]   (EAIO)
SHS .... Scottish History Society   (EA)
SHS .... Self-Propagating High-Temperature Synthesis [*Ceramic technolgy*]
SHS .... Senior High School
SHS .... Shaer Shoe Corp. [*AMEX symbol*]   (SPSG)
ShS............. Shakespeare Survey [*A publication*]
SHS .... Shares [*Stock exchange term*]
SHS .... Shashi [*China*] [*Airport symbol*]   (OAG)
SHS .... Shasta Dam [*California*] [*Seismograph station code, US Geological Survey*] [*Closed*]   (SEIS)
SHS .... Sheep Hemolyzate Supernatant
SHS .... Ship's Heading Servo
SHS .... Shire Horse Society [*British*]   (DI)
SHS .... Shop Television Network [*Vancouver Stock Exchange symbol*]
SHS .... Simulation Hardware System [*NASA*]   (MCD)
SHS .... Small Hydro Society   (EA)
SHS .... Smoothing Heading Spot   (SAA)
SHS .... Social History Society of the United Kingdom
SHS .... Societatis Historiae Socius [*Fellow of the Historical Society*] [*Latin*]
SHS .... Sod House Society   (EA)
SHS .... Sodium Hexadecyl Sulfate [*Organic chemistry*]
SHS .... Soil and Health Society [*Later, RI*]   (EA)
SHS .... Soviet Hydrometeorological Service
SHS .... Spartan Homing Sensor [*Missiles*]
SHS .... Spherical Harmonic Series   (SAA)
SHS .... Sports Hall of Shame   (EA)
SHS .... Square Hollow Section [*Metal industry*]
SHS .... Standard Heavy Spanwire [*Military*]   (CAAL)
SHS .... Superheated Steam
SHS .... Surveyors Historical Society   (EA)
SHS .... Systemhouse Ltd. [*Toronto Stock Exchange symbol*]
SHS .... University of Sheffield, Postgraduate Librarianship, Sheffield, England [*OCLC symbol*]   (OCLC)
SHSA........ Saint Hubert Society of America   (EA)
SHSA........ Scottish Harp Society of America   (EA)
SHSA........ Seaman Apprentice, Ship's Serviceman, Striker [*Navy rating*]
SHSA........ Southern Hardwood Square Association   (EA)
SHSAC...... Supreme Headquarters, Supreme Allied Commander [*World War II*]

SHSB......... Southern Home Savings Bank [*Pensacola, FL*] [*NASDAQ symbol*]   (NQ)
Sh Sc App .. Shaw's Scotch Appeal Cases, House of Lords [*A publication*]   (DLA)
SHSD .... Shiseido Co. [*NASDAQ symbol*]   (NQ)
SHS/DC..... Social and Human Sciences Documentation Centre [*UNESCO*]   (DUND)
SHSGS ...... Supreme Headquarters, Secretary General Staff [*World War II*]
ShSh .... Shomer Shabbat   (BJA)
SHSLB ...... Street and Highway Safety Lighting Bureau [*Defunct*]   (EA)
SHSLC ...... Siouxland Health Sciences Consortium [*Library network*]
SHSN .... Seaman, Ship's Serviceman, Striker [*Navy rating*]
SHSN .... Sod House Society of Nebraska [*Later, SHS*]   (EA)
SHSPB ...... Soviet Hydrology. Selected Papers [*A publication*]
SHSR .... Society for Humanity and Social Reform [*British*]
SHSS......... Stanford Hypnotic Susceptibility Scale [*Psychology*]
SHSTF .... Scout Helicopter Special Task Force   (MCD)
SHSTS .... Ship Status
ShStud .... Shakespeare Studies [*Tokyo*] [*A publication*]
SHSV........ Superstructure Heater Safety Valve   (DS)
SHSWD.... Society for Hospital Social Work Directors   (EA)
SHT .... Recycling [*Dusseldorf*] [*A publication*]
SHT .... Sheet   (AAG)
SHT .... Shetland Times [*A publication*]
SHT .... Sholia Resources Ltd. [*Vancouver Stock Exchange symbol*]
SHT .... Short   (MSA)
SH & T....... Shower and Toilet   (AAG)
SHT .... Sidi Hakoma Tuff [*Geology*]
SHT .... Simple Hypocalcemic Tetany [*Medicine*]
SHT .... Society for the History of Technology   (EA)
SHT .... Society of the Most Holy Trinity [*Anglican religious community*]
SHT .... Space Hand Tool [*NASA*]
SHT .... Subcutaneous Histamine Test [*Medicine*]   (MAE)
SHT .... Svensk Humanistisk Tidsskrift [*A publication*]
SHT .... Swansea Harbour Trust [*Wales*]
SHTC .... Short Time Constant   (MSA)
Sh Teind Ct ... Shaw's Scotch Teind [*Tithe*] Court Decisions [*A publication*]   (DLA)
SHTG .... Sheeting [*Freight*]
SHTG .... Shortage   (AFM)
SHTHG ..... Sheathing   (MSA)
SHT IRN... Sheet Iron [*Freight*]
SHT IRN STL ... Sheet Iron or Steel [*Freight*]
SHTL......... Shuttle   (MSA)
SHTL......... Small Heat-Transfer Loop [*Nuclear energy*]   (NRCH)
SHT MTL ... Sheet Metal [*Freight*]
SHTN .... Short Ton [*2000 lbs.*]
SHTPB ...... Saturated Hydroxy-Terminated Polybutadiene
SHTR .... Shutter   (AAG)
SHTSD...... Short Side
SHT STL WRE ... Sheet Steel Ware [*Freight*]
SHTT......... Sequential Headturn Test
SHU.......... Sacred Heart University, Library, Bridgeport, CT [*OCLC symbol*]   (OCLC)
SHU.......... Seton Hall University [*South Orange, NJ*]
SHU.......... Shoe-Town, Inc. [*NYSE symbol*]   (SPSG)
SHU.......... Shuyak Island [*Alaska*] [*Seismograph station code, US Geological Survey*]   (SEIS)
SHU.......... Skyhigh Resources Ltd. [*Vancouver Stock Exchange symbol*]
SHUJA....... Shujutsu [*A publication*]
SHum........ Studies in the Humanities [*A publication*]
S Hum Rev ... Southern Humanities Review [*A publication*]
SHUR........ Selected History Update and Reporting   (MCD)
SHUR........ System for Hospital Uniform Reporting
SHUSA...... Scottish Heritage USA   (EA)
SHUT .... Shuttle   (SSD)
SHUTDN .. Shutdown   (NASA)
Shuttle........ Shuttle, Spindle, and Dyepot [*A publication*]
Shuttle Spin and Dye ... Shuttle, Spindle, and Dyepot [*A publication*]
SHV .... Shavano Air, Inc. [*Poncha Springs, CO*] [*FAA designator*]   (FAAC)
SHV .... Sheave   (MSA)
SHV .... Shreveport [*Louisiana*] [*Airport symbol*]   (OAG)
SHV .... Shreveport, LA [*Location identifier*] [*FAA*]   (FAAL)
SHV .... Solenoid Hydraulic Valve
SHV .... Standard Havens, Inc. [*AMEX symbol*]   (SPSG)
SHV .... Sub Hoc Voce [*Under This Word*] [*Latin*]
SHVE .... Sammelblatt der Historischer Verein Eichstatt [*A publication*]
SHVF........ Sammelblatt der Historischer Verein Freising [*A publication*]
SHVG........ Shaving [*Freight*]
SHVHS ..... Sandy Hook Veterans Historical Society   (EA)
SHVI .... Sammelblatt der Historischer Verein Ingolstadt [*A publication*]
SHVSCE ... Shuttle Versus Current Expendable Launch Vehicle [*NASA*]   (KSC)
SHVSNE... Shuttle Versus New Expendable Launch Vehicle [*NASA*]   (KSC)
SHW .... Mount St. Helens [*Washington*] [*Seismograph station code, US Geological Survey*]   (SEIS)
SHW .... Sharurah [*Saudi Arabia*] [*Airport symbol*]   (OAG)

SHW.........	Sherwin-Williams Co. [*NYSE symbol*] (SPSG)
Sh W & C...	Shaw, Wilson, and Courtenay's Scotch Appeals Reports [*Wilson and Shaw's Reports*] [*A publication*] (DLA)
SHWDGP ...	Sherwood Group, Inc. [*Associated Press abbreviation*] (APAG)
SHWPA.....	Sheng Wu Hua Hsueh Yu Sheng Wu Wu Li Hsueh Pao [*A publication*]
SHWR	Shower (FAAC)
SHWS.......	Shoppers World Stores, Inc. [*San Antonio, TX*] [*NASDAQ symbol*] (NQ)
shwy	Showy [*Horticulture*]
SHWY	Super Highway (TEL)
SHX	Shageluk [*Alaska*] (OAG)
SHX	Shageluk, AK [*Location identifier*] [*FAA*] (FAAL)
SHX	Shaw Industries, Inc. [*NYSE symbol*] (SPSG)
SHY	Kaiser, MO [*Location identifier*] [*FAA*] (FAAL)
SHY	Sharon Energy Ltd. [*Vancouver Stock Exchange symbol*]
SHY	Shinyanga [*Tanzania*] [*Airport symbol*] (OAG)
SHY	Syllable Hyphen Character [*Data processing*]
SHYD	Sharon Energy Ltd. [*NASDAQ symbol*] (NQ)
SHZ	Seshute's [*Lesotho*] [*Airport symbol*] (OAG)
SHZ	Shizuoka [*Japan*] [*Seismograph station code, US Geological Survey*] (SEIS)
SHZ	Steelhead Resources Ltd. [*Vancouver Stock Exchange symbol*]
SHZAA	Shoyakugaku Zasshi [*A publication*]
SHZAAY...	Japanese Journal of Pharmacognosy [*A publication*]
SHZD	Steelhead Resources Ltd. [*NASDAQ symbol*] (NQ)
SI...............	ACM Government Spectrum Fund [*NYSE symbol*] (SPSG)
SI...............	Arab Wings Co. [*ICAO designator*] (FAAC)
SI...............	Sacroiliac [*Medicine*]
SI...............	Safety Injection [*Nuclear energy*] (NRCH)
SI...............	Safety Inspection (IEEE)
SI...............	Sailmakers Institute (EA)
SI...............	Saintpaulia International (EA)
SI...............	Saline Injection [*Abortion technique*]
SI...............	Salinity Indicator
SI...............	Salmon Institute [*Formerly, CSI*] (EA)
SI...............	Salt Institute (EA)
SI...............	Sample Interval
SI...............	Sandwich Islands
SI...............	Sanitary Inspector [*British*] (ROG)
SI...............	Saturation Index [*Chemistry*]
SI...............	Saturday Inspection [*Slang*]
SI...............	Save It [*Energy-saving campaign*] [*British*]
SI...............	Savings Institutions [*A publication*]
S of I..........	School of Infantry [*British military*] (DMA)
SI...............	School Inventory [*Psychology*]
SI...............	Scientific Instrument (NASA)
SI...............	Screen Grid Input
SI...............	Scuola Italiana [*A publication*]
SI...............	Secondary Injection
SI...............	Secondary Item [*Army*]
SI...............	Security Identity
SI...............	Seine Island [*Island off the coast of France*] (ROG)
SI...............	Selected Item (MCD)
SI...............	Selective Identification
SI...............	Self Incompatible
SI...............	Self Inflicted (MAE)
SI...............	Semi-Insulating
S-I	Sensation-Intuition [*Jungian psychology*]
SI...............	Sensitive Information (MCD)
SI...............	Sensory Integration
SI...............	Septic Inflammation [*Medicine*]
SI...............	Sergeant Instructor [*Military*] [*British*]
SI...............	Serial Input
SI...............	Seriously Ill [*Military*] (AABC)
SI...............	Serra International (EA)
SI...............	Sertoma International (EA)
SI...............	Serum Iron [*Serology*]
SI...............	Servas International (EA)
SI...............	Service Indicator [*Telecommunications*] (TEL)
SI...............	Service Instruction
SI...............	Service Interruption
SI...............	Sex Inventory [*Psychology*]
SI...............	Sexual Intercourse (ADA)
SI...............	Shared Information (PCM)
SI...............	Shetland Isles
SI...............	Shift-In Character [*Keyboard*] [*Data processing*]
SI...............	Ship Item (MCD)
SI...............	Shipping Instructions (AFM)
SI...............	Ship's Installation [*Navy*]
SI...............	Short Interest [*Brokerage*]
SI...............	Signal Intelligence (MCD)
SI...............	Signal Interface
S/I..............	Signal-to-Interference
SI...............	Signal-to-Intermodulation [*Ratio*]
SI...............	Signed Integer [*Data processing*]
SI...............	Silence [*Navigation*]
Si...............	Silicon [*Chemical element*]
Si...............	Silicone [*Organic chemistry*]
Si...............	Silty Soil [*Agronomy*]
SI...............	Silver Institute (EA)

SI...............	Similarity Index
Si...............	Simon de Bisignano [*Flourished, 1174-79*] [*Authority cited in pre-1607 legal work*] (DSA)
SI...............	Simple Interest [*Banking*]
SI...............	Simulator Initiation (MCD)
SI...............	Sinai (BJA)
SI...............	Sing Out [*A publication*]
si...............	Singapore [*MARC country of publication code*] [*Library of Congress*] (LCCP)
SI...............	Single Instruction
SI...............	Single Silk [*Wire insulation*] (AAG)
SI...............	Sinus Iridum [*Bay of Rainbows*] [*Lunar area*]
SI...............	Sirach [*Ecclesiasticus*] [*Old Testament book*]
Si...............	Sistema [*A publication*]
SI...............	Site, Inc. (EA)
SI...............	Site Investigation
SI...............	Skill Identifier [*Career development*] [*Army*] (RDA)
SI...............	Slaved Illuminator [*Military*] (CAAL)
SI...............	Small Inclusions [*Diamond clarity grade*]
SI...............	Small Intestine [*Anatomy*]
S/I.............	Smectite-Illite [*Clay mineral*]
SI...............	Smithsonian Institution
SI...............	Social Independiente [*Netherlands Antilles*] [*Political party*] (EY)
SI...............	Socialist International [*Political party*] [*British*] (EAIO)
SI...............	Society of Illustrators (EA)
SI...............	Society of Indexers (EAIO)
SI...............	Software Implementation
SI...............	Solar Inertial (MCD)
SI...............	Solidarity International (EA)
SI...............	Solubility Index [*Water*]
SI...............	Soluble Insulin
SI...............	Soroptimist International [*Cambridge, England*] (EAIO)
SI...............	Source Impedance
SI...............	Southeast Institute for Group and Family Therapy (EA)
SI...............	Southpaw's International (EA)
SI...............	Space Institute [*University of Tennessee*] [*Research center*] (RCD)
SI...............	Space Intelligence [*Parapsychology*]
SI...............	Spark Ignition
SI...............	Speaker Intercom
SI...............	Special Inquiry [*Classification system used by doctors on Ellis Island to detain, re-examine, and possibly deny entry to certain immigrants*]
SI...............	Special Inspection (MCD)
SI...............	Special Instruction
SI...............	Special Intelligence [*Army*] (AABC)
SI...............	Special Intervention [*Medicine*]
SI...............	Specialist Insectivore
SI...............	Specific Inventory (OA)
SI...............	Spectrum Index
SI...............	Speech Intelligibility (RDA)
SI...............	Speech Interpolation [*Telecommunications*] (TEL)
SI...............	Spettatore Italiano [*A publication*]
SI...............	Spokane International Railroad Co. [*AAR code*]
SI...............	Sponsor Identification [*Television*]
SI...............	Sports Illustrated [*A publication*]
SI...............	Spot Inspection [*Military*] (AFM)
SI...............	Spot Inventory
S und I........	Sprache und Information [*A publication*]
SI...............	Spratly Islands [*ANSI two-letter standard code*] (CNC)
SI...............	Square Inch (MCD)
SI...............	Staff Inspector
SI...............	Standardization and Interoperability
SI...............	Standards Institution [*Telecommunications*]
SI...............	Standing Instruction (MSA)
SI...............	Star of India
SI...............	Staten Island
SI...............	Station Identification
SI...............	Statutory Instruments [*Ireland*] [*A publication*]
SI...............	Steer, Inc. [*An association*] (EA)
SI...............	Steering Intelligence (MCD)
SI...............	Stereo Imaging (SSD)
SI...............	Stimulation Index [*Cytochemistry*]
S & I..........	Stocked and Issued (AFM)
SI...............	Storage Immediate
SI...............	Straight-In Approach [*Aviation*]
SI...............	Straight, Inc. (EA)
SI...............	Strathclyde Institute [*Glasgow, Scotland*]
SI...............	Stretch-Inactivated Ion Channel
SI...............	Stretch Inhibitor
S/I.............	Strike/Interdiction (MCD)
SI...............	Stroke Index
SI...............	Structure-of-Intellect [*Model*]
SI...............	Student Investigator (KSC)
S/I.............	Subject Issue
SI...............	Subscription Item
SI...............	Suitability Index [*Fishery science*]
SI...............	Sulphur Institute (EA)
SI...............	Sundance Institute (EA)
SI...............	Superimpose (MDG)

S of I.......... Superintendent of Instruction [*British military*]　(DMA)
SI.............. Supply Instruction [*Marine Corps*]
SI.............. Support Installation　(MCD)
SI.............. Surface Impoundment　(EG)
SI.............. Surface Integrity
SI.............. Surface Ionization [*Physics*]
SI.............. Surveillance Inspection [*Nuclear energy*]　(NRCH)
S & I.......... Surveillance and Inspection　(AAG)
S & I.......... Surveys and Investigation
SI.............. Survival International [*British*]　(EAIO)
SI.............. Suspect Index [*British*]
SI.............. Svizzera Italiana [*A publication*]
SI.............. Swap-In [*Data processing*]
SI.............. Symbolic Input [*Data processing*]
SI.............. System Information [*Data processing*]　(PCM)
SI.............. System Integration
SI.............. Systeme International d'Unites [*International System of Units*]
　　　　 [*Also, SIU*]
SIA............ Sailing Industry Association　(EA)
SIA............ San Francisco, CA [*Location identifier*] [*FAA*]　(FAAL)
SIA............ Sanitary Institute of America [*Later, IAWCM*]
SIA............ Sasquatch Investigations of Mid-America　(EA)
SIA............ Scaffold Industry Association　(EA)
SIA............ Science Information Association
SIA............ Scottish Island Area [*Council*]
SIA............ Securities Industry Association　(EA)
SIA............ Self-Insurers Association
SIA............ Self-Interstitial Atom
SIA............ Semiconductor Industry Association　(EA)
SIA............ Sensor Interface Assembly
SIA............ Serial Input Adapter
SIA............ Service in Information and Analysis [*Host*] [*British*]　(BUR)
SIA............ Shelter Oil & Gas Ltd. [*Toronto Stock Exchange symbol*]
SIA............ Shuttle Induced Atmosphere　(NASA)
SIA............ Sialic Acid [*Biochemistry*]
SIA............ Sian [*Republic of China*] [*Seismograph station code, US
　　　　 Geological Survey*] [*Closed*]　(SEIS)
SIA............ Sigma Immunoassay [*Test for rubella*]
SIA............ Signal Apparel Co., Inc. [*NYSE symbol*]　(SPSG)
SIA............ Singapore Airlines
SIA............ Singles in Agriculture [*An association*]　(EA)
SIA............ Ski Industries America　(EA)
SIA............ Societa Italiana di Agopuntura [*Italy*]
SIA............ Societe Internationale d'Acupuncture [*International Society of
　　　　 Acupuncture*]
SIA............ Societe Internationale Arthurienne, [*International Arthurian
　　　　 Society*] North American Branch　(EA)
SIA............ Society of Industrial Accountants of Canada
SIA............ Society for Industrial Archeology　(EA)
SIA............ Society of Insurance Accountants [*Crozet, VA*]　(EA)
SIA............ Software Impact Assessment [*NASA*]　(NASA)
SIA............ Software Institute of America [*Andover, MA*]
　　　　 [*Telecommunications*]　(TSSD)
SIA............ Solar Inertial Attitude　(NASA)
SIA............ Soroptimist International of the Americas　(EA)
SIA............ Speaker Intercom Assembly [*NASA*]
SIA............ Special Interest Automobiles [*A publication*]
SIA............ Special Investor Account [*Stock purchasing*]
SIA............ Spinal Injuries Association [*British*]
SIA............ Sprinkler Irrigation Association [*Later, IA*]　(EA)
SIA............ Standard Instrument Approach [*RADAR*] [*Aviation*]
SIA............ Standard Interface Adapter
SIA............ Station of Initial Assignment
SIA............ Station Interface Adapter　(SSD)
SIA............ Storage Instantaneous Audimeter [*Measures television viewing*]
SIA............ Strategic Industries Association　(EA)
SIA............ Stress-Induced Analgesia [*Medicine*]
SIA............ Structural Inventory and Appraisal [*Of roads and bridges*]
SIA............ Subaru-Isuzu Automotive
SIA............ Subminiature Integrated Antenna
SIA............ Survivors of Incest Anonymous　(EA)
SIA............ Synalbumin-Insulin Antagonism [*Medicine*]
SIA............ System Integration Area　(MCD)
SIA............ Xian [*China*] [*Airport symbol*]　(OAG)
SIABA....... Sindacato Italiano Artisti Belle Arti [*Italian Union of Fine Arts*]
SIABC....... Sociedad Iberoamericana de Biologia Celular [*Ibero-American
　　　　 Society for Cell Biology - IASCB*]　(EAIO)
SIAC......... Secretariat International des Artistes Catholiques
SIAC......... Securities Industry Automation Corp. [*NYSE/ASE*] [*New York,
　　　　 NY*]
SIAC......... Shock Isolator Air Compressor　(DWSG)
SIAC......... Societe Internationale des Artistes Chretiens [*International
　　　　 Society for Christian Artists*] [*Lydiate, Merseyside,
　　　　 England*]　(EAIO)
SIAC......... Southeastern Intercollegiate Athletic Association　(MCD)
SIAC......... Special Interest Auto Club　(EA)
SIAC......... State Industry Advisory Committee [*Civil Defense*]
SIAC......... Studies in Automation and Control [*Elsevier Book Series*] [*A
　　　　 publication*]
SIAC......... Submarine Integrated Attack Center　(MCD)
SIAC......... Support List Allowance Card

SIACI....... Societe Intercontinental d'Assurances pour le Commerce et
　　　　 l'Industrie [*Intercontinental Assurance Company of
　　　　 Commerce and Industry*] [*France*]
SIAD......... Chartered Society of Designers　(EAIO)
SIAD......... Sierra Army Depot [*California*]　(AABC)
SIAD......... Society of Industrial Artists and Designers [*British*]　(DI)
SIADH...... Syndrome of Inappropriate Antidiuretic Hormone
　　　　 [*Endocrinology*]
SIADS...... Sensor Integration and Display Sharing [*Military*]　(CAAL)
SIAE......... Scottish Institute of Adult Education　(DI)
SIAE......... Scottish Institute of Agricultural Engineering [*Research
　　　　 center*]　(IRC)
SIAF......... Service Indicator Associated Field
　　　　 [*Telecommunications*]　(TEL)
SIAF......... Small Independent Action Force [*Military*]
SIAGL....... Survey Instrument, Azimuth Gyroscope, Lightweight　(MCD)
SIAJ......... SIAJ: Singapore Institute of Architects. Journal [*A publication*]
SIAL......... Salon International de l'Alimentation [*World Food Fair*]
SIAL......... Sialagogue [*Promoting Flow of Saliva*] [*Medicine*]　(ROG)
SIAL......... Sigma-Aldrich Corp. [*NASDAQ symbol*]　(NQ)
SIAL......... Southeast Iowa Academic Libraries [*Library network*]
SIALON.... Silicon, Aluminum, Oxygen, and Nitrogen [*A ceramic*]
SIAM........ Self-Initiating Antiaircraft Munition [*ARPA*]
SIAM........ Separate Index Access Method [*Data processing*]　(BUR)
SIAM........ Signal Information and Monitoring Service [*American radio
　　　　 monitoring service*]
SIAM........ Society for Industrial and Applied Mathematics　(EA)
SIAM........ Strategic Impact and Assumptions Identification Method
SIAM........ System for Improved Acquisition of Material　(MCD)
SIAMA...... Society for Interests of Active Missionaries in Asia, Africa, and
　　　　 America　(EAIO)
SIAM AMS Proc ... SIAM [*Society for Industrial and Applied Mathematics*]-
　　　　 AMS [*American Mathematical Society*] Proceedings [*A
　　　　 publication*]
Siamese Vet Assoc J ... Siamese Veterinary Association. Journal [*A
　　　　 publication*]
SIAM J Algebraic Discrete Methods ... SIAM [*Society for Industrial and
　　　　 Applied Mathematics*] Journal on Algebraic and Discrete
　　　　 Methods [*A publication*]
SIAM J A Ma ... SIAM [*Society for Industrial and Applied Mathematics*]
　　　　 Journal on Applied Mathematics [*A publication*]
SIAM J Appl Math ... SIAM [*Society for Industrial and Applied
　　　　 Mathematics*] Journal on Applied Mathematics [*A
　　　　 publication*]
SIAM J App Math ... SIAM [*Society for Industrial and Applied
　　　　 Mathematics*] Journal on Applied Mathematics [*A
　　　　 publication*]
SIAM J Comput ... SIAM [*Society for Industrial and Applied Mathematics*]
　　　　 Journal on Computing [*A publication*]
SIAM J Cont ... SIAM [*Society for Industrial and Applied Mathematics*]
　　　　 Journal on Control [*A publication*]
SIAM J Control ... SIAM [*Society for Industrial and Applied Mathematics*]
　　　　 Journal on Control [*A publication*]
SIAM J Control Optim ... SIAM [*Society for Industrial and Applied
　　　　 Mathematics*] Journal on Control and Optimization [*A
　　　　 publication*]
SIAM J Control and Optimiz ... SIAM [*Society for Industrial and Applied
　　　　 Mathematics*] Journal on Control and Optimization [*A
　　　　 publication*]
SIAM J Control Optimization ... SIAM [*Society for Industrial and Applied
　　　　 Mathematics*] Journal on Control and Optimization [*A
　　　　 publication*]
SIAM J Math ... SIAM [*Society for Industrial and Applied Mathematics*]
　　　　 Journal on Mathematical Analysis [*A publication*]
SIAM J Math Anal ... SIAM [*Society for Industrial and Applied
　　　　 Mathematics*] Journal on Mathematical Analysis [*A
　　　　 publication*]
SIAM J Num ... SIAM [*Society for Industrial and Applied Mathematics*]
　　　　 Journal on Numerical Analysis [*A publication*]
SIAM J Numer Anal ... SIAM [*Society for Industrial and Applied
　　　　 Mathematics*] Journal on Numerical Analysis [*A
　　　　 publication*]
SIAM J Sci Stat Comput ... SIAM [*Society for Industrial and Applied
　　　　 Mathematics*] Journal on Scientific and Statistical
　　　　 Computing [*A publication*]
SIAM J Sci Statist Comput ... SIAM [*Society for Industrial and Applied
　　　　 Mathematics*] Journal on Scientific and Statistical
　　　　 Computing [*A publication*]
SIAM R ..... SIAM [*Society for Industrial and Applied Mathematics*] Review
　　　　 [*A publication*]
SIAM Rev ... SIAM [*Society for Industrial and Applied Mathematics*] Review
　　　　 [*A publication*]
SIAM Sci Bull ... SIAM [*Society for Industrial and Applied Mathematics*]
　　　　 Science Bulletin [*A publication*]
SIAM (Soc Ind Appl Math) SIMS (SIAM Inst Math Soc) Conf Ser ... SIAM
　　　　 (Society for Industrial and Applied Mathematics) SIMS
　　　　 (SIAM Institute for Mathematics and Society) Conference
　　　　 Series [*A publication*]
SIAM Stud Appl Math ... SIAM [*Society for Industrial and Applied
　　　　 Mathematics*] Studies in Applied Mathematics [*A
　　　　 publication*]

SIAM Studies in Appl Math ... SIAM [*Society for Industrial and Applied Mathematics*] Studies in Applied Mathematics [*A publication*]

SIAN......... Societe Industrielle et Agriculturelle du Niari [*Industrial and Agricultural Society of Niari*]

SIANM..... Special Inspection, Army Nuclear Matters (MCD)

SI/AO....... Smithsonian Institution/Astrophysical Observatory (KSC)

SIAON...... Silicon-Aluminum Oxynitride

SIAP......... Sociedad Interamericana de Planeficacion [*Inter-American Planning Society*] [*Mexico*]

SIAP......... Standard Instrument Approach Procedure [*Aviation*]

SIAP......... Standard-Italo Americana Petroli

SIAP......... Straight-In Approach [*Aviation*]

SIAR......... Small, Irregular, Agglutinated Rooms [*Architecture*]

SIAS......... Safety Injection Actuation Signal [*Nuclear energy*] (NRCH)

SIAS......... Scandinavian Institute of Asian Studies [*See also CINA*] [*Later, NIAS*] (EAIO)

SIAS......... Signals Intelligence Analysis System (MCD)

SIAS......... Submarine Integrated Antenna System (MCD)

SIASP....... Society for Italian-American Scientists and Physicians (EA)

SIA Surf Interface Anal ... SIA. Surface and Interface Analysis [*A publication*]

SIAT......... Single Integrated Attack Team

SIAT......... Synthesis of Impact Acceleration Technology (MCD)

SIATE-MTS ... Simulated Intermediate Automatic Test Equipment-Maintenance Training System [*Air Force*]

SIAU......... Seminario Internacional de Administracao Universitaria

SIAWS...... Satellite-Interrogated Automatic Weather Station (NOAA)

SIB............ Satellite Integrated Buoy

SIB............ Satellite Ionospheric Beacons [*Military*]

SIB............ Saudi International Bank

SIB............ Scale plus Index plus Base

SIB............ Scales of Independent Behavior [*Occupational therapy*]

SIB............ Screen Image Buffer [*Data processing*]

SIB............ Securities and Investments Board [*British*]

SIB............ Selection Interview Blueprint [*LIMRA*]

SIB............ Self-Injurious Behavior [*Abnormal psychology*]

SIB............ Serial Interface Board

SIB............ Ship Information Booklet [*Navy*]

SIB............ Shipbuilding Industry Board [*British*]

SIB............ Siberia

SIB............ Sibiti [*Congo*] [*Airport symbol*] (OAG)

Sib............ Sibling

SIB............ Sibola Mines Ltd. [*Vancouver Stock Exchange symbol*]

Sib............ Sibyllines (BJA)

SIB............ SIDPERS [*Standard Installation/Division Personnel System*] Interface Branch [*Military*] (INF)

SIB............ Simulation Interface Buffer (SSD)

SIB............ Sistema de Informacion Bursatil [*Stock Exchange Information System*] [*Madrid Stock Exchange*] [*Information service or system*] (IID)

SIB............ Situation Intelligence Brief (DNAB)

SIB............ Societe Internationale de Biometeorologie [*International Society of Biometeorology*] (EAIO)

SIB............ Special Intelligence Brief (MCD)

SIB............ Special Investigation Branch [*Army*] [*British*]

SIB............ Standard Index Base (DNAB)

SIB............ Standard Iron Bar (MSA)

SIB............ Subject Interface Box (KSC)

SIB............ System Integration Board (SSD)

SIB............ System Interconnect Bus [*Data processing*]

SIB............ Systems Information Bulletin [*Data processing*]

SIBA......... Small Independent Brewers' Association [*British*] (ECON)

SIBC......... Saudi Investment Banking Corp.

SIBC......... Societe Internationale de Biologie Clinique [*World Association of Anatomic and Clinical Pathology Societies*]

Sib Chem J ... Siberian Chemistry Journal [*A publication*]

Sib Chem J Engl Transl ... Siberian Chemistry Journal. English Translation [*A publication*]

SIBD......... Soviet Independent Business Directory [*A publication*]

SIBE......... Studies in Bayesian Econometrics [*Elsevier Book Series*] [*A publication*]

Sibelius...... Sibelius-Mitteilungen [*A publication*]

Siberian Math J ... Siberian Mathematical Journal [*A publication*]

SIBEX....... Second International BIOMASS Experiment

SIBEX....... Singapore International Building Exhibition

SIBH......... Salicylideniminobenzohydroxamic Acid [*Biochemistry*]

SIBIL......... System Informatise pour Biblitheques [*Information System for Libraries*] (EAIO)

SIBIL......... Systeme Integre pour les Bibliotheques Universitaires de Lausanne [*Integrated System for the University of Lausanne Libraries*] [*Switzerland*] (IID)

Sibirsk Mat Z ... Sibirskii Matematiceskii Zurnal [*A publication*]

Sibirsk Vrach Viedom ... Sibirskiia Vrachebnyia Viedomosti [*A publication*]

SIBIS......... Self-Injurious Behavior Inhibiting System [*Psychology*]

SIBIS......... Smithsonian Institution Bibliographic Information System

SIBL......... Separate Infantry Brigade Light (INF)

SIBM......... Societe Internationale de Biologie Mathematique [*International Society of Mathematical Biology*] (EAIO)

SIBMAS.... Societe Internationale des Bibliotheques et Musees des Arts du Spectacle [*International Association of Libraries and Museums of the Performing Arts*] (EAIO)

Sib Math J ... Siberian Mathematical Journal [*A publication*]

SIB-MIBOC ... Securities and Investments Board and the Marketing of Investments Board Organisation Commission [*British*]

SibOr......... Sibylline Oracles (BJA)

SIBOR...... Singapore Interbank Offered Rate

SIBR......... Styrene-Isoprene-Butadiene Rubber [*Materials science*]

SIBR......... Sybra, Inc. [*Atlanta, GA*] [*NASDAQ symbol*] (NQ)

SI/BRC..... Strategic Intelligence/Business Research Corp.

SIBS........... Salk Institute for Biological Studies

SIBS........... Semiconductor Industry & Business Survey [*Database*] [*HTE Management Resources*] [*Information service or system*] (CRD)

SIBS........... Stellar Inertial Bombing System

SIBTN...... Something Is Better than Nothing

SIC............ Covington/Cincinnati, OH [*Location identifier*] [*FAA*] (FAAL)

SIC............ High School Student Information Center (EA)

SIC............ Safety Information Center [*National Safety Council*] (IID)

SIC............ Sakharov International Committee (EA)

SIC............ Science Information Council [*National Science Foundation*]

SIC............ Scientific Information Center

SIC............ Second Pilot in Command [*Aviation*] (FAAC)

SIC............ Security Intelligence Centre [*British*] [*World War II*]

SIC............ Security Intelligence Corps

SIC............ Semiconductor Integrated Circuit

SIC............ Sept-Iles [*Quebec*] [*Seismograph station code, US Geological Survey*] (SEIS)

SIC............ Serial Interface Chip

SIC............ Service, Inc., Omaha NE [*STAC*]

SIC............ Servicio Informativo Continental [*Press agency*] [*Argentina*]

SIC............ Siccus [*Dry*] [*Latin*] (ADA)

SIC............ Sicily

SIC............ Sico, Inc. [*Toronto Stock Exchange symbol*]

SIC............ Silicon-Insulating Compound

SIC............ Silicon Integrated Circuit

SIC............ Simulated Interface Calibration

SIC............ Skills Inventory Coordinator

SIC............ Social Interaction Code

SIC............ Societe Internationale de Cardiologie [*International Society of Cardiology*]

SIC............ Societe Internationale de Chirurgie [*International Society of Surgery - ISS*] [*Basel, Switzerland*] (EA)

SIC............ Societe Internationale de Criminologie [*International Society of Criminology*] (EA)

SIC............ Society of Inkwell Collectors (EA)

SIC............ SONAR Information Center (NVT)

SIC............ Sorties per Inspection Cycle [*Air Force*] (AFIT)

SIC............ Special Information Center (MCD)

SIC............ Special Interest Committee

SIC............ Specific Inductive Capacitance

SIC............ Split Investment Company [*Generic term*]

SIC............ Standard Industrial Classification [*File indexing code*] [*Also, an information service or system*]

SIC............ Standard Industry Code (PCM)

SIC............ Standard Inspection Criteria

SIC............ Standard Interface Connector (SSD)

SIC............ States Information Center [*Council of State Governments*] (IID)

SIC............ Status of Implementation Chart

SIC............ Stock Item Catalog (MCD)

SIC............ Structural Influence Coefficient

SIC............ Studies in Inorganic Chemistry [*Elsevier Book Series*] [*A publication*]

SIC............ Supervisory Inventory on Communication [*Test*]

SIC............ Support Identification Code (SSD)

SIC............ Survey Information Center [*Military*]

SIC............ System Integration Computer (MCD)

SIC............ Systeme Informatique pour la Conjoncture [*Information System for the Economy*] [*INSEE*] [*France*] [*Information service or system*] (IID)

SIC............ Systems Integration Contractor

SICA......... Secondary Inventory Control Activity (MCD)

Sic A.......... Sicilia Archeologica [*A publication*]

SICA......... Soccer Industry Council of America (EA)

SICA......... Society of Industrial and Cost Accountants of Canada

SICA......... Subud International Cultural Association (EA)

SICAB...... Sichere Arbeit [*A publication*]

SICAC...... Society of Inter-Celtic Arts and Culture (EA)

SICAM..... Sex Information Council of America [*Later, CSIE*] (EA)

SICB......... Senior Interservice Control Board (DNAB)

SICBM...... Single-Warhead Intercontinental Ballistic Missile (MCD)

SICBM...... Small Intercontinental Ballistic Missile (MCD)

SICC......... Safeguard Inventory Control Center [*Army*] (AABC)

SICC......... Secondary Item Control Center

SICC......... Secours International de Caritas Catholica [*Belgium*] (EAIO)

SICC......... Service Inventory Control Center [*DoD*]

SICCM...... Supervisor Information on Civilian Career Management [*Navy*] (DNAB)

SICCS....... Social Interaction and Creativity in Communication System [*Educational test*]

SICD......... Serum Isocitric Dehydrogenase (MAE)

SICD.......... Supplier Interface Control Drawing   (MCD)
SIC & DH ... Scientific Instrument Computer and Data Handling   (SSD)
SICDOC.... Special Interest Committee on Program Documentation
　　　　　　　　[*Association for Computing Machinery*]
SICEA .... Steel Industry Compliance Extension Act of 1981
SICF .... Societe des Ingenieurs Civils de France
SICF .... Societe Ivoirienne des Chemins de Fer [*Railway system*] [*The
　　　　　　　　Ivory Coast*]   (EY)
SicG .... Siculorum Gymnasium [*A publication*]
Sic Gymn ... Siculorum Gymnasium [*A publication*]
Sich Arb..... Sichere Arbeit [*Austria*] [*A publication*]
SICHD...... Sicherheit [*A publication*]
SICHEJ..... Studies in Inorganic Chemistry [*A publication*]
Sicherheit... Wirtschaftsschutz und Sicherheitstechnik [*A publication*]
Sicherheit Chem Umwelt ... Sicherheit in Chemie und Umwelt [*A publication*]
Sicherheitspol Heute ... Sicherheitspolitik Heute [*A publication*]
SICJA........ Siberian Chemistry Journal [*English Translation*] [*A
　　　　　　　　publication*]
SIC/JIC..... Secondary Injection Control/Jet Interaction Control
Sick .... Sickels' Reports [*46-85 New York*] [*A publication*]   (DLA)
Sick .... Single Income, Couple of Kids [*Lifestyle classification*]
Sick Min Dec ... Sickels' United States Mining Laws and Decisions [*A
　　　　　　　　publication*]   (DLA)
Sick Op ...... Sickels' Opinions of the New York Attorneys-General [*A
　　　　　　　　publication*]   (DLA)
SICL .... Sampling Inspection Checklist
SICL .... Selected Item Configuration Log
SICL .... Self-Interview Checklist [*Navy*]   (NVT)
SICL .... Supplier Item Control List   (MCD)
SICM........ Scanning Ion-Conductance Microscope
SICM........ Scheduled Input Control Method   (MCD)
SICM........ Small Intercontinental Ballistic Missile   (MCD)
SICM........ Soybean Integrated Crop Management Model
SICMA ...... Special Initial Clothing Monetary Allowance
　　　　　　　　[*Military*]   (DNAB)
SICMA-CIV ... Special Initial Clothing Monetary Allowance - Civilian
　　　　　　　　[*Military*]   (DNAB)
SICMA-NAOC ... Special Initial Clothing Monetary Allowance - Naval
　　　　　　　　Aviation Officer Candidate [*Navy*]   (DNAB)
SICMA-NAVCAD ... Special Initial Clothing Monetary Allowance - Naval
　　　　　　　　Aviation Cadet [*Navy*]   (DNAB)
SICMAU... International Congress for Microbiology. Symposia [*A
　　　　　　　　publication*]
SICN.......... Syndicate for Fabrication of Fuel Elements [*French*] [*Acronym
　　　　　　　　is based on foreign phrase*]
SICO.......... Signal Control   (DEN)
SICO.......... Switched in for Checkout [*NASA*]   (KSC)
SICO.......... Systems Integration and Checkout
SICOB....... Salon International de l'Informatique, de la Communication, et
　　　　　　　　de l'Organisation du Bureau [*Business equipment
　　　　　　　　exhibition*]
SICOM...... Securities Industry Communication [*Western Union Corp.*]
　　　　　　　　[*Information service or system*]
SI COMMS ... Special Intelligence Communications   (MCD)
S Icon .... Studies in Iconography [*A publication*]
SICOT....... Societe Internationale de Chirurgie Orthopedique et de
　　　　　　　　Traumatologie [*International Society of Orthopaedic
　　　　　　　　Surgery and Traumatology*] [*Brussels, Belgium*]   (EAIO)
SICOVAM ... Societe Interprofessionnelle pour la Compensation des Valeurs
　　　　　　　　Mobilieres [*French depository body*]
SICP .... Selected Ion Current Profile [*Spectrometry*]
SICP .... Society of Indochina Philatelists   (EA)
SICPS....... Standardized Integrated Command Post System [*Army*]   (INF)
SICR .... Selected Item Configuration Record   (MCD)
SICR .... Specific Intelligence Collection Requirements
　　　　　　　　[*Military*]   (AFM)
SICR .... Supply Item Change Record
SICRI........ Substances Immunologically Cross-Reactive with Insulin
SICS .... Safety Injection Control System [*Nuclear energy*]   (NRCH)
SICS .... Secondary Infrared Calibration System
SICS .... Ships Integrated Communications System   (MCD)
SICSA....... Sicher Ist Sicher [*A publication*]
SICS-PACK ... Screw Integrated Control System - Pontoon Air Cushion Kit
　　　　　　　　[*Army*]   (RDA)
SICSVA..... Sequential Impaction Cascade Sieve Volumetric Air   (MAE)
SI & CTF ... Scottish Industry and Commerce Trade Fair   (ITD)
SICTLM.... Solomon Islands Cultural Traditional Leaders Movement
Sicu .... [*Abbas*] Siculus [*Deceased, 1445*] [*Authority cited in pre-1607
　　　　　　　　legal work*]   (DSA)
SICU......... Surgical Intensive Care Unit [*Medicine*]
Sicu Ab....... Abbas Siculus [*Deceased, 1445*] [*Authority cited in pre-1607
　　　　　　　　legal work*]   (DSA)
SID............. Doctor of Industrial Science
SID............. ICP [*International Computer Programs, Inc.*] Software
　　　　　　　　Information Database [*Information service or
　　　　　　　　system*]   (CRD)
SID............. Sal Island [*Cape Verde Islands*] [*Airport symbol*]   (OAG)
SID............. Scale of Institutional Differentiation   (AEBS)
SID............. Scheduled Issue Date [*Telecommunications*]   (TEL)
SID............. Seal-In Device   (MSA)
SID............. Security and Intelligence Service [*Army*]

SID............. Seismic Intrusion Detector [*Army*]
SID............. Selected Item Drawing   (MCD)
sid............. Semel in Die [*Once a Day*] [*Pharmacy*]
SID............. Sequence Information Data
SID............. Serial Input Data [*Data processing*]
SID............. Servizio Informazioni Difesa [*Defense Intelligence Service*]
　　　　　　　　[*Italy*]
SID............. Shuttle Integration Device [*NASA*]   (NASA)
SID............. Sida [*Iceland*] [*Seismograph station code, US Geological
　　　　　　　　Survey*]   (SEIS)
sid............. Sidamo [*MARC language code*] [*Library of Congress*]   (LCCP)
SID............. Side-Impact Dummy [*Collision testing device*]
Sid .... Siderfin's King's Bench Reports [*82 English Reprint*] [*A
　　　　　　　　publication*]   (DLA)
SID............. Silicon Imaging Device   (IEEE)
SID............. Silver Iodine Generator
SID............. Simulator Interface Device   (MCD)
SID............. Situation Display
SID............. Situation Information Display
SID............. Sketch-in-Depth [*Parthorn*] [*Software package*]   (NCC)
SIDD........ Skin Inserted Detonator   (MCD)
SID............. Slew-Induced Distortion
SID............. Society for Information Display   (EA)
SID............. Society for International Development   (EA)
SID............. Society for Investigative Dermatology   (EA)
SID............. Sodium Ionization Detector [*Nuclear energy*]   (NRCH)
SID............. Software Interface Document   (MCD)
SID............. Solubilization by Incipient Development   (OA)
SID............. Sound Ideas, Inc. [*Vancouver Stock Exchange symbol*]
SID............. Sound Interface Device [*Computer chip*]
SID............. Source Image Distortion
SID............. Space and Information Systems Division [*NASA*]
SID............. Space Intruder Detector [*Burglar alarm*]
SID............. Special Intelligence Detachment [*Military*]   (CINC)
SID............. Specific Infrared Detector
SID............. Specification Interpretation Documentation   (MCD)
SID............. Spiritus in Deo [*Spirit Rests in God*] [*Latin*]
SID............. Sports Information Director
SID............. Standard Instrument Departure [*RADAR*] [*Aviation*]
SID............. Standard Interface Document   (NASA)
SID............. Strategic Intelligence Digests [*Military*]   (AABC)
SID............. Subcontract Item Definition
SID............. Subject Identification Module [*NASA*]
SID............. Subscriber Identification   (CAAL)
SID............. Subsystem Identification [*Electronics*]
SID............. Sudden Infant Death [*Syndrome*] [*Medicine*]
SID............. Sudden Ionospheric Disturbance [*Geophysics*]
SID............. Surface-Induced Dissociation [*Physics*]
SID............. Surface Ionization Detector [*Instrumentation*]
S & ID........ Surveillance and Identification
SID............. SWIFT [*Society for Worldwide Interbank Financial
　　　　　　　　Telecommunications*] Interface Device
SID............. Synchronous Identification System   (DNAB)
SID............. Syntax Improving Device   (IEEE)
SID............. System Interface Document [*NASA*]   (NASA)
SID............. Systems Integration Demonstrator [*Aircraft*]
SID............. Systems Integration and Deployment [*Program*] [*Department
　　　　　　　　of Transportation*]
SIDA.......... 7th Infantry Division Association   (EA)
SIDA.......... SIOP [*Single Integrated Operations Plan*] Integrated Data
　　　　　　　　Base   (MCD)
SIDA.......... Societe Internationale Fernand de Vischer pour l'Histoire des
　　　　　　　　Droits de l'Antiquite   (EA)
SIDA.......... Swedish International Development Agency
SIDAC....... Single Integrated Damage Anaysis Capability   (MCD)
Sida Contrib Bot ... Sida Contributions to Botany [*A publication*]
Sid Apoll.... Sidonius Apollinaris [*Fifth century AD*] [*Classical
　　　　　　　　studies*]   (OCD)
SIDAR....... Selective Information Dissemination and Retrieval [*Data
　　　　　　　　processing*]   (DIT)
SIDAR....... Symposium on Image Display and Recording
SIDASE..... Significant Data Selection
SIDC......... Slaved Illuminator Data Converter [*Military*]   (CAAL)
SIDC......... Supply Item Design Change [*Navy*]   (NG)
SIDC......... Support Issue Development Committee [*Military*]   (CAAL)
SIDC......... Systems Identification Data Cost
SIDD......... Scientific Information and Documentation Division [*Later,
　　　　　　　　ESIC*]
SIDE......... Suprathermal-Ion-Detector Experiment [*Apollo*] [*NASA*]
SIDEC .... Stanford International Development Education Center
　　　　　　　　[*Stanford University*]
Side Eff Drugs ... Side Effects of Drugs [*A publication*]
Side Eff Drugs Annu ... Side Effects of Drugs. Annual [*A publication*]
SIDEFCOOP ... Sociedad Interamericana de Desarrollo de Financiamiento
　　　　　　　　Cooperativo [*Inter-American Society for the Development
　　　　　　　　of Cooperative Financing*] [*Buenos Aires,
　　　　　　　　Argentina*]   (EAIO)
Sid (Eng).... Siderfin's King's Bench Reports [*82 English Reprint*] [*A
　　　　　　　　publication*]   (DLA)
Sider Latinoam ... Siderurgia Latinoamericana [*A publication*]
SIDES........ Source Input Data Edit System

SIDF	Sinusoidal Input Describing Function [*Data processing*]
SIDFA	Senior Industrial Development Field Adviser [*United Nations*]
Sid Gov	Sidney on Government [*A publication*] (DLA)
SID J..........	SID [*Society for Information Display*] Journal [*A publication*]
SIDL..........	System Identification Data List [*Navy*] (NG)
SIDLOB	Side Lobe [*Entomology*]
SIDM........	Shipboard Identification Demolition Model [*Navy*]
SIDM........	Solar Internal Dynamics Mission (SSD)
SIDM........	Syndicat International des Debardeurs et Magasiniers [*International Longshoremen's and Warehousemen's Union - ILWU*] [*Canada*]
Sid Mess....	Sidereal Messenger [*A publication*]
SIDMS......	Status Inventory Data Management System (MCD)
SIDN	Small Industry Development Network [*Georgia Institute of Technology*]
SIDO	Societe Internationale pour le Developpement des Organisations [*International Society for the Development of Organizations*] (EAIO)
SIDOR.......	Siderurgica del Orinoco [*Government steel company*] [*Venezuela*]
SIDOS......	Site Document Order Section (SAA)
SIDP	Seed Industry Development Program [*UN Food and Agriculture Organization*]
SIDP	Sheep Industry Development Program (EA)
SIDPE	Sensing, Identitying, Deciding, Predicting, and Executing
SIDPERS ..	Standard Installation/Division Personnel System [*Military*] (AABC)
SIDS	Satellite Imagery Dissemination System (MCD)
SIDS	Sensor Interface Data System [*Military*] (CAAL)
SIDS	Ships Integrated Defense System
SIDS	Shrike Improved Display System [*Military*] (NVT)
SIDS	Societe Internationale de Defense Sociale [*International Society for Social Defence - ISSD*] [*Paris, France*] (EAIO)
SIDS	Societe Internationale de Droit Sociale
SIDS	Space Investigations Documentation System [*NASA*]
SIDS	Spares Integrated Data System (MCD)
SIDS	Specification Interpretation Documents (MCD)
SIDS	Standard Information Display System [*Military*] (CAAL)
SIDS	Stellar Inertial Doppler System
SIDS	Strike Improved Display System (MCD)
SIDS	Sudden Infant Death Syndrome [*Medicine*]
SIDS	Support Integrated Data System (MCD)
SIDSA	Sudden Infant Death Syndrome Act of 1974
SIDTC	Single Integrated Development Test Cycle
SIDTEC.....	Single Integrated Development Test Cycle (MCD)
SIDTS......	Single Integrated Development Test System
SIDY	Science Dynamics Corp. [*NASDAQ symbol*] (NQ)
SIDZD.......	Saitama Ika Daigaku Zasshi [*A publication*]
SIE	Science Information Exchange [*Later, SSIE*] [*Smithsonian Institution*]
SIE............	Sea Isle, NJ [*Location identifier*] [*FAA*] (FAAL)
SIE............	Select Information Exchange [*Information service or system*] (IID)
SIE............	Selected Inertial Equipment
SIE............	Selected Item Exchange (MCD)
SIE............	Sensory Isolation Experiment (SAA)
SIE............	Serum Immunoreative Erythropoietin [*Immunochemistry*]
SIE............	Servizio Informazioni Esercito [*Italy*] [*Forces Intelligence Service*]
SIE............	Shanell International Energy Corp. [*Vancouver Stock Exchange symbol*]
SIE............	Shuttle Interface Equipment [*NASA*] (NASA)
Sie............	Siemens [*Unit of electric conductance*]
SIE............	Siena [*Italy*] [*Seismograph station code, US Geological Survey*] (SEIS)
SIE............	Sierra Express [*Reno, NV*] [*FAA designator*] (FAAC)
SIE............	Sierra Health Services, Inc. [*AMEX symbol*] (SPSG)
SIE............	Single Instruction Execute
SIE............	Societe Internationale d'Electrochimie [*International Society of Electrochemistry*]
SIE............	Society of Industrial Engineers [*Later, SAM*]
SIE............	Soroptimist International d'Europe [*Soroptimist International of Europe*] (EAIO)
SIE............	Special Inspection Equipment
SIE............	Start Interpretive Execution (HGAA)
SIE............	Studies in International Economics [*Elsevier Book Series*] [*A publication*]
SIE............	Suicide Information and Education [*Suicide Information and Education Center*] [*Canada*] [*Information service or system*] (CRD)
SIE............	Surface Ionization Engine
SIE............	System Integration Equipment (KSC)
SIE............	System Investigation Equipment (KSC)
SIEA	Sensor Interface Electronics Assembly (MCD)
SIEB	Satellite-Interrogated Environmental Buoy
SIEBA7	Sieboldia Acta Biologica [*A publication*]
Siebel Tech Rev ...	Siebel Technical Review [*A publication*]
SIEC	Societe Internationale pour l'Enseignement Commercial [*International Society for Business Education*] [*Lausanne, Switzerland*] (EAIO)

SIEC	Suicide Information and Education Centre [*Canadian Mental Health Association*] [*Information service or system*] (IID)
SIECCAN ...	Sex Information and Education Council of Canada
SIECD	Societe Internationale d'Education Continue en Dentisterie [*International Society of Continuing Education in Dentistry - ISCED*] [*Brussels, Belgium*] (EAIO)
SIECOP.....	Scientific Information and Education Council of Physicians (EA)
SIECUS.....	Sex Information and Education Council of the US (EA)
SIED..........	Supplier Item Engineering Order (MCD)
SIEDS........	Societe Internationale d'Etude du Dix-Huitieme Siecle [*International Society for Eighteenth-Century Studies - ISECS*] (EAIO)
SIEF..........	Societe Internationale d'Ethnographie et de Folklore [*International Society for Ethnology and Folklore*]
SIEFA........	Source Inventory and Emission Factor Analysis [*Environmental Protection Agency*]
SIEGE	Simulated EMP [*Electromagnetic Pulse*] Ground Environment [*Air Force*]
Siego	Single, Intelligent, and Educated and Growing Old [*Lifestyle classification*]
Siemens-Albis Ber ...	Siemens-Albis Berichte [*A publication*]
Siemens Components (Engl Ed) ...	Siemens Components (English Edition) [*A publication*]
Siemens Electron Components Bull ...	Siemens Electronic Components Bulletin [*A publication*]
Siemens Energietech ...	Siemens Energietechnik [*West Germany*] [*A publication*]
Siemens Forsch Entwickl ...	Siemens Forschungs- und Entwicklungsberichte. Research and Development Reports [*A publication*]
Siemens Forsch Entwicklungsber ...	Siemens Forschungs- und Entwicklungsberichte [*A publication*]
Siemens Forsch Entwicklungsber Res Dev Rep ...	Siemens Forschungs- und Entwicklungsberichte. Research and Development Reports [*A publication*]
Siemens Power Eng ...	Siemens Power Engineering [*West Germany*] [*A publication*]
Siemens Res Dev Rep ...	Siemens Research and Development Reports [*A publication*]
Siemens Rev ...	Siemens Review [*A publication*]
sien............	Sienna [*Philately*]
SIEND......	Saiensu [*A publication*]
SIEP	Screening Inspection for Electronic Parts [*NASA*]
SIEPM	Societe Internationale pour l'Etude de la Philosophie Medievale [*International Society for the Study of Medieval Philosophy*] (EAIO)
SIER	Sierra On-Line, Inc. [*NASDAQ symbol*] (CTT)
SIERC	Sierra Capital Realty Trust Co. [*Associated Press abbreviation*] (APAG)
SIERHS.....	Sierra Health Services, Inc. [*Associated Press abbreviation*] (APAG)
SIERNEV ...	Sierra Nevada [*FAA*] (FAAC)
SierPac.......	Sierra Pacific Resources [*Associated Press abbreviation*] (APAG)
Sierra	Sierra Club. Bulletin [*A publication*]
Sierra Club B ...	Sierra Club. Bulletin [*A publication*]
Sierra Club Bull ...	Sierra Club. Bulletin [*A publication*]
Sierra Ed News ...	Sierra Educational News [*A publication*]
Sierra Leone Agric Div Minist Agric Nat Resour Rep ...	Sierra Leone Agricultural Division. Ministry of Agriculture and Natural Resources. Report [*A publication*]
Sierra Leone Fish Div Tech Pap ...	Sierra Leone Fisheries Division. Technical Paper [*A publication*]
Sierra Leone LR ...	Law Reports, Sierra Leone Series [*A publication*] (ILCA)
Sierra Leone L Rec ...	Law Recorder (Sierra Leone) [*A publication*] (ILCA)
Sierra Leone Rep Geol Surv Div ...	Sierra Leone. Report on the Geological Survey Division [*A publication*]
SIES..........	Ship Integrated Electronic System
SIES..........	Sobek's International Explorer's Society [*Commercial firm*] (EA)
SIES..........	Society of the Incarnation of the Eternal Son [*Anglican religious community*]
SIES..........	Supervision, Inspection, Engineering, and Services (NASA)
SIESC........	Secretariat International des Enseignants Secondaires Catholiques [*International Secretariat of Catholic Secondary School Teachers*] [*Acronym used in association name, SIESC Pax Romana*] [*Nijmegen, Netherlands*] (EAIO)
SIESTA	Silent Energy Sources for Tactical Applications (MCD)
SIETAR/INTL ...	International Society for Intercultural Education, Training, and Research (EA)
SIEUSE.....	Secretariat International de l'Enseignement Universitaire des Sciences de l'Education
SI/EW	Special Intelligence/Electronic Warfare (MCD)
SIF	Reidsville, NC [*Location identifier*] [*FAA*] (FAAL)
SIF	Salvo in Flight [*Military*] (CAAL)
SIF	Science Information Facility [*FDA*]
SIF	Scleroderma International Foundation (EA)
SIF	Scotch-Irish Foundation (EA)
SIF	Scott Industrial Foam
SIF	Secure Identification Feature

SIF .... Security and Intelligence Foundation [*Later, CIS*] (EA)
SIF .... Selective Identification Feature [*Military decoder modification*]
SIF .... Selective Interrogation Feature (MCD)
SIF .... Service Incroyance et Foi [*Canadian Catholic Conference*]
SIF .... Short-Intrusion Fuze (RDA)
SIF .... SIFCO Industries, Inc. [*AMEX symbol*] (SPSG)
SIF .... Signaling Information Field [*Telecommunications*] (TEL)
SIF .... Simra [*Nepal*] [*Airport symbol*] (OAG)
SIF .... Single Face
SIF .... Small Intensely Fluorescent [*Cytology*]
SIF .... Social Investment Forum (EA)
SIF .... Sociedad Iberoamericana de Filosofia [*Spain*] (EAIO)
SIF .... Society of International Friendship (EA)
SIF .... Sound Intermediate Frequency
SIF .... Storage Interface Facility
SIF .... Stress Intensity Factor (MCD)
SIF .... Switched In-Flight (KSC)
SIF .... Synthetic Interstitial Fluid [*Biochemistry*]
SIFA .... Society of Independent Financial Advisors [*Englewood, CO*] (EA)
SIFAD .... Separate Ion Formation and Drift
SIFAR .... Surveillance Imagery Fast Access Recording (MCD)
SIFAT .... Servants in Faith and Technology (EA)
SIFC .... Saskatchewan Indian Federated College [*University of Regina*]
SIFC .... Sparks International Official Fan Club (EAIO)
SIFCC .... Senate Interstate and Foreign Commerce Committee
SIFCO .... SIFCO Industries, Inc. [*Associated Press abbreviation*] (APAG)
SIFCS .... Sideband Intermediate Frequency Communications System (AAG)
SifDeut....... Sifrei Deuteronomy (BJA)
SIFE........... Sanitation Inspection Fish Establishment [*National Marine Fisheries Service*] (NOAA)
SIFE........... Students in Free Enterprise [*Bolivar, MO*] (EA)
SIFEA........ Silva Fennica [*A publication*]
SIFF.......... Stock Index Futures Fund
SIF/IFF ..... Selective Identification Feature/Identification Friend or Foe [*Military*] (AFM)
SIFJ .... Saskatchewan Indian Federated College. Journal [*A publication*]
SifNum....... Sifrei Numbers (BJA)
SIFO .... Societa Italiana di Farmacia Ospedaliera [*Italy*]
SIFO .... Svenska Institutet foer Opinionsundersoekningar
Si-Fo-An-Di ... Silica-Forsterite-Anorthite-Diopside [*Lunar geology*]
Si-Fo-Di..... Silica-Forsterite-Diopside [*Lunar geology*]
SIFPPS..... Shore Installations and Facilities Planning and Programming System [*Navy*] (MCD)
SIFR .... Simulated Instrument Flight Rules (AAG)
SIFR .... Sun-Improved Frequency Response
SIFT.......... Selected-Ion Flow Tube [*Instrumentation*]
SIFT.......... Share Internal FORTRAN Translator [*Data processing*] (IEEE)
SIFT.......... Simplified Input for Toss [*Data processing*]
SIFT.......... Software Implemented Fault Tolerance [*NASA*]
SIFT.......... Summary of Information on Film and Television [*British*]
SIFT.......... System Identification from Tracking (MCD)
SIFTOR..... Sifting of Information for Technology of Reactors [*MIT-AEC study*]
SIFX .... Simulated Installation Fixture (AAG)
SifZut........ Sifrei Zuta (BJA)
SIG............. San Juan/Isla Grande [*Puerto Rico*] [*Airport symbol*] (OAG)
SIG............. San Juan, PR [*Location identifier*] [*FAA*] (FAAL)
SIg............. Secretory Immunoglobin [*Immunology*]
SIG............. Senior Interagency Group [*Federal government*]
SIG............. Senior Interdepartmental Group [*Department of State*]
SIG............. Serum Immune Globulin [*Immunochemistry*]
SIG............. Ship Improvement Guide
SIG............. Sigmoidoscope [*or Sigmoidoscopy*] [*Medicine*] (AAMN)
SIG............. Signa [*Write*] [*Pharmacy*]
SIG............. Signal
SIG............. Signalman [*Navy rating*] [*British*]
SIG............. Signature (AFM)
SIG............. Signetur [*Let It Be Labelled*] [*Pharmacy*]
sig............... Significant
SIG............. Signifying (ROG)
SIG............. Signore [*or Signora*] (EY)
SIG............. Silicon-Insulated Gate
SIG............. Silver-Intensified Gold [*Biological stain*]
SIG............. Silver Ridge Resources, Inc. [*Vancouver Stock Exchange symbol*]
SIG............. Simplicity Is Greatness [*See also GIS*]
SIG............. Simplified Inertial Guidance
SIG............. Society for Integrative Graphology [*Inactive*] (EA)
SIG............. South Ingalls [*Colorado*] [*Seismograph station code, US Geological Survey*] [*Closed*] (SEIS)
SIG............. Southern Indiana Gas & Electric Co. [*NYSE symbol*] (SPSG)
SIG............. Special Interest Group
SIG............. Special Investigative Group [*DoD*]
SIG............. Starfield Image Generator
SIG............. State Implementation Grant
SIG............. Stellar Inertial Guidance Signal
SIG............. Strapdown Inertial Guidance
sIg .... Surface Immunoglobulin [*Immunochemistry*]

SIG............. Sylloge Inscriptionum Graecarum [*A publication*]
SIG............. Three Sigma Market Newspaper Audiences [*Three Sigma Research Center, Inc.*] [*Information service or system*] (CRD)
S-IgA .... Secretory Immunoglobulin A [*Immunology*]
Siga .... Signora [*Madam*] [*Italian*]
SIGAB .... Saigai Igaku [*A publication*]
SIGACT .... Special Interest Group on Automata and Computability Theory (EA)
SIGADA.... Special Interest Group on Ada (EA)
SIG/AH..... Special Interest Group/Arts and Humanities [*of the American Society for Information Science*]
SIG/ALP... Special Interest Group/Automated Language Processing [*American Society for Information Science*]
SIGAP .... Surrey Investigation Group into Aerial Phenomena [*British*]
SIGAPL..... Special Interest Group on APL Programming Language (EA)
SIGARCH ... Special Interest Group for Architecture of Computer Systems (EA)
SIGART .... Special Interest Group on Artificial Intelligence (EA)
SIGBAT .... Signal Battalion [*Army*]
SIG/BC...... Special Interest Group/Biological and Chemical Information Systems [*of the American Society for Information Science*]
SIGBDP .... Special Interest Group for Business Data Processing and Management (EA)
SIGBI .... Soroptimist International of Great Britain and Ireland (EAIO)
SIGBIO ..... Special Interest Group on Biomedical Computing (EA)
SIG/BSS.... Special Interest Group/Behavioral and Social Sciences [*of the American Society for Information Science*]
SIGC......... Signal Corps [*Later, Communications and Electronics Command*] [*Army*]
SIGC......... Signal Corps Engineering Laboratories [*Fort Monmouth, NJ*]
SIGCAPH ... Special Interest Group for Computers and the Physically Handicapped (EA)
SIGCAS..... Special Interest Group for Computers and Society (EA)
SIG/CBE... Special Interest Group/Costs, Budgeting, and Economics [*of the American Society for Information Science*]
SIGCEN .... Signal Center [*Military*] (AABC)
SIGCHI..... Special Interest Group on Computer and Human Interaction (EA)
SIGCLD .... Significant Clouds [*Aviation*] (FAAC)
SIGCOMM ... Special Interest Group on Data Communication (EA)
SIGCONDR ... Signal Conditioner (MCD)
SIGCOR.... Signal Corps [*Later, Communications and Electronics Command*] [*Army*]
SIGCOSIM ... Special Interest Group on Computer Systems, Installation Management [*Association for Computing Machinery*]
SIGCPR..... Special Interest Group for Computer Personnel Research (EA)
SIG/CR ..... Special Interest Group/Classification Research [*of the American Society for Information Science*]
SIGCS........ Special Interest Group for Computers and Society [*Association for Computing Machinery*] (EA)
SIG CSE .... Special Interest Group for Computer Science Education (EA)
SIGCUE .... Special Interest Group for Computer Uses in Education (EA)
SIG-D .... Simplified Inertial Guidance-Demonstration [*Army*] (RDA)
SIGDA .... Special Interest Group for Design Automation (EA)
SIGDIV ..... Signal Division [*SHAPE*] (NATG)
SIGDOC.... Special Interest Group for Systems Documentation (EA)
SIGE......... Silicon Germanium
SIGE......... Societe Internationale de Gastro-Enterologie
SIGEA .... Silvae Genetica [*A publication*]
SIG/ES...... Special Interest Group/Education for Information Science [*of the American Society for Information Science*]
SIGEX .... Signal Exercise (NATG)
SIGFIDET ... Special Interest Group on File Description and Translation [*Association for Computing Machinery*] [*Later, Special Interest Group on the Management of Data*]
SIG/FIS..... Special Interest Group/Foundations of Information Science [*of the American Society for Information Science*]
SIGG......... Signatures (WGA)
SIGGEN .... Signal Generator (IEEE)
SIGGRAPH ... Special Interest Group on Computer Graphics (EA)
Sight & S... Sight and Sound [*A publication*]
Sight-Sav R ... Sight-Saving Review [*A publication*]
Sight-Sav Rev ... Sight-Saving Review [*A publication*]
SIGI........... Selective Insurance Group, Inc. [*Branchville, NJ*] [*NASDAQ symbol*] (NQ)
SIGI........... System for Interactive Guidance and Information [*Computerized career-counseling service offered by the Educational Testing Service*] [*Princeton, NJ*]
SIG/IAC.... Special Interest Group/Information Analysis Centers [*of the American Society for Information Science*]
SIGILL...... Sigillum [*Seal*] [*Latin*] (WGA)
SIGINT ..... Signal Intelligence [*Military*] (AABC)
SIGINT/EW ... Signal Intelligence/Electronic Warfare (MCD)
SIGIR .... Special Interest Group on Information Retrieval (EA)
SIGIRD ..... Systeme Integre de Gestion Informatise des Ressources Documentaires [*Integrated System for the Management of Documentary Resources*] [*University of Quebec, Montreal*] [*Information service or system*] (IID)
SIG/IRG.... Senior Interdepartmental Group / Interdepartmental Regional Group (DNAB)

SIG/ISE .... Special Interest Group/Information Services to Education [*of the American Society for Information Science*]
Sig L........... Signal Lieutenant [*British military*]   (DMA)
SIG/LA...... Special Interest Group/Library Automation and Networks [*of the American Society for Information Science*]
SIGLASH ... Special Interest Group on Language Analysis and Studies in the Humanities [*Association for Computing Machinery*]
SIGLE .... System for Information on Grey Literature in Europe [*European Association for Grey Literature Exploitation*] [*Commission of the European Communities*] [*Information service or system*]   (IID)
SIGLEX..... Special Interest Group on Lexicography [*National Security Agency*]
SIGLINT... Signal Intelligence [*US surveillance satellite*]
Siglo Med .. Siglo Medico [*A publication*]
SIGM........ Sigma Designs, Inc. [*Fremont, CA*] [*NASDAQ symbol*]   (NQ)
SIGM........ Syndicat International des Gens de Mer du Canada
SIGMA...... Science in General Management [*British*]   (DI)
SIGMA...... Sealed Insulating Glass Manufacturers Association   (EA)
SIGMA...... Site Information Generation and Material Accountability Plan [*Army*]   (AABC)
SIGMA...... Society of In-Plant Graphics Management Associations
SIGMA...... Society of Independent Gasoline Marketers of America [*Washington, DC*]   (EA)
SIGMA...... Society of Inventors of Games and Mathematical Attractions [*British*]
SIGMA...... Standardized Inertial Guidance Multiple Application
SIGMALOG ... Simulation and Gaming Method for Analysis of Logistics [*Army*]
SIGMAP ... Special Interest Group for Mathematical Programming   (EA)
SIGMAS ... Signal Measurement and Analysis System
Sigma Ser Pure Math ... Sigma Series in Pure Mathematics [*A publication*]
Sigma Xi Q ... Sigma Xi Quarterly [*A publication*]
SIGMET ... Significant Meteorological Information [*Aviation*]   (FAAC)
SIGMETRICS ... Special Interest Group on Measurement and Evaluation   (EA)
SIGMICRO ... Special Interest Group on Microprogramming and Microarchitecture   (EA)
SIGMINI .. Special Interest Group on Minicomputers [*Later, SIGSMALL*] [*Association for Computing Machinery*]   (CSR)
Sig Mis ...... Signature Missing
SIGMN...... Signalman
sigmo.......... Sigmoidoscopy [*Medicine*]
SIGMOD .. Special Interest Group on Management of Data   (EA)
SIGMS ...... Signal Material Support   (DNAB)
SIGN .... Plasti-Line, Inc. [*NASDAQ symbol*]   (NQ)
SIGN .... Signa [*Label*] [*Pharmacy*]   (ROG)
SIGN .... Strapdown Inertial Guidance and Navigation   (MCD)
SIGNA....... Signora [*Madam*] [*Italian*]   (ROG)
Signa .... Signorina [*Miss*] [*Italian*]
SIGNA....... Species Iris Group of North America   (EA)
Signalmans J ... Signalman's Journal [*A publication*]
Signal Process ... Signal Processing [*A publication*]
SIGNCE .... Significance   (ROG)
SIGNE....... Signature
SIGNET .... Signal Network
Signet .... Signet Banking Corp. [*Associated Press abbreviation*]   (APAG)
SIGNF ...... Signify   (ROG)
Sign Lang Stud ... Sign Language Studies [*A publication*]
SIGN N P .. Signetur Nomine Proprio [*Let It Be Written Upon with the Proper Name*] [*Pharmacy*]   (ROG)
Signor de Homod ... Signorolus de Homodeis de Mediolano [*Flourished, 14th-15th century*] [*Authority cited in pre-1607 legal work*]   (DSA)
SIG/NPM ... Special Interest Group/Nonprint Media [*of the American Society for Information Science*]
Sig N Pro ... Signa Nomine Proprio [*Label with the Proper Name*] [*Pharmacy*]
SIGNRE .... Signature   (ROG)
Signs J Women Cult Soc ... Signs; Journal of Women in Culture and Society [*A publication*]
SIGNUM .. Special Interest Group on Numerical Control [*Military*]
SIGNUM .. Special Interest Group on Numerical Mathematics   (EA)
SIGO .... Signal Officer
Sigo .... Signorolus de Homodeis de Mediolano [*Flourished, 14th-15th century*] [*Authority cited in pre-1607 legal work*]   (DSA)
SIGOA....... Special Interest Group on Office Automation [*Later, SIGOIS*]
SIGOIS...... Special Interest Group on Office Information Systems   (EA)
SIGOP....... Signal Optimization Program [*Federal Highway Administration*]
SIGOPS..... Special Interest Group on Operating Systems   (EA)
SIGP .... Bicoastal Corp. [*NASDAQ symbol*]   (NQ)
SIGPC .... Special Interest Group on Personal Computing [*Association for Computing Machinery*]
SIGPLAN ... Special Interest Group on Programming Languages   (EA)
SIGPRAD ... Special Interest Group on Phobias and Related Anxiety Disorders   (EA)
SIGR.......... Sigma Research, Inc. [*NASDAQ symbol*]   (NQ)
SIGRAM... Sound Intensity Diagram   (MCD)
SIGREAL ... Special Interest Group on Real Time Processing [*Association for Computing Machinery*]

SIG/RT...... Special Interest Group/Reprographic Technology [*of the American Society for Information Science*]
SIGRTN .... Signal Return [*Electronics*]
SIGS .... Sandia Interactive Graphics System
SIGS .... Simplified Inertial Guidance System   (MCD)
SIGS .... Stellar Inertial Guidance System [*Air Force*]   (AAG)
SIGSAC.... Special Interest Group on Security, Audit, and Control   (EA)
SIGSAM ... Special Interest Group for Symbolic and Algebraic Manipulation   (EA)
SIGSCSA .. Special Interest Group on Small Computing Systems and Applications [*Later, SIGSMALL*] [*Association for Computing Machinery*]   (EA)
SIG/SDI .... Special Interest Group/Selective Dissemination of Information [*American Society for Information Science*]
SIGSEC..... Signal Security [*Military*]   (AABC)
SIG SEL .... Signal Selector   (DNAB)
SIGSIM..... Special Interest Group on Simulation   (EA)
SIGSMALL ... Special Interest Group on Small Computing Systems and Applications [*Formerly, SIGSCSA*] [*Association for Computing Machinery*]   (EA)
SIGSMALL/PC ... [*A*] Special Interest Group on Small and Personal Computing Systems and Applications [*An association for Computing Machinery*]   (HGAA)
SIGSOC .... Special Interest Group on Social and Behavioral Science Computing [*Association for Computing Machinery*]
SIGSOFT .. Special Interest Group on Software Engineering   (EA)
SIGSOP..... Signals Operator   (ADA)
SIGSPAC .. Special Interest Group on Urban Data Systems, Planning, Architecture, and Civil Engineering [*Association for Computing Machinery*]
SIGSPACE ... Senior Interagency Group (Space)
SIGSPCSA ... Special Interest Group on Small and Personal Computing Systems Applications   (EA)
Sig Sta........ Signal Station [*Nautical charts*]
SIGSTN .... Signal Station [*Navigation*]
SIGTRAN ... Special Interest Group on Translation [*National Security Agency*]
SIGTTO .... Society of International Gas Tanker and Terminal Operators [*British*]   (EAIO)
SIGUCCS ... Special Interest Group for University and College Computing Services   (EA)
Sig Unk...... Signature Unknown
SIG/UOI ... [*A*] Special Interest Group on User Online Interaction [*An association for Computing Machinery*]   (HGAA)
Sigurnost Rudn ... Sigurnost u Rudnicima [*A publication*]
SIGVOICE ... Special Interest Group on Voice [*National Security Agency*]
SIGZA .... Showa Igakkai Zasshi [*A publication*]
SIH .... Schweizerisches Institut fuer Hauswirtschaft
SIH .... Scinde Irregular Horse [*British military*]   (DMA)
SIH .... Seafarers and International House   (EA)
SIH .... Silgarhi Doti [*Nepal*] [*Airport symbol*]   (OAG)
SIH .... Societe Internationale d'Hematologie [*International Society of Hematology - ISH*] [*Buenos Aires, Argentina*]   (EA)
SIH .... Society for Italic Handwriting   (EA)
SIH .... South Irish Horse [*British military*]   (DMA)
SIH .... Studies in the Humanities [*A publication*]
SIH .... Sun Ice Ltd. [*Toronto Stock Exchange symbol*]
SIH .... Superstar Ice Hockey [*Computer game*]
SIHAG .... Experimental Farm, Agriculture Canada [*Ferme Experimentale, Agriculture Canada*], Indian Head, Saskatchewan [*Library symbol*] [*National Library of Canada*]   (BIB)
SIHED....... Sanitaer-Installateur und Heizungsbauer [*A publication*]
SIHR.......... Supervisory Inventory on Human Relations [*Test*]
SIHS.......... SI Handling Systems, Inc. [*NASDAQ symbol*]   (NQ)
SIHS.......... Society for Italian Historical Studies   (EA)
SIHT.......... Space Impact Hand Tool [*NASA*]
SIHW .... Society for Italic Handwriting   (EA)
SII .... School Interest Inventory [*Psychology*]
SII .... Security-Insecurity Inventory [*Psychology*]
SII .... Self-Interview Inventory [*Psychology*]
SII .... Short Interval Identification
SII .... Sitkinak Island [*Alaska*] [*Seismograph station code, US Geological Survey*]   (SEIS)
SII .... Smith International, Inc. [*NYSE symbol*]   (SPSG)
SII .... Space Industries, Inc.
SII .... Special Interest Items   (MCD)
SII .... Standard Identification for Individuals [*Social security*] [*American National Standards Institute*]
SII .... Statement of Intelligence Interest [*Army*]   (RDA)
SII .... Structural Impediments Initiative [*US-Japan trade negotiations*]
SII .... Sugar Information, Inc. [*Defunct*]   (EA)
SII .... Supervisory Immigrant Inspector [*Immigration and Naturalization Service*]
SIIA .... Self-Insurance Institute of America   (EA)
SIIAEC....... Secretariat International des Ingenieurs, des Agronomes, et des Cadres Economiques Catholiques [*International Secretariat of Catholic Technologists, Agriculturists, and Economists*] [*Paris, France*]   (EAIO)
SIIC .... Secretariat International des Groupements Professionnels des Industries Chimiques des Pays de la CEE

SIIC	Smith International, Inc. [*NASDAQ symbol*] (NQ)
SIIC	Special Interest Item Code [*Military*] (AABC)
SIIFT	Sociedad Internacional de Ingenieros Forestales Tropicales [*International Society of Tropical Foresters*] (EAIO)
SIINA	Silicates Industriels [*Belgium*] [*A publication*]
SIINC	Scientific Instrumentation Information Network and Curricula [*National Science Foundation*]
SIIR	Spares Item Inventory Record (MCD)
SIIRS........	Smithsonian Institution Information Retrieval System (DIT)
SIITO	Standard Installation Instruction Technical Order (SAA)
SIJ	Minneapolis, MN [*Location identifier*] [*FAA*] (FAAL)
SIJ	Sacroiliac Joint
SIJ	Siglufjordur [*Iceland*] [*Airport symbol*] (OAG)
SIJ	Small Industry Journal [*Quezon City*] [*A publication*]
SIJADEP ..	International Secretariat of Jurists for an Amnesty and Democracy in Paraguay [*Paris, France*] (EAIO)
SIJAU	Secretariat International des Juristes pour l'Amnistie en Uruguay [*France*]
SI/JI	Secondary Injection/Jet Interaction
SIJIC	Senior International Joint Intelligence Course (MCD)
SIK.............	Sikeston, MO [*Location identifier*] [*FAA*] (FAAL)
SIK.............	Silknit Ltd. [*Toronto Stock Exchange symbol*]
Sik..............	Single Income, Kids [*Lifestyle classification*]
SiK	Sztuka i Krytyka [*A publication*]
Sikh R	Sikh Review [*Calcutta*] [*A publication*]
SIKTA	Silikaty [*A publication*]
SIL.............	Ile a la Crosse Public Library, Saskatchewan [*Library symbol*] [*National Library of Canada*] (NLC)
SIL.............	Safety Information Letter (IEEE)
SIL.............	Scanner Input Language
SIL.............	Schedule Interface Log
SIL.............	SCN [*Stock Control Number*] Index and Log
SIL.............	Selected Item List
SIL.............	Semiconductor Injector LASER
SIL.............	Seriously Ill List [*Military*]
SIL.............	Service Information Letter
SIL.............	Set Indicators of the Left Half (SAA)
SIL.............	Shift Indicator Light [*Automotive engineering*]
SIL.............	Silcorp Ltd. [*Toronto Stock Exchange symbol*]
SIL.............	Silence (MSA)
SIL.............	Silicate
SIL.............	Silicon Systems, Inc. [*NYSE symbol*] (SPSG)
Sil..............	Silius Italicus [*First century AD*] [*Classical studies*] (OCD)
SIL.............	Sillimanite [*Mineralogy*]
SIL.............	Silurian [*Period, era, or system*] [*Geology*]
SIL.............	Silver (AAG)
Sil..............	Silver Tax Division (Internal Revenue Bulletin) [*A publication*] (DLA)
Sil..............	Silvester Godinho [*Deceased, 1244*] [*Authority cited in pre-1607 legal work*] (DSA)
SIL.............	Slidel, LA [*Location identifier*] [*FAA*] (FAAL)
SIL.............	Smithsonian Institution Information Leaflets
SIL.............	Smithsonian Institution Libraries
SIL.............	SNOBOL Implementation Language Reimplemented [*1974*] [*Data processing*] (CSR)
SIL.............	Societas Internationalis Limnologiae Theoreticae et Applicae [*International Association of Theoretical and Applied Limnology*]
SIL.............	Societe Internationale de la Lepre [*International Leprosy Association*]
SIL.............	Society for Individual Liberty (EA)
SIL.............	Sound Intensity Level
SIL.............	Sound Interference Level [*NASA*] (NASA)
SIL.............	Special Interest Launch [*Military*] (AFIT)
SIL.............	Specific Individual Licence [*Importing*] [*British*] (DS)
SIL.............	Speech Interference Level
SIL.............	Squamous Intraepithelial Lesion [*Medicine*]
SIL.............	Steam Isolation Line (IEEE)
SIL.............	Store Interface Link
SIL.............	Studies in Linguistics [*A publication*]
SIL.............	Summer Institute of Linguistics
SIL.............	Supply Information Letter (MCD)
SIL.............	Support Items List (MCD)
SIL.............	Surge Impedance Loading
SIL.............	System Implementation Language [*Data processing*]
SIL.............	Systems Integration Laboratory [*NASA*] (MCD)
SILA	Scientific Laboratories, Inc. [*NASDAQ symbol*] (NQ)
SILAD	Siderurgia Latinoamericana [*A publication*]
SILAF........	Sindacato Italiano Lavoratori Appalti Ferroviari [*Italian Union of Railroad Contract Workers*]
SILAP.......	Sindacato Nazionale Dipendenti Ministero del Lavori Pubblici [*National Union of Employees in the Ministry of Public Welfare*] [*Italy*]
SILAT.......	Society for Iberian and Latin American Thought (EA)
SILAT.......	Subionospheric Latitude
SILCA	Sindacato Italiano Lavoratori Cappellai ed Affini [*Italian Federation of Hat and Allied Workers*]
SilCLV.......	Silicon Liquid Crystal Light Valve [*NASA*]
SilcnGr.......	Silicon Graphics [*Associated Press abbreviation*] (APAG)
Sil (Ct of Ap) ...	Silvernail's New York Court of Appeals Reports [*A publication*] (DLA)

Silent Pic....	Silent Picture [*A publication*]
SILF..........	Societe Internationale de Linguistique Fonctionelle [*International Society of Functional Linguistics*] (EAIO)
SILG	Silencing (MSA)
SILI	Siliconix, Inc. [*NASDAQ symbol*] (NQ)
SILI	Sindacato Nazionale Lavoratori Italcable [*National Union of Cable Workers*] [*Italy*]
SILI	Standard Item Location Index
SILICA......	System for International Literature Information on Ceramics and Glass [*Fachinformationszentrum Werkstoffe*] [*Database*]
Silicates Indus ...	Silicates Industriels [*A publication*]
Silic Conf Proc ...	Silicate Conference. Proceedings [*A publication*]
Silicon Carbide Proc Int Conf ...	Silicon Carbide. Proceedings. International Conference on Silicon Carbide [*A publication*]
Silik...........	Silikaty [*A publication*]
Silik J.........	Silikat Journal [*A publication*]
SILJ	Survey of Inmates of Local Jails [*Department of Justice*] (GFGA)
SILK	Silk, Silk, Silk International, Inc. [*NASDAQ symbol*] (NQ)
Silk Artif Silk Mercury ...	Silk and Artificial Silk Mercury [*A publication*]
Silk Dig Wkly ...	Silk Digest Weekly [*A publication*]
Silk J.......	Silk Journal [*A publication*]
Silk J Rayon World ...	Silk Journal and Rayon World [*A publication*]
Silk Rayon Dig ...	Silk and Rayon Digest [*A publication*]
Silk Rayon Ind India ...	Silk and Rayon Industries of India [*A publication*]
Silkworm Inf Bull ...	Silkworm Information Bulletin [*A publication*]
Sill Comp ...	Sill on Composition in Bankruptcy [*A publication*] (DLA)
Silliman J ..	Silliman Journal [*A publication*]
Sillimans J Sci ...	Silliman's Journal of Science [*A publication*]
S Ill ULJ....	Southern Illinois University. Law Journal [*A publication*]
SILM	Single In-Line Module [*Data processing*]
SILMOD...	Silhouette Model [*Military*] (INF)
SILN........	Silicon General, Inc. [*NASDAQ symbol*] (NQ)
SILO	Security Intelligence Liaison Office [*Central Mediterranean Forces*] [*Navy*]
SILON......	Subionospheric Longitude
SILOP	Studies in Linguistics. Occasional Papers [*A publication*]
SILP.........	Section of International Law and Practice (EA)
SILP.........	Sindacato Italiano Lavoratori del Petrolio [*Italian Union of Oil Workers*]
SILP.........	Sindacato Italiano Lavoratori Postelegrafonici [*Italian Union of Postal and Telegraph Workers*]
SILP.........	Solomon Islands Liberal Party [*Political party*] (EY)
SILPWS	Sheet Iron and Light Plate Workers' Society [*A union*] [*British*]
SILS.........	Shipboard Impact Locator System
SILS.........	Shipley-Institute of Living Scale for Measuring Intellectual Impairment [*Psychology*]
SILS.........	Silver Solder
SILSP........	Safeguard Integrated Logistics Support Plan [*Army*] (AABC)
Sil (Sup Ct) ...	Silvernail's New York Supreme Court Reports [*A publication*] (DLA)
SILT	Stored Information Loss Tree
SILTF........	System Integration Laboratory and Test Facility
SILTS........	Shuttle Infrared Leeside Temperature Sensing [*NASA*] (NASA)
Silv	Silvae [*of Statius*] [*Classical studies*] (OCD)
SILV	Silver (ROG)
SILV	Silver King Mines, Inc. [*NASDAQ symbol*] (NQ)
Silv	Silvernail's New York Criminal Reports [*9-14 New York*] [*A publication*] (DLA)
Silv	Silvernail's New York Reports [*1886-92*] [*A publication*] (DLA)
Silv	Silvernail's New York Supreme Court Reports [*1889-90*] [*A publication*] (DLA)
Silv A	Silvernail's New York Court of Appeals Reports [*A publication*] (DLA)
Silvaecult Trop Subtrop ...	Silvaecultura Tropica et Subtropica [*A publication*]
Silvae Genet ...	Silvae Genetica [*A publication*]
Silva Fenn ...	Silva Fennica [*A publication*]
Silv App	Silvernail's New York Court of Appeals Reports [*A publication*] (DLA)
Silv Cit	Silvernail's New York Citations [*A publication*] (DLA)
Silv Ct App ...	Silvernail's New York Court of Appeals Reports [*A publication*] (DLA)
Silv Ct App (NY) ...	Silvernail's New York Court of Appeals Reports [*A publication*] (DLA)
Silve	Silvester Godinho [*Deceased, 1244*] [*Authority cited in pre-1607 legal work*] (DSA)
Silver Inst Lett ...	Silver Institute Letter [*A publication*]
Silvernail's NY Rep ...	Silvernail's New York Court of Appeals Reports [*A publication*] (DLA)
SILVIC......	Silviculture
Silvic Sao Paulo ...	Silvicultura em Sao Paulo [*A publication*]
Silv Notes Ont Dep Lds For ...	Silvicultural Notes. Ontario Department of Lands and Forests [*A publication*]
Silvr...........	Silvester Godinho [*Deceased, 1244*] [*Authority cited in pre-1607 legal work*] (DSA)
Silv Res Note (Tanz) ...	Silviculture Research Note (Tanzania) [*A publication*]
Silv Sup......	Silvernail's New York Supreme Court Reports [*A publication*] (DLA)

Silv (Sup Ct) ... Silvernail's New York Supreme Court Reports [*A publication*]   (DLA)
Silv Unrep ... Silvernail's New York Unreported Cases [*A publication*]   (DLA)
SIM............ SACLANT [*Supreme Allied Commander, Atlantic*] Staff Instruction Manual   (NATG)
SIM............ SAM [*Surface-to-Air Missile*] Intercept Missile   (DNAB)
SIM............ Scanning Ion Microscope
SIM............ School of Industrial Management [*MIT*]   (MCD)
SIM............ Scientific Instrument Module [*NASA*]
SIM............ Sclerite-Inducing Membrane [*Entomology*]
SIM............ Selected Inventory Management [*Military*]   (CAAL)
SIM............ Selected Ion Monitoring [*Chromatography*]
SIM............ Selected Item Management
SIM............ Sequential Inference Machine [*Data processing*]
SIM............ Sergeant Instructor of Musketry
SIM........... Service Instructions Message [*Telecommunications*]   (TEL)
SIM............ Service International de Microfilm, Paris, France [*Library symbol*] [*Library of Congress*]   (LCLS)
SIM............ Servicio Intelligencia Militar [*Military Intelligence Service*] [*Dominican Republic*]
SIM............ Servizio Informazioni Militare [*Military Intelligence Service*] [*Italy*]
SIM............ Set Interrupt Mask [*Data processing*]
SIM............ Shima Resources [*Vancouver Stock Exchange symbol*]
SIM............ Ship Instrumentation Manager   (KSC)
SIM............ Simbai [*Papua New Guinea*] [*Airport symbol*]   (OAG)
SIM............ Simferopol [*Former USSR*] [*Seismograph station code, US Geological Survey*]   (SEIS)
SIM............ Similar   (AAG)
SIM............ Simile [*In a Similar Manner*] [*Music*]
Sim............ Simmons' Reports [*95-97, 99 Wisconsin*] [*A publication*]   (DLA)
Sim............ Simons' English Chancery Reports [*57-60 English Reprint*] [*1826-50*] [*A publication*]   (DLA)
SIM............ Simplex
SIM............ Simposio Internacional de Macromoleculas [*International Symposium on Macromolecules*]
SIM............ Simulated [*or Simulation*]   (AABC)
SIM............ Simulator [*Data processing*]
SIM............ Small Intestine Metaplasia [*Medicine*]
SIM............ Societa di Intermediazione Mobiliare [*Finance*] [*Italy*]   (ECON)
SIM............ Societa Italiana di Metapsichica [*Italy*]
SIM............ Societe Internationale de la Moselle [*International Moselle Co.*]
SIM............ Societe Internationale de Musicologie [*International Musicological Society*]
SIM............ Society for Industrial Microbiology   (EA)
SIM............ Society for Information Management [*Chicago, IL*]   (EA)
SIM............ Solar Interplanetary Model
SIM............ Somali Islamic Movement [*Political party*]
SIM............ Space Interceptor Missile   (MCD)
SIM............ Stage Inert Mass
SIM............ Standard Injection Method [*Laboratory science*]
SIM............ Steatite Insulation Material
SIM............ Stellar Image Monitor
SIM............ Structural Integrity Monitoring   (MCD)
SIM............ Student Interracial Ministry [*Defunct*]
SIM............ Submarine Intended Movement   (NVT)
SIM............ Subsystem Interface Module
SIM............ Subtotal Integration Mode
SIM............ Sucrose-Isomaltose Deficiency [*Medicine*]
SIM............ Sudan Interior Mission
SIM............ Sulfide Production, Indole Production, and Motility [*Growth medium*]
SIM............ Surveillance Intelligence and Reconnaissance Mission [*Military*]   (CAAL)
SIM............ Synchronous Interface Module
SIM............ Systems Integration Model   (MCD)
SIMA........ Salon International de la Machine Agricole
SIMA........ Scientific Instrument Manufacturers' Association [*British*]
SIMA........ Shore Intermediate Maintenance Activity [*Navy*]   (NVT)
SIMA........ Steel Industry Management Association [*Trade union*] [*British*]
SIMA........ Studies in Mediterranean Archaeology [*A publication*]
SIMAC..... Sonic Instrument Measurement and Control   (AAG)
SIMAJ...... Scientific Instrument Manufacturers' Association of Japan
SIMArsbok ... Svenska Israels-Missionens Arsbok [*Stockholm*] [*A publication*]
SIMAS ...... Shuttle Information Management Accountability System [*NASA*]   (NASA)
SIMAS ...... SONAR In-Situ Mode Assessment System   (MSC)
SIMATS.... Supplementary Interim Medium Antitank System [*Army*]   (INF)
SIMBAD ... Simulation as a Basis for Social Agents' Decisions [*Data processing*]
SIMBAY ... Scientific Instrumentation Module Bay [*NASA*]   (KSC)
SIMC........ Silicon Integrated Monolithic Circuit
Sim & C...... Simmons and Conover's Reports [*99-100 Wisconsin*] [*A publication*]   (DLA)
SIMC......... Societe Internationale de Medecine de Catastrophe [*International Society for Disaster Medicine - ISDM*] [*Switzerland*]   (EA)

SIMC......... Societe Internationale de Medecine Cybernetique [*International Society of Cybernetic Medicine*]
SIMC......... Societe Internationale pour la Musique Contemporaine [*International Society for Contemporary Music*]
SIMC......... Syndicat International des Marins Canadiens [*Seafarers' International Union of Canada - SIU*]
SIMCA ...... Societe Industrielle de Mecanique et de Carrosserie Automobile [*French automobile manufacturer; acronym used as name of its cars*]
SIMCA ...... Soft Independent Modeling of Class Analogy [*Analytical chemistry technique*]
SIMCANSOC ... Simulated Canadian Society [*Simulation game*]
SIMCAP... Simulation, Corps Automated Procedures   (MCD)
SIMCE...... Simulation Communications Electronics [*Group of computer programs*] [*Army*]
SIMCEN ... Simulation Center [*Deep Space Network, NASA*]
SIMCERT ... Simulator Certification
SIMCHE.. Simulation and Checkout Equipment [*NASA*]   (KSC)
SIMCO...... Sea Ice Microbial Colony
SIMCOM ... Simulation Complex   (NASA)
SIMCOM ... Simulation and Computer [*Data processing*]
SIMCOM ... Simulator Compiler [*Computer*]
SIMCON... Scientific Inventory Management and Control
SIMCON... Simplified Control
SIMCON... Simulation Controller
Sim Ct M .. Simmons on Courts-Martial [*A publication*]   (DLA)
SIMD........ Single Instruction, Multiple Data   (IEEE)
SIMDEP ... Simulation Development Program [*DASA*]
Sim Des Pat ... Simonds' Law of Design Patents [*A publication*]   (DLA)
Sim Dig...... Simmons' Wisconsin Digest [*A publication*]   (DLA)
Sim Dig Pat Dec ... Simonds' Digest of Patent Office Decisions [*United States*] [*A publication*]   (DLA)
SIME......... Security Intelligence, Middle East [*Navy*]
SIME......... Studies in Mechanical Engineering [*Elsevier Book Series*] [*A publication*]
Sim Elect.... Simeon on Elections [*A publication*]   (DLA)
Sim (Eng)... Simons' English Chancery Reports [*57-60 English Reprint*] [*A publication*]   (DLA)
Simes & S Future Interests ... Simes and Smith on the Law of Future Interests [*A publication*]   (DLA)
SIMEX ...... Secondary Item Materiel Excess [*DoD*]
SIMFAC... Simulation Facility [*NASA*]
SIMFAR.... Simulated Frequency Analysis and Recording   (MCD)
SIMFIRE .. Simulated Fire
SIMFIRE .. Simulated Mission Firing
SIMG........ Sammelbaende. Internationale Musik Gesellschaft [*A publication*]
SIMG........ Societas Internationalis Medicinae Generalis [*International Society of General Practice*] [*Klagenfurt, Austria*]   (EAIO)
SIMGCA ... Similarity Graft Clustering Analysis [*Plant phylogeny*]
SIMHA ..... Societe Internationale de Mycologie Humaine et Animale [*International Society for Human and Animal Mycology - ISHAM*] [*British*]   (EA)
SIMI........ Scientific Imaging Instruments, Inc. [*NASDAQ symbol*]   (NQ)
SIMICOR ... Simultaneous Multiple Image Correlation
SIMILE..... Simulator of Immediate Memory in Learning Experiments
Sim Int ...... Simons' Law of Interpleader [*A publication*]   (DLA)
SIMIS........ SAIC [*Science Applications International Corp.*] Integrated Management Information System   (MCD)
SIMJA...... Singapore Medical Journal [*A publication*]
SIML......... Similar   (AAG)
Simla.......... All India Reporter, Simla [*1951*] [*A publication*]   (DLA)
SIMLR ...... Similar   (ROG)
SIMM........ Simmons Airlines, Inc. [*Chicago, IL*] [*NASDAQ symbol*]   (NQ)
SIMM........ Single In-Line Memory Module [*Data processing*]
SIMM........ Studies in Indo-Muslim Mysticism [*A publication*]
SIMM........ Symbolic Integrated Maintenance Manual   (MCD)
SIM M-R... Simulation Monitor-Recorder   (SAA)
SIMNET..... Simulation Network
Sim NS....... Simons' English Vice-Chancery Reports, New Series [*61 English Reprint*] [*A publication*]   (DLA)
SIMNS ...... Simulated Navigation Systems
Sim NS (Eng) ... Simons' English Vice-Chancery Reports, New Series [*61 English Reprint*] [*A publication*]   (DLA)
Simo........... [*Jacobus*] Simonetta [*Deceased, 1539*] [*Authority cited in pre-1607 legal work*]   (DSA)
SIMO .... Simultaneously   (NASA)
SIMO .... Special Items Management Office
SIMOBS ... Simultaneous Observations [*RADAR and optical*]
SIMOC...... Simulated Occupant [*People Machine*] [*Office of Civil Defense*]
Simon .... [*Jacobus*] Simonetta [*Deceased, 1539*] [*Authority cited in pre-1607 legal work*]   (DSA)
Simon........ Simonides [*Fifth century BC*] [*Classical studies*]   (OCD)
Simon's TC ... Simon's Tax Cases [*United Kingdom*] [*A publication*]   (DLA)
Simon's Town Hist Soc ... Simon's Town Historical Society [*A publication*]
SIMOP...... Simultaneous Operation
SIMOS ...... Space Imbalanced Military Occupational Specialty
SIMOX...... Separation by Implantation of Oxygen [*Semiconductor technology*]
SIMP......... Satellite Information Message Protocol

SIMP......... Shipboard Integrated Maintenance Program [*Navy*] (NG)
SIMP......... Simpleton (DSUE)
simp............ Simplex (MAE)
Simp........... Single Income, Money Problems [*Lifestyle classification*]
SIMP........... Societa Italiana di Medicina Psicosomatica [*Italy*]
SIMP......... Specific Impulse (MSA)
SIMPA ...... Rendiconti. Societa Italiana di Mineralogia e Petrologia [*A publication*]
SIMPAC.... Simplified Programming for Acquisition and Control (IEEE)
SIMPAC.... Simulation Package [*Data processing*]
Sim Pat L... Simond's Patent Law [*A publication*] (DLA)
Simp Inf ... Simpson on Infants [*4th ed.*] [*1926*] [*A publication*] (DLA)
SIMPL....... Simulation Implementation Machine Programming Languages (KSC)
SIMPL/1 ... Simulation Language Based on Programming Language, Version One
SIMPLAN ... Simple Modeling and Planning [*SIMPLAN Users Group*] [*New York, NY*] (CSR)
SIMPLAN ... Simplified Modeling and Planning [*Programming language*] [*1973*] (CSR)
SIMPLE.... Semi-Implicit Pressure-Linked Equation [*Algorithm*]
SIMPLE.... Simulation of Industrial Management Problems [*Program*] [*1958*] [*Data processing*] (CSR)
SIMPLE.... Solver for Implicit Equations [*Computer language*]
SIMPLE.... System for Integrated Maintenance and Program Language Extension
SIMPO...... Simulation of Personnel Operations [*Army Research Institute for the Behavioral and Social Sciences*] (RDA)
Simp Otlalennoi Gibrid Rast ... Simpozium po Otlalennoi Gibridizatsii Rastenii [*A publication*]
SIMPP....... Simple Image-Processing Package (BYTE)
SIMPP....... Society of Independent Motion Picture Producers
SIMPU....... Simulation Punch
SIMR......... Schenley Instant Market Reports
SIMR......... Simulator (AAG)
SIMR......... Societe Internationale de Mecanique des Roches [*International Society for Rock Mechanics - ISRM*] (EAIO)
SIMR......... Systems Integration Management Review [*NASA*] (MCD)
SIMRAND ... Simulation of Research and Development
SIMRDU... Survey of Immunologic Research [*A publication*]
Sim Ry Acc ... Simon's Law Relating to Railway Accidents [*1862*] [*A publication*] (DLA)
SIMS .... Secondary Ion Mass Spectrometry [*or Spectroscopy*]
SIMS .... Sedna Information Management System [*Sedna Corp.*] [*Information service or system*] (IID)
SIMS .... Selected Item Management System [*Military*] (AABC)
SIMS .... Selective Interference Modulation Spectrometer
SIMS .... Services Information Management System [*DoD*] (GFGA)
SIMS .... Shuttle Imaging Microwave System [*NASA*] (NASA)
SIMS .... Shuttle Inventory Management System [*NASA*] (NASA)
SIMS .... SIAM [*Society for Industrial and Applied Mathematics*] Institute for Mathematics and Society
Sim & S ...... Simons and Stuart's English Chancery Reports [*57 English Reprint*] [*A publication*] (DLA)
SIMS .... Single Item, Multisource (IEEE)
SIMS .... Skandinaviska Simuleringssaellskapet [*Scandinavian Simulation Society*] [*Also, SSS*] (EA)
SIMS .... Societal Institute of the Mathematical Sciences [*Research center*] (RCD)
SIMS .... Stable Isotope Mass Spectrometer
SIMS .... Stellar Inertial Measurement System [*NASA*]
SIMS .... Strategic Integrated Management System [*American Occupational Therapy Association*]
SIMS .... Students' International Meditation Society
SiMS......... Studier i Modern Sprakvetenskap [*A publication*]
SIMS .... Supply Information Management System [*Air Force*] (GFGA)
SIMS .... Symbolic Integrated Maintenance System
SIMSA ...... Savings Institutions Marketing Society of America
SIMSCRIPT ... [*A*] Simulation Programming Language [*1963*] [*Data processing*]
SIMSEP.... Simulation of Solar Electric Propulsion [*NASA*]
SIMSHO... Simulation Scheduled Order (SSD)
SIMSI....... Selective Inventory Management of Secondary Items [*Navy*]
SIMSIN.... Simulated Strapdown Inertial Navigation (MCD)
SIMSLIN .. Safety in Mines Scattered Light Instrument (ADA)
SIMSOC ... Simulated Society
Sim & St..... Simons and Stuart's English Chancery Reports [*57 English Reprint*] [*A publication*] (DLA)
SIMSTF .... Societe Internationale de Mecanique des Sols et de Travaux de Fondations [*International Society for Soil Mechanics and Foundation Engineering - ISSMFE*]
Sim & Stu... Simons and Stuart's English Vice-Chancery Reports [*57 English Reprint*] [*A publication*] (DLA)
Sim & Stu (Eng) ... Simons and Stuart's English Chancery Reports [*57 English Reprint*] [*A publication*] (DLA)
SIMSUP.... Simulation Supervisor
SIMS-X ..... Selected Items Management System - Expanded (MCD)
SIMSYS .... Simulated System (CAAL)
SIMTOS ... Simulated Tactical Operations Systems [*Army*] (RDA)
SIMTRACC ... Simulator Trainer Command and Control
SIMTS....... Scientific Instrument Makers Trade Society [*A union*] [*British*]

SIMU......... Simulated Inertial Measurement Unit (NASA)
SIMUA...... Simulation [*A publication*]
SIMUL...... Simultaneous (AABC)
SIMULA ... Simulation Language [*1964*] [*Data processing*]
Simulat Gam ... Simulation and Games [*A publication*]
Simulat & Games ... Simulation and Games [*A publication*]
Simulations Councils Proc ... Simulations Councils. Proceedings [*A publication*]
Simul Counc Proc Ser ... Simulation Councils. Proceedings Series [*A publication*]
Simul and Games ... Simulation and Games [*A publication*]
Simul Games Learn ... Simulation/Games for Learning [*A publication*]
Simul Today ... Simulation Today [*A publication*]
SIMUPOL ... Simulative Procedure Oriented Language (MCD)
SIN .... Salpingitis Isthmica Nodosum
SIN .... Scientific Information Notes [*A publication*]
SIN .... Security Information Network
SIN .... Sensitive Information Network
SIN .... Simultaneous Interpenetrating Networks [*Organic chemistry*]
SiN............ Sin Nombre [*A publication*]
SIN .... Sinagawa [*Japan*] [*Seismograph station code, US Geological Survey*] [*Closed*] (SEIS)
SIN .... Sinclair Community College, Dayton, OH [*OCLC symbol*] (OCLC)
SIN .... Sine [*Mathematics*]
SIN .... Sine [*Without*] [*Latin*]
SIN .... Sinecure (ROG)
Sin.............. Sinemurian [*Geology*]
SIN .... Singapore [*Airport symbol*] (OAG)
SIN .... Single Identifying Number
SIN .... Sinistra [*Left Hand*] [*Music*]
Sin.............. Sinter [*Record label*] [*Brazil*]
SIN .... Social Insurance Number [*Canada*]
SIN .... Society for International Numismatics (EA)
SIN .... [*The*] Spanish Information Network [*Later, Spanish International Network*] [*Cable- television system*] (WDMC)
SIN .... Spanish International Network [*Cable-television system*]
SIN .... Squamous Intraepithelial Neoplastic [*Oncology*]
SIN .... Stop Inflation Now [*Variation on the anti-inflation WIN slogan of President Gerald Ford*]
SIN .... Study Item Number [*Army*] (AABC)
S IN............ Sub Initio [*Towards the Beginning*] [*Latin*] (ROG)
SIN .... Subject Indication Number
SIN .... Support Information Network
SIN .... Symbolic Integrator
SIN .... Syngold Exploration, Inc. [*Toronto Stock Exchange symbol*]
SIN .... System Integrators, Inc. [*NYSE symbol*] (SPSG)
SINA......... Scheduling Information Not Available (KSC)
SINA......... Shellfish Institute of North America [*Also known as Oyster Growers and Dealers Association of North America*] (EA)
SINA......... Society for Indecency to Naked Animals [*A hoax association*]
SINACMA ... Sindacato Nazionale Dipendenti Corte dei Conti e Magistrature Amministrative [*National Union of General Accounting Office Employees*] [*Italy*]
SINAD....... Signal Plus Noise and Distortion
SINADIMID ... Sindacato Nazionale Dipendenti Ministero Difesa [*National Union of Ministry of Defense Employees*] [*Italy*]
SINAF .... Sindacato Nazionale Dipendenti Ministero Agricoltura e Foreste [*National Union of Ministry of Agriculture and Forestry Employees*] [*Italy*]
Sinai Hosp J ... Sinai Hospital. Journal [*A publication*]
SINAMAI ... Sindacato Nazionale e Dipendenti Ministero Africa Italiana [*National Union of Former Italian Employees of African Ministry*] [*Italy*]
SINAMIL ... Sindacato Nazionale Dipendenti Ministero del Lavoro e Previdenza Sociale [*National Union of Ministry of Labor and Social Security Employees*] [*Italy*]
SINAMN... Sindacato Nazionale Dipendenti Marina Mercantile [*National Union of Merchant Marine Workers*] [*Italy*]
SINAP .... Satellite Input to Numerical Analysis and Prediction [*National Weather Service*]
SINAP .... Sinapis [*Mustard*] [*Pharmacology*] (ROG)
SINAPI...... Sindacato Nazionale Ministero Pubblica Istruzione [*National Union of Ministry of Public Instructors*] [*Italy*]
SINASCEL ... Sindacato Nazionale Scuola Elementare [*National Union of Elementary School Teachers*] [*Italy*]
SINB.......... Southern Interstate Nuclear Board
SINC.......... Nicaraguan International Rescue from Communism (PD)
SINC.......... Seal, Inc. [*NASDAQ symbol*] (NQ)
SINCGARS ... Single-Channel Ground and Airborne Radio System [*or Subsystem*] (MCD)
SINCGARS-V ... Single-Channel Ground and Airborne Radio System, Very High Frequency
Sinclair....... Sinclair's Manuscript Decisions, Scotch Session Cases [*A publication*] (DLA)
SINCOE.... Sindacato Nazionale Dipendenti Ministero Industria e Commercio Estero [*National Union of Ministry of Industry and Foreign Commerce Employees*] [*Italy*]
SINCTRAC ... Single Channel Tactical Radio Communications [*Army*] (RDA)

Sind........... All India Reporter, Sind [*1914-50*] [*A publication*] (DLA)
Sind........... Indian Rulings, Sind Series [*A publication*] (DLA)
SIND........ Saskatchewan Indian [*A publication*]
SIND........ Satellite Inertial Navigation Determination (MCD)
SIND........ Southern Indiana Railway, Inc. [*AAR code*]
SIND........ Strobe Intersection Deghoster
SINDA....... Systems Improved Numerical Differencing Analyses [*Database*]
SINDAF.... Sindacato Nazionale Dipendenti Amministrazioni Finanziarie [*National Union of Financial Administration Employees*] [*Italy*]
Sindar Rep ... Sindar Reporter [*A publication*]
SINDB....... Science and Industry [*Karachi*] [*A publication*]
S Ind Stud.. Southern Indian Studies [*A publication*]
Sind Univ Res J Sci Ser ... Sind University Research Journal. Science Series [*A publication*]
SINE.......... Short Interspersed Nucleotide Element [*Genetics*]
Sinema....... Andere Sinema [*A publication*]
Sinet Ethiop J Sci ... Sinet: An Ethiopian Journal of Science [*A publication*]
SIN-ETH... Swiss Institute of Nuclear Research - Eidgenoessische Technische Hochschule
SINEWS.... Ship Integrated Electronic Warfare System
SINF......... Sinfonia [*Symphony*] [*Music*]
SINFDOK ... Statens Rad for Vetenskaplig Information och Dokumentation [*Swedish Council for Scientific Information and Documentation*] (IID)
SINFUB .... Skrifter Utgitt. Instituttet foer Nordisk Filologi. Universitetet i Bergen [*A publication*]
SING .... Singapore
SING .... Singular
SING .... Singulorum [*Of Each*] [*Pharmacy*]
SINGAN.... Singularity Analyzer [*Data processing*]
Singap........ Singapore Fund [*Associated Press abbreviation*] (APAG)
Singapore Bus ... Singapore Business [*A publication*]
Singapore Dent J ... Singapore Dental Journal [*A publication*]
Singapore J Obstet Gynaecol ... Singapore Journal of Obstetrics and Gynaecology [*A publication*]
Singapore J Phy ... Singapore Journal of Physics [*A publication*]
Singapore J Primary Ind ... Singapore Journal of Primary Industries [*A publication*]
Singapore J Trop Geogr ... Singapore Journal of Tropical Geography [*A publication*]
Singapore Lib ... Singapore Libraries [*A publication*]
Singapore L Rev ... Singapore Law Review [*A publication*]
Singapore Med J ... Singapore Medical Journal [*A publication*]
Singapore MJ ... Singapore Medical Journal [*A publication*]
Singapore Nat Acad Sci J ... Singapore National Academy of Science. Journal [*A publication*]
Singapore Natl Inst Chem Bull ... Singapore National Institute of Chemistry. Bulletin [*A publication*]
Singapore Statist Bull ... Singapore Statistical Bulletin [*A publication*]
Singer........ Singer Co. NV [*Associated Press abbreviation*] (APAG)
Singer Prob Cas (PA) ... Singer's Probate Cases [*Pennsylvania*] [*A publication*] (DLA)
Singers .... Singer's Probate Court [*Pennsylvania*] [*A publication*] (DLA)
Sing Kir..... Singende Kirche [*A publication*]
Single Cryst Prop ... Single Crystal Properties [*A publication*]
Sing LR...... Singapore Law Review [*A publication*]
Sing Med J ... Singapore Medical Journal [*A publication*]
Sing Pub Health B ... Singapore Public Health Bulletin [*A publication*]
SINGR....... Singular
Sing Shipbuild Rep Dir ... Singapore Shipbuilding and Repairing Directory [*A publication*]
Sing Stat B ... Singapore Statistical Bulletin [*A publication*]
Sing YB...... Singapore Year Book [*A publication*]
SINH........ Sine, Hyperbolic
SINIE .... Sistema Nacional de Informacion Documental en Educacion [*National System of Documentary Information on Education*] [*Information service or system*] (IID)
SINIST...... Sinister [*Left*] [*Latin*]
Sinister....... Sinister Wisdom [*A publication*]
Sink........... Single Income, No Kids [*Lifestyle classification*]
Sin N......... Sin Nombre [*A publication*]
SIN Newsl ... SIN [*Schweizerisches Institut fuer Nuklearforschung*] Newsletter [*A publication*]
SIno........... Thioinosine [*Also, Sno, M*] [*A nucleoside*]
Sino-Am Rels ... Sino-American Relations [*Taiwan*] [*A publication*]
Si Non Val ... Si Non Valeat [*If It Is Not Effective*] [*Pharmacy*]
Sinop Odontol ... Sinopse de Odontologia [*A publication*]
SINR......... Shoulder Internal Rotation [*Sports medicine*]
SINR......... Signal to Interference plus Noise Ratio (MCD)
SINR......... Swiss Institute for Nuclear Research
SINS .... Satellite Interceptor Navigation System [*Navy*] (CAAL)
SINS .... Ship Inertial Navigational System
SINS .... Sindacato Scuola non Statale [*Union of Private Schools' Employees*] [*Italy*]
SInstBB ..... Student of the Institute of British Bakers (DBQ)
SInstPet..... Student of the Institute of Petroleum [*British*] (DBQ)
SINSU .... Skrifter Utgivna. Institutionen foer Nordiska Sprak Vid. Uppsala Universitet [*A publication*]
SINSUU.... Skrifter Utgivna. Institutionen foer Nordiska Sprak Vid. Uppsala Universitet [*A publication*]

S INT........ Senza Interruzione [*Without Interruption or Pause*] [*Music*]
Sint Almazy ... Sinteticheskie Almazy [*A publication*]
Sint Anal Strukt Org Soedin ... Sintez, Analiz, i Struktura Organicheskikh Soedinenii [*Former USSR*] [*A publication*]
S INTER.... Senza Interruzione [*Without Interruption or Pause*] [*Music*] (ROG)
Sintesi Econ ... Sintesi Economica [*A publication*]
Sint Fiz-Khim Polim ... Sintez i Fiziko-Khimiya Polimerov [*A publication*]
Sint Org Soedin ... Sintezy Organicheskikh Soedinenij [*A publication*]
SI N VAL... Si Non Valeat [*If It Is Not Effective*] [*Pharmacy*] (ROG)
SIO .... Sacroiliac Orthosis [*Medicine*]
SIO .... Scripps Institution of Oceanography [*La Jolla, CA*] [*Research center*]
SIO .... Senior Information Officer (DCTA)
SIO .... Senior Instructor Operator [*Military*] (INF)
SIO .... Senior Intelligence Officer (MCD)
SIO .... Serial Input/Output (MCD)
SIO .... Ship's Information Officer [*Navy*]
SIO .... Simultaneous Interface Operation [*Printer technology*] [*Data processing*] (PCM)
SIO .... Sindacato Italiano Ostetriche [*Italian Union of Midwives*]
sio .... Siouan [*MARC language code*] [*Library of Congress*] (LCCP)
SIO .... Skidway Institute of Oceanography [*Georgia*] (NOAA)
SIO .... Smithton [*Australia*] [*Airport symbol*] (OAG)
SIO .... Sorting It Out (EA)
SIO .... Southern Union Resources [*Vancouver Stock Exchange symbol*]
SIO .... Special Inquiry Officer
SIO .... Special Intelligence Officer [*Military*] (NVT)
SIO .... Staged in Orbit
SIO .... Standard Input/Output (MCD)
SIO .... Start Input/Output
SIO .... Systems Integration Office [*NASA*] (NASA)
SIOA......... System Input/Output Adapter (CAAL)
SIOATH... Source Identification and Ordering Authorization [*DoD*]
SIOC......... Serial Input/Output Channel
SIOD .... Sindacato Italiano Odonototecnici Diplomati [*Italian Union of Odontotechnicians*]
SIOE......... Special Issue of Equipment
SIOFC ...... Sparks International Official Fan Club (EA)
SIOG .... Societe Internationale d'Ophtalmologie Geographique [*International Society of Geographic Opthalmology*] (EAIO)
SIOH .... Supervision, Inspection, and Overhead (AFM)
SIOMS ...... Surface Ionization Organic Mass Spectrometry
SIOP......... Secure Identification Operating Procedure
SIOP......... Selector Input/Output Processor [*Data processing*] (IEEE)
SIOP......... Single Integrated Operational [*or Operations*] Plan [*Military*] (AFM)
SIOP......... Societe Internationale d'Oncologie Pediatrique [*International Society of Pediatric Oncology*] [*Leeds, England*] (EAIO)
SIOP......... Strategic Integrated Operational Plan [*Nuclear warfare*]
SIOP-ESI.. Single Integrated Operational Plan - Extremely Sensitive Information [*Security level above Top Secret*]
SI OP SIT ... Si Opus Sit [*If There Be Occasion*] [*Pharmacy*] (ROG)
SIOR......... Society of Industrial and Office Realtors (EA)
SIOS......... Spectrophotometer Input-Output System
SIOSA ...... Sicula Oceanicas SA [*Shipping line*] [*Italy*] (EY)
SIOUX..... Sequential and Iterative Operation Unit X (IEEE)
SIP........... Safety Injection Pump (IEEE)
SIP........... Safety Instrumentation Package (MCD)
SIP........... Sampling Inspection Procedures
SIP........... Saskatchewan Institute of Pedology [*University of Saskatchewan*] [*Research center*] (RCD)
SIP........... Satellite Information Processor
SIP........... Satellite Inspector Program (AAG)
SIP........... SCANS [*Scheduling and Control by Automated Network Systems*] Implementation Plan (SAA)
SIP........... Schedule-Induced Polydipsia [*Psychology*]
SIP........... Schedule of Investment Projects
SIP........... Scientific Information [*or Instruction*] Processor [*Honeywell, Inc.*]
SIP........... Scientific Instrument Package [*NASA*] (KSC)
SIP........... Seat Index Point [*Automotive design*]
SIP........... Securities Investor Protection Corp.
SIP........... Selma [*Alabama*] Interreligious Project (EA)
SIP........... Senior Intensified Program [*Education*]
SIP........... Separation Instrument Package [*NASA*] (MCD)
SIP........... Sharebuilder Investment Plan [*Banking*]
SIP........... Sheet Metal Insert Process
SIP........... Shinkiari [*Pakistan*] [*Seismograph station code, US Geological Survey*] (SEIS)
SIP........... Ship Improvement Program
SIP........... Ship in Production
SIP........... Short Interval Plan [*Management principles*]
SIP........... Short Irregular Pulses
SIP........... Sickness Impact Profile [*National Institutes of Health*]
SIP........... Side Impact Protection [*Automotive safety system*] (PS)
SIP........... Simferopol [*Former USSR*] [*Airport symbol*] (OAG)
SIP........... Simulated Input Processor [*Data processing*]
SIP........... Sindacato Italiano Pescatori [*Italian Union of Fishermen*]

SIP .... Single In-Line Package [*Data processing*]
SIP .... Single In-Line PIN [*Data processing*]   (PCM)
SIP .... Sipald Resources [*Vancouver Stock Exchange symbol*]
Sip .... Sipario [*A publication*]
SIP .... Skill Improvement Program [*Bureau of Apprenticeship and Training*] [*Department of Labor*]
SIP .... Slow Inhibitory Potential [*Electrophysiology*]
SIP .... Small Interplanetary Probes   (SAA)
SIP .... Smithsonian Institution Press [*Publisher*]
SIP .... Sociedad Interamericana de Prensa [*Inter-American Press Association*]
SIP .... Sociedad Interamericana de Psicologia [*Interamerican Society of Psychology*]   (EAIO)
SIP .... Societa Italiana per l'Esercizio Telefonico [*Italian Society for Telephone Use*] [*Information service or system*]   (IID)
SIP .... Society of Indiana Pioneers   (EA)
SIP .... Society for Invertebrate Pathology   (EA)
SIP .... Society of Israel Philatelists   (EA)
SIP .... Sodium Iron Pyrophosphate [*Inorganic chemistry*]
SIP .... Software Instrumentation Package [*Sperry UNIVAC*] [*Data processing*]
SIP .... Software in Print [*Technique Learning*] [*Information service or system*]   (IID)
SIP .... Solar Instrument Probe   (MUGU)
SIP .... Solar and Interplanetary Programme [*International Council of Scientific Unions*]
SIP .... SPALT [*Special Projects Alterations*] Improvement Program
SIP .... Special Impact Program   (OICC)
SIP .... Standard Initial Provisioning System   (MCD)
SIP .... Standard Inspection Procedure [*Military*]
SIP .... Standard Interest Profile
SIP .... Standardization Instructor Pilot [*Military*]   (AABC)
SIP .... State Implementation Plan [*Environmental Protection Agency*]
SIP .... Step in Place
SIP .... Strain Isolator Pad [*Aerospace*]
SIP .... Strategic Information Plan   (SSD)
SIP .... Strongly Implicit Procedure
SIP .... Student Insurance Producers Association   (EA)
SIP .... Studies in Process [*Jet Propulsion Laboratory, NASA*]
SIP .... Subject Index to Periodicals [*A publication*]
SIP .... Submerged Injection Process [*Steelmaking*]
SIP .... Supermolecular Information Processor
SIP .... Supersonic Infantry Projectile
SIP .... Supplemental Income Plan
SIP .... Supply Improvement Program
SIP .... Svensk-Internationella Pressbyran [*Swedish-International Press Bureau*]   (EY)
SIP .... Symbolic Input Program [*Data processing*]   (BUR)
SIP .... System Improvement Plan   (INF)
SIP .... Systems Implementation Plan [*Military*]
SIPA .... Secondary Item Procurement Appropriation [*Army*]
SIPA .... Securities Investor Protection Act [*1970*]
SIPAAP ..... Escuela Nacional de Agricultura [*Chapingo*]. Serie de Investigaciones [*A publication*]
SIPAMA ... Servico de Inspecao dos Produtos Agropecuarios e Materiais Agricolas [*Brazil*]
SIPB .... Safety Injection Permissive Block   (IEEE)
SIPC .... Securities Investor Protection Corp. [*Government insurance agency for brok erage accounts*] [*Pronounced "sipic"*]
SIPC .... Stationing and Installations Planning Committee [*Military*]
SIPCO ...... Signal Processor Checkout   (CAAL)
SIPD .... Supply Item Provisioning Document [*Navy*]   (NG)
SIPDE ...... Sensing, Identifying, Predicting, Deciding, and Executing
SIPE .... Scientific Information Program on Eutrophication [*University of Wisconsin*]
SIPE .... Societe Internationale de Psychopathologie de l'Expression [*International Society of Art and Psychopathology*]
SIPE .... Soldier-Integrated Protective Ensemble [*Army*]   (INF)
SIPES ...... Society of Independent Professional Earth Scientists   (EA)
SIPG .... Societe Internationale de Pathologie Geographique [*International Society of Geographical Pathology*] [*Australia*]   (EAIO)
SIPG .... Special Intercept Priorities Group [*Armed Forces Security Agency*]
SIPI .... Scientists' Institute for Public Information   (EA)
SIPI .... Short Imaginal Process Inventory [*Personality development test*] [*Psychology*]
SIPI .... Sisterhood Is Powerful Institute   (EA)
SIPI .... Southwestern Indian Polytechnic Institute [*New Mexico*]
SIPI .... Supervisory Immigration Patrol Inspector [*Immigration and Naturalization Service*]
SIPL .... Seeley's Illustrated Pocket Library [*A publication*]
SIPL .... Studies in Philippine Linguistics [*A publication*]
SIPM .... Star Identification Program, Mariner [*NASA*]
SIPN .... Security Industry and Product News [*A publication*]
SIPN .... Semi-Interpenetrating Polymer Network [*Organic chemistry*]
SIPO .... Serial-In, Parallel-Out [*Telecommunications*]   (TEL)
SIPO .... Sicherheitspolizei [*Security Police*] [*NAZI*]   (BJA)
SIPO .... Soobshcheniia Imperatorskovo Pravoslavnovo Palestinskovo Obshchestva [*A publication*]
SIPO .... Spacecraft Integration Project Office

SIPO .... Swiss Intellectual Property Office [*Bern*] [*Information service or system*]   (IID)
SIPOA ...... Servico de Inspecao de Produtos de Origem Animal [*Brazil*]
SIPOP ...... Satellite Information Processor Operational Program   (AFM)
SIPOS ...... Semi-Insulating Polycrystalline Silicon [*Photovoltaic energy systems*]
SIPP .... Sodium Iron Pyrophosphate [*Organic chemistry*]
SIPP .... Standard Interline Passenger Procedures Manual [*Air Traffic Conference of America*] [*IATA*]   (DS)
SIPP .... Survey on Income and Program Participation [*Census Bureau, Department of Health and Human Services*]
SIPP .... System Information Processing Program   (MCD)
SIPPAP ..... Survey of Income and Program Participation Awareness Program [*Bureau of the Census*]   (GFGA)
SIPPS ...... System of Information Processing for Professional Societies
Sippy .... Senior Independent Pioneer [*Lifestyle classification*]
SIPR .... Special In-Process Review   (MCD)
SIPRA ...... Societa Italiana Pubblicita Per Azioni [*Italian radio and television advertising company*]
SIPRE ...... Snow, Ice, and Permafrost Research Establishment
SIPRI .... Stockholm International Peace Research Institute [*Solna, Sweden*]   (EAIO)
SIPROS ..... Simultaneous Processing Operation System [*Control Data Corp.*] [*Data processing*]
SIPS .... Shipbuilding Industries Pension Scheme [*British*]
SIPS .... Simulated Input Preparation System   (IEEE)
SIPS .... Small Instrument Pointing System   (MCD)
SIPS .... Societa Internazionale di Psicologia della Scrittura [*International Society of Psychology of Handwriting - ISPH*]   (EAIO)
SIPS .... Societe Internationale de Psychologie des Sports [*International Society of Sports Psychology*]   (EAIO)
SIPS .... Spartan Improved Performance Study [*Missiles*]   (AABC)
SIPS .... Sputter-Induced Photon Spectroscopy   (MCD)
SIPS .... State Implementation Plan System [*Environmental Protection Agency*]
SIPS .... Statistical Interactive Programming System
SIPSDE ..... Society of Independent and Private School Data Education [*Later, SDE*]   (EA)
SIPT .... Sensory Integration and Praxis Test [*Occupational therapy*]
SIPT .... Simulating Part   (AAG)
SIPTH ...... Serum Immunoreactive Parathyroid Hormone [*Endocrinology*]
SIPU .... Selective Inactivation Photodynamic Unit
SIQ .... Sick in Quarters
SIQ .... Social Intelligence Quotient [*In book title*]
SIQ .... Student Interests Quarterly [*A publication*]
SIQR .... Studies: An Irish Quarterly Review of Letters, Philosophy, and Science [*A publication*]
SIR .... Safari International Resources [*Vancouver Stock Exchange symbol*]
SIR .... Safe Integral Reactor [*Nuclear energy*]
SIR .... Safeguards Implementation Report [*Nuclear energy*]   (NRCH)
SIR .... Scientific Information Retrieval, Inc. [*Database management system*] [*Information service or system*]   (IID)
SIR .... Search, Inspection, and Recovery   (NVT)
SIR .... Secondary-Image-Registration [*Photography*]
SIR .... Segment Identification Register
SIR .... Selected Item Reporting
SIR .... Selected Item Review   (MCD)
SIR .... Selective Information Retrieval [*Data processing*]
SIR .... Selective Ion Recording [*Spectrometry*]
SIR .... Self-Indication Ratio
SIR .... Self-Insured Retention [*Insurance*]
SIR .... Semantic Information Retrieval [*Massachusetts Institute of Technology*] [*Data processing*]   (DIT)
SIR .... Semiannual Inventory Report [*Navy*]   (NVT)
SIR .... Serious Incident Report [*Military*]   (AFM)
SIR .... Serum Inducible Repeat [*Genetics*]
SIR .... Service International de Recherches [*International Tracing Service*] [*Red Cross*]
SIR .... Set Indicators of the Right Half   (SAA)
SIR .... Shipboard Intercept Receiver [*Navy*]
SIR .... Shuttle Imaging RADAR [*of earth's surface*] [*NASA*]
SIR .... Signal-to-Interference Ratio
SIR .... Silo Installation Refurbish   (SAA)
SIR .... Simultaneous Impact Rate   (AFM)
SIR .... Sinclair, WY [*Location identifier*] [*FAA*]   (FAAL)
SIR .... Single Imaging RADAR
SIR .... Single Isomorphous Replacement [*Crystallography*]
SIR .... Single Item Release
SIR .... Single Item Removal [*Maintenance*]
SIR .... Sion [*Switzerland*] [*Airport symbol*]
Sir .... Sirach [*Old Testament book*] [*Roman Catholic canon*]
SIR .... Siria [*Venezuela*] [*Seismograph station code, US Geological Survey*]   (SEIS)
Sir .... Sirius [*Record label*] [*Sweden*]
SIR .... Size Up, Interview, Rate [*Mnemonic used by Responsible Beverage Service in its bartender training program*]
SIR .... Small Intestine Rinse [*Physiology*]
SIR .... Snow and Ice on Runways [*Aviation*]   (FAAC)
SIR .... Societa Italiana Resine [*Italy*]

SIR............ Societe Rorschach Internationale [*International Rorschach Society*] [*Originally, Societe Internationale du Test de Rorschach et Autres Methodes Projectives*]

SIR............ Society for Individual Responsibility [*Defunct*] (EA)

SIR............ Society of Industrial Realtors [*Association name and designation awarded by this group*] [*Washington, DC*] (EA)

SIR............ Society of Insurance Research [*Appleton, WI*] (EA)

SIR............ Software Incident Report (MCD)

SIR............ Software Initiated Restart (NASA)

SIR............ Sound Isolation Room

SIR............ Spaceborne Imaging RADAR

SIR............ Special Information Retrieval

SIR............ Special Inspection Requirement

SIR............ Special Investigative Requirement (AFM)

SIR............ Specific Insulation Resistance

SIR............ Specification Information Retrieval System [*Data processing*] (MCD)

SIR............ Stable Isotopes Resource

SIR............ Standarization, Interoperability, and Readiness [*NATO*] (MCD)

SIR............ Staten Island Rapid Transit Railway Co. [*Later, SIRC*] [*AAR code*]

SIR............ Statistical Information Retrieval

SIR............ Statutory Invention Registration [*Patents*]

SIR............ Stratified Indexing and Retrieval [*Japan*] [*Data processing*]

SIR............ Struthers Industries [*AMEX symbol*] (SPSG)

SIR............ Student Instructional Report [*Test of teacher performance*]

SIR............ Studies in Romanticism [*A publication*]

SIR............ Styrene-Isoprene Rubber

SIR............ Subcontractor Information Request

SIR............ Submarine Intermediate Reactor [*Nuclear energy*]

SIR............ Subsurface Interface RADAR [*A trademark*]

SIR............ Supersonic Infantry Rocket

SIR............ Suppliers Information Request

SIR............ Symbolic Input Routine [*Data processing*] (DIT)

SIR............ Synthetic-Aperture Imaging RADAR [*System*]

SIR............ System Initialization Routine

SIR............ System Integration Receiver [*System*]

SIR............ System Interface Requirements (NASA)

SIR............ Systems Integration Review [*NASA*] (NASA)

SIRA......... Safety Investigation Regulations (IEEE)

SIRA......... Scientific Instrument Research Association [*British*]

SIRA......... Social Issues Research Associates (EA)

SIRA......... Sports Industries Representatives Association (EA)

SIRA......... Stable Isotope Ratio Analysis

SIRA......... Strapdown Inertial Reference Assembly (MCD)

SIRA......... Strategic Intelligence Research and Analysis

SIRA......... System for Instructional Response Analysis

SIRA Abstr Rev ... SIRA Abstracts and Reviews [*A publication*]

Sirag......... Sirag. Amsagir Grakanut ean ew Aruesdi [*A publication*]

SIRAP....... System of Information Retrieval and Analysis, Planning [*Army*] [*Information service or system*] (IID)

SIRAS....... Single Isomorphous Replacement, Anomalous Scattering [*Crystallography*]

SIRB......... Sintered Iron Rotating Band

SIRC......... Science Information Resource Center [*Harper & Row*] [*Information service or system*]

SIRC......... Sirco International Corp. [*NASDAQ symbol*] (NQ)

SIRC......... Socialist International Research Council [*British*]

SIRC......... Spares Integrated Reporting and Control [*System*]

SIRC......... Sport Information Resource Centre [*Coaching Association of Canada*] [*Database*] (IID)

SIRC......... [*The*] Staten Island Railroad Corp. [*AAR code*]

SIRC......... Styrene Information and Research Center (EA)

SIR(CICR) ... Service International de Recherches (du Comite International de la Croix-Rouge) [*International Tracing Service of the International Committee of the Red Cross*]

SIRCS....... Shipboard Intermediate Range Combat System [*Navy*]

SIRCULS.. San Bernardino-Inyo-Riverside Counties United Library Services [*Library network*]

SIRCUS..... Standard Information Retrieval Capability for Users [*Army*]

SIRD......... Shore-Based Interfare Requirement Date

SIRD......... Support Instrumentation Requirements Document [*NASA*]

SIRE......... Satellite Infrared Experiment (MCD)

SIRE......... Society for the Investigation of Recurring Events (EA)

SIREA....... SIAM [*Society for Industrial and Applied Mathematics*] Review [*A publication*]

SIREN....... Sanders Intact Reentry Encapsulation (MCD)

SIREN....... SIGSEC Resources and Equipment Needs (MCD)

SIREWS.... Shipboard Infrared Electronic Warfare System

SIRF......... System Information Reports Formatting (MCD)

SIRI.......... Societe Internationale pour la Readaptation des Invalides

SIRIC........ Soybean Insect Research Information Center [*University of Illinois*] [*Champaign, IL*]

SIRIN .... Single Readiness Information System [*NORRS*]

Siriraj Hosp Gaz ... Siriraj Hospital Gazette [*A publication*]

SIRIS........ Sputter-Initiated Resonance Ionization Spectrometry

SIRIS........ Sylloge Inscriptionum Religionis Isiacae et Sarapiacae [*A publication*] (BJA)

SIRIVS...... Spaceborne Intensified Radiometer for Imaging Vetroviolet Spectroscopy (MCD)

Sir JS......... [*Sir John*] Strange's English Reports [*A publication*] (DLA)

SIRL......... Site Installation Requirements List (AAG)

SIRL......... Support Item Requirement List (MCD)

SIRLEJ ..... Societe Internationale de Recherche en Litterature d'Enfance et de Jeunesse [*International Research Society for Children's Literature - IRSCL*] (EA)

Sir L Jenk .. Wynne's Life of Sir Leoline Jenkins [*1724*] [*A publication*] (DLA)

SIRLS....... Information Retrieval System for the Sociology of Leisure and Sport [*University of Waterloo*] [*Information service or system*] (IID)

SIRLS....... Southwest Idaho Regional Library System [*Library network*]

SIRLS....... Specialized Information Retrieval and Library Services (IID)

SIRM........ Saturation Isothermal Remanent Magnetization [*Paleomagnetics*]

SIRM........ Societe Internationale Robert Musil [*International Robert Musil Society - IRMS*] [*Saarbrucken, Federal Republic of Germany*] (EAIO)

SIRM........ Sterile Insect Release Method

SIRMA ...... Small Independent Record Manufacturers Association [*Stanford, CT*] (EA)

SIRMCE.... Societe Internationale pour la Recherche sur les Maladies de Civilisation et l'Environment [*International Society for Research on Civilization Diseases and Environment*] [*Brussels, Belgium*] (EAIO)

SIRMS....... Stable Isotope Ratio Mass Spectrometer [*or Spectrometry*]

SIROS ...... Specialized Operating System (DNAB)

SIROW...... Southwest Institute for Research on Women [*University of Arizona*] [*Research center*] (RCD)

Sirpur Ind J ... Sirpur Industries Journal [*A publication*]

SIRR......... Section on Individual Rights and Responsibilities (EA)

SIRR......... Small Integral Rocket/Ramjet (MCD)

SIRR......... Software Integration Readiness Review [*NASA*] (NASA)

SIRR......... Southern Industrial Railroad, Inc. [*AAR code*]

SIRRBJ ..... Institutionen foer Skogsforyngring Rapporter och Uppsatser [*A publication*]

SIRS .... Salary Information Retrieval System (IEEE)

SIRS .... Satellite Infrared Spectrometer [*NASA*]

SIRS .... Scheduled Issue Release System

SIRS .... Ship Installed RADIAC [*Radiation Detection, Indication, and Computation*] System (NATG)

SIRS .... Skills Inventory Retrieval System (MCD)

SIRS .... Small Independent Radio Stations [*An association*] [*British*]

SIRS .... Social Issues Resources Series [*A publication*]

SIRS .... Soils Information Retrieval Systems [*Database*] [*Army Corps of Engineers*]

SIRS .... Soluble Immune Response Suppressor [*Immunology*]

SIRS .... Special Issue Rating System [*Veterans Administration*]

SIRS .... Specification, Instrumentation, and Range Safety

SIRS .... Statewide Individual Referral System (OICC)

SIRS .... Student Information Record System (AEBS)

SIRS .... Supplemental Inflatable Restraint System [*Automotive engineering*]

SIRS .... System Integration Receiver System (MCD)

SIRSA....... Special Industrial Radio Service Association (EA)

SIRT......... Signaling Information Receiver/Transmitter (MCD)

SIRT......... Staten Island Rapid Transit Railway Co. [*Later, SIRC*]

SIRTF....... Space [*formerly, Shuttle*] Infrared Telescope Facility [*NASA*]

Sir TJ......... [*Sir Thomas*] Jones' English King's Bench and Common Pleas Reports [*A publication*] (DLA)

Sir T Ray.... Sir T. Raymond's English King's Bench Reports [*A publication*] (DLA)

SIRU......... Strapdown Inertial Reference Unit [*Navigation*]

SIRVES ..... SIGINT [*Signal Intelligence*] Requirements Validation and Evaluation Subcommittee

SIRW........ Safety Injection and Refueling Water [*Nuclear energy*] (NRCH)

SIRWT ...... Safety Injection and Refueling Water Tank [*Nuclear energy*] (NRCH)

SIRWT ...... Safety Injection Reserve Water Tank (IEEE)

SIS .... Canadian Security and Intelligence Service [*UTLAS symbol*]

SIS .... Naval Intelligence Service [*Italy*]

SIS .... Safety Information System [*Department of Transportation*]

SIS .... Safety Injection System [*Nuclear energy*] (NRCH)

SIS .... SAGE [*Semiautomatic Ground Environment*] Interceptor Simulator

SIS .... SAIL [*Shuttle Avionics Integration Laboratory*] Interface System [*NASA*] (NASA)

SIS .... Satellite Infrared Spectrometer [*NASA*]

SIS .... Satellite Interceptor System [*Military*] (AFM)

SIS .... Savage Information Services (IID)

SIS .... Scale for the Identification of School Phobia [*Test*]

SIS .... Scanning Image Spectrometer

SIS .... Science Information Service (EA)

SIS .... Science Information Services [*Franklin Institute*]

SIS .... Scientific Instruction Set

SIS .... Scientific Instrument Society (EA)

SIS .... Scotch-Irish Society of the United States of America (EA)

SIS .... Screening/Inspection System (DNAB)

SIs............. Scripta Islandica [*A publication*]

SIS	Secondary Injection System
SIS	Secret Intelligence Service [*British*]
SIS	Secretarial Information System (EPA)
SIS	Semiautomatic Imagery Screening Subsystem (MCD)
SIS	Semiconductor-Insulator-Semiconductor
SIS	Seminar Information Service Database [*Seminar Information Service, Inc.*] [*Information service or system*] (CRD)
SIS	Senior Intelligence Service [*CIA personnel*]
SIS	Sensor Image Simulator (MCD)
SIS	Sensor Integration System (DWSG)
SIS	Serial Input System (MCD)
SIS	Serving the Indigent Sick
SIS	Share Information Service [*British*] (DCTA)
SIS	Shared Information Service (CMD)
SIS	Shipping Instruction Sheet
SIS	Shock-Isolation Support
SIS	Shock-Isolation System
SIS	Short Interval Scheduling [*Quality control*]
SIS	Shut-In Society
SIS	Shuttle Information System [*NASA*] (MCD)
SIS	Shuttle Interface Simulator [*NASA*] (NASA)
SIS	Signal Intelligence Service [*Later, Army Security Agency*]
SIS	Signaling Interworking Subsystem [*Telecommunications*] (TEL)
SIS	Significant Indications Summary
SIS	Silicon of Insulating Substrate (MCD)
SIS	Silkridge Resources [*Vancouver Stock Exchange symbol*]
SIS	Simian Sarcoma Virus [*Oncology*]
SIS	Simulation Interface Subsystem (KSC)
SIS	Single Item Squawk Sheet
SIS	Singles in Service (EA)
SISES	Sino-Indian Studies [*A publication*]
SIS	Sion [*Switzerland*] [*Seismograph station code, US Geological Survey*] [*Closed*] (SEIS)
SIS	Sishen [*South Africa*] [*Airport symbol*] (OAG)
SIS	Sister
SIS	Societa Internazionale Scotista [*International Scotist Society - ISS*] (EAIO)
SIS	Society of International Secretaries
SISIR	Society for Iranian Studies (EA)
SIS	Software Implementation Specifications [*NASA*] (NASA)
SIS	Software Integrated Schedule [*NASA*] (NASA)
SIS	Somatic Inkblot Series [*Personality development test*] [*Psychology*]
SIS	Soviet Intelligence Services
SIS	Space and Information System
SIS	SPALT [*Special Projects Alterations*] Information Shut
SIS	SPALT [*Special Projects Alterations*] Information System
SIS	Spark Ignition System
SIS	Speaker Intercom System (KSC)
SIS	Special Industrial Services [*United Nations Industrial Development Organization*]
SIS	Special Information System (MCD)
SIS	Special Intelligence Service
SISR	Special Interest Sessions
SIS	Special Isotope Separation [*Physics*]
SIS	Specification Information System
SIS	Spectral Imaging Sensor
SIS	Spectral Index of Sample [*Experimentation*]
SIS	Spuria Iris Society (EA)
SIS	Stage Interface Substitute
SIS	Stall Inhibitor System [*Aviation*] (GFGA)
SIS	Stand-Alone Information System [*National Library of Medicine*]
SIS	Standard Indexing System [*DoD*]
SIS	Standard Instruction Set (MSA)
SIS	Standard Interface Specification [*NASA*] (GFGA)
SIS	Standards Information Service [*Standards Council of Canada*] [*Information service or system*] (IID)
SIS	Standards Information Service [*National Institute of Standards and Technology*] (IID)
SIS	Station Identification Store [*Bell Laboratories*]
SIS	Stator Interstage Seal
SIS	STEP [*Scientific and Technical Exploitation Program*] Information Subsystem
SIS	Sterile Injectable Suspension
SIS	Strategic Intelligence School [*Military*]
SIS	Strategic Intelligence Summary [*Military*] (NATG)
SIS	Strategic Intelligence Systems, Inc. [*Also, an information service or system*] (IID)
SIS	Streamlined Inspection System [*USDA meat standards*]
SIS	Student Instruction Sheet [*Military*]
SIS	Student International Service [*Foundation*]
SIS	Styrene-Isoprene-Styrene [*Organic chemistry*]
SIS	Submarine Integrated SONAR
SIS	Superconductivity Information System [*Department of Energy*] [*Information service or system*] (IID)
SIS	Superconductor-Insulator-Superconductor [*Transistor technology*]
SIS	Supervisory Inventory on Safety [*Test*]
SIS	Supplier Identification System [*London Enterprise Agency*] [*Information service or system*] (IID)
SIS	Supply Item Status
SIS	Surgical Infection Society (EA)
S & IS	Survey and Investigation Staff [*Navy*] (NVT)
SIS	Sveriges Standardiseringskommission [*Swedish Standards Institution*] [*Also, an information service or system*] (IID)
SIS	Swedish Standards Institution (IID)
SIS	Synchronous Identification System (MCD)
SIS	System Integration Schedule [*NASA*] (NASA)
SIS	System Integration Support
SIS	System Interrupt Supervisor
SISAC	Serials Industry Systems Advisory Committee [*Book Industry Study Group*] [*Information service or system*] (IID)
Sisal Rev	Sisal Review [*A publication*]
SISAM	Spectrometer with Interference Selective Amplitude Modulation [*Physics*]
SI/SAO......	Special Intelligence/Special Activities Office (MCD)
SISB..........	SIS Corp. [*NASDAQ symbol*] (NQ)
SISC	Single Screw
SISC	Statewide Information Steering Committee [*California*]
SISC	Stewart Information Services Corp. [*NASDAQ symbol*] (NQ)
SISCIS......	Subject Index to Sources of Comparative International Statistics [*A publication*]
SISCO	Special Inter-Departmental Selection Committee [*UN Food and Agriculture Organization*]
SISCON	Science in Social Context
SISD	Scientific Information Systems Department [*Information service or system*] (IID)
SISD	Single Instruction, Single Data (IEEE)
SISEX.......	Shuttle Imaging Spectrometer Experiment [*NASA*]
SISH	Societe Internationale de la Science Horticole [*International Society for Horticultural Science - ISHS*] (EAIO)
SISI...........	Short Increment Sensitivity Index [*Medicine*]
SISI...........	Surveillance and In-Service Inspection [*Nuclear energy*] (NRCH)
SI-SIC.......	Siliconized Silicon Carbide (SAA)
SISIMS	Say It So It Makes Sense [*A publication*]
SISIR	Singapore Institute of Standards and Industrial Research
SISKY.......	Siskiyou [*FAA*] (FAAC)
S Isl...........	Sandwich Islands
SISL..........	Sons of Italy Supreme Lodge (EA)
SISMS.......	Standard Integrated Support Management System [*Joint Chiefs of Staff*]
SISO	Science Information Services Organization [*Franklin Institute*] (IID)
Si & So	Sight and Sound [*A publication*]
SISO	Single-Input, Single-Output [*Process engineering*]
SISOR	Supply Item Status Order Reporting [*Army*]
SISORS	Supply Item Status and Order Reporting System
SISP..........	Sudden Increase of Solar Particles
SISP..........	Surface Imaging and Sounding Package
SISPA.......	Sequence-Independent Single Primer Amplification [*Genetics*]
SISR	Selected Items Status Report [*Army*] (AABC)
SISRBO.....	Institutionen foer Skogszoologi Rapporter och Uppsatser [*A publication*]
SISS..........	Second International Science Study [*International Association for the Evaluation of Educational Achievement*]
SISS..........	Semiconductor-Insulator-Semiconductor System
SISS..........	Sensory Integration Special Interest Section [*American Occupational Therapy Association*]
SIS-S.........	SENTRY [*Survey Entry*] Interceptor System Simulator
SISS..........	Single Item, Single Source (IEEE)
SISS..........	Societe Internationale de la Science du Sol
SISS..........	Sources of Information on Social Security [*British*]
SISS..........	Standoff Imaging Sensor System (MCD)
SISS..........	Submarine Integrated SONAR System
SISS..........	Synchronous Identification System Study
SISS..........	System Integration Support Service
SISSC	Special Interest Sections Steering Committee [*American Occupational Therapy Association*]
SIST..........	Self-Inflating Surface Target
SIST..........	Sentence Imitation Screening Test [*Speech and language test*]
SIST..........	Sister
Sist e Autom ...	Sistemi e Automazione [*A publication*]
Sist Avtom Nauchn Issled ...	Sistemy Avtomatisatsii Nauchnykh Issledovanii [*A publication*]
Sistem Metod Sovrem Nauka ...	Sistemnyj Metod i Sovremennaja Nauka [*A publication*]
SISTER	Special Institution for Scientific and Technological Education and Research [*In proposal stage, 1964, in Great Britain*]
Sisters	Sisters Today [*A publication*]
SISTM.......	Simulation by Incremental Stochastic Transition Matrices (MCD)
SISTMS	Standard Integrated Supply/Transportation Manifest System [*Military*] (AABC)
Sist Nerv	Sistema Nervoso [*A publication*]
SISTRAN ...	System for Information Storage and Retrieval and Analysis
SISUL........	Serials in Swaziland University Libraries [*A publication*]
SISUSA	Scotch-Irish Society of the United States of America (EA)

SiSV.......... Simian Sarcoma Virus [*Also, SSV*]
SISWG ...... STS [*Shuttle Test Station*] Integrated Schedule Working Group [*NASA*]   (GFGA)
SISWP....... Soroptimist International of the South West Pacific [*Sydney, NSW, Australia*]   (EAIO)
SIT............ Safety Injection Tank [*Nuclear energy*]   (NRCH)
SIT............ Safety Injection Transmitter [*Nuclear energy*]   (NRCH)
SIT............ Satellite Inspector Target   (MCD)
SIT............ Self-Ignition Temperature
SIT............ Sensory Integration Training
SIT............ Separation-Initiated Timer
SIT............ Sequential Interval Timer
SIT............ Serum Inhibitory Titer [*Clinical chemistry*]
SIT............ Shorr Imagery Test [*Personality development test*] [*Psychology*]
SIT............ Shuttle Integrated Test [*NASA*]   (NASA)
SIT............ Shuttle Interface Test [*NASA*]   (NASA)
SIT............ Silicon Intensifier Target
SIT............ Silicon Intensifier Tube
SIT............ Simulation Input Tape
sit .... Sino-Tibetan [*MARC language code*] [*Library of Congress*]   (LCCP)
SIT............ Sitka [*Alaska*] [*Seismograph station code, US Geological Survey*]   (SEIS)
SIT............ Sitka [*Alaska*] [*Geomagnetic observatory code*]
SIT............ Sitka [*Alaska*] [*Airport symbol*]   (OAG)
SIT............ Sitka, AK [*Location identifier*] [*FAA*]   (FAAL)
SIT............ Situation   (AFM)
SIT............ Slosson Intelligence Test
SIT............ Social Intelligence Test [*Psychology*]
SIT............ Society of Industrial Tutors [*British*]
SIT............ Society of Instrument Technology [*British*]
SIT............ Society of International Treasurers   (EAIO)
SIT............ Software Integrated Test [*NASA*]   (KSC)
SIT............ Space Impact Tool [*NASA*]
SIT............ Spaceborne Infrared Tracker
SIT............ Special Information Tones [*Telecommunications*]
SIT............ Sperm Immobilization Test [*Clinical chemistry*]
SIT............ Spontaneous Ignition Temperature
SIT............ SSV [*Space Shuttle Vehicle*] Integrated Test [*NASA*]   (NASA)
SIT............ Statement of Inventory Transaction [*Military*]
SIT............ Static Induction Transistor [*Telecommunications*]   (TEL)
SIT............ Stevens Institute of Technology [*Hoboken, NJ*]
SIT............ Stop Immorality on Television [*An association*]
SIT............ Stopping in Transit
SIT............ Storage Inspection Test [*Navy*]   (NG)
SIT............ Storage in Transit
SIT............ Structurally Integrated Thruster   (MCD)
SIT............ Sugar Industry Technologists   (EA)
SIT............ System Integration Test
SIT............ Systems Interface Test   (NVT)
SITA .... Sociedade Internacional de Trilogia Analitica [*International Society of Analytical Trilogy - ISAT*] [*Sao Paulo, Brazil*]   (EAIO)
SITA .... Societe Internationale des Telecommunications Aeronautiques [*International Society of Aeronautical Telecommunications*] [*London, England*]
SITA .... Students' International Travel Association
SITA .... System International Tinplate Area
SITAP....... Simulator for Transportation Analysis and Planning   (DNAB)
SITAR ...... Societa Incremento Turismo Aereo [*Italy*]
SITB .... Shipbuilding Industrial Training Board [*British*]
SITC .... Satellite International Television Center [*Telecommunications*]   (TEL)
SITC .... Single Integrated Test Cycle [*Army*]
SITC .... Standard Industrial Trade Classification [*United Nations*]
SITC .... Standard International Trade Classification
SITCA ...... Secretaria de Integracion Turistica Centroamericana
SITCEN .... Situation Center [*NATO*]   (NATG)
SITCOM.... Situation Comedy [*Television*]
Sit-Comm... Situation Commercial [*Advertisement imitating a TV sitcom*]
SITE .... Sample Instruction Test Exercise   (MCD)
SITE .... Satellite Instructional Television Experiment [*NASA/Indian Space Research Organization, 1974*]
SITE .... Sculpture in the Environment [*In Best by SITE, Inc.*]
SITE .... Search Information Tape Equipment
SITE .... Securities-Investment Trust Enterprise
SITE .... Shipboard Information, Training, and Education [*System*] [*Navy*]   (NVT)
SITE .... Situate   (ROG)
SITE .... Snow and Ice Traversing Equipment [*Army*]
SITE .... Society of Incentive Travel Executives [*New York, NY*]   (EA)
SITE .... Society of Insurance Trainers and Educators   (EA)
SITE .... Spacecraft Instrumentation Test Equipment
SITE .... Suction Infusion Tissue Extractor [*Ophthalmology*]
SITE .... Superfund Innovative Technologies Evaluation Program [*Environmental Protection Agency*]
S-ITED...... Superimposed Integrated Trajectory Error [*Aviation*]
SITES....... Smithsonian Institution Traveling Exhibition Service
Site Sel Hdbk ... Site Selection Handbook [*A publication*]

SITI .... Swiss Institute for Technical Information [*Information service or system*]   (IID)
SITIM .... Societe Internationale des Techniques d'Imagerie Mentals [*International Society for Mental Imagery Techniques in Psychotherapy and Psychology*] [*Paris, France*]   (EAIO)
SITK .... Sitka National Monument
SITKA ...... Silikattechnik [*East Germany*] [*A publication*]
SITL .... Southwestern Industrial Traffic League   (EA)
SITLILM .. Subcontractor Interceptor Transporter/Loader Intermediate Level Maintenance Course
SITMAP.... Situation Map   (MCD)
SITN......... Situation   (ROG)
SITO......... Senior Information Technology Officer
SITOR...... Simplex TELEX over Radio
SITP .... Scheduled into Production
SITP .... Shipyard Installation Test Procedure [*or Program*]
SITP .... Site Inspection and Test Procedure [*Nuclear energy*]   (NRCH)
SITP .... System Integration Test Program
SITPB....... Systems Integrated Test Plan [*Military*]   (CAAL)
SITPB....... System Integration Test Program Board
SITPRO..... Simplification of International Trade Procedures [*Committee or Board*] [*British*]
SITRAM ... Societe Ivoirienne de Transport Maritime [*The Ivorian national shipping industry*]
SITREP..... Situation Report
SITS.......... IEEE Social Implications of Technology Society   (EA)
SITS.......... SAGE [*Semiautomatic Ground Environment*] Intercept Target Simulation
SITS.......... Scientists in the Sea Program [*National Oceanic and Atmospheric Administration*]   (MSC)
SITS.......... Secondary Influent Treatment System
SITS.......... Secure Imagery Transmission System [*Military*]   (CAAL)
SITS.......... Societe Internationale de Transfusion Sanguine [*International Society of Blood Transfusion - ISBT*] [*Paris, France*]   (EA)
SITS.......... System Integration Test Service
SITS.......... System Integration Test Site [*Military*]   (CAAL)
SITSUM.... Situation Summary [*Military*]   (NVT)
SITTS........ Small-Inventory Top-Tier Site [*Industrial hazard designation*] [*British*]
SITU .... Society for the Investigation of the Unexplained   (EA)
SITU .... South India Teachers' Union
SITU .... Surgical Intensive Therapy Unit
SITV .... Southbrook International Television Co. Ltd. [*London, England*] [*NASDAQ symbol*]   (NQ)
SITV .... System Integration Test Vehicle
SITVC .... Secondary Injection Thrust Vector Control
Sitz............ Sitzungsberichte [*Proceedings*] [*German*]   (OCD)
Sitzungber Saechs Akad Wiss (Leipzig) Math-Natur Kl ... Sitzungsberichte. Saechsische Akademie der Wissenschaften (Leipzig). Mathematisch-Naturwissenschaftliche Klasse [*A publication*]
Sitzungsber d Akadem d Wiss ... Sitzungsberichte. Akademie der Wissenschaften [*A publication*]
Sitzungsber Akad Wiss DDR Math-Naturwiss-Tech Jahrgang 1977 ... Sitzungsberichte. Akademie der Wissenschaften der DDR. Mathematik-Naturwissenschaften-Technik. Jahrgang 1977 [*A publication*]
Sitzungsber Akad Wiss DDR Math-Naturwiss Tech Jahrgang 1979 ... Sitzungsberichte. Akademie der Wissenschaften der DDR. Mathematik-Naturwissenschaften-Technik. Jahrgang 1979 [*A publication*]
Sitzungsber Bayer Akad Wiss Math-Naturwiss Kl ... Sitzungsberichte. Bayerische Akademie der Wissenschaften. Mathematisch-Naturwissenschaftliche Klasse [*A publication*]
Sitzungsber Berl Ges Naturforsch Freunde ... Sitzungsberichte. Berlinische Gesellschaft Naturforschender Freunde [*A publication*]
Sitzungsber Deut Akad Landwirt Wiss Berlin ... Sitzungsberichte. Deutsche Akademie der Landwirtschaftswissenschaften zu Berlin [*A publication*]
Sitzungsber Deut Akad Wiss Berlin Kl Math Phys Tech ... Sitzungsberichte. Deutsche Akademie der Wissenschaften zu Berlin. Klasse fuer Mathematik, Physik, und Technik [*A publication*]
Sitzungsber Finn Akad Wiss ... Sitzungsberichte. Finnische Akademie der Wissenschaften [*A publication*]
Sitzungsber Ges Befoerd Ges Naturwiss Marburg ... Sitzungsberichte. Gesellschaft zur Befoerderung der Gesamten Naturwissenschaften zu Marburg [*West Germany*] [*A publication*]
Sitzungsber Ges Naturforsch Freunde Berlin ... Sitzungsberichte. Gesellschaft Naturforschender Freunde zu Berlin [*A publication*]
Sitzungsber Heidelb Akad Wiss Math-Natur Kl ... Sitzungsberichte. Heidelberg Akademie der Wissenschaften. Mathematisch-Naturwissenschaftliche Klasse [*A publication*]
Sitzungsber Heidelb Akad Wiss Math-Naturwiss Kl ... Sitzungsberichte. Heidelberg Akademie der Wissenschaften. Mathematisch-Naturwissenschaftliche Klasse [*A publication*]
Sitzungsber Oesterr Akad Wiss Math-Naturwiss Kl Abt II ... Sitzungsberichte. Oesterreichische Akademie der Wissenschaften. Mathematisch-Naturwissenschaftliche Klasse. Abteilung II. Mathematik, Astronomie, Physik, Meteorologie, und Technik [*A publication*]

Sitzungsber Preuss Akad Wiss ... Sitzungsberichte. Preussische Akademie der Wissenschaften [*A publication*]
Sitz Wien ... Sitzungsberichte der Akademie der Wissenschaften in Wien [*A publication*]   (OCD)
SIU .... Saturn Instrumentation [*NASA*]
SIU .... Seafarers' International Union of North America [*AFL-CIO*]
SIU .... Sequence Initiate Update
SIU .... Sets in Use [*Television rating*]   (WDMC)
SIU .... Shiloh Resources Ltd. [*Vancouver Stock Exchange symbol*]
SIU .... Signal Interface Unit   (MCD)
SIU .... Significant Industrial Use
SIU .... Simushir [*Former USSR*] [*Seismograph station code, US Geological Survey*]   (SEIS)
SIU .... Slide-In Unit [*Telecommunications*]   (TEL)
SIU .... Societe Internationale d'Urologie [*International Society of Urology - ISU*] [*Paris, France*]   (EAIO)
SIU .... Sonobuoy Interface Unit [*Navy*]   (CAAL)
SIU .... Southern Illinois University
SIU .... System [*or Subsystem*] Interface Unit
SIU .... Systeme International d'Unites [*International System of Units*] [*Also, SI*]
SIU-AGLI ... Seafarers' International Union of North America [*AFL-CIO*]; Atlantic, Gulf, Lakes, and Inland Waters District
SIU-AGLIW ... Seafarers' International Union of North America [*AFL-CIO*]; Atlantic, Gulf, Lakes, and Inland Waters District
SIUC .... Southern Illinois University, Carbondale
SIUCB .... Societa Italiana della Union Chimique Belge [*Italy*]
SIUFL .... Suspend Issue and Use of Following Lots
SIU-IUP .... Seafarers' International Union of North America [*AFL-CIO*]; Inlandboatmen's Union of the Pacific
SIU-IUPW ... Seafarers' International Union of North America [*AFL-CIO*]; International Union of Petroleum Workers
SIU-MCS .. Seafarers' International Union of North America [*AFL-CIO*]; Marine Cooks and Stewards' Union
SIU-MFOW ... Seafarers' International Union of North America [*AFL-CIO*]; Pacific Coast Marine Firemen, Oilers, Watertenders, and Wipers Association
SIUNA ...... Seafarers' International Union of North America   (EA)
SIUP .... Southern Illinois University Press
SIUPA ...... Solomon Islands United Party [*Political party*]   (PPW)
SIUSA .... Survival International, USA   (EA)
SIUSM ...... Suspend from Issue and Use as Suspect Material
SIU-SUP ... Seafarers' International Union of North America [*AFL-CIO*]; Sailors' Union of the Pacific
SIU-TSAW ... Seafarers' International Union of North America [*AFL-CIO*]; Transporation Services and Allied Workers
SIV .... Sieve   (NASA)
SIV .... Silicon Videcon [*TV system*]
SIV .... Silver Cloud Mines [*Vancouver Stock Exchange symbol*]
SIV .... Simian Immunodeficiency Virus
SIV .... Solar and Interplanetary Variability [*Meteorology*]
SIV .... Spectrum Identification Voltage [*Military*]   (CAAL)
SIV .... Sullivan, IN [*Location identifier*] [*FAA*]   (FAAL)
SIV .... Survey of Interpersonal Values [*Psychology*]
SIV .... Vierteljahrshefte zur Wirtschaftsforschung [*A publication*]
SIVB .... Silicon Valley Bancshares [*NASDAQ symbol*]   (NQ)
SIVD .... Spacecraft Information Viewing Device
SIVE .... Shuttle Interface Verification Equipment [*NASA*]   (NASA)
SI VIR PERM ... Si Vires Permittant [*If the Strength Will Bear It*] [*Pharmacy*]   (ROG)
SIVOMAR ... Societe Ivoirenne de Navigation Maritime [*Ivory Coast*]   (EY)
SIVP .... South Italian Vase Painting [*A publication*]
SIW .... Congregation of the Incarnate Word and the Blessed Sacrament [*Roman Catholic women's religious order*]
SIW .... Schmitt Industries, Inc. [*Vancouver Stock Exchange symbol*]
SIW .... Self-Inflicted Wound [*Military*]
SIW .... Serum Samples from Infertile Women [*Immunochemistry*]
SIW .... Socialist International Women   (EA)
SIW .... Strassburger Israelitisch Wochenschrift [*A publication*]   (BJA)
SIW .... Strategic Intelligence Wing   (MCD)
SIW .... Subpolar Intermediate Water [*Oceanography*]
SIWDR ...... Sidewinder [*Naval ordnance*]
SIWL .... Single Isolated Wheel Load [*Aviation*]   (FAAC)
SIX .... Motel 6 LP [*NYSE symbol*]   (SPSG)
SIX .... Sigma [*A publication*]
SIX .... Singleton [*Australia*] [*Airport symbol*]   (OAG)
Six .... Sixties [*A publication*]
SIXATAF .. Sixth Allied Tactical Air Force, Southeastern Europe [*NATO*]   (NATG)
Six Cent J .. Sixteenth Century Journal [*A publication*]
Six Circ ...... Cases on the Six Circuits [*1841-43*] [*Ireland*] [*A publication*]   (DLA)
Six Ct J ...... Sixteenth Century Journal [*A publication*]
SIXEP .... Site Ion Exchange Effluent Plant [*Nuclear energy*]
SIXFLT ...... Sixth Fleet [*Atlantic*] [*Navy*]
SIXP .... Sixpenny [*England*]
SIXPAC ..... System for Inertial Experiment Priority and Attitude Control   (MCD)
Sixteen Cent J ... Sixteenth Century Journal [*A publication*]
SIXTHFLT ... Sixth Fleet [*Atlantic*] [*Navy*]
SIY .... Montague, CA [*Location identifier*] [*FAA*]   (FAAL)

SIY .... Shropshire Imperial Yeomanry [*British military*]   (DMA)
SIY .... South of Ireland Yeomanry [*British military*]   (DMA)
SIY .... Staffordshire Imperial Yeomanry [*British military*]   (DMA)
SIY .... Sussex Imperial Yeomanry [*British military*]   (DMA)
SIZ .... Security Identification Zone
SIZ .... Sizeler Property Investors, Inc. [*NYSE symbol*]   (SPSG)
SiZ .... Studies in Zionism [*A publication*]
SizelerP ...... Sizeler Property Investors, Inc. [*Associated Press abbreviation*]   (APAG)
SIZSA .... Sapporo Igaku Zasshi [*A publication*]
Sizzler .... Sizzler International, Inc. [*Associated Press abbreviation*]   (APAG)
SJ .... Saalburg-Jahrbuch [*A publication*]
SJ .... Sales Journal [*Accounting*]
SJ .... Samuel Johnson [*Initials used as pseudonym*]
SJ .... San Juan [*Puerto Rico*]
SJ .... Saxophone Journal [*A publication*]
SJ .... Schistosoma Japonicum [*Parasitic fluke*]
SJ .... Scottish Jurist [*1829-73*] [*A publication*]   (DLA)
SJ .... Service Junior
SJ .... Shakespeare-Jahrbuch [*A publication*]
SJ .... Show Jumper [*or Jumping*] [*Horsemanship*] [*British*]   (DI)
SJ .... Side Judge [*Football*]
SJ .... Silliman Journal [*A publication*]
SJ .... Simulation Journal [*A publication*]
SJ .... Single Jewish [*Classified advertising*]
SJ .... SJ Huvudkontor [*Swedish State Railways*]   (DCTA)
SJ .... Slip Joint [*Technical drawings*]
SJ .... Sloppy Joe [*Sandwich*]
SJ .... Slovensky Jazyk [*A publication*]
SJ .... Societas Jesu [*Society of Jesus*] [*Jesuits*] [*Roman Catholic men's religious order*]
SJ .... Solicitors' Journal [*A publication*] [*A publication*]   (DLA)
SJ .... Source Jamming
SJ .... Southern Air Transport, Inc. [*ICAO designator*]   (FAAC)
SJ .... Statens Jaernvaegar [*Sweden*]
S-J .... Stevens-Johnson Syndrome [*Medicine*]   (AAMN)
SJ .... Sub Judice [*Under Consideration*] [*Latin*]
sj .... Sudan [*MARC country of publication code*] [*Library of Congress*]   (LCCP)
SJ .... Supersonic Jet [*Gas stream*]
SJ .... Svalbard and Jan Mayen Islands [*ANSI two-letter standard code*]   (CNC)
SJA .... San Juan Airlines [*Port Angeles, WA*] [*FAA designator*]   (FAAC)
SJA .... Service Job Analysis [*A publication*]
SJA .... Southwestern Journal of Anthropology [*A publication*]
SJA .... Staff Judge Advocate [*Military*]
SJAA .... Swedish Journalists Association of America   (EA)
SJAE .... Steam Jet Air Ejector [*Nuclear energy*]   (NRCH)
SJAEA .... Soviet Journal of Atomic Energy [*A publication*]
SJAnth .... Southwestern Journal of Anthropology [*A publication*]
SJAOI .... Staff Judge Advocate Office Institute   (SAA)
SJART .... San Jacinto Army Terminal
SJB .... St. Joseph Belt Railway Co. [*AAR code*]
SJB .... Society of Jewish Bibliophiles   (EA)
SJB .... Society of Journeymen Brushmakers [*A union*] [*British*]
SJB .... Surinaams Juristenblad [*A publication*]
SJB .... Westfield, MA [*Location identifier*] [*FAA*]   (FAAL)
SJBA .... Sephardic Jewish Brotherhood of America   (EA)
SJBC .... Saint John the Baptist, Clewer
SJBCD5 ..... Soviet Journal of Bioorganic Chemistry [*English translation of Bioorganicheskaya Khimiya*] [*A publication*]
SJC .... Saint John's College [*California; Kansas; Maryland*]
SJC .... Saint Joseph College [*West Hartford, CT*]
SJC .... Saint Joseph's College [*California; Indiana; Maine; New Jersey; New York, Pennsylvania*]
SJC .... San Javier [*Chile*] [*Seismograph station code, US Geological Survey*] [*Closed*]   (SEIS)
SJC .... San Jose [*California*] [*Airport symbol*]   (OAG)
SJC .... San Jose, CA [*Location identifier*] [*FAA*]   (FAAL)
SJC .... Sayre Junior College [*Oklahoma*]
SJC .... Snead Junior College [*Boaz, AL*]
SJC .... Society of Jews and Christians
SJC .... Southerland, J. C., Dearborn, MI [*STAC*]
SJC .... Standing Joint Committee
SJC .... Supreme Judicial Court
SJCC .... Cayey [*Puerto Rico*] [*Seismograph station code, US Geological Survey*]   (SEIS)
SJCC .... Saint John College of Cleveland [*Ohio*]
SJCC .... San Jose City College [*California*]
SJCC .... Scott Joplin Commemorative Committee   (EA)
SJCC .... Spring Joint Computer Conference [*American Federation of Information Processing Societies*]
SJCCA .... Stroke [*A publication*]
SJCLA .... Scandinavian Journal of Clinical and Laboratory Investigation [*A publication*]
SJCOA ...... SIAM [*Society for Industrial and Applied Mathematics*] Journal on Control [*A publication*]
SJCOD ...... SIAM [*Society for Industrial and Applied Mathematics*] Journal on Control and Optimization [*A publication*]

SJCPS .... Society of Jewish Composers, Publishers, and Songwriters [*Defunct*]   (EA)
SJCS .... Secretary Joint Chiefs of Staff   (MCD)
SJCT .... SJC Today. Sheldon Jackson College [*Sitka, AK*] [*A publication*]
SJCW .... Saint Joseph's College for Women [*Later, SJC*] [*New York*]
SJD .... Doctor of Juridical Science [*or Doctor of the Science of Jurisprudence or Doctor of the Science of Law*]
SJD .... Los Cabos [*Mexico*] [*Airport symbol*]   (OAG)
SJD .... St. Joseph's College, Philadelphia, PA [*OCLC symbol*]   (OCLC)
SJD .... Supervisory Job Discipline Test
SJDAOIIA ... Saint John of Damascus Association of Orthodox Iconographers, Iconologists, and Architects   (EA)
SJDBA ...... Soviet Journal of Developmental Biology [*A publication*]
SJDFC .... Spirit, John Denver Fan Club   (EA)
SJE .... St. Jude Express [*An association*]   (EA)
SJE .... San Jose Del Guaviaro [*Colombia*] [*Airport symbol*]   (OAG)
SJE .... Swedish Journal of Economics [*A publication*]
SJE .... Swiveling Jet Engine
SJECA .... Soviet Journal of Ecology [*English Translation*] [*A publication*]
SJER .... Scandinavian Journal of Educational Research [*A publication*]
SJF .... Japanese Finance and Industry [*A publication*]
SJF .... Saint John [*Virgin Islands*] [*Airport symbol*]   (OAG)
SJF .... Shortest Job First [*Data processing*]
SJF .... Single Jewish Female [*Classified advertising*]
SJF .... Sonny James and Friends [*An association*]   (EA)
SJF .... Supersonic Jet Flow
SJFC .... Saint John Fisher College [*Rochester, NY*]
SJFC .... Skidrow Joe Fan Club   (EA)
SJFMA ...... Soviet Journal of Non-Ferrous Metals [*English Translation*] [*A publication*]
SJFRE3 ..... Scandinavian Journal of Forest Research [*A publication*]
SJFT .... Svenska Jerusalems-Foereningens Tidskrift [*A publication*]
SJFTD8 ..... Sudan Journal of Food Science and Technology [*A publication*]
SJG .... St. Joe Gold Corp. [*AMEX symbol*] [*Toronto Stock Exchange symbol*]   (SPSG)
SJG .... San Juan [*Puerto Rico*] [*Seismograph station code, US Geological Survey*]   (SEIS)
SJG .... San Juan [*Puerto Rico*] [*Geomagnetic observatory code*]
SJGE .... St. Joseph Grain Exchange   (EA)
SJGHA ...... Sumitomo Jukikai Giho [*A publication*]
SJGRA ..... Scandinavian Journal of Gastroenterology [*A publication*]
SJH .... St. Joseph Seminary [*California*] [*Seismograph station code, US Geological Survey*]   (SEIS)
SJH .... San Juan Del Cesar [*Colombia*] [*Airport symbol*]   (OAG)
SJH .... Shakespeare-Jahrbuch (Heidelberg) [*A publication*]
SJHAA ...... Scandinavian Journal of Haematology [*A publication*]
SJI .... Mobile, AL [*Location identifier*] [*FAA*]   (FAAL)
SJI .... San Jose [*Philippines*] [*Airport symbol*]   (OAG)
SJI .... Society for Japanese Irises   (EA)
SJI .... South Jersey Industries, Inc. [*NYSE symbol*]   (SPSG)
SJI .... Steel Joist Institute   (EA)
SJI .... Supervisory Job Instruction Test
SJIA .... Saint Joan's International Alliance [*See also AIJA*]   (EAIO)
SJIFC .... Spike Jones International Fan Club   (EA)
SJIS .... State Judicial Information System   (OICC)
SJJ .... Sarajevo [*Former Yugoslavia*] [*Airport symbol*]   (OAG)
SJJC .... Sheldon Jackson Junior College [*Sitka, AK*] [*Later, Sheldon Jackson College*]
SJJR .... Societe Jean-Jacques Rousseau [*Switzerland*]   (EAIO)
SJJR .... Standard Jack and Jennet Registry of America   (EA)
SJK .... Sao Jose Dos Campos [*Brazil*] [*Airport symbol*]   (OAG)
SJK .... Steam-Jacketed Kettle
SJL .... St. Jude League   (EA)
SJL .... San Joaquin Valley Library System, Fresno, CA [*OCLC symbol*]   (OCLC)
SJL .... Semitic Journal of Linguistics [*A publication*]
SJL .... Slovensky Jazyk a Literatura v Skole [*A publication*]
SJL .... Southwest Journal of Linguistics [*US*] [*A publication*]
SJLA .... Studies in Judaism in Late Antiquity [*A publication*]
SJLAC .... Soviet Jewry Legal Advocacy Center   (EA)
SJLB .... Selected Judgments, Lower Burma [*A publication*]   (DLA)
SJLC .... St. Johnsbury & Lamoille County R. R. [*AAR code*]
SJLC .... Single Junction Latching Circulator
SJLR .... St. John's Law Review [*A publication*]
SJM .... San Jose De Maipo [*Chile*] [*Seismograph station code, US Geological Survey*] [*Closed*]   (SEIS)
SJM .... Single Jewish Male [*Classified advertising*]
SJM .... Smucker [*J. M.*] Co. [*NYSE symbol*]   (SPSG)
SJM .... Special Joint Meeting
SJM .... Svalbard and Jan Mayen Islands [*ANSI three-letter standard code*]   (CNC)
SJM .... System Junction Module [*Deep Space Instrumentation Facility, NASA*]
SJMAA ..... SIAM [*Society for Industrial and Applied Mathematics*] Journal on Mathematical Analysis [*A publication*]
SJMC .... Signed Judgments of the Military Courts in the Administered Territories [*Israel*]   (BJA)
SJMED ..... South African Journal of Hospital Medicine [*A publication*]
SJMJ .... Societe de Jesus, Marie et Joseph [*Society of Jesus, Mary and Joseph*] [*Netherlands*]   (EAIO)

SJMS .... Speculum [*A publication*]
SJMSE7 .... Suid-Afrikaanse Tydskrif vir Seewetenskap [*A publication*]
SJN .... St. Johns, AZ [*Location identifier*] [*FAA*]   (FAAL)
SJN .... San Juan [*Peru*] [*Seismograph station code, US Geological Survey*] [*Closed*]   (SEIS)
S/J + N ..... Signal-to-Jamming - plus Noise Ratio
SJN .... Supersonic Jet Noise
SJNAA ...... SIAM [*Society for Industrial and Applied Mathematics*] Journal on Numerical Analysis [*A publication*]
SJ24NACA ... San Juan 24 North American Class Association   (EA)
SJNB .... SJNB Financial Corp. [*San Jose, CA*] [*NASDAQ symbol*]   (NQ)
SJNCA ...... Soviet Journal of Nuclear Physics [*English Translation*] [*A publication*]
SJNTA ...... Soviet Journal of Nondestructive Testing [*English Translation*] [*A publication*]
SJO .... Jahrbuch. Deutsche Shakespeare-Gesellschaft Ost [*A publication*]
SJO .... San Jose [*Costa Rica*] [*Airport symbol*]   (OAG)
SJO .... Service Junior - Oil-Resistant
SJOJ .... Savez Jevrejskih Opstina Jugoslavije   (BJA)
SJOTB ...... Soviet Journal of Optical Technology [*English Translation*] [*A publication*]
SJP .... St. James Press [*Publisher*]
SJP .... St. Joe Paper Co. [*NYSE symbol*]   (SPSG)
SJP .... San Jose Public Library, San Jose, CA [*OCLC symbol*]   (OCLC)
SJP .... San Juan [*Puerto Rico*] [*Seismograph station code, US Geological Survey*] [*Closed*]   (SEIS)
SJP .... Sao Jose Do Rio Preto [*Brazil*] [*Airport symbol*]   (OAG)
SJP .... Scottish Journal of Political Economy [*A publication*]
SJP .... Serialized Job Processor
SJP .... Singapore Justice Party [*Political party*]   (PPW)
SJP .... Socialist Janata Party [*India*] [*Political party*]   (ECON)
SJP .... Southern Journal of Philosophy [*A publication*]
SJP .... Special Job Procedure [*Navy*]   (NG)
SJP .... Standard Jet Penetration [*Aviation*]
SJP .... Sun-Jupiter-Probe [*Angle*]
SJPC .... Standing Joint Pacifist Committee   (EAIO)
SJPE .... Scottish Journal of Political Economy [*A publication*]
S J Phil ...... Southern Journal of Philosophy [*A publication*]
SJ Philos .... Southern Journal of Philosophy [*A publication*]
SJPNA ...... Soviet Journal of Particles and Nuclei [*A publication*]
SJPRB .... Scandinavian Journal of Plastic and Reconstructive Surgery [*A publication*]
SJPS .... Saint John's Provincial Seminary [*Plymouth, MI*]
SJPSDL ...... Suid-Afrikaanse Tydskrif vir Sielkunde [*A publication*]
SJPYA .... Scandinavian Journal of Psychology [*A publication*]
SJQ .... San Joaquin Reservoir [*California*] [*Seismograph station code, US Geological Survey*] [*Closed*]   (SEIS)
SJR .... San Jose [*Costa Rica*] [*Seismograph station code, US Geological Survey*] [*Closed*]   (SEIS)
SJR .... San Juan Racing Association, Inc. [*NYSE symbol*]   (SPSG)
SJR .... Senate Joint Resolution
SJR .... Shinowara-Jones-Reinhard Unit [*Medicine*]   (MAE)
SJR .... Social Justice Review [*A publication*]
SJR .... Textile Month [*A publication*]
SJRB .... Soviet Jewry Research Bureau   (EA)
SJRDA ..... Scandinavian Journal of Respiratory Diseases [*A publication*]
SJRES .... Senate Joint Resolution   (AFIT)
SJRF .... Scott Joplin Ragtime Festival   (EA)
SJRMF ..... Senator Joseph R. McCarthy Foundation   (EA)
SJRT .... St. Johns River Terminal [*AAR code*]
SJS .... Saint John's Seminary [*Brighton, MA*]
SJS .... St. Johns Tracking Station [*Newfoundland*]
SJS .... Saint Joseph's Seminary [*Illinois; New York*]
SJS .... San Jose [*Costa Rica*] [*Seismograph station code, US Geological Survey*]   (SEIS)
SJS .... San Jose Studies [*A publication*]
SJS .... Search Jam System
SJS .... Secretary, Joint Staff [*Military*]   (CINC)
SJS .... Society of Jewish Science   (EA)
SJS .... Sunshine-Jr. Stores, Inc. [*AMEX symbol*]   (SPSG)
SJS .... Supervisory Job Safety Test
SJSC .... San Jose State College [*California*] [*Later, San Jose State University*]
SJSCDM ... Shimane Journal of Medical Science [*A publication*]
SJSD .... Soviet Jewry Solidarity Day   (BJA)
SJSS .... Saint Joseph's Seraphic Seminary [*New York*]
SJSU .... San Jose State University [*California*]
SJSUD ..... Science Journal. Shivaji University [*A publication*]
SJT .... St. Joseph Terminal Railroad Co. [*AAR code*]
SJT .... San Angelo [*Texas*] [*Airport symbol*]   (OAG)
SJT .... San Angelo, TX [*Location identifier*] [*FAA*]   (FAAL)
SJT .... San Juan Basin Royalty Trust [*NYSE symbol*]   (SPSG)
SJT .... Scottish Journal of Theology [*A publication*]
Sjt .... Serjeant [*Military*] [*British*]   (DMA)
SJT .... Service Junior - Thermoplastic
SJT .... Southwestern Journal of Theology [*A publication*]
SJT .... Subsonic [*or Supersonic*] Jet Transport
SJTCA .... San Juan 21 Class Association   (EA)

SJTCA.......	Scandinavian Journal of Thoracic and Cardiovascular Surgery [*A publication*]
SJTCC.......	State Job Training Coordinating Council (OICC)
SJTGD5	Singapore Journal of Tropical Geography [*A publication*]
SJTh..........	Scottish Journal of Theology [*A publication*] (BJA)
SJU...........	St. John's University [*Minnesota; New York*]
SJU...........	St. John's University, Division of Library and Information Science, Jamaica, NY [*OCLC symbol*] (OCLC)
SJU...........	San Juan [*Puerto Rico*] [*Airport symbol*] (OAG)
SJuanB	San Juan Basin Royalty Trust [*Associated Press abbreviation*] (APAG)
SJUF	Skandinavisk Jodisk Ungdomsforbund (BJA)
SJUMPS...	Shipboard Joint Uniform Military Pay System [*Navy*] (DNAB)
SJUNA......	Scandinavian Journal of Urology and Nephrology [*A publication*]
S Jur..........	Sirey. Jurisprudence [*France*] [*A publication*] (DLA)
S Just	Shaw's Scotch Justiciary Cases [*A publication*] (DLA)
SJV	Kyoto University. Jimbun Kagaku Kenkyu-sho. Silver Jubilee Volume [*A publication*]
SJV	St. John [*Virgin Islands*] [*Seismograph station code, US Geological Survey*] (SEIS)
SJV	Sharing Joint Venture
SjV	Sirp ja Vasar [*A publication*]
SJV	Societe Jules Verne [*France*] (EAIO)
SJVLS	San Joaquin Valley Library System [*Library network*]
SJVWGA ..	San Joaquin Valley Wine Growers Association (EA)
SJW	St. Louis, MO [*Location identifier*] [*FAA*] (FAAL)
SJW	Shakespeare-Jahrbuch (Weimar) [*A publication*]
SJW	Single Jewish Woman [*Classified advertising*]
SJW	SJW Corp. [*Associated Press abbreviation*] (APAG)
SJW	SJW Corp. [*AMEX symbol*] (SPSG)
SJWCP......	Skid Jacket Water Cooling Pump [*Nuclear energy*] (NRCH)
SJ(Weimar) ...	Shakespeare-Jahrbuch (Weimar) [*A publication*]
SJWVUSA ...	Sons of Jewish War Veterans of the United States of America (EA)
SJX	St. James, MI [*Location identifier*] [*FAA*] (FAAL)
SJX	Sartaneja [*Belize*] [*Airport symbol*] (OAG)
SJY	San Jacinto, CA [*Location identifier*] [*FAA*] (FAAL)
SJZ	Angola, IN [*Location identifier*] [*FAA*] (FAAL)
SJZ	Sao Jorge Island [*Azores*] [*Airport symbol*] (OAG)
SJZ	Selected Judgments, Zambia [*A publication*] (DLA)
SJZ	Sueddeutsche Juristenzeitung [*German*] (ILCA)
SK	Sack
SK	Safekeeping
SK	Safety-Kleen Corp. [*NYSE symbol*] (SPSG)
SK	Sanitaetskompanie [*Medical company*] [*German military - World War II*]
SK	Santa Klaus (ROG)
SK	Saskatchewan [*Canadian province, postal code*]
SK	Scandinavian Airlines System [*Sweden*] [*ICAO designator*] (OAG)
SK	Sealed Knot [*An association*] (EAIO)
SK	Seminarium Kondakovianum [*A publication*]
SK	Service Kit
SK	Sick
sk...............	Sikkim [*ii (India) used in records cataloged after January 1978*] [*MARC country of publication code*] [*Library of Congress*] (LCCP)
SK	Sikorsky Aircraft Division [*United Aircraft Corp.*] [*ICAO aircraft manufacturer identifier*] (ICAO)
SK	Sinclair-Koppers Co. [*Later, Arco Polymers, Inc.*]
SK	Sink (AAG)
SK	Skein
SK	Skeletals (DCTA)
SK	Sketch (AAG)
Sk..............	Skewness (WGA)
S & K........	Skills and Knowledges
SK	Skimmed
SK	Skinned (MSA)
SK	Skip
sk...............	Skot [*Unit of luminance*]
SK	Sloan-Kettering [*Cancer-treatment compound*] (MAE)
SK	Smack (ROG)
SK	Socket (DEN)
SK	Sonic Key (MCD)
SK	South Kensington [*District of London*] (ROG)
SK	South Korea
SK	Sovetskii Kollektsioner [*A publication*]
SK	Sovetskaya Kolonia [*Soviet Colony*]
SK	Station-Keeping
SK	Storekeeper [*Navy rating*]
SK	Streptokinase [*An enzyme*]
Sk..............	Strike [*or Stroke*]
SK	Substance K [*Biochemistry*]
SK	Sumerische Kultlieder aus Altbabylonischer Zeit [*A publication*] (BJA)
SK1	Storekeeper, First Class [*Navy rating*]
SK2	Storekeeper, Second Class [*Navy rating*]
SK3	Storekeeper, Third Class [*Navy rating*]
SKA	Sikes Corp. Class A [*AMEX symbol*] (SPSG)

SKA	Skalstugan [*Sweden*] [*Seismograph station code, US Geological Survey*] (SEIS)
SKA	Skandinaviska Enskilda Banken. Quarterly Review [*A publication*]
SKA	Skill, Knowledge, and Ability [*or Attitude*] [*Employment*]
SKA	Spokane, WA [*Location identifier*] [*FAA*] (FAAL)
SKA	Station-Keeping Assistance (DS)
S/KA	Submarine Kit Allowance [*British military*] (DMA)
SKA	Switchblade Knife Act
SKAC........	Sikes Corp. [*NASDAQ symbol*] (NQ)
SKAD........	Survival Kit Air-Droppable [*Military*] [*Canada*]
SKAI.........	Skylink America, Inc. [*NASDAQ symbol*] (NQ)
SKAMP	Station-Keeping and Mobile Platform [*Robot sailboat*]
SKAN	Skaneateles Savings Bank [*Skaneateles, NY*] [*NASDAQ symbol*] (NQ)
SKAN	Solidariteits Komitee Argentiniee [*Netherlands*]
Skand........	Skandinavistik [*A publication*]
Skand Bank ...	Skandinaviska Enskilda Banken [*A publication*]
Skand Ensk Bank Quart R ...	Skandinaviska Enskilda Banken. Quarterly Review [*A publication*]
Skandia......	Skandia America Corp. [*Associated Press abbreviation*] (APAG)
Skandia Int Symp ...	Skandia International Symposia [*A publication*]
Skandinavis ...	Skandinavistik [*A publication*]
Skandinaviska Enskilda Banken Q R ...	Skandinaviska Enskilda Banken. Quarterly Review [*A publication*]
Skand Numis ...	Skandinavisk Numismatik [*A publication*]
SKAND SF ...	Skandinaviska Seglarforbundet [*Scandinavian Yachting Association - SYA*] (EAIO)
Skand Vet Tidskr ...	Skandinavisk Veterinaertidskrift foer Bakteriologi, Patologi, samt Koettoch Mjoelkhygien [*A publication*]
SKAP........	Armedia/El Elden [*Colombia*] [*ICAO location identifier*] (ICLI)
SKAP........	Skills, Knowledge, Abilities, and Personnel [*Attributes*] (MCD)
SKAS	Puerto Asis [*Colombia*] [*ICAO location identifier*] (ICLI)
SKAT........	Kommentar zum Alten Testament [*A publication*] (BJA)
SKAT........	Sex Knowledge and Aptitude [*Test*]
SKATI	Skills, Knowledges, Aptitudes, Temperaments, Interests (OICC)
Skat Mag ...	Skating Magazine [*A publication*]
SKAWW....	Sitzungsberichte. Kaiserliche Akademie der Wissenschaften in Wien [*A publication*]
SKB...........	Saint Kitts [*Leeward Islands*] [*Airport symbol*] (OAG)
SKB...........	Skew Buffer
SKB...........	Skybridge International, Inc. [*Vancouver Stock Exchange symbol*]
SKB...........	SmithKline Beckman Corp. [*Formerly, SKL*] [*NYSE symbol*] (SPSG)
SKB...........	Wichita Falls, TX [*Location identifier*] [*FAA*] (FAAL)
SKBC........	El Banco/Los Flores [*Colombia*] [*ICAO location identifier*] (ICLI)
SKBF	Schweizerische Koordinationsstelle fuer Bildungsforschung [*Swiss Coordination Center for Research in Education*] [*Information service or system*] (IID)
SKBG........	Bucaramanga/Palo Negro Sur [*Colombia*] [*ICAO location identifier*] (ICLI)
SKBGD......	Sangyo Kogai Boshi Gijutsu [*A publication*]
SKBO........	Bogota/Eldorado [*Colombia*] [*ICAO location identifier*] (ICLI)
SKBQ........	Barranquilla/Ernesto Cortissoz [*Colombia*] [*ICAO location identifier*] (ICLI)
SKBS	Bahia Solano/Jose Celestino Mutis [*Colombia*] [*ICAO location identifier*] (ICLI)
SKBU........	Buenaventura [*Colombia*] [*ICAO location identifier*] (ICLI)
SKC..........	Services Kinema Corp. [*British military*] (DMA)
SKC..........	Sky Clear [*Meteorology*] (FAAC)
SKC..........	Suki [*Papua New Guinea*] [*Airport symbol*] (OAG)
SKC..........	Waukesha, WI [*Location identifier*] [*FAA*] (FAAL)
SKCATL....	South Korea Conventional Air Target List (MCD)
SKCB	Storekeeper, Construction Battalion, Stevedore [*Navy rating*]
SKCC........	Cucuta/Camilo Daza [*Colombia*] [*ICAO location identifier*] (ICLI)
SKCD........	Condoto/Mandinga [*Colombia*] [*ICAO location identifier*] (ICLI)
SKCG........	Cartagena/Rafael Nunez [*Colombia*] [*ICAO location identifier*] (ICLI)
SKCH	Skyline Chili, Inc. [*Cincinnati, OH*] [*NASDAQ symbol*] (NQ)
SKCL........	Cali/Alfonso Bonilla Aragon [*Colombia*] [*ICAO location identifier*] (ICLI)
SKCM.......	Master Chief Storekeeper [*Navy rating*]
SKCM.......	Society of King Charles the Martyr (EA)
SKCMA.....	Steel Kitchen Cabinet Manufacturers Association (EA)
SKCO	Tumaco/La Florida [*Colombia*] [*ICAO location identifier*] (ICLI)
SKCS	Senior Chief Storekeeper [*Navy rating*]
SKCZ........	Corozal/Las Brujas [*Colombia*] [*ICAO location identifier*] (ICLI)
SKD	St. Katherine's Dock [*Shipping*] [*British*] (ROG)
SKD	Samarkand [*Former USSR*] [*Airport symbol*] (OAG)
SKD	Selve-Kornbegel-Dornheim [*Name of a German small arms ammunition factory*] [*World War II*]
SKD	Semi Knocked Down [*Shipping*] (DS)

SKD .... Sitkalidak Island [*Alaska*] [*Seismograph station code, US Geological Survey*]   (SEIS)
SKD .... Skid
SKD .... Skilled   (MSA)
SKD .... Skirted
SKD .... Skyworld Resources & Development Ltd. [*Vancouver Stock Exchange symbol*]
SKD .... Station-Keeping Distance [*British military*]   (DMA)
SKD .... Storekeeper, Disbursing [*Navy rating*]
SKD .... Svenska Dagbladet [*A publication*]
SKDGQ ..... Sammlung Ausgewaehlter Kirchen- und Dogmengeschichtlichen Quellenschriften [*A publication*]
SKDH .... Shikimate Dehydrogenase [*An enzyme*]
SKDL .... Suomen Kansan Demokraattinen Liitto [*Finnish People's Democratic League*] [*Political party*]   (PPW)
SKDN .... Shakedown [*Navy*]   (NVT)
SKDNC ...... Shakedown Cruise [*Navy*]
SKDNCRU ... Shakedown Cruise [*Navy*]   (NVT)
SKDP .... Sambungan Komunikasi Data Packet [*Indonesia*] [*Telecommunications service*]   (TSSD)
SKDU .... Ship's Keyboard Display Unit
SKE .... Belleville, IL [*Location identifier*] [*FAA*]   (FAAL)
SKE .... Skeena Resources Ltd. [*Vancouver Stock Exchange symbol*]
SKE .... Skien [*Norway*] [*Airport symbol*]   (OAG)
SKE .... Sky Tours, Inc. [*Port Clinton, OH*] [*FAA designator*]   (FAAC)
SKE .... Station-Keeping Equipment
SKEC .... Barranquilla [*Colombia*] [*ICAO location identifier*]   (ICLI)
SKED .... Bogota [*Colombia*] [*ICAO location identifier*]   (ICLI)
SKED .... Schedule   (NG)
SKED .... Sort Key Edit [*Library of Congress*]
SKEDCON ... Schedule Conference [*Military*]   (NVT)
SKEIA .... Sanshi Kagaku Kenkyusho Iho [*A publication*]
SKEJ .... Barrancabermeja/Yariguis [*Colombia*] [*ICAO location identifier*]   (ICLI)
SKEL .... Skeletal   (AAG)
Skeletal Radiol ... Skeletal Radiology [*A publication*]
SKENAN ... Ecological Review [*A publication*]
Skene .... [*Sir John*] Skene's De Verborum Significatione [*Of the Signification of Words*] [*7 eds.*] [*1597-1683*] [*A publication*]   (DLA)
SKET .... Skeleton Key   (DSUE)
SKF .... San Antonio, TX [*Location identifier*] [*FAA*]   (FAAL)
SKF .... Skycraft, Inc. [*Seattle, WA*] [*FAA designator*]   (FAAC)
SKF .... SmithKline Corp. [*Formerly, Smith, Kline & French Co.*] [*Research code symbol*]
SKF .... Svenska Kullagerfabriken AB [*Swedish manufacturer, especially of ball bearings; active in many countries*]
SKFB .... S & K Famous Brands, Inc. [*NASDAQ symbol*]   (NQ)
SkFi .... Skandinavskaga Filologija [*A publication*]
SKFL .... Florencia/Capitolio [*Colombia*] [*ICAO location identifier*]   (ICLI)
SKF Psychiatr Rep ... SK and F [*Smith, Kline, and French*] Psychiatric Reporter [*A publication*]
SKFR .... SKF AB [*Goteborg, Sweden*] [*NASDAQ symbol*]   (NQ)
SkFx .... Skull Fracture [*Medicine*]
Skg .... Safekeeping
SKG .... Schriften. Koenigsberger Gelehrten-Gesellschaft [*A publication*]
SKG .... Sikaman Gold Resources Ltd. [*Toronto Stock Exchange symbol*]
SKG .... Srpski Knjizevni Glasnik [*A publication*]
SKG .... Thessaloniki [*Greece*] [*Airport symbol*]   (OAG)
SKGG .... Schriften. Koenigsberger Gelehrten-Gesellschaft [*A publication*]
SKGGD ..... Sammlung Kurzer Grammatiken Germanischer Dialekte [*A publication*]
SKGI .... Girardot/Santiago Vila [*Colombia*] [*ICAO location identifier*]   (ICLI)
SKGND ..... Sanup Kwahak Gisul Yeonguso Nonmunjip [*Inha University*] [*A publication*]
SKGP .... Guapi [*Colombia*] [*ICAO location identifier*]   (ICLI)
SKGSA ...... Sekiyu Gakkaishi [*A publication*]
SKH .... Selkirk Communications Ltd. [*Toronto Stock Exchange symbol*]
SKH .... Staatsblad van het Koninkrijk der Nederlanden [*A publication*]
SKH .... Surkhet [*Nepal*] [*Airport symbol*]   (OAG)
S-Kh Biol ... Sel'skokhozyaistvennaya Biologiya [*A publication*]
S-Kh Proizvod Urala ... Sel'skokhozyaistvennoe Proizvodstvo Urala [*A publication*]
S-Kh Rub Rastenievod ... Sel'skokhozyaistvo za Rubezhom Rastenievodstvo [*A publication*]
SKHS .... Sri Kapila Humanitarian Society   (EAIO)
SKHVL ...... Skrifter Utgivna av Kungliga Humanistiska Vetenskapssamfundet i Lund [*A publication*]
SkHVSU ... Skrifter Utgivna. Humanistiska Vetenskapssamfundet i Uppsala [*A publication*]
SKI .... Sac City, IA [*Location identifier*] [*FAA*]   (FAAL)
SKI .... St. Kitts [*St. Kitts*] [*Seismograph station code, US Geological Survey*]   (SEIS)
SKI .... Sex Knowledge Inventory [*Premarital and marital relations test*]
SKI .... Sister Kenny Institute   (EA)
SKI .... Skiff, Ice [*Coast Guard*]   (DNAB)

SKI .... Sloan-Kettering Institute for Cancer Research
SKI .... Spinal Kinematic Instrument [*Medicine*]
SKIB .... Ibague/Perales [*Colombia*] [*ICAO location identifier*]   (ICLI)
Skid Min ... Skidmore's Mining Statutes [*A publication*]   (DLA)
SKIF .... Social Security Number Key Index File [*IRS*]
SKIF .... Sotsyalistisher Kinder Farband   (BJA)
SKII .... S-K-I Ltd. [*Killington, VT*] [*NASDAQ symbol*]   (NQ)
SKIL .... Canterbury Educational Services, Inc. [*NASDAQ symbol*]   (NQ)
SKIL .... Scanner Keyed Input Language
SKILA ...... Southern Korean Interim Legislative Assembly
SKILL .... Satellite Kill
Skillings' Min Rev ... Skillings' Mining Review [*A publication*]
Skill Pol Rep ... Skillman's New York Police Reports [*A publication*]   (DLA)
Skil Mining ... Skillings' Mining Review [*A publication*]
Skin .... Skinner's English King's Bench Reports [*A publication*]   (DLA)
Skin Diver Mag ... Skin Diver Magazine [*A publication*]
Skinker ...... Skinker's Reports [*65-79 Missouri*] [*A publication*]   (DLA)
Skinner ...... Skinner's English King's Bench Reports [*90 English Reprint*] [*1681-98*] [*A publication*]   (DLA)
Skinner (Eng) ... Skinner's English King's Bench Reports [*90 English Reprint*] [*A publication*]   (DLA)
Skin Res ..... Skin Research [*A publication*]
SKINS .... Supplemental Knowledge Incentive Notes [*Scrip offered to students for good performance*] [*Experimental learning program*]
SKIP .... Ipiales/San Luis [*Colombia*] [*ICAO location identifier*]   (ICLI)
SKIP .... Sick Kids Need Involved People   (EA)
SKIP .... Skill/Knowledge Improvement Program [*Navy*]   (DNAB)
SKIP .... Skinner Investigation Platform
SKIP .... Skipper's, Inc. [*NASDAQ symbol*]   (NQ)
SKIPI .... Super Knowledge Information Processing Intelligence [*Data processing*]
SKJ .... Sitkinak Island, AK [*Location identifier*] [*FAA*]   (FAAL)
SKK .... Shaktoolik [*Alaska*] [*Airport symbol*]   (OAG)
SKK .... Shaktoolik, AK [*Location identifier*] [*FAA*]   (FAAL)
SKK .... Sikka [*Former USSR*] [*Seismograph station code, US Geological Survey*] [*Closed*]   (SEIS)
SKK .... Sowjetische Kontrollkommission
SKK .... Sydslesvigsk Kirkekalender [*A publication*]
SKKCA ..... Supreme Knight of the Knights of Columbus of America
SKKEA ..... Sklar a Keramik [*A publication*]
SKKNAJ ... Annual Report. Sankyo Research Laboratories [*A publication*]
SKKOA ...... Shin Kinzoku Kogyo [*A publication*]
SKL .... Isle Of Skye [*Scotland*] [*Airport symbol*]   (OAG)
SKL .... Skiff, Light [*Coast Guard*]   (DNAB)
SKL .... Skilak [*Cooper Landing*] [*Alaska*] [*Seismograph station code, US Geological Survey*]   (SEIS)
SKL .... Skill Level
SKL .... Skylight [*Technical drawings*]
SKL .... Smith, Kline & French Laboratories [*Canada*]   (IIA)
SKL .... Stackpool Resources Ltd. [*Vancouver Stock Exchange symbol*]
SKL .... Suomen Kristillinen Liitto [*Finnish Christian League*] [*Political party*]   (PPE)
SKLC .... Los Cedros/Uraba [*Colombia*] [*ICAO location identifier*]   (ICLI)
SKLM .... La Mina/Riohacha [*Colombia*] [*ICAO location identifier*]   (ICLI)
SKLT .... Leticia/Alfredo Vasquez Cobo [*Colombia*] [*ICAO location identifier*]   (ICLI)
S Kl V .... Sammlung Klinischer Vortraege [*A publication*]
SKM .... Fayette Flying Service & Scheduled Skyways System [*Fayetteville, AR*] [*FAA designator*]   (FAAC)
SKM .... Schuster-Kubelka-Munk [*Optics*]
SKM .... Sine-Kosine Multiplier
SKM .... Skiff, Medium [*Coast Guard*]   (DNAB)
SKMC .... Sickness due to Misconduct [*Military*]   (DNAB)
SKMG .... Magangue/Baracoa [*Colombia*] [*ICAO location identifier*]   (ICLI)
SkMg .... Sulfate of Potash Magnesia Export Association   (EA)
SKMQ .... Mariquita/Mariquita [*Colombia*] [*ICAO location identifier*]   (ICLI)
SKMR .... Monteria/Los Garzones [*Colombia*] [*ICAO location identifier*]   (ICLI)
SKMRA ..... Skillings' Mining Review [*A publication*]
SKMU ...... Mitu/Mitu [*Colombia*] [*ICAO location identifier*]   (ICLI)
SKMZ .... Manizales/La Nubia [*Colombia*] [*ICAO location identifier*]   (ICLI)
SKN .... Skaneateles [*New York*] [*Seismograph station code, US Geological Survey*]   (SEIS)
SKN .... Skein   (ROG)
SKN .... Skolniks, Inc. [*AMEX symbol*]   (SPSG)
SKN .... Skyline Aviation Service, Inc. [*Beaver Falls, PA*] [*FAA designator*]   (FAAC)
SKN .... Smithville, TN [*Location identifier*] [*FAA*]   (FAAL)
SKN .... Stokmarknes [*Norway*] [*Airport symbol*]   (OAG)
SKNEA7 .... Annual Report. Shionogi Research Laboratory [*A publication*]
SKNSAF ... Advances in Neurological Sciences [*A publication*]
SKNSB ..... Shokuhin Shosha [*A publication*]
SKNTO ..... St. Kitts-Nevis Tourist Office   (EA)
S/KNU ...... Steering Knuckle [*Automotive engineering*]

SKNV .... Neiva/La Manguila [*Colombia*] [*ICAO location identifier*] (ICLI)
SKO .... Deadhorse, AK [*Location identifier*] [*FAA*] (FAAL)
SKO .... Saskatchewan Oil & Gas Corp. [*Toronto Stock Exchange symbol*]
SKO .... Sets, Kits, and Outfits (MCD)
SKO .... Shopko Stores [*NYSE symbol*] (SPSG)
SKO .... Skopje [*Yugoslavia*] [*Seismograph station code, US Geological Survey*] (SEIS)
SKO .... Society of Kastorians "Omonoia" (EA)
SKO .... Sokoto [*Nigeria*] [*Airport symbol*] (OAG)
SKOC .... Ocana/Aguas Claras [*Colombia*] [*ICAO location identifier*] (ICLI)
Skoda Rev ... Skoda Review [*A publication*]
Skogshoegsk Inst Skogstek Rapp Uppsats Res Notes ... Skogshoegskolan, Institutionen foer Skogsteknik, Rapporter och Uppsatser. Research Notes [*Sweden*] [*A publication*]
Skogs-Lantbruksakad Tidskr ... Skogs- och Lantbruksakademiens Tidskrift [*A publication*]
Skogstradsforadling Inst Skogsforbattring ... Skogstradsforadling-Institutet foer Skogsforbattring [*A publication*]
SKOI .... Suomen Konsulttitoimistojen Liitto [*Finnish Association of Consulting Firms*] (EY)
SKOL .... Suomen Konsulttitoimistojen Liitto [*Finnish Association of Consulting Firms*] (EY)
SKOLD ...... Screening Kit of Language Development [*Child development test*]
SKOR .... Score Exploration Corp. [*NASDAQ symbol*] (NQ)
SKOR .... Sperry Kalman Optical Reset [*Ship's Inertial Navigation System*] [*Navy*] (DNAB)
SKOT .... Otu/Otu [*Colombia*] [*ICAO location identifier*] (ICLI)
Skoteys ...... Spoiled Kids of the Eighties [*Lifestyle classification*] [*Offspring of the Yuppies*]
SKP .... Skip (BUR)
SKP .... Skopje [*Former Yugoslavia*] [*Airport symbol*] (OAG)
SKP .... Station-Keeping Position
SKP .... Suomen Kommunistinen Puolue [*Communist Party of Finland*] [*Political party*] (PPW)
SKP .... Sveriges Kommunistiska Partiet [*Communist Party of Sweden*] [*Political party*] (PPE)
S-K-P's .... Escapees, Inc. (EA)
SKPanKr .... Sprawozdania z Posiedzen Komisji Pan. Oddzial w Krakowie [*A publication*]
SKPB .... Puerto Bolivar/Riohacha [*Colombia*] [*ICAO location identifier*] (ICLI)
SKPC .... Puerto Carreno [*Colombia*] [*ICAO location identifier*] (ICLI)
SKPE .... Pereira/Matecana [*Colombia*] [*ICAO location identifier*] (ICLI)
SKPI .... Pitalito [*Colombia*] [*ICAO location identifier*] (ICLI)
SKPI .... Super Knowledge, Processing Interaction [*Concept advanced by Timothy Leary*]
SK-PJ .... Savez Komunista - Pokret za Jugoslaviju [*League of Communists - Movement for Yugoslavia*] [*Political party*]
SKPL .... Sketch Pad Layout (MCD)
SKPP .... Popayan/Guillermo Leon Valencia [*Colombia*] [*ICAO location identifier*] (ICLI)
SKPS .... Pasto/Antonio Narino [*Colombia*] [*ICAO location identifier*] (ICLI)
SKPTA ...... Skipsteknikk [*A publication*]
SKPV .... Providencia/Providencia [*Colombia*] [*ICAO location identifier*] (ICLI)
SKQ .... Sekakes [*Lesotho*] [*Airport symbol*] (OAG)
SKQ .... Sexual Knowledge Questionnaire
SKR .... Bedford, MA [*Location identifier*] [*FAA*] (FAAL)
SKR .... Sanskrit [*Language, etc.*]
SKR .... Saskatchewan Regional Libraries [*UTLAS symbol*]
SKR .... Saturn Kilometer-Wave Radiation [*Planetary science*]
SKR .... Sea King Replacement [*Naval aircraft*] [*British*]
SKR .... Seeker
SKR .... Separator-Key Generator-Recombiner (MCD)
SKR .... Severo-Kurilsk [*Former USSR*] [*Seismograph station code, US Geological Survey*] (SEIS)
SKR .... Shaker Heights City School District, Shaker Heights, OH [*OCLC symbol*] (OCLC)
Skr .... Skipper [*Navy*] [*British*]
SKR .... Skylark Resources Ltd. [*Vancouver Stock Exchange symbol*]
SKR .... South Korea Republic
SKR .... Station-Keeping RADAR
SKR .... Substance-K Receptor [*Biochemistry*]
S KR .... Swedish Krona [*Monetary unit*]
SKRAD ..... Skeletal Radiology [*A publication*]
SKRG .... Rio Negro/Jose Maria Cordova [*Colombia*] [*ICAO location identifier*] (ICLI)
SKRH .... Rio Hacha, Guajira [*Colombia*] [*ICAO location identifier*] (ICLI)
Skriftser Roskilde Universitetsbibl ... Skriftserie. Roskilde Universitetsbibliotek [*A publication*]
Skr Lund .... Skrifter Utgivna. Vetenskaps-Societeten i Lund [*A publication*]
Skr Mineral Paleontol Geol Inst ... Skrifter fran Mineralogisk och Paleontologisk-Geologiska Institutionerna [*A publication*]

Skr Norske Vid-Akad Oslo I ... Skrifter Utgitt. Norske Videnskaps-Akademi i Oslo. I. Matematisk-Naturvidenskapelig Klasse [*A publication*]
Skr Nor Vidensk-Akad Oslo I ... Skrifter Utgitt. Norske Videnskaps-Akademi i Oslo. I. Matematisk-Naturvidenskapelig Klasse [*A publication*]
Skr Nor Vidensk-Akad Oslo I Mat-Naturvidensk Kl ... Skrifter. Norske Videnskaps-Akademi i Oslo. I. Matematisk-Naturvidenskapelig Klasse [*A publication*]
Skr Szk Gl Gospod Wiejsk-Akad Roln Warszawie Ogrod ... Skrypty Szkoly Glownej Gospodarstwa Wiejskiego-Akademii Rolniczej w Warszawie. Ogrodnictwo [*A publication*]
Skr Udgivet Univ Zool Mus (Kbh) ... Skrifter Udgivet. Universitetets Zoologiske Museum (Kobenhavn) [*A publication*]
Skr Uppsala ... Skrifter Utgivna av Kungliga Humanist. Vetenskaps-Samfundet i Uppsala [*A publication*]
SKS .... Career Development Center, Shaker Heights, OH [*OCLC symbol*] (OCLC)
SKS .... Savezna Komisija za Standardizacija [*Federal Commission for Standardization*] [*Yugoslavia*]
SKS .... Scanning Kinetic Spectroscopy
SKS .... Skrydstrup [*Denmark*] [*Airport symbol*] (OAG)
SKS .... Soren Kierkegaard Society [*Copenhagen, Denmark*] (EA)
SKS .... Sound Air Aviation [*Ronkonkoma, NY*] [*FAA designator*] (FAAC)
SKS .... Specialist Knowledge Services [*British organization for occult research*]
SKS .... Station-Keeping Ship
SKS .... Suomalainen Kirjallisuuden Seura [*A publication*]
SKS .... Svetoveho Kongresu Slovakov [*Canada*] (EAIO)
SKSA .... Saravena/Saravena El Eden [*Colombia*] [*ICAO location identifier*] (ICLI)
SKSA .... Seaman Apprentice, Storekeeper, Striker [*Navy rating*]
SKSD .... Streptokinase Streptodornase [*An enzyme mixture*] [*Medicine*]
SKSG .... Santagueda/Santagueda [*Colombia*] [*ICAO location identifier*] (ICLI)
SKSJ .... San Jose Del Guaviare/S. J. Del Guaviore [*Colombia*] [*ICAO location identifier*] (ICLI)
SKSL .... Skaneateles Short Line Railroad Corp. [*Later, SSL*] [*AAR code*]
SKSM .... Santa Marta/Simon Bolivar [*Colombia*] [*ICAO location identifier*] (ICLI)
SKSN .... Seaman, Storekeeper, Striker [*Navy rating*]
SKSODV ... Neurology. Series One. Neural Mechanisms of Movement [*A publication*]
SKSP .... San Andres/Sesquicentenario, San Andres [*Colombia*] [*ICAO location identifier*] (ICLI)
SKSS .... Stoleczny Komitet Samopomocy Spolecznej [*Warsaw*] (BJA)
SKSV .... San Vicente Del Caguan [*Colombia*] [*ICAO location identifier*] (ICLI)
SKT .... Sanskrit [*Afrikaans*]
SKT .... Saskatchewan Trust Co. [*Toronto Stock Exchange symbol*]
SKT .... Skill Knowledge Tests
SKT .... Skirt (MSA)
SKT .... Skwentna [*Alaska*] [*Seismograph station code, US Geological Survey*] (SEIS)
SKT .... Socket (MSA)
SKT .... Specialty Knowledge Test [*Military*] (AFM)
SKT .... Storekeeper, Technical [*Navy rating*]
SKT .... Svensk Kemisk Tidskrift [*A publication*]
SKT .... Tropical International, Inc. [*Miami, FL*] [*FAA designator*] (FAAC)
SKTC .... SK Technologies Corp. [*NASDAQ symbol*] (SPSG)
SKTD .... Trinidad [*Colombia*] [*ICAO location identifier*] (ICLI)
SKTEA ...... Sky and Telescope [*A publication*]
SKTF .... Spring Knife Trade Federation [*A union*] [*British*]
SKTM .... Tame [*Colombia*] [*ICAO location identifier*] (ICLI)
SKTU .... Turbo, Gonzalo Mejia [*Colombia*] [*ICAO location identifier*] (ICLI)
SKU .... Newburgh, NY [*Location identifier*] [*FAA*] (FAAL)
SKU .... Sakura [*Japan*] [*Seismograph station code, US Geological Survey*] [*Closed*] (SEIS)
SKU .... Stock Keeping Unit [*Merchandising system*]
SKUC .... Arauca/Santiago Perez [*Colombia*] [*ICAO location identifier*] (ICLI)
SKUI .... Quibdo/El Carano [*Colombia*] [*ICAO location identifier*] (ICLI)
SKV .... Santa Katarina [*Egypt*] [*Airport symbol*] (OAG)
SKV .... Skewing the Pitch Angle
SKV .... Skukum Gold [*Vancouver Stock Exchange symbol*]
SKV .... Storekeeper, Aviation [*Navy rating*]
SKVP .... Valledupar/Alfonso Lopez [*Colombia*] [*ICAO location identifier*] (ICLI)
SKVV .... Schweizerischer Katholischer Volksverein
SKVH .... Villavicencio/Vanguardia [*Colombia*] [*ICAO location identifier*] (ICLI)
SKW .... Shichikawa [*Japan*] [*Seismograph station code, US Geological Survey*] (SEIS)
SKW .... Skwentna, AK [*Location identifier*] [*FAA*] (FAAL)
SKW .... Sky West Aviation, Inc. [*St. George, UT*] [*FAA designator*] (FAAC)
SKW .... Sueddeutsche Kalkstickstoffwerke [*AG*]

SKW .... Syndicate of North Germany Electric Utilities [*Germany*] [*Acronym is based on foreign phrase*]
SKWKA ..... Sanop Kwa Kisul [*A publication*]
SKX .... Skyline Explorations Ltd. [*Vancouver Stock Exchange symbol*] [*Toronto Stock Exchange symbol*]
SKX .... Taos, NM [*Location identifier*] [*FAA*]   (FAAL)
SKY .... Sandusky, OH [*Location identifier*] [*FAA*]   (FAAL)
SKY .... Sky Flite, Inc. [*Tulsa, OK*] [*FAA designator*]   (FAAC)
SKY .... Skyline Corp. [*NYSE symbol*]   (SPSG)
SKY .... Skyrocket Exploration [*Vancouver Stock Exchange symbol*]
Sky .... Skywriting [*A publication*]
SKYBET.... Skylab Best Estimate of Trajectory [*NASA*]
SKYCAV ... Sky Cavalry
SKYCOM ... Skylab Communications Engineer [*NASA*]
Skyline....... Skyline Corp. [*Associated Press abbreviation*]   (APAG)
SKYOA...... Shikizai Kyokaishi [*A publication*]
SKYP .... Suomen Kansan Yhtenaeisyyden Puolue [*People's Unity Party*] [*Finland*] [*Political party*]   (PPW)
SKYP .... Yopal/Yopal [*Colombia*] [*ICAO location identifier*]   (ICLI)
Skyscraper Mgt ... Skyscraper Management [*A publication*]
Sky & Tel... Sky and Telescope [*A publication*]
Sky Telesc ... Sky and Telescope [*A publication*]
SKYW........ SkyWest, Inc. [*St. George, UT*] [*NASDAQ symbol*]   (NQ)
SKYX .... Sky Express, Inc. [*Valley Stream, NY*] [*NASDAQ symbol*]   (NQ)
SKZ........... Sukkur [*Pakistan*] [*Airport symbol*]   (OAG)
SL.............. Antares SpA [*ICAO designator*]   (FAAC)
SL.............. Large-Scale Disturbance Field
SL.............. Lloydminster Public Library, Saskatchewan [*Library symbol*] [*National Library of Canada*]   (NLC)
SL.............. Safe Locker   (AAG)
SL.............. Safety Level [*Army*]
SL.............. Safety Limit [*Nuclear energy*]   (NRCH)
S & L .... Sale and Leaseback
SL.............. Sales Letter
SL.............. Salt Loading
SL.............. Salvage Loss
SL.............. Sample Laboratory   (MCD)
SL.............. San Luis Obispo [*Mexican state; city and county in California*]
SL.............. Sand-Loaded [*Technical drawings*]
SL.............. Satellite-Like Virus
SL.............. Save Lebanon   (EA)
S & L .... Savings and Loan [*Association*]
SL.............. Savings and Loan [*Association*]
sl................ Scale Leaf [*Botany*]
SL.............. Scanning Slit   (MCD)
S & L .... Schoales and Lefroy's Irish Chancery Reports [*1802-06*] [*A publication*]   (DLA)
SL.............. School Leavers [*Department of Employment*] [*British*]
SL.............. Schutte Lanz [*World War I German aircraft designation*]
SL.............. Scientists for Life [*An association*] [*Defunct*]   (EA)
SL.............. Scottish Liturgy [*Episcopalian*]
SL.............. Sea Level
SL.............. Seal   (NASA)
SL.............. Searchlight
SL.............. Second Lieutenant
SL.............. Section Leader [*Nuclear energy*]   (NRCH)
SL.............. Section List   (MCD)
SL.............. Secundum Legem [*According to Law*] [*Latin*]
SL.............. Seditious Libeler
SL.............. Send Leg [*Telegraphy*]   (TEL)
SL.............. Sendero Luminoso [*Shining Path*] [*Peru*]   (PD)
SL.............. Sensation Level [*Audiometry*]
SL.............. Sensu Lato [*In a Broad Sense*] [*Latin*]
SL.............. Separate Lead [*Cables*]
SL.............. Sergeant-at-Law
SL.............. Service Letter   (MCD)
SL.............. Servomechanisms Laboratory [*MIT*]   (MCD)
SL.............. Session Laws   (DLA)
SL.............. Shear Layer [*or Load*]
SL.............. Shelf Life   (NASA)
SL.............. Shift Left
SL.............. Ship Library [*Maritime Data Network, Inc.*] [*Information service or system*]   (CRD)
SL.............. Ship-of-the-Line
S-of-L........ Ship-of-the-Line
SL.............. Shipowner's Liability [*Business term*]
S/L............ Shops and Labs [*NASA*]   (NASA)
SL.............. Short Landed [*Tea trade*]   (ROG)
SL.............. Short Lengths [*Construction*]
SL.............. Short Letter   (DCTA)
S-L .... Short-Long [*as of a signal light's flash cycle*]
SL.............. Sibley-Lehninger [*Unit*]   (MAE)
SL.............. Sick Leave   (AFM)
SL.............. Side Load   (AAG)
SL.............. Sidelobe   (CAAL)
sl................ Sierra Leone [*MARC country of publication code*] [*Library of Congress*]   (LCCP)
SL.............. Sierra Leone [*ANSI two-letter standard code*]   (CNC)
SL.............. Sigillo Locus [*Place for the Seal*] [*Latin*]   (ROG)
SL.............. Signal Level

S & L .... Signed and Limited Edition [*Publishing*]
SL.............. Significance Level
SL.............. Silicon Lacquer
SL.............. Silvaire [*ICAO aircraft manufacturer identifier*]   (ICAO)
SL.............. Silver Library [*A publication*]
SL.............. Simulation Language [*Data processing*]   (BUR)
SL.............. Sine Loco [*Without Place*] [*Latin*]
SL.............. Single Ledger [*Accounting*]
SL.............. Single Line
SL.............. Single-Locus [*Light flashes*]
SL.............. Sisters of Loretto at the Foot of the Cross [*Roman Catholic religious order*]
SL.............. Skill Level
SL.............. Skylab [*NASA*]   (KSC)
SL.............. SL Industries, Inc. [*NYSE symbol*]   (SPSG)
SL.............. Slain   (ROG)
SL.............. Slate   (AAG)
Sl................ Slavia [*A publication*]
SL.............. Slavica [*A publication*]
SL.............. Sleeve [*Technical drawings*]
SL.............. Slesvigske Parti [*Schleswig Party*] [*Denmark*] [*Political party*]   (PPE)
SL.............. Slide   (AAG)
SL.............. Slightly
SL.............. Slip [*Knitting*]
SL.............. Slit Lamp [*Instrumentation*]
Sl................ Slovo. Casopis Staroslavenskog Instituta [*A publication*]
SL.............. Slow [*Track condition*] [*Thoroughbred racing*]
SL.............. Small Light Seeds [*Botany*]
SL.............. Small Lymphocytes [*Hematology*]
SL.............. Small Lymphoma [*Oncology*]
SL.............. Societas Liturgica   (EA)
SL.............. Society of Limerents   (EA)
SL.............. Sockellafette [*Pedestal mount*] [*German military - World War II*]
SL.............. Sodium Lactate   (MAE)
SL.............. Soft Landing   (MCD)
SL.............. Soft LASER
SL.............. Solar Lobby [*An association*]   (EA)
SL.............. Sold
SL.............. Solicitor-at-Law
SL.............. Solidified Liquid   (MAE)
SL.............. Sonic Log
SL.............. Sons of Liberty   (EA)
SL.............. Sortie Lab [*NASA*]
SL.............. Sound Level   (NASA)
SL.............. Sound Locator [*Military*]
SL.............. Source Language [*Data processing*]   (BUR)
SL.............. Source Level
SL.............. South Latitude
SL.............. Southeast Airlines, Inc. [*ICAO designator*] [*Obsolete*]   (OAG)
SL.............. Southern Lumberman [*United States*] [*A publication*]
SL.............. Soviet Life [*A publication*]
SL.............. Soviet Literature [*A publication*]
S/L............ Space Laboratory   (KSC)
SL.............. Spacelab [*NASA*]   (NASA)
SL.............. Spartacist League   (EA)
SL.............. Special Layout   (MCD)
SL.............. Special Libraries [*A publication*]
SL.............. Special Linear [*Group theory, mathematics*]
SL.............. Speed Lock [*Data processing*]   (PCM)
S/L............ Speedletter
SL.............. Split Level [*Home*] [*Classified advertising*]
SL.............. Spool
SL.............. Sport Leicht [*Sports Lightweight (Car)*] [*German*]
SL.............. Sprache und Literatur [*A publication*]
SL.............. Sprinkler Leakage [*Insurance*]
SL.............. Squadron-Leader [*Military*]
SL.............. Stage Left [*A stage direction*]
SL.............. Stagnation Line
SL.............. Standard Label [*Data processing*]
SL.............. Standard Length
SL.............. Standard of Living
SL.............. Standard Load [*Automotive engineering*]
SL.............. Standard Location [*Civil Defense*]
S & L .... Standards and Limits
SL.............. Star Line
SL.............. Start Line
SL.............. Stationary Low-Power [*Reactor*] [*Dismantled*]   (NRCH)
SL.............. Statistical List
S/L............ Statute of Limitations   (OICC)
SL.............. Stern Loading
SL.............. Stock Length [*Construction or manufacturing materials*]
SL.............. Stock Level   (AFM)
SL.............. Stock List   (MCD)
SL.............. Stomodeal Lip [*Endocrinology*]
SL.............. Stoplamp [*Automotive engineering*]
SL.............. Storage Location
SL.............. Straight Line
SL.............. Streamline
SL.............. Streptolysin [*Hematology*]

SL...............	Stronnictwo Ludowe [*Peasant Party*] [*Poland*] [*Political party*] (PPE)
SL...............	Structures Laboratory [*Army*] (GRD)
SL...............	Studies in Linguistics [*A publication*]
SL...............	Studio Location
SL...............	Sub-Lieutenant [*British military*]
SL...............	Suberin Lamella [*Botany*]
SL...............	Sublingual [*Medicine*]
SL...............	Submarine Lightwave Cable [*AT & T*] [*Telecommunications*]
SL...............	Submarine Qualification Lapsed [*Navy*]
SL...............	Subscriber's Loop [*Telecommunications*] (TEL)
SL...............	Sue and Labor Charges [*Insurance*]
SL...............	Sumerian Laws (BJA)
SL...............	Sumerisches Lexikon [*Rome*] [*A publication*]
SL...............	Sunday League (EA)
sl................	Suo Loco [*In Its Place*] [*Latin*] (WGA)
SL...............	Superlattice [*Solid state physics*]
SL...............	Supplementary List [*Navy*] [*British*]
SL...............	Supplier Letter (MCD)
S & L..........	Supply and Logistics
SL...............	Support Line [*Military*]
SL...............	Surface Launch (MUGU)
SL...............	Surveillance Licence [*Importing*] [*British*] (DS)
SL...............	Svenska Landsmal och Svenskt Folkliv [*A publication*]
SL...............	Sydney & Louisburg Railway Co. [*AAR code*]
SL...............	Synchronous Line Medium Speed (BUR)
SL...............	Syria and Lebanon
SL...............	System Language
S & L..........	System and Logistics
SLA............	La Ronge Public Library, Saskatchewan [*Library symbol*] [*National Library of Canada*] (NLC)
SLA............	Left Sacroanterior Position [*of the fetus*] [*Obstetrics*]
SLA............	Sacrolaeva Anterior [*A fetal position*] (AAMN)
SLA............	Salta [*Argentina*] [*Airport symbol*] (OAG)
SLA............	San Lorenzo [*Argentina*] [*Seismograph station code, US Geological Survey*] (SEIS)
SLA............	Sandia Laboratories, Albuquerque (AABC)
SLA............	Saturn LM [*Lunar Module*] Adapter [*NASA*]
SLA............	Scanning LASER Altimeter (SSD)
SLA............	School Lecturers' Association [*British*]
SLA............	School Library Association
SLA............	Scott Library [*A publication*]
SLA............	Scottish Library Association
SLA............	Sealed Lead Acid [*Battery*] [*Automotive engineering*]
SLA............	Second Language Acquisition
SLA............	Sequential Launch Adapter [*Missiles*] (RDA)
SLA............	Shared Line Adapter
SLA............	Short and Long Arm [*Automotive engineering*]
SLA............	Showmen's League of America (EA)
SLA............	Side-Looking LASER Altimeter (RDA)
SLA............	Sierra Leone Airlines
SL & A.......	Sine Loco et Anno [*Without Place and Year*] [*Latin*]
SLA............	Single-Line Approach
Sla.............	Slavia [*A publication*]
sla.............	Slavic [*MARC language code*] [*Library of Congress*] (LCCP)
SLA............	Sleep-Learning Association (EA)
SLA............	Slide Latex Agglutination [*Clinical chemistry*] (AAMN)
SLA............	Slovak League of America (EA)
SLA............	Society for Linguistic Anthropology (EA)
SLA............	South Lebanon Army
SLA............	Southeastern Library Association (AEBS)
SLA............	Southwestern Library Association (AEBS)
SLA............	Spacecraft LM [*Lunar Module*] Adapter [*NASA*]
SLA............	Special Libraries Association (EA)
SLA............	Specific Leaf Area [*Botany*]
SLA............	Sports Lawyers Association (EA)
SLA............	Square Loop Antenna
SLA............	Stable Lads' Association [*British*] (ECON)
SLA............	Standard Life Association (EA)
SLA............	Standard Location Area [*Civil Defense*]
SLA............	State Liquor Authority
SLA............	Stereolithography [*Desktop manufacturing*]
SLA............	Stored Logic Array
SLA............	Strategic Logistics Agency [*Army*] (RDA)
SLA............	Stripline
SLA............	Studies in Linguistic Analysis [*Elsevier Book Series*] [*A publication*]
SLA............	Sulfur-Lead Analyzer
SLA............	Supplies in Liberated Areas [*British*] [*World War II*]
SLA............	Supply Loading Airfield
SLA............	Support and Logistics Areas [*NASA*] (MCD)
SLA............	Svenska Linne-Sallskapet Arsskrift [*A publication*]
SLA............	Switching Linear Amplifier
SLA............	Symbionese Liberation Army (EA)
SLA............	Synchronous Line Adapter
SLAA........	Sex and Love Addicts Anonymous (EA)
SLAA........	Society for Latin American Anthropology (EA)
SLAA........	State and Local Assistance Act
SLA Adv & Mkt Div Bul ...	Special Libraries Association. Advertising and Marketing Division. Bulletin [*A publication*]
SLA Alabama Chap Bul ...	Special Libraries Association. Alabama Chapter. Bulletin [*A publication*]
SLAAP	St. Louis Army Ammunition Plant
SLAAS......	Supersonic Low-Altitude Attack Aircraft System (MCD)
SLAB	Abopo [*Bolivia*] [*ICAO location identifier*] (ICLI)
SLAB	Sage Laboratories, Inc. [*NASDAQ symbol*] (NQ)
SLAB	Students for Labeling of Alcoholic Beverages [*Student legal action organization*]
SLABCON ...	Slab Construction
SLA Biol Sci Div Reminder ...	Special Libraries Association. Biological Sciences Division. Reminder [*A publication*]
Slaboproudy Obz ...	Slaboproudy Obzor [*Czechoslovakia*] [*A publication*]
SLA Bus & Fin Div Bul ...	Special Libraries Association. Business and Financial Division. Bulletin [*A publication*]
SLAC	Special Committee on Latin American Coordination
SLAC	Stanford Linear Accelerator Center [*Stanford, CA*] [*Department of Energy*]
SLAC	Stowage Launch Adapter Container
SLAC	Straight-Line (Linear) Accelerator [*Nuclear energy*]
SLAC	Support List Allowance Card (MCD)
SLAD........	Salon Litteraire, Artistique, et Diplomatique
SLAD........	Shipboard Landing Assist Device
SLAD........	SONAR Locator, Altimeter, and Depthometer
SLAD........	System Logic and Algorithm Development
Slade	Slade's Reports [*15 Vermont*] [*A publication*] (DLA)
SLADE.......	Society of Lithographic Artists, Designers, and Engineers [*British*]
SLAE	Standard Lightweight Avionics Equipment [*Army*] (RDA)
SLAET	Society of Licensed Aircraft Engineers and Technologists (EAIO)
SLA Fin Div Bul ...	Special Libraries Association. Financial Division. Bulletin [*A publication*]
SLAFRS	Southwestern Livestock and Forage Research Station [*Oklahoma State University*] [*Research center*] (RCD)
SLAG........	Monteagudo [*Bolivia*] [*ICAO location identifier*] (ICLI)
SLAG........	Safe Launch Angle Gate
SLAG........	Scottish Legal Action Group (ILCA)
SLAG........	Side-Looking Air-to-Ground [*RADAR*]
SLA GA Chap Bul ...	Special Libraries Association. Georgia Chapter. Bulletin [*A publication*]
SLA Geog & Map Div Bul ...	Special Libraries Association. Geography and Map Division. Bulletin [*A publication*]
SLA Geog and Map Div Bull ...	Special Libraries Association. Geography and Map Division. Bulletin [*A publication*]
SLAHF	Slovak League of America Heritage Foundation (EA)
SLAHTS ...	Stowage List and Hardware Tracking System [*NASA*] (MCD)
SLA Ind Chap Slant ...	Special Libraries Association. Indiana Chapter. Slant [*A publication*]
SLAIS........	School of Library, Archival, and Information Studies [*University of British Columbia, Vancouver*] [*Canada*]
SLAIT.......	Study Group on Legal Aspects of Intermodal Transportation [*National Research Council*]
SLAK	Spacelab Late Access Kit [*NASA*] (NASA)
SLAKSJ	Supreme Ladies Auxiliary Knights of St. John (EA)
SLAL	Stowage Launch Adapter, Lower
SLAM	Samuel Lyman Atwood Marshall [*American general and author, 1900-1977*]
SLAM.......	Scanning LASER Acoustic Microscope
SLAM.......	Sea-Launched Air Missile (NVT)
SLAM.......	Seeking, Locating, Annihilating, Monitoring [*Army project, Vietnam*]
SLAM.......	Short LOFAR [*Low-Frequency Acquisition and Ranging*] Alerting Message (NVT)
SLAM.......	Shoulder-Launched Antitank Missile [*Army*]
SLAM.......	Side Load Arresting Mechanism (KSC)
SLAM.......	Sierra Leone Alliance Movement (PD)
SLAM.......	Simulation Language for Alternative Modeling [*Data processing*] (CSR)
SLAM.......	Society's League Against Molestation (EA)
SLAM.......	Space-Launched Air Missile (MCD)
SLAM.......	Spares Level Activity Model (MCD)
SLAM.......	Standoff Land Attack Missile [*Military*]
SLAM.......	Stowage Launch Adapter, Middle
SLAM.......	Strategic Low Attitude Missile
SLAM.......	Stress Wave in Layered Arbitrary Media (SAA)
SLAM.......	Submarine-Launched Air Missile
SLAM.......	Supersonic Low-Altitude Missile [*Later, LASV*] [*NATO*] (NATG)
SLAM.......	Support List Allowance Master
SLAM.......	Surface-Launched Air Missile
SLAM.......	Surface Look-Alike Mine
SLAM.......	Symbolic Language Adapted for Microcomputers
SLA Metals Div News ...	Special Libraries Association. Metals Division. News [*A publication*]
SLAMEX ..	Submarine-Launched Assault Missile Exercise (NVT)
SLA Mich Chap Bul ...	Special Libraries Association. Michigan Chapter. Bulletin [*A publication*]
SLA Montreal Chap Bul ...	Special Libraries Association. Montreal Chapter. Bulletin [*A publication*]
SLAMS	Simplified Language for Abstract Mathematical Structures [*Data processing*] (IEEE)

SLAMS ..... State and Local Air Monitoring Stations [*Environmental Protection Agency*]
SLAMS ..... Successive Linear Approximation at Minimum Step   (SAA)
SLAMS ..... Surface Look-Alike Mine System   (MCD)
SLA Museum Div Bul ... Special Libraries Association. Museum Division. Bulletin [*A publication*]
SLAN......... Angora [*Bolivia*] [*ICAO location identifier*]   (ICLI)
SLAN......... Shock Landing Analysis   (MCD)
SLAN......... Sine Loco, Anno, vel Nomine [*Without Place, Year, or Name*] [*Latin*]
SLAN......... Slander [*or Slanderous*] [*FBI standardized term*]
SLA News ... SLA [*Scottish Library Association*] News [*A publication*]
SLANG...... Selected Letter and Abbreviated Name Guide [*Environmental Protection Agency*] [*A publication*]   (GFGA)
S Lang........ Studies in Language [*A publication*]
SLANG...... Systems Language
SLANT ...... Simulator Landing Attachment for Night Landing Training
SlAnt.......... Slavia Antiqua [*A publication*]
Slants Khim Prom-St ... Slantsevaya i Khimicheskaya Promyshlennost [*Estonian SSR*] [*A publication*]
SLAO........ Committee on Supply Questions in Liberated Areas (Official) [*World War II*]
SLAP .... Apolo [*Bolivia*] [*ICAO location identifier*]   (ICLI)
SLAP .... Office of State and Local Assistance Programs [*Department of Energy*]
SLAP .... Saboted Light Armor Penetrator [*Weaponry*]   (MCD)
SLAP .... Sandia-Livermore Aeroheating Program
SLAP .... Serum Leucine Aminopeptidase [*An enzyme*]   (MAE)
SLAP .... Service Life Assessment Program [*Military*]
SLAP .... Simplified Labor and Performance   (MCD)
SLAP .... Symbolic Language Assembly Program [*Data processing*]   (KSC)
SLAPC...... Studies in Latin American Popular Culture [*A publication*]
SLA Picture Div Picturescope ... Special Libraries Association. Picture Division. Picturescope [*A publication*]
SLA Pittsburgh Chap Bul ... Special Libraries Association. Pittsburgh Chapter. Bulletin [*A publication*]
SLAPN ...... Succinyl-L-alanyl-L-alanyl-L-alanine-p-nitroanilide [*Biochemistry*]
SLAPP...... Strategic Lawsuit Against Public Participation [*Term coined by George Pring and Penelope Canan*]
SLAPS...... Subscriber Loop Analysis Program System [*Bell System*]
SLAQ........ Aiquile [*Bolivia*] [*ICAO location identifier*]   (ICLI)
SLAR........ Select ADC [*Analog-to-Digital Converter*] Register [*Data processing*]   (MDG)
SLAR .... Senior Logistics Aviation Representative   (MCD)
SLAR .... Side-Looking Aerial [*or Airborne*] RADAR [*Military*]
SLAR .... Slant Range
SLAR .... Slargando [*Slackening*] [*Music*]   (ROG)
SLAR .... Steerable LASER Radiometer   (MCD)
SLARD...... Saskatchewan Law Review [*A publication*]
SLARF...... Slant Range Fuze   (NG)
SLARG...... Slargando [*Slackening*] [*Music*]
SLAS .... Ascencion De Guarayos [*Bolivia*] [*ICAO location identifier*]   (ICLI)
SLAS .... Society for Latin American Studies [*British*]
SLAS .... State Library Agency Section [*Association of Specialized and Cooperative Library Agencies*]
SLASC...... St. Louis Area Support Center [*Military*]   (MCD)
SLA Sci-Tech News ... Special Libraries Association. Science-Technology Division. News [*A publication*]
SLASER .... Space LASER   (SSD)
SLASH ...... Second Edition List of Australian Subject Headings [*A publication*]
SLASH ...... Seiler Laboratory ALGOL Simulated Hybrid [*Data processing*]
SLASH ...... Small Light Antisubmarine Helicopter
Slaski Kwar Hist Sobotka ... Slaski Kwartalnik Historyczny Sobotka [*A publication*]
SLAST...... Submarine-Launched Antiship Torpedo
SLAT .... Sample Lot Acceptance Testing
s lat........... Sensu Lato [*In a Wide Sense*] [*Latin*]
SLAT .... Ship-Launched Air Targeting   (MCD)
SLAT .... Sindacato Lavoratori Amministrativi e Technichi [*Union of Administration and Technical Workers*] [*Somalia*]
SLAT .... Slater Electric, Inc. [*NASDAQ symbol*]   (NQ)
SLAT .... South Latitude
SLAT .... Special Logistics Actions, Thailand   (AABC)
SLAT .... Supersonic Low Activities Target   (MCD)
SLAT .... Supersonic Low-Altitude Target [*Navy*]
SLAT .... Support List Allowance Tape   (MCD)
SLAT .... Surface Launcher Air-Targeted [*Weapon*]   (MCD)
SLATA ...... Secondary Learning Assistance Teachers' Association. Newsletter [*A publication*]
SLATE ...... Organization of campus activists at the University of California, Berkeley [*Name, although capitalized, is not an acronym but is instead derived from the group's founding in 1958, when it ran a slate of candidates for student government*]
SLATE ...... Ship-Launched ASW [*Antisubmarine Warfare*] Two-Way Expendable [*Buoy*] [*Navy*]   (CAAL)
SLATE ...... Small, Lightweight Altitude-Transmission Equipment [*FAA*]
SLATE ...... Stimulated Learning by Automated Typewriter Environment

SLA Texas Chap Bul ... Special Libraries Association. Texas Chapter. Bulletin [*A publication*]
SLATO...... Secretariado Latinamericano de Trotskismo Orthodoxo [*Peru*]
SLA Toronto Chap Bul ... Special Libraries Association. Toronto Chapter. Bulletin [*A publication*]
SLAU......... San Aurelio [*Bolivia*] [*ICAO location identifier*]   (ICLI)
SLAU......... Stowage Launch Adapter, Upper
SLAUGH .. Slaughter [*England*]
SLAV .... Avicaya [*Bolivia*] [*ICAO location identifier*]   (ICLI)
Slav .... Slavia [*A publication*]
SLAV .... Slavonic [*Language, etc.*]
SLAV .... Special Logistics Actions, South Vietnam   (CINC)
SlavA .... Slavia Antiqua [*A publication*]
SLAVCA ... Sindacato Nazionale Lavoratori Vetro e Ceramica [*National Union of Glass and Ceramics' Workers*] [*Italy*]
Slav East Eur Rev ... Slavonic and East European Review [*A publication*]
Slav E Eur ... Slavic and East European Journal [*A publication*]
SlavEnoch ... Slavic Book of Enoch   (BJA)
Slav Euro Educ Rev ... Slavic and European Education Review [*A publication*]
SlavF.......... Slavjanskaja Filologija [*A publication*]
Slav Goth ... Slavica Gothoburgensia [*A publication*]
Slav Helv ... Slavica Helvetica [*A publication*]
Slavia Ant .. Slavia Antiqua [*A publication*]
Slavic E Eu ... Slavic and East European Journal [*A publication*]
Slavic & E Eur J ... Slavic and East European Journal [*A publication*]
Slavic R..... Slavic Review [*A publication*]
Slavic Rev .. Slavic Review [*A publication*]
Slav Lund... Slavica Lundensia [*A publication*]
SlavO......... Slavica Othiniensia [*A publication*]
Slav Occ ... Slavia Occidentalis [*A publication*]
Slavon E Eu ... Slavonic and East European Review [*A publication*]
Slavon & E Eur R ... Slavonic and East European Review [*A publication*]
Slavonic & E Eur R ... Slavonic and East European Review [*A publication*]
Slavonic R ... Slavonic Review [*A publication*]
Slav Or....... Slavia Orientalis [*A publication*]
SlavP.......... Slavica Pragensia [*A publication*]
SlavR......... Slavic Review [*A publication*]
Slav R........ Slavische Rundschau [*A publication*]
SlavR......... Slavisticna Revija [*A publication*]
SLAVR ...... Slavonic Review [*A publication*]
SlavRev...... Slavisticna Revija [*A publication*]
SlavS.......... Slavica Slovaca [*A publication*]
SLAW....... Conference on the Sociology of the Languages of American Women [*1976*]
SLAW....... St. Lawrence Railroad [*Division of National Railway Utilization Corp.*] [*AAR code*]
SLA Western NY Chap Bul ... Special Libraries Association. Western New York Chapter. Bulletin [*A publication*]
SLAX......... Ay-Luri [*Bolivia*] [*ICAO location identifier*]   (ICLI)
SLB............ St. Louis Blueliners   (EA)
SLB............ Schaulade. Unabhaengiges Internationales Fachblatt fuer Porzellan, Keramik, Glas, Geschenkartikel, und Hausrat [*A publication*]
SLB............ Schlumberger Ltd. [*NYSE symbol*]   (SPSG)
SLB............ Self-Lubricating Bearing
SLB............ Short Leg Brace [*Medicine*]
SLB............ Side-Lobe Blanking [*RADAR*]
SLB............ Signal Light Bare   (MSA)
SLB............ Sintered Lead Bronze
SLB............ Solomon Islands [*ANSI three-letter standard code*]   (CNC)
SLB............ Southland Aviation, Inc. [*Destin, FL*] [*FAA designator*]   (FAAC)
SLB............ Steam Line Break   (NRCH)
SLB............ Storm Lake, IA [*Location identifier*] [*FAA*]   (FAAL)
SLBC .... Superannuation Law Bulletin [*A publication*]
SLBC .... Boca Chapare [*Bolivia*] [*ICAO location identifier*]   (ICLI)
SLBEDP.... Suicide and Life-Threatening Behavior [*A publication*]
SLBF......... Blanca Flor [*Bolivia*] [*ICAO location identifier*]   (ICLI)
SLBH........ Buena Hora [*Bolivia*] [*ICAO location identifier*]   (ICLI)
SLBJ......... Bermejo [*Bolivia*] [*ICAO location identifier*]   (ICLI)
SLBL .... Soluble   (MSA)
SLBM........ Sea [*or Submarine or Surface*]-Launched Ballistic Missile [*Navy*]   (CAAL)
SLBMD & W ... Sea-Launched Ballistic Missile Detection and Warning
SLBMDWS ... Submarine-Launched Ballistic Missile Detection and Warning System   (IEEE)
SLBN........ Bella Union [*Bolivia*] [*ICAO location identifier*]   (ICLI)
SLBP .... Spring-Loaded Ball Plunger
SLBR .... Slaughter Brothers, Inc. [*NASDAQ symbol*]   (NQ)
SLBS......... Sierra Leone Broadcasting Service
SLBtry .... Searchlight Battery [*Army*]
SLBU........ Baures [*Bolivia*] [*ICAO location identifier*]   (ICLI)
SLBV .... Villa Vista [*Bolivia*] [*ICAO location identifier*]   (ICLI)
SLBW .... Buena Vista [*Bolivia*] [*ICAO location identifier*]   (ICLI)
SLBY .... Boyuibe [*Bolivia*] [*ICAO location identifier*]   (ICLI)
SLC........... Salt Lake City [*Utah*] [*Seismograph station code, US Geological Survey*]   (SEIS)
SLC........... Salt Lake City [*Utah*]
SLC........... Salt Lake City [*Utah*] [*Airport symbol*]   (OAG)
SLC........... Salt Lake City, UT [*Location identifier*] [*FAA*]   (FAAL)
SLC........... [*The*] San Luis Central Railroad Co. [*AAR code*]

SLC........... Sarah Lawrence College [*Bronxville, NY*]
SLC........... Satellite LASER Communication [*Military*]
SLC........... Scottish Land Court Reports [*A publication*]   (DLA)
SLC........... Scottish Leaving Certificate
SLC........... Sea-Level Canal Study   (IID)
SLC........... Searchlight Control [*Military*]
SLC........... Secretarial Language Certificate [*British*]   (DI)
SLC........... Selector Channel
SLC........... Set Location Counter   (CMD)
SLC........... Shelf Life Code   (MCD)
SLC........... Shift Left and Count Instructions [*Data processing*]   (MDG)
SL & C....... Shipper's Load and Count [*Bills of lading*]
SLC........... Shuttle Launch Center [*Vandenberg Air Force Base, CA*] [*NASA*]
SLC........... Side-Lobe Cancellation [*RADAR*]
SLC........... Side-Lobe Clutter
SLC........... Signal Level Converter   (DWSG)
SLC........... Simulated Linguistic Computer
SLC........... Single Launch Contractor   (KSC)
SLC........... Single Line Control   (BUR)
SLC........... Slice   (MSA)
SLC........... Small Library Computing, Inc. [*Information service or system*]   (IID)
SLC........... Smith's Leading Cases [*A publication*]   (DLA)
SLC........... Songwriters and Lyricists Club   (EA)
SLC........... Sonobuoy Launch Container   (NVT)
SLC........... South London College [*London, England*]
SLCY.......... Southland Corp. [*NYSE symbol*]   (SPSG)
SLC........... Space Launch Complex [*NASA*]
SLC........... Spanish Literature Committee   (EA)
SLC........... Special Libraries Cataloguing, Inc. [*Information service or system*]   (IID)
SLC........... Sport Leicht Coupe [*Sports Lightweight Coupe*] [*German*]
SLC........... Standard Launch Complex   (KSC)
SLC........... Standard Location Codes
SLC........... Standby Liquid Control [*Nuclear energy*]   (NRCH)
SLC........... Standing Liaison Committee
SLC........... Stanford Linear Collider [*High-energy physics*]
SLC........... State Legislative Committee
SLC........... State Library of Ohio, Catalog Center, Columbus, OH [*OCLC symbol*]   (OCLC)
SLC........... State Line Airport [*Leawood, KS*] [*FAA designator*]   (FAAC)
SLC........... Stockage List Code [*Military*]   (AABC)
SLC........... Straight-Line Capacitance [*or Capacity*]
SLC........... Strategic LASER Communications [*Military*]   (CAAL)
SLC........... Stuart's Lower Canada Appeal Cases [*1810-35*] [*A publication*]   (DLA)
SLC........... Sublingual Cleft [*Medicine*]
SLC........... Submarine LASER Communications
SLC........... Subscriber Loop Carrier [*Telecommunications*]   (TEL)
SLC........... Sue and Labor Clause [*Business term*]
SLC........... Surgeon Lieutenant-Commander [*British military*]
SLC........... Susquehanna Library Cooperative [*Library network*]
SLC........... Sustained Load Crack [*Titanium alloy*]
SLC........... Synchro Loop Closure
SLC........... Synchronous Line Medium Speed with Clock   (BUR)
SLC........... Synchronous Link Control [*Data processing*]
SLC........... System Life Cycle
SLCA......... Camiri [*Bolivia*] [*ICAO location identifier*]   (ICLI)
SLC App.... Stuart's Lower Canada Appeal Cases [*A publication*]   (DLA)
SLCB........ Cochabamba/Jorge Wilsterman [*Bolivia*] [*ICAO location identifier*]   (ICLI)
SLCB........ Single-Line Color Bar   (IEEE)
SLCBMA .. Solid Leather Case and Bag Makers' Association [*A union*] [*British*]
SLCC........ Copacabana [*Bolivia*] [*ICAO location identifier*]   (ICLI)
SLCC........ Lincoln Cent Collectors Society   (EA)
SLCC........ Saturn Launch Control Computer [*NASA*]   (KSC)
SLCC........ Society of Local Council Clerks [*British*]
SLCD........ Surplus Land for Community Development
SLCG........ Charagua [*Bolivia*] [*ICAO location identifier*]   (ICLI)
SLCH........ Chapacura [*Bolivia*] [*ICAO location identifier*]   (ICLI)
SLCI......... Clara Rios [*Bolivia*] [*ICAO location identifier*]   (ICLI)
SLCJ......... Cavinas [*Bolivia*] [*ICAO location identifier*]   (ICLI)
SLCL........ Collpani [*Bolivia*] [*ICAO location identifier*]   (ICLI)
SLCL........ Shop/Lab Configuration Layout [*NASA*]   (MCD)
SLCL........ Sierra Leone Council of Labour
SLCL........ Small Lymphocyte Cell Lymphoma [*Oncology*]
SLCM........ Camiare [*Bolivia*] [*ICAO location identifier*]   (ICLI)
SLCM........ Sea-Launched Cruise Missile [*Pronounced "slick-em"*]   (AABC)
SLCM........ Ship Life-Cycle Management
SLCM........ Software Life Cycle Management
SLCM........ [*The*] Southland Corp. [*NASDAQ symbol*]   (NQ)
SLCM........ Structural Liquid Composite Molding [*Plastics technology*]
SLCM........ Submarine-Launched Cruise Missile   (IEEE)
SLCM........ Surface Launch Cruise Missile
SLCMP .... Software Life Cycle Management Plan   (DNAB)
SLCN........ Charana [*Bolivia*] [*ICAO location identifier*]   (ICLI)
SL Co........ Appendices of Proceedings of the Scottish Land Court [*A publication*]   (DLA)
SLCO........ Cobija [*Bolivia*] [*ICAO location identifier*]   (ICLI)

SL Co R...... Appendices of Proceedings of the Scottish Land Court [*A publication*]   (DLA)
SL Council Phila & Vicinity Bul ... Special Libraries Council of Philadelphia and Vicinity. Bulletin [*A publication*]
SLCP .... Concepcion [*Bolivia*] [*ICAO location identifier*]   (ICLI)
SLCP .... Saturn Launch Computer Program   (OA)
SLCP .... Ship's Loading Characteristics Pamphlet [*Navy*]   (NVT)
SLCP .... Standing Liaison Committee of Physiotherapists within the EEC [*European Economic Community*] [*See also CPLK*] [*Copenhagen, Denmark*]   (EAIO)
SLCQ........ Copaquilla [*Bolivia*] [*ICAO location identifier*]   (ICLI)
SLCR .... Comarapa [*Bolivia*] [*ICAO location identifier*]   (ICLI)
SLCR .... Salem Carpet Mills, Inc. [*NASDAQ symbol*]   (NQ)
SLCR .... Scottish Land Court Reports [*A publication*]   (DLA)
SLCRM ..... Ship Life-Cycle Reference Matrix [*Navy*]
SLCRS....... Supplementary Leak Collection and Release System [*Nuclear energy*]   (NRCH)
SLCS......... Cerdas [*Bolivia*] [*ICAO location identifier*]   (ICLI)
SLCS......... Standby Liquid Control System [*Nuclear energy*]   (NRCH)
SLCS......... Studies in Language. Companion Series [*A publication*]
SLCSAT .... Submarine LASER Communications Satellite   (MCD)
SLCT .... Choreti [*Bolivia*] [*ICAO location identifier*]   (ICLI)
SLCT .... Select   (FAAC)
SLCU......... Standard Landing Craft Unit [*Military*]
SLCU......... Synchronous Line Control Unit
SLCV .... Cavinas [*Bolivia*] [*ICAO location identifier*]   (ICLI)
SLCV .... Squash Leaf Curl Virus
SLCY .... Collpa [*Bolivia*] [*ICAO location identifier*]   (ICLI)
SLCZ .... Santa Cruz/El Trompillo [*Bolivia*] [*ICAO location identifier*]   (ICLI)
SLD........... Sailed
SLD........... San Luis Dam [*California*] [*Seismograph station code, US Geological Survey*]   (SEIS)
SLD........... Sea Landing Division [*NATO*]
SLD........... Sealed
SLD........... Secretarial Language Diploma [*British*]   (DI)
SLD........... Serum Lactate Dehydrogenase [*Also, SLDH*] [*An enzyme*]
SLD........... Shelf Life Data [*Army*]
SLD........... Shutdown Logic Diagram [*Nuclear energy*]   (NRCH)
SLD........... Simulated Launch Demonstration [*NASA*]   (KSC)
SLD........... Sliac [*Former Czechoslovakia*] [*Airport symbol*]   (OAG)
SLD........... Slide
SLD........... Sliding Door   (AAG)
SLD........... Slim Line Diffuser   (OA)
SLD........... Slowdown   (AAG)
SLD........... Slumber Lodge Development Corp. Ltd. [*Vancouver Stock Exchange symbol*]
SLD........... Social and Liberal Democrats [*British*] [*Political party*]   (ECON)
SLD........... Society of Loyalist Descendants   (EA)
SLD........... Sold
SLD........... Solder
SLD........... Solid   (FAAC)
SLD........... Solid Logic Dense   (BUR)
SLD........... Sonic Layer Depth   (NVT)
SLD........... Source Language Debug [*Data processing*]   (IEEE)
SLD........... Source-Level Debugger [*Motorola, Inc.*]
SLD........... Special Litigation Division [*Environmental Protection Agency*]   (GFGA)
SLD........... Specific Language [*or Learning*] Disability [*Education*]
SLD........... Square Law Detection
SLD........... Stiff-Leg Derrick   (NASA)
SLD........... Straight Line Depreciation [*Telecommunications*]   (TEL)
SLD........... Superluminescent Diode [*Tomography*]
SLD........... Synchronous Line Driver
SLDAA...... SACLANT [*Supreme Allied Commander, Atlantic*] Distributing and Accounting Agency   (NATG)
SLD CARB DI ... Solidified Carbon Dioxide [*Freight*]
SLDD........ Scientific Library and Documentation Division [*National Science and Technology Authority*] [*Philippines*] [*Information service or system*]   (IID)
SLDG........ Sliding
SLDH .... Serum Lactate Dehydrogenase [*Also, SLD*] [*An enzyme*]
SLDN .... El Desengano [*Bolivia*] [*ICAO location identifier*]   (ICLI)
SLDP .... Loma Del Porvenir [*Bolivia*] [*ICAO location identifier*]   (ICLI)
SLDP .... Sierra Leone Democratic Party [*Political party*]   (EY)
SLDPF....... Spacelab Data Processing Facility   (MCD)
SLDR .... Solder   (MSA)
SLDR .... Soldier
S/Ldr .... Squadron Leader [*British military*]   (DMA)
SLDR .... System Loader [*Data processing*]
SLDS .... Scanning LASER Doppler System [*NASA*]
SLDS .... Skylab Launch Data System [*NASA*]   (KSC)
SLDTF....... State and Local Documents Task Force [*Government Documents Round Table*] [*American Library Association*]
SLDTSS..... Single Language Dedicated Time-Sharing System
SLDVS ...... Scanning LASER Doppler Vortex System [*NASA*]
SLE.......... St. Louis Encephalitis [*Medicine*]
SLE........... Salem [*Oregon*] [*Airport symbol*]   (OAG)
SLE........... Salem, OR [*Location identifier*] [*FAA*]   (FAAL)
SLE........... Sara Lee Corp. [*NYSE symbol*]   (SPSG)

SLE .... Service Life Evaluation
SLE .... Shuttle Transport [*New York, NY*] [*FAA designator*]   (FAAC)
SLE .... Sierra Leone [*ANSI three-letter standard code*]   (CNC)
SLE .... Small Lattice Experiment
SLE .... Small Local Exchange [*Telecommunications*]   (TEL)
SLE .... Smith, Leland C., Oakland CA [*STAC*]
SLE .... Snap Lock Environmental [*Electrical engineering*]
SLE .... Societas Linguistica Europaea [*Linguistic Society of Europe*] [*Austria*]   (EAIO)
SLE .... Society of Logistics Engineers   (MCD)
SLE .... Spacelab Engineering [*European Research National Organization*]   (MCD)
SLE .... Station Liaison Engineer [*NASA*]
SLE .... Stochastic Liouville Equation [*Statistical mechanics*]
SLE .... Student Letter Exchange   (EA)
SLE .... Studio Lighting Equipment
SLE .... Sulphurets Gold [*Vancouver Stock Exchange symbol*]
SLE .... Superheat Limit Explosion
SLE .... Systemic Lupus Erythematosus [*Medicine*]
SLEC .... El Cairo [*Bolivia*] [*ICAO location identifier*]   (ICLI)
SLEC .... Southland Energy Corp. [*NASDAQ symbol*]   (NQ)
SLED .... El Dorado [*Bolivia*] [*ICAO location identifier*]   (ICLI)
SLED .... Single Large Expensive Disk [*Data processing*]   (PCM)
SLED .... State Level Electricity Demand [*Model*] [*Nuclear Regulatory Commission*]
SLED .... Surface Light Emitting Diode [*Electronics*]
SLED .... System-Level Engineering Document   (SSD)
SLEDGE .... Simulating Large Explosive Detonable Gas Experiments
SLEEC ...... Shingle Lap Extendable Exit Cone   (MCD)
SLEEP ...... Scanning Low-Energy Electron Probe   (IEEE)
SLEEP ...... Silent, Lightweight, Electric Energy Plant   (RDA)
SLEEP ...... Swedish Low-Energy Experimental Pile [*Nuclear energy*]
Sleep Sick Bureau Bull ... Sleeping Sickness Bureau. Bulletin [*A publication*]
SLEF .... El Triunfo [*Bolivia*] [*ICAO location identifier*]   (ICLI)
SLEH .... Stage Loose Equipment Hardware   (SAA)
SLEICC ..... Statue of Liberty - Ellis Island Centennial Commission   (EA)
SLEIF .... Statue of Liberty - Ellis Island Foundation   (EA)
SLEJ .... El Jovi [*Bolivia*] [*ICAO location identifier*]   (ICLI)
SLEL .... El Roseda [*Bolivia*] [*ICAO location identifier*]   (ICLI)
SLEM .... Solution of Linearized Equations of Motion
SLEMA ..... Schiffli Lace and Embroidery Manufacturers Association   (EA)
SLEMU ..... Spacelab Engineering Model Unit [*NASA*]   (MCD)
SLENT ...... Slentando [*Slackening*] [*Music*]   (ROG)
SLEO .... El Paraiso [*Bolivia*] [*ICAO location identifier*]   (ICLI)
SLEP .... El Peru [*Bolivia*] [*ICAO location identifier*]   (ICLI)
SLEP .... Second Large ESRO [*European Space Research Organization*] Project
SLEP .... Secondary Level English Proficiency Test
SLEP .... Service Life Extension Program [*Military*]   (MCD)
SLEP .... State Line End Point   (DNAB)
SLES .... Espiritu [*Bolivia*] [*ICAO location identifier*]   (ICLI)
SLESP .... Semilinear Erection System   (SAA)
SLESP .... Suplemento Literario do Estado de Sao Paulo [*A publication*]
Sleszky Num ... Sleszky Numismatik [*A publication*]
SLet .... Sestante Letterario [*A publication*]
SLEU .... Eucaliptos [*Bolivia*] [*ICAO location identifier*]   (ICLI)
SLEUTH ... UNIVAC 1108 Assembly Language
SLEV .... El Salvador [*Bolivia*] [*ICAO location identifier*]   (ICLI)
SLEV .... St. Louis Encephalitis Virus
SLEV .... Salaried Legal Expense Voucher
SLEVA ...... Slevarenstvi [*A publication*]
SLEW .... Static Load Error Washout
SLEZ .... La Esperanza [*Bolivia*] [*ICAO location identifier*]   (ICLI)
SLF .... Saturn Launch Facility [*NASA*]
SLF .... Savings and Loan Foundation [*Later, FSI*]   (EA)
SLF .... Scientific Laboratory Facility
SLF .... Shuttle Landing Facility [*NASA*]   (MCD)
SLF .... Skandinaviska Lackteknikers Forbund [*Federation of Scandinavian Paint and Varnish Technologists*] [*Sweden*]   (EAIO)
SLF .... Skrifter Utgivna av Svenska Litteratursaellskapet i Finland [*A publication*]
SLF .... Society of the Little Flower   (EA)
SLF .... South Luzon Force [*Army*] [*World War II*]
SLF .... Southwestern Legal Foundation   (DLA)
SLF .... Special Landing Forces [*Marine Corps*]
SLF .... Straight-Line Frequency
SLF .... Stress Loading Facility [*Fort Huachuca, AZ*] [*United States Army Electronic Proving Ground*]   (GRD)
SLF .... Suction Line Filter
SLF .... Super-Low-Frequency   (MCD)
SLF .... Svenska Litteratursaellskapet i Finland [*A publication*]
SLF .... System Library File [*Data processing*]   (BUR)
SLFA .... Fatima [*Bolivia*] [*ICAO location identifier*]   (ICLI)
SLFA .... Svensklaerarfoereningens Arsskrift [*A publication*]
SLFB .... Solid-Liquid Fluidized Bed [*Chemical engineering*]
SLFC .... Shoreline Financial Corp. [*NASDAQ symbol*]   (NQ)
SLFC .... Sierra Leone Full Court Reports [*A publication*]   (DLA)
SLFC .... Steve Long Fan Club   (EA)
SLFC .... Survivable Low-Frequency Communications [*Air Force*]
SLFCLN .... Self-Cleaning [*Engineering*]

SLFCS .... Survivable Low-Frequency Communications System [*Air Force*]
SLFD .... Steam Lava Flow Deflector   (MCD)
SLFGEN ... Self-Generating
SLFIA .... Substrate-Labeled Fluorescent Immunoassay
SLFIND..... Self-Indicating
S-LFL .... Short-Long Flashing Light [*Navigation signal*]
SLFLKG .... Self-Locking [*Engineering*]
SLFOEAMTMTS ... St. Louis Field Office, Eastern Area, Military Traffic Management and Terminal Service [*Army*]   (AABC)
SLFP .... Sri Lanka Freedom Party [*Political party*]   (PPW)
SLFSE .... Self-Sealing [*Engineering*]
SLFTPG .... Self-Tapping [*Screw*] [*Design engineering*]
SLFU .... Skrifter Utgivna. Genom Landsmals-och Folk-Minnesarkivet i Uppsala [*A publication*]
SLFX .... Selfix, Inc. [*NASDAQ symbol*]   (CTT)
SLG .... Community of the Sisters of the Love of God [*Anglican religious community*]
SLG .... Lander College, Larry A. Jackson Library, Greenwood, SC [*OCLC symbol*]   (OCLC)
SLG .... Sailing   (WGA)
SLG .... Satellite Landing Ground [*British military*]   (DMA)
SLG .... Scottish Law Gazette [*A publication*]
SLG .... Self-Launching Glider
SLG .... Seligman & Associates, Inc. [*AMEX symbol*]   (SPSG)
SLG .... Shorthand Typist (Lower Grade) [*British military*]   (DMA)
SLG .... Siloam Springs, AK [*Location identifier*] [*FAA*]   (FAAL)
SLG .... Sludge   (MSA)
SLG .... Slugger [*Percentage*] [*Baseball*]
SLG .... Soda Lime Glass
SLG .... Solid-Liquid-Gas [*Phase diagram line*]
SLG .... Southern Lights [*Vancouver Stock Exchange symbol*]
SLG .... State or Local Government
SLG .... Synchronous Line Group   (BUR)
SLGB .... Society of Local Government Barristers [*British*]   (DLA)
SLGJ .... Guadalajara [*Bolivia*] [*ICAO location identifier*]   (ICLI)
SLGM....... Surface-Launched Guided Missile
SLGP .... Student Loan Guaranty Program
SLGR .... Slinger
SLGT .... Slight   (FAAC)
SLGW....... Salt Lake, Garfield & Western Railway Co. [*AAR code*]
SLGY .... Guayaramerin [*Bolivia*] [*ICAO location identifier*]   (ICLI)
SLH .... Shearson Lehman Hutton [*NYSE symbol*]   (SPSG)
SLH .... Sociedade Latinoamericana de Hepatologia [*Latin American Society of Hepatology - LASH*]   (EAIO)
SLH .... Sola [*Vanuatu*] [*Airport symbol*]   (OAG)
SLHA .... Small Luxury Hotel Association   (EA)
SLHC........ Southlife Holding Co. [*NASDAQ symbol*]   (NQ)
SLHJ .... Huacaraje [*Bolivia*] [*ICAO location identifier*]   (ICLI)
SLHN........ Chane Bedoya [*Bolivia*] [*ICAO location identifier*]   (ICLI)
SLHR........ Society for Life History Research   (EA)
SLHRP....... Society for Life History Research in Psychopathology [*Later, SLHR*]   (EA)
SLHT........ Colquechaca [*Bolivia*] [*ICAO location identifier*]   (ICLI)
SLHU .... Huachi [*Bolivia*] [*ICAO location identifier*]   (ICLI)
SLHY .... Caquiaviri [*Bolivia*] [*ICAO location identifier*]   (ICLI)
SLI .... Los Alamitos, CA [*Location identifier*] [*FAA*]   (FAAL)
SLI .... St. Lucia [*Seismograph station code, US Geological Survey*] [*Closed*]   (SEIS)
SLI .... Sea-Level Indicator   (KSC)
SLI .... Seal and Label Institute
SLI .... Shelf Life Item [*Military*]   (AABC)
SLI .... Shropshire Light Infantry [*British military*]   (DMA)
SLI .... Signal Line Isolator
SLI .... Sikh Local Infantry [*British military*]   (DMA)
SLI .... Silver Hill Mines [*Vancouver Stock Exchange symbol*]
SLI .... Slick Airways, Inc.
SLI .... Slide Lobe Indicator
SLI .... Society for Louisiana Irises   (EA)
SLI .... Somatostatin-Like Immunoreactivity
SLI .... Somerset Light Infantry [*Military unit*] [*British*]
SLI .... Sound Level Indicator
SLI .... Spacelab Integration   (MCD)
SLI .... Special Libraries [*A publication*]
SLI .... Specific Language Impairment
SLI .... Splenic Localization Index [*Medicine*]   (MAE)
SLI .... Starting, Lighting, and Ignition [*Automobile system*]
SLI .... Stations Legers d'Infrastructures [*Light infrastructures*] [*French*]
SLI .... Steam Line Isolation [*Nuclear energy*]   (NRCH)
SLI .... Studies in the Literary Imagination [*A publication*]
SLI .... Suppress Length Indication   (BUR)
SLI .... Synchronous Line Interface
SL & I .... System Load and Initialization [*NASA*]   (NASA)
SLIA .... Spiritual Life Institute of America   (EA)
SLIAG .... State Legalization Impact Assistance Grant [*Department of Health and Human Services*]
SLIB .... Source Library [*Data processing*]
SLIB .... Subsystem Library [*Data processing*]   (IBMDP)
SLIC .... Coroico [*Bolivia*] [*ICAO location identifier*]   (ICLI)

SLIC .... [*Federal*] Savings and Loan Insurance Corp. [*Functions transferred to SAIF, 1989*]
SLIC .... Savings and Loan Insurance Corp. [*New Deal*]
SLIC .... School Libraries in Canada [*A publication*]
SLIC .... Search of the Library Information Collection [*Search system*]
SLIC .... Second Life Insurance of Georgia [*NASDAQ symbol*] (NQ)
SLIC .... Selective Letters [*or Listing*] in Combination
SLIC .... Signature Library Intelligence Catalogue
SLIC .... Simulation Linear Integrated Circuit [*Electronics*] (OA)
SLIC .... Subscriber's Line Interface Circuit [*Telecommunications*] (TEL)
SLIC .... System Line Image Composer
SLICB .... Sea-Launched Intercontinental Ballistic Missile (MUGU)
SLICBM.... Sea-Launched Intercontinental Ballistic Missile (SAA)
SLICE....... Source Label Indicating and Coding Equipment
SLICE....... Southwestern Library Interstate Cooperative Endeavor
SLICE....... Students Litigating Against Injurious Can Edges [*Student legal action organization*]
SLICE....... System Life Cycle Estimation
SLID .... Scanning Light Intensity Device
SLID .... Students League for Industrial Democracy [*Later, Students for a Democratic Society*]
SLIDE .... [*A*] Programming Language (CSR)
SLif .... Slovjans'ke Literaturoznavstvo i Fol'klorystyka [*A publication*]
SLIF.......... Student Loan Insurance Fund [*Department of Health and Human Services*] (GFGA)
SLIG .... Inglaterra [*Bolivia*] [*ICAO location identifier*] (ICLI)
SLIG .... Sucker, Low-Brow, Idiot, Goodwill-Buster [*Acronym used as word meaning "act of discourtesy or stupid criticism"*] [*World War II*]
SLIGO .... Sand Lake Irish Gatherings Organization
SLIH......... Samaihuate [*Bolivia*] [*ICAO location identifier*] (ICLI)
SLIH......... Second Level Interrupt Handler (CMD)
SLIJ.......... Iniguazu [*Bolivia*] [*ICAO location identifier*] (ICLI)
SLIM .... Saint Louis Institute of Music
SLIM .... Side Line Indexing Method [*Spectrometry*]
SLIM .... Simplified Logistics and Improved Maintenance (MCD)
SLIM .... Slewed-Launch Interceptor Missile
SLIM .... Standards Laboratory Information Manual (NG)
SLIM .... Submarine-Launched Inertial Missile
SLIMS...... Supply Line Inventory Management System [*Bell System*]
SLIN .... Standard Library Identification Number
SLIN .... Standard Line Item Number [*Army*] (AABC)
SLIN .... Sub-Line Item Number (MCD)
SLIN .... System Line Item Number (MCD)
S Lincolnshire Archaeol ... South Lincolnshire Archaeology [*A publication*]
SL Ind .... SL Industries, Inc. [*Associated Press abbreviation*] (APAG)
Slink.......... Single, Lots of Income, No Kids [*Lifestyle classification*]
SLIP.......... Self Leisure Interest Profile
SLIP.......... Serial Line Intermit Protocol
SLIP.......... Skills Level Improvement Program
SLIP.......... Symbolic List Processor
SLIP.......... Symmetric List Interpretive Program [*Data processing*]
SLIP.......... Symmetric List Processor [*FORTRAN extension*]
SLIPR .... Source Language Input Program
SLIQ .... Scott's Liquid Gold, Inc. [*NASDAQ symbol*] (NQ)
SLIQ .... Special Libraries in Queensland [*Australia*] [*A publication*]
SLIR .... Ibori [*Bolivia*] [*ICAO location identifier*] (ICLI)
SLIR .... School of Labor and Industrial Relations [*Michigan State University*] [*Research center*] (RCD)
SLIRBM.... Sea-Launched Intermediate-Range Ballistic Missile (MUGU)
SLIS.......... Shared Laboratory Information System
SLIS.......... Social Legislation Information Service (EA)
SLIT .... Itaguazurenda [*Bolivia*] [*ICAO location identifier*] (ICLI)
SLIT .... Serial/Lot Item Tracking (DNAB)
SLit .... Slovenska Literatura [*A publication*]
SLit .... Studies in Literature [*A publication*]
SLitI.......... Studies in the Literary Imagination [*A publication*]
S Lit J .... Southern Literary Journal [*A publication*]
SLIV .... Isla Verde [*Bolivia*] [*ICAO location identifier*] (ICLI)
S Liv .... Southern Living [*A publication*]
SLIV .... Steam Line Isolation Valve [*Nuclear energy*] (NRCH)
SLIX .... Ixiamas [*Bolivia*] [*ICAO location identifier*] (ICLI)
SLIZ .... Izozog [*Bolivia*] [*ICAO location identifier*] (ICLI)
SLJ .... Hattiesburg, MS [*Location identifier*] [*FAA*] (FAAL)
SLJ .... School Library Journal [*A publication*]
SLJ .... Scottish Law Journal [*Edinburgh*] [*A publication*] (DLA)
S/LJ.......... Semiconductor/Liquid Junction
SLJ .... Silly Little Job (DSUE)
SLJ .... Southern Literary Journal [*A publication*]
SLJ .... Southwestern Law Journal [*A publication*]
SLJ .... Straits Law Journal [*1888-92*] [*Malasia*] [*A publication*] (DLA)
SLJD .... El Jordan [*Bolivia*] [*ICAO location identifier*] (ICLI)
SLJE .... San Jose [*Bolivia*] [*ICAO location identifier*] (ICLI)
SLJM .... San Juan De Fribal [*Bolivia*] [*ICAO location identifier*] (ICLI)
SLJN .... San Juan (Estancias) [*Bolivia*] [*ICAO location identifier*] (ICLI)
SLJO .... San Joaquin [*Bolivia*] [*ICAO location identifier*] (ICLI)
SLJR......... Sudan Law Journal and Reports [*A publication*] (DLA)
SLJT......... Santa Juanita [*Bolivia*] [*ICAO location identifier*] (ICLI)
SLJV......... San Javier [*Bolivia*] [*ICAO location identifier*] (ICLI)

SLK........... Atlanta Skylark Club, Inc. [*Atlanta, GA*] [*FAA designator*] (FAAC)
SLK........... Kitsaki School/Public Library, La Ronge, Saskatchewan [*Library symbol*] [*National Library of Canada*] (BIB)
SLK........... Saranac Lake [*New York*] [*Airport symbol*] (OAG)
SLK........... Saranac Lake, NY [*Location identifier*] [*FAA*] (FAAL)
SLK........... Schwerpunkte Linguistik und Kommunikationswissenschaft [*A publication*]
SLK........... Slick (MCD)
SLK........... Superior Limbic Keratoconjunctivitis [*Ophthalmology*]
SLk........... Surface Linking Number [*Genetics*]
SLKC .... Superior Limbic Keratoconjunctivitis [*Ophthalmology*] (MAE)
SLKP........ Supreme Lodge Knights of Pythias (EA)
SLKPEN.... Slack and Penalty
SLKQ........ San Miguel [*Bolivia*] [*ICAO location identifier*] (ICLI)
SLKT .... Survivability, Lethality, and Key Technologies (SDI)
SLKW .... Schwerpunkte Linguistik und Kommunikationswissenschaft [*A publication*]
SLKY .... Puerto Yuca [*Bolivia*] [*ICAO location identifier*] (ICLI)
SLL........... La Loche Public Library, Saskatchewan [*Library symbol*] [*National Library of Canada*] (NLC)
SLL........... Salalah [*Oman*] [*Airport symbol*] (OAG)
SLL........... Sandia Laboratories, Livermore (AABC)
SLL........... Sandwell Swan Wooster, Inc. [*Toronto Stock Exchange symbol*]
SLL........... Shelf Life Limit (MCD)
SLL........... Signal Long Lines
SLL........... Skrifter Utgivna. Genom Landsmalsarkivet i Lund [*A publication*]
SLL........... Society for Libertarian Life (EA)
SLL........... Station List Publishing Co., St. Louis MO [*STAC*]
SLL........... Sterling Lord Literistic, Inc. [*Literary agency*] [*British*]
SLL........... Stollet [*Sweden*] [*Seismograph station code, US Geological Survey*] (SEIS)
SLL........... Studies in Language Learning [*A publication*]
SLL........... Suffolk University, Law Library, Boston, MA [*OCLC symbol*] (OCLC)
SLLA .... La Asunta [*Bolivia*] [*ICAO location identifier*] (ICLI)
SLLC .... La China [*Bolivia*] [*ICAO location identifier*] (ICLI)
SLLE .... La Ele [*Bolivia*] [*ICAO location identifier*] (ICLI)
SLLI .... La India [*Bolivia*] [*ICAO location identifier*] (ICLI)
SLLJ .... Laja [*Bolivia*] [*ICAO location identifier*] (ICLI)
SLLL......... Laguna Loa [*Bolivia*] [*ICAO location identifier*] (ICLI)
SLLL......... Synchronous Line, Low, Load (BUR)
SLLP......... La Paz/Kennedy Internacional [*Bolivia*] [*ICAO location identifier*] (ICLI)
SLLR .... Sierra Leone Language Review [*A publication*]
SLLR .... Sierra Leone Law Recorder [*A publication*] (DLA)
SLLS......... Snap Lock Limit Switch
SLLS......... Solid-State LASER Light Source
SLLT .... Los Tajibos [*Bolivia*] [*ICAO location identifier*] (ICLI)
SLLU .... San Lorenzo [*Cordillera*] [*ICAO location identifier*] (ICLI)
SLLV .... La Selva [*Bolivia*] [*ICAO location identifier*] (ICLI)
SLLZ .... San Lorenzo [*Bolivia*] [*ICAO location identifier*] (ICLI)
SLM.......... St. Louis [*Missouri*] [*Seismograph station code, US Geological Survey*] (SEIS)
SLM.......... Sales and Marketing Management [*A publication*]
SLM.......... School for Latin America [*Military*]
SLM.......... Sea-Launched Missile
SLM.......... Sealift Magazine [*A publication*]
SLM.......... Senior Level Management
SLM.......... Silver Life-Saving Medal [*Military decoration*] (GFGA)
SLM.......... Simulated Laboratory Module
SLM.......... Single Longitudinal Mode
SLM.......... Snow Lake Mines Ltd. [*Vancouver Stock Exchange symbol*]
SLM.......... Sound Level Meter
SLM.......... Southern Literary Messenger [*A publication*]
SLM.......... Spatial Light Modulator [*Instrumentation*]
SLM.......... Statistical Learning Model (IEEE)
SLM.......... Student Loan Marketing Association [*NYSE symbol*] (SPSG)
SLM.......... Submarine-Launched Missile
SLM.......... Subscriber Loop Multiplex [*Bell System*]
SLM.......... Supported Liquid Membrane [*Separation science and technology*]
SLM.......... Surface-Launched Missile [*Navy*] (CAAL)
SLM.......... Surinaamse Luchtvaart Maatschappij NV [*Surinam Airways*] (EY)
SLM.......... Surrey Local Militia [*British military*] (DMA)
SLM.......... Synchronous Line Module
SLMA........ Shoe Lace Manufacturers Association [*Defunct*] (EA)
SLMA........ Southeastern Lumber Manufacturers Association (EA)
SLMA........ Student Loan Marketing Association [*Government-chartered private corporation*] [*Nickname: "Sallie Mae"*]
SLMA........ Student Loan Marketing Association [*NASDAQ symbol*] (NQ)
SLMAB...... Single-Line Missile Assembly Building
SLMD....... Madidi [*Bolivia*] [*ICAO location identifier*] (ICLI)
SLMD(RA) ... Searchlight Militia Depot (Royal Artillery) [*British military*] (DMA)
SLME........ Select Manual Entry Switch
SLMG....... Magdalena [*Bolivia*] [*ICAO location identifier*] (ICLI)
SLMI .... SLM International [*NASDAQ symbol*] (SPSG)
SLML........ La Madre [*Bolivia*] [*ICAO location identifier*] (ICLI)

SLMM....... Simultaneous Compass Locator at Middle Marker [*Aviation*] (FAAC)
SLMM....... Submarine-Launched Mobile Mine (MCD)
SlMov .... Sloc'jans'ke Movoznavstvo [*A publication*]
SLMP .... Mapiri [*Bolivia*] [*ICAO location identifier*] (ICLI)
SLMP .... School Library Manpower Project [*American Association of School Librarians*] (EA)
SLMQ....... School Library Media Quarterly [*A publication*]
SLMR .... Memore [*Bolivia*] [*ICAO location identifier*] (ICLI)
SLMR .... Sailmaker [*Navy*] [*British*]
SLMS .... Scanning LASER Mass Spectrometry
SLMS .... Ship-Based Long-Range Missile System (DNAB)
SLMS .... Sound Level Measuring Set
SLMS .... Surface-Launched Missile System
SLMSC...... South London (Volunteers) Medical Staff Corps [*British military*] (DMA)
SLMV........ Monte Verde [*Bolivia*] [*ICAO location identifier*] (ICLI)
SLMW....... Mategua [*Bolivia*] [*ICAO location identifier*] (ICLI)
SLMX........ Monos Arana [*Bolivia*] [*ICAO location identifier*] (ICLI)
SLN .... Salena Research Corp. [*Vancouver Stock Exchange symbol*]
SLN .... Salina [*Kansas*] [*Airport symbol*] (OAG)
SLN .... Salina,,KS [*Location identifier*] [*FAA*] (FAAL)
SLN .... Salinas [*Chile*] [*Seismograph station code, US Geological Survey*] (SEIS)
SLN .... Santiago Library System, Orange, CA [*OCLC symbol*] (OCLC)
SLN .... Secretariat Linguistiques Nordiques [*Nordic Language Secretariat - NLS*] [*Oslo, Norway*] (EAIO)
SLN .... Section List Number (MCD)
SLN .... Selena Research [*Vancouver Stock Exchange symbol*]
SLN .... Sense Lights On (SAA)
SLN .... Sequence Line Number [*Army*]
SLN .... Service Link Network [*Bell Laboratories*]
SLN .... Sinclair Lewis Newsletter [*A publication*]
SLN .... Solution
SLN .... Southeastern Library Network [*Library network*]
SLN .... Sri Lanka Navy
SLN .... Statement of Logistical Needs [*Air Force*]
SLN .... Superior Laryngeal Nerve [*Neuroanatomy*]
SLN/ALN ... Archivos Latinoamericanos de Nutricion. Organo Oficial. Sociedad Latinoamericano de Nutricion [*A publication*]
SLNC........ Service Life Not Completed (DNAB)
SLND .... Sine Loco Nec Data [*Without Place or Date of Printing*] [*Latin*]
SLNE........ Nueva Era [*Bolivia*] [*ICAO location identifier*] (ICLI)
SLNK........ Satellink Corp. [*NASDAQ symbol*] (NQ)
SLNO .... Nuevo Mundo [*Bolivia*] [*ICAO location identifier*] (ICLI)
SLNP........ Nueva Esperanza [*Bolivia*] [*ICAO location identifier*] (ICLI)
SLNQ .... Nueva Esperanza (Marban) [*Bolivia*] [*ICAO location identifier*] (ICLI)
SLNS .... Department of Northern Saskatchewan, La Ronge, Saskatchewan [*Library symbol*] [*National Library of Canada*] (NLC)
SLNV........ Nieve [*Bolivia*] [*ICAO location identifier*] (ICLI)
SLO .... Salem, IL [*Location identifier*] [*FAA*] (FAAL)
SLO .... Scanning LASER Ophthalmoscope
SLO .... Searchlight Operator [*British military*] (DMA)
SLO .... Segment Limits Origin
SLO .... Shark Liver Oil
SLO .... Ship Liaison Officer [*Navy*] (CAAL)
SLO .... Single Loop Operation [*Nuclear energy*] (NRCH)
SLO .... Slavia Orientalis [*A publication*]
SLO .... Sligo [*County in Ireland*] (ROG)
SLO .... Slocan Development [*Vancouver Stock Exchange symbol*]
SLO .... Slocum Air, Inc. [*Miami, FL*] [*FAA designator*] (FAAC)
SLO .... Slough [*British depot code*]
slo.............. Slovak [*MARC language code*] [*Library of Congress*] (LCCP)
SLO .... Slow Lift-Off (MCD)
SLO .... Space Laboratory Operations
SLO .... Staff Legal Officer [*Navy*] (DNAB)
SLO .... State Liaison Officer
SLO .... State Library of Ohio
SLO .... Stop-Limit Order [*Business term*]
SLO .... Stop-Loss Order [*Business term*]
SLO .... Streptolysin O [*Hematology*]
SLO .... Submarine Liaison Officer [*Navy*] (NVT)
SLO .... Swept Local Oscillator (IEEE)
Sloan......... Sloan Management Review [*A publication*]
Sloan Leg Reg ... Sloan's New York Legal Register [*A publication*] (DLA)
Sloan L & T ... Sloan on Landlord and Tenant [*New York*] [*A publication*] (DLA)
Sloan Manag ... Sloan Management Review [*A publication*]
Sloan Manage Rev ... Sloan Management Review [*A publication*]
Sloan Mgmt Rev ... Sloan Management Review [*A publication*]
Sloan Mgt R ... Sloan Management Review [*A publication*]
SLOB......... Satellite Low-Orbit Bombardment
SLOB......... Strategic Low-Orbit Bomber (AAG)
SLOB......... Supplemental Layoff Benefits (MCD)
SLOB......... Supply Left of Baseline (MCD)
SLOC........ Sea Lines of Communication [*NATO*] (NATG)
SLOc......... Slavia Occidentalis [*A publication*]
SLOC........ Source Lines of Code (SSD)
SLOcc........ Slavia Occidentalis [*A publication*]

SLOCOP ... Specific Linear Optimal Control Program [*Hydrofoil*] [*Grumman Aerospace Corp.*]
SLOE........ Save Life on Earth (EA)
SLOE........ Special List of Equipment [*Air Force*]
SLOH .... Skylab Operations Handbook [*NASA*] (MCD)
SLOI......... Orialsa [*Bolivia*] [*ICAO location identifier*] (ICLI)
Slo L........ Slovo Lektora [*A publication*]
SLOM .... Simultaneous Compass Locator at Outer Marker [*Aviation*] (FAAC)
SLOMAR ... Space Logistics, Maintenance, and Rescue
SLON .... Sloan Technology Corp. [*NASDAQ symbol*] (NQ)
SLoP......... Slovansky Prehled [*A publication*]
SLOPE ...... Study of Lunar Orbiter Photographic Evaluation (MCD)
SLOR........ Oruro [*Bolivia*] [*ICAO location identifier*] (ICLI)
SLOR........ Simultaneous Line Over-Relaxation [*Nuclear energy*]
SLOR........ Slavia Orientalis [*A publication*]
SLOR........ Swept Local Oscillator Receiver (NG)
SLORC....... State Law and Order Restoration Council [*Myanmar*]
SLORV...... Structural Loads on Reentry Vehicles (MCD)
SLOS .... Scanning Line of Sight (KSC)
SLOS .... Secondary Line of Sight [*Sextants*]
SLOS .... Sierra Leone Organization Society
SLOS .... Star Line-of-Sight (MCD)
SLOS .... Sun Line-of-Sight
SLOS .... Swept Local Oscillator
SLOSH...... Sea Level and Overland Surge from Hurricanes [*National Oceanic and Atmospheric Administration*]
SLOSJ....... State and Local Officials for Soviet Jews (EA)
SLO/SRI ... Shift Left Out/Shift Right In
SLOT........ Sinaota [*Bolivia*] [*ICAO location identifier*] (ICLI)
SLOT........ Stabilized Line-of-Sight Tracker
SLOT........ Submarine-Launched One-Way Tactical [*Buoy*] (NVT)
SLOTH...... Suppressing Line Operands and Translating to Hexadecimal [*Telecommunications*] (TEL)
Slov .... Slovenia
Slov A .... Slovenska Archeologia [*A publication*]
Slov Akad Znan Umet Razred Prirodosl Vede Dela ... Slovenska Akademija Znanosti in Umetnosti. Razred za Prirodoslovne Vede. Dela [*A publication*]
Slovak Mus ... Slovak Musik [*A publication*]
Slov Arch ... Slovenska Archeologia [*A publication*]
Slov Archeol ... Slovenska Archeologia [*A publication*]
Slov Ceb ...... Slovenski Cebelar [*A publication*]
Slovenska Hud ... Slovenska Hudba [*A publication*]
Slov Etnogr ... Slovenski Etnograf [*A publication*]
Slov Hud .... Slovenska Hudba [*A publication*]
Slov Lit....... Slovenska Literatura [*A publication*]
SlovN .... Slovensky Narodopis [*A publication*]
Slov Num ... Slovenska Numizmatika [*A publication*]
Slov Numiz ... Slovenska Numizmatika [*A publication*]
SlovP......... Slovensky Pohl'ady [*A publication*]
Slov Preh ... Slovansky Prehled [*A publication*]
SlovS......... Slovene Studies [*A publication*]
Slow Learn ... Slow Learning Child [*A publication*]
Slow Learn Child ... Slow Learning Child [*A publication*] (APTA)
SLOWPOKE ... Safe Low-Power Critical Experiment [*Nuclear energy*]
SLOZA...... Slaboproudy Obzor [*A publication*]
SLP .... Left Sacroposterior Position [*of the fetus*] [*Obstetrics*]
SLP .... Sacrolaeva Posterior [*A fetal position*] (AAMN)
SLP .... St. Lucie Plant [*Nuclear energy*] (NRCH)
SLP .... School Lunch Program
SLP .... Scintilore Explorations Ltd. [*Toronto Stock Exchange symbol*]
SLP .... Scottish Labour Party [*Political party*] (PPW)
SLP .... Scottish Liberal Party [*Political party*]
SLP .... Scouting Landplane
SLP .... Sea-Level Pressure
SLP .... Secretary for Logistics Planning [*Air Force*]
SLP .... Sectional Linear Programming [*Data processing*]
SLP .... Segmented Level Programming [*Data processing*] (IEEE)
SLP .... Serie Linguistica Peruana [*A publication*]
SLP .... Sex-Limited Protein [*Immunology*]
SLP .... Shelby, NC [*Location identifier*] [*FAA*] (FAAL)
SLP .... Silicon Light Pulser
SLP .... Sine Legitima Prole [*Without Lawful Issue*] [*Latin*]
SLP .... Single Linear Polarization
SLP .... Sleep
SLP .... Slip (ADA)
SLP .... Sloop
SLP .... Slope (MSA)
SLP .... Slovansky Prehled [*A publication*]
SLP .... Slovensky Pohl'ady [*A publication*]
SLP .... Slovensky Porocevalec [*A publication*]
SLP .... Socialist Labor Party [*Egypt*] [*Political party*] (PPW)
SLP .... Socialist Labor Party of America [*Political party*] (EA)
SLP .... Soft Lander Probe [*Aerospace*]
SLP .... Sound Level Plot [*Military*] (CAAL)
SLP .... Source Language Processor [*Data processing*] (BUR)
SLP .... Spacelab Program Office [*European Research National Organization*] (MCD)
SLP .... Specific Line of Precipitin [*Immunology*]
SLP .... Spring-Loaded Pulley

SLP............ Stock List Price [*Military*] (AFIT)
S/LP.......... Stop Lamp [*Automotive engineering*]
SLP............ Strategic Locations Planning [*Information service or system*] (IID)
SLP............ Strategic Logistic Program [*Army*] (RDA)
SLP............ Street Legal Performance [*Auto model designation*]
SLP............ Sun Energy Partners LP [*NYSE symbol*] (SPSG)
SLP............ Super Long Play [*Video technology*]
SLP............ Supersonic Local Pressure
SLP............ Supplier Loaned Property (MCD)
SLP............ Surface Launch Platform (NVT)
SLP............ Systematic Layout Planning [*Industrial engineering*]
SLPA.......... Selected Legally Protected Animals [*Marine science*] (MSC)
SLPA.......... Silicon Light Pulser Array
SLPB........ Spacelab Program Board [*NASA*] (NASA)
SLPC........ St. Louis Production Center
SLPC........ Socialist Labour Party of Canada
SLPC........ Supported Liquid Phase Catalyst [*Chemical engineering*]
SLPD........ Skylab Program Directive [*NASA*] (KSC)
SLPD........ State and Local Planning Division [*Environmental Protection Agency*] (GFGA)
SLPH........ Seat Lock Pin Handle
SLPHR...... Sulphur
SLPI.......... Secretory Leukoprotease Inhibitor [*Biochemistry*]
SLPL.......... St. Louis Public Library [*Missouri*]
SLPL.......... Sea Loading Pipe Line [*Technical drawings*]
SLPM........ Palmira [*Bolivia*] [*ICAO location identifier*] (ICLI)
SLPM........ Selected List of Published Material [*Her Majesty's Stationery Office*] [*British*]
SLPM........ Silicon Light Pulser Matrix
SLPMS...... Single Level Power Management System
SLPO........ Potosi [*Bolivia*] [*ICAO location identifier*] (ICLI)
SLPO........ Skylab Program Office [*NASA*] (KSC)
SLPo.......... Slovensky Pohl'ady [*A publication*]
SLPoh....... Slovensky Pohl'ady [*A publication*]
SLPP.......... Paraparau [*Bolivia*] [*ICAO location identifier*] (ICLI)
SLPP.......... Serum Lipophosphoprotein [*Serology*]
SLPP.......... Sierra Leone People's Party [*Political party*] (PD)
SLPP.......... Sri Lanka People's Party [*Political party*] (PPW)
SLPR.......... Puerto Rico [*Bolivia*] [*ICAO location identifier*] (ICLI)
SLPR.......... Sidelobe Pulse Rejection [*Military*] (CAAL)
SLPr.......... Slavica Pragensia [*A publication*]
SLPR.......... Slavistic Printings and Reprintings [*A publication*]
SLPR.......... Supplier Loaned Property Request (MCD)
SLPRB...... Steroids and Lipids Research [*A publication*]
SLPRF....... Northern Teacher Education Program, Inc., La Ronge, Saskatchewan [*Library symbol*] [*National Library of Canada*] (NLC)
SLPS......... Puerto Suarez [*Bolivia*] [*ICAO location identifier*] (ICLI)
SLPS......... Sonobuoy Launcher Pneumatic System
SLPS......... State and Local Program Support [*Nuclear energy*] (NRCH)
SLPT .... Peta [*Bolivia*] [*ICAO location identifier*] (ICLI)
SLPT .... Scintilore Explorations Ltd. [*NASDAQ symbol*] (NQ)
SLPT .... Socialist Labor Party of Turkey [*Turkiye Sosyalist Isci Partisi*] [*Political party*] (PPW)
SLPTC....... Solid-Liquid Phase-Transfer Catalysis
SLPU......... Puchuni [*Bolivia*] [*ICAO location identifier*] (ICLI)
SLPV......... Puerto Villa-Roel [*Bolivia*] [*ICAO location identifier*] (ICLI)
SLPW........ Sloop-of-War
SLQ........... Saint Louis Quarterly [*Baguio City*] [*A publication*]
SLQ........... Sleetmute [*Alaska*] [*Airport symbol*] (OAG)
SLQ........... Sleetmute, AK [*Location identifier*] [*FAA*] (FAAL)
SLQ........... Surface Layer Quality
SLQY......... Curichi [*Bolivia*] [*ICAO location identifier*] (ICLI)
SLR........... Radcliffe College, Schlesinger Library, Cambridge, MA [*OCLC symbol*] (OCLC)
SLR........... Sales Letter Report
SLR........... Saskatchewan Law Reports [*A publication*] (DLA)
SLR........... Satellite LASER Ranging [*for geodetic and geophysical measurements*]
SLR........... Scottish Land Court Reports [*A publication*] (DLA)
SLR........... Scottish Law Reporter [*Edinburgh*] [*A publication*] (DLA)
SLR........... Scottish Law Review and Sheriff Court Reports [*1885-1963*] [*A publication*] (DLA)
SLR........... Sealer
SLR........... Self-Loading Rifle (MCD)
SLR........... Sense Line Register
SLR........... Service Level Reporter [*IBM Corp.*]
SLR........... Seychelles Law Reports [*1921-23*] [*A publication*] (DLA)
SL & R ...... Shop Order Load Analysis and Reporting [*IBM Corp.*]
SLR........... Side-Looking RADAR (AFM)
SLR........... Simple Left to Right [*Data processing*]
SLR........... Simple Linear Regression [*Statistics*]
SLR........... Sind Law Reporter [*India*] [*A publication*] (DLA)
SLR........... Singapore Law Reports [*1946-49, 1953-56*] [*A publication*] (DLA)
SLR........... Single-Lens Reflex [*Camera*]
SLR........... Skylab Rescue [*NASA*] (KSC)
SLR........... Slager. Vakblad voor de Vleesspecialist [*A publication*]
SLR........... Slavische Rundschau [*A publication*]
SLR........... Slavisticna Revija [*A publication*]

SLR........... Slavonic and East European Review [*A publication*]
SLR........... Slush on Runway [*Aviation*] (FAAC)
SLR........... Solar (AAG)
SLR........... Solectron Corp. [*NYSE symbol*] (SPSG)
SLR........... Sound Level Recorder
SLR........... South Lancashire Regiment [*British*]
SLR........... Southern Law Review [*St. Louis, MO*] [*A publication*] (DLA)
SLR........... Special Leave Refused
SLR........... Special Light Rifle (NATG)
SLR........... Specific Lung Resistance
SLR........... Spin Lattice Relaxation
SLR........... Sport Leicht Renn [*Sports Lightweight Racing (Car)*] [*German*]
SLR........... Stabell Resources [*Vancouver Stock Exchange symbol*]
SLR........... Stanford Law Review [*A publication*]
SLR........... Static Line Regulation
SLR........... Static Loaded Radius [*Automotive engineering*]
SLR........... Statute Law Revision [*A publication*] (DLA)
SLR........... Storage Limits Register
SLR........... Straight Leg Raising [*Medicine*]
SLR........... Streptococcus lactis R Factor [*Biochemistry*]
SLR........... Sulphur Springs, TX [*Location identifier*] [*FAA*] (FAAL)
SLR........... Sydney Law Review [*A publication*] (APTA)
SLR........... System Level Requirement [*Military*] (CAAL)
SLRA......... San Ramon [*Bolivia*] [*ICAO location identifier*] (ICLI)
SLRA......... Sierra Leone Royal Artillery [*British military*] (DMA)
SLRA......... Soviet Long-Range Air (MCD)
SLRA........ Suede and Leather Refinishers of America [*Defunct*] (EA)
SLRAAA ... Sprache und Literatur. Regensburger Arbeiten zur Anglistik und Amerikanistik [*A publication*]
SLRAP ...... Standard Low-Frequency Range Approach
SLRB........ Robore [*Bolivia*] [*ICAO location identifier*] (ICLI)
SLRB........ State Labor Relations Board
SLRB........ Steel Labor Relations Board [*New Deal*]
SLRC......... San Luis Rey College [*California*]
SLRC/MILO ... State Library Resource Center - Maryland Interlibrary Organization [*Library network*]
SLRD........ Searchlight RADAR
SLRE .... El Remate [*Bolivia*] [*ICAO location identifier*] (ICLI)
SLRec .... Slovenska Rec [*A publication*]
SL Rev .... Scottish Law Review and Sheriff Court Reports [*A publication*] (DLA)
SLRev .... Slavonic and East European Review [*A publication*]
SLRev .... Slavonic Review [*A publication*]
SLRH........ Rancho Alegre [*Bolivia*] [*ICAO location identifier*] (ICLI)
SLRI .... Riberalta [*Bolivia*] [*ICAO location identifier*] (ICLI)
SLRI .... Shipboard Long-Range Input
SLRJ.......... St. Louis University. Research Journal. Graduate School of Arts and Sciences [*A publication*]
SLR Leic .... Leicester's Straits Law Reports [*Malaya*] [*A publication*] (DLA)
SLR Leicester ... Leicester's Straits Law Reports [*Malaya*] [*A publication*] (DLA)
SLRN......... Select Read Numerically
SLRN......... Solaron Corp. [*NASDAQ symbol*] (NQ)
SL RNG ...... Slope Range
SLRNS ...... Straits Law Reports, New Series [*Malasia*] [*A publication*] (DLA)
SLRP .... Rosapata [*Bolivia*] [*ICAO location identifier*] (ICLI)
SLRP .... Society for Strategic and Long Range Planning [*Later, Strategic Planning Society - SP*] (EAIO)
SLRP .... State Loan Repayment Program [*Department of Health and Human Services*] (GFGA)
SLRQ........ Rurrenabaque [*Bolivia*] [*ICAO location identifier*] (ICLI)
SLRR .... Retiro [*Bolivia*] [*ICAO location identifier*] (ICLI)
SLRRB ..... Senior Logistics Readiness Review Board [*Fort Lewis*] (MCD)
SLRS .... Rio Seco [*Bolivia*] [*ICAO location identifier*] (ICLI)
SLRS .... Satellite LASER Ranging System
SLRS .... Sexual Law Reform Society [*British*]
SLRT .... Santa Rita [*Bolivia*] [*ICAO location identifier*] (ICLI)
SLRT .... Straight Leg Raising Test [*or Tenderness*] [*Medicine*]
SLRTB....... Saskatchewan Department of Tourism and Small Business, La Ronge, Saskatchewan [*Library symbol*] [*National Library of Canada*] (NLC)
SlRund .... Slavische Rundschau [*A publication*]
SLRV......... Sellersville Savings & Loan Association [*NASDAQ symbol*] (NQ)
SLRV......... Shuttle Launched Research Vehicle [*NASA*] (NASA)
SLRV......... South London Regiment of Volunteers [*British military*] (DMA)
SLRV......... Standard Light Rail Vehicle [*Mass transit*]
SLRV......... Strawberry Latent Ringspot Virus [*Plant pathology*]
SLRV......... Surveyor Lunar Roving Vehicle [*Aerospace*] (MCD)
SLRY........ Reyes [*Bolivia*] [*ICAO location identifier*] (ICLI)
SLS .... Annual Report. Society for Libyan Studies [*London*] [*A publication*]
SLS .... Saint Lawrence Seaway Development Corp. [*Department of Transportation*]
SLS .... Saint Lawrence Seminary [*Wisconsin*]
SLS .... Santiago Library System [*Library network*]
SLS .... Sassafras Loamy Sand [*Type of soil*]
SLS .... Saturn Longitude System [*Planetary science*]

SLS .... Scanning LASER System
SLS .... School of Library Service [*Columbia University*] [*Defunct*]
SLS .... School of Logistics Science [*Army*]
SLS .... Sea-Land Service, Inc. [*AAR code*]
SLS .... Sea Level, Standard Day
SLS .... Sea-Level Static
SLS .... Secondary Landing Site [*NASA*]   (NASA)
SLS .... Segment Long-Spacing Collagen Fiber
SLS .... Selas Corp. of America [*AMEX symbol*]   (SPSG)
SLS .... Selective LASER [*Light Amplification by Stimulated Emission of Radiation*] Sintering [*Desktop manufacturing*]
SLS .... Serra Cooperative Library System, San Diego, CA [*OCLC symbol*]   (OCLC)
SLS .... Shore Labourers Society [*A union*] [*British*]
SLS .... Side-Lobe Suppression RADAR
SLS .... Side-Looking SONAR
SLS .... Sign Language Studies [*A publication*]
SLS .... Signaling Link Selection [*Telecommunications*]   (TEL)
SLS .... Silicon Light Source
SLS .... Silistra [*Bulgaria*] [*Airport symbol*]   (OAG)
SLS .... Sindacato Lavoratori della Somalia [*Workers Union of Somalia*]
SLS .... Skylab Simulator [*NASA*]   (KSC)
SLS .... Slightly Soluble
SLS .... Slovenska Ljudska Stranka [*Slovene People's Party*] [*Former Yugoslavia*] [*Political party*]   (PPE)
SL'S .... Slovenska L'Udova Strana [*Slovak People's Party*] [*Also, HSL'S*] [*Political party*]   (PPE)
SLS .... So-Luminaire Systems [*Vancouver Stock Exchange symbol*]
SLS .... Society for Libyan Studies   (EAIO)
SLS .... Sodium Lauryl Sulfate [*Also, SDS*] [*Organic chemistry*]
SLS .... Soengei Langka [*Sumatra*] [*Seismograph station code, US Geological Survey*] [*Closed*]   (SEIS)
SLS .... Sonobuoy Localization System   (NVT)
SLS .... Sortie Lab Simulator [*NASA*]   (NASA)
SLS .... Sound Learning Society [*British*]
SLS .... Source Library System [*Data processing*]
SLS .... Space Laboratory Simulator [*NASA*]
SLS .... Space Launch System
SLS .... Spacecraft Landing Strut
SLS .... Specific Living Space   (AAG)
SLS .... Spoken Language Services, Inc.
SLS .... Standard Light Spanwire [*Military*]   (CAAL)
SLS .... Statement Level Simulator [*NASA*]   (NASA)
SLS .... Stores Locator System   (MCD)
SLS .... Strained-Layer Superlattices [*Crystalline materials*]
SLS .... Student Lesson Sheets
SLS .... Students for a Libertarian Society   (EA)
SLS .... Styles of Leadership Survey [*Test*]
SLS .... Suburban Library System [*Library network*]
SLS .... Sun-Load Sensor [*Automotive engineering*]
SLS .... Supplemental Loans for Students [*Department of Education*]
SLS .... Surface Laboratory System [*NASA*]   (KSC)
SLS .... SWALCAP Library Services Ltd. [*Information service or system*]   (IID)
SLS .... Symbolic Layout System   (MCD)
SLSA .... St. Lawrence Seaway Authority [*Canada*] [*See also AVMS*]
SLSA .... Santa Ana De Yacuma [*Bolivia*] [*ICAO location identifier*]   (ICLI)
SLSA .... Seamen's Loyal Standard Association [*A union*] [*British*]
SLSA .... Secondary Lead Smelters Association   (EA)
SLSA .... Shuttle Logistics Support Aircraft [*NASA*]   (MCD)
SLSA .... Slotting Saw
SLSA .... Svenska Linne-Sallskapet Arsskrift [*Uppsala*] [*A publication*]
SLSAC ...... Saint Lawrence Seaway Authority of Canada
SLSADJ .... Stores Locator System Adjustment   (MCD)
SLSB .... San Borja [*Bolivia*] [*ICAO location identifier*]   (ICLI)
SLSC .... Santa Clara (Moxos) [*Bolivia*] [*ICAO location identifier*]   (ICLI)
SLSc .... Studies in the Linguistic Sciences [*A publication*]
SLSD .... San Carlos Gutierrez [*Bolivia*] [*ICAO location identifier*]   (ICLI)
SLSDC ...... Saint Lawrence Seaway Development Corp. [*Department of Transportation*]
SLSF .... St. Louis-San Francisco Railway Co. [*AAR code*]
SLSF .... San Francisco (Moxos) [*Bolivia*] [*ICAO location identifier*]   (ICLI)
SLSF .... Sodium Loop Safety Facility [*Nuclear energy*]
SLSF .... Svenska Landsmal och Svenskt Folkliv [*Uppsala*] [*A publication*]
SLSG .... S-Locus-Specific Glycoprotein [*Botany*]
SLSG .... Sipuati [*Bolivia*] [*ICAO location identifier*]   (ICLI)
SLSH .... Santa Ana De Huachi [*Bolivia*] [*ICAO location identifier*]   (ICLI)
SLSH .... Short Length Super HIPPO [*High Internal Pressure Producing Orifice*]   (MCD)
SLSI .... San Ignacio De Velasco [*Bolivia*] [*ICAO location identifier*]   (ICLI)
SLSI .... Super Large-Scale Integration
SLSJ .... Salinas [*Bolivia*] [*ICAO location identifier*]   (ICLI)
SLSK .... Sauces [*Bolivia*] [*ICAO location identifier*]   (ICLI)

SLSL .... Santa Lucia (Cliza) [*Bolivia*] [*ICAO location identifier*]   (ICLI)
SLSL .... Statutory Long Service Leave   (ADA)
SLSM .... San Ignacio De Moxos [*Bolivia*] [*ICAO location identifier*]   (ICLI)
SLSM .... Silver Life-Saving Medal [*Military decoration*]
SLSM .... Simple Line Source Model [*Environmental Protection Agency*]   (GFGA)
SLSMGR... Sales Manager   (WGA)
SLSMN ..... Salesman   (WGA)
SLSMS ..... Spacelab Support Module Simulator [*NASA*]   (MCD)
SLSN .... Sanandita [*Bolivia*] [*ICAO location identifier*]   (ICLI)
SLSO .... Santa Barbara De Parra [*Bolivia*] [*ICAO location identifier*]   (ICLI)
SLSO .... Shipyard Labour Supply Officer [*British*]
SLSP .... SACLANT Scheduled Program   (MCD)
SLSp .... Slovensky Spisovatel [*A publication*]
SLSP .... Slow Speed
SLSQ .... Saahaqui [*Bolivia*] [*ICAO location identifier*]   (ICLI)
SLSR .... Santa Rosa De Yacuma [*Bolivia*] [*ICAO location identifier*]   (ICLI)
SLSS .... Sasasama [*Bolivia*] [*ICAO location identifier*]   (ICLI)
SLSS .... Secondary Life Support System [*NASA*]
SLSS .... Shuttle Launch Support System   (MCD)
SL-SS .... Spacelab Subsystem [*NASA*]   (NASA)
SLSS .... Swimmer Life Support System [*Navy*]   (CAAL)
SLSS .... Systems Library Subscription Service [*Data processing*]   (IBMDP)
SLSSM ..... Submerged Launched Surface-to-Surface Missile   (MCD)
SL-SSS ..... Spacelab Subsystem Segment [*NASA*]   (NASA)
SLST .... St. Louis, San Francisco & Texas Railway Co. [*AAR code*]
SLST .... San Antonio [*Bolivia*] [*ICAO location identifier*]   (ICLI)
Sl St .... Slade's Compilation of the Statutes of Vermont [*A publication*]   (DLA)
SLST .... Slightly Staining
SLST .... Slip Stitch [*Knitting*]
SLSU .... Sucre [*Bolivia*] [*ICAO location identifier*]   (ICLI)
SLSW .... St. Louis Southwestern Railway Co.   (IIA)
SLSW .... Santa Barbara (Versalles) [*Bolivia*] [*ICAO location identifier*]   (ICLI)
SLSX .... San Ramon De Senac [*Bolivia*] [*ICAO location identifier*]   (ICLI)
SLT .... Sacrolaeva Transversa [*A fetal position*]   (AAMN)
SLT .... Salant Corp. [*NYSE symbol*]   (SPSG)
SLT .... Salta [*Argentina*] [*Seismograph station code, US Geological Survey*] [*Closed*]   (SEIS)
SLT .... Scots Law Times [*A publication*]
SLT .... Searchlight
SLT .... Second Law of Thermodynamics
SLT .... Self-Loading Tape   (AFM)
SLT .... Sellectek Industries, Inc. [*Vancouver Stock Exchange symbol*]
SLT .... Sense Light Test   (SAA)
SLT .... Shiga-Like Toxin [*Biochemistry*]
SLT .... Ship Letter Telegram
SL & T ...... Shipper's Load and Tally [*Bills of lading*]
SLT .... Shuttle Loop Transit [*NASA*]
SLT .... Signaling Link Termination [*Telecommunications*]
SLT .... Simulated LASER Target
SLT .... Simulated Launch Test [*NASA*]   (KSC)
SLT .... Skylight   (AAG)
SLT .... Slate   (MSA)
SLT .... Slate Run, PA [*Location identifier*] [*FAA*]   (FAAL)
SLT .... Sleet [*Meteorology*]   (FAAC)
SLT .... Slit
SLT .... Solid Logic Technique [*Data processing*]   (IEEE)
SLT .... Solid Logic Technology
SLT .... Sonobuoy Launch Tube [*Navy*]   (CAAL)
SLT .... Special [*or Specific*] Launch Trajectory   (AFM)
SLT .... Spotlight   (MSA)
SLT .... Stockpile Laboratory Tests
SLT .... Stress Limit Tests
SLT .... Structured Learning Therapy
S Lt .... Sub-Lieutenant [*British military*]   (DMA)
SLT .... Svensk Litteraturtidskrift [*A publication*]
SLT .... Swing [*Parachute*] Landing Trainer [*Military*]   (INF)
SLT .... Switchman's Local Test [*Telecommunications*]   (TEL)
SLTB .... St. Lucia Tourist Board   (EA)
SLTB .... Society for Low Temperature Biology   (EA)
SLTC .... Siltec Corp. [*NASDAQ symbol*]   (NQ)
SLTC .... Society of Leather Technologists and Chemists [*British*]
SLTD .... Salted
SLTD .... Slotted   (MSA)
SLTDP ...... Special LASER Technology Development Program
SLTE .... Teoponte [*Bolivia*] [*ICAO location identifier*]   (ICLI)
SLTEA ...... Sheffield Lighter Trades Employers' Association [*British*]   (DCTA)
SLTerm..... Slavjanska Lingvisticna Terminologija [*A publication*]
SLTF .... San Telmo (Cordillera) [*Bolivia*] [*ICAO location identifier*]   (ICLI)
SLTF .... Shortest Latency Time First
SLTF .... Silo-Launch Test Facility
SLTG .... Santiago [*Bolivia*] [*ICAO location identifier*]   (ICLI)

SLTG.........	Sterner Lighting Systems, Inc. [*NASDAQ symbol*] (NQ)
SLTH........	Tumichucua [*Bolivia*] [*ICAO location identifier*] (ICLI)
SLTI.........	San Matias [*Bolivia*] [*ICAO location identifier*] (ICLI)
SLTI	Surgical Laser Technologies, Inc. [*NASDAQ symbol*] (NQ)
SLTJ.........	Tarija [*Bolivia*] [*ICAO location identifier*] (ICLI)
SLT (Lyon Ct) ...	Scots Law Times (Lyon Court Reports) [*A publication*] (DLA)
SLTM.......	Selecterm, Inc. [*NASDAQ symbol*] (NQ)
SLTM.......	Short Lead Time Material (DNAB)
SLTM.......	Standard Lap Turn Method (NVT)
SLTM.......	Storia delle Letteratura di Tutto il Mondo [*A publication*]
SLTM.......	Structural Lander Test Model
SLT (Notes) ...	Scots Law Times (Notes of Recent Decisions) [*A publication*] (DLA)
SLTO........	Sea-Level Takeoff
SLTP	Tipuani [*Bolivia*] [*ICAO location identifier*] (ICLI)
SLTR	Service Life Test Report (AAG)
SLTR	Trinidad [*Bolivia*] [*ICAO location identifier*] (ICLI)
SLTS.........	Todos Santos [*Bolivia*] [*ICAO location identifier*] (ICLI)
SLT & SDL ...	Searchlight and Sound Locator [*Navy*]
SLT (Sh Ct) ...	Scots Law Times Sheriff Court Reports [*A publication*] (DLA)
sLTSV.......	Satellite Lucerne Transient Streak Virus
SLTT	Total Bolivia [*Bolivia*] [*ICAO location identifier*] (ICLI)
SLTU.........	Tucavaca [*Bolivia*] [*ICAO location identifier*] (ICLI)
SLTUF	Sri Lanka Trade Union Federation [*Sri Lanka Vurthiya Samithi Sammelanaya*]
SLTV........	St. Lucia Television Service
SLTX	Sales Tax
SLTY	Tigüipa [*Bolivia*] [*ICAO location identifier*] (ICLI)
SLTZ	Tupiza [*Bolivia*] [*ICAO location identifier*] (ICLI)
SLU...........	Pavlovsk [*Former USSR*] [*Later, LNN*] [*Geomagnetic observatory code*]
SLU...........	Saint Lawrence University [*Canton, NY*]
SLU...........	St. Louis University [*Missouri*]
SLU...........	St. Louis University, Law Library, St. Louis, MO [*OCLC symbol*] (OCLC)
SLU...........	St. Lucia [*West Indies*] [*Airport symbol*] (OAG)
SLU...........	Secondary Logic Unit
SLU...........	Serial Line Unit
Slu..............	Slough [*Maps and charts*]
SLU...........	Slutsk [*Former USSR*] [*Later, LNN*] [*Geomagnetic observatory code*]
SLU...........	Source Library Update [*Data processing*]
SLU...........	Southern Labor Union
SLU...........	Special Liaison Unit [*Military intelligence*] [*World War II*]
SLU...........	Spil. Een Progressief Onafhankelijk Maandblad voor Zelfstandigen en Werknemers in het Middenbedrijf en Kleinbedrijf [*A publication*]
SLU...........	Subscriber Line Use [*Telecommunications*]
SLU...........	Svenska Litteratursaellskapet i Uppsala [*A publication*]
SLU...........	Switching Logic Unit (CAAL)
SLUC........	Standard Level User Charge
SLUC........	Uncia [*Bolivia*] [*ICAO location identifier*] (ICLI)
Sludge Mag ...	Sludge Magazine [*A publication*]
Sludge Manage Ser ...	Sludge Management Series [*A publication*]
SLUF	Short Little Ugly Feller [*Nickname for A-7 aircraft*] (MCD)
SLUFAE....	Surface-Launched Unit, Fire Area Equipment (MCD)
SLUFAE....	Surface-Launched Unit, Fuel-Air Explosive Mine Neutralizer [*Army*] (RDA)
SLUG........	Superconducting Low-Inductance Undulatory Galvanometer
SLULJ.......	St. Louis University. Law Journal [*A publication*]
SLUMA.....	Southern Lumberman [*United States*] [*A publication*]
SLUMINE ...	Surface-Launched Unit, Mine Layer (MCD)
SLUR........	Share Library User Report [*Data processing*] (OA)
SLURB	Slovenly Suburb
SLURJ.......	St. Louis University. Research Journal [*Baguio City*] [*A publication*]
SLURP	Self Leveling Unit for Removing Pollution [*Marine science*] (MSC)
SLURP	Spiny Lobster Undersea Research Project
SLURREX ...	Slurry Reactor Experiment
SLUS	Subscriber's Line Use System [*AT & T*] [*Telecommunications*] (TEL)
SLUV........	Uvas Verdes [*Bolivia*] [*ICAO location identifier*] (ICLI)
Sl UVAN ...	Slavistica. Praci Institutu Slov'janoznavstva Ukrajins'koji Vil'noji Akademiji Nauk [*A publication*]
SLUY........	Uyuni [*Bolivia*] [*ICAO location identifier*] (ICLI)
SLV...........	El Salvador [*ANSI three-letter standard code*] (CNC)
SLV...........	Federal Carriers, Inc. [*White Lake, NY*] [*FAA designator*] (FAAC)
SLV...........	Salivate (KSC)
SLV...........	San Jose, CA [*Location identifier*] [*FAA*] (FAAL)
SLV...........	Satellite Launching Vehicle [*Air Force*]
SLV...........	Satellite-Like Virus
SLV...........	Saturn Launch Vehicle [*NASA*] (KSC)
SLV...........	Seldovia [*Alaska*] [*Seismograph station code, US Geological Survey*] (SEIS)
SLV...........	Shallot Latent Virus [*Plant pathology*]
SLv.............	Sifra on Leviticus [*A publication*] (BJA)
SLV...........	Silver Lady Resources [*Vancouver Stock Exchange symbol*]
SLV...........	Silvercrest Industries [*AMEX symbol*] (SPSG)
SLV...........	Simulated Launch Vehicle (MCD)
SLV...........	Sleeve (AAG)
slv..............	Slovenian [*MARC language code*] [*Library of Congress*] (LCCP)
SLV...........	Soft Landing Vehicle [*NASA*]
SLV...........	Solvent (WGA)
SLV...........	Space Launch Vehicle [*NASA*]
SLV...........	Space-Like Vector
SLV...........	Standard Launch Vehicle
SLVA........	Villa Aroma [*Bolivia*] [*ICAO location identifier*] (ICLI)
SLVC........	Selvac Corp. [*NASDAQ symbol*] (NQ)
SLVD........	Covendo [*Bolivia*] [*ICAO location identifier*] (ICLI)
SLVE........	Venecia [*Bolivia*] [*ICAO location identifier*] (ICLI)
SLVG........	Sleeving [*Electricity*]
SLVG........	Special Launch Vehicle Group [*NASA*] (KSC)
SLVG........	Valle Grande [*Bolivia*] [*ICAO location identifier*] (ICLI)
SLVI	Caranavi [*Bolivia*] [*ICAO location identifier*] (ICLI)
SLVM.......	Villa Montes [*Bolivia*] [*ICAO location identifier*] (ICLI)
SLVN........	Sylvan Learning Corp. [*Montgomery, AL*] [*NASDAQ symbol*] (NQ)
SLVN........	Valencia [*Bolivia*] [*ICAO location identifier*] (ICLI)
SLVR	Silverado Mines Ltd. [*NASDAQ symbol*] (NQ)
SLVR	Viru Viru [*Bolivia*] [*ICAO location identifier*] (ICLI)
SLVRJ.......	Surface-Launched Low-Volume Ramjet
SLVS	San Luis Valley Southern Railroad (IIA)
SLVT	Solvent (MSA)
SLVY	Silvey Corp. [*NASDAQ symbol*] (NQ)
SLW...........	Silversword Corp. [*Vancouver Stock Exchange symbol*]
SLW...........	Single Line Working [*Railway engineering term*] (DCTA)
SLW...........	Sisters of the Living Word [*Roman Catholic religious order*]
SLW...........	Slow
SLW...........	Space-Based LASER Weapon (MCD)
SLW...........	Specific Leaf Weight [*Botany*]
SLW...........	Spectral Line Width
SLW...........	Store Logical Word
SLW...........	Straight-Line Wavelength
SLW...........	Wooster, OH [*Location identifier*] [*FAA*] (FAAL)
SLWA........	Santa Rosa De Abuna [*Bolivia*] [*ICAO location identifier*] (ICLI)
SLWD........	Seis De Agosto [*Bolivia*] [*ICAO location identifier*] (ICLI)
SLWL........	Straight-Line Wavelength (MSA)
SLWMS	Secondary Liquid Waste Management System [*Nuclear energy*] (NRCH)
SL-Wola Ludu ...	Stronnictwo Ludowe-Wola Ludu [*Peasant Party-People's Will*] [*Poland*] [*Political party*] (PPE)
SLWT	Side Loadable Warping Tug [*Navy*] (CAAL)
SLX...........	Salt Cay [*British West Indies*] [*Airport symbol*] (OAG)
SLX...........	Siltronics Ltd. [*Toronto Stock Exchange symbol*]
SLX...........	Slate Creek, AK [*Location identifier*] [*FAA*] (FAAL)
SLY...........	Hayward, WI [*Location identifier*] [*FAA*] (FAAL)
SLY...........	Safety, Liquidity, Yield
SLY...........	Skelly Resources Ltd. [*Vancouver Stock Exchange symbol*]
SLY...........	Slijtersvakblad. Vakblad voor de Drankenbranche [*A publication*]
SLY...........	Sloppy [*Horse racing*]
SLY...........	Southerly
SLYA........	Yacuiba [*Bolivia*] [*ICAO location identifier*] (ICLI)
SLYB	El Bato [*Bolivia*] [*ICAO location identifier*] (ICLI)
SLYI	Yapacani [*Bolivia*] [*ICAO location identifier*] (ICLI)
SLYP	Muyupampa [*Bolivia*] [*ICAO location identifier*] (ICLI)
SLYP	Short Leaf Yellow Pine [*Lumber*]
SLYY	San Yo Yo [*Bolivia*] [*ICAO location identifier*] (ICLI)
SLZ...........	Sao Luiz [*Brazil*] [*Airport symbol*] (OAG)
SLZ...........	Solidor Resources, Inc. [*Vancouver Stock Exchange symbol*]
SLZ...........	Suppress Leading Zero [*Data processing*]
SLZA	Scandinavian Lead Zinc Association [*Stockholm, Sweden*] (EAIO)
SLZB	San Pedro [*Bolivia*] [*ICAO location identifier*] (ICLI)
SLZF.........	San Francisco (Naciff) [*Bolivia*] [*ICAO location identifier*] (ICLI)
SLZG........	San Agustin [*Bolivia*] [*ICAO location identifier*] (ICLI)
SLZJ.........	San Pedro (Richard) [*Bolivia*] [*ICAO location identifier*] (ICLI)
SLZK........	San Lucas [*Bolivia*] [*ICAO location identifier*] (ICLI)
SLZR........	San Rafael (Isidoro) [*Bolivia*] [*ICAO location identifier*] (ICLI)
SLZX........	San Pedro (Salvatierra) [*Bolivia*] [*ICAO location identifier*] (ICLI)
SM	Altair Linee Aeree SpA [*Italy*] [*ICAO designator*] (FAAC)
SM	Dr. Schwarz Arzneimittelfabrik GmbH [*Germany*] [*Research code symbol*]
SM	Master of Science
SM	Medal of Service of the Order of Canada
SM	Meteorological Aids Station [*ITU designation*]
SM	Misericorde Sisters [*Roman Catholic religious order*]
SM	Sacred to the Memory of --- [*Epitaphs*] (ROG)
SM	Sacred Music [*A publication*]
S & M........	Sadism and Masochism
SM	St. Marys Railroad Co. [*AAR code*]
SM	Sales Management [*Later, Sales and Marketing Management*] [*A publication*]

SM	Sales Manager
SM	Sales and Marketing Management [*A publication*]
SM	Salvage Mechanic [*Navy*]
Sm	Samarium [*See Sa*] [*Chemical element*]
SM	Sammlung Metzler [*A publication*]
Sm	Samuel [*Old Testament book*]
SM	San Marco [*Satellite*] [*NASA/Italy*]
sm	San Marino [*MARC country of publication code*] [*Library of Congress*] [*IYRU nationality code*] (LCCP)
SM	San Marino [*ANSI two-letter standard code*] (CNC)
SM	Sanctae Memoriae [*Of Holy Memory*] [*Latin*]
S & M	Sappers and Miners [*British military*] .(DMA)
SM	Scheduled Maintenance (MCD)
SM	Schistosoma Mansoni [*A parasitic fluke*]
S of M	School of Musketry [*Military*] [*British*] (ROG)
S-M	Schuetzenmine [*Antipersonnel mine*] [*German military - World War II*]
SM	Schwarz/Mann [*Supply company in biochemistry and chemistry*]
SM	Schweizer Muenzblaetter [*Gazette Numismatique Suisse*] [*A publication*]
SM	Scientific Memorandum
SM	Scientific Monthly [*A publication*]
Sm	Sclerotinia minor [*A fungus*]
SM	Seamen [*British military*] (DMA)
SM	Seat Mile
SM	Second Mortgage [*Banking*]
SM	Secondary Market [*Investment term*]
SM	Secondary Memory [*Data processing*] (BUR)
SM	Secretary's Memorandum [*Military*]
SM	Security Manual (AAG)
SM	Security Monitor (AAG)
SM	Seed Mass [*Botany*]
Sm	Semahot (BJA)
SM	Semiconductor Memory
SM	Semimonthly
SM	Senior Magistrate
S/M	Sensory-to-Motor [*Ratio*]
SM	Sentence Modifier [*Linguistics*]
S & M	September and March [*Denotes semiannual payments of interest or dividends in these months*] [*Business term*]
SM	Sequence Monitor
S & M	Sequencer and Monitor (KSC)
SM	Sergeant Major
SM	Serious Music [*Canadian Broadcasting Corp. record series prefix*]
SM	Serratia Marcescens [*Bacterium*]
S & M	Service and Maintenance
S/M	Service/Maintenance (NASA)
SM	Service Manual
SM	Service Mark [*Trademarks*]
SM	Service Member [*Military*] (AABC)
SM	Service Module [*NASA*]
SM	Service Monitoring [*Telecommunications*] (TEL)
SM	Set Mode (BUR)
SM	Sewage Microparticulates [*Oceanography*]
SM	Sewing Machine
S & M	Sexton and Malone [*Comic book*] [*CBC TV series*]
SM	Sexual Myths [*Scale*]
SM	Shape Memory [*Metallurgy*]
SM	Shared Memory [*Data processing*] (BUR)
S & M	Shaw and Maclean's House of Lords Cases [*A publication*] (DLA)
SM	Sheet Metal
SM	Shell Model
SM	Shelter Management [*Civil Defense*]
SM	Ship Movement Library [*Maritime Data Network, Inc.*] [*Information service or system*] (CRD)
SM	Shipment Memorandum [*Navy*]
SM	Shipping Monthly Data [*Department of Commerce*] (GFGA)
SM	Ship's Manifest (ADA)
SM	Shock Mount
SM	Shop Manual [*Air Force*] (AAG)
SM	Short Meter [*Music*]
SM	Short Module [*NASA*] (NASA)
SM	Shuttle Management [*Kennedy Space Center*] [*NASA*] (NASA)
SM	SIAI-Marchetti SpA [*Italy*] [*ICAO aircraft manufacturer identifier*] (ICAO)
SM	Siam
S/M	Siemens per Meter
SM	Signaling Module [*Telecommunications*] (TEL)
SM	Signalman [*Navy rating*]
SM	Silver Medalist
SM	Silver Methenamine [*Biological stain*]
SM	Silver Mica [*Capacitor*]
SM	Simple Maintenance
SM	Simple Mastectomy [*Medicine*]
SM	Simpson's Multipliers [*Naval architecture*]
SM	Simulated Missile (AAG)
SM	Simulators [*JETDS nomenclature*] [*Military*] (CET)
SM	Single Manager [*Military*]

SM	Single Mode
SM	Sinistra Mano [*Left Hand*]
SM	Sinus Medii [*Central Bay*] [*Lunar area*]
SM	Sisters of Mercy [*Roman Catholic religious order*]
S de M	Sisters Servants of Mary [*Roman Catholic religious order*]
SM	Skim Milk (MAE)
SM	Slow Moving
SM	Small (AAG)
SM	Small Pica
SM	Smectic Phase [*Physical chemistry*]
Sm	Smectite [*Agronomy*]
S & M	Smedes and Marshall's Mississippi Chancery Reports [*A publication*] (DLA)
S & M	Smedes and Marshall's Mississippi Reports [*9-22 Mississippi*] [*1843-50*] [*A publication*] (DLA)
Sm	Smena [*Moscow*] [*A publication*]
Sm	Smith Antigen [*Immunology*]
Sm	Smith Collection. British Museum [*London*] (BJA)
Sm	Smithsonian [*A publication*]
SM	SMM Enterprises Ltd. [*Vancouver Stock Exchange symbol*]
SM	Smooth (MSA)
SM	Snell Motorcycle
SM	Sociaal Maandblad [*A publication*]
SM	Socially Maladjusted
SM	Societa Altair [*Italy*] [*ICAO designator*] (ICDA)
SM	Societas Mariae [*Congregation of Mary*] [*Marists*] [*Roman Catholic religious order*]
SM	Society of Medalists
S of M	Society of Metaphysicians (EA)
SM	Society of Miniaturists (EA)
SM	Soft Manual (NASA)
SM	Soil Mechanics
SM	Solar Magnetic [*System*] [*NASA*]
SM	Solar Magnetospheric
SM	Soldier's Manual
SM	Soldier's Medal [*Military decoration*]
SM	Solicitor's Memorandum, United States Internal Revenue Bureau [*A publication*] (DLA)
SM	Solid Measure (ROG)
SM	Somatomedin [*Biochemistry*]
SM	Song of Moses (BJA)
SM	Sons of Malta
SM	Sound Management [*Radio Advertising Bureau*] [*A publication*]
SM	Southern Minnesota Railroad
SM	Space Medicine (SAA)
SM	Spanish Moss
SM	Spawning Mark
SM	Special Memorandum
SM	Specification Memo (AAG)
SM	Speculative Masonry [*Freemasonry*]
SM	Speech Monographs [*A publication*]
SM	SpenderMenders [*An association*] (EA)
SM	Sphingomyelin [*Also, Sph*] [*Biochemistry*]
SM	Sports Medicine [*A publication*]
SM	Square Meter
SM	Stability Margin
SM	Stabilized Member [*NASA*] (KSC)
SM	Staff Manager [*Insurance*]
SM	Staff Memorandum
SM	Stage Manager
SM	Standard Matched
SM	Standard Memoranda (AAG)
SM	Standard Methods
SM	Standard Missile
SM	Standards Manual
SM	Staphylococcus Medium [*Microbiology*]
SM	State Militia [*e.g., NJSM - New Jersey State Militia*]
SM	Static Margin
SM	Station Manager [*Deep Space Instrumentation Facility, NASA*]
SM	Stationary Medium-Power [*Reactor*] [*Nuclear energy*]
SM	Statistical Multiplexer (MCD)
SM	Statistiske Meddelelser [*Denmark*]
SM	Statute Mile
SM	Stipendiary Magistrate
S & M	Stock and Machinery
SM	Stock Market
SM	Stock Material (SAA)
SM	Storage Mark [*Data processing*] (OA)
SM	Strategic Missile (NATG)
SM	Streptomycin [*An antibiotic*]
SM	Stria Medullaris [*Neuroanatomy*]
SM	Strip Mine
SM	Structural Mechanical (MCD)
SM	Structure Memory
S & M	Structures and Materials (MCD)
SM	Structures Memorandum
SM	Student Manual [*Civil Defense*]
SM	Studio SM [*Record label*] [*France*]
S/M	Submarine [*British*]
SM	[*Officer Qualified for*] Submarine Duties [*British*]

SM	Submarine Flag [*Navy*] [*British*]
SM	Submarine, Minelaying [*Obsolete*]
S/M	Submarine Pay
sm	Submetacentric [*Botany*]
sm	Submucous [*Medicine*] (MAE)
SM	Substitute Materials [*British*]
SM	Suckling Mice
SM	Suction Method [*Medicine*] (MAE)
SM	Sumerian Mythology [*S. N. Kramer*] [*A publication*] (BJA)
SM	Summary Memorandum
SM	Summer [*A publication*]
S & M	Sun and Moon [*A publication*]
SM	Super Maneuverable Aircraft
S/M	Super Mare [*On Sea*] [*In place names*] [*Latin*] (ROG)
S & M	Supply and Maintenance [*Army*] (AABC)
SM	Supply Manual [*Military*]
SM	Supply Module (SSD)
SM	Support Module [*NASA*] (NASA)
SM	Surface Measure
SM	Surface Missile (AAG)
S & M	Surfaced and Matched [*Lumber*]
SM	Surgeon Major
SM	Suspended Matter [*Chemistry*]
SM	Sustained Medication [*Pharmacology*]
SM	Sydney Mail [*A publication*] (APTA)
SM	Symbolic Manipulation [*Data processing*]
SM	Symptom [*Medicine*] (MAE)
S & M	SYNCH [*Synchronize*] and MUX [*Multiplex*] (MCD)
SM	Synchronous MODEM
SM	Synthetic Medium [*Microbiology*]
SM	System Manager [*Military*] (AFM)
SM	System Mechanics
SM	System Monitor
SM	Systema Malykh [*Small System*] [*Russian*] [*Data processing*]
SM	Systemic Mastocytosis [*Medicine*]
SM	Systems Management [*NASA*] (MCD)
SM	Systems Memory [*Data processing*] (BUR)
SM	Systolic Mean [*Cardiology*]
SM	Systolic Murmur [*Cardiology*]
SM1	Signalman, First Class [*Navy rating*]
SM2	Signalman, Second Class [*Navy rating*]
SM3	Signalman, Third Class [*Navy rating*]
SMA	Andreafsky/St. Marys, AK [*Location identifier*] [*FAA*] (FAAL)
SMA	Sa Majeste Aulique [*His, or Her, Austrian Majesty*] [*French*] (ROG)
SMA	Safe Manufacturers' Association
SMA	Saigon Mission Association (EA)
SMA	Salad Manufacturers Association (EA)
SMA	Salt Manufacturing Association [*British*]
SMA	San Manuel Arizona Railroad Co. [*AAR code*]
SMA	Santa Maria [*Azores*] [*Airport symbol*] (OAG)
SMA	Scale Manufacturers Association (EA)
SMA	Scheduled Maintenance Action
SMA	Screen Manufacturers Association (EA)
SMA	Scythe Makers' Association [*A union*] [*British*]
SMA	Semimajor Axis
SMA	Senior Marine Advisor
SMA	Senior Military Attache
SMA	Sequential Multiple Analysis [*or Analyzer*] [*Clinical chemistry*]
SMA	Sergeant Major Academy [*Army*]
SMA	Sergeant Major of the Army (AABC)
SMA	Service Merchandisers of America [*Later, NASM*] (EA)
SMA	Shape Memory Alloy (RDA)
SMA	Shelving Manufacturers Association (EA)
SMA	Shielded Metal Arc [*Nickel and alloy welding*]
SMA	Ship's Material Account
SMA	Simultaneous Multiphasic Analysis [*Medicine*]
SMA	Single Manager for Ammunition [*DoD*] (MCD)
SMA	Single Manager Approach
SMA	Site Maintenance Area (AAG)
SMA	Skymark Airlines (FAAC)
SMA	Slave Manipulator Arm [*Astronautics*]
SMA	Small Arms (NATG)
SMA	Smooth Muscle Antibody (AAMN)
SMA	Sociaal Maandblad Arbeid [*A publication*]
SMA	Social Maturity Age
SMA	Socialist Medical Association [*British*]
SMA	Societe des Missionnaires d'Afrique [*Society of Missionaries of Africa*] (EA)
SMA	Society of African Missions [*Roman Catholic men's religious order*]
SMA	Society of Management Accountants
SMA	Society of Manufacturer's Agents [*Later, SMR*] (EA)
SMA	Society of Marine Artists [*British*]
SMA	Society of Maritime Arbitrators (EA)
SMA	Society of Medical Administrators (EA)
SMA	Society for Medical Anthropology (EA)
SMA	Society for Medieval Archaeology (EA)
SMA	Society of Mineral Analysts (EA)
SMA	Society of Municipal Arborists (EA)
SMA	Software Maintenance Association (EA)

SMA	Solar Maximum Analysis [*Meteorology*]
SMA	Somatomedin A [*Biochemistry*]
SMA	Southern Marketing Association. Proceedings [*A publication*]
SMA	Southern Maryland Aviation, Inc. [*FAA designator*] (FAAC)
SMA	Soviet Military Administration
SMA	Special Miscellaneous Account
SMA	Special Mission Alteration
SMA	Spinal Muscular Atrophy [*Medicine*]
SMA	Spiritual Ministry for Adults (EA)
SMA	Spontaneous Motor Activity [*Neurophysiology*]
SMA	Squadron Maintenance Area
SMA	Stabilized Member Assembly [*NASA*]
SMA	Stage Management Association [*British*]
SMA	Standard Maintenance Allowance
SMA	Standard Methods Agar [*Microbiology*]
SMA	State Mutual Life Assurance Co. of America
SMA	Statutory Marketing Authority
SMA	Steatite Manufacturers Association [*Later, DPCSMA*] (EA)
SMA	Steel Manufacturers Association (EA)
SMA	Stichting Mondiaal Alternatief [*Foundation for Ecological Development Alternatives*] [*Netherlands*] (EAIO)
SMA	Stoker Manufacturers Association (EA)
SMA	Strategic Management Accounting (ADA)
SMA	Strategic Mobility Analysis [*Military*]
SMA	Stucco Manufacturers Association (EA)
S M (A)	Studies in Music (Australia) [*A publication*]
SMA	Stylomastoid Artery [*Anatomy*]
SMA	Styrene-Maleic Anhydride [*Organic chemistry*]
SMA	Subject Matter Area (AFM)
SMA	Submerged Metal Arc Welding
SMA	Subsequent Maintenance Assessment
SMA	Suggested for Mature Audiences [*Motion pictures*]
SMA	Sukuma Exploration [*Vancouver Stock Exchange symbol*]
SMA	Summerton [*South Carolina*] [*Seismograph station code, US Geological Survey*] [*Closed*] (SEIS)
SMA	Superior Mesenteric Artery [*Anatomy*]
SMA	Superplastic Metal Alloy
SMA	Supplemental Maintenance Appraisal
SMA	Supplementary Motor Area [*Anatomy*]
S & MA	Supply and Maintenance Agency [*System*] [*Army*]
SMA	Support Management Area [*Mission Control Center*] [*NASA*]
SMA	Surface Modulating Assembly [*Cytology*]
SMA	Surplus Marketing Administration [*New Deal*]
SMA	Syrie et Monde Arabe [*Damascus*] [*A publication*]
SMAA	Submarine Movement Advisory Authority (NVT)
SMAB	Solid Motor Assembly Building [*for Missiles*]
SMAB	Spartan Management Action Board [*Missiles*] (MCD)
SMAC	Scene Matching Area Correlator [*Navy*] (MCD)
SMAC	Science and Mathematics Analysis Center [*ERIC*]
SMAC	Scientific Machine Automation Corp.
SMAC	Senate Military Affairs Committee [*British*] (DAS)
SMAC	Serial Memory Address Counter [*Computer*]
SMAC	Shielded Metal Arc Cutting [*Welding*]
SMAC	Simulation, Manual and Computerized
SMAC	Single Manager for Ammunition, Conventional [*DoD*]
SMAC	Society of Management Accountants of Canada
SMAC	Spartan Material Availability Control [*Army*]
SMAC	Special Mission Attack Computer
SMAC	Striated Microtubule-Associated Components [*Botanical cytology*]
SMAC	Submicron Aerosol Collector
SMAC	System Management and Control
SMAC/CRC ...	Surface Modification and Characterization Collaborative Research Center [*Oak Ridge, TN*] [*Oak Ridge National Laboratory*] [*Department of Energy*] (GRD)
SMACH	Sounding Machine [*Engineering*]
SMACK	Society of Males Who Appreciate Cute Knees [*Group opposing below-the-knee fashions introduced in 1970*]
SMACNA ...	Sheet Metal and Air Conditioning Contractors' National Association (EA)
SMACRATRACEN ...	Small Craft Training Center
SMACS	Serialized Missile Accounting and Control System
SMACS	Simulated Message Analysis and Conversion Subsystem
Sm Act	Smith's Action at Law [*12th ed.*] [*1876*] [*A publication*] (DLA)
SMACTRACEN ...	Small Craft Training Center [*Navy*] (DNAB)
SMAD	Scaled Median Absolute Deviation [*Mathematics*]
SMAD	Solvated Metal Atom Dispersion [*Chemistry*]
SMAD	Sowjetische Militaeradministration
Sm Adm Pr ...	Smith's Admiralty Practice [*4th ed.*] [*1892*] [*A publication*] (DLA)
SMADS	Sault Sainte Marie Air Defense Sector (SAA)
SMAE	Sbornik Muzeia Antropologii i Etnografii [*A publication*] (BJA)
SMAE	Society of Model Aeronautical Engineers [*British*]
SMAE	Superior Mesenteric Artery Embolus [*Medicine*]
SMAE	System Management Application Entity
SMAF	Afobaka [*Surinam*] [*ICAO location identifier*] (ICLI)
SMAF	Shipboard Maintenance Action Form (DNAB)
SMAF	Smooth Muscle Activating Factor
SMAF	Special Mission Aircraft Flights (NATG)
SMAF	Specific Macrophage Arming Factor [*Hematology*]

SMAF....... Superior Mesenteric Artery Flow
SMAG....... Simulator Missile Airborne and Ground (MCD)
SMAG....... Star Magnitude (NASA)
SMAG....... Systems Management Analysis Group (MCD)
SMAGD .... Solaire 1 Magazine [*A publication*]
Sma & Giff ... Smale and Giffard's English Vice-Chancellors' Reports [*A publication*] (DLA)
SMAGOL ... Small Computer Algorithmic Language (DNAB)
SMAIL...... Source Mail [*Electronic mail*]
SMAJ .... Sergeant Major
SMAL........ Single Mode Alignment (CAAL)
SMAL....... Society for Musteline Arts and Literature (EA)
SMAL....... Structural Macroassembly Language
SMAL........ System Material Analysis List
SMALC..... Sacramento Air Logistics Center (MCD)
Smale & G ... Smale and Giffard's English Vice-Chancellors' Reports [*A publication*] (DLA)
SMALGOL ... Small Computer Algorithmic Language
Small Bus... Small Business Reporter [*A publication*]
Small Bus Bull ... Small Business Bulletin [*A publication*]
Small Bus Comp ... Small Business Computers Magazine [*A publication*]
Small Bus Comput ... Small Business Computers [*A publication*]
Small Bus Comput News ... Small Business Computer News [*A publication*]
Small Business ... Small Business Report [*A publication*]
Small Bus Reporter ... Small Business Reporter [*A publication*]
Small Bus Rt ... Small Business Report [*A publication*]
Small Comput Libr ... Small Computers in Libraries [*A publication*]
Small Gr B ... Small Group Behavior [*A publication*]
Small Group Behav ... Small Group Behavior [*A publication*]
Small Mamm Newsl ... Small Mammal Newsletters [*A publication*]
Small Pr..... Small Press Review [*A publication*]
Small Ruminant Res ... Small Ruminant Research [*A publication*]
Small Rural Hosp Rep ... Small and Rural Hospital Report [*A publication*]
Small-Scale Master Bldr ... Small-Scale Master Builder [*A publication*]
Small Sch For ... Small School Forum [*A publication*]
Small Stock Mag ... Small Stock Magazine [*A publication*]
Small Sys... Small Systems World [*A publication*]
Small Sys Soft ... Small Systems Software [*A publication*]
Small Syst Software ... Small Systems Software [*A publication*]
Small Syst World ... Small Systems World [*A publication*]
SMALLTALK ... [*A*] Programming Language (CSR)
SMAM ...... Amotopo [*Surinam*] [*ICAO location identifier*] (ICLI)
SMAM ...... Single Mission Air Medal (DNAB)
SMAMA ... Sacramento Air Materiel Area (KSC)
SMAME... Society of Marine Architects and Marine Engineers (EA)
SMAN .... Standard Medium-Accuracy Navigator
SMANCS .. Styrene Maleic Acid Neocarzinostatin [*Antineoplastic drug*]
Smap.......... Surprised Middle-Aged Person [*Lifestyle classification*]
SMAP........ System Management Application Process
SMAP....... Systems Management Analysis Project (MCD)
SMAR....... Sheet Metal Assembler Riveter (MCD)
S & Mar ..... Smedes and Marshall's Mississippi Reports [*9-22 Mississippi*] [*A publication*] (DLA)
SMAR........ Summary of Monthly Aerological Reports [*Navy*] (DNAB)
SMARC..... Survivable-MOS [*Metal-Oxide Semiconductor*] Array Computer [*Air Force*]
SM Arch.... SM [*Solid Mechanics*] Archives [*A publication*]
S & Mar Ch ... Smedes and Marshall's Mississippi Chancery Reports [*A publication*] (DLA)
SM Arch .... Solid Mechanics Archives [*A publication*]
SMART..... Salton's Magical Automatic Retriever of Texts [*Data processing*]
SMART..... Satellite Maintenance and Repair Techniques [*Air Force*]
SMART..... Scheduled Maintenance and Reliability Team (MCD)
SMART..... Science, Mathematics, and Related Technologies
SMART..... Selected Methods for Attracting the Right Targets [*Bombing system*] (AFM)
SMART..... Sensitive-Membrane-Antigen-Rapid-Test
SMART..... Sequential Mechanism for Automatic Recording and Testing
SMART..... Shuttle Meeting Action - Item Review Tracking [*NASA*] (NASA)
SMART..... Simplified Method to Achieve Regulated Training
SMART..... Small Firms Merit Award for Research and Technology [*British*]
SMART..... Socony Mobil Automatic Real Time (DIT)
SMART..... Sort Merge and Reduction Tapes (CAAL)
SMART..... Source Management of Resources and Time (DNAB)
SMART..... Space Maintenance and Repair Techniques
SMART..... Space Management and Retail Tracking System [*Information Resources, Inc.*]
SMART..... Spacesaver Material Accounting Resource Terminal [*Spacesaver Corp.*]
SMART..... Specific, Measurable, Agreed-To, Reachable, Time-Specific [*Management technique*]
SMART..... Stop Merchandising Alcohol on Radio and Television
SMART..... Structural Maintenance and Repair Team (MCD)
SMART..... Supersonic Military Air Research Track
SMART..... Supersonic Missile and Rocket Track
SMART..... Supply and Maintenance Assessment and Review Team [*Army*]
SMART..... System Malfunction Analysis Reinforcement Trainer

SMART..... System for Management and Allocation of Resources Technique [*Data processing*]
SMART..... System Management and Review Technique (HGAA)
SMART..... System for Manipulation and Retrieval of Text
SMART..... System for the Mechanical Analysis and Retrieval of Text
SMART..... System Monitoring and Reporting Tool (HGAA)
SMART..... Systems Management Analysis, Research, and Testing (MCD)
SMART..... Systems Managers Administrative Rating Test [*Simulation game*]
SMART..... University of Saskatchewan Libraries Machine-Assisted Reference Teleservices [*University of Saskatchewan Library*] [*Information service or system*] (IID)
SMARTee ... Smart End-Effector [*Robotics*] (ECON)
SMARTS... Selective Multiple Addresses Radio and Television Service [*A program delivery service introduced by RCA*]
SMARTS... Sport Management Art and Science Society [*Defunct*] (EA)
SMARTS... Status Memory and Real Time System [*AT & T*]
SMARTS... Submarine Advanced Reactive Tactical Training System
SMAS....... Subcontract Material Availability Schedule
SMAS....... Submuscular Aponeurotic System [*Medicine*]
SMAS........ Superficial Musculoaponeurotic System [*Plastic surgery*]
SMAS........ Switched Maintenance Access System [*Bell System*]
SMASF...... Servicemen's Mutual Aid and Savings Fund [*South Vietnam*]
SMASH..... Small Manned Anti-Submarine Helicopter (SAA)
SMASH..... Southeast Asia Multisensor Armed Surveillance Helicopter
SMASH..... Step-by-Step Monitor and Selector Hold [*Telecommunications*] (TEL)
SMASH..... Students Mobilizing on Auto Safety Hazards [*Student legal action organization*] (EA)
SMASHEX ... Search for Simulated Submarine Casualty Exercise [*Navy*] (NVT)
SMASHT .. Simple-Minded Approach to Squeezed Hollerith Text (SAA)
Smaskrift Landbruksdep Opplysningstjenesten ... Smaskrift-Norway. Landbruksdepartementet. Opplysningstjenesten [*A publication*]
SMAT....... School Motivation Analysis Test [*Personality development test*] [*Psychology*]
SMAT....... Superior Mesenteric Artery Thrombosis [*Medicine*]
SMATH .... Satellite Materials Hardening (MCD)
SMATS ..... Speed-Modulated Augmented Thrust System (NG)
SMATV..... Satellite Master Antenna Television
SMAW ...... Second Marine Aircraft Wing
SMAW ...... Shielded Metal Arc Welding
SMAW ...... Shoulder-Launched Multipurpose Assault Weapon (MCD)
SMAW ...... Shoulder-Mounted Assault Weapon (DWSG)
SMAW ...... Submerged Metal Arc Weld [*Nuclear energy*] (NRCH)
SMAWT.... Short-Range Man-Portable Antitank Weapons Technology
SMB.......... Bachelor of Sacred Music
SMB.......... Sa Majeste Britannique [*His or Her Britannic Majesty*] [*French*]
SMB.......... Samaipata [*Bolivia*] [*Seismograph station code, US Geological Survey*] [*Closed*] (SEIS)
SMB.......... Server Message Blocks (PCM)
SMB.......... Simba Resources, Inc. [*Vancouver Stock Exchange symbol*]
SMB.......... Small and Medium-Sized Businesses
SMB.......... Space Meteorology Branch [*NASA*]
SMB.......... Standard Merchants Bank [*British*]
SMB.......... Standard Mineral Base [*Medium*] [*Medicine*]
SMB.......... Static Memory Board [*Data processing*] (BYTE)
SMB.......... Steve Miller Band [*Pop music group*]
SMB.......... System Monitor Board
SMBA....... Scottish Marine Biological Association [*British*] (IRUK)
SMBA....... Slovenian Mutual Benefit Association [*Later, AMLA*] (EA)
Sm & Bat... Smith and Batty's Irish King's Bench Reports [*A publication*] (DLA)
SMBC....... Santuario Madre del Buon Consiglio [*Pious Union of Our Mother of Good Counsel - PUMGC*] [*Genazzano, Italy*] (EAIO)
SMBC....... Studien und Mitteilungen aus dem Benediktiner- und dem Cistercienser-Orden [*A publication*]
SMBCO..... Studien und Mitteilungen aus dem Benediktiner- und dem Cistercienser-Orden [*A publication*]
SMBCOZ.. Studien und Mitteilungen aus dem Benediktiner- und dem Cistercienser-Orden [*A publication*]
SMBD....... Stat'i Materialy po Bolgarskoj Dialektologii [*A publication*]
SMBDB..... Structural Margin Beyond Design Basis [*Nuclear energy*] (NRCH)
SMBF....... Superior Mesenteric Blood Flow [*Physiology*]
SMBFT ..... Small Bowel Follow-Through [*Medicine*]
SMBG....... Bakhuys [*Surinam*] [*ICAO location identifier*] (ICLI)
SMBG....... Self-Monitoring of Blood Glucose [*Medicine*]
SMBJ .... Style Manual for Biological Journals
SMBL....... Semimobile
SMBN ...... Albina [*Surinam*] [*ICAO location identifier*] (ICLI)
SMBO ...... Botopasie [*Surinam*] [*ICAO location identifier*] (ICLI)
Sm & BRR Cas ... Smith and Bates' American Railway Cases [*A publication*] (DLA)
SMBS....... Safeguard Material Balance Simulator
SMBW....... Bronsweg [*Surinam*] [*ICAO location identifier*] (ICLI)
SMBX....... Symbolics, Inc. [*NASDAQ symbol*] (NQ)
SMC .... Chief Signalman [*Navy rating*]

SMC	Medical University of South Carolina Library, Charleston, SC [*OCLC symbol*] (OCLC)
SMC	Sa Majeste Catholique [*His or Her Catholic Majesty*] [*of Spain*] [*French*]
SMC	SAGE [*Semiautomatic Ground Environment*] Maintenance Control
SMC	Saint Martin's College [*Washington*]
SMC	Saint Mary's College [*Indiana; Kansas; Michigan; Minnesota*]
SMC	Saint Michael's College [*Vermont*]
SMC	Sales and Marketing Management in Canada [*A publication*]
SMC	Save the Manatee Club (EA)
SMC	Scientific Manpower Commission (EA)
SMC	Secondary Mesenchyme Cell [*Cytology*]
SMC	Segmented Maintenance Cask [*Nuclear energy*] (NRCH)
SMC	Senior Medical Consultant
SMC	Senior Mission Controller (MCD)
SMC	Sensory Organ Mother Cell [*Genetics*]
SMC	Sequential Machine Controller [*Programming language*] [*1977-78*] (CSR)
SMC	Service Men's Center [*World War II*]
SMC	Sheet Molding Compound [*Plastics technology*]
SMC	Short-Run Marginal Cost Curve [*Economics*]
SMC	Silicon Monolithic Circuit
SMC	Silva Mind Control [*Psychic system*]
SMC	Single Mothers by Choice (EA)
SMC	Small Magellanic Cloud [*Astronomy*]
SMC	Smith [*A. O.*] Corp. [*AMEX symbol*] (SPSG)
SMC	Smithsonian Miscellaneous Collections [*A publication*]
SMC	Smooth Muscle Cell [*Cytology*]
SMC	Societe Mediterraneenne de Chimiotherapie [*Mediterranean Society of Chemotherapy - MSC*] [*Italy*] (EAIO)
SMC	Society of Marine Consultants (EA)
SMC	Soil and Moisture Conservation
SMC	Solar Monitor Constant (SSD)
SMC	Somatomedin C [*Biochemistry*]
SMC	Somerset [*Colorado*] [*Seismograph station code, US Geological Survey*] (SEIS)
SmC	Southern Microfilm Corporation, Houston, TX [*Library symbol*] [*Library of Congress*] (LCLS)
SMC	Southern Missionary College [*Tennessee*]
SMC	Southern Motor Carriers Rate Conference, Atlanta GA [*STAC*]
SMC	Spanish Music Center [*Commercial firm*] (EA)
SMC	Special Monthly Compensation (MAE)
SMC	Special Mouth Care [*Medicine*]
S-M-C	Sperm [*or Spore*] Mother-Cell
SMC	Squared Multiple Correlation [*Psychology*]
SMC	Squawk Mode Code (FAAC)
SMC	Staff Message Control [*Military*]
SMC	Standard Mean Chord [*Aviation*] (AIA)
SMC	Standard-Modern Technologies Corp. [*Toronto Stock Exchange symbol*]
SMC	Standard Molding Corp.
SMC	Standard Motorists Centre [*Automotive sales and service chain*] [*British*]
SMC	Station-Control and Monitor Console Subsystem [*Deep Space Instrumentation Facility, NASA*]
SMC	Stepper Motor Control
SMC	Storage Module Controller
SMC	Student Mobilization Committee [*to End the War in Vietnam*] [*Defunct*] (EA)
SMC	Studies in Medieval Culture [*A publication*]
SMC	Sub-Machine Carbine [*British military*] (DMA)
SMC	Succinylmonocholine [*Biochemistry*] (MAE)
SMC	Sunnybrook Medical Centre, Toronto [*UTLAS symbol*]
SMC	Super-Multi-Coating [*Camera lenses*]
SMC	Supply and Maintenance Command [*Army*]
SMC	Surface Movement Control [*Aviation*]
SMC	Switch Maintenance Center [*Telecommunications*] (TEL)
SMC	Synchronized Maneuver Countermeasures Model (MCD)
SMC	System Monitor Console (CAAL)
SMC	Systems, Man, and Cybernetics (MCD)
SMCA	Cayana [*Surinam*] [*ICAO location identifier*] (ICLI)
SMCA	Single Manager for Conventional Ammunition [*DoD*]
SMCA	Sodium Monochloroacetate [*Organic chemistry*]
SMCA	Suckling Mouse Cataract Agent [*Microbiology*]
SMCAF	Society of Medical Consultants to the Armed Forces (EA)
sm cap	Small Capitals [*Typography*] (WGA)
SMCC	Saint Mary's College of California
SMCC	Santa Monica City College [*California*]
SMCC	Schield Management Co. [*Denver, CO*] [*NASDAQ symbol*] (NQ)
SMCC	Shuttle Mission Control Center [*NASA*] (NASA)
SMCC	Simulation Monitor and Control Console (KSC)
SMCC	Society of Memorial Cancer Center
SMCC	Sport Medicine Council of Canada
SMCC	Standard Machinery Control Console [*Canadian Navy*]
SMCC	State Manpower Coordinating Committee [*Department of Labor*]
SMCC	Succinimidyl (Maleimidomethyl)cyclohexanecarboxylate [*Organic chemistry*]
SMC-CF	Smooth Muscle Cell-Chemotactic Factor [*Oncology*]
Sm CCM	Smith's Circuit Courts-Martial Reports [*Maine*] [*A publication*] (DLA)
SMC(Disp)	Spectacle Makers Co. (Dispenser) [*British*] (DI)
SMCE	Master of Science in Civil Engineering
SMCE	Sociedad Mexicana de Computacion Electronica [*Mexico*]
SMCG	Stuart McGuire Co. [*NASDAQ symbol*] (NQ)
SMCH	Service Merchandise Co., Inc. [*NASDAQ symbol*] (NQ)
S & M Ch	Smedes and Marshall's Mississippi Chancery Reports [*A publication*] (DLA)
SMCH	Standard Mixed Cargo Harness (NASA)
Sm Ch Pr	Smith's Chancery Practice [*7th ed.*] [*1862*] [*A publication*] (DLA)
S & M Ch R	Smedes and Marshall's Mississippi Chancery Reports [*A publication*] (DLA)
S & M Ch Rep	Smedes and Marshall's Mississippi Chancery Reports [*A publication*] (DLA)
S & M Chy	Smedes and Marshall's Mississippi Chancery Reports [*A publication*] (DLA)
SMCI	Coeroeni [*Surinam*] [*ICAO location identifier*] (ICLI)
Smckr	Smucker [*J.M.*] Co. [*Associated Press abbreviation*] (APAG)
SMCL	Secondary Maximum Contaminant Level (EG)
SMCL	Southeastern Massachusetts Cooperating Libraries [*Library network*]
SMCLN	Semicolon (AABC)
SMCM	Master Chief Signalman [*Navy rating*]
SMCN	Selective Myocardial Cell Necrosis [*Cardiology*]
SMCO	Coronie [*Surinam*] [*ICAO location identifier*] (ICLI)
SMCO	SAGE [*Semiautomatic Ground Environment*] Maintenance Control Office
Sm Com L	Smith's Manual of Common Law [*12th ed.*] [*1905*] [*A publication*] (DLA)
Sm Con	Smith on Contracts [*8th ed.*] [*1885*] [*A publication*] (DLA)
Sm Cond Ala	Smith's Condensed Alabama Reports [*A publication*] (DLA)
Sm Const Cons	Smith on Constitutional and Statutory Construction [*A publication*] (DLA)
Sm Conv	Smith on Conveyancing [*A publication*] (DLA)
SMCP	San Marino Communist Party
SMCP	Supply and Maintenance Career Program
SMCP	Supply and Maintenance Control Point
SMCPA	Simulation Councils. Proceedings Series [*A publication*]
SMCPCF	Fort Walsh National Historic Park, Parks Canada [*Parc Historique National Fort Walsh, Parcs Canada*] Maple Creek, Saskatchewan [*Library symbol*] [*National Library of Canada*] (NLC)
SMCPSTC	Supply and Maintenance Command Packaging Storage and Transportability Center [*Army*]
SMCR	Selected Marine Corps Reserve
SMCR	Society for Menstrual Cycle Research (EA)
SMCR	Summcorp [*Fort Wayne, IN*] [*NASDAQ symbol*] (NQ)
SMCRA	Surface Mining Control and Reclamation Act [*1977*]
SMCRC	Southern Motor Carriers Rate Conference
SMCRD8	Saunders Monographs in Clinical Radiology [*A publication*]
SMCS	IEEE Systems, Man, and Cybernetics Society (EA)
SMCS	Senior Chief Signalman [*Navy rating*]
SMCS	Separation Monitor and Control System [*NASA*] (MCD)
SMCS	Simulation Monitor and Control System (CAAL)
SMCS	Structural Mode Control System (MCD)
SMCSG	Special Military Construction Study Group (AABC)
SMCT	Cottica [*Surinam*] [*ICAO location identifier*] (ICLI)
SMCTG	Standard Missile Correlation Task Group [*Military*]
SMCTG	Surface Missile Compatibility Test Group [*Military*]
SMCU	Separation Monitoring Control Unit [*NASA*] (MCD)
SMD	Doctor of Sacred Music
SMD	Fort Wayne, IN [*Location identifier*] [*FAA*] (FAAL)
SMD	Saint Michael's College, Library, Winooski, VT [*OCLC symbol*] (OCLC)
SMD	Sauter Mean Diameter (KSC)
SMD	Scheduling Management Display
SMD	Scottish Malt Distillers [*British*]
SMD	Senile Macular Degeneration [*Medicine*]
SMD	Serum Malic Dehydrogenase [*An enzyme*]
SMD	Ship Manning Document [*Navy*]
SMD	Short Meter Double [*Music*]
SMD	Silicon Multiplier Detector
SMD	Singular Multinomial Distribution [*Statistics*]
SMD	Society of Medical-Dental Management Consultants (EA)
SMD	Spacelab Mission Development [*NASA*] (MCD)
SMD	Special Measuring Device (NASA)
SMD	Standardized Military Drawings [*Army*]
SMD	Statistical Methods Division [*Bureau of the Census*] (OICC)
SMD	Stop Motion Detector
SMD	Storage Module Device [*Data processing*]
SMD	Storage Module Drive
SMD	Structures and Mechanics Division [*NASA*]
SMD	Submanubrial Dullness [*Medicine*]
SMD	Submarine Mine Depot
SMD	Submersible Mining Device
SMD	Sunrise Medical, Inc. [*NYSE symbol*] (SPSG)
SMD	Surface Mounted Device [*Microelectronics*]

SMD .... Susceptor Meus Dominus [*God Is My Protector*] [*Latin*] [*Motto of Jacob, Margrave of Baden-Hochberg (1562-90); Georg Friedrich, Margrave of Baden-Hochberg (1573-1638)*]
SMD .... Symptom Medication Diary [*Medicine*]
SMD .... Synchronous Modulator-Demodulator (MCD)
SMD .... System Management Directive (AFM)
SMD .... Systems Display [*Vancouver Stock Exchange symbol*]
SMD .... Systems Manufacturing Division [*IBM Corp.*]
SMD .... Systems Measuring Device (KSC)
SMD .... Systems Monitor Display
SMDA ...... Drietabbetje [*Surinam*] [*ICAO location identifier*] (ICLI)
SMDA ...... Second Marine Division Association (EA)
SMDA ...... Sixth Marine Division Association [*Later, 6th MAR DIV*] (EA)
SMDA ...... State Medicaid Directors Association (EA)
SMDC ...... Saint Mary's Dominican College [*Louisiana*]
SMDC ...... Shielded Mild Detonating Cord
SMDC ...... Sisters of Mercy, Daughters of Christian Charity of St. Vincent de Paul [*Roman Catholic religious order*]
SMDC ...... Sodium Methyldithiocarbamate [*Fungicide*]
SMDC ...... Superconductive Materials Data Center (KSC)
SMDE .... Static Mercury Drop Electrode [*Electrochemistry*]
SM Dendrol ... Master of Science in Dendrology
SMDF .... SCATS [*Simulation, Checkout, and Training System*] Main Distributing Frame
SMDI .... Surface Miss Distance Indicator [*Navy*] (CAAL)
SMDJ .... Djoemoe [*Surinam*] [*ICAO location identifier*] (ICLI)
SMDK ...... Donderskamp [*Surinam*] [*ICAO location identifier*] (ICLI)
SMDL .... Standard Music Description Language [*Data processing*]
SMDL .... Stoff- und Motivgeschichte der Deutschen Literatur [*A publication*]
SMDL .... Subminiature Microwave Delay Line
SMDMC ... Society of Medical-Dental Management Consultants (EA)
SMDO ...... Ladoeanie [*Surinam*] [*ICAO location identifier*] (ICLI)
SMDO ...... Special Microwave Devices Operation [*Raytheon Co.*]
SMD, OCOFS ... Staff Management Division, Office, Chief of Staff [*Army*]
SMD OC of SA ... Staff Management Division, Office, Chief of Staff, Army (AABC)
SMD OCSA ... Staff Management Division, Office, Chief of Staff, Army (AABC)
SMDP .... Stock Management Description Pattern
SMDPL ..... Supply Management Date and Price List [*Navy*]
SMDPS ..... Service Module Deluge Purge System [*NASA*] (KSC)
SMDR .... Selected Management Data Report [*DoD*]
SMDR .... Station Message Detail Recording [*Formerly, MDR*] [*Telecommunications*]
SMDR .... Summary Management Data Report [*DoD*]
SMDS .... Switched Multimegabit Data Service [*Telecommunications*] (PCM)
SM & DSL ... Sector Management and Direct Support Logistics Center [*Navy*] (DNAB)
SMDT .... Shore Mode Data Transmitter (MCD)
SMDTB ..... School Musician. Director and Teacher [*A publication*]
SME .... Sales and Marketing Executives-International (EA)
SME .... Sancta Mater Ecclesia [*Holy Mother Church*] [*Latin*]
SME .... Scale Model Engineering [*Initialism is brand name of tone arm*]
SME .... School of Military Engineering
SME .... Semiconductor Manufacturing Equipment [*Sumitomo Metals*]
SME .... Service Merchandise Co., Inc. [*NYSE symbol*] (SPSG)
SME .... Shape Memory Effect [*Metal alloy property*]
SME .... Sheet Metal Enclosure
SME .... Shell Metal Extractant
SME .... Shipbuilding and Marine Engineering [*Department of Employment*] [*British*]
SME .... SHOWME [*VERALEX, Inc.*] [*Information service or system*] (CRD)
SME .... Singleton Materials Engineering Laboratories [*Tennessee Valley Authority*] (GRD)
SME .... Small and Medium-Size Enterprises
SME .... Society of Manufacturing Engineers (EA)
SME .... Society of Military Engineers (KSC)
SME .... Society for Mining, Metallurgy, and Exploration, Inc. [*In association name, SME, Inc.*] (EA)
SME .... Soil Mechanics Experiment [*NASA*]
SME .... Solar Mesosphere Explorer (MCD)
SME .... Somerset, KY [*Location identifier*] [*FAA*] (FAAL)
SME .... Sony Music Entertainment (ECON)
SME .... Spartan Missile Equipment [*Missiles*] (MCD)
SME .... Squadron Medical Element
SME .... Stalk Median Eminence [*Anatomy*]
SME .... Standard Medical Examination [*Military*]
SME .... Stellar Mass Ejection
SME .... Studies in Monetary Economics [*Elsevier Book Series*] [*A publication*]
SME .... Subject Matter Expert (NVT)
SME .... Surface Measuring Equipment
SME .... Surface Movement Element (AFIT)
SMEA .... Sun Marine Employees Association (EA)
SMEAC ..... Science, Mathematics, and Environmental Education Information Analysis Center

SMEADO ... Selected Major Exploratory Advanced Development Objective (MCD)
SMEAG ..... Research Station, Agriculture Canada [*Station de Recherches, Agriculture Canada*], Melfort, Saskatchewan [*Library symbol*] [*National Library of Canada*] (BIB)
SME of AIME ... Society of Mining Engineers of American Institute of Mining, Metallurgical, and Petroleum Engineers [*Later, SME, Inc.*] (EA)
SMEAR ..... SPAN [*Spacecraft Analysis*] Mission Evaluation Action Request [*NASA*] (GFGA)
SMEAT ..... Skylab Medical Experiments Altitude Test [*NASA*]
SMEC .... Single Module Engine Control [*Automotive engineering*]
SMEC .... Strategic Missile Evaluation Committee [*Air Force*]
Sm Ecc Cts ... Smith on Ecclesiastical Courts [*7th ed.*] [*1920*] [*A publication*] (DLA)
SMEC Mag ... SMEC [*Snowy Mountains Engineering Corporation*] Magazine [*A publication*] (APTA)
SME Collect Pap ... Society of Manufacturing Engineers. Collective Papers [*A publication*]
SME Creative Mfg Semin Tech Pap ... Society of Manufacturing Engineers. Creative Manufacturing Seminars. Technical Papers [*A publication*]
SMECTYMNUS ... Steven Marshall, Edward Calamy, Thomas Young, Matthew Newcomen, William Spurstow [*Collective author of 17th-century antiepiscopal tract*]
SMED .... Shared Medical Systems Corp. [*NASDAQ symbol*] (NQ)
Sm Ed .... Smith's Education for the English Bar [*A publication*] (DLA)
Sm E D ...... [*E. D.*] Smith's New York Common Pleas Reports [*A publication*] (DLA)
Smedes and Marshall's Chy Repts ... Smedes and Marshall's Mississippi Chancery Reports [*A publication*] (DLA)
Smedes & M Ch ... Smedes and Marshall's Mississippi Chancery Reports [*A publication*] (DLA)
Smedes & M (Miss) ... Smedes and Marshall's Mississippi Reports [*A publication*] (DLA)
Smed & M ... Smedes and Marshall's Mississippi Reports [*A publication*] (DLA)
Smed & M Ch ... Smedes and Marshall's Mississippi Chancery Reports [*A publication*] (DLA)
Smee .... Collection of Abstracts of Acts of Parliament [*A publication*] (DLA)
SMEE .... Master of Science in Electrical Engineering
SMEF .... Smooth Muscle-Derived Elastogenic Factor [*Biochemistry*]
SME-I .... Sales and Marketing Executives-International [*Cleveland, OH*] (EA)
SMEK .... Summary Message Enable Keyboard
Sm El .... Smith's Elements of Law [*A publication*] (DLA)
SMEMA ... Surface Mount Equipment Manufacturers Association (EA)
Sm Eng ...... Smith's English King's Bench Reports [*A publication*] (DLA)
SMEP .... Society of Multivariate Experimental Psychology (EA)
Sm Eq .... [*J. W.*] Smith's Manual of Equity [*A publication*] (DLA)
Sm Eq .... Smith's Principles of Equity [*A publication*] (DLA)
SMER .... Skylab Mission Evaluation Report [*NASA*] (MCD)
SM-ER ...... Surface Missile, Extended Range
SMERC ..... San Mateo Educational Resources Center [*San Mateo County Office of Education*] [*Information service or system*] (IID)
SMERE ..... SPRINT Missile Electromagnetic Radiation Evaluation [*Army*] (AABC)
SMERF ..... Social, Military, Ethnic, Religious, and Fraternal Groups [*Market segment*]
SMERFS ... Statistical Modeling and Estimation Review of Functioning Software [*Science Applications International Corp.*]
SMERP ..... Supplemental Medical Expense Reimbursement Plan
SMERSH .. Smert' Shpionam [*Russian phrase meaning "Death to the Spies," and name of a special division of USSR state security organizations charged with elimination of internal opposition to the regime from 1942 into postwar years*] [*Best known outside of USSR for role of its agents in the popular James Bond series of espionage stories*]
SMES .... Shuttle Mission Engineering Simulator [*NASA*] (NASA)
SMES .... Shuttle Mission Evaluation Simulation [*NASA*] (NASA)
SMES .... Strategic Missile Evaluation Squadron
SMES .... Superconducting Magnetic Energy Storage (NASA)
SME/SC.... SPRINT Missile Engineering/Service Course [*Army*] (AABC)
SMET .... SiMETCO, Inc. [*NASDAQ symbol*] (CTT)
SMET .... Simulated Mission Endurance Test (MCD)
SMET .... Spacecraft Maneuver Engine Transients [*Apollo program*] [*NASA*]
SMETC ..... Swiss Mouse Embryo Tissue Culture
SMETDS... Standard Message Trunk Design System [*Telecommunications*] (TEL)
SME Tech Pap ... Society of Manufacturing Engineers. Technical Paper [*A publication*]
SME Tech Pap Ser AD ... SME [*Society of Manufacturing Engineers*] Technical Paper. Series AD. Assembly Division [*A publication*]
SME Tech Pap Ser EE ... Society of Manufacturing Engineers. Technical Paper. Series EE (Electrical Engineering) [*A publication*]
SME Tech Pap Ser EM ... Society of Manufacturing Engineers. Technical Paper. Series EM (Engineering Materials) [*A publication*]

SME Tech Pap Ser FC ... Society of Manufacturing Engineers. Technical Paper. Series FC (Finishing and Coating) [*A publication*]
SME Tech Pap Ser MF ... Society of Manufacturing Engineers. Technical Paper. Series MF (Material Forming) [*A publication*]
SME Tech Pap Ser MR ... Society of Manufacturing Engineers. Technical Paper. Series MR (Material Removal) [*A publication*]
Smeth LS ... Smethurst on Locus Standi [*1867*] [*A publication*]   (DLA)
SMETO ..... Staff Meteorological Officer [*NATO*]   (NATG)
SME West Metal Tool Expos Conf Tech Pap ... Society of Manufacturing Engineers. Western Metal and Tool Exposition and Conference. Technical Papers [*A publication*]
SMEX .... Singapore International Monetary Exchange
Sm Ex Int ... Smith on Executory Interest [*A publication*]   (DLA)
SMF .... S-Band Multifrequency
SMF .... S & M Photolabels, Inc. [*Toronto Stock Exchange symbol*]
SMF .... Sacramento [*California*] [*Airport symbol*]   (OAG)
SMF .... Sacramento, CA [*Location identifier*] [*FAA*]   (FAAL)
SMF .... Sales Manpower Foundation   (EA)
SMF .... Sample Management Facility
SMF .... Saticon Mixed-Field [*Video technology*]
SMF .... Saw Machine Fixture   (MCD)
SMF .... Schumann Memorial Foundation [*Defunct*]   (EA)
SMF .... Scientific Marriage Foundation   (EA)
SMF .... Screw Machine Feeder
SMF .... Senior Management Forum [*Information Industry Association*]
SMF .... Service to Military Families [*Red Cross*]
SMF .... Shaker Museum Foundation   (EA)
SMF .... Signal De Mont [*France*] [*Seismograph station code, US Geological Survey*]   (SEIS)
SMF .... [*The*] Singer Co. [*NYSE symbol*]   (SPSG)
SMF .... Site Modification Facility
SMF .... Skrifter Utgivna. Modernsmalslararnas Forening [*A publication*]
Sm F .... Small Farm [*A publication*]
SMF .... Smart & Final, Inc. [*NYSE symbol*]   (SPSG)
SMF .... Snell Memorial Foundation, Inc.
SMF .... Society for the Maintenance of the Faith [*British*]
SMF .... Software Maintenance Function [*Data processing*]   (TEL)
SMF .... Solar Magnetic Field
SMF .... Space Manufacturing Facility
SMF .... Spar Material Factor [*Yacht racing regulation*]
SMF .... Special Modifying Factor   (DEN)
SMF .... Spectral Multilayer Filter
SMF .... Stable Matrix Form
SMF .... Standard MIDI [*Musical Instrument Digital Interface*] File
SMF .... Static Magnetic Field
SMF .... Streptozocin, Mitomycin C, Fluorouracil [*Antineoplastic drug regimen*]
SMF .... Student Missions Fellowship [*Later, IVMF*]   (EA)
SMF .... Swift Museum Foundation   (EA)
SMF .... Switchable Matched Filter
SMF .... Synthetic Mineral Fiber
SMF .... System Management Facility [*IBM Corp.*]
SMF .... System Measurement Facility [*Data processing*]   (IEEE)
SMFA ...... Simplified Modular Frame Assignment System [*Telecommunications*]   (TEL)
SMFAS ..... Simplified Mainframe Administration System   (MCD)
SMFAS ..... Simplified Modular Frame Assignment System [*Bell System*]
SMFC .... Shellee Morris Fan Club   (EA)
SMFG .... Stearns Manufacturing Co. [*NASDAQ symbol*]   (NQ)
SMFL .... Science, Mathematics, Foreign Languages
SmFlts .... Small Faults [*Philately*]
SMFMA .... Sprayed Mineral Fiber Manufacturers Association   (EA)
Sm For Med ... Smith on Forensic Medicine [*10th ed.*] [*1955*] [*A publication*]   (DLA)
Sm Forms ... Smith's Forms of Procedure [*A publication*]   (DLA)
SMFP .... State Medical Facilities Plan [*Generic term*]   (DHSM)
SMFP .... Systems Maintenance Field Party [*Aviation*]   (FAAC)
SMFR .... Service to Military Families Representative [*Red Cross*]
SMFT .... Semitrailer-Mounted Fabric Tank [*for water distribution*] [*Army*]
SMFW .... Society of Medical Friends of Wine   (EA)
SMG .... Megilot Genuzot [*E. L. Sukenik*] [*A publication*]   (BJA)
SMG .... San Miguel [*Portugal*] [*Geomagnetic observatory code*]
SMG .... School of Military Government [*World War II*]
SMG .... Science Management Corp. [*AMEX symbol*]   (SPSG)
SMG .... Seismocardiogram
SMG .... Senior Master Sergeant   (MCD)
SMG .... Sisters Poor Servants of the Mother of God [*Roman Catholic religious order*]
Sm & G ...... Smale and Giffard's English Vice-Chancery Reports [*A publication*]   (DLA)
Sm & G ...... Smith and Guthrie's Missouri Appeal Reports [*81-101 Missouri*] [*A publication*]   (DLA)
SMG .... Software Message Generator [*Data processing*]   (TEL)
SMG .... Solids Moisture Gauge
SMG .... Space Missions Group [*Ford Aerospace & Communications Corp.*] [*Detroit, MI*] [*Telecommunications service*]   (TSSD)
SMG .... Spacecraft Meteorology Group   (KSC)
SMG .... Spaceflight Meteorology Group [*NASA*]   (NASA)

SMG .... Speed Made Good [*Navy*]   (NVT)
SMG .... Submachine Gun
SMG .... Submandibular Gland [*Anatomy*]
SMGB .... Studien und Mitteilungen zur Geschichte des Benediktiner-Ordens und Seiner Zweige [*A publication*]
SMGBOZ ... Studien und Mitteilungen zur Geschichte des Benediktiner-Ordens und Seiner Zweige [*Salzburg*] [*A publication*]
SMGC .... Sun-Maid Growers of California   (EA)
SMGD .... Supply Management Grouping Designator [*Navy*]   (NG)
SM Geol ..... Master of Science in Geology
SMGO .... Senior Military Government Officer [*World War II*]
SMGP .... Strategic Missile Group [*Air Force*]
SMGS .... Southeastern Michigan Gas Enterprises, Inc. [*NASDAQ symbol*]   (NQ)
SMH .... St. Michael's Hospital, Toronto [*UTLAS symbol*]
SMH .... Scheduled Man-Hours   (MCD)
SMH .... Section for Metropolitan Hospitals   (EA)
SMH .... Semtech Corp. [*AMEX symbol*]   (SPSG)
SMH .... Societe Suisse de Microelectronique et d'Horlogerie [*Commercial firm*]   (ECON)
SMH .... Speelgoed en Hobby. Vakblad voor de Speelgoedbranche [*A publication*]
SMH .... Standard Mirror Hybrid   (MCD)
SMH .... Sydney Morning Herald [*A publication*]   (APTA)
SMH .... Sydney Morning Herald [*Database*]
SMHA .... Southern Mutual Help Association   (EA)
SMHC .... Sarcomeric Myosin Heavy Chain [*Muscle physiology*]
SMHE .... Selected Material Handling Equipment [*Army*]   (RDA)
SMH (Newspr) (NSW) ... Sydney Morning Herald Reports (Newspaper) (New South Wales) [*A publication*]   (APTA)
Sm Homest ... Smyth on the Law of Homesteads and Exemptions [*A publication*]   (DLA)
SMHR .... Smoking and Health Reporter [*A publication*]
SMHS .... Superstition Mountain Historical Society   (EA)
SM in Hyg ... Master of Science in Hygiene
SMI .... Sa Majeste Imperiale [*His or Her Imperial Majesty*] [*French*]
SMI .... Sales Method Index [*LIMRA*]
SMI .... Samos Island [*Greece*] [*Airport symbol*]   (OAG)
SMI .... Scanning Microscopy International   (EA)
SMI .... Secondary Metal Institute   (EA)
SMI .... Self-Metering Instrumentation
SMI .... Senior Medical Investigator
SMI .... Sergeant-Major Instructor [*British military*]   (DMA)
SMI .... Service at Military Installations [*Red Cross*]
SMI .... Severely Mentally Ill   (GFGA)
SMI .... Shelter Management Instructor [*Civil Defense*]
SMI .... Ship Missile Interface
SMI .... Simla [*India*] [*Seismograph station code, US Geological Survey*] [*Closed*]   (SEIS)
SMI .... Simulation of Machine Indexing
SMI .... Smithsonian Institution, Washington, DC [*OCLC symbol*]   (OCLC)
SMI .... Society for Machine Intelligence   (EA)
SMI .... Soldier-Machine Interface [*Army*]   (RDA)
SMI .... Sorptive Minerals Institute   (EA)
SMI .... Special Manufacturing Instruction
SMI .... Special Multiperil Insurance
SMI .... Spectrametrics, Inc.
SMI .... SpenderMenders International [*Inactive*]   (EA)
SMI .... Spring Manufacturers Institute   (EA)
SMI .... Springs Industries, Inc. [*Formerly, Springs Mills, Incorporated*] [*NYSE symbol*]   (SPSG)
SMI .... Standard Measuring Instrument
SMI .... Static Memory Interface [*Data processing*]   (MDG)
SMI .... Statute Miles
SMI .... Structure of Management Information
SMI .... Style of Mind Inventory [*Psychology*]
SMI .... Styles of Management Inventory [*Test*]
SMI .... Success Motivation Institute
SMI .... Super Market Institute [*Later, FMI*]   (EA)
SMI .... Supplementary Medical Insurance
SMI .... Supply Management Inspection   (NVT)
SMI .... Sustained Maximal Inspiration [*Physiology*]
SMI .... Swiss Market Index   (ECON)
SMI .... Synthetic Multiple-Interaction [*For chiral separation*]
SMI .... System Management Interrupt [*Data processing*]   (PCM)
SMI .... System Memory Interface [*Data processing*]
SMI .... Systems Measurement Instrument [*Data processing*]
SMIA .... Serial Multiplexer Interface Adapter   (NASA)
SMIA .... Social Marketing International Association [*Queretaro, Mexico*]   (EAIO)
SMIA .... Steel Management in Action [*Bethlehem Steel Co.*]
SMIA .... Studies in Mathematics and Its Applications [*Elsevier Book Series*] [*A publication*]
SMIAC ...... Soil Mechanics Information Analysis Center [*Army Corps of Engineers*]   (IID)
SMIAL ...... Software Manufacturing Industry in Australia [*Database*]
SMIAT ...... Special Military Intelligence Activities Team   (CINC)
Smi & Bat ... Smith and Batty's Irish King's Bench Reports [*A publication*]   (DLA)

SMIC......... Missionary Sisters of the Immaculate Conception of the Mother of God [*Roman Catholic religious order*]
SMIC......... Sorghum and Millets Information Center [*ICRISAT*] [*India*]
SMIC......... Special Material Identification Code
SMIC......... Study of Man's Impact on Climate
SMIC......... Submarine Material Identification and Control [*Navy*]   (DNAB)
SMIC......... Superior Manufacturing & Instrument Corp. [*NASDAQ symbol*]   (NQ)
SMIC......... Supply Management Information Center [*Military*]   (CAAL)
SMICBM .. Semimobile Intercontinental Ballistic Missile
SMID........ Semiconductor Memory Integrated Device   (MCD)
SMID......... Studies in Mycenaean Inscriptions and Dialect [*A publication*]
SMIDA...... Small Business Innovation Development Act [*1982*]
SMIEEE.... Senior Member of Institute of Electrical and Electronic Engineers
SMIER ...... Societe Medicale Internationale d'Endoscopie et de Radiocinematographie [*International Medical Society for Endoscopy and Radiocinematography*]
SMIG......... Sergeant-Major Instructor of Gunnery [*British military*]   (DMA)
SmIg........... Surface Membrane Immunoglobulin [*Immunochemistry*]
SMIIS....... Solar Microwave Interferometer Imaging System
SMIJA....... South African Mining and Engineering Journal [*A publication*]
SMIL........ Solidaritet med Israel
SMIL......... Statistical Methods in Linguistics [*A publication*]
SMIL......... Statistics and Market Intelligence Library [*Department of Trade*] [*British*]   (DCTA)
SMILAC.... Society for Music in the Liberal Arts College   (AEBS)
SMILE ...... Safe Military Infrared LASER Equipment
SMILE ...... Ship's Master Index Listing of Equipment   (MCD)
SMILE ...... Significant Milestone Integration Lateral Evaluation [*Data processing*]
SMILE ...... South Central Minnesota Interlibrary Exchange [*Library network*]
SMILE ...... Spherical Micro Integrated Lens
SMILE ...... Surface Mixed Layer Experiment   (NOAA)
SMI²LE..... Space Migration, Intelligence Increase, Life Extension [*Idea advanced by Timothy Leary, 1960's counterculture figure*]
SMILES .... Simplified Molecular Input Line Editor [*or Entry*] System [*Data processing*]
SMILS....... Sonobuoy Missile Impact Location System [*Navy*]   (CAAL)
SM/IM .... System Manager or Item Manager   (AFIT)
SMIN .... Southern Mineral Corp. [*NASDAQ symbol*]   (NQ)
Sm Ind........ Smith's Reports [*1-4 Indiana*] [*A publication*]   (DLA)
SMIO .... Spares Multiple Item Order   (AAG)
SMIP .... Ship's 3-M Improvement Plan [*Navy*]   (NVT)
SMIP......... Structure Memory Information Processor
SMIPE ...... Small Interplanetary Probe Experiment   (DNAB)
SMIPP....... Sheet Metal Industry Promotion Plan   (EA)
SMIPS....... Small Interactive Image Processing System [*NASA*]
SMIR......... Shuttle Multispectral Infrared Radiometer [*NASA*]   (GFGA)
SMIRE ...... Senior Member of the Institution of Radio Engineers
SMIRR ..... Shuttle Multispectral Infrared Radiometer [*NASA*]
SMIRS ...... School Management Information Retrieval Service [*University of Oregon*] [*Eugene, OR*]
SMIS .... Safeguard Management Information System [*Army*]   (AABC)
SMIS .... School of Management Information Systems [*Army*]
SMIS .... Ship Management Information System   (MCD)
SMIS .... Society for Management Information Systems   (EA)
SMIS .... Supply Management Information System
SMIS .... Survey Methodology Information System [*Inter-University Consortium for Political & Social Research*] [*Database*]
SMIS .... Symbolic Matrix Interpretation System
SMIS INC ... Societe de Microelectronique Industrielle de Sherbrooke, Inc. [*University of Sherbrooke*] [*Canada*] [*Research center*]   (RCD)
SMISOP.... Safeguard Management Information System Operating Program [*Army*]   (AABC)
SMIT......... Sherman Mental Impairment Test [*Psychology*]
SMIT......... Simulated Midcourse Interaction Test [*NASA*]
SMIT......... Spin Motor Interruption Technique
SMIT......... Submit   (ROG)
SMITE ...... Simulated Mechanical Impact Test Equipment   (MCD)
SMITE ...... Simulation Model of Interceptor Terminal Effectiveness
Smith .... Smith on English Registration [*A publication*]   (DLA)
Smith .... Smith, Reporter (7, 12 Heiskell's Tennessee Reports) [*A publication*]   (DLA)
Smith .... [*E. H.*] Smith's Court of Appeals Reports [*147-162 New York*] [*A publication*]   (DLA)
Smith .... [*E. P.*] Smith's Court of Appeals Reports [*15-27 New York*] [*A publication*]   (DLA)
Smith .... [*J. P.*] Smith's English King's Bench Reports [*A publication*]   (DLA)
Smith .... Smith's Indiana Reports [*A publication*]   (DLA)
Smith .... Smith's New Hampshire Reports [*A publication*]   (DLA)
Smith .... [*E. D.*] Smith's New York Common Pleas Reports [*A publication*]   (DLA)
Smith .... [*P. F.*] Smith's Pennsylvania State Reports [*A publication*]   (DLA)

Smith .... [*C. L.*] Smith's Registration Cases [*1895-1914*] [*A publication*]   (DLA)
Smith .... Smith's Reports [*2-4 South Dakota*] [*A publication*]   (DLA)
Smith .... Smith's Reports [*1-11 Wisconsin*] [*A publication*]   (DLA)
Smith .... Smith's Reports [*81-83 Missouri Appeals*] [*A publication*]   (DLA)
Smith .... [*E. B.*] Smith's Reports [*21-47 Illinois Appeals*] [*A publication*]   (DLA)
Smith .... Smith's Reports [*61-84 Maine*] [*A publication*]   (DLA)
Smith .... Smith's Reports [*54-62 California*] [*A publication*]   (DLA)
Smith .... Smithsonian [*A publication*]
Smith Act... Smith's Actions at Law [*A publication*]   (DLA)
Smith & B .. Smith and Bates' American Railway Cases [*A publication*]   (DLA)
Smith & B .. Smith and Batty's Irish King's Bench Reports [*A publication*]   (DLA)
Smith & Bat ... Smith and Batty's Irish King's Bench Reports [*A publication*]   (DLA)
Smith & BRRC ... Smith and Bates' American Railway Cases [*A publication*]   (DLA)
Smith CCM ... Smith's Circuit Courts-Martial Reports [*Maine*] [*A publication*]   (DLA)
Smith Ch Pr ... Smith's Chancery Practice [*A publication*]   (DLA)
Smith Coll ... Smith College. Studies in Social Work [*A publication*]
Smith Coll Mus Bul ... Smith College. Museum of Art. Bulletin [*A publication*]
Smith Coll Stud Social Work ... Smith College. Studies in Social Work [*A publication*]
Smith Com Law ... Smith's Manual of Common Law [*A publication*]   (DLA)
Smith Cond ... Smith's Condensed Alabama Reports [*A publication*]   (DLA)
Smith Cond Rep ... Smith's Condensed Alabama Reports [*A publication*]   (DLA)
Smith Cong Election Cases ... Smith's Election Cases [*United States*] [*A publication*]   (DLA)
Smith Cont ... Smith on Contracts [*A publication*]   (DLA)
Smith CP ... [*E. D.*] Smith's New York Common Pleas Reports [*A publication*]   (DLA)
Smith Ct App ... [*E. P.*] Smith's Court of Appeals Reports [*15-27 New York*] [*A publication*]   (DLA)
Smith De Rep Angl ... [*Sir Thomas*] Smith. De Republica Anglica [*The Commonwealth of England and the Manner of Government Thereof*] [*1621*] [*A publication*]   (DLA)
Smith Dict Antiq ... Smith's Dictionary of Greek and Roman Antiquities [*A publication*]   (DLA)
Smith E D .. [*E. D.*] Smith's New York Common Pleas Reports [*1850-58*] [*A publication*]   (DLA)
Smith E H ... [*E. H.*] Smith's Court of Appeals Reports [*147-162 New York*] [*A publication*]   (DLA)
Smith E P... [*E. P.*] Smith's Court of Appeals Reports [*15-27 New York*] [*A publication*]   (DLA)
Smith Ext Int ... Smith on Executory Interest [*A publication*]   (DLA)
Smith & G ... Smith and Guthrie's Missouri Appeal Reports [*81-101 Missouri*] [*A publication*]   (DLA)
Smith & H ... Smith and Heiskell [*Tennessee*] [*A publication*]   (DLA)
Smith-Hurd ... Smith-Hurd's Illinois Annotated Statutes [*A publication*]   (DLA)
Smith-Hurd Ann St ... Smith-Hurd's Illinois Annotated Statutes [*A publication*]   (DLA)
SmithIn...... Smith International, Inc. [*Associated Press abbreviation*]   (APAG)
Smith Ind... Smith's Indiana Reports [*A publication*]   (DLA)
Smith J P ... [*J. P.*] Smith's English King's Bench Reports [*A publication*]   (DLA)
Smith KB ... Smith's English King's Bench Reports [*A publication*]   (DLA)
Smith Laws PA ... Smith's Laws of Pennsylvania [*A publication*]   (DLA)
Smith LC ... Smith's Leading Cases [*A publication*]   (DLA)
Smith Lead Cas ... Smith's Leading Cases [*A publication*]   (DLA)
Smith LJ.... Smith's Law Journal [*A publication*]   (DLA)
Smith Man Eq Jur ... Smith's Manual of Equity Jurisprudence [*A publication*]   (DLA)
Smith ME.. Smith's Reports [*61-84 Maine*] [*A publication*]   (DLA)
Smith Merc Law ... Smith on Mercantile Law [*A publication*]   (DLA)
Smith NH .. Smith's New Hampshire Reports [*A publication*]   (DLA)
Smith NY... Smith's Court of Appeals Reports [*15-27, 147-162 New York*] [*A publication*]   (DLA)
Smith PA ... [*P. F.*] Smith's Pennsylvania State Reports [*A publication*]   (DLA)
Smith P F... [*P. F.*] Smith's Pennsylvania State Reports [*A publication*]   (DLA)
Smith Rec .. Smith's Law of Receivers [*A publication*]   (DLA)
Smith Reg .. [*C. L.*] Smith's Registration Cases [*England*] [*A publication*]   (DLA)
Smith Reg Cas ... [*C. L.*] Smith's Registration Cases [*England*] [*A publication*]   (DLA)
Smith Repar ... Smith's Law of Reparation [*A publication*]   (DLA)
Smith Rules ... Smith's Chancery Rules [*A publication*]   (DLA)
Smith's (Ind) R ... Smith's Indiana Reports [*A publication*]   (DLA)
Smith's Laws ... Smith's Laws of Pennsylvania [*A publication*]   (DLA)
Smith's Lead Cas ... Smith's Leading Cases [*A publication*]   (DLA)
Smithson Ann Flight ... Smithsonian Annals of Flight [*A publication*]
Smithson Contr Bot ... Smithsonian Contributions to Botany [*A publication*]

Smithson Contrib Anthropol ... Smithsonian Contributions to Anthropology [*A publication*]
Smithson Contrib Astrophys ... Smithsonian Contributions to Astrophysics [*A publication*]
Smithson Contrib Bot ... Smithsonian Contributions to Botany [*A publication*]
Smithson Contrib Earth Sci ... Smithsonian Contributions to the Earth Sciences [*A publication*]
Smithson Contrib Earth Sciences ... Smithsonian Contributions to the Earth Sciences [*A publication*]
Smithson Contrib Mar Sci ... Smithsonian Contributions to the Marine Sciences [*A publication*]
Smithson Contrib Paleobiol ... Smithsonian Contributions to Paleobiology [*A publication*]
Smithson Contrib Zool ... Smithsonian Contributions to Zoology [*A publication*]
Smithson Contr Zool ... Smithsonian Contributions to Zoology [*A publication*]
Smithson Inst Annu Rep ... Smithsonian Institution. Annual Report [*A publication*]
Smithson Inst Cent Short-Lived Phenom Annu Rep Rev Events ... Smithsonian Institution. Center for Short-Lived Phenomena. Annual Report and Review of Events [*A publication*]
Smithson Misc Colins ... Smithsonian Miscellaneous Collections [*A publication*]
Smithson Misc Collect ... Smithsonian Miscellaneous Collections [*A publication*]
Smithson Rep ... Smithsonian Institution. Annual Report [*A publication*]
Smithson Rept ... Smithsonian Institution. Reports [*A publication*]
Smithson Year ... Smithsonian Year [*A publication*]
Smith's R ... Smith's Indiana Reports [*A publication*] (DLA)
Smith Wealth Nat ... Smith's Inquiry into the Nature and Causes of the Wealth of Nations [*A publication*] (DLA)
Smith Wis ... Smith's Reports [*1-11 Wisconsin*] [*A publication*] (DLA)
SMIU......... Stove Mounters International Union of North America [*Later, Stove, Furnace, Allied Appliance Workers International Union of North America*]
SMIU......... Studies by Members of the Istanbul University English Department [*A publication*]
SMIZD...... Sei Marianna Ika Daigaku Zasshi [*A publication*]
SMJ.......... Moose Jaw Public Library, Saskatchewan [*Library symbol*] [*National Library of Canada*] (NLC)
SMJ.......... Santa Marina Gold [*Vancouver Stock Exchange symbol*]
SMJ.......... Sarawak Museum. Journal [*A publication*]
SMJ.......... Services Missionnaires des Jeunes [*Canada*]
SMJ.......... Siberian Mathematical Journal [*A publication*]
SMJ.......... Sim [*Papua New Guinea*] [*Airport symbol*] (OAG)
SMJ.......... Society of Malawi. Journal [*A publication*]
SMJ.......... Society of Medical Jurisprudence (EA)
SMJ.......... Strategic Management Journal [*A publication*]
SMJAEM ... Saskatchewan Department of Advanced Education and Manpower, Moose Jaw, Saskatchewan [*Library symbol*] [*National Library of Canada*] (NLC)
SMJC........ Saint Mary's Junior College [*Minnesota; Missouri; North Carolina*]
SMJC........ Service Module Jettison Controller [*NASA*] (MCD)
SM-JDCC ... Sunshine Music - Jan and Dean Collectors Club (EA)
SMJK........ Njoeng Jakob Kondre [*Surinam*] [*ICAO location identifier*] (ICLI)
SMJMA .... SIAM [*Society for Industrial and Applied Mathematics*] Journal on Applied Mathematics [*A publication*]
SMJOA..... Southern Medical Journal [*United States*] [*A publication*]
SMJP........ Palliser Regional Library, Moose Jaw, Saskatchewan [*Library symbol*] [*National Library of Canada*] (NLC)
Sm J St Comp ... Smith on Joint-Stock Companies [*A publication*] (DLA)
SMJT........ Saskatchewan Technical Institute, Moose Jaw, Saskatchewan [*Library symbol*] [*National Library of Canada*] (NLC)
SMK .... St. Michael [*Alaska*] [*Airport symbol*] (OAG)
SMK .... St. Michael, AK [*Location identifier*] [*FAA*] (FAAL)
SMK .... Sanmark-Stardust, Inc. [*Later, Movie Star, Inc.*] [*AMEX symbol*] (SPSG)
SMK .... Smack [*Ship*]
SMK .... Smoke (AAG)
SMK .... Software Migration Kit [*Microsoft, Inc.*] [*Data processing*] (PCM)
SMKA....... Kabalebo [*Surinam*] [*ICAO location identifier*] (ICLI)
Sm KB....... Smith's English King's Bench Reports [*A publication*] (DLA)
SMKD ...... Smoked (WGA)
SMKE....... Kayser [*Surinam*] [*ICAO location identifier*] (ICLI)
SMKHDI... Science Report. Shima Marineland [*A publication*]
SMKLS ..... Smokeless (AAG)
SMKR....... Sim-Kar Lighting Fixture Co., Inc. [*NASDAQ symbol*] (NQ)
SMKRA...... Stroitel'naya Mekhanika i Raschet Sooruzheniy [*A publication*]
SMKSTK... Smokestack[*s*] [*Freight*]
SMKW ...... Paramaribo/Kwatta [*Surinam*] [*ICAO location identifier*] (ICLI)
SML.......... CV Sportsmark International, Inc. [*Vancouver Stock Exchange symbol*]
SML.......... Montreal Lake Library, Saskatchewan [*Library symbol*] [*National Library of Canada*] (NLC)

SML......... Saluda Motor Lines [*AAR code*]
SML......... Sawmill [*Alaska*] [*Seismograph station code, US Geological Survey*] (SEIS)
SML......... Search Mode Logic
SML......... Security Market Line
SML......... Semantic-Meta-Language
SML......... Serials Master List
SML......... Simulator Load
SML......... Skylab Mobile Laboratory [*NASA*] (KSC)
SML......... Small (FAAC)
SML......... Software Master Library [*Data processing*] (TEL)
SML......... Southern Maine Library District, Portland, ME [*OCLC symbol*] (OCLC)
SML ...... Spartan Material List [*Missiles*] (MCD)
SML......... Spectrum Management Licence [*Telecommunications*] [*British*]
SML......... Spool Multileaving [*Data processing*] (IBMDP)
SML......... Standard Markup Language [*Data processing*]
SML......... States Marine Lines
SML......... Statistical Methods in Linguistics [*Stockholm*] [*A publication*]
SML......... Stella Maris [*Bahamas*] [*Airport symbol*] (OAG)
SML......... Stimmen aus Maria-Laach [*A publication*]
SML......... Structure Mold Line (MCD)
SML......... Subacute Myeloid Leukemia [*Oncology*]
SML......... Support Material List
SML......... Symbolic Machine Language [*Data processing*]
SMLA....... Kamala Soela [*Surinam*] [*ICAO location identifier*] (ICLI)
SMLAA.... Smokeless Air [*England*] [*A publication*]
Sm Lawy ... Smith's Lawyer and His Profession [*A publication*] (DLA)
SMLB........ Smith Laboratories, Inc. [*NASDAQ symbol*] (NQ)
SMLC....... Scottish Mountain Leadership Certificate (DI)
Sm LC .... Smith's Leading Cases [*A publication*] (DLA)
SMLC........ Southwest Michigan Library Cooperative [*Library network*]
Sm L Cas Com L ... Smith's Leading Cases on Commercial Law [*A publication*] (DLA)
SMLD....... Suckling Mouse Mean Lethal Dose [*Microbiology*]
SMLE........ Short Magazine Lee-Enfield Rifle
SMLE........ Small-Medium Local Exchange [*Telecommunications*] (TEL)
SMLF .... Skrifter Utgivna. Modernsmalslararnas Forening [*A publication*]
SMLI .... Space Microwave Laboratories, Inc. [*NASDAQ symbol*] (NQ)
SM Lit .... Studies in Mystical Literature [*A publication*]
Sm LJ .... Law Journal (Smith) [*England*] [*A publication*] (DLA)
SMLJ .... St. Mary's Law Journal [*A publication*]
SMLM...... Simple-Minded Learning Machine (IEEE)
SMLM...... Soviet Military Liaison Mission [*Army*]
SMLO....... Senior Military Liaison Officer
SMLR....... Stepwise Multiple Linear Regression [*Mathematics*]
SMLS .... Saint Mary of the Lake Seminary [*Mundelein, IL*]
SMLS .... Scimed Life Systems, Inc. [*NASDAQ symbol*] (NQ)
SMLS .... Sea-Based Mobile Logistics Supply [*Navy*] (CAAL)
SMLS .... Seamless (AAG)
SMLS .... Small and Medium-Sized Libraries Section [*Public Library Association*]
SMLT .... Langatabbetje [*Surinam*] [*ICAO location identifier*] (ICLI)
Sm L & T ... Smith's Landlord and Tenant [*A publication*] (DLA)
SMLV....... Standard Memory Loader Verifier (DWSG)
SMM .... Master of Sacred Music (BJA)
SMM .... Safeguards and Materials Management [*AEC*]
SMM .... Saigon Military Mission [*Vietnam*]
SMM .... Sancta Mater Maria [*Holy Mother Mary*] [*Latin*]
SMM .... Scanning Multichannel Microwave
SMM .... Scattering Matrix Method [*Materials research*]
SMM .... Secondary Mortgage Market (ADA)
SMM .... Semiconductor Memory Module
SMM .... Semporna [*Malaysia*] [*Airport symbol*] (OAG)
SMM .... Shared Multiport Memory
SMM .... Ship, Machinery, Marine Technology International Exhibition
Sm & M ... Smedes and Marshall's Mississippi Reports [*9-22 Mississippi*] [*A publication*] (DLA)
SMM .... Societas Mariae Montfortana [*Missionaries of the Company of Mary*] [*Montfort Fathers*] [*Roman Catholic religious order*]
SMM .... Solar Maximum Mission [*NASA*] (MCD)
SMM .... Sooty Mangabey Monkey
SMM .... Specially Meritorious Medal
SMM .... Spectral Matrix Method (KSC)
SMM .... Standard Method of Measurement (IEEE)
SMM .... Start of Manual Message (BUR)
SMM .... Stress Memo Manual
SMM .... Study of Media & Markets [*Simmons Market Research Bureau, Inc.*] [*Information service or system*] (CRD)
SMM .... Submarine Miners [*British military*] (DMA)
SMM .... Subsystem Measurement Management [*NASA*] (NASA)
SMM .... Summit Airlines [*Philadelphia, PA*] [*FAA designator*] (FAAC)
SMM .... Supervisory Middle Management
SMM .... Supplemental Minimal Medium [*Microbiology*]
SMM .... System Maintenance Manual
SMM .... System Management Mode [*Data processing*] (ECON)
SMM .... Systems Maintenance Management [*Data processing*]
SMMA ...... Small Motor Manufacturers Association [*Libertyville, IL*] (EA)

Sm Man Eq ... [*J. W.*] Smith's Manual of Equity [*A publication*]   (DLA)
SMMART ... Society for Mass Media and Resource Technology. Journal [*A publication*]   (APTA)
SMMAS.... Shipboard Maintenance Manpower Analysis System [*Navy*]   (DNAB)
SMMB....... Scottish Milk Marketing Board   (DI)
SMMB....... Stores Management Multiplex Bus [*Data processing*]   (MCD)
SMMC ...... System Maintenance Monitor Console [*FAA*]
Sm & M Ch ... Smedes and Marshall's Mississippi Reports [*9-22 Mississippi*] [*A publication*]   (DLA)
SMMD ...... Specimen Mass Measurement Device [*NASA*]   (KSC)
SMMDA ... Smaller Manufacturers Medical Device Association [*Inactive*]   (EA)
Sm ME ...... Smith's Reports [*61-84 Maine*] [*A publication*]   (DLA)
SMME....... Society for Mining, Metallurgy, and Exploration [*In association name, SMME, Inc.*]   (EA)
SMME....... Studies in Mathematical and Managerial Economics [*Elsevier Book Series*] [*A publication*]
Sm Merc L ... Smith on Mercantile Law [*13th ed.*] [*1931*] [*A publication*]   (DLA)
SMMH...... Scheduled Maintenance Man-Hours   (MCD)
SMMI........ El Senoussi Multiphasic Marital Inventory [*Psychology*]
SMMI........ Salesian Missionaries of Mary Immaculate [*See also SSMMI*] [*Gentilly, France*]   (EAIO)
S & MMIS ... Supply and Maintenance Management Information System [*Army*]
SMMO ...... Moengo [*Surinam*] [*ICAO location identifier*]   (ICLI)
SMMP....... Screw Machine Metal Part
SMMP....... Standard Methods of Measuring Performance   (IEEE)
SMMP....... System MANPRINT [*Manpower and Personnel Integration*] Management Plan [*Army*]
SMMR ...... Scanning Multichannel [*or Multifrequency or Multispectral*] Microwave Radiometer
SMMR ...... Simmons Major Market Research, Inc. [*New York, NY*] [*Information service or system*]   (IID)
SMMR ...... Specific Mobilization Material Requirement [*Military*]   (AFIT)
SMMR ...... Standard Missile Medium-Range   (SAA)
SM-MR ..... Surface Missile, Medium Range
SMMRT Journal ... Society for Mass Media and Resource Technology. Journal [*A publication*]   (APTA)
SMMS....... Shipbuilding Material Management Systems [*Navy*]   (NG)
Sm M & S .. Smith on Master and Servant [*8th ed.*] [*1931*] [*A publication*]   (DLA)
SMMS....... Standard Maintenance Management System [*Military*]   (CAAL)
SMMS....... Support Maintenance Management System [*Army*]
SMMT....... Society of Motor Manufacturers and Traders [*Defunct*]   (EA)
SMMT....... Strategic Missiles Materials Technology   (MCD)
SMMT....... Summit Savings Association [*NASDAQ symbol*]   (NQ)
SMMW ..... Submillimeter Wave   (MCD)
SMN .... Nazi Texts in the Semitic Museum [*Harvard*]   (BJA)
SMN .... Salmon, ID [*Location identifier*] [*FAA*]   (FAAL)
SMN .... Seaman [*Military*] [*British*]
SMN .... Seamen's Corp. [*AMEX symbol*]   (SPSG)
SMN .... Single Wire Multiplex Network [*Automotive engineering*]
SMN .... Sleeping Mountain [*Nevada*] [*Seismograph station code, US Geological Survey*] [*Closed*]   (SEIS)
SMN .... Spain-Morocco Network [*Armed Forces Radio-Television*]   (DNAB)
SMNA ...... Safe Manufacturers' National Association   (EA)
SMNA ...... Samna Corp. [*NASDAQ symbol*]   (NQ)
SMNC ...... Splenic Mononuclear Cell [*Cytology*]
Sm Neg ..... Smith on Negligence [*2nd ed.*] [*1884*] [*A publication*]   (DLA)
SMNI .... New Nickerie/Nickerie [*Surinam*] [*ICAO location identifier*]   (ICLI)
SMNI .... Satellite Music Network, Inc. [*Dallas, TX*] [*NASDAQ symbol*]   (NQ)
SMNK .... Smooth Neck
SMNO .... Singapore Malays National Organization [*Pertubohan Kebangsaan Melayu Singapore*] [*Political party*]   (PPW)
SMNRY ..... Seminary
SMNSA..... Soviet Mining Science [*English Translation*] [*A publication*]
SMO .... Santa Maria Resources Ltd. [*Toronto Stock Exchange symbol*]
SMO .... Santa Monica, CA [*Location identifier*] [*FAA*]   (FAAL)
SMO .... Sea Airmotive, Inc. [*Anchorage, AK*] [*FAA designator*]   (FAAC)
SMO .... Secondary Market Operation
SMO .... Senior Medical Officer [*Military*]
SMO .... Service Module Oxidizer [*NASA*]
SMO .... Slip Made Out   (MAE)
SMO .... Small Magnetospheric Observatory [*Satellite*] [*NASA*]
SMO .... Smoke
SMO .... So Much Of
SMO .... Society of Military Ophthalmologists   (EA)
SMO .... Society of Military Otolaryngologists [*Later, SMO-HNS*]   (EA)
SMO .... Sovereign Military Order [*British*]
SMO .... Special Military Operation
SMO .... Squadron Medical Officer
SMO .... Stabilized Master Oscillator
SMO .... State Maintenance Office [*or Officer*] [*Military*]
SMO .... Statistical Model of Overlap
SMO .... Stock Material Order   (SAA)

SMO .... Supermassive Object [*Cosmology*]
SMO .... Supplementary Meteorological Office   (FAAC)
SMO .... Supply Management Office [*Air Force*]   (AFM)
SMO .... Surface Mining Office [*Department of the Interior*]   (OICC)
SMO .... Survivability Management Office [*Adelphi, MD*] [*Army*]
SMO .... System Management Office   (AFIT)
SMO .... Systems Methodology Office
SMOA .... Ships Material Office, Atlantic
SMOA ...... Single-Manager Operating Agency [*Military*]
SMOA ...... Superfund Memorandum of Agreement [*Environmental Protection Agency*]
SMOBE..... Surveys of Minority-Owned Business Enterprises [*Bureau of the Census*]   (GFGA)
SMOBSMOD ... Strategic Mobility Simulation Model
SMOC .... Simulation Mission Operation Computer [*NASA*]   (MCD)
SMOC .... Submodule and Operator Controller [*For sequence of telephonic operations*]
SMOG .... Sales Management Organization Game
SMOG .... Save Me, Oh God
SMOG .... Smoke and Fog
SMOG .... Special Monitor Output Generator   (IEEE)
SMOG .... Sprite-Midget Owners Group   (EA)
SMOG .... Structural Modeling Oriented Graphics [*Module*]
SMOH...... Society of Medical Officers of Health [*British*]
SMOHI ...... Sheet Metal Occupational Health Institute   (EA)
SMO-HNS ... Society of Military Otolaryngologists - Head and Neck Surgeons   (EA)
SMOKE.... Surface Magnetooptic Kerr Effect [*Surface analysis*]
SMOL .... Oelemari [*Surinam*] [*ICAO location identifier*]   (ICLI)
SMOLANT ... Ships Material Office, Atlantic   (MCD)
SMOM ...... Sovereign Military Order of Malta   (EA)
SMON .... Subacute Myelo-Optic Neuropathy [*Medicine*]
SMON .... Subacute Myelooptic Neuropathy [*Medicine*]
SMONBK ... Santa Monica Bank [*Associated Press abbreviation*]   (APAG)
SMOP .... Ships Material Office, Pacific
SMOP .... So Much of Paragraph
SMOPAC ... Ships Material Office, Pacific   (MCD)
SMOPS..... School of Maritime Operations [*British*]
SMORG .... Senior Marketing Officers Research Group [*LIMRA*]
SMORZ..... Smorzando [*Slower and Softer*] [*Music*]
SMOS....... Secondary Military Occupational Specialty
SMOS....... Senior Marketing Officers Seminar [*LIMRA*]
SMOS....... Society of Military Orthopaedic Surgeons   (EA)
SMOSC..... Secondary Military Occupational Specialty Code   (AABC)
SMOTE..... Simulation of Turbofan Engine [*Air Force*]
SMOTEC.. Special Missions Operational Test and Evaluation Center [*Hurlburt Field, FL*]
Smoult....... Notes of Cases in Smoult's Collection of Orders [*Calcutta, India*] [*A publication*]   (DLA)
SMOW ...... Standard Mean Ocean Water
SMP.......... Sacred Music Press   (BJA)
SMP.......... St. Martin's Press
SMP.......... Saint Mary's Press [*Record label*] [*New York*]
SMP.......... Sampler   (DEN)
SMP.......... Santa Monica Public Library, Santa Monica, CA [*OCLC symbol*]   (OCLC)
SMP.......... Scanning and Measuring Projector
SMP.......... Scanning Microscope Photometer   (OA)
SMP.......... Scheduled Maintenance Program   (MCD)
SMP.......... School Mathematics Project [*British*]
SMP.......... See Me Please
SMP.......... Self-Maintenance Period [*British military*]   (DMA)
SMP.......... Sensitized Material Print   (MSA)
SMP.......... Servo Meter Panel   (AAG)
SMP.......... Shipboard Microfilm Program [*Navy*]   (DNAB)
SMP.......... Ship's Mission Profile [*Navy*]   (CAAL)
SMP.......... Silicon-Modified Polyether [*Organic chemistry*]
SMP.......... Simplon Resources Ltd. [*Vancouver Stock Exchange symbol*]
SMP.......... Simulation Management Plan
SMP.......... Simultaneous Macular Perception [*Ophthalmology*]
SMP.......... Simultaneous Membership Program [*Military*]
SMP.......... Sine Mascula Prole [*Without Male Issue*] [*Latin*]
SMP.......... Sisters of St. Mary of the Presentation [*Roman Catholic religious order*]
SMP.......... Skimmed Milk Powder   (ADA)
SMP.......... Slow-Moving Protease
SMP.......... Smudge Pot
SMP.......... Social Marginal Productivity
SMP.......... Society of Miniature Painters [*British*]   (ROG)
SMP.......... Sodium Mercaptopyruvate [*Organic chemistry*]
SMP.......... Software Management Plan [*NASA*]   (MCD)
SMP.......... Soldier Modernization Plan [*Army*]   (INF)
SMP.......... Somplago [*Italy*] [*Seismograph station code, US Geological Survey*] [*Closed*]   (SEIS)
SMP.......... Sound Motion Picture Technician [*Navy*]
SMP.......... Special Maintenance Project [*FAA*]
SMP.......... Special Manufacturing Procedure
SMP.......... Special Marketing Program [*Business*]
SMP.......... Special Multiperil [*Insurance*]
SMP.......... Stampede Pass, WA [*Location identifier*] [*FAA*]   (FAAL)
SMP.......... Standard Maintenance Procedure

SMP..........	Standard Motor Products, Inc. [*NYSE symbol*] (SPSG)
SMP..........	Standard Motor Pump
SMP..........	Standards, Methods, and Planning
SMP..........	Statutory Maternity Pay [*British*]
SMP..........	Stores Management Process (MCD)
SMP..........	Submitochondrial Particle [*Cytology*]
SMP..........	Sulfamethoxypyridazine [*Antimicrobial compound*]
SMP..........	Summary Maneuver Plan
SMP..........	Suomen Maaseudun Puolue [*Finnish Rural Party*] [*Political party*] (PPW)
SMP..........	Supply Master Plan
SMP..........	Symbolic Mathematics Program
SMP..........	Symmetric Multiprocessing
SMP..........	Syrtis Major Plantia [*A filamentary mark on Mars*]
SMP..........	System Management Plan
SMP..........	System Mechanical Performance
SMP..........	System Memory Pool (PCM)
SMP..........	System Modification Program [*Data processing*]
SMP..........	Systems Maintenance Procedure (MCD)
SMP..........	Systems Modernization Plan [*Social Security Administration*]
SMP..........	Systems Monitoring Panel (NVT)
SMPA.......	Paloemeu/Vincent Fajks [*Surinam*] [*ICAO location identifier*] (ICLI)
SMPA.......	Solid Motor Processing Area [*NASA*] (KSC)
SMPA.......	Switch Mode Power Amplifier (DWSG)
SMPAD.....	Society of Motion Picture Art Directors [*Later, SMPTAD*] (EA)
Sm Pat	Smith on Patents [*2nd ed.*] [*1854*] [*A publication*] (DLA)
SMPB........	Paramaribo [*Surinam*] [*ICAO location identifier*] (ICLI)
SMPB........	Succinimidyl (Maleimidophenyl)butyrate [*Organic chemistry*]
SMPC........	Saint Mary of the Plains College [*Dodge City, KS*]
SMPC........	Simplified Model Predictive Control [*Chemical engineering*] [*Data processing*]
SMPD.......	Ship Maintenance Planning Data (MCD)
Sm Pd........	Small Pond [*A publication*]
SMPD.......	Surface Missile Processing Description (MCD)
SMPE........	Society of Marine Port Engineers (EA)
SMPF	Scientific & Medical Publications of France, Inc.
SMPG.......	Poesoegroenoe [*Surinam*] [*ICAO location identifier*] (ICLI)
SMPG.......	Small Magazine Publishers Group (EA)
SMPG.......	Standardization Management Policy Group
SMPG.......	Successful Magazine Publishers Group (EA)
SMPI........	Sequential Multipoint Injection [*Automotive engineering*]
SMPI........	Surface Missile Proficiency Inspection (MCD)
SMPKA......	Sempaku [*A publication*]
SMPL........	Sample
Sm Pl.........	Somersetshire Pleas (Civil and Criminal), Edited by Chadwyck-Healey and Landon [*Somerset Record Society Publications, Vols. 11, 36, 41, 44*] [*A publication*] (DLA)
SMPLG	Sampling (MSA)
SMPM.......	Paramaribo [*Surinam*] [*ICAO location identifier*] (ICLI)
SMPM.......	Structural Materials Property Manual [*NASA*] (NASA)
SM/PM	System Management/Performance Monitor [*NASA*] (NASA)
SMPO	SEATO [*Southeast Asia Treaty Organization*] Military Planning Office (CINC)
SMPO	Sound Motion Picture Operator [*Navy*]
Sm Poor L ...	Smith's Scotch Poor Law [*A publication*] (DLA)
SMPP	Sintered Metal Powder Process (MCD)
S-MPR.......	Semimonthly Progress Reports [*Navy*]
SMPR.......	Supply and Maintenance Plan and Report [*Army*] (AABC)
Sm Pr Eq....	Smith's Principles of Equity [*A publication*] (DLA)
Sm Prob L ...	Smith's Probate Law and Practice [*A publication*] (DLA)
Sm Pr R......	Small Press Review [*A publication*]
SMPS	Simplified Message Processing Simulation (IEEE)
SMPS	Simpson Industries, Inc. [*NASDAQ symbol*] (NQ)
SMPS	Society for Marketing Professional Services [*Alexandria, VA*] (EA)
SMPS	Special Mobile Provost Section [*British military*] (DMA)
SMPSA	Solid Motor Processing and Storage Car
SMPT	Apentina [*Surinam*] [*ICAO location identifier*] (ICLI)
SMPT	Shuttle Main Propulsion Test (SSD)
SMPT	Sound Movie Projector Technician [*Navy*] (DNAB)
SMPTAD..	Society of Motion Picture and Television Art Directors (EA)
SMPTE	Society of Motion Picture and Television Engineers (EA)
SMPTE J ..	Society of Motion Picture and Television Engineers. Journal [*A publication*]
SMPTRB...	Shuttle Main Propulsion Test Requirement Board [*NASA*] (MCD) ·
SMPVS	Central Resource Centre, Prairie View School Division No. 74, Milestone, Saskatchewan [*Library symbol*] [*National Library of Canada*] (NLC)
SMQ	School Media Quarterly [*A publication*]
SMQ	Silvermaque Mining Ltd. [*Toronto Stock Exchange symbol*]
SMQ	Social Maturity Quotient
SMQ	Structure Module Qualification Test (MCD)
SMQ	Surface Metastable Quenching [*Surface analysis*]
SMR	Great Falls, MT [*Location identifier*] [*FAA*] (FAAL)
SMR	Midrash Rabbah [*H. Freedman and Maurice Simon*] [*A publication*] (BJA)
SMR	Sa Majeste Royale [*His, or Her, Royal Majesty*] [*French*]
SMR	San Marino [*ANSI three-letter standard code*] (CNC)

SMR	Santa Marta [*Colombia*] [*Airport symbol*] (OAG)
SMR	Saskatchewan Mounted Rifles (DMA)
SMR	Scheduled Maintenance Replacement
SMR	School of Materiel Readiness [*Formerly, SAM*] [*Army*] (RDA)
SMR	Secret Marriage Rite (BJA)
SMR	Semeru [*Java*] [*Seismograph station code, US Geological Survey*] [*Closed*] (SEIS)
SMR	Seminarians for Ministerial Renewal [*Later, NFCS*] (EA)
SMR	Senior Maintenance Rating [*British military*] (DMA)
SMR	Sensorimotor Rhythm [*Neurophysiology*]
SMR	Series Mode Rejection
SMR	Severely Mentally Retarded
SMR	Shared Mobile Radio [*Telecommunications*]
SMR	Sheffield and Midland Railway [*British*] (ROG)
SMR	Shield Mock-Up Reactor
S & MR......	Shire and Municipal Record [*A publication*] (APTA)
SMR	Side-Looking Mapping RADAR
SMR	Skeletal Muscle Relaxant [*Drug*]
SMR	Sloan Management Review [*A publication*]
SMR	Small Missile Range (MCD)
SMR	Society of Manufacturers' Representatives (EA)
SMR	Society of Mary Reparatrix [*Roman Catholic women's religious order*]
SMR	Solid Moderated Reactor [*Nuclear energy*]
SMR	Somnolent Metabolic Rate [*Medicine*]
SMR	Source, Maintenance, and Recoverability (MCD)
SM & R......	Source, Maintenance, and Recoverability (NG)
SMR	Spanish Mustang Registry (EA)
SMR	Special Money Requisition [*Military*]
SMR	Specialized Mobile Radio
SMR	St Mark's Review [*A publication*] (APTA)
SMR	Standard Malaysian Rubber [*Grade of natural rubber*]
SMR	Standard Morbidity Ratio (MAE)
SMR	Standard Mortality Rate
SMR	Standardized Mortality Ratio
SMR	Stanmar Resources Ltd. [*Vancouver Stock Exchange symbol*]
SMR	Statement of Material Requirements
SMR	Status Monitoring Routine
SMR	Statute Mile Radius (FAAC)
SMR	Statutory Minimum Remuneration [*British*] (DI)
SMR	Steam-Methane Reforming [*Chemical engineering*]
SMR	Stock Management Report [*Military*]
Smr	Streptomycin Resistance [*Genetics*]
SMR	Submucous Resection [*Medicine*]
SMR	Super-Metal Rich [*Astronomy*]
SMR	Supplemental Medical Report
SMR	Supply, Maintenance, and Recoverability Code [*Army*]
SMR	Supply Management Report
SMR	Supportability, Maintainability, and Repairability (SSD)
SMR	Surface Movement RADAR
SMR	Switching Mode Regulator
SMR	System Malfunction Report
SMR	Systems Management Responsibility (SAA)
SMRA.......	Raleighvallen [*Surinam*] [*ICAO location identifier*] (ICLI)
SMRA.......	Simultaneous Multicomponent Rank Annihilation [*Mathematics*]
SMRAS	Safeguard Maintenance and Reporting Analysis System [*Army*] (AABC)
SMRB.......	Simmons Market Research Bureau, Inc. [*New York, NY*] [*Database producer*]
SMRC.......	Silver Marten Rabbit Club (EA)
SMRC.......	Society of Miniature Rifle Clubs [*British*] (ROG)
SMRCS	Service Module Reaction Control System [*NASA*] (KSC)
SMRD	Spin Motor Rotation [*or Running*] Detector (MCD)
SMRD	Spin Motor Run Discrete (NASA)
SMRE.......	Safety in Mines Research Establishment [*British*]
SMRE.......	Societe de Marie Reine d'Ecosse [*Mary Queen of Scots Society*] (EAIO)
SMRE.......	Submerged Repeater Monitoring Equipment [*RADAR*]
S & M Record ...	Shire and Municipal Record [*A publication*] (APTA)
SMRF	Salvadoran Medical Relief Fund (EA)
SMRF	Small Materials Recovery Facility [*for recycling of glass, plastics, etc.*]
SMRGC.....	Sun-Maid Raisin Growers of California (EA)
SMRI........	Society for Magnetic Resonance Imaging (EA)
SMRI........	Solution Mining Research Institute (EA)
SMRIS	Soviet Missile Range Instrumented Ship (CINC)
SMRL.......	Stanford Magnetic Resonance Laboratory [*Stanford University*] [*Research center*] (RCD)
SMRL.......	Submarine Medical Research Laboratory
SMRLA	Southern Maryland Regional Library Resource Center [*Library network*]
SMRLH.....	Soldier's Mail, Rush Like Hell [*On correspondence*]
SMRM.......	Solar Maximum Repair Mission [*NASA*] (NASA)
SMR/MIS ...	Supply, Maintenance, and Readiness Management Information System [*Logistics Management Information System*] [*Military*] (AABC)
SMRP........	Society for Medieval and Renaissance Philosophy (EA)
SMRP........	Strategic Mobilization Requirements and Program (MCD)
Sm R & P Prop ...	Smith on the Law of Real and Personal Property [*A publication*] (DLA)

SMRR........ Submucous Resection and Rhinoplasty [*Medicine*]   (MAE)

SMRR........ Supplier Material Review Record   (MCD)

SMRRA..... Report. Saskatchewan Department of Mineral Resources [*A publication*]

SMRS........ Specialized Mobile Radio System

SMRS........ Specific Mobilization Reserve Stock [*Military*]   (AFIT)

SM/RSF.... Ammunition Stores Management and Remote Set Fuzing   (MCD)

SMRT........ Scheduled Maintenance Replacement Time

SMRT........ Single Message Rate Timing

SMRT........ SmartCard International, Inc. [*New York, NY*] [*NASDAQ symbol*]   (NQ)

SmrtFnl...... Smart & Final, Inc. [*Associated Press abbreviation*]   (APAG)

SMRU........ Sea Mammal Research Unit [*British*]   (ARC)

SMRV........ South Middlesex Rifle Volunteers [*British military*]   (DMA)

SMRV........ Squirrel Monkey Retravirus

SMRVA..... Sloan Management Review [*A publication*]

SMRVS...... Small Modular Recovery Vehicle System [*Nuclear energy*]

SMRX........ Summa RX Laboratories, Inc. [*NASDAQ symbol*]   (NQ)

SMRY........ Summary   (FAAC)

SMS........... Marine Service Squadron

SMS........... Sa Majeste Suedoise [*His, or Her, Swedish Majesty*] [*French*]   (ROG)

SMS........... Safety Manual Supplement

SMS........... Saint Marie [*Madagascar*] [*Airport symbol*]   (OAG)

SMS........... Saint Mary's Seminary [*Connecticut; Missouri; Ohio; Vermont*]

SMS........... Sales Motivation Survey [*Test*]

SMS........... Samos [*Greece*] [*Seismograph station code, US Geological Survey*] [*Closed*]   (SEIS)

SMS........... Sample Management System [*Laboratory science*]

SMS........... Satellite Motion Simulator

SMS........... Scandinavian Migraine Society   (EA)

SMS........... Scientific Mission Support

SMS........... Screen Management System [*Computer technology*]

SMS........... Semiconductor-Metal-Semiconductor

SMS........... Sensor Monitoring Set   (MCD)

SMS........... Separation Mechanism Subsystem [*NASA*]   (NASA)

SMS........... Sequence Milestone System

SMS........... Serial Motor Seizures [*Medicine*]

SMSI.......... Service Management System [*Telecommunications*]

SMS........... Service Manipulator System   (SSD)

SMS........... Shared Mass Storage

SMS........... Ship Motion Simulator

SMS........... Ship's Missile System   (MCD)

SMS........... Shoreline Modeling System [*US Army Corps of Engineers*]

SMS........... Shuttle Mission Simulator [*NASA*]   (NASA)

SMS........... Signal Messenger Service   (NATG)

SMS......... Signal Missile Support [*Air Force*]   (MUGU)

SMS......... Silane to Molten Silane [*Photovoltaic energy systems*]

SMS......... Silico-Manganese Steel

SMSA........ Sinatra Music Society   (EAIO)

SMS........... Skandinavisk Migraeneselskab [*Scandinavian Migraine Society*]   (EAIO)

SMS........... Small Magnetospheric Satellite [*NASA*]

Sm & S..... Smith and Sager's Drainage Cases [*Canada*] [*A publication*]   (DLA)

SMS........... Solar Maximum Satellite [*NASA*]   (MCD)

SMS........... Spanish Market Selection [*Cigars*]

SMS......... Spares Management System

SMS........... Special Mint Set [*Numismatics*]

SMS........... Spectronics Micro Sytems [*Data processing*]

SMS........... Spin Motor Supply

SMS........... SPRINT [*Solid-Propellant Rocket Intercept*] Missile Subsystem [*Army*]

SMS........... Standard Material Specification   (MCD)

SMS........... Standard Meteorological Station   (SAA)

SMS........... Standard Modular System

SMS........... Standard Molecular System

SMS........... Startling Mystery Stories [*A publication*]

SMS........... State Medical Society   (MAE)

SMS........... State Mutual Securities Trust [*NYSE symbol*]   (SPSG)

SMS........... Stationary Meteorological Satellite [*NASA*]

SMS........... Stiff-Man Syndrome [*Medicine*]

SMS........... Stores Management Sea [*Navy*]

SMS........... Stores Management System   (MCD)

SMS........... Strategic Management Society [*British*]

SMSTRS... Strategic Missile Squadron [*Air Force*]

SMS........... Structures and Mechanical System [*Skylab*] [*NASA*]

SMS........... Student Monitoring System [*Vocational guidance*]

SMS........... Studier i Modern Sprakvetenskap [*A publication*]

SMS........... Styrene Methylstyrene [*Organic chemistry*]

SMS........... Subject Matter Specialist

SMS........... Success Management System

SMS........... Sumter, SC [*Location identifier*] [*FAA*]   (FAAL)

SMS........... Surface Missile Ship   (MUGU)

SMS........... Surface Missile System [*NASA*]

SMS........... SURTASS Measurement System [*Navy*]   (CAAL)

SMS........... Suspended Maneuvering System [*McDonnell Douglas Corp.*]   (MCD)

SMS........... Switching and Maintenance Set

SMS........... Synchronous Meteorological Satellite [*NASA*]

SMS........... Synoptic Meteorological Sounding

SMS.......... Syro-Mesopotamian Studies [*Malibu, CA*] [*A publication*]   (BJA)

SMS.......... System Migration Section [*Social Security Administration*]

SMS.......... Systems Maintenance Sector [*Electronics*]   (FAAC)

SMS.......... Systems Maintenance Service   (MCD)

SM & S...... Systems Management and Sequencing   (NASA)

SMSA........ Seaman Apprentice, Signalman, Striker [*Navy rating*]

SMSA........ Shop Missile Assembly and Maintenance

SMSA........ Signal Missile Support Agency [*Air Force*]   (AAG)

SMSA........ Standard Metropolitan Statistical Area [*Later, MSA*] [*Census Bureau*]

SMSA........ Super-Cooled Infrared Multispectral Survey and Analysis [*Traces mineral deposits*]

SMSAE..... Surface Missile System Availability Evaluation [*NASA*]   (KSC)

SMSanE..... Master of Science in Sanitary Engineering

SMSB........ Strategic Missile Support Base [*Air Force*]   (AFM)

SMSC........ Service Module Sequence Controller [*NASA*]

SMSC........ Southeastern Missouri State College

SMSC........ Standard Microsystems Corp. [*NASDAQ symbol*]   (NQ)

SMSC........ Standard Modular System Card [*Data processing*]   (BUR)

SMSC........ State Manpower Service Council [*Department of Labor*]

SMSCC..... Shuttle Mission Simulator Computer Complex [*NASA*]   (MCD)

SMSD........ Ship Magnetic Submarine Detector

SMSE........ Systems Maintenance Sector Electronics   (FAAC)

SMSF........ Special Maintenance Support Facility   (MCD)

SMSG........ School Management Study Group   (EA)

SMSG........ School Mathematics Study Group   (IIA)

SMSG........ Self-Mutilators Support Group   (EA)

SMSG........ Survivability Management Steering Group [*DoD*]

SMSGT..... Senior Master Sergeant

SMSH........ Sisters of Sainte Marthe [*of St. Hyacinthe*] [*Roman Catholic religious order*]

SMSI.......... Scientific Micro Systems, Inc. [*Mountain View, CA*] [*NASDAQ symbol*]   (NQ)

SMSI......... Sipaliwini [*Surinam*] [*ICAO location identifier*]   (ICLI)

SMSI......... Standard Manned Space Flight Initiator [*Later, NSI-I*] [*NASA*]   (NASA)

SMSI......... State Microscopical Society of Illinois   (EA)

SMSI......... Strong Metal-Support Interaction [*Catalysis*]

SMSIP....... Space Mission Survivability Implementation Plan

SMSIP....... Surface Missile Ship Improvement Program   (MCD)

SMSJ......... Scott's Monthly Stamp Journal [*A publication*]

SMSM....... Kwamalasoemoetoe [*Surinam*] [*ICAO location identifier*]   (ICLI)

SMSM....... Soeurs Missionnaires de la Societe de Marie [*Missionary Sisters of the Society of Mary*]   (EAIO)

SMSMS.... Strategic Missile Squadron Munitions Section [*Air Force*]   (AAG)

SMSN........ Seaman, Signalman, Striker [*Navy rating*]

SMSNA..... Smithsonian [*A publication*]

SMSO....... Subcontract Material Sales Order

Sm & Sod L & T ... Smith and Soden on Landlord and Tenant [*2nd ed.*] [*1878*] [*A publication*]   (DLA)

SMSP........ St. Peter's Abbey and College, Muenster, Saskatchewan [*Library symbol*] [*National Library of Canada*]   (NLC)

SMSP........ Security Military Space Program   (MUGU)

SMSP........ Soil Moisture Strength Prediction [*Army*]

SMS/360PPE ... Software Management System/360 Problem Program Efficiency

SMSpr....... Studier i Modern Sprakvetenskap [*A publication*]

SMSq......... Strategic Missile Squadron [*Air Force*]

SMSRAH ... Institutionen foer Skoglig Matematisk Statistik Rapporter och Uppsatser [*A publication*]

SMS Report ... Socioeconomic Monitoring System Report [*A publication*]

SMSRL...... Sarah Mellon Scaife Radiation Laboratory [*University of Pittsburgh*]   (MCD)

SMSRS...... Shipboard Meteorological Satellite Readout Station

SMSS........ School of Management and Strategic Studies [*Founded 1982 by Richard Farson, offers a two-year management program through GTE Telenet*]

SMSS........ Strategic Mission Support Study [*DoD*]

SMSS........ Studies in Management Science and Systems [*Elsevier Book Series*] [*A publication*]

SMST........ Stoelmanseiland [*Surinam*] [*ICAO location identifier*]   (ICLI)

Sm Stat Law ... Smith's Statute Law [*A publication*]   (DLA)

SMSTRS... Seamstress   (WGA)

SMSV........ San Miguel Sea Lion Virus

SMT.......... S-Band Megawatt Transmit

SMT.......... Sacred Marriage Texts   (BJA)

SMT.......... Sample Mix Table [*Musical instrument digital interface*]

SMT.......... Samuel Manu-Tech, Inc. [*Toronto Stock Exchange symbol*]

SMT.......... Saturn Missile Test [*NASA*]

SMT.......... Scheduled Maintenance Time [*Automotive engineering*]

SMT.......... Segmented Mirror Telescope [*Astronomy*]

SMT.......... Selective Message Transaction   (NASA)

SMT.......... Senior Medical Technician

SMT.......... Service Module Technician [*NASA*]   (KSC)

SMT.......... Sexual Medicine Today [*A publication*]

SMT.......... Shelter Management Training [*Civil Defense*]

SMT........... Ship Maintenance Test

SMT.......... Shipboard Marriage Test
SMT.......... Ship's Mean Time [*Navigation*]
SMT.......... Shop Mechanic's Test
SMT.......... Small Missile Telecamera
SMT.......... Society of Metropolitan Treasurers [*British*]
SMT.......... South Dakota School of Mines and Technology, Rapid City, SD [*OCLC symbol*] (OCLC)
SMT.......... Square Mesh Tracking [*Air Force*]
SMT.......... Stabilized March Technique
SMT.......... Standard Measurement Technique [*Navy*]
SMT.......... Station Management
SMT.......... Studies in Modern Thermodynamics [*Elsevier Book Series*] [*A publication*]
SMT.......... Subject Matter Trainer (SAA)
SMT.......... Submit (FAAC)
SMT.......... Successful Meetings [*A publication*]
SMT.......... Sultan-Mazar [*Former USSR*] [*Seismograph station code, US Geological Survey*] [*Closed*] (SEIS)
SMT......... Summit (MCD)
SMT.......... Supermedial Thigh [*Flap for plastic surgery*]
SMT.......... Supplementary Monophonic Transmission (ADA)
SMT.......... Supply, Maintenance, and Transportation [*Directorate*] [*Army*] (RDA)
SMT.......... Surface Missile Test [*Navy*] (CAAL)
SMT.......... Surface-Mount Technology [*Electronics*]
SMT.......... System Maintenance Test
SMT.......... System Maintenance Trainer (MCD)
SMT.......... System Modulation Transfer [*Acutance*] [*Photography*]
SMT.......... Systems Manufacturing Technology [*San Marcos, CA*]
SMTA...... Sewing Machine Trade Association (EA)
SMTA........ Surface Mount Technology Association (EA)
SMTA..... Tabiki [*Surinam*] [*ICAO location identifier*] (ICLI)
SMTAS..... Shuttle Model Test and Analysis System [*NASA*] (NASA)
SMTB....... Tafelberg/Rudi Kappel [*Surinam*] [*ICAO location identifier*] (ICLI)
SmtBc .... SmithKline Beecham Ltd. [*Associated Press abbreviation*] (APAG)
SMTBIN ... Smith Barney Intermediate Quality Municipal Fund [*Associated Press abbreviation*] (APAG)
SmtBrn...... Smith Barney Municipal Fund [*Associated Press abbreviation*] (APAG)
SMTC........ Sa Majeste Tres Chretienne [*His, or Her, Most Christian Majesty*] [*French*]
SMTD........ Short Take-Off and Landing and Maneuvering Technology Demonstrator [*Air Force*]
SMTE........ Society for Music Teacher Education (EA)
SMTEBI.... Entomologische Abhandlungen [*Dresden*] [*A publication*]
SMTF .... Sa Majeste Tres Fidele [*His, or Her, Most Faithful Majesty*] [*French*]
SMTF .... Spacecraft Magnetic Test Facility [*Goddard Space Flight Center*] [*NASA*]
SMTFBL... Faunistische Abhandlungen [*Dresden*] [*A publication*]
SmtFD .... Smith's Food & Drug Centers, Inc. [*Associated Press abbreviation*] (APAG)
SMTG........ Solid-State and Molecular Theory Group [*MIT*] (MCD)
SMTG....... Somatogen, Inc. [*NASDAQ symbol*] (SPSG)
Smth.......... Smith [*A.O.*] Corp. [*Associated Press abbreviation*] (APAG)
SMTH .... Smooth (FAAC)
SmthBc ..... SmithKline Beecham Ltd. [*Associated Press abbreviation*] (APAG)
SMTI........ Selective Moving Target Indicator (IEEE)
SMTI........ Sodium Mechanisms Test Installation [*Nuclear energy*] (NRCH)
SMTI........ Southeastern Massachusetts Technological Institute [*Later, Southeastern Massachusetts University*]
SMTI........ Tibiti [*Surinam*] [*ICAO location identifier*] (ICLI)
SMTK....... Simtek Corp. [*NASDAQ symbol*] (SPSG)
SMTK....... Sump Tank
SMTLB .... Strength of Materials [*English Translation*] [*A publication*]
SMTM....... Sometime (FAAC)
SMTN ...... Smoky Mountain R. R. [*AAR code*]
SMTO ...... St. Maarten Tourist Office (EA)
SMTO ...... Senior Mechanical Transport Officer [*British military*] (DMA)
SMTP .... Simple Mail Transfer Protocol [*Data processing*] (PCM)
SMTP........ Tepoe [*Surinam*] [*ICAO location identifier*] (ICLI)
SMTRB ..... Ship and Marine Technology Requirements Board [*British*]
SMTS........ Simulated Maintenance Training System [*Air Force*]
SMTS........ Southern Manufacturing Technology Show and Conference (ITD)
SMTS........ Synchronous Meteorological Test Satellite [*NASA*]
SMTSDS... Annual Research Reviews. Somatostatin [*A publication*]
SMTS Journal ... Saskatchewan Mathematics Teachers' Society. Journal [*A publication*]
SMTT........ Small Bowel Transit Time [*Gastroenterology*]
SMU .... St. Mary's University Library [*UTLAS symbol*]
SMU .... Scottish Mothers' Union [*Episcopalian*]
SMU .... Secondary Multiplexing Unit
SMU .... Self-Maneuvering Unit [*Air Force*]
SMU .... Sheep Mountain, AK [*Location identifier*] [*FAA*] (FAAL)
SMU .... Single Motor Unit
SMU .... Soft Mock-Up [*NASA*] (MCD)

SMU .... Southeastern Massachusetts University [*North Dartmouth*]
SMU .... Southeastern Massachusetts University, North Dartmouth, MA [*OCLC symbol*] (OCLC)
SMU .... Southern Methodist University [*Texas*]
SMU .... Spectrum Monitoring Unit
SMU .... Store Monitor Unit
SMU .... Sunnyside Mine [*Utah*] [*Seismograph station code, US Geological Survey*] [*Closed*] (SEIS)
SMU .... Super-Module Unit [*Telecommunications*] (TEL)
SMU .... System Maintenance Unit [*Data processing*]
SMU .... System Monitoring Unit
SMUAP..... Simple Motor Unit Action Potential [*Medicine*]
SMUC .... Societe de Musique des Universites Canadiennes [*Canadian University Music Society - CUMS*]
SMUD .... Sacramento Municipal Utility District [*Photovoltaic energy systems*]
SMUD .... Standoff Munitions Disrupter System (MCD)
SMUG .... Smuggling [*FBI standardized term*]
S Mus D.... Doctor of Sacred Music
SMUSE ..... Socialist Movement for the United States of Europe
SMUT ...... Shrink Mock-Up Template (MSA)
SMUT .... Special Mission Utility Transport [*Aviation*]
SMV .... Samovar Hills, AK [*Location identifier*] [*FAA*] (FAAL)
SMV .... Samsville [*Illinois*] [*Seismograph station code, US Geological Survey*] (SEIS)
SMV .... Santa Maria Valley Railroad Co. [*AAR code*]
SMV .... Santa Monica Bank Voting Trust Certificates [*AMEX symbol*] (SPSG)
SMV .... Satellite Mutual Visibility
SMV .... Short Market Value [*Investment term*]
SMV .... Sinusoidal Membrane Vesicle [*Anatomy*]
SMV .... Skeletal Muscle Ventricle [*Medicine*]
SMV .... Slow Moving Vehicle [*Emblem to prevent rear-end collisions*]
SMV .... Soybean Mosaic Virus [*Plant pathology*]
SM/V........ Squared-Mean to Variance
SMV .... Superior Mesenteric Vein [*Anatomy*]
SMVH .... Service in Military and Veterans Hospitals [*Red Cross*]
SMVLF ..... Shipboard Mobile Very Low Frequency [*Navy*] (DNAB)
SMVO .... Avanavero [*Surinam*] [*ICAO location identifier*] (ICLI)
SMVP........ Shuttle Master Verification Plan [*NASA*] (NASA)
SMVRD.... Shuttle Master Verification Requirements Document [*NASA*] (NASA)
SMW .... Second Main Watch
SMW .... Sheet Metal Workers' International Association (EA)
SMW .... Simpatico Wines [*Vancouver Stock Exchange symbol*]
SMW .... Slotted Metal Window
SMW .... Smara [*Morocco*] [*Airport symbol*] (OAG)
SMW .... Society of Magazine Writers [*Later, ASJA*] (EA)
SMW .... Society of Military Widows (EA)
SMW .... South Mountain [*Washington*] [*Seismograph station code, US Geological Survey*] (SEIS)
SMW .... Standard Materials Worksheet [*NASA*] (NASA)
SMW .... Strategic Missile Wing [*Air Force*]
S Mw........ Studien zur Musikwissenschaft [*A publication*]
SMWA ...... Wageningen [*Surinam*] [*ICAO location identifier*] (ICLI)
SMWC....... Saint Mary-Of-The-Woods College [*Indiana*]
SMWDSEP ... Single, Married, Widowed, Divorced, Separated
SMWG ...... Strategic Missile Wing [*Air Force*]
SMWG ...... System Management Work Group
SMWHT ... Somewhat (DNAB)
SMWIA..... Sheet Metal Workers' International Association (EA)
SMWP........ Strategic Mobility Work Project [*Army*] (AABC)
SMWS....... Washabo [*Surinam*] [*ICAO location identifier*] (ICLI)
SMX .... Santa Maria [*California*] [*Airport symbol*] (OAG)
SMX .... Santa Maria, CA [*Location identifier*] [*FAA*] (FAAL)
SMX .... Semi-Micro Xerography
SMX .... Submultiplexer Unit
SMX .... Sulfamethoxazole [*Also, S, SMZ*] [*Antibacterial compound*]
SMX .... Systems Center, Inc. [*NYSE symbol*] (SPSG)
SMY .... Ark Valley Airways [*Arkansas City, KS*] [*FAA designator*] (FAAC)
SMY .... Marianna, FL [*Location identifier*] [*FAA*] (FAAL)
SMY .... Scientist-Man Year
SMY .... Shemya [*Alaska*] [*Seismograph station code, US Geological Survey*] (SEIS)
SMY .... Simenti [*Senegal*] [*Airport symbol*] (OAG)
SMY .... Smyrna Public Library, Smyrna, DE [*OCLC symbol*] (OCLC)
Smy .... Smythe's Irish Common Pleas Reports [*1839-40*] [*A publication*] (DLA)
SMY .... Solar Maximum Year [*August, 1979-February, 1981*]
SMY .... Summary (MSA)
Smy & B.... Smythe and Bourke's Irish Marriage Cases [*1842*] [*A publication*] (DLA)
Smy Home ... Smyth on the Law of Homestead and Exemptions [*A publication*] (DLA)
SMYRAD ... Smithsonian Year [*A publication*]
SMYS....... Specified Minimum Yield Strength
Smythe....... Smythe's Irish Common Pleas Reports [*1839-40*] [*A publication*] (DLA)
SMZ .... Southern Maritime Zone (DNAB)
SMZ .... Stoelmanseiland [*Surinam*] [*Airport symbol*] (OAG)

SMZ .... Sulfamethoxazole [*Also, S, SMX*] [*Antibacterial compound*]
SMZHA .... Sibirskii Matematiceskii Zurnal [*A publication*]
SMZO .... Paramaribo/Zorg en Hoop [*Surinam*] [*ICAO location identifier*] (ICLI)
SMZY .... Paramaribo/Zandery [*Surinam*] [*ICAO location identifier*] (ICLI)
sn----- .... Andean Area [*MARC geographic area code*] [*Library of Congress*] (LCCP)
SN .... Parke, Davis & Co. [*Research code symbol*]
SN .... Sacramento Northern Railway [*AAR code*]
SN .... Safety Notice (MCD)
SN .... Salomon Inc., [*Associated Press abbreviation*] (APAG)
SN .... Sample Name
SN .... SAN [*Societe Aeronautique Normande*] [*France*] [*ICAO aircraft manufacturer identifier*] (ICAO)
SN .... San
Sn .... Sanitary
SN .... Santa [*Saint*] [*Italian*]
SN .... Santo
SN .... Saponification Number [*Analytical chemistry*]
SN .... Saturday Night [*A publication*]
SN .... School of Nursing (AAMN)
SN .... Science News [*A publication*]
SN .... Scientific Note
S & N .... Scottish & Newcastle Breweries [*Commercial firm*] [*British*]
SN .... Seaman [*Navy rating*]
SN .... Secretary of the Navy
SN .... Sector Number (MUGU)
SN .... Secundum Naturam [*According to Nature*] [*Latin*]
SN .... See Note (ROG)
SN .... Semiconductor Network (IEEE)
SN .... Senegal [*ANSI two-letter standard code*] (CNC)
SN .... Senior Navigator [*Air Force*]
S/N .... Sequence Number
SN .... Sergeant Navigator [*British*]
SN .... Serial Number
SN .... Serum Neutralization Test
SN .... Service Note (MSA)
SN .... Service Number [*Military*]
SN .... Session Notes [*Scotland*] [*A publication*] (DLA)
SN .... Shakespeare Newsletter [*A publication*]
SN .... Shalom Network (EA)
SN .... Shaping Network (MCD)
Sn .... Shingle [*Quality of the bottom*] [*Nautical charts*]
SN .... Shipping Note [*Business term*]
S/N .... Shipping Number
SN .... Side Note
SN .... Sigma Nu [*A national fraternity*]
SN .... Sign (BUR)
SN .... Signal Node
S/N .... Signal to Noise Ratio [*Unweighted*] (CMD)
SN .... Silicon Nitrate
SN .... Sine [*Without*] [*Latin*]
SN .... Sine of the Amplitude (IEEE)
sn .... Sine Nomine [*Without Name*] [*Latin*] (WGA)
sn .... Sine Numero [*Without Number*] [*Latin*]
SN .... Sinoatrial Node [*Medicine*]
SN .... Siren
SN .... Slovensky Narodopis [*A publication*]
sn .... Small Nuclear
SN .... Small-Probe Nephelometer [*NASA*]
SN .... Smoke Number [*Emissions measurement*] (EG)
SN .... Snellen [*Test types*] [*Ophthalmology*]
SN .... Snow [*Meteorology*] (FAAC)
SN .... Societe Anonyme Belge d'Exploitation de la Navigation Aerienne [*Sabena Belgian World Airlines*] [*ICAO designator*] (FAAC)
SN .... Society for Neuroscience (EA)
SN .... Solid Neutral
S/N .... Sons of Norway (EA)
SN .... Sovetskaja Nauka [*A publication*]
SN .... Special Nuclear [*Material*]
S/N .... Speech/Noise [*Ratio*] [*Electronics*]
SN .... Sponsoring Agency [*Online database field identifier*]
SN .... Sporting News [*A publication*]
SN .... Standard Nomenclature
SN .... Standard Oil Co. (Indiana) [*NYSE symbol*] [*Toronto Stock Exchange symbol*] (SPSG)
Sn .... Stannum [*Tin*] [*Chemical element*]
S & N .... Statesman and Nation [*A publication*]
SN .... Stationing Flag [*Navy*] [*British*]
SN .... Statutes of Newfoundland [*A publication*] (ILCA)
SN .... Steam Navigation
sn .... Stereospecifically Numbered [*Biochemistry*]
SN .... Sterling Nuclear Plant (NRCH)
sn .... Sthene [*Absolute unit of force*]
SN .... Stock Number (MCD)
SN .... Story of the Nations [*A publication*]
S-N .... Stress Number (NASA)
SN .... Stronnictwo Narodowe [*Nationalist Party*] [*Poland*] [*Political party*] (PPE)

SN .... Strouhal Number [*Sound*]
SN .... Student Nurse
SN .... Subnormal
SN .... Substantia Nigra [*Brain anatomy*]
SN .... Sunday Nation [*A publication*]
SN .... Supernatant [*Chemistry*]
SN .... Supernova
SN .... Suprasternal Notch [*Anatomy*]
SN .... Survey Number
SN .... Syllable Number [*Entomology*]
SN .... Synchronizers [*JETDS nomenclature*] [*Military*] (CET)
SN .... Systems/Strategic Navigation [*Aviation*] (FAAC)
S-N (Plane) ... Sella Turcica-Nasion [*Plane that passes through these points*] [*Cephalometrics*]
SNA .... Orange County [*California*] [*Airport symbol*] (OAG)
SNA .... Sadr Nizamut Adalat Reports [*India*] [*A publication*] (DLA)
SNA .... Sanae [*Antarctica*] [*Geomagnetic observatory code*]
SNA .... Sanae [*Antarctica*] [*Seismograph station code, US Geological Survey*] (SEIS)
SNA .... Santa Ana, CA [*Location identifier*] [*FAA*] (FAAL)
SNA .... Santana Petroleum [*Vancouver Stock Exchange symbol*]
SNA .... Satellite Networking Associates, Inc. [*New York, NY*] [*Telecommunications*] (TSSD)
SNA .... Schlaraffia Nordamerika (EA)
SNA .... Sella, Nasion, A [*Anthropometric landmark*]
SNA .... Shakespeariana [*A publication*]
SNA .... Shaping Network Assembly (SSD)
SNA .... Snap-On Tools Corp. [*NYSE symbol*] (SPSG)
SNA .... Sodium Naphthalene Acetate (IIA)
SNa .... Sot la Nape [*A publication*]
SNA .... Soviet Naval Aviation
SNA .... Student Naval Aviator
SNA .... Suburban Newspapers of America (EA)
SNA .... Sudan News Agency (BJA)
SNA .... Surinaams Nieuws Agentschap [*Surinam News Agency*] (EY)
SNA .... Syrian News Agency (BJA)
SNA .... System of National Accounts [*United Nations*]
SNA .... Systems Network Architecture [*IBM Corp.*] [*Data processing*]
SNAA .... Syndicat National des Travailleurs de l'Amiante d'Asbestos [*Canada*]
SNAAQS ... Secondary National Ambient Air Quality Standards [*Environmental Protection Agency*] (GFGA)
SNAB........ Stock Number Action Bulletin
SNA Beng ... Sadr Nizamut Adalat Reports [*India*] [*A publication*] (DLA)
SNA Beng (NS) ... Sadr Nizamut Adalat Reports, New Series [*1851-59*] [*Bengal, India*] [*A publication*] (DLA)
SNACC...... Society of Neurosurgical Anesthesia and Critical Care (EA)
SNACMA ... Snack, Nut, and Crisp Manufacturers' Association [*British*]
SNACS...... Share News on Automatic Coding Systems [*Data processing*]
SNACS...... Single Nuclear Attack Case Study [*DoD*]
SNACS...... Stock Number Assignment Control System [*Air Force*] (AFM)
SNADIGC ... Sindacato Nazionale Dipendenti Ministero Grazia e Giustizia [*National Union of Ministry of Justice Employees*] [*Italy*]
SNAF........ Soviet Naval Air Force
SNAFU...... Situation Normal, All Fouled Up [*Military slang*] [*Bowdlerized version*]
SNAG .... Short Notes on Alaskan Geology. Alaska Department of Natural Resources. Geologic Report [*A publication*]
SNAG .... Society of North American Goldsmiths (EA)
SNagg....... Serum Normal Agglutinator [*Hematology*]
SNAI......... Standard Nomenclature of Athletic Injuries [*Medicine*] (MAE)
SNAIAS .... Ship's Navigation and Aircraft Inertial Alignment System [*Navy*] (NG)
SNAKE...... Stochastic Network Adaptive Kinematics Evaluator
SNAKE...... Super-Normal Attitude Kinetic Enhancement [*Later, Enhanced Fighter Maneuverability*] [*X-31 experimental aircraft under development by Rockwell International Corp. and Messerschmitt-Boelkow-Blohm GmbH*]
SNAL........ Site Number Assignment List (SAA)
SNAME..... Society of Naval Architects and Marine Engineers (EA)
SNaN .... Signaling Not a Number [*Computer programming*] (BYTE)
SNANSC... Society of Neurosurgical Anesthesia and Neurological Supportive Care [*Later, SNACC*] (EA)
SNA Nursery Res J South Nurserymen's Assoc ... SNA Nursery Research Journal. Southern Nurserymen's Association [*A publication*]
SNAO/CWC ... Sustained Naval Aviation Operations in Chemical, Biological, and Radiological Warfare Conditions [*Military*]
SNAP........ Sarawak National Party [*Malaysia*] [*Political party*] (PPW)
SNAP........ Satellite Nuclear Auxiliary Power [*Military*] (CAAL)
SNAP........ Selective Niobium Anodization Process [*Semiconductor technology*]
SNAP........ Senior Naval Aviator Present
SNAP........ Sensory Nerve Action Potential [*Neurophysiology*]
SNAP........ Sharp National Account Program [*Sharp Electronics Corp.*]
SNAP........ Shelter Neighborhood Action Project
SNAP........ Shielded Neutron Assay Probe [*Nuclear energy*] (NRCH)
SNAP........ Shipboard Nontactical ADP [*Automatic Data Processing*] Program [*Navy*] (CAAL)
SNAP........ Short Notice Annual Practice [*Military*]

SNAP......... Significant Noncompliance Action Program [*Environmental Protection Agency*]   (GFGA)
SNAP......... Simplified Needs Assessment Profile System [*Developed by Texas Instruments, Inc.*]
SNAP......... Simplified Numerical Automatic Programmer [*Data processing*]
SNAP......... Simulated Network Analysis Program   (SAA)
SNAP......... Single Number Access Plan [*Telecommunications*]   (TEL)
SNAP......... Six Node Averaging Program [*Data processing*]
SNAP......... Small Nuclear Adapted Power Source
SNAP......... Small Nuclear Auxiliary Power
snap........... Snapdragon [*Horticulture*]
SNAP......... Society of National Association Publications   (EA)
SNAP......... Soviet Nuclear Artillery Projectile   (MCD)
SNAP......... Space Nuclear Auxiliary Power
SNAP......... Special Night Answer Position [*Telecommunications*]
SNAP......... Specifications for Non-Heat-Set Advertising Printing
SNAP......... Staffing Needs Assessment Process
SNAP......... Standard Navy Accounting Procedures
SNAP......... Standard Network Access Protocol [*Data processing*]
SNAP......... Static Nibble Access Path [*Data processing*]
SNAP......... Steerable Null Antenna Processor   (RDA)
SNAP......... Sterile Nitrogen Atmosphere Processing
SNAP......... Structural Network Analysis Program
SNAP......... Student Naval Aviation Pilot
SNAP......... Student Nursing Assistant Program
SNAP......... Summary of Navy Approved Programs
SNAP......... Supersonic Nonequilibrium Analysis Program   (MCD)
SNAP......... Switching Network Analysis Program [*Bell System*]
SNAP......... System Network Activity Program [*Sperry UNIVAC*]
SNAP......... Systematic National Acquisitions Programme [*Public Archives of Canada*]
SNAP......... Systems Network Analysis Process [*Data processing*]   (AEBS)
SNAP......... Systems for Nuclear Auxiliary Power
SNAP(G)... Student Naval Aviation Pilot (Glider)
SnapOn...... Snap-On Tools Corp. [*Associated Press abbreviation*]   (APAG)
SNAPPS.... Short-Term Nuclear Annual Power Production Simulation Model [*Department of Energy*]   (GFGA)
SNAPS ...... Standard Notes and Parts Selection   (TEL)
SNAPS ...... State and National Apprenticeship Program Statistics [*Bureau of Apprenticeship and Training*] [*Department of Labor*]
SNAPS ...... Switching Node and Processing Sites [*ITT*]   (TEL)
SNAPTRAN ... Systems for Nuclear Auxiliary Power Transient
SNARE...... Sandia Nuclear Assembly for Reactor Experiments
SNARK...... Snake-Shark   (SAA)
SNARL...... Suggested No Adverse Risk Levels [*Environmental Protection Agency*]
SNAS........ Student Need Analysis System
SNASOR... Static Nonlinear Analysis of Shells of Revolution [*Computer program*]
SNAT........ Serotonin N-Acetyltransferase [*An enzyme*]
SNAT........ Southern National Corp. [*NASDAQ symbol*]   (NQ)
SNAV .... Sindacato Nazionale Attrazionisti Viaggianti [*National Union of Traveling Entertainers*] [*Italy*]
SNB .... Lakeland Library Region, North Battleford, Saskatchewan [*Library symbol*] [*National Library of Canada*]   (NLC)
SNB .... Scalene Node Biopsy [*Medicine*]
SNB .... Sella, Nasion, B [*Anthropometric landmark*]
SNB .... Sierra Nevada Batholith [*Geology*]
SNB .... Small Navigation Buoy   (DNAB)
SNB .... Snake Bay [*Australia*] [*Airport symbol*]   (OAG)
SNB .... Soviet News Bureau
SNB .... Spinal Nucleus of the Bulbocavernosus [*Neuroanatomy*]
SNB .... Statutes of New Brunswick [*Database*] [*Department of Justice*] [*Information service or system*]   (CRD)
SNB .... Sunbird, Inc. D/B/A Sunbird Airlines, Inc. [*Murray, KY*] [*FAA designator*]   (FAAC)
SNB .... Swiss National Bank
SNBH........ Battleford Union Hospital Memorial Library, North Battleford, Saskatchewan [*Library symbol*] [*National Library of Canada*]   (BIB)
SNBK........ Summit National Bank [*NASDAQ symbol*]   (NQ)
SNBL........ Sioux City & New Orleans Barge Line [*AAR code*]
SNBNK ..... Snowbank   (FAAC)
SNBR........ Snubber [*Mechanical engineering*]
SNBRTU... Screw, Nut, Bolt, and Rivet Trade Union [*British*]
SNBS........ Slovene National Benefit Society   (EA)
SNBU .... Switched Network Backup [*Data processing*]   (IBMDP)
SNC .... Apollo Airways, Inc. D/B/A Pacific Coast Airlines [*Goleta, CA*] [*FAA designator*]   (FAAC)
SNC .... Saint Norbert College [*Wisconsin*]
SNC .... San Antonio College, San Antonio, TX [*OCLC symbol*]   (OCLC)
SNC .... San Nicolas Island [*California*] [*Seismograph station code, US Geological Survey*] [*Closed*]   (SEIS)
SNC .... Sanitary Corps [*Army*]
snc............. Saskatchewan [*MARC country of publication code*] [*Library of Congress*]   (LCCP)
SNC .... Satellite News Channel [*Cable-television system*] [*Went off the air October, 1983*]
S/NC.......... Satisfactory/No Credit [*University grading system*]

SNC .... School of Naval Co-Operation [*Air Force*] [*British*]
SNC .... Scottish National Certificate
SNC .... Servo Nozzle Control   (MCD)
SNC .... Shawmut National Corp. [*NYSE symbol*]   (SPSG)
SNC .... Shergotty [*India*], Nakhla [*Egypt*], and Chassigny [*French*] [*Pronounced "snick"*] [*Classification for a group of meteorites recovered from these sites*]
SNC .... Shipped Not Credited [*Military*]   (AFIT)
SNC .... Significant Noncomplier [*Environmental Protection Agency*]   (GFGA)
SNC .... Skilled Nursing Care
SNC .... Standard Navigation Computer
SNC .... Submarine Net Controller   (MCD)
SNC .... Sunatco Development Corp. [*Vancouver Stock Exchange symbol*]
SNC .... Supreme National Council [*Cambodia*]
SNC .... Swiss Nonvaleurs Club [*Later, Scripophila Helvetica - SH*]   (EAIO)
SNC .... Syndicat National du Cinema [*National Syndicate of Motion Pictures*]
SNCA .... Seneca Oil Co. [*NASDAQ symbol*]   (NQ)
SNCC........ Student National Coordinating Committee [*Pronounced "snick"*]   (EA)
SNCC........ System Network Computer Center [*Louisiana State University*] [*Research center*]   (RCD)
SNCCDIPP ... Selected Non-Communist Countries Defense Intelligence Projection for Planning   (MCD)
SNCF........ SECOMO [*Software Engineering Cost Model*] Non-COCOMO [*Constructive Cost Model*] Factor
SNCF........ Societe Nationale des Chemins de Fer Francais [*French National Railways*]
SNCFA ...... Societe Nationale des Chemins de Fer Algeriens [*Algerian Railways*]
SN-CIE...... Statement of Need - Clothing and Individual Equipment [*Military*]
SNCL........ Serial Number Configuration List   (MCD)
SNCL........ Serial Number Conversion List
SNCLAR ... University of Santa Clara School of Law   (DLA)
SNCLF ...... Societe de Neuro-Chirurgie de Langue Francaise [*Society of French-Speaking Neurosurgeons - SFSN*]   (EA)
SNCM .... Second Nicaraguan Campaign Medal
SNCO .... Seaport Navigation Co. [*AAR code*]
SNCO .... Senior Noncommissioned Officer
SNCO .... Staff Noncommissioned Officer [*Military*]
SNCOC ...... Senior Noncommissioned Officer Course
SNCP........ Salem National Corp. [*NASDAQ symbol*]   (NQ)
SNCP........ Special Navy Control Program   (MCD)
SNCR........ Selective Noncatalytic Reduction [*Combustion technology*]
SNCUNESCO ... Swedish National Commission for UNESCO   (EAIO)
SND .... San Diego - College [*California*] [*Seismograph station code, US Geological Survey*]   (SEIS)
SND .... Sand   (FAAC)
SND .... Sanford, FL [*Location identifier*] [*FAA*]   (FAAL)
SND .... Sanfred Resources [*Vancouver Stock Exchange symbol*]
SND .... Sap No Defect
SND .... Scottish National Dictionary [*A publication*]
SND .... Scottish National Diploma
SND .... Second Class Passengers [*Shipping*] [*British*]
SND .... Selected Natural Diamond
SND .... Self-Powered Neutron Detector
SND .... Semiconductor Neutron Dosimeter
snd............. Sindhi [*MARC language code*] [*Library of Congress*]   (LCCP)
SND .... Sisters of Notre Dame [*Roman Catholic religious order*]
SND .... Sisters of Notre Dame de Namur [*Roman Catholic religious order*]
SND .... Society of Newspaper Design   (EA)
SND .... Sound   (AAG)
SND .... Standard Normal Distribution [*Mathematics*]
SND .... Standardized Normal Distribution
SND .... Static No Delivery
SNDA .... Scottish National Dictionary Association
SNDA .... Student National Dental Association   (EA)
SNDC .... Sand Technology Systems International, Inc. [*NASDAQ symbol*]   (NQ)
SNDC .... Serbian National Defense Council   (EA)
SNDG .... Sending   (MSA)
SNDG .... Sounding   (MSA)
SNDL .... Sandale R. R. [*AAR code*]
SNDL .... Standard Navy Distribution List
SNDL .... Standard Nomenclature List [*Military*]
SNDL .... Studienausgaben zur Neueren Deutschen Literatur [*A publication*]
SNDLF ...... Societe de Nutrition et de Dietetique de Langue Francaise [*French-Language Society of Nutrition and Dietetics - FLSND*] [*France*]   (EAIO)
SNDM .... Secretary of Navy Decision Memorandum
SND-MB ... Selected Natural Diamond - Metal Bond
SNDN........ Sisters of Notre Dame de Namur [*Roman Catholic religious order*] [*Rome, Italy*]   (EAIO)
SNDO........ Standard Nomenclature of Diseases and Operations [*Medicine*]
SNDPRF ... Soundproof   (MSA)

SNDR .... Shimane Daigaku Ronshu: Jinbun Kagaku [*Journal of the Shimane University: Humanistic Sciences*] [*A publication*]
SNDS........ [*The*] Sands Regent [*Reno, NV*] [*NASDAQ symbol*] (NQ)
SNDS........ Stillbirth and Neonatal Death Society [*British*] (EAIO)
SNDS........ Stock Number Data Section (MCD)
SNDSB ...... Sonderschule [*A publication*]
SNDT .... Shreemati Nathibai Domodar Thackersey Women's University [*India*]
SNDT .... Society for Nondestructive Testing [*Later, ASNT*] (KSC)
SNDT .... SunGard Data Systems, Inc. [*Wayne, PA*] [*NASDAQ symbol*] (NQ)
SNDV .... Strategic Nuclear Delivery Vehicle [*Army*] (AABC)
SNE .... Santa Elena, TX [*Location identifier*] [*FAA*] (FAAL)
SNE .... Sao Nicolau [*Cape Verde Islands*] [*Airport symbol*] (OAG)
SNE .... Severe Noise Environment
SNE .... Shawnee Airlines [*Orlando, FL*] [*FAA designator*] (FAAC)
SNE .... Society for Nutrition Education (EA)
SNE .... Sony Corp. America [*NYSE symbol*] [*Toronto Stock Exchange symbol*] [*Vancouver Stock Exchange symbol*] (SPSG)
SNE .... Spatial Nonemotional (Stimuli)
SNE .... Subacute Necrotizing Encephalomyelopathy [*Medicine*]
SNE .... Syndicat National de l'Edition [*French publishers' association*]
SNEA........ Student National Education Association (EA)
SNEC........ Saxton Nuclear Engineering Corp.
SNEC........ Secondary Navy Enlisted Classification (DNAB)
SNEC........ Subgroup on Nuclear Export Coordination [*Nuclear Regulatory Commission*] (GFGA)
SNECI .... Sindicato Nacional dos Empregados do Comercio e da Industria da Provincia de Mocambique [*National Union of Commercial and Industrial Workers of Mozambique*]
SNECIPA ... Sindicato Nacional dos Empregados do Comercio e da Industria da Provincia de Angola [*National Syndicate of Workers of Commerce and Industry of the Province of Angola*]
Sneed.......... Sneed's Kentucky Decisions [*2 Kentucky*] [*A publication*] (DLA)
Sneed.......... Sneed's Tennessee Reports [*33-37 Tennessee*] [*A publication*] (DLA)
Sneed Dec .. Sneed's Kentucky Decisions [*2 Kentucky*] [*A publication*] (DLA)
Sneed Tenn ... Sneed's Tennessee Reports [*A publication*] (DLA)
Sneed (Tenn) Rep ... Sneed's Tennessee Reports [*A publication*] (DLA)
SN(EF) ...... Seaman (Electronics Field) [*Navy rating*] (DNAB)
SNEFU ...... Situation Normal - Everything Fouled Up [*Bowdlerized version*] [*Obsolete*] (DSUE)
SNEG .... Syndicat National des Enseignants de Guinee [*National Union of Guinean Teachers*]
SNEI .... Societe Nouvelle d'Editions pour l'Industrie [*Industrial News Publishing Company*] (IID)
SNEIL .... Secretariat for the Nordic Energy Information Libraries (IID)
SNEL........ Snelling and Snelling, Inc. [*NASDAQ symbol*] (NQ)
SNEL........ Societe Nationale d'Electricite
SNEL........ Special Nuclear Effects Laboratory
Snell Eq...... Snell's Principles in Equity [*A publication*] (DLA)
SNELPIF .. Sindacato Nazionale Esperti Laureati Propagandisti Industrie Farmaceutiche [*National Union of University Graduated Experts for Propaganda in Pharmaceutical Industries*] [*Italy*]
SNEMSA .. Southern New England Marine Sciences Association
SNEP........ Saudi Naval Expansion Program (MCD)
SNEP FIT ... Saudi Naval Expansion Program, Fleet Introduction Team (DNAB)
SNEP PMT ... Saudi Naval Expansion Program, Project Management Team (DNAB)
SNEP PROJMGR ... Saudi Naval Expansion Program, Project Manager (DNAB)
SNEP PROJMGRT AFT ... Saudi Naval Expansion Program, Project Manager, Technical Assistance Field Team (DNAB)
SNEPT ...... Space Nuclear Electric Propulsion Test
SNERA ...... Statistica Neerlandica [*A publication*]
SNES........ Syndicat National de l'Enseignement Secondaire [*National Union of Secondary Schoolteachers*] [*France*]
SNET........ Southern New England Telecommunications Corp. [*New Haven, CT*] (TSSD)
SNET........ Syndicat National de l'Enseignement Technique [*National Union of Technical School Teachers*] [*France*]
SNETel...... Southern New England Telecommunications Corp. [*Associated Press abbreviation*] (APAG)
S New........ Sidney Newsletter [*A publication*]
SNF........... Secret - No Foreigners [*Security classification*]
SNF........... Selskab foer Nordisk Filologi Arsberetning [*A publication*]
SNF........... Serb National Federation (EA)
SNF........... Short-Range Nuclear Forces
SNF........... Silicon Nitride Film
SNF........... Skilled Nursing Facility
SNF........... Solids Not Fat
SNF........... Somali National Front [*Political party*] (EY)
SNF........... Spain Fund [*NYSE symbol*] (SPSG)
SNF........... Spent Nuclear Fuel
SNF........... Spot Noise Figure
SNF........... Sudanese National Front [*Political party*] (PD)
SNF........... System Noise Figure

SNFCC ...... Shippers National Freight Claim Council [*Later, TCPC*] (EA)
SNFL......... Standing Naval Force, Atlantic (MCD)
SNFLD ...... Secret - Limited Distribution - Not Releasable to Foreigners [*Security classification*]
SNFLK ...... Snowflake (FAAC)
SNFO .... Student Naval Flight Officer
SNFPP....... Syndicat National de la Fonction Publique Provinciale [*National Union of Provincial Government Employees - NUPGE*] [*Canada*]
SNFR .... Small-Probe Net Flux Radiometer [*NASA*]
SNFRC ...... Seattle National Fisheries Research Center [*Seattle, WA*] [*Department of the Interior*] (GRD)
SNFS......... Student Naval Flight Surgeon
SNFU........ Scottish National Farmers' Union
SNG .... San Ignacio De Velasco [*Bolivia*] [*Airport symbol*] (OAG)
SNG .... Sans Notre Garantie [*Without Our Guarantee*] [*French*] [*Business term*]
SNG .... Solidified Nitroglycerol [*or Nitroglycerin*] [*Explosive*]
SNG .... Songkhla [*Thailand*] [*Seismograph station code, US Geological Survey*] (SEIS)
SNG .... Southern New England Telecommunications Corp. [*NYSE symbol*] (SPSG)
SNG .... Stabilization Network Group
SNG .... Sterling Energy Corp. [*Vancouver Stock Exchange symbol*]
SNG .... Substitute [*or Synthetic*] Natural Gas
Sng .... Synagogue (BJA)
SNG .... Synthetic Natural Gas (IEEE)
SNGA .... Sodium N-Glycoloylarsanilic [*or N-Glycolylarsanilic*] Acid [*Pharmacology*]
SNGFR...... Single Nephron Glomerular Filtration Rate
SNGL........ Single
SNGN........ Segmental Necrotizing Glomerulonephritis [*Medicine*]
SNGOD..... Special NGO [*Nongovernmental Organization*] Committee on Disarmament (EA)
SNGRA ..... Sangre [*A publication*]
SNGS........ Salem Nuclear Generating Station (NRCH)
SNH.......... Savannah, TN [*Location identifier*] [*FAA*] (FAAL)
SNH.......... Signtech, Inc. [*Toronto Stock Exchange symbol*]
snh............. Sinhalese [*MARC language code*] [*Library of Congress*] (LCCP)
SNH.......... Skilled Nursing Home
SNH.......... Snatch [*Block*] [*Design engineering*]
SNH.......... Society for Nursing History (EA)
SNH.......... South Nottinghamshire Hussars [*British military*] (DMA)
SNH.......... Sunshine Point [*Alaska*] [*Seismograph station code, US Geological Survey*] (SEIS)
SNHA....... Shenandoah Natural History Association (EA)
SNHL....... Sensorineural Hearing Loss [*Medicine*] (MAE)
SNI .... National Intelligence Service [*Zaire*] (PD)
SNI .... San Nicolas Island
SNI .... Selective Notification of Information
SNI .... Sequence Number Indicator
SNI .... Signal-to-Noise Improvement [*Data transmission*] (IEEE)
S/N + I ...... Signal-to-Noise plus Interference Ratio
SNI .... Sinoe [*Liberia*] [*Airport symbol*] (OAG)
SNI .... Sistema Nacional de Informacion [*National Information System*] [*Colombia*] (IID)
SNI .... Sonor Investments Ltd. [*Toronto Stock Exchange symbol*]
SNI .... Sports Network, Inc. [*Later, HSN*]
SNI .... Staatsblad Nederlands-Indie [*A publication*]
SNI .... Standard Network Interconnection [*Telecommunications*]
SNI .... Sun City Industries, Inc. [*AMEX symbol*] (SPSG)
SNI .... Syndicat National des Instituteurs [*National Union of Teachers*] [*France*]
SNIC......... Sigmatron Nova, Inc. [*NASDAQ symbol*] (NQ)
SNIC Bull ... SNIC [*Singapore National Institute of Chemistry*] Bulletin [*A publication*]
SNIE......... Sindacato Nazionale Insegnanti Elementari [*National Union of Elementary Teachers*] [*Italy*]
SNIE's .... Special National Intelligence Estimates [*Summaries of foreign policy information and advice prepared for the president*] [*Known informally as "sneeze"*]
SNIF .... Short-Term Note-Issuance Facility [*Banking*]
SNIF .... Site-Specific Natural Isotope Fractionation [*Analytical chemistry*]
SNIF .... Standby Note Issuance Facility [*Finance*]
SNIF .... Syndicated Note-Issuance Facility [*Banking*] (ADA)
SNIFFEX .. Sniffer [*Exhaust trail indicator*] Exercise [*Military*] (NVT)
SNIFTIRS ... Subtractively Normalized Interfacial FTIR [*Fourier Transform Infrared*] Spectroscopy
SNIMOG .. Sustained Noninflationary Market-Oriented Growth
SNIP .... Single Net Information and Position [*Reporting procedures*] [*Navy*] (NVT)
SNIP .... Single Net Integrated Procedure [*Military*] (CAAL)
SNIPE .... SDI [*Strategic Defense Initiative*] Network Interface Processor Engine (SDI)
SNIPE .... Soviet Naval Interdiction Possibilities, Europe
SNIR......... Signal-to-Noise Plus Interference Ratio
SNIRD....... Supposedly Noiseless Infrared Detector
SNIT......... Stock Number Identification Table
SNIVT .... Society of Non-Invasive Vascular Technology (EA)

SNJ............ Everett, WA [*Location identifier*] [*FAA*]   (FAAL)
SNJ............ Sinj [*Yugoslavia*] [*Seismograph station code, US Geological Survey*] [*Closed*]   (SEIS)
SNJ............ Switching Network Junction [*Telecommunications*]   (OA)
SN(JC)...... Seaman (Junior College) [*Navy rating*]   (DNAB)
SN(JCE).... Seaman (Junior College Technical Electrician) [*Navy rating*]   (DNAB)
SN(JCNE) ... Seaman (Junior College Nuclear Field Electronics) [*Navy rating*]   (DNAB)
SN(JCNSET) ... Seaman (Junior College Nuclear Submarine Engineering Technician) [*Navy rating*]   (DNAB)
SN(JCPE) ... Seaman (Junior College Polaris Field Electronics) [*Navy rating*]   (DNAB)
SN(JCPL) ... Seaman (Junior College Polaris Field Launcher) [*Navy rating*]   (DNAB)
SN(JCT).... Seaman (Junior College Technical) [*Navy rating*]   (DNAB)
SNJM........ Sisters of the Holy Names of Jesus and Mary [*Roman Catholic religious order*]
SNK .... Shannock Corp. [*Vancouver Stock Exchange symbol*]
SNK .... Snyder, TX [*Location identifier*] [*FAA*]   (FAAL)
SNK .... Student-Newman-Keuls [*Statistical procedure*]
SNK .... Survey of Next of Kin [*Department of Health and Human Services*]   (GFGA)
SNK .... Swank, Inc. [*NYSE symbol*]   (SPSG)
SNKI.......... Swank, Inc. [*NASDAQ symbol*]   (NQ)
SNKL........ Snorkel   (MSA)
SNKORL... Subject to No Known or Reported Losses [*Insurance*]   (AIA)
SNL .... Department of State. Newsletter [*A publication*]
SNL .... Sample Noise Level
SNL .... Sandia National Laboratories [*Department of Energy*] [*Albuquerque, NM*]   (GRD)
SNL .... Satire Newsletter [*A publication*]
SNL .... Saturday Night Live [*Television program*]
SNL .... Selected Nodes List [*Telecommunications*]   (TEL)
SNL .... Seminole Resources, Inc. [*Vancouver Stock Exchange symbol*]
SNL .... Sevenhill [*Australia*] [*Seismograph station code, US Geological Survey*] [*Closed*]   (SEIS)
SNL .... Shakespeare Newsletter [*A publication*]
SNL .... Shawnee, OK [*Location identifier*] [*FAA*]   (FAAL)
SNL .... Snout Length [*Pisciculture*]
SNL .... Somali National League
SNL .... Soonair Lines, Inc. [*Tulsa, OK*] [*FAA designator*]   (FAAC)
SNL .... Spore Newsletter [*A publication*]
SNL .... Standard Name Line [*Military*]
SNL .... Standard Nomenclature List [*Military*]
SNL .... State Narcotic Law
SNL .... Stock Not Listed   (AAG)
SNLA........ Sandia National Laboratory (Albuquerque)
SNLB........ Second National Bancorporation [*NASDAQ symbol*]   (SPSG)
SNLC........ Senior NATO Logistician Conference   (NATG)
SNLC........ Service National des Liberations Conditionnelles [*Canada*]
SNLF........ SNL Financial Corp. [*NASDAQ symbol*]   (NQ)
SNLG........ Signaling   (MSA)
SNLN .... Saskatchewan Native Library Services Newsletter [*A publication*]
SNLR........ Services No Longer Required
SNLS........ Society for New Language Study   (EA)
SNLT........ Sunlite, Inc. [*NASDAQ symbol*]   (NQ)
SNLV........ Strategic Nuclear Launch Vehicle
SNM.......... Saint Mary's University, San Antonio, TX [*OCLC symbol*]   (OCLC)
SNM .... Satellite Navigation Map
SNM .... Senior Naval Member
SNM .... Signal-to-Noise Merit
SNM .... Society of Nuclear Medicine   (EA)
SNM .... Socorro [*New Mexico*] [*Seismograph station code, US Geological Survey*]   (SEIS)
SNM .... Somali National Movement [*Political party*]   (PD)
SNM .... Special Nuclear Material
SNM .... Spent Nuclear Material   (IEEE)
SNM .... Square Nautical Mile   (NVT)
SNM .... Subject Named Member   (NVT)
SNM .... Sulfanilamide [*Antimicrobial compound*]
SNM .... Sunmask Petroleum [*Vancouver Stock Exchange symbol*]
SNMA ...... Sonoma Vineyards [*NASDAQ symbol*]   (NQ)
SNMA ...... Student National Medical Association   (EA)
SNMAD .... Southwest Bulletin [*A publication*]
SNMCB..... Scheduled Not Mission Capable Both [*Maintenance and supply*]   (MCD)
SNMCM ... Scheduled Not Mission Capable Maintenance   (MCD)
SNMDCS ... Standard Navy Maintenance Data Collection System
SNMMMIS ... Standard Navy Maintenance and Material Management Information System
SNMMMS ... Standard Navy Maintenance and Material Management System
SNMP........ Simple Network Management Protocol [*Data processing*]
SNMP........ Spent Nuclear Material Pool   (IEEE)
SNMPAM ... Acta Musei Nationalis Pragae. Series B. Historia Naturalis [*A publication*]
SNMS........ Secondary Neutrals Mass Spectrometry
SNMS........ Sputtered Neutral Mass Spectrometry [*Surface analysis*]

SNMT .... Society of Nuclear Medical Technologists [*Defunct*]   (EA)
SNMV .... Solanum Nodiflorum Mottle Virus [*Plant pathology*]
SNN .... Sha Na Na   (EA)
SNN .... Shannon [*Ireland*] [*Airport symbol*]   (OAG)
SNN .... Shared Nearest Neighbor   (MCD)
SNN .... Sienna Resources Ltd. [*Toronto Stock Exchange symbol*]
SNN .... Sining [*Republic of China*] [*Seismograph station code, US Geological Survey*]   (SEIS)
SNN .... Smith College, Northampton, MA [*OCLC symbol*]   (OCLC)
SNN .... Structure-Nomenclature Notation [*Chemistry*]
SNNEB..... Scottish Nursery Nurses Examination Board   (DI)
SNNG .... Schakels Nederlands Nieuw Guinea [*A publication*]
SNNSB3.... Food Irradiation [*Japan*] [*A publication*]
SNNTS..... Studies in the Novel. North Texas State University [*A publication*]
SNO.......... Polaris Industries Partners Ltd. [*AMEX symbol*]   (SPSG)
SNO.......... Semiempirical Natural Orbital [*Physical chemistry*]
SNO.......... Senior Naval Officer
SNO.......... Senior Navigation Officer [*Air Force*] [*British*]
SNO.......... Senior Nursing Officer [*British*]
SNO.......... Serial Number   (MDG)
SNO.......... Special Naval Operations   (NVT)
SNO.......... Stock Number   (MSA)
SNO.......... Sudbury Neutrino Observatory [*Proposed joint US-Canadian project*]
Sno .... Thioinosine [*Also, SIno, M*] [*A nucleoside*]
SNOAD ..... Senior Naval Officer Adriatic [*British*]
SNOB .... Senior Naval Officer on Board
S Nob .... Sine Nobilitate [*Without Nobility*] [*Notation used at Oxford University to indicate that a student was untitled. This abbreviation is claimed to have acquired its present connotation when commoners at the university put on more airs than did their titled counterparts*] [*Latin*]
SNOBOL... String-Oriented Symbolic Language [*1963*] [*Data processing*]
SNODO..... Standard Nomenclature of Diseases and Operations [*Medicine*]   (DHSM)
SNOE .... Smart Noise Equipment [*RADAR jammer*] [*Air Force*]
SNoF........ Studier i Nordisk Filologi [*A publication*]
SNOINCR ... Snow Depth Increase in Past Hour [*Meteorology*]   (FAAC)
SNOK .... Secondary Next of Kin [*Army*]   (AABC)
SNOL .... Senior Naval Officer, Landings [*British*]
SNOMed ... Systematized Nomenclature of Medicine
SNOO....... Small Nonoverlapping Offset [*Oceanography*]
SNOOP ..... Students Naturally Opposed to Outrageous Prying [*Student legal action organization*]   (EA)
SNOOPE... System for Nuclear Observation of Possible Explosives [*Science Applications International Corp.*] [*Aviation*]
SNOOPI.... System Network Online Operations Information [*Suggested name for the Library of Congress computer system*]
SNOP .... Senior Naval Officer Present
SNOP .... Standard Nomenclature of Pathology [*College of American Pathologists*]
SNOP .... Systematized Nomenclature of Pathology [*NCI*]
SNOPG ..... Senior Naval Officer, Persian Gulf [*British military*]   (DMA)
SNORE ..... Self-Noise Reduction
SNORE ..... Signal-to-Noise Ratio Estimator
SNORKEX ... Snorkel Detection Exercise [*Military*]   (NVT)
SNORT ..... Supersonic Naval Ordnance Research Track [*China Lake, CA*]
SNOS .... Scottish National Orchestra Society
SNOTEL... Snow Survey Telemetry Network [*Department of Agriculture*]
SNov .... Seara Nova [*A publication*]
SNovel ...... Studies in the Novel [*A publication*]
Snow......... Snow's Reports [*3 Utah*] [*A publication*]   (DLA)
SNOW ...... Standard Normal Ocean Water
SNOWCAT ... Support of Nuclear Operations with Conventional Air Tactics   (NATG)
SNOWFLEX ... Field Exercise under Snow Conditions [*Military*]   (NVT)
SNOWI ..... Senior Naval Officer, West Indies [*British*]
Snow Revel ... Snow Revelry [*A publication*]   (APTA)
SNOW TIME ... SAC-NORAD [*Strategic Air Command - North American Air Defense*] Operational Weapons Test Involving Military Electronics
SNP .... St. Paul Island [*Alaska*] [*Airport symbol*]   (OAG)
SNP .... St. Paul Island, AK [*Location identifier*] [*FAA*]   (FAAL)
S-N-P........ Salt and Pepa [*Rap recording group*]
SNP .... Samnordisk Planteforedling [*Internordic plant breeding*] [*An association*] [*Sweden*]   (EAIO)
SNP .... School Nurse Practitioner
SNP .... Scottish National Party [*Political party*]   (PPW)
SNP .... Skagit Nuclear Project   (NRCH)
SNP .... Slovak National Party [*Former Czechoslovakia*] [*Political party*]   (EY)
SNP .... Society for Natural Philosophy   (EA)
SNP .... Sodium Nitroprusside [*A vasodilator*]
SNP .... Soluble Nucleoprotein
SNP .... Sonepat [*India*] [*Seismograph station code, US Geological Survey*] [*Closed*]   (SEIS)
SNP .... Space Nuclear Propulsion
SNP .... Statistical Network Processor
SNP .... Sudanese National Party [*Political party*]   (EY)
SNP .... Suspected, Not Proved

SNP	Synchro Null Pulse
SNP	Synchronous Network Processor
SNP	System Network Processor
SNPA........	Southern Newspaper Publishers Association
SN(PFE)....	Seaman (Polaris Field Electronics) [*Navy rating*] (DNAB)
SN(PFL)....	Seaman (Polaris Field Launcher) [*Navy rating*] (DNAB)
SNPJ	Slovene National Benefit Society (EA)
SNPM.......	Standard and Nuclear Propulsion Module
SNPMA.....	Student National Podiatric Medical Association (EA)
SNPO	Society for Nonprofit Organizations (EA)
SNPO	Space Nuclear Propulsion Office [*Later, Division of Space Nuclear Systems, of Energy Research and Development Administration*] [*AEC-NASA*]
SNPOA	Space Nuclear Propulsion Office, Albuquerque [*See SNPO*]
SNPOC......	Space Nuclear Propulsion Office, Cleveland [*See SNPO*]
SNPON	Space Nuclear Propulsion Office, Nevada [*See SNPO*]
SNPP	Sequoyah Nuclear Power Plant (NRCH)
SNPR........	Screen Print (AAG)
SNPRI	Selected Nonpriority List Item [*Military*]
SNPRM......	Supplemental Notice of Proposed Rulemaking
SNPS	Satellite Nuclear Power Station (OA)
SNPS	Shoreham Nuclear Power Station (NRCH)
SNPX........	SynOptics Communications, Inc. [*NASDAQ symbol*] (CTT)
SNQ..........	Scottish Notes and Queries [*A publication*]
SNQ..........	Sea-1 Aquafarms Ltd. [*Vancouver Stock Exchange symbol*]
SNQ..........	Sussex Notes and Queries [*A publication*]
SNR	Saint Nazaire [*France*] [*Airport symbol*] (OAG)
SNR	Schaffner Ranch [*California*] [*Seismograph station code, US Geological Survey*] (SEIS)
SNR	Schenectady Naval Reactors Office [*Energy Research and Development Administration*]
SNR	Selective Nitrogen Oxide Reduction [*Combustion technology*]
SNR	Selective Noncatalytic Reduction [*Combustion technology*]
SNR	Senior
SNR	Senior National Representatives SONAR [*Four Power Army*] (MCD)
SNR	Senor [*Mister*] [*Spanish*]
SNR	Service Not Required
SNR	Signal-to-Noise Ratio
SNR	Slow Neutron Reactor [*Nuclear energy*] (NRCH)
SNR	Society for Nautical Research [*British*] (EAIO)
SNR	SONAR
SNr	Substantia Nigra Pars Reticulata [*Brain anatomy*]
SNR	Sudan Notes and Records [*A publication*]
SNR	Sunair Electronics, Inc. [*AMEX symbol*] (SPSG)
SNR	Supernova Remnant [*Astronomy*]
SNR	Supplier Nonconformance Report [*Nuclear energy*] (NRCH)
SNRA	Sawtooth National Recreation Area [*Idaho*]
SNRA	Senora [*Mrs.*] [*Spanish*]
SNRAFU...	Situation Normal, Really All Fouled Up [*Military slang*] [*Bowdlerized version*]
SNRC........	Sudanese National Research Council
SNRE........	Small Nuclear Rocket Engine
SNRG	Scientific NRG, Inc. [*NASDAQ symbol*] (NQ)
SNRLTCS ...	Skilled Nursing and Related Long Term Care Services (EA)
snRNA	Ribonucleic Acid, Small Nuclear [*Biochemistry, genetics*]
snRNP	Ribonucleoprotein, Small Nuclear [*Biochemistry*]
SNRS........	Sunrise [*Meteorology*] (FAAC)
SNRS........	Sunrise Technologies, Inc. [*NASDAQ symbol*] (NQ)
SNRSA	Sunrise Savings & Loan Association of Florida Cl A [*NASDAQ symbol*] (NQ)
SNRT........	Sinus Node Recovery Time [*Cardiology*]
SNRTC......	Sinus Node Recovery Time Corrected [*Cardiology*]
SNS...........	Salinas, CA [*Location identifier*] [*FAA*] (FAAL)
SNS...........	Samarbeidsnemden for Nordisk Skogforskning [*Nordic Forest Research Cooperation Committee - NFRCC*] [*Finland*] (EAIO)
SNS...........	San Onofre [*California*] [*Seismograph station code, US Geological Survey*] (SEIS)
SNS...........	Scandinavian Neurosurgical Society (EA)
SNS...........	Seabrook Nuclear Station (NRCH)
SNS...........	Senior Nursing Sister [*Navy*] [*British*]
SNS...........	Sensorstat System [*Vancouver Stock Exchange symbol*]
SNS...........	Service National des Sauveteurs [*Canada*]
SNS...........	Simulated Network Simulations (KSC)
SNS...........	Skyline Network Service [*Satellite Business Systems*] [*McLean, VA*] [*Telecommunications*] (TSSD)
SNS...........	Slovo na Storozi [*A publication*]
SNS...........	Small Nuclear Stage (KSC)
SNS...........	Society of Neurological Surgeons (EA)
SNS...........	Somatic Nervous System
SNS...........	Space Navigation System (OA)
SNS...........	Space Nuclear System
SNS...........	Spallation Neutron Source
SNS...........	Spanish Economic News Service [*A publication*]
SNS...........	Special Night Squads [*Palestine*] (BJA)
SNS...........	Stabilized Night Sight
SNS...........	Sundstrand Corp. [*NYSE symbol*] (SPSG)
SNS...........	Superconductor/Normal Metal/Superconductor [*Physics*]
SNS...........	Switched Network Server [*Tylink Corp.*]
SNS...........	Sympathetic Nervous System [*Physiology*]
SN/SC	Stock Number Source Code (MCD)
SNSCNY ...	St. Nicholas Society of the City of New York (EA)
SNSE	Society of Nuclear Scientists and Engineers [*Defunct*]
SNSH	Snow Showers [*Meteorology*]
SNSL	Standard Navy Stock List
SNSL	Stock Number Sequence Listing (MSA)
SNSM.......	Sindacato Nazionale Scuola Media [*National Union of Intermediate School Teachers*] [*Italy*]
SNSN........	Standard Navy Stock Number
SNSO	Space Nuclear Systems Office [*AEC/NASA*]
SNSO	Superintending Naval Stores Officer [*British military*] (DMA)
SNSR........	Sensor (AAG)
SNSR........	Sensormatic Electronics Corp. [*NASDAQ symbol*] (NQ)
SNSS	School Natural Science Society [*British*]
SNSS	Skrifter Utgivna. Namnden foer Svensk Sprakvard [*A publication*]
SNST	Sonesta International Hotels Corp. [*NASDAQ symbol*] (NQ)
SNST	Sunset [*Meteorology*] (FAAC)
SNT	Saint
SNT	[*The*] Scrolls and the New Testament [*K. Stendahl*] [*A publication*] (BJA)
SNT	Sealant [*Technical drawings*]
SNT	Sears Point [*California*] [*Seismograph station code, US Geological Survey*] (SEIS)
SNT	Secretaria Nacional de Transportes [*Brazil*] (EY)
SNT	Selective Nuclear Transfer
SNT	Serial Number Tracking
SNT	Silicon Needle Transducer
SNT	Sindacato Nazionale Tabacchine [*National Union of Women Tobacco Workers*] [*Italy*]
SNT	Single Negotiating Text [*UN Law of the Sea Conference*]
SNT	Society for Nondestructive Testing [*Later, ASNT*] (EA)
SNT	Sonat, Inc. [*NYSE symbol*] (SPSG)
SNT	Supplements. Novum Testamentum [*Leiden*] [*A publication*]
SNT	Synthetic Navigation Trainer
SNT	System Noise Temperature
SNTA........	Sodium Nitrilotriacetate
SNTC........	Syndicat National des Transporteurs de Cameroun [*National Union of Cameroonese Transportation Workers*]
SNTC........	Syndicat National des Travailleurs Congolais [*National Union of Congolese Workers*] [*Leopoldville*]
SNTC........	Synetic, Inc. [*NASDAQ symbol*] (NQ)
SNTCC......	Simplified Neutron Transport Computer Code
SNTCDL...	INTA [*Instituto Nacional de Tecnologia Agropecuaria*] Estacion Experimental Agropecuaria Concordia. Serie Notas Tecnicas [*A publication*]
SNTE........	Santec Corp. [*NASDAQ symbol*] (NQ)
SNTF........	Special Navy Task Force (MUGU)
SNTFC	Special Navy Task Force Commander
SNTF(SMS) ...	Special Navy Task Force for Surface Missile Systems (MUGU)
SNTK........	Senetek Ltd. [*NASDAQ symbol*] (NQ)
SntO.........	Santander Overseas Bank, Inc. [*Associated Press abbreviation*] (APAG)
SNTO	Swiss National Tourist Office (EA)
SntOv........	Santander Overseas Bank, Inc. [*Associated Press abbreviation*] (APAG)
SNTPC......	Scottish National Town Planning Council (DAS)
SNTR........	Sinter [*Metallurgy*]
SNTS	Short-Length, Nonbuoyant Torpedo System
SNTS	Society for New Testament Study [*Exeter, Devonshire, England*] (EA)
SNTSB	Studiorum Novi Testamenti Societas. Bulletin [*A publication*]
SNTSMS...	Studiorum Novi Testamenti Societas. Monograph Series [*A publication*]
SNTZD......	Sensitized (MSA)
SNTZG......	Sensitizing (MSA)
SNu..........	Sifre on Numbers (BJA)
SNU..........	SNC Group, Inc. [*Toronto Stock Exchange symbol*]
SNU..........	Solar Neutrino Unit [*Astrophysics*]
SNU..........	Somali National Union
SNUB	Show Nothing Unless Bad
SNUCD	Software Newsletter [*A publication*]
SNUD........	Stock Number User Directory [*Air Force*] (AFM)
SNUJ........	Singapore National Union of Journalists
SNUM	Special Nuclear Material
SNUPPS....	Standardized Nuclear Unit Power Plant System [*Nuclear reactor combine*]
SNUR........	Significant New Use Rules [*Environmental Protection Agency*]
SNURP......	Small Nuclear Ribonucleoprotein Particle [*Genetics*]
SNV	Santa Elena [*Venezuela*] [*Airport symbol*] (OAG)
SNV	Spleen Necrosis Virus
SNV	Suneva Resources [*Vancouver Stock Exchange symbol*]
SNV	Synovus Financial Corp. [*NYSE symbol*] (SPSG)
SNV	Systema Nervosum Vegetativo [*Obsolete term for the autonomic nervous system*] [*Medicine*]
SNVAO	Skrifter Utgitt. Det Norske Videnskaps-Akademi i Oslo [*A publication*]
SNVB........	Society for Northwestern Vertebrate Biology (EA)
SNVO	Skrifter. Norske Videnskaps-Akademi i Oslo [*A publication*]
SNVPP	Simulated Night Vertical Pinpoint

SNVT.........	Short No-Voltage Tester [*Ground surveillance RADAR system*] (MCD)
SNW.........	Sandoway [*Myanmar*] [*Airport symbol*] (OAG)
S/Nw.........	Signal-to-Noise, Weighted
SNW.........	Snow [*Meteorology*] (FAAC)
SNW.........	Snowwater Resources Ltd. [*Vancouver Stock Exchange symbol*]
SNW.........	Stanwood Corp. [*AMEX symbol*] (SPSG)
SNW.........	Strategic Nuclear Weapon
SNW.........	Sun West Airlines [*Scottsdale, AZ*] [*FAA designator*] (FAAC)
Sn & W Ch ...	Snow and Winstanley's Chancery Practice [*A publication*] (DLA)
SNWFL.....	Snowfall (FAAC)
SNWS........	Shipboard Nuclear Weapon Security [*Navy*] (CAAL)
SNWT	Snowshoe. Newsletter. NWT [*Northwest Territories, Canada*] Library Association [*A publication*]
SNWT	Steel Non-Watertight [*Shipfitting*]
SNWTH	Sources for NWT [*Northwest Territory*] History. Prince of Wales Northern Heritage Centre [*Canada*] [*A publication*]
SNX	Sunburst Exploration Ltd. [*Toronto Stock Exchange symbol*]
SNY	Sidney [*Nebraska*] [*Airport symbol*] (OAG)
SNY	Snyder Oil Corp. [*NYSE symbol*] (SPSG)
SNY	Southern New York Railway [*AAR code*]
SNY	Spanish Navy
SNY	Sunny (MSA)
SNYC........	South Nottinghamshire Yeomanry Cavalry [*British military*] (DMA)
Snyder........	Snyder Oil Corp. [*Associated Press abbreviation*] (APAG)
Snyder Mines ...	Snyder on Mines and Mining [*A publication*] (DLA)
Snydr.........	Snyder Oil Corp. [*Associated Press abbreviation*] (APAG)
SNYK	Security New York State Corp. [*NASDAQ symbol*] (NQ)
Sny Not Man ...	Snyder's Notaries' and Commissioners' Manual [*A publication*] (DLA)
SNYPO......	Sold, Not Yet Paid Out
Sny Rel Corp ...	Snyder on Religious Corporations [*A publication*] (DLA)
SNZ	Senzan [*Japan*] [*Seismograph station code, US Geological Survey*] (SEIS)
SNZ	Shipping Corp. of New Zealand (CDA) [*Toronto Stock Exchange symbol*]
SNZO	South Karori [*New Zealand*] [*Seismograph station code, US Geological Survey*] (SEIS)
SO	Austrian Air Services [*Austria*] [*ICAO designator*] (ICDA)
SO	SAI Ambrosini SpA [*Italy*] [*ICAO aircraft manufacturer identifier*] (ICAO)
SO	Sail Only (CINC)
SO	Sales Order
SO	Salpingo-Oophorectomy [*Medicine*]
SO	Salvis Omissis [*Omissions Excepted*] [*Latin*]
SO	Saturdays Only [*British railroad term*]
SO	Saturn Orbiter [*NASA*]
SO	Schenectady Operation [*Energy Research and Development Administration*] (MCD)
SO	Scientific Officer [*Ministry of Agriculture, Fisheries, and Food*] [*Also, ScO*] [*British*]
SO	Scottish [*Communion*] Office [*Episcopalian*]
SO	Scouting-Observation Plane [*When prefixed to Navy aircraft designation*]
S(O)	Seaman (Operator) [*British military*] (DMA)
SO	Second Class Open [*Train ticket*] (DCTA)
SO	Second Opinion [*An association*] [*Defunct*] (EA)
SO	Secretary's Office [*Navy*]
SO	Secretary's Order
SO	Section Officer [*British military*] (DMA)
SO	Secure Operations (MCD)
SO	Security Office
SO	Seder 'Olam (BJA)
SO	Sell-Off (AAG)
SO	Seller's Option [*Stock exchange term*]
SO	Send Only
SO	Senior Officer [*Military, police*]
SO	Sensory Organ [*Anatomy*]
SO	Serial Output
SO	Service Order
SO	Sex Offender
SO	Sheriff's Office [*or Officer*] (ROG)
SO	Shift-Out Character [*Keyboard*] [*Data processing*]
SO	Shipment [*or Shipping*] Order
SO	Shipping Order (WGA)
SO	Ship's Option
SO	Ships-on-Order Library [*Maritime Data Network, Inc.*] [*Information service or system*] (CRD)
SO	Shop Order
SO	Shot
S-O............	Shut-Off (AAG)
SO	Shutout [*Sports*]
SO	Sibirskie Ogni [*A publication*]
S/O	Sign Off
SO	Signal Officer
SO	Signal Oscillator (OA)
SO	Significant Other [*Term for members of unmarried couples*]
SO	Silvered Optics
SO	Slavia Occidentalis [*A publication*]
SO	Sleepout (ADA)
SO	Slope Occurrence
SO	Slow Operate [*Relay*]
SO	Slow Oxidative [*Fibers*] [*Neuroanatomy*]
SO	Small Oocyte
So	Societa [*A publication*]
SO	Society (ROG)
So	Sojourner [*A publication*]
So	Sokrates [*A publication*]
SO	Sold Out (ADA)
SO	Solicitor's Opinion [*Legal term*] (DLA)
so	Somalia [*MARC country of publication code*] [*Library of Congress*] (LCCP)
SO	Somalia [*ANSI two-letter standard code*] (CNC)
S/O	Son Of [*Genealogy*]
SO	SONARman [*Navy*]
So	Sophia: Studies in Western Civilization and the Cultural Interaction of East and West [*Tokyo*] [*A publication*]
SO	Sorrel Resources Ltd. [*Toronto Stock Exchange symbol*]
SO	Sorting Office [*British*] (ROG)
S/O	Sound Off
So	Soundings [*A publication*]
SO	Source [*Online database field identifier*]
SO	South [*or Southern*]
SO	Southern Airways [*ICAO designator*]
SO	Southern Co. [*NYSE symbol*] (SPSG)
SO	Southern Oscillation [*Meteorology*]
So	Southern Reporter [*National Reporter System*] [*A publication*] (DLA)
SO	Special Olympics [*Later, SOI*] (EA)
SO	Special Operations
SO	Special Orders [*Military*]
SO	Spheno-Occipital [*Synchondrosis*] [*Medicine*]
SO	Spiracular Organ [*Fish anatomy*]
SO	Spring Opening
SO	Staff Officer
SO	Stamp Office [*British*] (ROG)
SO	Standing Order
SO	Station Officer [*British police*]
SO	Stationery Office [*British*]
SO	Statutes of Ontario [*QL Systems Ltd.*] [*Information service or system*] (CRD)
SO	Stay Out [*Official leave from Eton College*] [*British*]
SO	Stock Option [*Investment term*]
SO	Stock Order (AAG)
SO	Stock Outboard [*Powerboat*]
SO	Stockage Objectives [*Military*]
SO	Stop Order (MCD)
SO	Stopover [*Slang*]
SO	Stores Officer [*British military*] (DMA)
SO	Strategic Outline Chart [*Air Force*]
SO	Strikeouts [*Baseball*]
SO	Submarine Oscillator (DEN)
SO	Suboffice
S/O	Substance Of
SO	Superior Oblique [*Muscle*] [*Anatomy*]
SO	Superior Old [*Spirits*]
SO	Supply Officer
SO	Support Operations
SO	Surface Operations [*Navy*] (CAAL)
SO	Surveillance Officer
SO	Switching Oscilloscope
SO	Switchover
SO	Symbolae Osloenses [*A publication*]
SO	Symbolic Output [*Data processing*]
SO	Sympathetic Ophthalmia [*Medicine*]
SO	Symphony Orchestra
SO	System Override (AAG)
SO	Systems Orientation
SO1	SONARman First Class [*Navy*]
SO2	SONARman Second Class [*Navy*]
SO3	SONARman Third Class [*Navy*]
SO4	Science on 4 [*Radio program*] [*British*]
SOA	Safe Operating Area (IEEE)
SOA	Sales Order Authority (AAG)
SOA	Scandinavian Orthopaedic Association (EA)
SOA	School of the Air [*Army*] (TSSD)
SOA	Self-Optimizing and Adaptive
SOA	Senate Operating Agency (MCD)
SOA	Separate Operating Agency [*Air Force*] (AFM)
SOA	Serial Output Adapter
SOA	Shelby Owners of America (EA)
S-OA..........	Ship Operating Automation
SOA	Shipyard Overhaul Availability
SOA	Shuttle Orbital Application [*NASA*]
SOA	Smithsonian Office of Anthropology
SOA	Society of Actuaries (EA)
SOA	Society of Authors [*British*] (EAIO)
SOA	Sonora, TX [*Location identifier*] [*FAA*] (FAAL)
SOA	Sorata Development, Inc. [*Vancouver Stock Exchange symbol*]
SOA	Soundness of Approach (MCD)

SOA .... Source of Assignment (MCD)
SOA .... Southern Airways (MCD)
SOA .... Special Open Allotment [*Military*] (AABC)
SOA .... Special Operating Agency [*Military*] (AABC)
SOA .... Special Operations Aircraft
SOA .... Speed of Advance [*Military*]
SOA .... Speed of Approach
SOA .... Spirit of Adventure (EA)
SOA .... Staff Officer, Administration [*British military*] (DMA)
SOA .... Standardbred Owners Association (EA)
SOA .... Start of Address
SOA .... State of Alert
SOA .... State of the Art
SOA .... Statement of Assurance
SOA .... Stimulus Onset Asynchrony [*Psychology*]
SOA .... Student Orientation Assistant
SOA .... Superoxide Anion [*Chemistry*]
SOA .... Supplement on Aging [*to the 1984 National Health Interview Survey*] [*Department of Health and Human Services*] (GFGA)
SOA .... Switch Off Assembly (MCD)
SOA .... Sydsvenska Ortnamns-Saellskapets Arsskrift [*A publication*]
SOAA .... Signed Out Against Advice [*Medicine*]
SOAA .... Staff Officers Association of America (EA)
SoAB .... South Atlantic Bulletin [*A publication*]
SOAC .... State-of-the-Art Car [*Transit*] [*Department of Transportation*]
SOAC .... Submarine Officer Advanced Course [*Navy*] (DNAB)
SOAD .... Spectrometric Oil Analysis Device
SOAD .... Staff Officer, Air Defence [*British military*] (DMA)
SOAF .... South Atlantic Financial Corp. [*NASDAQ symbol*] (NQ)
SoAF .... Soviet Air Force
SOAF .... Sultanate of Oman Air Force
So Afr .... South Africa
So Africa .... Southern Africa [*A publication*]
So African L ... South African Law Reports [*A publication*]
So African LJ ... South African Law Journal [*A publication*]
So Afr LJ ... South African Law Journal [*A publication*]
So Afr LR... South African Law Reports [*A publication*]
So Afr LT... South African Law Times [*A publication*] (DLA)
So Afr Prize Cas ... South African Prize Cases (Juta) [*A publication*] (DLA)
SoAfrStJ... South African Statistical Journal [*A publication*]
SOAGD ..... Solar Age [*A publication*]
SOAI .... Service des Organisations Aeronautiques Internationales [*France*]
SOAIAG.... Annales Medicinae Militaris Fenniae [*A publication*]
SOAL .... Search Optical Augmentation LASER (MCD)
SOAMB.... Soviet Applied Mechanics [*English Translation*] [*A publication*]
SOA-MCA ... Superficial Occipital Artery to Middle Cerebral Artery [*Medicine*] (MAE)
SOAMUS ... Study of One-Atmosphere Manned Underwater Structures
SoANGr..... Soobscenija Akademiji Nauk Gruzinskoj SSR [*A publication*]
SOAP........ Pioneer Communications Network, Inc. [*Rocky Hill, CT*] [*NASDAQ symbol*] (NQ)
SOAP........ Sarnia Olefins and Aromatics Project [*Canadian ethylene project*]
SOAP........ Self-Optimizing Automatic Pilot
SOAP......... Shaft Optimum Alignment Procedure (DNAB)
SOAP........ Ship Overhaul Assistance Program (MCD)
SOAP........ Simplify Obscure ALGOL [*Algorithmic Language*] Programs (MCD)
SOAP........ Society of Airway Pioneers (EA)
SOAP........ Society for Obstetric Anesthesia and Perinatology (EA)
SOAP........ Society of Office Automation Professionals [*Later, AMS*] [*Telecommunications service*] [*Willow Grove, PA*] (TSSD)
SOAP........ Spectrochemical [*or Spectrographic, Spectrometric, or Spectroscopic*] Oil Analysis Program [*Air Force*]
SOAP........ Standing Order Advance Payment
SOAP........ Students Opposed to Advertised Pollutants [*Student legal action organization*]
SOAP........ Subjective, Objective, Assessment, and Plan [*Medicine*]
SOAP......... Submarine Overhaul Allowance Parts [*Navy*] (DNAB)
SOAP........ Supply Operations Assistance Program [*Military*]
SOAP........ Symbolic Optimum Assembly Programming [*IBM Corp.*] [*Data processing*]
SOAP........ Symptoms, Observations, Assessment, Plan
SOAP........ Systems Operational Analysis Plan
Soap Chem Spec ... Soap and Chemical Specialties [*Later, Soap/Cosmetics/Chemical Specialties*] [*A publication*]
Soap Cosmet ... Soap/Cosmetics/Chemical Specialties [*A publication*]
Soap/Cosmet/Chem Spec ... Soap/Cosmetics/Chemical Specialities [*A publication*]
SOAPD...... Southern Air Procurement District
Soap Perfum Cosmet ... Soap, Perfumery, and Cosmetics [*A publication*]
Soap Prf Cos ... Soap, Perfumery, and Cosmetics [*A publication*]
SOAPS ...... Suction, Oxygen, Apparatus, Pharmaceuticals, Saline [*Mnemonic device for anesthetists*] (AAMN)
Soap & San Chem ... Soap and Sanitary Chemicals [*A publication*]
SOAR .... Safe Operating Area
SOAR .... Save Our American Resources [*Boy Scout project*]
SOAR .... Seminars on Aeroanxiety Relief

SOAR .... Shuttle Orbital Applications and Requirements [*NASA*]
SOAR .... Simulation of Airlift Resources [*Air Force*]
SOAR .... Simulation of Apollo Reliability [*NASA*] (KSC)
SOAR .... Staff Organization and Regulation
SOAR .... State-of-the-Art Report [*Navy*]
SOAR .... State Operator and Result [*Computer program*]
SOAR .... Stress on Analytical Reasoning
SOARS ..... Satellite On-Board Attack Reporting System (MCD)
SOARS ..... Second Order Attitude Reference Set (MCD)
SOARS ..... Shuttle Operations Automated Reporting System [*NASA*] (NASA)
SOAS........ School of Oriental and African Studies [*University of London*]
So AS .... Somersetshire Archaeological and Natural History Society. Proceedings [*Later, Somerset Archaeology and Natural History*] [*A publication*]
SOASC(I) ... Senior Officer Assault Ships and Craft (India) [*British*]
SOase........ Sulfite Oxidase [*An enzyme*]
SOAS JLCR ... School of Oriental and African Studies. Jordan Lectures in Comparative Religion [*A publication*]
So Assn Q .. Southern Association Quarterly [*A publication*]
SOAS ULLOS ... School of Oriental and African Studies. University of London. London. Oriental Series [*A publication*]
So Atlan Bul ... South Atlantic Bulletin [*A publication*]
So Atlan Q ... South Atlantic Quarterly [*A publication*]
So Atl Quar ... South Atlantic Quarterly [*A publication*]
SOATS ...... Support Operations Automated Training System [*NASA*] (NASA)
So Aus Bul ... National Gallery of South Australia. Bulletin [*A publication*]
So Aus LR ... South Australian Law Reports [*A publication*] (APTA)
So Aust LR ... South Australian Law Reports [*A publication*]
So Austr L ... South Australian Law Reports [*A publication*]
So Austr St ... South Australian State Reports [*A publication*]
SOAW .... Sitzungsberichte. Oesterreichische Akademie der Wissenschaften in Wien. Philosophisch-Historische Klasse [*A publication*]
Sob .... De Sobrietate [*of Philo*] (BJA)
SOB .... Second Overtone Band
SOB .... Senate Office Building
SOB .... Service Observance Bureau [*A telephone-monitoring section of the Bell System*]
SOB .... Shipped on Board a Specified Vessel (DS)
SOB .... Shortness of Breath [*Cardiology*]
SOB .... Silly Old Bugger [*Officer over the age of 39*] [*British*] (DSUE)
SOB .... Son of a Bitch
SOB .... Souls on Board [*Aviation slang*] (FAAC)
SOB .... Space Orbital Bomber (AAG)
SOB .... Start of Block
SOB .... Sub-Occipito Bregma [*Medicine*] (ROG)
SOB .... Sudost-Bahn [*Swiss Southeastern Railway*]
SOB .... Sulfur Oxidizing Bacteria
SOB .... Superior Official Bureaucrat [*Satirical bureaucracy term*]
SOB's........ Sons of Bosses International [*An association*] [*Later, NFBC*] (EA)
SOB's......... South of Broad Street [*Reference is to residents of the historic and aristocratic section of Charleston, South Carolina*]
SOBA .... 605th Ordnance Battalion Association (EA)
SOBASSPIFTAGE ... Society of Beer and Sordid Sex Professional Invitational Fishing Tournament and Gastronomical Extravaganza
SOBC......... Save Our Barns Committee (EA)
SOBECOV ... Societe de Stockage et de Commercialisation des Produits Vivriers [*Development organization*] [*Burundi*] (EY)
SOBELAIR ... Societe Belge de Transports Pan Air [*Airline*] [*Belgium*]
SOBEP ...... Scale of Beliefs in Extraordinary Phenomena [*Research test*] [*Psychology*]
SOBIA .... Social Biology [*A publication*]
SOBIGM... Sign Off Brother, I've Got Mine [*Remark used by seamen who avoided risky assignments during World War II*] [*Also used as hoax by National Maritime Union for name of organization issuing pamphlet about low state of merchant marine service*]
So Biv......... Southern Bivouac [*A publication*]
SOBK........ Southern Bankshares, Inc. [*Beckley, WV*] [*NASDAQ symbol*] (NQ)
SOBLIN .... Self-Organizing Binary Logical Network [*OTS*]
SOBND ..... Southbound (WGA)
So Bod .... Sounding Board [*A publication*]
SOBP......... Sentral Organisasi Buruh Pantjasila [*Central Organization of Pantjasila Labor*] [*Indonesia*]
Sobre Deriv Cana Azucar ... Sobre los Derivados de la Cana de Azucar [*Cuba*] [*A publication*]
SOBS......... Scanning Ocean Bottom SONAR
SOBS......... Society for Office-Based Surgery [*Later, ASOS*] (EA)
SOBU .... Student Organization for Black Unity
SOC .... Chief SONARman [*Navy rating*] [*Obsolete*]
SOC .... Saint Olaf College [*Northfield, MN*]
SOC .... Satellite Operations Center [*Cape Kennedy*]
SOC .... Satellite Operations Complex
SOC .... Satellite Orbit Control
SOC .... Scene of Crime
SOC .... Schedule of Organizational Change [*Air Force*] (AFM)

SOC .... Scottish Ornithologists' Club [*British*]
SOC .... Sector Operations Center [*Air Force*]
SOC .... Self-Organized Criticality [*Physics*]
SOC .... Self-Organizing Control
SOC .... Separated Orbit Cyclotron (IEEE)
SOC .... Sequential Oral Contraceptive (HGAA)
SOC .... Service and Overhaul Change (MSA)
SOC .... Servicemen's Opportunity College [*DoD*]
SOC .... Set Overrides Clear (IEEE)
SOC .... Shop Order Control
SO-in-C ..... Signal Officer-in-Chief [*British military*] (DMA)
SOC .... Silicon on Ceramic [*Technique for producing solar cells*]
SOC .... Simulated Operational Computer (KSC)
SOC .... Simulation Operations Center [*NASA*] (KSC)
SOC .... Singer Owners Club (EA)
SOC .... Single Orbit Computation
SOC .... Soap, Perfumery, and Cosmetics [*A publication*]
SOC .... Sochi [*Former USSR*] [*Seismograph station code, US Geological Survey*] (SEIS)
SOC .... Social
SOC .... Socialist (EY)
Soc. .... Societas [*A publication*]
Soc. .... Society [*A publication*]
SOC .... Society
SOC .... Society of Cinematologists [*Later, SCS*] (EA)
SOC .... Sociology
SOC .... Socket (AAG)
SOC .... Socrates [*Greek philosopher, 470-399BC*] (ROG)
SOC .... Solo [*Indonesia*] [*Airport symbol*] (OAG)
SOC .... Somerset County College, Somerville, NJ [*OCLC symbol*] (OCLC)
So C........... South Carolina Reports [*A publication*] (DLA)
SOC .... South Coast Airways [*Nederland, TX*] [*FAA designator*] (FAAC)
SOC .... Southern Oregon College
SOC .... Space Operations Center
SOC .... Space Operations Controller
SOC .... Special Operations Command [*Military*] (AABC)
SOC .... Specialized Oceanographic Center [*National Oceanic and Atmospheric Administration*] (MSC)
SOC .... Specific Optimal Control
SOC .... Spin-Orbit Coupling [*Physical chemistry*]
SOC .... Spouse Observation Checklist
SOC .... Squadron Operations Center [*Air Force*]
SOC .... Standard Occupational Classifications (OICC)
SOC .... Standard Oil Co.
SOC .... Standards of Official Conduct [*A publication*] (DLA)
SOC .... Standing Order Confirmation [*Publishing*]
SOC .... Standing Orders Committee [*British*] (DCTA)
SOC .... Start of Construction [*Military*] (AFIT)
SOC .... Start of Conversion [*Navy*]
SOC .... State of Charge
SoC............ State of Consciousness
SOC .... State-Operated Contracts
SOC .... State-Owned Corporation
SOC .... Statement of Capability (MCD)
SOC .... Statement of Charges
SOC .... Statement of Conditions
SOC .... Station Operations Console (MCD)
SOC .... Strike Operations Coordinator [*Navy*] (NVT)
SOC .... Strike Options Comparison (MCD)
SOC .... Struck off Charge [*British military*] (DMA)
SOC .... Studies in Organic Chemistry [*Elsevier Book Series*] [*A publication*]
SOC .... Sunbeam-Oster [*NYSE symbol*] (SPSG)
SOC .... Superior Oil Co. [*Nevada*] [*NYSE symbol*] [*Delisted*] [*Toronto Stock Exchange symbol*] (SPSG)
SOC .... Superposition of Configuration [*Atomic physics*]
SOC .... Supply Overhaul Coordinator (MCD)
SOC .... Support Operations Center
SOC .... Suspended Organic Carbon [*Chemistry*]
SOC .... Synthetic Organic Chemical
SOC .... System Operational Complex
SOC .... System Operational Concept
SOC .... System Operations Control [*Canadian Airlines International*]
SOC .... System Option Controller [*NASA*] (NASA)
SOC .... Systems Operation Center
SOCA .... Cayenne/Rochambeau [*French Guiana*] [*ICAO location identifier*] (ICLI)
Soc A.......... Sociological Abstracts [*A publication*]
SOCA .... Soul and Calypso [*Music*]
SOCA .... Staff Officer for Civil Affairs [*British*] [*World War II*]
SocAb......... Sociological Abstracts [*A publication*]
SOCABU... Societe du Caoutchouc Butyl [*France*]
Soc Act....... Social Action [*A publication*]
Soc Action & L ... Social Action and the Law [*A publication*] (DLA)
Soc Act & L ... Social Action and the Law [*A publication*]
Soc Actuar Trans ... Society of Actuaries. Transactions [*A publication*]
SOCAD ..... Serviceman's Opportunity for College Associate Degree [*Military*] (MCD)

Soc Adv Electrochem Sci Technol Trans ... Society for the Advancement of Electrochemical Science and Technology. Transactions [*A publication*]
SOCAL...... Southern California [*Military*] (NVT)
SOCAL...... Standard Oil Co. of California
So Cal Bsn ... Southern California Business [*A publication*]
So Calif L Rev ... Southern California Law Review [*A publication*]
So Calif Q .. Southern California Quarterly [*A publication*]
So Calif Quar ... Southern California Quarterly [*A publication*]
So Calif Tax Inst ... University of Southern California School of Law Tax Institute (DLA)
So Cal LR .. Southern California Law Review [*A publication*]
Soc Alp Giulie Comm Grotte Eugenio Boegan Atti Mem ... Societa Alpina delle Giulie. Club Alpino Italiano. Sezione di Trieste. Commissione Grotte "Eugenio Boegan." Atti e Memorie [*A publication*]
SOCALSEC ... Southern California Sector, Western Sea Frontier
Soc Alt .... Social Alternatives [*A publication*]
Soc Altern.. Social Alternatives [*A publication*] (APTA)
Soc Alternatives ... Social Alternatives [*Australia*] [*A publication*]
Soc Am For .... Society of American Foresters. Proceedings [*A publication*]
Soc Anal..... Sociological Analysis [*A publication*]
Soc Anarc... Social Anarchism [*A publication*]
SOCAP...... Society of Consumer Affairs Professionals in Business [*Alexandria, VA*] (EA)
Soc Appl Bacteriol Symp Ser ... Society for Applied Bacteriology. Symposium Series [*A publication*]
Soc Appl Bacteriol Tech Ser ... Society for Applied Bacteriology. Technical Series [*A publication*]
SOCAR...... Shuttle Operational Capability Assessment Report [*NASA*] (MCD)
So Car .... South Carolina Reports [*A publication*] (DLA)
So Ca R ...... South Carolina Review [*A publication*]
SOCAR...... Statement of Condition and Recommendation [*Military*] (AABC)
SOCAR...... Systems Operational Compatibility Assessment Review [*NASA*]
So Car BA Rep ... South Carolina Bar Association Reports [*A publication*] (DLA)
So Car BJ... South Carolina Business Journal [*A publication*]
Soc Arch Hist J ... Society of Architectural Historians. Journal [*A publication*]
Soc Archit Hist J ... Society of Architectural Historians. Journal [*A publication*]
Soc Archtl Historians Jnl ... Society of Architectural Historians. Journal [*A publication*]
Soc of Archtl Historians Newsletter ... Society of Architectural Historians. Newsletter [*A publication*]
Soc of Archtl Historians Newsletter ... Society of Architectural Historians. Newsletter [*A publication*]
So Car Const ... South Carolina Constitutional Reports (Treadway, Mill, or Harper) [*A publication*] (DLA)
Soc Argent Cancerol Bol Trab ... Sociedad Argentina de Cancerologia. Boletines y Trabajos [*A publication*]
Soc Argent Cir Jornadas Quir ... Sociedad Argentina de Cirujanos Jornadas Quirurgicas [*A publication*]
So Car Hist Assoc Proc ... South Carolina Historical Association. Proceedings [*A publication*]
So Car Hist Mag ... South Carolina Historical and Genealogical Magazine [*A publication*]
So Car LJ... South Carolina Law Journal [*Columbia*] [*A publication*] (DLA)
So Car LQ ... South Carolina Law Quarterly [*A publication*]
So Car L Rev ... South Carolina Law Review [*A publication*]
Soc Army Hist Research Jour ... Society for Army Historical Research. Journal [*London*] [*A publication*]
So Car R..... South Carolina Law Reports [*A publication*] (DLA)
Soc Arts J .. Society of Arts. Journal [*A publication*]
SOCAS...... Subcommittee on Chemical Abstracts Service [*American Chemical Society*]
Soc Astron Ital Mem ... Societa Astronomica Italiana. Memorie [*A publication*]
SOCAT...... Student Occupational Competency Achievement Testing [*Educational test*]
SOCATOUR ... Societe Camerounaise de Tourisme (EY)
SOCATS ... Scenario Oriented Corps Area Training System (MCD)
Soc Auto Eng J ... Society of Automotive Engineers. Journal [*A publication*]
SOCB......... Shop Order Control Board
SoCB......... South Central Bulletin [*A publication*]
Soc Behav Pers ... Social Behavior and Personality [*A publication*]
Soc Behav Sci ... Social and Behavioral Sciences [*A publication*]
Soc Beh Per ... Social Behavior and Personality [*A publication*]
Soc Biol...... Social Biology [*A publication*]
Soc Biol Hum Aff ... Social Biology and Human Affairs [*A publication*]
Soc Bras Nematol Publ ... Sociedade Brasileira de Nematologia. Publicacao [*A publication*]
Soc Brotheriana Bol ... Sociedade Brotheriana. Boletim [*A publication*]
SOCC......... Salvage Operational Control Center [*On submarine rescue ship during salvage operation*]
SOCC......... Satellite Oceanic Control Center
SOCC......... Satellite Operations Control Center [*NASA*] (NASA)
SOCC......... Spacecraft Operations Control Center

SOCC......... Special Opportunities Counties and Cities Program [*Tennessee Valley Authority*]
SOCC......... Submarine Operations Control Center [*Navy*] (CAAL)
SOCC......... Subordinate Operations Control Center
Soc Casework ... Social Casework [*A publication*]
SOCCER ... SMART's Own Concordance Constructor, Extremely Rapid [*Cornell University*] [*Data processing*]
Soccer J...... Soccer Journal [*A publication*]
Soccer M.... Soccer Monthly [*A publication*]
Soc Chem Ind J ... Society of Chemical Industry. Journal [*A publication*]
Soc Chem Ind (Lond) Monogr ... Society of Chemical Industry (London). Monograph [*A publication*]
Soc Chem Ind Victoria Proc ... Society of Chemical Industry of Victoria. Proceedings [*A publication*]
Soc Cognit ... Social Cognition [*A publication*]
Soc Comp... Social Compass [*A publication*]
Soc Compass ... Social Compass [*A publication*]
Soc Con ...... Social Concept [*A publication*]
SOCCS ...... Summary of Component Control Status [*Nuclear energy*] (NRCH)
Soc Cubana Historia Nat Mem ... Sociedad Cubana de Historia Natural. Memorias [*A publication*]
SOCD .... Source Control Document (MCD)
SOCD .... Source Control Drawing
Soc Def...... Social Defence [*New Delhi*] [*A publication*]
Soc Dev ...... Social Development [*A publication*]
SOCDS ...... Source Codes (MCD)
Soc Dyers & Col J ... Society of Dyers and Colourists. Journal [*A publication*]
Soc Dyn...... Social Dynamics [*A publication*]
SOCE......... Staff Officer Construction Engineering
Soc Econ .... Social Economist [*A publication*]
Soc Econ Admin ... Social and Economic Administration [*A publication*]
Soc Econ Paleontol Mineral Pac Sect Guideb ... Society of Economic Paleontologists and Mineralogists. Pacific Section. Guidebooks [*A publication*]
Soc Econ Paleontol Mineral Paleontol Monogr ... Society of Economic Paleontologists and Mineralogists. Paleontological Monograph [*A publication*]
Soc Econ Paleontol Mineral Permian Basin Sect Publ ... Society of Economic Paleontologists and Mineralogists. Permian Basin Section. Publication [*A publication*]
Soc Econ Paleontol Mineral Repr Ser ... Society of Economic Paleontologists and Mineralogists. Reprint Series [*A publication*]
Soc Econ Paleontol Mineral Spec Publ ... Society of Economic Paleontologists and Mineralogists. Special Publication [*A publication*]
Soc Econ Paleontologists and Mineralogists Special Pub ... Society of Economic Paleontologists and Mineralogists. Special Publication [*A publication*]
Soc Econ Paleontologists and Mineralogists Spec Pub ... Society of Economic Paleontologists and Mineralogists. Special Publication [*A publication*]
Soc-Econ Plan Sci ... Socio-Economic Planning Sciences [*A publication*]
Soc Econ Rev ... Socialist Economic Review [*A publication*]
Soc Econ Stud ... Social and Economic Studies [*A publication*]
Soc Econ Wetgeving ... Social Economisch Wetgeving. Tijdschrift voor Europees en Economisch Recht [*A publication*] (DLA)
Soc Ed .... Social Education [*A publication*]
Soc of Ed .... Sociology of Education [*A publication*]
Soc Educ ... Social Education [*A publication*]
Soc Ekon Integrace ... Socialisticka Ekonomicka Integrace [*Czechoslovakia*] [*A publication*]
SOCELEX ... Society Against Elephant Exploitation (EA)
Soc Eng (London) J ... Society of Engineers (London). Journal [*A publication*]
Soc Espan Hist Nat Bol Secc Geol ... Sociedad Espanola de Historia Natural. Boletin. Seccion Geologica [*A publication*]
Soc Espanola H N An ... Sociedad Espanola de Historia Natural. Anales [*A publication*]
Soc Exp Biol Semin Ser ... Society for Experimental Biology. Seminar Series [*A publication*]
Soc Explor Geophys Annu Int Meet Abstr ... Society of Exploration Geophysicists. Annual International Meeting. Abstracts [*A publication*]
Soc Exp Stress Anal Pap ... Society for Experimental Stress Analysis. Papers [*A publication*]
SOCF........ Spacecraft Operations and Checkout Facility (AAG)
Soc Fauna Flora Fenn Flora Fenn ... Societas pro Fauna et Flora Fennica. Flora Fennica [*A publication*]
Soc Fauna Flora Fenn Memo ... Societatis pro Fauna et Flora Fennica. Memoranda [*A publication*]
Soc Forces ... Social Forces [*A publication*]
Soc F TV Arts J ... Society of Film and Television Arts. Journal [*A publication*]
Soc Gen Physiol Ser ... Society of General Physiologists. Series [*A publication*]
Soc Geog Fenniae Acta Geog ... Societas Geographica Fenniae. Acta Geographica [*A publication*]
Soc Geog Lima Bol ... Sociedad Geografica de Lima. Boletin [*A publication*]
Soc Geog Mex B ... Sociedad de Geografia y Estadistica de la Republica Mexicana. Boletin [*A publication*]
Soc Geogr Bol (Madrid) ... Sociedad Geografica. Boletin (Madrid) [*A publication*]
Soc Geol Ital Mem ... Societa Geologica Italiana. Memorie [*A publication*]

Soc Geol Mex Bol ... Sociedad Geologica Mexicana. Boletin [*A publication*]
Soc Geol Mexicana Bol ... Sociedad Geologica Mexicana. Boletin [*A publication*]
Soc Geol Peru Bol ... Sociedad Geologica del Peru. Boletin [*A publication*]
Soc Geol Port Bol ... Sociedade Geologica de Portugal. Boletim [*A publication*]
Soc G Italiana B ... Societa Geologica Italiana. Bollettino [*A publication*]
Soc Glass Technology Jour ... Society of Glass Technology. Journal [*A publication*]
Soc G Mex B ... Sociedad Geologica Mexicana. Boletin [*A publication*]
SOCH .... Spacelab Orbiter Common Hardware [*NASA*] (MCD)
SOCHINAFOR ... South China Force [*World War II*]
Soc Hist ..... Social History [*A publication*]
Soc Hist/Hist Soc ... Social History/Histoire Sociale [*A publication*]
So C Hist Mag ... South Carolina Historical Magazine [*A publication*]
Soc Hygiene ... Social Hygiene [*A publication*]
Soci .... [*Marianus*] Socinus [*Authority cited in pre-1607 legal work*] (DSA)
Social Biol ... Social Biology [*A publication*]
Social Case ... Social Casework [*A publication*]
Social Comp ... Social Compass [*A publication*]
Social en Democr ... Socialisme en Democratie [*A publication*]
Social Ec A ... Social and Economic Administration [*A publication*]
Social Econ ... Social and Economic Studies [*A publication*]
Social and Econ Admin ... Social and Economic Administration [*A publication*]
Social & Econ Stud ... Social and Economic Studies [*A publication*]
Social Educ ... Social Education [*A publication*]
Social Forc ... Social Forces [*A publication*]
Social Ind... Social Indicators Research [*A publication*]
Social Indicators Res ... Social Indicators Research [*A publication*]
Socialist Wkr ... Socialist Worker [*A publication*]
Social Pol... Social Policy [*A publication*]
Social Policy Admin ... Social Policy and Administration [*A publication*]
Social Prax ... Social Praxis [*A publication*]
Social Prob ... Social Problems [*A publication*]
Social Psy .. Social Psychiatry [*A publication*]
Social Psychol Q ... Social Psychology Quarterly [*A publication*]
Social Res .. Social Research [*A publication*]
Social Revol ... Socialist Revolution [*A publication*]
Social Sci ... Social Science Quarterly [*A publication*]
Social Scie ... Social Science [*A publication*]
Social Science J (Fort Collins) ... Social Science Journal (Fort Collins) [*A publication*]
Social Science Q ... Social Science Quarterly [*A publication*]
Social Sci Inf ... Social Science Information [*A publication*]
Social Sci Q ... Social Science Quarterly [*A publication*]
SOCIAL SCISEARCH ... Social Science Citation Index Search [*Database*]
Social Sc M ... Social Science and Medicine [*A publication*]
Social Sec... Social Security Bulletin [*US*] [*A publication*]
Social Security Bul ... Social Security Bulletin [*A publication*]
Social Se R ... Social Service Review [*A publication*]
Social Service R ... Social Service Review [*A publication*]
Social Services Abs ... Social Services Abstracts [*A publication*]
Social Services J ... Social Services Journal [*A publication*] (APTA)
Social St S ... Social Studies of Science [*A publication*]
Social Stud ... Social Studies [*A publication*]
Social Theor Pract ... Social Theory and Practice [*A publication*]
Social Trud ... Socialisticeskij Trud [*A publication*]
Social Wk Today ... Social Work Today [*A publication*]
Society........ Society Corp. [*Associated Press abbreviation*] (APAG)
SOCIM...... Society of Connoisseurs in Murder (EA)
Soc Indep Prof Earth Sci Bull ... Society of Independent Professional Earth Scientists. Bulletin [*A publication*]
Soc Indicators Res ... Social Indicators Research [*A publication*]
Soc Indic Res ... Social Indicators Research [*A publication*]
Soc Ind Res ... Social Indicators Research [*A publication*]
Soc Insects ... Social Insects [*A publication*]
Socin Sen ... Marianus Socinus, the Elder [*Deceased, 1467*] [*Authority cited in pre-1607 legal work*] (DSA)
Socio-Econ ... Socio-Economic Planning Sciences [*A publication*]
Socioecon Issues Health ... Socioeconomic Issues of Health [*A publication*]
Socioecon Newsletter ... Socioeconomic Newsletter [*A publication*]
Socio-Econ Planning Sciences ... Socio-Economic Planning Sciences [*A publication*]
Socio-Econ Plann Sci ... Socio-Economic Planning Sciences [*A publication*]
Socioecon Rep ... Socioeconomic Report. California Medical Association [*A publication*]
Sociol .... Sociologus [*Berlin*] [*A publication*]
Sociol .... Sociology [*A publication*]
SOCIOL ...... Sociology
Sociol Abstr ... Sociological Abstracts [*A publication*]
Sociol Anal ... Sociological Analysis [*A publication*]
Sociol Anal Theory ... Sociological Analysis and Theory [*A publication*]
Sociol B ... Sociological Bulletin (New Delhi) [*A publication*]
Sociol B (Bombay) ... Sociological Bulletin (Bombay) [*A publication*]
Sociol Bull ... Sociological Bulletin [*A publication*]
Sociol Cas .. Sociologicky Casopis [*A publication*]
Sociol Contemp ... Sociologie Contemporaine [*A publication*]
Sociol of Ed ... Sociology of Education [*A publication*]
Sociol Educ ... Sociology of Education [*A publication*]

Sociol Educ Abstr ... Sociology of Education Abstracts [*A publication*]
Sociol Focu ... Sociological Focus [*A publication*]
Sociol Fors ... Sociologisk Forskning [*A publication*]
Sociol Gids ... Sociologische Gids [*A publication*]
Sociol Health Illn ... Sociology of Health and Illness [*A publication*]
Sociol Health Illness ... Sociology of Health and Illness [*A publication*]
Socioling Newsl ... Sociolinguistics Newsletter [*A publication*]
Sociol Inq... Sociological Inquiry [*A publication*]
Sociol Inquiry ... Sociological Inquiry [*A publication*]
Sociol Int (Berlin) ... Sociologia Internationalis (Berlin) [*A publication*]
Sociol Issled (Moskva) ... Sociologiceskie Issledovanija (Moskva) [*A publication*]
Sociol Issled (Sverdlovsk) ... Sociologiceskie Issledovanija (Sverdlovsk) [*A publication*]
Sociol Lav .. Sociologia del Lavoro [*A publication*]
Sociol Law ... Sociology of Law [*A publication*]
Sociol Leis Sports Abstr ... Sociology of Leisure and Sport Abstracts [*A publication*]
Sociol Meddel ... Sociologiske Meddelelser [*A publication*]
Sociol Meth ... Sociological Methods and Research [*A publication*]
Sociol Methods & Res ... Sociological Methods and Research [*A publication*]
Sociol Neer ... Sociologia Neerlandica [*A publication*]
Sociological R ... Sociological Review [*A publication*]
Sociol Org ... Sociologia dell'Organizzazione [*A publication*]
Sociol Q ..... Sociological Quarterly [*A publication*]
Sociol Quart ... Sociological Quarterly [*A publication*]
Sociol R...... Sociological Review [*A publication*]
Sociol Rev .. Sociological Review [*A publication*]
Sociol Rev Monogr ... Sociological Review. Monograph [*A publication*]
Sociol R Mg ... Sociological Review. Monograph [*A publication*]
Sociol R NS ... Sociological Review. New Series [*A publication*]
Sociol Rur .. Sociologia Ruralis [*A publication*]
Sociol Ruralis ... Sociologia Ruralis [*A publication*]
Sociol Rural Life Minn Univ Agric Ext Serv ... Sociology of Rural Life. Minnesota University. Agricultural Extension Service [*A publication*]
Sociol Sela ... Sociologija Sela [*A publication*]
Sociol et Soc ... Sociologie et Societes [*A publication*]
Sociol Soc... Sociology and Social Research [*A publication*]
Sociol Soci ... Sociologie et Societes [*A publication*]
Sociol & Social Res ... Sociology and Social Research [*A publication*]
Sociol & Soc Res ... Sociology and Social Research [*A publication*]
Sociol Symp ... Sociological Symposium [*A publication*]
Sociol Theory ... Sociological Theory [*A publication*]
Sociol Trav ... Sociologie du Travail [*A publication*]
Sociol Wk Occupat ... Sociology of Work and Occupations [*A publication*]
Sociol W Oc ... Sociology of Work and Occupations [*A publication*]
Sociol Work Occ ... Sociology of Work and Occupations [*A publication*]
Sociol Yb Relig Britain ... Sociological Yearbook of Religion in Britain [*A publication*]
Sociom .... Sociometry [*A publication*]
Socio Meth ... Sociological Methodology [*A publication*]
Socio R...... Sociological Review [*A publication*]
Socio-Tech B ... Social-Technological Bulletin [*Quezon City*] [*A publication*]
Soc Isl .... Society Islands
SO Cist ...... Sacer Ordo Cisterciensis [*Order of Cistercians*] [*Roman Catholic men's religious order*]
Soc Italiana Sc Nat Milano Atti ... Societa Italiana di Scienze Naturali in Milano. Atti [*A publication*]
Soc Ital Sci Farm Doc ... Societa Italiana di Scienze Farmaceutiche Documento [*A publication*]
Soc Ital Sci Nat Mus Civ Stor Nat Milano Atti ... Societa Italiana di Scienze Naturali e Museo Civico di Storia Naturale di Milano. Atti [*A publication*]
Soc J.......... Soccer Journal [*A publication*]
Soc Jus R ... Social Justice Review [*A publication*]
SocJust ...... Social Justice Review [*A publication*]
Socker Handli ... Socker Handlingar [*A publication*]
SOCL......... Social
Soc Lab Bull ... Social and Labour Bulletin [*A publication*] (ILCA)
Soc Labour Bull ... Social and Labour Bulletin [*A publication*]
SOCLD...... Solar Cells [*A publication*]
Soc and Leisure ... Society and Leisure [*A publication*]
SOCLGY ... Sociology
Soc Ligustica Sc Nat Geog Atti ... Societa Ligustica di Scienze Naturali e Geografiche. Atti [*A publication*]
SOCM .... Master Chief SONARman [*Navy rating*]
SOCM .... Shanley Oil Co. [*NASDAQ symbol*] (NQ)
SOCM .... Standoff Cluster Munitions
SOCMA .... Scottish Operative Coach Makers' Association [*A union*]
SOCMA .... Synthetic Organic Chemical Manufacturers Association (EA)
Soc Maandbl Arb ... Sociaal Maandblad Arbeid [*A publication*]
SOCMAC ... Socially-Oriented Comprehensive Memory-Assist Computer (IIA)
Soc Malawi J ... Society of Malawi. Journal [*A publication*]
Soc Manuf Eng Tech Pap Ser AD ... Society of Manufacturing Engineers. Technical Paper. Series AD (Assembly Division) [*A publication*]
Soc Manuf Eng Tech Pap Ser EE ... Society of Manufacturing Engineers. Technical Paper. Series EE (Electrical Engineering) [*A publication*]

Soc Manuf Eng Tech Pap Ser EM ... Society of Manufacturing Engineers. Technical Paper. Series EM (Engineering Materials) [*A publication*]
Soc Manuf Eng Tech Pap Ser FC ... Society of Manufacturing Engineers. Technical Paper. Series FC (Finishing and Coating) [*A publication*]
Soc Manuf Eng Tech Pap Ser IQ ... Society of Manufacturing Engineers. Technical Paper. Series IQ (Inspection and Quality) [*A publication*]
Soc Manuf Eng Tech Pap Ser MF ... Society of Manufacturing Engineers. Technical Paper. Series MF (Material Forming) [*A publication*]
Soc Manuf Eng Tech Pap Ser MR ... Society of Manufacturing Engineers. Technical Paper. Series MR (Material Removal) [*A publication*]
Soc Manuf Eng Tech Pap Ser MS ... Society of Manufacturing Engineers. Technical Paper. Series MS [*A publication*]
Soc Mass Media Resour Technol J ... Society for Mass Media and Resource Technology. Journal [*A publication*] (APTA)
SOCMC..... Special Order of the Commandant of the Marine Corps
Soc Mean Leg Con ... Social Meaning of Legal Concepts [*A publication*] (ILCA)
Soc Med Tidskr ... Social-Medicinsk Tidskrift [*A publication*]
Soc Meth.... Sociological Methodology [*A publication*]
Soc Mex Geog Estadistica B ... Sociedad Mexicana de Geografia y Estadistica. Boletin [*A publication*]
Soc Mexicana Geografia y Estadistica Bol ... Sociedad Mexicana de Geografia y Estadistica. Boletin [*A publication*]
SOCMI...... Synthetic Organic Chemical Manufacturing Industry [*Environmental Protection Agency*]
Soc Min Eng AIME Trans ... Society of Mining Engineers of AIME [*American Institute of Mining, Metallurgical, and Petroleum Engineers*]. Transactions [*A publication*]
Soc Mining Engineers AIME Trans ... Society of Mining Engineers of AIME [*American Institute of Mining, Metallurgical, and Petroleum Engineers*]. Transactions [*A publication*]
SocN .... Sociolinguistics Newsletter [*A publication*]
SOCN .... Source Control Number
Soc Nat Resour ... Society and Natural Resources [*A publication*]
Soc Nav Architects Mar Eng Tech Res Bull ... Society of Naval Architects and Marine Engineers. Technical and Research Bulletin [*New York*] [*A publication*]
Soc Nav Architects Mar Eng Trans ... Society of Naval Architects and Marine Engineers of New York. Transactions [*A publication*]
Soc Nav Archit Mar Eng Trans ... Society of Naval Architects and Marine Engineers. Transactions [*United States*] [*A publication*]
Soc Nematol Spec Publ ... Society of Nematologists. Special Publication [*A publication*]
Soc Neurosci Abstr ... Society for Neuroscience. Abstracts [*A publication*]
Soc Neurosci Symp ... Society for Neuroscience. Symposia [*A publication*]
Soc Nucl Med Southeast Chapter Contin Educ Lect ... Society of Nuclear Medicine. Southeastern Chapter. Continuing Education Lectures [*A publication*]
Soc Num Mexico Bol ... Sociedad Numismatica de Mexico. Boletin [*A publication*]
Soc Nurs Hist Gaz ... Society for Nursing History. Gazette [*A publication*]
SOCO .... Scenes-of-the-Crime Officer [*Scotland Yard*]
SOCO .... Standard Oil Co. of California
SOCO .... Summit Oilfield Corp. [*NASDAQ symbol*] (NQ)
SOCO .... Switched out for Checkout [*NASA*] (KSC)
Soc Occup Medicine J ... Society of Occupational Medicine. Journal [*A publication*]
SOCOEE..... Social Cognition [*A publication*]
SOCOM .... Society and Commerce Publications
SOCOM .... Solar Communications
SOCOM .... Southern Command (MCD)
SOCOM .... Special Operations Command [*Military*]
SOCONY .. Standard Oil Co. of New York [*Socony Mobil is now official name of firm*]
SOCORICO ... Society of Costa Rica Collectors (EA)
SOCPAC ... Special Operations Center, Pacific Command (CINC)
Soc Paleontol Ital Boll ... Societa Paleontologica Italiana. Bollettino [*A publication*]
Soc Perspect ... Social Perspectives [*A publication*]
Soc Pet E J ... Society of Petroleum Engineers. American Institute of Mining, Metallurgical, and Petroleum Engineers. Journal [*A publication*]
Soc Pet Eng AIME Improv Oil Recovery Field Rep ... Society of Petroleum Engineers. American Institute of Mining, Metallurgical, and Petroleum Engineers. Improved Oil Recovery Field Reports [*A publication*]
Soc Pet Eng AIME J ... Society of Petroleum Engineers. American Institute of Mining, Metallurgical, and Petroleum Engineers. Journal [*A publication*]
Soc Pet Eng AIME Pap ... Society of Petroleum Engineers. American Institute of Mining, Metallurgical, and Petroleum Engineers. Papers [*A publication*]
Soc Pet Eng AIME Trans ... Society of Petroleum Engineers. American Institute of Mining, Metallurgical, and Petroleum Engineers. Transactions [*A publication*]

Soc Pet Eng J ... Society of Petroleum Engineers. American Institute of Mining, Metallurgical, and Petroleum Engineers. Journal [A publication]

Soc Pet Engr J ... Society of Petroleum Engineers. American Institute of Mining, Metallurgical, and Petroleum Engineers. Journal [A publication]

Soc Pet Engrs J ... Society of Petroleum Engineers. American Institute of Mining, Metallurgical, and Petroleum Engineers. Journal [A publication]

Soc Petrol Eng J ... Society of Petroleum Engineers. American Institute of Mining, Metallurgical, and Petroleum Engineers. Journal [A publication]

Soc Petrol Eng Trans ... Society of Petroleum Engineers. American Institute of Mining, Metallurgical, and Petroleum Engineers. Transactions [A publication]

Soc Petroleum Engineers AIME Trans ... Society of Petroleum Engineers. American Institute of Mining, Metallurgical, and Petroleum Engineers. Transactions [A publication]

Soc Petroleum Engineers Jour ... Society of Petroleum Engineers. American Institute of Mining, Metallurgical, and Petroleum Engineers. Journal [A publication]

Soc Petroleum Engrs Jol ... Society of Petroleum Engineers. Journal [A publication]

Soc Phot Instr Eng Newsletter ... Society of Photographic Instrumentation Engineers. Newsletter [A publication]

Soc Photo-Opt Instrum Eng Proc ... Society of Photo-Optical Instrumentation Engineers. Proceedings [United States] [A publication]

Soc Plan Policy Dev Abstr ... Social Planning, Policy, and Development Abstracts [A publication]

Soc Plant Prot North Jpn Spec Rep ... Society of Plant Protection of North Japan. Special Report [A publication]

Soc Plast Eng Div Tech Conf Tech Pap ... Society of Plastics Engineers. Divisional Technical Conference. Technical Papers [A publication]

Soc Plast Ind Struct Foam Conf Proc ... Society of the Plastics Industry. Structural Foam Conference. Proceedings [A publication]

SOCPO...... Society of Chief Personnel Officers [British]

Soc Pol .... Social Policy [A publication]

Soc Policy .. Social Policy [A publication]

Soc Pr......... Social Progress [A publication]

Soc Prax ...... Social Praxis [A publication]

Soc Prob..... Social Problems [A publication]

Soc Probl.... Social Problems [A publication]

Soc Promotion Agr Sc Pr ... Society for the Promotion of Agricultural Science. Proceedings of the Annual Meeting [A publication]

Soc Psichol Filos ... Social'naja Psichologija i Filosofija [A publication]

Soc Psychiatry ... Social Psychiatry [A publication]

Soc Psychol ... Social Psychology [A publication]

Soc Psychol Q ... Social Psychology Quarterly [A publication]

Soc Psych Q ... Social Psychology Quarterly [A publication]

Soc Psych Res Proc ... Society for Psychical Research. Proceedings [A publication]

SOCQ .... Stages of Concern Questionnaire [Educational test]

SOCR......... Scan-Optics, Inc. [NASDAQ symbol]　(NQ)

Soc R .... Social Research [A publication]

Soc R .... Socialist Review [A publication]

Soc R .... Sociological Review [A publication]

SoCR......... South Carolina Review [A publication]

SOCR........ Special Operational Contract Requirements　(AAG)

SOCR........ Sustained Operations Control Room [NASA]　(KSC)

SOCR........ Synchronous Orbit Communication Relay　(MCD)

Soc Radiol Prot J ... Society for Radiological Protection. Journal [A publication]

SOCRATES ... Service Order, Customer Records, and Terminal Entry System

SOCRATES ... System for Organizing Content to Review and Teach Educational Subjects

SOCRATES ... System for Organizing Current Reports to Aid Technology and Science

SOCRED... Social Credit Party [British]

SOCREDO ... Societe pour le Credit et le Developpement en Oceanie [Commercial bank] [French Polynesia]　(EY)

Soc Regis.... Socialist Register [A publication]

Soc Rehabil Rec ... Social and Rehabilitation Record [A publication]

Soc Res....... Social Research [A publication]

Soc Res....... Social Reserve [A publication]

Soc Res Child Devel Monogr ... Society for Research in Child Development. Monographs [A publication]

Soc Research Administrators J ... Journal. Society of Research Administrators [A publication]

Soc Resp .... Social Responsibility [A publication]

Soc Rev ...... Socialist Review [A publication]

Soc Revol .... Socialist Revolution [A publication]

Soc R di Nap Accad di Archeol Atti ... Societa Reale di Napoli. Accademia di Archeologia, Lettere, e Belle Arti. Atti [A publication]

Soc R di Nap Accad di Sci Mor e Pol Atti ... Societa Reale di Napoli. Accademia di Scienze Morali e Politiche. Atti [A publication]

Soc R di Napoli Accad di Archeol Atti ... Societa Reale di Napoli. Accademia di Archeologia, Lettere, e Belle Arti. Atti [A publication]

Soc R di Napoli Accad d Sci Fis e Mat Atti ... Societa Reale di Napoli. Accademia delle Scienze, Fisiche, e Matematiche. Atti [A publication]

SOC ROS.. Societas Rosicruciana [Freemasonry]

SOCS......... Satellite Operations Control System

SOCS......... School of Corresponding Studies [Military]　(INF)

SOCS......... Senior Chief SONARman [Navy rating]

SOCS......... Society for Savings Bancorp, Inc. [NASDAQ symbol]　(NQ)

SOCS......... Spacecraft-Orientation-Control System

SOCS......... Subsystem Operating and Checkout System [NASA]　(MCD)

SOCS......... Survey of Clerical Skills　(AEBS)

Soc Sci....... Social Sciences [A publication]

Soc Sci Citation Index ... Social Science Citation Index [A publication]

Soc Scientist ... Social Scientist [A publication]

Soc Sci Fenn Arsb-Vuosik ... Societas Scientiarum Fennicae. Arsbok-Vuosikirja [A publication]

Soc Sci Fenn Commentat Biol ... Societas Scientiarum Fennica. Commentationes Biologicae [A publication]

Soc Sci Fenn Commentat Phys-Math ... Societas Scientiarum Fennica. Commentationes Physico-Mathematicae [A publication]

Soc Sci Fenn Comment Phys-Math ... Societas Scientiarum Fennica. Commentationes Physico-Mathematicae [A publication]

Soc Sci Fennica Arsb ... Societas Scientiarum Fennica. Arsbok [A publication]

Soc Sci Fennica Commentationes Phys-Math ... Societas Scientiarum Fennica. Commentationes Physico-Mathematicae [A publication]

Soc Sci Humanit Index ... Social Sciences and Humanities Index [A publication]

Soc Sci Ind ... Social Sciences Index [A publication]

Soc Sci Index ... Social Sciences Index [A publication]

Soc Sci Inf ... Social Science Information [A publication]

Soc Sci Inform ... Social Science Information [A publication]

Soc Sci Inf Stud ... Social Science Information Studies [A publication]

Soc Sci J .... Social Science Journal [A publication]

Soc Sci Lodz Acta Chim ... Societatis Scientiarum Lodziensis. Acta Chimica [A publication]

Soc Sci Med ... Social Science and Medicine [A publication]

Soc Sci Med A ... Social Science and Medicine. Part A. Medical Sociology [A publication]

Soc Sci Med B ... Social Science and Medicine. Part B. Medical Anthropology [A publication]

Soc Sci Med C ... Social Science and Medicine. Part C. Medical Economics [A publication]

Soc Sci Med D ... Social Science and Medicine. Part D. Medical Geography [A publication]

Soc Sci Medic ... Social Science and Medicine [A publication]

Soc Sci Med (Med Anthropol) ... Social Science and Medicine (Medical Anthropology) [A publication]

Soc Sci Med Med Econ ... Social Science and Medicine. Part C. Medical Economics [A publication]

Soc Sci Med (Med Geogr) ... Social Science and Medicine (Medical Geography) [A publication]

Soc Sci Med (Med Psychol Med Sociol) ... Social Science and Medicine (Medical Psychology and Medical Sociology) [A publication]

Soc Sci & Med Part A Med Psychol & Med Sociol ... Social Science and Medicine. Part A. Medical Psychology and Medical Sociology [A publication]

Soc Sci & Med Part A Med Sociol ... Social Science and Medicine. Part A. Medical Sociology [A publication]

Soc Sci & Med Part B Med Anthropol ... Social Science and Medicine. Part B. Medical Anthropology [A publication]

Soc Sci & Med Part C Med Econ ... Social Science and Medicine. Part C. Medical Economics [A publication]

Soc Sci & Med Part D Med Geogr ... Social Science and Medicine. Part D. Medical Geography [A publication]

Soc Sci & Med Part E Med Psychol ... Social Science and Medicine. Part E. Medical Psychology [A publication]

Soc Sci & Med Part F Med & Soc Ethics ... Social Science and Medicine. Part F. Medical and Social Ethics [A publication]

Soc Sci Micro Rev ... Social Science Micro Review [A publication]

Soc Sci Monographs ... Social Science Monographs [A publication]　(APTA)

Soc Sci NL ... Social Science Newsletter [A publication]

Soc Sci Q.... Social Science Quarterly [A publication]

Soc Sci R.... Social Science Review [Bangkok] [A publication]

Soc Sci Res ... Social Science Research [A publication]

Soc Sci Res Council Bull ... Social Science Research Council. Bulletin [A publication]

Soc Sci (Winfield) ... Social Science (Winfield) [A publication]

Soc & Scl Res ... Sociology and Social Research [A publication]

SOCSE ...... Special Operations Communications Elements [Military]　(GFGA)

Soc Sec Bull ... Social Security Bulletin [US] [A publication]

Soc Sec J ... Social Security Journal [A publication]

Soc Sec Q... Social Security Quarterly [A publication]

Soc Sec Rep ... Social Security Reporter [A publication]　(APTA)

Soc Secur Bull ... Social Security Bulletin [A publication]

Soc Secur Bull Annu Stat Suppl ... Social Security Bulletin. Annual Statistical Supplement [US] [A publication]

Soc Ser Rev ... Social Service Review [A publication]

Soc Serv ..... Social Service [A publication]　(APTA)

Soc Services Rev ... Social Services Review [A publication]

Soc Serv J .. Social Services Journal [*A publication*] (APTA)
Soc Serv Q ... Social Service Quarterly [*A publication*]
Soc Serv R ... Social Service Review [*A publication*]
Soc Serv Rev ... Social Service Review [*A publication*]
Soc Soc Hist Med Bull ... Society for the Social History of Medicine. Bulletin [*A publication*]
Soc Soc Res ... Sociology and Social Research [*A publication*]
Soc Sport J ... Sociology of Sport Journal [*A publication*]
Soc St .... Social Studies [*A publication*]
Soc Stud ..... Social Studies [*A publication*]
Soc Studies ... Social Studies [*A publication*]
Soc Stud Sci ... Social Studies of Science [*United Kingdom*] [*A publication*]
Soc Study Amphib Reptiles Herpetol Circ ... Society for the Study of Amphibians and Reptiles. Herpetological Circular [*A publication*]
Soc Study Inborn Errors Metab Proc Symp ... Society for the Study of Inborn Errors of Metabolism. Proceedings of the Symposium [*A publication*]
Soc Sur .... Social Survey [*A publication*] (APTA)
Soc Surv ..... Social Survey [*A publication*] (APTA)
Soc Survey ... Social Survey [*A publication*] (APTA)
SOCTAP ... Sulfur Oxide Control Technology Assessment Panel [*Federal interagency committee*]
Soc Theory ... Sociological Theory [*A publication*]
Soc Theory & Pract ... Social Theory and Practice [*A publication*]
Soc Thought ... Social Thought [*A publication*]
Soc Thr ...... Socialist Theory and Practice [*A publication*]
Soc Toscana Sci Nat Atti Mem Ser A ... Societa Toscana di Scienze Naturali. Atti. Memorie. Serie A [*A publication*]
Soc Tr......... Socialisticeskij Trud [*A publication*]
Soc Trav..... Sociologie du Travail [*A publication*]
Soc Travail ... Sociologie du Travail [*A publication*]
Soc Trends ... Social Trends [*A publication*]
Soc Tss....... Social Tidsskrift [*A publication*]
Soc Vac Coaters Proc Annu Conf ... Society of Vacuum Coaters. Proceedings. Annual Conference [*A publication*]
Soc Venez Cienc Nat Bol ... Sociedad Venezolana de Ciencias Naturales. Boletin [*A publication*]
Soc Venezolana Ciencias Natur Bol ... Sociedad Venezolana de Ciencias Naturales. Boletin [*A publication*]
Soc Ven Sci Nat Lav ... Societa Veneziana di Scienze Naturali Lavori [*A publication*]
Soc W .... Social Work [*A publication*]
Soc Welfare ... Social Welfare [*A publication*]
Soc Welf Soc Plan Policy Soc Dev ... Social Welfare. Social Planning/Policy and Social Development [*A publication*]
Soc Wetensch ... Sociale Wetenschappen [*A publication*]
Soc Wk (Albany) ... Social Work (Albany) [*A publication*]
Soc Work ... Social Work [*A publication*]
Soc Work Health Care ... Social Work in Health Care [*A publication*]
Soc Work Lect ... Social Work Lectures [*New Zealand*] [*A publication*]
Soc Workr ... Socialist Worker [*A publication*]
Soc Work Res Abstr ... Social Work Research and Abstracts [*A publication*]
Soc Work Today ... Social Work Today [*A publication*]
SOCY........ Society (ROG)
SOCY........ Sociology (ROG)
SOCYA...... Society [*A publication*]
Soc Zemed ... Socialisticke Zemedelstvi [*A publication*]
Soc Zemes Ukis ... Socialistinis Zemes Ukis [*A publication*]
Soc Zemjod ... Socijalisticko Zemjodelstvo [*A publication*]
SOD.......... Sediment Oxygen Demand [*of water bodies*]
SOD.......... Sell-Off Date (AAG)
SOD.......... Seller's Option to Double [*Stock exchange term*]
SOD.......... Serial Output Data [*Data processing*]
SOD.......... Shorter Oxford Dictionary [*A publication*]
SOD.......... Shuttle Operational Data (MCD)
SOD.......... Small Object Detector
SOD.......... Socialisme en Democratie [*A publication*]
SOD.......... Society of Dismas (EA)
SOD......... Sodalite [*A zeolite*]
SOD.......... Sodankyla [*Finland*] [*Seismograph station code, US Geological Survey*] (SEIS)
SOD.......... Sodankyla [*Finland*] [*Geomagnetic observatory code*]
SOD......... Sodium (DHSM)
Sod .... Sodobnost [*A publication*]
SOD.......... Sodomy [*FBI standardized term*]
SOD.......... Soldier Orientation and Development (MCD)
SOD.......... Solitron Devices, Inc. [*NYSE symbol*] (SPSG)
SOD.......... Sons of the Desert (EA)
SOD.......... Sound-on-Disk (DEN)
SOD.......... Space Operation Directorate (SSD)
SOD.......... Special Operations Detachment [*Military*] (AABC)
SOD.......... Special Operations Division [*Office of Preparedness, General Services Administration*]
SOD.......... Special Order Discharge
SOD.......... Staff Operations Division [*NASA*] (MCD)
SOD.......... Superintendent of Documents [*US Government Printing Office*]
SOD.......... Superoxide Dismutase [*Also, SODI*] [*An enzyme*]
SOD.......... Surgical Operations Database [*Medicine*]
SOD.......... Sustained Operational Date (AFM)

SOD.......... Systems Operational Description [*or Design*]
So 2d .... Southern Reporter, Second Series [*A publication*] (DLA)
SODA .... A & W Brands, Inc. [*NASDAQ symbol*] (NQ)
SODA .... Source Oriented Data Acquisition
SODA .... Stamp Out Drug Addiction
SODA .... System Optimization and Design Algorithm (HGAA)
SODAA ..... Solnechnye Dannye [*A publication*]
SODAC ..... Source Data Collection
So Dak B Jo ... South Dakota Bar Journal [*A publication*] (DLA)
So Dak Hist ... South Dakota History [*A publication*]
So Dak Hist Coll ... South Dakota Historical Collections [*A publication*]
So Dak L Rev ... South Dakota Law Review [*A publication*]
So Dakota Lib Bul ... South Dakota Library Bulletin [*A publication*]
So Dak R.... South Dakota Review [*A publication*]
SODAR...... Sound Detecting and Ranging
SODAS...... Sandia Optical Disk Archival System [*Online map database*] [*Developed by Sandia National Laboratories for the USGS*]
SODAS...... Structure-Oriented Description and Simulation (IEEE)
SODAS...... Synoptic Oceanographic Data Acquisition System [*Marine science*] (MSC)
SODB .... Science Organization Development Board [*National Academy of Sciences*]
SODB .... Shuttle [*or Spacecraft*] Operational Data Book [*NASA*]
SODB .... Sodbury [*England*]
SODB .... Start of Data Block (MCD)
sod bicarb... Sodium Bicarbonate [*Inorganic chemistry*] (MAE)
SODC .... Siblings of Disabled Children (EA)
SODDS...... Submarine Oceanographic Digital Data System [*Navy*] (DNAB)
Sodep .... Social Democratic Party [*Turkey*] [*Political party*] (PPW)
SODEPALM ... Societe pour le Developpement et l'Exploitation du Palmier a Huile [*Ivory Coast*]
SODEPAX ... Committee on Society, Development, and Peace [*of the Roman Catholic Church and the World Council of Churches*] [*Defunct*] (EA)
SODEX...... Social Data Exchange Association [*Council for Community Services*] [*Information service or system*] (IID)
SODI .... Superoxide Dismutase [*Absorbed by SOD*] [*An enzyme*]
SODITAL ... Societe de Developpement de l'Industrie Touristique en Algerie (EY)
SODPAL... Social Democrat Party and Liberal [*British*]
SODRE...... Servicio Oficial de Difusion Radio Electrica [*Radio and television network*] [*Uruguay*]
SODRS...... Synchronous Orbit Data Relay Satellite
SODS........ Saturn Operational Display System [*NASA*]
SODS........ Shuttle Operational Data System [*NASA*] (MCD)
SODS........ Skylab Orbit-Deorbit System [*NASA*] (MCD)
SODS........ Subordinate Operations Data System (NVT)
SODT .... Scope Octal Debugging Tape
SODTICIOAP ... Special Ordnance Depot Tool Identification, Classification, Inventory, and Obsolescence Analysis Program [*Popularly called "Soda Cap"*]
SODU........ Screen Oriented Disk Utility [*Data processing*]
SOE .... Senior Officer Escort [*British military*] (DMA)
SOE .... Sequence of Events
SOE .... Short of Exchange [*Economics*]
SOE .... Significant Operating Experience (IEEE)
SOE .... Silver Oxide Electrode
SOE .... Skylab Operational Environment [*NASA*]
SOE .... Slater Orbital Exponents [*Atomic physics*]
SOE .... Socio-Economic Planning Sciences [*A publication*]
SOE .... Soft Drinks Trade Journal [*A publication*]
SOE .... Souanke [*Congo*] [*Airport symbol*] (OAG)
SOE .... Special Operations Executive [*British research unit corresponding to OSS*] [*World War II*]
SOE .... Stage Operations Engineer
SOE .... Start of Entry [*Data processing*]
SOE .... State-Owned Enterprise
SOE .... Status of Equipment [*Army*] (AABC)
SOE .... Summary of Engagements (MCD)
SOE .... Super Orbit Entry
SOEAP...... Summary of Effective Allowance Parts List [*Navy*]
SOEAPL... Summary of Effective Allowance Parts List [*Navy*] (DNAB)
SOEASTPAC ... Southeast Pacific Command [*Navy*]
So East Rep ... Southeastern Reporter [*A publication*] (DLA)
SOEBT...... Stationery and Office Equipment Board of Trade (EA)
SOEC...... Statistical Office of the European Communities (DCTA)
SOECA...... Soviet Electrochemistry [*English Translation*] [*A publication*]
So Econ J ... Southern Economic Journal [*A publication*]
SOED .... Shorter Oxford English Dictionary [*A publication*]
SOED .... Southern Educators Life Insurance Co. [*NASDAQ symbol*] (NQ)
So Educ Report ... Southern Education Report [*A publication*]
SOEEA...... Soviet Electrical Engineering [*English Translation*] [*A publication*]
SOEH........ Society for Occupational and Environmental Health (EA)
SOEMC..... Senior Officer Executive Management Course [*Naval War College*]
SOEMD ... Solar Energy Materials [*A publication*]
SOEND ..... Solar Engineering [*A publication*]

SOEP........ Solar-Oriented Experimental Package [*NASA*]
SOER........ Significant Operating Event Report   (IEEE)
SOERO ..... Small Orbiting Earth Resources Observatory   (IEEE)
SOES .... Special Operations Evaluation System   (DNAB)
SOES........ Station Operations and Engineering Squadron [*Marine Corps*]
SOE/SO .... Special Operations Executive, Special Operations [*British*]
            [*World War II*]
So Expose .. Southern Exposure [*A publication*]
SOF........... Safety of Flight [*NASA*]   (NASA)
SoF............ Samtid och Framtid [*A publication*]
SOF........... Satisfactory Operation Factor [*Telecommunications*]   (TEL)
SOF........... Secretary's Open Forum   (EA)
SOF........... Shortest Operation First
SOF........... Single Oriental Female [*Classified advertising*]
Sof............ Soferim   (BJA)
SOF........... Sofia [*Bulgaria*] [*Seismograph station code, US Geological
            Survey*]   (SEIS)
SOF........... Sofia [*Bulgaria*] [*Airport symbol*]   (OAG)
SOF........... Soldier of Fortune [*A publication*]
SOF........... Soluble Organic Fraction [*Environmental chemistry*]
SOF........... Sound on Film
SOF........... Special Operations Force [*Military*]
SOF........... Spillover Factor
SOF........... Spreading Ocean Floor
SOFAT........ Start-of-Format Control [*Data processing*]
SOF........... Start of Frame
SOF........... Status of Forces
SOF........... Storage Oscilloscope Fragments
SOF........... Strategic Offensive Forces [*Army*]   (AABC)
SOF........... Sub-Occipito Frontal [*Medicine*]   (ROG)
SOF........... Suedost-Forschungen [*A publication*]
SOF........... Superior Orbital Fissure [*Eye anatomy*]
SOF........... Supervisor of Flying   (MCD)
SOFA........ Bench Craft, Inc. [*NASDAQ symbol*]   (NQ)
SOFA........ Status of Forces Agreement [*International treaty*]
SOFA........ Student Overseas Flights for Americans
SOFAR ..... Sound Fixing and Ranging [*Navy underground sound system*]
SOFAR ..... Sound Fusing and Ranging
SOFAR/BF ... Sound Fixing and Ranging/Bomb Fuze [*Navy underground
            sound system*]   (SAA)
SOFAS ..... Suitable Occupation for a Sloane [*British*] [*Slang*]
SOFAS ..... Survivable Optical Forward Acquisition Sensor
SOFAS ..... Survivable Optical Forward Acquisition System   (MCD)
SOF ATS... Special Operations Force Aircrew Training System [*Military*]
SOFC........ Saturn Operational Flight Control [*NASA*]
SOFC........ Solid Electrolyte Fuel Cell [*Chemistry*]
SOFC........ Solid Oxide Fuel Cell [*Energy source*]
SOFCS ..... Self-Organizing Flight Control System
SofD........... Sons of David   (BJA)
SOFE........ Society of Financial Examiners   (EA)
SOFEX...... Southern Ocean Float Experiment [*Marine science*]   (MSC)
S/OFF ...... Sign Off [*Data processing*]   (MDG)
SOFFEX.... Swiss Options and Financial Futures Exchange
SOFI......... Spray-On Foam Insulation   (NASA)
SOFIA ...... Stratospheric Observatory for Infrared Astronomy [*NASA*]
Sofia Univ Geol-Geogr Fak God Kn 2 Geogr ... Sofia Universitet. Geologo-
            Geografski Fakultet. Godishnik. Kniga 2. Geografiya [*A
            publication*]
Sofia Univ Geol-Geogr Fak God Kniga 1 Geol ... Sofia Universitet. Geologo-
            Geografski Fakultet. Godishnik. Kniga 1. Geologiya [*A
            publication*]
Sofia Vissh Minno Geol Inst God ... Sofia Vissh Minno-Geolozhki Institut.
            Godishnik [*A publication*]
SOFIE .... Sources de Financement des Entreprises [*CCMC Informatique
            de Gestion*] [*Database*]
SOFIX ...... Software Fix [*NASA*]
So Fla BJ ... South Florida Business Journal [*A publication*]
SOFLAM .. Special Operations Force LASER Marker [*Military*]   (RDA)
SOFMA..... Soviet Fluid Mechanics [*English Translation*] [*A publication*]
SOFNET ... Solar Observing and Forecasting Network [*Air Force*]
SOFOA...... Social Forces [*A publication*]
So Folklore Q ... Southern Folklore Quarterly [*A publication*]
SOFPAC ... Special Operating Forces, Pacific [*Military*]
SOFRES.... Societe Francaise d'Enquetes par Sondages [*French opinion-
            polling organization*]
SOFT........ Signature of Fragmented Tanks
SOFT........ Simple Output Format Translator   (IEEE)
SOFT........ Society of Forensic Toxicologists   (EA)
SOFT........ SofTech, Inc. [*NASDAQ symbol*]   (NQ)
SOFT........ Software [*Data processing*]
SOFT........ Space Operations and Flight Techniques [*NASA*]   (NASA)
SOFT........ Special Operational Forces Taiwan   (CINC)
SOFT........ Status of Forces Treaty
SOFT 18/13 ... Support Organization for Trisomy 18/13   (EA)
SOFTA ...... Shippers Oil Field Traffic Association   (EA)
SOFTCON ... Software Conference [*Trademark*]
Soft Eng ..... IEEE. Transactions on Software Engineering [*A publication*]
Soft Eng Notes ... Software Engineering Notes [*A publication*]
Soft News... Software News [*A publication*]
Software..... Software: Practice and Experience [*A publication*]
Software Dig Rat Newsl ... Software Digest Ratings Newsletter [*A publication*]

Software N ... Software News [*A publication*]
Software Pract Exper ... Software: Practice and Experience [*A publication*]
Software Pub Rep ... Software Publishing Report [*A publication*]
Software Rev ... Software Review [*A publication*]
Software Tools Commun ... Software Tools Communications [*A publication*]
Softw Healthc ... Software in Healthcare [*A publication*]
Softw Newsl ... Software Newsletter [*A publication*]
Soft World ... Software World [*A publication*]
SOFTY ...... Southern Federation of Temple Youth
Sof Vr........ Sofijskij Vremennik [*A publication*]
SOG .... Same Output Gate [*Data processing*]   (AAG)
SOG .... Satellite Operations Group [*Military*]
SOG .... Seat of Government [*Washington, DC*]
SOG .... Second-Order Gradient
sog .... Sogdian [*MARC language code*] [*Library of Congress*]   (LCCP)
SOG .... Sogenannt [*So-Called*] [*German*]
SOG .... Sogndal [*Norway*] [*Airport symbol*]   (OAG)
SOG .... Special Operations Group [*Navy*]
SOG .... Speed Made Good Over the Ground   (NATG)
SOG .... Statement of Guidance
SOG .... Straits Oil & Gas [*Vancouver Stock Exchange symbol*]
SOG .... Studies and Observations Group [*Military*]
SOG .... Supraoesophageal Ganglion [*Invertebrate nuerology*]
SOGA .... Spouses of Gays Association   (EA)
SOGAT..... Society of Graphical and Allied Trades [*British*]
SOGEA...... Southeastern Geology [*United States*] [*A publication*]
SOGEAC... Societe de Gestion et d'Exploitation de l'Aeroport de Conakry
            [*Guinea*]   (EY)
SOGEB...... Soviet Genetics [*English Translation*] [*A publication*]
SOGEKO .. Korean-French Banking Corp. [*Acronym is based on foreign
            phrase*]   (EY)
Sog Iga .... Sogo Igaku [*A publication*]
SOGITS .... Senior Officials Group on IT [*Information Technologies*]
            Standardisation [*British*]
SOGLF ...... Shelter Oil & Gas Ltd. [*NASDAQ symbol*]   (NQ)
Sogo Hog ... Sogo Hogaku [*A publication*]
Sogo Ky Kenk Kiyo ... Sogo Kyodo Kenkyusho Kiyo [*A publication*]
SOGp......... Special Operations Group [*Air Force*]   (AFM)
Sog Rinsh... Sogo Rinsho [*A publication*]
SOGS......... Science Operations Ground System [*Space telescope software*]
Sog Shik Nenpo ... Sogo Shikensho Nenpo [*A publication*]
SOGWPIP ... Silly Old Grandmother with Pictures in Purse
SOH.......... Skylab Operations Handbook [*NASA*]
SOH.......... Southern Ohio Aviation Sales Co. [*West Carrollton, OH*] [*FAA
            designator*]   (FAAC)
SOH.......... Standard Oil Co. (Ohio) [*NYSE symbol*]   (SPSG)
SOH.......... Start of Header [*or Heading*] [*Transmission control character*]
            [*Data processing*]
SOH.......... Stichting Oecumenische Hulp aan Kerken en Vluchtelingen
            [*Netherlands*]
SOH.......... Supply Overhaul   (MCD)
SOHAM.... Southampton [*City in England*]   (ROG)
SOHC........ Single Overhead Camshaft [*Automotive engineering*]
SOHED ..... Sowjetunion Heute [*A publication*]
SOHF .... Sense of Humor Failure [*British*] [*Slang*]
SOHI .... Sponsors of Open Housing Investment [*Later, Fund for an
            Open Society*]   (EA)
SOHIC ...... Stress-Oriented Hydrogen-Induced Cracking [*Metallurgy*]
SOHID ...... Sohioan [*A publication*]
SOHIO ...... Standard Oil Co. (Ohio)
So His S ..... Southern Historical Society [*A publication*]
So Hist Pap ... Southern Historical Society. Papers [*A publication*]
SOHO........ Solar and Heliospheric Observatory [*European Space Agency*]
SoHo .... South of Houston Street [*See also NoHo, SoSo, TriBeCa*]
            [*Artists' colony in New York City*]
SOHR .... Solar Hydrogen Rocket Engine
SoHR .... Southern Humanities Review [*A publication*]
SOI .... Scientific and Optical Instruments
SOI .... Security and Operational Inspection [*Army*]
SOI .... Shoshoni Gold [*Vancouver Stock Exchange symbol*]
SOI .... Signal Operation Instructions
SOI .... Silicon-on-Insulator
SOI .... Simulating Oriented Language
SOI .... Solar Oscillations Imager [*Instrumentation*]
SOI .... South Molle Island [*Australia*] [*Airport symbol*]   (OAG)
SOI .... Southern Illinois University at Carbondale, Carbondale, IL
            [*OCLC symbol*]   (OCLC)
SOI .... Southern Indiana Railway, Inc. [*Later, SIND*] [*AAR code*]
SOI .... Southern Oscillation Index
SOI .... Space Object Identification   (AFM)
SOI .... Special Olympics International   (EA)
SOI .... Specific Operating Instruction   (AFM)
SOI .... SPEEDEX [*Systemwide Project for Electronic Equipment at
            Depots Extended*] Operating Instructions
SOI .... Sphere of Influence
SOI .... Standard Operating Instruction   (KSC)
SOI .... State of Stimulus Overinclusion [*Schizophrenia*]
SOI .... Statement of Intent
SOI .... Statistics of Income [*IRS*]
SOI .... Stimulus Onset Interval
SOI .... Surety and Operational Inspection [*Military*]   (AFIT)

SOIC.......... Small Outline Integrated Circuit [*Data processing*]
SOIC.......... Supply Officer-in-Command [*Military*]
SOICAS .... Space Object Identification Central Analysis System
SOICC........ State Occupational Information Coordinating Committee
SOICS ...... Special Operations Improved Crypto System [*Military*]   (RDA)
SOICS ...... Summary of Installation Control Status [*Nuclear
              energy*]   (NRCH)
SOID .... Shipboard Ordnance Infrared Decoy   (MCD)
SOIFA ...... Soils and Fertilizers [*A publication*]
SOIG .... Special Operations Industry Group [*Army*]
Soil Assoc Inf Bull Advis Serv ... Soil Association. Information Bulletin and
              Advisory Service [*England*] [*A publication*]
Soil Biochem ... Soil Biochemistry [*A publication*]
Soil Biol B ... Soil Biology and Biochemistry [*A publication*]
Soil Biol Biochem ... Soil Biology and Biochemistry [*A publication*]
Soil Biol Microbiol ... Soil Biology and Microbiology [*A publication*]
Soil Cons.... Soil Conservation [*A publication*]
Soil Conser ... Soil Conservation [*A publication*]
Soil Conserv ... Soil Conservation [*A publication*]
Soil Conserv US Soil Conserv Serv ... Soil Conservation. United States Soil
              Conservation Service [*A publication*]
Soil Cons Serv NSW J ... Soil Conservation Service of New South Wales.
              Journal [*A publication*]   (APTA)
Soil Crop Sci Soc Fla Proc ... Soil and Crop Science Society of Florida.
              Proceedings [*A publication*]
Soil Fert ..... Soils and Fertilizers [*A publication*]
Soil Fertil... Soils and Fertilizers [*A publication*]
Soil Fert Taiwan ... Soils and Fertilizers in Taiwan [*A publication*]
Soil Ld-Use Surv Br Caribb ... Soil and Land-Use Surveys of the British
              Caribbean [*A publication*]
So Ill LJ ..... Southern Illinois University. Law Journal [*A publication*]
So Ill ULJ ... Southern Illinois University. Law Journal [*A publication*]
Soil Mech Found Eng ... Soil Mechanics and Foundation Engineering [*A
              publication*]
Soil Mech Found Engng ... Soil Mechanics and Foundation Engineering [*A
              publication*]
Soil Mech Found Eng Reg Conf Afr Proc ... Soil Mechanics and Foundation
              Engineering. Regional Conference for Africa. Proceedings
              [*A publication*]
Soil Publ .... Soil Publication. Commonwealth Scientific and Industrial
              Research Organisation [*Australia*] [*A
              publication*]   (APTA)
Soil Publ CSIRO ... Soil Publication. Commonwealth Scientific and Industrial
              Research Organisation [*Australia*] [*A publication*]   (APTA)
Soils Bull FAO ... Soils Bulletin. Food and Agriculture Organization [*A
              publication*]
Soil Sci....... Soil Science [*A publication*]
Soil Sci Agrochem ... Soil Science and Agrochemistry [*A publication*]
Soil Sci Agrochem Plant Prot ... Soil Science, Agrochemistry, and Plant
              Protection [*A publication*]
Soil Sci Agron ... Soil Science and Agronomy [*A publication*]
Soil Sci Plant Nutr ... Soil Science and Plant Nutrition [*A publication*]
Soil Sci Plant Nutr (Tokyo) ... Soil Science and Plant Nutrition (Tokyo) [*A
              publication*]
Soil Sci Pl Nutr ... Soil Science and Plant Nutrition [*A publication*]
Soil Sci So ... Soil Science Society of America. Proceedings [*A publication*]
Soil Sci Soc Am Book Ser ... Soil Science Society of America. Book Series [*A
              publication*]
Soil Sci Soc America Proc ... Soil Science Society of America. Proceedings [*A
              publication*]
Soil Sci Soc Am J ... Soil Science Society of America. Journal [*A publication*]
Soil Sci Soc Am Proc ... Soil Science Society of America. Proceedings [*A
              publication*]
Soil Sci Soc Fla Proc ... Soil Science Society of Florida. Proceedings [*A
              publication*]
Soil Ser Dep Soil Sci Minnesota Univ ... Minnesota. University. Department
              of Soil Science. Soil Series [*A publication*]
Soil Ser Minn Univ Agr Ext Serv ... Soil Series. Minnesota University.
              Agriculture Extension Service [*A publication*]
Soils Fert.... Soils and Fertilizers [*England*] [*A publication*]
Soils Fertil ... Soils and Fertilizers [*A publication*]
Soils Fertil Taiwan ... Soils and Fertilizers in Taiwan [*A publication*]
Soils Found ... Soils and Foundations [*A publication*]
Soils Land Use Ser Div Soils CSIRO ... Soils and Land Use Series. Division of
              Soils. Commonwealth Scientific and Industrial Research
              Organisation [*A publication*]   (APTA)
Soils Ld Use Ser Div Soils CSIRO ... Soils and Land Use Series. Division of
              Soils. Commonwealth Scientific and Industrial Research
              Organisation [*A publication*]   (APTA)
Soils Rep Manitoba Soil Surv ... Soils Report. Manitoba Soil Survey [*A
              publication*]
Soil Surv Bull Samaru ... Soil Survey Bulletin. Samaru Institute for
              Agricultural Research [*A publication*]
Soil Surv Invest Rep ... Soil Survey Investigations. Report [*A publication*]
Soil Surv Pap Neth Soil Surv Inst ... Soil Survey Papers. Netherlands Soil
              Survey Institute [*A publication*]
Soil Tillage Res ... Soil and Tillage Research [*A publication*]
Soil Use Manage ... Soil Use and Management [*A publication*]
Soil and Water Conser News ... Soil and Water Conservation News [*A
              publication*]

Soil and Water Conserv Jour ... Soil and Water Conservation Journal [*A
              publication*]
SOINC...... Supply Officer-in-Charge [*Navy*]
SoInGs .... Southern Indiana Gas & Electric Co. [*Associated Press
              abbreviation*]   (APAG)
Soins Chir ... Soins. Chirurgie [*A publication*]
Soins Gynecol Obst Pueric ... Soins. Gynecologie, Obstetrique, Puericulture [*A
              publication*]
Soins Pathol Trop ... Soins. Pathologie Tropicale [*A publication*]
SOIP.......... Sell-Off Impact Prognosticator [*Aerospace*]   (AAG)
SOIP.......... Ship Overhaul Improvement Program [*Navy*]
SOIP.......... Sphere of Influence People
SOIS.......... Shipping Operations Information System   (OA)
SOIS.......... Space Object Identification System
SOIS.......... Spacelab/Orbiter Interface Simulator [*NASA*]   (NASA)
SOISCUM ... Space Object Identification Summary   (MCD)
SOITLM ... Subcontractor Organizational Intermediate Level Maintenance
SOJ........... Sea of Japan   (NVT)
SOJ........... Sorkjosen [*Norway*] [*Airport symbol*]   (OAG)
SOJ........... Standoff Jammer   (NVT)
SoJA .... Soviet Jewish Affairs [*A publication*]
SO Jb .... Suedosteuropa-Jahrbuch [*A publication*]
SoJerIn ...... South Jersey Industries, Inc. [*Associated Press
              abbreviation*]   (APAG)
So Jersey LS Dictum ... South Jersey Law School Dictum [*A
              publication*]   (DLA)
SOJIM ...... Standoff Jammer Interceptor Missile   (MCD)
SOJS .... Standoff Jammer Suppression   (MCD)
SOJS .... Standoff Jammer System   (MCD)
SOJSM ..... Standoff Jammer Suppression Missile   (MCD)
SOJT .... Structured On-the-Job Training   (MCD)
SOJT .... Supervised On-the-Job Training
SOJTA ...... State On-the-Job Training Agencies [*Department of Labor*]
Sojuzot Zdruzenijata Farm Farm Teh SR Maked Bilt ... Sojuzot na
              Zdruzenijata na Farmacevtite i Farmacevtskite Tehnicari
              na SR Makedonija. Bilten [*A publication*]
SOK .... American Sokol Educational and Physical Culture Organization
SOK .... Semongkong [*Lesotho*] [*Airport symbol*] [*Obsolete*]   (OAG)
Sok .... Sokrates [*A publication*]
SOK .... South Kauai, HI [*Location identifier*] [*FAA*]   (FAAL)
SOK .... Sprog og Kultur [*A publication*]
SOK .... Supply OK [*i.e., Authorized*]
SOKAB..... Sosei To Kako [*A publication*]
SOKS......... Sport of Kings Society   (EA)
SOKSI .... Sentral Organisasi Karyawan Sosialis Indonesia [*Central
              Organization of Indonesian Socialist Workers*]
SOL .... Safe Operating Limit
SOL .... Sasko Oil & Gas Ltd. [*Toronto Stock Exchange symbol*]
              [*Vancouver Stock Exchange symbol*]
SOL .... Saturation Output Level [*Recording tapes*]
SOL .... School of Living   (EA)
SOL .... Second Order Logic
SOL .... Secretary of Labor   (OICC)
SOL .... Senior Operator License [*Nuclear energy*]   (NRCH)
SOL .... Shipowner's Liability [*Business term*]
SOL .... Short of Luck   (DSUE)
SOL .... Shut-Off Lights   (SAA)
SOL .... Simulation Oriented Language [*Data processing*]
SOL .... Sisters of Our Lady [*Roman Catholic religious order*]
SOL .... Social Organisation Limited
SOL .... Solar   (AAG)
SOL .... Solder
sol.............. Soldier
SOL .... Soldier out of Luck [*Military slang*]
SOL .... Solenoid   (AAG)
SOL .... Soleus Muscle [*Anatomy*]
SOL .... Soliciting [*FBI standardized term*]
SOL .... Solicitor
Sol .... Solicitor [*A publication*]
SOL .... Solicitor of Labor [*Department of Labor*]
SOL .... Solid   (MSA)
Sol .... Solidarity [*Manila*] [*A publication*]
SOL .... Solitaire [*Jewelry*]   (ROG)
Sol .... Soloman's Court of Request Appeals [*Ceylon*] [*A
              publication*]   (DLA)
SOL .... Solomon [*Biblical king*]   (ROG)
SOL .... Solomon, AK [*Location identifier*] [*FAA*]   (FAAL)
Sol .... Solon [*of Plutarch*] [*Classical studies*]   (OCD)
SOL .... Solubilis [*Soluble*] [*Pharmacy*]
SOL .... Soluble
SOL .... Solutio [*Solution*] [*Pharmacy*]
SOL .... Solution
SOL .... Solve [*or Solutus*] [*Dissolve or Dissolved*] [*Pharmacy*]   (ROG)
SOL .... Southern Illinois University, School of Law Library,
              Carbondale, IL [*OCLC symbol*]   (OCLC)
So L .... Sowjetliteratur. Eine Monatsschrift [*A publication*]
SOL .... Space-Occupying Lesion [*Medicine*]
SOL .... Standard of Living
Sol .... Still Out of Luck [*Army*] [*Slang*]
SOL .... Strictly Out of Luck   (IIA)
SOL .... Substitute Optical Landing System   (NG)

SOL .... Sure out of Luck [*Bowdlerized version*]
SOL .... System Oriented Language
SOLA......... Selected Objects for Living Actively [*Commercial firm specializing in home furnishings for the elderly*]
SOLA......... Student Organization for Latin America [*University of Notre Dame*] [*Research center*] (RCD)
Sol Act .... Solar Activity [*A publication*]
Sol Age....... Solar Age [*A publication*]
SOLAIR .... Solomon Islands Airways Ltd. (FEA)
Solaire 1 Mag ... Solaire 1 Magazine [*France*] [*A publication*]
SOLAN ..... Solid Angles
SOLANT... South Atlantic Force [*Later, Command*] [*Navy*] [*World War II*]
SOLANTFOR ... South Atlantic Force [*Later, Command*] [*Navy*] [*World War II*]
SOLAR...... Sandel On-Line Automated Reference [*Information service or system*]
SOLAR...... Semantically Oriented Lexical Archive
SOLAR...... Serialized On-Line Automatic Recording [*Data processing*] (IEEE)
SOLAR...... Shop Operations Load Analysis Reporting
SOLAR...... Sociedad Latinoamericana de Estudios sobre America Latina y el Caribe [*Mexico*] (EAIO)
SOLAR...... Society of Loose Actors Revolving [*SOLAR Theater, Inc.*]
Solar 1985 ... Solar Energy Employment and Requirements, 1978-1985 [*A publication*]
Solar E D ... Solar Energy Digest [*A publication*]
Solar En D ... Solar Energy Digest [*A publication*]
Solar Energ ... Solar Energy [*A publication*]
Solar Intel ... Solar Energy Intelligence Report [*A publication*]
SOLARIS ... Submerged Object Locating and Retrieving Identification System
Solar L Rep ... Solar Law Reporter [*A publication*]
Solar Mag ... Solar Magazine [*A publication*]
SOLAR MAX ... Solar Maximum Mission Satellite
Solar Phys ... Solar Physics [*A publication*]
Solar Syst Res ... Solar System Research [*A publication*]
SOLAS ...... Safety of Life at Sea Conference [*Intergovernmental Maritime Consultative Organization*] (MSC)
SOLAT...... Style of Learning and Thinking [*Occupational therapy*]
So Law .... Southern Lawyer [*A publication*] (DLA)
So Law T.... Southern Law Times [*A publication*] (DLA)
SOLB........ Start of Line Block (CET)
Sol Cells..... Solar Cells [*A publication*]
SOLCGS ... Sisters of Our Lady of Charity of the Good Shepherd [*Roman Catholic religious order*] [*Rome, Italy*] (EAIO)
SOLCHEM ... Solar-Chemical [*Energy conversion process*]
Sol Cl Gaz ... Solicitors' Clerks' Gazette [*1921-40*] [*A publication*] (DLA)
SOLCR...... Solicitor
SOLD .... Simulation of Logic Design
SOLD .... Soldering
SOLD .... Symbolic Debugger [*Also, sdb, SYMDEB*] [*Data processing*]
SOLE....... Society of Logistics Engineers (EA)
SOLEC...... Stand on Leg, Eyes Closed [*Equilibrium test*]
Solectr........ Solectron Corp. [*Associated Press abbreviation*] (APAG)
Sol Energy ... Solar Energy [*A publication*]
Sol Energy Intell Rep ... Solar Energy Intelligence Report [*A publication*]
Sol Energy Intel Rep ... Solar Energy Intelligence Report [*A publication*]
Sol Energy Mater ... Solar Energy Materials [*Netherlands*] [*A publication*]
Sol Energy Prog Aust NZ ... Solar Energy Progress in Australia and New Zealand [*A publication*] (APTA)
Sol Energy R & D Eur Community Ser E Energy Biomass ... Solar Energy R and D [*Research and Development*] in the European Community. Series E. Energy from Biomass [*A publication*]
Sol Energy Res Dev Rep ... Solar Energy Research and Development Report [*A publication*]
Sol Energy Res Rep Univ Queensl ... Solar Energy Research Report. University of Queensland [*A publication*] (APTA)
Sol Energy Update ... Solar Energy Update [*A publication*]
Sol Eng....... Solar Engineering [*A publication*]
Sol Eng Mag ... Solar Engineering Magazine [*A publication*]
SOLF........ Southern Oregon Library Federation [*Library network*]
SOLFEAS ... Solar Energy System Economic Feasibility Program [*Army*] (RDA)
Sol G .... Solicitor General [*Legal term*] (DLA)
Sol-Gel...... Solution-Gelatin (SDI)
Sol Gen ...... Solicitor General [*Legal term*] (DLA)
Sol Heat Cool ... Solar Heating and Cooling [*A publication*]
SOLI......... Solitec, Inc. [*NASDAQ symbol*] (NQ)
SOLI......... Soviet Life [*A publication*]
SOLI......... Symphony Orchestra Library Information [*Sinfonia Software*] [*Piedmont, CA*]
SOLIC ...... Solicitation
Solic .... Solicitor [*A publication*]
SOLIC ...... Special Operations/Low Intensity Conflict [*Army*]
Solicitors' J ... Solicitors' Journal [*A publication*]
Solic J .... Solicitors' Journal [*A publication*]
SOLICO .... Sorenson Lighted Controls, Inc.
SOLIC PREP ... Solicitation Preparation
Solic Q .... Solicitor's Quarterly [*A publication*]

SOLID...... Self-Organizing Large Information Dissemination System (IEEE)
SOLID...... Simulation of Life Insurance Decisions [*Game*]
SOLID...... Solar Life [*A publication*]
Solid Fuel Chem ... Solid Fuel Chemistry [*English Translation of Khimiya Tverdogo Topliva*] [*A publication*]
Solid Fuel Chem (Engl Transl) ... Solid Fuel Chemistry (English Translation) [*A publication*]
Solid Mech Arch ... Solid Mechanics Archives [*A publication*]
Solid St Abstr ... Solid State Abstracts [*A publication*]
Solid Stat ... Solid State Technology [*A publication*]
Solid State Abstr J ... Solid State Abstracts Journal [*A publication*]
Solid State Commun ... Solid State Communications [*A publication*]
Solid-State Electron ... Solid-State Electronics [*A publication*]
Solid State J ... Solid State Journal [*A publication*]
Solid State Phys ... Solid State Physics [*A publication*]
Solid State Phys Chem ... Solid State Physics and Chemistry [*Japan*] [*A publication*]
Solid State Phys (New York) ... Solid State Physics. Advances in Research and Applications (New York) [*A publication*]
Solid State Surf Sci ... Solid State Surface Science [*A publication*]
Solid State Technol ... Solid State Technology [*A publication*]
Solid St Commun ... Solid State Communications [*A publication*]
Solid Waste Bull ... Solid Waste Bulletin [*A publication*]
Solid Wastes Manage ... Solid Wastes Management [*Later, World Wastes*] [*England*] [*A publication*]
Solid Wastes Manage Refuse Removal J ... Solid Wastes Management/Refuse Removal Journal [*Later, World Wastes*] [*A publication*]
Solid Wastes Mgmt ... Solid Wastes Management [*Later, World Wastes*] [*A publication*]
Solid Waste Syst ... Solid Waste Systems [*A publication*]
Solid WM .. Solid Wastes Management [*Later, World Wastes*] [*A publication*]
SOLIMPEX ... Societe Lao Import-Export (EY)
Sol Ind Ind ... Solar Industry Index [*A publication*]
SOLINET ... Southeastern Library Network [*Atlanta, GA*] [*Library network*]
SOLINEWS ... Southeastern Library Network. Newsletter [*A publication*]
SOLION.... Solution of Ions [*Office of Naval Research*]
SOLIS........ Sozialwissenschaftliches LiteraturInformationssystem [*Database*] [*Informationszentrum Sozialwissenschaften*] [*Social Sciences Literature Information System*] [*German*] [*Information service or system*] (CRD)
SOLIS........ Symbionics On-Line Information System [*Data processing*]
SOLISTRON ... Solid-State Klystron
So Lit J ...... Southern Literary Journal [*A publication*]
Sol J .... Solicitors' Journal [*A publication*]
So LJ......... Southern Law Journal and Reporter [*A publication*] (DLA)
SoLJ......... Southern Literary Journal [*A publication*]
Sol Jo (Eng) ... Solicitors' Journal (England) [*A publication*]
Sol J & R... Solicitors' Journal and Reporter [*A publication*] (DLA)
SOLL......... Special Operations, Low Level (MCD)
SOLLAR ... Soft Lunar Landing and Return (SAA)
Sol Law Rep ... Solar Law Reporter [*A publication*]
Sol Life....... Solar Life [*A publication*]
SOLM .... Sisters of Our Lady of Mercy [*Mercedarians*] [*Roman Catholic religious order*]
SOLM .... Soldier's Medal [*Military decoration*]
Sol Man Cl Gaz ... Solicitor's Managing Clerks' Gazette [*1941-62*] [*A publication*] (DLA)
SOLMC..... Senior Officer Logistics Management Course [*Military*] (INF)
SOLMD .... Solar Magazine [*A publication*]
SOLN .... Solution
Soln Akt..... Solnechnaya Aktivnost [*A publication*]
Soln Dannye ... Solnechnye Dannye [*Former USSR*] [*A publication*]
Sol News Int ... Solar News International [*West Germany*] [*A publication*]
SOLO .... Selective Optical Lock-On [*Sighting device*]
SOLO .... Senior Officer Legal Orientation (MCD)
SOLO .... Southeastern Ohio Library Organization [*Library network*]
SOLO .... Status of Logistics Offensive [*Military*] (AABC)
SOLO .... Supply On-Line Option [*IMS America Ltd.*] [*Database*]
SOLO .... System for Ordinary Life Operations [*Insurance*]
SOLOC...... Southern Line of Communications [*World War II*]
Solo Cent Acad "Luiz De Queiroz" Univ Sao Paulo ... Solo Centro Academico "Luiz De Queiroz." Universidade de Sao Paulo [*A publication*]
SOLOG ..... Standardization of Certain Aspects of Operations and Logistics [*Military*]
SOLOMON ... Simultaneous Operation Linked Ordinal Modular Network
Sol Op........ Solicitor's Opinion [*Especially of Internal Revenue Bureau*] [*United States*] (DLA)
Sol Phys..... Solar Physics [*A publication*]
Sol Q .... Solicitor Quarterly [*1962-65*] [*A publication*] (DLA)
Sol Q .... Solicitor's Quarterly [*A publication*]
So LQ......... Southern Law Quarterly [*A publication*] (DLA)
SOLQA...... Sociological Quarterly [*A publication*]
SOLR........ Applied Solar Energy Corp. [*NASDAQ symbol*] (NQ)
SOLR........ Sidetone Objective Loudness Rating [*of telephone connections*] (IEEE)
SOLR........ Solicitor
So LR .... Southern Law Review [*Nashville, TN*] [*A publication*] (DLA)
SOLRAD... Solar Radiation [*Satellite system*] [*Navy*]

SOLRAD-HI ... Solar Radiation - High-Altitude [*Satellite system*] [*Navy*]
SOL Rev .... School of Law. Review [*Canada*] [*A publication*] (DLA)
So L Rev ..... Southern Law Review [*A publication*] (DLA)
So L Rev NS ... Southern Law Review, New Series [*St. Louis, MO*] [*A publication*] (DLA)
So LRNS.... Southern Law Review, New Series [*St. Louis, MO*] [*A publication*] (DLA)
SOLS........ Substitute Optical Landing System (MCD)
Sols Afr...... Sols Africains [*A publication*]
SOL-SAL .. Solar Scientific Airlock
Sol St Comm ... Solid State Communications [*A publication*]
Sol-St Elec ... Solid-State Electronics [*A publication*]
Sol St Tech ... Solid State Technology [*A publication*]
Sol Syst Res ... Solar System Research [*A publication*]
So LT .... Southern Law Times [*A publication*] (DLA)
SOLTA...... Sotsialisticheskiy Trud [*A publication*]
Sol Terr Environ Res Jpn ... Solar Terrestrial Environmental Research in Japan [*A publication*]
Sol Therm Components ... Solar Thermal Components [*A publication*]
Sol Therm Energy Util ... Solar Thermal Energy Utilization [*A publication*]
Sol Therm Heat Cool ... Solar Thermal Heating and Cooling [*A publication*]
Sol Therm Power Gener ... Solar Thermal Power Generation [*A publication*]
Sol Therm Rep ... Solar Thermal Report [*A publication*]
Sol Times... Solar Times [*A publication*]
SOLTRAN ... Solar Spectrum and Transmittance [*Solar energy research*]
SOLU .... Solute (AAMN)
SOLUB...... Aqueous Solubility Database [*Chemical Information Systems, Inc.*] [*Information service or system*] (CRD)
SOL U/T ... Solicitor's Undertaking (DCTA)
SOLUT...... Solutus [*Dissolved*] [*Pharmacy*] (ROG)
SOLV........ Solenoid Valve [*Mechanical engineering*]
SOLV........ Solv-Ex Corp. [*NASDAQ symbol*] (NQ)
SOLV........ Solve [*Dissolve*] [*Pharmacy*]
SOLV........ Solvent
SOLV........ Super-Open-Frame Low Voltage (IEEE)
SOLVE C CAL ... Solve Cum Calore [*Dissolve by Heating*] [*Pharmacy*]
Solvent Ext ... Solvent Extraction and Ion Exchange [*A publication*]
Solvent Extr Ion Exch ... Solvent Extraction and Ion Exchange [*A publication*]
Solvent Extr Rev ... Solvent Extraction Reviews [*A publication*]
SOLW........ Society of Our Lady of the Way (EA)
SOLY........ Solubility
Som .... De Somniis [*of Philo*] (BJA)
SOM .... SACLANT [*Supreme Allied Commander, Atlantic*] Staff Organization Manual (NATG)
SOM .... San Tome [*Venezuela*] [*Airport symbol*] (OAG)
SOM .... Scanning Optical Microscope
SOM .... Secretory Otitis Media [*Medicine*] (MAE)
SOM .... Securities Order Matching [*Data processing*]
SOM .... See Our Message
SOM .... Self-Organizing Machine
SOM .... Send-Only-Multipoint (DNAB)
SOM .... Sensitivity-of-Method [*FDA*]
SOM .... Serous Otitis Media [*Ear inflammation*]
SOM .... Share of Market [*Advertising*]
SOM .... Share of Market [*Lundberg Survey, Inc.*] [*Information service or system*] (CRD)
SOM .... Shift Operations Manager (NRCH)
SOM .... Ship Operations Manager [*NASA*] (KSC)
SOM .... Simulator Operation and Maintenance Program (MCD)
SOM .... Single Oriental Male [*Classified advertising*]
SOM .... Skidmore, Owings & Merrill [*Architectural firm*]
SOM .... Small Office Microfilm
SOM .... Society of Medalists (EA)
SOM .... Society of Occupational Medicine [*British*]
som .... Somalia [*MARC language code*] [*Library of Congress*] (LCCP)
SOMM .... Somalia [*ANSI three-letter standard code*] (CNC)
SOM .... Somatostatin [*Biochemistry*]
SOM .... Somatotrophin [*Endocrinology*]
SOM .... Sombrero [*Chile*] [*Seismograph station code, US Geological Survey*] (SEIS)
SOM .... Somerset [*County in England*]
SOM .... Somerset County Library, Bridgewater, NJ [*OCLC symbol*] (OCLC)
Som .... Somerset Legal Journal [*Pennsylvania*] [*A publication*] (DLA)
SOM .... Somersetshire [*County in England*]
SOM .... Somnus [*Sleep*] [*Latin*] (ROG)
SOM .... SONARman [*Navy*]
SOM .... Sound of Music [*Dolls by Alexander*] [*Doll collecting*]
So M .... Southern Magazine [*A publication*]
So M .... Sovetskaja Muzyka [*A publication*]
SOM .... Spacecraft Operations Manual
SOM .... Spares Optimization Model [*NASA*] (NASA)
SOM .... Stage Operating Manual [*NASA*] (KSC)
SOM .... Standard Operating Manual [*NASA*] (NASA)
SOM .... Standoff Missile (MCD)
SOM .... Start-of-Message
SOM .... State Operations Manual [*Home Health Agency Program*] [*Department of Health and Human Services*] (GFGA)
SOM .... Steward of Meeting [*Auto racing*]
SOM .... Storage Operations Module [*SAILS*] (MCD)
SOM .... Strap-On Motor

SOM .... Suborbital Mission [*NASA*] (SAA)
SOM .... Sulfomethoxine [*Medicine*] (MAE)
SOM .... Superior Oblique Muscle [*Eye anatomy*]
SOM .... Superior Old Marsala
SOM .... Survivability Optimization Model (MCD)
SOM .... Sustained Operations Manual
SOM .... Sustained Operations Model
SOM .... System Object Model [*Data processing*] (PCM)
SOM .... System Operator Manual [*Military*] (CAAL)
SOMA .... Services to Ongoing Mature Aging [*Counseling group*]
SOMA .... Sharing of Missionaries Abroad [*Church of England*]
SOMA .... Signed Out Against Medical Advice
SOMA .... Soobscenija Otdela Machanizacii i Avtomatizacii Informacionnych Robot [*A publication*]
SoMa .... South of Market [*District of San Francisco*]
SOMA .... Student Osteopathic Medical Association (EA)
SOMA .... Survey of Market Absorption [*Department of Housing and Urban Development*] (GFGA)
SOMADA ... Self-Organizing Multiple-Access Discrete Address [*Data processing*] (IEEE)
Som A Natur Hist ... Somerset Archaeology and Natural History [*A publication*]
Somatic Cell Genet ... Somatic Cell Genetics [*A publication*]
Somatic Cell Mol Genet ... Somatic Cell and Molecular Genetics [*A publication*]
Somatosens Mot Res ... Somatosensory and Motor Research [*A publication*]
Somatosens Res ... Somatosensory Research [*A publication*]
SOMB .... Somerset Bancorp, Inc. [*Somerville, NJ*] [*NASDAQ symbol*] (NQ)
SOMBA..... Southern Medical Bulletin [*United States*] [*A publication*]
SOMC .... Shadow Open Market Committee
Som Cell G ... Somatic Cell Genetics [*A publication*]
SOMDA ... Southwestern Medicine [*United States*] [*A publication*]
SOME .... Secretary's Office, Management Engineer [*Navy*]
SOME .... Senior Ordnance Mechanical Engineer [*British military*] (DMA)
SOME .... State-o-Maine, Inc. [*New York, NY*] [*NASDAQ symbol*] (NQ)
SOMEA..... Sovetskaya Meditsina [*A publication*]
SOMEG to ADV ... Something to Advantage [*Legal term*] [*Advertising*]
Somerset Archaeol Natur Hist ... Somerset Archaeology and Natural History [*A publication*]
Somerset Arch Nat Hist ... Somerset Archaeology and Natural History [*A publication*]
Somerset Industrial Archaeology Soc Jnl ... Somerset Industrial Archaeology Society. Journal [*A publication*]
Somerset Levels Pap ... Somerset Levels Papers [*A publication*]
Somerset LJ ... Somerset Legal Journal [*A publication*] (DLA)
SOMET..... Sometimes
SOMF........ SIDPERS [*Standard Installation/Division Personnel System*] Organization Master File [*Military*] (AABC)
SOMF........ Start of Minor Frame (MCD)
SOMH...... SONARman Harbor Defense [*Navy*]
SOM-H ..... Start-of-Message - High Precedence (CET)
SOMI .... Sternal-Occipital-Mandibular Immobilization [*Medicine*]
SOMIEX ... Societe Malienne d'Importation et d'Exportation [*Malian Import Export Co.*]
SOMISA ... Sociedad Mixta Siderurgia Argentina [*Steel producer in Argentina*]
SOMISS .... Study of Management Information Systems Support [*Army*]
SOM-L ...... Start-of-Message - Low Precedence (CET)
Som Leg J (PA) ... Somerset Legal Journal [*Pennsylvania*] [*A publication*] (DLA)
SOM-LI..... Somatostatin-Like Immunoreactivity
Som LJ....... Somerset Legal Journal [*Pennsylvania*] [*A publication*] (DLA)
Som LR ...... Somalia Law Reports [*A publication*] (DLA)
SOMM .... Shift Operations Maintenance Manager (SSD)
Somn on Gav ... Somner on Gavelkind [*A publication*] (DLA)
SOMO ...... Semioccupied Molecular Orbital [*Physical chemistry*]
SOMO ...... Senior Officer Management Office [*Army*] (INF)
Somogyi Muesz Sz ... Somogyi Mueszaki Szemle [*Hungary*] [*A publication*]
SOM-P ...... Start-of-Message - Priority
SOMP .... Sydney Ocean Meeting Point [*Navy*]
SOMPA..... System of Multicultural Pluralistic Assessment [*Psychological and educational testing*]
Som Pl........ Somersetshire Pleas (Civil and Criminal), Edited by Chadwyck-Healey and Landon [*Somerset Record Society Publications, Vols. 11, 36, 41, 44*] [*A publication*] (DLA)
SOMR .... [*The*] Somerset Group, Inc. [*Indianapolis, IN*] [*NASDAQ symbol*] (NQ)
SOMRB..... Senior Officers Materiel Review Board [*Army*] (AABC)
SOMS........ Senior Officer, Minesweepers [*British military*] (DMA)
SOMS........ Service Order Mechanization [*or Mechanized*] System [*AT & T*]
SOMS........ Shuttle Orbiter Medical System [*NASA*] (MCD)
SOMS........ Standard Operations and Maintenance Squadron (DNAB)
SOMS........ Synchronous, Operational Meteorological Satellite
SOMSA..... Soviet Materials Science [*English Translation*] [*A publication*]
SOMST..... Somersetshire [*County in England*] (ROG)
SOMT .... Soldier Operator Maintainer Testing (MCD)
SOMTO .... Subversive Operations, Mediterranean Theatre of Operations [*World War II*]

SOMTS..... Division of Ship Operations and Marine Technical Support [*Research center*] (RCD)
SoMV .... Sowbane Mosaic Virus
SON.......... Espiritu Santo [*Vanuatu*] [*Airport symbol*] (OAG)
S/ON .... Sign On [*Data processing*] (MDG)
SON.......... Slovenske Odborne Nazvoslovie [*A publication*]
SON.......... Snijders-Oomen Non-Verbal Intelligence Scale (AEBS)
SON.......... Society of Nematologists (EA)
SON.......... Sonata [*Music*] (WGA)
son............. Songhai [*MARC language code*] [*Library of Congress*] (LCCP)
SON.......... Sonneberg [*Federal Republic of Germany*] [*Seismograph station code, US Geological Survey*] [*Closed*] (SEIS)
Son .... Sonnets [*Shakespearean work*]
Son .... Sonora [*Record label*] [*Sweden*]
SON .... Sonora Gold Corp. [*Toronto Stock Exchange symbol*] [*Vancouver Stock Exchange symbol*]
SON.......... Southern (WGA)
SON.......... Statement of Operational Need
SON.......... Submitting Office Number [*Navy*] (DNAB)
SON.......... Support of Other Nations [*Military support furnished certain nations and funded by the Air Force*]
SON .... Supraoptic Nucleus [*Brain anatomy*]
SONA .... School of Naval Administration, Leland Stanford University
SonA .... Stratford-on-Avon [*British*]
SONAC ..... SONAR Nacelle [*Sonacelle*]
SONAD ..... Sonic Azimuth Detector (MCD)
SONAD..... Speech-Operated Noise Adjusting Device [*Telecommunications*] (TEL)
SONAR ..... Sonic Azimuth and Ranging [*British military*] (DMA)
SONAR ..... Sound Navigation and Ranging
SONARRAY ... SONAR Array [*Sounding system*] [*Navy*]
Sonat......... Sonat, Inc. [*Associated Press abbreviation*] (APAG)
SoNat........ Southern National Corp. [*Associated Press abbreviation*] (APAG)
SoNatCp ... Southern National Corp. [*Associated Press abbreviation*] (APAG)
SONATRACH ... Societe Nationale de Transport et de Commercialisation des Hydrocarbures
SONB .... Sonobuoy
Sonc .... Soncino (BJA)
SONC .... Sonic Corp. [*NASDAQ symbol*] (SPSG)
SoncinoB.... [*The*] Soncino Books of the Bible (Bornemouth) [*A publication*] (BJA)
SONCM .... SONAR Countermeasures and Deception [*Military*]
SONCR ..... SONAR Control Room (MSA)
SOND........ Secretary's Office, Navy Department
Sonderb Naturwiss Ver Hamb ... Sonderbaende des Naturwissenschaftlichen Vereins in Hamburg [*A publication*]
Sonderdr Internist Welt ... Sonderdruck aus Internistische Welt [*West Germany*] [*A publication*]
Sonderh Bayer Landw Jb ... Sonderhefte. Bayerisches Landwirtschaftliches Jahrbuch [*A publication*]
Sonderhefte zum Allgemein Statist Arch ... Sonderhefte zum Allgemeinen Statistischen Archiv [*A publication*]
Sonderjydsk M-Skr ... Sonderjydsk Manedsskrift [*A publication*]
Sonenergie ... Sonnenenergie und Waermepumpe [*A publication*]
SONET...... Synchronous Optical Network [*Data processing*]
SONG........ Seeking of Noetic Goals Test [*Personality development test*] [*Psychology*]
Song .... Song of Songs [*Old Testament book*] [*Roman Catholic canon*]
SongCh ...... Song of the Three Children [*Old Testament book*] [*Apocrypha*] (BJA)
Song 3 Childr ... Song of the Three Children [*Old Testament book*] [*Apocrypha*]
Song Hits Mag ... Song Hits Magazine [*A publication*]
Songklanakarin J Sci Technol ... Songklanakarin Journal of Science and Technology [*A publication*]
SongR .... Song of Songs Rabbah (BJA)
SONGS...... San Onofre Nuclear Generating Station (NRCH)
Song Sol ... Song of Solomon [*Old Testament book*]
Song of Three Childr ... [*The*] Song of the Three Holy Children [*Apocrypha*]
Songwriter ... Songwriter Magazine [*A publication*]
Songwriters R ... Songwriter's Review [*A publication*]
SONIBANQUE ... Societe Nigerienne de Banque (EY)
SONIC....... SPAN [*Space Physics Analysis Network*] Ocean Network Information Center [*Database*]
SONIC....... System-Wide On-Line Network for Information Control [*Data processing*]
SONKA ..... Shonika [*A publication*]
SONM....... Sonoma International [*NASDAQ symbol*] (NQ)
SONN....... Sonning [*England*]
SONN........ Sonora Gold Corp. [*NASDAQ symbol*] (NQ)
SONNA..... Somali National News Agency
Sonnenenerg ... Sonnenenergie [*A publication*]
Sonnenenerg Waermepumpe ... Sonnenenergie und Waermepumpe [*A publication*]
SONO........ Satellite Object Number (MUGU)
SONO........ Sonobuoy
SONO........ Sonoco Products Co. [*NASDAQ symbol*] (NQ)
SONO........ Sonogram [*Medicine*] (DHSM)
SONOAN ... Sonic Noise Analyzer

SONOSW ... Sonoswitch
SONP .... Solid Organs Not Palpable [*Medicine*]
So NQ .... Somerset Notes and Queries [*A publication*]
SONRD ..... Secretary's Office, Office of Research and Development [*Navy*]
SONRES ... Saturated Optical Nonresonant Emission Spectroscopy
SONS .... Seek Out New Suppliers
SONS .... Society of Non-Smokers (EA)
SONS .... Statistics of Naval Shipyards
Sonsbec...... [*Franciscus*] Sonsbeccius [*Flourished, 16th century*] [*Authority cited in pre-1607 legal work*] (DSA)
Son Spec ... Sonorum Speculum [*A publication*]
SONV .... Sonchus Virus [*Plant pathology*]
SONWD..... Sonnenenergie und Waermepumpe [*A publication*]
SONX .... Sonex Research, Inc. [*Annapolis, MD*] [*NASDAQ symbol*] (NQ)
SonyCp ...... Sony Corp. America [*Associated Press abbreviation*] (APAG)
SOO.......... Sault Meadows Energy [*Vancouver Stock Exchange symbol*]
SOO.......... Schenectady Operations Office [*Energy Research and Development Administration*]
SOO.......... Songo [*Mozambique*] [*Airport symbol*] (OAG)
SOO.......... Soo Line Corp. [*NYSE symbol and AAR code*] (SPSG)
SOO.......... Staff Officer Operations [*British*]
SOO.......... State of Origin [*Soccer*]
Soob A N Gruz SSR ... Soobshcheniia Akademii Nauk Gruzinskoi SSR [*A publication*]
Soob Ermit ... Soobscenija Gosudarstvennogo Ordena Lenina Ermitaza [*A publication*]
Soob G Ermitazh ... Soobshcheniia Gosudarstvennogo Ermitazha [*A publication*]
Soob G Muz Izob Isk Pushkin ... Soobshcheniia Gosudarstvennyi Muzei Izobrazitel'nykh Iskusstv Imeni A. S. Pushkina [*A publication*]
Soob Kherson Muz ... Soobshcheniia Khersonnesskogo Muzeia [*Sebastopol*] [*A publication*]
Soobscenija Akad Nauk Gruz SSR ... Soobscenija Akademiji Nauk Gruzinskoj SSR [*A publication*]
Soobsc Gosud Russk Muz ... Soobscenija Gosudarstvennogo Russkogo Muzeja [*A publication*]
Soobsc Muz Isk Nar Vostoka ... Soobscenija Muzeja Iskusstva Narodov Vostoka [*A publication*]
Soobsc Vycisl Mat ... Soobscenija po Vychislitel noi Matematike [*A publication*]
Soobshch Akad Nauk Gruzin SSR ... Soobshcheniya Akademiya Nauk Gruzinskoi SSR [*A publication*]
Soobshch Akad Nauk Gruz SSSR ... Soobshcheniya Akademiya Nauk Gruzinskoi SSSR [*A publication*]
Soobshch Byurakan Obs Akad Nauk Arm SSR ... Soobshcheniya Byurakanskoi Observatorii Akademiya Nauk Armyanskoi SSR [*A publication*]
Soobshch Chuv Zon Agrokhim Lab ... Soobshcheniya Chuvashskoi Zonal'noi Agrokhimicheskoi Laboratorii [*A publication*]
Soobshch Dal'Nevost Fil Sib Otd Aka Nauk SSSR ... Soobshcheniya Dal'Nevostochnogo Filiala Sibirskogo Otdla Akademii Nauk SSSR [*A publication*]
Soobshch Inst Agrokhim Probl Gidroponiki Akad Nauk Arm SSR ... Soobshcheniya Instituta Agrokhimicheskikh Problem i Gidroponiki Akademiya Nauk Armyanskoi SSR [*Armenian SSR*] [*A publication*]
Soobshch Inst Lesa Akad Nauk SSSR ... Soobshcheniya Instituta Lesa Akademii Nauk SSSR [*A publication*]
SoobshchIPPO ... Soobshcheniia Imperialnovo Pravoslavnovo Palestinskavo Obshchestva [*A publication*]
Soobshch Mosk Otd Vses Bot Ova ... Soobshcheniya Moskovskogo Otdeleniya Vsesoyuznogo Botanicheskogo Obshchestva [*A publication*]
Soobshch Nauchno Issled Rab Kiev Politekh Inst ... Soobshcheniya o Nauchno-Issledovatel'skoi Rabote Kievskii Politekhnicheskii Institut [*A publication*]
Soobshch Ob'edin Inst Yad Issled (Dubna) ... Soobshcheniya Ob'edinennogo Instituta Yadernykh Issledovanii (Dubna) [*A publication*]
Soobshch Obshch Lab Agrokhim Akad Nauk Armyan SSR ... Soobshcheniya Obshchestvoi Laboratorii Agrokhimii Akademii Nauk Armyanskoi SSR [*A publication*]
Soobshch Sakhalin Fil Akad Nauk SSSR ... Soobshcheniya Sakhalinskogo Filiala Akademii Nauk SSSR [*A publication*]
Soobshch Shemakhinskoi Astrofiz Obs Akad Nauk Azerb SSR ... Soobshcheskoi Shemakhinskoi Astrofizicheskoi Observatorii Akademiya Nauk Azerbaidzhan SSR [*Azerbaidzhan SSR*] [*A publication*]
Soochow J Hum ... Soochow Journal of Humanities [*Taipei*] [*A publication*]
Soochow J Lit Soc Stud ... Soochow Journal of Literature and Social Studies [*Taipei*] [*A publication*]
Soochow J Math ... Soochow Journal of Mathematics [*Taipei*] [*A publication*]
Soochow J Math Natur Sci ... Soochow Journal of Mathematical and Natural Sciences [*Later, Soochow Journal of Mathematics*] [*A publication*]
SOOG........ Saint-Georges-De-L'Oyapock [*French Guiana*] [*ICAO location identifier*] (ICLI)
SOOM....... Saigon Officers Open Mess [*Vietnam*]
SOOM....... Saint-Laurent du Maroni [*French Guiana*] [*ICAO location identifier*] (ICLI)

SOON........ Sequence for Opportunities and Negatives [*Rand Corp.*]
SOON........ Solar Observing Optical Network [*Air Force*]
SOON........ Sooner Defense of Florida, Inc. [*NASDAQ symbol*] (NQ)
Soon Chun Hyang J Med ... Soon Chun Hyang Journal of Medicine [*Republic of Korea*] [*A publication*]
SOOP .... Ship of Opportunity Program [*National Oceanic and Atmospheric Administration*] (GFGA)
SOOP .... Special Old Oil Price
SOOP .... Submarine Oceanographic Observation Program
SOOR........ Regina [*French Guiana*] [*ICAO location identifier*] (ICLI)
SOOS .... Saul [*French Guiana*] [*ICAO location identifier*] (ICLI)
SOOSE...... Suborbital Offense Systems Group [*NASA*] (SAA)
SOOY .... Sinnamary [*French Guiana*] [*ICAO location identifier*] (ICLI)
SOPLA .... Pinehurst [*North Carolina*] [*Airport symbol*] (OAG)
SOP .... Safety Operating Plan
SOP .... Saturn Orbiter Probe [*NASA*]
SOP .... Scavenging, Oil Pump (MSA)
SOP .... Scented Orange Pekoe [*Tea trade*] (ROG)
SOP .... Seat of the Pants
SOP .... Second Opinion Program [*Later, NSOP*] (EA)
SOP .... Secondary Operation
SOP .... Secondary Oxygen Pack [*NASA*]
SOP .... Semiopen Position [*Dancing*]
SOP .... Semiorganic Polymer
SOP .... Senior Officer Present
SOP .... Ship's Operational Program [*Navy*] (NVT)
SOP .... Shop Overload Parts (AAG)
SOP .... Simulated Output Program [*Data processing*]
SOP .... Simulation Operations Plan [*NASA*] (KSC)
SOP .... Sleeping-Out Pass [*British armed forces*]
SOP .... Soprano
SOP .... Sopron [*Hungary*] [*Seismograph station code, US Geological Survey*] (SEIS)
SOP .... Southern Pines, NC [*Location identifier*] [*FAA*] (FAAL)
So P........... Sovjetckaja Pecat' [*A publication*]
SOP .... Spacelab Opportunity Payload [*NASA*] (MCD)
SOP .... Spares Order Processing (MCD)
SOP .... Special Operating Procedure (IEEE)
SOP .... Special Order Price
SOPUA........ Sphere of Positon (SAA)
SOP .... Staff Officer of Pensioners [*Army*] [*British*] (ROG)
SOP .... Standard Operating Plan (OICC)
SOP .... Standard [*or Standing*] Operating Procedure
SOP .... State-Operated Program [*Department of Education*] (GFGA)
SOP .... State of Polarization
SOP .... Statement of Policy [*SEC*]
SOP .... Statewide Operating Plan
SOP .... Station Operating Plan (AAG)
SOP .... Stock Option Plan
SOP .... Strategic Objectives Plan
SOPE .... Strategic Orbit Point (KSC)
SOP .... Study Organization Plan (BUR)
SOP .... Subsystem Operating Program (NASA)
SOP .... Subsystems Operating Procedure [*NASA*] (NASA)
SOP .... Successive Organization of Perception [*Pilot behavior*]
SOP .... Sulfate of Potash [*Fertilizer*]
SOP .... Sum-of-Products [*Data processing*] (OA)
SOP .... Supplemental Oxygen Package (MCD)
SOP .... Supplier Operating Procedure (MCD)
SOP .... Surface Oil Pickup
SOP .... Surgical Outpatient [*Medicine*]
SOP .... Survey of Use Permits [*Bureau of the Census*] (GFGA)
SOP .... Symbolic Optimum Program
SOP .... System Operations Panel (SSD)
SOP .... Systems Operation Plan [*NASA*] (KSC)
SOPA........ Senior Officer Present Afloat [*Navy*]
SOP(A)...... Senior Officer Present (Ashore) [*Navy*]
SOPA........ Society of Professional Archeologists (EA)
SOPA........ Standoff Precision Attack [*Military*] (CAAL)
SOPAA........ Soviet Physics. Acoustics [*English Translation*] [*A publication*]
SOPAC...... Joint CCOP/IOC Program of Research on the South Pacific [*Marine science*] (MSC)
SOPAC...... South Pacific Command [*Navy*]
SOPAC...... Southern Pacific Railroad Co.
SOPACBACOM ... South Pacific Base Command [*Navy*] [*World War II*]
SOPACCOMS ... South Pacific Communications [*Navy*]
SOPAD...... SOPA [*Senior Officer Present Afloat*] Administrative Duties [*Military*] (NVT)
SOPAD...... Summary of Proceedings and Debate [*of House of Representatives*]
SOPAG...... Societe des Participations Gardinier [*French fertilizer firm*]
SOPAT...... South China Patrol [*Navy*] [*World War II*]
SOPC......... Sales Operations Planning and Control [*Management*]
SOPC......... Shuttle Operations and Planning Center [*NASA*] (MCD)
SOPC......... Shuttle Operations Planning Complex (NASA)
SOPDOSS ... Submersible Oriented Platform for Deep Ocean Sediment Studies [*Marine science*] (MSC)
SOPE......... Simulated Off-the-Pad Ejection [*NASA*]
SO-PE........ Sodium Pentathol [*Nickname*]
Soph.......... Sopherim (BJA)
Soph.......... Sophia [*A publication*]

Soph .... Sophista [*of Plato*] [*A publication*] (OCD)
SOPH .... Sophister [*British*] (ROG)
SOPH .... Sophocles [*Greek poet, 496-406BC*] [*Classical studies*] (ROG)
SOPH .... Sophomore
Soph .... Sophonias [*Old Testament book*] [*Douay version*]
SOPH .... Starboard Out, Port Home [*Variation of POSH*]
SOPHE...... Society for Public Health Education (EA)
Soph El ...... Sophistici Elenchi [*of Aristotle*] [*Classical studies*] (OCD)
Sophia Econ R ... Sophia Economic Review [*Tokyo*] [*A publication*]
Sophia:T .... Sophia: Studies in Western Civilization and the Cultural Interaction of East and West (Tokyo) [*A publication*]
SOPI.......... Superintendent of Public Instruction (OICC)
SOPJA ..... Soviet Physics Journal [*English Translation*] [*A publication*]
SOPLA ..... Soviet Plastics [*English Translation*] [*A publication*]
SOPLASCO ... Southern Plastics Co.
SOPLC ...... Senior Officer Preventive Logistics Course (MCD)
SOPM .... Standard Orbital Parameter Message [*NASA*] (KSC)
SOPMET.. Standing Operating Procedure - Meteorological Plan (NATG)
SOP/MR ... Standard Operating Procedure/Maintenance Requirement (MCD)
SOPO .... Society of Oral Physiology and Occlusion
SOPODA .. Social Planning, Policy & Development Abstracts [*Sociological Abstracts, Inc.*] [*Database*]
SOPP......... Sodium Ortho-Phenylphenoxide [*Organic chemistry*]
SOPP......... Special Order Perfect Price [*for undamaged merchandise*]
SOPP......... Statement of Provisioning Policy [*Military*] (AFIT)
SOPPA ...... Soviet Plant Physiology [*English Translation*] [*A publication*]
SOPPC ...... Special Operations Photo Processing Cell (MCD)
SOPR........ South Pierce Railroad [*AAR code*]
SOPR........ Spanish Open Pool Reactor
SOPR........ Special Officer Personnel Requirements [*Military*]
SOPR........ Standing Operating Procedure Regulation [*Navy*] (MCD)
SOPS......... Shot Noise Optical Optimization Communication System with Stops [*NASA*]
S Op S........ Si Opus Sit [*If Needed*] [*Pharmacy*]
SOPS......... Spacecraft Operations Planning Section
SOPS......... Special Operations Power Source [*Military*] (RDA)
SOPSA ...... Shuttle Orbit-Injection Propulsion System Analysis [*NASA*]
SOPT........ Science Operations Planning Team
SOPUA...... Soviet Physics. Uspekhi [*English Translation*] [*A publication*]
SOPUS...... Senior Officer Present, United States Navy
SOPUSN... Senior Officer Present, United States Navy (SAA)
SOQ.......... Senior Officers' Quarters
SOQ.......... Sick Officer Quarters
Soq .... Soqotri (BJA)
SOQ.......... Sorong [*Indonesia*] [*Airport symbol*] (OAG)
So Q .... Southern Quarterly Review [*A publication*]
SOQ.......... Star One Resources, Inc. [*Vancouver Stock Exchange symbol*]
SOQ.......... System Optical Quality (MCD)
SOQAS..... Statement of Quality and Support (MCD)
SOQE .... Society for Optical and Quantum Electronics
SOQUEM ... Societe Quebecoise d'Exploration Miniere [*Quebec Mining Exploration Co.*]
SOQUIJ .... Societe Quebecoise d'Information Juridique [*Quebec Society for Legal Information*] [*Information service or system*] (IID)
SOR .... Sale or Return [*Business term*] (ADA)
SOR .... Sampling Oscilloscope Recorder
SOR .... Saxon Owners Registry (EA)
SOR .... Schedule Outlook Report (SAA)
SOR .... Seder 'Olam Rabbah (BJA)
SOR .... Sensor Operation Room (AFM)
SOR .... Serie Orientale Roma [*A publication*]
SOR .... Service Operational Requirement
SOR .... Single Order Release (MCD)
SOR .... Society of Rheology (EA)
SOR .... Sonor Petroleum Corp. [*Toronto Stock Exchange symbol*]
Sor............. Soria [*Record label*]
SOR .... Soroa [*Cuba*] [*Seismograph station code, US Geological Survey*] (SEIS)
SOR .... Source Capital, Inc. [*NYSE symbol*] (SPSG)
SOR .... Source of Repair (MCD)
So R........... Southern Review [*US*] [*A publication*]
SoR .... Southern Review: An Australian Journal of Literary Studies [*A publication*]
SOR .... Specific Operational Requirement [*Military*]
SOR .... Spilled Oil Research Team [*National Oceanic and Atmospheric Administration*] (MSC)
SOR .... Squadron Operational Report
SOR .... Stable-Orbit Rendezvous [*NASA*]
SOR .... Standard Operating Report
SOR .... Standard Operating Rules
SOR .... Standoff Range (MCD)
sor .... Starboard (DS)
SOR .... Starfire Optical Range [*Air Force*]
SOR .... Start of Record (MUGU)
SOR .... State of Readiness (MCD)
SOR .... Statement of Requirement [*Military*] (AFIT)
SOR .... Status or Operating Resources (MCD)
SOR .... Statutory Orders and Regulations of Canada [*Canada Department of Justice*] [*Information service or system*]
SOR .... Stearic/Oleic Acid Ratio [*Clinical chemistry*]

SOR .... Stephens Owners Registry [*Inactive*] (EA)
S-O-R........ Stimulus-Organism-Response
SOR .... Stockholder of Record
SOR .... Students for Origins Research (EA)
SOR .... Subcarrier Oscillator Rack
SOR .... Successive Overrelaxation
SOR .... Synchrotron Orbital Radiation [*High-energy physics*]
SOR .... Systems Operational Requirement
SOR .... Winfield/Arkansas City, KS [*Location identifier*]
          [*FAA*] (FAAL)
S Or A .... Sammlung Orientalistischer Arbeiten [*A publication*]
SORA .... Secretary's Office, Records Administration [*Navy*]
SORA .... Sorgento Rapido [*Reactor*] (NRCH)
SoRA .... Southern Review (Adelaide, Australia) [*A publication*]
So R A .... Southern Review: An Australian Journal of Literary Studies [*A publication*]
SORAD ..... Sonic Ranging and Detection (KSC)
SORAFOM ... Societe de Radiodiffusion de la France d'Outre-Mer [*Society for Radio Broadcasting of Overseas France*]
SORAK..... Special Operation Radio Antenna Kit [*Military*] (RDA)
SORAP...... Signature Overlap Range Prediction
SORAP...... Standard Omnirange Approach
SORAT...... Submarine Operational Readiness Assessment and Training
SORB........ Submarine Overhaul and Refueling Building [*Navy*] (DNAB)
SORB........ Subsistence Operations Review Board [*Military*] (AABC)
Sorb D........ Sorbitol Dehydrogenase [*Also, SDH*] [*An enzyme*]
SORC........ Signal Officers' Reserve Corps
SORC........ Simultaneous Oxidation-Reduction Catalyst [*Automotive engineering*]
SORC........ Sound Ranging Control
SORC........ Southern Ocean Racing Conference
SORC........ Station Operations Review Committee [*Nuclear energy*] (NRCH)
SORCS ..... Shipboard Ordnance Requirement Computer System [*Navy*]
SORD .... Society of Record Dealers of America
SORD .... Southwestern Order Retrieval and Distribution [*Southwest Bell Telephone Co.*]
SORD .... Submerged Object Recovery Device
SORD .... Systematic Organizational Design
SORDAC... Special Operations Research, Development, and Acquisition Center [*Military*]
SORDC...... Southwest Ohio Regional Data Center [*University of Cincinnati*] [*Research center*] (RCD)
SORE........ Stamp Out Regulatory Excesses [*An association*] (EA)
SOREL ...... Sun-Orbiting Relativity Experiment Satellite
SOREM..... Sleep-Onset REM [*Rapid Eye Movement*]
So Rep ...... Southern Reporter [*A publication*] (DLA)
So Repr ..... Southern Reporter [*A publication*] (DLA)
S O Rev ..... Sean O'Casey Review [*A publication*]
SORG .... Sorg Printing Co. [*NASDAQ symbol*] (NQ)
SORG .... Submarine Operations Research Group [*Navy*]
SORI........ Southern Research Institute (AAG)
SORIN...... Societa Ricerche Impianti Nucleari [*Italy*]
SORM .... Set-Oriented Retrieval Module
SORNE(I) ... Senior Officer, Royal Naval Establishment (India) [*British*] [*World War II*]
SORNG ..... Sound Ranging
So R NS ..... Southern Review: New Series [*US*] [*A publication*]
SORO .... Scan on Receive Only (MCD)
SORO .... Special Operations Research Office
SORP........ Signature Overlay Range Prediction (MCD)
SORP........ Statement of Recommended Practice [*Accounting*] [*British*]
SORPTR ... South Repeater [*NASA*] (MCD)
SORR .... SIGINT [*Signal Intelligence*] Operations Readiness Review [*Military*] (AABC)
SORR .... Submarine Operations Research Report [*Navy*]
SORRAT... Society for Research on Rapport and Telekinesis (EA)
SORS........ Shipboard Operational Readiness System [*Navy*] (CAAL)
SORS........ Spacecraft Oscillograph Recording System
SORSI ...... Sacro Occipital Research Society International (EA)
SORT........ Self-Observation and Report Technique
SORT........ Senior Officer Refresher Training
SORT........ Shippers of Recycled Textiles [*An association*] (EA)
SORT........ Ship's Operational Readiness Test
SORT........ Simulated Optical Range Target (MCD)
SORT........ Slosson Oral Reading Tests
SORT........ Special Operations Response Team [*Prison management*]
SORT........ Spilled Oil Response Team [*Marine science*] (MSC)
SORT........ Staff Organizations Round Table [*American Library Association*]
SORT........ Structured-Objective Rorschach Test [*Psychology*]
SORT........ Structures for Orbiting Radio Telescope (MCD)
SORT........ Supply Corps Officer Refresher Training [*Navy*] (DNAB)
SORT........ System Operational Readiness Test (MCD)
SORTE...... Summary of Radiation Tolerant Electronics
SORTEC ... Synchrotron Orbital Radiation Technology [*High-energy physics*]
SORTI....... Satellite Orbital Track and Intercept [*ARPA*]
SORTI....... Star-Oriented Real-Time Teaching Instrument (AAG)
SORTIE .... Simulation of Reentry Target Interceptor Endgame (MCD)
SORTIE .... Super-Orbital Reentry Test Integrated Environment (MUGU)

SORTS ...... Shipboard Organizational Troubleshooting System (MCD)
SORTS ...... Status of Resources and Training System Report [*Military*]
SORWUC ... Service, Office, and Retail Workers Union of Canada
SOS........... Coalition to Protect Social Security (EA)
SOS........... Congress of Scientists on Survival [*Inactive*]
SOS........... Safety Observation Station
SOS........... Safety on the Streets [*Project of National Safety Council*]
SoS............ Saga och Sed [*A publication*]
SOS........... Same Old Sludge [*Slang phrase used to describe television programming*]
SOS........... Same Old Stew [*Military slang*] [*Bowdlerized version*]
SOS........... Same Old Stuff [*Reference to the weather*]
SOS........... Same Only Softer [*Band leader's signal*] [*Slang*]
SOS........... Sanity on Sex [*Group opposing sex education in schools*]
SOS........... Satellite Observation System
SOS........... Save Our Schools (EA)
SOS........... Save Our Security (EA)
SOS........... Save Our Ship [*or Souls*] [*Popular explanation of Morse code letters used as a signal for extreme distress*]
SOS........... Save Our Shores (EA)
SOS........... Save Our Snails [*An association*]
SOS........... Save Our Sons [*Cancer information service*] [*British*]
SOS........... Save Our Strays (EA)
SOS........... [*Anatoly*] Scharansky, [*Yuri*] Orlov, and [*Andrei*] Sakharov [*Organization named after dissident Soviet scientists*] (EA)
SOS........... Scheduled Oil Sampling [*Automotive engineering*]
SOS........... Science of Survival
SOS........... Scientists for Sakharov, Orlov, and Shcharansky (EA)
SO & S....... Scouting, Observation, and Sniping [*British military*] (DMA)
SOS........... Secretary of State
SOS........... Secular Organizations for Sobriety (EA)
SOS........... Self-Opening Sack [*Paper bag*]
SOS........... Self-Organizing System
SOS........... Semitic and Oriental Studies [*A publication*]
SOS........... Send Out Succor
SOS........... Senior Opportunities and Services [*OEO*]
SOS........... Sentinel on Station
SOS........... Serial Output Special (MCD)
SOS........... Service Order System [*Telecommunications*] (TEL)
SOS........... Service on Sight [*Computer warranty program offered by Hyundai Electronics*] (PCM)
SOS........... Service of Supply [*Later, ASF*] [*Army*]
SOS........... Shakespeare Oxford Society (EA)
SOS........... Share Operating System [*Data processing*]
SOS........... Share Our Strength (EA)
SOS........... Ship Our Ships Program [*Navy*] (DNAB)
SOS........... Ships Operational Safety [*A publication*]
SOS........... Ships Ordnance Summary
SOS........... Shock-on-Shock
SOS........... Shop Order Shop (SAA)
SOS........... Shop Out of Stock (SAA)
SOS........... Si Opus Sit [*If Needed*] [*Pharmacy*]
SOS........... Signed-Off Sick
SOS........... Silicon-on-Sapphire [*Integrated circuit*]
SOS........... Simultaneous Oral Spelling [*Gillingham method*] [*Education*]
SOS........... Sisters of Service [*Roman Catholic religious order*]
SOS........... Slip on Show [*Indicates a woman's slip is showing*] (DSUE)
SOS........... Slum on a Shingle [*Army breakfast dish*] [*Bowdlerized version*]
SOS........... Sniping, Observation, and Scouting [*Course*] [*Military*] [*British*] [*World War I*]
SOS........... Society for Occlusal Studies (EA)
SOS........... Society of Operative Stonemasons [*A union*] [*British*]
SOS........... Society of Scribes (EA)
SOS........... Society of Separationists (EA)
SOS........... Society of Shuttlemakers [*A union*] [*British*]
SOS........... Society of Signalmen (EA)
SoS............ Song of Songs [*Old Testament book*] [*Roman Catholic canon*] (BJA)
SOS........... Sophisticated Operating System [*Apple III microcomputer*] [*Data processing*]
SOS........... Sostenuto [*Sustained*] [*Music*]
SOS........... Source of Supply
SOS........... Soviet Oceanographic Surveillance (MCD)
SOS........... Space Ordnance Systems, Inc. (MCD)
SOS........... Spare Operation Support
SOS........... Special Operations Squadron [*Air Force*]
SOS........... Special Organizational Services [*An association*] (EA)
SOS........... Speed of Service [*Telecommunications*] (TEL)
SOS........... Speed of Sound
SOS........... SPRINT Operations Shelter [*Army*]
SOS........... Squadron Officers School [*Air Force*]
SOS........... Squadron Operational Support [*Military*] (AFIT)
SOS........... Stabilized Optical Sight
SOS........... Stamp Out Stupidity [*Student group opposing drug abuse*]
SOS........... Start of Significance [*Data processing*] (BUR)
SOS........... Statement of Service [*Military*]
SOS........... Statement of Supply
SOS........... Station Operating Supervisor (IEEE)
SOS........... Stock Order Shipment
SOS........... Storage-on-Site [*Grolier Electronic Publishing, Inc.*]

SOS........... Store Overstocked [*Inventory*]
SOS........... Strategic Orbital System   (AAG)
SOS........... Struck off Strength [*British military*]   (DMA)
SOS........... Student Orientations Survey [*Student attitudes test*]
SOS........... Student-Originated Studies [*National Science Foundation*]
SOS........... Studies on Smoking, Inc. [*Research center*]   (RCD)
SOS........... Suborbital Sequence [*NASA*]
SOS........... Sum-of-the-Squares
SOS........... Sum over States [*Physics*]
SOS........... Supervisor of Shipbuilding [*Navy*]
SOS........... Supplemental Oxygen System   (MCD)
SOS........... Supplementary Ophthalmic Service [*Medicine*]
SOS........... Support Our Soldiers [*Network of antiwar-oriented coffee
               houses located near military bases*]   (EA)
SOS........... Supporters of Silkwood [*Inactive*]   (EA)
SOS........... Survivors of Sacrifice   (EA)
SOS........... Survivors of Suicide
SOS........... Suspend Other Service [*Business term*]
SOS........... Suspension of Service [*Pilots' strike*]
SOS........... Symbolic Operating System [*Data processing*]
SOS........... Symmetry, Orbitals, and Spectra [*Atomic physics*]
SoS............ Syn og Segn [*A publication*]
SOS........... Synchronous Orbit Satellite   (AAG)
SOS........... System Operational Specification [*Military*]   (CAAL)
SOS........... Systems, Objectives, Solutions [*A publication*]
SOSA......... Sell Overseas America, the Association of American Export
               [*Redondo Beach, CA*]   (EA)
SOSA......... Somerset Bankshares, Inc. [*NASDAQ symbol*]   (NQ)
SOSA......... Sustained Operations Support Area [*NASA*]   (KSC)
Sos Aikakausk ... Sosiaalinen Aikakauskirja [*A publication*]
SOSAL...... School of Systems and Logistics [*Military*]
SOSAT...... Submarine One-Way Satellite [*Navy*]   (CAAL)
SOSC......... Safety Observation Station Display Console
SOSC......... Smithsonian Oceanographic Sorting Center
SOSC......... Source of Supply Code
SOSCAR ... Supervisor of Shipbuilding, Conversion, and Repair
               [*Navy*]   (DNAB)
So School News ... Southern School News [*A publication*]
SOSCU...... Stamps on Stamps - Centenary Unit   (EA)
SOSD........ Spatial Operational Sequence Diagram
SOSE......... Science Operations Support Equipment
SOSE......... Silicon-on-Something-Else [*Telecommunications*]   (TEL)
SOSE......... Special Operations Support Element [*Military*]   (GFGA)
SOSEC...... Satellite Ocean Surveillance Evaluation Center
SOSED...... Secretary's Office, Shore Establishments Division [*Incorporated
               into SECP, 1944*] [*Navy*]
SOSH .... Search for the Odd Shape [*Neuropsychology test*]
SO SH ...... Somali Shilling [*Monetary unit*]
Sosh .... Soshioloji [*A publication*]
SOS:HRG ... SOS: Human Rights for Guyana   (EA)
SOSI......... Shift In, Shift Out   (IEEE)
SOSI......... Sippican, Inc. [*Formerly, Sippican Ocean Systems*] [*NASDAQ
               symbol*]   (NQ)
SOS Intl..... Society of Saunterers, International   (EA)
SOSIS........ Status of Support Information System
SOSK........ Squadron Operational Support Kit   (MCD)
SO/SL .... Saturn Orbiter Satellite Lander [*NASA*]
S Osl .... Symbolae Osloenses [*A publication*]
SOSM........ Ship Overhaul Schedule Milestone [*Navy*]
SOSM........ Source of Supply Modifier
SOSO .... Safety and Operating Systems Office [*NASA*]
SoSo........... South of SoHo [*See also NoHo, SoHo, TriBeCa*] [*Artists' colony
               in New York City*]
SOSO .... Synchronous Orbiting Solar Observatory
SOSP........ Squadron Operational Support Package [*Military*]   (AFIT)
SOSQ......... Special Operations Squadron
SOSR......... Spin on Straight Rail
SOSS......... Satellite Ocean Surveillance System
SOSS .... Satellite Optical Surveillance Station   (MCD)
SOSS .... Shipboard Oceanographic Survey System
SOSS .... SONAR Schoolship [*Navy*]   (NVT)
SOSS .... Sound Search Station
SOSS .... Soviet Ocean Surveillance System   (MCD)
SOSS .... Strategic Orbital System Study   (AAG)
SOSS .... Structurally Oriented Simulation System [*NASA*]
SOSSI........ Scouts on Stamps Society International   (EA)
SOSSI........ SOS Sahel International [*British*]   (EAIO)
SOSSPA.... Service of Supply, South Pacific Area [*Navy*] [*World War II*]
SOSSUS.... Study on Surgical Services in the United States [*Medicine*]
SOST........ Sostenuto [*Sustained*] [*Music*]
So St.......... Southern Studies [*A publication*]
SOST........ Special Operator Service Traffic [*Telecommunications*]   (TEL)
SOSTEL.... Solid-State Electric Logic   (NG)
SOSTEN ... Sostenuto [*Sustained*] [*Music*]
SOSU......... Scout Observation Service Unit [*Navy*]
SOSU......... Seattle Ocean Services Unit [*National Oceanic and
               Atmospheric Administration*]   (GFGA)
SOSU......... Ships on Stamps Unit   (EA)
SOSUS...... SONAR Surveillance System [*Military*]
SOSUS...... Sound Surveillance System   (MSA)
SOSUS...... Sound Surveillance Undersea   (MCD)

SOSUS...... Sound Surveillance Underwater System [*Navy*]
SOSVS ...... Sound Surveillance System
SOT .... Same Old Thing [*Slang*]
SOT .... Secretary of Transportation   (NATG)
SOT .... Sensation of Transcendence
SOT .... Shower over Tub [*Real estate*]
SOT .... Simulated Operational Training [*Navy*]   (DNAB)
SoT .... Slöejd och Ton [*A publication*]
SOT .... Snowbird, TN [*Location identifier*] [*FAA*]   (FAAL)
SOT .... Society of Ornamental Turners   (EA)
SOT .... Society of Toxicology   (EA)
SOT .... Solar Optical Telescope
SOT .... Son of Temperance [*A heavy drinker*] [*Slang*]
Sot............ Sotah   (BJA)
SOT .... Sound on Tape [*Videotape*]
SOT .... Sounds of Our Times, Cook Studio [*Record label*]
SOT .... South Omaha Terminal Railway Co. [*AAR code*]
SOT .... Soviet Orientation Team   (MCD)
SOT .... Spatial Orientation Trainer [*Air Force*]
SOT .... Special Operations Team   (ADA)
SOT .... SRO Entertainment [*Vancouver Stock Exchange symbol*]
SOT .... Start of Tape
SOT .... Start of Text
SOT .... State of Termination [*Telecommunications*]   (TEL)
S-O-T....... Stoke-On-Trent [*City in England*]
SOT .... Strap-On Tank [*NASA*]   (NASA)
SOT .... Stream of Thought
SOT .... Structural Operations Technology Group   (SSD)
SOT .... Subscriber Originating Trunk [*Telecommunications*]   (TEL)
SOT .... Syntax-Oriented Translator   (IEEE)
SOT .... Systems Operating Test
SOTA .... State of the Art
SOTA .... State of the Art, Inc. [*NASDAQ symbol*]   (SPSG)
SOTA .... Students Older than Average
SOTAC...... State-of-the-Art Car [*Transit*] [*Department of Transportation*]
SOTACA ... State-of-the-Art Contingency Analysis System [*Science
               Applications International Corp.*]   (MCD)
SOTAP...... Sophisticated Training Program
SOTARSS ... Standoff Target Acquisition Reconnaissance Surveillance
               System   (MCD)
SOTAS...... Standoff Target Acquisition/Attack System
SOTASS.... Standoff Target Acquisition and Surveillance System [*Army*]
SOTB........ Secretary's Office, Transportation Branch [*Navy*]
SOTCA...... Soudage et Techniques Connexes [*A publication*]
SOTD .... Stabilized Optical Tracking Device   (SAA)
SOTDAT... Source Test Data System [*Environmental Protection Agency*]
SOTE........ Standard Optical Test Equipment
SOTE........ System Operational Test Evaluation   (SAA)
SOTEAG... Shetland Oil Terminal Environmental Advisory Group
So Tex LJ .. Southern Texas Law Journal [*A publication*]   (DLA)
SOTF........ Special Operations Task Force [*Military*]   (GFGA)
SOTFE...... Special Operations Task Force, Europe [*Military*]
SOTG .... Sales Other than Gasoline [*Business term*]
Sothbys ...... Sotheby's Holdings, Inc. [*Associated Press
               abbreviation*]   (APAG)
SOTI.......... [*A*] Survey of Old Testament Introductions [*Gleason L. Archer*]
               [*A publication*]   (BJA)
SOTIB ...... Sotsialisticheskaya Industriya [*A publication*]
SOTID ...... Solar Times [*A publication*]
Sotilaslaak Aikak ... Sotilaslaaketieteellinen Aikakauslehti [*A publication*]
SOTIM...... Sonic Observation of the Trajectory and Impact of Missiles
SOTK........ Sono-Tek Corp. [*NASDAQ symbol*]   (NQ)
SOTP......... Saturn Orbiter/Titan Probe   (MCD)
SOTP......... Ship Overhaul Test Program
SOTP......... Shipyard Overhaul Test Program
SOTP......... System Overhaul Test Program
SOTR........ Single Object Tracking RADAR   (MCD)
SOTR........ SouthTrust Corp. [*NASDAQ symbol*]   (NQ)
SOTS........ Suborbital Tank Separation [*NASA*]   (MCD)
SOTS........ Synchronous Orbiting Tracking Stations   (MCD)
Sots Pollum ... Sotsialistik Pollumajandus [*A publication*]
Sots Sel'Khoz Azerb ... Sotsialisticheskoe Sel'skoe Khozyaistvo
               Azerbaidzhana [*A publication*]
Sots Sel'Khoz Uzbek ... Sotsialisticheskoe Sel'skoe Khozyaistvo Uzbekistana
               [*A publication*]
Sots Sel'sk Khoz Azerb ... Sotsialisticheskoe Sel'skoe Khozyaistvo
               Azerbaidzhana [*A publication*]
Sots Sel'sk Khoz Uzb ... Sotsialisticheskoe Sel'skoe Khozyaistvo Uzbekistana
               [*A publication*]
Sots Trud ... Sotsialisticheskiy Trud [*Former USSR*] [*A publication*]
Sots Tvarinnit ... Sotsialistichne Tvarinnitstvo [*A publication*]
Sots Tvarynnytstvo ... Sotsialistychne Tvarynnytstvo [*A publication*]
SOTT......... Second-Order Transition Temperature
SOTT......... Synthetic Medium Old Tuberculin Trichloroacetic Acid
               Precipitated [*Later, PPD, Purified Protein Derivative*]
               [*Immunology*]
SOTUS...... Sequentially Operated Teletypewriter Universal Selector
SOU.......... Scandinavian Ornithological Union [*Lund, Sweden*]   (EAIO)
SOU.......... Souchong [*Tea trade*]   (ROG)
SOU.......... Sources Public Library [*UTLAS symbol*]
SOU.......... South   (ROG)

SOU .... South. The Third World Magazine [*A publication*]
SOU .... Southampton [*England*] [*Airport symbol*] (OAG)
SOU .... Southern Airways [*Air carrier designation symbol*]
SOU .... Southern California Gas Co. [*AMEX symbol*] (SPSG)
SOU .... Southern Petroleum Corp. [*Vancouver Stock Exchange symbol*]
SOU .... Southern Railway System [*AAR code*]
SOU .... Statens Offentliga Utredningar [*Sweden*]
Sou Aus LR ... South Australian Law Reports [*A publication*]
SOUCO ..... Southern Union Co. [*Associated Press abbreviation*] (APAG)
Soudage Tech Connexes ... Soudage et Techniques Connexes [*A publication*]
Soud Lek.... Soudni Lekarstvi [*A publication*]
Soudwn....... Southdown, Inc. [*Associated Press abbreviation*] (APAG)
SOUL .... Studies of Ocean Upper Layers (MSC)
Soule Syn ... Soule's Dictionary of English Synonyms [*A publication*] (DLA)
Soul Il........ Soul Illustrated [*A publication*]
So U LR .... Southern University Law Review [*A publication*]
So U L Rev ... Southern University Law Review [*A publication*]
Soun .... Soundings [*A publication*]
Sound .... Soundings [*A publication*]
Sound Brass ... Sounding Brass and the Conductor [*A publication*]
Sound (Can) ... Sound (Canada) [*A publication*]
Sound Vib .. Sound and Vibration [*A publication*]
Sound Vis Broadc ... Sound and Vision Broadcasting [*A publication*]
So Univ L Rev ... Southern University Law Review [*A publication*]
SOUP .... Solar Optical Universal Polarimeter
SOUP .... Solid Uncured Propellant (MCD)
SOUP .... Students Opposed to Unfair Practices [*in advertising*] [*Student legal action organization*]
SOUP .... Submarine Operational Update Program [*Canadian Navy*]
SOUQAR .. Section d'Oceanographie d'Universite de Quebec a Rimouski [*Canada*] (MSC)
SOUR .... Sourdough Journal. Alaska Library Association [*A publication*]
SouR .... Southern Review [*US*] [*A publication*]
SourcC ...... Source Capital, Inc. [*Associated Press abbreviation*] (APAG)
SOURCE... Simulation of Utilization, Resources, Cost, and Efficiency
Sources Chr ... Sources Chretiennes [*A publication*]
Sources Hist Math Phys Sci ... Sources in the History of Mathematics and Physical Sciences [*A publication*]
Sources Sci ... Sources of Science [*A publication*]
Sources and Stud Hist Arabic-Islamic Sci Hist of Math Ser ... Sources and Studies in the History of Arabic-Islamic Science. History of Mathematics Series [*A publication*]
Sources Stud Hist Arabic-Islamic Sci Hist of Tech Ser ... Sources and Studies in the History of Arabic-Islamic Science. History of Technology Series [*A publication*]
Sources Stud Hist Arabic Math ... Sources and Studies in the History of Arabic Mathematics [*A publication*]
SOURS...... Subcommittee on Use of Radioactivity Standards [*National Research Council*]
SOUSAFE ... Status of United States Air Force Equipment
SOUSSA ... Steady, Oscillatory, and Unsteady, Subsonic, and Supersonic Aerodynamics [*NASA*]
SOUT .... SouthernNet, Inc. [*NASDAQ symbol*] (NQ)
SOUT .... Swap-Out [*Data processing*]
SOUTB...... Statens Offentliga Utredningar [*A publication*]
SOUTC...... Satellite Operators and Users Technical Committee (EA)
South.......... Southern Reporter [*National Reporter System*] [*A publication*] (DLA)
South Afr Archaeol B ... South African Archaeological Bulletin [*A publication*]
South Afr Arch B ... South African Archaeological Bulletin [*A publication*]
South Afr Geogr J ... South African Geographical Journal [*A publication*]
South African J African Affairs ... South African Journal of African Affairs [*A publication*]
South African J Econ ... South African Journal of Economics [*Suid-Afrikaanse Tydskrif vir Ekonomie*] [*A publication*]
South African Labour Bul ... South African Labour Bulletin [*A publication*]
South African Med J ... South African Medical Journal [*A publication*]
South African Med Rec ... South African Medical Record [*A publication*]
South African Min Eng Jour ... South African Mining and Engineering Journal [*A publication*]
South African MJ ... South African Medical Journal [*A publication*]
South African Statist J ... South African Statistical Journal [*A publication*]
South Afr Int Quart ... South Africa International Quarterly [*A publication*]
South Afr J Afr Aff ... South African Journal of African Affairs [*A publication*]
South Afr J Econ ... South African Journal of Economics [*Suid-Afrikaanse Tydskrif vir Ekonomie*] [*A publication*]
South Afr J Sci ... South African Journal of Science [*A publication*]
South Afr J Surg ... South African Journal of Surgery [*A publication*]
South Afr Law J ... South African Law Journal [*A publication*]
South Afr LJ ... South African Law Journal [*A publication*]
South Afr Text ... Southern Africa Textiles [*A publication*]
South Am J Bio-Sci ... South American Journal of Bio-Sciences [*A publication*]
South Am J Med ... South American Journal of Medicine [*A publication*]
Southard .... Southard's New Jersey Law Reports [*4-5 New Jersey*] [*A publication*] (DLA)
South Ariz Guideb ... Southern Arizona Guidebook [*A publication*]

South As Dig Reg Writ ... South Asian Digest of Regional Writing [*Heidelberg*] [*A publication*]
South Asian R ... South Asian Review [*A publication*]
South Asian Stud ... South Asian Studies [*A publication*]
South As Stud ... South Asian Studies [*Jaipur*] [*A publication*]
South As Surv ... South Asian Survey [*New Delhi*] [*A publication*]
South Atlan Q ... South Atlantic Quarterly [*A publication*]
South Atl Bull ... South Atlantic Bulletin [*A publication*]
South Atl Q ... South Atlantic Quarterly [*A publication*]
South Aus LR ... South Australian Law Reports [*A publication*]
South Aust Dep Agric Fish Agron Branch Rep ... South Australia. Department of Agriculture and Fisheries. Agronomy Branch. Report [*A publication*]
South Aust Dep Agric Fish Agron Bran Rep ... South Australia. Department of Agriculture and Fisheries. Agronomy Branch. Report [*A publication*] (APTA)
South Aust Dep Mines Miner Resour Rev ... South Australia. Department of Mines. Mineral Resources Review [*A publication*] (APTA)
South Aust Geol Surv Bull ... South Australia. Geological Survey. Bulletin [*A publication*] (APTA)
South Aust Geol Surv 1:250000 Geol Ser ... South Australia. Geological Survey. 1:250,000 Geological Series [*A publication*] (APTA)
South Aust Geol Surv Q Geol Notes ... South Australia. Geological Survey. Quarterly Geological Notes [*A publication*] (APTA)
South Aust Geol Surv Rep Invest ... South Australia. Geological Survey. Report of Investigations [*A publication*] (APTA)
South Aust Mot ... South Australian Motor [*A publication*] (APTA)
South Aust Nat ... South Australian Naturalist [*A publication*] (APTA)
South Aust Orn ... South Australian Ornithologist [*A publication*] (APTA)
South Aust Rep Mus Board ... South Australia. Report of the Museum Board [*A publication*]
South Bap Per Ind ... Southern Baptist Periodical Index [*A publication*]
South Baptist Period Index ... Southern Baptist Periodical Index [*A publication*]
South Birds ... Southern Birds [*A publication*]
South Bus... South Business [*A publication*]
South Calif Coastal Water Res Proj Annu Rep ... Southern California Coastal Water Research Project. Annual Report [*A publication*]
South Calif Coastal Water Res Proj Bienn Rep ... Southern California Coastal Water Research Project. Biennial Report [*A publication*]
South Calif L Rev ... Southern California Law Review [*A publication*]
South Calif Q ... Southern California Quarterly [*A publication*]
South Cal Law Rev ... Southern California Law Review [*A publication*]
South Canner Packer ... Southern Canner and Packer [*A publication*]
South Cant J ... South Canterbury Journal [*A publication*]
South Car... South Carolina Reports [*A publication*] (DLA)
South Carbonator Bottler ... Southern Carbonator and Bottler [*A publication*]
South Carolina Acad Sci Bull ... South Carolina Academy of Science. Bulletin [*A publication*]
South Carolina Div Geology Geol Notes ... South Carolina. Division of Geology. Geologic Notes [*A publication*]
South Carolina Div Geology Misc Rept ... South Carolina. Division of Geology. Miscellaneous Report [*A publication*]
South Carolina L Rev ... South Carolina Law Review [*A publication*]
South Car R ... South Carolina Review [*A publication*]
South Chem ... Southern Chemist [*A publication*]
South Chem Ind ... Southern Chemical Industry [*A publication*]
South China J Agric Sci ... South China Journal of Agricultural Science [*A publication*]
SouthCo ..... Southern Co. [*Associated Press abbreviation*] (APAG)
SOUTHCOM ... Southern Command [*Military*] (AFM)
South Conf Gerontol Rep ... Southern Conference on Gerontology. Report [*A publication*]
South Coop Ser Bull ... Southern Cooperative Series Bulletin [*A publication*]
South Corn Impr Conf Rep ... Southern Corn Improvement Conference. Report [*A publication*]
South Dairy Prod J ... Southern Dairy Products Journal [*A publication*]
South Dak L Rev ... South Dakota Law Review [*A publication*]
South Dakota Geol Survey Guidebook ... South Dakota. Geological Survey. Guidebook [*A publication*]
South Dakota Geol Survey Rept Inv ... South Dakota. Geological Survey. Report of Investigations [*A publication*]
South Dakota Geol Survey Spec Rept ... South Dakota. Geological Survey. Special Report [*A publication*]
South Dakota Geol Survey Water Resources Rept ... South Dakota Geological Survey and South Dakota Water Resources Commission. Water Resources Report [*A publication*]
South Dakota L Rev ... South Dakota Law Review [*A publication*]
Southeast Asia Bldg Materials & Equipment ... Southeast Asia Building Materials and Equipment [*A publication*]
South East Asia Iron Steel Inst Q ... South East Asia Iron and Steel Institute. Quarterly [*A publication*]
Southeast Asia J Theol ... Southeast Asia Journal of Theology [*A publication*]
Southeast Asian Conf Soil Eng Proc ... Southeast Asian Conference on Soil Engineering. Proceedings [*A publication*]
Southeast Asian Fish Dev Cent Aquacult Dep Q Res Rep ... Southeast Asian Fisheries Development Center. Aquaculture Department. Quarterly Research Report [*A publication*]
Southeast Asian J Soc Sci ... Southeast Asian Journal of Social Science [*A publication*]

Southeast Asian J Trop Med Public Health ... Southeast Asian Journal of Tropical Medicine and Public Health [*A publication*]
South East Asian Pac Congr Clin Biochem ... South East Asian and Pacific Congress of Clinical Biochemistry [*A publication*]
South East Asian Stud ... South East Asian Studies [*A publication*]
Southeast Asia Pet Explor Soc Proc ... Southeast Asia Petroleum Exploration Society. Proceedings [*A publication*]
Southeast Conf Appl Sol Energy Proc ... Southeast Conference on Application of Solar Energy. Proceedings [*A publication*]
Southeastcon Reg 3 (Three) Conf Proc ... Southeastcon Region 3 (Three) Conference Proceedings [*United States*] [*A publication*]
Southeast Drug J ... Southeastern Drug Journal [*A publication*]
Southeastern Geology Spec Pub ... Southeastern Geology. Special Publication [*A publication*]
Southeastern Rep ... South Eastern Reporter [*A publication*]   (DLA)
Southeast Geogr ... Southeastern Geographer [*A publication*]
Southeast Geol ... Southeastern Geology [*A publication*]
Southeast Geol Soc Field Conf Guideb ... Southeastern Geological Society. Field Conference Guidebook [*A publication*]
Southeast Geol Spec Publ ... Southeastern Geology. Special Publication [*A publication*]
Southeast Reg Conf Kraft Mill Process Prod Eng ... Southeast Regional Conference. Kraft Mill Process and Product Engineering [*A publication*]
Southeast Reg Water Resour Symp Proc ... Southeast Region Water Resources Symposium. Proceedings [*A publication*]
Southeast Semin Therm Sci ... Southeastern Seminar on Thermal Sciences [*A publication*]
Southeast Semin Therm Sci Proc ... Southeastern Seminar on Thermal Sciences. Proceedings [*A publication*]
South Econ ... Southern Economist [*Bangalore*] [*A publication*]
South Econ J ... Southern Economic Journal [*A publication*]
South Econ Jour ... Southern Economic Journal [*A publication*]
Southern .... Southern Reporter [*A publication*]   (DLA)
Southern Calif Acad Sci Bull ... Southern California Academy of Sciences. Bulletin [*A publication*]
Southern Econ J ... Southern Economic Journal [*A publication*]
Southern Folklore Q ... Southern Folklore Quarterly [*A publication*]
Southern H R ... Southern Humanities Review [*A publication*]
Southern Hum R ... Southern Humanities Review [*A publication*]
Southern J Med Phys Sc ... Southern Journal of the Medical and Physical Sciences [*A publication*]
Southern Lit J ... Southern Literary Journal [*A publication*]
Southern P R ... Southern Poetry Review [*A publication*]
Southern Pulp Paper Mfr ... Southern Pulp and Paper Manufacturer [*A publication*]
Southern R ... Southern Review [*US*] [*A publication*]
Southern Rep ... Southern Reporter [*A publication*]   (DLA)
Southern Rev ... Southern Review [*US*] [*A publication*]   (APTA)
South Exposure ... Southern Exposure [*United States*] [*A publication*]
South Fisherman ... Southern Fisherman [*A publication*]
South Florist Nurseryman ... Southern Florist and Nurseryman [*United States*] [*A publication*]
South Folkl Q ... Southern Folklore Quarterly [*A publication*]
South Folkl Quart ... Southern Folklore Quarterly [*A publication*]
South Folk Q ... Southern Folklore Quarterly [*A publication*]
South Food Process ... Southern Food Processor [*A publication*]
SOUTHFORNET ... Southern Forestry Information Network [*Forest Service*] (IID)
South Gen Pract Med Surg ... Southern General Practitioner of Medicine and Surgery [*A publication*]
South Hist Assoc Publ ... Southern Historical Association. Publications [*A publication*]
South Hist Soc Papers ... Southern Historical Society. Papers [*A publication*]
South Hort ... Southern Horticulture [*New Zealand*] [*A publication*]
South Hortic ... Southern Horticulture [*A publication*]
South Hosp ... Southern Hospitals [*A publication*]
South Hum Rev ... Southern Humanities Review [*A publication*]
South Ill Lab Trib ... Southern Illinois Labor Tribune [*A publication*]
South Ill ULJ ... Southern Illinois University. Law Journal [*A publication*]
South Indian Hortic ... Southern Indian Horticulture [*A publication*]
South Ind St ... Southern Indian Studies [*United States*] [*A publication*]
South J Agric Econ ... Southern Journal of Agricultural Economics [*A publication*]
South J Appl For ... Southern Journal of Applied Forestry [*A publication*]
South Jewel ... Southern Jeweler [*A publication*]
South Law J ... Southern Law Journal [*Tuscaloosa, AL*] [*A publication*]   (DLA)
South Law J & Rep ... Southern Law Journal and Reporter [*A publication*]   (DLA)
South Law Rev ... Southern Law Review [*A publication*]   (DLA)
South Law Rev NS ... Southern Law Review, New Series [*A publication*]   (DLA)
South Lit J ... Southern Literary Journal [*A publication*]
South Liv .... Southern Living [*A publication*]
South LJ .... Southern Law Journal [*A publication*]   (DLA)
South LJ & Rep ... Southern Law Journal and Reporter [*A publication*]   (DLA)
South L Rev ... Southern Law Review [*A publication*]   (DLA)
South L Rev NS ... Southern Law Review, New Series [*A publication*]   (DLA)
South Lumberman ... Southern Lumberman [*A publication*]

South M ..... South Magazine [*A publication*]
South Med ... Southern Medicine [*A publication*]
South Med Bull ... Southern Medical Bulletin [*A publication*]
South Med J ... Southern Medical Journal [*A publication*]
South Med Surg ... Southern Medicine and Surgery [*A publication*]
South Methodist Univ Inst Stud Earth Man Rep ... Southern Methodist University. Institute for the Study of Earth and Man. Reports of Investigations [*A publication*]
South MJ ... Southern Medical Journal [*A publication*]
SOUTHN ... Southampton [*City in England*]   (ROG)
South Pac ... South Pacific [*A publication*]
South Pac Bull ... South Pacific Bulletin [*A publication*]
South Pac Comm Handb ... South Pacific Commission. Handbook [*A publication*]
South Pac Comm Tech Pap ... Southern Pacific Commission. Technical Paper [*A publication*]
South Pacific B ... South Pacific Bulletin [*A publication*]
South Pacific Bul ... South Pacific Bulletin [*A publication*]   (APTA)
South Pacific J Ed ... South Pacific Journal of Education [*A publication*]   (APTA)
South Pac J Nat Sci ... South Pacific Journal of Natural Science [*A publication*]
South Pac J Teach Educ ... South Pacific Journal of Teacher Education [*A publication*]   (APTA)
South Pac Mar Geol Notes ... South Pacific Marine Geological Notes [*Suva*] [*A publication*]
South Petrochem Ind Corp Ind Eng Train Bull ... Southern Petrochemical Industries Corp. Industrial Engineering and Training Bulletin [*A publication*]
South Pharm J ... Southern Pharmaceutical Journal [*A publication*]
South Plast Chem ... Southern Plastics and Chemicals [*A publication*]
South Power Ind ... Southern Power and Industry [*A publication*]
South Power J ... Southern Power Journal [*A publication*]
South Pract ... Southern Practitioner [*A publication*]
South Pulp Pap ... Southern Pulp and Paper [*A publication*]
South Pulp Pap J ... Southern Pulp and Paper Journal [*A publication*]
South Pulp Pap Manuf ... Southern Pulp and Paper Manufacturer [*A publication*]
South Q ...... Southern Quarterly [*A publication*]
South Quar ... Southern Quarterly Review [*A publication*]
South Quart ... Southern Quarterly [*A publication*]
South Queensl Conf ... Southern Queensland Conference [*A publication*]
South R ...... South Carolina Review [*A publication*]
South R ...... Southern Review [*US*] [*A publication*]
South Rag .. Southern Rag [*A publication*]
South Res Inst Bull ... Southern Research Institute. Bulletin [*United States*] [*A publication*]
South Rhod Geol Surv Bull ... Southern Rhodesia. Geological Survey. Bulletin [*A publication*]
South Rhod Geol Surv Short Rep ... Southern Rhodesia. Geological Survey. Short Report [*A publication*]
South Seedsman ... Southern Seedsman [*A publication*]
South Speech Comm J ... Southern Speech Communication Journal [*A publication*]
South Stars ... Southern Stars [*A publication*]
South States Assoc Comm Agric Other Agric Work Proc ... Southern States Association of Commissioners of Agriculture and Other Agricultural Workers. Proceedings [*A publication*]
South Stud ... Southern Studies [*A publication*]
South Surg ... Southern Surgeon [*United States*] [*A publication*]
South Texas Geol Soc Bull ... South Texas Geological Society. Bulletin [*A publication*]
South Texas LJ ... South Texas Law Journal [*A publication*]
South Text Bull ... Southern Textile Bulletin [*A publication*]
South UL Rev ... Southern University Law Review [*A publication*]
SOUTHW ... Southwell [*City in England*]   (ROG)
South Weed Sci Soc Proc ... Southern Weed Science Society. Proceedings [*A publication*]
Southwest Afr Ann ... Southwest Africa Annual [*A publication*]
South West Afr Sci Soc J ... South West Africa Scientific Society. Journal [*A publication*]
Southwest Bull ... Southwest Bulletin [*United States*] [*A publication*]
Southwest Bus and Econ R ... Southwest Business and Economic Review [*United States*] [*A publication*]
Southwest Entomol ... Southwestern Entomologist [*A publication*]
Southwest Entomol Suppl ... Southwestern Entomologist. Supplement [*A publication*]
Southwestern As Petroleum G B ... Southwestern Association of Petroleum Geologists. Bulletin [*A publication*]
Southwestern LA Jour ... Southwestern Louisiana Journal [*A publication*]
Southwestern LJ ... Southwestern Law Journal [*A publication*]
Southwestern R Mgt and Econ ... Southwestern Review of Management and Economics [*United States*] [*A publication*]
Southwestern UL Rev ... Southwestern University. Law Review [*A publication*]
Southwestern Univ L Rev ... Southwestern University. Law Review [*A publication*]
Southwest Hist Q ... Southwestern Historical Quarterly [*A publication*]
Southwest IEEE Conf Exhib Rec ... Southwestern IEEE [*Institute of Electrical and Electronics Engineers*] Conference and Exhibition. Record [*A publication*]

Southwest J ... Southwest Journal [*A publication*]
Southwest J Anthropol ... Southwestern Journal of Anthropology [*A publication*]
Southwest Med ... Southwestern Medicine [*United States*] [*A publication*]
Southwest Miller ... Southwestern Miller [*A publication*]
Southwest Mus Paper ... Southwest Museum. Papers [*A publication*]
Southwest Nat ... Southwestern Naturalist [*A publication*]
Southwest Pet Short Course Proc Annu Meet ... Southwestern Petroleum Short Course. Proceedings of the Annual Meeting [*United States*] [*A publication*]
Southwest Reg Conf Astron Astrophys Proc ... Southwest Regional Conference for Astronomy and Astrophysics. Proceedings [*A publication*]
Southwest Tex Water Works J ... Southwest and Texas Water Works Journal [*A publication*]
Southwest UL Rev ... Southwestern University. Law Review [*A publication*]
Southwest Vet ... Southwestern Veterinarian [*United States*] [*A publication*]
Southwest Water Works J ... Southwest Water Works Journal [*A publication*]
Southw His Q ... Southwestern Historical Quarterly [*A publication*]
Southw Hist Quar ... Southwestern Historical Quarterly [*A publication*]
Southw Hist Quart ... Southwestern Historical Quarterly [*United States*] [*A publication*]
Southw J Anthrop ... Southwestern Journal of Anthropology [*United States*] [*A publication*]
Southw Jnl Philos ... Southwestern Journal of Philosophy [*A publication*]
SouthWJTh ... Southwestern Journal of Theology [*Fort Worth, TX*] [*A publication*]
Southw LJ ... Southwestern Law Journal [*United States*] [*A publication*]
Southw LJ ... Southwestern Law Journal and Reporter [*A publication*]   (DLA)
Southw Lore ... Southwestern Lore [*A publication*]
Southw Pol Sci Quar ... Southwest Political Science Quarterly [*A publication*]
Southw Pol and Soc Sci Q ... Southwestern Political and Social Science Quarterly [*A publication*]
Southw Rev ... Southwest Review [*A publication*]
Southw Soc Sci Quar ... Southwestern Social Science Quarterly [*A publication*]
SOV .... Sammons' Opuntia Virus [*Plant pathology*]
SOV .... Seldovia, AK [*Location identifier*] [*FAA*]   (FAAL)
SOV .... Sham Ovariectomy [*Endocrinology*]
SOV .... Share of Voice [*Advertising*]
SOV .... Shut-Off Valve
SOV .... Simulated Operational Vehicle   (MCD)
SOV .... Single-Occupancy Vehicle   (ECON)
SOV .... Solenoid-Operated Valve
SOV .... Somerset County Vocational and Technical School, Bridgewater, NJ [*OCLC symbol*]   (OCLC)
SOV .... Sovereign
SOV .... Soviet
SOV .... Sovran Financial Corp. [*NYSE symbol*]   (CTT)
SOV .... Study of Values
SOV .... Subjective Optical Vertical
SOVAC.... Software Validation and Control System   (MCD)
SovAE........ Soviet Antarctic Expedition [*1955-*]
Sov Aeronaut ... Soviet Aeronautics [*English Translation of Izvestiya VUZ. Aviatsionnaya Teknika*] [*A publication*]
Sov Agron .. Sovetskaya Agronomiya [*A publication*]
Sov Am Symp Compr Anal Environ ... Soviet-American Symposium on the Comprehensive Analysis of the Environment [*A publication*]
Sov Am Symp Theory Light Scattering Solids ... Soviet-American Symposium on the Theory of Light Scattering in Solids [*A publication*]
Sov Antarct Exped Inf Bull ... Soviet Antarctic Expedition. Information Bulletin [*A publication*]
Sov Antarct Exped Inf Bull (Engl Transl) ... Soviet Antarctic Expedition. Information Bulletin (English Translation) [*A publication*]
Sov Antarct Exped Inform Bull ... Soviet Antarctic Expedition. Information Bulletin [*A publication*]
Sov Antarkt Eksped Inform Byull ... Sovetskaya Antarkticheskaya Ekspeditsiya Informatsionnyy Byulletin [*A publication*]
Sov Anthr A ... Soviet Anthropology and Archeology [*A publication*]
Sov Anthro Arch ... Soviet Anthropology and Archeology [*New York*] [*A publication*]
Sov Appl Mech ... Soviet Applied Mechanics [*A publication*]
Sov Appl Mech (Engl Transl) ... Soviet Applied Mechanics (English Translation) [*A publication*]
Sov Arch .... Sovetskaja Archeologija [*A publication*]
Sov Arh ...... Sovetskie Arhivi [*A publication*]
Sov Arkh.... Sovetskie Arkhivy [*A publication*]
Sov Arkheol ... Sovetskaya Arkheologiya [*A publication*]
Sov Astron ... Soviet Astronomy [*A publication*]
Sov Astron (Engl Transl) ... Soviet Astronomy (English Translation) [*A publication*]
Sov Astron Lett ... Soviet Astronomy. Letters [*A publication*]
Sov Astron Lett (Engl Transl) ... Soviet Astronomy. Letters (English Translation) [*A publication*]
Sov At Energy ... Soviet Atomic Energy [*A publication*]
Sov At Energy (Engl Transl) ... Soviet Atomic Energy (English Translation) [*A publication*]
Sov At En R ... Soviet Atomic Energy (USSR) [*A publication*]
Sov Atom Energy ... Soviet Atomic Energy [*A publication*]
Sov Automat Contr ... Soviet Automatic Control [*A publication*]

Sov Autom Control ... Soviet Automatic Control [*A publication*]
Sov Autom Control (Engl Transl) ... Soviet Automatic Control (English Translation) [*A publication*]
Sov Bibliog ... Sovetskaya Bibliografia [*A publication*]
Sov Bibliotekov ... Sovetskaia Bibliotekovedenie [*A publication*]
Sov Bot...... Sovetskaya Botanika [*A publication*]
Sov Bus Trade ... Soviet Business and Trade [*A publication*]
Sov Chem Ind ... Soviet Chemical Industry [*A publication*]
Sov Chem Ind (Engl Transl) ... Soviet Chemical Industry (English Translation) [*A publication*]
Sov Cybern Rev ... Soviet Cybernetics Review [*A publication*]
SOVD .... Stabilized Optical Viewing Device
SOVEA...... Southwestern Veterinarian [*United States*] [*A publication*]
Sov East Eur China Bus Trade ... Soviet-Eastern Europe-China Business and Trade [*A publication*]
Sov East Europ For Trade ... Soviet and Eastern European Foreign Trade [*A publication*]
Sov Educ .... Soviet Education [*A publication*]
Sov E E For ... Soviet and Eastern European Foreign Trade [*A publication*]
Sov & E Eur For Tr ... American Review of Soviet and Eastern European Foreign Trade [*A publication*]   (DLA)
Sov Elec Eng ... Soviet Electrical Engineering [*A publication*]
Sov Electr Eng ... Soviet Electrical Engineering [*English Translation of Elektrotekhnika*] [*A publication*]
Sov Electr Eng (Engl Transl) ... Soviet Electrical Engineering (English Translation) [*A publication*]
Sov Electrochem ... Soviet Electrochemistry [*A publication*]
Sov Electrochem (Engl Transl) ... Soviet Electrochemistry (English Translation) [*A publication*]
Sov Eng J ... Soviet Engineering Journal [*A publication*]
Sov Engng Res ... Soviet Engineering Research [*A publication*]
Sov Eng Res ... Soviet Engineering Research [*A publication*]
SovEt......... Sovetskaya Etnografija [*A publication*]
Sovet Geol ... Sovetskaya Geologiya [*A publication*]
Sovet Geologiya ... Sovetskaya Geologiya [*A publication*]
Sovet Muz ... Sovetskaya Muzyka [*A publication*]
SovEtn...... Sovetskaya Etnografija [*A publication*]
Sov Etnogr ... Sovetskaja Etnografija [*A publication*]
Sovetskaya M ... Sovetskaya Muzyka [*A publication*]
Sovetskoe Bibl ... Sovetskoe Bibliotekovedenie [*A publication*]
Sov Export ... Soviet Export [*A publication*]
Sov Farm.... Sovetskaya Farmatsiya [*A publication*]
Sov Film..... Soviet Film [*A publication*]
Sov Finno-Ugroved ... Sovetskoje Finno-Ugrovedenie [*A publication*]
Sov Flour Milling Baking ... Soviet Flour Milling and Baking [*A publication*]
Sov Fluid Mech (Engl Transl) ... Soviet Fluid Mechanics (English Translation) [*A publication*]
Sov Foto ..... Sovetskoe Foto [*A publication*]
SovFU........ Sovetskoje Finno-Ugrovedenie [*A publication*]
Sov Genet... Soviet Genetics [*A publication*]
Sov Genet (Engl Transl) ... Soviet Genetics (English Translation) [*A publication*]
Sov Genet (Engl Transl Genetika) ... Soviet Genetics (English Translation of Genetika) [*A publication*]
Sov Geogr... Soviet Geography. Review and Translations [*A publication*]
Sov Geogr R ... Soviet Geography. Review and Translations [*A publication*]
Sov Geol..... Sovetskaya Geologiya [*A publication*]
Sov Geol Geophys ... Soviet Geology and Geophysics [*A publication*]
Sov Geol Geophys (Engl Transl) ... Soviet Geology and Geophysics (English Translation) [*A publication*]
Sov Gold Min Ind ... Soviet Gold Mining Industry [*A publication*]
Sov Gos Pravo ... Sovetskoe Gosudarstvo i Pravo [*A publication*]
SovH .... Sovetish Heymland [*A publication*]
Sov Health Prot Turkomen ... Soviet Health Protection in Turkomen [*A publication*]
Sov Hydrol ... Soviet Hydrology. Selected Papers [*A publication*]
Sov Hydrol Sel Pap ... Soviet Hydrology. Selected Papers [*A publication*]
SOVIA....... Sound and Vibration [*A publication*]
Soviet Aeronaut ... Soviet Aeronautics [*A publication*]
Soviet Agric Sci ... Soviet Agricultural Science [*A publication*]
Soviet Appl Mech ... Soviet Applied Mechanics [*A publication*]
Soviet Astronom ... Soviet Astronomy [*A publication*]
Soviet Automat Control ... Soviet Automatic Control [*A publication*]
Soviet Chem Ind ... Soviet Chemical Industry [*A publication*]
Soviet and Eastern Eur For Trade ... Soviet and Eastern European Foreign Trade [*A publication*]
Soviet Ed.... Soviet Education [*A publication*]
Soviet F...... Soviet Film [*A publication*]
Soviet Genet ... Soviet Genetics [*A publication*]
Soviet J Contemporary Math Anal ... Soviet Journal of Contemporary Mathematical Analysis [*A publication*]
Soviet J Ecol ... Soviet Journal of Ecology [*A publication*]
Soviet Jewry L Rev ... Soviet Jewry Law Review [*A publication*]   (DLA)
Soviet J Nuclear Phys ... American Institute of Physics. Soviet Journal of Nuclear Physics [*A publication*]
Soviet J Particles and Nuclei ... Soviet Journal of Particles and Nuclei [*A publication*]
Soviet Law and Govt ... Soviet Law and Government [*A publication*]
Soviet L & Govt ... Soviet Law and Government [*A publication*]
Soviet Lit.... Soviet Literature [*A publication*]
Soviet Math Dokl ... Soviet Mathematics. Doklady [*A publication*]

Soviet Math (Iz VUZ) ... Soviet Mathematics (Izvestija Vyssih Ucebnyh Zavedenii. Matematika) [*A publication*]
Soviet Phys Acoust ... Soviet Physics. Acoustics [*A publication*]
Soviet Phys Collection ... Soviet Physics. Collection [*English Translation*] [*A publication*]
Soviet Phys Cryst ... Soviet Physics. Crystallography [*A publication*]
Soviet Physics Acoust ... Soviet Physics. Acoustics [*A publication*]
Soviet Physics Dokl ... Soviet Physics. Doklady [*A publication*]
Soviet Physics J ... Soviet Physics Journal [*A publication*]
Soviet Phys J ... Soviet Physics Journal [*A publication*]
Soviet Phys JETP ... Soviet Physics. JETP [*Journal of Experimental and Theoretical Physics of the Academy of Sciences of the USSR*] [*A publication*]
Soviet Phys Uspekhi ... Soviet Physics. Uspekhi [*A publication*]
Soviet Plant Physiol ... Soviet Plant Physiology [*A publication*]
Soviet Pl Physiol ... Soviet Plant Physiology [*A publication*]
Soviet Sci Rev Sect C Math Phys Rev ... Soviet Scientific Reviews. Section C. Mathematical Physics Reviews [*A publication*]
Soviet Sociol ... Soviet Sociology [*A publication*]
Soviet Soil Sci ... Soviet Soil Science [*A publication*]
Soviet Stat & Dec ... Soviet Statutes and Decisions [*A publication*] (DLA)
Soviet Stud ... Soviet Studies [*A publication*]
Soviet Stud Phil ... Soviet Studies in Philosophy [*A publication*]
Soviet YB Int'l L ... Soviet Year-Book of International Law [*A publication*] (DLA)
SOVIII...... Third Survey of Veterans [*Veterans Administration*] (GFGA)
SOVIN...... Samenwerkingsverband voor Opleiding en Vorming op het Terrein van de Informatieverzorging via Netwerken [*Collective for Training and Education in Connection with Information Provision via Networks*] [*Netherlands*] [*Information service or system*] [*Ceased operation*] (IID)
Sov Indian Semin Catal ... Soviet-Indian Seminar on Catalysis [*A publication*]
Sov India Rubber ... Soviet India Rubber [*A publication*]
Sov Instrum & Control J ... Soviet Journal of Instrumentation and Control [*A publication*]
Sov Instrum Control J (Engl Transl) ... Soviet Instrumentation and Control Journal (English Translation) [*A publication*]
Sovistva At Yader ... Sovistva Atomnykh Yader [*Former USSR*] [*A publication*]
Sov Ital Symp Macromol Funct Cell ... Soviet-Italian Symposium on Macromolecules in the Functioning Cell [*A publication*]
SovJa .... Sovetska Jazykoveda [*A publication*]
Sov J At ..... Soviet Journal of Atomic Energy [*A publication*]
Sov J At Energy ... Soviet Journal of Atomic Energy [*A publication*]
Sov J Bioorganic Chem ... Soviet Journal of Bioorganic Chemistry [*A publication*]
Sov J Bioorg Chem (Engl Transl) ... Soviet Journal of Bioorganic Chemistry (English Translation of Bioorganicheskaya Khimiya) [*A publication*]
Sov J Bioorg Chem (Engl Transl Bioorg Khim) ... Soviet Journal of Bioorganic Chemistry (English Translation of Bioorganicheskaya Khimiya) [*A publication*]
Sov J Coord Chem (Engl Transl) ... Soviet Journal of Coordination Chemistry (English Translation) [*A publication*]
Sov J Coord Chem (Engl Transl Koord Khim) ... Soviet Journal of Coordination Chemistry (English Translation of Koordinatsionnaya Khimiya) [*A publication*]
Sov J Dev Biol (Engl Transl) ... Soviet Journal of Developmental Biology (English Translation) [*A publication*]
Sov J Dev Biol (Engl Transl Ontogenez) ... Soviet Journal of Developmental Biology (English Translation of Ontogenez) [*A publication*]
Sov J Ecol .. Soviet Journal of Ecology [*A publication*]
Sov J Ecol (Engl Transl) ... Soviet Journal of Ecology (English Translation) [*A publication*]
Sov J Ecol (Engl Transl Ekologiya) ... Soviet Journal of Ecology (English Translation of Ekologiya) [*A publication*]
Sov Jew Aff ... Soviet Jewish Affairs [*A publication*]
Sov J Glass Phys Chem ... Soviet Journal of Glass Physics and Chemistry [*A publication*]
Sov J Glass Phys Chem (Engl Transl) ... Soviet Journal of Glass Physics and Chemistry (English Translation) [*A publication*]
Sov J Instrum Control ... Soviet Journal of Instrumentation and Control [*A publication*]
Sov J Instrum Control (Engl Transl) ... Soviet Journal of Instrumentation and Control (English Translation) [*A publication*]
Sov J Low Temp Phys ... Soviet Journal of Low Temperature Physics [*A publication*]
Sov J Low Temp Phys (Engl Transl) ... Soviet Journal of Low Temperature Physics (English Translation) [*A publication*]
Sov J Mar Biol ... Soviet Journal of Marine Biology [*A publication*]
Sov J Mar Biol (Engl Transl) ... Soviet Journal of Marine Biology (English Translation) [*A publication*]
Sov J Mar Biol (Engl Transl Biol Morya) ... Soviet Journal of Marine Biology (English Translation of Biologiya Morya) [*A publication*]
Sov J Nondestr Test ... Soviet Journal of Nondestructive Testing [*A publication*]
Sov J Nondestr Test (Engl Transl) ... Soviet Journal of Nondestructive Testing (English Translation) [*A publication*]
Sov J Nondestruct Test ... Soviet Journal of Nondestructive Testing [*A publication*]

Sov J Non-Ferrous Met ... Soviet Journal of Non-Ferrous Metals [*A publication*]
Sov J Nucl Phys ... Soviet Journal of Nuclear Physics [*A publication*]
Sov J Nucl Phys (Engl Transl) ... Soviet Journal of Nuclear Physics (English Translation) [*A publication*]
Sov J Nuc R ... Soviet Journal of Nuclear Physics (USSR) [*A publication*]
Sov J Opt Technol ... Soviet Journal of Optical Technology [*A publication*]
Sov J Opt Technol (Engl Transl) ... Soviet Journal of Optical Technology (English Translation) [*A publication*]
Sov J Part Nucl ... Soviet Journal of Particles and Nuclei [*A publication*]
Sov J Part Nucl (Engl Transl) ... Soviet Journal of Particles and Nuclei (English Translation) [*A publication*]
Sov J Plasma Phys ... Soviet Journal of Plasma Physics [*A publication*]
Sov J Plasma Phys (Engl Transl) ... Soviet Journal of Plasma Physics (English Translation) [*A publication*]
Sov J Quant Electron ... Soviet Journal of Quantum Electronics [*A publication*]
Sov J Quantum Electron ... Soviet Journal of Quantum Electronics [*A publication*]
Sov J Quantum Electron (Engl Transl) ... Soviet Journal of Quantum Electronics (English Translation) [*A publication*]
Sov Khlopok ... Sovetskii Khlopok [*A publication*]
Sov Kino Fotopromst ... Sovetskaya Kino-Fotopromyshlennost [*A publication*]
SovKniga.... Sovetskaya Kniga [*A publication*]
Sov Krasnyi Krest ... Soveti Krasnyi Krest [*Former USSR*] [*A publication*]
SovL.......... Soviet Literature [*A publication*]
SOVLA..... Sovetskaya Latviya [*A publication*]
Sov Law Gov ... Soviet Law and Government [*A publication*]
Sov Law & Govt ... Soviet Law and Government [*A publication*]
Sov Lit........ Soviet Literature [*A publication*]
Sov M......... Sovetskaya Muzyka [*A publication*]
Sov Mater Sci ... Soviet Materials Science [*A publication*]
Sov Mater Sci (Engl Transl) ... Soviet Materials Science (English Translation of Fiziko-Khimicheskaya Mekhanika Materialov) [*A publication*]
Sov Math ... Soviet Mathematics [*A publication*]
Sov Math (Engl Transl) ... Soviet Mathematics (English Translation) [*A publication*]
Sov Med..... Sovetskaya Meditsina [*A publication*]
SOVMEDRON ... Soviet Mediterranean Squadron [*NATO*] (NATG)
Sovmestnaya Sov-Mong Nauchno-Issled Geol Eksped ... Sovmestnaya Sovetsko-Mongol'skaya Nauchno-Issledovatel'skaya Geologicheskaya Ekspeditsiya [*A publication*]
Sov Metall ... Sovetskaya Metallurgiya [*A publication*]
Sov Meteorol Hydrol ... Soviet Meteorology and Hydrology [*English translation of Meteorologiya i Gidrologiya*] [*A publication*]
Sov Meteorol Hydrol (Engl Transl) ... Soviet Meteorology and Hydrology (English Translation) [*A publication*]
Sov Microelectron ... Soviet Microelectronics [*A publication*]
Sov Min Sci ... Soviet Mining Science [*A publication*]
Sov Min Sci (Engl Transl) ... Soviet Mining Science (English Translation) [*A publication*]
Sov Ml Rev ... Soviet Military Review [*A publication*]
Sov Nauka ... Sovetskaya Nauka [*A publication*]
Sov Neurol Psychiatry ... Soviet Neurology and Psychiatry [*A publication*]
Sov Neur R ... Soviet Neurology and Psychiatry (USSR) [*A publication*]
Sov Non-Ferrous Met Res ... Soviet Non-Ferrous Metals Research [*A publication*]
Sov Non-Ferrous Met Res (Engl Transl) ... Soviet Non-Ferrous Metals Research (English Translation) [*A publication*]
Sov Oceanogr ... Soviet Oceanography [*A publication*]
SOVOG..... Sozialistische Volksorganisation [*Socialist National Community*] [*Lithuania*] [*Political party*] (PPE)
Sov Pedag .. Soviet Pedagogy [*A publication*]
Sov Ph Ac R ... Soviet Physics. Acoustics (USSR) [*A publication*]
Sov Pharm ... Soviet Pharmacy [*A publication*]
Sov Ph Se R ... Soviet Physics. Semiconductors (USSR) [*A publication*]
Sov Phys Acoust ... Soviet Physics. Acoustics [*A publication*]
Sov Phys Acoust (Engl Transl) ... Soviet Physics. Acoustics (English Translation) [*A publication*]
Sov Phys Collect ... Soviet Physics. Collection [*A publication*]
Sov Phys Collect (Engl Transl) ... Soviet Physics. Collection (English Translation) [*A publication*]
Sov Phys Coll (Engl Transl) ... Soviet Physics. Collection (English Translation) [*A publication*]
Sov Phys Cryst ... Soviet Physics. Crystallography [*A publication*]
Sov Phys Crystallogr ... Soviet Physics. Crystallography [*A publication*]
Sov Phys Crystallogr (Engl Transl) ... Soviet Physics. Crystallography (English Translation) [*A publication*]
Sov Phys Dokl ... Soviet Physics. Doklady [*A publication*]
Sov Phys Dokl (Engl Transl) ... Soviet Physics. Doklady (English Translation) [*A publication*]
Sov Physicians J ... Soviet Physicians' Journal [*A publication*]
Sov Phys J ... Soviet Physics Journal [*A publication*]
Sov Phys J (Engl Transl) ... Soviet Physics Journal (English Translation) [*A publication*]
Sov Phys JETP ... Soviet Physics. JETP [*Journal of Experimental and Theoretical Physics of the Academy of Sciences of the USSR*] [*A publication*]

Sov Phys Lebedev Inst Rep (Engl Transl) ... Soviet Physics. Lebedev Institute Reports (English Translation) [*A publication*]
Sov Phys Semicond ... Soviet Physics. Semiconductors [*A publication*]
Sov Phys Semicond (Engl Transl) ... Soviet Physics. Semiconductors (English Translation) [*A publication*]
Sov Phys Solid State ... Soviet Physics. Solid State [*English translation of Fizika Tverdogo Tela*] [*A publication*]
Sov Phys Solid State (Engl Transl) ... Soviet Physics. Solid State (English Translation) [*A publication*]
Sov Phys Sol St ... Soviet Physics. Solid State Physics [*A publication*]
Sov Phys Tech Phys ... Soviet Physics. Technical Physics [*A publication*]
Sov Phys Tech Phys (Engl Transl) ... Soviet Physics. Technical Physics (English Translation) [*A publication*]
Sov Phys Tech Phys Lett ... Soviet Physics. Technical Physics. Letters [*A publication*]
Sov Phys T P ... Soviet Physics. Technical Physics [*A publication*]
Sov Phys Usp ... Soviet Physics. Uspekhi [*A publication*]
Sov Phys Uspekhi ... Soviet Physics. Uspekhi [*A publication*]
Sov Phys Usp (Engl Transl) ... Soviet Physics. Uspekhi (English Translation) [*A publication*]
Sov Plant Ind Rec ... Soviet Plant Industry Record [*A publication*]
Sov Plant Physiol ... Soviet Plant Physiology [*A publication*]
Sov Plant Physiol (Engl Transl) ... Soviet Plant Physiology (English Translation) [*A publication*]
Sov Plant Physiol (Engl Transl Fiziol Rast) ... Soviet Plant Physiology (English Translation of Fiziologiya Rastenii) [*A publication*]
Sov Plast .... Soviet Plastics [*A publication*]
Sov Plast (Engl Transl) ... Soviet Plastics (English Translation) [*A publication*]
Sov Powder Metall Met Ceram ... Soviet Powder Metallurgy and Metal Ceramics [*A publication*]
Sov Powder Metall Met Ceram (Engl Transl) ... Soviet Powder Metallurgy and Metal Ceramics (English Translation) [*A publication*]
Sov Powder Met Metal Ceram ... Soviet Powder Metallurgy and Metal Ceramics [*A publication*]
Sov Power Eng ... Soviet Power Engineering [*A publication*]
Sov Power Eng (Engl Transl) ... Soviet Power Engineering (English Translation of Elektricheskie Stantsii) [*A publication*]
Sov Prog Chem ... Soviet Progress in Chemistry [*A publication*]
Sov Prog Chem (Engl Transl) ... Soviet Progress in Chemistry (English Translation) [*A publication*]
Sov Psikhonevrol ... Sovetskaya Psikhonevrologiya [*A publication*]
Sov Psychol ... Soviet Psychology [*A publication*]
Sov Psychoneurol ... Soviet Psychoneurology [*A publication*]
Sov Psyco R ... Soviet Psychology (USSR) [*A publication*]
Sov Public Health ... Soviet Public Health [*A publication*]
Sov Public Health (Engl Transl) ... Soviet Public Health (English Translation) [*A publication*]
SOVR .... Sovereign Corp. [*NASDAQ symbol*] (NQ)
SovR.......... Soviet Review [*A publication*]
Sov Radiochem ... Soviet Radiochemistry [*A publication*]
Sov Radiochem (Engl Transl) ... Soviet Radiochemistry (English Translation) [*A publication*]
Sov Radio Eng ... Soviet Radio Engineering [*A publication*]
Sov Radiophys ... Soviet Radiophysics [*A publication*]
Sov Radiophys (Engl Transl) ... Soviet Radiophysics (English Translation of Izvestiya Vysshikh Uchebnykh Zavedenii Radiofizika) [*A publication*]
Sovrem Metody Issled ... Sovremennye Metody Issledovaniya [*A publication*]
Sovrem Psikhotropnye Sredstva ... Sovremennye Psikhotropnye Sredstva [*A publication*]
Sovrem Zadachi Tochn Naukakh ... Sovremennye Zadachi v Tochnykh Naukakh [*A publication*]
Sov Res High Energy Fission ... Soviet Research in High Energy Fission [*A publication*]
Sov Res Nucl Phys ... Soviet Research in Nuclear Physics [*A publication*]
Sov Res Nucl Solid State Phys ... Soviet Research in Nuclear and Solid State Physics [*A publication*]
Sov Res Phys ... Soviet Research in Physics [*A publication*]
Sov Rubber Technol ... Soviet Rubber Technology [*A publication*]
Sov Rubber Technol (Engl Transl) ... Soviet Rubber Technology (English Translation) [*A publication*]
SOVS .... Sovereigns [*Monetary unit*] [*Obsolete*] [*British*]
SovS .... Soviet Studies [*A publication*]
SovS .... Soviet Survey [*A publication*]
Sov Sakhar ... Sovetskii Sakhar [*A publication*]
Sov Sci ..... Soviet Science [*A publication*]
Sov Sci (Engl Transl) ... Soviet Science (English Translation) [*A publication*]
Sov Sci Rev ... Soviet Science Review [*England*] [*A publication*]
Sov Sci Rev Sect A ... Soviet Scientific Reviews. Section A. Physics Reviews [*A publication*]
Sov Sci Rev Sect B ... Soviet Scientific Reviews. Section B. Chemistry Reviews [*A publication*]
Sov Sci Rev Sect D Biol Rev ... Soviet Scientific Reviews. Section D. Biology Reviews [*A publication*]
Sov Sci Rev Sect E ... Soviet Scientific Reviews. Section E. Astrophysics and Space Physics Reviews [*A publication*]
Sov Shakhtior ... Sovetskii Shakhtior [*Former USSR*] [*A publication*]
SovSlav ...... Sovetskoe Slavjanovedenie [*A publication*]
Sov Soc....... Soviet Sociology [*A publication*]

Sov Sociol... Soviet Sociology [*A publication*]
Sov Soil Sci ... Soviet Soil Science [*A publication*]
Sov Soil Sci (Engl Transl) ... Soviet Soil Science (English Translation of Pochvovedenie) [*A publication*]
Sov Soil Sci (Engl Transl Pochvovedenie) ... Soviet Soil Science (English Translation of Pochvovedenie) [*A publication*]
Sov Soil Sci Suppl ... Soviet Soil Science. Supplement [*A publication*]
Sov Stat & Dec ... Soviet Statutes and Decisions [*A publication*]
Sov St Hist ... Soviet Studies in History [*A publication*]
Sov St Lit ... Soviet Studies in Literature [*A publication*]
Sov St Phil ... Soviet Studies in Philosophy [*A publication*]
Sov Stud ..... Soviet Studies [*A publication*]
Sov Stud Hist ... Soviet Studies in History [*A publication*]
Sov Subtrop (Moscow) ... Sovetskie Subtropiki (Moscow) [*A publication*]
Sov Subtrop (Sukhumi USSR) ... Sovetskie Subtropiki (Sukhumi, USSR) [*A publication*]
Sov Sugar ... Soviet Sugar [*A publication*]
Sov Swed Symp Pollut Balt ... Soviet-Swedish Symposium on the Pollution of the Baltic [*A publication*]
SovT.......... Sovetskaja Tjurkologija [*A publication*]
Sov Tech Phys Lett ... Soviet Technical Physics. Letters [*A publication*]
Sov Tech Phys Lett (Engl Transl) ... Soviet Technical Physics. Letters (English Translation) [*A publication*]
Sov Tjurkolog ... Sovetskaja Tjurkologija [*A publication*]
Sov T P Lett ... Soviet Technical Physics. Letters [*A publication*]
Sov Union .. Soviet Union [*A publication*]
Sov Veda Chem ... Sovetska Veda. Chemie [*A publication*]
SovVo........ Sovetskoje Vostokovedenije [*A publication*]
SOVX .... Sham Ovariectomized [*Endocrinology*]
Sov Zdravookhr ... Sovetskoe Zdravookhranenie [*A publication*]
Sov Zdravookhr Kirg ... Sovetskoe Zdravookhranenie Kirgizii [*A publication*]
Sov Zdravookhr Turkm ... Sovetskoe Zdravookhranenie Turkmenii [*A publication*]
Sov Zootekh ... Sovetskaya Zootekhniya [*A publication*]
SOW .... Scope of Work (MCD)
SOW .... Scramble-on-Warning
SOW .... Show Low [*Arizona*] [*Airport symbol*] [*Obsolete*] (OAG)
SOW .... Skylab Orbital Workshop [*NASA*]
SOW .... Special Operations Wing [*Military*] (MCD)
SOW .... Standoff Weapons (MCD)
SOW .... Start of Word
SOW .... Start of Work
SOW .... Statement of Work (MCD)
SOW .... Subdivision of Work [*NASA*] (NASA)
SOW .... Sunflower Ordnance Works [*Military*]
SOW .... Synthetic Ocean Water
SOWA ...... Stock Option Writers Association (EA)
SOWC .... Senior Officers' War Course [*British*]
SOWESPAC ... Southwest Pacific Command [*Navy*]
SOWESSEAFRON ... Southwest Sea Frontier [*Navy*]
SOWESTDIVDOCKS ... Southwest Division, Bureau of Yards and Docks [*Navy*] (MUGU)
So West LJ ... Southwestern Law Journal [*A publication*]
SOWESTPACCOM ... Southwest Pacific Command [*Navy*] (DNAB)
So West Rep ... South Western Reporter [*A publication*] (DLA)
SOWETO ... Southwestern Townships [*South Africa*]
SOWg .... Special Operations Wing [*Air Force*] (AFM)
SOWIDOK ... Sozialwissenschaftliche Dokumentation [*Social Sciences Documentation Center*] [*Vienna Chamber of Labor*] [*Information service or system*] (IID)
Sowjetw Ges ... Sowjetwissenschaft Gesellschaft [*A publication*]
Sowjetwiss ... Sowjetwissenschaft [*A publication*]
SOWM ...... Special Ocean Wave Model
So Workm ... Southern Workman [*A publication*]
SOWP........ Society of Wireless Pioneers (EA)
SOWR .... Submarine Overhaul Work Requirement [*Navy*] (DNAB)
SOWRA ...... Submarine Overhaul Work Requirement Authorization [*Navy*] (DNAB)
SOWRBALL ... Southwest RADAR Balloon [*for illegal drug interdiction*]
SoWS .... Southern Writers Series [*A publication*]
SOW/S & D ... Statement of Work/Specifications and Design
SOX .... Sentry Resources Corp. [*Formerly, Sentry Oil & Gas*] [*Vancouver Stock Exchange symbol*]
SOX .... Solid Oxygen
SOX .... Sulfur Oxide
SOX .... Supercritical Oxygen [*NASA*] (KSC)
SOXP......... Southeast Explorations Corp. [*NASDAQ symbol*] (NQ)
SOY .... Sioux Center, IA [*Location identifier*] [*FAA*] (FAAL)
SOY .... SO Resources [*Vancouver Stock Exchange symbol*]
SOY .... Stronsay [*Scotland*] [*Airport symbol*] (OAG)
Soybean Dig ... Soybean Digest [*A publication*]
SOYD ...... Sum of the Years' Digits Method [*Finance*]
SOYDV ..... Soybean Dwarf Virus [*Plant pathology*]
SOYMV .... Soybean Mosaic Virus [*Plant pathology*]
SOYO .... Society of Orthodox Youth Organizations (EA)
Soy Protein Prev Atheroscler Proc Int Symp ... Soy Protein in the Prevention of Atherosclerosis. Proceedings. International Symposium [*A publication*]
SOZ .... Seder 'Olam Zuta (BJA)
SOZ .... Solo International Resources Ltd. [*Vancouver Stock Exchange symbol*]

SOZ .... Somerset, PA [*Location identifier*] [*FAA*]   (FAAL)
SOZ .... Soviet Occupied Zone   (NATG)
SoZ............. Sovremennye Zapiski [*A publication*]
Soz Arbeit .. Soziale Arbeit [*A publication*]
SOZDA ..... Sovetskoe Zdravookhranenie [*A publication*]
Soz Forstwirtsch ... Sozialistische Forstwirtschaft [*A publication*]
Soz Fortschritt ... Sozialer Fortschritt [*A publication*]
Sozialdemokr Pressedienst ... Sozialdemokratische Pressedienst [*A
            publication*]
Sozial Forstw ... Sozialistische Forstwirtschaft [*A publication*]
Sozialistische Arbeitswiss ... Sozialistische Arbeitswissenschaft [*A
            publication*]
Sozialistische Finwirt ... Sozialistische Finanzwirtschaft [*A publication*]
Sozialmed Paedagog Jugendkd ... Sozialmedizinische und Paedagogische
            Jugendkunde [*A publication*]
Sozial Polit ... Sozialistische Politik [*A publication*]
Soz Kommun ... Sozialisation und Kommunikation [*A publication*]
Soz- Praeventivmed ... Sozial- und Praeventivmedizin [*A publication*]
Soz Sicherheit ... Soziale Sicherheit [*A publication*]
Soz Welt..... Soziale Welt [*A publication*]
Soz und Wirtpol MSpiegel ... Sozial- und Wirtschaftspolitischer
            Monatsspiegel aus Zeitungen und Zeitschriften [*A
            publication*]
Soz Wiss Jb Polit ... Sozialwissenschaftliches Jahrbuch fuer Politik [*A
            publication*]
Sp .... Biblioteca Nacional, Madrid, Spain [*Library symbol*] [*Library
            of Congress*]   (LCLS)
SP............... Error in Spelling [*Used in correcting manuscripts, etc.*]
SP............... International Society of Philology
sp----- .... La Plata River and Basin [*MARC geographic area code*]
            [*Library of Congress*]   (LCCP)
SP............... Motor Patrol Boat [*Navy symbol*] [*Obsolete*]
Sp .... [*The*] New Testament of Our Lord and Saviour Jesus Christ
            (1937) (Francis Aloysius Spencer) [*A publication*]   (BJA)
SP............... Office of State Programs [*Nuclear energy*]   (NRCH)
SP............... Poland [*Aircraft nationality and registration mark*]   (FAAC)
SP............... Sacra Pagina [*Paris-Gembloux*] [*A publication*]   (BJA)
Sp .... Sacropubic [*Anatomy*]   (AAMN)
SP............... Safety Panel
S & P .... Salt and Pepper
SP............... Same Point   (ILCA)
SP............... Same Principle   (ILCA)
SP............... Sample Part
SP............... Sampling Point   (NRCH)
SP............... San Pedro [*California*]
SP............... Sanctissime Pater [*Most Holy Father*] [*Latin*]
SP............... Satellite Processor [*Data transmission*]
S & P .... Save & Prosper [*Financial services group*] [*British*]
SP............... Scalable Processing [*Northgate*] [*Data processing*]
SP............... Schering-Plough Corp. [*Commercial firm*]
SP............... Scholarly Publishing [*A publication*]
SP............... Schools of Philosophy [*A publication*]
SP............... Science Pilot
SP............... Science Press [*Information service or system*]   (IID)
SP............... Scientific Paper
SP............... Scientific Processor   (BUR)
S/P............. Scientific Products
SP............... Scottish Peer   (ROG)
SP............... Scratch Pad [*Data processing*]
SP............... Sea Platform   (MCD)
S/P............. Seaplane
SP............... Secretory Piece [*Superseded by SC, Secretory Component*]
            [*Immunology*]
SP............... Secretory Protein [*Endocrinology*]
SP............... Section Patrol [*Navy*]
SP............... Security Police [*Air Force*]   (AFM)
SP............... Security Procedure   (NRCH)
SP............... Security Publication [*Navy*]
SP............... Seed Production [*Agriculture*]
SP............... Seeing Problems [*Research test*] [*Psychology*]
SP............... Selective Purchases
SP............... Self Potential [*Log*]
SP............... Self-Powered [*Gun*]   (MCD)
SP............... Self-Propelled [*Military*]
SP............... Selling Price
SP............... Seminar Press
SP............... Semipostal
S/P............. Semiprivate [*Room*]
SP............... Semipublic [*Telecommunications*]   (TEL)
SP............... Send Processor
SP............... Senile Plaque [*Neurology*]
SP............... Senior Partner
SP............... Senior Pilot [*Air Force*]
SP............... Sensor Processor   (BUR)
Sp .... Senterpartiet [*Center Party*] [*Norway*] [*Political party*]   (PPE)
SP............... Senza Pedale [*Without Pedals*] [*Music*]
SP............... Septum Pellucidum [*Brain anatomy*]
SP............... Sequence Programmer [*Data processing*]   (AAG)
S-P............. Sequential-Phase   (CET)
SP............... Sequential Processor
S/P............. Serial to Parallel   (KSC)

SP............... Servants of the Holy Paraclete [*Roman Catholic men's religious
            order*]
SP............... Service Package   (OA)
SP............... Service Panel
SP............... Service Phase   (MCD)
SP............... Service Police [*British military*]   (DMA)
SP............... Service Processor   (IEEE)
SP............... Service Publications   (AAG)
SP............... Serving Point [*Telecommunications*]
SP............... Session of Peace [*Legal*] [*British*]   (ROG)
SP............... Set Point
SP............... Severely, Profoundly Handicapped   (OICC)
SP............... Sewer Pipe [*Telecommunications*]   (TEL)
SP............... Shanti Project   (EA)
SP............... Shear Plate [*Technical drawings*]
SP............... Shift Pulses
SP............... Shipping Port
SP............... Shore Party [*Navy*]
SP............... Shore Patrol [*Navy*]
SP............... Shore Police [*Navy*]
SP............... Shoreline Protection [*Type of water project*]
SP............... Short Page
SP............... Short Perforation [*Philately*]
SP............... Short Period
SP............... Short Persistence
SP............... Short Position [*Investment term*]
SP............... Short Pulse
SP............... Shortest Path
SP............... Shoulder Pitch   (MCD)
SP............... Shunt Procedure [*Medicine*]   (MAE)
SP............... Shuttle Projects Office [*Kennedy Space Center*]
            [*NASA*]   (NASA)
SP............... Sic Porro [*So Forth*] [*Latin*]
SP............... Sieve Pore [*Botany*]
SP............... Sign Post
S/P............... Signal Processor   (NASA)
SP............... Signal Publication [*British*]
SP............... Signaling Projector [*British*]
SP............... Signed Photograph
SP............... Sikkim Parishad [*India*] [*Political party*]   (PPW)
SP............... Silver Plate
SP............... Silver Protein [*An antiseptic*]
SP............... Simple Printing
SP............... Sine Prole [*Died Without Issue*] [*Latin*]
SP............... Singing Point [*Telecommunications*]   (TEL)
SP............... Single Particle
SP............... Single Payment   (ILCA)
SP............... Single-Phase
SP............... Single-Pole [*Switch*]
SP............... Single Precision   (NASA)
SP............... Single Programmer
SP............... Single Purpose
SP............... Sisters of the Presentation of Mary [*Roman Catholic religious
            order*]
SP............... Sisters of Providence [*Roman Catholic religious order*]
SP............... Skin Painting [*Method of administering experimental
            chemicals*]
SP............... Skin Potential   (MAE)
SP............... Skin Prick [*Immunology*]
SP............... Sloop   (ROG)
SP............... Slovansky Prehled [*A publication*]
SP............... Slugging Percentage [*Baseball*]
SP............... Small Packet
SP............... Small Paper [*Printing*]
SP............... Small Pica
SP............... Small Plaque
SP............... Small Premises [*Hairdressers, doctors, dentists, etc.*] [*Public-
            performance tariff class*] [*British*]
SP............... Smith Predictor [*Process control*]
SP............... Smokeless Powder
SP............... Smokeless Propellant   (NATG)
SP............... Smoki People   (EA)
SP............... Sniper's Post [*British military*]   (DMA)
SP............... Snow Pellets [*Meteorology*]   (FAAC)
SP............... Socialismo y Participacion [*A publication*]
SP............... Socialist Party
SP............... Socialistische Partij [*Socialist Party*] [*Belgium*] [*Political
            party*]   (PPW)
SP............... Sociedade Acoriana de Transportes Aereos Ltda.
            [*Portugal*]   (FAAC)
SP............... Society of Philaticians   (EA)
SP............... Society of Protozoologists   (EA)
SP............... Sociolinguistics Program   (EA)
SP............... Softening Point   (MCD)
SP............... Soil Pipe
SP............... Soil Pit
SP............... Soil Psychrometer
SP............... Solar Panel
SP............... Solar Physics   (NASA)
SP............... Soldiers for Peace   (EA)
SP............... Solid Propellant

S of P.........	Sons of Phoenix [*Freemasonry*] (ROG)
SP..............	Sosyalist Parti [*Socialist Party*] [*Turkey*] [*Political party*] (EY)
S/P.............	Sotto Protesto [*Under Protest*] [*Italian*]
SP..............	Sound Powered (CAAL)
SP..............	Soundproof [*Technical drawings*]
SP..............	South Pacific
SP..............	South Pole [*Also, PS*]
SP..............	South Proceeding [*Astronomy*]
SP..............	Southern Pacific Transportation Co. [*AAR code*]
SP..............	Southern Pine [*Utility pole*] [*Telecommunications*] (TEL)
sp..............	Space [*Crocheting*]
SP..............	Space Character [*Keyboard*] (AAG)
SP..............	Space Patrol (AAG)
SP..............	Space Platform (SSD)
SP..............	Space and Power
SP..............	Space Propulsion [*A publication*]
Sp..............	Spacers [*Electron transfer*]
sp..............	Spain [*MARC country of publication code*] [*Library of Congress*] (LCCP)
SP..............	Spain
SP..............	Spanish (ROG)
SP..............	Spare (AAG)
SP..............	Spare Part
SP..............	Spares Planning (AAG)
SP..............	Spark (AAG)
SP..............	Spartan Program [*Missiles*] (MCD)
Sp..............	Spears' South Carolina Law Reports [*1842-44*] [*A publication*] (DLA)
SP..............	Special (AFM)
Sp..............	Special Branch [*Navy*] [*British*]
SP..............	Special Paper
SP..............	Special Performance
SP..............	Special Planning (AAG)
SP..............	Special Product (MCD)
SP..............	Special Proficiency [*British military*] (DMA)
SP..............	Special Program
SP..............	Special Progress [*Program*] [*Education*]
SP..............	Special Projects
SP..............	Special Propellants
SP..............	Special Publication
SP..............	Special Purchase (ADA)
SP..............	Special Purpose
SP..............	Specialist (ADA)
SP..............	Species [*Also, sp*]
SP..............	Specific (AAG)
SP..............	Specific Power
SP..............	Specimen
SP..............	Speck (WGA)
Sp..............	Spectator [*A publication*]
SP..............	Spectral Pitch [*Neurophysiology*]
Sp..............	Speculum [*A publication*]
SP..............	Speech (WGA)
SP..............	Speech Pathologist
SP..............	Speed (MSA)
SP..............	Spelling
SP..............	Spelling Entertainment Group [*Formerly, Charter Co.*] [*NYSE symbol*] (SPSG)
SP..............	Spelling [*Aaron*] Entertainment, Inc. [*AMEX symbol*] (SPSG)
SP..............	Spherical [*Buoy*]
SP..............	Spherical Polar
sp..............	Spherical Tank [*Liquid gas carriers*]
Sp..............	[*Jacobus*] Spiegelius [*Flourished, 1483-1547*] [*Authority cited in pre-1607 legal work*] (DSA)
S/P.............	Spikes Plant [*Wheat*]
SP..............	Spin Polarized [*Physics*]
SP..............	Spine [*or Spinal*]
SP..............	Spine Point Bullet
sp..............	Spinel [*CIPW classification*] [*Geology*]
Sp..............	Spinks' English Admiralty Prize Cases [*164 English Reprint*] [*1854-56*] [*A publication*] (DLA)
Sp..............	Spinks' English Ecclesiastical and Admiralty Reports [*A publication*] (DLA)
Sp..............	Spirillum (MAE)
SP..............	Spirit
SP..............	Spirometry
SP..............	Spitze [*Point*] [*Music*]
SP..............	Splash Plate
SP..............	Splashproof (MSA)
SP..............	Splinting [*Dentistry*]
SP..............	Splitting [*Electronics*]
SP..............	Sponge (WGA)
Sp..............	Spontaneous
SP..............	Spontaneous Potential [*Log*]
SP..............	Spool (MSA)
SP..............	Spoon (WGA)
SP..............	Spore Plasma [*Botany*]
SP..............	Sport
SP..............	Sportavia Puetzer GmbH & Co. KG [*Germany*] [*ICAO aircraft manufacturer identifier*] (ICAO)
SP..............	Sports for the People (EA)
SP..............	Spot Price [*Investment term*]
SP..............	Sprague-Dawley [*Rat variety*]
SP..............	Spray Pressure [*Agriculture*]
SP..............	Spring [*A publication*]
Sp..............	Spring Tide
Sp..............	Sputnik [*Moscow*] [*A publication*]
SP..............	Square Planar [*Organic chemistry*]
SP..............	Square Punch
SP..............	Stable Platform
SP..............	Stack Pointer [*Data processing*]
SP..............	Staff Paymaster [*Navy*] [*British*] (ROG)
SP..............	Stained Pollen [*Botany*]
S & P.........	Stake and Platform [*Technical drawings*]
SP..............	Standard Holding Pattern [*Aviation*]
SP..............	Standard or Peculiar (NASA)
SP..............	Standard Pile [*Nuclear reactor*]
SP..............	Standard Play [*Video technology*]
S & P.........	Standard & Poor's Corp.
SP..............	Standard Practice [*or Procedure*]
SP..............	Standard Price
SP..............	Standard Program [*Data processing*] (BUR)
SP..............	Standby Power
SP..............	Standing Procedure (NATG)
SP..............	Standpipe (MSA)
SP..............	Start Permission (KSC)
SP..............	Starting Point
SP..............	Starting Price
SP..............	State Plan (OICC)
SP..............	Static Pointer [*Data processing*]
SP..............	Static Pressure
SP..............	Station Police [*British military*] (DMA)
SP..............	Station Pressure [*Meteorology*] (FAAC)
SP..............	Status Panel (CAAL)
S/P.............	Status Post [*Medicine*]
SP..............	Steady Potential (MAE)
SP..............	Stern Post
SP..............	Stipule [*Botany*]
SP..............	Stirrup Pump
SP..............	Stool Preservative [*Medicine*]
SP..............	Stop Payment [*Banking*]
SP..............	Stop Press (ADA)
SP..............	Storage Protein [*Food industry*]
SP..............	Straight Partners (EA)
SP..............	Strategic Planning Chart [*Air Force*]
SP..............	Strategic Planning Society [*See also SPS*] [*London, England*] (EAIO)
S & P.........	Strategy and Policy Group [*War Department*] [*World War II*]
SP..............	Street Price (ROG)
SP..............	Stretcher Party
SP..............	Stronnictwo Pracy [*Labour Party*] [*Poland*] [*Political party*] (EY)
SP..............	Structured Programming [*Data processing*] (BUR)
S-P.............	Studebaker-Packard [*Automobile manufacturer*]
SP..............	Studies in Philology [*A publication*]
SP..............	Study Plan
SP..............	Subject-Predicate
SP..............	Subliminal Perception
SP..............	Submarine Patrol [*Navy*]
S/P.............	Submarine Pay [*British military*] (DMA)
SP..............	Subplate [*Neurology*]
SP..............	Subprofessional [*Civil Service employees designation*]
SP..............	Substance P [*A peptide*] [*Biochemistry*]
SP..............	Successive Planometric [*A discrimination task*]
SP..............	Sugar Phosphate [*Biochemistry*]
SP..............	Suicide Precaution (MAE)
SP..............	Suisse Primitive [*A publication*]
SP..............	Sumatra Post [*A publication*]
SP..............	Sumerian Proverbs (BJA)
SP..............	Summary Plotter [*RADAR*]
SP..............	Summary Punch [*Data processing*] (OA)
SP..............	Summating Potential [*Hearing*]
SP..............	Summus Pontifex [*Supreme Pontiff, Pope*] [*Latin*]
SP..............	Sunlit Period
SP..............	Sun's Parallax [*Astronomy*] (ROG)
SP..............	Superficial Pineal Organ [*Neuroanatomy*]
SP..............	Superparamagnetic [*Fraction in rock*] [*Geophysics*]
SP..............	Superseded in Part [*New matter substituted for part of an existing regulation or order*] [*Used in Shepard's Citations*] [*Legal term*] (DLA)
Sp..............	Supertrust Trust Index Trust [*Associated Press abbreviation*] (APAG)
SP..............	Supervisory Package (OA)
SP..............	Supervisory Printer [*Data processing*] (OA)
SP..............	Supervisory Process [*Telecommunications*] (TEL)
SP..............	Supplement
SP..............	Supply Point [*Military*] (NATG)
SP..............	Support
SP..............	Support Plan (MCD)
SP..............	Support Publications (AAG)
SP..............	Supraprotest
SP..............	Suprapubic [*Medicine*]
SP..............	Surveillance Procedure (NRCH)

SP..............	Surviving Propagules [*Botany*]
SP..............	Suspicious Person
SP..............	Sustainer Pitch (AAG)
SP..............	Swelling Power [*Food technology*]
SP..............	Switch Panel
SP..............	Switch Port [*Telecommunications*]
SP..............	Syllable Period [*Entomology*]
SP..............	Symbol Programmer (MUGU)
SP..............	Symphonic Popular [*Armed Forces Radio-Televsion*] (DNAB)
SP..............	Symphysis Pubica [*Anatomy*]
SP..............	Synperiplanar [*Chemistry*]
SP..............	System Parameter (KSC)
SP..............	System Processor (IEEE)
S-P	Systems and Procedures
SP..............	Systolic Pressure [*Cardiology*]
SP4.............	Specialist 4 [*Army*]
SP5.............	Specialist 5 [*Obsolete*] [*Army*]
SP6.............	Specialist 6 [*Obsolete*] [*Army*]
SP7.............	Specialist 7 [*Army*]
SP8.............	Specialist 8 [*Obsolete*] [*Army*]
SP9.............	Specialist 9 [*Obsolete*] [*Army*]
SPA............	Dagblad Scheepvaart [*A publication*]
SPA............	Greenville/Spartanburg [*South Carolina*] Downtown [*Airport symbol*] (OAG)
SPA............	S-Band Power Amplifier
SPA............	Sacrum Palatium Apostolicum [*Sacred Apostolic Palace, Vatican, Quirinal*] [*Latin*]
SPA............	St. Maarten Patriotic Alliance [*Netherlands Antilles*] [*Political party*] (EY)
SPA............	Salt-Poor Albumin [*Medicine*]
SPA............	Salt Producers Association [*Later, SI*] (EA)
SPA............	Sample Preparation Accessory [*Laboratory analysis*]
SPA............	Satellite Personnel Activity [*Military*]
SPA............	Saudi Press Agency
SPA............	Scalable Processing Architecture [*Computer hardware*] [*Northgate*] (PCM)
SPA............	Scatter Propagation Antenna
SPA............	Science and Public Affairs [*A publication*]
SPA............	Science and Public Affairs. Bulletin of the Atomic Scientists [*A publication*]
SPA............	Scintillation Proximity Assay [*Analytical biochemistry*]
SPA............	Scottish Paraplegic (Spinal Injury) Association [*British*]
SPA............	Sea Photo Analysis [*Navy*]
SPA............	Seaplane Pilots Association (EA)
SPA............	Self-Phasing Array
SPA............	Semipermanently Associated [*Telecommunications*] (TEL)
SPA............	Service Pay and Allowances [*Military*] [*British*]
SPA............	Servo Power Amplifier (NASA)
SPA............	Servo Power Assembly (MCD)
SPA............	Servo Preamplifier
SPA............	Shared Peripheral Area (NASA)
SPA............	Sierra Pacific Airlines [*North Hollywood, CA*] [*FAA designator*] (FAAC)
SPA............	Signal Processor Assembly [*NASA*]
SPA............	Silicon Pulser Array
SPA............	Singapore People's Alliance
SPA............	Single Parameter Analysis
SPA............	Single Photon Absorptiometry [*Analytical chemistry*]
SPA............	Single Position Automatic [*Tester*]
SPA............	Singles Press Association (EA)
SPA............	Sitzungsberichte. Preussische Akademie der Wissenschaften [*A publication*]
SPA............	Skill Performance Aid [*Army*] (RDA)
SPA............	Small-Particle Aerosol
SPA............	Socialist Party of Albania [*Political party*] (EY)
SPA............	Socialist Party of Australia [*Political party*]
SPA............	Society of Participating Artists [*Record label*]
SPA............	Society for Personality Assessment (EA)
SPA............	Society for Personnel Administration [*Later, IPMA*] (EA)
SPA............	Society of Philatelic Americans [*Defunct*] (EA)
SPA............	Society of Philosophers in America (EA)
SPA............	Society of Professional Assessors [*Address unknown*]
SPA............	Society for Psychological Anthropology (EA)
SPA............	Society for Public Administration
SPA............	Sociological Practice Association (EA)
SPA............	Sodium Polyacrylate [*Organic chemistry*]
SPA............	Software Product Assurance (SSD)
SPA............	Software Publishers Association (EA)
SPA............	Solar Power Array
SPA............	Songwriters Protective Association [*Later, AGAC*]
SPA............	SOSUS Probability Area (NVT)
SPA............	South Pacific Area [*World War II*]
SPA............	South Pole [*Antarctica*] [*Seismograph station code, US Geological Survey*] (SEIS)
SPA............	Southeastern Peanut Association (EA)
SPA............	Southern Pine Association [*Later, SFPA*] (EA)
SPA............	Southwest Placement Association (AEBS)
SPA............	Southwestern Power Administration [*Department of Energy*]
SPA............	Space Processing Applications [*Program*] [*NASA*]
SPA............	Spade [*Freight*]
SPA............	Spanish
spa.............	Spanish [*MARC language code*] [*Library of Congress*] (LCCP)
SPA............	Spartanburg, SC [*Location identifier*] [*FAA*] (FAAL)
SPA............	Sparton Corp. [*NYSE symbol*] (SPSG)
SPA............	Special Project Activities (MCD)
SPA............	Special Public Assistance
SPA............	Special-Purpose Aircraft [*Drone vehicle*] [*Military*]
SPA............	Special Purpose Alteration (MCD)
SPA............	Specialist, Physical Training Instructor [*Navy rating*]
SPA............	Spectair Industry [*Vancouver Stock Exchange symbol*]
SPA............	Spectrum Analyzer
SPA............	Splice Plug Assembly
SPA............	Sportsman Pilots Association
SPA............	Standard Plate Agar [*Microbiology*] (OA)
SPA............	Standard Practice Amendment (AAG)
SPA............	Staphylococcal Protein A [*Immunochemistry*]
SPA............	State Planning Agency [*Department of Justice*]
SPA............	Sterile Preparation Area (MCD)
SPA............	Stimulation-Produced Analgesia
SPA............	Strategic Posture Analysis [*Army*] (AABC)
SPA............	Subject to Particular Average [*Insurance*]
SPA............	Submarine Patrol Area [*Navy*] (NVT)
SPA............	Subpoena [*Legal term*]
SPA............	Substance P Antagonist [*Biochemistry*]
SPA............	Substitute Part Authorization (AAG)
SPA............	Sudden Phase Anomaly [*Radio engineering*]
SPA............	Sundry Persons' Account [*Banking*]
SPA............	Superphosphoric Acid [*Fertilizer*]
SPA............	Supervisory Performance Appraisal [*Civil Service*]
SPA............	Supplemental Preclaims Assistance [*Department of Education*] (GFGA)
SPA............	Suprapubic Aspiration [*Medicine*]
SPA............	Supreme People's Assembly [*Political party*] [*North Korea*] (FEA)
SPA............	Surface Vehicle Power Adapter
SPA............	Surinaamse Partij van de Arvid [*Suriname Labour Party*] [*Political party*] (EY)
SPA............	SURTASS Probability Area [*Navy*] (CAAL)
SPA............	Survey of Personal Attitude [*Psychology*]
SPA............	Symbolic Processing Array [*Data processing*]
SPA............	System Performance Analyzer [*Motorola, Inc.*]
SPA............	System Problem Area (SAA)
SPA............	Systems and Procedures Association [*Later, ASM*] (EA)
SPAA.........	Caraz [*Peru*] [*ICAO location identifier*] (ICLI)
SPAA.........	Sage Public Administration Abstracts [*A publication*]
SPAA........	Spacecraft Performance Analysis Area
SPAAAX ..	Memoires Suisses de Paleontologie [*A publication*]
SPAAAX ..	Memorie Svizzere di Paleontologia [*A publication*]
SPAAC	Syndicat du Personnel Africain de l'Aeronautique Civile [*African Union for Civil Aviation Employees*]
SPAAG......	Self-Propelled Anti-Aircraft Gun [*Former Soviet Union*]
SPAALAL ...	Society for the Promotion of African, Asian, and Latin American Literature [*See also GFLAAL*] [*Germany*] (EAIO)
SPAAMFAA ...	Society for the Preservation and Appreciation of Antique Motor Fire Apparatus in America (EA)
SPAAN......	Societe Protectrice des Animaux en Afrique du Nord [*Society for the Protection of Animals in North Africa - SPANA*] [*British*] (EAIO)
SPAASS	Synod Office, Diocese of Saskatchewan, Angelican Church of Canada, Prince Albert, Saskatchewan [*Library symbol*] [*National Library of Canada*] (NLC)
SPAB........	Huancabamba [*Peru*] [*ICAO location identifier*] (ICLI)
SPAB........	Security Pacific Asian Bank
SPAB........	Society for the Protection of Ancient Buildings (EA)
SPAB........	Society of Psychologists in Addictive Behaviors [*Later, PAB*] (EA)
SPAB........	Supply, Priorities, and Allocations Board [*World War II*]
SPABH......	Society for the Preservation of American Business History (EA)
SPAC........	Ciro Alegria [*Peru*] [*ICAO location identifier*] (ICLI)
SPAC........	Saratoga Performing Arts Center [*Summer home of NYCB*] [*Saratoga Springs, NY*]
SPAC........	Secretary's Pesticide Advisory Committee [*HEW*]
SPAC........	Signal Programmer and Conditioner [*Air Force Eastern Test Range*]
S Pac.........	South Pacific [*A publication*] (APTA)
SPAC........	Space Program Advisory Council [*Terminated, 1977*] [*NASA*]
SPAC........	Spacecraft Performance Analysis and Command [*NASA*]
SPAC........	Spacious (ADA)
SPAC........	Spatial Computer
SPACA......	Spectrochimica Acta [*A publication*]
SPACCS	Space Command and Control System
SPACD8....	Israel. Agricultural Research Organization. Special Publication [*A publication*]
SPACE	Council of AFL-CIO Unions for Scientific, Professional, and Cultural Employees [*Later, Department for Professional Employees, AFL-CIO*]
SPACE	Sales Profitability and Contribution Evaluator [*Data processing*]
SPACE	Satellite Precipitation and Cloud Experiment [*National Oceanic and Atmospheric Administration*]

SPACE ...... Self-Programming Automatic Circuit Evaluator
SPACE ...... Sequential Position and Covariance Estimation (IEEE)
SPACE ...... Shuttle/Payload Contamination Evaluation Program (MCD)
SPACE ...... Sidereal Polar Axis Celestial Equipment
SPACE ...... Society for Private and Commercial Earth Stations [Telecommunications] [Information service or system] (EA)
SPACE ...... Space Program American Citizens' Effort
SPACE ...... Spacecraft Prelaunch Automatic Checkout Equipment [NASA]
SPACE ...... Special Political Agricultural Community Education [Milk cooperative trust fund]
SPACE ...... Sperry Program for Advancing Careers through Education
SPACE ...... Support Package for Aerospace Computer Emulation (MCD)
SPACE ...... Symbolic Programming Anyone Can Enjoy
Space/Aeronaut ... Space/Aeronautics [A publication]
Space Biol Aerosp Med ... Space Biology and Aerospace Medicine [A publication]
Space Biol Med (Engl Transl) ... Space Biology and Medicine (English Translation) [A publication]
Space Cit.... Space City News [A publication]
SPACECOM ... Space Command [Military]
SPACECOM ... Space Communications
Space Comm ... Space Commerce Bulletin [A publication]
Space Congr ... Space Congress [A publication]
Space Congr Proc ... Space Congress. Proceedings [United States] [A publication]
Spacecr Mater Space Environ Eur Symp Proc ... Spacecraft Materials in Space Environment. European Symposium. Proceedings [A publication]
Space Ind ... Space Industrialization [A publication]
Space Life Sci ... Space Life Sciences [A publication]
Space Marke ... Space Markets [A publication]
Space Res... Space Research [A publication]
Space Res Bulg ... Space Research in Bulgaria [A publication]
Space Res Eng ... Space Research and Engineering [A publication]
SPACES..... Saving and Preserving Arts and Cultural Environments (EA)
Space Sci Instrum ... Space Science Instrumentation [A publication]
Space Sci R ... Space Science Reviews [A publication]
Space Sci Rev ... Space Science Reviews [A publication]
Space Simul Proc Symp ... Space Simulation. Proceedings of a Symposium [A publication]
Space Sol Power Rev ... Space Solar Power Review [A publication]
Space Stn Autom ... Space Station Automation [A publication]
Space Stn Present Future Proc Int Astronaut Congr ... Space Stations Present and Future. Proceedings. International Astronautical Congress [A publication]
SPACETAC ... Space and Tactical System Corp. (MCD)
SPACETRACK ... Space Tracking System [Air Force] (MCD)
SPACG ...... Syndicat du Personnel de l'Aeronautique Civile du Gabon [Union of Civil Aviation Employees of Gabon]
S Pacific..... South Pacific [A publication] (APTA)
S Pacific Bull ... South Pacific Bulletin [A publication] (APTA)
SPACLALS ... South Pacific Association for Commonwealth Literature and Language Studies (EAIO)
SPACON... Space Control
SPACS....... Sodium Purification and Characterization System [Nuclear energy] (NRCH)
SPAD........ Satellite Position Prediction and Display
SPAD........ Satellite Protection for Area Defense [ARPA]
SPAD........ Scratch Pad Memory [Data processing]
SPAD........ Seaway Port Authority of Duluth
SPAD........ Shuttle Payload Accommodation Document [NASA] (MCD)
SPAD........ Simplified Procedures for Analysis of Data (OA)
SPAD........ Societe pour Aviation et ses Derives [France] [World War I airplane]
SPAD........ Space Patrol Active Defense
SPAD........ Space Patrol for Air Defense
SPAD........ Space Principles, Applications, and Doctrine [Air Force Systems Command]
SPAD........ Special Programs and Analysis Division [Environmental Protection Agency] (GFGA)
SPAD........ SPRINT Air-Directed Defense [Army]
SPAD........ Submarine Patrol Area Definition (MCD)
SPAD........ Subsystem Postioning Aid Device (NASA)
SPADATS ... Space Detection and Tracking System [Military]
SPADATSC ... Space Detection and Tracking System Center [Air Force]
SPADATSS ... Space Detection and Tracking System Sensors [Air Force]
SPADCCS ... Space Defense Command and Control System (MCD)
SPADE...... Signal Processing and Display Equipment
SPADE...... Single-Channel-per-Carrier, Pulse-Code-Modulation, Multiple-Access, Demand-Assignment Equipment [Telecommunications]
SPADE...... Small Portable Analysis and Diagnostic Equipment [Aircraft maintenance]
SPADE...... Spare Parts Analysis, Documentation, and Evaluation
SPADE...... Sparta Acquisition Digital Equipment (MCD)
SPADE...... Sperry Air Data Equipment
SPADE...... Strike Planning and Damage Estimator [Military]
SPADES.... Solar Perturbation and Atmospheric Density Measurement Satellite
SPADETS ... Space Detection Network [Military]

SPADL ...... Spare Parts Application Data List
SPADNS ... (Sulfophenylazo)dihydroxynaphthalene-disulfonate [Organic chemistry]
SPADOC... Space Defense Operations Center [DoD]
SPADS ...... Satellite Position and Display System
SPADS ...... Shuttle Problem Action [or Analysis] Data System [NASA] (NASA)
SPADS ...... SPRINT Air-Directed Defense System [Army] (AABC)
SPADS ...... STRATCOM Program Automated Data System [Army]
SPA DT .... Subpoena Duces Tecum [Legal] [Latin] (ROG)
SPAE........ Societe Planetaire pour l'Assainissement de l'Energie [Planetary Association for Clean Energy] (EAIO)
SPAEA ...... Space/Aeronautics [A publication]
SPAEF...... Societe des Petroles d'Afrique Equatoriale Francaise [French Equatorial African Petroleum Co.]
SPAEF...... Southern Public Administration Education Foundation (EA)
SPAEI....... South Pacific Association of Environmental Institutions
SPAF .... Forestry Branch, Saskatchewan Department of Natural Resources, Prince Albert, Saskatchewan [Library symbol] [National Library of Canada] (NLC)
SP-AF........ Shuttle Projects - Air Force Liaison Office [Kennedy Space Center] [NASA] (NASA)
SPAF .... Simulation Processor and Formatter (MCD)
SPAFA ...... Sports Afield [A publication]
SPAG........ South Plains Association of Governments
SPAG........ Space Radiation Analysis Group [NASA]
SPAG........ Spaghetti (DSUE)
SPAG........ Special Program/Analysis Guidance [DoD]
SPAG........ Standards Promotion Application Group [Telecommunications]
SPAH .... Society for the Preservation and Advancement of the Harmonica (EA)
SPAH .... Spacelab Payload Accommodations Handbook [NASA] (MCD)
SPAI .... Screen Printing Association International (EA)
SPAI .... Steroid Protein Activity Index [Medicine] (MAE)
SPAI .... Strategic Planning Associates, Inc. [Washington, DC] [NASDAQ symbol] (NQ)
SPAID ...... Sheffield Package Analysis and Identification of Data [Commercial & Industrial Development Bureau] [Software package] (NCC)
SPAID ...... Society for the Prevention of Asbestosis and Industrial Diseases [British] (DI)
SPAIN ...... Indian and Northern Affairs Canada [Affaires Indiennes et du Nord Canada] Prince Albert, Saskatchewan [Library symbol] [National Library of Canada] (NLC)
Spain......... Spain Fund [Associated Press abbreviation] (APAG)
Spain Estac Cent Ecol Bol ... Spain. Estacion Centro de Ecologia. Boletin [A publication]
Spain Inst Geol Min Bol Geol Min ... Spain. Instituto Geologico y Minero. Boletin Geologico y Minero [A publication]
Spain Inst Geol Min Mem ... Spain. Instituto Geologico y Minero. Memorias [A publication]
Spain Junta Energ Nucl Rep ... Spain. Junta de Energia Nuclear. Report [A publication]
Spain Pat Doc ... Spain. Patent Document [A publication]
SPA Jnl ..... School of Planning and Architecture. Journal [A publication]
SpAk .... Spisanie na Bulgarskata Akademiya na Naukite [A publication]
SPAL .... Simulator, Projectile, Airburst, Liquid [Chemical defense device] [Military] (RDA)
SPAL .... Stabilized Platform Airborne LASER (RDA)
SPAL .... Succinyl-poly-DL-alanine Poly-L-lysine [Biochemical analysis]
S & P (Ala) Rep ... Stewart and Porter's Alabama Reports [A publication] (DLA)
Spald Cop .. Spalding on Copyright [A publication] (DLA)
SPALT...... Single-Point Articulated Loading Tower [Engineering]
SPALT...... Special Projects Alterations [Navy]
SPALTRA ... Special Projects Alterations, Training [Navy]
SPAM........ Camana [Peru] [ICAO location identifier] (ICLI)
SPAM........ S-Parameter Acquisition and Manipulation [Computer software program] [General Motors Corp.]
SPAM........ Satellite Processor Access Method
SPAM........ Scanning Photoacoustic Microscopy
SPAM........ Search Pattern Assessment Model [Military] (CAAL)
SPAM........ Ship Position and Attitude Measurement (IEEE)
SPAM........ Shipment Planning and Movement [Army]
SPAM........ Shop Portable Aircraft Maintenance [Army]
SPAM........ Society for the Publication of American Music [Record label]
SPAM........ Soil-Plant-Atmosphere [Computer simulation model]
SPAM........ Sonobuoy Placement Assortment Model (MCD)
SPAM........ Special Aeronautical Material [Navy] (NG)
SPAM........ Spiced Ham [Hormel (George A.) & Co.]
SPAMA..... Spanish Air Materiel Area
SPAMAG ... Space Medicine Advisory Group (MCD)
SPAMF...... Seychelles Popular Anti-Marxist Front [Political party] (PD)
SPAMMER ... Space Hammer
SPAMS ..... Ship Position and Altitude Measurement System (MCD)
SPAN........ Social Policy and Administration Network [A publication]
SPAN........ Society of Philatelists and Numismatists (EA)
SPAN........ Solar Particle Alert Network [National Oceanic and Atmospheric Administration]

SPAN......... Solar Proton Alert Network
SPAN......... South Pacific Action Network
SPAN......... South Pacific Association for Commonwealth Literature and Language Studies. Newsletter [*A publication*]
SPAN......... Space Communications Network
SPAN......... Space Navigation
SPAN......... Space Physics Analysis Network [*Database*]
SPAN......... Space Plasma Analysis Network [*NASA*]
SPAN......... Spacecraft Analysis   (KSC)
SPAN......... Span-America Medical Systems, Inc. [*NASDAQ symbol*]   (NQ)
SPAN......... SPAN. Shell Public Health and Agricultural News [*A publication*]
SPAN......... SPAN: State Planning Authority News [*A publication*]   (APTA)
SPAN......... Spaniard   (ROG)
SPAN......... Spanish
Span........... Spanish (Patent Document) [*A publication*]
SPAN......... Statistical Processing and Analysis [*Data processing*]
SPAN......... Storage Planning and Allocation [*Data processing*]
SPAN......... Stored Program Alphanumerics [*FAA*]
SPAN......... Submarine Piloting and Navigation [*Navy*]
SPAN......... Successive, Proportionate, Additive Numeration [*Decision making*]
SPAN......... Sullana [*Peru*] [*ICAO location identifier*]   (ICLI)
SPAN......... System for Projection and Analysis
SPANA...... Society for the Protection of Animals in North Africa [*See also SPAAN*] [*British*]   (EAIO)
SPANAT ... Systems Planning Approach - North Atlantic [*FAA*]
SPANC...... Wapiti Regional Library, Prince Albert, Saskatchewan [*Library symbol*] [*National Library of Canada*]   (NLC)
SPAND...... Solar Proton Albedo Neutron Decay
SPANDAR ... Space and Range RADAR [*NASA*]
Spanet........ Secure Prioritized ATM [*Asynchronous Transfer Mode*] Network [*Telecommunications*]
SPANGLISH ... Spanish and English
SPANI...... Northern Institute of Technology, Prince Albert, Saskatchewan [*Library symbol*] [*National Library of Canada*]   (NLC)
SPANNER ... Special Analysis of Net Radio [*Study*]
SPAN Prog Agric ... SPAN [*Shell Public Health and Agricultural News*] Progress in Agriculture [*A publication*]
SPANRAD ... Superimposed Panoramic RADAR Display
SPANS ...... Sealift Procurement and National Security [*Study*]
SPANS ...... Small Passive Navigation System   (DNAB)
SPAO........ San Juan Aposento [*Peru*] [*ICAO location identifier*]   (ICLI)
SPAOPSUP ... Space Operations Support   (NVT)
SPAP......... Picota [*Peru*] [*ICAO location identifier*]   (ICLI)
SPAP .... Serum Prostatic Acid Phosphatase [*An enzyme*]
SPAP .... Special Package Auto Policy [*Insurance*]
SPAQUA... Sealed Package Quality Assurance   (IEEE)
SPAR........ Alerta [*Peru*] [*ICAO location identifier*]   (ICLI)
SPAR......... SAC [*Strategic Air Command*] Peacetime Airborne Reconnaissance
SPAR........ Satellite Position Adjusting Rocket   (SAA)
SPAR........ Seagoing Platform for Acoustic Research [*NOL*]
SPAR........ Semper Paratus [*Always Ready*] [*Coast Guard motto*]
SPAR........ Sensitivity Prediction from the Acoustic Reflex [*Audiometry*]
SPAR........ Society of Photographers and Artist Representatives   (EA)
SPAR........ Soil-Plant-Atmosphere-Research [*Agriculture*]
SPAS........ Space Precision Altitude Reference System   (MCD)
SPAR........ Space Processing Applications Rocket [*NASA*]
SPAR........ SPALT [*Special Projects Alterations*] Planning and Authorization Report
Spar............ Spartan
SPAR......... Spartan Motors, Inc. [*Charlotte, MI*] [*NASDAQ symbol*]   (NQ)
SPAR......... Special Prelaunch Analysis Request [*NASA*]   (KSC)
SPAR......... Special Progressive Aircraft Rework
SPAR......... Spelling and Reading Tests
SPAR......... Staff Payroll Allocation and Record   (OA)
SPAR......... Staff Procurement Activity Requirement [*Military*]
SPAR......... Stock Point ADP [*Automatic Data Processing*] Replacement Program [*Navy*]   (GFGA)
SPAR......... Student Profile and Assessment Record [*Student attitudes test*]
SPAR......... Submersible Pipe Alignment Rig [*Deep-sea diving*]
SPAR......... Super-Precision Approach RADAR
SPAR......... Surveillance and Precision Approach RADAR   (NATG)
SPAR......... Symbolic Program Assembly Routine [*Data processing*]
SPAR......... Synchronous Position Altitude Recorder
SPAR......... System Program Assessment Review [*Air Force*]
SPARC...... Scaleable Processor Architecture [*Data processing*]
SPARC...... Shore-Establishment Planning Analysis and Review Cooperation [*or Coordination*] [*Navy*]   (NG)
SPARC...... Short Planning Analysis and Review Cooperation
SPARC...... Slab Penetration and Reflection Calculation
SPARC...... Space Air Relay Communications   (MCD)
SPARC...... Space Program Analysis and Review Council [*Air Force*]
SPARC...... Space Research Capsule [*or Conic*] [*NASA*]
SPARC...... Spare Parts Provisioning for Combat
SPARC...... Spectral Analysis and Recognition Computer [*NASA*]
SPARC...... Standards Planning and Requirements Committee [*ANSI*]
SPARC...... Steam Plant Automation and Results Computer
SPARC...... Support Planning Analysis Reporting and Control [*Navy*]   (NG)

SPARC...... Sustainability Predictions for Army Spare Component Requirements for Combat   (RDA)
SPARC...... System Parametric Allocation of Resources and Cost   (MCD)
SPARCS.... Solar Pointing Aerobee Rocket Control System
SPARCS.... Statewide Planning and Research Cooperative System [*New York State Department of Health*] [*Albany*] [*Information service or system*]   (IID)
SPARD...... Sparkasse [*A publication*]
SPARE ...... Save Pound Animals from Research Experiments   (EA)
SPARE ...... System for Projecting Ammunition Repairable End Items [*Military*]
SPARES.... Space Radiation Evaluation System [*NASA*]   (KSC)
SPAREX.... Canada Regional Industrial Expansion [*Expansion Industrielle Regionale*], Prince Albert, Saskatchewan [*Library symbol*] [*National Library of Canada*]   (BIB)
SPARK ...... Saboteurs for a Philistine America Redeemed from Kultur [*From book, "Bringing Down the House," by Richard P. Brickner*]
SPARK ...... Screen Pattern Analyzer and Rescreening Key [*Printing process*]
SPARK ...... Seminars on Practical Applications of Research Knowledge [*Advertising Research Foundation*]
SPARK ...... Solid Propellant Advanced Ramjet Kinetic Energy   (MCD)
SPARK ...... Systematic Pulmono/Cardiac Anaphylaxis Resusitation Kit   (MCD)
Sparks........ Sparks' Reports [*British Burma*] [*A publication*]   (DLA)
Spark's Am Biog ... Spark's Library of American Biography [*A publication*]
SPARM ..... Solid-Propellant Augmented Rocket Motor [*Navy*]
SPARM ..... Sparrow Antiradiation Missile   (MCD)
SPARMIS ... Standard Police Automated Resource Management Information System
SPARMO ... Solar Particles and Radiations Monitoring Organization
SPARMO Bull ... SPARMO [*Solar Particles and Radiation Monitoring Organization*] Bulletin [*A publication*]
SPARPS.... Spares and Repair Parts Support [*Navy*]   (NG)
SPARS...... Semper Paratus [*US Coast Guard Women's Auxiliary; name taken from Coast Guard motto*]
SPARS...... Site Production and Reduction System
SPARS...... Society of Professional Audio Recording Services   (EA)
SPARS...... Space Precision Altitude [*or Attitude*] Reference System
SPARSA.... Sferics, Position [*or Pulse*], Azimuth, Rate, and Spectrum Analyzer
SPARSIM ... Spartan Simulation [*Missile system evaluation*]   (RDA)
SPART ...... Space Research and Technology [*Report*] [*NASA*]   (KSC)
SPART ...... Sunny Point Army Terminal
SPARTA.... Sequential Programmed Automatic Recording Transistor Analyzer
SPARTA.... Special Antimissile Research Tests in Australia
SPARTA.... System for Private Access for Reservations and Travel Agents [*British*]   (DI)
SPARTAN ... Shuttle-Pointed Autonomous Research Tool for Astronomy [*NASA*]
SPARTAN ... Special Proficiency at Rugged Training and Nation Building [*Training program for Green Berets*] [*Army*]
SPARTAN ... System for Personnel Automated Reports, Transactions, and Notices [*Census Bureau, NASA*]
SPARTCH ... Spartech Corp. [*Associated Press abbreviation*]   (APAG)
Sparton ...... Sparton Corp. [*Associated Press abbreviation*]   (APAG)
SPAS .... Security Police Automated System [*Air Force*]   (GFGA)
SPAS .... Shipboard Pollution Abatement System [*Navy*]   (CAAL)
SPAS .... Shuttle Pallet Satellite [*NASA*]
SPAS .... Skill Performance Aids
SPAS .... Social Service Department, Prince Albert, Saskatchewan [*Library symbol*] [*National Library of Canada*]   (NLC)
SPA-S........ Societa Prodotti Antibiotici [*Italy*] [*Research code symbol*]
SPAS .... Societatis Philosophicae Americanae Socius [*Member of the American Philosophical Society*]
SPAS .... Solar Proton Alpha Spectrometer
SPASE....... South Pole Air Shower Experiment [*Astronomy*]
SPASEP .... Secretaria Permanente del Acuerdo Sudamericano de Estupefacientes y Psicotropicos [*Permanent Secretariat of the South American Agreement on Narcotic Drugs and Psychotropic Substances - PSSAANDPS*] [*Argentina*]   (EAIO)
SPASM ..... Self-Propelled Air-to-Surface Missile   (MCD)
SPASM ..... Smithsonian Package for Algebra and Symbolic Mathematics   (MCD)
SPASM ..... Space Propulsion Automated Synthesis Modeling [*Program*]
SPASM ..... System Performance and Activity Software Monitor [*Data processing*]   (IEEE)
SPAST....... Special Assistant [*Navy*]
SPASUR.... Space Surveillance System [*Navy*]
SPASYN... Space-Syncromesh
SPAT .... Aguas Calientes [*Peru*] [*ICAO location identifier*]   (ICLI)
SPAT .... Self-Propelled Antitank Gun   (MCD)
SPAT .... Silicon Precision Alloy Transistor
SPAT .... Spleen Antigen [*Complement Fixation*] Test [*Immunology*]
SPAT .... Supplementary Pay Appeals Tribunal [*British*]   (DI)
SPAT .... Systems Programming Aptitude Test
SPATA ...... Society of Polish-American Travel Agents   (EA)
SPATE ...... Sergeant Production Automatic Test Equipment

SPATE ...... South Pacific Association for Teacher Education [*Later, ATEA*]   (EA)

SPATE ...... Student Personnel Association for Teacher Education [*Later, AHEAD*]   (EA)

SPA ad TEST ... Subpoena ad Testificandum [*Subpoena to Testify*] [*Latin*]   (ROG)

S Patriot..... Southern Patriot [*A publication*]

SPATS....... South Pacific Air Transportation Service [*Navy*]

Spat Vision ... Spatial Vision [*A publication*]

SPAU........ Signal Processing [*or Processor*] Arithmetic Unit [*Navy*]

SPAU........ Stable Platform Alignment Unit

Spaulding... Spaulding's Reports [*71-73 Maine*] [*A publication*]   (DLA)

SPAW........ Learning Resource Centre, Woodland Campus, Saskatchewan Institute of Applied Science and Technology, Prince Albert, Saskatchewan [*Library symbol*] [*National Library of Canada*]   (BIB)

SPAW........ Sitzungsberichte. Preussische Akademie der Wissenschaften [*A publication*]

Spawanie Ciecie Met ... Spawanie i Ciecie Metali [*A publication*]

SPAWAR .. Space and Naval Warfare Systems Command [*Washington, DC*] [*Navy*]   (GRD)

SPAWG..... Special Activity Wing   (MUGU)

SPAWN..... Salmon Protection Association of Western Newfoundland [*Canada*]   (ASF)

SPAYZ ...... Spatial Property Analyzer

SPAZD9 .... Agronomy Society of New Zealand. Special Publication [*A publication*]

SPB .... St. Thomas [*Virgin Islands*] Seaplane Base [*Airport symbol*]   (OAG)

SPB .... Scottish Prayer Book [*Episcopalian*]

SPB .... Seaplane Base

SPB .... Shergottite Parent Body [*Planetary science*]

SPB .... Ship's Plotting Board

SPB .... Silver-Plated Bronze

SPB .... Society of the Precious Blood [*Anglican religious community*]

SPB .... Solar Particle Beams

SPB .... Sotheby Parke Bernet [*Formerly, PB*] [*Manhattan art auction house*]

SPB .... Special Pathogens Branch [*Centers for Disease Control*]

SPB .... Spindle Pole Body [*Cell biology*]

SpB .... Sprakliga Bidrag [*Lund*] [*A publication*]

SPB .... Springboard Resources Ltd. [*Vancouver Stock Exchange symbol*]

SPB .... Standard Practice Bulletin   (MCD)

SPB .... Standardized Performance Battery [*Acoustics*]

SPB .... Stored Program Buffer

SPB .... Summary Plot Board   (SAA)

SPB .... Surplus Property Board

SPB .... Systems Personnel Branch   (SAA)

SPBA .... Society of Professional Benefit Administrators [*Washington, DC*]   (EA)

SPBA .... Specialty Paper and Board Affiliates [*Later, API*]   (EA)

SpBA......... Spisanie na Bulgarskata Akademiya na Naukite [*A publication*]

SPBAA ..... Spisanie na Bulgarskata Akademiya na Naukite [*A publication*]

SpBAN ...... Spisanie na Bulgarskata Akademiya na Naukite [*A publication*]

SpBaU .... Universidad de Barcelona, Biblioteca Universitaria y Provincal, Barcelona, Spain [*Library symbol*] [*Library of Congress*]   (LCLS)

SPBB .... Moyobamba [*Peru*] [*ICAO location identifier*]   (ICLI)

SPBC .... Caballococha [*Peru*] [*ICAO location identifier*]   (ICLI)

SPBC .... St. Paul Bancorp, Inc. [*NASDAQ symbol*]   (NQ)

SPBC .... Saint Paul Bible College [*Saint Bonifacius, MN*]

SPBC .... Society of Professional Business Consultants [*Chicago, IL*]   (EA)

SPBC .... South Pacific Base Command [*Navy*] [*World War II*]

SPBD........ Springboard   (NVT)

SPBD........ Springboard Software, Inc. [*Minneapolis, MN*] [*NASDAQ symbol*]   (NQ)

SPBE .... Service de Presse Baptiste Europeen [*European Baptist Press Service - EBPS*]   (EAIO)

SPBE .... Society of Parrot Breeders and Exhibitors   (EA)

SPBEC....... South Pacific Bureau for Economic Cooperation in Developing Uniform Maritime Standards for the Pacific Area [*Suva, Fiji*]   (EAIO)

SPBI .... Serikat Buruh Pertjetakan Indonesia [*Printing Workers' Union of Indonesia*]

SPBI .... Serum Protein-Bound Iodine [*Clinical chemistry*]   (AAMN)

SPBI .... Society for Proclaiming Britain in Israel

SPBK .... Speed Brake   (NASA)

SPBL .... Bellavista/Huallaga [*Peru*] [*ICAO location identifier*]   (ICLI)

SPBM .... Single Point Buoy Mooring [*Oil platform*]

SPBOT ...... Stationers and Publishers Board of Trade [*Later, Stationery and Office Equipment Board of Trade*]

SPBP .... Society for the Preservation of Birds of Prey   (EA)

SPBR .... Iberia [*Peru*] [*ICAO location identifier*]   (ICLI)

SPBR .... Speed Brake   (MCD)

SPBS......... Jeberos/Bellavista [*Peru*] [*ICAO location identifier*]   (ICLI)

SPBS.......... Schweizerische Partei der Behinderten und Sozialbenachteiligten [*Swiss Party of the Handicapped and Socially Disadvantaged*] [*Political party*]   (PPW)

SPBS......... Standard Property Book System [*Army*]

SPBSES..... Special Publications Series. British Ecological Society [*A publication*]

SPBS-R..... Standard Army Property Book System - Redesign

SPBT .... Obenteni [*Peru*] [*ICAO location identifier*]   (ICLI)

SPBU........ Vista Breau [*Peru*] [*ICAO location identifier*]   (ICLI)

SPBUA ...... SPARMO [*Solid Particles and Radiation Monitoring Organization*] Bulletin [*A publication*]

SPBW .... Society for the Preservation of Beers from the Wood [*British*]   (EAIO)

SPC .... IEEE. Spectrum [*A publication*]

SPC .... Institute for Studies of Destructive Behaviors and the Suicide Prevention Center of Los Angeles [*California*]   (EA)

SPC .... Political Committee at Senior Level [*NATO*]   (NATG)

SPC .... St. Paul's Cathedral [*London, England*]

SPC .... Saint Paul's College [*Missouri; Virginia; Washington, DC*]

SPC .... Saint Paul's College, Lawrenceville, VA [*OCLC symbol*]   (OCLC)

SPC .... Saint Peter College [*Maryland; New Jersey*]

SPC .... Saint Procopius College [*Illinois*]

SPC .... Salicylamide, Phenacetin [*Acetophenetidin*], and Caffeine [*Pharmacy*]

SPC .... Salkowski Positive Compound   (OA)

SPC .... Santa Cruz La Palma [*Canary Islands*] [*Airport symbol*]   (OAG)

SPC .... Saratoga Processing Co. Ltd. [*Vancouver Stock Exchange symbol*]

SPC .... Satellite Processing Center [*Military*]

SPC .... Seattle Pacific College [*Washington*]

SPC .... Security Pacific Corp. [*Later, BankAmerica Corp.*] [*NYSE symbol*]   (SPSG)

SPC .... Self-Polishing Copolymer [*Anti-fouling paint*]   (DS)

SPC .... Self-Programming Compiler [*Software*] [*Data processing*]

SPC .... Sequence Parameter Checking   (SAA)

SPC .... Set Point Controller

SPC .... Shipping and Packing Cost   (NASA)

SPC .... Shop Process Card [*Navy*]   (DNAB)

SPC .... Shuttle Pin Clutch

SPC .... Shuttle Processing Contractor [*NASA*]

SPC .... Silver-Plated Copper

SPC .... Simple Prose Coefficient [*Publishing*]

SPC .... Simultaneous Prism and Cover (Test) [*Ophthalmology*]

SPC .... Single Prime Contractor [*Weapon system procurement*] [*Air Force*]   (AAG)

SPC .... Site Programmer Course

SPC .... Size-Press Coated [*Publishing*]

SPC .... Skalnate-Pleso [*Czechoslovakia*] [*Seismograph station code, US Geological Survey*]   (SEIS)

SPC .... Small Peripheral Controller

SPC .... Soap Perfumery and Cosmetics [*A publication*]

SPC .... Socialist Party of Canada [*Political party*]

SPC .... Socialist Party of Chile

SPC .... Socialist Party of Croatia [*Political party*]   (EY)

SPC .... Socialist Party of Cyprus [*Political party*]   (EAIO)

SPC .... Society for Philosophy of Creativity   (EA)

SPC .... Society for the Prevention of Crime   (EA)

SPC .... Software Productivity Consortium   (MCD)

SPC .... Solar Pointing Control

SPC .... Solid-Propellant Combustion

SPC .... Solid-Propellant Conference

S/P/C......... Sotto Protesto per Mettere in Conto [*Under Protest to Place to Account*] [*Italian*]

SPC .... South Pacific Commission [*See also CPS*]   (EAIO)

SPC .... South Pacific Island Airways, Inc. [*Pago Pago, American Samoa*]   (FAAC)

SPC .... South Polar Cap [*A filamentary mark on Mars*]

SPC .... Southern Pacific Communications Corp.

SPC .... Southern Ports Foreign Committee, Chicago IL [*STAC*]

SPC .... Soy Protein Council   (EA)

SPC .... Space Development Conference

SPC .... Space Polymer Chemistry   (SSD)

SPC .... Space Projects Center [*NASA*]

SPC .... Spacer [*Technical drawings*]

SpC .... Spanish Columbia, San Sebastian [*Record label*] [*Spain*]

SPC .... Spare Parts Catalog

SPC .... Special Code

Sp C .... Special Commissioner   (DLA)

SPC .... Special Common [*Projectile*]

SPC .... Special Program Code [*Navy*]

SPC .... Special Project Code [*IRS*]

SPC .... Special Purpose Chaff [*Navy*]   (CAAL)

SPC .... Special Purpose Computer

SPC .... Specialist, Classification Interviewer [*Navy rating*]

SPC .... Specific Propellant Consumption

SPC .... Specification

SPC .... Standard Plate Count [*Microbiology*]

SPC .... Standard Products Committee [*Navy*]

SPC .... Standby Pressure Control [*Nuclear energy*]   (NRCH)

SPC .... Starting Point Code   (NASA)

SPC .... Static Power Conservers   (MCD)

SPC .... Static Pressure Compensation

SPC .... Station Program Cooperative [*Public television*]

SPC............	Statistical Process Control
SPC............	Sterilizable Potting Compound
SPC............	Stigmastanyl(phosphorylcholine) [*Biochemistry*]
SPC............	Still-Picture Camera (DNAB)
SPC............	Stockage Priority Code [*Military*] (AFIT)
SPC............	Storage Planning Centre [*Shipping*]
SPC............	Stored Program Command [*or Control*] [*Data processing*]
SPC............	Strategy and Planning Committee [*Military*]
SPC............	Subcontract Plans Committee
SPC............	Sucrose-Phosphate-Citrate [*A culture medium*]
SPC............	Sugar Packet Club (EA)
SPC............	Suicide Prevention Center (IIA)
SPC............	Supplemental Planning Card (AAG)
SPC............	Supplementary Patent Certificate [*European Community*]
SPC............	Suspended Plaster Ceiling [*Technical drawings*]
SPC............	Switching and Processing Center [*EFTS*] [*Banking*]
SPC............	Syndicat des Postiers du Canada [*Canadian Union of Postal Workers - CUPW*]
SPC............	Synoptic Properties Code (MCD)
SPC............	System Professional Computer (HGAA)
Sp3c...........	Specialist, Third Class (GFGA)
SPCA	Barraca [*Peru*] [*ICAO location identifier*] (ICLI)
SPCA	School Projectionist Club of America (EA)
SPCA	Serum Prothrombin Conversion Accelerator [*Factor VII*] [*Also, PPCA*] [*Hematology*]
SPCA	Society for the Prevention of Cruelty to Animals
SPCA	Southern Pulpwood Conservation Association [*Later, SFI*] (EA)
SPCA	Spark Plug Collectors of America (EA)
SPCA	Special-Purpose Cable Assembly
SPCAP......	Society of Professors of Child and Adolescent Psychiatry (EA)
SPCAT	Special Category (MSA)
SPCB	Aguas Blancas [*Peru*] [*ICAO location identifier*] (ICLI)
SPCC	Servo Pressure Control Console
SPCC	Ship's Parts Control Center
SPCC	Society for the Prevention of Cruelty to Children
SPCC	Southern Pacific Communications Corp.
SPCC	Space Parts Control Center (MUGU)
SPCC	Spill Prevention Control and Countermeasure [*Petroleum industry*]
SPCC	Staggered Phase Carrier Cancellation
SPCC	Standardization, Policy, and Coordination Committee [*NATO*] (NATG)
SPCC	Stored Program CAMAC [*Computer-Aided Measurement and Control*] Channel [*Data processing*]
SPCC	Strength Power and Communications Cable
SPCC	STS [*Shuttle Test Station*] Processing Control Center [*NASA*] (GFGA)
SPCC	Study Planning and Coordinating Committee [*Army*]
SPCC	Sugar Packet Collectors Club (EA)
SPCC	Super-Packed Capillary Column [*Spectroscopy*]
SPCC	System Performance Check Compound
SpcCh	Specialty Chemical Resources, Inc. [*Associated Press abbreviation*] (APAG)
SPCCS.......	Spill Prevention Control and Countermeasure System [*Environmental Protection Agency*] [*Information service or system*] [*No longer exists*] (IID)
SPCD........	Space Communications Division [*Military*]
SPCD........	Specification Control Drawing (MCD)
sp cd	Spinal Cord [*Medicine*] (MAE)
SPCDS.......	Small Permanent Communications and Display Segment (MCD)
SPCEC......	Stereo Photographers, Collectors, and Enthusiasts Club (EA)
SPCF	Special Project Control File [*IRS*]
Sp Ch	Spears' South Carolina Chancery Reports [*A publication*] (DLA)
SPCH........	Speech
SPCH........	Tocache [*Peru*] [*ICAO location identifier*] (ICLI)
SPC Handb ...	SPC [*South Pacific Commission*] Handbook [*A publication*]
SPCHB......	Soviet Progress in Chemistry [*English Translation*] [*A publication*]
SPCHDX...	Carnegie Museum of Natural History. Special Publication [*A publication*]
SPCHG.....	Supercharge
SPCHGR...	Supercharger (AAG)
SPCK	Society for Promoting Christian Knowledge [*Publisher*] [*British*]
SPCL	Pucallpa [*Peru*] [*ICAO location identifier*] (ICLI)
SPCL	Special (MSA)
SPCL	Spectrum Information Technologies, Inc. [*NASDAQ symbol*] (NQ)
SPCLASGN ...	Special Assignment [*Military*] (NVT)
SPCLN	Special Cleaning
SPCLY......	Especially (FAAC)
SPCM........	Contamana [*Peru*] [*ICAO location identifier*] (ICLI)
SPCM........	Master Chief Steam Propulsionman [*Navy rating*]
SPCM........	Spanish Campaign Medal
SPCM........	Special Court-Martial
SPCM........	Specialty Composites Corp. [*NASDAQ symbol*] (NQ)
SPCMO.....	Special Court-Martial Order
SPCMWOMJ ...	Special Court-Martial without a Military Judge (AFM)

SPCN.........	Stored Program Controlled Network [*Telecommunications*]
SPCNI	Society for Pacific Coast Native Irises (EA)
SPCO.........	Software Publishing Corp. [*Mountain View, CA*] [*NASDAQ symbol*] (NQ)
SPCO.........	Southern Pacific Co.
SPCOA	Spark Plug Collectors of America (EA)
SPCONV...	Speed Converter
SPCP	Pucacaca [*Peru*] [*ICAO location identifier*] (ICLI)
SPCP	Single Prime Contractor Policy [*Air Force*] (AAG)
SPCP	Society of Professors of Child Psychiatry [*Later, SPCAP*] (EA)
SPCP	Standardization and Parts Control Program
SPCP	Steam Propulsion Control Panel (DNAB)
SPCPB......	Space Congress. Proceedings [*A publication*]
SPCQB	SPC [*South Pacific Commission*] Quarterly Bulletin [*A publication*]
SPC Quart Bull ...	SPC [*South Pacific Commission*] Quarterly Bulletin [*A publication*]
SPCR	Spacer
SPCR	Spare Parts Change Request
Spcr...........	Spectinomycin Resistance
Sp Cr Ct	Special Criminal Court (DLA)
SPC Rep Sask Power Corp ...	SPC Report. Saskatchewan Power Corp. [*A publication*]
SpcRtl	Specialty Retailers, Inc. [*Associated Press abbreviation*] (APAG)
SPCS.........	Schedule Planning and Control System (MCD)
SPCS.........	Selective Paging Communications System
S & PCS	Silver and Pewter Collectors Society (EA)
SPCS.........	Standard & Poor's COMPUSTAT Services, Inc. [*Also, an information service or system*] (IID)
SPCS.........	State Plane Coordinate System [*National Geodetic Survey Division*] [*National Oceanic and Atmospheric Administration*]
SPCS.........	Static Power Conversion System
SPCS.........	Statistical Process Control Society (EA)
SPCS.........	Storage and Processing Control System
SPCS.........	Surgical Postcaval Shunt [*Medicine*]
SPCSDW...	Commonwealth Bureau of Soils. Special Publication [*A publication*]
SPC Soap Perfum Cosmet ...	SPC. Soap, Perfumery, and Cosmetics [*A publication*]
SPC/SQC ..	Statistical Process/Statistical Quality Control
SPCT	Chota [*Peru*] [*ICAO location identifier*] (ICLI)
SPCT	Spectra Pharmaceutical Services, Inc. [*Hanover, MA*] [*NASDAQ symbol*] (NQ)
SPCT	Statistical Process Control Toolbox (RDA)
SPC Tech Pap ...	SPC [*South Pacific Commission*] Technical Paper [*A publication*]
SPCTG	Spherical Cartridge
Sp Ct RRRA ...	Special Court Regional Railroad Reorganization Act [*A publication*] (DLA)
SpctSg........	Spectrum Signal Processing [*Associated Press abbreviation*] (APAG)
SPCTYS	Society for the Prevention of Cruelty to Young Singers
SPCU	Simulation Process Control Unit (MCD)
SPCU	Skylab Process Control Unit [*NASA*]
SPCUS	Sweet Potato Council of the United States (EA)
SPCW........	Specialist, Chemical Warfare [*Navy rating*]
SPCW........	Stored Program Command Word [*Data processing*] (NASA)
SPCZ	South Pacific Convergence Zone (MCD)
SPD............	Doctor of Political Science
SPD............	S-Band Polarization Diversity
SPD............	Safety Program Directive [*NASA*]
SPD............	Saidpur [*Bangladesh*] [*Airport symbol*] (OAG)
SPD............	St. Peter's Dome Lookout [*New Mexico*] [*Seismograph station code, US Geological Survey*] (SEIS)
SPD............	Salmon Poisoning Disease [*Medicine*] (AAMN)
SPD............	Salutem Plurimam Dicit [*He Wishes Much Health*] [*Latin*]
SPD............	Sample Preparation and DNA [*Deoxyribonucleic Acid*] Probe
SPD............	Sampled [*Tea trade*] (ROG)
SPD............	Scientific Passenger Pod (MCD)
SPD............	Seaplane Depot Ship
SPD............	Sedona Industries Ltd. [*Toronto Stock Exchange symbol*]
SPD............	Semipermeable Dressing [*Medicine*]
SPD............	Separation Program Designator [*Military*] (AABC)
SPD............	Service Project Drawing
SPD............	Shearing, Piling, and Disking [*Forest management*]
SPD............	Ship Performance Department [*David W. Taylor Naval Ship Research and Development Center*]
SPD............	Ship Planning Document (DNAB)
SPD............	Ship Project Directive [*Navy*]
SPD............	Sigma Phi Delta (EA)
SPD............	Silicon Photodiode
SPD............	Single Path Doppler [*RADAR*] (AAG)
SPD............	Situation Projected Display
SPD............	Skylab Program Directive [*NASA*] (KSC)
SPD............	Smokeless Powder, Diphenylamine (DNAB)
SPD............	Society for Pediatric Dermatology (EA)
SPD............	Society of Professional Drivers (EA)
SPD............	Society of Publication Designers (EA)
SPD............	South Pacific Division [*Army*] [*World War II*]

SPD........... South Polar Distance
SPD........... Southern Procurement Division [*Navy*]
SPD........... Sozialdemokratische Partei Deutschlands [*Social Democratic Party of Germany*] [*West Germany*]
SpD .... Spanish Decca, San Sebastian [*Record label*] [*Spain*]
SPD........... Spectral Power Density [*Electronics*]
SPD........... Spectral Power Distribution   (MCD)
SPD........... Speech Processing Device
SPD........... Speed   (AABC)
Spd .... Spermidine [*Biochemistry*]
SPD........... Sprayed   (WGA)
SPD........... Standard Periodical Database [*Oxbridge Communications, Inc.*] [*Information service or system*]   (CRD)
SPD........... Standard Periodical Directory [*A publication*]
SPD........... Standard Practice Directive [*NASA*]   (NASA)
SPD........... Standard Products Co. [*NYSE symbol*]   (SPSG)
SPD........... State Programs Division [*Environmental Protection Agency*]   (GFGA)
SPD........... Static Pressure Distribution
SPD........... Statistical Policy Division [*Office of Management and Budget*]
SPD........... Steamer Pays Dues [*Shipping*]
SPD........... Stick Positioning Device   (MCD)
SPD........... Storage Pool Disease
SPD........... Stored Program Decoder [*or Decommutation*]
SPD........... Strategic Posture Display   (MCD)
SPD........... Student Pilot Disposition   (DNAB)
SPD........... Subjective Probability Distribution
SPD........... Superheater Protection Device   (DNAB)
SPD........... Supplemental Program Directive   (AFIT)
SPD........... Supplementary Petroleum Duty [*Tax*] [*British*]
SPD........... Surge Protective Device   (MCD)
SPD........... Suspended-Particle Display [*Glazing technology*]
SPD........... Synchronized Parallel Displacement [*Automotive engineering*]
SPD........... Synchronizer for Peripheral Devices
SPD........... Synchronous Phase Demodulator
SPD........... System Performance Demonstration
SPD........... System Program Directive   (AFIT)
SPD........... System Program Director [*Air Force*]   (MCD)
SPD........... Systems Parameters Document   (AAG)
SPD........... Systems Program Documentation
SPDA........ Single-Premium Deferred Annuity [*Insurance*]
SPDB........ Subsystem Power Distribution Box   (MCD)
SPDBK ...... Speed Brake   (MCD)
SPDC........ S-P Drug Co. [*NASDAQ symbol*]   (NQ)
SPDC........ Spare Parts Distributing Center [*Navy*]
SPDCI ...... Standard Payload Display and Control Interface   (NASA)
SPDCU ...... Subsurface Probe Data and Control Unit
SPDF .... Smokeless Powder, Diphenylamine, Flashless   (DNAB)
SPDF .... Special Projects Data Facility
SPDF .... Swedish Post Defense Forces
SPDG........ Spectrum Digital Corp. [*Herndon, VA*] [*NASDAQ symbol*]   (NQ)
SPDG........ Spiral Point Drill Geometry
SPDHF...... Special Pay for Duty Subject to Hostile Fire [*Military*]
SPDI .... Special Discriminant   (CAAL)
SPDL........ Spin-Dependent Luminescence [*Physics*]
SPDL........ Spindle   (MSA)
SPDL........ Standard Page Description Language [*ISO/IEC*] [*Data processing*]
SPDLTR.... Speedletter
SPDM....... Special Purpose Dexterous Manipulator
SPDM....... Subprocessor with Dynamic Microprogramming
SPDMS ..... Shuttle Program Data Management System [*NASA*]   (SSD)
SPDN .... Smokeless Powder, Diphenylamine, Nonvolatile   (DNAB)
SPD NAV ... Speed Navigation   (MCD)
SPDO .... Mollendo [*Peru*] [*ICAO location identifier*]   (ICLI)
SPDOM .... Speedometer   (MSA)
SPDP........ Stored Program Data Processor   (KSC)
SPDP........ Succinimidyl(pyridyldithio)propionate [*Organic chemistry*]
SPDR........ Software Preliminary Design Review [*NASA*]   (NASA)
SPDR........ Special Drill [*Tool*]   (AAG)
SPDR........ Spider [*Engineering acoustics*]
SPDR........ Standard & Poors Depositary Receipts [*Associated Press abbreviation*]   (APAG)
SP/DR ...... Systems Performance/Design Requirements
SPDRAB ... Society for the Prevention of Disparaging Remarks about Brooklyn
SPDS .... Safe-Practice Data Sheet   (MSA)
SPDS .... Safety Parameter Display System [*Instrumentation*]
SPDS .... Sequential Payload Delivery System   (MCD)
SPDS .... Strategic Platform Defense Study [*DoD*]
SPDS .... Suggestion Program Data System [*Military*]
SPDT........ Single-Pole, Double-Throw [*Switch*]
SPDTDB ... Single-Pole, Double-Throw, Double-Break [*Switch*]
SPDTNCDB ... Single-Pole, Double-Throw, Normally-Closed, Double-Break [*Switch*]
SPDTNO... Single-Pole, Double-Throw, Normally-Open [*Switch*]
SPDTNODB ... Single-Pole, Double-Throw, Normally-Open, Double-Break [*Switch*]
SPDTSW... Single-Pole, Double-Throw Switch
SPDVB ...... Science Progres Decouverte [*A publication*]

SPDW........ Smokeless Powder, Diphenylamine, Reworked   (DNAB)
SPDW........ South Pacific Deep Water
SPDWY ..... Speedway
SPDY........ Spectradyne, Inc. [*NASDAQ symbol*]   (NQ)
Spe .... Durandi. Speculum Judiciale [*A publication*]   (DSA)
s-pe--- .... Peru [*MARC geographic area code*] [*Library of Congress*]   (LCCP)
SPE........... Secondary Particulate Emissions [*Environmental Protection Agency*]   (GFGA)
SPE........... Senior Project Engineer
SPE........... Serum Protein Electrophoresis
SPE........... Shaft Position Encoder
SPE........... Sian [*Republic of China*] [*Seismograph station code, US Geological Survey*]   (SEIS)
SPE........... Signal Processing Element [*Navy*]
SPE........... Sliding Padeye   (MCD)
SPE........... Small Processing Element [*Data processing*]
SPE........... Society of Petroleum Engineers   (EA)
SPE........... Society for Photographic Education   (EA)
SPE........... Society of Plastics Engineers   (EA)
SPE........... Society of Professors of Education   (EA)
SPE........... Society for Pure English
SPE........... Solar Proton Event [*Geophysics*]
SPE........... Solid-Phase Extraction
SPE........... Solid Polymer Electrolyte
SPE........... Space Processing Equipment [*Astronautics*]
SPE........... Special Libraries [*A publication*]
SPE........... Special Purpose Electronics   (MCD)
SPE........... Special-Purpose Equipment
SPE........... Specialty Equipment Companies [*NYSE symbol*]   (SPSG)
Spe .... Speculum. Journal of Medieval Studies [*A publication*]
SPE........... Sperry UNIVAC Information Center, Blue Bell, PA [*OCLC symbol*]   (OCLC)
SPe............ Spettatore Italiano [*A publication*]
SPE........... Spherical Probable Error
SPE........... Static Phase Error [*NASA*]
SPE........... Station Project Engineer [*NASA*]
SPE........... Stepped Potential Electrode [*Electrode chemistry*]
SPE........... Stop Project ELF [*Extremely Low Frequency system*]   (EA)
SPE........... Stored Program Element
SPE........... Streptococcal Enterotoxin [*Medicine*]
SPE........... Studies in Philosophy and Education [*A publication*]   (AEBS)
SPE........... Studies in Public Economics [*Elsevier Book Series*] [*A publication*]
SPE........... Subport of Embarkation
SPE........... Sucrose Polyester [*Pharmacology*]
SPE........... Sun-Planet-Earth [*Astronomy*]
SPE........... Suriname Post [*A publication*]
SPE........... System Performance Evaluation   (KSC)
SPE........... Systems Performance Effectiveness
SPE........... Unilabo [*France*] [*Research code symbol*]
SPEA .... Sales Promotion Executives Association [*Later, MCEI*]   (EA)
SPEA .... Scottish Physical Education Association [*British*]
SPEA .... Southeastern Poultry and Egg Association   (EA)
SPEAC ...... Selma Project Education Alternatives Center [*Alabama*]   (EA)
SPEAC ...... Solar Photovoltaic Energy Advisory Committee [*Terminated, 1986*]   (EGAO)
SPEAHR ... Society for the Protection of East Asians' Human Rights/ USA   (EA)
SPE of AIME ... Society of Petroleum Engineers of American Institute of Mining, Metallurgical, and Petroleum Engineers   (EA)
SPEAK ...... Society for Promoting and Encouraging the Arts and Knowledge of the Church   (EA)
SPEAKEASY ... [*An*] Information Retrieval System
SPEAL........ Special-Purpose Engineering Analysis Language   (MCD)
SPEAR ...... Signal Processing, Evaluation, Alert, and Report [*Navy*]   (NVT)
SPEAR ...... SLAC Positron-Electron Asymmetric Ring
SPEAR ...... Small Payload Ejection and Recovery for the Space Shuttle [*NASA*]   (MCD)
SPEAR ...... Source Performance Evaluation and Reporting
SPEAR ...... Spaceborne Earth Applications Ranging System   (MCD)
Spear.......... Spears' South Carolina Law Reports [*1842-44*] [*A publication*]   (DLA)
SPEAR ...... Squadron Performance Effectiveness Analysis Representation   (MCD)
SPEAR ...... Stanford Positron-Electron Axisymmetric Ring
SPEAR ...... Statistical Property Estimation and Regeneration   (MCD)
SPEAR ...... Supplier Performance Evaluation and Reporting [*or Review*] [*General Motors quality award*]
Spear Ch .... Spears' South Carolina Chancery Reports [*A publication*]   (DLA)
Spear Eq ... Spears' South Carolina Equity Reports [*A publication*]   (DLA)
Spear Ext ... Spear's Law of Extradition [*A publication*]   (DLA)
Spear High ... Spearman on Highways [*1881*] [*A publication*]   (DLA)
SPEARS .... Satellite Photoelectric Analog Rectification System
SPEARS .... Spaceborne Earth Applications Ranging System [*NASA*]
Spears .... Spears' South Carolina Equity Reports [*1842-44*] [*A publication*]   (DLA)
Spears .... Spears' South Carolina Law Reports [*A publication*]   (DLA)
Spears Eq... Spears' South Carolina Equity Reports [*A publication*]   (DLA)
SPEB .... Pebas [*Peru*] [*ICAO location identifier*]   (ICLI)

SPEBSQSA ... Society for the Preservation and Encouragement of Barber Shop Quartet Singing in America　(EA)
Spec............ De Specialibus Legibus [*of Philo*]　(BJA)
SPEC .... Scientific Pollution and Environmental Control Society
SPEC .... Simulation of Propulsion Engine Cycle [*NASA*]
SPEC .... Society of Professional Engineering Checkers
SPEC .... Special [*or Specialist*]　(KSC)
SPEC .... Species　(WGA)
SPEC .... Specific
SPEC .... Specification　(AFM)
SPEC .... Specimen　(AAG)
Spec............ Spectacle [*or Spectacular*]　(WGA)
Spec............ Spectator [*A publication*]
Spec............ Spectrum [*A publication*]
SPEC .... Spectrum
SPEC .... Spectrum Control, Inc. [*NASDAQ symbol*]　(NQ)
SPEC .... Speculation　(WGA)
Spec............ Speculation [*A publication*]
Spec............ Speculator [*Guillelmus Durandi*] [*Deceased, 1296*] [*Authority cited in pre-1607 legal work*]　(DSA)
Spec............ Speculum [*A publication*]
SPEC .... Speech Predictive Encoded Communications [*Telephone channels*]
SPEC .... Staff of the Production Executive Committee [*of the WPB*] [*Obsolete*]
SPEC .... Stored Program Educational Computer
SPEC .... Studies in the Political Economy of Canada [*Society*]
SPEC .... Systems and Procedures Exchange Center [*Association of Research Libraries*]
SPECA ...... Society for the Preservation and Enjoyment of Carriages in America　(EA)
SPECA ...... Spectrum [*Oxford*] [*A publication*]
SPECAN .... Spectral Analysis
Spec Aspects Nucl En Isot Appl Proc Int Conf Peace Use At En ... Special Aspects of Nuclear Energy and Isotope Applications. Proceedings. International Conference on the Peaceful Uses of Atomic Energy [*A publication*]
SPECASTSECNAV ... Special Assistant to the Secretary of the Navy　(DNAB)
SPECAT.... Special Category　(AABC)
Spec Bull Aichiken Agric Res Cent ... Special Bulletin. Aichi-ken Agricultural Research Center [*A publication*]
Spec Bull Coll Agric Utsunomiya Univ ... Special Bulletin. College of Agriculture. Utsunomiya University [*A publication*]
Spec Bull Coll Agr Utsunomiya Univ ... Special Bulletin. College of Agriculture. Utsunomiya University [*A publication*]
Spec Bull Dep Agric S Aust ... Special Bulletin. Department of Agriculture. South Australia [*A publication*]　(APTA)
Spec Bull Dep Agric South Aust ... Special Bulletin. Department of Agriculture. South Australia [*A publication*]　(APTA)
Spec Bull First Agron Div Tokai-Kinki Natl Agric Exp Stn ... Special Bulletin. First Agronomy Division. Tokai-Kinki National Agricultural Experiment Station [*A publication*]
Spec Bull Fukui Agric Exp Stn ... Special Bulletin. Fukui Agricultural Experiment Station [*A publication*]
Spec Bull Fukuoka Agric Res Cent ... Special Bulletin. Fukuoka Agricultural Research Center [*A publication*]
Spec Bull Hortic Stn Tokai Kinki Agric Exp Stn ... Special Bulletin. Horticultural Station. Tokai Kinki Agricultural Experiment Station [*A publication*]
Spec Bull Mich Agric Exp Stn ... Special Bulletin. Michigan Agricultural Experiment Station [*A publication*]
Spec Bull Mich State Univ Agr Exp Sta ... Special Bulletin. Michigan State University. Agricultural Experiment Station [*A publication*]
Spec Bull Okayama Agr Exp Sta ... Special Bulletin. Okayama Agricultural Experiment Station [*A publication*]
Spec Bull Okayama Prefect Agric Exp Stn ... Special Bulletin. Okayama Prefectural Agricultural Experiment Station [*A publication*]
Spec Bull Rehovot Nat Univ Inst Agr ... Special Bulletin. Rehovot. National and University Institute of Agriculture [*A publication*]
Spec Bull Taiwan For Res Inst ... Special Bulletin. Taiwan Forestry Research Institute [*A publication*]
Spec Bull Tottori Agric Exp Stn ... Special Bulletin. Tottori Agricultural Experiment Station [*A publication*]
Sp Ecc & Ad ... Spinks' English Ecclesiastical and Admiralty Reports [*164 English Reprint*] [*1853-55*] [*A publication*]　(DLA)
Spec Care Dentist ... Special Care in Dentistry [*A publication*]
Spec Ceram ... Special Ceramics [*A publication*]
Spec Chem ... Specialty Chemicals [*A publication*]
Spec Chem Oil Ind Proc Lect Ser ... Special Chemicals in the Oil Industry. Proceedings. Lecture Series [*A publication*]
Spec Circ Mass Ext Serv ... Special Circular. Massachusetts Extension Service [*A publication*]
Spec Circ Ohio Agr Exp Sta ... Special Circular. Ohio Agricultural Experiment Station [*A publication*]
Spec Circ Ohio Agric Res Dev Cent ... Special Circular. Ohio Agricultural Research and Development Center [*A publication*]
Spec Circ PA State Univ Coll-Agric Ext Serv ... Special Circular. Pennsylvania State University. College of Agriculture. Extension Service [*A publication*]

Spec Circ Univ Wis Coll Agr Ext Serv ... Special Circular. University of Wisconsin. College of Agriculture. Extension Service [*A publication*]
Spec Collect ... Special Collections [*A publication*]
Spec Colloq Ampere Appl Reson Methods Solid State Physics ... Specialized Colloque Ampere. Application of Resonance Methods in Solid State Physics [*A publication*]
Spec Conf Atmos Deposition Proc ... Specialty Conference on Atmospheric Deposition. Proceedings [*A publication*]
Spec Conf Contin Monit Stationary Air Pollut Sources Proc ... Specialty Conference on Continuous Monitoring of Stationary Air Pollution Sources. Proceedings [*A publication*]
Spec Conf Control Specific Toxic Pollut Proc ... Specialty Conference on Control of Specific Toxic Pollutants. Proceedings [*A publication*]
Spec Conf Control Technol Agric Air Pollut ... Specialty Conference on Control Technology for Agricultural Air Pollutants [*A publication*]
Spec Conf Dredging Its Environ Eff Proc ... Specialty Conference on Dredging and Its Environmental Effects. Proceedings [*A publication*]
Spec Conf Emiss Factors Inventories Proc ... Specialty Conference on Emission Factors and Inventories. Proceedings [*A publication*]
Spec Conf Emiss Inventories Air Qual Manage ... Specialty Conference on Emission Inventories and Air Quality Management [*A publication*]
Spec Conf Long Term Maint Clean Air Stand Proc ... Specialty Conference on Long Term Maintenance of Clean Air Standards. Proceedings [*A publication*]
Spec Conf Meas Monit Non Criter Toxic Contam Air ... Specialty Conference on Measurement and Monitoring of Non-Criteria, Toxic Contaminants in Air [*A publication*]
Spec Conf Ozone Oxid Interact Total Environ Proc ... Specialty Conference on Ozone/Oxidants. Interactions with the Total Environment. Proceedings [*A publication*]
Spec Conf Qual Assur Air Pollut Meas Proc ... Specialty Conference on Quality Assurance in Air Pollution Measurement. Proceedings [*A publication*]
Spec Conf Resid Wood Coal Combust Proc ... Specialty Conference on Residential Wood and Coal Combustion. Proceedings [*A publication*]
Spec Conf Tech Basis Size Specific Part Stand Proc ... Specialty Conference on the Technical Basis for a Size Specific Particulate Standard. Proceedings [*A publication*]
Spec Conf Toxic Subst Air Environ Proc ... Specialty Conference on Toxic Substances in the Air Environment. Proceedings [*A publication*]
Spec Conf User Fabric Filtr Equip Proc ... Specialty Conference on the User and Fabric Filtration Equipment. Proceedings [*A publication*]
Spec Conf View Visibility Regul Sci Proc ... Specialty Conference on View and Visibility. Regulatory and Scientific. Proceedings [*A publication*]
Spec Conf Waste Treat Disposal Aspects Combust Air Pollut ... Specialty Conference on Waste Treatment and Disposal Aspects. Combustion and Air Pollution Control Processes [*A publication*]
Spec Contrib Geophys Inst Kyoto Univ ... Special Contributions. Geophysical Institute. Kyoto University [*Japan*] [*A publication*]
Spec Contrib Inst Geophys Nat Cent Univ (Taiwan) ... Special Contributions. Institute of Geophysics. National Central University (Taiwan) [*A publication*]
Spec Contrib Inst Geophys Natl Cent Univ (Miaoli Taiwan) ... Special Contributions. Institute of Geophysics. National Central University (Miaoli, Taiwan) [*A publication*]
Spec Courses Fd Ind ... Specialist Courses for the Food Industry [*A publication*]　(APTA)
Spec Courses Food Ind ... Specialist Courses for the Food Industry [*Food Industry News*] [*A publication*]　(APTA)
SPECD ...... Specification Data Base
SPECD ...... Spectrum [*Berlin*] [*A publication*]
SPECDEVCEN ... Special Devices Center [*Navy*]
Spec Discuss Faraday Soc ... Special Discussions. Faraday Society [*A publication*]
Spec Econ Ser Maine Geol Surv ... Special Economic Series. Maine Geological Survey [*A publication*]
Spec Ed Counc News ... Special Education Council. Newsletter [*A publication*]
Spec Ed Inst Geol Hydrogeol Geophys Geotech Res ... Special Edition. Institute for Geological, Hydrogeological, Geophysical, and Geotechnical Research [*A publication*]
Spec Educ .. Special Education [*A publication*]
Spec Educ .. Special Education. Forward Trends [*A publication*]
Spec Educ Bull ... Special Education Bulletin [*A publication*]　(APTA)
Spec Educ Can ... Special Education in Canada [*A publication*]
Spec Educ Forward Trends ... Special Education. Forward Trends [*A publication*]
Spec Eng .... Specifying Engineer [*A publication*]
Spec Environ Rep ... Special Environmental Report [*A publication*]
Spec Environ Rep WMO ... Special Environmental Report. World Meteorological Organization [*A publication*]
SPECFORCOM ... Special Forces Command [*Navy*]　(DNAB)

SPECHNDLG ... Special Handling (MCD)
SPECI........ Specimen (DSUE)
Special Bull Univ Minnesota Agric Exten Div ... Special Bulletin. University of Minnesota. Agricultural Extension Division [*A publication*]
Special Ed ... Special Education [*A publication*]
Special Ed ... Special Education in Canada [*A publication*]
Specialised Nat Councils' M (Egypt) ... Specialised National Councils' Magazine (Egypt) [*A publication*]
Speciality Chem ... Speciality Chemicals [*A publication*]
Special Lib ... Special Libraries [*A publication*]
Special Rep Ser Med Research Com (London) ... Special Report Series. Medical Research Committee (London) [*A publication*]
Special Sch Bul (NT) ... Special Schools Bulletin (Northern Territory) [*A publication*] (APTA)
Special Sch Bul (Qld) ... Special Schools Bulletin (Queensland Department of Education) [*A publication*] (APTA)
SPECIF ..... Specific (WGA)
SPECIFD .. Specified (ROG)
Specif Eng ... Specifying Engineer [*A publication*]
Specif Engr ... Specifying Engineer [*A publication*]
SPECIFN .. Specification (ROG)
Spec Int ...... Specialties International [*A publication*]
SPECINVESDIST ... Special Investigations District [*Air Force*]
Spec Issue Bot Mag ... Special Issue. Botanical Magazine [*A publication*]
Spec Issue Plant Cell Physiol ... Special Issue of Plant and Cell Physiology [*A publication*]
SPECK ...... Safety, Pride, Efficiency, Compatibility, Knowledge (DNAB)
SPECL....... Special (ROG)
SPECL....... Specialize
Spec Law Dig Health Care Mon ... Specialty Law Digest. Health Care Monthly [*A publication*]
Spec Liaison Rep Commonw Geol Liaison Off ... Special Liaison Report. Commonwealth Geological Liaison Office [*London*] [*A publication*]
Spec Libr.... Special Libraries [*A publication*]
Spec Libr Ass Toronto Chapter Bull ... Special Libraries Association. Toronto Chapter. Bulletin [*A publication*]
SPECLST ... Specialist
SPECMAP ... Spectral Mapping
Spec Meet Int Combust Inst ... Specialists Meeting. International Combustion Institute [*A publication*]
SPECO ...... Steel Products Engineering Co.
SPECOL.... Special Customer-Oriented Language
SPECOM .. Special Command
SPECOMALT ... Special Communications Alteration
SPECOMDIV ... Special Communications Division [*Navy*] (DNAB)
SPECOMME ... Specified Command Middle East [*Military*]
SPECON ... Systems Performance Effectiveness Conference
SPECOPNSSq ... Special Operations Squadron [*Air Force*]
SPECOPS ... Special Operations [*Navy*] (NVT)
SPECOR ... Spectral Correlation RADAR (MCD)
Spec Pap Cent Precambrian Res Univ Adelaide ... Special Paper. Centre for Precambrian Research. University of Adelaide [*A publication*]
Spec Pap Dep Nat Resour (Qd) ... Special Papers. Department of Natural Resources (Queensland) [*A publication*]
Spec Pap Dep Nat Resour Que ... Special Paper. Department of Natural Resources. Quebec [*A publication*]
Spec Pap Geol Ass Can ... Special Paper. Geological Association of Canada [*A publication*]
Spec Pap Geol Assoc Can ... Special Paper. Geological Association of Canada [*A publication*]
Spec Pap Geol Soc Am ... Special Paper. Geological Society of America [*A publication*]
Spec Pap Palaeontol ... Special Papers in Palaeontology [*A publication*]
Spec Pap State Ore Dep Geol Min Ind ... Special Paper. State of Oregon Department of Geology and Mineral Industries [*A publication*]
Spec Pap Univ Adelaide Cent Precambrian Res ... Special Paper. University of Adelaide. Centre for Precambrian Research [*A publication*]
Spec Pap Univ Adelaide Cent Prec Res ... Special Paper. University of Adelaide. Centre for Precambrian Research [*A publication*]
Spec Period Rep Alicyclic Chem ... Specialist Periodical Reports. Alicyclic Chemistry [*A publication*]
Spec Period Rep Aliphatic Chem ... Specialist Periodical Reports. Aliphatic Chemistry [*A publication*]
Spec Period Rep Aliphatic Relat Nat Prod Chem ... Specialist Periodical Reports. Aliphatic and Related Natural Product Chemistry [*A publication*]
Spec Period Rep Alkaloids ... Specialist Periodical Reports. Alkaloids [*A publication*]
Spec Period Rep Amino-Acids Peptides Proteins ... Specialist Periodical Reports. Amino-Acids, Peptides, and Proteins [*A publication*]
Spec Period Rep Amino-Acids Pept Proteins ... Specialist Periodical Reports. Amino-Acids, Peptides, and Proteins [*A publication*]
Spec Period Rep Arom Heteroaromat Chem ... Specialist Periodical Reports. Aromatic and Heteroaromatic Chemistry [*A publication*]
Spec Period Rep Biosynth ... Specialist Periodical Reports. Biosynthesis [*A publication*]

Spec Period Rep Carbohydr Chem ... Specialist Periodical Reports. Carbohydrate Chemistry [*A publication*]
Spec Period Rep Catal ... Specialist Periodical Reports. Catalysis [*A publication*]
Spec Period Rep Chem Phys Solids Their Surf ... Specialist Periodical Reports. Chemical Physics of Solids and Their Surfaces [*A publication*]
Spec Period Rep Chem Thermodyn ... Specialist Periodical Reports. Chemical Thermodynamics [*A publication*]
Spec Period Rep Colloid Sci ... Specialist Periodical Reports. Colloid Science [*A publication*]
Spec Period Rep Dielectr Relat Mol Processes ... Specialist Periodical Reports. Dielectric and Related Molecular Processes [*A publication*]
Spec Period Rep Electrochem ... Specialist Periodical Reports. Electrochemistry [*A publication*]
Spec Period Rep Electron Spin Reson ... Specialist Periodical Reports. Electron Spin Resonance [*A publication*]
Spec Period Rep Electron Struct Magn Inorg Compd ... Specialist Periodical Reports. Electronic Structure and Magnetism of Inorganic Compounds [*A publication*]
Spec Period Rep Environ Chem ... Specialist Periodical Reports. Environmental Chemistry [*A publication*]
Spec Period Rep Fluorocarbon Relat Chem ... Specialist Periodical Reports. Fluorocarbon and Related Chemistry [*A publication*]
Spec Period Rep Foreign Compd Metab Mamm ... Specialist Periodical Reports. Foreign Compound Metabolism in Mammals [*A publication*]
Spec Period Rep Gas Kinet Energy Transfer ... Specialist Periodical Reports. Gas Kinetics and Energy Transfer [*A publication*]
Spec Period Rep Gen Synth Methods ... Specialist Periodical Reports. General and Synthetic Methods [*A publication*]
Spec Period Rep Heterocycl Chem ... Specialist Periodical Reports. Heterocyclic Chemistry [*A publication*]
Spec Period Rep Inorg Biochem ... Specialist Periodical Reports. Inorganic Biochemistry [*A publication*]
Spec Period Rep Inorg Chem Main Group Elem ... Specialist Periodical Reports. Inorganic Chemistry of the Main-Group Elements [*A publication*]
Spec Period Rep Inorg Chem Transition Elem ... Specialist Periodical Reports. Inorganic Chemistry of the Transition Elements [*A publication*]
Spec Period Rep Inorg React Mech ... Specialist Periodical Reports. Inorganic Reaction Mechanisms [*A publication*]
Spec Period Rep Macromol Chem ... Specialist Periodical Reports. Macromolecular Chemistry [*A publication*]
Spec Period Rep Mass Spectrom ... Specialist Periodical Reports. Mass Spectrometry [*A publication*]
Spec Period Rep Mol Struct Diffr Methods ... Specialist Periodical Reports. Molecular Structure by Diffraction Methods [*A publication*]
Spec Period Rep Nucl Magn Resonance ... Specialist Periodical Reports. Nuclear Magnetic Resonance [*A publication*]
Spec Period Rep Organomet Chem ... Specialist Periodical Reports. Organometallic Chemistry [*A publication*]
Spec Period Rep Organophosphorus Chem ... Specialist Periodical Reports. Organophosphorus Chemistry [*A publication*]
Spec Period Rep Org Compd Sulphur Selenium Tellurium ... Specialist Periodical Reports. Organic Compounds of Sulphur, Selenium, and Tellurium [*A publication*]
Spec Period Rep Photochem ... Specialist Periodical Reports. Photochemistry [*A publication*]
Spec Period Rep Radiochem ... Specialist Periodical Reports. Radiochemistry [*A publication*]
Spec Period Rep React Kinet ... Specialist Periodical Reports. Reaction Kinetics [*A publication*]
Spec Period Rep Saturated Heterocycl Chem ... Specialist Periodical Reports. Saturated Heterocyclic Chemistry [*A publication*]
Spec Period Rep Spectrosc Prop Inorg Organomet Compd ... Specialist Periodical Reports. Spectroscopic Properties of Inorganic and Organometallic Compounds [*A publication*]
Spec Period Rep Stat Mech ... Specialist Periodical Reports. Statistical Mechanics [*A publication*]
Spec Period Rep Surf Defect Prop Solids ... Specialist Periodical Reports. Surface and Defect Properties of Solids [*A publication*]
Spec Period Rep Terpenoids Steroids ... Specialist Periodical Reports. Terpenoids and Steroids [*A publication*]
Spec Period Rep Theor Chem ... Specialist Periodical Reports. Theoretical Chemistry [*A publication*]
Spec Prog News ... Special Programmes News [*A publication*]
SPECPROJOUK ... Special Projects Liaison Offices, United Kingdom [*Navy*] (DNAB)
Spec Pub Agric Res Org ... Special Publication. Agricultural Research Organization [*A publication*]
Spec Publ Acad Nat Sci Phila ... Special Publication. Academy of Natural Sciences. Philadelphia [*A publication*]
Spec Publ Agric Res Organ Volcani Cent (Bet Dagan) ... Special Publication. Agricultural Research Organization. Volcani Center (Bet Dagan) [*A publication*]
Spec Publ Am Concr Inst ... Special Publication. American Concrete Institute [*A publication*]

Spec Publ Am Littoral Soc ... Special Publication. American Littoral Society [*A publication*]
Spec Publ Am Soc Agron ... Special Publication. American Society of Agronomy [*A publication*]
Spec Publ Am Soc Mammal ... Special Publication. American Society of Mammalogists [*A publication*]
Spec Publ ARLCD SP US Army Armament Res Dev Command Large ... Special Publication ARLCD-SP. US Army Armament Research and Development Command. Large Caliber Weapon System Laboratory [*A publication*]
Spec Publ Assoc Explor Geochem ... Special Publication. Association of Exploration Geochemists [*A publication*]
Spec Publ Aust Conserv Fdn ... Special Publication. Australian Conservation Foundation [*A publication*] (APTA)
Spec Publ Aust Conserv Found ... Special Publication. Australian Conservation Foundation [*A publication*] (APTA)
Spec Publ BCRA Br Carbonization Res Assoc ... Special Publication. BCRA. British Carbonization Research Associaton [*A publication*]
Spec Publ Biochem Soc London ... Special Publication. Biochemical Society of London [*A publication*]
Spec Publ Br Carbonization Res Assoc ... Special Publication. British Carbonization Research Association [*A publication*]
Spec Publ Br Ceram Res Assoc ... Special Publication. British Ceramics Research Association [*A publication*]
Spec Publ Br Ecol Soc ... Special Publication. British Ecological Society [*A publication*]
Spec Publ Bur Mines Geol (Mont) ... Special Publication. Bureau of Mines and Geology (Montana) [*A publication*]
Spec Publ Chem Soc ... Special Publication. Chemical Society [*A publication*]
Spec Publ Chicago Acad Sci ... Special Publications. Chicago Academy of Science [*A publication*]
Spec Publ Coll Agric Natl Taiwan Univ ... Special Publication. College of Agriculture. National Taiwan University [*A publication*]
Spec Publ Coll Agr Nat Taiwan U ... Special Publications. College of Agriculture. National Taiwan University [*A publication*]
Spec Publ Coll Earth Miner Sci Pa State Univ ... Special Publication. College of Earth and Mineral Sciences. Pennsylvania State University [*A publication*]
Spec Publ Colo Geol Surv ... Special Publication. Colorado Geological Survey [*A publication*]
Spec Publ Colorado Geol Surv ... Special Publication. Colorado Geological Survey [*A publication*]
Spec Publ Commonw Bur Soils ... Special Publication. Commonwealth Bureau of Soils [*A publication*]
Spec Publ Cushman Found Foraminiferal Res ... Special Publication. Cushman Foundation for Foraminiferal Research [*A publication*]
Spec Publ Ecol Soc Am ... Special Publication. Ecological Society of America [*A publication*]
Spec Publ Entomol Soc Am ... Special Publication. Entomological Society of America [*A publication*]
Spec Publ Fla Bur Geol ... Special Publication. Florida Bureau of Geology [*A publication*]
Spec Publ Forintek Can Corp East Lab ... Special Publication. Forintek Canada Corporation. Eastern Laboratory [*A publication*]
Spec Publ Geochem Soc ... Special Publication. Geochemical Society [*A publication*]
Spec Publ Geol Soc Aust ... Special Publication. Geological Society of Australia [*A publication*] (APTA)
Spec Publ Geol Soc London ... Special Publication. Geological Society of London [*A publication*]
Spec Publ Geol Soc S Afr ... Special Publication. Geological Society of South Africa [*A publication*]
Spec Publ Geol Soc Zimbabwe ... Special Publication. Geological Society of Zimbabwe [*A publication*]
Spec Publ Geol Surv Indones ... Special Publication. Geological Survey of Indonesia [*A publication*]
Spec Publ Geol Surv S Afr ... Special Publications. Geological Survey of South Africa [*A publication*]
Spec Publ IEEE Power Eng Soc ... Special Publication. IEEE Power Engineering Society [*A publication*]
Spec Publ Int Assoc Sedimentol ... Special Publication. International Association of Sedimentologists [*A publication*]
Spec Publ Int Fert Dev Cent ... Special Publication. International Fertilizer Development Center [*A publication*]
Spec Publ (Isr) Agric Res Org ... Special Publication (Israel). Agricultural Research Organization [*A publication*]
Spec Publ KY Geol Surv ... Special Publication. Kentucky Geological Survey [*A publication*]
Spec Publ Montana Bur Mines Geol ... Special Publication. Montana Bureau of Mines and Geology [*A publication*]
Spec Publ Mont Bur Mines Geol ... Special Publication. Montana Bureau of Mines and Geology [*A publication*]
Spec Publ Mus Tex Tech Univ ... Special Publications. Museum. Texas Tech University [*A publication*]
Spec Publ Natl Bur Stand US ... Special Publication. United States National Bureau of Standards [*A publication*]
Spec Publ NC Dep Nat Econ Resour Geol Miner Resour Sect ... Special Publication. North Carolina Department of Natural and Economic Resources. Geology and Mineral Resources Section [*A publication*]

Spec Publ NC Geol Miner Resour Sect ... Special Publication. North Carolina. Geology and Mineral Resources Section [*A publication*]
Spec Publ NM Geol Soc ... Special Publication. New Mexico Geological Society [*A publication*]
Spec Publ Pa State Univ Coll Earth Min Sci ... Special Publication. Pennsylvania State University. College of Earth and Mineral Sciences [*A publication*]
Spec Publ R Numis Soc ... Special Publication. Royal Numismatic Society [*A publication*]
Spec Publ R Soc Chem ... Special Publication. Royal Society of Chemistry [*A publication*]
Spec Publ Sado Mar Biol Stn Niigata Univ ... Special Publication. Sado Marine Biological Station. Niigata University [*A publication*]
Spec Publ S Afr Assoc Adv Sci ... Special Publication. South African Association for the Advancement of Science [*A publication*]
Spec Publs Am Ass Econ Ent ... Special Publications. American Association of Economic Entomology [*A publication*]
Spec Publ Sask Geol Soc ... Special Publication. Saskatchewan Geological Society [*A publication*]
Spec Publ Ser Br Ecol Soc ... Special Publications Series. British Ecological Society [*A publication*]
Spec Publ Ser Geol Surv India ... Special Publication Series. Geological Survey of India [*A publication*]
Spec Publ Ser Int Atl Salmon Found ... Special Publication Series. International Atlantic Salmon Foundation [*A publication*]
Spec Publ Ser Minn Geol Surv ... Special Publication Series. Minnesota Geological Survey [*A publication*]
Spec Publ Ser Soil Sci Soc Amer ... Special Publication Series. Soil Science Society of America [*A publication*]
Spec Publ Seto Mar Biol Lab Ser IV ... Special Publications. Seto Marine Biological Laboratory. Series IV [*A publication*]
Spec Publ Soc Econ Paleontol Mineral ... Special Publication. Society of Economic Paleontologists and Mineralogists [*A publication*]
Spec Publ Soc Gen Microbiol ... Special Publications. Society for General Microbiology [*A publication*]
Spec Publ Soc Geol Appl Miner Deposits ... Special Publication. Society for Geology Applied to Mineral Deposits [*A publication*]
Spec Publ South Aust Dep Mines Energy ... Special Publication. South Australia Department of Mines and Energy [*A publication*]
Spec Publ Univ NM Inst Meteorit ... Special Publication. University of New Mexico. Institute of Meteoritics [*A publication*]
Spec Publ UNM Inst Meteorit ... Special Publication. UNM [*University of New Mexico*] Institute of Meteoritics [*A publication*]
Spec Publ US Bur Mines ... Special Publications. United States Bureau of Mines [*A publication*]
Spec Publ US Natn Bur Stand ... Special Publications. United States National Bureau of Standards [*A publication*]
Spec Publ Volcani Cent (Bet Dagan) ... Special Publication. Volcani Center (Bet Dagan) [*A publication*]
Spec Publ West Aust Mus ... Special Publication. Western Australian Museum [*A publication*] (APTA)
Spec Publ World Maric Soc ... Special Publication. World Mariculture Society [*A publication*]
Spec Pub R Soc Tasm ... Royal Society of Tasmania. Special Publications [*A publication*] (APTA)
Spec Rep Agric Exp Stn Coop Ext Serv Univ Arkansas ... Special Report. Agricultural Experiment Station. Cooperative Extension Service. University of Arkansas [*A publication*]
Spec Rep Agric Exp Stn Oreg State Univ ... Special Report. Agricultural Experiment Station. Oregon State University [*A publication*]
Spec Rep Alaska Div Geol Geophys Surv ... Special Report. Alaska Division of Geological and Geophysical Surveys [*A publication*]
Spec Rep Alaska Div Mines Geol ... Special Report. Alaska. Division of Mines and Geology [*A publication*]
Spec Rep APL/JHU SR Johns Hopkins Univ Appl Phys Lab ... Special Report. APL/JHU SR. Johns Hopkins University. Applied Physics Laboratory [*A publication*]
Spec Rep Arctic Inst N Am ... Special Report. Arctic Institute of North America [*A publication*]
Spec Rep Ark Agr Exp Sta ... Special Report. Arkansas Agricultural Experiment Station [*A publication*]
Spec Rep Ark Agric Exp Stn ... Special Report. Arkansas Agricultural Experiment Station [*A publication*]
Spec Rep Arkansas Agric Exp Stn ... Special Report. Arkansas Agricultural Experiment Station [*A publication*]
Spec Rep Br Inst Radiol ... Special Report. British Institute of Radiology [*A publication*]
Spec Rep Br J Radiol ... Special Report. British Journal of Radiology [*A publication*]
Spec Rep Calif Div Mines Geol ... Special Report. California Division of Mines and Geology [*A publication*]
Spec Rep Colo Dep Game Fish Parks ... Special Report. Colorado Department of Game, Fish, and Parks [*A publication*]
Spec Rep Colo Div Game Fish Parks ... Special Report. Colorado Division of Game, Fish, and Parks [*A publication*]
Spec Rep Colo Div Wildl ... Special Report. Colorado Division of Wildlife [*A publication*]

Spec Rep Commonw Exp Bldg Stn ... Special Report. Commonwealth Experimental Building Station [*A publication*]   (APTA)
Spec Rep Electr Power Res Inst EPRI AF ... Special Report. Electric Power Research Institute. EPRI AF [*A publication*]
Spec Rep Electr Power Res Inst EPRI EA ... Special Report. Electric Power Research Institute. EPRI EA [*A publication*]
Spec Rep Electr Power Res Inst EPRI EL ... Special Report. Electric Power Research Institute. EPRI EL [*A publication*]
Spec Rep Electr Power Res Inst EPRI EM ... Special Report. Electric Power Research Institute. EPRI EM [*A publication*]
Spec Rep Electr Power Res Inst EPRI ER (Palo Alto, Calif) ... Special Report. Electric Power Research Institute. EPRI ER (Palo Alto, California) [*A publication*]
Spec Rep Electr Power Res Inst EPRI FP (Palo Alto, Calif) ... Special Report. Electric Power Research Institute. EPRI FP (Palo Alto, California) [*A publication*]
Spec Rep Electr Power Res Inst EPRI NP ... Special Report. Electric Power Research Institute. EPRI NP [*A publication*]
Spec Rep Electr Power Res Inst EPRI SR ... Special Report. Electric Power Research Institute. EPRI SR [*A publication*]
Spec Rep EPRI SR Electr Power Res Inst (Palo Alto Calif) ... Special Report. Electric Power Research Institute. EPRI SR (Palo Alto, Califor nia) [*A publication*]
Spec Rep Fulmer Res Inst ... Special Report. Fulmer Research Institute [*A publication*]
Spec Rep GB For Prod Res ... Special Report. Great Britain Forest Products Research [*A publication*]
Spec Rep Geol Soc Lond ... Special Reports. Geological Society of London [*A publication*]
Spec Rep Geol Surv Jpn ... Special Report. Geological Survey of Japan [*A publication*]
Spec Rep Great Lakes Res Div Univ Mich ... Special Report. Great Lakes Research Division. University of Michigan [*A publication*]
Spec Rep ICSU Comm Data Sci Technol ... Special Report. International Council of Scientific Unions. Committee on Data for Science and Technology [*A publication*]
Spec Rep Indiana Geol Surv ... Special Report. Indiana Geological Survey [*A publication*]
Spec Rep Int Congr Reprogr Inf ... Specialists Reports. International Congress on Reprography and Information [*A publication*]
Spec Rep Iowa State Univ Coop Ext Serv ... Special Report. Iowa State University. Cooperative Extension Service [*A publication*]
Spec Rep Iron Steel Inst Jpn ... Special Report. Iron and Steel Institute of Japan [*A publication*]
Spec Rep Johns Hopkins Univ Appl Phys Lab ... Special Report. Johns Hopkins University. Applied Physics Laboratory [*A publication*]
Spec Rep Miner Resour GB ... Special Reports on the Mineral Resources of Great Britain [*A publication*]
Spec Rep Mo Agric Exp Stn ... Special Report. Missouri. Agricultural Experiment Station [*A publication*]
Spec Rep Natl Inst Anim Ind ... Special Report. National Institute of Animal Industry [*A publication*]
Spec Rep Nat Res Counc Highw Res Board ... Special Report. National Research Council. Highway Research Board [*A publication*]
Spec Rep Nat Res Counc Transp Res Board ... Special Report. National Research Council. Transportation Research Board [*A publication*]
Spec Rep Nat Timber Res Inst CSIR(SA) ... Special Report. National Timber Research Institute. Council for Scientific and Industrial Research (South Africa) [*A publication*]
Spec Rep NCASI Nat Counc Pap Ind Air Stream Improv ... Special Report. NCASI. National Council of the Paper Industry for Air and Stream Improvement [*A publication*]
Spec Rep Nebr Agr Exp Sta ... Special Report. Nebraska Agricultural Experiment Station [*A publication*]
Spec Rep NJ Div Water Resour ... Special Report. New Jersey Division of Water Resources [*A publication*]
Spec Rep NY State Agric Exp Stn (Geneva) ... Special Report. New York State Agricultural Experiment Station (Geneva) [*A publication*]
Spec Rep Oreg For Prod Lab ... Special Report. Oregon Forest Products Laboratory [*A publication*]
Spec Rep (Oregon) Agric Exp Stn ... Special Report (Oregon). Agricultural Experiment Station [*A publication*]
Spec Rep Oreg State Coll Agr Exp Sta ... Special Report. Oregon State College Agricultural Experiment Station [*A publication*]
Spec Rep Packag Inst ... Special Report. Packaging Institute [*A publication*]
Spec Rep Robert Wood Johnson Foundation ... Special Report. Robert Wood Johnson Foundation [*A publication*]
Spec Rep S Afr CSIR ... Special Report. South African Council for Scientific and Industrial Research [*A publication*]
Spec Rep SD Geol Surv ... Special Report. South Dakota Geological Survey [*A publication*]
Spec Rep Ser Indian Counc Med Res ... Special Report Series. Indian Council of Medical Research [*A publication*]
Spec Rep Ser Med Res Counc (UK) ... Special Report Series. Medical Research Council (United Kingdom) [*A publication*]

Spec Rep Ser Nat Open Hearth Steel Comm Iron Steel Div Met ... Special Report Series. National Open Hearth Steel Committee. Iron and Steel Division. Metals Branch. American Institute of Mining, Metallurgical, and Petroleum Engineers [*A publication*]
Spec Rep Soc Plant Prot North Jpn ... Special Report. Society of Plant Protection of North Japan [*A publication*]
Spec Rep Univ Ill Urbana Champaign Water Resour Cent ... Special Report. University of Illinois at Urbana-Champaign. Water Resources Center [*A publication*]
Spec Rep Univ Minn Agr Ext Serv ... Special Report. University of Minnesota. Agricultural Extension Service [*A publication*]
Spec Rep Univ MO Coll Agr Exp Sta ... Special Report. University of Missouri. College of Agriculture. Experiment Station [*A publication*]
Spec Rep Univ MO Columbia Agric Exp Stn ... Special Report. University of Missouri, Columbia. Agricultural Experiment Station [*A publication*]
Spec Rep Univ Wis Milwaukee Cent Great Lakes Stud ... Special Report. University of Wisconsin, Milwaukee. Center for Great Lakes Studies [*A publication*]
Spec Rep Wood Res Lab VA Polyt Inst ... Special Report. Wood Research Laboratory. Virginia Polytechnic Institute [*A publication*]
SPECS....... Spectacles   (ROG)
Spec Sci Rep FL Dep Nat Resour Mar Res Lab ... Special Scientific Report. Florida Department of Natural Resources. Marine Research Laboratory [*A publication*]
Spec Sci Rep Wildlife US Fish Wildlife Serv ... Special Scientific Report. Wildlife. United States Fish and Wildlife Service [*A publication*]
Spec Sci Rep Wildl US Fish Wildl Serv ... Special Scientific Report. Wildlife. US Fish and Wildlife Service [*A publication*]
Spec Ser Fla Dep Agric ... Special Series. Florida Department of Agriculture [*A publication*]
Spec Ser Int Assoc Volcanol Chem Earths Inter ... Special Series. International Association of Volcanology and Chemistry of the Earth's Interior [*A publication*]
Spec Sess Cotton Dust Proc ... Special Session on Cotton Dust. Proceedings [*A publication*]
Spec Sess Cotton Dust Res Proc ... Special Session on Cotton Dust Research. Proceedings [*A publication*]
Spec Steel... Special Steel [*Japan*] [*A publication*]
Spec Steels Rev ... Special Steels Review [*A publication*]
Spec Steels Tech Rev (Sheffield) ... Special Steels Technical Review (Sheffield) [*A publication*]
Spec Steel (Tokyo) ... Special Steel (Tokyo) [*A publication*]
Spec Stud Utah Geol Miner Surv ... Special Studies. Utah Geological and Mineral Survey [*A publication*]
Spec Symp Am Soc Limnol Oceanogr ... Special Symposia. American Society of Limnology and Oceanography [*A publication*]
Spec Symp Nat Radiat Environ ... Special Symposium on Natural Radiation Environment [*A publication*]
SPECT....... Single Photon Emission Computed Tomography
Spect .... Spectacula [*of Martial*] [*Classical studies*]   (OCD)
Spect .... Spectator [*A publication*]
SPECT....... Spectrograph
SPECT....... Spectrometer   (NASA)
Spect Act A ... Spectrochimica Acta. Part A. Molecular Spectroscopy [*A publication*]
Spect Act B ... Spectrochimica Acta. Part B. Atomic Spectroscopy [*A publication*]
Spec Tech Assoc Publ ... Special Technical Association. Publication [*A publication*]
Spec Tech Assoc Publ TAPPI ... Special Technical Association Publication. TAPPI [*Technical Association of the Pulp and Paper Industry*] [*A publication*]
Spec Tech Publs Am Soc Test Mater ... Special Technical Publications. American Society for Testing Materials [*A publication*]
Spect Lett... Spectroscopy Letters [*A publication*]
SPECTNG ... Specialist Training [*Navy*]   (NVT)
Spec Top Endocrinol Metab ... Special Topics in Endocrinology and Metabolism [*A publication*]
Spectr .... Spectroscopy [*A publication*]
Spectral Evol Galaxies Proc Workshop Adv Sch Astron Ettore ... Spectral Evolution of Galaxies. Proceedings. Workshop. Advanced School of Astronomy of the "Ettore Majorana" Centre for Scientific Culture [*A publication*]
Spectral Line Shapes Proc Int Conf ... Spectral Line Shapes. Proceedings. International Conference [*A publication*]
Spec Transp Plann Practice ... Specialized Transportation Planning and Practice [*A publication*]
Spectra Phys Laser Tech Bull ... Spectra-Physics Laser Technical Bulletin [*A publication*]
SPECTRE ... Special Executive for Counterintelligence, Terrorism, Revenge, and Extortion [*Fictitious organization whose agents were characters in the late Ian Fleming's "James Bond" mysteries*]
Spectrochim Acta ... Spectrochimica Acta [*A publication*]
Spectrochim Acta A ... Spectrochimica Acta. Part A. Molecular Spectroscopy [*A publication*]

Spectrochim Acta B ... Spectrochimica Acta. Part B. Atomic Spectroscopy [*A publication*]
Spectrochim Acta Part A ... Spectrochimica Acta. Part A. Molecular Spectroscopy [*A publication*]
Spectrochim Acta Part A Mol Spectrosc ... Spectrochimica Acta. Part A. Molecular Spectroscopy [*A publication*]
Spectrochim Acta Part B ... Spectrochimica Acta. Part B. Atomic Spectroscopy [*A publication*]
Spectrochim Acta Part B At Spectrosc ... Spectrochimica Acta. Part B. Atomic Spectroscopy [*A publication*]
Spectrochim Acta Suppl ... Spectrochimica Acta. Supplement [*A publication*]
SPECTROL ... Scheduling, Planning, Evaluation, and Cost Control [*Air Force*]
Spectrom Tech ... Spectrometric Techniques [*A publication*]
Spectrosc Charact Tech Semicond Technol ... Spectroscopic Characterization Techniques for Semiconductor Technology [*A publication*]
Spectrosc Int J ... Spectroscopy. International Journal [*A publication*]
Spectrosc Lett ... Spectroscopy Letters [*A publication*]
Spectrosc Mol ... Spectroscopia Molecular [*A publication*]
Spectrosc Sci Ind ... Spectroscopy in Science and Industry [*A publication*]
Spectros Prop Inorg Organomet Compd ... Spectroscopic Properties of Inorganic and Organometallic Compounds [*A publication*]
Spectrum Int ... Spectrum International [*A publication*]
Specu .... Speculator [*Guillelmus Durandi*] [*Deceased, 1296*] [*Authority cited in pre-1607 legal work*] (DSA)
Specu .... Speculum [*A publication*]
Specula ...... Speculator [*Guillelmus Durandi*] [*Deceased, 1296*] [*Authority cited in pre-1607 legal work*] (DSA)
Speculations Sci and Technol ... Speculations in Science and Technology [*A publication*]
Speculations Sci Technol ... Speculations in Science and Technology (Complete Edition) [*A publication*]
Specul Sci Technol ... Speculations in Science and Technology [*Switzerland*] [*A publication*]
SPECVER ... Specification Verification [*Data processing*] (IEEE)
Spec Vol Can Inst Min Metall ... Special Volume. Canadian Institute of Mining and Metallurgy [*A publication*]
Spec Vol Ont Geol Surv ... Special Volume. Ontario Geological Survey [*A publication*]
SPED .... Sir Speedy Printing Centres [*NASDAQ symbol*] (NQ)
SPED .... Special Education Director
Sp Ed .... Specialist in Education [*Academic degree*]
SPED .... Sulfur, Phosphorus, Emission Detector [*Chromatograph accessory*]
SPED .... Supersonic Planetary Entry Decelerator (KSC)
SPEDA ...... Special Education [*A publication*]
SPEDAC ... Solid-State, Parallel, Expandable, Differential Analyzer Computer
SPEDCO ... Southeastern Pennsylvania Development Corp.
SPEDE ...... System for Processing Educational Data Electronically
SPEDIAT ... Special Diary Transcript [*Military*]
SPEDTAC ... Stored Program Educational Transistorized Automatic Computer
SPEDY ...... Summer Program for Economically Disadvantaged Youth [*Department of Labor*]
SPEE .... Society for the Promotion of Engineering Education [*Later, ASEE*]
SPEE .... Special Purpose End Effector (MCD)
SPEE .... Studies in Production and Engineering Economics [*Elsevier Book Series*] [*A publication*]
Speech Commun ... Speech Communication [*A publication*]
Speech Commun Abstr ... Speech Communication Abstracts [*A publication*]
Speech Found Am Publ ... Speech Foundation of America. Publication [*A publication*]
Speech Mon ... Speech Monographs [*A publication*]
Speech Monogr ... Speech Monographs [*A publication*]
Speech Pathol Ther ... Speech Pathology and Therapy [*A publication*]
Speech Teac ... Speech Teacher [*A publication*]
Speech Technol ... Speech Technology [*A publication*]
SPEED ...... Scheduled Procurement of Essential Equipment Deliveries [*US Postal Service*]
SPEED ...... Self-Programmed Electronic Equation Delineator
SPEED ...... Signal Processing in Evacuated Electronic Devices
SPEED ...... Single-Point Emergency Equipment Divestment
SPEED ...... Special Procedures for Expediting Equipment Development (MCD)
SPEED ...... Study and Performance Efficiency in Entry Design
SPEED ...... Subsistence Preparation by Electronic Energy Diffusion
SPEED ...... Systematic Plotting and Evaluation of Enumerated Data [*National Institute of Standards and Technology*] [*Data processing*]
SPEED ...... Systems Planning and Effectiveness Evaluation Device (MCD)
SPEED ...... Systemwide Project for Electronic Equipment at Depots [*Military*] (AABC)
SPEEDEX ... Systemwide Project for Electronic Equipment at Depots Extended [*Military*] (AABC)
SPEEDO ... Speedometer [*Automotive engineering*]
SPEEDX .... Society to Preserve the Engrossing Enjoyment of DXing (EA)
SPEEL .... Shore Plant Electronic Equipment List (MUGU)

SPEER ...... Scientists and Professional Engineers Employment Registry [*Career Technologies Corp. - CTC*] [*Andover, MA*] [*Information service or system*] (IID)
SPEEREBRA ... Speech Research Branch [*Navy*] (DNAB)
Speers .... Speers' [*or Spears'*] South Carolina Law Reports [*A publication*] (DLA)
Speers Eq ... Speers' [*or Spears'*] South Carolina Equity Reports [*A publication*] (DLA)
Speers Eq (SC) ... Speers' [*or Spears'*] South Carolina Equity Reports [*A publication*] (DLA)
Speers L (SC) ... Speers' [*or Spears'*] South Carolina Law Reports [*A publication*] (DLA)
SPEF .... Single Program Element Funding [*Military*] (AABC)
SPEF .... Student Performance Evaluation Form
SPE Form Eval ... SPE [*Society of Petroleum Engineers*] Formation Evaluation [*A publication*]
SPEG .... Serum Protein Electrophoretogram [*Clinical chemistry*]
SPEG .... Spencerville & Elgin Railroad Co. [*AAR code*]
SPEG .... Staff Planning Evaluation Group (AAG)
SPEJ .... Society of Petroleum Engineers. American Institute of Mining, Metallurgical, and Petroleum Engineers. Journal [*A publication*]
SPE J .... SPE [*Society of Plastics Engineers*] Journal [*A publication*]
SPEJA ...... SPE [*Society of Plastics Engineers*] Journal [*A publication*]
SPEJ Soc Pet Eng J ... SPEJ. Society of Petroleum Engineers [*of AIME*] Journal [*United States*] [*A publication*]
SPEK .... Spec's Music, Inc. [*Miami, FL*] [*NASDAQ symbol*] (NQ)
Spektrum Wiss ... Spektrum der Wissenschaft [*German Federal Republic*] [*A publication*]
SPELD ...... Specific Learning Disability (ADA)
SPELEOL ... Speleological
Speleol Abstr ... Speleological Abstracts [*A publication*]
Speleol Biul Speleoklubu Warsz ... Speleologia Biuletyn Speleoklubu Warszawskiego [*A publication*]
Spel Feuds ... Spelman on Feuds [*A publication*] (DLA)
Spel Gl .... Spelman's Glossarium Archaiologicum [*A publication*] (DLA)
SPELL .... Society for the Preservation of English Language and Literature (EA)
SpellEnt ..... Spelling Entertainment, Inc. [*Associated Press abbreviation*] (APAG)
Spell Extr Rel ... Spelling on Extraordinary Relief in Equity and in Law [*A publication*] (DLA)
Spell Extr Rem ... Spelling's Treatise on Injunctions and Other Extraordinary Remedies [*A publication*] (DLA)
Spel LT ...... Spelman's Law Tracts [*A publication*] (DLA)
Spelm .... Spelman's Glossarium Archaiologicum [*3 eds.*] [*1626-87*] [*A publication*] (DLA)
Spelman ..... Spelman's Glossarium Archaiologicum [*3 eds.*] [*1626-87*] [*A publication*] (DLA)
SPELPAT ... Spelling Patterns
Spel Rep ..... Spelman's Reports, Manuscript, English King's Bench [*A publication*] (DLA)
SPEM .... Sindacato Petrolieri e Methanieri [*Union of Oil and Methane Gas Workers*] [*Italy*]
SPEMS ...... Self-Propelled Elevated Maintenance Stand (MCD)
SPEMU ..... Stable-Price Economic and Monetary Union [*Europe*]
SPEN .... Iscozacin [*Peru*] [*ICAO location identifier*] (ICLI)
SPENAVO ... Special Naval Observer
Spenc .... Spencer's Law Reports [*20 New Jersey*] [*A publication*] (DLA)
Spenc .... Spencer's Reports [*10-20 Minnesota*] [*A publication*] (DLA)
Spence Ch .. Spence's Equitable Jurisdiction of the Court of Chancery [*A publication*] (DLA)
Spence Cop ... Spence on Copyright of Designs [*A publication*] (DLA)
Spence Eq Jur ... Spence's Equitable Jurisdiction of the Court of Chancery [*A publication*] (DLA)
Spence Or L ... Spence's Origin of Laws [*A publication*] (DLA)
Spence Pat Inv ... Spence on Patentable Inventions [*1851*] [*A publication*] (DLA)
Spencer ...... Spencer's Law Reports [*20 New Jersey*] [*A publication*] (DLA)
Spencer ...... Spencer's Reports [*10-20 Minnesota*] [*A publication*] (DLA)
SPEND ...... Specifying Engineer [*A publication*]
Spen (NJ) .. Spencer's Law Reports [*20 New Jersey*] [*A publication*] (DLA)
Spenser St ... Spenser Studies [*A publication*]
Spens Sel Cas ... Spens' Select Cases [*Bombay, India*] [*A publication*] (DLA)
SPEO .... Chimbote [*Peru*] [*ICAO location identifier*] (ICLI)
SPEOPT .... Special Optical Tracking System [*NASA*]
SPEP .... Puerto Esperanza [*Peru*] [*ICAO location identifier*] (ICLI)
SPEP .... Serum Protein Electrophoresis [*Clinical chemistry*]
SPEP .... Society for Phenomenology and Existential Philosophy (EA)
SPEPD ...... Space Power and Electric Propulsion Division [*Formerly, Nuclear Systems and Space Power Division*] [*NASA*]
SPEPOS .... Society of Petroleum Engineers Production Operations Symposium and Exhibition (ITD)
SPE Prod Eng ... SPE [*Society of Petroleum Engineers*] Production Engineering [*A publication*]
SPEPS .... Specialist, Motion Picture Service - Booker [*Navy rating*]
SPEQ .... Moquegua [*Peru*] [*ICAO location identifier*] (ICLI)
Sp Eq .... Spears' South Carolina Equity Reports [*A publication*] (DLA)
SPEQ .... Special Equipment (AAG)
SPER .... Sperti Drug Products, Inc. [*NASDAQ symbol*] (NQ)
SPERA ...... Sperimentale [*A publication*]

Sper Arch Biol Norm Patol ... Sperimentale. Archivio di Biologia Normale e Patologica [*A publication*]
SPERDVAC ... Society to Preserve and Encourage Radio Drama, Variety, and Comedy (EA)
SPE Reg Tech Conf Tech Pap ... SPE [*Society of Plastics Engineers*] Regional Technical Conference. Technical Papers [*A publication*]
SPE Repr Ser ... Society of Petroleum Engineers. American Institute of Mining, Metallurgical, and Petroleum Engineers. Reprint Series [*United States*] [*A publication*]
Spe Rep Ser Ohio Agr Exp Sta ... Special Report Series. Ohio Agricultural Experiment Station [*A publication*]
SPE Reservoir Eng ... SPE [*Society of Petroleum Engineers*] Reservoir Engineering [*A publication*]
Sperimentale Arch Biol Norm e Patol ... Sperimentale. Archivio di Biologia Normale e Patologica [*A publication*]
Sperimentale Sez Chim Biol ... Sperimentale. Sezione di Chimica Biologica [*A publication*]
SPERM ..... Secret Paper Reconstitution Mechanism [*Device to reclaim documents that have been inadvertently shredded*]
SPERMFLOW ... Society for the Preservation and Enhancement of the Recognition of Millard Fillmore, Last of the Whigs (EA)
Sperry Technol ... Sperry Technology [*A publication*]
SPERT .... Schedule Performance Evaluation and Review Technique
SPERT .... Short Pulse Experimental RADAR Techniques (MCD)
SPERT .... Simplified Program Evaluation and Review Technique [*Trademark*]
SPERT .... Special Power Excursion Reactor Test [*US reactor facilities*]
SPERTTT ... Society for Promotion of Educational Reform through Teacher Training [*British*]
SPERW ..... Specialist, Recreation and Welfare Assistant [*Navy rating*]
SPES .... Servico de Propaganda e Educacao Sanitaria [*Brazil*]
SPES .... South Place Ethical Society [*British*]
SPES .... Stored Program Element System [*Data processing*] (IEEE)
SPE Soc Pet Eng AIME Publ ... SPE. Society of Petroleum Engineers of AIME [*American Institute of Mining, Metallurgical, and Petroleum Engineers*] Publications [*A publication*]
SPESS .... Stored Program Electronic Switching System [*Telecommunications*] (TEL)
SPET .... Single Photon Emission Tomography
SPET .... Solid-Propellant Electric Thruster [*Aerospace*]
SPET .... Super Power Electron Tube
SPETE .... Special Purpose Electronic Test Equipment [*Military*] (CAAL)
SPE Tech Pap ... SPE [*Society of Plastics Engineers*] Technical Papers [*A publication*]
SPETERL ... Ship Portable Electrical/Electronic Test Equipment Requirement List [*Navy*] (CAAL)
SPE Trans ... SPE [*Society of Plastics Engineers*] Transactions [*A publication*]
Spets Stali Splavy ... Spetsial'nye Stali Splavy [*Former USSR*] [*A publication*]
Spettatore Int ... Spettatore Internazionale [*A publication*]
Spettatore M ... Spettatore Musicale [*A publication*]
SPEX .... Small and Specialists Publishers Exhibition
SPEX .... Sozialwissenschaftliche Experten und Gutachter [*Social Science Experts*] [*NOMOS Datapool*] [*Database*] (IID)
SPEX .... Space Plasma Experiment [*NASA*] (SSD)
SPEX .... Special Exercise [*Navy*] (NVT)
SPEX .... Spex Group, Inc. [*NASDAQ symbol*] (NQ)
SPEZ .... Puerto Bermudez [*Peru*] [*ICAO location identifier*] (ICLI)
SPF .... St. Paul-En-Foret [*France*] [*Seismograph station code, US Geological Survey*] (SEIS)
SPF .... St. Photios Foundation (EA)
SPF .... Science Policy Foundation [*Later, ISPF*] [*British*]
SPF .... Scottish Pharmaceutical Federation [*British*]
SPF .... Security Police Flight [*Air Force*]
SPF .... Service Publication Form (AAG)
SPF .... SIDPERS [*Standard Installation/Division Personnel System*] Personnel File [*Military*] (AABC)
SPF .... Single Point Failure (NASA)
SPF .... Single Project Funding (MCD)
SPF .... Site Population Factor [*Nuclear energy*] (NRCH)
SPF .... Skin Protection Factor [*Medicine*]
SPF .... Society of Phantom Friends (EA)
SPF .... Society for the Propagation of the Faith (EA)
SPF .... Software Production Facility [*NASA*] (NASA)
SPF .... Somali Patriotic Front [*Political party*] (EY)
SPF .... Soy Protein Flour [*Food technology*]
SPF .... Space Power Facility
SPF .... Space Science Fiction Magazine [*A publication*]
SPF .... Spacelab Processing Facility [*NASA*] (NASA)
SPF .... Spearfish, SD [*Location identifier*] [*FAA*] (FAAL)
SPF .... Special Purpose Force (MCD)
SPF .... Specialist, Firefighter [*Navy rating*]
SPF .... Specific-Pathogen Free [*Medicine*]
SPF .... Spectrophotofluorometer
SPF .... Spinning Form (MCD)
SPF .... Split Product of Fibrin (MAE)
Spf. .... Sprachforum [*A publication*]
SPF .... Springfield Resources [*Vancouver Stock Exchange symbol*]
SPF .... Standard-Pacific Corp. [*NYSE symbol*] (SPSG)
SPF .... Standard Pesticide File [*Derwent Publications Ltd.*] [*Database*]
SPF .... Standard Project Flood [*Nuclear energy*] (NRCH)
SPF .... Start-Promoting Factor [*Cytology*]

SPF .... Strategic Protection Force
SPF .... Stressed Panel Fasteners
SPF .... Structured Programming Facility [*Data processing*]
SPF .... Studded Panel Fastener (DNAB)
SPF .... Subscriber Plant Factor [*Telecommunications*]
SPF .... Sun-Protection Factor [*Cosmetics industry*]
SPF .... Superplastic Forming [*Materials science*]
SPF .... Surrogate Parent Foundation (EA)
SPF .... Survival Probability Function
SPF .... Synthetic Phenolic Foam
SPF .... System Performance Factor [*Telecommunications*] (TEL)
SPF .... System Productivity Facility [*Data processing*]
SPFA .... Single-Point Failure Analysis (KSC)
SPFA .... Societe des Professeurs Francais et Francophones en Amerique (EA)
SPFA .... Steel Plate Fabricators Association (EA)
SPFC .... Site Peculiar Facility Change (AAG)
SPFC .... Society for the Parents of Fugitive Children [*Fictional organization in film "Taking Off"*]
SPFC .... Solid Polymer Fuel Cell [*Energy source*]
SPF/DB ..... Superplastic Forming/Diffusion Bonding [*Materials science*]
Spfdr .... Springfielder [*A publication*]
SpFest .... Spanish Festival [*Record label*]
SPFFA .... South Pacific Forum Fisheries Agency [*Honiara, Solomon Islands*] (EAIO)
SPFFC .... Southern Ports Foreign Freight Committee
SP-FGS ..... Shuttle Projects - Flight and Ground Systems Office [*Kennedy Space Center*] [*NASA*] (NASA)
SPFL .... Southern Philippines Federation of Labor
sp fl .... Spinal Fluid [*Medicine*] (MAE)
SPFLA .... Spaceflight [*A publication*]
SPFM .... Society for the Preservation of Film Music (EA)
SPFM .... Society of Priests for a Free Ministry (EA)
SPFM .... Spinning Form [*Tool*] (AAG)
SPFMV ..... Sweet Potato Feather Mottle Virus
SPFP .... Single Pass Fit Program (MCD)
SPFP .... Single-Point Failure Potential (KSC)
SPFP .... Single-Precision Floating Point [*Data processing*]
SPFP .... Sudanese People's Federal Party [*Political party*] [*Sudan*] (MENA)
SPFPAD .... Spacecraft Performance and Flight Path Analysis Directorate [*NASA*]
SPFS .... Soldier Physical Fitness School [*Army*] (INF)
SPFT .... Single-Pedestal Flat-Top [*Desk*]
SPFW .... Single-Phase Full Wave
SPFWBR .... Single-Phase Full-Wave Bridge (DWSG)
SPFX .... Special Effects [*Filmmaking*]
SPG .... Saint Paul Guild (EA)
SPG .... St. Petersburg, FL [*Location identifier*] [*FAA*] (FAAL)
SPG .... Salicyl Phenolic Glucuronide [*Organic chemistry*]
SPG .... Saxifrage Publications Group (EA)
SPG .... Scan Pattern Generator
SPG .... Screen Producers Guild [*Later, PGA*] (EA)
SPG .... Security Police Group [*Air Force*]
SPG .... Seed Pea Group [*Defunct*] (EA)
SPG .... Self-Propelled Gun [*British military*] (DMA)
SPG .... Shift Pattern Generator [*Automotive engineering*]
SPG .... Short Pulse Generator
SPG .... Signal Point Ground (NASA)
SPG .... Silver Spring Mining [*Vancouver Stock Exchange symbol*]
SPG .... Simple Phrase Grammar
SPG .... Single-Point Ground (MCD)
SPG .... Sinusoidal Pressure Generator
SPG .... Society for the Propagation of the Gospel [*Later, USPG*] [*British*]
SPG .... Sort Program Generator [*Data processing*] (BUR)
SPG .... Source Power Gain
SPG .... Special Patrol Group [*of the London Metropolitan Police, providing protection for public figures*]
SPG .... Special Performance Group [*In automobile name SAAB 900 Turbo SPG*]
SPG .... Special Project Group [*DoD*]
SPG .... Specialist, Gunnery [*Navy rating*]
SPG .... Specific Gravity [*Also, SP, SPGR*]
SPG .... Spiroglycol [*Organic chemistry*]
Spg .... Sponge [*Quality of the bottom*] [*Nautical charts*]
SPG .... Spooling (MSA)
SPG .... Spring (AAG)
SPG .... Stereophotogrammetry [*Medicine*]
SPG .... STI Group [*Formerly, Sprague Technologies*] [*NYSE symbol*] (SPSG)
SPG .... Study Planning Guide (MCD)
SPG .... Sucrose, Phosphate, Glutamate [*A culture medium*]
SPG .... System Phasing Group (MCD)
SPGA .... Southeastern Pecan Growers Association
SPGA .... Southwestern Peanut Growers Association (EA)
SPGB .... Socialist Party of Great Britain (PPW)
SPGCA ...... Survey of Progress in Chemistry [*A publication*]
SPGCPS .... Senior Policy Group for Canadian Production Sharing
SPGD .... Self-Powered Gamma Detector [*Nuclear energy*] (NRCH)
SPGE .... Steam Plant Gauge (DNAB)

SPGFP....... Society for the Propagation of the Gospel in Foreign Parts [*British*]   (DAS)
SPGG......... Solid-Propellant Gas Generator   (AAG)
SPGH .... Society for the Preservation of the Greek Heritage   (EA)
SPGJ .... Society for the Propagation of the Gospel among the Jews [*British*]
SPGKA ..... Senpaku Gijutsu Kenkyujo Hokoku [*A publication*]
SPGL .... Spiegel, Inc. [*NASDAQ symbol*]   (NQ)
SPGL .... Studien zur Poetik und Geschichte der Literatur [*A publication*]
Sp Glos...... Spelman's Glossarium Archaiologicum [*A publication*]   (DLA)
SPGM........ Specialist, Gunnery, Aviation Free Gunnery Instructor [*Navy rating*]
SPGM........ Tingo Maria [*Peru*] [*ICAO location identifier*]   (ICLI)
SPGN........ Specialist, Gunnery, Antiaircraft Gunnery Instructor [*Navy rating*]
SPGN........ Sympathetic Post-Ganglionic Neurone [*Neurology*]
SPGPM ..... Shots per Gun.per Minute [*Military*]   (NVT)
SPGR........ Specific Gravity [*Also, SG, SPG*]
SPGS .... Lagunas [*Peru*] [*ICAO location identifier*]   (ICLI)
SPGS .... Spare Guidance System
SPGS .... Springs   (MCD)
SPGT .... Puerto Victoria [*Peru*] [*ICAO location identifier*]   (ICLI)
SPGT .... Springfield Terminal Railway Co. [*Later, ST*] [*AAR code*]
SPGU........ Bagua [*Peru*] [*ICAO location identifier*]   (ICLI)
SPGWRE .. Spaghetti Warehouse, Inc. [*Associated Press abbreviation*]   (APAG)
SPH .... San Pedro Hill [*California*] [*Seismograph station code, US Geological Survey*] [*Closed*]   (SEIS)
SPH .... Scans per Hour [*Photocopying, Microfilming*]
SPH .... Secondary Pulmonary Hemosiderosis [*Medicine*]   (MAE)
SPH .... Self-Propelled Howitzer   (MCD)
SPH .... Severely and Profoundly Handicapped
SPH .... Sheets per Hour   (WDMC)
SPH .... Singapore Press Holdings   (ECON)
S-Ph .... Single-Phase
SPH .... Smoothed-Particle Hydrodynamics [*Statistical mechanics*]
SPH .... Social Process in Hawaii [*A publication*]
SPH .... Society of Public Health   (EAIO)
SPH .... Soy Protein Hydrolyzate
SPH .... Space Heater   (KSC)
SPH .... Special Psychiatric Hospital [*Former USSR*]
SPH .... Spherical   (ROG)
SPH .... Spherical Lens [*Ophthalmology*]
Sph............. Sphingosine [*Also, SM*] [*Biochemistry*]
SPH .... SPI Holdings, Inc. [*AMEX symbol*]   (SPSG)
SPH .... Springhill, LA [*Location identifier*] [*FAA*]   (FAAL)
SPH .... Stable Platform Housing
SPH .... Statement of Personal History [*Military*]
SPh .... Studiea Phonetica [*A publication*]
SPh .... Studies in Philology [*A publication*]
S in Ph ...... Studies in Philology [*A publication*]
SPHA .... Chincha [*Peru*] [*ICAO location identifier*]   (ICLI)
SPHC......... Chala [*Peru*] [*ICAO location identifier*]   (ICLI)
SPHCA...... Soviet Physics. Crystallography [*English Translation*] [*A publication*]
SPHCT...... Simplified Perturbed Hard Chain Theory [*Equation of state*]
SPHD .... Special Pay for Hostile Duty [*Military*]   (AFM)
SP/Hd........ Spool Piece Head [*Nuclear energy*]   (NRCH)
SPHDA ..... Soviet Physics. Doklady [*English Translation*] [*A publication*]
SPHE......... Society of Packaging and Handling Engineers [*Later, IoPP*]   (EA)
SPHER...... Small-Particle Heat-Exchange Receiver [*Solar energy technology*]
SPHER...... Spherical
SPHERE ... Scientific Parameters for Health and the Environment, Retrieval and Estimation [*Environmental Protection Agency*] [*Washington, DC*] [*Database*]
SPHF......... Spin-Polarized Hartree-Fock [*Atomic wave-function*]
SPHF......... Spontaneous Hole Filling [*Spectrometry*]
SPHG .... Speed and Heading [*Navy Navigation and Satellite System*]   (DNAB)
SPHI.......... Chiclayo/Cap. Jose Abelardo Quinones Gonzalez [*Peru*] [*ICAO location identifier*]   (ICLI)
SPHINX.... Space Plasma High-Voltage Interaction Experiment.[*Spacecraft*] [*NASA*]
SPHINX.... Survival Probability Hazard in a Nuclear Exchange
SPHJA ...... Soviet Physics. JETP [*Journal of Experimental and Theoretical Physics of the Academy of Sciences of the USSR*] [*English Translation*] [*A publication*]
SPHL......... Self-Propelled Hyperbaric Lifeboat   (DS)
SP-HL .... Sun Present - Horizon Lost
SPHN .... Siphon   (MSA)
SPhNC....... Studies in Philology. University of North Carolina [*A publication*]
SPHO .... Ayacucho/Coronel FAP Alfredo Mendivil Duarte [*Peru*] [*ICAO location identifier*]   (ICLI)
SPhP.......... Symbolae Philologorum Posnaniensium [*A publication*]
SPHQ .... Shore Patrol Headquarters
SPHQ......... Swedish Pioneer Historical Quarterly [*A publication*]
SPHS......... Society for the Promotion of Hellenic Studies   (EA)
SPHS......... Swedish Pioneer Historical Society   (EA)

SP/HT .... Specific Heat
SPHT......... Super Pressure - High Temperature
SPHU........ Huancayo [*Peru*] [*ICAO location identifier*]   (ICLI)
SPHV........ Huanuco Viejo [*Peru*] [*ICAO location identifier*]   (ICLI)
SPHW .... Single-Phase Half Wave
SPHX........ Sphinx Pharmaceuticals [*NASDAQ symbol*]   (SPSG)
SPHY......... Andahuaylas [*Peru*] [*ICAO location identifier*]   (ICLI)
SPHZ......... Anta/Comdte. FAP German Arias Grazziani [*Peru*] [*ICAO location identifier*]   (ICLI)
SPI .... Die Sprache der Palmyrenischen Inschriften [*Leipzig*] [*A publication*]   (BJA)
SPI .... Illinois State Library, Springfield, IL [*OCLC symbol*]   (OCLC)
SPI .... St. Paul Island [*Alaska*] [*Seismograph station code, US Geological Survey*] [*Closed*]   (SEIS)
SPI .... Scanning Pulse Immobilization
SPI .... Schedule Performance Index   (MCD)
SPI .... School Psychology International [*A publication*]
SPI .... Scottish Provident Institution [*Commercial firm*]
SPI .... Secretariats Professionnels Internationaux
SPI .... Selective Population Inversion [*Physics*]
SPI .... Self-Paced Instruction   (IEEE)
SPI .... Self-Perception Inventory [*Personality development test*] [*Psychology*]
SPI .... Senior Patrol Inspection [*Immigration and Naturalization Service*]
SPI .... Septum-Equipped Programmable Injector [*Gas chromatography*]
SPI .... Sequence of Pulse Intervals
SPI .... Series-Parallel Interface [*Data processing*]
SPI .... Serum Precipitable Iodine [*Serology*]
SPI .... Service Pedalogique Interafricain
SPI .... Service Publication Instruction   (AAG)
SPI .... Severely and Profoundly Impaired
SPI .... Share Price Index   (ADA)
SPI .... Shared Peripheral Interface
SPI .... Ship's Plan Index
SPI .... Signal Presence Indicator   (CAAL)
SPI .... Single Point Injection [*Automotive engineering*]
SPI .... Single Processor Interface
SPI .... Single Program Initiation [*Data processing*]
SPI .... Site Peculiar Interference   (AAG)
SPI .... Site Population Index [*Nuclear energy*]   (NRCH)
SPI .... Smoke Point Improvement [*Petroleum refining*]
SPI .... Smoking Policy Institute   (EA)
SPI .... Societe pour l'Informatique [*Company for Informatics*] [*Information service or system*] [*Defunct*]   (IID)
SPI .... Society of Photographic Illustrators   (EA)
SPI .... Society of the Plastics Industry   (EA)
SPI .... Society of Professional Investigators   (EA)
SPI .... Solid Propellant Information
SPI .... South Pacific Island Airways, Inc. [*Pago Pago, American Samoa*] [*FAA designator*]   (FAAC)
SPI .... Soy Protein Isolate [*Food technology*]
SPI .... Spanish Paprika Institute   (EA)
SPI .... Special Position Identification
SPI .... Specialist, Punched Card Accounting Machine Operator [*Navy rating*]
SPI .... Specific Productivity Index   (IEEE)
SPI .... SPI Holdings, Inc. [*AMEX symbol*]   (SPSG)
SPI .... SPI Holdings, Inc. [*Associated Press abbreviation*]   (APAG)
Spi............. Spicules [*Quality of the bottom*] [*Nautical charts*]
Spi................ [*Jacobus*] Spiegelius [*Flourished, 1483-1547*] [*Authority cited in pre-1607 legal work*]   (DSA)
SPI .... Sports Philatelists International   (EA)
SPI .... Springfield [*Illinois*] [*Airport symbol*]   (OAG)
SPI .... Standard Performance Indicator [*Army*]
SPI .... Standard Practice Instructions   (MCD)
SPI .... Standard Protective Item
SPI .... Statement of Policy or Interpretation [*Food and Drug Administration*]
SPI .... Station Program Identification [*Telecommunications*]   (TEL)
SPI .... Storage Protein Isolate [*Food industry*]
SPI .... Strategic Planning Initiative [*Environmental Protection Agency*]   (GFGA)
SPI .... Strategic Planning Institute [*Cambridge, MA*]
SPI .... Superintendent of Public Instruction   (DNAB)
SPI .... Supervisory Practices Inventory [*Test*]
SPI .... Surface Position Indicator   (NASA)
SPI .... Symbolic Pictorial Indicator   (MCD)
SPI .... Synergy Power Institute   (EA)
SPI .... Synthetic Phase Isolation [*Telemetry*]
SPI .... System Performance Indicator
SPIA .... Ica [*Peru*] [*ICAO location identifier*]   (ICLI)
SPIA .... Solid Propellant Information Agency [*Air Force*]
SPIAM ...... Sodium Purity In-Line Analytical Module [*Nuclear energy*]   (NRCH)
SPI Annu Struct Foam Conf Proc ... SPI [*Society of the Plastics Industry*] Annual Structural Foam Conference. Proceedings [*A publication*]
SPI Annu Tech Conf ... SPI [*Society of the Plastics Industry*] Annual Technical Conference [*A publication*]

SPI Annu Urethane Div Tech Conf Proc ... SPI [*Society of the Plastics Industry*] Annual Urethane Division Technical Conference. Proceedings [*A publication*]
SPIAP........ Shuttle/Payload Integration Activities Plan (NASA)
SPIB .... Scripta Pontificii Instituti Biblici [*A publication*] (BJA)
SPIB .... Shetland Pony Identification Bureau
SPIB .... Social and Prevocational Information Battery
SPIB .... Society of Power Industry Biologists (EA)
SPIB .... Southern Pine Inspection Bureau (EA)
SPIBS...... Satellite Positive-Ion-Beam System [*Air Force*] (MCD)
SPIC .... Ship Position Interpolation Computer
SPIC .... Sisters of Providence and of the Immaculate Conception [*Roman Catholic religious order*]
SPIC .... Society of the Plastics Industry of Canada
SPIC .... Standard and Poor's Index - Composite [*Stock market*]
SPIC .... Students for Promotion of Identity on Campus [*New York group promoting ethnic pride among Latin American students*]
SPIC .... Summary Punch IBM [*International Business Machines*] Collector
SPICE....... Sales-Point Information Computing Equipment [*Merchandising*]
SPICE....... Simulation Program with Integrated Circuit Emphasis (MCD)
SPICE....... Solar Particle Intensity Composition Experiment [*NASA*]
SPICE....... Space Power Internal Combustion Engine (MCD)
SPICE........ Spacelab Payload Integration and Coordination in Europe [*NASA*] (NASA)
SPICE....... Special Programs Incorporating Custom Elective
SPICE....... Special Programs Increasing Counseling Effectiveness [*Pennsylvania State Department of Public Instruction*]
SPICE....... Stanford Program on International and Cross Cultural Education [*Stanford University*] [*Research center*] (RCD)
SPICI........ SPI [*Society of the Plastics Industry*] Composites Institute (EA)
SPIC Ind Eng Train Bull ... SPIC [*Southern Petrochemical Industries Corp.*] Industrial Engineering and Training Bulletin [*A publication*]
SPID .... SIS [*Superconductivity Information System*] Published Information Database [*Office of Scientific and Technical Information*] [*Department of Energy*]
SPID .... Standard Performance Indicator Dictionary [*Army*]
SPID .... Submersible Portable Inflatable Dwelling
SPID .... Sum of Pain Intensity Differences
SPIDAC .... Specimen Input to Digital Automatic Computer
SPIDE .... Short Planning Identification File
SPIDER..... Smokeless Propellant in Demonstration Experimental Rocket (KSC)
SPIDER..... Sonic Pulse-Echo Instrument Designed for Extreme Resolution (IEEE)
SPIDER..... Systematic Planning for the Integration of Defense Engineering and Research [*Program*]
SPIDF....... Support Planning Identification File [*NASA*] (MCD)
SPIDO....... Shuttle Payload Integration and Development Program Office [*NASA*]
SPIDOT .... Self-Propelled Immersible Drive-Off Trolley [*British*] (DI)
SPIDPO .... Shuttle Payload Integration and Development Program Office [*Johnson Space Center*] (NASA)
SPIDR .... Society of Professionals in Dispute Resolution (EA)
SPIE .... Scavenging-Precipitation-Ion Exchange (IEEE)
SPIE .... Secretariat Professionnel International de l'Enseignement [*International Federation of Free Teachers' Unions - IFFTU*] [*Amsterdam, Netherlands*] (EAIO)
SPIE .... Self-Programmed Individualized Education (IEEE)
SPIE .... Ships Precise Identification Emitter (MCD)
SPIE .... Simulated Problem Input Evaluation
SPIE .... Society of Photo-Optical Instrumentation Engineers [*International Society for Optical Engineering*]
SPIE .... Society of Political Item Enthusiasts (EA)
SPIE .... Special Patrol Insertion/Extraction (MCD)
SPIE .... SPIE - the International Society for Optical Engineering (EA)
Spie .... [*Jacobus*] Spiegelius [*Flourished, 1483-1547*] [*Authority cited in pre-1607 legal work*] (DSA)
SPIE Annu Tech Symp Proc ... SPIE [*Society of Photo-Optical Instrumentation Engineers*] Annual Technical Symposium. Proceedings [*A publication*]
SPIEC....... Proceedings. Society of Photo-Optical Instrumentation Engineers [*A publication*]
Spieg .... [*Jacobus*] Spiegelius [*Flourished, 1483-1547*] [*Authority cited in pre-1607 legal work*] (DSA)
Spiegel Hist ... Spiegel Historical [*A publication*]
Spiegel Let ... Spiegel der Letteren [*A publication*]
SPIE Int Soc Opt Eng Proc ... SPIE [*Society of Photo-Optical Instrumentation Engineers*] International Society for Optical Engineering. Proceedings [*A publication*]
SPIE J .... SPIE [*Society of Photo-Optical Instrumentation Engineers*] Journal [*Later, Optical Engineering*] [*A publication*]
SPIE Journal ... Society of Photographic Instrumentation Engineers. Journal [*A publication*]
SPIE Newsl ... SPIE [*Society of Photo-Optical Instrumentation Engineers*] Newsletter [*A publication*]

SPIE Proc ... SPIE [*Society of Photo-Optical Instrumentation Engineers*] Proceedings [*A publication*]
SPIE Semin Proc ... SPIE [*Society of Photo-Optical Instrumentation Engineers*] Seminar Proceedings [*A publication*]
SPIE Vol.... SPIE [*Society of Photo-Optical Instrumentation Engineers*] Volume [*United States*] [*A publication*]
SPIF.......... School Practices Information File [*BRS Information Technologies*] [*Information service or system*] [*Defunct*]
SPIF.......... Sequential Prime Implicant Form
SPIF.......... Shuttle Payload Integration Facility [*NASA*] (MCD)
SPIF.......... Standard Payload Interface Facility [*NASA*] (MCD)
SPIFC........ Southern Pacific International Fan Club (EA)
SPIFDA..... South Pacific Islands Fisheries Development Agency [*Noumea, New Caledonia*] (EAIO)
SPIFDN..... International Commission for the Northwest Atlantic Fisheries. Selected Papers [*A publication*]
SPIG Invited Lect ... SPIG [*Symposium on Physics of Ionized Gases*] Invited Lectures [*A publication*]
SPII .... Shuttle Program Implementation Instruction [*NASA*] (NASA)
SPII .... Standard and Poor's Index - Industrials [*Stock market*]
SPIIN .... Supplemental Procurement Instrument Identification Number [*DoD*]
SPI Int Cell Plast Conf Proc ... SPI [*Society of the Plastics Industry*] International Cellular Plastics Conference. Proceedings [*A publication*]
SPI Int Tech Mark Conf ... SPI [*Society of the Plastics Industry*] International Technical/Marketing Conference [*A publication*]
Spike M & S ... Spike on Master and Servant [*3rd ed.*] [*1872*] [*A publication*] (DLA)
SPIL.......... Quincemil [*Peru*] [*ICAO location identifier*] (ICLI)
SPIL.......... Self-Rating Psychiatric Inventory List [*Personality development test*] [*Psychology*]
SPIL.......... Sensitive Projects and Installation List (MCD)
SPIL.......... Ship's Parts Integration List
SPIL.......... SPI-Suspension & Parts Industries Ltd. [*New York, NY*] [*NASDAQ symbol*] (NQ)
SPILA........ Sports Illustrated [*A publication*]
SPILB........ Spiegel [*A publication*]
SP-ILS....... Shuttle Projects - Integrated Logistics Support [*Kennedy Space Center*] [*NASA*] (NASA)
SPIM .... Lima-Callao/Internacional Jorge Chavez [*Peru*] [*ICAO location identifier*] (ICLI)
SPIM .... Service de Previsions Ionospherique Militaire
SPIMD ...... Siauliu Pedagoginio Instituto Mokslo Darbai [*A publication*]
SPIMS....... Shuttle Program Information Management System [*NASA*]
SPIN.......... School Practices Information Network [*Bibliographic Retrieval Services*] [*Information service or system*] (IID)
SPIN.......... Science Procurement Information Network [*Canada*]
SPIN.......... Searchable Physics Information Notices [*American Institute of Physics*] [*New York, NY*] [*Bibliographic database*]
SPIN.......... Service Parts Information Notice
SPIN.......... Space Inspection
SPIN.......... Space Intercept (SAA)
SPIN.......... Special Inquiry [*FBI term*]
SPIN.......... Spinster (ADA)
SPIN.......... Standard & Poor's 500 Index Subordinated Notes
SPIN.......... Standard Procedure Instructions (KSC)
SPIN.......... Strategies and Policies for Informatics [*Intergovernmental Bureau for Informatics*]
SPIN.......... Submarine Program Information Notebook
SPIN.......... Superconductive Precision Inertial Navigation
SPINAL..... Stimulator, Planetary Instrument Alignment
SPINAR ... Spinning Star [*Astronomy*]
sp indet....... Species Indeterminata [*Species Indeterminate*] [*Latin*] (MAE)
SPINDEX ... Selective Permutation Indexing [*Library of Congress*]
SPINDEX ... Subject Profile Index [*Computer-based*]
SPINE .... Simulated Program for Investigation of Nuclear Effects
SPINE .... Space Informatics Network Experiment [*European Space Agency*]
SPINES..... Science and Technology Policies Information Exchange System [*UNESCO*] [*Bibliographic database*] (IID)
Spinks........ Spinks' English Ecclesiastical and Admiralty Reports [*164 English Reprint*] [*A publication*] (DLA)
Spinks Eccl & Adm (Eng) ... Spinks' English Ecclesiastical and Admiralty Reports [*164 English Reprint*] [*A publication*] (DLA)
Spinks PC ... Spinks' English Admiralty Prize Cases [*A publication*] (DLA)
Spinks Prize Cas ... Spinks' English Admiralty Prize Cases [*164 English Reprint*] [*A publication*] (DLA)
Spinks Prize Cas (Eng) ... Spinks' English Admiralty Prize Cases [*164 English Reprint*] [*A publication*] (DLA)
Spinner Weber Textilveredl ... Spinner, Weber, Textilveredlung [*A publication*]
sp inquir ..... Species Inquirendae [*Species of Doubtful Status*] [*Latin*] (MAE)
SPINS........ Ship Passive Integrated Navigation System (DNAB)
SPINSTRE ... Spencer Information Storage and Retrieval System (DIT)
SPINT .... Special Intelligence (MCD)
SPINTAC ... Special Interest Aircraft (NVT)
SPINTCOM ... Special Intelligence Communications [*Later, DIN/DSSCS*]
SPINTCOMM ... Special Intelligence Communications [*Later, DIN/DSSCS*] (CET)

SPINVESWG ... Special Investigation Wing (MUGU)
SPIO......... Systems Planning and Integration Office [*NASA*]
SPIP........... Satipo [*Peru*] [*ICAO location identifier*] (ICLI)
SPIP........... Special Position Identification Pulse (CET)
SPIPA....... Scientific Papers. Institute of Physical and Chemical Research [*A publication*]
SPIPE....... Spin-Polarized Inverse Photoemission [*Physics*]
S'PIPE....... Standpipe
SPI PH ...... SPI Pharmaceuticals, Inc. [*Associated Press abbreviation*] (APAG)
SPIR .... Patria [*Peru*] [*ICAO location identifier*] (ICLI)
SPIR .... Search Program for Infrared Spectra [*Canada Institute for Scientific and Technical Information*] [*Information service or system*]
SPIR .... Sears Point International Raceway [*California*]
SPIR .... Spiral
SPIR .... Spire Corp. [*NASDAQ symbol*] (NQ)
SPIR .... Spiritoso [*With Animation*] [*Music*]
SPIR .... Spiritus [*Spirit*] [*Pharmacy*]
SPIR .... Standard and Poor's Index - Rails [*Stock market*]
SPIR .... Standardized Proportional Incidence Ratio [*Epidemiology*]
SPIR .... Student Project for International Responsibility
SPIRAL..... Sperry Inertial RADAR Altimeter
SPIRBM.... Solid-Propellant Intermediate Range Ballistic Missile (AAG)
SPIRE....... Spatial Inertial Reference Equipment
SPI Reinf Plast Compos Inst Annu Conf Proc ... SPI [*Society of the Plastics Industry*] Reinforced Plastics/Composites Institute. Annual Conference. Proceedings [*A publication*]
SPIREP..... Spot Intelligence Report [*Air Force*]
SPIRES .... Standard Personnel Information Retrieval System [*Military*]
SPIRES ..... Stanford Public Information Retrieval System [*Stanford University Libraries*] [*Stanford, CA*] [*Bibliographic database management system*] [*Information service or system*]
SPIRIT ...... Sales Processing Interactive Real-Time Inventory Technique [*NCR Corp. trademark*]
SPIRIT ...... Sensible Policy in Information Resources and Information Technology [*Defunct*] (EA)
Spirit......... Spirit That Moves Us [*A publication*]
SPIRIT ...... Spiritoso [*With Animation*] [*Music*]
SPIRIT ...... Spiritus [*Spirit*] [*Latin*] (ROG)
Spirit Mis .. Spirit of Missions [*A publication*]
Spirit Pilg .. Spirit of the Pilgrims [*A publication*]
Spirit Verkauf ... Spirituosen-Verkauf [*A publication*]
Spir Life..... Spiritual Life [*A publication*]
SPIRO .... Students Protesting Illegal Real Estate Operators [*Student legal action organization*] (EA)
SPIRT........ Short Path Infrared Tester (KSC)
SPIRT........ Stock Point Interrogation/Requirements Technique
Spir Tod ..... Spirituality Today [*A publication*]
Spirto Vodochn Promst ... Spirto-Vodochnaya Promyshlennost [*A publication*]
Spirt Prom-St' ... Spirtovaya Promyshlennost' [*A publication*]
SPIS........... Pias [*Peru*] [*ICAO location identifier*] (ICLI)
SPIS........... Senate Permanent Investigating Subcommittee (AAG)
SPIS........... Space Philatelists International Society (EA)
Spis Bulg Akad Nauk ... Spisanie na Bulgarskata Akademiya na Naukite [*Bulgaria*] [*A publication*]
Spis Bulg Geol Druzh ... Spisanie na Bulgarskoto Geologichesko Druzhestvo [*A publication*]
Spis Bulg Geol Druzhu ... Spisania na Bulgarsoto Geologichesko Druzhestvo [*A publication*]
SPISE........ Special Projects in Science Education
Spis Nauchno-Issled Inst Minist Zemed Gorite ... Spisanie na Nauchno-Issledovatelskite Instituti pri Ministerstvata na Zemedelete i Gorite [*A publication*]
Spis Nauchnoizsled Inst Minist Zemed (Bulg) ... Spisanie na Nauchnoizsledovatelskite Instituti pri Ministerstvoto na Zemedelieto (Bulgaria) [*A publication*]
SPISS .... Spissus [*Dried*] [*Pharmacy*]
SPI Struct Foam Conf Proc ... SPI [*Society of the Plastics Industry*] Structural Foam Conference. Proceedings [*A publication*]
Spisy Lek Fak Masaryk Univ (Brno) ... Spisy Lekarske Fakulty Mesarykovy University (Brno) [*A publication*]
Spisy Pedagog Fak Ostrave ... Spisy Pedagogicke Fakulty v Ostrave [*A publication*]
Spisy Prir Fak Univ Brne ... Spisy Prirodovedecke Fakulty Universita v Brne [*Czechoslovakia*] [*A publication*]
Spisy Prirodoved Fak Univ JE Purkyne Brne ... Spisy Prirodovedecke Fakulty University J. E. Purkyne v Brne [*A publication*]
Spisy Priroved Fak Univ J E Purkyne Brne ... Spisy Prirodovedecke Fakulty University J. E. Purkyne v Brne [*A publication*]
Spisy Vydavane Prirodoved Fak Massarkovy Univ ... Spisy Vydavane Prirodovedeckou Fakultou Massarykovy University [*A publication*]
SPIT .... Paita [*Peru*] [*ICAO location identifier*] (ICLI)
SPIT .... Secondary Power Integration Test (MCD)
SPIT .... Selective Printing of Items from Tape [*Data processing*]
SPITS........ Scan Platform Inertial Thermal Simulator
SPIU......... Ship Position Interpolation Unit
SPIU......... Standard and Poor's Index - Utilities [*Stock market*]

SPIW......... ESCAP [*Economic and Social Commssion for the Asia and Pacific*] Division for Shipping, Ports, and Inland Waterways (EAIO)
SPIW......... Special-Purpose Individual Weapon [*A rifle that fires flechettes or darts*] [*Pronounced "spew"*]
SPIY .... Yauri [*Peru*] [*ICAO location identifier*] (ICLI)
SPIZ .... Uchiza [*Peru*] [*ICAO location identifier*] (ICLI)
SPJ .... Austria [*Republic of*] Stock Index Growth Notes [*NYSE symbol*] (SPSG)
SPJ .... Senior Puisne Judge [*British*] (ILCA)
SPJ .... Socialist Party of Japan [*Nikon Shakaito*] [*Political party*] (PPW)
SPJ .... Socijalisticka Partija Jugoslavije [*Socialist Party of Yugoslavia*] [*Political party*] (PPE)
SPJ .... Sparta [*Greece*] [*Airport symbol*] [*Obsolete*] (OAG)
SPJ .... Special Purpose Jammer [*Military*] (CAAL)
SPJA......... Rioja [*Peru*] [*ICAO location identifier*] (ICLI)
SPJB......... Cajabamba/Pampa Grande [*Peru*] [*ICAO location identifier*] (ICLI)
SPJC......... St. Petersburg Junior College [*Clearwater, FL*]
SP-JFI .... School Principal Job Functions Inventory [*Test*]
SPJI......... Juanjui [*Peru*] [*ICAO location identifier*] (ICLI)
SPJJ .... Jauja [*Peru*] [*ICAO location identifier*] (ICLI)
SPJL......... Juliaca [*Peru*] [*ICAO location identifier*] (ICLI)
SPJN......... San Juan [*Peru*] [*ICAO location identifier*] (ICLI)
SPJR......... Cajamarca/Mayor General FAP Armando Revoredo Iglesias [*Peru*] [*ICAO location identifier*] (ICLI)
SPJ SDX ... Society of Professional Journalists, Sigma Delta Chi (EA)
SPJSEY..... South Pacific Journal of Natural Science [*A publication*]
SPJTG....... Secondary Plant Joint Test Group (DNAB)
SPK........... Reno, NV [*Location identifier*] [*FAA*] (FAAL)
SPK........... Saporamean Kampuchea News Agency [*Cambodia*]
SPK........... Sapporo [*Japan*] [*Airport symbol*] (OAG)
SPK........... Scotts Peak [*Tasmania*] [*Seismograph station code, US Geological Survey*] (SEIS)
SPK........... Silver Tusk Mines [*Vancouver Stock Exchange symbol*]
SPK........... Socialist Party of Kurdistan [*Iraq*] [*Political party*] (MENA)
SPK........... Spare Parts Kit
SPK........... Spark (MSA)
spk........... Speckled [*Quality of the bottom*] [*Nautical charts*]
SPK........... Spike (MSA)
SPK........... Spinnbarkheit [*With reference to cervical mucus*] [*Medicine*]
SPK........... Superficial Punctate Keratitis [*Ophthalmology*]
SPKL .... Sprinkle (FAAC)
SPKP .... Suomen Perustuslaillinen Kansanpuolue [*Finnish Constitutional People's Party*] [*Political party*] (PPW)
SPKR........ Speaker (AAG)
SPKR........ Spinnaker Software Corp. [*NASDAQ symbol*] (NQ)
SPKR........ Sprinkler (WGA)
SPKT........ Sprocket
SPKYB ..... Shih P'in Kung Yeh [*A publication*]
SPL........... Airspur Helicopters, Inc. [*Huntington Beach, CA*] [*FAA designator*] (FAAC)
SPL........... Saskatoon Public Library [*UTLAS symbol*]
SPL........... Scott Paper Ltd. [*Toronto Stock Exchange symbol*] [*Vancouver Stock Exchange symbol*]
SPL........... Scratch Pad Line [*NASA*] (MCD)
SPL........... Self-Propelled Launcher [*British military*] (DMA)
SPL........... Separate Parts List (MSA)
SPL........... Serialized Parts List [*NASA*] (MCD)
SPL........... Service Priority List (BUR)
SPL........... Signal Processing Language [*Data processing*] (CSR)
SPL........... Signature and Propagation Laboratory [*Army*] (RDA)
SPL........... Simple Phrase Language [*Data processing*]
SPL........... Simple Programming Language [*Data processing*]
SPL........... Simulation Programming Language [*Data processing*]
SPL........... Sine Prole Legitima [*Without Legitimate Issue*] [*Latin*]
SPL........... Single Pet Lover
SPL........... Single-Premium Life [*Insurance*]
SPL........... Single-Premium Whole Life [*Insurance*]
SPL........... Single Propellant Loading (AFM)
SPL........... Skin Potential Level
SPL........... Sloane Physics Laboratory [*Yale*] (MCD)
SPL........... Smoke Puff Limiter [*Automotive engineering*]
SPL........... Software Parts List [*Data processing*] (TEL)
SPL........... Software Programming Language [*Data processing*] (IEEE)
SPL........... Solar Pumped LASER (SSD)
SPL........... Sound Power Level [*Acoustics*]
SPL........... Sound Pressure Level [*Acoustics*]
SPL........... Source Program Library
SPL........... Space Physics Laboratory [*Aerospace corporation*]
SPL........... Space Programming Language [*Data processing*]
SPL........... Space Programs Laboratory [*Fort Belvoir, VA*] [*United States Army Engineer Topographic Laboratories*] (GRD)
SPL........... Spare Parts List
SPL........... Spartanburg County Public Library, Spartanburg, SC [*OCLC symbol*] (OCLC)
SPL........... Special (AAG)
SPL........... Special-Purpose Language [*Data processing*]
SPL........... Speed Phase Lock
SPL........... Spermatophore Length

SpL............ Spiegel der Letteren [*A publication*]
SPL............ Spiral (MSA)
SPL............ Spiridon Lake [*Alaska*] [*Seismograph station code, US Geological Survey*] (SEIS)
SPL............ Splice [*Telecommunications*] (TEL)
SPL............ Splice Junction Mutation [*Genetics*]
SPL............ Spontaneous Lesion [*Medicine*] (MAE)
SPL............ Sporulation per Lesion [*Plant pathology*]
SPL............ Spritsail [*Ship's rigging*] (ROG)
SPL............ Standard Pulse LASER
SPL............ Standards Parts Listing (MCD)
SPL............ Staphylococcal Phage Lysate [*Biochemistry*]
SPL............ Student Pilot's Licence (AIA)
SPL............ Succinyl-Poly-L-Lysine [*Biochemical analysis*]
SPL............ Summary Parts List
SPL............ Sun Pumped LASER (MCD)
SPL............ Superior Parietal Lobule [*Neuroanatomy*]
Spl............ Supplement (BJA)
SPL............ Supplementary Flight Plan Message [*Aviation code*]
SPL............ Support Platoon Leader [*Military*] (INF)
SPL............ Swiss Party of Labour
SPL............ System Program Loader
SPL............ System Programming Language [*Data processing*] (NASA)
SPLA........ Louisiana [*Peru*] [*ICAO location identifier*] (ICLI)
SPLA........ Special-Purpose Lead Azide (MCD)
SPLA........ Sudan People's Liberation Army
SPLAASH ... Spacecraft Protective Landing Area for the Advancement of Science and Humanities [*Landing zone for flying saucers near Mt. Rainier, WA*]
SPLAN...... Support Plan (MCD)
SPLANCH ... Split-Level Ranch [*House*]
SPLASH.... Shipboard Platforms for Landing and Servicing Helicopters
SPLASH.... Special Program to List Amplitudes of Surges from Hurricanes
SPLAT...... Simplified Programming Language for Artists [*1978*] [*Data processing*] (CSR)
SPLAT...... Student Potential Life Achievement Test [*Parody of Scholastic Aptitude Test preparation books*]
SPLATT .... Single Pedestrians League Against Taxes and Traffic [*British*] (DI)
Sp Laws ..... Spirit of the Laws (Montesquieu) [*A publication*] (DLA)
SPLC .... Ship Program Life Cycle [*Navy*]
SPLC .... Simulated Planetary Landing Capsule (DNAB)
SPLC .... Southern Poverty Law Center (EA)
SPLC .... Spare Parts List for Codification
SPLC .... Splice
SPLC .... Standard Point Location Code [*American Trucking Association and Association of American Railroads*]
SPLC .... Student Press Law Center (EA)
SPLD........ Celendin [*Peru*] [*ICAO location identifier*] (ICLI)
SPLEB...... Spectroscopy Letters [*A publication*]
SPLEE2..... Studies in Plant Ecology [*A publication*]
SPLF.......... [*The*] Sporting Life, Inc. [*Alexandria, VA*] [*NASDAQ symbol*] (NQ)
S/PLF .... Station/Platform LIDAR Facility (SSD)
SPLHC...... Sgt. Pepper's Lonely Hearts Club (EA)
SPLI.......... Lima [*Peru*] [*ICAO location identifier*] (ICLI)
SPLI.......... Spermatophore Length Index
SPLI.......... Substance P-Like Immunoreactivity
Sp Lib........ Special Libraries [*A publication*]
SPLICE ..... Stock Point Logistics Integrated Communications Environment Project [*Navy*]
SPLID....... SpeciaList [*A publication*]
SPLIT....... Space Program Language Implementation Tool (KSC)
SPLIT....... Sundstrand Processing Language Internally Translated
SPLK .... Jones Spacelink Ltd. [*NASDAQ symbol*] (NQ)
SPLK .... Studie Prazskeho Linguistickeho Krouzku [*A publication*]
SPLL.......... Self-Propelled Launcher Loader (MCD)
SPLL.......... Standard Phase-Locked Loop
SPLLG....... Stable Production Low Leach Glass [*For nuclear wastes*]
SPLM .... Space Programming Language Machine
SP-LMO.... Shuttle Projects - Logistics Management Office [*NASA*] (GFGA)
SPLN .... Rodriguez de Mendoz/San Nicolas [*Peru*] [*ICAO location identifier*] (ICLI)
SPLN .... Spline [*Engineering*]
SPLNS....... South Plains [*FAA*] (FAAC)
SPLO........ Ilo [*Peru*] [*ICAO location identifier*] (ICLI)
SPLP.......... Las Palmas [*Peru*] [*ICAO location identifier*] (ICLI)
SPLS.......... Staples, Inc. [*NASDAQ symbol*] (NQ)
SPLS.......... Zorrillos [*Peru*] [*ICAO location identifier*] (ICLI)
SPLSA....... Space Life Sciences [*A publication*]
SPLT .... Lobitos [*Peru*] [*ICAO location identifier*] (ICLI)
SPLT .... Specialist, Link Trainer Instructor [*Navy rating*]
SPLTR....... Splitter
SPLTRK .... Special Tracker [*Military*] (CAAL)
SPLTY....... Specialty (WGA)
SPLV .... Lago Verde [*Peru*] [*ICAO location identifier*] (ICLI)
SPLV .... Spinach Latent Virus [*Plant pathology*]
SPLV .... Stable Plurilamellar Vesicle [*Pharmacology*]
SPLX .... Simplex [*Mathematics*]
SPLY .... Spa Lady Corp. [*NASDAQ symbol*] (NQ)

SPLY .... Supply (MSA)
SPM........... St. Philips Marsh [*Bristol*] [*British depot code*]
SPM........... St. Pierre and Miquelon [*ANSI three-letter standard code*] (CNC)
SPM........... Salud Publica de Mexico [*A publication*]
SPM........... Scanning Photoemission Microscope
SPM........... Scanning Probe Microscopy
SPM........... Scratch Pad Memory [*Data processing*] (BUR)
SPM........... Scripture Press Ministries (EA)
SPM........... Security Program Manager [*Military*] (GFGA)
SPM........... Sedimentary Phosphate Method
SPM........... Self-Propelled Mount [*Military*]
SPM........... Semipermeable Membrane
SPM........... Senior Project Manager
SPM........... Sequential Processing Machine (DIT)
SPM........... Short Particular Metre [*Music*]
SPM........... Shots per Minute [*Military*] (RDA)
SPM........... Significant Probability Mapping
SPM........... Sine Prole Mascula [*Without Male Issue*] [*Latin*]
SPM........... Single-Point Management
SPM........... Single-Point Mooring [*Oil platform*]
SPM........... Single Program Manager [*Air Force*]
SPM........... Six Point Mooring [*Oil platform*]
SPM........... Smaller Profit Margin
SPM........... Societas Patrum Misericordiae [*Fathers of Mercy*] [*Roman Catholic religious order*]
SPM........... Society for Policy Modeling (EA)
SPM........... Society of Pragmatic Mysticism (EA)
SPM........... Society of Prospective Medicine (EA)
SPM........... Software Programmer's Manual
SPM........... Solar Polar Mission (MCD)
SPM........... Solar Power Module
SPM........... Solar Proton Monitor
SPM........... Somali Patriotic Movement [*Political party*] (EY)
SPM........... Sound-Powered Microphone
SPM........... Source Program Maintenance [*IBM Corp.*]
SPM........... South Pacific Mail [*A publication*]
SPM........... Special-Purpose Materials (MCD)
SPM........... Specialist, Mail Clerk [*Navy rating*]
SPM........... Spectrophosphorimeter
SPM........... Spectrum Industrial Resources [*Vancouver Stock Exchange symbol*]
Sp M.......... Spicilegio Moderno [*A publication*]
SpM........... Spiriformis Medialis Nucleus [*Brain anatomy*]
SPM........... Split Phase Motor
SPM........... Standard Payload Module (MCD)
SPM........... Standard Practice Memo (MCD)
SPM........... Standard Procedure Manual (AAG)
SPM........... Standard Process Manual
SPM........... Static Presentation Mode
SPM........... Stationary Plasma Motor
SPM........... Strokes per Minute
SPM........... Subscriber's Private Meter [*Telecommunications*] (TEL)
SPM........... Subsystem Project Manager [*NASA*] (NASA)
SPM........... Sun Probe-Mars [*NASA*]
SPM........... Superparamagnetic [*Fraction in rock*] [*Geophysics*]
SPM........... Supervisory Management [*A publication*]
SPM........... Support Program Management
SPM........... Surface Plasmon Microscopy [*Physics*]
SPM........... Suspended Particulate Matter
SPM........... Symbol Processing Machine (IEEE)
SPM........... Synaptic Plasma Membrane [*Neurophysiology*]
SPM........... Synaptosomal Plasma Membrane [*Neurobiology*]
SPM........... Synthetic Plasma Membrane [*Biochemistry*]
SPM........... System Performance Model
S/PM......... System/Project Management
SPM........... Systems Program Manager
SPMA....... Rio Maranon [*Peru*] [*ICAO location identifier*] (ICLI)
SPMA....... Shoe Pattern Manufacturers Association [*Inactive*] (EA)
SPMA....... Society for Post-Medieval Archaeology [*British*]
SPMA....... Soda Pulp Manufacturers Association [*Defunct*] (EA)
SPMA....... Southwest Parks and Monuments Association (EA)
SPMA....... Spinal Progressive Muscular Atrophy [*Medicine*] (AAMN)
SPMA....... Sump Pump Manufacturers Association [*Later, SSPMA*] (EA)
SPMB....... Strong Partial Maternal Behavior [*Psychology*]
SPMC........ Shannon Park Marine Center [*West Washington University*] [*Anacortes, WA*]
SPMC........ Society of Paper Money Collectors (EA)
SPMC........ Society of Professional Management Consultants [*Association name and designation awarded by this group*] [*Englewood, NJ*] (EA)
SPMC........ Special Machine [*Tool*] (AAG)
SPMCA...... Soviet Powder Metallurgy and Metal Ceramics [*English Translation*] [*A publication*]
SPMD....... Spectramed, Inc. [*NASDAQ symbol*] (NQ)
SPME....... Tumbes/Pedro Canga [*Peru*] [*ICAO location identifier*] (ICLI)
SPMEA....... Sulfate of Potash Magnesia Export Association (EA)
SPMGA...... Speech Monographs [*A publication*]
SPML........ Special Meal [*Diabetic, low-cholesterol, low-calorie, hypoglycemic, or gluten-free*] [*Airline notation*] (ADA)
SPML........ Supermail International, Inc. [*NASDAQ symbol*] (NQ)

SPMLF...... Societe de la Psychologie Medicale de Langue Francaise [*French-Language Society of Medical Psychology - FLSMP*] (EA)
SPMM....... Society for the Promotion of Mohammedan Missions [*Defunct*] (EA)
SPMMV.... Sweet Potato Mild Mottle Virus [*Plant pathology*]
SPMO .... SAMMS [*Standard Automated Materiel Management System*] Program Management Office [*DoD*]
SPMO ...... Senior Principal Medical Officer [*British*] (DI)
SPMOL..... Source Program Maintenance Online
Sp Mon ...... Speech Monographs [*A publication*]
SPMP .... Special-Purpose Multiprocessor [*Data processing*]
SP-MPC .... Shuttle Projects - Management Planning and Control Office [*Kennedy Space Center*] [*NASA*] (NASA)
SPMR....... Southern Provinces Mounted Rifles [*British military*] (DMA)
SPMR....... Sub Postmaster [*British*] (DCTA)
SPMRL ..... Sulphite Pulp Manufacturers' Research League (EA)
SPMS .... Sine Prole Mascula Superstite [*Without Surviving Male Issue*] [*Latin*] (ADA)
SPMS .... Solar Particle Monitoring System [*NASA*] (KSC)
SPMS .... Special-Purpose Manipulator System [*NASA*] (NASA)
SPMS .... Special-Purpose Monitoring Station [*Environmental Protection Agency*]
SPMS .... Strategic Planning and Management System [*Environmental Protection Agency*] (GFGA)
SPMS .... Suppression Pool Makeup System [*Nuclear energy*] (NRCH)
SPMS .... Surveyor Payload Mechanism Section
SPMS .... System Program Management Surveys [*Air Force*]
SPMS .... Yurimaguas [*Peru*] [*ICAO location identifier*] (ICLI)
Sp Msgr ...... Special Messenger [*Army*]
SPMV .... Satellite Panicum Mosaic Virus
SPMXA ..... Salud Publica de Mexico [*A publication*]
SPMY....... Dos De Mayo [*Peru*] [*ICAO location identifier*] (ICLI)
SPN .... Cape Shipunski [*Former USSR*] [*Seismograph station code, US Geological Survey*] (SEIS)
SPN .... Pelican Narrows Public Library, Saskatchewan [*Library symbol*] [*National Library of Canada*] (NLC)
SPN .... Saipan [*Mariana Islands*] [*Airport symbol*] (OAG)
SPN .... Satellite Programming Network [*Cable-television system*]
SPN .... Savanna Pastoral Neolithic [*Archeology*]
SPN .... School Product News [*A publication*]
SPN .... Secretariado da Propaganda Nacional [*Portugal*]
SPN .... Separation Program Number [*Military*]
SPN .... Service Part Number
SPN .... Shipment/Performance Notification [*DoD*]
SPN .... Shuttle Project Notice [*Kennedy Space Center*] [*NASA*] (NASA)
SPN .... Sparton Resources, Inc. [*Toronto Stock Exchange symbol*]
SPN .... Special Program Number (MUGU)
SPN .... Specimen (WGA)
SPN .... Sponsor Program Number [*Military*]
SPN .... Standard Precision Navigator
SPN .... Student Practical Nurse (AAMN)
SPN .... Subscriber Premises Network [*Telecommunications*]
SPNA .... Sympathetic Preganglionic Neuron [*Anatomy*]
SPNA .... Punta De Lomas [*Peru*] [*ICAO location identifier*] (ICLI)
SPNC........ Huanuco/Alferez FAP David Figuerao Fernandini [*Peru*] [*ICAO location identifier*] (ICLI)
SPNC........ Spectranetics Corp. [*NASDAQ symbol*] (SPSG)
SPND .... Self-Powered Neutron Detector [*Nuclear energy*] (NRCH)
SPND .... Suspend (NASA)
SPNEA ...... Society for the Preservation of New England Antiquities (EA)
SPNF .... Shot Peening Fixture (MCD)
SPNFT ...... South Pacific Nuclear Free Treaty
SPNG........ Society for Provincial Notaries General [*British*]
SPNG........ Sponge
SPN/GEANS ... Standard Precision Navigator/Gimbaled Electrostatic-Gyro Aircraft Navigation System (MCD)
SPN/GEANS ... Standard Precision Navigator/Gimballed Electrostatic Aircraft Navigation System
SPNH .... Laguna Choclococha [*Peru*] [*ICAO location identifier*] (ICLI)
SPNI......... Societe pour la Protection de la Nature en Israel [*Society for the Protection of Nature in Israel*] [*Tel Aviv*] (EAIO)
S/PNL .... Side Panel [*Automotive engineering*]
SPNM........ Society for the Promotion of New Music [*British*]
SPNO .... Ancon [*Peru*] [*ICAO location identifier*] (ICLI)
sp nov .... Species Nova [*New Species*] [*Biology*]
SPNP........ Puno [*Peru*] [*ICAO location identifier*] (ICLI)
SPNR........ Ricran [*Peru*] [*ICAO location identifier*] (ICLI)
SPNR........ Spanner (AAG)
SPNR........ System Peculiar Non-Repairable
SPNS .... Spoons (ROG)
SPNS .... Switched Private Network Service [*ITT service mark*]
SPNSF....... Sapiens International NV [*NYSE symbol*] (SPSG)
SPNSN ...... Suspension (MSA)
SPNT .... Intuto [*Peru*] [*ICAO location identifier*] (ICLI)
SPNU .... Manu [*Peru*] [*ICAO location identifier*] (ICLI)
SPNX........ Sphinx Mining, Inc. [*NASDAQ symbol*] (NQ)
SPNZ........ Santa Cruz [*Peru*] [*ICAO location identifier*] (ICLI)
SPNZ........ Socialist Party of New Zealand [*Political party*] (PPW)
SPO .... Denver, CO [*Location identifier*] [*FAA*] (FAAL)

SPO .... Sacramento Peak Observatory
SPO .... Salomon Phibro Oil Trust [*AMEX symbol*] (SPSG)
SPO .... Sandia Pulse Reactor
SPO .... Saturn Program Office [*NASA*] (KSC)
SPO .... Sausages, Potatoes, and Onions [*Meaning a cheap restaurant that specializes in these*] [*British slang*]
SPO .... Sea Post Office
SPO .... Senate Post Office
SPO .... SENTRY [*Survey Entry*] Project Office
SPO .... Separate Partition Option
SPO .... Shore Patrol Officer [*Navy*]
SPO .... Short Period Oscillation
SPO .... Shuttle Project Office [*NASA*] (KSC)
SPO .... Signal Property Office [*Military*]
SPO .... Single Pickle Ordinary [*Metal industry*]
SPO .... Slaving Pick-Off
SPO .... Society of Planning Officials
SPO .... Sozialdemokratische Partei Oesterreichs [*Social Democratic Party of Austria*] [*Political party*]
SPO .... Spacelab Program Office [*NASA*]
SPO .... Spare Parts Order [*NASA*] (NASA)
SPO .... Special Placement Officer (ADA)
SP & O .... Special Plans and Operation [*Military*]
SPO .... Special Projects Office [*Navy*]
SPO .... Specialist, Inspector of Naval Material [*Navy rating*]
SPO .... Spokane [*Washington*] [*Seismograph station code, US Geological Survey*] [*Closed*] (SEIS)
SPO .... Spooner Mines & Oils Ltd. [*Toronto Stock Exchange symbol*]
SPO .... Spotlight [*A publication*]
SPO .... Srpski Pokret Obnove [*Serbian Renaissance Movement*] [*Political party*] (EY)
SPO .... Stoker Petty Officer [*Navy*] [*British*] (DSUE)
SPO .... Subpurchase Order (AAG)
SPO .... Supplemental Production Order (AAG)
SPO .... Surplus Property Office [*Transferred to War Assets Administration, 1947*]
SPO .... System Program [*or Project*] Office [*Military*]
SPOA........ Les Sagesses du Proche-Orient Ancien. Colloque de Strasbourg [*1962*]. Travaux du Centre d'Etudes Superieurs Specialise d'Histoire des Religions de Strassbourg [*Paris*] [*A publication*] (BJA)
SPOA........ Saposoa [*Peru*] [*ICAO location identifier*] (ICLI)
SPOA........ Soviet Panorama [*A publication*]
SPOAV...... Specialist, Inspector of Aviation Material [*Navy rating*]
SPOBS...... Special Observer [*US Army group in London*] [*World War II*]
SPOC........ Shuttle Payload Operations Contractor (NASA)
SPOC........ Shuttle Payload Opportunity Carrier
SPOC........ Shuttle Portable Onboard Computer [*NASA*]
SPOC........ Single Point of Contact (GFGA)
SPOC........ Single-Point Orbit Calculator
SPOC........ Solid-Propulsion Optimization Code (MCD)
SPOC........ Spacecraft Oceanography Project [*Navy*]
SPOC........ Special Projects Operations Center [*Allied Force Headquarters*] [*World War II*]
SPOC........ Systems Program Office Cadre (MCD)
SPOCK...... Simulated Procedure for Obtaining Common Knowledge
SPOCK...... Special Purpose Operational Computing Kernel [*Pilot training device developed at Georgia Institute of Technology*]
SPOCM..... Society for the Preservation of Old Mills (EA)
SPOCN..... Subpurchase Order Change Notice (AAG)
SPOD .... Seaports of Debarkation (MCD)
SPOD .... Ship's Plan of the Day [*Navy*] (DNAB)
SpOd.......... Spanish Odeon, Barcelona [*Record label*] [*Spain*]
SPODA...... Society for the Prevention of Drug Addiction
SPODAC... SITS [*SAGE Intercept Target Simulation*] Probability of Detection and Conversion (MCD)
SPODP...... Single Precision Orbit Determination Program [*NASA*]
SPOE........ Seaports of Embarkation (MCD)
SPOE........ Society of Post Office Engineers [*Pronounced "spowee"*] [*British*] (DCTA)
SPOE........ Sozialistische Partei Oesterreichs [*Socialist Party of Austria*]
SPOEN...... Specialist, Engineering Inspector [*Navy rating*]
SPOFOR ... Sportwissenschaftliche Forschungsprojekte [*Bundesinstitut fuer Sportwissenschaft*] [*Germany*] [*Information service or system*] (CRD)
SPOG .... Sales of Products Other than Gasoline
Spokane Bs ... Spokane Business Examiner [*United States*] [*A publication*]
SPOL.......... Collique [*Peru*] [*ICAO location identifier*] (ICLI)
SPol.......... Storia e Politica [*A publication*]
Spold Kwartal Nauk ... Spoldzielczy Kwartalnik Naukomy [*A publication*]
Spolia Zeylan ... Spolia Zeylanica [*A publication*]
Spolia Zool Mus Haun ... Spolia Zoologica Musei Hauniensis [*A publication*]
SPOLIT..... Sportliteratur [*Bundesinstitut fuer Sportwissenschaft*] [*Germany*] [*Information service or system*] (CRD)
SPOM .... Society of Post Office Managers [*A union*] [*British*]
SPOM .... STS [*Shuttle Test Station*] Planning and Operations Management [*NASA*] (GFGA)
SPOM .... Suspended Particulate Organic Material [*Environmental chemistry*]
SPOMCUS ... Selective Prepositioning of Materiel Configured to Unit Sets [*Army*] (AABC)

S Pomp....... Sextus Pomponius [*Flourished, 2nd century*] [*Authority cited in pre-1607 legal work*] (DSA)
SpomSAN ... Spomenik Srpske Akademije Nauka [*A publication*]
SPON .... Sponsor (AFM)
SPON .... Spontaneous (WGA)
SPON .... Statistical Profile of Old Norse
SPONT....... Spontaneous
Spont Ab .... Spontaneous Abortion [*Medicine*] (MAE)
SPOOF...... Society for the Protection of Old Fishes (EA)
SPOOF...... Structure and Parity Observing Output Function
SPOOFS.... Society for the Promotion of Otherwise Overlooked Football Scores
SPOOK...... Supervisor Program Over Other Kinds [*Data processing*]
SPOOL...... Simultaneous Peripheral Operation Online [*Data processing*] (MCD)
SPOOL...... Simultaneous Processing of Off-Line Item
SPOOL...... Simultaneous Production Operation Online
SPOOM ... Society for the Preservation of Old Mills (EA)
Spoon .... Spooner's Reports [*12-15 Wisconsin*] [*A publication*] (DLA)
Spooner...... Spooner's Reports [*12-15 Wisconsin*] [*A publication*] (DLA)
SPOOR...... Specialist, Ordnance Inspector [*Navy rating*]
SPOP........ Poto [*Peru*] [*ICAO location identifier*] (ICLI)
SPOP........ Scan Platform Operations Program
SPOPE ...... Specialist, Petroleum Technician [*Navy rating*]
SP-OPI ...... Shuttle Projects - Operations Planning and Integration [*NASA*] (GFGA)
SP-OPN..... Shuttle Projects - Operations Planning Office [*Kennedy Space Center*] [*NASA*] (NASA)
SPO-PO .... System Program Office/Project Office [*Air Force*] (AFIT)
SPOPS...... Special Operations
Spore Res ... Spore Research [*A publication*]
SPORK...... Spoon and Fork
SPORS ...... Slosson Pre-Observational Record Screen [*Educational test*]
SPORT ...... St. Petersburg [*Florida*] Olympic Regatta Training
SPORT ...... Space Probe Optical Recording Telescope [*Army*]
SPORT ...... Sporting (ROG)
Sportarzt Sportmed ... Sportarzt Sportmedizin [*A publication*]
Sport Fish Abstr ... Sport Fisheries Abstracts [*A publication*]
Sport Fit Ind ... Sport and Fitness Index [*A publication*]
SPORTFOR ... Support Force
Sport Leis .. Sport and Leisure [*A publication*]
Sport Med J ... Sport-Medical Journal [*A publication*]
Spor Tr....... Sporting Traditions [*A publication*]
Sport Rec ... Sport and Recreation [*A publication*]
Sport Rec Ind ... Sport and Recreation Index [*A publication*]
Sports and Ath ... Sports and Athletes [*A publication*]
Sports Ill.... Sports Illustrated [*A publication*]
Sports Illus .. Sports Illustrated [*A publication*]
Sports Med ... Sports Medicine [*A publication*]
Sports Med (Auckland) ... Sports Medicine (Auckland) [*A publication*]
Sport Sociol Bul ... Sport Sociology Bulletin [*A publication*]
Sports Ret .. Sports Retailer [*A publication*]
Sports 'n Spokes ... Sports 'n Spokes Magazine [*A publication*]
Sports Turf Bull ... Sports Turf Bulletin [*A publication*]
Sport es Testn ... Sport es Testneveles [*A publication*]
Sporulation Germination Proc Int Spore Conf ... Sporulation and Germination. Proceedings. International Spore Conference [*A publication*]
SPOS .... Strong Point/Obstacle System [*Military*] (NVT)
SPOS .... Zorritos [*Peru*] [*ICAO location identifier*] (ICLI)
SP-OSO..... Shuttle Projects - Off-Site Offices [*NASA*] (GFGA)
Sposoby Zap Inf Besserebr Nositelyakh ... Sposoby Zapisi Informatsii na Besserebryanykh Nositelyakh [*A publication*]
SPOSS...... Society for the Promotion of Science and Scholarship (EA)
SPOT........ Satellite and Physicians Office Testing
SPOT........ Satellite Positioning and Tracking
SPOT........ Simulated Pave Penny Omnidirectional Target (MCD)
SPOT........ Skill in Personnel through On-Site Training [*Department of Labor*]
SPOT........ Smithsonian Precision Optical Tracking
SPOT........ Speed Position and Track (MCD)
Spot........... Spotlight [*Record label*] [*Australia*]
SPOT........ Symptom Pattern Observation Technique [*Aviation*]
SPOTR...... Special Projects Officer, Technical Representative [*Navy*] (DNAB)
SPOTREP ... Spot Report [*Military*] (NVT)
SPOTS ...... Sikorsky Program Operations Tracking System (MCD)
SPOTS ...... Slosson Post-Observational Testing Screen [*Educational test*]
Spott.......... Spottiswoode's Equity [*Scotland*] [*A publication*] (DLA)
Spott Eq Rep ... Spottiswoode's English Equity Reports [*A publication*] (DLA)
Spottis........ [*R.*] Spottiswoode's Scotch Court of Session Reports [*A publication*] (DLA)
Spottis CL & Eq Rep ... Common Law and Equity Reports, Published by Spottiswoode [*A publication*] (DLA)
Spottis Eq .. Spottiswoode's Equity [*Scotland*] [*A publication*] (DLA)
Spottis Pr ... Spottiswoode's Practices [*Scotland*] [*A publication*] (DLA)
Spottis St ... Spottiswoode's Styles [*Scotland*] [*A publication*] (DLA)
Spottisw .... Spottiswoode's Equity [*Scotland*] [*A publication*] (DLA)
Spottisw Eq ... Spottiswoode's Equity [*Scotland*] [*A publication*] (DLA)
SPOTY ...... Single Parent of the Year

SPOUT...... System Peripheral Output Utility [*Nuclear energy*] (NRCH)
SPOV......... Leon Velarde/Shiringayoc O Hda. Mejia [*Peru*] [*ICAO location identifier*] (ICLI)
SPOY........ Atico [*Peru*] [*ICAO location identifier*] (ICLI)
SPP .... Menongue [*Angola*] [*Airport symbol*] (OAG)
SPP .... New York Society for the Prevention of Pauperism
SPP .... Peace Corps School Partnership Program [*Later, PCPP*] (EA)
SPP .... Safe-Practice Procedure (MCD)
SPP .... St. Paul [*Alaska*] [*Seismograph station code, US Geological Survey*] [*Closed*] (SEIS)
SPP .... St. Paul Public Library, St. Paul, MN [*OCLC symbol*] (OCLC)
SPP .... St. Philips Resources [*Vancouver Stock Exchange symbol*]
SPP .... Scientific Passenger Pod [*NASA*]
SPP .... Sclerosing Papillomatous Pattern [*Medicine*]
SPP .... Scott Paper Co. [*NYSE symbol*] (SPSG)
SPP .... Secular Periodic Perturbation
SPP .... Sensor-Pointing Platform (SSD)
SPP .... Sequenced Packet Protocol [*Data processing*] (PCM)
SPP .... Severe Parental Punishment
SPP .... Sexuality Preference Profile
SPP .... Signal Processing Peripheral
SPP .... Signal Processing Program [*BV Engineering*] [*Data processing*]
SPP .... Simulation Planning Panel [*NASA*] (NASA)
SPP .... Society for Pediatric Psychology (EA)
SPP .... Society of Private Printers [*Middlesex, England*]
SPP .... Society of Professional Pilots (EA)
SPP .... Sodium Pentachlorophenoxide [*Insecticide*]
SPP .... Soeurs de la Providence de Portieux (EAIO)
SPP .... Solar Photometry Probe (AAG)
SPP .... Solar Physics Payload [*NASA*] (MCD)
SPP .... Solar Pumped Plasma (SSD)
SPP .... Sole Parent's Pension
SPP .... Soluble Protein Preparation [*Biochemistry*]
SPP .... Song Position Pointer [*Data processing*] (PCM)
SPP .... Southwest Power Pool [*Regional power council*]
SPP .... Spare Parts Provisioning
SPP .... Special Proficiency Pay [*British military*] (DMA)
SPP .... Special Purpose Processor
SPP .... Specialist, Photographic Specialist [*Navy rating*]
SPP .... Specially Promoted Programme [*British*]
SPP .... Species [*Plural form*] [*Also, spp*]
SPP .... Sponsor Program Proposal (MCD)
SPP .... Spot Product Prices [*Database*] [*Petroleum Intelligence Weekly*] [*Information service or system*] (CRD)
SPP .... Standard Practice Procedures (MCD)
SPP .... Still Picture Projector (MSA)
SPP .... Stock Purchase Plan [*Offered by a company to its employees*]
SPP .... Straight Path Penetration
SPP .... Suprapubic Prostatectomy [*Medicine*]
SPP .... Surplus Personal Property
SPP .... Swaziland Progressive Party
SPP .... System Package Plan [*or Program*] [*Military*]
SPPA .... Puerto Ocopa [*Peru*] [*ICAO location identifier*] (ICLI)
SPPA .... Screen Process Printing Association [*Later, SPAI*] (EA)
SPPA .... Society for Philosophy and Public Affairs (EA)
SPPA .... Society for the Preservation of Poultry Antiquities (EA)
SP-PAI ...... Shuttle Projects - Project Assessment and Integration Staff [*NASA*] (GFGA)
SPPAY ...... Semipost-Pay, Pay-Station [*Telecommunications*] (TEL)
SP-PAY ..... Shuttle Projects - Payload Integration Office [*Kennedy Space Center*] [*NASA*] (NASA)
SPPB .... Sodium Pyrophosphate Buffer [*Analytical chemistry*]
SPPB .... Statens Psykologisk-Pedagogiska Bibliotek [*National Library for Psychology and Education*] [*Information service or system*] [*Sweden*] (IID)
SPPC .... Spare Parts Provisioning Card
SP-PCO ..... Shuttle Projects - Program Control Office [*NASA*] (GFGA)
SPPD .... Space Propulsion and Power Division [*NASA*]
SPPD......... Spin-Polarized Photoelectron Diffraction [*Physics*]
SPPE .... State per Pupil Expenditure [*Education*] (GFGA)
SPPF......... Seychelles People's Progressive Front (PPW)
SPPF......... Solid-Phase Pressure Forming [*Shell Chemical Co.*]
SPPG .... Paramonga [*Peru*] [*ICAO location identifier*] (ICLI)
SPPG .... Space Plasma Physics Payload Group [*NASA*] (SSD)
SPPGA ...... Society of Economic Paleontologists and Mineralogists. Pacific Section. Guidebooks [*A publication*]
SPPI .... Southern Production Program, Inc.
SPPI .... Symposium on the Preventability of Perinatal Injury
SPPIL........ Shuttle Preferred Pyrotechnic Items List [*NASA*] (NASA)
SPPK .... Studien zur Palaeographie und Papyruskunde [*C. Wessely*] [*A publication*] (BJA)
SPPL......... Spare Parts Provisioning List [*NASA*] (NASA)
SPPL......... Spark Plug
SPPL......... Statewide Public Library Interlibrary Loan and Reference Network [*Library network*]
SPPLB....... Science and Public Policy [*A publication*]
SPPLB....... Specialist, Photographer, Laboratory [*Navy rating*]
SPPLITT... Southern Pacific Pipelines and International Tank Terminals [*Two companies jointly building deepwater port to accommodate outsize oil carriers*]

SpPm	Biblioteca Publica, Palma De Mallorca, Spain [*Library symbol*] [*Library of Congress*] (LCLS)
SPPM	Pomacocha [*Peru*] [*ICAO location identifier*] (ICLI)
SPPM	Safe Passage Path Map (SAA)
SPPMA	Southern Pulp and Paper Manufacturer [*United States*] [*A publication*]
SPPMP	Specialist, Motion Picture Production [*Navy rating*]
SP-PMS	Shuttle Projects - Performance Management Systems Office [*NASA*] (GFGA)
SPPN	Society of Private and Pioneer Numismatics (EA)
SPPO	Scheduled Program Printout (NATG)
SPPO	Spacelab Payload Project Office [*NASA*]
SPPO	Special Projects Program Order (AAG)
SPPP	Huanacopampa [*Peru*] [*ICAO location identifier*] (ICLI)
SPPP	Spacelab Payloads Processing Project (NASA)
SPPP	Superior Performance Proficiency Pay (MCD)
SPPPA	Spartan Potential Production Problem Analysis [*Missiles*] (MCD)
SPPPA	Spartan Production Program Producibility Analysis [*Missiles*] (MCD)
SPPPG	Specialist, Photogrammetry [*Navy rating*]
SPPPM	Surveyor Project Policy and Procedure Manual [*NASA*]
SPPR	Special Peacetime Program Requirements [*DoD*]
SPPR	Specialist, Public Relations [*Coast Guard*]
Sp Pr Cas	Spinks' English Admiralty Prize Cases [*1854-56*] [*A publication*] (DLA)
SPPS	Semipost-Pay, Pay-Station [*Telecommunications*] (TEL)
SPPS	Solid-Phase Peptide Synthesis [*Biochemistry*]
SPPS	Special Products and Program Support
SPPS	Specialist, Port Security [*Coast Guard*]
SPPS	Stable Plasma Protein Solution [*Medicine*]
SPPS	Subsystem Program Preparation Support [*Programming language*] [*Data processing*]
SPPT	Southern Pacific Petroleum NL [*NASDAQ symbol*] (NQ)
SPPVM	Specialist, V-Mail [*Navy rating*]
SPPY	Chachapoyas [*Peru*] [*ICAO location identifier*] (ICLI)
SPQ	Memphis, TN [*Location identifier*] [*FAA*] (FAAL)
SPQ	San Pedro [*California*] [*Airport symbol*] [*Obsolete*] (OAG)
SPQ	Sandpiper Oil & Gas [*Vancouver Stock Exchange symbol*]
SPQ	Stanford Parent Questionnaire [*Psychology*]
SPQCR	Specialist, Communications Specialist, Cryptographer [*Navy rating*]
SPQIN	Specialist, Communications Specialist, Radio Intelligence [*Navy rating*]
SPQJ	Jaqui [*Peru*] [*ICAO location identifier*] (ICLI)
SPQN	Requena [*Peru*] [*ICAO location identifier*] (ICLI)
SPQR	Selected Product Quality Review [*DoD*]
SPQR	Senatus Populusque Romanus [*The Senate and People of Rome*] [*Latin*]
SPQR	Small Profits, Quick Returns
SPQR	Speed, Power, Quietness, and Reliability [*Automotive engineering*]
SPQRP	Specialist, Communications Specialist, Registered Publication Clerk [*Navy rating*]
SPQS	Self Profile Q-Sort [*Child development test*]
SPQT	Iquitos/Coronel FAP Francisco Secada Vignetta [*Peru*] [*ICAO location identifier*] (ICLI)
SPQTE	Specialist, Communications Specialist, Technician [*Navy rating*]
SPQU	Arequipa/Rodriguez Ballon [*Peru*] [*ICAO location identifier*] (ICLI)
SPR	Puerto Rico Reports, Spanish Edition [*A publication*] (DLA)
SPR	S-Band Planetary RADAR
SPR	St. Pierre [*Quebec*] [*Seismograph station code, US Geological Survey*] [*Closed*] (SEIS)
SPR	Sampling with Partial Replacement
SPR	San Pedro [*Belize*] [*Airport symbol*] (OAG)
SPR	Sandia Pulsed Reactor [*Nuclear energy*]
SPR	Sapper [*Military*]
SPR	Satellite Parametric Reduction
SPR	Scientific Process & Research, Inc. [*Information service or system*] (IID)
SPR	Seal Pressure Ratio
SPR	Seconds per Revolution [*or Rotation*] (NVT)
SPR	Secretary of the Air Force Program Review (MCD)
SPR	Semipermanent Repellent (ADA)
SPR	Send Priority and Route Digit [*Telecommunications*] (TEL)
SPR	Sense Printer
SPR	Sequential Probability Ratio [*Statistics*]
SPR	Serial Probe Recognition [*Psychometrics*]
SPR	Shock Position Ratio
SPR	Shortest Possible Route (MCD)
SPR	Silicon Power Rectifier
SPR	Simplified Practice Recommendation
SPR	Single-Ply Roofing
SPR	Single-Point Refueling (MCD)
SPR	Skin Potential Response [*Physiology*]
SPR	Slavistic Printings and Reprintings [*A publication*]
SPR	Society of Patient Representatives [*Later, NSPR*] (EA)
SPR	Society for Pediatric Radiology (EA)
SPR	Society for Pediatric Research (EA)

SPR	Society for Philosophy of Religion (EA)
SPR	Society for Psychical Research [*British*]
SPR	Society for Psychophysiological Research (EA)
SPR	Society for Psychosomatic Research (EAIO)
SPR	Software Problem Report [*NASA*] (NASA)
SPR	Solid-Phase Reactor
SPR	Solid Phase Receptacle [*Laboratory testing*]
SPR	Solid-Propellant Rocket
SPR	South Polar Region
SPR	Southern Poetry Review [*A publication*]
SPR	Spacer (AAG)
SPR	Spare [*Telecommunications*] (TEL)
SPR	Special Program Requirement (AFM)
SPR	Special Program Review [*Army*] (RDA)
SPR	Special Project Report
SPR	Special-Purpose RADAR
SPR	Special-Purpose Requirements [*Army*]
SPR	Specialist, Recruiter [*Navy rating*]
SPR	Specific Price Reduction
SPR	Spinster
SPR	Sponsor
Spr	Sprache [*A publication*]
Spr	Sprague's United States District Court (Admiralty) Decisions [*A publication*] (DLA)
SPR	Spratly Islands [*ANSI three-letter standard code*] (CNC)
SPR	Spring (MSA)
SPR	Springer Resources [*Vancouver Stock Exchange symbol*]
SPR	Sprinkler (AAG)
SPR	Statement of Procedural Rules [*A publication*] (DLA)
SPR	Sterling Capital Corp. [*AMEX symbol*] (SPSG)
SPR	Storage Protection Register
SPR	Strategic Petroleum Reserve [*Department of Energy*]
SPR	Strategic Planning Review (SSD)
SPR	Stroposcopic Pulse Radiolysis [*Physical chemistry*]
SPR	Structure-Property Relationship [*Chemistry*]
SPR	Sub Petito Remissionis [*With Request for Return*] [*Latin*]
SPR	Subcontractor Performance Review [*NASA*] (NASA)
SPR	Substance P Receptor [*Biochemistry*]
SPR	Sudden Pressure Relay
SPR	Sun Protection Required [*Identification system for heat-sensitive cargo*] [*Shipping*] (DCTA)
SPR	Supervisory Printer Read [*Data processing*] (OA)
SPR	Supplementary Progress Report
SPR	Supply Performance Report (CINC)
SPR	Support Period Requirement
SPR	Support Plans and Requirements
SPR	Surface Plasmon Resonance [*Physics*]
SPR	System Parameter Record [*Data processing*] (IBMDP)
SPR	System Performance Rating
SPR	System Problem Report (MCD)
SPR	System Program Review [*Military*] (AABC)
SPR's	Small Parcels and Rolls [*Postal Service*]
SPRA	Space Probe RADAR Altimeter (KSC)
SPRA	Special-Purpose Reconnaissance Aircraft [*Navy*]
SPRA	Sponsor's Profit and Risk Allowance [*Department of Housing and Urban Development*] (GFGA)
SPRACAY	Society for Prevention of Rock and Roll and Corruption of American Youth [*Organization in 1956 movie "Shake, Rattle and Roll"*]
Sprache und Datenverarb	Sprache und Datenverarbeitung [*A publication*]
Sprache Tech Zeit	Sprache im Technischen Zeitalter [*A publication*]
SPRAG	Spray Arrester Gear (MCD)
SPRAG	STS Payload Requirements and Analysis Group [*NASA*] (NASA)
Sprague	Sprague's United States District Court (Admiralty) Decisions [*A publication*] (DLA)
Sprague's J ME His	Sprague's Journal of Maine History [*A publication*]
Sprakvetensk Sallsk i Uppsala Forhandl	Sprakvetenskapliga Sallskapets i Uppsala Foerhandlingar [*A publication*]
SPRANS	Special Projects of Regional and National Significance [*HHS*]
SPRAT	Small Portable RADAR Torch
Spraw	Sprawozdania [*A publication*]
Spraw A	Sprawozdania Archeologiczne [*A publication*]
Spraw Kom Jez AU	Sprawozdania z Posiedzen Komisji Jezykowej Akademii Umietjetnosci [*A publication*]
Spraw Opolskie Tow Przyj Nauk Wydz Nauk Med	Sprawozdania Opolskie Towarzystwo Przyjaciol Nauk. Wydzial Nauk Medycznych [*A publication*]
Sprawozdania Kom Nauk PAN	Sprawozdania z Posiedzen Komisji Naukowych. Polskiej Akademii Nauk [*A publication*]
Spraw Posied Tow Nauk Warsz	Sprawozdania z Posiedzen Towarzystwa Naukowego Warszawskiego [*A publication*]
Spraw Poznan Tow Przyj Nauk	Sprawozdania Poznanskiego Towarzystwa Przyjaciol Nauk [*A publication*]
Spraw TNW	Sprawozdania z Posiedzen Towarzystwa Naukowego Warszawskiego [*A publication*]
Spraw Tow Nauk Lwowie	Sprawozdania Towarzystwa Naukowego we Lwowie [*A publication*]
Spraw Tow Nauk Toruniu	Sprawozdania Towarzystwa Naukowego w Toruniu [*A publication*]

Spraw Wroclaw Tow Nauk ... Sprawozdania Wroclawskiego Towarzystwa Naukowego [*A publication*]
Spraw Wroclaw Tow Nauk Ser A ... Sprawozdania Wroclawskiego Towarzystwa Naukowego. Seria A [*A publication*]
Spraw Wroclaw Tow Nauk Ser B ... Sprawozdania Wroclawskiego Towarzystwa Naukowego. Seria B [*A publication*]
SprB.......... Sprakliga Bidrag [*A publication*]
SPR BOG .. Springender Bogen [*Bouncing Bow*] [*Music*]
SPRC .... Seafood Products Research Center [*Public Health Service*] (GRD)
SPRC .... Self-Propelled Robot Craft (IEEE)
SPRC .... Society of Public Relations Counsellors
SPRCHTB ... Senior Parachutist Badge [*Military decoration*] (GFGA)
SPRCS....... Safe Passage Route Creation Sheet (SAA)
SPRD........ Science Policy Research Division [*of Congressional Research Service, Library of Congress*]
SPRD......... Spread (FAAC)
SPRD......... Survey of Primary Reading Development (AEBS)
SPRDA...... Solid Pipeline Research and Development Association (HGAA)
SPRDNG... Spreading [*Freight*]
SPRDR ...... Spreader (MSA)
SPRDS ...... Steam Pipe Rupture Detector System (IEEE)
SPRE .... Society of Park and Recreation Educators (EA)
SPRE .... Solid-Propellant Rocket Engine
SPRE .... Special Prefix Code [*Northern Telecom*] [*Telecommunications*]
SPREAD ... Spring Evaluation Analysis and Design (MCD)
SPREAD ... Supercomputer Project Research Experiment in Advanced Development [*Lawrence Livermore Laboratory, Los Alamos National Laboratory, and SRI*]
SPREC....... Specular Reflection Computer Program (MCD)
Sprechsaal Keram Glas Silik ... Sprechsaal fuer Keramik, Glas, Email, Silikate [*A publication*]
SPREE....... Solid-Propellant Exhaust Effects (MCD)
SPREE....... Structure Preserving Estimation (ADA)
SPREG ...... Speed Regulator
SPREP....... South Pacific Regional Environment Programme [*of the South Pacific Commission*] [*New Caledonia*]
SPRES....... Star Present (NASA)
S & P RES DIS ... Severn and Potomac Reserve District [*Marine Corps*]
SPRF .... Sandia Pulsed Reactor Facility [*Nuclear energy*]
SPRF .... Space Propulsion Research Facility (AAG)
SPRF .... Special-Purpose Receiving Facility
SPRG........ San Regis [*Peru*] [*ICAO location identifier*] (ICLI)
SPRG........ Social Policy Research Group, Inc. [*Information service or system*] (IID)
SPRG........ Spring
SPRG........ Sprinkling (MSA)
SPRH........ Spearhead Industries, Inc. [*NASDAQ symbol*] (NQ)
SPRI .... Scott Polar Research Institute [*Cambridge, England*]
SPRI .... Single Ply Roofing Institute (EA)
SPRI .... Social Problems Research Institute [*University of South Carolina at Columbia*] [*Research center*] (RCD)
SPRI .... Social Process Research Institute [*Research center*] (RCD)
SPRI .... Social Psychiatry Research Institute (EA)
SPRI .... Sperm Reservoir Length Index
SPRI .... Sugar Processing Research, Inc.
SPRIA .... Solid-Phase Radioimmunoassay [*or Radioimmunoprecipitation Assay*] [*Clinical medicine*]
Springer Proc Phys ... Springer Proceedings in Physics [*A publication*]
Springer Semin Immunopathol ... Springer Seminars in Immunopathology [*A publication*]
Springer Ser Biophys ... Springer Series in Biophysics [*A publication*]
Springer Ser Chem Phys ... Springer Series in Chemical Physics [*A publication*]
Springer Ser Electrophys ... Springer Series in Electrophysics [*A publication*]
Springer Ser Health Care Soc ... Springer Series on Health Care and Society [*A publication*]
Springer Ser Inform Sci ... Springer Series in Information Sciences [*A publication*]
Springer Ser Optical Sci ... Springer Series in Optical Sciences [*A publication*]
Springer Ser Opt Sci ... Springer Series in Optical Sciences [*A publication*]
Springer Ser Solid-State Sci ... Springer Series in Solid-State Sciences [*A publication*]
Springer Ser Statist ... Springer Series in Statistics [*A publication*]
Springer Ser Synergetics ... Springer Series in Synergetics [*A publication*]
Springer Tracts Modern Phys ... Springer Tracts in Modern Physics [*A publication*]
Springer Tracts Mod Phys ... Springer Tracts in Modern Physics [*A publication*]
Springer Tracts Nat Philos ... Springer Tracts in Natural Philosophy [*A publication*]
Springs....... Spring Industries, Inc. [*Associated Press abbreviation*] (APAG)
SPRINT..... Selective Printing [*Data processing*]
SPRINT..... Solid-Propellant Rocket Intercept Missile [*ARPA/AMC*]
SPRINT..... Southern Pacific Communications' Switched Long Distance Service [*Telecommunications*] (TEL)
SPRINT..... Spare Parts Review Initiatives [*Army*] (RDA)
SPRINT..... Special Police Radio Inquiry Network [*New York City*]
Sprint........ Sprint Corp. [*Associated Press abbreviation*] (APAG)
SPRINT..... Strategic Programme for Innovation and Technology Transfer [*European Commission*]

SPRINTER ... Specification of Profits with Interaction under Trial and Error Response
Spr Int L .... Sprague on International Law [*A publication*] (DLA)
SPRITE..... Signal Processing in the Element (MCD)
SPRITE..... Solid-Propellant Rocket Ignition Test and Evaluation (KSC)
SPRITE..... Surveillance, Patrol, Reconnaissance, Intelligence Gathering, Target Designation, and Electronic Warfare [*Unmanned aircraft*] [*Military*]
SPRJ......... Self-Powered Reference Junction
SPRK .... Sparkman Producing Co. [*NASDAQ symbol*] (NQ)
SprKJ........ Sprawozdania z Posiedzen Komisji Jezykowej Towarzystwa Naukowego Warszawskiego [*A publication*]
SPRKLG.... Sprinkling [*Freight*]
SPRKT ...... Sprocket (MSA)
SprKUL..... Sprawozdania z Czynnosci Wydawniczej i Posiedzen Naukowych Oraz Kronika Towarzystwa Naukowego Katolockiego Uniwersytetu Lubelskiego [*A publication*]
SPRL .... Space Physics Research Laboratory [*University of Michigan*] [*Research center*] (RCD)
SPRL .... Spiral (FAAC)
SprLTN ..... Sprawozdania z Czynnosci i Posiedzen Lodzkiego Towarzystwa Naukowego [*A publication*]
SPRM........ San Ramon/Capitan Alvarino [*Peru*] [*ICAO location identifier*] (ICLI)
SPRM........ Special Reamer [*Tool*] (AAG)
Spr Miedzyn ... Sprawy Miedzynarodowe [*A publication*]
Spr Miedzynar ... Sprawy Miedzynarodowe [*A publication*]
SPRO......... Services Public Relations Officer [*British military*] (DMA)
SPROE...... Software Protection [*A publication*]
S-P/ROM ... Slave Programmable Read-Only Memory
SPROM..... Switched Programmable Read-Only Memory
SPROPS..... Section Properties [*Camutek*] [*Software package*] (NCC)
SprPAUm.. Sprawozdania z Czynnosci i Posiedzen Polskiej Akademii Umiejetnosci [*A publication*]
SprPTPN... Sprawozdania Poznanskiego Towarzystwa Przyjaciol Nauk [*A publication*]
SPRR .... Selective Paramagnetic Relaxation Reagent [*Chemistry*]
SPRR .... Self-Propelled Recoilless Rifle [*British military*] (DMA)
SPRRS...... Southern Plains Range Research Station [*Oklahoma State University*] [*Research center*] (RCD)
SPRS .... Single Passenger Reservation System [*DoD*]
SPRS .... Society for the Promotion of Roman Studies (EAIO)
SPRS .... Special-Purpose RADAR Set
SPRS .... Student Proficiency Rating Scale
SPRS .... Sublime Power of the Royal Secret [*Freemasonry*] (ROG)
SprSUF...... Sprakvetenskapliga Sallskapets i Uppsala Foerhandlingar [*A publication*]
SPRT .... Rio Tigre [*Peru*] [*ICAO location identifier*] (ICLI)
SPRT .... Sequential Probability Ratio Test [*Statistics*]
SPRT .... Sportecular, Inc. [*Penfield, NY*] [*NASDAQ symbol*] (NQ)
SPRT .... Standard Platinum Resistance Thermometer
SPRT .... Support (MSA)
SPRT .... System Performance and Repeatability Test [*Military*] (CAAL)
SPRTAP..... Specially Prepared Tape Program (SAA)
SprTNW.... Sprawozdania z Posiedzen Towarzystwa Naukowego Warszawskiego [*A publication*]
SPRTSUP ... Sport Supply Group [*Associated Press abbreviation*] (APAG)
SprTT .... Sprawozdania Towarzystwa Naukowego w Toruniu [*A publication*]
SPRU......... Science Policy Research Unit [*Research center*] [*British*] (IRC)
SPRU......... Trujillo/Capitan Carlos Martinez de Pinillos - Huanchaco [*Peru*] [*ICAO location identifier*] (ICLI)
SPRUCE ... Special Programs and Rehabilitation under Unemployment Compensation [*Department of Labor*]
SprV.......... Sprachkunst (Vienna) [*A publication*]
SPS .... St. Patrick's Missionary Society [*Roman Catholic men's religious order*]
SPS .... Saint Patrick's Seminary [*Menlo Park, CA*]
SPS .... Samples per Second
SPS .... San Pedro De Poas [*Costa Rica*] [*Seismograph station code, US Geological Survey*] (SEIS)
SPS .... Satellite Power System (MCD)
SPS .... Satellite and Production Services [*Tallahassee, FL*] [*Telecommunications*] (TSSD)
SPS .... Saturn Parts Sales [*NASA*]
SPS .... Saturn Propulsion System [*NASA*]
SPS .... Scene per Second (MCD)
SPS .... Schedule Promulgated Separately [*Navy*] (NVT)
SPS .... Scheduled Passenger Service (IIA)
SPS .... School of Practical Science
SPS .... Scientific Power Switching
SPS .... Seamen's Protection Society [*A union*] [*British*]
SPS .... Second Preferred Stock [*Investment term*]
SPS .... Secondary Plant System [*Nuclear energy*] (NRCH)
SPS .... Secondary Power Source
SPS .... Secondary Power System [*or Subsystem*] (MCD)
SPS .... Secondary Propulsion System [*NASA*]
SPS .... Security Police Squadron [*Air Force*]
SPS .... Sekcja Pracy Spolecznej [*A publication*] (BJA)
SPS .... Self Protection System (MCD)
SPS .... Senior Private Secretary

SPS	Series-Parallel-Serial Configuration [*Electronics*] (MDG)
SPS	Service Propulsion System [*or Subsystem*] [*NASA*]
SPS	Servo Parameter Shift
SPS	Set Point Station
SpS............	Sharpshooter [*Military decoration*] (AABC)
SPS	Ship Planning System
SPS	Ship Program Schedule
SPS	Shipping/Production Scheduling
SPS	Shuttle Procedures Simulator [*NASA*] (NASA)
SPS	Signal Processing System (KSC)
SPS	Silent Propulsion System (MCD)
SPS	Simple Phrase System
SPS	Simplified Processing Station (MCD)
SPS	Simulated Parts Sketch (MCD)
SPS	Simulator Panel Set (MCD)
SPS	Sine Prole Superstite [*Without Surviving Issue*] [*Latin*]
SPS	Single-Pole Switch
SPS	Social Problems Series [*A publication*]
SPS	Socialist Party of Slovenia [*Political party*] (EY)
SPS	Socialistische Partij Suriname [*Surinam Socialist Party*] [*Political party*] (PPW)
SPS	Society of Pelvic Surgeons (EA)
SPS	Society for Pentecostal Studies (EA)
SPS	Society of Physics Students (EA)
SPS	Socijalisticka Partija Srbije [*Socialist Party of Serbia*] [*Political party*] (EY)
SPS	Sodium Polyanetholesulfonate [*Analytical biochemistry*]
SPS	Sodium Polystyrene Sulfonate [*Organic chemistry*]
SPS	Soft Particle Spectrometer [*Geophysics*]
SPS	Software Procurement Specification
SPS	Software Product Specification
SPS	Software Products Scheme [*Data processing*] (DCTA)
SPS	Solar Panel Substrate
SPS	Solar Power Satellite [*NASA*]
SPS	Solar Power System (MCD)
SPS	Solar Probe Spacecraft [*Pioneer satellite*]
SPS	Solar Proton Stream [*Geophysics*] (SAA)
SPS	Solid Phase Synthesis [*Chemistry*]
SPS	Soluble Polysaccharide of Soybean [*Food technology*]
SPS	SONAR Phase Shifter
SPS	South Pole Station [*National Weather Service*]
SPS	Southwestern Public Service Co. [*NYSE symbol*] (SPSG)
SPS	Sozialdemokratische Partei der Schweiz [*Social Democratic Party of Switzerland*] [*Political party*] (PPE)
SPS	Sozialdemokratische Partei Suedtirols [*Social Democratic Party of South Tirol*] [*Political party*] (PPE)
SPS	Space Planning System [*Applied Research of Cambridge Ltd.*] [*Software package*] (NCC)
SPS	Space Power System (CET)
SPS	Space Stories [*A publication*]
SPS	Spacecraft Propulsion System (AAG)
SP & S........	Special Processes and Sequencing (NASA)
SPS	Special-Purpose SONAR (MCD)
SPS	Special Services [*Military*]
SPS	Specialist, Personnel Supervisor [*Women's Reserve*] [*Navy rating*]
SPS	Specialist, Shore Patrol and Security [*Navy rating*]
SPS	Specimina Philologiae Slavicae [*A publication*]
SPS	Spectrum Planning Subcommittee [*FCC*]
SPS	Speed Switch (IEEE)
SPS	Spokane, Portland & Seattle Railway System [*AAR code*]
SPS	SPS Technologies, Inc. [*Formerly, Standard Pressed Steel Co.*] (MCD)
SPS	Stabilized Platform Subsystem (KSC)
SPS	Standard Pipe Size
SPS	Standard Port System (MCD)
SPS	Standard Positioning Service
SPS	Standard Process Specification (MCD)
SPS	Standard Project Storm [*Nuclear energy*] (NRCH)
SPS	Standby Power Source [*Electronics*]
SPS	State Permit System [*Environmental Protection Agency*] (GFGA)
SPS	Statement of Prior Submission (NASA)
SPS	Static Power System
SPS	Static Pressure System
SPS	Statistical Performance Standards [*Navy*] (NG)
SPS	Stator Pivot Seal
SPS	Status Projection System
SPS	Steady Potential Shift
SPS	Steampipe Survey
SPS	Stereo Photographic System
SPS	Stichting Plurale Samenlevingen [*Foundation for the Study of Plural Societies - FSPS*] (EAIO)
SPS	Stored Program Simulator
SPS	Strategic Planning Society [*Formerly, Society for Strategic and Long Range Planning*] (EA)
SPS	Strategic Planning Staff [*Social Security Administration*]
SPS	Strategical Planning Section [*Joint Planning Staff*] [*World War II*]
SPS	Stratford Papers on Shakespeare [*A publication*]
SPS	String Processing System [*Word processing software*]

SPS	Student Profile Section [*of the American College Testing Test Battery*]
SPS	Submarine Piping System
SPS	Submerged Production System [*Deepwater platform*] [*Humble Oil*]
SPS	Subsea Production System [*Petroleum technology*]
SPS	Sucrose-Phosphate Synthase [*An enzyme*]
SPS	Suicide Probability Scale [*Personality development test*] [*Psychology*]
SPS	Sulfite-Polymyxin-Sulfadiazine [*Agar*] [*Microbiology*]
SPS	Summit Power Station [*Nuclear energy*] (NRCH)
SPS	Super Proton Synchrotron [*Particle physics*]
SPS	Supplementary Protection System [*Nuclear energy*] (NRCH)
SPS	Supply Point Simulation (MCD)
SPS	Symbolic Programming System [*Data processing*]
SPS	Symbols per Second [*Data processing*]
SPS	System Performance Score [*Telecommunications*] (TEL)
SPS	System Performance Simulation
SPS	Systemic Progressive Sclerosis [*Medicine*] (AAMN)
SPS	Wichita Falls [*Texas*] [*Airport symbol*] (OAG)
SPSA	Casma [*Peru*] [*ICAO location identifier*] (ICLI)
SPSA	Senate Press Secretaries Association (EA)
SPSA	Society of Philippine Surgeons in America (EA)
SPSA	Special Projects School for Air
SpSAG	Archivo General de Indias [*Archives of the Indies*], Seville, Spain [*Library symbol*] [*Library of Congress*] (LCLS)
SPSBDR	Special Publications. Seto Marine Biological Laboratory. Series IV [*A publication*]
SPSC.........	Saharan People's Support Committee (EA)
SPSC.........	Seventy Plus Ski Club (EA)
SP/SC.......	Shield Plug/Support Cylinder [*Nuclear energy*] (NRCH)
SPSC.........	Signal Processing and Spectral Control
SPSC.........	Space Power Systems Conference
SPSC.........	Standard Performance Summary Charts (AAG)
SPSCR	Special Screw
SPSD	Space Power Systems Division [*NASA*]
SPSDC......	Surface and Defect Properties of Solids [*A publication*]
SP-SDF	Socialist Party - Social Democratic Federation [*Later, Socialist Party of the United States of America*] (EA)
SPSDM	Society for the Philosophical Study of Dialectical Materialism (EA)
SPSDS	Ship's Passive Surveillance and Detection System [*Navy*] (CAAL)
SPSE.........	Society of Photographic Scientists and Engineers (EA)
SPSE.........	Special Purpose Support Equipment
SPSEA	Soviet Physics. Semiconductors [*English translation*] [*A publication*]
SPSEE3	Special Publication. South Australia Department of Mines and Energy [*A publication*]
Sp & Sel Cas ...	Special and Selected Law Cases [*1648*] [*England*] [*A publication*] (DLA)
SPSF.........	Self-Propagating-Star Formation [*Galactic science*]
SPSF.........	Society of the President Street Fellows (EA)
SPSFM	St. Patrick's Society for the Foreign Missions [*See also SSPME*] [*Kiltegan, County Wicklow, Republic of Ireland*] (EAIO)
SP/SHLD ...	Splash Shield [*Automotive engineering*]
SPSHP	Special Shaped
SPSHS	Stanford Profile Scales of Hypnotic Susceptibility [*Psychology*]
SPSI.........	Serikat Pelajaran Seluruh Indonesia [*Sailors' Union of Indonesia*]
SPSI.........	Society for the Promotion of Scientific Industry [*British*]
SPSJ	San Jose De Sisa [*Peru*] [*ICAO location identifier*] (ICLI)
SPSL.........	Lamas [*Peru*] [*ICAO location identifier*] (ICLI)
SPSL.........	Socialist Party of Sri Lanka
SPSL.........	Society for the Philosophy of Sex and Love (EA)
SPSL.........	Society for the Protection of Science and Learning [*British*]
SPSL.........	Spare Parts Selection List
SPSLGI	Society for the Psychological Study of Lesbian and Gay Issues (EA)
SPSM	Socialist Party of San Marino [*Political party*] (EAIO)
SPSM	Society for the Philosophical Study of Marxism (EA)
SPSM	Supply Point Simulation Model (MCD)
SPSMDQ ..	Special Publications. Society for General Microbiology [*A publication*]
SPSME......	Spacelab Payload Standard Modular Electronics (MCD)
SP-SMO....	Shuttle Projects - Site Management Office [*NASA*] (GFGA)
SPSN	Submitted Package Sequence Number (MCD)
SPSO	Pisco [*Peru*] [*ICAO location identifier*] (ICLI)
SPSO	Senior Personnel Staff Officer [*Air Force*] [*British*]
SPSO	Senior Principal Scientific Officer [*Ministry of Agriculture, Fisheries, and Food*] [*British*]
SPSP........	St. Peter and St. Paul [*The Papal seal*]
SPSP........	Solid-Propellant Surveillance Panel [*Military*]
SPSP.........	Spare Parts Support Package
SPSP-AGE ...	Spare Parts Support Package for Aerospace Ground Equipment (MCD)
SPSPCY	Specialist Periodical Reports. Spectroscopic Properties of Inorganic and Organometallic Compounds [*A publication*]
SPSPS	Specialist, Personnel Supervisor, V-10 [*Navy rating*]
SPSQ	Satisfaction with Performance Scaled Questionnaire

SpsQualBad ... Sharpshooter Qualification Badge [*Military decoration*]   (AABC)
SPSRA....... Space Science Reviews [*A publication*]
SPSS......... Masisea [*Peru*] [*ICAO location identifier*]   (ICLI)
SPSS......... Shield Plug Storage Station [*Nuclear energy*]   (NRCH)
SPSS......... Single Pulse Selection System
SPSS......... Society of the Priests of St. Sulpice [*See also CPSS*] [*Paris, France*]   (EAIO)
SPSS......... Statistical Package for the Social Sciences [*Programming language*] [*1970*]
SPS-SCWG ... Spanish Philatelic Society Spanish Civil War Study Group [*Defunct*]   (EA)
SPSSI........ Society for the Psychological Study of Social Issues   (EA)
Sp St........... Private and Special Laws [*A publication*]   (DLA)
SPST......... Single-Pole, Single-Throw [*Switch*]
SPST......... Symonds Picture-Story Test [*Psychology*]
SPST......... Tarapoto [*Peru*] [*ICAO location identifier*]   (ICLI)
SPSTec...... SPS Technologies, Inc. [*Associated Press abbreviation*]   (APAG)
SPSTNC... Single-Pole, Single-Throw, Normally-Closed [*Switch*]
SPSTNO ... Single-Pole, Single-Throw, Normally-Open [*Switch*]
SPSTNODM ... Single-Pole, Single-Throw, Normally-Open, Double-Make [*Switch*]
SPSTP....... Solid-Propellant Rocket Static Test Panel [*Military*]
SPS Tr....... SPS Transaction Services, Inc. [*Associated Press abbreviation*]   (APAG)
SPSTSW ... Single-Pole, Single-Throw Switch
SPSW........ Single-Pole Switch
S/PSWO ... Service/Parts Sales Work Order   (MCD)
SPSWO..... Spare Parts Sales Work Order
S Psy.......... Social Psychology Quarterly [*A publication*]
SPT............ Albuquerque, NM [*Location identifier*] [*FAA*]   (FAAL)
SPT............ Openbaar Vervoer [*A publication*]
SPT............ Piedmont Technical College, Greenwood, SC [*OCLC symbol*]   (OCLC)
SPT............ Scaled-Particle Theory
SPT............ School of Physical Training [*British*]
SPT............ Scientist-Pilot [*NASA*]   (KSC)
SPT............ Seaport
SPT............ Sectors per Track
SPT............ Selective Population Transfer [*Physics*]
SPT............ Sense Printer Test   (SAA)
Spt.............. September   (CDAI)
SPT............ Septic [*Classified advertising*]   (ADA)
SPT............ Septuple   (MSA)
SPT............ Shaft Position Transducer
SPT............ Shared Page Table [*Data processing*]   (OA)
SPT............ Ship Position Transmitter
SPT............ Shipper Pays Taxes
SPT............ Silicon Planar Transistor
SPT............ Silicon-Powered Transistor
SPT............ Skin Prick Test [*Immunology*]
SPT............ Slowest Processing Time
SPT............ Small Perturbation Theory
SPT............ Socialist Party of Thailand [*Political party*]   (FEA)
SPT............ Society of Painters in Tempera   (EA)
SPT............ Society for Philosophy and Technology   (EA)
SPT............ Society of Photo-Technologists   (EA)
SPT............ Society of Projective Techniques [*Later, SPA*]   (EA)
SPT............ Sodium Pyridinethione [*Organic chemistry*]
SPT............ Sogepet Ltd. [*Toronto Stock Exchange symbol*]
SPT............ Solar Panel Technology   (SSD)
SPT............ Sound-Powered Telephone
SPT............ South Point [*Hawaii*] [*Seismograph station code, US Geological Survey*]   (SEIS)
SPT............ Space Power Tool
SPT............ Space Travel [*A publication*]
SPT............ Span East Airlines, Inc. [*Miami, FL*] [*FAA designator*]   (FAAC)
SpT............ Spanish Telefunken [*Record label*]
SPT............ Spare Parts Transfer
SPT............ Special Perishable Tool   (MCD)
SPT............ Special Purpose Test [*Nuclear energy*]   (NRCH)
SP T........... Special Term [*Legal term*]   (DLA)
SPT............ Specialist, Teacher [*Navy rating*]
SpT............ Speech Teacher [*A publication*]
SPT............ Spirit
spt.............. Spiritus [*Spirit*] [*Latin*] [*Pharmacy*]   (MAE)
SPT............ Split   (MSA)
SPT............ Spraytight
Spt.............. Spritsail [*Ship's rigging*]   (DS)
SPT............ Sputum
SPT............ Standard Penetration Test [*Nuclear energy*]   (NRCH)
SPT............ Star Point Transfer [*Photography*]   (OA)
SPT............ Static Pressure Transducer
SPT............ Streptomycin Phosphotransferase [*An enzyme*]
SPT............ Structural Programming Technique
SPT............ Supervisory Potential Test
SPT............ Support   (AFM)
SPT............ Symbolic Play Test [*Child development test*]
SPT............ Symbolic Program Tape [*Data processing*]   (IEEE)
SPT............ Symbolic Program Translator [*Data processing*]   (IEEE)

SPT............ System Page Table [*Telecommunications*]   (TEL)
SPT............ System Parameter Table [*Data processing*]   (IBMDP)
SPT............ System Planning Team [*Military*]   (AFIT)
SP3T......... Single-Pole, Triple-Throw [*Switch*]   (IEEE)
SP4T......... Single-Pole, Quadruple-Throw [*Switch*]   (IEEE)
SPTA......... Nauta [*Peru*] [*ICAO location identifier*]   (ICLI)
SPTA .... Southern Paper Trade Association [*Defunct*]   (EA)
SPTA .... Southern Pressure Treaters Association   (EA)
Sp Tax Rul ... Special Tax Ruling [*Internal Revenue Service*] [*United States*] [*A publication*]   (DLA)
SPTC .... Share-Purchase Tax Credit [*Canada*]
SPTC .... Specified Period of Time Contract
SPTC .... Studies in Physical and Theoretical Chemistry [*Elsevier Book Series*] [*A publication*]
SPTCDZ.... Studies in Physical and Theoretical Chemistry [*Elsevier Book Series*] [*A publication*]
SPTCEN.... Support Center [*Army*]
SPTD........ Signal Processor Techniques Department
SPTD........ Supplemental Provisioning Technical Documentation [*NASA*]   (NASA)
SPTE......... Special Purpose Test Equipment   (MCD)
SPTE .... Teresita [*Peru*] [*ICAO location identifier*]   (ICLI)
SPTEA ..... Single Persons for Tax Equality Association   (EAIO)
SPTF......... Screen Printing Technical Foundation   (EA)
SPTF......... Signal Processing Test Facility
SPTF......... Social Progress Trust Fund [*Inter-American Development Bank*]
SPTF......... Sodium Pump Test Facility [*Energy Research and Development Administration*]
SPTF......... Support Flight [*Military*]
SPTG .... Support Group [*Military*]
SPTH........ Systolic Threshold Pressure [*Cardiology*]
SPT-HP..... Scholastic Proficiency Test - Higher Primary Level [*Educational test*] [*South Africa*]
SPTI .... Puerto Inca [*Peru*] [*ICAO location identifier*]   (ICLI)
SPTI .... Senior Physical Training Instructor [*British military*]   (DMA)
SPTK .... Sports-Tech, Inc. [*Formerly, Bristol Holdings, Inc.*] [*NASDAQ symbol*]   (SPSG)
SPTL .... Society of Public Teachers of Law [*British*]   (DLA)
SPTL .... Support Line [*Military*]
SPTM .... Spectrum Laboratories, Inc. [*NASDAQ symbol*]   (NQ)
SPTN .... Spill Technology Newsletter [*A publication*]
SPTN .... Tacna [*Peru*] [*ICAO location identifier*]   (ICLI)
SPTO .... Sporto Corp. [*Boston, MA*] [*NASDAQ symbol*]   (NQ)
SPTP .... Special-Purpose Test Program   (MCD)
SPTP .... Talara/El Pato [*Peru*] [*ICAO location identifier*]   (ICLI)
SPT & PA ... Society for Projective Techniques and Personality Assessment [*Later, SPA*]
SPTPA....... Soviet Physics. Technical Physics [*English Translation*] [*A publication*]
SPTPN ...... Sprawozdania Poznanskiego Towarzystwa Przyjaciol Nauk [*A publication*]
SP(TR)...... Specialist (Transportation) [*Coast Guard*]
SPTR .... SpecTran Corp. [*NASDAQ symbol*]   (NQ)
SPTR .... Tournavista [*Peru*] [*ICAO location identifier*]   (ICLI)
SPTRJ....... Self-Powered Thermocouple Reference Junction
Sp Trs .... Special Troops [*Army*]
SPTS......... Spirits
SPTS......... Sport's Restaurants [*NASDAQ symbol*]   (NQ)
S & PTS..... Standard & Poor's Trading Systems [*Standard & Poor's Corp.*] [*Information service or system*]   (IID)
SPTS......... Stock Positioning and Transportation Study [*DoD*]
SPTS......... Support Squadron [*Air Force*]
SPTSq....... Support Squadron [*Air Force*]
SptSu .... Sport Supply Group [*Associated Press abbreviation*]   (APAG)
SPTT......... Single-Pole, Triple-Throw [*Switch*]   (CET)
SPTU......... Puerto Maldonado/Padre Aldamiz [*Peru*] [*ICAO location identifier*]   (ICLI)
SPTUF ...... South Pacific Trade Union Forum [*14-nation group opposed to nuclear testing and dumping in the Pacific*]
SPTW........ Single-Pedestal Typewriter [*Desk*]
SPTWC ..... Salle Palasz and Tri-Weapon Club   (EA)
SPU........... Mount Spur [*Alaska*] [*Seismograph station code, US Geological Survey*]   (SEIS)
SPU........... S-Band Polar Ultra
SPU........... Salinas Public Library, Salinas, CA [*OCLC symbol*]   (OCLC)
SPU........... School Personnel Utilization
SPU........... Service Propulsion Unit
SPU........... Signal Processing Unit
SPU........... Slave Processing Unit
SPU........... Smallest Publishable Unit
SPU........... Society for Pediatric Urology   (EA)
SPU........... Southeast Airmotive Corp. [*Charlotte, NC*] [*FAA designator*]   (FAAC)
SPU........... Specialist, Utility [*Women's Reserve*] [*Navy rating*]
SPU........... Split [*Former Yugoslavia*] [*Airport symbol*]   (OAG)
SPU........... Statutes of Practical Utility [*A publication*]   (APTA)
SPU........... Student Peace Union [*Defunct*]   (EA)
SPU........... Subsurface Propulsion Unit
SPU........... Supertech Industries [*Vancouver Stock Exchange symbol*]
SPU........... System Partitioning Unit [*Data processing*]

SPUC......... Huamachuco [*Peru*] [*ICAO location identifier*]   (ICLI)
SPUC......... Society for the Protection of Unborn Children   (EA)
SPUD......... One Potato 2, Inc. [*NASDAQ symbol*]   (NQ)
SPUD......... St. Paul Union Depot Co. [*AAR code*]
SPUD......... Sniff, Paw, Urinate, and Defecate [*Ungulate territorial marking procedure*]
SPUD......... Society for Prevention of Unwholesome Diet [*National Potato Council*]
SPUD......... Solar Power Unit Demonstrator
Spud........... Spudasmata [*A publication*]
SPUD......... Stored Program Universal Demonstrator
SPUK......... Special Projects, United Kingdom
SPUN........ Society for the Protection of the Unborn through Nutrition   (EA)
SPUP......... Seychelles People's United Party [*Political party*]   (PPW)
SPUR......... Piura/Capitan Concha [*Peru*] [*ICAO location identifier*]   (ICLI)
SPUR......... San Francisco Planning and Urban Research Association [*California*] [*Information service or system*]   (IID)
SPUR......... Single Precision Unpacked Rounded [*floating-point package*] [*Computer program system*] [*Sperry Rand Corp.*]
SPUR......... Software Package for Unique Reports   (GFGA)
SPUR......... Source Program Utility Routine
SPUR......... Space Power Unit Reactor [*Air Force*]
SPUR......... Special Purchase Office [*DoD*]
SPUR......... Support for Projects Under Research [*British*]
SPUR......... Support for Promoting the Utilization of Resources [*Esso Education Foundation*]
SPUR......... Symbolic Processing Using RISC [*Reduced Instruction Set Computer*]
SPURM..... Special Purpose Unilateral Repetitive Modulation   (IEEE)
SPURT...... Small Primate Unrestrained Test
SPURT...... Spinning Unguided Rocket Trajectory
SPURV...... Self-Propelled Underwater Research Vehicle
SP-USA..... Socialist Party of the United States of America   (EA)
SP-USA..... Student Pugwash (USA)   (EA)
SPUTA...... Scientific Papers. College of General Education. University of Tokyo [*A publication*]
SPV............ Sa-Pa [*Vietnam*] [*Seismograph station code, US Geological Survey*]   (SEIS)
SPV............ Sensor Payload Vehicle
SPV............ Shope Papilloma Virus
SPV............ Slow-Phase Velocity [*Ophthalmology*]
SPV............ Space Adventures [*A publication*]
SpV............ Spanish RCA Victor [*Record label*]
SPV............ Special-Purpose Vehicle [*Military*]
SPV............ Specialist, Transport Airman [*Navy rating*]
SPV............ Specification Performance Validation [*Military*]   (CAAL)
SPV............ Split-Product Vaccine [*Immunology*]
SPV............ STN Shop Television Network Ltd. [*Vancouver Stock Exchange symbol*]
SPV............ Storage Process Vent [*Nuclear energy*]   (NRCH)
SPV............ Storage Protect Violation   (CMD)
SPV............ Sulfophosphovanillin (Reaction) [*Clinical chemistry*]
SPV............ Sun Probe near Limb of Venus [*Angle*]
SPV............ Surface Photovoltage [*Photovoltaic energy systems*]
SPV............ Survey of Personal Values [*Psychology*]
SPVA......... Society for the Preservation of Variety Arts   (EA)
SPVEA...... Superintendencia do Plano de Valorizacao Economica da Amazonia [*Brazil*]
SPVIEU..... Spatial Vision [*A publication*]
SPVL......... Caraveli [*Peru*] [*ICAO location identifier*]   (ICLI)
SPVLI........ Single Premium Variable Life Investment [*Insurance*]
SPVN........ Society of Peripheral Vascular Nursing   (EA)
SPVN........ Supervision   (MSA)
SPVOL...... Specific Volume   (DEN)
SPVPF....... Shuttle Payload Vertical Processing Facility [*NASA*]   (MCD)
SPVR........ Storage Process Vent Room [*Nuclear energy*]   (NRCH)
SPVR........ Vitor/San Isidro [*Peru*] [*ICAO location identifier*]   (ICLI)
Spvry Mgt ... Supervisory Management [*A publication*]
SPVS......... Supervisors Section [*American Association of School Librarians*]
Spvsr......... Supervisor
SPW.......... Self-Protection Weapon
SPW.......... Seward Park [*Washington*] [*Seismograph station code, US Geological Survey*]   (SEIS)
SPW.......... Shipment Planning Worksheet
SPW.......... Shipping World and Shipbuilder [*A publication*]
SPW.......... Spaceway Science Fiction [*A publication*]
SPW.......... Spare Parts Withdrawal   (MCD)
SPW.......... Special Warfare   (NVT)
SPW.......... Specialist, Chaplain's Assistant [*Navy rating*]
SPW.......... Spencer [*Iowa*] [*Airport symbol*]   (OAG)
SPW.......... SPX Corp. [*Formerly, Sealed Power Corp.*] [*NYSE symbol*]   (SPSG)
SPW.......... Surface Plasma Wave
SPW.......... Wofford College, Spartanburg, SC [*OCLC symbol*]   (OCLC)
SPWA....... Southern Peanut Warehousemen's Association   (EA)
SPWA....... Steel Products Warehouse Association
SPWAO..... Small Press Writers and Artists Organization   (EA)
SPWAR..... Special Warfare
SPWC....... Society for the Punishment of War Criminals   (EA)

SPWG........ Space Parts Working Group
SPWL........ Single Premium Whole Life Insurance Policy
SPWLA ..... Society of Professional Well Log Analysts   (EA)
SPWLA Logging Symp Trans ... SPWLA [*Society of Professional Well Log Analysts*] Logging Symposium. Transactions [*A publication*]
SPWM....... Single-Sided Pulse Width Modulation [*Telecommunications*]
SPWP........ Society of Prayer for World Peace   (EAIO)
SPWR........ Small Pressurized Water Reactor
SPWS........ Self-Protection Weapon System
SPWS .... Shipment Planning Worksheet   (MCD)
SPWSM..... Spanish War Service Medal
SPWVSRA ... Selected Papers. West Virginia Shakespeare and Renaissance Association [*A publication*]
SPWWIII.. Society for the Prevention of World War III [*Defunct*]
SPX............ League City, TX [*Location identifier*] [*FAA*]   (FAAL)
SPX............ Simplex Circuit
SPX............ Simplex Instrument [*Telegraphy*]
SPX............ Spirit Petroleum [*Vancouver Stock Exchange symbol*]
SPX............ Superheat Power Experiment [*Nuclear energy*]
SPXAC ...... Specialist, Archivist [*Navy rating*]
SPXAR ..... Specialist, Artist [*Navy rating*]
SPXBL...... Specialist, Ballistics [*Navy rating*]
SPXCC ...... Specialist, Cable Censor [*Navy rating*]
SPXCG ...... Specialist, Crystal Grinder [*Navy rating*]
SPX Cp ...... SPX Corp. [*Formerly, Sealed Power Corp.*] [*Associated Press abbreviation*]   (APAG)
SPXCT....... Specialist, Cartographer [*Navy rating*]
SPXDI ...... Specialist, Discharge Interviewer [*Navy rating*]
SPXED ...... Specialist, Engineering Draftsman [*Navy rating*]
SPXFP....... Specialist, Fingerprint Expert [*Navy rating*]
SPXGU ..... Specialist, Gauge Specialist [*Navy rating*]
SPXID ...... Specialist, Intelligence Duties [*Navy rating*]
SPXIR....... Specialist, Interpreter [*Navy rating*]
SPXJO....... Specialist, Journalist [*Navy rating*]
SPXKP...... Specialist, Key Punch Operator and Supervisor [*Navy rating*]
SPXNC ..... Specialist, Naval Correspondent [*Navy rating*]
SPXOP...... Specialist, Special Project [*Navy rating*]
SPXPC...... Specialist, Position Classifier [*Navy rating*]
SPXPI....... Specialist, Pigeon Trainer [*Navy rating*]
SPXPL...... Specialist, Plastic Expert [*Navy rating*]
SPXPR...... Specialist, Public Information [*Navy rating*]
SPXQM..... Specialist, Operations - Plotting and Chart Work [*Navy rating*]
SPXRL...... Specialist, Research Laboratory [*Navy rating*]
SPXRS....... Specialist, Armed Forces Radio Service and Special Naval Radio Units [*Navy rating*]
SPXSB....... Specialist, Telephone Switchboard Operator and Supervisor [*Navy rating*]
SPXST....... Specialist, Strategic Services [*Navy rating*]
SPXTD...... Specialist, Topographic Draftsman [*Navy rating*]
SPXTS....... Specialist, Air Stations Operations Desk - Time Shack [*Navy rating*]
SPXVA ..... Specialist, Visual Training Aids [*Navy rating*]
s-py---........ Paraguay [*MARC geographic area code*] [*Library of Congress*]   (LCCP)
SPY........... Saint Paul Island, AK [*Location identifier*] [*FAA*]   (FAAL)
SPY........... San Pedro [*Ivory Coast*] [*Airport symbol*]   (OAG)
SPY........... Spectra-Physics, Inc. [*NYSE symbol*]   (SPSG)
SPY........... Square Pyramidal [*Organic chemistry*]
SPY........... Standard & Poor's Deposit Receipts [*AMEX symbol*]   (SPSG)
SPYA......... Luya [*Peru*] [*ICAO location identifier*]   (ICLI)
SPYC......... Yarinacocha [*Peru*] [*ICAO location identifier*]   (ICLI)
SPYL .... Talara/Capitan Montes [*Peru*] [*ICAO location identifier*]   (ICLI)
SPYO......... Pacasmayo [*Peru*] [*ICAO location identifier*]   (ICLI)
SPYR .... Sprayer   (MSA)
SPYU........ Yauca [*Peru*] [*ICAO location identifier*]   (ICLI)
SPZ........... Spar Aerospace Ltd. [*Toronto Stock Exchange symbol*]
SPZ........... Springdale [*Arkansas*] [*Airport symbol*]   (OAG)
SPZ........... Submarine Patrol Zone [*Navy*]   (NVT)
SPZ........... Sulfinpyrazone [*Uricosuric compound*]
SPZA......... Nazca [*Peru*] [*ICAO location identifier*]   (ICLI)
SPZH......... Pachiza [*Peru*] [*ICAO location identifier*]   (ICLI)
SPZK .... Sotziki [*Peru*] [*ICAO location identifier*]   (ICLI)
SPZO......... Cuzco/Velazco Astete [*Peru*] [*ICAO location identifier*]   (ICLI)
SPZT .... Chazuta [*Peru*] [*ICAO location identifier*]   (ICLI)
SQ.............. E. R. Squibb & Sons [*Research code symbol*]
SQ.............. Safety Quotient
SQ.............. Sequens [*Following*] [*Latin*]
SQ.............. Shakespeare Quarterly [*A publication*]
SQ.............. Sick Quarters [*Navy*] [*British*]
SQ.............. Singapore Airlines Ltd. [*ICAO designator*]   (FAAC)
SQ.............. Situation Questionnaire
SQ.............. Social Quotient [*Psychology*]
SQ.............. Southern Quarterly [*A publication*]
SQ.............. Specialist Qualifications [*British military*]   (DMA)
SQ.............. Squadron
SQ.............. Squall [*Meteorology*]
SQ.............. Squamous [*Cell*] [*Oncology*]
SQ.............. Square   (EY)
sq................ Square Tank [*Liquid gas carriers*]

SQ .... Squeezed Files [*Data processing*]
Sq .... Squire (WGA)
SQ .... Staff Qualified [*Military*] [*British*]
SQ .... Stereoquadraphonic [*Record playing system*] [*CBS*]
S-Q .... Stock Quality [*Pisciculture*]
SQ .... Subcutaneous [*Beneath the Skin*] [*Medicine*]
SQ .... Superquick [*Fuse*]
SQ .... Survival Quotient (ADA)
sq .... Swaziland [*MARC country of publication code*] [*Library of Congress*] (LCCP)
SQA .... Sequa Corp. [*NYSE symbol*] (SPSG)
SQA .... Software Quality Assurance [*Data processing*] (IEEE)
SQA .... South Queensland Airways [*Australia*]
SQA .... Sparrevohn, AK [*Location identifier*] [*FAA*] (FAAL)
SQA .... Squaring Amplifier
SQA .... Stina Resources Ltd. [*Vancouver Stock Exchange symbol*]
SQA .... Supplier Quality Assurance
SQA .... Surveyor Quality Assurance
SQA .... System Queue Area [*Data processing*] (BUR)
SQAD .... Surveyor Quality Assurance Directive
SQAI .... Square Industries, Inc. [*NASDAQ symbol*] (NQ)
SQAL......... Squall [*Meteorology*] (FAAC)
SQAP......... Supplemental Quality Assurance Provision [*Military*]
SQAPP ...... Software Quality Assurance Program Plan [*Data processing*]
SQAR .... Supplier Quality Assurance Representative
SQAT........ Ship's Qualification Assistance Team [*Navy*]
SQAW .... Schriften und Quellen der Alten Welt [*A publication*]
SQB .... Space Qualified Booster
SQB .... Squibb Corp. [*NYSE symbol*] (SPSG)
SQBC........ Space Qualified Booster Charger
SQBE......... Small Quantity Burner Exemption [*Environmental Protection Agency*] (EPA)
SQC .... Self-Quenching Control
SQC .... Sierra Madre Resources [*Vancouver Stock Exchange symbol*]
SQC .... Southern Cross [*Australia*] [*Airport symbol*] (OAG)
SQC .... Station Quality Control [*RADAR*]
SQC .... Statistical Quality Control
sq cell ca... Squamous Cell Carcinoma [*Medicine*] (MAE)
SQCG .... Squirrel Cage [*Electricity*]
SQCM .... Square Centimeter (MSA)
SQCP........ Statistical Quality Control Procedure
SQD .... Self-Quenching Detector
SQD .... Signal Quality Detector
SQD .... Silicone Quadrant Detector (MCD)
SQD .... Social Questions of Today [*A publication*]
SQD .... Squad (AABC)
SQD .... Squadron (NVT)
SQD .... Square D Co. [*NYSE symbol*] (SPSG)
SQDC........ Special Quick Disconnect Coupling
SQ-DEL..... Superquick and Delay [*Fuse*] (SAA)
SQDN....... Squadron (AAG)
Sqdn Ldr ... Squadron-Leader [*British military*] (DMA)
SQE .... Signal Quality Error [*Data processing*] (PCM)
SQE .... Software Quality Evaluation (MCD)
SQE .... Startec Marketing [*Vancouver Stock Exchange symbol*]
SQE .... Supplier Quality Engineering (MCD)
SQEP........ Software [*Firmware*] Quality Evaluation Plan
SQF........... Cleveland, OH [*Location identifier*] [*FAA*] (FAAL)
SQF........... Seligman Quality Municipal Fund [*NYSE symbol*] (SPSG)
SQF........... Semiquantitative Fibrinogen [*Hematology*]
SQF........... Socialist Thought and Practice [*A publication*]
SQF........... Subjective Quality Factor (OA)
SQFT .... Square Foot (MSA)
SQG .... Small Quantity Generator [*Automotive engineering*] [*Environmental Protection Agency*]
SQH.......... Ford-Aire [*Sidney, NY*] [*FAA designator*] (FAAC)
SQ/H .... Square of the Hatch [*Stowage*] (DNAB)
SQH.......... Square Head [*Bolt*]
SQHA .... Standard Quarter Horse Association (EA)
SQI .... Skill Qualification Identifier [*Army*] (INF)
SQI .... Special Qualifications Identifiers [*Army*] (AABC)
SQI .... Sterling/Rock Falls [*Illinois*] [*Airport symbol*] (OAG)
SQIC......... Suppliers Quality Identification Classification
SQIN .... Square Inch (MSA)
SQKM .... Square Kilometer (MSA)
SQL........... San Carlos, CA [*Location identifier*] [*FAA*] (FAAL)
SQL........... School Quota Letter
SQL........... Space Qualified LASER
SQL........... Squelch
SQL........... Standard High-Level Query Language
SQL........... Standard Quantum Limit [*Physics*]
SQL........... Strand Resources [*Vancouver Stock Exchange symbol*]
SQL........... Structured Query Language [*IBM Corp.*]
SQL/DS .... Structured Query Language/Data System [*IBM Corp.*]
SQLN .... Squall Line [*Meteorology*] (FAAC)
SQLW........ Sinclair QL World [*A publication*]
SQM .... Level Island, AK [*Location identifier*] [*FAA*] (FAAL)
SQM .... Sao Miguel Do Araguaia [*Brazil*] [*Airport symbol*] (OAG)
SQM .... Square Meter
SQMC .... Squadron Quartermaster-Corporal [*British military*] (DMA)
SQMD .... Squadron Manning Document (NVT)

sq mi.......... Square Mile (CDAI)
sq mm........ Square Millimeter (MAE)
SQMS........ Squadron Quartermaster-Serjeant [*Military*] [*British*] (ROG)
SQMS....... Staff Quartermaster Sergeant
SQMV ...... Squash Mosaic Virus
SQN .... Sanana [*Indonesia*] [*Airport symbol*] (OAG)
SQN .... School Quota Number
SQN .... Spin Quantum Number [*Atomic physics*]
SQN .... Squadron (NATG)
SQN .... Susquehanna Corp. [*AMEX symbol*] (SPSG)
SQNA .... Squadron Airfield (NATG)
Sqn Ldr ..... Squadron-Leader [*British military*] (DMA)
Sqn Obs .... Squadron Observer [*British military*] (DMA)
Sqn Offr .... Squadron-Officer [*British military*] (DMA)
SQNT .... Sequent Computer Systems, Inc. [*NASDAQ symbol*] (NQ)
SQO .... Senior Quarters Officer [*British military*] (DMA)
SQO .... Squadron Officer
SQORD ..... Separation, Quality Analysis of RADAR Data (SAA)
SQP........... Secret Pass Mine [*Vancouver Stock Exchange symbol*]
SQP........... Shippensburg State College, Shippensburg, PA [*OCLC symbol*] (OCLC)
SQP........... Successive Quadratic Programming [*Algorithm*] [*Data processing*]
SQPD........ Super Quick Point Detonating
SQPN .... Staggered Quadriphase Pseudorandom Noise (MCD)
SQPP .... Software Quality Program Plan
SQQ .... San Quentin Quail [*A minor female*] [*Slang*]
SQQ .... Sequentibus [*In the Following Places*] [*Latin*]
SQR .... Sequence Relay (KSC)
SQR .... Sequoia Resources Ltd. [*Vancouver Stock Exchange symbol*]
SQR .... Soroako [*Indonesia*] [*Airport symbol*] (OAG)
SQR .... Square
SQR .... Square Root [*Data processing*]
SQR .... State Reports (Queensland) [*A publication*]
SQR .... Supplier Quality Rating
SQR .... Supplier Quality Representative [*Nuclear energy*] (NRCH)
SQ3R .... Survey, Question, Read, Review, Recite [*Psychology*]
sq rd .... Square Rod (CDAI)
SQRT......... Seismic Qualification Review Team [*Nuclear energy*] (NRCH)
SQRT........ Square Root
SQS........... Skill Qualification Score [*Military*] (AABC)
SQS........... Statistische Quellenwerke der Schweiz [*Switzerland*]
SQS........... Stochastic Queuing System
SQS........... Stratford American Corp. [*Vancouver Stock Exchange symbol*]
SQS........... Superquick Sensor (MCD)
SQ/SD........ Special Qualifications/Special Designation (NVT)
SQSPM ...... Software Quality Standards and Procedures Manual
SQSSE...... Supplier Quality System Survey Evaluations (MCD)
SQT .... Melbourne, FL [*Location identifier*] [*FAA*] (FAAL)
SQT .... Queensland State Reports [*A publication*] (DLA)
SQT .... Ship Qualification Test [*or Trial*] [*Navy*]
SQT .... Silverquest Resources [*Vancouver Stock Exchange symbol*]
SQT .... Skill Qualification Test [*Army*]
SQT .... Soldier Qualification Test (MCD)
SQT .... Sterilization Qualification Tests
SQT .... System Qualification Tests
SQTIPT...... Ship Qualification Trials in Port [*Navy*] (NVT)
SQTNG ..... Squadron Training (NVT)
SQTT........ Ship Qualification Trial Team [*Navy*] (NG)
SQT(WC).. Skill Qualification Test (Written Component) [*Army*] (INF)
SQU .... E. R. Squibb & Sons, Princeton, NJ [*OCLC symbol*] (OCLC)
Squ .... Square (BJA)
SQU .... Squaw Peak [*Utah*] [*Seismograph station code, US Geological Survey*] (SEIS)
SQUAD ..... Squadron
SQUADEX ... Squadron Exercises [*Canadian Navy*]
SQUAF...... Sonobuoy Qualification Facility [*Navy*] (CAAL)
SQUALL..... Salary Quotient at Lower Limits [*Business term*]
SQUAP...... Supplementary Quality Assurance Provisions
SQUAPP... Software Quality Assurance Program Plan
SQUARE... Specifying Queries as Relational Expressions [*Programming language*] [*1973*] [*Data processing*] (CSR)
S Quart ...... Southern Quarterly [*A publication*]
Squibb Abstr Bull ... Squibb Abstract Bulletin [*A publication*]
Squibb Auc ... Squibb on Auctioneers [*2nd ed.*] [*1891*] [*A publication*] (DLA)
SQUID ...... Semiconducting Quantum Interference Device (MCD)
SQUID ...... Sperry Quick Updating of Internal Documentation (IEEE)
SQUID ...... Submerged Quick Intervention Device [*Human-powered submarine*]
SQUID ...... Superconducting Quantum Interference Detector [*or Device*] [*For study of magnetic fields*]
SQUIRE .... Submarine Quickened Response
SQUO........ Squadron-Officer [*British military*] (DSUE)
SQUOD..... Selected Quantile Output Device [*Electronics*]
SQUOFF... Squadron-Officer [*British military*] (DSUE)
SQW .... Squarewave (MSA)
SQWV ...... Squarewave
SQX .... Sulfaquinoxaline [*or (Sulfanilamido)quinoxaline*] [*Animal antibiotic*]
sq yd .... Square Yard (CDAI)
SQZE......... Stark Quadratic Zeeman Effect [*Physics*]

SQZGR......	Squeeze Grip
SR	Air-Cushion Vehicle built by Saunders Roe [*England*] [*Usually used in combination with numerals*]
SR	Air Search RADAR Receiver [*Shipborne*]
SR	General Society, Sons of the Revolution (EA)
SR	New South Wales State Reports [*A publication*]
SR	New York State Reporter [*A publication*] (DLA)
SR	Partiia Sotsialistov Revolyutsionerov [*Socialist Revolutionary Party*] [*Russian*] [*Political party*] (PPE)
SR	Regina Public Library, Saskatchewan [*Library symbol*] [*National Library of Canada*] (NLC)
SR	Saarlandischer Rundfunk [*Radio network*] [*West Germany*]
SR	Safety Recommendation (AAG)
SR	Safety Release [*Army*]
S/R.............	Safety Relief Valve [*Nuclear energy*] (NRCH)
S/R.............	Safety Representative [*Insurance*]
SR	Safety Rod [*Nuclear energy*] (NRCH)
SR	Salva Ratificatione [*On Condition of Ratification*] [*Latin*]
SR	Sample Rate
SR	Sanctioned Ritual [*British*] [*Slang*]
SR	Sarcoplasmic Reticulum [*Anatomy*]
SR	Saturable Reactor
SR	Saturation Recovery [*NMR imaging*]
SR	Saturday Review [*A publication*]
SR	Saudi Riyal [*Monetary unit*] (BJA)
SR	Savannah River Test Pile [*Nuclear energy*] (NRCH)
SR	Sawyer Rifle
SR	Scan Radius
SR	Scan Rate
SR	Scan Ratio (MCD)
SR	Scanning Radiometer
SR	Schooner [*Shipping*] (ROG)
SR	Schumann Runge [*Spectral region*]
SR	Sciences Religieuses [*A publication*]
SR	Scientific Report
SR	Scientific Research
SR	Scoring Reliability (MCD)
SR	Scottish Regional [*Council*]
SR	Scottish Rifles [*Military unit*] [*British*]
SR	Scripture Reader (ROG)
SR	Seaman Recruit [*Navy*]
SR	Seaplane Reconnaissance Aircraft
SR	Search RADAR
SR	Search and Reconnaissance [*Air Force*]
SR	Search and Recovery [*Military*]
SR	Search and Rescue
SR	Second-Harmonic Resonance (MCD)
SR	Second Routing (MCD)
SR	Secretion Rate [*Endocrinology*]
SR	Section Report
SR	Sedimentation Rate
SR	Seer (WGA)
SR	Selective Ringing
SR	Selenium Rectifier [*Electronics*]
SR	Self-Rectifying
SR	Semantic Reaction
SR	Senate Recedes
SR	Senate Report
SR	Senate Resolution
SR	Send and Receive
SR	Senior
SR	Senior Registrar
SR	Senior Reviewer
SR	Senor [*Mister*] [*Spanish*]
SR	Sensibility Reciprocal (WGA)
SR	Sensitivity Ratio
SR	Sensitivity Response [*Cell*] [*Radiology*]
SR	Sensitization Response
SR	Sensory Rhodopsin [*Biochemistry*]
SR	Separate Rations [*Military*]
S & R.........	Sergeant and Rawle's Pennsylvania Reports [*1824-28*] [*A publication*] (DLA)
SR	Series Number [*Online database field identifier*]
SR	Service Record [*Military*]
SR	Service Report
SR	Service Rifle [*British military*] (DMA)
S-R.............	Set-Reset [*Flip-Flop*] [*Data processing*]
SR	Settlement Register [*Data processing*]
SR	Severe, Right-Moving [*Thunderstorm*]
SR	Sewanee Review [*A publication*]
SR	Sex Ratio [*Biology*]
SR	Shaft Rate (NVT)
SR	Sharpened Romberg [*Equilibrium*]
SR	Shift Register
SR	Shift Reverse
SR	Shift Right
SR	Ship Repair Ratings
SR	Ship-to-Shore RADAR [*or Radio*] (DEN)
SR	Shipment [*or Shipping*] Request
S/R.............	Shipper/Receiver [*Difference*]
SR	Shipping Receipt [*Business term*]
SR	Ships Records (MCD)
SR	Shock Related
SR	Shock Resistance
SR	Short Range
SR	Short Rate
SR	Short Run [*Economics*]
SR	Shutdown Request [*NASA*] (KSC)
SR	Side Rails [*On a bed*] [*Medicine*]
SR	Sierra Railroad Co. (IIA)
SR	Sigma Reaction
SR	Signor [*Mister*] [*Italian*]
SR	Silicon Rectifier
SR	Silicon Rubber
SR	Simian Rotavirus [*Pathology*]
SR	Simla Rifles [*British military*] (DMA)
SR	Simulation Report
SR	Single Reduction
SR	Sinus Rhythm [*Medicine*]
SR	Sinus Roris [*Bay of Dew*] [*Lunar area*]
SR	Sir
SR	Sister
SR	Skagit River Railroad (IIA)
SR	Skeleton Records [*Army*]
SR	Skin Resistance [*Physiology*] (MAE)
SR	Skywave Synchronization (DEN)
SR	Slant Range
SR	Slave River Journal [*Fort Smith, Northwest Territory*] [*A publication*]
SR	Slavic Review [*A publication*]
SR	Slavonic Review [*A publication*]
SR	Slew Rate
SR	Sling Ring
SR	Slip Ring [*Electricity*]
SR	Sloane Ranger [*Member of a British social set satirized in "The Official Sloane Ranger Handbook, The First Guide to What Really Matters in Life"*] [*Name is derived from Sloane Square in Chelsea*]
SR	Slovenska Rec [*A publication*]
SR	Slow Release [*Electronics*]
SR	Small Ring
S-R.............	Smooth-Rough Variation [*Medicine*] (MAE)
SR	Social Register
SR	Social Research [*A publication*]
SR	Socialist Revolutionary [*Former USSR*]
SR	Society of Radiographers (EAIO)
SR	Society of Rheology [*Later, SoR*] (EA)
SR	Society of Rosicrucians (EA)
SR	Sociologia Religiosa [*A publication*]
SR	Solar Radiation
SR	Solar Reference
SR	Solicitor's Recommendation [*Internal Revenue Bureau*] [*United States*] [*A publication*] (DLA)
SR	Solid Rocket
SR	Soluble, Repository [*With reference to penicillin*]
SR	Songwriter's Review [*A publication*]
SR	Soror [*Sister*]
SR	Sorter Reader
SR	Sortie Rate (MCD)
SR	Sound Ranging
SR	Sound Rating (IEEE)
SR	Sound Recordings [*US Copyright Office class*]
SR	Sound Report
SR	Source Range [*Nuclear energy*] (NRCH)
SR	Southern Railway Co. [*NYSE symbol*] (SPSG)
SR	Southern Review [*US*] [*A publication*]
SR	Southern Rhodesia [*Later, Zimbabwe*]
SR	Southern Rhodesia High Court Reports [*A publication*] (DLA)
SR	Southwest Review [*A publication*]
SR	Sovjetskaja Rossija [*A publication*]
SR	Sparebanken Rogaland [*Rogaland Savings Bank*] [*Norway*]
SR	Spares Requirement
SR	Special Register
SR	Special Regulations [*Military*]
SR	Special Report
S-R.............	Special Reserve
SR	Specific Range
SR	Specification Requirement
SR	Spectral Recording
SR	Speculative Resource [*Minerals*]
SR	Speech Recognition
SR	Speed Recorder (IEEE)
SR	Speed Regulator
SR	Spelling Reform (ADA)
SR	Spin-Rotation [*Physics*]
SR	Split Ring [*Technical drawings*]
SR	Spontaneous Discharge Rate [*Audiology*]
S/R.............	Spotter Reconnaissance [*Air Force*] [*British*]
S-R.............	Spring Inflow-River Inflow [*Geology*]
SR	Square [*Ship's rigging*] (ROG)
SR	Stable Recipient [*Medicine*]
SR	Staff Report

SR .... Stage of Resistance [*in General-Adaptation Syndrome*]
SR .... Stage Right [*A stage direction*]
SR .... Standard Range Approach [*Aviation*]
SR .... Standard Repair   (AAG)
SR .... Standard Requirement
SR .... Standardization Report
SR .... Star Route [*A type of rural postal delivery route*]
SR .... Starting Relay   (DEN)
SR .... State Register
SR .... Statement of Requirements [*NASA*]   (MCD)
SR .... Stateroom   (MSA)
SR .... Station Radio [*British*]
SR .... Station Regulation
SR .... Stationery Request   (MCD)
SR .... Statistical Reporter [*Manila*] [*A publication*]
SR .... Statstjanstemannens Riksforbund [*National Association of Salaried Employees in Government Service*] [*Sweden*]
SR .... Status Register [*Data processing*]
SR .... Status Report
SR .... Status Review [*NASA*]   (NASA)
SR .... Statutes Revised [*A publication*]   (DLA)
SR .... Statutory Regulations [*New Zealand*] [*A publication*]
SR .... Statutory Rule   (ADA)
SR .... Steep Rock Resources, Inc. [*Toronto Stock Exchange symbol*]
sr .... Steradian [*Symbol*] [*SI unit of solid angle*]
SR .... Stereo Review [*A publication*]
S-R .... Steroid Receptor [*Endocrinology*]
S-R .... Stimulus-Response
SR .... Stock Replacement   (AAG)
SR .... Stock Report
SR .... Stoichiometric Ratio [*Chemistry*]
SR .... Stomach Rumble [*Medicine*]   (AAMN)
SR .... Storage Rack
SR .... Storage Register
SR .... Storage and Repair   (MCD)
S/R .... Storage/Retrieval [*Data processing*]
S & R .... Storage and Retrieval [*Data processing*]
SR .... Storage Room
SR .... Stove or Range
S & R .... Stowage and Repair
SR .... Strategic Research   (MCD)
SR .... Stress-Rupture   (MCD)
SR .... Stretch Reflex   (MAE)
SR .... Strike Rate   (ADA)
SR .... Stripe Rot [*Plant pathology*]
Sr .... Strontium [*Chemical element*]
Sr .... Strouhal Number [*IUPAC*]
SR .... Studies in Religion [*A publication*]
SR .... Studies in the Renaissance [*A publication*]
SR .... Studies and Reports. Ben-Zvi Institute [*Jerusalem*] [*A publication*]
SR .... Studies in Romanticism [*A publication*]
SR .... Study Regulation   (MCD)
SR .... Study Requirement [*Air Force*]
SR .... Styrene Rubber
SR .... Su Remesa [*Your Remittance*] [*Spanish*] [*Business term*]
SR .... Subject Ratio
SR .... Submarine Recorder [*British military*]   (DMA)
SR .... Subroutine [*Data processing*]   (AAG)
SR .... Subscriber Register
SR .... Sugar Requirements and Quotas
SR .... Sulfonamide-Resistant [*Microbiology*]
SR .... Summary Report
SR .... Sunrise [*Meteorology*]   (FAAC)
SR .... Superior Rectus [*Ophthalmology*]   (MAE)
SR .... Supervisor   (TEL)
SR .... Supplemental Report
SR .... Supplementary Regulation
SR .... Supplementary Reserve [*British military*]   (DMA)
SR .... Supply Room
SR .... Support Reaction Load   (NRCH)
SR .... Support Request [*or Requirement*]   (KSC)
SR .... Support Room   (MCD)
SR .... Supporting Research [*Military*]
SR .... Suppressor Receptor [*Embryology*]
SR .... Supreme Court of Quebec, Reports [*A publication*]   (DLA)
SR .... Surface Roughness
sr .... Surinam [*MARC country of publication code*] [*Library of Congress*]   (LCCP)
SR .... Surinam [*ANSI two-letter standard code*]   (CNC)
SR .... Surveillance RADAR [*Air Force*]
SR .... Surveillance Requirement [*Nuclear Regulatory Commission*]   (GFGA)
SR .... Surveying Recorder [*Navy rating*] [*British*]
SR .... Surveyor [*British military*]   (DMA)
SR .... Sustained Release [*Pharmacy*]
SR .... Sveriges Radio
SR .... Swissair [*Airline*] [*ICAO designator*]
SR .... Switch Register
SR .... Synchrotron Radiation [*High-energy physics*]
SR .... System Requirement   (SSD)

SR .... Systematische Sammlung des Bundesrechts [*Switzerland*] [*A publication*]
SR .... Systemic Resistance [*Medicine*]   (MAE)
SR .... Systems Review [*Medicine*]
SR .... Union of Soviet Socialist Republics [*IYRU nationality code*]   (IYR)
SR-11 .... Sapporo Rat (Virus)
SRA............ Journal. Society of Research Administrators [*A publication*]
SRA............ Sair Aviation [*Syracuse, NY*] [*FAA designator*]   (FAAC)
SRA............ San Ramon [*Costa Rica*] [*Seismograph station code, US Geological Survey*]   (SEIS)
SRA............ Saskatchewan Archives, Regina, Saskatchewan [*Library symbol*] [*National Library of Canada*]   (NLC)
SRA............ Saturday Review of the Arts [*A publication*]
SRA............ Science Research Associates   (AEBS)
SRA............ Scottish Rifle Association   (DI)
SRA............ Screw Research Association   (EA)
SRA............ Scuba Retailers Association   (EA)
SRA............ Sea Rangers' Association [*British*]   (DI)
SRA............ Seatrade [*A publication*]
SRA............ Selective Restricted Availability   (MCD)
SRA............ Self-Regulatory Agency [*Securities*] [*British*]
SrA............ Senior Airman
SRA............ Senior Residential Appraiser [*Designation awarded by Society of Real Estate Appraisers*]
SRA............ Separate Reporting Activities [*Army*]
SRA............ Service and Regulatory Announcement, Department of Agriculture [*A publication*]   (DLA)
SRA............ Servicemen's Readjustment Act
SRA............ Ship Radio Authorization [*Army*]   (AABC)
SRA............ Ship Replaceable Assembly   (MCD)
SRA............ Shipyard Restricted Availability [*Navy*]   (CAAL)
SRA............ Shop-Replaceable Assembly [*NASA*]
SRA............ Short-Range Acquisition   (MCD)
SRA............ Short Reflex Arc
SRA............ Significant Regulatory Action [*Office of Management and Budget*]   (GFGA)
SRA............ Simultaneous Range Adcock Antenna [*Military RADAR*]
SRA............ Small, Replaceable Assembly   (RDA)
SRA............ Smoker's Rights Alliance   (EA)
SRA............ Social Research and Applications [*Research center*]   (RCD)
SRA............ Social Research Association [*British*]
SRA............ Social Responsibility Auditing   (ADA)
SRA............ Society of Research Administrators   (EA)
SRA............ Society of Residential Appraisers [*Later, AI*]
SRA............ Society for Risk Analysis   (EA)
SRA............ Sociological Research Association   (EA)
SRA............ Software Requirements Analysis
SRA............ Southern Rhodesia Artillery [*British military*]   (DMA)
SRA............ Southern Rural Action, Inc.
SRA............ Spanish Refugee Aid   (EA)
SRA............ Special Refractories Association [*Defunct*]   (EA)
SRA............ Special Repair Activity   (MCD)
SRA............ Special Rules Area
SRA............ Specialized Repair Activity
SRA............ Specular Reflectance Accessory [*Spectrophotometry*]
SRA............ Spherical Radiation Absorber   (MCD)
SRA............ Spin Reference Axis   (KSC)
SRA............ Squash Rackets Association [*British*]
SRA............ Standards of Readiness and Availability   (NATG)
SRA............ State and Regional Associations of the United States [*A publication*]
SRA............ Station Representatives Association   (EA)
SRA............ Stearman Restorers Association   (EA)
SRA............ Stock Record Account   (AFM)
SR & A ...... Strategy, Research & Action [*Commercial firm*] [*British*]
SRA............ Stratus Computer, Inc. [*NYSE symbol*]   (SPSG)
SRA............ Structures Research Associates
SRA............ Subminiature Rotary Actuator
SRA............ Sugar Rationing Administration [*Department of Agriculture*] [*Ceased functions, 1948*]
SRA............ Sulforicinoleic Acid [*Organic chemistry*]
SRA............ Sun's Right Ascension [*Astrology*]   (ROG)
SRA............ Supplemental Retirement Annuities
SRA............ Support Requirements Analysis [*NASA*]   (NASA)
SRA............ Surgeon Rear-Admiral [*British military*]
SRA............ Surveillance RADAR Approach
SRA............ System Reaction Analysis [*Bell System*]
SRA............ System Reliability Analysis
SRA............ System Requirements Analysis
SRA............ Systems Research and Applications Corp. [*Arlington, VA*]   (TSSD)
SRAA........ Scholastic Rowing Association of America   (EA)
SRAA........ Senior Army Advisor   (AABC)
SRAAG...... Senior Army Advisor, Army National Guard   (AABC)
SRAAM..... Short-Range Air-to-Air Missile   (MCD)
SRAAR...... Senior Army Advisor, Army Reserve   (AABC)
SRAB........ Allan Blair Memorial Clinic, Regina, Saskatchewan [*Library symbol*] [*National Library of Canada*]   (NLC)

SRAC......... Alcoholism Commission of Saskatchewan, Regina, Saskatchewan [*Library symbol*] [*National Library of Canada*] (NLC)
SRAC......... Safe Return Amnesty Committee (EA)
SRAC......... Sears Roebuck Acceptance Corp.
SRAC......... Short Run Average Costs
SRAC......... Societe Royale d'Astronomie du Canada
SRACCMB ... Senior Aircraft Crewman Badge [*Military decoration*] (GFGA)
SrAcftCrmnBad ... Senior Aircraft Crewman Badge [*Military decoration*] (AABC)
SR-ACK..... Service Request Acknowledgment [*Air Force*] (CET)
SRACR...... Southern Rhodesia Armoured Car Regiment [*British military*] (DMA)
SRAD........ Ship's Restricted Availability Date [*Navy*] (DNAB)
SRAD........ Solar Radiation (NOAA)
SRAD........ Steerable Right-Angle Drive (DNAB)
SR/AD...... Supporting Research and Advanced Development
SRAD........ Surveillance RADAR (MCD)
SRAE........ Solar Radio Astronomy Experiment
SRAEL...... Labour Market Planning and Information Resource Centre, Saskatchewan Department of Advanced Education and Manpower, Regina, Saskatchewan [*Library symbol*] [*National Library of Canada*] (NLC)
SRAEN...... Systeme de Reference pour la Determination de l'Affaiblissement Equivalent pour la Nettete [*Master telephone transmission reference system*]
SRAEW..... Women's Services Branch, Saskatchewan Department of Advanced Education and Manpower, Regina, Saskatchewan [*Library symbol*] [*National Library of Canada*] (NLC)
SRAF......... Archibald Foundation, Regina, Saskatchewan [*Library symbol*] [*National Library of Canada*] (NLC)
SRAF......... Social Revolutionary Anarchist Federation (EA)
SRAF......... Standby Reserve of the Armed Forces
SRAFO...... Senior Royal Air Force Officer [*British military*] (DMA)
SRAG........ Saskatchewan Department of Agriculture, Regina, Saskatchewan [*Library symbol*] [*National Library of Canada*] (NLC)
SRAG........ Semiactive RADAR Antiair Guidance System
SRAG........ Space Radiation Analysis Group [*NASA*] (NASA)
SRAGE...... Shared Services, Agriculture Canada [*Services en Commun, Agriculture Canada*] Regina, Saskatchewan [*Library symbol*] [*National Library of Canada*] (NLC)
SRAGR...... Research Station, Agriculture Canada [*Station de Recherches, Agriculture Canada*] Regina, Saskatchewan [*Library symbol*] [*National Library of Canada*] (NLC)
SRAI......... Soybean Research Advisory Institute [*Terminated, 1984*] (EGAO)
SRAI......... Supercat Race Association International (EA)
SRA-J Soc R ... SRA - Journal of the Society of Research Administrators [*A publication*]
SRAM........ Semirandom Access Memory
SRAM........ Short-Range Attack Missile [*Military*]
SRAM........ Skill Qualification Test Requirements Alert Message
SRAM........ Some Remarks on Abstract Machines [*Data processing*]
SRAM........ SQT [*Ship's Qualification Trial*] Requirements Alert Message
SRAM........ Static Random Access Memory [*Data processing*]
SRAM........ System Rehabilitation and Modernization (MCD)
SRAMA..... Spring Research and Manufacturers' Association (EAIO)
SRAM(T).. Short-Range Attack Missile (Tactical) [*Military*]
SRAN .... Short-Range Aids to Navigation [*Navy*]
SRAN .... Skill Qualification Test Requirements Alert Notice
SRAN .... Stock Record Account Number (AFM)
SRANA..... Shrine Recorders Association of North America (EA)
SRANC...... Southern Rhodesia African National Congress
SRAO .... Supplemental Recreational Activities Overseas [*Red Cross*]
SRAP........ Service Record and Allied Papers [*Military*]
SRAP........ Slow Response Action Potentials [*Neurophysiology*]
SRAP........ Standard Range Approach [*Aviation*]
SRAPMA .. Science Research Associates Primary Mental Abilities [*Psychology*] (AEBS)
SRARAV ... Senior Army Aviator (AABC)
SRARAVB ... Senior Army Aviator Badge [*Military decoration*] (GFGA)
SrArAvBad ... Senior Army Aviator Badge [*Military decoration*]
SRARM..... Short-Range Antiradiation Missile
SR Arts ...... Saturday Review of the Arts [*A publication*]
SRAS .... Albert South Library, Regina, Saskatchewan [*Library symbol*] [*National Library of Canada*] (NLC)
SRASM ...... Short-Range Air-to-Surface Missile (MCD)
SRAT........ Search RADAR Alignment Test [*Military*] (CAAL)
SRAT........ Short-Range Applied Technology
SRAT-B..... Self-Report Assertiveness Test for Boys
SRATC...... Short-Run Average Total Cost [*Economics*]
SRATS...... Solar Radiation and Thermospheric Structure [*Japanese satellite*]
SRATUC ... Southern Rhodesian African Trade Union Congress
Sr Autobahn ... Strasse und Autobahn [*A publication*]
SRAVC...... Short-Run Average Variable Cost [*Economics*]
SRAW........ Short-Range Antitank Weapon
SRaw......... Specific Resistance, Airway [*Medicine*]
SRAX......... Southern Air Transport, Inc. [*Air carrier designation symbol*]

SRB........... Safety Review Board [*Nuclear energy*] (NRCH)
SRB........... Schilpp, Reed B., Los Angeles CA [*STAC*]
SRB........... Scientific Review Board [*Intergovernmental Oceanographic Commission*] (GFGA)
SRB........... Scurry-Rainbow Oil Ltd. [*AMEX symbol*] (SPSG)
SRB........... Seaplane Repair Base
SRB........... Selective Reenlistment Bonus [*Military*] (AABC)
SRB........... Self-Retaining Bolt
SRB........... Service Record Book [*Military*]
SRB........... Service Request Block [*Data processing*] (BUR)
SRB........... Sheftall Record Book [*A publication*] (BJA)
SRB........... Sky Ranch for Boys (EA)
SRB........... Solar Reflectory Beacon
SRB........... Solid-Rocket Booster [*NASA*]
SRB........... Sorter Reader Buffer
SRB........... Source-Route Bridge [*Data processing*] (PCM)
SRB........... Sparta, TN [*Location identifier*] [*FAA*] (FAAL)
SRB........... Special Research Bureau [*Department of External Affairs*] [*Canada*]
SRB........... Special Review Board [*Military*] (INF)
SRB........... Specification Review Board [*Navy*] (DNAB)
SRB........... Spherical Roller Bearing
SRB........... State Research Bureau [*Secret police*] [*Uganda*]
SRB........... Styrene Rubber Butadiene (NG)
SRB........... Subspecialty Requirements Board [*Navy*] (DNAB)
SRB........... Sulfate Reducing Bacteria
SRB........... Support Research Branch [*Springfield Armory*]
SRB........... Survey and Reports Branch [*Division of Biometry and Applied Sciences, National Institute of Mental Health*] (GFGA)
SRB........... System Review Board (MCD)
SRBA........ Statistical Record of Black America [*A publication*]
SRBA........ Students for the Right to Bear Arms (EA)
SRBAB...... Solid-Rocket Booster Assembly Building [*NASA*] (NASA)
SRBC........ Serum-Treated Red Blood Cell [*Clinical chemistry*]
SRBC........ Sheep Red Blood Cell[s] [*Also, SRC*]
SRBC........ Sunrise Bancorp [*NASDAQ symbol*] (NQ)
SRBC........ Susquehanna River Basin Commission [*Federal government*] (EGAO)
SRBC........ Susquehanna River Basin Compact [*Maryland, Pennsylvania, New York*]
SRBCSS .... Scales for Rating the Behavioral Characteristics of Superior Students [*Educational test*]
SRBDF ...... Solid-Rocket Booster Disassembly Facility [*NASA*] (NASA)
SRBDM..... Short-Range Bomber Defense Missile
SRBM........ Short-Range Ballistic Missile
SRBMI ...... BMI Finance, Regina, Saskatchewan [*Library symbol*] [*National Library of Canada*] (NLC)
SRBOC...... Super Rapid Bloom Off Board Chaff [*Navy*] (NVT)
SRBPF...... Solid-Rocket Booster Processing Facility [*NASA*] (NASA)
SRBT .... Single-Rod Burst Test [*Nuclear energy*] (NRCH)
SRBUC...... Scientific Research in British Universities and Colleges [*Later, RBUPC*] [*British Library*]
SRBUD...... Space Research in Bulgaria [*A publication*]
SRC........... AMF Sunfish Racing Class Association (EA)
SRC........... Richland County Library, Columbia, SC [*OCLC symbol*] (OCLC)
SRC........... Sacra Rituum Congregatio [*Sacred Congregation of Rites*] [*Latin*]
SRC........... Safety Research Center [*Bureau of Mines*]
SRC........... Salinas Road [*California*] [*Seismograph station code, US Geological Survey*] (SEIS)
SRC........... Sample Recovery Container [*NASA*] (KSC)
SRC........... Sample Return Container [*NASA*] (NASA)
SRC........... Sample Rock Container [*NASA*]
SRC........... Sarcoma
SRC........... Saskatchewan Research Council [*University of Saskatchewan*] [*Research center*] (RCD)
SRC........... Saturable Reactor Coil
SRC........... Schedule Request Confirmation (SSD)
SRC........... Scheduled Removal Component (MCD)
SRC........... Science Research Council [*Later, SERC*] [*British*]
SRC........... Scleroderma Renal Crisis [*Medicine*]
SRC........... Scott's Hospitality, Inc. [*Toronto Stock Exchange symbol*]
SRC........... Se Ruega Contestacion [*The Favor of a Reply Is Requested*] [*Spanish*]
SRC........... Searcy, AR [*Location identifier*] [*FAA*] (FAAL)
SRC........... Secured Returns Code [*IRS*]
SRC........... Securities Research Co.
SRC........... Sedimented Red Cell [*Hematology*] (MAE)
SRC........... Semiconductor Research Cooperative
SRC........... Senate Rail Caucus (EA)
S/RC......... Send/Receive Center (FAAC)
SRC........... Send Register Control [*Data processing*]
SRC........... Servants of Our Lady Queen of the Clergy [*Roman Catholic women's religious order*]
SRC........... Sheep Red Cell[s] [*Also, SRBC*]
SRC........... Shop Resident Control (SAA)
SRC........... Shutdown Reactor Cooling [*Nuclear energy*] (NRCH)
SRC........... Signal Reserve Corps
SRC........... Silicon Readout Cell
SRC........... Silicon Rectifier Column

SRC........... Single Round Container [*for toxic chemicals*] [*Army*]
SRC........... Ski Retailers Council [*Inactive*]   (EA)
SRC........... Slow-Recovery Capsules [*Pharmacy*]
SRC........... Snyder Research Co. [*Information service or system*]   (IID)
SRC........... Social Rehabilitation Clinic   (EA)
SRC........... Societe Royale du Canada [*Royal Society of Canada - RSC*]
SRC........... Society of Friends Community Relations Committee [*British*]
SRC........... Solvent-Refined Coal
SRC........... Sound Ranging Control
SRC........... Sound Recording Co. [*Record label*]
SRC........... Source
SRC........... Source Range Channel   (IEEE)
SRC........... Southeast Asia Resource Center   (EA)
SRC........... Southern Regional Council   (EA)
SRC........... Southwest Radio Church [*An association*]
SRC........... Southwest Research Corp.
SRC........... Space Research Council [*British*]
SRC........... Spares Receiving Checklist   (NRCH)
SRC........... Special Regular Commissions [*Army*] [*British*]
SRC........... Specific Reactant Consumption [*Engine*]
SRC........... Specimen Research Centrifuge   (SSD)
SRC........... Specimen Return Container   (SAA)
SRC........... Specimen Return Control   (SAA)
SRC........... Speech Recognition Computer
SRC........... Standard Requirements Code [*Military*]
SRC........... Standards Review Committee [*American Occupational Therapy Association*]
SRC........... Station Reliability Coordinator
SRC........... Statuts Revises du Canada [*Revised Statutes of Canada*] [*Database*] [*Federal Department of Justice*] [*Information service or system*]   (CRD)
SRC........... Sterility Research Center [*Public Health Service*]   (GRD)
SRC........... Stock Record Card [*Military*]
SRC........... Strasburg Railroad Co. [*AAR code*]
SRC........... Stray Radiation Chamber
SRC........... Stuart's Lower Canada Reports [*A publication*]   (DLA)
SRC........... Student Reaction to College [*Student attitudes test*]
SRC........... Students' Representative Council [*British*]
SRC........... Studies in Religion: A Canadian Journal [*A publication*]
SRC..... Subject-Field Reference Code   (ADA)
SRC........... Submarine Rescue Chamber   (MCD)
SRC........... Support Review Code   (MCD)
SRC........... Survey Research Center [*University of Kentucky*] [*Research center*]   (RCD)
SRC........... Survey Research Center [*Oregon State University*] [*Research center*]   (RCD)
SRC........... Sustained-Release Capsule [*Pharmacology*]
SRC........... Swiss Red Cross
SRC........... Synchronous Remote Control
SRC........... Synchrotron Radiation Center [*University of Wisconsin - Madison*] [*Research center*]   (RCD)
SRC........... Syracuse Research Corp. [*New York*] [*Information service or system*]   (IID)
SRC........... Systems Release Certification [*Social Security Administration*]
SRC........... Systems Research Configuration
SRCA........ Saskatchewan Department of Consumer Affairs, Regina, Saskatchewan [*Library symbol*] [*National Library of Canada*]   (NLC)
SRCA........ Slovenian Research Center of America   (EA)
SRCA........ Specific Red Cell Adherence [*Test*] [*Clinical chemistry*]
SRCAS ..... Safety-Related Control Air System [*Nuclear energy*]   (NRCH)
SRCB........ Canadian Bible College, Regina, Saskatchewan [*Library symbol*] [*National Library of Canada*]   (NLC)
SRCB........ Software Requirements Change Board [*NASA*]   (NASA)
SRCB........ Software Requirements Control Board [*NASA*]   (NASA)
SRCBD...... Software Requirements Change Board Directive [*NASA*]   (NASA)
SRCBD...... Software Requirements Control Board Directive [*NASA*]   (NASA)
SRCC......... Senior Control Center [*Air Force*]
SRCC......... Sensor Referenced and Computer Controlled [*For remote manipulators*]
SRCC......... Simplex Remote Communications Central
SRCC......... Solar Rating and Certification Corp.   (EA)
SR & CC .... Strikes, Riots, and Civil Commotions [*Insurance*]
SRCC .... Strikes, Riots, and Civil Commotions [*Insurance*]
SrcCp....... Source Capital, Inc. [*Associated Press abbreviation*]   (APAG)
SRCD........ Set-Reset Clocked Data [*Data processing*]
SRCD........ Society for Research in Child Development   (EA)
SRCD......... Society of Richmond County Descendants   (EA)
SRCE......... First Source Corp. [*NASDAQ symbol*]   (NQ)
SR-CEF..... Schmidt-Ruppin Chick Embryo Fibroblast[*s*]
SRCH .... Search   (AAG)
SRCH .... Search Natural Resources, Inc. [*NASDAQ symbol*]   (NQ)
SRCI .... Safety-Related Controls and Instrumentation [*Nuclear energy*]   (NRCH)
SRCI .... Survey Research Consultants International, Inc. [*Information service or system*]   (IID)
SRCL........ Security Requirements Check List   (MCD)
SRCM........ Savonius Rotor Current Meter

SRCM........ Sisters of Reparation of the Congregation of Mary [*Roman Catholic religious order*]
SRCMLT... Standing Representative Committee for Medical Laboratory Technology in the EEC [*European Econommic Community*] [*England*]   (EAIO)
SRCMP ..... Southern Rhodesia Corps of Military Police [*British military*]   (DMA)
SRCNET ... Science and Engineering Research Council Network [*Later, SERCNET*]
SRCO........ Sealright Co., Inc. [*Kansas City, MO*] [*NASDAQ symbol*]   (NQ)
SRCO......... Selected Regardless of Race, Color, Creed, or National Orgin   (SAA)
SRCP .... Short Range Construction Program [*Military*]
SRCP .... Society of Retired Catholic Persons   (EA)
SRCP .... Special Reserve Components Program [*Military*]
SRC Publ ... SRC [*Saskatchewan Research Council*] Publication
SRCR........ Saskatchewan Culture and Recreation, Regina, Saskatchewan [*Library symbol*] [*National Library of Canada*]   (NLC)
SRCR........ SONAR Control Room
SRCR........ Stability Regulated Controlled Rectifier
SRCR........ System Run Control Record
SRCRA ...... Shipowners Refrigerated Cargo Research Association [*Research center*] [*British*]   (IRUK)
SRCRC ...... Snake River Conservation Research Center [*University of Idaho*] [*Research center*]   (RCD)
SRCT........ Standard Recovery Completion Time
SRCU........ Credit Union Central, Regina, Saskatchewan [*Library symbol*] [*National Library of Canada*]   (NLC)
SRCU........ Secretary's Records Correspondence Unit [*Department of Labor*]
SRD .... Safety and Reliability Directorate [*England*]   (IID)
SRD .... San Andres [*Colombia*] [*Seismograph station code, US Geological Survey*]   (SEIS)
SRD .... Satellite Racing Development [*British*]
SRD .... Scheduled Release Date   (MCD)
SRD .... Secret - Restricted Data [*Security classification*]
SRD .... Seldom Reaches Destination
SRD .... Selective Radiation Detector
SRD .... Self-Reading Dosimeter   (IEEE)
SRD .... Serous Retinal Detachment [*Ophthalmology*]
SRD .... Service Revealed Deficiency [*or Difficulty*]
SRD .... Service Rum Diluted [*British military*]   (DMA)
SRD .... Shift Register Drive
S-RD .... Shipper-Receiver Difference   (NRCH)
SRD .... Shuttle Requirements Definition [*NASA*]   (NASA)
SRD .... Shuttle Requirements Document [*NASA*]   (NASA)
SRD .... Silver Drake Resources [*Vancouver Stock Exchange symbol*]
SRD .... Single Radial Diffusion [*or Immunodiffusion*] [*Analytical biochemistry*]
SRD .... Small Rigid Dome
SRD .... Society for the Relief of Distress [*British*]
SRD .... Society for the Right to Die   (EA)
SRD .... Software Requirements Document [*Data processing*]
SRD .... Special Research Detachment [*Army*]
SRD .... Stafford Road [*Wolverhampton*] [*British depot code*]
SRD .... [*The*] Standard Oil Co. [*NYSE symbol*]   (SPSG)
SRD .... Standard Reference Data
SRD .... Standard Repair Design [*Navy*]   (MCD)
SRD .... Standard Reporting Designator   (MCD)
SRD .... State Registered Dietitian
SRD .... Statistical Research Division [*Census*]   (OICC)
SRD .... Step Recovery Diode
SRD .... Studio Reference Disc [*Prosonus*] [*Electronic music*]
SRD .... Super-Radiant Diode
SRD .... Sutherland Resources [*Vancouver Stock Exchange symbol*]
SRD .... Systems Requirements Document [*NASA*]
Srd............. Thiouridine [*Also, S, SU*] [*A nucleoside*]
SRDA........ Dunlop Art Gallery, Regina, Saskatchewan [*Library symbol*] [*National Library of Canada*]   (NLC)
SRDA........ Search RADAR Designation Alignment   (MCD)
SRDA........ Sodium Removal Development Apparatus [*Nuclear energy*]   (NRCH)
SRDAS ..... Service Recording and Data Analysis System   (IEEE)
SRDB........ Scientific Research and Development Branch [*Home Office*] [*British*]   (IRUK)
SRDC......... Standard Reference Data Center
SRDCS ...... Simulation Reconfiguration Data Collection Subsystem   (SSD)
SRDDD ..... Solar Energy R and D in the European Community. Series D [*A publication*]
SRDE........ Signals Research and Development Establishment [*British*]
SRDE........ Smallest Replaceable Defective Element
SRDG........ Software Research and Development Group [*University of Calgary*] [*Research center*]   (RCD)
SRDH .... Subsystems Requirements Definition Handbook [*NASA*]   (NASA)
SRDI.......... Safety-Related Display Instrumentation [*Nuclear energy*]   (NRCH)
SRDL........ Saskatchewan Department of Labour, Regina, Saskatchewan [*Library symbol*] [*National Library of Canada*]   (NLC)

SRDL......... Signals Research and Development Laboratory [*Army*] [*British*]
SRDM .... Subrate Data Multiplexer [*Telecommunications*] (TEL)
SRDRD...... Solar Energy Research and Development Report [*A publication*]
SRDS......... Shop Repair Data Sheets
SRDS......... Single Requirements Determination System
SRDS......... Standard Rate and Data Service, Inc. [*Information service or system*] (MCD)
SRDS......... Standard Reference Data System (DIT)
SRDS......... Systems Research and Development Service [*FAA*] (MCD)
SRDT......... Single Rotating Directional Transmission [*Military*] (CAAL)
SRE........... Sancta Romana Ecclesia [*Most Holy Roman Church*] [*Latin*]
SRE........... Sanctae Romanae Ecclesiae [*Of the Most Holy Roman Church*] [*Latin*]
SRE........... Saskatchewan Department of the Environment, Regina, Saskatchewan [*Library symbol*] [*National Library of Canada*] (NLC)
SRE........... Saturday Review of Education [*A publication*]
SRE........... Scanning Reference Electrode (MCD)
SRE........... Schedule of Recent Experience [*Psychometrics*]
SRe............ Science Review [*Manila*] [*A publication*]
SRE........... Seminole, OK [*Location identifier*] [*FAA*] (FAAL)
SRE........... Send Reference Equivalent, Search RADAR [*Telecommunications*] (TEL)
SRE........... Series Relay [*Electronics*]
SRE........... Serum Response Element [*Genetics*]
SRE........... Serum-Response Enhancer [*Genetics*]
SRE........... Shelby's Rabbit Eater [*In model name Omni SRE, proposed for Dodge car designed by Carroll Shelby*]
SRE........... Signaling Range Extender [*Telecommunications*] (TEL)
SRE........... Single Region Execution
SRE........... Single Round Effectiveness (NATG)
SRE........... Single Rural Eligible [*Classified advertising*]
SRE........... Site Resident Engineer [*Telecommunications*] (TEL)
SRE........... Society of Recreation Executives (EA)
SRE........... Society of Relay Engineers [*British*]
SRE........... Society of Reliability Engineers (EA)
SRE........... Society of Reproduction Engineers [*Later, IA VCM*] (EA)
SRE........... Society of Reproductive Endocrinologists (EA)
SRE........... Society for Reproductive Surgeons (EA)
SRE........... Sodium Reactor Experiment [*Nuclear energy*]
SRE........... Sound Reproduction Equipment (DEN)
SRE........... Special Re-Education
SRE........... Srednekan [*Former USSR*] [*Later, MGD*] [*Geomagnetic observatory code*]
SRE........... Standard RADAR Environment
SRE........... Statistical Record of the Environment [*A publication*]
SRE........... Statistical Reporter [*A publication*]
SRE........... STDN [*Space Tracking and Data Network*] Ranging Equipment [*NASA*] (GFGA)
SRE........... Sterol Regulatory Element [*Genetics*]
SRE........... Stray Radiant Energy
SRE........... Sucre [*Bolivia*] [*Airport symbol*] (OAG)
SRE........... Surveillance RADAR Element
SRE........... Surveillance RADAR Equipment
SREA......... Senior Real Estate Analyst [*Designation awarded by Society of Real Estate Appraisers*]
SREA........ Society of Real Estate Appraisers [*Later, AI*] (EA)
SREA........ Street Rod Equipment Association (EA)
SREAE ...... AES Regina Weather Office, Environment Canada [*Bureau Meteorologique du SEA de Regina, Environnement Canada*] Saskatchewan [*Library symbol*] [*National Library of Canada*] (NLC)
SREB........ Southern Regional Educational Board
SREC........ Executive Council, Regina, Saskatchewan [*Library symbol*] [*National Library of Canada*] (NLC)
SREC........ Southern Rice Export Corp. (EA)
SRED........ Saskatchewan Department of Education, Regina, Saskatchewan [*Library symbol*] [*National Library of Canada*] (NLC)
Sred Med Rab ... Sreden Medicinski Rabotnik [*A publication*]
SREEP...... Environmental Protection Service, Environment Canada [*Service de la Protection de l'Environnement, Environnement Canada*] Regina, Saskatchewan [*Library symbol*] [*National Library of Canada*] (NLC)
SR(EF)...... Seaman Recruit (Electronics Field) [*Navy rating*] (DNAB)
SREG......... [*The*] Standard Register Co. [*NASDAQ symbol*] (NQ)
SREG......... Standing Register [*Civil Service*]
SREHP...... Serine-Rich Entamoeba Histolytica Protein [*Biochemistry*]
SREI......... Student Role Expectation Inventory
SREIW ...... Inland Waters Directorate, Environment Canada [*Direction Generale des Eaux Interieures, Environnement Canada*] Regina, Saskatchewan [*Library symbol*] [*National Library of Canada*] (NLC)
SREL........ Savannah River Ecology Laboratory [*Department of Energy*] [*Aiken, SC*]
SREL........ Southwest Regional Educational Laboratory (AEBS)
SREL........ Space Radiation Effects Laboratory [*Langley, VA*] [*NASA*]
S Rel Sc Rel ... Studies in Religion/Sciences Religieuses [*A publication*]
SREM........ Scanning Reflection Electron Microscopy
S-REM ...... Sleep with Rapid Eye Movement

SREM....... Software Requirements Engineering Methodology
SREM....... Sound Ranging Evaluation Model (MCD)
SREMP ..... Source Region Electromagnetic Pulse
SRen......... Studies in the Renaissance [*A publication*]
SREND7.... Science Research News [*Kanpur*] [*A publication*]
SREODB.... Senior Explosive Ordnance Disposal Badge [*Military decoration*] (GFGA)
S Rep.......... Senate Reports [*A publication*] (DLA)
S Rep.......... Southern Reporter [*A publication*] (DLA)
SREPT...... Senate Committee Report (AFIT)
SRES .... Senate Resolution (AFIT)
SRES .... Senores [*Sirs, Gentlemen*] [*Spanish*]
SRES .... Sierra Resources [*NASDAQ symbol*] (NQ)
SRES .... Southern Railway Employees' Sangh [*India*]
S Res .... United States Senate Resolution [*A publication*] (DLA)
SRET .... Satellite de Recherches et d'Environment Technique [*Satellite for Environmental and Technical Research*] [*France*]
SRET .... Scanning Reference Electrode [*Corrosion testing*]
SRev.......... Sayers Review [*A publication*]
SRev.......... School Review [*A publication*]
SRE(V) ...... Singapore Royal Engineers (Volunteers) [*British military*] (DMA)
SRev.......... Slavic Review [*A publication*]
SRev.......... Southwest Review [*A publication*]
S Rev (Adel) ... Southern Review (Adelaide, Australia) [*A publication*]
S Rev (Baton) ... Southern Review (Baton Rouge) [*A publication*]
S Rev Lit .... Saturday Review of Literature [*A publication*]
S Rev Pub Adm ... Southern Review of Public Administration [*A publication*]
SRF .... S-Band Receiver Filter
SRF .... Salmonellosis-Resistance Factor
SRF .... Sam Rayburn Foundation
SRF .... San Rafael, CA [*Location identifier*] [*FAA*] (FAAL)
SRF .... Scleroderma Research Foundation (EA)
SRF .... Seal Rescue Fund (EA)
SRF .... Secure Reserve Forces [*Military*] (MCD)
SRF .... Selected Reserve Force [*Units*] [*of Army National Guard*] [*Discontinued, 1969*]
SR & F .... Selection, Referral, and Followup
SRF .... Self-Realization Fellowship (EA)
SRF .... Self-Referenced Fringe (MCD)
SRF .... Self-Resonant Frequency
SRF .... Semireinforcing Furnace [*Carbon black manufacture*]
SRF .... Serum Response Factor [*Biochemistry*]
SRF .... Ship Repair Facility [*Navy*] (NVT)
SRF .... Shuttle Refurbish Facility [*NASA*] (NASA)
SRF .... Sido, Robert F., Edwardsville IL [*STAC*]
SRF .... Skin Reactive Factor [*Immunochemistry*]
SRF .... Skin Respiratory Factor [*Physiology*]
SRF .... Slovak Relief Fund (EA)
SRF .... Snake Ranch Flats [*New Mexico*] [*Seismograph station code, US Geological Survey*] [*Closed*] (SEIS)
SRF .... Software Recording Facility
SRF .... Software Recovery Facility [*Data processing*] (IBMDP)
SRF .... Solar Radiation Flux
SRF .... Somatotrophin-Releasing Factor [*Endocrinology*]
SRF .... Sorter Reader Flow
SRF .... Space Requirement Forms (AAG)
SRF .... Spacecraft Research Foundation [*Inactive*] (EA)
SRF .... Special Reporting Facility [*Department of State*]
SRF .... Split Renal Function [*Medicine*] (MAE)
SRF .... Stable Radio Frequency
SRF .... State Revolving Fund [*Environmental Protection Agency*] (GFGA)
SRF .... Strategic Reserve Forces (MCD)
SRF .... Strategic Retaliatory Forces (AAG)
SRF .... Strategic Rocket Forces (MCD)
SRF .... Submarine Range-Finder
SRF .... Submarine Repair Facility
SRF .... Subretinal Fluid [*Ophthalmology*] (MAE)
SRF .... Sun River Gold Corp. [*Vancouver Stock Exchange symbol*]
SRF .... Supported Ring Frame
SRF .... Surface Roughness Factor [*Telecommunications*] (TEL)
SRF .... Survival Research Foundation (EA)
SRF .... System Recovery Factor
SRFB .... Space Research Facilities Branch [*National Research Council of Canada*]
SRFC .... Sheep Red Cell Rosette Forming Cells (AAMN)
SRFC .... Shotgun Red Fan Club (EA)
SRFCEE .... Fox Chase Cancer Center. Scientific Report [*A publication*]
SRFCS...... Self-Repairing Flight Control System
SRFD........ Society for the Rehabilitation of the Facially Disfigured [*Later, National Foundation for Facial Reconstruction*] (EA)
SRFF......... Set-Reset Flip-Flop [*Data processing*]
SRFI .... Self-Rising Flour Institute [*Later, HBA*]
SRFI .... Sugar Research Foundation, Inc. [*Later, ISRF*] (EA)
SRFI .... Super Rite Foods, Inc. [*NASDAQ symbol*] (NQ)
SRFLANT ... Ships Repair Facility, Atlantic (DNAB)
SRFLSBAD ... Senior Flight Surgeon Badge [*Military decoration*] (GFGA)
SrFltSurgBad ... Senior Flight Surgeon Badge [*Military decoration*] (AABC)
SRFM .... Source Range Flux Monitoring [*Nuclear energy*] (NRCH)
SRFPAC.... Ships Repair Facility, Pacific (DNAB)

SRFS......... Split Renal Function Study [*Medicine*]   (MAE)
SRFT .... Shortest Remaining First Time   (HGAA)
SRFTL....... Secure Resource Force Target List   (MCD)
SRFU........ Seal Research and Fisheries Unit [*British*]
SRG .... Regina General Hospital, Saskatchewan [*Library symbol*] [*National Library of Canada*]   (NLC)
SRG .... Santa Sarita Mining [*Vancouver Stock Exchange symbol*]
SRG .... Schering-Plough Corp. [*Research code symbol*]
SRG .... Schriften. Raabe-Gesellschaft [*A publication*]
SRG .... Semarang [*Indonesia*] [*Airport symbol*]   (OAG)
SRG .... Servomotor Rate Generator
SRG .... Short Range   (FAAC)
SRG .... Sine-Random Generator
SRG .... Social Research Group [*George Washington University*] [*Research center*]   (RCD)
SRG .... Society of Remedial Gymnasts   (EA)
SRG .... Sorg, Inc. [*AMEX symbol*]   (SPSG)
SRG .... Sound Ranging
SRG .... Statistical Research Group [*Princeton University*]   (MCD)
SRG .... Stimulated Raman Gain [*Spectroscopy*]
SRG .... Stock Removal Grinding   (MCD)
SRg .... Studies in Religion [*A publication*]
SRG .... Surge   (MSA)
SRG .... System Routing Guide [*Military*]   (CAAL)
SRG .... Systems Research Group   (CINC)
SRGA........ Stable Reactor, General, Atomic
SRGD .... Gabriel Dumont Institute, Regina, Saskatchewan [*Library symbol*] [*National Library of Canada*]   (NLC)
SRGE........ Saskatchewan Government Employees Association, Regina, Saskatchewan [*Library symbol*] [*National Library of Canada*]   (NLC)
SRGH .... Pasqua Hospital, Regina, Saskatchewan [*Library symbol*] [*National Library of Canada*]   (NLC)
SRGI......... Saskatchewan Government Insurance, Regina, Saskatchewan [*Library symbol*] [*National Library of Canada*]   (NLC)
SRGM .... Super Rapid Gun Mounting [*Military*]
SRGMF ..... Santa Sarita Mining [*NASDAQ symbol*]   (NQ)
SRGR........ Short-Range Guided Rocket
SRGS........ St. Rosalie Generating Station [*Nuclear energy*]   (NRCH)
SRGS........ Saskatchewan Genealogical Society, Regina, Saskatchewan [*Library symbol*] [*National Library of Canada*]   (NLC)
SRGS........ Survivable Radio Guidance System [*Military*]
SRGSC ...... Southern Rhodesia General Service Corps [*British military*]   (DMA)
SRGY........ American Surgery Centers Corp. [*NASDAQ symbol*]   (NQ)
SRH .... Saskatchewan Housing Corp., Regina, Saskatchewan [*Library symbol*] [*National Library of Canada*]   (BIB)
SRH .... Secretaria de Recursos Hidraulicos [*Mexico*]
SRH .... Sequential Rough Handling   (MCD)
SRH .... Single Radial Hemolysis [*Immunochemistry*]
SRH .... Smith, R. H., Minneapolis MN [*STAC*]
SRH .... [*A*] Social and Religious History of the Jews [*S. W. Baron*] [*A publication*]   (BJA)
SRH .... Somatotropin-Releasing Hormone [*Endocrinology*]   (MAE)
SRH .... Spontaneously Responding Hyperthyroidism [*Endocrinology*]
SRH .... Stigmata of Recent Hemorrhage [*Medicine*]
SRH .... Strathcona Resources Industries Ltd. [*Toronto Stock Exchange symbol*]
SRH .... Structural Repair Handbook   (DNAB)
SRH .... Subsystems Requirements Handbook [*NASA*]   (NASA)
SRH .... Supply Railhead
SRH .... Switchyard Relay House [*Nuclear energy*]   (NRCH)
SRHA .... Statistical Record of Hispanic Americans [*A publication*]
SRHB .... Society for Research into Hydrocephalus and Spina Bifida   (EA)
SRHC .... Shutdown Reactor Head Cooling [*Nuclear energy*]   (NRCH)
SR HCR..... Southern Rhodesia High Court Reports [*1911-55*] [*A publication*]   (DLA)
SRHE .... Society for Religion in Higher Education [*Later, SVHE*]   (EA)
SRHE .... Society for Research into Higher Education [*Guildford, Surrey, England*]   (EAIO)
SRHE Bull ... Society for Research into Higher Education. Bulletin [*A publication*]
SRHE Newsl ... Society for Research into Higher Education. Newsletter [*A publication*]
SRHIT....... Small RADAR-Homing Interceptor Technology
SRHJ......... [*A*] Social and Religious History of the Jews [*S. W. Baron*] [*A publication*]   (BJA)
SRHL........ Small RADAR Homing Interceptor
SRHL........ Southwestern Radiological Health Laboratory [*HEW*]
S Rhodesia Geol Surv Bull ... Southern Rhodesia. Geological Survey. Bulletin [*A publication*]
SRHP........ Planning Branch, Saskatchewan Department of Highways and Transportation, Regina, Saskatchewan [*Library symbol*] [*National Library of Canada*]
SRHP........ Section for Rehabilitation Hospitals and Programs [*American Hospital Association*]   (EA)
SRHQ........ Subregional Headquarters [*Military*] [*British*]
SRHS........ Health Sciences Library, Plains Health Centre, Regina, Saskatchewan [*Library symbol*] [*National Library of Canada*]   (NLC)
SR(HS)....... Seaman Recruit (High School) [*Navy rating*]   (DNAB)

SRHSB ..... Society for Research into Hydrocephalus and Spina Bifida   (EA)
SRI........... British Steel [*A publication*]
SRI........... Sacrum Romanum Imperium [*The Holy Roman Empire*] [*Latin*]
SRI............ Samarinda [*Indonesia*] [*Airport symbol*]   (OAG)
SRI............ Scholarly Resources, Incorporated, Wilmington, DE [*Library symbol*] [*Library of Congress*]   (LCLS)
SRI............ Sefid-Roud [*Iran*] [*Seismograph station code, US Geological Survey*]   (SEIS)
SRI............ Selective Retention Indicators   (NVT)
SRI............ Senior Resident Inspector [*Nuclear energy*]   (NRCH)
SRI............ Servo Repeater Indicator
SRI............ Severe Renal Insufficiency [*Medicine*]
SRI............ Signal Routing and Interface   (MCD)
SRI............ Silicon Rubber Insulation
SRI............ Ski Retailers International   (EA)
SRI............ Social Research Institute [*University of Utah*] [*Research center*]   (RCD)
SRI............ Society for Rational Individualism [*Later, SIL*]   (EA)
SRI............ Sorry [*Communications operator's procedural remark*]
SRI............ Southeastern Reservoir Investigation [*Department of the Interior*]   (GRD)
SRI............ Southern Research Institute
SRI............ Southwest Research Institute
SRI............ Space Research Institute [*Defunct*]   (EA)
SRI............ Spalling Resistance Index   (IEEE)
SRI............ Special Recreation, Inc.   (EA)
SRI............ Spectrum Resolver Integrator
SRI............ Spectrum Resources, Inc. [*St. Charles, MO*] [*Telecommunications*]   (TSSD)
SRI............ Speech Rehabilitation Institute   (EA)
SRI............ Spring Research Institute   (EA)
SRI............ Standard Research Institute   (MCD)
SRI............ Standby Request for Information [*Military*]   (AABC)
SRI............ Standing Request for Information   (MCD)
SRI............ Stanford Research Institute [*Later, SRI International*] [*Databank originator*]
SRI............ Statistical Reference Index [*A publication*]
SRI............ Stick to Rudder Interconnect   (MCD)
SRI............ Storeroom Item   (DNAB)
SRI............ Supply Requisition Inquiry
SRI............ Surface Roughness Indicator
SRI............ Sveriges Runinskrifter [*A publication*]
SRI............ Swiss Radio International
SRI............ Syllable Repetition Interval [*Entomology*]
SRIA .... Saskatchewan Intergovernmental Affairs, Regina, Saskatchewan [*Library symbol*] [*National Library of Canada*]   (NLC)
SRIA .... State and Regional Indicators Archive [*University of New Hampshire*] [*Information service or system*]   (IID)
SRIAER..... Scientific Research Institute for Atomic Energy Reactors [*Former USSR*]
SRIB .... Strike Route Information Book [*Strategic Air Command*]   (AABC)
SRIC .... Short-Run Incremental Cost   (ADA)
SRIC .... Southwest Research and Information Center   (EA)
SRIC .... SRI Corp. [*NASDAQ symbol*]   (NQ)
SRICDS..... Inter-American Tropical Tuna Commission. Special Report [*A publication*]
SRID......... Search RADAR Input Device   (MCD)
SRIELA..... Selected Reports: Publication of the Institute of Ethnomusicology of the University of California at Los Angeles [*A publication*]
SRIF .... Somatotrophin-Releasing Inhibiting Factor [*Also, GH-RIF, GH-RIH, GRIF, SS*] [*Endocrinology*]
SRIF .... Special Risk Insurance Fund [*Federal Housing Administration*]
SRIFC....... Saskatchewan Indian Federated College, Regina, Saskatchewan [*Library symbol*] [*National Library of Canada*]   (NLC)
SRIH......... Somatostatin [*Biochemistry*]
SRIIA .... Silk and Rayon Industries of India [*A publication*]
SRI J........ SRI [*Stanford Research Institute*] Journal [*A publication*]
Sri Lan J Hum ... Sri Lanka Journal of Humanities [*Peradeniya*] [*A publication*]
Sri Lanka Assoc Adv Sci Proc Annu Sess ... Sri Lanka Association for the Advancement of Science. Proceedings of the Annual Session [*A publication*]
Sri Lanka For ... Sri Lanka Forester [*A publication*]
Sri Lanka Geol Surv Dep Econ Bull ... Sri Lanka. Geological Survey Department. Economic Bulletin [*A publication*]
Sri Lanka Lab Gaz ... Sri Lanka Labour Gazette [*A publication*]
SriLJH ...... Sri Lanka Journal of the Humanities [*A publication*]
SRILTA...... Stanford Research Institute Lead Time Analysis
SR-IM........ Office of Strategic Research, Intelligence Memoranda [*CIA*]
SRIM .... Selected Research in Microfiche [*A publication*]
SRIM .... Short-Range Intercept Missile   (MCD)
SRIM .... Standing Order Microfiche Service
SRIM .... Structural Reaction Injection Molding [*Plastics*]
SRIN......... Indian and Northern Affairs Canada [*Affaires Indiennes et du Nord Canada*], Regina, Saskatchewan [*Library symbol*] [*National Library of Canada*]   (BIB)
SRIO......... Systems Research Integration Office [*Army Air Mobility Research and Development Laboratory*] [*St. Louis, MO*]

SRIP .... Selected Reserve Incentive Program [*Army*]
SRIP .... Ship Readiness Improvement Plan [*Navy*]   (NG)
SRIP .... Short-Range Impact Point   (MUGU)
SRIP .... Soldier/Robot Interface Program Vehicle [*Military*]   (RDA)
SRIP .... Specification Review and Improvement Program [*Navy*]   (NG)
SRIP .... Supplier Rating Incentive Program
SRI Pestic Res Bull ... SRI [*Stanford Research Institute*] Pesticide Research Bulletin [*A publication*]
SRIS .... Safety Recommendation Information System [*Database*]
SRIS .... Safety Research Information Service [*National Safety Council*]   (IID)
SRIS .... Science Reference and Information Service   (IID)
SRISP .... Interprovincial Steel & Pipe Corp. Ltd., (IPSCO), Regina, Saskatchewan [*Library symbol*] [*National Library of Canada*]   (NLC)
SRIT .... Service and Repair Identification Tag   (MCD)
Srita .... Senorita [*Miss*] [*Spanish*]
SRIY .... Sherwood Rangers Imperial Yeomanry [*British military*]   (DMA)
SRJ .... San Borja [*Bolivia*] [*Airport symbol*]   (OAG)
SRJ .... Scorcorp Industries, Inc. [*Vancouver Stock Exchange symbol*]
SRJ .... Self-Restraint Joint
SRJ .... Short Run Job   (MCD)
SRJ .... Standard-Range Juno [*Survey meter for radiation*]
SRJ .... Static Round Jet
SRJC .... Communications Policy Branch, Saskatchewan Department of Justice, Regina, Saskatchewan [*Library symbol*] [*National Library of Canada*]   (NLC)
SRJC .... Santa Rosa Junior College [*California*]
SRJKAK.... Annual Report. Sado Marine Biological Station. Niigata University [*A publication*]
SRK........... Soave-Redlich-Kwong [*Equation of state*]
SRK........... Spirit Lake, IA [*Location identifier*] [*FAA*]   (FAAL)
SRK........... Sredniy Kalar [*Former USSR*] [*Seismograph station code, US Geological Survey*]   (SEIS)
SRK........... Stralak Resources [*Vancouver Stock Exchange symbol*]
SRKN .... Single Rotating Knife
SRL........... HRIN [*Human Resource Information Network*] Special Reports Library [*Executive Telecom System, Inc.*] [*Information service or system*]   (CRD)
SRL........... Legislative Library of Saskatchewan, Regina, Saskatchewan [*Library symbol*] [*National Library of Canada*]   (NLC)
SRL........... Santa Rosalia [*Mexico*] [*Seismograph station code, US Geological Survey*] [*Closed*]   (SEIS)
SRL........... Saturday Review of Literature [*A publication*]
SRL........... Savannah River Laboratory [*Department of Energy*] [*Aiken, SC*]
SRL........... Save-the-Redwoods League   (EA)
SRL........... Sceptre Resources Ltd. [*AMEX symbol*] [*Toronto Stock Exchange symbol*]   (SPSG)
SRL........... Scheme Representation Language [*Artificial intelligence*]
SRL........... Scientific Research Laboratory   (AAG)
SRL........... Screwworm Research Laboratory [*Department of Agriculture*]   (GRD)
SRL........... Securities Regulation Law Journal [*A publication*]
SRL........... Seiler Research Laboratory [*Air Force*]   (MCD)
SRL........... Service Rights Layer [*Data processing*]
SRL........... Singing Return Loss [*Telecommunications*]   (TEL)
SRL........... Skin Resistance Level [*Physiology*]
SRL........... Society of Romance Linguistics [*Nancy, France*]   (EAIO)
SRL........... Sonobuoy Receiver Logic [*Navy*]   (CAAL)
SRL........... Sound Reference Laboratory [*Orlando, FL*] [*Navy*]
SRL........... Sound Research Laboratories Ltd. [*Research center*] [*British*]   (IRUK)
SRL........... Spares Recommendation List   (MCD)
SRL........... Stability Return Loss [*Telecommunications*]   (TEL)
SRL........... Standard Reference Library
SRL........... Strangeways Research Laboratory [*British*]   (IRUK)
SRL........... Stress Relieving Liner   (KSC)
SRL........... Structural Return Loss [*Telecommunications*]   (TEL)
SRL........... Student Religious Liberals [*Later, SRL, A Free Religious Fellowship*] [*Defunct*]
SRL........... Studies in Romance Languages [*A publication*]
SRL........... Study Reference List   (AFM)
SRL........... Summary Requirements List   (MCD)
SRL........... Support Requirements Letter   (CET)
SRL........... Survey Research Laboratory [*University of Illinois*] [*Information service or system*]   (IID)
SRL........... System Reference Library   (HGAA)
SRL........... Systems Research Laboratory
SRLC .... Luther College, Regina, Saskatchewan [*Library symbol*] [*National Library of Canada*]   (NLC)
SRLD........ Small Rocket Lift Device
SRLF .... Saggi e Ricerche di Letteratura Francese [*A publication*]
SRLP .... Leader-Post Ltd., Regina, Saskatchewan [*Library symbol*] [*National Library of Canada*]   (NLC)
SRLP .... Socialist and Revolutionary Labour Party [*Gambia*] [*Political party*]   (PD)
SRLR .... Securities Regulation and Law Reports [*Bureau of National Affairs*] [*A publication*]

SRLS .... Law Society of Saskatchewan Libraries, Regina [*Library symbol*] [*National Library of Canada*]   (BIB)
Sr LS .... Senior Life Saving [*Red Cross*]
SRLS .... Starved Rock Library System [*Library network*]
SRLUDT ... Scientific Report. Laboratory for Amphibian Biology. Hiroshima University [*A publication*]
SRLY .... Series Relay   (IEEE)
SRM .... Safety, Reliability, and Maintainability   (SSD)
SRM .... Schedule Request Message   (MCD)
SRM .... Scrim-Reinforced Material [*Nonwoven sheets*]
SRM .... Secretory Rate Maximum [*Physiology*]
SRM .... Sensor Response Model
SRM .... Sensormatic Electronics Corp. [*NYSE symbol*]   (SPSG)
SRM .... Serbian Renaissance Movement [*Political party*]   (EY)
SRM .... Service Repair Manual
SRM .... Shared Resource Management [*Data processing*]
SRM .... Shift Register Memory
SRM .... Ship Repair and Maintenance [*National Shipping Authority*]
SRM .... Shock Remanent Magnetization   (OA)
SRM .... Short-Range Missile [*Projected; not to be confused with SRAM*]
SRM .... Short-Range MODEM
SRM .... Single Register Machine
SRM .... Smokeless Rocket Motor   (MCD)
SRM .... Snowmelt-Runoff Model [*Hydrology*]
SRM .... Society for Range Management   (EA)
SRM .... Socorro - La Joya [*New Mexico*] [*Seismograph station code, US Geological Survey*] [*Closed*]   (SEIS)
SRM .... Solid-Rocket Motor
SRM .... Source Range Monitor [*Nuclear energy*]   (NRCH)
SRM .... Specific Repair Methods [*Boeing*]
SRM .... Specification Requirements Manual [*NASA*]   (NASA)
SRM .... Speed of Relative Movement
SRM .... Spiritual Regeneration Movement [*Foundation of America*]   (EA)
SRM .... Square Root Mode [*Data processing*]
SRM .... Standard Reference Material [*National Institute of Standards and Technology*]
SRM .... Standard Reference Module
SRM .... Standard Repair Manual   (MCD)
SRM .... Strategic Reconnaissance Missile
SRM .... Structural Repair Manual
SRM .... Superior Rectus Muscle [*Eye anatomy*]
SRM .... System Resource Manager [*IBM Corp.*]   (BUR)
SRM .... System for Resources Management [*Jet Propulsion Laboratory, NASA*]
SRMA....... Silk and Rayon Manufacturers Association [*Defunct*]   (EA)
SRMA....... Ski Resort Marketing Association   (EA)
SRMBDB .. Marine Sciences Research Center [*Stony Brook*]. Special Report [*A publication*]
SRMBR ..... Senior Member   (DNAB)
SRMC........ Society of Risk Management Consultants [*Baton Rouge, LA*]   (EA)
SRMC........ Specification Requirements Manual   (MCD)
SRMC....... Stimulus/Response Measurements Catalog   (NASA)
SRMCASE ... Symmetry-Restricted-Multiconfiguration Annihilation of Single Excitations [*Physics*]
SRMD .... Stress-Related Mucosal Damage [*Medicine*]
SRMF........ Short-Run Manufacturing Facility   (MCD)
SRML........ Short-Range Missile Launcher
SRMP........ Supply Readiness Milestone Plan [*Military*]   (CAAL)
SRM & QA ... Safety, Reliability, Maintainability, and Quality Assurance [*NASA*]   (SSD)
SRMR........ Saskatchewan Department of Mineral Resources, Regina, Saskatchewan [*Library symbol*] [*National Library of Canada*]   (NLC)
SRMS........ Scheduling and Resource Management System [*Tymshare UK*] [*Software package*]   (NCC)
SRMS........ Ships Records Management System   (MCD)
SRMS........ Shuttle Remote Manipulator System   (SSD)
SRMS........ Strategic Research and Management Service
SRMS........ Structure Resonance Modulation Spectroscopy
SRMSDS... Montana. Forest and Conservation Experiment Station. Study Report [*A publication*]
SRMT........ Southern Rock Mountain Trench [*Geology*]
SRN .... Sabine River & Northern Railroad Co. [*AAR code*]
SRN .... Saskatchewan Registered Nurses Association, Regina, Saskatchewan [*Library symbol*] [*National Library of Canada*]   (NLC)
SRN .... Satellite Radio Navigation   (DNAB)
SRN .... Saturn Science Fiction and Fantasy [*A publication*]
SRN .... Serial Reference Number
SRN .... Simulation Reference Number
SRN .... Software Release Notice [*NASA*]   (NASA)
SRN .... Southern
SRN .... Southern Air Transport, Inc.
SRN .... Souvenir Nieuws [*A publication*]
SRN .... Specification Revision Notice   (MCD)
SRN .... State Registered Nurse [*British*]
SRN .... Strathearn House Group Ltd. [*Toronto Stock Exchange symbol*]
SRN .... Stretch Receptor Neuron
SRN .... Student Registered Nurse   (MAE)

sRNA	Ribonucleic Acid, Soluble [*Replaced by tRNA*] [*Biochemistry, genetics*]
SRNB.........	Sociology. Reviews of New Books [*A publication*]
SRNC........	Severn River Naval Command
SRND	Surround (FAAC)
S & R Neg ..	Shearman and Redfield on the Law of Negligence [*A publication*] (DLA)
S & R on Neg ...	Shearman and Redfield on the Law of Negligence [*A publication*] (DLA)
SRNFC......	Source Range Neutron Flux Channel (IEEE)
SR(NFE)....	Seaman Recruit (Nuclear Field Electronics) [*Navy rating*] (DNAB)
SRNG	Syringe
SRNLS	Northern Library Services, Saskatchewan Library, Regina, Saskatchewan [*Library symbol*] [*National Library of Canada*] (NLC)
SRNR........	Stock Request Number
SRNS........	Steroid-Responsive Nephrotic Syndrome [*Medicine*]
SRNS........	Surveyor Retro Nozzle Structure
SR(NSET) ...	Seaman Recruit (Nuclear Submarine Engineering Technician) [*Navy rating*] (DNAB)
SR (NSW) ...	State Reports (New South Wales) [*A publication*] (APTA)
SR (NSW) B & P ...	State Reports (New South Wales). Bankruptcy and Probate [*A publication*] (APTA)
SR (NSW) Eq ...	State Reports (New South Wales). Equity [*A publication*] (APTA)
Sr Nurse.....	Senior Nurse [*A publication*]
SRNV	Subretinal Neovascularization [*Ophthalmology*]
SRO	S-Band RADAR Operational
SRO	Safety Recall Order (MCD)
SRO	Sales Release Order
SRO	Saskatchewan Oil Co., Regina, Saskatchewan [*Library symbol*] [*National Library of Canada*] (NLC)
SRO	Savannah River Operation [*Office*] [*Energy Research and Development Administration*]
SRO	Scarboro Resources Ltd. [*Toronto Stock Exchange symbol*]
SRO	Scottish Record Office
SRO	Self-Regulatory Organisation [*Financial Services Act of 1986*] [*British*]
SRO	Senior Range Officer
SRO	Senior Reactor Operator [*Nuclear energy*] (NRCH)
SRO	Senior Research Officer [*Ministry of Agriculture, Fisheries, and Food*] [*British*]
SRO	Sex-Ratio Organism [*Entomology*]
SRO	Shakespearean Research Opportunities [*A publication*]
SRO	Sharable and Read Only [*Data processing*] (PCM)
SRO	Shop Repair Order
SRO	Short-Range Order [*Solid state physics*]
SRO	Shrobarova [*Czechoslovakia*] [*Seismograph station code, US Geological Survey*] (SEIS)
SRO	Single-Room Occupancy [*Housing*]
SRO	Singly Resonant Oscillator (IEEE)
SRO	Society of Radio Operators
SRO	Solar Radio Observatory
SRO	Southern Airlines, Inc. [*West Palm Beach, FL*] [*FAA designator*] (FAAC)
SRO	Spares Requirement Order
SRO	Special Rate Order [*Business term*]
SRO	Special Regional Operations (NATG)
SRO	Specification Release Order [*Nuclear energy*] (NRCH)
SRO	Squadron Recreation Officer [*Navy*] [*British*]
SRO	Standing Room Only [*Theater*]
SRO	Standing Route Order [*Army*] (AABC)
SR & O.......	Statutory Rules and Orders [*England*] [*A publication*] (DLA)
SRO	Statutory Rules and Orders
SRO	Steele-Richardson-Olszewski Syndrome [*Medicine*]
SRO	Stock Record Officer
SRo	Studia Rosenthaliana [*A publication*] (BJA)
SRO	Superintendent [*or Supervisor*] of Range Operations [*NASA*]
SRO	Supervisor Range Operations (MCD)
SRO	Supplementary Reserve of Officers [*Military*] [*British*]
SRO	System Readiness Objective
SRO	Systems Reproduction Order (MCD)
SROA	Safety-Related Operator Action [*Nuclear energy*] (NRCH)
SROA	Society for Radiation Oncology Administrators (EA)
SROB........	Short-Range Omnidirectional Beacon [*Aerospace*]
SROD........	Stove Rod
SROE.........	[*Shipboard*] Satellite Readout Equipment (MCD)
SROE.........	Statistical Record of the Environment [*A publication*]
SROEQ......	Selected References on Environmental Quality as It Relates to Health [*A publication*]
SROF........	Self-Renewal Occupational Field
SROF........	Sustained Rate of Fire [*Military*] (INF)
SROH.........	Societe de Recherche en Orientation Humaine [*Canada*]
SROKA......	Second Republic of Korea Army
SROP.........	Senior Registered Options Principal [*Investment term*]
SROS........	Seybold Report on Office Systems (HGAA)
SR & O and SI Rev ...	Statutory Rules and Orders and Statutory Instruments Revised [*England*] [*A publication*] (DLA)
SROTC......	Senior Reserve Officers' Training Corps [*Military*] (AABC)
SROTS	Superficial Rays of the Sun [*In reference to suntanning, supposedly occuring before 10am and after 2pm*] [*See also BROTS*]
SROWW ...	Statistical Record of Women Worldwide [*A publication*]
SRP...........	Safeguard Readiness Posture [*Army*] (AABC)
SRP...........	Salary Reduction Plan [*Business term*]
SRP...........	Saskatchewan Library and Union Catalogue, Regina, Saskatchewan [*Library symbol*] [*National Library of Canada*] (NLC)
SRP...........	Saskatchewan Provincial Library [*UTLAS symbol*]
SRP...........	Savannah River Plant [*Department of Energy*]
SRP...........	Savings and Retirement Plan
SRP...........	Scientific Research Proposal (AAG)
SRP...........	Sealift Readiness Program [*Military*]
SRP...........	Seat Reference Point
SRP...........	Seismic Reflection Profile [*Marine science*] (MSC)
SRP...........	Selective Reenlistment Program [*Air Force*]
SRP...........	Self-Recording Penetrometer
SRP...........	Sensor Reporting Post
SRP...........	Serbian Radical Party [*Political party*]
SRP...........	Shags Rocks Passage [*Oceanography*]
SRP...........	Shark Research Panel [*Navy*] (DNAB)
SRP...........	Ship's Repair Party [*Navy*] [*British*]
SRP...........	Short Ragweed Pollen [*Immunology*]
SRP...........	Sierra Pacific Resources [*NYSE symbol*] (SPSG)
SRP...........	Signal Recognition Particle [*Biochemistry*]
SRP...........	SIOP Reconnaissance Plan (MCD)
SRP...........	Small Rotating Plug [*Nuclear energy*] (NRCH)
SRP...........	Socialist Revolution Party [*Turkey*] [*Political party*] (PPW)
SRP...........	Socialist Revolutionary Party [*India*] [*Political party*] (PPW)
SRP...........	Socialist Revolutionary Party [*Former USSR*] [*Political party*]
SRP...........	Socialisticka Radnicka Partija Jugoslavije [*Socialist Workers' Party of Yugoslavia*] [*Political party*] (PPE)
SRP...........	Society for Radiological Protection [*British*] (DEN)
SRP...........	Software Renewal Program [*Food and Nutrition Service*] [*Department of Agriculture*] (GFGA)
SRP...........	Solar Radiation Pressure
SRP...........	Solicitation Review Panel [*Air Force*]
SRP...........	Sonobuoy Referenced Position [*Navy*] (NG)
SRP...........	Source Record Punch
SRP...........	Sozialistische Reichspartei [*Socialist Reich Party*] [*Germany*] [*Political party*] (PPE)
SRP...........	Space Requirement Program (MCD)
S & RP	Spares and Repair Parts [*Navy*]
SRP...........	Spin Recovery Parachute
SRP...........	Stabilization Reference Package (MCD)
SRP...........	Standard Relative Power
SRP...........	Standard Repair Procedures
SRP...........	Standard Review Plan [*Nuclear energy*] (NRCH)
SRP...........	Start Rendezvous Point (MCD)
SRP...........	State Registered Physiotherapist [*British*]
SR & P	Station Resources and Planning [*Navy*] (DNAB)
SRP...........	Status Report Panels (SAA)
SRP...........	Stern Reference Point [*Navy*] (DNAB)
SRP...........	Stratospheric Research Program
SRP...........	Stray Radiant Power
SRP...........	Suggested Retail Price
SRP...........	Supply Readiness Program [*Air Force*]
SRP...........	Supply Refuelling Point [*Air Force*] [*British*]
SRP...........	Supply and Repair Parts (DNAB)
SRP...........	Traverse City, MI [*Location identifier*] [*FAA*] (FAAL)
SRPA	Senior Real Property Appraiser [*Designation awarded by Society of Real Estate Appraisers*]
SRPA	Spherical Retarding Potential Analyzer (MCD)
Srp Akad Nauka Umet Od Prir-Mat Nauka (Glas) ...	Srpska Akademija Nauka i Umetnosti Odeljenje Prirodno-Matematickikh Nauka (Glas) [*A publication*]
Srp Akad Nauka Umet Posebna Izdan Od Prir Mat Nauka ...	Srpska Akademija Nauka i Umetnosti Posebna Izdanja Odeljenje Prirodno-Matematickikh Nauka [*A publication*]
SRPARABAD ...	Senior Parachutist Badge [*Military decoration*]
Srp Arh Celok Lek ...	Srpski Arhiv za Celokupno Lekarstvo [*A publication*]
Srp Arkh Tselok Lek ...	Srpski Arkhiv za Tselokupno Lekarstvo [*A publication*]
SRPB	Scottish River Purification Board
SRPBA	Scottish River Purification Boards Association
SRPC........	SaskPower, Regina, Saskatchewan [*Library symbol*] [*National Library of Canada*] (NLC)
SRPC........	Sulphate Resisting Portland Cement
SRPCRD ...	Research and Development Center Library, SaskPower, Regina, Saskatchewan [*Library symbol*] [*National Library of Canada*] (NLC)
SRPD........	System Research and Planning Division [*NASA*] (KSC)
SRPDAA ...	Silk and Rayon Printers and Dyers Association of America (EA)
SR(PFE)	Seaman Recruit (Polaris Field Electronics) [*Navy rating*] (DNAB)
SR(PFL)	Seaman Recruit (Polaris Field Launcher) [*Navy rating*] (DNAB)
SRPG........	Scraping

SRPH......... Saskatchewan Department of Health, Regina, Saskatchewan [*Library symbol*] [*National Library of Canada*] (NLC)
SRPI .... Scrap Rubber and Plastics Institute (EA)
SRPI .... Silk and Rayon Print Institute [*Defunct*] (EA)
SRPIS........ Southern Regional Plant Introduction Station [*University of Georgia*] [*Research center*] (RCD)
SRPJ......... Self-Restraining Pipe Joint
SRPM....... Shaft Revolutions per Minute (DNAB)
SRPM....... Stated Redemption Price at Maturity [*of debt instruments*]
SRPMME ... Society for Research in the Psychology of Music and Music Education [*British*]
SRPN........ Special Requisition Priority Number
SRPO......... Science Resources Planning Office [*National Science Foundation*]
SRPO......... Soobchtcheniia Russkago Palestinskago Obchtshestva [*A publication*]
SR & PO .... Station Resources and Planning Office [*Navy*] (DNAB)
SRPP .... Public Participation Library, Regina, Saskatchewan [*Library symbol*] [*National Library of Canada*] (BIB)
SRPP .... Skeletal Rod of Palp
SRPR .... Saskatchewan Parks and Renewable Resources, Regina, Saskatchewan [*Library symbol*] [*National Library of Canada*] (NLC)
SRPR .... Scraper
SRPR .... Stray Radiant Power Ratio
SRPR .... Surtsey Research Progress Report [*A publication*]
SrPrchtBad ... Senior Parachutist Badge [*Military decoration*]
SRPS .... Saskatchewan Public Service Commission, Regina, Saskatchewan [*Library symbol*] [*National Library of Canada*] (NLC)
SRPS .... Scientific Research Project Support [*National Science Foundation*]
SRPS .... Secure Record and Playback System (MCD)
SRPS .... Sensor-Referenced Positioning System
SR/PS......... Shipping Request/Packing Sheet (MCD)
SRPS .... Supply and Repair Parts Specification (DNAB)
Srpsko Hem Drus Bull ... Srpsko Hemiskog Drustvo. Bulletin [*A publication*]
SRPV .... Stationary Remotely Piloted Vehicle (MCD)
SRPW........ Savannah River Plant - Well DRB-10 [*South Carolina*] [*Seismograph station code, US Geological Survey*] (SEIS)
SR & Q ...... Safety, Reliability, and Quality (NASA)
SRQ .... Sarasota/Bradenton [*Florida*] [*Airport symbol*]
SRQ .... Service Request
SRQ .... State Reports (Queensland) [*A publication*] (APTA)
SR & QA .... Safety, Reliability, and Quality Assurance (NASA)
SRR............ Central New York Library Resources Council, Syracuse, NY [*OCLC symbol*] (OCLC)
SRR............ Schuh Kurier. Das Wirtschaftmagazin der Schuhbranche [*A publication*]
SRR............ Scots Revised Reports [*A publication*] (DLA)
SRR............ Search and Range RADAR
SRR............ Search and Rescue Region [*Aviation*] (FAAC)
SRR............ Seastar Resource Corp. [*Vancouver Stock Exchange symbol*]
SRR............ Security Rules and Regulations
srr.............. Serer [*MARC language code*] [*Library of Congress*] (LCCP)
SRR............ Serially Reusable Resource [*Data processing*]
SRR............ Service Representative Report (MCD)
SRR............ Shift Register Recognizer (IEEE)
SRR............ Short-Range RADAR
SRR............ Short-Range Recovery (IEEE)
SRR............ Shuttle Requirements Review [*NASA*] (MCD)
SRR............ Site Readiness Review [*NASA*] (NASA)
SRR............ Skin Resistance Response [*Physiology*]
SRR............ Slow Rotation Room [*NASA*]
SRR............ Socialist Republic of Romania
SRR............ Society for Reformation Research (EA)
SRR............ Software Requirements Review [*NASA*] (NASA)
SRR............ Sound Recorder-Reproducer (MSA)
SRR............ Source-Receptor Relation [*Environmental chemistry*]
SRR............ Special Reimbursement Rate (AFM)
SRR............ Special Report Writer [*NASA*]
SRR............ Spurious Response Rejection
SRR............ Stain Release Rating [*Textile technology*]
SRR............ State Regulation Report: Toxics [*Business Publishers, Inc.*] [*Information service or system*] (CRD)
SRR............ Steering Reversal Rate
SRR............ Strategic Ready Reserve [*Military*]
SRR............ Stride Rite Corp. [*NYSE symbol*] (SPSG)
SRR............ Subsystem Requirements Review
SRR............ Supplementary Reserve Regulations [*Army*] [*British*]
SRR............ Supplier Rating Report (SAA)
SRR............ Support Requirements Records [*Navy*] (NG)
SRR............ Surplus Review Record (SAA)
SRR............ Survival, Recovery, and Reconstitution [*Military*] (AFM)
SRR............ System Readiness Review (MCD)
SRR............ System Requirements Review [*NASA*]
SRRA .... Sage Race Relations Abstracts [*A publication*]
SRRB .... Search and Rescue Radio Beacon
SRRC........ Resource Centre, RCMP [*Royal Canadian Mounted Police*] Academy, Regina, Saskatchewan [*Library symbol*] [*National Library of Canada*] (NLC)

SRRC........ Scottish Reactor Research Centre (DEN)
SRRC......... Southern Regional Research Center [*Department of Agriculture*] [*New Orleans, LA*] (GRD)
SRRC......... Sperry Rand Research Center (MCD)
SRRC......... Standing Results Review Committee [*Nuclear energy*] (NRCH)
SRRCP ...... Petroleum Division, Saskatchewan Research Council, Regina [*Library symbol*] [*National Library of Canada*] (BIB)
SRRCS...... Surface Raid Reporting Control Ship [*Navy*] (NVT)
SRRE .... Prairie Farm Rehabilitation Administration, Agriculture Canada [*Administration du Retablissement Agricole des Prairies, Agriculture Canada*] Regina, Saskatchewan [*Library symbol*] [*National Library of Canada*] (NLC)
SRREEC.... Institute of Soil Science. Academia Sinica. Soil Research Report [*A publication*]
SRRI .... Wascana Campus, Saskatchewan Institute of Applied Science and Technology, Regina, Saskatchewan [*Library symbol*] [*National Library of Canada*] (NLC)
SRRS .... Social Readjustment Rating Scale [*Psychometrics*]
SR-RSV .... Rous Sarcoma Virus, Schmidt-Ruppin Strain
SRRT .... Simultaneous Rotating and Reciprocating Technique (DNAB)
SRRT .... Social Responsibilities Round Table [*American Library Association*] (EA)
SRS........... Sales Relations Survey [*Test*]
SRS........... Salzburg Renaissance Studies [*A publication*]
SRS........... Saskoil, Regina, Saskatchewan [*Library symbol*] [*National Library of Canada*] (NLC)
SRS........... Satellite RADAR Station (NATG)
SRS........... Satellite Readout Station (MCD)
SRS........... Satellite Receiving Station
SRS........... Scandinavian Radiological Society (EA)
SRS........... Science Requirements Strategy [*Viking lander mission*] [*NASA*]
SRS........... Scientific Reference Service [*HEW*]
SRS........... Scientific Research Society of America [*Later, Sigma XI, The Scientific Research Society of America*] (AAG)
SRS........... Scottish Record Society [*Glasgow*] (EA)
SRS........... Search and Rescue Ship (KSC)
SRS........... Second Readiness State (AAG)
SRS........... Secondary RADAR System
SRS........... Secondary Recovery Ships [*NASA*] (KSC)
SRS........... Secure Range Safety [*NASA*] (KSC)
SRS........... Segment Ready Storage
SRS........... Seismic Recording System
SRS........... Selenium Rectifier Stack
SRS........... Self-Rating Scale [*Psychology*]
SRS........... Senate Recording Studio
SRS........... Series [*Deltiology*]
SRS........... Shakespeare Recording Society [*Commercial firm*] (EA)
SRS........... Shipboard RADAR System
SRS........... Short-Range Search (MCD)
SRS........... Shorter Range Scheduling
SRS........... Side-Looking RADAR System
SRS........... Sight Restoration Society (EA)
SRS........... Silent Running Society (EA)
SRS........... Silver-Russell Syndrome [*Medicine*]
SRS........... Simple Random Sample [*Statistics*]
SRS........... Simulated Raman Scattering
SRS........... Simulated Remote Sites [*NASA*] (KSC)
SRS........... Simulated Remote Station [*NASA*]
SRS........... Slave Register Set
SRS........... Sleep Research Society (EA)
SRS........... Slippery Rock State College, Slippery Rock, PA [*OCLC symbol*] (OCLC)
SRS........... Slow-Reacting Substance [*of anaphylaxis*] [*Leukotriene C*] [*Immunology*]
SRS........... Small Research Satellite (KSC)
SRS........... Social and Rehabilitation Service [*Abolished, 1977*] [*HEW*]
SRS........... Social and Rehabilitation Service. Publications [*A publication*]
SRS........... Society for Romanian Studies (EA)
SRS........... Sodium Removal Station [*Nuclear energy*] (NRCH)
SRS........... Software Requirements Specification [*NASA*] (NASA)
SRS........... Solar Radiation Simulator
SRS........... Solid RADWASTE [*Radioactive Waste*] System [*Nuclear energy*] (NRCH)
SRS........... Songwriters Resources and Services [*Later, NAS*] (EA)
SRS........... Sonobuoy Reference System [*Navy*] (CAAL)
SRS........... Sound Ranging Set
SRS........... Sound Recordings Specialists [*Record label*]
SRS........... Sound Retrieval System [*Hughes Aircraft Co.*]
SRS........... Sounding Rocket System
SRS........... Southern Railway System (MCD)
SRS........... Space Recovery Systems (KSC)
SRS........... Spaceborne Reconnaissance System
SRS........... Spares Recommendation Sheet (MCD)
SRS........... Spares Requirement Schedule (MCD)
SRS........... Special Revenue Sharing (OICC)
SRS........... Specification Requirement Sheet (RDA)
SRS........... Specification Revision Sheet [*NASA*] (NASA)
SRS........... Speech Reinforcement System
SRS........... Splenorenal Shunt [*Medicine*]
SRS........... Squad Radio Set

SRS .... Srpska Radikalna Stranka [*Serbian Radical Party*] [*Former Yugoslavia*] [*Political party*] (PPE)
S/RS .... Staff Returns [*Marine Corps*]
SRS .... Standard Random Sample
SRS .... Standard Reference Section
SRS .... Standard Repair Specification (MCD)
SRS .... State Revenue Society (EA)
SRS .... Statistical Reporting Service [*Later, ESCS*] [*Department of Agriculture*]
SRS .... Stimulated Raman Scattering [*Spectrometry*]
SRS .... Strange Stories [*A publication*]
SRS .... Strategic Reconnaissance Squadron (MCD)
SRS .... Strike Reporting System
SRS .... Structural Research Series
SRS .... Student Response System [*Automated group instruction*]
SRSA .... Submarine Reactor Small
SRS .... Subscriber-Response System [*Study of cable television*] [*Hughes Aircraft Co.*]
SRS .... Substitute Route Structure
SRS .... Sum of All Repairable Subassemblies
SRS .... Sunrise Metals [*Vancouver Stock Exchange symbol*]
SRS .... Supplemental Restraint System [*Automotive engineering*]
SRS .... Supply Response Section [*Navy*]
SRS .... Support Requirement System [*NASA*] (NASA)
SRS .... Surgical Research Society [*British*]
SRS .... Surveillance RADAR Station
SRS .... Survey Research Service [*National Opinion Research Center, University of Chicago*] [*Research center*]
SRS .... Survey Research Singapore (Pte) Ltd. [*Information service or system*] (IID)
SRS .... Synchronous Relay Satellite [*Telecommunications*] (TEL)
SRS .... Synchrotron Radiation Source [*High-energy physics*]
SRS .... System Requirements Specification (MCD)
SRSA .... Saskatchewan Arts Board, Regina, Saskatchewan [*Library symbol*] [*National Library of Canada*] (NLC)
SRSA .... Scientific Research Society of America [*Later, Sigma XI, The Scientific Research Society of America*]
SRS-A .... Slow-Reacting Substance of Anaphylaxis [*Immunology*]
SR SATSIM ... Search RADAR Satellite Simulation [*Military*] (CAAL)
SRSC .... Safety Railway Services Corp. [*NASDAQ symbol*] (NQ)
SRSC .... Saturday Review of the Sciences [*A publication*]
SRSC .... Slippery Rock State College [*Pennsylvania*]
SRSC .... Space Remote Sensing Center
SRSC .... Sul Ross State College [*Later, SRSU*] [*Texas*]
SRSC .... System Centre, Saskatchewan Revenue Supply and Services, Regina, Saskatchewan [*Library symbol*] [*National Library of Canada*] (NLC)
SRSCC .... Simulated Remote Station Control Center
SRSCCD .... Saskatchewan Co-Operation and Co-Operative Development, Regina, Saskatchewan [*Library symbol*] [*National Library of Canada*] (NLC)
Sr Sch .... Senior Scholastic [*A publication*]
Sr Schol ..... Senior Scholastic [*A publication*]
SR-Sci .... Saturday Review of the Sciences [*A publication*]
Sr Sci .... Senior Science [*A publication*]
SRSCU ...... Saskatchewan Computer Utility Corp. [*SaskComp*], Regina, Saskatchewan [*Library symbol*] [*National Library of Canada*] (NLC)
SRSD .... Saturday Review of Society [*A publication*]
SRSEM ..... Saskatchewan Department of Energy and Mines, Regina, Saskatchewan [*Library symbol*] [*National Library of Canada*] (NLC)
SRSEMG .. Geological Laboratory, Saskatchewan Department of Energy and Mines, Regina, Saskatchewan [*Library symbol*] [*National Library of Canada*] (NLC)
SRSF .... Saskatchewan Finance, Regina, Saskatchewan [*Library symbol*] [*National Library of Canada*] (NLC)
SRSF .... SRB [*Solid-Rocket Booster*] Receiving [*or Refurbishment*] and Subassembly Facility [*NASA*] (NASA)
SRSG .... Search RADAR Simulation Group [*Military*] (CAAL)
SRSG .... Subsurface Geological Laboratory, Regina, Saskatchewan [*Library symbol*] [*National Library of Canada*] (NLC)
SRSH .... Wascana Hospital, Regina, Saskatchewan [*Library symbol*] [*National Library of Canada*] (NLC)
SRSI .... Sikh Religious Studies Information [*A publication*]
SRSI .... Specialty Retail Services, Inc. [*NASDAQ symbol*] (NQ)
SRSIB .... Salt Research and Industry [*A publication*]
SRSK .... Short-Range Station Keeping (NG)
SRSL .... Sunrise Bancorp, Inc. [*NASDAQ symbol*] (NQ)
SRSM .... Special Research Study Memorandum
SRSNY ..... Stockholder Relations Society of New York (EA)
SRSO .... Saturday Review of Society [*A publication*]
SRSO .... Scoliosis Research Society (EA)
SR-Soc ...... Saturday Review of Society [*A publication*]
SRSP .... Stockpile Reliability/Survivability Program
SRSPMC ... Saskatchewan Property Management Corp., Regina, Saskatchewan [*Library symbol*] [*National Library of Canada*] (NLC)
SR Sq .... Strategic Reconnaissance Squadron
SRSR .... Schedule and Resources Status Report [*NASA*] (NASA)

SRSRDL .... Soviet Scientific Reviews. Section D. Biology Reviews [*A publication*]
SRSS .... Resource Centre, Saskatchewan Department of Social Services, Regina, Saskatchewan [*Library symbol*] [*National Library of Canada*] (NLC)
SRSS .... Shuttle Range Safety System [*NASA*] (NASA)
SRSS .... Simulated Remote Sites Subsystem [*NASA*] (KSC)
SRSS .... Sociological Resources for Secondary Schools (AEBS)
SRSS .... Sociological Resources for Social Studies [*Project of American Sociological Association*]
SRSS .... Solar Radiation Simulator System
SRSS .... Square Root of the Sum of the Squares (NRCH)
SRST .... SASK TEL Corporate Library, Regina, Saskatchewan [*Library symbol*] [*National Library of Canada*] (NLC)
SRST .... Speed Reading Self-Taught [*Learning International*]
SRSTA .... Society of Roller Skating Teachers of America (EA)
SRSU .... Satellite Readout Station Upgrade (DWSG)
SRSU .... Sul Ross State University [*Texas*]
SRSUE .... Studies in Regional Science and Urban Economics [*Elsevier Book Series*] [*A publication*]
SRT .... S-Band Radio Transmitter
SRT .... Sagittal Ray Trace
SRT .... Sarafotoxin [*Biochemistry*]
SRT .... Sarutani [*Japan*] [*Seismograph station code, US Geological Survey*] (SEIS)
SRT .... Scarlet Energy, Inc. [*Vancouver Stock Exchange symbol*]
SRT .... School Readiness Test [*Child development test*]
SRT .... Science Recommendation Team
SRT .... Science, Research, and Technology
SRT .... Search RADAR Terminal
SRT .... Security Response Team [*Military*]
SRT .... Sedimentation Rate Test
SRT .... Self-Repair Technique
SRT .... Serials Round Table [*Later, RTSD*] [*American Library Association*]
SRT .... Short-Range Transport [*Aircraft*] (NATG)
SRT .... Shuttle Requirements Traceability [*NASA*] (MCD)
SRT .... Silica RADOME Technique
SRT .... Simple Reaction Time [*Psychometry*]
SRT .... Single Requesting Terminal [*Data processing*] (IBMDP)
SRT .... Slow-Run-Through Trials [*Navy*] (NG)
SRT .... Social Relations Test [*Psychology*]
SRT .... Solar Radiation Test
SRT .... Solar Radio Telescope
SRT .... Solids Retention Time [*Water pollution*]
SRT .... Soroti [*Uganda*] [*Airport symbol*] (OAG)
SRT .... Source Routing Transparent [*Telecommunications*]
SRT .... Special Rated Thrust [*Aerospace*] (MCD)
SRT .... Special Real-Time Command (MCD)
SRT .... Special Review Team [*Nuclear energy*] (NRCH)
SRT .... Specification Requirements Table [*NASA*] (NASA)
SRT .... Speech Reception Test [*Audiometry*] (MAE)
SRT .... Speech Reception Thresholds [*Audiometry*]
SRT .... Spent Resin Tank [*Nuclear energy*] (NRCH)
SRT .... Spousal Remainder Trust [*Banking*]
SRT .... Standard Rate Turn (NVT)
SRT .... Standard Remote Terminal
SRT .... Station Readiness Test
SRT .... Step Recovery Transistor
SRT .... Strategic Relocatable Target [*DoD*]
SRT .... Strategic Rocket Troops (NATG)
SRT .... Stress Relief Tool
SRT .... Stroke Rehabilitation Technician (MAE)
SRT .... Subcaliber Rocket Trainer [*Army*] (INF)
SRT .... Supply Response Time
SRT .... Supporting Research and Technology (MCD)
SR & T ...... Supporting Research and Technology
SRT .... Surface Recording Terminal (MCD)
SRT .... Sustained Release Theophylline [*Medicine*]
SRT .... Synchro and Resolver Transmission
SRT .... System Reaction Time (KSC)
SRT .... System Reliability Test
SRT .... Systems Readiness Test (KSC)
SRTA .... Senorita [*Miss*] [*Spanish*]
SRTA .... Single Relaxation Time Approximation [*Physics*]
SRTBM ..... Short-Range Tactical Ballistic Missile
SRTC .... Scientific Research Tax Credit [*Canada*]
SRTC .... Search RADAR Terrain Clearance (NG)
SRTC .... Society of Ration Token Collectors (EA)
SRTC .... Southern Rhodesia Transport Corps [*British military*] (DMA)
SRTC .... Special Real-Time Command (KSC)
SRTC .... Stored Program Real-Time Commands (MCD)
SRTD .... Sorted (MCD)
SRTF .... Short-Range Task Force
SRTF .... Shortest Remaining Time First [*Data processing*]
SRTG-A ..... Science Reports. Tohoku University. Seventh Series. Geography [*Japan*] [*A publication*]
SRTN .... Sensor Return [*Automotive engineering*]
SRTN .... Solar Radio Telescope Network
SRTN .... Special Representative for Trade Negotiations [*Later, USTR*] [*Executive Office of the President*]

SRTP	Sensitized Room Temperature Phosphorescence
SRTR	Short-Range Training Round [*Army*] (INF)
SRTS	Scaled Range Target System (MCD)
SRTS	Science Research Temperament Scale [*Psychology*]
SRTS	Short-Range Thermal Sight [*Army*] (INF)
SRTS	Strategic Reconnaissance Training Squadron
SRTS	Surveillance RADAR Test Set
SRTSB	Business Library, Saskatchewan Department of Tourism and Small Business, Regina, Saskatchewan [*Library symbol*] [*National Library of Canada*] (NLC)
SRTU	Ship Repair Training Unit
SRTUAW ...	Acta Geologica Taiwanica [*A publication*]
SRTUC	Southern Rhodesian Trade Unions Congress
SRTVM	Short-Range Track via Missile [*Military*] (CAAL)
SRU	Santa Cruz, CA [*Location identifier*] [*FAA*] (FAAL)
SRU	Scottish Rugby Union (DAS)
SRU	Seaplane Reconnaissance Unit
SRU	Secondary Replaceable Unit
SRU	Selective Reserve Unit [*Navy*] (NVT)
SRU	Self-Representing Unit (GFGA)
SRU	Sensor Readout Unit (MCD)
SRU	Servo Repeater Unit
SRU	Ship Repair Unit
SRU	Shop-Replaceable Unit [*NASA*] (NASA)
SRU	Signal Responder Unit (AAG)
SRU	Silver Recovery Unit
SRU	Smallest Replaceable Unit (MCD)
SRU	Societe de Raffinage d'Uranium [*France*]
SRU	Space Replaceable Unit (MCD)
SRU	Structural Repeating Unit [*Polymer nomenclature system*]
SRU	Subassembly Repairable Unit (MCD)
SRU	Submarine Repair Unit
SRU	Sulfur Recovery Unit [*Chemical engineering*]
SRU	Support Resource Unit (MCD)
SRU	Suspension and Release Units (AFM)
SRU	System Replaceable Unit
SRU	System Resource Unit [*Environmental Protection Agency*] (GFGA)
SRU	University of Regina, Saskatchewan [*Library symbol*] [*National Library of Canada*] (NLC)
SRU	University of Scranton, Scranton, PA [*OCLC symbol*] (OCLC)
SRUA	Saskatchewan Urban Affairs, Regina, Saskatchewan [*Library symbol*] [*National Library of Canada*] (NLC)
SRUC	Regina Campus, Campion College, University of Saskatchewan, Saskatchewan [*Library symbol*] [*National Library of Canada*] (NLC)
SRUE	Education Library, University of Regina, Saskatchewan [*Library symbol*] [*National Library of Canada*] (BIB)
SRUEA	Structural Engineer [*A publication*]
SRUFA	Faculty of Fine Arts, University of Regina, Saskatchewan [*Library symbol*] [*National Library of Canada*] (NLC)
SRUG	Department of Geography, University of Regina, Saskatchewan [*Library symbol*] [*National Library of Canada*] (NLC)
SRUNM	Norman MacKenzie Art Gallery, University of Regina, Saskatchewan [*Library symbol*] [*National Library of Canada*] (NLC)
SRUTA	Soviet Rubber Technology [*English Translation*] [*A publication*]
SRV	Executive Air Services, Inc. [*Jacksonville, FL*] [*FAA designator*] (FAAC)
SRV	Safety Relief Valve [*Nuclear energy*] (NRCH)
SRV	Saline Retention Value
SRV	Satellite Reentry Vehicle
SRV	Service Corp. International [*NYSE symbol*] (SPSG)
SRV	Short-Range Viewer
SRV	Simulated Reentry Vehicle
SRV	Sirius Resources [*Vancouver Stock Exchange symbol*]
SRV	Socialist Republic of Vietnam
SRV	Society of Russian Veterans of the World War (EA)
SRv	Southwest Review [*A publication*]
SRV	Space Recovery [*or Rescue*] Vehicle
SRV	Step Recovery Varactor
SRV	Stony River [*Alaska*] [*Airport symbol*] (OAG)
SRV	Submerged Research Vehicle
SRV	Surface Recombination Velocity (DEN)
SRV	Surface Roving Vehicle [*NASA*] (KSC)
SRV	Surrogate Research Vehicle [*Army Tank-Automotive Command*]
SRV	System Readiness Verification
Srvc	Service
SRVC	Sine-Random Vibration Control
SRVCLG ...	Service Ceiling [*Aerospace engineering*]
SRVDL	Safety/Relief Valve Discharge Line [*Nuclear energy*] (NRCH)
Srve	Service
SRVEILOPS ...	Surveillance Operations [*Military*] (NVT)
SRVI	Servico, Inc. [*NASDAQ symbol*] (NQ)
SRVL	Survival (MSA)
SRVLSCH ...	Survival School [*Air Force*]
SRVSB	Saturday Review of the Sciences [*A publication*]
SRW	Salisbury, NC [*Location identifier*] [*FAA*] (FAAL)

SRW	Saskatchewan Wheat Pool, Regina, Saskatchewan [*Library symbol*] [*National Library of Canada*] (NLC)
SRW	Saturday Review/World [*A publication*]
SRW	Short Ragweed [*Immunology*]
SRW	Silenced Reconnaissance Weapon (MCD)
SRW	Strategic Reconnaissance Wing [*Air Force*] (MCD)
SR (WA)	State Reports (Western Australia) [*A publication*] (APTA)
SRWA	Swiss Review of World Affairs [*A publication*]
SRWBR	Short-Range Wideband Radio (MCD)
SRWD	South Saskatchewan Committee for World Development, Regina, Saskatchewan [*Library symbol*] [*National Library of Canada*] (NLC)
SRWg.........	Strategic Reconnaissance Wing [*Air Force*] (AFM)
SRWL	Speeded Reading of Word List [*Neuropsychology test*]
SRW Nachr ...	SRW [*Siemens-Reiniger-Werke*] Nachricht [*West Germany*] [*A publication*]
SR/World ..	Saturday Review/World [*A publication*]
SRWR	Saskatchewan Water Resources Commission, Regina, Saskatchewan [*Library symbol*] [*National Library of Canada*] (NLC)
SRWS	Simplified and Regularized Writing System
SRWS	Solid Radioactive Waste System [*Nuclear energy*] (NRCH)
SRWS	Standard Reference Water Sample [*US Geological Survey*]
SRWSDA ..	World Fertility Survey. Scientific Reports [*A publication*]
SRX	Sert [*Libya*] [*Airport symbol*] [*Obsolete*] (OAG)
SRX	SR Telecom, Inc. [*Toronto Stock Exchange symbol*]
SRY	Sherwood Rangers Yeomanry [*Military unit*] [*British*]
SRY	Ship Repair Yard (CINC)
SRY	Shiroyama [*Japan*] [*Seismograph station code, US Geological Survey*] (SEIS)
SRY	Stryker Resources Ltd. [*Vancouver Stock Exchange symbol*]
SRZ	San Marcos, TX [*Location identifier*] [*FAA*] (FAAL)
SRZ	Santa Cruz [*Bolivia*] [*Airport symbol*] (OAG)
SRZ	Satz Rechen Zentrum [*Computer Composition Center*] [*Hartmann & Heenemann*] [*Information service or system*] (IID)
SRZ	Special Rules Zone
SRZ	Stratas Corp. [*Vancouver Stock Exchange symbol*]
SRZF	Synchro Resolver Zeroing Fixture
SRZLO	Supreme Royal Zuanna, Ladies of the Orient [*Defunct*] (EA)
SS	Aerolineas Dominicanas SA [*Dominican Republic*] [*ICAO designator*] (FAAC)
SS	Attack Submarine, Conventional Powered [*Navy symbol*]
SS	Faulty Sentence Structure [*Used in correcting manuscripts, etc.*]
SS	Passing Stop Sign [*Traffic offense charge*]
SS	Royal Statistical Society [*British*]
SS	Sa Saintete [*His Holiness*] [*The Pope*] [*French*]
SS	Sa Seigneurie [*His Lordship*] [*French*]
SS	Saccharin Sodium [*Sweetening agent*]
SS	Sacred Scripture
SS	Safe Shutdown [*Nuclear energy*] (NRCH)
SS	Safer Sex
SS	Safety Services [*Red Cross*]
SS	Safety Supervisor (MUGU)
SS	Safety Supplements [*Air Force*]
SS	Sagittal Sinus [*Anatomy*]
SS	Saint-Sacrement [*Blessed Sacrament*] [*French*]
SS	Saints [*as in "SS Peter and Paul"*]
SS	Saline Soak
SS	Saliva Sample (MAE)
SS	Salmonella-Shigella [*Microbiology*]
SS	Salt-Sensitive
SS	Same Size [*Photography, publishing*]
SS	Sample Sink [*Nuclear energy*] (NRCH)
SS	Sample Station [*Nuclear energy*] (NRCH)
SS	Sampled Servo [*Formatting scheme*] [*Data processing*] (PCM)
S/S	Samples per Second (KSC)
SS	Sampling System (NRCH)
SS	Sancti [*Saints*] [*Latin*]
SS	Sanctissimus [*Most Holy*] [*Latin*]
SS	Sanctum Sanctorum [*Holy of Holies*] [*Latin*] [*Freemasonry*]
SS	Sand Springs Railway Co. [*AAR code*]
SS	Sandstone [*Lithology*]
S & S	Saratoga & Schuylerville Railroad (IIA)
SS	Sartre Society (EA)
SS	Saskatoon Public Library, Saskatchewan [*Library symbol*] [*National Library of Canada*] (NLC)
SS	Satellite-Switched
SS	Satellite System
SS	Saturated Solution [*Pharmacy*]
S & S	Sausse and Scully's Irish Rolls Court Reports [*1837-40*] [*A publication*] (DLA)
SS	Sawin Society (EA)
SS	Scandinavian Seminar (EA)
SS	Scandinavian Studies [*A publication*]
SS	Scanning Slit
SS	Schempp-Hirth KG [*Germany*] [*ICAO aircraft manufacturer identifier*] (ICAO)
S en S	Schip en Schade [*A publication*]
S & S	Schleicher & Schuell [*Filter-paper company*]
SS	School and Society [*A publication*]

SS.............. Schutzstaffel [*Elite Guard*] [*NAZI Germany*]
SS.............. Schwab Safe Co. [*AMEX symbol*]   (SPSG)
SS.............. Science Service
SS.............. Science and Society [*A publication*]
SS.............. Scilicet [*Namely*] [*Legal term*] [*Latin*]
SS.............. Scintiscanning [*Medicine*]
SS.............. Sclerotinia sclerlatiorum (Causative Agent of Peanut Blight)
SS.............. Screw Steamer
SS.............. Sea Scout - Nonrigid Airship [*Royal Naval Air Service*] [*British*]
SS.............. Sea Service [*British military*]   (DMA)
SS.............. Sea State
S & S .... Searle and Smith's English Probate and Divorce Reports [*1859-60*] [*A publication*]   (DLA)
SS.............. Second Stage
SS.............. Secondary School
SS.............. Secondary Sources
SS.............. Secondary Surveillance
SS.............. Secret Service
SS.............. Secretary for Scotland
SS.............. Secretary of State
S of S .... Secretary of State
S of S .... Secretary of State for Defence [*British*]   (RDA)
SS.............. Secretary of State Department [*Canada*]
SS.............. Sections   (ADA)
SS.............. Security Service
SS.............. Security Systems, Inc. [*In TV series "Max Headroom"*]
SS.............. See a Solicitor [*British*]
SS.............. Seingalt Society   (EA)
SS.............. Selden Society   (EA)
SS.............. Select Standby
SS.............. Selective Service
SS.............. Selective Signaling
SS.............. Selector Switch   (IEEE)
SS.............. Self Simulation
SS.............. Selling Short [*or Short Sale*] [*Investment term*]
SS.............. Semifinal Splice [*Telecommunications*]   (TEL)
SS.............. Semis [*One-Half*] [*Pharmacy*]
SS.............. Semisteel
SS.............. Semisubmersible [*Drilling unit*]
SS.............. Sempervivium Society [*Burgess Hill, West Sussex, England*]   (EAIO)
SS.............. Senior Scholars   (EA)
SS.............. Senior Scholastic [*A publication*]
SS.............. Senior Security [*Investment term*]
S & S .... Sense and Sensibility [*Novel by Jane Austen*]
SS.............. Sensor [*Genetics*]
SS.............. Sensor Supervisor [*Military*]   (CAAL)
SS.............. Sensu Stricto [*In a Narrow Sense*] [*Latin*]
SS.............. Sentence Suspended
SS.............. Senza Sordini [*Without Mutes*] [*Music*]
SS.............. Sequentia [*What Follows*] [*Latin*]   (ROG)
SS.............. Sequential Switch
SS.............. Serials Section [*Resources and Technical Services Division*] [*American Library Association*]
SS.............. Series Separate
Ss .... Serum Serologic [*Immunochemistry*]
SS.............. Serum Sickness [*Medicine*]
SS.............. Service Sink   (MSA)
SS.............. Service Squadron   (AAG)
SS.............. Service Structure   (KSC)
SS.............. Sessions
SS.............. Set Screw [*Technical drawings*]
SS.............. Set Steering
S & S .... Sex and Shopping [*Themes of Judith Krantz's novels*]
SS.............. Sezary Syndrome [*Dermatology*]
SS.............. Shackamaxon Society   (EA)
SS.............. Shakespeare Survey [*A publication*]
SS.............. Sharpshooter [*Marine Corps*]
SS.............. Shear Strength   (AAG)
SS.............. Shelf Stock
SS.............. Shell Shock
SS.............. Shift Supervisor   (IEEE)
SS.............. Shimmy Showing [*From one girl to another, in reference to dress disarrangement*]
SS.............. Ship Service
S/S .... Ship-to-Shore   (MUGU)
SS.............. Ship Station
SS.............. Ship System
SS.............. Shipmasters' Society [*A union*] [*British*]
SS.............. Shipping Situation [*British*]
S & S .... Shipping and Storage
SS.............. Shipside
SS.............. Shomrim Society   (EA)
SS.............. Shoot Tip Abscission Scar [*Botany*]
SS.............. Shop Steward
SS.............. Short Sight   (ADA)
SS.............. Short Sleeves
SS.............. Shortstop
SS.............. Shosin Society   (EA)
SS.............. Shrinking Stock [*Corporate investment*]

SS.............. Shuttle System [*NASA*]   (MCD)
SS.............. Side Scatter
SS.............. Side Seam
SS.............. Side to Side
SS.............. Side by Side   (AAG)
SS.............. Side Slip   (MCD)
SS.............. Sidestream Smoke [*from cigarettes*]
SS.............. Sight and Sound [*A publication*]
S/S .... Sign Signature   (AAG)
SS.............. Signal Selector   (DEN)
SS.............. Signal Strength [*Broadcasting*]   (KSC)
SS.............. Signaling System [*Telecommunications*]   (TEL)
SS.............. Signed and Sealed
S & S .... Signs and Symptoms [*Medicine*]
S/S .... Silk Screen   (ADA)
SS.............. Silver Spur Resources [*Vancouver Stock Exchange symbol*]
SS.............. Silver Standard [*Vancouver Stock Exchange symbol*]
SS.............. Silver Star [*Military decoration*]
SS.............. Silvernail's New York Supreme Court Reports [*A publication*]   (DLA)
S & S .... Simon & Schuster [*Publisher*]
S de S .... Simon de Southwell [*Flourished, 1184-1209*] [*Authority cited in pre-1607 legal work*]   (DSA)
S & S .... Simons and Stuart's English Vice-Chancellors' Reports [*1822-26*] [*A publication*]   (DLA)
SS.............. Simple Spike
SS.............. Simplified Spelling
SS.............. Simulated Strike   (SAA)
SS.............. Simulation Supervisor   (SAA)
SS.............. Single Scan
SS.............. Single Scattering [*Photonics*]
SS.............. Single Seated
SS.............. Single Shot
SS.............. Single Sideband
SS.............. Single Signal
SS.............. Single Stout [*Beer*]   (ROG)
SS.............. Single-Stranded [*or ss*] [*Genetics*]
SS.............. Single Strength [*Citrus juices*]
SS.............. Single String   (MCD)
SS.............. Sinistral Sig   (EA)
SS.............. Sinner Saved [*Pseudonym used by William Huntington*]
SS.............. Site Safety [*Nuclear energy*]   (NRCH)
SS.............. Site Suitability [*Nuclear energy*]   (NRCH)
SS.............. Sjoegren's Syndrome [*Medicine*]
SS.............. Skid Strip   (KSC)
SS.............. Skinners' Society [*A union*] [*British*]
SS.............. Slaters' Society [*A union*] [*British*]
SS.............. Sliding Scale   (AAG)
SS.............. Slocum Society   (EA)
SS.............. Slop Sink
SS.............. Slovo a Slovesnost [*A publication*]
SS.............. Slow Setting [*Asphalt grade*]
SS.............. Small Signal
SS.............. Small Subcompact [*Car size*]
SS.............. Smallest Subunit [*Genetics*]
SS.............. Smoke Stand   (MSA)
SS.............. Smokeshop [*A publication*]
SS.............. Soap Solution
SS.............. Soapsuds
SS.............. Social Science
SS.............. Social Security
SS.............. Social Service
SS.............. Social Shopper
SS.............. Social Studies [*A publication*]
SS.............. Social Surveys
SS.............. Society of St. Sulpice [*Sulpicians*] [*Roman Catholic men's religious order*]
SS.............. Society of Separationists   (EA)
SS.............. Society of Shuttlemakers [*A union*] [*British*]
SS.............. Society of Signalmen   (EA)
SS.............. Society of the Silurians   (EA)
SS.............. Society for Strings   (EA)
SS.............. Sociological Studies [*A publication*]
SS.............. Sodium Salicylate [*Organic chemistry*]   (OA)
SS.............. Soft Sarcoma [*Oncology*]
SS.............. SoftSearch, Inc. [*Information service or system*]   (IID)
SS.............. Software Systems
SS.............. Solar Simulator   (MCD)
SS.............. Sole Source   (SAA)
SS.............. Solid Shield   (MCD)
SS.............. Solid Solution   (OA)
SS.............. Solid State
SS.............. Soluble Solids [*Chemistry*]
SS.............. Somatics Society [*Commercial firm*]   (EA)
SS.............. Somatostatin [*Also, GH-RIF, GH-RIH, GRIF, SRIF*] [*Endocrinology*]
S of S .... Song of Solomon [*Old Testament book*]
SS.............. Song Sparrow [*Ornithology*]
SS.............. Songsmith Society   (EA)
SS.............. Sonneck Society   (EA)
SS.............. Soprano Saxophone

SS.............	Sound and Sense [*Baguio City*] [*A publication*]
SS.............	Sound System
SS.............	Source Selection (MCD)
S/S.............	Source/Sink [*Data processing*] (IBMDP)
SS.............	Source/Source [*Inspection/Acceptance point*] (MCD)
SS.............	Source and Special [*Material*] [*Nuclear energy*]
SS.............	Source of Supply (AFM)
SS.............	South Saxon (ROG)
SS.............	Souvenir Sheet [*Philately*]
SS.............	Space Segment (SSD)
SS.............	Space Shuttle [*NASA*] (KSC)
SS.............	Space Simulator (IEEE)
SS.............	Space Station (AAG)
SS.............	Space Switch [*Telecommunications*] (TEL)
ss.............	Spanish Sahara [*Western Sahara*] [*MARC country of publication code*] [*Library of Congress*] (LCCP)
SS.............	Sparingly Soluble
SS.............	Special Series
SS.............	Special Service [*Vessel load line mark*]
SS.............	Special Session
SS.............	Special Settlement [*Business term*]
SS.............	Special Source Materials [*Nuclear energy*] (NRCH)
SS.............	Special Staff
SS.............	Special Strike (NATG)
SS.............	Special Study
SS.............	Special Subjects
SS.............	Special Survey [*Lloyd's Register of Shipping*] (DS)
SS.............	Specification for Structure
S/S.............	Spectrum Signature (NG)
SS.............	Speed Sensor (NRCH)
SS.............	Spenser Society (EA)
SS.............	Spherical Symmetry
S & S.........	Spigot and Socket
SS.............	Spin-Stabilized [*Rockets*]
SS.............	Spiral to Spiral
SS.............	Spore Surface [*Immunology*]
S o S.........	Sprak och Stil [*A publication*]
SS.............	Spread Spectrum (CET)
SS.............	Squawk Sheet (KSC)
SS.............	Stabilization System (AAG)
SS.............	Stack Segment [*Data processing*]
SS.............	Staff Sergeant [*Military*] [*British*] (ROG)
SS.............	Staff Specialist [*Military*]
SS.............	Staff Surgeon
SS.............	Stainless Steel
SS.............	Standard Frequency Station [*ITU designation*]
SS.............	Standard Score [*Psychology*]
SS.............	Standard Size (ADA)
SS.............	Standardized Solution [*Pharmacy*]
SS.............	Starlight Scope
S & S.........	Stars & Stripes [*A publication*]
S/S.............	Start/Stop
SS.............	Startling Stories [*A publication*]
SS.............	State School (ADA)
SS.............	State Supervisor
S/S.............	Statement of Service [*Military*]
SS.............	Statesman Series [*A publication*]
SS.............	Static Stretching [*Medicine*]
SS.............	Station Set [*NASA*] (NASA)
S to S.........	Station to Station
SS.............	Station Supervision
SS.............	Statistical Standards
SS.............	Statistically Significant (MAE)
SS.............	Statistics Sources [*A publication*]
sS.............	Statsiemens [*Also, statS*] [*Unit of electric conductance, admittance, and susceptance*]
SS.............	Steady State
SS.............	Steamship
SS.............	Steel Sash
SS.............	Steering Safety
SS.............	Steering System
SS.............	Stereoscopic Society [*Chessington, Surrey, England*] (EAIO)
SS.............	Stereoscopic Society - American Branch (EA)
SS.............	Sterile Solution
SS.............	Steroid Score [*Immunology*]
SS.............	Steroid Sulfurylation (AAMN)
SS.............	Stimulator Substance [*Liver regeneration*]
SS.............	Storage to Storage (MCD)
SS.............	Straight Shank [*Screw*]
SS.............	Straight Sided
SS.............	Straits Settlements [*in Malaya*]
SS.............	Strategic Squadron
SS.............	Strategic Study [*Military*]
Ss.............	Striped Shiner [*Ichthyology*]
SS.............	Strong Safety [*Football*]
SS.............	Structure-Superstructure [*Economics*]
SS.............	Student at Staff College [*Army*] [*British*] (ROG)
SS.............	Stumpwork Society (EA)
SS.............	Style Sac
SS.............	Subaortic Stenosis [*Medicine*] (MAE)
SS.............	Subject-Subject [*Education of the hearing-impaired*]
SS.............	Subliminal Self [*Psychical research*]
SS.............	Submarine [*Navy symbol*]
SS.............	Submarine Qualification [*Navy*]
SS.............	Submarine Scout
SS.............	Submarine Studies [*SORG*]
SS.............	Subsagittal [*Medicine*]
SS.............	Subscale
SS.............	Subscriber Switching [*Telecommunications*] (TEL)
SS.............	Subsolar [*NASA*] (KSC)
SS.............	Substitutes [*Sports*]
ss.............	Substructure [*Data processing*]
SS.............	Subsystem (AAG)
SS.............	Successive Stereometric [*A discrimination task*]
SS.............	Suction Socket (AAMN)
SS.............	Sugar Series [*Elsevier Book Series*] [*A publication*]
SS.............	Sum-of-the-Squares
SS.............	Summary Sheet
SS.............	Summation Sound
SS.............	Summing Selector (MSA)
SS.............	Summons (ROG)
SS.............	Sun Seeker (AAG)
SS.............	Sun Sensor
SS.............	Sun Simulator (MCD)
SS.............	Sunday School
SS.............	Sunday Sport [*A publication*]
SS.............	Sunset [*Meteorology*] (FAAC)
SS.............	Super Search (MCD)
SS.............	Super Speed
SS.............	Super Sport [*In automobile model name*]
SS.............	Super Symmetric [*Particle physics*]
SS.............	Superfund Surcharge [*Environmental Protection Agency*] (GFGA)
SS.............	Superintending Scientist [*British*] (ADA)
SS.............	Superintending Sister [*Navy*] [*British*]
SS.............	Supersaturated (MAE)
SS.............	Supersensitive (AAG)
SS.............	Supersonic
SS.............	Supervisors Section [*American Association of School Librarians*]
S & S.........	Supply and Service [*Army*] (AABC)
SS.............	Supply Ship (MCD)
SS.............	Support System [*Air Force*]
SS.............	Supportive Service (OICC)
SS.............	Supra Scriptum [*Written Above*] [*Latin*]
SS.............	Surface Ship
SS.............	Surface-Sized [*Paper*]
SS.............	Surface-to-Surface (NATG)
SS.............	Surratt Society (EA)
SS.............	Surveillance Station [*RADAR*]
SS.............	Suspended Sentence
SS.............	Suspended Solids [*Wastewater treatment*]
S & S.........	Swan and Sayler's Revised Statutes of Ohio [*A publication*] (DLA)
SS.............	Swedish Society, Discofil [*Record label*] [*Sweden*]
SS.............	Switch Selector (KSC)
S & S.........	Sword and Sorcery
SS.............	Sworn Statement
SS.............	Sympathetically Stimulated [*Physiology*]
SS.............	Syn og Segn [*A publication*]
SS.............	Synchro Standard
SS.............	Synergetic Society (EA)
SS.............	Synopsis Series of the United States Treasury Decisions [*A publication*] (DLA)
S & S.........	Syntax and Semantics [*A publication*]
SS.............	System Segment (MCD)
SS.............	System Sensitivity
SS.............	System Software [*NASA*] (MCD)
SS.............	System Summary [*NASA*] (MCD)
SS.............	System Supervisor
SS.............	Systems Specifications [*NASA*] (NG)
S1S.............	Surfaced or Dressed One Side [*Technical drawings*]
S2S.............	Surfaced or Dressed Two Sides [*Technical drawings*]
S4S.............	Surfaced or Dressed Four Sides [*Technical drawings*]
SSA.............	Associate in Secretarial Science
SSA.............	Cargo Submarine [*Navy symbol*] [*Obsolete*]
SSA.............	First Soprano, Second Soprano, and Alto [*in all-women choral groups*]
SSA.............	S-Band Single Access (MCD)
SSA.............	Salicylsalicylic Acid [*Organic chemistry*] (MAE)
SSA.............	Salisbury Sound Association (EA)
SSA.............	Salsalate [*Anti-inflammatory drug*]
SSA.............	Salvador [*Brazil*] [*Airport symbol*] (OAG)
SSA.............	Saskatchewan Archives Office, Saskatoon, Saskatchewan [*Library symbol*] [*National Library of Canada*] (NLC)
SSA.............	SATCOM [*Satellite Command*] Signal Analyser (DWSG)
SSA.............	Sauna Society of America (EA)
SSA.............	Scandinavian Society of Anaesthesiologists (EA)
SSA.............	Scandinavian Sociological Association (EA)
SSA.............	Schools Sailing Association [*British*]
SSA.............	Scottish Schoolmasters Association [*British*]
SSA.............	Scottish Shipmasters' Association [*A union*]

SSA............ Secretary of State for Air [*British*]
SS of A....... Secular Society of America [*Defunct*]
SSA............ Security Support Activity
SSA............ Security Supporting Assistance [*US government program for promoting economic and political stability in areas of strategic interest*]
SSA............ Segment Search Argument [*Data processing*] (BUR)
SSA............ Seismological Society of America (EA)
SSA............ Selective Service Act
SSA............ Semiconductor Safety Association (EA)
SSA............ Semiotic Society of America (EA)
SSA............ Senior Scientific Assistant [*Ministry of Agriculture, Fisheries, and Food*] [*British*]
SSA............ Sensat Technologies Ltd. [*Vancouver Stock Exchange symbol*]
SSA............ Sequential Spectrometer Accessory [*Instrumentation*]
SSA............ Series of Standard Additions
SSA............ Service Support Arrangement
SSA............ Shakespeare Society of America (EA)
SSA............ Shan State Army [*Myanmar*] [*Political party*] (EY)
SSA............ Shaw Society of America [*Defunct*] (EA)
SSA............ Sheath of Skeletal Axis
SSA............ Ship's Stores Ashore [*Navy*]
SSA............ Shuttle Simulation Aircraft [*NASA*] (NASA)
SSA............ Signal Security Agency [*Later, Army Security Agency*]
SSA............ Signal Supply Agency
SSA............ Silo Subassembly (SAA)
SSA............ Simian Society of America (EA)
SSA............ Simpler Spelling Association [*Later, PSC*] (EA)
SSA............ Sinatra Society of America (EA)
SSA............ Single Line Synchronous Adapter (MCD)
SSA............ Singular-Spectrum Analysis [*Meteorology*]
SSA............ Sisters of St. Ann of Providence [*Roman Catholic religious order*]
SS-A........... Sjogren's Syndrome A [*Medicine*]
SSA............ Skin Sensitizing Antibody (AAMN)
SSA............ Slaving Signal Amplifier
SSA........... Sleeve Stub Antenna
SSA............ Slovak Studies Association (EA)
SSA............ Small Search Area (SAA)
SSA............ Soaring Society of America (EA)
SSA............ Social Science Abstracts [*A publication*]
SSA............ Social Security Act [*1935*] [*Also, SSACT*]
SSA............ Social Security Administration [*Department of Health and Human Services*]
SSA............ Social Security Administration. Publications [*A publication*]
SSA............ Society of Security Analysts
SSA............ Society for the Study of Addiction to Alcohol and Other Drugs (EAIO)
SSA............ Software Support Activity (SSD)
SSA............ Solid-State Abstracts
SSA............ Solid-State Amorphization [*Metallurgy*]
SSA............ Sommelier Society of America (EA)
SSA............ Source Selection Activity [*or Authority*] [*Military*]
SSA............ Space Structure Assembly (SSD)
SSA............ Space Suit Assembly (KSC)
SS & A........ Space Systems and Applications [*NASA*] (NASA)
SSA............ Spanish-Surnamed American
SSA............ Spatial Sound Around [*Acoustics*]
SSA............ Special Service Agreement [*UN Food and Agriculture Organization*]
SSA............ Special Survey Automated Controls [*Lloyd's Register of Shipping*] (DS)
SSA............ Sportswear Salesmen's Association (EA)
SSA............ Staff Supply Assistant [*Military*] (AABC)
SSA............ Staff Support Agencies [*Military*]
SSAJ........... Staging and Support Area [*NASA*] (KSC)
SSA............ Standard Single Account (INF)
SSA............ Standard Spending Assessment [*Department of the Environment*] [*British*]
SSA............ Standard System Applications [*Military*]
SSA............ Stars of the Stage [*A publication*]
SSA............ Steuben Society of America (EA)
SSA............ Stick Sensor Assembly (MCD)
SSA............ Stratford Public Library, Stratford, CT [*OCLC symbol*] (OCLC)
SSA............ Student Ski Association (EA)
SSA............ Studio Suppliers Association (EA)
SSA............ Style Sac Artery
ssa .... Sub-Saharan African [*MARC language code*] [*Library of Congress*] (LCCP)
SSA............ Sub-Saharan African Country
SSA............ Subterranean Sociological Association (EA)
SSA............ Sulfite Sensitive Asthmatic
SSA............ Sulfosalicylic Acid [*Organic chemistry*]
SSA............ Sumi-E Society of America (EA)
SSA............ Supply Support Activity [*Military*] (AABC)
SSA............ Supply Support Arrangements [*A bilateral agreement between the United States and a friendly foreign government*]
SSA............ Support Services Alliance [*Schoharie, NY*] (EA)
SSA............ Survey of School Attitudes [*Student attitudes test*]
SSA............ Survival Surface-to-Air (MCD)

SSA............ Suspension Specialists Association (EA)
SSA............ Symbol Synchronizer Assembly [*NASA*]
SSA............ Synchro Signal Amplifier
SSA............ System Safety Assessment [*Army*]
SSAA........ Salzburger Studien zur Anglistik und Amerikanistik [*A publication*]
SSAA........ Saskatchewan Institute of Applied Arts, Saskatoon, Saskatchewan [*Library symbol*] [*National Library of Canada*] (NLC)
SSAA........ Shoe Suppliers Association of America (EA)
SSAA........ Skate Sailing Association of America (EA)
SSAA........ Social Security Acts Amendments [*A publication*] (DLA)
SSAA........ Space Science Analysis Area [*Space Flight Operations Facility, NASA*]
SSAAII...... Ses Altesses Imperiales [*Their Imperial Highnesses*] [*French*] (ROG)
SSAAT ...... Sun Sensor Attitude Angle Transducer
SSAB........ Special Surveys and Analysis Branch [*National Center for Education Statistics*] [*Department of Education*] (GFGA)
SSAC........ Armak Chemicals, Saskatoon, Saskatchewan [*Library symbol*] [*National Library of Canada*] (NLC)
SSAC........ Auxiliary Submarine [*Navy symbol*]
SSAC........ Secondary School Admissions Center [*Defunct*] (EA)
SSAC........ Social Security Advisory Committee [*British*]
SSAC........ Society for the Study of Architecture in Canada [*Established 1974*]
SSAC........ Solid-State Audio Clock (DWSG)
SSAC........ Source Selection Advisory Council [*Military*] (AFM)
SSAC........ Space Science Analysis and Command [*Team*] [*NASA*]
SSAC........ Sponsors' Standards Advisory Committee [*American National Standards Institute*]
SSAC........ Standing State Advisory Committee [*Terminated, 1977*] [*of Water Resources Council*] (EGAO)
SSAC........ Sterling Savings Association [*NASDAQ symbol*] (NQ)
SSAC........ Suprasellar Arachnoid Cyst [*Medicine*]
SSAC........ Suspended Sprayed Acoustical Ceiling [*Technical drawings*]
SSACT...... Social Security Act [*1935*] [*Also, SSA*]
SSADARS ... Social Security Administration Data Acquisition and Response System
SSADC...... Solid-State Air Data Computer (MCD)
SSADH...... Succinate-Semialdehyde Dehydrogenase [*An enzyme*]
SSADM..... Structured Systems Analysis and Design Method [*British*]
SSADP ...... Soldier's, Sailor's, and Airmen's Deposit Program (DNAB)
SSADP ...... Support Site Activation Data Package (MCD)
SSAE........ Society of Senior Aerospace Executives (EA)
SSAEA ...... Safety Series. IAEA [*International Atomic Energy Agency*] [*A publication*]
SSAEC...... Society for the Study of Alchemy and Early Chemistry [*British*]
SSAEPL .... Space Station Approved EEE [*Electrical, Electronic, and Electromechanical*] Parts List (SSD)
SSAF........ S-Band, Single Access Forward (SSD)
SSAF........ Standard Single Account File [*Number*] (MCD)
SSAFA...... Soldiers, Sailors, and Airmen's Family Association [*British*]
SSAG........ Single-Step Acidulation Granulation [*Fertilizer technology*]
SSAG........ Strategic Studies Advisory Group [*Army*] (AABC)
SSAGA ...... Animal Pathology Laboratory, Food Production and Inspection Branch, Agriculture Canada [*Laboratoire de Pathologie Veterinaire, Direction Generale de la Production et de l'Inspection des Aliments, Agriculture Canada*], Saskatoon, Saskatchewan [*Library symbol*] [*National Library of Canada*] (BIB)
SSAGR ...... Research Station, Agriculture Canada [*Station de Recherches, Agriculture Canada*] Saskatoon, Saskatchewan [*Library symbol*] [*National Library of Canada*] (NLC)
SSAIS........ Senior South African Individual Scale [*Intelligence test*]
SSAJ.......... Sweep Stop Alarm Jam (MCD)
SSAL .... Scientific Serials in Australian Libraries [*A publication*] (APTA)
SSAL .... Shelton Savings Bank [*NASDAQ symbol*] (NQ)
SSAL .... Simplified Short Approach Light [*Aviation*]
S-SAL....... Solar Scientific Airlock (MCD)
SSALF....... Simplified Short ALS [*Approach Light System*] with Sequenced Flashers [*Aviation*]
SSALR...... Simplified Short ALS [*Approach Light System*] with Runway Alignment Indicator Lights [*Aviation*]
SSALS....... Simplified Short Approach Light System [*Aviation*]
SSALSR .... Simplified Short Approach Light System with Runway Alignment Indicator Lights [*Aviation*]
SSAL Suppt ... SSAL [*Scientific Serials in Australian Libraries*] Supplement [*A publication*] (APTA)
SSAM........ Seismic Spectral Amplitude Measurement
SSAMR ..... John Dolan Resource Library, Saskatchewan Association for the Mentally Retarded, Saskatoon, Saskatchewan [*Library symbol*] [*National Library of Canada*] (NLC)
SSAN........ Social Security Account Number
SSAO........ Semicarbazide-Sensitive Amine Oxidase [*Biochemistry*]
SSAO........ Solid-State Audio Oscillator
SSAOA...... Soobshcheniya Shemakhinskoi Astrofizicheskoi Observatorii Akademiya Nauk Azerbaidzhanskoi SSR [*A publication*]
SSAP .... Source Service Access Point
SSAP .... Statement of Standard Accounting Practice

SSAP .... Survival Stabilator Actuator Package [*Hydraulic power*]
SSAPD ...... Symposium on Salt. Proceedings [*A publication*]
SSAPEA .... Swedish Society Against Painful Experiments on Animals (EAIO)
SSAR .... S-Band, Single Access Return (SSD)
S-SAR .... Secret - Special Access Required [*Security classification*] (MCD)
SSAR .... Site Safety Analysis Report [*Nuclear energy*] (NRCH)
SSAR .... Society for the Study of Amphibians and Reptiles (EA)
SSAR .... Spin-Stabilized Aircraft Rocket
SSAR .... Standard Safety Analysis Report [*Nuclear energy*] (NRCH)
SSAR .... Steady State Adiabatic Reactor [*Chemical engineering*]
SSAR .... Stereo Synthetic Aperture RADAR (SSD)
SSARB ...... Sassar [*A publication*]
SSARR ...... Streamflow Synthesis and Reservoir Regulation [*Data processing*]
SSAS .... Salzburg Seminar in American Studies (EA)
SSAS .... Searchless Self-Adjusting System
SSAS .... Self-Scoring Answer Sheet (DNAB)
SSAS .... Signal Security Assessment System [*Military*] (CAAL)
SSAS .... Small Sample Assay System [*Nuclear energy*] (NRCH)
SSAS .... Small Self-Administered Scheme [*Pensions*] [*British*]
SSAS .... Society for South Asian Studies (EAIO)
SSAS .... Special Signal Analysis System [*Electronic countermeasures system*]
SSAS .... Static Stability Augmentation System [*Aviation*]
SSAS .... Station Signaling and Announcement Subsystem [*Telecommunications*] (TEL)
SSAT .... Screening Speech Articulation Test [*Educational test*]
SSAT .... Secondary School Admission Test Board (EA)
SSAT .... Shuttle Service and Access Tower [*NASA*] (NASA)
SSAT .... Society for Surgery of the Alimentary Tract (EA)
SSAT .... Space Shuttle Access Tower [*NASA*] (MCD)
SSAT .... Space Station Assembly Technology (SSD)
SSAT .... Sweep Stop Alarm Target [*Military*] (CAAL)
SSATB ...... Secondary School Admission Test Board (EA)
SSAU .... Submarine Search Attack Unit (NVT)
SSAV .... Shoreline Savings Bank [*NASDAQ symbol*] (NQ)
SSAV .... Simian Sarcoma Associated Virus
SSAW .... Saatchi & Saatchi Advertising Worldwide (ECON)
SSAWL ..... Sitzungsberichte. Saechsische Akademie der Wissenschaften (Leipzig). Philologisch-Historische Klasse [*A publication*]
SSAWS ...... Single Seat Attack Weapon System [*Military*]
SSAWV ...... Sons of Spanish American War Veterans (EA)
SSAX .... System Software Associates, Inc. [*NASDAQ symbol*] (NQ)
SSB .... Ballistic Missile Submarine [*Navy symbol*]
SSB .... Cave Junction, OR [*Location identifier*] [*FAA*] (FAAL)
SSB .... Fleet Ballistic Submarine [*Navy symbol*]
SSB .... Reserve Bank of Australia. Statistical Bulletin [*A publication*]
SSB .... St. Croix [*Virgin Islands*] Seaplane Base [*Airport symbol*] (OAG)
SSB .... St. Sauveur Badole [*France*] [*Seismograph station code, US Geological Survey*] (SEIS)
SSB .... Scots Styles Book [*A publication*] (ILCA)
SSB .... Scottish Society of Boilermakers [*A union*]
SSB .... Security Screening Board [*Army*]
SSB .... Selective Service Board
SSB .... Signal Sight Back (SAA)
SSB .... Single Sideband
SSB .... Single-Strand Break [*Genetics*]
SSB .... Single-Stranded DNA [*Deoxyribonucleic Acid*] Binding Protein [*Biochemistry*]
SSB .... Sino-Soviet Bloc
SS-B .... Sjogren's Syndrome B [*Medicine*]
SSB .... Social Security Bank [*Ghana*] (EY)
SSB .... Social Security Board [*Abolished, 1946*]
SSB .... Social Security Bulletin [*US*] [*A publication*]
SSB .... Society for the Study of Blood (EA)
SSB .... Soft Service Building (SAA)
SSB .... Source Selection Board [*NASA*]
SSB .... Space Science Board [*National Research Council*]
SSB .... Special Service Battalion [*British military*] (DMA)
SSB .... Special Studies Branch [*Supreme Headquarters Allied Powers Europe*] (NATG)
SSB .... Spontaneous Symmetry Breaking [*Physics*]
SSB .... Standard Software Base (MCD)
SSB .... Submarine, Ballistic Missile [*Diesel*] [*NATO*]
SSB .... Subscriber Busy [*Telecommunications*] (TEL)
SSB .... Subsystem Status Block (MCD)
SSB .... Swimmer Support Boat
SSBA .... Seacoast Savings Bank [*NASDAQ symbol*] (NQ)
SSBA .... Sons of Scotland Benevolent Association (EA)
SSBA .... Surface Supplied Breathing Apparatus
SSBAM ..... Single Sideband Amplitude Modulation (KSC)
SSBB .... Southington Savings Bank [*Southington, CT*] [*NASDAQ symbol*] (NQ)
SSBC .... Shelton Bancorp, Inc. [*NASDAQ symbol*] (NQ)
SSBC .... Solar System Barycenter [*Astronomy*]
SSBC .... Stock Status Balance Card (NG)
SSBC .... Summary Sheet Bar Chart [*NASA*] (NASA)
SSBD .... Single-Sideboard (IEEE)

SSBD .... Society for the Study of Breast Disease (EA)
SSB/DPUT ... Serikat Sekerdja Biro/Dinas Pembangunan Usaha Tani [*Agricultural Development Service Workers' Union*] [*Indonesia*]
SSBE .... Saskatoon Board of Education, Saskatchewan [*Library symbol*] [*National Library of Canada*] (NLC)
SSBF .... Single Sideband Filter
SSBF .... Solid Surface Burning Facility (SSD)
SSBFH ...... Star-Spangled Banner Flag House Association (EA)
SSBFM ...... Single Sideband Frequency Modulation (IEEE)
SSBG .... Sex Steroid Binding Globulin [*Endocrinology*]
SSBG .... Single Sideband Generator
SSBG .... Social Services Block Grant [*Department of Health and Human Services*]
SSBG .... Southern Starr Broadcasting Group, Inc. [*NASDAQ symbol*] (NQ)
SSB/GP .... Source Selection Board/General Procurement (MCD)
SSBIC .... Specialized Small Business Investment Company
SSBK .... Suffield Savings Bank [*Suffield, CT*] [*NASDAQ symbol*] (NQ)
SSBKD ...... Serikat Sekerdja/Buruh Ketapradja Djakarta Raja [*General Union of Government Officials of Greater Djakarta*] [*Indonesia*]
SSBKTN .... Serikat Sekerdja Bank Koporasi, Tani dan Nelajan Disingkat [*Cooperative, Farmers and Fishers Bank Employees' Union*] [*Indonesia*]
SSB/L .... Steamship Bill of Lading [*Shipping*]
SSBLA ...... Sel'skokhozyaistvennaya Biologiya [*A publication*]
SSBM .... Single Sideband Modulation
SSBMA ..... Students to Save Baltic and Mediterranean Avenues (EA)
SSBN .... Fleet Ballistic Missile Submarine (Nuclear powered) [*Navy symbol*]
SSBN .... Ships Submersible Ballistic Nuclear [*British military*] (DMA)
SSBO .... Single Swing Blocking Oscillator (MSA)
SSBPI .... Serikat Sekerdja Bank Pembangunan Indonesia [*Indonesian Development Bank Employees' Union*]
SSBPS ...... Social Security Benefit Protection Service (EA)
SSBPT ...... Serikat Sekerdja Balai Penelitian Tekstil [*Textile Research Institute Workers' Union*] [*Indonesia*]
SSBR .... Smooth-Surface Built-Up Roof [*Technical drawings*]
SSBR .... Solid Strand Burning Rate (KSC)
SSBR .... Solution-Based Styrene-Butadiene Rubber [*Materials science*]
SSBS .... Sisters Servants of the Blessed Sacrament [*Roman Catholic religious order*]
SSBSC ...... Single Sideband Suppressed Carrier [*Telecommunications*]
SSBSCOM ... Single Sideband Suppressed Carrier Optical Modulator
SSBSEF .... Scientia Sinica. Series B. Chemical, Biological, Agricultural, Medical, and Earth Sciences [*A publication*]
SSBUS ...... South Slavic Benevolent Union Sloga [*Later, Sloga Fraternal Life Insurance Society*] (EA)
SSBUV ...... Shuttle Solar Backscatter Ultraviolet Instrument (MCD)
SSBWM .... Society of Scale Beam and Weighing Machinists [*A union*] [*British*]
SSC .... Co-Operative College of Canada, Saskatoon, Saskatchewan [*Library symbol*] [*National Library of Canada*] (NLC)
SSC .... Coastal Submarine [*Navy symbol*]
SSC .... Cruiser Submarine [*Navy symbol*] [*Obsolete*]
SSC .... Missionary Sisters of St. Columban [*Roman Catholic religious order*]
SSC .... Naval Service School Command
SSC .... Safeguard System Command [*Obsolete*] [*Army*] (MCD)
SSC .... St. Sauveur De Carouges [*Seismograph station code, US Geological Survey*] (SEIS)
SSC .... Saline Sodium Citrate [*Clinical chemistry*]
SSC .... Salisbury State College, Salisbury, MD [*OCLC symbol*] (OCLC)
SS & C ..... Same Sea and Country [*or Coast*] [*Shipping*] (DS)
SSC .... Sandford's New York Superior Court Reports [*A publication*] (DLA)
SSC .... Sarawak Supreme Court Reports [*A publication*] (DLA)
SSC .... Satellite Systems Corp. [*Virginia Beach, VA*] [*Telecommunications*] (TSSD)
S & Sc ...... Sausse and Scully's Irish Rolls Court Reports [*A publication*] (DLA)
SSC .... Savannah State College [*Georgia*]
SSC .... Scan-to-Scan Correlation
SSC .... Scotch Session Cases [*A publication*] (DLA)
SSC .... Sculptors Society of Canada
SSC .... Sea-State Correction [*Doppler navigation*] (DEN)
SSC .... Sea Systems Command [*Also, NSSC*] [*Navy*]
SSC .... Second-Stage Conduit
SSC .... Sector Switching Center [*Telecommunications*] (TEL)
SSC .... Secure Systems Corp. [*Manassas, VA*] [*Telecommunications*] [*Defunct*] (TSSD)
SSC .... Security Classification Code (MCD)
SSC .... Selector Subchannels
SSC .... Senate Staff Club (EA)
SSC .... Senate Steel Caucus (EA)
SSC .... Senior Service College [*Army*] (AABC)
SSC .... Sensor Signal Conditioner
SSC .... Sequential Subsystem Controllers (MCD)

SSC .... Serendipitous Survey Catalog [*Infrared Astronomical Satellite*] [*Astronomy*]
SSC .... Serial Shift Counter [*Data processing*]
SSC .... Service Schools Command (MCD)
SSC .... Servicing Support Center (SSD)
SSC .... Seton Shrine Center (EA)
SSC .... Seven Springs Center [*An association*] (EA)
SSC .... Ship Structure Committee (EA)
SSC .... Ship Systems Command [*Navy*]
SSC .... Shipbuilding Stabilization Committee [*World War II*]
SSC .... Shipment Status Correlation
SSC .... Ship's Speed Converter (MCD)
SSC .... Short Segmented Cask [*Nuclear energy*] (NRCH)
SSC .... Short Service Commissions [*Army*] [*British*]
SSC .... Short Story Criticism [*A publication*]
SSC .... Shuttle System Contractor [*NASA*] (NASA)
SSC .... Siblings for Significant Change (EA)
SSC .... Side-Stick Controller
SSC .... Signaling and Supervisory Control
SSC .... Silver Star Citation [*Military award*]
SSC .... Simulated Spacecraft [*NASA*]
SSC .... Single Silk-Covered [*Wire insulation*]
SSC .... Single-Stage Command (NASA)
SSC .... Sintered Silicon Carbide (MCD)
SSC .... Sisters of St. Casimir [*Roman Catholic religious order*]
SSC .... Site Selection Criteria (AAG)
S & SC ...... Sized and Supercalendered [*Paper*]
SSC .... Skill Specialty Code (MCD)
SSC .... Small Saver Certificate [*Banking*]
SSC .... Social Sciences Center [*University of Nevada*] [*Research center*] (RCD)
SSC .... Socialist Scholars Conference (EA)
SSC .... Societas Sanctae Crucis [*Society of the Holy Cross*] [*Latin*]
SSC .... Society of the Sacred Cross [*Anglican religious community*]
SSC .... Society of Silver Collectors (EA)
SSC .... Society for the Study of Caucasia (EA)
SSC .... Sodium Chloride-Sodium Citrate [*Analytical chemistry*]
SSC .... Software Support Center [*Army*] (RDA)
SSC .... Software System Change (MCD)
SSC .... Solar Stabilization Computer
SSC .... Soldier Support Center
SSC .... Solicitor, Supreme Court
SSC .... Solid-Solution CERMET [*NASA*] (NASA)
SSC .... Solid-State Circuit
SSC .... Solid-State Computer
SSC .... Soluble Solids Content [*Analytical chemistry*]
SSC .... Southeastern Simulation Council
SSC .... Southeastern State College [*Later, Southeastern Oklahoma State University*]
SSC .... Southern State College [*Arkansas; South Dakota*]
SSC .... Space Science Committee [*Formerly, Provisional Space Science Advisory Board for Europe*] [*of the European Science Foundation*] (EA)
SSC .... Space Suit Communicator [*Apollo*] [*NASA*]
SSC .... Space Systems Center
SSC .... Spacecraft System Console
SSC .... Special Service Center [*Bell System*]
SSC .... Special Service Clergyman [*Church of England*]
SSC .... Speciality Shopping Centre [*British*]
SSC .... Spectroscopy Society of Canada [*Societe de Spectroscopie du Canada*]
SSC .... Spin Synchronous Clock
SSC .... Squadron Supervisory Console [*Air Force*]
SSC .... Squadron Support Center (AAG)
SSC .... Squib Simulator Console
SSC .... Staff Selection Committee [*UN Food and Agriculture Organization*]
SSC .... Staff Service Center (MCD)
SSC .... Standard Saline Citrate
SSC .... Saskatoon Systems Center [*Military*]
SSC .... Standardization Status Code [*DoD*]
SSC .... Standards Steering Committee [*ANSI*]
SSC .... State Superfund Contract [*Environmental Protection Agency*]
SSC .... Static Standby Computer [*Mission Control Center*] [*NASA*]
SSC .... Station Selection Code [*Western Union*] (BUR)
SSC .... Statistical Society of Canada [*Societe Statistique du Canada*]
SSC .... Stellar Simulation Complex (OA)
SSC .... Stepping Switch Counter (AAG)
SSC .... Stock Shortage Control (SAA)
SSC .... Stores Stock Catalog
SSC .... Structures, Systems, and Components [*Nuclear energy*] (NRCH)
SSC .... Submarine Supply Center
SSC .... Subsystem Computer (MCD)
SSC .... Subsystem Sequence Controller [*NASA*] (NASA)
SSC .... Sudden Storm Commencement [*Physics*]
SSC .... Sumter, SC [*Location identifier*] [*FAA*] (FAAL)
SSC .... Sunshine Mining Co. [*NYSE symbol*] (SPSG)
SSC .... Super Serial Card [*Apple Computer, Inc.*]
SSC .... Super System Code (NRCH)
SSC .... Superconducting Super Collider [*Particle accelerator*]

SS & C ..... Supersized and Calendered [*Paper*]
SSC .... Supply and Services Canada
SSC .... Supply Status Code [*Army*] (AABC)
SSC .... Supply Support Center [*Navy*]
SSC .... Supply System Command [*Navy*] (MCD)
SSC .... Support Software Center
SSC .... System Simulation Center
SSC .... Systems Science and Cybernetics (MCD)
SSC .... Systems Support Center (BUR)
SSCA .... Scottish Stone Cutters' Association [*A union*]
SSCA .... Seven Seas Cruising Association (EA)
SSCA .... Southern Speech Communication Association (EA)
SSCA .... Spray System Compressed Air [*Nuclear energy*] (NRCH)
SSCA .... Standard Schnauzer Club of America (EA)
SSCA .... Stockholm Studies in Classical Archaeology [*A publication*]
SSCA .... Strobed Single Channel Analyzer [*Electronics*] (OA)
SSCA .... Super Sunfish Class Association (EA)
SSCA .... Surface Sampler Control Assembly [*NASA*] (NASA)
SSCAEU ... Social Service Commission of the American Ethical Union (EA)
SSCAG ...... Research Station, Agriculture Canada [*Station de Recherches, Agriculture Canada*] Swift Current, Saskatchewan [*Library symbol*] [*National Library of Canada*] (NLC)
SSCATS .... Skylab Simulation, Checkout, and Training System [*NASA*]
SSCB .... SCB Restaurant Systems [*NASDAQ symbol*] (NQ)
SSCB .... Space Station Control Board (SSD)
SSCB .... Super Small-Scale Cook-Off Bomb (MCD)
SSCB(B) .... Submarine Safety Certification Boundary (Book) [*Navy*] (DNAB)
SSCBD ...... Space Station Control Board Directive (SSD)
SSCC .... Common Channel Signaling System [*Telecommunications*] (TEL)
SSCC .... Congregation of the Sacred Hearts of Jesus and Mary [*Rome, Italy*] (EAIO)
SSCC .... IEEE Solid-State Circuits Council (EA)
SSCC .... Salt Shaker Collectors Club [*Later, AAGSSCS*] (EA)
SSCC .... SATCOM System Control Center (KSC)
SSCC .... Sea Surface Chlorophyll Concentration
SSCC .... Second-Stage Conduit Container
SSCC .... Sound Surveillance System Control Center (MCD)
SSCC .... Space Surveillance Control Center
SSCC .... Spin-Scan Cloud Camera [*NASA*]
SSCC .... Sulfide Stress Corrosion Cracking (MCD)
SSCC .... Support Services Control Center [*NASA*] (MCD)
SSCCB .... Safeguard System Configuration Control Board [*Army*] (AABC)
SSCCS .... Solid State Component Control System [*Nuclear energy*] (NRCH)
SSCD .... Society of Small Craft Designers (EA)
SSCD .... Start Sample Command Delayed
SSCD .... Stationary Source Compliance Division [*Environmental Protection Agency*] (GFGA)
SSCD .... Superheated Superconducting Colloid Detector [*Particle physics*]
SSCD .... Support System Concept Document
SSCDR ...... Subsystem Critical Design Review
SSCDS .... Small Ship Combat Data System
SSCE .... Silver/Silver Chloride Electrode
SSCE .... Sodium Chloride Calomel Electrode
SSCE .... Squadron Supervisory and Control Equipment (SAA)
SSCE .... Study Skills Counseling Evaluation Reading (AEBS)
SSCES .... Stanford Studies in the Civilizations of Eastern Asia [*A publication*]
SS/CF .... Signal Strength, Center Frequency [*Broadcasting*]
SSCF .... Space Subsystem Control Facility (NATG)
SSCF .... Stress/Strain Controlled Fatigue (MCD)
SSCH .... Sisters of Ste. Chretienne [*Roman Catholic religious order*]
SSCHS ...... Space Shuttle Cargo Handling System [*NASA*] (NASA)
SSCI .... Sanitation Suppliers and Contractors Institute (EA)
SSCI .... Saskatoon Collegiate Institute, Saskatchewan [*Library symbol*] [*National Library of Canada*] (NLC)
SSCI .... Senate Select Committee on Intelligence (MCD)
SSCI .... Social Sciences Citation Index [*Institute for Scientific Information*] [*Database*] [*A publication*]
SSCI .... Solar Satellite Communications, Inc. [*Denver, CO*] [*NASDAQ symbol*] (NQ)
SSCI .... Steel Service Center Institute (EA)
SSCI .... Steel Shipping Container Institute (EA)
SSCJ .... Sorores a Sacro Corde Jesus [*Sisters of the Sacred Heart of Jesus*] [*Roman Catholic religious order*]
SSCJ .... Southern Speech Communication Journal [*A publication*]
SSCK .... Sister Servants of Christ the King [*Roman Catholic religious order*]
SSCL .... Shuttle System Commonality List [*NASA*] (NASA)
SSCL .... Social Science Computing Laboratory [*University of Western Ontario*] [*Information service or system*] (IID)
SSCM .... Scattering Structural Contour Map [*Surface analysis*]
SSCM .... Servants of the Holy Heart of Mary [*Roman Catholic women's religious order*]
SSCM .... Sisters of Saints Cyril and Methodius [*Roman Catholic religious order*]

SSCMA.....	Special Supplementary Clothing Monetary Allowance [*Military*]
SSCN.........	Nuclear Cruise Missile Submarine (MCD)
SSCN.........	Scotts Seaboard Corp. [*NASDAQ symbol*] (NQ)
SSC-NCR..	Soldier Support Center - National Capitol Region [*Army*]
SSCND......	Senate Special Committee on National Defence [*Canada*]
SSCNS......	Ship's Self-Contained Navigation System
SSCO.........	Shipper Service Control Office [*Military*] (AABC)
SSCO.........	Sunstyle Corp. [*NASDAQ symbol*] (NQ)
SSCO.........	System Security Control Officer [*Military*] (GFGA)
SSCP.........	School Science Curriculum Project
SSCP.........	Single-Strand Conformation Polymorphism [*Genetics*]
SSCP.........	Small Self-Contained Payload (NASA)
SSCP.........	Standard Saline Citrate Phosphate [*A buffer*]
SSCP.........	State Service Center Program (OICC)
SSCP.........	System Services Control Point [*Data processing*]
SSCQT.....	Selective Service College Qualifying Test
SSCR.........	Set Screw
SSCR.........	Sind Sadr Court Reports [*India*] [*A publication*] (DLA)
SSCR.........	Space Station Change Request (SSD)
SSCR.........	Spectral Shift Control Reactor [*Nuclear energy*]
SSCr..........	Stainless Steel Crown [*Dentistry*]
SSCRA......	School Science Review [*A publication*]
SSCRA......	Soldiers' and Sailors' Civil Relief Act [*1940*]
SSCRI........	Social Science Computer Research Institute [*University of Pittsburgh*] [*Pennsylvania*] [*Information service or system*] (IID)
SSCRN......	Silkscreen (MSA)
SSCS.........	Sea Shepherd Conservation Society (EA)
SSCS.........	Shipboard Satellite Communications System
SS & CS....	Ship's Stores and Commissary Stores [*Navy*]
SSCS.........	Side-Stick Control System
SSCS.........	Single Sideband Communications System
SSCS.........	Southern Signal Corps School
SSCS.........	Space Station Communication System (SSD)
SSCS.........	Space Suit Communications System (MCD)
SSCS.........	Standards and Security Compliance Section [*Social Security Administration*]
SSCS.........	Steep-Spectrum Compact Sources [*of galactic radio waves*]
SSCS.........	Submarine SONAR Calibration Set
SSCS.........	Synchronous Satellite Communications System
SSCSDJ	SIAM [*Society for Industrial and Applied Mathematics*] SIMS [*SIAM Institute for Mathematics and Society*] Conference Series [*A publication*]
SSCSP.......	Space Shuttle Crew Safety Panel [*NASA*] (NASA)
SSCT.........	Shipboard Communications Terminal
SSCT.........	Solid-State Celestial Tracker
SSCT.........	Solid-State Control Transformer
SSCTS......	Space Station Communication and Tracking System (SSD)
SSCU.........	Soil Sampler Control Unit
SSCU.........	Spacecraft Systems Controller Unit [*NASA*] (KSC)
SSCU.........	Special Signal Conditioning Unit
SSCU.........	Store Station Control Unit (MCD)
SSCV.........	Semisubmersible Crane Vessel
SSCX.........	Solid-State Control Transformer
SSD...........	Doctor of Sacred Scripture
SSD...........	Institute of the Sisters of St. Dorothy [*Roman Catholic religious order*]
SSD...........	Safe Separation Device
SSD...........	Sanctissimus Dominus [*Most Holy Lord*] [*Latin*]
SSD...........	Scrap Salvage Division [*Navy*]
SSD...........	SDC Sydney Development Corp. [*Toronto Stock Exchange symbol*] [*Vancouver Stock Exchange symbol*]
SSD...........	Second-Degree Stochastic Dominance [*Statistics*]
SSD...........	Security Support Detachment (MCD)
SSD...........	Seize Signal Detector
SSD...........	Semiconductor Silicon Detector
SSD...........	Separation Systems Division [*Energy Research and Development Administration*]
SSD...........	Sequence Switch Driver
S & SD......	Sewerage and Sewage Disposal (DCTA)
SSD...........	Signal Seeking Device
SSD...........	Single-Station DOVAP [*Doppler, Velocity, and Position*]
SSD...........	Smoothing by Spectral Dispersion [*LASER technology*]
SSD...........	Social Security Disability
SSD...........	Software System Design [*Data processing*]
SSD...........	Soldiers Service Dress [*British military*] (DMA)
SSD...........	Solid-State Detector
SSD...........	Solid-State Disk [*Data processing*]
SSD...........	Solid-State Dosimeter
SSD...........	Solid-State Storage Device [*Data processing*]
SSD...........	Source-to-Skin [*or -Surface*] Distance [*Radiology*]
SSD...........	Space Sciences Division [*Jet Propulsion Laboratory*]
SSD...........	Space Shuttle Display [*NASA*]
SSD...........	Space Systems Division [*Air Force*]
SSD...........	Spacecraft Software Division [*NASA*] (NASA)
SSD...........	Special Service Division [*Army Services Forces*] [*World War II*]
SSD...........	Specialized Storage Depot
SSD...........	Specialized Support Department [*Air Force*] (AFM)
SSD...........	Specialized Support Depot [*Army*] (AABC)
SSD...........	Specific Surface Diameter

SSD...........	Split-Screen Display
SSD...........	Split Stage Demonstrator (MCD)
SSD...........	Squared Successive Differences [*Data processing*]
SSD...........	Staatssicherheitsdienst [*State Security Service*] [*Germany*]
SSD...........	Stabilized Ship Detector [*Navy*]
SSD...........	Standards Support Document [*Environmental Protection Agency*] (GFGA)
SSD...........	Stock Split-Down [*Investment term*]
SSD...........	Subsoil Drain [*Technical drawings*]
SSD...........	Sum of Square Deviation (MAE)
SSD...........	Sum-of-the-Squares of the Differences [*Mathematics*]
SSD...........	Sun Shadow Device
SSD...........	Support Software Documentation (MCD)
SSD...........	Surface Sampler Device [*NASA*]
SSD...........	Surveillance Situation Display
SSD...........	Survival Support Device (NVT)
SS & D......	Synchronization Separator and Digitizer
SSD...........	System Status Display
SSD...........	System Summary Display [*NASA*] (MCD)
SSD...........	Systems Support Division [*Air Force*]
SSDA.........	Sequential Similarity Detection Algorithm
SSDA.........	Service Station Dealers of America (EA)
SSDA.........	Social Science Data Archive [*Carleton University*] [*Canada*] [*Information service or system*] (IID)
SSDA.........	Social Science Data Archive [*University of Iowa*] [*Iowa City*] [*Information service or system*] (IID)
SSDA.........	Synchronous Serial Data Adapter
SSDB.........	Shore Station Development Board
SSDC.........	Sclerosing Sweat Duct Carcinoma [*Oncology*]
SSDC.........	Signal Source Distribution Center (AAG)
SSDC.........	Social Science Data Center [*University of Connecticut*] [*Research center*] (IID)
SSDC.........	Social Science Data Center [*University of Pennsylvania*] [*Philadelphia*] [*Information service or system*] (IID)
SSDC.........	Social Science Documentation Centre [*UNESCO*] (IID)
SSDC.........	Social Science Documentation Centre [*Indian Council of Social Science Research*] [*Information service or system*] (IID)
SSDC.........	Society of Stage Directors and Choreographers (EA)
SSDC.........	Space Science Data Center [*NASA*] (MCD)
SSDC.........	Synoptic-Scale Subprogramme Data Centre [*Marine science*] (MSC)
SSDD.........	Single-Sided, Double-Density Disk [*Magnetic disk*] [*Data processing*]
SSDD.........	Software System Design Document (MCD)
SSDD.........	System Segment Design Document
SSDF.........	Space Science Development Facility (SAA)
SSD(F)......	Submarine Support Division (Fleet Support) [*Navy*] (DNAB)
SSDF-NAA ...	Space Science Development Facility-North American Aviation (SAA)
SSDG.........	Ship Service Diesel Generator [*Navy*] (CAAL)
SSDG.........	Society for the Study of Development and Growth [*Later, SDB*] (EA)
SSDH........	Subsystem Data Handbook [*NASA*] (NASA)
SSDHPER ...	Society of State Directors of Health, Physical Education, and Recreation (EA)
SSDI.........	Social Security Disability Insurance
SSDI.........	Support System Design Integration (AAG)
SSDK.........	Savannah State Docks Railroad Co. [*AAR code*]
SSDL.........	Secondary Standard Dosimetry Laboratory
SSDL.........	Social Science Data Library [*University of North Carolina*] [*Chapel Hill*] [*Information service or system*] (IID)
SSDL.........	Society for the Study of Dictionaries and Lexicography [*Later, DSNA*] (EA)
SSDM........	Shielding Standard Design Method (MCD)
SSDMIC....	Secretariat State-Defense Military Information Control Committee
SSDMS	Space Station Data Management System [*NASA*] (SSD)
SSDN.........	Sanctissimus Dominus Noster [*Our Most Holy Lord, Jesus Christ*] [*Latin*]
SSDN.........	Solar Systems by Sun Dance, Inc. [*Hialeah Gardens, FL*] [*NASDAQ symbol*] (NQ)
SSD/N.......	Sun Synchronous Day/Night (SSD)
ssDNA	Deoxyribonucleic Acid, Single-Stranded [*Biochemistry, genetics*]
SSDP.........	Standard Source Data Package (AFIT)
SSDP.........	Suomen Sosialidemokraattinen Puolue [*Finnish Social Democratic Party*] [*Political party*] (PPW)
SSDPA	Soft-Serv Dairy Products Association [*Later, NSSFFA*] (EA)
SSDPE.......	Society for the Systematic Documentation of Paranormal Experiments (EA)
SSDPS.......	Solar System Data Processing System
SSDR.........	Satellite Situation Display Room
SSDR.........	SIGINT/SIGSEC Facilities Data Reporting System (MCD)
SSDR.........	Species Specific Defense Reaction
SSDR.........	Steady State Determining Routine
SSDR.........	Subsystem Design Review
SSDR.........	Subsystem Development Requirement (AFM)
SSDR.........	Supermarket Subsystem Definition Record [*Data processing*] (IBMDP)
SSDRS.......	Safeguard System Design Release Schedule [*Army*] (AABC)
SSDS.........	Small Ship Data System (MUGU)

SSDS .... Space Shuttle Display and Simulation [*NASA*]
SSDS .... Space Station Data System   (NASA)
SSD(S)...... Submarine Support Division (Shore Facilities) [*Navy*]   (DNAB)
SSDS .... Surface-Supported Diving System   (CAAL)
SSDSA....... Solomon Schecter Day School Association   (EA)
SSDSG ...... Special State Defense Study Group [*Military*]
SSD(ST).... Submarine Support Division (Staff Support) [*Navy*]   (DNAB)
SSDT .... Society of Soft Drink Technologists   (EA)
SSDVOR ... Single Sideband Doppler Very-High-Frequency
                   Omnidirectional Range [*FAA*]
SSE .... North-Holland Series in Systems Science and Engineering
                   [*Elsevier Book Series*] [*A publication*]
SSE .... Safe Shutdown Earthquake [*Nuclear energy*]   (NRCH)
SSE .... Safety System Engineering   (MCD)
SSE .... Saline Solution Enema [*Medicine*]
SSE .... Salvador Society of Engineers
SSE .... Satellite Systems Engineering, Inc. [*Bethesda, MD*]
                   [*Information service or system*]   (TSSD)
SSE .... Scale of Socio-Egocentrism [*Psychology*]
SSE .... Schick Shaving Experience [*Advertising slogan*]
SSE .... Scuola de Sviluppo Economico [*Italy*]
SSE .... Sector Scan Engagement [*Military*]   (CAAL)
SSE .... Security and Safety Equipment   (IMH)
SSE .... Seed Savers Exchange   (EA)
SSE .... Self-Sustained Emission
SSE .... Separated Statistical Ensemble [*Physical chemistry*]
SSE .... SIGINT Support Element   (MCD)
SSE .... Signal Security Element [*Military*]   (AABC)
SSE .... Single Sideband Exciter
SSE .... Single Silk Covering over Enamel Insulation
                   [*Telecommunications*]   (TEL)
SSE .... Sisters of St. Elizabeth [*Roman Catholic religious order*]
SSE .... Skin Self Examination [*Medicine*]
SSE .... Soap Suds Enema [*Medicine*]
SSE .... Society of St. Edmund [*Roman Catholic men's religious order*]
SSE .... Society for Scientific Exploration   (EA)
SSEng .... Society for the Study of Evolution   (EA)
SSE .... Software Support Environment   (SSD)
SSE .... Solid-State Electronics
SSE .... South-Southeast
SSE .... Southeastern Stock Exchange
SSE .... Southwest Semiconductor and Electronics Exposition   (TSPED)
SSE .... Space Shuttle Engines [*NASA*]   (MCD)
SSE .... Special Support Equipment
SSE .... Spokane Stock Exchange [*Washington*]
SSE .... Squared Sum of Errors [*Statistics*]
SSE .... Stage Systems Engineer
SSE .... Stateside Energy Corp. [*Vancouver Stock Exchange symbol*]
SSE .... Straight to Services Economy
SSE .... Strangest Stories Ever Told [*A publication*]
SSE .... Submarine Scout Experimental [*British military*]   (DMA)
SSE .... Subsystem Element [*NASA*]   (NASA)
SSE .... Subsystem Support Equipment [*NASA*]   (MCD)
SSE .... Sum of Squared Errors [*Statistics*]
SSE .... Summary Status Entry   (SAA)
SSE .... Supplemental Support Evaluation
SSE .... Support System Evaluation
SSE .... Support Systems Engineering [*Boeing*]
SSE .... Surface Support Equipment
SSE .... Sydney Stock Exchange [*Australia*]   (ADA)
SSE .... System Safety Engineering   (AFM)
SSE .... System Status Evaluation [*Army*]   (AABC)
SSE .... System Support Engineering
SSE .... System Support Equipment
S1S1E .... Surfaced or Dressed One Side and One Edge [*Technical
                   drawings*]
SSEA .... Sentinel System Evaluation Agency [*DoD*]
SSEA .... Separate Sampling and Excitation Analysis [*Spectroscopy*]
SSEA .... Stage-Specific Embryonic Antigen [*Immunology*]
SSEA .... System Safety Engineering Analysis   (MCD)
SSEAM ..... Ship Systems Equipment Acquisition Manual   (MCD)
SSEAT...... Surveyor Scientific Evaluation Advisory Team [*NASA*]
SSEB .... Source Selection Evaluation Board [*Military*]   (AFM)
SSEB .... South of Scotland Electricity Board   (ECON)
SSEC .... Selective Sequence Electronic Calculator [*Data processing*]
SSEC .... Social Science Education Consortium   (EA)
SSEC .... Society for the Study of Early China   (EA)
SSEC .... Solar System Exploration Committee [*NASA*]
SSEC .... Solid-State Electronic Chronograph
SSEC .... Sound Surveillance Evaluation Center [*Navy*]   (NVT)
SSEC .... Space Science and Engineering Center [*University of Wisconsin
                   - Madison*] [*Research center*]   (RCD)
SSEC .... Static Source Error Correction
SSECF...... Stateside Energy Corp. [*NASDAQ symbol*]   (NQ)
SSECO ...... Second-Stage Engine Cutoff
SSECS...... Space Station Environmental Control System
SSECW ..... Prairie Migratory Bird Research Centre, Canadian Wildlife
                   Service, Environment Canada [*Centre de Recherches sur
                   les Oiseaux Migrateurs des Prairies, Service Canadien de la
                   Faune, Environnement Canada*] Saskatoon, Saskatchewan
                   [*Library symbol*] [*National Library of Canada*]   (NLC)

SSEDF....... Software Support Environment Development Facility   (SSD)
SSEE .... Standing-Shock Equilibrium Expansion
S-SEED .... Symmetric Self-Electro-Optic Effect Device
S-SEED .... Symmetric Self Electrooptic Effect Device [*Optical Computing*]
SSE/EWE ... SIGINT [*Signal Intelligence*] Support Element/Electronic
                   Warfare Element [*Military*]   (AABC)
SSEF.......... Solid-State Electro-Optic Filter
SSEF.......... Support Squadron Eastern Flank [*British military*]   (DMA)
SSEG .... Ship System Engineering Group [*British*]
SSEG .... System-Segment [*Data processing*]
SSEH .... National Hydrology Research Centre, Environment Canada
                   [*Centre National de Recherche en Hydrologie,
                   Environnement Canada*] Saskatoon, Saskatchewan
                   [*Library symbol*] [*National Library of Canada*]   (NLC)
SSEIF .... Software Support Environment Integration Facility   (SSD)
SSEIP....... Special Stockpile Engineering Investigation Program   (MCD)
SSEIS .... Standard Support and Environmental Impact Statement
                   [*Environmental Protection Agency*]   (GFGA)
SSEIS .... Stationary Source Emissions and Inventory System
                   [*Environmental Protection Agency*]   (GFGA)
SSEKP...... Single Shot Engagement Kill Probability   (MCD)
SSEL.......... Solid-State Electronics Laboratory [*Stanford
                   University*]   (MCD)
SSEL.......... Space Science and Engineering Laboratory [*Pennsylvania State
                   University*]
SSEL.......... Standard Statistical Establishment List [*Bureau of the Census*]
SSEL.......... Stockholm Studies in English Literature [*A publication*]
SSELA....... Standing Committee on Social Sciences, Economic, and Legal
                   Aspects [*Great Lakes Research Advisory Board*]
SSELER .... Salzburg Studies in English Literature. Elizabethan and
                   Renaissance [*A publication*]
SSELRR .... Salzburg Studies in English Literature. Romantic Reassessment
                   [*A publication*]
SSEM .... Solid State Extended Memory   (MCD)
SSEM .... Space System Effectiveness Model
SSEM .... Supply Support Element Manager
SSEng .... Sydney Studies in English [*A publication*]
SSEO .... SEABEE Support and Equipment Office [*Navy*]
SSEOF....... Software Support Environment Operation Facility   (SSD)
SSEOS...... Space Shuttle Engineering and Operations Support
                   [*NASA*]   (MCD)
SSEP......... Somatosensory Evoked Potential [*Neurophysiology*]
SSEP......... Source Selection Evaluation Plan
SSEP......... Steady State Evoked Potential [*Neurophysiology*]
SSEP......... Submarine Surveillance Equipment Program   (NVT)
SSEP......... System Safety Engineering Plan   (AFM)
SSEPA...... Society of Spanish Engineers, Planners, and Architects   (EA)
SSEPF....... Software Support Environment Production Facility   (SSD)
SSER .... Site Safety Evaluation Report [*Nuclear energy*]   (NRCH)
SSER .... Somatosensory Evoked Response [*Neurophysiology*]
SSER .... Supplement to Safety Evaluation Report [*Nuclear
                   energy*]   (NRCH)
SSERN ...... South-Southeastern [*Meteorology*]   (FAAC)
SSES.......... Ship Signals Exploitation Space [*Navy*]   (CAAL)
SSES.......... Shipboard Signal Exploration System   (MCD)
SSES.......... Single Strip Engine System
SSES.......... Special Signal Exploitation Spaces   (NVT)
SSES.......... Susquehanna Steam Electric Station [*Nuclear energy*]   (NRCH)
SSESC....... College of Emmanuel and St. Chad, Saskatoon, Saskatchewan
                   [*Library symbol*] [*National Library of Canada*]   (NLC)
SSESI .... Statistical and Social Enqiry Society of Ireland
SSESM...... Spent Stage Experimental Support Module   (KSC)
SSESPF..... Software Support Environment Software Production
                   Facility   (SSD)
SSESS .... Soviet Space Event Support Ships   (CINC)
SSET .... Source Selection Evaluation Test
SSET .... State Science, Engineering, and Technology Program [*National
                   Science Foundation*]
SSEU .... System Selector Extension Unit
SS EVAL ... Skill Specialty Evaluation Code [*Army*]
SSEWD ..... South-Southeastward [*Meteorology*]   (FAAC)
SSF .... Congregation of the Sisters of the Family [*Roman Catholic
                   religious order*]
SSF .... S-Band Shuttle Forward   (SSD)
SSF .... Safe Shutdown Facility [*Nuclear energy*]   (NRCH)
SSF .... Saint Saulge [*France*] [*Seismograph station code, US Geological
                   Survey*]   (SEIS)
SSF .... Samantha Smith Foundation   (EA)
SSF .... San Antonio, TX [*Location identifier*] [*FAA*]   (FAAL)
SSF .... Saybolt Seconds Furol [*Oil viscosity*]
SSF .... Scottish Spring Fair   (ITD)
SSF .... Service Storage Facility [*Military*]
SSF .... Service Support Force [*Military*]
SSF .... Ship's Service Force [*Navy*]
SSF .... Simulated Spinal Fluid [*Medicine*]
SSF .... Single-Seated Fighter
SSF .... Single Sideband Filter
SSF .... Single Sided Frame [*Telecommunications*]   (TEL)
SSF .... Single Solar Flare
SSF .... Single-Stage Fan
SSF .... Sjogren's Syndrome Foundation   (EA)

SSF	Small, Shelly Fauna [*Paleontology*]
SSF	Society of St. Francis [*Anglican religious community*]
SSF	Society for the Study of Fertility [*British*]
SSF	Sodium Silicofluoride [*Inorganic chemistry*]
SSF	Software Support Facility (MCD)
SSF	Solid-State Fermentation
SSF	Solid Substrate Fermentation
SSF	Soluble Suppressor Factor [*Immunology*]
SSF	Somali Salvation Front (PD)
SSF	Sona Systems Ltd. (Canada) [*Vancouver Stock Exchange symbol*]
SSF	Space Simulation Facility (AAG)
SSF	Special Security Facility
SSF	Special Service Force [*Canadian and US troops under combined command*] [*World War II*]
SSF	Spin Stretch Factor [*Textile technology*]
SSF	Spun Soy Fiber [*Food technology*]
SSF	SRB [*Solid-Rocket Booster*] Storage Facility [*NASA*] (NASA)
SSF	Stainless Steel Fiber
SSF	Standard Saybolt Furol [*Oil viscosity*]
SSF	Standby Shutdown Facility [*Nuclear energy*] (NRCH)
SS/F	Starboard Side/Forward [*Stowage*] (DNAB)
SSF	Structured Surfactant Formulation [*Solvent technology*]
SSF	Studies in Short Fiction [*A publication*]
SSF	Style Sac Flap
SSF	Super Science Fiction [*A publication*]
SSF	Supply Status File (MCD)
SSF	Symmetrical Switching Function
SSF	System Support Facility
SSFC	Sequential Single Frequency Code System [*Telecommunications*] (TEL)
SSFC	Social Science Federation of Canada [*Research center*] (IRC)
SSFC	Solid State Frequency Changer [*Military*] (CAAL)
SSFC	Susanne Severeid Fan Club (EA)
SSF CHL...	Societas Scientiarum Fennicae. Commentationes Humanarum Litterarum [*A publication*]
SSFD	Sisters of St. Francis of Dillingen [*See also SFD*] [*Rome, Italy*] (EAIO)
SSFE	Scandinavian Society of Forest Economics (EAIO)
SSFF	Scholastic Science Fiction Federation [*Defunct*] (EA)
SSFF	Space Shuttle Furnace Facility [*NASA*] (SSD)
SSFGSS.....	Space Shuttle Flight and Ground System Specification [*NASA*] (NASA)
SSFI	Scaffolding, Shoring, and Forming Institute (EA)
SSFL	Santa Susana Field Laboratory [*NASA*] (NASA)
SSFL	Steady-State Fermi Level
SSFLC	Surface Stabilized Ferroelectric Liquid Crystal [*Physical chemistry*]
SSFM	Single Sideband Frequency Modulation
SSFN	Solidarity: A Socialist-Feminist Network (EA)
SSFO	Scandinavian Society of Forensic Odontology (EA)
SSFO	Simultaneous Single Frequency Outlet
SS & FO ...	Specialized Safety and Flight Operations
SSFR	Safety Services Field Representative [*Red Cross*]
SSFS	Samlingar Utgivna av Svenska Fornskriftssallskapet (Stockholm) [*A publication*]
SSFS	Space Shuttle Functional Simulator [*NASA*] (KSC)
SSFS	Special Services Forecasting System [*Telecommunications*] (TEL)
SSFS	Steven Spielberg Film Society (EA)
SSFT	Scientific Software-Intercomp, Inc. [*NASDAQ symbol*] (NQ)
SSFT	Self-Sealing Fuel Tank
SSFU	Scottish Sea Fishers' Union
SSFVT	Subsystems Functional Verification Test [*NASA*]
SSG	Guided Missile Submarine [*Navy symbol*]
SSG	Malabo [*Equatorial Guinea*] [*Airport symbol*] (OAG)
SSG	Safety Study Group (MCD)
SSG	Schriften. Theodor-Storm-Gesellschaft [*A publication*]
SSG	Science Steering Group [*NASA*]
SSG	Scleroderma Support Group (EA)
SSG	Search Signal Generator
SSG	Security Service Guide (SAA)
SSG	Senior Savers Guide Publishing, Inc. [*Vancouver Stock Exchange symbol*]
SSG	Shuttle Support Group (MCD)
SSG	Single Sideband Generator
SSG	Small Signal Gain (IEEE)
SSG	Solution-Sol-Gel [*Materials science*]
SSG	South Sydney Greens [*Political party*] [*Australia*]
SSG	Southern Society of Genealogists (EA)
SSG	Special Security Group (MCD)
SSG	Special Studies Group [*Joint Chiefs of Staff*] [*Military*]
SSG	Special Support Group [*FBI*] (CINC)
SSG	Staff Sergeant [*Army*] (AABC)
SSG	State Services Group [*Information service or system*] (IID)
SSG	Stonehenge Study Group (EA)
SSG	Subsystem Software Group
SSG	Supply Spectrum Generator
SSG	Sweep Signal Generator
SSG	Symbolic Stream Generator [*Data processing*]
SSG	System Safety Group [*Air Force*]
SSGA	Scottish Salmon Growers' Association
SSGA	Society of St. Gregory of America [*Later, CMAA*] (EA)
SSGA	Sterling Silversmiths Guild of America (EA)
SSGA	Swordsmen and Sorcerers' Guild of America (EA)
SSGB	Suore di San Giovanni Baptista [*Sisters of St. John the Baptist - SSJB*] [*Rome, Italy*] (EAIO)
SSGC	Saskatoon Gallery and Conservatory, Saskatchewan [*Library symbol*] [*National Library of Canada*] (NLC)
SSGC	Short System Ground Check
SSGD	Smoke Screen Generative Device
SSGED	Seikei-Saigai Geka [*A publication*]
SSGJ	Single Strength Grapefruit Juice
SSGJ	Supersonic Gas Jet
SSGL	Studies in Slavic and General Linguistics [*A publication*]
SSGM	Service Station & Garage Management [*Canada*] [*A publication*]
SSGN	Guided Missile Submarine (Nuclear Propulsion) [*Navy symbol*]
SSGP	Spin Stabilized Guided Projectile (MCD)
SSGp	System Safety Group [*Air Force*] (AFM)
SSGS	Solid-State Gamma Switch
SSGS	Standard Space Guidance System
SSGS	Stanford Studies in Germanics and Slavics [*A publication*]
SSGT	Ship Service Gas Turbine [*Navy*] (CAAL)
SSGT	Small-Scale Gap Test [*Explosive*]
SSGT	Staff Sergeant [*Military*]
SSGT	Subsystem Ground Test (MCD)
SSGTG	Ship's Service Gas Turbine Generator [*Navy*] (NVT)
SSGW	Sitzungsberichte. Saechsische Gesellschaft der Wissenschaften (Leipzig) [*A publication*]
SSGW	Surface-to-Surface Guided Weapon (NATG)
SSH	S-Band Shuttle (SSD)
SSH	Schwartz-Slawsky-Herzfeld [*Theory*] [*Chemical kinetics*]
SSH	Second-Stage Hydraulics
SSH	Sharm E Sheikh [*Israel*] [*Airport symbol*] (OAG)
SSH	Site Selection Handbook [*A publication*]
SSH	Skytteanska Samfundets Handlinger [*A publication*]
SSH	Small-Scale Hydroelectric Project
SSH	Snowshoe Hare
SSH	Social Sciences and Humanities Index [*A publication*]
SSH	Social Sciences and Humanities Research Council of Canada [*UTLAS symbol*]
SSH	Social Service Handbooks [*A publication*]
SSH	South Shore [*AAR code*]
SSH	Special Survey of the Hull [*Lloyd's Register of Shipping*] (DS)
SSH	Studies in Society and History [*A publication*]
SSH	Substantial Stockholder
SSH	Sunshine [*Alaska*] [*Seismograph station code, US Geological Survey*] (SEIS)
SSHA	Subsystem Hazard Analysis
SSHA	Survey of Study Habits and Attitudes [*Education*]
SSHACS...	Small Ships Accounting System (DNAB)
SSHB	Society for the Study of Human Biology (EA)
SSHB	Stainless Steel Helium Bottle
SSHB	Station Set Handbook [*NASA*] (NASA)
SSHC	Single-Stage Hydrocracker [*Chemical engineering*]
SSHCG	Students' Series of Historical and Comparative Grammars [*A publication*]
SSHD	Single-Silo Hardsite Defense
SSHE	Scraped-Surface Heat Exchanger [*Process engineering*]
SSHJM	Sisters of the Sacred Hearts of Jesus and Mary [*Roman Catholic religious order*]
SSHJP.......	Servants of the Sacred Heart of Jesus and of the Poor [*Roman Catholic women's religious order*]
S/SHLD	Side Shield [*Automotive engineering*]
SSHM	Society for the Social History of Medicine [*Oxford, England*] (EAIO)
SSHMA.....	Senior Secondary Headmasters' Association [*British*]
SSHP........	Single-Shot Hit Probability
SSHPF.......	Space Station Hazardous Processing Facility (SSD)
SSHR........	Social Systems and Human Resources [*National Science Foundation*] (MCD)
SSHR........	Spartan Safety Hazard Report [*Missiles*] (MCD)
SSHRC	Social Sciences and Humanities Research Council of Canada
SSHRCC ...	Social Sciences and Humanities Research Council of Canada [*Pronounced "sherk"*] [*See also CRSHC*]
SSHS........	Stainless Steel Helium Sphere
SSHSA	Steamship Historical Society of America (EA)
SSHum	Social Sciences and Humanities Index [*A publication*]
SSI	Brunswick, GA [*Location identifier*] [*FAA*] (FAAL)
SSI	Safe Shutdown Impoundment [*Nuclear energy*] (NRCH)
SSI	SafeCard Services, Inc. [*NYSE symbol*] (SPSG)
SSI	Safeway Stores, Inc.
SSI	Satellite Services, Inc. [*Houston, TX*] [*Telecommunications*] (TSSD)
SSI	Scaffolding and Shoring Institute [*Later, SSFI*] (EA)
SSI	Scientific Systems, Inc.
SSI	Second-Stage Ignition
SSI	Sector Scan Indicator
SSI	Security Systems, Inc. [*In TV series "Max Headroom"*]
SSI	Security Systems Inspectorate [*Established in 1987*] [*British*]
SSI	Segmental Sequential Irradiation (AAMN)

SSI .... Seismic Survival Indicator [*Earthquake analysis program*] [*Data processing*]
SSI .... Semisopochnoi Island [*Alaska*] [*Seismograph station code, US Geological Survey*] [*Closed*]   (SEIS)
SSI .... Service Social International [*International Social Service - ISS*] [*Geneva, Switzerland*]   (EAIO)
SSI .... Shaft Speed Indicator
SSI .... Ship and Shore Installation   (MCD)
SSI .... Short Story International [*A publication*]
SSI .... Shoulder Sleeve Insignia [*Military*]   (AABC)
SSI .... Significant Structural Item   (NASA)
SSI .... Single Service Institute [*Later, FPI*]   (EA)
SSI .... Single System Image
SSI .... Site of Special Scientific Interest [*Great Britain*]
SSI .... Size Selective Inlet [*Environmental Protection Agency*]   (GFGA)
SSI .... Skill Speciality Identifier   (MCD)
SSI .... Sky Survey Instrument
SSI .... Slater Industries, Inc. [*Toronto Stock Exchange symbol*]
SSI .... Slater Steels Corp. [*Formerly, Slater Steel Industries*] [*Toronto Stock Exchange symbol*]
SSI .... Small-Scale Integration
SSI .... Smart Set International [*Program to discourage drug abuse*] [*Defunct*]   (EA)
SSI .... Social Science Information [*A publication*]
SSI .... Social Science Institute [*Washington University*] [*Research center*]   (RCD)
SSI .... Social Security Information
SSI .... Society of Saunterers, International   (EA)
SSI .... Society of Scribes and Illuminators   (EA)
SSI .... Society for Siberian Irises   (EA)
SSI .... Society for the Study of Internationalism   (EA)
SSI .... Solid-State Inverter
SSI .... Space Studies Institute   (EA)
SSI .... Spacecraft System Integration
SSI .... Spares Status Inquiry   (AAG)
SSI .... Special Subject for Inspection [*DoD*]
SSI .... Special Surveillance Inspection   (MCD)
SSI .... Specialty Skill Identifier [*Military*]   (AABC)
SSI .... Specific Searching Image [*Tendency of birds to select prey of the color to which they have been accustomed*]
SSI .... Staff Sergeant Instructor [*Military*] [*British*]
SSI .... Standing Signal Instructions [*Military*]
SSI .... Start Signal Indicator [*Telecommunications*]   (TEL)
SSI .... Steady-State Irradiation [*Nuclear energy*]   (NRCH)
SSI .... Stockpile Surveillance Inspection
SSI .... Storage-to-Storage Instruction   (IEEE)
SSI .... Strategic Studies Institute   (MCD)
SSI .... Structural Significant Item   (MCD)
SSI .... Student/Supervisor Instructions [*Army Training Extension Course*]   (INF)
SSI .... Sucro-Sac-Ologists Society International [*Defunct*]   (EA)
SSI .... Supplemental Security Income [*Social Security Administration*]
SSI .... Supplemental Security Insurance [*Program*]
SSI .... Supply Support Index   (CAAL)
SSI .... Surprise Security Inspection [*Navy*]   (NVT)
SSI .... Survey Sampling, Inc. [*Information service or system*]   (IID)
SSI .... Sustaining Support Increment [*Military*]
SSI .... Symptom Sign Inventory [*Psychology*]
SSI .... Synchronous Systems Interface
SSI .... System Science Institute [*IBM Corp.*]
SSI .... System Status Indicator [*Bell System*]
SSIA .... Scottish Society for Industrial Archaeology   (EA)
SSIA .... Shiprepairers and Shipbuilders Independent Association [*British*]   (DS)
SSIA .... Shoe Service Institute of America   (EA)
SSIA .... Specification Serial of Individual Assigned
SSIA .... Stockholder Systems, Inc. [*Norcross, GA*] [*NASDAQ symbol*]   (NQ)
SSIAM ...... Structured and Scaled Interview to Assess Maladjustment [*Psychometrics*]
SSIB .... Shop Stock Items Bin   (MCD)
SSIBD .... Shuttle System Interface Block Diagram [*NASA*]   (NASA)
SSIC .... Saskatchewan Indian Cultural College, Saskatoon, Saskatchewan [*Library symbol*] [*National Library of Canada*]   (NLC)
SSIC .... Small-Scale Integrated Circuit
SSIC .... Southern States Industrial Council [*Later, USIC*]   (EA)
SSIC .... Standard Subject Identification Code   (NVT)
SSICM ...... Spin-Stabilized Impulsively Controlled Missile   (MCD)
SSID .... Ship Systems Integration Data   (MCD)
SSID .... Shuttle Stowage Installation Drawing   (NASA)
SSIDS .... Siblings of Sudden Infant Death Syndrome Victims [*Medicine*]
SSIE .... Skylab Systems Integration Equipment [*NASA*]   (MCD)
SSIE .... Smithsonian Science Information Exchange [*National Technical Information Service*] [*Later, FEDRIP*]
SSIE .... Solid Surface Interaction Experiment
SSIEM ...... Society for the Study of Inborn Errors of Metabolism [*Middleway, England*]   (EAIO)
SSIF .... [*The*] Southeastern Savings Institutions Fund, Inc. [*NASDAQ symbol*]   (NQ)

SSIFC .... Saskatoon Campus, Saskatchewan Indian Federated College, Saskatchewan [*Library symbol*] [*National Library of Canada*]   (BIB)
SSIFC .... Sharon Smith International Fan Club   (EA)
SSIG .... Single Signal   (IEEE)
SSIG .... State Student Incentive Grant [*Department of Education*]
SSIGS .... Special Survey of Inert Gas System [*Lloyd's Register of Shipping*]   (DS)
S Sig Sta .... Storm Signal Station [*Nautical charts*]
SSII .... Solid-State Image Intensifier
SSII .... Specialized Systems, Inc. [*NASDAQ symbol*]   (NQ)
SSI/ISS ..... Social Science Information/Information sur les Sciences Sociales [*A publication*]
SSIK .... Shipboard SONAR Bouy Interface Kit   (DWSG)
SSIL .... Supply Significant Items List   (MCD)
SSILS .... Solid State Instrument Landing System   (MCD)
S-SIM .... S-Band Simulator   (SSD)
SSIM .... Scientific Systems, Inc. [*Cambridge, MA*] [*NASDAQ symbol*]   (NQ)
SSIM .... Static Secondary Ion Mass Spectroscopy
SSIM .... Statistical, Sampling Inventory Method [*Military*]   (AABC)
SSIMS ...... Static Secondary Ion Mass Spectroscopy
SSINA ...... Scientia Sinica [*English Edition*] [*A publication*]
SSINI .... System Input Unit I [*Data processing*]   (AEBS)
SSIOD .... Solid State Ionics [*A publication*]
SSIP .... Secondary Students Information Press [*A publication*]   (APTA)
SSIP .... Ship Support Improvement Program [*DoD*]
SSIP .... Shuttle Student Involvement Project [*NASA*]
SSIP .... Solvent-Separated Ion-Pair [*Physical chemistry*]
SSIP .... Specific, Sincere, Immediate, Private, and Personal [*Management technique*]
SSIP .... Standard Systems Improvement Program
SSIP .... Subsystems Integration Program [*or Project*] [*NATO*]   (NATG)
SSIP .... System Setup Indicator Panel
SSIP .... Systems Software Interface Processing [*NASA*]   (MCD)
SSIPL .... Support and Sustaining Implications of Increased POMCUS Levels [*Military*]
SSIR .... Soil Survey Investigations Report
SSIR .... Special Security Investigation Requirement   (AFM)
SSIS .... Social Security Information System [*ILO*] [*United Nations*]   (DUND)
SSIS.......... Society for South India Studies   (EA)
SSIS .... Space Station Information System   (NASA)
SSIS .... Spacecraft System Integration Support
SSISS .... Spacecraft System Integration Support Service
SSITF .... Standard Shipboard Inspection and Testing Form [*Navy*]   (DNAB)
SSITP .... Shuttle System Integrated Test Plan [*NASA*]   (NASA)
SSIU .... Subsystem Interface Unit   (MCD)
SSIUL .... Social Sciences Information Utilization Laboratory
SSIUS .... Specialty Steel Industry of the United States   (EA)
SSIWA ...... Shipwrights' and Shipwrights Iron Workers' Association [*A union*] [*British*]
SSIX .... Scribe Systems, Inc. [*NASDAQ symbol*]   (NQ)
SSIX .... Submarine Satellite Information Exchange [*Geosynchronous communications satellite*]
SSIXS .... Submarine Satellite Information Exchange System   (MCD)
SSJ............ Sandnessjoen [*Norway*] [*Airport symbol*]   (OAG)
SSJ............ Savez Sindikata Jugoslavije [*Yugoslavia Federation of Trade Unions*]
SSJ............ Self-Aligning Swivel Joint
SSJ............ Self-Screening Jammer   (MCD)
SSJ............ Sequential Spot Jamming [*Military*]   (CAAL)
SSJ............ Servo Summing Junction
SSJ............ Shinshu-Shinmachi [*Japan*] [*Seismograph station code, US Geological Survey*]   (SEIS)
SSJ............ Side-Support Jack
SSJ............ Sinatra Society of Japan [*Tokyo*]   (EAIO)
SSJ............ Single Subsonic Jet
SSJ............ Sisters of St. Joseph [*Roman Catholic religious order*]
SSJ............ Sisters of St. Joseph of the Third Order of St. Francis [*Roman Catholic religious order*]
SSJ............ Societas Sancti Joseph Sanctissimi Cordis [*St. Joseph's Society of the Sacred Heart*] [*Josephites*] [*Roman Catholic men's religious order*]
SSJ............ Socijalisticka Stranka Jugoslavije [*Yugoslav Socialist Party*] [*Political party*]   (EAIO)
SSJ............ Solid-State Jammer
SSJ............ Southern Speech Journal [*A publication*]
SSJB .... Sisters of St. John the Baptist [*See also SSGB*] [*Roman Catholic religious order*] [*Rome, Italy*]   (EAIO)
SSJC .... Southern Seminary and Junior College [*Virginia*]
SSJD .... Society of St. John the Divine [*Anglican religious community*]
SSJE .... Society of St. John the Evangelist [*Anglican religious community*]
SS-JFI .... School Superintendent Job Functions Inventory [*Test*]
SSJG .... Sisters of St. John of God [*Wexford, Republic of Ireland*]   (EAIO)
SSJM .... United States Embassy. Summary of Selected Japanese Magazines [*A publication*]

SSJSM	Sisters of St. Joseph of St. Mark [*Roman Catholic religious order*]
SSK............	Antisubmarine Submarine [*Navy symbol*]
SSK............	Keethanou School/Public Library, Stanley Mission, Saskatchewan [*Library symbol*] [*National Library of Canada*] (BIB)
SSK............	Service Sink [*Technical drawings*]
SSK............	Softkey Software Products, Inc. [*Toronto Stock Exchange symbol*]
SSK............	Soil Stack
SSKAT	Socio-Sexual Knowledge and Attitudes Test [*Psychology*]
SSKDN	Serikat Sekerdja Kementerian Dalam Negeri [*Union of Workers in the Department of Interior*] [*Indonesia*]
SSKI	Saturated Solution of Potassium Iodide [*Medicine*]
SSKIL........	Library Technician Program, Kelsey Institute of Applied Arts & Sciences, Saskatoon, Saskatchewan [*Library symbol*] [*National Library of Canada*] (NLC)
SSKP	Serikat Sekerdja Kementerian Pertaganan [*Ministry of Defense Workers' Unions*] [*Indonesia*]
SSKP	Single-Shot Kill Probability
SSKPS	Solid-State Klystron Power Supply
SSKY	Super Sky International, Inc. [*NASDAQ symbol*] (NQ)
SSL	Licentiate of Sacred Scripture
SSL	Safety Systems Laboratory [*Formerly, Office of Vehicle Systems Research*] [*Department of Transportation*]
SSL	Scandoslavica [*Copenhagen*] [*A publication*]
SSL	School of Systems and Logistics [*Military*]
SSL	Scientific Subroutine Library
SSL	Scientific Support Laboratory [*CDEC*] (MCD)
SSL	Seattle, WA [*Location identifier*] [*FAA*] (FAAL)
SSL	Seismograph Service Ltd. [*British*]
SSL	Selected Source List (AAG)
SSL	Serpentine Superlattice [*Physics*]
SSL	Service Security Layer [*Data processing*]
SSL	Shift and Select [*Data processing*] (MDG)
SSL	Ship Shortage Log (AAG)
SSL	Shop Stock List (MCD)
SSL	Skaneateles Short Line Railroad Corp. [*AAR code*]
SSL	Skin Surface Lipid [*Physiology*]
SSL	Social Security Administration Library, Baltimore, MD [*OCLC symbol*] (OCLC)
SSL	Sociosystem Laboratory
SSL	Sodium Stearoyl Lactylate
SSL	Soeurs de Saint Louis [*Sisters of Saint Louis*] (EAIO)
SSL	Software Sciences Ltd. [*British*]
SSL	Software Slave Library [*Data processing*] (TEL)
SSL	Software Specification Language
SSL	Solid State Lamp (MCD)
SSL	Solid-State LASER
SSL	Solid Statement Library (HGAA)
SSL	Source Statement Library [*Data processing*]
SSL	Southern Star Resources Ltd. [*Vancouver Stock Exchange symbol*]
SSL	Space Sciences Laboratory [*University of California, Berkeley*] [*Research center*] [*NASA*] (MCD)
SSL	Space Simulation Laboratory
SSL	Special Sensor-Lightning
SSL	Spent Sulfite Liquor [*Papermaking*]
SSL	Storage Structure Language
SSL	Studies in Scottish Literature [*A publication*]
SSL	Studies in Semitic Languages and Linguistics [*A publication*]
SSL	Sunset Lake [*Pennsylvania*] [*Seismograph station code, US Geological Survey*] [*Closed*] (SEIS)
SSL	Support Status List (MCD)
SSL	System Software Loader (NASA)
SSL	System Specification Language
SSL	System Stock List (NATG)
SSLA	Star Savings & Loan Association [*Sayre, PA*] [*NASDAQ symbol*] (NQ)
SSlav.........	Symbolae Slavicae [*A publication*]
SSLC.........	Ship System Life Cycle [*Navy*]
SSLC.........	Society of Savings and Loan Controllers [*Later, Financial Managers Society*] (EA)
SSLC.........	Synchronous Single-Line Controller
SSLE.........	Subacute Sclerosing Leukoencephalitis [*Medicine*]
SSLF.........	Skrifter Utgivna. Svenska Litteratursallskapet i Finland [*A publication*]
SSLF.........	Southern Sudan Liberation Front (BJA)
SSLH.........	Society for the Study of Labour History [*Sheffield, England*] (EA)
SSLI..........	Serum Sickness-Like Illness [*Medicine*]
SSLI..........	Society of School Librarians International (EA)
SSLI..........	Southern Security Life Insurance Co. [*NASDAQ symbol*] (NQ)
SSLI..........	Studies in Semitic Languages and Linguistics [*A publication*]
SS Lit........	Soviet Studies in Literature [*A publication*]
SSLL.........	Stanford Studies in Language and Literature [*A publication*]
SSLM	Solid-Supported Liquid Membrane [*Chemical engineering*]
SSLN	Security Investments Group, Inc. [*NASDAQ symbol*] (NQ)
SSLO	Solid-State Local Oscillator
SSLORAN ...	Skywave Synchronized Long-Range Aid to Navigation
SSLP.........	Simple-Sequence Length Polymorphism [*Genetics*]
SSLP.........	Transport Submarine (MCD)
SSL-POW/MIA ...	Seaside Support League - POW/MIA [*Prisoner of War/ Missing in Action*] (EA)
SSLPS	Solid-State Logic Protection System [*Nuclear energy*] (NRCH)
SSLR	Straits Settlements Law Reports [*A publication*] (DLA)
SSLR Supp ...	Straits Settlements Law Reports, Supplement [*1897-99*] [*Malasia*] [*A publication*] (DLA)
SSLS.........	Solid-State LASER System
SSLS.........	Standard Space Launch System [*BSD*]
SSLSM......	Single Service Logistics Support Manager (MCD)
SSLSN.......	Skrifter Utgivna. Svenska Litteratursallskapet Studier i Nordisk Filologi [*A publication*]
SSLT.........	Solid-State Logic Timer
SSLT.........	Starboard Side Light (MCD)
SSLT.........	Stock Status Lag Time (AABC)
SSLV	Southern San Luis Valley Railroad Co. [*AAR code*]
SSLV	Standard Space Launch Vehicle
SSM...........	Midget Submarine [*Navy symbol*]
SSM...........	St. Thomas More College, Saskatoon, Saskatchewan [*Library symbol*] [*National Library of Canada*] (NLC)
SSM...........	Satellite Stratospheric Monitor (NOAA)
SSM...........	Sault Ste. Marie [*Michigan*] [*Airport symbol*] (OAG)
SSM...........	School in Sales Management [*LIMRA*]
S & Sm	Searle and Smith's English Probate and Divorce Reports [*A publication*] (DLA)
SSM...........	Second-Stage Motor
SSM...........	Second Surface Mirror
SSM...........	Second-Tier Securities Market [*Investment term*]
SSM...........	Self-Sterilizing-Material [*Pharmacology*]
SSM...........	Semiconductor Storage Module
SSM...........	Seminaire St. Martial [*Haiti*] [*Seismograph station code, US Geological Survey*] [*Closed*] (SEIS)
SSM...........	Serum-Supplemented Medium [*Microbiology*]
SSM...........	Sesquiterpenoid Stress Metabolite [*Plant physiology*]
SSM...........	Set Sign Minus (SAA)
SSM...........	Set System Mask (HGAA)
SSM...........	Ship Simulation Model [*Navy*]
SSM...........	Signal Strength Monitor [*Broadcasting*]
SSM...........	Silver Star Medal [*Military decoration*]
SSM...........	Single Sideband Modulation
SSM...........	Single Sideband Signal Multiplier [*Telecommunications*]
SSM...........	Sisters of St. Mary of the Third Order of St. Francis [*Roman Catholic religious order*]
SSM...........	Sisters of the Sorrowful Mother [*Third Order of St. Francis*] [*Roman Catholic religious order*]
SSM...........	Small Semiconductor Memory
SSM...........	Society of the Sacred Mission [*Anglican religious community*]
SSM...........	Society of St. Margaret [*Anglican religious community*]
SSM...........	Society of St. Monica (EA)
SSM...........	Society of the Servants of Mary [*Anglican religious community*]
SSM...........	Solar Simulation Module
SSM...........	Solar Stereoscopic Mission [*NASA*]
SSM...........	Solid-State Materials (CET)
SSM...........	Southlands Mining [*Vancouver Stock Exchange symbol*]
SSM...........	Space Science Fiction Magazine [*A publication*]
SSM...........	Space Station Module [*NASA*] (KSC)
SSM...........	Spacecraft Systems Monitor [*NASA*] (MCD)
SSM...........	Spark Source Mass Spectroscopy
SSM...........	Special Safeguarding Measures [*Telecommunications*] (TEL)
SSM...........	Special Survey of the Machinery [*Lloyd's Register of Shipping*] (DS)
SSM...........	Spread Spectrum Modulation (NATG)
SSM...........	Squadron Sergeant Major
SSM...........	SSMC, Inc. [*NYSE symbol*] (SPSG)
SSM...........	Staff Sergeant Major [*Military*]
SSM...........	Staff Squadron Major [*Military*] [*British*]
SSM...........	Stage Scanning Microscope
SSM...........	Standard Surfacing Mat [*Fiberglass*]
SSM...........	Studies in Statistical Mechanics [*Elsevier Book Series*] [*A publication*]
SSM...........	Subsynaptic Membrane [*Anatomy*]
SSM...........	Subsystem Manager [*NASA*] (NASA)
SSM...........	Superficial Spreading Melanoma [*Oncology*]
SSM...........	Supply Support Management
SSM...........	Support Subsystem Manager
SSM...........	Support Systems Module [*NASA*]
SSM...........	Surface-to-Surface Missile
SSM...........	System Security Manager [*Military*] (GFGA)
SSM...........	System Supply Manager
SSM...........	System Support Machine [*Telecommunications*]
SSM...........	System Support Management [*or Manager*] [*Military*] (AFM)
SSM...........	Systems Support Module [*NASA*] (MCD)
SSMA........	School Science and Mathematics Association (EA)
SSMA........	Soldiers, Sailors, Marines, and Airmen's Club [*Washington, DC*]
SSMA........	Solid-State Microwave Amplifier
SSMA........	Southwest Spanish Mustang Association (EA)
SSMA........	Spread-Spectrum Multiple Access [*Satellite communications*]
SSMB........	Ship's Serviceman, Barber [*Navy rating*]
SSMB........	Space Shuttle Maintenance Baseline [*NASA*] (MCD)

SSMB........ Special Services Management Bureau
              [*Telecommunications*]   (TEL)
SSMC....... Second-Stage Motor Container
SSMC....... Ship's Serviceman, Cobbler [*Navy rating*]
SSMC....... Silver State Mining Corp. [*NASDAQ symbol*]   (NQ)
SSMCC ..... Space Shuttle Mission Control Center [*NASA*]   (SSD)
SSMCIS .... Secondary School Mathematics Curriculum Improvement
              Study [*National Science Foundation*]
SSMCNP .. Safeguard System Management Communications Network
              Program [*Army*]   (AABC)
SSMCO..... SPARTAN Santa Monica Checkout [*NASA*]
SSMCS..... Synchronous Satellite Military Communication System
SSMD........ Saskatchewan Mining Development Corp., Saskatoon,
              Saskatchewan [*Library symbol*] [*National Library of
              Canada*]   (NLC)
SSMD....... Silicon Stud-Mounted Diode
SSME........ Satellite System Monitoring Equipment
SSME........ Society for the Study of Medical Ethics [*British*]
SSME........ Space Shuttle Main Engine [*NASA*]
SSME........ Spread Spectrum Modulation Equipment [*NATO*]   (MCD)
SSMEC ..... Space Shuttle Main Engine Controller [*NASA*]   (MCD)
SSMECA... Space Shuttle Main Engine Controller Assembly
              [*NASA*]   (NASA)
SSMES...... Systems Support Module Equipment Section [*NASA*]   (SSD)
SSMF .... Symbol Sink - Matched Filter
SSMG........ Satellite Systems Monitoring Group [*INTELSAT*]
SSMG........ Ship's Service Motor Generator [*Navy*]   (NVT)
SSMH .... Scottish Society for the Mentally Handicapped   (EAIO)
SSMHRC .. Spanish Speaking Mental Health Research Center [*Public
              Health Service*] [*Research center*]   (RCD)
SSM/I....... Sensor System Microwave/Imager
SSMI .... Sister Servants of Mary Immaculate [*Roman Catholic religious
              order*]
SSMIF & G ... Squadron Sergeant-Major Instructor in Fencing and
              Gymnastics [*Military*] [*British*]   (ROG)
SSM/IM.... System Support Manager/Inventory Manager   (MCD)
SSMIMA .. Scissor, Shear, and Manicure Implement Manufacturers
              Association [*Later, National Association of Scissors and
              Shears Manufacturers*]   (EA)
SSMIS...... Support Services Management Information System [*Army*]
SSML .... Shaped Substrata Meanderline   (MCD)
SSML .... Ship's Serviceman, Laundryman [*Navy rating*]
SSML .... Society for the Study of Midwestern Literature   (EA)
SSMLL...... Society for the Study of Medieval Languages and Literature
              [*British*]
SSMLN ..... Society for the Study of Midwestern Literature. Newsletter [*A
              publication*]
SSMM....... Space Station Mathematical Model
SSMMA.... Staple and Stapling Machine Manufacturers Association
              [*Defunct*]
SSMMI ..... Soeurs Salesiennes Missionnaires de Marie Immaculee [*Salesian
              Missionaries of Mary Immaculate - SMMI*] [*Gentilly,
              France*]   (EAIO)
SSMN........ Sisters of St. Mary of Namur [*Roman Catholic religious order*]
SSMO........ Sisters of St. Mary of Oregon [*Roman Catholic religious order*]
SSMO........ Summary of Synoptic Meteorological Observations [*National
              Oceanic and Atmospheric Administration*]   (MSC)
SSMOB..... Surface-to-Surface Missile Order of Battle   (MCD)
SSMP .... Safeguard System Master Plan [*Army*]   (AABC)
SSMP .... Stockholm Studies in Modern Philology [*A publication*]
SSMP .... Supply Support Management Plan [*Military*]   (CAAL)
SSMPP...... Society for the Study of Male Psychology and Physiology   (EA)
SSMRP...... Seismic Safety Margins Research Program [*Nuclear Regulatory
              Commission*]
SSMS .... Solid-State Mass Spectrometer
SSMS .... Sons of Sherman's March to the Sea   (EA)
SSMS .... Spark Source Mass Spectroscopy
SSMS .... Submarine Safety Monitoring System
SSMSDZ... Social Science and Medicine. Part A. Medical Psychology and
              Medical Sociology [*A publication*]
SSMSN ..... Surface-to-Surface Mission [*Military*]   (AABC)
S SMS N CLSD ... Side Seams Not Closed [*Freight*]
SSMT .... Salvage Sales Material Transfer
SSM/T ...... Sensor System Microwave/Temperature
SSMT .... Ship's Serviceman, Tailor [*Navy rating*]
SSMT .... Site Security Maintenance Team
SSMT .... Society for the Study of Myth and Tradition   (EA)
SSMTG ..... Solid-State and Molecular Theory Group [*MIT*]   (MCD)
SSMTS...... Spade and Shovel Makers' Trade Society [*A union*] [*British*]
SSMV .... Single-Shot Multivibrator
SSMVP ..... Space Station Master Verification Plan [*NASA*]   (SSD)
SSMVR ..... Space Station Master Verification Requirement [*NASA*]   (SSD)
SSN........... Romulus, NY [*Location identifier*] [*FAA*]   (FAAL)
SSN........... Samson Gold Corp. [*Vancouver Stock Exchange symbol*]
SSN........... San Juan Del Sur [*Nicaragua*] [*Seismograph station code, US
              Geological Survey*]   (SEIS)
SSN........... Scandinavian Studies and Notes [*A publication*]
SSN........... Season and Sunspot Number   (DNAB)
SSN........... Segment Stack Number
SSN........... Senior Security Network   (EA)
SSN........... Severely Subnormal

SSN........... Ship, Submersible (Nuclear-Powered)
SSN........... Social Security Number   (AABC)
SSN........... Soviet Sciences in the News [*A publication*]
SSN........... Space Surveillance Network
SSN........... Specification Serial Number [*Military*]
SSN........... Standard Serial Numbers   (DIT)
SSN........... Standard Study Number [*Military*]
SSN........... Station Serial Number   (CET)
SSN........... Stock Segregation Notice [*DoD*]
SSN........... Submarine (Nuclear-Powered) [*Navy symbol*]   (NVT)
SSN........... Switched Service Network [*Telecommunications*]
SSN........... Sykepleiernes Samarbeid i Norden [*Northern Nurses Federation
              - NNF*]   (EAIO)
SSNAP ..... Single Seat Night Attack Program   (MCD)
SSNCHK... Social Security Number Check
SSND....... School Sisters of Notre Dame   (IIA)
SSND........ Solid-State Neutral Dosimeter
SSN(DS)... Submarine (Nuclear-Powered) in Direct Support [*Navy
              symbol*]   (NVT)
SSNDT...... Scottish School of Non-Destructive Testing [*Research
              center*]   (IRUK)
SSNF .... Source Spot Noise Figure
SSNJ .... Self-Screening Noise Jammer   (MCD)
SSNLO ...... Shan State Nationalities Liberation Organization
              [*Myanmar*]   (PD)
SSNM....... Strategic Special Nuclear Materials
SSNMH ... Scipio Society of Naval and Military History   (EA)
SSNPP...... Small-Size Nuclear Power Plant
SSNS .... Scottish Society for Northern Studies
SSNS .... Standard Study Numbering System [*Military*]   (AABC)
SSNW....... Social Scientists Against Nuclear War   (EA)
SSNY........ Swiss Society of New York   (EA)
SSO........... Safety/Security Officer [*Military*]   (AABC)
SSO........... Safety Significant Operation [*Aerospace*]
SSO........... San Simon, AZ [*Location identifier*] [*FAA*]   (FAAL)
SSO........... Saturn Systems Office [*NASA*]   (SAA)
SSO........... Security System Organization
SSO........... Self-Sustained Outlet   (FAAC)
SSO........... Senior Safety Officer [*Navy*]   (CAAL)
SSO........... Senior Scientific Officer [*Ministry of Agriculture, Fisheries, and
              Food*] [*British*]
SSO........... Senior Staff Officer [*Military*] [*British*]
SSO........... Senior Supply Officer [*Military*] [*British*]
SSO........... Ship Safety Officer
SSO........... Simosato [*Japan*] [*Later, HTY*] [*Geomagnetic observatory
              code*]
SSO........... Single Sweep Operation
SSO........... Single System Operator   (WDMC)
SSO........... Society of Surgical Oncology   (EA)
SSO........... Solid-State Oscillator
SSO........... Source Selection Official   (NASA)
sso .... Southern Sotho [*MARC language code*] [*Library of
              Congress*]   (LCCP)
SSO........... Space Shuttle Orbiter [*NASA*]   (RDA)
SSO........... Space Station Office [*NASA*]   (SSD)
SSO........... Spacecraft Systems Officer   (SAA)
SSO........... Spares Shipping Order
SSO........... Special Security Office [*or Officer*] [*Military*]   (CINC)
SSO........... Special Service Officer [*Military*]
SSO........... Squadron Signals Officer [*Navy*] [*British*]
SSO........... Srednee Spetsial'noe Obrazovanie [*Moscow*] [*A publication*]
SSO........... Staff Security Officer   (AAG)
SSO........... Staff Signals Officer [*British military*]   (DMA)
SSO........... Station Staff Officer [*British military*]   (DMA)
SSO........... Statistical Service Office [*Military*]
SSO........... Steady-State Oscillation
SSO........... Studier fra Sprog- og Oldtidsforskning [*A publication*]
SSO........... Submarine Oiler [*Navy ship symbol*]
SSO........... Submarine Supply Office
SSO........... Subsystem Operation [*in Spacelab*] [*NASA*]   (MCD)
SSO........... Sunflower Seed Oil
SSO........... Support Services Office [*Environmental Protection
              Agency*]   (GFGA)
SSO........... Support System for OEX [*Orbiter Experiments*]   (NASA)
SSO........... System Security Officer
SSO........... System Service Order [*Bell System*]
SSO........... System Staff Office
SSOA......... Software Services of America, Inc. [*NASDAQ symbol*]   (NQ)
SSOA......... Submarine Operating Area [*Navy*]
SSOA......... Subsurface Ocean Area   (NVT)
SSOB......... Senior Scientist on Board [*Navy*]
SSOC......... Southern Student Organizing Committee [*Defunct*]
SSOC......... Space Station Operations Center [*NASA*]   (SSD)
SSOC......... Space Surveillance Operations Center   (SAA)
SSOC......... Switching Service Operations Center [*Telecommunications*]
SSOCA ..... Senior Staff Officer for Civil Affairs [*British*] [*World War II*]
SSOCC ...... Space Station Operations and Control Center [*NASA*]   (SSD)
SSOD........ Solid-State Optical Detector
SSOD........ Special Session on Disarmament [*A special session of the UN
              General Assembly held from May 23 to June 28, 1978*]
SSODCM ... Space Systems Operational Design Criteria Manual [*NASA*]

SSODIA	Special Security Office, Defense Intelligence Agency　(CINC)
SSOE........	Special Subject Operational Evaluation
SSOEC	Ship Suppliers' Organization of the European Community [*Hague, Netherlands*]　(EAIO)
SSOED3....	Southwestern Entomologist. Supplement [*A publication*]
SSOFS.......	Smiling Sons of the Friendly Shillelaghs
SSOG........	Satellite Systems Operations Guide [*INTELSAT*]
SSOG........	Scandinavian Association of Obstetricians and Gynaecologists　(EA)
SSOG........	Spur Stepover Gear
SSOJ	Savez Socialisticke Omladine Jugoslavije [*League of Socialist Youth of Yugoslavia*] [*Political party*]　(PPE)
SSOJ	Single Strength Orange Juice
S of Sol....	Song of Solomon [*Old Testament book*]　(ROG)
SSOL........	Space Station Operations Language [*NASA*]　(SSD)
SSOM.......	Solid-State Optical MASER
SSOM.......	[*The*] Space Shuttle Operator's Manual
SSOO	Satellite Supply Operations Officer [*Military*]　(AFIT)
SSOP........	Satellite Systems Operations Plan [*INTELSAT*]
SSOP........	Space Systems Operating Procedures [*NASA*]　(MCD)
SSOP........	Standard Security Operating Procedure　(SSD)
SSOR........	Ship Systems Operational Requirements
S SORD	Senza Sordini [*Without Mutes*] [*Music*]
SSORD......	Software Review [*A publication*]
SSORM.....	Standard Ship's Organization and Regulations Manual [*Navy*]　(NVT)
SSORM.....	Standing Submarine Operations and Repair Manual [*Navy*]　(DNAB)
SSORT	Ship's Systems Operational Readiness Test　(MCD)
SSORT	Ships Systems Operational Requirements
SSOS	One Sky, the Saskatchewan Cross Cultural Centre, Saskatoon, Saskatchewan [*Library symbol*] [*National Library of Canada*]　(NLC)
SSOS	Single Source of Supply　(MCD)
SSOSMFC ...	Simply Simon - The Official Simon MacCorkindale Fan Club　(EA)
SSOT........	Special Session of Oyer and Terminer [*Legal*] [*British*]　(ROG)
SSOTC	Skinner's School Officers Training Corps [*British military*]　(DMA)
SSOU1.......	System Output Unit 1 [*IBM Corp.*]　(MDG)
SSOW........	Subcontractor Statement of Work　(MCD)
SSOWSJ ...	Supreme Shrine of the Order of the White Shrine of Jerusalem　(EA)
SSP	Association of the Sons of Poland　(EA)
SSP	Petroleum Air Transport, Inc. [*Lafayette, LA*] [*FAA designator*]　(FAAC)
SSP	Plant Biotechnology Institute, National Research Council Canada [*Institut de Biotechologie des Plantes, Conseil National de Recherches Canada*], Saskatoon, Saskatchewan [*Library symbol*] [*Obsolete*] [*National Library of Canada*]　(NLC)
SSP	SACEUR [*Supreme Allied Commander, Europe*] Schedule Program [*Army*]　(AABC)
SSP	Sagittal Sinus Pressure [*Medicine*]
SSP	St. Philip's College, San Antonio, TX [*OCLC symbol*]　(OCLC)
SSP	Salt Soluble Protein [*Food industry*]
SSP	Schwartzman-Sanarelli Phenomenon [*Medicine*]　(MAE)
SSP	Scientific Services Program [*Army Research Office*]　(RDA)
SSP	Scientific Software Products, Inc. [*Information service or system*]　(IID)
SSP	Scientific Subroutine Package [*Data processing*]
SSP	Scouting Seaplane
SSP	Scripps [*E.W.*] Co. [*NYSE symbol*]　(SPSG)
SSP	Secondary Stock Point　(DNAB)
SSP	Seguro Resources [*Vancouver Stock Exchange symbol*]
SSP	Seismic Section Profiler
SSP	Selected Topics in Solid State Physics [*Elsevier Book Series*] [*A publication*]
SSP	Semi-Annual Service Program [*Army*]　(INF)
SSP	Sensor Select Panel　(MCD)
SSP	Sentence Synthesizing Program
SSP	Serbian Socialist Party [*Political party*]
SS & P......	Service, Supply, and Procurement [*Military*]
SSP	Set Sign Plus　(SAA)
SSP	Ship Speed
SSP	Ship's Stores Profit [*Navy*]
SSP	Shortage Specialty Pay [*Navy*]　(NVT)
SSP	Shoshone Peak [*Nevada*] [*Seismograph station code, US Geological Survey*]　(SEIS)
SSP	SIGINT Support Plan　(MCD)
SSP	Silo Support Plan　(SAA)
SSP	Simulation Support Processor
SSP	Single-Shot Probability [*Military*]
SSP	Single Stock Point [*Military*]　(AFIT)
SSP	Site Survey Payload　(MCD)
SSP	Skylab Student Project [*NASA*]
SSP	Small Sortie Payload [*NASA*]　(NASA)
SSP	Society of St. Paul for the Apostolate of Communications [*Pauline Fathers*] [*Roman Catholic religious order*]
SSP	Society of Satellite Professionals [*Later, SSPI*]　(EA)
SSP	Society for Scholarly Publishing　(EA)

SSP	Sodium Sampling Package [*Nuclear energy*]　(NRCH)
SSP	Solid-State Photodiode
SSP	Solid-State Pneumatic
SSP	Solid-State Preamplifier
SSP	SONAR Signal Processor
SSP	Sorghum Soy Pellet　(OA)
SSP	Source Selection Plan
SSP	South Simpson, AK [*Location identifier*] [*FAA*]　(FAAL)
SSP	Space Shuttle Program [*NASA*]　(NASA)
SSP	Space Station Program [*NASA*]　(SSD)
SSP	Special Services Protection [*Telecommunications*]　(TEL)
SSP	Special Session of Peace [*Legal*] [*British*]　(ROG)
SSP	Species Survival Plans [*Program sponsored by the American Association of Zoological Parks and Aquariums to protect certain endangered species*]
SSP	Sporozoite Surface Protein [*Biochemistry*]
SSP	Staff Site Position [*Nuclear energy*]　(NRCH)
SSP	Stainless Steel Propeller　(DS)
SSP	Standard Shop Practice　(MCD)
SSP	Standard Stability Prediction　(MCD)
SSP	Standard Subroutine Package
SSP	Standard Switch Panel　(MCD)
SSP	Standby Status Panel
SSP	State Supplementary Payment [*Department of Health and Human Services*]
SSP	Static Sodium Pot [*Nuclear energy*]　(NRCH)
SSP	Statutory Sick Pay [*British*]
SSP	Steam Service Pressure
SSP	Stores Select Panel　(SAA)
SSP	Stores Stressed Platform [*Military*] [*British*]
SSP	Strategic Systems Project [*Office*] [*Navy*]
SSP	Submarine Scout Patrol　(DMA)
SSP	Submarine Transport [*Navy symbol*] [*Obsolete*]
SSP	Subsatellite Point [*Telecommunications*]　(TEL)
SSP	Subsolar Point [*Aerospace*]
SSP	Subspecies [*Also, ssp*]
S/SP	Subsystem Software Program　(MCD)
SSP	Supersensitivity Perception
SSP	Supervisory Surveillance Program [*DoD*]
SSP	Supplemental Standard Practice　(AAG)
SSP	Support Software Package　(MCD)
SSP	Surgical Specialist
SSP	Sustained Superior Performance [*Military*]
SSP	System Safety Plan　(MCD)
SSP	System Security Plan
SSP	System Status Panel
SSP	System Support Program　(AFM)
SSPA	Senescent-Soybean-Pod Agar [*Microbiology*]
SSPA	Social Security Pensions Act [*1975*] [*British*]　(DCTA)
SSPA	Society of St. Peter Apostle　(EA)
SSPA	Solid State Phased Array　(MCD)
SSPA	Southern Sudanese Political Association [*Political party*] [*Sudan*]　(MENA)
SSPANC....	Society of St. Peter the Apostle for Native Clergy [*Later, SSPA*]　(EA)
SSPB..........	Socket Screw Products Bureau [*Defunct*]　(EA)
SSPB..........	Swedish State Power Board [*Nuclear energy*]
SSPC.........	Solid-State Power Controller [*NASA*]
SSPC.........	Spacelab Stored Program Command [*NASA*]　(MCD)
SSPC.........	Steel Structures Painting Council　(EA)
SSPCL.......	System Software Package Component List　(MCD)
SSPCL.......	System Support Package Component List　(MCD)
SSPCP	Shipboard Signal Processing Control Program [*Navy*]　(CAAL)
SSPCT.......	Technical Library, Potash Corp. of Saskatchewan, Saskatoon, Saskatchewan [*Library symbol*] [*National Library of Canada*]　(NLC)
SSPD	Shuttle System Payload Data [*NASA*]　(NASA)
SSPD	Shuttle System Payload Definition Study [*NASA*]　(NASA)
SSPD	Shuttle System Payload Description [*NASA*]　(NASA)
S/SPD.......	Single Speed [*Automotive engineering*]
SSPDA	Space Shuttle Payload Data Activity [*NASA*]　(NASA)
SSPDA	Surface Sampler Processing and Distribution Assembly
SSPDB.......	Subsystem Power Distribution Box　(MCD)
SSPDPT	Salzburg Studies. Poetic Drama and Poetic Theory [*A publication*]
SSPDR	Subsystem Preliminary Design Review
SSPDS.......	Space Shuttle Payload Data Study [*NASA*]　(NASA)
SSPE.........	Software Spectrum [*NASDAQ symbol*]　(SPSG)
SSPE.........	Space Station Program Element [*NASA*]　(SSD)
SSPE.........	Subacute Sclerosing Panencephalitis [*Medicine*]
SSPE.........	Support System Project Engineer
S Speech Commun J ...	Southern Speech Communication Journal [*A publication*]
SSPF.........	Signal Structure Parametric Filter [*Telecommunications*]　(OA)
SSPF.........	Software Support Production Facility　(SSD)
SSPF.........	Space Station Processing Facility [*NASA*]　(SSD)
SSPF.........	Structured Soy Protein Fiber [*Food industry*]
SSPFC.......	Stainless Steel Plumbing Fixture Council [*Defunct*]　(EA)
SSPGSE	Space Shuttle Program Ground Support Equipment [*NASA*]　(GFGA)
SSPHA	Solid State Physics [*A publication*]

SSPHS......	Society for Spanish and Portuguese Historical Studies (EA)
SSPI.........	Sight System Passive Infrared [*Sensor*] [*Army*]
SSPI.........	Society of Satellite Professionals International (TSSD)
SSPIF.......	Software Support Production Integration Facility (SSD)
SSpJ.........	Southern Speech Journal [*A publication*]
SSPK........	Single Shot Probability of Kill [*Military*]
SSPL.........	Saturation Sound Pressure Level
SSPL.........	Solid-State Pneumatic Logic
SSPL.........	Steady-State Power Level (IEEE)
SSPL.........	System Support Package List (MCD)
SSPM.......	Schedule Statusing and Performance Measurement (SSD)
SSPM.......	Single Strokes per Minute (MSA)
SSPM.......	Software Standards and Procedures Manual (SSD)
SSPM.......	Space Shuttle Program Manager [*NASA*] (NASA)
SSPMA.....	Sump and Sewage Pump Manufacturers Association (EA)
SSPME......	Societa di San Patrizio per le Missioni Estere [*St. Patrick's Society for the Foreign Missions - SPSFM*] [*Kiltegan, County Wicklow, Republic of Ireland*] (EAIO)
SSPMO.....	SONAR Systems Project Management Office
SSPN.........	Satellite System for Precise Navigation [*Air Force*]
SSPN.........	Ship's Stores and Profit, Navy
SSPN.........	System for Precise Navigation [*Later, DNSS*] (MCD)
ssp nov......	Subspecies Nova [*New Subspecies*] [*Biology*]
SSPO.........	Space Shuttle Program Office [*NASA*] (KSC)
SSPO.........	Strategic Systems Project Office [*Navy*]
SSPOTR....	Strategic Systems Project Office, Technical Representative [*Navy*] (DNAB)
SSPP.........	POS Pilot Plant Corp., University of Saskatchewan Campus, Saskatoon, Saskatchewan [*Library symbol*] [*National Library of Canada*] (NLC)
SSPP.........	Sancti Patres [*Holy Fathers*] [*Latin*]
SSPP.........	Schedule Status Preprocessor (MCD)
SSPP.........	Serikat Sekerdja Pamong Pradja [*Public Officials' Union*] [*Indonesia*]
SSPP.........	Shan State Progressive Party [*Myanmar*] [*Political party*] (EY)
SSPP.........	Society for the Study of Process Philosophies (EA)
SSPP.........	Solar Sea Power Plant [*NASA*]
SSPP.........	Space Station Program Participant [*NASA*] (SSD)
SSPP.........	Subspecies [*Plural form*] [*Also, sspp*]
SSPP.........	Subsynaptic Plate Perforation [*Neurophysiology*]
SSPP.........	System Safety Program Plan [*Navy*]
SSPPSG....	Space Shuttle Payload Planning Steering Group [*NASA*] (NASA)
SSPR........	Space Solar Power Review [*A publication*]
SSPR........	Subcontract Schedule and Procurement Request
SSPRO......	Space Shuttle Program Resident Office [*NASA*] (NASA)
SSPS.........	Satellite Solar Power Station [*or System*] [*NASA*]
SSPS.........	Sheffield Sawmakers' Protection Society [*A union*] [*British*] (DCTA)
SSPS.........	Silver/Somatostatin Positive Structure [*Anatomy*]
SSP-S........	Single Source Processor-SIGINT [*Signal Intelligence*]
SSPS.........	Solar-Based Solar Power Satellite
SSPS.........	Solar Satellite Power Station
SSPS.........	Solid-State Protection System [*Nuclear energy*] (IEEE)
SSPS.........	Space Shuttle Program Schedule [*NASA*] (NASA)
SSPS.........	Spacecraft Support Planning Section
SSPSF......	Stochastic Self-Propagating Star Formation
SSPSG......	Science and Public Policy Studies Group [*Newsletter*]
SSPSM......	Serikat Sekerdja Pabrik Sendjata dan Mesiu [*Armaments' Union*] [*Indonesia*]
SSPTF.......	Santa Susana Propulsion Test Facility [*NASA*] (NASA)
SSPTS.......	Security Support Squadron
SSPTT.......	Serikat Sekerdja Pos, Telegrap dan Telepon [*National Postal, Telegraph and Telephone Employees' Union*] [*Indonesia*]
SSPU........	Ship's Service Power Unit [*Navy*] (CAAL)
SSPW........	Sun Sportswear, Inc. [*NASDAQ symbol*] (NQ)
SSPWB......	Studium Spraw Polskich (Wielka Brytania) [*Information Centre for Polish Affairs*] (EAIO)
SSPWR......	Small-Size Pressurized Water Reactor [*Nuclear energy*]
SSQ...........	Shell Lake, WI [*Location identifier*] [*FAA*] (FAAL)
SSQ...........	Simple Sinusoidal Quantity
SSQ...........	Social Science Quarterly [*A publication*]
SSQ...........	Society for Software Quality (EA)
SSQ...........	Station Sick Quarters
SSQTA......	Social Science Quarterly [*A publication*]
SSR...........	RADAR Picket Submarine [*Navy symbol*]
SSR...........	S-Band Shuttle Return (SSD)
SSR...........	SACEUR [*Supreme Allied Commander, Europe*] Strategic Reserve [*Army*] (NATG)
SSR...........	Safe Secure Railcar [*Army*]
SSR...........	Safety Services Representative [*Red Cross*]
SSR...........	Saskatchewan Research Council, Saskatoon, Saskatchewan [*Library symbol*] [*National Library of Canada*] (NLC)
SSR...........	SATCOM Station Reports (MCD)
SSR...........	Satellite Situation Report (AAG)
SSR...........	Schedule Shipment Record (MCD)
SSR...........	Seal Steam Regulator [*Nuclear energy*] (NRCH)
SSR...........	Secondary Surveillance RADAR
SSR...........	Security Services [*Vancouver Stock Exchange symbol*]
SSR...........	Security Survey Report [*Nuclear energy*]
SSR...........	Seek-Storm RADAR
SSR...........	Selenium Stack Rectifier
SSR...........	Self-Sufficiency Ratio [*Business term*]
SSR...........	Separate Superheater Reactor [*Nuclear energy*]
SSR...........	Shipbuilding and Ship Repair [*Department of Employment*] [*British*]
SSR...........	Shop Support Request [*NASA*] (NASA)
SSR...........	SIA [*Semiconductor Industry Association*] Statistical Review [*A publication*] (EAAP)
SSR...........	Signal-Sequence Receptor [*Biochemistry*]
SSR...........	Sink to Source Relation
SSR...........	Sisters Island, AK [*Location identifier*] [*FAA*] (FAAL)
SSR...........	Site Suitability Report [*Nuclear energy*] (NRCH)
SSR...........	Slate-Shingle Roof [*Technical drawings*]
SSR...........	Slow Strain Rate [*Tensile test*]
SSR...........	Social Security Reporter [*Australia*] [*A publication*]
SSR...........	Social Security Rulings [*on Old Age, Survivors, and Disability Insurance*] [*US*] [*A publication*]
SSR...........	Societe Suisse de Radiodiffusion et Television [*Radio and television network*] [*Switzerland*]
SSR...........	Society for the Study of Reproduction (EA)
SSR...........	Sociology and Social Research [*A publication*]
SSR...........	Software Specification Review
SSR...........	Solid State Relay (IEEE)
SSR...........	South Staffordshire Regiment [*Military unit*] [*British*]
SSR...........	Soviet Socialist Republic
SSR...........	Special Scientific Report
SSR...........	Special Services Request [*Travel industry*]
SSR...........	Special Survey of Refrigerated Machinery [*Lloyd's Register of Shipping*] (DS)
SSR...........	Specification Status Report [*Nuclear Regulatory Commission*] (GFGA)
SSR...........	Spin-Stabilized Rockets
SSR...........	Spotted Swine Record [*Later, National Spotted Swine Record*] (EA)
SSR...........	Staff Support Room [*NASA*]
SSR...........	Static Shift Register
SSR...........	Static Squelch Range
SSR...........	Station Set Requirement [*NASA*] (NASA)
SSR...........	Statistical Summary Report (AAG)
SSR...........	Steady-State Rate [*of production*] [*Medicine*]
SSR...........	Stock Status Report
SSR...........	Students for Social Responsibility (EA)
SSR...........	Subsynchronous Resonance (IEEE)
SSR...........	Sum of the Squared Residuals [*Econometrics*]
SSR...........	Summarized Spares Requirement
SSR...........	Supplemental Security Record [*Social Security Administration*] (GFGA)
SSR...........	Supplementary Statement Required [*Civil Service*]
SSR...........	Supply Support Request [*or Requirement*] [*Military*] (AFM)
SSR...........	Support Staff Rooms (SAA)
SSR...........	Surface Search RADAR (SAA)
SSR...........	Surface Slip Resistance
s-sr---........	Surinam [*MARC geographic area code*] [*Library of Congress*] (LCCP)
SSR...........	Susara [*Romania*] [*Seismograph station code, US Geological Survey*] (SEIS)
SSR...........	Synchronous Stable Relaying (IEEE)
SSR...........	System Status Report
SSR...........	System Status Review
SSR...........	System Study Requirement (AAG)
SSR...........	System Subroutines (SAA)
SSR...........	System Support Record
SSRA.........	Scottish Squash Rackets Association (EAIO)
SSRA.........	Spread Spectrum Random Access System [*Telecommunications*] (TEL)
SSRA.........	System Safety Risk Analysis [*Army*]
SSRB.........	Sole Source Review Board (MCD)
SSRBD......	Solid State RADAR Beacon Decoder (DWSG)
SSRC........	Social Science Research Center [*Mississippi State University*] [*Research center*] (RCD)
SSRC........	Social Science Research Council (EA)
SSRC........	Social Systems Research Center [*California State University, Dominguez Hills*] [*Research center*] (RCD)
SSRC........	Society for the Study of Religion and Communism (EA)
SSRC........	Structural Stability Research Council (EA)
SSRC........	Swedish Space Research Committee
SSRCA......	Super Sunfish Racing Class Association (EA)
SSRCC......	Social Sciences Research Council of Canada [*See also CCRSS*] [*Later, SSHRCC*]
SSRC Newsl...	SSRC [*Social Science Research Council*] Newsletter [*A publication*]
SSRCR.......	Suggested State Regulations for the Control of Radiation [*Nuclear Regulatory Commission*] (NRCH)
SSRD........	Station Set Requirements Document [*NASA*] (NASA)
SSREA.......	Sight-Saving Review [*A publication*]
SSREIU.....	Shipbuilding, Ship Repairing, and Engineering Industrial Union [*British*]
SSREX......	Canada Department of Regional Industrial Expansion [*Ministere de l'Expansion Industrielle Regionale*] Saskatoon, Saskatchewan [*Library symbol*] [*National Library of Canada*] (NLC)

SSRF.........	Shell-Supported Ring Frame
SSRF.........	Small-Scale Raiding Force [*Military*]
SSR-F.......	Special Scientific Report - Fisheries
SSRFC.......	Social Science Research Facilities Center [*University of Minnesota*] [*Research center*] (RCD)
SSRG........	Selective Service Regulations
SSRG........	Simple Shift Register Generator
SSRH.........	General Constituency Section for Small or Rural Hospitals (EA)
SSRI	Social Science Research Institute [*University of Maine at Orono*] [*Research center*] (RCD)
SSRI	Social Science Research Institute [*of CRESS*] [*University of Hawaii at Manoa*] [*Research center*] (RDA)
SSRI	Social Systems Research Institute [*University of Wisconsin - Madison*] [*Research center*] (RCD)
SSRL	Stanford Synchrotron Radiation Laboratory [*Stanford, CA*] [*Department of Energy*]
SSRL	Stockholm Studies in Russian Literature [*A publication*]
SSRL	Systems Simulation Research Laboratory
SSRM........	Second-Stage Rocket Motor
SSRMS.....	Space Station Remote Manipulator System [*NASA*] (SSD)
SSRN.........	RADAR Picket Submarine (Nuclear Powered) [*Navy symbol*] [*Obsolete*]
SSRN........	Service Shop Requirement Notice
SSRN........	System Software Reference Number [*NASA*] (NASA)
SSRNJ.......	Socijalisticka Savez Radnog Naroda Jugoslavije [*Socialist Alliance of Working People of Yugoslavia - SAWPY*] [*Political party*] (PPE)
SSRP	Single Shot Kill Probability (MCD)
SSRP	Somali Socialist Revolutionary Party
SSRP	Stanford Synchrotron Radiation Project
SSRPOS....	Space Station Rendezvous and Proximity Operations Simulator [*NASA*] (SSD)
SSRR	Social Service Reporting Requirements [*HEW*]
SSRR	Station Set Requirements Review [*NASA*] (NASA)
SSRR	System Software Requirement Review (MCD)
SSRS........	SIGINT Surveillance and Reporting System (MCD)
SSRS........	Society for Social Responsibility in Science (EA)
SSRS........	Start-Stop-Restart System [*NASA*] (KSC)
SSRS........	Submarine Sand Recovery System
SSRSB.......	Safety and Special Radio Services Bureau [*of FCC*]
SSRSJC.....	Saudi-Sudanese Red Sea Joint Commission [*Commercial firm*] [*Jeddah, Saudi Arabia*] (EAIO)
SSRT	Subsystem Readiness Test (KSC)
SSRTP.......	Solid Substrate Room Temperature Phosphorescence
SS-RTP......	Solid-Surface, Room-Temperature Phosphorescence [*Physics*]
SSRWA	Soviet Science Review [*A publication*]
SSS	MSA Realty Corp. [*AMEX symbol*] (SPSG)
SSS	Safeguard Spartan System [*Aerospace*] (MCD)
SSS	San Salvador [*El Salvador*] [*Seismograph station code, US Geological Survey*] (SEIS)
SSS	Satellite Surveillance System (MCD)
SSS	Satellite Syndicated Systems [*Douglasville, GA*] [*Cable TV programming service*] [*Telecommunications*]
SSS	Sauna - Swimming Pool - Storage Area [*Key fitting those locks in apartment complex*]
SSS	Scalded Skin Syndrome [*Medicine*] (MAE)
SSS	Scandinavian Surgical Society (EAIO)
SSS	Scene Storage System (MCD)
SSS	School of Social Studies [*British*]
SSS	Scientific Subroutine System [*Data processing*] (BUR)
SSS	Secondary Sampling System [*Nuclear energy*] (NRCH)
S/SS...........	Sector/Subsector
SSS	Selective Service System
SSS	Self-Service Store
SSS	Semitic Study Series [*A publication*] (BJA)
SSS	Senior Service School [*Military*] (AFM)
SSS	Sensitized Stainless Steel (NRCH)
SSS	Sentinel-Spartan System (MCD)
SSS	Shevchenko Scientific Society (EA)
SSS	Shield and Seismic Support [*Nuclear energy*] (NRCH)
SSS	Shift Ship Superintendent [*Navy*] (DNAB)
SSS	Ship's Service Stores
SSS	Shnat Sherut Scheme (BJA)
SSS	Shore Signal Service [*British Royal Navy*]
SSS	Siassi [*Papua New Guinea*] [*Airport symbol*] (OAG)
SSS	Sick Sinus Syndrome [*Medicine*]
SSS	Signal Switching System
SSS	Signature Security Service [*DoD*]
SSS	Silicon-Symmetrical Switch (CET)
SSS	Simplified Spelling Society (EA)
SSS	Simulation Study Series (KSC)
SSS	Single Screw Ship
SSS	Single Signal Supersonic [*Heterodyne*] (DEN)
SSS	Sisters of Social Service [*Roman Catholic religious order*]
SSS	Site Security Supervisor (AFM)
SSS	Skills Support System [*Education*]
SSS	Small Scientific Satellite [*NASA*]
SSS	Small Solar Satellite [*NASA*]
SSS	Small Starlight Scope [*Light-intensifying device*]
SSS	Small Structures Survey [*Civil Defense*]
SSS	Social Science Series [*A publication*]
SSS	Social Status Study [*Psychology*]
SSS	Societas Sanctissimi Sacramenti [*Congregation of the Blessed Sacrament*] [*Roman Catholic men's religious order*]
SSS	Societe Scandinave de Simulation [*Scandinavian Simulation Society*] [*Finland*] (EAIO)
SSS	Society of St. Stephen (EA)
SSS	Society for the Second Self (EA)
SSS	Society for Slovene Studies (EA)
SSS	Society for Socialist Studies [*Canada*] [*See also SES*]
SSS	Society for the Suppression of Speculative Stamps [*Defunct*]
SSS	Software/Segment Specification
SSS	Software Service System [*Anti-piracy device invented by Ryoichi Mori of the Japan Electronics Industry Development Association*] (BYTE)
SSS	Software Staging Section [*Social Security Administration*]
SSS	Solid-State Spectrometer
SSS	Solid-State Switching (NG)
SSS	Solid-State System
SSS	SONAR Signal Simulator
SSS	Sortie Support System (MCD)
SSS	Sound Suppression System (NASA)
SSS	Southern Satellite Systems, Inc. [*Tulsa, OK*] [*Telecommunications*] (TSSD)
SSS	Space Settlers' Society (EAIO)
SSS	Space Shuttle Simulation [*NASA*]
SSS	Space Shuttle System [*NASA*] (KSC)
SSS	Space Station Simulator
SSS	Space Surveillance System [*Navy*] (MCD)
SSS	Spacecraft System Support
SSS	Special Safeguards Study [*Nuclear energy*] (NRCH)
SSS	Special Safety Safeguards (NRCH)
SSS	Special Security Squadron
SSS	Special Support Services
SSS	Specific Soluble Substance [*Polysaccharide hapten*]
SSS	Spin-Stabilized Spacecraft
SSS	Spinning Space Station
SSS	Stabilized Sighting System
SSS	Staff Summary Sheet (MCD)
SSS	Stage Separation Subsystem [*NASA*] (NASA)
SSS	Stainless Steel Sink [*Classified advertising*] (ADA)
SSS	Standard Scratch Score [*Golf*]
SSS	Standard Seawater Service [*British*]
SSS	Standard Supply System [*Army*] (AABC)
SSS	Stanford Sleepiness Scale
SSS	Station Set Specification [*NASA*] (NASA)
SSS	Stepping Switch Scanner
SSS	Sterile Saline Soak
SSS	Stockholders Sovereignty Society [*Later, FFSR*] (EA)
SSS	STOL Support Ship [*Navy*] (CAAL)
SSS	Storage Serviceability Standard [*Army*]
SSS	Strategic Satellite System (MCD)
SSS	Strategic Studies Staff [*Environmental Protection Agency*] (GFGA)
SSS	Strategic Support Squadron [*Air Force*]
SSS	Stratum Super Stratum [*Layer Over Layer*] [*Latin*]
SSS	Strike Support Ship [*Navy*] (NVT)
SSS	Strong Soap Solution
SSS	Structures Subsystem (KSC)
SSS	Student Support Services Program [*Department of Education*] (GFGA)
SSS	Study Skills Surveys [*Educational test*]
SSS	Subject Specialists Section [*Association of College and Research Libraries*]
SSS	Subjective Stress Scale
SSS	Subscribers' Switching Subsystem [*Telecommunications*] (TEL)
SSS	Substructure Search System [*Later, SANSS*] [*NIH/EPA*]
SSS	Subsystem Segment [*NASA*] (NASA)
SSS	Subsystem Support Service (BUR)
SSS	Sunday Shakespeare Society [*British*]
SSS	Super Science Stories [*A publication*]
SSS	Superior Shore Systems [*An association*] (EA)
SSS	Supply Screening Section [*Navy*]
SSS	Survivable Satellite System (MCD)
SSS	Symbolic Shorthand System
SSS	System Safety Society (EA)
SSS	System Segment Specification (MCD)
SSS	Systems, Science, and Software
SSS	Trois Fois Salut [*Thrice Greeting*] [*French*] [*Freemasonry*] (ROG)
SSSA..........	St. Andrew's College, Saskatoon, Saskatchewan [*Library symbol*] [*National Library of Canada*] (NLC)
SSSA..........	Self-Service Storage Association [*Later, SSA*] (EA)
SSSA..........	Soil Science Society of America (EA)
SSSA..........	Sotos Syndrome Support Association (EA)
SSSA..........	Submarine SONAR Subjective Analysis (NVT)
SSSAS	Society of Spanish and Spanish-American Studies (EA)
SSSAS	Space Station Systems Analysis Study [*NASA*] (SSD)
SSSA Spec Publ ...	SSSA [*Soil Science Society of America*] Special Publication [*A publication*]

SSSA Spec Publ Ser ... SSSA [*Soil Science Society of America*] Special Publication Series [*A publication*]
SSSB......... Society for the Study of Social Biology (EA)
SSSB......... System Source Selection Board [*Air Force*]
SSSBCR .... Star, Starling, Stuart, and Briton Car Register (EA)
SSSBP ...... System Source Selection Board Procedure [*Air Force*]
SSSC......... Self-Service Supply Center [*Military*] (AFIT)
SSSC......... Single Sideband Suppressed Carrier
SSSC......... Soft-Sized Super-Calendered [*Paper*]
SSSC......... Solid-State Sciences Committee [*National Research Council*] [*Physics*]
SSSC......... Space Science Steering Committee
SSSC......... Space Station Support Center [*NASA*] (SSD)
SSSC......... Special Spectrum Study Committee
SSSC......... Stainless Steel Sink Council [*Defunct*] (EA)
SSSC......... Studies in Surface Science and Catalysis [*Elsevier Book Series*] [*A publication*]
SSSC......... Surface/Subsurface Control [*Navy*] (CAAL)
SSSC......... Surface/Subsurface Surveillance Center [*Navy*] (NVT)
SSSC......... Surface/Subsurface Surveillance Coordinator [*Navy*]
SSSCA...... Soviet Soil Science [*English translation*] [*A publication*]
SSSCAE .... Soviet Soil Science [*English translation of Pochvovedenie*] [*A publication*]
SSSCD...... Social Studies of Science [*A publication*]
SSSCP ...... Single Supply Support Control Point (MCD)
SSSD .... Second-Stage Separation Device
SSSD .... Single-Sided, Single-Density Disk [*Magnetic disk*] [*Data processing*]
SSSD .... Solid-State Solenoid Driver
SSSD .... Space Shuttle Simulation Display [*NASA*]
SSSEDA .... Aerospace Products Division, SED Systems Ltd., Saskatoon, Saskatchewan [*Library symbol*] [*National Library of Canada*] (NLC)
SSSERC .... Scottish Schools Science Equipment Research Centre (CB)
SSSF.......... Stationary Source Simulator Facility [*Environmental science*]
SSSG .... SLCM [*Sea-Launched Cruise Missile*] Survivability Steering Group [*Navy*] (CAAL)
SSSI.......... Kelsey Institute of Applied Arts and Sciences, Saskatoon, Saskatchewan [*Library symbol*] [*National Library of Canada*] (NLC)
SSSI.......... Servamatic Solar Systems [*NASDAQ symbol*] (NQ)
SSSI.......... Site of Special Scientific Interest [*British*]
SSSI.......... Society for the Study of Symbolic Interaction (EA)
SSSI.......... Special Steel Summary Invoice [*International Trade Administration*]
SSSI.......... Steel Scaffolding and Shoring Institute [*Later, SSFI*] (EA)
SSSJ.......... Single Subsonic Jet
SSSJ.......... Student Struggle for Soviet Jewry (EA)
SSSJD .... Soil Science Society of America. Journal [*A publication*]
SSS Journal ... State Shipping Service of Western Australia. Journal [*A publication*] (APTA)
SSSL.......... Society for the Study of Southern Literature (EA)
SSSL.......... Sun State Savings & Loan Association [*Phoenix, AZ*] [*NASDAQ symbol*] (NQ)
SSSL.......... Supersonic Split Line (KSC)
SSSLF .... South Slavonian Socialist Labor Federation [*Defunct*] (EA)
SSSM .... Site Space Surveillance Monitor (AFM)
SSSM .... South Street Seaport Museum (EA)
SSSM .... Subset-Specified Sequential Machine [*Air Force*]
SSSM .... Systems Support Service Module (SSD)
SSSMP...... Surface Ship SONAR Modernization Program (MCD)
SSSN......... Satellite Syndicated Systems [*NASDAQ symbol*] (NQ)
SSSN......... Secondary Social Security Number
S/S/SN...... System/Subsystem/Subject Number (MCD)
SSSO .... Specialized Satellite Service Operators [*British*]
SSSO .... Specialized Surplus Sales Office [*Military*]
SSSP.......... Society for the Study of Social Problems (EA)
SSSP.......... Space Settlement Studies Program (EA)
SSSP.......... Space Shuttle Synthesis Program [*National Academy of Sciences*]
SSSP.......... Station to Station Send Paid [*Telecommunications*] (TEL)
SSSP.......... Stockholm Studies in Scandinavian Philology [*A publication*]
SSSP.......... System Source Selection Procedure [*Air Force*]
SSSQ .... McCarron-Dial Street Survival Skills Questionnaire [*Occupational therapy*]
SSSQ .... Southwestern Social Science Quarterly [*A publication*]
SS/SR........ Safety Standdown/Safety Review (MCD)
SSSR......... SAGE [*Semiautomatic Ground Environment*] System Status Report
SSSR......... Smallest Set of Smallest Rings [*Organic chemistry*]
SSSR......... Social Sciences Services and Resources (EA)
SSSR......... Society for the Scientific Study of Religion (EA)
SSSR......... Southwestern Social Science Review [*A publication*]
SSSR......... Soyuz Sovetskikh Sotsialisticheskikh Respublik [*Union of Soviet Socialist Republics*]
SSSR......... Syracuse Scales of Social Relations [*Education*]
SSSS......... Shallow Spherical Sandwich Shell
SSSS......... Society for the Scientific Study of Sex (EA)
SSSS......... Space Shuttle System Segment (MCD)
SSSS......... Space Shuttle System Specification [*NASA*] (NASA)
SSSS......... Space Systems Support Squadron

SSSS......... Spaceborne Software Systems Study (DNAB)
SSSS......... Staphylococcal Scalded Skin Syndrome [*Medicine*]
SSSS......... Stewart & Stevenson Services, Inc. [*NASDAQ symbol*] (NQ)
SSSSC .... Surface/Subsurface Surveillance Coordinator [*Navy*] (CAAL)
SSSST .... Subscale Subsonic Targets (MCD)
SSSST .... S-Band Spread Spectrum Transponder (MCD)
SSST......... Site Suitability Source Term [*Nuclear energy*] (NRCH)
SSST......... Solid-State Silicon Target
SSST......... Space Station Simulator Trainee [*or Trainer*] [*NASA*] (SSD)
SSST......... Spectroscopic Survey Telescope [*Proposed*] [*Joint project of the University of Texas and Pennsylvania State University*]
SSStJ......... Serving Sister, Order of St. John of Jerusalem [*British*]
SSSV......... Scientific Systems Services, Inc. [*NASDAQ symbol*] (NQ)
SSSV......... Superior Sagittal Sinus Blood Velocity [*Medicine*] (AAMN)
SSSW .... Surface/Subsurface Warfare [*Navy*] (CAAL)
SSSYDF .... Synergetics [*Berlin*] [*A publication*]
SST .... Safe Secure Trailer [*For transporting nuclear materials*]
SST .... Safe Separate/Timing (CINC)
SST .... Saskatchewan Teachers' Federation Saskatoon, Saskatchewan [*Library symbol*] [*National Library of Canada*] (NLC)
SST .... Satellite-to-Satellite Tracking
SST .... Satellite Servicing Technology (SSD)
SST .... Saturated Suction Temperature [*Refrigeration*]
SST .... Saturn Systems Test [*NASA*]
SST .... Science Stories [*A publication*]
SST .... Sea Surface Temperature [*Oceanography*]
SST .... Seaplane Shuttle Transport [*New York-Philadelphia air-link*]
SST .... Secondary Surge Tank [*Nuclear energy*] (NRCH)
SST .... Semi-Submerged Trimaran [*Tri-hull ship design invented by Calvin Gongwer*]
SST .... Serviceability Self-Test (MCD)
SST .... Set Strobe Time [*Data processing*] (OA)
SST .... Shakespeare Studies (Tokyo) [*A publication*]
SST .... Shelter Components Corp. [*AMEX symbol*] (SPSG)
SST .... Shipboard [*Weapon*] Suitability Test [*Navy*] (NG)
SST .... Ships Service Turbine (MCD)
SST .... Shore Survey Team (DNAB)
SST .... Sideways-Spinning Tube [*Spectrometry*]
SST .... Sight, Sound, and Touch [*Ways to identify proper belt tension*] [*Automotive engineering*]
SST .... Silver Sceptre Resources [*Vancouver Stock Exchange symbol*]
SST .... Simulated Structural Test (KSC)
SST .... Single Sideband Transmission [*Telecommunications*] (TEL)
SST .... Single Subscriber Terminal [*Army*] (RDA)
SST .... Single Systems Trainer [*NASA*] (MCD)
SST .... Slide, Script, and Tape
SST .... Social Security Tax Ruling [*Internal Revenue Bulletin*] [*A publication*] (DLA)
SST .... Society for the Study of Theology [*British*]
SST .... Society of Surveying Technicians (EAIO)
SST .... Solid-State Transmitter (MCD)
SST .... SONAR Signaling (NVT)
SST .... Soviet Science and Technology [*IFI/Plenum Data Corp.*] [*Information service or system*] (IID)
SSt .... Sowjet Studien [*A publication*]
SST .... Space Selector Terminal (SAA)
SST .... Space Surveillance Technology
SST .... Spacecraft System Test [*NASA*]
SST .... Special Strike Teletype (NATG)
SST .... Spectroscopic Survey Telescope [*Proposed*] [*Joint project of the University of Texas and Pennsylvania State University*]
SSt .... Spenser Studies [*A publication*]
SST .... Split Second Timing
SST .... Stainless Steel
SST .... Station Service Transformer [*Nuclear energy*] (NRCH)
SS/T .... Steady-State/Transient Analysis [*Nuclear energy*] (NRCH)
SST .... Stiffened Super-Tough [*Polymer technology*]
SST .... Stock Size Template (MCD)
SST .... Stream Support Team (MCD)
SST .... Structural Static Test [*NASA*] (NASA)
SST .... Student Science Training [*Program*] [*National Science Foundation*] [*Defunct*]
SST .... Subject Standardized Test
SST .... Submarine Scout Twin-Type [*British military*] (DMA)
SST .... Subscriber Transferred [*Telecommunications*] (TEL)
SST .... Subsystem Terminal on Spacelab [*NASA*] (MCD)
SST .... Subsystems Test (KSC)
SST .... Super Smoothing Technology [*Apple Computer, Inc.*]
SST .... Superficial Spreading Type (Melanoma) [*Oncology*]
SS/T .... Supersonic Telegraphy [*British military*] (DMA)
SST .... Supersonic Transport
SST .... Supplementary Service Tariff [*British*] (DCTA)
SST .... Susitna [*Alaska*] [*Seismograph station code, US Geological Survey*] [*Closed*] (SEIS)
SST .... Synchronous System Trap
SST .... System Segment Table
SST .... System Survey Team [*Military*] (AFIT)
SST .... Systems Support Tape
SST .... Target and Training Submarine [*Self-propelled*] [*Navy symbol*]
SST .... Training Submarine [*Navy symbol*]
SSTA .... Scottish Secondary Teachers' Association (DI)

SSTA	Secondary School Theatre Association [*Inactive*] (EA)
SSTA	Support System Task Analysis (AAG)
SSTADS....	Small Ship Typhoon Air Defense System (MCD)
SSTAR.......	Society for Sex Therapy and Research (EA)
SSTC	Secondary School Theatre Conference [*Later, SSTA*] (EA)
SSTC	Ship System Test Contractor (MCD)
SSTC	Single-Sideband Transmitted Carrier (IEEE)
SSTC	Solid-State Timer-Controller
SSTC	Space Shuttle Test Conductor [*NASA*] (NASA)
SSTC	Spacecraft System Test Console [*NASA*]
SSTC	Specialized System Test Contractor
SSTC	Summary of Supplemental Type Certificates
SSTCWN ..	Specifications Subject to Change without Notice
SSTD	Solid State Track Detector [*Instrumentation*]
SSTD.........	Surface Ship Torpedo Defense [*Navy*] (CAAL)
SSTDC	Society of Stage Directors and Choreographers (EA)
SST-DMA ...	Satellite Switched Time Division Multiple Access
SSTDMA ..	Spacecraft Switched Time Division Multiple Access [*Telecommunications*]
SS/TDMA ...	Spread Spectrum/Time Division Multiple Access (MCD)
SSTDS.......	Small Ship Tactical Data System [*Navy*] (CAAL)
SSTEP.......	System Support Test Evaluation Program
SSTF..........	Saturn Static Test Facility [*NASA*]
SSTF..........	Shortest Seek Time First
SSTF..........	Space Shuttle Task Force [*NASA*]
SSTF..........	Space Simulation Test Facility (AAG)
SSTF..........	Space Station Task Force [*NASA*]
SSTF..........	Space Station Training Facility [*NASA*] (SSD)
SSTG	Ship Service Turbo Generator (MSA)
SSTG	Space Shuttle Task Group [*NASA*] (KSC)
SSTG	Special Service Training Group [*World War II*]
SSTI...........	Serikat Sekerdja Topografi Indonesia [*Indonesian Topography Employees' Union*]
SSTIR........	Sea Surface Temperature Imaging Radiometer
SSTIXS	Small Ship Teletype Information Exchange System [*or Subsystem*] (MCD)
SSTJA	Solid State Journal [*A publication*]
SSTL..........	Sector System Training Leader (SAA)
SSTL..........	Solid State Track Link [*TOW*] (MCD)
SSTLA.......	Strip Shunt Transmission Line Antenna [*Aviation*] (AIA)
SSTM	SAGE [*Semiautomatic Ground Environment*] System Training Mission
SSTM	Single Service Training Manager (MCD)
SSTM	System Support Technical Manager [*Navy*] (NG)
SSTMS......	Standard Supply Transportation Manifest System
SSTO.........	Single Stage to Orbit [*NASA*]
SSTO.........	Superintending Sea Transport Officer [*British military*] (DMA)
SSTO.........	Systonetics, Inc. [*Fullerton, CA*] [*NASDAQ symbol*] (NQ)
SSTP..........	Software Support Transition Plan [*Army*]
SSTP..........	Student Science Training Program [*National Science Foundation*] [*Defunct*]
SSTP..........	Subsystems Test Procedure (KSC)
SSTP..........	Supersonic Transport Panel [*International Civil Aviation Organization*]
SSTR	Senior Staff Technical Representative (MCD)
s str.............	Sensu Stricto [*In a Narrow Sense*] [*Latin*] (MAE)
SSTRA.......	Successive Subtraction with Total Recognition Accuracy [*Algorithm*]
SSTRD	Special Steels Technical Review [*A publication*]
SSTS..........	Signaling and Supervision Techniques Study
SSTS..........	Space Surveillance and Tracking System [*Military*]
SST Sver Skogsvaardsfoerb Tidskr ...	SST. Sveriges Skogsvaardsfoerbunds Tidskrift [*A publication*]
SSTT	Specialized Systems Test Teams (SAA)
SST-T-T	Sound, Sense, Today, Tomorrow, Thereafter [*Teacher's Guide, published by Department of Transportation, for promoting supersonic travel*]
SSTU	SAGE [*Semiautomatic Ground Environment*] System Training Unit
SSTU	Seamless Steel Tubing
SStud	Shakespeare Studies [*A publication*]
SSTV	Congregation of Sisters of St. Thomas of Villanova [*Roman Catholic religious order*]
SSTV	Sea Skimming Test Vehicles
SSTV	Slow-Scan Television
SSTV	Submarine Shock Test Vehicle
SStW..........	Synoptische Studien fuer A. Wikenhauser [*1953*] [*A publication*] (BJA)
SSU............	Safety Sequence Unit (MCD)
SSU............	San Pedro Sula [*Honduras*] [*Seismograph station code, US Geological Survey*] (SEIS)
SSU............	Saybolt Seconds Universal [*Oil viscosity*]
SSU............	Self-Service Unit
SSU............	Semiconductor Storage Unit [*Data processing*]
SSU............	Sensor Simulator Unit
SSU............	Sight Survey Unit
SSU............	Signal Summing Unit [*Aviation*]
SSU............	Single Signaling Unit [*Telecommunications*] (TEL)
SSU............	Solvent Service Unit
SSU............	Source Resources Ltd. [*Vancouver Stock Exchange symbol*]
SSU............	Spacecraft Support Unit

SSU............	Special Service Unit [*Military*]
SSU............	Squadron Service Unit [*Aircraft*]
SSU............	Stabilized Sight Unit (MCD)
SSU............	Standard Saybolt Universal [*Oil viscosity*]
SSU............	Statistical Service Unit [*Military*]
SSU............	Sterile Supply Unit (MAE)
SSU............	Strategic Services Unit [*Formerly, OSS*]
SSU............	Stratospheric Sounding Unit [*Telecommunications*] (TEL)
SSU............	Subscriber Switching Unit [*Telecommunications*] (TEL)
SSU............	Subsequent Signal Unit [*Group of BITS*] [*Telecommunications*] (TEL)
SSU............	Sunday School Union
SSU............	Surface Screen Unit [*Navy*] (NVT)
SSU............	Switch Selector Update
SSU............	System Selector Unit
SSU............	System Support Unification (MCD)
SSU............	University of Saskatchewan, Saskatoon, Saskatchewan [*Library symbol*] [*National Library of Canada*] (NLC)
SSU............	White Sulphur Springs, WV [*Location identifier*] [*FAA*] (FAAL)
SSUEM	Uranerz Exploration & Mining Ltd., Saskatoon, Saskatchewan [*Library symbol*] [*National Library of Canada*] (NLC)
SSUF	Sprakvetenskapliga Sallskapets i Uppsala Foerhandlingar [*A publication*]
SSUGP	Government Publications, University of Saskatchewan, Saskatoon, Saskatchewan [*Library symbol*] [*National Library of Canada*] (NLC)
SSUIS........	Space Station User Information System [*NASA*] (SSD)
SSUJD	[*The*] Right Honourable John G. Diefenbaker Centre, University of Saskatchewan, Saskatoon, Saskatchewan [*Library symbol*] [*National Library of Canada*] (NLC)
SSUL	Law Library, University of Saskatchewan, Saskatoon, Saskatchewan [*Library symbol*] [*National Library of Canada*] (NLC)
SSULS.......	Lutheran Seminary, University of Saskatchewan, Saskatoon, Saskatchewan [*Library symbol*] [*National Library of Canada*] (NLC)
SSUM.......	Medical Library, University of Saskatchewan, Saskatoon, Saskatchewan [*Library symbol*] [*National Library of Canada*] (NLC)
SSUMC.....	Ukrainian Museum of Canada, Saskatoon, Saskatchewan [*Library symbol*] [*National Library of Canada*] (NLC)
SSUR........	Springfield Sunday Union and Republican [*A publication*]
SSURADS ...	Shipboard Surveillance RADAR System (MCD)
SSURO......	Stop Sale, Use and Removal Order [*Environmental Protection Agency*] (GFGA)
SSUS	Spin-Stabilized Upper Stage [*NASA*] (NASA)
SSUS	Spinning Solid Upper Stage (RDA)
SSUS	System Support Unification Subsystem (MCD)
SSUSA	Special Staff, United States Army
SSUS-A	Spinning Solid Upper Stage - Atlas Class Spacecraft (MCD)
SSUS-D.....	Spinning Solid Upper Stage - Delta Class Spacecraft (MCD)
SSUSN	Society of Sponsors of the United States Navy (EA)
SSUSP......	Spinning Solid Upper Stage Project (MCD)
SSUTC	Special Service Unit Training Center [*World War II*]
SSV............	Satellite Servicing Vehicle
SSV............	Seraphic Society for Vocations [*Defunct*] (EA)
SSV............	Sheep Seminal Vesicle
SSV............	Ship-to-Surface Vessel
SSV............	Simian Sarcoma Virus [*Also, SiSV*]
SSV............	Small Synaptic Vesicle [*Neurobiology*]
SSV............	Space Shuttle Vehicle [*NASA*]
SSV............	Special Surveillance Vehicle [*Navy*] (DNAB)
SSV............	Spool Selector Valve
SSV............	SPRINT [*Solid-Propellant Rocket Intercept*] Service Vehicle [*Army*]
SSV............	Static Self-Verification
SSV............	Sub Signo Veneni [*Under a Poison Label*] [*Pharmacy*]
SSV............	Subjective Scale Value
SSV............	Sumac Ventures, Inc. [*Vancouver Stock Exchange symbol*]
SSV............	Supersatellite Vehicle
SSV............	Supersonic Test Vehicles
SSV............	Sydslesvigsk Vaelgerforening [*South Schleswig Voters' Association*] [*Also, SSW*] [*Germany*] [*Political party*] (PPW)
SSVA	Signal Susceptibility and Vulnerability Assessment [*Military*] (CAAL)
SSVB	Security Savings Bank FSB [*NASDAQ symbol*] (NQ)
SSVC	Selective Service [*Military*]
SSVC	Services Sound and Video Corp. [*British*]
SSVE	Subacute Spongiform Virus Encephalopathies [*Medicine*]
SSVF..........	Straits Settlements Volunteer Force [*British military*] (DMA)
SSV/GC & N ...	Space Shuttle Vehicle/Guidance, Control, and Navigation [*NASA*]
SSVM........	Self-Scaling Variable Metric [*Algorithms*] [*Data processing*]
SSVN.........	Subsystem and Vehicle Number (SAA)
SsvOA........	Sydsvenska Ortnamns-Saellskapets Arsskrift [*A publication*]
SSVP	Society of St. Vincent De Paul [*Paris, France*] (EAIO)
SSVP	Soviet Ship Vulnerability Program
SSVS..........	Slow-Scan Video Simulator

SSV-SSAV ...	Simian Sarcoma Virus-Simian Sarcoma Associated Virus [*Complex*]
SSW..........	Safety Switch
SSW..........	St. Louis Southwestern Railway Co. [*AAR code*]
SSW..........	Save the Strippers Wells (EA)
SSW..........	Scramble Status and Weather (SAA)
SSW..........	Secretary of State for War [*British*]
SSW..........	Senior Social Worker (ADA)
SSW..........	Sense Switch [*Military*] (AFIT)
SSW..........	Shipboard Safety Watch [*Navy*] (DNAB)
SSW..........	Siemens-Schuckert Werke [*Germany*]
SSW..........	Solid-State Welding
SSW..........	South-Southwest
SSW..........	Space Support Wing [*Military*]
SSW..........	Space Switch [*Telecommunications*] (TEL)
SSW..........	Staggered Spondaic Word
SSW..........	Standby Service Water [*Nuclear energy*] (NRCH)
SSW..........	Sterling Software, Inc. [*NYSE symbol*] (SPSG)
SSW..........	Suedschleswigscher Waehlerverband [*South Schleswig Voter's League*] [*Also, SSV*] [*Germany*] [*Political party*] (PPE)
SSW..........	Support Software (MCD)
SSW..........	Surface Science Western [*University of Western Ontario*] [*Research center*] (RCD)
SSW..........	Surface Strike Warfare [*Navy*] (CAAL)
SSW..........	Swept Square Wave (MCD)
SSW..........	Synchro Switch [*Electronics*]
SSW..........	Systems West Consultants Ltd. [*Vancouver Stock Exchange symbol*]
SSW..........	Wheatland Regional Library, Saskatoon, Saskatchewan [*Library symbol*] [*National Library of Canada*] (NLC)
SSWA.......	Sanitary Supply Wholesalers Association (EA)
SSWC.......	Surface/Subsurface Warfare Coordinator [*Navy*] (CAAL)
SSWD.......	Single, Separated, Widowed, or Divorced
SSWD.......	Western Development Museum, Saskatoon, Saskatchewan [*Library symbol*] [*National Library of Canada*] (NLC)
SSWF	Sudden Shortwave Fade
SSWG.......	System Safety Working Group
SSWLH.....	Society for the Study of Women in Legal History (EA)
SSWM.......	Standing Spin Wave Mode (MCD)
SSWM.......	Superimposed Surface Wave Modes
SSWO.......	Special Service Work Order [*Telecommunications*] (TEL)
SSWP	Space Station Work Package [*NASA*] (SSD)
SSWP	Station Service Water Pump [*Nuclear energy*] (NRCH)
SSWRN.....	South-Southwestern [*Meteorology*] (FAAC)
SSWS	Standby Service Water System [*Nuclear energy*] (NRCH)
SSWU.......	Singapore Sawmill Workers' Union
SSWWD....	South-Southwestward [*Meteorology*] (FAAC)
SSWWS....	Seismic Sea-Wave Warning System
SSX..........	Samsun [*Turkey*] [*Airport symbol*] (OAG)
SSX..........	Space Ship Experimental
SSX..........	SS1 [*Nevada*] [*Seismograph station code, US Geological Survey*] [*Closed*] (SEIS)
SSX..........	Submarines, Experimental
SSX..........	Sulfisoxazole [*An antibiotic*]
SSXBT.......	Submarine Expendable Bathythermograph [*Marine science*] (MSC)
S & Sx Yeo ...	Surrey and Sussex Yeomanry [*British military*] (DMA)
SSY..........	M'Banza Congo [*Angola*] [*Airport symbol*] (OAG)
SSY..........	Sharpshooters Yeomanry [*British military*] (DMA)
SSY..........	Silver Strike Resources [*Vancouver Stock Exchange symbol*]
SSY..........	South Somerset Yeomanry [*British military*] (DMA)
SSYS........	Sterling Medical Systems, Inc. [*NASDAQ symbol*] (NQ)
S/SYS.......	Subsystem (NASA)
SSZ..........	Pocket Submarine (NATG)
SSZ..........	Saigon Special Zone [*Military*]
SSZ..........	Samos Resources, Inc. [*Vancouver Stock Exchange symbol*]
SSZ..........	Sea Scout Zero - Nonrigid Airship [*Royal Naval Air Service*] [*British*]
SSZ..........	Society of Systematic Zoology (EA)
SSZ..........	Specified Strike Zone [*Army*] (AABC)
SSZ..........	Supra-Subduction Zone [*Geology*]
St..............	C. H. Boehringer Sohn, Ingelheim [*Germany*] [*Research code symbol*]
St..............	E. Merck AG [*Germany*] [*Research code symbol*]
ST	Esotropia [*Ophthalmology*] (MAE)
ST	Journal of Structural Engineering [*A publication*]
ST	Missionarii Servi Sanctissimae Trinitatis [*Missionary Servants of the Most Holy Trinity*] [*Roman Catholic men's religious order*]
ST	Saddle Tank [*Trains*] [*British*]
ST	Safety Tool (MCD)
ST	Saint (EY)
ST	St. Lawrence Cement, Inc. [*Toronto Stock Exchange symbol*]
ST	Sainte
ST	Sales Tax
ST	Sales Tax Branch, United States Internal Revenue Bureau (DLA)
ST	Sales Tax Rulings, United States Internal Revenue Bureau [*A publication*] (DLA)
ST	Sample Tube
ST	Sanitary Towel [*British*] (DSUE)
ST	Sao Tome and Principe [*ANSI two-letter standard code*] (CNC)
ST	Save the Theaters (EA)
ST	Sawtooth [*Architecture*]
ST	Scalar Totalizer
ST	Scalloped Tinned [*Configuration*] (MCD)
ST	Schmitt Trigger [*Electronics*]
ST	Schuler Tuning
S & T.........	Science and Technology (NATG)
ST	Science Train
ST	Sclerotherapy [*Medicine*]
ST	Screw Terminal
ST	Seaman Torpedoman [*Obsolete*] [*Navy*]
S/T............	Search/Track
ST	Seat
ST	Secretary/Treasurer [*or Secretary and Treasurer*]
ST	Sedimentation Time
ST	Segment Table [*Data processing*] (OA)
ST	Self-Test
ST	Self-Toning [*Paper*] [*Photography*] (ROG)
ST	Semitendinosus [*Muscle*]
ST	Senior Teacher (ADA)
ST	Sensitivity Training
ST	Senza Tempo [*Without Regard to Time*] [*Music*]
ST	Sequence Timer
ST	Service Tabulating (AAG)
ST	Service Test [*Military*]
ST	Service Tools (AAG)
ST	Set Trigger
ST	Shares Time With [*Broadcasting term*]
S/T............	Shelter Taxi [*NASA*] (KSC)
ST	Ship Trial (MCD)
ST	Shipping Ticket [*Military*]
ST	Shock Tube
ST	Shock Tunnel
ST	Shoot Tip [*Botany*]
ST	Short-Term Stay [*in hospital*] [*British*]
ST	Short Ton [*2000 lbs.*]
ST	Short Tour [*Military*]
ST	Shorthand Writer [*British military*] (DMA)
ST	Shrink Template
ST	Side Tank [*on a ship*] (DS)
ST	Sidetone [*Telecommunications*] (TEL)
ST	Sigma Tau [*Later, Tau Beta Pi Association*]
ST	Signes du Temps [*A publication*]
ST	Silent [*Films, television, etc.*]
ST	Silicon Tube
ST	Silicotungstate [*Inorganic chemistry*]
ST	Simhat Torah (BJA)
ST	Simplification Task (MCD)
S & T.........	Simulation and Training
ST	Simulator Training
st...............	Sine Tempore [*At the Time Announced*] [*Latin*]
ST	Single Throw [*Switch*]
ST	Single Tire
ST	Single Turn (MSA)
ST	Sinus Tachycardia [*Cardiology*]
ST	Skill Technical (INF)
ST	Skin Temperature (OA)
ST	Skin Test
ST	Skin Track (MUGU)
S & T.........	Sky and Telescope [*A publication*]
ST	Sleeping Time
ST	Slide and Tape
ST	Slight Trace
ST	Slovo a Tvar [*A publication*]
ST	Small Tug [*Army*]
ST	Societe Theosophique [*Theosophical Society*]
ST	Society for Theriogenology (EA)
ST	Solar Thermal [*Energy source*]
ST	SONAR Technician [*Navy rating*]
S/T............	Sonic Telegraphy
S of T.........	Sons of Temperance
ST	Sons of Temperance
ST	Sound Trap (OA)
ST	Sounding Tube
ST	Space Telescope [*NASA*]
ST	Space-Time
ST	Spaced Triplet (SAA)
ST	Spacelab Technology [*NASA*] (NASA)
ST	Spasmodic Torticollis [*Medicine*]
ST	Special Test
ST	Special Text [*Military*]
ST	Special Tooling (GFGA)
ST	Special Translation
ST	Speech Teacher [*A publication*]
ST	Speech Therapist
ST	Speed Transmitter (NRCH)
ST	Sphincter Tone [*Medicine*] (MAE)
ST	Springfield Terminal Railway Co. [*AAR code*]
ST	SPS Technologies, Inc. [*Formerly, Standard Pressed Steel Co.*] [*NYSE symbol*] (SPSG)

ST	Stable
ST	Stage
ST	Stain (WGA)
St	Stair's Decisions, Scotch Court of Session [*A publication*] (DLA)
St	Stair's Institutes [*5th ed.*] [*1832*] [*A publication*] (DLA)
St	Stamen [*Botany*]
ST	Stamped [*Stock exchange term*] (SPSG)
ST	Stand (WGA)
ST	Standard
ST	Standard Time
ST	Standardized Test [*Psychology*]
ST	Standby Time (MCD)
St	Stanton Number [*IUPAC*]
ST	Stanza
St	Star [*Johannesburg*] [*A publication*]
ST	Star Tracker [*NASA*] (AAG)
ST	Starboard Flag [*Navy*] [*British*]
ST	Starsky Operupolnomochennyy [*Senior Case Officer*] [*Soviet military rank*]
ST	Start
S/T	Start Tank (AAG)
ST	Start Timing
ST	Starter (MCD)
ST	State
ST	State Trials [*Legal*] [*British*]
ST	Static (KSC)
ST	Static Test
ST	Static Thrust
ST	Statim [*Immediately*] [*Latin*] (ROG)
ST	Station [*Medicine*]
ST	Statsoekonomisk Tidsskrift [*A publication*]
ST	Statue (WDMC)
ST	Status
ST	Statute
ST	Steam (AAG)
ST	Steam Tanker
ST	Steam Trawler
ST	Steam Tug
ST	Steam Turbine (MCD)
ST	Steamer (ROG)
ST	Steel [*Technical drawings*]
ST	Steel Truss [*Bridges*]
ST	Stem [*Linguistics*] [*Botany*]
ST	Stencil
ST	Stenographer [*British military*] (DMA)
S & T	Stenographer and Typist [*Examination*] [*Civil Service Commission*]
st	Stent [*Let Them Stand*] [*Latin*] (MAE)
st	Stere [*Metric measure of volume*]
ST	Stereo [*A publication*]
St	Stereo Review [*A publication*]
ST	Stereocilia [*Zoology*]
ST	Stern Thruster [*Type of ship*] (DS)
ST	Sternothyroid [*Anatomy*]
ST	Sternotomy [*Medicine*]
ST	Stet [*Let It Stand*] [*Latin*]
ST	Stichting Tool [*Tool Foundation - TF*] [*Amsterdam, Netherlands*] (EAIO)
ST	Sticky Type [*Bomb*]
ST	Stigma [*Botany*]
ST	Stimulus [*Medicine*]
ST	Stinson [*ICAO aircraft manufacturer identifier*] (ICAO)
ST	Stitch
ST	Stock Transfer
St	Stokes [*Unit of kinematic viscosity*]
St	Stomach (MAE)
ST	Stone [*Unit of weight*]
ST	Stone Roller [*Ichthyology*]
St	Stones [*Quality of the bottom*] [*Nautical charts*]
ST	Stony Soil [*Agronomy*]
ST	Stop Tap
ST	Stop-Transfer [*Genetics*]
ST	Storage Tube
ST	Store (AAG)
ST	Stored Time
S & T	Storm and Tempest (ADA)
ST	Story (ROG)
St	Story's United States Circuit Court Reports [*A publication*] (DLA)
ST	Stotinki [*Monetary unit*] [*Bulgaria*]
ST	Strad [*A publication*]
st	Straight (AAMN)
S/T	Straight Time
ST	Strait
ST	Straps [*JETDS nomenclature*] [*Military*] (CET)
ST	Strategic Transport [*Aircraft*] [*Military*]
S & T	Strategy and Tactics [*A publication*]
St	Stratosphere
ST	Stratus [*Meteorology*]
ST	Street (EY)
ST	Stress Testing [*Medicine*]
ST	Strict [*Medicine*]
S-T	Strip-Tin (MSA)
ST	Stroma [*Medicine*]
ST	Strophe [*Poetry*] (ROG)
ST	Structural (NASA)
ST	Structure Tee (AAG)
St	Stuart, Milne, and Peddie's Scotch Court of Session Cases [*A publication*] (DLA)
ST	Student's t-Test [*Statistical mathematics*]
St	Studies [*A publication*]
ST	Studies in Theology [*A publication*]
St	Studium [*A publication*]
ST	Stumped [*Cricket*]
St	Styrene [*Also, Sty*] [*Organic chemistry*]
ST	Substitution Theorem [*Logic*]
ST	Subtalar [*Medicine*] (MAE)
st	Subtelocentric [*Botany*]
ST	Subtentacular [*Zoology*]
ST	Subtotal (MAE)
St	Subtype (MAE)
ST	Sucrose Tallowate (OA)
ST	Sudan [*Aircraft nationality and registration mark*] (FAAC)
ST	Sulfotransferase [*An enzyme*]
ST	Summer Time [*Daylight saving time*]
ST	Sunday Telegraph [*A publication*] (APTA)
ST	Sunday Times [*United Kingdom*] [*A publication*]
ST	Super Tampella [*Explosive*] (INF)
S of T	Superintendent of Transportation
ST	Superintendent of Transportation
ST	Supplementary Term [*Online database field identifier*]
S & T	Supply and Transport [*Military*]
S & T	Supply and Transport Corps [*British*] (DMA)
ST	Supporting Technologies [*Military*] (RDA)
ST	Surface Target [*Navy*] (CAAL)
ST	Surface Tension
ST	Surface Tracker [*Navy*] (CAAL)
ST	Surgical Technician
ST	Surveillance Test (NATG)
ST	Survival Time
ST	Svensk Tidskrift [*A publication*]
S & T	Swabey and Tristram's Probate and Divorce Reports [*1858-65*] [*A publication*] (DLA)
ST	Swept Tone
ST	Symmetrical TOKAMAK
ST	System Response Time [*Computer order entry*]
ST	System Test
ST	Szondi Test [*Psychology*]
ST	Tradewinds Pte. Ltd. [*Great Britain*] [*ICAO designator*] (FAAC)
St	United States Statutes at Large [*A publication*] (DLA)
ST1	SONAR Technician, First Class [*Navy rating*]
ST2	SONAR Technician, Second Class [*Navy rating*]
ST3	SONAR Technician, Third Class [*Navy rating*]
STA	S-Band Test Antenna
STA	Sail Training Association (EA)
STA	Sales Transaction Audit [*Test*]
STA	Santa [*Saint*] [*Italian*]
STA	Satara [*India*] [*Seismograph station code, US Geological Survey*] [*Closed*] (SEIS)
STA	Satellite Test Annex (SAA)
STA	Satellite Tracking Annex (MUGU)
STA	Science and Technology Agent (SDI)
STA	Securities Transfer Association (EA)
STA	Security Traders Association (EA)
STA	Serum Thrombotic Accelerator [*Serology*]
STA	Serum Thymic-Like Activity [*Biochemistry*]
STA	Servico des Transportes Aereos [*Portuguese West Africa*]
STA	Shift Technical Adviser [*Nuclear energy*] (NRCH)
STA	Shipboard Transmitting Antenna
STA	Shore-Based Transmitting Antenna
STA	Short-Term Arrangements [*Department of State*]
STA	Short-Term Averaging (CAAL)
STA	Short-Terms Abroad
STA	Shuttle Training Aircraft [*NASA*]
STA	Sialyltransferase Activity [*Medicine*]
STA	Single Target Attack
STA	Skills Training Agency [*British*]
STA	Slaving Torquer Amplifier
STA	Slurry Technology Association [*Later, CSTA*] (EA)
STA	Small Tactical Airlifter [*Military*] [*British*]
STA	Society of Typographic Arts [*Later, ACD*] (EA)
STA	Softening Temperature of Ash
STA	Solution Treat and Age [*Metals*]
STA	Southern Textile Association (EA)
STA	Space Technology Applications
STA	Spanning Tree Algorithm [*Data processing*] (PCM)
STA	Spark Thrust Augmenter (SAA)
STA	Special Temporary Authorization [*FCC*]
STA	Stacia Ventures [*Vancouver Stock Exchange symbol*]
STA	Staff Training Assistant [*Army*] (AABC)

STA............ Stagger Tuned Antenna
STA............ Staley Continental, Inc. [*NYSE symbol*] (SPSG)
STA............ Stamped
STA............ Star Aviation Corp. [*Denver, CO*] [*FAA designator*] (FAAC)
STA............ Stara Dala [*Czechoslovakia*] [*Later, HRB*] [*Geomagnetic observatory code*]
STA............ State Technical Assistance (OICC)
Sta.............. Statham's Abridgment [*A publication*] (DSA)
STA............ Static Test Article (NASA)
STA............ Station [*Telecommunications*]
STA............ Stationary (MSA)
STA............ Stator (WGA)
STA............ Status [*Online database field identifier*] (AABC)
STA............ Statute (WGA)
STA............ Stauning [*Denmark*] [*Airport symbol*] (OAG)
STA............ Steel Carriers Tariff Association, Inc., East Riverdale MD [*STAC*]
STA............ Steel Tape Armored [*Cables*]
STA............ Stock Transfer Association [*New York, NY*] (EA)
STA............ Store Accumulator
STACOL...... Store Address (SAA)
STA............ Straight-In Approach [*Aviation*] (FAAC)
STA............ Strange Adventures [*A publication*]
STA............ Structural Test Article (NASA)
STA............ Submarine Tender Availability
STA............ Sunday Telegraph (Australia) [*A publication*]
STA............ Superficial Temporal Artery [*Anatomy*]
STA............ Superior Temporal Artery [*Anatomy*]
STA............ Supersonic Tunnel Association (EA)
STA............ Survival in Target Area (MCD)
STA............ Swedish Telecommunications Administration [*Telecommunications*]
STA............ Swimming Teachers' Association [*British*]
STA............ Syrie et Monde Arabe. Etude Mensuelle Economique, Politique, et Statistique [*A publication*]
STA............ Systems Test Area
STA............ University of Santa Clara, Orradre Library, Santa Clara, CA [*OCLC symbol*] (OCLC)
STAA........ Soldiers Total Abstinence Association [*British military*] (DMA)
STAA........ Staar Surgical Co. [*NASDAQ symbol*] (NQ)
STAA........ Surface Transportation Assistance Act [*1978*]
STAA........ Survey Test of Algebraic Aptitude [*Education*] (AEBS)
STAACT J ... STAACT [*Science Teachers Association of the Australian Capital Territory*] Journal [*A publication*] (APTA)
STAAD...... Submarine Tender Availability Arrival/Departure [*Obsolete*]
STAAF ...... Study to Align AMC [*Now DAR COM*] Functions (MCD)
STAAG...... Standard Tachymetric Anti-Aircraft Gun [*British military*] (DMA)
STAAS ...... Surveillance and Target Acquisition Aircraft System (AFM)
Staat u Recht ... Staat und Recht [*A publication*]
Staatsanz Baden-Wuerttemb ... Staatsanzeiger fuer Baden-Wuerttemberg [*A publication*]
Staatsanz Rheinl-Pfalz ... Staatsanzeiger fuer Rheinland-Pfalz [*German Federal Republic*] [*A publication*]
Staatsbl...... Belgisch Staatsblad [*A publication*]
Staatsblad K Ned ... Staatsblad van het Koninkrijk der Nederlanden [*A publication*]
Staatsbl Koninkrijk Ned ... Staatsblad van het Koninkrijk der Nederlanden [*A publication*]
Staatsbuerger-Beil Bayer Staatsztg ... Staatsbuerger-Beilage der Bayerischen Staatszeitung [*A publication*]
Staatsverw ... Roemische Staatsverwaltung [*A publication*] (OCD)
Staat und Wirt in Hessen ... Staat und Wirtschaft in Hessen [*A publication*]
STAB........ Space, Time, and Beyond [*Dance work choreographed by Marie Chouinard*]
STAB........ Squadron Tactical Analysis Board [*Military*] (CAAL)
STAB........ Stabilize [*or Stabilizer*] [*Aviation*] (AAG)
Stab........... Stable [*Army*]
STAB........ Standby Advisory Board [*Army*] (INF)
St Ab .... Statham's Abridgment [*A publication*] (DLA)
STAB........ Strike Assault Boat [*Navy symbol*]
STAB........ Supersonic Tests of Aerodynamic Bombs (MUGU)
STAB........ Supersonic Transport Advisory Board
STAB AUG ... Stability Augmentation [*Aviation*] (MCD)
STABEX.... Stabilization of Export Earnings [*Program of the EEC*]
StAbs .... Status Absolutus
STABS....... Suinn Test Anxiety Behavior Scale [*Psychology*]
Sta Bull Oreg State Coll Agr Exp Sta ... Station Bulletin. Oregon State College. Agricultural Experiment Station [*A publication*]
Sta Bull Univ Minn Agr Exp Sta ... Station Bulletin. University of Minnesota. Agricultural Experiment Station [*A publication*]
STABY ...... Stability (MSA)
STAC........ Science and Technology Advisory Committee [*NASA*] (MCD)
STAC........ Software Timing and Control
STAC........ Southern Technology Applications Center [*NASA*] [*University of Florida*] [*Gainesville*] [*Information service or system*] (IID)
STAC........ Staccato [*Detached, Distinct*] [*Music*]
STAC........ Standard Tariff Agents Code
STAC.......... Submarine-to-Aircraft Communications

STAC........ Surface Target Attack Comparison Model (MCD)
STACAP.... Status and Capability (SAA)
STACC ...... Staccato [*Detached, Distinct*] [*Music*]
Sta Circ Wash Agr Exp Sta ... Station Circular. Washington Agricultural Experiment Station [*A publication*]
STACO...... Standing Committee for the Study of Scientific Principles of Standardization [*ISO*]
STACOM ... Standard Army Commissary Operating Manual
STACOM ... Standard Computer Output Microform [*Army*]
STACOM ... State Criminal Justice Communications
Sta Com ..... Station Complement [*Army*]
STACRES ... Standing Committee on Research and Statistics [*UN Food and Agriculture Organization*]
STACS...... Subtropical Atlantic Climate Studies [*National Oceanic and Atmospheric Administration*]
STACWV .. Standing Technical Advisory Committee on Water Quality [*Department of the Environment*] [*British*]
STAD........ Start Address [*Telecommunications*] (TEL)
STAD........ Submarine Tender Availability Document
STADAC... Station Data Acquisition and Control [*NASA*] (NASA)
STADACOL ... Statistical Data Collection Program
STADAD... Satellite Tracking and Data Acquisition Department
STADAN... Satellite Tracking and Data Acquisition Network [*Later, STDN*]
STADAN... Space Tracking and Data Acquisition Network
STADD...... Ship-Towed Acoustic Deception Device (MCD)
Staden-Jb... Staden-Jahrbuch [*A publication*]
STADES... Standard Army Data Elements Systems (MCD)
STADES... Standard Data Elements System (MCD)
STADIN.... Standing Administrative Instruction for Army Attaches (AABC)
STADINAIR ... Standing Administrative Instruction for Air Attaches (AFM)
Stadler Genet Symp ... Stadler Genetics Symposia [*A publication*]
St Adm NS ... Stuart's Lower Canada Vice-Admiralty Reports, New Series [*A publication*] (DLA)
STADMR ... Station Administrator [*Aviation*] (FAAC)
STADN...... Space Tracking and Acquisition Data Network
Stadt- Gebaeudetech ... Stadt- und Gebaeudetechnik [*German Democratic Republic*] [*A publication*]
Stadt-LB .... Stadt- und Landesbibliothek [*A publication*]
Stadt (Wien) ... Informationsdienst der Stadt (Wien) [*A publication*]
STADU...... System Termination and Display Unit (MCD)
STA-DYNULSIMU ... Static-Dynamic Ullage Simulation Unit
STAE........ Second Time Around Echo
STAE........ Specify Task Asynchronous Exit [*Data processing*]
Staedel Jb .. Staedel-Jahrbuch [*A publication*]
Sta Eng ..... Stationary Engineer
STAEP ...... Scientific and Technical Assessment of Environmental Pollutants [*Marine science*] (MSC)
STAESA.... Society of Turkish Architects, Engineers, and Scientists in America (EA)
STAF .... St. Thomas Aquinas Foundation (EA)
STAF .... Science Team Analysis Facility [*NASA*]
STAF .... Scientific and Technical Application Forecasts
STAF .... Staff Builders, Inc. [*NASDAQ symbol*] (NQ)
STA/F........ Standard Access and Format [*Reference Technology, Inc. software*]
STAF .... Standard Test and Administrative Form (SAA)
STAFDA ... Specialty Tools and Fasteners Distributors Association (EA)
STAFEX... Staff Exercises [*NATO*] (NATG)
STAFF....... Smart Target-Activated Fire and Forget [*Antitank weapon system*] (RDA)
STAFF....... Society for Techno-Innovation of Agriculture, Forestry and Fisheries [*Japan*]
STAFF....... Staffordshire [*County in England*]
STAFF...... Stellar Acquisition Flight Feasibility
Staff J (University of Reading) ... Staff Journal (University of Reading) [*A publication*]
Stafford...... Stafford's Reports [*69-71 Vermont*] [*A publication*] (DLA)
Staffordshire Archaeol ... Staffordshire Archaeology [*A publication*]
Staff Pap .... Staff Papers [*A publication*]
Staff Pap P Minn Univ Dep Agric Appl Econ ... Staff Paper P. Minnesota University. Department of Agricultural and Applied Economics [*A publication*]
Staff Pap Univ Florida Food Resour Econ Dep ... Staff Paper. University of Florida. Food and Resources Economics Department [*A publication*]
STAFFS .... Staffordshire [*County in England*]
STAFS...... Standard Automated Financial System [*Navy*] (GFGA)
STAFS...... Sugar, Tobacco, Alcohol, Fat, and Salt
STAFT...... Steerable Antenna Focusing Technique
STAG........ Security Tag Systems, Inc. [*NASDAQ symbol*] (NQ)
STAG........ Shuttle Turnaround Analysis Group [*NASA*] (NASA)
STAG........ Skills Training Adjustment Group [*Educational project sponsored by The Hartford*]
STAG........ Special Task Air Group
STAG........ Standards Technical Advisory Group
STAG........ Steam and Gas [*Turbine*]
STAG........ Straight-Talking American Government [*Comedian Pat Paulsen's political party*]

STAG......... Strategy and Tactics Analysis Group [*Later, Concepts Analysis Agency*] [*Army*]   (KSC)
STAG......... Student Agitation [*FBI*]
STAG......... Submarine-Rocket Technical Advisory Group
STAGD...... Syndicat des Travailleurs de l'Administration Generale du Dahomey [*Dahomean Union of General Administration Workers*]
STAGE...... Simulated Total Atomic Global Exchange [*DoD*]
STAGE...... Stage II Apparel Corp. [*Associated Press abbreviation*]   (APAG)
STAGG...... Small-Turbine Advanced Gas Generator
STAG-MAG ... Stage Manager [*Theater term*]   (DSUE)
STAGN...... Stagnation [*Meteorology*]   (FAAC)
STAGS ...... Simulated Tank and Antiarmor Gunnery System   (INF)
STAGS ...... Structural Analysis of General Shells
STAGS ...... Swedish Tank Agility/Survivability Test   (MCD)
STAGS-D.. Simulated Tank Antiarmor Gunnery System - Dragon [*Army*]   (INF)
St A H .... Studies in American Humor [*A publication*]
STAHA ..... Stahlbau [*A publication*]
Stahlbau Rundsch ... Stahlbau Rundschau [*Austria*] [*A publication*]
Stahlbau Tech ... Stahlbau-Technik [*A publication*]
Stahlia Misc Pap ... Stahlia Miscellaneous Papers [*A publication*]
STAI......... Simulation Tape Alarm Indicator   (SAA)
STAI......... State-Trait Anxiety Inventory [*Psychology*]
STAI......... Subtask ABEND [*Abnormal End*] Intercept [*Data processing*]   (BUR)
STAI......... Systems Technology Associates, Inc. [*Sterling, VA*] [*NASDAQ symbol*]   (NQ)
STAIC ...... State-Trait Anxiety Inventory for Children [*Psychology*]
STAID...... Station Identification
Stainless Steel Ind ... Stainless Steel Industry [*A publication*]
Stainl Steel ... Stainless Steel [*South Africa*] [*A publication*]
Stain Tech ... Stain Technology [*A publication*]
Stain Technol ... Stain Technology [*A publication*]
Stair .... Stair's Decisions of the Lords of Council and Session [*1661-81*] [*Scotland*] [*A publication*]   (DLA)
STAIR ...... Structural Analysis Interpretive Routine
Stair I........ Stair's Institutes [*5 eds.*] [*1681-1832*] [*A publication*]   (DLA)
Stair Inst.... Stair's Institutes [*5 eds.*] [*1681-1832*] [*A publication*]   (DLA)
Stair Prin ... Stair's Principles of the Laws of Scotland [*A publication*]   (DLA)
Stair Rep.... Stair's Decisions, Scotch Court of Session [*A publication*]   (DLA)
STAIRS..... Standard Advanced Infrared Sensor [*Military*]
STAIRS..... Storage and Information Retrieval System [*IBM Corp.*]
STAIRS/VS ... Storage and Information Retrieval System/Virtual Storage [*IBM Corp.*]
STAJ .... Short-Term Anti-Jam   (MCD)
STAK........ Short Takes, Inc. [*NASDAQ symbol*]   (NQ)
STAL........ Screening Test of Adolescent Language [*Educational test*]
STAL........ Stalactite/Stalagmite Formation   (DSUE)
STALAG ... Stammlager [*Prisoner-of-war camp*] [*German*]
STALAGLUFT ... Stammlagerluft [*Prisoner-of-war camp for airmen*] [*German*]
STALAS.... Stationary LASER Site [*NASA*]
Stal Elect ... Stalman on Election and Satisfaction [*1827*] [*A publication*]   (DLA)
Staleplavil'n Proizvod ... Staleplavil'noe Proizvodstvo [*A publication*]
Staleplavil'n Proizvod (Moscow) ... Staleplavil'noe Proizvodstvo (Moscow) [*A publication*]
Stal Nemet Vklyucheniya ... Stal'e Nemetallicheskie Vklyucheniya [*A publication*]
STALO...... Stabilized Local Oscillator [*RADAR*]
STALOG... Study of Automation of the Logistic System [*Military*]
STALOS.... Stabilized Tunable Local Oscillator
STALPETH ... Steel, Aluminum, Polyethylene [*Components of a type of telecommunications cable*]
STAL Sci Tech Anim Lab ... STAL. Sciences et Techniques de l'Animal de Laboratoire [*A publication*]
St Altaeg Kul ... Studien zur Altaegyptischen Kultur [*A publication*]
STaM........ Sefer Torah. Tefillin. Mezuzah
STAM........ Shared Tape Allocation Manager
STAM........ Statistics in Medicine [*A publication*]
STAM........ Submarine Tactical Advanced Missile   (MCD)
STAM........ Superintendent of Technical Applications of Metals [*Ministry of Supply*] [*British*] [*World War II*]
STAM........ Surface Target Acquisition Model   (MCD)
STAM........ System Telecommunications Access Method [*NCR Corp.*]
STAMAT .. Schaie-Thurstone Adult Mental Abilities Test [*Intelligence test*] [*Psychology*]
STA-MCA ... Superficial Temporal Artery to Middle Cerebral Artery [*Anatomy*]   (MAE)
Sta Mi........ Statute Mile
STAMIC ... Set Theory Analysis and Measure of Information Characteristics
STAMIDS ... Standoff Minefield Detection System [*Military*]   (INF)
STAMINRQ ... Status During Minimize Required   (MCD)
STAMIS.... Standard Army Management Information System
STAMM.... Systematic Teaching and Measuring Mathematics [*Education*]
STAMMIS ... Standard Army Multicommand Management Information System   (MCD)
STAMNI... Sonic True Airspeed and Mach Number Indicator

STAMO..... Stable Master Oscillator
STAMOS .. Sortie Turn Around Maintenance Operations Simulation [*NASA*]   (KSC)
STAMP .... Satellite Telecommunications Analysis and Modeling Program
STAMP ..... Small Tactical Aerial Mobility Platform [*Proposed*] [*Marine Corps*]
STAMP ..... Space Technology Analysis and Mission Planning   (MCD)
STAMP ..... Standard Air Munitions Package
STAMP ..... Systems Tape Addition and Maintenance Program [*Data processing*]   (IEEE)
STAMPED ... Size, Temperature, Application, Material, Pressure, Ends, and Delivery [*To aid selection of industrial hose*]
STAMPEX ... National Stamp Exhibition [*British*]   (ITD)
STAMPS... Spectrophotometric Transient Analysis Method for Multiple Positions and Species
St Am Renaissance ... Studies in the American Renaissance [*A publication*]
StaMSe...... State Mutual Securities Trust [*Associated Press abbreviation*]   (APAG)
STAN........ Selectable Two-Area Nozzle   (MCD)
STAN........ Stanchion
STAN........ Standard   (WGA)
STAN........ Stanline, Inc. [*Norwalk, CA*] [*NASDAQ symbol*]   (NQ)
STAN........ Stanstead [*England*]
STAN........ Sum Total and Nosegear   (MCD)
STANA...... Statistics on the North Atlantic [*Fisheries*] [*UN Food and Agriculture Organization*]
STANAG... Standardization Agreement [*NATO*]
STANAVFORCHAN ... Standing Naval Force, Channel [*NATO*]   (NATG)
STANAVITO ... Syndicat des Travailleurs de Transport et de la Navigation du Togo [*Union of Transport and Navigation Workers of Togo*]
STANB...... Stanborough [*England*]
STANCAL ... Standard Oil Co. of California
STANCHART ... Standard Chartered [*International bank*] [*British*]
STANCIB ... State-Army-Navy Communications Intelligence Board [*Later, USCIB*]
STAND...... Standard
Standard Chartered R ... Standard Chartered Review [*A publication*]
Stand Ass Aust Aust Stand ... Standards Association of Australia. Australian Standard [*A publication*]   (APTA)
Stand Ass Aust Commercial Stand ... Standards Association of Australia. Commercial Standard [*A publication*]   (APTA)
Stand Ass Aust Miscell Pub ... Standards Association of Australia. Miscellaneous Publication [*A publication*]   (APTA)
Stand Bank ... Standard Bank Review [*A publication*]
Stand Chart Rev ... Standard Chartered Review [*London*] [*A publication*]
Standex...... Standex International Corp. [*Associated Press abbreviation*]   (APAG)
Stand Ex Prof Tax Rep ... Standard Excess Profits Tax Reporter [*Commerce Clearing House*] [*A publication*]   (DLA)
Stand Fed Tax Rep ... Standard Federal Tax Reporter [*Commerce Clearing House*] [*A publication*]   (DLA)
Stand Fed Tax Rep CCH ... Standard Federal Tax Reports. Commerce Clearing House [*A publication*]
Stand GA Prac ... Standard Georgia Practice [*A publication*]   (DLA)
Stan Dig..... Stanton's Kentucky Digest [*A publication*]   (DLA)
Stand Kach ... Standarty i Kachestvo [*A publication*]
Stand Methods Clin Chem ... Standard Methods of Clinical Chemistry [*A publication*]
Stand News ... Standardization News [*A publication*]
Stand PA Prac ... Standard Pennsylvania Practice [*A publication*]   (DLA)
Stand Philip Per Ind ... Standard Philippine Periodicals Index [*A publication*]
Stand Phys Fitness Tests Magglinger Symp ... Standardization of Physical Fitness Tests. Magglinger Symposium [*A publication*]
Stand Qual ... Standardisierung und Qualitaet [*German Democratic Republic*] [*A publication*]
St Andrew Univ Sociol R ... St. Andrew's University. Sociological Review [*A publication*]
Stan Env't Ann ... Stanford Environmental Law Annual [*A publication*]
STAN/EVAL ... Standardization/Evaluation
STANFINS ... Standard Financial System [*Military*]   (AABC)
STANFINS-R ... Standard Finance System Redesign [*DoD*]   (GFGA)
Stanf J Int ... Stanford Journal of International Studies [*A publication*]
STANFLT ... Standardization Flight [*Naval Air Training and Operating Procedures Standardization*]   (DNAB)
Stanford ..... Stanford's English Pleas of the Crown [*A publication*]   (DLA)
Stanford Fr ... Stanford French Review [*A publication*]
Stanford Ichthyol Bull ... Stanford Ichthyological Bulletin [*A publication*]
Stanford J Internat Law ... Stanford Journal of International Law [*A publication*]
Stanford J Internat Studies ... Stanford Journal of International Studies [*A publication*]
Stanford J Int'l Stud ... Stanford Journal of International Studies [*A publication*]
Stanford J Int Stud ... Stanford Journal of International Studies [*A publication*]
Stanford La ... Stanford Law Review [*A publication*]
Stanford Law R ... Stanford Law Review [*A publication*]
Stanford Law Rev ... Stanford Law Review [*A publication*]
Stanford L Rev ... Stanford Law Review [*A publication*]
Stanford M Bull ... Stanford Medical Bulletin [*A publication*]

Stanford Med Bull ... Stanford Medical Bulletin [*A publication*]
Stanford Research Inst Jour ... Stanford Research Institute. Journal [*A publication*]
Stanford Stud Med Sci ... Stanford Studies in Medical Sciences [*A publication*]
Stanford Stud Psychol ... Stanford Studies in Psychology [*A publication*]
Stanford Univ Dep Civ Eng Tech Rep ... Stanford University. Department of Civil Engineering. Technical Report [*A publication*]
Stanford Univ Dep Mech Eng Tech Rep ... Stanford University. Department of Mechanical Engineering. Technical Report [*A publication*]
Stanford Univ Publ Geol ... Stanford University Publications in the Geological Sciences [*A publication*]
Stanford Univ Publ Geol Sci ... Stanford University. Publications in the Geological Sciences [*A publication*]
Stanford Univ Publ Univ Ser Biol Sci ... Stanford University. Publications. University Series. Biological Sciences [*A publication*]
Stanford Univ Publ Univ Ser Eng ... Stanford University. Publications. University Series. Engineering [*A publication*]
Stanford Univ Publ Univ Ser Math Astron ... Stanford University. Publications. University Series. Mathematics and Astronomy [*A publication*]
Stanford Univ Publ Univ Ser Med Sci ... Stanford University. Publications. University Series. Medical Sciences [*A publication*]
Stanhm....... Stanhome, Inc. [*Associated Press abbreviation*]   (APAG)
STANINE ... Standard Nine Score [*Military*]
Stan J Intl L ... Stanford Journal of International Law [*A publication*]
Stan J Intl St ... Stanford Journal of International Studies [*A publication*]
Stan J Int'l Stud ... Stanford Journal of International Studies [*A publication*]
Stanki i Instrum ... Stanki i Instrument [*A publication*]
Stanki Rezhushchie Instrum ... Stanki i Rezhushchie Instrumenty [*A publication*]
STANLANCRU ... Standard Landing Craft Unit [*Military*]
Stan Law.... Stanford Lawyer [*A publication*]
Stan LR...... Stanford Law Review [*A publication*]
Stan L Rev ... Stanford Law Review [*A publication*]
StanlWk..... [*The*] Stanley Works [*Associated Press abbreviation*]   (APAG)
STANO ..... Surveillance, Target Acquisition, and Night Observation [*DoD*]
STANOC... Surveillance, Target Acquisition, Night Observation, and Counter - Surveillance [*British*]   (MCD)
STANOLIND ... Standard Oil Co. (Indiana)
STANORD ... Standardization Order [*Navy*]   (NG)
Sta Note For Exp Sta (Idaho) ... Station Note. Forest, Wildlife, and Range Experiment Station (Moscow, Idaho) [*A publication*]
Stan PA Prac ... Standard Pennsylvania Practice [*A publication*]   (DLA)
STANS...... Soviet Tactical Nuclear Study   (MCD)
STANS...... Standard Aircraft Navigation System
STANS...... Standard Army Nonappropriated System   (MCD)
StAns .... Studia Anselmiana [*Rome*] [*A publication*]
STANSM .. STANO [*Surveillance, Target Acquisition, and Night Observation*] System Manager [*Army*]   (RDA)
StANT .... Studien zum Alten und Neuen Testament [*Munich*] [*A publication*]
STANTEC ... Standard Telephones Electronic Computer   (MCD)
St Anth....... St. Anthony Messenger [*A publication*]
Stanton...... Stanton's Reports [*11-13 Ohio*] [*A publication*]   (DLA)
Stanton's Rev St ... Stanton's Revised Kentucky Statutes [*A publication*]   (DLA)
STANVAC ... Standard Vacuum Oil Co.
STANY...... Security Traders Association of New York
STAP .... Science and Technology Advisory Panel
STAP .... Scientific and Technical Analysis and Programs Directorate
STAP .... Screening Test for Auditory Perception
STAP .... Shipbuilding Temporary Assistance Program
STAP .... Ships Towed Acoustic Project   (DWSG)
STAP .... Special Technical Assistance Program   (EA)
STAP .... Stapleton [*England*]
STAP .... Staploe [*England*]
STAP .... Survivability Test Advisory Panel [*Military*]   (CAAL)
Sta Pap For Exp Sta (Idaho) ... Station Paper. Forest, Wildlife, and Range Experiment Station (Moscow, Idaho) [*A publication*]
Sta P C .... Staundeforde's Pleas of Crown [*A publication*]   (DSA)
STAPFUS ... Stable Axis Platform Follow-Up System
STAPH...... Staphylococcus [*Medicine*]
STAPL....... SIGPLAN Technical Committee on APL [*A Programming Language*] [*Association for Computing Machinery*]   (CSR)
STAPLAN ... Status, Time, Attrition, Planning Methodology
STAPP...... Simulation Tape Print Program
STAPP...... Single-Thread All-Purpose Program
STAPPA.... State and Territorial Air Pollution Program Administrators   (EA)
Stapp Car Crash Conf Proc ... Stapp Car Crash Conference. Proceedings [*A publication*]
Sta Pr .... Staundeforde's Exposition of the King's Prerogative [*A publication*]   (DSA)
STAPRC.... Scientific and Technical Association of the People's Republic of China
STAQ........ Security Traders Automated Quotation [*System*]
STAQ........ Student Teachers' Attitude Questionnaire
STAQC...... Statistical Quality Control System [*Military*]
STAR......... Safe Teenage Rocketry

St A R........ St. Andrews Review [*A publication*]
STAR........ San Clemente 3-D Acoustic Range   (MCD)
STAR........ Satellite Telecommunications Automatic Routing
STAR........ Satellite Television Asia Region [*Hong Kong*]
STAR........ Satellite Transponder Addressable Receiver
STAR........ Satellites for Telecommunications, Applications, and Research [*Consortium*]
STAR........ Science Teaching Achievement Recognition
STAR........ Scientific and Technical Aerospace Reports [*NASA*] [*Information service or system*] [*A publication*]
STAR........ Score, Teach, and Record [*Teaching machine*]
STAR........ Screening Test of Academic Readiness [*Child development test*]
STAR........ Second Time Around Racers [*Car racing*]
STAR........ Selective Training and Retention [*Navy*]
STAR........ Self-Test Antenna Radiation [*Military*]   (CAAL)
STAR........ Self-Test Automatic Readout
STAR........ Self-Testing and Repairing [*Computer self-repair*]
STAR........ Self-Training and Assessment of Readiness
STAR........ Serials Titles Automated Records [*US National Agricultural Library*] [*Beltsville, MD*] [*A publication*]
STAR........ Shell Transient Asymmetric Response
STAR........ Shield Test Air Reactor [*Nuclear energy*]
STAR........ Ship-Tended Acoustic Relay [*Military*]
STAR........ Shipboard Tactical Airborne Remote Piloted Vehicle [*Navy*]   (CAAL)
STAR........ Shock Thermodynamics Applied Research [*Department of Energy*]
STAR........ Shuttle Turnaround Analysis Report [*NASA*]   (NASA)
STAR........ Simple Test Approach for Readability [*General Electric*]
STAR........ Simulation of Tactical Alternative Responses   (MCD)
STAR........ Simultaneous Temperature Alarm Readout
STAR........ Simultaneous Transmission and Reception RADAR [*DoD*]   (ECON)
STAR........ Sled Towed Array   (MCD)
STAR........ Societe de Transport Aerien du Rwanda [*Airline*]   (FAAC)
STAR........ Society for Test Anxiety Research   (EA)
STAR........ Space Technology and Advanced Research
STAR........ Space Technology and Research Center [*Research center*]   (RCD)
STAR........ Space Thermionic Auxiliary Reactor [*Nuclear energy*]
STAR........ Space-Time Autoregressive [*Statistics*]
STAR........ Special Treatment and Review [*Navy*]   (NG)
STAR........ Special Tube Analyzing Recorder
STAR........ Specialized Training for Army Readiness [*Army Reserve*]
STAR........ Specialized Training and Reassignment [*Military*]
STAR........ Spectral Technology and Applied Research
STAR........ Speed through Aerial Resupply [*Air Force*]
STAR........ Sport, Travel, Art, and Recreation
STAR........ Standard Instrument Arrival [*Aviation*]   (FAAC)
STAR........ Standard Telecommunications Automatic Recognizer [*Data processing*]
STAR........ Standard Tensioned Alongside Receiver [*Navy*]   (NVT)
STAR........ Standard Terminal Arrival Route [*Aviation*]
STAR........ Standard Test Authorization and Report System [*Navy*]
Star .... Starkie's English Nisi Prius Reports [*A publication*]   (DLA)
STAR........ Stars to Go, Inc. [*NASDAQ symbol*]   (NQ)
Star .... Starship. The Magazine about Science Fiction [*A publication*]
STAR........ State Acid Rain Projects [*Environmental Protection Agency*]   (GFGA)
STAR........ Statistical Table Assembly and Retrieval System [*Proposed for Social Security Administration*]
STAR........ Statistical Treatment of Aircraft Returns   (MCD)
STAR........ Status Application Resource   (HGAA)
STAR........ Steerable Array RADAR
STAR........ Stellar Attitude Reference
STAR........ Steps to Abstract Reasoning
STAR........ STING [*Swift Target Identification Notification Grid*] Array [*Computer system*]
STAR........ Stock Technical Analysis Reports [*Innovest Systems, Inc.*] [*Database*]
STAR........ Stop the Arms Race [*Women's International League for Peace and Freedom*]
STAR........ Strategic Technologies for the Army
STAR........ Streamlined Acquisition Requirements System [*DoD*]
STAR........ Strike, Transfers, Acquisitions, or Removals [*Navy*]   (NG)
STAR........ String Array [*Computer system*]   (MCD)
STAR........ String Array Processor
STAR........ Structural Testing, Analysis, and Reporting
STAR........ Students Taught Awareness and Resistance [*An association*]
STAR........ Submarine Test and Research   (MCD)
STAR........ [*The*] Sunday Times Atlantic Riband [*Award offered by a London newspaper to any sailboat beating the 1905 record for a transatlantic crossing*]
STAR........ Supplementary Teaching Assistance in Reading   (AEBS)
STAR........ Supplier Transmittal and Approval Request   (MCD)
STAR........ Surface-to-Air Recovery
STAR........ Surveillance, Target Acquisition, and Reconnaissance
STAR........ Swedish Tactical Attack RADAR
STAR........ System for Telephone Administrative Response [*Data processing*]
STAR........ System Threat Assessment Report [*Army*]

STAR......... System for Time and Accomplishment Reporting   (MCD)
STAR......... System Training Application Requirements
STAR......... Systems Test Bed for Avionics Research
STARAD... Starfish Radiation [*Satellite*] [*NASA*]
STARAN... Stellar Attitude Reference and Navigation
STARC...... Solar Thermal Advanced Research Center [*University of Houston*] [*Research center*]   (RCD)
STARC...... State Area Commands   (MCD)
Star Ch Ca ... Star Chamber Cases [*1477-1648*] [*England*] [*A publication*]   (DLA)
Star Ch Cas ... Star Chamber Cases [*1477-1648*] [*England*] [*A publication*]   (DLA)
Starchroom Laundry J ... Starchroom Laundry Journal [*A publication*]
STARCIPS ... Standard Army Civilian Pay System
STARCIPS-R ... Standard Army Civilian Pay System Redesign   (GFGA)
STARCOM ... Strategic Army Command Network
STARCOM ... Strategic Army Communications System
STARD...... Starch/Staerke [*A publication*]
STARE...... Scandinavian Twin Auroral RADAR Experiment [*Ionospheric science*]
STARE...... Steerable Telemetry Antenna Receiving Equipment
STA Rept Abstr ... Scientific and Technical Aerospace Reports Abstract [*A publication*]
STARFIARS ... Standard Army Financial Inventory Accounting and Reporting System
STARFIRE ... System to Accumulate and Retrieve Financial Information with Random Extraction [*Data processing*]
STARIMAR ... Space-Time Autoregressive Integrated Moving Average [*Statistics*]
Stark .... Starkie's English Nisi Prius Reports [*1815-22*] [*A publication*]   (DLA)
Stark CL.... Starkie's Criminal Law [*A publication*]   (DLA)
Stark Cr Pl ... Starkie's Criminal Pleading [*A publication*]   (DLA)
Stark Ev..... Starkie on Evidence [*A publication*]   (DLA)
Starkie ...... Starkie's English Nisi Prius Reports [*A publication*]   (DLA)
Starkie (Eng) ... Starkie's English Nisi Prius Reports [*171 English Reprint*] [*A publication*]   (DLA)
Starkie Ev .. Starkie on Evidence [*A publication*]   (DLA)
Starkie's..... English Nisi Prius Reports [*171 English Reprint*] [*A publication*]   (DLA)
Starkie Sland & L ... Starkie on Slander and Libel [*A publication*]   (DLA)
Stark Jury Tr ... Starkie on Trial by Jury [*A publication*]   (DLA)
Stark Lib.... Starkie on Libel [*A publication*]   (DLA)
Stark NP.... Starkie's English Nisi Prius Reports [*A publication*]   (DLA)
Stark Sl & L ... Starkie on Slander and Libel [*A publication*]   (DLA)
STARLAB ... Space Technology Applications and Research Laboratory [*NASA*]
Starl I Cr Law ... Starling's East India Criminal Law and Procedure [*A publication*]   (DLA)
STARLO... Special Test Army Reserve Limited Objective
St Arm Leg Pow ... St. Armand on the Legislative Power of England [*A publication*]   (DLA)
STARNET ... Sustaining Base Army Network   (GFGA)
STARP ...... Supplemental Training and Readiness Program
STARPAHC ... Space Technology Applied to Rural Papago Advanced Health Care   (SSD)
STARPUBS ... Standard Army Publications System
STARR...... Schedule, Technical, and Resources Report [*NASA*]   (NASA)
STARR...... Scientific and Technical Annual Reference Review [*A publication*]
STARR...... Staff Assessment of Readiness Report   (MCD)
STARR...... Study Techniques for Advanced RADAR Requirements
Starr & C Ann St ... Starr and Curtis' Annotated Statutes [*Illinois*] [*A publication*]   (DLA)
Starret ...... Starrett [*L.S.*] Co. [*Associated Press abbreviation*]   (APAG)
STARRTH ... Starrett Housing Corp. [*Associated Press abbreviation*]   (APAG)
STARS...... Satellite Telemetry Automatic Reduction System [*NASA*]
STARS...... Satellite Transmission and Reception Specialists [*Houston, TX*] [*Telecommunications*]   (TSSD)
STARS...... Seaborne Tracking and Ranging Station
STARS...... Sealink Ticket and Reservation System [*Sealink UK Ltd.*] [*Information service or system*]   (IID)
STARS...... Shell Theory Automated for Rotational Structures
STARS...... Short-Term Auction-Rate Stock [*Investment term*]
STARS...... Short-Term Auditory Retrieval and Storage Test
STARS...... Short Track Auto Racing Series [*Car racing*]
STARS...... Short Track Auto Racing Stars [*An association*]
STARS...... Silent Tactical Attack Reconnaissance System
STARS...... Simmons Teen-Age Research Study [*Simmons Market Research Bureau, Inc.*] [*Information service or system*]   (CRD)
STARS...... Simulation and Training Advanced Research System [*Air Force*]
STARS...... Software Technology for Adaptable, Reliable Systems [*Military*]
STAR(S).... Specialized Training and Reassignment (Student) [*Military*]
STARS...... Stabilized Twin-Gyro Attitude Reference System
STARS...... Standard Accounting and Reporting Systems   (MCD)
STARS...... Standard Terminal Arrival Routes [*Aviation*]   (MCD)
STARS...... Standard, TRADOC Automated Retrieval System   (MCD)
STARS...... Star Shot   (SAA)
STARS...... Stationary Automotive Road Simulator

STARS...... Stellar Tracking Attitude Reference System
STARS...... Strategic Target System [*Rocket*]
STARS...... Study of Tactical Airborne RADAR System
STARS...... Support Tracking Analysis Reporting Systems   (MCD)
STARS...... Surface-to-Air Recovery System
STARS...... Surveillance Target Attack RADAR System
STARS...... Synchronized Time, Automated Reporting System
STARS...... System Test and Astronaut Requirement Simulation
STARS...... System Thermal Air Platform Reconnaissance Signature   (MCD)
Star SC ...... Star Session Cases [*1824-25*] [*A publication*]   (DLA)
STARS II.. Shell Theory Automated for Rotational Structures - II   (MCD)
START ...... Safety Technology Applied to Rapid Transit [*Committee*] [*American Public Transit Association*]
START ...... Selection to Activate Random Testing [*Module*] [*NASA*]
START ...... Service Technician Advancement, Recruitment, and Training
START ...... Space Test and Reentry Technology
START ...... Space Transport and Reentry Tests
START ..... Spacecraft Technology and Advanced Reentry Tests [*Air Force*]
START ...... Special Treatment and Rehabilitative Training [*Prisons project*]
START ...... Spend Today and Retire Tomorrow [*Consumer pension plan*]
START ...... Sports Technique and Reaction Trainer [*Computerized training program for baseball and tennis*]
START ...... State of the Total Army Report Team
START ...... Story-Telling Automatic Reading Tutor
START ...... Strategic Arms Reduction Talks
START ...... Summary Tape Assistance, Research, and Training
START ...... System of Transportation Applying Rendezvous Technique   (MCD)
START ...... Systematic Tabular Analysis of Requirements Technique   (IEEE)
STARTEX ... Start of the Exercise   (MCD)
STARTLE ... Surveillance and Target Acquisition RADAR for Tank Location and Engagement [*Army*]   (MCD)
STARTS... Software Tools for Application to Real Time Systems[*British*]
STARUTE ... Stable Parachute
STAS .... Safe-to-Arm Signal
STAS .... Safe-to-Arm System   (MUGU)
STAS .... Short Term Analysis Services [*Scientific Services Program*] [*Army*]   (RDA)
STAS .... Startel Corp. [*NASDAQ symbol*]   (NQ)
STAS .... Statutes
STASD ...... Stainless Steel [*A publication*]
STASH ...... Student Association for the Study of Hallucinogens [*Defunct*]   (EA)
STASHIP ... Station Ship [*Navy*]   (NVT)
Sta Sper Maiscolt (Bergamo) ... Stazione Sperimentale di Maiscoltura (Bergamo) [*A publication*]
STASS...... Submarine Tactical Array SONAR System
STASS...... Submarine Towed Array SONAR System [*Navy*]
STASS...... Submarine-Towed Array Surveillance System   (NVT)
STAT .... SEABEE Technical Assistance Team [*Navy*]
STAT .... SEABEE Training Advisory Team [*Navy*]
STAT .... Seeing through Arithmetic Tests   (AEBS)
STAT .... Small Transport Aircraft Technology   (MCD)
STAT .... Society of Teachers of the Alexander Technique   (EAIO)
Stat............ Stat. Bulletin of the Wisconsin Nurses' Association [*A publication*]
STAT .... Static   (AAG)
STAT .... Statim [*Immediately*] [*Latin*]
STAT .... Station ·
STAT .... Stationary [*Chemistry*]
STAT .... Stationery Office [*British*]
STAT .... Statistic   (AFM)
Stat............ Statius [*First century AD*] [*Classical studies*]   (OCD)
Stat............ Stative   (BJA)
STAT .... Statuary
STAT .... Status   (MSA)
STAT .... Statute
STAT .... Statutory Tenant   (DSUE)
STAT .... Stop Teen-Age Addiction to Tobacco   (EA)
Stat............ United States Statutes at Large [*A publication*]
STATA ...... Stata Corp. Cl A [*NASDAQ symbol*]   (NQ)
statA.......... Statampere [*Also, sA*] [*Unit of electric current*]
Stat Ab (NZ) ... Monthly Abstract of Statistics (New Zealand) [*A publication*]
Stat Abs ..... Statistical Abstract. United States [*A publication*]
STAT AN .. Statistical Annals   (DLA)
Stat Bull..... Statistical Bulletin. Metropolitan Life Insurance Co. [*A publication*]
Stat Bull Metrop Life Found ... Statistical Bulletin. Metropolitan Life Foundation [*A publication*]
Stat Bull Metrop Life Insur Co ... Statistical Bulletin. Metropolitan Life Insurance Co. [*A publication*]
Stat Bull Metropol Life Ins Co ... Statistical Bulletin. Metropolitan Life Insurance Co. [*A publication*]
Stat Bull US Farm Credit Admin Econ Anal Div ... Statistical Bulletin. United States Farm Credit Administration. Economic Analysis Division [*A publication*]
statC.......... Statcoulomb [*Also, sC*] [*Unit of electric charge*]
StatCan...... Statistics Canada [*Statistics Canada Library*] [*Information service or system*]

STATCAT ... Statistical Context-Aided Testing [*North-Holland Publishing Co.*] [*Software package*] (NCC)
StatConst ... Status Constructus (BJA)
Stat Def ...... Statutory Definition [*Legal term*] (DLA)
STATE ...... Simplified Tactical Approach and Terminal Equipment
STATE ...... Simulation for Tank/Antitank Evaluation (NATG)
STATE ...... Space Transportation Air-Breathing Technology Evaluation [*DoD*]
State Agric Coll Oreg Eng Exp Stn Circ ... State Agricultural College of Oregon. Engineering Experiment Station. Circular [*A publication*]
State of the Art Rev Occup Med ... State of the Art Reviews. Occupational Medicine [*A publication*]
State Court J ... State Court Journal [*A publication*]
State Dept Bull ... United States State Department. Bulletin [*A publication*] (DLA)
State Fish Chief Secr Dep NSW Res Bull ... State Fisheries Chief. Secretary's Department. New South Wales. Research Bulletin [*A publication*]
State Geol Nat Hist Surv Conn Rep Invest ... State Geological and Natural History Survey of Connecticut. Report of Investigation [*A publication*]
State Geologists Jour ... State Geologists Journal [*A publication*]
State Gov ... State Government [*A publication*]
State Govt .. State Government [*A publication*]
State Govt News ... State Government News [*A publication*]
State Hortic Assoc PA Proc ... State Horticultural Association of Pennsylvania. Proceedings [*A publication*]
State Ill Div State Geol Surv Bull ... State of Illinois. Division of the State Geological Survey. Bulletin [*A publication*]
State Legis ... State Legislatures [*A publication*]
State Libn .. State Librarian [*A publication*]
State Libr ... State Librarian [*A publication*]
State and Local Govt R ... State and Local Government Review [*A publication*]
State Locl & Urb L Newsl ... State, Local, and Urban Law Newsletter [*A publication*]
State Loc and Urb L Newsl ... State, Local, and Urban Law Newsletter [*A publication*]
STATEM .. Shipment Status System [*Military*] (AABC)
State Miner Profiles US Bur Mines ... State Mineral Profiles. United States Bureau of Mines [*A publication*]
State Mont Bur Mines Geol Mem ... State of Montana. Bureau of Mines and Geology. Memoir [*A publication*]
State Mot Carr Guide ... State Motor Carrier Guide [*Commerce Clearing House*] [*A publication*] (DLA)
Staten Island As Pr ... Staten Island Association of Arts and Sciences. Proceedings [*A publication*]
Staten Island Inst Arts Sci Proc ... Staten Island Institute of Arts and Sciences. Proceedings [*A publication*]
Statens Inst Byggnadsforsk Handl (Trans) ... Statens Institut foer Byggnadsforskning. Handlingar (Translations) [*A publication*]
Statens Inst Byggnadsforsk Natl Swedish Bldg Res Doc ... Statens Institut foer Byggnadsforskning. National Swedish Building Research Document [*A publication*]
Statens Lantbrukskem Kontrollanst Medd ... Statens Lantbrukskemiska Kontrollanstalt. Meddelande [*A publication*]
Statens Lantbrukskem Lab Medd ... Statens Lantbrukskemiska Laboratorium. Meddelande [*A publication*]
Statens Naturvetensk Forskningsrad Ekologikomm Bull ... Statens Naturvetenskapliga Forskningsrad Ekologikommitter Bulletin [*A publication*]
Statens Offentliga Utredn ... Statens Offentliga Utredningar [*A publication*]
Statens Provingsanst (Stockholm) Cirk ... Statens Provningsanstalt (Stockholm). Cirkulaer [*A publication*]
Statens Provingsanst (Stockholm) Medd ... Statens Provningsanstalt (Stockholm). Meddelande [*A publication*]
Statens Skadedyrlab Arsberet ... Statens Skadedyrlaboratorium Arsberetning [*A publication*]
Statens Vaeginst (Swed) Medd ... Statens Baeginstitut (Sweden). Meddelande [*A publication*]
Statens Vaeginst (Swed) Rapp ... Statens Vaeginstitut (Sweden). Rapport [*A publication*]
Statens Vaxtskyddsanst Medd ... Statens Vaxtskyddsanstalt Meddelanden [*A publication*]
State Nurse Legis Q ... State Nursing Legislation. Quarterly [*A publication*]
State Plann and Environ Comm Tech Bull ... State Planning and Environment Commission. Technical Bulletin [*A publication*] (APTA)
State R ...... New York State Reporter [*A publication*] (DLA)
State Rep .... New York State Reporter [*A publication*] (DLA)
State Res .... State Research [*A publication*]
STATES ...... Simplified Tactical Approach and Terminal Equipment System
states .... Statesman [*or Stateswoman*]
State Tax Cas Rep ... State Tax Cases Reporter [*Commerce Clearing House*] [*A publication*] (DLA)
State Tax Guide CCH ... State Tax Guide. Commerce Clearing House [*A publication*]
State Tr ...... State Trials (Howell) [*England*] [*A publication*] (DLA)
State Tr NS ... State Trials, New Series, Edited by Macdonell [*England*] [*A publication*] (DLA)

State Univ Coll For Syracuse Univ Tech Publ ... State University College of Forestry. Syracuse University. Technical Publication [*A publication*]
State Univ NY Mar Sci Res Cent (Stony Brook) Tech Rep Ser ... State University of New York. Marine Sciences Research Center (Stony Brook). Technical Report Series [*A publication*]
State Vet J ... State Veterinary Journal [*A publication*]
State Wash Dep Fish Res Div Inf Bkl ... State of Washington. Department of Fisheries. Research Division. Information Booklet [*A publication*]
State Wash Dep Fish Res Div Inf Booklet ... State of Washington. Department of Fisheries. Research Division. Information Booklet [*A publication*]
statF .... Statfarad [*Also, sF*] [*Unit of capacitance*]
Stat Glo ...... Statute of Gloucester [*First statute to give costs in actions*] [*A publication*]
statH .... Stathenry [*Also, sH*] [*Unit of inductance*]
Stath Abr ... Statham's Abridgment [*A publication*] (DLA)
STATIC ..... Student Taskforce Against Telecommunication Information Concealment [*Student legal action organization*]
Stat ICJ ..... Statute of the International Court of Justice [*A publication*] (DLA)
STATINDEX ... Stationery Industry Exhibition [*British*] (ITD)
STATINF ... Statistical Information System [*Bundesamt fuer Statistik*] [*Switzerland*] [*Information service or system*] (CRD)
Stat Inst ..... Statutory Instruments [*A publication*] (DLA)
Stat Instrum (Lond) ... Statutory Instrument (London) [*A publication*]
STATIS ..... Statistics
Statis .... Statistiques [*A publication*]
Statis Affaires Socs ... Statistiques des Affaires Sociales [*A publication*]
Statis Agric ... Statistique Agricole [*A publication*]
Statis and Econ Info Bul Africa ... Statistical and Economic Information Bulletin for Africa [*A publication*]
Statis Enseignements ... Statistiques des Enseignements [*A publication*]
Statis et Etud Fins (Ser Bleue) ... Statistiques et Etudes Financieres (Serie Bleue) [*A publication*]
Statis et Etud Fins (Ser Orange) ... Statistiques et Etudes Financieres (Serie Orange) [*A publication*]
Statis et Etud Fins (Ser Rouge) ... Statistiques et Etudes Financieres (Serie Rouge) [*A publication*]
Statis et Etud Midi Pyrenees ... Statistiques et Etudes Midi-Pyrenees [*A publication*]
Statis Judiciaires ... Statistiques Judiciaires [*A publication*]
Statis Mhefte Rheinland-Pfalz ... Statistische Monatshefte Rheinland-Pfalz [*A publication*]
Statis Nachr (Austria) NF ... Statistische Nachrichten (Austria). Neue Folge [*A publication*]
Statis Neerl ... Statistica Neerlandica [*Netherlands*] [*A publication*]
Statis Reporter ... Statistical Reporter [*A publication*]
Statist Abstr US ... Statistical Abstract. United States [*A publication*]
Statist Anal Donnees ... Statistique et Analyse des Donnees. Bulletin de l'Association des Statisticiens Universitaires [*A publication*]
Statist Bull USDA ... Statistical Bulletin. United States Department of Agriculture [*A publication*]
Statist Canad Consumpt Prodn Invent Rubb ... Statistics Canada. Consumption. Production Inventories of Rubber and Other Selected Sections [*A publication*]
Statist Decisions Econom ... Statistique et Decisions Economiques [*Paris*] [*A publication*]
Statist et Develop Loire ... Statistique et Developpement Pays de la Loire [*A publication*]
Statist Distributions Sci Work ... Statistical Distributions in Scientific Work [*A publication*]
Statist Ecology Ser ... Statistical Ecology Series [*A publication*]
Statist Econ Normande ... Statistiques pour l'Economie Normande [*A publication*]
Statist i Elektron-Vycisl Tehn v Ekonom ... Statistika i Elektronno-Vycislitel'naja Tehnika v Ekonomike Naucno-Issledovatel'skii Institut po Proektirovanija Vycislitel'nyh Centrov i Sistem Ekonomiceskoi Informacii CSU SSSR [*A publication*]
Statist Et Finance Et Econ (Ser Orange) ... Statistiques et Etudes Financieres. Etudes Economiques (Serie Orange) [*A publication*]
Statist Et Financ (Ser Bleue) ... Statistiques et Etudes Financieres (Serie Bleue) [*A publication*]
Statist Et Financ (Ser Rouge) ... Statistiques et Etudes Financieres (Serie Rouge) [*A publication*]
Statist Et Midi-Pyrenees ... Statistiques et Etudes Midi-Pyrenees [*A publication*]
Statist Foreign Trade B ... Statistics of Foreign Trade. Series B. Annual. Tables by Reporting Countries [*A publication*]
Statist Hefte ... Statistische Hefte [*A publication*]
Statistical Register of SA ... Statistical Register of South Australia [*A publication*] (APTA)
Statistical Register of WA ... Statistical Register of Western Australia [*A publication*] (APTA)
Statist M L ... Statistical Methods in Linguistics [*A publication*]
Statist Neerlandica ... Statistica Neerlandica [*A publication*]
Statist Newslett Abstr ... Statistical Newsletter and Abstracts. Indian Council of Agricultural Research [*A publication*]

Statist Paper ... Statistics of Paper [*A publication*]
Statist Probab Lett ... Statistics and Probability Letters [*A publication*]
Statist R (Beograd) ... Statisticka Revija (Beograd) [*A publication*]
Statist Sect Pap For Comm (Lond) ... Statistics Section Paper. Forestry Commission (London) [*A publication*]
Statist Theory Method Abstracts ... Statistical Theory and Method Abstracts [*A publication*]
Statist Trav Suppl B Mens ... Statistiques du Travail. Supplement au Bulletin Mensuel [*A publication*]
Statiszt Szle ... Statisztikai Szemle [*A publication*]
Stat Jahr .... Statistisches Jahrbuch fuer die Bundesrepublik Deutschland [*A publication*]
Stat Japan ... Statistics on Japanese Industries 1982 [*A publication*]
Statl............. Statistical [*Army*]
Stat at L ..... United States Statutes at Large [*A publication*]   (DLA)
STATLIB .. Statistical Computing Library [*Bell System*]
Stat Local ... Governments Statute of Local Governments [*A publication*]   (DLA)
Stat LR ...... Statute Law Review [*A publication*]
Stat Marl ... Statute of Marlbridge [*A publication*]   (DLA)
Stat Mech .. Statistical Mechanics [*A publication*]
Stat Med ... Statistics in Medicine [*A publication*]
Stat Mer..... Statute of Merton [*A publication*]   (DLA)
Stat Mert ... Statute of Merton [*A publication*]   (DLA)
STATNET ... Statistical Analysis of Network
STAT News ... Science Teachers Association of Tasmania. Newsletter [*A publication*]   (APTA)
Stat News Lett (New Delhi) ... Statistical News Letter (New Delhi) [*A publication*]
Statni Tech Knih Praze Vymena Zkusenosti ... Statni Technicka Knihovna v Praze. Vymena Zkusenosti [*A publication*]
Statni Vyzk Ustav Sklarsky Kradec Kralove Inf Prehl ... Statni Vyzkumny Ustav Sklarsky. Kradec Kralove. Informativni Prehled [*A publication*]
Stat Notes Health Plann ... Statistical Notes for Health Planners [*A publication*]
Stat NZ ...... Statutes of New Zealand [*A publication*]   (DLA)
Stat O & R ... Statutory Orders and Regulations [*Canada*] [*A publication*]   (DLA)
Stato Soc .... Stato Sociale [*A publication*]
STATPAC ... Statistics Package [*Computer program*]   (IEEE)
STATRAFO ... Standard Transfer Order
Stat Realm ... Statutes of the Realm [*England*] [*A publication*]   (DLA)
Stat Reg NZ ... Statutory Regulations [*New Zealand*] [*A publication*]   (DLA)
STATREP ..... Advise Present Grade, Status, Physical Condition, and Mailing Address of Following Named [*Military*]
Stat Rep ..... Statistical Reporter [*A publication*]
Stat Rep Pollen Mold Comm Am Acad Allergy ... Statistical Report. Pollen and Mold Committee. American Academy of Allergy [*A publication*]
Stat Rev Wld Oil Ind ... Statistical Review of the World Oil Industry [*A publication*]
Stat R & O ... Statutory Rules and Orders [*1890-1947*] [*England*] [*A publication*]   (DLA)
Stat R & ONI ... Statutory Rules and Orders of Northern Ireland [*A publication*]   (DLA)
Stat R & O N Ir ... Statutory Rules and Orders of Northern Ireland [*A publication*]
Stat R & O & Stat Inst Rev ... Statutory Rules and Orders and Statutory Instruments Revised [*England*] [*A publication*]   (DLA)
Stat Rptr .... Statistical Reporter [*A publication*]
STATS....... Simulated Tax and Transfer System [*Social Security Administration*]   (GFGA)
STATS...... Stationary Tank Automatic Target System   (MCD)
statS.......... Statsiemens [*Also, sS*] [*Unit of electric conductance, admittance, and susceptance*]
STATS...... Strategic/Tactical Area Test System   (MCD)
STATSBOBP ... Scale of Teacher Attitudes toward Selective Behavior of Boy Pupils [*Satirical*]
Stats Can ... Statistics Canada
STAT-SEL ... Status Select [*Army*]
STATSERVOFF ... Statistical Service Office [*Supreme Headquarters Allied Powers Europe*]   (NATG)
Statsokon Tss ... Statsoekonomisk Tidsskrift [*A publication*]
Stat Sum Can Gas Assoc ... Statistical Summary. Canadian Gas Association [*A publication*]
Statsvet Ts ... Statsvetenskaplig Tidskrift [*A publication*]
STATSVS ... Statistical Services   (MUGU)
STATT ...... Statement
statT.......... Stattesla [*Unit of magnetic flux density*]
Stat Textb Monogr ... Statistics Textbooks and Monographs [*A publication*]
Stat Theor Meth Abstr ... Statistical Theory and Method Abstracts [*A publication*]
Stat Theory Method Abstr ... Statistical Theory and Method Abstracts [*A publication*]
Stat Tidskr ... Statistisk Tidskrift [*A publication*]
Stat Tidskrift ... Statistick Tidskrift [*A publication*]
STATTS...... Stationary Automatic Tank Target System   (MCD)
Stat Use Radiat Jpn ... Statistics on the Use of Radiation in Japan [*A publication*]
Statute L Rev ... Statute Law Review [*A publication*]

Statutory Invent Regist ... Statutory Invention Registration [*A publication*]
statV........... Statvolt [*Also, sV*] [*Electrostatic unit of potential difference*]
statWb .... Statweber [*Unit of magnetic flux*]
Stat Westm ... Statute of Westminster [*A publication*]   (DLA)
Stat Winch ... Statute of Winchester [*A publication*]   (DLA)
STATY ...... Stationary   (WGA)
STATY ...... Statutory   (ROG)
Staub J .... Staub Journal [*A publication*]
Staub-Reinhalt Luft ... Staub, Reinhaltung der Luft [*A publication*]
Staundef..... Staundeforde's Exposition of the King's Prerogative [*A publication*]   (DLA)
Staundf Prerog ... Staundeforde's Exposition of the King's Prerogative [*A publication*]   (DLA)
Staund Pl ... Staundeforde's Pleas of Crown [*A publication*]   (DLA)
Staunf Pr.... Staundeforde's Exposition of the King's Prerogative [*A publication*]   (DLA)
St Autobahn ... Strasse und Autobahn [*A publication*]
STAVA ...... Stavivo [*Czechoslovakia*] [*A publication*]
Stavby Jadrovej Energ ... Stavby Jadrovej Energetiky [*Supplement to Inzenyrske Stavby*] [*Czechoslovakia*] [*A publication*]
Stavebnicky Cas ... Stavebnicky Casopis [*A publication*]
STAVRA ... Supreme High Command of the Soviet Armed Forces [*Russian*]   (MCD)
STAX........ Sludge Tracking Acoustical Experiment [*Marine science*]   (MSC)
STB............ Bachelor of the Science of Theology
StB .... Kommentar zum Neuen Testament aus Talmud und Midrasch (H. L. Strack - F. Billerbeck) [*A publication*]   (BJA)
STB............ St. Blazey [*British depot code*]
STB............ Santa Barbara [*Venezuela*] [*Airport symbol*]   (OAG)
STB............ Scan True Bearing   (NVT)
STB............ Scandinavian Tourist Boards   (EA)
STB............ Scottish Tourist Board   (EAIO)
STB............ Segment Tag BITS [*Binary Digits*]
STB............ September Resources Ltd. [*Vancouver Stock Exchange symbol*]
STB............ Shore Terminal Box   (MSA)
STB............ Signal Training Brigade   (MCD)
STB............ Soprano, Tenor, Bass
STB............ Southeast Banking Corp. [*NYSE symbol*]   (SPSG)
STB............ Southern Tourist Board [*British*]   (DCTA)
STB............ Special Tax Bond
Stb.............. Staatsblad [*Official Bulletin*] [*Netherlands*]   (ILCA)
STB............ Stable   (MSA)
STB............ Staged Turbulent Bed Process [*Chevron Corp.*] [*Oil shale pyrolysis*]
STB............ Standard Torsion Bar   (MCD)
STB............ Steinbach [*Federal Republic of Germany*] [*Seismograph station code, US Geological Survey*]   (SEIS)
StB .... Stenografische Berichte. Fuenf Hauptversammlungen. Verband der Deutschen Juden [*A publication*]
Stb.............. Steuerberater [*A publication*]
STB............ Stillborn [*Medicine*]
STB............ Stock-Tank Barrel [*Petroleum industry*]
STB............ Stourbridge [*British depot code*]
STB............ Streaming Tape Backup Unit
STB............ Stretch Block   (MCD)
STB............ Subsystems Test Bed   (MCD)
STB............ Sun's True Bearing [*Navigation*]
STB............ Supertropical Bleach [*Sanitizing agent*]
STB............ System [*or Subsystem*] Test Bed [*NASA*]   (KSC)
STB............ Systems Testing Branch [*Social Security Administration*]
STBA .... Selective Top-to-Bottom Algorithm   (DIT)
St Barbara Mus Nat Hist Contrib Sci ... Santa Barbara Museum of Natural History. Contributions in Science [*A publication*]
St Bar Rev ... State Bar Review [*A publication*]   (DLA)
STBC .... School Readiness Tests for Blind Children
STBD......... Standard-Bred Pacers & Trotters, Inc. [*NASDAQ symbol*]   (NQ)
STBD......... Starboard
St Ber G ..... Steuerberatungsgesetz [*A publication*]
sTBG.......... Slow Thyroxine-Binding Globulin [*Endocrinology*]
STBGA ...... Structure and Bonding [*Berlin*] [*A publication*]
St Bibl Theol ... Studies in Biblical Theology [*A publication*]
St Bi Franc ... Studium Biblicum Franciscanum Liber Annuus [*A publication*]
Stb Jb........ Steuerberater-Jahrbuch [*A publication*]
STBK .... State Street Boston Corp. [*NASDAQ symbol*]   (NQ)
STBL .... Stable   (FAAC)
St Bl .... Steuer und Zollblatt fuer Berlin [*A publication*]
STBLN ...... Stabilization   (MSA)
St Bl Nds.... Steuerblatt fuer das Land Niedersachsen [*A publication*]
St Bl Schl H ... Steuerblatt fuer das Land Schleswig-Holstein [*A publication*]
STBLZ .... Stabilize   (AABC)
StBM........ Shaft-to-Bore Misalignment
StBN......... Stuttgarter Biblische Monographien [*A publication*]
STBN......... Southern Bancorp, Inc. [*NASDAQ symbol*]   (NQ)
St Bonaventure Sci Stud ... St. Bonaventure Science Studies [*A publication*]
StBoT........ Studien zu den Bogazkoey-Texten [*Wiesbaden*] [*A publication*]
STBR .... Stater Brothers, Inc. [*NASDAQ symbol*]   (NQ)
St BRD....... Statistik der Bundesrepublik Deutschland [*A publication*]
STBRIAV ... Saint Briavels [*England*]

St Brown .... Stewart-Brown's Cases in the Court of the Star Chamber [*1455-1547*] [*A publication*]   (DLA)
STBSCP .... Stroboscope [*Engineering*]
StBSt......... Stuttgarter Bibelstudien [*Stuttgart*] [*A publication*]
STBT .... Steamboat   (ADA)
STBT .... Straits Times. Business Times [*A publication*]
STBT .... Subcaliber Tracer Bullet Trainer [*Army*]   (INF)
STBU........ Statistical Bulletin
STBY .... Standby   (AAG)
STBY .... Stansbury Mining Corp. [*NASDAQ symbol*]   (NQ)
STC........... Chief SONAR Technician [*Navy rating*]
STC........... Sacramento Test Center   (MCD)
STC........... Said to Contain [*Cargo manifest description*]
STC........... St. Cloud, MN [*Location identifier*] [*FAA*]   (FAAL)
STC........... Sales Tax Cases [*A publication*]   (APTA)
STC........... Samuel Taylor Coleridge [*Nineteenth-century British poet*]
STC........... Satellite Television Corp. [*Washington, DC*] [*Telecommunications*]   (TSSD)
STC........... Satellite Test Center [*Air Force*]
STC........... Satellite Tracking Center [*Sunnyvale, CA*]
STC........... Satellite Tracking Committee [*Military*]
STC........... Scandinavian Travel Commission [*Later, Scandinavian National Travel Offices*]   (EA)
STC........... Science and Technology Center [*National Science Foundation*]
STC........... Science and Technology Corp.   (RDA)
STC........... Security Time Control
STC........... Security Training Center
STC........... Senate Tourism Caucus   (EA)
STC........... Senior Training Corps [*British*]
STC........... Sensitivity-Time Control [*RADAR*]
STC........... Serum Theophylline Concentration [*Clinical chemistry*]
STC........... Service to Chapters [*Red Cross*]
STC........... Service to Claimants [*Unemployment Insurance Service*] [*Department of Labor*]
STC........... Service Technology Corp. [*of Ling-Temco-Vought, Inc.*]
STC........... Serving Test Center [*Bell System*]
STC........... Set Carry
STC........... [*The*] Seven Tablets of Creation [*L. W. King*] [*A publication*]   (BJA)
STC........... SHAPE [*Supreme Headquarters Allied Powers Europe*] Technical Center [*Formerly, SADTC*] [*The Hague, Netherlands*] [*NATO*]
STC........... Short Time Constant
STC........... Short Title Catalog [*A publication*]
STC........... Signal Training Centre [*British military*]   (DMA)
STC........... Simon's Tax Cases [*United Kingdom*] [*A publication*]
STC........... Simulation Tape Conversion
STC........... Single-Trip Container
STC........... Ski Touring Council   (EA)
STC........... Slow Time Constant   (MCD)
STC........... Smokeless Tobacco Council   (EA)
STC........... Society for Technical Communication   (EA)
STC........... Society of Telecommunications Consultants   (EA)
STC........... Society of Theatrical Carpenters [*A union*] [*British*]
STC........... Soft Tissue Calcification [*Medicine*]
STC........... Solidaridad de Trabajadores Cristianos [*Nicaragua*] [*Political party*]   (EY)
STC........... Sound Transmission Class [*Followed by number, indicates FHA rating of sound insulating quality of a partition construction*]
STC........... Source Telecomputing Corp. [*McLean, VA*] [*Telecommunications*]   (TSSD)
STC........... South Thames College [*London, England*]
STC........... Space Technology Center
STC........... Space Test Center [*Air Force*]
STC........... Space-Time Continuum
STC........... Spacecraft Test Conductor [*NASA*]   (KSC)
STC........... Specialists Training Center
STC........... Specific Taste Changes
STC........... Specific Thermal Capacity
STC........... Spectral Transfer Coefficient
STC........... Standard Telephone and Cable [*IT & T affiliate*] [*Research center*] [*British*]
STC........... Standard Test Chamber   (MCD)
STC........... Standard Test Configuration [*NASA*]   (NASA)
STC........... Standard Transmission Code [*Data processing*]
STC........... Standing Technical Committee [*British*]   (DCTA)
STC........... State Tax Cases [*Commerce Clearing House*] [*A publication*]   (DLA)
STC........... State Teachers College
STC........... Station Technical Control [*Telecommunications*]   (TEL)
STC........... Station Test and Calibration
StC........... Status Constructus   (BJA)
STC........... Step Timing Control [*Truck engineering*]
STC........... Stepchild
St C........... Stephen's Commentaries on the Laws of England [*21st ed.*] [*1950*] [*A publication*]   (DLA)
STC........... Stereo Tape Club of America
STC........... Stern Telecommunications Corp. [*New York, NY*] [*Telecommunications*]   (TSSD)
STC........... Stewart, Tabori & Chang [*Publisher*]

STC........... Stock Trust Certificate [*Investment term*]
STC........... Stone Canyon Observatory [*California*] [*Seismograph station code, US Geological Survey*]   (SEIS)
STC........... Storage Container   (MCD)
STC........... Stored Time Command
STC........... Straight Cactus [*Horticulture*]
STC........... Streamtube Curvature
STC........... Subtropical Convergence [*Oceanography*]
STC........... Summit Technical Center [*Celanese Research Co.*]
STC........... Supplemental Type Certificate
STC........... Synthetic Turf Council   (EA)
STC........... System Technical Control
STC........... System Test Configuration
STC........... System Test Console
STC........... System Transfer Constant
STC........... Systems Test Complex [*NASA*]
STCA .... Scottish Terrier Club of America   (EA)
STCA .... Short Tests of Clerical Ability
STCA .... Silky Terrier Club of America   (EA)
STCA .... Skye Terrier Club of America   (EA)
STCA .... Sodium Trichloroacetate [*Organic chemistry*]
STCA .... Staffordshire Terrier Club of America   (EA)
STCA .... Stockbridge Capital Ltd. [*Dallas, TX*] [*NASDAQ symbol*]   (NQ)
S/TCAC..... Scientific/Technical Careers Advisory Committee [*Environmental Protection Agency*]   (GFGA)
St Can Lit... Studies in Canadian Literature [*A publication*]
St Cas........ Stillingfleet's English Ecclesiastical Cases [*A publication*]   (DLA)
StCath .... Studia Catholica [*Nijmegen*] [*A publication*]   (BJA)
STCB .... Subtask Control Block [*Data processing*]   (IBMDP)
STCC .... Spacecraft Technical Control Center   (MDG)
STCC .... Springfield Technical Community College [*Massachusetts*]
STCC .... Standard Transportation Commodity Classification [*or Code*]
STCC .... Standards Council of Canada [*See also CCNO*]
STCC .... Syndicat des Travailleurs en Communication du Canada
STCC .... Syndicat des Travailleurs en Communication, Electronique, Electricite, Techniciens, et Salaries du Canada [*Communications, Electronic, Electrical, Technical, and Salaried Workers of Canada - CWC*]
STCDHS ... Spacecraft Telemetry Command Data Handling System
STCDS ...... System Test Complex Data System
STCDSS .... Standing Technical Committee on Disposal of Sewage Sludge [*British*]   (DCTA)
STCE .... System Test Complex Equipment
STCFEO.... Science and Technology Center, Far East Office [*Army*]   (AABC)
STCH .... Shared Technologies, Inc. [*NASDAQ symbol*]   (NQ)
STCH .... Stitch   (MSA)
St Ch Cas... Star Chamber Cases [*England*] [*A publication*]   (DLA)
STCI .... Siebert Telecommunications Consulting, Inc. [*Cincinnati, OH*] [*Telecommunications*]   (TSSD)
STCICS ..... Strike Command Integrated Communications System [*British*]
STCL .... Source-Term Control Loop [*Nuclear energy*]   (NRCH)
STCLB ...... Start Climb [*Aviation*]   (FAAC)
St Clem ..... St. Clement's Church Case [*Philadelphia, PA*] [*A publication*]   (DLA)
STCM .... Master Chief SONAR Technician [*Navy rating*]
STCO........ StratAmerica Corp. [*NASDAQ symbol*]   (NQ)
STCO........ Supervisor Training Conference Outline [*Air Force*]   (MCD)
STCOL...... Steel Column [*Camutek*] [*Software package*]   (NCC)
St Comp Int Devel ... Studies in Comparative International Development [*A publication*]
St Cons....... Studies in Conservation [*A publication*]
STCP .... Short-Term Cost Plan [*NASA*]   (NASA)
STCP .... Society of Tympanuchus Cupido Pinnatus   (EA)
STCR .... Solar Thermal Central Receiver
StCrN........ Stephen Crane Newsletter [*A publication*]
STCRS....... Solar Thermal Central Receiver System
STCS .... Senior Chief SONAR Technician [*Navy rating*]
St CS .... Studies in Contemporary Satire [*A publication*]
STCS .... Surveyor Thermal Control Section
STCT .... Small Transportable Communications Terminal
STCT .... System Technical Coordinator Technician   (SAA)
St Ct J .... State Court Journal [*A publication*]
StCu .... Stratocumulus [*Cloud*] [*Meteorology*]   (AIA)
STCV .... Strawberry Crinkle Virus [*Plant pathology*]
STCW .... Standard of Training, Certification, and Watchkeeping Convention   (DS)
STCW .... Stichting Technisch Centrum Waalsteen [*Research center*] [*Netherlands*]   (IRC)
STCW .... System Time Code Word
STCY .... Stacy Industries, Inc. [*Wood-Ridge, NJ*] [*NASDAQ symbol*]   (NQ)
STD .... Banco de Santander SA [*NYSE symbol*]   (SPSG)
STD .... Doctor of the Science of Theology
STD .... Sacrae Theologiae Doctor [*Doctor of Sacred Theology*] [*Latin*]
STD .... Safety Topic Discussion   (AAG)
STD .... Salinity/Temperature/Density [*or Depth*] [*Oceanography*]
std............. Saturated   (MAE)
STD .... Schools of Theology in Dubuque [*Library network*]

STD	Sea Transport Department [*British military*] (DMA)
STD	Seated (WGA)
STD	Servo Tape Display
STD	Set Driver (SAA)
STD	Sexually Transmitted Disease [*Medicine*]
STD	Ship Training Detachment
STD	Short-Term Disability
STD	Shuttle Test Director [*NASA*] (MCD)
STD	Skin Test Dose
STD	Skin to Tumor Distance [*Medicine*] (MAE)
STD	Sledborne Time Digitizer
STD	Society for Theological Discussion [*Defunct*] (EA)
STD	Society of Typographic Designers [*British*] (EAIO)
STD	Sodium Thermionic Detector (SAA)
STD	Software Test Description [*DoD*]
STD	Spacecraft Technology Division [*NASA*] (KSC)
STD	Sports Trainers Digest [*A publication*]
STD	Standaard. Dagblad voor Staatkundige, Matschappelijke, en Economische Belangen [*A publication*]
STD	Standard (AFM)
STD	Standard Airways [*El Paso, TX*] [*FAA designator*] (FAAC)
STD	Standard Test Dose
STD	Standard Trustco Ltd. [*Toronto Stock Exchange symbol*]
STD	Standing (AABC)
STD	Started (ADA)
STD	State-Transition Diagram [*Data processing*]
STD	Stepwise Thermal Desorption [*Surface analysis*]
STD	Steward [*British*]
ST D..........	Stopped Diapason [*Organ stop*] [*Music*]
STD	Storage Target Date
STD	Storage Tube Display
STD	Store Decrement (SAA)
STD	Strain Gauge Transient Dosimetry
STD	Stripline Tunnel Diode
StD............	Studies and Documents [*A publication*]
STD	Subscriber Toll Dialing [*Telecommunications*] (TSSD)
STD	Subscriber Trunk Dialing [*Telephone communications*]
STD	Sunbeam-Talbot-Darracq [*Automobile manufacturer*]
STD	Supporting Technology Development (KSC)
STD	Synopsis Series of the United States Treasury Decisions [*A publication*] (DLA)
STD	System Technology Demonstration Program (RDA)
STD	Training and Development Journal [*A publication*]
S-TDA.......	Selenium-Tellurium Development Association (EA)
STDA........	Steward's Assistant [*Navy*]
STDA........	StreetTalk Directory Assistance [*VINES*] [*Data processing*] (PCM)
STDA........	Stripline Tunnel Diode Amplifier
STD Abstr Bib ...	Sexually Transmitted Diseases. Abstracts and Bibliography [*A publication*]
STDB........	Steward's Branch [*Marine Corps*]
STDBY......	Standby (NVT)
STDC........	Southern Travel Directors Council
STDC........	Standards Council of Canada [*See also CCNO*]
STDCF	Space Telescope Data Capture Facility [*NASA*] (SSD)
StdCm........	Standard Commercial Corp. [*Associated Press abbreviation*] (APAG)
STD/DEV ...	Standard Deviation (MCD)
STDDS......	Submarine Tactical Data Display Subsystem (MCD)
STDE........	Standard Energy Corp. [*NASDAQ symbol*] (NQ)
St Dept.......	State Department Reports [*A publication*] (DLA)
STDF........	Sodium Taurodihydrofusidate [*Organic chemistry*]
STDF........	Standoff
STDHA......	Staedtehygiene [*A publication*]
ST DIAP....	Stopped Diapason [*Organ stop*] [*Music*]
STDJ........	Studies on the Texts of the Desert of Judah [*A publication*]
St DKG	Studien zur Deutschen Kunstgeschichte [*A publication*]
STDL........	Standard Distribution List [*NASA*] (NASA)
STDL........	Standard Logic, Inc. [*NASDAQ symbol*] (NQ)
STDL........	Submarine Tactical Data Link (NVT)
STDM........	Statistical Time-Division Multiplexer [*or Multiplexing*]
STDM........	Synchronous Time-Division Multiplexing [*Data processing*] (MDG)
STDN	Set the Date Now [*Association supporting the end of US military involvement in Indochina*] [*Defunct*] (EA)
STDN	Space Flight Tracking and Data Network [*Formerly, STADAN*] [*NASA*]
STDN	Standardization (AFM)
STDNA......	ASTM [*American Society for Testing and Materials*] Standardization News [*A publication*]
STDO	Standard Oil & Exploration of Delaware, Inc. [*NASDAQ symbol*] (NQ)
Std Obraztsy Chern Metall ...	Standartnye Obraztsy v Chernoi Metallurgii [*A publication*]
STDP........	Short-Term Dynamic Psychotherapy
STDP........	Special Training Devices Program (AFM)
StdPac........	Standard-Pacific Corp. [*Associated Press abbreviation*] (APAG)
StdPrd........	Standard Products Co. [*Associated Press abbreviation*] (APAG)
STDR........	Science and Technology Desk Reference [*A publication*]
STDR........	Space Technology Data Report

St DR	Statistik des Deutschen Reichs [*A publication*]
STDS	Snake Torpedo Destruction System
STDS	Standards [*Timber measurement*] (EY)
STDS	Strategic Target Data System (SSD)
STDS	Submarine Tactical Data System (MCD)
STDS	Survey of Teacher Demand and Shortage [*Department of Education*] (GFGA)
STDS	System for Thermal Diagnostic Studies
STDST	Start Descent [*Aviation*] (FAAC)
STDV......	Start Tank Discharge Valve (KSC)
STDVG......	Stern Diving
STDWN	Stand Down (MCD)
STDY........	Saturday
STDY........	Steady (MSA)
STDZN......	Standardization (AABC)
STE............	Sainte [*French*] (EY)
ST & E	Security Test and Evaluation [*Military*] (GFGA)
STE...........	Segment Table Entry [*Data processing*] (MDG)
STE...........	Self-Trapped Exciton [*Physical chemistry*]
STE...........	Shield Test Experiment [*Nuclear energy*] (NRCH)
STE...........	Shift Technical Engineer [*Nuclear energy*] (NRCH)
STE...........	[*The*] Simplified Test Equipment [*Army*] (INF)
Ste	Societe [*Company*] [*French*] [*Business term*]
STE...........	Society of Telecom Executives [*Trade union*] [*British*]
STE...........	Society of Tractor Engineers [*Later, SAE*]
STE...........	Spacecraft Test Engineering [*NASA*] (KSC)
STE...........	Span Terminating Equipment [*Telecommunications*] (TEL)
STE...........	Special Temporary Enlistment [*Coast Guard*]
STE...........	Special Test Equipment
STE...........	Special-Type Ellipsometer
STE...........	Specific Temperature Excursion
STE...........	Standard Terminal Equipment [*Data processing*] (HGAA)
STE...........	Star Tracker Electronics [*Apollo*] [*NASA*]
STE...........	Station Test Equipment [*Deep Space Instrumentation Facility, NASA*]
STE...........	Statute
Ste	Steaua [*A publication*]
STE	Stelco, Inc. [*Toronto Stock Exchange symbol*] [*Vancouver Stock Exchange symbol*]
STE...........	Stepanavan [*Former USSR*] [*Seismograph station code, US Geological Survey*] [*Closed*] (SEIS)
Ste	Stephanus Provincialis [*Flourished, 1290-97*] [*Authority cited in pre-1607 legal work*] (DSA)
Ste	Stephanus Tornacensis [*Deceased, 1203*] [*Authority cited in pre-1607 legal work*] (DSA)
STE...........	Stevens Point [*Wisconsin*] [*Airport symbol*] [*Obsolete*] (OAG)
STE...........	Stockton Terminal & Eastern Railroad [*AAR code*]
STE...........	Stop Transfer Effector [*Genetics*]
St E	Studienreihe Englisch [*A publication*]
STE...........	Suitability Test Evaluation (AAG)
STE...........	Supergroup Translation Equipment
STE...........	Support Test Equipment (MCD)
STE...........	Syrian Telecommunications Establishment [*Syrian Arab Republic*] (TSSD)
STE...........	System Test Engineer [*NASA*] (NASA)
STE...........	System Test and Evaluation
STE...........	System Training Exercise (SAA)
STEA	Short-Term Emergency Assistance
STEA	Surveyor Test Equipment Assembly
STEA	System Test, Evaluation, and Assembly
STEADG...	Sciences et Techniques de l'Eau [*A publication*]
STEADY ...	Simulation Tables - Environment and Dynamic (SAA)
STEAG......	Steinkohlen-Elektrizitaet AG [*West Germany*]
STEAM.....	Department of Science, Technology, Energy, and Materials [*Proposed Cabinet department*]
STEAM.....	Sensor Technology as Applied to the Marine Corps
STEAM.....	Standard Towing Equipment for Aircraft Maintenance (MCD)
STEAM.....	Streptonigrin, Thioguanine, Endoxan [*Cyclophosphamide*], Actinomycin, Mitomycin C [*Antineoplastic drug regimen*]
Steam Eng ...	Steam Engineer [*A publication*]
Steam Fuel Users J ...	Steam and Fuel Users' Journal [*A publication*]
Steam Heat Eng ...	Steam and Heating Engineer [*A publication*]
Steam Heat Engr ...	Steam and Heating Engineer [*A publication*]
Steam Plant Eng ...	Steam Plant Engineering [*A publication*]
Steam Pwr ...	Steam Power [*A publication*]
Steamusers Fuel Users J ...	Steamusers' and Fuel Users' Journal [*A publication*]
STEAP	Simulated Trajectories Error Analysis Program [*NASA*]
Stearns RA ...	Stearn's Real Actions [*A publication*] (DLA)
Stearns Real Act ...	Stearn's Real Actions [*A publication*] (DLA)
STEC........	Serv-Tech, Inc. [*NASDAQ symbol*] (NQ)
STEC........	Solar Thermal Electric Conversation (MCD)
STEC........	Syndicat des Travailleurs de l'Energie et de la Chimie [*Energy and Chemical Workers Union - ECWU*] [*Canada*]
St Eccl Cas ...	Stillingfleet's English Ecclesiastical Cases [*A publication*] (DLA)
Stecher Agency & Partnership ...	Stecher's Cases on Agency and Partnership [*A publication*] (DLA)
Stechert-Hafner Bk News ...	Stechert-Hafner Book News [*A publication*]
STECR	Ships Tactical Environmental Control Receiver

STECS....... Software Technology and Engineering Center Staff [*Social Security Administration*]
STED......... Science, Technology, and Economic Development
STED......... Standard Technical Equipment Development Division [*Obsolete*] [*National Security Agency*]
STEDA...... Steroids [*A publication*]
STEDBAC ... Stearyldimethylbenzylammonium Chloride [*Organic chemistry*]
STEDI .... Space Thrust Evolution and Disposal Investigation [*Air Force*]
STEDMIS ... Ships Technical Data Management Information System [*Navy*]
STEDMIS ... Standard Technical Data Management Information System (CAAL)
STEEG...... Scanned Topographic Electroencephalograph
STEEL....... Simulation Test Environment to Evaluate Team Load (SAA)
Steel Const ... Steel Construction [*A publication*] (APTA)
Steel Constr ... Steel Construction [*A publication*] (APTA)
Steel Fabric J ... Steel Fabrication Journal [*A publication*] (APTA)
Steel Fabr J ... Steel Fabrication Journal [*A publication*] (APTA)
STEELFACTS ... Materials Database Steel and Iron [*German Iron and Steel Engineers Association*] [*Information service or system*] [*Ceased operation*] (IID)
Steel Founders' Res J ... Steel Founders' Research Journal [*A publication*]
Steel Furn Mon ... Steel Furnace Monthly [*A publication*]
Steel Horiz ... Steel Horizons [*A publication*]
Steel Ind..... World Steel Industry. Into and Out of the 1990's [*A publication*]
Steel Ind Environ Proc CC Furnas Meml Conf ... Steel Industry and the Environment. Proceedings. C.C. Furnas Memorial Conference [*A publication*]
Steel Ind Jpn Annu ... Steel Industry of Japan Annual [*A publication*]
Steel Int ..... Steel International [*A publication*]
Steel Met Int ... Steels and Metals International [*A publication*]
Steel Process ... Steel Processing [*A publication*]
Steel Process Convers ... Steel Processing and Conversion [*A publication*]
Steel Rev .... Steel Review [*A publication*]
Steel Stat.... Steel Statistics for Europe [*A publication*]
Steel Stat Q ... Quarterly Bulletin of Steel Statistics for Europe [*A publication*]
Steel Times Int ... Steel Times International [*England*] [*A publication*]
Steenth....... Sixteenth [*Stock and commodity price quotes*]
STEEP....... Safety Training for the Execution of Emergency Procedures [*NASA*]
STEEP....... Shock Two-Dimensional Eulerian Elastic Plastic [*Computer code*]
STEEP....... Solution to Environmental and Economic Problems
Steer PL..... Steer on Parish Law [*6th ed.*] [*1899*] [*A publication*] (DLA)
STEG......... Staatliche Gesellschaft zur Erfassung von Ruestungsgut [*German Public Corporation for the Collection and Distribution of War Materials*]
STEG......... Supersonic Transport Evaluation Group
STEI .... Stewart Enterprises [*NASDAQ symbol*] (SPSG)
STEIA .... Stahl und Eisen [*A publication*]
STE/ICE ... Simplified Test Equipment for Internal Combustion Engines (RDA)
STE/ICEPM ... Simplified Test Equipment for Internal Combustion Engine Powered Material (MCD)
STEIN .... System Test Environment Input
Steinbeck M ... Steinbeck Monograph Series [*A publication*]
Steinbeck Q ... Steinbeck Quarterly [*A publication*]
SteinbQ...... Steinbeck Quarterly [*A publication*]
S Teind....... Shaw's Scotch Teind [*Tithe*] Cases [*A publication*] (DLA)
Steiner Tb .. Rudolf Steiner Taschenbuchausgaben [*A publication*]
Steinind Steinstrassenbau ... Steinindustrie und Steinstrassenbau [*A publication*]
Stein-Ind Strassenbau ... Stein-Industrie und -Strassenbau [*A publication*]
Steinkohlenbergbauver Kurznachr ... Steinkohlenbergbauverein Kurznachrichten [*A publication*]
SteiQ.......... Steinbeck Quarterly [*A publication*]
Steirische Beitr Hydrogeol ... Steirische Beitraege zur Hydrogeologie [*A publication*]
Steirisch Imkerbote ... Steirischer Imkerbote [*A publication*]
St Ek .... Studiea Ekonomiczne [*A publication*]
Steklo Sitally Silik Mater ... Steklo, Sitally, i Silikatnye Materialy [*Belorussian SSR*] [*A publication*]
Stekolnaya Keram Promst ... Stekol'naya i Keramicheskaya Promyshlennost [*A publication*]
Stekol'naya Prom-St ... Stekol'naya Promyshlennost [*Former USSR*] [*A publication*]
STEL .... Satelco, Inc. [*NASDAQ symbol*] (NQ)
STEL .... Short-Term Exposure Limit [*Environmental chemistry*]
STEL .... Society of Telegraphic Engineers [*British*]
STEL .... Structure Tests, English Language [*Educational test*]
STEL .... Studenta Tutmonda Esperantista Liga [*World League of Esperanto-Speaking Students*]
STEL .... Sunday Telegraph [*United Kingdom*] [*A publication*]
STELB....... Stereo Review [*A publication*]
STELCO ... Steel Co. of Canada
STELDF.... Science and Technology Libraries [*A publication*]
STELLA .... Satellite Transmission Experiment Linking Laboratories [*European Space Agency*]
STELLA .... Structural Thinking Experiential Learning Laboratory with Animation [*Software*]

STELLAR ... Star Tracker for Economical Long Life Attitude Reference [*NASA*]
Stellenbosse Stud ... Stellenbosse Student [*A publication*]
STEM....... Scanning Transmission Electron Microscope
STEM....... Science and Technology Employment [*Longman Cartermill Ltd.*] [*Scotland*] [*Information service or system*] (CRD)
STEM....... SEABEE Tactical Equipment Management [*Navy*]
STEM....... Searching Together Educational Ministries (EA)
STEM....... Shaped Tube Electrolytic Machining [*GE*]
STEM....... Shoplifters Take Everybody's Money
STEM....... Situated Atop an Extendable Mast (SAA)
STEM....... Society of Teachers of Emergency Medicine (EA)
STEM....... Socio-Technological-Economic-Military [*DoD*]
STEM....... Solar-Terrestrial Environment Model [*to predict the terrestrial effects of solar events*]
STEM....... Special Technical and Economic Mission
STEM....... Special Telemetry Equipped Missile
STEM....... Statistically-Tensioned Extension Mast (DNAB)
STEM....... Stay Time Extension Module [*NASA*]
STEM....... Stellar Tracker Evaluation Missile
STEM....... Storable Tubular Extendable Member
STEM....... System Test Equipment Mission [*NASA*] (KSC)
STEM....... Systems for Tools and Equipment Management [*Military*] (AFIT)
STEM....... Systems Training and Exercise Module (MCD)
STEMFAB ... Storable Tubular Extendable Member Fabrication
STEMS..... Small Terminal Evasive Missile System (MCD)
STEMS..... Society to Encourage Miniskirts [*New York group opposing below-the-knee fashions introduced in 1970*]
STEMS..... Structural Tracking and Engine Monitoring System (MCD)
STEM-TEM ... Scanning Transmission Electron Microscopy - Transmission Electron Microscopy
STEN........ Sheppard-Turpin-England [*Machine carbine codesigned by Sheppard and Turpin*]
STEN........ Stencil
STEN........ Stenographer
St Enc........ Study Encounter [*A publication*]
STENCH.. Society to Exterminate Neo-Communist Harbingers
Stendhal Cl ... Stendhal Club [*A publication*]
ST-ENDOR ... Special Triple-Electron Nuclear Double Resonance [*Spectroscopy*]
St Engl Lit ... Studies in English Literature [*A publication*]
STENO...... Stenographer (MUGU)
STENS ...... Standard Terrestrial Navigation System (MCD)
STENS ...... STD Terrestrial Navigation System (MCD)
Stenton....... Stenton. Rolls of the Justices in Eyre [*A publication*] (ILCA)
Stenton G ... Rolls of the Justices in Eyre for Gloucestershire, Worcestershire, and Staffordshire [*A publication*] (ILCA)
Stenton Y ... Rolls of the Justices in Eyre in Yorkshire [*A publication*] (ILCA)
STEO........ Special Test Equipment Order (MCD)
STEP .... Safeguard Test and Evaluation Program [*Army*] (AABC)
STEP .... Safety Test Engineering Program [*AEC*]
STEP .... Sales Tax Exemption Processing System [*Software*]
STEP .... School to Employment Program
STEP .... Scientific and Technical Exploitation Program (AFM)
STEP .... Selective Traffic Enforcement Program [*Department of Transportation*]
STEP .... Self-Teaching Exportable Package
STEP .... Sensitivity Temperature Error Program (MCD)
STEP .... Sequential Tests of Educational Progress [*of ETS; given in 10th and 12th grades*]
STEP .... Sequentially Timed Events Plotting [*In publication title, "Investigating Accidents with STEP"*] [*Marcel Decker, Inc.*]
STEP .... Shell Technology Enterprise Programme [*British*]
STEP .... Ship Type Electronics Plan [*Navy*] (NG)
STEP .... Short Term Enrichment Program [*of US Information Agency*]
STEP .... Simple Transition to Economical Processing (IEEE)
STEP .... Simple Transition to Electronic Processing
STEP .... Simulated Tracking Evaluation Program (SAA)
STEP .... Software T & E Panel (RDA)
STEP .... Software Test and Evaluation Process [*DoD*]
STEP .... Solutions to Employment Problems [*A program of National Association of Manufacturers*]
STEP .... Space Technology Experiments Platform
STEP .... Space Terminal Evaluation Program
STEP .... Special Training Enlistment Program
STEP .... Special Training Equipment Program Document (AFIT)
STEP .... Staff Training Extramural Programs [*National Institutes of Health*]
STEP .... Standard Tape Executive Package [*or Program*] [*NCR Corp.*]
STEP .... Standard Terminal Program [*Data processing*] (IEEE)
STEP .... Standard Test Equipment Procedure (NG)
STEP .... State Technology Extension Program [*National Institute of Standards and Technology*]
STEP .... Statistical Trajectory Estimation Program [*NASA*]
STEP .... Stratosphere-Troposphere Exchange Project [*NASA*]
STEP .... Structures Technology Experiments Platform (MCD)
STEP .... Student Education Program

STEP .... Student Transfer Education Plan [*Defunct*] [*National Urban League*]
STEP .... Students toward Environmental Participation [*UNESCO and National Park Service*]
STEP .... Summer Training Employment Program   (MCD)
STEP .... Supervisory Tape Executive Program [*Data processing*]
STEP .... Supplemental Training and Employment Program   (OICC)
STEP .... System for Testing Evaluation of Potential [*Employee evaluation software*] [*London House, Inc.*]
STEP .... Systematic Training for Effective Parenting
STEP .... Systems Test Equipment Program   (MCD)
Stepan .... Stephan Co. [*Associated Press abbreviation*]   (APAG)
Steph .... Stephanus Pragensis [*Flourished, 14th century*] [*Authority cited in pre-1607 legal work*]   (DSA)
Steph .... Stephanus Tornacensis [*Deceased, 1203*] [*Authority cited in pre-1607 legal work*]   (DSA)
Steph .... Stephens' Supreme Court Decisions [*1774-1923*] [*Jamaica*] [*A publication*]
Stepha Bertrand ... Stephanus Bertrandus [*Flourished, 16th century*] [*Authority cited in pre-1607 legal work*]   (DSA)
Steph Cl ..... Stephens on Clergy [*1848*] [*A publication*]   (DLA)
Steph Com ... Stephen's Commentaries on the Laws of England [*A publication*]   (DLA)
Steph Comm ... Stephen's Commentaries on the Laws of England [*A publication*]   (DLA)
Steph Const ... Stephens on the English Constitution [*A publication*]   (DLA)
Steph Cr ..... Stephen's Digest of the Criminal Law [*A publication*]   (DLA)
Steph Crim Dig ... Stephen's Digest of the Criminal Law [*A publication*]   (DLA)
Steph Cr L ... Stephen's General View of the Criminal Law [*9 eds.*] [*1877-1950*] [*A publication*]   (DLA)
Steph Cr Law ... Stephen's General View of the Criminal Law [*A publication*]   (DLA)
Steph Dig... Stephen's Digest, New Brunswick Reports [*A publication*]   (DLA)
Steph Dig Cr L ... Stephen's Digest of the Criminal Law [*A publication*]   (DLA)
Steph Dig Cr Law ... Stephen's Digest of the Criminal Law [*A publication*]   (DLA)
Steph Dig Ev ... Stephen's Digest of the Law of Evidence [*A publication*]   (DLA)
Steph Elect ... Stephens on Elections [*1840*] [*A publication*]   (DLA)
Stephen F Austin State Coll Sch For Bull ... Stephen F. Austin State College. School of Forestry. Bulletin [*A publication*]
Stephen HCL ... Stephen's History of Criminal Law [*A publication*]   (DLA)
Stephens .... Supreme Court Decisions, by J. E. R. Stephens [*A publication*]   (DLA)
Steph Ev..... Stephen's Digest of the Law of Evidence [*A publication*]   (DLA)
Steph Gen View ... Stephen's General View of the Criminal Law [*2nd ed.*] [*1890*] [*A publication*]   (DLA)
Steph J St Comp ... Steph's Joint-Stock Companies in Canada [*A publication*]   (DLA)
Steph Lect ... Stephen's Lectures on the History of France [*A publication*]   (DLA)
Steph NP ... Stephen's Law of Nisi Prius [*A publication*]   (DLA)
Steph Pl ..... Stephen on Pleading [*A publication*]   (DLA)
Steph Proc ... Stephens on Procurations [*A publication*]   (DLA)
Steph Slav ... Stephens on Slavery [*A publication*]   (DLA)
STEPP .... Society of Teachers in Education of Professional Photography   (EA)
STEPR .... Saturation Transfer Electron Paramagnetic Resonance [*Physics*]
STEPS .... Science and Technology Evaluation and Prioritization System [*Program*]   (RDA)
STEPS .... Ships Technical Publication System [*Navy*]
STEPS .... Solar Thermionic Electrical Power System
STEPS .... Staff Training Exercise for Programming Supervisor   (SAA)
STEPS .... Stored Thermal Energy Propulsion System
STER .... Seater
STER .... Steradian
STER .... Stereotype
STER .... Sterilize   (AABC)
STER .... Sterling
STER .... Sterna [*A publication*]
STER .... Successively Truncated Expectation of the Reciprocal [*Statistics*]
STER .... System Training Equipment Requirement
Stereo .... Stereo Review [*A publication*]
STEREO ... Stereophonic   (MSA)
STEREO ... Stereoscope [*or Stereoscopic*]
STEREO ... Stereotype [*Refers to old news*] [*Slang*]   (DSUE)
Stereochem Fundam Methods ... Stereochemistry. Fundamentals and Methods [*A publication*]
Stereo R ..... Stereo Review [*A publication*]
Stereotactic Funct Neurosurg ... Stereotactic and Functional Neurosurgery [*A publication*]
STERF....... Special Test Equipment Repair Facility
STERL...... Sterling   (ADA)
STERLEL ... Sterling Electronics Corp. [*Associated Press abbreviation*]   (APAG)
SterlSft....... Sterling Software, Inc. [*Associated Press abbreviation*]   (APAG)
STERNUT ... Sternutamentum [*Snuff*] [*Pharmacy*]

Steroid Horm ... Steroid Hormones [*A publication*]
Steroids Lipids Res ... Steroids and Lipids Research [*A publication*]
Steroids Suppl ... Steroids. Supplement [*A publication*]
STES .... Solar Thermal Energy System
STES Newsl ... STES [*Seasonal Thermal Energy Storage*] Newsletter [*United States*] [*A publication*]
STESTG.... Space Test Group [*Military*]
STE-T....... Simplified Test Equipment - Transitional [*Army*]
STET .... Specialized Technique for Efficient Typesetting
STET .... Steward, Technical [*Marine Corps*]
STET .... Submaximal Treadmill Exercise Test   (AAMN)
STET .... System Test Experiments Tape
STETF....... Solar Total Energy Test Facility [*Energy Research and Development Administration*]
STETS....... Solar-Terrestrial Energy Transfer Studies [*Meteorology*]
Stetson L Rev ... Stetson Law Review [*A publication*]
Stettin Ent Ztg ... Stettiner Entomologische Zeitung [*A publication*]
STEUA...... Steuerungstechnik [*A publication*]
STEV .... Spinach Temperate Virus [*Plant pathology*]
STEV .... Stevedore
STEV .... Stevia Co., Inc. [*Arlington Heights, IL*] [*NASDAQ symbol*]   (NQ)
Stev Arb..... Stevens on Arbitration [*2nd ed.*] [*1835*] [*A publication*]   (DLA)
Stev Av....... Stevens on Average [*5th ed.*] [*1835*] [*A publication*]   (DLA)
Stev & Ben Ins ... Stevens and Benecke on Insurance [*A publication*]   (DLA)
Stev Dig ...... Stevens' New Brunswick Digest [*A publication*]   (DLA)
STEVE ...... Space Tool for Extravehicular Emergencies
Stevens & G ... Stevens and Graham's Reports [*98-139 Georgia*] [*A publication*]   (DLA)
Stevens Ind ... Stevens Indicator [*A publication*]
Stevens Inst Technol (Hoboken NJ) Davidson Lab Rep ... Stevens Institute of Technology (Hoboken, New Jersey). Davidson Laboratory. Report [*A publication*]
Stev & G..... Stevens and Graham's Reports [*98-139 Georgia*] [*A publication*]   (DLA)
STEVS...... Spartan Tactical Equipment Verification Site [*Missiles*]   (MCD)
STEVS...... Subsystem Tactical Equipment Verification Site
STEW........ Stewart Sandwiches, Inc. [*NASDAQ symbol*]   (NQ)
Stew........... Stewart's Alabama Reports [*1827-31*] [*A publication*]   (DLA)
Stew........... Stewart's Equity Reports [*28-45 New Jersey*] [*A publication*]   (DLA)
Stew........... Stewart's Nova Scotia Admiralty Reports [*A publication*]   (DLA)
Stew........... Stewart's Reports [*1-10 South Dakota*] [*A publication*]   (DLA)
Stew Adm... Stewart's Nova Scotia Vice-Admiralty Reports [*1803-13*] [*A publication*]   (DLA)
Stew Admr ... Stewart's Nova Scotia Admiralty Reports [*A publication*]   (DLA)
Stew (Ala).. Stewart's Alabama Reports [*A publication*]   (DLA)
Stew Ans .... Stewart's Answers to Dirleton's Doubts [*2 eds.*] [*1715, 1762*] [*Scotland*] [*A publication*]   (DLA)
Stewart....... Stewart's Alabama Reports [*1827-31*] [*A publication*]   (DLA)
Stewart....... Stewart's Equity Reports [*28-45 New Jersey*] [*A publication*]   (DLA)
Stewart....... Stewart's Nova Scotia Admiralty Reports [*A publication*]   (DLA)
Stewart....... Stewart's Reports [*1-10 South Dakota*] [*A publication*]   (DLA)
Stewart (Ala) ... Stewart's Alabama Reports [*A publication*]   (DLA)
Stewart-Brown ... Stewart-Brown's Lancashire and Cheshire Cases in the Court of Star Chamber [*A publication*]   (DLA)
Stewart R ... Stewart's Alabama Reports [*A publication*]   (DLA)
Stew Dig..... Stewart's Digest of Decisions of Law and Equity [*New Jersey*] [*A publication*]   (ILCA)
Stew Eq...... Stewart's Equity Reports [*28-45 New Jersey*] [*A publication*]   (DLA)
Stew N Sc... Stewart's Nova Scotia Admiralty Reports [*A publication*]   (DLA)
Stew & P ... Stewart and Porter's Alabama Supreme Court Reports [*1831-34*] [*A publication*]   (DLA)
Stew and Porter ... Stewart and Porter's Alabama Reports [*A publication*]   (DLA)
Stew & P Rep ... Stewart and Porter's Alabama Reports [*A publication*]   (DLA)
STEWS...... Shipboard Tactical Electronic Warfare System [*Navy*]
Stewt Rep... Stewart's Alabama Reports [*A publication*]   (DLA)
Stew VA..... Stewart's Nova Scotia Vice-Admiralty Reports [*A publication*]   (DLA)
STE-X....... Simplified Test Equipment-Expandable [*Army*]   (RDA)
STEX .... Statute Expired [*IRS*]
S Texas LJ ... South Texas Law Journal [*A publication*]
S Tex LJ ..... South Texas Law Journal [*A publication*]
STeZ......... South Temperate Zone
STF .... S-Band Temperature Fahrenheit
STF .... S-Band Transmit Filter
STF .... Safety Test Facility [*Nuclear energy*]
STF .... Satellite Tracking Facility [*Air Force*]
STF .... Service Tabulating Form   (AAG)
STF .... Shield Test Facility [*Nuclear energy*]   (GFGA)
STF .... Signal Tracking Filter
STF .... Sociedad Colombiana de Transporte Ferroviario SA [*Public rail services*]   (EY)

STF	Software Test Facility [*NASA*] (MCD)
STF	Soviet Studies. A Quarterly Journal on the USSR and Eastern Europe [*A publication*]
STF	Space Track Facility
STF	Spacecraft Test Facility
STF	Special Task Force [*Army*]
STF	Special Technical Factors (MCD)
STF	Special Tube Feeding [*Medicine*]
STF	Spin Test Facility [*NASA*]
STF	Staff (AFM)
STF	Standardized Test of Fitness [*Canadian Association of Sports Sciences*]
STF	Stanford Resources Ltd. [*Toronto Stock Exchange symbol*]
St F	Starch-Free [*Pharmacy*]
STF	Starkville, MS [*Location identifier*] [*FAA*] (FAAL)
STF	Static Test Facility (KSC)
stf	Stiff [*Quality of the bottom*] [*Nautical charts*]
STF	Stirred-Tank Fermentors [*Chemical engineering*]
STF	Strange Fantasy [*A publication*]
STF	Stratiform [*Meteorology*] (FAAC)
STF	Structural Fatigue Test (MCD)
STF	Subject to Finance (ADA)
STF	Subjective Transfer Function (MCD)
STF	Summary Tape File [*Bureau of the Census*] (GFGA)
STF	Supervisory Time Frame
STF	System Test Facility
STF	Systems Technology Forum [*Fairfax, VA*] [*Telecommunications*] (TSSD)
STFAS	Support to Total Force Analysis [*TRADOC*] (MCD)
STFC	State Auto Financial Corp. [*NASDAQ symbol*] (SPSG)
STFD	Standard Federal Savings and Loan Association [*NASDAQ symbol*] (NQ)
StFdBk	Standard Federal Bank [*Associated Press abbreviation*] (APAG)
STF DDC	System Test Facility Data Display Control (SAA)
STFF	Safeguard Tactical Field Force [*Army*] (AABC)
STFG	Staffing Guides [*Army*] (AABC)
STFG	Stuffing (MSA)
STFM	Society of Teachers of Family Medicine (EA)
STFM	Stretcher Form [*Tool*] (AAG)
St Form Sp	Studies in Formative Spirituality [*A publication*]
St For Note Calif Div For	State Forest Notes. California Division of Forestry [*A publication*]
STFPA	Strahlenschutz in Forschung und Praxis [*A publication*]
STFR	Stratus Fractus [*Meteorology*] (FAAC)
STFRM	Stratiform [*Meteorology*] (FAAC)
STFSGT	Staff Sergeant [*Marine Corps*]
STFT	Stray Field Test (NVT)
St Furrow	Straight Furrow [*A publication*]
STG	Saint George Island [*Alaska*] [*Airport symbol*] (OAG)
STG	Satellite Terminal Guidance
Stg	Sea-Tangle [*Nautical charts*]
STG	Seating [*Technical drawings*]
STG	Sedalia, Marshall, Boonville Stage Line, Inc. [*Des Moines, IA*] [*FAA designator*] (FAAC)
STG	SONAR Technician, Ground [*Navy rating*] (DNAB)
STG	Souther Gold Resources [*Vancouver Stock Exchange symbol*]
STG	Space Task Group [*Later, Manned Spacecraft Center*] [*NASA*]
STG	Space Telescope Guidance [*NASA*]
STG	Special Technology Group [*National Technical Information Service*] (MCD)
STG	Special Training Group [*Military*]
STG	Split Thickness Graft [*Medicine*]
STG	Staging (AABC)
STG	Standing [*Numismatics*]
STG	Starting (MSA)
STG	State Government [*A publication*]
STG	Steego Corp. [*Formerly, Sterling Precision Corp.*] [*NYSE symbol*] (SPSG)
STG	Steering Task Group
STG	Sterling
STG	Stomatogastric Ganglion [*Neuroanatomy*]
STG	Storage
STG	Storage Triacylglycerol [*Biochemistry*]
STG	Strathgordon [*Tasmania*] [*Seismograph station code, US Geological Survey*] (SEIS)
STG	Strong (FAAC)
StG	Studium Generale [*Heidelberg*] [*A publication*]
STG	Study Group [*NATO*]
STG	Sturmgewehr [*Storm Rifle*] [*German military - World War II*]
STG	Sydney Tourist Guide [*A publication*] (APTA)
STGA	Saratoga Standardbreds, Inc. [*North Salem, NY*] [*NASDAQ symbol*] (NQ)
STGAA	Shade Tobacco Growers Agricultural Association (EA)
StGAK	Studien zur Germanistik, Anglistik und Komparatistik [*A publication*]
STGAR	Staging Area [*Military*]
STGB	Staging Base [*Military*]
StGB	Strafgesetzbuch [*Penal Code*] [*German*]
STGC	Secure Task Group, Common (MCD)
STGE	Storage
STGEA	Studium Generale [*A publication*]
STGEN	Steam Generator
St Ger D & S	St. German's Doctor and Student [*A publication*] (DLA)
STGG	Staging (AAG)
STGH	Stang Hydronics [*NASDAQ symbol*] (NQ)
STGHT	Straight
StGKA	Studien zur Geschichte und Kultur des Altertums [*A publication*]
St Gloc	Statute of Gloucester [*First statute to give costs in actions*] [*A publication*] (DLA)
STGM	Status Game Corp. [*NASDAQ symbol*] (NQ)
STGO	Star-Glo Industries [*NASDAQ symbol*] (NQ)
STGP	Subcontract Task Group Procurement
STGR	Steiger Tractor, Inc. [*NASDAQ symbol*] (NQ)
STGR	Stringer (AAG)
STGS	Strings Ltd. [*NASDAQ symbol*] (NQ)
STGSA	SONAR Technician, Ground, Seaman Apprentice [*Navy rating*] (DNAB)
STGSN	SONAR Technician, Ground, Seaman [*Navy rating*] (DNAB)
STG/STF	Special Task Group/Special Task Force [*Army*] (MCD)
STGT	Secondary Target [*Military*]
StGThK	Studien zur Geschichte der Theologie und der Kirche [*A publication*]
S Th	Scholar in Theology [*British*]
STH	Seton Hall University, South Orange, NJ [*OCLC symbol*] (OCLC)
STH	Somatotrophic [*Growth*] Hormone [*Also, GH, SH*] [*Endocrinology*]
STH	South
STH	Stanhome, Inc. [*NYSE symbol*] (SPSG)
STH	Stoney Hill [*Jamaica*] [*Seismograph station code, US Geological Survey*] (SEIS)
STH	Stray Horse Resources, Inc. [*Vancouver Stock Exchange symbol*]
STH	Student in Theology [*British*]
STh	Subthalamus [*Anatomy*]
STH	Subtotal Hysterectomy [*Medicine*]
STH	Toronto School of Theology Library, University of Toronto [*UTLAS symbol*]
St & H Abor	Storer and Heard on Criminal Abortion [*A publication*] (DLA)
Sth Afr Rep	South African Republic High Court Reports [*A publication*] (DLA)
SThB	Sacrae Theologiae Baccalaureus [*Bachelor of Sacred Theology*]
SthCor	Smith Corona Corp. [*Associated Press abbreviation*] (APAG)
SThD	Sacrae Theologiae Doctor [*Doctor of Sacred Theology*]
STHEA	Steam and Heating Engineer [*A publication*]
StHefte	Statistische Hefte [*A publication*]
Sthen	Sthenoboea [*of Euripides*] [*Classical studies*] (OCD)
STHEST	Southeast
STHESTN	Southeastern
STHF	Stanley Interiors Corp. [*Stanleytown, VA*] [*NASDAQ symbol*] (NQ)
S ThL	Sacrae Theologiae Lecentiatus [*Licentiate in Sacred Theology*]
STHLY	Southerly [*A publication*]
STHMPN	Southampton [*England*]
STHN	Southern
Sthn Afr Fam Pract	Southern African Family Practice [*A publication*]
Sthn Afr Text	Southern Africa Textiles [*A publication*]
Sthn Birds	Southern Birds [*A publication*]
STHP	Shih-Ta Hsueh-Pao [*Bulletin of Taiwan Normal University*] [*A publication*]
STHPD	Shih-Ta Hsueh-Pao [*Bulletin of Taiwan Normal University*] [*A publication*]
StHR	Stress Hypertensive Rats
STHRD	Solar Thermal Report [*A publication*]
STHS	Scottish Thoracic Society
St Hum	Studies in the Humanities [*A publication*]
STHV	Science, Technology, and Human Values [*A publication*]
STHWST	Southwest
STHWSTN	Southwestern
STI	Mountain Home, ID [*Location identifier*] [*FAA*] (FAAL)
STI	St. Thomas Institute [*Research center*] (RCD)
STI	Santiago [*Dominican Republic*] [*Airport symbol*] (OAG)
STI	Saskatoon Technical Institute [*UTLAS symbol*]
STI	Saxton Industries [*Vancouver Stock Exchange symbol*]
STI	Scientific and Technical Information [*System*] [*Canada*]
STI	Scientific and Technical Information [*Facility*] [*NASA*]
S & TI	Scientific and Technical Intelligence [*Military*] (RDA)
STI	Screw Thread Insert
STI	Self-Test Index [*Electronics*]
STI	Serum Trypsin Inhibitor [*Serology*]
STI	Server Technology, Inc. [*Information service or system*] (IID)
STI	Service Tools Institute [*Later, HTI*] (EA)
STI	Sexually-Transmitted Infection [*Medicine*] (DI)
STI	Short-Term Integration (CAAL)
STI	Silicon Target Intensifier
STI	Single Tooth Indexer
STI	Small Towns Institute (EA)
STI	Software Tool Information Database [*Air Force Systems Command*] [*Information service or system*] (CRD)

STI............. Soybean Trypsin Inhibition [*Biochemistry*]
STI............. Space Technology, Inc.   (MCD)
STI............. Special Test Instructions   (SAA)
STI............. Specifications Technology, Inc.
STI............. Speech Transmission Index
STI............. Standard Technical Institute   (SSD)
STI............. Star Valley [*Idaho*] [*Seismograph station code, US Geological Survey*]   (SEIS)
STI............. State Technical Institute
STI............. Steel Tank Institute   (EA)
STI............. Steel Tube Institute
STI............. Stem Tolerance Index [*Botany*]
STI............. Stilbite [*A zeolite*]
Sti.............. Stinson [*Record label*]
STI............. Store Indicators   (SAA)
StI .... Studies: An Irish Quarterly Review of Letters, Philosophy, and Science [*A publication*]
STI............. SunTrust Banks, Inc. [*NYSE symbol*]   (SPSG)
STI............. Surface Targets of Interest   (MCD)
STI............. Survive Tomorrow, Inc. [*Commercial firm*]   (EA)
STI............. Systolic Time Interval [*Cardiology*]
STIA .... Scientific, Technological, and International Affairs Directorate [*National Science Foundation*]
STIAP........ Standard Instrument Approach [*RADAR*] [*Aviation*]
STIB .... Stimulus Train-Induced Bursting [*Neuroscience*]
STIC .... Scientific and Technical Intelligence Center [*DoD*]
STIC .... Solid-State Transducer Intercompartmental Catheter [*Instrumentation*]
STIC .... Space Technical Information Control   (MCD)
STIC .... Space Toy Information Center   (EA)
STICAP..... Stiff Circuit Analysis Program [*Data processing*]
STICEC..... Special Travel Industry Council on Energy Conservation
ST/ICERD ... Suntory Toyota International Centre for Economics and Related Disciplines [*London School of Economics and Political Science*] [*British*]   (CB)
Stich.......... Stichus [*of Plautus*] [*Classical studies*]   (OCD)
Sticht Bosbouwproefsta "Dorschkamp" Ber ... Stichting Bosbouwproefstation "De Dorschkamp." Berichten [*A publication*]
Sticht Bosbouwproefsta "Dorschkamp" Korte Meded ... Stichting Bosbouwproefstation "De Dorschkamp." Korte Mededelingen [*A publication*]
Sticht Bosbouwproefsta "Dorschkamp" Uitv Versl ... Stichting Bosbouwproefstation "De Dorschkamp." Uitvoerige Verslagen [*A publication*]
Sticht Bosbouwproefstn "De Dorschkamp" Korte Meded ... Stichting Bosbouwproefstation "De Dorschkamp." Korte Mededeling [*A publication*]
Sticht Coord Cult Onderz Broodgraan Jaarb ... Stichting voor Coordinate van Cultuur en Onderzoek van Broodgraan Jaarboekje [*A publication*]
Sticht Energieonderz Cent Ned Rep ... Stichting Energieonderzoek Centrum Nederland. Report [*A publication*]
Sticht Fundam Onderz Mater Jaarb ... Stichting voor Fundamenteel Onderzoek der Materie. Jaarboek [*A publication*]
Sticht Inst Kernphys Onderz Jaarb ... Stichting Instituut voor Kernphysisch Onderzoek. Jaarboek [*A publication*]
Sticht Inst Pluimveeonderz Het Spelderholt Jaarversl ... Stichting Instituut voor Pluimveeonderzoek "Het Spelderholt" Jaarverslag [*A publication*]
Sticht Inst Pluimveeonderz Spelderholt Jaarversl ... Stichting Instituut voor Pluimveeonderzoek "Het Spelderholt" Jaarverslag [*A publication*]
STICTION ... Static Friction
STID.......... Scientific and Technical Information Dissemination [*NASA*]
STID.......... Scientific and Technical Information Division [*NASA*]   (IEEE)
STID.......... Ship's Test and Inspection Department [*Navy*]   (DNAB)
STIDAS..... Speech Transmission Index Device [*Using*] Artificial Signals
STIF.......... Scientific and Technical Information Facility [*NASA*]
STIF.......... Short-Term Irradiation Facility [*Nuclear energy*]   (NRCH)
STIF.......... Spectral Transmission Interference Filter
STIF.......... Stiffener [*Civil engineering*]
STIFC........ Space Track Interim Fire Control
Stifel.......... Stifel Financial Corp. [*Associated Press abbreviation*]   (APAG)
STIFS .... Short-Term Integrated Forecasting System [*Department of Energy*]   (GFGA)
STIG .... Steam-Injected Gas Turbine
STII .... Science and Technology Information Institute [*Information service or system*]   (IID)
STII .... Stanford Telecommunications, Inc. [*NASDAQ symbol*]   (NQ)
St I I .... Studien zur Indologie und Iranistik [*A publication*]
Stiinta Sol .. Stiinta Solului [*A publication*]
STIL .... Short-Term Inhalation Limits [*of air pollutants*]
STIL .... Software Test and Integration Laboratory [*NASA*]   (NASA)
STIL .... Statistical Interpretive Language [*Data processing*]   (MDG)
Stil............. Stillingfleet's English Ecclesiastical Cases [*1702-04*] [*A publication*]   (DLA)
StIL........... Studi. Istituto Linguistico [*A publication*]
Stiles .... Stiles' Reports [*22-29 Iowa*] [*A publication*]   (DLA)
Stiles (IA) .. Stiles' Reports [*22-29 Iowa*] [*A publication*]   (DLA)
STILLAT .. Stillatim [*By Drops or In Small Quantities*] [*Pharmacy*]
STILLB ..... Stillborn [*Medicine*]

Still Ecc Law ... Stillingfleet's Discourse on Ecclesiastical Law [*A publication*]   (DLA)
Still Eccl Cas ... Stillingfleet's English Ecclesiastical Cases [*A publication*]   (DLA)
STILO .... Scientific and Technical Intelligence Liaison Officer   (MCD)
STILS........ Stinger Launch Simulator   (MCD)
STIM .... Scanning Transmission Ion Microscopy
STIM .... Sensitivity Training Impact Model
STIM .... Stimulant   (DSUE)
STIM .... Stimulating   (ROG)
stim .... Stimulus
STIM .... Subsystem: Short-Term Integrating Model [*Department of Energy*]   (GFGA)
S Times ...... Sunday Times [*A publication*]
Stim Gloss ... Stimson's Law Glossary [*A publication*]   (DLA)
Stim Law Gloss ... Stimson's Law Glossary [*A publication*]   (DLA)
Stim L Gl ... Stimson's Law Glossary [*A publication*]   (DLA)
Stimm Zeit ... Stimmen der Zeit [*A publication*]
STIMS....... Scientific and Technical Information Modular System [*NASA*]   (MCD)
Stimson .... Stimson's Law Glossary [*A publication*]   (DLA)
STIMU...... Stimutech, Inc. Uts [*NASDAQ symbol*]   (NQ)
Stimul Newsl ... Stimulation Newsletter [*A publication*]
STINA ...... Stanki i Instrument [*A publication*]
STINA ...... Steel Tube Institute of North America   (EA)
STINCOM ... Scientific and Technical Information and Communication   (SAA)
Stiness....... Stiness' Reports [*20-34 Rhode Island*] [*A publication*]   (DLA)
STINFO ..... Scientific and Technical Information Office [*Army*]
STING....... Swift Target Identification Notification Grid   (MCD)
STINGER ... SEABEE Tactically Installed, Navy Generated, Engineer Resources [*System*] [*Navy*]   (NVT)
STINGS .... Stellar Inertial Guidance System [*Air Force*]
St Inst .... Stair's Institutes [*5th ed.*] [*1832*] [*A publication*]   (ILCA)
STIO......... Scientific and Technical Information Office [*NASA*]
STIP .... Scientific and Technical Information Program   (MCD)
STIP .... Skill Training Improvement Program [*Department of Labor*]
STIP .... Solar Technical Information Program [*Solar Energy Research Institute*] [*Information service or system*]   (IID)
STIP .... Stipend [*or Stipendiary*]
STIP .... Stipulation   (DAS)
STIP .... Study of Travelling Interplanetary Phenomena [*Meteorology*]
STIPE....... Stipendiary Magistrate [*British*]   (DSUE)
STIPIS ...... Scientific, Technical, Intelligence, and Program Information System [*HEW*]
STIR .... Scientific and Technical Intelligence Register   (AFM)
STIR .... Separate Track and Illumination RADAR [*Military*]   (CAAL)
STIR .... Shield Test and Irradiation Reactor [*Nuclear energy*]
STIR .... Signal Track and Illuminating RADAR [*Canadian Navy*]
STIR .... SNAP [*Systems for Nuclear Auxiliary Power*] Shield Test Irradiation Reactor
StIR........... Stanford Italian Review [*A publication*]
STIR .... Stirrup   (WGA)
STIR .... Surplus to Immediate Requirements   (ADA)
STIRD .... SAIL [*Shuttle Avionics Integration Laboratory*] Test Implementation Requirements Document [*NASA*]   (NASA)
Stirling E N ... Stirling Engine Newsletter [*A publication*]
STIRS........ Self-Training Interpretive Retrieval System
STIS.......... Science and Technology Information System [*National Science Foundation*]
STIS.......... Scientific & Technical Information Services, Inc. [*Information service or system*]   (IID)
STIS.......... Silicon Target Image Sensor
STIS.......... Specialized Textile Information Service
STIS.......... Sumika Technical Information Service, Inc. [*Information service or system*]   (IID)
Sti Solului .. Stiinta Solului [*A publication*]
STIT .... Scientific and Technical Information Team [*Army*]   (GFGA)
STIT .... Signal Technical Intelligence Team [*Army*]   (AABC)
STIT .... Simulated Time in Turn   (SAA)
STIT .... Sweet's Technical Information Test [*Vocational guidance test*]
STIT-CONUS ... Scientific and Technical Information Team, Continental United States [*Army*]   (AABC)
STIT-EUR ... Scientific and Technical Information Team, Europe [*Army*]   (AABC)
STIT-FE.... Scientific and Technical Information Team, Far East [*Army*]   (AABC)
STIV .... Silicon Target Intensifier Vidicon
STIZ .... Scientific Technologies, Inc. [*NASDAQ symbol*]   (NQ)
StiZ .... Stimmen der Zeit [*A publication*]   (BJA)
STIZ .... Submarine Transit Identification Zones   (NVT)
STJ .... St. John's [*Newfoundland*] [*Seismograph station code, US Geological Survey*]   (SEIS)
STJ .... St. John's [*Newfoundland*] [*Geomagnetic observatory code*]
STJ .... Saint Joseph College, West Hartford, CT [*OCLC symbol*]   (OCLC)
STJ .... St. Joseph, MO [*Location identifier*] [*FAA*]   (FAAL)
StJ............. St. Joseph Railway
STJ .... Series Tee Junction
STJ .... Severn Tunnel Junction [*British depot code*]

STJ .... Special Trial Judge [*US Tax Court*]
STJ .... Steel Today and Tomorrow [*A publication*]
STJ .... Subtropical Jet Stream   (ADA)
STJA(NC) ... St. John Ambulance (Nursing Cadets) [*British*]
StJb............ Stifter-Jahrbuch [*A publication*]
STJCA....... Strojnicky Casopis [*A publication*]
St J LR ...... St. John's Law Review [*A publication*]
STJM .... St. Jude Medical, Inc. [*NASDAQ symbol*]   (NQ)
St J MO PUC ... St. Joseph, Missouri, Public Utilities Commission Reports [*A publication*]   (DLA)
STJO .... St. Joseph Bancorporation, Inc. [*South Bend, IN*] [*NASDAQ symbol*]   (NQ)
StJoe .... St. Joe Paper Co. [*Associated Press abbreviation*]   (APAG)
St John's L Rev ... St. John's Law Review [*A publication*]
StJoLP....... St. Joseph Light & Power Co. [*Associated Press abbreviation*]   (APAG)
STJU .... St. John's University [*Minnesota; New York*]
STJW .... Stretcher Jaws [*Tool*]   (AAG)
stk .... Scotland [*MARC country of publication code*] [*Library of Congress*]   (LCCP)
STK........... Single Tone Keying
STK........... Situation Track Display
STK........... Soiuz Trudovogo Krest'ianstva [*Union of Working Peasantry*] [*Russian*]
STK........... Stack   (MSA)
STK........... Stakes Race [*Horse racing*]
STK........... Standard Test Key [*Data processing*]
STK........... Stephens Creek [*Australia*] [*Seismograph station code, US Geological Survey*]   (SEIS)
STK........... Sterling, CO [*Location identifier*] [*FAA*]   (FAAL)
stk .... Sticky [*Quality of the bottom*] [*Nautical charts*]
STK........... Stock   (AAG)
STK........... Storage Technology Corp. [*NYSE symbol*]   (SPSG)
STK........... Strake [*Mining engineering*]
STK........... Streptokinase [*An enzyme*]   (AAMN)
STK........... Sturmkanone [*Self-propelled assault gun*] [*German military - World War II*]
STK........... Svensk Teologisk Kvartalskrift [*A publication*]
STKAB ...... Standarty i Kachestvo [*A publication*]
STKC .... [*The*] Stanwick Corp. [*NASDAQ symbol*]   (NQ)
STKD........ Stockade   (AABC)
STK EX ..... Stock Exchange
STKF .... Stock Fund [*Military*]
STKFA ...... Stock Fund Accounting [*Military*]
STKFS...... Stock Fund Statement [*Military*]
STKG........ Sturzkampfgeschwader [*Dive-bomber wing*] [*German military - World War II*]
STKL .... Stake Technology Ltd. [*Oakville, ON*] [*NASDAQ symbol*]   (NQ)
STKM....... Storm King Mines [*NASDAQ symbol*]   (NQ)
STKMBC .. Mammalogical Informations [*A publication*]
STKMBC .. Saugetierkundliche Mitteilungen [*A publication*]
STKN........ Stockton Savings & Loan Association [*Stockton, CA*] [*NASDAQ symbol*]   (NQ)
STK NO..... Stock Number
St u Komm V ... Staats und Kommunalverwaltung [*A publication*]
STKR........ Stocker & Yale, Inc. [*NASDAQ symbol*]   (NQ)
STKR........ Stockroom   (AABC)
STKR........ Stoker [*Navy*] [*British*]
STKRA ..... Steklo i Keramika [*A publication*]
STKS........ Stakes   (ROG)
STKv........ Svensk Teologisk Kvartalskrift [*A publication*]
StkVC .... Stokely-Van Camp, Inc. [*Associated Press abbreviation*]   (APAG)
STKY .... Stokely USA, Inc. [*Oconomowoc, WI*] [*NASDAQ symbol*]   (NQ)
STL........... Bibliotheque Municipale de Saint-Laurent [*UTLAS symbol*]
STL........... Sacrae Theologiae Lector [*Reader in Sacred Theology*] [*Latin*]
STL........... Sacrae Theologiae Licentiatus [*Licentiate in Sacred Theology*] [*Latin*]
STL........... Safe Tow Length
STL........... St. Louis [*Missouri*] [*Airport symbol*]
STL........... Santa Lucia [*Chile*] [*Seismograph station code, US Geological Survey*] [*Closed*]   (SEIS)
STL........... Satellite
STL........... Schottky Transistor Logic   (IEEE)
STL........... Seatrain Lines, Inc. [*AAR code*]
STL........... Self-Test Logic [*Navy Navigation Satellite System*]   (DNAB)
STL........... Sequential Table Lookup
STL........... Short Term Leaflet. Ministry of Agriculture, Fisheries, and Food [*A publication*]
STL........... Short-Term Loan   (ADA)
STL........... Simulated Tape Load
STL........... Site Team Leader [*Nuclear energy*]   (NRCH)
STL........... Southern Traffic League
STL........... Southern Transportation League   (EA)
STL........... Space Technology Laboratories [*of TRW Group*]
STL........... Special Tool List
STL........... Stall   (WGA)
STL........... Standard Telegraph Level [*Telecommunications*]   (TEL)
STL........... Startling Stories [*A publication*]

STL........... Status and Telling   (SAA)
STL........... Steel   (KSC)
STL........... Step-Through Latencies
STL........... Stereo Lithography
STL........... Sterling Bancorp [*NYSE symbol*]   (SPSG)
STL........... Stile   (WGA)
STL........... Stock, Time Limitation   (DNAB)
STL........... Stockage List [*Military*]
STL........... STOL Air Commuter [*San Rafael, CA*] [*FAA designator*]   (FAAC)
STL........... Storage Time Limit   (DNAB)
St L .... Student Lawyer [*A publication*]
StL .... Studies on the Left [*A publication*]
STL........... Studies in Logic and the Foundations of Mathematics [*Elsevier Book Series*] [*A publication*]
STL........... Studio-Transmitter Link
STL........... Sunday Times (London) [*A publication*]
STL........... Supersonic Transition Locus [*Galactic winds*]
STL........... Support Table Load
STL........... Suppressor T Lymphocyte [*Immunology*]
STL........... Swelling, Tenderness, Limitation of Movement [*Medicine*]
STL........... Synchronous Transistor Logic   (MDG)
STL........... System Test Loop   (IEEE)
STL........... Systems Techniques Laboratory [*Stanford University*]   (MCD)
STLA .... Strip Transmission Line Adapter [*or Assembly*]
StLAR....... St. Lawrence & Atlantic Railway
St at Large ... Statutes at Large [*A publication*]   (DLA)
St Law....... Loughborough's Digest of Statute Law [*Kentucky*] [*A publication*]   (DLA)
STLB & M ... St. Louis, Brownsville & Mexico [*Railway*]
STLC .... Sequence Thin-Layer Chromatography
STLC .... Short-Term Lethal Concentration [*of air pollutants*]
STLC .... Soluble Threshold Limit Concentration [*Environmental chemistry*]
STLD........ Support Teacher Learning Difficulties
STLDD...... Software Top Level Design Document [*Army*]
STLF......... Southern Troops and Landing Force
STLG .... Sterling   (WGA)
STLI .... Statue of Liberty National Monument
STLI .... Stockage List Item [*Military*]
St Lim .... Statute of Limitations [*A publication*]   (DLA)
StLIM & S ... St. Louis, Iron Mountain & Southern Railway
StLing .... Studies in Linguistics [*A publication*]
S T L J .... South Texas Law Journal [*A publication*]
STLJD...... South Texas Law Journal [*A publication*]
St L J Th.... St. Luke's Journal of Theology [*A publication*]
STLL .... Submarine Tender Load List
STLM .... Safeguard Tactical Logistics Management
St L M....... Studien zur Literatur der Moderne [*A publication*]
St Lngst....... Statistical Methods in Linguistics [*A publication*]
STLO........ St. Louis Steel Casting [*NASDAQ symbol*]   (NQ)
STLO........ Scientific and Technical Liaison Office [*AFSC*]
St & Loc Taxes (BNA) ... State and Local Taxes (Bureau of National Affairs) [*A publication*]   (DLA)
St & Loc Tax Serv (P-H) ... State and Local Tax Service (Prentice-Hall, Inc.) [*A publication*]   (DLA)
StL & OR.... St. Louis & Ohio River Railroad
STLOS ..... Star Line-of-Sight   (KSC)
St Lou Com ... St. Louis Commerce [*United States*] [*A publication*]
St Louis B .. St. Louis Business Journal [*United States*] [*A publication*]
St Louis Commer ... St. Louis Commerce [*A publication*]
St Louis L Rev ... St. Louis Law Review [*A publication*]   (DLA)
St Louis Metropol Med ... St. Louis Metropolitan Medicine [*A publication*]
St Louis Mus Bul ... St. Louis City Art Museum. Bulletin [*A publication*]
St Louis U L J ... St. Louis University. Law Journal [*A publication*]
St Louis Univ B ... St. Louis University. Bulletin [*A publication*]
St Louis Univ Public Law Forum ... St. Louis University. Public Law Forum [*A publication*]
St Louis U Res J ... St. Louis University. Research Journal [*Baguio City*] [*A publication*]
St Lou Mgr ... St. Louis Manager [*United States*] [*A publication*]
St Lou Pos ... St. Louis Post-Dispatch [*United States*] [*A publication*]
St Lou ULJ ... St. Louis University. Law Journal [*A publication*]
STL-QPSR ... Speech Transmission Laboratory. Royal Institute of Technology. Stockholm. Quarterly Progress and Status Reports [*A publication*]
STLR .... Semitrailer
STLS......... Ship's Transducer Location System   (DNAB)
STLS......... South Texas Library System [*Library network*]
STLS......... Southern Tier Library System [*Library network*]
STLS......... Stinger Training Launch Simulator   (MCD)
STL-SF...... St. Louis-San Francisco Railway Co.
STL-SF & T ... St. Louis, San Francisco & Texas Railway Co.
STL STL and WD ... Steel or Steel and Wood [*Freight*]
StL & SW .. St. Louis & South Western Railway
STLSW of T ... St. Louis Southwestern Railway Co. of Texas
STLT .... Satellite   (FAAC)
STLT .... Small Transportable Link Terminal
STLT .... Stellite [*Metallurgy*]
STLT .... Stolt Tankers & Terminals (Holdings) SA [*NASDAQ symbol*]   (NQ)

STLT	Studio-Transmitter Link-Television
STLTA	Steel Times [*A publication*]
STLU	St. Louis University [*Missouri*]
St LU Intra L Rev ...	St. Louis University. Intramural Law Review [*A publication*] (DLA)
St Luke J ...	St. Luke's Journal of Theology [*A publication*]
St Luke's Hosp Gaz ...	St. Luke's Hospital Gazette [*A publication*]
St LU LJ ...	St. Louis University. Law Journal [*A publication*]
STLV	Simian T-Cell Lymphotropic Virus
STL WD	Steel or Wood [*Freight*]
STL WI....	Steel or Wire [*Freight*]
STM	Groupement International d'Editeurs Scientifiques, Techniques, et Medicaux [*International Group of Scientific, Technical, and Medical Publishers*] (EAIO)
STM	International Group of Scientific, Technical, and Medical Publishers (EAIO)
STM	Master of Arts in Theology
STM	Master of the Science of Theology
STM	Sacrae Theologiae Magister [*Master of Sacred Theology*]
STM	Safety Test Missile (MCD)
STM	St. Martin Hospitals Group [*British*]
STM	Santarem [*Brazil*] [*Airport symbol*] (OAG)
STM	Satellite Technology Management, Inc. [*Torrance, CA*] [*Telecommunications*] (TSSD)
STM	Save the Manatee Club (EA)
STM	Scanning Tunneling Microscope
STM	Scientific, Technical, and Medical
STM	Screened through Matching [*Parapsychology*]
STM	Section Technical Manual [*Jet Propulsion Laboratory, NASA*]
STM	Send Test Message (AAG)
STM	Service Technique Militaire [*Switzerland*]
STM	Service Test Model (NG)
STM	Shielded Tunable Magnetron
STM	Short-Term Memory
STM	Signal Termination Module [*NASA*] (NASA)
STM	Significant Technical Milestone (SDI)
STM	Slate Mountain [*Nevada*] [*Seismograph station code, US Geological Survey*] [*Closed*] (SEIS)
STM	Society for Traditional Music (EA)
STM	Sonet Transmission Manager [*Adaptive Corp.*]
STM	Southam, Inc. [*Toronto Stock Exchange symbol*] [*Vancouver Stock Exchange symbol*]
STM	Special Test Missile
STM	Specialized Trade Mission [*Department of Commerce*]
STM	Specification Test Material (MCD)
STM	Spin Tuned Magnetron
STM	Spore Tip Mucilage [*Mycology*]
STM	Standard Test Methods Bulletins [*A publication*] (EAAP)
STM	Standard Type Material (MCD)
STM	Standards Tool Master (MCD)
STM	State Transition Matrix
STM	Static Test Model (MCD)
STM	Statistical Multiplexing [*Telecommunications*]
STM	Statute Mile
STM	Steam
STM	Steward's Mate [*Navy rating*]
STM	Store Multiple [*Computer command*] (PCM)
STM	Storm (FAAC)
STM	Strategic Mortgage Investments, Inc. [*NYSE symbol*] (SPSG)
STM	Stream [*Board on Geographic Names*]
STM	Streptomycin [*An antibiotic*] (AAMN)
STM	Structural Test Model
StM	Studien zur Musikwissenschaft [*A publication*]
STM	Subject to Mortgage (ADA)
STM	Supersonic Tactical Missile (MCD)
STM	Supplementary Technical Manual [*Military*]
STM	Support Test Manager (NASA)
STM	Surface-to-Target-to-Missile
STM	Synthetic Timing Mode
STM	System Training Mission (AFM)
STMA	Space-Time Moving Average [*Statistics*]
STMA	Sports Turf Managers Association [*Defunct*] (EA)
STMA	Statistical Theory and Method Abstracts [*A publication*]
STMA	Stuffed Toy Manufacturers Association
STMAF	Stampede International Resources Cl A [*NASDAQ symbol*] (NQ)
St Marianna Med J ...	St. Marianna Medical Journal [*Japan*] [*A publication*]
St Mark	St. Mark's Church Case [*Philadelphia, PA*] [*A publication*] (DLA)
St Mark R ...	St. Mark's Review [*A publication*]
St Mark Rev ...	St. Mark's Review [*A publication*] (APTA)
St Marks R ...	St. Mark's Review [*A publication*] (APTA)
St Marks Rev ...	St. Mark's Review [*A publication*] (APTA)
St Marlb	Statute of Marlbridge [*A publication*] (DLA)
St Mary's L J ...	St. Mary's Law Journal [*A publication*]
StMBC.......	Studien und Mitteilungen aus dem Benediktiner- und dem Cistercienser-Orden [*A publication*]
STMC	Standard Metals Corp. [*NASDAQ symbol*] (NQ)
STMCGMW ...	Subcommission for Tectonic Maps of the Commission for the Geological Map of the World (EAIO)
STME	Stellar Television Monitor Equipment

St Mert......	Statute of Merton [*A publication*] (DLA)
STMEV	Storm Evasion [*Navy*] (NVT)
S T Mf.......	Svensk Tidskrift foer Musikforskning [*A publication*]
STMFR	Steamfitter (WGA)
STMG	Steaming (MSA)
STMGA.....	Salmon and Trout Magazine [*A publication*]
STMGA3....	Salmon and Trout Magazine [*A publication*]
StMGB	Studien und Mitteilungen zur Geschichte des Benediktiner-Ordens [*A publication*]
STMGR.....	Station Manager [*Aviation*] (FAAC)
St Mi	Statute Mile [*Nautical charts*]
STMIS	System Test Manufacturing Information System (IEEE)
STML	Separate Transporter and Mobile Launcher
STML	Sindicato de Trabajadores Mineros de Llallagua
STML	Stimulate (MSA)
STMLA	Stomatologia [*Bucharest*] [*A publication*]
St M LJ	St. Mary's Law Journal [*A publication*]
St Mot Carr Guide (CCH) ...	State Motor Carrier Guide (Commerce Clearing House) [*A publication*] (DLA)
StMotr	Standard Motor Products, Inc. [*Associated Press abbreviation*] (APAG)
STMP	Ship Test Management Plan [*Navy*] (CAAL)
STMP	System Training Management Plan (MCD)
STMR	Steamer
S/T-MR.....	Surplus Termination Material Requisition (MCD)
STMS	St. Thomas More Society (EA)
STMS	Scientific and Technical Modular System
STMS	Scottish Tramway Museum Society (DCTA)
STMS	Spring Trap Makers' Society [*A union*] [*British*]
STMS	State Tax Management System [*Price Waterhouse & Co.*] (PCM)
St MS........	Steinbeck Monograph Series [*A publication*]
STMT	Statement (AFM)
STMTA	Stomatologica [*Genoa*] [*A publication*]
STMT of SVC ...	Statement of Service [*Military*]
STMU	Special Test and Maintenance Unit
STMW	Subtropical Mode Water [*Oceanography*]
STMX	SyStemix, Inc. [*NASDAQ symbol*] (SPSG)
STMYA	Stomatologiya [*A publication*]
STN	SAC [*Strategic Air Command*] Telephone Net
St N............	St. Nicholas [*A publication*]
STN	Satellite Television Network [*Telecommunications*] [*Defunct*] (TSSD)
STN	Satellite Theater Network [*Falls Church, VA*] (TSSD)
STN	Satellite Tracking Network (MCD)
STN	Saturn Airways, Inc. (MCD)
STN	Scientific and Technical Information Network
STN	Seatoun [*New Zealand*] [*Seismograph station code, US Geological Survey*] [*Closed*] (SEIS)
STN	Software Trouble Note [*NASA*] (NASA)
STN	Solar Telescope Network
STN	Solitary Tract Nucleus [*Also, NST*] [*Anatomy*]
STN	Special Traffic Notice [*British*] (DCTA)
STN	Specification Transmittal Notice (MCD)
STN	Staff Papers [*A publication*]
STN	Stain [*Deltiology*]
STN	Stainless
STN	Stansted [*England*] [*Airport symbol*] (OAG)
STN	Statement of Technology Needs [*Air Force*]
STN	Station
STN	Stevens [*J. P.*] & Co., Inc. [*NYSE symbol*] (SPSG)
STN	Stone [*Unit of weight*] (AAG)
STN	Subthalamic Nucleus [*Neurobiology*]
STN	Switched Telecommunications Network
STNA........	Sons of Temperance of North America (EA)
STNA........	Stanadyne, Inc. [*NASDAQ symbol*] (NQ)
STNAG.....	Standardization Agreement [*NATO*]
Stn Biol Mar Grande Riviere Que Rapp Annu ...	Station de Biologie Marine. Grande Riviere, Quebec. Rapport Annuel [*A publication*]
Stn Bull Agric Exp Stn Univ Minn ...	Station Bulletin. Minnesota Agricultural Experiment Station [*A publication*]
Stn Bull Dep Agri Econ Agric Exp Stn Purdue Univ ...	Station Bulletin. Department of Agricultural Economics. Agricultural Experiment Station. Purdue University [*A publication*]
Stn Bull New Hamps Agric Exp Stn ...	Station Bulletin. Agricultural Experiment Station. University of New Hampshire [*A publication*]
Stn Bull Ore Agric Exp Stn ...	Station Bulletin. Oregon Agricultural Experiment Station [*A publication*]
Stn Bull Univ Minn Agric Exp Stn ...	Station Bulletin. Univerity of Minnesota. Agricultural Experiment Station [*A publication*]
STnC..........	Skeletal Troponin C [*Biochemistry*]
Stn Chim Agrar Sper Torino Annu ...	Stazione Chimico-Agraria Sperimentale di Torino. Annuario [*A publication*]
Stn Circ Ore Agric Exp Stn ...	Station Circular. Oregon Agricultural Experiment Station [*A publication*]
STND	Stained (WGA)
STNEA........	Sterne [*A publication*]
StNeerla.....	Statistica Neerlandica [*A publication*]
StneWb.......	Stone & Webster, Inc. [*Associated Press abbreviation*] (APAG)

StNF .... Studier i Nordisk Filologi [*A publication*]
Stn Fed Essais Agric (Lausanne) Publ ... Stations Federales d'Essais Agricoles (Lausanne). Publication [*A publication*]
STNG .... Sustaining
STNI .... Stendig Industries, Inc. [*Fairfield, NJ*] [*NASDAQ symbol*] (NQ)
STNI .... Subtotal Nodal Irradiation [*Oncology*]
Stn L .... Stanford Law Review [*A publication*]
STNLB ...... Stimulation Newsletter [*A publication*]
STNLS ...... Stainless (MSA)
STNR .... Stationary
Stn Rep Hort Res Stn (Tatura) ... Station Report. Horticultural Research Station (Tatura) [*A publication*]
STNRY ...... Stationary (FAAC)
Stns Circ Wash Agric Exp Stns ... Stations Circular. Washington Agricultural Experiment Stations [*A publication*]
Stn Sper Agrar Ital ... Stazione Sperimentali Agrarie Italiane [*A publication*]
Stn Sper Vitic Enol (Conegliano Italy) Annu ... Stazione Sperimentale di Viticoltura e di Enologia (Conegliano, Italy). Annuario [*A publication*]
STNT .... Sprawozdania Towarzystwa Naukowego w Toruniu [*A publication*]
StNT .... Studien zum Neuen Testament [*A publication*]
Stn Tech Bull Ore Agric Exp Stn ... Station Technical Bulletin. Oregon Agricultural Experiment Station [*A publication*]
STNV .... Satellite Tobacco Necrosis Virus
STNWA ..... Sci-Tech News [*A publication*]
STNWRE .. Stoneware [*Freight*]
STNYA ...... Science and Technology [*New York*] [*A publication*]
StO .... St. Olaf [*Record label*]
STO .... Science and Technology Objectives (MCD)
STO .... Sea Transport Officer
STO .... Segment Table Origin
STO .... Self-Test Output [*Automotive engineering*]
STO .... Service du Travail Obligatoire [*French labor force*] [*World War II*]
STO .... Ship Test Organization (DNAB)
STO .... Short Takeoff (MCD)
STO .... Short-Term Objective
STO .... Slater-Type Orbital [*Atomic structure*]
STO .... Small-Time Operator [*Slang*]
STO .... Soft Target of Opportunity [*Terrorism*] (DI)
STO .... Sojourner Truth Organization (EA)
STO .... Solar Terrestrial Observatory (SSD)
STO .... Standard Transfer Order
STO .... Standing Order [*Business term*] (DCTA)
STO .... Standing Tool Order (KSC)
StO .... Steuerordnung [*Tax Law*] [*German*] (ILCA)
StO .... Stimmen des Orients [*A publication*]
STO .... Stockholm [*Sweden*] [*Airport symbol*] (OAG)
STO .... Stoker [*Navy*] [*British*]
STO .... Stone Container Corp. [*NYSE symbol*] (SPSG)
STO .... Stonehill College, North Easton, MA [*OCLC symbol*] (OCLC)
STO .... Stonyhurst [*Blackburn*] [*England*] [*Seismograph station code, US Geological Survey*] [*Closed*] (SEIS)
STO .... Storage Processor
STO .... Storekeeper [*Coast Guard*]
Sto .... Storey's Delaware Reports [*A publication*] (DLA)
STO .... Story (WGA)
Sto .... Story's United States Circuit Court Reports [*A publication*] (DLA)
STO .... Stow (NASA)
STO .... Strategic Technology Office [*Arlington, VA*] [*DoD*] (GRD)
STO .... Swedish Trade Office (EA)
STO .... System Test Objectives
STOAA ...... Stomatologiya [*Moscow*] [*A publication*]
Sto Abr Const ... Story's Abridgment of the Constitution [*A publication*] (DLA)
STOAD ..... Scientific and Technical Organizations and Agencies Directory [*A publication*]
Sto Ag .... Story on Agency [*A publication*] (DLA)
STOAL ...... Short Takeoff Arrested Landing (MCD)
Sto Att Lien ... Stokes on Lien of Attorneys and Solicitors [*1860*] [*A publication*] (DLA)
Sto Bailm ... Story on Bailments [*A publication*] (DLA)
Sto Bills ..... Story on Bills [*A publication*] (DLA)
STobRV ..... Satellite Tobacco Ringspot Virus
STOC .... Standard Tactical Operating Condition
STOC .... Systems for Test Output Consolidation [*Data processing*]
STOCC ...... Space Telescope Operations Control Center [*NASA*] (NASA)
Sto CC .... Story's United States Circuit Court Reports [*A publication*] (DLA)
STOCD ...... Software Tools Communications [*A publication*]
Stochastic Processes Appl ... Stochastic Processes and Their Applications [*A publication*]
Stoch Processes Appl ... Stochastic Processes and Their Applications [*A publication*]
Stock .... Stockton's New Brunswick Vice-Admiralty Reports [*1879-91*] [*A publication*] (DLA)
Stock .... Stockton's New Jersey Equity Reports [*A publication*] (DLA)

Stock Adm ... Stockton's New Brunswick Vice-Admiralty Reports [*A publication*] (DLA)
Stockett ...... Stockett's Reports [*27-53 Maryland*] [*A publication*] (DLA)
STOCKH... Stockholmia [*Stockholm*] [*Imprint*] (ROG)
Stockh Contrib Geol ... Stockholm Contributions in Geology [*A publication*]
Stockholm Contrib Geol ... Stockholm Contributions in Geology [*A publication*]
Stockholm Tek Hogsk Avh ... Stockholm. Tekniska Hogskolan. Avhandling [*A publication*]
Stockholm Tek Hogsk Handl ... Stockholm. Tekniska Hogskolan. Handlingar [*Transactions*] [*A publication*]
Stock Non Com ... Stock on Non Compotes Mentis [*A publication*] (DLA)
Stockt .... Stockton's New Jersey Equity Reports [*9-11 New Jersey*] [*A publication*] (DLA)
Stockt Ch ... Stockton's New Jersey Equity Reports [*9-11 New Jersey*] [*A publication*] (DLA)
Stockton ..... Stockton's New Brunswick Vice-Admiralty Reports [*A publication*] (DLA)
Stockton Adm (New Br) ... Stockton's New Brunswick Vice-Admiralty Reports [*A publication*] (DLA)
Stockt Vice-Adm ... Stockton's New Brunswick Vice-Admiralty Reports [*A publication*] (DLA)
Sto Comm .. Story's Commentaries on the Constitution of the United States [*A publication*] (DLA)
Sto Con ...... Story on Contracts [*A publication*] (DLA)
Sto Conf Law ... Story on Conflict of Laws [*A publication*] (DLA)
Sto Const .... Story's Commentaries on the Constitution of the United States [*A publication*] (DLA)
Sto Const Cl B ... Story's Constitutional Class Book [*A publication*] (DLA)
Sto Cont ...... Story on Contracts [*A publication*] (DLA)
StocProc ...... Stochastic Processes and Their Applications [*A publication*]
STOCS ...... South Texas Outer Continental Shelf
STOD .... Stodden [*England*]
Sto Eq Jur ... Story on Equity Jurisprudence [*A publication*] (DLA)
Sto Eq Pl ..... Story on Equity Pleadings [*A publication*] (DLA)
St Offenbach ... Studien und Forschungen. Stadt- und Landkreis Offenbach Am Main [*A publication*]
STOG .... Science and Technology Objectives Guide (MCD)
Sto & G ...... Stone and Graham's Private Bills Decisions [*1865*] [*A publication*] (DLA)
STOGW ..... Short Takeoff Gross Weight [*Aviation*]
Sto & H Cr Ab ... Storer and Heard on Criminal Abortion [*A publication*] (DLA)
STOIAC .... Strategic Technology Office Information Analysis Center [*Battelle Memorial Institute*] (MCD)
STOIIP...... Stock Tank Oil Initially in Place [*Petroleum technology*]
Stokes L of Att ... Stokes on Liens of Attorneys [*A publication*] (DLA)
STOL........ Saturn Test Oriented Language [*NASA*]
STOL........ Short Takeoff and Landing [*Aviation*]
STOL........ Standing Operating and Landing
STOL........ Systems Test and Operation Language
STOLAND ... STOL Navigation and Landing System (MCD)
Sto Laws .... Story's Laws of the United States [*A publication*] (DLA)
Stolport ...... Short Takeoff and Landing Airport [*London, England*]
STOM .... Safe Transport of Munitions (MCD)
STOM .... Stomachic [*To Strengthen the Stomach*] [*Medicine*] (ROG)
STOM .... System Test and Operations Manual
Stomach Intest ... Stomach and Intestine [*Japan*] [*A publication*]
S Tomas Nurs J ... Santo Tomas Nursing Journal [*A publication*]
Stomatol DDR ... Stomatologie der DDR [*East Germany*] [*A publication*]
Stomatol Glas Srb ... Stomatoloski Glasnik Srbije [*A publication*]
Stomatol Vjesn ... Stomatoloski Vjesnik [*Stomatological Review*] [*A publication*]
Stomatol Zpr ... Stomatologicke Zpracy [*A publication*]
Sto Miscel Writ ... Story's Miscellaneous Writings [*A publication*] (DLA)
STOMPER ... Soil Test Ordnance Multipurpose Exploration Rocket (SAA)
STON .... Daylight Industries, Inc. [*NASDAQ symbol*] (NQ)
STON .... Short Ton [*2000 lbs.*] (AABC)
StonC .... Stone Container Corp. [*Associated Press abbreviation*] (APAG)
Stone .... Stone's Justices' Manual (Annual) [*A publication*] (DLA)
STONE4.... Strahlentherapie und Onkologie [*A publication*]
Stone Ben Bdg Soc ... Stone's Benefit Building Societies [*1851*] [*A publication*] (DLA)
StoneC .... Stone Container Corp. [*Associated Press abbreviation*] (APAG)
Stone C .... Stone Country [*A publication*]
Stone D .... Stone Drum [*A publication*]
STONEH .. Stonehouse [*England*]
Stone Ind.... Stone Industries [*A publication*]
Stone Just Man ... Stone's Justices' Manual (Annual) [*A publication*] (DLA)
Stony .... Stony Hills [*A publication*]
STOP........ Save the Oppressed People Committee [*Defunct*] (EA)
STOP........ Selected Test Optimization Program (MCD)
STOP........ Ship's Toxicological Protective System
STOP........ Single Title Order Plan [*Formerly, SCOP*] [*ABA*]
STOP........ Society that Opposes Pornography
STOP........ Software Theft Opposition Project [*Project STOP*] [*Information service or system*] (CRD)
STOP........ Stable Ocean Platform
STOP........ Stable Tubule Only Polypeptide [*Biochemistry*]
STOP........ Start Tromping on Pedal [*Facetious interpretation of the traffic sign*]

STOP......... Stop forced busing; Teach children, not bus them; Operate neighborhood schools for those in the neighborhood wishing to attend them; Put an end to government interference in the parent-child relationship   (EA)

STOP......... Stop the Oil Profiteers [*Antioil price slogan*]

STOP......... Stop the Olympic Prison [*Lake Placid Olympics, 1980*] [*Opposed possible later use of an Olympic building as a prison*] [*Defunct*]

STOP......... Stop This Outrageous Purge [*Group opposed to extremist measures used by segregationists in Arkansas; opposed by CROSS*]

STOP......... Strategic Orbit Point   (AFM)

STOP......... Strategic Talks on Prevention [*of accidental atomic war and nuclear weapons proliferation*] [*Proposed by Sen. Gary Hart, 1982*]

STOP......... Student/Teacher Organization to Prevent Nuclear War   (EA)

STOP......... Students Tackle Ocean Plastics

STOP......... Supersonic Transport Optimization Program [*NASA*]

STOP ABC ... Stop Abuse by Counselors   (EA)

Sto Part...... Story on Partnership [*A publication*]   (DLA)

Sto Pl .... Story's Civil Pleading [*A publication*]   (DLA)

STOP-NSA ... Students to Oppose Participation in the National Student Association   (EA)

STOPP ...... Society of Teachers Opposed to Physical Punishment

STOPP ...... Society of Teachers of Professional Photography [*Later, STEPP*]   (EA)

Stop Pregl .. Stopanski Pregled [*A publication*]

STOPPS.... Standard Transportation Operations Personnel Property   (MCD)

Sto Pr .... Story on Prize Courts [*A publication*]   (DLA)

Sto Pr Notes ... Story on Promissory Notes [*A publication*]   (DLA)

STOPS ...... Shipboard Toxicological Operational Protective System [*Navy*]

STOPS ...... Stability Operations

STOPS ...... Stabilized Terrain Optical Position Sensor [*Army*]

STOPS ...... Standard Transportation Operations Property System   (MCD)

STOPS ...... Supreme Temple Order Pythian Sisters   (EA)

StopSh .... [*The*] Stop & Shop Companies, Inc. [*Associated Press abbreviation*]   (APAG)

STOQ .... Storage Queue

STOR........ Scripps Tuna Oceanographic Research

STOR........ Segment Table Origin Register [*Data processing*]   (BUR)

STOR........ Storage   (AFM)

STOR........ Summary Tape Operations Rental [*Bureau of the Census*]

STOR........ System Test and Operations Report

STORAD... Stored Address [*Data processing*]

STORADS ... Site Tactical Optimized Range Air Defense System

Storage Handl Distrib ... Storage Handling Distribution [*A publication*]

Stor Art..... Storia dell'Arte [*A publication*]

Stor Arte .... Storia dell'Arte [*A publication*]

STORC...... Self-Ferrying Trans-Ocean Rotary-Wing Crane [*Helicopter*]

Stor Dict..... Stormouth's Dictionary of the English Language [*A publication*]   (DLA)

STORE...... Storage Technology for Operational Readiness

STORE...... Students to Observe Retail Establishments [*Student legal action organization*]   (EA)

Stor Ebr It ... Storia dell'Ebraismo in Italia. Sezione Toscana [*A publication*]

Storefront... Storefront Classroom [*A publication*]

StorEq........ Storage Equities, Inc. [*Associated Press abbreviation*]   (APAG)

STORES... Syntactic Tracer Organized Retrospective Enquiry System [*Instituut voor Wiskunde, Informatiewerk, en Statistiek*] [*Data processing*] [*Netherlands*]

STORET ... Storage and Retrieval [*Data processing*]

STORET ... Storage and Retrieval for Water Quality Data [*Environmental Protection Agency*] [*Databank*]   (MSC)

Stor & H Abor ... Storer and Heard on Criminal Abortion [*A publication*]   (DLA)

Storia e Polit ... Storia e Politica [*A publication*]

STORLAB ... Space Technology Operations and Research Laboratory   (IEEE)

STORM..... Safe Transport of Munitions Project   (MCD)

STORM..... Sensor, Tank, Off-Route Mine   (MCD)

STORM..... Somali, Tigray, and Ormo Resistance Monitor [*British*]

STORM..... Statistically Oriented Matrix Program   (IEEE)

STORM..... Stormscale Operational and Research Meteorology [*National Oceanic and Atmospheric Administration*]

STORMS.. Standardized Operation Research Management System   (MCD)

STORMSAT ... Storm Satellite   (MCD)

STORPR ... Storage Properties, Inc. [*Associated Press abbreviation*]   (APAG)

STORS ...... Sludge to Oil Reactor System [*Battelle Memorial Institute*]

StorTch ...... Storage Technology Corp. [*Associated Press abbreviation*]   (APAG)

STORW..... Storer Communications Wts [*NASDAQ symbol*]   (NQ)

Story........... Story on Equity Jurisprudence [*1836-1920*] [*A publication*]   (DLA)

Story........... Story's United States Circuit Court Reports [*A publication*]   (DLA)

Story Ag..... Story on Agency [*A publication*]   (DLA)

Story Bailm ... Story on Bailments [*A publication*]   (DLA)

Story Comm Const ... Story's Commentaries on the Constitution of the United States [*A publication*]   (DLA)

Story Confl Laws ... Story on Conflict of Laws [*A publication*]   (DLA)

Story Const ... Story's Commentaries on the Constitution of the United States [*A publication*]   (DLA)

Story Cont ... Story on Contracts [*A publication*]   (DLA)

Story Eq Jur ... Story on Equity Jurisprudence [*A publication*]   (DLA)

Story Eq Pl ... Story's Equity Planning [*A publication*]   (DLA)

Story Laws ... Story's Laws of the United States [*A publication*]   (DLA)

Story Merchants ... Abbott's Merchant Ships and Seamen, by Story [*A publication*]   (DLA)

Story Partn ... Story on Partnership [*A publication*]   (DLA)

Story Prom Notes ... Story on Promissory Notes [*A publication*]   (DLA)

Story R....... Story's United States Circuit Court Reports [*First Circuit*] [*A publication*]   (DLA)

Story Sales ... Story on Sales of Personal Property [*A publication*]   (DLA)

Story's Circuit CR ... Story's United States Circuit Court Reports [*First Circuit*] [*A publication*]   (DLA)

Story's Laws ... Story's United States Laws [*A publication*]   (DLA)

Story's Rep ... Story's United States Circuit Court Reports [*A publication*]   (DLA)

Story US Laws ... Story's Laws of the United States [*A publication*]   (DLA)

STOS......... Santos Ltd. [*NASDAQ symbol*]   (NQ)

STOS......... Space Test Operations Section

Sto Sales ... Story on Sales of Personal Property [*A publication*]   (DLA)

STOT........ Scheduled Time over Target   (AFM)

STOT........ Stockpile-to-Target   (AFM)

STOTINS ... Standoff Techniques for Parachute Insertion   (MCD)

StOTPr... Studies in Old Testament Prophecy Presented to T. H. Robinson [*A publication*]   (BJA)

Stotz-Kontakt-Roemmler Nachr ... Stotz-Kontakt-Roemmler Nachrichten [*A publication*]

StOU.......... Stimmen Orient und Uebersee [*A publication*]   (BJA)

Sto US Laws ... Story's Laws of the United States [*A publication*]   (DLA)

Stov Hors... Stovins' Law Respecting Horses [*A publication*]   (DLA)

STOVL...... Short Takeoff and Vertical Landing   (MCD)

STOW ...... Side Transfer Optimum Warehousing

STOW ...... Stowage   (AAG)

STOW ...... Swim the Ontario Waterways [*Personal incentive program for fitness swimmers*] [*Ontario Masters Swimming Club*]

STOW ...... System for Takeoff Weight

STP........... NAVAS [*Nederlandse Aannemersvereniging van Afbouwen Stukadoorswerken*] 77 [*A publication*]

STP........... North-Holland Studies in Theoretical Poetics [*Elsevier Book Series*] [*A publication*]

STP........... Sacrae [*or Sacrosanctae*] Theologiae Professor [*Professor of Sacred Theology*]

STP........... SAGE [*Semiautomatic Ground Environment*] System Training Program

STP........... St. Paul, MN [*Location identifier*] [*FAA*]   (FAAL)

STP........... Saint Peter's College, Jersey City, NJ [*OCLC symbol*]   (OCLC)

STP........... Sao Tome and Principe [*ANSI three-letter standard code*]   (CNC)

STP........... Satellite Ticket Printer [*Travel industry*]

STP........... Satellite Tracking Program [*of the Smithsonian Institution's Astrophysical Observatory*]

STP........... Save the Tallgrass Prairie [*An association*]   (EA)

STP........... Scientifically Treated Petroleum [*A motor fuel oil additive*] [*Initials reported, by extension of meaning, also to stand for a hallucinogenic drug, DOM*]

STP........... Sea Test Phase [*Navy*]   (CAAL)

STP........... Seal to Parents [*Genealogy*]   (PCM)

STP........... Selective Tape Print

STP........... Self-Test Program   (MCD)

STP........... Sent to Printer [*Publishing*]

STP........... Serenity, Tranquility, Peace   (IIA)

STP........... Sewage Treatment Plant

STP........... Shielded Twisted-Pair [*Data processing*]   (PCM)

STP........... Short-Term Program [*Nuclear energy*]   (NRCH)

STP........... Short Term Projections [*Townsend, Greenspan & Co., Inc.*] [*Information service or system*] [*No longer available online*]

STP........... Shuttle Technology Panel [*NASA*]   (NASA)

STP........... Signal Transfer Point [*Telecommunications*]   (TEL)

STP........... Simultaneous Test Procedure [*Statistics*]

STP........... Simultaneous Track Processor

STP........... Singing Tree Press [*Publisher's imprint*]

ST-P.......... Small Transmitter Coated with Paraffin

STP........... Socialism: Theory and Practice [*A publication*]

STP........... Society of Telecommunications Professionals   (TSSD)

STP........... Society of Television Pioneers   (EA)

STP........... Society for Thai Philately   (EA)

STP........... Society of Toxicologic Pathologists   (EA)

STP........... Sodium Triphosphate [*or Sodium Tripolyphosphate*] [*Also, STPP*] [*Inorganic chemistry*]

STP........... Software Test Plan [*DoD*]

STP........... Solar-Terrestrial Physics   (IID)

STP........... Solar-Terrestrial Probe [*NASA*]

STP........... Soldier Training Publications [*Military*]   (INF)

STP........... South Texas Project [*Nuclear energy*]   (NRCH)

STP........... Space Technology Payload [*NASA*]   (MCD)

STP........... Space Test Program [*Air Force*]

STP........... Special Technical Publication   (MCD)

STP........... Special Tool Production

STP...........	Spectrum of Time Project [*Astronomy*]
STP...........	Stamp (MSA)
STP...........	Standard Temperature and Pressure
STP...........	Standard [*Normal*] Temperature and Pulse [*Medicine*]
STP...........	Standard Test Procedure
STP...........	Standard Thermal Profile
STP...........	Standard Type Process (MCD)
STP...........	Standardized Test Program
St P	State Papers [*A publication*] (DLA)
STP...........	Stepping (WGA)
STP...........	Sterilization Test Program
St & P........	Stewart and Porter's Alabama Reports [*A publication*] (DLA)
STP...........	Stop Character [*Data processing*]
STP...........	Stop the Pentagon/Serve the People (EA)
STP...........	Stoppage (AABC)
STP...........	Storage Tube Processor
STP...........	Storm Track Prediction (MCD)
STP...........	Strength, Toughness, Pride
STP...........	Strip
St u P ...	Studium und Praxis [*A publication*]
STP...........	Subsystem Test Plan [*NASA*] (NASA)
STP...........	Supracondylar Tibial Prosthesis [*Medicine*]
STP...........	Sustainment Training Program [*Army*] (INF)
STP...........	Sycamore Test Procedure [*Aerospace*] (AAG)
STP...........	System Test Plan
STP...........	System Test Procedure [*Nuclear energy*] (GFGA)
STP...........	System Test Program [*Navy*] (CAAL)
STP...........	Systems Technology Program (MCD)
STP...........	Systems Training Program [*RADAR*]
STPA	Statistical Training Programme for Africa [*United Nations*] (EY)
StPaul	[*The*] St. Paul Companies, Inc. [*Associated Press abbreviation*] (APAG)
St Paul Med J ...	St. Paul Medical Journal [*A publication*]
St Pauls Rev Sci ...	St. Paul's Review of Science [*A publication*]
St P Brook ...	Staff Papers. Brookings Institution [*A publication*]
StPCyRy....	St. Paul City Railway
StP & D......	St. Paul & Duluth Railroad
STPD........	Stamped (ROG)
STPD........	Standard Temperature and Pressure, Dry
STPD........	Stripped (MSA)
STPD........	Stumped (WGA)
STPD........	System Training Production Department (SAA)
STPDN......	Stepdown
STPDS......	Scientific and Technical Personnel Data System [*National Science Foundation*] (GFGA)
St Petersb Med Wchnschr ...	St. Petersburger Medizinische Wochenschrift [*A publication*]
STPF.........	Shield Test Pool Facility [*Nuclear energy*]
STPF.........	Stabilized Temperature Platform Furnace
STPFM......	Subsystem: Short-Term Price Forecasting Model [*Department of Energy*] (GFGA)
STPG........	Spare-Time Production for Gain [*FAO*]
STPG........	Stamping (ROG)
STPG........	Stepping (MSA)
STPGA	Steel Processing [*A publication*]
STPH........	Static Phase Error [*NASA*] (NASA)
STPHB......	Springer Tracts in Modern Physics [*A publication*]
STPI	Science and Technology Policy Implementation [*Project*]
STPI	Static Power Inverter (DWSG)
STPL	[*The*] St. Paul Companies, Inc. [*NASDAQ symbol*] (NQ)
STPL	Short-Term Public Exposure Limit (MCD)
STPL	Sidetone Path Loss [*Telecommunications*] (TEL)
STPL	Steeple (DS)
STPL	Stern Plane
St Pl Cr	Staundeforde's Pleas of Crown [*A publication*] (DLA)
STP-M	Solar-Terrestrial Physics - Meteorology
STPM........	Syndicat Togolais du Personnel de la Meteorologie [*Togolese Union of Meteorological Personnel*]
STP-MET ...	Solar-Terrestrial Physics - Meteorology [*International Council of Scientific Unions*]
StPM & M ...	St. Paul, Minneapolis & Manitoba Railway
STPNG......	Stopping (MSA)
STPO.........	Science and Technology Policy Office [*Supersedes OST*] [*National Science Foundation*]
STPO........	Systems Technology Project Office
St and Port ...	Stewart and Porter's Alabama Reports [*A publication*] (DLA)
StP & P......	St. Paul & Pacific Railroad
STPP	Sodium Tripolyphosphate [*Also, STP*] [*Inorganic chemistry*]
STPP	Student Teacher Performance Profile
STPR	Semiannual Technical Progress Report
STPR	Software Test Procedure
St Pr...........	Staundeforde's Exposition of the King's Prerogative [*A publication*] (DLA)
STPR	Stepper [*Motor*] [*Electronics*]
STPR	Stripper
STPR	Stumper [*Freight*]
St Pr Reg ...	Style's Practical Register [*England*] [*A publication*] (DLA)
STPS.........	Solar Thermal Power System
STPS.........	Stern Teacher Preference Schedule
STPS.........	Summary Task Planning Sheet
STPS.........	Systems Test Planning Section (SAA)
StP & SC...	St. Paul & Sioux City Railroad
STPST.......	Stop-Start [*Telecommunications*] (TEL)
STPT	Society of Town Planning Technicians [*British*]
STPT	Starpointe Savings Bank [*Plainfield, NJ*] [*NASDAQ symbol*] (NQ)
STPTC......	Standardization of Tar Products Test Committee
STPUB	Stem Pubescence [*Botany*]
StPUD	St. Paul Union Depot
StPUSY	St. Paul Union Stock Yards Co.
STPV	Semitrailer Petroleum Van (DWSG)
STPX	Systems Training Program Exercise (AABC)
STQ	Society of Translators of Quebec [*Canada*]
StQ...........	Steinbeck Quarterly [*A publication*]
STQ...........	Streator, IL [*Location identifier*] [*FAA*] (FAAL)
STR..........	Questar Corp. [*NYSE symbol*] (SPSG)
STR..........	Scientific Technical Report
STR..........	Scientific and Technological Research (DEN)
STR..........	Sea Test Range (MUGU)
STR..........	Search and Track RADAR
STR..........	Seater (ADA)
STR..........	Segment Table Register
STR..........	Senior Technical Representative
STR..........	Service Test Review
STR..........	Service Trouble Report
STR..........	Short-Term Returns
STR..........	Sidetone Reduction [*Telecommunications*] (TEL)
STR..........	Society for Theatre Research (EA)
STR..........	Society of Thoracic Radiology (EA)
STR..........	Software Test Report
STR..........	Software Trouble Report (MCD)
STR..........	Soul-Taehakkyo Ronmunjip. Inmun-Sahoe-Kwahak [*Seoul University Journal. Humanities and Social Sciences*] [*A publication*]
STR..........	Spacecraft Telemetry Regenerator (MCD)
STR..........	Special Theory of Relativity
STR..........	Special Trade Representative
STR..........	Speed Tolerant Recording [*Electronic Processors, Inc.*]
St u R	Staat und Recht [*A publication*]
STR..........	Staff Technical Representative
STR..........	Standard Broadcasting Corp. Ltd. [*Toronto Stock Exchange symbol*]
STR..........	Standard Taxiway Routing
STR..........	Standard Tool Request
STR..........	Standard Training Requirements [*Navy*] (NVT)
STR..........	Star Science Fiction [*A publication*]
STR..........	Status Register [*Data processing*]
STR..........	Steamer
STR..........	Stereo Review [*A publication*]
STR..........	Storage Rack (MCD)
STR..........	Store
STR..........	Straight (AAG)
STR..........	Strainer (AAG)
STR..........	Strait [*Maps and charts*]
Str	Strange's Cases of Evidence [*1698-1732*] [*England*] [*A publication*] (DLA)
Str	Strange's English King's Bench Reports [*1716-49*] [*A publication*] (DLA)
STR..........	Strasbourg [*France*] [*Seismograph station code, US Geological Survey*] (SEIS)
STR..........	Strasse [*Street*] [*German*]
Str	Strategemata [*of Frontinus*] [*Classical studies*] (OCD)
STR..........	Strategic Training Range (MCD)
STR..........	Streak
str	Streaky [*Quality of the bottom*] [*Nautical charts*]
STR..........	Stream [*Maps and charts*]
STR..........	Street
STR..........	Streichinstrumente [*Stringed Instruments*] [*Music*]
STR..........	Strength (AFM)
STR..........	Streptococcus [*Medicine*]
STR..........	Stretch [*Horse racing*]
Str	Striatum [*Brain anatomy*] [*Also, ST*]
STR..........	Striking (WGA)
STR..........	String
STR..........	Stringendo [*Hastening*] [*Music*]
STR..........	Strings [*of an orchestra*]
STR..........	Strip (AAG)
STR..........	Stroke
STR..........	Strophe [*Classical studies*] (OCD)
STR..........	Structural [*Lumber*]
St R	Stuart's Lower Canada Appeal Cases [*Quebec*] [*A publication*] (DLA)
StR	Studie o Rukopisech [*A publication*]
STR..........	Stuttgart [*Germany*] [*Airport symbol*] (OAG)
STR..........	Subject Terminal Control Release [*Aviation*] (FAAC)
STR..........	Submarine Test Reactor
STR..........	Submarine Thermal Reactor [*Nuclear energy*]
STR..........	Submersible Test Rack
STR..........	Summary Technical Report
STR..........	Super Transportable RADAR
STR..........	Surplus to Requirements (ADA)

STR........... Synchronous Transmitter Receiver [*Data processing*]
STR........... System Test Review [*NASA*]   (NASA)
STR........... Systems Technology RADAR   (MCD)
STR........... Systems Technology Report   (MCD)
STRA......... Supply and Training Mission [*Military*]   (CINC)
STRAA....... Strahlentherapie [*A publication*]
STRAAD... Special Techniques Repair Analysis Aircraft Damage
               [*Navy*]   (NVT)
STRAB...... Strabismus [*Medicine*]
Strab......... Strabo [*First century BC*] [*Classical studies*]   (OCD)
STRAB...... Strain [*A publication*]
STRABAD... Strategic Base Air Defense [*Military*]   (AABC)
STRAC...... Standards in Training Commission [*Army*]   (INF)
STRAC...... Strategic Army Corps [*Acronym has come to mean "ordered" or
               "neat"*]
STRACOS ... Strategic Air Combat Operations Staff
STRACS... Small Transportable Communications Stations
STRACS... Surface Traffic Control System   (MCD)
STRAD...... Signal Transmission Reception and Distribution   (IEEE)
Strad......... Stradivari [*Record label*]
STRAD...... Stradivarius Violin [*Music*]   (DSUE)
STRAD...... Strategic Aerospace Division [*Air Force*]   (AFM)
STRAD...... Switching, Transmitting, Receiving, and Distribution
STRADAP... Storm RADAR Data Processor [*ESD*]
STRAF...... Special Therapeutic and Rehabilitation Activities Fund
               [*Department of Veterans Affairs*]
STRAF...... Strategic Army Forces
STRAFE... Students Resisting Aerosol Flurocarbon Emissions [*Student
               legal action organization*]   (EA)
Strafford .... Smith's New Hampshire Reports [*A publication*]   (DLA)
STRAFIP .. Strategic Army Forces Readiness Improvement
               Program   (AABC)
STRAFLO ... Straight-Flow [*Water turbine*]
STRAFPOA ... Strategic Air Force, Pacific Ocean Area
STRAG..... Straggler
STRAGL ... Straggler Line [*Military*]
Strahan...... Strahan's Reports [*19 Oregon*] [*A publication*]   (DLA)
Strah Domat ... Strahan's Domat's Civil Law [*A publication*]   (DLA)
Strahlenschutz Forsch Prax ... Strahlenschutz in Forschung und Praxis [*West
               Germany*] [*A publication*]
Strahlenthe ... Strahlentherapie [*A publication*]
Strahlenther Sonderb ... Strahlentherapie. Sonderbaende [*A publication*]
STRAIN .... Structural Analytical Interpreter
STRAIRPOA ... Strategic Air Force, Pacific Ocean Area
Straits LJ & Rep ... Straits Law Journal and Reporter [*A publication*]   (DLA)
Straits Times A ... Straits Times Annual [*Singapore*] [*A publication*]
STRAM..... Synchronous Transmit Receive Access Method   (CMD)
Strand .... Strand Magazine [*A publication*]
Strand (Lond) ... Strand Magazine (London) [*A publication*]
Strand (NY) ... Strand Magazine (New York) [*A publication*]
STRANGE ... SAGE [*Semiautomatic Ground Environment*] Tracking and
               Guidance Evaluation System
Strange....... Strange's English Court Reports [*A publication*]   (DLA)
Strange (Eng) ... Strange's English Courts Reports [*93 English Reprint*] [*A
               publication*]   (DLA)
Strange Madras ... Strange's Notes of Cases, Madras [*A publication*]   (DLA)
STRAP ...... SCAR Team Report Analysis Program   (MCD)
STRAP ...... Simplified Transient Radiation Analysis Program   (MCD)
STRAP ...... Simultaneous Transmission and Recovery of Alternating
               Pictures [*TV system*]
STRAP ...... Sonobuoy Thinned Random Array Program [*Navy*]   (CAAL)
STRAP ...... Star [*or Stellar*] Tracking Rocket Attitude Positioning [*System*]
               [*NASA*]
STRAP ...... Stretch Assembly Program [*IBM Corp.*]
STRAP ...... Structural Analysis Package
STRAP ...... System Training Plan
STRAPP.... Standard Tanks, Racks, Adapter, and Pylon Packages   (MCD)
STRASB.... Strasbourg [*Imprint*]   (ROG)
Strasb Med ... Strasbourg Medical [*A publication*]
STRAT ...... Strategic   (AFM)
STRAT ...... Stratigraphic
STRAT ...... Stratton [*England*]
STRATAD ... Strategic Aerospace Division [*Air Force*]
STRATANALSUPPGRU ... Strategic Analysis Support Group
               [*Navy*]   (DNAB)
STRATCOM ... Strategic Air Command [*Air Force*]
STRATCOM ... Strategic Communications Command [*Army*]   (RDA)
STRATCOM ... Stratospheric Composition   (MCD)
Strateg Anal ... Strategic Analysis [*India*] [*A publication*]
Strategic Dig ... Strategic Digest [*A publication*]
Strategic R ... Strategic Review [*A publication*]
Strateg Manage J ... Strategic Management Journal [*A publication*]
STRATF.... Stratford [*England*]
Strathclyde Bioeng Semin ... Strathclyde Bioengineering Seminars [*A
               publication*]
STRATMAS ... Strategic Mobility [*Planning and*] Analysis System
               [*Military*]   (NVT)
STRATMID... Strategic Military Intelligence Detachment [*Army*]   (MCD)
STRATO... Stratosphere   (AFM)
Strat R........ Strategic Review [*Washington, DC*] [*A publication*]
Strat Rev .... Strategic Review [*A publication*]

STRATSAT ... Strategic Satellite System [*Air Force*]
               [*Telecommunications*]   (TEL)
Strat Svy .... Strategic Survey [*A publication*]
Stratton...... Stratton's Reports [*12-14 Oregon*] [*A publication*]   (DLA)
Stratus .... Stratus Computer, Inc. [*Associated Press
               abbreviation*]   (APAG)
STRATWARM ... Stratospheric Warming
Strauss .... Internationale Richard-Strauss-Gesellschaft. Mitteilungen [*A
               publication*]
Str Autobahn ... Strasse und Autobahn [*A publication*]
STRAW..... Simultaneous Tape Read and Write
STRB .... Strobe   (NASA)
STRB .... [*The*] Strober Organization, Inc. [*Brooklyn, NY*] [*NASDAQ
               symbol*]   (NQ)
STRBK ...... Strongback
STRC......... Science and Technology Research Center [*North
               Carolina*]   (MCD)
STRC......... Scientific and Technical Research Centres in Australia
               [*Information service or system*] [*A publication*]   (APTA)
STRC......... Scientific, Technical, and Research Commission   (EY)
STRC......... Society of Traditional Roman Catholics   (EA)
STRC......... Stratford American Corp. [*NASDAQ symbol*]   (CTT)
STRC......... Switch Tail Ring Counter
Str Cas Ev ... Strange's Cases of Evidence ("Octavo Strange") [*A
               publication*]   (DLA)
STRCH...... Stretch   (AAG)
STRC-IVS ... STRC [*Science and Technology Research Center*] Inverted File
               Search System [*Search system*]
STRD......... Short Tour Return Date [*Military*]
STRD......... Stored
STRD......... Strand [*Engineering*]
STRE......... Specialist Teams Royal Engineers [*Military*] [*British*]
STREAM .. Standard Tensioned Replenishment Alongside Method
               [*Military*]   (NVT)
S Treaty Doc ... Senate Treaty Documents [*A publication*]   (DLA)
Street Ry Rep ... Street Railway Reports [*A publication*]   (DLA)
StRel/ScRel ... Studies in Religion/Sciences Religieuses [*A publication*]
Strem Chem ... Strem Chemiker [*A publication*]
St Ren .... Studies in the Renaissance [*A publication*]
Streng and H ... Strength and Health [*A publication*]
STRENGTHD ... Strengthened   (ROG)
Strength Mater ... Strength of Materials [*A publication*]
Strenna Stor Bolognese ... Strenna Storica Bolognese [*A publication*]
STREP...... Ship's Test and Readiness Evaluation Procedure
STREP....... Space Trajectory Radiation Exposure Procedure
St Rep .... State Reporter [*A publication*]   (DLA)
St Rep .... State Reports [*A publication*]   (DLA)
STREP...... Status Report [*IRS*]
Strep.......... Strepsiptera [*Entomology*]
STREP...... Streptococcus [*Medicine*]
STREP...... Systems Technology Reentry Experiment Program [*Military*]
St Rep (NSW) ... State Reports (New South Wales) [*A publication*]
STREPTO ... Streptomycin [*An antibiotic*]   (DSUE)
StrEq.......... Storage Equities, Inc. [*Associated Press abbreviation*]   (APAG)
STRES........ Store Release Evaluation System   (MCD)
STRESS .... Satellite Transmission Effects Simulation   (MCD)
STRESS .... Stop the Robberies, Enjoy Safe Streets [*Detroit police unit*]
               [*Disbanded*]
STRESS .... Structural Engineering Systems Solver [*Programming language*]
               [*1962*]
STRETCH ... [*An*] Early Large Computer [*IBM 7030*]
STRETCH ... Space Technology Requirements Engineering Test of
               Component Hardware [*NASA*]   (KSC)
Str Ev .... Strange's Cases of Evidence [*1698-1732*] [*England*] [*A
               publication*]   (DLA)
STRF .... Sea Turtle Rescue Fund   (EA)
STRFLD.... Star Field   (MCD)
STRG........ Steering   (AAG)
STRG........ String   (NASA)
STRG........ Strong   (MSA)
StrGlob ...... Strategic Global Income Fund [*Associated Press
               abbreviation*]   (APAG)
STRG WND ... String or Wind [*Freight*]
STRHA...... Staub, Reinhaltung der Luft [*A publication*]
Str & HC.... Streets and Highways Code [*A publication*]   (DLA)
Str HL........ Strange's Hindoo Law [*A publication*]   (DLA)
STRI .... Smithsonian Tropical Research Institute [*Miami, FL*]
STRI .... Sports Turf Research Institute [*British*]   (IRUK)
STRI .... Stones River National Battlefield
Strick Ev .... Strickland on Evidence [*1830*] [*A publication*]   (DLA)
STRICOM ... Simulation, Training, and Instrumentation Command
               [*Army*]   (RDA)
STRICOM ... Strike Command [*Military*]
STRIDE..... Science and Technology for Regional Innovation and
               Development in Europe [*EC*]   (ECED)
STRIDE..... Standard Reactor Island Design [*Nuclear energy*]   (NRCH)
STRIDE..... System to Retrieve Information from Drug Evidence [*Drug
               Enforcement Administration*]
StrideRt ..... Stride Rite Corp. [*Associated Press abbreviation*]   (APAG)
STRIKEOPS ... Strike Operations [*Military*]   (NVT)
STRIKEX.. Strike Exercise [*Navy*] [*NATO*]   (NATG)

STRIKFLTLANT ... Striking Fleet Atlantic [*Military*]
STRIKFORSOUTH ... Striking and Support Forces Southern Europe [*Navy*]
STRIKFTLANTREPEUR ... Striking Fleet Atlantic Representative in Europe [*NATO*]   (NATG)
STRING .... Stringendo [*Hastening*] [*Music*]
Stringf........ Stringfellow's Reports [*9-11 Missouri*] [*A publication*]   (DLA)
Stringfellow ... Stringfellow's Reports [*9-11 Missouri*] [*A publication*]   (DLA)
STRINGS ... Stellar Inertial Guidance System   (DNAB)
STRINO.... Stringendo [*Hastening*] [*Music*]   (ROG)
STRIP........ Select Technical Requirements Information Program
STRIP........ Specification Technical Review and Improvement Program [*Navy*]   (NG)
STRIP........ Standard Requisition and Issue Procedures [*Military*]   (CINC)
STRIP........ Standard Taped Routines for Image Processing [*National Institute of Standards and Technology*]
STRIP........ Stock Turn-In and Replenishment Invoicing Procedures
STRIP........ String Processing Language [*Data processing*]   (DIT)
STRIPE...... Swap Transferring Risk with Participating Element [*Finance*]
STRIPS ..... Separate Trading of Registered Interest and Principal of Securities [*Investment term*]
STRIVE..... Standard Techniques for Reporting Information on Value Engineering
St Riv Wat Supply Comm Tech Bull ... Victoria. State Rivers and Water Supply Commission. Technical Bulletin [*A publication*]   (APTA)
STRJ.......... Self-Powered Thermocouple Reference Junction
STRJA....... Strojirenstvi [*A publication*]
STRK........ Star Tracker   (NASA)
STRK........ Stroke   (MSA)
STRKA ...... Staerke [*A publication*]
STRKR ...... Striker [*Automotive engineering*]
STRL.......... Sea Trials [*Navy*]   (NVT)
STRL........ Sterling, Inc. [*Akron, OH*] [*NASDAQ symbol*]   (NQ)
STR L .... Straight Line [*Freight*]
STRL........ Structural
StrlBcp....... Sterling Bancorp [*Associated Press abbreviation*]   (APAG)
STRLCAP ... Sterling Capital Corp. [*Associated Press abbreviation*]   (APAG)
StrlCh .... Sterling Chemicals, Inc. [*Associated Press abbreviation*]   (APAG)
STR LGTHS ... Straight Lengths [*Freight*]
STRLN ...... Streamline   (MSA)
STRM........ Storeroom   (MSA)
STR M .... Strand Magazine [*A publication*]
STRM........ Stream
STRMD..... Strategic Missile Division [*Military*]
STRN........ Standard Technical Report Number
STRN........ Strength   (AAG)
STRN........ Sutron Corp. [*NASDAQ symbol*]   (NQ)
Str NC .... [*Sir T.*] Strange's Notes of Cases [*Madras*] [*A publication*]   (DLA)
STRND...... Sternenbote [*A publication*]
STRNG...... Steering
STRNR...... Strainer   (AAG)
STRO......... Scandinavian Tire and Rim Organization   (EA)
STRO......... Stereo Routes   (FAAC)
Strob .... Strobhart's South Carolina Law Reports [*1846-50*] [*A publication*]   (DLA)
Strob Ch..... Strobhart's South Carolina Equity Reports [*A publication*]   (DLA)
STROBE ... Satellite Tracking of Balloons and Emergencies
STROBE ... Stroboscopic   (MSA)
Strob Eq..... Strobhart's South Carolina Equity Reports [*1846-50*] [*A publication*]   (DLA)
STROBES ... Shared-Time Repair of Big Electronic Systems [*Data processing*]
Strobh Eq (SC) ... Strobhart's South Carolina Equity Reports [*A publication*]   (DLA)
Strobh L (SC) ... Strobhart's South Carolina Law Reports [*A publication*]   (DLA)
Stroemungsmech Stroemungsmasch ... Stroemungsmechanik und Stroemungsmaschinen [*A publication*]
Stroezh Funkts Mozuka ... Stroezh i Funktsii na Mozuka [*A publication*]
STROFAC ... Stabilized Routing for Afloat Commands   (MCD)
STR OFF FIXT ... Store or Office Fixture[*s*] [*Freight*]
Stroit Alyum Konstr ... Stroitel'nye Alyuminievye Konstruktsii [*A publication*]
Stroit Arkhit Leningrada ... Stroitel'stvo i Arkhitektura Leningrada [*A publication*]
Stroit Arkhit Uzb ... Stroitel'stvo i Arkhitektura Uzbekistana [*A publication*]
Stroit Dorog ... Stroitel'stvo Dorog [*A publication*]
Stroit Dorozhn Mash ... Stroitel'nye i Dorozhnye Mashiny [*A publication*]
Stroit Keram ... Stroitel'naya Keramika [*A publication*]
Stroit Konstr ... Stroitel'nye Konstruktsii [*A publication*]
Stroit Konstr Alyum Splavov ... Stroitel'nye Konstruktsii iz Alyuminievkh Splavov [*A publication*]
Stroit Mater ... Stroitel'nye Materialy [*A publication*]
Stroit Mater (1929-32) ... Stroitel'nye Materialy (1929-32) [*A publication*]
Stroit Mater (1933-38) ... Stroitel'nye Materialy (1932-38) [*A publication*]
Stroit Mater Betony ... Stroitel'nye Materialy i Betony [*A publication*]
Stroit Mater Detali Izdeliya ... Stroitel'nye Materialy. Detali i Izdeliya [*A publication*]

Stroit Mater Izdeliya Konstr ... Stroitel'nye Materialy. Izdeliya i Konstruktsii [*A publication*]
Stroit Mater Konstr ... Stroitel'nye Materialy i Konstruktsii [*A publication*]
Stroit Mater Silik Prom-St ... Stroitelni Materiali i Silikatna Promishlenost [*Bulgaria*] [*A publication*]
Stroit Mekh Raschet Sooruz ... Stroitel'naya Mekhanika i Raschet Sooruzheniy [*Former USSR*] [*A publication*]
Stroit Predpr Neft Promsti ... Stroitel'stvo Predpriyatii Neftyanoi Promyshlennosti [*A publication*]
Stroit Promst ... Stroitel'naya Promyshlennost [*A publication*]
Stroit Truboprovodov ... Stroitel'stvo Truboprovodov [*Former USSR*] [*A publication*]
Strojir Vyroba ... Strojirenska Vyroba [*A publication*]
Strojnicky Cas ... Strojnicky Casopis [*Czechoslovakia*] [*A publication*]
Stroke Suppl ... Stroke. Supplement [*A publication*]
Strom .... Stromateis [*of Clemens Alexandrinus*] [*Classical studies*]   (OCD)
STROM..... Stromberg [*Automotive engineering*]
StRom .... Studies in Romanticism [*A publication*]
Stromprax ... Strompraxis [*A publication*]
Stroud Sl.... Stroud on Slavery [*A publication*]   (DLA)
STRP .... Strap
STRP .... Striker Petroleum Corp. [*NASDAQ symbol*]   (NQ)
St R (Q)..... State Reports (Queensland) [*A publication*]   (APTA)
St R (Qd).... State Reports (Queensland) [*A publication*]   (APTA)
St R (Queensl) ... State Reports (Queensland) [*A publication*]
STRR .... Star Technologies, Inc. [*Sterling, VA*] [*NASDAQ symbol*]   (NQ)
STRS .... SAGE [*Semi-Automatic Ground Equipment*] Training Requirements Section   (SAA)
STRS .... Sprouse-Reitz Stores, Inc. [*Portland, OR*] [*NASDAQ symbol*]   (NQ)
STRS .... Submarine Technical Repair Standard [*Navy*]   (DNAB)
STRSPH... Stratosphere   (WGA)
STRT .... [*The*] Stewartstown Railroad Co. [*AAR code*]
STRT .... Strait [*Board on Geographic Names*]
Str Tiefbau ... Strassen- und Tiefbau [*A publication*]
STRTL...... Structural
STRTR ...... Starter [*Automotive engineering*]
STRU .... Structofab, Inc. [*NASDAQ symbol*]   (NQ)
STRU......... Styrelserepresentationsutredningen [*Sweden*]
STRUBAL ... Structured Basic Language [*Data processing*]   (CSR)
STRUC....... Structure   (AABC)
Struc Rev.... Structuralist Review [*A publication*]
STRUCT ... Structure   (AAG)
Struct Bonding ... Structure and Bonding [*A publication*]
Struct Chem ... Structural Chemistry [*A publication*]
Struct Concr ... Structural Concrete [*A publication*]
Struct Eng ... Structural Engineer [*A publication*]
Struct Engnr ... Structural Engineer. Parts A and B [*A publication*]
Struct Engr ... Structural Engineer [*A publication*]
Struct Foam Conf Proc ... Structural Foam Conference. Proceedings [*A publication*]
Struct Funct Brain ... Structure and Functions of the Brain [*A publication*]
Struct Glass ... Structure of Glass [*A publication*]
Struct Mater Note Aust Aeronaut Res Lab ... Australia. Department of Supply. Aeronautical Research Laboratories. Structures and Materials Note [*A publication*]   (APTA)
Struct Mater Rep Aust Aeronaut Res Lab ... Australia. Aeronautical Research Laboratories. Structures and Materials Report [*A publication*]   (APTA)
Struct Note Aust Aeronaut Res Lab ... Australia. Aeronautical Research Laboratories. Structures Note [*A publication*]   (APTA)
Struct Rep ... Structure Reports [*A publication*]
Struct Rep Aust Aeronaut Res Lab ... Australia. Aeronautical Research Laboratories. Structures Report [*A publication*]   (APTA)
Struct Rep Dep Archit Sci Syd Univ ... Structures Report. Department of Architectural Science. University of Sydney [*A publication*]   (APTA)
Struct Saf... Structural Safety [*A publication*]
Struct Surv ... Structural Survey [*A publication*]
STRUDL... Structural Design Language [*Data processing*]   (MCD)
STRUDLDYNAL ... Structural Design Language Dynamic Analysis [*Data processing*]
STRUDLPLOTS ... Structural Design Language Output Plots
STRUDLTOWER ... Structural Design Language for Transmission Tower
STRUFO ... Structural Formula [*Data processing*] [*Chemistry*]
Strukt Funkts Fermentov ... Struktura i Funktsiya Fermentov [*A publication*]
Strukt Modif Khlopk Tsellyul ... Struktura i Modifikatsiya Khlopkovoi Tsellyulozy [*A publication*]
Strukt Rol Vody Zhivom Org ... Struktura i Rol Vody v Zhivom Organizme [*A publication*]
Strukt Svoistva Krist ... Struktura i Svoistva Kristallov [*A publication*]
Strukt Svoistva Litykh Splavov ... Struktura i Svoistva Litykh Splavov [*A publication*]
Strukturn i Mat Lingvistika ... Strukturnaja i Matematiceskaja Lingvistika [*A publication*]
ST Rulings ... Sales Tax Rulings [*Australia*] [*A publication*]
Strum Crit ... Strumenti Critici [*A publication*]
Strum una Nuova Cultur Guida e Manual ... Strumenti per una Nuova Cultura. Guida e Manuali [*A publication*]

STRUTHER ... Struthers Industries [*Associated Press abbreviation*] (APAG)
Struve........ Struve's Washington Territory Reports [*1854-88*] [*A publication*] (DLA)
Str Verkehr ... Strasse und Verkehr [*A publication*]
STRW........ Strawbridge & Clothier [*NASDAQ symbol*] (NQ)
STRX........ Syntrex, Inc. [*NASDAQ symbol*] (NQ)
STRY......... Stryker Corp. [*NASDAQ symbol*] (NQ)
STRYCH... Strychnina [*Strychnine*] [*Pharmacy*] (ROG)
St Ry Rep... Street Railway Reports [*United States*] [*A publication*] (DLA)
STrZ.......... South Tropical Zone [*Planet Jupiter*]
STRZ.......... Star Banc Corp. [*NASDAQ symbol*] (NQ)
STS........... Office of State Technical Services [*Also, OSTS*] [*Abolished, 1970*] [*Department of Commerce*]
STS........... S-Band Transmitter System
STS........... SAGE [*Semi-Automatic Ground Equipment*] Training Specialist (SAA)
STS........... Saint Thomas Seminary [*Colorado; Connecticut; Kentucky*]
STS........... Santa Rosa [*California*] [*Airport symbol*] (OAG)
STS........... Santiago [*Spain*] [*Seismograph station code, US Geological Survey*] (SEIS)
STS........... Satellite-to-Satellite (CET)
STS........... Satellite Tracking Station
STS........... Satellite Transmission Systems, Inc. [*Hauppauge, NY*] [*Telecommunications*] (TSSD)
STS........... Scheduled Truck Service [*Army*]
STS........... School-to-School [*Red Cross Youth*]
STS........... School Television Service
STS........... Science Talent Search (EA)
STS........... Science and Technology Section [*Association of College and Research Libraries*]
STS........... Science, Technology, and Society
STS........... Science of To-Day Series [*A publication*]
STS........... Scottish Tartans Society (EA)
STS........... Scottish Text Society [*A publication*]
STS........... Sea Training Staff [*Canadian Navy*]
STS........... Security Termination Statement [*Military*] (AFM)
STS........... Self-Test Select
STS........... Seminex [*Concordia Seminary in Exile*] Library, St. Louis, MO [*OCLC symbol*] (OCLC)
STS........... Sequence-Tagged Site [*Genetics*]
STS........... Serological Test for Syphilis [*Medicine*]
STS........... Servo Test System
STSH........ Servocylinder Test Set (MCD)
STS........... Seville Touring Sedan [*General Motors Corp.*]
STS........... Sewage Treatment System [*Navy*] (CAAL)
STS........... Shared Tenant Services [*Telecommunications*] (TSSD)
STS........... Ship-to-Shore
STS........... Shuttle Test Station (NASA)
STS........... Shuttle Transportation System (MCD)
STS........... Siltstone [*Lithology*]
STSN........ Simulator Test Set (CAAL)
STS........... Skaggs Telecommunications Service [*Salt Lake City, UT*] [*Telecommunications*] (TSSD)
STS........... Skylab Terminal System [*NASA*]
STS........... Society for Textual Scholarship (EA)
STS........... Society of Thoracic Surgeons (EA)
STS........... Socio-Technical Systems [*Management technique*]
STS........... Sodium Tetradecyl Sulfate [*Organic chemistry*]
STS........... Sodium Thiosulfate [*Inorganic chemistry, biochemistry*]
STS........... Soft Tissue Sarcoma [*Oncology*]
STS........... Solar Tracking System
STSS........ SONAR Technician, Submarine [*Navy rating*] (DNAB)
STS........... SONAR Test System
STS........... Sonic Telex System [*Sonicair*] [*Phoenix, AZ*] [*Telecommunications*] (TSSD)
STS........... Space-Time-Space [*Digital switching structure*] [*Telecommunications*] (TEL)
STS........... Space Transportation System
STS........... Spacecraft Telecommunications System
STS........... Spacecraft Tracking Station [*NASA*] (KSC)
STS........... Special Task Stores [*Military*] [*British*]
STS........... Special Test System [*Air Force*] (AFM)
STSV........ Special Training Standard [*Air Force*] (AFM)
STS........... Special Treatment Steel
STS........... Specialty Training System
STS........... Specific Tensile Strength
STS........... Spring Trapmakers' Society [*British*] (DCTA)
STS........... Stabilized Telescope System
StS........... Stamp Seal (BJA)
STS........... Standard (Galilean) Telescopes [*Instrumentation*]
STS........... Standard Technical Specifications [*Nuclear energy*] (NRCH)
STS........... Standard Test for Syphilis [*Medicine*]
STS........... Standard Threshold Shift
STS........... State Technical Services [*Abolished, 1970*]
STS........... Static Test Stand
STS........... Station to Station
STS........... Stationary Time Series
STS........... Sterol-sulphatase [*An enzyme*]
STS........... Stimulated Thermal Scattering [*Photonics*]
STS........... Stirring Science Stories [*A publication*]
STS........... Stock Trading System

STS........... Stockpile-to-Target Sequence [*Military*]
STS........... Stomatogastric Nervous System [*Neuroanatomy*]
STS........... Strategic Technical Service (CINC)
STS........... Strategic Training Squadron (MCD)
STS........... Structural Transition Section [*NASA*] (MCD)
STS........... Student Travel School
STS........... Superior Temporal Sulcus [*Brain anatomy*]
STS........... Supersonic Target System
STS........... Supplementary Test Site [*Nuclear energy*] (IID)
STS........... Surface Target Simulator [*Navy*] (DNAB)
STS........... Surveillance Test Set (MCD)
STS........... Survey Tabulation Services, Inc. [*Information service or system*] (IID)
STS........... Synchronous Transport Signal [*Data processing*]
STS........... Synchrony Service and Transport System [*Ascom Timeplex, Inc.*]
STS........... System Technical Services
STS........... System Test Set
STS........... System Test Software (CAAL)
STS........... System Test Station (SAA)
STS........... System Training Section (SAA)
STS........... System Training Specialist (SAA)
STS........... System Trouble Shooting
STS........... System Trouble Survey (CET)
STSA........ Seaman Apprentice, SONAR Technician, Striker [*Navy rating*]
STSA........ Southern Thoracic Surgical Association (EA)
STSA........ State Technical Services Act
STSALV.... Standby Salvage Ship [*Navy*] (NVT)
ST-SAS..... Septic Tank-Subsurface Absorption System
STSB........ Seattle Trust & Savings Bank [*NASDAQ symbol*] (NQ)
STSC........ Scientific Time Sharing Corp. [*Host*] [*Information service or system*] (IID)
STSC........ Scottish Teachers Salaries Committee [*British*]
STSC........ Shipboard Tactical Satellite Communications (DNAB)
ST SCI...... Space Telescope Science Institute [*Johns Hopkins University*] [*Research center*] (RCD)
STSCM..... Space Transportation System Cost Model [*NASA*] (KSC)
STSD........ Society of Teachers of Speech and Drama [*British*]
STSFSC.... Scarf Trailers Science Fiction Social Club [*Inactive*] (EA)
STSG........ Shuttle Test Group [*NASA*] (NASA)
STSG........ Space Topics Study Group (EA)
STSG........ Split Thickness Skin Graft
STSH........ Stabilized Shunt [*Electricity*]
STSI......... Space Telescope Science Institute [*NASA*]
STSK........ Scandinavian Committee for Satellite Communications [*Telecommunications*] (TEL)
StSLL....... Studies in Semitic Languages and Linguistics [*A publication*]
STSM........ Statesman (WGA)
STSM........ Surface-to-Target-to-Surface-to-Missile
STSN........ Seaman, SONAR Technician, Striker [*Navy rating*]
STSN........ Set-and-Test-Sequence-Number [*Data processing*] (IBMDP)
STSO........ Senior Technical Staff Officer [*British*]
STSOC...... Space Transportation System Operations Contact [*NASA*] (SSD)
STSODQ... Annual Report. Natural Products Research Institute. Seoul National University [*A publication*]
STSOPO... Shuttle Transportation Systems Operations Program Office [*Johnson Space Center*] (NASA)
ST & SP.... Start and Stop
ST-SR....... Small Transmitter Coated with Silicon Rubber
STSR........ System Test Summary Report [*NASA*] (NASA)
STSS......... Sensitive Thrust Stand System
STSS......... Society for Traumatic Stress Studies (EA)
STSS......... Star States Corp. [*NASDAQ symbol*] (NQ)
STSSA...... SONAR Technician, Submarine, Seaman Apprentice [*Navy rating*] (DNAB)
STSSN...... SONAR Technician, Submarine, Seaman [*Navy rating*] (DNAB)
STSSPF.... Space Transportation System Spacelab Processing Facility [*NASA*] (SSD)
Ststcian..... Statistician [*A publication*]
ST/STE..... Special Tooling / Special Test Equipment [*Navy*] (DNAB)
STSV........ Satellite-to-Space Vehicle (SAA)
STT........... Charlotte Amalie, VI [*Location identifier*] [*FAA*] (FAAL)
STT........... Saigon Transportation Terminal Command [*Republic of Vietnam Armed Forces*]
STT........... St. Thomas [*Virgin Islands*] [*Airport symbol*]
STT........... Save the Theatres (EA)
STT........... School of Tank Technology [*British military*] (DMA)
STT........... School of Technical Training [*British military*] (DMA)
STT........... Science Stories [*A publication*]
STT........... Seattle - Marshall [*Washington*] [*Seismograph station code, US Geological Survey*] [*Closed*] (SEIS)
STT........... Seek Time per Track
STT........... Semitendinosus Tendon [*Anatomy*]
STT........... Sensitization Test
STT........... Sent to Typesetter [*Publishing*]
STT........... Serial Thrombin Time [*Medicine*] (MAE)
STT........... Ship Turn Transmitter
STT........... Shock Tube Test
STT........... Shore Targeting Terminal [*Navy*] (CAAL)

STT........... Short-Term Test [*Toxicology*]
STT........... Signal Tracing Tester
STT........... Single Target Track [*Navy*] (NG)
STT........... Skid-to-Turn
STT........... Skin Temperature Test [*Physiology*]
STT.......... Spacecraft Terminal Thrust
STT.......... Spacelab Transfer Tunnel (NASA)
STT.......... Spade Tongue Terminal
STT.......... Standard Triple Therapy [*For hypertension*]
STT.......... Stenographer, Medical [*Navy*]
STT.......... Store Tag (SAA)
STT........... Strain-Transport-Time [*Geology*]
STT.......... Strange Tales of Mystery and Terror [*A publication*]
STT........... Superior Teletec Corp. [*AMEX symbol*] (SPSG)
STT........... Sutton Resources Ltd. [*Vancouver Stock Exchange symbol*]
STT........... Svensk Traevaru- och Pappersmassetidning [*A publication*]
STT........... Syndicat des Travailleurs en Telecommunications
[*Telecommunications Workers Union - TWU*] [*Canada*]
St Tax Cas CCH ... State Tax Cases. Commerce Clearing House [*A publication*]
St Tax Cas Rep (CCH) ... State Tax Cases Reporter (Commerce Clearing
House) [*A publication*] (DLA)
St Tax Cas Rep CCH ... State Tax Cases Reports. Commerce Clearing House
[*A publication*]
St Tax Rep (CCH) ... State Tax Reporter (Commerce Clearing House) [*A
publication*] (DLA)
St Tax Rep CCH ... State Tax Reports. Commerce Clearing House [*A
publication*]
STTBA ...... Strassen- und Tiefbau [*A publication*]
STTC .... Scottish Textile and Technical Centre Ltd. [*British*] (IRUK)
STTC .... Sheppard Technical Training Center (AFM)
StTCL .... Studies in Twentieth-Century Literature [*A publication*]
StTDJ .... Studies on the Texts of the Desert of Judah [*J. Van Der Ploeg*]
[*Leiden*] [*A publication*] (BJA)
ST & TE..... Special Tools and Test Equipment (MCD)
STTE .... Special Tools and Test Equipment
STTEA .... Stain Technology [*A publication*]
StTEstmatn ... Statistical Theory of Estimation [*A publication*]
STTF .... Sanskrittexte aus den Turfanfunden [*A publication*]
STTF .... Service to the Fleet [*A publication*] (DNAB)
STTF .... SONAR Test Tower Facility
STTF .... Special Tank Task Force (MCD)
STTF .... System Technology Test Facility (MCD)
STT-FNB .. Suomen Tietotoimisto-Finska Notisbyran [*Press agency*]
[*Finland*]
STTG .... [*The*] Statesman Group, Inc. [*NASDAQ symbol*] (NQ)
S/TTL........ Schottky Transistor-Transistor Logic
STTL .... Sit Tibi Terra Levis [*May the Earth Lie Light on Thee*] [*Letters
found on Roman tombs*] [*Latin*]
STTM .... Stabilized Tracking Tripod Module (RDA)
STTNG....... Star Trek, the Next Generation [*Television program*]
STTO....... Sawtooth Timing Oscillator (DEN)
STTO........ Staking Tool (AAG)
St Tomas J Med ... Santo Tomas Journal of Medicine [*A publication*]
St Tomas Nurs J ... Santo Tomas Nursing Journal [*A publication*]
STTOT...... Single Target Track on Target [*Navy*]
St Tr........... Howell's English State Trials [*1163-1820*] [*A
publication*] (DLA)
STTR .... Stator
STTRA ...... Stroitel'stvo Truboprovodov [*A publication*]
St Tri........ State Trials [*A publication*] (DLA)
St Tr NS ... Macdonell's State Trials [*1820-58*] [*A publication*] (DLA)
STTS .... S-Band Transponder Test Set (MCD)
STTS .... Shipboard Target Tracking System
STTSRA.... Scoot-Tours Touring Scooter Riders Association (EA)
STTT .... Space Telescope Task Team [*NASA*]
St Twen Ct ... Studies in Twentieth-Century Literature [*A publication*]
STTX .... Steel Technologies, Inc. [*Louisville, KY*] [*NASDAQ
symbol*] (NQ)
STU .... Secure Telephone Unit [*Data processing*]
STU .... Seeker Test Unit (MCD)
STU .... Service Trials Unit
STU .... Servo Test Unit
STU .... Short Ton Unit
STU .... Signal Transfer Unit
STU .... Skin Test Unit
STU .... Space-Time Unit [*Computer*]
STU .... Special Test Unit (CET)
STU .... Special Training Unit
STU .... Star Tracker Unit [*NASA*] (MCD)
STU .... Static Test Unit (KSC)
STU .... Step Up
STU .... Stuart (ROG)
STU .... Stuart [*D. A.*] Ltd. [*Toronto Stock Exchange symbol*]
STU .... Student (AFM)
STU .... Student Loan Corp. [*NYSE symbol*] (SPSG)
STU .... Studies on International Relations [*Warsaw*] [*A publication*]
Stu............. Studium [*A publication*]
STU .... Stuttgart [*Federal Republic of Germany*] [*Seismograph station
code, US Geological Survey*] (SEIS)

STU .... Styrelsen foer Teknisk Utveckling [*Swedish Board for Technical
Development*]
STU .... Submarine Test Unit
STU .... Submersible Test Unit [*Navy*]
STU .... Subscribers' Trunk Unit [*Telecommunications*] (TEL)
STU .... System Timing Unit
STU .... System Transition Unit [*Data processing*]
STU .... Systems Test Unit (KSC)
STU .... University of Steubenville, Steubenville, OH [*OCLC
symbol*] (OCLC)
STUA........ Stuart Entertainment [*NASDAQ symbol*] (SPSG)
Stu Adm..... Stuart's Lower Canada Vice-Admiralty Reports [*A
publication*] (DLA)
Stu Adm NS ... Stuart's Lower Canada Vice-Admiralty Reports, New Series [*A
publication*] (DLA)
Stu Ap .... Stuart's Lower Canada King's Bench Reports, Appeal Cases [*A
publication*] (DLA)
Stuart .... Stuart, Milne, and Peddie's Scotch Court of Session Cases [*A
publication*] (DLA)
Stuart .... Stuart's Lower Canada Reports [*A publication*] (DLA)
Stuart .... Stuart's Lower Canada Vice-Admiralty Reports [*A
publication*] (DLA)
Stuart Adm NS ... Stuart's Lower Canada Vice-Admiralty Reports, New Series
[*A publication*] (DLA)
Stuart Beng ... Stuart's Select Cases [*1860*] [*Bengal, India*] [*A
publication*] (DLA)
Stuart KB... Stuart's Lower Canada King's Bench Reports [*1810-25*]
[*Quebec*] [*A publication*] (DLA)
Stuart KB (Quebec) ... Stuart's Lower Canada King's Bench Reports [*Quebec*]
[*A publication*] (DLA)
Stuart LCKB ... Stuart's Lower Canada King's Bench Reports [*A
publication*] (DLA)
Stuart LCVA ... Stuart's Lower Canada Vice-Admiralty Reports [*A
publication*] (DLA)
Stuart M & P ... Stuart, Milne, and Peddie's Scotch Court of Session Cases
[*1851-53*] [*A publication*] (DLA)
Stuart & Por ... Stuart [*or Stewart*] and Porter's Alabama Reports [*A
publication*] (DLA)
Stuart & Porter ... Stuart [*or Stewart*] and Porter's Alabama Reports [*A
publication*] (DLA)
Stuart's Adm ... Stuart's Lower Canada Vice-Admiralty Reports [*A
publication*] (DLA)
Stuart's R... Stuart's Lower Canada King's Bench Reports, Appeal Cases
[*Quebec*] [*A publication*] (DLA)
Stuart Vice-Adm ... Stuart's Lower Canada Vice-Admiralty Reports [*A
publication*] (DLA)
STUB........ Stadt- und Universitaetsbibliothek Frankfurt [*Database
producer*]
Stubbs CH ... Stubb's Constitutional History [*A publication*] (DLA)
Stubbs Sel Ch ... Stubb's Select Charters [*A publication*] (DLA)
STUC........ Sarawak Trade Union Congress
STUC........ Scottish Trades Union Congress
STUC........ Singapore Trade Union Congress
STUD .... Standard Tractor, Universal with Dozer [*Army*]
STUD .... Student
Stud............ Studien [*A publication*]
Stud............ Studies [*A publication*]
STUD .... Studies
Stud........... Studies: An Irish Quarterly Review of Letters, Philosophy, and
Science [*A publication*]
Stud Account ... Studies in Accountancy [*A publication*]
Stud Afr Linguist ... Studies in African Linguistics [*A publication*]
Stud Age Chaucer ... Studies in the Age of Chaucer [*A publication*]
Stud Ag Econ ... Stanford University Food Research Institute Studies in
Agricultural Economics, Trade, and Development [*A
publication*]
Stud Algebra Anwendungen ... Studien zur Algebra und Ihre Anwendungen [*A
publication*]
Stud Am Fic ... Studies in American Fiction [*A publication*]
Stud Anc Technol ... Studies in Ancient Technology [*A publication*] (OCD)
Stud Angew Wirtschaftsforsch Statist ... Studien zur Angewandten
Wirtschaftsforschung und Statistik [*A publication*]
Stud Appl M ... Studies in Applied Mathematics [*A publication*]
Stud Appl Math ... Studies in Applied Mathematics [*A publication*]
Stud Appl Mech ... Studies in Applied Mechanics [*A publication*]
Stud Art Ed ... Studies in Art Education [*A publication*]
Stud Art Educ ... Studies in Art Education [*A publication*]
Stud Automat Control ... Studies in Automation and Control [*A publication*]
Stud Bank Fin ... Studies in Banking and Finance [*A publication*]
Stud Bayesian Econometrics ... Studies in Bayesian Econometrics [*A
publication*]
Stud Bibliog ... Virginia University. Bibliographical Society. Studies in
Bibliography [*A publication*]
Stud Bibliog & Bklore ... Studies in Bibliography and Booklore [*A publication*]
Stud Biol .... Studies in Biology [*A publication*]
Stud Black Lit ... Studies in Black Literature [*A publication*]
Stud Brain Funct ... Studies in Brain Function [*A publication*]
Stud Br His ... Studies in British History and Culture [*A publication*]
Stud Broadcast ... Studies of Broadcasting [*A publication*]
Stud Brown ... Studies in Browning and His Circle [*A publication*]
Stud Burke Time ... Studies in Burke and His Time [*A publication*]

Stud Chemother Inst Med Res ... Studies. Chemotherapeutic Institute for Medical Research [*Japan*] [*A publication*]
Stud Ch G P ... Studies in Chinese Government and Politics [*A publication*]
Stud Church Hist ... Studies in Church History. American Society of Church History [*A publication*]
Stud Class ... Studies of Classical India [*A publication*]
Stud Com Co ... Studies in Comparative Communism [*A publication*]
Stud Com I D ... Studies in Comparative International Development [*A publication*]
Stud Com L G ... Studies in Comparative Local Government [*A publication*]
Stud Comm R ... Studies in Communism, Revisionism, and Revolution [*A publication*]
Stud Comp Com ... Studies in Comparative Communism [*Los Angeles*] [*A publication*]
Stud Comp Commun ... Studies in Comparative Communism [*A publication*]
Stud Comp Communism ... Studies in Comparative Communism [*A publication*]
Stud Comp Int Dev ... Studies in Comparative International Development [*New Jersey*] [*A publication*]
Stud Comp Int Develop ... Studies in Comparative International Development [*A publication*]
Stud in Comp Local Govt ... Studies in Comparative Local Government [*A publication*]
Stud Comp R ... Studies in Comparative Religion [*A publication*]
Stud Comp Relig ... Studies in Comparative Religion [*A publication*]
Stud Conserv ... Studies in Conservation [*A publication*]
Stud Cont Ed ... Studies in Continuing Education [*A publication*]
Stud in Contin Educ ... Studies in Continuing Education [*A publication*] (APTA)
Stud Cosmic Ray ... Studies of Cosmic Ray [*Japan*] [*A publication*]
Stud Design Educ Craft Technol ... Studies in Design Education, Craft, and Technology [*A publication*]
Stud Develop ... Middle East Technical University. Studies in Development [*A publication*]
Stud Develop Special Issue ... Studies in Development. Special Issue. Middle East Technical University [*A publication*]
Stud Doc Hist Iur ... Studia et Documenta Historiae et Iuris [*Rome*] [*A publication*] (OCD)
Stud Docum Asian Docum ... Studies and Documents. Asian Documentation and Research Center [*A publication*]
STUDE...... Studebaker [*Automotive engineering*]
Stud Ecol ... Studies in Ecology [*A publication*]
Stud Ed ...... Studies in Education [*A publication*]
Stud Educ Adults ... Studies in the Education of Adults [*A publication*]
Stud Eight ... Studies in Eighteenth-Century Culture [*A publication*]
Stud Eighteenth-Century Cult ... Studies in Eighteenth-Century Culture [*A publication*]
Stud Engl L ... Studies in English Literature, 1500-1900 [*A publication*]
Stud Engl Lit ... Studies in English Literature [*A publication*]
Stud Engl Phil ... Studien zur Englischen Philologie [*A publication*]
Stud Engl (T) ... Studies in English Literature (Tokyo) [*A publication*]
Student Adv ... Student Advocate [*A publication*]
Studente Vet ... Studente Veterinario [*A publication*]
StudentIElecIE ... Student of the Institution of Electrical and Electronic Incorporated Engineers [*British*] (DBQ)
StudentIWHTE ... Student of the Institution of Works and Highways Technician Engineers [*British*] (DBQ)
Student Law ... Student Lawyer [*A publication*]
Student Law J ... Student Lawyer Journal [*A publication*] (DLA)
Student L Rev ... Student Law Review [*A publication*] (DLA)
Student Musicol ... Student Musicologists at Minnesota [*A publication*]
Student Q J Instn Elec Engrs ... Institution of Electrical Engineers. Student Quarterly Journal [*A publication*]
Students'ky Nauk Pratsi Kyyv Derzh Unyv ... Students'ky Naukovi Pratsi Kyyivs'kyyi Derzhavnyyi Unyversytet [*A publication*]
Stud Environ Sci ... Studies in Environmental Science [*A publication*]
Stud Etr...... Studi Etruschi [*Firenze*] [*A publication*] (OCD)
Stud Europ Soc ... Studies in European Society [*A publication*]
Stud Fam Pl ... Studies in Family Planning [*A publication*]
Stud Fam Plann ... Studies in Family Planning [*A publication*]
Stud Fauna Curacao Other Caribb Isl ... Studies on the Fauna of Curacao and Other Caribbean Islands [*A publication*]
Stud Fauna Suriname Other Guyanas ... Studies of the Fauna of Suriname and Other Guyanas [*A publication*]
Stud Filol ... Studime Filologjike [*A publication*]
Stud Form Spir ... Studies in Formative Spirituality [*A publication*]
Stud Found Methodol Philos Sci ... Studies in the Foundations, Methodology, and Philosophy of Science [*A publication*]
Stud Gen .... Studium Generale [*A publication*]
Stud Genet ... Studies in Genetics [*A publication*]
Stud Geogr ... Studies in Geography [*A publication*]
Stud Geol Mineral Inst Tokyo Univ Educ ... Studies from the Geological and Mineralogical Institute. Tokyo University of Education [*A publication*]
Stud Geol (Tulsa Okla) ... Studies in Geology (Tulsa, Oklahoma) [*A publication*]
Stud Gesch Akad Wiss DDR ... Studien zur Geschichte der Akademie der Wissenschaften der Deutsche Demokratische Republik [*A publication*]
Stud Gesch Kult Alt ... Studien zur Geschichte und Kultur des Altertums [*A publication*] (OCD)

Stud Gr Rom Hist ... Studies in Greek and Roman History [*A publication*] (OCD)
Stud H Art ... Studies in the History of Art [*A publication*]
Stud High Educ ... Studies in Higher Education [*A publication*]
Stud High Temp Supercond ... Studies of High Temperature Superconductors. Advances in Research and Applications [*A publication*]
Stud Hist.... Studies in History, Economics, and Public Law [*A publication*] (DLA)
Stud Hist.... Studime Historike [*A publication*]
Stud Hist Art ... Studies in the History of Art [*A publication*]
Stud Hist Biol ... Studies in History of Biology [*A publication*]
Stud Hist Math Phys Sci ... Studies in the History of Mathematics and Physical Sciences [*A publication*]
Stud Hist Med ... Studies in History of Medicine [*A publication*]
Stud Hist Modern Sci ... Studies in the History of Modern Science [*A publication*]
Stud Hist P ... Studies in History and Philosophy of Science [*A publication*]
Stud Hist Philos Sci ... Studies in History and Philosophy of Science [*A publication*]
Stud Hist & Soc ... Studies in History and Society [*A publication*]
Studia Ser Math ... Studia. Series Mathematica [*A publication*]
Studia Univ Babes-Bolyai Math ... Universitatis Babes-Bolyai. Studia. Series Mathematica [*A publication*]
Studiecent TNO Scheepsbouw Navig Commun ... Studiecentrum TNO [*Toegepast Natuurwetenschappelijk Onderzoek*] voor Scheepsbouw en Navigatie. Communication [*A publication*]
Studiecent TNO Scheepsbouw Navig Rep ... Studiecentrum TNO [*Toegepast Natuurwetenschappelijk Onderzoek*] voor Scheepsbouw en Navigatie. Report [*A publication*]
Studienb Naturwiss Tech ... Studienbuecher Naturwissenschaft und Technik [*A publication*]
Studien und Mitteilungen ... Studien und Mitteilungen aus dem Benediktiner- und dem Cistercienser-Orden [*A publication*]
Studienskripten zur Soziol ... Studienskripten zur Soziologie [*A publication*]
Studies .... Studies in Political Economy [*A publication*]
Studies Appl Math ... Studies in Applied Mathematics [*A publication*]
Studies App Math ... Studies in Applied Mathematics [*A publication*]
Studies in Art Ed ... Studies in Art Education [*A publication*]
Studies in Aust Bibliog ... Studies in Australian Bibliography [*A publication*] (APTA)
Studies of Bcasting ... Studies of Broadcasting [*Japan*] [*A publication*]
Studies in Can Lit ... Studies in Canadian Literature [*A publication*]
Studies Conserv ... Studies in Conservation [*A publication*]
Studies Crim L ... Studies in Criminal Law and Procedure [*A publication*] (DLA)
Studies Econ Analysis ... Studies in Economic Analysis [*A publication*]
Studies Hum ... Studies in the Humanities [*A publication*]
Studies Internat Relations (Warsaw) ... Studies on International Relations (Warsaw) [*A publication*]
Studies L & Econ Develop ... Studies in Law and Economic Development [*A publication*]
Studies Mus ... Studies in Music [*A publication*]
Studies Parasitol and Gen Zool ... Studies in Parasitology and General Zoology [*A publication*]
Studies Philol ... Studies in Philology [*A publication*]
Studies Pol Economy ... Studies in Political Economy [*A publication*]
Studies Zool Lab Univ Nebr ... Studies. Zoological Laboratory. University of Nebraska [*A publication*]
Studijni Inform Lesnictyi ... Studijni Informace. Lesnictyi [*A publication*]
StudIManf ... Student Member of the Institute of Manufacturing [*British*] (DBQ)
StudIMS.... Student of the Institute of Management Specialists [*British*] (DBQ)
Stud Indo-As Art Cult ... Studies in Indo-Asian Art and Culture [*New Delhi*] [*A publication*]
Stud Inorg Chem ... Studies in Inorganic Chemistry [*A publication*]
Stud In Relat ... Studies on International Relations [*A publication*]
StudInstBTM ... Student Member of the Institute of Business and Technical Management [*British*] (DBQ)
Stud Inst Divi Thomae ... Studies. Institutum Divi Thomae [*A publication*]
Stud Inst Med Res (Malaya) ... Studies. Institute for Medical Research (Malaya) [*A publication*]
Stud Int ...... Studio International [*A publication*]
Stud Intellectual Precocity ... Studies of Intellectual Precocity [*A publication*]
Stud Intell Obs ... Student and Intellectual Observer [*A publication*]
Stud & Intel Obs ... Student and Intellectual Observer [*A publication*]
Stud Int'l Fiscal L ... Studies on International Fiscal Law [*A publication*] (DLA)
Studio......... Studio International [*A publication*]
Studio Int... Studio International [*A publication*]
Studio Intl ... Studio International [*A publication*]
Studi Stor... Studi Storici per l'Antichita Classica [*A publication*] (OCD)
Stud Ital..... Studi Italiani di Filologia Classica [*A publication*] (OCD)
Stud J Inst Electron Telecommun Eng ... Students' Journal. Institution of Electronics and Telecommunication Engineers [*A publication*]
Stud Jugendzahn A ... Student und Jugendzahnarzt [*A publication*]
Stud Kulturkunde ... Studien zur Kulturkunde [*A publication*]
Stud Labour Hist ... Studies in Labour History [*A publication*]
Stud Lang... Studies in Language. International Journal [*A publication*]

Stud Lang C ... Studies in Language. Companion Series [*A publication*]
Stud Law Lex ... Students' Pocket Law Lexicon [*A publication*]   (DLA)
Stud L & Econ Dev ... Studies in Law and Economic Development [*A publication*]   (DLA)
Stud Ling ... Studies in Linguistics [*A publication*]
Stud Ling Lang Learn ... Studies in Linguistics and Languages Learning
Stud Ling Sci ... Studies in the Linguistic Sciences [*Urbana*] [*A publication*]
Stud Lit Im ... Studies in the Literary Imagination [*A publication*]
Stud Logic Foundations Math ... Studies in Logic and the Foundations of Mathematics [*A publication*]
Stud M ... Studies in Music [*A publication*]
Stud Management Sci ... Studies in the Management Sciences [*A publication*]
Stud Management Sci Systems ... Studies in Management Science and Systems [*A publication*]
Stud Materialien Geschichte Philos ... Studien und Materialien zur Geschichte der Philosophie [*A publication*]
Stud Mater Weiterbild Med Tech Laborassistenten ... Studien-Material zur Weiterbildung Medizinisch-Technischer Laborassistenten [*A publication*]
Stud Math Appl ... Studies in Mathematics and Its Applications [*A publication*]
Stud Math Managerial Econom ... Studies in Mathematical and Managerial Economics [*A publication*]
Stud Med ... Student Medicine [*A publication*]
Stud Med Geogr ... Studies in Medical Geography [*A publication*]
Stud Mediev ... Studies in Medieval Culture [*A publication*]
Stud Microbiol ... Studies in Microbiology [*A publication*]
Stud Mitt Bened Cisterc ... Studien und Mitteilungen aus dem Benediktiner- und dem Cistercienser-Orden [*A publication*]
Stud Mitt Gesch Benediktinerorden ... Studien und Mitteilungen zur Geschichte des Benediktiner-Ordens und Seiner Zweige [*A publication*]
Stud Modern Thermodynamics ... Studies in Modern Thermodynamics [*A publication*]
Stud MW ... Studien zur Musikwissenschaft [*A publication*]
Stud Mycol ... Studies in Mycology [*A publication*]
Stud Nakamura Gakuin Univ ... Studies. Nakamura Gakuin University [*A publication*]
Stud Nat Sci ... Studies in the Natural Sciences [*A publication*]
Stud Nat Sci (Portales NM) ... Studies in Natural Sciences (Portales, New Mexico) [*A publication*]
Stud Nauchno Issled Rab Sib Tekhnol Inst ... Studencheskie Nauchno-Issledovatel'skie Raboty. Sibirskii Tekhnologicheskii Institut [*A publication*]
Stud Nauchn Rab Univ Druzhby Nar ... Studencheskie Nauchnye Raboty. Universitet Druzhby Narodov [*A publication*]
Stud Nauk Pr Kiiv Derzh Univ ... Students'ki Naukovi Pratsi Kiivs'kii Derzhavnii Universitet [*A publication*]
Stud Neotrop Fauna ... Studies on the Neotropical Fauna [*Later, Studies on the Neotropical Fauna and Environment*] [*A publication*]
Stud Neotrop Fauna Environ ... Studies on the Neotropical Fauna and Environment [*A publication*]
Stud Neuro Anat ... Studies in Neuro-Anatomy [*A publication*]
Stud Niger Lang ... Studies in Nigerian Languages [*A publication*]
Stud No Phil ... Studies and Notes in Philology and Literature [*A publication*]
Stud Novel ... Studies in the Novel [*A publication*]
StudNT ... Studien zum Neuen Testament [*Guetersloh*] [*A publication*]
Stud Nurs Man ... Studies in Nursing Management [*A publication*]
Stud Ov ... Studium Ovetense [*A publication*]
Stud Pac Lang Cult ... Studies in Pacific Languages and Cultures in Honour of Bruce Biggs [*A publication*]
Stud Paint (Osaka) ... Studies in Paint (Osaka) [*Japan*] [*A publication*]
StudPal ... Studien zur Palaeographie und Papyruskunde [*Leipzig*] [*A publication*]
Stud Person Psychol ... Studies in Personnel Psychology [*A publication*]
Stud Pers P ... Studies in Personnel Psychology [*A publication*]
Stud Pers Psych ... Studies in Personnel Psychology [*A publication*]
Stud Phil ... Studies in Philology [*A publication*]
Stud Phil E ... Studies in Philosophy and Education [*A publication*]
Stud Phil & Ed ... Studies in Philosophy and Education [*A publication*]
Stud Phil H ... Studies in Philosophy and the History of Philosophy [*A publication*]
Stud Phil Hist Phil ... Studies in Philosophy and the History of Philosophy [*A publication*]
Stud Phil Ling ... Studies in Philippine Linguistics [*Manila*] [*A publication*]
Stud Philol ... Studies in Philology [*A publication*]
Stud Philos ... Studies in Philosophy [*The Hague*] [*A publication*]
Stud Philos & Educ ... Studies in Philosophy and Education [*A publication*]
Stud Philos Med ... Studies in Philosophy of Medicine [*A publication*]
Stud Phys Anthropol ... Studies in Physical Anthropology [*A publication*]
Stud Phys Theor Chem ... Studies in Physical and Theoretical Chemistry [*A publication*]
Stud Plant Ecol ... Studies in Plant Ecology [*A publication*]
Stud Psychol Psychiat Cath Univ Amer ... Studies in Psychology and Psychiatry. Catholic University of America [*A publication*]
Stud Q J Inst Electr Eng ... Students Quarterly Journal. Institution of Electrical Engineers [*England*] [*A publication*]
Stud QJ Inst El Eng ... Students Quarterly Journal. Institution of Electrical Engineers [*A publication*]
Stud Radiat Eff Solids ... Studies in Radiation Effects in Solids [*A publication*]

Stud Regional Sci Urban Econom ... Studies in Regional Science and Urban Economics [*A publication*]
Stud Rel ... Studies in Religion [*Ontario*] [*A publication*]
Stud Relig ... Studies in Religion [*A publication*]
Stud Ren ... Studies in the Renaissance [*A publication*]
Stud Rep Hydrol IAHS - UNESCO ... Studies and Reports in Hydrology. International Association of Hydrological Sciences - United Nations Educational, Scientific, and Cultural Organization [*A publication*]
Stud Res Inst Meteorol Hydrol Part 2 ... Studies and Research. Institute of Meteorology and Hydrology. Part 2. Hydrology [*A publication*]
Stud Roman ... Studies in Romanticism [*A publication*]
Stud Romant ... Studies in Romanticism [*A publication*]
Stud Romanticism ... Studies in Romanticism [*A publication*]
Stud Rsch ... Studentische Rundschau [*A publication*]
Stud Sci Educ ... Studies in Science Education [*A publication*]
Stud Sc Lit ... Studies in Scottish Literature [*A publication*]
Stud Scott Lit ... Studies in Scottish Literature [*A publication*]
StudSCP ... Student of the Society of Certified Professionals [*British*]   (DBQ)
StudSE ... Student of the Society of Engineers [*British*]   (DBQ)
Stud Sh Fic ... Studies in Short Fiction [*A publication*]
Stud Short Fict ... Studies in Short Fiction [*A publication*]
Stud Short Fiction ... Studies in Short Fiction [*A publication*]
StudSLAET ... Student of the Society of Licensed Aircraft Engineers and Technologists [*British*]   (DBQ)
Stud Soc Li ... Studies in Social Life [*A publication*]
Stud Soc Wk ... Studies on Social Work [*A publication*]
Stud Solid Phys Chem ... Studies on Solid State Physics and Chemistry [*Japan*] [*A publication*]
Stud Sov Th ... Studies in Soviet Thought [*A publication*]
Stud Sov Thought ... Studies in Soviet Thought [*A publication*]
Stud Spelaeol ... Studies in Spelaeology [*A publication*]
Stud Speleol ... Studies in Speleology [*A publication*]
Stud Statist Mech ... Studies in Statistical Mechanics [*A publication*]
Stud Stat Mech ... Studies in Statistical Mechanics [*A publication*]
Stud Stn Fish Res Board Can ... Studies. Stations of the Fisheries Research Board of Canada [*A publication*]
Stud Stobi ... Studies in the Antiquities of Stobi [*A publication*]
Stud Surf Sci Catal ... Studies in Surface Science and Catalysis [*Netherlands*] [*Elsevier Book Series*] [*A publication*]
Stud TC ... Studies in the Twentieth Century [*A publication*]
Stud Third World Soc ... Studies in Third World Societies [*Williamsburg*] [*A publication*]
Stud Tokugawa Inst ... Studies. Tokugawa Institute [*A publication*]
Stud Tour Rep Dep Prim Ind (Queensl) ... Study Tour Report. Department of Primary Industries (Queensland) [*A publication*]   (APTA)
Stud Trade Unionists ... Studies for Trade Unionists [*A publication*]
Stud Trop Oceanogr Inst Mar Sci Univ Miami ... Studies in Tropical Oceanography. Institute of Marine Science. University of Miami [*A publication*]
Stud Trop Oceanogr (Miami) ... Studies in Tropical Oceanography (Miami) [*A publication*]
Stud Urb ... Studi di Urbanistica Antica [*A publication*]   (OCD)
Stud Vis Com ... Studies in Visual Communication [*A publication*]
Stud Voltaire ... Studies on Voltaire and the Eighteenth Century [*A publication*]
Stud Voltaire Eighteenth Century ... Studies on Voltaire and the Eighteenth Century [*A publication*]
Stud VT Geol ... Studies in Vermont Geology [*A publication*]
Stud W ... Student World [*A publication*]
Stud W Aust Hist ... Studies in Western Australian History [*A publication*]
StudWeldI ... Student of the Welding Institute [*British*]   (DBQ)
Stud Women Abstr ... Studies on Women Abstracts [*A publication*]
Study Elem Particles ... Study of Elementary Particles [*Japan*] [*A publication*]
Study of Soc ... Study of Society [*A publication*]   (APTA)
Study Tea ... Study of Tea [*A publication*]
StudzumAuNT ... Studien zum Alten und Neuen Testament [*Munich*] [*A publication*]
STUF ... Student Flight [*Military*]
STUF ... Stuff Yer Face, Inc. [*NASDAQ symbol*]   (NQ)
STUFF ... System to Uncover Facts Fast
STUFT ... Ships Taken Up from Trade
STUG ... Student Group [*Military*]
STUG ... Sturmgeschuetz [*Self-propelled assault gun*] [*German military - World War II*]
STUH ... Stuart Hall Co., Inc. [*NASDAQ symbol*]   (NQ)
STU-IIM ... Secure Terminal Unit-II Militarized
STUK ... Sturmkanone [*Self-propelled assault gun*] [*German military - World War II*]
STUKA ... Sturzkampfflugzeug [*Dive bomber*] [*German military - World War II*]
Stu KB ... Stuart's Lower Canada King's Bench Reports [*1810-35*] [*A publication*]   (DLA)
Stu LC ... Stuart's Lower Canada King's Bench Reports [*1810-35*] [*A publication*]   (DLA)
StuLnC ... Student Loan Corp. [*Associated Press abbreviation*]   (APAG)
Stu Mil & Ped ... Stuart, Milne, and Peddie's Scotch Court of Sessions Reports [*A publication*]   (DLA)

Stu M & P ...	Stuart, Milne, and Peddie's Scotch Court of Sessions Reports [*A publication*] (DLA)
StUmwNT ...	Studien zur Umwelt des Neuen Testament [*Goettingen*] [*A publication*]
Stun............	Serial Tunneling [*Data processing*]
St UNT	Studien zur Umwelt des Neuen Testament [*A publication*]
STUP......	Spinning Tubular Projectile (MCD)
STUPID	Simulation of the Underlying Processes in Decisions (MCD)
Stu Prob & St ...	Studies in Probability and Statistics [*A publication*]
STURAA...	Surface Transportation and Uniform Relocation Assistance Act [*1987*]
S Turb........	Steam Turbine (DS)
Sturg BL	Sturgeon. Bankrupt Acts [*A publication*] (ILCA)
Sturg Ins D ...	Sturgeon's Insolvent Debtors Act [*1842*] [*A publication*] (DLA)
STURM.....	Sturminster [*England*]
SturmR.....	Sturm Ruger & Co. [*Associated Press abbreviation*] (APAG)
STURP......	Shroud of Turin Research Project (EA)
Stur & Porter ...	Stuart [*or Stewart*] and Porter's Alabama Reports [*A publication*] (DLA)
STUS........	Stuarts Department Stores, Inc. [*Hopkinton, MA*] [*NASDAQ symbol*] (NQ)
STUS........	Student Squadron
StuTC........	Studies in the Twentieth Century [*A publication*]
STUTNG...	Student Training [*Navy*] (DNAB)
Stutt Beitr Naturk ...	Stuttgarter Beitraege zur Naturkunde [*A publication*]
Stuttgarter Beitraege ...	Stuttgarter Beitraege zur Geschichte und Politik [*A publication*]
Stuttg Beitr Naturkd ...	Stuttgarter Beitraege zur Naturkunde [*A publication*]
Stuttg Beitr Naturkd Ser A (Biol) ...	Stuttgarter Beitraege zur Naturkunde. Serie A (Biologie) [*A publication*]
Stuttg Beitr Naturkd Ser B (Geol Palaeontol) ...	Stuttgarter Beitraege zur Naturkunde. Serie B (Geologie und Palaeontologie) [*A publication*]
Stuttg Beitr Naturk Ser C Allg Aufsaetze ...	Stuttgarter Beitraege zur Naturkunde. Serie C. Allgemeinverstaendliche Aufsaetze [*A publication*]
Stuttg Geogr Stud ...	Stuttgarter Geographische Studien [*A publication*]
Stu VA	Stuart's Lower Canada Vice-Admiralty Reports [*A publication*] (ILCA)
STUWA.....	Sterne und Weltraum [*A publication*]
STV...........	Santa Anna Di Valdieri [*Italy*] [*Seismograph station code, US Geological Survey*] (SEIS)
STV...........	Scottish Television (DI)
STV...........	Separation Test Vehicle
STV...........	Short-Tube Vertical [*Evaporator*]
STV...........	Single Transferable Vote
STV...........	Small Test Vessel [*Nuclear energy*] (NRCH)
STV...........	Solar Thermal Vacuum
STV...........	Solidaridad de Trabajadores Vascos [*Solidarity of Basque Workers*] [*In exile*] [*Spain*]
STV...........	Southern Television [*British*] (DI)
STV...........	Space Test Vehicle [*NASA*] (KSC)
STV...........	Special Test Vehicle
STV...........	Standard Test Vehicle
STV...........	Steam Tank Vessel (DNAB)
STV...........	Stikine Silver [*Vancouver Stock Exchange symbol*]
STV...........	Stonewall, TX [*Location identifier*] [*FAA*] (FAAL)
STV...........	Stove [*Classified advertising*] (ADA)
STV...........	Structural Test Vehicle [*NASA*] (KSC)
StV	Studies on Voltaire and the Eighteenth Century [*A publication*]
STV...........	Submarine Target Vessel (NVT)
STV.........	Subscription Television
STV...........	Supersonic Test Vehicle (AAG)
STV...........	Surveillance Television (AFM)
STVA........	Self-Tuning Vibration Absorber [*Navy*] (CAAL)
Stva	Stvaranje [*A publication*]
STVA........	Subscription Television Association [*Defunct*] (EA)
STVA........	Subtotal Villose Atrophy [*Medicine*] (MAE)
STV Bull	STV [*Schweizerischer Technischer Verband*] Bulletin [*A publication*]
STVC........	Space Thermal Vacuum Chamber (SAA)
STVC........	Sumerian Texts of Varied Context [*E. Chiera*] [*A publication*]
STVCA........	Stavebnicky Casopis [*A publication*]
STVD........	Spacecraft Television Video Data
stvdr	Stevedore (DS)
St Vd VUB ...	Studies en Voordrachten. VUB [*Vrije Universiteit te Brussel*] [*A publication*]
STVE.........	Steve's Homemade Ice Cream, Inc. [*Lindenhurst, NY*] [*NASDAQ symbol*] (NQ)
STVFB.......	Samoletostroenie i Tekhnika Vozdushnogo Flota [*A publication*]
St VG	Straphenverrkehrsgesetz [*A publication*]
StvGp	Stevens Graphics Corp. [*Associated Press abbreviation*] (APAG)
STVI	STV Engineers, Inc. [*NASDAQ symbol*] (NQ)
St Vj	Statistische Vierteljahrsschrift [*A publication*]
St VK	Studien und Voelkerkunde [*A publication*]
STVL	Stereo Village, Inc. [*Decatur, GA*] [*NASDAQ symbol*] (NQ)
StVladSemQ ...	St. Vladimir's Seminary. Quarterly [*New York*] [*A publication*]

St Vl Th Q ...	Saint Vladimir's Theological Quarterly [*A publication*]
STVM........	Semitrailer Van Mount
St VO	Strafvollstreckungsordnung [*A publication*]
St VO	Strassenverkehrsordnung [*A publication*]
St Vollstr O ...	Strafvollstreckungsordnung [*A publication*]
STVP........	Short-Term Vehicle Park (DS)
STVS	Short-Term Visual Storage [*or Store*] [*Psychophysiology*]
STVS	Surinaamse Televisie Sichting [*Television network*] [*Surinam*]
STVS	Surinaamse Televisie Stichtig (EY)
STVT.........	Sterivet Laboratories Ltd. [*NASDAQ symbol*] (NQ)
St VZO	Strassenverkehrszulassungsordnung [*A publication*]
STW...........	Save the Whales (EA)
STW...........	Sewage Treatment Works
STW...........	Southwest Tech [*Vancouver Stock Exchange symbol*]
STW...........	Speed Made Good Through the Water (NATG)
STW...........	Standard Commercial Tobacco Co. [*NYSE symbol*] (SPSG)
STW...........	Star Trek Welcommittee (EA)
STW...........	Stern Wheel [*of a ship*] (DS)
STW...........	Stillwater, NJ [*Location identifier*] [*FAA*] (FAAL)
STW...........	Stillwater Public Library, Stillwater, OK [*OCLC symbol*] (OCLC)
STW...........	Storm Water
STW...........	Striped Peak [*Washington*] [*Seismograph station code, US Geological Survey*] (SEIS)
STW...........	Subtropical Water
ST. WAPNIACL ...	State, Treasury, War, Attorney General, Postmaster General, Navy, Interior, Agriculture, Commerce, Labor [*Pre-1947 mnemonic guide to names of the departments in the President's Cabinet, in order of creation*] [*Obsolete*]
STWB........	Statewide Bancorp [*NASDAQ symbol*] (NQ)
STWBRD ..	Strawboard [*Shipping*]
STWD........	Steward (FAAC)
STWE........	Society of Technical Writers and Editors [*Later, STWP, STC*]
St Westm ...	Statute of Westminster [*A publication*] (DLA)
STWG........	Stowage (MSA)
St u Wi	Steuer und Wirtschaft [*A publication*]
STWP........	Society of Technical Writers and Publishers [*Formerly, STWE*] [*Later, STC*] (EA)
STWP........	Steam Working Pressure (MSA)
STWS	Stewardess (FAAC)
STWY........	Stairway (AAG)
STWY........	Stopway (FAAC)
STX...........	Christiansted, St. Croix, VI [*Location identifier*] [*FAA*] (FAAL)
STX...........	St. Croix [*Virgin Islands*] [*Airport symbol*]
STX...........	Saxitoxin [*A neurotoxin*]
STX...........	Situational Training Exercise [*Army*] (INF)
STX...........	Spherical Torus Experiment [*Oak Ridge National Laboratory*]
STX...........	Starrex Mining Corp. Ltd. [*Toronto Stock Exchange symbol*]
STX...........	Start of Text Character [*Keyboard*] [*Data processing*]
STX...........	Station 2 [*Nevada*] [*Seismograph station code, US Geological Survey*] [*Closed*] (SEIS)
STX...........	Sterling Chemicals, Inc. [*NYSE symbol*] (CTT)
STX...........	Stewart-Warner Corp. [*NYSE symbol*] (SPSG)
STXL.........	Sports-Tech International, Inc. [*NASDAQ symbol*] (NQ)
STXM........	Scanning Transmission X-Ray Microscopy (MCD)
STXRF.......	Source-Tuned X-Ray Fluorescence [*Spectroscopy*]
STY...........	Salto [*Uruguay*] [*Airport symbol*] (OAG)
STY...........	Space-Time Yield [*Chemical engineering*]
StY	Standard Yiddish (BJA)
STY...........	Sterling Drug, Inc. [*NYSE symbol*] (SPSG)
STY...........	Stony River [*Alaska*] [*Seismograph station code, US Geological Survey*] (SEIS)
Sty..............	Story [*Journalism*]
Sty..............	Style's English King's Bench Reports [*1646-55*] [*A publication*] (DLA)
Sty..............	Styrene [*Also, St*] [*Organic chemistry*]
Style	Style's English King's Bench Reports [*A publication*] (DLA)
Style Pr Reg ...	Style's Practical Register [*A publication*] (DLA)
STYP........	Styptic [*Stopping Bleeding*] [*Medicine*] (ROG)
Sty Pr Reg ...	Style's Practical Register [*1657-1710*] [*A publication*] (DLA)
Styr Tek Utveckling Inf Energitek ...	Styrelsen foer Teknisk Utveckling Informerar om Energiteknik [*Sweden*] [*A publication*]
STZ............	Santa Terezinha [*Brazil*] [*Airport symbol*] (OAG)
STZ............	Schweizerische Theologische Zeitschrift [*Zurich*] [*A publication*] (BJA)
STZ............	Serum-Treated Zymosan [*Clinical chemistry*]
STZ............	Southern Transgressive Zone [*Geology*]
STZ............	Sprache im Technischen Zeitalter [*A publication*]
STZ............	Stallion Resources Ltd. [*Vancouver Stock Exchange symbol*]
STZ............	Stratford [*New Zealand*] [*Seismograph station code, US Geological Survey*] [*Closed*] (SEIS)
STZ............	Streptozocin [*Antineoplastic drug*]
St ZA	Steuer-Zentralarchiv [*A publication*]
STZED.......	Stimmen der Zeit [*A publication*]
SU............	AEROFLOT [*Aero Flotilla*] [*Former USSR*] [*ICAO designator*] (FAAC)
Su...............	Ciba-Geigy Corp. [*Research code symbol*]
SU.............	Optical Device [*JETDS nomenclature*] [*Military*] (CET)
SU.............	Salicyluric Acid [*Also, SUA*] [*Biochemistry*]
SU.............	Salmon Unlimited (EA)

SU .... Samostijna Ukraina [*Independent Ukraine*] [*A publication*]
su .... Saudi Arabia [*MARC country of publication code*] [*Library of Congress*]   (LCCP)
SU .... Savings Unit
SU .... Schriften des Urchristentums [*A publication*]
SU .... Scorable Unit
SU .... Scripture Union [*British*]
SU .... Seamen's Union [*British*]
SU .... Selectable Unit   (BUR)
SU .... Sensation Units
SU .... Separation Ullage
SU .... Service Unit [*Military*]
SU .... Set Up [*Freight*]
SU .... Shipment Unit [*Army*]
SU .... Siemens Unit
SU .... Sigma Units
SU .... Signaling Unit
SU .... Single Uptake [*Boilers*]
SU .... Single User [*The military activity that has the sole interest in an item of supply*] [*DoD*]
SU .... Society of the Sisters of St. Ursula of the Blessed Virgin [*Roman Catholic religious order*]
SU .... Somogyi Unit [*of amylase*] [*Clinical chemistry*]
SU .... Sonics and Ultrasonics   (MCD)
SU .... Sosialistisk Ungdom [*Norway*]
SU .... Soviet Union [*The USSR*]
SU .... Space Unit   (EA)
SU .... Special Unitary [*Algebra*]
SU .... Standard Upkeep
SU .... Stanford University [*California*]
SU .... Start Up [*of a relay, power switchgear*]   (IEEE)
S/U .... Startup [*Nuclear energy*]   (NRCH)
SU .... Station Unit [*Telecommunications*]   (OA)
SU .... Statistical Unit [*UNRISD*] [*United Nations*]   (DUND)
SU .... Storage Unit [*Data processing*]
SU .... Stripers Unlimited   (EA)
SU .... Strontium Units [*Nuclear energy*]
SU .... Student Union
SU .... Stunts Unlimited   (EA)
SU .... Sub-Unit   (DNAB)
SU .... Subject [*Online database field identifier*]
SU .... Submarine School Graduate [*Navy*]   (DNAB)
SU .... Subscriber Unit [*RADA*] [*Army*]   (RDA)
Su .... Sufentanil [*or Sulfentanyl*] [*An analgesic*]
su .... Sugary [*A gene in sweet corn*]
SU .... Suit   (DNAB)
Su .... Suite
SU .... Sukhoy [*Aircraft*]
Su .... Sulcus [*Brain anatomy*]
Su .... Sumarstvo [*A publication*]
Su .... Sumet [*Let Him, or Her, Take*] [*Pharmacy*]
SU .... Suncor, Inc. [*Toronto Stock Exchange symbol*]
SU .... Sunday
SU .... Super Unleaded (Gasoline)
Su .... Superb [*Philately*]
SU .... Supercommutation   (SAA)
Su .... Superior Court   (DLA)
SU .... Supply [*Business term*]
SU .... Support Unit [*NASA*]   (NASA)
SU .... Suppressor [*Electronics*]   (MDG)
SU .... Switching Unit
SUCH ...... Syne Unit [*Telecommunications*]   (OA)
SU .... Syracuse University [*New York*]
SU .... Thiouridine [*Two-letter symbol; see Srd*]
SU .... Union of Soviet Socialist Republics [*ANSI two-letter standard code*]   (CNC)
SU .... United Arab Republic [*Aircraft nationality and registration mark*]   (FAAC)
SUA .... Salicyluric Acid [*Also, SU*] [*Biochemistry*]
SUA .... Satellite Unfurlable Antenna
SUA .... Serum Uric Acid [*Clinical chemistry*]
SUA .... Silver Users Association   (EA)
SUA .... Single Umbilical Artery [*Medicine*]   (MAE)
SUA .... Small Unit Action [*Military*]   (CINC)
SUA .... Society for Urban Anthropology   (EA)
SUA .... Standard Unit of Accounting [*Data processing*]
SUA .... State Universities Association [*Later, NASULGC*]
SUA .... Stuart [*Florida*] [*Airport symbol*]   (OAG)
SUA .... Stuart, FL [*Location identifier*] [*FAA*]   (FAAL)
SUA ,......... Summit Tax Exempt Bond Fund Ltd. [*AMEX symbol*]   (SPSG)
SUA .... Superior Acceptance Corp. Ltd. [*Toronto Stock Exchange symbol*]
SUA .... Supplemental Unemployment Assistance
SUA .... Supply/Utilization Accounts [*FAO*] [*Information service or system*] [*United Nations*]   (DUND)
SUA .... Susitna [*Alaska*] [*Seismograph station code, US Geological Survey*]   (SEIS)
SUA .... Sweetener Users Association   (EA)
SUAA .... Montevideo/Angel S. Adami [*Uruguay*] [*ICAO location identifier*]   (ICLI)

SUAB .... Svenska Utvecklingsaktiebolaget [*Swedish Corporation for Development*]
SUADPS ... Shipboard Uniform Automatic Data Processing System [*Navy*]
SUAEWICS ... Soviet Union Airborne Early Warning and Interceptor Control System   (MCD)
SUAG .... Artigas/Aeropuerto Deptal [*Uruguay*] [*ICAO location identifier*]   (ICLI)
SUAGDL... Sulphur in Agriculture [*A publication*]
SUALM..... Submerged Anchor Leg Mooring [*Engineering*]
SUAR .... Start Unload Address Register
Suar........... [*Rodericus*] Suarez [*Flourished, 15th century*] [*Authority cited in pre-1607 legal work*]   (DSA)
Suara Ekon ... Suara Ekonomi [*Singapore*] [*A publication*]
Suas........... Suasoriae [*of Seneca the Elder*] [*Classical studies*]   (OCD)
SUAS........ System for Upper Atmosphere Sounding   (MCD)
SuavSh..... Suave Shoe Corp. [*Associated Press abbreviation*]   (APAG)
SUAWACS ... Soviet Union Airborne Warning and Control System   (MCD)
SUB .... Scandinavian University Books [*A publication*]
SUB .... Student Union Building [*Canada*]
SUB .... Subaltern
SUB .... Subaud [*Understand*] [*Latin*]
Sub .... Subcommittee   (DLA)
SUB .... Subcontractor   (WGA)
SUB .... Subeditor
SUB .... Subject
SUB .... Subjunctive [*Grammar*]
SUB .... Submarine   (AFM)
SUB .... Submerged
SUB .... Subordinate   (DSUE)
SUB .... Subroutine
Sub .... Subscriber [*Finance*]
SUB .... Subscription [*Finance*]
SUB .... Subsidiary [*Business term*]
SUB .... Substitute
SUB .... Substitute Character [*Keyboard*]   (AFM)
SUB .... Substratum
SUB .... Subtract
SUB .... Subtract Binary Number [*Data processing*]
SUB .... Suburban
SUB .... Subway   (AAG)
SUB .... Supplemental Unemployment Benefits
SUB .... Surabaya [*Indonesia*] [*Airport symbol*]   (OAG)
SUBACLANT ... Submarine Allied Command, Atlantic [*NATO*]   (NATG)
SUBACS ... Submarine Advanced [*or Active*] Combat System
SUBAD..... Submarine Air Defense
SUBAD..... Submarine Force, Pacific Fleet Administration
SUBADMI ... Submarine Force, Pacific Fleet Administration, Mare Island
SUBASE.... Submarine Base [*Navy*]
SUBASELANT ... Submarine Bases, Atlantic [*Navy*]
SUBASEPAC ... Submarine Bases, Pacific [*Navy*]
SUBASSY ... Subassembly
SUBASWEX ... Submarine-Antisubmarine Warfare Exercise   (NVT)
SUBB........ Suburban Bancorp, Inc. [*Palatine, IL*] [*NASDAQ symbol*]   (NQ)
SUB-BELL ... Submarine Fog Bell [*Mechanical*]
SUBC........ Subler, Carl, Agent, Versailles OH [*STAC*]
SUBCAL ... Subcaliber
SUBCAP ... [*Rescue*] Submarine Combat Air Patrol [*Navy*]   (DNAB)
Sub-Cell Bi ... Sub-Cellular Biochemistry [*A publication*]
Sub-Cell Biochem ... Sub-Cellular Biochemistry [*A publication*]
SUBCERT ... Submarine Safety Certification [*Navy*]   (DNAB)
SUBCH ...... Subchapter   (DNAB)
SUBCOM ... Subcommittee
SUBCOM ... Subordinate Command, Service Force, Pacific Fleet
SUBCOMNELM ... Subordinate Command, [*US*] Naval Forces, Eastern Atlantic and Mediterranean
SUBCOR... Subject to Correction   (DNAB)
subcrep....... Subcrepitant [*Medicine*]
SUBCU...... Subcutaneous [*Beneath the Skin*] [*Medicine*]
subcut......... Subcutaneous [*Beneath the Skin*] [*Medicine*]
Subd.......... Subdivision   (DLA)
SUBDEVGRUONE ... Submarine Development Group One [*San Diego*]
SUBDEVGRUTWO ... Submarine Development Group Two [*New York*]
SUBDIV ..... Submarine Division [*Navy*]
SUBDIZ .... Submarine Defense Identification Zone
SUBEASTLANT ... Submarine Force, Eastern Atlantic [*NATO*]
SUBED...... Submarine Electromagnetic Deception System
SUBEX...... Submarine Exercise   (NATG)
SUBFIN COCT ... Sub Finem Coctionis [*When the Boiling Is Nearly Finished*]   (ROG)
SUBFIX..... We Forward Subject to Correction [*Code*]   (FAAC)
SUBFLOT ... Submarine Flotilla [*Navy*]
subg........... Subgenus
SUBGEN... Subgenus
SUBGRU... Submarine Group
SUBH .... Scripta Universitatis atque Bibliotecae Hierosolymitanarum Jerusalem [*A publication*]   (BJA)
SUBIC...... Submarine Integrated Control Systems
Sub Ind Child Mag ... Subject Index to Children's Magazines [*A publication*]
SUBINSURV ... Inspection and Survey Board Sub Board [*Navy*]
SUBJ .... Subject   (AFM)

SUBJ .... Subjective (ROG)
SUBJ .... Subjunctive [*Grammar*]
Subj of Day ... Subject of the Day [*A publication*]
Subj Index Child Mag ... Subject Index to Children's Magazines [*A publication*]
Subj Index Period ... Subject Index to Periodicals [*A publication*]
Subj Index Sel Period Lit ... Subject Index to Select Periodical Literature [*A publication*]
SUBJV ...... Subjunctive [*Grammar*] (WGA)
SUBK .... Suffolk Bancorp [*Riverhead, NY*] [*NASDAQ symbol*] (NQ)
SUBL .... Sublime [*or Subliming*]
SUBLANT ... Submarine Force, Atlantic Fleet
Sub Life ...... Suburban Life [*A publication*]
subling .... Sublingual [*Medicine*]
Sub-Lt .... Sub-Lieutenant [*British military*] (DMA)
SUBM .... Submarine (WGA)
SUBM ...... Submerged
SUBM ...... Submission [*or Submit*] (AFM)
SUBMACOM ... Major Army Subcommand (AABC)
submand ..... Submandibular [*Medicine*]
SUBMED ... Submarines Mediterranean [*NATO*] (NATG)
SUBMEDCEN ... Submarine Medical Center [*Navy*]
SUBMEDNOREAST ... Submarines Northeast Mediterranean [*NATO*] (NATG)
SUBMG .... Submerged (MSA)
SUBMIN ... Subminiature
SUBMISS ... Submarine Missing [*Navy*] (NVT)
SUBMIS/SUBSUNK ... Submarine Missing/Presumed Sunk [*Navy*]
SUBMON ... Submission (ROG)
Subm W ..... Submerged Well [*Nautical charts*]
SUBN .... [*The*] Summit Bancorporation [*NASDAQ symbol*] (NQ)
SUBNAVPERS ... Submit to Naval Personnel (DNAB)
SUBNEWSTA ... Submit New Duty Station [*Navy*] (DNAB)
SUBNO ..... Substitutes Not Desired [*Military*]
sub nom ...... Sub Nomine [*Under the Name*] [*Latin*] (DLA)
SUBNOT ... Submarine Notice (MCD)
SUBNOTE ... Submarine Notice [*Navy*] (NVT)
Subnucl Ser ... Subnuclear Series [*A publication*]
SUBOK ..... Substitution Acceptable [*Military*]
SUBOPAUTH ... Submarine Operating Authority [*Navy*] (NVT)
sub opn ...... Subsequent Opinion (HGAA)
SUBOR ...... Subordinate (AFM)
SUBORCOM ... Subordinate Command
SUBORCOMDSERVLANT ... Subordinate Command, Service Force, Atlantic Fleet
SUBORCOMDSERVPAC ... Subordinate Command, Service Force, Pacific Fleet
SUBORD ... Subordinate [*Linguistics*]
SUB-OSC ... Submarine Oscillator
SUBPA ...... Antisubmarine Warfare Barrier Submarine Patrol Area [*Navy*] (NVT)
SUBPAC ... Submarine Force, Pacific Fleet
SUBPACAD ... Submarine Force, Pacific Fleet, Administrative Command
SUBPACSUBORDCOM ... Submarine Force, Pacific Fleet, Subordinate Command
Subpar .... Subparagraph (DLA)
SUBPARA ... Subparagraph
SUBPDJ .... Annual Research Reviews. Substance P [*A publication*]
SUBPZ ...... Antisubmarine Warfare Barrier Submarine Patrol Zone [*Navy*] (NVT)
SUB Q .... Subcutaneous [*Beneath the Skin*] [*Medicine*]
SUBQ .... Subsequent (AABC)
SUBRAP ... Submarine Range Prediction System [*Navy*] (NVT)
SUBRO ...... Subrogation
SUBROC ... Submarine Rocket
SUBRON ... Submarine Squadron [*Navy*]
SUBRPIO ... Sub-Registered Publications Issuing Office
SUBRQMT ... Subrequirement
SUBRU ...... Submarine Repair Unit
SUBS .... Salford University Business Services [*British*]
SUBS .... Subscription (WGA)
SUBS .... Subsidiary [*Business term*]
SUBS .... Subsistence (AABC)
SUBS .... Substantive [*Grammar*]
SUBS .... Substitute
SUBSAFE ... Submarine Safety [*Program*]
SUBSAFECEN ... Submarine Safety Center [*Navy*]
SUBSALVEX ... Submarine Salvage Exercise [*Navy*] (DNAB)
Subsc .... Subscription (DLA)
SUBSCD ... Subscribed (ROG)
SUBSCOFOR ... Submarines Scouting Force [*Pacific Fleet*]
SUBSCR .... Subscription [*Finance*] (ROG)
SUBSCRON ... Subscription [*Finance*] (ROG)
SUBSEC ... Subsection
SUBSELS ... Subsisting Elsewhere
SUBSEQ ... Subsequent (ROG)
Subser Optical Sci Engrg ... Subseries on Optical Science and Engineering [*A publication*]
SUBSET .... Subscriber Set (CET)
SUBSID .... Subsidiary [*Business term*] (ROG)
Subsidia Med ... Subsidia Medica [*A publication*]

SUBSIS ..... Subsistence (AFM)
SUBSLANT ... Submarines, Atlantic Fleet
SUBSLY .... Subsequently (ROG)
SUBSP .... Subspecies
SUBSPAC ... Submarines, Pacific Fleet
subspp .... Subspecies [*Plural form*]
SUBSQ ...... Subsequently (ADA)
SUB-SRA .. Sub-Shop Replaceable Assembly
SUBSS .... Submarine Schoolship [*Navy*] (NVT)
SUBSSOWESPAC ... Submarines, Southwest Pacific Force
SUBST ...... Substance (ROG)
SUBST ...... Substantive (ROG)
SUBST ...... Substitute (AAG)
SUBSTA ... Substation
Subst Alcohol Actions Misuse ... Substance and Alcohol Actions/Misuse [*A publication*]
Substand .... Substandard (WGA)
SUB-STD .. Substitute Standard [*Army*]
SUBSTD .. Substituted (ROG)
SUBSTG ... Substituting (AAG)
SUBSTN ... Substitution
SUBSTR ... Substructure (AAG)
SUBSTTD ... Substituted
SUBSUNK ... Submarine Sunk [*Navy*] (NVT)
SUBSYS ... Subsystem (AAG)
SUBTACGRU ... Submarine Tactical Group [*NATO*] (NATG)
SUBTAG ... Submarine Tactics Analysis Group
Sub Torg .... Sovetskaya Torgovlya [*A publication*]
SUBTR .... Subtraction (MSA)
SUBTRAFAC ... Submarine Training Facility
SUBTRAP ... Submersible Training Platform [*Marine science*] (MSC)
subtrop .... Subtropical
Subtrop Kul't ... Subtropicheskie Kul'tury [*A publication*]
Subtrop Kul't Min Sel'Khoz SSSR ... Subtropicheskie Kul'tury. Ministerstvo Sel'skogo Khozyaistva SSSR [*A publication*]
SUBV .... Subversion (AABC)
Sub Vol ...... Submarine Volcano [*Nautical charts*]
SUBWESTLANT ... Submarine Force, Western Atlantic Area [*NATO*] (NATG)
Suby .... Subsidiary [*Business term*]
SUC .... Saggi di Umanismo Cristiano [*A publication*]
SUC .... Society of University Cartographers [*British*]
SUC .... Southern Union College [*Wadley, AL*]
SUC .... Succeeding (MSA)
SUC .... Successor (ADA)
Suc .... Succinoyl [*Biochemistry*]
SUC .... Succus [*Juice*] [*Pharmacy*]
SUC .... Sucre [*Bolivia*] [*Seismograph station code, US Geological Survey*] [*Closed*] (SEIS)
SUC .... Sucrose [*Organic chemistry*]
SUC .... Suction (ADA)
SUC .... Suncoast Petroleum [*Vancouver Stock Exchange symbol*]
SUC .... Sundance, WY [*Location identifier*] [*FAA*] (FAAL)
SUC .... University of South Carolina, Columbia, SC [*OCLC symbol*] (OCLC)
SUCA .... Colonia/Aeropuerto Deptal. [*Uruguay*] [*ICAO location identifier*] (ICLI)
SUCC .... State University Computation Center [*Iowa State University*] [*Research center*] (RCD)
SUCC .... Succentor [*Ecclesiastical*] (ROG)
SUCC .... Successor (ROG)
SUCC .... Succinate
SUCC .... Succinum [*Amber*] [*Latin*] (ROG)
Success Farming ... Successful Farming [*A publication*]
Success Farm South ... Successful Farming in the South [*A publication*]
Successful F ... Successful Farming [*A publication*]
Success Mtg ... Successful Meetings [*A publication*]
SUCCN ...... Succession (ROG)
SUCCON .. Succession
SUCCR ...... Successor
SUCE .... South Universal Commodity Exchange [*Ukraine*] (EY)
SUCEC ...... Setting Up a Company in the European Community [*Monograph*] [*A publication*]
SUCEE ...... Socialist Union of Central and Eastern Europe (PD)
Suc Farm .... Successful Farming [*A publication*]
SUCHTRANS ... Such Transportation as Command Indicated Designates
SUCHTRANSAVAIL ... Such Transportation as Available
SUCI .... Socialist Unity Center of India [*Political party*] (PPW)
SUCKER ... Society for Understanding Cats, Kangaroos, Elks, and Reptiles [*Slang*]
SUCL .... Set Up in Carloads [*Freight*]
SUCL .... Stetson University College of Law (DLA)
SUCO .... Service Universitaire Canadien Outre-Mer [*Canadian University Service Overseas - CUSO*]
SUCR .... Successor (WGA)
SUCR .... Sunset Crater National Monument
Sucr Belg Sugar Ind Abstr ... Sucrerie Belge and Sugar Industry Abstracts [*A publication*]
SUCT .... Suction (AAG)
Su Ct Rev .. Supreme Court Review [*A publication*] (ILCA)
SuD .... Sprache und Dichtung [*A publication*]

SUD .... Stretched Upper Deck (AIA)
SUD .... Stroud, OK [Location identifier] [FAA] (FAAL)
SUD .... Sudbury [Ontario] [Seismograph station code, US Geological Survey] (SEIS)
SUD .... Sudbury Board of Education [UTLAS symbol]
SUD .... Sudbury Contact Mines Ltd. [Toronto Stock Exchange symbol]
SUD .... Sudden Unexpected [or Unexplained] Death [Medicine]
SUD .... Sudestasie. Magazine d'Information [A publication]
SUD .... Sudorific [Causing Sweat] [Pharmacy] (ROG)
SUDAER... Stanford University, Department of Aeronautics and Astronautics (MCD)
SUDAM .... Editorial Sudamericana, BA [A publication]
SUDAM .... Sunk or Damaged [Navy]
Sudan Eng Soc J ... Sudan Engineering Society. Journal [A publication]
Sudan Geol Surv Dep Bull ... Sudan. Geological Survey Department. Bulletin [A publication]
Sudan J Econ and Social Studies ... Sudan Journal of Economic and Social Studies [A publication]
Sudan J Food Sci Technol ... Sudan Journal of Food Science and Technology [A publication]
Sudan J Vet Sci Anim Husb ... Sudan Journal of Veterinary Science and Animal Husbandry [A publication]
Sudan LJ & Rep ... Sudan Law Journal and Reports [Khartoum] [A publication] (DLA)
Sudan Notes ... Sudan Notes and Records [A publication]
Sudan Notes Rec ... Sudan Notes and Records [A publication]
Sudan Soc .. Sudan Society [A publication]
SUDAP...... Superintendencia da Agricultura e Producao [Brazil]
Sud Dew Ad ... Sudder Dewanny Adawlut [or Sadr Diwani Adalat] Reports [India] [A publication] (DLA)
Sud Dew Rep ... Sudder Dewanny [or Sadr Diwani] Reports, Northwest Province [India] [A publication] (DLA)
Sudebno-Med Ekspert ... Sudebno-Meditsinskaya Ekspertiza [A publication]
SUDEC...... Superintendencia do Desenvolvimento Economico e Cultural [Brazil]
SUDEL...... Groupe Regional pour la Coordination de la Production et du Transport de l'Energie Electrique entre l'Autriche, la Grece, l'Italie et la Yougoslavie (EA)
SUDENE... Superintendencia do Desenvolvimento do Nordeste [Brazil]
SUDENE Bol Recur Nat ... SUDENE [Superintendencia do Desenvolvimento do Nordeste] Boletim do Recursos Naturais [A publication]
SUDI .... State Unemployment Disability Insurance (AAG)
SUDIC...... Sulfur Development Institute of Canada
SUDIC...... Sulphur Development Institute of Canada
Sud Inform Econ Provence-Cote D'Azur-Corse ... Sud. Information Economique Provence-Cote D'Azur-Corse [A publication]
Sud Med Chir ... Sud Medical et Chirurgical [A publication]
Sud-Med Ekspert ... Sudebno-Meditsinskaya Ekspertiza [A publication]
Sud Med Ekspert Krim Sluzhbe Sledstviya ... Sudebno-Meditsinskaya Ekspertiza i Kriminalistika na Sluzhbe Sledstviya [A publication]
Sud Med J ... Sudan Medical Journal [A publication]
Su Doc........ Superintendent of Documents, Government Printing Office (DLA)
SUDOSAT ... Sudanian Satellite
SUDS......... Satellite Undetected Duds
SUDS......... Silhouetting Underwater Detecting System
SUDS......... Single-Use Diagnostic System [Trademark of the Murex Corp.]
SUDS......... Small Unit Delivery System (MCD)
SUDS......... Software Update and Distribution System [Frye Computer Systems] (PCM)
SUDS......... State's Urban Development Something-or-Other [Slang for Urban Development Corporation, New York]
SUDS......... Steps Up Developmental Screening Program [Child development test] [Psychology]
SUDS......... Subjective Units of Disturbance
SUDS......... Submarine Detecting System
SUDS......... Sudbury, Inc. [NASDAQ symbol] (NQ)
SUDT .... Silicon Unilateral Diffused Transistor
SUDU .... Durazno/Santa Bernardina Internacional de Alternativa [Uruguay] [ICAO location identifier] (ICLI)
SUE .... Sahara Upwelling Experiment [US, Spain] (MSC)
SUE .... Seismic Underwater Explorer
SUE .... Servants' United Effort [Lemonade] [Slang] [British] (DSUE)
SUE .... Shuttle Unique Equipment (MCD)
SUE .... Signal Underwater Exploding [British military] (DMA)
SUE .... Significantly Underutilized Employee Program [DoD]
SUE .... Skylab Upwelling Experiment [Marine science] (MSC)
SUE .... Strontium Unit Equivalent
SUE .... Sturgeon Bay, WI [Location identifier] [FAA] (FAAL)
SUE .... Sub-Unit Evaluation (MCD)
SUE .... Sudden Expansion
SUE .... Suzie Mining Exploration [Vancouver Stock Exchange symbol]
SuedA .... Suedostdeutsches Archiv [A publication]
Sueddt Ap Zt ... Sueddeutsche Apothekerzeitung [A publication]
Sueddt Mh ... Sueddeutsche Monatshefte [A publication]
Sueddtsch Ztg ... Sueddeutsche Zeitung [A publication]
SUEDE...... Surface Evaluation and Definition
SuedoA...... Suedostdeutsches Archiv [A publication]
Suedost Eur Jb ... Suedosteuropa-Jahrbuch [A publication]

Suedosteur Mitt ... Suedosteuropa Mitteilungen [A publication]
Suedost F ... Suedost-Forschungen [A publication]
Suedwestdt Imker ... Suedwestdeutscher Imker [A publication]
SUEL........ Sperry Utah Engineering Laboratory (MCD)
Suelos Ecuat ... Suelos Ecuatoriales [A publication]
SUEM .... Syndicat Unique des Enseignants de Mauritanie [Unitary Union of Mauritanian Teachers]
SUEO .... Montevideo [Uruguay] [ICAO location identifier] (ICLI)
SUEOTU... Supreme Unsurpassable Engineers of the Universe [Rank in Junior Woodchucks organization mentioned in Donald Duck comic by Carl Barks]
SUERF ...... Societe Universitaire Europeenne de Recherches Financieres (EAIO)
SUET........ Small Unit Evaluation and Training (MCD)
Suet .... Suetonius [First century AD] [Classical studies] (OCD)
SUF........... Lametia-Terme [Italy] [Airport symbol] (OAG)
SUF........... Scottish Union of Fishermen
SuF........... Sinn und Form [A publication]
SUF........... Socialist Unity Front [Romania] [Political party] (PPW)
SUF........... Southernera Resources Ltd. [Toronto Stock Exchange symbol]
SUF........... Sufficient (AFM)
SUF........... Suffolk University, Boston, MA [OCLC symbol] (OCLC)
SUF........... Swaziland United Front
SUFF .... Sufficient
SUFF .... Sufficit [Suffices] [Latin]
SUFF .... Suffix (AAG)
SUFF .... Suffolk [County in England]
SUFF .... Suffragan [Ecclesiastical] (ROG)
SUFFER.... Save Us from Formaldehyde Environmental Repercussions [Later, CURE Formaldehyde Poisoning Association] (EA)
SUFFER.... System Utility Facility for Easy Recovery [NASA]
Suffolk Transnatl LJ ... Suffolk Transnational Law Journal [A publication]
Suffolk U L Rev ... Suffolk University. Law Review [A publication]
Suffolk Univ L Rev ... Suffolk University. Law Review [A publication]
SUFFR ...... Suffragan [Ecclesiastical] (WGA)
SUFFT...... Sufficient
Suff Trans LJ ... Suffolk Transnational Law Journal [A publication]
SUFFTY.... Sufficiently (ROG)
Suff U LR... Suffolk University. Law Review [A publication]
SUFPAC... Surface Force Pacific (MCD)
SUFSW .... Small Unit Fire Support Weapon (MCD)
SUG .... Asheville, NC [Location identifier] [FAA] (FAAL)
SUG .... Sell Under the Guise of Market Research [Marketing] [British]
SUG .... Smartmac User Group (EA)
SUG .... Southern Union Co. [Formerly, Southern Union Gas Co.] [NYSE symbol] (SPSG)
SuG .... Sprache und Gemeinschaft [A publication]
SUG .... Sugar
SUG .... Sugar Island [Michigan] [Seismograph station code, US Geological Survey] [Closed] (SEIS)
SUG .... Suggest (AFM)
SUG .... Surigao [Philippines] [Airport symbol] (OAG)
Sugaku .... Sugaku. Mathematical Society of Japan [A publication]
SUGAR ..... Software Users Guide to Available Resources [Australia] [A publication]
Sugar.......... Sugar y Azucar [A publication]
Sugarbeet Grow ... Sugarbeet Grower [A publication]
Sugar Beet J ... Sugar Beet Journal [A publication]
Sugar Bul ... Sugar Bulletin [A publication]
Sugar Bull ... Sugar Bulletin [United States] [A publication]
Sugarcane Breed Newsl ... Sugarcane Breeders' Newsletter [A publication]
Sugarcane Var Tests Fla ... Sugarcane Variety Tests in Florida [A publication]
Sugar Ind Abstr ... Sugar Industry Abstracts [A publication]
Sugar J....... Sugar Journal [A publication]
Sugar Mol ... Sugar Molecule [A publication]
Sugar Technol Rev ... Sugar Technology Reviews [A publication]
Sug Azuc ... Sugar y Azucar [A publication]
Sugd Powers ... Sugden on Powers [A publication] (DLA)
Sugd Vend ... Sugden on Vendors and Purchasers [A publication] (DLA)
SUGEND .. Sugendus [To Be Sucked] [Pharmacy]
Sug Est....... Sugden on the Law of Estates [A publication] (DLA)
SUGG .... Suggestion (ROG)
Sug Hd Bk ... Sugden's Hand-Book of Property Law [A publication] (DLA)
SUGI......... SAS [Statistical Analysis System] Users Group International (EA)
Sug J .... Sugar Journal [A publication]
SUGMAW ... Glas. Srpska Akademija Nauka i Umetnosti Odeljenje Medicinskih Nauka [A publication]
Sug Pow ..... Sugden on Powers [8 eds.] [1808-61] [A publication] (DLA)
Sug Pr .... Sugden on the Law of Property [A publication] (DLA)
Sug Prop .... Sugden on the Law of Property as Administered by the House of Lords [A publication] (DLA)
Sug Pr St ... Sugden on Property Statutes [A publication] (DLA)
SUGR........ Summagraphics Corp. [NASDAQ symbol] (NQ)
Sug Vend .... Sugden on Vendors and Purchasers [A publication] (DLA)
Sug V & P .. Sugden on Vendors and Purchasers [14 eds.] [1805-62] [A publication] (DLA)
SUH .... Rockland, ME [Location identifier] [FAA] (FAAL)
SUHC........ Summit Holding Corp. [Beckley, WV] [NASDAQ symbol] (NQ)

SUHL........ Sylvania Ultrahigh-Level Logic (IEEE)
SUHS .... Susitna Hydro Studies [*A publication*]
SUI .... Safe Use Instructions [*General Motors Corp.*]
SUI .... Speleological Union of Ireland (EAIO)
SUI .... Standard Universal Identifying Number
SUI .... Stanford University Institute for Plasma Research
SUI .... State University of Iowa [*Later, University of Iowa*]
SUI .... Suihwa [*Republic of China*] [*Seismograph station code, US Geological Survey*] (SEIS)
SUI .... Summit Resources Ltd. [*Toronto Stock Exchange symbol*]
SUIAP ...... Simplified Unit Invoice Accounting Plan
SUIC........ Salford University Industrial Centre Ltd. [*British*] (IRUK)
SUICA...... Soul Uitae Chapchi [*A publication*]
Suicide Life Threat Behav ... Suicide and Life-Threatening Behavior [*A publication*]
Suicide Life Threatening Behav ... Suicide and Life Threatening Behavior [*A publication*]
SUID .... Sudden Unexpected Infant Death [*Medicine*]
Suid-Afrikaanse Tydskr Natuurwetenskap Tegnol ... Suid-Afrikaanse Tydskrif vir Natuurwetenskap en Tegnologie [*A publication*]
Suid Afr Tyd Geneesk ... Suid-Afrikaanse Tydskrif vir Geneeskunde [*A publication*]
Suid-Afr Tydskr Geneesk ... Suid-Afrikaanse Tydskrif vir Geneeskunde [*A publication*]
Suid-Afr Tydskr Landbouwetenskap ... Suid-Afrikaanse Tydskrif vir Landbouwetenskap [*A publication*]
SUIP......... Support Unit Improvement Program (MCD)
SUIS .... Smoloskyp, Ukrainian Information Service (EA)
SUIT......... Sight Unit Infantry Trilux [*British*]
SUIV......... Suivant [*Following*] [*French*]
SUJ .... Satu Mare [*Romania*] [*Airport symbol*] (OAG)
SUJ .... Side Upset Jaw (MSA)
SUJ .... Suntac Minerals [*Vancouver Stock Exchange symbol*]
SUJB .... Southern Universities Joint Board [*for school examinations*] [*British*] (DCTA)
SUK .... Suckling Hill [*Alaska*] [*Seismograph station code, US Geological Survey*] (SEIS)
Suk............ Sukkah (BJA)
suk............. Sukuma [*MARC language code*] [*Library of Congress*] (LCCP)
SUK .... Sumitomo Bank Review [*A publication*]
SUKGA .... Sumitomo Kikai Giho [*A publication*]
SUKLO..... Senior United Kingdom Liaison Officer [*Later, BJSM*] [*British*]
SUKUA ..... Subtropicheskie Kul'tury [*A publication*]
SUL........... Per lo Studio e l'Uso del Latino [*A publication*]
SUL........... Simplified User Logistics [*Military*] (AABC)
SUL........... Small University Libraries
SUL........... Sophia University [*UTLAS symbol*]
SuL............ Sprache und Literatur [*A publication*]
SUL........... Standard User Labels [*Data processing*]
SUL........... State University of New York, Union List of Serials, Albany, NY [*OCLC symbol*] (OCLC)
SUL........... Sui [*Pakistan*] [*Airport symbol*] (OAG)
SUL........... Sulcus Computer Corp. [*AMEX symbol*] (SPSG)
SUL........... Sulpetro Ltd. [*Toronto Stock Exchange symbol*]
SUL........... Sulphur Creek [*New Britain*] [*Seismograph station code, US Geological Survey*] (SEIS)
SULAAL ... Surinam Agriculture [*A publication*]
SULCL...... Set Up in Less than Carloads [*Freight*]
Sulcus........ Sulcus Computer Corp. [*Associated Press abbreviation*] (APAG)
SuLEXCo... Sulphur Export Corp. [*An association*] (EA)
SULF .... Southern United Life Insurance Co. [*NASDAQ symbol*] (NQ)
SULF .... Speedball Up-Range Launch Facility [*Army*] (AABC)
Sulfuric Acid Ind ... Sulfuric Acid and Industry [*Japan*] [*A publication*]
SULI......... Skrifter Utgivna av Litteraturvetenskapliga Institutionen Vid. Uppsala Universitet [*A publication*]
SULINAC ... Super Linear Accelerator [*Space flight simulator*]
SULIS........ Syracuse University Libraries Information System [*Syracuse University Libraries*][*New York*] [*Information service or system*] (IID)
Sull............ Pro Sulla [*of Cicero*] [*Classical studies*] (OCD)
Sull............ Sulla [*of Plutarch*] [*Classical studies*] (OCD)
Sullivan...... Smith's New Hampshire Reports [*A publication*] (DLA)
Sull Ld Tit ... Sullivan's Land Titles in Massachusetts [*A publication*] (DLA)
Sull Lect..... Sullivan's Lectures on Constitution and Laws of England [*A publication*] (DLA)
Sulphur Agric ... Sulphur in Agriculture [*A publication*]
Sulphur Inst J ... Sulphur Institute. Journal [*A publication*]
Su LR ... Suffolk University. Law Review [*A publication*]
SUL Rev .... Southern University Law Review [*A publication*]
SULS .... Maldonado/Base Aeronaval C/C Carlos A. Curbelo [*Uruguay*] [*ICAO location identifier*] (ICLI)
SULT......... Sultan
Sulzer Tech Rev ... Sulzer Technical Review [*A publication*]
Sulz Tech Rev ... Sulzer Technical Review [*A publication*]
Sum .... Hale's Summary of the Pleas of the Crown [*England*] [*A publication*] (DLA)
SUM .... Saturn Umbilical Maintenance [*NASA*]
SUM .... Save Uganda Movement
SUM .... Servicio Universitario Mundial [*World University Service*]
SUM .... Set-Up [*Control*] Module [*Telecommunications*] (TEL)

SUM .... Shallow Underwater Missile
SUM .... Socialist Unionist Movement [*Al Haraka at Tawhidiyya al Ishtirakiyya*] [*Syria*] [*Political party*] (PPW)
SUM .... Software User's Manual [*Army*]
SUM .... Solar Ultraviolet Monitor (MCD)
SUM .... Sullivan Mines, Inc. [*Toronto Stock Exchange symbol*]
Sum........... Sumatra
SUM .... Sume [*Take*] [*Pharmacy*]
Sum .... Sumer. A Journal of Archaeology and History in Iraq [*A publication*]
Sum......... Sumerian (BJA)
SUM .... Summary (AABC)
SUM .... Summation (AAMN)
SUM .... Summer
SUM .... Summing
Sum .... Summit: Journal of the Liturgical Commission [*of the Archdiocese of Melbourne*] [*A publication*] (APTA)
SUM .... Summoned
Sum .... Sumner's United States Circuit Court Reports [*A publication*] (DLA)
SUM .... Sumoto [*Japan*] [*Seismograph station code, US Geological Survey*] (SEIS)
SUM .... Sumter [*South Carolina*] [*Airport symbol*] (OAG)
SUM .... Surface-to-Underwater Missile
SUM .... System Check and Utility Master (MCD)
SUM .... System Utilization Monitor [*Data processing*]
SUM .... Systems Unit Method [*Medical transcription*]
SUM .... University of South Carolina, School of Medicine, Columbia, SC [*OCLC symbol*] (OCLC)
SUMA ...... Summa Medical Corp. [*NASDAQ symbol*] (NQ)
SUMAC..... Sheffield University Metals Advisory Centre [*British*] (IRUK)
SUMARPI ... Supplemental Maintenance and Repair Parts Instruction
Sumatra Res B ... Sumatra Research Bulletin [*A publication*]
SUMC....... Space Ultrareliable Modular Computer
SUMCA..... Summer & Co. Cl A [*NASDAQ symbol*] (NQ)
SUMCM ... Summary Court-Martial
SUMCMO ... Summary Court-Martial Order
Sum Dec ... Summary Decisions [*Bengal, India*] [*A publication*] (DLA)
SUME .... Mercedes/Ricardo de Tomasi [*Uruguay*] [*ICAO location identifier*] (ICLI)
SUMED ... Suez-Mediterranean [*Pipeline*]
SUMEX..... Stanford University Medical Experimental Computer Project [*Stanford University*] [*Research center*] (RCD)
SUMH....... Summit Health Ltd. [*NASDAQ symbol*] (NQ)
SUMI....... Sumitomo Bank of California [*NASDAQ symbol*] (NQ)
SUMIT...... Standard Utility Means for Information Transformation [*Data processing*]
Sumitomo... Sumitomo Bank Review [*A publication*]
Sumitomo Bank R ... Sumitomo Bank Review [*A publication*]
Sumitomo Bull Ind Health ... Sumitomo Bulletin of Industrial Health [*A publication*]
Sumitomo Elec Tech Rev ... Sumitomo Electric Technical Review [*A publication*]
Sumitomo Electr Rev ... Sumitomo Electric Review [*Japan*] [*A publication*]
Sumitomo Electr Tech Rev ... Sumitomo Electric Technical Review [*A publication*]
Sumitomo Light Metal Tech Rep ... Sumitomo Light Metal Technical Reports [*A publication*]
Sumitomo Light Met Tech Rep ... Sumitomo Light Metal Technical Reports [*A publication*]
Sumitomo Mach ... Sumitomo Machinery [*Japan*] [*A publication*]
Sumitomo Met ... Sumitomo Metals [*A publication*]
Sumitomo Q ... Sumitomo Quarterly [*A publication*]
Sum List ... Sumarski List [*A publication*]
SUMM ...... Summary
SUMM ...... Summer
SUMM ...... Summitatis [*Summits or Tops*] [*Pharmacy*] (ROG)
SUMMA ... Superconducting Magnetic Mirror Apparatus
SUMMAC ... Stanford University Modified Markers and Cell Method
Summa Phytopathol ... Summa Phytopathologica [*A publication*]
SUMMCO ... Summary Court-Martial Order
Summ Dec ... Summary Decisions [*Bengal, India*] [*A publication*] (ILCA)
Summer Comput Simul Conf Proc ... Summer Computer Simulation Conference. Proceedings [*A publication*]
Summerfield... Summerfield's Reports [*21 Nevada*] [*A publication*] (DLA)
Summerfield S ... S. Summerfield's Reports [*21 Nevada*] [*A publication*] (DLA)
Summer Inst Part Phys Proc ... Summer Institute on Particle Physics. Proceedings [*A publication*]
SUMMIT ... Sperry UNIVAC Minicomputer Management of Interactive Terminals
SUMMIT ... Supervisor of Multiprogramming, Multiprocessing, Interactive Time Sharing [*Data processing*] (IEEE)
Summit Mag ... Summit Magazine [*A publication*]
Summ NP .. Summary of the Law of Nisi Prius [*A publication*] (DLA)
Summ Proc Aust Conf Nucl Tech Anal ... Australian Conference on Nuclear Techniques of Analysis. Summary of Proceedings [*A publication*] (APTA)
Summ Proc West Cotton Prod Conf ... Summary of Proceedings. Western Cotton Production Conference [*A publication*]

Summ Prog Geol Surv Div (Nigeria) ... Summary of Progress. Geological Survey Division (Nigeria) [*A publication*]
Summ Rep Electrotech Lab ... Summary Reports. Electrotechnical Laboratory [*Japan*] [*A publication*]
Summ World Broadcasts Part 1 ... Summary of World Broadcasts. Part 1. The USSR Weekly Economic Report [*A publication*]
Summ World Broadcasts Part 2 ... Summary of World Broadcasts. Part 2. Eastern Europe Weekly Economic Report [*A publication*]
Summ World Broadcasts Part 3 ... Summary of World Broadcasts. Part 3. The Middle East, Africa, and Latin America Weekly Economic Report [*A publication*]
Sumn .... Sumner's United States Circuit Court Reports [*A publication*] (DLA)
Sumner .... Sumner's United States Circuit Court Reports [*A publication*] (DLA)
SUMNS ..... Summons (ROG)
Sumn Ves ... Sumner's Edition of Vesey's Reports [*A publication*] (DLA)
SUMO .... Melo/Aeropuerto Deptal de Cerro Largo [*Uruguay*] [*ICAO location identifier*] (ICLI)
SUMPAC .. Southampton University Man-Powered Aircraft [*British*]
SUMPM .... Summary Performance Measure (MCD)
Sum Proc Soil Sci Soc NC ... Summary of Proceedings. Soil Science Society of North Carolina [*A publication*]
Sum Rep ..... Sumner's United States Circuit Court Reports [*A publication*] (DLA)
Sum Rep Electrotech Lab (Tokyo Japan) ... Summaries of Reports. Electrotechnical Laboratory (Tokyo, Japan) [*A publication*]
SUMS .... Shuttle Upper-Atmosphere Mass Spectrometer [*NASA*] (MCD)
SUMS .... Specialized Unit Maintenance Support (MCD)
SUMS .... Sperry UNIVAC Material System
SUMS .... Standard USAREUR Munitions System
SUMS .... Summons (ROG)
SUMSTAT ... Summary Statistical Data [*Federal government*]
SUMT .... Sequential Unconstrained Minimization Technique
SUM TAL ... Sumat Talem [*Take One Like This*] [*Pharmacy*]
SUMTTX .. Summit Tax Exempt Bond Fund Ltd. [*Associated Press abbreviation*] (APAG)
SUMU .... Montevideo/Carrasco Internacional [*Uruguay*] [*ICAO location identifier*] (ICLI)
Sum UCCR ... Sumner's United States Circuit Court Reports [*A publication*] (DLA)
Sum Ves ..... Sumner's Edition of Vesey's Reports [*A publication*] (DLA)
SUN .... Hailey, ID [*Location identifier*] [*FAA*] (FAAL)
SUN .... OPTEVFOR [*Operational Test and Evaluation Force*] Detachment, Sunnyvale, CA [*Navy*] (CAAL)
SUN .... Serum Urea Nitrogen [*Clinical medicine*]
SUN .... Spanish Universal Network [*Cable-television system*]
SUN .... Spiritual Unity of Nations [*An association*]
SUN .... Standard Units and Nomenclature (MCD)
SUN .... State University of Nebraska
SUN .... Sun Aire Lines [*Palm Springs, CA*] [*FAA designator*] (FAAC)
SUN .... Sun Co., Inc. [*NYSE symbol*] (SPSG)
SUN .... Sun Life Assurance Co. of Canada [*UTLAS symbol*]
SUN .... Sun Valley [*Idaho*] [*Airport symbol*] (OAG)
sun .... Sundanese [*MARC language code*] [*Library of Congress*] (LCCP)
SUN .... Sunday (AFM)
SUN .... Sundstrand-Turbo Division (AAG)
SUN .... Sunnyside [*Utah*] [*Seismograph station code, US Geological Survey*] [*Closed*] (SEIS)
SUN .... Sunset Railway Co. [*AAR code*]
SUN .... Suntec Ventures Ltd. [*Vancouver Stock Exchange symbol*]
SUN .... Suntech Library and Information Center, Marcus Hook, PA [*OCLC symbol*] (OCLC)
SUN .... Switching Unit
SUN .... Symbols, Units, and Nomenclature [*Commission*] [*IUPAC*]
SUN .... Symphony for United Nations (EA)
SUN .... Union of Soviet Socialist Republics [*ANSI three-letter standard code*] (CNC)
SUNA .... Seafarers' International Union of North America [*AFL-CIO*] (EA)
SUNA .... Sudan News Agency
SUNA .... Sunworld International Airways, Inc. [*Las Vegas, NV*] [*NASDAQ symbol*] (NQ)
SUNA .... Switchmen's Union of North America [*Later, United Transportation Union*]
Sunair .... Sunair Electronics, Inc. [*Fort Lauderdale, FL*] [*Associated Press abbreviation*] (APAG)
SUNAT ..... Scandinavian Union for Non-Alcoholic Traffic (EA)
SUnBH ...... Scripta Universitatis atque Bibliotecae Hierosolymitanarum Jerusalem [*A publication*] (BJA)
SunCo .... Sun Co., Inc. [*Associated Press abbreviation*] (APAG)
SUNCOR .. Sun Oil Co. of Radnor [*Pennsylvania*]
SUNCTY ... Sun City Industries, Inc. [*Associated Press abbreviation*] (APAG)
SUND .... Sound Advice, Inc. [*NASDAQ symbol*] (NQ)
SUND .... Sunday
SUND .... Sundries
SUNDAE ... Stanford University Division of Aero Engineering (AAG)
Sunday M .. Sunday Magazine [*A publication*]
Sunday Rev ... Sunday Review [*A publication*]

Sun Demo & Ch ... Sunday Democrat and Chronicle [*A publication*]
Sund H .... Sunday Herald [*Melbourne*] [*A publication*]
SunDist ...... Sun Distributors Ltd. [*Associated Press abbreviation*] (APAG)
Sund M .... Sunday Magazine [*A publication*]
SUNDS ...... Sudden Unexpected Nocturnal Death Syndrome [*Medicine*] (ECON)
SUNDS ...... Sundries (ROG)
SUNEC .... Seaborne Supply of the Northeast Command (DNAB)
SunEn .... Sunrise Energy Services [*Associated Press abbreviation*] (APAG)
SunEng ...... Sun Energy Partners Ltd. [*Associated Press abbreviation*] (APAG)
SUNF .... SUNF, Inc. [*NASDAQ symbol*] (NQ)
SUNFED ... Special United Nations Fund for Economic Development
Sun Gaz-Ma ... Sunday Gazette-Mail [*A publication*]
Sung Kyun Kwan Univ J ... Sung Kyun Kwan University. Journal [*A publication*]
Sung Stud Newsl ... Sung Studies Newsletter [*A publication*]
SUNI .... Southern Universities Nuclear Institute
SUNI .... Sun Coast Plastics, Inc. [*NASDAQ symbol*] (NQ)
SUNIST ..... Serveur Universitaire National de l'Information Scientifique et Technique [*Online service*]
Sunk .... Single, Unemployed, No Kids [*Lifestyle classification*]
Sun M .... Sun and Moon [*A publication*]
SunM .... Sunshine Mining Co. [*Associated Press abbreviation*] (APAG)
SunMed ...... Sunrise Medical, Inc. [*Associated Press abbreviation*] (APAG)
SunMn .... Sunshine Mining Co. [*Associated Press abbreviation*] (APAG)
SUNN .... SunGroup, Inc. [*NASDAQ symbol*] (NQ)
SUNNUR .. Sunbelt Nursery Group, Inc. [*Associated Press abbreviation*] (APAG)
SUNO .... Southern University in New Orleans
SUNOCO ... Sun Oil Co. [*Later, Sun Co., Inc.*]
Sun Oklahom ... Sunday Oklahoman [*A publication*]
SunOst .... Sunbeam Oster Co. [*Associated Press abbreviation*] (APAG)
SUNR .... Sunrise Preschools, Inc. [*NASDAQ symbol*] (NQ)
SUNS .... Small Unit Navigation System
SUNS .... Sunshine Mining Co. [*NASDAQ symbol*] (NQ)
SUNSAT ... Sun-Energy Collecting Satellite
Sunset Mag ... Sunset Magazine [*A publication*]
Sunshine St Agric Res Rep ... Sunshine State Agricultural Research Report [*A publication*]
Sunshine State Agric Res Rep ... Sunshine State Agricultural Research Report [*A publication*]
Sunshine State Agr Res Rep ... Sunshine State Agricultural Research Report. Florida University Agricultural Experiment Station [*A publication*]
SUNSPOT ... Study of Utilization Systems, Policies, and Techniques (MCD)
SUNSTAR ... Stanford University Network for Space Telescience Applications Research [*Research center*] (RCD)
Sunstrnd .... Sundstrand Corp. [*Associated Press abbreviation*] (APAG)
SUNT .... Studien zur Umwelt des Neuen Testament [*Goettingen*] [*A publication*]
SunT .... Sunday Times [*A publication*]
SUNT .... Sunward Technologies, Inc. [*NASDAQ symbol*] (SPSG)
Sun Times ... Sunday Times [*A publication*]
SunTrst ...... SunTrust Banks, Inc. [*Associated Press abbreviation*] (APAG)
SUNW .... Sun Microsystems, Inc. [*Mountain View, CA*] [*NASDAQ symbol*] (NQ)
SUNWACD ... Swaleureniddwharfeairecalderdon [*British town*]
Sun Wld ...... Sun World [*A publication*]
Sun Work Br ... Sun at Work in Britain [*A publication*]
SUNX .... Sunbelt Exploration [*NASDAQ symbol*] (NQ)
SUNY .... State University of New York [*Computer retrieval and control projects*] [*Albany, NY*]
SUNYA ..... State University of New York at Albany
SUNYAB ... State University of New York at Buffalo
SUNY BCN ... State University of New York Biomedical Communication Network (EA)
SUNY/OCLC ... State University of New York Online Computer Library Center [*Library network*]
SunyP .... State University of New York Press, Albany, NY [*Library symbol*] [*Library of Congress*] (LCLS)
SUO .... Senior Under-Officer [*Royal Military Academy*] [*British*] (ROG)
SUO .... Shell Oil Co. [*Toronto Stock Exchange symbol*] (SPSG)
SUO .... Society of University Otolaryngologists [*Later, SOU-HNS*] (EA)
SUO .... Sun River [*Oregon*] [*Airport symbol*] [*Obsolete*] (OAG)
SUO-HNS ... Society of University Otolaryngologists - Head and Neck Surgeons (EA)
Suom Elainlaakaril ... Suomen Elainlaakarilehti [*A publication*]
Suomen Elainlaakril Fin Veterinartidskr ... Suomen Elainlaakarilehti. Finsk Veterinartidskrift [*A publication*]
Suomen Kem A B ... Suomen Kemistilehti A, B [*A publication*]
Suomen Kemistil A ... Suomen Kemistilehti A [*A publication*]
Suomen Maatalous Seura Maatalousk Aikakausk ... Suomen Maataloustieteellinen Seura. Maataloustieteellinen Aikakauskirj [*A publication*]
Suomen Maatalous Seuran Julk ... Suomen Maataloustieteellisen Seuran Julkaisuja [*A publication*]
Suomen M Vuosikirja ... Suomen Musukin Vuosikirja [*A publication*]

Suom Hammaslaak Toim ... Suomen Hammaslaakariseuran Toimituksia [*A publication*]
Suom Hammaslaak Toimi ... Suomen Hammaslaakariseuran Toimituksia [*A publication*]
Suom Hyonteistiet Aikak ... Suomen Hyonteistieteellinen Aikakauskirja [*A publication*]
Suom Kalatalous ... Suomen Kalatalous [*A publication*]
Suom Kemistil A ... Suomen Kemistilehti A [*A publication*]
Suom Kemistil B ... Suomen Kemistilehti B [*A publication*]
Suom Kemistiseuran Tied ... Suomen Kemistiseuran Tiedonantoja [*A publication*]
Suom Kemistis Tied ... Suomen Kemistiseuran Tiedonantoja [*A publication*]
Suom Maataloustiet Seuran Julk ... Suomen Maataloustieteellisen Seuran Julkaisuja [*A publication*]
Suom Maatal Seur Julk ... Suomen Maataloustieteellisen Seuran Julkaisuja [*A publication*]
Suom Naishammaslaak Julk ... Suomen Naishammaslaakarit Ryhma Julkaisu [*A publication*]
Suom Psykiatr ... Suomalaista Psykiatriaa [*A publication*]
SUOT .... Spacelab Ultraviolet Telescope
SUP .... ABC Airlines, Inc. [*DFW Airport*] [*Mesquite, TX*] [*FAA designator*]   (FAAC)
SUP .... Sabah United Party [*Political party*] [*Malaysia*]
SUP .... Sailors' Union of the Pacific   (EA)
SUP .... Single Unit Pack [*for vehicles*]
SUP .... Single Unit Package [*Pharmacy*]
SUP .... Single Unit Parameter
SUP .... Special Utility Program [*NASA*]   (KSC)
SUP .... Spisy University J. E. Purkyne [*A publication*]
SUP .... Standard Unit of Processing [*Data processing*]
SUP .... Statistical Utility Program
SUP .... Super
SUP .... Superannuation
SUP .... Superficial   (AAMN)
SUP .... Superfine
SUP .... Superior   (AFM)
SUP .... Superior Industries International, Inc. [*NYSE symbol*]   (SPSG)
SUP .... Superior Oil Co., Exploration Library, Houston, TX [*OCLC symbol*]   (OCLC)
SUP .... Superlative
SUP .... Supersede   (WGA)
SUP .... Supervision [*A publication*]
SUP .... Supine
SUP .... Supplement   (AFM)
SUP .... Supply [*Business term*]   (AFM)
SUP .... Support
SUP .... Suppress   (DEN)
SUP .... Supra [*Above*] [*Latin*]
Sup .... Supraphon [*Record label*] [*Former Czechoslovakia*]
SUP .... Supreme
SUP .... Supreme Resources, Inc. [*Vancouver Stock Exchange symbol*]
SUP .... Sydney University Press [*Australia*]   (ADA)
SUP .... System Utilization Procedure
SUPA .... Society of University Patent Administrators   (EA)
SUPAD ...... Supplementary Address   (MCD)
SUPADS ... Suppression of Air Defense System   (MCD)
SUPANX ... Supply Annex
SUPARCO ... Space and Upper Atmospheric Research Committee [*Pakistan*]
SUPARS .... Supply Acquisition Regulation Supplement [*Navy*]
SUPCE ...... Syracuse University Publications in Continuing Education   (EA)
SUPCEN ... Supply Center
SUPCHG ... Supercharge   (FAAC)
SUPCOM ... Support Command [*Army*]
SUPCOM ... Supreme Command
SUPCON ... Superintending Constructor
SUPCOSTINS ... Supervisory Cost Inspector [*Navy*]
Sup Court Rep ... Supreme Court Reporter [*A publication*]   (DLA)
SUPCRIT ... Super Critical   (MCD)
Sup Ct .... Supreme Court   (DLA)
Sup Ct .... Supreme Court Reporter [*National Reporter System*] [*A publication*]   (DLA)
Sup Ct App ... Supreme Court Appeals [*India*] [*A publication*]   (DLA)
Sup Ct Hist Socy YB ... Supreme Court Historical Society. Yearbook [*US*] [*A publication*]
Sup Ct J ..... Supreme Court Journal [*India*] [*A publication*]   (DLA)
Sup Ct L Rev ... Supreme Court Law Review [*A publication*]
Sup Ct MR ... Supreme Court Monthly Review [*India*] [*A publication*]   (DLA)
Sup Ct Pr ... Supreme Court Practice [*A publication*]   (DLA)
Sup Ct R ..... Supreme Court Reports [*India*] [*A publication*]   (DLA)
Sup Ct R ..... United States Supreme Court Rule [*A publication*]   (DLA)
Sup Ct Rep ... Supreme Court Reporter [*A publication*]   (DLA)
Sup Ct Repr ... Supreme Court Reporter [*A publication*]   (DLA)
Sup Ct Rev ... Supreme Court Review [*A publication*]
Sup Ct R (NY) ... New York Supreme Court Reports [*A publication*]   (DLA)
SUPCUR ... Superimposed Current
SUPD .... Supradur Companies, Inc. [*NASDAQ symbol*]   (NQ)
SUPDEP ... Supply Depot
SUPDIV .... Supervisor of Diving [*Navy*]
SUPDIVE ... Supervisor of Diving [*Navy*]

SUPDT ...... Superintendent   (ADA)
SUPE .... Punta Del Este/Aeropuerto Deptal de Maldonado [*Uruguay*] [*ICAO location identifier*]   (ICLI)
SUPE .... [*The*] Superior Electric Co. [*NASDAQ symbol*]   (NQ)
SUPER ...... Superannuation
SUPER ...... Superficial
SUPER ...... Superfine
SUPER ...... Superimpose
SUPER ...... Superintendent
SUPER ...... Superior
Super .... Superior Court   (DLA)
Super .... Superior Court Reports [*A publication*]   (DLA)
SUPER ...... Supernumerary
SUPER ...... Supersede   (MUGU)
SUPER ...... Supervisor   (DSUE)
Super Bsns ... Supermarket Business [*A publication*]
Super Ct ...... Superior Court   (DLA)
Super Ct App Div ... Superior Court, Appellate Division   (DLA)
Super Ct Ch Div ... Superior Court, Chancery Division   (DLA)
Super Ct Law Div ... Superior Court, Law Division   (DLA)
Super Ct Rep ... Superior Court Reports [*New York, Pennsylvania, etc.*] [*A publication*]   (DLA)
Super Ct (RI) ... Rhode Island Superior Court   (DLA)
SUPERFL ... Superficial   (ROG)
SUPERHET ... Superheterodyne
SUPERL .... Superlative
Superlatt M ... Superlattices and Microstructures [*A publication*]
SUPERMAG ... Superconducting Magnet   (SSD)
Supermark Retail ... Supermarket and Retailer [*A publication*]
Super Mgt ... Supervisory Management [*A publication*]
Supermkt ... Supermarketing [*A publication*]
Supermkt Bus ... Supermarket Business [*A publication*]
Super News ... Supermarket News [*A publication*]
SUPERNOVA ... [*A*] NOVA Computer [*Data General Corp.*]
Superphosphat-Mitt ... Superphosphat-Mitteilungen [*A publication*]
SUPERSTR ... Superstructure
Superv Manage ... Supervisory Management [*A publication*]
Superv Nurse ... Supervisor Nurse [*A publication*]
Supery Manage ... Supervisory Management [*A publication*]
SUPF .... Superior Foods, Inc. [*NASDAQ symbol*]   (NQ)
SUPG .... System Utilization Procedural Guide
SUP GOSSYP ... Super Gossypium [*On Cotton Wool*] [*Pharmacy*]
SUPHTD ... Superheated   (AAG)
SUPHTR ... Superheater   (AAG)
SUPIER ..... Supply Pier [*Navy*]
SupInd .... Superior Industries International, Inc. [*Associated Press abbreviation*]   (APAG)
SUPINSMAT ... Supervising Inspector of Naval Material
SUPINSP ... Supply Inspection [*Navy*]   (NVT)
SUPINTREP ... Supplementary Intelligence Report [*Military*]   (AABC)
SUPIR ...... Supplementary Photographic Interpretation Report [*Military*]
Sup Jud Ct ... Supreme Judicial Court [*Massachusetts*]   (DLA)
Supl Antropol ... Suplemento Antropologico [*A publication*]
SUP LINT ... Super Linteum [*On Lint*] [*Pharmacy*]
SUPLO ...... Scottish Union of Power Loom Overlookers
SUPLS ...... Supplies   (WGA)
SUPMG ..... Southern University Press Marketing Group [*Acronym is pronounced "soupmug"*]
SUPMTL .. Supplemental
SUPNZ ...... Socialist Unity Party of New Zealand
SUPO .... Super Power [*Water boiler*] [*Nuclear reactor*]
SUPO .... Supply Officer
SUPOH DI ... Supply on Hand or Due In
SUPOHDU ... Supply from Stock on Hand or Due In
SUPOPS ... Supply Operations [*DoD*]
Supp .... New York Supplement Reports [*A publication*]   (DLA)
SUPP .... Sarawak United People's Party [*Malaysia*] [*Political party*]   (PPW)
Supp .... Supplement   (KSC)
Supp .... Supplices [*of Euripides*] [*Classical studies*]   (OCD)
Supp .... Supplices Contra Thebas [*of Aeschylus*] [*Classical studies*]   (OCD)
SUPP .... Supply
SUPP .... Support   (AAG)
SUPP .... Suppositorium [*Suppository*] [*Pharmacy*]
supp .... Suppurative [*Medicine*]
SUPPACT ... Support Activity
Supp Aesch ... Supplementum Aeschyleum [*A publication*]   (OCD)
SUPP BAS ... Supplemental Basic Allowance for Subsistence [*Military*]   (DNAB)
SUPPL ...... Supplement   (AABC)
Suppl .... Supplementary   (DLA)
Suppl Acta Agric Scand ... Acta Agriculturae Scandinavica. Supplementum [*A publication*]
Suppl Acta Univ Carol Biol ... Supplementum. Acta Universitatis Carolinae. Biologica [*A publication*]
Suppl Agrokem Talajt ... Supplementum. Agrokemia es Talajtan [*A publication*]
Suppl Annls Agric Fenn ... Annales Agriculturae Fenniae. Supplementum [*A publication*]
Suppl Annls Gembloux ... Supplement. Annales de Gembloux [*A publication*]

Suppl Annls Inst Pasteur (Paris) ... Supplement. Annales de l'Institut Pasteur (Paris) [*A publication*]
Suppl Certif Eng ... Supplement. Certificated Engineer [*A publication*]
Suppl Collect Sci Works Charles Univ Fac Med Hradec Kralove ... Supplement to Collection of Scientific Works. Charles University Faculty of Medicine. Hradec Kralove [*A publication*]
Suppl For Rep (Sixth) Discuss Meet (Edinb) ... Supplement to Forestry. Report of the Sixth Discussion Meeting (Edinburgh) [*A publication*]
Suppl Geophys ... Supplement. Geophysics [*A publication*]
Suppl Israel J Bot ... Supplement. Israel Journal of Botany [*A publication*]
Suppl J Phys Soc Jap ... Supplement. Journal of the Physical Society of Japan [*A publication*]
Suppl LC Subj Head ... Supplement. LC [*United States Library of Congress*] Subject Headings [*A publication*]
Suppl Nord Jordbrforsk ... Nordisk Jordbrugsforskning. Supplement [*A publication*]
SUPPLOT ... Supplemental Plot   (MCD)
Suppl Prog Theor Phys ... Supplement. Progress of Theoretical Physics [*A publication*]
Suppl Ric Biol Selvaggina ... Supplemento alle Ricerche di Biologia della Selvaggina [*A publication*]
Suppl Ric Sci ... Supplemento a la Ricerca Scientifica [*A publication*]
Suppl Sb Ved Pr Lek Fak Univ Karlovy (Hradci Kralove) ... Supplementum. Sborniku Vedeckych Praci Lekarske Fakulty University Karlovy (Hradci Kralove) [*A publication*]
SUPPLT.... Supply Platoon [*Military*]   (DNAB)
Supplta Ent ... Supplementa Entomologica [*A publication*]
Sup Pop Sci Mo ... Supplement. Popular Science Monthly [*A publication*]
SUPPOS ... Suppository [*Pharmacy*]
Supp Pr T P ... Supplement. Progress of Theoretical Physics [*A publication*]
SUPPR ... Suppression   (MSA)
SUPPREP ... Supplemental Reporting Code
Supp Rev.... Supplement to the Revision [*A publication*]   (DLA)
Supp Rev St ... Supplement to the Revised Statutes [*A publication*]   (DLA)
Supp Rev Stat ... Supplement to the Revised Statutes [*A publication*]   (GFGA)
SUPPS...... Regional Supplementary Procedures [*Aviation code*]
SUPPT ... Supply Point [*Military*]
Supp Ves Jun ... Supplement to Vesey, Junior's, Reports [*A publication*]   (DLA)
SUPR........ Super Rite [*NASDAQ symbol*]   (SPSG)
SUPR........ Supercomputing Solutions, Inc. [*NASDAQ symbol*]   (NQ)
SUPR........ Superintendent   (ROG)
SUPR........ Superior   (AABC)
SUPR........ Supervisor
SUPR........ Suppress
SUPR........ Supreme
SUPRA...... Suppression Pool Retention Analysis [*Nuclear energy*]
SUPRAD... Supplementary Radio   (NG)
Supr Court ... Supreme Court Review [*A publication*]
Supr Ct....... Pennsylvania Superior Court Reports [*A publication*]   (DLA)
Supr Ct LR ... Supreme Court Law Review [*A publication*]
Supr Ct Rep ... Supreme Court Reporter [*A publication*]   (DLA)
Supreme Court LR ... Supreme Court Law Review [*A publication*]
Supreme Court Rev ... Supreme Court Review [*A publication*]
SuprFd .... Super Food Services, Inc. [*Associated Press abbreviation*]   (APAG)
SuprMd...... Supra Medical [*Associated Press abbreviation*]   (APAG)
SUPRN...... Suppression
SUPROX... Successive Approximation   (IEEE)
SUPRSTR ... Superstructure   (AAG)
SUPS .... Seamen's United Protection Society [*A union*] [*British*]
SUPS .... Supply Squadron
SUPSAL.... Supervisor of Salvage [*Navy*]
SUPSALREPWCOAST ... Supervisor of Salvage Representative, West Coast [*Navy*]   (DNAB)
SUPSALV ... Supervisor of Salvage [*Navy*]
SUPSD...... Supersede   (AFM)
SUPSENS ... Supersensitive
SUPSGT.... Supply Sergeant [*Marine Corps*]
SUPSHIP ... Supervisor of Shipbuilding [*Navy*]
SUPSTARS ... Supply Selective Treatment and Review System
Sup Stud..... Superior Student [*A publication*]
SUPSUR ... Superior Surgical Manufacturing Co., Inc. [*Associated Press abbreviation*]   (APAG)
SUPSYSCOM ... Supply System Command [*Navy*]
SUPSYSECGRU ... Supply System, Security Group [*Navy*]   (DNAB)
SUPT......... Specialized Undergraduate Pilot Training [*Air Force*]
SUPT......... Superintendent   (EY)
SUPT......... Support   (CINC)
SUPTG...... Supporting   (AAG)
SUPTLTK ... Superior Teletec, Inc. [*Associated Press abbreviation*]   (APAG)
SUPTNAVOBSY ... Superintendent, Naval Observatory
SUPU .... Paysandu/Aeropuerto Deptal [*Uruguay*] [*ICAO location identifier*]   (ICLI)
SUPUSLL ... Stanford University. Publications. University Series. Languages and Literatures [*A publication*]
SUPV........ Supervisor   (AAG)
SupVal .... Super Valu Stores, Inc. [*Associated Press abbreviation*]   (APAG)

SUPVR...... Supervisor   (AFM)
Supvry Mgmt ... Supervisory Management [*A publication*]
SUPVSN ... Supervision
SUPWB.... Socialist Unity Party of West Berlin [*Germany*]
SUPX........ Supertex, Inc. [*NASDAQ symbol*]   (NQ)
SUPY........ Supervisory   (DEN)
SUR .... SCOR US Corp. [*NYSE symbol*]   (SPSG)
SUR .... Seemingly Unrelated Regression [*Statistics*]
SUR .... Small Unit Radio [*Military*]   (INF)
SUR .... Speech Understanding Research
SUR .... Start-Up Rate   (NRCH)
SUR .... State University Railroad Co. [*AAR code*]
SUR .... Sul Ross State University, Library, Alpine, TX [*OCLC symbol*]   (OCLC)
SUR .... Supervisory Union Relations Test
Sur............. Sural Nerve
SUR .... Surcharge [*Business term*]   (ROG)
Sur............. Surety   (DLA)
SUR .... Surface   (AABC)
SUR .... Surgery
SUR .... Surinam [*ANSI three-letter standard code*]   (CNC)
SUR .... Surlari [*Romania*] [*Geomagnetic observatory code*]
SUR .... Surplus [*Business term*]
SUR .... Surrender   (DNAB)
SUR .... Surrendered   (WGA)
SUR .... Surround
SUR .... Survey of Current Affairs [*A publication*]
SUR .... Survivor   (DNAB)
SUR .... Sutherland [*South Africa*] [*Seismograph station code, US Geological Survey*]   (SEIS)
Sur............. Thiouracil [*Also, SUra*] [*Biochemistry*]
SURA .... Shan United Revolutionary Army [*Myanmar*]   (PD)
SUra.......... Thiouracil [*Also, Sur*] [*Biochemistry*]
SURAB...... Surgery Annual [*A publication*]
SURANO .. Surface RADAR and Navigation Operation
SURBAT ... Simultaneous Unlimited Rigorous Block Analytical Triangulation [*Apollo program*] [*NASA*]
SURC........ Syracuse University Research Corp.
SURCAL... Surveillance Calibration Satellite
SURCAP .. Surviving Capability Plan [*Military*]
SURCO ..... State University Research Center at Oswego [*State University College at Oswego*] [*Research center*]   (RCD)
Sur Ct........ Surrogate's Court   (DLA)
SURE........ Sensor Upgrade and Refurbishment Effort [*Marine Corps*]   (MCD)
SURE........ Shuttle Users Review and Evaluation [*NASA*]   (NASA)
SURE........ Simplicity, Useability, Reliability, Economy
SURE........ Space Ultraviolet Radiation Environment   (MCD)
SURE........ Subsystem Replacement
SURE........ Sulphate Regional Experiment [*Electric Power Research Institute*]
SURE........ Symbolic Utilities Revenue Environment [*IBM Corp.*]
SUREJ ...... Surface Ship Electromagnetic Jammer
SUREPI..... Surface Ship Electromagnetic Passive Intercept System
SUREQ .... Submit Requisition   (NOAA)
SURF........ Antisubmarine Warfare Barrier Surface Patrol Ship [*Navy*]   (NVT)
SURF........ Single Unit Retrieval Format
SURF........ Standard UNREP [*Underway Replenishment*] Receiving Fixture [*Navy*]   (NVT)
SURF........ Support of User Records and Files [*Data processing*]
SURF........ Surface
surf .... Surfactant
SURF........ Synchrotron Ultraviolet Radiation Facility [*National Institute of Standards and Technology*]
SURF........ System Utilization Reporting Facility   (HGAA)
SURFAC ... Surveillance Facility [*Navy*]
Surface Sci ... Surface Science [*A publication*]
Surface Techn ... Surface Technology [*A publication*]
Surfacing J ... Surfacing Journal [*United Kingdom*] [*A publication*]
Surfactant Sci Ser ... Surfactant Science Series [*A publication*]
SURFCO... Surf Code   (DNAB)
Surf Coat.... Surface Coatings [*A publication*]
Surf Coat Aust ... Surface Coatings Australia [*A publication*]
Surf Colloid Sci ... Surface and Colloid Science [*A publication*]
Surf Defect Prop Solids ... Surface and Defect Properties of Solids [*A publication*]
SURF DET TRKR ... Surface Detector/Tracker [*Navy*]   (CAAL)
SUR/FIN... American Electroplaters' and Surface Finishers Society Exposition   (ITD)
Surf Interface Anal ... Surface and Interface Analysis [*A publication*]
Surf J .... Surfacing Journal [*A publication*]
Surf Min Law ... Surface Mining Law [*A publication*]
Surf Min Reclam Symp ... Surface Mining and Reclamation Symposia [*A publication*]
SURFPA.... Antisubmarine Warfare Barrier Surface Patrol Area [*Navy*]   (NVT)
SURFPZ.... Antisubmarine Warfare Barrier Surface Patrol Zone [*Navy*]   (NVT)
Surf Sci ...... Surface Science [*A publication*]
Surf Sci R... Surface Science Reports [*A publication*]

Surf Sci Rep ... Surface Science Reports [*A publication*]
SURFSIDE ... Small Unified Reactor Facility Systems for Isotopes, Desalting, and Electricity [*Nuclear energy*]
Surf Tech ... Surface Technology [*A publication*]
Surf Technol ... Surface Technology [*A publication*]
SURFWARDEVGRU ... Surface Warfare Development Group [*Also, SWDG*] [*Navy*]
Surf Warf ... Surface Warfare [*A publication*]
SURG .... International Surgical and Pharmaceutical Corp. [*NASDAQ symbol*] (NQ)
SURG .... Surgeon [*or Surgery or Surgical*] (AFM)
SurgAf .... Surgical Care Affiliates, Inc. [*Nashville, TN*] [*Associated Press abbreviation*] (APAG)
Surg Annu ... Surgery Annual [*A publication*]
SURGAZ ... Surgery [*Saint Louis*] [*A publication*]
Surg Bus ..... Surgical Business [*A publication*]
Surg Cdr ..... Surgeon-Commander [*British military*]
Surg Clin N Am ... Surgical Clinics of North America [*A publication*]
Surg Clin North Am ... Surgical Clinics of North America [*A publication*]
Surg Cl NA ... Surgical Clinics of North America [*A publication*]
SURGE ...... SEASAT Users Group of Europe (MSC)
SURGE ...... Sorting, Updating, Report Generating, Etc. [*IBM Corp.*] [*Data processing*]
SURGEN ... [*The*] Surgeon General [*Army, Air Force*]
Surg Forum ... Surgical Forum [*A publication*]
Surg Gastroenterol ... Surgical Gastroenterology [*A publication*]
Surg Gen .... Surgeon General (GFGA)
Surg Gynec and Obst ... Surgery, Gynecology, and Obstetrics [*A publication*]
Surg Gynecol Obstet ... Surgery, Gynecology, and Obstetrics [*A publication*]
Surg Gyn Ob ... Surgery, Gynecology, and Obstetrics [*A publication*]
Surgical ...... Surgical Business [*A publication*]
Surg Ital ..... Surgery in Italy [*A publication*]
Surg Lt .... Surgeon Lieutenant [*British military*]
SURGN ..... Surgeon
Surg Neurol ... Surgical Neurology [*A publication*]
Surg Radiol Anat ... Surgical and Radiologic Anatomy [*A publication*]
Surg Technol ... Surgical Technologist [*A publication*]
Surg Ther ... Surgical Therapy [*Japan*] [*A publication*]
SURI .... Syracuse University Research Institute (MCD)
SURIC ...... Surface Integrated Control (MCD)
SURIC ...... Surface Ship Integrated Control System [*Obsolete*] [*Navy*]
Surinaam ... Surinaamse Landbouw [*A publication*]
Surinam Agric ... Surinam Agriculture [*A publication*]
SURISS ..... Sheffield Urban and Regional Instructional Simulation System [*British*]
SURM .... Standard Usage Rate Modifier
SURMAC ... Surface Magnetic Confinement (MCD)
SUROB ...... Surf Observation Report [*Navy*] (NVT)
SURORDTECH ... Surface Ordnance Technician [*Navy*] (DNAB)
Surowce Miner ... Surowce Mineralne [*A publication*]
SURP .... Submerged Unmanned Recovery Platform (NVT)
SURPIC ...... Surface Picture [*AMVER*] [*Coast Guard*]
Surps .... Surplus
SURR .... Surrender (AABC)
SURR .... Surrey [*County in England*]
SURR .... Surrogate
SURRC ...... Scottish Universities Research and Reactor Centre [*Research center*] (IRC)
Surr Ct Proc Act ... Surrogate's Court Procedure Act [*A publication*] (DLA)
SURRD ...... Surrendered (ROG)
Surrey AC ... Surrey Archaeological Collections [*A publication*]
Surrey Archaeol Collect ... Surrey Archaeological Collections [*A publication*]
Surrey Arch Coll ... Surrey Archaeological Collections [*A publication*]
SURRO ..... Surrogate (ADA)
Surry A Coll ... Surrey Archaeological Collections [*A publication*]
SURS .... Standard Umbilical Retraction System (NASA)
SURS .... Surface Export Cargo System [*Military*] (AABC)
SURS .... Surveillance Squadron
SURSAN ... Superintendencia de Urbanizacao e Saneamento [*Brazil*]
SURSAT ... Satellite Surveillance Program [*Canada*] (MSC)
SURSAT ... Survey Satellite [*NASA*]
SUR/SATCOM ... Survivable Satellite Communications
SURTAC ... NORAD Surveillance and Tactical Network (MCD)
SURTAC ... Surveillance Tactical (MCD)
SURTASS ... Surveillance Towed Array SONAR System
SURTEMS ... Surface Temperature Measuring System
SURTOPS ... Surveillance Training and Operating Procedures Standardization [*Military*] (CAAL)
Surtsey Res Prog Rep ... Surtsey Research Progress Report [*A publication*]
SURV .... Rivera/Aeropuerto Deptal [*Uruguay*] [*ICAO location identifier*] (ICLI)
SURV .... Standard Underwater Research Vehicle
SURV .... Surveillance (AAG)
SURV .... Survey (AABC)
SURV .... Surveyor
SURV .... Survival (AFM)
Surv .... Survival [*A publication*]
SURV .... Survival Technology, Inc. [*NASDAQ symbol*] (NQ)
SURV .... Surviving
Surv .... Survivor
SURVAL ... Simulator Universal Radio Variability Library

Surv Anesthesiol ... Survey of Anesthesiology [*A publication*]
Surv Biol Prog ... Survey of Biological Progress [*A publication*]
Surv Bus ..... Survey of Business [*United States*] [*A publication*]
Surv Cur Bus ... Survey of Current Business [*A publication*]
Surv Curr Affairs ... Survey of Current Affairs [*London*] [*A publication*]
Surv Curr Bus ... Survey of Current Business [*A publication*]
Surv Curr Busin ... Survey of Current Business [*A publication*]
Surv Dig Dis ... Survey of Digestive Diseases [*A publication*]
Surv Drug Res Immunol Dis ... Survey of Drug Research in Immunologic Disease [*A publication*]
Survey Bus (Univ Tenn) ... Survey of Business (University of Tennessee) [*A publication*]
Survey Calif L ... Survey of California Law [*A publication*] (DLA)
Survey Cur Bus ... Survey of Current Business [*A publication*]
Survey Current Bus ... Survey of Current Business [*A publication*]
Survey G .... Survey Graphic [*A publication*]
Surveying Tech ... Surveying Technician [*A publication*]
Survey Progr Chem ... Survey of Progress in Chemistry [*A publication*]
Surveys Reference Works Math ... Surveys and Reference Works in Mathematics [*A publication*]
SURVFOR ... Surveillance Force (DNAB)
Surv High Energy Phys ... Surveys in High Energy Physics [*Switzerland*] [*A publication*]
SURVI ...... Surveillance
SURVIAC ... Survivability/Vulnerability Information Analysis Center [*DoD*] [*Wright-Patterson Air Force Base, OH*] (MCD)
Surv Immunol Res ... Survey of Immunologic Research [*A publication*]
Surv Immun Res ... Survey of Immunologic Research [*A publication*]
SURVL ...... Surveillance (AFM)
Surv-Local Gov Technol ... Surveyor-Local Government Technology [*A publication*]
SURVM ..... Surveillance and Maintenance [*Army*] (AABC)
Surv & Map ... Surveying and Mapping [*A publication*]
Surv Mapp ... Surveying and Mapping [*A publication*]
Surv Munic Cty Eng ... Surveyor and Municipal and County Engineer [*A publication*]
Surv Notes Utah Geol Miner Surv ... Survey Notes. Utah Geological and Mineral Survey [*A publication*]
Surv Ophthalmol ... Survey of Ophthalmology [*A publication*]
SURVOPS ... Survey Operations [*Navy*] (NVT)
SURVOR ... Survivor
Surv Pap Horace Lamb Centre Oceanogr Res ... Survey Paper. Horace Lamb Centre for Oceanographical Research. Flinders University of South Australia [*A publication*] (APTA)
Surv Prog Chem ... Survey of Progress in Chemistry [*A publication*]
SURVR ..... Surveyor
SURVR ..... Survivor (AAG)
SURVRAP ... Surveillance Range Acoustics Prediction System (MCD)
SURVSA ... Survivable Satellite Communications System (MCD)
SURVSAT ... Survivable Satellite
SURVSATCOM ... Survivable Satellite Communications System
SURVSUM ... Surveillance Summary Reports (NVT)
Surv Synth Pathol Res ... Survey and Synthesis of Pathology Research [*A publication*]
SURWAC ... Surface Water Automatic Computer (AAG)
SUS .... St. Louis [*Missouri*] Spirit of St. Louis Airport [*Airport symbol*] [*Obsolete*] (OAG)
SUS .... Samband Ungra Sjalfstaedismanna [*National Youth Organization of the Independence Party*] [*Iceland*] [*Political party*] (EAIO)
SUS .... Saybolt Universal Seconds [*Oil viscosity*]
SUS .... Scottish Union of Students (AEBS)
SUS .... Semiconductor Unilateral Switch (MSA)
SUS .... Signal Underwater Sound
SUS .... Silicon Unilateral Switch
SUS .... Single Underwater Sound (MCD)
SUS .... Small Ultimate Size [*Telecommunications*] (TEL)
SUS .... Society of University Surgeons (EA)
SUS .... Society for Utopian Studies (EA)
SUS .... Sound Underwater Source [*Navy*] (CAAL)
SUS .... Special Urban Survey 1987 [*Bureau of the Census*] (GFGA)
SUS .... Speech Understanding System
SUS .... Stained Urinary Sediment [*Medicine*] (MAE)
SUS .... Startup System [*Nuclear energy*] (NRCH)
SUS .... Stop Unnecessary Spending
SUS .... Suesswaren. Die Fachzeitschrift der Suesswaren Industrie. Produktion, Verpackung, Verkauf [*A publication*]
SUS .... Suit Umbilical System (MCD)
SUS .... Sunshine Columbia [*Vancouver Stock Exchange symbol*]
SUS .... Sunstates Corp. [*AMEX symbol*] (SPSG)
SUS .... Susaki [*Mitsui*] [*Japan*] [*Seismograph station code, US Geological Survey*] [*Closed*] (SEIS)
Sus .... Susanna [*Apocrypha*] (BJA)
SUS .... Suspect
SUS .... Suspended [*Technical drawings*]
SUS .... Suspense [*A publication*]
SUS .... Suspicion Law [*Statute permitting policemen to detain individuals suspected of criminal activity*] [*British*]
SUS .... Susquehanna University, Selinsgrove, PA [*OCLC symbol*] (OCLC)
SUS .... Susquehanna University. Studies [*A publication*]

Sus .... Susreti [*A publication*]
SUS............ Sustainer   (AAG)
sus............ Susu [*MARC language code*] [*Library of Congress*]   (LCCP)
SUSA........ Sage Urban Studies Abstracts [*A publication*]
SUSA........ Service Industries USA [*A publication*]
SUSA........ Seventh United States Army
SUSAFFS ... Society of United States Air Force Flight Surgeons
SUSAI .... SIAMA [*Society for Interest of Active Missionaries Abroad*] USA, Inc.   (EA)
SUSAN...... System Utilizing Signal-Processing for Automatic Navigation   (MCD)
SUSAT ...... Sight Unit Small Arms Trilux [*British*]
SUSC........ Religieuses de la Sainte-Union des Sacres-Coeurs de Jesus et Marie [*Religious of the Holy Union of the Sacred Hearts*] [*Roman Catholic women's religious order*]
SUS per COLL ... Suspensio per Collum [*Hanged by the Neck*] [*Latin*]
SUSD........ State University of South Dakota
SUS DUP .. Suspected Duplicate
SUSEME .. Superintendencia de Servicos Medicos [*Brazil*]
SUSF .... Samlingar Utgivna av Svenska Fornskriftssallskapet [*A publication*]
SUSF .... State University System of Florida   (NOAA)
SUSFU ...... Situation Unchanged, Still Fouled Up [*Military slang*] [*Bowdlerized version*]
SUSGR...... Southwestern Union for the Study of Great Religions   (EA)
SUSH .... Set-Up Sheet   (AAG)
SUSIE .... Stock Updating Sales Invoicing Electronically   (IEEE)
SUSIE .... Surface/Underwater Ship Intercept Equipment   (DNAB)
SUSIM ...... Solar Ultraviolet Spectral Irradiance Monitor   (MCD)
SUSIO .... [*Florida*] State University Institute of Oceanography   (MCD)
SUSIO .... State University System of Florida Institute of Oceanography   (NOAA)
SUSIS........ Sport und Sportwissenschaftliche Informationssystem [*Sport and Sports-Scientific Information System*] [*West Germany*]   (IID)
Sus Leg Chron ... Susquehanna Legal Chronicle [*Pennsylvania*] [*A publication*]   (DLA)
SUSLO ...... Senior United States Liaison Officer [*National Security Agency*]
SUSM....... Scottish United Services Museum [*British military*]   (DMA)
SUSMOP.. Senior United States Military Observer Palestine
SUSNO ...... Senior United States Naval Officer
SUSO........ Salto/Aeropuerto Deptal [*Uruguay*] [*ICAO location identifier*]   (ICLI)
SUSOPS.... Sustained Operations [*Study of soldier performance in extended combat situation*] [*Army*]
SUSP .... Suspected [*Passage or line of a work*] [*Literary criticism*]   (ROG)
SUSP .... Suspend [*or Suspension*]   (AFM)
SUSP........ Suspicion [*FBI standardized term*]
SUSPD...... Suspended
SUSPDNG ... Suspending [*Freight*]
SUSP L...... Suspecta Lectio [*Double Reading*] [*Latin*]   (ROG)
SUSQ........ Susquehanna Bancshares, Inc. [*Lititz, PA*] [*NASDAQ symbol*]   (NQ)
Susq LC ..... Susquehanna Leading Chronicle [*Pennsylvania*] [*A publication*]   (DLA)
Susq L Chron ... Susquehanna Legal Chronicle [*Pennsylvania*] [*A publication*]   (DLA)
Susq Legal Chron ... Susquehanna Legal Chronicle [*Pennsylvania*] [*A publication*]   (DLA)
Susq Leg Chron ... Susquehanna Legal Chronicle [*Pennsylvania*] [*A publication*]   (DLA)
Susquehanna Leg Chron (PA) ... Susquehanna Legal Chronicle [*Pennsylvania*] [*A publication*]   (DLA)
SUSRA ...... Steel in the USSR [*A publication*]
SUSREP.... Senior United States Representative to Defense Production Board [*NATO*]   (NATG)
SUSS .... Shuttle Upper-Stage System   (SSD)
SUSS .... Signalmen's United and Sick Society [*A union*] [*British*]
SUSS .... Sound Underwater Signal Source   (MCD)
SUSS .... Submarine Schoolship [*Navy*]   (NVT)
SUSS .... Sussex [*County in England*]
Sussex AC ... Sussex Archaeological Collections [*A publication*]
Sussex A Coll ... Sussex Archaeological Collections [*A publication*]
Sussex Arch Coll ... Sussex Archaeological Collections Relating to the Antiquities of the County [*A publication*]
SUST........ Sustainer
SUSTD...... Sustained [*Legal*]   (ROG)
SUSTN...... Sustain [*Legal*]   (ROG)
SUSTN...... Sustentation [*Ecclesiastical*]   (ROG)
SuSu........ Suomalainen Suomi [*A publication*]
SuSuomi...... Suomalainen Suomi [*A publication*]
SuSuV .... Suomalainen Suomi. Kulttuuripolittinen Aikakauskirja/Valvoja [*A publication*]
SUSV........ Small Unit Support Vehicle [*Military*]   (RDA)
SUSY's ...... Supersymmetric Theories [*Particle physics*]
SUT .... Satellite under Test
SUT .... Set-Up Time
SUT .... Small Unit Transceiver [*Military*]   (INF)
SUT .... Society for Underwater Technology   (EA)
SUT .... Southport, NC [*Location identifier*] [*FAA*]   (FAAL)

SUT .... Start-Up Transformer   (NRCH)
SUT .... State Unemployment Tax   (MCD)
SUT .... Subunit Test
SUT .... Surface and Underwater Target   (MCD)
SUT .... Suttsu [*Japan*] [*Seismograph station code, US Geological Survey*]   (SEIS)
SUT .... Syndicat Uni du Transport [*United Transportation Union - UTU*] [*Canada*]
SUT .... System under Test   (AAG)
SUTAGS ... Shuttle Uplink Text and Graphics Scanner   (NASA)
SUTARS .... Search Unit Tracing and Recording System
SUTB........ Tacuarembo [*Uruguay*] [*ICAO location identifier*]   (ICLI)
SUTD .... Soviet Union Today [*A publication*]
SUTEC ..... Seneca Underwater Test and Evaluation Center
SUTH .... Sutherland [*County in Scotland*]
Suth........... Sutherland's Calcutta Reports [*India*] [*A publication*]   (DLA)
Suth App.... Sutherland's Appeal Reports, Small Causes Court [*1861-65*] [*Bengal, India*] [*A publication*]   (DLA)
Suth Bengal ... Sutherland's Bengal High Court Reports [*India*] [*A publication*]   (DLA)
Suth Dam ... Sutherland on the Law of Damages [*A publication*]   (DLA)
Suth FBR ... Sutherland's Bengal Full Bench Reports [*India*] [*A publication*]   (DLA)
Suth Mis .... India Weekly Reporter, Miscellaneous Appeals [*A publication*]   (DLA)
Suth PCA... Sutherland's Privy Council Appeals [*A publication*]   (DLA)
Suth PCJ ... Sutherland's Privy Council Judgments [*A publication*]   (DLA)
Suth Sp N .. Full Bench Rulings [*Calcutta*] [*A publication*]   (DLA)
Suth Sp N .. Sutherland's Special Number of Weekly Reporter [*A publication*]   (DLA)
Suth Stat Const ... Sutherland on Statutes and Statutory Construction [*A publication*]   (DLA)
Suth St Const ... Sutherland on Statutes and Statutory Construction [*A publication*]   (DLA)
Suth WR .... Sutherland's Weekly Reporter, Calcutta [*1864-76*] [*A publication*]   (DLA)
Suth WR Mis ... Sutherland's Weekly Reports, Miscellaneous Appeals [*India*] [*A publication*]   (DLA)
SUTR........ Treinta Y Tres [*Uruguay*] [*ICAO location identifier*]   (ICLI)
SUTRA...... Saturated-Unsaturated Transport [*Ground-water modeling*]
SUTRASFCO ... Sindicato Unificado de Trabajadores de la Standard Fruit Co. [*Honduras*]
SUTT........ Small Unit Training Team [*Military*]
Sutton........ Sutton on Personal Actions at Common Law [*A publication*]   (DLA)
SUU .... Fairfield, CA [*Location identifier*] [*FAA*]   (FAAL)
SUU .... Santaquin Canyon [*Utah*] [*Seismograph station code, US Geological Survey*]   (SEIS)
SUU .... Society of University Urologists   (EA)
SUU .... Suspension Unit   (AFM)
SUU .... Suspension Unit Universal [*Weaponry*] [*Air Force*]   (INF)
SUV .... Small Unilamellar Vesicle [*Pharmacy*] [*Biochemistry*]
SUV .... Socicated Unilamellar Vesicles
SUV .... Sport-Utility Vehicle [*Type of truck*]
SUV .... Sumpter Valley Railway [*AAR code*]
SUV .... Suva [*Fiji*] [*Seismograph station code, US Geological Survey*]   (SEIS)
SUV .... Suva [*Fiji*] [*Airport symbol*]   (OAG)
SUVAT...... Support Unit Vehicle Automatic Tester
SUVCW..... Sons of Union Veterans of the Civil War   (EA)
SUVI......... Strong Ultraviolet Index
SUVO .... Student Voice [*A publication*]
Suvrem Med ... Suvremenna Meditsina [*Bulgaria*] [*A publication*]
Suvrem Probl Endokrinol ... Suvremenni Problemi na Endokrinologiyata [*A publication*]
SUVSL ...... Skrifter Utgivna. Vetenskaps-Societeten i Lund [*A publication*]
SUW .... Struthers Wells Corp. [*AMEX symbol*]   (SPSG)
SUW .... Superior, WI [*Location identifier*] [*FAA*]   (FAAL)
SUW .... Surface Warfare   (NVT)
SUWC....... Surface Warfare Coordinator [*Also, SWC*]   (NVT)
SUWU....... Skilled and Unskilled Workers' Union - Somali Republic
SUX .... Sioux City [*Iowa*] [*Airport symbol*]   (OAG)
sux............. Sumerian [*MARC language code*] [*Library of Congress*]   (LCCP)
SUY .... State University Railroad Co. [*Later, SUR*] [*AAR code*]
SUY .... Sudureyri [*Iceland*] [*Airport symbol*]   (OAG)
s-uy---....... Uruguay [*MARC geographic area code*] [*Library of Congress*]   (LCCP)
SUYR........ Southampton University Yacht Research Group [*British*]
SUZ .... Suez Petroleum Corp. [*Vancouver Stock Exchange symbol*]
SUZ .... Suria [*Papua New Guinea*] [*Airport symbol*]   (OAG)
SV .... El Salvador [*ANSI two-letter standard code*]   (CNC)
SV .... Safety Valve   (AAG)
SV .... Sailing Vessel
SV .... Sales Voucher [*Business term*]   (DCTA)
SV .... Sancta Virgo [*Holy Virgin*] [*Latin*]
SV .... Sanctitas Vestra [*Your Holiness*] [*Latin*]
SV .... Saponification Value [*Organic analytical chemistry*]
SV .... Sapper Vehicle [*Military*]
SV .... Sarcoma Virus [*Medicine*]   (MAE)
SV .... Satellite Virus

SV	Saudi Arabian Airlines [*ICAO designator*] (FAAC)
SV	Saves [*Baseball*]
SV	Savings Transfer [*Banking*]
SV	Scalp Vein [*Medicine*]
SV	Schedule Variance (MCD)
SV	Schweizer Volkskunde [*A publication*]
SV	Schweizerische Volkspartei [*Swiss People's Party*] [*Political party*]
SV	Scuola e Vita [*A publication*]
SV	Secondary Valve
SV	Secular Variation [*Geophysics*]
SV	Security Violation (AAG)
SV	Selecta Vision [*RCA brand name for tape cartridges of TV programs*]
SV	Selective Volunteer [*Navy*]
SV	Selenoid Valve (MCD)
SV	Self-Ventilated (MSA)
SV	Self Verification
SV	Seminal Vesicle [*Anatomy*]
SV	Service
SV	Service Vehicle
S/V	Servovalve
SV	Set Value
SV	Severe (MAE)
S & V	Shock and Vibration
SV	Shuttle Vehicle [*NASA*] (NASA)
S de V	Sicardus Fabri de Vauro [*Deceased, 1323*] [*Authority cited in pre-1607 legal work*] (DSA)
SV	Side Valve [*Automotive engineering*]
SV	Side View (MSA)
SV	Sieve
Sv	Sievert [*SI unit for radioactive dose equivalent*]
SV	Silicone Varnish
SV	Silvercraft SpA [*Italy*] [*ICAO aircraft manufacturer identifier*] (ICAO)
SV	Simian Virus
SV	Simulated Video (MCD)
SV	Single Silk Varnish [*Wire insulation*] (AAG)
SV	Single Value
SV	Single Vibrations [*Half cycles*]
SV	Sinus Venosus [*Anatomy*]
SV	Siste, Viator [*Stop, Traveller*] [*Latin*] (ROG)
SV	Slide Valve
SV	Slovesna Veda [*A publication*]
SV	Slowed-Down Video [*RADAR*] (CET)
SV	Sluice [*or Stop*] Valve
SV	Snake Venom [*Medicine*]
SV	Sodium Vapor
SV	Soft Valve
SV	Solenoid Valve (KSC)
SV	Solicited Volunteer [*In drug studies*]
SV	Sons of Veterans
SV	Sophisticated Vocabulary (AAG)
SV	Sosialistisk Valgforbund [*Socialist Electoral Alliance*] [*Norway*] [*Political party*] (PPE)
SV	Sosialistisk Venstreparti [*Socialist Left Party*] [*Norway*] [*Political party*] (PPE)
SV	Sotto Voce [*In an Undertone*] [*Music*]
S/V	Sound and Vibration [*A publication*]
SV	Sovetskaia Vostokovedenie [*A publication*]
SV	Space Vehicle
SV	Space Velocity [*Chemical engineering*]
SV	Space Visualization [*Visual perception*]
SV	Specified Value (MCD)
SV	Spiritus Vinosus [*Ardent Spirit*] [*Pharmacy*] (ROG)
SV	Star of Valour [*British*] (ADA)
SV	State Vector (KSC)
SV	Status Valid
sV	Statvolt [*Also, statV*] [*Electrostatic unit of potential difference*]
SV	Steam Valve
SV	Stimulation Value [*Psychology*]
SV	Storm Vulcan
SV	Stripping Voltammetry [*Electroanalytical chemistry*]
SV	Stroke Volume [*Physiology*]
SV	Study of Values [*Psychology*]
SV	Sub Verbo [*or Sub Voce*] [*Under the Word*] [*Latin*]
SV	Subclavian Vein [*Cardiology*]
SV	Subdivision Flag [*Navy*] [*British*]
SV	Subject-Verb [*Education of the hearing-impaired*]
SV	Subjective Vertical [*Neurology*]
SV	Super Volkswagen [*Auto racing*]
S/V	Supply Valve (MCD)
SV	Support Vehicle [*British military*] (DMA)
SV	Supraventricular [*Cardiology*]
SV	Supravital [*Medicine*] (MAE)
SV	Surface Vessel
S/V	Surface/Volume [*Ratio*]
S/V	Surrender Value [*Insurance*]
S/V	Survivability/Vulnerability [*Applied to ability of weapon systems to survive attacks*] [*Military*]
SV	Suvaguq. Pond Inlet [*A publication*]
sv	Swan Islands [*used in records cataloged after January 1978*] [*MARC country of publication code*] [*Library of Congress*] (LCCP)
SV	Swept Volume
SV	Symptomatic Volunteer [*In drug studies*]
SV	Synaptic Vesicle [*Neurobiology*]
SV	Synchronous Voltage (OA)
SVA	Sample Valve Assembly
SVA	Savoonga [*Alaska*] [*Airport symbol*] (OAG)
SVA	School of Visual Arts [*New York, NY*]
SVA	SEABEE Veterans of America (EA)
SVA	Sectionalized Vertical Antenna
SVA	Security and Vulnerability Analysis (MCD)
SVA	Selective Visceral Angiography [*Medicine*] (AAMN)
SVA	Shared Virtual Area [*Data processing*]
SVA	Shareholder Valuation Analysis
SVA	Singapore Volunteer Artillery [*British military*] (DMA)
SVA	Single-Valve First-Actuation [*Nuclear energy*] (NRCH)
SVA	Singular-Value Analysis [*Industrial control*]
SVA	Society for Visual Anthropology (EA)
SVA	Solar Vane Actuators
SVA	Statistical Vibration Analysis
SVA	Stock Valuation Adjustment [*Business term*] (ADA)
SVA	Sun Valley Airlines (FAAC)
SVA	Suva [*Fiji*] [*Seismograph station code, US Geological Survey*] (SEIS)
SVAA	Super Vernier Auto Alert [*Military*] (CAAL)
SVAB	Shuttle Vehicle Assembly Building [*NASA*] (NASA)
SVAC	Acarigua, Portuguesa [*Venezuela*] [*ICAO location identifier*] (ICLI)
SVAC	Senate Veterans Affairs Committee
SVA & C	Shuttle Vehicle Assembly and Checkout [*NASA*] (NASA)
SVAC	Shuttle Vehicle Assembly and Checkout [*NASA*] (GFGA)
SVAC	Singapore Volunteer Artillery Corps [*British military*] (DMA)
SVAD	Savanna Army Depot [*Illinois*] (AABC)
SVADA	Savanna Army Depot Activity (AABC)
Sv Aeroplan Ab SAAB Tech Notes ...	Svenska Aeroplan Aktiebolaget [*Linkoping, Sweden*]. SAAB Technical Notes [*A publication*]
SVAFB	South Vandenberg Air Force Base [*California*] (NASA)
SVALC	Sangamon Valley Academic Library Consortium [*Library network*]
SVAN	Anaco, Anzoategui [*Venezuela*] [*ICAO location identifier*] (ICLI)
SVAO	Service at Veterans Administration Offices [*Red Cross*]
SVAPA	Svarochnoe Proizvodstvo [*A publication*]
SVAR	Stuart's Lower Canada Vice-Admiralty Reports [*A publication*] (DLA)
Svarka Vzryvom Svoistva Svarnykh Soedin ...	Svarka Vzryvom i Svoistva Svarnykh Soedinenii [*A publication*]
Svar Proizvod ...	Svarochnoe Proizvodstvo [*A publication*]
SVAS	Supravalvular Aortic Stenosis [*Cardiology*] (MAE)
SVAT	San Fernando De Atabapo, T. F. Amazonas [*Venezuela*] [*ICAO location identifier*] (ICLI)
SVAT	Standard Version Acceptance Test (MCD)
SVB	Sambava [*Madagascar*] [*Airport symbol*] (OAG)
SVB	Savin Corp. [*NYSE symbol*] (SPSG)
SVB	Shuttle Vehicle Booster [*NASA*] (NASA)
SVB	Space Vehicle Booster [*NASA*] (MCD)
SVB	Sterivet Laboratories Ltd. [*Toronto Stock Exchange symbol*]
SV:B	Study of Values: British Edition [*Psychology*]
SVBC	Barcelona/Gral. Jose Antonio Anzoategui Internacional Anzoategui [*Venezuela*] [*ICAO location identifier*] (ICLI)
SVBEEQV ...	Si Vales, Bene Est; Ego Quoque Valeo [*I Hope You're Well; I Am*] [*Latin*]
SVBI	Barinas, Barinas [*Venezuela*] [*ICAO location identifier*] (ICLI)
SVBL	Maracay/El Libertador, Base Aerea Aragua [*Venezuela*] [*ICAO location identifier*] (ICLI)
SVBM	Barquisimeto/Internacional, Lara [*Venezuela*] [*ICAO location identifier*] (ICLI)
SVBP	Single-Variable Bypass Program [*DoD*]
SVBS	Maracay/Mariscal Sucre, Base Aerea Aragua [*Venezuela*] [*ICAO location identifier*] (ICLI)
SVBSA	Sivilt Beredskap [*A publication*]
SVBT	Space Vehicle Booster Test (AAG)
SVBUA	Shock and Vibration Bulletin [*A publication*]
SVBV	Strawberry Vein Banding Virus [*Plant pathology*]
SVBZ	Bruzual, Apure [*Venezuela*] [*ICAO location identifier*] (ICLI)
SVC	Saint Vincent College [*Latrobe, PA*]
SVC	Selective Venous Catheterization [*Cardiology*]
SVC	Service (AFM)
SVC	Service Command [*Army*]
SVC	Service Message [*Aviation code*]
SVC	Silver City [*New Mexico*] [*Airport symbol*] (OAG)
SVC	Silver Creek [*California*] [*Seismograph station code, US Geological Survey*] (SEIS)
SVC	Sine Vibration Control
SVC	Singapore Volunteer Corps [*British military*] (DMA)
SVC	Single Variable Control
SVC	Slow Vital Capacity [*Medicine*] (MAE)
SVC	Society of Vacuum Coaters (EA)

SVC............ Space Vehicle Code
SVC............ Spiroplasmavirus citri [*Bacteriology*]
SVC............ Spring Viremia of Carp
SVC............ Still Video Camera
SVC............ Stokely-Van Camp, Inc. [*NYSE symbol*]   (SPSG)
SVC............ Superior Vena Cava [*Anatomy*]
SVC............ Supervisor Call   (NASA)
SVC............ Suprahepatic Vena Cava [*Medicine*]   (AAMN)
SVC............ Switched Virtual Circuit
SVCA........ Caracas Maiquetia Distrito Federal [*Venezuela*] [*ICAO location identifier*]   (ICLI)
SVCAB...... Saphenous Vein Coronary Artery Bypass [*Cardiology*]
SVCB........ Ciudad Bolivar, Bolivar [*Venezuela*] [*ICAO location identifier*]   (ICLI)
SVCBL...... Serviceable
SVCBV...... Solenoid Valve-Carburetor Bowl Vent [*Automotive engineering*]
SVCC........ Caracas Ciudad Distrito Federal [*Venezuela*] [*ICAO location identifier*]   (ICLI)
SVCD........ Caicara De Orinoco, Bolivar [*Venezuela*] [*ICAO location identifier*]   (ICLI)
SVCE........ Service
SvceCp....... Service Corp. International [*Associated Press abbreviation*]   (APAG)
SVCG........ Spatial Vectorcardiogram [*Cardiology*]
SVCH........ Achaguas, Apure [*Venezuela*] [*ICAO location identifier*]   (ICLI)
SVCI......... Cachipo, Monagas [*Venezuela*] [*ICAO location identifier*]   (ICLI)
SVCIA....... Soviet Chemical Industry [*English Translation*] [*A publication*]
SVCJ........ San Carlos, Cojedes [*Venezuela*] [*ICAO location identifier*]   (ICLI)
SVCL........ Calabozo, Guarico [*Venezuela*] [*ICAO location identifier*]   (ICLI)
SVCMN..... Service Man   (NVT)
Svcmst....... ServiceMaster Ltd. [*Associated Press abbreviation*]   (APAG)
SVCN........ Canaima, Bolivar [*Venezuela*] [*ICAO location identifier*]   (ICLI)
SVCO .... Carora, Lara [*Venezuela*] [*ICAO location identifier*]   (ICLI)
SVCO .... Shillelagh Ventures, Chartered [*NASDAQ symbol*]   (NQ)
SVCP........ Carupano/Gral. en Jefe Jose Francisco Bermudez, Sucre [*Venezuela*] [*ICAO location identifier*]   (ICLI)
SVCP........ Special Virus Cancer Program [*National Cancer Institute*]
SVCR........ Coro/Internacional, Falcon [*Venezuela*] [*ICAO location identifier*]   (ICLI)
SVC-RPA .. Superior Vena Cava - Right Pulmonary Artery Shunt [*Anatomy*]   (MAE)
SVCS .... Caracas/Internacional del Centro Miranda [*Venezuela*] [*ICAO location identifier*]   (ICLI)
SVCS .... Star Vector Calibration Sensor [*Aviation*]   (OA)
SVCS .... Superior Vena Caval Syndrome [*Medicine*]
SvcStrs....... Service Stars [*Military decoration*]
SVCU........ Cumana, Sucre [*Venezuela*] [*ICAO location identifier*]   (ICLI)
SVCU........ Space Visualization Contralateral Use [*Occupational therapy*]
SVD .... St. Vincent [*Windward Islands*] [*Airport symbol*]   (OAG)
SVD .... Seismic Velocity Discontinuity [*Geology*]
SVD .... Share Valuation Division [*Inland Revenue*] [*British*]
SVD .... Silver Talon Mines Ltd. [*Vancouver Stock Exchange symbol*]
SVD .... Simple Vertex Delivery [*Medicine*]
SVD .... Simplified Vapor Detector
SVD .... Simultaneous Voice/Data
SVD .... Singular Value Decomposition [*Mathematics*]
SVD .... Societas Verbi Divini [*Society of the Divine Word*] [*Roman Catholic men's religious order*]
SVD .... Soviet Export. Soviet Foreign Trade Bimonthly [*A publication*]
SVD .... Space Vehicles Division [*NASA*]   (MCD)
SVD .... Spontaneous Vaginal Delivery [*Gynecology*]
SVD .... Surveyor Vehicle Department
SvD .... Svenska Dagbladet [*A publication*]
SVD .... Sverdlovsk [*Former USSR*] [*Geomagnetic observatory code*]
SVD .... Swine Vesicular Disease
SVDA .... Savanna Depot Activity [*Army*]
SVDF .... Segmented Virtual Display File
SVDI........ Serie de Vocabularios y Diccionarios Indigenas [*A publication*]
SVDP........ La Divina Pastora, Bolivar [*Venezuela*] [*ICAO location identifier*]   (ICLI)
SVDP........ Saint Vincent de Paul   (ADA)
SVDP........ Skylab Video Documentation Project [*NASA*]   (KSC)
SVDS........ Space Vehicle Dynamic Simulator [*NASA*]   (NASA)
SVE .... Secure Voice Equipment   (NATG)
SVE .... Seminal Vesicle Epithelium [*Anatomy*]
SVE .... Severide Resources, Inc. [*Vancouver Stock Exchange symbol*]
SVE .... Society for Vector Ecology   (EA)
SVE .... Society for Veterinary Ethology [*See also SEV*] [*Edinburgh, Scotland*]   (EAIO)
SVE .... Society for Visual Education, Inc.   (AEBS)
SVE .... Space Vehicle Electronics   (SAA)
SVE .... Special Vehicle Engineering [*Ford Motor Co.*]
SVE .... Supraventricular Ectopic [*Beat*] [*Cardiology*]
SVE .... Susanville, CA [*Location identifier*] [*FAA*]   (FAAL)

SVE........... Sverdlovsk [*Ekaterinburg*] [*Former USSR*] [*Seismograph station code, US Geological Survey*]   (SEIS)
SVE........... Swept Volume Efficiency [*Air Force*]
SVE........... System Valve Engineering
s-ve--- .... Venezuela [*MARC geographic area code*] [*Library of Congress*]   (LCCP)
SVEA........ Schweizerischer Verband Evangaelischer Arbeitnehmer [*A union*] [*Switzerland*]   (DCTA)
SVEA........ Supplemental Vocational Education Assistance   (OICC)
SvEA.......... Svensk Exegetisk Arsbok [*A publication*]
SVEAA...... Schweizerischer Verband Evangelischer Arbeiter und Angestellter [*Swiss Federation of Protestant Trade Unions*]
SVEAD...... State Variable Estimation and Accuracy Determination
SVEC........ Studies on Voltaire and the Eighteenth Century [*A publication*]
SVED........ El Dorado, Bolivar [*Venezuela*] [*ICAO location identifier*]   (ICLI)
Sved Zemed ... Svedeniya po Zemedelieto [*A publication*]
SVEN........ Shipboard Voice-Enhanced Navigation System [*for blind sailors*]
Sven Bot Tidskr ... Svensk Botanisk Tidskrift [*A publication*]
Sven Bryggarefoeren Manadsbl ... Svenska Bryggarefoereningens Manadsblad [*A publication*]
Sven Bryggeritidskr ... Svensk Bryggeritidskrift [*A publication*]
Sven Faerg Tek Tidskr ... Svensk Faerg-Teknisk Tidskrift [*A publication*]
Sven Farm Tidskr ... Svensk Farmaceutisk Tidskrift [*A publication*]
Sven Farm Tidskr Sci Ed ... Svensk Farmaceutisk Tidskrift. Scientific Edition [*A publication*]
Sven Foerfattningssaml ... Svensk Foerfattningssamling [*A publication*]
Sven Forskningsinst Cem Betong K Tek Hoegsk Stockholm Handl ... Svenska Forskningsinstitutet foer Cement och Betong vid Kungliga Tekniska Hoegskolan i Stockholm. Handlingar [*A publication*]
Sven Forskningsinst Cem Betong K Tek Hoegsk Stockholm Medd ... Svenska Forskningsinstitutet foer Cement och Betong vid Kungliga Tekniska Hoegskolan i Stockholm. Meddelanden [*A publication*]
Sven Forskningsinst Cem Betong K Tek Hoegsk Stockholm Saertr ... Svenska Forskningsinstitutet foer Cement och Betong vid Kungliga Tekniska Hoegskolan i Stockholm. Saertryck [*A publication*]
Sven Forskningsinst Cem Betong K Tek Hoegsk Stockholm Utredn ... Svenska Forskningsinstitutet foer Cement och Betong vid Kungliga Tekniska Hoegskolan i Stockholm. Utredningar [*A publication*]
Sven Forskningsinst Cem Betong K Tek Hogsk ... Svenska Forskningsinstitutet foer Cement och Betong vid Kungliga i Stockholm. Meddelanden Tekniska Hoegskolan [*Sweden*] [*A publication*]
Sven Fotogr Tidskr ... Svensk Fotografisk Tidskrift [*A publication*]
Sven Frotidn ... Svensk Froetidning [*A publication*]
Sven Gasfoeren Manadsbl ... Svenska Gasfoereningens Manadsblad [*A publication*]
Sven Gasverksfoeren Aarsb ... Svenska Gasverksfoereningens Aarsbok [*A publication*]
Sven Hydrogr Biol Komm Skr Ny Ser Biol ... Svenska Hydrografisk-Biologiska Kommissionens Skrifter. Ny Serie. Biologi [*A publication*]
Sven Inst Konserveringsforsk Publ ... Svenska Institutet foer Konserveringsforskning. Publikation [*A publication*]
Sven Kem Tidskr ... Svensk Kemisk Tidskrift [*A publication*]
Sven Kraftverksfoeren Publ ... Svenska Kraftverksfoereningens Publikationer [*A publication*]
Sven Kraftverksfoeren Publ Medd ... Svenska Kraftverksfoereningens Publikationer Meddelande [*A publication*]
Sven Laekaresaellsk Foerh ... Svenska Laekaresaellskapets Foerhandlingar [*A publication*]
Sven Laekartidn ... Svenska Laekartidningen [*A publication*]
Sven Linne-SallskArsskr ... Svenska Linne-Sallskapet Arsskrift [*A publication*]
Sven Mejeriernas Riksfoeren Produkttek Avd Medd ... Svenska Mejeriernas Riksfoerening. Produkttekniska Avdelningen. Meddelande [*A publication*]
Sven Mejeritidn ... Svenska Mejeritidningen [*A publication*]
Sven Mosskulturfoeren Tidskr ... Svenska Mosskulturfoereningens Tidskrift [*A publication*]
Sven Naturvetensk ... Svensk Naturvetenskap [*A publication*]
Sven Papperfoeraedlingstidskr ... Svensk Pappersfoeraedlingstidskrift [*A publication*]
Sven Pappersmassetidn ... Svensk Pappersmassetidning [*A publication*]
Sven Papperstidn ... Svensk Papperstidning [*A publication*]
Svensk Bot Tidskr ... Svensk Botanisk Tidskrift [*A publication*]
Svensk Froetidn ... Svensk Froetidning [*A publication*]
Svensk Geog Arsbok ... Svensk Geografisk Arsbok [*A publication*]
Svensk Kem Tidskr ... Svensk Kemisk Tidskrift [*A publication*]
Svensk Litt ... Svensk Litteraturtidskrift [*A publication*]
Sven Skogsvardsforen Tidskr ... Svenska Skogsvardsforeningens Tidskrift [*A publication*]
SvenskPapr ... Svensk Papperstidning [*A publication*]
Svensk Teol Kvartalskr ... Svensk Teologisk Kvartalskrift [*A publication*]
Svensk Tid ... Svensk Tidskrift foer Musikforskning [*A publication*]

Svenskt MHistoriskt ... Svenskt Musikhistoriskt Arkiv. Bulletin [*A publication*]

Svensk Travarutidn ... Svensk Traevaru- och Pappersmassetidning [*A publication*]

Svensk Vet-Tidskr ... Svensk Veterinaertidskrift [*A publication*]

Svens Pap T ... Svensk Papperstidning Tidskrift [*A publication*]

Sven Tandlaek Tidskr ... Svensk Tandlaekare Tidskrift [*A publication*]

Sven Tandlakareforb Tidn ... Svensk Tandlaekareforbunds Tidning [*Sweden*] [*A publication*]

Sven Tandlak Tidskr ... Svensk Tandlaekare Tidskrift [*A publication*]

Sven Tids M ... Svensk Tidskrift foer Musikforskning [*A publication*]

Sven Traevaru-Tidn ... Svensk Traevaru-Tidning [*A publication*]

Sven Vall Mosskulturfoeren Medd ... Svenska Vall- och Mosskulturfoereningens Meddelanden [*A publication*]

Sven Vattenkraftfoeren Publ ... Svenska Vattenkraftforeningens Publikationer [*A publication*]

Sven Veterinartidn ... Svensk Veterinaertidning [*A publication*]

SVER .... Spatial Visual Evoked Response   (OA)

SVER .... State Veterans Employment Representative [*Department of Labor*]

Sver Geol Unders Arsb ... Sveriges Geologiska Undersoekning. Arsbok [*A publication*]

Sver Geol Unders Arsb Ser C Avh Uppsatser ... Sveriges Geologiska Undersoekning. Arsbok. Serie C. Avhandlingar och Uppsatser [*A publication*]

Sver Gummitek Foren Publ ... Sveriges Gummitekniska Foerening. Publicerande [*A publication*]

Sveriges Geol Unders Ser C ... Sveriges Geologiska Undersoekning. Arsbok. Serie C. Avhandlingar och Uppsatser [*A publication*]

Sveriges Riksbank Q R ... Sveriges Riksbank. Quarterly Review [*A publication*]

Sveriges Skogsvforb Tidskr ... Sveriges Skogsvardsfoerbunds Tidskrift [*A publication*]

Sveriges Utsaedesfoer Tidskr ... Sveriges Utsaedesfoerenings Tidskrift [*A publication*]

Sver Lantbruksuniv Inst Biom Skogsindelning Rapp ... Sveriges Lantbruksuniversitet Institutionen foer Biometri och Skogsindelning. Rapport [*A publication*]

Sver Lantbruksuniv Inst Lantbrukets Byggnadstek Rapp ... Sveriges Lantbruksuniversitet Institutionen foer Lantbrukets Byggnadsteknik. Rapport [*A publication*]

Sver Lantbruksuniv Inst Mikrobiol Rapp ... Sveriges Lantbruksuniversitet Institutionen foer Mikrobiologi. Rapport [*A publication*]

Sver Lantbruksuniv Inst Tradgardsvetensk Rapp ... Sveriges Lantbruksuniversitet Institutionen foer Tradgardsvetenskap. Rapport [*A publication*]

Sver Lantbruksuniv Konsulentavd Rapp Landskap ... Sveriges Lantbruksuniversitet Konsulentavdelningens Rapporter Landskap [*A publication*]

Sver Lantbruksuniv Vaxtskyddsrapp Avh ... Sveriges Lantbruksuniversitet Vaxtskyddsrapporter Avhandlingar [*A publication*]

Sver Lantbruksuniv Vaxtskyddsrapp Tradg ... Sveriges Lantbruksuniversitet Vaxtskyddsrapporter Tradgard [*A publication*]

Sver Mekanforb Mekanresult ... Sveriges Mekanforbund, Mekanresultat [*A publication*]

Sver Nat ..... Sveriges Natur [*A publication*]

Sver Nat Arsb ... Sveriges Natur Arsbok [*A publication*]

Sver Off Stat Bergshantering ... Sveriges Officiella Statistik Bergshantering. Statistika Centralbyran [*Stockholm*] [*A publication*]

Sver Pomol Foeren Arsskr ... Sveriges Pomologiska Foerening Arsskrift [*A publication*]

Sver Skogsvardsfoerbunds Tidskr ... Sveriges Skogsvardsfoerbunds Tidskrift [*A publication*]

Sver Skogsvardsforb Tidskr ... Sveriges Skogsvardsfoerbunds Tidskrift [*A publication*]

SVERT ...... Subvert   (ROG)

Svertyvayushchaya Sist Krovi Akush Ginekol ... Svertyvayushchaya Sistema Krovi v Akusherstve i Ginekologii [*A publication*]

Sver Utsadesforen Tidskr ... Sveriges Utsaedesfoerenings Tidskrift [*A publication*]

Sver Utsadesfoer Tidskr ... Sveriges Utsaedesfoerenings Tidskrift [*A publication*]

Svetotekh ... Svetotekhnika [*A publication*]

Svetotekhnika Svetotekh Kom Akad Nauk SSSR ... Svetotekhnika. Svetotekhnicheskaya Komissiya Akademii Nauk SSSR [*A publication*]

Svetsaren Dtsch Ausg ... Svetsaren. Deutsche Ausgabe [*A publication*]

Svetsaren Ed Fr ... Svetsaren. Edition Francaise [*A publication*]

Svetsaren Weld Rev ... Svetsaren: A Welding Review [*A publication*]

SvExAb ...... Svensk Exegetisk Arsbok [*A publication*]

SvExArsb ... Svensk Exegetisk Arsbok [*A publication*]

SVEZ .... Elorza, Apure [*Venezuela*] [*ICAO location identifier*]   (ICLI)

SVF .... Save [*Benin*] [*Airport symbol*]   (OAG)

SVF .... Services Flight [*Military*]

SVF .... Silverleaf Resources Ltd. [*Vancouver Stock Exchange symbol*]

SVF .... Standard Vented Furnace

SVF .... State Variable Filter

SVF .... Stoicorum Veterum Fragmenta [*A publication*]   (OCD)

Sv Farm Tid ... Svensk Farmaceutisk Tidskrift [*A publication*]

SVF Fachorgan Textilveredl ... SVF [*Svetstekniska Foereningen*] Fachorgan fuer Textilveredlung [*A publication*]

SVFM .... Caracas/Generelisimo Francisco De Miranda Base Aerea La Carlota, Miranda [*Venezuela*] [*ICAO location identifier*]   (ICLI)

SVFR .... Special Visual Flight Rules [*Aviation*]

SVG .... Gids voor Personeelsbeleid. Arbeidsvraagstukken en Sociale Verzekering [*A publication*]

SVG .... Saphenous Vein Graft [*Cardiology*]

SVG .... Sauvagine [*A polypeptide*]

SVG .... Servicing

SVG .... Spiritus Vini Gallici [*Brandy*] [*Pharmacy*]   (ROG)

SVG .... Stavanger [*Norway*] [*Airport symbol*]   (OAG)

SVG .... Stevens Graphics, Inc. [*AMEX symbol*]   (SPSG)

SVG .... Sun Valley Gold Mines Ltd. [*Vancouver Stock Exchange symbol*]

SVGA .... Super Video Graphics Array [*Data processing*]

SVGC .... Secure Voice and Graphic Conferencing   (MCD)

SVGD .... Guasdualito, Apure [*Venezuela*] [*ICAO location identifier*]   (ICLI)

SVGI .... Guiria, Sucre [*Venezuela*] [*ICAO location identifier*]   (ICLI)

SVGI .... Silicon Valley Group, Inc. [*NASDAQ symbol*]   (NQ)

SVGLA ...... Sovetskaya Geologiya [*A publication*]

SVGS .... Savings

SVGT .... Guasipati, Bolivar [*Venezuela*] [*ICAO location identifier*]   (ICLI)

SVGU .... Guanare, Portuguesa [*Venezuela*] [*ICAO location identifier*]   (ICLI)

SVGU .... Sveriges Geologiska Undersoekning [*A publication*]

SVH .... Seven Mile High Resources, Inc. [*Vancouver Stock Exchange symbol*]

SVH .... Severely Handicapped

SVH .... Solar Vacuum Head [*Astronomy*]   (OA)

SVH .... Statesville, NC [*Location identifier*] [*FAA*]   (FAAL)

SVHE .... Society for Values in Higher Education   (EA)

SVHG .... Higuerote, Miranda [*Venezuela*] [*ICAO location identifier*]   (ICLI)

SVHS .... Super Video Home System [*Japan Victor Co.*]

SVI .... St. Vincent [*St. Vincent*] [*Seismograph station code, US Geological Survey*] [*Closed*]   (SEIS)

SVI .... San Vincente Del Caguan [*Colombia*] [*Airport symbol*]   (OAG)

SVI .... Service Interception [*Telecommunications*]   (TEL)

SVI .... Singapore Volunteer Infantry [*British military*]   (DMA)

SVI .... Single Vendor Integrity   (MCD)

SVI .... Single Vibrational Level [*Physics*]

SVI .... Sludge Volume Index [*Wastewater treatment*]

SVI .... Sound Velocity Indicator

SVI .... Spiritus Vini Industrialis [*Industrial Alcohol*] [*Pharmacy*]

SVI .... Stroke Volume Index [*Medicine*]

SVI .... Sveriges Riksbank. Quarterly Review [*A publication*]

SvI .... Svizzera Italiana [*A publication*]

SVI .... System Verification Installation

SVIA .... Specialty Vehicles Institute of America   (EA)

SVIB .... Strong Vocational Interest Blank [*Psychology*]

SVIC .... Icabaru, Bolivar [*Venezuela*] [*ICAO location identifier*]   (ICLI)

SVIC .... Shock and Vibration Information Center [*Terminated*] [*Navy*]   (MCD)

SVIC .... Silicon Valley Information Center [*Database producer*]   (IID)

SVIC .... Sweet Victory, Inc. [*New York, NY*] [*NASDAQ symbol*]   (NQ)

SVICLC ..... Shenandoah Valley Independent College Library Cooperative [*Library network*]

SVIE .... Isla De Coche, Nueva Esparta [*Venezuela*] [*ICAO location identifier*]   (ICLI)

SVIF .... Svenski Indianska Foerbundet [*Sweden*]

SVIL .... Seville Energy Corp. [*NASDAQ symbol*]   (NQ)

SVIMS ...... Short Vehicle Integrated Management System

Svinovod ..... Svinovodstvo [*A publication*]

SVIO .... Superintending Veterinary Investigation Officer [*Ministry of Agriculture, Fisheries, and Food*] [*British*]

SVIP .... Secure Voice Improvement Program [*DoD*]

SVIPA .... Swiss Videotex Industry Association [*Information service or system*]   (IID)

SVIPA .... Swiss Viewdata Information Providers Association [*Zurich*] [*Telecommunications*]

SVITA .... Spectravideo, Inc. Cl A [*NASDAQ symbol*]   (NQ)

SVJ .... Lompoc, CA [*Location identifier*] [*FAA*]   (FAAL)

SVJ .... Sovetska Veda. Jazykoveda [*A publication*]

SVJ .... Steed Ventures Corp. [*Formerly, Poney Explorations Ltd.*] [*Vancouver Stock Exchange symbol*]

SVJ .... Svolvaer [*Norway*] [*Airport symbol*]   (OAG)

SVJC .... Paraguana/Josefa Camejo Internacional, Falcon [*Venezuela*] [*ICAO location identifier*]   (ICLI)

SvJerTs ...... Svenska Jerusalems-Foereningens Tidskrift [*Uppsala*] [*A publication*]

SVK .... Secure Voice Kit   (DWSG)

SVKA .... Kavanayen, Bolivar [*Venezuela*] [*ICAO location identifier*]   (ICLI)

SVKM .... Kamarata, Bolivar [*Venezuela*] [*ICAO location identifier*]   (ICLI)

Sv Kraftverksforen Publ ... Svenska Kraftverksfoereningens Publikationer [*A publication*]

SVKTA ...... Strassenverkehrstechnik [*A publication*]

SVL .... Sapphire Vacuum Lens

SVL............ Savonlinna [*Finland*] [*Airport symbol*] (OAG)
SVL............ Scripps Visibility Laboratory
SVL............ Silver Lake Resources, Inc. [*Toronto Stock Exchange symbol*]
SVL............ Snout-to-Vent Length [*Biometry*]
SVL............ Star Valley Resources [*Vancouver Stock Exchange symbol*]
SVL............ Studien zur Vergleichenden Literaturgeschichte [*A publication*]
SVL............ Support Validation Laboratory [*Army*]
SVLA........ Steered Vertical Line Array [*Military*] (CAAL)
SVLAA...... Svenska Laekartidningen [*A publication*]
SVLB........ Sapphire Vacuum Lens Blank
SVLF........ La Fria, Tachira [*Venezuela*] [*ICAO location identifier*] (ICLI)
SVLF........ Shipboard Very Low Frequency [*Navy*] (NG)
SVLH........ Surma Valley Light Horse [*British military*] (DMA)
SVLKAO... Collection of Scientific Works. Faculty of Medicine. Charles University (Hradec Kralove) [*A publication*]
SVLL........ Short Vertical Lower Left
SvLm........ Svenska Landsmal och Svenskt Folkliv [*A publication*]
SVLO........ La Orchila - Dependencia Federal [*Venezuela*] [*ICAO location identifier*] (ICLI)
SVLOG...... Servicing Log [*Telecommunications*] (TEL)
SVLP........ Special Virus Leukemia Program [*National Cancer Institute*]
SVLR........ Short Vertical Lower Right
SVLTE...... Services Valve Life Test Establishment [*British*] (MCD)
SVLW....... Sectoraal Verband Landbouwwetenschappen [*Committee on International Education in Agricultural Sciences*] [*Netherlands*] (EAIO)
SVM .... Salem, MI [*Location identifier*] [*FAA*] (FAAL)
SVM .... Seminal Vesicle Mesenchyme [*Anatomy*]
SVM .... Seminal Vesicle Microsome [*Anatomy*]
SVM .... Semitrailer Van Mount
SVM .... Service Volontaire Mennonite [*Mennonite Voluntary Service*]
SVM .... ServiceMaster Ltd. [*NYSE symbol*] (SPSG)
SVM .... Ship Vulnerability Model (MCD)
SVM .... Ship's Value Manual (DNAB)
SVM .... Silicon Video Memory
SVM .... Silver City [*New Mexico*] [*Seismograph station code, US Geological Survey*] (SEIS)
SVM .... Silver Hart Mines Ltd. [*Vancouver Stock Exchange symbol*]
SVM .... Sisters of the Visitation of the Congregation of the Immaculate Heart of Mary [*Roman Catholic religious order*]
SVM .... Special Vehicle Management [*Automotive engineering*]
SVM .... Spiritus Vini Methylatus [*Methylated Spirit*] [*Pharmacy*]
SVM .... Stamp Vending Machine (DCTA)
SvM .... Svensk Missionstidskrift [*A publication*]
SVM .... Syncytiovascular Membrane [*Medicine*] (MAE)
SVM .... System Validation Model (NVT)
SVMA........ Space Vehicle Mission Analysis
SVMC........ Maracaibo/La Chinita Internacional, Zulia [*Venezuela*] [*ICAO location identifier*] (ICLI)
SVMCD8... Sciences Veterinaires Medecine Comparee [*A publication*]
SVMD .... Merida/Alberto Carnevalli, Merida [*Venezuela*] [*ICAO location identifier*] (ICLI)
SvMer .... Service Merchandise Co., Inc. [*Associated Press abbreviation*] (APAG)
SVMG .... Margarita/Internacional del Caribe Gral Santiago Marino, Neuva Esparta [*Venezuela*] [*ICAO location identifier*] (ICLI)
SVMH .... Silver Hart Mines Ltd. [*NASDAQ symbol*] (NQ)
SVMI........ Caracas/Simon Bolivar Internacional Maiquetia Distrito Federal [*Venezuela*] [*ICAO location identifier*] (ICLI)
SVML........ Standard Vehicle Mounted Launcher [*Army*]
SVMP........ Caracas/Metropolitano Internacional, Miranda [*Venezuela*] [*ICAO location identifier*] (ICLI)
SVMPCG .. Grasslands National Park, Parks Canada [*Parc National Grasslands, Parcs Canada*] Val Marie, Saskatchewan [*Library symbol*] [*National Library of Canada*] (NLC)
SVMR........ Maracay/Centro Nacional de Comunicaciones/Meteorologicos, Aragua [*Venezuela*] [*ICAO location identifier*] (ICLI)
SVMT........ Maturin/Internacional, Monagas [*Venezuela*] [*ICAO location identifier*] (ICLI)
SVMTR ..... Servomotor [*Control systems*]
SVN .... Savannah, GA [*Location identifier*] [*FAA*] (FAAL)
SVN .... South Vietnam (CINC)
SVNAB...... Svensk Naturvetenskap [*A publication*]
SVNESE.... South Vietnamese
SVNM ...... St. Vincent National Movement [*Political party*] (PPW)
SVNRF ...... State of Vietnam Ribbon of Friendship [*Military decoration*] (AABC)
SVNVAC... Sunny Von Bulow National Victim Advocacy Center [*Later, NVC*] (EA)
SVO .... Moscow [*Former USSR*] Sheremetyevo Airport [*Airport symbol*] (OAG)
SVO .... Scottish Variety Orchestra (DI)
SVO .... Senior Veterinary Officer [*British military*] (DMA)
SVO .... Servo (KSC)
SVO .... Space Vehicle Operations (MCD)
SVO .... Special Vehicle Operation [*Ford Motor Co.*]
SVO .... Subject-Verb-Object [*Education of the hearing-impaired*]
SVOIR....... Specification Verification Open Item Report
Svoista Veshchestv Str Mol ... Svoistva Veshchestv i Stroenie Molekul [*A publication*]

Svojstva At Yader ... Svojstva Atomnykh Yader [*A publication*]
SVP........... Bie [*Angola*] [*Airport symbol*] (OAG)
SVP........... St. Louis Public Library, St. Louis, MO [*OCLC symbol*] (OCLC)
SVP........... Security Vehicle Patrol [*Air Force*] (AFM)
SVP........... Seminal Vesicle Protein [*Biochemistry*]
SVP........... Senior Vice President
SVP........... Service Processor (BUR)
SVP........... Services Vegetable Production [*British military*] (DMA)
SVP........... Sewer Vent Pipe
SVP........... S'il Vous Plait [*If You Please*] [*French*]
SVP........... Silver Princess Resources [*Vancouver Stock Exchange symbol*]
SVP........... Small Volume Parenteral [*Pharmacy*]
SVP........... Snake Venom Phosphodiesterase [*Also, SVPDE*] [*An enzyme*]
SVP........... Societe pour Vaincre la Pollution [*Canada*]
SVP........... Society of St. Vincent de Paul
SVP........... Society of Vertebrate Paleontology (EA)
SVP........... Sound Velocity Profile
SVP........... Specific Vocational Preparation [*US Employment Service*] [*Department of Labor*]
SVP........... Star-Vaporizing Millisecond Pulsar [*Cosmology*]
SVP........... Steam Vacuum Pulse
SVP........... Sudtiroler Volkspartei [*South Tyrolean People's Party*] [*Italy*] [*Political party*] (EAIO)
SVP........... Supplemental Vacation Plan
SVPA........ Puerto Ayacucho, T. F. Amazonas [*Venezuela*] [*ICAO location identifier*] (ICLI)
SVPB .... Supraventricular Premature Beats [*Cardiology*]
SVPC .... Puerto Cabello/Gral. Bartolome Salom Internacional, Carabobo [*Venezuela*] [*ICAO location identifier*] (ICLI)
SVPDE ...... Snake Venom Phosphodiesterase [*Also, SVP*] [*An enzyme*]
SVPIA ...... Surface and Vacuum Physics Index [*A publication*]
SVPM........ San Cristobal/Paramillo, Tachira [*Venezuela*] [*ICAO location identifier*] (ICLI)
SVPM........ Small Vehicles, Program Manager
SVPP .... Schweizerische Vereinigung fuer Parapsychologie
SVPP/A..... Archivos Venezolanas de Puericultura y Pediatria. Sociedad Venezolana de Puericultura y Pediatria [*A publication*]
SVPR .... Guayana/Puerto Ordaz Internacional, Bolivar [*Venezuela*] [*ICAO location identifier*] (ICLI)
SVPT .... Palmarito, Apure [*Venezuela*] [*ICAO location identifier*] (ICLI)
SVQ .... Seville [*Spain*] [*Airport symbol*] (OAG)
SVR........... Severe (FAAC)
SVR........... Singapore Volunteer Rifles [*British military*] (DMA)
SVR........... Slant Visual Range
SVR........... Society of Vietnamese Rangers (EA)
SVR........... Spiritus Vini Rectificatus [*Rectified Spirit of Wine*] [*Pharmacy*]
SVR........... Super Video Recorder
SVR........... Supply-Voltage Rejection (IEEE)
SVR........... Surface/Volume Ratio
SVR........... Systemic Vascular Resistance [*Medicine*]
SVRA........ Sportscar Vintage Racing Association (EA)
SVRA........ State Vehicular Recreation Area
SVRB........ Supervisor Request Block [*Data processing*] (BUR)
SVRD........ Silicon Voltage Reference Diode
SVRDA...... Soviet Radiochemistry [*English Translation*] [*A publication*]
SVREP ...... Southwest Voter Registration Education Project (EA)
SVRI .... Systemic Vascular Resistance Index
SVRL........ Several (FAAC)
SVRL........ Silvar-Lisco [*NASDAQ symbol*] (NQ)
SVRN .... Sovereign Bancorp, Inc. [*NASDAQ symbol*] (NQ)
SVRR .... Software Verification Readiness Review [*NASA*] (NASA)
SVRS .... Los Roques, Dependencia Federal [*Venezuela*] [*ICAO location identifier*] (ICLI)
SVS........... Eastern Commuter, Inc. [*Hasbrouck Heights, NJ*] [*FAA designator*] (FAAC)
SVS........... Saga-Book. Viking Society for Northern Research [*A publication*]
SVS........... Schedule Visibility System (AAG)
SVS........... Secure Voice Switch
SVS........... Secure Voice System [*Telecommunications*]
SVS........... Service School [*Military*]
SVS........... Services Squadron
SVS........... Silverside Resources, Inc. [*Toronto Stock Exchange symbol*]
SVS........... Single Virtual Storage [*IBM Corp.*] [*Data processing*]
SVS........... Slandsville [*South Carolina*] [*Seismograph station code, US Geological Survey*] (SEIS)
SVS........... Society for Vascular Surgery (EA)
SVS........... Soil Vapor Survey [*Environmental chemistry*]
SVS........... Sound Velocity Structure
SVS........... Space Vehicle Simulator (AAG)
SVS........... Spectroradiometer Visible System
SVS........... Spinning Vehicle Simulator
SVS........... Stabilized Viewing System
SVS........... Statistica Neerlandica [*A publication*]
SVS........... Stevens Village [*Alaska*] [*Airport symbol*] (OAG)
SVS........... Still-Camera Video System [*Canon, Inc.*]
SVS........... Suit Ventilation System [*Aerospace*] (MCD)
SVS........... Synthetic Vision Systems, Inc.

SVSA	San Antonio, Tachira [*Venezuela*] [*ICAO location identifier*] (ICLI)
SVSB	Santa Barbara De Barinas, Barinas [*Venezuela*] [*ICAO location identifier*] (ICLI)
SVSC	San Carlos De Rio Negro, T. F. Amazonas [*Venezuela*] [*ICAO location identifier*] (ICLI)
SVSC	Space Vehicle Sectoring Code
SVSE	Santa Elena de Uairen, Bolivar [*Venezuela*] [*ICAO location identifier*] (ICLI)
SVSHA	Sovetskii Shakhtior [*A publication*]
SVSHKG	Schriften. Verein fuer Schleswig-Holsteinische Kirchengeschichte [*A publication*]
SVSL	Skrifter Utgivna. Vetenskaps-Societeten i Lund [*A publication*]
SVSO	Santo Domingo/Mayor Buenaventura Vivas A. B., Tachira [*Venezuela*] [*ICAO location identifier*] (ICLI)
SVSO	Superintending Victualling Stores Officer [*British*]
S V Sound Vib	S. V. Sound and Vibration [*A publication*]
SVSP	San Felipe/Subteniente Nestor Arias, Yaracuy [*Venezuela*] [*ICAO location identifier*] (ICLI)
SVSP	School Volunteer Services Program
SV-SP	Spray Volume - Spray Pressure
SVSQ	St. Vladimir's Seminary Quarterly [*A publication*]
SVSR	San Fernando De Apure, Apure [*Venezuela*] [*ICAO location identifier*] (ICLI)
SVSR	Silverside Resources, Inc. [*NASDAQ symbol*] (NQ)
SVSS	Sprague Voltage-Sensitive Switch
SVST	San Tome, Anzoategui [*Venezuela*] [*ICAO location identifier*] (ICLI)
SVSThR	Sammlung Gemeinverstaendlicher Vortraege und Schriften aus dem Gebiet der Theologie und der Religionsgeschichte [*A publication*]
SVSZ	Santa Barbara Del Zulia, Zulia [*Venezuela*] [*ICAO location identifier*] (ICLI)
SVT	St. Vincent [*St. Vincent*] [*Seismograph station code, US Geological Survey*] (SEIS)
SVT	Secure Voice Terminal (MCD)
SVT	Self Valuation Test [*Psychology*]
SVT	Servotronics, Inc. [*AMEX symbol*] (SPSG)
SVT	Silicon Vidicon Target
SVT	Silverton Resources Ltd. [*Toronto Stock Exchange symbol*]
SVT	Solar Vacuum Telescope
SVT	Space Vehicle Test
SVT	Space Visualization Test
SVT	Spiritus Vini Tenuis [*Proof Spirit of Wine*] [*Pharmacy*]
SVT	Stray Voltage Tester
SVT	Supplements. Vetus Testamentum [*Leiden*] [*A publication*]
SVT	Supralaryngeal Vocal Tract [*Anatomy*]
SVT	Supraventricular Tachycardia [*Cardiology*]
SvT	Svenska Texter [*A publication*]
SVT	System Validation Testing
SVTC	Surrey Volunteer Training Corps [*British military*] (DMA)
SVTC	Tucupita, T. F. Delta Amacuro [*Venezuela*] [*ICAO location identifier*] (ICLI)
SVTFDI	Sugarcane Variety Tests in Florida [*A publication*]
SvTK	Svensk Teologisk Kvartalskrift [*A publication*]
SvTKv	Svensk Teologisk Kvartalskrift [*A publication*]
SVTL	Semivital
SVTL	Services Valve Test Laboratory [*British*] (NATG)
SVTM	Shielded Voltage Tunable Magnetron
SVTM	Tumeremo, Bolivar [*Venezuela*] [*ICAO location identifier*] (ICLI)
S/VTOL	Short/Vertical Takeoff and Landing [*Aviation*] (NATG)
SVTP	Sound, Velocity, Temperature, Pressure
SVTQ	St. Vladimir's Theological Quarterly [*A publication*]
Sv Trav Pap	Svensk Traevaru- och Pappersmassetidning [*A publication*]
SVT(S)	Space Vehicle Test (Supervisor)
SvTs	Svensk Tidskrift [*A publication*]
SVTSV	Space-Vehicle-to-Space-Vehicle (SAA)
SVTT	Surface Vessel Torpedo Tube (NVT)
SVU	Savusavu [*Fiji*] [*Airport symbol*] (OAG)
S/VU	Sound/Video Unlimited
SVU	Spur Ventures [*Vancouver Stock Exchange symbol*]
SVU	Supervalu, Inc. [*NYSE symbol*] (SPSG)
SVU	Surface Vehicular Unit
SVU	System Verification Unit
SVUL	Short Vertical Upper Left
SVUL	Suomen Valtakunnan Uhreiluliitto [*Finnish Central Sports Federation*]
SVUM	Uriman, Bolivar [*Venezuela*] [*ICAO location identifier*] (ICLI)
SVUOJ	Sri Venkateswara University. Oriental Journal [*A publication*]
SVUQ	Uonquen, Bolivar [*Venezuela*] [*ICAO location identifier*] (ICLI)
SVUR	Short Vertical Upper Right
SVV	Sit Venia Verbo [*Forgive the Expression*] [*Latin*]
SVV	Solenoid Vent Valve [*Automotive engineering*]
SVVA	Valencia/Internacional, Carabobo [*Venezuela*] [*ICAO location identifier*] (ICLI)
SVVL	Valera/Dr. Antonio Nicolas Briceno, Trujillo [*Venezuela*] [*ICAO location identifier*] (ICLI)
SVVP	Valle De La Pascua, Guarico [*Venezuela*] [*ICAO location identifier*] (ICLI)

SVW	Silverhawk Resources [*Vancouver Stock Exchange symbol*]
SVW	Sparrevohn [*Alaska*] [*Seismograph station code, US Geological Survey*] (SEIS)
SVW	Sparrevohn, AK [*Location identifier*] [*FAA*] (FAAL)
SVX	Socanav, Inc. [*Toronto Stock Exchange symbol*]
SVY	Survey
Svy Sports	Survey on Sports Attendance [*A publication*]
SVZ	San Antonio [*Venezuela*] [*Airport symbol*] (OAG)
SVZ	Sisters of Charity of St. Vincent de Paul [*Roman Catholic religious order*]
SVZM	Maiquetia [*Venezuela*] [*ICAO location identifier*] (ICLI)
SVZZ	Maiquetia [*Venezuela*] [*ICAO location identifier*] (ICLI)
SW	Methylphosphonous Dichloride [*Toxic compound*] [*Army symbol*]
SW	Namib Air (Pty) Ltd. [*South Africa*] [*ICAO designator*] (FAAC)
Sw	Royal Swedish Library (Kungl. Biblioteket), Stockholm, Sweden [*Library symbol*] [*Library of Congress*] (LCLS)
SW	Sadler's Wells Theatre [*London*]
SW	Salt Water
SW	Sandwich-Wound (DEN)
SW	Sapwood [*Botany*]
SW	Satan Worship
SW	Schwartz-Watson Test [*Medicine*] (MAE)
SW	Science Wonder Stories [*A publication*]
SW	Seaboard World Airlines, Inc.
SW	Seawater
S/W	Seaworthy (ADA)
SW	Secret Writing [*Espionage*]
SW	Secretary of War [*Obsolete*]
SW	Security Watch
SW	Semiweekly
SW	Senior Warden [*Freemasonry*]
SW	Senior Wolf [*An accomplished philanderer*] [*Slang*]
SW	Senior Woodward [*Ancient Order of Foresters*]
SW	Sent Wrong [*i.e., misdirected*]
SW	Series Winding [*Wiring*] (DNAB)
SW	Service Water [*Nuclear energy*] (NRCH)
SW	Sewing Machine Repair Program [*Association of Independent Colleges and Schools specialization code*]
SW	Shallow Water Attack Craft [*Navy symbol*]
SW	Shallow Water Diver [*British military*] (DMA)
SW	Shelter Warden [*British Home Defence*] [*World War II*]
SW	Shipper's Weights [*Bills of lading*]
SW	Ship's Warrant [*Marine Corps*]
SW	Shirl J. Winter [*Designer's mark when appearing on US coins*]
SW	Short Weight
SW	Shortwave [*Electronics*]
SW	Shotgun Wedding [*Forced marriage*] [*Slang*]
SW	Side Wheel
SW	Sidewinder
SW	Simple Wear
SW	Single Wall (AAG)
SW	Single Weight
SW	Slavic Word [*A publication*]
SW	Slow Wave [*Electroencephalograph*]
S & W	Smith and Wesson (MCD)
SW	Smith's Weekly [*A publication*]
SW	Snow [*Ship's rigging*] (ROG)
SW	Snow Showers [*Meteorology*] (FAAC)
S & W	Soap and Water [*Enema*] [*Medicine*]
SW	Social Work [*or Worker*]
SW	Socialist Worker [*A publication*] (APTA)
SW	Socket Weld
SW	Software [*Data processing*]
SW	Softwood
SW	Solar Wing (MCD)
SW	Solid Waste
SW	Son of a Witch (EA)
SW	Sound Whistle [*British railroad term*]
SW	South Wales
SW	South and West [*A publication*]
SW	South Western Reporter [*National Reporter System*] [*A publication*] (DLA)
SW	Southwest
SW	Southwest Africa (MCD)
SW	Southwestern Musician - Texas Music Educator [*A publication*]
SW	Special Warfare
SW	Special Weapon
SW	Specific Weight
SW	Sperm Whale
SW	Spiral Wound [*Medicine*] (MAE)
SW	Spontaneous Swallows [*Gastroenterology*]
SW	Spore Wall [*Botany*]
SW	Spores Injected into Wounded Kernels [*Plant pathology*]
SW	Spotweld [*Technical drawings*]
SW	Stab Wound [*Medicine*] (MAE)
SW	Stall Warning System (MCD)
SW	Standard Winter
SW	Standby Service Water [*Nuclear energy*] (NRCH)
SW	Station Wagon [*Car*]

SW .... Status of Women [*Canada*]
SW .... Status Word
SW .... Steam Wagon [*British*]
SW .... Steelworker [*Navy rating*]
SW .... Stenciled Weight
SW .... Sterile Water
SW .... Stewart-Warner Corp.
SW .... Stock Width [*Construction or manufacturing materials*]
SW .... Stone & Webster, Inc. [*NYSE symbol*]   (SPSG)
SW .... Strafwetboek [*A publication*]
SW .... Strategic Warning   (MCD)
SW .... Strategic Wing [*Military*]
SW .... Stroke Work [*Cardiology*]
SW .... Stud-Arc Welding
SW .... Subjective Weakness [*Medicine*]
SW .... Surface Warfare   (MCD)
Sw.............. Swabey's English Admiralty Reports [*A publication*]   (DLA)
Sw.............. Swabey's English Ecclesiastical Reports [*1855-59*] [*A publication*]   (DLA)
SW .... Swamp   (ROG)
sw .... Swamp [*Maps and charts*]
Sw.............. Swann [*Blood group*]
Sw.............. Swan's Tennessee Reports [*31, 32 Tennessee*] [*A publication*]   (DLA)
Sw.............. Swanston's English Chancery Reports [*A publication*]   (DLA)
SW .... Swash
SW .... Swatch   (WGA)
SW .... Swear
SW .... Swearingen Aircraft [*ICAO aircraft manufacturer identifier*]   (ICAO)
sw .... Sweden [*MARC country of publication code*] [*Library of Congress*]   (LCCP)
SW .... Sweden
Sw.............. Sweeney's New York Superior Court Reports [*A publication*]   (DLA)
SW .... Swell Organ
Sw.............. Swinton's Scotch Justiciary Cases [*A publication*]   (DLA)
SW .... Swiss
SW .... Switch   (AAG)
SW .... Switchband Wound [*Relay*]
SW .... Switzerland
S1W .... Security of the First World [*Rap music group*]
SW1 .... Steelworker, First Class [*Navy rating*]
SW2 .... Steelworker, Second Class [*Navy rating*]
SW3 .... Steelworker, Third Class [*Navy rating*]
SWA .... Reports of the High Court of South-West Africa [*1920-46*] [*A publication*]   (DLA)
SWA .... Scheduler Work Area [*Data processing*]   (IBMDP)
SWA .... Scope of Word Addendum   (MCD)
SWA .... Seriously Wounded in Action [*Military*]
SWA .... Shallow Water Acoustics
SWA .... Shantou [*China*] [*Airport symbol*]   (OAG)
SWA .... Shayna International Industry [*Vancouver Stock Exchange symbol*]
SWA .... Single Wire Armored [*Cables*]
SWA .... Sitzungsberichte. Wiener Akademie [*A publication*]
SWA .... Solo Wargamers Association   (EAIO)
SWA .... Southern Water Authority [*British*]   (DCTA)
SWA .... Southern Wholesalers Association [*Atlanta, GA*]   (EA)
SWA .... Southern Woodwork Association   (EA)
SWA .... Southwest Africa
SWA .... Southwest Airlines Co. [*San Antonio, TX*] [*FAA designator*]   (FAAC)
SWA .... Southwest Approach   (DNAB)
SWA .... Southwest Art [*A publication*]
SWA .... Southwest Asia
SWA .... Specialty Wire Association [*Later, AWPA*]
SWA .... Standing Wave Apparatus
SWA .... State Welfare Agency [*Social Security Administration*]   (OICC)
SWA .... Straight Wire Antenna
SWA .... Stunt Women of America [*Later, SAMP*]   (EA)
SWA .... Superwomen's Anonymous   (EA)
SWA .... Support Work Authorization [*NASA*]   (MCD)
swa .... Swahili [*MARC language code*] [*Library of Congress*]   (LCCP)
SWA .... Swan Island [*Seismograph station code, US Geological Survey*] [*Closed*]   (SEIS)
SWA .... Swedish Warmblood Association   (EA)
SWA .... Swissair [*Airline*]   (MCD)
SWA .... System Work Area
SWAA .... Slovak Writers and Artists Association   (EA)
SWAA .... Spacelab Window Adapter Assembly   (NASA)
Swab........... Swabey's English Ecclesiastical Reports [*1855-59*] [*A publication*]   (DLA)
Swab Admr ... Swabey's English Admiralty Reports [*166 English Reprint*] [*A publication*]   (DLA)
Swab Div.... Swabey on Divorce and Matrimonial Causes [*3rd ed.*] [*1859*] [*A publication*]   (DLA)
Swabey Adm ... Swabey's English Admiralty Reports [*166 English Reprint*] [*1855-59*] [*A publication*]   (DLA)
Swabey Adm (Eng) ... Swabey's English Admiralty Reports [*166 English Reprint*] [*A publication*]   (DLA)

Swabey & T (Eng) ... Swabey and Tristram's Probate and Divorce Reports [*164 English Reports*] [*A publication*]   (DLA)
Swab & T ... Swabey and Tristram's Probate and Divorce Reports [*164 English Reprint*] [*A publication*]   (DLA)
Swab & Tr ... Swabey and Tristram's Probate and Divorce Reports [*164 English Reprint*] [*A publication*]   (DLA)
SWAC....... Shallow Water Attack Craft, Light   (MCD)
SWAC....... Special Warhead Arming Control   (AFM)
SWAC....... Specification Writers Association of Canada
SWAC....... Spotweld Accessory [*Tool*]   (AAG)
SWAC....... Standards Western Automatic Computer [*National Institute of Standards and Technology*]
SWACHA ... Southwestern Automated Clearing House Association
SWACS ..... Space Warning and Control System [*NORAD*]
SWAD .... Special Warfare Aviation Detachment [*Army*]
SWAD .... Subdivision of Work Authorization Document [*NASA*]   (NASA)
SWADE..... Second Wives of America Demanding Equality
SWADS.... Scheduler Work Area Data Set [*IBM Corp.*]   (MCD)
SW Af....... South-West Africa
SWAFAC .. Southwest Atlantic Fisheries Advisory Commission [*FAO*]
SWAG ...... Scientific Wild Aim Guess [*Bowdlerized version*]
SWAG ...... Standard Written Agreement [*Military*]
SWAG ...... Systems Work Assignment Group   (SAA)
SWAGS..... Scientific Wild-Aim Guess System [*Bowdlerized version*]   (MCD)
SWAH...... Studies in Western Australian History [*A publication*]
SwAirl........ Southwest Airlines Co. [*Associated Press abbreviation*]   (APAG)
SWAJB...... South and Western Australia Judgements Bulletin [*A publication*]
SWAK....... Sealed with a Kiss [*Correspondence*]
SWAK....... Spinners and Weavers Association of Korea [*Defunct*]   (EA)
SWAL....... Shallow Water Attack Craft, Light [*Navy symbol*]   (NVT)
SwAL........ Southwestern American Literature [*A publication*]
SWAL....... StatesWest Airlines, Inc. [*Phoenix, AZ*] [*NASDAQ symbol*]   (NQ)
SWALC ..... Southwest Academic Library Consortium [*Library network*]   (IID)
SWALCAKWS ... Sealed with a Lick 'Cause a Kiss Won't Stick [*Correspondence*]   (DSUE)
SWALK ..... Sealed with a Loving Kiss [*Correspondence*]
SWALM.... Switch Alarm   (AAG)
SWAM ...... Shallow Water Attack Craft, Medium [*Navy symbol*]   (NVT)
SWAM ...... Sine Wave Amplitude Modulation
SWAMI.... Software-Aided Multiform Input [*Software*] [*Data processing*]
SWAMI.... Speech with Alternating Masking Index [*Discrimination test*]
SWAMI.... Stall Warning and Margin Indicator
SWAMI.... Standing Wave Area Monitor Indicator   (MUGU)
SWAMI.... Stanford Worldwide Acquisition of Meteorological Information [*Weather prediction system*]
SWAN ...... Second Wives Association of North America   (EA)
SWAN ...... Severe Weather Avoidance Nationwide [*National Oceanic and Atmospheric Administration*]
SWAN ...... Swan Resources Ltd. [*NASDAQ symbol*]   (NQ)
Swan........... Swan's Tennessee Supreme Court Reports [*1851-53*] [*A publication*]   (DLA)
Swan........... Swanston's English Chancery Reports [*A publication*]   (DLA)
Swan Ch...... Swanston's English Chancery Reports [*A publication*]   (DLA)
Swan & CR St ... Swan and Critchfield's Revised Statutes [*Ohio*] [*A publication*]   (DLA)
Swan Eccl C ... Swan's Ecclesiastical Courts [*1830*] [*A publication*]   (DLA)
Swan Just... Swan's Justice [*Ohio*] [*A publication*]   (DLA)
SWANK ..... Sealed with a Nice Kiss [*Correspondence*]
Swank .... Single Woman and No Kids [*Lifestyle classification*]
Swan Pl & Pr ... Swan on Pleading and Practice [*Ohio*] [*A publication*]   (DLA)
Swan Pr...... Swan on Practice [*Ohio*] [*A publication*]   (DLA)
SWANS..... State Wildlife Advisory News Service [*A publication*]   (APTA)
Swan's....... Swan's Tennessee Reports [*A publication*]   (DLA)
Swans........ Swanston's English Chancery Reports [*A publication*]   (DLA)
Swansea Coll Fac Ed J ... University College of Swansea. Collegiate Faculty of Education. Journal [*A publication*]
Swan's R ... Swan's Tennessee Reports [*A publication*]   (DLA)
Swan & S St ... Swan and Sayler's Supplement to the Revised Statutes [*Ohio*] [*A publication*]   (DLA)
Swan's St ... Swan's Ohio Statutes [*A publication*]   (DLA)
Swanst........ Swanston's English Chancery Reports [*36 English Reprint*] [*A publication*]   (DLA)
Swanst (Eng) ... Swanston's English Chancery Reports [*36 English Reprint*] [*A publication*]   (DLA)
Swan Tr...... Swan's Ohio Treatise [*A publication*]   (DLA)
SWANU .... South West Africa National Union [*Namibia*] [*Political party*]   (PPW)
SWAP........ Section on Women and Psychology [*Canadian Psychology Association*]
SWAP........ Severe Weather Avoidance Plan   (FAAC)
SWAP........ Smith-Winnick-Abrams-Prausnitz [*Vapor pressure correlation equation*]
SWAP........ Society for Wang Applications and Programs   (CSR)
SWAP........ Standard Wafer Array Programming

SWAP........ Stress Wave Analyzing Program
SWAP........ Student Woodlawn Area Project [*Chicago, IL*]
SWAP........ Surface Water Acidification Project [*Joint venture involving Norway, Sweden, and Great Britain*]
SWAP........ SWAP [*Salesmen with a Purpose*] Club International [*Arvada, CO*] (EA)
SWAP........ Systems Worthiness Analysis Program [*FAA*]
SWAPDOP ... Southwest Asia Petroleum Distribution Operation Project [*Army*]
SWAPO..... South West Africa People's Organization [*Namibia*] (PD)
SWAPS ..... Ship Workload and Priority Systems [*Navy*]
SWAPS ..... Special Wire Assembly Planning System (MCD)
SWAR........ Schwartz Brothers, Inc. [*NASDAQ symbol*] (NQ)
Swarajya A ... Swarajya. Annual Number [*Madras*] [*A publication*]
SWARK..... Southwark [*Borough of London*] (ROG)
SWARM.... Southwestern and Rocky Mountain Division [*AAAS division*]
SWARMS ... Small Warhead and Reentry Multiple System
SWAS........ Slim Whitman Appreciation Society of the United States (EA)
SWASG..... Submarine Sensor to Weapon Alignment Steering Group
SWASGB .. Slim Whitman Appreciation Society of Great Britain (EAIO)
SWASS..... Screwworm Adult Suppression System [*Medicine*]
SWASS..... Slim Whitman Appreciation Society of Scotland (EAIO)
SWAT........ Secure Wire Access Terminal (MCD)
SWAT........ Service Weapons Acceptability Tests
SWAT........ Sidewinder Acquisition Track (IEEE)
SWAT........ Sidewinder Angle Tracking [*Missiles*] (NG)
SWAT........ Simultaneous Wide Area Telecommunications Service (TSSD)
SWAT........ Sipay Word Analysis Test [*Educational test*]
SWAT........ Solid Waste Assessment Test
SWAT........ Special Warfare Armored Transporter [*A vehicle*]
SWAT........ Special Weapons and Tactics [*Police*]
SWAT........ Special Wrenches and Techniques [*Automotive repair*]
SWAT........ Squad Weapon Analytical Trainer (MCD)
SWAT........ Strengths, Weaknesses, Alternatives, Threats [*Analysis*] (ADA)
SWAT........ Stress Wave Analysis Technique
SWATCH ... Swiss Watch
SWATH .... Small Waterplane Area Twin Hull [*Ship*] [*Navy*]
SWATM.... Shallow Water Antitraffic Mine [*Military*]
SWATS ..... Shallow Water Acoustic Tracking System [*Navy*] (CAAL)
SWATT .... Simulator for Antitank Tactical Training [*Army*] (INF)
SWAW ...... Sitzungsberichte. Wiener Akademie der Wissenschaften [*A publication*]
SWAX........ Southwest Airlines Co. [*Air carrier designation symbol*]
Swazil......... Swaziland
Swaziland Annu Rep Geol Surv Mines Dep ... Swaziland. Annual Report. Geological Survey and Mines Department [*A publication*]
Swaziland Geol Surv Mines Dep Annu Rep ... Swaziland. Annual Report. Geological Survey and Mines Department [*A publication*]
SWB.......... Sandia Wind Balloon (MUGU)
SWB.......... Scheduled Weather Broadcast (FAAC)
SWN.......... Short Wheelbase
SWB.......... Single with Bath [*Hotel room*]
SWB.......... Single Weight Baryta [*Photography*] (OA)
SWB.......... South Wales Borderers [*Military unit*] [*British*]
SWB.......... South Westchester BOCES [*Boards of Cooperative Educational Services*] [*UTLAS symbol*]
SWB.......... Southwest Bancorp [*AMEX symbol*] (SPSG)
SWB.......... Southwestern Motor Freight Bureau, Dallas TX [*STAC*]
SWB.......... Stichting Weg. Bulletin [*A publication*]
SWB.......... Summary of World Broadcasts [*British Broadcasting Corporation*]
SWB.......... Switchboard (NATG)
SWBD....... Switchboard (AAG)
SwBell........ Southwestern Bell Corp. [*Associated Press abbreviation*] (APAG)
SWBHD .... Swash Bulkhead
SWB & IE ... South West Business and Industry Exhibition [*British*] (ITD)
SWBP........ Service Water Booster Pump [*Nuclear energy*] (IEEE)
SWBRD..... Sun at Work in Britain [*A publication*]
SWBS....... Ship Work Breakdown Structure [*Navy*] (CAAL)
SWBS....... Software Work Breakdown Structure (MCD)
SWBS........ Solid Waste Barrel Storage [*Nuclear energy*] (NRCH)
SWbS........ Southwest by South
SWBS....... Subcontract Work Breakdown Structure (MCD)
SWbW ...... Southwest by West
SWC .... Chief Steelworker [*Navy rating*]
SWC .... Omaha, NE [*Location identifier*] [*FAA*] (FAAL)
SWC .... Safe Water Coalition (EA)
SWC .... Saline Water Conversion (MCD)
SWC .... Scan-with-Composition (MCD)
SWC .... Scanning with Compensation
SWC .... Second Wives Coalition (EA)
SWC .... Semi-Wadcutter [*Ammunition*]
SWC .... Senate Wine Caucus (EA)
SWC .... Settlement with Conditions [*Environmental Protection Agency*] (GFGA)
SWC .... Share the Work Coalition (EA)
SWC .... Ship Weapon Coordinator (NVT)
SWC .... Shock Wave Control
SWC .... Shortwave Converter
SWC .... Signals Warfare Center [*Army*] [*Warrenton, VA*]

SWC .... Simon Wiesenthal Center (EA)
SWC .... Single Wire Connector
SWC .... Skywave Correction [*Aircraft navigation*]
SWC .... Slovak World Congress (EAIO)
SWC .... Social Work and Christianity [*A publication*]
SWC .... Soil and Water Conservation Research Division [*of ARS, Department of Agriculture*]
SWC .... Solar Wind Compensator [*or Composition*] [*Apollo 11*] [*NASA*]
SWC .... Solid Wastes Cask [*Nuclear energy*] (NRCH)
SWC .... Southwest Conference [*College sports*]
SWC .... Southwestern Connecticut Library Council, Bridgeport, CT [*OCLC symbol*] (OCLC)
SWC .... Special Warfare Center [*Later, J. F. Kennedy Center for Special Warfare*] [*Army*]
SWC .... Special Warfare Craft [*Navy*] (CAAL)
SWC .... Special Weapons Center [*or Command*]
SWC .... Sportscar World Championship [*Auto racing*]
SWC .... Stall Warning Computer (MCD)
SWC .... Stawell [*Australia*] [*Airport symbol*] (OAG)
SWC .... Step-Wise Cracking (MCD)
SWC .... Stormwater Channel
SWC .... Submersible Work Chamber
SWC .... Superior White Crystal [*Sugar*]
SWC .... Supreme War Council [*World War II*]
SWC .... Surewin Resources Corp. [*Vancouver Stock Exchange symbol*]
SWC .... Surface Warfare Coordinator [*Also, SUWC*] (NVT)
SWC .... Surface Weapons Control
SWC .... Surface Weapons Coordinator [*Navy*] (CAAL)
SWC .... Surge Withstand Capability (IEEE)
SWC .... System Weapons Coordinator [*Navy*] (CAAL)
SWCA....... Constructionman Apprentice, Steelworker, Striker [*Navy rating*]
SWCA....... Silver Wyandotte Club of America (EA)
SWCB........ [*The*] Sandwich Co-Operative Bank [*Sandwich, MA*] [*NASDAQ symbol*] (NQ)
SWCC....... Southwest Capital Corp. [*Albuquerque, NM*] [*NASDAQ symbol*] (NQ)
SWCEL ..... Southwestern Cooperative Educational Laboratory
SWCENT .. Switching Central [*Telecommunications*] (AABC)
SWCH ...... Switch (MCD)
SWCHMN ... Switchman (WGA)
SWCL........ Seawater Conversion Laboratory (KSC)
SWCL........ Special Warfare Craft, Light [*Navy symbol*]
SWCL........ State Worker's Compensation Law (OICC)
SWCLR ..... Southwest Council of La Raza [*Mexican-American organization*] (EA)
SWCM...... Master Chief Steelworker [*Navy rating*]
SW/CM..... Software Configuration Management (MCD)
SWCM...... Special Warfare Craft, Medium [*Navy symbol*]
SWCN ...... Constructionman, Steelworker, Striker [*Navy rating*]
SWCP....... Saline Water Conversion Program [*Department of the Interior*]
SWCP........ Salt-Water Circulating Pump (MSA)
SWCP....... Society of the War of 1812 in the Commonwealth of Pennsylvania (EA)
SWCPI ...... Solid Waste Council of the Paper Industry (EA)
SWCS .... SAC Warning and Control System (MCD)
SWCS .... Salt-Water Cooling System [*Nuclear energy*] (NRCH)
SWCS .... Senior Chief Steelworker [*Navy rating*]
SWCST ..... Saturn Workshop Cockpit Simulation Trainer [*NASA*]
SWD .... Self-Wiring Data [*Telecommunications*] (TEL)
SWD .... Senior Weapon Director [*Air Force*]
SWD .... Seward, AK [*Location identifier*] [*FAA*] (FAAL)
SWD .... Sewed
SWD .... Short-Wave Diathermy [*Medicine*]
SWD .... Side Water Depth
SWD .... Sideward (WGA)
SWD .... Single Word Dump
SWD .... Sliding Watertight Door
SWD .... Smaller Word
SWD .... Softwood
SWD .... Soil Water Deficit [*Soil science*]
SWD .... Southwestern Division [*Army Corps of Engineers*]
SWD .... Special Water Dispenser [*British military*] (DMA)
SWD .... Standing Wave Detector
SWD .... Stormwater Drain
SWD .... Submarine Wire Dispenser
SWD .... Sun, Wind, Dust [*Goggles*] (MCD)
SWD .... Surface Wave Dielectrometer
SWD .... Swaziland [*Swaziland*] [*Seismograph station code, US Geological Survey*] (SEIS)
SWD .... Synchronous Wave Device
SW 2d ...... South Western Reporter, Second Series [*A publication*] (DLA)
SWDA ...... Solid Waste Disposal Act [*1965*]
SWDA ...... Step-Wise Discriminant Analysis
SWDB....... Special Weapons Development Board
SWDC....... Shock Wave Data Center [*Lawrence Radiation Laboratory*]
SWDG .... Surface Warfare Development Group [*Also, SURFWARDEVGRU*] [*Navy*]
SWDL........ Safe Winter Driving League (EA)
SWDL........ Surface Wave Delay Line

SWDS....... Scrolls from the Wilderness of the Dead Sea. Smithsonian Institution Exhibit Catalogue [*Washington, DC*]　(BJA)
SWDS........ Software Development System　(MCD)
SWDVS..... Software Development and Verification System [*NASA*]
SWDYN .... Single-Wheel Dynamometer
SWE........... Scalar Wave Equation
SWE........... Shift Word, Extracting
SWE........... Simulated Work Experience
SWE........... Society of Wine Educators　(EA)
SWE........... Society of Women Engineers　(EA)
SWE........... Solar Wind Experiment [*NASA*]　(KSC)
SWE........... Spherical Wave Expansion [*Telecommunications*]　(TEL)
SWE........... Status Word Enable
SWE........... Steelworker Erector [*Navy rating*]
SWE........... Stress Wave Emission
SWE........... Sweden [*ANSI three-letter standard code*]　(CNC)
swe .... Swedish [*MARC language code*] [*Library of Congress*]　(LCCP)
SWE........... Swensen's, Inc. [*Vancouver Stock Exchange symbol*]
SWEA....... Swedish Women's Educational Association, International　(EA)
SWECS ..... Small Wind Energy Conversion Systems
SWED....... Sweden [*or Swedish*]
SWED....... Swedlow, Inc. [*NASDAQ symbol*]　(NQ)
SwedAE ..... Swedish Antarctic Expedition [*1901-04*]
Swed Am TN ... Swedish American Trade News [*A publication*]
Swed Bud ... Swedish Budget [*A publication*]
Swed Dent J ... Swedish Dental Journal [*A publication*]
Swed Dent J (Suppl) ... Swedish Dental Journal (Supplement) [*A publication*]
Swed Foersvarets Forskningsanst FOA Rep ... Sweden. Foersvarets Forskningsanstalt. FOA Report [*A publication*]
Swed Geol Unders Ser Ae Geol Kartbl 1:50000 ... Sweden. Geologiska Undersoekning. Serie Ae. Geologiska Kartblad i Skala 1:50,000 [*A publication*]
Swed Geol Unders Ser C ... Sweden. Geologiska Undersoekning. Serie C [*A publication*]
Swed Geol Unders Ser Ca Avh Uppsatser ... Sweden. Geologiska Undersoekning. Serie Ca. Avhandlingar och Uppsatser [*A publication*]
Swed Geotech Inst Proc ... Swedish Geotechnical Institute. Proceedings [*A publication*]
Swed Geotech Inst Rep ... Swedish Geotechnical Institute. Report [*A publication*]
Swed Inst Agric Eng Circ ... Swedish Institute of Agricultural Engineering. Circular [*A publication*]
SWEDIS.... Swedish Drug Information System [*Swedish National Board of Health and Welfare*] [*Databank*]　(IID)
Swedish Aust & Swedish NZ Trade J ... Swedish-Australian and Swedish-New Zealand Trade Journal [*A publication*]　(APTA)
Swedish Deep-Sea Expedition Repts ... Swedish Deep-Sea Expedition. Reports [*A publication*]
Swedish Ec ... Swedish Economy [*A publication*]
Swedish Econ ... Swedish Economy [*A publication*]
Swedish Hist Soc Yearbook ... Swedish Historical Society. Yearbook [*A publication*]
Swedish J Econ ... Swedish Journal of Economics [*A publication*]
Swed J Agric Res ... Swedish Journal of Agricultural Research [*A publication*]
Swed J Econ ... Swedish Journal of Economics [*A publication*]
SWEDL..... Southwest Educational Development Laboratory
Swed Pap J ... Swedish Paper Journal [*A publication*]
Swed State Shipbuild Exp Tank Report ... Swedish State Shipbuilding Experiment Tank. Report [*A publication*]
SWEDTEL ... Swedish Telecoms International AB [*Telecommunications*]
Swed Univ Agric Sci Dep Agric Eng Rep ... Swedish University of Agricultural Sciences. Department of Agricultural Engineering. Report [*A publication*]
Swed Univ Agric Sci Dep Farm Build Rep ... Swedish University of Agricultural Sciences. Department of Farm Buildings. Report [*A publication*]
Swed Univ Agric Sci Dep Hortic Sci Rep ... Swedish University of Agricultural Sciences. Department of Horticultural Science. Report [*A publication*]
Swed Univ Agric Sci Dep Microbiol Rep ... Swedish University of Agricultural Sciences. Department of Microbiology. Report [*A publication*]
Swed Univ Agric Sci Dep Plant Husb Rep ... Swedish University of Agricultural Sciences. Department of Plant Husbandry. Report [*A publication*]
Swed Univ Agric Sci Rep For Ecol For Soils ... Swedish University of Agricultural Sciences. Reports in Forest Ecology and Forest Soils [*A publication*]
Swed Weed Conf Rep ... Swedish Weed Conference. Reports [*A publication*]
Swed Wildl Res (Viltrevy) ... Swedish Wildlife Research (Viltrevy) [*A publication*]
SWEE........ Southwest Electronic Exhibit
Sween......... Sweeney's New York Superior Court Reports [*31-32 New York*] [*1869-70*] [*A publication*]　(DLA)
Sweeney (NY) ... Sweeney's New York Superior Court Reports [*31-32 New York*] [*A publication*]　(DLA)
Sweeny....... Sweeney's New York Superior Court Reports [*31-32 New York*] [*A publication*]　(DLA)
SWEEP ..... Structures with Error Expurgation Program
SWEET ...... Stay at Work, Earn Extra Time [*United Auto Workers*]

Sweet.......... Sweet on the Limited Liability Act [*A publication*]　(DLA)
Sweet.......... Sweet on Wills [*A publication*]　(DLA)
Sweet.......... Sweet's Law Dictionary [*A publication*]　(DLA)
Sweet.......... Sweet's Marriage Settlement Cases [*A publication*]　(DLA)
Sweet.......... Sweet's Precedents in Conveyancing [*A publication*]　(DLA)
Sweet LD ... Sweet's Dictionary of English Law [*1882*] [*A publication*]　(DLA)
Sweet LL.... Sweet on the Limited Liability Act [*A publication*]　(DLA)
Sweet M Sett Cas ... Sweet's Marriage Settlement Cases [*England*] [*A publication*]　(DLA)
Sweet Pr Conv ... Sweet's Precedents in Conveyancing [*4th ed.*] [*1886*] [*A publication*]　(DLA)
SWEFCO .. Special Weapons Ferry Control Office [*or Officer*]
SWEHO .... Scandinavian Journal of Work Environment and Health [*A publication*]
SWEIA ...... Studies in Wind Engineering and Industrial Aerodynamics [*Elsevier Book Series*] [*A publication*]
SWEJDFC ... Sing with the Earth John Denver Fan Club　(EA)
SWEL........ Southwestern Electric Service Co. [*NASDAQ symbol*]　(NQ)
SWEL........ Special Weapons Equipment List
Swell .... Single Woman Earning Lots in London [*Lifestyle classification*]
SWELSTRA ... Special Weapons Equipment List Single Theater Requisitioning Agency
SWEMED ... Swedish Medical Literature [*Database*] [*Karolinska Institute Library and Information Center/Medical Information Center*] [*Information service or system*]　(CRD)
SWEMS .... Soil, Water, Estuarine Monitoring [*Environmental Protection Agency*]　(GFGA)
Swen.......... Sweeney's New York Superior Court Reports [*31-32 New York*] [*A publication*]　(DLA)
SWEN .... Swensen's, Inc. [*NASDAQ symbol*]　(NQ)
SwEnr .... Southwestern Energy Co. [*Associated Press abbreviation*]　(APAG)
SW Entomol ... Southwestern Entomologist [*A publication*]
SWEPS...... Safety Weather Probability Study
SWERD..... Solid Waste and Emergency Response [*Environmental Protection Agency*]　(GFGA)
SWES .... Southwest Leasing Corp. [*NASDAQ symbol*]　(NQ)
SWESS...... Special Weapons Emergency Separation System　(AFM)
SWESSAR ... Stone and Webster Standard Safety Analysis Report [*Nuclear energy*]　(NRCH)
SWest Entomologist ... Southwestern Entomologist [*A publication*]
SWest Nat ... Southwestern Naturalist [*A publication*]
SWET........ Simulated Water Entry Test [*Nuclear energy*]
SWET........ Special Weapon Equipment Test　(SAA)
SWETS...... Solid Waste Engineering Transfer System
SWETTU .. Special Weapons Experimental Tactical Test Unit
SWF.......... Newburgh [*New York*] [*Airport symbol*]　(OAG)
SWF.......... Seawater Feed
SWF.......... Shortwave Fadeouts
SWF.......... Silver Wings Fraternity　(EA)
SWF.......... Single White Female [*Classified advertising*]
SWF.......... Southwest Folklore [*A publication*]
SWF.......... Southwest Forest Industries, Inc. [*NYSE symbol*]　(SPSG)
SWF.......... Special Warning Function　(MCD)
SWF.......... Special Weapons Facility [*Navy*]
SWF.......... Steelworker Fabricator [*Navy rating*]
SWF.......... Stelway Food [*Vancouver Stock Exchange symbol*]
SWF.......... Still Waters Foundation　(EA)
SWF.......... Sturge-Weber Foundation　(EA)
SWF.......... Suedwestfunk [*Radio network*] [*West Germany*]
SWFB .... Southwestern Freight Bureau
SWFC .... Southwest Fisheries Center [*Department of Commerce*] [*La Jolla, CA*]
SWFC .... Surface Weapons Fire Control
SWFG........ Secondary Waveform Generator [*Telecommunications*]　(TEL)
SWFPA ..... Structural Wood Fiber Products Association [*Later, SCFPA*]　(EA)
SWFR .... Slow Write, Fast Read [*Data processing*]　(IEEE)
SWFTENG ... Swift Energy Co. [*Associated Press abbreviation*]　(APAG)
SWFX .... Spotweld Fixture [*Tool*]
SWG .... Salam-Weinberg-Glashow [*One unified field theory in physics*]
SWG .... Scientific Working Group [*EXAMETNET*]
SWG .... Shock Wave Generator
SWG .... Shuttle Working Group [*NASA*]　(MCD)
SWG .... Sine Wave Generator
SWG .... Slotted Waveguide
SWG .... Society of Woman Geographers　(EA)
SWG .... Software Working Group [*NASA*]　(NASA)
SWG .... Songwriters Guild of Great Britain
SWG .... South-West Gold Corp. [*Vancouver Stock Exchange symbol*]
SWG .... Space Wing [*Military*]
SWG .... Special Wireless Group [*World War II*] [*British*]
SWG .... Special Working Group
SWG .... Squarewave Generator
SWG .... Staff Working Group
SWG .... Standard Wire Gauge [*Telecommunications*]
SWG .... Standard/Working Group　(MCD)
SWG .... Strictly Wild Guess　(SAA)
SWG .... Stubs Wire Gauge
SWG .... Swing　(MSA)

SWG	Switching (WGA)
SWGD	Swinging Door
SWGM	Spanish World Gospel Mission (EA)
SWGR	Switchgear
SWGS	Surface Wire Grounding System [*Electronics*] (RDA)
SwGU	Goteborgs Universitítsbibliotek, Goteborg, Sweden [*Library symbol*] [*Library of Congress*] (LCLS)
SWH	Scottish Women's Hospital [*British military*] (DMA)
SWH	Seaway Multi-Corp Ltd. [*Toronto Stock Exchange symbol*]
SWH	Significant Wave Height [*Oceanography*]
SWH	Sociale Wetenschappen [*A publication*]
SWH	Solar Water Heating
SWH	Spaghetti Warehouse, Inc. [*NYSE symbol*] (SPSG)
SWHA	Social Welfare History Archives Center [*University of Minnesota*] [*Research center*] (RCD)
SWHC	Social Work in Health Care [*A publication*]
SwHelv.	Swiss Helvetia Fund, Inc. [*Associated Press abbreviation*] (APAG)
SWHG	Social Welfare History Group [*Western Michigan University*] [*Kalamazoo*] (EA)
SWHI	Sound Warehouse, Inc. [*Dallas, TX*] [*NASDAQ symbol*] (NQ)
SW Hist Q	Southwestern Historical Quarterly [*A publication*]
SWHQ	Southwestern Historical Quarterly [*A publication*]
SWHS	Scissor Workboard Hands' Society [*A union*] [*British*]
SWI	Salt-Water Igniter
SWI	Scottish Woollen Industry
SWI	Sealant and Waterproofers Institute (EA)
SWI	Seawind Resources, Inc. [*Vancouver Stock Exchange symbol*]
SWI	Seaworthiness Impairment (NVT)
SWI	Service World International [*A publication*]
SWI	Sherman [*Texas*] [*Airport symbol*] (OAG)
SWI	Shock Wave Interaction
SWI	Sine Wave Inverter
SWI	Software Interrupt [*Data processing*]
SWI	Special Weather Intelligence (MCD)
SWI	Special World Intervals
SWI	Stall Warning Indicator
SWI	Standing Wave Indicator
SWI	Steel Window Institute (EA)
SWI	Stroke Work Index [*Neurology*]
SWI	Sunworld International Airways, Inc. [*Las Vegas, NV*] [*FAA designator*] (FAAC)
SWICA	Self Winding Clock Association (EA)
SWICS	Solar Wind Ion Composition Spectrometer (MCD)
SWIDOC	Sociaal-Wetenschappelijk Informatie- en Documentatiecentrum [*Social Science Information and Documentation Center*] [*Netherlands*] [*Information service or system*] (IID)
SWIFT	Significant Word in the Full Title [*Data processing*] (DIT)
SWIFT	Society for Worldwide Interbank Financial Telecommunication [*Belgium*] [*Banking network*]
SWIFT	Software Implemented Friden Translator [*Data processing*]
SWIFT	Stored Wave Inverse Fourier Transform [*Spectrometry*]
SWIFT	Strength of Wings Including Flutter
SWIFT	Swept Wing with Inboard Flap for Trim [*Hang glider*] (PS)
SWIFT	System Workshops in Forecasting Techniques [*Bell System*]
SWIFT-ANSWER	Special Word Indexed Full Text Alpha Numeric Storage with Easy Retrieval [*Software*]
Swift Dig	Swift's Connecticut Digest [*A publication*] (DLA)
Swift Ev	Swift on Evidence, and Bills and Notes [*A publication*] (DLA)
SWIFT LASS	Signal Word Index of Field and Title - Literature Abstract Specialized Search (DIT)
SWIFT SIR	Signal Word Index of Field and Title - Scientific Information Retrieval (DIT)
Swift Sys	Swift's System of the Laws of Connecticut [*A publication*] (DLA)
SWIG	Southwestern Irrigated Cotton Growers Association
SWIM	San Juan Fiberglass Pools, Inc. [*NASDAQ symbol*] (NQ)
SWIM	Sea Warfare Interim Model (CINC)
SWIM	Ship Weapons Installation Manual (MCD)
SWIM	Sperm-Washing Insemination Method
SWIM	Standard Wozniak Integrated Machine [*Data processing*]
SWIM	Super Wozniak Integrated Machine [*Data processing*]
SWIM	Surface Water Improvement and Management (MCD)
SWIM	Switch Tail Interceptor Missile (MCD)
SWIMCRIT	Swim Criteria
Swimm Tech	Swimming Technique [*A publication*]
Swimm World Jun Swimm	Swimming World and Junior Swimmer [*A publication*]
SWIMS	Serialized Weapons Information Management System [*Navy*]
Swim Wld	Swimming World and Junior Swimmer [*A publication*]
Swin	Swinburne on Wills [*10 eds.*] [*1590-1803*] [*A publication*] (DLA)
SWIN	Swinehead [*England*]
Swin	Swinton's Scotch Justiciary Reports [*1835-41*] [*A publication*] (DLA)
Swinb Desc	Swinburne on Descents [*1825*] [*A publication*] (DLA)
Swinb Mar	Swinburne on Married Women [*1846*] [*A publication*] (DLA)
Swinb Spo	Swinburne on Spousals [*A publication*] (DLA)
Swinb Wills	Swinburne on Wills [*A publication*] (DLA)
SWINE	Students Wildly Indignant about Nearly Everything [*Group in "L'il Abner" comic strip*]

Swine Day Univ Calif	Swine Day. University of California [*A publication*]
Swine Rep Univ Hawaii Coop Ext Serv	Swine Report. University of Hawaii. Cooperative Extension Service [*A publication*]
SWINGR	Sweep Integrator (AAG)
Swin Jus Cas	Swinton's Scotch Justiciary Cases [*A publication*] (DLA)
Swin Reg App	Swinton's Scotch Registration Appeal Cases [*1835-41*] [*A publication*] (DLA)
Swint	Swinton's Scotch Justiciary Cases [*A publication*] (DLA)
SWINTER	Service Women in Non-Traditional Environmental Roles [*Canadian armed forces*]
SWIO	SACLANT [*Supreme Allied Commander, Atlantic*] War Intelligence Organization (NATG)
SWIP	Secret Work in Process (MCD)
SWIP	Society for Women in Philosophy (EA)
SWIP	Soil-Wheel Interaction Performance
SWIP	Standing Wave Impedance Probe [*Geophysical instrument*]
SWIP	Stichting Werkgroep Indianen Projekt [*Netherlands*]
SWIP	Super-Weight Improvement Program [*Navy*] (NG)
SWIPMD	Society for Women in Philosophy, Midwest Division (EA)
SWIR	Shortwave Infrared
SWIR	Special Weapons Inspection Report
SWIRL	South Western Industrial Research Ltd. [*British*] (ARC)
SWIRLS	Southwest Regional Library System [*Library network*]
SWIRS	Solid Waste Information Retrieval System [*Environmental Protection Agency*]
SWIS	St. Ives Laboratories Corp. [*NASDAQ symbol*] (NQ)
SWIS	Satellite Weather Information System [*National Oceanic and Atmospheric Administration*]
SWIS	Sensitive Wildlife Information System [*Army*] (IID)
SWIS	Special Weapons Integration Subcommittee (SAA)
SWIS	Swiss Wildlife Information Service [*Zurich*] [*Information service or system*] (IID)
Swiss Credit Bank Bul	Swiss Credit Banking Bulletin [*A publication*]
Swiss J Hydrol	Swiss Journal of Hydrology [*A publication*]
Swiss News	Swiss Economic News [*A publication*]
Swiss R Wld Aff	Swiss Review of World Affairs [*A publication*]
SWIT	Switzerland
SWITL	Southwestern Industrial Traffic League (EA)
SWITT	Surface Wave Independent Tap Transducer (IEEE)
SWITZ	Switzerland
SWJ	Single Wire Junction
SWJ	Socket Wrench Joint
SW J Anthrop	Southwestern Journal of Anthropology [*A publication*]
SW J Phil	Southwestern Journal of Philosophy [*A publication*]
Sw J T	Southwestern Journal of Theology [*A publication*]
SW J Th	Southwestern Journal of Theology [*A publication*]
SWK	Southwark [*England*]
SWK	[*The*] Stanley Works [*NYSE symbol*] (SPSG)
SWK	Stewart Lake Resources, Inc. [*Toronto Stock Exchange symbol*]
SW KR	Swedish Krona [*Monetary unit*]
SWL	Safe Working Load [*Shipping*]
SWL	Short Wavelength LASER
SWL	Short Wavelength Limit
SWL	Shortwave Listener [*Radio*]
SWL	Signals Warfare Laboratory [*Army*] (RDA)
SWL	Single-Wheel Loading [*Aviation*]
SWL	Snow Hill, MD [*Location identifier*] [*FAA*] (FAAL)
SWL	Solid Waste Litter
SWL	South West Air Ltd. [*Windsor, ON, Canada*] [*FAA designator*] (FAAC)
SWL	Southwest Realty Ltd. [*Later, Southwestern Property Trade*] AM (SPSG)
SWL	Special Weapons Loading (SAA)
SWL	Still Water Level
SWL	Strategic Weapons Loader (DWSG)
SWL	Sulfite Waste Liquor
SWL	Surface Wave Line
SWLA	Southwestern Library Association
SW Law J	Southwestern Law Journal [*A publication*]
SWLC	South West London College [*London, England*]
SWLC	Southwestern Connecticut Library Council [*Library network*]
SWLDG	Socket Welding
Sw Legal Found Inst on Oil and Gas L and Tax	Southwestern Legal Foundation. Institution on Oil and Gas Law and Taxation [*United States*] [*A publication*]
SWLF	Southwestern Legal Foundation (EA)
SWLG	Swelling (FAAC)
SWLG	SWLG Corp. [*NASDAQ symbol*] (NQ)
SWLIN	System Work List Item Number (DNAB)
SW L J	Southwestern Law Journal [*A publication*]
SWL Rev	Southwestern Law Review [*A publication*] (DLA)
SwLU	Lunds Universitet [*University of Lund*], Lund, Sweden [*Library symbol*] [*Library of Congress*] (LCLS)
SWLY	Southwesterly [*Meteorology*] (FAAC)
SWM	Sawmill [*California*] [*Seismograph station code, US Geological Survey*] [*Closed*] (SEIS)
SWM	Serber-Wilson Method [*Nuclear energy*] (NRCH)
SWM	Shipboard Wave Meter
SWM	Single White Male [*Classified advertising*]
SwM	Southwest Microfilm, Inc., El Paso, TX [*Library symbol*] [*Library of Congress*] (LCLS)

SWM	Special Warfare Mission (AABC)
SWM	Spotweld Machine [*Tool*]
SWM	Stan West Mining Corp. [*Toronto Stock Exchange symbol*]
SWM	Suia-Missu [*Brazil*] [*Airport symbol*] (OAG)
SWM	Surface Wave Mode
SWMA	Society of Women in Military Aviation (EA)
SWMA	Solid Waste Management Association
SWMA	Southwestern Monuments Association [*Later, SPMA*] (EA)
SWMAT....	Switch Matrix (MCD)
SWMC....	Stan West Mining Corp. [*NASDAQ symbol*] (NQ)
SWMCA....	Schweizer Maschinenmarkt [*A publication*]
SWMCCS ...	Standard Weather Messages Command and Control System (MCD)
SWMF......	South Wales Miners' Federation (DAS)
SWMFB....	Southwestern Motor Freight Bureau
SWMGA ...	Solid Wastes Management [*Later, World Wastes*] [*A publication*]
SWMO	Solid Waste Management Office [*Later, Office of Solid Waste Management Programs*] [*Environmental Protection Agency*]
SWMS......	Solid Waste Management System [*Nuclear energy*] (NRCH)
SW Musician ...	Southwestern Musician [*A publication*]
SWN	Leadville, CO [*Location identifier*] [*FAA*] (FAAL)
SWN	Notre Dame College, Wilcox, Saskatchewan [*Library symbol*] [*National Library of Canada*] (NLC)
SWN	Southwestern Energy Co. [*NYSE symbol*] (SPSG)
SWN	Sworn (ROG)
SWNAA	Southwestern Naturalist [*United States*] [*A publication*]
SWNCC	State, War, Navy Coordinating Committee [*Later, SANAAC*]
SWND......	Social Workers for Nuclear Disarmament (EA)
SWNJ........	Southwest New Jersey Consortium for Health Information Services [*Library network*]
SWNS........	Sprawozdanie z Prac Naukowych Wydzialu Nauk Spolecznych Pan [*A publication*]
SWO	Senior Watch Officer [*Navy*] (NVT)
SWO	Shallow Resources, Inc. [*Vancouver Stock Exchange symbol*]
SWO	Solid Waste Office [*Later, Office of Solid Waste Management Programs*] [*Environmental Protection Agency*]
SWO	Southwestern Oregon Community College, Coos Bay, OR [*OCLC symbol*] (OCLC)
SWO	Squadron Wireless Officer [*Navy*] [*British*]
SWO	Squarewave Oscillator
SWO	Staff Watch Officer (NVT)
SWO	Staff Weather Officer [*Military*]
SWO	Station Warrant Officer [*Air Force*] [*British*]
SWO	Stillwater [*Oklahoma*] [*Airport symbol*] (OAG)
SWO	Stop Work Order
SWO	Stud Welding Outfit
SWO	Support Work Order (AAG)
SWO	Surface Warfare Officer [*Navy*] (NVT)
SW/O	Switchover
SWOAPQS ...	Surface Warfare Officer, Personnel Qualification Standards [*Navy*] (DNAB)
SWOB	Salaries, Wages, Overhead, and Benefits (NASA)
SWOB	Ship Waste Off-Loading Barge [*Navy*] (CAAL)
SWOC	Special Weapons Operation Center [*Army*] (AABC)
SWOC	Steel Workers Organizing Committee [*Became United Steelworkers of America*]
SWOC	Subject Word out of Context [*Data processing*] (DIT)
SWOD......	Special Weapons Ordnance Devices
SWOG......	Special Weapons Overflight Guide (AFM)
SWOP......	Service Weapons Operational Procedures (MCD)
SWOP.......	Special Leave Without Pay
SWOP.......	Special Weapons Ordnance Publication [*Navy*] (NVT)
SWOP.......	Specifications for Web Offset Publications [*Printing technology*]
SWOP.......	Stop without Pay
SWOP.......	Structural Weight Optimization Program [*NASA*] (KSC)
SWOP.......	Switchboard Operator [*British military*] (DMA)
SWOPS......	Single Well Oil Production Ship [*British*]
SWOPSI....	Stanford Workshop on Political and Social Issues [*Stanford University*]
SWORD	Separated, Widowed, or Divorced [*New York City association*]
SWORD	Shallow Water Oceanographic Research Data [*System*] [*Naval Ordnance Laboratory and Naval Oceanographic Office*]
SWORD	Small Wars Operational Research Division [*Military*] (INF)
SWORDS ...	Standard Work Ordering and Reporting Data System [*Army*]
SWORL.....	Southwestern Ohio Rural Libraries [*Library network*]
SwOrM......	Regionsjukhuset, Medicinska Biblioteket [*Regional Hospital, Medical Library*], Orebro, Sweden [*Library symbol*] [*Library of Congress*] (LCLS)
SWOS........	Surface Warfare Officer's School [*Navy*] (NVT)
SWOSCOLCOM ...	Surface Warfare Officer's School Command [*Navy*] (NVT)
SWOSCOLCOMDET ...	Surface Warfare Officer's School Command Detachment [*Navy*] (DNAB)
SWOT	Strengths, Weaknesses, Opportunities, Threats [*Analysis for organizations*]
SWOV	Switchover (MSA)
SWP..........	Safe Working Pressure
SWP..........	Salt-Water Pump (MSA)
SWP..........	Science Working Panel [*NASA*]

SWP..........	Scientific Word Processor [*Data processing*]
SWP..........	Sector Working Party [*British*] (DCTA)
SWP..........	Semi-Tech Microelectronics, Inc. [*Toronto Stock Exchange symbol*]
SWP..........	Service Water Pump [*Nuclear energy*] (NRCH)
SWP..........	Shock Wave Profile
SWP..........	Short Wavelength Prime [*Camera for spectra*]
SWP..........	Socialist Workers' Party [*British*] [*Political party*] (PPW)
SWP..........	Society of Wireless Pioneers
SWP..........	Society for Women in Plastics (EA)
SWP..........	Soil-Test Water Probe
SWP..........	Solid Waste Packaging [*Nuclear energy*] (NRCH)
SWP..........	Solid Waste Processing [*Nuclear energy*] (NRCH)
SWP..........	Southwest Pacific
SWP..........	Southwestern Property Trade [*Formerly, Southwest Realty*] [*AMEX symbol*] (SPSG)
SWP..........	Space, Weight, and Power
SWP..........	Special Weapons Project [*Military*]
SWP..........	Special Working Party [*Military*]
SWP..........	Standard Work Procedure (SAA)
SWP..........	Standby Warning Panel (MCD)
SWP..........	State Water Project [*California*] (ECON)
SWP..........	Stichting Waakzaamheid Persoonregistratie [*Netherlands*]
SWP..........	Stiftung Wissenschaft und Politik [*Foundation for Science and Politics*] [*Information service or system*] (IID)
SWP..........	Submersible Water Pump
SWP..........	Summer Work Program
SWP..........	Supply Working Party of Official Committee on Armistice Terms and Civil Administration [*World War II*]
SWP..........	Surface Warfare Plan [*Navy*] (CAAL)
SWP..........	Surface Wave Phenomena
SWP..........	Survey of Western Palestine [*C. R. Conder et al*] [*A publication*] (BJA)
SWP..........	Swamp (ADA)
SWP..........	Swamp Creek [*Montana*] [*Seismograph station code, US Geological Survey*] [*Closed*] (SEIS)
SWP..........	Sweep
SWPA.......	Section for Women in Public Administration (EA)
SWPA.......	Southwest National Corp. [*Greensburg, PA*] [*NASDAQ symbol*] (NQ)
SWPA.......	Southwest Pacific Area [*World War II*]
SWPA.......	Southwest Placement Association (AEBS)
SWPA.......	Southwestern Power Administration [*Department of Energy*]
SWPA.......	Southwestern Psychological Association (MCD)
SWPA.......	Spotweld Pattern [*Tool*] (AAG)
SWPA.......	Submersible Wastewater Pump Association (EA)
SWPA.......	Surplus War Property Administration [*Terminated, 1944*]
SW Pacific ...	South West Pacific [*A publication*] (APTA)
SWPAN.....	Special Weapons Project Analysis (SAA)
SWPB	Surplus War Property Board [*Terminated, 1945*]
SWPC........	Short Wing Piper Club (EA)
SWPC........	Smaller War Plants Corp. [*World War II*]
SWPC........	Southwest Pacific Command [*Navy*]
SWPCP	Prince Albert National Park, Parks Canada [*Parc National Prince Albert, Parcs Canada*] Waskesiu Lakes, Saskatchewan [*Library symbol*] [*National Library of Canada*] (NLC)
SWPF	Southwest Pacific Force [*Later, Southwest Pacific Command*] [*Navy*]
SW Phil Stud ...	Southwest Philosophical Studies [*United States*] [*A publication*]
SWPIA	Southwest Pacific Island Arc [*Oceanography*]
SWPJ	Study of Western Palestine: Jerusalem [*C. Warren and C. R. Conder*] [*A publication*] (BJA)
SWPM.......	Survey of Western Palestine: Memoirs [*C. R. Conder*] [*A publication*] (BJA)
SW Pol Sci Q ...	Southwestern Political Science Quarterly [*A publication*] (DLA)
SWPP	Service Water Pressurization Pump [*Nuclear energy*] (IEEE)
SWPP	Southwest Power Pool [*Regional power council*] (NRCH)
SWPPD	Society for Women in Philosophy, Pacific Division (EA)
SWPR........	Swedish Polar Research [*A publication*]
SwPrp	Southwestern Property Trust, Inc. [*Associated Press abbreviation*] (APAG)
SWP(S)......	Solid Waste Processing System [*Nuclear energy*] (NRCH)
SWPS	Strategic War Planning System [*Air Force*]
SWPSA	Southwestern Peanut Shellers Association (EA)
SWPSD	Society for Women in Philosophy, Southwest Division (EA)
SWPSP......	Survey of Western Palestine: Special Papers [*A publication*] (BJA)
SWPT	Service Weapons Test (NVT)
SWR	Serum Wassermann Reaction [*Clinical chemistry*]
SWR	Service Water Reservoir [*Nuclear energy*] (NRCH)
SwR...........	Sewanee Review [*A publication*]
SWR	Short Wavelength Radiation (KSC)
SWR	Shortwave Ratio (DEN)
SWR	Sine Wave Response
SWR	Siphon Withdrawal Response
SWR	Sodium-Water Reaction [*Nuclear energy*] (NRCH)
SWR	Sons of the Whiskey Rebellion (EA)
SWR	South Western Reporter [*A publication*] (DLA)

SWR .... Southwest Review [*A publication*]
SWR .... Southwestern Railway [*British*] (ROG)
SWR .... Special Warning Receiver (MCD)
SWR .... Standing Wave Ratio [*Voltage*] [*Electronics*]
SWR .... Steel Wire Rope
SWR .... Stonewall Resources [*Vancouver Stock Exchange symbol*]
SWR .... Stress Wave Riveter [*Metal forming*]
SWR .... Submarine Water Reactor [*Nuclear energy*] (NRCH)
SWR .... Switch Rails
SWR2 .... Scaled Weapons Radius Squared (SAA)
SWRA........ Selected Water Resources Abstracts [*US Geological Survey*] [*Information service or system*] (CRD)
SWRA........ Social Work Research and Abstracts [*A publication*]
SWRB........ Sadler's Wells Royal Ballet [*British*]
SWRB........ Standing Wave Ratio Bridge [*Electronics*]
SW Rep..... South Western Reporter [*A publication*] (DLA)
SW Repr .... South Western Reporter [*A publication*] (DLA)
SWRF........ Sine Wave Response Filter [*Program*]
SWRHL..... Southwestern Radiological Health Laboratory [*HEW*]
SWRI......... Scottish Women's Rural Institutes (DI)
SWRI......... Southwestern Research Institute [*San Antonio, TX*] [*Research center*]
SWRJ .... Split Wing Ramjet
SWRL........ Southwest Regional Laboratory [*Research center*] (RCD)
SWRL........ Southwest Regional Laboratory for Educational Research and Development
SWRLSS ... Southwest Regional Library Service System [*Library network*]
SWRM ...... Standing Wave Ratio Meter [*Electronics*]
SWRMPAC ... Southwestern Regional Manpower Advisory Committee [*Terminated, 1974*] [*Department of Labor*] (EGAO)
SWRN .... Southwestern [*Meteorology*] (FAAC)
SWROM .... Standing Wave Read-Only Memory [*Data processing*]
SWROSS... Southwest Regional Office for Spanish Speaking (EA)
SWRP....... Satellite Wildlife Research Project
SWRP....... Sectionalized Work Requirements Package (MCD)
SWRPRS... Sodium-Water Reaction Pressure Relief Subsystem [*Nuclear energy*] (NRCH)
SWRSIC.... Southern Water Resources Scientific Information Center [*Raleigh, NC*]
SWRVDT .. Swedish Wildlife Research Viltrevy [*A publication*]
SWS.......... Saturn Workshop [*NASA*]
SWS.......... Seam Welding System
SWS.......... Service Water System [*Nuclear energy*] (NRCH)
SWS.......... Service-Wide Supply
SWS.......... Shallow Water SONAR
SWS.......... Shift Word, Substituting
SWS.......... Shock Wave Sensor (RDA)
SWS.......... Shore Wireless Service [*British military*] (DMA)
SWS.......... Short-Wave Sleep (OA)
SWS.......... Single White Silk-Covered [*Wire insulation*]
SWS.......... Slow-Wave Sleep
SWS.......... Smart Weapons Systems [*Army*] (RDA)
SWS.......... Sniper Weapon Sight (INF)
SWS.......... Sniper Weapon System (INF)
SWS.......... Sociologists for Women in Society (EA)
SWS.......... Solar Wind Spectrometer
SWS.......... Solid Waste System [*Nuclear energy*] (NRCH)
SwS .... Solidarity with Solidarity [*See also SzS*] [*British*] (EAIO)
SWS.......... Southwest Writers Series [*A publication*]
SWS.......... Southwestern Studies [*University of Texas, El Paso*] [*A publication*]
SWS.......... Space Weapon Systems [*Air Force*]
SWS.......... Special Weapon Systems [*Military*]
SWS.......... Standard Weapon Station [*Nuclear arms control*]
SWS.......... Static Water Supply (ADA)
SWS.......... Still Water Surface
SWS.......... Strategic Warning Staff
SWS.......... Strategic Weapon System [*Military*] (CAAL)
SWS.......... Swansea [*Wales*] [*Airport symbol*] (OAG)
SWS.......... Swift Minerals Ltd. [*Vancouver Stock Exchange symbol*]
SWS.......... Switch Scan (MCD)
SWS.......... Switch Stand
SWS.......... Systolic Wall Stress [*Cardiology*]
SWSA........ Southern Wood Seasoning Association
SWSD....... Special Weapons Supply Depot
SWSE .... Southeast Regional Library, Weyburn, Saskatchewan [*Library symbol*] [*National Library of Canada*] (NLC)
SWSF .... Society for a World Service Federation (EA)
SWSG....... Security Window Screen and Guard
SWSI .... Single Width, Single Inlet (OA)
SWSI .... Stanley Well Service [*NASDAQ symbol*] (NQ)
SWSI .... Surface Water Supply Index [*to measure drought*]
SWSIR....... Ship Weapons System Integration Requirements [*Navy*]
SWSJ .... Son of WSFA Journal [*A publication*]
SwSK .... Kungliga Tekniska Hoegskolan [*Royal Institute of Technology*], Stockholm, Sweden [*Library symbol*] [*Library of Congress*] (LCLS)
SwSKB....... Kungliga Biblioteket, Bibliotheca Regia Holmiensis, Stockholm, Sweden [*Library symbol*] [*Library of Congress*] (LCLS)
SwSKM ..... Kungliga Karolinska Mediko-Kirurgiska Institutes, Stockholm, Sweden [*Library symbol*] [*Library of Congress*] (LCLS)

SwSL.......... Latinamerika-Institutet, Stockholm, Sweden [*Library symbol*] [*Library of Congress*] (LCLS)
SWSM...... Special Weapons Supply Memorandum [*Army*] (AABC)
SW Social Sci Q ... Southwestern Social Science Quarterly [*A publication*]
SWSR........ Solid Waste Shipping Room [*Nuclear energy*] (NRCH)
SWST .... Service Water Storage Tank [*Nuclear energy*] (IEEE)
SWST .... Society of Wood Science and Technology (EA)
SWST .... Southwest Securities Group [*NASDAQ symbol*] (SPSG)
SW St (UTEP) ... Southwestern Studies (University of Texas, El Paso) [*A publication*]
SwSU .... Stockholms Universitetsbiblioteket, Stockholm, Sweden [*Library symbol*] [*Library of Congress*] (LCLS)
SWSVC ..... Souris Valley Regional Care Center, Weyburn, Saskatchewan [*Library symbol*] [*National Library of Canada*] (NLC)
SW-SWIP ... Society for Women in Philosophy, Southwestern Division (EA)
SWSWTU ... Sheffield Wool Shear Workers' Trade Union [*British*] (DCTA)
SWT.......... Safe Women's Transport [*British*]
SWT.......... Scottish Wildlife Trust [*British*]
SWT.......... Search-while-Track (CAAL)
SWT.......... Seward, NE [*Location identifier*] [*FAA*] (FAAL)
SWT.......... Shortwave Transmitter
SWT.......... Silent Witness [*Vancouver Stock Exchange symbol*]
SWT.......... Single-Weight [*Paper*]
SWT.......... Special Weapons Test
SWT.......... Spiral Wrap Tubing
SWT.......... Spotweld Template (MCD)
SWT.......... Steel Watertight [*Shipfitting*]
SWT.......... Supersonic Wind Tunnel (MCD)
SWT.......... Sweat
SWT.......... Swept Frequency Transform (CAAL)
SWT.......... Swift Aire Lines, Inc. [*San Luis Obispo, CA*] [*FAA designator*] (FAAC)
SWT.......... Switch Ties
SWT.......... System Work Team (MCD)
SWTA....... Special Weapons Training Allowance
SWTC....... Special Weapon Technical Command [*Navy*] (MCD)
SWTC....... Stop War Toys Campaign (EA)
SWTED ..... Solar Waerme Technik [*A publication*]
SWTG....... Switching (WGA)
SwtGas...... Southwest Gas Corp. [*Associated Press abbreviation*] (APAG)
SWTI .... Special Weapons Technical Instructions [*Army*] (AABC)
SWTL........ Surface Wave Transmission Line
SWTN ...... Sprawozdania Wroclawskiego Towarzystwa Naukowego [*A publication*]
SWTN ...... Swanton Corp. [*NASDAQ symbol*] (NQ)
SwtPS .... Southwestern Public Service Co. [*Associated Press abbreviation*] (APAG)
SWTR....... Southern California Water Co. [*NASDAQ symbol*] (NQ)
SWTR....... Surface Water Treatment Rule [*Environmental Protection Agency*]
Sw & Tr...... Swabey and Tristram's Probate and Divorce Reports [*164 English Reprint*] [*A publication*] (DLA)
SWTS .... Secondary Waste Treatment System [*Nuclear energy*] (NRCH)
SWTT .... Single-Well Tracer Test [*Petroleum technology*]
SWTTEU .. Special Weapons Test and Tactical Evaluation Unit
SWTX....... Southwall Technologies, Inc. [*NASDAQ symbol*] (NQ)
SWTZ....... Switzerland
SWU .... Idaho Falls, ID [*Location identifier*] [*FAA*] (FAAL)
SWU .... Sagami Women's University [*UTLAS symbol*]
SWU .... Separative Work Unit [*Measure of uranium enrichment capability*]
SWU .... Slovenian Women's Union (EA)
SWU .... Standard Work Unit (EG)
SWU .... Steelhawk Resources Ltd. [*Vancouver Stock Exchange symbol*]
SWULANT ... Special Weapons Unit, Atlantic [*Navy*] (DNAB)
Sw U LR .... Southwestern University. Law Review [*A publication*]
Sw U L Rev ... Southwestern University. Law Review [*A publication*]
SwUmU ..... Umea Universitetsbibliotek, Umea, Sweden [*Library symbol*] [*Library of Congress*] (LCLS)
SWUPAC.. Special Weapons Unit, Pacific [*Navy*] (DNAB)
SWUS....... Southwest United States
SWUSL ..... Southwestern University School of Law (DLA)
SwUU .... Universitet i Uppsala [*University of Uppsala*], Uppsala, Sweden [*Library symbol*] [*Library of Congress*] (LCLS)
SWV .... Squarewave Voltammetry [*Electrochemistry*]
SWV .... Suave Shoe Corp. [*NYSE symbol*] (SPSG)
SWV .... Swan View [*Australia*] [*Seismograph station code, US Geological Survey*] (SEIS)
SWV .... Swivel (AAG)
SWVA....... Scottish War Veterans of America (EA)
SWVA....... Shemya WWII Veterans Association (EA)
SWVA....... Steel of West Virginia, Inc. [*NASDAQ symbol*] (NQ)
SWVB....... Social Work Vocational Bureau (EA)
SWVL........ Swivel (MSA)
SWW .... Hotels and Restaurants International [*A publication*]
SWW .... Severe Weather Warning (KSC)
SWW .... Soft White Winter [*Wheat*] (OA)
SWW .... Stow Resources [*Vancouver Stock Exchange symbol*]
SWW .... Sweetwater, TX [*Location identifier*] [*FAA*] (FAAL)
SWW .... Winthrop College, Rock Hill, SC [*OCLC symbol*] (OCLC)
SWWA ...... South-West Water Authority [*British*] (DCTA)

SWWBDS ... Software Work Breakdown Structure (MCD)
SWWBS .... Software Work Breakdown Structure
SWWC .... Southwest Water Co. [*La Puente, CA*] [*NASDAQ symbol*] (NQ)
SWWF .... Speed-Welding Wire Feeder
SWWG ...... Social Work with Groups [*A publication*]
SWWOAH ... Society of World War One Aero Historians (EA)
SWWU ...... Singapore Wood Workers' Union
SWX .... Southwest Gas Corp. [*NYSE symbol*] (SPSG)
SWXO .... Staff Weather Officer [*NASA*] (KSC)
SWY .... Albemarle, NC [*Location identifier*] [*FAA*] (FAAL)
SWY .... Safeway, Inc. [*NYSE symbol*] (SPSG)
SWY .... Stopway
SWY .... Stornaway Resources Corp. [*Vancouver Stock Exchange symbol*]
SWY .... Swedish Economy [*A publication*]
SWY .... Swiss Yiddish (BJA)
SWZ .... Smyrna, TN [*Location identifier*] [*FAA*] (FAAL)
SWZ .... Special Watch Zone [*Navy*] (NVT)
SWZ .... Swaziland [*ANSI three-letter standard code*] (CNC)
SWZ .... Swiss Helvetia Fund [*NYSE symbol*] (SPSG)
SWZBA ..... Schweizer Buch [*A publication*]
SX .... Greece [*Aircraft nationality and registration mark*] (FAAC)
SX .... Pia Societas Sancti Francisci Xaverii pro Exteris Missionibus [*St. Francis Xavier Foreign Mission Society*] [*Xaverian Missionary Fathers*] [*Roman Catholic religious order*]
SX .... Sacks
SX .... Sigma Xi [*Society*]
SX .... Simplex [*Transmission direction*] (CET)
SX .... Society of St. Francis Xavier for the Foreign Missions [*Also known as Xaverian Missionaries*] (EAIO)
SX .... Solvent Extraction (DEN)
sx .... South West Africa [*Namibia*] [*MARC country of publication code*] [*Library of Congress*] (LCCP)
SX .... Stability Index [*Aviation*] (FAAC)
SX .... Sterling Philippines Airways, Inc. [*ICAO designator*] (FAAC)
SX .... Sussex [*County in England*]
SX .... SXT Resources Ltd. [*Vancouver Stock Exchange symbol*]
Sx .... Symptoms [*Medicine*] (WGA)
SX .... Union of Soviet Socialist Republics [*Later, FC*] [*License plate code assigned to foreign diplomats in the US*]
SX-1980 ..... Model number used by U.S. Pioneer Electronic Corp. [*Name is derived from "S" in "stereo amplifier" and "X" in "TX tuner"*]
SXA .... Stored Index to Address
SXAD .... Sioux Army Depot
SXAPS .... Soft X-Ray Appearance Potential Spectrometer [*or Spectroscopy*]
SXB .... Strasbourg [*France*] [*Airport symbol*] (OAG)
SXBT .... Shipboard Expendable Bathythermograph [*System*] [*Naval Oceanographic Office*]
SXC .... Saint Xavier College [*Chicago, IL*]
SXC .... Santa Catalina, CA [*Location identifier*] [*FAA*] (FAAL)
SXCO .... Switchco, Inc. [*NASDAQ symbol*] (NQ)
SXD .... Notes et Etudes Documentaires [*A publication*]
SXD .... Springfield, VT [*Location identifier*] [*FAA*] (FAAL)
SXD .... Store Index in Decrement (SAA)
SXE .... Sale [*Australia*] [*Airport symbol*] (OAG)
SXE .... Soft X-Ray Experiment [*Also, SXX*]
SXE .... Spencar Explorations Ltd. [*Vancouver Stock Exchange symbol*]
SXEW .... Solvent Extraction and Electrowinning [*Metallurgy*]
SXF .... Berlin [*Germany*] [*Airport symbol*] (OAG)
SXF .... Solvent Extraction Feed [*Nuclear energy*] (NRCH)
SXG .... Senanga [*Zambia*] [*Airport symbol*] (OAG)
SXH .... Sehulea [*Papua New Guinea*] [*Airport symbol*] (OAG)
SXI .... Singapore Business [*A publication*]
SXI .... Software Extraordinaire, Inc. [*Telecommunications service*] (TSSD)
SXI .... Standex International Corp. [*NYSE symbol*] (SPSG)
SXI .... Synex International, Inc. [*Toronto Stock Exchange symbol*]
SXIS .... Scattered X-Ray Internal Standard [*for surface analysis*]
SXL .... Sexless [*Connector*]
SXL .... Short-Arc Xenon Lamp
SXL .... Soft X-Ray LASER
SXL .... Summersville, WV [*Location identifier*] [*FAA*] (FAAL)
SXM .... St. Maarten [*Netherlands Antilles*] [*Airport symbol*]
SXM .... Scanning X-Ray Microscopy (MCD)
SXM .... Sphinx Mining Inc. [*Vancouver Stock Exchange symbol*]
SXML .... San Xavier Mining Laboratory [*University of Arizona*] [*Research center*] (RCD)
SXN .... Sao Jose Do Xingu [*Brazil*] [*Airport symbol*] (OAG)
SXN .... Section (MDG)
SXNP .... Saxton Products [*NASDAQ symbol*] (NQ)
SXO .... Senior Experimental Officer [*Also, SEO, SExO*] [*Ministry of Agriculture, Fisheries, and Food*] [*British*]
SXP .... Sheldon Point [*Alaska*] [*Airport symbol*] (OAG)
SXP .... Sunnyvale Public Library, Sunnyvale, CA [*OCLC symbol*] (OCLC)
SXQ .... Soldotna, AK [*Location identifier*] [*FAA*] (FAAL)
SXR .... Soft X-Ray Region
SXR .... Srinagar [*India*] [*Airport symbol*] (OAG)

SXRB .... Soft X-Ray Background [*Astronomy*]
SXRF .... Synchrotron X-Ray Fluorescence [*Spectrometry*]
SXRT .... Soft X-Ray Telescope (SSD)
SXS .... Sigma Xi Society
SXS .... Stellar X-Ray Spectra
SxS .... Step-by-Step Switching System [*Telecommunications*]
SXS .... Surface X-Ray Scattering [*Physics*]
SXSKA .... Sakura X-Rei Shashin Kenkyu [*A publication*]
SXT .... Sextant (NASA)
SXT .... Sexton Summit, OR [*Location identifier*] [*FAA*] (FAAL)
SXT .... Sextuple (MSA)
SXT .... Soft X-Ray Telescope [*Astronomy*] (PS)
SXT .... Stable X-Ray Transmitter
SXTF .... Satellite X-Ray Test Facility
SXTN .... Sextant (MSA)
SXX .... Secolul XX [*A publication*]
SXX .... Soft X-Ray Experiment [*Also, SXE*]
SXY .... Sidney [*New York*] [*Airport symbol*] (OAG)
SY .... Air Alsace [*France*] [*ICAO designator*] (FAAC)
SY .... School Year (AABC)
SY .... Security
SY .... Sefer Yezirah (BJA)
SY .... Seychelles
SY .... Shelby Williams Industries, Inc. [*NYSE symbol*] (SPSG)
SY .... Shipyard
SY .... Shoulder Yaw (MCD)
SY .... Shropshire Yeomanry [*British military*] (DMA)
SY .... Sloppy [*Track condition*] [*Thoroughbred racing*]
SY .... Southern Yiddish (BJA)
SY .... Spring Yearling
SY .... Square Yard
SY .... Staff Years (OICC)
SY .... Steam Yacht (ROG)
SY .... Sticky (WGA)
SY .... Stripping Yield [*Agriculture*] (OA)
SY .... Supply [*Business term*]
SY .... Surrey [*County in England*]
SY .... Survey
SY .... Sussex Yeomanry [*British military*] (DMA)
SY .... Sustainer Yaw (AAG)
Sy .... Symmachus (BJA)
SY .... Symposium [*A publication*]
Sy .... Symptoms [*Medicine*]
SY .... Synchronized (MDG)
Sy .... Synchronous System [*on a ship*] (DS)
SY .... Synthesis [*A publication*]
SY .... Syphilis [*Medicine*]
sy .... Syria [*MARC country of publication code*] [*Library of Congress*] (LCCP)
SY .... Syria [*or Syrian Arab Republic*] [*ANSI two-letter standard code*] (CNC)
SY .... Syrup (WGA)
SY .... System
SYA .... Save Your Afterdeck [*Bowdlerized version*]
SYA .... Scandinavian Yachting Association [*See also SKAN SF*] (EAIO)
SYA .... Shemya Island [*Alaska*] [*Airport symbol*] (OAG)
SYA .... Subud Youth Association (EA)
SYADS ...... Syracuse Air Defense Sector (SAA)
SYAH .... Aishalton [*Guyana*] [*ICAO location identifier*] (ICLI)
SYAN .... Annai [*Guyana*] [*ICAO location identifier*] (ICLI)
SYAP .... Apoteri [*Guyana*] [*ICAO location identifier*] (ICLI)
SYAW .... Awaruwaunawa [*Guyana*] [*ICAO location identifier*] (ICLI)
SYB .... Seal Bay [*Alaska*] [*Airport symbol*] (OAG)
SYB .... Sybron Corp. [*NYSE symbol*] (SPSG)
SYB .... Syracuse University, Syracuse, NY [*OCLC symbol*] (OCLC)
SYBF .... Share Your Birthday Foundation (EA)
SyblTc .... Symbol Technologies, Inc. [*Associated Press abbreviation*] (APAG)
SYBR .... Baramita [*Guyana*] [*ICAO location identifier*] (ICLI)
Sybrn .... Sybron Corp. [*Associated Press abbreviation*] (APAG)
SYBS .... Sybase, Inc. [*NASDAQ symbol*] (SPSG)
SYBT .... Bartica [*Guyana*] [*ICAO location identifier*] (ICLI)
SyBU .... Symbolae Biblicae Upsalienses [*A publication*]
SYC .... Seychelles [*ANSI three-letter standard code*] (CNC)
SYC .... Sycamore (AAG)
SYC .... Symbol Correspondence Element [*Data processing*] (PCM)
SYC .... Symbolic Corrector (SAA)
SYC .... Synco Development [*Vancouver Stock Exchange symbol*]
SYCATE ..... Symptom-Cause-Test
SYCLOPS ... SYFA Concurrent Logic Operating System
SYCOM ..... Synchronous Communications [*Satellite*] [*GSFC*]
SYCOM ..... Systems Command
SYCOSPARE ... Shipyard Checkout Spare
SYCOT ...... Shipyard Checkout Test
SYCP .... Syncom Corp. [*NASDAQ symbol*] (NQ)
SYD .... Casper, WY [*Location identifier*] [*FAA*] (FAAL)
SYD .... Scheer Energy Development Corp. [*Vancouver Stock Exchange symbol*]
SYD .... Scotland Yard
SYD .... Shipyard

SYD .... South Yemen Dinar (BJA)
SYD .... [*Release*] Subject Your Discretion (FAAC)
SYD .... Sum of the Year's Digits [*Statistics*]
SYD .... Sydney [*Australia*] [*Seismograph station code, US Geological Survey*] [*Closed*] (SEIS)
SYD .... Sydney [*Australia*] [*Airport symbol*] (OAG)
SYDAS ..... System Data Acquisition System
SYDEC ...... Selective Yield Delayed Coking [*Foster Wheeler USA Corp. process*]
SYDIA .... System Developer Interface Activity [*Data processing*]
Syd Inst Crim Proc ... University of Sydney Faculty of Law. Proceedings of the Institute of Criminology [*A publication*]
Syd Jaycee ... Sydney Jaycee [*A publication*] (APTA)
Syd Jewish News ... Sydney Jewish News [*A publication*] (APTA)
Syd Law R ... Sydney Law Review [*A publication*] (APTA)
Syd LR .... Sydney Law Review [*A publication*] (APTA)
Syd L Rev... Sydney Law Review [*A publication*] (APTA)
SYDMF ..... Scheer Energy Development Corp. [*NASDAQ symbol*] (NQ)
Syd Morning Her ... Sydney Morning Herald [*A publication*]
Syd Morning Herald ... Sydney Morning Herald [*A publication*] (APTA)
Sydney GCN ... Sydney Gay Community News [*A publication*] (APTA)
Sydney Law R ... Sydney Law Review [*A publication*] (APTA)
Sydney Law Rev ... Sydney Law Review [*A publication*] (APTA)
Sydney L Rev ... Sydney Law Review [*A publication*]
Sydney Q Mag ... Sydney Quarterly Magazine [*A publication*] (APTA)
Sydney Univ Gaz ... Sydney University. Gazette [*A publication*]
Sydney Univ Med J ... Sydney University. Medical Journal [*A publication*] (APTA)
Sydney Univ Rev ... Sydney University. Review [*A publication*]
Sydney Univ Sch Civ Eng Res Rep ... Sydney University. School of Civil Engineering. Research Report [*A publication*] (APTA)
Sydney Water Bd J ... Sydney Water Board. Journal [*A publication*] (APTA)
Sydowia Ann Mycol ... Sydowia. Annales Mycologici [*A publication*]
Sydowia Ann Mycolog Beih ... Sydowia. Annales Mycologici. Beihefte [*A publication*]
Syd R.......... Sydney Review [*A publication*]
Syd Stud..... Sydney Studies in English [*A publication*] (APTA)
Sydsven Medicinhist ... Sydsvenska Medicinhistoriska Saellskapets Arsskrift [*A publication*]
Sydsvenska Ortnamns-Sallsk Arsskr ... Sydsvenska Ortnamns-Saellskapets Arsskrift [*A publication*]
Syd Univ Ag Economics Res Bul ... University of Sydney. Department of Agricultural Economics. Research Bulletin [*A publication*] (APTA)
Syd Univ Civ Engng Schl Res Rep ... University of Sydney. School of Civil Engineering. Research Report [*A publication*] (APTA)
Syd Univ Dep Agric Econ Mimeo Rep ... University of Sydney. Department of Agricultural Economics. Mimeographed Report [*A publication*] (APTA)
Syd Univ Gaz ... Sydney University. Gazette [*A publication*] (APTA)
Syd Univ Med J ... Sydney University. Medical Journal [*A publication*] (APTA)
Syd Univ Post Grad Comm Med Bul ... University of Sydney. Postgraduate Committee in Medicine. Bulletin [*A publication*] (APTA)
Syd Univ Post Grad Comm Med Oration ... University of Sydney. Postgraduate Committee in Medicine. Annual Postgraduate Oration [*A publication*] (APTA)
Syd Univ Sch Agric Rep ... University of Sydney. School of Agriculture. Report [*A publication*] (APTA)
Syd Wat Bd J ... Sydney Water Board. Journal [*A publication*] (APTA)
Syd Water Bd J ... Sydney Water Board. Journal [*A publication*] (APTA)
Syd Water Board J ... Sydney Water Board. Journal [*A publication*] (APTA)
SYE............. Sa'Dah [*Yemen Arab Republic*] [*Airport symbol*] (OAG)
SYE .... Symbol Element [*Data processing*] (PCM)
SYEB .... Ebini [*Guyana*] [*ICAO location identifier*] (ICLI)
SYENDM ... Systematic Entomology [*A publication*]
SYEP .... Summer Youth Employment Program [*Department of Labor*]
SYEP .... Symmetrical Disubstituted Ethoxy Propane [*Organic chemistry*] (MCD)
SYES .... Syesis [*A publication*]
SYF............ St. Francis, KS [*Location identifier*] [*FAA*] (FAAL)
SYFA .... System for Application [*Data processing*]
SYFANET ... System for Access Network [*Wespac*] (TSSD)
SYG .... Arcola, TX [*Location identifier*] [*FAA*] (FAAL)
SYG .... Secretary-General (NATG)
SYG .... Symbol Graph [*Data processing*] (PCM)
SYG .... Synergy International [*Vancouver Stock Exchange symbol*]
SYGA........ Systems Gauge [*Tool*] (AAG)
SYGC........ Georgetown [*Guyana*] [*ICAO location identifier*] (ICLI)
SYGH .... Good Hope [*Guyana*] [*ICAO location identifier*] (ICLI)
SYGN .... Synergen, Inc. [*Boulder, CO*] [*NASDAQ symbol*] (NQ)
SYGO .... Ogle [*Guyana*] [*ICAO location identifier*] (ICLI)
SYGT........ Georgetown [*Guyana*] [*ICAO location identifier*] (ICLI)
SYH .... Scottish & York Holdings Ltd. [*Toronto Stock Exchange symbol*]
SYH .... See You Home [*Teen slang*]
Syh .... Syrohexapla (BJA)
SYHA .... Scottish Youth Hostels Association
SYI............. Shelbyville, TN [*Location identifier*] [*FAA*] (FAAL)
SYI............. Symes Resources [*Vancouver Stock Exchange symbol*]
SYI............. Systems Industries, Inc. [*AMEX symbol*] (CTT)

SYIB .... Imbaimadai [*Guyana*] [*ICAO location identifier*] (ICLI)
Sy J Int L... Syracuse Journal of International Law and Commerce [*A publication*]
SYK............ Skyhawk Resources, Inc. [*Vancouver Stock Exchange symbol*]
SYK............ Stykkisholmur [*Iceland*] [*Airport symbol*] (OAG)
SYKA .... Kaieteur [*Guyana*] [*ICAO location identifier*] (ICLI)
SYKE .... Sykes Datatronics, Inc. [*NASDAQ symbol*] (NQ)
SYKI .... Kaow Island [*Guyana*] [*ICAO location identifier*] (ICLI)
SYKK .... Kurukabaru [*Guyana*] [*ICAO location identifier*] (ICLI)
SYKM........ Kamarang [*Guyana*] [*ICAO location identifier*] (ICLI)
SYKR .... Karanambo [*Guyana*] [*ICAO location identifier*] (ICLI)
SYKS .... Karasabai [*Guyana*] [*ICAO location identifier*] (ICLI)
SYKT......... Kato (Karto) [*Guyana*] [*ICAO location identifier*] (ICLI)
SYKW .... Kwakwani [*Guyana*] [*ICAO location identifier*] (ICLI)
SYL............ San Miguel, CA [*Location identifier*] [*FAA*] (FAAL)
SYL............ Somali Youth League [*Political party*] (AF)
SYL............ Spartacus Youth League (EA)
Syl.............. [*The*] Syllabi [*A publication*] (DLA)
SYL............ Syllable (ADA)
SYLD........ Linden [*Guyana*] [*ICAO location identifier*] (ICLI)
SY & LI..... Sherwood Yeomanry and Light Infantry [*British military*] (DMA)
SYLK........ Symbolic Link [*Data format*]
SYLL.......... Syllable
SYLL.......... Syllogeus [*A publication*]
SYLP .... Lumid Pau [*Guyana*] [*ICAO location identifier*] (ICLI)
SYLP .... Support Your Local Police
Sy LR .... Syracuse Law Review [*A publication*]
SYLT .... Lethem [*Guyana*] [*ICAO location identifier*] (ICLI)
Sylvatrop Philipp For Res J ... Sylvatrop. The Philippine Forest Research Journal [*A publication*]
SYM .... Salesian Youth Movement (EA)
SYM .... Secondary Yield Measurement
SYM .... Seymour Resources [*Vancouver Stock Exchange symbol*]
SYM .... Simao [*China*] [*Airport symbol*] (OAG)
SYM .... Simmons Aviation [*Negaunee, MI*] [*FAA designator*] (FAAC)
SYM .... Symbiont
SYM .... Symbol [*or Symbolic*] (AAG)
Sym .... Symmachus' Greek Translation of the Bible [*A publication*] (BJA)
sym............ Symmetrical [*Also, s*] [*Chemistry*]
SYM .... Symmetry
SYM .... Symphony
Sym........... Symphony Recording Co. [*Record label*]
Sym............ Symposium [*A publication*]
SYM .... Syms Corp. [*NYSE symbol*] (SPSG)
SYM .... System (MDG)
SYMAN .... Symbol Manipulation [*Data processing*]
SYM/ANNOT ... Symbology Annotation (MCD)
SYMAP ..... Synagraphic Mapping System [*Computer-made maps*]
SYMB........ Mabaruma [*Guyana*] [*ICAO location identifier*] (ICLI)
SYMB........ Symbion, Inc. [*NASDAQ symbol*] (NQ)
SYMB........ Symbol
SYMBA ..... Symbioses [*A publication*]
SYMBAL .. Symbolic Algebraic Language [*Data processing*]
SYMBAS... Symbolization All Series (ADA)
SYMBOLANG ... Symbolic Manipulation Language [*Data processing*] (CSR)
SymbOsl .... Symbolae Osloenses [*A publication*]
Symb Oslo ... Symbolae Osloenses [*A publication*]
Symb Philol Danielsson ... Symbolae Philologicae [*O. A.*] Danielsson Octogenario Dicatae [*Uppsala*] [*A publication*] (OCD)
SYMC........ Symantec Corp. [*NASDAQ symbol*] (NQ)
SYMCA..... Symposium (International) on Combustion. Proceedings [*A publication*]
Sym Code... Syms' Code of English Law [*1870*] [*A publication*] (DLA)
SYMD .... Mahdia [*Guyana*] [*ICAO location identifier*] (ICLI)
SYMD .... Systemed, Inc. [*Salt Lake City, UT*] [*NASDAQ symbol*] (NQ)
SYMDEB .. Symbolic Debugger [*Also, sdb, SOLD*] [*Data processing*]
Syme .... Syme's Scotch Justiciary Reports [*1826-30*] [*A publication*] (DLA)
SYMED..... Synthetic Metals [*A publication*]
SYMEVETOPHARSA ... Syndicat des Medecins, Veterinaires, Pharmaciens, et Sages Femmes Africains du Mali [*Union of African Doctors, Pharmacists, Midwives, and Veterinarians of the Mali Federation*]
Symf.......... Symfoni & Artist [*Record label*] [*Sweden*]
SYMK........ Sym-Tek Systems, Inc. [*NASDAQ symbol*] (NQ)
SYMM ...... Monkey Mountain [*Guyana*] [*ICAO location identifier*] (ICLI)
SYMM ...... Symmetrical (MSA)
Sym Mag ... Symphony Magazine [*A publication*]
SYMMOD ... Symbolic Modeling [*Data processing*]
SYMMTRAC ... Sylvania Multimode Tracking [*Aerospace*] (MCD)
SYMN .... Manari [*Guyana*] [*ICAO location identifier*] (ICLI)
Sym News .. Symphony News [*A publication*]
SYMP........ Mountain Point [*Guyana*] [*ICAO location identifier*] (ICLI)
SYMP........ Symposium (MSA)
Symp .... Symposium [*of Xenophon*] [*Classical studies*] (OCD)
Symp .... Symposium [*of Plato*] [*Classical studies*] (OCD)
Symp .... Symposium [*of Lucian*] [*Classical studies*] (OCD)
SYMP........ Symptom [*Medicine*] (AAMN)

SYMPA ..... Symposia on Theoretical Physics and Mathematics [*A publication*]
Symp Abnorm Subsurf Pressure Proc ... Symposium on Abnormal Subsurface Pressure. Proceedings [*A publication*]
SYMPAC .. Symbolic Program for Automatic Control
Symp Angiol Sanitoriana ... Symposia Angiologica Sanitoriana [*A publication*]
sympat........ Sympathetic [*Neurology*]
Symp Biol Hung ... Symposia Biologica Hungarica [*A publication*]
Symp Br Soc Dev Biol ... Symposium. British Society for Developmental Biology [*A publication*]
Symp Br Soc Parasitol ... Symposia. British Society for Parasitology [*A publication*]
Symp Cell Biol ... Symposia for Cell Biology [*Japan*] [*A publication*]
Symp Chem Nat Prod Symp Pap ... Symposium on the Chemistry of Natural Products. Symposium Papers [*A publication*]
Symp Coal Manag Tech Pap ... Symposium on Coal Management Techniques. Papers [*A publication*]
Symp Coal Mine Drain Res Pap ... Symposium on Coal Mine Drainage Research. Papers [*A publication*]
Symp Coal Prep Pap ... Symposium on Coal Preparation. Papers [*A publication*]
Symp Coal Util Pap ... Symposium on Coal Utilization. Papers [*A publication*]
Symp Ecol Res Humid Trop Vegtn ... Symposium on Ecological Research in Humid Tropics Vegetation [*A publication*]
Symp Eng Appl Mech ... Symposium on Engineering Applications of Mechanics [*A publication*]
Symp Eng Geol Soils Eng Proc ... Symposium on Engineering Geology and Soils Engineering. Proceedings [*A publication*]
Symp Faraday Soc ... Symposia. Faraday Society [*A publication*]
Symp Foods ... Symposium of Foods [*A publication*]
Symp Freq Control Proc ... Symposium on Frequency Control. Proceedings [*A publication*]
Symp Fundam Cancer Res ... Symposium on Fundamental Cancer Research [*A publication*]
Symp Fundam Cancer Res Collect Pap ... Symposium on Fundamental Cancer Research. Collections of Papers [*A publication*]
Symp Genet Biol Ital ... Symposia Genetica et Biologica Italica [*A publication*]
Symp Genet Breed Wheat Proc ... Symposium on Genetics and Breeding of Wheat. Proceedings [*A publication*]
SYMPH ..... Symphony (ADA)
Symp (Int) Combust Proc ... Symposium (International) on Combustion. Proceedings [*A publication*]
Symp Int Soc Cell Biol ... Symposia. International Society for Cell Biology [*A publication*]
Symp Int Union Biol Sci Proc ... Symposium. International Union of Biological Sciences. Proceedings [*A publication*]
Symp Maize Prod Southeast Asia ... Symposium on Maize Production in Southeast Asia [*A publication*]
Symp Med Hoechst ... Symposia Medica Hoechst [*A publication*]
Symp Microb Drug Resist ... Symposium on Microbial Drug Resistance [*A publication*]
Symp Mine Prep Plant Refuse Disposal Pap ... Symposium on Mine and Preparation Plant Refuse Disposal. Papers [*A publication*]
Symp Moessbauer Eff Methodol Proc ... Symposium on Moessbauer Effect Methodology. Proceedings [*A publication*]
Symp Natl Phys Lab (UK) ... Symposium. National Physical Laboratory (United Kingdom) [*A publication*]
Symp Neurosci ... Symposia in Neuroscience [*A publication*]
Symp Ocul Ther ... Symposium on Ocular Therapy [*A publication*]
Symp Oral Sens Percept ... Symposium on Oral Sensation and Perception [*A publication*]
Symposium ... Symposium: A Quarterly Journal in Modern Foreign Literatures [*A publication*]
Sympos Math ... Symposia Mathematica [*A publication*]
Symposum Jun Bar ... Symposium. Association de Jeune Barreau de Montreal [*A publication*] (DLA)
Sympos Univ Upsaliensis Annum Quingentesimum Celebrantis ... Symposia Universitatis Upsaliensis Annum Quingentesimum Celebrantis [*A publication*]
Symp Pap Symp Chem Nat Prod ... Symposium Papers. Symposium on the Chemistry of Natural Products [*A publication*]
Symp Particleboard Proc ... Symposium on Particleboard. Proceedings [*A publication*]
Symp Pharmacol Ther Toxicol Group ... Symposium. Pharmacology, Therapeutics, and Toxicology Group. International Association for Dental Research [*A publication*]
Symp Priv Invest Abroad ... Symposium. Private Investors Abroad [*A publication*]
Symp Pyrrolizidine Senecio Alka ... Symposium on Pyrrolizidine Senecio Alkaloids. Toxicity [*A publication*]
Symp Regul Enzyme Act Synth Norm Neoplast Tissues Proc ... Symposium on Regulation of Enzyme Activity and Syntheses in Normal and Neoplastic Tissues. Proceedings [*A publication*]
Symp R Entomol Soc Lond ... Symposia. Royal Entomological Society of London [*A publication*]
Symp R Entomol Soc London ... Symposia. Royal Entomological Society of London [*A publication*]
Symp Salivary Gland ... Symposium for the Salivary Gland [*A publication*]

Symp Ser Australas Inst Min Metall ... Symposia Series. Australasian Institute of Mining and Metallurgy [*A publication*]
Symp Ser Immunobiol Stand ... Symposia Series in Immunobiological Standardization [*A publication*]
Symp Ser Inst Fuel (London) ... Symposium Series. Institute of Fuel (London) [*A publication*]
Symp Soc Dev Biol ... Symposia. Society for Developmental Biology [*A publication*]
Symp Soc Exp Biol ... Symposia. Society for Experimental Biology [*A publication*]
Symp Soc Gen Microbiol ... Symposium. Society for General Microbiology [*A publication*]
Symp Soc Study Dev Growth ... Symposium. Society for the Study of Development and Growth [*A publication*]
Symp Soc Study Hum Biol ... Symposia. Society for the Study of Human Biology [*A publication*]
Symp Soc Study Inborn Errors Metab ... Symposium. Society for the Study of Inborn Errors of Metabolism [*A publication*]
Symp Surf Min Reclam Pap ... Symposium on Surface Mining and Reclamation. Papers [*A publication*]
Symp Surf Phenom Enhanced Oil Recovery ... Symposium on Surface Phenomena in Enhanced Oil Recovery [*A publication*]
Symp Swed Nutr Found ... Symposia. Swedish Nutrition Foundation [*A publication*]
sympt .... Symptom [*Medicine*]
Symp Theor Phys Math ... Symposia on Theoretical Physics and Mathematics [*United States*] [*A publication*]
Symp Turbul Liq Proc ... Symposium on Turbulence in Liquids. Proceedings [*A publication*]
Symp Underground Min Pap ... Symposium on Underground Mining. Papers [*A publication*]
Symp Zool Soc Lond ... Symposia. Zoological Society of London [*A publication*]
SYMR .... Matthews Ridge [*Guyana*] [*ICAO location identifier*] (ICLI)
SYMRO .... System Management Research Operation (DIT)
SYMS .... Secondary Yield Measurement System
SymsCp .... Syms Corp. [*Associated Press abbreviation*] (APAG)
SYMT .... Symetrics Industries, Inc. [*NASDAQ symbol*] (NQ)
SYMW .... Maruranawa [*Guyana*] [*ICAO location identifier*] (ICLI)
SYMWAR ... System for Estimating Wartime Attrition and Replacement Requirements (AABC)
SYMX .... Symix Systems [*NASDAQ symbol*] (SPSG)
SYN .... Stanton, MN [*Location identifier*] [*FAA*] (FAAL)
SYN .... Synagogue
SYN .... Synaptec, a Knowledge Engineering Corp. [*Vancouver Stock Exchange symbol*]
Syn .... Synbiotics Corp.
SYN .... Synchronous (AAG)
SYN .... Synchronous Idle [*Transmission control character*] [*Data processing*]
SYN .... Syndicate (ROG)
SYN .... Synergist (WGA)
SYN .... Synod
SYN .... Synonym
Syn .... Synopsis (DLA)
syn .... Synovial [*Fluid*] [*Medicine*]
syn .... Synovitis [*Medicine*]
SYN .... Syntex Corp. [*NYSE symbol*] (SPSG)
SYN .... Syntex Corp., Palo Alto, CA [*OCLC symbol*] (OCLC)
Syn .... Syntheses [*A publication*]
SYN .... Synthesizer
SYN .... Synthetic (AAG)
SYN .... Syntype
SYNA .... New Amsterdam [*Guyana*] [*ICAO location identifier*] (ICLI)
SYNAC .... Synthesis of Aircraft (MCD)
SYNAPSE ... CUEA Synthesis and Publication Segment [*Marine science*] (MSC)
SYNBAPS ... Synthetic Bathymetric Profiling System [*Naval Oceanographic Office*]
SYNC .... Synchromechanism
SYNC .... Synchronize (AAG)
sync .... Synchrony
SYNCD ...... Synchronized (AAG)
SYNCELL ... Synthetic Cell [*Biological research*]
SYNCG ...... Synchronizing (AAG)
SYNCH ...... Synchronize
SYNCH ...... Synchronous Transmission [*Data processing*] (TSSD)
SYNCOM ... Synchronous Communications [*Hughes Aircraft Co.*]
SYNCOM ... Synchronous-Orbiting Communications Satellite [*GSFC*]
Syn Commun ... Synthetic Communications [*A publication*]
SYNCR .... Synchronizer (AAG)
SYNCRO ... Synchromesh [*Automotive engineering*]
SYNCRUDE ... Synthetic Crude
SYNCS .... Synchronous (AAG)
SYND .... Syndicate
synd .... Syndrome [*Medicine*]
SYNDARC ... Standard Format for Exchange of MAPMOPP Data among Data Centers (MSC)
SYNDETS ... Synthetic Detergents
SYNDEX ..... Syndicated Exclusivity [*FCC*]
SYNE .... Syntech International, Inc. [*NASDAQ symbol*] (NQ)

SYNED...... Synerjy [*A publication*]
SYNEE7.... Symposia in Neuroscience [*A publication*]
SYNESCI.. Syndicat National des Enseignants du Second Degre de Cote d'Ivoire
syn fl.......... Synovial Fluid [*Medicine*]　(MAE)
SYNFRQ... Synthesizer Frequency
SYNFUELS ... Synthetic Fuels
SYNG .... Synergetics International, Inc. [*NASDAQ symbol*]　(NQ)
SYNG .... Synergy. Syncrude Canada [*A publication*]
Syn Hist L ... Synthese Historical Library [*A publication*]
Syn Inorg Met-Org Chem ... Synthesis in Inorganic and Metal-Organic Chemistry [*Later, Synthesis and Reactivity in Inorganic and Metalorganic Chemistry*] [*A publication*]
SYNMAS.. Synchronous Missile Alarm System
SYNON..... Synonym　(ROG)
SYNOP...... Synopsis　(AABC)
Synop Br Fauna New Ser ... Synopses of the British Fauna. New Series [*A publication*]
Synopsis Swedish Bldg Res ... Synopsis of Swedish Building Research [*A publication*]
Syn Org...... Synthetische Methoden der Organischen Chemie [*Synthetic Methods of Organic Chemistry*] [*A publication*]
Synovs........ Synovus Financial Corp. [*Associated Press abbreviation*]　(APAG)
Synpt.......... Synoptic [*or Synoptist*]　(BJA)
SYNR......... Synercom Technology, Inc. [*NASDAQ symbol*]　(NQ)
SYNRAMS ... Synoptic Random Access Measurement System　(NOAA)
Syn Reac In ... Synthesis and Reactivity in Inorganic and Metalorganic Chemistry [*A publication*]
Syn Reactiv Inorg Metal Org C ... Synthesis and Reactivity in Inorganic and Metalorganic Chemistry [*A publication*]
SYNROC... Synthetic Rock [*For storage of nuclear waste*]
SYNS........ Synopsis　(MSA)
SYNSCP.... Synchroscope　(KSC)
SYNSEM .. Syntax and Semantics　(IEEE)
Syn Ser....... Synopsis Series of the United States Treasury Decisions [*A publication*]　(DLA)
SYNSPADE ... Symposium on the Numerical Solution of Partial Differential Equations [*Book title, Academic Press*]
SYNT........ Syntro Corp. [*NASDAQ symbol*]　(NQ)
SYNTAC... Synthetic Tactics
SYNTEEDISETO ... Syndicat des Travailleurs de l'Energie Electrique et de Distribution d'Eau du Togo [*Union of Electrical and Water Distribution Workers of Togo*]
Syntex........ Syntex Corp. [*Associated Press abbreviation*]　(APAG)
Synth.......... Syntheses. An International Quarterly for the Logical and Psychological Study of the Foundations of the Sciences [*A publication*]
SYNTH ..... Synthesizer
SYNTH ..... Synthetic
Synth Commun ... Synthetic Communications [*A publication*]
Synthesis (C) ... Synthesis (Cambridge) [*A publication*]
Synth Fuels ... Synthetic Fuels [*A publication*]
Synth Fuels Update ... Synthetic Fuels Update [*A publication*]
Synth Libr ... Synthese Library [*A publication*]
Synth Met ... Synthetic Metals [*Switzerland*] [*A publication*]
Synth Methods Org Chem Yearb ... Synthetic Methods of Organic Chemistry Yearbook [*A publication*]
Synth Pipeline Gas Symp Proc ... Synthetic Pipeline Gas Symposium. Proceedings [*A publication*]
Synth React Inorg Metorg Chem ... Synthesis and Reactivity in Inorganic and Metalorganic Chemistry [*A publication*]
Synth Rubber ... Synthetic Rubber [*A publication*]
Synth Rubber Ind (Lanzhou People's Repub China) ... Synthetic Rubber Industry (Lanzhou, People's Republic of China) [*A publication*]
SYNTI....... Synchro Tie
SYNTIRT ... Syndicat des Travailleurs des Industries Reunies du Togo [*Union of Workers of United Industries of Togo*]
SYNTOL.... Syntagmatic Organization Language [*Data processing*]
SYNTRAN ... Syntax Translation [*Data processing*]　(DIT)
SYNV .... Sonchus Yellow Net Virus [*Plant pathology*]
SYNZYMES ... Synthetic Enzymes
SYO .... Sayre, OK [*Location identifier*] [*FAA*]　(FAAL)
SYO .... Skygold Resources [*Vancouver Stock Exchange symbol*]
SYO .... Synalloy Corp. [*AMEX symbol*]　(SPSG)
SYO .... Syowa [*Ongul*] [*Antarctica*] [*Seismograph station code, US Geological Survey*]　(SEIS)
SYO .... Syowa Base [*Antarctica*] [*Geomagnetic observatory code*]
SYOR .... Orinduik [*Guyana*] [*ICAO location identifier*]　(ICLI)
Syoyak Zass ... Syoyakugaku Zasshi. Japanese Journal of Pharmacognosy [*A publication*]
SYP........... Parkland Regional Library, Yorkton, Saskatchewan [*Library symbol*] [*National Library of Canada*]　(NLC)
SYP........... Santa Ynez Peak [*California*] [*Seismograph station code, US Geological Survey*]　(SEIS)
SYP........... Southern Yellow Pine
SYP........... Spiritualist Yoga Fellowship　(EAIO)
SYP........... Suomen Yksityisyrittaejaein Puoluejaerjesto [*Finnish Private Entrepreneurs' Party*] [*Political party*]　(PPE)
Syp............ Syropalaestinum　(BJA)

SYPH........ Syphilis　(DSUE)
Sy PO........ Supply Petty Officer [*British military*]　(DMA)
SYPR........ Paruima [*Guyana*] [*ICAO location identifier*]　(ICLI)
SYQT........ SyQuest Technology [*NASDAQ symbol*]　(SPSG)
syr .... Sirop [*Syrup*] [*Pharmacy*]
SYR.......... Smyrna [*Washington*] [*Seismograph station code, US Geological Survey*]　(SEIS)
SYR.......... South Yorkshire Railway [*British*]　(ROG)
SYR.......... Syracuse [*New York*] [*Airport symbol*]
SYR.......... Syria [*or Syrian Arab Republic*] [*ANSI three-letter standard code*]　(CNC)
syr .... Syriac [*MARC language code*] [*Library of Congress*]　(LCCP)
SYR.......... Syrian [*Language, etc.*]　(ROG)
SYR.......... Syringe [*Medicine*]
SYR.......... Syrupus [*Syrup*] [*Pharmacy*]
SYRA........ Syracuse Supply Co. [*NASDAQ symbol*]　(NQ)
Syrac Law R ... Syracuse Law Review [*A publication*]
SYRACUSE ... System of Radio Communications Using a Satellite [*Telecommunications*]　(TSSD)
Syracuse HA ... Syracuse Herald-America and Post-Standard [*A publication*]
Syracuse HJ ... Syracuse Herald Journal [*A publication*]
Syracuse Int'l L & Com ... Syracuse Journal of International Law and Commerce [*A publication*]
Syracuse J Int'l L ... Syracuse Journal of International Law [*A publication*]　(DLA)
Syracuse L Rev ... Syracuse Law Review [*A publication*]
Syr D.......... De Syria Dea [*of Lucian*] [*Classical studies*]　(OCD)
SyrH.......... Hexaplaric Syriac　(BJA)
Syrian J Stomatol ... Syrian Journal of Stomatology [*A publication*]
Syr J Intl.... Syracuse Journal of International Law and Commerce [*A publication*]
Syr J Intl L & Com ... Syracuse Journal of International Law and Commerce [*A publication*]
Syr LR........ Syracuse Law Review [*A publication*]
Syr Mesop St ... Syro-Mesopotamian Studies [*A publication*]
SYRP........ Summer Youth Recreation Program
SYRUCL ... Syracuse University College of Law　(DLA)
SyrW......... Syriac Version in Walton's Polyglot　(BJA)
SYS........... ISI Systems [*AMEX symbol*]　(SPSG)
SYS........... See Your Service　(FAAC)
SYS........... Sobeys Stores Ltd. [*Toronto Stock Exchange symbol*]
SYS........... Somerset, PA [*Location identifier*] [*FAA*]　(FAAL)
SYS........... Sweet Yet Simple [*Data processing*]
Sy S.......... Syn og Segn. Norsk-Tidsskrift [*A publication*]
SYS........... Synthesewerk Schwarzheide [*Former East German chemical company*]　(ECON)
SYS........... System　(AFM)
SYSAD...... Systems Adviser
SYSADMIN ... System Administrator [*Data processing*]
SYSCAP.... System of Circuit Analysis Program
Sysco......... Sysco Corp. [*Associated Press abbreviation*]　(APAG)
SYSCOM .. System Communications
SYSCOM .. Systems Command [*Navy*]
SYSCON... Systems Control [*Military*]　(AABC)
SYSDEV.... Systems Development　(NOAA)
SYSE........ Systems Equipment Corp. [*NASDAQ symbol*]　(NQ)
SYSEC....... System Synthesizer and Evaluation Center
SYSG .... Systematics General Corp. [*NASDAQ symbol*]　(NQ)
SYSGEN ... Systems Generator [*or Generation*] [*Data processing*]
SYSIN .... System Input [*Data processing*]　(MDG)
SYSLIB .... System Library [*Data processing*]　(MDG)
SYSLOG ... System Log [*Data processing*]
SYSMIN ... System for Safeguarding and Developing Mineral Production [*EC*]　(ECED)
SYSOP ...... System Operator [*Computer networking*]
SYSOUT ... System Output [*Data processing*]　(IBMDP)
SYSP .... Sixth-Year Specialist Program [*Library science*]
SYSPLLTM ... System Purchase of Long Lead Time Material
SYSPM...... System Performance Measure　(MCD)
SYSPOP ... System Programmed Operators [*Data processing*]　(MDG)
Sys Proced ... Systems and Procedures [*A publication*]
SYSRES .... System Residence [*Data processing*]
Sys and Soft ... Systems and Software [*A publication*]
SYST .... System
SYST .... Systematics, Inc. [*NASDAQ symbol*]　(NQ)
syst............ Systemic [*Medicine*]
Syst .... Systems [*A publication*]
syst............ Systolic [*Cardiology*]
Syst Appl Microbiol ... Systematic and Applied Microbiology [*A publication*]
Syst Assoc Publ ... Systematics Association. Publication [*A publication*]
Syst Assoc Spec Vol ... Systematics Association. Special Volume [*A publication*]
Syst Ass Spec Vol ... Systematics Association. Special Volume [*A publication*]
Syst Bot...... Systematic Botany [*A publication*]
Syst-Comput-Controls ... Systems-Computers-Controls [*A publication*]
Syst & Control ... Systems and Control [*A publication*]
Syst and Control Lett ... Systems and Control Letters [*A publication*]
SystCtr....... Systems Center, Inc. [*Associated Press abbreviation*]　(APAG)
Systematics Assoc Pub ... Systematics Association. Publication [*A publication*]
Systems-Comput-Controls ... Systems-Computers-Controls [*A publication*]

Systems Control Lett ... Systems and Control Letters [*A publication*]
Systems & Proc J ... Systems and Procedures Journal [*A publication*]
Systems Sci ... Systems Science [*A publication*]
Systems Theory Res ... Systems Theory Research [*A publication*]
Syst Entomol ... Systematic Entomology [*A publication*]
SYSTEP .... Systems Test and Evaluation Plan [*Military*]   (AABC)
SYSTIN..... System Industries, Inc. [*Associated Press abbreviation*]   (APAG)
Syst Int...... Systems International [*A publication*]
Syst Logiques ... Systemes Logiques [*A publication*]
SYSTO ...... System Staff Office [*or Officer*]
Syst Objectives Solutions ... Systems, Objectives, Solutions [*A publication*]
Syst Parasitol ... Systematic Parasitology [*A publication*]
SYSTRAN ... Systems Analysis Translator [*Data processing*]
Syst Sci...... Systems Science [*A publication*]
Syst Technol ... Systems Technology [*A publication*]
Syst Theory Res ... Systems Theory Research [*A publication*]
Syst Zool.... Systematic Zoology [*A publication*]
Sys User..... Systems User [*A publication*]
SYSVER.... System Specification Verification   (IEEE)
SYT........... Sweet Young Thing [*An attractive girl*] [*Slang*]
SYTA........ Sustained-Yield Tropical Agroecosystem
SYTM........ Georgetown/Timehri Internacional [*Guyana*] [*ICAO location identifier*]   (ICLI)
SYU .... Sudanese Youth Union
SYU .... Synchronization Signal Unit [*Telecommunications*]
SYU .... Syuhurei [*South Korea*] [*Seismograph station code, US Geological Survey*] [*Closed*]   (SEIS)
SYUBAT ... Science Reports. Yokohama National University. Section II. Biology and Geology [*A publication*]
SYUS........ Specialized Youth Units [*Canada*]
SYV........... Saynor Varah, Inc. [*Toronto Stock Exchange symbol*]
SYV........... Society for Young Victims [*Later, SYV/MCC*]   (EA)
SYV........... Solanum Yellows Virus [*Plant pathology*]
SYV........... Sylvester, GA [*Location identifier*] [*FAA*]   (FAAL)
SYV........... Symbol Value [*Data processing*]   (PCM)
SYV........... Syva Research Library, Palo Alto, CA [*OCLC symbol*]   (OCLC)
SYV/MCC ... Society for Young Victims, Missing Children Center   (EA)
Syvrem Med ... Syvremenna Meditsina [*A publication*]
SYVV........ Sowthistle Yellow Vein Virus
SYW .... Skyway Resources Ltd. [*Vancouver Stock Exchange symbol*]
SYWI........ Wichabai [*Guyana*] [*ICAO location identifier*]   (ICLI)
SYY........... Stornoway [*Scotland*] [*Airport symbol*]   (OAG)
SYY........... Sysco Corp. [*NYSE symbol*]   (SPSG)
SYZ........... Shelbyville, IL [*Location identifier*] [*FAA*]   (FAAL)
SYZ........... Shiraz [*Iran*] [*Airport symbol*]   (OAG)
SZ .... Aerolineas de El Salvador [*ICAO designator*]   (FAAC)
SZ .... Sceptre Investment Counsel Ltd. [*Toronto Stock Exchange symbol*]
sz .... Schizophrenia [*Psychology*]
Sz .... Schweizerische Landesbibliothek [*Swiss National Library*], Bern, Switzerland [*Library symbol*] [*Library of Congress*]   (LCLS)
SZ .... Secondary Zone
sz .... Seizure [*Medicine*]
SZ .... Seizure [*Telecommunications*]   (TEL)
SZ .... Sha'arei Zedek   (BJA)
SZ .... Shigaku Zasshi [*A publication*]
SZ .... Size   (MDG)
SZ .... Sizzler International [*NYSE symbol*]   (SPSG)
SZ .... Sovremennye Zapiski [*A publication*]
SZ .... Splash Zone
SZ .... Stimmen der Zeit [*A publication*]
SZ .... Streptozocin [*Antineoplastic drug*]
SZ .... Subduction Zone [*Geology*]
SZ .... Sueddeutsche Zeitung [*A publication*]
SZ .... Surface Zero [*Navy*]   (NVT)
SZ .... Swaziland [*ANSI two-letter standard code*]   (CNC)
sz .... Switzerland [*MARC country of publication code*] [*Library of Congress*]   (LCCP)
SZA........... Solar Zenith Angle [*Geophysics*]
SZA........... Soyo [*Angola*] [*Airport symbol*]   (OAG)
Szakserv Szle ... Szakszervezeti Szemle [*A publication*]
Szamki Koezlem ... Szamki Koezlemenyek [*A publication*]
Szamki Tanulmanyok ... Szamitogepalkalmazasi Kutato Intezet. Tanulmanyok [*A publication*]
Szamvit Uegyviteltech ... Szamvitel es Ugyviteltechnika [*A publication*]
SZB........... Silver-Zinc Battery
SZB........... Sintered Zinc Battery
SzBaL........ Lonza Aktiengesellschaft, Zentralbibliothek, Basel, Switzerland [*Library symbol*] [*Library of Congress*]   (LCLS)
SzBaM....... Museum fur Volkerkunde und Schweizerisches Museum fur Volkskunde, Basel, Switzerland [*Library symbol*] [*Library of Congress*]   (LCLS)
SzBaU........ Universitat Basel, Basel, Switzerland [*Library symbol*] [*Library of Congress*]   (LCLS)
SzBaU-IO ... Institut fur Organische Chemie der Universitat Basel, Basel, Switzerland [*Library symbol*] [*Library of Congress*]   (LCLS)
SZC........... Silver-Zinc Cell
SZCSAV.... Annual Review of the Schizophrenic Syndrome [*A publication*]

SZD .... St. George, SC [*Location identifier*] [*FAA*]   (FAAL)
SZD .... Sovetski Zhelezno-Dorozhni [*Soviet railways*] [*Former USSR*]
S Zd........... Sovetskoe Zdravoochranenie [*A publication*]
SZDKA...... Sovetskoe Zdravookhranenie Kirgizii [*A publication*]
SzDL......... Studien zur Deutschen Literatur [*A publication*]
SzDP......... Magyarorszagi Szocialdemokrata Part [*Hungarian Social-Democratic Party*] [*Political party*]   (EY)
SZDSZ ...... Alliance of Free Democrats [*Hungary*] [*Political party*]
SzDSz .... Szabad Demokratak Szovetsege [*Alliance of Free Democrats*] [*Hungary*] [*Political party*]   (EY)
SZE........... Szeged [*Hungary*] [*Seismograph station code, US Geological Survey*] [*Closed*]   (SEIS)
SZEC .... Silver-Zinc Electrochemical Cell
SZECC ...... Silver-Zinc Electrochemical Cell
S Zek......... Sociale Zekerheidsgids [*A publication*]
SzEP .... Studien zur Englischen Philologie [*A publication*]
SZG .... Salzburg [*Austria*] [*Airport symbol*]   (OAG)
SZG .... Soviet Zone Germany   (NATG)
SzGB......... Bibliotheque Battelle, Centre de Recherche, Geneve, Switzerland [*Library symbol*] [*Library of Congress*]   (LCLS)
SzGBNU.... Bibliotheque des Nations Unies, Geneve, Switzerland [*Library symbol*] [*Library of Congress*]   (LCLS)
SzGE......... Ecole de Chimie, Geneva, Switzerland [*Library symbol*] [*Library of Congress*]   (LCLS)
SzGPAr...... Archives Jean Piaget, Geneve, Switzerland [*Library symbol*] [*Library of Congress*]   (LCLS)
SzGSI........ Societe Generale pour l'Industrie, Geneve, Switzerland [*Library symbol*] [*Library of Congress*]   (LCLS)
SZI............ Seattle, WA [*Location identifier*] [*FAA*]   (FAAL)
Szigma Mat-Koezgazdasagi Folyoirat ... Szigma. Matematikai-Koezgazdasagi Folyoirat [*A publication*]
SZJ............ Atlanta, GA [*Location identifier*] [*FAA*]   (FAAL)
SZK........... Roanoke, VA [*Location identifier*] [*FAA*]   (FAAL)
SZK........... Skukuza [*South Africa*] [*Airport symbol*]   (OAG)
SZKKB ...... Shimizu Kensetsu Kenkyusho-Ho [*A publication*]
Szklo Ceram ... Szklo i Ceramika [*A publication*]
SZL........... Knob Noster, MO [*Location identifier*] [*FAA*]   (FAAL)
SzL............ Schriften zur Literatur [*A publication*]
SZL........... Spielzeug. Internationales Fachblatt fuer Spielmittel, Hobby- und Modellbau-Artikel, Christbaumschmuck, Fest- und Scherzartikel, Rohstoffe, Halbteile, Werkzeuge, Maschinen, und Verpackung [*A publication*]
SZL........... SZL Sportsight [*Vancouver Stock Exchange symbol*]
SzLaCU ..... Bibliotheque Cantonal et Universitaire de Lausanne, Lausanne, Switzerland [*Library symbol*] [*Library of Congress*]   (LCLS)
SzLaS........ Station Federale d'Essais Agricoles, Lausanne, Switzerland [*Library symbol*] [*Library of Congress*]   (LCLS)
SZLGD...... Sozialgerichtsbarkeit [*A publication*]
SZM .... Stereo Zoom Microscope
SZM .... Synthetic Zeolite Molecule
SZN .... Santa Barbara, CA [*Location identifier*] [*FAA*]   (FAAL)
SZN .... Streptozocin [*Antineoplastic drug*]
SZO .... Student Zionist Organization [*Defunct*]   (EA)
SZOG .... Soviet Zone of Occupation of Germany   (NATG)
Szolesz Boraszat ... Szoleszet es Boraszat [*A publication*]
SZOR......... Sintered Zinc Oxide Resistor
SZOT......... Szakszervezetek Orszagos Tanacsa [*National Trade Union Council*] [*Hungary*]
SZP........... Santa Paula, CA [*Location identifier*] [*FAA*]   (FAAL)
SZP........... Surf Zone Process
SZP........... Synchro Zeroing Procedure
SZPMA ..... Sozial- und Praeventivmedizin [*A publication*]
SZPMAA .. Medecine Sociale et Preventive [*A publication*]
SZR........... Sintered Zinc Resistor
SZR........... Stargazer Resources Ltd. [*Vancouver Stock Exchange symbol*]
SZR........... University of South Carolina, Regional Campus Processing Center, Columbia, SC [*OCLC symbol*]   (OCLC)
SzS............ Solidarnosc z Solidarnoscia [*Solidarity with Solidarity - SwS*] [*British*]   (EAIO)
SZS........... Srpska Zemljoradnicka Stranka [*Serbian Agrarian Party*] [*Former Yugoslavia*] [*Political party*]   (PPE)
SZS........... Staatliche Zentrale fuer Strahlenschutz Berlin [*East Germany*]
SZS........... Stewart Island [*New Zealand*] [*Airport symbol*]   (OAG)
SZSB .... Silver-Zinc Secondary [*or Storage*] Battery
SzStg......... Stadtbibliothek Vadiana, St. Gallen, Switzerland [*Library symbol*] [*Library of Congress*]   (LCLS)
SZT........... Sandpoint, ID [*Location identifier*] [*FAA*]   (FAAL)
SzT............ Schriften zur Theaterwissenschaft [*A publication*]
SZutNu....... Sifre Zuta on Numbers   (BJA)
SZVR......... Silicon Zener Voltage Regulator
SZY........... Selmer, TN [*Location identifier*] [*FAA*]   (FAAL)
SZZ........... Szczecin [*Poland*] [*Airport symbol*]   (OAG)
SzZ............ Zentralbibliothek Zurich, Zurich, Switzerland [*Library symbol*] [*Library of Congress*]   (LCLS)
SzZE .... Eidgenoessische Technische Hochschule, Zurich, Switzerland [*Library symbol*] [*Library of Congress*]   (LCLS)
SzZU........ Universitat Zurich, Universitatsspital-Bibliothek, Kantonsspital, Zurich, Switzerland [*Library symbol*] [*Library of Congress*]   (LCLS)

T

T................	Absolute Temperature [Symbol] [IUPAC]
T................	Aerotec [Sociedade Aerotec Ltda.] [Brazil] [ICAO aircraft manufacturer identifier] (ICAO)
T................	Air Temperature Correction
T................	American Telephone & Telegraph Co. [NYSE symbol] [Wall Street slang name: "Telephone"] (SPSG)
t------	Antarctic [MARC geographic area code] [Library of Congress] (LCCP)
T................	Backhoe Trench [Archaeology]
t................	Celsius Temperature [Symbol] [IUPAC]
T................	Cleared Through for Landing and Takeoff [Aviation] (FAAC)
T................	Internal Transmittance [Symbol] [IUPAC]
T................	Kinetic Energy [Symbol] [IUPAC]
t................	Marginal Propensity to Tax [Economics]
T................	Meridian Angle
T................	Military Sealift Command Ship [When precedes vessel classification] [Navy symbol]
T................	Octodecimo [Book from 12-1/2 to 15 centimeters in height] [Bibliography]
T................	Ribothymidine [One-letter symbol; see Thd]
T................	Shape Descriptor [T-bar and T-square, for example. The shape resembles the letter for which it is named]
T................	Table
T................	Tablespoon [Measure]
T................	Tablet (WGA)
T................	Tablet-Shaped [As in "T-grains"] [Photography]
t................	Tabula [Plate] [Latin]
T................	Tabulated [or Charted] LORAN [Long-Range Aid to Navigation] Reading
T................	Tace [Be Silent]
T................	Tackle [Football]
T................	Tactical Organization
T................	Tactual
T................	Taenia [Medicine] (MAE)
T................	Taken
T................	Takeoff [Aviation] (FAAC)
T................	Tala [Monetary unit in Western Samoa]
T................	Talc
T................	Talk/Monitor (NASA)
T................	Talon [Heel of the Bow] [Music]
T................	Tamoxifen [Antineoplastic drug]
T................	Tan (FAAC)
T................	Tango [Phonetic alphabet] [International] (DSUE)
T................	Tanhuma (BJA)
T................	Tank [Trains] [British]
T................	Tanna (BJA)
T................	Taped Commentary [On a bus tour] [British]
T................	Taper
T................	Tapered Hatchway [on a ship] (DS)
T................	Tappan's Ohio Common Pleas Reports [A publication] (DLA)
T................	Tare [Phonetic alphabet] [World War II] (DSUE)
T................	Target
T................	Tasto [Touch, Key, Fingerboard] [Music]
T................	Taxation [Economics]
T................	Taxes (DLA)
T................	Teacher
T................	Tear [Phonetic alphabet] [World War II]
t................	Teaspoon [Measure]
T................	Teatar [Sofia] [A publication]
T................	Teatr [A publication]
T................	Technical [or Technician]
T................	Technical College [British]
T................	Technological Service [Queen's Award] [British]
T................	Tee [Piping joint, etc.] [Technical drawings]
T................	Teeth [Technical drawings]
T................	Teich [Pond] [German military]
T................	Telefunken [Record label] [Germany, etc.]
T................	Telegram (BJA)
T................	Telegraph (ROG)
T................	Telegrapher [Navy]
T................	Telephone
T................	Telephone Trunk Call [British] (ROG)
T................	Teletype
t................	Telocentric
T................	Temperance [i.e., entitled to a daily rum ration but voluntarily not drawing it and receiving money instead] [See also G, UA] [Navy] [British]
T................	Temperature
T................	Tempo
T................	Temporal
T................	Temporary
T................	Tempore [In the Time of] [Latin]
T................	Tender [Horticulture]
T................	Tendre [Tender] [Music]
T................	Tenero [Tender]
T................	Tennessee State Library and Archives, Nashville, TN [Library symbol] [Library of Congress] (LCLS)
T................	Tenor [Genotype of Phlox paniculata]
T................	Tenor
T................	Tense
T................	Tension
T................	Tensor
T................	Tentative Target
T................	Ter [Three Times] [Pharmacy]
T................	Tera [A prefix meaning multiplied by 10^{12}] [SI symbol]
T................	Teracycle (BUR)
T................	Term [Medicine]
T................	Terminal
T................	Terminal Area Chart [Followed by identification] [Aviation]
T................	Termination
T................	Terminator [Genetics]
T................	Terminus [Biochemistry]
T................	Terrain
T................	Territory
t................	Tertiary [Also, tert] [Chemistry]
T................	Tesla [Symbol] [SI unit of flux density]
T................	Test (MSA)
T................	Test Equipment (NG)
T................	Test Reactor
T................	Test Set
t................	Test of Significance [Medicine] (MAE)
T................	Testament (ROG)
T................	Testator [Legal term]
T................	Tetracycline [Antibiotic compound]
T................	Teuthonista [A publication]
T................	Texana [A publication]
T................	Thaler [or Talari] [Monetary unit] [Ethiopia]
T................	Than
T................	That
T................	Theatres [Public-performance tariff class] [British]
T................	Theft
T................	Theology [A publication]
T................	Theophylline [Pharmacology]
T................	Thermodynamic Temperature [Symbol] [IUPAC]
T................	Thermometer
T................	Thermoplastic [Also, TP] [Plastics technology] (MSA)
T................	Thermostabilized (NASA)
T................	Thickness
T................	Thief
T................	Thioguanine [Also, TG] [Antineoplastic drug]
T................	Thiopental [An anesthetic]
T................	Third Word Designator [Data processing]
T................	Thomas Mieres [Flourished, 1429-39] [Authority cited in pre-1607 legal work] (DSA)
T................	Thoracic [Anatomy]
T................	Thorax [Anatomy] (MAE)
T................	Thread
T................	Threonine [One-letter symbol; see Thr] [An amino acid]
T................	Thromboxane [Also, TA, Tx, TX] [Biochemistry]
T................	Throttle Command (NASA)
T................	Thrust of Propeller [Naval engineering] (DAS)
T................	Thruster [of a ship] (DS)

T................	Thunderstorm [*Meteorology*]
T................	Thursday (WGA)
T................	Thymidine [*Medicine*] (MAE)
T................	Thymine [*Also, Thy*] [*Biochemistry*]
T................	Thymus [*Medicine*]
T................	Thymus Derived [*Hematology*]
T................	Thyroid [*Medicine*]
T................	Tidal Gas [*Respiration*] [*Medicine*]
T................	Tide Rips [*Navigation*]
T................	Tie [*Sports*]
T................	Tier [*Psychology*]
T................	Tiler [*Freemasonry*]
T................	Tilic Subgroup [*Ilmenite, titanite, perofskite, rutile*] [*CIPW classification*] [*Geology*]
T................	Time
t................	Time [*Symbol*] [*IUPAC*]
T................	Time [*A publication*]
T................	Time Consumed in Playing Game [*Baseball*]
T+............	Time Postintegration (NASA)
T................	Time Prior to Launch [*Usually followed by a number*] [*NASA*] (KSC)
T................	Time-Reversal [*Atomic physics*]
t................	Time in Seconds [*Aerospace*]
T................	Time Trial
T................	Timekeeper [*Sports*]
T................	Times [*London*] [*A publication*]
T................	Tip [*Switchboard plug*] [*Telecommunications*] (TEL)
T................	Tipper [*Shipping*] (DS)
T................	Tithing [*Geographical division*] [*British*]
T................	Title [*Bibliography*]
T................	Toarcian [*Geology*]
T................	Tobacco Tax Ruling, Internal Revenue Bureau [*United States*] [*A publication*] (DLA)
T................	Toc [*Phonetic alphabet*] [*Pre-World War II*] (DSUE)
T................	Tocopherol [*Biochemistry*]
T................	Toe
T................	Toilet (MSA)
T................	Toll
T................	Tommy [*Phonetic alphabet*] [*Royal Navy*] [*World War I*] (DSUE)
T................	Tomo [*Volume*] [*Italian*] (ILCA)
T................	Tomus [*Volume*]
T................	Ton
T................	Tonnage [*Shipping*]
t................	Tonne [*Metric*]
T................	Tooth
T................	Top
t................	Top [*or Truth*] (Quark) [*Atomic physics*]
T................	Top Secret
T................	Topical (ADA)
T................	Toronto Stock Exchange
T................	Torpedo [*Obsolete*] [*Navy*] [*British*] (ROG)
T................	Torpedoman [*Navy*] [*British*]
T................	Torque
T................	Tosefta (BJA)
T................	Total
T................	Tourist [*Rate*] [*Value of the English pound*]
T................	Toward [*Altitude difference*]
T................	Town
T................	Township
T................	Toxicity (MAE)
T................	Trace of Precipitation [*Less than 0.005 inch of rain or 0.05 inch of snow*]
T................	Tracer [*Ammunition*] (NATG)
T................	Trachea [*Anatomy*]
T................	Track
T................	Tracker [*British military*] (DMA)
T................	Traded
T................	Tradesman [*British military*] (DMA)
T................	Traditio [*A publication*]
T................	Traditional (BJA)
T................	Trafalgar [*On army list*] [*British*] (ROG)
T................	Traffic Cases [*A publication*] (DLA)
T................	Traffic Headquarters
T................	Trainer [*Designation for all US military aircraft*]
T................	Training (FAAC)
t................	Trans [*Chemical conformation*]
T................	Transaction
T................	Transcription
T................	Transducer
t................	Transfer [*Genetics*]
T................	Transferred [*Navy*]
T................	Transferrin [*Also, TF, TRF*] [*Biochemistry*]
T................	Transformation Rule [*Linguistics*]
T................	Transformer
T................	Transfusion [*Medicine*]
T................	Transient [*Bureau of the Census*]
T................	Transit
T................	Transition
T................	Transitive
T................	Translated (ROG)
T................	Translation
T................	Translocation
T................	Transmit [*or Transmitting*]
T................	Transmitter
T................	Transpiration [*Botany*]
T................	Transport (NATG)
t................	Transport Number [*Symbol*] [*Electrochemistry*]
T................	Transvaal Provincial Division Reports [*South Africa*] [*A publication*] (DLA)
T................	Transverse (AAMN)
T................	Transverse Tubule [*Muscle neurobiology*]
T................	Trawling
T................	Tread [*Stair details*] [*Technical drawings*]
T................	Treasurer
T................	Treasury [*As in T-Bill, T-Bond, T-Note*]
T................	Treated
T................	Treatment
T................	Treble [*Music*] (ROG)
T................	Treponema [*Microbiology*] (AAMN)
T................	Triangle
T................	Trichome [*Botany*]
T................	Trichophyton [*Medicine*] (MAE)
T................	Triggered [*Cardiology*]
T................	Trillion [10^{12}]
T................	Trillo [*Trill*] [*Music*]
T................	Trimethoprim [*Also, TMP*] [*Antibacterial compound*]
T................	Trinitas [*The Trinity*]
T................	Triode
T................	Triple
T................	Tritium [*Also, H_3*] [*Radioisotope of hydrogen*]
t................	Triton [*A nuclear particle*]
T................	Triton Industries, Inc. [*Toronto Stock Exchange symbol*]
T................	Tropical [*Load line mark, or air mass*]
T................	Trotter
T................	Troy [*A system of weights for precious metals*]
T................	Truce
T................	True [*Direction*]
T................	Truss (AAG)
T................	Trypanosoma [*Medicine*] (MAE)
T................	Tubulin [*A protein*]
T................	Tuesday
T................	Tufa [*Quality of the bottom*] [*Nautical charts*]
T................	Tug [*Navy*]
T................	Tumor [*Oncology*]
T................	Tun [*Unit of liquid capacity*]
T................	Turbocharged [*Automotive engineering*]
T................	Turin [*A publication*]
T................	Turkish
T................	Turn [*or Turning*]
T................	Turner [*Navy rating*] [*British*]
T................	Turnover Index [*Botany*]
T................	Tutti [*Sing or Play Together*] [*Music*]
T................	Twentyfourmo [*Book up to 15 centimeters in height*]
T................	Twin Screw [*Shipping*] (DS)
T................	Type
T................	Typed [*Manuscript descriptions*]
T................	Typhlosole [*Biology*]
T................	Typhoid
T................	Wrong Tense of Verb [*Used in correcting manuscripts, etc.*]
T-0............	Time Zero (MCD)
T-1............	Carrier which identifies the all-digital communications links (TSSD)
T1...............	First Transcript [*Genetics*]
T_1	Tricuspid First Heart Sound [*Cardiology*]
T_2	Diiodothyronine [*Endocrinology*]
T2...............	Second Transcript [*Genetics*]
T2...............	Terminator 2 [*Motion picture*]
T2...............	Time of Flight to Intercept [*Military*] (CAAL)
T_2	Tricuspid Second Heart Sound [*Cardiology*]
T3...............	Tank Track Test [*Army*]
T-3.............	Tocotrienol [*Biochemistry*]
T_3	Triiodothyronine [*Also, TITh*] [*Endocrinology*]
3T...............	Triple Throw [*Switch*]
T4...............	Thyroxine [*Also, Thx, Ty*] [*An amino acid*] [*Endocrinology*]
5T...............	Mauritania [*Aircraft nationality and registration mark*] (FAAC)
T/5.............	Technician Fifth Grade [*Army*]
T-10...........	Codename used by Ronald Reagan while serving as an FBI informant during his term as president of the Screen Actors Guild
T (Bird)......	Thunderbird [*Automobile*] (DSUE)
T (Colds)....	Toxic Colds [*Medicine*]
T (Day).......	Transition Day [*Based on the expected transition from a two-front to a one-front war*] [*World War II*]
T (Day).......	Truce Day
TA	Chinese Taipei [*IYRU nationality code*] (IYR)
Ta	Ta'anith (BJA)
TA	Table of Allowances (MCD)
TA	Table of Authorization
TA	Tabled Agreement [*in labor relations*]
TA	Tablet (ADA)

TA	TACA International Airlines SA [El Salvador] [ICAO designator] (ICDA)
TA	TACAN [Tactical Air Navigation] Approach (FAAC)
TA	Tactical Air Missile
TA	Tactical Aircraft
T/A	Tactical Airlift [Tactical Air Command]
TA	Tailhook Association (EA)
TA	Talanta [A publication]
TA	Talmudical Academy (BJA)
TA	Talmudische Archaeologie [A publication] (BJA)
TA	Tanabe Seiyaku Co. Ltd. [Japan] [Research code symbol]
TA	Tangible Asset
TA	Tank Army (MCD)
TA	Tank Tainers [Shipping] (DCTA)
TA	Tanker [Shipping] (DCTA)
Ta	Tantalum [Chemical element]
TA	Tape Adapter
TA	Tape Advance (AAG)
TA	Tape Armored [Telecommunications] (TEL)
TA	Target (DEN)
TA	Target Acquisition (MCD)
TA	Target Aircraft (MUGU)
TA	Target Area [Military] (AFM)
TA	Targeting Agent [Medicine]
TA	Tariff Act [1930]
TA	Tartana [Ship's rigging] (ROG)
TA	Task Analysis
TA	Task Assignment (AAG)
TA	Tax Abatement
TA	Tax Agent
TA	Tax Amortization [Plan]
TA	Tea Association of the USA (EA)
TA	Teaching Assistant [in a university]
TA	Technical Advisor (MCD)
TA	Technical Analysis (NG)
TA	Technical Assessor
TA	Technical Assistance [or Assistant]
TA	Technology Assessment Database [Fachinformationszentrum Karlsruhe GmbH] [Germany] [Information service or system] (CRD)
TA	Technonet Asia (EA)
TA	Teichoic Acids [Biochemistry]
TA	Tel Aviv [Israel] (BJA)
TA	Telegraphic Address
TA	Teleoperator Assembler (SSD)
TA	Telephone Apparatus [JETDS nomenclature] [Military] (CET)
TA	Telescope Assembly (KSC)
TA	Television Associates [Mountain View, CA] (TSSD)
TA	Television/Radio Age [A publication]
TA	Tell-Amarna [Egypt] (BJA)
TA	Tell Asmar [Iraq] (BJA)
TA	Telluride Association (EA)
TA	Temperature, Axillary
TA	Temple Autobiographies [A publication]
TA	Temporal Arteritis [Medicine]
TA	Tension by Applanation [Ophthalmology]
TA	Tension Arterielle [Blood Pressure] [Medicine]
TA	Tenuazonic Acid [Biochemistry]
TA	Teologinen Aikakauskirja [Helsinki] [A publication] (BJA)
TA	Terephthalic Acid [Also, TPA] [Organic chemistry]
TA	Terminal Adapter [Telecommunications]
T of A	Terms of Agreement (NATG)
TA	Terrain Avoidance [Helicopter]
TA	Terrarium Association (EA)
TA	Territorial Army
TA	Test Access [Telecommunications] (TEL)
TA	Test Accessory (AAG)
T & A	Test and Adjust (SSD)
TA	Test Article (NASA)
TA	Testantibus Actis [As the Records Show] [Latin]
TA	Theater Army
TA	Theatre Annual [A publication]
TA	Theatre Arts [A publication]
TA	Theatre Authority (EA)
TA	Therapeutic Abortion [Medicine]
TA	Thermal Activation [Physics]
TA	Thermal Analysis
TA	Thermophilic Actinomyces [Microbiology]
TA	Third Attack [Men's lacrosse position, until 1933]
TA	Threat Analysis (MCD)
TA	Threat Axis [Military] (NVT)
TA	Thromboxane [Also, T, Tx, TX] [Biochemistry]
TA	Thromboxane A [Also, TxA, TXA] [Biochemistry]
TA	Throw Away
TA	Thunderbirds of America (EA)
TA	Thyroglobulin Auto-Precipitation [Endocrinology] (AAMN)
TA	Tibialis Anterior [A muscle]
TA	Time Actual (NASA)
T & A	Time and Allowance
T & A	Time and Attendance (AFM)
T & A	Time and Attendance
TA	Tippers Anonymous (EA)
TA	Tithe Annuity
TA	Titratable Acid [Clinical chemistry]
TA	Titration Alkalinity [Oceanography]
TA	Tnu'at 'Aliyah (BJA)
TA	Tobacco Associates (EA)
T & A	Tonsillectomy and Adenoidectomy [or Tonsils and Adenoids] [Medicine]
TA	Tool Available
T & A	Tops and Accessories [Show business slang] [Bowdlerized version]
TA	Torah Atmosphere (BJA)
TA	Total Aboard [Aviation] (FAAC)
TA	Total Adenine [Nucleotide pool] [Medicine]
TA	Total Alkaloids [Medicine]
TA	Total Audience [Television ratings]
TA	Toward
TA	Toxin-Antitoxin [Also, TAT] [Immunology]
TA	Tracers Association [A union] [British]
TA	Track Accelerator [Missile simulator]
TA	Traction Assist [Automotive engineering]
T/A	Trade Acceptance [Business term]
TA	Trade Agreements Act
TA	Trade Association (DCTA)
TA	Trading As
TA	Traduction Automatique [A publication]
TA	Traffic Agent [or Auditor]
T/A	Traffic Analysis [National Security Agency]
TA	Trained Aide [Medicine]
TA	Training Allowance [British military] (DMA)
TA	Training Analyst (HGAA)
T/A	Training As
TA	Trans Am [Model of automobile]
TA	Transactional Analysis [System of psychotherapy developed by Eric Berne, MD]
TA	Transaldolase [An enzyme] (AAMN)
TA	Transalta Resources Corp. [Toronto Stock Exchange symbol]
TA	Transamerica Corp. [NYSE symbol] (SPSG)
TA	Transantral [Medicine] (AAMN)
T/A	Transfer of Accountability
TA	Transfer Agent [Business term]
TA	Transfer Aisle (NRCH)
TA	Transfusion Associated
TA	Transient Alert (MCD)
TA	Transit Authority
TA	Transition Agreement
TA	Transition Altitude
TA	Transition Area [For chart use only] [Aviation]
TA	Transmission Authenticator [Telecommunications] (TEL)
TA	Transplantation Antigen [Medicine]
TA	Transportability Approval [Army]
TA	Transportation Agent
TA	Transportation Alternatives (EA)
TA	Transportation Authorization (AAG)
T of A	Transposition of Aorta [Cardiology] (MAE)
TA	Transverse Acoustic
TA	Travel Allowance
TA	Travel [or Trip] Authorization (MCD)
TA	Traveler's Advisory [Weather information]
TA	Triacetin [Antifungal compound] [Organic chemistry]
TA	Triamcinolone Acetonide [Also, TAA] [Synthetic steroidal drug]
TA	Tribunal Administratif [Administrative Court] [French] (ILCA)
TA	Tricuspid Atresia [Cardiology]
TA	Trierisches Archiv [A publication]
TA	Trinidad Artillery [British military] (DMA)
TA	Trip Authorization
TA	Triple Antigen [Medicine]
TA	Triplex Annealed
TA	Trophoblast Antigen [Immunochemistry]
TA	Truck Assembly
TA	True Altitude [Height] [Navigation]
TA	True Anomaly
TA	Trunnion Angle (KSC)
TA	Trustee under Agreement [Legal term] (DLA)
TA	Truth in Advertising [An association] [Defunct] (EA)
TA	Tryptophane Acid (AAMN)
TA	Tube Agglutination [Medicine] (MAE)
TA	Tuberculin, Alkaline [Medicine]
TA	Tubular Atrophy [Nephrology]
T/A	Turboalternator
TA	Turbulence Amplifier
TA	Turkish Army (NATG)
T/A	Turnaround (NASA)
T & A	Turnbull & Asser [Men's fashions]
TA	Turning Angle [Automotive engineering]
TA	Type Americain [World War I troop train in France made according to US specifications]
TA	Type Approval
TA	Type Availability

TA .... VEB Fahlberg-List [*East Germany*] [*Research code symbol*]
TA1 .... Trophoblast Antigen One [*Immunochemistry*]
TA₄ .... Tetraiodothyroacetic Acid [*Medicine*]   (MAE)
TAA .... Tactical Air Army   (NATG)
TAA .... Tactical Army Automation   (MCD)
TAA .... Tactical Automation Appraisal   (MCD)
TAA .... Taiwanese Association of America   (EA)
TAA .... Tamburitza Association of America   (EA)
TAA .... Tannic Acid Agar [*Culture media*]
TAA .... Technical Assistance Administration [*United Nations*]
TAA .... Technical Assistance Agreement [*NASA*]   (NASA)
TAA .... Technology Assessment Annex   (MCD)
TAA .... Telephone Artifacts Association   (EA)
TAA .... Television Appliance Association
TAA .... Temporary Access Authorization   (NASA)
TAA .... Terre Adelie [*Antarctica*] [*Seismograph station code, US Geological Survey*] [*Closed*]   (SEIS)
TAA .... Territorial Army Association [*British*]
TAA .... Tertiary-Amyl Alcohol [*Organic chemistry*]
TAA .... Texas Armadillo Association [*Commercial firm*]   (EA)
TAA .... Textbook Authors Association   (EA)
TAA .... Thioacetamide [*Organic chemistry*]
TAA .... Thoracic Aortic Aneurysm [*Cardiology*]
TAA .... Three-Axis Accelerometer
TAA .... Ticket Agents' Association [*British*]
TAA .... Tobacconists' Association of America   (EA)
TAA .... Total Aerospace Vehicle [*or Aircraft*] Authorization
TAA .... Total Aircraft Authorized   (MCD)
TAA .... Total Army Analysis   (AABC)
TAA .... Trade Adjustment Act
TAA .... Trade Adjustment Assistance [*Department of Commerce*]
TAA .... Trade Agreements Act
TAA .... Trans-American Airline
TAA .... Trans-Antarctic Association [*British*]
TAA .... Trans-Australia Airlines   (ADA)
TAA .... Transactions and Proceedings. American Philological Association [*A publication*]
TAA .... Transcript of Absentee's Account
TAA .... Transferable Account Area [*Business term*]   (DCTA)
TAA .... Transient Absorption Anisotropy [*Physics*]
TAA .... Transit Advertising Association [*Washington, DC*]   (EA)
TAA .... Transportation Association of America   (EA)
TAA .... Triamcinolone Acetonide [*Also, TA*] [*Synthetic steroidal drug*]
TAA .... Tumor-Associated Antigen [*Immunology*]
TAA .... Turbine Alternator Assembly
TAA .... Turkish-American Associations   (EA)
TAAA .... Teen-Age Assembly of America   (EA)
TAAA .... Thoracoabdominal Aortic Aneurysm [*Cardiology*]
TAAA .... Total Active Aircraft Authorized   (MCD)
TAAA .... Travelers Aid Association of America   (EA)
TAABS ..... [*The*] Army Automated Budget System
TAAC .... Target Area Advisory Council   (OICC)
TAAC .... Technology Assessment Advisory Council [*Washington, DC*]   (EGAO)
TAAC .... Trade Adjustment Assistance Center [*Department of Commerce*]
TAAC .... Training Ammunition Authorization Committee   (MCD)
TAAC .... Troubles d'Apprentissage - Association Canadienne [*Learning Disabilities Association of Canada*]   (EAIO)
TAACOM ... Theater Army Area Command   (AABC)
TAAD .... Task Assignment and Directive   (MCD)
TAAD .... Terrain Avoidance Accessory Device
TAADC ..... Theater Army Air Defense Command   (AABC)
TAADCOM ... Theater Army Air Defense Command   (AABC)
TAADS ...... [*The*] Army Authorization Document System
TAAF .... Test, Analyze, and Fix Program [*Navy*]   (MCD)
TAAF .... Thromboplastic Activity of Amniotic Fluid [*Medicine*]
TAAFA ..... Territorial Army and Air Force Association [*British military*]   (DMA)
TAAFFEE ... Tactical Air Against First and Following Enemy Echelons   (MCD)
TAAG .... Technical Analysis and Advisory Group [*Navy*]   (MCD)
TAAG .... Tropical Africa Advisory Group [*British Overseas Trade Board*]   (DS)
TAAGA ..... Transactions. American Association of Genito-Urinary Surgeons [*A publication*]
TAAI .... Total Active Aircraft Inventory   (MCD)
TAALODS ... [*The*] Army Automated Logistic Data System
TAALS ...... [*The*] American Association of Language Specialists   (EA)
TAALS ...... [*The*] Judge Advocate General Automated Army Legal System
TAALS ...... Tactical Army Aircraft Landing Systems
TAAM .... Tomahawk Air Field Attack Missile   (MCD)
TAAM .... Transportation Army Aviation Maintenance
Ta'an .... Ta'anith   (BJA)
TAAN .... Transworld Advertising Agency Network [*Englewood, CO*]   (EA)
TAANA ..... [*The*] American Association of Nurse Attorneys   (EA)
TAAOA ..... Transactions. American Academy of Ophthalmology and Oto-Laryngology [*A publication*]
TAAP .... Three-Axis Antenna Positioner

TAAP .... Trade Adjustment Assistance Program [*Department of Commerce*]
TAAP .... Transient Analysis Array Program
TAAPA ..... Transactions. Association of American Physicians [*A publication*]
TAAR .... Target Area Analysis-RADAR
TAAR .... Target Area Analysis-Repair   (MCD)
TAARS ..... [*The*] Army Ammunition Reporting System   (AABC)
TAAS .... Tactical Air Armament Study   (MCD)
TAAS .... Terminal Advanced Automation System [*Aviation*]
TAAS .... Thorotrast-Associated Angiosarcoma [*Oncology*]
TAAS .... Three-Axis Attitude Sensor   (IEEE)
TAAS .... Traffic Account Analysis System [*Military*] [*British*]
TAASC ...... [*The*] Association of American Sword Collectors   (EA)
TAASP ..... [*The*] Association for the Anthropological Study of Play   (EA)
TAB .... Airborne Tanker, Boom   (NVT)
TAB .... Tabaktueel Magazine [*A publication*]
TAB .... Tabella [*Tablet*] [*Pharmacy*]
TAB .... Table
Tab .... Tablet. A Weekly Newspaper and Review [*A publication*]
TAB .... Tabloncillo [*Race of maize*]
TAB .... Tabriz [*Iran*] [*Seismograph station code, US Geological Survey*]   (SEIS)
TAB .... Tabular Language [*Data processing*]   (IEEE)
TAB .... Tabulate   (AAG)
TAB .... Tactical Air Base   (AFM)
TAB .... Tactical Analysis Branch [*Military*]   (DNAB)
TAB .... Tamper Attempt Board
TAB .... Tape Automated Bonding [*Integrated circuit technology*]
TAB .... Target Acquisition Battalion [*Military*]
TAB .... Target Acquisition Battery   (MCD)
TAB .... Tax Anticipation Bill [*Obligation*] [*Department of the Treasury*]
TAB .... Technical Abstract Bulletin [*ASTIA*] [*A publication*]
TAB .... Technical Activities Board   (MCD)
TAB .... Technical Assistance Board [*United Nations*]
TAB .... Technology Assessment Board [*Washington, DC*]   (EGAO)
TAB .... Telecommunications Advisory Board
TAB .... Temporarily Able-Bodied
TAB .... Testing, Adjusting, and Balancing [*Heating and cooling technology*]
TAB .... Tetraaminobiphenyl [*Organic chemistry*]
T-AB .... Thai-American Business [*A publication*]   (IMH)
TAB .... Thermactor Air Bypass [*Automotive engineering*]
TAB .... Thiolacetoxybenzanilide [*Organic chemistry*]
TAB .... Title Announcement Bulletin
TAB .... Tobago [*Trinidad and Tobago*] [*Airport symbol*]   (OAG)
TAB .... Total Abstinence Brotherhood
TAB .... Traffic Audit Bureau [*Later, TABMM*]   (EA)
TAB .... Training Aid Bulletins [*Navy*]
TAB .... Transatlantic Broadcasting Co. [*In TV series "W.E.B."*]
TAB .... Transports Aeriens du Benin [*Benin*]   (EY)
TAB .... Truck, Airplane, Boat   (SAA)
TAB .... Typhoid, Paratyphoid A and B [*Vaccine*]
TABA .... [*The*] American Book Award [*Later, ABA*]
TABA .... Transcaribe [*Airline*] [*Colombia*]
TABA .... Transportes Aereos da Bacia Amazonica [*Airline*] [*Brazil*]
TABAMLN ... Tampa Bay Medical Library Network [*Library network*]
TABBSS .... Tactical Bare Base Support Study [*Air Force*]
TABC .... Total Aerobic Bacteria Counts
TABCASS ... Tactical Air Beacon Command and Surveillance System   (MCD)
TAB-CD .... Tabulating Card
TABE .... Tests of Adult Basic Education [*Achievement test*]
TABEL ...... Tabella [*Tablet*] [*Pharmacy*]   (ROG)
TABL .... Tropical Atlantic Biological Laboratory
TABLASER ... Trace Element Analyzer Based on LASER Ablation and Selectivity   (MCD)
Table Gov Order ... Table of Government Orders [*A publication*]
TableR .... La Table Ronde [*Paris*] [*A publication*]
TABMM ... Traffic Audit Bureau for Media Measurement   (EA)
TABP .... Tetraaminobenzophenone [*Organic chemistry*]
TABPM ..... Transportation Authorized in Accordance with BUPERS Manual, Article _____
TABPRD ... Tab Products Co. [*Associated Press abbreviation*]   (APAG)
TabR .... La Table Ronde [*Paris*] [*A publication*]
TABS .... Tabulator Stops   (AAG)
TABS .... Tactical Airborne Beacon System   (AFM)
TABS .... Tangential Bomb Suspension   (MCD)
TABS .... Team Approach to Better Schools [*National Education Association program*]
TABS .... Technical and Business Service
TABS .... Telephone Area Billing System
TABS .... Terminal Access to Batch Service [*Data processing*]   (BUR)
TABS .... Tests of Achievement in Basic Skills [*Educational test*]
TABS .... Theater Air Base Survivability [*Air Force*]
TABS .... Theological Abstracting and Bibliographical Services [*A publication*]
TABS .... Time Analysis and Billing System   (BUR)
TABS .... Total Automatic Banking System [*Trademark of Diebold, Inc.*]
TABS .... Transatlantic Book Service [*British*]

TABS......... TRIS-Acetate-Buffered Saline [*Clinical chemistry*]
TABSIM ... Tabulator Simulator
TABSOL ... Tabular Systems-Oriented Language [*General Electric Co.*]
        [*British*]
TABSTONE ... Target and Background Signal-to-Noise Evaluation   (MUGU)
TAB Tyres Access Batt ... TAB. Tyres, Accessories, Batteries [*A publication*]
TABU .... Typical Army Ball-Up [*Slang for a military muddle*]
Tabulae Biol ... Tabulae Biologicae [*A publication*]
Tabul Biol .. Tabulae Biologicae [*A publication*]
TABV......... Theater Air Base Vulnerability [*Air Force*]   (AFM)
TAB VEE .. Theater Air Base Vulnerability [*Air Force*]
TABWAG ... Tank Battle War Game
TABWDS.. Tactical Air Base Weather Dissemination System [*Air Force*]
TABWE.... Tactical Air Base Weather Element [*Air Force*]
TABWS..... Tactical Airborne Weather Stations   (MCD)
TABWX..... Tactical Air Base Weather
TAC .... [*The*] Aeroplane Collection [*British*]
TAC .... [*The*] Alien Critic [*A publication*]
TAC .... [*The*] Architects Collaborative [*Design firm*]
TAC .... [*The*] Athletics Congress [*Track*] [*An association*]
TAC .... Austin Community College, Austin, TX [*OCLC*
        symbol]   (OCLC)
Tac .... Tacitus [*First century AD*] [*Classical studies*]   (OCD)
TAC .... Tacloban [*Philippines*] [*Airport symbol*]   (OAG)
TAC .... Tacon [*Flamenco dance term*]
TAC .... Tactical   (AAG)
TAC .... Tactical Air Command [*Air Force*]
TAC .... Tactical Air Controller   (NVT)
TAC .... Tactical Air Coordinator   (SAA)
TAC .... Tactical Air Cover
TAC .... Tactical Assignment Console
TAC .... Tactical Coordinator   (NATG)
TAC .... Tacubaya [*Mexico*] [*Later, TEO*] [*Geomagnetic observatory*
        code]
TAC .... Tacubaya [*Mexico*] [*Seismograph station code, US Geological*
        Survey]   (SEIS)
TAC .... Tamoxifen, Adriamycin, Cyclophosphamide [*Antineoplastic*
        drug regimen]
TAC .... Tandycrafts, Inc. [*NYSE symbol*]   (SPSG)
TAC .... Target Acquisition Center [*Army*]
TAC .... Target Acquisition Console [*Military*]   (CAAL)
TAC .... Targeted Amortization-Class Bond [*Investment term*]
TAC .... Tax Court of the United States Reports [*A publication*]
TAC .... Team Activity Chart
TAC .... Technical Activities Committee   (SAA)
TAC .... Technical Advisory Center [*National Bureau of Standards*]
TAC .... Technical Advisory Committee
TAC .... Technical Applications Center [*Air Force*]
TAC .... Technical Area Coordinator
TAC .... Technical Assignment Control [*Nuclear energy*]   (NRCH)
TAC .... Technical Assistance Center [*State University College at*
        Plattsburgh] [*Research center*]   (RCD)
TAC .... Technical Assistance Center [*Telecommunications*]
TAC .... Technical Assistance Committee [*of the Economic and Social*
        Council of the United Nations]
TAC .... Technical Assistance Contract [*Nuclear energy*]   (NRCH)
TAC .... Technology Application Center [*University of New Mexico*]
        [*Albuquerque, NM*]
TAC .... Teleconference Association of Canada [*Toronto, ON*]
        [*Information service or system*]   (TSSD)
TAC .... Telemetry and Command   (MCD)
TAC .... TELENET Access Controller
TAC .... Television Advisory Committee [*British*]   (DEN)
TAC .... Temperature Altitude Chamber
TAC .... Terminal Access Controller [*Advanced Research Projects*
        Agency Network] [*DoD*]
TAC .... Terminal Area Chart [*FAA*]   (FAAC)
TAC .... Terrain Analysis Center [*Army*]   (RDA)
TAC .... Test Access Control [*Telecommunications*]   (TEL)
TAC .... Test Advisory Committee   (MUGU)
TAC .... Test of Auditory Comprehension
TAC .... Thai Airways Co. Ltd. [*Later, Thai Airways International*]
TAC .... Theatres Advisory Committee [*British*]
TAC .... Thermostatic Air Cleaner [*Automotive engineering*]
TAC .... Time Action Calendar [*Management*]
TAC .... Time-to-Amplitude Converter
TAC .... Time at Completion   (MCD)
TAC .... Tobacco Advisory Council [*British*]
TAC .... Total Alkaloids of Cinchona [*Medicine*]
TAC .... Total Allowable Catch [*Fishing regulation proposed by EEC*]
TAC .... Total Annualized Cost
TAC .... Total Average Cost   (KSC)
TAC .... Toxic Air Contaminant
TAC .... Tracking Accuracy Control
TAC .... Trade Agreements Committee [*An interagency committee of the*
        executive branch of US government] [*Terminated, 1963*]
TAC .... Traders and Contacts
TAC .... Trades Advisory Council [*British*]
TAC .... Training Alarm Controller
TAC .... Trans-Aminocrotonic Acid [*Also, TACA*] [*Organic chemistry*]

TAC .... TRANSAC [*Transistorized Automatic Computer*] Assembler
        Compiler
TAC .... Transformer Analog Computer
TAC .... Transistor-Assisted Circuit   (ADA)
TAC .... Transistorized Automatic Control
TAC .... Translations Activities Committee [*Special Libraries*
        Association]
TAC .... Translator, Assembler, Compiler
TAC .... Transonic Aerodynamic Characteristics
TAC .... Transportation Account Code [*Military*]   (AFM)
TAC .... Transportes, Aduanas, y Consignaciones SA [*Shipping*
        company] [*Spain*]   (EY)
TAC .... Trapped Air Cushion
TAC .... Traskei Airways Corp. [*South Africa*]   (EY)
TAC .... Travel Air Club   (EA)
TAC .... Travelcraft Ambassadors Club   (EA)
TAC .... Trialkoxycitrate [*Organic chemistry*]
TAC .... Triallyl Cyanurate [*Organic chemistry*]
TAC .... Triamcinolone Cream [*Anti-inflammatory steroid*]
TAC .... Trouble Analysis Chart
TAC .... True Airspeed Computer
TAC .... Turboalternator Compressor
TAC .... Type of Activity Code [*Military*]
TAC .... Type Address Code
TAC .... Types of Assistance Code [*Army*]
TACA .... [*The*] Association of Comedy Artists   (EA)
TAC(A)..... Tactical Air Coordinator (Airborne) [*Military*]   (NVT)
TACA .... Tactical Airborne Controller Aircraft [*Military*]   (CAAL)
TACA .... TELECOMS Authorities Cryptographic Algorithm [*Bell*
        Telephone encryption chip]
TACA .... Test of Adult College Aptitude
TACA .... Trans-Aminocrotonic Acid [*Also, TAC*] [*Organic chemistry*]
TACA .... Tucker Automobile Club of America   (EA)
TACAC..... Theater Army Civil Affairs Command   (AABC)
TACAD .... Tactical Advisory [*Military*]   (CAAL)
TACAD .... Traffic Alert and Collision Avoidance Detection [*Aviation*]
TACADE... Teachers' Advisory Council on Alcohol and Drug Education
        [*British*]
TACADS ... Tactical Automated Data Processing System
TAC/AFSC ... Tactical Air Command/Air Force Systems Command
TACAID.... Tactical Airborne Information Document   (NVT)
TACAIR.... Tactical Air [*Military*]   (AABC)
TACAIRLIFTSq ... Tactical Airlift Squadron [*Air Force*]
TACAIRLIFTTNGSq ... Tactical Airlift Training Squadron [*Air Force*]
TACAIR TED ... Tactical Air Threat Environment Description   (MCD)
TACAMO ... Take Charge and Move Out Aircraft [*Military*]
TACAN ... Tactical Air Navigation [*System*]
TACANCEN ... Tactical Air Navigation Control Center   (DNAB)
TACAN-DME ... Tactical Air Navigation Distance Measuring Equipment
TACAP...... Tactical Air Command Aircraft Profiler Capability [*Air Force*]
TACAV...... Linea Aerea TACA de Venezuela
TACAV...... Tactical Aviation Model
TACAWS .. [*The*] Army Counter-Air Weapons System
TACBOMBSq ... Tactical Bomb Squadron [*Air Force*]
TACC........ [*The*] Australian Comic Collector [*A publication*]   (APTA)
TACC........ Tactical Air Command Center [*Air Force*]   (NVT)
TACC........ Tactical Air Command, Central
TACC........ Tactical Air Command and Control [*Air Force*]
TACC........ Tactical Air Control Center [*Air Force*]
TACC........ Tactical Air Coordination Center [*Military*]   (CAAL)
TACC........ Thorotrast-Associated Cholangiocarcinoma [*Oncology*]
TACC........ Time Averaged Clutter Coherent   (MCD)
TACC........ Total Army Career Counselor [*Inservice recruiter*]   (INF)
TACCAR ... Time Averaged Clutter Coherent Airborne RADAR
TACCIMS ... Theater Automated Command and Control Information
        Management System   (MCD)
TACCO ..... Tactical Air Control Coordinator
TACCO ..... Tactical Control Officer [*Army*]   (AABC)
TACCOM ... Tactical Communications   (MCD)
TACCOMSIM ... Tactical Communications Simulator
TACCONSq ... Tactical Control Squadron [*Air Force*]
TACCOPS ... Tactical Air Control Center Operations   (NVT)
TAC COUNT ... Tactical Countermeasure
TACCP...... Tactical Command Post [*Army*]
TACCS ...... Tactical Air Command Control System   (MCD)
TACCS ...... Tactical Air Control Center Squadron
TACCS ...... Tactical Airborne Command, Control, and Surveillance
TACCS ...... Tactical Army Combat Service Support Computer System
TACCSF.... Theater Air Command and Control Simulator Facility [*Air*
        Force]
TACCS-K .. Theater Automated Command and Control System - Korea
TACCTA ... Tactical Commander's Terrain Analysis [*Military*]   (AABC)
TAC-D....... Tactical Deception   (MCD)
TACD .... Transport and Communications Division, United Nations
        ESCAP [*Economic and Social Commission for Asia and*
        the Pacific] [*Thailand*]   (EAIO)
TACDA ..... [*The*] American Civil Defense Association   (EA)
TACDACS ... Target Acquisition and Data Collection System
TACDAS... Target Acquisition and Data Collection System
TAC D & E ... Tactical Development and Evaluation [*Military*]   (CAAL)
TACDEN... Tactical Data Entry Unit [*Army*]

TACDEW ... Tactical Advanced Combat Direction and Electronic Warfare (MCD)
TACDEW/EGCS ... Tactical Advanced Combat Direction and Electronic Warfare Environmental Generation Control System [*Navy*]
TACDIFINSPRO ... Temporary Active Duty under Instruction in a Flying Status Involving ProficiencyFlying [*Navy*] (DNAB)
TACDIFPRO ... Temporary Active Duty in a Flying Status Involving Proficiency Flying [*Navy*] (DNAB)
TACE......... Tactical Air Coordination Element
TAC-E .... Tactical Emergency [*Army*]
TACE......... Talos Conversion Equipment (MCD)
TACE......... Tri-para-anisylchloroethylene [*Estrogen*]
TACED...... Tank Appended Crew Evaluation Device (MCD)
TACELECRON ... Tactical Electronic Warfare Squadron [*Air Force*] (DNAB)
TACELECRONDET ... Tactical Electronic Warfare Squadron Detachment [*Air Force*] (DNAB)
TACELIS .. Tactical Communications Emitter Location and Identification System [*Army*] (MCD)
TACES ...... Tactical Electronics Squadron
TACESS.... Tactical Communications-Electronics Simulation and Support System
TACEST.... Tactical Test [*Military*] (NVT)
TACEVAL ... Tactical Evaluation (MCD)
TACEXEC ... Tactical Executive
TACFAX .... Tactical Digital Facsimile Equipment (MCD)
TACFDC .... Tactical Fire Direction Center [*Army*] (AABC)
TACFIRE ... Tactical Fire [*Military*]
TACFO...... TASAMS [*The Army Supply and Maintenance System*] Coordination Field Office (AABC)
TACFTRRSq ... Tactical Fighter Replacement Squadron [*Air Force*]
TACG .... Tactical Air Control Group [*Military*]
TACG .... Tactical Group [*Military*]
TACGP ...... Tactical Air Control Group [*Military*]
TACGRU... Tactical Air Control Group [*Military*] (NVT)
TACH........ Athens Community Hospital, Athens, TN [*Library symbol*] [*Library of Congress*] (LCLS)
TACH .... Tachometer (AAG)
TACHA ..... Tennessee Automated Clearing House Association
TACHO..... Tachometer (DSUE)
TACHY ..... Tachycardia [*Cardiology*] (AAMN)
TACI........ Test Access Control Interface [*Telecommunications*] (TEL)
TACIMPS ... Tactical Integrated Mission Planning Station (MCD)
TACINTEL ... Tactical Intelligence Information Exchange System (NVT)
TACIT .... Technical Advisory Committee on Inland Transport
TACIT .... Time-Authenticated Cryptographic Identity Transmission [*Military*]
TACJAM .. Tactical Jamming
TACL........ Tactical Air Command Letter [*Air Force*]
TACL........ Tank-Automotive Concepts Laboratory [*Army*] (RDA)
TACL........ Theater Authorized Consumption List [*Army*] (AABC)
TACL........ Time and Cycle Log [*NASA*] (KSC)
TACLAND ... Tactical Instrument Landing (MCD)
TACLET.... Tactical Law Enforcement Teams [*Coast Guard*]
TACLO...... Tactical Air Command Liaison Officer [*Air Force*] (FAAC)
TACLOG... Tactical-Logistical [*Army*] (AABC)
TACLOG GP ... Tactical-Logistics Control Group [*Military*]
TACM .... Tactical Air Command Manual [*Air Force*]
TACM .... Transit Air Cargo Manifest
TACMAN ... Tactical Manuals [*Aircraft*] (MCD)
TACMAR ... Tactical Multifunction Array RADAR [*Air Force*]
TACMAS .. Tactical Computer Modeling Analysis and Simulation (SSD)
TACMIS ... Tactical Management Information System [*Army*] (RDA)
TACMS .... Tactical Missile System [*Provisional*] [*Army*] (RDA)
TACNAV... Tactical Navigation System
TACNAVMOD ... Tactical/Navigational Modernization [*Navy*]
TACNOTE ... Tactical Notice (NVT)
TACO .... Good Taco Corp. [*NASDAQ symbol*] (NQ)
TACO .... Tactical Coordinator (NG)
TACO .... Tamoxifen, Adriamycin, Cyclophosphamide, Oncovin [*Vincristine*] [*Antineoplastic drug regimen*]
TACO .... Test and Checkout Operations [*NASA*] (NASA)
TAC-OA .... Tactical Air Command Office of Operations Analysis [*Langley Air Force Base, VA*]
TACOC ..... Tactical Air Control Operation Center
TACODA .. Target Coordinate Data (IEEE)
TACOL...... Thinned Aperture Computed Lens (IEEE)
TACOM .... Tactical Area Communications System (MCD)
TACOM .... Tactical Communications (AFM)
TACOM .... Tank-Automotive Command [*Army*] [*Warren, MI*] (MCD)
TACOMM ... Tactical Communications [*Military*] (AABC)
TACOMPLAN ... Tactical Communications Plan [*NATO*]
TACOMSAT ... Tactical Communications Satellite [*Also, TACSAT*] [*DoD*]
TACON..... Tactical Control [*Military*] (CAAL)
TACOPNSSq ... Tactical Operations Squadron [*Air Force*]
TACOPS ... Tactical Air Combat Operations Staff (MCD)
TACOR ..... Threat Assessment and Control Receiver [*Air Force*]
TACOS...... Tactical Air Combat Operations Staff
TACOS...... Tactical Air Combat Simulation (NATG)
TACOS...... Tactical Airborne Countermeasures or Strike [*Air Force*]

TACOS...... Tactical Communications System
TACOS...... Talos Adaptable Computer System [*Navy*]
TACOS...... Tool for Automatic Conversion of Operational Software
TACOS...... Travel Agents Computer Society (EA)
TACOSS ... Tactical Container Shelter System [*Rockwell International Corp.*]
TACP........ Tactical Air Command Pamphlet [*Air Force*]
TACP........ Tactical Air Command Post [*Air Force*] (MCD)
TACP........ Tactical Air Control Party [*Air Force*]
TACP........ Tactical Air Control Point
TACP........ Technical Analysis of Cost Proposals [*DoD*]
TACPACS ... Tactical Packet Switching System [*Army*] (RDA)
TACPOL... Tactical Procedure Oriented Language [*Data processing*] (CSR)
TACPOL... Tactile Procedure-Oriented Language (CSR)
TACR........ TACAN [*Tactical Air Navigation*] Collocated with VOR [*Very-High-Frequency Omnidirectional Range*] (FAAC)
TACR........ Tactical Air Command Regulation [*Air Force*]
TAC/R...... Tactical Reconnaissance
TACR........ Time and Cycle Record [*NASA*] (KSC)
TAC/RA ... TACAN [*Tactical Air Navigation*] RADAR Altimeter (NASA)
TACRAC... Tactical Warfare Research Advisory Committee [*Military*] (RDA)
TACRAPS ... Tactical Range Prediction System
TACREACT ... Tactical Reconnaissance Reaction Aircraft (MCD)
TACREDD ... Tactical Readiness Drill [*Military*] (DNAB)
TAC RISE ... Tactical Reconnaissance Intelligence System Enhancement [*Air Force*]
TACRON .. Tactical Air Control Squadron [*Military*]
TACRV...... Tracked Air-Cushion Research Vehicle [*DoD*]
TACS........ Auxiliary Crane Ship [*Navy symbol*]
TACS........ Tactical Air Control System [*Air Force*]
TACS........ Technical Assignment Control System [*Nuclear energy*] (NRCH)
TACS........ Telemetry and Command System (MCD)
TACS........ Test Assembly Conditioning Station [*Nuclear energy*] (NRCH)
TACS........ Theater Area Communications Systems [*Military*]
TACS........ Theater Army Communications System (MCD)
TACS........ Thruster Attitude Control System [*NASA*]
TACS........ Total Access Communications System [*Commercial firm*] [*British*]
TACSAT ... Tactical Communications Satellite [*Also, TACOMSAT*] [*DoD*]
TACSATCOM ... Tactical Satellite Communications [*Military*]
TACSI ...... Tactical Air Communications [*or Control*] System Improvements [*Air Force*] (MCD)
TACSIM ... Tactical Simulation
TACSOP ... Tactical Standing Operating Procedure [*Army*] (INF)
TACSQ ..... Tactical Air Control Squadron [*Air Force*]
TACSS....... Tactical Schoolship [*Navy*] (NVT)
TACS/TADS ... Tactical Air Control System/Tactical Air Defense System
TACSYR ... Tactical Communications Systems Requirements (MCD)
TACT........ [*The*] Association of Corporate Trustees [*British*] (EAIO)
Tact........... Tactica [*of Arrian*] [*Classical studies*] (OCD)
TACT........ Tactical
TACT........ Tactical Air Control Training
TACT........ Tactical Transport [*Aircraft*]
TACT........ Television Action Committee for Today and Tomorrow [*Later, American Council for Better Broadcasts*] (AEBS)
TACT........ Terminal Activated Channel Test
TACT........ Tories Against Cruise and Trident [*Missiles*] [*British*] (DI)
TACT........ Transact International, Inc. [*NASDAQ symbol*] (NQ)
TACT........ Transactional Analysis Control Technique [*Training program*] [*American Airlines*]
TACT........ Transistor and Component Tester
TACT........ Transonic Aircraft Technology [*Program*] [*NASA and Air Force*]
TACT........ Truth about Civil Turmoil (EA)
TAC/TADS ... Tactical Air Control/Tactical Air Defense System [*Military*] (CAAL)
TACTAN... Tactical Air Control and Navigation
TACTAS ... Tactical Towed Array Sensor [*Formerly, ETAS*] [*Navy*]
TACTAS ... Tactical Towed Array SONAR [*Navy*]
TACTASS ... Tactical Tone and Acoustic Surveillance System [*Military*] (CAAL)
TACTEC ... Tactical Technology Information Analysis Center [*Columbus, OH*] [*DoD*] (GRD)
TACTEC ... Totally Advanced Communications Technology
TACTECS ... Tables and Charts through Extended Character Sets [*Data processing*]
TACTIC .... Technical Advisory Committee to Influence Congress [*Federation of American Scientists*]
TACTICS.. Technical Assistance Consortium to Improve College Services [*Defunct*] (EA)
TACTL...... Tactical (AAG)
TACTLASS ... Tactical Towed Array Surveillance System [*Military*] (MCD)
TAC T MR ... Tactical Transport Medium Range [*Aircraft*]
TACTOOL ... Tactical [*Software*] Tools
TACTRAGRULANT ... Tactical Training Group, Atlantic [*Military*] (DNAB)
TACTRAGRUPAC ... Tactical Training Group, Pacific [*Military*] (DNAB)
TACTRUST ... [*The*] Athletics Congress/USA Trust Fund
TACTS ...... Tactical Aircrew Combat Training System (NVT)

TACTS/ACMI ... Tactical Aircrew Combat Training System/Air Combat Maneuvering Instrumentation (MCD)
TAC T SR ... Tactical Transport Short Range [*Aircraft*]
TACUDC... Tests of Agrochemicals and Cultivars [*A publication*]
TAC/USA ... [*The*] Athletics Congress/USA (EA)
TACV......... Tracked Air-Cushion Vehicle [*High-speed ground transportation*]
TACVA...... Tactical Vulnerability Assessment [*Military*] (MCD)
TACVA/CEWIS ... Tactical Communications Vulnerability Assessment of Combat Electronics Warfare Intelligence System (MCD)
TACWE..... Tactical Weather System (MCD)
TAD........... Air Traffic Control Tower, Approach Control, and Departure Control Facility [*Aviation*] (FAAC)
TAD........... Airborne Tanker, Drogue (NVT)
TAD........... [*The*] Armchair Detective [*A publication*]
TAD........... Tactical Action Display [*SAGE*]
TAD........... Tactical Air Defense (MCD)
TAD........... Tactical Air Direction [*Military*]
TAD........... Tactical Atomic Demolition [*Munitions*] [*Obsolete*] [*Military*] (NG)
TAD........... Tadiran Limited [*NYSE symbol*] (SPSG)
TAD........... Tadotu [*Japan*] [*Seismograph station code, US Geological Survey*] [*Closed*] (SEIS)
TAD........... Target Acquisition Data
TAD........... Target Activation Date (AAG)
TAD........... Target Area Designator [*Air Force*]
TAD........... Target Audience Description [*Army*]
TAD........... Task Assignment Directive (KSC)
TAD........... Task Assignment Drawing (MCD)
TAD........... Tax Advisor [*A publication*]
TAD........... Technical Acceptance Date (AAG)
TAD........... Technical Analysis Division [*National Bureau of Standards*]
TAD........... Technical Approach Demonstration
TAD........... Technical Approval Demonstration (AAG)
TAD........... Technology Area Description (MCD)
TAD........... Technology Availability Date (MCD)
TAD........... Telecommunications Automation Directorate [*Army*] (RDA)
TAD........... Telemetry Analog to Digital [*Information converter*]
TAD........... Telephone Answering Device
TAD........... Television Advertising Duty
TAD........... Temperature and Dew Point (NASA)
TAD........... Temporary Additional Duty [*Military*]
TAD........... Temporary Attached Duty
TAD........... Terminal Address Designator
TAD........... Test and Development (MCD)
TAD........... Thermactor Air Diverter [*Automotive engineering*]
TAD........... Thermal Analysis Data
TAD........... Thioguanine, ara-C, Daunomycin [*Daunorubicin*] [*Antineoplastic drug regimen*]
TAD........... Thomas Aloysius Dorgan [*Satirical cartoonist*]
TAD........... Thoracic Asphyxiant Dystrophy [*Medicine*] (MAE)
TAD........... Throw Away Detector [*Space shuttle*] [*NASA*]
TAD........... Thrust-Augmented Delta [*NASA*]
TAD........... Time Available for Delivery (CET)
TAD........... Tobyhanna Army Depot, Library, Tobyhanna, PA [*OCLC symbol*] (OCLC)
TAD........... Tooele Army Depot [*Utah*]
TAD........... Top Assembly Drawing
TAD........... Toward Affective Development [*Educational tool*]
TAD........... Traffic Accident Data [*Project*] [*National Safety Council*]
TAD........... Trailing-Arm-Drive
TAD........... Training Aids Division [*Navy*]
TAD........... Traitement Automatique des Donnees [*Automatic Data Processing*] [*French*]
TAD........... Transaction Application Drive [*Computer Technology, Inc.*]
TAD........... Traveling Around Drunk
TAD........... Trinidad [*Colorado*] [*Airport symbol*] [*Obsolete*] (OAG)
TAD........... Trio Archean Developments [*Vancouver Stock Exchange symbol*]
TAD........... Turk Arkeoloji Dergisi [*Ankara*] [*A publication*]
TAD........... Twin and Add (SAA)
TADAAS... TEMPEST Automated Data Acquisition and Analysis System
TADAC ..... Therapeutic Abortion, Dilation, Aspiration, Curettage [*Medicine*] (MAE)
TADAR ..... Tactical Area Defense Alerting RADAR (MCD)
TADARS... Target Acquisition/Designation Aerial Reconnaissance System (MCD)
TADAS...... Tactical Air Defense Alerting System [*Army*]
TADC .... Tactical Air Direction Center [*Military*]
TADC .... Training and Distribution Center [*Navy*]
TADD .... Tangential Abrasive Dehulling Device [*for grains*]
TADD .... Target Alert Data Display Set (MCD)
TADD .... Termite and Ant Detection Dog [*In TADD Services Corp.*]
TADD .... Truckers Against Drunk Drivers (EA)
TADDS ..... Target Alert Data Display Set (RDA)
TADE .... Tetraaminodiphenylether [*Organic chemistry*]
TADF........ Thermally Activated Delayed Fluorescence [*Analytical chemistry*]
TADF........ Thomas A. Dooley Foundation [*Later, Dooley Foundation/ Intermed-USA*]
TADGC ..... Tactical Air Designation Grid System [*Tactical Air Command*]

TADI .... Time Assigned Data Interpolation (HGAA)
TADIC....... Telemetry Analog-Digital Information Converter
TADIL....... Tactical Data Information Link [*Tactical Air Command*]
TADIL....... Tactical Digital Information Link
TADIL-J ... Tactical Data Information Link-JTIDS [*Joint Tactical Information Distribution System*] [*DoD*]
TADIL-J ... Tactical Digital Information Link - Joint
TADILS..... Tactical Automatic Data Information Links (MCD)
Tadiran ..... Tadiran Ltd. [*Associated Press abbreviation*] (APAG)
TADIXS .... Tactical Data Information Exchange Subsystem
TAD J........ Technical Aid to the Disabled Journal [*A publication*] (APTA)
TADJET.... Transport Air Drop and Jettison Test [*Air Force, Army*]
TADLR...... Tooling Automated Direct Labor Reporting (MCD)
TADM .... Tactical Atomic Demolition Munitions [*Obsolete*] [*Military*] (AABC)
TADO....... Tactical Airlift Duty Officer (AFM)
TADOR .... Table Data Organization and Reductions
TADP .... Tactical Air Direction Post [*Military*]
TAD/P....... Terminal Area Distribution Processing
TADP .... Toronto Anti-Draft Programme [*Defunct*] (EA)
TA3DPT.... Twitchell-Allen Three-Dimensional Personality Test [*Psychology*]
TADR .... Tabulated Drawing (MSA)
TADR .... Test Answer Document Reader
TADREPS ... Tactical Data Replay System (NVT)
TADRS...... Target Acquisition/Designation Reconnaissance System (MCD)
TADS........ Tactical Air Defense Systems (RDA)
TADS........ Tactical Automatic Digital Switch [*Military*]
TADS........ Target Acquisition Designation Sight [*Army*]
TADS........ Target Acquisition and Designation System (MCD)
TADS........ Target and Activity Display System [*Military*]
TADS........ Target Designation System [*Navy*]
TADS........ Technical Assistance Data
TADS........ Teletypewriter Automatic Dispatch System
TADS........ Test and Debug System (HGAA)
TADS........ Thermal Analysis Data Station
TADS........ Tracking and Display System
TADS........ Type [*Command*] Automated Data System [*Navy*]
TADSO ..... Tactical Digital Systems Office [*Navy*] (MCD)
TADS/PNVS ... Target Acquisition Designation System/Pilot Night Vision System [*Army*] (RDA)
TADSS...... Tactical Automatic Digital Switching System
TADSYS... Turbine Automated Design System
TADYL...... Tom Dooley Youth League [*Defunct*]
TadzhSSR ... Tadzhik Soviet Socialist Republic
TAE .... Tactical Aeromed Evacuation (CINC)
TAE .... Taegu [*South Korea*] [*Seismograph station code, US Geological Survey*] [*Closed*] (SEIS)
TAE .... Tannic Acid Equivalent [*Analytical chemistry*]
TAE .... Test and Evaluation (MCD)
TAE .... Textes Arameens d'Egypte [*A publication*] (BJA)
TAE .... Transantarctic Expedition (ADA)
TAE .... Transcatheter Arterial Embolization [*Medicine*]
TAE .... Transoceanic Airborne Environment
TAE .... Tris-Acetate-EDTA [*Ethylenediaminetetraacetate*] [*Buffer*]
TAEA........ Tangipahoa & Eastern [*AAR code*]
TAEAS...... Tactical ASW [*Antisubmarine Warfare*] Environmental Acoustic Support [*Navy*] (CAAL)
TAeB......... Tuebinger Aegyptologische Beitraege [*A publication*]
TAEC........ Thailand Atomic Energy Commission for Peace
TAEC........ Turkish Atomic Energy Commission
TAED .... Tetraacetylethylenediamine [*Laundry bleaching agent*]
TAEDA Newsl ... TAEDA [*Technology Assessment of Energy Development in Appalachia*] Newsletter [*United States*] [*A publication*]
TAEDP...... Total Army Equipment Distribution Program (AABC)
TAEDS...... Total Army Equipment Distribution System (MCD)
TAEG .... Training Analysis and Evaluation Group [*Navy*]
TAEG .... Training and Evaluation Group [*Navy*] (MCD)
TAEM .... Terminal Area Energy Management [*NASA*] (NASA)
TAEMS..... Transportable Automated Electromagnetic Measurement System (MCD)
TAEO .... Test Article Engineering Order (MCD)
TAER........ Time, Azimuth, Elevation, and Range [*Aerospace*]
TAERS ...... [*The*] Army Equipment Record System [*Later, TAMMS*]
TAES........ Tactical Aeromedical Evacuation System
TAES........ Texas Agricultural Experiment Station [*Texas A & M University*] [*Research center*] (RCD)
TAETGM ... Test and Evaluation Task Group Manager (MCD)
TAF........... Aerodrome Forecast [*Aviation*] (FAAC)
TAF........... Arnold Engineering Development Center, Arnold Air Force Station, TN [*OCLC symbol*] (OCLC)
TAF........... [*The*] Asia Foundation (EA)
TAF........... Oran-Tafaraoui [*Algeria*] [*Airport symbol*] (OAG)
TAF........... Stores Ship [*Military Sea Transportation Service*] (CINC)
TAF........... Tactical Air Force
TAF........... Tactical Area Files [*Military*] (CAAL)
TAF........... Taforalt [*Morocco*] [*Seismograph station code, US Geological Survey*] (SEIS)
TAF........... Task Analysis Form
TAF........... Technology Access Fund [*Chrysler Corp.*]

TAF........... Terminal Aerodrome Forecast [*Also, TAFOR*]
TAF........... Test, Analyze, Fix   (MCD)
TAF........... Third Air Force
TAF........... Thousand Acre-Feet [*Measurement*]
TAF........... Top of Active Fuel [*Nuclear energy*]   (NRCH)
TAF........... Toxoid-Antitoxin Floccules [*Immunology*]
TAF........... Traditional Acupuncture Foundation   (EA)
TAF........... Training Analysis and Feedback   (MCD)
TAF........... Transaction Facility
TAF........... Trim after Forming   (MSA)
TAF........... Trypsin-Aldehyde-Fuchsin [*Medicine*]   (MAE)
TAF........... Tuberculin Albumose-Frei [*Albumose-Free Tuberculin*] [*German*] [*Medicine*]
TAF........... Tumor-Angiogenesis Factor [*Medicine*]
TAF........... Turkish Air Force   (NATG)
TAFA........ Territorial and Auxiliary Forces Association [*British military*]   (DMA)
TAFAD...... Task Force Air Defense   (MUGU)
TAFB........ Travis Air Force Base [*California*]
TAFB........ Tyndall Air Force Base [*Florida*]
TAFCSD.... Total Active Federal Commissioned Service to Date [*Military*]
TAFD........ Test for Auditory Figure-Ground Discrimination
TAFDS...... Tactical Airfield Fuel Dispensing System   (NG)
TAFE........ Telemetry Auto Following Equipment
TAFE........ Transverse Alternating Field Electrophoresis
TAFEQ...... TAFE [*New South Wales Department of Technical and Further Education*] Quarterly [*A publication*]   (APTA)
TAFF........ Thermally Activated Flux Flow [*Physics*]
TAFF........ Timer, Actuator, Fin, Fuze   (DWSG)
TAFFE....... Tactical Air Against First and Follow-On Eschelon   (MCD)
Taffie........ Technologically Advanced Family [*Lifestyle classification*]
TAFFS...... [*The*] Army Functional Files System
TAFFTS.... [*The*] Army Functional Files Test System   (MCD)
TAFG........ Two-Axis Free Gyro   (AAG)
TAFHQ...... Tactical Air Force Headquarters
TAFI........ Technical Association of the Fur Industry
TAFI......... Turnaround Fault Isolation [*Aviation*]
TAFIES..... Tactical Air Forces Intelligence Exploitation System
TAFIG....... Tactical Air Forces Interoperability Group [*Air Force*]
TAFIIS...... Tactical Air Force Integrated Information Systems   (MCD)
TAFIM...... Turnaround Fault Isolation Manual
TAFIN....... Tactical Air Force Initiative   (MCD)
TAFIS........ TCATA [*TRADOC Combined Arms Test Activity*] Automated Field Instrumentation System   (MCD)
TAFIS....... TEXCOM [*Test and Experimentation Command*] Automated Field Instrumentation System[*Army*]
TAFMM.... Tactical Air Force Maintenance Management   (MCD)
TAFMS ..... Total Active Federal Military Service   (DNAB)
TAFMSD .. Total Active Federal Military Service to Date
TAFNORNOR ... Allied Tactical Air Force, Northern Norway [*NATO*]
TAFO........ Theater Accounting and Finance Office [*Military*]   (AFM)
TAFOR...... Terminal Aerodrome Forecast [*Also, TAF*]
TAFPD...... Technical Assessment and Fraud Prevention Division [*Environmental Protection Agency*]   (GFGA)
TAFR........ Total Age-Specific Fertility Rate [*Population studies*]
TAFR........ Trouble and Failure Report [*Army*]
TAFROC.... Tactical Air Force Required Operational Capability   (MCD)
TAFS........ Stores Ship
TAFS......... Training Aid Feasibility Studies   (AAG)
TAFSA...... Transactions. American Fisheries Society [*A publication*]
TAFSD...... Technical Report. AFWAL-TR. United States Air Force Wright Aeronautical Laboratories [*A publication*]
TAFSEA.... Technical Applications for Southeast Asia [*Air Force*]
TAFSEG.... Tactical Air Force Systems Engineering Group   (MCD)
TAFSONOR ... Allied Tactical Air Force, South Norway [*NATO*]   (NATG)
TAFSUS.... Turkish American Friendship Society of the United States   (EA)
TAFT........ Technical Assistance Field Team   (MCD)
TAFUBAR ... Things Are Fouled Up Beyond All Recognition [*Military slang*] [*Bowdlerized version*]
TAFVER ... Terminal Aerodrome Forecast Verification
TAFX........ Tapping Fixture
TAFY........ American Theatre Arts for Youth   (EA)
TAG .... [*The*] Acronym Generator [*An RCA computer program*]
TAG .... [*The*] Acrylonitrile Group   (EA)
TAG .... [*The*] Adjutant General [*Army*]
TAG .... Airborne Tanker, General   (NVT)
TAG .... American Group of CPA Firms [*Lombard, IL*]   (EA)
TAG .... [*The*] Association for the Gifted   (EA)
TAG .... [*The*] Attorneys Group   (EA)
TAG .... [*The*] Audiotex Group [*Princeton, NJ*] [*Telecommunications service*]   (TSSD)
TAG .... Orion Air, Inc. [*Chapel Hill, NC*] [*FAA designator*]   (FAAC)
TAG .... Tactical Airlift Group   (MCD)
TAG .... Tactical Analysis Group [*Military*]   (CAAL)
tag .... Tagalog [*MARC language code*] [*Library of Congress*]   (LCCP)
TAG .... Tagbilaran [*Philippines*] [*Army*]   (OAG)
Tag .... Tagoro [*A publication*]
TAG .... Target Attaching Globulin [*Medicine*]   (AAMN)
TAG .... Target Attitude Group [*Advertising*]
TAG .... Tavern and Guild Association [*Division of Homophile Effort for Legal Protection*]   (EA)

TAG .... Taxi Air Group, Inc.
TAG .... Technical Air-to-Ground   (NASA)
TAG .... Technical Art Group
TAG .... Technical Assessment Group [*Navy*]
TAG .... Technical Assistance Grant
TAG .... Technical Assistance Group [*NASA*]   (KSC)
TAG .... Technical Assistance Guides   (OICC)
TAG .... Technician Affiliate Group [*of American Chemical Society*]
TAG .... Telecomputer Applications Group
TAG .... Telegraphist Air Gunner [*British military*]   (DMA)
TAG .... Telemetry System Analysis Group
TAG .... Tennessee, Alabama & Georgia Railway Co. [*AAR code*]
TAG .... Terminal Applications Group, Inc.
TAG .... Terminating and Grounding
TAG .... Test Analysis Guide
TAG .... Test Assembly Grapple [*Nuclear energy*]   (NRCH)
TAG .... Test Automation Growth
TAG .... Texas A & M University at Galveston, Galveston, TX [*OCLC symbol*]   (OCLC)
TAG .... Thomson Advisory Group [*NYSE symbol*]   (SPSG)
TAG .... Time Arrive Guarantee   (AAG)
TAG .... Time Automated Grid
TAG .... Training Aids Guide [*Navy*]
TAG .... Trans-Atlantic Geotraverse [*Project*] [*National Oceanic and Atmospheric Administration*]
TAG .... Transient Analysis Generator
TAG .... Transport Air Group [*Joint Army, Navy, and Marine Corps*]
TAG .... Trauma Action Group   (EA)
TAG .... Tree-Adjoining Grammar [*Artificial intelligence*]
TAG .... Triacylglycerol [*Food technology*]
TAGA .... Technical Association of the Graphic Arts   (EA)
TAGA .... Telegraphist Air Gunner's Association [*Navy*] [*British*]
TAGA .... Trace Atmospheric Gas Analyser [*Instrument*]
TAGA .... Travel Agents Guild of America   (EA)
TAGAMET ... Antagonist Cimetidine [*Ulcer medicine manufactured by SmithKline Beckman Corp.*]
TAGBDUSA ... [*The*] Adjutant General's Board, United States Army
Tagber Dt Akad Landw-Wiss Berl ... Tagungsberichte. Deutsche Akademie der Landwirtschaftswissenschaften zu Berlin [*A publication*]
TAGC .... Tripped Automatic Gain Control
TAGCEN... [*The*] Adjutant General Center [*Army*]   (AABC)
TAGER...... [*The*] Association for Graduate Education and Research
TAGEX...... Travel at Government Expense [*Aviation*]   (FAAC)
TAGI .... Terminal Applications Group, Inc. [*NASDAQ symbol*]   (NQ)
TAGIS .... Tracking and Ground Instrumentation System   (DNAB)
TAGIU ...... Tracking and Ground Instrumentation Unit [*NASA*]
TAGLA...... Tropical Agriculture [*A publication*]
TAGM ...... Range Instrumentation Ship
TAGM ...... Table and Art Glassware Manufacturers [*Defunct*]   (EA)
Tag Muellerei-Technol Ber ... Tagung ueber die Muellerei-Technologie. Bericht [*A publication*]
TAGN........ Triaminoguanidine Nitrate [*Propellant ingredient*]
TAGO........ [*The*] Adjutant General's Office [*Army*]
TAGO........ Tago, Inc. [*NASDAQ symbol*]   (NQ)
TAGOTA .. TACFIRE [*Tactical Fire*] Ad Hoc Group on Testing and Analysis   (MCD)
TAGRDCUSA ... [*The*] Adjutant General's Research and Development Command, United States Army
TAGS........ FBM [*Fleet Ballistic Missile*] Support Ship
TAGS........ Tactical Aircraft Guidance System [*Air Force*]
TAGS........ Teledyne Airborne Geophysical Services
TAGS........ Text and Graphics System [*or Subsystem*]   (NASA)
TAGS........ Theater Air-Ground Warfare Simulation   (MCD)
TAGS........ Tower Automated Ground Surveillance System   (MCD)
TAGSRWC .. [*The*] Andy Griffith Show Rerun Watchers Club   (EA)
TAGSUSA ... [*The*] Adjutant General's School [*United States*], Army
TAGUA ..... Transactions. American Geophysical Union [*A publication*]
Tagungsber Akad Landwirtschaftswiss Dtsch Demokr Repub ... Tagungsbericht. Akademie der Landwirtschaftswissenschaften der Deutschen Demokratischen Republik [*A publication*]
Tagungsber Deut Akad Landwirt Wiss Berlin ... Tagungsberichte. Deutsche Akademie der Landwirtschaftswissenschaften zu Berlin [*A publication*]
Tagungsber Ges Inn Med DDR ... Tagungsbericht. Gesellschaft fuer Innere Medizin der DDR [*A publication*]
TAH........... [*The*] American Hispanist [*A publication*]
TAH........... Hospital Ship
Tah............ Taehti [*Record label*] [*Finland*]
TAH............ Tahiti [*Society Islands*] [*Seismograph station code, US Geological Survey*] [*Closed*]   (SEIS)
TAH........... Tanna Island [*Vanuata*] [*Airport symbol*]   (OAG)
TAH........... Tell Abu Huwam   (BJA)
TAH........... Total Abdominal Hysterectomy [*Medicine*]
TAH........... Total Artificial Heart
TAH........... Transabdominal Hysterectomy [*Medicine*]   (MAE)
TAHA........ Tapered Aperture Horn Antenna
TAHCD..... Taehan Ankwa Hakhoe Chapchi [*A publication*]
TAHE........ Thin Line Array Handling Equipment   (DWSG)
TAHFDQ .. Allan Hancock Foundation. Technical Reports [*A publication*]

TAHOE.....	TOW Against Helicopter Operational Equipment (RDA)
TAHOP.....	Tank/Attack Helicopter Operational Performance (MCD)
TAHQ.......	Theater Army Headquarters
TAI	National Organization for Travelers Aid Societies [*Also known as Travelers Aid International*] (EA)
TAI	T. A. Informations [*Formerly, Traduction Automatique*] [*A publication*]
TAI	Tactical Area of Interest [*Military*] (INF)
TAI	Tainan [*Republic of China*] [*Seismograph station code, US Geological Survey*] (SEIS)
Tai.............	Taiwan
TAI	Taiz [*Yemen Arab Republic*] [*Airport symbol*] (OAG)
TAI	Target Area of Interest [*Army intelligence matrix*] (INF)
TAI	Tax Management International Journal [*A publication*]
TAI	Teacher Attitude Inventory [*Teacher evaluation test*]
TAI	Temps Atomique International [*International Atomic Time*] [*Telecommunications*]
TAI	Test Anxiety Inventory [*Educational test*]
TAI	Thai Airways International (MCD)
TAI	Therapy Attitude Inventory [*Test*] [*Psychology*]
TAI	Time-to-Autoignition [*NASA*] (KSC)
TAI	Total Active Inventory (MCD)
TAI	Total Aircraft Inventory
TAI	Traditionally Administered Instruction (BUR)
TAI	Transamerica Income Shares, Inc. [*NYSE symbol*] (SPSG)
TAI	Transports Aeriens Intercontinentaux [*Privately owned French airline*]
TAI	Turnaround Index [*Data processing*]
TAI	Tuskegee Airmen, Inc. (EA)
TAIB..........	Trans-Arabian Investment Bank (MENA)
TAIC..........	Technical Air Intelligence Center [*Navy*]
TAIC..........	Tokyo Atomic Industrial Consortium
TAIC..........	Triallylisocyanurate [*Organic chemistry*]
TAICH	Technical Assistance Information Clearing House [*of ACVAFS*] [*Information service or system*] (EA)
TAID	Thrust-Augmented Improved Delta [*Launch vehicle*] [*NASA*]
TAID	Thunderbird American Indian Dancers (EA)
TAIDB.......	Tank-Automotive Integrated Database (MCD)
TAIDET	Triple Axis Inertial Drift Erection Test
TAIDHS....	Tactical Air Intelligence Data Handling System (NATG)
TAik..........	Teologinen Aikakauskirja. Teologisk Tidskrift [*Helsinki*] [*A publication*]
Taikomoji Branduoline Fiz ...	Taikomoji Branduoline Fizika [*A publication*]
TAILRATS ...	Tail RADAR Acquisition and Tracking System (MCD)
TAILS........	Tactical Automatic Landing System [*Aviation*] (NG)
TAIM	Technical Area Integration Manager (SSD)
TA Inf	Traduction Automatique Informations [*A publication*]
TAINS......	TERCOM [*Terrain Contour Mapping*]-Assisted Inertial Navigation System (MCD)
TAIP.........	Terminal Area Impact Point (MUGU)
TAIR.........	Terminal Area Instrumentation RADAR (MCD)
TAIR.........	Test Assembly Inspection Record [*NASA*] (NASA)
TAIRCF.....	Tactical Air Control Flight [*Military*]
TAIRCG	Tactical Air Control Group [*Military*] (AFIT)
TAIRCS.....	Tactical Air Control Squadron [*Air Force*]
TAIRCW ...	Tactical Air Control Wing [*Air Force*]
TAIS	Tactical Air Intelligence System [*Military*] (MCD)
TAISSA.....	Travelers Aid - International Social Service of America [*Later, ISS/AB*]
Tait............	Tait's Edinburgh Magazine [*A publication*]
Tait............	Tait's Index to Morison's Dictionary [*Scotland*] [*A publication*] (DLA)
Tait............	Tait's Index to Scotch Session Cases [*1823*] [*A publication*] (DLA)
Tait............	Tait's Manuscript Decisions, Scotch Session Cases [*A publication*] (DLA)
Tait Ev	Tait on Evidence [*A publication*] (DLA)
Tait Ind	Tait's Index to Scotch Session Cases [*1823*] [*A publication*] (DLA)
Tait JP	Tait's Justice of the Peace [*A publication*] (DLA)
TAIU	Technical Aircraft Instrument Unit [*Navy*]
Taiwan	Taiwan Fund, Inc. [*Associated Press abbreviation*] (APAG)
Taiwan Agric Bimon ...	Taiwan Agriculture Bimonthly [*A publication*]
Taiwan Agr Res J ...	Taiwan Agricultural Research Journal [*A publication*]
Taiwan Environ Sanit ...	Taiwan Environmental Sanitation [*A publication*]
Taiwan Fish Res Inst Fish Cult Rep ...	Taiwan. Fisheries Research Institute. Fish Culture. Report [*A publication*]
Taiwan Fish Res Inst Lab Biol Rep ...	Taiwan. Fisheries Research Institute. Laboratory of Biology. Report [*A publication*]
Taiwan Fish Res Inst Lab Fish Biol Rep ...	Taiwan. Fisheries Research Institute. Laboratory of Fishery Biology. Report [*A publication*]
Taiwan J Th ...	Taiwan Journal of Theology [*A publication*]
Taiwan J Vet Med Anim Husb ...	Taiwan Journal of Veterinary Medicine and Animal Husbandry [*A publication*]
Taiwan Sugar Exp Stn Annu Rep ...	Taiwan. Sugar Experiment Station. Annual Report [*A publication*]
Taiwan Sugar Exp Stn Res Rep ...	Taiwan. Sugar Experiment Station. Research Report [*A publication*]
Taiwan Sugar Res Inst Annu Rep ...	Taiwan. Sugar Research Institute. Annual Report [*A publication*]

Taiwan Trade Mo ...	Taiwan Trade Monthly [*A publication*]
Taiw Ind.....	Taiwan Industrial Panorama [*A publication*]
Taiw Stat....	Taiwan Statistical Data Book [*A publication*]
Taiw Svy	Monthly Economic Survey. Taiwan [*A publication*]
TAJ............	Tadji [*Papua New Guinea*] [*Airport symbol*] (OAG)
taj	Tajik [*MARC language code*] [*Library of Congress*] (LCCP)
TAJ............	Tanegashima [*Ryukyu Islands*] [*Seismograph station code, US Geological Survey*] (SEIS)
TAJ............	Thermal Arc Jet
TAJ............	Turbulent Air Jet
TAJA..........	The Abibi Jazz Artists [*British*]
TAJAG......	[*The*] Assistant Judge Advocate General [*Army*] (AABC)
TAK	Cargo Ship [*Military Sea Transportation Service*] (CINC)
TAK	Takaka [*New Zealand*] [*Seismograph station code, US Geological Survey*] [*Closed*] (SEIS)
TAK	Takamatsu [*Japan*] [*Airport symbol*] (OAG)
TAK	Taken
TAK	Tonan Ajia Kenkyu [*Southeast Asia Studies*] [*A publication*]
TAK	Trainer Appraisal Kit
TAK	Transparent Armor Kit
TAKAAN ..	Japanese Journal of Physical Fitness and Sports Medicine [*A publication*]
TAKC........	Taking Care. Newsletter of the Center for Consumer Health Education [*A publication*]
TAKC........	Theological Associate, King's College [*London*]
TAKCAL...	Tachometer Calibration (DNAB)
TAKEAZ...	Japanese Journal of Physical Education [*A publication*]
TAKEAZ...	Research Journal of Physical Education [*A publication*]
Takenaka Tech Res Rep ...	Takenaka Technical Research Report [*A publication*]
TAKIS	Tutmonda Asocio pri Kibernetiko, Informatiko, kaj Sistemiko [*World Association of Cybernetics, Computer Science, and System Theory*] (EAIO)
TAKIT	Teaching Aids Kit [*Red Cross Youth*]
TAKR	Vehicle Cargo Ship
TAKRX......	Fast Sealift Ship
TAKV	Cargo Ship and Aircraft Ferry [*Military Sea Transportation Service*] (CINC)
TAKX	Maritime Prepositioning Ship
TAL	[*The*] Apocryphal Literature: A Brief Introduction [*1945*] [*A publication*] (BJA)
Tal..............	Cases Tempore Talbot, English Chancery [*1734-38*] [*A publication*] (DLA)
TAL	Tailor (MSA)
TAL	Taiwan Industrial Panorama [*A publication*]
TAL	Talara [*Peru*] [*Seismograph station code, US Geological Survey*] (SEIS)
Tal..............	Talbot's Cases in Equity [*1734-38*] [*A publication*] (DLA)
TAL............	Talcorp Ltd. [*Toronto Stock Exchange symbol*]
Tal..............	Taliesin [*England*] [*A publication*]
TAL	Talis [*Such*] [*Pharmacy*]
Tal..............	Talisman [*A publication*]
TAL	Talladega College, Talladega, AL [*OCLC symbol*] (OCLC)
TAL	Talley Industries, Inc. [*NYSE symbol*] (SPSG)
TAL	Talmud
TAL	Tanana [*Alaska*] [*Airport symbol*] (OAG)
TAL	Target Acquisition Laboratory
TAL	Taxation for Lawyers [*A publication*]
TAL	Technische Akademie der Luftwaffe [*Germany*] (MCD)
TAL	Telecommunications Access Language
TAL	TEPI [*Technical Equipment Planning Information*] Approved Letter
TAL	Terminal Application Language
TAL	Territory Airlines [*Australia*]
TAL	Tetraalkyllead [*Organic chemistry*]
TAL	Thymic Alymphoplasia [*Medicine*] (MAE)
TAL	Timeslips III Accounting Link [*Data processing*]
TAL	Training Aids Library [*Navy*]
TAL	TransAlpine [*Pipeline*] [*Western Europe*]
TAL	Transatlantic (SSD)
TAL	Transatlantic Landing
TAL	Transocean Air Lines
TAL	Transoceanic Abort Landing (NASA)
TAL	Transporter Air Lock [*Nuclear energy*] (NRCH)
TALA........	Teacher Author League of America [*Formerly, TALNY*] (EA)
TALA........	Textile Association of Los Angeles (EA)
TALAFIT ..	Tank, Laying, Aiming, and Firing Trainer (MCD)
TALANT...	Thiokol Nuclear Development Center; Allison Division, General Motors; Linde Division, Union Carbide; and Nuclear Development Corp. Team (SAA)
TALAR......	Tactical Approach and Landing RADAR [*NASA*]
TALAR......	Talos Activity Report (MCD)
Talb...........	Cases Tempore Talbot, English Chancery [*1734-38*] [*A publication*] (DLA)
Talb...........	Talbot's Cases in Equity [*1734-38*] [*A publication*] (DLA)
TALBE	Talk and Listen Beacon [*Radio*]
TALC.........	Tactical Airlift Center (AFM)
TALC.........	Take-a-Look-See (MCD)
TALC.........	Tank-Automotive Logistics Command [*Army*]
TALCM.....	Tactical Air-Launched Cruise Missile (MCD)

TALC-OA ... Tactical Airlift Center Office of Operations Analysis [*Pope Air Force Base, NC*]
TALDT...... Total Administrative and Logistics Downtime   (MCD)
TALF......... Take a Look Foundation   (EA)
TALFF....... Total Allowable Level of Foreign Fishing
TALIA .... Transactions. Association of Life Insurance Medical Directors of America [*A publication*]
TALIS....... Topics in Australasian Library and Information Studies [*A publication*]
TALISMAN ... Transfer Accounting, Lodging for Investments, and Stock Management for Jobbers [*Stock exchange term*] [*British*]
TALISSI.... Tactical Light Shot Simulation   (MCD)
TALK........ Titles Alphabetically Listed by Keyword   (KSC)
T-ALL........ T-Cell Acute Lymphoblastic Leukemia [*Oncology*]
Talley......... Talley Industries, Inc. [*Associated Press abbreviation*]   (APAG)
Tallin Polueteh Inst Toim ... Tallinna Poluetehnilise Instituudi Toimetised [*A publication*]
Tall Timbers Res Stn Misc Publ ... Tall Timbers Research Station. Miscellaneous Publication [*A publication*]
TALM....... Tactical Air-Launched Missile   (MCD)
TALMIS.... Technology-Assisted Learning Market Information Services [*Educational Programming Systems, Inc.*]
TALMS ..... Tangier American Legation Museum Society   (EA)
TALMS ..... Tunable Atomic Line Molecular Spectroscopy
TALNY...... Teacher Author League of New York [*Later, TALA*]   (EA)
TALO .... Tactical Air Liaison Officer [*Air Force*]
TALO .... Time after Lift-Off
TALO .... Total Audience Listening Output [*Television ratings*]   (WDMC)
TALOG ...... Theater Army Logistical Command
TALON ..... South Central Regional Medical Library Program [*Library network*]
TALON ..... Tactical Air-Land Operations   (MCD)
TALONS... Tactical Airborne LORAN Navigation System [*Model*]   (MCD)
TALOP...... Terminology, Administrative, Logistical, and Operational Procedures [*Military*]
TALPS...... Transactional Analysis Life Position Survey [*Psychology*]
TAL QUAL ... Talis Qualis [*Such As It Is*] [*Latin*]   (ROG)
TALR........ Law Reports of the District Court of Tel Aviv [*A publication*]   (BJA)
TALS .... [*The*] American Lupus Society   (EA)
TALS .... [*The*] Army Language School
TALS .... Barge Cargo Ship
TALS .... Transport Approach and Landing Simulator
TALT......... Tracking Altitude   (MCD)
TALTC ...... Test Access Line Termination Circuit [*Telecommunications*]   (TEL)
TALTT....... Thrust Augmented Long Tank Thor   (MCD)
TALUS...... Transportation and Land Use Study [*Michigan*]
TAm........... [*The*] Americas: A Quarterly Review of Inter-American Cultural History [*A publication*]
TAM .... [*The*] Associated Missions   (EA)
TAM .... Tactical Air Missile
TAM .... Tactical Air Mission [*Air Force*]
TAM .... Tactical Airlift Modernization
TAM .... Tamanrasset [*Algeria*] [*Geomagnetic observatory code*]
TAM .... Tamanrasset [*Algeria*] [*Seismograph station code, US Geological Survey*]   (SEIS)
TAM .... Tamara Resources, Inc. [*Vancouver Stock Exchange symbol*]
TAM .... Tamerton [*England*]
Tam........... Tamid   (BJA)
tam .... Tamil [*MARC language code*] [*Library of Congress*]   (LCCP)
TAM .... Tamil [*Language, etc.*]   (ROG)
Tam........... Tamlyn's English Rolls Court Reports [*48 English Reprint*] [*A publication*]   (DLA)
TAM .... Tamoxifen [*Antineoplastic drug*]
TAM .... Tampico [*Mexico*] [*Airport symbol*]   (OAG)
TAM .... Tangent Approximating Manifold
TAM .... Target Acquisition Model [*Military*]
TAM .... Target Activated Munition [*Air-delivered land mines*]
TaM .... Tarybine Mokykla [*A publication*]
TAM .... Taxes. The Tax Magazine [*A publication*]
TAM .... Technical Acknowledgment Message [*Aviation*]
TAM .... Technical Ammunition
TAM .... Technical Area Manager
TAM .... Techniques of Alcohol Management [*Campaign, sponsored in part by the National Licensed Beverage Association, to prevent drunk driving*]
TAM .... Telecommunications Access Method
TAM .... Telephone Answering Machine   (IEEE)
TAM .... Television Audience Measurement
TAM .... Teresian Apostolic Movement [*See also MTA*] [*Italy*]   (EAIO)
TAM .... Terminal Access Method
TAM .... Test Access Multiplexer [*Telecommunications*]   (TEL)
TAM .... Texas A & M University [*College Station, TX*]
TAM .... Theatre Arts Magazine [*A publication*]
TAM .... Theatre Arts Monthly [*A publication*]
TAM .... Thermal Analytical Model [*Apollo*] [*NASA*]
TAM .... Throw Away Maintenance
TAM .... Time and Materials   (MCD)
TAM .... Tituli Asiae Minoris [*Vienna*] [*A publication*]   (OCD)
TAM .... Total Active Motion [*Orthopedics*]

TAM .... Toxoid-Antitoxin Mixture [*Immunology*]
TAM .... Trajectory Application Method   (MCD)
TAM .... Transistor-Amplifier-Multiplier   (IIA)
TAM .... Transparent Anatomical Manikin [*An exhibit at the Chicago Museum of Science and Industry*]
TAM .... Trialkylamine [*Organic chemistry*]
TAM .... Triangle Amplitude Modulation
TAM .... Tubos de Acero de Mexico [*AMEX symbol*]   (SPSG)
TAM .... Tumor-Associated Macrophages [*Immunology*]
TAM .... Twentieth Anniversary Mobilization   (EA)
TAM .... Type-Approval Model
TAMA .... Technical Assistance and Manufacturing Agreement
TAMA ...... Training Aids Management Agency [*Army*]   (AABC)
TAMAC ...... Three-Axis Manual Attitude Controller
Tamarack R ... Tamarack Review [*A publication*]
Tamb.......... Tambyah's Reports [*Ceylon*] [*A publication*]   (DLA)
Tambd........ Tambrands, Inc. [*Associated Press abbreviation*]   (APAG)
TAMC .... Tactical Aviation Maintenance Co. [*Army*]
TamC .... Tamil Culture [*A publication*]
TAMC .... Transportation Aircraft Maintenance Company [*Army*]
TAMC .... Tripler Army Medical Center   (AABC)
TAMCO .... Training Aid for MOBIDIC Console Operations
TAME .... Tactical Air-to-Air Mission Evaluation   (MCD)
TAME .... Tactical Missile Encounter [*Air Force*]   (KSC)
TAME .... Tertiary-Amyl Methyl Ether [*Gasoline additive*]
TAME .... Toluene-Sulfo-Trypsin Arginine Methyl Ester [*Organic chemistry*]   (MAE)
TAME .... Tosyl-L-arginine Methyl Ester [*Also, TosArgOMe*] [*Biochemical analysis*]
TAMED .... Totally Automated Method Development [*High-performance liquid chromatography*]
TAMF........ Tactical Automated Maintenance Facility
T Am Fish S ... Transactions. American Fisheries Society [*A publication*]
T Am Geophy ... Transactions. American Geophysical Union [*A publication*]
TAMI .... Tanks and Mechanized Infantry Experiment   (MCD)
TAMI .... Tip Air Mass Injection [*Helicopter*]
TAMICSS ... TAFIES [*Tactical Air Force Intelligence Exploitation System*] Microfilm Subsystem   (MCD)
Tamil Nadu J Coop ... Tamil Nadu Journal of Co-operation [*A publication*]
TAMIRAD ... Tactical Mid-Range Air Defense Program [*Army*]   (AABC)
TAMIS ...... Telemetric Automated Microbial Identification System
TAMIS ...... Training Ammunition Management Information System   (MCD)
Tamkang J Math ... Tamkang Journal of Mathematics [*Taipei*] [*A publication*]
Tamkang R ... Tamkang Review [*A publication*]
Tamkang Rev ... Tamkang Review [*A publication*]
TamkR....... Tamkang Review [*A publication*]
Taml.......... Tamlyn's English Rolls Court Reports [*48 English Reprint*] [*A publication*]   (DLA)
TAML....... Taunton Municipal Lighting Plant [*Nuclear energy*]   (NRCH)
TAMLA..... Technical Assistance and Manufacturing License Agreement
Taml Ev ..... Tamlyn's Evidence in Chancery [*2nd ed.*] [*1846*] [*A publication*]   (DLA)
Taml TY .... Tamlyn's Terms of Years [*1825*] [*A publication*]   (DLA)
Tamlyn....... Tamlyn's English Rolls Court Reports [*48 English Reprint*] [*A publication*]   (DLA)
Tamlyn Ch ... Tamlyn's English Rolls Court Reports [*48 English Reprint*] [*A publication*]   (DLA)
Tamlyn (Eng) ... Tamlyn's English Rolls Court Reports [*A publication*]   (DLA)
TAMM ...... Tetrakis(acetoxymercuri)methane [*Organic chemistry*]
T Am Math S ... Transactions. American Mathematical Society [*A publication*]
TAMMC ... Theater Army Materiel Management Center
T Am Micros ... Transactions. American Microscopical Society [*A publication*]
TAMMIS.. Theater Army Medical Management Information System   (GFGA)
TAMMIS-D ... Theater Army Medical Management Information System - Division
TAMMS.... [*The*] Army Maintenance Management System [*Formerly, TAERS*]   (AABC)
T Am Nucl S ... Transactions. American Nuclear Society [*A publication*]
TAMO....... Tooling Advance Material Order   (MCD)
TAMO....... Training Aids Management Office [*Army*]   (AABC)
TAMOS.... Terminal Automatic Monitoring System
TAMP....... Tactical Armament Master Plan   (MCD)
TAMP....... Tampering [*FBI standardized term*]
TAMP....... Tertiary-Amylphenol [*Disinfectant*]
TAMP....... Thailand Ammunition Manufacturing Plant   (CINC)
TAMP....... Tufts Assessment of Motor Performance [*Occupational therapy*]
Tampa........ Transportes Aereos Mercantiles Panamericanos [*National airlines*] [*Colombia*]   (EY)
Tampa Bay ... Tampa Bay Business [*A publication*]
Tampa Trib ... Tampa Tribune [*A publication*]
Tampa Tr & Ti ... Tampa Tribune and Times [*A publication*]
TAMPD..... TAPPI [*Technical Association of the Pulp and Paper Industry*] Annual Meeting. Proceedings [*United States*] [*A publication*]

TAMPER .. Tables for Approximation of Midpoints for Exponential Regression (MCD)
T Am Phil S ... Transactions. American Philosophical Society [*A publication*]
TAMPS ..... Teaming Analysis Model Personnel Selector (MCD)
TamR .... Tamarack Review [*Toronto*] [*A publication*]
TAMR ...... Teen Association of Model Railroading (EA)
TAMRA .... Technical and Miscellaneous Revenue Act of 1988
TAMS .... Tactical Avionics Maintenance Simulation (KSC)
TAMS .... Tandem Accelerator Mass Spectrometry
TAMS .... Target Activated Munitions System
TAMS .... Technical Assistance and Management Services [*General Services Administration*] (GFGA)
TAMS .... Test and Monitoring System (MCD)
TA-MS ..... Thermal Analysis Mass Spectrometry
TAMS .... Thruster-Assisted Mooring System [*of a ship*] (DS)
TAMS .... Token and Medal Society (EA)
TAMS .... Total Active Military Service (AFM)
TAMS ...... Total Automotive Management Service
TAMS .... Toxic Air Monitoring System [*Environmental Protection Agency*] (GFGA)
TAMS .... Trade Action Monitoring System [*Office of the United States Trade Representative*] (GFGA)
TAMS .... Training Ammunition Management Study [*Army*] (MCD)
TAMSA ..... Transactions. American Microscopical Society [*A publication*]
TAMSA ..... Transportes Aereos Mexicano, Sociedad Anonima
T Am S Art ... Transactions. American Society for Artificial Internal Organs [*A publication*]
TAMSJ ..... TAMS [*Token and Medal Society*] Journal [*A publication*]
Tamsui Oxford Coll Lecture Notes Ser ... Tamsui Oxford College. Lecture Notes Series [*A publication*]
TAMT ...... [*The*] American Mime Theatre (EA)
TAMTA ..... Transactions. American Mathematical Society [*A publication*]
TAMTAC ... Toxic Air Monitoring Technical Advisory Committee [*Environmental Protection Agency*] (GFGA)
TAMU ...... Texas A & M University
TAMV ...... Tulare Apple Mosaic Virus [*Plant pathology*]
TAMVEC ... Texas A & M University Variable Energy Cyclotron
TAN .... Tactical Air Navigational Aid (FAAC)
TAN .... Tananarive [*Madagascar*] [*Seismograph station code, US Geological Survey*] (SEIS)
TAN .... Tananarive [*Madagascar*] [*Geomagnetic observatory code*]
Tan .... Tancredus [*Deceased circa 1236*] [*Authority cited in pre-1607 legal work*] (DSA)
TAN .... Tandem (AAG)
TAN .... Tandy Corp. [*NYSE symbol*] (SPSG)
Tan .... Taney's United States Circuit Court Reports [*A publication*] (DLA)
TAN .... Tangent [*Mathematics*]
TAN .... Tangential Cell [*Neurology*]
TAN .... Tanglewood Consolidated Resources, Inc. [*Toronto Stock Exchange symbol*]
Tan .... Tanhuma (BJA)
TAN .... Tanned (MSA)
TAN .... Task Authorization Notice
TAN .... Taunton, MA [*Location identifier*] [*FAA*] (FAAL)
TAN .... Tax Administrators News [*Federation of Tax Administrators*] [*A publication*]
TAN .... Tax Anticipation Note [*Obligation*] [*State or local government*]
TAN .... Technische Arbeitsnorm
TAN .... Teletype Alert Network (NVT)
TAN .... Test Area North [*AEC*]
TAN .... Thiazolylazonaphthol [*An indicator*] [*Chemistry*]
TAN .... Title Analytic [*Bibliography*]
TAN .... Total Acid Number [*Oil analysis*]
TAN .... Total Adenine Nucleotide [*Medicine*]
TAN .... Total Ammonia Nitrogen
TAN .... Trainable Adaptive Network
TAN .... Transall-Normen (MCD)
TAN .... Transonic Aerodynamic Nozzle
TAN .... Transportes Aereos Nacionales, SA [*TAN Airlines*]
TAN .... Transportes Aeros Nacionales [*National Air Line*] [*Honduras*] (PDAA)
TAN .... Twilight All Night
TANAA ..... Transactions. American Neurological Association [*A publication*]
Tanc .... Tancredus [*Deceased circa 1236*] [*Authority cited in pre-1607 legal work*] (DSA)
TANC .... Through-Axis Navigational Control
TANC .... Total Absorption Nuclear Cascade
TANCAV ... Tactical Navigation and Collision Avoidance [*Military*] (CAAL)
T Anc Monum ... Ancient Monuments Society. Transactions [*A publication*]
Tanc QW ... Tancred. Quo Warranto [*A publication*] (ILCA)
Tancre .... Tancredus [*Deceased circa 1236*] [*Authority cited in pre-1607 legal work*] (DSA)
Tancred ...... Tancredus [*Deceased circa 1236*] [*Authority cited in pre-1607 legal work*] (DSA)
TAND .... Tandem (FAAC)
TANDA ..... Time and Attendance Report (FAAC)
Tandem ...... Tandem Computers, Inc. [*Associated Press abbreviation*] (APAG)

TANDEM ... Tibi Aderit Numen Divinum, Expecta Modo [*God Will Help Thee - Only Wait*] [*Latin*] [*Motto of Elisabeth Ernestine Antonie, Duchess of Saxony (1681-1766)*]
TANDOC .. Tanzania National Documentation Centre [*National Central Library*] [*Information service or system*] (IID)
Tandy .... Tandy Corp. [*Associated Press abbreviation*] (APAG)
TANE .... Transportes Aereos Nacionales Ecuatorianas [*Airline*] [*Ecuador*]
TANESCO ... Tanzania Electric Supply Co.
Taney .... Taney's United States Circuit Court Reports [*A publication*] (DLA)
TANEYCOMO ... Taney County, MO [*A lake at Branson, MO*]
Taney's CC Dec ... Taney's United States Circuit Court Reports [*A publication*] (DLA)
Taney's Dec (USCC) ... Taney's United States Circuit Court Reports [*A publication*] (DLA)
TANG .... Tangential (AAG)
TANGLE ... Angle at Tip of Leaf [*Botany*]
TANH .... Tangent, Hyperbolic
Tanh .... Tanhuma (BJA)
TANi .... Recueil de Jurisprudence des Tribunaux de l'Arrondissement de Nivelles [*A publication*]
TANI .... Total Axial Lymph Node Irradiation [*Medicine*]
TANJUG ... Telegrafska Agencija Nove Jugoslavije [*Press agency*] [*Yugoslavia*]
TANK .... Floatation Tank Association (EA)
TANK .... Tanknology Environmental [*NASDAQ symbol*] (SPSG)
TANKBAT ... Tank Battalion [*Army*]
Tank Bulk Marit Manage ... Tanker and Bulker Maritime Management [*England*] [*A publication*]
Tanker Bulk Carr ... Tanker and Bulk Carrier [*A publication*]
Tanker Bulker Int ... Tanker and Bulker International [*England*] [*A publication*]
TANKEX ... Tank Field Exercise (NVT)
TANKOPINS ... Tanker Operating Instructions (DNAB)
Tan Lect HV ... Tanner Lectures on Human Values [*A publication*]
Tan LR .... Tanganyika Territory Law Reports [*A publication*] (DLA)
Tann .... Tanner's Reports [*8-14 Indiana*] [*A publication*] (DLA)
Tann .... Tanner's Reports [*13-17 Utah*] [*A publication*] (DLA)
TANN .... Taqrimiut Nipingat News [*Salluit, Quebec*] [*A publication*]
Tanner .... Tanner's Reports [*8-14 Indiana*] [*A publication*] (DLA)
Tanner .... Tanner's Reports [*13-17 Utah*] [*A publication*] (DLA)
TANO .... Tano Corp. [*NASDAQ symbol*] (NQ)
TANO .... Triacetoneamine Nitroxide [*Organic chemistry*]
TANREM ... Tactical Nuclear Weapons Requirements Methodology
TANS .... Tactical Air Navigation System [*Helicopter*]
TANS .... Tax Anticipation Notes
TANS .... Terminal Area Navigation System
TANS .... Territorial Army Nursing Service [*British*]
TA-NS ...... Total Abstinence - No Smoking [*On social invitations*]
TANSA ...... Transactions. American Nuclear Society [*A publication*]
TANSTAAFL ... There Ain't No Such Thing As a Free Lunch [*Principle of economics indicating that one cannot get something for nothing*] [*See also TINSTAAFL*]
TANT .... Tennant Co. [*NASDAQ symbol*] (NQ)
TANU .... Tanganyika African National Union [*Political party*]
Tanulmanyok Magy Tud Akad Szamitastech es Autom Kut Intez ... Tanulmanyok Magyar Tudomanyos Akademia Szamitastechnikai es Automatizalasi Kutato Intezet [*A publication*]
Tanulmanyok MTA Szamitastechn Automat Kutato Int (Budapest) ... Tanulmanyok. MTA [*Magyar Tudomanyos Akademia*] Szamitastechnikai es Automatizalasi Kutato Intezet (Budapest) [*A publication*]
TANWERE ... Tactical Nuclear Weapons Requirements (CINC)
TANY .... Typographers Association of New York (EA)
Tanz .... Tanzania
TAN-ZAM ... Tanzania-Zambia [*Railway*]
Tanzania Miner Resour Power Annu Rep Geol Surv Div ... Tanzania. Ministry of Industries. Mineral Resources and Power. Annual Report of the Geological Survey Division [*A publication*]
Tanzania Rec Geol Surv Tanganyika ... Tanzania. Records of the Geological Survey of Tanganyika [*A publication*]
Tanzania Silvic Res Note ... Tanzania Silviculture Research Note [*A publication*]
Tanzania Silvic Res Stn Tech Note (New Ser) ... Tanzania. Silviculture Research Station. Technical Note (New Series) [*A publication*]
TAO .... Auxiliary Oiler [*Military Sea Transportation Service*]
TAO .... Hammond, LA [*Location identifier*] [*FAA*] (FAAL)
TAO .... Qingdao [*China*] [*Airport symbol*] (OAG)
TAO .... TACAN [*Tactical Air Navigation*] Only (FAAC)
TAO .... Tactical Action Observer [*Military*] (CAAL)
TAO .... Tactical Action Officer [*Navy*] (NVT)
TAO .... Tactical Air Observation [*or Observer*] (NATG)
TAO .... Tactical Air Officer (NVT)
TAO .... Tactical Air Operations
TAO .... Technical Analysis Office (MCD)
TAO .... Technical Analysis Order
TAO .... Technical Assistance Office
TAO .... Technical Assistance Operations [*United Nations*]

TAO.......... Technical Assistance Order   (KSC)
TAO.......... Technology Applications Office [*NASA*]
TAO.......... Technology Assistance Officer [*Small Business Administration*]
TAO.......... Telephone Area Office [*British*]
TAO.......... Terrain Avoidance Override   (MCD)
TAO.......... Test Analysis Outline
TAO.......... Thromboangitis Obliterans [*Cardiology*]
TAO.......... Time and Altitude Over [*Aviation*]   (FAAC)
TAO.......... Tokyo Astronomical Observatory
TAO.......... Total Acid Output [*Clinical chemistry*]
TAO.......... Transition Assistance Office [*Army*]   (INF)
TAO.......... Transportation Applications Office [*Jet Propulsion Laboratory, NASA*]
TAO.......... Troleandomycin [*Formerly, Triacetyloleandomycin*] [*Antibacterial compound*]
TAO.......... TSCA [*Toxic Substances Control Act*] Assistance Office [*Environmental Protection Agency*]   (GFGA)
TAOBBATED ... [*The*] Adventures of Buckaroo Banzai across the Eighth Dimension [*1984 movie title*]
TAOC........ [*The*] Army Operations Center
TAOC........ Tactical Air Operations Center
TAOC........ Train Axis Optical Cube
TAOCC ..... Tactical Air Operations Control Center   (NATG)
TAOG........ Gasoline Tanker [*Military Sea Transportation Service*]   (CINC)
TAOI .... Tactical Area of Interest [*Military*]
TAOM/MCE ... Tactical Air Operations Module/Modular Control Equipment [*Military*]   (RDA)
TAOO........ Tactical Air Operations Officer [*Tactical Air Command*]
TAOR .... Tactical Area of Responsibility [*Military*]   (AFM)
TAOS .... Thrust-Assisted Orbiter Shuttle [*NASA*]
TAOS .... Travel Allowance on Separation [*Military*]
TA/OSD.... Task Analysis/Operational Sequence Diagram
TAOT .... Transport Oiler Ship
TAP .... Amarillo Public Library, Amarillo, TX [*OCLC symbol*]   (OCLC)
TAP .... [*The*] Angel Planes   (EA)
TAP .... [*The*] Army Plan
TAP .... Onitap Resources, Inc. [*Toronto Stock Exchange symbol*]
TAP .... T-Cell-Activating Protein [*Biochemistry*]
TAP .... Tabaksplant. Maandblad voor de Sigaren, Sigaretten, en Tabakshandel en Industrie [*A publication*]
TAP .... Table of Authorized Personnel   (NATG)
TAP .... Tackled Attempting to Pass [*Football*]
TAP .... Tactical Action Programs
TAP .... Tactical Armament Plan   (MCD)
TAP .... Taipei [*Taihoku*] [*Taiwan*] [*Seismograph station code, US Geological Survey*]   (SEIS)
TAP .... Taipei [*Taiwan*] [*Later, LNP*] [*Geomagnetic observatory code*]
TAP .... Tapachula [*Mexico*] [*Airport symbol*]   (OAG)
TAP .... Tapestry   (ADA)
Tap........... Tappan's Ohio Common Pleas Reports [*A publication*]   (DLA)
TAP .... Target Aim Points
TAP .... Target Analysis and Planning [*Computer system*] [*Military*]
TAP .... Target Angular Position [*Photonics*]
TAP .... Target Assignment Panel
TAP .... Task Area Plan
TAP .... Teacher's Aide Program
TAP .... Technical Achievement Plan [*NASA*]   (NASA)
TAP .... Technical Action Panel [*Department of Agriculture*]
TAP .... Technical Action Program   (OICC)
TAP .... Technical Advisory Panel [*United Nations*]
TAP .... Technical Area Plan [*Navy*]   (MCD)
TAP .... Technical Assistance Program [*Environmental Protection Agency*]   (GFGA)
TAP .... Technical Assistance Project   (EA)
TAP .... Technological Adjustment Pay
TAP .... Technological American Party   (EA)
TAP .... Technology Adaptation Program [*Massachusetts Institute of Technology*] [*Research center*]   (RCD)
TAP .... Technology Applications Program [*NASA*] [*University of Kentucky*] [*Lexington, KY*]
TAP .... Technology Assistance Program [*Army*]
TAP .... Telemetry Acceptance Pattern   (KSC)
TAP .... Telemetry Antenna Pedestal
TAP .... Temporal Analysis of Products [*System developed by Monsanto Chemical Co.*]
TAP .... Tension by Applanation [*Ophthalmology*]
TAP .... Terminal Access Processor
TAP .... Terminal Applications Package   (IEEE)
TAP .... Terrain Analysis Program [*Military*]
TAP .... Terrestrial Auxiliary Power
TAP .... Test Administration Plan   (NASA)
TAP .... Test Anxiety Profile [*Educational test*]
TAP .... Test Assistance Program [*Sperry UNIVAC*]
TAP .... Test of Auditory-Perceptual Skills
TAP .... Tests of Achievement and Proficiency [*Educational test*]
TAP .... Theater of All Possibilities [*International touring company of actor-authors*]
TAP .... Thermal Analysis Program [*Nuclear energy*]
TAP .... Thermosiphoning Air Pan
TAP .... Thermoviscoelastic Analysis Program   (MCD)

TAP .... Thesaurus at Play [*Acronym is trademark for word game*]
TAP .... Thiol Alkaline Phosphatase [*An enzyme*]
TAP .... Three-Axis Package
TAP .... Tibetan Aid Project   (EA)
TAP .... Time-Sharing Assembly Program [*Data processing*]   (DIT)
TAP .... Total Action Against Poverty [*A federal government program*]
TAP .... Total Air Pressure   (NASA)
TAP .... Total Annualized Profit
TAP .... Toxic Air Pollutant
TAP .... Toxicological Agent Protective Item   (MCD)
TAP .... Tracking Alarms Processor [*Space Flight Operations Facility, NASA*]
TAP .... Trajectory Analysis Program   (MCD)
TAP .... Trans-Alaska Pipeline
TAP .... Transaction Application Program [*Data processing*]
TAP .... Transcription Activating Protein [*Biochemistry*]
TAP .... Transferable Assets Program
TAP .... Transformation-Associated Protein [*Biochemistry*]
TAP .... Transition Assistance Program [*Military*]
TAP .... Transmission Access Processor [*Newbridge Networks, Inc.*]
TAP .... Transponder Access Program [*Satellite Business Systems*] [*McLean, VA*] [*Telecommunications*]   (TSSD)
TAP .... Transport Ship [*Military Sea Transportation Service*]   (CINC)
TAP .... Transportes Aereos Portugueses, SARL [*Portuguese Air Transport*]
TAP .... Trend Analysis Program [*American Council of Life Insurance*] [*Washington, DC*] [*Information service or system*]   (IID)
TAP .... Triaminopyrimidine [*Organic chemistry*]
TAP .... Trickle Ammonia Process [*for drying grain feedstuffs*]
TAP .... Trimethylaminoethylpiperazine [*Organic chemistry*]
TAP .... Truck Assembly Plants
TAP .... Trustee, Administration, and Physician's Institute [*Seminar*]
TAP .... Tunis-Afrique Presse [*Press agency*] [*Tunisia*]
TAPA........ St. Johns/V. C. Bird [*Antigua Island*] [*ICAO location identifier*]   (ICLI)
TAPA........ (Tetranitrofluorylideneaminooxy)propionic Acid
TAPA........ Three-Dimensional Antenna Pattern Analyzer [*Air Force*]
TAPA........ Total Army Personnel Agency   (INF)
TAPA........ Trans-Alaska Pipeline Authorization Act
TAPA........ Transactions and Proceedings. American Philological Association [*A publication*]
TAPA........ Turkish American Physicians Association   (EA)
TAPAC...... Tape Automatic Positioning and Control
TAPAC...... Transportation Allocations, Priorities, and Controls Committee [*Military*]
TAPAK...... Tape-Pack
TAPAT...... Tape Programmed Automatic Tester
TAPATS.... Threat Artillery Preparation Against Thermal Sights   (MCD)
TAPC........ [*Department of the*] Treasury Administrative Processing Center   (GFGA)
TAPCC...... Technology and Pollution Control Committee [*Environmental Protection Agency*]
TAPCHAN ... Tapered Channel [*Wave power technology*]
Tap Chi Toan Hoc ... Tap Chi Toan Hoc. Progress of Mathematical Sciences [*A publication*]
Tap CM .... Tapping's Copyholder's Manual [*A publication*]   (DLA)
TAPCO...... Thompson Products, Inc. [*Later, Thompson Ramo Woolridge, Inc.*]
TAP-D...... Test of Articulation Performance - Diagnostic
TAPDB...... Total Army Personnel Database   (GFGA)
TAPDS...... Toxic Air Pollutant Data System [*Environmental Protection Agency*]   (GFGA)
TAPE........ Magnetech Corp. [*NASDAQ symbol*]   (NQ)
TAPE........ Tactical Air Power Evaluation [*Air Force*]
TAPE........ Tape Automatic Preparation Equipment
TAPE........ Target Profile Examination Technique [*RADAR analysis concept*] [*Air Force*]
TAPE........ Technical Advisory Panel for Electronics [*Air Force*]
TAPE........ Television Audience Program Evaluation
TAPE........ Tentative Annual Planning Estimate   (NVT)
TAPE........ Timed Access to Pertinent Excerpts
TAPE........ Total Application of Prerecorded Evidence
TAPE........ Totally Automated Programming Equipment
TAPE........ Transactional Analysis of Personality and Environment [*Psychology*]   (AEBS)
TAPER...... [*The*] Army Plan for Equipment Records
TAPER...... Tailored Performance Test Vehicle   (SAA)
TAPER...... Temporary Appointment Pending Establishment of a Register [*Civil Service*]
TAPER...... Theater Army Personnel   (MCD)
TAPER...... Turbulent Air Pilot Environment Research [*NASA-FAA project*]
TAPEX...... Tape Executive Program   (SAA)
TAPFOR ... [*The*] Army Portion of Force Status and Identify Report [*Force Status Report*]
TAPH .... Codrington [*Barbuda Island*] [*ICAO location identifier*]   (ICLI)
TAPH .... Toluic Acid Phenylhydrazide [*Organic chemistry*]
TAPhA ...... Transactions and Proceedings. American Philological Association [*A publication*]
TA Philos Soc ... Transactions. American Philosophical Society [*A publication*]

TAPhS.......	Transactions. American Philosophical Society [*A publication*]
TAPIO.......	Tape Input and Output [*Data processing*] (DNAB)
TAPIT	Tactical Photographic Image Transmission
TAPITS.....	Tactical Airborne Processing, Interpretation, and Transmission System [*Military*]
TAPITS.....	Tactical Photographic Image Transmission System
TAPLF......	Trans-Alaska Pipeline Liability Fund
TAPLINE ..	Trans-Alaska Pipeline
TAPLINE ..	Trans-Arabian Pipeline
TAPM........	Technology Application Program Management [*Air Force*]
Tap Man	Tapping on the Writ of Mandamus [*1848*] [*A publication*] (DLA)
TAPO	Termination Accountable Property Officer
TAPO	Tris(l-aziridinyl) Phosphine Oxide [*Organic chemistry*]
TAPOC......	Theater Army Personnel Operations Center
TAPOL......	Comite de Defense des Prisonniers en Indonesie [*France*]
Tapp..........	Tappan's Ohio Common Pleas Reports [*A publication*] (DLA)
TAPP........	Time and Attendance, Payroll, and Personnel (GFGA)
TAPP........	Total Assets Protection, Inc. [*Arlington, TX*] [*NASDAQ symbol*] (NQ)
TAPP........	Trade Association of Proprietary Plants (EA)
TAPP........	Tumor Acquisition, Processing, and Preservation [*Oncology*]
TAPP........	Two-Axis Pneumatic Pickup (IEEE)
Tappan.......	Tappan's Ohio Common Pleas Reports [*A publication*] (DLA)
Tappan (Ohio) ...	Tappan's Ohio Common Pleas Reports [*A publication*] (DLA)
Tappan's Ohio Rep ...	Tappan's Ohio Common Pleas Reports [*A publication*] (DLA)
Tappan's R ...	Tappan's Ohio Common Pleas Reports [*A publication*] (DLA)
TAPPI	TAPPI [*Technical Association of the Pulp and Paper Industry*] Journal [*A publication*]
TAPPI	Technical Association of the Pulp and Paper Industry (EA)
TAPPI Alkaline Pulping Conf Prepr ...	TAPPI [*Technical Association of the Pulp and Paper Industry*] Alkaline Pulping Conference Preprint [*A publication*]
TAPPI Annu Meet Prepr ...	TAPPI [*Technical Association of the Pulp and Paper Industry*] Annual Meeting. Preprint [*A publication*]
TAPPI Annu Meet Proc ...	TAPPI [*Technical Association of the Pulp and Paper Industry*] Annual Meeting. Proceedings [*A publication*]
TAPPI Bibl ...	TAPPI [*Technical Association of the Pulp and Paper Industry*] Bibliography of Pulp and Paper Manufacture [*A publication*]
TAPPI Coat Conf Prepr ...	TAPPI [*Technical Association of the Pulp and Paper Industry*] Coating Conference. Preprint [*A publication*]
TAPPI Environ Conf Proc ...	TAPPI [*Technical Association of the Pulp and Paper Industry*] Environmental Conference. Proceedings [*A publication*]
TAPPI For Biol Wood Chem Conf Conf Pap ...	TAPPI [*Technical Association of the Pulp and Paper Industry*] Forest Biology - Wood Chemistry Conference. Conference Papers [*A publication*]
TAPPI J Tech Assoc Pulp Paper Ind ...	TAPPI. Journal of the Technical Association of the Pulp and Paper Industry [*A publication*]
TAPPI Monogr Ser ...	TAPPI [*Technical Association of the Pulp and Paper Industry*] Monograph Series [*A publication*]
Tapping......	Tapping on the Writ of Mandamus [*A publication*] (DLA)
TAPPI Papermakers Conf Pap ...	TAPPI [*Technical Association of the Pulp and Paper Industry*] Papermakers Conference. Papers [*A publication*]
TAPPI Papermakers Conf Proc ...	TAPPI [*Technical Association of the Pulp and Paper Industry*] Papermakers Conference. Proceedings [*A publication*]
TAPPI Special Rept ...	TAPPI [*Technical Association of the Pulp and Paper Industry*] Special Reports [*A publication*]
TAPPI Spec Tech Assoc Publ ...	TAPPI [*Technical Association of the Pulp and Paper Industry*] Special Technical Association. Publication [*A publication*]
Tapp M & Ch ...	Tapp on Maintenance and Champerty [*1861*] [*A publication*] (ILCA)
TAPPS.......	[*The*] Automated Procurement Planning System
TAPR.........	Tactical Automation Program Review [*Military*]
TAPR.........	Toxic Altitude Propulsion Research (MCD)
TAPRE......	Tracking in an Active and Passive RADAR Environment
TAPS........	Tactical Area Positioning System [*Military*]
TAPS........	Tactical Protective Structures (MCD)
TAPS........	Tarapur Atomic Power Station [*India*]
TAPS........	Teachers Audio Placement System
TAPS........	Technical Analysis Positions System
TAPS........	Telemetry Antenna Positions System [*Military*] (CAAL)
TAPS........	TERCOM [*Terrain Contour Mapping*] Aircraft Positioning Systems [*Air Force*]
TAPS........	Terminal Application Processing System
TAPS........	Terminal Application Program System [*Data processing*]
TAPS........	Terminal Area Positive Separation [*FAA*]
TAP-S.......	Test of Articulation Performance - Screen
TAPS........	Time Analysis of Program Status
TAPS........	Total Atoll Production System (NOAA)
TAPS........	Trajectory Accuracy Prediction System [*Air Force*]
TAPS........	Trans-Alaska Pipeline System [*Department of Energy*]
TAPS........	Transactions. American Philosophical Society [*A publication*]
TAPS.........	Tris(hydroxymethyl)methylamino Propanesulfonic Acid
TAPS.........	Turboalternator Power System (IEEE)
TAPS.........	Turret-Anchored Production System [*Petroleum engineering*]
TAPSC	Trans-Atlantic Passenger Steamship Conference [*Later, IPSA*] (EA)
TAPSYS...	Total Army Personnel System
TAPU	Tanganyika African Postal Union
TAPVC	Total Anomalous Pulmonary Venous Connection [*Cardiology*]
TAPVD......	Total Anomalous Pulmonary Venous Drainage [*Cardiology*] (AAMN)
TAPVR	Total Anomalous Pulmonary Venous Return [*Cardiology*]
Taq............	Thermus Aquaticus [*Bacteria*]
TAQ..........	Trans Asian Resources [*Vancouver Stock Exchange symbol*]
TAQ..........	Transient Airman Quarters [*Air Force*] (AFM)
TAQK........	Taqralik [*A publication*]
TAQL	Taqralik [*Montreal*] [*A publication*]
TAQO........	Tawow. Canadian Indian Cultural Magazine [*A publication*]
TAQT	Task Assignment Queue Table (MCD)
TAQTD	Task Assignment Queue Table Display (MCD)
TAQTU	Task Assignment Queue Table Update (MCD)
TAQW	Transient Abnormal Q Waves [*Medicine*] (AAMN)
TAR	Tactical Air Reconnaissance (AFM)
TAR	Tactical Air Request (NVT)
TAR	Tactical Aircraft Recovery (CINC)
tar..............	Tadzhik Soviet Socialist Republic [*MARC country of publication code*] [*Library of Congress*] (LCCP)
TAR	Tansy Resources, Inc. [*Vancouver Stock Exchange symbol*]
TAR	Tape Address Register [*Demography*]
TAR	Tape Address Register File [*Bureau of the Census*] (GFGA)
TAR	Tara Exploration & Development Co. Ltd. [*Toronto Stock Exchange symbol*]
TAR	Taranto [*Italy*] [*Seismograph station code, US Geological Survey*] (SEIS)
TAR	Target
tar..............	Tatar [*MARC language code*] [*Library of Congress*] (LCCP)
TAR	Tax Advance Rulings [*Database*] [*Taxation Canada*] [*Information service or system*] (CRD)
TAR	Team Acceptance Review (SAA)
TAR	Technical Action Request [*Army*] (AABC)
TAR	Technical Amendment Regulation [*Federal government*] (EG)
TAR	Technical Analysis Request [*NASA*] (KSC)
TAR	Technical Assistance Request [*Nuclear energy*] (NRCH)
TAR	Teen Age Republican [*Lifestyle classification*]
TAR	Temporary Active Reserve (DNAB)
TAR	Terminal Address Register
TAR	Terminal Area Surveillance RADAR
TAR	Terrain Avoidance RADAR
TAR	Terrier Advanced RADAR (DNAB)
TAR	Territorial Army Regulations [*British military*] (DMA)
TAR	Test Action Requirement (NASA)
TAR	Test Agency Report (NASA)
TAR	Test Analysis Report
TAr	Theater Arts [*A publication*]
TAR	Therm Advanced Research (SAA)
TAR	Threat Avoidance Receiver (MCD)
TAR	Thrombocytopenia with Absent Radii [*Medicine*]
TAR	Thrust-Augmented Rocket [*NASA*]
TAR	Total Accomplishment Requirement (DNAB)
TAR	Total Assets Reporting (MCD)
TAR	Towed Array RADAR
TAR	Track Address Register
TAR	Training and Administration of the Reserve
TAR	Trajectory Analysis Room [*NASA*] (KSC)
TAR	Trans-Acting Responsive Sequence [*Genetics*]
TAR	Trans-Activator Response Element [*Genetics*]
TAR	Transactivator-Responsive Region [*Genetics*]
TAR	Transportes Aereos Regionais [*Airline*] [*Brazil*]
TAR	Triannual Review (NATG)
TAR	Truck and Rail
TAR	Turnaround Ratio
TAR	Two-Axis Rate (SAA)
TARA	Taurus Resources Ltd. [*NASDAQ symbol*] (NQ)
TARA	Technical Assistant, Royal Artillery [*British military*] (DMA)
TA/RA	Technical Availability/Restricted Availability [*Navy*] (NVT)
TARA	Territorial Army Rifle Association [*British military*] (DMA)
TARA	Total Articular Replacement Arthroplasty [*Orthopedics*]
TARA	Truck-Frame and Axle Repair Association (EA)
TARA	Tumor-Associated Rejection Antigen [*Immunology*] (MAE)
TARABS ...	Tactical Air Reconnaissance and Aerial Battlefield Surveillance System [*Military*]
TARADCOM ...	Tank-Automotive Research and Development Command [*Army*]
TARAN	Tactical Attack RADAR and Navigation
TARAN	Test and Repair [*or Replace*] as Necessary
Tarb	Tarbiz. Jerusalem (BJA)
Tar Bak Orm Gen Mud Yay ...	Tarim Bakanligi. Orman Genel Mudurlugu Yayinlarindan [*A publication*]
TARC........	[*The*] Army Research Council
TARC........	Tactical Air Reconnaissance Center [*Shaw Air Force Base*]
TARC........	Television Allocation Research Committee [*or Council*]
TARC........	Theater Army Replacement Command

TARC......... Through Axis Rotational Control [*Aerospace*] (MCD)
TARC......... Thru-Axis Rotational Control
TARC......... Total Available Residual Chlorine [*Water quality*]
TARC......... Toxics Testing and Assessment Research Committee [*Terminated, 1984*] [*Environmental Protection Agency*] (EGAO)
TARC......... TransAtlantic Resources [*NASDAQ symbol*] (NQ)
TARC......... Transport Airworthiness Reports Committee [*AIA*] (MCD)
TARCAP ... Target Combat Air Patrol [*Navy*]
TARC-OA ... Tactical Air Reconnaissance Center Office of Operations Analysis [*Shaw Air Force Base, SC*]
TARCOG .. Top of Alabama Regional Council of Governments
TARCOM ... Tank-Automotive Materiel Readiness Command [*Army*]
TARCOMSA ... Tank-Automotive Materiel Readiness Command, Selfridge Activity (MCD)
TArDC....... Arlington Development Center, Arlington, TN [*Library symbol*] [*Library of Congress*] (LCLS)
TARDEC..... Tank-Automotive Research, Development, and Engineering Center [*Army*] (RDA)
TARDIS ... Time and Relative Dimensions in Space [*Acronym is name of spaceship in British TV series "Dr. Who"*]
TARDIS .... Tropical Analysis and Real-Time Display [*National Oceanic and Atmospheric Administration*]
TARE......... Telegraphic Automatic Relay [*or Routing*] Equipment (NG)
TARE......... Telemetry Automatic Reduction Equipment
TARE......... Transistor Analysis Recording Equipment
TAREA...... Terminal Leaf Area [*Botany*]
TAREWS .. Tactical Air Reconnaissance and Electronic Warfare Support (MCD)
TAREX...... Target Exploitation [*Military*] (AABC)
TARF......... [*The*] Acid Rain Foundation (EA)
TARF......... Tracking and Reporting Format [*Military*] (CAAL)
TARFU...... Things Are Really Fouled Up [*Military slang*] [*Bowdlerized version*]
TARFX ...... Tracking and Reporting Format Extended [*Military*] (CAAL)
Targ .... Targum (BJA)
TARGA ...... Truevision Advanced Raster Graphics Adapter [*AT & T*]
TARGET ... Team to Advance Research for Gas Energy Transformation [*Group of US gas and gas-electric companies*]
TARGET ... Thermal Advanced Reactor, Gas-Cooled, Exploiting Thorium [*Nuclear energy*]
TARGET ... Transportability Analysis Reports Generator [*Military*] (MCD)
TARGET ... Transportation Accident Research Graduate Education and Training
Targeted Diagn Ther Ser ... Targeted Diagnosis and Therapy Series [*A publication*]
Target Mark ... Target Marketing [*A publication*]
TargJer...... [*The*] Jerusalem Targum of the Pentateuch (BJA)
TargJon ..... Targum Jonathan (BJA)
TargOnk .... Targum Onkelos (BJA)
TargYer...... Targum Yerusahlmi (BJA)
TARIC....... Texas American Resources [*NASDAQ symbol*] (NQ)
TARIF .... Telegraphic Automatic Routing in the Field (MCD)
Tarl .... Tarleton Term Reports [*A publication*] (APTA)
TARL......... Training Aids Research Laboratory [*Air Force*] (MCD)
TARLOCS ... Target Locating System [*Military*] (MCD)
Tarl Term R .. Tarleton Term Reports [*A publication*] (APTA)
TARMAC ... Tar Macadam
TARMAC ... Terminal Area RADAR/Moving Aircraft (KSC)
TARMOCS ... [*The*] Army Operations Center System
TARN .... Team Acceptance Review Notice (SAA)
TArnA........ ARO, Inc., AEDC Library, Arnold Air Force Station, TN [*Library symbol*] [*Library of Congress*] (LCLS)
TARND ..... Turnaround (FAAC)
TARO .... Taro-Vit Industries Ltd. [*NASDAQ symbol*] (NQ)
TARO .... Territorial Army Reserve of Officers [*British*]
TAROM ..... Transporturi Aeriene Romane [*Romanian Air Transport*]
TAROT ..... [*The*] Associated Readers of Tarot International (EA)
TARP........ Tactical Airborne Reconnaissance Pod
TARP........ Tactical Airborne Recording Package
TARP........ Tarpaulin (AAG)
TARP........ Test and Repair Processor [*Data processing*]
TARP........ Theater Army Repair Program
TARP........ Total Army Requirements Program
TARP........ Tour Advisory Review Panel [*Army National Guard*] (INF)
TARP........ Transient Acoustic Radiation Program
TARP........ Typical Airland Resupply Profile (MCD)
TARPAC ... Television and Radio Political Action Committee [*National Association of Broadcasters*]
TARPS ...... Tactical Aerial Reconnaissance Pod System (MCD)
TARPTOLA ... Theologiae Apud Remonstrantes Professorem, Tyrannidis Osorem, Limburgium Amstelodamensem [*Pseudonym used by John Locke*]
TARS........ [*The*] Arthur Ransome Society [*British*] (EAIO)
TARS........ Tactical Air Reconnaissance School [*Air Force*]
TARS........ Tactical Air Research and Survey Office [*Air Force*]
TARS........ Target Acquisition Reconnaissance and Surveillance System (SAA)
TARS........ Technical Assistance Recruitment Service [*United Nations*]
TARS........ Teen Age Republicans
TARS........ Terminal Automated RADAR Services [*Aviation*] (FAAC)

TARS........ Terrain Analog RADAR Simulator
TARS........ Terrain Avoidance RADAR System (MCD)
TARS........ Test and Repair Station
TARS........ Theater Army Replacement System (AABC)
TARS........ Three-Axis Reference System [*Used in reference to Titan missile*]
TARS........ Training and Administrative Reserves [*on permanent active duty*]
TARS........ Transportation Aircraft Rebuild Shops [*National Guard*] (MCD)
TARS........ Turnaround Ranging Station [*Telecommunications*] (TEL)
TARS-75.... Tactical Reconnaissance and Surveillance - 1975 [*Army*]
TARSA ...... Transportes Aereos Ranquetes, Sociedad Anonima [*Argentina*]
Tarsad Szle ... Tarsadalmi Szemle [*A publication*]
TARSCC ... Three-Axis Reference System Checkout Console [*Used in reference to Titan missile*]
TARSD...... Tropical Agriculture Research Series [*A publication*]
TARSLL.... Tender and Repair Ship Load List [*Navy*] (NG)
TARS OCUL ... Tarsis Oculorum [*To the Eyelids*] [*Pharmacy*]
TARS/SEA ... Theater Army Replacement System / Southeast Asia (SAA)
TART........ Tactical Antiradiation Tracker [*Military*] (CAAL)
TART........ Tartarum [*Tartar*] [*Pharmacy*] (ROG)
TART........ Tartrate
TART........ Task Analysis Reduction Technique [*Navy*]
TART........ Theodore Army Terminal
TART........ Transonic Armament Technology (MCD)
TART........ Twin Accelerator Ring Transfer (IEEE)
TARTA ...... Tactical RADAR Target Analysis [*Military*] (CAAL)
TARTC...... Theater Army Replacement and Training Command
TArts.......... Theater Arts [*A publication*]
Tartu Riikl Ul Toimetised ... Tartu Riikliku Uelikooli Toimetised [*A publication*]
TARU Research Note ... New South Wales. Traffic Accident Research Unit. TARU Research Note [*A publication*] (APTA)
TARVAN... Truck and Rail Van
TARWI...... Target Weather Information
TAS........... [*The*] Air Surgeon [*Army*]
TAS........... [*The*] Army Staff
TAS........... TACAN [*Tactical Air Navigation*] Antenna System (DWSG)
TAS........... Tactical Advisory Service [*Department of Commerce*]
TAS........... Tactical Air Support [*Tactical Air Command*]
TAS........... Tactical Airlift Squadron [*Air Force*]
TAS........... Tactical Area Switching
TAS........... Tactical Automated System (MCD)
TAS........... Tactical Automatic Switch [*Military*] (AABC)
TAS........... Taiwanese-American Society (EA)
TAS........... Tallow Alkyl Sulfate [*Surfactant*]
TAS........... Tampa Southern Railroad [*AAR code*]
TAS........... Taos, NM [*Location identifier*] [*FAA*] (FAAL)
TAS........... Tape Alteration Subroutine
TAS........... Target Acquisition System
TAS........... Tashkent [*Former USSR*] [*Seismograph station code, US Geological Survey*] (SEIS)
TAS........... Tashkent [*Former USSR*] [*Airport symbol*] (OAG)
TAS........... Tasmania
TAS........... Tasu Resources Ltd. [*Vancouver Stock Exchange symbol*]
TAS........... Tax Administration System [*Internal Revenue Service*]
TAS........... Technical Advisory Services [*Army*] (RDA)
TAS........... Telecom Analysis Systems, Inc.
TAS........... Telecommunications Authority Singapore
TAS........... Telemetry Antenna Subsystem (NASA)
TAS........... Telephone Answering Service [*or System*]
TAS........... Telephone Area Staff [*British*]
TAS........... Tempelhof Automatic System (DWSG)
TAS........... Temperature-Actuated Switch (IEEE)
TAS........... Terminal Access System (MCD)
TAS........... Terminal Address Selector
TAS........... Test Access Selector [*Telecommunications*] (TEL)
TAS........... Test Answer Sheets
TAS........... Test Article Specification (NASA)
TAS........... Test and Set [*Data processing*]
TAS........... Texture Analysis System [*Image analysis for biochemistry*]
TAS........... Theatre Arts Society [*British*]
TAS........... Three-Axis Stabilization (AAG)
TAS........... Time Air Speed (NATG)
TAS........... Torpedo and Antisubmarine [*Obsolete*] [*Navy*] [*British*]
TAS........... Towed Array SONAR
TAS........... Tracking Adjunct System [*I-HAWK*] (MCD)
TAS........... Tracking Antenna System
TAS........... Traditional Acupuncture Society [*Stratford-Upon-Avon, Warwickshire, England*] (EAIO)
TAS........... Traffic Analysis Survey (MCD)
TAS........... Training Aids Section [*Navy*]
TAS........... Transfer Alignment Set (DNAB)
TAS........... Transportes Aereos Salvador [*Brazil*]
TAS........... Transverse Air Spring
TAS........... Tribunal Arbitral du Sport [*Court of Arbitration of Sport - CAS*] [*Switzerland*] (EAIO)
TAS........... Triple Axis Spectrometer [*Biochemistry*]
TAS........... Troop Airlift Squadron (CINC)

TAS............ True Airspeed
TAS............ Tychon's Assembler (MCD)
TAS3.......... Transportation Aviation Supply Support System
TASA......... [*The*] Aircraft Service Association
TASA......... [*The*] Antique Stove Association (EA)
TASA......... [*The*] Assistant Secretary of the Army
TASA......... Tactical Air Support Aircraft
TASA......... Task and Skill Analysis [*Military*] (AABC)
TASA......... Teaching Atypical Students in Alberta [*A publication*]
TASA......... Technical Advisory Service for Attorneys [*Technical Advisory Service, Inc.*] [*Information service or system*]
TASA......... Television Audio Support Activity [*Army*]
TASA......... Test Area Support Assembly
TASA......... Tumor-Associated Surface Antigen [*Immunology*]
TASAE...... Training and Audio-Visual Support Activity - Europe (MCD)
T ASAE..... Transactions. ASAE [*American Society of Agricultural Engineers*] [*A publication*]
TASAG...... TACOM [*Tank Automotive Command*] Scientific Advisory Group [*DoD*] (EGAO)
TASAMS .. [*The*] Army Supply and Maintenance System (AABC)
TASAP ..... [*The*] Army Scientific Advisory Panel
TASAPS.... [*The*] Army Security Assistance Program Study Group
Tas Arch .... Tasmanian Architect [*A publication*] (APTA)
Tas Architect ... Tasmanian Architect [*A publication*] (APTA)
TASB......... Texas Archaeological Society. Bulletin [*A publication*]
Tas Bldg App R ... Tasmanian Building Appeal Reports [*A publication*] (APTA)
Tas Build ... Tasmanian Builder [*A publication*]
Tas Build J ... Tasmanian Building Journal [*A publication*]
TASC......... [*The*] Analytic Sciences Corp.
TASC......... Tabular Sequence Control
TASC......... Tactical Air Support Center (CINC)
TASC......... Tactical Articulated Swimmable Carrier (OA)
TASC......... Target Area Sequential Correlator (MCD)
TASC......... Teaching as a Career [*British*]
TASC......... Technical Activity Steering Committee [*Nuclear energy*] (NRCH)
TASC......... Tehran Area Support Center [*Military*] (MCD)
TASC......... Telecommunication Alarm Surveillance and Control [*AT & T*]
TASC......... Terminal Area Sequencing and Control
TASC......... Test Anxiety Scale for Children [*Psychology*]
TASC......... Total Absorption Shower Cascade
TASC......... Total Avionic Support Capability
TASC......... Training Aids Support Center [*Army*]
TASC......... Training and Audiovisual Support Center [*Army*]
TASC......... Treatment Alternatives to Street Crime [*Antidrug program*]
TASC......... True Airspeed Computer
TASCC ...... Tactical Air Support Coordination Center (MCD)
TASCC ...... Test Access Signaling Conversion Circuit [*Telecommunications*] (TEL)
Tasch Cr Acts ... Taschereau's Criminal Law Acts [*Canada*] [*A publication*] (DLA)
TASCO...... Tactical Automatic Switch Control Office
TASCOM ... Theater Army Support Command [*Terminated, 1975*] [*West Germany*] (AABC)
TASCOM(S) ... Theater Army Support Command (Supply)
TASCON... Television Automatic Sequence Control
TASC/SC .. Training and Audiovisual Support Center/Subcommunity [*Army*]
TASD......... Tactical Action Situation Display
TASD......... Terminal Railway, Alabama State Docks [*AAR code*]
TASDA...... [*The*] American Safe Deposit Association (EA)
TASDA...... Tactical Airborne SONAR Decision Aid
TASDC...... Tank-Automotive Systems Development Center [*Army*]
Tas Dep Agric Bull ... Bulletin. Department of Agriculture (Tasmania) [*A publication*] (APTA)
Tas Div Bul ... Institution of Engineers of Australia. Tasmania Division. Bulletin [*A publication*] (APTA)
TASE......... Tactical Air Support Element [*Military*] (AABC)
TASE......... Tactical Support Equipment
TASE......... Tel Aviv Stock Exchange [*Israel*] (IMH)
Tas Ed....... Tasmanian Education [*A publication*] (APTA)
Tas Ed Gaz ... Tasmanian Education Gazette [*A publication*] (APTA)
Tas Ed Rec ... Educational Record. Tasmania Education Department [*A publication*] (APTA)
Tas Educ.... Tasmanian Education [*A publication*] (APTA)
TASER ...... Teleactive Shock Electronic Repulsion [*Nonlethal weapon*]
TASER ...... Tom Swift and His Electric Rifle [*Electronic "stun gun"*] [*A trademark*]
TASES....... Tactical Airborne Signal Exploitation System (MCD)
TASF .... Tactical Air Strike Force [*Air Force*]
Tas Fish ..... Tasmanian Fisheries Research [*A publication*] (APTA)
TASFMA ... Target Acquisition Systems Force Mix Analysis [*Military*]
TASFMEA ... Target Acquisition Systems Force Mix Evaluation Analysis
Tas Fruitgrower and Farmer ... Tasmanian Fruitgrower and Farmer [*A publication*] (APTA)
TASFUIRA ... Things Are So Fouled Up It's Really Amazing [*Military slang*] [*Bowdlerized version*]
TASG......... Tactical Air Support Group [*Air Force*] (AFIT)
Tas Geol Surv Geol Atlas 1 Mile Ser ... Tasmanian Geological Survey. Geological Atlas. 1 Mile Series [*A publication*] (APTA)

Tas Govt Gaz ... Tasmanian Government Gazette [*A publication*] (APTA)
TASH .... [*The*] Association for the Severely Handicapped [*Later, TASH: the Association for Persons with Severe Handicaps*] (EA)
Tas Hist Research Assoc Papers & Proc ... Tasmanian Historical Research Association. Papers and Proceedings [*A publication*] (APTA)
Tas Hotel R ... Tasmanian Hotel Review [*A publication*] (APTA)
TAS/I .... Target Acquisition System / Integrated [*Military*] (DNAB)
TASI .... Time Assignment Speech Interpolation [*Timesharing technique*] [*Telecommunications*]
TASI .... Torpedo and Anti-Submarine Instructor [*British military*] (DMA)
TASI .... Transactional Analysis Systems Institute
Tas Ind...... Tasmanian Industry [*A publication*] (APTA)
TAS/IRAS ... Target Acquisition System / Infrared Automatic System [*Military*] (DNAB)
Tas Irreg Notes ... Tasmanian Irregular Notes [*A publication*]
TASIS........ [*The*] American School in Switzerland
TASJ .... Transactions. Asiatic Society of Japan [*A publication*]
Tas J Ag.... Tasmanian Journal of Agriculture [*A publication*] (APTA)
Tas J Agric ... Tasmanian Journal of Agriculture [*A publication*] (APTA)
Tas J Ed.... Tasmanian Journal of Education [*A publication*] (APTA)
TASK........ Temporary Assigned Skeleton [*Data processing*]
Taskent Inst Narod Hoz Naucn Zap ... Taskentskii Institut Narodnogo Hozjaistva Naucnye Zapiski [*A publication*]
Taskent Inst Narod Hoz Naucn Zap Mat v Prilozen ... Taskentskii Institut Narodnogo Hozjaistva Naucnye Zapiski. Matematika v Prilozenijah [*A publication*]
Taskent Politehn Inst Naucn Trudy ... Taskentskii Politehniceskii Institut Naucnye Trudy. Novaja Serija [*A publication*]
Taskent Politehn Inst Naucn Trudy NS ... Taskentskii Politehniceskii Institut Naucnye Trudy. Novaja Serija [*A publication*]
TASKFLOT ... Task Flotilla
TASKFORNON ... Allied Task Force, North Norway [*NATO*] (NATG)
Tasks Veg Sci ... Tasks for Vegetation Science [*A publication*]
TASL........ Theater Authorized Stockage List [*Military*] (AABC)
Tas Lab & Ind Bul ... Tasmania. Department of Labour and Industry. Bulletin [*A publication*] (APTA)
Tas LN...... Tasmanian Law Newsletter [*A publication*]
Tas LR ...... Tasmanian Law Reports [*A publication*] (APTA)
Tas L Rev... University of Tasmania. Law Review [*A publication*] (APTA)
TASM....... Tactical Air-to-Surface Missile (NATG)
TASM....... Tactical Antiship Missile (MCD)
TASM....... Tasmania (ROG)
Tasm .... Tasmanian State Reports [*A publication*]
TASM....... Tomahawk Antiship Missile (MCD)
TASM....... Trialkylstannylmaleate [*Organic chemistry*]
TASM........ Turbo Assembler [*Data processing*]
Tasm Acts ... Tasmania Acts of Parliament [*A publication*] (DLA)
Tasmania Build J ... Tasmanian Building Journal [*A publication*] (APTA)
Tasmania Dep Agric Annu Rep ... Tasmania. Department of Agriculture. Annual Report [*A publication*]
Tasmania Dep Mines Geol Atlas 1:250000 Ser SK ... Tasmania. Department of Mines. Geological Atlas. 1:250,000 Series SK [*A publication*]
Tasmania Dep Mines Geol Surv Bull ... Tasmania. Department of Mines. Geological Survey. Bulletin [*A publication*] (APTA)
Tasmania Dep Mines Geol Surv Rec ... Tasmania. Department of Mines. Geological Survey. Record [*A publication*] (APTA)
Tasmania Dep Mines Geol Surv Rep ... Tasmania. Department of Mines. Geological Survey. Report [*A publication*] (APTA)
Tasmania Dep Mines Tech Rep ... Tasmania. Department of Mines. Technical Report [*A publication*] (APTA)
Tasmania Dep Mines Underground Water Supply Pap ... Tasmania. Department of Mines. Underground Water Supply Paper [*A publication*] (APTA)
Tasmania For Comm Bull ... Tasmania. Forestry Commission. Bulletin [*A publication*]
Tasmania Geol Surv Bull ... Tasmania. Geological Survey. Bulletin [*A publication*] (APTA)
Tasmania Geol Surv Explanatory Rep ... Tasmania. Geological Survey. Explanatory Report [*A publication*]
Tasmania Geol Surv Explan Rep Geol Atlas 1 Mile Ser ... Tasmania. Geological Survey. Explanatory Report. Geological Atlas. 1 Mile Series [*A publication*]
Tasmania Geol Surv Rec ... Tasmania. Geological Survey. Record [*A publication*] (APTA)
Tasmania Geol Surv Rep ... Tasmania. Geological Survey. Report [*A publication*] (APTA)
Tasmania Geol Surv Underground Water Supply Pap ... Tasmania. Geological Survey. Underground Water Supply Paper [*A publication*] (APTA)
Tasmania Inland Fish Comm Rep ... Tasmania. Inland Fisheries Commission. Report [*A publication*]
Tasmania LR ... University of Tasmania. Law Review [*A publication*] (DLA)
Tasmania Mines Dep Bull ... Tasmania. Department of Mines. Bulletin [*A publication*]
Tasmanian Dep Agric Insect Pest Surv ... Tasmanian Department of Agriculture. Insect Pest Survey [*A publication*]
Tasmanian Dep Agric Pamp ... Tasmanian Department of Agriculture. Pamphlet [*A publication*]

Tasmanian Fish Res ... Tasmanian Fisheries Research [*A publication*]
Tasmanian Fis Res ... Tasmanian Fisheries Research [*A publication*]
Tasmanian For Comm Bull ... Tasmanian Forestry Commission. Bulletin [*A publication*]
Tasmanian J ... Tasmanian Journal of Natural Science [*A publication*]
Tasmanian J Agr ... Tasmanian Journal of Agriculture [*A publication*]
Tasmanian J Agric ... Tasmanian Journal of Agriculture [*A publication*]
Tasmanian U L Rev ... Tasmanian University. Law Review [*A publication*]
Tasmanian Univ L Rev ... Tasmanian University. Law Review [*A publication*]
Tasmania Parl Dir Mines Annu Rep ... Tasmania. Parliament. Director of Mines. Annual Report [*A publication*]
Tasm Dep Agric Bull ... Tasmania. Department of Agriculture. Bulletin [*A publication*] (APTA)
Tasm Dep Agric Res Bull ... Tasmania. Department of Agriculture. Research Bulletin [*A publication*] (APTA)
TASME ..... Tosyl-L-arginyl Sarcosine Methyl Ester [*Biochemistry*]
Tasm Fmr .. Tasmanian Farmer [*A publication*] (APTA)
Tasm Fruitgr Fmr ... Tasmanian Fruitgrower and Farmer [*A publication*] (APTA)
Tasm Fruitgrow Fmr ... Tasmanian Fruitgrower and Farmer [*A publication*] (APTA)
Tasm Geol Surv Bull ... Tasmania. Geological Survey. Bulletin [*A publication*] (APTA)
Tasm Geol Surv Geol Atlas 1 Mile Ser ... Tasmania. Geological Survey. Geological Atlas. 1 Mile Series [*A publication*] (APTA)
Tasm Geol Surv Undergr Wat Supply Pap ... Tasmania. Geological Survey. Underground Water Supply Paper [*A publication*] (APTA)
TASMGS .. Tomahawk Antiship Missile Guidance Set (MCD)
Tasm Hist Res Ass Pap Proc ... Tasmanian Historical Research Association. Papers and Proceedings [*A publication*] (APTA)
Tasm J Agr ... Tasmanian Journal of Agriculture [*A publication*]
Tasm J Agric ... Tasmanian Journal of Agriculture [*A publication*]
Tasm Nat ... Tasmanian Naturalist [*A publication*] (APTA)
TASMO ..... Tactical Air Support for Maritime Operations [*Navy*] (NVT)
TASMOL .. Tactical Aircraft Support Model (MCD)
Tas Motor Trade & Transport J ... Tasmanian Motor Trade and Transport Journal [*A publication*] (APTA)
Tasm SR .... Tasmanian State Reports [*A publication*]
Tasm St R .. Tasmanian State Reports [*A publication*]
Tasm UL Rev ... Tasmanian University. Law Review [*A publication*]
Tasm Univ Law Rev ... University of Tasmania. Law Review [*A publication*] (APTA)
Tas Nat ... Tasmanian Naturalist [*A publication*] (APTA)
Tas News ... Tasmanian Motor News [*A publication*] (APTA)
Tas News ... Tasmanian News Reports [*A publication*] (APTA)
Tas Nurse .. Tasmanian Nurse [*A publication*] (APTA)
TASO .... Television Allocations Study Organization [*Defunct*]
TASO .... Terminal Area Security Officer [*Military*] (AABC)
TASO .... Training Aids Service Office [*Army*] (AABC)
TASO .... Training and Audiovisual Support Officer [*Military*]
TASOS ...... Towed Array SONAR System
TASOSC ... Theater Army Special Operations Support Command
TASP .... [*The*] Army Studies Program (AABC)
TASP .... Target Antisubmarine Patrol (NVT)
TASP .... Telemetry Analysis and Simulation Program [*Spacecraft*] [*NASA*]
TASP .... Template-Assisted Synthetic Protein [*Biochemistry*]
TASP .... Tentative Acceptance Sampling Procedure [*Army*]
TASP .... Texas Archaeological Society. Papers [*A publication*]
TASP .... Toll Alternatives Studies Program [*Telecommunications*] (TEL)
TAS-PAC .. Total Analysis System for Production, Accounting, and Control [*Data processing*]
TASPR ...... Technical and Schedule Performance Report [*NASA*] (NASA)
TASQ .... Tactical Airlift Squadron [*Air Force*]
Tas R .... Tasmanian Reports [*A publication*] (APTA)
Tas R .... Tasmanian State Reports [*A publication*]
TASR .... Terminal Area Surveillance RADAR
TASR .... Torque Arm Speed Reducer
TASRA ..... Tabular System Reliability Analysis
TASRA ..... Thermal Activation-Strain Rate Analysis
TAS/RAS .. Target Acquisition System / RADAR Automatic System [*Military*] (DNAB)
TAS/RMS ... Target Acquisition Sytem / RADAR Manual System [*Military*] (DNAB)
TASROCO ... Tactical Aerial Surveillance and Reconnaissance Operational Capability Objectives [*1995*] (MCD)
TASS .... [*The*] Army Study System
TASS .... Tactical Air Support Section [*Military*]
TASS .... Tactical Air Support Squadron [*Military*]
TASS .... Tactical Avionics System Simulator [*Army*] (MCD)
TASS .... Tactical Signal Simulator [*Canadian Astronautics Ltd. RADAR threat simulation system*]
TASS .... Technical, Administrative, and Supervisory Section [*Amalgamated Union of Engineering Workers - Engineering Section*] [*British*]
TASS .... Technical Assembly System
TASS .... Telegraphnoye Agentstvo Sovyetskovo Soyuza [*Telegraph Agency of the Soviet Union*] [*News agency*]
TASS .... Terminal Application Support System (MCD)
TASS .... Terrain Analyst's Synthesizer Station [*Army*] (RDA)

TASS .... Towed Acoustic Surveillance System [*Marine science*] (MSC)
TASS .... Towed Array SONAR System
TASS .... Towed Array Surveillance System [*Navy*] (CAAL)
TASS .... Trouble Analysis System or Subsystem [*Telecommunications*] (TEL)
TASSA ...... [*The*] Army Signal Supply Agency
TASSC ...... [*The*] American Specialty Surety Council [*Later, ASA*] (EA)
TASSEL .... Three-Astronaut Space System Experimental Laboratory (MCD)
TASSI .... Tactical Airborne SIGINT Support Improvement Acquisition Plan (MCD)
TASSO ..... Tactical Special Security Office [*Army*] (AABC)
TASSO ..... Transatlantic Air Safety Service Organization
TASSO ..... Two-Arm Spectrometer Solenoid (MCD)
TASSq .... Tactical Air Support Squadron [*Military*] (AFM)
Tas S R ..... Tasmanian State Reports [*A publication*] (APTA)
TASSRAP ... Towed Array Surveillance Range Prediction (MCD)
TASST .... Tentative Airworthiness Standards for Supersonic Transports
TAST .... Tactical Assault Supply Transport (MCD)
TAST .... Test Article Signal Translator (MCD)
TAST .... Thermoacoustic Sensing Technique (IEEE)
TASTA ...... [*The*] Administrative Support Theaters Army
TASTE ...... Thermal Accelerated Short Time Evaporator [*Facetious term used in orange juice industry*]
Tas Teach .. Tasmanian Teacher [*A publication*] (APTA)
Tas Teacher ... Tasmanian Teacher [*A publication*] (APTA)
TASTG ...... Tactical Air Support Training Group [*Air Force*]
TASTNGSq ... Tactical Air Support Training Squadron [*Air Force*]
Tas Trader ... Tasmanian Trader and Successful Independent [*A publication*] (APTA)
Tas Tramp ... Tasmanian Tramp [*A publication*] (APTA)
TASTS ...... Tactical Air Support Training Squadron [*Air Force*]
TASTY ...... Tasty Baking Co. [*Associated Press abbreviation*] (APAG)
Tas Univ Gaz ... University of Tasmania. Gazette [*A publication*] (APTA)
Tas Univ Law R ... University of Tasmania. Law Review [*A publication*] (APTA)
Tas Univ Law Rev ... University of Tasmania. Law Review [*A publication*] (APTA)
Tas Univ L Rev ... Tasmanian University. Law Review [*A publication*] (APTA)
TASWD ..... Torpedo, Anti-Submarine, and Mine Warfare Division [*British military*] (DMA)
Tasw Lang Hist ... Taswell-Langmead's English Constitutional History [*10th ed.*] [*1946*] [*A publication*] (DLA)
TASWM .... Test ASW [*Antisubmarine Warfare*] Missile [*Navy*] (CAAL)
TAT .... [*The*] Absolute Truth [*In Julian Barnes' novel "Staring at the Sun"*]
TAT .... [*The*] Associated Turtles [*Defunct*] (EA)
TAT .... Tactical Analysis Team [*Military drug interdiction program*]
TAT .... Tactical Armament Turret (NG)
T & AT ...... Tank and Antitank [*Artillery and ammunition*] (NATG)
TAT .... Target Abilities Test [*Psychometrics*]
TAT .... Target Aircraft Transmitter
TAT .... Task Assignment Table (MCD)
TAT .... Tateyama [*Japan*] [*Seismograph station code, US Geological Survey*] (SEIS)
TAT .... Tatry/Poprad [*Former Czechoslovakia*] [*Airport symbol*] (OAG)
TAT .... Technical Acceptance Team [*NASA*] (AAG)
TAT .... Technical Approval Team
TAT .... Technical Assistance Team [*Air Force*] (AFM)
TAT .... Technical Assistance and Training
TAT .... Technology Application Team [*NASA*]
TAT .... Television Awareness Training
TAT .... Temporary Ambulance Train [*British military*] (DMA)
TAT .... Tensile Adhesion Test [*for coatings*]
TAT .... Terrorist Action Team [*Military*] (MCD)
TAT .... Tetanus Antitoxin [*Medicine*]
TAT .... Thematic Apperception Test [*Psychology*]
TAT .... Thinned Aperture Telescope
TAT .... Thromboplastin Activation Test [*Clinical chemistry*]
TAT .... Thrust-Augmented Thor [*NASA*]
TAT .... To Accompany Troops
TAT .... Tochas Affen Tish [*In television production company name "TAT Productions." Words are Yiddish and translate figuratively as "Let's Be Honest"*]
TAT .... Torpedo Attack Teacher [*Navy*]
TAT .... Total Air Temperature (NASA)
TAT .... Total Aircraft Time (MCD)
TAT .... Total Alert Time
TAT .... Total Antitryptic Activity [*Medicine*] (MAE)
TAT .... Touraine Air Transport [*Private airline*] [*French*] (EY)
TAT .... Tourist Authority of Thailand (ECON)
TAT .... Toxin-Antitoxin [*Also, TA*] [*Immunology*]
TAT .... Trace Acceptance Tester
TAT .... Training and Technology
TAT .... Trans-Activator [*Genetics*]
TAT .... Trans Atlantic Resources, Inc. [*Vancouver Stock Exchange symbol*]
TAT .... Transatlantic Telephone [*Cable*]
TAT .... Transcontinental Air Transport
TAT .... Transportes Aeroside Timor [*Portuguese Timor*]

TAT	Triaminotrinitrobenzene [*Organic chemistry*]
TAT	Triamterene [*Diuretic*]
TAT	True Air Temperature (AFM)
TAT	Turnaround Time
TAT	Two-Axis Tracking
TAT	Type-Approval Test
TAT	Tyrosine Aminotransferase [*An enzyme*]
Tatabanyai Szenbanyak Musz Kozgazdasagi Kozl ... Tatabanyai Szenbanyak Muszaki Kozgazdasagi Kozlemenyei [*Hungary*] [*A publication*]
TATAC......	Temporary Air Transport Advisory Committee [*NATO*] (NATG)
Tata Inst Fund Res Lectures on Math and Phys ... Tata Institute of Fundamental Research. Lectures on Mathematics and Physics [*A publication*]
Tata Inst Fund Res Studies in Math ... Tata Institute of Fundamental Research. Studies in Mathematics [*A publication*]
Tatar Neft ... Tatarskaya Neft [*A publication*]
TATAWS ..	Tank, Antitank, and Assault Weapons Study [*or System*] [*Army*]
TATB........	Theater Air Transportation Board
TATB........	Triaminotrinitrobenzene [*Organic chemistry*]
TATC.........	Tactical Air Traffic Control (NVT)
TATC.........	Terminal Air Traffic Control
TATC.........	Transatlantic Telephone Cable (IEEE)
TATCA......	Trialkoxytricarballylate [*Organic chemistry*]
TATCE	Terminal Air Traffic Control Element
TATCF	Terminal Air Traffic Control Facility
TATCO......	Tactical Automatic Telephone Central Office [*Military*]
TATCS	Terminal Air Traffic Control System
TATD	Task Assignment Table Display (MCD)
TATDL	Tabulated Assembly Technical Data List
TATE.........	Ashton-Tate Corp. [*NASDAQ symbol*] (NQ)
TATE.........	Tank Arrangement Thermal Efficiency [*Computer program*] (KSC)
TATEJ......	Tasmanian Association for the Teaching of English. Journal [*A publication*] (APTA)
TATER......	Talos-Terrier-Recruit [*Flight-test vehicle*]
Tate's Dig ..	Tate's Digest of Laws [*Virginia*] [*A publication*] (DLA)
TATG	Tactical Airlift Training Group [*Air Force*]
TATG	Tuned Anode Tuned Grid (DEN)
TATHS......	Tool and Trades History Society (EAIO)
TATI.........	Total Air Temperature Indicator
TATI.........	Tumor-Associated Trypsin Inhibitor [*Medicine*]
Tatigkeitsber Bundesanst Geowiss Rohst ... Taetigkeitsbericht. Bundesanstalt fuer Geowissenschaften und Rohstoffe [*A publication*]
Tatigkeitsber Geol Landsamt Nordrhein-Westfal ... Taetigkeitsbericht. Geologisches Landesamt Nordrhein-Westfalen [*A publication*]
Tatigkeitsber Niedersach Landsamt Bodenforsch ... Taetigkeitsbericht. Niedersachsisches Landesamt fuer Bodenforschung [*A publication*]
TATM	Tatum Petroleum Corp. [*Downey, CA*] [*NASDAQ symbol*] (NQ)
TATO	Taipei [*Taiwan*] [*Seismograph station code, US Geological Survey*] (SEIS)
TATP.........	TACFIRE [*Tactical Fire*] Advanced Training Program [*Army*]
TATP.........	Two-Axis Tracking Pedestal
TATR........	Tactical Air Target Recommender
TATr.........	Tyrosine Aminotransferase Regulator
TATRC......	Type-Approval Test Review Committee
TATS.........	Tactical Aerial Targets Squadron (MCD)
TATS.........	Tactical Airlift Training Squadron [*Air Force*]
TATS.........	Tactical Armament Turret System
TATS........	Tactical Transmission System Summary (KSC)
TATS........	Target Acquisition and Track System (MUGU)
TATS........	Technical Assistance and Training Survey [*Department of Labor*] (OICC)
TATS........	Test and Training Satellite [*Also, TETR, TTS*] [*NASA*]
TATSA......	Transportation Aircraft Test and Support Activity [*Military*]
Tatslil........	Tatslil [*The Chord*]. Forum for Music Research and Bibliography [*A publication*]
TATST	Tetanus Antitoxin Skin Test [*Medicine*] (MAE)
TATSU......	Transportation Aviation Test and Support
Tatsuta Tech Rev ... Tatsuta Technical Review [*A publication*]
TATT........	Technical Assistance and Technology Transfer (NOAA)
TATTE.......	Talos [*Missile*] Tactical Test Equipment
TATU........	Technical Advanced Training for Units (MCD)
TAU..........	Fort Meade, MD [*Location identifier*] [*FAA*] (FAAL)
TAU..........	Tasmania University [*Tasmania*] [*Seismograph station code, US Geological Survey*] (SEIS)
Tau	Taurus [*Constellation*]
TAU..........	Technical Advisory Unit (OICC)
TAU..........	Tel Aviv University [*Israel*]
TAU..........	Temporary Authorization [*Personnel*] (OICC)
TAU..........	Test Access Unit [*Telecommunications*] (TEL)
TAU..........	Thousand Astronomical Units
TAU..........	Transalta Utilities Corp. [*Toronto Stock Exchange symbol*]
TAU..........	Triton Acid Urea
TAU..........	Trunk Access Unit
TAU..........	Twin Agent Unit [*Fire fighting*] (NVT)

Taubmn......	Taubman Centers Co., Inc. [*Associated Press abbreviation*] (APAG)
TauCA	Taurus Municipal California Holdings [*Associated Press abbreviation*] (APAG)
TAUCH.....	Tauchnitz [*Bibliography*] (ROG)
TAUF........	Test Assembly Unloading Fixture [*Nuclear energy*] (NRCH)
TAUM.......	Groupe de Recherches pour la Traduction Automatique [*Universite de Montreal*] [*Canada*] [*Research center*]
Taun..........	Taunton's English Common Pleas Reports [*A publication*] (DLA)
TAUN........	Technical Assistance of the United Nations
Taunt (Eng) ... Taunton's English Common Pleas Reports [*127, 129 English Reprint*] [*A publication*] (DLA)
TauNY	Taurus Municipal New York Holdings [*Associated Press abbreviation*] (APAG)
TAUPDJ ...	Trends in Autonomic Pharmacology [*A publication*]
Taur	Taurus [*Constellation*]
TAUR	Taurus Petroleum, Inc. [*Denver, CO*] [*NASDAQ symbol*] (NQ)
TAUS........	Tobacco Association of United States (EA)
TAUSA......	Trans-Atlantic Universities Speech Association
Taut..........	Taunton's English Common Pleas Reports [*A publication*] (DLA)
TAUT	Tautology (ADA)
TAUTDV...	Texas A & M University. Sea Grant College. TAMU-SG [*A publication*]
TAV	Tau [*American Samoa*] [*Airport symbol*] (OAG)
TAV	Tavern (ROG)
TAV	Tavistock [*England*]
TAV	Tavurvur [*New Britain*] [*Seismograph station code, US Geological Survey*] (SEIS)
TAV	Technical Assistance Visit (MCD)
TAV	Technical Availability [*Navy*] (NG)
TAV	Temperature-Activated Vacuum [*Automotive engineering*]
TAV	Tender Availability [*Navy*]
TAV	Test and Validation (KSC)
TAV	Tomato Aspermy Virus
TAV	Toward, Away, versus Selection System [*Psychology*] (AEBS)
TAV	Transatmospheric Vehicle [*Proposed futuristic plane capable of flying at hypersonic speeds*]
TAVC........	Total Active Vitamin C [*Nutrition*]
TAVD	Trans-Atlantic Video, Inc. [*NASDAQ symbol*] (NQ)
TAVE........	Average Temperature (NRCH)
TAVE........	Thor-Agena Vibration Experiment [*NASA*]
TAVERNS ... Test and Verification Environment for Remote Network Systems (SSD)
TAVET......	Temperature Acceleration Vibration Environmental Tester
TAVI.........	Thorn Apple Valley, Inc. [*Southfield, MI*] [*NASDAQ symbol*] (NQ)
TAVIP.......	Tahun Vivere Pericoloso [*The Year of Living Dangerously*] [*President Sukarno's national policy in 1964*] [*Indonesia*]
T & AVR ... Territorial and Army Volunteer Reserve [*British*]
TAVRA......	Territorial Auxiliary and Volunteer Reserve Association [*British Armed Forces*]
TAVS........	Turbine Area Ventilation System [*Nuclear energy*] (NRCH)
TAVSC	Training and Audiovisual Support Center [*Army*]
TAW	Tactical Air [*or Airlift*] Wing
TAW	Tactical Assault Weapon
TAW	Tawu [*Republic of China*] [*Seismograph station code, US Geological Survey*] (SEIS)
TAW	Tennessee Wesleyan College, Athens, TN [*Library symbol*] [*Library of Congress*] (LCLS)
TAW	Terrawest [*Vancouver Stock Exchange symbol*]
TAW	Thrust-Augmented Wing [*NASA*] (MCD)
TAW	[*The*] Toledo, Angola & Western Railway Co. [*AAR code*]
TAW	Troop Airlift Wing (CINC)
TAW	Twice a Week [*Advertising frequency*]
TAWACS ..	Tactical Airborne Warning and Control System (AFM)
TAWAR	Tactical All Weather Attack Requirements [*Air Force*] (MCD)
TAWB	Through Air Waybill [*Shipping*] (DS)
TAWC	Tactical Air Warfare Center [*Air Force*]
TAWC	Tactical Armored Weapons Carrier (MCD)
TAWCS	Tactical Air Weapons Control System
TAWDS.....	Target Acquisition Weapon Delivery System [*Air Force*] (MCD)
TAWDS.....	Terminal Area Weapon Delivery Simulator (MCD)
TAWG	Tactical Air Warfare Group
TAWG	Target Acquisition Working Group [*Air Force*]
TAWOG	Travel Arrangements without Government Expense (FAAC)
TAWRS......	Tower Aviation Weather Reporting Station (NOAA)
TAWS........	Tactical Area Weather Sensor (MCD)
TAWS........	Tactical Automatic Weather Station [*Buoy*] (MSC)
TAWS........	Tactical Warfare Center [*Army*] (AABC)
TAWS........	Technical Analysis Work Sheet (AAG)
TAWS........	Terrain Analyst Work Station [*Army*] (RDA)
TAWS........	Total Airborne Weapon Systems (MUGU)
TAWS........	Total Armament Weapons System (MUGU)
TAWS........	Transonabuoy Automatic Weather System (SAA)
TAWT	Tawton [*England*]
TAX	Madison, WI [*Location identifier*] [*FAA*] (FAAL)
TAX	Tactical Air Exercise (CINC)

TAX .... Tarxien International, Inc. [*Toronto Stock Exchange symbol*]
Tax............. Taxandria [*A publication*]
Tax............. Taxation [*A publication*]
TAX .... Taxation for Accountants [*A publication*]
TAX .... Taxiing [*Aviation*]
TAX .... Training Assessment Exercise
Tax ABC.... Canada Tax Appeal Board Cases [*A publication*] (DLA)
Tax Acct..... Taxation for Accountants [*A publication*] (DLA)
Tax Ad .... Tax Advisor [*A publication*]
Tax Adm'rs News ... Tax Administrators News [*A publication*] (DLA)
Tax Adv ..... Tax Advisor [*A publication*]
Tax Aust .... Taxation in Australia [*A publication*]
Tax Cas...... Tax Cases [*A publication*] (DLA)
Tax Conf .... Tax Conference [*A publication*]
Tax Coun Q ... Tax Counselor's Quarterly [*A publication*]
Tax Ct Mem Dec ... Tax Court Memorandum Decisions [*Commerce Clearing House*] [*A publication*] (DLA)
Tax Ct Mem Dec CCH ... Tax Court Memorandum Decisions. Commerce Clearing House [*A publication*]
Tax Ct Mem Dec P-H ... Tax Court Memorandum Decisions. Prentice-Hall [*A publication*]
Tax Ct Rep ... Tax Court Reporter [*Commerce Clearing House*] [*A publication*] (DLA)
Tax Ct Rep CCH ... Tax Court Reports. Commerce Clearing House [*A publication*]
Tax Ct Rep Dec ... Tax Court Reported Decisions [*Prentice-Hall, Inc.*] [*A publication*] (DLA)
Tax Ct Rep Dec P-H ... Tax Court Reported Decisions. Prentice-Hall [*A publication*]
Tax Ct Rep & Mem Dec (P-H) ... Tax Court Reported and Memorandum Decisions (Prentice-Hall, Inc.) [*A publication*] (DLA)
Taxes .... Tax Magazine [*A publication*] (DLA)
Tax Exec.... Tax Executive [*A publication*]
Tax-Exempt Org P-H ... Tax-Exempt Organizations. Prentice-Hall [*A publication*]
Tax Expend ... Tax Expenditures. Budget Control Options and 5-Year Projections for Fiscal Years 1983-1987 [*A publication*]
Tax Fin and Est Pl ... Tax, Financial, and Estate Planning for the Owner of a Closely Held Corporation [*A publication*]
TAXI.......... Transparent Asynchronous Transceiver Interface
TAXIR....... Taxonomic Information Retrieval [*Data processing*] (DIT)
Tax Law..... Tax Lawyer [*A publication*]
Tax for Law ... Taxation for Lawyers [*A publication*]
Tax Law R ... Tax Law Review [*A publication*]
Tax Law Rep ... Tax Law Reporter [*A publication*] (DLA)
TAXLE ...... Tandem Cantilevered Axle
Tax LR....... Tax Law Reporter [*A publication*] (DLA)
Tax LR .... Tax Law Review [*A publication*]
Tax L Rep .. Tax Law Reporter [*A publication*] (DLA)
Tax L Rev .. Tax Law Review [*A publication*]
Tax Mag .... Tax Magazine [*A publication*] (DLA)
Tax Man.... Tax Management [*A publication*] (DLA)
Tax Management Int'l ... Tax Management International Journal [*A publication*]
Tax Mgmt (BNA) ... Tax Management (Bureau of National Affairs) [*A publication*] (DLA)
Tax Mgmt Int'l J ... Tax Management International Journal [*A publication*] (DLA)
Tax Mngm't ... Tax Management [*Bureau of National Affairs*] [*A publication*] (DLA)
Tax Mo (Manila) ... Tax Monthly (Manila) [*A publication*]
TAXN .... Taxation (ROG)
Taxn in Aust ... Taxation in Australia [*A publication*] (APTA)
TAXON ..... Taxonomy
Taxon Index ... Taxonomic Index [*A publication*]
Taxpayers Bul ... Taxpayers' Bulletin [*A publication*] (APTA)
Tax Pl Int... Tax Planning International [*A publication*] (DLA)
Tax Pl Rev ... Tax Planning Review [*A publication*] (DLA)
Tax Pract Forum ... Tax Practitioners Forum [*A publication*] (DLA)
Tax R .... Tax Review [*A publication*]
Tax R .... Taxation Reports [*England*] [*A publication*] (DLA)
Tax Rev...... Tax Review [*A publication*]
Tax & Rev ... Taxation and Revenue (DLA)
t-ay--- .... Antarctica [*MARC geographic area code*] [*Library of Congress*] (LCCP)
TAY .... Taylor, FL [*Location identifier*] [*FAA*] (FAAL)
Tay............. Taylor's North Carolina Reports [*1 North Carolina*] [*1798-1802*] [*A publication*] (DLA)
Tay............. Taylor's Supreme Court Reports [*1847-48*] [*Bengal, India*] [*A publication*] (DLA)
Tay............. Taylor's Upper Canada King's Bench Reports [*1823-1827*] [*A publication*] (DLA)
Tay............. Tayside [*Scotland*] (WGA)
TAY .... Tule Lake Aster Yellows [*Plant pathology*]
Tay & B...... Taylor and Bell's Bengal Reports [*India*] [*A publication*] (DLA)
Tay Bank L ... Taylor on the Bankruptcy Law [*A publication*] (DLA)
Tay Bk R... Taylor's Book of Rights [*1833*] [*A publication*] (DLA)
Tay Civ L... Taylor's Elements of Civil Law [*A publication*] (DLA)
TAYD .... Taylor Devices, Inc. [*NASDAQ symbol*] (NQ)
Tay Eq Jur ... Taylor on Equity Jurisprudence [*A publication*] (DLA)

Tay Ev........ Taylor on Evidence [*12th ed.*] [*1931*] [*A publication*] (DLA)
Tay Glos ..... Taylor's Law Glossary [*2nd ed.*] [*1823*] [*A publication*] (DLA)
Tay Gov..... Taylor on Government [*A publication*] (DLA)
Tay J L....... [*J. L.*] Taylor's Reports [*1 North Carolina*] [*A publication*] (DLA)
Tayl Civil Law ... Taylor on Civil Law [*A publication*] (DLA)
Tayl Corp... Taylor on Private Corporations [*A publication*] (DLA)
Tayl Ev....... Taylor on Evidence [*A publication*] (DLA)
Tay L Gl..... Taylor's Law Glossary [*A publication*] (DLA)
Tayl Gloss ... Taylor's Law Glossary [*A publication*] (DLA)
Tayl Hist Gav ... [*Silas*] Taylor's History of Gavelkind [*A publication*] (DLA)
Tayl Landl & Ten ... Taylor's Landlord and Tenant [*A publication*] (DLA)
Tayl Med Jur ... Taylor's Medical Jurisprudence [*A publication*] (DLA)
Tayl NC ..... Taylor's North Carolina Reports [*1 North Carolina*] [*A publication*] (DLA)
Taylor .... Taylor's Customary Laws of Rembau [*1903-28*] [*Malaya*] [*A publication*] (DLA)
Taylor .... Taylor's North Carolina Reports [*1 North Carolina*] [*A publication*] (DLA)
Taylor .... Taylor's North Carolina Term Reports [*4 North Carolina*] [*A publication*] (DLA)
Taylor .... Taylor's Reports [*Bengal, India*] [*A publication*] (DLA)
Taylor .... Taylor's Upper Canada King's Bench Reports [*A publication*] (DLA)
Taylor KB (Can) ... Taylor's Upper Canada King's Bench Reports [*A publication*] (DLA)
Taylor (Malaya) ... Taylor's Customary Laws of Rembau [*1903-28*] [*Malaya*] [*A publication*] (DLA)
Taylor Soc Bul ... Taylor Society. Bulletin [*A publication*]
Taylor UC ... Taylor's Upper Canada King's Bench Reports [*A publication*] (DLA)
Tayl Priv Corp ... Taylor on Private Corporations [*A publication*] (DLA)
Tayl St .... Taylor's Revised Statutes [*Wisconsin*] [*A publication*] (DLA)
Tay L & T .. Taylor's Landlord and Tenant [*A publication*] (DLA)
Tay Med Jur ... Taylor's Medical Jurisprudence [*12th ed.*] [*1966*] [*A publication*] (DLA)
TAYMEL.. Taylor Woodrow Management & Engineering Ltd. [*British*] (IRUK)
Tay NC ...... Taylor's North Carolina Reports [*1 North Carolina*] [*A publication*] (DLA)
Tay Poi...... Taylor on Poisons [*3rd ed.*] [*1875*] [*A publication*] (DLA)
Tay Rep...... Taylor's North Carolina Reports [*1 North Carolina*] [*A publication*] (DLA)
TAYS........ Taylor [*S.*] Companies, Inc. [*Columbus, GA*] [*NASDAQ symbol*] (NQ)
Tay Tit .... Taylor on Tithe Commutation [*1876*] [*A publication*] (DLA)
Tay UC ...... Taylor's Upper Canada King's Bench Reports [*1 vol.*] [*1823-27*] [*A publication*] (DLA)
Tay Wills ... Taylor's Precedents of Wills [*A publication*] (DLA)
Tay Wis Stat ... Taylor's Wisconsin Statutes [*A publication*] (DLA)
TAZ .... Tabak Zeitung. Fachorgan der Tabakwirtschaft [*A publication*]
TAZ .... Tactical Alert Zone (NATG)
TAZ .... Taylorville, IL [*Location identifier*] [*FAA*] (FAAL)
TAZ .... Theater Administrative Zone [*Military*]
TAZ .... Traffic Analysis Zone [*Bureau of the Census*] (GFGA)
TAZ .... Triazolam [*Tranquilizer*]
TAZARA... Tanzania-Zambia Railway
TB .... Aerospatiale (SOCATA) Stark KG [*Germany*] [*ICAO aircraft manufacturer identifier*] (ICAO)
TB .... Automotive Engine Rebuilders Association. Technical Bulletin [*A publication*] (EAAP)
Tb............... Body Temperature [*Medicine*]
tb............... Tablespoon [*Measure*] (WGA)
TB .... Tabulation Block (MSA)
TB .... Tail Back [*Football*]
TB .... Talk Back [*NASA*] (KSC)
TB .... Talmud Bavli (BJA)
TB .... Tangential Bracket
TB .... Tank Battalion [*Army*]
TB .... Tape Backup Unit
TB .... Tapes for the Blind [*Defunct*] (EA)
TB .... Tariff Bureau
T & B......... Taylor and Bell's Calcutta Supreme Court Reports [*India*] [*A publication*] (DLA)
TB .... Techbyte, Inc. [*Vancouver Stock Exchange symbol*]
TB .... Technical Bulletin [*Military*]
TB .... Telegraph Bureau
TB .... Temple Biographies [*A publication*]
TB .... Tempo Brasileiro [*A publication*]
TB .... Temporary Buoy [*Nautical charts*]
TB .... Tenor, Bass (CDAI)
Tb............... TeraBIT [*Binary Digit*] [*10^{12} BITs*]
TB .... Terabyte [*10^{12} bytes*]
Tb............... Terbium [*Chemical element*]
TB .... Terminal Base (MCD)
TB .... Terminal Block
TB .... Terminal Board
TB .... Terminal Bronchiole [*Medicine*] (MAE)
TB .... Test Bed (MCD)
TB .... Test Bulletin
TB .... Theologische Blaetter [*Leipzig*] [*A publication*]

TB	Thermobarometer
TB	Thexylborane [*Organic chemistry*]
TB	Thoroughbred
TB	Thrill Book [*A publication*]
TB	Thromboxane B [*Also, TxB, TXB*] [*Biochemistry*]
TB	Throttle Body [*Automotive engineering*]
T/B	Thunderbird [*Automobile*]
TB	Thymol Blue [*An indicator*]
TB	Tile Base [*Technical drawings*]
T/B	Tile Block [*Technical drawings*]
TB	Time-Bandwidth
TB	Time Base
TB	Time Duration of Burn (MCD)
TB	Time between Points [*Experimentation*]
TB	Times at Bat [*Baseball*]
T/B	Title Block (SAA)
Tb	Tobit [*Old Testament book*] [*Roman Catholic canon*]
TB	Toggle Buffer (MCD)
TB	Toluidine Blue [*Organic chemistry*]
TB	Tone Burst
T & B	Top and Bottom [*Technical drawings*]
T/B	Top to Bottom
TB	Top Boy [*British*] (DSUE)
TB	Torch Bible Commentaries [*A publication*] (BJA)
TB	Torch Brazing
TB	Torpedo Boat [*Navy symbol*] [*Obsolete*]
TB	Torpedo Bomber [*or Bombing*]
TB	Torsion Bar [*Automotive engineering*]
TB	Total Bases
TB	Total Bilirubin [*Clinical chemistry*]
TB	Total Blank [*Entertainment slang for poor show town*]
TB	Total Body [*Nuclear energy*] (NRCH)
TB	Total Bouts [*Boxing*]
TB	Total Burn
TB	Tourism Brisbane [*Australia*]
TB	Towel Bar [*Technical drawings*]
TB	Tracer Bullet
TB	Tracheal-Bronchiolar [*Region*] [*Medicine*]
TB	Tracheobronchitis [*Medicine*]
TB	Tractor Biplane
TB	Trading Bank
TB	Trafalgar Brookmount [*British*]
TB	Traffic Bureau
TB	Training Back [*Main parachute*]
TB	Training Battalion [*British military*] (DMA)
TB	Tranquility Base [*Moon landing site*]
TB	Transfer Building
TB	Transmitter-Blocker (DEN)
TB	Trapezoid Body [*Audiometry*]
TB	Travelair [*Cargo*] BV [*Netherlands*] [*ICAO designator*] (FAAC)
TB	Treasury Bill
TB	Treasury Board Secretariat [*Canada*]
TB	Trial Balance [*Bookkeeping*]
TB	Trial Balloon
TB	Triple-Braided (CET)
TB	Troop Basis [*Military*]
T & B	Truck and Bus
TB	True Bearing [*Navigation*]
TB	True Blue [*A fluorescent dye*]
TB	Tryptone Broth [*Culture medium*]
TB	Tubercle Bacillus [*Bacteriology*]
TB	Tuberculin [*or Tuberculosis*] (AABC)
TB	Tumor-Bearing [*Animal*]
TB	Tundra Biome [*Ecological biogeographic study*]
TB	Turbine Building [*Nuclear energy*] (NRCH)
T & B	Turn-and-Bank Indicators
T and B	Turned and Bored
TB	Tvorba [*A publication*]
TB	Twin Branch Railroad Co. [*AAR code*]
TB	Twirly Birds (EA)
TB	Tyndale Bulletin [*A publication*]
TBA	[*The*] Bettmann Archive [*A publication*]
TBA	Tabibuga [*Papua New Guinea*] [*Airport symbol*] (OAG)
TBA	Tables of Basic Allowances [*Previously, Basic Tables of Commissioning Allowances*] [*Navy*]
TBA	Task Budget Allocation (MCD)
TBA	Taurine Bibliophiles of America (EA)
TBA	Television Bureau of Advertising
TBA	Terminal Board Assembly (MSA)
TBA	Tertiary Butyl Acetate [*Organic chemistry*]
TBA	Tertiary Butyl Alcohol [*Gasoline additive*]
TBA	Tertiary-Butylamine [*Organic chemistry*]
TBA	Tertiary-Butylarsine [*Organic chemistry*]
TBA	Test of Basic Assumptions [*Psychology*]
TBA	Test Bed Aircraft
TBA	Test Boring Association (EA)
TBA	Testosterone-Binding Affinity [*Endocrinology*] (MAE)
TBA	Thiobarbituric Acid [*Organic chemistry*]
TBA	Thyroxine-Binding Albumin [*Biochemistry*] (MAE)
TBA	Tires, Batteries, and Accessories

TBA	To Be Activated [*Military*]
TBA	To Be Added (AAG)
TBA	To Be Agreed (AIA)
TBA	To Be Announced
TBA	To Be Assigned
TBA	To Be Avoided [*Slang*]
TBA	Torsional Braid Analysis [*Instrumentation*]
TBA	Towed Buoy Antenna
TBA	Tributylamine [*Organic chemistry*]
TBA	Trichlorobenzoic Acid [*Herbicide*] [*Organic chemistry*]
TBA	Tuba [*Music*]
TBA	Tumor-Bearing Animal (AAMN)
TBA	Twin Bonanza Association (EA)
TBAB	Tetrabutylammonium Bromide [*Organic chemistry*]
TBAB	Theosophical Book Association for the Blind (EA)
TBAC........	Tertiary-Butylacetyl Chloride [*Organic chemistry*]
TBACC......	Tetrabutylammonium Chlorochromate [*Organic chemistry*]
TBAC/FLM ...	Treasury Board Advisory Committee on Federal Land Management [*Canada*]
TBAD	To Be Advised (AIA)
TBAF	Tetrabutylammonium Fluoride [*Organic chemistry*]
TBAF	Tetrabutylammonium Fluoroborate [*Organic chemistry*]
TBAG	To Be Agreed (AIA)
TBAH	Tetrabutylammonium Hydroxide [*Organic chemistry*]
TBAHS......	Tetrabutylammonium Hydrogen Sulfate [*Organic chemistry*]
TBAI	Temporary Base Activation Instruction (AAG)
TBAI.........	Tidbit Alley, Inc. [*New York, NY*] [*NASDAQ symbol*] (NQ)
TBAM	Tone Burst Amplitude Modulation
TBAN	To Be Announced [*Army*] (AABC)
TBAP........	Tetrabutylammoniumperchlorate [*Photovoltaic energy systems*]
TBARA......	Trakehner Breed Association and Registry of America [*Defunct*] (EA)
TBAS........	[*The*] Band Appreciation Society (EAIO)
TBAT........	Tow/Bushmaster Armored Turret [*Military*]
TBAWRBA ...	Travel by Military Aircraft, Military and/or Naval Water Carrier, Commercial Rail and/or Bus Is Authorized [*Army*] (AABC)
TBAX........	Tube Axial
TBAZFCA ...	Toledo Bird Association, Zebra Finch Club of America (EA)
TBB...........	Columbus, MS [*Location identifier*] [*FAA*] (FAAL)
TBB...........	Die Tempel von Babylon und Borsippa [*A publication*] (BJA)
TBB...........	Temporal Bone Banks [*Otology*] (EA)
TBB...........	Tenor, Baritone, Bass
TBB...........	Tobex Resources Ltd. [*Vancouver Stock Exchange symbol*]
T & BB.......	Top and Bottom Bolt [*Technical drawings*]
TBB...........	Transbronchial Biopsy [*Medicine*]
TBB...........	Trolleybus Bulletin [*A publication*] (EAAP)
TB & B	Tuberculosis and Brucellosis [*Medicine*] (ADA)
TBBA........	Terephthalyl Bis(butylaniline) [*Organic chemistry*]
TBBF	Top Baseband Frequency
TBBM.......	Total Body Bone Mineral
TBBPA	Tetrabromobisphenol-A [*Organic chemistry*]
TBBS	[*The*] Bread Board System [*eSoft, Inc.*] [*Data processing*] (PCM)
TBBSA	Transactions. British Bryological Society [*A publication*]
TBC...........	Belmont College, Nashville, TN [*OCLC symbol*] (OCLC)
TBC...........	Confederation College of Applied Arts and Technology [*UTLAS symbol*]
TBC...........	Taiwan Base Command (CINC)
TBC...........	Tanker and Bulk Carrier
TBC...........	Tasty Baking Co. [*AMEX symbol*] (SPSG)
TBC...........	Technology & Business Communications, Inc. [*Information service or system*] (IID)
TBC...........	Television Briefing Console
TBC...........	Tembec Inc. [*Toronto Stock Exchange symbol*]
TBC...........	Terminal Buffer Controller (NASA)
TBC...........	Tertiary-Butylcatechol [*Organic chemistry*]
TBC...........	Theatre Ballet of Canada
TBC...........	Thermal Barrier Coating (RDA)
TBC...........	Thyroxine-Binding Capacity [*Biochemistry*]
TBC...........	Thyroxine-Binding Coagulin [*Biochemistry*] (MAE)
TBC...........	Time Base Corrector [*Videotape recording element*] [*Early processing device*]
TBC...........	To Be Cooked [*Food*]
TBC...........	Token Bus Controller [*Motorola, Inc.*]
TBC...........	Torch Bible Commentaries [*New York/London*] [*A publication*] (BJA)
TBC...........	Torrey Botanical Club (EA)
TBC...........	Toss Bomb Computer
TBC...........	Total Body Calcium
TBC...........	Total Body Carbon
TBC...........	Trinidad Base Command [*World War II*]
TBC...........	Trunk Block Connector
TBC...........	Tuba City, AZ [*Location identifier*] [*FAA*] (FAAL)
TBC...........	Tube Bending Chart
TBC...........	Tubercle Bacillus [*Bacteriology*]
TBC...........	Tuberculosis
TBC...........	Turbulent Bed Contactor [*Chemical engineering*]
TBCA........	Test Boring Contractors Association [*Later, TBA*] (EA)
TBCA........	Transportation Brokers Conference of America (EA)

TBCC......... TBC Corp. [*NASDAQ symbol*]   (NQ)
TBCC......... Tom Baker Cancer Centre [*University of Calgary*] [*Formerly, Southern Alberta Cancer Centre*] [*Research center*]   (RCD)
TBCCW..... Turbine-Building Closed Cooling Water [*Nuclear energy*]   (NRCH)
TBCR........ Times British Colonies Review [*London*] [*A publication*]
TBCX........ [*The*] Banking Center [*Waterbury, CT*] [*NASDAQ symbol*]   (NQ)
TBD .... Tactical Battle Drill [*Army*]   (INF)
TBD .... Target Bearing Designator [*Navy*]
TBD .... Terminal Bomber Defense [*Army*]   (AABC)
TBD .... Thibodaux, LA [*Location identifier*] [*FAA*]   (FAAL)
TBD .... Thousand Barrels per Day [*Also, KBD*]
TBD .... To Be Declassified   (AAG)
TBD .... To Be Defined
TBD .... To Be Designated   (MCD)
TBD .... To Be Determined   (AFM)
TBD .... To Be Developed   (NASA)
TBD .... To Be Disbanded
TBD .... To Be Done   (AAG)
TBD .... Too Badly Decomposed
TBD .... Torpedo-Boat Destroyer [*Obsolete*]
TBD .... Total Body Density [*Medicine*]   (MAE)
TBD .... Trans Border Energy [*Vancouver Stock Exchange symbol*]
TBD .... Triazabicydo-decene [*Organic chemistry*]
TBD .... Troubleshooting Block Diagram
TBD .... Tube Bending Data   (MCD)
TBD .... Twin Boundary Diffusion
TBDA .... Thexylborane-N, N-Diethylaniline [*Organic chemistry*]
TBDD .... Tetrabromodibenzo-p-dioxin [*Organic chemistry*]
TBDF........ Transborder Data Flows [*Also, TDF*] [*Telecommunications*]
TBDL........ To Be Designated Later   (CINC)
TBDL........ Total Bile-Duct Ligation [*Medicine*]
TBDMIM ... Tertiary-Butyldimethylsilylimidazole [*Organic chemistry*]
TBDMS...... Tertiary-Butyldimethylsilyl [*Organic chemistry*]
TBDMSCI ... Tertiary-Butyldimethylsilyl Chloride [*Also, TBSCI*] [*Organic chemistry*]
TBDPS ...... Tertiary-Butyldiphenysilyl [*Also, TBDMS, TBS*] [*Organic chemistry*]
TBDS........ Test Base Dispatch Service   (AAG)
TBD/TDA ... Too Badly Decomposed/Technician Destroyed Animal [*Laboratory testing*]
TBE........... Federation Europeenne des Fabricants de Tuiles et de Briques [*European Association of Brick and Tile Manufacturers*]   (EAIO)
TBE........... Tetrabromoethane [*Microscopy*]
TBE........... Texas Business Executive [*A publication*]
TBE........... Thread Both Ends   (MSA)
TBE........... Tiber Energy Corp. [*Toronto Stock Exchange symbol*]
TBE........... Tick-Borne Encephalitis
TBE........... Time Base Error
TBE........... To Be Evaluated   (NASA)
TBE........... To Be Expended   (AAG)
TBE........... Tobe, CO [*Location identifier*] [*FAA*]   (FAAL)
TBE........... Toronto Board of Education, Professional Library [*UTLAS symbol*]
TBE........... Total Body Ergometer
TBE........... Total Breech Extraction [*Gynecology*]
TBE........... Trade Opportunities in Taiwan [*A publication*]
TBE........... Transmitter Buffer Empty [*Data processing*]
TBE........... Tris-Borate Buffer Electrophoresis
TBE........... Tris-Borate-EDTA [*Ethylenediaminetetraacetate*] [*Buffer*]
TBE........... Tuberculin Bacillen Emulsion [*Medicine*]
TBEA........ Truck Body and Equipment Association   (EA)
TBE Class ... Timber Bulletin for Europe. Classification and Definitions of Forest Products [*A publication*]
TBEM........ Terminal-Based Electronic Mail
TBeP......... Polk County High School, Benton, TN [*Library symbol*] [*Library of Congress*]   (LCLS)
TBEP........ Tri(butoxyethyl) Phosphate [*Organic chemistry*]
TBESC....... Technology Base Executive Steering Commitee [*Army*]   (RDA)
TBESI....... Turbine-Building Exhaust System Isolation [*Nuclear energy*]   (NRCH)
TBEX........ Tube Expander
TBF.......... Tabiteuea North [*Kiribati*] [*Airport symbol*]   (OAG)
TBF.......... Tail Bomb Fuse   (KSC)
TBF.......... Test de Bon Fonctionnement [*Spacelab*]   (MCD)
TBF.......... Testicular Blood Flow [*Physiology*]
TBF.......... Tie Bus Fault
TBF.......... Time between Failures [*Quality control*]   (AFIT)
TBF.......... To Be Funded [*Contracting*] [*Military*]
TBF.......... Torpedo Bomber Fighter   (NATG)
TBF.......... Total Body Fat
TBF.......... Tour Basing Fare [*Air travel term*]
TBF.......... Tributyl Phosphate [*Organic chemistry*]
TBF.......... Two-Body Force
TBFC........ Teresa Brewer Fan Club   (EA)
TBFC........ Tom Burford Fan Club   (EA)
TBFC........ Tony Booth Fan Club   (EA)
TBFG........ Tom Baker Friendship Group   (EAIO)

TBFU......... Twin-Ball Fire Fighting Unit [*Navy*]   (DNAB)
TBFX .... Tube Fixture [*Tool*]   (AAG)
TBG .... Tabubil [*Papua New Guinea*] [*Airport symbol*]   (OAG)
TBG .... Testosterone-Binding Globulin [*Endocrinology*]
TBG .... Teubners Bibliotheca Scriptorum Graecorum et Romanorum   (BJA)
TBG .... Thyroxine-Binding Globulin [*Biochemistry*]
TBG .... Thyssen-Bornemisza Group NV [*Netherlands*]
TBG .... Tipping Bucket Gauge   (NOAA)
TBG .... Tubing   (MSA)
TBGAA...... Travel by Government Automobile Authorized
TBGP........ Tactical Bomb Group [*Air Force*]
TBGP........ Total Blood Granulocyte Pool [*Hematology*]
TBGTA...... Travel by Government Transportation Authorized [*Military*]   (AABC)
TBH.......... Tablas [*Philippines*] [*Airport symbol*]   (OAG)
TBH .... Technical Benzene Hexachloride [*Organic chemistry*]
TBH .... Test Bed Harness   (MCD)
TBH .... Test Bench Harness   (NG)
TBH .... Total Body Hematocrit [*Medicine*]   (MAE)
TBH .... TourBase Hotel-/Unterkunftsdaten [*Jaeger-Verlag GmbH*] [*Germany*] [*Information service or system*]   (CRD)
TBH .... Trinidad [*Brigand Hill*] [*Trinidad-Tobago*] [*Seismograph station code, US Geological Survey*]   (SEIS)
TBHBA ..... Tribromo(hydroxy)benzoic Acid [*Organic chemistry*]
TBHP .... Tertiary-Butyl Hydroperoxide [*Organic chemistry*]
TBHP .... Trihydroxybutyrophenone [*Antioxidant*] [*Organic chemistry*]
TBHQ........ Tertiary-Butylhydroquinone [*Also, MTBHQ*] [*Organic chemistry*]
TBI............ Ink and Print [*A publication*]
TBI............ Target Bearing Indicator [*Military*]
TBI............ Telecom Broadcasting, Inc. [*Oceanside, CA*] [*Telecommunications service*]   (TSSD)
TBI............ Test Bed Installation   (MCD)
TBI............ Test Bench Installation   (NG)
TBI............ Thomson Business Information [*The Thomson Corp.*] [*Publishing*]
TBI............ Threaded Blind Insert
TBI............ Throttle Body Fuel Injection [*Automotive engineering*]
TBI............ Through-Bulkhead Initiator [*Military*]   (MCD)
TBI............ Thyroxine-Binding Index [*Biochemistry*]   (MAE)
TBI............ Time, Bulb, Instantaneous [*Initials on certain Kodak cameras*]
TBI............ Time between Inspections [*Quality control*]
TBI............ To Be Inactivated
TBI............ To Be Indicated   (AIA)
TBI............ Total Body Irradiation [*Medicine*]
TBI............ Training [*A publication*]
TBI............ Traumatic Brain Injury [*Medicine*]
TBI............ Trinity Bible Institute, Ellendale, ND [*OCLC symbol*]   (OCLC)
TBI............ Tromboni [*Trombones*]
TBI............ Tubuai [*Tubuai Islands*] [*Seismograph station code, US Geological Survey*]   (SEIS)
TBIFC........ Thom Bierdz International Fan Club   (EA)
TbIG .... Terbium Iron Garnet   (IEEE)
TBII .... Thyrotropin-Binding Inhibitor Immunoglobulin
TBIL.......... Total Bilirubin [*Clinical chemistry*]
T Bili.......... Total Bilirubin [*Clinical chemistry*]   (MAE)
Tbilisis Univ Sromebi ... Stalinis Sacheolobis Tbilisis Universitatis Sromebi [*A publication*]
TBIRD....... Terrestrial Background Infrared Detection   (SAA)
T-BIRD...... Terrestrial Ballistic Infrared Development   (SAA)
TBIS .... Technology Base Investment Strategy [*Army*]
TBJ .... Turbulent Bounded Jet
TBJT .... Turbojet   (FAAC)
TBK .... TEFLON Bonding Kit
TBK .... Tolland Bank [*AMEX symbol*]   (SPSG)
TBK .... ToolBook [*Computer format*]   (PCM)
TBK .... Total Body Potassium [*Clinical chemistry*]
TBK .... Toyo Bungaku Kenkyu [*Studies on Oriental Literature*] [*A publication*]
T/BKL ...... Turn Buckle [*Automotive engineering*]
TBL........... Tabele [*Papua New Guinea*] [*Seismograph station code, US Geological Survey*]   (SEIS)
TBL........... Table
TBL........... Tactical Bomb Line   (NVT)
TBL........... [*The*] Tamarind Book of Lithography
TBL........... Terminal Ballistics Laboratory [*Army*]
TBL........... Thin Base Laminate
TBL........... Thomas Branigan Memorial Library, Las Cruces, NM [*OCLC symbol*]   (OCLC)
TBL........... Through Back of Loop [*Knitting*]
TBL........... Through Bill of Lading [*Shipping*]
TBL........... Timberland Co. [*NYSE symbol*]   (SPSG)
TBL........... Tombill Mines Ltd. [*Toronto Stock Exchange symbol*]
TBL........... Tootal Broadhurst Lee [*Textile testing*] [*Obsolete*]
TBL........... Trouble [*Telecommunications*]   (TEL)
TBL........... True Blood Loss
TBL........... Turbulent Boundary Layer
TBLC........ Term Birth, Living Child [*Medicine*]
TBLE......... Top Blacks in Law Enforcement [*Later, BLE*]   (EA)
T/BLK ...... Terminal Block [*Automotive engineering*]

TBLN......... Tracheobronchial Lymph Node [*Anatomy*]
TBLR......... Tumbler (MSA)
TBLS .... Trail Blazer Library System [*Library network*]
TBLSP....... Tablespoon
TBM .... School of Aerospace Medicine, Brooks AFB, TX [*OCLC symbol*] (OCLC)
TBM .... Tactical Ballistic Missile [*Military*] (CAAL)
TBM .... Tax Board Memorandum [*Internal Revenue Bulletin*] [*United States*] [*A publication*] (DLA)
TBM .... TBM NT Corp. [*Toronto Stock Exchange symbol*]
TBM .... Tell Beit Mirsim (BJA)
TBM .... Temporary Bench Mark
TBM .... TeraBIT [*Binary Digit*] Memory [*Data processing*]
TBM .... Tertiary Butyl Mercaptan [*Organic chemistry*]
TBM .... Theater Ballistic Missile
TBM .... Theater Battle Model (MCD)
TBM .... Tone Burst Modulation
TB & M...... Tracewell, Bowers, and Mitchell's United States Comptroller's Decisions [*A publication*] (DLA)
TBM .... Tuberculous Meningitis [*Medicine*]
TBM .... Tubular Basement Membrane
TBM .... Tunnel Boring Machine
TBMA .... Textile Bag Manufacturers Association (EA)
TBMAA ..... Travel by Military Aircraft Authorized
TBMAC..... Tributylmethylammonium Chloride [*Organic chemistry*]
TBMC....... Test Bed Mode Control
TBMD .... Terminal Ballistic Missile Defense [*Army*] (AABC)
TBMO .... Test Base Material Operation (AAG)
T B Mon..... T. B. Monroe's Kentucky Supreme Court Reports [*17-23 Kentucky*] [*1824-28*] [*A publication*] (DLA)
T B Mon (KY) ... T. B. Monroe's Kentucky Reports [*17-23 Kentucky*] [*A publication*] (DLA)
TBMOS..... TeraBIT Memory Operating System (NOAA)
TBMS........ Text-Based Management Systems [*Data processing*]
TBMSDT .. Mississippi. Agricultural and Forestry Experiment Station. Technical Bulletin [*A publication*]
TBMT....... Transmitter Buffer Empty [*Data processing*]
TBMX....... Tactical Ballistic Missile Experiment
TBN .... Fort Leonard Wood [*Missouri*] [*Airport symbol*] (OAG)
TBN .... Tertiary-Butylnaphthalene [*Organic chemistry*]
TBN .... Tetrabenzonaphthalene [*Organic chemistry*]
TBN .... Thailand Business [*A publication*]
TBN .... Titratable Base Number [*Analytical chemistry*]
TBN .... To Be Negotiated (NASA)
TBN .... To Be Nominated
TBN .... Total Base Number [*Automotive engineering*]
TBN .... Traveling Businesswomen's Network (EA)
TBN .... Trinity Broadcasting Network [*Cable-television system*]
TBNA .... Total Body Neutron Activation (AAMN)
TBNA .... Treated but Not Admitted [*Medicine*]
TBNAA .... Total Body Neutron Activation Analysis
TBNHL ..... Tippecanoe Battleground National Historical Landmark (EA)
Tbnl........... Tribunal
TBO .... Tabora [*Tanzania*] [*Airport symbol*] (OAG)
TBO .... Tacoma Boatbuilding Co. [*NYSE symbol*] (SPSG)
TBO .... Thermal Bakeout
TBO .... Time between Overhauls [*of engine, or other equipment*]
TBO .... Total Blackout (IIA)
TBO .... TourBase Ortsdaten [*Jaeger-Verlag GmbH*] [*Germany*] [*Information service or system*] (CRD)
TBO .... Transactions by Others [*Military*]
TBOA .... T-18 Builders and Owners Association (EA)
TBOA .... Tuna Boat Owners' Association [*Defunct*] (EA)
t-Boc......... Butoxycarbonyl [*or t-BOC*]
t-BOC........ tert-Butyloxycarbonyl [*Also, t-Boc*] [*Organic chemistry*]
TBOI........ Tentative Basis of Issue [*Army*] (AABC)
TBOIP...... Tentative Basis of Issue Plan [*Army*] (AABC)
TBOIPFD .. Tentative Basis of Issue Plan Feedback Data [*Army*]
TBolMH.... Western Mental Health Institute, Boliver, TN [*Library symbol*] [*Library of Congress*] (LCLS)
TBON........ [*The*] Bank of Nashville [*NASDAQ symbol*] (NQ)
TBOS........ [*The*] Bank of Southington [*NASDAQ symbol*] (NQ)
TBP........... Tab Products Co. [*AMEX symbol*] (SPSG)
TbP .... Tampa Blue Print Co., Tampa, FL [*Library symbol*] [*Library of Congress*] (LCLS)
TBP........... Tat-Binding Protein [*Genetics*]
TBP........... Tau Beta Pi Association
TBP........... Tertiary Butyl Phosphine [*Organic chemistry*]
TBP........... Testosterone-Binding Protein [*Endocrinology*] (MAE)
TBP........... Tethered Buoyed Platform [*Petroleum engineering*]
TBP........... Tetraphenylboron [*Analytical chemistry*]
TBP........... Thiobisdichlorophenol [*Pharmacology*]
TBP........... Thyroxine-Binding Protein [*Biochemistry*]
TBP........... Timing Belt Pulley
TBP........... To Be Planned (MCD)
TBP........... To Be Provided (NASA)
TBP........... To be Published
TBP........... Trainable Bow Propeller
TBP........... Tributyl Phosphate [*Organic chemistry*]
TBP........... Tributyl Phosphine [*Organic chemistry*]
TBP........... Trigonal Bipyramidal [*Geometry of molecular structure*]

TBP........... True Boiling Point
TBP........... Tumbes [*Peru*] [*Airport symbol*] (OAG)
TBP........... Twisted Bonded Pair
TBP........... Two-Body Problem
TBPA .... Tetrabromophthalic Anhydride [*Flame retardant*] [*Organic chemistry*]
TBPA .... Textile Bag and Packaging Association (EA)
TBPA .... Thyroxine-Binding Prealbumin [*Biochemistry*]
TBPA .... Transatlantic Brides and Parents Association (EA)
TBPB .... Bridgetown/Grantley Adams Internacional [*Barbados*] [*ICAO location identifier*] (ICLI)
TBPC......... Text-Books of Physical Chemistry [*A publication*]
TBPI .... Thigh Brachial Pressure Index
TBPO......... Bridgetown [*Barbados*] [*ICAO location identifier*] (ICLI)
TBPS......... Tert-Butylbicyclophosphorothionate [*Biochemistry*]
TBPU......... To Be Picked Up [*Postal service marking*] [*British*]
TBQ .... Addison, TX [*Location identifier*] [*FAA*] (FAAL)
TBR .... Advisory Tax Board Recommendation [*Internal Revenue Bureau*] [*United States*] [*A publication*] (DLA)
TBR .... New York Times Book Review [*A publication*]
TBR .... Statesboro, GA [*Location identifier*] [*FAA*] (FAAL)
TBR .... T-Bar, Inc. [*AMEX symbol*] (SPSG)
TBR .... Table Base Register
TBR .... Table Rock [*New York*] [*Seismograph station code, US Geological Survey*] (SEIS)
TBR .... Test of Behavioral Rigidity [*Psychology*]
TBR .... Three Banks Review [*A publication*]
TBR .... Tilt Board Reach [*Test*] [*Occupational therapy*]
TBR .... To be Released (SAA)
TBR .... To be Resolved (SSD)
TBR .... Torpedo Bomber Reconnaissance Aircraft [*Navy*]
TBR .... Training Base Review (MCD)
TBR .... Trickle Bed Reactor [*Chemical engineering*]
TBR .... Tumor-Bearing Rabbit Serum [*Immunology*]
TBR .... Turbo Resources Ltd. [*Toronto Stock Exchange symbol*]
TBRC........ Time-Based Recurring Cost
TBRC........ Top-Blown Rotary Converter [*Nonferrous metallurgy*]
TBRD .... Taxation Board of Review Decisions [*A publication*] (APTA)
TBRD .... Taxation Board of Review Decisions. New Series [*Australia*] [*A publication*] (DLA)
TB-RD .... Tuberculosis - Respiratory Disease (MAE)
TBRD (NS) ... Taxation Board of Review Decisions (New Series) [*A publication*] (APTA)
TBRG......... Thomson Book/Reference Group [*The Thomson Corp.*] [*Publishing*]
TBRI.......... Technical Book Review Index
TBriH .... Bristol Memorial Hospital, Bristol, TN [*Library symbol*] [*Library of Congress*] (LCLS)
TBriK........ King College, Bristol, TN [*Library symbol*] [*Library of Congress*] (LCLS)
T Br Mycol ... Transactions. British Mycological Society [*A publication*]
TBroH........ Haywood Park General Hospital, Brownsville, TN [*Library symbol*] [*Library of Congress*] (LCLS)
TBRV......... Tomato Black Ring Virus [*Plant pathology*]
TBS........... Sir Thomas Beecham Society (EA)
TBS........... Tablespoon
TBS........... Tactical Bomb Squadron [*Air Force*]
TBS........... Talk-between-Ships [*which are tactically maneuvering; also, the VHF radio equipment used for this purpose*]
TBS........... Tall Building Syndrome
TBS........... Tape and Buffer System [*Data processing*]
TBS........... Task Breakdown Structure (NASA)
TBS........... Tbilisi [*Former USSR*] [*Airport symbol*] (OAG)
TBS........... Temple, Barker & Sloane, Inc. [*Lexington, MA*] [*Telecommunications service*] (TSSD)
TBS........... Tertiary-Butyldimethylsilyl [*Also, TBDMS, TBDPS*] [*Organic chemistry*]
TBS........... Tertiary Butylphenyl Salicylate [*Food packaging*]
TBS........... Tertiary-Butylstyrene [*Organic chemistry*]
TBS........... Test Bench Set (MCD)
TBS........... Tetrapropylene Alkylbenesulfonate [*Surfactant*] [*Organic chemistry*]
TBS........... Text-Books of Science [*A publication*]
TBS........... Tight Building Syndrome [*Air quality*]
TBS........... Tired Bureaucrat Syndrome
TBS........... To Be Selected (KSC)
TBS........... To Be Specified (NASA)
TBS........... To Be Superseded (NASA)
TBS........... To Be Supplied (KSC)
TBS........... Tobacco Black-Shank Nematode [*Plant pathology*]
TBS........... Tokyo Broadcasting System
TB & S ...... Top, Bottom, and Sides [*Lumber*]
TBS........... Toronto Baptist Seminary
TBS........... Toronto Board of Education, Secondary Schools [*UTLAS symbol*]
TBS........... Torsion Bar Spring [*Automotive engineering*]
TBS........... Total Body Solute [*Biochemistry*]
TBS........... Total Body Surface [*Medicine*]
TBS........... Training and Battle Simulation [*SAGE*]
TBS........... Translator Bail Switch
TBS........... Treasury Board Secretariat [*Canada*]

TBS............ Tribromosalicylanilide [*or Tribromsalan*] [*Organic chemistry*]
TBS............ Triethanolamine-Buffered Saline [*Organic chemistry*] (MAE)
TBS............ Trinitarian Bible Society [*British*]
TBS............ TRIS-Buffered Saline [*Solution*]
TBS............ Tubeshaft (DS)
TBS............ Turbine Bypass System [*Nuclear energy*] (NRCH)
TBS............ Turner Broadcasting System, Inc. [*AMEX symbol*] (SPSG)
TBSA........ Total Body Surface Area [*Medicine*]
TBSA........ Total Serum Bile Acid [*Clinical chemistry*]
TBSA........ TRIS-Buffered Saline Azide [*Culture media*]
TBSCCW... Turbine Building Secondary Closed Cooling Water [*Nuclear energy*] (NRCH)
TBSCI....... Tertiary-Butyldimethylsilyl Chloride [*Also, TBDMSCI*] [*Organic chemistry*]
TBSG........ Test Base Support Group (AAG)
TBSM........ Tributylstannylmaleate [*Organic chemistry*]
TBSP........ Tablespoon
TBST'G..... Troubleshooting
TBSV........ Time between Scheduled Visits (MCD)
TBSV........ Tomato Bushy Stunt Virus
TBT............ Mid American Baptist Theological Seminary, Memphis, TN [*OCLC symbol*] (OCLC)
TBT............ Tabatinga [*Brazil*] [*Airport symbol*] (OAG)
TBT............ Taburiente [*Canary Islands*] [*Seismograph station code, US Geological Survey*] (SEIS)
TBT............ Target Bearing Transmitter
TBT............ Tax-Benefit Transfer (WGA)
TBT............ Terminal Ballistic Track
TBT............ Tetrabutyl Titanate [*Organic chemistry*]
TBT............ Thallium Beam Tube
TBT............ Tilt Board Tip [*Test*] [*Occupational therapy*]
TBT............ Tolbutamide - Tolerance Test [*Clinical chemistry*] (MAE)
TBT............ Tracheobronchial Toilet [*Medicine*] (MAE)
TBT............ Trends in Biotechnology [*A publication*]
TBT............ Tributyltin [*Anitimicrobial agent*]
TBTC........ Transportable Blood Transfusion Shipment Center (DWSG)
TBTD........ Tetrabutylthiuram Disulfide [*Organic chemistry*]
TBTF........ Tributyltin Fluoride [*Antimicrobial agent*]
TBTH........ Tributyltin Hydride [*Organic chemistry*]
TBTI......... Telebyte Technology, Inc. [*NASDAQ symbol*] (NQ)
TBTO........ Tributyltin Oxide [*Organic chemistry*]
TBTP........ Tributyl Trithiophosphate [*Defoliant*] [*Organic chemistry*]
TBTS........ Tributyltin Sulfide [*Organic chemistry*]
TBTU........ Tributylthiourea [*Organic chemistry*]
TBU.......... Hong Kong Enterprise [*A publication*]
TBU.......... Telemetry Buffer Unit (SSD)
TBU.......... Terminal Buffer Unit [*Telecommunications*] (TEL)
TBU.......... Test Before Using (MCD)
TBU.......... Time Base Unit
TBU.......... Tongatapu [*Tonga Island*] [*Airport symbol*] (OAG)
TBUP........ Tributylphosphine [*Organic chemistry*]
TBV.......... Thermal Bypass Valve
TBV.......... Total Blood Volume [*Physiology*]
TBV.......... Trabecular Bone Volume
TBV.......... Tubercle Bacillus Vaccine [*Medicine*]
TBV.......... Tulip Breaking Virus [*Plant pathology*]
TBV.......... Turbine Building Ventilation [*Nuclear energy*] (NRCH)
TBVD........ Torsional-Bending Vibration Damper [*Mechanical engineering*]
TBVE........ Two-Point Boundary Value Equation [*Mathematics*]
TBW.......... [*The*] Business World [*A publication*]
TBW.......... Tampa Bay-Ruskin, FL [*Location identifier*] [*FAA*] (FAAL)
TBW.......... That Bloody Woman [*Nickname given to British Prime Minister Margaret Thatcher*]
TBW.......... Titanium Butt Weld
TBW.......... To Be Withheld
TBW.......... Tobacco Bud Worm [*Agronomy*]
TBW.......... Total Bandwidth
TBW.......... Total Body Water [*Man*]
TBW.......... Total Body Weight [*Medicine*]
TBW.......... Tracking Band Width (MCD)
TBWCA...... Texas Barbed Wire Collectors Association (EA)
TBWEP..... Trial Boll Weevil Eradication Program [*Department of Agriculture*]
TBWG........ Tactical Bomb Wing [*Air Force*]
TBWO........ Tuned Backward Wave Oscillator
TBX.......... Tactical Ballistic Missile, Experimental
TBY.......... Oxford, CT [*Location identifier*] [*FAA*] (FAAL)
TBY.......... TCBY Enterprises, Inc. [*NYSE symbol*] (CTT)
TBY.......... Terrace Bay Resources [*Vancouver Stock Exchange symbol*]
TBZ............ Istanbul [*Trabzon*] [*Turkey*] [*Seismograph station code, US Geological Survey*] (SEIS)
TBZ............ Tabriz [*Iran*] [*Airport symbol*] (OAG)
TBZ............ Tetrabenazine [*Tranquilizer*]
TBZ............ Thiabendazole [*or Thiazolyl*] Benzimidazole [*Pesticide*]
TC............ 13 Coins Restaurants Ltd. [*Vancouver Stock Exchange symbol*]
TC............ Air Tanzania [*ICAO designator*] (FAAC)
TC............ All India Reporter, Travancore-Cochin [*1950-57*] [*A publication*] (DLA)
TC............ Chattanooga-Hamilton County Bicentennial Library, Chattanooga, TN [*Library symbol*] [*Library of Congress*] (LCLS)

TC............ Chronicle (Toowoomba) [*A publication*] (APTA)
TC............ Cold Leg Temperature [*Nuclear energy*] (NRCH)
Tc............ Core Temperature [*Medicine*]
TC............ [*The*] Courier [*Code name for Robert W. Owen, participant in the Iran-Contra affair during the Reagan Administration*]
TC............ Journal of Technical Topics in Civil Engineering [*A publication*]
TC............ Order of the Trinity Cross [*Trinidad and Tobago*]
TC............ Reports of English Tax Cases [*A publication*] (DLA)
TC............ Reports of Tax Cases [*United Kingdom*] [*A publication*]
TC............ T-Carrier [*Telecommunications*] (TEL)
TC............ Table of Contents (IT)
TC............ Tablettes Cappadociennes [*Paris*] [*A publication*] (BJA)
TC............ Tabulating Card (AAG)
TC............ Tactical Command (NATG)
TC............ Tactical Communications [*Military*] (DWSG)
TC............ Tactical Computer (IEEE)
T/C........... Tactical Coordinator (NVT)
TC............ Tactile Communicator [*Device which aids the deaf by translating certain sounds into coded vibrations*]
TC............ Tail Clamp
TC............ Talk[*ing*] Club
TC............ Tamil Culture [*A publication*]
TC............ Tank Car
TC............ Tank Commander (RDA)
TC............ Tank Company [*Military*] (MCD)
TC............ Tank Corps
TC............ Tantalum Capacitor (IEEE)
TC............ Tape Command
TC............ Tape Core
TC............ Target Cell [*Immunology*]
TC............ Target Control (MCD)
TC............ Tariff Circular
TC............ Tariff Commission [*Later, International Trade Commission*]
TC............ Taurocholate [*Microbiology*] (MAE)
TC............ Tax Cases [*Legal*] [*British*]
TC............ Tax Certificate
TC............ Tax Council (EA)
TC............ Tax Court [*of the United States*] [*Also, TCUS*] [*Later, United States Tax Court*]
TC............ Taxpayers' Committee (EA)
TC............ Taylorcraft [*ICAO aircraft manufacturer identifier*] (ICAO)
TC............ Tayu Center (EA)
TC............ Tea Council of the United States of America (EA)
TC............ Teacher's Certificate [*British*]
TC............ Teachers College
TC............ Teardown Compliance
Tc............ Technetium [*Chemical element*]
TC............ Technical Center [*Environmental Protection Agency*] (GFGA)
TC............ Technical Characteristics [*Military*] (AABC)
TC............ Technical Circular
TC............ Technical College
TC............ Technical Committee
TC............ Technical Communication
TC............ Technical Control (MSA)
TC............ Technical Cooperation
TC............ Technician's Certificate [*British*] (DI)
TC............ Technicolor (KSC)
T & C........ Technology and Culture [*A publication*]
TC............ Tekakwitha Conference National Center [*Later, TCNC*] (EA)
T/C........... Telecine
TC............ Telecommunications
TC............ Telecommunications Counselor [*Voice & Data Resources, Inc.*] [*Information service or system*] [*Defunct*] (IID)
TC............ TeleCommuting Report [*Electronic Services Unlimited*] [*Information service or system*] (CRD)
T & C........ Telemetry and Command (SSD)
TC............ Telescoping Collar (OA)
TC............ Temperament Comparator [*Psychology*]
TC............ Temperature Capability
TC............ Temperature Change [*Refrigeration*]
TC............ Temperature Coefficient
TC............ Temperature Compensating (MSA)
TC............ Temperature Control
TC............ Temperature Controller [*Nuclear energy*] (NRCH)
TC............ Temple Classics [*A publication*]
TC............ Temporary Chaplain [*British military*] (DMA)
TC............ Temporary Constable
TC............ Temporary Correction
TC............ Tennessee Central Railway Co. [*AAR code*]
TC............ Tennis Club
TC............ Teracycle
TC............ Terciarios Capuchinos de Nostra Signora de los Dolores [*Tertiary Capuchins of Our Lady of Sorrows*] [*Italy*] (EAIO)
TC............ Terminal Computer (BUR)
TC............ Terminal Concentrator
TC............ Terminal Congestion [*Telecommunications*] (TEL)
TC............ Terminal Controller
T/C........... Termination Check [*NASA*] (NASA)
T/C........... Termination for Convenience [*DoD*]

T & C..........	Terms and Conditions
TC............	Terra Cotta [*Technical drawings*]
TC............	Terrain Clearance [*Military*] (NG)
TC............	Terrain Correlation (MCD)
TC............	Test Chief
TC............	Test Collection [*Educational Testing Service*] [*Information service or system*] (IID)
TC............	Test Conductor (AAG)
TC............	Test Console
TC............	Test Controller
TC............	Test Coordinator
TC............	Testing Complete (CAAL)
TC............	Tetracycline [*Antibiotic compound*]
TC............	Tetrahedral Cubic [*Metallography*]
TC............	Texas Central Railroad Co.
TC............	Thai Capital Fund, Inc. [*NYSE symbol*] (SPSG)
TC............	Theory of Computation Series [*Elsevier Book Series*] [*A publication*]
TC............	Therapeutic Concentration [*Pharmacology*]
TC............	Thermal Conductivity
TC............	Thermal Control (KSC)
TC............	Thermal Cracker [*Chemical engineering*]
TC............	Thermal Cutting [*Welding*]
TC............	Thermocouple
TC............	Thermocurrent (IEEE)
TC............	Thickness Chord Wing [*Aviation*] (AIA)
TC............	Thinking Cap [*Layman's term for neocortex*]
TC............	Thomas C. Calvin [*Character in TV series "Magnum, P.I."*]
T & C..........	Thompson and Cook's New York Supreme Court Reports [*A publication*] (DLA)
TC............	Thoracic Cage [*Medicine*]
TC............	Thread Cutting (MSA)
TC............	Threshold Circuit [*Telecommunications*] (OA)
TC............	Throat Culture [*Clinical chemistry*]
TC............	Thrust Chamber [*Air Force, NASA*]
TC............	Thyrocalcitonin [*Endocrinology*] (MAE)
TC............	Tical [*Monetary unit in Thailand*]
TC............	Tidal Constants [*Marine science*] (MSC)
TC............	Tie Connector (MCD)
TC............	Tierce [*Unit of measurement*]
T/C............	Till Counterbalanced
TC............	Till Countermanded
TC............	Tilt Covered [*Truck*] (DCTA)
Tc............	Time Called [*Baseball*]
TC............	Time Certificate of Deposit [*Banking*]
T & C..........	Time and Charges [*Telecommunications*] (TEL)
T/C............	Time Charter [*Shipping*]
TC............	Time Check
TC............	Time to Circular (MCD)
TC............	Time Clock
TC............	Time Closing (MSA)
TC............	Time Compensation
TC............	Time to Computation
TC............	Time Constant (MSA)
TC............	Timing Channel
TC............	Timing Cover Gasket [*Automotive engineering*]
TC............	Tinned Copper
TC............	Tissue Culture [*Microbiology*]
TC............	To Contain [*Pipet calibration*]
TC............	Tobramycin-Clindamycin [*Antibiotic compound*]
TC............	Today's Computers [*A publication*]
TC............	Togoland Congress [*Ghana*] [*Political party*]
TC............	Toilet Case (MSA)
TC............	Toll Center [*Telecommunications*]
TC............	Toll Completing [*Telecommunications*]
TC............	Toluene-Cellosolve [*Scintillation solvent*]
TC............	Top Carnivore
TC............	Top Cat [*Cartoon character*]
TC............	Top Center [*Valve position*]
TC............	Top Chord
TC............	Top of Column
TC............	Top Contact [*Valve*] (DEN)
TC............	Topographic Center [*Defense Mapping Agency*]
TC............	Torpedo Control [*British military*] (DMA)
TC............	Torpedo Coxswain [*British military*] (DMA)
TC............	Total Capacity [*Lung*]
TC............	Total Carbon
TC............	Total Chances
TC............	Total Cholesterol [*Medicine*]
TC............	Total Colonoscopy [*Proctoscopy*]
TC............	Total Control (PCM)
TC............	Total Cost
TC............	Touring Club
T of C..........	Tournament of Champions
Tc............	Towing Chock [*Shipfitting*]
TC............	Town Clerk [*or Councillor*]
T & C..........	Town & Country [*A publication*]
TC............	Toxicity Characteristic [*Environmental Protection Agency*]
TC............	Traceability Code (NASA)
TC............	Track Circuit (DCTA)
TC............	Track Commander [*Army*] (INF)
TC............	Tracking Camera
TC............	Tracking Console
TC............	Trade Cases [*Commerce Clearing House*] [*A publication*] (DLA)
TC............	Traffic Collision
TC............	Traffic Commissioner [*or Consultant*]
TC............	Traffic Consultant (WGA)
TC............	Traffic Controller (CAAL)
TC............	Training Center [*Military*]
TC............	Training Chest [*Emergency parachute*]
TC............	Training Circular [*Military*]
TC............	Training Command (AAG)
TC............	Training Corps [*British military*] (DMA)
TC............	Transaction Code [*Military*]
TC............	Transceiver Code [*Navy*]
TC............	Transcobalamin [*Biochemistry*]
TC............	Transcutaneous
TC............	Transfer Canal [*Nuclear energy*] (NRCH)
TC............	Transfer Clerk
TC............	Transfer Control (HGAA)
TC............	Transistorized Carrier
TC............	Transit Canal (NVT)
TC............	Translation Controller
TC............	Transmission Controller
TC............	Transmitting Circuit [*Telecommunications*] (OA)
TC............	Transpersonal Consciousness [*Parapsychology*]
TC............	Transponder Component (MCD)
TC............	Transport Canada [*Government regulatory agency*]
TC............	Transport Cargo (NATG)
TC............	Transport Combine [*Combined Transport*] [*French*] [*Business term*]
TC............	Transport Command [*British military*] (DMA)
TC............	Transport and Communications [*Department of Employment*] [*British*]
TC............	Transportation Corps [*Military*]
TC............	Transporte Combinado [*Combined Transport*] [*Spanish*] [*Business term*]
TC............	Transporto Combinato [*Combined Transport*] [*Italian*] [*Business term*]
TC............	Transvaal Cadets [*British military*] (DMA)
TC............	Travellers Cheque [*British*] (ADA)
TC............	Tre Corde [*With Three Strings, or Release the Soft Pedal*] [*Music*]
TC............	Treasury Circular
T/C............	Treated Versus Cured [*Medicine*]
T/C............	Treatment Charge [*Metallurgy*]
TC............	Trial Counsel [*Military*]
TC............	Tribology Centre [*British*]
TC............	Tribunal des Conflits [*Tribunal of Conflicts*] [*French*] (ILCA)
TC............	Tricuspid Closure [*Cardiology*]
TC............	Tricycle Club [*British*]
TC............	Triennial Cycle (BJA)
TC............	Trierische Chronik [*A publication*]
TC............	Trilateral Commission (EA)
TC............	Trim Coil (AAG)
TC............	[*Order of the*] Trinity Cross [*Trinidad and Tobago*]
TC............	Trip Coil
TC............	Triplet Connection (EA)
TC............	Triton Corp. (EA)
TC............	Troop Carrier [*Air Force*]
TC............	Tropical Continental [*American air mass*]
TC............	Tropical Cyclone (ADA)
TC............	Truck Commander [*Military*] (INF)
T/C............	True Complement
TC............	True Course
TC............	Truncated Cone [*Golf balls*]
TC............	Trunk Control
TC............	Trusteeship Council [*of the United Nations*]
TC............	Tuberculosis, Contagious [*Medicine*] (AAMN)
TC............	Tubing Connector [*Instrumentation*]
TC............	Tubocurarine [*Muscle relaxant*]
TC............	Turbocharger [*Automotive engineering*]
TC............	Turf Course [*Horse racing*]
TC............	Turkey [*Aircraft nationality and registration mark*] (FAAC)
TC............	Turkey Coryza [*Pathology*]
tc............	Turks and Caicos Islands [*MARC country of publication code*] [*Library of Congress*] (LCCP)
TC............	Turks and Caicos Islands [*ANSI two-letter standard code*] (CNC)
TC............	Turn-Cock (ROG)
T & C..........	Turn and Cough [*Medicine*]
TC............	Turning Circle [*Automotive engineering*]
TC............	Turnip Crinkle Virus
TC............	Turret Captain [*Navy*]
TC............	Twentieth Century [*A publication*]
TC............	[*The*] Twentieth Century New Testament [*A publication*] (BJA)
TC............	Twin Camshaft [*Automotive engineering*]
TC............	Twin Carburetor [*Automotive engineering*]
TC............	Two Cycle [*Mechanics*]
TC............	Tworczosc [*A publication*]

TC .... Type Certificate
TC .... Type Classification
TC .... Type and Crossmatch [*of blood*]
TC .... United States Tax Court Cases [*A publication*]   (DLA)
TC3 .... Telecommunications, Command, Control, and Computer System
T4C .... Technology for Children [*Vocational program*]
TCA .... Adventist Network of Georgia, Cumberland Elementary Library, Collegedale, TN [*OCLC symbol*]   (OCLC)
TCA .... [*The*] Canadian Amateur [*A publication*]
TCA .... Tactical Combat Aircraft   (IEEE)
TCA .... Tactical Communications Area
TCA .... Tandem Club of America   (EA)
TCA .... Tanner's Council of America [*Later, LIA*]   (EA)
TCA .... Tanzer 22 Class Association   (EA)
TCA .... Target Class Assignment
TCA .... Tattoo Club of America   (EA)
TCA .... Teach Cable Assembly [*Robot technology*]
TCA .... Teaching Curriculum Association [*A generic term; not the name of a specific organization*]
TCA .... Technical Change Analysis   (MCD)
TCA .... Technical Contract Administrator
TCA .... Technical Cooperation Administration [*Transferred to Foreign Operations Administration, 1953*]
TCA .... Technician in Costing and Accounting [*British*]   (DBQ)
TCA .... Tele-Communications Association   (EA)
TCA .... Telemarketing Corp. of America [*Phoenix, AZ*]   (TSSD)
TCA .... Telemetering Control Assembly   (AAG)
TCA .... Telephone Consultants of America [*Bergenfield, NJ*] [*Telecommunications*]   (TSSD)
TCA .... Television Critics Association   (EA)
TCA .... Tempelhof Central Airport [*West Berlin*]
TCA .... Temperance Collegiate Association [*British*]   (AEBS)
TCA .... Temperature Control Assembly   (KSC)
TCA .... Temperature-Controlled Animal
TCA .... Temporary Care Arrangement
TCA .... Ten Class Association   (EA)
TCA .... Tennant Creek [*Australia*] [*Airport symbol*]   (OAG)
TCA .... Tennessee Code Annotated [*A publication*]
TCA .... Terminal Cancer [*Medicine*]
TCA .... Terminal Communication Adapter
TCA .... Terminal Control Area [*Aviation*]   (AFM)
TCA .... Tetracyanoanthracene [*Organic chemistry*]
TCA .... Textile Converters Association   (EA)
TCA .... Theater Commander's Approval [*Military*]
TCA .... Therapeutic Communities of America   (EA)
TCA .... Thermal Critical Assembly [*Nuclear energy*]
TCA .... Thermo Cardiosystems, Inc. [*AMEX symbol*]   (SPSG)
TCA .... Thermocentrifugometric Analysis [*Analytical chemistry*]
TCA .... Thermochimica Acta [*A publication*]
TCA .... Thiocarbanilide [*Organic chemistry*]
TCA .... Thistle Class Association   (EA)
TCA .... Thoroughbred Club of America   (EA)
TCA .... Thrust Chamber Assembly [*Missile technology*]
TCA .... Thyrocalcitonin [*Also, CT, TCT*] [*Endocrinology*]
TCA .... Tiger Cat Association [*Defunct*]   (EA)
TCA .... Tile Council of America   (EA)
TCA .... Tilt-Up Concrete Association   (EA)
TCA .... Time of Closest Approach [*Aerospace*]
TCA .... Tissue Culture Association   (EA)
TCA3 .... Tithe Commutation Act [*British*]
TCA .... To Come Again [*in a given number of days*] [*Medicine*]
TCA .... TOKAMAK [*Toroidal Kamera Magnetic*] Chauffage Alfven [*Plasma physics instrumentation*]
TCa .... Total Calcium [*Clinical chemistry*]
TCA .... Trace Contamination Analysis
TCA .... Track Continuity Area   (NATG)
TCA .... Track Crossing Altitude [*or Attitude*]
TCA .... Track Crossing Angle
TCA .... Traffic Control Area [*Aviation*]
TCA .... Trailer Coach Association [*Later, Manufactured Housing Institute*]   (EA)
TCA .... Train Collectors Association   (EA)
TCA .... Trans-Canada Airlines [*Facetious translation: "Two Crashes Apiece"*]
TCA .... Trans-Caribbean Airways   (IIA)
TCA .... Transfer Control A Register   (SAA)
TCA .... Translation Controller Assembly   (NASA)
TCA .... Transluminal Coronary Angioplasty [*Cardiology*]
TCA .... Travellers Cheque Association Ltd. [*British*]
TCA .... Tricalcium Aluminate [*Inorganic chemistry*]   (MAE)
TCA .... Tricarboxylic Acid [*Cycle*] [*Biochemistry*]
TCA .... Trichloroacetate [*Organic chemistry*]
TCA .... Trichloroacetic Acid [*Also, TCAA*] [*Organic chemistry*]
TCA .... Trichloroanisole [*Organic chemistry*]
TCA .... Trichosanic Acid [*Biochemistry*]
TCA .... Tricyclic Antidepressant [*Medicine*]
TCA .... Turbulent Contacting Absorber
TCA .... Turks and Caicos Islands [*ANSI three-letter standard code*]   (CNC)
TCA .... Two Hundred Contemporary Authors [*A publication*]

TCA .... Typographic Communications Association   (EA)
TCAA .... Tile Contractors' Association of America   (EA)
TCAA .... Trichloroacetic Acid [*Also, TCA*] [*Organic chemistry*]
TCAAP ...... Twin Cities Army Ammunition Plant   (AABC)
TCAAS ...... Transactions. Connecticut Academy of Arts and Sciences [*A publication*]
TCAB......... Temperature of Cabin [*Aerospace*]   (MCD)
TCAB......... Tetrachloroazobenzene [*Organic chemistry*]
TCABG...... Triple Coronary Artery Bypass Graft [*Cardiology*]
TCAC........ Technical Control and Analysis Center
TC ACCIS ... Transportation Coordination Automated Command and Control Information System [*Military*]
TCAC-D .... Technical Control and Analysis Center - Division
TCAD .... Technology Computer-Aided Design [*Data processing*]
TCAE......... Technical Control and Analysis Element   (INF)
TCAF......... TEFLON-Coated Aluminum Foil
TCAI......... Tutorial Computer-Assisted Instruction   (IEEE)
TCAL........ Total Calorimeter   (KSC)
TCAM .... Telecommunications Access Method [*IBM Corp.*] [*Data processing*]
TCAM .... Thinking Creatively in Action and Movement [*Test*]
TCA Man .. TCA [*Tissue Culture Association*] Manual [*A publication*]
TCaMH..... Smith County Memorial Hospital, Carthage, TN [*Library symbol*] [*Library of Congress*]   (LCLS)
TCANAQ .. Commonwealth Bureau of Animal Nutrition. Technical Communication [*A publication*]
TCAOB...... Tetrachloroazoxybenzene [*Organic chemistry*]
TCAP......... Tactical Channel Assignment Panel [*Military radio*]
T/CAP ...... Thermal Capacitor   (MCD)
TCAP......... Tricyanoaminopropene [*Organic chemistry*]
TCAP......... Trimethylcetylammonium Pentachlorphenate [*Organic chemistry*]
TCAPE ...... Truck Computer Analysis of Performance and Economy
TCARC...... Tropical Cyclone Aircraft Reconnaissance Coordinator [*Navy*]   (DNAB)
TCaS .... Smith County High School Library, Carthage, TN [*Library symbol*] [*Library of Congress*]   (LCLS)
TCAS......... T-Carrier Administration System [*Minicomputer*] [*Bell System*]
TCAS........ Technical Control and Analysis System   (MCD)
T/CAS .... Threat Alert Collision Avoidance System
TCAS........ Three Counties Agricultural Society [*British*]
TCAS........ Traffic Alert and Collision Avoidance System [*Aviation*]
TCASNY ... Turkish Cypriot Aid Society of New York   (EA)
TCAT........ Tape-Controlled Automatic Testing
TCAT........ TCA Cable TV, Inc. [*NASDAQ symbol*]   (NQ)
TCAT........ Test Coverage Analysis Tool   (IEEE)
TCATA ...... Textile Care Allied Trades Association   (EA)
TCATA ...... TRADOC Combined Arms Test Activity [*Army*]   (MCD)
TCATA ...... TRADOC [*Training and Doctrine Command*] Combined Arms Test Agency [*Army*]
TCAus....... Twentieth Century (Australia) [*A publication*]
TCAX........ Trans Continental Air Transport [*Air carrier designation symbol*]
TCB............ [*The*] College Board   (EA)
TCB............ [*The*] Conference Board   (EA)
TCB............ Fort Worth, TX [*Location identifier*] [*FAA*]   (FAAL)
TCB............ Take Care of Business [*Slang*]
TCB............ Taking Care of Business [*Brand name of Alberto-Culver Co.*]
TCB............ Tantalum Carbon Bond
TCB............ Target Control Box [*Army*]
TCB............ Task Control Block [*Data processing*]
TCB............ Task Force for Community Broadcasting   (EA)
TCB............ Taylor-Carlisle Bookseller [*ACCORD*] [*UTLAS symbol*]
TCB............ TCF Financial Corp. [*NYSE symbol*]   (SPSG)
TCB............ Technical Coordinator Bulletin [*NASA*]   (KSC)
TCB............ TEN Private Cable Systems, Inc. [*Vancouver Stock Exchange symbol*]
TCB............ Tent City Bravo [*Area near Tan Son Nhut Air Base, formerly site of USAR headquarters*]
TCB............ Terminal Control Block [*Data processing*]   (OA)
TCB............ Tetrachlorobiphenyl [*Organic chemistry*]
TCB............ Themes Concerning Blacks [*Personality development test*] [*Psychology*]
TCB............ Thermal Compression Bond
TCB............ Time Correlation Buffer   (MCD)
TCB............ Title Certificate Book [*A publication*]   (DLA)
TCB............ TMIS [*Technical and Management Information System*] Control Board [*NASA*]   (SSD)
TCB............ Total Cardiopulmonary Bypass [*Medicine*]   (MAE)
TCB............ Trans-Continental Freight Bureau, Chicago IL [*STAC*]
TCB............ Transfer Control Block
TCB............ Treasure Cay [*Bahamas*] [*Airport symbol*]   (OAG)
TCB............ Trichlorobenzene [*Organic chemistry*]
TCB............ Truss Connector Bulletin [*Department of Housing and Urban Development*] [*A publication*]   (GFGA)
TCB............ Trusted Computing Base
TCB............ Tulare County Free Library System, Visalia, CA [*OCLC symbol*]   (OCLC)
TCB............ Tumor Cell Burden [*Oncology*]
TCBA......... Tesla Coil Builders Association   (EA)

T-CBA	Transfluxor, Constant Board Assembly (AAG)
TCBAAQ...	Commonwealth Bureau of Animal Breeding and Genetics. Technical Communication [*A publication*]
TCBC........	Trichlorobenzyl Chloride [*Organic chemistry*]
TCBC........	[*The*] TrustCompany Bancorp. [*Jersey City, NJ*] [*NASDAQ symbol*] (NQ)
TCBC........	Twin Cities Biomedical Consortium [*Library network*]
TCBCO......	Thallium Calcium Barium Copper Oxide [*Inorganic chemistry*]
TCBCS	Blue Cross and Blue Shield of Tennessee, Chattanooga, TN [*Library symbol*] [*Library of Congress*] (LCLS)
TCBE........	Thermocompression Bonding Equipment
TCBEFC....	TCB [*Taking Care of Business*] for Elvis Fan Club (EA)
TCBG........	Training Centre Brigade of Gurkhas [*British military*] (DMA)
TCBHHA ..	[*The*] Church of the Brethren Homes and Hospitals Association [*Later, BHOAM*] (EA)
TCBI.........	Television Center for Business and Industry
TCBM........	Transcontinental Ballistic Missile [*Air Force*]
TCBO	Trichlorobutylene Oxide [*Organic chemistry*]
TCBS	Thiosulfate-Citrate-Bile Salt Sucrose [*Growth medium*]
TCBS	Transactions. Cambridge Bibliographical Society [*A publication*]
TCBT........	[*The*] Circuit Board Thermometer [*Data processing*]
TCBV........	Temperature Coefficient of Breakdown Voltage
TCBY........	[*The*] Country's Best Yogurt [*Store franchise*]
TCBY........	TCBY Enterprises, Inc. [*Associated Press abbreviation*] (APAG)
TCC	[*The*] Cesarean Connection (EA)
TCC	[*The*] Coin Coalition (EA)
TCC	[*The*] Cola Clan [*Later, Coca-Cola Collectors Club International*] (EA)
TCC	[*The*] Comedy Channel
TCC	[*The*] Computer Co. [*Information service or system*] (IID)
TCC	[*The*] Conservative Caucus (EA)
TCC	[*The*] Creative Coalition
TCC	[*The*] Curwood Collector [*A publication*] (EA)
TCC	New Mexico Institute of Mining and Technology Computer Center [*Research center*] (RCD)
TCC	T-Cell Clone [*Cytology*]
TCC	Tactical Command Control (MCD)
TCC	Tactical Communications Center
TCC	Tactical Control Center [*Military*]
TCC	Tactical Control Computer (AAG)
TCC	Tactical Control Console (NATG)
TCC	Tag Closed Cup [*Flash point test*]
TCC	Tagliabue Closed Cup [*Analytical chemistry*]
TCC	Tara Collectors Club (EA)
TCC	Target Coordination Center
TCC	Task Control Character (CMD)
TCC	Teachers College of Connecticut
TCC	Technical Change Centre [*British*] (CB)
TCC	Technical Computing Center (IEEE)
TCC	Technical Control Center
TCC ...	Technology Commercialization Center [*Minority Business Development Administration*]
TCC	Telecommunications Center (CET)
TCC	Telecommunications Consumer Coalition (EA)
TCC	Telecommunications Coordinating Committee [*Department of State*]
TCC	Teleconcepts in Communications, Inc. [*New York, NY*] [*Telecommunications*] (TSSD)
TCC	TeleConcepts Corp. [*Later, Virology Testing Systems*] [*AMEX symbol*] (SPSG)
TCC	Telemetry Standards Coordination Committee (HGAA)
TCC	Television Control Center
TCC	Temperature Coefficient of Capacitance
TCC	Temperature Control Circuit
TCC	Temporary Council Committee [*NATO*]
TCC	Terminal Control Corridor [*Aviation*]
TCC	Test Conductor Console (AAG)
TCC	Test Control Center [*NASA*]
TCC	Test Control Commission [*NATO*]
TCC	Test Controller Computer (MCD)
TCC	Test Controller Console (KSC)
TCC	Test Coordinating Center [*Army*]
TCC	Test Coordinator Console (CAAL)
TCC	Tetrachlorocatechol [*Organic chemistry*]
TCC	Theater Communications Center (MCD)
TCC	Theater Communications Command (MCD)
TCC	Thermal Control Coating
TCC	Therofor Catalytic Cracking
TCC	Thiamine Cobalt Chlorophyllin [*Antiulcer*]
TCC	Thiokol Chemical Corp. [*Later, Thiokol Corp.*] (AAG)
TCC	Third Continental Congress (EA)
TCC	Thromboplastic Cell Component [*Hematology*]
TCC	Through-Connected Circuit [*Telecommunications*] (TEL)
TCC	Time Compression Coding
TCC	Toroidal Combustion Chamber
TCC	Torque Converter Clutch [*Automotive engineering*]
TCC	TOS [*TIROS Operational Satellite*] Checkout Center [*Goddard Space Flight Center*] (NOAA)
TCC	Total Car Coefficient [*Formula*] [*Automobile analysis*]

TCC	Total Comparative Costs [*Army*]
TCC	Tracking and Communication Component
TCC	Tracking Computer Controls (MCD)
TCC	Tracking and Control Center
TCC	Traffic Control Center
TCC	Traffic Control Complex (SAA)
TCC	Transcontinental Corps [*Amateur radio*]
TCC	Transfer Channel Control (IEEE)
TCC	Transient Combustion Chamber [*Analysis*] (MCD)
TCC	Transit Control Center (SAA)
TCC	Transitional Cell Carcinoma
TCC	Transmission Control Character [*Telecommunications*] (TEL)
TCC	Transmit Carry and Clear
TCC	Transparent Conductive Coating [*Organic chemistry*]
TCC	Transport Control Center [*Air Force*]
TCC	Transportation Commodity Classification Code
TCC	Transportation Control Card [*Military*]
TCC	Transportation Control Center
TCC	Transportation Control Committee [*Navy*]
TCC	Travel Classification Code
TCC	Travel Correction Calculator (MSA)
TCC	Travelers' Century Club (EA)
TCC	Triactor Resources Corp. [*Vancouver Stock Exchange symbol*]
TCC	Trichlorocarbanilide [*Organic chemistry*]
TCC	Triclocarban [*Pharmacology*]
TCC	Trilobita-Crustacea-Chelicerata [*Evolution history*]
TCC	Triple Cotton-Covered [*Wire insulation*]
TCC	Troop Carrier Command [*World War II*]
TCC	Tucumcari, NM [*Location identifier*] [*FAA*] (FAAL)
TCC	Turbine Close Coupled (MSA)
TCC	Turnbull Canyon [*California*] [*Seismograph station code, US Geological Survey*] [*Closed*] (SEIS)
TCC	Type of Changed Code [*Army*]
TCCA........	Teachers' Committee on Central America (EA)
TCCA........	Textile Color Card Association of the US [*Later, CAUS*]
TCCA........	Thermometer Collectors Club of America (EA)
TCCA........	Tin Container Collectors Association (EA)
TCCA........	Trichloroisocyanuric Acid [*Organic chemistry*]
T & CCA	Turks and Caicos Canadian Association
TCCB........	Test and County Cricket Board [*British*]
TCCBL	Tons of Cubic Capacity Bale Space [*Shipping*]
TCCC........	Tower Control Computer Complex [*Aviation*]
TCCCS	Tactical Command, Control, and Communications System [*Canada*]
TCC/CT	Telecommunications/Communications Terminal (MCD)
TCCDC......	Chattem Drug and Chemical Co., Chattanooga, TN [*Library symbol*] [*Library of Congress*] (LCLS)
TCCF	Tactical Communications Control Facility [*Air Force*] (MCD)
TCCFU	Typical Coastal Command Foul Up [*RAF slang*] [*World War II*]
TCCH	Tracer Control Chassis
TCCM	Thermal Control Coating Material
TCCND5 ...	Commonwealth Bureau of Nutrition. Technical Communication [*A publication*]
TCCO	Technical Communications Corp. [*NASDAQ symbol*] (NQ)
TCCO	Temperature-Compensated Crystal Oscillator (MCD)
TCCOB......	Textile Chemist and Colorist [*A publication*]
TC-CON....	Type Classification - Contingency
T & CCP	Telecommunications and Command and Control Program [*Air Force*] (AFIT)
TCCP	Tissue Culture for Crops Project [*Colorado State University*] [*Research center*] (RCD)
TCCPSWG ...	Tactical Command and Control Procedures Standardization Working Group [*Army*] (AABC)
TCCRAEF ...	[*The*] Conservative Caucus Research, Analysis, and Education Foundation (EA)
TCCS	Technical Committee on Communications Satellites
TCCS	Tide Communication Control Ship (NATG)
TCCS	Toyota's Computer-Controlled System (ADA)
TCCS	Trace Contaminant Control System
TCC/SCA ...	Tai Chi Chuan/Shaolin Chuan Association (EA)
TCCT........	Tactical Communications Control Terminal (MCD)
TCCT........	Tooling Contour Check Tool (MCD)
TCD	Chad [*ANSI three-letter standard code*] (CNC)
TCD	Consolidated Companies [*AMEX symbol*] (SPSG)
TCD	Department of Technical Cooperation for Development [*United Nations*]
TCD	Tactical Communications Division [*Military*]
TCD	Tapetochoroidal Dystrophy [*Ophthalmology*]
TCD	Target Center Display
TCD	Task Completion Date (AAG)
TCD	Technical Contracts Department
TCD	Telemetry and Command Data (KSC)
TCD	Teletype Conversion Device (DWSG)
TCD	Tentative Classification of Damage
TCD	Tentative Classification of Defects (NG)
TCD	Tentative Classification of Documents
TCD	Terminal Countdown Demonstration
TCD	Test Communications Division (SAA)
TCD	Test Completion Date (NASA)
TCD	Test Control Document [*NASA*] (MCD)

TCD .... Test Control Drawings (MCD)
TCD .... Thermal Conductivity Detector [*Analytical instrumentation*]
TCD .... Thermochemical Deposition
TCD .... Three-Channel Decoder
TCD .... Thyratron Core Driver
TCD .... Time Compliance Directive [*Air Force*] (MCD)
TCD .... Time Correlation Data
T & CD ...... Timing and Countdown [*NASA*] (NASA)
TCD .... Tissue Culture Dose (AAMN)
TCD .... Tor-Cal Resources Ltd. [*Toronto Stock Exchange symbol*]
TCD .... Total Cost Approach to Distribution
TCD .... Tour Completion Date
TCD .... TOXLINE Chemical Dictionary [*A publication*]
TCD .... Transistor Chopper Driver
TCD .... Transistor-Controlled Delay (MCD)
TCD .... Transportability Clearance Diagram (MCD)
TCD .... Trinity College, Dublin [*Ireland*]
TCD .... Tumor Control Dose [*Oncology*]
TCD .... Type Classification Date [*Army*]
TCD$_{50}$ .... Tissue Culture Dose, 50% Infectivity
TC & DB ... Turn, Cough, and Deep Breathe [*Medicine*]
TCDC .... Taurochenodeoxycholate [*Biochemistry*]
TCDC .... Technical Cooperation among Developing Countries [*United Nations*]
TCDC .... Two Count Holding Co. [*NASDAQ symbol*] (NQ)
TCDC/INRES ... Information Referral System for Technical Co-operation among Developing Countries [*United Nations Development Programme*] [*Information service or system*] (IID)
TCDD .... Tetrachlorodibenzodioxin [*Organic chemistry*]
TCDF .... Temporary Container Discharge Facility
TCDF .... Tetrachlorodibenzofuran [*Organic chemistry*]
TCDF .... TIN [*Taxpayer Identification Number*] Control Number/DLN [*Document Locator Number*] File [*IRS*]
TCDMS ..... Telecommunication/Data Management System
TCDN .... Techdyne, Inc. [*Hialeah, FL*] [*NASDAQ symbol*] (NQ)
TCDP .... Transmitter Control and Display Panel
TCDR .... Cedar Income Fund 2, Ltd. [*NASDAQ symbol*] (NQ)
TCDS........ Tryptamine Chemical Delivery System [*Pharmacology*]
TCDU .... Transport Command Development Unit [*British military*] (DMA)
TCE............ 20th Century-Energy [*Vancouver Stock Exchange symbol*]
TCE............ [*The*] Chemical Engineer [*A publication*]
TCE............ Taking Care of Elvis [*Motto of Elvis Presley fans*]
TCE............ Talker Commission Error (MUGU)
TCE............ Tax Counseling for the Elderly [*Internal Revenue Service*]
TCE............ Teachers' Centers Exchange (EA)
TCE............ Telemetry Checkout Equipment (KSC)
TCE............ Telephone Co. Engineered [*Telecommunications*] (TEL)
TCE............ Temperature Coefficient of Expansion
TCE............ Terminal Control Element (CAAL)
TCE............ Terminal Cretaceous Event [*Geology*]
TCE............ Terrace (ROG)
TCE............ Tetrachloroethylene [*Also, P*] [*Organic chemistry*]
TCE............ Thermal Canister Experiment [*Space shuttle*] [*NASA*]
TCE............ Thermal Coefficient of Expansion
TCE............ Thomson's Loss-Making Consumer-Electronics [*France*] (ECON)
TCE............ Tons of Coal Equivalent
TCE............ Total Composite Error
TCE............ Total Concept Engineering
TCE............ TOW [*Tube-Launched, Optically Tracked, Wire-Guided (Weapon)*] Crew Evaluator [*Military*] (INF)
TCE............ Trans-Colorado Airlines, Inc. [*Gunnison, CO*] [*FAA designator*] (FAAC)
TCE............ Transportation-Communication Employees Union [*Later, TCIU*]
TCE............ Trichloroethanol [*Organic chemistry*]
TCE............ Trichloroethylene [*Also, TRI*] [*Organic chemistry*]
TCE............ Tubular Carbon Electrode
TCE............ Tulcea [*Romania*] [*Airport symbol*] (OAG)
TCE............ Tyumen Commodity Exchange [*Russian Federation*] (EY)
TCEA........ Theoretical Chemical Engineering Abstracts [*A publication*]
TCEA........ Training Center for Experimental Aerodynamics [*NATO*]
TCEA........ Trichloroethane [*Organic chemistry*]
TCEBA ...... Tribune. CEBEDEAU [*Centre Belge d'Etude et de Documentation des Eaux et de l'Air*] [*A publication*]
TCEC........ Erlanger Medical Center, Medical Library, Chattanooga, TN [*Library symbol*] [*Library of Congress*] (LCLS)
TCEC-N .... Erlanger Medical Center, Nursing School, Chattanooga, TN [*Library symbol*] [*Library of Congress*] (LCLS)
TCEC-P..... Erlanger Medical Center, I. C., Thompson's Children's Pediatric Library, Chattanooga, TN [*Library symbol*] [*Library of Congress*] (LCLS)
TCED........ Thrust Control Exploratory Development (KSC)
TCEL........ T Cell Sciences, Inc. [*Cambridge, MA*] [*NASDAQ symbol*] (NQ)
TCEL........ Thought Currents in English Literature [*A publication*]
TCEO .... Theatre Committee for Eugene O'Neill (EA)
TCEP .... Tris(chloroethyl)phosphite [*Organic chemistry*]
TCEP .... Tris(cyanoethoxy)propane [*Organic chemistry*]

TCert........ Teacher's Certificate [*British*] (DBQ)
TCES .... [*Romberg*] Tiburon Center for Environmental Studies [*San Francisco State University*] [*Research center*]
TCES .... Transcutaneous Cranial Electrical Stimulation [*Medicine*]
TCESOM .. Trichlorethylene-Extracted Soybean Oil Meal
TCET........ Transcerebral Electrotherapy
TCF........... [*The*] Children's Foundation (EA)
TCF........... [*The*] Compassionate Friends (EA)
TCF........... T-Lymphocyte Chemotactic Factor
TCF........... Tactical Control Flight
TCF........... Tank Checkout Facility [*NASA*] (NASA)
TCF........... Technical Control Facility [*or Function*]
TCF........... Temporary Chaplain to the Forces [*British*]
TCF........... Terminal Communication Facility [*Telecommunications*] (TSSD)
TCF........... Terminal Configuration Facility [*Data processing*]
TCF........... Territorial Cadet Force [*British military*] (DMA)
TCF........... Test Control Fixture (MCD)
TCF........... Time Correction Factor (ADA)
TCF........... To Be Called For [*British Rail parcel service*] [*Obsolete*] (DI)
TCF........... Total Coronary Flow [*Medicine*] (MAE)
TCF........... Toulx Ste. Croix [*France*] [*Seismograph station code, US Geological Survey*] (SEIS)
TCF........... Training Check Frame [*Data processing*]
TCF........... Transparent Computing Facility
TCF........... Treacher Collins Foundation (EA)
TCF........... Trillion Cubic Feet
TCF........... Troop Carrier Forces [*Military*]
TCF........... Tunable Control Frequency
TCF........... Twentieth Century Fiction [*A publication*]
TCF........... Twentieth Century Fund (EA)
TCFB........ Trans-Continental Freight Bureau
TCFC........ [*The*] Cars Fan Club (EA)
TCFC........ Thom Christopher Fan Club (EA)
TCFC........ Tom Cruise Fan Club (EA)
TCFC........ Tommy Cash Fan Club (EA)
TCFC........ Turkish Children Foster Care (EA)
TCF Fn ...... TCF Financial Corp. [*Associated Press abbreviation*] (APAG)
TCFIC .... Textile, Clothing, and Footwear Industries Committee [*British*] (DCTA)
TCFlt .... Tactical Control Flight
TCFM....... Teilhard Centre for the Future of Man (EAIO)
TCFM....... Temperature Control Flux Monitor [*NASA*]
TCFNO ..... [*The*] Common Fund for Nonprofit Organizations [*Ford Foundation*]
TCFP .... Thrust Chamber Fuel Purge (SAA)
TCFS .... Turkish Cypriot Federated State
TCFU........ Tumor Colony-Forming Unit [*Oncology*]
TCG .... [*The*] Crimson Group [*Cambridge, MA*] [*Telecommunications*] (TSSD)
TCG .... Tactical Control Group [*Air Force*]
TCG .... Technical Coordination Group (MCD)
TCG .... Telecommunications Consulting Group, Inc. [*Washington, DC*] (TSSD)
TCG .... Telecommunications Group [*Range Commanders Council*] [*NASA*]
TCG .... Territorial College of Guam
TCG .... Test Call Generator [*Telecommunications*] (TEL)
TCG .... Test Control Group [*NASA*] (NASA)
TCG .... Theatre Communications Group (EA)
TCG .... Threat Coordinating Group [*DoD*]
TCG .... Time Code Generator
TCG .... Time-Compensated Gain [*Cardiology*]
TCG .... Time Controlled Gain (AAG)
TCG .... Tooling Coordination Group (AAG)
TC/G .... Total Fielding Chances per Game [*Baseball*]
TCG .... Trans Canada Glass Ltd. [*Toronto Stock Exchange symbol*] [*Vancouver Stock Exchange symbol*]
TCG .... Transponder Control Group
TCG .... Tritocerebral Commissure, Giant [*Zoology*]
TCG .... Tucson, Cornelia & Gila Bend Railroad Co. [*AAR code*]
TCG .... Tune-Controlled Gain
TCGCB....... Transactions. Caribbean Geological Conference [*A publication*]
TCGE....... Tool and Cutter Grinding Equipment (MCD)
TCGE-G .... Technika Hronika (Greece) [*A publication*]
TCGF........ T-Cell Growth Factor [*Biochemistry*] [*See also IL-2*]
TCGF........ Thymus Cell Growth Factor [*Cytology*]
TCGH........ Downtown General Hospital, Chattanooga, TN [*Library symbol*] [*Library of Congress*] (LCLS)
TCGp......... Tactical Control Group [*Air Force*] (AFM)
TCGS......... Terak Corp. [*NASDAQ symbol*] (NQ)
TCGT......... Georgia-Tennessee Regional Health Commission, Chattanooga, TN [*Library symbol*] [*Library of Congress*] (LCLS)
TCGT........ Tool and Cutter Grinding Tool (MCD)
TCGU .... Texaco Continuous Grease Unit
TCH.......... Chattanooga-Hamilton County Bicentennial Library, Chattanooga, TX [*OCLC symbol*] (OCLC)
TCH.......... Compania de Telefonos de Chile SA ADS [*NYSE symbol*] (SPSG)
TCH.......... Tchibanga [*Gabon*] [*Airport symbol*] (OAG)

TCH.......... Tchimkent [*Former USSR*] [*Seismograph station code, US Geological Survey*] [*Closed*]   (SEIS)
TCH.......... Tchoupitoulas [*Virus*]
TCH.......... Tec Tech [*Vancouver Stock Exchange symbol*]
TCH.......... TechAmerica Group, Inc. [*AMEX symbol*]   (SPSG)
TCH.......... Technologie-Centrum Hannover GmbH [*Database producer*]   (IID)
TCH.......... Technovation [*Netherlands*] [*A publication*]
TCh............ Temoignage Chretien [*A publication*]
TCH.......... Temporary Construction Hole [*Technical drawings*]
TCH.......... Tetrachlorohydroquinone [*Organic chemistry*]
TCH.......... Thiocarbohydrazide [*Organic chemistry*]
TCH.......... Threshold Crossing Height [*Aviation*]   (FAAC)
TCH.......... Total Circulating Hemoglobin [*Medicine*]   (MAE)
TCH.......... Trade Channel [*A publication*]
TCH.......... Trans-Canada Highway
TCH.......... Transfer in Channel
TCH.......... Trust Chamber [*NASA*]   (KSC)
TCH.......... Turn, Cough, Hyperventilate [*Medicine*]
TCHCB...... Chattanooga-Hamilton County Bicentennial Library, Chattanooga, TN [*Library symbol*] [*Library of Congress*]   (LCLS)
TCHD....... Threshold Crossing Height Downwind [*Aviation*]   (FAAC)
TCHEP...... Technical Committee on High Energy Physics [*of the Federal Council for Science and Technology*]
TCHG....... Teaching
TCHHC...... Ti Ch'iu Hua Hsueh [*A publication*]
TCHHW.... Tropic Higher High Water [*Tides*]
TCHHWI.. Tropic Higher High-Water Interval [*Tides*]
TCHK....... Text Check [*Data processing*]
TCHLW .... Tropic Higher Low Water [*Tides*]
TCHMA .... Technika v Chemii [*A publication*]
TCHNG..... Teaching
TChO......... Olin Corp., D. B. Beene Technical Information Center, Charleston, TN [*Library symbol*] [*Library of Congress*]   (LCLS)
TCHOG..... Technical Operations Group [*Air Force*]
TCHOS ..... Technical Operations Squadron [*Air Force*]
TCHPAX... Acta Geologica Sinica [*A publication*]
TCHR....... Teacher
T Christ Wet ... Tydskrif vir Christelike Wetenskap [*A publication*]
TchSym...... Tech-Sym Corp. [*Associated Press abbreviation*]   (APAG)
TCHT .... Tanned-Cell Hemagglutination Test [*Immunology*]
TCHTS...... Technical Training Squadron [*Air Force*]
TCHTW .... Technical Training Wing [*Air Force*]
TCHU....... Threshold Crossing Height Upwind [*Aviation*]   (FAAC)
TCI............ Tall Clubs International   (EA)
TCI............ TDRS Command Interface   (MCD)
TCI............ Technical Component Industries [*Aerospace*] [*British*]
TCI............ Technical Critical Item   (NASA)
TCI............ Technology Catalysts, Inc. [*Information service or system*]   (IID)
TCI............ Technology Communications, Inc.
TCI............ Technology for Communications International
TCI............ Technology Concepts, Inc. [*Sudbury, MA*] [*Telecommunications*]   (TSSD)
TCI............ Tele-Communications, Inc. [*Brookpark, OH*]   (TSSD)
TCI............ Teleconferencing Systems International, Inc. [*Elk Grove Village, IL*] [*Telecommunications*]   (TSSD)
TCI............ Telemetry Components Information   (KSC)
TCI............ Telephone Collectors International   (EA)
TCI............ Temperature Control Instrument
TCI............ Temporary Customs Impost [*British*]
TCI............ Tenerife [*Canary Islands*] [*Airport symbol*]   (OAG)
TCI............ Terminal Communications Interface
TCI............ Terrain Clearance Indicator
TCI............ Test Control Instruction   (KSC)
TCI............ Theoretical Chemistry Institute [*University of Wisconsin - Madison*] [*Research center*]   (RCD)
TCI............ Thermo Cardiosystems, Inc.   (PS)
TCI............ Thimble Collectors International   (EA)
TCI............ Thomson CEA Industries [*France*]   (ECON)
TCI............ Time Change Item   (MCD)
TCI............ To Come In [*to hospital*] [*Medicine*]
TCI............ Torque Control Isolation [*Automotive engineering*]
TCI............ Total Cerebral Ischemia
TCI............ Traffic Clubs International   (EA)
TCI............ Transcontinental Realty Investors [*NYSE symbol*]   (SPSG)
TCI............ Transient Cerebral Ischemia [*Medicine*]
TCI............ Transportation Clubs International   (EA)
TCI............ Travel Consultants, Inc.
TCI............ Trunk Cut-In
TCI............ Twentieth Century Interpretations [*A publication*]
TCIA......... Truck Cap Industry Association   (EA)
TCIC......... Technical Coatings, Inc. [*Lubbock, TX*] [*NASDAQ symbol*]   (NQ)
TCIC......... Technical Committee on Industrial Classification [*Office of Management and Budget*] [*Washington, DC*]   (EGAO)
TCID......... Terminal Computer Identification   (KSC)
TCID......... Test Configuration Identifier   (NASA)
TCID......... Tissue Culture Infectious [*or Infective*] Dose

Tc-IDA ...... Technetium Iminodiacetic Acid [*Clinical chemistry*]
TCIE .... Transient Cerebral Ischemic Episode [*Medicine*]   (MAE)
TCIF .... Telecommunications Industry Forum   (EA)
TCII.......... TCI International, Inc. [*NASDAQ symbol*]   (NQ)
TCIR......... Technical Command Informal Reports [*Army*]   (MCD)
TCIS .... TELEX Computer Inquiry Service
TCITA .... Transactions. Chalmers University of Technology [*Gothenburg, Sweden*] [*A publication*]
TCITP .... Terminal Communications Interface Test Program   (MCD)
TCIU......... Transportation Communications International Union   (EA)
TCJ .... Tactical Communications Jamming [*Military*]   (CAAL)
TCJ .... Tarrant County Junior College, Hurst, TX [*OCLC symbol*]   (OCLC)
TCJ .... Thermocouple Junction
TCJ .... Town and Country Journal [*A publication*]   (APTA)
TCJ .... Turbulent Confined Jet
TCJAA ...... Telecommunication Journal of Australia [*A publication*]
TCJCC...... Trades Councils' Joint Consultative Committee [*British*]   (DCTA)
TCJOA ...... Telecommunication Journal [*A publication*]
TCK .... F.A. Tucker Group [*AMEX symbol*]   (SPSG)
TCK .... Thermochemical-Kinetic
TCK .... Tilletia controversa Kuehn [*Wheat fungus*]
TCK .... TOW [*Tube-Launched, Optically-Tracked, Wire-Guided Weapon*] Cooler Kit   (DWSG)
TCK .... Track   (AAG)
TCK .... Two-Cavity Klystron
TCKHA ..... Ti Chih Ko Hsueh [*A publication*]
TCL........... [*The*] Command Language [*Data processing*]   (PCM)
TCL........... Takeoff Cruise Landing [*Aviation*]
TCL........... Telecommunication Laboratories [*Taiwan*]
TCL........... Telephone Cables Ltd. [*British*]
TCL........... Terminal Command Language [*Applied Digital Data Systems*]
TCL........... Terminal Control Language
TCL........... Textes Cuneiformes. Departement des Antiquites Orientales. Musee du Louvre [*A publication*]   (BJA)
TCL........... Thin Charcoal Layer
TCL........... Through-Camera-Lens
TCL........... Time and Cycle Log [*NASA*]   (KSC)
TCL........... Toll Circuit Layout [*Telecommunications*]   (TEL)
TCL........... Tool Command Language [*Data processing*]
TCL........... Tool Control List [*Military*]   (AFIT)
TCL........... Transcon, Inc. [*NYSE symbol*]   (SPSG)
TCL........... Transfer Chemical LASER   (IEEE)
TCL........... Transistor Contact Land
TCL........... Transistor Coupled Logic
TCL........... Transport Canada Library, Ottawa [*UTLAS symbol*]
TCL........... Transportable Calibration Laboratory
TCL........... Trap Control Line
TCL........... Trinity College, London
TCL........... Troposcatter Communications Link
TCL........... Tulane Computer Laboratory [*Tulane University*] [*Research center*]   (RCD)
TCL........... Tuscaloosa [*Alabama*] [*Airport symbol*]   (OAG)
TCL........... Tusculum College, Greenville, TN [*OCLC symbol*] [*Inactive*]   (OCLC)
TCL........... Twentieth Century Literature [*A publication*]
TClA .... Austin Peay State University, Clarksville, TN [*Library symbol*] [*Library of Congress*]   (LCLS)
TCLAS ...... Type Classification [*Military*]   (AABC)
TCLBRP..... Tank Cannon Launched Beam Rider Projectile   (MCD)
TCLBS....... Tropical Constant-Level Balloon System [*Meteorology*]
TCLC......... Travaux. Cercle Linguistique de Copenhague [*A publication*]
TCLC........ Tri-State College Library Cooperative [*Rosemont College Library*] [*Rosemont, PA*] [*Library network*]
TCLC........ Twentieth-Century Literary Criticism [*A publication*]
TC/LD....... Thermocouple/Lead Detector [*Nuclear energy*]   (NRCH)
TCle .... Cleveland Public Library, Cleveland, TN [*Library symbol*] [*Library of Congress*]   (LCLS)
TCLE......... Thermal Coefficient of Linear Expansion [*Rocket motor stress*]
TCleB........ Bradley Memorial Hospital, Cleveland, TN [*Library symbol*] [*Library of Congress*]   (LCLS)
TCleC........ Cleveland State Community College, Cleveland, TN [*Library symbol*] [*Library of Congress*]   (LCLS)
TCleL........ Lee College, Cleveland, TN [*Library symbol*] [*Library of Congress*]   (LCLS)
TClH......... Clarksville Memorial Hospital, Clarksville, TN [*Library symbol*] [*Library of Congress*]   (LCLS)
TCLHW .... Tropic Lower High Water [*Tides*]
TCLL........ T-Cell Chronic Lymphocytic Leukemia [*Oncology*]
TCLLW ..... Tropic Lower Low Water [*Tides*]
TCLLWI... Tropic Lower Low-Water Interval [*Tides*]
TCLN........ Techniclone International Corp. [*NASDAQ symbol*]   (NQ)
TCLNA...... Tall Cedars of Lebanon of North America   (EA)
TCLP .... Toxic Characteristics Leaching Procedure [*Environmental Protection Agency*]
TCLP .... Toxicity Characteristic Leaching Procedure [*Environmental Protection Agency*]
TCLP .... Travaux. Cercle Linguistique de Prague [*A publication*]
TCLP .... Type Classification, Limited Procurement
TC-LP........ Type Classification - Limited Production

TC-LPT ..... Type Classified - Limited Production Test
TC-LPU ..... Type Classification - Limited Production Urgent
TCLR .... Toll Circuit Layout Record [*Telecommunications*]   (TEL)
TCLSC .... Theater COMSEC [*Communications Security*] Logistic Support Center [*Army*]   (AABC)
TCLSC-E ... Theater COMSEC Logistics Support Center - Europe   (MCD)
TCM .... T/SF Communications Corp. [*AMEX symbol*]   (SPSG)
TCM .... Tacoma, WA [*Location identifier*] [*FAA*]   (FAAL)
TCM .... Tactical Cruise Missile   (MCD)
TCM .... Tax Court Memorandum Decisions [*Commerce Clearing House or Prentice-Hall, Inc.*] [*A publication*]   (DLA)
TCM .... Teaching Career Month
TCM .... Technical Committee Minutes [*Military*]   (AFIT)
TCM .... Technical Coordination Meeting   (MCD)
TCM .... Telecommunications Monitor
TCM .... Teledyne Continental Motors [*Muskegon, MI*] [*FAA designator*]   (FAAC)
TCM .... Telemetry Code Modulation
TC & M ...... Telemetry Control and Monitoring
TCM .... Telephone Channel Monitor
TCM .... Temperature Control Model
TCM .... Teratogenesis, Carcinogenesis, and Mutagenesis [*A publication*]
TCM .... Terminal Capacity Matrix   (OA)
TCM .... Terminal-to-Computer Multiplexer
TCM .... Termination of Centralized Management   (MCD)
TCM .... Terrain Clearance Measurement
TCM .... Terrestrial Carbon Model [*Earth science*]
TCM .... Test Call Module [*Telecommunications*]   (TEL)
TCM .... Tetrachloromercurate [*Inorganic chemistry*]
TCM .... Texas Climatological Model [*Environmental Protection Agency*].   (GFGA)
TCM .... Textil-Mitteilungen. Unabhangige Textil Zeitung fuer Handel und Industrie [*A publication*]
TCM .... Theater Combat Model   (NATG)
TCM .... Thermal Conduction Module [*IBM Corp.*]
TCM .... Thermoplastic Cellular Molding [*Plastics technology*]
TCM .... Tissue Culture Medium
TCM .... Toroidal Carbohydrate Module [*i.e., doughnut*] [*Slang*]
TCM .... Torpedo Countermeasures   (NVT)
TCM .... Total Downtime for Corrective Unscheduled Maintenance [*Quality control*]   (MCD)
TCM .... Toxic Chemical Munitions [*Army*]
TCM .... Trade and Commerce [*A publication*]
TCM .... Trajectory Correction Maneuver
TCM .... Transcutaneous [*Oxygen*] Monitoring [*Medicine*]
TCM .... Transfluxor Constants Matrix   (AAG)
TCM .... Translator Command Module [*Fluorescence technique*]
TCM .... Transportation Control Measure [*Environmental Protection Agency*]   (GFGA)
TCM .... Travel Cost Method
TCM .... Trellis-Coded Modulation [*Data transmission*]   (BYTE)
TCM .... Troop Corporal-Major [*British military*]   (DMA)
TCM .... Truck Components Marketing [*Eaton Corp.*]
TCM .... Tubing Connector Manifold [*Instrumentation*]
TCM .... Tucuman [*Argentina*] [*Seismograph station code, US Geological Survey*] [*Closed*]   (SEIS)
TCM .... Twentieth Century Monthly [*A publication*]
TCM .... Twin-Cartridge Machine
TCMA .... Tabulating Card Manufacturers Association [*Later, IOSA*]   (EA)
TCMA .... Textile Chemical Manufacturers Association [*Later, IOSA*]   (EA)
TCMA .... Theater Container Management Agency
TCMA .... Third Class Mail Association   (EA)
TCMA .... Tooling Component Manufacturers Association   (EA)
TCM/A ...... Toxic Chemical Munitions/Agents   (MCD)
TCMB .... Turkiye Cumhuriyet Merkez Bankasi [*The Central Bank of the Republic of Turkey*]
TCM (CCH) ... Tax Court Memorandum Decisions (Commerce Clearing House) [*A publication*]   (DLA)
TCMD .... Transportation Cargo Manifest Document
TCMD .... Transportation Control and Movement Document [*Military*]
TCMDBN ... Handelinge van die Kollege van Geneeskunde van Suid-Afrika [*A publication*]
TC Memo .. Tax Court Memorandum Decisions [*Commerce Clearing House or Prentice-Hall, Inc.*] [*A publication*]   (DLA)
TCMF .... Touch Calling Multifrequency   (IEEE)
TCMH .... Memorial Hospital, Chattanooga, TN [*Library symbol*] [*Library of Congress*]   (LCLS)
TCMI .... Moccasin Bend Mental Health Institute, Chattanooga, TN [*Library symbol*] [*Library of Congress*]   (LCLS)
TCMIS ...... Trade Control Measures Information System [*UNCTAD*] [*United Nations*]   (DUND)
T C MITS ... [*The*] Common Man in the Street [*The average man*] [*See also MITS*]
TCMP .... Taxpayer Compliance Measurement Program [*IRS*]
TCM (P-H) ... Tax Court Memorandum Decisions (Prentice-Hall, Inc.) [*A publication*]   (DLA)
TCMS .... Technical Control and Management Subsystem   (MCD)
TC-MS ...... Thermal Chromatography/Mass Spectrometry

TCMS .... Toll Centering and Metropolitan Sectoring [*AT & T*] [*Telecommunications*]   (TEL)
TCMS .... Track Combat Status   (SAA)
TCMS .... Training Certification Management System [*NASA*]
TCMTA ..... Technometrics [*A publication*]
TCMTB ..... (Thiocyanomethylthio)benzothiazole [*Fungicide*] [*Organic chemistry*]
TCMUA .... Telecommunications [*English Translation*] [*A publication*]
TCMUD8 .. Teratogenesis, Carcinogenesis, and Mutagenesis [*A publication*]
TCMUE9 .. Topics in Chemical Mutagenesis [*A publication*]
TCMZ .... Trichloromethiazide [*Diuretic*]
TCN .... Carson-Newman College, Jefferson City, TN [*OCLC symbol*]   (OCLC)
TCN .... Telecommunications Cooperative Network   (EA)
TCN .... Teleconference Network [*University of Nebraska Medical Center*] [*Omaha, NE*] [*Telecommunications*]   (TSSD)
TCN .... Territorial Command Net
TCN .... Test Change Notice [*NASA*]   (MCD)
TCN .... Tetracycline [*Antibiotic*]
TCN .... Texcan Technology Corp. [*Vancouver Stock Exchange symbol*]
TCN .... Tobacco Cyst Nematode [*Plant pathology*]
TCN .... Toconce [*Chile*] [*Seismograph station code, US Geological Survey*]   (SEIS)
TCN .... Tracing Change Notice
TCN .... Track Channel Number   (SAA)
TCN .... Trade Commission of Norway   (EA)
TCN .... Trans Continental Airlines [*Ypsilanti, MI*] [*FAA designator*]   (FAAC)
TCN .... Transfer on Channel Not in Operation   (SAA)
TCN .... Transportation Control Number [*Air Force*]   (AFM)
TCN .... Trolley Coach News [*A publication*]   (EAAP)
TCNA .... Tube Council of North America   (EA)
TCNB .... Tetracyanobenzene [*Organic chemistry*]
TC-NBT .... Thiocarbamyl-nitro-blue Tetrazolium [*Organic chemistry*]
TCNC .... Tekakwitha Conference National Center   (EA)
TCNCO ..... Test Control Noncommissioned Officer   (AFM)
TCNE .... Tetracyanoethylene [*Organic chemistry*]
TCNEO ..... Tetracyanoethylene Oxide [*Organic chemistry*]
TCNJ .... Trust Co. of New Jersey [*NASDAQ symbol*]   (NQ)
TCNL .... Tecnol Medical Products [*NASDAQ symbol*]   (SPSG)
TCNM .... Trimethylcyclopropenyl(nitrophenyl)malononitrile [*Organic chemistry*]
TCNOA ...... Technology [*Sindri, India*] [*A publication*]
TCNPEX ... Bulletin. Taichung District Agricultural Improvement Station [*A publication*]
TCNQ .... Tetracyanoquinodimethane [*Organic chemistry*]
TCNRS ...... Transactions. Canadian Numismatic Research Society [*A publication*]
TCNS .... Transcutaneous Nerve Stimulation [*Medicine*]   (MAE)
TCNSB ...... Technos [*A publication*]
TCNT .... Transpiration-Cooled Nose Tip
TCNTL ...... Transcontinental   (FAAC)
TCO .... Tactical Combat Operations
TCO .... Tactical Control Officer [*Army*]
TCO .... Taken Care Of   (MCD)
TCO .... Taubman Centers, Inc. [*NYSE symbol*]   (SPSG)
TCO .... Technical Checkout [*Nuclear*]   (MCD)
TCO .... Technical Contracting Office [*Navy*]
TCO .... Technical Cooperation Officer [*British*]
TCO .... Telecommunications Certifying Officer [*Air Force*]   (AFIT)
TCO .... Telemetry and Command Subsystem [*Deep Space Instrumentation Facility, NASA*]
TCO .... Terminal Control Office [*or Officer*]
TCO .... Termination Contracting Officer [*Military*]
TCO .... Test and Checkout [*NASA*]   (GFGA)
T & C/O .... Test and Checkout [*NASA*]   (KSC)
TCO .... Test Control Officer [*Military*]
TCO .... Thrust Cutoff   (NVT)
TCO .... Tillamook County Library, Tillamook, OR [*OCLC symbol*]   (OCLC)
TCO .... Time and Charges, Operate
TCO .... Tjaenstemaennens Centralorganisation [*Central Organization of Salaried Employees*] [*Sweden*]
TCO .... Tool Change Order   (MCD)
TCO .... Torpedo Control Officer [*British military*]   (DMA)
TCO .... Train Conducting Officer [*British military*]   (DMA)
TCO .... Trans Canada Options [*Stock exchange network of VSE, TSE, and MSE*]
TCO .... Trans-Canada Resources Ltd. [*Toronto Stock Exchange symbol*]
TCO .... Translational Control   (SAA)
TCO .... Translocation Crossover [*Geology*]
TCO .... Transparent Conductive Oxide [*Photovoltaic energy systems*]
TCO .... Transportation Co. [*Army*]
TCO .... Transportation Control Officer [*Air Force*]   (AFM)
TCO .... Trinity College, Oxford [*British*]   (DAS)
TCO .... Triode Cavity Oscillator
TCO .... Trunk Cutoff
TCO .... Tumaco [*Colombia*] [*Airport symbol*]   (OAG)
TCOA .... Telephone Contract Officers' Association [*A union*] [*British*]
TCOBS ...... Type Classification - Obsolete   (MCD)

TCOC .... Transverse Cylindrical Orthomorphic Chart
TColISM.... Southern Missionary College, Collegedale, TN [*Library symbol*] [*Library of Congress*] (LCLS)
TCOM .... Tele-Communications, Inc. [*NASDAQ symbol*] (NQ)
TCOM .... Terminal Communications (FAAC)
TCOM .... Terminal or Computer Originated Mail Systems, Inc. [*Washington, DC*] (TSSD)
TCOM .... Tethered Communications, Inc. [*Westinghouse subsidiary*]
TCOM .... Texas College of Osteopathic Medicine
T-Comm .... Terret Communications [*Whitehouse Station, NJ*] (TSSD)
TCOMP..... Tape Compare Processor [*Data processing*]
T/COMP.... Trimmed Complete [*Automotive engineering*]
T/CONT.... Throttle Control [*Automotive engineering*]
T/CONV ... Torque Converter [*Automotive engineering*]
TCoo .... Putnam County Public Library, Cookeville, TN [*Library symbol*] [*Library of Congress*] (LCLS)
TCooH .... Cookeville General Hospital, Stephen Farr Health Sciences Library, Cookeville, TN [*Library symbol*] [*Library of Congress*] (LCLS)
TCooP .... Tennessee Technological University, Cookeville, TN [*Library symbol*] [*Library of Congress*] (LCLS)
TCOP .... Test and Checkout Plan [*NASA*] (KSC)
TCOP .... Thrust Chamber Oxidizer Purge (SAA)
TCOR .... Chrysler Town and Country Owners Registry (EA)
TCORA ..... Teacher's College Record [*A publication*]
TCOS........ Trunk Class of Service [*Telecommunications*] (TEL)
TCOT .... Tension Control Optimisation Theory [*Tire manufacturing*]
T-COUNT ... Terminal Count [*Flight readiness count*] (MCD)
TCovH .... Tipton County Hospital, Covington, TN [*Library symbol*] [*Library of Congress*] (LCLS)
TCP........... Tactical Computer Processor
TCP........... Tactical Control Panel (MCD)
TCP........... Tactical Cryptologic Program [*DoD*]
TCP........... Tape Conversion Program [*Data processing*] (MDG)
TCP........... Task Change Proposal (AAG)
TCP........... Task Control Packet (NASA)
TCP........... Task Control Program
TCP........... Teachers College Press
TCP........... Technical Change Proposal
TCP........... Technical Coordination Program [*Military*] (AFIT)
TCP........... Technical Cost Proposal (AAG)
TCP........... Technology Coordinating Paper
TCP........... Telemetry and Command Processor Assembly [*Deep Space Instrumentation Facility, NASA*]
TCP........... Temple Cyclopaedic Primers [*A publication*]
TCP........... Temporary Change Procedure (AAG)
TCP........... Terminal Control Program
TCP........... Test Change Proposal (CAAL)
TCP........... Test Checkout Panel
TCP........... Test and Checkout Procedure [*NASA*] (KSC)
T & CP .... Test and Checkout Procedure [*NASA*] (GFGA)
TCP........... Test Control Package (NASA)
TCP........... Test of Creative Potential
TCP........... Tetrachlorobiphenyl [*Organic chemistry*]
TCP........... Tetrachlorophenol [*Organic chemistry*]
TCP........... Tetracyanoplatinate [*Inorganic chemistry*]
TCP........... Tetracyanopyrazine [*Organic chemistry*]
TCP........... Therapeutic Continuous Penicillin [*Medicine*] (MAE)
TCP........... Thienyl(cyclohexyl)piperidine [*Biochemistry*]
TCP........... Thrust Chamber Pressure [*Aerospace*] (IEEE)
TCP........... Time, Cost, and Performance
TCP........... Time Limited Correlation Processing
TCP........... Timing and Control Panel
TCP........... Tocopilla [*Chile*] [*Seismograph station code, US Geological Survey*] [*Closed*] (SEIS)
TCP........... Tool Center Point [*Robotics*]
TCP........... Torpedo Certification Program [*Military*] (CAAL)
TCP........... Total Clottable Protein [*Clinical chemistry*]
TC + P ...... Total Colonoscopy plus Polypectomy [*Proctoscopy*]
TCP........... Town and Country Planning Act [*British*]
TCP........... Traffic Control Point [*or Post*] [*Military*]
TCP........... Trainer Change Proposal [*Military*] (AFIT)
TCP........... Training Controller Panel
TCP........... Transmission Control Program
TCP........... Transmission Control Protocol [*Advanced Research Projects Agency Network*] [*DoD*]
TCP........... Transparent Conducting Polymers [*Photovoltaic energy systems*]
TCP........... Transport Command Police [*British military*] (DMA)
TCP........... Transport Control Protocol [*Telecommunications*]
TCP........... Transportation Control Plan [*Environmental Protection Agency*] (GFGA)
TCP........... Tranylcypromine [*Organic chemistry*]
TCP........... Tricalcium Phosphate [*Inorganic chemistry*]
TCP........... Trichlorophenol [*Organic chemistry*]
TCP........... (Trichlorophenoxy)acetic Acid [*Also known as 2,4,5-T*] [*Herbicide*]
TCP........... Trichloropropane [*Organic chemistry*]
TCP........... Tricresyl Phosphate [*Organic chemistry*]
TCP........... Tropical Canine Pancytopenia (RDA)
TCP........... True Conservative Party [*British*] (ECON)

TCP........... Trust Chamber Pressure [*Missile technology*] (KSC)
TCPA........ Tetrachlorophthalic Anhydride [*Flame retardant*] [*Organic chemistry*]
TCPA........ Time to Closest Point of Approach [*Navigation*]
TCPA........ Town and Country Planning Association [*British*]
TCPA........ Trichlorophenylacetic Acid [*Herbicide*] [*Organic chemistry*]
TCPAM..... Tentative CNO [*Chief of Naval Operations*] Program Analysis Memorandum (NVT)
TCPC........ Tab Card Punch Control
TCPC........ Time-Correlated Photon Counting [*Spectrometry*]
TCPC........ Transportation Claims and Prevention Council (EA)
TCP(CC)R ... Town and Country Planning (Compensation and Certificates) Regulations [*British*]
TCP(CPRW)R ... Town and Country Planning (Churches, Places of Religious Worship, and Burial Grounds) Regulations [*British*]
TCP-E........ Thermal Case Penetrator - External (MCD)
T C Peirce .. Transactions. Charles S. Peirce Society [*A publication*]
TCPGR....... Town and Country Planning General Regulations [*British*]
TCPH .... Toluoyl Chloride Phenylhydrazine [*Drug for sheep*]
TCP-I........ Thermal Case Penetrator - Internal (MCD)
TCPI .... "To Complete" Performance Index (MCD)
TCPI .... Transportation Club of the Petroleum Industry (EA)
TCP/IP...... Transmission Control Protocol and Internet Protocol (PCM)
TCPL........ TransCanada Pipelines Ltd. [*Commercial firm*]
TCPLA ...... Town and Country Planning [*A publication*]
TCP(M)R .. Town and Country Planning (Minerals) Regulations [*British*]
TCPO .... bis(Trichlorophenyl) Oxalate [*Organic chemistry*]
TCPO .... Third-Class Post Office
TCPP .... (Tetrachlorophenyl)pyrrole [*Organic chemistry*]
TCPPA ...... (Trichlorophenoxy)propionic Acid [*Plant hormone*] [*Herbicide*]
TCPS .... Trailerless Collective Protection Station [*Military*]
TCPS .... Transportable Collective Protection System (DWSG)
TCPTF....... Target Cost plus Target Fee
TC Pub...... Tariff Commission Publications [*A publication*] (DLA)
TCpY .... Transcarpathian Yiddish (BJA)
TCQ .... Tacna [*Peru*] [*Airport symbol*] (OAG)
TCQ .... Tax Counselor's Quarterly [*A publication*]
TCQ .... Trichlorobenzoquinoneimine [*Reagent*]
TCQC .... Tank Crew Qualification Course [*Army*]
TCQM .... [*The*] Chief Quartermaster [*Military*]
TCQM .... Tetracyanoquionodimethane [*Organic chemistry*] (SAA)
TCR .... Central Air Transport, Inc. [*Nashville, TN*] [*FAA designator*] (FAAC)
TCR .... T-Cell Reactivity
TCR .... T-Cell Receptor [*Immunology*]
TCR .... T-Cell Recovery Column [*Chromatography*]
TCR .... Tab Card Reader
TCR .... Tantalum-Controlled Rectifier
TCR .... Tape Cassette Recorder
TCR .... Task Change Request [*Army*]
TCR .... Teacher's College Record [*A publication*]
TCR .... Technical Change Request
TCR .... Technical Characteristics Review
TCR .... Technical Compliance Record
TCR .... Technical Cost Review (SSD)
TCR .... Technology Review [*A publication*]
TCR .... Telemetry Compression Routine
TCR .... Temperature Coefficient of Resistance
TCR .... Temperature Control Reference
TCR .... Tentative Cancellation Request
TCR .... Terrain Clearance RADAR
TCR .... Test Compare Results (MCD)
TCR .... Test Condition Requirements [*Army*]
TCR .... Test Conductor (MCD)
TCR .... Test Constraints Review [*NASA*] (MCD)
TCR .... Tetrachlororesourcinol [*Organic chemistry*]
TCR .... Thalamocortical Relay [*Neurology*]
TCR .... Thermal Concept Review (NASA)
TCR .... Thermochemical Recuperator [*Proposed heat recovery system*]
TCR .... Thitec Recovery [*Vancouver Stock Exchange symbol*]
TCR .... Tie Control Relay (MCD)
TCR .... Time Code Reader
TCR .... Time Critical Requirements (MCD)
TCR .... Tonecraft Realty, Inc. [*Toronto Stock Exchange symbol*]
TCR .... Tool Completion Report
TCR .... Tooling Change Request
TCR .... Total Contractual Requirements (MCD)
TCR .... Total Control Racing [*Road-racing game*] [*Ideal Toy Corp.*]
TCr............ Total Creatine [*Pool*]
TCR .... Tracer (AAG)
TCR .... Traffic Control RADAR
TCR .... Trainer Change Request [*Military*]
TCR .... Training/Conversion/Replacement (MCD)
TCR .... Trammell Crow Real Estate Investment [*NYSE symbol*] (SPSG)
TCR .... Transceiver (AABC)
TCR .... Transfer Control Register
TCR .... Transit Commission Reports [*New York*] [*A publication*] (DLA)
TCR .... Transmittal Control Record [*Data processing*]

TCR .... Transportation Corps Release [*Military*]
TCR .... Travaux. Centre de Recherche sur le Proche-Orient et la Grece
     Antiques. Universite de Sciences Humaines de Strasbourg
     [*A publication*] (BJA)
TCR .... Tubing Connector Reducer [*Instrumentation*]
TCR .... Two-Color Radiometer
TCrA........... Art Circle Public Library, Crossville, TN [*Library symbol*]
     [*Library of Congress*] (LCLS)
TCRA........ Telegraphy Channel Reliability Analyzer
     [*Telecommunications*] (OA)
TCRC........ Time and Cycle Record Card [*NASA*] (KSC)
TCRD .... Telecredit, Inc. [*NASDAQ symbol*] (NQ)
TCRD .... Test and Checkout Requirements Document [*NASA*] (KSC)
TCRE........ Temperature-Compensated Reference Element
TCREA...... Telecommunications and Radio Engineering [*English
     Translation*] [*A publication*]
TCREC........ Transportation Research Command [*Army*] (MCD)
TCRF........ Toxic Chemical Release Form
T Crit .... Texto Critico [*A publication*]
TCRJ .... Thermocouple Reference Junction
TCRM .... Thermochemical Remanent Magnetization
TCRMG .... Tripartite Commission for the Restitution of Monetary Gold
     [*Belgium*] (EAIO)
TCRN .... Temporary Chaplain to the Royal Navy [*British*]
tcRNA........ Translation Control Ribonucleic Acid (MAE)
TCRP........ Tactical Command Readiness Program [*Army*]
TCRPA...... Trans-Continental Railroad Passenger Association
     [*Defunct*] (EA)
TCRPC ...... Tri-County Regional Planning Commission [*Information
     service or system*] (IID)
TCRSD...... Test and Checkout Requirements Specification Documentation
     [*NASA*] (NASA)
TCRUA ..... Technische Rundschau [*A publication*]
TCS........... [*The*] Classification Society (EA)
TCS........... [*The*] Coastal Society (EA)
TCS........... [*The*] Computer Store [*NASDAQ symbol*] (NQ)
TCS........... [*The*] Constant Society (EA)
TCS........... [*The*] Cousteau Society (EA)
TCS........... [*The*] Crustacean Society (EA)
TCS........... [*The*] Cybele Society (EA)
TCS........... Tactical Computer System [*Army*] (MCD)
TCS........... Tactical Control Squadron
TCS........... Tanking Control System (AAG)
TCS........... Target Control System
TCS........... Target Cost System
TCS........... TCS Enterprises, Inc. [*AMEX symbol*] (SPSG)
TCS........... TCS Enterprises, Inc. [*Associated Press abbreviation*] (APAG)
TCS........... Teacher Characteristics Schedule
TCS........... Teaching Company Scheme [*British*]
TCS........... Technical Change Summary [*NASA*] (MCD)
TCS........... Technical Concurrence Sheets [*NASA*] (NASA)
TCS........... Technical Countdown Sequences (KSC)
TCS........... Telecommunications Consulting Services [*Richard A. Eisner &
     Co.*] [*New York, NY*] (TSSD)
TCS........... Telecommunications Control System [*Toshiba Corp.*] [*Data
     processing*]
TCS........... Telecommunications System
TCS........... Teleconference System [*Memorial University of
     Newfoundland*] [*St. John's, NF*]
     [*Telecommunications*] (TSSD)
TCS........... Telemetry and Command Station [*Aerospace*] (MCD)
TCS........... Telephone Conference Summary (NRCH)
TCS........... Television Camera System
TCS........... Television Control Set
TCS........... Temperature Control Subsystem (KSC)
TCS........... Temperature Controlled Storage and Distribution [*A
     publication*]
TCS........... Temporary Change of Station [*Military*]
TCS........... Temporary Conditioning Station [*Nuclear energy*] (NRCH)
TCS........... Temporary Correction Sheet (MCD)
TCS........... Terminal Communications Subsystem
TCS........... Terminal Computer System (BUR)
TCS........... Terminal Control System [*Hewlett-Packard Co.*]
TCS........... Terminal Countdown Sequencer [*or Sequences*]
     [*NASA*] (KSC)
TCS........... Ternary Compound Semiconductor
TCS........... Test of Cognitive Skills [*Achievement test*]
TCS........... Test Control Supervisor (NASA)
TCS........... Test Control System (NASA)
TCS........... Texas Centennial Society (EA)
TCS........... Texts from Cuneiform Sources [*A publication*] (BJA)
TCS........... Theater Communications System (MCD)
TCS........... Thermal Conditioning System (KSC)
TCS........... Thermal Control System [*or Subsystem*]
TCS........... Thermally Stimulated Charge [*Analytical chemistry*]
TCS........... Timing Cover and Seal Set [*Automotive engineering*]
TCS........... Tin Can Sailors (EA)
TCS........... Tool Clearance Slip (AAG)
TCS........... Tool Coordinate System
TCS........... Total Communication Systems [*Pittsburgh, PA*]
     [*Telecommunications service*] (TSSD)

TCS........... Trac Industries, Inc. [*Toronto Stock Exchange symbol*]
     [*Vancouver Stock Exchange symbol*]
TCS........... Tracheal Cellular Score [*Medicine*]
TCS........... Traction Control System [*Alfred Teves GmbH*] [*Automotive
     engineering*]
TCS........... Trade Commission of Spain (EA)
TCS........... Traffic Control Satellite
TCS........... Traffic Control Station
TCS........... Traffic Control System [*Army*]
TCS........... Transaction Control System [*Hitachi Ltd.*]
TCS........... TransCanada Telephone System [*Later, Telecom
     Canada*] (TSSD)
TCS........... Transcutaneous Stimulation
TCS........... Transducer Calibration System
TCS........... Transfer Carry Subtract
TCS........... Transmission Controlled Spark (MCD)
TCS........... Transmission-Controlled Speed (IIA)
TCS........... Transportable Communications System
TCS........... Transportation and Communications Service [*of GSA*]
     [*Abolished, 1972*]
TCS........... Transportation Consulting & Service Corp., Chicago IL [*STAC*]
TCS........... Transportation Costing Service [*Database*] [*A. T. Kearney,
     Inc.*] [*Information service or system*] (CRD)
TCS........... Trichlorosilane [*Inorganic chemistry*]
TCS........... Trim Control System
TCS........... Troop Carrier Squadron [*Military*] (CINC)
TCS........... Troposcatter Communications System
TCS........... Truth Or Consequences, NM [*Location identifier*]
     [*FAA*] (FAAL)
TCS........... Tube Cooling Supply
TCS........... Turbine Control System [*Nuclear energy*] (NRCH)
TCS........... Two-Photon Coherent States (MCD)
TCSA........ Tetrachlorosalicylanilide [*Organic chemistry*]
TCSA........ Trunk Cross Sectional Area [*of a tree*]
TCSAA...... Twentieth Century Spanish Association of America (EA)
TCSC........ Time-Critical Shipment Committee [*Defunct*] (EA)
TCSC........ Toyota Celica Supra Club (EA)
TCSC........ Trainer Control and Simulation Computer
TCSC........ Two-Channel Scan Camera (NOAA)
TCSCLC.... Two-Carrier Space-Charge-Limited Current
TCSD........ Telemetry and Communications Systems Division [*Apollo*]
     [*NASA*]
TCS & D .... Temperature Controlled Storage and Distribution Exhibition
     [*British*] (ITD)
TCSE........ TCS Enterprises, Inc. [*NASDAQ symbol*] (NQ)
TCSEC ...... Trusted Computer System Evaluation Criteria (MCD)
T C Ser Soil Conserv Auth (Vic) ... T C Series. Soil Conservation Authority
     (Victoria) [*A publication*] (APTA)
T C Ser Soil Conserv Auth (Vict) ... T C Series. Soil Conservation Authority
     (Victoria) [*A publication*] (APTA)
TCSF .... Thomson-CSF [*France*] [*NASDAQ symbol*]
TCSF .... Total Counts of Successive Fractions [*Chromatography*]
TCSG........ [*The*] Center for Social Gerontology (EA)
TCSI .... Teknekron Communications Systems [*NASDAQ
     symbol*] (SPSG)
TCSL .... Tri-County Savings & Loan Association [*NASDAQ
     symbol*] (NQ)
TCSM....... Test of Cognitive Style in Mathematics [*Educational test*]
TCSM....... Transactions. Colonial Society of Massachusetts [*A publication*]
TCSM....... Tropospheric Chemistry Systems Model (MCD)
TCSMC ..... Transportation Corps Supply Maintenance Command [*Army*]
TCSP .... Tactical Communications Satellite Program [*DoD*] (MCD)
TCSP .... Tandem Cross-Section Program [*Bell System*]
TCSP .... Test Checkout Support Plan (KSC)
TCSPr........ Second Presbyterian Church Library, Chattanooga, TN [*Library
     symbol*] [*Library of Congress*] (LCLS)
TCSq.......... Troop Carrier Squadron [*Air Force*] (AFM)
TCSR........ Tri-Comp Sensors [*NASDAQ symbol*] (NQ)
TCSR........ Typographic Council for Spelling Reform (EA)
TCSS .... Tactical Control Surveillance System
TCSS .... Tri-Cone Support Structure [*NASA*]
TCSSS...... Thermal Control Subsystem Segment [*NASA*] (NASA)
TCST .... Chattanooga State Technical Community College, Chattanooga,
     TN [*Library symbol*] [*Library of Congress*] (LCLS)
TCST .... Telecast, Inc. [*Fraser, MI*] [*NASDAQ symbol*] (NQ)
TC STD ..... Type Classification - Standard (MCD)
TCSTE....... Triangle Coalition for Science and Technology Education (EA)
TCSUH ..... Texas Center for Superconductivity, University of Houston
     [*Research center*] (RCD)
TCSW........ Thinking Creatively with Sounds and Words [*Educational test*]
TCT........... Tactical Communications Terminal
TCT........... Tactical Computer Terminal [*Army*] (MCD)
TCT........... Takotna [*Alaska*] [*Airport symbol*] (OAG)
TCT........... Takotna, AK [*Location identifier*] [*FAA*] (FAAL)
T Ct .... Tax Court of the United States, Reports [*A publication*] (DLA)
TCT........... Telemetry-Computer Translator [*Bell Laboratories*]
TCT........... Tennessee Temple Schools, Chattanooga, TN [*Library symbol*]
     [*Library of Congress*] (LCLS)
TCT........... Tennessee Temple University, Chattanooga, TN [*OCLC
     symbol*] (OCLC)
TCT........... Terracotta Tile [*Classified advertising*] (ADA)

TCT........... Texas City Terminal Railway Co. [*AAR code*]
TCT........... Thrombin Clotting Time [*Clinical chemistry*]
TCT........... Thyrocalcitonin [*Also, CT, TCA*] [*Endocrinology*]
TCT........... Time Code Translator
TCT........... Tin Can Tourists of the World   (EA)
Tct............. Tinctura [*Tincture*] [*Latin*]
TCT........... Toll Connecting Trunk [*Telecommunications*]   (TEL)
TCT........... Tool Change Time
TCT........... Total Composite Tolerance
TCT........... Traffic Control Transponder
TCT........... Translator and Code Treatment Frame   (IEEE)
TCT........... Tricentrol Ltd. [*NYSE symbol*] [*Toronto Stock Exchange symbol*]   (SPSG)
TCT........... True Centerline Tested
TCT........... Trunk Coin Telephone   (OA)
TCT........... Two-Component TOKAMAK
TCTA......... Teaching Certificate for Teachers of Art [*British*]
T & CTB .... Thames and Chilterns Tourist Board [*British*]   (DCTA)
Tctbl.......... Tractatenblad [*A publication*]
TCTC........ Temperature-Controlled Test Chamber [*EPA engine test*]
TCTC........ Tompkins County Trust Co. [*Ithaca, NY*] [*NASDAQ symbol*]   (NQ)
TCTC........ Transportation Corps Technical Committee [*Army*]
TCTFE ...... Trichlorotrifluoroethane [*Organic chemistry*]
TCTI.......... Time Compliance Technical Instruction   (NASA)
TCTL......... Tactical   (AAG)
TCTL......... Tectel, Inc. [*NASDAQ symbol*]   (NQ)
TCTM....... Aircraft Time Compliance Technical Manuals
T Ct Mem .. Tax Court of the United States, Memorandum [*A publication*]   (DLA)
TCTNB...... Trichlorotrinitrobenzene [*Organic chemistry*]
TCTO .... Technical Changes to Technical Orders
TCTO .... Time Compliance Technical Order [*NASA*]   (AAG)
TCTOA...... Tectonophysics [*A publication*]
TCTP........ Tetrachlorothiophene [*Organic chemistry*]
TCTP........ Tricapped Triangular Prism
TCTS .... Tactical Communications Systems Technical Standards [*Military*]
TCTS .... Tank Crew Turret Simulator   (MCD)
TCTS .... Trans-Canada Telephone System   (MCD)
TCTU .... Turkish Confederation of Trade Unions
TCTV........ Telemedia Communication Television [*Cable-television system*]
TCTV........ Today's Child, Tomorrow's Victim [*Book title*]
TCTVA...... Tennessee Valley Authority, Technical Library, Chattanooga, TN [*Library symbol*] [*Library of Congress*]   (LCLS)
TCTY........ Twin City Barge, Inc. [*NASDAQ symbol*]   (NQ)
TCU .... Tactical Control Unit   (MCD)
TCU .... Taichung [*Taityu*] [*Republic of China*] [*Seismograph station code, US Geological Survey*]   (SEIS)
TCU .... Tape Control Unit
TCU .... Tecumseh, MI [*Location identifier*] [*FAA*]   (FAAL)
TCU .... Teletype Communications Unit   (NVT)
TCU .... Teletypewriter Control Unit   (CET)
TCU .... Temperature Control Unit
TCU .... Tentative Clean Up   (MCD)
TCU .... Terminal Cluster Unit
TCU .... Terminal Control Unit   (MCD)
TCU .... Test Computer Unit
TCU .... Test of Concept Utilization [*Psychometrics*]
TCU .... Test Control Unit
TCU .... Texas Christian University [*Fort Worth, TX*]
TCU .... Thermal Control Unit
TCU .... Threshold Control Unit   (CET)
TCU .... Thrust Control Unit
TCU .... Time Change Unit   (MCD)
TCU .... Timing Control Unit
TCU .... Topping Control Unit   (AAG)
TCU .... Torpedo Control Unit
TCU .... Towering Cumulus [*Meteorology*]
TCU .... Transmission Control Unit
TCU .... Transport Conversion Unit [*British military*]   (DMA)
TCU .... Transportable Computer Unit
TCU .... Transportation-Communication Employees Union [*Later, TCIU*]
TCU .... Transportation, Communications, and Utilities
TCU .... Tri-College University Library Consortium [*Library network*]
TCU .... Turbine Control Unit
TCU .... University of Tennessee at Chattanooga, Chattanooga, TN [*Library symbol*] [*Library of Congress*]   (LCLS)
TCUA .... [*The*] Committee to Unite America [*Inactive*]   (EA)
TCUA .... Time-Critical, Unspecified Area
TCUCC...... Texas Christian University Computer Center [*Research center*]   (RCD)
TCUL........ Tap Changing Under Load   (MSA)
TC(UN) ..... Trusteeship Council of the United Nations
TCUS........ Tax Court of the United States [*Also, TC*] [*Later, United States Tax Court*]
TCUSA...... Trans Am Club USA   (EA)
TCV .... Tank Cleaning Vessel   (ADA)
TCV .... Temperature Coefficient of Voltage

TCV .... Temperature Control Valve   (AAG)
TCV .... Terminal-Configured Vehicle [*NASA*]
TCV .... Thoracic Cage Volume [*Medicine*]
TCV .... Throttle Control Valve
TCV .... Thrust Chamber Valve   (MCD)
TCV .... Thrust Control Valve
TCV .... TOKAMAK [*Toroidal Kamera Magnetic*] Chauffage Variable [*Plasma physics instrumentation*]
TCV .... Total Containment Vessel   (CAAL)
TCV .... Tracked Combat Vehicle   (MCD)
TCV .... Troop Carrying Vehicle
TCV .... Turbine Control Valve [*Nuclear energy*]   (NRCH)
TCV .... Turnip Crinkle Virus
TCV .... Twentieth Century Views [*A publication*]
TCVA........ Terminal-Configured Vehicles and Avionics [*Program*] [*NASA*]
TCVC........ Tape Control via Console
TCVR........ Transceiver   (CET)
TCW .... Tactical Control Wing [*Air Force*]
TCW .... TCW Convertible Security Fund [*Associated Press abbreviation*]   (APAG)
TCW .... Time Code Word
TCW .... Tinned Copper Weld
TCW .... Tocumwal [*Australia*] [*Airport symbol*]   (OAG)
TCW .... Today's Christian Woman [*A publication*]
TCW .... Track Confirmation Word [*Data processing*]
TCW .... Triple-Crown Resources [*Vancouver Stock Exchange symbol*]
TCW .... Troop Carrier Wing [*Military*]   (CINC)
TCWA ...... Transactions. Cumberland and Westmorland Antiquarian and Archaeological Society [*A publication*]
TCWC....... Texas Cooperative Wildlife Collections [*Texas A & M University*] [*Research center*]   (RCD)
TCW/DW ... TCW/DW Term Trust [*Associated Press abbreviation*]   (APAG)
TCWG .... Telecommunication Working Group
TCWg .... Troop Carrier Wing [*Air Force*]   (AFM)
T-CW & IB ... Trans-Continental Weighing and Inspection Bureau
TCWSA .... T'ai-Wan Huan Ching Wei Sheng [*A publication*]
TCX .... Transfer of Control Cancellation Message [*Aviation*]
TCXO .... Temperature-Compensated Crystal Oscillator
TCXO .... Temperature-Controlled Crystal Oscillator
TCYAW .... Twentieth Century Young Adult Writers [*A publication*]
TCYC....... Tropical Cyclone   (FAAC)
TCZD .... Temperature-Compensated Zener Diode
TD............. Area Training Director [*Red Cross*]
TD............. Chad [*ANSI two-letter standard code*]   (CNC)
Td............. Dorsal Touch Neurons [*of a leech*]
Td............. T-Cell, Delayed Type [*Immunology*]
TD............. T-Dependent [*Immunology*]
TD............. Table of Distribution [*Military*]
TD............. Tabular Data   (BUR)
TD............. Tactical Director [*Military*]   (GFGA)
TD............. Tactical Division [*Air Force*]
TD............. Tank Destroyer [*Military*]
TD............. Tank Division   (MCD)
TD............. Tape Degausser
TD............. Tape Drive
TD............. Tardive Dyskinesia [*Medicine*]
TD............. Target Designator   (MCD)
TD............. Target Discrimination
TD............. Target Drone
TD............. Task Description   (AAG)
TD............. Task Directive   (AAG)
TD............. Teacher's Diploma [*British*]
TD............. Teachta Dala [*Member of Parliament*] [*Ireland*]
TD............. Tealto Dail [*Member of the Dail*] [*Irish*]   (ILCA)
TD............. Technical Data
TD............. Technical Demonstration   (AAG)
TD............. Technical Design   (AAG)
TD............. Technical Direction [*or Directive*]
TD............. Technical Director [*Television*]
TD............. Technical Discussion
TD............. Technical Division
TD............. Technical Drawing
TD............. Technician's Diploma [*British*]   (DI)
TD............. Technological Dependence
TD............. Technology Document   (KSC)
TD............. Telegraph Department
TD............. Telegraphist Detector [*British military*]   (DMA)
TD............. Telemetry Data
TD............. Telephone Department
TD............. Telephone Directory
T/D............ Temperature Datum   (NG)
TD............. Temperature Differential   (MSA)
TD............. Temporarily Discontinued [*Fog signal*]
TD............. Temporary Disability
TD............. Temporary Duty
TD............. Ter in Die [*Three Times a Day*] [*Pharmacy*]
TD............. Terminal Device [*of a prosthesis*]
TD............. Terminal Digit [*Telecommunications*]   (TEL)
TD............. Terminal Display   (BUR)
TD............. Terminal Distributor   (KSC)
T (for) D..... Termination for Default   (MCD)

TD.............	Territorial Decoration [*Military*] [*British*]
TD.............	Test Data
TD.............	Test Design Specification (IEEE)
TD.............	Test Directive (AAG)
TD.............	Test Director
TD.............	Test Distributor [*Telecommunications*] (TEL)
TD.............	Test Drawing (MCD)
TD.............	Testing and Development Division [*Coast Guard*]
TD.............	Testing Device (MSA)
TD.............	Tetanus and Diphtheria [*Toxoids*] [*Medicine*]
Td.............	Tetrahedral [*Molecular geometry*]
TD.............	Theatre Documentation [*A publication*]
TD.............	Theology Digest [*St. Mary's, KS*] [*A publication*]
TD.............	Theoretical Density [*Nuclear energy*] (NRCH)
TD.............	Therapy [*or Treatment*] Discontinued [*Medicine*]
TD.............	Thermal Desorption [*from surfaces*]
TD.............	Thermodilution
TD.............	Thiamine Deficient (OA)
TD.............	Thioredoxin [*Also, TR, Trx*] [*Biochemistry*]
TD.............	Third Defense [*Men's lacrosse position, until 1933*]
TD.............	Thor-Delta [*Satellite*]
TD.............	Thoracic Duct [*Anatomy*]
TD.............	Thoria Dispersed [*Nickel*]
TD.............	Threat Determination (MCD)
TD.............	Threshold Detection
TD.............	Threshold of Discomfort [*Medicine*] (MAE)
TD.............	Threshold Dose [*Medicine*]
TD.............	Thymus Dependent [*Cells*] [*Hematology*]
TD.............	Tibial Dyschondroplasia [*Medicine*]
TD.............	Tidal Disruption [*Astronomy*]
TD.............	Tied
TD.............	Tilbury Docks (ROG)
TD.............	Tile Drain [*Technical drawings*]
TD.............	Time Delay
TD.............	Time of Departure
TD.............	Time Deposit [*Banking*]
TD.............	Time Difference [*or Differential*]
TD.............	Time Division (SAA)
TD.............	Timed Disintegration [*Pharmacy*]
TD.............	Timing Device
TD.............	Tinned
TD.............	To Deliver [*Pipet calibration*]
TD.............	Tod [*Unit of weight*]
TD.............	Tolerance Detector
TD.............	Tone Decay [*Audiometry*] (MAE)
TD.............	Tons per Day
TD.............	Tool Design
TD.............	Tool Disposition
TD.............	Tool Drawing (MCD)
TD.............	Top Down
TD.............	Topographic Draftsman [*Navy*]
TD.............	Toronto Dominion Bank [*Toronto Stock Exchange symbol*] [*Vancouver Stock Exchange symbol*]
TD.............	Torpedo Dive Bomber Aircraft
TD.............	Torsion Dystonia [*Medicine*] (AAMN)
T and D......	[*Jayne*] Torvill and [*Christopher*] Dean [*British ice dancers*]
TD.............	Total Damage [*Meteorology*]
TD.............	Total Denier [*Textile technology*]
TD.............	Total Depth
TD.............	Total Dictatorship
TD.............	Total Disability [*Medicine*]
TD.............	Total Discectomy [*Medicine*]
TD.............	Total Dose [*of radiation*]
T/D.............	Touchdown [*NASA*] (NASA)
TD.............	Touchdown [*Football*]
TD.............	Toxic Dose (EG)
TD.............	Tracing Dye (OA)
TD.............	Track Data
TD.............	Track Display
TD.............	Track Dog [*Dog show term*]
TD.............	Tractor-Drawn
TD.............	Trade Dispute (OICC)
TD.............	Trade Division [*British military*] (DMA)
TD.............	Tradesman [*British military*]
TD.............	TRADEVMAN [*Training Devices Man*] [*Navy rating*]
TD.............	Traffic Decisions [*Interstate Commerce Commission*]
TD.............	Traffic Department [*Scotland Yard*]
TD.............	Traffic Director
TD.............	Training Detachment
T & D.........	Training and Detention (ADA)
TD.............	Training Developments
TD.............	Training Device (MCD)
TD.............	Training of Documentalists
TD.............	Trajectory Diagram [*Army*] (MCD)
TD.............	Transaction Diaries [*Bureau of the Census*] (GFGA)
TD.............	Transfer Dolly [*Bottom-loading transfer cask*] [*Nuclear energy*] (NRCH)
TD.............	Transform Domain
TD.............	Transient Detector
T & D.........	Transmission and Distribution
TD.............	Transmit Data (IEEE)

T-D...........	Transmitter-Distributor
TD.............	Transport Driver (NOAA)
TD.............	Transportation Department
TD.............	Transportation and Docking (MCD)
TD.............	Transporte Aereo de Cargo SA [*Venezuela*] [*ICAO designator*] (FAAC)
T & D.........	Transposition and Docking [*NASA*] (KSC)
TD.............	Transverse Diameter [*Of heart*] [*Anatomy*]
TD.............	Transverse Direction
TD.............	Transverse Division [*Cytology*]
TD.............	Treasury Decision [*In references to rulings*]
TD.............	Treasury Department
TD.............	Treatment Day
T/D.............	Treatment Discontinued [*Medicine*]
TD.............	Trinidad and Tobago
TD.............	Tropical Depression [*Meteorology*]
TD.............	Tropical Deterioration Committee Reports [*of NDRC*] [*World War II*]
TD.............	Truck Driving Program [*Association of Independent Colleges and Schools specialization code*]
TD.............	True Depth [*Diamond drilling*]
TD.............	Trust Deed
TD.............	Tuberoinfundibular Dopaminergic [*Neurons*] [*Neurology*]
TD.............	Tundra Drums [*A publication*]
TD.............	Tunnel Diode
TD.............	Turbine Direct
TD.............	Turbine Drive [*or Driven*]
TD.............	Turbodiesel [*Automotive engineering*]
TD.............	Turntable Desk (DEN)
TD.............	Tyne Division [*British military*] (DMA)
TD.............	Typhoid Dysentery (AAMN)
TD.............	Typographic Draftsman [*Navy*]
TD1...........	TRADEVMAN [*Training Devices Man*], First Class [*Navy rating*]
TD2...........	TRADEVMAN [*Training Devices Man*], Second Class [*Navy rating*]
TD3...........	TRADEVMAN [*Training Devices Man*], Third Class [*Navy rating*]
TDA..........	American Train Dispatchers Association
TDA..........	[*The*] Disposables Association
TDA..........	Table of Distribution and Allowances [*Military*] (AABC)
TDA..........	Table of Distribution-Augmentation [*Military*]
TDA..........	Tactical Decision Aid
TDA..........	Tactical Development Agent [*Military*] (CAAL)
TDA..........	Taking and Driving Away [*Motoring offense*] [*British*] (DI)
TDA..........	Target Docking Adapter [*NASA*] (KSC)
TDA..........	Tax Deferred Annuity [*Insurance*]
TDA..........	Taxpayer Delinquent Account [*IRS*]
TDA..........	Technical Directing Agency
TDA..........	Telecommunications Dealers Association (EA)
TDA..........	Telemetric Data Analyzer
TDA..........	Test Development Activity [*Army*]
TDA..........	Test Development Agent (CAAL)
TDA..........	Tetradecenyl Acetate [*Organic chemistry*]
TDA..........	Textile Distributors Association (EA)
TDA..........	Thermal Depolarization Analysis
TDA..........	Thermodifferential Analysis
TDA..........	Time Delay Amplifier
TDA..........	Titanium Development Association (EA)
TDA..........	Today (FAAC)
TDA..........	Toll Dial Assistance [*Telecommunications*] (TEL)
TDA..........	Toluenediamine [*Organic chemistry*]
TDA..........	Tombs of the Double Axes and Associated Group [*A publication*]
TDA..........	Torpedo Danger Area (NVT)
TDA..........	Total Dissolved Arsenic
TDA..........	Town Development Act [*Town planning*] [*British*]
TDA..........	Tracking and Data Acquisition
T & DA.....	Tracking and Data Acquisition (CET)
TDA..........	Tracking Data Analysis
TDA..........	Training Development Advisors (MCD)
TDA..........	Training and Development Alert [*Advanced Personnel Systems*] [*Information service or system*] (CRD)
TDA..........	Transport Distribution Analysis (DCTA)
TDA..........	Transportation Development Agency [*British*]
TDA..........	Trigger Distribution Amplifier [*Aviation*] (FAAC)
TDA..........	Trunnion Drive Axis (SAA)
TDA..........	Tundra Gold Mines [*Vancouver Stock Exchange symbol*]
TDA..........	Tuning Device Assembly
TDA..........	Tunnel-Diode Amplifier
TDA..........	Tyrosine-D-Arginine [*Biochemistry*]
TDAA........	Airman Apprentice, TRADEVMAN [*Training Devices Man*], Striker [*Navy rating*]
TDA/AE....	Tracking and Data Acquisition/Advanced Engineering
TDaB........	William Jennings Bryan University, Dayton, TN [*Library symbol*] [*Library of Congress*] (LCLS)
TDA Bull...	Timber Development Association. Bulletin [*A publication*]
TDAC.......	Training Data and Analysis Center
TDAC.......	Tropical Deterioration Administrative Committee [*of NDRC*] [*World War II*]
TDAC.......	Tumor-Derived Activated Cell [*Oncology*]

TDAD........ Trade Development Assistance Division [*Bureau of East-West Trade*] [*Former USSR*] (IMH)
TDAE........ Tactics Development and Evaluation [*Military*] (MCD)
TDAE........ Test Design and Evaluation (MCD)
TDAE........ Tetrakis Dimethylamino Ethylene [*Organic chemistry*]
TDAE........ Tetrakis(dimethylamino)ethylene [*Also, TKDE, TMAE*] [*Organic chemistry*]
TDAFP...... Turbine-Driven Auxiliary Feed Pump [*Nuclear energy*] (NRCH)
TDAFWP.. Turbine-Driven Auxiliary Feedwater Pump [*Nuclear energy*] (NRCH)
TDAG........ Technology Development Advocacy Group [*NASA*] (SSD)
TDAIR....... Taxpayer Delinquent Account Information Record [*IRS*]
TDAL....... Tetradecenal [*Biochemistry*]
TDAMM... Training Device Acquisition Management Model (MCD)
TDAMTB... Tables of Distribution and Allowances Mobilization Troop Basis [*Army*] (AABC)
TDAN....... Airman, TRADEVMAN [*Training Devices Man*], Striker [*Navy rating*]
TDANA...... Time-Domain Automatic Network Analyzer [*National Institute of Standards and Technology*]
TDAR .... Tactical Defense Alerting RADAR
TDARA ..... Threat Determination and Resource Allocation (MCD)
TDAS........ Thermal Decomposition Analytical System [*For study of incineration*]
TDAS........ Thermocouple Data Acquisition System
TDAS........ Thickness Data Acquisition System [*Southwest Research Institute*]
TDAS........ Tracking and Data Acquisition Satellite (SSD)
TDAS........ Tracking and Data Acquisition System
TDAS........ Traffic Data Administration System [*Bell System*]
TDAS........ Training Device Acquisition Strategy
TDAS........ Tunnel-Diode Amplifier System
TDASS...... Tracking and Data Acquisition Satellite System (SSD)
TDAT........ Teradata Corp. [*NASDAQ symbol*] (NQ)
TDAZA ..... Tautsaimnieciba Derigie Augi [*A publication*]
TDB .... Technical Directive Bulletin (MCD)
TDB .... Temporary Disability Benefits [*Insurance*]
TDB .... Temps Dynamique Barycentrique [*Barycentric Dynamical Time*] [*French*]
TDB .... Terminological Data Bank
TDB .... Terrestrial Dust Belt
TDB .... Test Documentation Booklet [*Navy*] (CAAL)
TDB .... Tetebedi [*Papua New Guinea*] [*Airport symbol*] (OAG)
TDB .... Top Drawing Breakdown (AAG)
TDB .... Total Disability Benefit (DLA)
TDB .... Toxicology Data Bank [*National Library of Medicine*] [*Information service or system*] (IID)
TDB .... Track Database (MCD)
TDB .... Trade Development Bank [*Subsidiary of American Express Bank*]
TDB .... Trade and Development Board [*United Nations Conference on Trade and Development*]
TDB .... Transportable Database [*Telecommunications*]
TDB .... Turbine-Driven Blower
TdbE .... Tanna di-be Eliahu (BJA)
TDBG .... Training Depot Brigade of Gurkhas [*British military*] (DMA)
TDBI .... Training Directory for Business and Industry [*A publication*]
TDBMS..... Tactical Database Management System
TDBP........ Tris(dibromopropyl) Phosphate [*Also, TDBPP, Tris, Tris-BP*] [*Flame retardant, mutagen*]
TDBPP ...... Tris(dibromopropyl) Phosphate [*Also, TDBP, Tris, Tris-BP*] [*Flame retardant, mutagen*]
TDC .... Chief TRADEVMAN [*Training Devices Man*] [*Navy rating*]
TDC .... Dallas Christian College, Dallas, TX [*OCLC symbol*] (OCLC)
TDC .... [*The*] Developing Child [*A publication*] (APTA)
TDC .... [*The*] Discovery Channel [*Television*]
TDC .... Tactical Data Converter
TDC .... Tactical Digital Computer (MCD)
TDC .... Tactical Document Copier (MCD)
TDC .... Taiwan Defense Command (MCD)
TDC .... Tank Destroyer Center [*Army*]
TDC .... Target Data Collection
TDC .... Target Data Communicator (DWSG)
TDC .... Target Designator Control (MCD)
TDC .... Tarif Douanier Commun [*Common Customs Tariff*]
TDC .... Taurodeoxycholate [*or Taurodeoxycholic*] Acid [*Biochemistry*]
TDC .... Technical Data Center [*Department of Labor*] [*Information service or system*] (IID)
TDC .... Technical Development Center
TDC .... Technical Development Contractor
TDC .... Technical Directive Compliance (MCD)
TDC .... Technical Document Center
TDC .... Technical Document Change (MCD)
TDC .... Technology Development Corp.
TDC .... TEFLON Dielectric Capacitor
TDC .... Teledyne Canada Ltd. [*Toronto Stock Exchange symbol*]
TDC .... Temperature Density Computer
TDC .... Temporary Detective Constable [*Scotland Yard*]
TDC .... Terminal Data Corp. [*Information service or system*] (IID)
TDC .... Termination Design Change

TDC .... Test Director Console
TDC .... Thermal Diffusion Chamber
TDC .... Thermal Diffusion Coefficient [*Nuclear energy*] (NRCH)
TDC .... Through Deck Cruisers [*British*]
TDC .... Time Data Card (AAG)
TDC .... Time Delay Closing
TDC .... Time-to-Digital Converter [*Instrumentation*]
TDC .... Time Distribution Card (AAG)
TDC .... Time-Domain Coding
TDC .... Tooling Design Change
TDC .... Top Dead Center
TDC .... Torpedo Data Computer [*Navy*] (NVT)
TDC .... Total Design Concept [*Sarcastic reference to a completely coordinated wardrobe, decorating scheme, etc.*] [*Slang*]
TDC .... Total Distributed Control [*Data processing*]
TDC .... Tourist Development Corp. of Malaysia
TDC .... Track Data Center
TDC .... Track Data Central
TDC .... Track Data Corp. [*Software firm*] [*Information service or system*] (IID)
TDC .... Track Detection Circuit [*Electronics*] (OA)
TDC .... Training Device Center
T & DC....... Training and Distribution Center [*Navy*]
TDC .... Transferable Development Credit
TDC .... Transportation Development Center [*Cambridge, MA*] [*Department of Transportation*] [*Formerly, NASA Electronic Research Center*]
TDC .... Transportation Development Centre [*Transport Canada*] [*Research center*] (RCD)
TDC .... Transportation Development Centre Library [*UTLAS symbol*]
TDC .... Treasury Department Circular [*A publication*] (DLA)
TDC .... Tridecylcyclohexane [*Organic chemistry*]
TDC .... Trinidad [*Colorado*] [*Seismograph station code, US Geological Survey*] [*Closed*] (SEIS)
TDC .... Tube Deflection Coil
TDC .... Type Directors Club (EA)
TDC .... Tyrosine Decarboxylase [*An enzyme*]
TDCB........ Tapered Double Cantilever Beam (MCD)
TDCC .... Tactical Data Communications Center
TDCC .... Transportation Data Coordinating Committee [*Later, EDIA*]
TDCC/EDIA ... TDCC [*Transportation Data Coordinating Committee*]: the Electronic Data Interchange Association [*Telecommunications service*] (TSSD)
TDCE........ Technical Direction Contract Effort
TDCF......... Technical Directive Compliance Form (NVT)
TDCH....... Tridecylcyclohexane [*Organic chemistry*]
TDCK .... Technisch Documentatie Centrum voor der Krijgsmacht [*Netherland Armed Services Technical Documentation and Information Center*] (MCD)
TDCM .... Master Chief TRADEVMAN [*Training Devices Man*] [*Navy rating*]
TDCM .... Transistor Driver Core Memory
TD/CMS ... Technical Data/Configuration Management System (MCD)
TDCN .... Technical Data Change Notice (MCD)
TDCN .... Time Delay Compression Network
TDCO........ Test Director Console Operator [*Navy*] (CAAL)
TDCO........ Thermal Dilution Cardiac Output
TDCO........ Torpedo Data Computer Operator [*Navy*]
TDCR .... Teacher's Diploma of the College of Radiographers [*British*] (DBQ)
TDCR .... Technical Data Change Request [*NASA*] (KSC)
TDCR .... Technical Data Contract Requirement (MCD)
TDCR .... Test Deficiency Change Request [*Nuclear energy*] (NRCH)
TDCS........ Senior Chief TRADEVMAN [*Training Devices Man*] [*Navy rating*]
TDCS......... Tactical Deployment Control Squadron
TDCS......... Tape Data Control Sheet [*Data processing*]
TDCS......... Target Detection-Conversion Sensor
TDCS......... Time-Division Circuit Switching [*Telecommunications*]
TDCS......... Traffic Data Collection System (MCD)
TDCSP ...... Tactical Defense Communications Satellite Program (MCD)
TDCT........ Time-Domain Coding Technique
TDCT........ Track Data Central Tables (SAA)
TDCT........ Tunnel-Diode Charge Transformer
TDCTL...... Tunnel-Diode Charge-Transformer Logic
TDCU .... Target Data Control Unit (AAG)
TDCU .... Target Designator Control Unit (MCD)
TDCU .... Threat Display Control Unit (MCD)
TDCU .... Tinned Copper
TDCX .... Technology Development Corp. [*NASDAQ symbol*] (NQ)
TDD.......... Tactical Data Display
TDD.......... Target Detecting Device
TDD.......... Task Description Document (NASA)
TDD.......... Teardown Deficiency (MCD)
TDD.......... Technical Data Digest [*Air Force*]
TDD.......... Technical Documents Division [*Naval Air Systems Command*]
TDD.......... Telecommunications Device for the Deaf
TDD.......... Telemetry Data Digitizer
TDD.......... Telephone Device for the Deaf
TDD.......... Test Data Division (SAA)
TDD.......... Test Definition Document

TDD.......... Test Design Description [*Nuclear energy*] (NRCH)
TDD.......... Test Development Director
TDD.......... Tetradecadiene [*Organic chemistry*]
TDD.......... Thedford, NE [*Location identifier*] [*FAA*] (FAAL)
TDD.......... Thoracic Duct Drainage [*Medicine*]
TDD.......... Three D Departments, Inc. [*AMEX symbol*] (SPSG)
TDD.......... Timing Defense Depot (SAA)
TDD.......... Tracy Defense Depot (SAA)
TDD.......... Treasury Department Decision (AFIT)
TDD.......... Trinidad [*Bolivia*] [*Airport symbol*] (OAG)
TDD.......... Tuberculous Diseases Diploma [*British*]
TDDA....... Tetradecadienyl Acetate [*Biochemistry*]
TDDL........ Time-Division Data Link [*Radio*]
TDDM....... Time Division Digital Multiplexer (MCD)
TDDM....... Training Device Development Management [*Model*] (MCD)
TDDn........ Tank Destroyers Division [*Army*]
TDDO........ Time Delay Dropout [*Relay*] (AAG)
TDDR....... Technical Data Department Report [*NASA*] (KSC)
TDDR....... Transdermal Drug Delivery Research
TDDRS..... Total Dose/Dose Rate Simulator
TDDS .... Tactical Data Display System (MCD)
TDDS .... Teacher Development in Desegregating Schools [*Office of Education*]
TDDS .... Television Data Display System (KSC)
TDE .... Tactical Deception Element (NVT)
TD & E...... Tactics Development and Evaluation
TDE .... Tactics Development Evaluation (MCD)
TDE .... Technical Data Engineer (MCD)
TDE .... Technical Data Evaluation
TD & E...... Test Design and Evaluation
TDE .... Testing Difficulty Estimator
TDE .... Tetrachlorodiphenylethane [*Also, DDD*] [*Insecticide*]
TDE .... Three Day Event [*Horseriding*] [*British*] (DI)
TDE .... Toluene-Dioxane-Ethanol [*Scintillation solvent*]
TDE .... Total Data Entry
TDE .... Total Differential Equation
TDE .... Total Digestible Energy [*Nutrition*]
TDE .... Trans-Dominion Energy Corp. [*Toronto Stock Exchange symbol*]
TDE .... Transdermal Estradiol [*Pharmacology*]
TD & E...... Transposition, Docking, and Ejection [*NASA*] (KSC)
TDE .... Triethylene Glycol Diglycidyl Ether [*Medicine*]
TDE .... Two-Dimensional Equilibrium
TDEC....... Technical Development Evaluation Center
TDEC....... Technical Division and Engineering Center [*FAA*] (MCD)
TDEC....... Telephone Line Digital Error Checking
TDECC..... Tactical Display Engagement Control Console [*Military*] (RDA)
TDED .... Istanbul Universitesi Edegiyat Fakultesi Turk Dili ve Edebiyati Dergisi [*A publication*]
TDED .... Trade Data Elements Directory (DS)
TDEFWP .. Turbine-Driven Emergency Feedwater Pump [*Nuclear energy*] (NRCH)
TDEL....... Time Delay (FAAC)
TDEN .... Total Density [*Ecology*]
TDEP........ Tracking Data Editing Program [*NASA*]
TDES........ [*The*] Duke Ellington Society (EA)
TDF .... Tactical Digital Facsimile (MCD)
TDF .... Tape Data Family
TDF .... Target Development Facility [*Proposed, 1986, for fusion research*]
TDF .... Task Deletion Form [*Nuclear energy*] (NRCH)
TDF .... Telediffusion de France [*Broadcasting agency*] [*French*]
TDF .... Temporary Detention Facility
TDF .... Testis-Determining Factor [*Genetics*]
TDF .... Theatre Development Fund (EA)
TDF .... Thin Dielectric Film
TDF .... Thoracic Duct Fistula [*Medicine*] (MAE)
TDF .... Thoracic Duct Flow [*Medicine*] (MAE)
TDF .... Time-Domain Filter
TDF .... Time Dose Fractionation Factor [*Roentgenology*]
TDF .... Tonga Defence Force [*British military*] (DMA)
TDF .... Training Directors' Forum [*An association*] (EA)
TDF .... Transborder Data Flows [*Also, TBDF*] [*Telecommunications*]
TDF .... Transkei Defence Force [*South Africa*]
TDF .... Trial-Dependent-Forgetting [*Process*] [*Psychology*]
TDF .... Trim and Drill Fixture (MCD)
TDF .... Trunk Distribution Frame (DEN)
TDF .... Two Degrees of Freedom
TDFC........ Thomas Dolby Fan Club (EA)
TDFCHB... Telemetry Data Format Control Handbook (KSC)
TDFR....... Total Duration-Specific Fertility Rate [*Population studies*]
TDFS........ Terminal Digit Fitting System [*Military*] (AABC)
TDG.......... Tactical Development Group [*Military*] (CAAL)
TDG.......... Tactical Drone Group (MCD)
TD & G ...... Tall, Dark, and Gruesome [*Slang*]
TDG.......... Talladega, AL [*Location identifier*] [*FAA*] (FAAL)
TDG.......... Tandag [*Philippines*] [*Airport symbol*] (OAG)
TDG.......... Technical Design Guide
TDG.......... Technical Developing Group [*of the Publishers' Association*] [*British*]

TDG.......... Telemetry Data Generation
TDG.......... Test Data Generator (BUR)
TDG.......... Test Display Generator
TDG.......... Test Documentation Group
TDG.......... Tetradecanylglutarate [*Biochemistry*]
TDG.......... Textile Designers Guild (EA)
TDG.......... Thio(deaza)guanine [*Antineoplastic drug*]
TDG.......... Thiodigalactoside [*Organic chemistry*]
TDG.......... Time Delay Generator
TDG.......... Timesharer Developers' Group [*British*]
TDG.......... Toodoggone Gold [*Vancouver Stock Exchange symbol*]
TDG.......... Top-Down Greedy
TDG.......... TOTAL Energold Corp. [*Toronto Stock Exchange symbol*]
TDG.......... Trading (DCTA)
TDG.......... Transport Development Group Ltd. [*British*]
TDG.......... Transportation of Dangerous Goods [*International symposium*]
TDG.......... Twist Drill Gauge
TD & GS...... Technical Documentation and Graphic Services
TDGS....... Test Data Generation Section [*Social Security Administration*]
TD & H ..... Tall, Dark, and Handsome [*Slang*]
TDH.......... Terre des Hommes [*An international organization*]
TDH.......... Total Dynamic Head (AAG)
TDH.......... Toxic Dose High (OA)
TDH.......... Tracking Data Handling
TDH.......... Transport Disengaging Height [*Fluidized beds of particles*]
TDHGA..... Travel of Dependents and Household Goods Authorized [*Military*] (AABC)
TDHL........ Transdihydrolisuride [*Biochemistry*]
TDHS........ Tape Data Handling System
TDHYA ..... Tohoku Daigaku Hisuiyoeki Kagaku Kenkyusho Hokoku [*A publication*]
TDI .... [*The*] Democracy International (EA)
TDI .... TACAN [*Tactical Air Navigation*] Distance Indicator
TDI .... Target Data Inventory [*Military*] (AFM)
TDI .... Target Doppler Indicator [*RADAR*]
TDI .... Task Description Item (MCD)
TDI .... Taxpayer Delinquent Investigation [*IRS*]
TDI .... Teardown Inspection
TDI .... Technical Data International [*Information service or system*] (IID)
TD & I....... Technology Development and Integration
TDI .... Technology Dynamics Institute [*Telecommunications service*] (TSSD)
TDI .... Telecommunications Data Interface
TDI .... Telecommunications for the Deaf, Inc. (EA)
TDI .... Telegraphist Detector Instructor [*British military*] (DMA)
TDI .... Teletec Development, Inc. [*Vancouver Stock Exchange symbol*]
TDI .... Temporary Disability Insurance [*Unemployment*]
TDI .... Test Data Interpolation
TDI .... Textile Dye Institute [*Later, American Dye Manufacturers Institute*]
TDI .... Therapeutic Donor Insemination [*Obstetrics*]
TDI .... Therapy Dogs International (EA)
TDI .... Time Delay and Integration (MCD)
TDI .... Toluene [*or Tolylene*] Diisocyanate [*Organic chemistry*]
T & DI....... Tool and Die Institute (EA)
TDI .... Tool and Die Institute (KSC)
TDI .... Total Domestic Incomes [*Department of Employment*] [*British*]
TDI .... Total Dose Infusion [*Medicine*] (MAE)
TDI .... Trade Data Interchange (DS)
TDI .... Training Development and Improvement Program [*Department of Education*]
TDI .... Training Developments Institute [*Army*]
TDI .... TSH [*Thyroid-Stimulating Hormone*] Displacing Immunoglobulin [*Endocrinology*]
TDI .... Turbine Disk Integrity [*Nuclear energy*] (NRCH)
TDI .... Twin Disc, Inc. [*NYSE symbol*] (SPSG)
TDI .... Tymnet DTS, Inc. [*San Jose, CA*] [*Telecommunications*] (TSSD)
TDIC........ Target Data Input Computer
TDIC........ Total Dissolved Inorganic Carbon [*Environmental chemistry*]
TDIL........ Target Detection, Identification, and Location
TDINF....... Taxpayer Delinquency Investigation Notice File [*IRS*]
TDIO....... Timing Data Input-Output
TDIP........ Total Disability Income Provisions [*Military*] (AABC)
TDIPR....... Test Design In-Process Review (MCD)
TDIS........ Technical Data Impact Summary (MCD)
TDIS........ Terminal Data Input System (MCD)
TDIS........ Terminal Defense Interceptor Subsystem [*DoD*]
TDIS........ Thai Development Information Service (EAIO)
TDIS........ Time Distance [*Military*] (AABC)
TDIS........ Time Distance Terminal Data Input System (MCD)
TDIS........ Training Development Information System [*Army*]
TDIS........ Travel Document and Issuance System [*US passport*] [*Department of State*]
TDISTR..... Tape Distributor (MSA)
TDIU .... Target Data Input Unit
TDJ.......... Dallas County Community College District, Dallas, TX [*OCLC symbol*] (OCLC)

TDJ............ Tadjoura [*Djibouti*] [*Seismograph station code, US Geological Survey*] (SEIS)
TDJ............ Tadjoura [*Djibouti*] [*Airport symbol*] (OAG)
TDJ............ Training and Development Journal [*A publication*]
TDJC........ Technical Data Justification Code [*Army*]
TDJKA...... Tokyo Daigaku Jishin Kenkyusho Iho [*A publication*]
TDK.......... TDK Corp. [*NYSE symbol*] (SPSG)
TDK .... TDK Corp. [*Associated Press abbreviation*] (APAG)
TDK .... Test of Diabetes Knowledge
TDK .... Tokyo Denki Kagaku [*Tokyo Electronics and Chemical Co.*] [*Initialism is now name of recording tape manufacturer and brand name of its products*]
TDK .... Toyo Daigaku Kiyo [*Bulletin. Department of Liberal Arts. Tokyo University*] [*A publication*]
TDKF........ Fahrzeugtestdatenbank [*Dokumentation Kraftfahwesen eV*] [*Germany*] [*Information service or system*] (CRD)
TDKIB....... Tokai Daigaku Kiyo Kogakubu [*A publication*]
TDKNAF... Annual Report. Takeda Research Laboratories [*A publication*]
TDKP........ Turkish Revolutionary Communist Party [*Political party*] (PD)
TDL .... David Lipscomb College, Nashville, TN [*OCLC symbol*] (OCLC)
TDL .... Tactical Data Link
TDL .... Tandil [*Argentina*] [*Airport symbol*] (OAG)
TDL .... Tapped Delay Line
TDL .... Target Development Laboratory [*Eglin AFB*] (AAG)
TDL .... Task-Directed Learning
TDL .... Technical Data Laboratory [*National Weather Service*]
TDL .... Technical Document List
TDL .... Test Description Log (MCD)
TDL .... Test and Diagnostic Language (MCD)
TDL .... Thoracic Duct Lymphocyte [*Immunochemistry*]
TDL .... Threshold Damage Level
TDL .... Threshold Detection Level
TDL .... Thymus-Dependent Lymphocyte [*Hematology*]
TDL .... Topographic Developments Laboratory [*Fort Belvoir, VA*] [*United States Army Engineer Topographic Laboratories*] (GRD)
TDL .... Toxic Dose Low (OA)
TDL .... Transaction Definition Language
TDL .... Transformation Definition Language [*Data processing*] (IBMDP)
TDL .... Translation Definition Language
TDL .... Transparent Data Link (SSD)
TDL .... Tunable Diode LASER [*Also, SDL*]
TDL .... Tunnel-Diode Logic
TDLAS ...... Tunable Diode LASER Absorption Spectrometry
TDLBAI .... Deutsche Akademie der Landwirtschaftwissenschaften zu Berlin. Tagungsberichte [*A publication*]
TDLCA...... Thoracic Duct Lining Cells Antigen [*Immunology*]
TDLOA ..... Training Device Letter of Agreement
TDLR........ Terminal Descent and Landing RADAR
TDLR........ Training Device Letter Requirement [*Military*]
TDLS........ Topographic Data Library System
TDLU........ Terminal Duct Lobular Unit [*Of mammary gland*]
TDM.......... Mount Alvernia Friary, Wappingers Falls, NY [*OCLC symbol*] [*Inactive*] (OCLC)
TDM.......... Tandem (AAG)
TDM.......... Tandem Computers, Inc. [*NYSE symbol*] (SPSG)
TDM.......... Tandem Resources [*Vancouver Stock Exchange symbol*]
TDM.......... Tank Destroyer Armed with Missiles (INF)
TDM.......... Task Description Memo (MCD)
TDM.......... Technical Division Manager
TDM.......... Technology Development Mission [*NASA*] (SSD)
TDM.......... Telecommunications Data-Link Monitor (CET)
TDM.......... Teledifusao de Macau [*Radio and television broadcasting company*] [*Macau*] (FEA)
TDM.......... Telemetric Data Monitor
TDM.......... Template Descriptor Memory
TDM.......... Ternary Delta Modulation
TDM.......... Tertiary Dodecyl Mercaplan (OA)
TDM.......... Test Data Memorandum (AAG)
TDM.......... Test Development Manager [*Military*] (CAAL)
TDM.......... Text and Date Messaging (HGAA)
TDM.......... Therapeutic Drug Monitoring
TDM.......... Thermal Development Model
TDM.......... Thermal Diffusion Method
TDM.......... Thermodynamic Molding
TDM.......... Time-Division Multiplexing [*Telecommunications*]
TDM.......... Time Duration Modulation (DEN)
TDM.......... Tire Degradation Monitor (MCD)
TDM.......... Tool Design Manual (MCD)
TDM.......... Torpedo Detection Modification [*SONAR*]
TDM.......... Total Dissolvable Manganese [*Chemistry*]
TDM.......... Tracking Data Message (SSD)
TDM.......... Trehalose Dimycolate [*Biochemistry*]
TDM.......... Trouble Detection and Monitoring
TDM.......... Tunnel-Diode Mixer
TDMA....... Tape Direct Memory Access
TDMA....... Time-Division [*or Time-Domain*] Multiple Access [*Computer control system*]

TDMA....... Trophy Dealers and Manufacturers Association (EA)
TDMAC .... Tridodecylmethylammonium Chloride [*Organic chemistry*]
TDMC .... Technical Data Management Center [*Department of Energy*] [*Information service or system*] [*Defunct*] (IID)
TDMD....... Time-Division Multiplex Device [*Radio*]
TDME....... Test, Diagnostic, and Measurement Equipment (MCD)
TDMG....... Telegraph and Data Message Generator (MCD)
TDMM...... International Union of Tool, Die, and Mold Makers
TDMO....... Technical Data Management Office [*Navy*]
TDMOD.... Therapeutic Drug Monitoring [*A publication*]
TDMP....... Technical Data Management Program [*Navy*]
TDMP .... Technology Development Mission Polar [*Canada*] (SSD)
TDMR .... Technical Division Memo Report [*Army*] [*World War II*]
TDMRA ..... Texas Delaine-Merino Record Association [*Later, TDSA*] (EA)
TDMS........ Telegraph Distortion Measuring System
TDMS........ Telemetry Data Monitor Set
TDMS........ Thermal Desorption Mass Spectroscopy
TDMS........ Time-Division Multiplex System [*Radio*] (MCD)
TDMS........ Time-Shared/Data Management System
TDMS........ Toxicology Data Management System [*Department of Health and Human Services*] (GFGA)
TDMS........ Transmission Distortion Measuring Set
TDMTB..... Tables of Distribution Mobilization Troop Basis [*Army*] (AABC)
TDM-VDMA ... Time-Division Multiplex - Variable Destination Multiple Access [*Telecommunications*] (TEL)
TDMWG... Technology Development Missions Working Group [*NASA*] (SSD)
TDN.......... Target Doppler Nullifier [*RADAR*]
TDN.......... Tendances de la Conjoncture. Graphiques Mensuels [*A publication*]
TDN.......... Total Digestible Nutrients
TDN.......... Touchdown [*Aviation*] (FAAC)
TDN.......... Travel as Directed Is Necessary in the Military Service (MUGU)
TDN.......... Trimethyldihydronapthalene [*Organic chemistry*]
T-DNA....... Transfer-Deoxyribonucleic Acid
TDNCA ..... Texas Date Nail Collectors Association (EA)
TDNN........ Time Delay Neural Network [*Data processing*]
TDNS .... Total Data Network System (TEL)
TDNS .... Training Device Needs Statement [*Army*]
TDNT .... Theological Dictionary of the New Testament [*A publication*] (BJA)
TDO.......... Technical Development Objective
TDO.......... Technical Directives Ordnance (NG)
TDO.......... Technical Divisions Office [*Jet Propulsion Laboratory, NASA*]
TDO.......... Telegraph Delivery Order
TDO.......... Time Delay Opening
TDO.......... Toledo, WA [*Location identifier*] [*FAA*] (FAAL)
TDO.......... Tornado
TDO.......... Training Development Office [*Army*]
TDO.......... Training Development Officer [*British*]
TDO.......... Treasury Department Order [*A publication*] (DLA)
TDO.......... Tuesday Downtown Operators and Observers [*An association*] (EA)
TDOA .... Time Delay of Arrival (MCD)
TDOA .... Time Deposit, Open Account [*Banking*]
TDOA .... Time Difference of Arrrival
TDOA/DD ... Time Difference of Arrival and Differential Doppler (MCD)
TDOC........ Technical Document (DNAB)
TDOD........ Training and Development Organizations Directory [*A publication*]
TDOL........ Tetradecanol [*Organic chemistry*]
TDOP .... Time Dilution of Precision
TDOP .... Truck Design Optimization Project [*Railroads*]
TDOS .... Tape Disk Operating System [*Data processing*]
TDOT .... Thorndike Dimensions of Temperament [*Psychology*]
TDP .... Tank Development Program [*Military*]
TDP .... Target Data Processor (NVT)
TDP .... Target Director Post [*RADAR*] [*Military*]
TDP .... Technical Data Package [*Military*]
TDP .... Technical Development Plan
TDP .... Technical Documentation for Provisioning [*Military*] (AFIT)
TDP .... Teledata Processing
TDP .... Temperature Density Plotter
TDP .... Temperature and Dew Point (KSC)
TDP .... Temporary Detention of Pay
TDP .... Terminal Defense Program [*Military*]
TDP .... Test Design Plan [*Army*]
TDP .... Thermal Death-Point
TDP .... Thermistor Detector Package
TDP .... Thiamine Diphosphate [*Also, DPT, TPP*] [*Biochemistry*]
TDP .... Thiodiphenol [*Organic chemistry*]
TDP .... Thoracic Duct Pressure [*Medicine*] (MAE)
TDP .... Thymidine Diphosphate [*Biochemistry*]
TDP .... Toluene Disproportionation Process [*Organic chemistry*]
TDP .... Total Development Plan
TDP .... Touchdown Protection [*Military*] (MCD)
TDP .... Tracking Data Processor
TDP .... Tracking and Display Processor (CAAL)

TDP .... Trade and Development Program [*US International Development Cooperation Agency*]
TDP .... Traffic Data Processing
TDP .... Traffic Demand Predictor [*Aviation*]
TDP .... Trainee Discharge Program [*Army*]
TDP .... Trim and Drain Pump [*Navy*]   (CAAL)
TDPA .... Textile Data Processing Association [*Later, ATMI*]   (EA)
TDPA .... Thiodipropionic Acid [*Organic chemistry*]
TDPAC...... Time Differential Perturbed Angular Correlation [*Physics*]
TDPB........ Tactical Display Plotting Board
TDPD .... Dominica/Melville Hall [*Dominica*] [*ICAO location identifier*]   (ICLI)
TDPD .... Technical Data Package Depository [*Army*]
TDPF........ Tail Damping Power Factor [*Aviation*]
TDPF......... Target Data Planning File   (SAA)
TDPFO...... Temporary Duty Pending Further Orders [*Military*]
TDPJ .... Truck Discharge Point Jet   (NATG)
TDPL........ Technical Data Package List [*Military*]   (AABC)
TDPL......... Top-Down Parsing Language
TDPM .... Truck Discharge Point Mogas   (NATG)
TDPMP.... Technical Data Package Management Plan [*Army*]
TDPP......... Traffic Data Processing Program   (MCD)
TDPR........ Roseau [*Dominica*] [*ICAO location identifier*]   (ICLI)
TDPRha .... Thymidine Diphosphorhamnose [*Biochemistry*]
TDPS........ Tracking Data Processor System   (MCD).
TDPSK ...... Time Differential Phase-Shift Keying
TDPU .... Telemetry Data Processing Unit   (CAAL)
TDQP .... Trimethyldihydroquinoline Polymer [*Organic chemistry*]
TDR .... Drama Review [*Formerly, Tulane Drama Review*] [*A publication*]
TDR .... Tail Damping Ratio [*Aviation*]
TDR .... Talos Discrepancy Report   (MCD)
TDR .... Tape Data Register
TDR .... Target Detection and Recognition   (MCD)
TDR .... Target Discrimination RADAR   (IEEE)
TDR .... Teacher Demonstration Rating   (OA)
TDR .... Teardown Deficiency Report
TDR .... Technical Data Relay   (IEEE)
TDR .... Technical Data Report
TDR .... Technical Data Requests
TDR .... Technical Deficiency Report
TDR .... Technical Design Review   (NASA)
TDR .... Technical Development Requirement
TDR .... Technical Directive Records   (NG)
TDR .... Technical Documentary Report
TDR .... Technology Review [*A publication*]
TDR .... Temperature-Dependent Resistor   (BYTE)
TDR .... Temperature Depth Recorder
TDR .... Temporarily Disconnected at Subscriber's Request [*Telecommunications*]   (TEL)
TDR .... Tender [*Navy*]   (NVT)
TDR .... Terminal Digit Requested [*Telecommunications*]   (TEL)
TDR .... Test Data Recorder
TDR .... Test Data Report   (AAG)
TDR .... Test Deficiency Report [*Nuclear energy*]   (NRCH)
TD/R .... Test Disable/Reset   (AAG)
TDR .... Test Discount Rate
TDR .... Test Discrepancy Report   (MCD)
TDR .... Thailand Development Report [*Bangkok*] [*A publication*]
TDR .... Threat Detection RADAR [*Military*]   (CAAL)
TDR .... Time Delay Relay
TDR .... Time-Domain Reflectometry
TDR .... Todoroki [*Japan*] [*Seismograph station code, US Geological Survey*] [*Closed*]   (SEIS)
TDR .... Tone Dial Receiver
TDR .... Tool Design Request   (KSC)
TDR .... Torque-Differential Receiver   (MUGU)
TDR .... Total Defect Rate
TDR .... Track Data Request   (CAAL)
TDR .... Tracking and Data Relay [*NASA*]
TDR .... Training Device Requirement [*Army*]   (AABC)
TDR .... Transferable Development Rights [*Community planning*]
TDR .... Transistorized Digital Readout
TDR .... Transmit Data Register [*Data processing*]   (MDG)
TDR .... Transnational Data and Communicative Report [*A publication*]   (TSSD)
TDR .... Trap Designator Register
TDR .... Treasury Deposit Receipt
TDR .... Triplet-Doublet Resonance [*Physics*]
TDR .... Tropical Disease Research [*WHO*]
TDR .... Tudor Corp. Ltd. [*Toronto Stock Exchange symbol*]
TDR .... Turndown Ratio
TD & RA .... Threat Determination and Resource Allocation
TDRC........ Total Diet Research Center [*Public Health Service*]   (GRD)
TDRCAH .. Contributions. Institute of Geology and Paleontology. Tohoku University [*A publication*]
TDRE .... Tracking and Data Relay Experiment [*Telecommunications*]   (TEL)
TDRF......... Target Doppler Reference Frequency
TDRI.......... Tropical Development and Research Institute [*Research center*] [*British*]   (IRC)

TDRL........ Temporary Disability Retired List [*Military*]
TDRL........ Tudor Corp. Ltd. [*NASDAQ symbol*]   (NQ)
T/DRLY .... Time Delay Relay
TDRM .... Time-Domain Reflectometry Microcomputer
TDRR .... Test Data Recording and Retrieval   (NASA)
TDRRB...... Technical Data Requirement Review Board
TDRRC...... Training Device Requirements Review Committee [*Army*]
TDRS........ Technical Data Requirements Sheet
TDRS........ Telemetering Data Recording Set   (CAAL)
TDRS........ Telemetry Downlist Receiving Site   (NASA)
TDRS........ Tracking and Data Relay Satellite [*NASA*]
TDRS........ Traffic Data Recording System [*Bell System*]
TDRS........ Transnational Data Reporting Service, Inc. [*Springfield, VA*] [*Telecommunications service*]   (TSSD)
TDRS........ Travelers, Defect Route Sheet   (DNAB)
TDRSS ...... Tracking and Data Relay Satellite Services [*or System*] [*NASA*]
TDRTC..... Tank Destroyer Replacement Training Center
TDS .... 3-D Systems [*Vancouver Stock Exchange symbol*]
TDS .... Tactical Data System
TDS .... Tactical Deployment Support
TDS .... Tactical Display System   (CAAL)
TDS .... Tactical Drone Squadron
TDS .... Tape Data Selector
TDS .... Tape Decal System
TDS .... Target Data Sheet   (MCD)
TDS .... Target Designation System [*Navy*]
TDS .... Teacher Demand and Shortage Survey [*Department of Education*]   (GFGA)
TDS .... Technical Data Specialist
TDS .... Technical Data System   (KSC)
TDS .... Technical Database Services, Inc. [*Information service or system*]   (IID)
TDS .... Technical Description Sheet
TDS .... Technical Directive System   (MCD)
TDS .... Technology Demonstration Satellite [*NASA*]   (NASA)
TDS .... Teleflora Delivery Service   (EA)
TDS .... Telemetry Decommutation System
TDS .... Telephone & Data Systems, Inc. [*AMEX symbol*]   (SPSG)
TDS .... Temperature-Depth-Salinity [*Oceanography*]
TDS .... Temporary Duty Station [*Air Force*]   (AFM)
TDS .... Ter in Die Sumendum [*To Be Taken Three Times a Day*] [*Pharmacy*]
TDS .... Tertiary Data Set [*Data processing*]   (OA)
TDS .... Test Data Sheet   (KSC)
TDS .... Test Data System   (NASA)
TDS .... Thermal Degradation Sample [*Apollo*]
TDS .... Thermal Desorption Spectroscopy
TDS .... Time Delay Switch
TDS .... Time, Distance, Speed
TDS .... Time Distribution System   (MCD)
TDS .... Time-Division Switching [*Telecommunications*]
TDS .... Time-Domain Spectroscopy   (IEEE)
TDS .... Tool Data Sheet   (MCD)
TDS .... Tool Design Service   (MCD)
TDS .... Tool Design Study   (MCD)
TDS .... Torpedo Deflection Sight
TDS .... Torpedo Destruction System
TDS .... Total Dissolved Solids
TDS .... Track Data Simulator
TDS .... Track Data Storage
T & DS ...... Tracking and Data System [*NASA*]
TDS .... Tracking and Data System [*NASA*]
TDS .... Training Depot Station [*British military*]   (DMA)
TDS .... Training Developments Study
TDS .... Training Directors Seminar [*LIMRA*]
TDS .... [*Annual*] Training Duty Status [*Navy Reserve*]
TDS .... Transaction Distribution System
TDS .... Transaction Driven System [*Honeywell, Inc.*]
TDS .... Transistor Display and Data-Handling System [*Data processing*]   (MDG)
TDS .... Translation and Docking Simulator [*Navy*]   (KSC)
TDS .... Trap Designator Set
TDS .... Trash Disposal System
TDS .... Traverse des Sioux Library System, Mankato MN [*OCLC symbol*]   (OCLC)
TDS .... [*US*] Treasury Daily Statement
TDS .... Tunnel Destruct System
TDSA........ Technical Data Status Accounting   (MCD)
TDSA........ Technical Directive Status Accounting
TDSA........ Telegraph and Data Signals Analyzer   (MCD)
TD & SA .... Telephone, Data, and Special Audio   (NASA)
TDSA........ Texas Delaine Sheep Association   (EA)
TDSA........ TRADEVMAN [*Training Devices Man*], Seaman Apprentice [*Navy rating*]
TDSC........ Tesdata Systems Corp. [*NASDAQ symbol*]   (NQ)
TDSC........ Training Device Support Center [*Army*]
TDSCC...... Tidbinbilla Deep Space Communications Complex
TDSDT...... Tactical Data System Development Testbed
TDSF........ Technical Data Support Facility
TDSIC .... Theatre/Drama, and Speech Information Center   (IID)

TDSKB ...... Reports. Research Institute for Strength and Fracture of Materials. Tohoku University [*A publication*]
TDSMO .... Tactical Data Systems Management Office [*Army*] [*Fort Leavenworth*]   (MCD)
TDSN .... TRADEVMAN [*Training Devices Man*], Seaman [*Navy rating*]
TDSO .... Training Device Supply Office [*Navy*]   (DNAB)
TDSP .... Technical Data Support Package [*Navy*]
TDSQB ...... Time Delay Squib [*Navy*]
TDSS .... 3-D Systems, Inc. [*NASDAQ symbol*]   (NQ)
TDSS .... Telemetry Data Signal Simulator   (MCD)
TDSS .... Time Dividing Spectrum Stabilization [*Electronics*]   (OA)
TDSS .... Turret Drive Subsystem   (DWSG)
TDST .... Track Data Storage   (MSA)
TDSTP ...... Trainer Digital Self-Test Program
TDT .... Tactical Data Terminal   (MCD)
TDT .... Tank Driver Trainer [*Army*]
TDT .... Target Designation Transmitter
TDT .... Target Docking Trainer [*NASA*]   (KSC)
TDT .... Task Dispatch Table [*Data processing*]   (OA)
TDT .... Tavil-Dara [*Former USSR*] [*Seismograph station code, US Geological Survey*] [*Closed*]   (SEIS)
TDT .... Terminal Death Time   (OA)
TDT .... Terminal Deoxynucleotidyl Transferase [*An enzyme*]
TDT .... Terrestrial Dynamic Time   (WGA)
TDT .... Test Direction Team
TDT .... Test Dwell Time
TDT .... Thermal Death Time [*Bacteriological testing*]
TDT .... Thiodiethanethiol [*Organic chemistry*]
TDT .... This Day Tonight   (ADA)
TDT .... Tidioute, PA [*Location identifier*] [*FAA*]   (FAAL)
TDT .... Tone Decay Test [*Audiometry*]
TDT .... Toronto Dance Theatre
TDT .... Total Delay Time
TDT .... Total Downtime
TDT .... Tower Disconnect Technician   (SAA)
TDT .... Translation and Docking Trainer
TDT .... Transonic Dynamic Tunnel [*NASA*]
TDT .... Tumor Doubling Time [*Cytology*]
TDT .... Tunnel-Diode Transducer
TDT .... Turret Director Trainer [*British military*]   (DMA)
TDT and CU ... Target Designation Transmitter and Control Unit
TD/TDNA ... Tardive Dyskinesia/Tardive Dystonia National Association   (EA)
TDT/FC .... Tank Destroyer Tactical and Firing Center
TDTG .... True Date-Time Group [*Military*]
TDTL .... Tunnel-Diode Transistor Logic
TDTS .... Tactical Data Transfer System   (NATG)
TDU .... Tactical Deception Unit   (NVT)
TDU .... Tactical Display Unit   (NVT)
TDU .... Talos Defense Unit   (SAA)
TDU .... Target Detection Unit
TDU .... Teamsters for a Democratic Union   (EA)
TDU .... Threat Display Unit   (MCD)
TDU .... Time Display Unit   (NASA)
TDU .... Tondu [*British depot code*]
TDU .... Torpedo Development Unit [*Ministry of Technology*] [*British*]
TDU .... Towed Unit [*Aerial Target*]   (CAAL)
TDU .... Tracking Display Unit
TDU .... Trash Disposal Unit   (DNAB)
TDU .... Traverse Displacement Unit   (DNAB)
TDU .... Trigger Delay Unit
TDU .... Tropendienstunfaehig [*Unfit for service in tropics*] [*German military - World War II*]
TDUKA ..... Tokyo Daigaku Uchu Koku Kenkyusho Hokoku [*A publication*]
TDUM .... Tape Dump and Utility Monitor [*Data processing*]
TDUP .... Technical Data Usage Program
TDV .... Technology Development Vehicle   (IEEE)
TDV .... Terminal Delivered Vehicle [*Army*]
TDV .... Test Data Van   (NASA)
TDV .... Test Data Variation
TDV .... Touchdown Velocity [*Aviation*]
TDV .... Tumbleweed Diagnostic Vehicle
TDVA .... 37th Division Veterans Association   (EA)
TDW .... Amarillo, TX [*Location identifier*] [*FAA*]   (FAAL)
TDW .... Tidewater, Inc. [*NYSE symbol*]   (SPSG)
TDW .... Tons Deadweight   (DS)
TDW .... Trunk Destination Words   (CET)
TDW .... Turbo Debugger for Windows [*Data processing*]   (PCM)
TDWO .... Test and Development Work Order
TDWR .... Terminal Doppler Weather RADAR   (DWSG)
TDWT .... Transonic Dynamic Wind Tunnel [*NASA*]   (KSC)
TDWU .... Transport and Dock Workers' Union [*India*]
TDX .... Thermal Demand Transmitter   (MSA)
TDX .... Time-Division Exchange
TDX .... Torque-Differential Transmitter   (MUGU)
TDX .... Transportation Data Xchange, Inc.   (IID)
TDX .... Tridex Corp. [*AMEX symbol*]   (SPSG)
TDY .... Teledyne, Inc. [*NYSE symbol*]   (SPSG)
TDY .... Temporary Duty
TDY .... Trading Bay, AK [*Location identifier*] [*FAA*]   (FAAL)

TDYKA ..... Tokushima Daigaku Yakugaku Kenkyu Nempo [*A publication*]
TDYKA8 ... Annual Reports. Faculty of Pharmaceutical Sciences. Tokushima University [*A publication*]
TDYN .... Thermodynetics, Inc. [*NASDAQ symbol*]   (NQ)
TDZ .... Thioridazine [*Tranquilizer*]
TDZ .... Thymus-Dependent Zone [*Hematology*]   (MAE)
TDZ .... Toledo, OH [*Location identifier*] [*FAA*]   (FAAL)
TDZ .... Torpedo Danger Zone   (NVT)
TDZ .... Touchdown Zone [*Aviation*]   (FAAC)
TDZ .... Trade Development Zone   (ADA)
TDZ .... Transcontinental Dislocation Zone [*Geology*]
TDZ .... Tridel Enterprises, Inc. [*Toronto Stock Exchange symbol*]
TDZ/CL .... Touchdown Zone/Centerline [*Aviation*]   (DNAB)
TDZL .... Touchdown Zone Lights [*Aviation*]   (FAAC)
TE .... Air New Zealand Ltd. [*International*] [*New Zealand*] [*ICAO designator*]   (FAAC)
TE .... Electron Temperature [*Plasma physics*]   (OA)
TE .... [*The*] Engelettes [*An association*]   (EA)
TE .... Journal of Transportation Engineering [*A publication*]
TE .... Light Temporarily Extinguished [*Navigation*]
TE .... Ling-Temco-Vought [*LTV*] [*ICAO aircraft manufacturer identifier*]   (ICAO)
TE .... Table of Equipment [*Army*]
T/E .... Tactical Emergency [*Army*]
TE .... Tageseinfluesse [*Weather factors, a gunnery term*] [*German military - World War II*]
TE .... Talmudic Encyclopedia [*A publication*]   (BJA)
TE .... Tamper Evident
TE .... Tangent Elevation   (MSA)
TE .... Task Element
TE .... Tatin Experimental [*British military*]   (DMA)
TE .... Teacher Education [*A publication*]
TE .... Teacher of Electrotherapy [*British*]
Te .... Teatr [*Moscow*] [*A publication*]
TE .... Technical Engineer
TE .... Technical Evaluation [*Army*]
TE .... Technical Exchange
TE .... Technician [*Communications*] [*Navy rating*]
TE .... Technological Engineer [*A publication*]
TE .... TECO Energy, Inc. [*NYSE symbol*]   (SPSG)
TE .... Tele-Engineering Corp. [*Telecommunications service*]   (TSSD)
TE .... Telecom Eireann [*Dublin, Ireland*] [*Telecommunications service*]   (TSSD)
TE .... Telegram
TE .... Teleman [*Navy rating*] [*British*]
TE .... Teller of the Exchequer [*British*]   (ROG)
Te .... Tellurium [*Chemical element*]
TE .... Temperature Element [*Nuclear energy*]   (NRCH)
Te .... Tempo [*A publication*]
TE .... Tenants by the Entirety [*Legal term*]
TE .... Tension Equalizer [*Electrical*] Wave
TE .... Teologia Espiritual [*A publication*]
TE .... Terminal Equipment
TE .... Terminal Exchange   (MCD)
TE .... Test and Engineering   (MCD)
TE .... Test Equipment
T & E .... Test and Evaluation [*Navy*]   (NG)
TE .... Test Exception [*Nuclear energy*]   (NRCH)
TE .... Test Explicit
Te .... Tetanus [*Medicine*]   (WGA)
TE .... Tetlit Tribune [*Fort McPherson*] [*A publication*]
TE .... Tetracycline [*Antibiotic compound*]
TE .... Text Editor [*Data processing*]
TE .... Theatre in Education   (EA)
TE .... Theistic Evolutionist
TE .... Theological Educator [*A publication*]
TE .... Theological Examination
TE .... Thermactor Emission [*Automotive engineering*]
TE .... Thermal Efficiency
TE .... Thermal Element   (KSC)
TE .... Thermal Expansion Load [*Nuclear energy*]   (NRCH)
TE .... Thermoelectric
TE .... Threat Evaluation   (NVT)
TE .... Threshold Energy [*Medicine*]   (MAE)
TE .... Thromboembolic [*Medicine*]
TE .... Throughput Efficiency   (CAAL)
TE .... Thunder Engines Corp. [*Vancouver Stock Exchange symbol*]
TE .... Tiger's Eye [*A publication*]
TE .... Tight End [*Football*]
Te .... Tigre   (BJA)
TE .... Time Earliest/Expected   (NASA)
TE .... Time to Echo [*Medicine*]
TE .... Time Electronics   (GFGA)
TE .... Time Error in Psychophysical Judgments [*Psychology*]
T & E .... Time and Events   (AAG)
T/E .... Time Expired   (ADA)
TE .... Timing Electronics   (KSC)
TE .... Tissue-Equivalent [*Medicine*]   (MAE)
TE .... Tocopherol Equivalent [*Nutrition*]
TE .... Today's Education [*A publication*]
TE .... Toluene-Ethanol [*Scintillation solvent*]

TE .... Tooth Extracted   (MAE)
TE .... Topographical Engineer
TE .... Tornisterempfaenger [*Pack-type portable receiver*] [*German military - World War II*]
TE .... Total Estrogen [*Medicine*]   (MAE)
TE .... Total Expenditure
TE .... Totally Enclosed   (MSA)
TE .... Tracheary Element [*Botany*]
TE .... Tracheoesophageal [*Also, TOE*] [*Medicine*]
TE .... Tracking Enhancement   (MCD)
TE .... Traction Engine [*British*]
TE .... Trade Expenses [*Business term*]
TE .... Trailing Edge [*Aviation*]
T & E .... Training and Education
TE .... Training Equipment
TE .... Training Establishment [*British military*]   (DMA)
TE .... Training and Evaluation   (OICC)
TE .... Trajectory Engineer
TE .... Transearth   (SAA)
TE .... Transequatorial [*Scatter*]
TE .... Transient Eddy
TE .... Transient Event [*Nuclear energy*]   (NRCH)
TE .... Transitional Engineering   (MCD)
TE .... Transmission Error [*Automotive engineering*]
TE .... Transport Empty
TE .... Transportation Engineer Magazine [*A publication*]   (EAAP)
T/E .... Transporter-Erector [*NASA*]   (KSC)
TE .... Transposable Element [*Genetics*]
TE .... Transverse Electric [*or Electrostatic*] [*Wave propagation mode*]
TE .... Travaux. Musee d'Etat de l'Ermitage [*A publication*]
T & E .... Travel and Entertainment [*IRS*]
T & E .... Traverse and Elevation [*Weapons*] [*Army*]   (INF)
TE .... Trial and Error
T & E .... Trial and Error   (AAMN)
TE .... Triple Expansion   (DS)
TE .... Trunk Equalizer [*Telecommunications*]   (OA)
TE .... Tuning Eye
TE .... Turbine Electric Drive
TE .... Twin Engine
TE .... Type Equipment   (MCD)
TE2 .... That's Entertainment, Part 2 [*Initialism is shortened form of movie title*]
TEA .... T Early Alpha [*Genetics*]
TEA .... Targeted Export Assistance Program [*Later, MAP*] [*Department of Agriculture*]
TEA .... Task Equipment Analysis
Tea .... Tea Boards of Kenya, Uganda, and Tanganyika. Journal [*A publication*]
TEA .... Tea and Coffee Trade Journal [*A publication*]
TEA .... Technical Engineers Association   (EA)
TEA .... Technical Exchange Agreement
TEA .... Tegra Enterprises, Inc. [*Vancouver Stock Exchange symbol*]
TEA .... Temporary Employment Assistance
TEA .... Tensile Energy Absorption [*Physics*]
TEA .... Test Engineer's Assistant [*Computer-aided design tool*]
TEA .... Test Equipment Accessory   (MCD)
TEA .... Test Equipment Analysis
TEA .... Test and Evaluation Agency
TEA .... Tetraethylammonium [*Organic chemistry*]
TEA .... Textile Export Association of the US   (EA)
TEA .... Thai Exiles Association   (CINC)
TEA .... Theatre Equipment Association   (EA)
TEA .... Thermal Energy Analysis [*or Analyzer*]
TEA .... Thiazoylethylamine [*Organic chemistry*]
TEA .... Tiselius Electrophoresis Apparatus
TEA .... Titanic Enthusiasts of America [*Later, THS*]   (EA)
TEA .... Torque Equilibrium Attitude   (SSD)
TEA .... Trade Expansion Act [*1962*]
TEA .... Training Effectiveness Analysis
TEA .... Trans European Airways [*Belgium*]   (EY)
TEA .... Transferred Electron Amplifier
TEA .... Transportability Engineering Analysis [*Army*]
TEA .... Transversely Excited Atmospheric [*LASER*]   (RDA)
TEA .... Treasury Enforcement Agent
TEA .... Triethanolamine [*Organic chemistry*]
TEA .... Triethylaluminum [*Organic chemistry*]
TEA .... Triethylamine [*Organic chemistry*]
TEA .... Triethylammonium [*Organic chemistry*]
TEA .... Tunnel-Emission Amplifier   (IEEE)
TEAA.......... Triethylammonium Acetate [*Organic chemistry*]
TEAAC...... Trade Expansion Act Advisory Committee [*Terminated, 1975*]   (EGAO)
TEAB........ Tetraethylammonium Bromide [*Organic chemistry*]
TEAC........ Test and Evaluation Advisory Council [*Military*]   (CAAL)
TEAC........ Tetraethylammonium Chloride [*Organic chemistry*]
TEAC........ Tokyo Electro Acoustical Co. [*Acronym is now name of electronics company and brand name of its products*]
TEAC........ Turbine Engine Analysis Check   (AABC)
TEACH ..... [*The*] Equity and Choice Act
Teach .... Teacher [*A publication*]
TEACH ..... Teacher Equity and Choice Act [*Proposed*]

TEACH ..... Teaching Each Other about Conquering Handicaps   (EA)
TEACH ..... Training and Education Activities Clearing House [*Military*]
Teach Adults ... Teaching Adults [*A publication*]
Teach Aids News ... Teaching Aids News [*A publication*]   (APTA)
TEACHCERT ... Teaching Certificate
Teach Coll Rec ... Teacher's College Record [*A publication*]
Teach Col R ... Teacher's College Record [*A publication*]
Teach Deaf ... Teacher of the Deaf [*A publication*]
Teach Dist ... Teaching at a Distance [*A publication*]
Teach Ed.... Teacher Education [*A publication*]
Teach Educ ... Teacher Education [*A publication*]
Teach Eng ... Teaching of English [*A publication*]   (APTA)
Teach Engl ... Teaching of English [*A publication*]   (APTA)
Teach Engl Deaf ... Teaching English to the Deaf [*A publication*]
Teacher Ed ... Teacher Education in New Countries [*A publication*]
Teacher Librn ... Teacher-Librarian [*A publication*]
Teachers J ... Teachers' Journal [*A publication*]   (APTA)
Teach Excep Child ... Teaching Exceptional Children [*A publication*]
Teach Feedback ... Teacher Feedback [*A publication*]   (APTA)
Teach Guild NSW Proc ... Teachers Guild of New South Wales. Proceedings [*A publication*]   (APTA)
Teach Hist ... Teaching History [*A publication*]   (APTA)
Teaching Engl ... Teaching of English [*A publication*]
Teaching Polit Sci ... Teaching Political Science [*A publication*]
Teach J ...... Teachers' Journal [*A publication*]   (APTA)
Teach J and Abst ... Teachers' Journal and Abstract [*A publication*]
Teach J Spec Educ ... Teachers' Journal of Special Education [*A publication*]   (APTA)
Teach J Vic ... Teachers' Journal (Victorian Teachers Union) [*A publication*]   (APTA)
Teach Lib... Teacher-Librarian [*A publication*]   (APTA)
Teach Lond Kids ... Teaching London Kids [*A publication*]
Teach Math ... Teaching Mathematics [*A publication*]   (APTA)
Teach Meth Page ... Teaching Methods Page [*A publication*]
Teach News Birm ... Teaching News. University of Birmingham [*A publication*]
Teach Newsl ... Teaching Newsletter [*A publication*]
Teach Phil ... Teaching Philosophy [*A publication*]
Teach Pol S ... Teaching Political Science [*A publication*]
Teach Pol Sci ... Teaching Political Science [*A publication*]
Teach Socio ... Teaching Sociology [*A publication*]
Teach Sociol ... Teaching Socioiogy [*A publication*]
Teach Train ... Teaching and Training [*A publication*]
Tea & Coff ... Tea and Coffee Trade Journal [*A publication*]
TEAD .... Tooele Army Depot [*Utah*]   (AABC)
TE/AE........ Tigers East/Alpines East   (EA)
TEAE........ Triethylaminoethyl [*Organic chemistry*]
Tea East Afr ... Tea in East Africa [*A publication*]
TEA-ER.... Traffic Executives Association, Eastern Railroads [*Later, ERA*]
TEAF........ Total Environmental Action Foundation   (EA)
TEAF........ Triethylammonium Formate [*Organic chemistry*]
TEAHA ..... Trans-East African Highway Authority   (EA)
TEAL........ Tactics, Equipment, and Logistics Conference [*between US, Great Britain, Australia, and Canada*] [*Developed "duck" designations for Mallard and Gander military communications systems*]
TEAL........ Tasman Empire Airways Ltd. [*Australia*]   (ADA)
TEAL........ Transversely Excited Atmospheric LASER   (RDA)
Tea Lib....... Teacher-Librarian [*A publication*]   (APTA)
TEAL Occ Pap ... Teachers of English as an Additional Language. Occasional Papers [*A publication*]
TEALS ...... Triethanolamine Lauryl Sulfate [*Organic chemistry*]
TEAM .... [*The*] European-Atlantic Movement [*British*]
TEAM .... [*The*] Evangelical Alliance Mission   (EA)
TEAM .... National TechTeam, Inc. [*NASDAQ symbol*]   (NQ)
TEAM .... Teacher Education and Media [*Project*]
TEAM .... Team, Inc. [*Associated Press abbreviation*]   (APAG)
TEAM .... Teamster Economic Action Mobilization
TEAM .... Tech-Base Enhancement for Autonomous Machines [*Military*]   (RDA)
TEAM .... Technical Engineer-Architect Management   (MCD)
TEAM .... Technical Engineering and Maintenance
TEAM .... Technique for Evaluation and Analysis of Maintainability
TEAM .... Technology Evaluation and Acquisition Method
TEAM .... Teleterminals Expandable Added Memory
TEAM .... Terminology Evaluation and Acquisition Method
TEAM .... Test and Evaluation of Air Mobility
TEAM .... Test, Evaluation, Analysis, and Modeling [*Army*]   (RDA)
TEAM .... Top European Advertising Media
TEAM .... Torpedo Evasive Maneuvering   (MCD)
TEAM .... Total Exposure Assessment Methodology [*or Monitoring*] [*Environmental chemistry*]
TEAM .... Training and Education in Adoption Methods [*Conference sponsored by the North American Council on Adoptable Children*]
TEAM .... Training/Employment of Automotive Mechanics [*Project*]
TEAM .... Training in Expanded Auxiliary Management
TEAM .... Trend Evaluation and Monitoring [*Congressional Clearinghouse on the Future*]   (EA)
TEAM .... Truck Expense Analysis and Management [*Data processing*]
TEAM .... Tube Earphone and Microphone   (DNAB)

TEAM A.... Theological Education Association of Mid-America, Library Section [Library network]
TEAMMATE ... Total Electronic Advanced Microprocessing Maneuvers and Tactics Equipment [A game]
TEAMS..... Technical Evaluation and Acquisition Management Support [Air Force]
TEAMS..... Test Evaluation and Monitoring System
TEAMS..... Tests of Engineering Aptitude, Mathematics, and Science
TEAMS..... Trend and Error Analysis Methodology System   (MCD)
TEAM-UP ... Test, Evaluation, Analysis, and Management Uniformity Plan [or Procedure] [Army]
TEAP........ Tetraethylammonium Perchlorate [Organic chemistry]
TEAP........ Trajectory Error Analysis Program [NASA]
TEAP........ Transversely Excited Atmospheric Pressure
TEAP........ Triethylammonium Phosphate [Organic chemistry]
TEAPA...... Technikas Apskats [A publication]
TEAPA...... Triethanolamine Phosphoric Acid [Organic chemistry]
Tea Q .... Tea Quarterly [A publication]
TEAR........ [The] Evangelical Alliance Relief [of The TEAR Fund]   (EA)
TEAR........ Time, Elevation, Azimuth, Range   (MCD)
TEARA...... Terapevticheskii Arkhiv [A publication]
Tea Res Assoc Annu Sci Rep ... Tea Research Association. Annual Scientific Report [A publication]
Tea Res Inst Ceylon Annu Rep ... Tea Research Institute of Ceylon. Annual Report [A publication]
Tea Res Inst Sri Lanka Tech Rep ... Tea Research Institute of Sri Lanka. Technical Report [A publication]
Tea Res J ... Tea Research Journal [A publication]
TEARR...... Times, Elevations, Azimuths, Ranges, and Range Rates [Aerospace]
TEARS ...... [The] Exeter Abstract Reference System [Exeter University] [Information service or system]   (IID)
TEAS........ Technical and Engineering Acquisition Support [Air Force]
TEAS........ Test and Evaluation, Aircraft Survivability
TEAS........ Threat Evaluation and Action Selection [Civilian defense program]
TEAS........ Twayne's English Author Series [A publication]
TEASE ...... Tracking Errors and Simulation Evaluation [RADAR]
TEASER.... Tunable Electron Amplifier for Stimulated Emission of Radiation   (MCD)
teasp.......... Teaspoonful
TEAT........ Obras de Teatro Estrenadas en Espana [Ministerio de Cultura] [Spain] [Information service or system]   (CRD)
TEA-TOW ... Training Effectiveness Analysis - Tube-Launched Optically Tracked Wire-Guided   (MCD)
TEB........... Tax-Exempt Bond [Investment term]
TEB........... Teterboro, NJ [Location identifier] [FAA]   (FAAL)
TEB........... Textile Economics Bureau
TEB........... Tone Encoded Burst
TEB........... Transient Electric Birefringence [Physics]
TEB........... Triethylbenzene [Organic chemistry]
TEB........... Triethylborane [Organic chemistry]
TEB........... Tropical Experiment Board [of World Meteorological Organization and International Council on Scientific Unions]
TEBA........ Tutmonda Esperantista Biblioteka Asocio [International Association for Esperanto in Libraries - IAEL]   (EAIO)
TEBAC...... Triethylbenylammonium Chloride [Organic chemistry]
TEBDA...... Truck Equipment and Body Distributor Association [Later, NTEA]   (EA)
TeBG.......... Testosterone Binding Globulin [Endocrinology]   (AAMN)
TeBG.......... Testosterone-Estradiol Binding Globulin [Endocrinology]
Tebiwa J Idaho Mus Nat Hist ... Tebiwa Journal. Idaho Museum of Natural History [A publication]
Tebiwa Misc Pap Idaho State Univ Mus Nat Hist ... Tebiwa Miscellaneous Papers. Idaho State University. Museum of Natural History [A publication]
TEBOL...... Terminal Business-Oriented Language
TEBPP....... Theoretical and Experimental Beam-Plasma Physics
TEBUTATE ... Tertiary Butyl Acetate [Organic chemistry] [USAN]
TEC........... Blacksburg, VA [Location identifier] [FAA]   (FAAL)
TEC........... [The] Electrification Council   (EA)
TEC........... [The] Entertainment Channel [Pay-television network] [Obsolete]
TEC........... [The] Executive President's Council [New Deal]
TEC........... Tactical Electromagnetic Coordinator   (IEEE)
TEC........... Tactical Exercise Controller [Marine Corps]   (MCD)
TEC........... Target Engagement Console
TEC........... Target Entry Console
TEC........... Tarif Exterieur Commun [Common External Tariff] [for EEC countries]
TEC........... Technical
TEC........... Technical Education Center
TEC........... Technical Escort Center [Army]   (RDA)
TEC........... Technical Evaluation Committee [Environmental Protection Agency]   (GFGA)
TEC........... Technician Education Council [British]   (DI)
Tec .... Technischord [Record label]
TEC........... Technological Excellence Commission
TEC........... Technology for Energy Corporation   (NRCH)

TEC........... Tele-Engineering Corp. [Framingham, MA] [Telecommunications]   (TSSD)
TEC........... Telecommunications Policy [A publication]
TEC........... Telemetry and Command
TEC........... Telephone Engineering Center [Telecommunications]   (TEL)
TEC........... Temporary Engineering Change   (AAG)
TEC........... Temporary Extended Compensation [Labor]
TEC........... Ternary Eutectic Chloride [Fire extinguishing agent]
TEC........... Test Equipment Center [NASA]   (NASA)
TEC........... Test Equipment Committee   (AAG)
T & EC...... Test and Evaluation Command [Army]
TEC........... Test and Evaluation Committee [DoD]   (RDA)
TEC........... Thermal End Cover
TEC........... Thermal Expansion Coefficient
TEC........... Thermal Unit End Cover   (MCD)
TEC........... Thermionic Energy Converter   (RDA)
TEC........... Thymic Epithelial Cell [Cytology]
TEC......... Tlemcen [Algeria] [Seismograph station code, US Geological Survey]   (SEIS)
TEC........... Tokyo Electronics Corp.
TEC........... Ton Equivalent of Coal
TEC........... Topographic Engineering Center [Ft. Belvoir, VA] [Army]   (RDA)
TEC........... TOS [TIROS Operational Satellite] Test Evaluation Center [Goddard Space Flight Center]   (NOAA)
TEC........... Total Electron Content   (MCD)
TEC........... Total Eosinophil Count [Hematology]
TEC........... Total Estimated Cost
TEC........... Tower En-Route Control [Aviation]   (FAAC)
TEC........... Track Entry Console   (MCD)
TEC........... Tract Evaluation Computer   (NATG)
TEC........... Training and Enterprise Council [British]
TEC........... Training Evaluation and Control
TEC........... Training Exercise Coordinator [Military]   (NVT)
TEC........... Training Extension Course [Army]
TEC........... Transearth Coast [AEC]
TEC........... Transient Early Curvature [Orthopedics]
TEC........... Transient Erythroblastopenia of Childhood [Hematology]
TEC........... Transmission Electronic Control [Bradley Fighting Vehicle] [Army]   (DWSG)
TEC........... Transport Environment Circulation [A publication]
T & EC....... Trauma and Emergency Center [Medicine]
TEC........... Tripartite Engineering Committee [Allied German Occupation Forces]
TEC........... Triple Erasure Correction
TEC........... Tropical Experiment Council [of World Meteorological Organization and International Council on Scientific Unions]
TEC........... Truck Electrical Center [Volvo White Truck Corp.]
TEC........... Type Equipment Code   (MCD)
TECA........ Tartan Educational and Cultural Association   (EA)
TECA........ Technical Evaluation and Countermeasures Assignment
TECA........ Temporary Emergency Court of Appeals
TECA........ Totally Enclosed - Closed-Air Circuit
TECA........ Tower En-Route Control Area [Aviation]   (FAAC)
TECAD..... Technical Advisory [Military]   (CAAL)
TECADS ... Techniques to Counter Air Defense Suppression   (MCD)
Tec Agr ..... Tecnica Agricola [A publication]
Tec Agric (Catania) ... Tecnica Agricola (Catania) [A publication]
Tec Autom ... Tecniche dell'Automazione [A publication]
TECC......... Technology Education for Children Council   (EA)
TECC......... Texas Education Computer Cooperative [Houston] [Information service or system]   (IID)
TECC......... Texas Educational Computer Courseware Database [Texas Education Computer Cooperative] [Information service or system] [Defunct]   (CRD)
TECC........ Thermal Exploration Co. [NASDAQ symbol]   (NQ)
TECCE ...... Tactical Exploitation Collection and Coordination Element   (MCD)
TECD......... Tech Data Corp. [Clearwater, FL] [NASDAQ symbol]   (NQ)
TECD........ Training Equipment Change Directives [Navy]
TECE........ Teleprinter Error Correction Equipment
TECED...... Techniques de l'Energie [A publication]
TECEPT.... Training Equipment Cost Effectiveness Prediction Techniques [Navy]
TECG........ Test and Evaluation Coordinating Group [Military]   (CAAL)
TECH .... Teach Each Customer How [Tire repair training seminar] [Technical Rubber Co.]
TECH .... Technical   (AAG)
TECH .... Technician
TECH .... Technique
TECH .... Technological Education Clearinghouse
TECH .... Technology   (AAG)
Tech .... Technology [A publication]   (APTA)
TECH .... Techtran Industries, Inc. [NASDAQ symbol]   (NQ)
TECH .... Toxic, Explosive, Corrosive, Hazardous Cargo [Shipping]   (DS)
Tech Abstr Bull ... Technical Abstract Bulletin [A publication]
TECHAD .. Technical Advisor [Navy]
Tech Adj .... Technical Adjutant [British military]   (DMA)
Tech Adv Shikoku Agric ... Technical Advances in Shikoku Agriculture [A publication]

Tech Agri... Technique Agricole [*France*] [*A publication*]
Tech Appl Pet ... Techniques et Applications du Petrole [*France*] [*A publication*]
Tech Apskats ... Technikas Apskats [*United States*] [*A publication*]
Tech Assn Pa ... Technical Association Papers [*A publication*]
TECHAUTHIND ... Technical Paper / Author Cross-Index System   (DNAB)
TECHAV... Technical Availability [*Navy*]   (NVT)
Tech Bau.... Technik am Bau [*West Germany*] [*A publication*]
Tech Belge Prothese Dent ... Technicien Belge en Prothese Dentaire [*A publication*]
Tech Ber Heinrich-Hertz Inst (Berlin-Charlottenburg) ... Technischer Bericht. Heinrich-Hertz Institut (Berlin-Charlottenburg) [*A publication*]
Tech Ber Sticht Nederl Graan-Cent ... Technisch Bericht. Stichting Nederlands Graan-Centrum [*A publication*]
Tech Bibliogr Birmingham Public Lib ... Technical Bibliographies. Birmingham Public Libraries [*A publication*]
Tech Bibliogr Ser Birmingham Cent Lib ... Technical Bibliographies Series. Birmingham Central Libraries [*A publication*]
Tech Biochem Biophys Morphol ... Techniques of Biochemical and Biophysical Morphology [*A publication*]
Tech Bul Dep Agric (Malaysia) ... Technical Bulletin. Department of Agriculture (Malaysia) [*A publication*]
Tech Bull Agric Exp Stn Ore St Univ ... Technical Bulletin. Agricultural Experiment Station. Oregon State University [*A publication*]
Tech Bull Agric Exp Stn Univ Ariz ... Technical Bulletin. Arizona Agricultural Experiment Station. University of Arizona [*A publication*]
Tech Bull Agric Exp Stn Wash St ... Technical Bulletin. Agricultural Experiment Station. Washington State Institute of Agricultural Sciences [*A publication*]
Tech Bull Agric Res Inst (Cyprus) ... Technical Bulletin. Agricultural Research Institute (Cyprus) [*A publication*]
Tech Bull Amersham Buchler ... Technisches Bulletin - Amerisham Buchler [*A publication*]
Tech Bull Anim Ind Agric Branch NT ... Technical Bulletin. Animal Industry and Agricultural Branch. Department of the Northern Territory [*A publication*]   (APTA)
Tech Bull Anim Ind Agric Br NT ... Technical Bulletin. Animal Industry and Agriculture Branch. Northern Territory [*A publication*]   (APTA)
Tech Bull Ariz Agr Exp Sta ... Technical Bulletin. Arizona Agricultural Experiment Station [*A publication*]
Tech Bull Ariz Agric Exp Stn ... Technical Bulletin. Arizona Agricultural Experiment Station [*A publication*]
Tech Bull At Energy Organ Iran ... Technical Bulletin. Atomic Energy Organization of Iran [*A publication*]
Tech Bull Banana Res Adv Comm ... Technical Bulletin. Banana Research Advisory Committee [*A publication*]   (APTA)
Tech Bull Can Inland Waters Dir ... Technical Bulletin. Canada Inland Waters Directorate [*A publication*]
Tech Bull Colo Agric Exp Stn ... Technical Bulletin. Colorado Agricultural Experiment Station [*A publication*]
Tech Bull Colo State Univ Agr Exp Sta ... Technical Bulletin. Colorado State University. Agricultural Experiment Station [*A publication*]
Tech Bull Commonwealth Inst Biol Contr ... Technical Bulletin. Commonwealth Institute of Biological Control [*A publication*]
Tech Bull Commonw Inst Biol Control ... Technical Bulletin. Commonwealth Institute of Biological Control [*A publication*]
Tech Bull Cyprus Agr Res Inst ... Technical Bulletin. Cyprus Agricultural Research Institute [*A publication*]
Tech Bull Dep Agric NSW ... New South Wales. Department of Agriculture. Technical Bulletin [*A publication*]   (APTA)
Tech Bull Dep Agric Vict ... Technical Bulletin. Department of Agriculture. Victoria [*A publication*]   (APTA)
Tech Bull Dep Agric West Aust ... Technical Bulletin. Department of Agriculture. Western Australia [*A publication*]   (APTA)
Tech Bull Exp For Taiwan Univ ... Technical Bulletin. Experimental Forest. National Taiwan University [*A publication*]
Tech Bull Fac Agric Kagawa Univ ... Technical Bulletin. Faculty of Agriculture. Kagawa University [*A publication*]
Tech Bull Fac Agr Kagawa Univ ... Technical Bulletin. Faculty of Agriculture. Kagawa University [*A publication*]
Tech Bull Fac Hort Chiba Univ ... Technical Bulletin. Faculty of Horticulture. Chiba University [*A publication*]
Tech Bull Fac Hortic Chiba Univ ... Technical Bulletin. Faculty of Horticulture. Chiba University [*A publication*]
Tech Bull Fla Agric Exp Stn ... Technical Bulletin. Florida Agricultural Experiment Station [*A publication*]
Tech Bull GA Agr Exp Sta ... Technical Bulletin. Georgia Agricultural Experiment Stations. University of Georgia. College of Agriculture [*A publication*]
Tech Bull Gt Brit Min Agr Fish Food ... Technical Bulletin. Great Britain Ministry of Agiculture, Fisheries, and Food [*A publication*]
Tech Bull Harper Adams Agr Coll ... Technical Bulletin. Harper Adams Agricultural College [*A publication*]
Tech Bull Hawaii Agric Exp Stn ... Technical Bulletin. Hawaii Agricultural Experiment Station [*A publication*]

Tech Bull Hokkaido Agric Exp Stn ... Technical Bulletin. Hokkaido Agricultural Experiment Station [*A publication*]
Tech Bull Inst Ld Wat Mgmt Res ... Technical Bulletin. Institute for Land and Water Management Research [*A publication*]
Tech Bull Kagawa Agr Coll ... Technical Bulletin. Kagawa Agricultural College [*A publication*]
Tech Bull Kans Agr Exp Sta ... Technical Bulletin. Kansas Agricultural Experiment Station [*A publication*]
Tech Bull Kans Agric Exp Stn ... Technical Bulletin. Kansas Agricultural Experiment Station [*A publication*]
Tech Bull Land Resour Div Dir Overseas Surv ... Technical Bulletin. Land Resources Division. Directorate of Overseas Surveys [*A publication*]
Tech Bull Life Sci Agric Exp Stn (Maine) ... Technical Bulletin. Life Sciences and Agriculture Experiment Station (Maine) [*A publication*]
Tech Bull Life Sci Agric Exp Stn Univ Maine ... Technical Bulletin. Life Sciences and Agriculture Experiment Station. University of Maine at Orono [*A publication*]
Tech Bull Mich State Univ Agr Exp Sta ... Technical Bulletin. Michigan State University. Agricultural Experiment Station [*A publication*]
Tech Bull Mich St Coll Agric Exp Stn ... Technical Bulletin. Michigan State College. Agricultural Experiment Station [*A publication*]
Tech Bull Minist Agric E Niger ... Technical Bulletin. Ministry of Agriculture of Eastern Nigeria [*A publication*]
Tech Bull Minist Agric Fish Fd ... Technical Bulletin. Ministry of Agriculture, Fisheries, and Food [*A publication*]
Tech Bull Minist Agric Fish Food (GB) ... Technical Bulletin. Ministry of Agriculture, Fisheries, and Food (Great Britain) [*A publication*]
Tech Bull Minn Agric Exp Sta ... Technical Bulletin. University of Minnesota. Agricultural Experiment Station [*A publication*]
Tech Bull Minn Agric Exp Stn ... Technical Bulletin. Minnesota Agricultural Experiment Station [*A publication*]
Tech Bull Miss Agr Exp Sta ... Technical Bulletin. Mississippi Agricultural Experiment Station [*A publication*]
Tech Bull Miss Agric For Exp Stn ... Technical Bulletin. Mississippi Agricultural and Forestry Experiment Station [*A publication*]
Tech Bull Miyagi Prefect Agr Exp Sta ... Technical Bulletin. Miyagi Prefectural Agricultural Experiment Station [*A publication*]
Tech Bull Mont Agr Exp Sta ... Technical Bulletin. Montana Agricultural Experiment Station [*A publication*]
Tech Bull NC Agr Exp Sta ... Technical Bulletin. North Carolina Agricultural Experiment Station [*A publication*]
Tech Bull NC Agric Exp Sta ... Technical Bulletin. North Carolina Agricultural Experiment Station [*A publication*]
Tech Bull N Carol Agric Exp Stn ... Technical Bulletin. North Carolina Agricultural Experiment Station [*A publication*]
Tech Bull N Carol St Coll Agric Exp Stn ... Technical Bulletin. North Carolina State College. Agricultural Experiment Station [*A publication*]
Tech Bull N Carol St Univ Agric Exp Stn ... Technical Bulletin. North Carolina State University. Agricultural Experiment Station [*A publication*]
Tech Bull Okla State Univ Agr Exp Sta ... Technical Bulletin. Oklahoma State University. Agricultural Experiment Station [*A publication*]
Tech Bull Ore Agric Exp Stn ... Technical Bulletin. Oregon Agricultural Experiment Station [*A publication*]
Tech Bull Oreg State Coll Agr Exp Sta ... Technical Bulletin. Oregon State College. Agricultural Experiment Station [*A publication*]
Tech Bull Regist Med Technol ... Technical Bulletin. Registry of Medical Technologists [*A publication*]
Tech Bull Rhodesia Agric J ... Technical Bulletin. Rhodesia Agricultural Journal [*A publication*]
Tech Bull SC Agric Exp Stn ... Technical Bulletin. South Carolina Agricultural Experiment Station [*A publication*]
Tech Bull S Dak Agr Exp Sta ... Technical Bulletin. South Dakota Agricultural Experiment Station [*A publication*]
Tech Bull Sug Manufact Ass ... Technical Bulletin. Sugar Manufacturers' Association [*A publication*]
Tech Bull Sulphur Inst ... Technical Bulletin. Sulphur Institute [*A publication*]
Tech Bull Taiwan Agric Res Inst ... Technical Bulletin. Taiwan Agricultural Research Institute [*A publication*]
Tech Bull Taiwan Fertil Co ... Technical Bulletin. Taiwan Fertilizer Co. [*A publication*]
Tech Bull TARC (Trop Agric Res Cent) ... Technical Bulletin. TARC (Tropical Agriculture Research Center) [*A publication*]
Tech Bull Tex Eng Exp Stn ... Technical Bulletin. Texas Engineering Experiment Station [*A publication*]
Tech Bull Tokushima Bunri Univ ... Technical Bulletin. Tokushima Bunri University [*A publication*]
Tech Bull Trop Agric Res Cent ... Technical Bulletin. Tropical Agriculture Research Center [*A publication*]
Tech Bull UAR Minist Agric Agrar Reform ... Technical Bulletin. United Arab Republic Ministry of Agriculture and Agrarian Reform [*A publication*]

Tech Bull Univ Maine Life Sci Agric Exp Stn ... Technical Bulletin. University of Maine. Life Sciences and Agriculture Experiment Station [*A publication*]

Tech Bull Univ Minn Agr Exp Sta ... Technical Bulletin. University of Minnesota. Agricultural Experiment Station [*A publication*]

Tech Bull Univ Nev Agr Exp Sta ... Technical Bulletin. University of Nevada. Agricultural Experiment Station [*A publication*]

Tech Bull Univ Philippines Coll Agr ... Technical Bulletin. University of the Philippines. College of Agriculture [*A publication*]

Tech Bull USDA ... Technical Bulletin. United States Department of Agriculture [*A publication*]

Tech Bull US Dep Agric ... Technical Bulletin. United States Department of Agriculture [*A publication*]

Tech Bull US Dep Agric Agric Res Serv ... Technical Bulletin. United States Department of Agriculture. Agricultural Research Service [*A publication*]

Tech Bull US For Serv ... Technical Bulletin. United States Forest Service [*A publication*]

Tech Bull VA Agr Exp Sta ... Technical Bulletin. Virginia Agricultural Experiment Station [*A publication*]

Tech Bull Vic Ctry Rd Bd ... Technical Bulletin. Victoria Country Roads Board [*A publication*] (APTA)

Tech Bull Wash Agr Exp Sta ... Technical Bulletin. Washington Agricultural Experiment Station [*A publication*]

Tech Bull Wash Agric Exp Stn ... Technical Bulletin. Washington Agricultural Experiment Station [*A publication*]

Tech Bull Wash State Univ Coll Agric Res Cent ... Technical Bulletin. Washington State University. College of Agriculture. Research Center [*A publication*]

Tech Bull West Aust Dep Agric ... Technical Bulletin. Western Australian Department of Agriculture [*A publication*]

Tech Bul VIUS Agric Exp Stn ... Technical Bulletin. Virgin Islands of the United States Agricultural Experiment Station [*A publication*]

Tech(CEI) ... Technician (Council of Engineering Institutions) [*British*] (DI)

Tech CEM ... Techniques CEM [*Compagnie Electro-Mecanique*] [*A publication*]

Tech Chem (Prague) ... Technika v Chemii (Prague) [*A publication*]

Tech Chron ... Technika Chronika [*A publication*]

Tech Circ Maurit Sug Ind Res Inst ... Technical Circular. Mauritius Sugar Industry Research Institute [*A publication*]

Tech Commun ... Technical Communications [*A publication*]

Tech Commun Bur Sugar Exp Stn (Queensl) ... Technical Communication. Bureau of Sugar Experiment Stations (Queensland) [*A publication*] (APTA)

Tech Commun Bur Sug Exp Stns (Qd) ... Technical Communication. Bureau of Sugar Experiment Stations (Queensland) [*A publication*] (APTA)

Tech Commun Central Inform Libr Edit Sect CSIRO ... Technical Communication. Central Information, Library, and Editorial Section. Commonwealth Scientific and Industrial Research Organisation [*A publication*] (APTA)

Tech Commun CILES CSIRO ... Technical Communication. Central Information, Library, and Editorial Section. Commonwealth Scientific and Industrial Research Organisation [*A publication*] (APTA)

Tech Commun CSIRO (Aust) ... Technical Communication. Minerals Research Laboratories. Commonwealth Scientific and Industrial Research Organisation (Australia) [*A publication*]

Tech Commun CSIRO Div Mineral ... Australia. Commonwealth Scientific and Industrial Research Organisation. Division of Mineralogy. Technical Communication [*A publication*] (APTA)

Tech Commun CSIRO Div Miner Chem ... Australia. Commonwealth Scientific and Industrial Research Organisation. Division of Mineral Chemistry. Technical Communication [*A publication*] (APTA)

Tech Commun CSIRO Inst Earth Resour ... CSIRO [*Commonwealth Scientific and Industrial Research Organisation*] Institute of Earth Resources. Technical Communication [*A publication*] (APTA)

Tech Commun CSIRO Miner Res Lab ... CSIRO [*Commonwealth Scientific and Industrial Research Organisation*] Minerals Research Laboratories. Technical Communication [*A publication*] (APTA)

Tech Commun Dept Agr Tech Serv Repub S Afr ... Technical Communication. Department of Agricultural Technical Services. Republic of South Africa [*A publication*]

Tech Commun Div Miner Chem CSIRO ... Technical Communication. Division of Mineral Chemistry. Commonwealth Scientific and Industrial Research Organisation [*A publication*] (APTA)

Tech Commun Div Miner CSIRO ... Technical Communication. Division of Mineralogy. Commonwealth Scientific and Industrial Research Organisation [*A publication*] (APTA)

Tech Commun For Bur (Oxf) ... Technical Communication. Commonwealth Forestry Bureau (Oxford) [*A publication*]

Tech Commun Miner Res Lab CSIRO ... Technical Communication. Minerals Research Laboratories. Commonwealth Scientific and Industrial Research Organisation [*A publication*] (APTA)

Tech Commun R Sch Mines ... Technical Communications. Royal School of Mines [*A publication*]

Tech Commun S Afr Dep Agric Fish ... Technical Communication. South Africa Department of Agriculture and Fisheries [*A publication*]

Tech Commun S Afr Dep Agric Tech Serv ... Technical Communications. South Africa Department of Agricultural Technical Services [*A publication*]

Tech Commun Woodld Ecol Unit CSIRO ... Technical Communication. Woodland Ecology Unit. Commonwealth Scientific and Industrial Research Organisation [*A publication*] (APTA)

Tech Conf Proc Irrig Assoc ... Technical Conference Proceedings. Irrigation Association [*A publication*]

Tech & Cult ... Technology and Culture [*A publication*]

Tech & Culture ... Technology and Culture [*A publication*]

Tech Cybern USSR ... Technical Cybernetics USSR [*A publication*]

TECHDATA ... Technical Data [*DoD*]

Tech Data Dig ... Technical Data Digest [*A publication*]

Tech Data Digest ... Technical Data Digest [*United States*] [*A publication*]

Tech Dig .... Technical Digest [*A publication*]

Tech Doc FAO Plant Prot Comm Southeast Asia Pac Reg ... Technical Document. Food and Agriculture Organization of the United Nations. Plant Protection Committee for the South East Asia and Pacific Region [*A publication*]

Tech Eau.... Technique de l'Eau et de l'Assainissement [*A publication*]

Tech Econ Publ Tatabanyai Szenbanyak ... Technical-Economical Publication. Tatabanyai Szenbanyak [*A publication*]

Tech Econ Stud Inst Geol Geophys Ser I ... Technical and Economical Studies. Institute of Geology and Geophysics. Series I. Mineralogy-Petrology [*A publication*]

Tech Educ.. Technical Education [*A publication*]

Tech Educ Abstr ... Technical Education Abstracts [*A publication*]

Tech Educ Yrbk ... Technician Education Yearbook [*A publication*]

Tech Electrochem ... Techniques of Electrochemistry [*A publication*]

Tech Electron Son Telev ... Techniques Electroniques - Son - Television [*A publication*]

Tech Energ ... Techniques de l'Energie [*France*] [*A publication*]

Tech Energie ... Techniques de l'Energie [*A publication*]

Tech Energ (Paris) ... Techniques de l'Energie (Paris) [*A publication*]

Tech Environ ... Technology and Environment [*A publication*]

TECHEVAL ... Technical Evaluation [*Navy*] (NG)

Tech Fore... Technology Forecasts and Technology Surveys [*A publication*]

Tech Forum Soc Vac Coaters ... Technical Forum. Society of Vacuum Coaters [*A publication*]

Tech Gem... Technische Gemeinschaft [*A publication*]

Tech Gemeindebl ... Technisches Gemeindeblatt [*West Germany*] [*A publication*]

TechGeol.... Technical Associate of the Geological Society [*British*] (DBQ)

Tech Gesch ... Technik-Geschichte [*A publication*]

Tech Gids Ziekenhuis Instelling ... Technische Gids voor Ziekenhuis en Instelling [*A publication*]

TECHGL... Technological

Tech Gospod Morsk ... Technika i Gospodarka Morska [*Poland*] [*A publication*]

Tech Heute ... Technik Heute [*German Federal Republic*] [*A publication*]

Tech Hogesch Delft Afd Werktuigbouwkd (Rep) WTHD ... Technische Hogeschool Delft. Afdeling der Werktuigbouwkunde (Report) WTHD [*A publication*]

Tech Illus... Technology Illustrated [*A publication*]

Tech-Index Plasmaphys Forsch Fusionreakt ... Technik-Index ueber Plasmaphysikalische Forschung und Fusionsreaktoren [*West Germany*] [*A publication*]

Tech Inf Bull ... Technical Information Bulletin. National Information Service on Drug Abuse [*A publication*]

Tech Inf GRW ... Technische Information GRW [*Geraete- und Regler Werke*] [*East Germany*] [*A publication*]

TECHINFO ... Technical Information [*DoD*]

Tech Info Service ... Technical Information Service [*A publication*]

Tech Ing Genie Chim ... Techniques de l'Ingenieur. Genie Chimique [*A publication*]

TECHINT ... Technical Intelligence [*Spy satellites, etc.*]

Tech Jahrb ... Technica Jahrbuch [*A publication*]

Tech J Ankara Nucl Res Cent ... Technical Journal. Ankara Nuclear Research Center [*A publication*]

Tech J Ankara Nucl Res Train Cent ... Technical Journal. Ankara Nuclear Research and Training Center [*A publication*]

Tech J Jap Broadcast Corp ... Technical Journal. Japan Broadcasting Corp. [*A publication*]

Tech J Jpn Broadcast Corp ... Technical Journal. Japan Broadcasting Corp. [*A publication*]

Tech Knih.. Technicka Knihovna [*A publication*]

Tech Knihovna ... Technicka Knihovna [*A publication*]

Tech Kurir ... Technikai Kurir [*Hungary*] [*A publication*]

TECHL...... Technical

Tech Lab Cent Res Inst Electr Power Ind Rep ... Technical Laboratory. Central Research Institute of the Electrical Power Industry. Report [*Japan*] [*A publication*]

Tech Landwirt ... Technik und Landwirtschaft. Landtechnischer Ratgeber [*A publication*]
Tech Life Sci Biochem ... Techniques in the Life Sciences. Biochemistry [*A publication*]
Tech Lotnicza Astronaut ... Technika Lotnicza i Astronautyczna [*Poland*] [*A publication*]
TECHMAN ... Technical Manual (DNAB)
Tech Manpower ... Technical Manpower [*A publication*] (APTA)
Tech Meas Med ... Techniques of Measurement in Medicine [*A publication*]
Tech Mem Calif Inst Technol Jet Propul Lab ... Technical Memorandum. California Institute of Technology. Jet Propulsion Laboratory [*A publication*]
Tech Memo Daresbury Lab ... Technical Memorandum. Daresbury Laboratory [*A publication*]
Tech Memo Daresbury Nucl Phys Lab ... Technical Memorandum. Daresbury Nuclear Physics Laboratory [*A publication*]
Tech Memo Div Appl Geomech CSIRO ... Technical Memorandum. Division of Applied Geomechanics. Commonwealth Scientific and Industrial Research Organisation [*A publication*] (APTA)
Tech Memo Div Land Use Res CSIRO ... Technical Memorandum. Division of Land Use Research. Commonwealth Scientific and Industrial Research Organisation [*A publication*] (APTA)
Tech Memo Div Wildl Res CSIRO ... Technical Memorandum. Division of Wildlife Research. Commonwealth Scientific and Industrial Research Organisation [*A publication*] (APTA)
Tech Memo Jet Propul Lab Calif Inst Technol ... Technical Memorandum. Jet Propulsion Laboratory. California Institute of Technology [*A publication*]
Tech Memor Plant Protection Ltd ... Technical Memoranda. Plant Protection Ltd. [*A publication*]
Tech Mess ATM ... Technisches Messen ATM [*Archiv fuer Technisches Messen*] [*A publication*]
Tech Mess-TM ... Techinsches Messen-TM [*A publication*]
Tech Methods Polym Eval ... Techniques and Methods of Polymer Evaluation [*A publication*]
Tech Meun ... Technique Meuniere [*A publication*]
Tech Mitt ... Technische Mitteilungen [*A publication*]
Tech Mitt AEG-Telefunken ... Technische Mitteilungen AEG- [*Allgemeine Elektrizitaets-Gesellschaft*] Telefunken [*A publication*]
Tech Mitteil Krupp Forschungsber ... Technische Mitteilungen Krupp. Forschungsberichte [*A publication*]
Tech Mitteil Krupp Werksber ... Technische Mitteilungen Krupp. Werksberichte [*A publication*]
Tech Mitt (Essen) ... Technische Mitteilungen (Essen) [*A publication*]
Tech Mitt Krupp ... Technische Mitteilungen Krupp [*West Germany*] [*A publication*]
Tech Mitt Krupp Forschungsber ... Technische Mitteilungen Krupp. Forschungsberichte [*A publication*]
Tech Mitt Krupp Werksber ... Technische Mitteilungen Krupp. Werksberichte [*A publication*]
Tech Mitt PTT ... Technische Mitteilungen PTT [*A publication*]
Tech Mitt RFZ ... Technische Mitteilungen. RFZ [*Rundfunk- und Fernsehtechnisches Zentralamt*] [*A publication*]
TechMIWPC ... Technician Member of the Institute of Water Pollution Control [*British*] (DI)
Tech Mod ... Technique Moderne [*A publication*]
TECHMOD ... Technology Modernization Program [*DoD*]
Tech Motoryzacyjna ... Technika Motoryzacyjna [*A publication*]
TECHN ..... Technical (EY)
TECHN ..... Technician
TECHN ..... Technology
Techn Agric Int ... Technique Agricole Internationale [*A publication*]
Techn Archit ... Techniques et Architecture [*A publication*]
Techn Ber Lorenz ... Technische Berichte der C. Lorenz [*A publication*]
Techn Bull Reg Med Technol ... Technical Bulletin. Registry of Medical Technologists [*A publication*]
Techn Chron ... Technika Chronika [*A publication*]
Techn Cult ... Technology and Culture [*A publication*]
Techn Dict ... Crabb's Technological Dictionary [*A publication*] (DLA)
Tech News ... Technical News [*A publication*]
Tech Newslett For Prod Res Inst (Ghana) ... Technical Newsletter. Forest Products Research Institute (Kumasi, Ghana) [*A publication*]
Tech News Serv Sarabhai M Chem ... Technical News Service. Sarabhai M. Chemicals [*A publication*]
Techn Hosp ... Techniques Hospitalieres, Medico-Sociales, et Sanitaires [*A publication*]
Technical J ... Technical Journal [*A publication*]
Technic Int ... Technic International [*West Germany*] [*A publication*]
Techn Ind Rd ... Technische und Industrielle Rundschau [*A publication*]
Technion Isr Inst Technol Dep Chem Eng Rep CE ... Technion-Israel Institute of Technology. Department of Chemical Engineering. Report CE [*A publication*]
Techniques Phys ... Techniques of Physics [*A publication*]
Techn Lab ... Techniques de Laboratoire [*A publication*]
Technmcs ... Technometrics [*A publication*]
Techn Mitt Krupp ... Technische Mitteilungen Krupp [*A publication*]
Techn Mod ... Technique Moderne [*A publication*]
TECHNOL ... Technologic
Technol ...... Technology [*A publication*] (APTA)
Technol Conserv ... Technology and Conservation [*A publication*]

Technol Cul ... Technology and Culture [*A publication*]
Technol Dev Rep EPS (Can Environ Prot Serv) ... Technology Development Report EPS (Canada Environmental Protection Service) [*A publication*]
Technol For ... Technological Forecasting and Social Change [*A publication*]
Technol Forecast ... Technological Forecasting [*Later, Technological Forecasting and Social Change*] [*A publication*]
Technol Forecasting ... Technological Forecasting [*Later, Technological Forecasting and Social Change*] [*United States*] [*A publication*]
Technol Forecasting Soc Change ... Technological Forecasting and Social Change [*A publication*]
Technol Forecast and Soc Change ... Technological Forecasting and Social Change [*A publication*]
Technol Index Plasmaphys Res Fusion React ... Technology Index for Plasmaphysics Research and Fusion Reactors [*West Germany*] [*A publication*]
Technol Inf (Sapporo) ... Technology and Information (Sapporo) [*A publication*]
Technol Ireland ... Technology Ireland [*A publication*]
Technol Japan ... Science and Technology of Japan [*A publication*]
Technol J Natl Sci Dev Board (Philip) ... Technology Journal. National Science Development Board (Philippines) [*A publication*]
Technol-Nachr Manage Inf ... Technologie-Nachrichten. Management-Informationen [*West Germany*] [*A publication*]
Technol-Nachr Programm-Inf ... Technologie-Nachrichten Programm-Informationen [*A publication*]
Technol-Nachr Sonderdienst-Programme ... Technologie-Nachrichten Sonderdienst-Programme [*German Federal Republic*] [*A publication*]
Technol News ... Technology News. Bureau of Mines [*United States*] [*A publication*]
Technol News Bur Mines ... Technology News. Bureau of Mines [*United States*] [*A publication*]
Technolog Pap Div Forest Prod CSIRO ... Technological Paper. Division of Forest Products. Commonwealth Scientific and Industrial Research Organisation [*A publication*] (APTA)
Technol Pap Div Forest Prod CSIRO ... Technological Paper. Division of Forest Products. Commonwealth Scientific and Industrial Research Organisation [*A publication*] (APTA)
Technol Pap Forest Prod Lab Div Appl Chem CSIRO ... Technological Paper. Forest Products Laboratory. Division of Applied Chemistry. Commonwealth Scientific and Industrial Research Organisation [*A publication*]
Technol Pap Forest Prod Lab Div Bldg Res CSIRO ... Technological Paper. Forest Products Laboratory. Division of Building Research. Commonwealth Scientific and Industrial Research Organisation [*A publication*] (APTA)
Technol Pap For Prod Lab Div Appl Chem CSIRO ... Technological Paper. Forest Products Laboratory. Division of Applied Chemistry. Commonwealth Scientific and Industrial Research Organisation [*A publication*] (APTA)
Technol Pap For Prod Lab Div Build Res CSIRO ... Technological Paper. Forest Products Laboratory. Division of Building Research. Commonwealth Scientific and Industrial Research Organisation [*A publication*] (APTA)
Technol R ... Technology Review [*Boston*] [*A publication*]
Technol Rep Iwate Univ ... Technology Reports. Iwate University [*A publication*]
Technol Rep Kansai Univ ... Technology Reports. Kansai University [*A publication*]
Technol Rep Kyushu Univ ... Technology Reports. Kyushu University [*A publication*]
Technol Rep Osaka Univ ... Technology Reports. Osaka University [*A publication*]
Technol Rep Seikei Univ ... Technology Reports. Seikei University [*A publication*]
Technol Rep Tohoku Univ ... Technology Reports. Tohoku University [*Sendaik, Japan*] [*A publication*]
Technol Rep Tohoku Univ (Jpn) ... Technology Reports. Tohoku University (Japan) [*A publication*]
Technol Rep Yamaguchi Univ ... Technology Reports. Yamaguchi University [*A publication*]
Technol Respir ... Technologie Respiratoire [*A publication*]
Technol Rev ... Technology Review [*A publication*]
Technol Rev Chonnam Natl Univ ... Technological Review. Chonnam National University [*Republic of Korea*] [*A publication*]
Technols .... Technologies
Technol Sci Chung Ang Univ ... Technologies and Sciences. Chung-Ang University [*A publication*]
Technol Soc ... Technology and Society [*A publication*]
Technol (Syd) ... Technology (Sydney) [*A publication*] (APTA)
Technol Use Lignite ... Technology and Use of Lignite. Proceedings of a Symposium [*A publication*]
Technol Utiliz Prog Rep ... Technology Utilization Program Report [*A publication*]
Technomet ... Technometrics [*A publication*]
Technop ..... Technopaegnion [*of Ausonius*] [*Classical studies*] (OCD)
TECHNOTE ... Technical Note [*or Notice*] (DNAB)
Tech Note Aust Def Stand Lab ... Technical Note. Australia Defence Standards Laboratories [*A publication*]

Tech Note Brick Manuf Assoc NSW ... Technical Note. Brick Manufacturers Association of New South Wales [*A publication*] (APTA)
Tech Note Brick Mf Assoc NSW ... Technical Note. Brick Manufacturers Association of New South Wales [*A publication*] (APTA)
Tech Note Charles Kolling Res Lab ... Technical Note. Charles Kolling Research Laboratory. Department of Mechanical Engineering. University of Sydney [*A publication*] (APTA)
Tech Note Def Stand Lab Aust ... Australia. Defence Standards Laboratories. Technical Note [*A publication*] (APTA)
Tech Note Dep For Res (Nigeria) ... Technical Note. Department of Forest Research (Nigeria) [*A publication*]
Tech Note E Afr Agric For Res Organ ... Technical Note. East African Agriculture and Forestry Research Organization [*A publication*]
Tech Note For Dep (Brit Solomon Islands Protect) ... Technical Note. Forestry Department (British Solomon Islands Protectorate) [*A publication*]
Tech Note For Dep (Kenya) ... Technical Note. Forest Department (Nairobi, Kenya) [*A publication*]
Tech Note For Dep (Uganda) ... Technical Note. Forest Department (Uganda) [*A publication*]
Tech Note For Prod Res Ind Dev Comm (Philipp) ... Technical Note. Forest Products Research and Industries Development Commission (Philippines) [*A publication*]
Tech Note For Prod Res Inst (Ghana) ... Technical Note. Forest Products Research Institute (Ghana) [*A publication*]
Tech Note For Timb Bur ... Technical Note. Bureau of Forestry and Timber [*A publication*] (APTA)
Tech Note Harbour Tech Res Inst Minist Transp (Jpn) ... Technical Note. Port and Harbour Technical Research Institute. Ministry of Transportation (Japan) [*A publication*]
Tech Note Mater Res Lab Aust ... Australia. Materials Research Laboratories. Technical Note [*A publication*] (APTA)
Tech Note Oji Inst For Tree Impr ... Technical Note. Oji Institute for Forest Tree Improvement [*A publication*]
Tech Note Quetico-Sup Wild Res Cent ... Technical Note. Quetico-Superior Wilderness Research Center [*A publication*]
Tech Note Res Inst Ind Saf ... Technical Note. Research Institute of Industrial Safety [*A publication*]
Tech Notes Clay Prod ... Technical Notes on Clay Products [*Brick Development Research Institute*] [*A publication*] (APTA)
Tech Notes For Comm NSW ... Technical Notes. Forestry Commission of New South Wales [*A publication*]
Tech Notes NSW For Comm Div Wood Technol ... New South Wales. Forestry Commission. Division of Wood Technology. Technical Notes [*A publication*] (APTA)
Tech Note Sol Energy Stud CSIRO ... Technical Note. Solar Energy Studies. Commonwealth Scientific and Industrial Research Organisation [*A publication*] (APTA)
Tech Notes Rubber Ind ... Technical Notes for the Rubber Industry [*A publication*]
Tech Notes Rubb Ind ... Technical Notes for the Rubber Industry [*A publication*]
Techn Pharm ... Technique Pharmaceutique [*A publication*]
TECHNQ .. Technique
Techn Rd.... Technische Rundschau [*A publication*]
Techn Rep Brit El All Ind Res Ass ... Technical Report. British Electrical and Allied Industries Research Association [*A publication*]
Techn Rep Ser Wld Hlth Org ... Technical Report Series. World Health Organisation [*A publication*]
Techn Rep Tohoku ... Technology Reports. Tohoku Imperial University [*A publication*]
Techn Rundschau ... Technische Rundschau [*A publication*]
Techn Sci Munic ... Techniques et Sciences Municipales [*A publication*]
Techn Soc .. Technology and Society [*A publication*]
Techn Ueberw ... Technische Ueberwachung [*A publication*]
TECHOPEVAL ... Technical Operational Evaluation
Tech Pap Agric Exp Stn (P Rico) ... Technical Paper. Agricultural Experiment Station (Puerto Rico) [*A publication*]
Tech Pap Amer Pulpw Ass ... Technical Papers. American Pulpwood Association [*A publication*]
Tech Pap Anim Res Lab CSIRO ... Technical Paper. Animal Research Laboratories. Commonwealth Scientific and Industrial Research Organisation [*A publication*] (APTA)
Tech Pap Anim Res Labs CSIRO ... Technical Paper. Animal Research Laboratories. Commonwealth Scientific and Industrial Research Organization [*A publication*]
Tech Pap (Aust) CSIRO Div Appl Geomech ... Technical Paper. (Australia) Commonwealth Scientific and Industrial Research Organisation. Division of Applied Geomechanics [*A publication*]
Tech Pap (Aust) CSIRO Div Mineragraphic Invest ... Technical Paper. (Australia) Commonwealth Scientific and Industrial Research Organisation. Division of Mineragraphic Investigation [*A publication*]
Tech Pap Aust Water Resour Coun ... Technical Paper. Australian Water Resources Council [*A publication*] (APTA)
Tech Pap Aust Wat Resour Coun ... Technical Paper. Australian Water Resources Council [*A publication*] (APTA)
Tech Pap Calif Dep Agric ... Technical Papers. California Department of Agriculture [*A publication*]

Tech Pap Canad Pulp Pap Ass ... Technical Paper. Canadian Pulp and Paper Association [*A publication*]
Tech Pap Dep For (Qd) ... Technical Paper. Department of Forestry (Queensland) [*A publication*]
Tech Pap Dep For (Queensl) ... Technical Paper. Department of Forestry (Queensland) [*A publication*] (APTA)
Tech Pap Div Appl Chem CSIRO ... Technical Paper. Division of Applied Chemistry. Commonwealth Scientific and Industrial Research Organisation [*A publication*] (APTA)
Tech Pap Div Appl Geomech CSIRO ... Technical Paper. Division of Applied Geomechanics. Commonwealth Scientific and Industrial Research Organisation [*A publication*] (APTA)
Tech Pap Div Appl Miner CSIRO ... Technical Paper. Division of Applied Mineralogy. Commonwealth Scientific and Industrial Research Organisation [*A publication*] (APTA)
Tech Pap Div Appl Org Chem CSIRO ... Technical Paper. Division of Applied Organic Chemistry. Commonwealth Scientific and Industrial Research Organisation [*A publication*] (APTA)
Tech Pap Div Atmosph Phys CSIRO ... Technical Paper. Division of Atmospheric Physics. Commonwealth Scientific and Industrial Research Organisation [*A publication*] (APTA)
Tech Pap Div Atmos Phys CSIRO ... Technical Paper. Division of Atmospheric Physics. Commonwealth Scientific and Industrial Research Organisation [*A publication*] (APTA)
Tech Pap Div Bldg Res CSIRO ... Technical Paper. Division of Building Research. Commonwealth Scientific and Industrial Research Organisation [*A publication*] (APTA)
Tech Pap Div Build Res CSIRO ... Technical Paper. Division of Building Research. Commonwealth Scientific and Industrial Research Organisation [*A publication*] (APTA)
Tech Pap Div Chem Technol CSIRO ... Technical Paper. Division of Chemical Technology. Commonwealth Scientific and Industrial Research Organisation [*A publication*] (APTA)
Tech Pap Div Ent CSIRO ... Technical Paper. Division of Entomology. Commonwealth Scientific and Industrial Research Organisation [*A publication*] (APTA)
Tech Pap Div Fd Preserv CSIRO ... Technical Paper. Division of Food Preservation. Commonwealth Scientific and Industrial Research Organisation [*A publication*] (APTA)
Tech Pap Div Fd Res CSIRO ... Technical Paper. Division of Food Research. Commonwealth Scientific and Industrial Research Organisation [*A publication*] (APTA)
Tech Pap Div Fd Res CSIRO (Aust) ... Technical Paper. Division of Food Research. Commonwealth Scientific and Industrial Research Organisation (Australia) [*A publication*]
Tech Pap Div Fish Oceanogr CSIRO ... Technical Paper. Division of Fisheries and Oceanography. Commonwealth Scientific and Industrial Research Organisation [*A publication*] (APTA)
Tech Pap Div Food Res CSIRO ... Technical Paper. Division of Food Research. Commonwealth Scientific and Industrial Research Organisation [*A publication*] (APTA)
Tech Pap Div Land Resour Manage CSIRO ... Technical Paper. Division of Land Resources Management. Commonwealth Scientific and Industrial Research Organisation [*A publication*] (APTA)
Tech Pap Div Land Use Res CSIRO ... Technical Paper. Division of Land Use Research. Commonwealth Scientific and Industrial Research Organisation [*A publication*] (APTA)
Tech Pap Div Ld Res CSIRO ... Technical Paper. Division of Land Research. Commonwealth Scientific and Industrial Research Organisation [*A publication*] (APTA)
Tech Pap Div Ld Res Reg Surv CSIRO (Aust) ... Technical Papers. Division of Land Research and Regional Survey. Commonwealth Scientific and Industrial Research Organisation (Australia) [*A publication*]
Tech Pap Div Ld Use Res CSIRO ... Technical Paper. Division of Land Use Research. Commonwealth Scientific and Industrial Research Organisation [*A publication*] (APTA)
Tech Pap Div Math Stat CSIRO ... Technical Paper. Division of Mathematics and Statistics. Commonwealth Scientific and Industrial Research Organisation [*A publication*] (APTA)
Tech Pap Div Math Statist CSIRO ... Technical Paper. Division of Mathematical Statistics. Commonwealth Scientific and Industrial Research Organisation [*A publication*]
Tech Pap Div Mat Statist CSIRO ... Technical Paper. Division of Mathematical Statistics. Commonwealth Scientific and Industrial Research Organisation [*A publication*] (APTA)
Tech Pap Div Meteorol Phys CSIRO ... Technical Paper. Division of Meteorological Physics. Commonwealth Scientific and Industrial Research Organisation [*A publication*] (APTA)
Tech Pap Div Met Phys CSIRO ... Technical Paper. Division of Meteorological Physics. Commonwealth Scientific and Industrial Research Organisation [*A publication*] (APTA)
Tech Pap Div Plant Ind CSIRO ... Technical Paper. Division of Plant Industry. Commonwealth Scientific and Industrial Research Organisation [*A publication*] (APTA)
Tech Pap Div Pl Ind CSIRO ... Technical Paper. Division of Plant Industry. Commonwealth Scientific and Industrial Research Organisation [*A publication*] (APTA)

Tech Pap Div Pl Ind CSIRO (Aust) ... Technical Papers. Division of Plant Industry. Commonwealth Scientific and Industrial Research Organisation (Australia) [*A publication*]
Tech Pap Div Soil Mechanics CSIRO ... Technical Paper. Division of Soil Mechanics. Commonwealth Scientific and Industrial Research Organisation [*A publication*] (APTA)
Tech Pap Div Soils CSIRO ... Technical Paper. Division of Soils. Commonwealth Scientific and Industrial Research Organisation [*A publication*] (APTA)
Tech Pap Div Tech Conf Soc Plast Eng ... Technical Papers. Divisional Technical Conference. Society of Plastics Engineers [*A publication*]
Tech Pap Div Trop Agron CSIRO ... Technical Paper. Division of Tropical Agronomy. Commonwealth Scientific and Industrial Research Organisation [*A publication*] (APTA)
Tech Pap Div Trop Crops Pastures CSIRO ... Technical Paper. Division of Tropical Crops and Pastures. Commonwealth Scientific and Industrial Research Organisation [*A publication*] (APTA)
Tech Pap Div Trop Pastures CSIRO ... Technical Paper. Division of Tropical Pastures. Commonwealth Scientific and Industrial Research Organisation [*A publication*] (APTA)
Tech Pap Div Wildl Res CSIRO ... Technical Paper. Division of Wildlife Research. Commonwealth Scientific and Industrial Research Organisation [*A publication*] (APTA)
Tech Pap For Comm NSW ... Technical Paper. Forestry Commission of New South Wales [*A publication*]
Tech Pap For Res Inst NZ For Serv ... Technical Paper. Forest Research Institute. New Zealand Forest Service [*A publication*]
Tech Pap Hydrol ... Technical Papers in Hydrology [*A publication*]
Tech Pap Inst Pet ... Technical Papers. Institute of Petroleum [*London*] [*A publication*]
Tech Pap Intersoc Energy Convers Eng Conf ... Technical Papers. Intersociety Energy Conversion Engineering Conference [*A publication*]
Tech Pap Natl Meas Lab CSIRO ... Technical Paper. National Measurement Laboratory. Commonwealth Scientific and Industrial Research Organisation [*A publication*] (APTA)
Tech Pap Natn Stand Lab CSIRO ... Technical Paper. National Standards Laboratory. Commonwealth Scientific and Industrial Research Organisation [*A publication*] (APTA)
Tech Pap NY State Dep Environ Conserv ... Technical Paper. New York State Department of Environmental Conservation [*A publication*]
Tech Pap SME Ser EE ... Technical Paper. Society of Manufacturing Engineers. Series EE (Electrical Engineering) [*A publication*]
Tech Pap Soc Manuf Eng Ser AD ... Technical Paper. Society of Manufacturing Engineers. Series AD (Assembly Division) [*A publication*]
Tech Pap Soc Manuf Eng Ser EE ... Technical Paper. Society of Manufacturing Engineers. Series EE (Electrical Engineering) [*A publication*]
Tech Pap Soc Manuf Eng Ser EM ... Technical Paper. Society of Manufacturing Engineers. Series EM (Engineering Materials) [*A publication*]
Tech Pap Soc Manuf Eng Ser FC ... Technical Paper. Society of Manufacturing Engineers. Series FC (Finishing and Coating) [*A publication*]
Tech Pap Soc Manuf Eng Ser IQ ... Technical Paper. Society of Manufacturing Engineers. Series IQ (Inspection and Quality) [*A publication*]
Tech Pap Soc Manuf Eng Ser MF ... Technical Paper. Society of Manufacturing Engineers. Series MF (Material Forming) [*A publication*]
Tech Pap Soc Manuf Eng Ser MR ... Technical Paper. Society of Manufacturing Engineers. Series MR (Material Removal) [*A publication*]
Tech Pap Univ PR Agr Exp Sta ... Technical Paper. University of Puerto Rico. Agricultural Experiment Station [*A publication*]
Tech Pet ..... Techniques du Petrole [*France*] [*A publication*]
Tech Phot... Technical Photography [*A publication*]
Tech-Phys Monogr ... Technisch-Physikalische Monographien [*A publication*]
Tech Phys Ser ... Techniques of Physics Series [*A publication*]
Tech Poszukiwan ... Technika Poszukiwan [*A publication*]
Tech Poszukiwan Geol ... Technika Poszukiwan Geologicznych [*A publication*]
Tech Poszukiwan Geol Geosynoptyka Geoterm ... Technika Poszukiwan Geologicznych, Geosynoptyka, i Geotermia [*A publication*]
Tech Prat Agr ... Technique et Pratique Agricoles [*A publication*]
Tech Prepr Am Soc Lubr Eng ... Technical Preprints. American Society of Lubrication Engineers [*A publication*]
Tech Prog Rep US Bur Mines ... Technical Progress Report. United States Bureau of Mines [*A publication*]
Tech Progr Rep Hawaii Agr Exp Sta ... Technical Progress Report. Hawaii Agricultural Experiment Station. University of Hawaii [*A publication*]
Tech Publ Aust Soc Dairy Technol ... Australian Society of Dairy Technology. Technical Publication [*A publication*] (APTA)

Tech Publ Div Wood Technol For Comm NSW ... Technical Publication. Division of Wood Technology. Forestry Commission of New South Wales [*A publication*]
Tech Publ NY St Coll For ... Technical Publication. New York State University. College of Forestry [*A publication*]
Tech Publs ... Technical Publications [*A publication*]
Tech Publs Aust Soc Dairy Technol ... Technical Publications. Australian Society of Dairy Technology [*A publication*] (APTA)
Tech Publs Dep Agric (Vict) ... Technical Publications. Department of Agriculture (Victoria) [*A publication*] (APTA)
Tech Publs Div Wood Technol NSW For Comm ... Technical Publications. Division of Wood Technology. New South Wales Forestry Commission [*A publication*] (APTA)
Tech Publs NSW For Comm Div Wood Technol ... Technical Publications. New South Wales Forestry Commission. Division of Wood Technology [*A publication*] (APTA)
Tech Publ State Biol Surv Kans ... Technical Publications. State Biological Survey of Kansas [*A publication*]
Tech Publ State Univ Coll For Syracuse Univ ... Technical Publication. State University College of Forestry. Syracuse University [*A publication*]
Tech Q .... Technology Quarterly and Proceedings. Society of Arts [*A publication*]
Tech Quart Master Brew Ass Amer ... Technical Quarterly. Master Brewers Association of America [*A publication*]
Tech R........ Technology Review [*A publication*]
Tech Radia & Telew ... Technika Radia i Telewizji [*A publication*]
Tech Rdsch (Bern) ... Technische Rundschau (Bern) [*Switzerland*] [*A publication*]
Tech Refrig Air Cond ... Technics of Refrigeration and Air Conditioning [*A publication*]
Tech Release Amer Pulpw Ass ... Technical Release. American Pulpwood Association [*A publication*]
TECHREP ... Technical Representative [*Military*]
Tech Rep AFAPL TR Air Force Aero Propul Lab (US) ... Technical Report. AFAPL-TR. Air Force Aero Propulsion Laboratory (United States) [*A publication*]
Tech Rep AFFDL TR Air Force Flight Dyn Lab (US) ... Technical Report. AFFDL-TR. Air Force Flight Dynamics Laboratory (United States) [*A publication*]
Tech Rep AFML TR Air Force Mater Lab (US) ... Technical Report. AFML-TR. Air Force Materials Laboratory (United States) [*A publication*]
Tech Rep AFWAL-TR US Air Force Wright Aeronaut Lab ... Technical Report. AFWAL-TR. United States Air Force Wright Aeronautical Laboratories [*A publication*]
Tech Rep Agric Chem Branch (Queensl) ... Technical Report. Agricultural Chemistry Branch (Queensland) [*A publication*]
Tech Rep Agric Eng Res Stn Min Agric For Ser F ... Technical Report. Agricultural Engineering Research Station. Ministry of Agriculture and Forestry. Series F. General [*Japan*] [*A publication*]
Tech Rep Agric Ld Serv Minist Agric Fish Fd ... Technical Report. Agricultural Land Service. Ministry of Agriculture, Fisheries, and Food [*A publication*]
Tech Rep Air Pollut Yokohama-Kawasaki Ind Area ... Technical Report on Air Pollution in Yokohama-Kawasaki Industrial Area [*Japan*] [*A publication*]
Tech Rep Aust Weapons Res Establ ... Technical Report. Australia Weapons Research Establishment [*A publication*]
Tech Rep Bur Met ... Technical Report. Bureau of Meteorology [*A publication*] (APTA)
Tech Rep Bur Meteorol ... Technical Report. Bureau of Meteorology [*A publication*] (APTA)
Tech Rep Cent Res Inst Electr Power Ind ... Technical Report. Central Research Institute of the Electrical Power Industry [*Japan*] [*A publication*]
Tech Rep Cent Res Water Resour Univ Tex Austin ... Technical Report. Center for Research in Water Resources. University of Texas at Austin [*A publication*]
Tech Rep Constr Eng Res Lab ... Technical Report. Construction Engineering Research Laboratory [*United States*] [*A publication*]
Tech Rep Dep Mines Tas ... Technical Report. Department of Mines. Tasmania [*A publication*] (APTA)
Tech Rep Desert Locust Control Organ East Afr ... Technical Report. Desert Locust Control Organization for Eastern Africa [*A publication*]
Tech Rep Div Appl Geomech CSIRO ... Technical Report. Division of Applied Geomechanics. Commonwealth Scientific and Industrial Research Organisation [*A publication*] (APTA)
Tech Rep Div Mech Eng CSIRO ... Technical Report. Division of Mechanical Engineering. Commonwealth Scientific and Industrial Research Organisation [*A publication*] (APTA)
Tech Rep Div Mech Engng CSIRO ... Technical Report. Division of Mechanical Engineering. Commonwealth Scientific and Industrial Research Organisation [*A publication*] (APTA)
Tech Rep Div Soil Mech CSIRO ... Technical Report. Division of Soil Mechanics. Commonwealth Scientific and Industrial Research Organisation [*A publication*] (APTA)
Tech Rep Eng Res Inst Kyoto Univ ... Technical Reports. Engineering Research Institute. Kyoto University [*A publication*]

Tech Rep Fac For Univ Toronto ... Technical Report. Faculty of Forestry. University of Toronto [*A publication*]

Tech Rep Grassld Res Inst ... Technical Report. Grassland Research Institute [*A publication*]

Tech Rep Inst At Energy Kyoto Univ ... Technical Reports. Institute of Atomic Energy. Kyoto University [*A publication*]

Tech Rep Inst Atom Energy Kyoto Univ ... Technical Reports. Institute of Atomic Energy. Kyoto University [*A publication*]

Tech Rep Inst Printed Circuits ... Technical Report. Institute of Printed Circuits [*A publication*]

Tech Rep ISSP (Inst Solid State Phys) Ser A ... Technical Report. ISSP (Institute for Solid State Physics). Series A [*A publication*]

Tech Rep Jet Propul Lab Calif Inst Technol ... Technical Report. Jet Propulsion Laboratory. California Institute of Technology [*A publication*]

Tech Rep JSS Proj ... Technical Report. JSS [*Japanese, Swiss, Swedish*] Project [*A publication*]

Tech Rep Kansai Univ ... Technology Reports. Kansai University [*A publication*]

Tech Rep Nanyang Univ Coll Grad Stud Inst Nat Sci ... Technical Report. Nanyang University. College of Graduate Studies. Institute of Natural Sciences [*A publication*]

Tech Rep Natl Space Dev Agency Jpn ... Technical Report. National Space Development Agency of Japan [*A publication*]

Tech Rep Nisshin Steel Co Ltd ... Technical Report. Nisshin Steel Co. Ltd. [*Japan*] [*A publication*]

Tech Rep Off Nav Res (USA) ... Technical Report. Office of Naval Research (USA) [*A publication*]

Tech Reports Osaka Univ ... Technology Reports. Osaka University [*A publication*]

Tech Rep Osaka Univ ... Technology Reports. Osaka University [*A publication*]

Tech Rep Reg Res Sta (Samaru) ... Technical Report. Regional Research Station (Samaru) [*A publication*]

Tech Repr Graver Water Cond Co ... Technical Reprint. Graver Water Conditioning Co. [*A publication*]

Tech Rep Sch For Resour NC St Univ ... Technical Report. School of Forest Resources. North Carolina State University [*A publication*]

Tech Rep Ser ARL/TR Aust Radiat Lab ... Australia. Australian Radiation Laboratory. Technical Report Series ARL/TR [*A publication*] (APTA)

Tech Rep Ser Carcinog Nat Cancer Inst (US) ... Technical Report Series: Carcinogenesis. National Cancer Institute (United States) [*A publication*]

Tech Rep Ser Int Atom Energy Ag ... Technical Reports Series. International Atomic Energy Agency [*A publication*]

Tech Rep Ser Victoria Dep Agric ... Victoria. Department of Agriculture. Technical Report Series [*A publication*] (APTA)

Tech Rep Soil Res Inst Ghana Acad Sci ... Technical Report. Soil Research Institute. Ghana Academy of Sciences [*A publication*]

Tech Rep Syst Am Soc Met ... Technical Report System. American Society for Metals [*A publication*]

Tech Rep Syst ASM ... Technical Report System. American Society for Metals [*A publication*]

Tech Rep Tasmania Dep Mines ... Tasmania. Department of Mines. Technical Report [*A publication*] (APTA)

Tech Rep Tasm Dep Mines ... Technical Report. Tasmania Department of Mines [*A publication*] (APTA)

Tech Rep Tex For Serv ... Technical Report. Texas Forest Service [*A publication*]

Tech Rep Toyo Kohan Co Ltd ... Technical Reports. Toyo Kohan Co. Ltd. [*Japan*] [*A publication*]

Tech Rep Univ Tex Austin Cent Res Water Resour ... Technical Report. University of Texas at Austin. Center for Research in Water Resources [*A publication*]

Tech Rep US Army Eng Waterw Exp Stn ... Technical Report. United States Army Engineers. Waterways Experiment Station [*A publication*]

Tech Rep Water Resour Res Cent Hawaii Univ ... Technical Report. Hawaii University. Water Resource Research Center [*A publication*]

Tech Rep Yale Sch For ... Technical Report. Yale University. School of Forestry [*A publication*]

Tech Res Cent Finland Electr and Nucl Technol Publ ... Technical Research Centre of Finland. Electrical and Nuclear Technology Publication [*A publication*]

Tech Res Cent Finland Mater and Process Technol Publ ... Technical Research Centre of Finland. Materials and Processing Technology Publication [*A publication*]

Tech Res Cent Finl Build Technol Community Dev Publ ... Technical Research Centre of Finland. Building Technology and Community Development Publication [*A publication*]

Tech Res Cent Finl Electr Nucl Technol Publ ... Technical Research Centre of Finland. Electrical and Nuclear Technology Publication [*A publication*]

Tech Res Cent Finl Gen Div Publ ... Technical Research Centre of Finland. General Division Publication [*A publication*]

Tech Res Cent Finl Mater Process Technol Publ ... Technical Research Centre of Finland. Materials and Processing Technology Publication [*A publication*]

Tech Res Cent Finl Publ ... Technical Research Centre of Finland. Publications [*A publication*]

Tech Res Cent Finl Res Rep ... Technical Research Centre of Finland. Research Reports [*A publication*]

Tech Rev .... Technology Review [*A publication*]

Tech Rev Mitsubishi Heavy-Ind (Jpn Ed) ... Technical Review. Mitsubishi Heavy-Industries (Japanese Edition) [*A publication*]

Tech Rev Sumitomo Heavy Ind Ltd ... Technical Review. Sumitomo Heavy Industries Ltd. [*A publication*]

TechRMS .. Technological Qualification in Microscopy, Royal Microscopical Society [*British*] (DBQ)

Tech Routiere ... Technique Routiere [*Belgium*] [*A publication*]

Tech Rundsch ... Technische Rundschau [*A publication*]

Tech Rundsch Sulzer ... Technische Rundschau Sulzer [*Switzerland*] [*A publication*]

TECHS ...... Technical School [*Air Force*]

TECHSAT ... Technology Satellite (MCD)

Tech Sci Aeronaut Spat ... Technique et Science Aeronautiques et Spatiales [*France*] [*A publication*]

Tech et Sci Inf ... Technique et Science Informatiques [*A publication*]

Tech Sci Munic ... Techniques et Sciences Municipales [*France*] [*A publication*]

Tech Sci Munic Eau ... Techniques et Sciences Municipales/l'Eau [*A publication*]

Tech Ser Bur Ent US ... Technical Series. Bureau of Entomology. United States Department of Agriculture [*A publication*]

Tech Ser Fla Dep Nat Resour Mar Res Lab ... Technical Series. Florida Department of Natural Resources. Marine Research Laboratory [*A publication*]

Tech Serv Newsl ... Technical Services Newsletter [*A publication*]

Tech Skoda ... Technika Skoda [*A publication*]

Tech Smarownicza ... Technika Smarownicza [*A publication*]

Tech Smarownicza Trybol ... Technika Smarownicza. Trybologia [*A publication*]

Tech Soc Pacific Coast Tr ... Technical Society of the Pacific Coast. Transactions [*A publication*]

Tech Stud Common Exp Bldg Stn ... Technical Studies. Commonwealth Experimental Building Station [*A publication*] (APTA)

Tech Stud Commonw Exp Bldg Stn ... Technical Studies. Commonwealth Experimental Building Station [*A publication*] (APTA)

TECHSVS ... Technical Services [*Army*]

TECHTAF ... Technical Training Air Force

Tech Teach ... Technical Teacher [*A publication*] (APTA)

Tech Timber Guide ... Technical Timber Guide [*A publication*] (APTA)

Tech Timb Guide ... Technical Timber Guide [*A publication*] (APTA)

Tech Times ... Technology Transfer Times [*A publication*]

TECHTNG ... Technical Training (NVT)

TECHTNGSq ... Technical Training Squadron [*Air Force*]

TECHTRA ... Air Technical Training [*Navy*]

Tech Trans Bull ... Technical Translation Bulletin [*A publication*]

Tech Transl ... Technical Translations [*A publication*]

TECHTRL ... Technitrol, Inc. [*Associated Press abbreviation*] (APAG)

Tech Tworczego Myslenia ... Techniki Tworczego Myslenia [*A publication*]

Tech Ueberwach ... Technische Ueberwachung [*Technological Supervising*] [*A publication*]

Tech Umweltschutz ... Technik und Umweltschutz [*East Germany*] [*A publication*]

Tech Univ Muenchen Jahrb ... Technische Universitaet Muenchen. Jahrbuch [*A publication*]

Tech W ...... Technical World [*Chicago*] [*A publication*]

Tech W ...... Technology Week [*A publication*]

TechWeldI ... Technician of the Welding Institute [*British*] (DBQ)

Tech Wk ...... Technology Week [*A publication*]

Tech Wlok ... Technik Wlokienniczy [*A publication*]

Tech World ... Technical World Magazine [*A publication*]

Tech Zukunft ... Techniken der Zukunft [*A publication*]

TECIB .... Technic International [*A publication*]

Tec Ind (Madrid) ... Tecnica Industrial (Madrid) [*A publication*]

Tec Ital...... Tecnica Italiana [*A publication*]

TECL .... Test Equipment Configuration Log [*NASA*] (KSC)

TECL .... Transmission-Engine Communication Link [*Automotive engineering*]

TECLA ...... Tecnica (Lisbon) [*A publication*]

TECM .... Test Equipment Commodity Manager

TECMA ..... Technical Ceramics Manufacturers Association (EA)

Tec Metal ... Tecnica Metalurgica [*Spain*] [*A publication*]

Tec Met (Barcelona) ... Tecnica Metalurgica (Barcelona) [*A publication*]

Tec Mit K F ... Technische Mitteilungen Krupp. Forschungsberichte [*A publication*]

Tec Mit K W ... Technische Mitteilungen Krupp. Werksberichte [*A publication*]

TECMOD ... Technology Modernization (MCD)

Tec Molit ... Tecnica Molitoria [*A publication*]

TECN .... Technalysis Corp. [*NASDAQ symbol*] (NQ)

TEC-NACS ... Teachers Educational Council - National Association Cosmetology Schools

TECNET ... Technologies Network [*Database*] [*EC*] (ECED)

Tecnica Ital ... Tecnica Italiana [*A publication*]

Tecn Ital ..... Tecnica Italiana [*A publication*]

Tecnol Aliment ... Tecnologia Alimentaria [*A publication*]

Tecnol Elettr ... Tecnologie Elettriche [*A publication*]

Tecnopolim Resine ... Tecnopolimeri e Resine [*A publication*]
TECO .... Technical Co-Operation Committee [*OECD*]   (DS)
TECO .... TECO Energy, Inc. [*Associated Press abbreviation*]   (APAG)
TECO .... Terra Cotta [*Pronounced "tee-ko"*] [*Type of American art pottery*]
TECO .... Tesco American, Inc. [*NASDAQ symbol*]   (NQ)
TECO .... Tooling Expenditure Control Order   (MCD)
TECO .... Trinity Engineering Co. [*Huxley, IA*] [*Telecommunications service*]   (TSSD)
TECO .... Turbine Engine Checkout
TECOGEN ... Tecogen, Inc. [*Associated Press abbreviation*]   (APAG)
TECOM .... Test and Evaluation Command [*Army*] [*Aberdeen Proving Ground, MD*]
TECOMAP ... Technical Conference of the Observation and Measurement of Atmospheric Pollution [*Helsinki, 1973*]
TECOPS ... Tech/Ops Sevcon, Inc. [*Associated Press abbreviation*]   (APAG)
TECP .... Training Equipment Checkout Procedure
TECPD ...... TAPPI [*Technical Association of the Pulp and Paper Industry*] Environmental Conference. Proceedings [*A publication*]
Tec Pecuar Mex ... Tecnica Pecuaria en Mexico [*A publication*]
Tec Pecu Mex ... Tecnica Pecuaria en Mexico [*A publication*]
TECR .... Technical Reason [*Aviation*]
TECR .... Technical Requirement   (AABC)
Tec R .... Technology Review [*A publication*]
TECR .... Test Equipment Change Requirement   (NATG)
TECRAS .... Technical Reconnaissance and Surveillance   (MCD)
Tec Regul & Mando Autom ... Tecnica de la Regulacion y Mando Automatico [*A publication*]
TECS .... Television Confirming Sensor   (MCD)
TECS .... Total Environmental Control System [*Army*]   (RDA)
TECS .... Treasury Enforcement Communications System [*Customs Service*]
Tec Sint Spec Org ... Tecniche e Sintesi Speciali Organiche [*A publication*]
TECSTAR ... Technical Missions, Structures and Career Development [*Military*]
Tectonophys ... Tectonophysics [*A publication*]
TECTRA ... Technology Transfer Data Bank [*California State University*] [*Sacramento*] [*Information service or system*]   (IID)
TECU .... Tecumseh Products Co. [*NASDAQ symbol*]   (NQ)
TECU .... Thermoelectric Environmental Control Unit
TECU .... Transportation Employees' Canadian Union
TED .... Electrical Distributor [*A publication*]   (EAAP)
TED .... International Association for Training and Education in Distribution
TED .... Tasks of Emotional Development Test [*Psychology*]
TeD .... Te Deum [*Music*]
TED .... Teacher Education Division [*Council for Exceptional Children*]
TeD .... Telefunken-Decca [*Video disk system*]
TED .... Tenders Electronic Daily [*Office for Official Publications of the European Communities*] [*Database*] [*Luxembourg*]
TED .... Terminal Editor   (ADA)
TED .... Test Engineering Division [*Navy*]
TED .... Test Engineering Documentation   (MCD)
TED .... Test, Evaluation, and Development   (MUGU)
TED .... Test and Evaluation Division [*National Weather Service*]
T Ed .... Theological Educator [*A publication*]
TED .... Thermionic Emission Detector [*For gas chromatography*]
TED .... Thermoelectric Device
TED .... Thisted [*Denmark*] [*Airport symbol*]   (OAG)
TED .... Thomas Edmund Dewey [*Republican candidate for President, 1948*]
TED .... Threshold Erythema Dose [*Medicine*]
TED .... Threshold Extension Demodulator
TED .... Thromboembolic Disease [*Medicine*]
TED .... Toledo Edison Co. [*NYSE symbol*]   (SPSG)
TED .... Total Energy Detector
TED .... Trace Element Doping
TED .... Tracking Error Detector   (MCD)
TED .... Trailing Edge Down [*Aviation*]   (MCD)
TED .... Training Equipment Development [*Military*]
TED .... Traitement Electronique des Donnees [*Electronic Data Processing - EDP*] [*French*]
TED .... Transfer Effective Date [*Military*]   (AFM)
TED .... Transferred Electron Device [*Air Force*]
TED .... Translation Error Detector   (DIT)
TED .... Transmission Electron Diffraction   (MCD)
TED .... Troop Exercise Director   (CINC)
TED .... True Economic Depreciation
TED .... Trunk Encryption Device [*Telecommunications*]   (TEL)
TED .... Turbine Electric Drive
TED .... Turbine Engine Division [*Air Force*]
TED .... Turtle Exclusion Device [*Tool attached to shrimp boats in the Gulf of Mexico which allows the endangered Kemp's ridley turtle to escape the shrimp nets*] [*Facetious translations: "Trawler Extinction Device," "Trawling Efficiency Device"*]
TEDA .... Theatre Equipment Dealers Association [*Later, TEA*]   (EA)
TEDA .... Triethylenediamine [*Organic chemistry*]
TEDAR ...... Telemetered Data Reduction   (AAG)
TEDC .... Technical Education Center

TEDC .... Tellurium Diethyldithiocarbamate [*Organic chemistry*]
TEDDS ...... Tactical Environmental Dissemination and Display System [*MCD*]
TEDE .... Temperature-Enhanced Displacement Effect
TEDES ..... Telemetry Data Evaluation System
TEDGA ..... Technical Digest [*A publication*]
TEDL .... Transferred-Electron-Device Logic   (MSA)
TEDMA .... Triethylene Dimethacrylate [*Organic chemistry*]
TEDP .... Tetraethyl Dithionopyrophosphate [*Organic chemistry*]
TEDPAS .. Technical Data Package Automated System
TEDS .... Tactical Expendable Drone System   (MCD)
TEDS .... Target Effluent Detection System   (MCD)
TEDS .... Teleteach Expanded Delivery System [*US Air Force*] [*Wright-Patterson AFB, OH*] [*Telecommunications*]   (TSSD)
TEDS .... Turbine-Electric Drive Submarine   (DNAB)
TEDSCO ... Test Equipment Documentation Scheduling Committee
TEE .... [*The*] Entrepreneurial Economy [*Corporation for Enterprise Development*] [*A publication*]
TEE .... Tape Editing Equipment
TEE .... Tbessa [*Algeria*] [*Airport symbol*]   (OAG)
TEE .... Teeples Ranch [*Montana*] [*Seismograph station code, US Geological Survey*] [*Closed*]   (SEIS)
TEE .... Teeshin Resources Ltd. [*Vancouver Stock Exchange symbol*]
TEE .... Telecommunications Engineering Establishment [*British*]
TEE .... Terminal Effects and Experimentation   (MCD)
TEE .... Test Equipment Engineering   (AAG)
TEE .... Tex-Textilis. Technisch Wetenschappelijk Maandblad voor de Benelux Textielindustrie [*A publication*]
TEE .... Theological Education by Extension [*Church of England*]
TEE .... Torpedo Experimental Establishment [*British*]
TEE .... Total Effective Exposure [*Advertising*]
TEE .... Training Effectiveness Evaluation
TEE .... Trans-Europ-Express [*Continental high-speed train*]
TEE .... Transesophageal Echocardiography
TEE .... Triaxial Earth Ellipsoid
TEE .... Tyrosine Ethyl Ester [*Organic chemistry*]   (MAE)
TeeCm .... Tee-Comm Electronics, Inc. [*Associated Press abbreviation*]   (APAG)
TEEF .... Tax-Exempt Equity Fund
TEEL .... Temporary Expedient Equipment List [*Army*]   (AABC)
TEEM .... Test for Examining Expressive Morphology [*Educational test*]
TEEM .... Trans-Europ-Express-Marchandises [*Continental high-speed train*]
TEES .... Texas Engineering Experiment Station [*Texas A & M University*] [*Research center*]
TEES .... Thermochemical Environmental Energy System [*Service mark*] [*Battelle Development Corp.*]
TEESS ...... Tank Engine Exhaust Smoke System   (MCD)
TEES Tech Bull ... TEES [*Texas Engineering Experiment Station*] Technical Bulletin [*A publication*]
TEEZI .... Threat Evaluation Equipment Zone of Interior   (SAA)
TEF .... [*The*] Eagle Foundation [*Defunct*]   (EA)
TEF .... [*The*] Environmental Fund [*Later, PEB*]   (EA)
TEF .... Tear Efficiency Factor [*Textiles*]
Tef .... Tefillin   (BJA)
TEF .... Telefonica de Espana ADS [*NYSE symbol*]   (SPSG)
TEF .... Telex Africa [*A publication*]
TEF .... Telfer [*Australia*] [*Airport symbol*]   (OAG)
TEF .... Temperance Education Foundation [*Defunct*]   (EA)
TEF .... Test and Evaluation Flight [*Military*]
TEF .... Total Environment Facility   (SAA)
TEF .... Tracheoesophageal Fistula [*Medicine*]
TEF .... Transfer on End of File   (SAA)
TEF .... Transverse Electric Field
TEF .... Tunable Etalon Filter
TEF .... Turkey Embryo Fibroblast [*Biochemistry*]
TEFA .... Total Essential Fatty Acid [*of foodstuffs*]
TEFA .... Total Esterified Fatty Acid
TEFA .... Tube-Excited X-Ray Fluorescence Analyzer
TEFAP ...... Temporary Emergency Food Assistance Program [*Department of Agriculture*]
TEFC .... Totally Enclosed - Fan Cooled
TEFL .... Teaching English as a Foreign Language
TEFLON ... Tetrafluoroethylene Resin [*Du Pont*]
TEFL/TESL Newsl ... TEFL [*Teaching English as a Foreign Language*]/TESL [*Teaching English as a Second Language*] Newsletter [*A publication*]   (APTA)
TEFO .... Technological Forecasting and Social Change [*A publication*]
TEFORS .... Technological Forecasting and Simulation for Program Selection   (MCD)
TEFP .... Transportability Engineering Focal Point
TEFRA ...... Tax Equity and Fiscal Responsibility Act of 1982
TEG .... Tactical Employment Guide [*Military*]   (CAAL)
Teg .... Tegula [*Entomology*]
TEG .... Templar Mining [*Vancouver Stock Exchange symbol*]
TEG .... Test Element Group
TEG .... Tetraethylene Glycol [*Organic chemistry*]
TEG .... Thermoelectric Generator
TEG .... Thromboelastogram [*or Thromboelastograph*] [*Medicine*]
TEG .... Top Edge Gilt [*Bookbinding*]
TEG .... Triethyl Gallium [*Organic chemistry*]

TEG .... Triethylene Glycol [*Organic chemistry*]
TEGAS...... Test Generation and Simulation
TEGAS...... Time Generation and Simulation [*Telecommunications*] (TEL)
TEGD .... Technical Enforcement Guidance Document [*Environmental Protection Agency*]
TEGDME ... Tetraethylene Glycol Dimethyl Ether [*Organic chemistry*]
TEGDN ..... Triethylene Glycol Dinitrate [*An explosive*]
TEGG .... Thermogrip Electric Glue Gun
TEGMA ..... Terminal Elevator Grain Merchants Association (EA)
TEGMA .... Triethylene Glycol Dimethacrylate [*Organic chemistry*] (MCD)
Teg Meded S Afr Dep Landbou Viss ... Tegniese Mededeling. Suid Afrika Departement van Landbou en Visserye [*A publication*]
TEGNA ..... Tegnikon [*A publication*]
TEGO .... Taylor's Encyclopedia of Government Officials [*A publication*]
TEGTA...... Technische Gemeinschaft [*A publication*]
TEGWAR ... [*The*] Exciting Game Without Any Rules [*Card game*]
TEH .... Blare Lake, AK [*Location identifier*] [*FAA*] (FAAL)
Teh .... Tehillim (BJA)
TEH .... Tehran [*Iran*] [*Seismograph station code, US Geological Survey*] (SEIS)
TEH .... Tehran [*Iran*] [*Geomagnetic observatory code*]
TEH .... Tehua [*Race of maize*]
TEH .... Topics in Environmental Health [*Elsevier Book Series*] [*A publication*]
TEH .... Twin-Engined Helicopter (MCD)
TEHBA ..... Tehnika (Belgrade) [*A publication*]
Teh Fiz...... Tehnicka Fizika [*A publication*]
Teh Hronika ... Tehnika Hronika [*A publication*]
TEHP .... Thermoelectric Heat Pump (MCD)
Teh Rud Geol Metal ... Tehnika Rudarstvo Geologiya i Metalurgija [*A publication*]
Teh Tootmine ... Tehnika ja Tootmine [*Estonian SSR*] [*A publication*]
TEI............. [*The*] Entrepreneurship Institute (EA)
TEI............. Tax Executives Institute (EA)
TEI............. Technical Engineering Item (MCD)
TE & I....... Technology Evaluation and Integration (MCD)
TEI............. Telecommunications Engineering, Inc. [*Dallas, TX*] (TSSD)
TEI............. Temporary Engineering Instruction [*Navy*] (NG)
TEI............. Texas International Co. [*NYSE symbol*] [*Toronto Stock Exchange symbol*]
TEI............. Text Encoding Initiative [*Data processing*]
TEI............. Thorne Ecological Institute (EA)
TEI............. Trait Evaluation Index [*Psychology*]
TEI............. Transearth Injection [*AEC*]
TEI............. Transfer on Error Indication
TEI............. Trucking Employers, Inc. [*Later, TMI*]
TEIB .... Triethyleneiminobenzoquinone [*Organic chemistry*] (MAE)
TEIC .... Tissue Equivalent Ionization Chamber
TEICA ...... Transactions. Engineering Institute of Canada [*A publication*]
TEIGA ...... Teishin Igaku [*A publication*]
TEIGN...... Teignmouth [*Urban district in England*]
TEIGNBR ... Teignbridge [*England*]
Teilhard Rev ... Teilhard Review [*London*] [*A publication*]
Teilhard St ... Teilhard Studies [*A publication*]
TEIM........ Travel Economic Impact Model [*Department of Commerce*]
Teint Apprets ... Teinture et Apprets [*A publication*]
TEIP .... Tax-Exempt Investor Program [*Investment term*]
TEIR......... Thomas Edison Inns, Inc. [*NASDAQ symbol*] (NQ)
TEIRD....... Technology Ireland [*A publication*]
TEIRDC .... Tamil Eelaam International Research and Documentation Centre [*Canada*]
TEIS .... Training Equipment Item Specification (MCD)
Teiss.......... Teisser's Court of Appeal. Parish of Orleans Reports [*A publication*]
Teiss.......... Teissler's Court of Appeal, Parish of Orleans, Reports [*1903-17*] [*A publication*] (DLA)
Teissler ...... Teissler's Court of Appeal, Parish of Orleans, Reports [*1903-17*] [*A publication*] (DLA)
TEJ .... Emmanuel School of Religion, Johnson City, TN [*OCLC symbol*] (OCLC)
TEJ .... Tejas Gas Corp. [*NYSE symbol*] (SPSG)
TEJ .... Transverse Expansion Joint [*Technical drawings*]
TEJA .... Tutmonda Esperantista Jurnalista Asocio [*World Association of Esperanto Journalists - WAEJ*] (EAIO)
TEJAC ...... Trade Effluent Joint Advisory Committee [*British*] (DCTA)
Tejas .... Tejas Gas Corp. [*Associated Press abbreviation*] (APAG)
TEJAS...... Tejas Power [*Associated Press abbreviation*] (APAG)
TEJIA........ Transport Engineer [*A publication*]
TEJNR...... Tejon Ranch Co. [*Associated Press abbreviation*] (APAG)
TEJO .... Tutmonda Esperantista Junulara Organizo [*World Organization of Young Esperantists*] (EAIO)
TEJPA...... Tejipar [*A publication*]
TEK .... Teck Corp. [*Toronto Stock Exchange symbol*] [*Vancouver Stock Exchange symbol*]
TEK .... Teekin [*Tonga*] [*Seismograph station code, US Geological Survey*] (SEIS)
TEK .... Tektronix, Inc. [*NYSE symbol*] (SPSG)
TEK .... Test Equipment Kit
TeK .... Text und Kontext [*A publication*]

TEK .... Truppenentgiftungskompanie [*Personnel decontamination company*] [*German military - World War II*]
Tek Aikak ... Teknillinen Aikakauslehti [*A publication*]
Tek Bul Petkim Petrokimya A S Arastirma Mudurlugu ... Teknik Bulten. Petkim Petrokimya A. S. Arastirma Mudurlugu [*A publication*]
TEKE........ Tau Kappa Epsilon [*Fraternity*] (EA)
Tek Forum ... Tekniskt Forum [*Finland*] [*A publication*]
TEKHA ..... Teoreticheskaya i Eksperimental'naya Khimiya [*A publication*]
Tekh Dokl Gidrol ... Tekhnicheskie Doklady po Gidrologii [*A publication*]
Tekh Ekon Izv Tatabanyai Szenbanyak ... Tekhnichesko Ekonomicheskie Izvestiya Tatabanyai Szenbanyak [*A publication*]
Tekh Estetika ... Tekhnicheskaya Estetika [*Former USSR*] [*A publication*]
Tekh Inf Sov Nar Khoz Kuibyshev Ekon Adm Raiona ... Tekhnicheskaya Informatsiya. Sovet Narodnogo Khozyaistva Kuibyshevskogo Ekonomicheskogo Administrativnogo Raiona [*A publication*]
Tekh Kibern ... Tekhnicheskaya Kibernetika [*A publication*]
Tekh Kino Telev ... Tekhnika Kino i Televideniya [*A publication*]
Tekh Mis'l ... Tekhnicheska Mis'l [*A publication*]
Tekh Misul ... Tekhnicheska Misul [*Bulgaria*] [*A publication*]
Tekh Molodezhi ... Tekhnika Molodezhi [*A publication*]
Tekhnol Legk Splavov ... Tekhnologiya Legkikh Splavov [*A publication*]
Tekhnol Mashinostr (Moscow) ... Tekhnologiya Mashinostroeniya (Moscow) [*A publication*]
Tekhnol Mater ... Tekhnologiya Materialov [*A publication*]
Tekhnol Neorg Veshchestv ... Tekhnologiya Neorganicheskikh Veshchestv [*A publication*]
Tekhnol Organ Mekh Liteinogo Proizvod ... Tekhnologiya, Organizatsiya, i Mekhanizatsiya Liteinogo Proizvodstva [*A publication*]
Tekhnol Organ Proizvod ... Tekhnologiya i Organizatsiya Proizvodstva [*A publication*]
Tekhnol Proizvod Sukhikh Diagn Pitatel'nykh Sred ... Tekhnologiya Proizvodstva Sukhikh Diagnosticheskikh Pitatel'nykh Sred [*A publication*]
Tekhnol Stroit Proizvod ... Tekhnologiya Stroitel'nogo Proizvodstva [*A publication*]
Tek Hoegsk Handl ... Tekniska Hoegskolan Handlingar [*A publication*]
Tek Hogsk Helsingfors Vetensk Publ ... Tekniska Hoegskolan i Helsingfors Vetenskapliga Publikationer [*A publication*]
Tekh Sel'Khoz ... Tekhnika v Sel'skom Khozyaistve [*A publication*]
Tekh Usloviya Metody Opred Vrednykh Veshchestv Vozdukhe ... Tekhnicheskie Usloviya na Metody Opredeleniya Vrednykh Veshchestv v Vozdukhe [*A publication*]
Tekh Vooruzhenie ... Tekhnika i Vooruzhenie [*Former USSR*] [*A publication*]
Tekh Vozdushn Flota ... Tekhnika Vozdushnogo Flota [*A publication*]
Tekh Zhelezn Dorog ... Tekhnika Zheleznykh Dorog [*A publication*]
Tek Inf .... Teknisk Information [*Sweden*] [*A publication*]
TEKKA...... Tekkokai [*A publication*]
Tek Kem Aikak ... Teknillisen Kemian Aikakauslehti [*Finland*] [*A publication*]
Tek Medd .. Tekniska Meddelanden [*Sweden*] [*A publication*]
Tekn Forsknstift Skogsarb ... Teknik Forskningsstiftelsen Skogsarbeten [*A publication*]
Tekn Kino Televid ... Tekhnika Kino i Televideniya [*A publication*]
Teknol Avtom Mashinostr ... Tekhnologiya i Avtomatizatsiya Mashinostroeniya [*A publication*]
TEKSA ...... Tekhnika (Sofia) [*A publication*]
Tek Samf Hand ... Tekniska Samfundets Handlingar [*A publication*]
TEKSIF ..... Turkiye Tekstil ve Orme Sanayii Iscileri Sendikalari Federasyonu [*National Federation of Textile Unions*] [*Turkey*]
Tekstil Prom ... Tekstil'naya Promyshlennost [*A publication*]
Tekst Ind ... Tekstilna Industrija [*A publication*]
Tekst Prom (Moscow) ... Tekstil'naya Promyshlennost (Moscow) [*A publication*]
Tekst Prom (Sofia) ... Tekstilna Promishlennost (Sofia) [*A publication*]
Tekst Prom-St ... Tekstil'naya Promyshlennost [*A publication*]
TEKTA...... Tekstil [*A publication*]
Tek Tidskr ... Teknisk Tidskrift [*A publication*]
Tek Tidsskr Text Beklaedning ... Teknisk Tidsskrift for Textil og Beklaedning [*A publication*]
Tektonika Sib ... Tektonika Sibiri [*A publication*]
Tektrnx...... Tektronix, Inc. [*Associated Press abbreviation*] (APAG)
Tek Ukebl ... Teknisk Ukeblad [*A publication*]
Tek Vetensk Forsk ... Teknisk Vetenskaplig Forskning [*Sweden*] [*A publication*]
Tek Yay Kavak Arast Enst (Izmit) ... Teknik Yayinlar. Kavakcihk Arastirma Enstitusu (Izmit, Turkey) [*A publication*]
TEL............ Task Execution Language
TEL............ Taxpayers Education Lobby (EA)
TEL............ TeleCom Corp. [*NYSE symbol*] (SPSG)
TEL............ Telecommunications (FAAC)
TEL............ Telegraaf [*A publication*]
TEL............ Telegram
TEL............ Telegraph
TEL............ Telemetry (KSC)
TEL............ Telephone (AAG)
TEL............ Telescope (AAG)
Tel.............. Telescopium [*Constellation*]
TEL............ Teletypewriter [*Telecommunications*] (NOAA)

TEL............. Tell City, IN [*Location identifier*] [*FAA*] (FAAL)
tel.............. Telugu [*MARC language code*] [*Library of Congress*] (LCCP)
TEL............. Terex Equipment Ltd.
TEL............. Test of Economic Literacy [*Educational test*]
TEL............. Test Log
TEL............. Tests for Everyday Living [*Educational test*]
TEL............. Tetraethyllead [*Organic chemistry*]
TEL............. Thalner Electronic Laboratories, Inc. [*Ann Arbor, MI*] (TSSD)
TEL............. Thomas Edward Lawrence [*Lawrence of Arabia*] [*British archaeologist, soldier, and writer, 1888-1935*]
TEL............. Training Equipment List
TEL............. Transporter-Erector-Launcher [*Air Force*]
Tel Add ...... Telegraphic Address (DS)
Telan .... Telenoticiosa Americana [*Press agency*] [*Argentina*]
TELAR ...... Transporter-Erector-Launcher and RADAR (MCD)
TELATS.... Tactical Electronic Locating and Targeting System (MCD)
Tel Aviv J Inst A ... Tel Aviv. Journal of the Tel Aviv University Institute of Archaeology [*A publication*]
Tel Aviv Univ Stud L ... Tel Aviv University Studies in Law [*Tel-Aviv, Israel*] [*A publication*] (DLA)
Tel-Aviv U Stud L ... Tel-Aviv University Studies in Law [*Tel-Aviv, Israel*] [*A publication*] (DLA)
TELB......... Telephone Booth
TELC......... Telco Systems, Inc. [*NASDAQ symbol*] (NQ)
TELC......... Teleglobe Canada
TELCAM .. Telecommunication Equipment Low-Cost Acquisition Method [*Navy*]
TelcNZ....... Telecom Corp. of New Zealand [*Associated Press abbreviation*] (APAG)
TELCO...... Tata Engineering & Locomotive Co. [*India*]
TELCO...... Telephone Operating Co. [*Also, TELOP*]
Telcom ...... TeleCom Corp. [*Associated Press abbreviation*] (APAG)
TELCOM ... Telecommunications (NASA)
Telcom Rep ... Telcom Report [*A publication*]
TELCON.... Telephone Conference [*or Conversation*] (AAG)
TELD......... Test of Early Language Development
TELDTA ... Telephone & Data Systems, Inc. [*Associated Press abbreviation*] (APAG)
Teldyn....... Teledyne, Inc. [*Associated Press abbreviation*] (APAG)
TELE......... Telegram
TELE......... Telegraph
TELE......... Telephone
Tele .... Telescopium [*Constellation*]
TELE......... Television (ADA)
TELE......... TPI Enterprises [*Formerly, Telecom Plus International*] [*NASDAQ symbol*] (SPSG)
TELEA ...... Tetrahedron Letters [*A publication*]
TELEC ...... Telecommunication
TELEC ...... Teleglobe Canada
TELEC ...... Thermoelectronic LASER Energy Converter
TELECAMRA ... Television Camera (MDG)
TELECAR ... Telemetry Carrier Acquisition and Recovery (MCD)
TELECAST ... Television Broadcasting (CET)
TELECC.... Telecommunication
Telecom...... Telecommunications [*A publication*]
TELECOM ... Telecommunications (AFM)
Telecom Aust Res Q ... Telecom Australia Research Quarterly [*A publication*] (APTA)
Telecom J... Telecommunication Journal of Australia [*A publication*] (APTA)
Telecom J Aust ... Telecommunication Journal of Australia [*A publication*] (APTA)
Telecomm... Telecommunications [*A publication*]
Telecomm J ... Telecommunication Journal [*A publication*]
Telecomm J Aust ... Telecommunication Journal of Australia [*A publication*] (APTA)
Telecom ML ... Telecom Market Letter [*A publication*]
Telecomm Po ... Telecommunications Policy [*A publication*]
Telecomm Prod ... Telecommunications Products and Technology [*A publication*]
Telecomms ... Telecommunications [*International Edition*] [*A publication*]
Telecommun J ... Telecommunication Journal [*A publication*]
Telecommun J Aust ... Telecommunication Journal of Australia [*A publication*]
Telecommun J (Engl Ed) ... Telecommunication Journal (English Edition) [*A publication*]
Telecommun Policy ... Telecommunications Policy [*A publication*]
Telecommun Radio Eng ... Telecommunications and Radio Engineering [*A publication*]
Telecommun and Radio Eng Part 1 ... Telecommunications and Radio Engineering. Part 1. Telecommunications [*A publication*]
Telecommun and Radio Eng Part 2 ... Telecommunications and Radio Engineering. Part 2. Radio Engineering [*A publication*]
Telecommun Radio Eng (USSR) Part 1 ... Telecommunications and Radio Engineering. Part 1. Telecommunications (USSR) [*A publication*]
Telecommun Radio Eng (USSR) Part 2 ... Telecommunications and Radio Engineering (USSR). Part 2. Radio Engineering [*A publication*]
TELECOMS ... Telecommunications Authority of Singapore (TSSD)
TELECON ... Telephone [*or Teletype*] Conference [*or Conversation*] (AFM)

TELECONV ... Telephone Conversation
TELEDAC ... Telemetric Data Converter
TELEDAQ ... Television Data Acquisition System (MCD)
TELEDIS.. Teletypewriter Distribution (NATG)
Tele (Engl Ed) ... Tele (English Edition) [*A publication*]
Telef.......... Telefonica de Espana SA [*Associated Press abbreviation*] (APAG)
TELEFAC ... Telecommunications Facility
TELEFLEX ... Teleflex, Inc. [*Associated Press abbreviation*] (APAG)
TELEFLORA ... Telegraph Florists Delivery Service
Telefon Rep ... Telefon Report [*A publication*]
Telef Rep.... Telefon Report [*A publication*]
Telefunken-Ztg ... Telefunken-Zeitung [*West Germany*] [*A publication*]
TELEG ...... Telegram
TELEG ...... Telegraph
Telegen Ann Rev ... Telegen Annual Review [*A publication*]
Telegen Doc Sourceb ... Telegen Document Sourcebook [*A publication*]
Telegr & Telef ... Telegraaf en Telefoon [*A publication*]
TELEMAN ... Telephone Management System
Telem Ant ... Telemetry Antenna
Telemktg.... Telemarketing [*A publication*]
TELENET ... Cooperative Extension Service Telephone Network [*University of Illinois at Champaign-Urbana*] [*Telecommunications service*] (TSSD)
TELENET ... TELENET Communications Corp. [*GTE*] (TEL)
Tele News .. Telephone News [*A publication*]
TELEPAK ... Telemetering Package
TELEPH ... Telephone
Teleph Eng & Manage ... Telephone Engineer and Management [*A publication*]
Telephone .. Telephone Engineer and Management [*A publication*]
TELER ...... Telecommunications Requirements (MCD)
TELERAN ... Television and RADAR Navigation System (MUGU)
TELESAT ... Telecommunications Satellite
TELESUN ... Telecommunications Software User's Network [*Telesun Corp.*] [*Englewood, OH*] (TSSD)
Tele (Swed Ed) ... Tele (Swedish Edition) [*A publication*]
Telesys J.... Telesystems Journal [*A publication*]
TELETECH ... National Telecommunications & Technology Fund, Inc. [*New York, NY*] (TSSD)
Tele-Tech & Electronic Ind ... Tele-Tech and Electronic Industries [*A publication*]
Teleteknik Engl Ed ... Teleteknik. English Edition [*A publication*]
Telettra Rev ... Telettra Review [*A publication*]
TELETYPE ... Teletypewriter [*Telecommunications*]
Telev Eng... Television Engineering [*A publication*]
Televerket.. National Swedish Telecommunications Administration [*Stockholm*] [*Information service or system*] (IID)
Television JR Telev Soc ... Television. Journal of the Royal Television Society [*A publication*]
Telev Quart ... Television Quarterly [*A publication*]
Telev/Radio Age ... Television/Radio Age [*A publication*]
TELEX ...... Automatic Teletypewriter Exchange Service [*of Western Union*]
TELF .... Tamil Eelam Liberation Front [*Sri Lanka*] [*Political party*] (PPW)
TELFAD ... Telephone Executive Leader for a Day [*New England Telephone Co. program for high school students*]
TELG......... Telegram
Telhan Patrica Oilseeds J ... Telhan Patrica/Oilseeds Journal [*A publication*]
TELID ...... Teletypewriter Identification (NOAA)
TELIDON ... [*A*] television terminal-based interactive information retrieval system
TELINT .... Telemetry Intelligence
TELIS....... Test Equipment Logistics Information Source [*Army*]
TELISA ..... Thermometric Enzyme-Linked Immunosorbent Assay [*Analytical biochemistry*]
TELIST ..... Telegraphist (DSUE)
TELL......... [*The*] Excellent Lodge Leader [*Freemasonry*]
TELL......... Teleci, Inc. of Texas [*NASDAQ symbol*] (NQ)
TELLA ...... Tellus [*Sweden*] [*A publication*]
TELL-A-GRAF ... [*A*] Programming Language [*1978*] (CSR)
Tellus Ser A ... Tellus. Series A. Dynamic Meteorology and Oceanography [*A publication*]
Tellus Ser A Dyn Meteorol Oceanogr ... Tellus. Series A. Dynamic Meteorology and Oceanography [*A publication*]
Tellus Ser B ... Tellus. Series B. Chemical and Physical Meteorology [*A publication*]
Tellus Ser B Chem Phys Meteorol ... Tellus. Series B. Chemical and Physical Meteorology [*A publication*]
TELM....... Telegram (ROG)
TelMex ...... Telefonos de Mexico SA [*Associated Press abbreviation*]
TelMex ...... Telefonos de Mexico SA de CV [*Associated Press abbreviation*] (APAG)
TELMTR .. Telemotor
TELNET ... Georgia Telecommunications Network [*Georgia Hospital Association*] [*Atlanta, GA*] [*Telecommunications*] (TSSD)
TELO........ Tamil Eelam Liberation Organization [*Sri Lanka*] [*Political party*]
TELO........ Tel Offshore Trust [*NASDAQ symbol*] (NQ)
Tel Off .... Telegraph Office

TELOP...... Telephone Operating Co. [*Also, TELCO*]
TELOPS.... Telemetry Online Processing System [*Data processing*]
TELPAK.... Telephone Package
TelQ.......... Tel Quel [*A publication*]
TELQ.......... TeleQuest, Inc. [*San Diego, CA*] [*NASDAQ symbol*]   (NQ)
TELR........ Teleram Communications [*NASDAQ symbol*]   (NQ)
Tel Rad E R ... Telecommunications and Radio Engineering (USSR) [*A publication*]
TELRY .... Telegraph Reply   (FAAC)
TELS .... TEL Electronics, Inc. [*American Fork, UT*] [*NASDAQ symbol*]   (NQ)
TELS .... Test of Early Learning Skills [*Child development test*]
TELS .... Turbine Engine Loads Simulator
TELSAM... Telephone Service Attitude Measurement [*Telephone interviews*] [*AT & T*]
TELSCAR ... Transmit Electronically Location Shippers' Car Advice Reports
TELSCOM ... Telemetry-Surveillance-Communications
TELSCPD ... Telescoped
TELSIM.... Teletypewriter Simulation
TELSUN ... Television Series for United Nations [*A foundation formed to produce, and telecast on a commercial basis, dramatized descriptions of UN activities*]
TEL SUR... Telephone Survey   (MUGU)
TEL-SYS... Telephone System
TELT........ Teltronics, Inc. [*NASDAQ symbol*]   (NQ)
TELTA ...... Tethered Lighter-than-Air   (KSC)
TELUQ...... Tele-Universite [*University of Quebec*] [*Telecommunications service*]   (TSSD)
TELUQ...... Tele-Universite (University of Quebec) [*Quebec, PQ*] [*Telecommunications*]   (TSSD)
TELUS ..... Telemetric Universal Sensor
TELV........ TeleVideo Systems, Inc. [*NASDAQ symbol*]   (NQ)
Tel Vaani ... Telugu Vaani [*Hyderabad*] [*A publication*]
TEM .... Exporter. Malta's Monthly Export Journal [*A publication*]
TEM .... Memphis University School, Hyde Library, Memphis, TN [*OCLC symbol*]   (OCLC)
TeM .... O Tempo e o Modo [*A publication*]
TEM .... Officers for Temporary Service [*Navy*] [*British*]   (ROG)
TEM .... Roswell Park Memorial Institute [*Research code symbol*]
TEM .... Target Engagement Message   (NVT)
TEM .... Target Evaluation Maintenance   (MCD)
TEM .... Technical Error Message [*Aviation*]
TE & M...... Telephone Engineer and Management [*Harcourt Brace Jovanovich Publications, Inc.*] [*Geneva, IL*] [*Information service or system*] [*A publication*]
TEM .... Temco National Corp. [*AMEX symbol*]   (SPSG)
TEM .... Temiskaming & Northern Ontario Railway [*AAR code*]
tem .... Temne [*MARC language code*] [*Library of Congress*]   (LCCP)
TEM .... Temora [*Australia*] [*Airport symbol*]   (OAG)
TEM .... Temperature   (DEN)
TEM .... Tempered   (DEN)
Tem............ [*The*] Templar [*1788-79*] [*London*] [*A publication*]   (DLA)
TEM .... Template   (DEN)
TEM .... Tempo [*Music*]
Tem............ Tempo [*Record label*] [*Germany*]
Tem............ Tempore [*In the Time Of*] [*Latin*]   (DLA)
TEM .... Temuco [*Chile*] [*Seismograph station code, US Geological Survey*] [*Closed*]   (SEIS)
TeM .... Tennessee Microfilms, Nashville, TN [*Library symbol*] [*Library of Congress*]   (LCLS)
TEM .... Terramar Resources Corp. [*Toronto Stock Exchange symbol*] [*Vancouver Stock Exchange symbol*]
TEM .... Texas Episodic Model [*Environmental Protection Agency*]   (GFGA)
TEM .... Thermal Expansion Molding   (MCD)
TEM .... Thermoelectric Module
TEM .... Tomato Extract Medium   (OA)
TEM .... Torpedo Evasive Maneuvering [*Navy*]
TEM .... Transmission Electron Micrograph
TEM........ Transmission Electron Microscope [*or Microscopy*]
TEM .... Transverse Electromagnetic [*Wave*] [*Radio*]
TEM .... Triethylenemelamine [*Organic chemistry*]
TEM .... Typical Egg Mass
TEMA .... Telecommunication Engineering and Manufacturing Association [*British*]
TEMA .... Test of Early Mathematics Ability
TEMA .... Test and Evaluation Management Agency [*Army*]   (RDA)
TEMA .... Trace Elements in Man and Animals [*An international symposium*]
TEMA .... Training, Education, and Mutual Assistance in the Marine Sciences [*IOC working committee*]   (MSC)
TEMA .... Tubular Exchanger Manufacturers Association   (EA)
TEMAC...... Temporary Active Duty
TEMAC..... Turbine Engine Monitoring and Control [*ASMAP Electronics Ltd.*] [*Software package*]   (NCC)
TEMACDIFOT ... Temporary Active Duty in a Flying Status Involving Operational or Training Flights [*Navy*]
TEMACDIFOTINS ... Temporary Active Duty under Instruction in a Flying Status Involving Operational or Training Flights [*Navy*]
TEMACDU ... Temporary Active Duty [*Navy*]
TEMACINS ... Temporary Active Duty under Instruction [*Navy*]

TEMADD ... Temporary Additional Duty [*Navy*]
TEMADDCON ... Temporary Additional Duty in Connection with [*Specified activity*] [*Navy*]
TEMADDINS ... Temporary Additional Duty under Instruction [*Navy*]
TEMARS .. Transportation Environmental Measurement and Recording System   (MCD)
Temas Odontol ... Temas Odontologicos [*A publication*]
Temas Quim Bibliogr Quim Argent ... Temas de Quimica y Bibliografia Quimica Argentina [*A publication*]
Temas Socs ... Temas Sociales [*A publication*]
TEMAW ... Tactical Effectiveness of Minefields in Antiarmor Warfare Systems [*Army*]   (INF)
TEMAWS ... Tactical Effectiveness of Minefields in Antiarmor Warfare Systems [*Army*]
TEMC........ Temco Home Health Care Products, Inc. [*NASDAQ symbol*]   (NQ)
TEMC........ Test and Evaluation Management Course   (MCD)
TEM-CAS ... Temporary-Casuality Pay Record [*Navy*]   (DNAB)
TEMCON ... Temporary Duty Connection [*Navy*]   (DNAB)
TEMDIFOT ... Temporary Duty in a Flying Status Involving Operational or Training Flights [*Navy*]
TEMDIFOTINS ... Temporary Duty under Instruction in a Flying Status Involving Operational or Training Flights [*Navy*]
TEMDIFPRO ... Temporary Duty in a Flying Status Involving Proficiency Flying [*Navy*]   (DNAB)
TEMDU .... Temporary Duty [*Navy*]
TEMDUCON ... Temporary Duty in Connection With [*Specified activity*] [*Navy*]
TEMDU DIS ... Temporary Duty Pending Disciplinary Action [*Navy*]   (DNAB)
TEMDU FFA ... Temporary Duty for Further Assignment [*Navy*]   (DNAB)
TEMDU FFT ... Temporary Duty for Further Transfer [*Navy*]   (DNAB)
TEMDUINS ... Temporary Duty under Instruction [*Navy*]
TEMDU PAT ... Temporary Duty as a Patient [*Navy*]   (DNAB)
TEMDU PSI ... Temporary Duty - Programmed Student Input [*Navy*]   (DNAB)
TEMDU SEP ... Temporary Duty Pending Separation [*Navy*]   (DNAB)
TEMEC..... Translational Electromagnetic Environment Chamber   (MCD)
TEMED..... Tetramethylethylenediamine [*Also, TMED, TMEDA*] [*Organic chemistry*]
TEMFLY... Temporary Duty Involving Flying [*Navy*]
TEMFLYINS ... Temporary Duty Involving Flying under Instruction [*Navy*]
TEM-GEN ... Temporary-General [*Navy*]   (DNAB)
TEMIA...... Technische Mitteilungen [*A publication*]
TEMIC...... Telecommunications Executive Management Institute of Canada   (TSSD)
TEMINS ... Temporary Duty under Instruction [*Navy*]
TEMIS ...... TRADOC [*Training and Doctrine Command*] Engineer Management Information System [*Army*]
TEMMF ...... Tax-Exempt Money Market Fund [*Investment term*]
TEMO ...... Test and Evaluation Management Office [*Army*]   (RDA)
TEMOA .... Tecnica Molitoria [*Italy*] [*A publication*]
TEMOD .... Test, Measurement, and Diagnostic Equipment Modernization [*Military*]   (RDA)
TEMP........ Electrical Resistance Temperature   (MCD)
TEMP........ [*The*] Expanded Memory Print Program   (SAA)
TEMP........ Tachyelectromagnetic Pulse
TEMP........ Taxation Employment Number [*Canada*]
TEMP........ Technique for Econometric Modeling Program   (BUR)
TEMP........ Temp-Stik Corp. [*NASDAQ symbol*]   (NQ)
TEMP........ Temperance   (ADA)
TEMP........ Temperate Zone
TEMP........ Temperature   (AAG)
TEMP........ Tempered   (AAG)
TEMP........ Template   (AAG)
TEMP........ Tempo [*Music*]
TEMP........ Temporal
TEMP........ Temporary
Temp.......... Temporary Light [*Navigation signal*]
TEMP........ Temporary Worker
TEMP........ Test and Evaluation Management Plan [*Army*]
TEMP........ Test Evaluation Master Plan   (MCD)
TEMP........ Texas Educational Microwave Project
TEMP........ Thermal Energy Management Process   (MCD)
TEMP........ Total Energy Management Professionals [*Defunct*]   (EA)
TEMPATT ... Temporarily Attached [*Navy*]   (DNAB)
Temp Bar ... Temple Bar [*A publication*]
TEMPDETD ... Temporary Detached Duty [*Navy*]   (DNAB)
TEMP DEXT ... Tempus Dextra [*Right Temple*] [*Medicine*]
Temp Emer Ct App ... Temporary Emergency Court of Appeals [*United States*]   (DLA)
TEMPER .. Technological, Economic, Military, and Political Evaluation Routine [*Computer-based simulation model*]
TEMPER .. Tent, Extendable, Modular, Personnel [*DoD*]
TEMPEST ... Transient Electromagnetic Pulse Emanation Standard   (MCD)
Temp Geo II ... Cases in Chancery Tempore George II [*England*] [*A publication*]   (DLA)
TEMPISTORS ... Temperature Compensating Resistors   (NATG)
TEMPL ..... Template [*Engineering*]
TemplE ...... Templeton Emerging Markets Fund, Inc. [*Associated Press abbreviation*]   (APAG)

Temple Dent Rev ... Temple Dental Review [*A publication*]
Temple Law ... Temple Law Quarterly [*A publication*]
Temple L Quart ... Temple Law Quarterly [*A publication*]
Temple & M ... Temple and Mew's English Crown Cases [*A publication*] (DLA)
Temple & M (Eng) ... Temple and Mew's English Crown Cases [*A publication*] (DLA)
TemplI .... Temple-Inland, Inc. [*Associated Press abbreviation*] (APAG)
Temp L Q ... Temple Law Quarterly [*A publication*]
Temp & M ... Temple and Mew's English Crown Cases [*1848-51*] [*A publication*] (DLA)
TEMPO ..... Tactical Electromagnetic Project Office [*Military*] (CAAL)
TEMPO ..... Technical Electronic Management Planning Organization
TEMPO ..... Technical Military Planning Operation (AAG)
TEMPO ..... Technique for Extreme Point Optimization (BUR)
TEMPO ..... Temporary (AAG)
TEMPO ..... Tetramethylpiperidinol N-oxyl [*Organic chemistry*]
TEMPO ..... Time and Effort Measurement through Periodic Observation (MCD)
TEMPO ..... Total Evaluation of Management and Production Output
TEMPOS .. Timed Environment Multipartitioned Operating System
TEMP PRIM ... Tempo Primo [*Original Tempo*] [*Music*]
TEMPRO ... Template-Assisted Intelligence Report Fusion Process
TEMPROX ... Temporary Duty Will Cover Approximately [*Navy*]
TEMPS ..... Transportable Electromagnetic Pulse Simulator (RDA)
TEMPSAL ... Temperature-Salinity Data [*Oceanography*] (MCD)
TEMP SINIST ... Tempori Sinistro [*To the Left Temple*] [*Pharmacy*] (ADA)
Temps Mod ... Temps Modernes [*A publication*]
Temp Univ LQ ... Temple University. Law Quarterly [*A publication*] (DLA)
TEMPUS .. Trans-European Mobility Scheme for Unversity Students [*EC*] (ECED)
Temp Wood ... Manitoba Reports Tempore Wood [*Canada*] [*A publication*] (DLA)
TEMPY ..... Temporary
TEM-RET ... Temporary Pay Record for a Retired Member [*Called to Active Duty*] [*Navy*] (DNAB)
TEMS .... Technical Engineering Management Support [*Air Force*]
TEMS .... Test Equipment Maintenance Set
TEMS .... Thermal Elastic Model Study
TEMS .... Toyota Electronically Modulated Suspension [*Automotive engineering*]
TEMS .... Transport Environment Monitoring System [*NASA*] (MCD)
TEMS .... Turbine Engine Monitoring System
TEMSEPRAD ... Temporary Duty Connection, Separation Processing. Upon Completion and When Directed Detach; Proceed Home for Release from Active Duty in Accordance with Instructions [*Navy*]
TEMSS ...... Total Emergency Medical Services System
TEMWAIT ... Temporary Duty Awaiting [*Specified event*] [*Navy*]
TEN .... Canarias [*Formerly, Tenerife*] [*Spain*] [*Geomagnetic observatory code*]
Ten .... Littleton's Tenures [*A publication*] (DSA)
TEN .... Tee-Comm Electronics, Inc. [*Toronto Stock Exchange symbol*]
ten .... Tenacious [*Quality of the bottom*] [*Nautical charts*]
TEN .... Tenerife [*Canary Islands*] [*Seismograph station code, US Geological Survey*] (SEIS)
TEN .... Tennessee (ROG)
TEN .... Tennessee Airways [*Alcoa, TN*] [*FAA designator*] (FAAC)
Ten .... Tennessee Reports [*A publication*] (ILCA)
TEN .... Tenor
TEN .... Tenuto [*Held, Sustained*] [*Music*]
TEN .... Total Enteral Nutrition
TEN .... Total Excreted [*or Excretory*] Nitrogen
TEN .... Toxic Epidermal Necrolysis [*Medicine*]
tenac .... Tenaculum [*Medicine*] (MAE)
Tenakh .... Torah, Veni'im, Ketubim (BJA)
Ten App ..... Tennessee Appeals Reports [*A publication*] (DLA)
Tenc .... Tenneco, Inc. [*Formerly, Tennessee Gas Transmission Co.*] [*Associated Press abbreviation*] (APAG)
TENCA ...... Traffic Engineering and Control [*England*] [*A publication*]
TENCAP ... Tactical Exploitation of National Space Capabilities
Ten Cas ..... Shannon's Tennessee Cases [*A publication*] (DLA)
Ten Cas ...... Thompson's Unreported Tennessee Cases [*A publication*] (DLA)
TENCY ...... Tenancy (ROG)
Tendances Conjonct ... Tendances de la Conjoncture [*A publication*]
Tendances Polit Act Dom ... Tendances et Politiques Actuelles dans le Domaine de l'Habitation de la Construction et de la Planification [*A publication*]
TENDR ..... Tendring [*England*]
TENEMT ... Tenement (ROG)
TENERA ...... Tenera Ltd. [*Associated Press abbreviation*] (APAG)
TENES ..... Teaching English to the Non-English Speaking
TEng .... Teaching English [*A publication*]
TENG .... Technical Engineers Association
TEng .... Technician Engineer [*British*] (DBQ)
TEngAMIN ... Technician Engineer of the Institution of Metallurgists [*British*] (DBQ)
Ten Mag .... Tennis Magazine [*A publication*]
TENN .... Tennessee (AAG)

TENN .... Tennessee Natural Resources [*NASDAQ symbol*] (NQ)
TENN .... Tennessee Railway Co. [*AAR code*]
Tenn .... Tennessee Reports [*A publication*]
Tenn .... Tennessee Supreme Court Reports [*A publication*] (DLA)
Tenn Admin Comp ... Official Compilation of the Rules and Regulations of the State of Tennessee [*A publication*] (DLA)
Tenn Admin Reg ... Tennessee Administrative Register [*A publication*] (DLA)
Tenn Ag Exp ... Tennessee. Agricultural Experiment Station. Publications [*A publication*]
Tenn Agric Exp Stn Annu Rep ... Tennessee. Agricultural Experiment Station. Annual Report [*A publication*]
Tenn Agric Exp Stn Bull ... Tennessee. Agricultural Experiment Station. Bulletin [*A publication*]
Tenn Agric Exp Stn Farm Econ Bull ... Tennessee. Agricultural Experiment Station. Farm Economics Bulletin [*A publication*]
Tenn Apiculture ... Tennessee Apiculture [*A publication*]
Tenn App ... Tennessee Appeals [*A publication*]
Tenn App ... Tennessee Appeals Reports [*A publication*] (DLA)
Tenn App ... Tennessee Appellate Bulletin [*A publication*] (DLA)
Tenn App ... Tennessee Civil Appeals Reports [*A publication*] (DLA)
Tenn App Bull ... Tennessee Appellate Bulletin [*A publication*] (DLA)
Tenn Appeals ... Tennessee Appeals Reports [*A publication*] (DLA)
Tenn App R ... Tennessee Appeals Reports [*A publication*] (DLA)
Tenn Bar J ... Tennessee Bar Journal [*A publication*]
Tenn BJ ..... Tennessee Bar Journal [*A publication*]
Tenn Cas .... Shannon's Unreported Tennessee Cases [*1847-1894*] [*A publication*] (DLA)
Tenn Cas (Shannon) ... [*R. T.*] Shannon's Tennessee Cases [*A publication*] (DLA)
Tenn Cas (Shannon) ... Thompson's Unreported Tennessee Cases [*1847-69*] [*A publication*] (DLA)
Tenn CCA ... Tennessee Court of Civil Appeals (DLA)
Tenn CCA (Higgins) ... Higgins' Tennessee Court of Civil Appeals Reports [*A publication*] (DLA)
Tenn Ch ..... Cooper's Tennessee Chancery Reports [*A publication*] (DLA)
Tenn Ch A ... Tennessee Chancery Appeals [*A publication*] (DLA)
Tenn Chancery ... Tennessee Chancery Reports (Cooper) [*A publication*] (DLA)
Tenn Chancery App ... Tennessee Chancery Appeals Reports (Wright) [*A publication*] (DLA)
Tenn Ch App ... Tennessee Chancery Appeals (Wright) [*A publication*] (DLA)
Tenn Ch App Dec ... Tennessee Chancery Appeals Decisions [*1895-1907*] [*A publication*] (DLA)
Tenn Ch Ap Reps ... Wright's Tennessee Chancery Appeals Reports [*A publication*] (DLA)
Tenn Ch R ... Tennessee Chancery Reports (Cooper) [*A publication*] (DLA)
Tenn Civ A ... Tennessee Civil Appeals [*A publication*] (DLA)
Tenn Civ App ... Tennessee Civil Appeals [*A publication*] (DLA)
Tennco .... Tenneco, Inc. [*Formerly, Tennessee Gas Transmission Co.*] [*Associated Press abbreviation*] (APAG)
Tenn Code Ann ... Tennessee Code, Annotated [*A publication*] (DLA)
Tenn Comp R & Regs ... Official Compilation Rules and Regulations of the State of Tennessee [*A publication*]
Tenn Conservationist ... Tennessee Conservationist [*A publication*]
Tenn Cr App ... Tennessee Criminal Appeals [*A publication*] (DLA)
Tenn Crim App ... Tennessee Criminal Appeals Reports [*A publication*] (DLA)
Tenn Dep Conserv Div Geol Bull ... Tennessee. Department of Conservation. Division of Geology. Bulletin [*A publication*]
Tenn Dep Conserv Div Geol Inf Circ ... Tennessee. Department of Conservation. Division of Geology. Information Circular [*A publication*]
Tenn Dept Labor Ann Rept ... Tennessee. Department of Labor. Annual Report [*A publication*]
Tenn Div Geol Bull ... Tennessee. Division of Geology. Bulletin [*A publication*]
Tenn Div Geol Environ Geol Ser ... Tennessee. Division of Geology. Environmental Geology Series [*A publication*]
Tenn Div Geol Inf Circ ... Tennessee. Division of Geology. Information Circular [*A publication*]
Tenn Div Geol Inform Circ ... Tennessee. Division of Geology. Information Circular [*A publication*]
Tenn Div Geol Rep Invest ... Tennessee. Division of Geology. Report of Investigations [*A publication*]
Tenn Div Water Resour Water Resour Ser ... Tennessee. Division of Water Resources. Water Resources Series [*A publication*]
Tenn Eng ... Tennessee Engineer [*A publication*]
Tennessee Acad Sci Jour ... Tennessee Academy of Science. Journal [*A publication*]
Tennessee Div Geology Geol Map ... Tennessee. Division of Geology. Geologic Map [*A publication*]
Tennessee Div Geology Rept Inv ... Tennessee. Division of Geology. Report of Investigations [*A publication*]
Tennessee R ... Tennessee Reports [*A publication*] (DLA)
Tennessee Rep ... Tennessee Reports [*A publication*] (DLA)
Tennessees Bus ... Tennessee's Business [*A publication*]
TENNEY ... Tenney Engineering, Inc. [*Associated Press abbreviation*] (APAG)
Tenn Farm & Home Sci ... Tennessee Farm and Home Science [*A publication*]

Tenn Farm Home Sci Progr Rep ... Tennessee Farm and Home Science. Progress Report. University of Tennessee. Agricultural Experiment Station [*A publication*]
Tenn Fm Home Sci Prog Rep ... Tennessee Farm and Home Science. Progress Report [*A publication*]
Tenn Folk S ... Tennessee Folklore Society. Bulletin [*A publication*]
Tenn G S Res Tenn B ... Tennessee State Geological Survey. Resources of Tennessee. Bulletin [*A publication*]
Tenn His M ... Tennessee Historical Magazine [*A publication*]
Tenn Hist Mag ... Tennessee Magazine of History [*A publication*]
Tenn Hist Q ... Tennessee Historical Quarterly [*A publication*]
Tenn Jur .... Tennessee Jurisprudence [*A publication*]   (DLA)
Tenn Juris ... Tennessee Jurisprudence [*A publication*]   (DLA)
Tenn Law ... Tennessee Lawyer [*A publication*]   (DLA)
Tenn Law Rev ... Tennessee Law Review [*A publication*]
Tenn Leg Rep ... Tennessee Legal Reporter [*A publication*]   (DLA)
Tenn Libn .. Tennessee Librarian [*A publication*]
Tenn Libr .. Tennessee Librarian [*A publication*]
Tenn Librn ... Tennessee Librarian [*A publication*]
Tenn L R .... Tennessee Law Review [*A publication*]
Tenn L Rev ... Tennessee Law Review [*A publication*]
Tenn Mag .. Tennessee Magazine [*A publication*]
Tenn Priv Acts ... Private Acts of the State of Tennessee [*A publication*]   (DLA)
Tenn Pub Acts ... Public Acts of the State of Tennessee [*A publication*]   (DLA)
Tenn R .... Tennessee Reports [*A publication*]   (DLA)
Tenn Rep .... Tennessee Reports [*A publication*]   (DLA)
Tenn St Bd Health B Rp ... Tennessee State Board of Health. Bulletin. Report [*A publication*]
Tenn Surv Bus ... Tennessee Survey of Business [*A publication*]
TENN-TOM ... Tennessee-Tombigbee [*Proposed waterway*]
Tenn Univ Eng Exp Sta Bull ... Tennessee University. Engineering Experiment Station. Bulletin [*A publication*]
Tenn Univ Water Resour Res Cent Res Rep ... Tennessee University. Water Resources Research Center. Research Report [*A publication*]
Tenn Val Auth Chem Eng Bul ... Tennessee Valley Authority. Chemical Engineering Bulletin [*A publication*]
Tenn Val Auth Natl Fert Dev Cent Bull Y ... Tennessee Valley Authority. National Fertilizer Development Center. Bulletin Y [*A publication*]
Tenn Valley Perspect ... Tennessee Valley Perspective [*A publication*]
Tenn Wildl ... Tennessee Wildlife [*A publication*]
TENOC ..... Ten-Year Oceanographic Program [*Navy*]
TENR .... Technically Enhanced Naturally Radioactive   (NRCH)
TENRAP ... Technically Enhanced Naturally Radioactive Product   (NRCH)
TENS .... Tensile
TENS .... Tension   (AAG)
TENS .... Training Element Need Statement
TENS .... Transcutaneous Electrical Nerve Stimulation [*Also, TES, TNS*] [*A method of pain control*] [*Medicine*]
Tensai Kenkyu Hokoku Suppl ... Tensai Kenkyu Hokoku. Supplement [*Japan*] [*A publication*]
TENSEGRITY ... Tensional Integrity [*Construction principle named by Buckminster Fuller*]
Tenside ...... Tenside-Detergents [*A publication*]
Tenside-Deterg ... Tenside-Detergents [*A publication*]
TENT .... Tenant   (ROG)
TENT .... Tenement   (ROG)
TENT .... Tentative   (AAG)
TENV .... Totally Enclosed - Nonventilated
TEO .... Teal Industry Ltd. [*Vancouver Stock Exchange symbol*]
TEO .... Technical Electronic Office [*Data General Corp.*]
TEO .... Telephone Equipment Order [*Telecommunications*]   (TEL)
TEO .... Teoloyucan [*Mexico*] [*Geomagnetic observatory code*]
TEO .... Terapo [*Papua New Guinea*] [*Airport symbol*]   (OAG)
TEO .... Terato Resources Ltd. [*Toronto Stock Exchange symbol*]
TEO .... Test Equipment Operator
TEO .... To Expiry Only   (AIA)
TEO .... Total Extractable Organic [*Analytical chemistry*]
T & EO ...... Training and Evaluation Outline
TEO .... Transferred Electron Oscillator
TEO .... Transmittal Engineering Order
TEOA .... Test and Evaluation Objectives Annex   (MCD)
TEOA .... Triethanolamine [*Organic chemistry*]
TEOC .... Texas Eagle Oil Co. [*NASDAQ symbol*]   (NQ)
TEOF .... Triethyl Orthoformate [*Organic chemistry*]
Teolisuuden Keskuslab Tied ... Teolisuuden Keskuslaboratorion Tiedonantoja [*A publication*]
Teollis Tiedottaa ... Teollisuuslitto Tiedottaa [*A publication*]
Teol Vida ... Teologia y Vida [*A publication*]
TEOM .... Tapered Element Oscillating Microbalance
TEOM .... Transformer Environment Overcurrent Monitor   (IEEE)
Teor Ehlektrotekh ... Teoreticheskaya Ehlektrotekhnika [*A publication*]
Teor Eksp Biofiz ... Teoreticheskaya i Eksperimental'naya Biofizica [*A publication*]
Teor & Eksp Khim ... Teoreticheskaya i Eksperimental'naya Khimiya [*A publication*]
Teoret Elektrotekhn ... L'vovskii Gosudarstvennyi Universitet. Teoreticheskaya Elektrotekhnika [*A publication*]
Teoret Mat Fiz ... Teoreticeskaja i Matematiceskaja Fizika [*A publication*]

Teoret i Prikladna Meh ... Teoreticna i Prikladna Mehanika Harkivs'kii Derzavnii Universitet Imeni O. M. Gor'kogo [*A publication*]
Teoret Prikl Mat ... Teoreticna i Prikladna Matematika [*A publication*]
Teoret i Prikl Mekh ... Belorusskii Politekhnicheski Institut. Teoreticheskaya i Prikladnaya Mekhanika [*A publication*]
Teoret Priloz Meh ... B'lgarska Akademija na Naukite. Teoreticna i Prilozna Mehanika [*A publication*]
Teoret i Priloz Meh ... Teoreticna i Prilozna Mehanika [*A publication*]
Teor Funktsii Funktsional Anal i Prilozhen ... Khar'kovskii Ordena Trudovogo Krasnogo Znameni Gosudarstvennyi Universitet Imeni A. M. Gor'kogo Teoriya Funktsii Funktsional'nyi Analiz i Ikh Prilozheniya [*A publication*]
Teor Prakt Metall (Dnepropetrovsk) ... Teoriya i Praktika Metallurgii (Dnepropetrovsk) [*A publication*]
Teor Prakt Podgot Koksovaniya Uglei ... Teoriya i Praktika Podgotovki i Koksovaniya Uglei [*A publication*]
Teor Prakt Stomatol ... Teoriya i Praktika Stomatologii [*A publication*]
Teor Prakt Szhiganiya Gaza ... Teoriya i Praktika Szhiganiya Gaza [*Former USSR*] [*A publication*]
Teor Prilozh Mekh ... Teoretichna i Prilozhna Mekhanika [*A publication*]
Teor Primen Meh ... Jugoslovensko Drustvo za Mehaniku. Teorijska i Primenjena Mehanika [*A publication*]
TEORS ..... Transient Electro-Optic Raman Scattering [*Physics*]
Teor Verojatn Mat Stat ... Teoriya Verojatnostej i Matematicheskaya Statistika [*A publication*]
Teor Verojatnost i Mat Statist ... Teorija Verojatnostei i Matematiceskaja Statistika [*A publication*]
Teor Veroya ... Teoriya Veroyatnostei i Ee Primeneniya [*A publication*]
Teor Veroyatn Primen ... Teoriya Veroyatnostei i Ee Primeneniya [*A publication*]
Teor Veroyat Primen ... Teoriya Veroyatnostei i Ee Primeneniya [*Former USSR*] [*A publication*]
TEOS .... Tetraethoxysilane [*Organic radical*]
TEOS .... Tetraethyl Orthosilicate [*Organic chemistry*]   (NASA)
TEOS .... Tillotson Equation of State [*Physical chemistry*]
TEOSS ..... Tactical Emitter Operational Support System   (MCD)
TEOTA ...... [*The*] Eyes of the Army   (AAG)
TEP .... Table Editing Process
TEP .... Tactical ELINT Processor   (MCD)
TEP .... Tape Edit Processor [*Data processing*]
TEP .... Tau Epsilon Phi [*Fraternity*]
TEP .... Technical Education Program   (OICC)
TEP .... Technical Evaluation Panel [*In various federal government agencies*]   (NASA)
TEP .... Temperature Extreme Pressure   (DNAB)
TEP .... Tepecintle [*Race of maize*]
TEP .... Teptep [*Papua New Guinea*] [*Airport symbol*]   (OAG)
TEP .... Terminal Error Program
TEP .... Territory Enterprises Proprietary
TEP .... Test and Evaluation Plan [*Military*]   (CAAL)
TEP .... Tetraethoxypropane [*Organic chemistry*]
TEP .... Thermal Enzyme Probe
TEP .... Thermoelectric Power [*Thermodynamics*]
TEP .... Thromboendophlebectomy [*Medicine*]   (MAE)
TEP .... Token Economy Program [*Psychiatry*]
TEP .... Tons Equivalent of Petroleum [*Fuel measure*]
TEP .... Torpedo Ejection Pump   (DNAB)
TEP .... Total Extractable Protein [*Food technology*]
TEP .... Toxicant Extraction Procedure
TEP .... Trace Element Pattern   (KSC)
TEP .... Tracheo-Esophageal Puncture [*Medicine*]
TEP .... Transmitter Experiment Package
TEP .... Transparent Electrophotography [*Proposed archival storage medium*]
TEP .... Transportable Equation Program   (DNAB)
TEP .... Triethyl-Phosphine [*Organic chemistry*]
TEP .... Tube Evaluation Program
TEP .... Tucson Electric Power Co. [*NYSE symbol*]   (SPSG)
TEP .... Turbine Extreme Pressure   (MCD)
TEP .... Turkiye Emekci Partisi [*Workers' Party of Turkey*] [*Political party*]   (PPW)
TEP .... Tyrone Energy Park   (NRCH)
TEPA .... Roswell Park Memorial Institute [*Research code symbol*]
TEPA .... Tetraethylenepentamine [*Organic chemistry*]
TEPA .... Triethylenephosphoramide [*Also, APO*] [*Organic chemistry*]
TEPAC ...... Tube Engineering Panel Advisory Council   (EA)
TEPC .... Test and Evaluation Planning Committee [*Military*]   (CAAL)
Tepco .... Teppco Partners Ltd. [*Associated Press abbreviation*]   (APAG)
TEPD .... Trademark Examining Procedure Directives [*A publication*]
TEPE .... Target Engagement Proficiency Exercise [*Military*]
TEPG .... Test Evaluation Planning Group   (MCD)
TEPG .... Thermionic Electrical Power Generator   (IEEE)
TEPI .... Technical Equipment Planning Information
TEPI .... Terminal Phase Intercept
TEPI .... Training Equipment Planning Information [*Military*]   (AFM)
TEPI .... Triadal Equated Personality Inventory [*Psychology*]
TEPIAC ..... Thermophysical and Electronic Properties Information Analysis Center [*Later, HTMIAC*] [*Purdue University*]
TEPIC .... Tris(epoxypropyl)isocyanurate [*Organic chemistry*]
TEPID .... Tepidus [*Lukewarm*] [*Pharmacy*]   (ROG)

TEPIGEN ... Television Picture Generator (MCD)
Tepl Naprazh Elem Konstr ... Teplovye Napryazheniya v Elementakh Konstruktsii [*A publication*]
Teploehnerg ... Teploehnergetika [*A publication*]
Teploenergetika Akad Nauk SSSR Energ Inst ... Teploenergetika Akademiya Nauk SSSR. Energeticheskii Institut [*A publication*]
Teplofiz Kharakt Veshchestv ... Teplofizicheskie Kharakteristiki Veshchestv [*Former USSR*] [*A publication*]
Teplofiz Optim Tepl Protsessov ... Teplofizika i Optimizatsiya Teplovykh Protsessov [*A publication*]
Teplofiz Svoistva Veshchestv ... Teplofizicheskie Svoistva Veshchestv [*A publication*]
Teplofiz Svoistva Veshchestv Mater ... Teplofizicheskie Svoistva Veshchestv i Materialov [*A publication*]
Teplofiz Teplotekh ... Teplofizika i Teplotekhnika [*A publication*]
Teplofiz Vys Temp ... Teplofizika Vysokikh Temperatur [*A publication*]
Teploprovodnost Diffuz ... Teploprovodnost i Diffuziya [*A publication*]
Teplosi Khoz ... Teplosilovoc Khozyaistvo [*A publication*]
TEPOS ...... Test Program Operating System
TEPP .... Tetraethyl Pyrophosphate [*Insecticide*] [*Pharmacology*]
TEPP .... Turbine Engine Power Plant (DWSG)
TEPPS .... Technique for Establishing Personnel Performance Standards [*Navy*]
TEPR .... Tomahawk Experimental Reaction [*Navy*]
TEPR .... Training Equipment Progress Report
TEPRSSC ... Technical Electronic Product Radiation Safety Standards Committee (MCD)
TEPS .... National Commission on Teacher Education and Professional Standards [*Defunct*]
TEPSA ...... Trans European Policy Studies Association (EA)
TEQ .... Toxicity Equivalent
TEQ .... Trian Equities Ltd. [*Vancouver Stock Exchange symbol*]
TEQ .... Turner Equity Investors, Inc. [*AMEX symbol*] (SPSG)
TEQ .... Twenty-Foot Equivalent [*Shipping*]
TEQE .... Trian Equities Ltd. [*NASDAQ symbol*] (NQ)
TER .... Tau Epsilon Rho [*Fraternity*]
TeR .... Te Reo [*A publication*]
TER .... Technical Evaluation Report [*Nuclear energy*] (NRCH)
TER .... Tera Mines Ltd. [*Toronto Stock Exchange symbol*]
TER .... Teradyne, Inc. [*NYSE symbol*] (SPSG)
TER .... Terceira [*Azores*] [*Airport symbol*] (OAG)
TER .... Tere [*Rub*] [*Pharmacy*]
Ter .... Terence [*Second century BC*] [*Classical studies*] (OCD)
ter .... Tereno [*MARC language code*] [*Library of Congress*] (LCCP)
TER .... Terra Mines Ltd. [*Toronto Stock Exchange symbol*] [*Vancouver Stock Exchange symbol*]
TER .... Terrace
TER .... Terranova [*Guatemala*] [*Seismograph station code, US Geological Survey*] (SEIS)
TER .... Terrazzo
TER .... Territory
Ter .... Terry's Delaware Reports [*A publication*] (DLA)
TER .... Tertiary (KSC)
Ter .... Terumot (BJA)
TER .... Test Effectiveness Ratio [*Data processing*]
TER .... Test Equipment Readiness [*NASA*] (NASA)
TER .... Test Evaluation Report [*NASA*] (KSC)
TER .... Thermal Enhancement Ratio
TE-R .... Thermostable E-Rosetting [*Cells*] [*Medicine*]
TER .... Time Estimating Relationship (NASA)
TER .... Time and Event Recorder
TER .... Total Endoplasmic Reticulum [*Cytology*]
TER .... Total External Reflection
TE/R .... Trailing Edge Radius (MSA)
TER .... Training Equipment Requirements Plan
TER .... Transcapillary Escape Rate
TER .... Transfer Effectiveness Ratio
TER .... Transmission Equivalent Resistance (IEEE)
TER .... Travel Expense Report (SAA)
TER .... Triple Ejection Rack (NVT)
TER .... True Height Above Aerodrome Level [*Aviation*] (AIA)
TERA .... Teradyne, Inc. [*NASDAQ symbol*] (NQ)
TERA .... Terminal Effects Research and Analysis Group [*New Mexico Institute of Mining and Technology*] [*Research center*] (RCD)
TERA .... Test of Early Reading Ability
TERA .... Tradable Emission Reduction Assessments [*Environmental Protection Agency*]
TERA .... TSCA [*Toxic Substances Control Act*] Experimental Release Application [*Environmental Protection Agency*]
TERAA ...... Terapia [*A publication*]
TERAC ...... Tactical Electromagnetic Readiness Advisory Council (MCD)
TERAG ...... Transportable Electronic Receiving Antenna Group (DWSG)
Ter Arkh .... Terapevticheskii Arkhiv [*A publication*]
TERAS ...... Tactical Energy Requirements and Supply System (MCD)
TERAT ...... Teratology (ROG)
Teratog Carcinog Mutagen ... Teratogenesis, Carcinogenesis, and Mutagenesis [*A publication*]
Teratogenesis Carcinog Mutagen ... Teratogenesis, Carcinogenesis, and Mutagenesis [*A publication*]
TERB .... Terrazzo Base

TERC .... Technical Education Research Centers, Inc. [*Cambridge, MA*] [*Research center*]
TERCOM ... Terrain Contour Mapping (MCD)
TERCOM ... Terrain Contour Matching [*Navigation system*] [*Air Force*]
TERCOM ... Terrain Correlation Method
TERD .... Turbine Electric Reduction Drive
Terdyn .... Terradyne, Inc. [*Associated Press abbreviation*] (APAG)
TEREA ...... Technology Review [*A publication*]
TEREBINTH ... Terebinthinae Oleum [*Oil of Turpentine*] [*Pharmacology*] (ROG)
TEREC ...... Tactical Electronic Reconnaissance [*Aircraft*]
Terent .... Terentius Clemens [*Flourished, 2nd century*] [*Authority cited in pre-1607 legal work*] (DSA)
TERENVSVC ... Terrestrial Environmental Services [*Army*] (AABC)
Terex .... Terex Corp. [*Associated Press abbreviation*] (APAG)
TERF .... Trudeau Early Retirement Fund [*Defunct*] [*Established 1982 by Canadians who hoped that the money would persuade their prime minister to retire from office*]
TERG .... Training Equipment Requirements Guide (KSC)
TERI .... Torpedo Effective Range Indicator
TERL .... Test Engineer Readiness List [*NASA*] (NASA)
TERL .... Test Equipment Readiness List [*NASA*] (NASA)
TERLS ...... Thumba Equatorial Launching Station [*Indian rocket station*]
TERM .... Temporary Equipment Recovery Mission (CINC)
Term .... Term Reports [*North Carolina*] [*1816-18*] [*A publication*] (DLA)
Term .... Term Reports, English King's Bench (Durnford and East's Reports) [*A publication*] (DLA)
TERM .... Terminal (AAG)
TERM .... Terminal Data Corp. [*NASDAQ symbol*] (NQ)
TERM .... Terminate (AFM)
TERM .... Terminology
TERM .... Termite (ADA)
TERMA ..... Termotecnica [*A publication*]
Termeloeszoevet Tanacsadoja ... Termeloeszoevetkezetek Tanacsadoja [*A publication*]
Termes de la Ley ... Terms of the Common Laws and Statutes Expounded and Explained by John Rastell [*1685*] [*A publication*] (DLA)
Termeszettud Koezloeny ... Termeszettudomanyi Koezloeny [*A publication*]
TERMIA ..... Association Internationale de Terminologie [*International Association of Terminology*] [*Quebec, PQ*] (EAIO)
TERMINACTRAORD ... Directed to Request Termination of Inactive Duty Training Orders [*Navy*]
TERMINON ... Termination (ROG)
TERMINOQ ... Banque de Terminologie de Quebec [*Terminology Bank of Quebec*] [*French Language Board*] [*Information service or system*]
TERMN .... Termination
Term NC .... Taylor's North Carolina Term Reports [*A publication*] (DLA)
TERMNET ... International Network for Terminology [*INFOTERM*] [*Vienna, Austria*]
Term Obrab Fiz Met ... Termicheskaya Obrabotka i Fizika Metallov [*A publication*]
Termodin Fiz Kinet Strukturoobra Svoista Chuguna Stali ... Termodinamika i Fizicheskaya Kinetika Strukturoobrazovaniya i Svoistva Chuguna i Stali [*A publication*]
Termodin Fiz Kinet Strukturoobraz Stali Chugune ... Termodinamika i Fizicheskaya Kinetika Strukturoobrazovaniya v Stali i Chugune [*A publication*]
Termodin Fiz Kinet Strukturoobraz Svoistva Chuguna Stali ... Termodinamika i Fizicheskaya Kinetika Strukturoobrazovaniya i Svoistva Chuguna i Stali [*A publication*]
Termoprochn Mater Konstr Elem ... Termoprochnost Materialov i Konstruktivnykh Elementov [*Former USSR*] [*A publication*]
Termotecnica Suppl ... Termotecnica. Supplemento [*Italy*] [*A publication*]
TERM PWR ... Terminator Power [*Data processing*]
Term R .... Term Reports, English King's Bench (Durnford and East's Reports) [*A publication*] (DLA)
Term Rep ... Term Reports, English King's Bench (Durnford and East's Reports) [*England*] [*A publication*] (DLA)
Term Rep (NC) ... Taylor's North Carolina Term Reports [*4 North Carolina*] [*A publication*] (DLA)
TERMS ..... Terminal Management System [*Military*] (AABC)
TERMTRAN ... Terminal Translator (KSC)
TERN .... Transnational European Rural Network [*Belgium*] (EAIO)
TERO .... Tribal Employment Rights Office
Ter Ortop Stomatol ... Terapevticheskaya i Ortopedicheskaya Stomatologiya [*A publication*]
TERP .... Terminal Equipment Replacement Program [*Electronic communications system*] [*Department of State*]
TERP .... Terminal Instrument Procedure [*Aviation*]
TERP .... Terrain Elevation Retrieval Program (IEEE)
TERPACIS ... Trust Territory of the Pacific Islands
TERPE ...... Tactical Electronic Reconnaissance Processing and Evaluation [*Air Force*] (MCD)
TERPES .... Tactical Electronic Reconnaissance Processing and Evaluation System (MCD)
TERPROM ... Terrain Profile Matching [*British*]
TERPS .... Terminal Enquiry/Response Programming System [*British*]

TERPS....... Terminal Instrument Procedures [*Military*]
TERPS....... Terminal Planning System [*Military*]
TERR......... Terrace
Terr............ Terrell's Reports [*38-71 Texas*] [*A publication*]   (DLA)
TERR.......... Territory   (AFM)
Terr............ Terrorist [*Slang term used by whites in Zimbabwe to refer to a black nationalist guerrilla*]
Terra.......... Terra Industries, Inc. [*Associated Press abbreviation*]   (APAG)
TERRA...... Terricide-Escape by Rethinking, Research, Action [*An association*]
Terra Amer ... Terra America [*A publication*]
TERRAP ... TERRAP [*Territorial Apprehensiveness*] Programs [*Commercial firm*]   (EA)
Terra Trent ... Terra Trentina [*A publication*]
TERREL....... Terrain Elevation   (SAA)
Terre Maroc ... Terre Marocaine [*A publication*]
TERRES.... Territorial Residents
TERRESTAR ... Terrestrial Application of Solar Technology and Research   (MCD)
TERRHICO ... Territorial Rhine Coordination [*NATO*]   (NATG)
Territ.......... Territorian [*A publication*]   (APTA)
TERRIT..... Territory
Terr L.......... Territories Law [*Northwest Territories*] [*A publication*]   (DLA)
Terr L (Can) ... Territories Law Reports [*1885-1907*] [*Canada*] [*A publication*]   (DLA)
Terr LJ........ Territory Law Journal [*A publication*]   (APTA)
Terr LR...... Territories Law Reports [*1885-1907*] [*Canada*] [*A publication*]   (DLA)
Terr Magn ... Terrestrial Magnetism and Atmospheric Electricity [*A publication*]
Terr Magn Atmos Electr ... Terrestrial Magnetism and Atmospheric Electricity [*A publication*]
Terror......... Terrorism [*A publication*]
Terrorilla ... Terrorism and Guerrilla Warfare [*Israel*]
Terr & Wal ... Terrell and Walker's Reports [*38-51 Texas*] [*A publication*]   (DLA)
Terr & Walk ... Terrell and Walker's Reports [*38-51 Texas*] [*A publication*]   (DLA)
TERS......... Tactical Electronic Reconnaissance System   (IEEE)
TerS.......... Terra Santa [*Jerusalem*]   (BJA)
TER SIM... Tere Simul [*Rub Together*] [*Latin*]   (ADA)
TERSSE.... Total Earth Resources System for the Shuttle Era [*NASA*]
Ter Stomatol ... Terapevticheskaya Stomatologiya [*A publication*]
tert.............. Tertiary [*Also, t*] [*Chemistry*]
TERT........ Tertiary [*Period, era, or system*] [*Geology*]
TERT........ Tertius [*Third*] [*Latin*]
Tert............ Tertullian [*160-240AD*] [*Classical studies*]   (OCD)
TERT........ Tracking/Erosion Resistance Tester
Tertiary Res Spec Pap ... Tertiary Research Special Papers [*A publication*]
TERTM..... Thermal Expansion Resin Transfer Molding
TERTSD ... Tertiary Sand [*Agronomy*]
Tertul........ Tertullianus [*Flourished, 2nd-3rd century*] [*Authority cited in pre-1607 legal work*]   (DSA)
TERU .... Teruletrendezes [*Hungary*] [*A publication*]
Teruv.......... Teruvenkatachariar's Railway Cases [*India*] [*A publication*]   (DLA)
TES............ [*The*] Engineers School   (MCD)
TES............ Tableaux Entrees-Sorties [*Database*] [*EC*]   (ECED)
TES............ Tactical Environment Simulator [*Navy*]   (MCD)
TES............ Tactical Environment System [*Navy*]
TES............ Target Engagement Simulator [*Military*]   (MCD)
TES............ Team Effectiveness Survey [*Test*]
TES............ Technical Enforcement Support [*Environmental Protection Agency*]   (GFGA)
TES............ Technical Engagement Simulation
TES............ Technical Enquiry Service [*British*]   (DCTA)
TES............ Telemetry Evaluation Station
TES............ Temporary Employment Subsidy [*British*]   (DCTA)
TES............ Terminal Encounter System
TeS............ Terre Sainte   (BJA)
TES............ Territorial Experiment Stations Division [*of ARS, Department of Agriculture*]
Tes .... Tesaur [*A publication*]
TES............ Test and Evaluation Squadron
TES............ Test and Evaluation Support
TES............ Test Squadron [*Air Force*]
TES............ Tetraethylsulfamide [*Organic chemistry*]
TES........ Text Editing System
TES............ Theatre Education Society   (EA)
TES............ Thermal Energy Storage
TES............ Thin Elastic Shell
TES........... Thymic Epithelial Supernatant [*Endocrinology*]
TES........... Tidal Electric Station
TES........... Time Encoded Speech [*Telecommunications*]   (TEL)
TES........... Times Educational Supplement [*A publication*]
TES........... Training Equipment Summary   (MCD)
TES........... Transcutaneous Electrical Stimulation [*Also, TENS, TNS*] [*A method of pain control*] [*Medicine*]
TES........... Transmural Electrical Stimulation
TES........... Transportable Earth Station [*British*]
TES........... Triethylsilyl [*Organic chemistry*]

TES........... Tris(hydroxymethyl)methylaminoethanesulfonic Acid [*A buffer*]
TES............ Tungsten Electron Snatcher
TES............ Twelve English Statesmen [*A publication*]
TESA .... Television and Electronics Service Association
TESAC ...... Temperature-Salinity-Currents [*Oceanography*]   (IID)
TESDA ...... Tenside [*Later, Tenside-Detergents*] [*A publication*]
TESE .... Tactical Exercise Simulator and Evaluator   (NVT)
TESEM ..... Television Esmeraldena Compania de Economia Mixta [*Ecuador*]   (EY)
TE(S)FC .... Totally-Enclosed (Separately) Fan-Cooled [*Reactor*]   (DEN)
TESG .... Target Echo Signature Generator [*SONAR*]
TESH......... Technical Shop   (NASA)
TESI .... Thermal Energy Storage [*NASDAQ symbol*]   (NQ)
TESI .... Transfer of Electrostatic Images [*Electrophotography*]
TESICO .... Threshold Electron Secondary Ion Coincidence [*Spectroscopy*]
TESL .... Teaching English as a Second Language
TESLAC.... Testolactone [*Antineoplastic drug*]
Tesla Electron ... Tesla Electronics [*A publication*]
Tesla Electron Q Rev Czech Electron Telecommun ... Tesla Electronics. Quarterly Review of Czechoslovak Electronics and Telecommunications [*A publication*]
TESL Can J ... TESL [*Teaching English as a Second Language*] Canada Journal [*A publication*]
TESM........ Triethylstannylmaleate [*Organic chemistry*]
TESMA ..... Theatre Equipment and Supply Manufacturers Association [*Later, TEA*]   (EA)
TESOB ...... Terra e Sole [*A publication*]
TESOL ...... Teachers of English to Speakers of Other Languages   (EA)
TESOL Newsl ... TESOL [*Teachers of English to Speakers of Other Languages*] Newsletter [*A publication*]
TESOLQ ... TESOL [*Teachers of English to Speakers of Other Languages*] Quarterly [*A publication*]
TESOL Quart ... TESOL [*Teachers of English to Speakers of Other Languages*] Quarterly [*A publication*]
Tesor .... Tesoro Petroleum Corp. [*Associated Press abbreviation*]   (APAG)
Tesoro .... Tesoro Petroleum Corp. [*Associated Press abbreviation*]   (APAG)
Tesoro Sacro M ... Tesoro Sacro-Musical [*A publication*]
TESP .... Telephone Specialists, Inc. [*NASDAQ symbol*]   (NQ)
TESR .... Tactical Environment Satellite Readout   (MCD)
TESR .... Test Equipment Status Report
TESR .... Time of Sunrise
TESRP....... Test and Evaluation Support Resource Plan   (MCD)
TESS .... Tactical Electromagnetic Systems Study   (IEEE)
TESS .... Tactical Engagement Simulation System [*Developed by Sandia National Laboratories for the Defense Nuclear Agency*]
TESS .... Tactical and Environmental Support System [*Military*]   (CAAL)
TESS .... Temporary Employment Subsidy Scheme [*Department of Employment*] [*British*]
TESS .... Time of Sunset
TESS .... Top Electronic Security Systems [*Commercial firm*] [*British*]
TESS .... Total Engineering Support System   (HGAA)
TESSA...... Tax-Exempt Special Savings Account [*British*]
TESSA...... Total Energy Suppression Shield Array [*Nuclear structure*]
Tessaur ...... [*Antonius*] Tessaurus [*Flourished, 17th century*] [*Authority cited in pre-1607 legal work*]   (DSA)
TEST .... Tanner Eclectic Stuttering Therapy Program
TEST .... Teen-Age Employment Skills Training, Inc.
TEST .... Testament
Test .... Testamentary [*Legal term*]   (DLA)
TEST .... Testator   (ADA)
TEST .... Testimonial   (ADA)
TEST .... Thesaurus of Engineering and Scientific Terms [*A publication*]
TEST .... Track Evaluation System [*Canadian National Railways*]
TEST .... Transamerica Electronic Scoring Technique [*Credit risk evaluation*]
TEST .... Two Element Synthesis Telescope   (ADA)
TestAbr...... Testament of Abraham [*Pseudepigrapha*]   (BJA)
TestAsh ..... Testament of Asher [*Pseudepigrapha*]   (BJA)
TestBen...... Testament of Benjamin [*Pseudepigrapha*]   (BJA)
testco .... Terra Sancta Tourist Co. Ltd. [*Jordan*]
TESTCOMDNA ... Test Command Defense Nuclear Agency [*Military*]   (AABC)
Test Eng Manage ... Test Engineering and Management [*A publication*]
TESTFAC ... Test Facility
TESTG .... Test Group [*Military*]
Test Instrum Controls ... Testing, Instruments, and Controls [*Australia*] [*A publication*]
TestIss .... Testament of Issachar [*Pseudepigrapha*]   (BJA)
TestJos ...... Testament of Joseph [*Pseudepigrapha*]   (BJA)
TestJud ...... Testament of Judah [*Pseudepigrapha*]   (BJA)
TestLevi ..... Testament of Levi [*Pseudepigrapha*]   (BJA)
Test Memor Timb Res Developm Ass ... Test Memorandum. Timber Research and Development Association [*A publication*]
TestNaph... Testament of Naphtali [*Pseudepigrapha*]   (BJA)
TESTO ...... Testigo [*Witness*] [*Latin*]   (ADA)
TESTOR ... Testator   (ROG)
Test Polym ... Testing of Polymers [*A publication*]
TESTRAN ... Test Translator [*Data processing*]

Test Rec Timb Res Developm Ass ... Test Record. Timber Research and Development Association [*A publication*]
TestReub.... Testament of Reuben [*Pseudepigrapha*] (BJA)
TESTRIX .. Testatrix (ROG)
TESTS...... Technical-Engineering-Science Training for Secretaries
TESTS...... Test Squadron (MCD)
Tests Agrochem Cultiv ... Tests of Agrochemicals and Cultivars [*A publication*]
TestSim...... Testament of Simeon [*Pseudepigrapha*] (BJA)
TESTT...... Testament
TESTW...... Test Wing [*Military*]
TestXII ..... Testaments of the Twelve Patriarchs [*Pseudepigrapha*] (BJA)
TESTY ...... Testamentary (ROG)
TestZeb..... Testament of Zebulun [*Pseudepigrapha*] (BJA)
TESV .... Tephrosia Symptomless Virus [*Plant pathology*]
TET............ East Tennessee State University, Johnson City, TN [*OCLC symbol*] (OCLC)
TeT .... Taal en Tongval [*Antwerpen*] [*A publication*]
TET............ Teacher Effectiveness Training [*A course of study*]
TET............ Teacher of Electrotherapy [*British*]
TET............ Technical Evaluation Team (MCD)
TET............ Technical Evaluation Test (MCD)
TET............ Telescope and Electron Telescope
TET.......... Test Equipment Team (AAG)
TET.......... Test Equipment Tool (AAG)
TET.......... Test Evaluation Team [*NASA*] (KSC)
Tet............ Tetanus [*Medicine*]
TET............ Tete [*Mozambique*] [*Seismograph station code, US Geological Survey*] (SEIS)
TET............ Tete [*Mozambique*] [*Airport symbol*] (OAG)
TET............ Tetrachloride [*Chemistry*] (AAG)
Tet.............. Tetracycline [*Antibiotic compound*]
TET............ Tetrahedron (FAAC)
Tet.............. Tetralogy [*Medicine*]
TET............ Tetrode [*Electronics*]
TET............ Texas Eastern Corp. [*Formerly, Texas Eastern Transmission Corp.*] [*NYSE symbol*] [*Toronto Stock Exchange symbol*] (SPSG)
TET............ Thermionic Emission Technique
TET............ Thermometric Enthalpy Titration [*Analytical chemistry*]
TET............ Titanium Elevon Track
TET............ Total Elapsed Time (KSC)
TET............ Transistor Evaluation Test
TET............ Transportable Electronic Tower (MCD)
TET............ Troop Evaluation Tests [*Army*]
TET............ Turbine Entry Temperature [*Aviation*]
TET............ Turbo-Electric Tanker
TETA........ Test Equipment Technical Adviser
TETA......... Travelers Emergency Transportation Association [*Sought to pool transportation of salesmen traveling similar routes*] [*World War II*]
TETA......... Triethylenetetramine [*Organic chemistry*]
TETAM..... Tactical Effectiveness Testing of Antitank Missiles [*DoD*]
TETB......... Tetbury [*England*]
TETC......... Teroson Europe Technical Centre [*Research center*] [*Germany*]
TETD......... Tetraethylthiuram Disulfide [*Also, TTD*] [*Organic chemistry*]
TETEP ...... Test for Entrance into Teacher Education Programs [*Achievement test*]
TETF .... Terminal Equipment Test Facility [*Army*] (RDA)
TETFLEYNE ... Tetrafluorethylene [*Organic chemistry*]
T & ETGM ... Test and Evaluation Task Group Manager
TETHB...... Tethys [*A publication*]
Tethys Suppl ... Tethys. Supplement [*A publication*]
TETM........ Tetraethylthiuram Monosulfide [*Organic chemistry*]
TETM........ Thermal Effects Tests Model
TETOC...... Council for Technical Education and Training for Overseas Countries [*British*]
TETR........ Test and Training Satellite [*Also, TATS, TTS*] [*NASA*]
TETR........ Tetragonal
TETRA..... Terminal Tracking Telescope
TETRA...... Tetrahedron [*A publication*]
tetra........... Tetraploid [*Genetics*]
TETRAC ... Tension Truss Antenna Concept
Tetrahedr L ... Tetrahedron Letters [*A publication*]
Tetrahedron Lett ... Tetrahedron Letters [*A publication*]
Tetrahedron Suppl ... Tetrahedron. Supplement [*A publication*]
TETROON ... Tetrahedral Balloon [*Meteorology*]
TETSS....... Test and Evaluation Technical Support Services [*Army*]
Tetsu Hagan ... Tetsu To Hagane Journal. Iron and Steel Institute of Japan [*A publication*]
TEU .... Te Anau [*New Zealand*] [*Airport symbol*] (OAG)
TEU .... Technical Edit Unit [*Navy*] (DNAB)
TEU .... Technical Escort Unit [*Army*] (AABC)
TeU .... Tekst en Uitleg (BJA)
TEU .... Telemetry Equipment Unit
TEU .... Temple University, Philadelphia, PA [*OCLC symbol*] (OCLC)
TEU .... Ter Elfder Ure [*A publication*]
TEU .... Test of Economic Understanding
TEU .... Tetraethyl Urea [*Organic chemistry*]
TEU .... Transducer Excitation Unit
TEU .... Tropical Experimental Unit [*British military*] (DMA)

TEU .... Twenty-Foot Equivalent Unit [*Used to compare capacity of containerships*]
Teubner Studienskr ... Teubner Studienskripten [*A publication*]
Teubner-Texte zur Math ... Teubner-Texte zur Mathematik [*A publication*]
TEUC .... TADS [*Target Acquisition Designation Sight*] Electronics Unit Card [*Army*]
TEUC .... Temporary Extended Unemployment Compensation [*Labor*]
TEUN .... Trust for Education on the United Nations (EA)
Teut............ Teuthonista [*A publication*]
TEUT........ Teuton
TEV .... Talipes Equinovarus [*Anatomy*]
T Ev.......... Taylor on Evidence [*12th ed.*] [*1931*] [*A publication*] (DLA)
TEV .... Terminal Equipment Vehicle [*British military*] (DMA)
TeV............ Tetra-Electron Volt
TEV .... Thermo Environmental [*AMEX symbol*] (SPSG)
TEV .... Thermoelectric Voltage
TEV .... Thermostatic Expansion Valve [*Refrigeration*]
TEV .... Time Expanded Video
TEV .... Tobacco Etch Virus
TEV .... Today's English Version [*of the Bible*]
TEV .... Tomato Etch Virus
TEV .... Total Economic Value
TEV .... Total Evaporative Emissions [*Automotive engineering*]
TeV .... Trillion Electron Volts
TEV .... Turbo-Electric Vessel
TEV .... Victoria College, Victoria, TX [*OCLC symbol*] (OCLC)
TEVA........ Tennessee Virginia Energy Corp. [*NASDAQ symbol*] (NQ)
TEVA......... Tutmonda Esperantista Vegetara Asocio [*World Esperantist Vegetarian Association - WEVA*] (EAIO)
TEVAL...... Target Engagement Evaluation [*Military*]
TEVI......... Teva Pharmaceutical Industries Ltd. [*NASDAQ symbol*] (NQ)
TEVROC... Tailored Exhaust Velocity Rocket
TEVROK.. Tailored Exhaust Velocity Rocket
TEW .... Tactical Early Warning
TEW .... Tactical Electronic Warfare [*Aircraft*] (NATG)
TEW .... Total Equivalent Weight
TE/W......... Tractive Effort to Weight Ratio (MCD)
TEWA .... Target Evaluation and Weapon Assignment (MCD)
TEWA .... Threat Evaluation and Weapons Assignment (NVT)
TEWC....... Totally-Enclosed Water-Cooled [*Reactor*] (DEN)
TEWDS...... Tactical Electronic Warfare Deception System (MCD)
TEWG .... Tactical Electronic Warfare Group [*Military*]
TEWG .... Test and Evaluation Work Group [*Military*] (CAAL)
TEWGp ...... Tactical Electronic Warfare Group [*Air Force*] (AFM)
TEWK....... Tewkesbury [*Municipal borough in England*]
TEWL....... Transepidermal Water Loss [*Physiology*]
TEWP....... Williams [*T. E.*] Pharmaceuticals, Inc. [*NASDAQ symbol*] (NQ)
TEWS....... Tactical Effectiveness of Weapons Systems [*Army*] (AABC)
TEWS....... Tactical Electronic Warfare Set
TEWS....... Tactical Electronic Warfare Squadron [*Air Force*]
TEWS....... Tactical Electronic Warfare Support (MCD)
TEWS....... Threat Evaluation and Weapon Selection [*Military*] (CAAL)
TEWSq....... Tactical Electronic Warfare Squadron [*Air Force*]
TEWT....... Tactical Exercise without Troops
TEW Tech Ber ... TEW [*Technische Edelstahlwerke*] Technische Berichte [*Later, Thyssen Edelstahl Technische Berichte*] [*A publication*]
TEWTS ..... Tactical Electronic Warfare Training Squadron
TEX .... Air Texana [*Beaumont, TX*] [*FAA designator*] (FAAC)
TEX .... Automatic Teleprinter Exchange Service [*of Western Union Corp.*]
TEX .... Teletype Exchange
TEX .... TELEX
TEX .... Terex Corp. [*NYSE symbol*] (SPSG)
tex .... Tex [*Formerly, den*] [*Linear density*] [*SI unit*]
TEX .... Texas (AAG)
TEX .... Texas Airlines, Inc. [*Galveston, TX*] [*FAA designator*] (FAAC)
Tex .... Texas Reports [*A publication*]
Tex .... Texas Supreme Court Reports [*A publication*] (DLA)
TEX .... Textile (AABC)
TEX .... Transaction Exception Code [*Military*] (AFIT)
TEX .... Tumbling Explorer [*Aerospace*]
TEX .... University of Texas at Tyler, Tyler, TX [*OCLC symbol*] (OCLC)
Tex A Civ ... White and Wilson's [*or Willson's*] Civil Cases, Texas Court of Appeals [*A publication*] (DLA)
Tex A Civ Cas ... White and Wilson's [*or Willson's*] Civil Cases, Texas Court of Appeals [*A publication*] (DLA)
Tex A Civ Cas (Wilson) ... Texas Court of Appeal Civil Cases (Wilson) [*or Willson*] [*A publication*] (DLA)
Texaco........ Texaco, Inc. [*Associated Press abbreviation*] (APAG)
TEXACO... Texas Co.
Tex Admin Code ... Texas Administrative Code [*A publication*] (DLA)
Tex Ag Exp ... Texas. Agricultural Experiment Station. Publications [*A publication*]
Tex Agric Exp Stn Bull ... Texas. Agricultural Experiment Station. Bulletin [*A publication*]
Tex Agric Exp Stn Leafl ... Texas. Agricultural Experiment Station. Leaflet [*A publication*]

Tex Agric Exp Stn Misc Publ ... Texas. Agricultural Experiment Station. Miscellaneous Publication [*A publication*]
Tex Agric Exp Stn Prog Rep ... Texas. Agricultural Experiment Station. Progress Report [*A publication*]
Tex Agric Exp Stn Res Monogr ... Texas. Agricultural Experiment Station. Research Monograph [*A publication*]
Tex Agric Exp Stn Tech Monogr ... Texas. Agricultural Experiment Station. Technical Monograph [*A publication*]
Tex Agric Ext Serv Fish Dis Diagn Lab ... Texas. Agricultural Extension Service. Fish Disease Diagnostic Laboratory [*A publication*]
Tex Agric Prog ... Texas Agricultural Progress [*A publication*]
Tex Agric Prog Tex Agric Exp Stn ... Texas Agricultural Progress. Texas Agricultural Experiment Station [*A publication*]
Tex Agr Progr ... Texas Agricultural Progress [*A publication*]
Tex A & M Univ Dep Civ Eng Rep ... Texas A & M University. Department of Civil Engineering. Report [*A publication*]
Tex A M Univ Oceanogr Stud ... Texas A & M University. Oceanographic Studies [*A publication*]
Tex A & M Univ Sea Grant Coll TAMU-SG ... Texas A & M University Sea Grant College. TAMU-SG [*A publication*]
Tex A & M Univ Syst Tex Agric Ext Serv Fish Dis Diagn Lab ... Texas A & M University System. Texas Agricultural Extension Service. Fish Disease Diagnostic Laboratory [*A publication*]
Tex A M Univ Syst Tex Agric Ext Serv Fish Dis Diagn Lab FDDL ... Texas A & M University System. Texas Agricultural Extension Service. Fish Disease Diagnostic Laboratory. FDDL [*A publication*]
Tex A & M Univ Tex Eng Exp Stn Tech Bull ... Texas A & M University. Texas Engineering Experiment Station. Technical Bulletin [*A publication*]
Tex App ..... Texas Appeals Reports [*A publication*]
Tex App ..... Texas Civil Appeals Cases [*A publication*] (DLA)
Tex App ..... Texas Court of Appeals Reports (Criminal Cases) [*A publication*] (DLA)
Tex App Civ Cas (Wilson) ... White and Wilson's [*or Willson's*] Civil Cases, Texas Court of Appeals [*A publication*] (DLA)
TEXAS ...... Tactical Exchange Automation System (MCD)
Texas Acad of Sci Trans ... Texas Academy of Sciences. Transactions [*A publication*]
Texas Archeol Paleont Soc Bull ... Texas Archeological and Paleontological Society. Bulletin [*A publication*]
Texas BJ .... Texas Bar Journal [*A publication*]
Texas Board of Water Engineers Bull ... Texas. Board of Water Engineers. Bulletin [*A publication*]
Texas Bus Rev ... Texas Business Review [*A publication*]
Texas Civ ... Texas Civil Appeals Reports [*A publication*] (DLA)
Texas Civ App ... Texas Civil Appeals Reports [*A publication*] (DLA)
Texas Cour Rec Med ... Texas Courier Record of Medicine [*A publication*]
Texas Cr App ... Texas Court of Appeals Reports [*A publication*] (DLA)
Texas Crim ... Texas Criminal Reports [*A publication*] (DLA)
Texas Crim App ... Texas Criminal Appeals Reports [*A publication*] (DLA)
Texas Crim Rep ... Texas Criminal Reports [*A publication*] (DLA)
Texas Cr Rep ... Texas Criminal Reports [*A publication*] (DLA)
Texas Ct App ... Texas Court of Appeals Reports [*A publication*] (DLA)
Texas Ct of App ... Texas Court of Appeals Reports [*A publication*] (DLA)
Texas Ct App Civ Cas ... Texas Civil Cases [*A publication*] (DLA)
Texas Ct Rep ... Texas Court Reporter [*1900-1908*] [*A publication*] (DLA)
Texas Dig... Texas Digest [*A publication*] (DLA)
Texas Eng Expt Sta Research Rept ... Texas. Engineering Experiment Station. Research Report [*A publication*]
Texas Internat L Forum ... Texas International Law Forum [*A publication*]
Texas Internat LJ ... Texas International Law Journal [*A publication*]
Texas Int'l LF ... Texas International Law Forum [*A publication*]
Texas Int'l LJ ... Texas International Law Journal [*A publication*]
Texas Jour Sci ... Texas Journal of Science [*A publication*]
Texas J Sci ... Texas Journal of Science [*A publication*]
Texas L Rev ... Texas Law Review [*A publication*]
Texas Med ... Texas Medicine [*A publication*]
Texas Memorial Mus Pearce-Sellards Ser ... Texas Memorial Museum. Pearce-Sellards Series [*A publication*]
Texas MJ .. Texas Medical Journal [*A publication*]
Texas Mo... Texas Monthly [*A publication*]
Texas Nurs ... Texas Nursing [*A publication*]
Texas Oil Jour ... Texas Oil Journal [*A publication*]
Texas Petroleum Research Comm Bull ... Texas Petroleum Research Committee. Bulletin [*A publication*]
Texas R...... Texas Reports [*A publication*] (DLA)
Texas Rep.. Texas Reports [*A publication*] (DLA)
Texas Rep Biol Med ... Texas Reports on Biology and Medicine [*A publication*]
Texas South UL Rev ... Texas Southern University. Law Review [*A publication*]
Texas Tech L Rev ... Texas Tech Law Review [*A publication*]
Texas Univ Austin Bur Econ Geology Geol Circ ... Texas University at Austin. Bureau of Economic Geology. Geological Circular [*A publication*]
Texas Univ Austin Bur Econ Geology Geol Quad Map ... University of Texas at Austin. Bureau of Economic Geology. Geologic Quadrangle Map [*A publication*]

Texas Univ Austin Bur Econ Geology Guidebook ... Texas University at Austin. Bureau of Economic Geology. Guidebook [*A publication*]
Texas Univ Austin Bur Econ Geology Rept Inv ... University of Texas at Austin. Bureau of Economic Geology. Report of Investigations [*A publication*]
Texas Univ Pub Bur Econ Geology Mineral Res Circ Rept Inv ... Texas University. Publication. Bureau of Economic Geology. Mineral Resource Circular. Report of Investigations [*A publication*]
Texas Water Devel Board Rept ... Texas. Water Development Board. Report [*A publication*]
Tex B J ...... Texas Bar Journal [*A publication*]
Tex Board Water Eng Bull ... Texas. Board of Water Engineers. Bulletin [*A publication*]
Tex Board Water Eng Chem Compos Tex Surf Waters ... Texas. Board of Water Engineers. Chemical Composition of Texas Surface Waters [*A publication*]
Tex Bus Corp Act Ann ... Texas Business Corporation Act, Annotated [*A publication*] (DLA)
Tex Bus Corp Act Ann (Vernon) ... Texas Business Corporation Act Annotated (Vernon) [*A publication*]
Tex Bus Exec ... Texas Business Executive [*A publication*]
Tex Busin Rev ... Texas Business Review [*A publication*]
Tex Bus R .. Texas Business Review [*A publication*]
Tex Bus Rev ... Texas Business Review [*A publication*]
TEXC......... Texas Central Railroad Co. [*AAR code*]
Tex Civ App ... Texas Civil Appeals Reports [*A publication*] (DLA)
Tex Civ Cas ... Texas Court of Appeals Decisions. Civil Cases [*A publication*]
Tex Civ Cas ... Texas Court of Appeals Decisions, Civil Cases (White and Wilson) [*or Willson*] [*1876-92*] [*A publication*] (DLA)
Tex Civ Rep ... Texas Civil Appeals Reports [*A publication*] (DLA)
Tex Coach ... Texas Coach [*A publication*]
Tex Code Ann ... Texas Codes, Annotated [*A publication*] (DLA)
Tex Code An (Vernon) ... Texas Codes Annotated (Vernon) [*A publication*]
Tex Code Crim Proc Ann ... Texas Code of Criminal Procedure, Annotated [*A publication*] (DLA)
Tex Code Crim Proc Ann (Vernon) ... Texas Code of Criminal Procedure Annotated (Vernon) [*A publication*]
TEXCOM ... Test and Experimentation Command [*TRADOC*] [*Fort Hood, TX*]
Tex Cr .... Texas Criminal [*A publication*] (DLA)
Tex Cr App ... Texas Criminal Appeals Reports [*A publication*] (DLA)
Tex Crim.... Texas Criminal Reports [*A publication*] (DLA)
Tex Crim Rep ... Texas Criminal Reports [*A publication*] (DLA)
Tex Cr R .... Texas Criminal Appeals Reports [*A publication*] (DLA)
Tex Cr Rpts ... Texas Criminal Reports [*A publication*] (DLA)
Tex Ct App ... Texas Court of Appeals Reports [*A publication*] (DLA)
Tex Ct App Civ ... Texas Civil Cases [*A publication*] (DLA)
Tex Ct App Dec Civ ... Texas Civil Cases [*A publication*] (DLA)
Tex Ct App R ... Texas Court of Appeals Reports [*A publication*] (DLA)
Tex Ct Rep ... Texas Court Reporter [*A publication*] (DLA)
TEXDEALAM ... Textile Dealers Association of America (EA)
Tex Dec...... Texas Decisions [*A publication*] (DLA)
Tex Dent Assist Assoc Bull ... Texas Dental Assistants Association. Bulletin [*A publication*]
Tex Dent J ... Texas Dental Journal [*A publication*]
Tex Dig Op Att'y Gen ... Digest of Opinions of the Attorney General of Texas [*A publication*] (DLA)
Tex Elec Code Ann ... Texas Election Code, Annotated [*A publication*] (DLA)
Tex Energy ... Texas Energy [*A publication*]
Tex Energy Miner Resour ... Texas Energy and Mineral Resources [*A publication*]
Tex Eng Exp Stn Bull ... Texas. Engineering Experiment Station. Bulletin [*A publication*]
Tex Eng Exp Stn News ... Texas. Engineering Experiment Station. News [*A publication*]
Tex Eng Exp Stn Res Rep ... Texas. Engineering Experiment Station. Research Report [*A publication*]
TEXF .... TGIF Texas, Inc. [*NASDAQ symbol*] (NQ)
Texfi.......... Texfi Industries, Inc. [*Associated Press abbreviation*] (APAG)
Tex For Pap ... Texas Forestry Paper [*A publication*]
Tex Gen Laws ... General and Special Laws of the State of Texas [*A publication*] (DLA)
Tex Geogr Mag ... Texas Geographic Magazine [*A publication*]
TEXGRP ... Texas Group [*Navy*] (DNAB)
Tex G S Rp Prog ... Texas. Geological Survey. Report of Progress [*A publication*]
Tex Heart Inst J ... Texas Heart Institute. Journal [*A publication*]
Tex His Q .. Texas State Historical Association. Quarterly [*A publication*]
Tex Hist Assoc Q ... Texas State Historical Association. Quarterly [*A publication*]
Tex Hosp ... Texas Hospitals [*A publication*]
Tex Hospitals ... Texas Hospitals [*A publication*]
TEXIN....... Texas Intersection Air Quality Model [*Environmental Protection Agency*] (GFGA)
TexInd .... Texas Industries, Inc. [*Associated Press abbreviation*] (APAG)
Tex Ins Code Ann ... Texas Insurance Code, Annotated [*A publication*] (DLA)

Tex Ins Code Ann (Vernon) ... Texas Insurance Code Annotated (Vernon) [*A publication*]
Tex Inst...... Texas Institutes [*A publication*]
TexInst ...... Texas Instruments, Inc. [*Associated Press abbreviation*] (APAG)
Tex Int L Forum ... Texas International Law Forum [*A publication*]
Tex Int L J .. Texas International Law Journal [*A publication*]
Tex Intl LJ ... Texas International Law Journal [*A publication*]
Tex J......... Texas Journal [*A publication*]
Tex J Pharm ... Texas Journal of Pharmacy [*A publication*]
Tex J Sci.... Texas Journal of Science [*A publication*]
Tex J Sci Spec Publ ... Texas Journal of Science. Special Publication [*A publication*]
Tex Jur ...... Texas Jurisprudence [*A publication*] (DLA)
Tex Jur 2d ... Texas Jurisprudence [*2nd ed.*] [*A publication*] (DLA)
Tex Law..... Texas Lawman [*A publication*] (DLA)
Tex Law & Leg ... Texas Law and Legislation [*A publication*] (DLA)
Tex Law Rev ... Texas Law Review [*A publication*]
TexLex....... Texas Lexicon [*Slang*]
Tex Lib....... Texas Libraries [*A publication*]
Tex Lib J ... Texas Library Journal [*A publication*]
Tex Libr...... Texas Libraries [*A publication*]
Tex LJ ...... Texas Law Journal [*A publication*] (DLA)
Tex L R...... Texas Law Review [*A publication*]
Tex L Rep .. Texas Law Reporter [*1882-84*] [*A publication*] (DLA)
Tex L Rev... Texas Law Review [*A publication*]
Tex Med .... Texas Medicine [*A publication*]
Tex Mem Mus Misc Pap ... Texas Memorial Museum. Miscellaneous Papers [*A publication*]
TEXMER .. Texas Meridian Resources Ltd. [*Associated Press abbreviation*] (APAG)
TEX MEX ... Texas Mexican Railway Co.
TexMex ..... Texas and Mexico [*Refers to fashion, food, language, or lifestyle that has characteristics of these two regions*]
Tex Mo ...... Texas Monthly [*A publication*]
Tex Nurs.... Texas Nursing [*A publication*]
Tex Nutr Conf Proc ... Texas Nutrition Conference. Proceedings [*A publication*]
Tex Outl..... Texas Outlook [*A publication*]
TEXP......... Time Exposure [*Photography*]
Tex Parks Wildl ... Texas Parks Wildlife [*A publication*]
Tex Pharm ... Texas Pharmacy [*A publication*]
Tex Prob Code Ann (Vernon) ... Texas Probate Code Annotated (Vernon) [*A publication*]
Tex Q .... Texas Quarterly [*A publication*]
Tex R Civ P Ann (Vernon) ... Texas Rules of Civil Procedure Annotated (Vernon) [*A publication*]
Tex Reg...... Texas Register [*A publication*]
Tex Rep Bio ... Texas Reports on Biology and Medicine [*A publication*]
Tex Rep Biol Med ... Texas Reports on Biology and Medicine [*A publication*]
Tex Res...... Textile Research [*A publication*]
Tex Res J ... Textile Research Journal [*A publication*]
Tex Rev...... Texas Review [*A publication*]
Tex Rev Civ Stat Ann (Vernon) ... Texas Revised Civil Statutes, Annotated (Vernon) [*A publication*] (DLA)
TEXS .... Tactical Explosive System [*Military*] (RDA)
Tex S.......... Texas Supreme Court Reports, Supplement [*A publication*] (DLA)
TEXSCN ... Texscan Corp. [*Associated Press abbreviation*] (APAG)
Tex S Ct..... Texas Supreme Court Reporter [*A publication*] (DLA)
Tex Sess Law Serv ... Texas Session Law Service (Vernon) [*A publication*] (DLA)
Tex Sess Law Serv (Vernon) ... Texas Session Law Service (Vernon) [*A publication*]
Tex So Intra L Rev ... Texas Southern Intramural Law Review [*A publication*] (DLA)
Tex So LR ... Texas Southern Law Review [*A publication*]
Tex So U L Rev ... Texas Southern University. Law Review [*A publication*]
Tex Stat Ann ... Texas Statutes, Annotated [*A publication*] (DLA)
Tex State Hist Assoc Quar ... Texas State Historical Association. Quarterly [*A publication*]
Tex State J Med ... Texas State Journal of Medicine [*A publication*]
Tex St Lit... Texas Studies in Literature and Language [*A publication*]
Tex Stud Lit & Lang ... Texas Studies in Literature and Language [*A publication*]
Tex SUL Rev ... Texas Southern University. Law Review [*A publication*]
Tex Sup Ct J ... Texas Supreme Court Journal [*A publication*]
Tex Supp.... Texas Supplement [*A publication*] (DLA)
Tex Suppl.. Texas Supplement [*A publication*] (DLA)
TEXT......... Intex Software Systems International Ltd. [*New York, NY*] [*NASDAQ symbol*] (NQ)
TEXT......... Texas Experimental TOKAMAK [*Atomic physics*]
TEXT......... Textile
TEXTA ...... Technical Extracts of Traffic [*National Security Agency*] [*A publication*]
Text Abstr ... Textile Abstracts [*A publication*]
Text Age .... Textile Age [*A publication*]
Text Am .... Textile American [*A publication*]
Text Argus ... Textile Argus [*A publication*]
Text Asia ... Textile Asia [*A publication*]
Tex Tax-Gen Ann ... Texas Tax-General, Annotated [*A publication*] (DLA)

Text Beklaedning ... Textil og Beklaedning [*A publication*]
Text Betr (Poessneck Ger) ... Textil-Betrich (Poessneck, Germany) [*A publication*]
Text Bull .... Textile Bulletin [*A publication*]
Text Chem Color ... Textile Chemist and Colorist [*A publication*]
Text Chim ... Textiles Chimiques [*A publication*]
Text Color ... Textile Colorist [*A publication*]
Text Color Converter ... Textile Colorist and Converter [*A publication*]
Text Cordage Q ... Textile and Cordage Quarterly [*A publication*]
Text Dyer Printer ... Textile Dyer and Printer [*A publication*]
Tex Tech LR ... Texas Tech Law Review [*A publication*]
Tex Tech L Rev ... Texas Tech Law Review [*A publication*]
Texte Kritisch Psych ... Texte zur Kritischen Psychologie [*A publication*]
TexteM...... Texte Metzler [*A publication*]
Textes et Doc (Bruxelles) ... Textes et Documents (Bruxelles) [*A publication*]
Textes Math ... Textes Mathematiques [*A publication*]
Tex-Text.... Tex-Textilis [*A publication*]
Text Faerberei Ztg ... Textil und Faerberei-Zeitung [*A publication*]
Text Faserstofftech ... Textil und Faserstofftechnik [*A publication*]
Text Forsch ... Textil-Forschung [*A publication*]
Text Hist.... Textile History [*A publication*]
Text Horizons ... Textile Horizons [*A publication*]
Text I Ind... Textile Institute and Industry [*A publication*]
Textilchem Color ... Textilchemiker und Colorist [*A publication*]
Textile Ind ... Textile Industries [*A publication*]
Textile Inst ... Textile Institute and Industry [*A publication*]
Textile Inst Ind ... Textile Institute and Industry [*A publication*]
Textile J Aust ... Textile Journal of Australia [*A publication*] (APTA)
Textile Jl.... Textile Research Journal [*A publication*]
Textile Mfr ... Textile Manufacturer [*A publication*]
Textile Progr ... Textile Progress [*A publication*]
Textile Res J ... Textile Research Journal [*A publication*]
Textile Technol Dig ... Textile Technology Digest [*A publication*]
Textil Ind.... Textile Industries [*A publication*]
Textil Mnth ... Textile Month [*A publication*]
Textil Prax ... Textil Praxis International [*A publication*]
Textil Rent ... Textile Rental [*A publication*]
Textil Rep.. America's Textiles Reporter Bulletin [*A publication*]
Textilvered ... Textilveredelung [*A publication*]
Textil-W .... Textil-Wirtschaft [*A publication*]
Textil Wld ... Textile World [*A publication*]
Textil Wld ... Textile World Buyer's Guide/Fact File [*A publication*]
Text Ind ..... Textile Industries [*A publication*]
Text Ind Dyegest Sthn Afr ... Textile Industries Dyegest Southern Africa [*A publication*]
Text Ind Exporter ... Textile Industry and Exporter [*A publication*]
Text Ind (Moenchen Gladbach Ger) ... Textil-Industrie (Moenchen Gladbach, Germany) [*A publication*]
Text Ind (Munich) ... Textil-Industrie (Munich) [*A publication*]
Text Ind Sthn Afr ... Textile Industries Southern Africa [*A publication*]
Text Ind (Zurich) ... Textil-Industrie (Zurich) [*A publication*]
Text Inf Users Coun Proc Meet ... Textile Information Users Council. Proceedings of the Meeting [*A publication*]
Text Inst Ind ... Textile Institute and Industry [*A publication*]
TEXTIR..... Text Indexing and Retrieval [*Data processing*]
Text J Aust ... Textile Journal of Australia [*A publication*]
Text Konfekt ... Textil och Konfektion [*A publication*]
Text Krit .... Text und Kritik [*A publication*]
Text Mag ... Textile Magazine [*A publication*]
Text Manuf J ... Textile Manufacturer's Journal [*A publication*]
Text Mercury Int ... Textile Mercury International [*A publication*]
Text Metod Mat ... Textos de Metodos Matematicos [*A publication*]
Text Mfr .... Textile Manufacturer [*A publication*]
Text MJ..... Textile Museum Journal [*A publication*]
Text Mon ... Textile Month [*A publication*]
TEXTOR ... TOKAMAK [*Toroidal Kamera Magnetic*] Experiment for Technical Oriented Research [*Oak Ridge National Laboratory*]
Text-Prax .. Textil-Praxis [*Later, Textil Praxis International*] [*A publication*]
Text Prax Int ... Textil Praxis International [*A publication*]
Text Prog ... Textile Progress [*A publication*]
Text Q........ Textile Quarterly [*A publication*]
Textr .... Textron, Inc. [*Associated Press abbreviation*] (APAG)
Tex Transp Res ... Texas Transportation Researcher [*A publication*]
Text Rec..... Textile Recorder [*A publication*]
TEXT REC ... Textus Receptus [*The Received Text*] [*Latin*]
Text Rent ... Textile Rental [*A publication*]
Text Res J ... Textile Research Journal [*A publication*]
Text Ring ... Textil-Ring [*A publication*]
Textron ..... Textron, Inc. [*Associated Press abbreviation*] (APAG)
Text Rundsch ... Textil-Rundschau [*A publication*]
Texts Monographs Phys ... Texts and Monographs in Physics [*A publication*]
Text Tech Dig ... Textile Technology Digest [*A publication*]
Text Technol Dig ... Textile Technology Digest [*A publication*]
Texture Cryst Solids ... Texture of Crystalline Solids [*A publication*]
Textures Microstruct ... Textures and Microstructures [*A publication*]
Text Wkly ... Textile Weekly [*A publication*]
Text World ... Textile World [*A publication*]
Text World J ... Textile World Journal [*A publication*]
Text World R ... Textile World Record [*A publication*]

Tex Univ B Min S B ... Texas University. Bulletin. Mineral Survey Bulletin [*A publication*]
Tex Univ Bur Econ Geol Geol Circ ... Texas University. Bureau of Economic Geology. Geological Circular [*A publication*]
Tex Univ Bur Econ Geol Miner Resour Circ ... Texas University. Bureau of Economic Geology. Mineral Resource Circular [*A publication*]
Tex Univ Bur Econ Geol Publ ... Texas University. Bureau of Economic Geology. Publication [*A publication*]
Tex Univ Bur Econ Geol Rep Invest ... Texas University. Bureau of Economic Geology. Report of Investigations [*A publication*]
Tex Univ Bur Econ Geol Res Note ... Texas University. Bureau of Economic Geology. Research Note [*A publication*]
Tex Univ Bur Eng Res Circ ... Texas University. Bureau of Engineering Research. Circular [*A publication*]
Tex Univ Cent Res Water Resour Tech Rep ... Texas University. Center for Research in Water Resources. Technical Report [*A publication*]
Tex Univ Publ ... Texas University. Publication [*A publication*]
Tex Unrep Cas ... Posey's Unreported Cases [*Texas*] [*A publication*]   (DLA)
TexUtil ...... Texas Utilities Co. [*Associated Press abbreviation*]   (APAG)
TE (XVIII) ... Textos y Estudios del Siglo XVIII [*A publication*]
Tex Water Comm Bull ... Texas Water Commission. Bulletin [*A publication*]
Tex Water Comm Circ ... Texas Water Commission. Circular [*A publication*]
Tex Water Comm Mem Rep ... Texas Water Commission. Memorandum Report [*A publication*]
Tex Water Dev Board Rep ... Texas. Water Development Board. Report [*A publication*]
TEY .... Thingeyri [*Iceland*] [*Airport symbol*]   (OAG)
TeZ .... Texte und Zeichen [*A publication*]
TEZ........... Tezpur [*India*] [*Airport symbol*]   (OAG)
Tez Doklad Nauch Konf Zootech Sek ... Tezisy Dokladov Nauchnoi Konferentsii. Zootekhnicheskaya Sektsiya [*A publication*]
TEZG........ Tribological Experiments in Zero Gravity
Tezhka Prom ... Tezhka Promishlenost [*A publication*]
Tezisy Dokl Vses Nauchno Metod Konf Vet Patoloanat ... Tezisy Dokladov Vsesoyuznoi Nauchno-Metodicheskoi Konferentsii Veterinarnykh Patologoanatomov [*A publication*]
TF .... [*The*] FORUM [*Foundation of Research for Understanding Man*] (EA)
TF .... Iceland [*Aircraft nationality and registration mark*]   (FAAC)
TF .... Tabulating Form   (AAG)
TF .... Tactical Fighter   (AFM)
TF .... Tactile Fremitus [*Medicine*]
TF .... Taeria Foundation   (EA)
Tf............... Tafel   (BJA)
TF .... Tallulah Falls Railway Co. [*AAR code*]
TF .... Tank Farm   (NATG)
TF .... Tape Feed
TF .... Target File   (MCD)
TF .... Task Force
TF .... Tax Foundation   (EA)
TF .... Tayu Fellowship   (EA)
TF .... Teaching Fellow
TF .... Tear Fund [*An association*]   (EA)
TF .... Teased Fibers [*Neurology*]
TF .... Technical File   (MCD)
TF .... Technological Forecasting
TF .... Telegram for Delivery by Telephone
TF .... Telegraph Form   (ROG)
TF .... Telephone   (NATG)
TF .... Temperature Factor
TF .... Temporary Fix   (AAG)
TF .... Terminal Forecast
TF .... Terminal Frame   (NATG)
TF .... Terrain-Following [*Helicopter*]
TF .... Territorial Force [*Military*] [*British*]
TF .... Test Facility [*NASA*]   (NASA)
TF .... Test to Failure   (SAA)
TF .... Test Fixture   (KSC)
TF .... Test Flight [*Air Force*]
TF .... Test Frame [*Telecommunications*]   (TEL)
TF .... Tetralogy of Fallot [*Cardiology*]
TF .... Text-Fiche
TF .... THEOS [*They Help Each Other Spiritually*] Foundation   (EA)
TF .... Thin Film
TF .... Thoreau Fellowship   (EA)
TF .... Thread Forming   (MSA)
TF .... Threshold Factor   (OA)
TF .... Thymidine Factor [*Endocrinology*]
TF .... Thymol Flocculation [*Clinical chemistry*]
TF .... Tibet Fund   (EA)
T & F......... Ticknor & Fields [*Publisher*]
TF .... Tile Floor [*Technical drawings*]
TF .... Till Forbidden [*i.e., repeat until forbidden to do so*] [*Advertising*]
TF .... Time Factor   (CAAL)
T/F............ Time of Fail   (MSA)
T/F............ Time of Fall   (SAA)
TF .... Time of Flight [*Ballistics*]
TF .... Time Frame

TF .... Time to Function
TF .... Tissue-Damaging Factor [*Medicine*]   (MAE)
TF .... Tissue Factor [*Clinical chemistry*]
TF .... To Fill
TF .... To Follow
TF .... Tolkien Fellowships   (EA)
TF .... Tolstoy Foundation   (EA)
TF .... Tool Fabrication   (SAA)
TF .... Tool Foundation [*See also ST*] [*Amsterdam, Netherlands*]   (EAIO)
TF .... Toroidal Field   (MCD)
TF .... Torpedo Fighter Aircraft [*Navy*]
TF .... Total Flow   (MAE)
TF .... Total Flowers [*Plant pathology*]
TF .... Total Forfeiture [*of all pay and allowances*] [*Army*]   (AABC)
TF .... Toward Freedom   (EA)
TF .... Toxicology Forum   (EA)
TF .... Tracking Filter
TF .... Trailfinders [*Travel agency*] [*British*]
TF .... Trainer Fighter
TF .... Training Film [*Military*]
TF .... Training Flight [*British military*]   (DMA)
TF .... TransAfrica Forum   (EA)
TF .... Transcription Factor [*Genetics*]
TF .... Transfer Factor [*Immunochemistry*]
TF .... Transfer Fee [*Banking*]
TF .... Transfer Function   (AAG)
T/F .... Transfer of Function [*Military*]   (AFM)
TF .... Transferrin [*Also, T, TRF*] [*Biochemistry*]
TF .... Transformation [*A publication*]
TF .... Transformers [*JETDS nomenclature*] [*Military*]   (CET)
TF .... Transfrontal   (AAMN)
TF .... Transmitter Frequency
TF .... Transportation Factor   (MCD)
TF .... Transportes Aereos Regionais (TAR) SA [*Brazil*] [*ICAO designator*]   (ICDA)
TF .... Trap Flag [*Computer memory language*]   (PCM)
TF .... Travail Force [*Penal Servitude*] [*French*]
TF .... Travellers Fare [*Train catering service*] [*British*]
TF .... Trench Feet [*or Fever*]
TF .... Trench Fighter [*British military*]   (DMA)
TF .... Trichloroethylene Finishing
TF .... Triple Frequency
TF .... Triple Fronted [*Classified advertising*]   (ADA)
TF .... Tritium Fluoride
TF .... Tropical Fresh Water [*Vessel load line mark*]
T/F............ True/False   (CDAI)
TF .... Trunk Frame [*Telecommunications*]   (TEL)
TF .... Trust Fund
TF .... Tuberculin Filtrate [*Medicine*]
TF .... Tubular Fluid [*Medicine*]   (MAE)
TF .... Tuning Fork   (AAMN)
TF .... Turbofan [*Engine*]
TF .... Twentieth Century-Fox Film Corp. [*NYSE symbol*]   (SPSG)
TF .... Twins Foundation   (EA)
TF .... Type of Flight   (SAA)
TF .... Type of Foundation [*IRS*]
TF1 .... Channel One [*French television station*]
TFA............ [*The*] Ferroalloys Association   (EA)
TFA............ Target Factor Analysis [*Statistical technique*]
TFA............ Task Force A
TFA............ Task Force Alpha [*DoD*]
TFA............ Tax Free America   (EA)
TFA............ Taxation for Accountants [*A publication*]
TFA............ Tie Fabrics Association [*Defunct*]   (EA)
TFA............ Timing Filter Analyzer
TFA............ Top Farmers of America Association [*Milwaukee, WI*]   (EA)
TFA............ Total Fatty Acids
TFA............ Transaction Flow Auditing   (ADA)
TFA............ Transfer Function Analyzer
TFA............ Transistor Feedback Amplifier
TFA............ Transverse Fascicular Area [*Neuroanatomy*]
TFA............ Transverse Film Attenuator
TFA............ Trifluoroacetic [*or Trifluoroacetyl*] Acid [*Organic chemistry*]
TFA............ Trifluoroacetic Anhydride [*Organic chemistry*]
TFA............ Trifluoroacetyl [*Organic chemistry*]
TFA............ Tube Failure Alarm
TFA............ Two-Way Finite Automata
TFA............ United States Trout Farmers Association
TFAA.......... Track and Field Athletes of America
TFAA.......... Trifluoroacetic Anhydride [*Organic chemistry*]
TFAG........ Tropical Forest Action Group   (EA)
TFAI.......... Territoire Francaise des Afars et des Issas [*French Territory of the Afars and Issas*]
TFAI.......... Trifluoroacetylimidazole [*Organic chemistry*]
TFAIP....... Task Force on Alternatives in Print   (EA)
TFANP..... Task Force Against Nuclear Pollution   (EA)
TFAP........ Tropical Forestry Action Plan [*World Bank, UN, and other groups*]
TFAR........ Tentative Findings and Recommendations
TFAT......... Technology for Alaskan Transportation [*A publication*]

TFA/USA ... Track and Field Association of the United States of America (EA)
TFB............ Taft Broadcasting Co. [*NYSE symbol*] (SPSG)
TFB............ Testing Facilities Branch [*Social Security Administration*]
TFB............ Thai Farmers' Bank
TFB............ Thin-Film Barrier
TFB............ Trifascicular Block [*Medicine*] (AAMN)
TFBA........ Textile Fibers and By-Products Association [*Charlotte, NC*]
TFBPA ...... Textile Fibers and By-Products Association (EA)
TFBR........ Technical Feedback Report (DNAB)
TFC........... [*The*] Felician College [*Chicago, IL*]
TFC........... [*The*] Freedom Council (EA)
TFC........... Tactical Fire Control (MCD)
TFC........... Tactical Flag Commander (MCD)
TFC........... Tactical Flight Control
TFC........... Tactical Fusion Center (MCD)
TFC........... Tank Fire Control
TFC........... Tantalum Foil Capacitor
TFC........... Task Force Commander [*Navy*] (DNAB)
TFC........... Terminal Flight Control (NATG)
TFC........... Territorial Fund Campaign [*Red Cross*]
TFC........... Thin-Film Capacitor
TFC........... Thin-Film Cell
TFC........... Thin-Film Circuit
TFC........... Time from Cutoff [*NASA*] (NASA)
TFC........... Time of First Call [*Navy*]
TFC........... Toccoa Falls College [*Georgia*]
TFC........... Top Flight Club [*Northwest Airlines' club for frequent flyers*] (EA)
TFC........... Torpedo Fire Control
TFC........... Total Fixed Cost
TFC........... Total Flow Control [*Automotive engineering*]
TFC........... Total Fuel Consumption (KSC)
TFC........... Traffic
TFC........... Traffic Control (NG)
TFC........... Transcapital Financial Corp. [*NYSE symbol*] (SPSG)
TFC........... Transfer Function Computer
TFC........... Transfer Function, Cumulative
TFC........... Transistorized Frequency Converter
TFC........... Transmission Fault Control [*Telecommunications*] (TEL)
TFC........... Transparent Ferroelectric Ceramics [*Physics*]
TFC........... Transport for Christ International (EA)
TFC........... Transportation Facilitation Center [*Department of Transportation*]
TFC........... Trifluoromethyldichlorocarbanilide [*Organic chemistry*]
TFC........... Trigonometric Function Computer
TFC........... Trilon Financial Corp. [*Toronto Stock Exchange symbol*] [*Vancouver Stock Exchange symbol*]
TFC........... Trustees for Conservation [*Defunct*] (EA)
TFC........... Turret Fire Control
TFC........... United States Overseas Tax Fairness Committee (EA)
TFC........... US-Japan Trade Facilitation Committee (IMH)
TFCA........ Thin-Film Cell Array
TF-CAS ..... Time Frequency Collision Avoidance System
TFCB........ Thanks for Coming By [*Exxon slogan*]
TFCC........ Tactical Flag Command Center [*Navy*]
TFCC........ Tank Fire Combat Computer
TFCC........ Triangular Fibrocartilage Complex [*Anatomy*]
TFCCS...... Tactical Flag Command Center System [*Navy*]
TFCF .... Twenty-First Century Foundation (EA)
TFCG........ Thin Film Crystal Growth
TFCM .... Three Factor Contribution Method [*Insurance*]
TFCNN...... Task Force Commander, North Norway [*NATO*] (NATG)
TFCOS ..... Task Force on Children Out of School (EA)
TFCP .... Technical Facility Change Procedure (AAG)
TFCS .... Tank Fire Control System
TFCS .... Task Force for Child Survival (EA)
TFCS .... TFC Teleservices Corp. [*Fort Lauderdale, FL*] [*NASDAQ symbol*] (NQ)
TFCS .... Torpedo Fire Control System
TFCS .... Treasury Financial Communication System [*Department of the Treasury*]
TFCS .... Triplex Flight Control System [*or Subsystem*] [*NASA*] (NASA)
TFCSD ...... Total Federal Commissioned Service to Date [*Military*]
TFCU........ Transportable Field Calibration Unit
TFCX........ TOKAMAK [*Toroidal Kamera Magnetic*] Fusion Core Experiment [*Plasma physics*]
TFCYC ...... Terry Fox Canadian Youth Centre
TFD .... Tactical Fighter Dispenser (MCD)
TFD .... Target-to-Film Distance [*X-Ray machine*] [*Navy*]
TFD .... Television Feasibility Demonstration [*NASA*] (KSC)
TFD .... Terrain-Following Display
TFD .... Test Flow Diagram (MCD)
TFD .... Thin-Film Distillation
TFD .... Time Frequency Digitizer (MCD)
TF/D......... Time-Frequency Dissemination (IEEE)
TFD .... Total Frequency Deviation (AAG)
TFD .... Tube Flood and Drain
TFD .... Tube Form Die (MCD)
TFDA........ Textile Fabric Distributors Association [*Later, TDA*] (EA)
TFDD .... Text File Device Driver [*Data processing*] (PCM)

TFDM .... Tactical Fighter Defense Munitions [*Air Force*]
TFDM .... Tactical Fighter Dispensing Munition (AFM)
TFDM .... Technical Feasibility Demonstration Model
TFDOP..... Total Field Detection Only Processor (CAAL)
TFDRL ...... Trustees of the Franklin Delano Roosevelt Library [*Abolished, 1958*] [*Library is now operated by the General Services Administration*]
TFDS .... Tactical Ferret Display System
TFDS .... Tactical Fighter Display Systems [*Air Force*]
TFDS .... Tactical Flag Data System (NG)
TFDS .... Troms Fylkes Dampskipsselskap [*Shipping line*] [*Norway*]
TFDTB ...... Tactical Fighter Dispenser Test Bed
TFDU .... Thin Film Deposition Unit
TFE .... Orlando, FL [*Location identifier*] [*FAA*] (FAAL)
TFE .... Terminal Flight Evaluation
TFE .... Terrain-Following Evaluator
TFE .... Tetrafluoroethylene [*Organic chemistry*]
TFE .... Thermionic Fuel Element [*Nuclear energy*]
TFE .... Thin-Film Electrode [*Electrochemistry*]
TFE .... Time from Event [*NASA*] (KSC)
TFE .... Total Fly-By Energy
TFE .... Trainer Flight Equipment (MCD)
TFE .... Transform Fault Effect [*Geology*]
TFE .... Transportation Feasibility Estimator
TFE .... Trifluoroethanol [*Organic chemistry*]
TFE .... Turbofan Engine
TFE .... Two-Fraction Fast Exchange [*Biophysics*]
TFECB ...... Task Force on Emphysema and Chronic Bronchitis [*Public Health Service and National Lung Association*] (EA)
TFECS...... Theater Force Evaluation by Combat Simulation (MCD)
TFEDSA.... Tetrafluoroethanedisulfonic Acid [*Organic chemistry*]
TFEL .... Thin-Film Electroluminescence
TFEO......... Tetrafluoroethylene-Epoxide [*Organic chemistry*]
TFEO......... Tetrafluoroethylene Oxide [*Organic chemistry*]
TFER .... Transfer
TFEWJ...... Task Force on Equality of Women in Judaism (EA)
TFF .... Fletcher School of Law and Diplomacy, Tufts University, Medford, MA [*OCLC symbol*] (OCLC)
TFF .... Tactical Fighter Force (ADA)
TFF .... Tangential Flow Filtration
TFF .... Tefe [*Brazil*] [*Airport symbol*] (OAG)
TFF .... Terrain-Following Flight
TFF .... Time of Free Fall [*NASA*] (KSC)
TFF .... Total Feedwater Flow
TFF .... Transverse Flow Fan
TFF .... Tuning Fork Filter
TFF .... Turbine Flow Function
TFFA .... Desirade/Grande-Anse, Guadeloupe [*French Antilles*] [*ICAO location identifier*] (ICLI)
TFFASF .... Temporaries Food for All Seasons Foundation (EA)
TFFB .... Basse-Terre/Baillif [*French Antilles*] [*ICAO location identifier*] (ICLI)
TFFC .... [*The*] Fixx Fan Club (EA)
TFFC .... Saint-Francois [*French Antilles*] [*ICAO location identifier*] (ICLI)
TFFC .... Task Force on Families in Crisis (EA)
TFFC .... Twenty-First Century Film Corp. [*NASDAQ symbol*] (NQ)
TFFD .... Fort-De-France, Martinique [*French Antilles*] [*ICAO location identifier*] (ICLI)
TFFE .... Terrain-Following Flight Evaluator
Tf-Fe........ Transferrin-Bound Iron [*Biochemistry*] (MAE)
TFFF......... Fort-De-France/Le Lamentin, Martinique [*French Antilles*] [*ICAO location identifier*] (ICLI)
TFFG .... Saint-Martin/Grand'Case, Guadeloupe [*French Antilles*] [*ICAO location identifier*] (ICLI)
TFFJ .... Saint-Barthelemy [*French Antilles*] [*ICAO location identifier*] (ICLI)
TFFLU ...... Trimmers, Firemen, and Foundry Labourers Union [*British*]
TFFM .... Grand-Bourg/Marie-Galante [*French Antilles*] [*ICAO location identifier*] (ICLI)
TFFR .... Pointe-A-Pitre/Le Raizet, Guadeloupe [*French Antilles*] [*ICAO location identifier*] (ICLI)
TFFR .... Task Force Final Report [*DoD*]
TFFS......... Les Saintes/Terre-De-Haut [*French Antilles*] [*ICAO location identifier*] (ICLI)
TFFS......... Thermoform, Fill, and Seal [*Pharmaceutical packaging*]
TFG .... [*The*] Fashion Group (EA)
TFG .... [*The*] Futures Group [*Commercial firm*] (EA)
TFG .... Tactical Fighter Group [*Air Force*]
TFG .... Tentative Fiscal Guidance (MCD)
TFG .... Tentative Force Guidance (NG)
TFG .... Terminal Facilities Guide [*DoD*]
TFG .... Test File Generator [*Data processing*]
TFG .... Textile Foremen's Guild
TFG .... Transmit Format Generator
TFG .... Typefounding (ADA)
TFGM....... Tank-Fired Guided Missile (MCD)
TFGM....... Tentative Fiscal Guidance Memorandum [*Military*] (AFIT)
TFGP......... Tactical Fighter Group [*Air Force*]
TFH .... Thick-Film Hybrid
TFH .... Touch for Health Foundation (EA)

TFH	Transfer Function Hazard
TFH	Transit Financial Holdings, Inc. [*Toronto Stock Exchange symbol*]
TFH	Tufts University, Health Sciences Library, Boston, MA [*OCLC symbol*] (OCLC)
TFHSA	Tennessee Farm and Home Science [*A publication*]
TFI...........	Deutsches Teppich-Forschungsinstitut [*German Carpet Research Institute - GCRI*] (EAIO)
TFI............	[*The*] Fertilizer Institute (EA)
TFI............	Table Fashion Institute (EA)
TFI............	Taurus Footwear, Inc. [*Toronto Stock Exchange symbol*]
TFI............	Tax Foundation, Inc.
TFI............	Textile Foundation, Inc.
TFI............	Theatre for Ideas (EA)
TFI............	Thick Film Ignition [*System*] [*Ford Motor Co.*] [*Automotive engineering*]
TFI............	Time from Ignition [*Apollo*] [*NASA*]
tfi..............	Travel for Industry [*Commercial firm*] [*British*]
TFI............	True Fibrous Involution [*Medicine*]
TFI............	Tufi [*Papua New Guinea*] [*Airport symbol*] (OAG)
TFIB	Thin-Film Interface Barrier
TFIC	Times Fiber Communications [*NASDAQ symbol*] (NQ)
TFI-I.........	Thin Film Ignition [*Automotive engineering*]
TFIM.........	Tool Fabrication Instruction Manual (MCD)
TFIN.........	TecFin Corp. [*NASDAQ symbol*] (NQ)
TFIS..........	Theft from Interstate Shipment [*FBI standardized term*]
TFIT	To-Fitness, Inc. [*NASDAQ symbol*] (NQ)
TfK...........	Tidskrift foer Konstvetinskap [*A publication*]
TFKVA	Teplofizicheskie Kharakteristiki Veshchestv [*A publication*]
TFL...........	Tail-Flick Latency
TFL...........	Taiwan Federation of Labor [*Nationalist China*]
TFL...........	Tanganyika Federation of Labor
TFL...........	Telemetry Format Load (MCD)
TFL...........	Tensor Fascia Lata [*Anatomy*]
TFL...........	Through Flow Line
TFL...........	Time to Failure Location
TFL...........	Time from Launch [*NASA*]
TFL...........	Training for Life [*Young Men's Christian Association*] [*British*]
TFL...........	Transient Fault Locator
TFL...........	Trees for Life [*An association*] (EA)
TFLAC	Fellowship of Reconciliation Task Force on Latin America and Caribbean (EA)
TFLC	Tulane Factors of Liberalism-Conservatism [*Psychology*]
TFLX	Termiflex Corp. [*NASDAQ symbol*] (NQ)
TFM	Tactical Flight Management (MCD)
TFM	Tape File Management
TFM	Teaching Family Model [*Psychology*]
TFM	Telefomin [*Papua New Guinea*] [*Airport symbol*] (OAG)
TFM	Tentative Final Monograph [*Food and Drug Administration*]
TFM	Terminal Forecast Manual
TFM	Testicular Feminization [*Endocrinology*]
TFM	Textes Francais Modernes [*A publication*]
TFM	Thin-Film Microelectronics
TFM	Tool Fabrication Manual (MCD)
TFM	Toronto International Furniture Market [*Canada*] (ITD)
TFM	Transmit Frame Memory
TFM	Transmitter Frequency Multiplier
TFM	Transportation Financial Management [*Army*]
TFM	Transverse Field Modulator
TFM	Trifluoromethylnitrophenol [*Organic chemistry*]
TFM	Turbine Flow Meter (KSC)
TFM	Two-Fluid Manometer
TFMA	Technical Facility Modification Authorization (AAG)
TFME........	Thin-Film Mercury Electrode [*Electrochemistry*]
TFMG........	Tank Force Management Group [*Army*]
TFMMS	Total Force Manpower Management System [*Navy*] (GFGA)
TFMO	Tank Forces Management Office [*Army*]
TFMP........	Test Facility Master Plan [*DoD*] (RDA)
TFMPP......	Trifluoromethyl(phenyl)piperazine [*Organic chemistry*]
TFMRA......	Top Fuel Motorcycle Riders Association (EA)
TFMRC....	Thermo-Fluid Mechanics Research Centre [*University of Sussex*] [*British*] (CB)
TFMS	Tactical Frequency Management System (MCD)
TFMS	Text and File Management System
TFMS	Trunk and Facilities Maintenance System [*Telecommunications*] (TEL)
TFMSA	Transactions. Free Museum of Science and Art. University of Pennsylvania [*A publication*]
TFMSA	Trifluoromethanesulfonic Acid [*Organic chemistry*]
TFN	Till Further Notice
TFN	Total Fecal Nitrogen
TFN	Total Fixed Nitrogen [*Chemistry*]
TFN	Total Fruit Number [*Botany*]
TFN	Track File Number (CAAL)
TFNA	Tennis Foundation of North America [*Later, ATF*] (EA)
TFNG	Thirty-Five New Guys [*Group of new astronauts*] [*NASA*]
TFNS.........	Territorial Force Nursing Service
TFO	Telemedicine for Ontario [*Toronto, ON*] [*Telecommunications*] (TSSD)
TFO	Tiffany Resources, Inc. [*Vancouver Stock Exchange symbol*]

TFO	Tonto Forest Array [*Arizona*] [*Seismograph station code, US Geological Survey*] [*Closed*] (SEIS)
TFO	Transactions for Others [*Military*]
TFO	Tuning Fork Oscillator
TFOA	Things Falling Off Aircraft (MCD)
TFOCA	Tactical Fiber Optic Cable Assembly [*Army*]
TFOE.........	Task Force on the Environment [*American Library Association*]
TFOL.........	Tape File Octal Load
TFON	Telefonos de Mexico SA de CV [*NASDAQ symbol*] (NQ)
TFOPS	Task Force Operations [*Navy*] (NVT)
TFORA	Tekniskt Forum [*A publication*]
TFORMR ...	Transformer
TFOS	Total Federal Officer Service [*Military*] (AABC)
TFOTB	[*The*] Friends of Tom Baker (EA)
TFOUT......	Thin-Film Oxygen Uptake Test
TFOV.........	Total Field of View (MCD)
TFP...........	American Society for the Defense of Tradition, Family and Property (EA)
TFP...........	[*The*] Feminist Press (EA)
TFP...........	[*The*] Friends Program (EA)
TFP...........	[*The*] Fund for Peace [*An association*] (EA)
TFP...........	Teachers Freedom Party (EA)
TFP...........	Teachers for Peace (EAIO)
TFP...........	Temporary Forfeiture of Pay
TFP...........	Test Facility Program [*NASA*] (KSC)
TFP...........	Total Factor Productivity [*Economics*]
TFP...........	Total Finish Positions [*Horse racing*]
TFP...........	Total Force Policy [*DoD*]
TFP...........	Trans-Fiberoptic-Photographic [*Electron microscopy*]
TFP...........	Transportability Focal Point [*Army*] (MCD)
TFP...........	Travaux. Faculte de Philosophie et Lettres. Universite Catholique de Louvain [*A publication*] (BJA)
TFP...........	Trifluoperazine [*Also, Trifluoroperazine*] [*Organic chemistry*]
TFP...........	Trifluoroperazine [*Also, Trifluoperazine*] [*Organic chemistry*]
TF/P	Tubular Fluid Plasma [*Medicine*] (MAE)
TFPA	Tubular Finishers and Processors Association (EA)
TFPC	Thin-Film Photovoltaic Cell
TFPCA	Thin-Film Photovoltaic Cell Array
TFPCTS	Thin-Film Personal Communications and Telemetry System (MCD)
TFPECTS ...	Thin-Film Personal Communications and Telemetry System (MCD)
TFPG	Task Force Planning Group [*DoD*]
TFPIA.......	Textile Fiber Products Identification Act [*1960*]
TFPL.........	Task Force Pro Libra Ltd. (IID)
TFPL.........	Texas Forest Products Laboratory
TFPL	Training Film Production Laboratory [*Military*]
T and F Q Rev ...	Track and Field Quarterly Review [*A publication*]
TFR...........	Pueblo, CO [*Location identifier*] [*FAA*] (FAAL)
TFR...........	Tape-to-File Recorder
TFR...........	Technological Forecasting and Social Change. An International Journal [*A publication*]
TFR...........	Television Film Recorder
TFR...........	Terrain-Following RADAR
TFR...........	Territorial Force Reserve [*British*]
TFR...........	Test Failure Report (CAAL)
TFR...........	Theoretical Final Route [*Telecommunications*] (TEL)
TFR...........	Thin-Film Resist
TFR...........	TOKAMAK [*Toroidal Kamera Magnetic*] at Fontenay-aux-Roses
T/FR	Top of Frame (AAG)
TFR...........	Torus Fontenay AWY-Roses
TFR...........	Total Fertility Rate [*Medicine*]
TFR...........	Total Final Reports
TFR...........	Total Follicular Response (OA)
TFR...........	Trafalgar Resources, Inc. [*Vancouver Stock Exchange symbol*]
TFR...........	Trainer Facilities Report [*Army*]
TFR...........	Transaction Formatting Routines
TFR...........	Transfer
TFR...........	Transfer Function Response
TfR.............	Transferrin Receptor [*Immunology*]
TFR...........	Traveler/Failure Report [*Deep Space Instrumentation Facility, NASA*]
TFR...........	Trouble and Failure Report [*NASA*]
TFR...........	Tubular Flow Reactor
TFR...........	Tunable Frequency Range
TFR/CAR ...	Trouble and Failure Report/Corrective Action Report
TFRCD......	Traffic Received (FAAC)
TFRD........	Test Facilities Requirements Document
TFRE........	International 800 Telecom Corp. [*NASDAQ symbol*] (NQ)
TFS...........	Tactical Fighter Squadron [*Air Force*]
TFS...........	Tape File Supervisor
TFS...........	Tax Free Shopping
TFS...........	Tbilisi [*Former USSR*] [*Geomagnetic observatory code*]
TFS...........	Teacher Follow-Up Survey [*Department of Education*] (GFGA)
TFS...........	Technological Forecasting and Social Change [*A publication*]
TFS...........	Telemetry Format Selection (NASA)
TFS...........	Tenerife-Reina Sofia [*Canary Islands*] [*Airport symbol*] (OAG)
TFS...........	Tennessee Folklore Society (EA)

TFS	Terrain-Following System
TFS	Testicular Feminization Syndrome [*Endocrinology*]
TFS	Thomson Financial Services [*The Thomson Corp.*] [*Publishing*]
TFS	Three-Five Systems [*AMEX symbol*] (SPSG)
TFS	Thrombus-Free Surface [*Hematology*]
TFS	Time and Frequency Standard
TFS	Tin-Free Steel
TFS	Torpedo Firing System (DNAB)
TFS	Traffic Flow Security [*Telecommunications*] (TEL)
TFS	Traffic Forecasting System [*Telecommunications*] (TEL)
TFS	Transport Ferry Service [*English Channel*]
TFS	Transverse Feed System
TFS	Trim Fuel System (MCD)
TFS	Trunk Forecasting System [*Telecommunications*] (TEL)
TFS	Tuliptree Flower Spiroplasma [*Plant pathology*]
TFS	Tunable Frequency Source
TFS	Turbine First Stage [*Nuclear energy*] (NRCH)
TFS	Turbine Flow Sensor
TFS	Type Finish Specification (MCD)
TFSA	304th Fighter Squadron Association (EA)
TFSA	Thin-Film Spreading Agent [*For enhanced oil recovery*]
TFSB	[*The*] Federal Savings Bank [*NASDAQ symbol*] (NQ)
TFSB	Tennessee Folklore Society. Bulletin [*A publication*]
TFSC	[*From the Latin for*] Franciscan Tertiaries of the Holy Cross
TFSC	Turkish Federated State of Cyprus
TFSCB	Technological Forecasting and Social Change [*A publication*]
TFSO	Tonto Forest Seismological Observatory [*Arizona*]
TFSOA	Transactions. Faraday Society [*A publication*]
TFSOA4	Faraday Society. Transactions [*A publication*]
TFSP	Task Force on Service to the Public [*Canada*]
TFSP	Texas Folklore Society. Publications [*A publication*]
TFSQ	Tactical Fighter Squadron [*Air Force*]
TFSS	Technical Facilities Subsystem [*Space Flight Operations Facility, NASA*]
TFST	Thin Films Science and Technology [*Elsevier Book Series*] [*A publication*]
TFSUSS	Task Force on Scientific Uses of the Space Station [*NASA*]
TFT	Tabular Firing Table [*Military*] (AABC)
TFT	Tangential Flow Torch [*For plasma generation*]
TFT	Technical Feasibility Testing [*Army*]
TFT	Temporary Facility Tool (SAA)
TFT	Temporary Full-Time (GFGA)
TFT	Termo Fibertek [*AMEX symbol*] (SPSG)
TF & T	Theatre, Film, and Television Biographies Master Index [*A publication*]
TFT	Thermal Fatigue Test
TFT	Thin-Film Field-Effect Transistor
TFT	Thin-Film Technique
TFT	Thin-Film Technology
TFT	Thin-Film Transducer
TFT	Thin-Film Transistor
TFT	Threshold Failure Temperatures
TFT	Tight Fingertip [*Medicine*]
TFT	Time-to-Frequency Transformation [*Electronics*] (OA)
TFT	Tit for Tat [*Slang*]
TFT	Trifluorothymidine [*Pharmacology*]
TF/TA	Terrain Following/Terrain Avoidance (MCD)
TFTAS	Tactical Fighter Training Aggressor Squadron [*Air Force*]
TFTASq	Tactical Fighter Training Aggressor Squadron [*Air Force*]
TFTB	Taping for the Blind (EA)
TFTE	Temporary Full-Time Equivalent (GFGA)
TFTG	Tactical Fighter Training Group [*Military*]
TF/TG	Task Force/Task Group
TFTNGSq	Tactical Fighter Training Squadron [*Air Force*]
TFTP	Task Force on Teaching as a Profession [*Defunct*] (EA)
TFTP	Television Facility Test Position [*Telecommunications*] (TEL)
TFTP	Trivial File Transfer Protocol (BYTE)
TFTR	TOKAMAK [*Toroidal Kamera Magnetic*] Fusion Test Reactor [*Princeton, NJ*]
TFTR	Toroidal Fusion Test Reactor [*Nuclear energy*] (MCD)
TFTS	Tactical Fighter Training Squadron [*Air Force*] (MCD)
TFTS	TOW [*Tube-Launched, Optically Tracked, Wire-Guided (Weapon)*] Field Test Set (MCD)
TFTTA	Teplofizika i Teplotekhnika [*A publication*]
TFTW	Tactical Fighter Training Wing [*Air Force*] (MCD)
TFTY	Thrifty Rent-a-Car System, Inc. [*NASDAQ symbol*] (NQ)
TFU	Tactical Forecast Unit
TFU	Telecommunications Flying Unit [*British*]
TFU	Test Facility Utilization [*NASA*] (NASA)
TFU	Theoretical First Unit [*Economics*]
TFUC	Theoretical First Unit Cost
TFV	Twin Falls Victory [*Tracking ship*] [*NASA*]
TFW	Tactical Fighter Wing [*Air Force*]
TFW	Tethered Free-Floating Worker
TFW	Thermoplastic Fan Wheel
TFW	Tokyo Financial Wire [*COMLINE International Corp.*] [*Japan*] [*Information service or system*] (CRD)
TFW	Tropical Fresh Water
TFW	Tufts University, Medford, MA [*OCLC symbol*] (OCLC)
TFW	Turbulent Far Wake

TFWC	Tactical Fighter Weapons Center [*Air Force*] (AFM)
TFWCRG	Tactical Fighter Weapons Center Range Group [*Military*]
TFWG	Tactical Fighter Wing [*Air Force*]
TFWRR	Task Force on Women's Rights and Responsibilities [*National Council on Family Relations*] (EA)
TFWS	Tactical Fighter Weapon School [*Air Force*] (MCD)
TFWS	Task Force on Women in Sports [*of NOW*] (EA)
TFX	Tactical Fighter Experimental [*Air Force*]
TFX	Teleflex, Inc. [*AMEX symbol*] (SPSG)
TFX	Thymic Factor X [*Endocrinology*]
TFX	Tri-Service Fighter, Experimental (MCD)
TFXA	Time-Focused Crystal Analyzer [*Spectrometer*]
TFX-N	Tactical Fighter Experimental - Navy
TFX-O	Tactical Fighter Experimental - Offensive
TFX-R	Tactical Fighter Experimental - Reconnaissance
TFY	Target Fiscal Year (MCD)
TFYAP	Tobacco Free Young America Project (EA)
TFYQA	Think for Yourself and Question Authority [*Term coined by Dr. Timothy Leary*]
TFZ	Tail Fuze (MSA)
TFZ	Traffic Zone (FAAC)
TFZ	Trifluroperazine [*Tranquilizer*]
TFZ	Tropospheric Frontal Zone
Tg	Glass Transition
TG	Guatemala [*Aircraft nationality and registration mark*] (FAAC)
TG	Positioning Devices [*JETDS nomenclature*] [*Military*] (CET)
TG	Tail Gear
TG	Tangent Group (EA)
TG	Tape Gauge
TG	Target Gate (CAAL)
TG	Task Group [*Military*]
TG	Task Guidance
TG	Technology Gap
TG	Telegram
TG	Telegraph
TG	Teleilaet Ghassul (BJA)
TG	Temporary Gentleman [*British slang term for officer for duration of the war*] [*World War I*]
TG	Terminal Guidance
TG	Terminator Group
TG	Test Group
TG	Test Guaranteed
TG	Testamentsgesetz [*Law on Wills*] [*German*] (ILCA)
TG	Testosterone Glucuronide [*Medicine*] (MAE)
TG	Text Change [*Data processing*] (PCM)
TG	Thai Airways International [*ICAO designator*] (FAAC)
TG	Thapsigargin [*Organic chemistry*]
TG	Theatre Guild (EA)
TG	Theologie und Glaube [*A publication*]
TG	Therapeutic Gazette [*Philadelphia*] [*A publication*]
TG	Thermogravimetry
TG	Thioglucose [*Biochemistry*]
TG	Thioglycolate [*Biochemistry*]
TG	Thioguanine [*Also, T*] [*Antineoplastic drug*]
TG	Third Generation (EA)
TG	Thoracic Ganglion [*Neuroanatomy*]
TG	Thromboglobulin [*Clinical chemistry*]
TG	Thyroglobulin [*Also, Thg*] [*Endocrinology*]
TG	Timing Gate (AAG)
TG	Tithing [*Church of England*]
tg	Togo [*MARC country of publication code*] [*Library of Congress*] (LCCP)
TG	Togo [*ANSI two-letter standard code*] (CNC)
TG	Toho Gakuho [*A publication*]
TG	Tollgate [*Maps and charts*]
T & G	Tongue and Groove [*Lumber*]
T & G	Tonopah & Goldfield Railroad (IIA)
TG	Top Grille (OA)
TG	Torpedo Group
TG	Total Graph (OA)
T & G	Touch and Go [*Landings*] [*Aviation*] (MCD)
TG	Toxic Goiter [*Medicine*] (MAE)
TG	Track Geometry [*In TG-01, an Austrian built subway inspection car*]
TG	Tracking and Guidance
TG	Traders Group Ltd. [*Toronto Stock Exchange symbol*] [*Vancouver Stock Exchange symbol*]
TG	Traffic Guidance [*Aviation*]
T-G	Transformational-Generative [*Linguistics*]
TG	Transgenic [*Genetics*]
TG	Transglutaminase [*An enzyme*]
TG	Transgranular [*Metallurgy*]
TG	Transmissible Gastroenteritis [*Virus*]
TG	Tredegar Industries, Inc. [*NYSE symbol*] (SPSG)
T & G	Tremont & Gulf Railroad (IIA)
TG	Tribune de St. Gervais [*A publication*]
TG	Trigeminal Ganglion [*Neuroanatomy*]
TG	Triglyceride [*Biochemistry*]
TG	Tropical Gulf [*American air mass*]
TG	Tuned Grid (KSC)
TG	Turbine Generator (NRCH)

TG.............. Turbogenerator
TG.............. TV Guide [*A publication*]
TG.............. Tying Goals [*Sports*]
TG.............. Type Genus
T & G .... Tyrwhitt and Granger's English Exchequer Reports [*1835-36*] [*A publication*] (DLA)
T2G............ Technician, Second Grade [*Military*]
TGA .... Antibody Thyroglobulin [*Immunology*]
TGA .... [*The*] Generation After [*An association*] (EA)
TGA .... [*The*] Glutamate Association - United States (EA)
TGA .... Taurocholate-Gelatin Agar [*Microbiology*]
T/GA .... Temperature Gauge [*Automotive engineering*]
TGA .... Thermogravimetric [*or Thermogravimetry*] Analysis [*Instrumentation*]
TGA .... Thioglycolic Acid [*Organic chemistry*]
TGA .... Toilet Goods Association [*Later, CTFA*] (EA)
TGA .... Tolmetin Glycine Amide [*Biochemistry*]
TGA .... Total Glycoalkaloids [*Analytical biochemistry*]
TGA .... Touristische Gemeinschaft der Alpenlander [*Alpine Tourist Commission - ATC*] [*Zurich, Switzerland*] (EAIO)
TGA .... Trace Gas Analysis
TGA .... Trade with Greece (Athens) [*A publication*]
TGA .... Transient Global Amnesia [*Medicine*]
TGA .... Transposition of Great Arteries [*Cardiology*]
TGA .... Treasury General Account [*Department of the Treasury*]
TGA .... Triglycollamic Acid [*Organic chemistry*]
TGA .... Tropical Growers' Association (EAIO)
TGA .... Tuebinger Germanistische Arbeiten [*A publication*]
TGAb .... Thyroglobulin Antibody
TGAJA8 .... TGA [*Toilet Goods Association*] Cosmetic Journal [*A publication*]
TGAL......... Teledyne Geotech Alexandria Laboratories
T-GAM..... Training - Guided Air Missile (MUGU)
TGANA ..... Tsitologiya i Genetika [*A publication*]
TGAOTU .. [*The*] Great Architect of the Universe [*Freemasonry*]
TGAR .... Total Graft Area Rejected [*Medicine*] (MAE)
TGARQ ...... Telegraphic Approval Requested (NOAA)
TGAS........ TACAN [*Tactical Air Navigation*] Guidance Augmentation System [*Military*] (CAAL)
TGAS........ Trace Gas Acquisition System
TGA (Toilet Goods Assoc) Cosmet J ... TGA (Toilet Goods Association) Cosmetic Journal [*A publication*]
TG-ATS..... Theatre Guild-American Theatre Society (EA)
TGaV .... Volunteer State Community College, Learning Resources Center, Gallatin, TN [*Library symbol*] [*Library of Congress*] (LCLS)
TGB .... Tongued, Grooved, and Beaded [*Lumber*]
TGB .... Torpedo Gunboat (ROG)
TGB .... Turbine Generator Building [*Nuclear energy*] (NRCH)
TGB .... Twist-Grain-Boundary [*Liquid crystal science*]
TGBL......... Through Government Bill of Lading [*Military*] (AABC)
TGBR........ Trans-Global Resources NL [*NASDAQ symbol*] (NQ)
TGC .... [*The*] Grantsmanship Center (EA)
TGC .... Teleglobe Canada
TGC .... Theater Ground Command [*Military*]
TGC .... Thermocouple Gauge Control
TGC .... Throttle Governor Control
TGC .... Tomato Genetics Cooperative (EA)
TGC .... Total Gas-Phase Carbon [*Environmental chemistry*]
TGC .... Tougaloo College, Tougaloo, MS [*OCLC symbol*] (OCLC)
TGC .... Transfer Gear Case (MCD)
TGC .... Transmit Gain Control (MSA)
TGC .... Travel Group Charter [*Airline fare*]
TGC .... Trenton, TN [*Location identifier*] [*FAA*] (FAAL)
TGCA .... Texas Gun Collectors Association
TGCA .... Transportable Group Control Approach (NG)
TGCGA ..... Transactions. Gulf Coast Association of Geological Societies [*A publication*]
TGCO........ Transidyne General Corp. [*NASDAQ symbol*] (NQ)
TGCR .... Tactical Generic Cable Replacement
TGCS........ Transportable Ground Communications Station
TGD.......... Task Group Delta (MCD)
TGD.......... Technical Guidance Directions
TGD.......... Titograd [*Former Yugoslavia*] [*Airport symbol*] (OAG)
TGD.......... Trajectory and Guidance Data
TGDDM... Tetraglycidyl(diaminodiphenyl)methane [*Organic chemistry*]
TGDG........ TOTAL Energold Corp. [*NASDAQ symbol*] (NQ)
TGDR .... Tokyo Gailkokugo Daigaku Ronshu [*Area and Cultural Studies*] [*A publication*]
TGE .... Transmissible Gastroenteritis [*Virus*]
TGE .... Traverse Gravimeter Experiment (KSC)
TGE .... Trialkoxyglyceryl Ether [*Organic chemistry*]
TGE .... Tryptone Glucose Extract [*Cell growth medium*]
TGE .... Tuskegee, AL [*Location identifier*] [*FAA*] (FAAL)
TGEEP ...... Terminal Guidance Environmental Effects Program (MCD)
T Geesteswet ... Tydskrif vir Geesteswetenskappe [*A publication*]
TGegw....... Theologie der Gegenwart [*A publication*]
TGEN .... Technology General Corp. [*NASDAQ symbol*] (NQ)
TGEOD .... Technika Poszukiwan Geologicznych [*A publication*]
TGEP........ Turbine Generator Emergency Power [*Nuclear energy*] (NRCH)

TGET........ Target Ground Elapsed Time
TGEV........ Transmissible Gastroenteritis Virus [*Virology*]
TGF .... Therapeutic Gain Factor [*Medicine*]
TGF .... Through Group Filter [*Telecommunications*] (TEL)
TGF .... Top Groove Fill [*Lubricating oil test*]
TGF .... Tragicorum Graecorum Fragmenta [*A publication*] (OCD)
TGF .... Transforming Growth Factor
TGF .... Transonic Gasdynamics Facility [*Air Force*]
TGF .... Treasury Guard Force
TGF .... Triglycine Fluoberyllate [*Ferroelectrics*]
TGF .... Tumor Growth Factor [*Oncology*]
TGF-A .... Transforming Growth Factor - Alpha
TGFA......... Triglyceride Fatty Acid [*Biochemistry*]
TGFC........ Tammy Graham Fan Club (EA)
TGFC........ Terri Gibbs Fan Club (EA)
TGG .... Kuala Trengganu [*Malaysia*] [*Airport symbol*] (OAG)
TGG .... Templeton Global Government Income Trust [*NYSE symbol*] (CTT)
TGG .... Temporary Geographic Grid
TGG .... Third Generation Gyro (MCD)
TGG .... Turkey Gamma G [*Immunology*]
TGH .... Tongoa [*Vanuatu*] [*Airport symbol*] (OAG)
TGH.......... Tripler General Hospital [*Army*] (GFGA)
TGI .... Instellingen [*A publication*]
TGI .... Tactics Guide Issued (CAAL)
TGI .... Taghi Ghambar [*Iran*] [*Seismograph station code, US Geological Survey*] (SEIS)
TGI .... Tangier, VA [*Location identifier*] [*FAA*] (FAAL)
TGI .... Target Group Index [*British Market Research Bureau Ltd.*] [*Information service or system*]
TGI .... Target Intensifier
TGI .... Telco Group, Inc. [*Telecommunications service*] (TSSD)
TGI .... Textbuch zur Geschichte Israels [*A publication*] (BJA)
TGI .... TGI Friday's [*NYSE symbol*] (SPSG)
TGI .... Tingo Maria [*Peru*] [*Airport symbol*] (OAG)
TGI .... Tournament Golf International
TGIC........ Tobacco Growers' Information Committee (EA)
TGIC........ Triglycidyl Isocyanurate [*Organic chemistry*]
TGID........ Trunk Group Identification [*Telecommunications*] (TEL)
TGIF........ Terminal Guidance Indirect Fire (MCD)
TGIF........ Thank God It's Friday [*Meaning work-week is nearly over*]
TGIF......... Toe Goes in First [*As is "You're so dumb you have TGIF on your shoes"*]
TGIF......... Transportable Ground Intercept Facility
TGIF-OTMWDUM ... Thank God It's Friday - Only Two More Work Days Until Monday [*Pentagon saying*]
TGIS .... Thank God It's Summer
TGJ............ Tiga [*Loyalty Islands*] [*Airport symbol*] (OAG)
TGKHA ..... Takenaka Gijutsu Kenkyu Hokoku [*A publication*]
TGL+........ [*The*] Graphics Link Plus [*Printer software*] [*TerraVision*] (PCM)
TGL .... Tagula [*Papua New Guinea*] [*Airport symbol*] (OAG)
TGL .... Tangent Oil & Gas [*Vancouver Stock Exchange symbol*]
TGL .... Task Group Leader
TGL .... Temperature Gradient Lamp [*Spectroscopy*]
T Gl........... Theologie und Glaube [*A publication*]
TGL .... Thin Glass Laminate
TGL .... Toggle (AAG)
TGL .... Touch and Go Landings [*Aviation*]
TGL .... Treasury Gold License (MCD)
TGL .... Triangular Guide Line
TGL .... Triglyceride [*Biochemistry*] (MAE)
TGL .... Triglyceride Lipase [*Clinical chemistry*]
TGL .... Triglycerides [*Clinical chemistry*]
TGL .... Triton Group Ltd. [*NYSE symbol*] (SPSG)
TGLC........ Total Gate Leakage Current
TGLM .... Task Group Lung Model [*ICRP*]
TG-LORAN ... Traffic-Guidance Long-Range Aid to Navigation (DEN)
TGLS .... Tongueless
TGLVQ ...... Terminal Guidance for Lunar Vehicles [*Aerospace*] (AAG)
TGM.......... Tactical Generic Multiplex
TGM.......... Task Group Manager (CAAL)
TGM.......... Telegram (ROG)
TGM.......... Theatre Guild Magazine [*A publication*]
TGM.......... Tirgu Mures [*Romania*] [*Airport symbol*] (OAG)
TGM.......... Torpedo Gunner's Mate [*Obsolete*] [*Navy*] [*British*]
TGM.......... Total Gaseous Mercury [*Environmental chemistry*]
TGM.......... Training Guided Missile [*Air Force*]
TGM.......... Transportability Guidance Manual
TGM.......... Trunk Group Multiplexer [*Telecommunications*] (TEL)
TGM.......... Turbine Generator Management
TGMA .... Tone Generator and Master Alarm (KSC)
TGMD....... Test of Gross Motor Development [*Sensorimotor skills test*]
TGMEA .... Tropical and Geographical Medicine [*A publication*]
TG-MS...... Thermogravimetry - Mass Spectrometry
TGMTS..... Tank Gunnery and Missile Tracking System
TGMV....... Tomato Golden Mosaic Virus
TGN.......... Anchorage, AK [*Location identifier*] [*FAA*] (FAAL)
TGN.......... Tecogen, Inc. [*AMEX symbol*] (SPSG)
TGN.......... Tournigan Mining Explorations Ltd. [*Vancouver Stock Exchange symbol*]

TGN........... Trans Golgi Network [*Cytology*]
TGN........... Trigeminal Neuralgia [*Medicine*]
TGN........... Trunk Group Number [*Telecommunications*] (TEL)
TGNMO..... Total Gaseous Non-Methane Organic [*Environmental chemistry*]
TGNR....... Tactics Guide Not Required (CAAL)
TGNU....... Transitional Government of National Unity [*South Africa*]
TGNX....... Tournigan Mining Explorations Ltd. [*NASDAQ symbol*] (NQ)
TGO........... Time to Go [*Apollo*] [*NASA*]
TGO........... Togo [*ANSI three-letter standard code*] (CNC)
TGO........... Tongliao [*China*] [*Airport symbol*] (OAG)
TGO........... Tuned Grid Oscillator
TGOPS..... Task Group Operations [*Navy*] (NVT)
TGOWG.... Teleoperator Ground Operations Working Group [*NASA*] (NASA)
TGP .... [*The*] Giraffe Project [*An association*] (EA)
TGP .... Tasmanian Government Publications [*A publication*] (APTA)
TGP .... Technigen Platinum Corp. [*Vancouver Stock Exchange symbol*]
TGP .... Theft of Government Property [*FBI standardized term*]
TGP .... Timothy Grass Pollen [*Immunology*]
TGP .... Tobacco Glycoprotein [*Biochemistry*]
TGP .... Tone Generator Panel
TGP .... Transcontinental Gas Pipe Line Corp. [*NYSE symbol*] (SPSG)
TGPA........ Technigen Corp. [*NASDAQ symbol*] (NQ)
TGPG .... St. Georges [*Grenada*] [*ICAO location identifier*] (ICLI)
TGPSG ...... Tactical Global Positioning System Guidance (MCD)
TGPWU .... Transport, General and Port Workers' Union [*Aden*]
TGPY........ Point Saline [*Grenada*] [*ICAO location identifier*] (ICLI)
TGR .... Tiger International, Inc. [*Formerly, FLY*] [*NYSE symbol*] (SPSG)
TGR .... Tohoku Gakuin Daigaku Ronshu [*North Japan College Review: Essays and Studies in English Language and Literature*] [*A publication*]
TGR .... Touggourt [*Algeria*] [*Airport symbol*] (OAG)
TGRLSS.... Two-Gas Regenerative Lift Support System
TGrT......... Tusculum College, Greeneville, TN [*Library symbol*] [*Library of Congress*] (LCLS)
TGS........... [*The*] Galactic Society (EA)
TGS........... Gulf States Utilities Co., Beaumont, TX [*OCLC symbol*] (OCLC)
TGS........... Target Generating System
TGS........... Taxiing Guidance System [*Aviation*]
TGS........... Telemetry Ground Station
TGS........... Telemetry Ground System (NASA)
TGS........... Telemetry Guidance System [*From computer game "Hacker II"*]
TGS........... Terminal Guidance Sensor [*or System*]
TGS........... Thermogravimetric [*or Thermogravimetry*] System [*Instrumentation*]
TGS........... Ticket-Granting Server
TGS........... Tide Gauge System
TGS........... Traite de Grammaire Syriaque [*A publication*] (BJA)
TGS........... Transcontinental Geophysical Survey (NOAA)
TGS........... Translator Generator System (IEEE)
TGS........... Transportable Ground Station
TGS........... Triglycine Sulfate [*Ferroelectrics*]
TGS........... Turbine Generator System [*Nuclear energy*] (NRCH)
TGS........... Turkish General Staff (NATG)
TGSDA...... Tulsa Geological Society. Digest [*A publication*]
TGSE........ Tactical Ground Support Equipment
TGSE........ Telemetry Ground Support Equipment [*NASA*] (KSC)
TGSF .... Test Group Support Facility
TGSG .... Transactions. Gaelic Society of Glasgow [*A publication*]
TGSI......... Transactions. Gaelic Society of Inverness [*A publication*]
TGSIFC..... T. G. Sheppard International Fan Club (EA)
TGSM....... Terminally Guided Submissile (MCD)
TGSM....... Terminally Guided Submunitions (MCD)
TGSR........ Triglyceride Secretion Rate [*Physiology*]
TGSS .... Terminal Guidance Sensor System
TGSS .... Turbine Gland Sealing System [*Nuclear energy*] (NRCH)
TGSSA ...... Transactions. Geological Society of South Africa [*A publication*]
TGSS/UGS ... Tactical Ground Sensor System/Unattended Ground Sensor (MCD)
TGT .... German Tribune [*A publication*]
TGT .... Tail Gate
TGT .... Tanga [*Tanzania*] [*Airport symbol*] (OAG)
TGT .... Target (AAG)
TGT .... Tenneco, Inc. [*Formerly, Tennessee Gas Transmission Co.*] [*NYSE symbol*] [*Toronto Stock Exchange symbol*] (SPSG)
TGT .... Thermocouple Gauge Tube
TGT .... Thromboplastin Generation Test [*Hematology*]
TGT .... Thromboplastin Generation Time [*Hematology*] (MAE)
TGT .... True Ground Track (MCD)
TGT .... Turbine Gas Temperature (NATG)
TGTM .... Transportability Guidance Technical Manual
TGTU .... Tail-Gas Treating Unit [*Petroleum engineering*]
TGU.......... Technical Guidance Unit (NVT)
TGU.......... Tegucigalpa [*Honduras*] [*Airport symbol*] (OAG)
TGU.......... Templeton Global Utilities, Inc. [*AMEX symbol*] (SPSG)

TGU........... Tri Gold Industry [*Vancouver Stock Exchange symbol*]
TGU........... Triglycidylurazol [*Antineoplastic drug*]
TG or UA... Temperance, Grog, or Underage [*British military*]
TGUBA ..... Bulletin. Tokyo Gakugei University [*A publication*]
TGUOS ..... Transactions. Glasgow University Oriental Society [*A publication*]
TGURG ...... Telegraphic Authority Requested (NOAA)
TGV .... Targovishte [*Bulgaria*] [*Airport symbol*] (OAG)
TGV .... Thomson Gold Co. [*Vancouver Stock Exchange symbol*]
TGV .... Thoracic Gas Volume [*Medicine*] (AAMN)
TGV .... Train a Grande Vitesse [*High-speed train*]
TGV .... Transposition of the Great Vessels [*Cardiology*]
TGV .... Turbine Governor Valve [*Nuclear energy*] (NRCH)
TGV .... Two Gentlemen of Verona [*Shakespearean work*]
TGW .... Terminally Guided Warhead [*or Weapon*]
TGW .... Theologie der Gegenwart [*A publication*]
TGW .... Things Gone Wrong [*Measure of automobile customer satisfaction*]
TGWU ...... Transport and General Workers' Union [*British*]
TGX .... Tube-Generated X-Ray
TGY .... Tryptone Glucose Yeast [*Cell growth medium*] (MAE)
TGZ .... Tuxtla Gutierrez [*Mexico*] [*Airport symbol*] (OAG)
TGZIA ...... Technische Gids voor Ziekenhuis en Instelling [*A publication*]
TGZM ...... Temperature-Gradient Zone-Melting [*Chemistry*]
Th.............. C. H. Boehringer Sohn, Ingelheim [*Germany*] [*Research code symbol*]
TH.............. Harriman Public Library, Harriman, TN [*Library symbol*] [*Library of Congress*] (LCLS)
TH.............. Hot Leg Temperature [*Nuclear energy*] (NRCH)
TH.............. Reports of the Witwatersrand High Court [*Transvaal, South Africa*] [*A publication*] (DLA)
Th.............. T-Cell, Helper Type [*Immunology*]
Th.............. T-Helper [*Immunology*]
T-H .... Taft-Hartley [*Act*]
TH.............. Tally Ho [*Air Force*]
TH.............. Teacher of Hydrotherapy [*British*]
TH.............. Teaching History [*A publication*] (APTA)
TH.............. Teaching Hospital [*British*]
TH.............. Technische Hochschule [*Technical College*] [*German*]
TH.............. Teki Historyczne [*A publication*]
TH.............. Telegraph Apparatus [*JETDS nomenclature*] [*Military*] (CET)
TH.............. Tell Halaf (BJA)
TH.............. Temporary Hold
TH.............. Terrain Height (MCD)
TH.............. Territory of Hawaii [*to 1959*]
T & H .... Test and Handling [*Equipment*] (NG)
TH.............. Tetrahydrocortisol (MAE)
TH.............. Thai Airways Co. Ltd. [*Later, TG*] [*ICAO designator*] (FAAC)
th .... Thailand [*MARC country of publication code*] [*Library of Congress*] (LCCP)
TH.............. Thailand [*ANSI two-letter standard code*] [*IYRU nationality code*] (CNC)
T & H .... Thames & Hudson [*Publisher*]
TH.............. Tharsis Region [*A filamentary mark on Mars*]
TH.............. Theatre (ROG)
TH.............. Their Highnesses (ADA)
Th.............. Themis. Verzameling van Bijdragen tot de Kennis van het Publiek- en Privaatrecht [*A publication*]
Th.............. Thenar [*Anatomy*]
th .... Thenardite [*CIPW classification*] [*Geology*]
Th.............. Theodotion (BJA)
Th.............. Theogonia [*of Hesiod*] [*Classical studies*] (OCD)
Th.............. Theologia [*A publication*]
TH.............. Theology
Th.............. Theology [*A publication*]
TH.............. Theraplix [*France*] [*Research code symbol*]
TH.............. Therapy [*Medicine*] (DHSM)
TH.............. Thermal
T/H........... Thermal and Hydraulic [*Nuclear energy*] (NRCH)
TH.............. Thermoid (SAA)
Th.............. Thessalonians [*New Testament book*] (BJA)
TH.............. Thick [*Automotive engineering*]
Th.............. Thin [*Philately*]
Th.............. Things [*A publication*]
TH.............. Thionine [*Organic chemistry*]
Th.............. Thiopental [*An anesthetic*]
Th.............. Thomas de Piperata [*Flourished, 1268-72*] [*Authority cited in pre-1607 legal work*] (DSA)
th .... Thoracic [*Anatomy*] (MAE)
TH.............. Thoracic Surgery [*Medicine*]
Th.............. Thorium [*Chemical element*]
Th.............. Thoroughbred (WGA)
Th.............. Thought [*A publication*]
Th.............. Threshold (WGA)
TH.............. Through-Hole [*Data processing*]
TH.............. Thunder
TH.............. Thursday
TH.............. Thyrohyoid [*Medicine*] (MAE)
TH.............. Thyroid Hormone [*Thyroxine*] [*Endocrinology*]
TH.............. Today's Health [*A publication*]
TH.............. Toilet-Paper Holder

TH.............. Toluene-Hyamine [*Scintillation solvent*]
TH.............. Tommy Hilfiger [*Fashion designer*]
TH.............. Total Hysterectomy [*Medicine*]
TH.............. Town Hall   (ROG)
TH.............. Townhouse
TH.............. Toy and Hobby Retailer [*A publication*]
TH.............. Tracing-Hold
T-H............ Transhydro   (AABC)
TH.............. Transient Hyperphosphatasemia [*Medicine*]
TH.............. Transmission Header [*Data processing*]   (IBMDP)
TH.............. Transponder-Hopping
T/H............ Transportation and Handling [*Army*]
TH.............. True Heading
TH.............. Trust House [*British*]
TH.............. Two Hands
TH.............. Tyrosine Hydroxylase [*An enzyme*]
TH.............. Tzivos Hashem   (EA)
ThA............ Associate in Theology   (ADA)
THA........... Taft-Hartley Act [*1947*]
T-HA .... Terminal High Altitude
THA........... Tetrahydroamino-Acridine [*Drug being tested for treatment of Alzheimer's disease*]
THA........... Tetrahydroaminoacridine [*Pharmacology*]
tha .... Thai [*MARC language code*] [*Library of Congress*]   (LCCP)
THA........... Thailand [*ANSI three-letter standard code*]   (CNC)
THA........... Thames Ontario Library Service Board [*UTLAS symbol*]
ThA........... Theatre Annual [*A publication*]
ThA........... Thoracic Aorta [*Medicine*]
THA........... Thorcheron Hunter Association   (EA)
THA........... Total Hip Arthroplasty [*Orthopedics*]
THA........... Total Hydrocarbon Analyzer
THA........... Total Hydroxyapatite [*Clinical chemistry*]   (MAE)
THA........... Tower Hill School, Wilmington, DE [*OCLC symbol*]   (OCLC)
THA........... Transvaal Horse Artillery [*British military*]   (DMA)
THA........... Treasury Historical Association   (EA)
THA........... Tullahoma, TN [*Location identifier*] [*FAA*]   (FAAL)
THA........... Turk Haberler Ajansi [*Press agency*] [*Turkey*]
THAA....... Tourist House Association of America   (EA)
THAAD..... Theater High-Altitude Area Defense [*Military*]
THAB........ Tetrahexylammonium Benzoate [*Organic chemistry*]
THABTS.... Thereabouts [*Legal term*] [*British*]
Thac Cr Cas ... Thacher's Criminal Cases [*1823-42*] [*Massachusetts*] [*A publication*]   (DLA)
Thach Cr.... Thacher's Criminal Cases [*Massachusetts*] [*A publication*]   (DLA)
Thacher Cr ... Thacher's Criminal Cases [*Massachusetts*] [*A publication*]   (DLA)
Thacher Cr Cas ... Thacher's Criminal Cases [*Massachusetts*] [*A publication*]   (DLA)
Thacher Crim Cas (Mass) ... Thacher's Criminal Cases [*Massachusetts*] [*A publication*]   (DLA)
Thack........ Thackeray Corp. [*Associated Press abbreviation*]   (APAG)
THAE........ Transcatheter Hepatic Artery Embolization [*Medicine*]
THAI........ Thai Airways International
Thai........... Thai Fund [*Associated Press abbreviation*]   (APAG)
Thai........... Thailand
(Thai) Bus R ... Business Review (Thailand) [*A publication*]
ThaiCF....... Thai Capital Fund, Inc. [*Associated Press abbreviation*]   (APAG)
Thai J Agric Sci ... Thai Journal of Agricultural Science [*A publication*]
Thai J Dev Adm ... Thai Journal of Development Administration [*Bangkok*] [*A publication*]
Thai J Nurs ... Thai Journal of Nursing [*A publication*]
Thai J Surg ... Thai Journal of Surgery [*A publication*]
Thail .... Thailand
Thailand Dep Miner Resour Ground Water Bull ... Thailand. Department of Mineral Resources. Ground Water Bulletin [*A publication*]
Thailand Dep Miner Resour Rep Invest ... Thailand. Department of Mineral Resources. Report of Investigation [*A publication*]
Thailheimer's Synth Methods of Org Chem Yearb ... Thailheimer's Synthetic Methods of Organic Chemistry Yearbook [*A publication*]
Thail Plant Prot Serv Tech Bull ... Thailand Plant Protection Service. Technical Bulletin [*A publication*]
Thai Natl Sci Pap Fauna Ser ... Thai National Scientific Papers. Fauna Series [*A publication*]
Thai Nurses Assoc J ... Thai Nurses Association Journal [*A publication*]
Thai Sci Bull ... Thai Science Bulletin [*A publication*]
THAJ......... Tasmania House of Assembly - Journals [*A publication*]
Thal........... Thalassemia [*Medicine*]
Thalassia Jugosl ... Thalassia Jugoslavica [*A publication*]
THAM....... Tris(hydroxymethyl)aminomethane [*Also, TRIS*] [*Biochemical analysis*]
THAMA.... Toxic and Hazardous Materials Agency [*Army*]   (RDA)
THAP........ Tactical High-Altitude Penetration   (MCD)
THAQ........ Tetrahydroanthraquinone [*Organic chemistry*]
Tharandter Forstl Jahrb ... Tharandter Forstliches Jahrbuch [*A publication*]
Tharandt Forstl Jb ... Tharandter Forstliches Jahrbuch [*A publication*]
Thar Forstl Jb ... Tharandter Forstliches Jahrbuch [*A publication*]
THARIES ... Total Hip Articular Replacement with Internal Eccentric Shells [*Orthopedics*]

THaroL...... Lincoln Memorial University, Harrogate, TN [*Library symbol*] [*Library of Congress*]   (LCLS)
THART ..... Theodore Army Terminal
ThArts .... Theatre Arts [*A publication*]
THAS .... Tumbleweed High-Altitude Samples   (MUGU)
ThAT .... Theologie des Alten Testaments [*A publication*]   (BJA)
THAT .... Theologisches Handwoerterbuch zum Alten Testament [*A publication*]
THAT .... Twenty-Four-Hour Automatic Teller [*Trademark for self-service banking display panel*]
Th Aust ...... Theatre Australia [*A publication*]   (APTA)
THAWS .... Tactical Homing and Warning System
Thayer........ Thayer's Reports [*18 Oregon*] [*A publication*]   (DLA)
Thayer Prelim Treatise Ev ... Thayer's Preliminary Treatise on Evidence [*A publication*]   (DLA)
THB........... Thaba Tseka [*Lesotho*] [*Airport symbol*]   (OAG)
Th B .... Theologiae Baccalaureas [*Bachelor of Theology*]
ThB .... Theologische Blaetter [*A publication*]
ThB .... Theologische Buecherei. Neudrucke und Berichte aus dem 20 Jahrhundert [*Munich*] [*A publication*]   (BJA)
THB........... Third-Harmonic Band
THB........... Today's Housing Briefs [*A publication*]
THB........... [*The*] Toronto, Hamilton & Buffalo Railway Co. [*AAR code*]
TH & B ...... [*The*] Toronto, Hamilton & Buffalo Railway Co. [*Nickname: To Hell and Back*]
THB........... Trierer Heimatbuch [*A publication*]
Th Ber .... Theologische Berichte [*A publication*]
THBF........ Total Hepatic Blood Flow
THBF........ Traditional Hi-Bye Function [*Army*]
THBI .... Thyroid Hormone Binding Inhibitor [*Clinical chemistry*]
Thbilis Sahelmc Univ Gamoqeneb Math Inst Srom ... Thbilisis Sahelmcipho Universiteti Gamoqenebithi Mathematikis Instituti. Sromebi [*A publication*]
Thbilis Univ Srom ... Thbilisis Universitetis. Phizika-Mathematikisa de Sabunebismetqvelo Mecnierebani. Sromebi [*A publication*]
Thbilis Univ Srom A ... Thbilisis Universitetis. Phizika-Mathematikisa de Sabunebismetqvelo Mecnierebani. Sromebi. A [*A publication*]
THbl .... Trierische Heimatblaetter [*A publication*]
ThBNL ...... National Library, Bangkok, Thailand [*Library symbol*] [*Library of Congress*]   (LCLS)
THBP .... Tetrahydrobenzopyrene [*Organic chemistry*]
Th Br.......... Thesaurus Brevium [*2 eds.*] [*1661, 1687*] [*A publication*]   (DLA)
THBR .... Thoroughbred Half-Bred Registry   (EA)
THBR .... Thyroid Hormone Binding Ratio [*Clinical chemistry*]
THBY .... Thereby
Th C .... Candidate of Theology
THC........... Houston Community College System, Learning Resource Center, Houston, TX [*OCLC symbol*]   (OCLC)
THC........... Target Homing Correlator
THC........... Tchien [*Liberia*] [*Airport symbol*]   (OAG)
TH & C ...... Terpin Hydrate and Codeine [*Medicine*]
THC........... Tetrahydrocannabinol [*Active principle of marijuana*]
THC........... Tetrahydrocortisol
THC........... Thermal Converter   (MSA)
THC........... Thermohaline Circulation [*Oceanography*]
THC........... Thiocarbanidin [*Pharmacology*]
Th & C ...... Thompson and Cook's New York Supreme Court Reports [*1873-75*] [*A publication*]   (DLA)
THC........... Thrust Hand Controller [*NASA*]   (KSC)
THC........... Topics in Health Care Financing [*A publication*]
THC........... Total Hydrocarbon
THC........... Transhepatic Cholangiogram [*Medicine*]
THC........... Translation Hand Controller [*NASA*]
THC........... Tridont Health Care, Inc. [*Toronto Stock Exchange symbol*]
THC........... True Heading Computer   (DNAB)
THC........... Tube Humidity Control
T & HCA ... Towboat and Harbor Carriers Association of New York and New Jersey   (EA)
T-HCA....... Trans-Hydroxycrotonic Acid [*Organic chemistry*]
THCA .... Trihydroxycholestanoic Acid [*Biochemistry*]
THCA .... Trihydroxycoprostanic Acid [*Biochemistry*]
Th Ca Const Law ... Thomas' Leading Cases in Constitutional Law [*A publication*]   (DLA)
THCAR ..... Thermo Cardiosystems, Inc. [*Associated Press abbreviation*]   (APAG)
THCARDIO ... Thermo Cardiosystems, Inc. [*Associated Press abbreviation*]   (APAG)
Th CC .... Thacher's Criminal Cases [*1823-42*] [*Massachusetts*] [*A publication*]   (DLA)
THCC........ Tube Heating and Cooling Control
Th C Const Law ... Thomas' Leading Cases on Constitutional Law [*A publication*]   (DLA)
THCF .... Thompson-Huston Co. of France
THCF .... Topics in Health Care Financing [*A publication*]
THCHDM ... Specialist Periodical Reports. Theoretical Chemistry [*A publication*]
THCN....... Tetrahydrocorynantheine [*Biochemistry*]
THCO........ [*The*] Hammond Co. [*NASDAQ symbol*]   (NQ)
THCOL ..... Thorn Color [*Botany*]

THCS .... Temperature of Hot-Channel Sodium [*Nuclear energy*] (NRCH)
THCUR ..... Thorn Curvature [*Botany*]
ThD .... Doctor of Thinkology [*Honorary degree awarded the scarecrow by the wizard in 1939 film "The Wizard of Oz"*]
Thd .... Ribothymidine [*Also, T*] [*A nucleoside*]
THD .... Testicular Hypothermia Device [*Medicine*]
Th D .... Theologiae Doctor [*Doctor of Theology*]
ThD .... Theology Digest [*St. Mary's, KS*] [*A publication*]
THD .... Third Canadian General Investment Trust Ltd. [*Toronto Stock Exchange symbol*]
THD .... Thread (AAG)
THD .... Thunander Corp. [*AMEX symbol*] (SPSG)
THD .... Thunderhead (FAAC)
THD .... Total Harmonic Distortion [*Electronics*]
THD .... Tube Heat Dissipator
THD .... University of Houston, Downtown College, Houston, TX [*OCLC symbol*] (OCLC)
THDA .... Telluraheptadecanoic Acid [*Organic chemistry*]
THDA .... Thermal Hydrodealkylation [*Petroleum technology*]
THDA .... Toluene Hydrodealkylation [*Organic chemistry*]
THDC .... Technical Handbook Distribution Code (MCD)
THDI .... Thread Die
ThDig .... Theology Digest [*St. Mary's, KS*] [*A publication*]
ThDip .... Diploma in Theology (ADA)
THDNK .... Threaded Neck
THDOC ..... Tetrahydrodeoxycorticosterone [*Biochemistry*]
THDPC ...... Threadpiece
THDr .... Doctor of Theology
THDR .... Thunder (FAAC)
THDS .... Thermal Helium Desorption Spectrometry (MCD)
THDS .... Time Homogenous Data Set (MCD)
THE .... T & H Resources Ltd. [*Toronto Stock Exchange symbol*]
THE .... Tape-Handling Equipment
THE .... Technical Help to Exporters [*British Standards Institution*]
THE .... Teresina [*Brazil*] [*Airport symbol*] (OAG)
THE .... Tetrahydrocortisone [*Endocrinology*]
ThE .... Theologische Existenz Heute [*Munich*] [*A publication*] (BJA)
THE .... Thomas Hewett Edward Cat [*In TV series "T.H.E. Cat"*]
THE .... Total Height Expansion
THE .... Transhepatic Embolization [*Medicine*]
THE .... Transportable Helicopter Enclosure (RDA)
THE .... Tube Heat Exchanger
THEA .... Theata [*A publication*]
THEAT ..... Theatrical
Theat Ann ... Theatre Annual [*A publication*]
Theat C ...... Theatre Crafts [*A publication*]
Theat Craft ... Theatre Crafts [*A publication*]
Theat Heute ... Theater Heute [*A publication*]
Theat J ...... Theatre Journal [*A publication*]
Theat Note ... Theatre Notebook [*A publication*]
Theat Q ...... Theatre Quarterly [*A publication*]
Theat Quart ... Theatre Quarterly [*A publication*]
Theatre Arts M ... Theatre Arts Magazine [*A publication*]
Theatre/Drama Abstr ... Theatre/Drama Abstracts [*A publication*]
Theatre J ... Theatre Journal [*A publication*]
Theatre M ... Theatre Magazine [*A publication*]
Theatre Notebk ... Theatre Notebook [*A publication*]
Theatre Pol ... Theatre en Pologne - Theatre in Poland [*A publication*]
Theatre Q... Theatre Quarterly [*A publication*]
Theatre Res Int ... Theatre Research International [*A publication*]
Theatre S ... Theatre Studies [*A publication*]
Theatre S ... Theatre Survey [*A publication*]
Theat Res I ... Theatre Research International [*A publication*]
Theat Stud ... Theatre Studies [*A publication*]
Theat Surv ... Theatre Survey [*A publication*]
Theat Zeit .. Theater der Zeit [*A publication*]
Theb .... Thebais [*of Statius*] [*Classical studies*] (OCD)
THEBES ... [*The*] Electronic Banking Economics Society [*New York, NY*] (EA)
THECC ...... Truck and Heavy Equipment Claims Council (EA)
Th Ed .... Theological Education [*A publication*]
T Heden Rom-Holl Reg ... Tydskrif vir Hedendaagse Romeins-Hollandse Reg [*A publication*]
Th Educ ..... Theological Education [*A publication*]
THEED ..... Tetrahydroxyethylethylenediamine [*Organic chemistry*]
THEG .... [*The*] Group, Inc. [*NASDAQ symbol*] (SPSG)
THEI .... Today Home Entertainment, Inc. [*NASDAQ symbol*] (NQ)
THEIC .... Tris(hydroxyethyl)isocyanurate [*Organic chemistry*]
THE J .... THE [*Technological Horizons in Education*] Journal [*A publication*]
THE Jrnl ... THE [*Technological Horizons in Education*] Journal [*A publication*]
Thel .... Theloall's Le Digest des Briefs [*2 eds.*] [*1579, 1687*] [*A publication*] (DLA)
Them .... American Themis [*A publication*] (DLA)
Them .... La Themis [*A publication*] (DLA)
Them .... Themelios [*A publication*]
Them .... Themistocles [*of Plutarch*] [*Classical studies*] (OCD)
Themis .... Rechtsgeleerd Magazijn Themis [*A publication*]

THEN .... Those Hags Encourage Neuterism [*Organization opposed to NOW (National Organization for Women)*]
THEO .... Theology
THEO .... Theophylline [*Pharmacology*]
THEO .... Theoretical
Theo Am A ... Theobald's Act for the Amendment of the Law [*A publication*] (DLA)
Theobald.... Theobald on Wills [*11 eds.*] [*1876-1954*] [*A publication*] (DLA)
Theoc .... Theocritus [*Third century BC*] [*Classical studies*] (OCD)
Theod .... Theodotion (BJA)
Theo Ecl ... Theological Eclectic [*A publication*]
Theog .... Theogonia [*of Hesiod*] [*Classical studies*] (OCD)
Theokr ...... Theokratia [*Leiden/Cologne*] [*A publication*]
Theol .... Theologia [*A publication*]
THEOL ..... Theological
Theol .... Theology [*London*] [*A publication*]
Theol Akad ... Theologische Akademie [*A publication*]
TheolArb ... Theologische Arbeiten [*A publication*] (BJA)
Theol Dgst ... Theology Digest [*A publication*]
Theol Evang ... Theologia Evangelica [*A publication*]
Theol Geg .. Theologie der Gegenwart [*A publication*]
Theol Gl..... Theologie und Glaube [*A publication*]
Theo & Lit J ... Theological and Literary Journal [*A publication*]
Theol Jb.... Theologisches Jahrbuch [*A publication*]
Theol Lit Z ... Theologische Literaturzeitung [*A publication*]
Theol LZ.... Theologische Literaturzeitung [*A publication*]
THEOLOG ... Theology Student (DSUE)
Theol Phil .. Theologie und Philosophie [*A publication*]
Theol Pract ... Theologia Practica [*A publication*]
Theol Pr Q Schr ... Theologisch-Praktische Quartalschrift [*A publication*]
Theol Pr Qu Schr ... Theologisch-Praktische Quartalschrift [*A publication*]
Theol Quart ... Theologische Quartalschrift [*A publication*]
Theol Quart-Schrift ... Theologische Quartalschrift [*A publication*]
Theol Relig Index ... Theological and Religious Index [*A publication*]
Theol & Rel Ind ... Theological and Religious Index [*A publication*]
Theol Ru ... Theologische Rundschau [*A publication*]
Theol St ..... Theological Studies [*A publication*]
Theol St ..... Theologische Studien [*A publication*]
Theol Stds ... Theological Studies [*A publication*]
Theol St Krit ... Theologische Studien und Kritiken [*A publication*]
Theol Stud ... Theological Studies [*A publication*]
Theol Today ... Theology Today [*A publication*]
Theol Via ... Theologia Viatorum [*A publication*]
Theom L..... Theomonistic Licensee
Theo Mo .... Theological Monthly [*A publication*]
Theophil..... Theophilus [*Flourished, 6th century*] [*Authority cited in pre-1607 legal work*] (DSA)
Theophr ..... Theophrastus [*Third century BC*] [*Classical studies*] (OCD)
Theopomp ... Theopompus Historicus [*Fourth century BC*] [*Classical studies*] (OCD)
Theo Pres Pr ... Theory of Presumptive Proof [*A publication*] (DLA)
Theo Pr & S ... Theobald's Principal and Surety [*1832*] [*A publication*] (DLA)
Theo R .... Theological Review [*A publication*]
THEOR ..... Theorem (ROG)
THEOR ..... Theoretical (AAG)
Theor A Gen ... Theoretical and Applied Genetics [*A publication*]
Theor Appl Genet ... Theoretical and Applied Genetics [*A publication*]
Theor Appl Mech (Sofia) ... Theoretical and Applied Mechanics (Sofia) [*A publication*]
Theor Chem ... Theoretical Chemistry [*A publication*]
Theor Chem Adv Perspect ... Theoretical Chemistry. Advances and Perspectives [*A publication*]
Theor Chem Eng Abstr ... Theoretical Chemical Engineering Abstracts [*A publication*]
Theor Chem Engng Abstr ... Theoretical Chemical Engineering Abstracts [*A publication*]
Theor Chem (NY) ... Theoretical Chemistry (New York) [*A publication*]
Theor Chem Period Chem Biol ... Theoretical Chemistry. Periodicities in Chemistry and Biology [*A publication*]
Theor Chim ... Theoretica Chimica Acta [*A publication*]
Theor Chim Acta ... Theoretica Chimica Acta [*A publication*]
Theor Comput Sci ... Theoretical Computer Science [*A publication*]
Theor Decis ... Theory and Decision [*A publication*]
Theo Repos ... Theological Repository [*A publication*]
Theoret Appl Genet ... Theoretical and Applied Genetics [*A publication*]
Theoret Chim Acta ... Theoretica Chimica Acta [*A publication*]
Theoret Comput Sci ... Theoretical Computer Science [*A publication*]
Theoret Linguist ... Theoretical Linguistics [*A publication*]
Theoret and Math Phys ... Theoretical and Mathematical Physics [*A publication*]
Theoret Population Biol ... Theoretical Population Biology [*A publication*]
Theoret Population Biology ... Theoretical Population Biology [*A publication*]
Theor Exp Biol ... Theoretical and Experimental Biology [*A publication*]
Theor Exp Biophys ... Theoretical and Experimental Biophysics [*A publication*]
Theor Exp Chem ... Theoretical and Experimental Chemistry [*A publication*]
Theor Exper Chem ... Theoretical and Experimental Chemistry [*A publication*]

Theor Exp Methoden Regelunstech ... Theoretische und Experimentelle Methoden der Regelungstechnik [*A publication*]
Theor Foundations Chem Engng ... Theoretical Foundations of Chemical Engineering [*A publication*]
Theor Found Chem Eng ... Theoretical Foundations of Chemical Engineering [*A publication*]
Theorie et Polit ... Theorie et Politique [*A publication*]
Theor Klin Med Einzeldarst ... Theoretische und Klinische Medizin in Einzeldarstellungen [*A publication*]
Theor Klin Med Einzeldarstell ... Theoretische und Klinische Medizin in Einzeldarstellungen [*West Germany*] [*A publication*]
Theor Math ... Theoretical and Mathematical Physics [*A publication*]
Theor Math Phys ... Theoretical and Mathematical Physics [*A publication*]
Theor Med ... Theoretical Medicine [*A publication*]
Theor Pop B ... Theoretical Population Biology [*A publication*]
Theor Popul Biol ... Theoretical Population Biology [*A publication*]
Theor Probability Appl ... Theory of Probability and Its Applications [*A publication*]
Theor Theor ... Theoria to Theory [*A publication*]
Theory Exp Exobiol ... Theory and Experiment in Exobiology [*A publication*]
Theory Probab Appl ... Theory of Probability and Its Applications [*A publication*]
Theory Probability and Math Statist ... Theory of Probability and Mathematical Statistics [*A publication*]
Theory Probab Math Statist ... Theory of Probability and Mathematical Statistics [*A publication*]
Theory Sci Dev ... Theory of Science Development [*A publication*]
Theory Soc ... Theory and Society [*A publication*]
THEOS ..... Theosophy
THEOS ..... They Help Each Other Spiritually [*Motto of THEOS Foundation*]
Theosophy in Aust ... Theosophy in Australia [*A publication*] (APTA)
Theos Q ..... Theosophical Quarterly [*A publication*]
THEOS R ... Theosophical Review [*A publication*] (ROG)
Theo Today ... Theology Today [*A publication*]
Theo Wills ... Theobald on Wills [*13th ed.*] [*1971*] [*A publication*] (DLA)
THer .... Ladies Hermitage Association, Hermitage, TN [*Library symbol*] [*Library of Congress*] (LCLS)
THER .... Therapeutic
Ther .... Theriaca [*of Nicander*] [*Classical studies*] (OCD)
THERAP... Therapeutic
Therap .... Therapie [*A publication*]
Therapeutic Ed ... Therapeutic Education [*A publication*]
Therap Gegenw ... Therapie der Gegenwart [*A publication*]
Therap Halbmonatsh ... Therapeutische Halbmonatshefte [*A publication*]
Therap Hung ... Therapia Hungarica [*Hungarian Medical Journal*] [*A publication*]
Therapie Gegenw ... Therapie der Gegenwart [*A publication*]
Therap Monatsh Vet-Med ... Therapeutische Monatshefte fuer Veterinaermedizin [*A publication*]
Therap Umschau ... Therapeutische Umschau und Medizinische Bibliographie [*A publication*]
Ther Ber ..... Therapeutische Berichte [*A publication*]
Ther Drug Monit ... Therapeutic Drug Monitoring [*A publication*]
THERE ...... [*The*] Heterogeneous Environment for Remote Execution [*Data processing*]
The Rep ..... [*The*] Reporter, Phi Alpha Delta [*A publication*] (DLA)
The Rep ..... [*The*] Reports, Coke's English King's Bench [*A publication*] (DLA)
Ther Gaz .... Therapeutic Gazette [*A publication*]
Ther Ggw ... Therapie der Gegenwart [*A publication*]
Ther Halbmonatsh ... Therapeutische Halbmonatshefte [*A publication*]
Ther Hung ... Therapia Hungarica [*A publication*]
THERM .... Thermal (DEN)
THERM .... Thermometer (AAG)
Therm .... Thermonews [*A publication*]
THERM .... Thermostat (DEN)
THERMA ... Transfer of Heat Reduced Magnetically
Therm Abstr ... Thermal Abstracts [*A publication*]
THERMD ... Thermedics, Inc. [*Associated Press abbreviation*] (APAG)
Therm Eng ... Thermal Engineering [*A publication*]
Therm Engng ... Thermal Engineering [*A publication*]
Therm Engr ... Thermal Engineering [*A publication*]
Therm Eng (USSR) ... Thermal Engineering (USSR) [*A publication*]
THERMISTOR ... Thermal Resistor
Therm Nucl Power ... Thermal and Nuclear Power [*Japan*] [*A publication*]
THERMO ... Thermal and Hydrodynamic Experiment Research Module in Orbit (MCD)
THERMO ... Thermodynamic Property Values Database [*Chemical Information Systems, Inc.*] [*Information service or system*] (CRD)
THERMO ... Thermostat (AAG)
Thermoc Act ... Thermochimica Acta [*A publication*]
Thermochim Acta ... Thermochimica Acta [*A publication*]
THERMODYN ... Thermodynamics (AAG)
Ther Monatsh ... Therapeutische Monatshefte [*A publication*]
Therm Power Conf Proc ... Thermal Power Conference. Proceedings [*United States*] [*A publication*]
Therm Power Gener ... Thermal Power Generation [*A publication*]
Ther Nervensys ... Therapie ueber das Nervensystem [*A publication*]
Ther Nervensyst ... Therapie ueber das Nervensystem [*A publication*]

THerP .... [*The*] Papers of Andrew Jackson, Hermitage, TN [*Library symbol*] [*Library of Congress*] (LCLS)
THERP ...... Technique for Human Error Rate Prediction
Ther Probl Today ... Therapeutic Problems of Today [*A publication*]
Ther Recreation J ... Therapeutic Recreation Journal [*A publication*]
Ther Recr J ... Therapeutic Recreation Journal [*A publication*]
Ther R J ... Therapeutic Recreation Journal [*A publication*]
Ther Sem Hop ... Therapeutique. Semaine des Hopitaux [*A publication*]
Ther Umsch ... Therapeutische Umschau [*A publication*]
Thes .... Thesaurus [*A publication*]
THES .... Theses of Economics and Business in Finland [*Helsinki School of Economics Library*] [*Information service or system*] (CRD)
Thes .... Theseus [*of Plutarch*] [*Classical studies*] (OCD)
THES .... Thesis (ADA)
Thes .... Thessalonians [*New Testament book*]
THES .... Times Higher Education Supplement [*A publication*]
THESA N ... Teachers of Home Economics Specialist Association. Newsletter [*A publication*]
Theses Cathol Med Coll ... Theses. Catholic Medical College [*A publication*]
Theses Cathol Med Coll (Seoul) ... Theses. Catholic Medical College (Seoul) [*A publication*]
Theses Collect Chonnam Univ Chonnam Univ ... Theses Collection of Chonnam University. Chonnam University [*A publication*]
Theses Collect Incheon Jr Coll ... Theses Collection. Incheon Junior College [*A publication*]
Theses Collect Kyungnam Ind Jr Coll ... Theses Collection. Kyungnam Industrial Junior College [*Republic of Korea*] [*A publication*]
Theses Collect Kyungnam Univ ... Theses Collection. Kyungnam University [*Republic of Korea*] [*A publication*]
Theses Collect Sookmyung Women's Univ ... Theses Collection. Sookmyung Women's University [*A publication*]
Theses Collect Yeungnam Univ ... Theses Collection. Yeungnam University [*Republic of Korea*] [*A publication*]
Theses Collect Yeungnam Univ Nat Sci ... Theses Collection. Yeungnam University. Natural Sciences [*Republic of Korea*] [*A publication*]
Theses Doct Ing Univ Dakar Ser Sci Nat ... Theses de Docteur-Ingenieur. Universite de Dakar. Serie Sciences Naturelles [*A publication*]
Theses Zool ... Theses Zoologicae [*A publication*]
THESIS ..... [*The*] Honeywell Engineering Status Information System (SAA)
Thesis .... Thesis Eleven [*A publication*]
Thesis Theo Cassettes ... Thesis Theological Cassettes [*A publication*]
THESLA ... Tennessee Health Science Library Association [*Library network*]
Thesm .... Thesmophoriazusae [*of Aristophanes*] [*Classical studies*] (OCD)
Thess .... Thessalonians [*New Testament book*]
THETA ..... [*The*] Handicapped and Elderly Travelers Association [*Defunct*] (EA)
THETA ..... Teenage Health Education Teaching Assistants [*National Foundation for the Prevention of Oral Disease*]
THETA ..... Tunneling Hot-Electron Transfer Amplifier [*Semiconductor technology*]
Theta NR ... Theta News Release [*A publication*]
T Heth .... Text der Hethiter [*A publication*]
THEX .... [*The*] Hitech Engineering Co. [*McLean, VA*] [*NASDAQ symbol*] (NQ)
Th Ex H ..... Theologische Existenz Heute [*A publication*]
ThExNF .... Theologische Existenz Heute. Neue Folge [*A publication*] (BJA)
THF .... Freelance Research Service, Houston, TX [*OCLC symbol*] (OCLC)
THF .... Target Height Finding (MCD)
THF .... Tetrahydrofluorenone [*Organic chemistry*]
THF .... Tetrahydrofolate [*Biochemistry*]
THF .... Tetrahydrofolic Acid [*Also, THFA*] [*Organic chemistry*]
THF .... Tetrahydrofuran [*Organic chemistry*]
ThF .... Theologische Forschung [*Hamburg*] [*A publication*]
THF .... Thermal Hysteresis Factor
THF .... Thymic Humoral Factor [*Endocrinology*]
THF .... Thymic Hypocalcemic Factor [*Biochemistry*]
THF .... Tian Hua Fen [*Chinese herbal medicine*]
THF .... Tremendously High Frequency [*Telecommunications*] (TEL)
THF .... Trust Houses Forte Ltd. [*Hotel empire*]
THFA .... Tetrahydrofolic Acid [*Biochemistry*]
THFA .... Tetrahydrofurfuryl Alcohol [*Organic chemistry*]
THFA .... Three-Conductor, Heat and Flame Resistant, Armor Cable
THFC .... Troy Hess Fan Club (EA)
THFI .... Plymouth Five Cents Savings Bank [*Plymouth, MA*] [*NASDAQ symbol*] (NQ)
Th F Jb ...... Tharandter Forstliches Jahrbuch [*A publication*]
THFM .... Therefrom [*Legal term*] [*British*]
THFOR ...... Therefor [*Legal term*] [*British*] (ROG)
THFR .... Thetford Corp. [*NASDAQ symbol*] (NQ)
THFR .... Three-Conductor, Heat and Flame Resistant, Radio Cable
THFROM ... Therefrom [*Legal term*] [*British*] (ROG)

THG........... Biloela [*Australia*] [*Airport symbol*]
ThG........... Theologie der Gegenwart [*A publication*]
ThG........... Theologie und Glaube [*A publication*]
Th G........... Therapie der Gegenwart [*A publication*]
THG........... Third-Harmonic Generation [*Physics*]
THG........... Thomson, GA [*Location identifier*] [*FAA*]   (FAAL)
Thg........... Thyroglobulin [*Also, TG*] [*Endocrinology*]
THGA....... Thread Gauge
THGA....... Trihydroxyglutamic Acid [*Organic chemistry*]
THGA....... Trihydroxyglutaric Acid [*Organic chemistry*]
TH GAZ..... Therapeutic Gazette [*Philadelphia*] [*A publication*]   (ROG)
THGEA..... Therapie der Gegenwart [*A publication*]
THGG....... Transportable Horizontal Gravity Gradiometer
THHF....... Tetrahydrohomofolate [*Organic chemistry*]
ThHK....... Theologischer Hand-Kommentar zum Neuen Testament [*A publication*]   (BJA)
THHN ...... Thermoplastic, Heat-Resistant, High-Temperature, Nylon-Jacketed [*Electric cable*]
THHP....... Target Health Hazard Program [*Occupational Safety and Health Administration*]
THHP....... Tung-Hai Hsueh-Pao [*Tunghai Journal*] [*A publication*]
THI........... Telehop, Inc. [*Fresno, CA*] [*Telecommunications*]   (TSSD)
THI........... Temperature-Humidity Index
THi .... Tennessee Historical Society, Nashville, TN [*Library symbol*] [*Library of Congress*]   (LCLS)
THI........... Terre Haute [*Indiana*] [*Seismograph station code, US Geological Survey*]   (SEIS)
THI........... Texas Heart Institute [*University of Texas*] [*Research center*]   (RCD)
THI........... Theodor Herzl Institute   (EA)
THI........... Thermo Instrument Systems, Inc. [*AMEX symbol*]   (SPSG)
THI........... Thios Resources, Inc. [*Vancouver Stock Exchange symbol*]
THI........... Time Handed In [*Navy*]
THI........... Total Height Index   (OA)
THI........... Travelers Health Institute [*Later, ITHI*]
THI........... Trihydroxyindol [*Organic chemistry*]
THIEF....... [*The*] Human-Initiated Equipment Failures
Thiemig-Taschenb ... Thiemig-Taschenbuecher [*A publication*]
Thiemig Tb ... Thiemig-Taschenbuecher [*A publication*]
Thieraerzt Mitth (Carlsruhe) ... Thieraerztliche Mittheilungen (Carlsruhe) [*A publication*]
Thiermed Rundschau ... Thiermedicinische Rundschau [*A publication*]
THIJDO.... Texas Heart Institute. Journal [*A publication*]
THilfgr....... Tommy Hilfiger Sportwear, Inc. [*Associated Press abbreviation*]   (APAG)
THINGS.... Totally Hilarious Incredibly Neat Games of Skill [*Milton-Bradley product*]
Thin Sol Fi ... Thin Solid Films [*A publication*]
THIO........ Thiopental [*An anesthetic*]
Thiokl....... Thiokol Corp. [*Associated Press abbreviation*]   (APAG)
THioTEPA ... Triethylenethiophosphoramide [*Also, TSPA*] [*Antineoplastic drug*]
THIP .... Tetrahydroisooxazolopyridineol [*Organic chemistry*]
THIR .... Temperature-Humidity Infrared Radiometer
TH-IR........ Tyrosine Hydroxylase-Immunoreactivity [*Physiology*]
THIRA ...... Thorium High-Temperature Reactor Association
Third Wld .. Third World Forum [*A publication*]
Third Wld Agric ... Third World Agriculture [*A publication*]
Third World Planning R ... Third World Planning Review [*A publication*]
Third World Q ... Third World Quarterly [*A publication*]
Third World Soc ... Third World Socialists [*A publication*]
Thirties Soc Jnl ... Thirties Society. Journal [*A publication*]
Thirty-3...... 33 Magazine [*A publication*]
Thirty-Three/33 Mag Met Prod Ind ... Thirty-Three/33. Magazine of the Metals Producing Industry [*A publication*]
THIS.......... [*The*] Hospitality and Information Service [*For diplomatic residents and families in Washington, DC*]
This Mag ... This Magazine Is about Schools [*Later, This Magazine: Education, Culture, Politics*] [*A publication*]
THJ .... Laurel, MS [*Location identifier*] [*FAA*]   (FAAL)
ThJ .... Theologische Jahrbuecher [*A publication*]
THJ .... Thermal Joining
Th Jb....... Theologisches Jahrbuch [*A publication*]
THJCS ...... Tsing Hua Journal of Chinese Studies [*A publication*]
THJUA ..... Thalassia Jugoslavica [*A publication*]
THK.......... Taiheiyo Hoso Kyokai [*Pacific Broadcasting Association*] [*Japan*]   (EAIO)
THK.......... Thackeray Corp. [*NYSE symbol*]   (SPSG)
THK.......... Thick [*or Thickness*]   (AAG)
THKF .... Thick Film   (MSA)
THKNS...... Thickness
THKR....... Thicker   (MSA)
THKSA...... Taiki Hoshano Kansoku Seiseki [*A publication*]
Th L......... Licentiate in Theology
'tHL........... 'T Heiling Land [*Nijmegen*] [*A publication*]   (BJA)
THL.......... Tachilek [*Myanmar*] [*Airport symbol*]   (OAG)
THL.......... Tally-Ho Explorations Ltd. [*Vancouver Stock Exchange symbol*]
ThL.......... Theologisches Literaturblatt [*Leipzig*] [*A publication*]
THL.......... Thermoluminescence [*Also, TL*]
THL.......... Thule [*Denmark*] [*Geomagnetic observatory code*]

THL.......... Transhybrid Loss [*Telecommunications*]   (TEL)
THL.......... Tuned Hybrid Lattice
THL.......... University of Houston, Law Library, Main, Houston, TX [*OCLC symbol*]   (OCLC)
ThLB........ Theologisches Literaturblatt [*A publication*]
ThlBer....... Theologischer Literaturbericht [*A publication*]   (BJA)
ThLBI....... Theologisches Literaturblatt [*Leipzig*] [*A publication*]
THLD....... Threshold
THLEN ..... Thorn Length [*Botany*]
Th Life .... Theology and Life [*A publication*]
Th Lit .... Theologische Literaturzeitung [*A publication*]
Th Lit Z ..... Theologische Literaturzeitung [*A publication*]
ThLL......... Thesaurus Linguae Latinae [*A publication*]
THLM .... Lehman [*T. H.*] & Co., Inc. [*New York, NY*] [*NASDAQ symbol*]   (NQ)
Th (Lond)... Theology (London) [*A publication*]
THLR........ Thaler [*Numismatics*]
THLRA ..... Taft-Hartley Labor Relations Act   (OICC)
THLS........ Turret Head Limit Switch
ThLZ .... Theologische Literaturzeitung [*A publication*]
THM.......... Tapia House Movement [*Trinidad and Tobago*] [*Political party*]   (PPW)
THM.......... Textos Hispanicos Modernos [*A publication*]
Th M......... Theologiae Magister [*Master of Theology*]
THM.......... Therm   (MSA)
THM.......... Thermwood Corp. [*AMEX symbol*]   (SPSG)
Thm.......... Thomist [*A publication*]
THM.......... Thompson Falls, MT [*Location identifier*] [*FAA*]   (FAAL)
THM.......... Thomson Newspapers Ltd. [*Toronto Stock Exchange symbol*]
THM.......... Tien Hsia Monthly [*A publication*]
THM.......... Topics in Health Care Materials Management [*A publication*]
THM.......... Total Heme Mass [*Medicine*]   (MAE)
THM.......... Traveling Heater Method
THM.......... Trihalomethane [*Organic chemistry*]
THM.......... TRIS, HEPES, Mannitol [*A buffer*]
THM.......... Trotting Horse Museum   (EA)
THM.......... University of Tennessee at Martin, Martin, TN [*OCLC symbol*]   (OCLC)
THMA...... Trailer Hitch Manufacturers Association   (EA)
ThmAd....... Thomson Advisory Group [*Associated Press abbreviation*]   (APAG)
Th Markings ... Theological Markings [*A publication*]
Thmbet....... Thomas & Betts Corp. [*Associated Press abbreviation*]   (APAG)
ThmFib....... Thermo Fibertek, Inc. [*Associated Press abbreviation*]   (APAG)
THMFP..... Trihalomethane Formation Potential [*Environmental chemistry*]
THMF-TS-TGSE ... Teachers Have More Fun - They Should - They Get Stewed Enough [*Slogan*] [*Bowdlerized version*]
THMOV.... Thistle Mottle Virus [*Plant pathology*]
THMP ...... Tetrahydromethanopterin [*Biochemistry*]
THMP ...... Thermal Industries, Inc. [*NASDAQ symbol*]   (NQ)
THMS ...... Thermistor [*Electronics*]
Th M S...... Thomas Mann-Studien [*A publication*]
THMTG ... Target Holding Mechanism, Tank Gunnery
THMZ....... Three Hundred Mile Zone
THN .... Thin   (FAAC)
THN .... Trihydroxynaphthalene [*Organic chemistry*]
THN .... Trollhattan [*Sweden*] [*Airport symbol*]   (OAG)
Th Nb......... Theatre Notebook. A Quarterly of Notes and Research [*A publication*]
THNR....... Thinner [*Freight*]
THNR T..... Thinner Than [*Freight*]
THO........... Thogoto Virus [*Virology*]
Tho........... Thomas Aquinas [*Deceased, 1274*] [*Authority cited in pre-1607 legal work*]   (DSA)
Tho........... Thomas Mieres [*Flourished, 1429-39*] [*Authority cited in pre-1607 legal work*]   (DSA)
Tho........... Thomas de Piperata [*Flourished, 1268-72*] [*Authority cited in pre-1607 legal work*]   (DSA)
THO .... Thomsonite [*A zeolite*]
THO .... Thor Industries, Inc. [*NYSE symbol*]   (SPSG)
THO .... Thorco Resources, Inc. [*Toronto Stock Exchange symbol*]
THO .... Thorshofn [*Iceland*] [*Airport symbol*]   (OAG)
THO .... Though
Tho........... Thought. A Review of Culture and Idea [*A publication*]
THO .... Thursdays Only [*British railroad term*]
THO .... Tonto Hills Observatory [*Arizona*] [*Seismograph station code, US Geological Survey*] [*Closed*]   (SEIS)
THOF....... Thereof
Tho For ...... Thomas de Formaginis [*Flourished, 1331-38*] [*Authority cited in pre-1607 legal work*]   (DSA)
Tho de For ... Thomas de Formaginis [*Flourished, 1331-38*] [*Authority cited in pre-1607 legal work*]   (DSA)
Tho Form ... Thomas de Formaginis [*Flourished, 1331-38*]   (DSA)
Tho Foroli ... Thomas Foroliviensis [*Authority cited in pre-1607 legal work*]   (DSA)
Tho Grama ... Thomas Grammaticus [*Flourished, 16th century*] [*Authority cited in pre-1607 legal work*]   (DSA)
THOLD..... Threshold   (NASA)
Thol Ed ...... Theological Educator [*A publication*]

Tho de Lya ... Thomas de Elya [*Authority cited in pre-1607 legal work*]　(DSA)

Thom.......... Thomas' Reports [*1 Wyoming*] [*A publication*]　(DLA)

Thom.......... Thomist [*A publication*]

Thom.......... Thomson's Nova Scotia Reports [*A publication*]　(DLA)

Thomas ...... Thomas' Reports [*1 Wyoming*] [*A publication*]　(DLA)

Thomas Mortg ... Thomas on Mortgages [*A publication*]　(DLA)

Thomas Negl ... Thomas on Negligence [*A publication*]　(DLA)

Thomas Say Found ... Thomas Say Foundation [*A publication*]

Thomas Say Found Monogr ... Thomas Say Foundation. Monographs [*A publication*]

Thom BBS ... Thompson. Benefit Building Societies [*A publication*]　(ILCA)

Thom Bills ... Thomson on Bills and Notes [*A publication*]　(DLA)

Thom B & N ... Thomson on Bills and Notes [*A publication*]　(DLA)

Thom Camp ... Thomas Campegius [*Deceased, 1564*] [*Authority cited in pre-1607 legal work*]　(DSA)

THOMCAT ... Thomas Register Catalog File [*A publication*]

Thom Co Lit ... Thomas' Edition of Coke upon Littleton [*A publication*]　(DLA)

Thom Co Litt ... Thomas' Edition of Coke upon Littleton [*A publication*]　(DLA)

Thom Const L ... Thomas' Leading Cases on Constitutional Law [*A publication*]　(DLA)

Thom Dec .. Thomson's Nova Scotia Reports [*1834-52*] [*A publication*]　(DLA)

Thom & Fr ... Thomas and Franklin's Chancery Reports [*1 Maryland*] [*A publication*]　(DLA)

ThomIn ...... Thomas Industries, Inc. [*Associated Press abbreviation*]　(APAG)

THOMIS... Total Hospital Operating and Medical Information System

Thom LC.... Thomas' Leading Cases on Constitutional Law [*A publication*]　(DLA)

Thom de Mar ... [*Johannes*] Thomas de Marinis [*Flourished, 16th century*] [*Authority cited in pre-1607 legal work*]　(DSA)

Thom Mort ... Thomas on Mortgages [*A publication*]　(DLA)

Thom N Sc ... Thomson's Nova Scotia Reports [*1834-51, 1856-59*] [*Canada*] [*A publication*]　(DLA)

Thomp & C ... Thompson and Cook's New York Supreme Court Reports [*A publication*]　(DLA)

Thomp Cal ... Thompson's Reports [*39, 40 California*] [*A publication*]　(DLA)

Thomp Car ... Thompson on Carriers [*A publication*]　(DLA)

Thomp Cas ... Thompson's Cases [*Tennessee*] [*A publication*]　(DLA)

Thomp Ch Jur ... Thompson on Charging the Jury [*A publication*]　(DLA)

Thomp Cit ... Thompson's Ohio Citations [*A publication*]　(DLA)

Thomp & Cook ... Thompson and Cook's New York Supreme Court Reports [*A publication*]　(DLA)

Thomp Corp ... Thompson's Commentaries on Law of Private Corporations [*A publication*]　(DLA)

Thomp Dig ... Thompson's Digest of Laws [*Florida*] [*A publication*]　(DLA)

Thomp Ent ... Thompson's Entries [*A publication*]　(DLA)

Thomp Farm ... Thompson's Law of the Farm [*A publication*]　(DLA)

Thomp H & Ex ... Thompson on Homesteads and Exemptions [*A publication*]　(DLA)

Thomp High ... Thompson on the Law of Highways [*A publication*]　(DLA)

Thomp Liab Off ... Thompson on Liability of Officers of Corporations [*A publication*]　(DLA)

Thomp Liab St ... Thompson on Liability of Stockholders [*A publication*]　(DLA)

Thomp Liab Stockh ... Thompson on Liability of Stockholders [*A publication*]　(DLA)

Thomp & M Jur ... Thompson and Merriam on Juries [*A publication*]　(DLA)

Thomp NB Cas ... Thompson's National Bank Cases [*A publication*]　(DLA)

Thomp Neg ... Thompson's Cases on Negligence [*A publication*]　(DLA)

Thomp Pat ... Thompson on Patent Laws of All Countries [*13th ed.*] [*1905*] [*A publication*]　(DLA)

Thomp Prov Rem ... Thompson's Provisional Remedies [*A publication*]　(DLA)

Thomps Cas ... Thompson's Tennessee Cases [*A publication*]　(DLA)

Thompson.. Thompson's Reports [*39, 40 California*] [*A publication*]　(DLA)

Thompson & C ... Thompson and Cook's New York Supreme Court Reports [*A publication*]　(DLA)

Thompson's Fla Dig ... Thompson's Digest of Laws [*Florida*] [*A publication*]　(DLA)

Thompson Unrep (PA) ... Thompson's Unreported Cases (Pennsylvania) [*A publication*]　(DLA)

Thompson Yates and Johnston Lab Rep ... Thompson, Yates, and Johnston Laboratories Reports [*A publication*]

Thompson Yates Lab Rep ... Thompson-Yates Laboratories Reports [*A publication*]

Thomp & St ... Thompson and Steger's Code [*Tennessee*] [*A publication*]　(DLA)

Thomp & St Code ... Thompson and Steger's Code [*Tennessee*] [*A publication*]　(DLA)

Thomp Tenn Cas ... Thompson's Unreported Tennessee Cases [*A publication*]　(DLA)

Thomp Trials ... Thompson on Trials [*A publication*]　(DLA)

Thom Rep .. Thomson's Nova Scotia Reports [*A publication*]　(DLA)

Thom Sc Acts ... Thomson's Scotch Acts [*A publication*]　(DLA)

Thom Sel Dec ... Thomson's Nova Scotia Select Decisions [*A publication*]　(DLA)

Thoms Jud Fac ... Thoms' Judicial Factors [*A publication*]　(DLA)

Thomson's Process Chem Eng ... Thomson's Process and Chemical Engineering [*Australia*] [*A publication*]

Thom St Sum ... Thomas' Leading Statutes Summarized [*A publication*]　(DLA)

Thom Un Jur ... Thomas' Universal Jurisprudence [*2nd ed.*] [*1829*] [*A publication*]　(DLA)

THON .... Thereon [*Legal term*] [*British*]

Tho Parpal ... Thomas Parpalea [*Flourished, 16th century*] [*Authority cited in pre-1607 legal work*]　(DSA)

THOPS...... Tape Handling Operational System [*Data processing*]　(IEEE)

THOR........ Tandy [*Corp.*] High-Performance Optical Recording System [*Dye-polymer technology*]　(PCM)

THOR........ Tape-Handling Optional Routines [*Honeywell, Inc.*]

THOR........ Thesaurus-Oriented Retrieval [*Information service or system*]

Thor .... Thorax [*British Medical Association*] [*A publication*]

Thor .... Thorington's Reports [*107 Alabama*] [*A publication*]　(DLA)

THOR....... Thought Organizer [*Computer program produced by Fastware, Inc.*]

THOR....... Trace Hierarchy of Requirements [*Science Applications International Corp.*]

THOR....... Transistorized High-Speed Operations Recorder

THOR....... Tsing Hua Open-Pool Reactor [*Formosa*]

THORAC .. Thoraci [*To the Throat*] [*Pharmacy*]

Thorac Cardiovasc Surg ... Thoracic and Cardiovascular Surgeon [*A publication*]

THORAD ... Thor-Agena D [*Rocket*] [*NASA*]

Thorax Chir ... Thoraxchirurgie und Vaskulaere Chirurgie [*A publication*]

Thoraxchir Vask Chir ... Thoraxchirurgie und Vaskulaere Chirurgie [*A publication*]

Thor Bank ... Thorborn on Bankers' Law [*A publication*]　(DLA)

Thoreau JQ ... Thoreau Journal Quarterly [*A publication*]

Thoreau Q ... Thoreau Quarterly [*A publication*]

THOREN ... Thor Energy Resources, Inc. [*Associated Press abbreviation*]　(APAG)

ThorIn........ Thor Industries, Inc. [*Associated Press abbreviation*]　(APAG)

Thorn .... Thornton's Notes of Ecclesiastical and Maritime Cases [*1841-50*] [*A publication*]　(DLA)

THORNB ... Thornbury [*England*]

Thorn Conv ... Thornton's Conveyancing [*A publication*]　(DLA)

Thornt & Bl Bldg & Loan Ass'ns ... Thornton and Blackledge's Law Relating to Building and Loan Associations [*A publication*]　(DLA)

Thornton Gifts ... Thornton on Gifts and Advancements [*A publication*]　(DLA)

Thoro .... Thoroughfare [*Maps and charts*]

Thoroton Soc Rec Ser ... Thoroton Society. Record Series [*A publication*]

THORP ..... Thermal Oxide Reprocessing Plant [*Nuclear energy*]

Thorpe .... Thorpe's Annual Reports [*52 Louisiana*] [*A publication*]　(DLA)

Thorpe Anc L ... Thorpe's Ancient Laws of England [*A publication*]　(DLA)

THORS ..... Thermal-Hydraulic Out-of-Reactor Safety Facility [*Department of Energy*]

Thos Co Lit ... Thomas' Edition of Coke upon Littleton [*A publication*]　(DLA)

THOT........ Thought

Thoth Res .. Thoth Research Journal [*A publication*]

THOU .... Thousand　(AFM)

THOUS..... Thousand　(NASA)

THP .... [*The*] Hunger Project　(EA)

THP .... Terminal Handling Processor

THP .... Terminal Holding Power [*Advertising*]　(IIA)

TH & P ...... Terre Haute & Peoria Railroad [*Nickname: Take Hold and Push*]

THP .... Tetrahydropalmatine [*Organic chemistry*]

THP .... Tetrahydropapaveroline [*Biochemistry*]

thp .... Tetrahydropyranyl [*Organic chemistry*]

THP .... Tetrakis(hydroxymethyl)phosphonium [*Organic chemistry*]

THP .... Thermopolis, WY [*Location identifier*] [*FAA*]　(FAAL)

THP .... Through Hole Probe

THP .... Thrust Horsepower [*Jet engines*]

THP .... Total Hydroxyproline [*Clinical chemistry*]　(MAE)

T & HP ...... Transportation and Handling Procedure

THP .... Triangle Home Products, Inc. [*AMEX symbol*]　(SPSG)

THP .... Trihydroxypropane [*Organic chemistry*]

THP .... (Trimethylhydrazinium) Propionate [*Biochemistry*]

THP .... Tris(hydroxymethyl)phosphine [*Organic chemistry*]

THPA .... Tetrahydrophthalic Anhydride [*Organic chemistry*]

THPA .... Tetrahydropteric Acid [*Organic chemistry*]　(MAE)

THPC .... Tetrakis(hydroxymethyl)phosphonium Chloride [*Flame retardant*]

THPDX ..... Tetrahydropyranyldoxorubicin [*Antineoplastic drug*]

THPF........ Total Hepatic Plasma Flow [*Physiology*]

THPFB...... Treated Hard-Pressed Fiberboard [*Technical drawings*]

Th & Ph ...... Theologie und Philosophie [*A publication*]

THPO........ Tris(hydroxymethyl)phosphine Oxide [*Organic chemistry*]

Th P Q .... Theologisch-Praktische Quartalschrift [*A publication*]

THPR .... Thermal Profiles, Inc. [*NASDAQ symbol*]　(NQ)

T & H Prac ... Troubat and Haly's Pennsylvania Practice [*A publication*]　(DLA)

Th Pract..... Theologia Practica [*A publication*]

ThPract...... Theologie en Practijk [*Rotterdam*] [*A publication*]　(BJA)

ThPrM....... Theologisch-Praktische Monatsschrift [*A publication*]　(BJA)

Th Pr Ma St ... Theory of Probability and Mathematical Statistics [*A publication*]
Th Prob Ap ... Theory of Probability and Its Applications [*A publication*]
ThPrQSchr ... Theologisch-Praktische Quartalschrift [*Linz, Austria*] [*A publication*]
THPS......... Tetrakis(hydroxymethyl)phosphonium Sulfate [*Flame retardant*] [*Organic chemistry*]
THQ .... Tennessee Historical Quarterly [*A publication*]
THQ .... Tetrahydroxyquinone [*Chemical indicator*]
THQ .... Theater Headquarters [*Military*]
ThQ........... Theatre Quarterly [*A publication*]
THQ........... Theologische Quartalschrift [*A publication*]
THQ .... Troop Headquarters
ThQ........... Tuebinger Theologische Quartalschrift [*A publication*]
ThQR......... Theological Quarterly Review [*A publication*]
Th QS .... Theologische Quartalschrift [*A publication*]
THR.......... Target Heart Rate [*Exercise*]   (INF)
THR.......... Tehran [*Iran*] [*Airport symbol*]   (OAG)
ThR............ Theatre Research [*A publication*]
THR.......... Their   (ROG)
THR......... Their Royal Highnesses [*British*]   (ROG)
ThR............ Theological Review [*Princeton, NJ*] [*A publication*]
ThR............ Theologische Rundschau [*A publication*]
THR.......... There   (ROG)
THR.......... Thor Energy Resources, Inc. [*AMEX symbol*]   (SPSG)
Thr .... Threni   (BJA)
Thr .... Threonine [*Also, T*] [*An amino acid*]
THR.......... Threshold
THR.......... Through   (ADA)
THR.......... Throughput
THR.......... Throughput Rate
THR.......... Thrust   (AAG)
THR.......... Thrust. Journal for Employment and Training Professionals [*A publication*]
THR.......... Total Hip Replacement [*Medicine*]
THR.......... Total Hydrocarbon Reforming [*Hydrogen production*]
THR.......... Transmittal Header Record [*Data processing*]
THR.......... Transmitter Holding Register
THR.......... Turbine Heat Rate   (DNAB)
THRA......... Theratech Corp. [*NASDAQ symbol*]   (NQ)
THRABTS ... Thereabouts [*Legal term*] [*British*]   (ROG)
THRAP ..... Tasmanian Historical Research Association. Papers and Proceedings [*A publication*]   (ADA)
THRAPP... Tasmanian Historical Research Association. Papers and Proceedings [*A publication*]
THRAR ..... Thereafter [*Legal term*] [*British*]   (ROG)
THRAT ..... Thereat [*Legal term*] [*British*]   (ROG)
THRB......... Theodore Roosevelt Birthplace National Historic Site
Th Rd .... Theologische Rundschau [*A publication*]
THRD........ Thread
ThrD .... Three D Departments, Inc. [*Associated Press abbreviation*]   (APAG)
Th Rdschau ... Theologische Rundschau [*A publication*]
Three Bank ... Three Banks Review [*A publication*]
Three Banks R ... Three Banks Review [*A publication*]
Three Banks Rev ... Three Banks Review [*A publication*]
Three Forks ... Three Forks of Muddy Creek [*A publication*]
ThreeFS..... Three-Five Systems, Inc. [*Associated Press abbreviation*]   (APAG)
Three R Int ... Three R International [*West Germany*] [*A publication*]
TH Rep Eindhoven Univ Technol Dep Electr Eng ... TH-Report-Eindhoven University of Technology. Department of Electrical Engineering [*A publication*]
THRF .... Thyrotrophic Hormone-Releasing Factor [*Endocrinology*]
THRFTR ... Thereafter   (FAAC)
Thr Hist Tr ... Thrupp's Historical Law Tracts [*A publication*]   (DLA)
Th RI.......... Theatre Research International [*A publication*]
THRIC...... Treasure Hunter Research and Information Center   (EA)
THRILLO ... Transfer to Higher Rated Job in Lieu of Layoff   (MCD)
THRIN....... Therein
THRINAR ... Thereinafter [*Legal term*] [*British*]   (ROG)
THRINBEFE ... Thereinbefore [*Legal term*] [*British*]   (ROG)
Thring J St Com ... Thring on Joint Stock Companies [*5th ed.*] [*1889*] [*A publication*]   (DLA)
Thring LD ... Thring on the Land Drainage Act [*1862*] [*A publication*]   (DLA)
THRINS.... Thermo Instrument Systems, Inc. [*Associated Press abbreviation*]   (APAG)
THRIP....... Thriplow [*England*]
Th Ri Po..... Three Rivers Poetry Journal [*A publication*]
THRM....... Thermal   (AAG)
ThrmEl...... Thermo Electron Corp. [*Associated Press abbreviation*]   (APAG)
THRMP .... Thermo Process Systems, Inc. [*Associated Press abbreviation*]   (APAG)
THRMST ... Thermostat
THRMSTC ... Thermostatic   (MSA)
Thrmtx....... Thermotrex Corp. [*Associated Press abbreviation*]   (APAG)
THRMWD ... Thermwood Corp. [*Associated Press abbreviation*]   (APAG)
ThRNF ...... Theologische Rundschau. Neue Folge [*Tuebingen*] [*A publication*]
THRO........ Theodore Roosevelt National Memorial Park

THRO........ Through
THRO....... Throw the Hypocritical Rascals Out [*An association*]
ThroBL...... Through Bill of Lading [*Shipping*]
THROF ..... Thereof
THROM.... Thrombosis   (AAMN)
Thromb Diat ... Thrombosis et Diathesis Haemorrhagica [*A publication*]
Thromb Diath Haemorrh ... Thrombosis et Diathesis Haemorrhagica [*A publication*]
Thromb Diath Haemorrh Suppl ... Thrombosis et Diathesis Haemorrhagica. Supplementum [*A publication*]
Thromb Haemost ... Thrombosis and Haemostasis [*A publication*]
Thromb Haemostas ... Thrombosis and Haemostasis [*A publication*]
Thromb Res ... Thrombosis Research [*A publication*]
Thromb Res Suppl ... Thrombosis Research. Supplement [*A publication*]
THRON.... Thereon [*Legal term*] [*British*]   (ROG)
Throop Pub Off ... Throop's Treatise on Public Officers [*A publication*]   (DLA)
THROT ..... Throttle   (AAG)
THROUT ... Thereout [*Legal term*] [*British*]   (ROG)
THRP .... Therapist
THRPY..... Therapy
Th Rsch ...... Theologische Rundschau [*A publication*]
THRSHL.... Thrust Shell
THRSUM ... Threat Summary Message   (MCD)
THRT .... Threat [*or Threatening*] [*FBI standardized term*]
THRT .... Throat
THRU........ I am connecting you to another switchboard [*Telecommunications*]   (FAAC)
ThRu.......... Theologische Rundschau [*A publication*]
THRU........ Through   (AAG)
THRU........ Thrust [*A publication*]
THRU........ Toxic Hazards Research Unit [*NASA*]   (KSC)
THRUPON ... Thereupon [*Legal term*] [*British*]   (ROG)
THRUSH .. Technological Hierarchy for the Removal of Undesirables and the Subjugation of Humanity [*Fictitious organization in "The Man from UNCLE" television series*]
THRUT ..... Throughout   (FAAC)
Thr Verb Agr ... Throop on the Validity of Verbal Agreements [*A publication*]   (DLA)
ThrVolt...... Thermo Voltek Corp. [*Associated Press abbreviation*]   (APAG)
Thr Wld Q ... Third World Quarterly [*A publication*]
THRX........ Theragenics Corp. [*NASDAQ symbol*]   (NQ)
THS .... [*The*] Hydrographic Society [*Dagenham, Essex, England*]   (EAIO)
THS .... St. Thomas, PA [*Location identifier*] [*FAA*]   (FAAL)
THS .... Target Homing System
THS .... Technical High School   (ADA)
THS .... Tenement House Smell [*British*]   (ROG)
THS Tetrahydro-11-Deoxycortisol
THS .... Tetrahydro-Compound S [*Organic chemistry*]   (MAE)
THS .... Textes pour l'Histoire Sacree [*A publication*]
THS .... Textile History Society [*Defunct*]   (EA)
THS .... Theatre Historical Society   (EA)
ThS .... Theatre Survey [*A publication*]
ThS .... Theological Studies [*A publication*]
ThS .... Theologische Studien und Kritiken [*A publication*]
THS .... Thermostat Switch
THS .... Thomas Hardy Society   (EAIO)
THS .... Three-Stage Least Squares [*Econometrics*]
ThS .... Thymidylate Synthase [*Also, TS*] [*An enzyme*]
THS .... Times Health Supplement [*London*] [*A publication*]
THS .... Titanic Historical Society   (EA)
THS .... Tourist Hospitality Service [*British*]
THS .... Transparent Hull Submersible [*Navy*]
THS .... Trimmable Horizontal Stabilizer [*Aviation*]
THS .... Tube Heating Supply
THSA .... Thomas Hardy Society of America   (EA)
THSA .... Traveling Hat Salesmen's Association [*Defunct*]   (EA)
THSAM .... Topographie Historique de la Syrie Antique et Medievale [*A publication*]   (BJA)
THSC .... Totipotent Hematopoietic Stem Cell [*Hematology*]   (MAE)
THSC .... Transactions. Honourable Society of Cymmrodorion [*A publication*]
THSD .... Thousand   (FAAC)
THSG .... Transactions. Historical Society of Ghana [*A publication*]
THSI......... Thermal Systems, Inc. [*NASDAQ symbol*]   (NQ)
ThSK......... Theologische Studien und Kritiken [*Hamburg/Berlin*] [*A publication*]
THSP........ Temporary-Help Supplier Personnel
THSP........ Thermal Spray [*Also, TS*] [*Coating technology*]
THSRB...... Tufts Health Science Review [*A publication*]
ThSt .... Theological Studies [*A publication*]
Th St .... Theologische Studien [*A publication*]
Th St B....... Theologische Studien. Karl Barth [*A publication*]
ThStKr....... Theologische Studien und Kritiken [*Hamburg/Berlin*] [*A publication*]
ThSzemle... Theologiai Szemle [*Budapest*] [*A publication*]   (BJA)
THT .... Papeete [*Orstom*] [*Society Islands*] [*Seismograph station code, US Geological Survey*]   (SEIS)
THT .... Teacher of Hydrotherapy [*British*]
THT .... Tetrahydrothiophene [*Organic chemistry*]

Tht	Theaetetus [*of Plato*] [*Classical studies*] (OCD)
Th T	Theology Today [*A publication*]
THT...........	Thrust Resources, Inc. [*Vancouver Stock Exchange symbol*]
THT...........	Total Homing Time
THTA	Thread Tap
THTAD	Thiemig-Taschenbuecher [*A publication*]
THTD........	Too Hard to Do (CAAL)
THTF........	Thermal Hydraulic Test Facility [*Nuclear energy*] (NRCH)
THTH.......	Too Hot to Handle
THTMS.....	Tetramethylthiuram Monosulfide [*Also, TMTD*] [*Organic chemistry*]
THTN........	Threaten (FAAC)
THTO........	Thereto
THTO........	Threading Tool (AAG)
Th Today ...	Theology Today [*A publication*]
THTR	Theater (AFM)
THTR	Thorium High-Temperature Reactor [*Nuclear energy*]
THU	Tetrhydrouridine [*Biochemistry*]
THU	Thule [*Greenland*] [*Seismograph station code, US Geological Survey*] [*Closed*] (SEIS)
THU	Thunder Explorations [*Vancouver Stock Exchange symbol*]
THU	Thursday (AFM)
Thuc...........	De Thucydide [*of Dionysius Halicarnassensis*] [*Classical studies*] (OCD)
THUC........	Thucydides [*Greek historian, c. 460-400BC*] [*Classical studies*] (ROG)
THUD	Thorium, Uranium, Deuterium
THUDD	Thermal Uplink Data Display [*Data processing*]
ThuGl........	Theologie und Glaube [*A publication*]
Thule Int Symp ...	Thule International Symposia [*A publication*]
THUMB....	Tiny Humans Underground Military Bureau [*Government organization in TV cartoon series "Tom of T.H.U.M.B."*]
THUMS	Texaco, Humble, Union, Mobil, and Shell [*Petroleum companies*]
Thur	Thursday (WGA)
Thurg B......	Thurgauische Beitraege zur Vaterlaendischen Geschichte [*A publication*]
THURIS....	[*The*] Human Role in Space [*Study*] (SSD)
Thur Mar L Rev ...	Thurgood Marshall Law Review [*A publication*] (DLA)
Thur Marsh LJ ...	Thurgood Marshall Law Journal [*A publication*]
THURS	Thursday
THURST...	Thurstable [*England*]
THUT........	Thyroid Hormone Uptake Test [*Clinical chemistry*]
THV	Terminal Homing Vehicle
ThV	Theologia Viatorum. Jahrbuch der Kirchlichen Hochschule [*Berlin*] [*A publication*]
THV	Thoracic Vertebra [*Medicine*]
THV	Tool Handling Vehicle (MCD)
THV	Total Heart Volume [*Physiology*]
THV	York, PA [*Location identifier*] [*FAA*] (FAAL)
ThViat........	Theologia Viatorum. Jahrbuch der Kirchlichen Hochschule [*Berlin*] [*A publication*]
ThW	Theologisches Woerterbuch zum Neuen Testament [*A publication*] (BJA)
THW..........	Therewith [*Legal term*] [*British*] (ROG)
THW..........	Thermoplastic, Heat-Resistant, Wet-Location [*Electric cable*]
Thw	Thwartship (DS)
THW..........	Torsion Head Wattmeter
ThWAT	Theologisches Woerterbuch zum Alten Testament [*A publication*] (BJA)
ThWB	Theologisches Woerterbuch zum Neuen Testament [*A publication*] (BJA)
ThWBNT ..	Theologisches Woerterbuch zum Neuen Testament [*A publication*] (BJA)
Th Wiss	Theologische Wissenschaft [*A publication*]
THWITH..	Therewith [*Legal term*] [*British*] (ROG)
THWM.....	Trinity High-Water Mark
THWN.......	Thermoplastic, Heat-Resistant, Wet-Location, Nylon-Jacketed [*Electric cable*]
ThWNT	Theologisches Woerterbuch zum Neuen Testament [*A publication*] (BJA)
THWR.......	Thrower
THWT	Throwout [*Mechanical engineering*]
THX...........	Thor Explorations [*Vancouver Stock Exchange symbol*]
THX...........	Three Rivers, TX [*Location identifier*] [*FAA*] (FAAL)
THX...........	Thyroxine [*Also, T4, Ty*] [*An amino acid*] [*Endocrinology*]
THX...........	Tomlinson-Holman Cross-Over [*Motion picture theater sound system*]
THX...........	Total Hypophysectomy [*Medicine*]
THY..........	Thomas Hardy Yearbook [*A publication*]
Thy.............	Thymine [*Also, T*] [*Biochemistry*]
THY..........	Thymocyte [*Clinical chemistry*]
THY..........	Turk Hava Yollari AO [*Turkish Airlines, Inc.*]
THYB	Tai Hei Yo Bashi [*Bridge over the Great Ocean*] (EA)
THYMD....	Thymus [*A publication*]
THYMOTRO ...	Thyratron Motor Control [*Electronics*] (MCD)
THYMOTROL ...	Thyratron Motor Control [*Electronics*]
THYP	Total Hydroxyproline [*Clinical chemistry*]
THYR	Thyristor [*Electronics*]
Thyssen Edelstahl Tech Ber ...	Thyssen Edelstahl Technische Berichte [*A publication*]

Thyssen Forsch Ber Forsch Betr ...	Thyssen Forschung. Berichte aus Forschung und Betrieb [*A publication*]
Thyssen Tech Ber ...	Thyssen Technische Berichte [*A publication*]
THZ...........	Tahoua [*Niger*] [*Airport symbol*] (OAG)
THz............	Terahertz
Th Z	Theater der Zeit [*A publication*]
THZOEN..	Theses Zoologicae [*A publication*]
TI	Costa Rica [*Aircraft nationality and registration mark*] (FAAC)
TI	Table Indicator [*Data processing*]
TI	Tamarind Institute (EA)
TI	Tamiment Institute (EA)
TI	Tape Inverter
TI	Target Identification
TI	Target Indicator
TI	Target Intelligence (MCD)
TI	Tariff Item
T & I	Tax and Insurance Payment [*Banking*]
TI	Taxable Income
TI	Teardown Inspection
ti	Technical Indexes Ltd. [*Information service or system*] (IID)
TI	Technical Information (CINC)
TI	Technical Information for Industry [*A publication*]
TI	Technical Inspection [*Military*]
TI	Technical Institute
TI	Technical Instruction [*or Instructor*]
TI	Technical Integration [*NASA*] (NASA)
TI	Technical Intelligence [*Military*]
TI	Technical Interchange (KSC)
TI	Technology Insertion [*Military*] (RDA)
TI	Tehrik-i-Istiqlal [*Solidarity Party*] [*See also TIP*] [*Political party*] [*Pakistan*] (FEA)
TI	Telecommunication Industry
TI	Teleos Institute (EA)
TI	Temperature Indicator
Ti...............	Temperature of Injectate
TI	Temporary Instruction [*Nuclear energy*] (NRCH)
TI	Teresian Institute (EA)
TI	Terminal Interface
TI	Terminal Island [*San Pedro*] [*Navy base*]
TI	Termination Instruction
TI	Terrestrial Interference (WDMC)
TI	Test Implicit
TI	Test Index (CAAL)
TI	Test Instruction (MCD)
TI	Test Instrumentation
TI	Texas Instruments, Inc.
TI	Textile Institute [*Manchester, England*] (EAIO)
TI	Thalassemia Intermedia [*Hematology*]
TI	Think Ink [*An association*] (EA)
TI	Thoracic Index [*Medicine*] (MAE)
TI	Thread Institute [*Defunct*] (EA)
TI	Thymidine-Labeling Index [*Biochemical analysis*]
TI	Thymus Independent [*Cells*] [*Hematology*]
TI	TI Travel International, Inc. [*Vancouver Stock Exchange symbol*]
TI	Tie In (MCD)
TI	Tiferet Israel (BJA)
TI	TII Industries, Inc. [*AMEX symbol*] (SPSG)
Ti...............	Timaeus [*of Plato*] [*Classical studies*] (OCD)
Ti...............	Timarit Pjooreknisfelags Islendinga 1957 [*A publication*]
Ti...............	Timberman. An International Lumber Journal [*A publication*]
TI	Time Index
TI	Time-to-Intercept
TI	Time Interval (IEEE)
TI	Tippers International (EA)
Ti...............	Titanium [*Chemical element*]
TI	Title [*Online database field identifier*] [*Data processing*]
TI	Title Information [*Publishing*]
Ti...............	Titus [*New Testament book*]
TI	Toastmasters International (EA)
TI	Tobacco Institute (EA)
TI	Tobacco Intelligence [*A publication*]
TI	Tobacco International [*A publication*]
TI	Together, Inc. (EA)
TI	Together International/Anti-Soviet Research Center (EA)
TI	Tonic Immobility [*Neurophysiology*]
TI	Torpedo Instructor [*British military*] (DMA)
T/I.............	Torque/Inertia
TI	Total Immersion [*Language study*]
T/I.............	TPFDD Interface
TI	Track Identity
TI	Track Initiator
TI	Trade and Industry Index [*Information Access Corp.*] [*Information service or system*] (IID)
TI	Traditional Instruction
TI	Traffic Identification
TI	Training Instructor
TI	Training Integrator [*or Integration*] (MCD)
TI	Trajectory Integration (CAAL)
TI	Transaction Interpretation (MCD)
TI	Transfer Impedance (IEEE)

TI .... Transfrigoroute International (EA)
TI .... Transillumination
TI .... Transmission Identification (NG)
TI .... Transportation Institute [*Camp Springs, MD*] (EA)
TI .... Transportes Aereos Internacionales, SA [*TAISA*] [*Peru*] [*ICAO designator*] (FAAC)
TI .... Transverse Inlet [*Medicine*] (MAE)
TI .... Treasure Island [*San Francisco Bay*] [*Navy base*]
TI .... Treasury Instruction (ADA)
TI .... Trial Installation (MCD)
TI .... Tricuspid Incompetence [*Cardiology*] (MAE)
TI .... Tricuspid Insufficiency [*Cardiology*]
TI .... Troop Information
TI .... Trusteeship Institute (EA)
TI .... Trypsin Inhibitor [*Food technology*]
TI .... Tube Investments Ltd. [*British*]
Ti .... Tumor-inducing [*Plasmids*] [*Plant cytology*]
TI .... Tungsten Institute [*Defunct*] (EA)
TI .... Tuning Indicator (DEN)
ti .... Tunisia [*MARC country of publication code*] [*Library of Congress*] (LCCP)
TI .... Turbine Intelligence [*A publication*]
TI .... Turing Institute [*British*] (IRUK)
TI .... Type Item [*Military*]
T2000I .... Transport 2000 International [*British*] (EAIO)
TIA .... [*The*] International Alliance, an Association of Executive and Professional Women [*Baltimore, MD*] (EA)
TIA .... Tactical Identification and Acquisition [*Navy*] (NG)
TIA .... Taian [*Republic of China*] [*Seismograph station code, US Geological Survey*] (SEIS)
TI & A .... Task Identification and Analysis
TIA .... Task Item Authorization (MCD)
TIA .... Tax Institute of America [*Later, NTA-TIA*] (EA)
TIA .... Taxation in Australia [*A publication*] (APTA)
TIA .... Teacher Investigator Awards
TIA .... Telecommunications Industry Association (EA)
TIA .... Test Interface Assembly
TIA .... Thallium Acetate
TIA .... Thin-Layer Immunoassay [*Analytical biochemistry*]
TIA .... Tiaprofenic Acid
TIA .... Tilapia International Association (EAIO)
TIA .... Tin International [*London*] [*A publication*]
TIA .... Tirana [*Albania*] [*Airport symbol*] (OAG)
TIA .... Tortilla Industry Association (EA)
TIA .... Total Inactive Aerospace Vehicle [*or Aircraft*] Authorization
TIA .... Trans International Airlines
TIA .... Transient Ischemic Attack [*Medicine*]
TIA .... Transimpedance Amplifier [*Instrumentation*]
TIA .... Transportation Intelligence Agency (AAG)
TIA .... Travel Industry Association of America (EA)
TIA .... Treaties and Other International Acts
TIA .... Trend Impact Analysis [*The Futures Group, Inc.*] [*Information service or system*] (IID)
TIA .... Trends, Indicators, and Analyses [*on the Southeast Asia war*] [*Classified Air Force document*]
TIA .... Tri-Basin Resources Ltd. [*Vancouver Stock Exchange symbol*]
TIA .... Tricot Institute of America [*Defunct*] (EA)
TIA .... Trouser Institute of America [*Absorbed by NOSA*] (EA)
TIA .... Trypsin Inhibitor Activity [*Food technology*]
TIA .... Tumor-Induced Angiogenesis [*Immunology*]
TIA .... Turbidimetric Immunoassay [*Immunology*]
TIA .... Typographers International Association (EA)
TIAA .... Task Identification and Analysis (MCD)
TIAA .... Teachers Insurance and Annuity Association [*New York, NY*] (EA)
TIAA .... Timber Importers Association of America
TIAA .... Travel Industry Association of America
TIAC .... Technical Information Advisory Committee [*AEC*]
TIAC .... Technical Information Analysis Centers
TIAC .... Techniques and Instrumentation in Analytical Chemistry [*Elsevier Book Series*] [*A publication*]
TIAC .... Texas Instruments Automatic Computer
TIAC .... Tourism Industry Association of Canada
TIAC .... Travel [*later, Tourism*] Industry Association of Canada
TIACS .... TEWS [*Tactical Electronic Warfare System*] Intermediate Age Commercial System
TIAFT .... [*The*] International Association of Forensic Toxicologists [*Newmarket, Suffolk, England*] (EAIO)
TI Agree..... Treaties and Other International Agreements of the United States of America [*A publication*] (DLA)
TIAH .... Totally Implantable Artificial Heart
TIALD....... Thermal Imaging, Airborne LASER Designator [*Royal Air Force*] [*British*]
Tianjin J Oncol ... Tianjin Journal of Oncology [*A publication*]
Tianjin Med J ... Tianjin Medical Journal [*A publication*]
TIARA....... Tactical Intelligence and Related Activity
TIARA....... Target Illumination and Recovery Aid
TIARA....... Telephone Installation and Requisition Application (MCD)
TIARA....... There Is a Radical Alternative [*Parliamentary slang*] [*British*] (DI)
TIAS .... Target Identification and Acquisition System

TIAS .... Treaties and Other International Acts Series [*A publication*]
TIAVSC..... [*The*] International Assets Valuation Standards Committee [*of the American Institute of Real Estate Appraisers*] [*British*] (EAIO)
TIAX......... Trans International Airlines [*Air carrier designation symbol*]
TIB............ Tasmanian Imperial Bushmen [*British military*] (DMA)
TIB............ Technical Information Base (MCD)
TIB............ Technical Information Branch [*US Public Health Service*] [*Information service or system*] (IID)
TIB............ Technical Information Bulletin [*Cincinnati, OH*] (AAG)
TIB............ Technical Information Bureau [*British*]
TIB............ Technische Informationsbibliothek [*Technical Information Library*] [*Germany*]
TIB............ Temporary Importation Bond (MCD)
TIB............ This I Believe Test [*Education*]
Tib............. Tiberius [*of Suetonius*] [*Classical studies*] (OCD)
tib............. Tibetan [*MARC language code*] [*Library of Congress*] (LCCP)
Tib............. Tibullus [*First century BC*] [*Classical studies*] (OCD)
TIB............ Training Improvement Board [*Military*] (CAAL)
TIB............ Treasury Indexed Bond (ADA)
TIB............ Triisopropylbenzene [*Also, TIPB*] [*Organic chemistry*]
TIB............ Trimmed in Bunkers [*Shipping*] (DS)
TIB............ Tuck in Back [*Sit up straight*] [*Slang*] [*British*] (DI)
TIBA......... Triiodobenzoic Acid [*Plant growth regulator*]
TIBA......... Triisobutylaluminum [*Organic chemistry*]
TIBA......... Triisobutylamine [*Organic chemistry*]
TIBALD .... Tibaldstone [*England*]
TIBC......... [*The*] International Beverage Corp. [*NASDAQ symbol*] (NQ)
TIBC......... Total Iron-Binding Capacity [*Hematology*]
Tibetan R ... Tibetan Review [*New Delhi*] [*A publication*]
Tibet J........ Tibet Journal [*Dharmasala*] [*A publication*]
Tibet Soc B ... Tibet Society. Bulletin [*United States*] [*A publication*]
TIB and FIB ... Tibia and Fibula (DSUE)
TIBI .... [*The*] Image Bank, Inc. [*NASDAQ symbol*] (NQ)
TIBL.......... Thermal Internal Boundary Layer (GFGA)
TIBO.......... Tetrahydroimidazobenzodiazepin [*Antiviral*]
TIBOE....... Transmitting Information by Optical Electronics (KSC)
T I Br Geog ... Transactions. Institute of British Geographers [*A publication*]
TIBS .... Trends in Biochemical Sciences [*A publication*]
TIBTPG..... Texas Instruments Bourdon Tube Pressure Gauge
TIC............ [*The*] Interchurch Center (EA)
TIC............ International Financial Law Review [*A publication*]
TIC............ Tactical Intelligence Concepts (MCD)
TIC............ Tactical Intercom Systems (MCD)
TIC............ Taken into Consideration
TIC............ Tantalum Producers International Study Center [*Later, Tantalum-Niobium International Study Center*] (EAIO)
TIC............ Tape Identification Card
TIC............ Tape Intersystem Connection [*Data processing*]
TIC............ Target Integration Center (MCD)
TIC............ Target Intercept Computer [*Military*]
TIC............ Teacher in Charge (ADA)
TIC............ Teacher Information Center (EA)
TIC............ Technical Information Capability
TIC............ Technical Information Center [*Department of Energy*]
TIC............ Technical Information Coordinator [*Environmental Protection Agency*] (GFGA)
TIC............ Technical Institute Council (EA)
TIC............ Technical Instructors Course [*Air Force*] (AFM)
TIC............ Technical Intelligence Center [*Navy*]
TIC............ Technical Interface Concepts (RDA)
TIC............ Technicon Integrator/Calculator
TIC............ Technology Innovation Center [*University of Iowa*] [*Research center*] (RCD)
TIC............ Technology and Innovation Council [*Information Industry Association*]
TIC............ Telecommunications Information Center [*George Washington University*] [*Information service or system*] (IID)
TIC............ Telemetry Instruction Conference (KSC)
TIC............ Telemetry Instrumentation Controller
TIC............ Temperature Indicator Controller
TIC............ Terminal Identification Code
TIC............ Texas Instruments Co.
TIC............ Thai Information Center (EA)
TIC............ Thermionic Integrated Circuit [*Electronics*]
TIC............ Thermostatic Ignition Control [*Automotive engineering*]
TIC............ Time Interval Counter
TIC............ Tinak [*Marshall Islands*] [*Airport symbol*] (OAG)
TIC............ Token Ring Interface Coupler (PCM)
TIC............ Tool Issue Center [*Military*] (AFIT)
TIC............ Total Inorganic Carbon [*Chemistry*]
TIC............ Total Installed Cost [*Engineering*]
TIC............ Total Ion Chromatography
TIC............ Total Ion Current [*Spectroscopy*]
TIC............ Total Item Change (NASA)
TIC............ Toumodi [*Ivory Coast*] [*Seismograph station code, US Geological Survey*] (SEIS)
TIC............ Trade Information Committee [*Department of State*] (EA)
TIC............ Transaction Identification Code [*Military*] (AFIT)
TIC............ Transducer Information Center (MCD)
TIC............ Transfer-In Channel (CMD)

TIC............	Transport Industries Committee [*Trades Union Congress*] [*British*] (DCTA)
TIC............	Transvaal Indian Congress [*South Africa*] (PD)
TIC............	Travel Information Center [*An association*] (EA)
TIC............	Travelers Corp. [*NYSE symbol*] (SPSG)
TIC............	Troops-in-Contact
TIC............	True Interest Cost [*Finance*]
TIC............	Trypsin Inhibitory Capacity [*Biochemistry*]
TIC............	Tuned Integrated Circuit
TICA.........	[*The*] International Cat Association (EA)
TICA.........	Tactical Intercom Assembly [*Ground Communications Facility, NASA*]
TICA.........	Technical Information Center Administration [*Conference*]
TICA.........	Timpanogos Cave National Monument
TICACE	Technical Intelligence Center Allied Command Europe [*NATO*] (NATG)
TICAF	[*The*] Industrial College of the Armed Forces [*Later, UND*]
TICAS	Taxonometric Intra-Cellular Analytic System (OA)
TICC	Technical Industrial Cooperation Contract
TICC.........	Technical Intelligence Coordination Center [*NATO*] (NATG)
TICCIH	[*The*] International Committee for the Conservation of the Industrial Heritage (EA)
TICCIT......	Time-Shared Interactive Computer-Controlled Information Television [*System*] [*Mitre Corp.*] [*Brigham Young University*] [*1971*]
TICE	Time Integral Cost Effectiveness
TICER	Temporary International Council for Educational Reconstruction (DLA)
TICF	Transient Installation Confinement Facility [*Military*] (AABC)
Tichb Tr...	Report of the Tichborne Trial [*London*] [*A publication*] (DLA)
T I Chem En ...	Transactions. Institution of Chemical Engineers and the Chemical Engineer [*A publication*]
TICI..........	TIC International Corp. [*NASDAQ symbol*] (NQ)
TICKS	Two Incomes, Kids [*Lifestyle classification*]
TICL.........	Topics in Culture Learning [*A publication*]
TICLER.....	Technical Input Checklist/Evaluation Report (MCD)
TICM........	Test Interface and Control Module (MCD)
TICM........	Thermal Imaging Common Modules
TICM........	Trust Investment Committee Memorandum [*A publication*] (DLA)
TICO	Technical Information Contact Officer [*Navy*] (DNAB)
TICO	Transactions. International Congress of Orientalists [*A publication*] (BJA)
TICOA.......	Testing, Instruments, and Controls [*A publication*]
TICODS	Time Compression Display System (NVT)
TICOJ	Transactions. International Conference of Orientalists in Japan [*A publication*]
TICOM	Texas Institute for Computational Mechanics [*University of Texas at Austin*] [*Research center*] (RCD)
TICOS.......	Truncated Icosahedra [*Crystallography*]
TICP.........	Theater Inventory Control Point [*Military*] (AABC)
TICP.........	Travaux. Institut Catholique de Paris [*A publication*] (BJA)
TICS	Teacher Interactive Computer System (IEEE)
TICS	Telecommunication Information Control System
TICS	Turret Interaction Crew Simulator (MCD)
TICT	Tactical Intelligence Collection Team [*Military*] (AFM)
TICT	Twisted Intramolecular Charge Transfer [*Biochemistry*]
TICTAC	Time Compression Tactical Communications
TICUS.......	Tidal and Current Survey (NOAA)
TICUS.......	Tidal Current Survey System [*National Oceanic and Atmospheric Administration*]
TICWAN...	Trailerable Intracoastal Waterway Aids to Navigation [*Boat*]
TID	Tactical Information Display
TID	Tactical Intrusion Detectors (MCD)
TID	Target Identification Device [*Military*] (CAAL)
TID	Technical Information Division [*Romar Consultants, Inc.*] [*Information service or system*] (IID)
TID	Technical Information Document [*A publication*]
TID	Technology Information Division [*Department of Energy, Mines, and Resources*] (IID)
TID	Ter in Die [*Three Times a Day*] [*Pharmacy*]
TID	Test Identify (CAAL)
TID	Thermal Imaging Devices (MCD)
TID	Thermionic Ionization Detector [*Instrumentation*]
TID	Thread Identifier [*Data processing*]
TID	Ticket Information Data
TID	Time Interval Distribution
TID	Titrated Initial Dose (AAMN)
TID	Total Integrated Dose [*Nuclear energy*] (NRCH)
TID	Total Ion Detector (OA)
TID	Touch Information Display
TID	Traitement Integre des Donnees [*Integrated Data Processing - IDP*] [*French*]
TID	Traveling Ionospheric Disturbance
TID	Trifluoromethyl(iodophenyl)deazirine [*Biochemistry*]
TID	Turn-In Document [*DoD*]
TIDA	30th Infantry Division Association (EA)
TIDAR......	Texas Instruments Digital Analog Readout
TIDAR......	Time Delay Array RADAR
Tidd...........	Tidd's Costs [*A publication*] (DLA)
Tidd...........	Tidd's Practice [*A publication*] (DLA)
TIDDAC....	Time in Deadband Digital Attitude Control
Tidd App....	Appendix to Tidd's Practice [*A publication*] (DLA)
Tidd Co	Tidd's Costs [*A publication*] (DLA)
Tid Dok.....	Tidskrift foer Dokumentation [*A publication*]
Tidd Pr......	Tidd's Practice [*A publication*] (DLA)
Tidd Prac ...	Tidd's Practice [*A publication*] (DLA)
Tidd's Pract ...	Tidd's Practice [*A publication*] (DLA)
TIDE.........	Tactical International Data Exchange (NG)
TIDE.........	Technical Intelligence Data Extraction (MCD)
TIDE.........	Tide West Oil Co. [*NASDAQ symbol*] (NQ)
TIDE.........	Timer Demodulator
TIDE.........	Travel Industry and Disabled Exchange (EA)
TIDES	Time-Division Electronics Switching System (KSC)
Tidewtr VA ...	Tidewater Virginian [*A publication*]
TIDF.........	Trunk Intermediate Distribution Frame [*Telecommunications*] (TEL)
TIDL.........	Test Instrumentation Data Link
TIDMA	Tape Interface Direct Memory Access
Tidn Byggnadskonst ...	Tidning foer Byggnadskonst [*A publication*]
TIDOC	Technical Information Documentation Center [*Advisory Group for Aerospace Research and Development*] (NATG)
TIDOS.......	Table and Item Documentation System
TIDP.........	Technical Interface Design Plans
TIDP-TE ...	Technical Interface Design Plan - Test Edition (RDA)
TIDR.........	Tool Investigation and Disposition Report (SAA)
TIDS.........	Tactical Information Distribution Systems [*Army*] (RDA)
TIDS.........	Technical Information Distribution Service [*Publisher*]
Tidsk Dokum ...	Tidskrift foer Dokumentation [*A publication*]
Tidskr Dok ...	Tidskrift foer Dokumentation [*A publication*]
Tidskr Hushallningssaellsk Skogsvardsstyr Gaevleborgs Laen ...	Tidskrift foer Hushallningssaellskapet och Skogsvardsstyrelsen i Gaevleborgs Laen [*A publication*]
Tidskr Lantmaen Andelsfolk ...	Tidskrift foer Lantmaen och Andelsfolk [*A publication*]
Tidskr Lantm Andelsfolk ...	Tidskrift foer Lantmaen och Andelsfolk [*A publication*]
Tidskr Mil Halsov ...	Tidskrift i Militar Halsovard [*Sweden*] [*A publication*]
Tidskr Sjukvardspedagog ...	Tidskrift foer Sjukvardspedagoger [*A publication*]
Tidskr Skogbruk ...	Tidsskrift foer Skogbruk [*A publication*]
Tidskr Skog Lantbruksakad ...	Tidskrift. Skogs- och Lantbruksakademien [*A publication*]
Tidskr Sver Sjukskot ...	Tidskrift foer Sveriges Sjukskoterskor [*A publication*]
Tidskr Sver Skogvardsforb ...	Tidskrift Sveriges Skogsvardsforbund [*A publication*]
Tidskr Sver Utsadesforen ...	Tidskrift. Sveriges Utsaedesfoereningen [*A publication*]
Tidskr Varme- Vent- Sanitetstek ...	Tidskrift foer Varme-, Ventilations-, och Sanitetsteknik [*Sweden*] [*A publication*]
Tids Samfun ...	Tidsskrift foer Samfunnsforskning [*A publication*]
Tidssk Kjemi Bergves Metall ...	Tidsskrift foer Kjemi. Bergvesen og Metallurgi [*A publication*]
Tidsskr Biavl ...	Tidsskrift foer Biavl [*A publication*]
Tidsskr Froavl ...	Tidsskrift foer Froavl [*A publication*]
Tidsskr Hermetikind ...	Tidsskrift foer Hermetikindustri [*A publication*]
Tidsskr Kemi ...	Tidsskrift foer Kemi [*A publication*]
Tidsskr Kemi Farm Ter ...	Tidsskrift foer Kemi. Farmaci og Terapi [*A publication*]
Tidsskr Kjemi Bergv ...	Tidsskrift foer Kjemi og Bergvesen [*A publication*]
Tidsskr Kjemi Bergves ...	Tidsskrift foer Kjemi og Bergvesen [*A publication*]
Tidsskr Kjemi Bergvesen Met ...	Tidsskrift foer Kjemi. Bergvesen og Metallurgi [*A publication*]
Tidsskr Landokon ...	Tidsskrift foer Landokonomi [*A publication*]
Tidsskr Nor Laegeforen ...	Tidsskrift foer den Norske Laegeforening [*A publication*]
Tidsskr Nor Landbruk ...	Tidsskrift foer det Norske Landbruk [*A publication*]
Tidsskr Norske Laegeforen ...	Tidsskrift foer den Norske Laegeforening [*A publication*]
Tidsskr Norske Landbruk ...	Tidsskrift foer det Norske Landbruk [*A publication*]
Tidsskr Papirind ...	Tidsskrift foer Papirindustri [*A publication*]
Tidsskr Plant ...	Tidsskrift foer Planteavl [*A publication*]
Tidsskr Planteavl ...	Tidsskrift foer Planteavl [*A publication*]
Tidsskr Plavl ...	Tidsskrift foer Planteavl [*A publication*]
Tidsskr Prakt Tandlaeg ...	Tidsskrift foer Praktiserende Tandlaeger [*A publication*]
Tidsskr Samfunnsforskning ...	Tidsskrift foer Samfunnsforskning [*A publication*]
Tidsskr Skogbr ...	Tidsskrift foer Skogbruk [*A publication*]
Tidsskr Skogbruk ...	Tidsskrift foer Skogbruk [*A publication*]
Tidsskr Textiltek ...	Tidsskrift foer Textilteknik [*A publication*]
Tid Tann ...	Tidens Tann [*A publication*]
TIDUP......	Technical Information Directive Update Panel
Tidwtr	Tidewater, Inc. [*Associated Press abbreviation*] (APAG)
TIDY.........	Teletypewriter Integrated Display (NVT)
TIDY.........	Track Identity
TIE............	[*The*] Information Exchange (EA)
TIE............	[*The*] Information Exchange on Young Adult Chronic Patients (EA)
TIE............	[*The*] Institute of Ecology [*Defunct*]
TIE............	[*The*] Issue Exchange (EA)

TIE............. Target Identification Equipment (MCD)
TIE............. Technical Idea Exchange (MCD)
TIE............. Technical Independent Evaluator [*Army*]
TIE............. Technical Information Exchange [*National Bureau of Standards*]
TIE............. Technical Integration and Evaluation [*Apollo*] [*NASA*]
TIE............. Technology Information Exchange (IID)
TIE............. Temporary/Intermittent Employee
TIE............. Terminal Interface Equipment
TIE............. Texas Information Exchange
TIE............. Texas Israel Exchange [*A trade and research venture*]
TIE............. Threshold Ignition Energy (MCD)
TIE............. TIE/Communications, Inc. [*AMEX symbol*] (SPSG)
TIE............. TIE/Communications, Inc. [*Associated Press abbreviation*] (APAG)
TIE............. Tientsin [*Republic of China*] [*Seismograph station code, US Geological Survey*] (SEIS)
TIE............. Time Interval Error [*Telecommunications*] (TEL)
TIE............. Tippi [*Ethiopia*] [*Airport symbol*] (OAG)
TIE............. Toxicity Identification Evaluation
TIE............. Toyota Industrial Equipment
TIE............. Training ICON Environment
TIE............. Training Instrumentation Evaluation (MCD)
TIE............. Transient Ischemic Episode [*Medicine*]
TIE............. Transnationals Information Exchange
TIE............. Travel Industry for the Environment
TI & E........ Troop Information and Education
TIEA.......... Tax Information Exchange Agreement (ECON)
TIED.......... Troop Information and Education Division
Tiedeman Real Prop ... Tiedeman on Real Property [*A publication*] (DLA)
Tied Lim Police Power ... Tiedeman's Treatise on the Limitations of Police Power in the United States [*A publication*] (DLA)
Tied Metsateho ... Tiedotus Metsateho [*A publication*]
Tied Mun Corp ... Tiedeman's Treatise on Municipal Corporations [*A publication*] (DLA)
Tied Valt Tekn Tutkimusl ... Tiedotus. Valtion Teknillinen Tutkimuslaitos [*A publication*]
Tied Valt Tek Tutkimuskeskus Poltto Voiteluainelab ... Tiedonanto-Valtion Teknillinen Tutkimuskeskus, Poltto-, ja Voiteluainelaboratorio [*Finland*] [*A publication*]
TIEED....... Transactions. Institute of Electronics and Communication Engineers of Japan. Section E (English) [*A publication*]
TIEG.......... Teen International Entomology Group [*Later, YES*] (EA)
TIE-IN....... Technology Information Exchange-Innovation Network [*Ohio State Department of Development*] [*Information service or system*] (IID)
TIEO.......... Toyota Industrial Engine Operations [*Torrance, CA*]
TIER.......... Tierce [*Unit of measurement*] (ROG)
TIER.......... [*The*] Tierco Group, Inc. [*NASDAQ symbol*] (NQ)
Tieraerztl Prax ... Tieraerztliche Praxis [*A publication*]
Tieraerztl Rd ... Tieraerztliche Rundschau [*A publication*]
Tieraerztl Rundsch ... Tieraerztliche Rundschau [*A publication*]
Tieraerztl Rundschau ... Tieraerztliche Rundschau [*A publication*]
Tieraerztl Umsch ... Tieraerztliche Umschau [*A publication*]
Tierernaehr Fuetter ... Tierernaehrung und Fuetterung [*A publication*]
Tier Erzeu.. Viehbestand und Tierische Erzeugung Land und Forstwirtschaft Fischerei [*A publication*]
Tierphysiol Tierernaehr Futtermittelk ... Tierphysiologie, Tierernaehrung, und Futtermittelkunde [*A publication*]
Tierra y Soc ... Tierra y Sociedad [*A publication*]
TIERS........ Title I Evaluation and Reporting System [*Department of Education*]
TIES .... [*The*] Interactive Encyclopedia System [*University of Maryland research project*] (PCM)
TIES .... Tactical Information Exchange System [*Navy*] [*United Nations*] (MCD)
TIES .... Technological Information Exchange System [*UNIDO*] [*United Nations*]
TIES .... Textbook Information and Exchange Service [*Regional clearinghouses for used textbooks*]
TIES .... Theater Information and Engagement System [*Military*] (MCD)
TIES .... Torpedo Installation and Exercise System [*Military*] (DWSG)
TIES .... Total Information for Educational Systems [*Saint Paul, MN*] (BUR)
TIES .... Total Integrated Engineering System
TIES .... Translators' and Interpreters' Educational Society (EA)
TIES .... Transmission and Information Exchange System
Tieteel Tutk ... Tietyeellisiae Tutkimuksia [*A publication*]
Tiet Julk Helsingin Tek Korkeakoulu ... Tieteellisia Julkaisuja. Helsingin Teknillinen Korkeakoulu [*A publication*]
TIEYACP ... [*The*] Information Exchange on Young Adult Chronic Patients (EA)
TIF............. [*The*] International Foundation (EA)
TIF............. Tagged Image File [*Data processing*] (PCM)
TIF............. Taif [*Saudi Arabia*] [*Airport symbol*] (OAG)
TIF............. Tape Inventory File (IEEE)
TIF............. Target Intelligence File (CINC)
TIF............. Task Initiation Force [*Nuclear energy*] (NRCH)
TIF............. Task Initiation Form [*Nuclear energy*] (NRCH)
TIF............. Tax Increment Financing

TIF............. Taxpayer Information File [*IRS*]
TIF............. Technical Information File
TIF............. Telecommunication Interference Filter [*Data processing*]
TIF............. Telephone Influence Factor
TIF............. Telephone Interference Factor (DEN)
TIF............. Terminal Independent Format
TIF............. Thin Iron Film
TIF............. Tiffany & Co. [*NYSE symbol*] (SPSG)
TIF............. Tiflis [*Tbilisi*] [*Former USSR*] [*Seismograph station code, US Geological Survey*] (SEIS)
TIF............. Tilapia International Foundation (EA)
TIF............. Tomato Intercellular Fluid
TIF............. Transfer if Indicators Off (SAA)
TIF............. Transport International par Fer [*International Transport of Goods by Railway*] [*French*]
TIF............. Treaties in Force [*A publication*] (DLA)
TIF............. Treaties in Force. US State Department [*A publication*]
TIF............. True Involute Form
TIF............. Tumor-Inducing Factor [*Oncology*]
TIF............. Tumor-Infiltrating Lymphocyte [*Immunotherapy*]
TIF............. Tumor Inhibitory Factor [*Oncology*]
TIFA .... Tourist Information Facts and Abstracts [*Economic Documentation and Information Ltd.*] [*Ringmer Near Lewes, East Sussex, England*] [*Information service or system*] (IID)
Tifany........ Tiffany & Co. [*Associated Press abbreviation*] (APAG)
Tif & Bul Tr ... Tiffany and Bullard on Trusts and Trustees [*A publication*] (DLA)
TIFF .... [*The*] Integrated FORSTAT [*Force Status and Identity Reporting System*] File
TIFF .... Tagged Image File Format [*Data processing*]
Tiff .... Tiffany's Reports [*28-39 New York Court of Appeals*] [*A publication*] (DLA)
TIFF .... Tokyo International Film Festival [*Japan*]
Tiffany .... Tiffany's Reports [*28-39 New York Court of Appeals*] [*A publication*] (DLA)
Tiffany Landlord & Ten ... Tiffany on Landlord and Tenant [*A publication*] (DLA)
Tiffany Landl & T ... Tiffany on Landlord and Tenant [*A publication*] (DLA)
Tiffany Real Prop ... Tiffany on Real Property [*A publication*] (DLA)
Tif Gov .... Tiffany on Government and Constitutional Law [*A publication*] (DLA)
TIFI .... Titus Foods, Inc. [*NASDAQ symbol*] (NQ)
TIFO.......... Technical Inspection Field Office, Office of the Inspector General
TIFO.......... Technische Informationen [*A publication*]
TIFR .... Tata Institute for Fundamental Research [*British*]
TIFR .... Total Improved Frequency Response
TIFS........... Total In-Flight Simulation [*or Simulator*] [*Air Force*]
Tif & Sm Pr ... Tiffany and Smith's New York Practice [*A publication*] (DLA)
TIG .... [*The*] Inspector General [*Army*]
TIG .... Tactical Intelligence Group [*Military*]
TIG .... Target Image Generator
TIG .... Taxicab Industry Group (EA)
TIG .... Telegram Identification Group [*Telecommunications*] (TEL)
TIG .... Teletype Input Generator
TIG .... Tetanus Immune Globulin [*Immunology*]
tig .... Tigre [*MARC language code*] [*Library of Congress*] (LCCP)
TIG .... Tigris Minerals [*Vancouver Stock Exchange symbol*]
TIG .... Time in Grade [*Air Force*]
TIG .... Time of Ignition
TIG .... Transearth Injection Geometry (SAA)
TIG .... Tungsten-Inert-Gas
TIGA .... TI [*Texas Instruments, Inc.*] Graphics Architecture [*Data processing*]
TIGC.......... Topics in Inorganic and General Chemistry [*Elsevier Book Series*] [*A publication*]
TIGER .... Terrorist Intelligence Gathering Evaluation and Review [*British*]
TIGER .... Topologically Integrated Geographic Encoding and Referencing [*Bureau of the Census*]
TIGER .... Total Information Gathering and Executive Reporting [*International Computers Ltd.*]
TIGER .... Traveling Industrial Gaseous Emission Research [*Vehicle*] [*Exxon Corp.*]
TIG(H) ...... Tetanus Immune Globulin (Human) [*Immunology*]
TIGN.......... Time of Ignition
TIGR.......... Institute for Genomic Research (ECON)
TIGR.......... Transmission Integrated Rotor
TIGR.......... Treasury Investment Growth Receipts [*Merrill Lynch & Co.*] [*Finance*]
TIGR.......... Turbine-Integrated Geared Rotor
Ti Gracch ... Tiberius Gracchus [*of Plutarch*] [*Classical studies*] (OCD)
TIGRB....... Technische Information GRW [*Geraete- und Regler Werke*] [*A publication*]
TIGRIS...... Televised Images of Gaseous Region in Interplanetary Space
TIGS.......... Terminal Independent Graphics System
TIGS.......... Transactions. Inverness Gaelic Society [*A publication*]
TIGT.......... Turbine Inlet Gas Temperature [*Aviation*]
TIGZD....... Teikyo Igaku Zasshi

TIH	Technical Information Handbook
TIH	Their Imperial Highnesses
TIH	Tikehau [*French Polynesia*] [*Airport symbol*] (OAG)
TIH	Time in Hold (SAA)
TIH	Toromont Industries Ltd. [*Toronto Stock Exchange symbol*]
TIH	Total Installed Horsepower
TIH	Trinity International Holdings [*British*]
TIH	Trunk Interface Handler
Tihanyi Biol Kutatointezetenek Evkoen ... Tihanyi Biologiai Kutatointezetenek Evkoenyve [*A publication*]
TIHB	Target Intelligence Handbook (MCD)
TIHP	Total Installed Horsepower
TII.............	European Association for the Transfer of Technologies, Innovation, and Industrial Information [*Information service or system*] (IID)
TII.............	[*The*] Independent Institute [*An association*] (EA)
TII.............	Table and Item Inventory (SAA)
TII.............	Talos Integration Investigation
TII.............	Texas Instruments, Inc.
TII.............	Texas Instruments, Incorporated, IS & S Library, Dallas, TX [*OCLC symbol*] (OCLC)
TII.............	Thomas Industries, Inc. [*NYSE symbol*] (SPSG)
TII.............	Tiffin, OH [*Location identifier*] [*FAA*] (FAAL)
TII.............	TII Industries, Inc. [*Associated Press abbreviation*] (APAG)
TII.............	Tooling Inspection Instrumentation (NASA)
TII.............	Total Inactive Aerospace Vehicle [*or Aircraft*] Inventory
TII.............	Trusteeship Institute, Inc. (EA)
TIIAL	[*The*] International Institute of Applied Linguistics
TIIC...........	Technical Industrial Intelligence Committee [*US Military Government, Germany*]
TIID...........	Technical Industrial Intelligence Division [*Allied Board set up to send experts into Germany to ferret out Germany's war-developed scientific secrets*] [*Post-World War II*]
TIIF	Tactical Imagery Interpretation Facility [*Military*]
TIIPS........	Technically Improved Interference Prediction System (IEEE)
TIJ	Tijuana [*Mexico*] [*Airport symbol*] (OAG)
Tijd............	Onze Tijd [*A publication*]
TIJI...........	Tribune Internationale des Jeunes Interpretes [*International Rostrum of Young Performers - IRP*] (EAIO)
TIK.............	Oklahoma City, OK [*Location identifier*] [*FAA*] (FAAL)
TIK.............	Target Indicator Kit
TIK.............	Thermal Imagery Kit (DWSG)
TIK.............	Tiara Enterprises Ltd. [*Vancouver Stock Exchange symbol*]
TIK.............	Tiksi [*Former USSR*] [*Seismograph station code, US Geological Survey*] (SEIS)
TIK.............	Tixie [*Former USSR*] [*Geomagnetic observatory code*]
TIKP	Turkiye Isci Koylu Partisi [*Worker-Peasant Party of Turkey*] [*Political party*] (PD)
TIL.............	Technical Information and Library Services [*Ministry of Technology*] [*British*]
TIL.............	Temperature Indicating Label
TIL.............	Temporary Instructor Lieutenant [*Navy*] [*British*]
TIL.............	Tilco Aviation Co., Inc. [*Baton Rouge, LA*] [*FAA designator*] (FAAC)
Til..............	Tilskueren [*A publication*]
TIL.............	Travaux. Institut de Linguistique [*A publication*]
TIL.............	Tree Island Industries Ltd. [*Toronto Stock Exchange symbol*] [*Vancouver Stock Exchange symbol*]
TIL.............	Tumor Infiltrating Lymphocyte [*Oncology*]
TIL.............	Until (FAAC)
TILA	Telemail International Licensees' Association (TSSD)
TILA	Truth-in-Lending Act [*1968*]
TILAS........	Travaux. Institut d'Etudes Latino-Americaines. Universite de Strasbourg [*A publication*]
TILE	Color Tile, Inc. [*NASDAQ symbol*] (NQ)
TILF	Tactical Integrity Loss Factor
TILL	Total Initial Lamp Lumens
Tillman	Tillman's Reports [*68, 69, 71, 73, 75 Alabama*] [*A publication*] (DLA)
TILLO	Transfer in Lieu of Layoff (MCD)
Till & Yates App ... Tillinghast and Yates on Appeals [*A publication*]   (DLA)
TILMC	Tobacco Industry Labor/Management Committee (EA)
TILO.........	Technical Industrial Liaison Office
Til Prec	Tillinghast's Precedents [*A publication*] (DLA)
TILRA	Tribal Indian Land Rights Association (EA)
TILS	Tactical Instrument Landing System
TILS	Technical Information & Liaison Service [*Information service or system*] (IID)
Til & Sh Pr ... Tillinghast and Shearman's New York Practice [*A publication*]   (DLA)
TILSRA.....	Truth-in-Lending Simplification and Reform Act [*1980*]
Tils St L.....	Tilsley on Stamp Laws [*3rd ed.*] [*1871*] [*A publication*] (DLA)
TILT	Taxpayer Inquiry Lookup Table [*IRS*]
TILT	Transmission Intercept and Landing Terminated (MCD)
TIM	Table Input to Memory
TIM	Tactical Instrumental Missile (MCD)
TIM	Tangential Inlet Manifold
TIM	Target Intelligence Material (MCD)
TIM	Technical Information Manager [*Environmental Protection Agency*] (GFGA)
TIM	Technical Information Manual

TIM	Technical Information on Microfilm [*British*] (DIT)
TIM	Technical Interchange Meeting (NASA)
TIM	TEFLON Insulation Material
TIM	Tembagapura [*Indonesia*] [*Airport symbol*] (OAG)
TIM	Temperature Indicator Monitor
TIM	Test Instrumented Missile [*Army*]
TIM	Test Interface Module (CAAL)
TIM	Test Item Malfunction (MCD)
TIM	Texas Instruments, Inc., Central Library Services, Dallas, TX [*OCLC symbol*] (OCLC)
TIM	Thailand Independence Movement [*Communist-directed activity outside Thailand*] [*Merged with TPF*]
TIM	Ticket Issue Machines
TIM	Time [*A publication*]
TIM	Time Indicator, Miniature (MUGU)
TIM	Time Initiator Monitor (SAA)
TIM	Time Interval Measurement
TIM	Time Interval Meter
TIM	Time Interval Monitor (NASA)
TIM	Time Meter (AAG)
TIM	Time in Mode (EG)
Tim............	Timely [*Record label*]
TIM	Timisoara [*Romania*] [*Seismograph station code, US Geological Survey*] (SEIS)
TIM	Timminco Ltd. [*Toronto Stock Exchange symbol*]
Tim............	Timoleon [*of Plutarch*] [*Classical studies*] (OCD)
Tim............	Timon of Athens [*Shakespearean work*]
Tim............	Timothy [*New Testament book*]
TIM	Titanium Mesh [*Medicine*]
TIM	Token/Net Interface Module [*Telecommunications*] (TSSD)
TIM	Topic Indexing Matrix
TIM	Total Ion Scanning Mode [*Spectroscopy*]
TIM	Track Imitation (MSA)
TIM	Track Initiator Monitor (CAAL)
TIM	Tracking Information Memorandum
TIM	Tracking Instruction Manual
TIM	Tracking Instrument Mount (MUGU)
TIM	Transient Intermodulation [*Distortion*]
TIM	Transistor Information Microfile
TIM	Trigger Inverter Module
TIM	Triose Phosphate Isomerase [*An enzyme*]
TIMA	Technical Illustrators Management Association [*Later, IG*]
TIMA	Truth in Mileage Act of 1986
TIMAR......	Near-Term Improvement in Materiel Asset Reporting [*Military*] (AABC)
Timarit Hjukrunarfel Isl ... Timarit Hjukrunarfelags Islands [*Reykjavik*] [*A publication*]
Timarit Verkfraedingafelags Is ... Timarit Verkfraedingafelags Islands [*A publication*]
TIMASS....	Time Interval Miss Distance Acoustical Scoring System (MCD)
TIMATION ... Time Location System [*Navy*]
TIMB........	Timballes [*Kettle drum*]
TIMB........	Timber (ADA)
TIMB........	Timberland Industries, Inc. [*NASDAQ symbol*] (NQ)
Timb Bull Eur ... Timber Bulletin for Europe [*A publication*]
Timb Bull Europe FAO ... Timber Bulletin for Europe. Food and Agricultural Organization [*A publication*]
TIMBCO...	Timberland Co. [*Associated Press abbreviation*] (APAG)
Timber B....	Timber Bulletin for Europe [*A publication*]
Timber BAR ... Timber Bulletin for Europe. Annual Forest Products Market Review [*A publication*]
Timber BFS ... Timber Bulletin for Europe. Forest Fire Statistics [*A publication*]
Timber B (Hu) ... Timber Bulletin for Europe. Forest and Forest Products Country Profile (Hungary) [*A publication*]
Timber B Pr ... Timber Bulletin for Europe. Monthly Prices for Forest Products. Supplement [*A publication*]
Timber BWP ... Timber Bulletin for Europe. Survey of the Wood-Based Panels Industries [*A publication*]
Timber Dev Assoc Inf Bull A/IB ... Timber Development Association. Information Bulletin A/IB [*A publication*]
Timber Dev Assoc Inf Bull B/IB ... Timber Development Association. Information Bulletin B/IB [*A publication*]
Timber Dev Assoc Inf Bull G/IB ... Timber Development Association. Information Bulletin G/IB [*A publication*]
Timber Dev Assoc Res Rep C/RR ... Timber Development Association. Research Report C/RR [*A publication*]
Timber Res Dev Assoc Res Rep C/RR ... Timber Research and Development Association. Research Report C/RR [*A publication*]
Timber Sit ... An Analysis of the Timber Situation in the United States 1952-2030 [*A publication*]
Timber Supp Rev ... Timber Supply Review [*A publication*]   (APTA)
Timber Technol ... Timber Technology [*A publication*]
Timber Trades J ... Timber Trades Journal and Woodworking Machinery [*Later, Timber Trades Journal and Wood Processing*] [*A publication*]
Timb Grower ... Timber Grower [*A publication*]
Timb Leafl For Dep (Brit Solomon Islands Protect) ... Timber Leaflet. Forestry Department (British Solomon Islands Protectorate) [*A publication*]

Timb Leafl For Dep (Kenya) ... Timber Leaflet. Forest Department (Nairobi, Kenya) [*A publication*]
Timb Leafl For Dep (Uganda) ... Timber Leaflet. Forest Department (Uganda) [*A publication*]
Timb & Plyw Ann ... Timber and Plywood Annual [*A publication*]
Timb Pres Assoc Aust ... Timber Preservers' Association of Australia. Pamphlet [*A publication*]   (APTA)
Timb Trades J Wood Process ... Timber Trades Journal and Wood Processing [*A publication*]
Timb Tr J... Timber Trades Journal [*A publication*]
TIM/DL .... Trunk Interface Module for Data Links [*Telecommunications*]
TIME........ Technique for Information Management and Employment
TIME........ Technology, Immediate-Diagnosis, Mammography Effective Treatment
TIME........ Terminal Instruction (System) for Managed Education
TIME........ Time Energy Systems [*NASDAQ symbol*]   (NQ)
Time A ... Time Australia [*A publication*]   (APTA)
TIMEA...... Transactions. Institute of Marine Engineers [*A publication*]
Time (Can) ... Time (Canada) [*A publication*]
Timely Turf Top ... Timely Turf Topics [*A publication*]
Time-Picay ... Times-Picayune [*A publication*]
Times Br Col R ... Times British Colonies Review [*A publication*]
Times Ednl Supp ... Times Educational Supplement [*A publication*]
Times Educ Supp ... Times Educational Supplement [*A publication*]
Times Higher Ed Supp ... Times Higher Education Supplement [*A publication*]
Times Higher Educ Supp ... Times Higher Education Supplement [*A publication*]
Times Higher Educ Suppl ... Times Higher Education Supplement [*A publication*]
Times Ind A ... Times of India Annual [*Bombay*] [*A publication*]
Times L...... Times Literary Supplement [*A publication*]
Times L (Eng) ... Times Law Reports [*England*] [*A publication*]   (DLA)
Times Lit Supp ... Times Literary Supplement [*A publication*]
Times Lit Suppl ... Times Literary Supplement [*A publication*]
Times (Lond) ... Times (London) [*A publication*]
Times LR ... Times Law Reports [*England*] [*A publication*]   (DLA)
Times LR ... Times Law Reports [*Ceylon*] [*A publication*]   (DLA)
Times L Rep ... Times Law Reports [*England*] [*A publication*]   (DLA)
Times L Rep ... Times Law Reports [*Ceylon*] [*A publication*]   (DLA)
Times Rev Ind ... Times Review of Industry [*A publication*]
Times R Ind ... Times Review of Industry [*A publication*]
Times R Ind & Tech ... Times Review of Industry and Technology [*A publication*]
Times Sci Rev ... Times Science Review [*A publication*]
Times Trib ... Times Tribune [*A publication*]
TimeW....... Time Warner, Inc. [*Associated Press abbreviation*]   (APAG)
TIMFA...... Transactions. Institute of Metal Finishing [*A publication*]
TIMI.......... Technical Information Maintenance Instruction
TIMI.......... Thrombolysis in Myocardial Infarction (Study) [*Medicine*]
TIMIG....... Time in Grade [*Army*]
TIMINT .... Time Interval   (AABC)
Timisoara Inst Politeh Traian Vuia Bul Stiint Teh Ser Chim ... Timisoara. Institutul Politehnic "Traian Vuia." Buletinul Stiintific si Tehnic. Seria Chimie [*A publication*]
Timisoara Med ... Timisoara Medicala [*Romania*] [*A publication*]
TIMIX....... [*The*] International Microcomputer Information Exchange   (EA)
TiMixE...... TI-MIX [*Texas Instruments Mini/Microcomputer Information Exchange*] Europe   (EA)
Timken....... [*The*] Timken Co. [*Associated Press abbreviation*]   (APAG)
TIMM ...... Thermionic Integrated Micromodule
TIMM ...... Timberline Minerals, Inc. [*NASDAQ symbol*]   (NQ)
TIMMS.... Total Integrated Manpower Management System
TIMOT...... Track, Initiation, Monitoring Overlap Technician   (SAA)
TIMP........ Tavistock Institute of Medical Psychology [*British*]
TIMP........ Texas Instructional Media Project [*Education*]
TIMP........ Timpani [*Kettle drum*]
TIMP........ Tissue Inhibitor of Metalloproteinases [*Biochemistry*]
TIMS........ [*The*] Institute of Management Sciences [*Providence, RI*]   (EA)
TIMS........ [*The*] International Molinological Society   (EA)
TIMS........ Tactical Incapacitating Munitions System   (MCD)
TIMS........ Technology Integration of Missile Subsystems   (MCD)
TIMS........ Telephone Information and Management Systems   (ADA)
TIMS........ Test Interactive Management System
TIMS........ Text Information and Management System [*Data processing*]
TIMS........ Thermal Infrared Mapping Spectrometer   (SSD)
TIMS........ Thermal Infrared Multispectral Scanner [*Airborne instrument for geological applications*]
TIMS........ Thermal Ionization Mass Spectrometry
TIMS........ Time Sharing Resources, Inc. [*NASDAQ symbol*]   (NQ)
TIMS........ Total Ion Measurement Source
TIMS........ Transmission Impairment Measuring Set [*Telecommunications*]   (TEL)
TIN .... Ebanewsletter. Daily Economic and Political News Indicators from Turkey [*A publication*]
TIN .... Taro Industries Ltd. [*Toronto Stock Exchange symbol*]
TIN .... Task Implementation Notice
TIN .... Taxpayer Identification Number [*IRS*]
TIN .... Temperature Independent [*Ferrite computer memory core*]
TIN .... Temple-Inland, Inc. [*NYSE symbol*]   (SPSG)

TIN .... Temporary Identification Number [*Military*]
TIN .... Temporary Instruction Notice
TIN .... Ter in Nocte [*Three Times a Night*] [*Pharmacy*]
Tin.............. [*Alfanus*] Tindarus [*Flourished, 15th century*] [*Authority cited in pre-1607 legal work*]   (DSA)
TIN .... Tindouf [*Algeria*] [*Airport symbol*]   (OAG)
TIN .... Tinemaha [*California*] [*Seismograph station code, US Geological Survey*]   (SEIS)
TIN .... Tooling Impound Notice
TIN .... Transaction Identification Number   (AFM)
TIN .... Tubulointerstitial Nephritis [*Nephrology*]
TINA .... [*The*] Integrated Nozzle Assembly   (MCD)
TINA .... There Is No Alternative [*Nickname given to British Prime Minister Margaret Thatcher because she so often uses this phrase to defend her government's economic policies*]
TINC .... Tincture   (ADA)
TINCT....... Tinctura [*Tincture*] [*Pharmacy*]
Tind........... [*Alfanus*] Tindarus [*Flourished, 15th century*] [*Authority cited in pre-1607 legal work*]   (DSA)
TINDECO ... Tin Decorating Co.
TINDX ...... Texas Instruments Index Access Method
TINE.......... There Is No Excuse   (ECON)
TI-NET...... Transparent Intelligent Network
TINET....... Travel Industry Network, Inc. [*Winter Springs, FL*] [*Telecommunications*]   (TSSD)
TINFO....... Tieteellisen Informoinnin Neuvosto [*Finnish Council for Scientific Information and Research Libraries*]   (EAIO)
TIN/FS....... Taxpayer Identification Number/File Source [*IRS*]
Tingo Maria Peru Est Exp Agric Bol ... Tingo Maria, Peru. Estacion Experimental Agricola. Boletin [*A publication*]
Tin Int........ Tin International [*A publication*]
Tin Inter...... Tin International [*A publication*]
Tin Intern.... Tin International [*A publication*]
Tink .... Two Incomes, No Kids [*Lifestyle classification*]
TINKER .... Timber Information Keyword Retrieval [*Timber Research and Development Association*] [*Information service or system*]   (IID)
TINNER.... Tea and Dinner [*Slang*] [*British*]   (DSUE)
TINO......... There Is No Opposition [*Parliamentary slang*] [*British*]   (DI)
TINOP....... Transponder Inoperative [*Aviation*]   (FAAC)
TINPOT.... There Is No Possible Other Tactic [*Parliamentary slang*] [*British*]   (DI)
Tin Print Box Mkr ... Tin-Printer and Box Maker [*A publication*]
TINR .... Target Identification Navigation RADAR
Tin Res Inst (Greenford Engl) Publ ... Tin Research Institute (Greenford, England). Publication [*A publication*]
TINS.......... Tax Identification Number System [*IRS*]
TINS.......... Thermal Imaging Navigation Set [*Hughes Aircraft Co.*] [*Navy*]   (ECON)
TINS.......... Trends in Neurosciences [*A publication*]
Tinsley ...... Tinsley's Magazine [*A publication*]
TINSTAAFL ... There Is No Such Thing as a Free Lunch [*Principle of economics indicating that one cannot get something for nothing*] [*See also TANSTAAFL*]
TINS Trends Neurosci ... TINS. Trends in Neurosciences [*A publication*]
TINSY .... Treasure Island Naval Shipyard [*San Francisco Bay*]
TINT......... Target Intercept Timer   (MCD)
TINTM...... Triisononyl Trimellitate [*Organic chemistry*]
TINTS ...... Tactical Intelligence Transfer System
TINTS ...... Turret Integrated Night Thermal Sight
Tin Uses..... Tin and Its Uses [*A publication*]
Tinw........... Tinwald's Reports, Scotch Court of Session [*A publication*]   (DLA)
TIO .... Target Indication Officer [*Navy*]
TIO .... Technical Information Office
TIO .... Technology Integration Office [*Army*]   (RDA)
TIO .... Television Information Office [*Defunct*]   (EA)
TIO .... Test Input/Output [*Data processing*]
TIO .... Time Interval Optimization   (IEEE)
TIO .... Tiouine [*Morocco*] [*Seismograph station code, US Geological Survey*]   (SEIS)
TIO .... Transistorized Image Orthicon
TIO .... Troop Information Officer
TIOC .... Terminal Input/Output Coordinator [*Data processing*]   (IBMDP)
TIOC .... Triumph International Owners Club   (EA)
TIOF .... [*The*] International Osprey Foundation   (EA)
TIOH......... [*The*] Institute of Heraldry [*Military*]
TIOLR...... Texas Instruments Online Reporting System [*Data processing*]
TIOM .... Telegraph Input-Output Multiplexer [*Telecommunications*]   (OA)
TIOM .... Terminal Input/Output Module [*Data processing*]
TIOOA ...... Transactions. Indiana Academy of Ophthalmology and Otolaryngology [*A publication*]
TIOS.......... Tactical Integrated Ocean Surveillance [*Military*]   (CAAL)
TIOT......... Task Input/Output Table [*Data processing*]   (BUR)
TIOTM...... Triisooctyl Trimellitate [*Organic chemistry*]
TIOWQ..... Terminal Input/Output Wait Queue [*Data processing*]
TIP............. [*The*] Information Partnership [*Information service or system*]   (IID)
TIP............. [*The*] Information Place [*Information service or system*]   (IID)

TIP............. TACAMO [*Take Charge and Move Out*] Improvement
 Program
TIP............. Tactical Implementation Time
TIP............. Tactical Improvement Program [*Military*]
TIP............. Tactile Information Presentation [*Biotechnology*]
TIP............. Target Identification Point   (NATG)
TIP............. Target Impact Point
TIP............. Target Industries Program [*Occupational Safety and Health
 Administration*]
TIP............. Target Input Panel
TIP............. Target Intelligence Package   (MCD)
TIP............. Task Initiation and Prediction
TIP............. Tax-Based Incomes Policy
TIP............. Taxpayer Information Processing [*IRS*]
TIP............. Teachers Instructional Plan
TIP............. Technical Improvement Program
TIP............. Technical Information Panel [*AEC*] [*Terminated, 1971*]
TIP............. Technical Information Pilot [*A publication*] [*Obsolete*]
TIP............. Technical Information Pool
TIP............. Technical Information Processing   (IEEE)
TIP............. Technical Information Program
TIP............. Technical Information Project [*MIT*]
TIP............. Technical Integration Panel [*NASA*]   (SSD)
TIP............. Technology Internship Program [*Oak Ridge National
 Laboratory*]
TIP............. Tehrik-i-Istiqlal [*Solidarity Party*] [*See also TI*] [*Political party*]
 [*Pakistan*]   (FEA)
TIP............. TELENET Interface Processor
TIP............. Telephone Information Processing   (MCD)
TIP............. Teletype Input Processing
TIP............. Temperature-Independent Paramagnetism
TIP............. Terminal Impact Prediction
TIP............. Terminal Interface Package [*Data processing*]
TIP............. Terminal Interface [*Message*] Processor [*Data processing*]
 [*DoD*]
TIP............. Tests in Print [*A publication*]
TIP............. Theory into Practice [*A publication*]
TIP............. Thrust Inlet Pressure   (MCD)
TIP............. Tiburon Petroleum [*Vancouver Stock Exchange symbol*]
TIP............. Tilt Isolation Platform
TIP............. Times of Increased Probability [*Earthquake prediction*]
Tip............. Tipperary [*County in Ireland*]   (WGA)
TIP............. TIROS [*Television and Infrared Observation Satellite*]
 Information Processor [*Telecommunications*]
TIP............. To Insure Promptness
TIP............. Tool Inventors Program [*Automobile tool design*]
TIP............. Total Information Processing   (BUR)
TIP............. Total Isomerization Process [*Petroleum refining*]
TIP............. Toxic Integration Program [*Environmental Protection Agency*]
TIP............. Toxicology Information Program [*National Library of
 Medicine*] [*Bethesda, MD*]
TIP............. Track Initiation and Prediction [*RADAR*]
TIP............. Tracking Impact Prediction [*of satellites*]
TIP............. Training Implementation Plan [*Military*]
TIP............. Trans-Israel Pipeline
TIP............. Transaction Interface Package [*Sperry UNIVAC*] [*Data
 processing*]
TIP............. Transaction Interface Processor
TIP............. Transient [*or Traveling or Traversing*] In-Core Probe [*Nuclear
 energy*]   (NRCH)
TIP............. Transit Improvement Program [*Satellite*]   (MCD)
TIP............. Translation Inhibitory Protein
TIP............. Transponder Interrogator Processor
TIP............. Transport Individuel Publique [*Also known as PROCOTIP*]
 [*French auto cooperative*]
TIP............. Transportation Improvement Program
TIP............. Traverisng In-Core Probe
TIP............. Tripoli [*Libya*] [*Airport symbol*]   (OAG)
TIP............. Troop Information Program
TIP............. Truth in Press [*An association*]   (EA)
TIP............. Tumor-Inducing Principle [*Plant cytology*]
TIP............. Tumor Inhibitory Principle [*Oncology*]
TIP............. Turbine Inlet Pressure   (MSA)
TIP............. Turbine Integral Propellant   (MCD)
TIP............. Turn In a Pusher [*Organization combating drug traffic*]
TIP............. Until Past [*Followed by place*]   (FAAC)
TIPA......... Triisopropanolamine [*Organic chemistry*]
TIPACS..... Texas Instruments Planning and Control System
TIPAT....... Technical Information on Patents [*Swiss Intellectual Property
 Office*] [*Bern*] [*Information service or system*]   (IID)
TIPB......... Triisopropylbenzene [*Also, TIB*] [*Organic chemistry*]
TIPC......... Texas Instruments Pressure Controller
TIPCC....... TI [*Texas Instruments*] Programmable Calculator Club   (EA)
TIPE......... Transponder, Interrogator, Pinger, and Echo Sounder
TIPEM...... Toolkit for Interoperable Privacy-Enhanced Messaging [*RSA
 Data Security, Inc.*]
Tip Fak Mecm ... Tip Fakultesi Mecmuasi. Istanbul Universitesi [*A
 publication*]
TIPG......... Thomson Information/Publishing Group [*The Thomson Corp.*]
Tiphok .... Tiphook Ltd. [*Associated Press abbreviation*]   (APAG)

TIPI .... Tactical Information Processing and Interpretation
 [*Military*]   (AFM)
TIPI .... Transportable Automated Intelligence Processing and
 Interpretation System   (MCD)
TIPIC........ Turkish Investment Promotion and Information Center
 [*Subdivision of the Union of Chambers of Commerce,
 Industry, and Commodity Exchanges of Turkey*]
TIPIT........ TDRSS [*Tracking and Data Relay Satellite System*] Interface
 Prepocessor Into TELOPS [*Telemetry Online Processing
 System*]
TIPITEF.... Tactical Information Processing and Interpretation Total
 Environment Facility   (MCD)
TIPL .... Tactical Imagery Processing Laboratory [*Army*]   (MCD)
TIPL .... Tactical Information Processing Laboratory [*Army*]   (MCD)
TIPL .... Teach Information Processing Language
TIPMG...... [*The*] International Project Management Group, Inc. [*Glyndon,
 MD*] [*Telecommunications*]   (TSSD)
TIPN......... International Platinum Corp. [*NASDAQ symbol*]   (NQ)
TIPP .... Target Intelligence Production Program
TIPP .... Technology and Information Policy Program [*Syracuse
 University*] [*Research center*]   (RCD)
TIPP .... Time Phasing Program [*NASA*]   (KSC)
TIPP .... Tipperary [*County in Ireland*]
Tippery ...... Tipperary Corp. [*Associated Press abbreviation*]   (APAG)
TIPPS........ Tetraiodophenolphthalein Sodium [*Pharmacology*]
TIPPS........ Total In-House Publication Production System   (MCD)
TIPR .... Tactical Inertial Performance Requirements
TIPR .... Tactics Inspection Procedures Report
TIPR .... Tipperary Corp. [*NASDAQ symbol*]   (NQ)
TIPRE .... Tactical Inertial Performance Requirements   (MCD)
TIPRO....... Texas Independent Producers and Royalty Owners
 Association   (EA)
TIPRO Rep ... TIPRO [*Texas Independent Producers and Royalty Owners
 Association*] Reporter [*A publication*]
TIPS .... Intrahepatic Portosystemic Shunt [*Medicine*]
TIPS .... [*The*] Italia Philatelic Society   (EA)
TIPS .... Tactical Imagery Processing Set
TIPS .... Tactical Information about Perilous Situations [*New York City
 Fire Department program*]
TIPS .... Tactical Information Processing System [*Military*]   (CAAL)
TIPS .... Teaching Individual Protective Strategies and Teaching
 Individual Positive Solutions [*In association name TIPS
 Program*]   (EA)
TIPS .... Teaching Information Processing System
TIPS .... Technical Information Periodicals Service [*General Electric
 Co.*]
TIPS .... Technical Information Processing System [*Rockwell
 International Corp.*] [*Downey, CA*]   (AFM)
TIPS .... Technical Information for Product Safety [*Consumer Product
 Safety Commission*]   (IID)
TIPS .... Technical Information and Product Service
TIPS .... Technical Interest Profiles   (SAA)
TIPS .... Techniques in Product Selection [*National Association of
 Manufacturers*]
TIPS .... Telemetry Impact Prediction System [*Air Force*]
TIPS .... Telemetry Integrated Processing System [*Air Force*]
TIPS .... Terminal Information Processing System [*Aviation*]   (FAAC)
TIPS .... Test Information Processing System [*Air Force*]
TIPS .... Text Information Processing System
TIPS .... Textile Industry Product Safety [*A publication*]
TIPS .... Thermally Induced Phase Separation [*Chemistry*]
Tips .... Tiny Income, Parents Supporting [*Lifestyle classification*]
TIPS .... Total Information Processing System [*Veterans
 Administration*]
TIPS .... Total Integrated Pneumatic System   (MCD)
TIPS .... Transistorized Inverter Power Supply
TIPS .... Transportation Induced Pollution Surveillance [*Marine
 science*]   (MSC)
TIPS .... Trends in Pharmacological Sciences [*A publication*]
TIPS .... Truevision Image Processing Software [*AT & T*]
TIPSY........ Task Input Parameter Synthesizer
TIPT .... Tipton Centers, Inc. [*St. Louis, MO*] [*NASDAQ symbol*]   (NQ)
TIP/TAP ... Target Input Panel and Target Assign Panel
TIPTOP ... Tape Input - Tape Output [*Honeywell, Inc.*] [*Data processing*]
TIP TOP.... Tax Information Plan and Total Owed Purchase Accounting
TIQ .... Paris, TN [*Location identifier*] [*FAA*]   (FAAL)
TIQ .... Task Input Queue [*Data processing*]   (IBMDP)
TIQ .... Tetrahydroisoquinoline [*Biochemistry*]
TIQ .... Tinian [*Mariana Islands*] [*Airport symbol*]   (OAG)
TI/QC....... Technical Inspection/Quality Control   (MCD)
TIQRC....... Toxicology Information Query Response Center [*National
 Library of Medicine*]
TIR............. Target Illuminating RADAR [*Air Force*]
TIR............. Target Indication Room [*Navy*]
TIR............. Target Industries [*Industry segments which have been selected
 by the US Department of Commerce for special trade
 promotion emphasis*]
TIR............. Target Instruction Register
TIR............. Technical Information Release
TIR............. Technical Information Report   (IEEE)
TIR............. Technical Intelligence Report

TIR............. Telecommunications Industry Research [*British*]   (ECON)
TIR............. Terminal Imaging RADAR [*Military*]   (RDA)
TIR............. Terminal Innervation Ratio [*Psychiatry*]
TIR............. Test Incidence and Reporting System
tir............. Tigrina [*MARC language code*] [*Library of Congress*]   (LCCP)
TIR............. Time in Rate
TIR............. Tirana [*Albania*] [*Seismograph station code, US Geological Survey*]   (SEIS)
TIR............. Tirupati [*India*] [*Airport symbol*]   (OAG)
TIR............. Tolerance in Radius
TIR............. Tooling Investigation Report
TIR............. Total Image Readout
TIR............. Total Immunoreaction [*Immunochemistry*]
TIR............. Total Indicated Runout
TIR............. Total Indicator Reading
TIR............. Total Internal Reflecting
TIR............. Total Item Record   (MCD)
TIR............. Transaction Item Report [*Navy*]   (NG)
TIR............. Transmission Infrared [*Spectroscopy*]
TIR............. Transport International Routier [*International Transport of Goods by Road*] [*French*]
TIRA.......... Thrift Industry Recovery Act [*1987*]
TIRA.......... Thrift Institutions Restructuring Act [*1982*]
TIRACS..... Telecommanded Inertially Referenced Attitude Control System   (MCD)
Tiraq .... [*Andreas*] Tiraquellus [*Deceased, 1558*] [*Authority cited in pre-1607 legal work*]   (DSA)
Tiraquel ..... [*Andreas*] Tiraquellus [*Deceased, 1558*] [*Authority cited in pre-1607 legal work*]   (DSA)
TIRAS .... Technical Information Retrieval and Analysis System   (CAAL)
Tiraspol Gos Ped Inst Ucen Zap ... Tiraspol'skii Gosudarstvennyi Pedagogiceskii Institut Imeni T. G. Sevcenko. Ucenyi Zapiski [*A publication*]
TIRB.......... Transportation Insurance Rating Bureau [*Later, AAIS*]   (EA)
TIRC.......... T Tauri Infrared Companion [*Object believed to be first planet sighted that is not in our solar system*]
TIRC.......... Tobacco Industry Research Committee   (EA)
TIRC.......... Toxicology Information Research Center [*Department of Energy*] [*Oak Ridge National Laboratory*] [*Oak Ridge, TN*]
TIRC.......... Toxicology Information Response Center [*Information service or system*]   (IID)
TIRC.......... TRADOC [*Training and Doctrine Command*] Instrumentation Review Committee [*Army*]
TIRC.......... Transimpedence Receiver Circuit
TIRE.......... One Liberty Firestone [*NASDAQ symbol*]   (NQ)
TIRE.......... Tank Infrared Elbow [*Night vision device*] [*Army*]   (RDA)
TIRE.......... Tires as Imaginative Recreation Equipment
TIREC .... TIROS [*Television and Infrared Observation Satellite*] Ice Reconnaissance [*NASA*]
Tire Dealr .. Modern Tire Dealer [*A publication*]
TIREM...... Terrain Integration Rough Earth Model
Tire Rev .... Tire Review [*A publication*]
Tire Rev D ... Tire Review. 1986 Sourcebook and Directory [*A publication*]
Tire Sci Technol ... Tire Science and Technology [*A publication*]
TIRF .... Total Internal Reflection Fluorescence
TIRF .... Traffic Injury Research Foundation of Canada [*Research center*]   (RCD)
TIR-FPL.... Total Internal Reflection Face-Pumped LASER
TIRH .... Theoretical Indoor Relative Humidity
TIRIS......... Traversing Infrared Inspection System   (MCD)
TIRKS .... Trunks Integrated Record Keeping System [*Bell System*]
TIRM........ Transparent Infrared Material
TIRMMS .. Technical Information Reports for Music-Media Specialists [*Music Library Association publication series*]
TIROD ...... Test Instruction Record of Discussion   (MCD)
T Iron St I ... Transactions. Iron and Steel Institute of Japan [*A publication*]
TIROS....... Television and Infrared Observation Satellite [*NASA*]
TIROS .... Topographical Infrared Operations Satellite   (NASA)
TIROS-M ... Television and Infrared Observation Satellite - Meteorological [*NASA*]   (DNAB)
TIRP .... Total Internal Reflection Prism
TIRPF........ Total Integrated Radial Peaking Factor   (IEEE)
TIRR .... [*The*] Institute for Rehabilitation and Research [*Houston, TX*]
TIRR .... Tactics Inspection Results Report
TIRR.......... Tradestar Corp. [*Formerly, Tierra Energy Corp.*] [*NASDAQ symbol*]   (NQ)
TIRR.......... Trainer Installation Requirements Report
TIRS .... Tactical Information Recording System [*Military*]   (CAAL)
TIRS .... Thermal Infrared Scanner   (RDA)
TIRS .... Travaux. Institut de Recherches Sahariennes [*A publication*]
TIR/SLIT ... Transaction Item Reporting / Serial Lot Item Tracking [*Navy*]   (DNAB)
TIRT .... Tidelands Royalty Trust "B" [*NASDAQ symbol*]   (NQ)
TIRT.......... Total Internal Reflection Technique
TIRU .... Service du Traitement Industriel des Residus Urbains [*France*]
TIRU .... Trade Information Research Unit [*ITC*] [*United Nations*]   (DUND)
TIRVB ...... Toronto University. Institute for Aerospace Studies. UTIAS Review [*A publication*]
TIS............. [*The*] Infantry School [*Army*]

TIS............. Tactical Intelligence Squadron   (MCD)
TIS............. Tactical Interdiction System
TIS............. Taft Information System [*Provides information on private foundations*]   (IID)
TIS............. Target Identification Software [*Military*]   (CAAL)
TIS............. Target Information Sheet [*Air Force*]
TIS............. Target Information System
TIS............. Technical Information Section [*Navy*]
TIS............. Technical Information Service [*American Institute of Aeronautics and Astronautics*]   (IID)
TIS............. Technical Information Service [*Caribbean Industrial Research Institute*] [*Trinidad and Tobago*]
TIS............. Technical Information Services [*Acurex Corp.*]   (IID)
TIS............. Technical Information Staff [*Environmental Protection Agency*]   (GFGA)
TIS............. Technical Information Systems [*Department of Agriculture*]
TIS............. Technical Interface Specification   (NATG)
TIS............. Technical Research Centre of Finland, Espoo, Finland [*OCLC symbol*]   (OCLC)
TIS............. Technology, Information, and Society
TIS............. Technology Information System [*Lawrence Livermore National Laboratory*] [*University of California*]   (IID)
TIS............. Telemetry Input System
TIS............. Telephone Information Services [*Commercial firm*] [*British*]
TIS............. Temperature Indicating Switch
TIS............. Terminal Interface Subsystem [*Telecommunications*]   (TEL)
TIS............. Termination Inventory Schedule   (SAA)
TIS............. Tern Island Station   (SAA)
TIS............. Terrain Information System
TIS............. Test Information Sheet   (MCD)
TIS............. Test Instrumentation System
TIS............. Test Interface Subsystem   (NASA)
TIS............. Test Interface Summary   (MCD)
TIS............. Test Item Simulator [*Fort Huachuca, AZ*] [*United States Army Electronic Proving Ground*]   (GRD)
TIS............. Tetracycline-Induced Steatosis [*Medicine*]
TIS............. Tetrahydroisoquinoline Sulfonamide [*A drug*]
TIS............. Theater Intelligence Section [*Navy*]
TIS............. Thermal Imaging Scanner
TIS............. Thermal Imaging Sight [*Artillery*] [*Army*]   (INF)
TIS............. Thermal Insulation System
TIS............. Thursday Island [*Australia*] [*Airport symbol*]   (OAG)
TIS............. Time Resources Corp. [*Vancouver Stock Exchange symbol*]
TIS............. Time in Service   (FAAC)
TIS............. Times [*London*] [*A publication*]
TIS............. TIS Mortgage Investment Co. [*NYSE symbol*]   (CTT)
TIS............. TIS Mortgage Investors Co. [*Associated Press abbreviation*]   (APAG)
TIS............. Tissue   (ADA)
TIS............. Tobacco Inspection Service [*Philippines*]
TIS............. Tops in Science Fiction [*A publication*]
TIS............. Total Information System [*Data processing*]
TIS............. Track Initiation Supervisor   (SAA)
TIS............. Tracking and Injection Station
TIS............. Tracking Instrumentation Subsystem   (MCD)
TIS............. Trade Information Service [*ESCAP*] [*United Nations*]   (DUND)
TIS............. Trading Information System [*AutEx Systems*] [*Information service or system*]   (CRD)
TIS............. Traffic Information System
TIS............. Transponder Interrogation SONAR
TIS............. Travel Information Service   (EA)
TIS............. Travelers Information Service [*Oracle Corp.*] [*Information service or system*]   (IID)
TIS............. Triskaidekaphobia Illuminatus Society   (EA)
TIS............. Trypsin-Insoluble Segment [*Cytochemistry*]
TIS............. Tumor in Situ [*Oncology*]
TIS............. Two-Impinging-Stream Reactor [*Chemical engineering*]
TISA .... Technical Information Support Activities [*Army*]
TISA .... Technique for Interactive Systems Analysis   (NVT)
TISA .... Troop Issue Subsistence Activity [*Military*]   (AABC)
TISA .... Troop Issue Support Agency   (MCD)
TISAL........ Tactical Instrument Steep Approach and Landing System   (MCD)
TISAP........ Technical Information Support Activities Project [*Army*]   (DIT)
TISAP........ Totalized Interface Subroutine and Post Processor [*Data processing*]   (BUR)
TISC .... Technology Integration Steering Committee [*Army*]   (RDA)
TISC .... Tire Industry Safety Council   (EA)
TISC .... Treasury Inter-Services Committee [*British military*]   (DMA)
TISCA .... Technical Information System for Carrier Aviation [*Navy*]   (MCD)
TISCO .... TISCO [*Tata Iron & Steel Co.*] Technical Journal [*A publication*]
TISCO Rev ... TISCO [*Tata Iron & Steel Co.*] Review [*A publication*]
TISE .... Technical Information Service Extension   (SAA)
TISEO .... Target Identification System, Electro-Optical [*Air Force*]
TISI .... Tenet Information Services, Inc. [*NASDAQ symbol*]   (NQ)
TISK .... Thailand Informations und Solidaritaetskomitee [*Germany*]

TISL	Telecommunications and Information Systems Laboratory [*University of Kansas*] [*Research center*] (RCD)
TISL	Thomson Information Services Ltd. [*The Thomson Corp.*] [*Publishing*]
TISO.........	Threat Integrated Staff Officer [*Army*]
TISO.........	TRADOC [*Training and Doctrine Command*] Integration Staff Officer [*Army*]
TISO.........	Troop Issue Subsistence Officer [*Military*] (AABC)
TISP	Technical Information Support Personnel [*Department of Labor*]
TISP	Thickness-Insensitive Solar Paint [*Coating technology*]
TISPOC.....	Trent Institute for the Study of Popular Culture [*Trent University*] [*Canada*] [*Research center*] (RCD)
TISq.........	Tactical Intelligence Squadron [*Air Force*]
TIS-RET....	Thermal Imaging System - Reticle
TISS.........	Tactical Intermediate Support System [*Military*] (MCD)
TISS..........	Trans-Ionospheric Sensing System (DWSG)
TISS.........	Troop Issue Support System [*Army*]
TISSG........	Travel Industry Systems Standards Group [*British*]
Tissue Anti ...	Tissue Antigens [*A publication*]
Tissue React ...	Tissue Reactions [*A publication*]
TIST	St. Thomas/Harry S. Truman [*Virgin Islands*] [*ICAO location identifier*] (ICLI)
TISTHR	Tool Inspection Small Tools Historical Record (MCD)
TISU	Trade Information Supply Unit [*ITC*] [*United Nations*] (DUND)
TISX	St. Croix/Alexander Hamilton [*Virgin Islands*] [*ICAO location identifier*] (ICLI)
Tit	Divus Titus [*of Suetonius*] [*Classical studies*] (OCD)
TIT............	Technician-in-Training (ADA)
TIT............	Technology in Training [*DoD*]
TIT............	Terminal Interface Table (MCD)
TIT............	Test Item Taker
TIT............	Thermal Inactivation Time
TIT............	Thermoisolation Technique
Tit	Titan [*Record label*]
Tit	Tithe (ILCA)
TIT............	Title [*Bibliography*]
Tit	Titus [*New Testament book*]
Tit	Titus Andronicus [*Shakespearean work*]
TIT............	Total Indication Time (MCD)
TIT............	Total Insertion Time
TIT............	Treponema Immobilization Test [*Clinical chemistry*]
TIT............	Triiodothyronine [*Endocrinology*] (MAE)
TIT............	Turbine Inlet Temperature
TIT............	Turbine Interstage Temperature
TIT............	Tustin Institute of Technology [*California*]
Titan	[*The*] Titan Corp. [*Associated Press abbreviation*] (APAG)
TITC.........	Toxic Substances Control Act Interagency Testing Committee [*Environmental Protection Agency*] (GFGA)
TITC..........	Traction-Immune Track Circuits [*Railway signals system*] [*British*]
TITE.........	Technologies and Innovations in Training Equipment
TITE.........	TEWS [*Tactical Electronic Warfare System*] Intermediate Test Equipment [*Military*]
TITE.........	Tijuana & Tecate Railway Co. [*Later, TTR*] [*AAR code*]
TI Tech Inf Ind ...	TI. Technical Information for Industry [*South Africa*] [*A publication*]
TITh.........	Triiodothyronine [*Also, T₃*] [*Endocrinology*]
TIT J Lif....	TIT [*Tower International Technomedical*] Journal of Life Sciences [*A publication*]
TIT J Life Sci ...	TIT [*Tower International Technomedical*] Journal of Life Sciences [*A publication*]
TITLA	Tecnica Italiana [*A publication*]
TITO..........	Troops In, Troops Out
TITPG	Taft Institute for Two-Party Government [*Later, TTI*] (EA)
titr	Titrate [*Analytical chemistry*]
TI/TTR......	Target Illumination/Target Tracking RADAR (MCD)
TITUS	Textile Information Treatment Users' Service [*French Textile Institute*] [*Bibliographic database*] [*Information service or system*] (IID)
TIU	Tape Identification Unit
TIU	Target Indication Unit [*Navy*]
TIU	Telecommunications International Union (EA)
TIU	Telephone Interface Unit [*Telecommunications*]
TIU	Terminal Interface Unit [*Bell System*]
TIU	Timaru [*New Zealand*] [*Airport symbol*] (OAG)
TIU	Time Isolation Unit
TIU	Toxicologically Insignificant Usage
TIU	Trigger Inverter Unit
TIU	Trypsin Inhibitory Unit [*Food analysis*]
TIUC.........	Textile Information Users Council (EA)
TIUV	Total Intrauterine Volume [*Gynecology*]
TIV............	Target Intensifier Vidicon
TIV............	Time in View
TIV............	Tivat [*Former Yugoslavia*] [*Airport symbol*] (OAG)
TIV............	Tiverton [*Municipal borough in England*]
TIV............	Tiverton Petroleums Ltd. [*Toronto Stock Exchange symbol*]
TIV............	Tivoli Music Hall [*London*] (DSUE)
TIVC.........	Thoracic Inferior Vena Cava [*Medicine*] (MAE)
TIVS	Thermally Initiated Venting System (MCD)
TIW	Tacoma, WA [*Location identifier*] [*FAA*] (FAAL)
TIW	Tactical Intelligence Wing [*Military*]
TIW	Tamarind Institute Workshop [*Graphic arts school*] [*New Mexico*]
TIW	TEFLON-Insulated Wire
tiw..............	Three Times a Week [*Pharmacology*]
TIW	Today's Insurance Woman [*National Association of Insurance Women (International)*] [*A publication*]
TIWG	Terrorism Incident Working Group [*Bureau of Diplomatic Security*] [*Department of State*] (EGAO)
TIWG	Test Integration Working Group [*Military*] (GFGA)
TIWSS......	Theater Integrated Warfare Scenarios Study
TIX...........	Timeplex, Inc. [*NYSE symbol*] (SPSG)
TIX...........	Titusville, FL [*Location identifier*] [*FAA*] (FAAL)
TIXA.........	Thioxanthone [*Organic chemistry*]
TIXI	Turret Integrated Xenon Illuminator
TIY...........	Tidjikja [*Mauritania*] [*Airport symbol*] (OAG)
TIY............	Tir Systems Ltd. [*Vancouver Stock Exchange symbol*]
TIYADG....	Tianjin Medical Journal [*A publication*]
TIZ............	Tari [*Papua New Guinea*] [*Airport symbol*] (OAG)
TIZZY	Tinny and Buzzing [*Sounds*]
TJ..............	Air Traffic GmbH [*ICAO designator*] (FAAC)
TJ..............	Cameroun [*Aircraft nationality and registration mark*] (FAAC)
TJ..............	East Germany [*License plate code assigned to foreign diplomats in the US*]
TJ..............	Tait's Justice of the Peace [*A publication*] (DLA)
TJ..............	Talk Jockey [*Radio*]
TJ..............	Talmud Jerushalmi (BJA)
TJ..............	Targum Jonathan (BJA)
TJ..............	Technical Journal · (MCD)
TJ..............	Telephone Jack (DEN)
TJ..............	Temperature Junction (MCD)
TJ..............	Terajoule [*SI unit of energy*]
TJ..............	Test Jack (DEN)
TJ..............	Theatre Journal [*A publication*]
TJ..............	Thermal Junction (KSC)
TJ..............	Thomas Jefferson [*US president, 1743-1826*]
TJ..............	Tijuana [*Mexico*]
TJ..............	Today's Japan [*A publication*]
TJ..............	Tolkien Journal [*A publication*]
TJ..............	Tomato Juice
TJ..............	Tommy John [*Baseball pitcher*]
TJ..............	Trajectory (AABC)
TJ..............	Trans-Jordan (BJA)
TJ..............	Triceps Jerk
TJ..............	Trinity Journal [*A publication*]
TJ..............	Turbojet
TJA............	Focus Japan (Tokyo) [*A publication*]
TJA............	Tarija [*Bolivia*] [*Airport symbol*] (OAG)
TJA............	Telecommunication Journal of Australia [*A publication*] (APTA)
TJA............	Trial Judge Advocate [*Army*]
TJA............	Turbojet Aircraft
TJADA......	Teratology [*A publication*]
TJADC......	Theater Joint Air Defense Command [*Military*] (AABC)
TJAETDS ...	Turbine and Jet Aircraft Engine Type Designation System
TJAG........	[*The*] Judge Advocate General [*Army*]
TJAGC......	[*The*] Judge Advocate General's Corps [*Army*]
TJaGH	Jackson-Madison County General Hospital, Learning Center, Jackson, TN [*Library symbol*] [*Library of Congress*] (LCLS)
TJAGSA....	[*The*] Judge Advocate General's School, Army
TJaL	Lane College, Jackson, TN [*Library symbol*] [*Library of Congress*] (LCLS)
TJaLam	Lambuth College, Jackson, TN [*Library symbol*] [*Library of Congress*] (LCLS)
TJaLaw......	Tennessee State Law Library, Jackson, TN [*Library symbol*] [*Library of Congress*] (LCLS)
T Jap I Met ...	Transactions. Japan Institute of Metals [*A publication*]
TJAS	Tom Jones Appreciation Society (EAIO)
TJASA.......	Transactions. Japan Society for Aeronautical and Space Sciences [*A publication*]
TJaU..........	Union University, Jackson, TN [*Library symbol*] [*Library of Congress*] (LCLS)
TJB	Theologischer Jahresbericht [*A publication*]
TJB	Tijuana Brass [*Musical group*]
TJB	Tilting Journal Bearing
TJB	Time-Sharing Job Control Block [*Data processing*] (IBMDP)
TJB	Trench Junction Box
TJBQ.........	Aguadilla/Borinquen [*Puerto Rico*] [*ICAO location identifier*] (ICLI)
T J Br Cer ...	Transactions and Journal. British Ceramic Society [*A publication*]
TJC...........	[*The*] Jockey Club (EA)
TJC...........	Targeted Jobs Credit [*Tax credit*]
TJC...........	Temple Junior College [*Texas*]
TJC...........	Thomas Jefferson Center (EA)
TJC...........	Thornton Junior College [*Illinois*]
TJC...........	Tower Jettison Command (SAA)
TJC...........	Trajectory Chart

TJC .... Trinidad [*Colorado*] [*Seismograph station code, US Geological Survey*] (SEIS)
TJC .... Tyler Junior College [*Texas*]
TJC .... Vanderbilt University Library, Nashville, TN [*OCLC symbol*] (OCLC)
TJCDR ...... Temporary Joint Committee on Deficit Reduction
TJCG .... Vieques/Camp Garcia Airstrip [*Puerto Rico*] [*ICAO location identifier*] (ICLI)
TJCK .... Timberjack Corp. [*NASDAQ symbol*] (NQ)
TJCO .... TJ International, Inc. [*NASDAQ symbol*] (NQ)
TJCP .... Culebra [*Puerto Rico*] [*ICAO location identifier*] (ICLI)
TJD .... Trajectory Diagram
TJE .... Trojan Energy Corp. [*Vancouver Stock Exchange symbol*]
TJE .... Turbojet Engine
TJEDS ...... Trainer Jet Exhaust Decontamination System
TJefC .... Carson-Newman College, Jefferson City, TN [*Library symbol*] [*Library of Congress*] (LCLS)
TJEMA ..... Tohoku Journal of Experimental Medicine [*A publication*]
TJEMD ...... Tokai Journal of Experimental and Clinical Medicine [*A publication*]
TJETS .... Thomas Jefferson Equal Tax Society (EA)
TJF .... Time-to-Jitter Flag
TJFA .... Fajardo [*Puerto Rico*] [*ICAO location identifier*] (ICLI)
TJFC .... [*The*] Johnsons Fan Club (EA)
TJFC .... Tex Jones Fan Club (EA)
TJFC .... Tom Jones Fan Club (EA)
TJFC .... Tomy Jennings Fan Club (EA)
TJFF .... Ramey [*Puerto Rico*] [*ICAO location identifier*] (ICLI)
TJFF .... Trans-Jordan Frontier Force [*British military*] (DMA)
TJFS .... T. J.'s [*Tom Jones'*] Fans of Soul (EA)
TJG .... Tom Jones Gadabouts (EA)
TJG .... Travel Journalists Guild (EA)
TJGTOI .... [*The*] Judge GTO International (EA)
TJHC .... Theology. Journal of Historic Christianity [*A publication*]
TJHPA ...... T'u Jang Hsueh Pao [*A publication*]
TJHPAE ... Acta Pedologica Sinica [*A publication*]
TJI .... Tabak Journal International [*A publication*]
TJI .... Tex Johnston, Inc.
TJI .... Trus-Joist I-Beam
TJID .... Terminal Job Identification (BUR)
TJIDA ...... Tokyo Jikeikai Ika Daigaku Zasshi [*A publication*]
TJIG .... San Juan/Isla Grande [*Puerto Rico*] [*ICAO location identifier*] (ICLI)
TJISRF ...... Thomas Jefferson Institute for the Study of Religious Freedom (EA)
TJIZA .... Tokyo Joshi Ika Daigaku Zasshi [*A publication*]
TJL .... [*The*] Jonxis Lectures [*Elsevier Book Series*] [*A publication*]
TJM .... Tower Jettison Motor
TJM .... Vanderbilt Medical Center, Nashville, TN [*OCLC symbol*] (OCLC)
TJMZ .... Mayaguez [*Puerto Rico*] [*ICAO location identifier*] (ICLI)
TJNR .... Roosevelt Roads Naval Air Station [*Puerto Rico*] [*ICAO location identifier*] (ICLI)
T Jo .... T. Jones' English King's Bench Reports [*84 English Reprint*] [*A publication*] (DLA)
TJOC .... Theater Joint Operations Center [*Military*]
TJoE .... Emmanuel School of Religion, Johnson City, TN [*Library symbol*] [*Library of Congress*] (LCLS)
TJoMC ...... Johnson City Medical Center Hospital, Learning Resources Center, Johnson City, TN [*Library symbol*] [*Library of Congress*] (LCLS)
T Jones ...... T. Jones' English King's Bench Reports [*84 English Reprint*] [*A publication*] (DLA)
T Jones (Eng) ... T. Jones' English King's Bench Reports [*84 English Reprint*] [*A publication*] (DLA)
TJoS .... East Tennessee State University, Johnson City, TN [*Library symbol*] [*Library of Congress*] (LCLS)
TJoS-M ..... East Tennessee State University, Medical Library, Johnson City, TN [*Library symbol*] [*Library of Congress*] (LCLS)
TJoV .... United States Veterans Administration Center, Johnson City, TN [*Library symbol*] [*Library of Congress*] (LCLS)
TJP .... Tactical Jamming Pod [*Military*] (CAAL)
TJP .... Turbojet Propulsion
TJPDA ...... Turkish Journal of Pediatrics [*A publication*]
TJPOI .... Twisted Jute Packing and Oakum Institute [*Defunct*] (EA)
TJPS .... Ponce/Mercedita [*Puerto Rico*] [*ICAO location identifier*] (ICLI)
TJQ .... Tanjung Pandan [*Indonesia*] [*Airport symbol*] (OAG)
TJQ .... Thoreau Journal Quarterly [*A publication*]
TJR .... Tactical Jammer [*Military*] (CAAL)
TJR .... Tajee Resources Ltd. [*Vancouver Stock Exchange symbol*]
TJR .... Tenri Journal of Religion [*A publication*]
TJR .... Trunk and Junction Routing [*Telecommunications*] (TEL)
TJRC .... Thomas Jefferson Research Center [*Later, TJC*] (EA)
TJS .... Tactical Jamming System
TJS .... Target Jamming System
TJS .... Tenajon Resources Corp. [*Formerly, Tenajon Silver*] [*Vancouver Stock Exchange symbol*]
TJS .... Terminal Junction System

TJS .... Timber Trades Journal and Woodworking Machinery [*Later, Timber Trades Journal and Wood Processing*] [*London*] [*A publication*]
TJS .... Transverse Junction Stripe (MCD)
TJSCA ...... Texas Journal of Science [*A publication*]
TJSF .... Temperature Jump-Stopped Flow [*Spectroscopy*]
TJSJ .... San Juan/Puerto Rico International [*Puerto Rico*] [*ICAO location identifier*] (ICLI)
TJSUDJ .... Thai Journal of Surgery [*A publication*]
TJT .... Tactical Jamming Transmitter [*Navy*]
TJT .... Tough Jeans Territory [*Sears, Roebuck & Co. advertising slogan*]
TJTA .... Taylor-Johnson Temperament Analysis [*Psychology*]
TJTC .... Targeted Jobs Tax Credits [*Federal program*]
TJTCC ...... Targeted Jobs Tax Credit Coalition (EA)
TJTTFC .... Tom Jones "Tom Terrific" Fan Club (EA)
Tju .... Tjuringa: an Australasian Benedictine Review [*A publication*] (APTA)
TJVQ .... Vieques [*Puerto Rico*] [*ICAO location identifier*] (ICLI)
TJW .... North Haven, ME [*Location identifier*] [*FAA*] (FAAL)
TJX .... TJX Companies [*NYSE symbol*] (SPSG)
TJX .... TJX Companies [*Associated Press abbreviation*] (APAG)
TJY .... Tulsa, OK [*Location identifier*] [*FAA*] (FAAL)
TJZS .... San Juan [*Puerto Rico*] [*ICAO location identifier*] (ICLI)
Tk .... Milli Kutuphane [*National Library*], Ankara, Turkey [*Library symbol*] [*Library of Congress*] (LCLS)
Tk .... T-Cell, Killer Type [*Immunology*]
TK .... Taegu [*South Korea*] (ECON)
TK .... Tank (AAG)
TK .... Tanker
TK .... Tekawennake. Six Nations. New Credit Reporter [*A publication*]
TK .... Tetzugaku-Kenkyu [*Tokyo*] [*A publication*]
T und K ..... Text und Kontext [*A publication*]
TK .... Text und Kritik [*A publication*]
TK .... Thick (ROG)
TK .... Through Knee [*Medicine*]
TK .... Thymidine Kinase [*An enzyme*]
TK .... To Kum [*i.e., To Come*] [*Publishing*]
TK .... Tokelau Islands [*ANSI two-letter standard code*] (CNC)
TK .... Tool Kits [*JETDS nomenclature*] [*Military*] (CET)
TK .... Torath Kohanim (BJA)
TK .... Track
TK .... Transducer Kit (MCD)
TK .... Transketolase [*An enzyme*]
TK .... Truck (AAG)
TK .... Trunk Equipment [*Telecommunications*] (TEL)
TK .... Turk Hava Yollari AO [*Turkish Airlines, Inc.*] [*ICAO designator*] (FAAC)
TK .... Turkey [*IYRU nationality code*]
TK .... Tuskegee R. R. [*AAR code*]
TK .... Tyrosine Kinase Domain [*Genetics*]
TKA .... Talkeetna, AK [*Location identifier*] [*FAA*] (FAAL)
TKA .... Tanaka [*New Britain*] [*Seismograph station code, US Geological Survey*] (SEIS)
TKA .... Terminator Kit Assembly [*Robot*]
TKA .... Thermokinetic Analysis
TKA .... Tonka Corp. [*NYSE symbol*] (SPSG)
TKA .... Total Knee Arthroplasty [*Medicine*]
TKA .... Toy Knights of America (EA)
TKA .... Transketolase Activity [*Medicine*] (MAE)
TKAI .... Teknowledge, Inc. [*Palo Alto, CA*] [*NASDAQ symbol*] (NQ)
TKAM ...... Knoxville Academy of Medicine, Knoxville, TN [*Library symbol*] [*Library of Congress*] (LCLS)
TKAT .... Technology 80, Inc. [*Minneapolis, MN*] [*NASDAQ symbol*] (NQ)
TKB .... Kingsville, TX [*Location identifier*] [*FAA*] (FAAL)
TKBD .... Tackboard [*Technical drawings*]
TKBN .... Tank Battalion [*Marine Corps*]
TKBRAS ... Transactions. Korean Branch. Royal Asiatic Society [*A publication*]
TKC .... Thiokol Corp. [*NYSE symbol*] (SPSG)
TKCR .... TakeCare, Inc. [*NASDAQ symbol*] (SPSG)
TKCS .... Knoxville City School, Knoxville, TN [*Library symbol*] [*Library of Congress*] (LCLS)
TKD .... Takada [*Japan*] [*Seismograph station code, US Geological Survey*] (SEIS)
TKD .... Tokodynamometer
TKD .... Top Kit Drawing
TKDE .... Tetrakis(dimethylamino)ethylene [*Organic chemistry*]
TkDtyr .... Tank Destroyer [*Military*]
TKE .... Tau Kappa Epsilon [*Fraternity*] [*Later, TEKE*]
TKE .... Tenakee [*Alaska*] [*Airport symbol*] (OAG)
TKE .... Tenakee Springs, AK [*Location identifier*] [*FAA*] (FAAL)
TKE .... Total Kinetic Energy
TKE .... Track Angle Error
TKE .... Turbulent Kinetic Energy
TKEBH...... East Tennessee Baptist Hospital, Knoxville, TN [*Library symbol*] [*Library of Congress*] (LCLS)
TKESB ...... Tekhnicheskaya Estetika [*A publication*]

TKETHi .... East Tennessee Historical Society, Knoxville, TN [*Library symbol*] [*Library of Congress*] (LCLS)

TKF........... Turkish Investment Fund [*NYSE symbol*] (SPSG)

TKFN........ Telkwa Foundation. Newsletter [*Telkwa, British Columbia*] [*A publication*]

TKFSM ..... Fort Sanders Regional Medical Center, Knoxville, TN [*Library symbol*] [*Library of Congress*] (LCLS)

TKG........... Bandar Lampung [*Indonesia*] [*Airport symbol*] (OAG)

TKG........... Capsule Technology Group, Inc. [*Toronto Stock Exchange symbol*]

TKG........... Tanking (AAG)

TKG........... Tokodynagraph

TKG........... Tongkang [*Ship's rigging*] (ROG)

TKGA....... [*The*] Knitting Guild of America (EA)

TKGJA...... Taisei Kensetsu Gijutsu Kenkyusho-Ho [*A publication*]

TKGS........ Church of Jesus Christ of Latter-Day Saints, Genealogical Society Library, Knoxville Branch, Knoxville, TN [*Library symbol*] [*Library of Congress*] (LCLS)

TKH........... Tikhaya Bay [*Former USSR*] [*Later, HIS*] [*Geomagnetic observatory code*]

TKi........... Kingsport Public Library, Kingsport, TN [*Library symbol*] [*Library of Congress*] (LCLS)

TKI............ McKinney, TX [*Location identifier*] [*FAA*] (FAAL)

TKI............ Trial Kit Installation (CAAL)

TKIBU....... Transmission-Keying Indicator Buffer (DNAB)

TKIF .... Training Name and Address Key Index File [*IRS*]

TKiH.......... Holston Valley Community Hospital, Health Science Library, Kingsport, TN [*Library symbol*] [*Library of Congress*] (LCLS)

TKimJ....... Johnson Bible College, Knoxville, TN [*Library symbol*] [*Library of Congress*] (LCLS)

TKIO .... [*The*] Tokio Marine & Fire Insurance Co. Ltd. [*NASDAQ symbol*] (NQ)

Tk J........... Tamkang Journal [*A publication*]

TKJ............ Tok, AK [*Location identifier*] [*FAA*] (FAAL)

TKK .... Token Kenkyu Kai (EA)

TKK .... Toyo Kogyo Co. [*Auto manufacturer*]

TKK .... Truk [*Caroline Islands*] [*Airport symbol*] (OAG)

TKKTFSLB ... [*The*] Kandy-Kolored Tangerine-Flake Streamline Baby [*Title of book by Tom Wolfe*]

TKL........... Knoxville-Knox County Public Library, Knoxville, TN [*OCLC symbol*] (OCLC)

TKL........... Public Library of Knoxville and Knox County, Knoxville, TN [*Library symbol*] [*Library of Congress*] (LCLS)

TKL........... Tackle [*Mechanical engineering*]

TKL........... Taku Lodge, AK [*Location identifier*] [*FAA*] (FAAL)

TKL........... Tanker Oil & Gas [*Vancouver Stock Exchange symbol*]

TKL........... Tokelau Islands [*ANSI three-letter standard code*] (CNC)

TKLaw....... Tennessee State Law Library, Knoxville, TN [*Library symbol*] [*Library of Congress*] (LCLS)

TKLC........ TEKELEC [*Calabasas, CA*] [*NASDAQ symbol*] (NQ)

TKLMI...... Lakeshore Mental Health Institute, Staff Library, Knoxville, TN [*Library symbol*] [*Library of Congress*] (LCLS)

TKLN .... Toklan Oil Corp. [*NASDAQ symbol*] (NQ)

TKM .... Takamatsu [*Japan*] [*Seismograph station code, US Geological Survey*] (SEIS)

TKM .... TRIS, Potassium Chloride, Magnesium Chloride [*A buffer*]

TKMEB..... Theoretische und Klinische Medizin in Einzeldarstellungen [*A publication*]

TKMSB..... Tekhnicheska Misul [*A publication*]

TKN........... Tek-Net International Ltd. (Canada) [*Vancouver Stock Exchange symbol*]

TKN........... Thermotrex Corp. [*AMEX symbol*] (SPSG)

TKN........... Tokuno Shima [*Japan*] [*Airport symbol*] (OAG)

TKN........... Total Kjeldahl Nitrogen [*Organic analysis*]

TKN........... Tractatenblad van het Koninkrijk der Nederlanden [*A publication*]

TKN........... University of Tennessee, Knoxville, TN [*OCLC symbol*] (OCLC)

TKNA .... Tekna-Tool, Inc. [*NASDAQ symbol*] (NQ)

TKNGMP ... Tijdschrift. Koninklijk Nederlandsch Genootschap voor Munt en Penningkunde [*A publication*]

TKNKB...... Tekniikka [*A publication*]

TKO........... Mankato, KS [*Location identifier*] [*FAA*] (FAAL)

TKO........... Taseko Mines Ltd. [*Vancouver Stock Exchange symbol*]

TKO........... Technical Knockout [*Boxing*]

TKO........... Technieuws Tokio. Korte Berichten op Technisch Wetenschappelijk Gebied [*A publication*]

TKO........... Technische Kontrollorganisation

TKO........... To Keep Open [*Medicine*]

TKO........... Trunk Offer [*Telecommunications*] (TEL)

TKOF........ Takeoff [*Aviation*]

TKP........... [*The*] Knapp Press [*Book publisher*]

TKP........... Takapoto Island [*French Polynesia*] [*Airport symbol*] (OAG)

TKP........... Theta Kappa Phi [*Fraternity*]

TKP........... Ton-Kilometer Performed

TKP........... Toplumcu Kurtulus Partisi [*Communal Liberation Party*] [*Cyprus*] [*Political party*] (EY)

TKP........... Trans Korea Pipeline

TKP........... Turkiye Komunist Partisi

TKPH .... Park West Hospital, Knoxville, TN [*Library symbol*] [*Library of Congress*] (LCLS)

TKPK........ Basseterre/Golden Rock [*St. Kitts Island*] [*ICAO location identifier*] (ICLI)

TKP-ML.... People's Revolutionary Union - Marxist-Leninist [*Turkey*] (PD)

TKPN .... Charlestown/Newcastle [*Nevis Island*] [*ICAO location identifier*] (ICLI)

TKPS .... Tuvalu and Kiribati Philatelic Society (EA)

TKQ .... Kigoma [*Tanzania*] [*Airport symbol*] (OAG)

TKR .... [*Telephone*] Talker

TkR .... Tamkang Review [*A publication*]

TKR .... Tanker (AAG)

TKR .... Terrestrial Kilometric Radiation [*Physics*]

TKR .... [*The*] Timken Co. [*Formerly, TDX*] [*NYSE symbol*] (SPSG)

TKR .... Total Knee Replacement [*Medicine*]

tkr............... Turkmen Soviet Socialist Republic [*MARC country of publication code*] [*Library of Congress*] (LCCP)

TKRAS ...... Transactions. Korean Branch. Royal Asiatic Society [*A publication*]

TKS .... Knoxville City School, Knoxville, TN [*OCLC symbol*] (OCLC)

TKS........... Tackstrip [*Technical drawings*]

TKS........... Tamavack Resources, Inc. [*Vancouver Stock Exchange symbol*]

TKS........... Thanks (ADA)

TKS........... Throttle Kicker Solenoid [*Automotive engineering*]

TKS........... Tokushima [*Japan*] [*Seismograph station code, US Geological Survey*] (SEIS)

TKS........... Tokushima [*Japan*] [*Airport symbol*] (OAG)

TKS........... Tokyo Kikai Seisakusho [*Japan*]

TKSBB ..... Tektonika Sibiri [*A publication*]

TK-SC....... Tennessee State Supreme Court Law Library, Knoxville, TN [*Library symbol*] [*Library of Congress*] [*Obsolete*] (LCLS)

TKSGB..... Tektonika i Stratigrafiya [*A publication*]

TKSMC..... Saint Mary's Medical Center, Medical Library, Knoxville, TN [*Library symbol*] [*Library of Congress*] (LCLS)

TKSMC-N ... Saint Mary's Medical Center, Nursing School Library, Knoxville, TN [*Library symbol*] [*Library of Congress*] (LCLS)

TKST .... Tukisiviksat [*A publication*]

TK SUP ..... Track Supervisor (CAAL)

TKT .... Tashkent [*Former USSR*] [*Geomagnetic observatory code*]

TKT .... Ticker Tape Resources Ltd. [*Vancouver Stock Exchange symbol*]

TKT .... Ticket

TKTEA...... Tekhnika Kino i Televideniya [*A publication*]

TKTF........ Tanker Task Force

TKTRANSR ... Tank Transporter [*Military*] (AABC)

TKTS........ Thermodynamic Kelvin Temperature Scale

TKTU .... Thymidine Kinase (Activity) Transforming Unit [*Biochemistry*]

TKTVA...... Tennessee Valley Authority, Knoxville, TN [*Library symbol*] [*Library of Congress*] (LCLS)

TKU .... Takayasuyama [*Japan*] [*Seismograph station code, US Geological Survey*] (SEIS)

TKU .... Turku [*Finland*] [*Airport symbol*] (OAG)

TKUN........ TMK/United, Inc. [*Birmingham, AL*] [*NASDAQ symbol*] (NQ)

TKV .... Tatakoto [*French Polynesia*] [*Airport symbol*] (OAG)

TKVD .... Techvend, Inc. [*NASDAQ symbol*] (NQ)

TKW .... Thermal Kilowatts

TKX .... Kennett, MO [*Location identifier*] [*FAA*] (FAAL)

TKY .... Takayama [*Japan*] [*Seismograph station code, US Geological Survey*] (SEIS)

TKZRA...... Taika Zairyo [*A publication*]

TL .... Central African Republic [*Aircraft nationality and registration mark*] (FAAC)

Tl................. Lateral Touch Neuron [*of a leech*]

TL .... Reports of the Witwatersrand High Court [*Transvaal, South Africa*] [*A publication*] (DLA)

TL .... Tackline [*British naval signaling*]

T/L............. Tactical Landing

TL .... Tail-Lift [*of trucks and vans*] (DCTA)

T/L............. Talk/Listen (NASA)

TL .... Tank Lease (ADA)

TL .... Tape Library (BUR)

TL .... Target Language

TL .... Target Loss (OA)

TL .... Task Leader (NRCH)

T/L............. Task List (KSC)

TL .... Team Leader (AABC)

TL .... Technical Letter

TL .... Technical Library

TL .... Technical Limit

TL .... Telegraphist-Lieutenant [*Navy*] [*British*]

T-L............. Tennessee State Law Library, Nashville, TN [*Library symbol*] [*Library of Congress*] (LCLS)

TL .... Terminal Limen

TL .... Terra Lliure [*Free Land*] [*Spanish terrorist group*]

TL .... Test Laboratory (AFM)

TL .... Test Link

TL .... Test Load

TL	Test Log (IEEE)
TL	Testolactone [*Biochemistry*]
TL	Texas League [*Baseball*]
Tl	Thallium [*Chemical element*]
TL	Theologische Literaturzeitung [*A publication*]
TL	Theologisches Literaturblatt [*Leipzig*] [*A publication*]
TL	Theoretical Linguistics [*Berlin*] [*A publication*]
TL	Therapeutic Level [*Medicine*]
TL	Thermal Liquefaction [*Chemical engineering*]
TL	Thermoluminescence [*Also, THL*]
TL	Thoreau Lyceum (EA)
T & L	Thrift & Loans [*Industrial loan company*]
TL	Throws Left-Handed [*Baseball*]
TL	Thrust Level (NASA)
TL ...	Thrust Line
TL	Thymic Lymphoma [*Medicine*]
TL	Thymus-Derived Lymphocyte [*Hematology*]
TL	Thymus Leukemia [*Hematology*]
TL	Ticket of Leave (ADA)
TL	Tie Line [*Communication channel*]
TL	Time, Inc. [*NYSE symbol*] [*Later, TWX*] (SPSG)
TL	Time of Landing
TL	Time Lapse (MAE)
TL	Time Latest (NASA)
TL	Time to Launch [*Navy*] (CAAL)
TL	Time Lengths
T-L	Time-Life Books [*Publisher*]
TL	Time Limit
TL	Time Line
T/L	Time Loan [*Banking*]
TL	Timeline (MCD)
TL	Title List
tl	Tokelau Islands [*MARC country of publication code*] [*Library of Congress*] (LCCP)
TL	Ton Load
TL	Tool Life
TL	Tool List
TL	Tools [*JETDS nomenclature*] [*Military*] (CET)
TL	Torpedo Lieutenant [*Navy*] [*British*]
TL	Torus Longitudinalis [*Anatomy*]
TL	Total
TL	Total Body Length [*Of Crustacea*]
TL	Total Length
TL	Total Lipids [*Clinical chemistry*]
TL	Total Load [*Engineering*]
TL	Total Loss [*Insurance*]
TL	Total Luminescence [*Spectroscopy*]
TL	Tower of London
TL	Tracker Lock [*NASA*] (KSC)
TL	Trade-Last
TL	Trade List (IIA)
TL	Trading Limit
T/L	Training Literature
TL	Trans Mediterranean Airlines [*Lebanon*] [*ICAO designator*] (FAAC)
TL	Transaction Language
TL	Transaction Listing (AFM)
TL	Transfer Line [*Manufacturing*]
T/L	Transformer Load (NASA)
TL	Transforming Lens
TL	Transient Load (MCD)
TL	Translocation Defect [*Medicine*]
TL	Transmission Level [*or Line*]
TL	Transmittal Letter (AAG)
TL	Transmitter Location
T/L	Transporter/Launcher [*NASA*] (KSC)
T/L	Transporter/Loader (MCD)
TL	Trial
TL	Triboluminescence [*Atomic physics*]
TL	Triple-Layer [*Pharmacy*]
TL	Triple Lindy [*Dance step*]
TL	Truck Lock [*Nuclear energy*] (NRCH)
TL	Truckload [*24,000 pounds or more*]
T-i-L	Truth-in-Lending Act [*1968*]
TL	Trybuna Literacka [*A publication*]
TL	Tubal Ligation [*Medicine*]
TL	Turkish Lira (BJA)
T²L	Turntable Ladder
T²L	Transistor-Transistor Logic [*Also, TTL*]
TLA	A-A-A Air Enterprises, Inc. [*Omaha, NE*] [*FAA designator*] (FAAC)
TLA	Tatlar Resources Ltd. [*Vancouver Stock Exchange symbol*]
TLA	Tax Lawyer [*A publication*]
TLA	Teller [*Alaska*] [*Airport symbol*] (OAG)
TLA	Teller, AK [*Location identifier*] [*FAA*] (FAAL)
TLA	Temporary Lodging Allowance [*Military*]
TLA	Terminal Low Altitude
TLA	Textile Labor Association [*India*]
TLA	Theatre Library Association (EA)
TLA	Throttle Lever Angle (MCD)
TLA	Time Line Analysis

TLA	Toy Libraries Association [*British*]
TLa	Transition Layer
TLA	Translumbar Aortogram [*Medicine*]
TLA	Transmission Line Adapter [*or Assembly*]
TLA	Transportation Lawyers Association (EA)
TLA	Travel and Living Allowance [*Military*] (AABC)
TLA	Trunk Line Association
TLAB	Tellabs, Inc. [*NASDAQ symbol*] (NQ)
TLAB	Translation Lookaside Buffer [*Data processing*] (CMD)
TLAC	Test Listening Accuracy in Children [*Educational test*]
TLAC	Top Loading Air Cleaner (MCD)
TLACV	Track-Laying Air-Cushion Vehicle
TLAM	Tomahawk Land Attack Missile (MCD)
TLAM	Tony Lama Co., Inc. [*NASDAQ symbol*] (NQ)
TLAM-N ...	Tomahawk Land Attack Missile - Nuclear (MCD)
TLAR	Tele-Art, Inc. [*NASDAQ symbol*]
TLAS	Tactical Logical and Air Simulation
TLAT	TOW [*Tube-Launched, Optically Tracked, Wire-Guided (Weapon)*] Light Antitank Battalion (MCD)
T Lawyr.....	Tax Lawyer [*A publication*] (ILCA)
TLAY	Tule Lake Aster Yellows [*Plant pathology*]
TLB...........	Temporary Lighted Buoy [*Maps and charts*]
TLB...........	Texas-Louisiana Freight Bureau, St. Louis MO [*STAC*]
TLB...........	Theologisches Literaturblatt [*A publication*]
TLB...........	Time-Life Books
TLB...........	Tractor/Loader/Backhoe
TLB...........	Trailer Launch Bridge (DWSG)
TLB...........	Translation Lookaside Buffer [*Data processing*] (BUR)
TLBAA	Texas Longhorn Breeders Association of America (EA)
TL/BBC.....	Tax Limitation/Balanced Budget Coalition (EA)
TLBID......	TLB [*Translation - Lookaside - Buffers*] Identifier
TLBl.........	Theologisches Literaturblatt [*A publication*]
TLBR........	Tactical LASER Beam Recorder (MCD)
TLC...........	[*The*] Learning Channel [*Cable-television system*]
TLC...........	Lee College, Cleveland, TN [*OCLC symbol*] (OCLC)
TLC...........	T-Lymphocyte Clones [*Immunology*]
TLC...........	Tactical Leadership Course [*Army*] (INF)
TLC...........	Tangent Latitude Computer
TLC...........	Tank Landing Craft [*Army*] [*British*]
TLC...........	Task Level Controller
TLC...........	Tele-Link, Inc. [*Miami, FL*] [*Telecommunications service*] (TSSD)
TLC...........	Telecommand (NASA)
TLC...........	Teletype, Line Printer, Card Reader Controller (NOAA)
TLC...........	Television Licensing Center (EA)
TLC...........	Tender Loving Care
TLC...........	Test of Language Competence [*Educational test*]
TLC...........	Texas Lutheran College
TLC...........	Textile Laundry Council (EA)
TLC...........	Thin-Layer Chromatography [*Analytical chemistry*]
TLC...........	Tillicum Industry [*Vancouver Stock Exchange symbol*]
TLC...........	Time-Lapse Cinematography
TLC...........	Time Line Controller
TLC...........	Tom's Love Connection (EA)
TLC...........	Total L-Chain Concentration
TLC...........	Total Load Control (MCD)
TLC...........	Total Lung Capacity [*Physiology*]
TLC...........	Total Lung Compliance [*Medicine*]
TLC...........	Total Lymphocyte Count [*Clinical chemistry*]
TLC...........	Touch and Learn Computer
TLC...........	Transferable Loan Certificate
TLC...........	Transient Late Curvature [*Orthopedics*]
TLC...........	Translunar Coast [*Aerospace*]
TLC...........	Tri-County Library Council, Inc. [*Library network*]
TLC...........	Trilateral Commission [*International study group*]
TLC...........	Troubles/Requests Logging and Coordination [*Staff*] [*Data processing*]
TLC...........	Type and Learn Concept [*Minolta Corp. office system*]
TLCA........	Tangent Latitude Computer Amplifier
TLCC.........	Telecalc, Inc. [*Bellevue, WA*] [*NASDAQ symbol*] (NQ)
TLCC.........	Thin-Line Communications Connectivity
TLC(C)......	Trades and Labour Congress of Canada [*1883-1956*]
TLCCP......	Total Life Cycle Competition Plan [*Army*]
TLCCS......	Total Life Cycle Competition Strategy [*Army*]
TLCE........	Transmission Line Conditioning Equipment (MCD)
TLCF........	Tactical Link Control Facility [*Military*] (CAAL)
TLCI........	Tea Leaf Club International (EA)
TLCI.........	Tender Loving Care Health Care, Inc. [*NASDAQ symbol*] (NQ)
TLC/IR......	Thin-Layer Chromatography/Infrared [*Analytical chemistry*]
TLCK........	Tosyllysine Chloromethyl Ketone [*Biochemistry*]
T-LCL.......	T-Cell Lymphosarcoma Cell Leukemia [*Oncology*]
TLCN........	Talcon LP [*NASDAQ symbol*] (NQ)
TLCO........	Teleco Oilfield Service [*NASDAQ symbol*] (NQ)
TLCOA......	Telecommunications [*Dedham, MA*] [*A publication*]
TLCPC......	Trunk Line-Central Passenger Committee
TLCR........	Telecrafter Corp. [*NASDAQ symbol*] (NQ)
TLCSC......	Top Level Computer Software Component
TLCT........	Total Life Cycle Time
TL-CTR.....	Trunk Line-Central Territory Railroad Tariff Bureau
TLCV.........	Tobacco Leaf Curl Virus [*Plant pathology*]

TLD .... [*The*] Living Daylights [*A publication*] (APTA)
TLD .... Technical Logistics Data [*Army*] (AABC)
TLD .... Thermoluminescent Device
TLD .... Thermoluminescent Dosimeter [*or Dosimetry*]
TLD .... Thoracic Lymph Duct [*Medicine*] (MAE)
TLD .... Tiled [*Classified advertising*] (ADA)
TLD .... Traffic Loading Device (CAAL)
TLD .... Tumor Lethal Dose [*Medicine*] (MAE)
TLDB........ Transportation Legislative Data Base [*Department of Energy*] [*Battelle Memorial Institute*] [*Information service or system*] (IID)
TLDC......... Taiwan Land Development Corp.
TLDF......... Thomas Legal Defense Fund (EA)
TLDI .... Technical Logistics Data and Information [*Army*] (AABC)
TLDIP .... Technical Logistics Data Information Program
TLDP........ Technical Logistics Data Program [*Navy*] (DNAB)
TLE............ [*The*] Learning Exchange (EA)
TLE............ Target Location Error [*Military*] (AABC)
TLE............ Technical Liaison Engineer
TLE............ Temperature-Limited Emission
TLE............ Temporal Lobe Epilepsy [*Medicine*]
TLE............ Thin-Layer Electrophoresis [*Analytical chemistry*]
TLE............ Thin Leading Edge
TLE............ Total Erickson Resources Ltd. [*Toronto Stock Exchange symbol*] [*Vancouver Stock Exchange symbol*]
TLE............ Total Lipid Extract [*Biochemistry*]
TLE............ Toward Liberal Education [*In book title*]
TLE............ Tower Lighting Equipment
TLE............ Tracking Light Electronics (KSC)
TLE............ Traffic Law Enforcement
TLE............ Transferline Heat Exchanger [*Chemical engineering*]
TLE............ Tulear [*Madagascar*] [*Airport symbol*] (OAG)
TLebC........ Cumberland College of Tennessee, Lebanon, TN [*Library symbol*] [*Library of Congress*] (LCLS)
TLEICS ..... Treasury Law Enforcement Information and Communications System
T Letterkd ... Tydskrif vir Letterkunde [*A publication*]
TLEV......... Transitional Low-Emission Vehicle
TLEX........ Total Erickson Resources Ltd. [*North Vancouver, BC*] [*NASDAQ symbol*] (NQ)
TLF........... Temporary Loading Facilities (MCD)
TLF........... Temporary Lodging Facility
TLF........... Terminal Launch Facility
TLF........... Textes Litteraires Francais [*A publication*]
TLF........... Thrust Required for Level Flight [*Aviation*] (MCD)
TLF........... Time Line Form
TLF........... Trunk Link Frame [*Telecommunications*] (TEL)
TLFB .... Texas-Louisiana Freight Bureau
TLFC .... Terri LaVelle Fan Club (EA)
TLFC .... Traci Lords Fan Club (EA)
TLFN........ Tunison Laboratory of Fish Nutrition [*Department of the Interior*] [*Cortland, NY*] (GRD)
TLG .... Consolidated Thompson-Lundmark Gold Mines Ltd. [*Toronto Stock Exchange symbol*]
TLG .... Tail Landing Gear
TLG .... Talgar [*Also, AAB*] [*Alma-Ata*] [*Former USSR*] [*Seismograph station code, US Geological Survey*] (SEIS)
TLG .... Telegraph (AAG)
TLG .... Tentative Logistics Guidance (MCD)
TLG .... Thin-Layer Gel [*Filtration*] [*Analytical chemistry*]
TLG .... Tilting
TLGB .... Tube-Launched Guided Projectiles (MCD)
TLH .... Tallahassee [*Florida*] [*Airport symbol*] (OAG)
TLH .... Tulloch Resources [*Vancouver Stock Exchange symbol*]
TLHS........ Thin Line Handling System (DWSG)
TLHT .... Total Health Systems, Inc. [*Great Neck, NY*] [*NASDAQ symbol*] (NQ)
TLI............ T-Logic, Inc. [*Information service or system*] (IID)
TLI............ Tank Level Indicator (DNAB)
TLI............ Telephone Line Interface (IEEE)
TLI............ Term Life Insurance
TLI............ Theoretical Lethality Index (MCD)
TLI............ Thymidine-Labeling Index [*Oncology*]
TLI............ Time-Life International
tli.............. Tlingit [*MARC language code*] [*Library of Congress*] (LCCP)
TLI............ Tolitoli [*Indonesia*] [*Airport symbol*] (OAG)
TLI............ Total Lymphoid Irradiation
TLI............ Translunar Injection [*Aerospace*]
TLI............ Transport Layer Interface [*Data processing*] (PCM)
TLI............ Triangle Resources, Inc. [*Vancouver Stock Exchange symbol*]
TLI............ Trinidad Light Infantry [*British military*] (DMA)
TLI............ True Life Institute (EA)
TLIB .... Tape Library [*National Center for Atmospheric Research*]
TLIB .... Transportation Library [*National Academy of Sciences*] [*Information service or system*] (IID)
TLIEF....... Thin-Layer Isoelectric Focusing [*Analytical chemistry*]
TLIG......... Tasmanian Legal Information Guide [*A publication*] (APTA)
TLII .... Trans Leasing International, Inc. [*Northbrook, IL*] [*NASDAQ symbol*] (NQ)
TLJ .... Laredo Junior College, Laredo, TX [*OCLC symbol*] (OCLC)
TLJ .... Tatalina [*Alaska*] [*Airport symbol*] (OAG)

TLJ .... Tatalina, AK [*Location identifier*] [*FAA*] (FAAL)
TLJ .... Transportation Law Journal [*A publication*]
TLJ .... Travancore Law Journal [*India*] [*A publication*] (DLA)
TLK........... New York, NY [*Location identifier*] [*FAA*] (FAAL)
TLK........... Talkeetna Mountains [*Alaska*] [*Seismograph station code, US Geological Survey*] (SEIS)
TLK........... Talking [*Telecommunications*] (TEL)
TLK........... Teaching London Kids [*A publication*]
TLK........... Test Link (IEEE)
TLK........... University of Tennessee, Law Library, Knoxville, TN [*OCLC symbol*] (OCLC)
T-LL......... T-Cell Lymphoblastic Lymphoma [*Oncology*]
TLL........... Tallinn [*Former USSR*] [*Airport symbol*] (OAG)
TLL........... Tank Lighter
TLL........... Television LASER Link
TLL........... Tender Load List
TLL........... Threshold Lactose Load [*Clinical chemistry*]
TLL........... Tololo Astronomical Observatory [*Chile*] [*Seismograph station code, US Geological Survey*] (SEIS)
TLL........... Tom's Look of Love (EA)
TLL........... Transporter, Loader, Launcher
TLLD........ Total Load
TLLM........ Temperature and Liquid Level Monitor [*Nuclear energy*] (NRCH)
TLLS........ Tellus Industries, Inc. [*Sacramento, CA*] [*NASDAQ symbol*] (NQ)
TLLW....... Tank Lighter (Medium Tank-Well Type)
TLM .... Technical Liaison Memo
TLM .... Telemeter [*or Telemetry*] (AAG)
TLM .... Thin Lipid Membrane (OA)
TLM .... Tilimsen [*Algeria*] [*Airport symbol*] (OAG)
TLM .... Toledo-Lucas County Public Library, Toledo, OH [*OCLC symbol*] (OCLC)
TLM .... Tolmezzo [*Italy*] [*Seismograph station code, US Geological Survey*] (SEIS)
TLM .... Transmission Line Method [*Photovoltaic energy systems*]
TLM .... Transmitted Light Microscope
TLM .... Trillium Telephone Systems, Inc. [*Toronto Stock Exchange symbol*]
TLM .... Tube-Launched Missile (MCD)
TLMA....... Trial Lawyers Marketing Association (EA)
TLMB....... Telemetry Data Buffer
TLMD .... Telemundo Group, Inc. [*NASDAQ symbol*] (NQ)
TLMG .... Telemetering (AAG)
TLMI......... Tag and Label Manufacturers Institute (EA)
TLMMDD ... Malaysia. Ministry of Agriculture. Technical Leaflet [*A publication*]
TLMN .... Talman Home Federal Savings & Loan Association of Illinois [*NASDAQ symbol*] (NQ)
TLMS....... Tape Library Management System
TLMT....... Telemation, Inc. [*NASDAQ symbol*] (NQ)
TLMY....... Telemetry (MSA)
TLN .... Talang [*Sumatra*] [*Seismograph station code, US Geological Survey*] [*Closed*] (SEIS)
TLN .... Tasmanian Law Newsletter [*A publication*]
TLN .... Thermolysin [*An enzyme*]
TLN .... Title plus Last Name
TLN .... Torque-Limiting Nut
TLN .... Toulon/Hyeres [*France*] [*Airport symbol*] (OAG)
TLN .... Transmittal Locator Number [*Data processing*]
TLN .... Trunk Line Network
TLNDA ..... Telonde [*France*] [*A publication*]
TLO .... [*The*] Last One [*A microcomputer program manufactured by DJ-AI*]
TLO .... [*The*] Lifestyles Organization (EA)
TLO .... Technical Liaison Office [*Military*]
TLO .... Terminal Learning Objective
TLO .... Tol [*Papua New Guinea*] [*Airport symbol*] (OAG)
TLO .... Toledo [*Spain*] [*Seismograph station code, US Geological Survey*] (SEIS)
TLO .... Total Loss Only
TLO .... Tracking Local Oscillator
TLO .... Training Liaison Officer [*Ministry of Agriculture, Fisheries, and Food*] [*British*]
TLOBS ...... Tailored List of Base Spares [*Military*] (AFIT)
TLOCC...... Tomlinson Oil [*NASDAQ symbol*] (NQ)
TLOG .... Transform Logic Corp. [*Scottsdale, AZ*] [*NASDAQ symbol*] (NQ)
TLOP........ [*The*] Language of Poetry [*A publication*]
TLOS........ Tailored List of Spares [*Military*] (AFIT)
TLOS........ Telos Corp. [*Santa Monica, CA*] [*NASDAQ symbol*] (NQ)
TLOS........ Troop List for Operations and Supply
TLO(S)..... Turbine Lube Oil (System) [*Nuclear energy*] (NRCH)
TLOST ...... Turbine Lube Oil Storage Tank [*Nuclear energy*] (NRCH)
TLP........... Tabular List of Parts (AAG)
TLP........... Tactical Leadership Program [*Military*]
T/LP......... Tail Lamp [*Automotive engineering*]
TLP........... Tapered Link Pin
TLP........... Target Letter Position [*Psychology*]
TLP........... Telegraph Line Pair (BUR)
TLP........... Telephone Line Patch

TLP........... Tenera Ltd. [*AMEX symbol*] (SPSG)
TLP........... Tension-Leg Platform [*Oil exploration*]
TLP........... Term-Limit Pricing [*Agreement*] [*Price Commission*]
TLP........... Therapeutic Learning Program [*Psychology*]
TLP........... Threshold Learning Process (IEEE)
TLP........... Top Load Pad (NRCH)
TLP........... Top Load Plane [*Nuclear energy*] (NRCH)
TLP........... Torpedo Landplane [*Navy*]
TLP........... Total Language Processor [*Data processing*] (IEEE)
TLP........... Total Liquid Product [*Chemical engineering*]
TLP........... Total Loss of Pay [*Court-martial sentence*] [*Military*]
TLP........... Transient Lunar Phenomena
TLP........... Transmission Level Point [*Telecommunications*]
TLP........... Tribal Liaison Program [*Bureau of the Census*] (GFGA)
TLP........... Troop-Leading Procedure [*Military*] (INF)
TLP........... Trouble Location Problem (AAG)
TLP........... Truck Loading Point (NATG)
0TLP......... Zero Transmission Level Point (IEEE)
TLPC........ Castries/Vigie [*St. Lucia*] [*ICAO location identifier*] (ICLI)
TLPC........ Tailpiece
TLPJ......... Trial Lawyers for Public Justice (EA)
TLPL......... Vieux-Fort/Hewanorra International [*St. Lucia*] [*ICAO location identifier*] (ICLI)
TLPR......... Terrestrial Low-Power Reactor
TLPWD..... Tory Legacy Plus World Depression [*British*] (DI)
TLQ.......... Temple Law Quarterly [*A publication*]
TLQ.......... Temporary Lodging Quarters [*Military*] (DNAB)
TLQ.......... Tender Load Quantities (DNAB)
TLQ.......... Total Living Quotient (MAE)
TLR........... Tailor
TLR........... Tally Resources [*Vancouver Stock Exchange symbol*]
TLR........... Tanganyika Law Reports [*1921-52*] [*A publication*] (DLA)
TLR........... Tanzania Gazette Law Reports [*A publication*] (DLA)
TLR........... Tape Loop Recorder
TLR........... Tasmanian Law Reports [*A publication*] (APTA)
TLR........... Tax Law Review [*A publication*]
TLR........... Telerate, Inc. [*NYSE symbol*] (SPSG)
TLR........... Teller
TLR........... Tiler [*Freemasonry*]
TLR........... Tiller (MSA)
TLR........... Times Law Reports [*1884-1952*] [*England*] [*A publication*] (DLA)
TLR........... Toll Line Release
TLR........... Tool Liaison Request (AAG)
TLR........... Top Level Requirements [*Navy*]
TLR........... Topped Long Resid [*Petroleum technology*]
TLR........... Trailer (AAG)
TLR........... Travancore Law Reports [*India*] [*A publication*] (DLA)
TLR........... Triangulation-Listening-Ranging [*SONAR*]
TLR........... Tulane Law Review [*A publication*]
TLR........... Tulare, CA [*Location identifier*] [*FAA*] (FAAL)
TLR........... Twin Lens Reflex [*Camera*] (MCD)
TLRB........ Textile Labor Relations Board [*Terminated, 1937; functions absorbed by US Conciliation Service, Department of Labor*]
TLRC........ Technology and Livelihood Resource Center [*Philippines*] [*Information service or system*] (IID)
TLRG........ Target List Review Group (CINC)
TLRMTD.. Trailer Mounted
TLRNC...... Tolerance (FAAC)
TLRP........ Track Last Reference Position
TLR (R)..... Tanganyika Law Reports (Revised) [*1921-52*] [*A publication*] (DLA)
TLR/S........ Total Logistic Readiness/Sustainability Analysis [*Military*]
TLRS......... Transportable LASER Ranging Station [*for measurement of earth movement*]
TLRT........ Telerent Leasing Corp. [*NASDAQ symbol*] (NQ)
TLRV........ Tracked Levitated Research Vehicle
TLS........... Laredo State University, Laredo, TX [*OCLC symbol*] (OCLC)
TLS........... Tactical Landing System
TLS........... Talasea [*New Britain*] [*Seismograph station code, US Geological Survey*] (SEIS)
TLS........... Tank LASER Sight (MCD)
TLS........... Tape Librarian System
TLS........... Target Location System
TLS........... Technical Library Service (IID)
TLS........... Telecommunication Liaison Staff (IEEE)
TLS........... Telemetry Listing Submodule
TLS........... Telepanel Systems [*Toronto Stock Exchange symbol*] (SPSG)
TLS........... Telescope (KSC)
TLS........... Terminal Landing System (KSC)
TLS........... Territorial Long Service Medal [*Military*] [*British*]
TLS........... Testing the Limits for Sex [*Psychology*]
TLS........... Theater Level Scenario [*Military*]
TLS........... Thin Liquid Stillage [*Fermentation byproduct*]
TLS........... Throttle Lever Setting (KSC)
TLS........... Tifton Loamy Soil [*Agronomy*]
TLS........... Time-Limited Signal
TLS........... Time Line Sheet [*NASA*]
TLS........... Times Literary Supplement [*London*] [*A publication*]
TLS........... Top Left Side (MCD)

TLS........... Top Level Specification [*Military*] (CAAL)
TLS........... Total Library System [*OCLC*]
TLS........... Total Logic Solution
TLS........... Total Luminescence Spectroscopy
TLS........... Toulouse [*France*] [*Airport symbol*] (OAG)
TLS........... Training Launch Station (MCD)
TLS........... Two-Level System [*Physics*]
TLS........... Typed Letter Signed
TLSA........ Torso Limb Suit Assembly (MCD)
TLSA........ Transparent Line Sharing Adapter
TLSC........ Target Logistics Support Costs
TLSC......... TLS Co. [*NASDAQ symbol*] (NQ)
TLSCP....... Telescope (MSA)
TLSD........ Torque-Limiting Screwdriver
TLSFT....... Tailshaft
TLSG........ Turret Lathe Stop Gauge
TLSGT...... Tactical Landing System Guidance Techniques (MCD)
TLSM....... Talouselama [*A publication*]
TLSO........ Thoracolumbosacral Orthosis [*Medicine*]
TLSP........ Telecommunications Specialists, Inc. [*NASDAQ symbol*] (NQ)
TLSP........ Transponder Location by Surface Positioning [*RADAR*]
TLSS......... Tactical Life Support System [*G-suit developed by Boeing Co.*]
TLSS......... Technical Library Services Section
TLSS......... Telesis Systems Corp. [*Chelmsford, MA*] [*NASDAQ symbol*] (NQ)
TLT........... LeTourneau College, Longview, TX [*OCLC symbol*] (OCLC)
TLT........... Teleprinter Load Tables (KSC)
TLT........... Telstar Resource Corp. [*Vancouver Stock Exchange symbol*]
TLT........... Toilet
TLT........... Transportable Link Terminal [*AMC*]
TLT........... Travancore Law Times [*India*] [*A publication*] (DLA)
TLT........... Tuluksak [*Alaska*] [*Airport symbol*] (OAG)
TLT........... Tuluksak, AK [*Location identifier*] [*FAA*] (FAAL)
TLTA........ Thin Line Towed Array [*Navy*] (CAAL)
TLTA........ Two-Loop Test Apparatus [*Nuclear energy*] (NRCH)
TLTB........ Trunk Line Tariff Bureau
TLTC........ Ta-Lu Tsa-Chih [*Continent Magazine*] [*Taiwan*] [*A publication*]
TLTK........ Teletek, Inc. [*NASDAQ symbol*] (NQ)
TLTK........ Tool Truck
TL to TL... Tangent Line to Tangent Line [*Engineering*]
TLTL........ Teaching Language through Literature [*A publication*]
TLTM....... Teletimer International, Inc. [*NASDAQ symbol*] (NQ)
TLTM....... Third Level Thermal Margin [*Nuclear energy*] (NRCH)
TLTP........ Too Long to Print [*Strip marking*] [*Aviation*] (FAAC)
TLTP........ Trunk Line Test Panel [*Telecommunications*] (TEL)
TLTR........ Translator (AFM)
TLTS........ Tracking Loop Test Set
TLU.......... Table Look Up [*Data processing*]
TLU.......... Terminal Logic Unit [*Telecommunications*] (TEL)
TLU.......... Threshold Logic Unit
TLU.......... Time of Last Update
TLU.......... Tolu [*Colombia*] [*Airport symbol*] (OAG)
TLU.......... Transportable LASER Unit
TLU.......... Tropical Livestock Unit [*Ratio of livestock to humans*]
TLV.......... Talemon Investments Ltd. [*Vancouver Stock Exchange symbol*]
TLV.......... Target Launch Vehicle [*NASA*]
TLV.......... Tel Aviv-Yafo [*Israel*] [*Airport symbol*] (OAG)
TLV.......... Test Launch Vehicle (MCD)
TLV.......... Threshold Limit Value [*Industrial hygiene*]
TLV.......... Total Lung Volume [*Physiology*]
TLV.......... Track Levitated Vehicle [*Department of Transportation*]
TLv.......... Transition Level
TLV.......... Transporter - Loader Vehicle [*NASA*] (NASA)
TLV.......... Two-Lung Ventilation [*Medicine*]
TLW.......... [*The*] Lighted Way [*An association*] (EA)
TLW.......... Test Load Wire
TLW.......... Torpedo Lieutenant's Writer [*British military*] (DMA)
TLWD....... Tail Wind (FAAC)
TLWM...... Trinity Low-Water Mark
TLWS........ Terrier Land Weapon System
T Lwyr..... Tax Lawyer [*A publication*]
TLX........... TELEX [*Automated Teletypewriter Exchange Service*] [*Western Union Corp.*]
TLX........... Thin-Layer Explosive (MCD)
TLX........... Trans-Lux Corp. [*AMEX symbol*] (SPSG)
TLX........... Transfer-Line Exchanger [*Manufacturing technology*]
TLX........... Tri-Line Expressways Ltd. [*Toronto Stock Exchange symbol*]
TLX........... Trophoblast/Lymphocyte Cross-Reactive (Antigens) [*Immunochemistry*]
TLXN........ Telxon Corp. [*NASDAQ symbol*] (NQ)
TLY.......... Tally
TLYYA4.... Co-Operative Bulletin. Taiwan Forestry Research Institute [*A publication*]
TLZ........... Target Launch Zone
TLZ........... Theologische Literaturzeitung [*A publication*]
TLZ........... Titanium-Lead-Zinc
TLZ........... Transfer on Less than Zero
TM............ Linhas Aereas de Mocambique [*LAM*] [*Mozambique*] [*ICAO designator*] (FAAC)

TM..............	[*The*] Maccabees [*Southfield, MI*] (EA)	TM.............	Track Monitor (CAAL)
TM..............	Memphis-Shelby County Public Library and Information Center, Memphis, TN [*Library symbol*] [*Library of Congress*] (LCLS)	TM.............	Tractor Monoplane
		TM.............	Trade Mission
		TM.............	Trademark
TM..............	National Income Tax Magazine [*A publication*] (DLA)	TM.............	Traffic Management [*A publication*]
TM..............	T-Cell Marker [*Biochemistry*]	TM.............	Traffic Manager
TM..............	Table Maintenance (NASA)	TM.............	Traffic Model (NASA)
TM..............	Tactical Manager [*Military*] (CAAL)	TM.............	Trager's Medium [*Chemically defined culture medium*]
TM..............	Tactical Missile [*Air Force*]	TM.............	Trained Man [*British military*] (DMA)
TM..............	Tactical Monitor	TM.............	Training Manual [*Military*]
TM..............	Tailor-Made (DSUE)	TM.............	Training Memorandum (DAS)
TM..............	Take-Off Mass (SAA)	TM.............	Training Missions [*Air Force*]
TM..............	Talking Machine	TM.............	Trainmaster [*Railroading*]
TM..............	Tangent Mechanism	TM.............	Transantarctic Mountains
TM..............	Tape Mark [*Data processing*] (BUR)	TM.............	Transcendental Meditation
TM..............	Tape Module (DEN)	TM.............	Transfer Memorandum
TM..............	Target Mechanism (MCD)	TM.............	Transition Management
TM..............	Taurine Mustard [*Antineoplastic drug*]	TM.............	Transition Metal (MCD)
TM..............	Tax Magazine [*A publication*] (DLA)	TM.............	"Transitional" Mucosa [*Oncology*]
TM..............	Tax Management [*A publication*] (DLA)	TM.............	Transmedullary [*Anatomy*]
TM..............	Tax Memo [*A publication*] (DLA)	TM.............	Transmembrane Domain [*Genetics*]
TM..............	Tax Module [*IRS*]	TM.............	Transmembrane Substitution Mutants [*Genetics*]
TM..............	Team (AABC)	TM.............	Transmetatarsal [*Anatomy*]
TM..............	Team Member	TM.............	Transmission Matrix (IEEE)
TM..............	Technical Manager	TM.............	Transmittal Memorandum (MCD)
TM..............	Technical Manual	TM.............	Transport Mechanism [*Physiology*]
TM..............	Technical Memorandum	TM.............	Transverse Magnetic
TM..............	Technical Minutes	TM.............	Travelwriter Marketletter [*Information service or system*] (IID)
TM..............	Technical Monograph		
TM..............	Tectorial Membrane [*of the cochlea*] [*Ear anatomy*]	TM.............	Trench Mortar
TM..............	Tele-Metropole, Inc. [*Toronto Stock Exchange symbol*]	TM.............	Trial Modification (SAA)
TM..............	Telegramme Multiple [*Telegram with Multiple Addresses*] [*French*] (ROG)	TM.............	Trombone, Muted
		TM.............	Tropical Maritime
TM..............	Telemetry	TM.............	Tropical Medicine
TM..............	Telephone Museum (EA)	TM.............	Tropomyosin [*Biochemistry*]
TM..............	Temperature, Mean	TM.............	True Mean
TM..............	Temperature Meter	TM.............	True Motion [*RADAR*] (DEN)
TM..............	Temperature Monitor (NRCH)	TM.............	Truncation Mutant
TM..............	Temple Magazine [*A publication*] (ROG)	TM.............	Tuberal Magnocellular [*Nuclei, neuroanatomy*]
TM..............	Temple of Man (EA)	TM.............	Tunicamycin [*Biochemistry*]
T & M	Temple and Mew's English Criminal Appeal Cases [*A publication*] (DLA)	TM.............	Tuning Meter (DEN)
		TM.............	Turing Machine [*Mathematical model*] [*Data processing*]
T & M	Temple and Mew's English Crown Cases [*1848-51*] [*A publication*] (DLA)	TM.............	Turkiyat Mecmuasi [*A publication*]
		TM.............	Twisting Moment
TM..............	Temporomandibular [*Anatomy*]	TM.............	Tygodnik Morski [*A publication*]
TM..............	Temps Modernes [*A publication*]	TM.............	Tympanic Membrane [*Anatomy*]
TM..............	Tennessee Musician [*A publication*]	TM1	Torpedoman's Mate, First Class [*Navy rating*]
TM..............	Tenu'at Ha-Moshavim (BJA)	T/M²	Metric Tons per Square Meter
TM..............	Test Manual	TM2	Torpedoman's Mate, Second Class [*Navy rating*]
T & M	Test and Measurement [*Quality control*]	T/M³	Metric Tons per Cubic Meter
TM..............	Test Mode	TM3	Torpedoman's Mate, Third Class [*Navy rating*]
TM..............	Test Model [*NASA*]	TMA..........	Memphis Academy of Arts, Memphis, TN [*Library symbol*] [*Library of Congress*] (LCLS)
T & M	Test and Monitor (CAAL)		
TM..............	Texas Mexican Railway Co. [*AAR code*]	TMA..........	Memphis State University, Memphis, TN [*OCLC symbol*] (OCLC)
TM..............	Textus Minores [*A publication*]		
TM..............	Thalassemia Major [*Hematology*]	TMA..........	[*The*] Money Advocate [*A publication*]
TM..............	Thames Measurement [*Formula for rating yachts*] [*British*]	TMA..........	[*The*] Mosquito Association (EA)
		TMA..........	Taiwan Maintenance Agency [*Military*] (AABC)
TM..............	Theatre Magazine [*A publication*]	TMA..........	Target Motion Analyzer
TM..............	Their Majesties	TMA..........	Technical Manual Management Agent
TM..............	Thematic Mapper [*Satellite technology*]	TMA..........	Telecommunications Managers Association [*Orpington, England*] (TSSD)
TM..............	Thermal Mapper		
TM..............	Third Market [*Securities*]	TMA..........	TeleManagement Associates [*Telecommunications service*] (TSSD)
TM..............	Thompson Medical Co., Inc. [*NYSE symbol*] (SPSG)		
Tm..............	Thulium [*Chemical element*]	TMA..........	Telephone Management and Accounting (HGAA)
Tm..............	Time [*A publication*]	TMA..........	Temperature Monitoring Apparatus
TM..............	Time Management (MCD)	TMA..........	Tennis Manufacturers Association [*Later, ATF*] (EA)
T & M	Time and Materials	TMA..........	Terminal Control Area [*Aviation*] (FAAC)
TM..............	Time, Mission	TMA..........	Terminal Maneuvering Area [*Aviation*]
TM..............	Time Modulation	TMA..........	Tetramethylammonium [*Organic chemistry*]
TM..............	Time Monitor	TMA..........	Theatrical Mutual Association (EA)
TM..............	Time Motion Technique	TMA..........	Thermomagnetic Analysis [*Analytical chemistry*]
TM..............	Timing of Movements [*Physiology*]	TMA..........	Thermomechanical Analysis [*or Analyzer*]
Tm..............	Timothy [*New Testament book*]	TMA..........	Thienylmalonic Acid [*Organic chemistry*]
TM..............	Titanium Chloride [*Inorganic chemistry*]	TMA..........	Thiomalic Acid [*Organic chemistry*]
TM..............	Tlalocan: A Journal of Source Materials on the Native Cultures of Mexico [*A publication*]	TMA..........	Thomas More Association (EA)
		TMA..........	Thomson McKinnon, Inc. [*NYSE symbol*] (SPSG)
TM..............	Toastmaster, Inc. [*NYSE symbol*] (SPSG)	TMA..........	Thrombotic Microangiopathy [*Nephrology*]
TM..............	Tobramycin [*An antibiotic*]	TMA..........	Thyroid Microsomal Antibody [*Immunology*]
TM..............	Toelichting-Meijers [*A publication*]	TMA..........	Tifton, GA [*Location identifier*] [*FAA*] (FAAL)
TM..............	Tolerant Majority (EA)	TMA..........	Tile Manufacturers Association (EA)
TM..............	Ton-Miles	TMA..........	Time-Modulated Antenna
TM..............	Tone Modulation	TMA..........	Tobacco Mechanics' Association [*A union*] [*British*] (DCTA)
TM..............	Tons per Minute	TMA..........	Tobacco Merchants Association of United States (EA)
TM..............	Top Man	TMA..........	Toiletry Merchandising Association [*Later, NASM*] (EA)
TM..............	Top Management	TMA..........	Tooling and Manufacturing Association (EA)
TM..............	Torpedoman's Mate [*Navy rating*]	TMA..........	Top Management Abstracts [*A publication*]
T/M	Torque Meter (NG)	TMA..........	Torpedo Main Assembly
TM..............	Torque Motor	TMA..........	Total Maintenance Actions (MCD)
TM..............	Tour du Monde [*World Tour*] [*French*] (BJA)	TMA..........	Total Materiel Assets [*Military*]
TM..............	Tourism Management [*A publication*]	TMA..........	Toy Manufacturers of America (EA)
TM..............	Town Major [*British military*] (DMA)		

TMA .... Toyota Manufacturing Australia Ltd.
TMA .... Trace Metals Analyzer
TMA .... Traffic Management [*A publication*]
TMA .... Traffic Management Agency (CINC)
TMA .... Trailer Manufacturers Association [*Later, NAMPS*] (EA)
TMA .... Training Media Association (EA)
TMA .... Trans-Mediterranean Airways (BJA)
TMA .... Trans Mo Airlines [*Jefferson City, MO*] [*FAA designator*] (FAAC)
TMA .... Transistor Magnetic-Pulse Amplifier
TMA .... Translater Mixer Amplifier (DWSG)
TMA .... Transmetatarsal Amputation [*Medicine*]
TMA .... Transport Museum Association (EA)
TMA .... Transportation Management Association
TMA .... Trimac Ltd. [*Toronto Stock Exchange symbol*]
TMA .... Trimellitic Anhydride [*Chemistry*]
TMA .... Trimethoxyamphetamine [*Organic chemistry*] (MAE)
TMA .... Trimethoxyphenyl Aminopropane [*Organic chemistry*] (MAE)
TMA .... Trimethyladenine [*Biochemistry*]
TMA .... Trimethylaluminum [*Organic chemistry*]
TMA .... Trimethylamine [*Organic chemistry*]
TMA .... Trimethylammonium [*Organic chemistry*]
TMaab .... Thyroid Microsomal Autoantibody [*Immunology*]
TMAB ...... Telecommunications Managers Association - Belgium
TMAB ...... Temporary Missile Assembly Building (AAG)
TMAB ...... Tetramethylammonium Borohydride [*Organic chemistry*]
TMA BITS ... TMA [*Tobacco Merchants Association*] Bibliographic Index to the Tobacco Scene [*Database*]
TMAC .... Agrico Chemical Co., Memphis, TN [*Library symbol*] [*Library of Congress*] (LCLS)
TMAC .... Telecommunication Management and Control [*AT & T*]
T-MAC ...... Test of Minimal Articulation Competence [*Speech evaluation test*]
TMAC .... Trimellitic Anhydride Chloride [*Organic chemistry*]
TMACA .... Telecommunications Managers Association of the Capital Area (TSSD)
TMACS ..... Tone Multiplex Apollo Command System [*NASA*] (KSC)
TMACS ..... Training Management Control System [*Army*] (INF)
TMAD ...... Tank Main Armament Development (MCD)
TMAD ...... Target Marker Air Droppable (MCD)
TMAD ...... Target Marker and Dispenser (MCD)
TMadH ..... Nashville Memorial Hospital, Madison, TN [*Library symbol*] [*Library of Congress*] (LCLS)
TMadM ..... Madison Academy, Madison College, TN [*Library symbol*] [*Library of Congress*] (LCLS)
TMADWG ... Tank Main Armament Development Working Group [*Army*]
TMAE .... Tetrakis(dimethylamino)ethylene [*Organic chemistry*]
TMAG .... Travel More Advantageous to the Government (AAG)
TMAGD .... Tennessee Magazine [*A publication*]
TMAH .... Tetramethylammonium Hydroxide [*Organic chemistry*]
TMAI .... Tetramethylammonium Iodide [*Organic chemistry*]
TMAIC ..... Trimethallyl Isocyanurate [*Organic chemistry*]
TMAM ...... Training and Doctrine Command Mission Area Manager [*Army*]
TMAMAP ... Ezhegodnik Instituta Eksperimental'noi Meditsiny Akademii Meditsinskikh Nauk SSSR [*A publication*]
TMAN .... Tel/Man, Inc. [*Greenville, SC*] [*NASDAQ symbol*] (NQ)
TMAO .... Trimethylamine Oxide [*Organic chemistry*]
TMAO .... Troop Movement Action Officer
TMAO .... Troop Movement Assignment Order
TMAP .... Tactical Multipurpose Automated Platform [*Military*]
TMAP .... Teleoperated Mobile Antiarmor Platform [*Army*] (INF)
TMAP .... Temporary Mortgage Assistance Payments Program [*HUD*]
TMARS ..... Technical Manual Audit and Requirement Reporting System (MCD)
TMaryB ..... Blount Memorial Hospital, Medical Library, Maryville, TN [*Library symbol*] [*Library of Congress*] (LCLS)
TMaryC ..... Maryville College, Maryville, TN [*Library symbol*] [*Library of Congress*] (LCLS)
TMAS .... Tank Main Armament Systems (RDA)
TMAS .... Taylor Manifest Anxiety State [*Psychology*]
TMAS .... Technical and Management Advisory Service [*ADPA*] (MCD)
TMATB ..... Technische Mitteilungen AEG- [*Allgemeine Elektrizitaets-Gesellschaft*] Telefunken [*A publication*]
TMaU .... University of Tennessee at Martin, Martin, TN [*Library symbol*] [*Library of Congress*] (LCLS)
TMAX .... Maximum Time [*Telecommunications*] (TEL)
TMAX .... Telematics International, Inc. [*NASDAQ symbol*] (NQ)
TMB .... David W. Taylor Model Basin [*Also, DATMOBAS, DTMB*] [*Later, DTNSRDC, NSRDC*]
TMB .... Iemootsies [*A publication*]
TMB .... Miami, FL [*Location identifier*] [*FAA*] (FAAL)
TMB .... Tambrands, Inc. [*NYSE symbol*] (SPSG)
TMB .... Task Maintenance Burden
TMB .... Taylor Model Basin [*Navy*]
TMB .... Tetramethylbenzidine [*Organic chemistry*]
TMB .... Textes Mathematiques Babyloniens [*A publication*] (BJA)
TMB .... Thimble
TMB .... Tide-Measuring Buoy
TMB .... Time Maintenance Began [*Military*] (AFIT)
TMB .... Transient Monocular Blindness [*Medicine*]

TMB .... Transportation Management Bulletin [*NASA*] (NASA)
TMB .... Trench Mortar Battery [*British military*] (DMA)
TMB .... Trimethoxyboroxine [*Organic chemistry*]
TMB .... Trimethylbenzene [*Organic chemistry*]
TMB .... Tumble (MSA)
TMB .... University of Texas, Medical Branch Library, Galveston, TX [*OCLC symbol*] (OCLC)
TMBA .... Brooks Art Gallery, Memphis, TN [*Library symbol*] [*Library of Congress*] (LCLS)
TMBA .... Tetramethylene-bis-Acetamide [*Biochemistry*]
TMBA .... Trimethylbenzaldehyde [*Organic chemistry*]
TMBA .... Trimethylbenzanthracene [*Carcinogen*]
TMBAC ..... Trimethylbenzylammonium Chloride [*Also, BTM*] [*Organic chemistry*]
TMBC .... Buckeye Cellulose Corp., Technical Division Library, Memphis, TN [*Library symbol*] [*Library of Congress*] (LCLS)
TMBDA .... Tetramethylbutanediamine [*Organic chemistry*]
TMBDB .... Thermal Margin beyond Design Basis [*Nuclear energy*] (NRCH)
TMBGIC ... They Might Be Giants Information Club (EA)
TMBH ...... Baptist Memorial Hospital, Memphis, TN [*Library symbol*] [*Library of Congress*] (LCLS)
TMBH-N ... Baptist Memorial Hospital, School of Nursing, Memphis, TN [*Library symbol*] [*Library of Congress*] (LCLS)
TMBL .... Buckman Laboratories, Inc., Memphis, TN [*Library symbol*] [*Library of Congress*] (LCLS)
TMBO .... Tacoma Municipal Belt Line Railway [*AAR code*]
TMBO .... Team Management by Objectives [*Management technique*] (ADA)
TMBP .... (Tetramethylbutyl)phenol [*Organic chemistry*]
TMBR .... Timber (AAG)
TMBR .... Tom Brown, Inc. [*NASDAQ symbol*] (NQ)
TMBS .... Timberline Software Corp. [*NASDAQ symbol*] (NQ)
TMBS .... Torque Motor Beam Steerer (MCD)
TMBU .... Table Maintenance Block Update (NASA)
TM Bull .... Trade Mark Bulletin, New Series [*A publication*] (DLA)
TMC .... Chief Torpedoman's Mate [*Navy rating*]
TMC .... Houston Academy of Medicine for Texas Medical Center, Houston, TX [*OCLC symbol*] (OCLC)
TMC .... Indo-Pacific International [*Tamuning, GU*] [*FAA designator*] (FAAC)
TMC .... [*The*] Maintenance Council of the American Trucking Associations (EA)
TMC .... [*The*] Mouse Club (EA)
TMC .... [*The*] Movie Channel [*Cable-television system*]
TMC .... Table Mountain [*California*] [*Seismograph station code, US Geological Survey*] [*Closed*] (SEIS)
TMC .... Tactical Medical Center
T/MC .... Talker per Megacycle (SAA)
TMC .... Tambolaka [*Indonesia*] [*Airport symbol*] (OAG)
TMC .... Tape Management Catalog
TMC .... Telamarketing Communications, Inc. [*Louisville, KY*] [*Telecommunications*] (TSSD)
TMC .... Telecommunications Management Corp. [*Needham Heights, MA*] (TSSD)
TMC .... Telecommunications Marketing Corp. [*Bay Shore, NY*] (TSSD)
TMC .... TeleMonteCarlo [*Private television operation*] [*Italy*]
TMC .... Temporary Minor Change (MCD)
TMC .... Terramycin Capsule [*Antibacterial, trademark of Pfizer, Inc.*]
TMC .... Terrestrial Microcosm Chamber [*For environmental studies*]
TMC .... Test, Monitor, and Control [*Aviation*]
TMC .... Test Monitoring Console (NASA)
TMC .... Thermal Micrometeoroid Cover (MCD)
TMC .... Thick Molding Compound [*Plastics technology*]
TM-C .... Thomas Micro-Catalogs
TMC .... Three-Mode Control (AAG)
TMC .... Threshold Management Center [*Environmental Protection Agency*] (GFGA)
TMC .... Thrust Magnitude Control (KSC)
TMC .... [*The*] Times Mirror Co. [*NYSE symbol*] (SPSG)
TMC .... Titan Missile Contractor (AAG)
TMC .... Tool Management Culture
TMC .... Total Market Coverage [*Advertising*]
TMC .... Transition Metal Chemistry [*A publication*]
TMC .... Transmedia Enterprises, Inc. [*Vancouver Stock Exchange symbol*]
TMC .... Transmission Maintenance Center [*Telecommunications*] (TEL)
TMC .... Transport Movement Control [*Military*] (AFM)
TMC .... Transportation Materiel Command [*AMC - Mobility*]
TMC .... Travel Management Center [*General Services Administration*] (GFGA)
TMC .... Triamcinolone [*Synthetic steroidal drug*]
TMC .... Trimethylcyclohexanol [*Organic chemistry*]
TMC .... Trinity Ministries Center (EA)
TMC .... Triple Molecular Collision
TMC .... Tube Moisture Control
TMC .... Type Maintenance Code (MCD)
TMCA ...... Thrust Management Control Analysis
TMCA .... Titanium Metals Corp. of America

TMCA .... Toxic Materials Control Activity [*General Motors Corp.*]
TMCA .... Trimethyl Colchicinic Acid [*Organic chemistry*] (MAE)
TMCBC.... Christian Brothers College, Memphis, TN [*Library symbol*] [*Library of Congress*] (LCLS)
TMCC .... Chapman Chemical Co., Memphis, TN [*Library symbol*] [*Library of Congress*] (LCLS)
TMCC .... Theater Movement Control Center [*Military*] (AABC)
TMCC .... Time-Multiplexer Communications Channels
TMCDT..... Trimethylcyclododecatriene [*Organic chemistry*]
TMCF........ Campbell Foundation, Memphis, TN [*Library symbol*] [*Library of Congress*] (LCLS)
TMCH....... City of Memphis Hospital, Memphis, TN [*Library symbol*] [*Library of Congress*] (LCLS)
TMCHD... Transition Metal Chemistry [*A publication*]
TM CHG ... Technical Manual Change Number [*Army*]
TMCI........ Telemetering Control Indicator
TMCI........ TM Century [*NASDAQ symbol*] (NQ)
TMCIA..... Temperature. Its Measurement and Control in Science and Industry [*A publication*]
TMCIOB... Technician Member of the Chartered Institute of Building [*British*] (DI)
TMckB ...... Bethel College, McKenzie, TN [*Library symbol*] [*Library of Congress*] (LCLS)
TMckB-C .. Cumberland Presbyterian Theological Seminary, Bethel College, McKenzie, TN [*Library symbol*] [*Library of Congress*] (LCLS)
TMCL........ Target Map Coordinate Locator [*Military*]
TMCM ...... Master Chief Torpedoman's Mate [*Navy rating*]
TMCM ...... Tooling Machine Control Medium (MCD)
TMCN .... Technical Management Requirements Document Change Notice (MCD)
TMCO .... Time Management Corp. [*NASDAQ symbol*] (NQ)
TMCOMP ... Telemetry Computation
TMCOT ..... Tetramethylcyclooctatetraene [*Organic chemistry*]
TMCP........ Trimethylcyclopentanone [*Organic chemistry*]
TMCR .... Technical Manual Change Request [*or Requirement*]
TMCR .... Technical Manual Contract Requirement
TMCRL..... Tailored Master Cross Reference List [*Military*] (AABC)
TMCS........ Memphis City Schools Professional Library, Memphis, TN [*Library symbol*] [*Library of Congress*] (LCLS)
TMCS........ Senior Chief Torpedoman's Mate [*Navy rating*]
TMCS........ Tactical Maintenance Control System
TMCS........ Toshiba Minicomputer Complex System
TMCS........ Trimethylchlorosilane [*Organic chemistry*]
TMD......... Meharry Medical College, Nashville, TN [*OCLC symbol*] (OCLC)
TMD......... Tactical Metrology Device (DWSG)
TMD......... Tactical Mission Data [*Military*] (AFM)
TMD......... Tactical Munitions Dispenser (MCD)
TMD......... Tagged Material Detector (DWSG)
TMD......... Technical Manual Designation
TMD......... Telemedia, Inc. [*Toronto Stock Exchange symbol*]
TMD......... Telemetered Data (AAG)
TMD......... Temperature of Maximum Density
TMD......... Tensor Meson Dominance [*Physics*] (OA)
TMD......... Tetramethyldioxetane [*Organic chemistry*]
TMD......... Theater Missile Defense
TMD......... Theoretical Maximum Density
TMD......... Thermedics, Inc. [*AMEX symbol*] (SPSG)
TMD......... Timed (MSA)
TMD......... Toluene-Methanol-Dioxane [*Scintillation solvent*]
TMD......... Toxicology and Microbiology Division [*Cincinnati, OH*] [*Environmental Protection Agency*] (GRD)
TMD......... Training Media Database [*Access Innovations, Inc.*] [*Information service or system*] (CRD)
TMD......... Transient Mass Distribution Code [*Nuclear energy*] (NRCH)
TMD......... Transmembrane Domain [*Genetics*]
TMD......... Trimethylhexamethylene Diamine [*Organic chemistry*]
TMDA .... Training Media Distributors Association [*Later, TMA*] (EA)
TMDAG .... This Mode of Transportation has been Determined to be More Advantageous to the Government
TMDC .... Technical Manual Data Cards [*DoD*] (MCD)
TMDC .... TIME-DC, Inc. [*NASDAQ symbol*] (NQ)
TMDC .... Transportation Movement Document Control (MCD)
TMDE .... Test Management and Diagnostic Equipment [*Army*]
TM & DE... Test, Measuring, and Diagnostic Equipment [*Later, TMDE*] [*Army*] (AABC)
TMDE .... Test, Measuring, and Diagnostic Equipment [*Formerly, TM & DE*] [*Army*] (AABC)
TMDESE .. Test, Measurement, and Diagnostic Equipment Support Equipment [*Army*]
TMDESG ... Test, Management, and Diagnostic Equipment Support Group [*Army*] (MCD)
TMDI .... Transponder Miss Distance Indicator
TMDI .... Trimethylhexamethylene Diisocyanate [*Organic chemistry*]
TMDI .... United States Defense Industrial Plant Equipment Center, Memphis, TN [*Library symbol*] [*Library of Congress*] (LCLS)
TMDL .... Technical Manual Data List [*DoD*]
TMDL .... Total Maximum Daily Load [*Environmental Protection Agency*]

TMDO....... Training Management Development Office [*Army*]
TMDP .... Technetium Methylene Diphosphonate [*Organic chemistry*]
TMDR .... Technical Manual Data Record [*DoD*] (MCD)
TMDS........ Test, Measurement, and Diagnostic Systems [*Army*] (RDA)
TMDS........ Tetramethyldisilazane [*Organic chemistry*]
TMDS........ Trilineage Myelodysplasia Syndrome [*Medicine*]
TMDT .... Total Mean Downtime
TMDT .... Trace Metals Detection Technique
TMDT .... Trimethyldodecatetraene [*Organic chemistry*]
TME .... Eastwood Hospital, Memphis, TN [*Library symbol*] [*Library of Congress*] (LCLS)
TME .... [*The*] Main Event [*A publication*]
TME .... Tame [*Colombia*] [*Airport symbol*] (OAG)
TME .... Teacher of Medical Electricity [*British*]
TME .... Termex Resources, Inc. [*Vancouver Stock Exchange symbol*]
TME .... Test Maintenance Equipment [*Data processing*]
TME .... Test Marketing Exemption [*Environmental Protection Agency*]
TME .... Test and Measurement Equipment (MCD)
TME .... Tetramethylethylene [*Organic chemistry*]
TME .... Theatre Mask Ensemble
TME .... Thermal Marrow Expansion [*Roentgenology*]
TME .... Thermal/Mechanical Enzyme [*Fermentation*]
TME .... Thrust Monopropellant Engine
TME .... TME Resources, Inc. [*Vancouver Stock Exchange symbol*]
TME .... Torpedoman's Mate, Electrical [*Navy rating*]
TME .... Total Market Estimate (ADA)
TME .... Total Metabolizable Energy [*Nutrition*]
TME .... Transmissible Mink Encephalopathy
TME .... Transmural Enteritis [*Medicine*]
TME .... Transverse-Mounted Engine
TME .... Trimethylolethane [*Organic chemistry*]
TMEA .... Typewriter Manufacturers Export Association [*Defunct*]
TMEC....... TRADOC [*Training and Doctrine Command*] Materiel Evaluation Committee [*Army*]
TMECO .... Time of Main Engine Cutoff [*Aerospace*] (MCD)
TMED .... Tetramethylethylenediamine [*Also, TEMED, TMEDA*] [*Organic chemistry*]
TMED .... Trimedyne, Inc. [*NASDAQ symbol*] (NQ)
T2 Med ...... T2 Medical, Inc. [*Associated Press abbreviation*] (APAG)
TMEDA .... Tetramethylethylenediamine [*Also, TEMED, TMED*] [*Organic chemistry*]
TMEDA .... Trimethylenediamine [*Organic chemistry*]
TME/FH... Total Maintenance Effort per Flight Hour [*Navy*] (NG)
TMEL........ Tender Master Equipment List
TMEL........ Trimethylethyllead [*Organic chemistry*]
TMEMC... Test and Measurement Equipment for Maintenance Calibration
TM-ENG... Technical Manual - Engineering [*Marine Corps*]
TMEP........ Trademark Manual of Examining Procedure [*A publication*] (DLA)
TMeP........ Trimethylpsoralen [*Photochemotherapeutic compound*]
TMEPS ...... Transverse-Mounted Engine Propulsion System
TMER .... Technical Manual Evaluation Record (MCD)
TMES........ Tactical Missile Electrical Simulator [*Obsolete*]
TMESS...... Telemessage (DS)
TMETN...... Trimethylolethane Trinitrate [*Organic chemistry*]
TMEV .... Theiler's Murine Encephalitis Virus
TMEX........ Terra Mines Ltd. [*NASDAQ symbol*] (NQ)
TMF .... Technical Transmitter Holding Fixture
TMF .... Technical Transmitter Holding Future (MCD)
TMF .... Telemetry Module Facility
TMF .... Test Mode Fail [*Apollo*] [*NASA*]
TMF .... Time Marker Frequency
TMF .... Transaction Monitoring Facility [*Tandem Computers*]
TMF .... Transfer Mold Forming (MCD)
TMF .... Transporter Maintenance Facility [*NASA*] (NASA)
TMF .... Trunk Maintenance Files [*Telecommunications*] (TEL)
TMF .... Tyler Cabot Mortgage Securities [*NYSE symbol*] (SPSG)
TMFC........ Ted McGinley Fan Club (EA)
TMFGCC.... Technical Manual Functional Group Code
TMFL........ Time of Flight (MSA)
TMFZA ...... Teoreticheskaya i Matematicheskaya Fizika [*A publication*]
TMG .... Goodwyn Institute, Memphis, TN [*Library symbol*] [*Library of Congress*] (LCLS)
TMG .... Tactical Missile Group [*Air Force*]
TMG .... Tetramethylguanidine [*Organic chemistry*]
TMG .... Thermal Meteoroid [*or Micrometeoroid*] Garment [*NASA*] (KSC)
TMG .... Thermomagnetometry [*Analytical chemistry*]
TMG .... Thiomethylgalactoside [*Organic chemistry*]
TMG .... Time Mark Generator
TMG .... Timing
TMG .... Tomanggong [*Malaysia*] [*Airport symbol*] (OAG)
TMG .... Track Made Good [*Aviation*]
TMG .... Trimethylgallium [*Organic chemistry*]
TMG .... Trimethylguanosine [*Biochemistry*]
TMGA .... Tetramethyleneglutaric Acid [*Organic chemistry*]
TMGC .... W. R. Grace & Co., Agricultural Chemicals Group, Memphis, TN [*Library symbol*] [*Library of Congress*] (LCLS)
TMGD....... Timing Devices (MSA)
TMGE .... Thermomagnetic-Galvanic Effect
TMGFC..... [*The*] Mel Gibson Fan Club [*Defunct*] (EA)

TMGG....... Goldsmith Civic Garden Center, Memphis, TN [*Library symbol*] [*Library of Congress*] (LCLS)

TMGRS..... Trace Material Generation Rate Simulator

TMGS........ Church of Jesus Christ of Latter-Day Saints, Genealogical Society Library, Memphis Branch, Memphis, TN [*Library symbol*] [*Library of Congress*] (LCLS)

TMGS....... Terrestrial Magnetic Guidance System [*Aerospace*] (AAG)

TMGS....... Transportable Mobile Ground Station (MCD)

TMH.......... Harding Graduate School of Religion, Memphis, TN [*Library symbol*] [*Library of Congress*] (LCLS)

TMH.......... Tanahmerah [*Indonesia*] [*Airport symbol*] (OAG)

TMH.......... Texas Military History [*A publication*]

TMH.......... Texte und Materialien der Frau Professor Hilprecht Collection of Babylonian Antiquities im Eigentum der Universitaet Jena (BJA)

TMH.......... Tomahawk Resources [*Vancouver Stock Exchange symbol*]

TMH.......... Tons per Man-Hour

TMH.......... Trainable Mentally Handicapped

TMH.......... Trimethylhexane [*Organic chemistry*]

TMH.......... Trolley-Mounted Hoist (NRCH)

TMHA....... Memphis Housing Authority, Memphis, TN [*Library symbol*] [*Library of Congress*] (LCLS)

TMHA....... [*The*] Military Housing Association

TMHB....... Harland Bartholomew & Associates, Memphis, TN [*Library symbol*] [*Library of Congress*] (LCLS)

TMHI....... Holiday Inns of America, Memphis, TN [*Library symbol*] [*Library of Congress*] (LCLS)

TMHI-U.... Holiday Inn University, Olive Branch, MS [*Library symbol*] [*Library of Congress*] (LCLS)

TMHL....... Triplet Metastable Helium Level

TMI .... International Harvester Co., Memphis, TN [*Library symbol*] [*Library of Congress*] (LCLS)

TMI .... [*The*] Media Institute (EA)

TMI .... Midwestern State University, George Moffett Library, Wichita Falls, TX [*OCLC symbol*] (OCLC)

TMI .... [*The*] Monroe Institute (EA)

TMI .... [*The*] Mortgage Index, Inc. [*Remote Computing Corp.*] [*Information service or system*] (IID)

TMI .... Tax Management International Journal [*A publication*]

TMI .... Taylor Mountain [*Idaho*] [*Seismograph station code, US Geological Survey*] (SEIS)

TMI .... Team, Inc. [*AMEX symbol*] (SPSG)

TMI .... Technical Management Items (NASA)

TMI .... Technical Manual Index [*Navy*]

TMI .... Teen Missions International (EA)

TMI .... Telecommunications Management, Inc. [*Oakbrook, IL*] [*Telecommunications*] (TSSD)

TmI .... Telematica, Inc. [*Telecommunications service*] (TSSD)

TMI .... Thornicroft's Mounted Infantry [*Military*] [*British*] (ROG)

TMI .... Three Mile Island [*Pennsylvania*] [*Site of nuclear reactor accident, 1979*]

TMI .... Time Air Corp. [*Toronto Stock Exchange symbol*]

TMI .... Time Manager International [*Commercial firm*] [*British*]

TMI .... Tolyl(mono)isocyanate [*Organic chemistry*]

TMI .... Tool Manufacturing Instruction (AAG)

TMI .... Tracking Merit Interception

TMI .... Trans-Mars Injection [*Aerospace*]

TMI .... Transfer on Minus (SAA)

TMI .... Transmural Myocardial Infarction [*Cardiology*]

TMI .... Travel Managers International (EA)

TMI .... Trucking Management, Inc. (EA)

TMI .... Tumlingtar [*Nepal*] [*Airport symbol*] (OAG)

TMI .... Tune-Up Manufacturers Institute (EA)

TMIA .... Three Mile Island Alert (EA)

TMIC........ Thomas Marketing Information Center [*Thomas Publishing Co.*] [*Information service or system*] (IID)

TMIC........ Toxic Materials Information Center [*Oak Ridge National Laboratory*] (IID)

TMICP..... Topographic Map Inventory Control Point [*Army*] (AABC)

TMIF....... Tumor-Cell Migratory Inhibition Factor [*Immunology*]

TMIFC...... Tom Mix International Fan Club (EA)

TMIG .... [*The*] Marketing Information Guide [*A publication*]

TMIG .... Time in Grade [*Navy*]

TMilM....... Milligan College, Milligan College, TN [*Library symbol*] [*Library of Congress*] (LCLS)

TMIMGTechE ... Technician Member of the Institution of Mechanical and General Technician Engineers [*British*] (DI)

TMIMIS ... Technical Manual Integrated Management Information Systems [*DoD*]

TMIN .... Minimum Time [*Telecommunications*] (TEL)

TMiNA...... United States Naval Air Station Library, Millington, TN [*Library symbol*] [*Library of Congress*] (LCLS)

TMINDCD ... Technical Manual Indenture Code [*Army*]

TMiNH ..... United States Naval Hospital, Millington, TN [*Library symbol*] [*Library of Congress*] (LCLS)

TMINS...... Technical Manual Identification Numbering System (MCD)

TMINS...... Three Mile Island Nuclear Station (NRCH)

TMIP........ Training Management Instruction Packet

TMIS........ Tank Management Information System (MCD)

TMIS........ Technical and Management Information System (SSD)

TMIS........ Technical Meetings Information Service

TMIS......... Television Measurement [*or Metering*] Information System (OA)

TMIS......... Total Management Information System

TMIU .... Teletype Modulator Interface Units (MCD)

TMJ.......... Temporomandibular Joint Disorder [*Medicine*]

TMJ.......... Trade Marks Journal [*A publication*]

TMJS......... Temporomandibular Joint Syndrome [*Medicine*]

TMK .... Kimberly-Clark Corp., Memphis, TN [*Library symbol*] [*Library of Congress*] (LCLS)

TMK .... Timiskaming [*Quebec*] [*Seismograph station code, US Geological Survey*] [*Closed*] (SEIS)

TMK .... Tiravita Munnerrat Kalam

TMK .... Tomahawk Airways, Inc. [*Alcoa, TN*] [*FAA designator*] (FAAC)

TMK .... Tomsk [*Former USSR*] [*Geomagnetic observatory code*]

TMK .... Tonnage Mark [*Found on each side of the ship aft*] (DS)

TMK .... Torchmark Corp. [*NYSE symbol*] (SPSG)

TMK .... Transistor Mounting Kit

TMK .... Trumark Resource Corp. [*Vancouver Stock Exchange symbol*]

TMKFA..... Technische Mitteilungen Krupp. Forschungsberichte [*A publication*]

TMKPR..... Timekeeper (WGA)

TMKT .... Technology Marketing, Inc. [*NASDAQ symbol*] (NQ)

TMKWA ... Technische Mitteilungen Krupp. Werksberichte [*A publication*]

TML .... Lakeside Hospital, Memphis, TN [*Library symbol*] [*Library of Congress*] (LCLS)

TML .... Tamale [*Ghana*] [*Airport symbol*] (OAG)

TML .... Tandem Matching Loss [*Telecommunications*] (TEL)

TML .... Technical Manual List (MCD)

TML .... Terminal (AABC)

TML .... Terrestrial Microwave Link

TML .... Tetramethyl Lead (MCD)

TML .... Tetramethyllead [*Organic chemistry*]

TML .... Texas Tech University, School of Medicine at Lubbock, Library of the Health Science, Lubbock, TX [*OCLC symbol*] (OCLC)

TML .... Thermomechanical Loading

TML .... Three-Mile Limit

TML .... Titanium Metallurgical Laboratory (MCD)

TML .... Transmanche-Link [*Eurotunnel*] (ECON)

TML .... Transportable Moisture Limit [*Shipping*] (DS)

TMLBC ..... Le Bonheur Children's Medical Center, Health Sciences Library, Memphis, TN [*Library symbol*] [*Library of Congress*] (LCLS)

TMLE........ Transient-Mode Liquid Epitaxy

TMLG .... Memphis Light, Gas, and Water Division Library, Memphis, TN [*Library symbol*] [*Library of Congress*] (LCLS)

TMLJ .... Thurgood Marshall Law Journal [*A publication*] (DLA)

TMLO .... LeMoyne-Owen College, Memphis, TN [*Library symbol*] [*Library of Congress*] (LCLS)

TM/LP ...... Thermal Margin/Low Pressure [*Nuclear energy*] (NRCH)

TML Rev ... Thurgood Marshall Law Review [*A publication*] (DLA)

TMM........ Memphis State University, Memphis, TN [*Library symbol*] [*Library of Congress*] (LCLS)

TMM........ Tamatave [*Madagascar*] [*Airport symbol*] (OAG)

TMM........ Tank Master Mechanic (MCD)

TMM........ Tax Management Memorandum [*Bureau of National Affairs*] [*A publication*] (DLA)

TMM........ Technocrat. A Monthly Review of Japanese Technology and Industry [*A publication*]

TMM........ Technologico De Monterrey [*Mexico*] [*Seismograph station code, US Geological Survey*] (SEIS)

TMM........ Test Message Monitor

TMM........ Thermal Mathematical Model

TMM........ Times Mirror Magazine [*A publication*]

TMM........ Too Many Metaphors [*Used in correcting manuscripts, etc.*]

TMM........ Transition Metal-Metalloid [*Physical chemistry*]

TMM........ Transportacion Maritima ADS [*NYSE symbol*] (SPSG)

TMM........ Trimethylenemethane [*Organic chemistry*]

TMM........ Trimethylolmelamine [*Organic chemistry*]

TMMAB ... Mid-America Baptist Theological Seminary, Memphis, TN [*Library symbol*] [*Library of Congress*] (LCLS)

TMM-B..... Memphis State University, Bureau of Business Research Library, Memphis, TN [*Library symbol*] [*Library of Congress*] (LCLS)

TMMB ...... Truck Mixer Manufacturers Bureau (EA)

TMMBC.... Mid-South Bible College, Memphis, TN [*Library symbol*] [*Library of Congress*] (LCLS)

TMMC ...... Tetramethylammonium Manganese Chloride [*Organic chemistry*]

TMMC ...... Theater Materiel Management Center [*Military*] (AABC)

TMMD...... Tactical Moving Map Display (MCD)

TMM-E..... Memphis State University, Engineering Library, Memphis, TN [*Library symbol*] [*Library of Congress*] (LCLS)

TMMEE.... Memphis Eye and Ear Hospital, Memphis, TN [*Library symbol*] [*Library of Congress*] (LCLS)

TMMG ...... Teacher of Massage and Medical Gymnastics [*British*]

TMMH...... Methodist Hospital, Stratton Medical Library, Memphis, TN [*Library symbol*] [*Library of Congress*] (LCLS)

TMMH-P ... Methodist Hospital, Pathology Library, Memphis, TN [*Library symbol*] [*Library of Congress*] (LCLS)

TmMir .... [*The*] Times Mirror Co. [*Associated Press abbreviation*] (APAG)

TMMIS ..... Technical Manual Management Information System [*Navy*] (DNAB)

TMM-L ..... Memphis State University, School of Law, Memphis, TN [*Library symbol*] [*Library of Congress*] (LCLS)

TMMM ..... Textes et Monuments Figures Relatifs aux Mysteres de Mithra [*A publication*] (BJA)

TMMP ...... Technical Manual Management Program [*Navy*] (NVT)

TMMS ...... Tactical Missile Maintenance Squadron [*Air Force*]

TMM-SH ... Memphis State University, Speech and Hearing Center, Memphis, TN [*Library symbol*] [*Library of Congress*] (LCLS)

TMMT ...... Technical Manual Management Team [*DoD*]

TMMxA .... Transportacion Maritima Mexicana [*Associated Press abbreviation*] (APAG)

TMN .... Charlotte Amalie, St. Thomas, VI [*Location identifier*] [*FAA*] (FAAL)

TMN .... Memphis and Shelby County Public Library and Information Center, Memphis, TN [*OCLC symbol*] (OCLC)

TMN .... National Cotton Council of America, Memphis, TN [*Library symbol*] [*Library of Congress*] (LCLS)

TMN .... Tamana [*Kiribati*] [*Airport symbol*] (OAG)

TMN .... Tax Matters Newsletter [*Australia*] [*A publication*]

TMN .... Technical and Management Note (IEEE)

TMN .... Telecommunications Management Network (MCD)

TMN .... Timber Mountain [*Nevada*] [*Seismograph station code, US Geological Survey*] (SEIS)

TMN .... Transmission (AFM)

TMN .... Trigeminal Mesencephalic Nucleus [*Neuroanatomy*]

TMN .... True Mach Number

TMNI .... Transmedia Network, Inc. [*New York, NY*] [*NASDAQ symbol*] (NQ)

TMNP ...... [*The*] Mystery Readers Newsletter [*A publication*]

TMNT ...... Teen-Age Mutant Ninja Turtles [*Name of comic book and cartoon characters and line of toys by Playmates Toys*]

TMo .... O Tempo e o Modo [*A publication*]

TMO .... Targets Management Office [*MIRCOM*] (RDA)

TMO .... Technology Management Office [*Army*]

TMO .... Telegraph Money Order

TMO .... Test Manufacturing Order (NASA)

TMO .... Thermo Electron Corp. [*NYSE symbol*] (SPSG)

TMO .... Thermomagnetic Optical Disk

TMO .... Thermomagneto-Optic (MCD)

TMO .... Time Out

TMO .... Tool Manufacturing Order [*NASA*] (NASA)

TMO .... Tooling Manufacturing Outline

TMO .... Total Materiel Objective [*Military*]

TMO .... Traffic Management Office [*or Officer*] [*Air Force*] (AFM)

TMO .... Trans MO Airlines [*Jefferson City, MO*] [*FAA designator*] (FAAC)

TMO .... Transition Metal Oxide (MCD)

TMO .... Transportation Movements Office [*or Officer*] [*Military*]

TMO .... Treminco Resources Ltd. [*Toronto Stock Exchange symbol*] [*Vancouver Stock Exchange symbol*]

TMO .... Trimethylamine N-Oxide [*Organic chemistry*]

TMO .... Tumeremo [*Venezuela*] [*Airport symbol*] (OAG)

TMOB ...... Trade Marks Opposition Board [*Information service or system*] (IID)

TMOD ...... TMDE [*Test, Measuring, and Diagnostic Equipment*] Modernization [*Army*] (RDA)

TMOP ...... Trimethylolpropane [*Organic chemistry*]

TMOR ...... Technical Manual Ordtask Requirement (MCD)

TMorM ..... Morristown College, Morristown, TN [*Library symbol*] [*Library of Congress*] (LCLS)

TMorNR.... Nolichucky Regional Library Center, Morristown, TN [*Library symbol*] [*Library of Congress*] (LCLS)

TMOS ...... Tetramethoxysilane [*Organic chemistry*]

TMOS ...... Thermosetting (MSA)

T-MOS ..... Trench-Metal Oxide Silicon [*Transistor*]

TMOS ..... Two Main Orbiting Spacecraft (SAA)

TMOT ...... Target [*or Total*] Maximum Operating Time

TMOTFSM ... [*The*] Master of the Free School, Margate [*Pseudonym used by Zachariah Cozens*]

TMP .... East Timor [*ISO three-letter standard code*] (CNC)

TMP .... [*The*] Madison Project (EA)

TMP .... [*The*] Management Processor (MCD)

TMP .... Tampere [*Finland*] [*Airport symbol*] (OAG)

TMP .... Target Materials Program [*DoD*]

TMP .... Technical Manual Parts [*Army*] (AABC)

TMP .... Technical Manual Plan [*DoD*]

TMP .... Teleprinter Message Pool

TMP .... Temazepam [*Tranquilizer*]

TMP .... Temperature (BUR)

Tmp .... [*The*] Tempest [*Shakespearean work*]

TMP .... Terminal Monitor Program [*Data processing*] (BUR)

TMP .... Terminal Panel (NASA)

TMP .... Ternary Mobile Phase [*Physical chemistry*]

TMP .... Terrain Mortar Positioning [*Military*] (INF)

TMP .... Test Maintenance Panel [*Data processing*]

TMP .... Test Methods and Procedures

TMP .... Tetramethylpiperidine [*Organic chemistry*]

TMP .... Theodolite Measuring Point (MUGU)

TMP .... Thermal Mass Penalty (KSC)

TMP .... Thermal Modeling Program

TMP .... Thermo Magnetic Printing (HGAA)

TMP .... Thermomechanical Processing

TMP .... Thermomechanical Pulps

TMP .... Thermomicrophotometry

TMP .... Thymidine Monophosphate [*Biochemistry*]

TMP .... Thymolphthalein Monophosphate [*Biochemistry*]

TMP .... Time Management Processor (NASA)

TMP .... Times Mirror Press

TMP .... Total Material Package [*Military*] (DNAB)

TMP .... Total Milk Proteinate [*Trademark of New Zealand Milk Products, Inc.*]

TMP .... Traditional Medical Practice

TMP .... Trans Mountain Pipe Line Co. Ltd. [*Toronto Stock Exchange symbol*] [*Vancouver Stock Exchange symbol*]

TMP .... Transistor Mounting Pad

TMP .... Transitional Manpower Program [*Navy*] (DNAB)

TMP .... Transmembrane Potential [*Biochemistry*]

TMP .... Transmembrane Protein [*Biochemistry*]

TMP .... Transportable Measurement Package (MCD)

TMP .... Transportation Motor Pool [*Military*] (AABC)

TMP .... Transversely Magnetized Plasma

TMP .... Trimetaphosphate [*Organic chemistry*]

TMP .... Trimethoprim [*Also, T*] [*Antibacterial compound*]

TMP .... Trimethyl Phosphate [*Organic chemistry*]

TMP .... Trimethylolpropane [*Organic chemistry*]

TMP .... Trimethylpentane [*Organic chemistry*]

TMP .... Trimethylphosphine [*Organic chemistry*]

TMP .... Trimethylpsoralen [*Photochemotherapeutic compound*] (AAMN)

TMPA....... Transocean Marine Paint Association [*Netherlands*] (EAIO)

TMPA....... Trimethylphosphoramide [*Organic chemistry*]

Tmpah....... Tubular Maximum for Para-Aminohippuric Acid [*Biochemistry*] (MAE)

TMPC....... Memphis Planning Commission, Memphis, TN [*Library symbol*] [*Library of Congress*] (LCLS)

TMPD ...... Tempered (MSA)

TMPD ...... Tetramethyl-para-phenylenediamine [*Analytical chemistry*]

TMPD ...... Trimethylpentanediol [*Organic chemistry*]

TmpGlb...... Templeton Global Income Fund [*Associated Press abbreviation*] (APAG)

TMPGU .... Templeton Global Utilities, Inc. [*Associated Press abbreviation*] (APAG)

TMPI........ Plough, Inc., Memphis, TN [*Library symbol*] [*Library of Congress*] (LCLS)

TMPI........ Target Material Production Instruction [*Air Force*]

TMPN ...... Tetramethylpiperidinol N-oxyl [*Organic chemistry*]

TMPO ...... Total Materiel Procurement Objective [*Military*]

TMPO ...... Traffic Management and Proceedings Office [*CONUS*] (MCD)

TMPRG.... Tempering

TMPRLY .. Temporarily (MDG)

TMPROC ... Telemetry Processing

TMPRY..... Temporary (AFM)

TMPS....... Temperature Monitoring Power Supply

TMPS....... Test Maintenance Panel Subassembly [*Data processing*]

TMPS....... Theater Mission Planning System [*Military*] (CAAL)

TMPS....... Tracking Modifier Power Supply

TMPS....... Trans-Mississippi Philatelic Society (EA)

TMP/SMX ... Trimethoprim-Sulfamethoxazole [*Antibacterial*] [*Antineoplastic drug*]

TMPSS...... Trailer-Mounted Power Support System (DWSG)

TMPT....... Tactical Marine Petroleum Terminal (MCD)

TMPTA..... Technische Mitteilungen PTT [*A publication*]

TMPTA..... Trimethylolpropane Triacrylate [*Organic chemistry*]

TMPTMA ... Trimethylolpropane Trimethacrylate [*Organic chemistry*]

TMPV....... Torque Motor Pilot Valve (NASA)

TMPZ....... Tetramethylpyrazine [*Biochemistry*]

TMQAP .... Technical Manual Quality Assurance Plan [*Navy*] (DNAB)

TMR .... Tactical Microwave Radio

TMR .... Tactical Missile Receiver

TMR .... Tamanrasset [*Algeria*] [*Airport symbol*] (OAG)

TMR .... Tandem Mirror Reactor (MCD)

TMR .... Technical Memorandum Report

TMR .... Technology Management Review [*Military*] (AFIT)

TMR .... Telecommunications Marketing Resource Ltd. [*Telecommunications service*] (TSSD)

TMR .... Telemanagement Resources, Inc. [*Charlotte, NC*] [*Telecommunications*] (TSSD)

TMR .... Temo Resources Ltd. [*Vancouver Stock Exchange symbol*]

TMR .... Terrestrial Myriametric Radiation [*Physics*]

TMR .... Test Malfunction Report

TMR .... Tetramethylrhodamine [*Fluorescent dye*]

TMR .... Texas Meridian Resources Ltd. [*AMEX symbol*] (SPSG)

TMR .... Thermistor Micropower Resistor

TMR .... Timber Management Research [*Department of Agriculture*] (GRD)

TMR .... Time Meter Reading

TMR.......... Timer (AAG)

TMR .... Tomakomai [*Japan*] [*Seismograph station code, US Geological Survey*] (SEIS)
TMR .... Topical Magnetic Resonance [*Medical diagnostic technique*]
TMR .... Total Materiel Requirement [*Military*] (AABC)
TMR .... Total Metal Removed
TMR .... Total Mission Recorder [*Navy*]
TMR .... Trade-Mark Reporter [*A publication*]
TMR .... Trainable Mentally Retarded
TMR .... Transportation Movements Release [*Military*] (AABC)
TMR .... Transvaal Mounted Rifles [*British military*] (DMA)
Tmr .... Trimmer [*British military*] (DMA)
TMR .... Triple Modular Redundancy [*Data processing*]
TMR .... True Money Rate [*Finance*]
TMRA ...... Texas Meridian Resources Ltd. [*NASDAQ symbol*] (NQ)
TMRAO .... Table Mountain Radio Astronomy Observatory
TMRBM.... Transportable Medium-Range Ballistic Missile
TMRC .... Technical Maintenance Repair Center (MCD)
TMRC .... Theoretical Maximum Residue Contribution [*to acceptable daily intake*] [*Environmental Protection Agency*]
TMRD ...... Technical Management Requirements Document
TMRD ...... Transportation Movement Requirements Data (MCD)
TM Rec...... Trade Mark Record [*United States*] [*A publication*] (DLA)
TM Rep .... Trade-Mark Reporter [*A publication*]
TM/RF ...... Telemetry/Radio Frequency
TMRI......... RAMCON, Inc., Environmental Engineering Library, Memphis, TN [*Library symbol*] [*Library of Congress*] (LCLS)
TMRI......... Tetramethylrhodamine Isothiocyanate [*Analytical biochemistry*]
TMRK .... Canadian Trade Marks [*Canada Systems Group*] [*Information service or system*] (IID)
TMRK .... Trimark Holdings [*NASDAQ symbol*] (SPSG)
TMRKH .... Tromura. Tromsoe Museum Rapportserie. Kulturhistorie [*A publication*]
TMRN .... [*The*] Mystery Readers Newsletter [*A publication*]
TMRNV .... Tromura. Tromsoe Museum Rapportserie. Naturvitenskap [*A publication*]
TMRP........ Technology Mobilization and Reemployment Program [*Department of Labor*]
TMR Prac ... Trademark Rules of Practice [*A publication*] (DLA)
TMRS........ Traffic Measuring and Recording System [*Telecommunications*] (TEL)
TMRSDT .. Tropical Medicine Research Studies Series [*A publication*]
TmRSV...... Tomato Ringspot Virus
TMRVDP ... Terminal-Modified RADAR Video Data Processor [*Noise control*]
TMS.......... [*The*] Magnolia Society (EA)
TMS.......... [*The*] Manufacturing System [*Burroughs Machines Ltd.*] [*Software package*] (NCC)
TMS.......... [*The*] Masonry Society (EA)
TMS.......... Minerals, Metals, and Materials Society (EA)
TMS.......... Sao Tome Island [*Sao Tome Islands*] [*Airport symbol*] (OAG)
TMS.......... Siena College, Memphis, TN [*Library symbol*] [*Library of Congress*] (LCLS)
TMS.......... Southern Missionary College, Collegedale, TN [*OCLC symbol*] (OCLC)
TMS.......... Tactical Missile Squadron [*Air Force*]
TMS.......... Tape Management System (MCD)
TMS.......... Target Marking System
TMS.......... Target Materials Squadron (MCD)
TMSIM...... Technisonic [*Record label*]
TMS.......... Technological Market Segmentation
TMS.......... Telecommunications Message Switcher
TMS.......... Telemetry Modulation System
TMS.......... Telemetry Multiplex System
TMS.......... Teleoperator Maneuvering System (MCD)
TMS.......... Telephone Management System (HGAA)
TMS.......... Temperature Management Station
TMS.......... Temperature Measurement Society
TMS.......... Temporomandibular Syndrome [*Medicine*]
TMS.......... Temsco Helicopters, Inc. [*Ketchikan, AK*] [*FAA designator*] (FAAC)
TMS.......... Tesla Memorial Society (EA)
TMS.......... Test Monitor System
TMS.......... Test and Monitoring Station
TMS.......... Tetramethoxysilane [*Organic chemistry*]
TMS.......... Tetramethylsilane [*Organic chemistry*]
TMS.......... Text Message System (MCD)
TMS.......... Textile Market Studies [*British*]
TMS.......... Thallium Myocardial Scintigraphy [*Cardiology*]
TMS.......... Thematic Mapper Simulator [*for aerial photography*]
TMS.......... Thermal Maneuvering System (SSD)
TMS.......... Thermomechanical System [*Instrumentation*]
TMS.......... Thread Mate System [*Dentistry*]
TMS.......... Thrust Measuring System
TMS.......... Tight Model Series (MCD)
TMS.......... Time and Motion Study (NG)
TMS.......... Time Multiplexed Switching [*Telecommunications*]
TMS.......... Time-Shared Monitor System [*Data processing*] (IEEE)
TMS.......... Times Square Energy Resource Ltd. [*Vancouver Stock Exchange symbol*]

TMS.......... Tissu Musculaire Specifique [*Medicine*] [*France*]
TMS.......... Tlalocan: A Journal of Source Materials on the Native Cultures of Mexico [*A publication*]
TMS.......... Tomisaki [*Mera*] [*Japan*] [*Seismograph station code, US Geological Survey*] [*Closed*] (SEIS)
TMS.......... Top Management Simulation [*Game*]
TMS.......... TOW [*Tube-Launched, Optically Tracked, Wire-Guided (Weapon)*] Missile System (RDA)
TMS.......... Toyota Motor Sales, Inc.
TMS.......... Trademark Section, Official Gazette [*Federal government*]
TMS.......... Trademark Society (EA)
TMS.......... Traffic Measurement System
TM/S .... Trained in Minesweeping [*British military*] (DMA)
TMS.......... Trainee Management System (MCD)
TMS.......... Training Material Support
TMS.......... Training Media Services
TMS.......... [*The*] Tramway Museum Society [*British*] (DCTA)
TMS.......... Transaction Management System (BUR)
TMS.......... Transmatic Money Service
TMS.......... Transmission Measuring Set [*Bell Laboratories*]
TMS.......... Transport Management Survey (MCD)
TMS.......... Transportation Management School [*Navy*]
TMS.......... Treasury Management Services [*British*]
TMS.......... TriMas Corp. [*NYSE symbol*] (SPSG)
TMS.......... Trimethylsilyl [*Organic chemistry*]
TMS.......... Truth-Maintenance System [*Artificial intelligence*] (ECON)
TMS.......... Turbine Management Station
TMS.......... Turbulence Measuring System
TMS.......... Type, Model, and Series
TMSA....... Technical Marketing Society of America (EA)
TMSA....... Telecommunications Marketing/Sales Association [*Defunct*] (EA)
TMSA....... Thomas More Society of America (EA)
TMSA....... Trimethylsilyl Azide [*Organic chemistry*]
TMSAA..... Transactions. Metallurgical Society of AIME [*American Institute of Mining, Metallurgical, and Petroleum Engineers*] [*A publication*]
TMSAN..... Trimethylsilylacetonitrile [*Organic chemistry*]
TMSB........ Memphis and Shelby County Bar Association, Memphis, TN [*Library symbol*] [*Library of Congress*] (LCLS)
TMSC........ Southwestern at Memphis, Memphis, TN [*Library symbol*] [*Library of Congress*] (LCLS)
TMSC........ Talcott Mountain Science Center for Student Involvement, Inc. [*Avon, CT*] [*Telecommunications service*] (TSSD)
TMSC........ Texas Male Sterility Cytoplasm [*Agriculture*] (OA)
TMSCH..... Memphis and Shelby County Health Department, Memphis, TN [*Library symbol*] [*Library of Congress*] (LCLS)
TMSCJ...... Trade Movement Society of Carpenters and Joiners [*A union*] [*British*]
TMSCl....... Trimethylsilyl Chloride [*Organic chemistry*]
TMSCN..... Trimethylsilylcyanide [*Organic chemistry*]
TMS-CPG ... Trimethylsilylated Controlled-Pore Glass [*Packing for chromatography*]
TMSCS ..... Memphis and Shelby County Safety Council, Memphis, TN [*Library symbol*] [*Library of Congress*] (LCLS)
TMSD........ Total Military Service to Date
TMSD........ Training Material Support Detachment [*Army*]
TMSDC..... Thermomechanical Model Software Development Center [*Research center*] (RCD)
TMSDEA .. Trimethylsilyldiethylamine [*Organic chemistry*]
TMSIM...... (Trimethylsilyl)imidazole [*Also, TSIM*] [*Organic chemistry*]
TMSM....... Shiloh Military Trail Library, Memphis, TN [*Library symbol*] [*Library of Congress*] (LCLS)
TMSM....... Trimethylstannylmaleate [*Organic chemistry*]
TMSMC.... Semmes-Murphey Clinic, Memphis, TN [*Library symbol*] [*Library of Congress*] (LCLS)
TMSN .... Tomsun Foods International [*Greenfield, MA*] [*NASDAQ symbol*] (NQ)
TMSO .... Southern College of Optometry, Memphis, TN [*Library symbol*] [*Library of Congress*] (LCLS)
TMSq........ Tactical Missile Squadron [*Air Force*]
TMSR........ Technical Manual Status Report (MCD)
TMSS........ Shelby State Community College, Memphis, TN [*Library symbol*] [*Library of Congress*] (LCLS)
TMSS .... Technical Manual Specifications and Standards [*Military*] (AFIT)
TMSS .... Technical Munitions Safety Study [*Air Force*]
TMSS .... Tecmar Music Synthesis System
TMSS .... Towanda-Monroeton Shippers Lifeline, Inc. [*AAR code*]
TMSSR ...... Technical Manual Status and Schedule Report (MCD)
TMST........ Thomaston Mills, Inc. [*NASDAQ symbol*] (NQ)
TMStF .... Saint Francis Hospital, Medical Library, Memphis, TN [*Library symbol*] [*Library of Congress*] (LCLS)
TMStJ .... Saint Jude Children's Research Hospital, Memphis, TN [*Library symbol*] [*Library of Congress*] (LCLS)
TMStJo ..... Saint Joseph Hospital, Memphis, TN [*Library symbol*] [*Library of Congress*] (LCLS)
TMSVCS... TOW [*Tube-Launched, Optically Tracked, Wire-Guided (Weapon)*] Missile Sight Video Camera System (MCD)
TMT .... Tactical Marine Terminal (MCD)

TMT	Talcott Mountain [*Connecticut*] [*Seismograph station code, US Geological Survey*] [*Closed*] (SEIS)
TMT	Temperature (MDG)
TMT	Terminal Monitor Program [*Data processing*] (MDG)
TMT	Testing Methods and Techniques [*Telecommunications*] (TEL)
TMT	Tetramethylthiourea [*Also, TMTU*] [*Organic chemistry*]
TMT	Thermal Measurement Treatment
TMT	Thermomechanical Treatment
TMT	Thousand Metric Tons (IMH)
TMT	Tire Management Terminal [*Automotive engineering*]
TMT	Total Maintenance Time (MCD)
TMT	Total Mission Time
TMT	TOW [*Tube-Launched, Optically Tracked, Wire-Guided (Weapon)*] Missile Transporter
TMT	Toxic Materials Transport [*Business Publishers, Inc.*] [*Information service or system*] (CRD)
TMT	Trans Midwest Airlines, Inc. [*Columbus, GA*] [*FAA designator*] (FAAC)
TMT	Transmit (FAAC)
TMT	Transonic Model Tunnel [*NASA*]
TMT	Transportation Motor Transport [*Military*] (AABC)
TMT	Treatment [*Medicine*]
TMT	Troy Mineral & Tech [*Vancouver Stock Exchange symbol*]
TMT	Tudomanyos es Muszaki Tajekoztatas [*A publication*]
TMT	Turret Maintenance Trainer (MCD)
TMTBL	Transmittable (FAAC)
TMTC	Thru-Mode [*or Tri-Mode*] Tape Converter
TMTD	Tetramethylthiuram Disulfide [*Also, THTMS, TMTDS*] [*Organic chemistry*]
TMTD	Transmitted (FAAC)
TMTDS	Tetramethylthiuram Disulfide [*Also, TMTD, THTMS*] [*Organic chemistry*]
TMTF	Tile, Marble, and Terrazzo Finishers and Shopmen International Union
TMTG	Tactical Missile Training Group [*Military*]
TMTG	Transmitting (FAAC)
TMTI	State Technical Institute at Memphis, Memphis, TN [*Library symbol*] [*Library of Congress*] (LCLS)
TMTN	Transmission (FAAC)
TMTNO	No Transmitting Capability (FAAC)
TMTP	Tennessee Psychiatric Hospital and Institute, Memphis, TN [*Library symbol*] [*Library of Congress*] (LCLS)
TMTR	Thermistor (AAG)
TMTR	Transmitter
TMTS	Memphis Theological Seminary of the Cumberland Presbyterian Church, Memphis, TN [*Library symbol*] [*Library of Congress*] (LCLS)
TMTS	Tactical Missile Training Squadron [*Air Force*]
TMTSF	Tetramethyltetraselenafulvene [*Organic chemistry*]
TMTU	Tetramethylthiourea [*Also, TMT*] [*Organic chemistry*]
TMTX	Temtex Industries, Inc. [*NASDAQ symbol*] (NQ)
TMU	Groton, CT [*Location identifier*] [*FAA*] (FAAL)
TMU	Tactical Mobile Unit [*Police*]
TMU	Temperature Measurement Unit (NASA)
TMU	Temuco [*Chile*] [*Seismograph station code, US Geological Survey*] (SEIS)
TMU	Test Maintenance Unit [*Data processing*]
TMU	Tetramethylurea [*Organic chemistry*]
TMU	Thermal-Mechanical Unit
TMU	Time Measurement Unit [*Industrial engineering*]
TMU	Transmission Message Unit
TMU	Turret Mock-Up (MCD)
TMUP	Union Planters National Bank, Memphis, TN [*Library symbol*] [*Library of Congress*] (LCLS)
TMurH	Highland Rim Regional Library Center, Murfreesboro, TN [*Library symbol*] [*Library of Congress*] (LCLS)
TMurS	Middle Tennessee State University, Murfreesboro, TN [*Library symbol*] [*Library of Congress*] (LCLS)
TMUS	Temporarily Mounted User Set [*Data processing*] (ADA)
TMUS	Toy Manufacturers of the United States
TMUSAE	United States Army Engineers Library, Memphis, TN [*Library symbol*] [*Library of Congress*] (LCLS)
TMUSDC	United States Department of Commerce, Memphis, TN [*Library symbol*] [*Library of Congress*] (LCLS)
TMV	Tanker Motor Vessel [*Shipping*] (DS)
TMV	Telemetry Van
TMV	Texas A & M University, Medical Sciences Library, College Station, TX [*OCLC symbol*] (OCLC)
TMV	Tobacco Mosaic Virus
TMV	Todd Memorial Volumes [*A publication*]
TMV	Torpedoman's Mate, Aviation [*Navy rating*]
TMV	Total Molecular Volume [*Chemistry*]
TMV	True Mean Value
TMV	Turnip Mosaic Virus
TMV	United States Veterans Administration Hospital, Memphis, TN [*Library symbol*] [*Library of Congress*] (LCLS)
TMV-C	Turnip Mosaic Virus - Common
TMV-L	Turnip Mosaic Virus - Legume
TMVP	Tobacco Mosaic Virus Protein

TMVS	Times Mirror Videotex Services, Inc. [*Information service or system*] [*Inactive*] (IID)
TMW	Tactical Missile Wing [*Air Force*]
TMW	Tamworth [*Australia*] [*Airport symbol*] (OAG)
TMW	Thermal Megawatt [*Also, Mwt*]
TmW	Time Warner, Inc. [*Associated Press abbreviation*] (APAG)
TMW	Tomorrow (FAAC)
TMW	Toyota Motor Workers' Union
TMW	Transverse Magnetic Wave [*Radio*]
TMW	Welzijnsweekblad [*A publication*]
TMWR	Tax Management Weekly Report [*Bureau of National Affairs*] [*Information service or system*] (CRD)
TMWR	Technical Manual Work Request
TMWR	Technical Manual Work Requirement (MCD)
TMX	Tamoxifen [*Antineoplastic drug*]
TMX	Tandem Mirror Experiment [*Atomic fusion*]
TMX	Telemeter Transmitter
TMXDI	Tetramethylxylene Diisocyanate [*Organic chemistry*]
TMXDI	Trimethylxylene Diisocyanate [*Organic chemistry*]
TMXO	Tactical Miniature Crystal Oscillator
TMXRT	Three-Mirror X-Ray Telescope [*NASA*]
TMZ	Houston, TX [*Location identifier*] [*FAA*] (FAAL)
TMZ	Textile Magazine. Vakblad voor de Handel in Textiel, Kleding, en Woningtextiel [*A publication*]
TN	Congo (Brazzaville) [*Aircraft nationality and registration mark*] (FAAC)
TN	[*The*] Navigators (EA)
TN	Public Library of Nashville and Davidson County, Nashville, TN [*Library symbol*] [*Library of Congress*] (LCLS)
TN	Stewardsman [*Nonrated enlisted man*] [*Navy*]
TN	Tagesarbeitsnormen [*Workday Standards*] [*German*]
TN	Talking Newspaper News [*A publication*]
T/N	Tar and Nicotine [*In cigarettes*]
TN	Tariff Number
TN	Tarragon Oil & Gas Ltd. [*Toronto Stock Exchange symbol*]
TN	Taunton [*British depot code*]
TN	TDRSS [*Tracking and Data Relay Satellite System*] Network [*NASA*] (SSD)
TN	Team Nursing
TN	Technical Note
TN	Technology Needs (MCD)
TN	Telephone (NATG)
TN	Telephone Number
TN	Tell en-Nasbeh (BJA)
TN	Temperature Normal [*Medicine*]
TN	Temple Name (BJA)
TN	Tennessee [*Postal code*]
TN	Tennessee Reports [*A publication*] (DLA)
TN	Terminal Node
TN	Test Narrative (CAAL)
TN	Test Negative [*Clinical chemistry*]
TN	Test Number (AAG)
TN	Texas & Northern Railway Co. [*AAR code*]
TN	Theatre Notebook [*A publication*]
TN	Thermonuclear
TN	Tin
tn	Titanite [*CIPW classification*] [*Geology*]
TN	Title News [*A publication*]
TN	Ton
TN	Tone (MSA)
TN	Top of the News [*A publication*]
TN	Total Negative (MAE)
TN	Total Nitrogen [*Analytical chemistry*]
TN	Town
TN	Track Number
TN	Trade Name (DEN)
TN	Train (AAG)
TN	Trans-Australia Airlines [*ICAO designator*] (FAAC)
TN	Transfer on Negative
TN	Transferable Notice [*Business term*]
TN	Transfield (NSW) Pty. Ltd. [*Transavia Division*] [*Australia*] [*ICAO aircraft manufacturer identifier*] (ICAO)
TN	Translator's Note
TN	Transport
TN	Transportation
TN	Transverse Nerve [*Neuroanatomy*]
TN	Travel News [*A publication*]
TN	Triafol
TN	Troponin [*Biochemistry*]
T/N	True Name
TN	True Negative [*Medicine*]
TN	True North
Tn	Tukulti-Ninurta (BJA)
TN	Tuning Units [*JETDS nomenclature*] [*Military*] (CET)
TN	Tunisia [*ANSI two-letter standard code*] [*IYRU nationality code*] (CNC)
TN	Twelfth Night [*Shakespearean work*]
TN	Twisted Nematic [*Telecommunications*] (TEL)
TN²	[*The*] News Is the News [*Television comedy program*]
TNA	Jinan [*China*] [*Airport symbol*] (OAG)

TNA........... [*The*] National Alliance of Professional and Executive Women's Networks [*Later, TIA*] (EA)
TNA........... [*The*] National Archives [*of the United States*]
TNA........... Office of Terrorism and Narcotics Analysis [*Washington, DC*] [*Bureau of Intelligence and Research*] [*Department of State*] (GRD)
TNA........... Telecommunications Network Architects [*Telecommunications service*] (TSSD)
TNA........... Telocator Network of America (EA)
TN A......... Tennessee Appeals Reports [*A publication*] (DLA)
TNA........... Tetranitroadamantane [*Explosive*] [*Organic chemistry*]
TNA........... Tetranitroaniline [*Organic chemistry*]
TNA........... Thermal Neutron Activation [*FAA*]
TNA........... Thermal Neutron Analysis [*For detection of explosives*]
TNA........... Thermal Nuclear Analyzer
TNA........... Thomas Nelson - Australia [*Publisher*]
TNA........... Tidsskrift foer Norron Arkeologi [*A publication*]
Tna............ Tigrinya (BJA)
TNA........... Time of Nearest Approach
TNA........... Tin City [*Alaska*] [*Seismograph station code, US Geological Survey*] (SEIS)
TNA........... Total Nucleic Acid
TNA........... Trans National Airlines [*South San Francisco, CA*] [*FAA designator*] (FAAC)
TNA........... Transient Network Analyzer (IEEE)
TNA........... Trigeminal Neuralgia Association (EA)
TNA........... Trinitroaniline [*Organic chemistry*]
TNA........... Tropicana Development Corp. [*Vancouver Stock Exchange symbol*]
TNAC....... Turkish News Agency of Cyprus (EAIO)
TNAE........ United States Army Engineer District, Nashville, Nashville, TN [*Library symbol*] [*Library of Congress*] (LCLS)
TNAEA ..... Teplovye Napryazheniya v Elementakh Konstruktsii [*A publication*]
TNAF .... Training Name and Address File [*IRS*]
TNAM....... Theater Network Analysis Model [*Europe*] (MCD)
TNAN....... Texas Numismatic Association. News [*A publication*]
TNAUK..... Talking Newspaper Association, United Kingdom
TNB .... Tanabu [*Japan*] [*Seismograph station code, US Geological Survey*] [*Closed*] (SEIS)
TNB .... Technical News Bulletin [*National Bureau of Standards*]
TNB .... Technion News Bulletin [*Haifa*] [*A publication*] (BJA)
TNB .... Thio(nitro)benzoic Acid [*Analytical biochemistry*]
TNB .... Thomas & Betts Corp. [*NYSE symbol*] (SPSG)
TNB .... Transnasal Butorphanol [*Analgesic*]
TNB .... Trinitrobenzene [*Explosive*]
TNBA .... Tri-Normal-Butylaluminum [*Organic chemistry*]
TNBA .... Tri-normal-butylamine [*Organic chemistry*]
TNBe .... Belmont College, Nashville, TN [*Library symbol*] [*Library of Congress*] (LCLS)
TNBH....... Baptist Hospital, Medical Library, Nashville, TN [*Library symbol*] [*Library of Congress*] (LCLS)
TNBMD .... Bureau of Mines. Technology News [*United States*] [*A publication*]
TNBP........ Tri-N-Butyl Phosphate [*Organic chemistry*] (AAMN)
TNBS........ Trinitrobenzenesulfonic Acid [*Biochemistry*]
TNBT .... American Baptist Theological Seminary, Nashville, TN [*Library symbol*] [*Library of Congress*] (LCLS)
TNBT .... Tetranitro Blue Tetrazolium [*A dye*] [*Organic chemistry*]
TNC........... Country Music Foundation Library and Media Center, Nashville, TN [*Library symbol*] [*Library of Congress*] (LCLS)
TNC........... [*The*] National Crossbowmen (EA)
TNC........... [*The*] Nature Conservancy (EA)
TNC........... [*The*] Nerve Center (EA)
TNC........... Tail Number Change [*Air Force*] (AFIT)
TNC........... Tekniska Nomenklaturcentralen [*Swedish Center for Technical Terminology*] [*Information service or system*] (IID)
T & NC ...... Tennessee & North Carolina Railroad (IIA)
TNC........... Terminal Network Controller
TNC........... Terminal Node Controller [*Data processing*]
TNC........... Texas Nuclear Corp. (KSC)
TNC........... Theater Naval Commander
TNC........... Thymic Nurse Cell [*Cytology*]
TNC........... Tide Net Controller (NATG)
TNC........... Tin City [*Alaska*] [*Airport symbol*] (OAG)
TNC........... Tin City, AK [*Location identifier*] [*FAA*] (FAAL)
TNC........... Too Numerous to Count
TNC........... Town & Country Corp. [*AMEX symbol*] (SPSG)
TNC........... Track Navigation Computer
TNC........... Track No Conversion
TNC........... Trans-National Communications, Inc.
TNC........... Transnational Corp.
TNC........... Transport Network Controller
TNC........... Trevecca Nazarene College [*Tennessee*]
TNC........... Trinitrocellulose [*Organic chemistry*]
TNC........... Trionics Technology Ltd. [*Vancouver Stock Exchange symbol*]
TNC........... Tripartite Naval Commission [*Allied German Occupation Forces*]
TnC............ Troponin C [*Biochemistry*]

TNCA .... Oranjestad/Reina Beatrix, Aruba Island [*Netherlands Antilles*] [*ICAO location identifier*] (ICLI)
TNCA .... Thionaphthenecarboxylic Acid [*Organic chemistry*]
TNCB .... Kralendijk/Flamingo, Bonaire Island [*Netherlands Antilles*] [*ICAO location identifier*] (ICLI)
TNCC .... Tripartite Nuclear Cross-Sections Committee [*British, Canadian, and US*]
TNCC .... Willemstad/Hato, Curacao Island [*Netherlands Antilles*] [*ICAO location identifier*] (ICLI)
TNCD........ Ten Nation Committee on Disarmament [*Defunct, 1960*]
TNCE .... Oranjestad/F. D. Roosevelt, Sint Eustatius Island [*Netherlands Antilles*] [*ICAO location identifier*] (ICLI)
TNCF........ Curacao [*Netherlands Antilles*] [*ICAO location identifier*] (ICLI)
TNCL........ Tail Number Configuration List [*Navy*] (NG)
TNCM .... Philipsburg/Prinses Juliana, Sint Maarten Island [*Netherlands Antilles*] [*ICAO location identifier*] (ICLI)
TN Cr........ Tennessee Criminal Appeals Reports [*A publication*] (DLA)
TNCS........ Saba/Yrausquin [*Netherlands Antilles*] [*ICAO location identifier*] (ICLI)
TNCSDT ... North Carolina. Agricultural Research Service. Technical Bulletin [*A publication*]
TnCSI .... Technician of the Construction Surveyor's Institute [*British*] (DBQ)
TNCSS ...... Temporary National Commission on Supplies and Shortages [*Initiated 1974*]
TNCV .... Televisao Nacional de Cabo Verde [*National Television of Cape Verde*] (EY)
TND.......... Telecommunications Network for the Deaf
TND.......... Term Normal Delivery [*Obstetrics*] (MAE)
TND.......... Tinned
TND.......... Todwind Development Corp. [*Vancouver Stock Exchange symbol*]
TND.......... Trace Narcotics Detector
TND.......... Trade Names Database [*Information service or system*] (IID)
TND.......... Trade Names Dictionary [*Later, BTC*] [*A publication*]
TND.......... Traditional Neighborhood Development Ordinance
TND.......... Transnational Data Report. Information Politics and Regulation [*A publication*]
TND.......... Turned (AAG)
TNDC........ Disciples of Christ Historical Society, Nashville, TN [*Library symbol*] [*Library of Congress*] (LCLS)
TNDC........ Thai National Documentation Center (IID)
TNDC........ Trade Negotiations among Developing Countries (IMH)
TND:CI ..... Trade Names Dictionary: Company Index [*Later, CTB*] [*A publication*]
TNDCY ..... Tendency (FAAC)
Tnd Hotel... Trends in the Hotel-Motel Industry [*A publication*]
TNDNA ..... Tokyo Nogyo Daigaku Nogaku Shuho [*A publication*]
TNDNAG ... Journal of Agricultural Science. Tokyo Nogyo Daigaku [*A publication*]
TNDP .... Tetranitrodiphenyl [*Organic chemistry*]
TNDS .... Tactical Navigational Display System
TNDS .... Total Network Data System [*Bell System*]
TNDS .... TS Industries, Inc. [*Huntington Beach, CA*] [*NASDAQ symbol*] (NQ)
TNDSA ...... Trends [*A publication*]
TNDU........ Technodyne, Inc. [*NASDAQ symbol*] (NQ)
TNDV .... Tobacco Necrotic Dwarf Virus [*Plant pathology*]
Tndycft....... Tandycrafts, Inc. [*Associated Press abbreviation*] (APAG)
TNDZR .... Tenderizer
TNE .... Tanegashima [*Japan*] [*Airport symbol*] (OAG)
TNE .... Terra Nova Energy [*Vancouver Stock Exchange symbol*]
TNE .... TRIS, Sodium Chloride, EDTA [*A buffer*]
TNEC .... Temporary National Economic Committee [*Congressional committee which studied the American economic system*] [*World War II*]
TNEF .... Trinitroethyl Formal [*An explosive*]
TNEL........ Nelson [*Thomas*], Inc. [*NASDAQ symbol*] (NQ)
TNEMBJ .. Annals. Research Institute of Epidemiology and Microbiology [*A publication*]
TNEOC ..... Trinitroethyl Orthocarbonate [*An explosive*]
TNEOF...... Trinitroethyl Orthoformate [*An explosive*]
TNET .... Telenetics Corp. [*NASDAQ symbol*] (NQ)
TNF .... Fisk University, Nashville, TN [*Library symbol*] [*Library of Congress*] (LCLS)
TNF .... Tactical Nuclear Force (MCD)
TNF .... Theater Nuclear Forces
TNF .... Thin Nickel Film
TNF .... Third Normal Form [*Databases*]
TNF .... Timing Negative Film
TNF .... Trainfire
TNF .... Transfer on No Overflow
TNF .... Trinitrofluorenone [*Organic chemistry*]
TNF .... True North Film [*Vancouver Stock Exchange symbol*]
TNF .... Tumor Necrosis Factor [*Antineoplastic drug*] [*Immunology*]
TNF-A ...... Tumor Necrosis Factor-Alpha
TNFB........ Free-Will Baptist Bible College, Nashville, TN [*Library symbol*] [*Library of Congress*] (LCLS)
TNF/S .... Theater Nuclear Forces Security [*DoD*]
TNFS......... Theater Nuclear Forces Survivability (MCD)

TNFS3.......	Theater Nuclear Forces, Survivability, Security, and Safety (MCD)
TNFSS......	Theater Nuclear Forces Survivability and Security (MCD)
TNG..........	[*The*] Newspaper Guild (EA)
TNG..........	Tanger [*Morocco*] [*Airport symbol*] (OAG)
TNG..........	Tangerang [*Java*] [*Seismograph station code, US Geological Survey*] (SEIS)
TNG..........	Tangerang [*Java*] [*Geomagnetic observatory code*]
TNG..........	Tongue (MSA)
TNG..........	Training (AAG)
TNG..........	Transdermal Nitroglycerine Patch [*Medicine*]
TNG..........	Tungco Resources Corp. [*Vancouver Stock Exchange symbol*]
TNGANCH ...	Training Anchorage [*Navy*] (NVT)
TNGE........	Tonnage [*Shipping*]
TNGLIT	Training Literature [*Military*]
TngS	Training Subject
TNGSUP...	Training Support [*Navy*] (NVT)
TNGSVCS ...	Training Services [*Navy*] (NVT)
TNGT	Tonight (FAAC)
TNH	Tampa-Hillsborough County Public Library, Tampa, FL [*OCLC symbol*] (OCLC)
TNH	Tax Notes Highlights [*Tax Analysts*] [*Information service or system*] (CRD)
TNH	Tienshui [*Republic of China*] [*Seismograph station code, US Geological Survey*] (SEIS)
TNHCA.....	Hospital Corp. of America, Research/Information Services, Nashville, TN [*Library symbol*] [*Library of Congress*] (LCLS)
TNHCA.....	Taehan Naekwa Hakhoe Chapchi [*A publication*]
TNHQ	Theater Navy Headquarters
TNI	[*The*] Network, Inc. [*An association*] (EA)
TNI	[*The*] Networking Institute [*Commercial firm*] (EA)
TNI	Peipeinimaru, TT [*Location identifier*] [*FAA*] (FAAL)
TNI	Thin Nickel Iron
TNI	Tin News. Accurate Information on World Tin Production, Prices, Marketing Developments, and New Uses and Applications [*A publication*]
TNI	Total Nodal Irradiation [*Oncology*]
TNI	Traffic Noise Index [*Department of Transportation*]
TNI	Trans International Gold [*Vancouver Stock Exchange symbol*]
TNI	Transcisco [*AMEX symbol*] (SPSG)
TNI	Transnational Institute [*Netherlands*]
TnI	Troponin I [*Biochemistry*]
TNIA	[*The*] Network Inc. of America [*Information service or system*] (IID)
TNIF.........	Thin Nickel Iron Film
TNII..........	Telecommunications Network, Inc. [*NASDAQ symbol*] (NQ)
TnIMBM...	Technician of the Institute of Municipal Building Management [*British*] (DBQ)
TNIP.........	TDRSS/NASCOM [*Tracking and Data Relay Satellite System/ NASA Communications Network*] Interface Panel (SSD)
TNJ...........	Joint University Libraries, Nashville, TN [*Library symbol*] [*Library of Congress*] (LCLS)
TNJ...........	Tanjung Pinang [*Indonesia*] [*Airport symbol*] (OAG)
TNJ-L.......	Joint University Libraries, Vanderbilt School of Law, Nashville, TN [*Library symbol*] [*Library of Congress*] (LCLS)
TNJ-M	Joint University Libraries, Vanderbilt Medical Center, Nashville, TN [*Library symbol*] [*Library of Congress*] (LCLS)
TNJ-P........	Joint University Libraries, George Peabody College for Teachers, Nashville, TN [*Library symbol*] [*Library of Congress*] (LCLS)
TNJ-R........	Joint University Libraries, Vanderbilt School of Religion, Nashville, TN [*Library symbol*] [*Library of Congress*] (LCLS)
TNJ-S........	Joint University Libraries, Scarritt College for Christian Workers, Nashville, TN [*Library symbol*] [*Library of Congress*] (LCLS)
TNK..........	Tank (AAG)
TNK..........	Tinkers Knob [*California*] [*Seismograph station code, US Geological Survey*] (SEIS)
TNK..........	Tunkwa Copper Mining [*Vancouver Stock Exchange symbol*]
TNK..........	Tununak [*Alaska*] [*Airport symbol*] (OAG)
TNK........	[*The*] Two Noble Kinsmen [*Shakespearean work*]
TNKR	Tanker (FAAC)
TNKUL	Towarzystwo Naukowe Katolickiego Uniwersytet Lubelskiego [*A publication*]
TNKULWP ...	Towarzystwo Naukowe Katolickiego Uniwersytet Lubelskiego. Wyklady i Przemowienia [*Lublin*] [*A publication*]
TNL	David Lipscomb College, Nashville, TN [*Library symbol*] [*Library of Congress*] (LCLS)
TNL	Technical Newsletter
TNL	Technitrol, Inc. [*AMEX symbol*] (SPSG)
TN L	Tennessee Law Review [*A publication*]
TNL	Terminal Net Loss
TNL	Times Newspapers Ltd. [*British*]
TNL	Tunnel (MSA)
TnL	Tunnel Luminescence [*Physics*]
TNLAAH ..	Tidsskrift foer den Norske Laegeforening [*A publication*]
TNLDIO....	Tunnel Diode [*Electronics*]
TNLG	Technology, Inc. [*NASDAQ symbol*] (NQ)

TNLR	Railroad Tunnel [*Board on Geographic Names*]
TN LR.......	Tennessee Law Review [*A publication*]
TNLRA......	Tennessee Law Review [*A publication*]
TNLS	Trans-National Leasing, Inc. [*NASDAQ symbol*] (NQ)
TNM.........	Meharry Medical College, Nashville, TN [*Library symbol*] [*Library of Congress*] (LCLS)
TNM.........	Tashota-Nipigon Mines [*Vancouver Stock Exchange symbol*]
TNM.........	Tetranitromethane [*Organic chemistry*]
TNM.........	Texas-New Mexico Railway Co. [*AAR code*]
TNM.........	Topical Nitrogen Mustard [*Dermatology*]
TNM.........	Tumor classification system derived from symbols: T for Primary Tumor; N for Regional Lymph Node Metastasis; M for Remote Metastasis [*Medicine*]
TNMH	Metro General Hospital, Nashville, TN [*Library symbol*] [*Library of Congress*] (LCLS)
TNMPH....	Methodist Publishing House Library, Nashville, TN [*Library symbol*] [*Library of Congress*] (LCLS)
TNMR	Tritium Nuclear Magnetic Resonance [*Spectrometry*]
TNN..........	[*The*] Nashville Network [*Cable-television system*]
TNN..........	Nashville Public Library, Nashville, TN [*OCLC symbol*] (OCLC)
TNN..........	Tainan [*Taiwan*] [*Airport symbol*] (OAG)
TNN..........	Tanana [*Alaska*] [*Seismograph station code, US Geological Survey*] (SEIS)
TNN..........	Teleconnect Co. [*NYSE symbol*] (SPSG)
TNN..........	TermNet News [*A publication*]
TNO..........	Nederlandse Centrale Organisatie voor Toegepast Natuurwetenschappelijk Onderzoek [*Netherlands Institute for Applied Scientific Research*]
TNO..........	Tamarindo [*Costa Rica*] [*Airport symbol*] (OAG)
TNO..........	Tenore Oil & Gas [*Vancouver Stock Exchange symbol*]
TNO..........	Texas & New Orleans R. R. [*AAR code*]
TNO..........	Torino [*Italy*] [*Seismograph station code, US Geological Survey*] (SEIS)
TNO..........	Transfer on No Overflow (SAA)
TNOC.......	Threads No Couplings
TNO Div Nutr Food Res TNO Rep ...	TNO [*Nederlands Centrale Organisatie voor Toegepast-Natuurwetenschappelijk Onderzoek*] Division for Nutrition and Food Research TNO. Report [*A publication*]
TNOP........	Total Network Operations Plan [*Telecommunications*] (TEL)
TNO Proj...	TNO [*Nederlands Centrale Organisatie voor Toegepast-Natuurwetenschappelijk Onderzoek*] Project [*A publication*]
TNOR........	Temiskaming & Northern Ontario Railway
TNOSA	Tunnels et Ouvrages Souterrains [*A publication*]
TNOT.......	Total Not Operating Time
TNP	[*The*] National Party [*Grenada*] [*Political party*] (EY)
TNP	[*The*] New Party [*Australia*] [*Political party*]
TNP	Thailand National Police (CINC)
TNP	Theatre National Populaire [*France*]
TNP	TNP Enterprises, Inc. [*NYSE symbol*] (SPSG)
TNP	TNP Enterprises, Inc. [*Associated Press abbreviation*] (APAG)
TNP	Tonopah [*Nevada*] [*Seismograph station code, US Geological Survey*] (SEIS)
TNP	Transkei National Party [*Political party*] (EY)
TNP	Trinitrophenol [*or Trinitrophenyl*] [*Organic chemistry*]
TNP	Trojan Nuclear Plant (NRCH)
TNP	Twentynine Palms [*California*] [*Airport symbol*] (OAG)
TNP	Twentynine Palms, CA [*Location identifier*] [*FAA*] (FAAL)
TNPA	Tri-Normal-Propylaluminum [*Organic chemistry*]
TNPA	Tri-normal-propylamine [*Organic chemistry*]
TNPF........	Tidewater Nicaragua Project Foundation (EA)
TNPG	[*The*] Nuclear Power Group [*British*]
TNPH........	Tennessee Department of Public Health, Nashville, TN [*Library symbol*] [*Library of Congress*] (LCLS)
TNPK	Turnpike
TNP-KLH ...	Trinitrophenyl Keyhole Limpet Hemocyanin [*Immunology*]
Tn Plann Rev ...	Town Planning Review [*A publication*]
TNPO	Terminal Navy Post Office (AFM)
TNPP........	Planned Parenthood of Nashville, Nashville, TN [*Library symbol*] [*Library of Congress*] (LCLS)
TNPP........	Tris(nonylphenyl) Phosphite [*Organic chemistry*]
TNPZOW ...	Towarzystwo Niesienia Pomocy Zydom Ofiarom Wojny [*A publication*] (BJA)
TNR..........	Antananarivo [*Madagascar*] [*Airport symbol*] (OAG)
TNR..........	[*The*] New Repertory
TNR..........	[*The*] New Republic [*A publication*]
TNR..........	Non-RADAR Transfer of Control Message [*Communications*] (FAAC)
TNR..........	Tanganyika Notes and Records [*A publication*]
TNR..........	Tanzania Notes and Records [*A publication*]
TNR..........	Thinner
TNR..........	Titan Resources Ltd. [*Vancouver Stock Exchange symbol*]
TNR..........	Tone Not Relevant
TNR..........	Tonic Neck Reflex [*Physiology*]
TNR..........	Trainer (AAG)
TNR..........	Transit Nuclear Radiation
TNRE........	Transit Nuclear Radiation Effect
TNRIS	Texas Natural Resources Information System [*Austin*] [*Information service or system*] (IID)

TNRIS....... Transportation Noise Research Information Service [*Department of Transportation*]

TNRT .... TNR Technical, Inc. [*Farmingdale, NY*] [*NASDAQ symbol*]   (NQ)

TNRY .... Tannery

TNS .... [*The*] Names Society   (EA)

TNS .... [*The*] National Switchboard [*Phoenix, AZ*] [*Telecommunications*]   (TSSD)

TNS .... [*The*] New Salesmanship [*Book by Steve Salerno*]

TNS .... [*The*] Next Step [*Physics*]

TNS .... Tactical Navigation System   (DWSG)

TNS .... Tank Nitrogen Supply   (AAG)

TNS .... Tanos Petroleum Corp. [*Vancouver Stock Exchange symbol*]

TNS .... Taunus [*Federal Republic of Germany*] [*Seismograph station code, US Geological Survey*]   (SEIS)

TNS .... Telecommunications Network Services [*Data Resources*] [*Information service or system*]   (CRD)

TNS .... Tennessee State Library and Archives, Nashville, TN [*OCLC symbol*]   (OCLC)

TNS .... Thames Navigation Service [*British*]   (DS)

TNS .... Thermal Night Site

TNS .... Thomas Nast Society   (EA)

TNS .... Timber Trade Review [*Kuala Lumpur*] [*A publication*]

TNS .... Toluidinylnaphthalene Sulfonate [*Organic chemistry*]

TNS .... Topical Numismatic Society   (EA)

TNS .... Toronto Normal School

TNS .... Track Number Sorted Table   (SAA)

TNS .... Transaction Network Service [*AT & T*]

TNS .... Transcutaneous Nerve Stimulation [*Also, TENS, TES*] [*A method of pain control*] [*Medicine*]

TNS .... Triple Nine Society   (EA)

TNS .... Tunable Noise Source

TNSA........ [*The*] National Spiritual Alliance of the United States of America

TNSA........ Technical Nuclear Safety   (MCD)

TNSB........ Southern Baptist Convention Historical Commission, Nashville, TN [*Library symbol*] [*Library of Congress*]   (LCLS)

TNSCDR... TINS. Trends in Neurosciences [*A publication*]

TNSDUNSPHI ... [*The*] National Society to Discourage Use of the Name Smith for Purposes of Hypothetical Illustration

TNSI.......... [*A*] Text-Book of North-Semitic Inscriptions [*A publication*]   (BJA)

TNSKA...... Tohoku Nogyo Shikenjo Kenkyu Hokoku [*A publication*]

TNSL........ Tensile

TNSL........ Tinsley Laboratories, Inc. [*NASDAQ symbol*]   (NQ)

TNSN .... Tension   (MSA)

TNSP .... Transportation   (CINC)

TNSRA...... Tensor [*A publication*]

TNStT .... Saint Thomas Hospital, Health Sciences Library, Nashville, TN [*Library symbol*] [*Library of Congress*]   (LCLS)

TN Stud Lit ... Tennessee Studies in Literature [*A publication*]

TNSX........ Taniisix. Aleutian Regional School District [*A publication*]

TNT .... Miami, FL [*Location identifier*] [*FAA*]   (FAAL)

TNT .... [*The*] Next Trend

TNT .... Tax Notes Today [*Database*] [*Tax Analysts*] [*Information service or system*]   (CRD)

TNT .... Teleconference Network of Texas [*University of Texas*] [*San Antonio*] [*Telecommunications*]   (TSSD)

TNT .... Tinto Gold Corp. [*Vancouver Stock Exchange symbol*]

TNT .... Titles Now Troublesome [*School books*] [*American Library Association*]

TNT .... TNT Tariff Agents, Inc., New York NY [*STAC*]

TNT .... Tobramycin-Nafcillin-Ticarcillin [*Antibiotic combination*]

TNT .... Toronto [*Ontario*] [*Seismograph station code, US Geological Survey*] [*Closed*]   (SEIS)

TNT .... Torque, Nip, and Tension [*Winding technology*]

TNT .... Towarzystwo Naukowe w Toruniu [*A publication*]

TNT .... Transient Nuclear Test

TNT .... Transnational Terrorism   (ADA)

TNT .... Transportation News Ticker [*Knight-Ridder Business Information Services*] [*Information service or system*]   (CRD)

TNT .... Trim, Neat, and Terrific [*Slang*]

TNT .... Trinitrotoluene [*Explosive*]

TnT .... Troponin T [*Biochemistry*]

TNT .... Turner Network Television [*Cable-television system*]

TNTBP ..... Trinitrotoluene and Black Powder   (SAA)

TNTC .... Too Numerous to Count [*Microbiology*]

TNTC .... Tyndale New Testament Commentary [*A publication*]   (BJA)

TNTDL ..... Tabulated Numerical Technical Data List

TNTDR ..... Thermonuclear TOKAMAK Demonstration Reactor [*Particle physics*]

TNTHA ..... Tennessee Hospital Association, Nashville, TN [*Library symbol*] [*Library of Congress*]   (LCLS)

TNTN .... Trevecca Nazarene College, Nashville, TN [*Library symbol*] [*Library of Congress*]   (LCLS)

TNTO .... Tintoretto, Inc. [*New York, NY*] [*NASDAQ symbol*]   (NQ)

TNTU .... University of Tennessee, Nashville, TN [*Library symbol*] [*Library of Congress*]   (LCLS)

TNTV .... Tentative   (AFM)

TNU.......... Newton, IA [*Location identifier*] [*FAA*]   (FAAL)

tnu .... Tennessee [*MARC country of publication code*] [*Library of Congress*]   (LCCP)

TNU.......... Upper Room Devotional Library and Museum, Nashville, TN [*Library symbol*] [*Library of Congress*]   (LCLS)

TNUK....... Thomas Nelson - United Kingdom [*Publisher*]

TNUM....... United Methodist Publishing House, Nashville, TN [*Library symbol*] [*Library of Congress*]   (LCLS)

TNV.......... Navasota, TX [*Location identifier*] [*FAA*]   (FAAL)

TNV.......... Tobacco Necrosis Virus

TNV.......... Total Net Value

TNV.......... Total Nonvolatile [*Chemistry*]

TNV.......... Trinova Corp. [*NYSE symbol*]   (SPSG)

TNVS........ Thermal Night Vision System

TNW........ Tactical Nuclear Warfare   (MCD)

TNW........ Tactical Nuclear Weapon

TNW........ Talking Newspaper Week [*British*]

TNW........ Theater Nuclear Weapon

TNW........ Towarzystwo Naukowe Warszawskie [*A publication*]

TNW/CW ... Tactical Nuclear Warfare/Chemical Warfare   (MCD)

TNWRRI... Tennessee Water Resources Research Center [*Knoxville, TN*] [*Department of the Interior*]   (GRD)

TNX.......... Thanks [*Communications operator's procedural remark*]

TNX.......... Tonopah, NV [*Location identifier*] [*FAA*]   (FAAL)

TNX.......... Transfer on No Index   (SAA)

TNX.......... Trinitroxylene [*Organic chemistry*]

TNY.......... Tenney Engineering, Inc. [*AMEX symbol*]   (SPSG)

TNY.......... Trans New York [*New York, NY*] [*FAA designator*]   (FAAC)

TNY.......... Trinity University, Library, San Antonio, TX [*OCLC symbol*]   (OCLC)

T NY Ac Sci ... Transactions. New York Academy of Sciences [*A publication*]

TNYTI...... [*The*] New York Times Index

TNZ.......... Tarata [*New Zealand*] [*Seismograph station code, US Geological Survey*]   (SEIS)

TNZ.......... Thermoneutral Zone

TNZ.......... Transfer on Nonzero

TNZ.......... Tranzonic Cos. [*AMEX symbol*]   (SPSG)

TO............. Games Taken Out [*Baseball*]

TO............. [*The*] Medina Aviation Co. [*ICAO designator*]   (FAAC)

TO............. Oak Ridge Public Library, Oak Ridge, TN [*Library symbol*] [*Library of Congress*]   (LCLS)

TO............. People's Republic of South Yemen [*Aircraft nationality and registration mark*]   (FAAC)

TO............. Table of Organization

TO............. Tactical Observer

TO............. Tactical Officer [*Military*]   (RDA)

TO............. Take One [*A publication*]

T/O .... Take Over   (MCD)

T & O .... Taken and Offered [*Sporting*] [*British*]

TO............. Takeoff [*Aviation*]

TO............. Tandem Outlet

T/O .... Target of Opportunity

TO............. Target Organ [*Medicine*]   (AAMN)

TO............. Targum Onkelos   (BJA)

TO............. Task Order   (MCD)

TO............. TDRS [*Tracking and Data Relay Satellite*] Operations [*NASA*]   (SSD)

TO............. Technical Objective

TO............. Technical Observer

TO............. Technical Officer [*Military*] [*British*]

TO............. Technical Order

TO............. Telegraph Office

TO............. Telephone Office

TO............. Telephone Order [*Medicine*]

TO............. Tell el-Obed   (BJA)

TO............. Temperature, Oral [*Medicine*]

TO............. Test Operation   (AAG)

T & O .... Test and Operation [*NASA*]   (KSC)

TO............. Test Outline   (CAAL)

TO............. Theater of Operations [*Military*]

TO............. Theiler's Original [*Strain of mouse encephalitis virus*]

TO............. Thiazole Orange [*Organic chemistry*]

TO............. Through Ownership [*Shipping*]

TO............. Ticked Off [*Slang*]

T-O .... Time of Launch [*NASA*]   (KSC)

TO............. Time Opening

TO............. Time-Out

TO............. Tinctura Opii [*Tincture of Opium*]

T/O .... To Oblige   (AIA)

TO............. Tobacco Observer [*A publication*]

to .... Tonga [*MARC country of publication code*] [*Library of Congress*]   (LCCP)

TO............. Tonga [*ANSI two-letter standard code*]   (CNC)

TO............. Tonnage Opening   (DS)

TO............. Tool Order

TO............. Tops Order   (MCD)

TO............. Toronto

TO............. Torpedo Officer [*Obsolete*] [*Navy*] [*British*]

TO............. Township

TO............. Traded Options Market [*London Stock Exchange*]

TO............. Traditional Orthography [*Writing system*]

TO............. Traffic Officer
TO............. Trained Operator [*British military*]   (DMA)
T & O........ Training and Operations [*Military*]
TO............. Transfer Order
TO............. Transistor Outline   (IEEE)
TO............. Transmission Only [*Telecommunications*]
TO............. Transmitter Oscillator
TO............. Transportation Officer [*Military*]
TO............. Transverse Optic
TO............. Travel Order
TO............. Treasury Obligation [*Finance*]
TO............. Treasury Order [*British*]   (ROG)
TO............. Tricuspid Valve Opening [*Cardiology*]
TO............. Troy Ounce
TO............. Tryptophan Oxygenase [*Also, TP, TPO*] [*An enzyme*]
TO............. Tuberculin Ober [*Supernatant portion*] [*Medicine*]
TO............. Tuberculin Old [*or Original*] [*Also, OT*] [*Medicine*]
TO............. Tubo-Ovarian [*Medicine*]   (MAE)
TO............. Tuesdays Only [*British railroad term*]
TO............. [*A*] Turn Over [*A prospective customer who cannot be sold by one clerk and is turned over to another*] [*Merchandising slang*]
T/O........... Turned Out [*for Examination*] [*Tea trade*]   (ROG)
TO............. Turnout   (AAG)
TO............. Turnover [*Number*] [*With reference to enzyme activity*]
TO............. Type of Organization Code [*IRS*]
TO............. Tyrosine Oxidase [*An enzyme*]
TOA........... Table of Allowances
TOA........... Table of Organization and Allowance
TOA........... Terms of Agreement [*Army*]   (AABC)
TOA........... Theatre Owners of America [*Later, NATO*]   (EA)
TOA........... Thermal Optical Analysis
TOA........... Time of Arrival   (AFM)
TOA........... Time Out of Area   (MCD)
TOA........... Tolsona [*Alaska*] [*Seismograph station code, US Geological Survey*]   (SEIS)
TOA........... Top of the Atmosphere [*Meterology*]
TOA........... Torrance, CA [*Location identifier*] [*FAA*]   (FAAL)
TOA........... Total Obligational Authority [*Military*]
TOA........... Toyota Owners Association   (EA)
TOA........... Trace Organic Analysis [*Environmental Protection Agency*]   (GFGA)
TOA........... Trade-Off Analysis [*Military*]
TOA........... Trans Oceanic Airways Ltd. [*British*]
TOA........... Transportation Operating Agencies   (AFM)
TOA........... Transportation Operations Authority   (MCD)
TOA........... Trim on Assembly   (MCD)
TOA........... Truck Operation Analysis
TOA........... Tubo-Ovarian Abscess [*Medicine*]
TOA........... Type of Agent
TOAA....... Total Overall Aerospace Vehicle [*or Aircraft*] Authorization
TOAC....... Tool Accessory   (AAG)
TOAD....... Take Off and Die [*Surfers' slang for a very dangerous wave*]
TOAD....... Tobyhanna Army Depot [*Pennsylvania*]   (AABC)
TOAD....... Towed Optical Assessment Device [*Marine science*]   (MSC)
TOADS ..... Terminal-Oriented Administrative Data System
TOAI....... Total Overall Aerospace Vehicle [*or Aircraft*] Inventory
TOAL....... Test of Adolescent Language
TOAL....... Total Ordnance Alteration Application List [*Navy*]
TOAMAC ... [*The*] Optimum Army Materiel Command   (RDA)
TOAP........ Thioguanine, Oncovin [*Vincristine*], ara-C, Prednisone [*Antineoplastic drug regimen*]
Toast.......... Toastmaster, Inc. [*Associated Press abbreviation*]   (APAG)
TOB.......... Takeoff Boost [*Aviation*]
TOB.......... Telemetry Output Buffer [*Data processing*]
TOB.......... Test One BIT [*Binary Digit*]   (SAA)
TOB.......... Tobacco   (ADA)
Tob........... Tobacco [*A publication*]
Tob............. Tobacco Branch, Internal Revenue Bureau [*United States*]   (DLA)
TOB.......... Tobias [*Old Testament book*] [*Douay version*]
TOB.......... Tobit [*Old Testament book*] [*Roman Catholic canon*]   (ROG)
TOB.......... Toboggan
TOB.......... Tobruk [*Libya*] [*Airport symbol*]   (OAG)
TOB.......... Tow Bar   (MCD)
TOB.......... Transistor Output Buffer   (DNAB)
TOB.......... Tube over Bar [*Suspension*]   (MCD)
TOB.......... Type of Blast
TOBA .... Theater Owners Booking Association [*Vaudeville*]
TOBA .... Thoroughbred Owners and Breeders Association   (EA)
TOBA .... Tough on Black Actors [*Facetious translation of acronym for Theater Owners Booking Association*]
TOBAA8 ... Tobacco [*New York*] [*A publication*]
Tob Abstr... Tobacco Abstracts [*A publication*]
Tob Abstracts ... Tobacco Abstracts [*A publication*]
Tobacco...... Tobacco International [*A publication*]
Tobacco J... Tobacco Journal [*A publication*]   (APTA)
TOBE .... Test of Basic Experiences [*Child development test*]
TOBEDI.... [*Vessel*] To Be Disposed of [*Navy*]   (DNAB)
TOBELE ... [*Vessel*] To Be Leased [*Navy*]   (DNAB)
TOBELN... [*Vessel*] To Be Loaned [*Navy*]   (DNAB)

Tobey .... Tobey's Reports [*9, 10 Rhode Island*] [*A publication*]   (DLA)
TOBI......... Test of Basic Information [*Education*]
TOBI......... Toxicity Bibliography [*MEDLARS*]
Tob Int (NY) ... Tobacco International (New York) [*A publication*]
Tob Leaf..... Tobacco Leaf [*A publication*]
Tob Manuf Standing Comm Res Pap ... Tobacco Manufacturers' Standing Committee. Research Papers [*A publication*]
Tob Res ...... Tobacco Research [*A publication*]
Tob Res Board Rhod Bull ... Tobacco Research Board of Rhodesia. Bulletin [*A publication*]
Tob Res Counc Res Pap ... Tobacco Research Council. Research Paper [*England*] [*A publication*]
TobRV .... Tobacco Ring Spot Virus
TOBS......... Telemetering Ocean Bottom Seismometer [*Marine science*]   (MSC)
Tob Sci .... Tobacco Science [*A publication*]
TOBWE..... Tactical Observing Weather Element [*Air Force*]
TOC.......... [*The*] Operations Council of the American Trucking Associations   (EA)
TOC.......... Table of Coincidences [*Telecommunications*]   (TEL)
TOC.......... Table of Contents
TOC.......... Tactical Operations Center [*Military*]
TOC.......... Tag Open Cup [*Flash point test*]
TOC.......... Tagliabue Open Cup [*Analytical chemistry*]
TOC.......... Tanker Operational Circular
TOC.......... Task Order Contract
TOC.......... Task-Oriented Costing [*Telecommunications*]   (TEL)
TOC.......... Tech/Ops Sevcon [*AMEX symbol*]   (SPSG)
TOC.......... Technical Operating Center [*Telecommunications*]   (TSSD)
TOC.......... Technical Order Compliance [*Military*]
TOC.......... Television Operating Center
TOC.......... Television Operators Caucus   (EA)
TOC.......... Test of Cure [*Medicine*]
TOC.......... Test Operations Center [*NASA*]   (NASA)
TOC.......... Test Operations Change [*NASA*]   (NASA)
TOC.......... Theater of Operations Command [*Military*]
TOC.......... Tiers Ordre Carmelitaine [*Carmelite Third Order*] [*An association*] [*Italy*]   (EAIO)
TOC.......... Timber Operators Council   (EA)
TOC.......... Time of Correlation   (MCD)
TOC.......... Time Optimal Control   (MCD)
TOC.......... Timing Operation Center
TOC.......... Tinctura Opii Camphorata [*Paregoric Elixir*] [*Pharmacy*]   (ROG)
TOC.......... To Be Continued, Circuit Time Permitting   (FAAC)
TOC.......... Toccoa, GA [*Location identifier*] [*FAA*]   (FAAL)
TOC.......... Tocklai [*India*] [*Seismograph station code, US Geological Survey*]   (SEIS)
TOC.......... Tooling Order Change
TOC.......... Top of Climb [*Aviation*]
TOC.......... TOS [*TIROS Operational Satellite*] Operations Center   (NOAA)
TOC.......... Total Operational Cost [*Engineering*]
TOC.......... Total Optical Color [*Photography*]   (OA)
TOC.......... Total Organic Carbon
TOC.......... Traditional Organized Crime
TOC.......... Traffic Order Change   (SAA)
TOC.......... Trainer Operator Console   (SAA)
TOC.......... Transfer of Control
TOC.......... Turn-On Command   (KSC)
TOCA .... [*The*] Order of the Crown in America   (EA)
TOCAP..... Terminal-Oriented Control Applications Program
TOCC .... TDRSS [*Tracking and Data Relay Satellite System*] Operations Control Center [*NASA*]
TOCC .... Technical and Operations Control Center [*INTELSAT*]
TOCC .... Test Operations Control Center [*NASA*]
TOCC .... Transfer of Control Card
TOC/CP.... Tactical Operations Center/Command Post [*Military*]
TOCCWE ... Tactical Operations Control Center Weather Element [*Air Force*]
TOC/ECP ... Technical Order Compliance/Engineering Change Proposal [*Military*]   (AFIT)
TOCED ..... Table of Contents Editor Processor [*Data processing*]
Tocklai Exp Stn Advis Bull ... Tocklai Experimental Station. Advisory Bulletin [*A publication*]
Tocklai Exp Stn Advis Leafl ... Tocklai Experimental Station. Advisory Leaflet [*A publication*]
TOCl......... Total Organic Chlorine [*Analytical chemistry*]
TOCM....... Tocom, Inc. [*NASDAQ symbol*]   (NQ)
TOCM....... Trust Officers Committee Minutes [*A publication*]   (DLA)
TOCN....... Technical Order Change Notice [*Air Force*]   (MCD)
Tocn i Nadezn Kibernet Sistem ... Tocnost i Nadeznost Kiberneticeskih Sistem [*A publication*]
TOCOM.... Tokyo Commodity Exchange for Industry [*Japan*]   (ECON)
TOCP .... Tri-ortho-cresyl Phosphate [*Organic chemistry*]
TOCR .... Tocor, Inc. [*NASDAQ symbol*]   (NQ)
TOCS........ Oriental Ceramic Society. Transactions [*A publication*]
TOCS........ Terminal Operations Control System
TOCS........ Terminal-Oriented Computer System
TOCS........ Textile Operational Control System [*Data processing*]
TOCS........ Tool Order Control System   (MCD)
TOCSY....... Total Correlated Spectroscopy

TOCSY	Total Correlation Spectroscopy
TOCU	Tornado Operational Conversion Unit [*British military*] (DMA)
TOD	Technical Objective Directive [*or Document*] [*Air Force*] (MCD)
TOD	Technical Operations Department
TOD	Technical Order Dilemma (SAA)
TOD	Test Operations Directorate (RDA)
TOD	Theater-Oriented Depot [*Military*]
TOD	Theoretical Oxygen Demand [*Analytical biochemistry*]
TOD	Time of Day
TOD	Time of Delivery
TOD	Time of Departure (NVT)
TOD	Time of Despatch [*British*]
TOD	Tioman [*Malaysia*] [*Airport symbol*] (OAG)
TOD	Top of Duct (OA)
TOD	Total Oxygen Demand [*Analytical chemistry*]
TOD	Tourist-Oriented-Directional [*Traffic sign*]
TOD	Trade-Off Determination [*Military*] (AABC)
TOD	Turnover Device
TODA	Takeoff Distance Available [*Aviation*] (FAAC)
TODA	Technical Order Distribution Activity
TODA	Third-Octave Digital Analyzer
Toda Educ	Today's Education [*A publication*]
TODARS	Terminal-Oriented Data Analysis and Retrieval System [*National Institute of Standards and Technology*]
TODAS	Towed Oceanographic Data Acquisition System (MSC)
TODAS	Typewriter-Oriented Documentation-Aid System
Today	Today for Tomorrow [*A publication*]
Today Min	Today's Ministry [*A publication*]
Todays Chiro	Today's Chiropractic [*A publication*]
Today's Ed	Today's Education [*A publication*]
Todays Educ	Today's Education [*A publication*]
Todays Exec	Today's Executive [*A publication*]
Today's Fmkr	Today's Filmmaker [*A publication*]
Todays Nurs Home	Today's Nursing Home [*A publication*]
Today's Sec	Today's Secretary [*A publication*]
Todays VD Vener Dis Control Probl	Today's VD. Venereal Disease Control Problem [*A publication*]
Today Technol	Today Technology [*A publication*]
Today & Tomorrow Educ	Today and Tomorrow in Education [*A publication*]
TODC	Technical Order Distribution Code [*Air Force*]
TODC	Theater-Oriented Depot Complex [*Military*] (AABC)
Tod Cath Teach	Today's Catholic Teacher [*A publication*]
TODD	[*The*] Todd-AO Corp. [*NASDAQ symbol*] (NQ)
TODD-AO	Todd-American Optical Co. [*Wide-screen system used by producer Michael Todd and the American Optical Co.*]
ToddS	Todd Shipyards Corp. [*Associated Press abbreviation*] (APAG)
TODE	Transcript of Data Extraction (DNAB)
TODES	Transcript of Data Extraction System (MCD)
TODN	Telephone Order Dispatch Notice
TODO	Technical Order Distribution Office [*or Officer*]
Tod Parish	Today's Parish [*A publication*]
TODR	Takeoff Distance Required [*Aviation*] (AIA)
TODS	Test-Oriented Disk System (IEEE)
TODS	Transactions on Database Systems
TODT	Tool Detail (AAG)
TOE	Epidermatophyton
TOE	Table of Organization Equipment
TOE	Tables of Organization and Equipment [*Military*]
TO & E	Tables of Organization and Equipment [*Military*] (AAG)
TOE	Talker Omission Error (MUGU)
T & OE	Tentage and Organizational Equipment Branch [*US Army Natick Research, Development, and Engineering Center*]
TOE	Term of Enlistment [*Military*]
TOE	Texas, Oklahoma & Eastern Railroad Co. [*AAR code*]
TOE	Theory of Everything [*Cosmology*]
TOE	Thread One End (MSA)
TOE	Time of Entry (MCD)
TOE	Time of Event [*Military*] (CAAL)
TOE	Tons of Oil Equivalent
TOE	Tony, Oscar, Emmy [*Refers to actors who have won these three major awards, for stage, film, and television work, respectively*]
TOE	Top of Edge (AAG)
TOE	Total Operating Expense
TOE	Tozeur [*Tunisia*] [*Airport symbol*] (OAG)
TOE	Tracheoesophageal [*Also, TE*] [*Medicine*]
TOE	Trainborne Operational Equipment
TOE	Tryout Employment [*Job Training and Partnership Act*] (OICC)
TOE	United States Energy Research and Development Administration, Technical Information, Oak Ridge, TN [*Library symbol*] [*Library of Congress*] (LCLS)
TOEFL	Teaching of English as a Foreign Language
TOEFL	Test of English as a Foreign Language
TOEIC	Test of English for International Communication
TOEL	Time Only Emitter Location System (MCD)
TOELA	Toute l'Electronique [*A publication*]

TOEMTB	Tables of Organization and Equipment Mobilization Troop Basis [*Army*] (AABC)
TOES	Trade-Off Evaluation System
TOESD	Test of Early Socioemotional Development [*Child development test*]
TOES-NA	[*The*] Other Economic Summit of North America (EA)
TOEWG	Table of Organization and Equipment Working Group [*Army*]
TOF	Beverly, MA [*Location identifier*] [*FAA*] (FAAL)
TOF	[*The*] Obesity Foundation (EA)
TOF	Tales of the Frightened [*A publication*]
TOF	Test Operations Facility [*NASA*] (MCD)
TOF	Tetralogy of Fallot [*Cardiology*]
TOF	Time of Filing
TOF	Time of Fire [*Military*] (CAAL)
TOF	Time of Flight
TOF	To Order From
TOF	Today's Office [*A publication*]
TOF	Tofutti Brands, Inc. [*AMEX symbol*] (SPSG)
TOF	Tone Off [*Telecommunications*] (TEL)
TOF	Top of File
TOF	Top of Form [*Data processing*]
TOF	Transfer of Function (MCD)
TOF	Turnover Frequency [*Chemical engineering*]
TOFA	Tall Oil Fatty Acids [*Organic chemistry*]
TOFABS	Time-of-Flight Aerosol Beam Spectrometry
TOFC	Tony Orlando Fan Club [*Defunct*] (EA)
TOFC	Trailer on Flatcar [*Railroad*]
TOFCN	Technical Order Field Change Notice [*Air Force*] (MCD)
TOFDC	Total Operational Flying Duty Credit [*Military*] (AABC)
TOFI	Time-of-Flight Isochronous Spectrometer
TOFL	Takeoff Field Length [*Aviation*]
TOFM	Tooling Form (AAG)
TOFMS	Time-of-Flight Mass Spectrometer
To de For	Thomas de Formaginis [*Flourished, 1331-38*] [*Authority cited in pre-1607 legal work*] (DSA)
To For	Thomas de Formaginis [*Flourished, 1331-38*] [*Authority cited in pre-1607 legal work*] (DSA)
TOFS	Time-of-Flight Spectrometer [*or Spectroscopy*]
TOFSARS	Time-of-Flight Scattering and Recoiling Spectrometry
TOFSIMS	Time-of-Flight Secondary Ion Mass Spectrometry
TOFU	Tofu Time, Inc. [*NASDAQ symbol*] (NQ)
TOFUTTI	Tofutti Brands, Inc. [*Associated Press abbreviation*] (APAG)
TOG	Skyway of Ocala [*Ocala, FL*] [*FAA designator*] (FAAC)
TOG	Takeoff Gross [*Weight*] [*Aviation*]
TOG	Target-Observer-Gun [*Method*] [*Army*]
TOG	Target Opportunity Generator (KSC)
TOG	Technical Operations Group [*Air Force*]
TOG	Temagami Oil & Gas Ltd. [*Toronto Stock Exchange symbol*]
TOG	Togane [*Japan*] [*Seismograph station code, US Geological Survey*] [*Closed*] (SEIS)
TOG	Together
TOG	Toggle
TOG	Togiak [*Alaska*] [*Airport symbol*] (OAG)
TOG	Togiak Village, AK [*Location identifier*] [*FAA*] (FAAL)
TOG	Top of Grade (MCD)
TOG	Toronto Game [*Simulation game*]
TOG	Total Canada Oil & Gas [*AMEX symbol*] (SPSG)
TOGA	Take Off/Go Around (MCD)
TOGA	Tests of General Ability [*Education*] (AEBS)
TOGA	Tooling Gauge (AAG)
TOGA	Tropical Oceans and Global Atmosphere Project [*World Meteorological Organization*]
TOGAD2	Topics in Gastroenterology [*A publication*]
Tog Cand	Oratio in Senatu in Toga Candida [*of Cicero*] [*Classical studies*] (OCD)
TOGI	Target Oil & Gas, Inc. [*NASDAQ symbol*] (NQ)
TOGI	Trans-Oceanic Geophysical Investigations [*Marine science*] (MSC)
TOGLA	Tea Operators' and General Labourers' Association [*A union*] [*British*]
TOGMV	Tomato Golden Mosaic Virus [*Plant pathology*]
TOGO	Time to Go (SAA)
(Togo) Plan	Fourth Plan of Economic and Social Development. Summary 1981-1985 (Togo) [*A publication*]
TOGR	Together (ROG)
TOGS	Thermal Observation and Gunnery Sights [*British*]
TOGW	Takeoff Gross Weight [*Aviation*]
TOH	Natchitoches, LA [*Location identifier*] [*FAA*] (FAAL)
TOH	Oak Ridge Hospital, Oak Ridge, TN [*Library symbol*] [*Library of Congress*] (LCLS)
TOH	Time Overhead (NVT)
Toh	Tohoroth [*or Toharoth*] (BJA)
TOH	Tyrosine Hydroxylase [*An enzyme*]
T & OHI	Truck & Off-Highway Industries [*A publication*]
Toh J Ex Me	Tohoku Journal of Experimental Medicine [*A publication*]
TOHM	Terohmmeter (IEEE)
Toho	Tohoroth [*or Toharoth*] (BJA)
Tohoku Agr Res	Tohoku Agricultural Research [*A publication*]
Tohoku Geophys J Sci Rep Tohoku Univ Fifth Ser	Tohoku Geophysical Journal. Science Reports of the Tohoku University. Fifth Series [*A publication*]

Tohoku Imp Univ Technol Rep ... Tohoku Imperial University Technology Reports [*Japan*] [*A publication*]
Tohoku J Agric Res ... Tohoku Journal of Agricultural Research [*A publication*]
Tohoku J Agr Res ... Tohoku Journal of Agricultural Research [*A publication*]
Tohoku J Exp Med ... Tohoku Journal of Experimental Medicine [*A publication*]
Tohoku Math ... Tohoku Mathematical Journal [*A publication*]
Tohoku Math J ... Tohoku Mathematical Journal [*A publication*]
Tohoku Math J 2 ... Tohoku Mathematical Journal. Second Series [*A publication*]
Tohoku Med J ... Tohoku Medical Journal [*A publication*]
Tohoku Psychol Folia ... Tohoku Psychologica Folia [*A publication*]
Tohoku Univ Inst Agric Res Rep ... Tohoku University. Institute for Agricultural Research. Reports [*A publication*]
Tohoku Univ Sci Rep Ser 2 ... Tohoku University. Science Reports. Series 2. Geology [*A publication*]
Tohoku Univ Sci Rep Ser 3 ... Tohoku University. Science Reports. Series 3. Mineralogy, Petrology, and Economic Geology [*A publication*]
Tohoku Univ Sci Rep Ser 5 ... Tohoku University. Science Reports. Series 5 [*A publication*]
Tohoku Univ Sci Repts Geology ... Tohoku University. Science Reports. Geology [*A publication*]
TOHP .... Takeoff Horsepower [*Aviation*]
TOI .... Target of Interest [*Military*]   (CAAL)
TOI .... Technical Operation Instruction   (KSC)
TOI .... Technical Operations, Inc.   (MCD)
TOI .... Term of Induction [*Military*]
TOI .... Time of Intercept [*Military*]   (CAAL)
TOI .... Transfer Orbital Insertion [*NASA*]
TOI .... Troy, AL [*Location identifier*] [*FAA*]   (FAAL)
TOID .... Technical Order Identification   (MCD)
TOIL .... Time Off in Lieu
Toim Eesti NSV Tead Akad Fuus Mat ... Toimetised. Eesti NSV Teaduste Akadeemia. Fuusika. Matemaatika [*A publication*]
TOJ .... Telecommunications of Jamaica [*Commercial firm*]   (ECON)
TOJ .... Track on Jamming
To Jo .... [*Sir Thomas*] Jones' English King's Bench Reports [*A publication*]   (DLA)
TOK .... Thrust Okay [*NASA*]   (KSC)
TOK .... Toeristenkampioen [*A publication*]
TOK .... Tokheim Corp. [*NYSE symbol*]   (SPSG)
TOK .... Tokyo [*Japan*] [*Seismograph station code, US Geological Survey*]   (SEIS)
TOK .... Tokyo [*Japan*] [*Later, KAK*] [*Geomagnetic observatory code*]
TOK .... Torokina [*Papua New Guinea*] [*Airport symbol*]   (OAG)
Tokai J Exp Clin Med ... Tokai Journal of Experimental and Clinical Medicine [*Japan*] [*A publication*]
Tokai-Kinki Natl Agric Exp Stn Res Prog Rep ... Tokai-Kinki National Agricultural Experiment Station. Research Progress Report [*A publication*]
Tokai Technol J ... Tokai Technological Journal [*Japan*] [*A publication*]
TOKAMAK ... Toroidal Kamera Magnetic [*Thermonuclear-fusion system*] [*Acronym formed from the Russian*]
Tokhem ...... Tokheim Corp. [*Associated Press abbreviation*]   (APAG)
Tokoginecol Prac ... Toko-Ginecologia Practica [*A publication*]
Toko-Ginecol Pract ... Toko-Ginecologia Practica [*A publication*]
TOKSA ...... Tokushuko [*A publication*]
Toksikol Nov Prom Khim Veshchestv ... Toksikologiya Novykh Promyshlennykh Khimicheskikh Veshchestv [*A publication*]
TOKTA ..... Teoreticheskie Osnovy Khimicheskoi Tekhnologii [*A publication*]
TOKTEN ... Transfer of Know-How through Expatriate Nationals [*British*]   (DI)
TOKTEN ... Transfer of Know-How Through Expatriate Nationals [*Council of Scientific and Industrial Research*] [*India*]
Tokushima J Exp Med ... Tokushima Journal of Experimental Medicine [*A publication*]
Tokyo Astron Bull ... Tokyo Astronomical Bulletin [*A publication*]
Tokyo Astron Bull Ser II ... Tokyo Astronomical Bulletin. Series II [*A publication*]
Tokyo Astron Obs Kiso Inf Bull ... Tokyo Astronomical Observatory. Kiso Information Bulletin [*A publication*]
Tokyo Astron Obs Rep ... Tokyo Astronomical Observatory. Report [*A publication*]
Tokyo Astron Obs Time and Latitude Bull ... Tokyo Astronomical Observatory. Time and Latitude Bulletins [*A publication*]
Tokyo Bk Dev Centre Newsl ... Tokyo Book Development Centre. Newsletter [*A publication*]
Tokyo Fin R ... Tokyo Financial Review [*A publication*]
Tokyo Inst Technol Bull ... Tokyo Institute of Technology. Bulletin [*A publication*]
Tokyo Jikeika Med J ... Tokyo Jikeika Medical Journal [*A publication*]
Tokyo J Math ... Tokyo Journal of Mathematics [*A publication*]
Tokyo J Med Sci ... Tokyo Journal of Medical Sciences [*A publication*]
Tokyo Kyoiku Daigaku Sci Rep Sec C ... Tokyo Kyoiku Daigaku. Science Reports. Section C. Geology, Mineralogy, and Geography [*A publication*]

Tokyo Metrop Isot Cent Annu Rep ... Tokyo Metropolitan Isotope Centre. Annual Report [*A publication*]
Tokyo Metrop Res Inst Environ Prot Annu Rep Engl Transl ... Tokyo Metropolitan Research Institute for Environmental Protection. Annual Report. English Translation [*A publication*]
Tokyo Metrop Univ Geogr Rep ... Tokyo Metropolitan University. Geographical Reports [*A publication*]
Tokyo Munic News ... Tokyo Municipal News [*A publication*]
Tokyo Natl Sci Mus Bull ... Tokyo National Science Museum. Bulletin [*A publication*]
Tokyo Tanabe Q ... Tokyo Tanabe Quarterly [*A publication*]
Tokyo Univ Coll Gen Educ Sci Pap ... Tokyo University. College of General Education. Scientific Papers [*A publication*]
Tokyo Univ Earthquake Research Inst Bull ... Tokyo University. Earthquake Research Institute. Bulletin [*A publication*]
Tokyo Univ Fac Eng J Ser B ... Tokyo University. Faculty of Engineering. Journal. Series B [*A publication*]
Tokyo Univ Faculty Sci Jour ... Tokyo University. Faculty of Science. Journal [*A publication*]
TOL .... Tailored Outfitting List   (MCD)
TOL .... Test-Oriented Language [*Data processing*]
TOL .... Ticket of Leave
TOL .... Toledo [*Spain*] [*Seismograph station code, US Geological Survey*]   (SEIS)
TOL .... Toledo [*Spain*] [*Geomagnetic observatory code*]
TOL .... Toledo [*Ohio*] [*Airport symbol*]   (OAG)
TOL .... Tolerance   (AAG)
TOL .... Toll Brothers, Inc. [*NYSE symbol*]   (SPSG)
TOL .... Tower of London
TOL .... Trial of Labor [*Gynecology*]
TOL .... Trucial Oman Levies [*British military*]   (DMA)
TOL .... University of Toledo, Toledo, OH [*OCLC symbol*]   (OCLC)
TOLA .... Takeoff and Landing Analysis [*Air Force*]
TOLA .... Theatre of Latin America   (EA)
TOLAR ...... Terminal On-Line Availability Reporting
TOLCAT ... Takeoff and Landing Clear Air Turbulence [*Aviation*]
TOLCAT ... Takeoff and Landing Critical Atmosphere Turbulence [*Aviation*]   (MCD)
TOLD .... TELECOMS On-Line Data System [*Telecommunications*]   (TEL)
TOLD .... Test of Language Development [*Education*]
TolE .... Toledo Edison Co. [*Associated Press abbreviation*]   (APAG)
Toledo L Rev ... University of Toledo. Law Review [*A publication*]
Toledo Mus N ... Toledo Museum of Art. Museum News [*A publication*]
Toledo Univ Inst Silicate Research Inf Circ ... Toledo University. Institute of Silicate Research. Information Circular [*A publication*]
TOLIP .... Trajectory Optimization and Linearized Pitch [*Computer program*]
TOLL .... Tollerford [*England*]
TOLLAND ... Tolland Bank [*Associated Press abbreviation*]   (APAG)
TollBro ...... Toll Brothers, Inc. [*Associated Press abbreviation*]   (APAG)
Toller .... Toller on Executors [*A publication*]   (DLA)
Toll Ex .... Toller on Executors [*A publication*]   (ILCA)
Tol LR .... University of Toledo. Law Review [*A publication*]
TOLM .... Toledo Mining [*NASDAQ symbol*]   (NQ)
TOLO .... Time of Lockout   (SAA)
TOLO .... Tool and Operation Liaison Order   (AAG)
TOLO .... Tooling Layout   (AAG)
TOLP .... Test for Oral Language Production [*Educational test*]
TOLR .... Toll Restricted [*Telecommunications*]   (TEL)
TOLR .... Transmitting Objective Loudness Rating [*of telephone connections*]   (IEEE)
To LR .... University of Toledo. Law Review [*A publication*]
TOLS .... Times On-Line Services [*Information service or system*]   (IID)
Tolst Div .... Tolstoy on Divorce and Matrimonial Causes [*A publication*]   (DLA)
TOLT .... Towing Light   (AAG)
TOLTEP ... Teleprocessing On-Line Test Executive Program [*IBM Corp.*]
TOLTS .... Total On-Line Testing System [*Honeywell, Inc.*]
Tolvmandsbl ... Tolvmandsbladet [*A publication*]
TOM .... GMT [*Greenwich Mean Time*] of Orbital Midnight
TOM .... [*The*] Old Man
TOM .... Table of Organization and Management
TOM .... Technical Operations Manager [*Navy*]
TOM .... Terz'Ordine dei Minimi [*Third Order of Minimi*] [*Italy*]   (EAIO)
TOM .... Texas College of Osteopathic Medicine, Fort Worth, TX [*OCLC symbol*]   (OCLC)
TOM .... Text on Microform [*Information Access Co. - IAC*] [*Information service or system*]   (IID)
TOM .... Third Order of Mary   (EA)
TOM .... Thompson-Lundmark Gold Mines Ltd. [*Toronto Stock Exchange symbol*]
TOM .... Time of Maximum [*Particle physics*]
TOM .... Tombouctou [*Mali*] [*Airport symbol*]   (OAG)
TOM .... Tomie [*Japan*] [*Seismograph station code, US Geological Survey*] [*Closed*]   (SEIS)
TOM .... Tommy Hilfiger Sportswear, Inc. [*NYSE symbol*]   (SPSG)
TOM .... Topological Optimization Module [*Data processing*]   (OA)

TOM.......... Toronto, Ottawa, Montreal [*Derogatory reference to people in these cities; used by other Canadians who think people living in these cities "run things"*]
TOM.......... Totem Capital Corp. [*Vancouver Stock Exchange symbol*]
TOM.......... Tracking Operation Memorandum [*Obsolete*]
TOM.......... Translator Octal Mnemonic
TOM.......... Typical Ocean Model [*Oceanography*]
TOMA....... Technical Order Management Agency [*Military*]   (AFIT)
TOMA....... Test of Mathematical Abilities
TOMA....... Turn Off My Addiction [*Proposed clinic*]
TOMAC .... Toroidal Magnetic Chamber   (DI)
TOMARA ... Texas Outlaw Midget Automobile Racing Association [*Car racing*]
TOMB .... Technical Organizational Memory Bank   (RDA)
TOMCAT ... Telemetry On-Line Monitoring Compression and Transmission
TOMCAT ... Teleoperator for Operations, Maintenance, and Construction Using Advanced Technology
TOMCAT ... Theater of Operations Missile Continuous-Wave Antitank Weapon
TOMH ...... Regional Mental Health Center of Oak Ridge, Oak Ridge, TN [*Library symbol*] [*Library of Congress*]   (LCLS)
Toming....... [*Jacobus*] Tomingius [*Deceased, 1576*] [*Authority cited in pre-1607 legal work*]   (DSA)
Tom Inst .... Tomkins' Institutes of Roman Law [*A publication*]   (DLA)
Tom & J Comp ... Tomkins and Jenckens' Compendium of the Modern Roman Law [*A publication*]   (DLA)
Tomkins & J Mod Rom Law ... Tomkins and Jencken's Compendium of the Modern Roman Law [*A publication*]   (DLA)
TOMKY .... Tomkins Ltd. ADS [*NASDAQ symbol*]   (SPSG)
Toml.......... Tomlins' Election Cases [*1689-1795*] [*A publication*]   (DLA)
Toml Cas.... Tomlins' Election Cases [*1689-1795*] [*A publication*]   (DLA)
Toml Cr L .. Tomlin's Criminal Law [*A publication*]   (DLA)
Tom & Lem Gai ... Tomkins and Lemon's Translation of Gaius [*A publication*]   (DLA)
Tomlins...... Tomlins' Law Dictionary [*A publication*]   (DLA)
Toml Law Dict ... Tomlins' Law Dictionary [*A publication*]   (DLA)
Toml LD .... Tomlins' Law Dictionary [*A publication*]   (DLA)
Toml Supp Br ... Tomlins' Supplement to Brown's Parliamentary Cases [*A publication*]   (DLA)
TOMM..... Time-Oriented Metropolitan Model   (MCD)
TOMMI .... Total Online Medical Material Integration [*Data processing*]
TOMMS ... Terminal Operations and Movements Management System   (MCD)
TomNDV ... Tomato Necrotic Dwarf Virus
TOMR....... Tomorrow   (ROG)
TomRSV .... Tomato Ringspot Virus
TomRSV-S ... Tomato Ringspot Virus - Seed Borne
TOMS .... Torus Oxygen Monitoring System   (IEEE)
TOMS .... Total Ozone Mapping Spectrometer   (MCD)
TOMS .... Total Ozone Mapping System [*Meteorology*]
TOMS .... Total Ozone Measurement Scanner   (SSD)
TOMS .... Transactions on Mathematical Software
TOMSI...... Transfer of Master Scheduled Item
TOMSS..... Theater of Operations Medical Support System [*Military*]   (MCD)
TOMT .... Target Organizational Maintenance Trainer   (MCD)
TOMUS .... [*The*] On-Line Multi-User System [*Carlyle Systems, Inc.*] [*Information service or system*]   (IID)
TOMV....... Tomato Mosaic Virus [*Plant pathology*]
TON.......... Threshold Odor Number [*Water analysis*]
TON.......... Tone On [*Telecommunications*]   (TEL)
TON.......... Tonga [*ANSI three-letter standard code*]   (CNC)
TON.......... Tongariro [*New Zealand*] [*Seismograph station code, US Geological Survey*] [*Closed*]   (SEIS)
TON.......... Tonic [*Permanently Strengthening*] [*Pharmacy*]   (ROG)
TON.......... Tonopah Resources, Inc. [*Vancouver Stock Exchange symbol*]
TON.......... Top of the News [*A publication*]
TON.......... Tyrone, PA [*Location identifier*] [*FAA*]   (FAAL)
TONAC..... Technical Order Notification and Completion System   (AAG)
TONE........ [*The*] One Bancorp [*Portland, ME*] [*NASDAQ symbol*]   (NQ)
TON/FT² .. Tons per Square Foot
TONI........ Test of Nonverbal Intelligence
Tonind Zeitung ... Tonindustrie-Zeitung [*A publication*]
Tonind-Ztg Keram Rundsch ... Tonindustrie-Zeitung und Keramische Rundschau [*A publication*]
Tonka........ Tonka Corp. [*Associated Press abbreviation*]   (APAG)
TONL........ Union Carbide Nuclear Co., Oak Ridge National Laboratories, Oak Ridge, TN [*Library symbol*] [*Library of Congress*]   (LCLS)
TONLAR .. Tone-Operated Net Loss Adjuster Receiving
TONL-B .... Union Carbide Nuclear Co., Oak Ridge National Laboratories, Biology Library, Oak Ridge, TN [*Library symbol*] [*Library of Congress*]   (LCLS)
TONL-T .... Union Carbide Nuclear Co., Oak Ridge National Laboratories, Thermal-Nuclear Library, Oak Ridge, TN [*Library symbol*] [*Library of Congress*]   (LCLS)
TONL-Y .... Union Carbide Nuclear Co., Oak Ridge National Laboratories, Y-12 Technical Library, Oak Ridge, TN [*Library symbol*] [*Library of Congress*]   (LCLS)
TONN .... Tonnage [*Shipping*]
TONS........ Tons of Toys, Inc. [*NASDAQ symbol*]   (NQ)

TONS .... Topical Numismatic Society   (EA)
TONS .... Transportation Office Network System [*Department of Transportation*]   (GFGA)
TONT .... Tonto National Monument
TONT .... Toronto Native Times [*A publication*]
TOO.......... 2001 Resource Industries Ltd. [*Vancouver Stock Exchange symbol*]
TOO.......... La Tour de l'Orle d'Or [*A publication*]
TOO.......... Target of Opportunity [*Military*]   (CAAL)
TOO.......... Test Operations Order [*NASA*]
TOO.......... Threshold of Odor   (NASA)
TOO.......... Time of Origin [*Communications*]
TOO.......... Toolangi [*Australia*] [*Seismograph station code, US Geological Survey*]   (SEIS)
TOO.......... Toolangi [*Australia*] [*Geomagnetic observatory code*]
TOOIS....... Transactions on Office Information Systems [*A publication*]
TOOL........ Easco Hand Tools, Inc. [*NASDAQ symbol*]   (NQ)
TOOL........ Teams of Our Lady [*See also END*]   (EAIO)
TOOL........ Test-Oriented Operated Language [*Programming language*] [*Data processing*]
TOOL CD ... Tool Requirement Code [*Army*]
Tool Die J .. Tool and Die Journal [*A publication*]
Tool Eng .... Tool Engineer [*A publication*]
Tooling P ... Tooling and Production [*A publication*]
Tool Mfg Eng ... Tool and Manufacturing Engineer [*A publication*]
Tool Prod ... Tooling and Production [*A publication*]
TOOS .... Torque Overload Switch   (NRCH)
TOOT........ 202 Data Systems. Inc. [*NASDAQ symbol*]   (NQ)
TOOTJFC ... [*The*] One and Only Tom Jones Fan Club   (EA)
TootRl........ Tootsie Roll Industries, Inc. [*Associated Press abbreviation*]   (APAG)
TOP .... [*The*] Olympic Programme   (ECON)
TOP .... [*The*] Opportunity Prospector [*A publication*]
TOP .... [*The*] Option Process [*HUD*]
TOP .... Table of Output Products
TOP .... Tactical Operations Plot [*Military*]   (CAAL)
TOP .... Target Occulting Processor   (MCD)
TOP .... Targeted Outreach Program [*Department of Labor*]
TOP .... Tax-Offset Pension [*Account*]
TOP .... Teacher Organizing Project   (EA)
TOP .... Technical, Office, and Professional Department [*UAW*]
TOP .... Technical and Office Protocol [*Data communications standards*]
TOP .... Technical Operating Procedure
TOP .... Temple Opportunity Program [*Temple University*]   (EA)
TOP .... Temporarily Out of Print
TOP .... Termination of Pregnancy   (MAE)
TOP .... Tertiary Operation
TOP .... Test Operating Procedure
TOP .... Test and Operations Plan
TOP .... Test Outline Plan [*Army*]   (AABC)
TOP .... Topeka [*Kansas*] [*Airport symbol*]   (OAG)
TOP .... Topeka, KS [*Location identifier*] [*FAA*]   (FAAL)
Top .... Topic [*Record label*] [*Great Britain*]
Top .... Topica [*of Aristotle*] [*Classical studies*]   (OCD)
Top .... Topica [*of Cicero*] [*Classical studies*]   (OCD)
top .... Topical
TOP .... Topographic
TOP .... Topoisomerase [*An enzyme*]
TOP .... Topology
TOP .... Topolovo [*Former USSR*] [*Seismograph station code, US Geological Survey*]   (SEIS)
TOP .... Toponymic [*Anatomy*]
TOP .... Torque Oil Pressure [*Air Force*]
TOP .... Total Obscuring Power [*Smoke cloud*]
TOP .... Total Office Products Group [*Commercial firm*] [*British*]
TOP .... Trade Opportunities Program [*Departments of State and Commerce*]
TOP .... Training Operation Plan [*Military*]   (CAAL)
TOP .... Transient Overpower Accident [*Nuclear energy*]
TOP .... Transovarial Passage [*Virology*]
TOP .... Transverse Optical Pumping   (MCD)
TOP .... Trinity Occasional Papers [*A publication*]
TOP .... Turn Out Perfection [*US Air Force Southern Command's acronym for the Zero Defects Program*]
TOP .... Turn Over, Please [*Correspondence*]   (ROG)
TOPA........ Tooling Pattern
Top Allerg Clin Immun ... Topics in Allergy and Clinical Immunology [*A publication*]
T-OPAM ... Tentative OMA [*Operations and Maintenance Army*] Program Analysis Memorandum
Top Antibiot Chem ... Topics in Antibiotic Chemistry [*A publication*]
Top Appl Phys ... Topics in Applied Physics [*A publication*]
Top Astrophys Space Phys ... Topics in Astrophysics and Space Physics [*A publication*]
Top Autom Chem Anal ... Topics in Automatic Chemical Analysis [*A publication*]
Top Bioelectrochem Bioenerg ... Topics in Bioelectrochemistry and Bioenergetics [*A publication*]
TOPCAP ... Total Objective Plan for Career Airmen Personnel [*Air Force*]   (AFM)

TOPCAT ... Trajectory Optimization Program for Comparing Advanced Technology (MCD)
Top Chem Mutagen ... Topics in Chemical Mutagenesis [*A publication*]
Top Clin Nurs ... Topics in Clinical Nursing [*A publication*]
Top Curr Chem ... Topics in Current Chemistry [*A publication*]
Top Curr Phys ... Topics in Current Physics [*A publication*]
Top Emerg Med ... Topics in Emergency Medicine [*A publication*]
Top Environ Health ... Topics in Environmental Health [*A publication*]
Top Enzyme Ferment Biotechnol ... Topics in Enzyme and Fermentation Biotechnology [*A publication*]
TOPES ...... Telephone Office Planning and Engineering System [*Telecommunications*] (TEL)
TOPEX ...... Topographic Experiment [*Proposed oceanographic satellite*]
TOPEX ...... Typhoon Operational Experiment [*Meteorology*]
TOPF .... Transplant Organ Procurement Foundation (EA)
TOPG .... Topping (MSA)
Top Gastroenterol ... Topics in Gastroenterology [*A publication*]
Top Geriatr ... Topics in Geriatrics [*A publication*]
TOPHAT .. Terrier Operation Proof High-Altitude Target (MUGU)
Top Health Care Financ ... Topics in Health Care Financing [*A publication*]
Top Health Rec Manage ... Topics in Health Record Management [*A publication*]
Top Horm Chem ... Topics in Hormone Chemistry [*A publication*]
Top Hosp Pharm Manage ... Topics in Hospital Pharmacy Management [*A publication*]
T Ophth Soc ... Transactions. Ophthalmological Societies of the United Kingdom [*A publication*]
Top Hum Genet ... Topics in Human Genetics [*A publication*]
TOPIC .... [*The*] Objective Personnel Inventory - Civilian [*Air Force*]
TOPIC .... Time-Ordered Programmer Integrated Circuit [*NASA*]
TOPICS ..... Test of Performance in Computational Skills [*Educational test*]
TOPICS ..... Total On-Line Program and Information Control System [*Japan*]
TOPICS ..... Traffic Operations to Increase Capacity and Safety [*Department of Transportation*]
TOPICS ..... Transcripts of Parlibs Information Classification System [*Queensland Parliamentary Library*] [*A publication*] (APTA)
Topics Appl Phys ... Topics in Applied Physics [*A publication*]
Topics Clin Nurs ... Topics in Clinical Nursing [*A publication*]
Topics Current Phys ... Topics in Current Physics [*A publication*]
Top Infect Dis ... Topics in Infectious Diseases [*A publication*]
TOPIX .... Tokyo Stock Price Index [*Japan*] (ECON)
TOPLAS ... Transactions on Programming Languages and Systems (MCD)
TOPLINE ... Total Officer Personnel Objective Structure for the Line Officer Force (DNAB)
Top Lipid Chem ... Topics in Lipid Chemistry [*A publication*]
TOPM .... Top Air Manufacturing, Inc. [*NASDAQ symbol*] (NQ)
Top Manage Abstr ... Top Management Abstracts [*A publication*]
Top Math Phys ... Topics in Mathematical Physics [*A publication*]
Top Med Chem ... Topics in Medicinal Chemistry [*A publication*]
Top Mol Struct Biol ... Topics in Molecular and Structural Biology [*A publication*]
Top News ... Top of the News [*A publication*]
TOPNS ...... Theater of Operations [*Military*]
T of OPNS ... Theater of Operations [*Military*]
TOPO .... Test Operations and Policy Office [*TECOM*] (RDA)
TOPO .... Topography (AFM)
TOPO .... Tri-n-Octyl Phosphine Oxide [*Organic chemistry*]
TOPO .... Trioctylphosphine Oxide [*Organic chemistry*]
TOPOCOM ... Topographic Command [*Army*]
Top Ocular Pharmacol Toxicol ... Topics in Ocular Pharmacology and Toxicology [*A publication*]
TOPOENGR ... Topographical Engineer
TOPOG ..... Topography
Topology Appl ... Topology and Its Applications [*A publication*]
Topology Proc ... Topology Proceedings [*A publication*]
TOPO-MIBK ... Trioctylphosphorine Oxide/Methyl Isobutyl Keton [*Solvent mixture*]
TOPOPLT ... Topographic Platoon (DNAB)
TOPP .... [*The*] Organization of Plastics Processors (EA)
TOPP .... Terminal-Operated Production Program (BUR)
TOPP .... Threat Orientation Protection Posture [*Military equipment*]
TOPP .... [*The*] Topps Co., Inc. [*NASDAQ symbol*] (NQ)
Top Paediatr ... Topics in Paediatrics [*A publication*]
TOPPER ... Toy Press Publishers, Editors, and Reporters
Top Perinat Med ... Topics in Perinatal Medicine [*A publication*]
Top Pharm Sci ... Topics in Pharmaceutical Sciences [*A publication*]
Top Phosphorus Chem ... Topics in Phosphorus Chemistry [*A publication*]
Top Photosynth ... Topics in Photosynthesis [*A publication*]
Top Probl Psychiatry Neurol ... Topical Problems in Psychiatry and Neurology [*A publication*]
Top Probl Psychother ... Topical Problems of Psychotherapy [*A publication*]
TOPR .... Taiwan Open Pool Reactor
TOPRA ...... Tooling and Production [*A publication*]
TOPREP ... Total Objective Plan for Reserve Personnel [*Air Force*] (AFM)
Top Rep NB Miner Resour Branch ... Topical Report. New Brunswick Mineral Resources Branch [*A publication*]
Top Rev Haematol ... Topical Reviews in Haematology [*A publication*]
TOPS .... [*The*] Operational PERT System
TOPS .... [*The*] Optimum Publishing System [*IBM Corp.*]

TOPS .... Tactical Optical Projection System (NVT)
TOPS .... Tailored Owner Protection System [*Automotive optional warranty*]
TOPS .... Take Off Pounds Sensibly (EA)
TOPS .... Technical Order Page Supplement [*Air Force*]
TOPS .... Telemetry On-Line Processing System [*Data processing*]
TOPS .... Telephone Order Personalities and Smiles [*Organization of chief telephone operators*]
TOPS .... Telephone Order Processing System
TOPS .... Telephone Order Purchasing System (MCD)
TOPS .... Teleregister Omni Processing and Switching [*Data processing*]
TOPS .... Teletype Optical Projection System (IEEE)
TOPS .... Terminal-Oriented Planning System (MCD)
TOPS .... Test Operations Procedures [*Army*] (RDA)
TOPS .... Test of Problem Solving [*Intelligence test*]
TOPS .... Tested Overhead Projection Series [*Education*]
TOPS .... Testing and Operating System
TOPS .... Theatre Organ Preservation Society [*British*]
TOPS .... Thermal Noise Optical Optimization Communication System [*NASA*]
TOPS .... Thermodynamic Ocean Prediction System [*Navy*] (GFGA)
TOPS .... Thermoelectric Outer Planet Spacecraft [*NASA*]
TOPS .... Time-Sharing Operating System
TOPS .... Top One Percent Society (EA)
TOPS .... Top Sound International, Inc. [*NASDAQ symbol*] (NQ)
TOPS .... Total Operations Processing System [*Data processing*]
TOPS .... Total Organ Perfusion System
TOPS .... Total Personnel Service
TOPS .... Toward Other Planetary Systems [*NASA*]
TOPS .... Traffic Operator Position System [*Telecommunications*] (TEL)
TOPS .... Training Operations and Planning Station (MCD)
TOPS .... Training Opportunities Schemes [*Department of Employment*] [*British*]
TOPS .... Transcendental Network [*Centram Systems West, Inc.*] [*Berkeley, CA*] [*Telecommunications*] (TSSD)
TOPS .... Transistorized Operational Phone System (MCD)
TOPS .... Transportation Operational Personal Property System [*Army*]
TOPS .... Truck Ordering and Pricing System
TOPS .... United States Travelers' Overseas Personalized Service [*Also known as USTOPS*]
TOPSEC ... Top Secret [*Security classification*]
TOPSEP .... Targeting/Optimization for Solar Electric Propulsion [*NASA*]
TOPSI .... Topside Sounder, Ionosphere [*NASA*]
TopSrce ... Top Source, Inc. [*Associated Press abbreviation*] (APAG)
TOPSTAR ... [*The*] Officer Personnel System, The Army Reserve (AABC)
Top Stereochem ... Topics in Stereochemistry [*A publication*]
Top Sulfur Chem ... Topics in Sulfur Chemistry [*A publication*]
TOPSY ...... Test Operations Planning System
TOPSY ...... Thermally Operated Plasma System
TOPT .... Tele-Optic, Inc. [*NASDAQ symbol*] (NQ)
Top Therap ... Topics in Therapeutics [*A publication*]
TOPTS ...... Test-Oriented Paper-Tape System [*Data processing*] (IEEE)
TOPV .... Trivalent Oral Poliomyelitis Vaccine [*Medicine*]
TOR .... Tactical Operational Requirement [*Military*] (CAAL)
TOR .... Tactical Operations Room [*Air Force*]
TOR .... Tall Oil Rosin [*Organic chemistry*]
TOR .... Technical Operating Report
TOR .... Technical Operations Research (KSC)
TOR .... Technical Override
TOR .... Telegraph on Radio [*Telecommunications*] (TEL)
TOR .... Teleprinter on Radio [*Telecommunications*] (TSSD)
TOR .... Tentative Operational Requirement
TOR .... Terms of Reference [*Army*] (AABC)
TOR .... Test Operation Report (KSC)
TOR .... Third Order Regular of St. Francis [*Roman Catholic men's religious order*]
TOR .... Time of Receipt [*Military*] (AABC)
TOR .... Time of Reception [*Communications*]
TOR .... Time on Risk [*Insurance*] (AIA)
TOR .... Tool Order Release (SAA)
TOR .... Torhsen Energy Corp. [*Vancouver Stock Exchange symbol*]
TOR .... Torishima [*Japan*] [*Seismograph station code, US Geological Survey*] [*Closed*] (SEIS)
TOR .... Toronto (ROG)
TOR .... Toronto Airways Ltd. [*Markom, ON*] [*FAA designator*] (FAAC)
Tor .... Torpedo [*Army*]
TOR .... Torque (AAG)
TOR .... Torrance [*California*]
Tor .... Torre [*A publication*]
TOR .... Torrington, WY [*Location identifier*] [*FAA*] (FAAL)
TOR .... Totalizing Relay
TOR .... Tournament of Roses Association (EA)
TOR .... Traffic on Request [*Aviation*] (FAAC)
TOR .... Turn-On Rate (CAAL)
TORA .... Takeoff Run Available [*Aviation*] (FAAC)
TORAC ..... Torpedo Acquisition
TORACCS ... Tool Order-Reporting and Cost Control System (SAA)
TORAH ..... Tough Orthodox Rabbis and Hassidim [*An association*]
TORC .... Test of Reading Comprehension
TORC .... Traffic Overload Reroute Control

TORCH..... Toxoplasma, Other [*Viruses*], Rubella, Cytomegaloviruses, Herpes [*Virus*]
TOREA ..... Toshiba Review [*A publication*]
TOREADOR ... Torero-Matador [*Said to have been coined by Georges Bizet for opera "Carmen"*]
TORES .... Toxicological Research (SAA)
TORF........ Time of Retrofire [*NASA*] (KSC)
Torf Delo.... Torfyanoe Delo [*A publication*]
Torfnachrichten Forsch Werbestelle Torf ... Torfnachrichten der Forschungs-und Werbestelle fuer Torf [*A publication*]
Torf Promst ... Torfyanaya Promyshlennost [*A publication*]
Tori Bull Ornithol Soc Jpn ... Tori. Bulletin of the Ornithological Society of Japan [*A publication*]
Torino Univ Ist Geol Pub ... Torino Universita. Istituto Geologico. Pubblicazioni [*A publication*]
Tor Life...... Toronto Life [*A publication*]
TORM .... Torquemeter
TORNL ...... Torsional
Toro............ Toro Corp. [*Associated Press abbreviation*] (APAG)
Toronto U Faculty L Rev ... Toronto University. Faculty Law Review [*Canada*] [*A publication*] (DLA)
Toronto Univ Dep Mech Eng Tech Publ Ser ... Toronto University. Department of Mechanical Engineering. Technical Publication Series [*A publication*]
Toronto Univ Inst Aerosp Stud UTIAS Rep ... Toronto University. Institute for Aerospace Studies. UTIAS Report [*A publication*]
Toronto Univ Inst Aerosp Stud UTIAS Rev ... Toronto University. Institute for Aerospace Studies. UTIAS Review [*A publication*]
Toronto Univ Inst Aerosp Stud UTIAS Tech Note ... Toronto University. Institute for Aerospace Studies. UTIAS Technical Note [*A publication*]
Toronto Univ Studies G S ... Toronto University Studies. Geological Series [*A publication*]
TORP .... Test of Orientation for Rehabilitation Patients [*Occupational therapy*]
TORP .... Torpedo (AABC)
TORP .... Total Ossicular Replacement Prosthesis
TORPA...... Torfyanaya Promyshlennost [*A publication*]
TORPCM ... Torpedo Countermeasures and Deception
TORPEX ... Torpedo Exercise (NVT)
TORPRON ... Torpedo Squadron
TORQ........ Torquay [*England*]
TORQ........ Torque [*Automotive engineering*]
TORQUE .. Tests of Reasonable Quantitative Understanding of the Environment [*Education*]
TORQUE .. Truck Operators Road Qualifying Exam [*National Highway Traffic Safety Administration*]
TORR .... Takeoff Run Required [*Aviation*] (AIA)
TORR .... Torricelli [*Unit of pressure*]
TORR .... Torrington [*England*]
Torreia Nueva Ser ... Torreia Nueva Serie [*A publication*]
Torrey Bot Club Bull ... Torrey Botanical Club. Bulletin [*A publication*]
Torry Res... Torry Research [*A publication*]
Torry Res Stn (Aberdeen Scotl) Annu Rep ... Torry Research Station (Aberdeen, Scotland). Annual Report [*A publication*]
Torry Res Stn Annu Rep Handl Preserv Fish Fish Prod ... Torry Research Station. Annual Report on the Handling and Preservation of Fish and Fish Products [*A publication*]
TORS........ Time-Ordered Reporting System (MCD)
TORS........ Torsion [*Automotive engineering*]
TORS........ Trade Opportunity Referral Service [*Department of Agriculture*] [*Information service or system*] (IID)
TORSEN ... Torque Sensing Differential [*Audi*] [*Automotive engineering*]
TORSV...... Tomato Ringspot Virus [*Plant pathology*]
TORT .... Tactical Operational Readiness Trainer
TORT .... Truck Operator Road Test [*Part of TORQUE*]
TORTEL ... Torotel, Inc. [*Associated Press abbreviation*] (APAG)
TOS .... Tactical Offense Subsystem
TOS .... Tactical Operation Simulator
TOS .... Tactical Operations Squadron [*Air Force*]
TOS .... Tactical Operations System [*ADSAF*]
TOS .... Taken Out of Service [*Telecommunications*] (TEL)
TOS .... Taken on Strength [*British military*] (DMA)
TOS .... Tape Operating System [*IBM Corp.*] [*Data processing*]
TOS .... Technical Operational Support
TOS .... Technical Operations Squadron [*Air Force*]
TOS .... Temporarily Out of Service (DEN)
TOS .... Temporarily Out of Stock [*Business term*]
TOS .... Term of Service [*Military*]
TOS .... Terminal-Oriented Software [*Data processing*] (IEEE)
TOS .... Terminal-Oriented System [*Data processing*] (IEEE)
TOS .... Test Operating System (MCD)
TOS .... Texas Ornithological Society. Bulletin [*A publication*]
TOS .... Thermally and Oxidatively Stable
TOS .... Thoracic Outlet Syndrome [*Medicine*]
TOS .... Time-Ordered System (MCD)
TOS .... Time-on-Station [*Military*] (INF)
TOS .... TIROS [*Television and Infrared Observation Satellite*] Operational Satellite [*NASA*]
TOS .... Top of Stack [*Data processing*]
TOS .... Top of Steel [*Flooring*] (AAG)

TOS .... Torque Overload Switch [*Nuclear energy*] (NRCH)
Tos .... Tosafoth (BJA)
TOS .... Tosco Corp. [*NYSE symbol*] (SPSG)
TOS .... Tosco Corp., Los Angeles, CA [*OCLC symbol*] (OCLC)
Tos .... Tosefta (BJA)
Tos .... Tosyl [*Also, Ts*] [*Organic chemistry*]
TOS .... Toxic Oil Syndrome [*Medicine*]
TOS .... Tramiel Operating System [*Atari, Inc.*]
TOS .... Transfer Orbit Stage [*Satellite booster*]
TOS .... Tromso [*Norway*] [*Airport symbol*] (OAG)
TOS .... Trucial Oman Scouts [*British military*] (DMA)
TOS .... Turkiye Ogretmenler Sendikasi
TOS .... Type of Shipment
TOS2 .... Tactical Operations System Operable Segment (MCD)
Tosaf.......... Tosafoth (BJA)
TosArgOMe ... Tosylarginine Methyl Ester [*Also, TAME*] [*Biochemistry*]
TOSBAC ... Toshiba Scientific and Business Automatic Computer [*Toshiba Corp.*]
TOSC........ Tactical Ocean Surveillance Coordinator [*Military*] (CAAL)
TOSC........ To Other Service Center [*IRS*]
TOSC........ Touch-Operated Selector Control
TOSCA...... Test of Scholastic Abilities [*Achievement test*]
TOSCA...... Tobacco Science [*A publication*]
TOSCA...... Total On-Line Searching and Cataloging Activities [*Information service or system*]
TOSCA...... Toxic Substances Control Act [*1976*]
Tosco.......... Tosco Corp. [*Associated Press abbreviation*] (APAG)
TOSCOM ... TOS [*TIROS Operational Satellite*] Communications System (NOAA)
TOSD .... Telephone Operations and Standards Division [*Rural Electrification Administration*] [*Telecommunications*] (TEL)
TOSD .... Third Order of Saint Dominic [*Rome, Italy*] (EAIO)
TOSE........ Tooling Samples
Tosef .... Tosefta (BJA)
Toseph .... Tosephta (BJA)
TOSF .... Tertiary of Third Order of St. Francis [*Later, SFO*] [*Roman Catholic religious order*]
TOSF .... Test of Oral Structures and Functions [*Speech evaluation test*]
Toshiba Rev ... Toshiba Review [*Japan*] [*A publication*]
Toshiba Rev (Int Ed) ... Toshiba Review (International Edition) [*A publication*]
Tosh-Kai... Toshokan-Kai [*A publication*]
Tosh Kenk ... Toshokan Kenkyu [*A publication*]
Tosh Zass .. Toshokan Zasshi [*A publication*]
TOSI......... Technical On-Site Inspection
TOSL........ Terminal-Oriented Service Language
TOSMIC ... Toluenesulfonylmethyl Isocyanide [*or Tosylmethylisocyanide*] [*Organic chemistry*]
TOSMIC ... Tosylmethyl Isocyanide [*Organic chemistry*]
TOS/OITDS ... Tactical Operations System/Operations and Intelligence Tactical Data Systems [*Military*] (RDA)
TOSPDR ... Technical Order System Publication Deficiency Report [*Military*] (AFIT)
TosPheCH₂Cl ... Tosylphenylalanine Chloromethyl Ketone [*Biochemistry*]
TOSR........ Technical Order Status Report (MCD)
TOSR........ Thermally and Oxidatively Stable Resin
TOSS........ Tactical Operational Scoring System (MCD)
TOSS........ Tactical Operations Support System (MCD)
TOSS........ Television Ordnance Scoring System (MCD)
TOSS........ Terminal-Oriented Support System
TOSS........ Test Operation Support Segment
TOSS........ Tethered Orbiting Satellite Simulator
TOSS......... TIROS [*Television and Infrared Observation Satellite*] Operational Satellite System [*NASA*]
TOSS........ Total Office Support System (HGAA)
TOS-S....... Transfer Orbit Stage - Shortened Version [*Space technology*]
TOSS........ Transient and/or Steady State [*Nuclear energy*] (NRCH)
TOSS........ Turbine-Operated Suspension System [*NASA*]
TOSSA ...... Transient or Steady-State Analysis [*Data processing*]
TOSSG ...... TACS/TADS OED [*Tactical Air Control System/Tactical Air Defense System Operational Effectiveness Demonstration*] Special Study Group [*Military*]
TOST........ Turbine Oxidation Stability Test (OA)
Tosyl .... Tolylsulfonyl [*Organic chemistry*]
TOT .... Denver, CO [*Location identifier*] [*FAA*] (FAAL)
T/OT .... Table of Organization (Tentative)
TOT .... Takeoff Trim [*Aviation*] (MCD)
TOT .... Tales of Tomorrow [*A publication*]
TOT .... Task Oriented Training (MCD)
TOT .... Terms of Trade
TOT .... Texaco Overseas Tankerships
TOT .... Texas Opera Theatre
TOT .... Theatrum Orbis Terrarum [*Dutch firm*]
TOT .... Time of Takeoff [*Air Force*] (AFIT)
TOT .... Time on Tape [*Military*]
TOT .... Time over Target [*Air support*]
TOT .... Time on Target [*Artillery support*]
TOT .... Time on Track
TOT .... Time of Transmission [*Communications*]
TOT .... Time of Travel (MCD)

TOT .... Tincture of Time [*Medical slang for treatment of problems that are better left alone*]
TOT .... Tip-of-Tongue Phenomenon [*Medicine*]
TOT .... Toe-Out-in-Turns [*Automotive engineering*]
TOT .... Total   (AAG)
TOT .... Totem Industries [*Vancouver Stock Exchange symbol*]
Tot.............. Tothill's English Chancery Reports [*A publication*]   (DLA)
Tot.............. Tothill's Transactions in Chancery [*21 English Reprint*] [*A publication*]   (DLA)
TOT .... Totnes [*Municipal borough in England*]
TOT .... Tottori [*Japan*] [*Seismograph station code, US Geological Survey*]   (SEIS)
TOT .... Tourist Organization of Thailand   (DS)
TOT .... Trade-Off and Technology
TOT .... Transfer of Technology [*Telecommunications*]   (TEL)
TOT .... Transfer-of-Training
TOT ...... Transovarial Transmission [*Virology*]
TOT .... Transportation Office Will Furnish the Necessary Transportation [*Military*]
TOT .... Tris-ortho-thymotide [*Organic chemistry*]
TOT .... Turbine Outlet Temperature   (NG)
TOT .... Turn-On Time
TOT .... Type of Transport [*Shipping*]   (DS)
Total.......... Total [*Associated Press abbreviation*]   (APAG)
Total Inf..... Total Information [*A publication*]
TOTCDA... Total Canada Oil & Gas Ltd. [*Associated Press abbreviation*]   (APAG)
TOTE .... Autotote Corp. [*NASDAQ symbol*]   (NQ)
TOTE .... Teleprocessing On-Line Test Executive [*Data processing*]   (IBMDP)
TOTE .... Test-Operator-Test-Exit [*Unit*] [*Psychology*]
TOTE .... Time Out to Enjoy   (EA)
TOTEM .... Theater Operations and Tactical Evaluation Model
TOTEM .... Tomahawk Test Missile   (MCD)
TOTES...... Time-Ordered Techniques Experiment System
TOTFORF ... Total Forfeiture [*of all pay and allowances*] [*Army*]   (AABC)
TOTH .... Toth Aluminum Corp. [*NASDAQ symbol*]   (NQ)
Toth........... Tothill's English Chancery Reports [*A publication*]   (DLA)
Toth........... Tothill's Transactions in Chancery [*21 English Reprint*] [*A publication*]   (DSA)
Tothill (Eng) ... Tothill's English Chancery Reports [*A publication*]   (DLA)
Tothill (Eng) ... Tothill's Transactions in Chancery [*21 English Reprint*] [*A publication*]   (DLA)
TOTJ .... Training on the Job
TOTL........ Test Operating Time Log
TOTL........ Total Research Corp. [*NASDAQ symbol*]   (NQ)
TOTLPET ... Total Petroleum (North America) Ltd. [*Associated Press abbreviation*]   (APAG)
TotlSys....... Total System Services, Inc. [*Associated Press abbreviation*]   (APAG)
TOTLZ...... Totalize
TOTM .... Totalmed Associates [*NASDAQ symbol*]   (NQ)
TOTM .... Trioctyl Trimellitate [*Chemistry*]
TOTO .... Tongue of the Ocean [*Area of the Bahama Islands*] [*Navy*]
TOTO .... Totable Tornado Observatory [*National Oceanic and Atmospheric Administration*]
TOTP........ Tooling Template
TOTP........ Top of the Pops [*Television program*] [*British*]
TOTP........ Triorthotolylphosphate [*Organic chemistry*]
TOTPAR... Total Pain Relief [*Medicine*]
tot prot ...... Total Protein   (MAE)
TotPt.......... Total Petroleum (North America) Ltd. [*Associated Press abbreviation*]   (APAG)
TOTR .... Test Observation and Training Room [*Military*]   (CAAL)
TOTRAD .. Tape Output Test Rack Autonetics Diode
TOTS........ Total Operating Traffic System [*Bell System*]
TOTS........ Tower Operator Training System [*Air traffic control*]
TOTS........ Turn Off Television Saturday [*of Action for Children's Television organization*]
TOU.......... Neah Bay, WA [*Location identifier*] [*FAA*]   (FAAL)
TOU.......... Oak Ridge Associated Universities, Oak Ridge, TN [*Library symbol*] [*Library of Congress*]   (LCLS)
TOU.......... Time of Use [*Utility rates*]
TOU.......... Touho [*New Caledonia*] [*Airport symbol*]   (OAG)
TOU.......... Trace Operate Unit
Touch .... Sheppard's Touchstone [*A publication*]   (DLA)
Toull........... Toullier's Droit Civil Francais [*A publication*]   (DLA)
Toulouse Med ... Toulouse Medical [*A publication*]
TOUR....... Tourist Class Passengers [*British*]
TOUR........ WorldGroup Companies, Inc. [*Evergreen, CO*] [*NASDAQ symbol*]   (NQ)
Tourbe Philos ... Tourbe Philosophique [*A publication*]
Tourg Dig... Tourgee's North Carolina Digest [*A publication*]   (DLA)
Tourism Aust ... Tourism Australia [*A publication*]   (APTA)
Tourism Engl ... Tourism in England [*A publication*]
Tourism Intell Q ... Tourism Intelligence Quarterly [*A publication*]
TOURN..... Tournament
TOUS .... Test on Understanding Science
TOUS .... Transmission Oscillator Ultrasonic Spectrometer
Toute Electron ... Toute l'Electronique [*A publication*]
TOV .... El Indio, TX [*Location identifier*] [*FAA*]   (FAAL)

TOV .... El Tocuyo [*Venezuela*] [*Seismograph station code, US Geological Survey*]   (SEIS)
TOV .... Telemetering Oscillator Voltage
TOV .... Time out of View
TOV .... Tooele Valley Railway Co. [*AAR code*]
Tov .... Tovaris [*A publication*]
TOVA .... [*The*] Other Victims of Alcoholism   (EA)
TOVALOP ... Tanker Owners Voluntary Agreement on Liability for Oil Pollution
Tovar Poshir Polit Nauk Znan Ukr SSR ... Tovaristvo dlya Poshirennya Politichnikh i Naukovikh Znan Ukrains'koi SSR [*A publication*]
TOVC .... Top of Overcast [*Aviation*]   (FAAC)
TOVD .... Transistor-Operated Voltage Divider
TOVR .... Turnover   (NVT)
TOVS........ TIROS [*Television and Infrared Observation Satellite*] Operational Vertical Sounder [*NASA*]
TOW.......... Cooperstown, ND [*Location identifier*] [*FAA*]   (FAAL)
TOW.......... Takeoff Weight [*Aviation*]
TOW.......... Tales of Wonder [*A publication*]
TOW.......... Tank and Orbiter Weight [*NASA*]   (MCD)
TOW.......... Target on Wire [*British military*]   (DMA)
TOW.......... Time of Week   (SSD)
TOW.......... Towards   (ROG)
TOW.......... Tube-Launched, Optically Tracked, Wire-Guided [*Weapon*]
TOWA .... Terrain and Obstacle Warning and Avoidance
TOW CAP ... TOW [*Tube-Launched, Optically Tracked, Wire-Guided (Weapon)*] Cover Artillery Protection
TOWER .... Testing Orientation and Work Evaluation for Rehabilitation
Tower Hamlets Local Trade Dev ... Tower Hamlets Local Trade Development [*A publication*]
TO WHD... Two Wheeled [*Freight*]
TOWL .... Test of Written Language
TOWL .... Towle Manufacturing Co. [*NASDAQ symbol*]   (NQ)
Towle Const ... Towle's Analysis of the United States Constitution [*A publication*]   (DLA)
TOWN....... Towne-Paulsen, Inc. [*NASDAQ symbol*]   (NQ)
Town Cntry Plann ... Town and Country Planning [*A publication*]
Town Co..... Townshend's Code [*A publication*]   (DLA)
Town Com Law ... Townsend on Commercial Law [*A publication*]   (DLA)
Town & Country Plan ... Town and Country Planning [*A publication*]
Town Ctry Plan ... Town and Country Planning [*A publication*]
TOWNCTY ... Town & Country Jewelry Corp. [*Associated Press abbreviation*]   (APAG)
Town Jud ... Townsend's Judgment [*A publication*]   (DLA)
Town Pl ...... Townshend's Pleading [*A publication*]   (DLA)
Town Plan Inst J ... Town Planning Institute. Journal [*A publication*]
Town Planning R ... Town Planning Review [*United Kingdom*] [*A publication*]
Town Plann Inst J ... Town Planning Institute. Journal [*A publication*]
Town Plann Q ... Town Planning Quarterly [*New Zealand*] [*A publication*]
Town Plann Rev ... Town Planning Review [*A publication*]
Town Plann Today ... Town Planning Today [*A publication*]
Town Plan R ... Town Planning Review [*A publication*]
Town Pr ...... Townshend's Practice [*A publication*]   (DLA)
Town Pr Pl ... Townshend's Precedents of Pleading [*A publication*]   (DLA)
Townsh Pl ... Townshend's Pleading [*A publication*]   (DLA)
Townsh Sland & L ... Townshend on Slander and Libel [*A publication*]   (DLA)
Town Sl & Lib ... Townshend on Slander and Libel [*A publication*]   (DLA)
Town St Tr ... Townsend's Modern State Trials [*1850*] [*A publication*]   (DLA)
Town Sum Proc ... Townshend's Summary Landlord and Tenant Process [*A publication*]   (DLA)
Townsville Nat ... Townsville Naturalist [*A publication*]   (APTA)
TOWPROS ... TOW [*Tube-Launched, Optically Tracked, Wire-Guided (Weapon)*] Protective Shelters   (MCD)
TOWR....... Tower Federal Savings Bank [*NASDAQ symbol*]   (NQ)
TOX.......... Total Oxidants
TOX.......... Toxicology
Tox Appl Ph ... Toxicology and Applied Pharmacology [*A publication*]
TOXBACK ... TOXLINE Back-File
TOXBIB .... Toxicity Bibliography [*MEDLARS*]
TOXIA .... Toxicon [*A publication*]
Toxic Appl Pharmac ... Toxicology and Applied Pharmacology [*A publication*]
Toxic Hazard Waste Disposal ... Toxic and Hazardous Waste Disposal [*A publication*]
TOXICOL ... Toxicology
Toxicol Annu ... Toxicology Annual [*A publication*]
Toxicol Appl Pharmacol ... Toxicology and Applied Pharmacology [*A publication*]
Toxicol Appl Pharmacol Suppl ... Toxicology and Applied Pharmacology. Supplement [*A publication*]
Toxicol Environ Chem ... Toxicological and Environmental Chemistry [*A publication*]
Toxicol Environ Chem Rev ... Toxicological and Environmental Chemistry Reviews [*A publication*]
Toxicol Eur Res ... Toxicological European Research [*A publication*]
Toxicol Ind Health ... Toxicology and Industrial Health [*A publication*]
Toxicol Lett ... Toxicology Letters [*A publication*]
Toxicol Lett (Amst) ... Toxicology Letters (Amsterdam) [*A publication*]

Toxicol Pathol ... Toxicologic Pathology [*A publication*]
TOXICON ... Toxicology Information Conversational On-Line Network [*National Library of Medicine*] [*Later, TOXLINE*]
Toxic Subst J ... Toxic Substances Journal [*A publication*]
TOXLINE ... Toxicology Information On-Line [*National Library of Medicine, MD*] [*Bibliographic database*]
TOXLIST ... Toxic Regulatory Listings [*American Petroleum Institute*] [*Information service or system*] (CRD)
TOXNET... Toxicology Data Network [*National Library of Medicine*] [*Information service or system*] (IID)
TOXO........ Toxoplasmosis [*Medicine*]
TOXREP... Toxic Incident Report
TOXREPT ... Toxic Incident Report (MUGU)
TOXT .... Toxteth (ROG)
TOXY .... Tri Coast Environmental Corp. [*NASDAQ symbol*] (NQ)
TOY .... Toyama [*Japan*] [*Seismograph station code, US Geological Survey*] (SEIS)
TOY .... Toys R Us, Inc. [*NYSE symbol*] (SPSG)
TOY .... Troy, IL [*Location identifier*] [*FAA*] (FAAL)
TOYCOM ... [*A*] Programming Language [*1971*] (CSR)
TOYDV ..... Tomato Yellow Dwarf Virus [*Plant pathology*]
TOYM .... Ten Outstanding Young Men of America [*Jaycees' program*]
TOYMV .... Tomato Yellow Mosaic Virus [*Plant pathology*]
TOYO .... Toyota Motor Corp. [*NASDAQ symbol*] (NQ)
Toyo Bunka Kenkyu Kiyo ... Toyo Bunka Kenkyusho Kiyo [*A publication*]
Toyo Junior Coll Food Technol Toyo Inst Food Technol Res Rep ... Toyo Junior College of Food Technology and Toyo Institute of Food Technology. Research Report [*Japan*] [*A publication*]
Toyo Ongaku ... Toyo Ongaku Kenkyu [*A publication*]
Toyota Eng ... Toyota Engineering [*Japan*] [*A publication*]
ToyRU .... Toys R Us, Inc. [*Associated Press abbreviation*] (APAG)
TOYS........ Toys Plus, Inc. [*St. Charles, MO*] [*NASDAQ symbol*] (NQ)
TOZ .... Harvard University, Tozzer Library, Cambridge, MA [*OCLC symbol*] (OCLC)
TOZ .... Touba [*Ivory Coast*] [*Airport symbol*] (OAG)
TOZ .... Towarzystwo Ochrony Zdrowia [*A publication*] (BJA)
TP .... East Timor [*ISO two-letter standard code*] (CNC)
TP .... Palestinian Talmud (BJA)
TP .... [*The*] Prosperos (EA)
T-P .... Tabloncillo Perla [*Race of maize*]
TP .... Tail-Pinch Stress
TP .... Tank Parliament [*British*]
TP .... Tank Piercing [*Ammunition*] [*Military*]
TP .... Tank Pressure (DS)
T & P .... Tank and Pump Unit [*Mechanized infantry battalion*] (DWSG)
TP .... Tape (BUR)
TP .... Target Point
TP .... Target Population
TP .... Target Practice [*Military*]
TP .... Task Processor [*Telecommunications*] (TSSD)
TP .... Tax Planning [*A publication*] (DLA)
TP .... Taxpayer
TP .... Teaching Practice
TP .... Technical Pamphlet
TP .... Technical Paper
TP .... Technical Performance (MCD)
TP .... Technical Problem
TP .... Technical Proposal
TP .... Technical Publication
TP .... Technographic Publication
TP .... Technology Parameter
TP .... Technophility Index [*Mining technology*]
TP .... Telemetry Processor
TP .... Telephone (CET)
TP .... Teleprensa [*Press agency*] [*Colombia*]
TP .... Teleprinter
TP .... Teleprocessing [*Data processing*] (MCD)
T/P............ Temperature to Precipitation Ratio [*Botany*]
TP .... Temperature and Pressure [*Medicine*]
TP .... Temperature Probe (AAG)
T + P .... Temperature and Pulse [*Medicine*]
TP .... Tempo Presente [*A publication*]
TP .... Tempo Primo [*Original Tempo*] [*Music*]
TP .... Temporary Patient [*British*]
TP .... Tempore Paschale [*At Easter Time*] [*Latin*]
TP .... Tensile Properties (MCD)
TP .... Tentative Pamphlet
TP .... Term Pass (AAG)
TP .... Terminal Phalanx [*Anatomy*]
TP .... Terminal Point (NATG)
TP .... Terminal Pole [*Telecommunications*] (TEL)
TP .... Terminal Processor
TP .... Terrestrial Plants
TP .... Territorial Party [*Northern Marianas*] (PPW)
TP .... Terza Posizione [*Third Position*] [*Italy*]
TP .... Terzo Programma [*Roma*] [*A publication*]
T/P............ Test Panel (AAG)
TP .... Test Plan
TP .... Test Point
TP .... Test Port (KSC)
TP .... Test Position

TP .... Test Positive [*Clinical chemistry*]
TP .... Test Pressure [*Nuclear energy*] (NRCH)
TP .... Test Procedure (NATG)
TP .... Test Program
TP .... Testosterone Propionate [*Endocrinology*]
TP .... [*The*] Texas & Pacific Railway Co. [*Absorbed into Missouri Pacific System*] [*AAR code*]
T and P....... [*The*] Texas & Pacific Railway Co. [*Absorbed into Missouri Pacific System*]
TP .... Text Processor
T and P....... Theft and Pilferage
TP .... Thermoplastic [*Also, T*] [*Plastics technology*]
TP .... Thermosphere Probe
TP .... Thiamphenicol [*Antimicrobial compound*]
TP .... Thiopental [*An anesthetic*]
T/P............ Third Party (ADA)
TP .... Thomas Power [*"Tay Pay"*] O'Connor [*Irish journalist and politician, 1848-1929*]
TP .... Thomson Press (India) Ltd. [*Publisher*]
TP .... Thought Patterns [*A publication*]
TP .... Threshold Potential (MAE)
TP .... Thrombocytopenic Purpura [*Medicine*]
TP .... Thrombophlebitis [*Medicine*]
TP .... Throttle Positioner [*Automotive engineering*]
TP .... Thymic Polypeptide [*Endocrinology*]
TP .... Thymidine Phosphorylase [*An enzyme*]
TP .... Thymolphthalein [*Organic chemistry*]
TP .... Thymopentin [*Biochemistry*]
TP .... Thymopoietin
TP .... Thymus Protein
TP .... Tibialis Posterior [*Anatomy*]
TP .... Tie Plate [*Technical drawings*]
TP .... Tie Point
T-P .... Timbre Poste [*Postage Stamp*] [*French*]
TP .... Time to Perigee (MCD)
TP .... Time Pulse
TP .... Timing Point (AFM)
TP .... Timpano [*Music*]
TP .... Tin Plate
TP .... Title Page [*Bibliography*]
TP .... To Pay (ADA)
TP .... Toilet Paper [*Slang*] [*To be "TP'd" is to have your yard covertly decorated with unrolled toilet paper*]
TP .... Toll Point [*Telecommunications*] (TEL)
TP .... Toll Prefix [*Telecommunications*] (TEL)
TP .... Toothpick
TP .... Top
TP .... Top Priority
TP .... Topics in Photosynthesis [*Elsevier Book Series*] [*A publication*]
TP .... Torpedo Part of Beam (MSA)
TP .... Total Parts
TP .... Total Phenolic Levels [*Chemistry*]
TP .... Total Phosphorus [*Analytical chemistry*]
TP .... Total Points
TP .... Total Power
TP .... Total Pressure
TP .... Total Production [*or Product*] [*Ecology*]
TP .... Total Protein
TP .... Totally Positive
TP .... Touchdowns Passing [*Football*]
TP .... T'oung Pao [*A publication*]
TP .... Township
TP .... Toxic Pregnancy [*Gynecology*]
TP .... Tracking Program (MUGU)
TP .... Trade Protection Service [*or Society*] [*British*]
TP .... Traffic Post
TP .... Training Period [*Military*] (AFM)
TP .... Training Plan (NASA)
TP .... Training, Practicing [*Ammunition*]
TP .... Transaction Processing [*Data processing*]
TP .... Transaction Program [*Data processing*] (BYTE)
TP .... Transaction Provider (WDMC)
TP .... Transannular Patch [*Cardiology*]
TP .... Transfer on Positive
TP .... Transforming Principle [*Bacteriology*]
TP .... Transition Period (NASA)
TP .... Transition Plans (MCD)
TP .... Translucent Paper (ADA)
TP .... Transnational Prospectives [*A publication*]
TP .... Transplant
TP .... Transport Pack
TP .... Transport Pilot
TP .... Transport Protein [*Superseded by SC, Secretory Component*] [*Immunology*]
TP .... Transport Protocol [*Data processing*]
TP .... Transportation Priority [*Military*] (AFM)
TP .... Transporter (DCTA)
TP .... Transportes Aereos Portugueses [*ICAO designator*] (FAAC)
TP .... Transvaal Province [*Republic of South Africa*]
TP .... Transvaal Supreme Court Reports [*South Africa*] [*A publication*] (DLA)

TP	Travaux Forces a Perpetuite [*Penal Servitude for Life*] [*French*]
TP	Travaux Publics [*Public Works*] [*French*]
TP	Travers Pensions [*Formerly, Naval Knights of Windsor*] [*Military*] [*British*] (ROG)
TP	Treaty Port
TP	Tree Project (EA)
TP	TreePeople (EA)
TP	Treponema Pallidum [*A spirochete*] [*Clinical chemistry*]
TP	Trigonometrischer Punkt [*Triangulation Point*] [*German military - World War II*]
TP	Triphosphate (MAE)
TP	Triple Play [*Baseball*]
TP	Triple Pole [*Switch*]
TP	Troop
TP	Troop Program [*Military*] (AABC)
TP	Tropical Pacific [*American air mass*]
TP	True Position
TP	True Positive [*Medicine*]
TP	True Profile [*Technical drawings*]
TP	Trumpet
TP	Tryptophan [*An amino acid*] (MAE)
TP	Tryptophan Pyrrolase [*Also, TPO*] [*An enzyme*]
TP	Tuberculin Precipitation [*Medicine*]
TP	Tuned Plate (DEN)
TP	Turboprop (AAG)
TP	Turbopump (AAG)
T & P	Turner and Phillips' English Chancery Reports [*A publication*] (DLA)
TP	Turning Point
TP	Tyndale Paper [*A publication*] (APTA)
TP	Type (NASA)
TPA	Austin Peay State University, Clarksville, TN [*OCLC symbol*] (OCLC)
TPA	Taildragger Pilots Association (EA)
TPA	Tala Pozo [*Argentina*] [*Seismograph station code, US Geological Survey*] [*Closed*] (SEIS)
TPA	Tallgrass Prairie Alliance (EA)
TPA	Tampa Air Center [*Tampa, FL*] [*FAA designator*] (FAAC)
TPA	Tampa/St. Petersburg/Clearwater [*Florida*] [*Airport symbol*]
TPA	Tannic Acid, Phosphomolybdic Acid, Amido Acid Black [*A staining technique*]
TPA	Tantalum Producers Association (EA)
TPA	Tape Pulse Amplifier
TPA	Target Position Analyzer [*Military*] (CAAL)
TPA	Tariff Programs and Appraisals [*Canada Customs*]
TPA	TASS [*Towed Array SONAR System*] Probability Area (NVT)
TPA	Technical Practice Aid (ADA)
TPA	Technical Publications Agent (MCD)
TPA	Technical Publications Announcement
TPA	Telemetry Power Amplifier
TPA	Telepanel, Inc. [*Vancouver Stock Exchange symbol*]
TPA	Telephone Pioneers of America (EA)
TPA	Temperature-Programmed Analysis
TPA	Tennis Professionals Association [*Canada*]
TPa	Terapascal [*Pressure unit*]
TPA	Terephthalic Acid [*Also, TA*] [*Organic chemistry*]
TPA	Test Plans and Analysis
TPA	Test Preparation Area [*NASA*] (KSC)
TPA	Test Project Agreement (NG)
TPA	Tetradecanoylphorbolacetate [*Also, PMA, PTA*] [*Organic chemistry*]
TPA	Tetrapropylammonium [*Chemical radical*]
TPA	Texture Profile Analysis [*Food technology*]
TPA	Theta Phi Alpha [*Sorority*]
TPA	Third Party Administrator
TPA	Timber Producers Association of Michigan and Wisconsin (EA)
TPA	Time-Phased Allocation (MCD)
TPA	Tissue Plasminogen Activator [*Anticlotting agent*]
TPA	Tissue Polypeptide Antigen [*Immunochemistry*]
TPA	Toll Pulse Accepter [*Telecommunications*] (TEL)
TPA	Tons per Annum (ADA)
TPA	Top Pumparound [*Chemical engineering*]
TPA	T'oung Pao. Archives [*A publication*]
TPA	Tournament Players Association (EA)
TPA	Track Production Area [*Air Force*]
TPA	Traffic Pattern Altitude [*Aviation*]
TPA	Training Problem Analysis (MCD)
TPA	Trans-Pacific Airlines Ltd.
TPA	Transfer of Pay Account [*Military*]
TPA	Transient Program Area
TPA	Transmission Products Association (EA)
TPA	Travel by Personal Auto Authorized [*Military*]
TPA	Travel Professionals Associate (EA)
TPA	Travelers Protective Association of America [*St. Louis, MO*] (EA)
TPA	Trim Power Assembly
TPA	Triphenylamine [*Organic chemistry*]
TPA	Truck Performance Analysis
TPA	Tunable Parametric Amplifier
TPA	Turboprop Aircraft
TPA	Turbopump Assembly (KSC)
TPA	Tutmonda Parolspuro-Asocio [*Universal Association for Speech Tracing - UAST*] (EAIO)
TPA	Type of Professional Activity
TPAA........	Travelers Protective Association of America (EA)
TPAC........	Technology Policy and Assessment Center [*Georgia Institute of Technology*] [*Research center*] (RCD)
TPAC........	Telescope Precision Angle Counter
TP-AD	Technical Publications - Administration [*Naval Facilities Engineering Command Publications*]
TPAD	Trunnion Pin Attachment Device [*NASA*]
TPAEDP...	Topics in Paediatrics [*A publication*]
TPAM.......	Teleprocessing Access Method
TPAM.......	Three-Phase Aquatic Microcosms [*Technique for study of waters*]
TPAMF	Transpacific Asbestos Capital Shares [*NASDAQ symbol*] (NQ)
TPAOH	Tetrapropylammonium Hydroxide [*Organic chemistry*]
TPAP	Time-Phased-Action Plan [*DoD*]
TPAPA	Transactions and Proceedings. American Philological Association [*A publication*]
TP A Ph A ...	Transactions and Proceedings. American Philological Association [*A publication*]
TPAPOABITCOS ...	[*The*] Precentor and Prebendary of Alton Borealis in the Church of Sarum [*Pseudonym used by Arthur Ashley Sykes*]
TPAR........	Tactical Penetration Aids Rocket
TPARR......	TRADOC Program Analysis and Resource Review [*Military*] (MCD)
TPAT........	Test Point Algorithm Technique (MCD)
TPAX........	Tampax, Inc. [*NASDAQ symbol*] (NQ)
TPB...........	Nebraska Library Commission, Lincoln, NE [*OCLC symbol*] (OCLC)
TPB...........	Tape Playback BIT [*Binary Digit*] [*Data processing*]
TPB...........	Tarnished Plant Bug [*Entomology*]
TPB...........	Tennessee Philological Bulletin [*A publication*]
TPB...........	Tetraphenylbutadiene [*Organic chemistry*]
TPB...........	Tetraphenylbutane [*Organic chemistry*]
TpB...........	Trypan Blue [*Biological stain*]
TPB...........	Tryptone Phosphate Broth
T(PBEIST) ...	Transport - Planning Board European Inland Surface Transport (NATG)
TPBF	Total Pulmonary Blood Flow [*Physiology*]
TPBI	Third Party Bodily Injury [*Insurance*] (AIA)
TPBK........	Tape Block
T(PBOS)....	Transport - Planning Board Ocean Shipping (NATG)
TPBR	Top Brass Enterprises, Inc. [*Merrick, NY*] [*NASDAQ symbol*] (NQ)
TPBS	Tetrapropylenbenzenesulfonate [*Organic chemistry*]
TPBT	Technical Papers for the Bible Translator [*A publication*] (BJA)
TPBVP	Two-Point Boundary Value Problem
TPC...........	Nebraska Library Commission, Lincoln, NE [*OCLC symbol*] (OCLC)
TPC...........	Tactical Pilotage Chart
TPC...........	Tangential Period Correction
TPC...........	Technical Performance Criteria (SSD)
TPC...........	Technical Prime Contractor
TPC...........	Technical Progress Committee [*British*] (DCTA)
TPC...........	Technical Protein Colloid
TPC...........	Tejas Power Corp. [*AMEX symbol*] (SPSG)
TPC...........	Telecommunications Planning Committee [*Civil Defense*]
TPC...........	Telemetry Preprocessing Computer (MCD)
TPC...........	Telephone Pickup Coil
TPC...........	Territorial Production Complex [*Russian*]
TPC...........	Test Point Controller
TPC...........	Texas Petroleum Corp. [*Vancouver Stock Exchange symbol*]
TPC...........	Thermafor Pyrolytic Cracking [*A chemical process developed by Surface Combustion*]
TP & C	Thermal Protection and Control (NASA)
TPC...........	Thermally Protected Composite
TPC...........	Thromboplastic Plasma Component [*Factor VIII*] [*Also, AHF, AHG, PTF*] [*Hematology*]
TPC...........	Thymolphthalein complexone [*Analytical reagent*]
TPC...........	Time Polarity Control
TPC...........	Time Projection Chamber [*High-energy physics*]
TPC...........	Tire Performance Criteria [*General Motors Corp.*]
TPC...........	Tons per Centimeter (DCTA)
TPC...........	Topical Pulmonary Chemotherapy [*Medicine*]
TPC...........	Topographic Center [*Defense Mapping Agency*]
TPC...........	Total Package Contract
TPC...........	Total Plasma Cholesterol [*Clinical chemistry*]
TPC...........	Total Program Costs (KSC)
TPC...........	Total Protein Concentration
TPC...........	Tournament Players Championship
TPC...........	Trade Policy Committee [*Advisory to President*] [*Abolished, 1963*]
TPC...........	Trade Practices Cases [*A publication*] (APTA)
TPC...........	Training Plans Conference
TPC...........	Trans-Pacific Freight Conference of Japan/Korea Agent, San Francisco CA [*STAC*]
TPC...........	Transaction Processing Performance Council (EA)

Acronyms, Initialisms & Abbreviations Dictionary • 1994

TPC........... Transistor Photo Control
TPC........... Transport Plane Commander
TPC........... Transvascular Protein Clearance [*Medicine*]
TPC........... Travaux Publics Canada [*Public Works Canada - PWC*]
TPC........... Travel by Privately-Owned Conveyance Permitted for Convenience [*Military*]   (AFM)
TPC........... Treated Paper Copier [*Reprography*]
TPC........... Treponema Pallidum Complement [*Clinical chemistry*]   (MAE)
TPC........... Tricalcium Phosphate Ceramic [*Inorganic chemistry*]
TPC........... Triple Paper-Covered [*Wire insulation*]   (DEN)
TPC........... Triple-Product Convolver [*Acousto-optic technology*]   (RDA)
TPC........... Turbopump Control
TPC........... Turns per Centimeter [*Yarn*]
TPC........... Twentynine Palms [*California*] [*Seismograph station code, US Geological Survey*]   (SEIS)
TPC........... Twisted Pair Cable
TPCA........ Test Procedure Change Authorization   (NATG)
TPCA........ Total Pharmaceutical Care [*NASDAQ symbol*]   (SPSG)
TPCB........ [*The*] Personal Computer Book
TPCC........ TPC Communications, Inc. [*NASDAQ symbol*]   (NQ)
TPCCA...... Topics in Current Chemistry [*A publication*]
TPCCOA... Telephone Provincial Clerical and Contract Officers' Association [*A union*] [*British*]
TPCD........ Tetraphenylcyclopentadienone [*Organic chemistry*]
TPCD........ Trade Practices Commission. Decisions and Determinations [*A publication*]   (APTA)
TPCDD...... Trade Practices Commission. Decisions and Determinations [*A publication*]   (APTA)
TPCF......... Treponema Pallidum Complement Fixation [*Clinical chemistry*]
TPCK........ Tosyl Phenylalanine Chloromethyl Ketone [*Biochemistry*]
TPCK........ Tosylaminophenylethyl Chloromethyl Ketone [*Organic chemistry*]
TPCN........ Task Plan Change Notice   (MCD)
TPCO........ Teleprinter Coordinator
TPCP........ Trainer Power Control Panel
TPCR........ Task Plan Change Request   (MCD)
TPCRP...... Tool and Production Change Planning Record   (SAA)
TPCS......... Torquay Pottery Collectors' Society   (EA)
TPCU......... Thermal Preconditioning Unit
TPCV........ Turbine Power Control Valve
TPCWDL.. Colorado. Division of Wildlife. Technical Publication [*A publication*]
TPD .... Five Associated University Libraries, Rochester, NY [*OCLC symbol*]   (OCLC)
TPD .... South African Law Reports, Transvaal Provincial Division [*South Africa*] [*A publication*]   (DLA)
T/PD .... Table of Personnel Distribution   (NATG)
TPD .... Tape Playback Discriminator
TPD .... Tapped   (MSA)
TPD .... Technical Programs Division [*Environmental Protection Agency*]   (GFGA)
TPD .... Technical Publications Documentation [*Army*]
TPD .... Temperature-Programmed Desorption [*Catalysis*]
TPD .... Temporary Partial Disablement [*Insurance*]   (AIA)
TPD .... Terminal Protective Device   (MSA)
TPD .... Terracamp Development [*Vancouver Stock Exchange symbol*]
TPD .... Test Plasma Produced by Discharge   (MCD)
TPD .... Test Point Data
TPD .... Test Procedure Deviation [*Nuclear energy*]   (NRCH)
TPD .... Test Procedure Drawing [*NASA*]   (KSC)
TPD .... Theophylline, Proxyphylline, and Dyphylline [*Antineoplastic drug regimen*]
TPD .... Thermoplastic Photoconductor Device
TPD .... Thiamine Propyl Disulfide   (MAE)
TPD .... Time Pulse Distributor   (MCD)
TPD .... Toilet Paper Dispenser [*Technical drawings*]
TPD .... Tons per Day
TPD .... Torque Proportioning Differential [*Automotive engineering*]
TPD .... Total Permanent Disability [*or Disablement*] [*Insurance*]   (AIA)
TPD .... Total Purity by Difference [*Gas analysis*]
TPD .... Tournament Players Division of the Professional Golfers Association of America [*Later, TPA*]
TPD .... Toxics and Pesticides Division [*Environmental Protection Agency*]   (GFGA)
TPD .... Training Programs Directorate [*Army*]
TPD .... Transient Photodichroism [*Physics*]
TPD .... Tumor-Producing Dose [*Virology*]
TPDB........ Tape Deblock
TPDC........ Training and Performance Data Center [*Military*]
TPDLRI..... Textile Printers and Dyers Labor Relations Institute   (EA)
TPDRS ...... Time-Phased Downgrading and Reclassification System [*Military*]   (DNAB)
TPDS........ Tape Playback Discriminator System
TPDS........ Test Procedures Development System   (NASA)
TPDSASR ... Tooling Project Data Sheet Assembly Sequence Record
TPDS-T..... Target Practice Discarding Sabot-Tracer [*Projectile*]   (MCD)
TPDT........ Triple-Pole, Double-Throw [*Switch*]
TPE........... Five Associated University Libraries, Rochester, NY [*OCLC symbol*]   (OCLC)

TPE........... T-Pulse Effectiveness [*Neurology*]
TPE........... Tactical Performance Evaluation
TPE........... Taipei [*Taiwan*] [*Airport symbol*]   (OAG)
TPE........... Task of Public Education Questionnaire   (AEBS)
TPE........... Technology, People, Environment [*National Science Foundation project*]
TP & E ...... Test Planning and Evaluation   (MCD)
TPE........... Test Planning and Evaluation
TPE........... Test Project Engineer   (NASA)
TPE........... Tetraphenylethylene [*Organic chemistry*]
TPE........... Thermoplastic Elastomer [*Plastics technology*]
TPE........... Threshold Photoelectron [*Spectroscopy*]
TPE........... Total Potential Energy
TPE........... Transaction Processing Executive   (MCD)
TPE........... Transport Planning and Economics [*British*]
TPE........... Triple Crown Electronics, Inc. [*Toronto Stock Exchange symbol*]
TPE........... Turbopropeller Engine
TPE........... Twisted-Pair Ethernet [*Intel Corp.*]
TPE........... Two-Photon Excitation [*Fluorescence spectrometry*]
TPE........... Two Pion Exchange [*Nuclear physics*]   (OA)
TPEA .... Television Program Export Association   (EA)
TPED......... Trade and Professional Exhibits Directory [*Later, TSW*] [*A publication*]
T-PEES .... Triplane Elevated Evaluation System [*Army*]   (RDA)
TPEMA..... Telephone Engineer and Management [*A publication*]
TPEMDZ.. Topics in Perinatal Medicine [*A publication*]
TPEN........ Tetrakis(pyridylmethyl)ethylenediamine [*Organic chemistry*]
TPer .... Tetradi Perevodcika [*A publication*]
TPES .... Threshold Photoelectron Spectroscopy [*Physics*]
TPESP...... Technical Panel on the Earth Satellite Program
TPET......... Terrapet Energy Corp. [*NASDAQ symbol*]   (NQ)
TPETA ...... Techniques du Petrole [*A publication*]
TPEX .... TPEX Exploration, Inc. [*NASDAQ symbol*]   (NQ)
TPEY........ Tellurite-Polymyxin-Egg Yolk [*Agar*] [*Microbiology*]
TPF .... [*The*] Pygmy Fund   (EA)
TPF .... Tactical Patrol Force [*Police*]
TPF .... Tailored Probability Forecast
TPF .... Tampa, FL [*Location identifier*] [*FAA*]   (FAAL)
TPF .... Telemetry Processing Facility   (MCD)
TPF .... Temporary Program File [*Data processing*]
TPF .... Terminal Phase Finalization [*or Finish*] [*NASA*]   (KSC)
TPF .... Tetraphenylfuran [*Organic chemistry*]
TPF .... Thai Patriotic Front [*Communist-directed activity outside Thailand*] [*Merged with TIM*]
TPF .... Theoretical Point of Fog   (MSA)
TPF .... Thymus Permeability Factor
TPF .... Time Prism Filter [*Telecommunications*]   (TEL)
TPF .... Total Package Fielding [*Army*]
TPF .... Total Peaking Factor [*Nuclear energy*]   (NRCH)
TPF .... Trainer Parts Fabrication   (AAG)
TPF .... Transaction Processing Facility   (HGAA)
TPF .... Transfer Phase Final   (MCD)
TPF .... Tri-Pacific Resources Ltd. [*Vancouver Stock Exchange symbol*]
TPF .... Tube and Pipe Fabricators Association, International   (EA)
TPF .... Tug Processing Facility [*NASA*]   (NASA)
TPF .... Two-Phase Flow
TPF .... Two Photon Fluorescence [*Electronics*]   (OA)
TPFA .... Tube and Pipe Fabricators Association, International   (EAIO)
TPFC .... [*The*] Platters Fan Club   (EA)
TPF & C..... Towers, Perrin, Forster & Crosby [*Compensation and actuarial consulting company*]
TPFDD...... Time-Phased Force Deployment Data [*Military*]   (AABC)
TPFDL ...... Time-Phased Force Deployment List [*Military*]   (AFM)
TPFDL ...... Troop Program Field Deployment List [*Military*]
TPFI .... Terminal Pin Fault Insertion
TPFP .... Transkei People's Freedom Party [*South Africa*] [*Political party*]   (PPW)
TPFR .... Time to Peak Filling Rate [*Cardiology*]
TPFW .... Thermoplastic Fan Wheel
TPFW .... Three-Phase Full Wave
TPG .... Tapping
TPG .... Technology Planning Guide [*Military*]   (AFIT)
TPG .... Telecom Publishing Group   (IID)
TPG .... Telecommunication Program Generator
TPG .... Teletype Preamble Generator
TPG .... Thermionic Power Generator
TPG .... Timing Pulse Generator
TPG .... Topping   (FAAC)
TPG .... Total Pressure Gauge
TPG .... Town Planning and Local Government Guide [*A publication*]   (APTA)
TPG .... Transplacental Gradient [*Obstetrics*]   (MAE)
TPG .... Trinity Peninsula Group [*Geology*]
TPG .... Triphenylguanidine [*Organic chemistry*]
TPG .... Trypticase, Peptone, Glucose
TPGC........ Temperature-Programmed Gas Chromatography
TpGGv .... Templeton Global Governments Income Trust [*Associated Press abbreviation*]   (APAG)
TPGS .... [*The*] Pennsylvania German Society   (EA)
TPGS......... Tocopherol Polyethylene Glycol Succinate [*Organic chemistry*]

TPH	Telephony [*A publication*]
TPH	Theosophical Publishing House
TPH	Thromboembolic Pulmonary Hypertension [*Medicine*]
TPH	Tiphook [*NYSE symbol*] (SPSG)
TPH	Tonopah [*Nevada*] [*Seismograph station code, US Geological Survey*] (SEIS)
TPH	Tonopah, NV [*Location identifier*] [*FAA*] (FAAL)
TPH	Tons per Hour
TPH	Total Petroleum Hydrocarbon [*Analytical chemistry*]
TPH	Total Possessed Hours (MCD)
TPH	Transplacental Hemorrhage [*Obstetrics*] (MAE)
TPH	Triumph Resources Corp. [*Vancouver Stock Exchange symbol*]
TPH	University of Texas, Health Science Center at Houston, School Public Health, Houston, TX [*OCLC symbol*] (OCLC)
TPHA	Treponema Pallidum Hemagglutination
TPHA	Truman Philatelic and Historical Association (EA)
TPHASAP ...	Telephone as Soon as Possible (NOAA)
TPHAT.....	Telephone at [*Followed by time*] (NOAA)
TPHAYC...	Telephone at Your Convenience (NOAA)
TPHC	Time-to-Pulse Height Converter
TPhI	Turfan Pahlavi (BJA)
TPHO	Telephotograph
TPHR	Tons per Hour
TPhS	Transactions. Philological Society [*A publication*]
TPhS	Transactions. Philosophical Society [*London and Strassburg*] [*A publication*]
TPHSDY ...	Trends in Pharmacological Sciences [*A publication*]
TPHSG	Troop Housing [*Army*] (AABC)
TPHW	Three-Phase Half Wave
TPI	[*The*] Progress Interview
TPI	Tape Phase Inverter
TPI	Tape-Position Indicator (DEN)
TPI	Tapini [*Papua New Guinea*] [*Airport symbol*] (OAG)
TPI	Target Position Indicator
TPI	Task Parameter Interpretation
TPI	Tax Planning Ideas [*A publication*] (DLA)
TPI	Tax and Price Index
TPI	Taxpayer Inquiry [*IRS*]
TPI	Teatro Popolare Italiano [*Italian theatrical troupe*]
TPI	Technical Proficiency Inspection [*Military*]
TPI	Teeth per Inch [*of cog wheels*]
TPI	Tennessee Polytechnic Institute
TPI	Terminal Phase Ignition [*NASA*]
TPI	Terminal Phase Initiate [*NASA*] (KSC)
TPI	Terminal Phase Insertion [*NASA*]
TPI	Test Program Instruction (MCD)
TPI	Test Program Interaction (MCD)
TPI	Thermal Protection Investigation
TPI	Thermo Process Systems, Inc. [*AMEX symbol*] (SPSG)
TPI	Threads per Inch
TPI	Time Perception Inventory [*Test*]
TPI	Timing Pulse Idler
TPI	Tire Pressure Indicating System (MCD)
TPI	Title, Page, and Index
TPI	Tons per Inch
TPI	Total Positive Income [*IRS*]
T & PI	Totally and Permanently Incapacitated [*Insurance*] (ADA)
TPI	Totally and Permanently Incapacitated [*Insurance*] (ADA)
TPI	Town Planning Institute [*Later, Royal Town Planning Institute*] [*British*] (ILCA)
TPI	Tracks per Inch [*Magnetic storage devices*] [*Data processing*]
TPI	TRADOC Procurement Instruction (MCD)
TPI	Training Plan Information (MCD)
TPI	Transmission Performance Index [*Telecommunications*] (TEL)
TPI	Treponema Immobilization Test [*Clinical chemistry*] (MAE)
TPI	Treponema Pallidum Immobilization [*or Immobilizing*] [*Clinical chemistry*]
TPI	Trim Position Indicator
TPI	Triosephosphate Isomerase [*An enzyme*]
TPI	Triphosphoinositide [*Biochemistry*]
TPI	Tropical Products Institute [*Overseas Development Administration*] [*British*] (DS)
TPI	Truss Plate Institute (EA)
TPI	Tuned Port Fuel Injection
TPI	Turns per Inch
TPIA	Take Pride in America Program [*Forest Service*] (GFGA)
TPIA	Treponema Pallidum Immune Adherence [*Clinical chemistry*]
TPIC	Town Planning Institute of Canada
TPID.........	Telecommunications Performance and Interface Document (MCD)
TPIE	TPI Enterprises, Inc. [*NASDAQ symbol*] (NQ)
TPIF	Thornton Pacific Investment Fund
TPIM.........	Tool Process Instruction Manual (MCD)
TPIN.........	True Personal Identification Number [*Banking*]
TPI Rep Trop Prod Inst ...	TPI Report. Tropical Products Institute [*A publication*]
TPIS	Tire Pressure Indicating System (MCD)
TPIX.........	Telepictures Corp. [*NASDAQ symbol*] (NQ)
TPJ	Tangkuban-Prahu [*Java*] [*Seismograph station code, US Geological Survey*] [*Closed*] (SEIS)
TPJ	Tennessee Poetry Journal [*A publication*]
TPJSL	Transactions and Proceedings. Japan Society (London) [*A publication*]
TPK...........	Test of Practical Knowledge
TPK...........	Tulare Free Public Library, Tulare, CA [*OCLC symbol*] (OCLC)
TPK...........	Turnpike
TPK...........	Turns per Knot [*Navy*] (CAAL)
TPKE........	Turnpike (MCD)
TPKrR	Theologicka Priloha (Krestanske Revue) [*A publication*] (BJA)
TPL...........	Table Producing Language [*1971*] [*Data processing*] (IID)
TPL...........	Tabular Parts List
TPL...........	Target Position Location (MCD)
TPL...........	Technical Publications Library (MCD)
TPL...........	Temple [*Texas*] [*Airport symbol*] (OAG)
TPL...........	Temple, TX [*Location identifier*] [*FAA*] (FAAL)
TPL...........	Terminal per Line [*Telecommunications*]
TPL...........	Terminal Processing Language
TPL...........	Test Parts List
TPL...........	Test Plan (CAAL)
TPL...........	Test Plan Log (MCD)
TPL...........	Test Point Logic
TPL...........	Texas Pacific Land Trust [*NYSE symbol*] (SPSG)
TPL...........	Text Processing Language [*Data processing*]
TPL...........	THERE Programming Language [*Data processing*]
TPL...........	Tocopilla [*Chile*] [*Seismograph station code, US Geological Survey*] (SEIS)
TPL...........	Toll Pole Line [*Telecommunications*] (TEL)
TPL...........	Tons Poids Lourd [*Deadweight Tons*] [*French*]
TPL...........	Topsail [*Ship's rigging*] (ROG)
TPL...........	Toronto Public Library [*UTLAS symbol*]
TPL...........	Training Parts List (AAG)
TPL...........	Transfer on Plus (SAA)
TPL...........	Transistorized Portable Laboratory
TPL...........	Trap Processing Line
TPL...........	Triple (MSA)
TPL...........	Triumph Petroleums Ltd. [*Vancouver Stock Exchange symbol*]
TPL...........	Troop Program List [*Army*]
TPL...........	Tropicalized (MSA)
TPL...........	Trust for Public Land (EA)
TPL...........	Tunable Pulsed LASER
TPL...........	Turns per Layer
TPL...........	Twyford Plant Laboratories Ltd. [*British*] (IRUK)
TPLA	[*The*] Product Liability Alliance (EA)
TPLA	Triphenyllead Acetate [*Organic chemistry*]
TPLA	Turkish People's Liberation Army (PD)
TPLAAV ...	Tidsskrift foer Planteavl [*A publication*]
TPLAB	Tape Label [*Data processing*]
TPLAF.......	Thai People's Liberation Armed Forces [*Thailand*]
TPLC.........	Test Program Logic Computer (DWSG)
TPLD.........	Test Planning Liaison Drawing (AAG)
TPLF	Tigre People's Liberation Front [*Ethiopia*] [*Political party*] (PD)
TPLG.........	Topologix, Inc. [*NASDAQ symbol*] (NQ)
TPLGG......	Town Planning and Local Government Guide [*A publication*] (APTA)
T-PLL........	T-Cell Prolymphocytic Leukemia [*Oncology*]
TPLOA......	Teploenergetika [*Moscow*] [*A publication*]
TPLP	Teeco Properties LP [*NASDAQ symbol*] (NQ)
TPLP	Tobacco Products Liability Project (EA)
TPLP	Turkish People's Liberation Party [*Political party*] (PD)
TPLP/F......	Turkish People's Liberation Party/Front
TPLQ-A.....	Town Planning Quarterly [*New Zealand*] [*A publication*]
TPLR-A.....	Town Planning Review [*United Kingdom*] [*A publication*]
TPLS	Technology in Public Libraries Section [*Public Library Association*]
TPLS	Terminal Position Location System
TPLS	Texas Panhandle Library System [*Library network*]
TPLS	Tunable Pulsed LASER System
T/PLT........	Tapping Plate [*Automotive engineering*]
TPLW........	Triple Wall
TPM	Tape Preventive Maintenance
TPM	Tape Processing Machine
TPM	Technical Performance Management
TPM	Technical Performance Measurement System [*NASA*]
TPM	Technical Performance Module (MCD)
TPM	Telemetry Processor Module
TPM	Tepoztlan [*Mexico*] [*Seismograph station code, US Geological Survey*] (SEIS)
TPM	Terminal Phase Maneuver [*Aerospace*] (MCD)
TPM	Terminal Phase Midcourse [*Aerospace*] (MCD)
TPM	Test Performance Management [*Army*]
TPM	Test Planning Manager [*NASA*] (KSC)
TPM	Theoretical Platers per Meter [*Chromatography*]
TPM	Thermal Power Monitor [*Nuclear energy*] (NRCH)
TPM	Thermal Protection Material
TPM	Timber Products Manufacturers (EA)
TPM	Title Page Mutilated
TPM	Tons per Minute
TPM	Tons per Month

TPM .... Torpedo Prize Money [*British military*] (DMA)
TPM .... Total Active Preventive Maintenance Time (MCD)
TPM .... Total Downtime for Preventive Scheduled Maintenance
            [*Quality control*] (MCD)
TPM .... Total Particulate Matter [*The "tar" of cigar and cigarette
            smoke*]
TPM .... Total Passive Motion
TPM .... Total Polar Material [*Analytical chemistry*]
TPM .... Total Population Management [*Department of Agriculture*]
TPM .... Total Productive Maintenance [*Japanese industrialization
            theory*]
TPM .... Tours par Minute [*Revolutions per Minute*] [*French*]
TPM .... Transfer Phase Midcourse [*Aerospace*] (MCD)
TPM .... Transfiguration Prison Ministries (EA)
TPM .... Transmission and Processing Model
TPM .... Trigger Pricing Mechanism
TPM .... Triphenylmethane [*Class of organic dyes*] [*Organic chemistry*]
TPM .... Triplate Module
TPM .... Tubular Products Manual [*A publication*] (EAAP)
TPMA .... Thermodynamic Properties of Metals and Alloys (KSC)
TPMA .... Timber Products Manufacturers Association [*Later, TPM*]
TPMAD5... Tropical Pest Management [*A publication*]
TP-MAU ... Twisted-Pair Medium Attachment Unit (PCM)
TPMF .... Tax Practitioner Master File [*IRS*]
TPMG .... [*The*] Provost Marshal General [*Army*]
TPMGA..... Teoriya i Praktika Metallurgii [*A publication*]
TPMM ...... Teleprocessing Multiplexer Module
TPMM ...... Triphenylmethyl Methacrylate [*Organic chemistry*]
TP-MO...... Technical Publications - Maintenance Operation [*Naval
            Facilities Engineering Command Publications*]
TPMP....... Tender Production Management Program
TPMP....... Texas Pacific-Missouri Pacific Terminal [*Railroad of New
            Orleans*] [*AAR code*]
TPMR....... Transfer of Program Management Responsibility
TPMR....... Trunked Private Mobile Radio
TPMV....... Tomato (Peru) Mosaic Virus
TPMXA..... Tecnica Pecuaria en Mexico [*A publication*]
TPN .... Pan American University, Library, Edinburg, TX [*OCLC
            symbol*] (OCLC)
TPN .... Sandoz Pharmaceuticals [*Research code symbol*]
TPN .... Tapini [*Papua New Guinea*] [*Seismograph station code, US
            Geological Survey*] [*Closed*] (SEIS)
TPN .... Tetrachlorophthalodinitrile [*Organic chemistry*]
TPN .... Thalamic Projection Neurons [*Neurology*]
TPN .... Total Parenteral Nutrition
TPN .... Total Petroleum (North America) Ltd. [*AMEX symbol*]
            [*Toronto Stock Exchange symbol*] (SPSG)
TPN .... Triphosphopyridine Nucleotide [*See NADP*] [*Biochemistry*]
TP & N....... Triple Pole and Neutral [*Switch*]
TPN .... Two-Position Nozzle (MCD)
TP & ND.... Theft, Pilferage, and Nondelivery [*Insurance*] (ADA)
TPND .... Theft, Pilferage, and Nondelivery [*Insurance*]
TPNEG...... Travel Will Be Performed at No Expense to the Government
            [*Military*]
TPNG .... Territory of Papua and New Guinea
TPNG .... Topping (AAG)
TPNH....... Triphosphopyridine Nucleotide (Reduced) [*See NADPH*]
            [*Biochemistry*]
TPNL........ Townsend Plan National Lobby (EA)
T/PNL....... Trim Panel [*Automotive engineering*]
TPNO .... Tree Planters' Notes [*A publication*]
TPNS......... Teleprocessing Network Simulator
TPO .... Nederlands Transport [*A publication*]
TPO .... Sandoz Pharmaceuticals [*Research code symbol*]
TPO .... Tanalian Point, AK [*Location identifier*] [*FAA*] (FAAL)
TPO .... Tank Pressurizing Orifice (KSC)
TPO .... Technical Planning Office
TPO .... Technical Project Officer
TPO .... Technology Planning Objectives (MCD)
TPO .... Telecommunications Program Objective [*Army*] (AABC)
TPO .... Temperature-Programmed Oxidation [*For surface analysis*]
Tpo .... Tempo [*Record label*] [*Germany*]
TPO .... TEMPO Enterprises, Inc. [*AMEX symbol*] (SPSG)
TPO .... Tentative Program Objectives [*Navy*]
TPO .... Test of Perceptual Organization [*Neuropsychology test*]
TPO .... Test Program Outline [*Military*]
TPO .... Thermoplastic Olefinic [*Elastomer*]
TPO .... Thyroid Peroxidase [*An enzyme*]
TPO .... Track Production Officer [*NATO Air Defense Ground
            Environment*] (NATG)
TPO .... Transportation Packaging Order (AFM)
TPO .... Traveling Post Office
TPO .... Tree Preservation Order [*Town planning*] [*British*]
TPO .... Tryptophan Oxygenase [*Also, TO, TP*] [*An enzyme*]
TPO .... Tryptophan Peroxidase [*An enzyme*] (AAMN)
TPO .... Tuned Plate Oscillator
TPOCP...... Turbopump Oxidizer Cavity Purge (SAA)
TPOD .... Test Plan of the Day
TPOH....... [*The*] Pursuit of Happiness [*Rock music group*]
TPOM ...... Tentative Program Objectives Memorandum
            [*Military*] (CAAL)

TPOM .... Tube Propagation d'Ondes Magnetron
TPorH....... Highland Hospital, Portland, TN [*Library symbol*] [*Library of
            Congress*] (LCLS)
TPORT...... Transport
TPOS........ Track Position
TPow........ Tygodnik Powszechny [*A publication*]
TPP........... Tarapoto [*Peru*] [*Airport symbol*] (OAG)
TPP........... Technical Performance Parameter (MCD)
TPP........... Technology Program Plan [*Military*] (AFIT)
TPP........... Telephony Preprocessor [*Telecommunications*] (TEL)
TPP........... Teletype Page Printer
TPP........... Teppco Partners LP [*NYSE symbol*] (SPSG)
TPP........... [*US*] Terminal Procedures Publication [*Aviation*]
TPP........... Test Point Pace (KSC)
TPP........... Test Program Plan (MCD)
TPP........... Tetraphenylporphine [*Organic chemistry*]
TPP........... Tetraphenylporphyrin [*Biochemistry*]
TPP........... Textured Peanut Protein [*Food industry*]
TPP........... Thermal Power Plant (CINC)
TPP........... Thermal Protection Panel
TPP........... Thermally Protected Plastic
TPP........... Thiamine Pyrophosphate [*Also, DPT, TDP*] [*Biochemistry*]
TPP........... Thomson Professional Publishing [*The Thomson Corp.*]
TP & P....... Time, Place, and Person
TPP........... Toledo Progressive Party [*Belize*] [*Political party*] (PPW)
TPP........... Tool and Production Planning (SAA)
TPP........... Total Package Procurement [*Government contracting*]
TPP........... Total Program Planning/Procurement
TPP........... Trained Profile Panel [*Sensory testing*]
TPP........... Training Program and Planning
TPP........... Trans-Pluto Probe
TPP........... Transducer Power Programmer
TPP........... Transients, Patients, and Prisoners [*Military*]
TP & P....... Transients, Patients, and Prisoners [*Military*]
TPP........... Transport Policies and Programme [*British*] (DCTA)
TPP........... Transuranium Processing Plant
TPP........... Tri-Power Petroleum Corp. [*Toronto Stock Exchange symbol*]
TPP........... Trinidad [*Pointe-A-Pierre*] [*Trinidad-Tobago*] [*Seismograph
            station code, US Geological Survey*] (SEIS)
TPP........... Triphenyl Phosphite [*Organic chemistry*]
TPP........... Triphenylphosphine [*Organic chemistry*]
TPP........... Tripolyphosphate [*Food industry*]
TPP........... True Path Party [*Turkey*] [*Political party*]
TPP........... Two-Phase Principle
TPPADK .. Trends and Perspectives in Parasitology [*A publication*]
TPPC .... Total Package Procurement Concept [*Government contracting*]
TPPC .... Trans-Pacific Passenger Conference [*Later, PCC*] (EA)
TPPCR ...... Tool and Production Planning Change Record (SAA)
TPPD........ Technical Program Planning Division [*Air Force*] (MCD)
TPPE .... Two-Photon Photoemission Spectroscopy
TPPEP...... Turkey Point Performance Enforcement Program [*Nuclear
            energy*] (NRCH)
TPPG .... Training Program and Planning Guidance
TPPGM..... Tentative Planning and Programming Guidance Memorandum
            [*Navy*] (NVT)
TPPha........ Transactions. College of Physicians of Philadelphia [*A
            publication*]
TPPIS........ Treasury Payroll/Personnel Information System
TP-PL........ Technical Publications - Planning [*Naval Facilities Engineering
            Command Publications*]
TPPN........ Total Peripheral Parenteral Nutrition
TPPP .... Third Party Prescription Program
TPPS .... Tape Post-Processing System
TPPS .... Tetraphenylporphinesulfonate [*Reagent*]
TPPS .... Tops Markets, Inc. [*Buffalo, NY*] [*NASDAQ symbol*] (NQ)
TP-PU ...... Technical Publications - Public Utilities [*Naval Facilities
            Engineering Command Publications*]
TPPYA ..... Topical Problems of Psychotherapy [*A publication*]
TPPYAL... Aktuelle Fragen der Psychotherapie [*A publication*]
TPQ .... AMIGOS [*Access Method for Indexed Data Generalized for
            Operating System*] Bibliographic Council, Dallas, TX
            [*OCLC symbol*] (OCLC)
TPQ .... Government of Quebec [*Canada*] [*FAA designator*] (FAAC)
TPQ .... Tepic [*Mexico*] [*Airport symbol*]
T P Q......... Theologisch-Praktische Quartalschrift [*A publication*]
TPQ .... Threshold Planning Quantity [*Hazardous substances*]
TPQI......... Teacher-Pupil Question Inventory
TPQS....... Theologisch-Praktische Quartalschrift [*A publication*]
TPR........... AMIGOS [*Access Method for Indexed Data Generalized for
            Operating System*] Bibliographic Council, Dallas, TX
            [*OCLC symbol*] (OCLC)
TPR........... Tamper-Protected Recording [*3M Co.*]
TPR........... Tape Programmed Row [*Data scanner*]
TPR........... Taper (MSA)
TPR........... Target Practice Round (SAA)
TPR........... Team Power Rating [*Hockey*]
TPR........... Technical Program Review
TPR........... Technical Progress Report
TPR........... Technical Proposal Requirement (MCD)
TPR........... Telecommunications Product Review [*A publication*]
TPR........... Teleprinter (AAG)

TPR...........	Telescopic Photographic Recorder
TPR...........	Temperature Profile Recorder (AAG)
TPR...........	Temperature-Programmed Reaction [*Chemistry*]
TPR...........	Temperature-Programmed Reduction [*For analysis of surfaces*]
TPR...........	Temperature, Pulse, Respiration [*Medicine*]
TPr...........	Tempo Presente [*A publication*]
TPR...........	Temporary Price Reduction
TPR...........	Terrain Profile Recorder
TPR...........	Test Performance Recorder
TPR...........	Test Phase Report
TPR...........	Test Problem Report [*NASA*] (NASA)
TPR...........	Test Procedure Record (NATG)
TPR...........	Test Program Report
TPR...........	Testosterone Production Rate [*Endocrinology*] (MAE)
TPR...........	Tetratricopeptide Repeat [*Genetics*]
TPR...........	Thermoplastic Recording
TPR...........	Thermoplastic Rubber
TPR...........	Three Penny Review [*A publication*]
TPR...........	Tom Price [*Australia*] [*Airport symbol*]
TPR...........	Tool Performance Report [*Navy*] (DNAB)
TPR...........	Total Peripheral Resistance
TPR...........	Total Pulmonary Resistance [*Cardiology*]
TPR...........	Trade Practices Reports [*Australia*] [*A publication*]
TPR...........	Trained Personnel Requirements [*Air Force*]
TPR...........	Transmitter Power Rating
TPR...........	Trapped Pressure Ratio [*Gas analysis*]
TPR...........	Trooper
TPRA........	Target Practice Round, Aerobee (SAA)
TPRC........	Thermophysical Properties Research Center [*DoD*]
TPRC........	Trade Policy Research Centre [*British*] (ECON)
TPRC........	Transition Program for Refugee Children [*Department of Education*] (GFGA)
TPRD........	Technology Planning and Research Division [*Central Electricity Generating Board*] [*British*] (IRUK)
TPRG........	Technology Performance Requirements Guideline
TPRI.........	Teacher-Pupil Relationship Inventory
TPRI.........	Time Problems Inventory [*Test*]
TPRI.........	Total Peripheral Resistance Index
TPRI.........	Training Priority Requirements Index
TPRL........	Thermophysical Properties Research Laboratory [*Purdue University*] [*Research center*] (RCD)
TPRR........	Test Procedures and Results Report
TPRRD......	Technik-Index ueber Plasmaphysikalische Forschung und Fusionsreaktoren [*A publication*]
TPRS........	Temperature-Programmed Reaction Spectroscopy
TPRS........	Temperature-Programmed Reaction System
TPRS........	Trade Practices Reporting Service [*A publication*] (APTA)
TPRSL.......	Transactions and Proceedings. Royal Society of Literature [*A publication*]
TPRU........	Technical Processing and Reporting Unit (CAAL)
TPRU........	Tropical Pesticides Research Unit [*Later, Centre for Overseas Pest Research*] [*British*]
TPRV........	Transient Peak Reverse Voltage
TPS...........	Bibliographic Center for Research, Denver, CO [*OCLC symbol*] (OCLC)
TPS...........	[*The*] Planetary Society
TPS...........	[*The*] Pope Speaks [*A publication*]
TPS...........	Tactical Paint Scheme (MCD)
TPS...........	Tactical Probe System (SAA)
TPS...........	Tandem Propeller Submarine
TPS...........	Tangent Plane System (MUGU)
TPS...........	Tank Pressure Sensing (AAG)
TPS...........	Tape Plotting System
TPS...........	Tape Processing System (CMD)
TPS...........	Tape Punch Subassembly
TPS...........	Task Parameter Synthesizer
TPS...........	Technical Publishing Society [*Later, STC*]
TPS...........	Technical Publishing Software [*Interleaf, Inc.*]
TPS...........	Technology Policy Statement [*1982*] [*India*]
TPS...........	Technopolymer Structure [*Engineering plastics*]
TPS...........	Telecommunications Programming System
TPS...........	Telemation Program Services
TPS...........	Telemetry Processing System [*Space Flight Operations Facility, NASA*]
TPS...........	Terminal Performance Specification
TPS...........	Terminal Polling System
TPS...........	Terminals per Station [*Telecommunications*]
TPS...........	Test Pilot School [*Navy*]
TPS...........	Test Plotting System
TPS...........	Test Point Selector
TPS...........	Test Preparation Sheet [*NASA*] (AAG)
TPS...........	Test Procedure Specification [*NASA*] (KSC)
TPS...........	Test Program Set [*Aviation*] (MCD)
TPS...........	Theater Production Service (AEBS)
TPS...........	Theologie Pastorale et Spiritualite [*A publication*]
TPS...........	Thermal Protection System [*or Subsystem*]
TPS...........	Thermoplastic Storage
TPS...........	Thomas Paine Society [*Nottingham, England*] (EAIO)
TPS...........	Threat Platform Simulator [*Military*] (CAAL)
TPS...........	Throttle Position Sensor [*Automotive engineering*]
TPS...........	Total Parameter Space [*Statistics*]
TPS...........	Total Product Support
TPS...........	Tough Plastic-Sheathed
TPS...........	TPA of America [*AMEX symbol*] (SPSG)
TPS...........	Track Processing Special (SAA)
TPS...........	Tracks per Second (WGA)
TPS...........	Trade Promotion Services Group [*British*]
TPS...........	Trail Pilot Sensor
TPS...........	Tramp Power Supply
TPS...........	Trans Rampart Industry [*Vancouver Stock Exchange symbol*]
TPS...........	Transaction Processing System [*Trademark of Software Consulting Service, Inc.*]
TPS...........	Transactions. Philological Society [*London*] [*A publication*]
TPS...........	Transactions per Second
TPS...........	Transduodenal Pancreatic Sphincteroplasty
TPS...........	Translunar Propulsion Stage [*Aerospace*] (AAG)
TPS...........	Trapani [*Italy*] [*Airport symbol*] (OAG)
TPS...........	Tree Pruning System
TPS...........	Trigger-Price System [*Department of the Treasury*]
TPS...........	Triphenylsulfonium Chloride [*Organic chemistry*]
TPS...........	Troops [*Military*] [*British*]
TPS...........	Trypsin (MAE)
TPS...........	Tube Pin Straightener
TPS...........	Tumor Polysaccharidal Substance [*Oncology*]
TPS...........	Turkey Point Station [*Nuclear energy*] (NRCH)
TPS...........	Turner Program Services [*Broadcasting*]
TPS...........	Tuvalu Philatelic Society (EA)
TPS...........	Twisted Pair Shielded
TPSB	Telemetry Processing System Buffer [*Space Flight Operations Facility, NASA*]
TPSB	Thomas Paine Society. Bulletin [*A publication*]
TPSC	Test Planning and Status Checker [*Data processing*]
TPSC	Trade Policy Staff Committee [*Federal interagency group*]
TPSE	Thermal Protection Subsystem Experiments (NASA)
TPSE	(Tritylphenyl)sulfonylethanol [*Organic chemistry*]
TPSF	Telephonie sans Fil [*Wireless Telephony*]
TPSF	Terminal Profile Security File [*IRS*]
TPSFA.......	Tohoku Psychologica Folia [*A publication*]
TPSI	Torque Pressure in Pounds per Square Inch
TPSL	Tyoevaeen ja Pienviljelijaein Sosialidemokraattinen Liitto [*Social Democratic League of Workers and Smallholders*] [*Finland*] [*Political party*] (PPE)
TPSM	Tepatshimuwin. Journal d'Information des Attikamekes et des Montagnais [*A publication*]
TPSMP	Test Program Set Management Plan
TPSN........	Transposition (AAG)
TPSN........	Troop Program Sequence Number [*Military*]
TPSO	Triphenylstibine Oxide [*Organic chemistry*]
TPSP	Tape Punch Subassembly Panel
TPSRS.......	Theologie Pastorale et Spiritualite. Recherches et Syntheses [*A publication*]
TPSS........	Thermal Protection System Selection
TPST	Training and Personnel Systems Technology (MCD)
TPST	Triple-Pole, Single-Throw [*Switch*]
TPSTe........	Triisopropylbenzenesulfonyl Tetrazolide [*Organic chemistry*]
TPSY	Task Parameter Synthesizer (SAA)
TPT...........	Air Transport Corp. [*Detroit, MI*] [*FAA designator*] (FAAC)
TPT...........	Bibliographic Center for Research, Denver, CO [*OCLC symbol*] (OCLC)
TPT...........	Tactical Petroleum Terminal
TPT...........	Tail Pipe Temperature (NG)
TPT...........	Tappet [*Mechanical engineering*]
TPT...........	Tappit Resources [*Vancouver Stock Exchange symbol*]
TPT...........	Target Practice [*Ammunition*] with Tracer
TPT...........	Telecommunication Products Plus Technology [*Pennwell Publishing Co.*] [*Littleton, MA*] (TSSD)
TPT...........	Teleprinter Planning Table
TPT...........	Temporary Part Time [*Personnel*] (MCD)
TPT...........	Test Pilot Training
TPT...........	Test Program Tape (MCD)
TPT...........	Tetraisopropyl Titanate [*Organic chemistry*]
TPT...........	Tetraphenyl Tetrazolium [*Histochemical stain*] (AAMN)
TPT...........	Third-Party Transaction [*Business term*]
TPT...........	Time to Peak Tension
TPT...........	Time Period Tape [*Database*] [*Arbitron Ratings Co.*] [*Information service or system*] (CRD)
TPT...........	Time Priority Table
TPT...........	Tiputa [*Tuamotu Archipelago*] [*Seismograph station code, US Geological Survey*] (SEIS)
TPT...........	Total Pressure Transducer
TPT...........	Total Prime Time (WDMC)
TPT...........	Total Protein Tuberculin [*Medicine*] (MAE)
TPT...........	Totul pentru Tara ["*All for the Fatherland*"] [*Romania*] [*Political party*] (PPE)
TPT...........	Toy Preference Test [*Psychology*] (AEBS)
TPT...........	Training Proficiency Test [*Army*] (INF)
TPT...........	Transonic Pressure Tunnel [*NASA*]
TPT...........	Transport
TPT...........	Trenton-Princeton Traction Co. [*Absorbed into Consolidated Rail Corp.*] [*AAR code*]
TPT...........	Troop Proficiency Trainer
TPT...........	Trumpet

TPT............ Typhoid-Paratyphoid [*Medicine*]
TPTA......... Thiophosphoryl Triamide [*Fertilizer technology*]
TPTA......... Tin Triphenyl [*or Triphenyltin*] Acetate [*Organic chemistry*]
TPTC......... Triphenyltin Chloride [*Organic chemistry*]
TPTD......... Test Pilot Training Division
TPTD......... Transported
TPTE......... (Tritylphenyl)thioethanol [*Organic chemistry*]
TPTF......... Tributyl Phosphate Task Force   (EA)
TPTG......... Terminal Program Testing Guide
TPTG......... Tuned Plate Tuned Grid [*Electronic tube*]
TPTH......... Triphenyltin Hydroxide [*Organic chemistry*]
TPTHS..... Total Parathyroid Hormone Secretion [*Endocrinology*]   (MAE)
TPTN......... Toilet Partition [*Technical drawings*]
TPTOL...... True Position Tolerance   (MSA)
TPTR......... Topps and Trousers [*NASDAQ symbol*]   (NQ)
TPTR......... Transporter
TPTR......... Trumpeter
TPTRL...... Time-Phased Transportation Requirements List [*Military*]   (AABC)
TPTS .... Two-Phase Thermosyphon [*Heat exchanger*]
TPTX......... Thyroparathyroidectomized [*Medicine*]
TPTZ......... Triphenyltetrazolium Chloride [*Also, RT, TTC*] [*Chemical indicator*]
TPTZ......... Tris(pyridyl)-s-triazine [*Analytical chemistry*]
TPU .... Capitol Consortium Network, Washington, DC [*OCLC symbol*]   (OCLC)
TPU .... Tank and Pump Unit [*Mechanized infantry battalion*]   (INF)
TPU .... Tape Preparation Unit
TPU .... Tarn Pure Technology Corp. [*Vancouver Stock Exchange symbol*]
TPU .... Task Processing Unit
TPU .... Telecommunications Processing Unit
TPU .... Text Processing Utility [*Data processing*]
TPU .... Thermoplastic Urethane [*Plastics technology*]
TPU .... Transient Personnel Unit [*Navy*]   (DNAB)
TPU .... Troop Program Unit [*Army*]   (AABC)
TPU .... Trunk Processing Unit [*Bell System*]
TPU .... Turbo Pascal Unit [*Borland International*] [*Data processing*]   (PCM)
TPU .... Turbopower Unit
TPUC......... Telephone Pickup Coil
TPUG .... Toronto PET Users Group [*Canada*]
TP/UMF ... Total Package/Unit Materiel Fielding [*Army*]   (RDA)
TPUN......... Test Procedure Update Notice   (NASA)
TPUS......... Transportation and Public Utilities Service [*Later, part of Transportation and Communication Service, GSA*]
TPV............ Capitol Consortium Network, Washington, DC [*OCLC symbol*]   (OCLC)
TPV............ Thermophotovoltaic
TPV............ Thermoplastic Vulcanizate [*Plastics technology*]
TPV............ Time to Peak Flow Velocity [*Cardiology*]
TPV............ Tonopah [*Nevada*] [*Seismograph station code, US Geological Survey*] [*Closed*]   (SEIS)
TPV............ Total Pore Volume [*Geology*]
TPV............ Transverse Pallial Vein
TPV............ Triple Polio Vaccine [*Medicine*]
TPVR......... Total Pulmonary Vascular Resistance   (AAMN)
TPW .... Tenth-Power Width
TPW .... Title Page Wanting
TP & W...... Toledo, Peoria & Western Railroad Co.
TPW .... Toledo, Peoria & Western Railroad Co. [*AAR code*]
TPW .... Tons per Week
TPW .... True Polar Wandering [*Geophysics*]
TPW .... Turbo Pascal for Windows [*Data processing*]
TPWBH .... Tax Paid Wine Bottling House
TPWG .... Test Planning Working Group [*Military*]
TPWIC ...... Theater Prisoner of War Information Center
TPWU .... Tanganyika Plantation Workers Union
TPWU .... Tea Plantation Workers' Union [*Kenya*]
TPX........... Total Pancreatectomy [*Medicine*]
TPX........... Transponder   (KSC)
TPY........... FEDLINK [*Federal Library and Information Network*], Washington, DC [*OCLC symbol*]   (OCLC)
TPY........... Tapestry   (ADA)
TPY........... Tipperary Corp. [*AMEX symbol*]   (SPSG)
TPY........... Tons per Year
TPY........... Trans-Provincial Airlines Ltd. [*Prince Rupert, BC*] [*FAA designator*]   (FAAC)
TPZ............ FEDLINK [*Federal Library and Information Network*], Washington, DC [*OCLC symbol*]   (OCLC)
TPZ............ Thioperazine [*or Thioproperazine*] [*Tranquilizer*]
TQ.............. [*The*] Questers   (EA)
TQ.............. Tale Quale [*Of Conditions on Arrival*] [*Latin*]
TQ.............. Texas Quarterly [*A publication*]
TQ.............. Theatre Quarterly [*A publication*]
TQ.............. Theologische Quartalschrift [*Tuebingen*] [*A publication*]
TQ.............. Thought Quality [*Psychology*]
TQ.............. Three-Quarter Midget [*Horse racing*]
TQ.............. Three-Quarter Size [*Car racing*]
TQ.............. Tocopherolquinone [*Vitamin E*] [*Biochemistry*]
TQ.............. Toronto Quarterly [*A publication*]

TQ.............. Total Quality
Tq............... Tourniquet [*Medicine*]   (MAE)
TQ.............. Track Quality
TQ.............. Trans Oceanic Airways Ltd. [*Great Britain*] [*ICAO designator*]   (FAAC)
TQ.............. Transition Quarter [*Between fiscal years 1976 and 1977*]
TQ.............. Tri-Quarterly [*A publication*]
TQ.............. Turf Quality   (OA)
TQ.............. Tyrolean Airways [*Austria*] [*ICAO designator*]   (ICDA)
TQ-3 .... Tocotrienolquinone [*Biochemistry*]
TQA.......... Abilene, TX [*Location identifier*] [*FAA*]   (FAAL)
TQA.......... ILLINET [*Illinois Library Information Network*], Springfield, IL [*OCLC symbol*]   (OCLC)
TQA.......... Total Quality Assurance   (OA)
TQAGA ..... Technique Agricole [*A publication*]
TQB .... ILLINET [*Illinois Library Information Network*], Springfield, IL [*OCLC symbol*]   (OCLC)
TQC .... Indiana Cooperative Library Services Authority, Indianapolis, IN [*OCLC symbol*]   (OCLC)
TQC .... Technical Quality Control [*Telecommunications*]   (TEL)
TQC .... Time, Quality, Cost
TQC .... Total Quality Control
TQCA .... Textile Quality Control Association   (EA)
TQCM .... Thermoelectric Quartz Crystal Microbalance
TQD.......... Indiana Cooperative Library Services Authority, Indianapolis, IN [*OCLC symbol*]   (OCLC)
TQD.......... Ter Quaterve in Die [*Three or Four Times a Day*] [*Pharmacy*]
TQD.......... Total Quality Design   (RDA)
TQE .... Michigan Library Consortium, Detroit, MI [*OCLC symbol*]   (OCLC)
TQE .... Technical Quality Evaluation [*Polaris*]
TQE .... Technique de l'Eau et de l'Assainissement [*A publication*]
TQE .... Tekamah, NE [*Location identifier*] [*FAA*]   (FAAL)
TQE .... Timer Queue Element
TQF .... Michigan Library Consortium, Detroit, MI [*OCLC symbol*]   (OCLC)
TQF .... Threshold Quality Factor
TQG .... MIDLNET [*Midwest Regional Library Network*], St. Louis, MO [*OCLC symbol*]   (OCLC)
TQG .... Tactical Quiet Generator   (RDA)
TQH .... MIDLNET [*Midwest Regional Library Network*], St. Louis, MO [*OCLC symbol*]   (OCLC)
TQH .... Tahlequah, OK [*Location identifier*] [*FAA*]   (FAAL)
TQI .... MINITEX [*Minnesota Interlibrary Teletype Exchange*], Minneapolis, MN [*OCLC symbol*]   (OCLC)
TQI .... Training Quality Index [*Military*]   (CAAL)
TQJ........... MINITEX [*Minnesota Interlibrary Teletype Exchange*], Minneapolis, MN [*OCLC symbol*]   (OCLC)
TQK .... NELINET [*New England Library Information Network*], Newton, MA [*OCLC symbol*]   (OCLC)
TQL .... NELINET [*New England Library Information Network*], Newton, MA [*OCLC symbol*]   (OCLC)
TQM.......... OCLC [*Online Computer Library Center*] Western Services Center, Claremont, CA [*OCLC symbol*]   (OCLC)
TQM.......... Total Quality Management
TQM.......... Transport Quartermaster
TQMG....... [*The*] Quartermaster General [*Army*]
TQMS ...... Technical Quartermaster Sergeant
TQMS ...... Total Quality Management System   (MCD)
TQMS ...... Triple Quadrupole Mass Spectrometer
TQMS ...... Troop Quartermaster-Sergeant [*British military*]   (DMA)
TQN.......... OCLC [*Online Computer Library Center*] Western Services Center, Claremont, CA [*OCLC symbol*]   (OCLC)
TQO.......... OHIONET, Columbus, OH [*OCLC symbol*]   (OCLC)
TQP .... OHIONET, Columbus, OH [*OCLC symbol*]   (OCLC)
TQP .... Transistor Qualification Program
TQPF........ [*The*] Valley/Wall Blake [*Anguilla Island*] [*ICAO location identifier*]   (ICLI)
TQPP........ Total Quality Planning and Producibility   (MCD)
TQQ......... Pennsylvania Area Library Network, Philadelphia, PA [*OCLC symbol*]   (OCLC)
TQQPRI.... Tentative Qualitative Quantitative Personnel Requirements Information [*Army*]
TQR.......... Pennsylvania Area Library Network, Philadelphia, PA [*OCLC symbol*]   (OCLC)
TQR.......... Saginaw, MI [*Location identifier*] [*FAA*]   (FAAL)
TQR.......... Tenquille Resources Ltd. [*Vancouver Stock Exchange symbol*]
TQS .... Pittsburgh Regional Library Center, Pittsburgh, PA [*OCLC symbol*]   (OCLC)
TQS .... Theologische Quartalschrift [*A publication*]
TQS .... Tres Esquinas [*Colombia*] [*Airport symbol*]   (OAG)
TQT .... Pittsburgh Regional Library Center, Pittsburgh, PA [*OCLC symbol*]   (OCLC)
TQT .... Transistor Qualification Test
TQTP........ Transistor Qualification Test Program
TQTYREC ... Total Quantity Recommended [*Army*]
TQU.......... Southeastern Library Network, Atlanta, GA [*OCLC symbol*]   (OCLC)
TQV .... Southeastern Library Network, Atlanta, GA [*OCLC symbol*]   (OCLC)
TQW......... Pittsburgh, PA [*Location identifier*] [*FAA*]   (FAAL)

TQW..........	State University of New York, OCLC [*Online Computer Library Center*], Albany, NY [*OCLC symbol*] (OCLC)
TQX..........	State University of New York, OCLC [*Online Computer Library Center*], Albany, NY [*OCLC symbol*] (OCLC)
TQY..........	Tanquery Resources Ltd. [*Vancouver Stock Exchange symbol*]
TQY..........	Wisconsin Library Consortium, Madison, WI [*OCLC symbol*] (OCLC)
TQZ..........	Wisconsin Library Consortium, Madison, WI [*OCLC symbol*] (OCLC)
TR.............	Caines' Term Reports [*New York*] [*A publication*] (DLA)
TR.............	Compania de Aviacion Trans-Europa [*Spain*] [*ICAO designator*] (ICDA)
TR.............	Gabon [*Aircraft nationality and registration mark*] (FAAC)
TR.............	Stewardsman Recruit [*Navy*]
TR.............	Table Ronde [*A publication*]
TR.............	Tactical Reconnaissance (NATG)
TR.............	Talyllyn Railway [*Wales*]
TR.............	Tank Regiment (MCD)
TR.............	Tape Reader
TR.............	Tape Recorder
TR.............	Tape Register
TR.............	Tape Resident
TR.............	Tare (ROG)
TR.............	Target Recognition (AFM)
TR.............	Tariff Reform
TR.............	Task Register [*Data processing*] (BYTE)
TR.............	Tax Rate
TR.............	Taxa Referencial de Juros [*Brazil*] (ECON)
TR.............	Taxation Reports [*England*] [*A publication*] (DLA)
TR.............	Teaching and Research [*Medicine*]
TR.............	Teaching Resources (AEBS)
TR.............	Team Recorder [*Sports*]
TR.............	Tear [*Deltiology*]
TR.............	Technical Readiness
TR.............	Technical Regulation
TR.............	Technical Report
TR.............	Technical Reporter [*World Council of Credit Unions*] [*A publication*]
TR.............	Technical Representative
TR.............	Technical Requirement (MCD)
TR.............	Technical Review [*Nuclear energy*] (NRCH)
TR.............	Technology Review [*A publication*]
TR.............	Telegraphe Restant [*Telegram to Be Called for at a Telegraph Office*] [*French*] (ROG)
TR.............	Telephone Rentals [*Commercial firm*]
TR.............	Tell-Rimah (BJA)
TR.............	Temperature Range
TR.............	Temperature Recorder
TR.............	Temperature, Rectal [*Medicine*]
TR.............	Temporary Resident
TR.............	Tempore Regis [*In the Time of the King*] [*Latin*]
TR.............	Terbium [*Chemical element*] [*Symbol is Tb*] (ROG)
TR.............	Term Reports [*Legal*] [*British*]
TR.............	Term Reports, English King's Bench [*Durnford and East's Reports*] [*England*] [*A publication*] (DLA)
TRW............	Terminal Ready [*Data processing*]
TR.............	Terminal Rendezvous
TRW............	Terminal Repeat [*Genetics*]
TRX............	Terminalischer Reiz [*Terminal Stimulus*] [*German*] [*Psychology*]
TR.............	Terms of Reference
TR.............	Territorial Reserve [*British military*] (DMA)
TR.............	Test Regulation (MCD)
TRZ............	Test Report
TR.............	Test Request
TR.............	Test-Retest
TR.............	Test Routine (AAG)
TR.............	Test Run
T & R.........	Testing and Regulating Department [*Especially, in a wire communications maintenance division*]
TR.............	Tetrazolium Reduction (MAE)
TR.............	Textus Receptus (BJA)
TR.............	Thalamic Radiation [*Neurology*]
TR.............	Theatre Research [*A publication*]
TR.............	Theatre Royal (ROG)
TR.............	Thematic Resource Nomination [*National Register of Historic Places*]
TR.............	Theodore [*Teddy*] Roosevelt [*US president, 1858-1919*]
TR.............	Theologische Rundschau [*A publication*]
TR.............	Therapeutic Radiology
TR.............	Thioredoxin [*Also, TD, Trx*] [*Biochemistry*]
TR.............	Thioredoxin Reductase [*An enzyme*]
TR.............	Threaded Rod
TR.............	Threat Reaction [*Military*] (CAAL)
TR.............	Throws Right-Handed [*Baseball*]
TR.............	Thrust Reverser (MCD)
TR.............	Thyroid Hormone Receptor [*Endocrinology*]
TR.............	Time Rate [*Payment system*]
TR.............	Time Record (MCD)
TR.............	Time Release (MAE)
TR............	Time to Repetition [*Medicine*]
TR.............	Time Resolved [*Fluoroscopy*]
TR.............	Time to Retrofire
TR.............	Time-to-Retrograde [*NASA*] (KSC)
T/R............	Time of Rise (MSA)
TR.............	Timed-Release [*Pharmacy*]
TR.............	Tinctura [*Tincture*] [*Pharmacy*]
TR.............	Tirailleur Regiments [*Military*]
TR.............	Tobacco Reporter [*A publication*]
TR.............	Tone Relevant
TR.............	Tons Registered [*Shipping*]
TR.............	Tool Resistant [*Rating for safes*]
TR.............	Toothed Ring [*Technical drawings*]
TR.............	Tootsie Roll Industries, Inc. [*NYSE symbol*] (SPSG)
TR.............	Top Register (OA)
TR.............	Topical Report [*Nuclear energy*] (NRCH)
TR.............	Torpedo Reconnaissance Aircraft [*Navy*]
TR.............	Torque Synchro Receiver (MUGU)
TR.............	Total Regulation
TR.............	Total Resistance (MAE)
TR.............	Total Response [*Medicine*] (MAE)
TR.............	Total Revenue
TR.............	Touchdowns Running [*Football*]
TR.............	Touche Remnant [*Investment firm*] [*British*]
TR.............	Towel Rack (MSA)
TR.............	Tower
TR.............	Trace
TR.............	Tracer
TR.............	Track
TR.............	Tracking RADAR
TR.............	Tract
TR.............	Trade
TR.............	Traffic Route [*Telecommunications*] (TEL)
TR.............	Tragedy
TR.............	Trailer (AAG)
TR.............	Train (ADA)
TR.............	Trainer (AAG)
TR.............	Training (ROG)
TR.............	Training Regulations [*Military*]
TR.............	Training Requirements
TR.............	Tramway (ROG)
TR.............	Transaction
TR.............	Transaction Record
TR.............	Transatlantic Review [*A publication*]
TR.............	Transbrasil SA Linhas Aereas [*Brazil*] [*ICAO designator*] (FAAC)
T/R............	Transceiver
TR.............	Transcontinental Resources [*Vancouver Stock Exchange symbol*]
Tr..............	Transcript (DLA)
TR.............	Transducers [*JETDS nomenclature*] [*Military*] (CET)
TR.............	Transfer (DEN)
TR.............	Transfer Register
TR.............	Transfer Reset
TR.............	Transferable Rouble [*International Bank for Economic Co-Operation*] (EY)
TR.............	Transformation Ratio
TR.............	Transformer (DEN)
T-R............	Transformer-Rectifier
TR.............	Transfusion Reaction [*Medicine*]
TR.............	Transfusion Receptors [*Oncology*]
TR.............	Transient Response (IEEE)
TR.............	Transilluminator [*Chromatography*]
TR.............	Transitive
TR.............	Translate [*or Translation, or Translator*]
TR.............	Translation Register
tr...............	Translator
TR.............	Transmission Report [*Telecommunications*] (TEL)
T-R............	Transmit-Receive
TR.............	Transmitter
TR.............	Transom (MSA)
TR.............	Transport
TR.............	Transportability Report [*Army*]
TR.............	Transportation [*or Travel*] Request [*Military*]
TR.............	Transportation Science [*A publication*] (EAAP)
TR.............	Transpose
TR.............	Transverse (DEN)
TR.............	Travel and Relocation
T/R............	Travel Request
TR.............	Travel Required [*Civil Service*]
TR.............	Trawler
TR.............	Tray (WGA)
TR.............	Tread (WGA)
TR.............	Treasurer
TR.............	Treasury Receipt
TR.............	Treatise (ROG)
TR.............	Treatment [*Medicine*] (AAMN)
TR.............	Treaty (ROG)
TR.............	Treble [*Knitting*]
TR.............	Treble [*Music*]
TR.............	Trees [*Ecology*]
TR.............	Tremor [*Medicine*] (AAMN)

TR .... Triad [*A publication*]
TR .... Trial (ROG)
TR .... Trial Report
TR .... Tributary (ROG)
TR .... Tricuspid Regurgitation [*Cardiology*]
TR .... Trident Aircraft Ltd. [*Canada*] [*ICAO aircraft manufacturer identifier*] (ICAO)
TR .... Trigonal [*Molecular geometry*]
TR .... Trillo [*Trill*] [*Music*]
tr .... Trinidad and Tobago [*MARC country of publication code*] [*Library of Congress*] (LCCP)
TR .... Trip Report
TR .... Triple Reduction (DS)
TR .... Triple Screw [*Shipping*] (DS)
Tr .... Tristia [*of Ovid*] [*Classical studies*] (OCD)
Tr .... Tristram's Consistory Judgments [*England*] [*A publication*] (DLA)
TR .... Tritium Ratio [*Measure of tritium activity*] [*AEC*]
TR .... Tritium Recovery [*Nuclear energy*] (NRCH)
Tr .... Trityl [*Organic chemistry*]
Tr .... Trivium [*A publication*]
TR .... Troop
TR .... Trouble Report
TR .... Trough (ADA)
TR .... Troupe (ROG)
TR .... Truck
TR .... True (FAAC)
TR .... Trumpet
TR .... Trunnion [*Pivot*]
TR .... Truro [*British depot code*]
TR .... Truss (MSA)
TR .... Trust
T/R .... Trust Receipt [*Banking*]
TR .... Trustee
TR .... Tubercular Rueckstand [*Medicine*]
TR .... Tuberculin Residue [*Medicine*]
TR .... Tubular Reabsorption [*Medicine*] (MAE)
TR .... Tunnel Rectifier
TR .... Turbidity Reducing (AAMN)
TR .... Turbine Rate (NVT)
TR .... Turkey [*ANSI two-letter standard code*] (CNC)
TR .... Turkish Reactor
TR .... Turn Rule (WDMC)
TR .... Turnaround Requirements (MCD)
T & R .... Turner and Russell's English Chancery Reports [*1822-25*] [*A publication*] (DLA)
Tr .... Y Traethodydd [*A publication*]
1TR .... One Turn Right [*Dance terminology*]
Tra .... Epistulae ad Traianum [*of Pliny the Younger*] [*Classical studies*] (OCD)
TRA .... La Tuyere a Reverse Aval [*Concorde*]
TRA .... RADAR Transfer of Control Message [*Communications*] (FAAC)
TRA .... Tackle Representatives Association (EA)
TRA .... Tandem Rotary Activator
TRA .... Tape Recorder Amplifier
TRA .... Taramajima [*Japan*] [*Airport symbol*] (OAG)
TRA .... Tax Reform Act [*1969, 1976, 1984, 1986*]
TRA .... Technical Requirement Analysis (OA)
TRA .... Technical Review and Analysis
TRA .... Technical Risk Assessment (MCD)
TRA .... Television/Radio Age [*A publication*]
TRA .... Temporary Restricted Area [*Former USSR*] (NATG)
TRA .... Terminal Repeat Array [*Genetics*]
TRA .... Terra Industries, Inc. [*Formerly, Inspiration Resources Corp.*] [*NYSE symbol*] (SPSG)
TRA .... Terrain-Related Accident [*Aviation*]
TRA .... Test Requirement Analysis (CAAL)
TRA .... Textile Refinishers Association (EA)
TRA .... Theodore Roosevelt Association (EA)
TRA .... Thoroughbred Racing Associations (EA)
TRA .... Thrace Requirements Analysis [*Military*]
TRA .... Throttle Resolver Angle (MCD)
TRA .... Tinctura [*Tincture*] [*Pharmacy*] (ROG)
TRA .... Tire and Rim Association (EA)
TRA .... Tournament of Roses Association [*Later, TOR*] (EA)
TRA .... Toward Revolutionary Art [*A publication*]
TRA .... Tracan Oil & Gas [*Vancouver Stock Exchange symbol*]
TRA .... Trade Readjustment Allowance [*or Assistance*]
TRA .... Trade Recovery Act
TRA .... Trade Relations Association (EA)
TrA .... Traduction Automatique [*The Hague*] [*A publication*]
TRA .... Training [*A publication*]
TRA .... Training
TRA .... Training Readjustment Allowance (OICC)
TRA .... Training Requirements Analysis [*NASA*] (NASA)
TRA .... Transaldolase [*An enzyme*] (MAE)
TRA .... Transfer
TRA .... Transportation Reform Alliance
TRA .... Transracial Adoption

TRA .... Travnik [*Yugoslavia*] [*Seismograph station code, US Geological Survey*] [*Closed*] (SEIS)
TrA .... Triangulum Australe [*Constellation*]
TRA .... Triaxial Recording Accelerometer
TRA .... Tripoli Rocketry Association (EA)
TRA .... Triumph Register of America (EA)
TRA .... Tubular Reactor Assembly [*Nuclear energy*] (NRCH)
TRA .... Turkish Reactor Assembly (SAA)
TRA .... Turnaround Requirements Analysis [*NASA*] (NASA)
TRA .... United States Army TRADOC, Institute for Military Assistance, Library, Fort Bragg, NC [*OCLC symbol*] (OCLC)
TRAA .... Towing and Recovery Association of America (EA)
TRAAC ...... Transit Research and Attitude Control [*Navy satellite*]
TRAACS ... Transit Research and Attitude Control Satellite [*Navy*] (IEEE)
Tr A Am Physicians ... Transactions. Association of American Physicians [*A publication*]
TRAB........ Triaminobenzene [*Organic chemistry*]
Trabajos Estadist ... Trabajos de Estadistica [*A publication*]
Trabajos Estadist Investigacion Oper ... Trabajos de Estadistica y de Investigacion Operativa [*A publication*]
Trab Antrop Etnol ... Trabalhos. Sociedade Portuguesa de Antropologia e Etnologia [*A publication*]
Trab Antropol Etnol ... Trabalhos de Antropologia e Etnologia [*A publication*]
Trab Cent Bot Junta Invest Ultramar ... Trabalhos. Centro de Botanica. Junta de Investigacoes do Ultramar [*A publication*]
Trab Compostelanos Biol ... Trabajos Compostelanos de Biologia [*A publication*]
Trab 5 Cong Med Latino-Am ... Trabajos Presentados al Quinto Congreso Medico Latino-Americano [*A publication*]
TrabEsta .... Trabajos de Estadistica [*A publication*]
Trab Estac Agric Exp Leon ... Trabajos. Estacion Agricola Experimental de Leon [*A publication*]
Trab Estadistica ... Trabajos de Estadistica y de Investigacion [*A publication*]
Trab Geol... Trabajos de Geologia [*A publication*]
Trab Geol Oviedo Univ Fac Cienc ... Trabajos de Geologia. Oviedo Universidad. Facultad de Ciencias [*A publication*]
Trab Inst Cajal Invest Biol ... Trabajos. Instituto Cajal de Investigaciones Biologicas [*A publication*]
Trab Inst Econ Prod Ganad Ebro ... Trabajos. Instituto de Economia y Producciones Ganaderas del Ebro [*A publication*]
Trab Inst Esp Entomol ... Trabajos. Instituto Espanol de Entomologia [*A publication*]
Trab Inst Esp Oceanogr ... Trabajos. Instituto Espanol de Oceanografia [*A publication*]
Trab Inst Fisiol Fac Med Univ Lisboa ... Trabajos. Instituto de Fisiologia. Faculdade de Medicina. Universidade do Lisboa [*A publication*]
Trab Inst Nac Cienc Med (Madrid) ... Trabajos. Instituto Nacional de Ciencias Medicas (Madrid) [*A publication*]
Trab Inst Oceanogr Univ Recife ... Trabalhos. Instituto Oceanografico. Universidade do Recife [*A publication*]
Trab Investigacao 79 ... Trabalhos de Investigacao 79 [*A publication*]
Trab Investigacao 80 ... Trabalhos de Investigacao 80 [*A publication*]
Trab Lab Bioquim Quim Apl Inst Alonso Barba ... Trabajo. Laboratorio de Bioquimica y Quimica Aplicada. Instituto "Alonso Barba" [*A publication*]
Trab Oceanogr Univ Fed Pernambuco ... Trabalhos Oceanograficos. Universidade Federal de Pernambuco [*A publication*]
TRABOT... Terrier RADAR and Beacon Orientation Test (MUGU)
Trab Pesqui Inst Nutr Univ Bras ... Trabalhos e Pesquisas. Instituto de Nutricao. Universidade do Brasil [*A publication*]
Trab Pr Hist ... Trabajos de Prehistoria [*A publication*]
TRAC........ DTIC [*Defense Technical Information Center*] Technical Awareness Circular [*Information service or system*] (CRD)
TRAC........ Tandem Razor and Cartridge [*Gillette Co.*]
TRAC........ Target Research Analysis Center (CINC)
TRAC........ Tax Reform Action Coalition (EA)
TRAC........ Technical Reports Announcement Checklist
TRAC........ Telecommunications Research and Action Center [*Washington, DC*] [*Information service or system*] [*Telecommunications*] (TSSD)
TRAC........ Teleprocessing Recording for Analysis by the Customer
TRAC........ Telescoping Rotor Aircraft Concept (MCD)
TRAC........ Test of Reading Affective Cues [*Psychology*]
TRAC........ Texas Reconfigurable Array Computer
TRAC........ Text Reckoning and Compiling [*Data processing*]
TRAC........ Thermally Regenerative Alloy Cell
TRAC........ Total Record Access Control (SAA)
TRAC........ Tracer (AABC)
TRAC........ Tractor (AAG)
TRAC........ Trade Reform Action Coalition [*Washington, DC*] (EA)
TRAC........ TRADOC Analysis Command
TRAC........ TRADOC [*Training and Doctrine Command*] Research and Analysis Center [*Army*]
TRAC........ Transaction Reporting and Control System (MCD)
TRAC........ Transient Radiation Analysis by Computer (KSC)
TRAC........ Transient Reactor Analysis Code (NRCH)
TRAC........ Transportation Account Code (AFM)
TrAC.......... Trends in Analytical Chemistry [*A publication*]

TRACAB... Terminal RADAR Approach Control Cab [*Aviation*] (FAAC)
TRACAD... Training for [*US Military Academy*] Cadets (NVT)
TRACALS ... Traffic Control Approach and Landing System [*Aviation electronics*]
TRACAP... Transient Circuit Analysis Program [*Data processing*]
TRACC...... Target Review and Adjustment for Continuous Control (MCD)
TRACDR... Tractor-Drawn
TRACE...... Tactical Readiness and Checkout Equipment
TRACE...... Tactical Resources and Combat Effectiveness Model (MCD)
TRACE...... Tape-Controlled Recording Automatic Checkout Equipment [*Component of automatic pilot*] [*Aviation*]
TRACE...... Task Reporting and Current Evaluation
TRACE...... Taxiing and Routing of Aircraft Coordinating Equipment (MCD)
TRACE...... Taxiway Routing and Coordination Equipment [*Aviation*]
TRACE...... Technical Report Analysis, Condensation, Evaluation
TRACE...... Teleprocessing Recording for Analysis by the Customer (IEEE)
TRACE...... Test Equipment for Rapid Automatic Checkout and Evaluation [*Pan American Airways*]
TRACE...... Time-Shared Routines for Analysis, Classification, and Evaluation (DIT)
TRACE...... Tolls Recording and Computing Equipment (IEEE)
TRACE...... Toronto Region Aggregation of Computer Enthusiasts [*Canada*]
TRACE...... Total Resource Allocation Cost Estimating (RDA)
TRACE...... Total Risk Assessing Cost Estimate [*Army*] (RDA)
TRACE...... Trace Remote Atmospheric Chemical Evaluation [*National Center for Atmospheric Research*]
TRACE...... Track Retrieve and Account for Configuration of Equipment [*A publication*] (DLA)
TRACE...... Tracking and Communications, Extraterrestrial
TRACE...... Traffic Routing and Control Equipment (MCD)
TRACE...... Trane Air Conditioning Economics [*The Trane Co.*]
TRACE...... Transistor Radio Automatic Circuit Evaluator
TRACE...... Transport and Atmospheric Chemistry Near the Equator
TRACE...... Transportable Automated Control Environment
Trace Anal ... Trace Analysis [*A publication*]
Trace & M ... Tracewell and Mitchell's United States Comptroller's Decisions [*A publication*] (DLA)
TRACEN... Training Center
TRACE-P.. Total Risk Assessing Cost Estimate - Production [*Army*] (RDA)
TRACER ... Technical Reporting of Automated Configuration Electrical Requirements
TRACER ... Turnaround Time, Repair Survival Rate and Cost Evaluation Report [*Navy*] (DNAB)
TRACERS ... Teleprocessed Record and Card Entry Reporting System (MCD)
Tracers Exogram Oil Gas Rev ... Tracer's Exogram and Oil and Gas Review [*A publication*]
TRACES.... Technology in Retrospect and Critical Events in Science [*IITRI*]
Trace Subst Environ Health ... Trace Substances in Environmental Health [*A publication*]
Trace Subst Environ Health Proc Univ Mo Annu Conf ... Trace Substances in Environmental Health. Proceedings. University of Missouri. Annual Conference [*A publication*]
TRACEX ... Amphibious Tractor Exercise [*Navy*] (NVT)
Tracey Evidence ... Tracey's Cases on Evidence [*A publication*] (DLA)
TRAC-F..... TRADOC [*Training and Doctrine Command*] Analysis Command - Fort Leavenworth [*Kansas*] [*Army*]
TRACH ..... Trachea [*or Tracheotomy*] [*Medicine*]
Trach......... Trachiniae [*of Sophocles*] [*Classical studies*] (OCD)
TRACHY... Tracheotomy (DSUE)
TRACINFO ... Tracer, Number as Indicated. Furnish Information Immediately or Advise
TRACIRS ... [*The*] Recording and Controlling of In-Transit Requisition System [*Army*]
TRACIS..... Traffic Records Criminal Justice Information System (OICC)
TRACKEX ... Tracking Exercise [*Navy*] (NVT)
Track Field Q Rev ... Track and Field Quarterly Review [*A publication*]
Track Tech ... Track Technique [*A publication*]
TRAC-MTRY ... TRADOC [*Training and Doctrine Command*] Analysis Command-Monterey [*California*] [*Army*] (GRD)
TRACOMD ... Training Command [*Navy*] (DNAB)
TRACOMDLANT ... Training Command, Atlantic Fleet [*Navy*]
TRACOMDPAC ... Training Command, Pacific Fleet [*Navy*]
TRACOMDSUBPAC ... Training Command, Submarines, Pacific Fleet [*Navy*]
TRACOMDWESTCOAST ... Training Command, West Coast [*Navy*]
TRACOMP ... Tracking Comparison
TRACON .. Terminal RADAR Approach Control [*FAA*]
TRACOPS ... Trailerless Collective Protection System (DWSG)
TRACS...... Teleprocessing Remote Access Control System (HGAA)
TRACS...... Tool Record Accountability System [*NASA*] (NASA)
TRACS...... Travel Accounting Control System [*Citicorp Diners Club*]
TRACS...... Triangulation Ranging and Crossfix System [*Military*] (CAAL)
tract........... Traction
TRACT...... Triggered Reconnection Adiabatically Compressed Torus (MCD)
Tract Sel Khozmashiny ... Tractory i Sel Khozmashiny [*A publication*]

Tracts Math Nat Sci ... Tracts in Mathematics and Natural Science [*A publication*]
TRAC-WSMR ... TRADOC [*Training and Doctrine Command*] Analysis Command - White Sands Missile Range [*New Mexico*] [*Army*]
TRACY...... Technical Reports Automated Cataloging - Yes [*National Oceanic and Atmospheric Administration*]
TRAD .... Terminal RADAR [*Aviation*] (FAAC)
Trad .... Traditio [*A publication*]
TRAD .... Tradition
TRAD .... Traditional Industries, Inc. [*NASDAQ symbol*] (NQ)
TRADA ..... Timber Research and Development Association [*Research center*] [*British*] (IRC)
TRADAC... Trajectory Determination and Acquisition Computation
TRADAD .. Trace to Destination and Advise [*Military*]
TRADAR... Transaction Data Recorder (DNAB)
TRADAT... Transit Data Transmission System (SAA)
TrADAT ... (Triazolyl-Azo) diaminotoluene [*Organic chemistry*]
TRADCOM ... Transportation Corps Research and Development Command [*Army*]
Trad Dep Exploit Util Bois Univ Laval ... Traduction. Departement d'Exploitation et Utilisation des Bois. Universite Laval [*A publication*]
TRADE...... Tracking RADAR Angle Deception Equipment (NG)
TRADE...... Training Devices (RDA)
TRADE...... Training Devices and Equipment
TRADEC... Training Device Computer (DNAB)
Trade Cas .. Trade Cases [*Commerce Clearing House*] [*A publication*] (DLA)
Trade Cas CCH ... Trade Cases. Commerce Clearing House [*A publication*]
Trade and Commer ... Trade and Commerce [*A publication*]
Trade Commod Mark Summaries C Exports ... Trade by Commodities. Market Summaries. Series C. Exports [*A publication*]
Trade Commod Mark Summaries C Imports ... Trade by Commodities. Market Summaries. Series C. Imports [*A publication*]
Trade D...... Trade Digest [*A publication*] (APTA)
Trade Dig ... Trade Digest [*A publication*] (APTA)
Trade Ind ... Trade and Industry [*A publication*]
Trade Ind Bul ... Trade and Industry Bulletin [*A publication*]
Trade Ind Index ... Trade and Industry Index [*A publication*]
Trademark Bull ... Bulletin. United States Trademark Association Series [*A publication*] (DLA)
Trademark Bull (NS) ... Trademark Bulletin. United States Trademark Association (New Series) [*New York*] [*A publication*] (DLA)
Trade-Mark Rep ... Trade-Mark Reporter [*A publication*]
Trademark Rptr ... Trademark Reporter [*A publication*]
Trade Mks J ... Trade Marks Journal [*A publication*]
Trade News N ... Trade News North [*A publication*]
Trade R ...... Trade Review. Swedish Chamber of Commerce for Australia [*A publication*] (APTA)
TRADER... Training Devices Requirements Office [*TRADOC*] (MCD)
TRADER... Transient Radiation Effects Recorder (MCD)
Trade Reg Rep ... Trade Regulation Reporter [*Commerce Clearing House*] [*A publication*] (DLA)
Trade Reg Rep CCH ... Trade Regulation Reporter. Commerce Clearing House [*A publication*]
Trade Reg Rev ... Trade Regulation Review [*A publication*] (DLA)
TRADES ... Technology Requirement and Definition Study
TRADES ... TRADOC Data Evaluation Study (MCD)
Trades Union D ... Trades Union Digest [*A publication*] (APTA)
TRADET ... Training Detachment [*Navy*]
TRADEVCO ... Trading & Development Bank Ltd. [*Liberia*]
Tra Devel Aust ... Training and Development in Australia [*A publication*]
TRADEVMAN ... Training Devices Man [*Navy rating*]
TRADEX... Target Resolution and Discrimination Experiment [*ARPA*]
TRADEX... Trade Data Element Exchange
Trad Greec ... Trade with Greece [*A publication*]
TRADIC.... Transistor Digital Computer
TRADIC.... Transistorized Airborne Digital Computer [*Air Force*]
TRADIS .... Tape Repeating Automatic Data Integration System
TRADIS .... Tropical Resources for Agricultural Development Information System [*Overseas Development Natural Resources Institute*] [*British*] [*Information service or system*] (IID)
Traditional Kent Bldgs ... Traditional Kent Buildings [*A publication*]
Trad Mus... Traditional Music [*A publication*]
TRADOC .. Training and Doctrine Command [*Army*]
TRADOC-R ... Training and Doctrine Command Regulation [*Army*]
TRADR...... Tactical Radio Analysis, Division Restructuring [*Army*]
TRADSTAT ... World Trade Statistics Database [*Data-Star*] [*British*] [*Information service or system*] (IID)
Trad Un Dig ... Trades Union Digest [*A publication*]
TRAE......... Transport Airlift Estimator [*Air Force*]
TRAEA...... Technical Report Series. IAEA [*International Atomic Energy Agency*] [*A publication*]
TRAEX...... Training and Experience [*Military*] (AFM)
TRAF......... Traffic
TRAFAC ... Training Facility [*Navy*] (DNAB)
TRAFCO... Television, Radio and Film Communications [*of the Methodist Church*]
TRAFF ...... Traffic (ROG)

Traff Cas.... Railway, Canal, and Road Traffic Cases [*A publication*] (DLA)
Traff Educ ... Traffic Education [*A publication*]
Traff Engng ... Traffic Engineering [*A publication*]
Traff Engng Control ... Traffic Engineering and Control [*A publication*]
TRAFFIC .. Trade Records Analysis of Flora and Fauna in Commerce [*An association*]
Traffic Dig Rev ... Traffic Digest and Review [*A publication*]
Traffic Eng ... Traffic Engineering [*A publication*]
Traffic Eng Contr ... Traffic Engineering and Control [*A publication*]
Traffic Eng & Control ... Traffic Engineering and Control [*A publication*]
Traffic Manage ... Traffic Management [*A publication*]
Traffic Q .... Traffic Quarterly [*A publication*]
Traffic Qly ... Traffic Quarterly [*A publication*]
Traffic Saf ... Traffic Safety [*A publication*]
Traffic Saf Ann Rep ... Traffic Safety Annual Report [*A publication*]
Traffic Saf Res Rev ... Traffic Safety Research Review [*A publication*]
Traff Q....... Traffic Quarterly [*A publication*]
TRAFOLPERS ... Transfer Following Enlisted Personnel
TRAG .... Traffic Responsive Advance Green [*Control strategy*]
TRAG .... Tragedy
Trag .... Tragoedopodagra [*of Lucian*] [*Classical studies*] (OCD)
TRAI......... Tackle Representatives Association International [*Later, TSSAA*] (EA)
TRAIF .... Torso Restraint Assembly with Integrated Flotation
TRAIN...... Telerail Automated Information Network [*Association of American Railroads*]
TRAIN...... To Restore American Independence Now [*An association*]
TRAIN....... Tourist Railway Association, Inc. (EA)
train.......... Training
Train .... Training [*A publication*]
Train Agric Rural Dev ... Training for Agriculture and Rural Development [*A publication*]
TRAINBASEFOR ... Training Base Force, Pacific Fleet [*Navy*]
TRAINCON ... Training Conference (MCD)
Train Dev Aust ... Training and Development in Australia [*A publication*] (APTA)
Train & Devel J ... Training and Development Journal [*A publication*]
Train Dev J ... Training and Development Journal [*A publication*]
TRAINDIV ... Training Division [*Canadian Navy*]
Training & Dev J ... Training and Development Journal [*A publication*]
TRAINLANT ... Training Atlantic Fleet [*Navy*]
TRAINMAN ... Training Management [*Navy*] (DNAB)
Train Off.... Training Officer [*A publication*]
TRAINPACHQ ... Training Group Pacific Headquarters [*Canadian Navy*]
TRAINRON ... Training Squadron [*Later, SERRON*] [*Navy*]
Train Sch B ... Training School Bulletin [*A publication*]
TRA INT'L ... Tackle Representatives Association International [*Later, TSSAA*] (EA)
TRAIS .... Transportation Research Activities Information Service [*Department of Transportation*]
Trait Surf... Traitements de Surface [*A publication*]
Trait Therm ... Traitement Thermique [*A publication*]
TRAJ .... Trajectory (AAG)
TRAJ/PS... Trajectory/Parametric Study (SAA)
Trak Sel'khozmashiny ... Traktory i Sel'khozmashiny [*Former USSR*] [*A publication*]
Trakt Landmasch ... Traktor und die Landmaschine [*A publication*]
TRAK TROL ... Trackless Trolley [*Freight*]
Trakt Sel'khozmash ... Traktory i Sel'khozmashiny [*A publication*]
TRALA...... Truck Renting and Leasing Association (EA)
TRALANT ... Fleet Training Command, Atlantic [*Navy*]
TRALINET ... TRADOC Library Information Network (MCD)
TRAM .... Target Recognition Attack Multisensor [*DoD*]
TRAM .... Tensioned Replacement Alongside Method (MCD)
TRAM .... Test Reliability and Maintenance Program [*Navy*] (NVT)
TRAM .... Tracking RADAR Automatic Monitoring (AFM)
TRAM .... Training Readiness Analysis Monitor (MCD)
TRAM .... Transputer Module [*Data processing*]
TRAM .... Treatment Rating Assessment Matrix [*Medicine*] (MAE)
TRAM .... Treatment Response Assessment Method [*Medicine*] (MAE)
Tr Am Acad Ophth ... Transactions. American Academy of Ophthalmology and Otolaryngology [*A publication*]
Tr Am Ass Genito-Urin Surg ... Transactions. American Association of Genito-Urinary Surgeons [*A publication*]
Tramel .... Trammell Crow Real Estate Investment [*Associated Press abbreviation*] (APAG)
Tr Am Fish Soc ... Transactions. American Fisheries Society [*A publication*]
TRAMID... Training for [*US Naval Academy/Naval Reserve Officers Training Corps*] Midshipmen (NVT)
TRAMIS ... TRADOC [*Training and Doctrine Command*] Management Information System [*Army*]
TRAMIT ... Especialidades Farmaceuticas en Tramite de Registro [*Ministerio de Sanidad y Consumo*] [*Spain*] [*Information service or system*] (CRD)
Tr Am Micr Soc ... Transactions. American Microscopical Society [*A publication*]
Tr Am Neurol A ... Transactions. American Neurological Association [*A publication*]
TRAMOD ... Training Requirements Analysis Model (MCD)
Tr Am Ophth Soc ... Transactions. American Ophthalmological Society [*A publication*]

TRAMP..... Temperature Regulation and Monitor Panel
TRAMP..... Test Retrieval and Memory Print [*Data processing*]
TRAMP..... Time-Shared Relational Associative Memory Program [*Data processing*] (IEEE)
TRAMPCO ... Thioguanine, Rubidomycin [*Daunorubicin*], ara-C, Methotrexate, Prednisolone, Cyclophosphamide, Oncovin [*Vincristine*] [*Antineoplastic drug regimen*]
TRAMPCOL ... Thioguanine, Rubidomycin [*Daunorubicin*], ara-C, Methotrexate, Prednisolone, Cyclophosphamide, Oncovin [*Vincristine*], L-Asparaginase [*Antineoplastic drug regimen*]
TRAMPL .. TRADOC Master Priority List (MCD)
TRAMPS .. Temperature Regulator and Missile Power Supply
TRAMPS .. Traffic Measure and Path Search [*Telecommunications*] (TEL)
TRAMPS .. Transportation Movement Planing System (SAA)
Tr Am Soc Artific Int Organs ... Transactions. American Society for Artificial Internal Organs [*A publication*]
Tr Am Soc Trop Med ... Transactions. American Society of Tropical Medicine [*A publication*]
TRAN .... Transaction
TRAN .... Transformer
TRAN .... Transient (AABC)
TRAN .... Transit
TRAN .... Transmit
TRAN .... Transport
TRANA ..... Transfusion [*Philadelphia*] [*A publication*]
TRANC ..... Transient Center [*Marine Corps*]
TRAND ..... Tone Reproduction and Neutral Determination [*Chart*] [*Printing technology*]
TRANDIR ... Translation Director (IEEE)
TRANET .. Tracking [*or Transit*] Network [*Navy*]
TRANET... Transnational Network for Appropriate/Alternative Technologies
TranEx....... Transco Exploration Partners Ltd. [*Associated Press abbreviation*] (APAG)
TranInc...... Transamerica Income Shares, Inc. [*Associated Press abbreviation*] (APAG)
TRAN-PRO ... Transaction Processing [*Data processing*]
Tranq .... De Tranquillitate Animi [*of Seneca the Younger*] [*Classical studies*] (OCD)
TRANQ ..... Tranquillo [*Quietly*] [*Music*] (ROG)
TRANS..... Telemetry Redundancy Analyzer System
TRANS..... Transaction
Trans......... Transactions. Institute of Professional Engineers [*New Zealand*] [*A publication*]
TRANS..... Transcript (ADA)
TRANS..... Transfer (AAG)
TRANS..... Transformer (AFM)
TRANS..... Transient (AFIT)
TRANS..... Transistor (ADA)
TRANS..... Transition (ROG)
TRANS..... Transitive
TRANS..... Transitory
TRANS..... Translation
Trans......... Translator (DLA)
TRANS..... Transmission
TRANS..... Transmittance (AAG)
TRANS..... Transparent (MSA)
TRANS..... Transport [*or Transportation*] (AAG)
TRANS..... Transpose [*Proofreading*]
TRANS..... Transverse
TRANSA ..... Transaction (MSA)
Trans AACE ... Transactions. American Association of Cost Engineers [*A publication*]
TRANSAC ... Transistorized Automatic Computer
Trans Acad Sci St Louis ... Transactions. Academy of Science of St. Louis [*A publication*]
Transact Am Phil Ass ... Transactions and Proceedings. American Philological Association [*A publication*]
Transact Cumb Ant ... Transactions. Cumberland and Westmorland Antiquarian and Archaeological Society [*A publication*]
Transact Dumfries ... Transactions. Dumfriesshire and Galloway Natural History and Antiquarian Society [*A publication*]
Transact Essex ... Essex Archaeology and History. The Transactions of the Essex Archaeological Society [*A publication*]
Transact Lond ... Transactions. London and Middlesex Archaeological Society [*A publication*]
Transact Roy Soc Canada ... Transactions. Royal Society of Canada [*A publication*]
Trans Act Soc Aust & NZ ... Transactions. Actuarial Society of Australia and New Zealand [*A publication*] (APTA)
Transact South Stafford ... Transactions. South Staffordshire Archaeological and Historical Society [*A publication*]
Trans Actuar Soc S Afr ... Transactions. Actuarial Society of South Africa [*A publication*]
Transact Worc ... Transactions. Worcestershire Archaeological Society [*A publication*]
Trans Agric Engng Soc (Tokyo) ... Transactions. Agricultural Engineering Society (Tokyo) [*A publication*]
Trans AIChE ... Transactions. AIChE [*American Institute of Chemical Engineers*] [*A publication*]

Trans AIME Metall Soc ... Transactions. AIME [*American Institute of Mining, Metallurgical, and Petroleum Engineers*] Metallurgical Society [*A publication*]

Trans All-India Inst Ment Health ... Transactions. All-India Institute of Mental Health [*A publication*]

Trans All Union Sci Res Inst Confect Ind ... Transactions. All-Union Scientific Research Institute of the Confectionery Industry [*A publication*]

Trans All Union Sci Res Inst Veg Oils Margarine ... Transactions. All-Union Scientific Research Institute for Vegetable Oils and Margarine [*A publication*]

Trans Am Acad Ophthalmol Oto-Laryngol ... Transactions. American Academy of Ophthalmology and Oto-Laryngology [*A publication*]

Trans Am Assoc Cost Eng ... Transactions. American Association of Cost Engineers [*A publication*]

Trans Am Assoc Genito-Urin Surg ... Transactions. American Association of Genito-Urinary Surgeons [*A publication*]

Trans Am Assoc Obstet Gynecol ... Transactions. American Association of Obstetricians and Gynecologists [*A publication*]

Trans Am Assoc Obstet Gynecol Abdom Surg ... Transactions. American Association of Obstetricians, Gynecologists, and Abdominal Surgeons [*A publication*]

Trans Am Brew Inst ... Transactions. American Brewing Institute [*A publication*]

Trans Am Broncho-Esophagol Assoc ... Transactions. American Broncho-Esophagological Association [*A publication*]

Trans Am Ceram Soc ... Transactions. American Ceramic Society [*A publication*]

Trans Am Clin Climatol Assoc ... Transactions. American Clinical and Climatological Association [*A publication*]

Trans Am Coll Cardiol ... Transactions. American College of Cardiology [*A publication*]

Trans Am Crystallogr Assoc ... Transactions. American Crystallographic Association [*A publication*]

Trans Am Electroch Soc ... Transactions. American Electrochemical Society [*A publication*]

Trans Am Entomol Soc (Phila) ... Transactions. American Entomological Society (Philadelphia) [*A publication*]

Trans Am Ent Soc ... Transactions. American Entomological Society [*A publication*]

Trans Amer Acad Ophthalmol Otolaryngol ... Transactions. American Academy of Ophthalmology and Otolaryngology [*A publication*]

Trans Amer Ass Cereal Chem ... Transactions. American Association of Cereal Chemists [*A publication*]

Trans Amer Electro-Chem Soc ... Transactions. American Electrochemical Society [*A publication*]

Trans Amer Foundrymen's Soc ... Transactions. American Foundrymen's Society [*A publication*]

Trans Amer Geophys Union ... Transactions. American Geophysical Union [*A publication*]

Trans Amer Math Soc ... Transactions. American Mathematical Society [*A publication*]

Trans Amer Microscop Soc ... Transactions. American Microscopical Society [*A publication*]

Trans Amer Nucl Soc ... Transactions. American Nuclear Society [*A publication*]

Trans Am Fisheries Soc ... Transactions. American Fisheries Society [*A publication*]

Trans Am Fish Soc ... Transactions. American Fisheries Society [*A publication*]

Trans Am Foundrymen's Assoc Q ... Transactions. American Foundrymen's Association [*Later, American Foundrymen's Society*]. Quarterly [*A publication*]

Trans Am Geophys Union ... Transactions. American Geophysical Union [*A publication*]

Trans Am Goiter Assoc ... Transactions. American Goiter Association [*A publication*]

Trans Am Gynecol Soc ... Transactions. American Gynecological Society [*A publication*]

Trans Am Inst Chem Eng ... Transactions. American Institute of Chemical Engineers [*A publication*]

Trans Am Inst Electr Eng ... Transactions. American Institute of Electrical Engineers [*A publication*]

Trans Am Inst Electr Eng Part 1 ... Transactions. American Institute of Electrical Engineers. Part 1. Communication and Electronics [*A publication*]

Trans Am Inst Electr Eng Part 2 ... Transactions. American Institute of Electrical Engineers. Part 2. Applications and Industry [*A publication*]

Trans Am Inst Electr Eng Part 3 ... Transactions. American Institute of Electrical Engineers. Part 3. Power Apparatus and Systems [*A publication*]

Trans Am Inst Ind Eng ... Transactions. American Institute of Industrial Engineers [*A publication*]

Trans Am Inst Min Eng ... Transactions. American Institute of Mining Engineers [*A publication*]

Trans Am Inst Min Metall Eng ... Transactions. American Institute of Mining and Metallurgical Engineers [*A publication*]

Trans Am Inst Min Metall Pet Eng ... Transactions. American Institute of Mining, Metallurgical, and Petroleum Engineers [*A publication*]

Trans Am Math Soc ... Transactions. American Mathematical Society [*A publication*]

Trans Am Microsc Soc ... Transactions. American Microscopical Society [*A publication*]

Trans Am Neurol Assoc ... Transactions. American Neurological Association [*A publication*]

Trans Am Nucl Soc ... Transactions. American Nuclear Society [*A publication*]

Trans Am Nucl Soc Suppl ... Transactions. American Nuclear Society. Supplement [*A publication*]

Trans Am Ophthalmol Soc ... Transactions. American Ophthalmological Society [*A publication*]

Trans Am Otol Soc ... Transactions. American Otological Society [*A publication*]

Trans Am Philos Soc ... Transactions. American Philosophical Society [*A publication*]

Trans Am Soc Agric Eng Gen Ed ... Transactions. American Society of Agricultural Engineers. General Edition [*A publication*]

Trans Am Soc Agric Engrs ... Transactions. American Society of Agricultural Engineers [*A publication*]

Trans Am Soc Agric Engrs Gen Edn ... Transactions. American Society of Agricultural Engineers. General Edition [*A publication*]

Trans Am Soc Artif Intern Organs ... Transactions. American Society for Artificial Internal Organs [*A publication*]

Trans Am Soc Art Int Org ... Transactions. American Society for Artificial Internal Organs [*A publication*]

Trans Am Soc Civ Eng ... Transactions. American Society of Civil Engineers [*A publication*]

Trans Am Soc Heat Air-Cond Eng ... Transactions. American Society of Heating and Air-Conditioning Engineers [*A publication*]

Trans Am Soc Met ... Transactions. American Society for Metals [*A publication*]

Trans Am Soc Ophthalmol Otolaryngol Allergy ... Transactions. American Society of Ophthalmologic and Otolaryngologic Allergy [*A publication*]

Trans Am Soc Steel Treat ... Transactions. American Society for Steel Treating [*A publication*]

Trans Am Ther Soc ... Transactions. American Therapeutic Society [*A publication*]

Trans Am Urol Assoc ... Transactions. American Urological Association [*A publication*]

Trans Ancient Monuments Soc ... Transactions. Ancient Monuments Society [*A publication*]

Trans Anglesey Antiq Soc Fld Club ... Transactions. Anglesey Antiquarian Society and Field Club [*A publication*]

Trans Ann Anthracite Conf Lehigh Univ ... Transactions. Annual Anthracite Conference of Lehigh University [*A publication*]

Trans Ann Meet Am Laryngol Assoc ... Transactions. Annual Meeting. American Laryngological Association [*A publication*]

Trans Annu Conf Can Nucl Soc ... Transactions. Annual Conference. Canadian Nuclear Society [*A publication*]

Trans Annu Meet Allen O Whipple Surg Soc ... Transactions. Annual Meeting. Allen O. Whipple Surgical Society [*A publication*]

Trans Annu Tech Conf Am Soc Qual Control ... Transactions. Annual Technical Conference. American Society for Quality Control [*A publication*]

Trans Annu Tech Conf ASQC ... Transactions. Annual Technical Conference. American Society for Quality Control [*A publication*]

Trans Annu Tech Conf Soc Vac Coaters ... Transactions. Annual Technical Conference. Society of Vacuum Coaters [*A publication*]

Trans Ap .... Transcript Appeals [*New York*] [*1867-68*] [*A publication*]   (DLA)

Trans A Ph A ... Transactions. American Philological Association [*A publication*]

Trans App ... Transcript Appeals [*New York*] [*A publication*]   (DLA)

Trans Appeal R ... New York Transcript Appeals Reports [*A publication*]   (DLA)

Trans Architect Archaeol Soc Durham Northumberland ... Transactions. Architectural and Archaeological Society of Durham and Northumberland [*A publication*]

Trans Architect Inst Jpn ... Transactions. Architectural Institute of Japan [*A publication*]

Trans ASAE ... Transactions. ASAE [*American Society of Agricultural Engineers*] [*A publication*]

Trans ASME ... Transactions. American Society of Mechanical Engineers [*A publication*]

Trans ASME J Appl Mech ... Transactions. American Society of Mechanical Engineers. Journal of Applied Mechanics [*A publication*]

Trans ASME J Biomech Eng ... Transactions. ASME [*American Society of Mechanical Engineers*] Series K. Journal of Biomechanical Engineering [*A publication*]

Trans ASME J Biomech Engng ... Transactions. American Society of Mechanical Engineers. Journal of Biomechanical Engineering [*A publication*]

Trans ASME J Dyn Syst Meas & Control ... Transactions. American Society of Mechanical Engineers. Journal of Dynamic Systems Measurement and Control [*A publication*]

Trans ASME J Energy Resour Technol ... Transactions. American Society of Mechanical Engineers. Journal of Energy Resources Technology [*A publication*]

Trans ASME J Eng Gas Turbines Power ... Transactions. ASME [*American Society of Mechanical Engineers*] Journal of Engineering for Gas Turbines and Power [*A publication*]

Trans ASME J Eng Ind ... Transactions. ASME [*American Society of Mechanical Engineers*] Series B. Journal of Engineering for Industry [*A publication*]

Trans ASME J Eng Mater and Technol ... Transactions. ASME [*American Society of Mechanical Engineers*] Series H. Journal of Engineering Materials and Technology [*A publication*]

Trans ASME J Engng Ind ... Transactions. American Society of Mechanical Engineers. Journal of Engineering for Industry [*A publication*]

Trans ASME J Engng Mater & Technol ... Transactions. American Society of Mechanical Engineers. Journal of Engineering Materials and Technology [*A publication*]

Trans ASME J Engng Power ... Transactions. American Society of Mechanical Engineers. Journal of Engineering for Power [*A publication*]

Trans ASME J Eng Power ... Transactions. ASME [*American Society of Mechanical Engineers*] Series A. Journal of Engineering for Power [*A publication*]

Trans ASME J Fluids Eng ... Transactions. ASME [*American Society of Mechanical Engineers*] Series I. Journal of Fluids Engineering [*A publication*]

Trans ASME J Fluids Engng ... Transactions. American Society of Mechanical Engineers. Journal of Fluids Engineering [*A publication*]

Trans ASME J Heat Transfer ... Transactions. American Society of Mechanical Engineers. Journal of Heat Transfer [*A publication*]

Trans ASME J Lubr Technol ... Transactions. American Society of Mechanical Engineers. Journal of Lubrication Technology [*A publication*]

Trans ASME J Mech Des ... Transactions. American Society of Mechanical Engineers. Journal of Mechanical Design [*A publication*]

Trans ASME J Pressure Vessel Technol ... Transactions. American Society of Mechanical Engineers. Journal of Pressure Vessel Technology [*A publication*]

Trans ASME J Sol Energy Eng ... Transactions. ASME [*American Society of Mechanical Engineers*] Journal of Solar Energy Engineering [*A publication*]

Trans ASME J Sol Energy Engng ... Transactions. American Society of Mechanical Engineers. Journal of Solar Energy Engineering [*A publication*]

Trans ASME J Tribol ... Transactions. ASME [*American Society of Mechanical Engineers*] Journal of Tribology [*A publication*]

Trans ASME Ser A ... Transactions. ASME [*American Society of Mechanical Engineers*] Series A. Journal of Engineering for Power [*A publication*]

Trans ASME Ser A J Eng Power ... Transactions. ASME [*American Society of Mechanical Engineers*] Series A. Journal of Engineering for Power [*A publication*]

Trans ASME Ser B ... Transactions. ASME [*American Society of Mechanical Engineers*] Series B. Journal of Engineering for Industry [*A publication*]

Trans ASME Ser B J Eng Ind ... Transactions. ASME [*American Society of Mechanical Engineers*] Series B. Journal of Engineering for Industry [*A publication*]

Trans ASME Ser C ... Transactions. ASME [*American Society of Mechanical Engineers*] Series C. Journal of Heat Transfer [*A publication*]

Trans ASME Ser C J Heat Transfer ... Transactions. ASME [*American Society of Mechanical Engineers*] Series C. Journal of Heat Transfer [*A publication*]

Trans ASME Ser D ... Transactions. ASME [*American Society of Mechanical Engineers*] Series D [*A publication*]

Trans ASME Ser E ... Transactions. ASME [*American Society of Mechanical Engineers*] Series E. Journal of Applied Mechanics [*A publication*]

Trans ASME Ser E J Appl Mech ... Transactions. ASME [*American Society of Mechanical Engineers*] Series E. Journal of Applied Mechanics [*A publication*]

Trans ASME Ser F ... Transactions. ASME [*American Society of Mechanical Engineers*] Series F. Journal of Lubrication Technology [*A publication*]

Trans ASME Ser F J Lubr Technol ... Transactions. ASME [*American Society of Mechanical Engineers*] Series F. Journal of Lubrication Technology [*A publication*]

Trans ASME Ser G ... Transactions. ASME [*American Society of Mechanical Engineers*] Series G. Journal of Dynamic Systems. Measurement and Control [*A publication*]

Trans ASME Ser GJ Dynamic Systems ... Transactions. ASME [*American Society of Mechanical Engineers*] Series G. Journal of Dynamic Systems. Measurement and Control [*A publication*]

Trans ASME Ser G J Dynamic Systems Measurement and Control ... Transactions. ASME [*American Society of Mechanical Engineers*] Series G. Journal of Dynamic Systems. Measurement and Control [*A publication*]

Trans ASME Ser G J Dyn Syst Meas and Control ... Transactions. ASME [*American Society of Mechanical Engineers*] Series G. Journal of Dynamic Systems. Measurement and Control [*A publication*]

Trans ASME Ser H ... Transactions. ASME [*American Society of Mechanical Engineers*] Series H. Journal of Engineering Materials and Technology [*A publication*]

Trans ASME Ser H J Eng Mater and Technol ... Transactions. ASME [*American Society of Mechanical Engineers*] Series H. Journal of Engineering Materials and Technology [*A publication*]

Trans ASME Ser I ... Transactions. ASME [*American Society of Mechanical Engineers*] Series I. Journal of Fluids Engineering [*A publication*]

Trans ASME Ser I J Fluids Eng ... Transactions. ASME [*American Society of Mechanical Engineers*] Series I. Journal of Fluids Engineering [*A publication*]

Trans ASME Ser J J Pressure Vessel Technol ... Transactions. ASME [*American Society of Mechanical Engineers*] Series J. Journal of Pressure Vessel Technology [*A publication*]

Trans ASME Ser K ... Transactions. ASME [*American Society of Mechanical Engineers*] Series K [*A publication*]

Trans ASME Ser K J Biomech Eng ... Transactions. ASME [*American Society of Mechanical Engineers*] Series K. Journal of Biomechanical Engineering [*A publication*]

Trans Assoc Am Physicians ... Transactions. Association of American Physicians [*A publication*]

Trans Assoc Ind Med Off ... Transactions. Association of Industrial Medical Officers [*A publication*]

Trans Assoc Life Ins Med Dir Am ... Transactions. Association of Life Insurance Medical Directors of America [*A publication*]

Transatl R ... Transatlantic Review [*A publication*]

Trans Aust Coll Ophthalmol ... Transactions. Australian College of Ophthalmologists [*A publication*]

Trans Aust Med Congress ... Transactions. Australian Medical Congress [*A publication*]

Trans B'ham Warwks Arch Soc ... Transactions. Birmingham and Warwickshire Archaeological Society [*A publication*]

Trans Biochem Soc ... Transactions. Biochemical Society [*A publication*]

Trans Birmingham Arch Soc ... Transactions. Birmingham and Warwickshire Archaeological Society [*A publication*]

Trans Birmingham Warwickshire Archaeol Soc ... Transactions. Birmingham and Warwickshire Archaeological Society [*A publication*]

Trans Bose Res Inst ... Transactions. Bose Research Institute [*A publication*]

Trans Bose Res Inst (Calcutta) ... Transactions. Bose Research Institute (Calcutta) [*A publication*]

Trans Bot Soc Edinb ... Transactions and Proceedings. Botanical Society of Edinburgh [*A publication*]

Trans Br Bryol Soc ... Transactions. British Bryological Society [*A publication*]

Trans Br Ceram Soc ... Transactions. British Ceramic Society [*A publication*]

Trans Bristol and Glos AS ... Transactions. Bristol and Gloucestershire Archaeological Society [*A publication*]

Trans Bristol Gloucestershire Archaeol Soc ... Transactions. Bristol and Gloucestershire Archaeological Society [*A publication*]

Trans Bristol Gloucestershire Arch Soc ... Transactions. Bristol and Gloucestershire Archaeological Society [*A publication*]

Trans Brit Mycol Soc ... Transactions. British Mycological Society [*A publication*]

Trans Br Mycol Soc ... Transactions. British Mycological Society [*A publication*]

Trans Br Soc Hist Pharm ... Transactions. British Society for the History of Pharmacy [*A publication*]

Trans Br Soc Study Orthod ... Transactions. British Society for the Study of Orthodontics [*A publication*]

Transc A .... Transcript Appeals [*New York*] [*A publication*] (DLA)

TRANSCAER ... Transportation Community Awareness and Emergency Response

Trans Caernarvonshire Hist Soc ... Transactions. Caernarvonshire Historical Society [*A publication*]

Trans Cambridge Philos Soc ... Transactions. Cambridge Philosophical Society [*A publication*]

Trans Can Inst Mining Soc NS ... Transactions. Canadian Institute of Mining and Metallurgy and Mining Society of Nova Scotia [*A publication*]

Trans Can Inst Min Metall ... Transactions. Canadian Institute of Mining and Metallurgy and Mining Society of Nova Scotia [*A publication*]

Trans Can Inst Min Metall Min Soc NS ... Transactions. Canadian Institute of Mining and Metallurgy and Mining Society of Nova Scotia [*A publication*]

Trans Can Min Inst ... Transactions. Canadian Mining Institute [*A publication*]

Trans Can Nucl Soc ... Transactions. Canadian Nuclear Society [*A publication*]

Trans Can Soc Mech Eng ... Transactions. Canadian Society of Mechanical Engineers [*A publication*]

Trans Can Soc Mech Engrs ... Transactions. Canadian Society of Mechanical Engineers [*A publication*]
Trans Cardiff Nat Soc ... Transactions. Cardiff Naturalists Society [*A publication*]
Trans Cardiff Natur Soc ... Transactions. Cardiff Naturalists Society [*A publication*]
Trans Cave Res Group GB ... Transactions. Cave Research Group of Great Britain [*A publication*]
TRANSCEIVER ... Transmitter-Receiver　(NATG)
Trans Cent Sci Res Inst Confect Ind ... Transactions. Central Scientific Research Institute of the Confectionery Industry [*A publication*]
Trans Ceylon Coll ... Transactions. Ceylon College of Physicians [*A publication*]
Trans Chalmers Univ Technol (Gothenburg) ... Transactions. Chalmers University of Technology (Gothenburg) [*Sweden*] [*A publication*]
Trans Chem Div Am Soc Qual Control ... Transactions. Chemical Division. American Society for Quality Control [*A publication*]
Trans Chin Assoc Adv Sci ... Transactions. Chinese Association for the Advancement of Science [*A publication*]
Trans Citrus Eng Conf ... Transactions. Citrus Engineering Conference [*A publication*]
Transcn ...... Transcon, Inc. [*Associated Press abbreviation*]　(APAG)
Transco ...... Transco Energy Co. [*Associated Press abbreviation*]　(APAG)
Trans Coll Med S Afr ... Transactions. College of Medicine of South Africa [*A publication*]
Trans Coll Physicians Philadelphia ... Transactions. College of Physicians of Philadelphia [*A publication*]
TRANSCOM ... Transportable Communications
TRANSCOM ... Transportation Command [*Army*]
TRANSCON ... Transcontinental　(MCD)
Trans Conf Cold Inj ... Transactions. Conference on Cold Injury [*A publication*]
Trans Conf Glaucoma ... Transactions. Conference on Glaucoma [*A publication*]
Trans Conf Group Processes ... Transactions. Conference on Group Processes [*A publication*]
Trans Conf Group Soc Adm Hist ... Transactions. Conference Group for Social and Administrative History [*A publication*]
Trans Conf Neuropharmacol ... Transactions. Conference on Neuropharmacology [*A publication*]
Trans Conf Physiol Prematurity ... Transactions. Conference on Physiology of Prematurity [*A publication*]
Trans Conf Polysaccharides Biol ... Transactions. Conference on Polysaccharides in Biology [*A publication*]
Trans Conn Acad Arts Sci ... Transactions. Connecticut Academy of Arts and Sciences [*A publication*]
Trans Corn Inst Eng ... Transactions. Cornish Institute of Engineers [*A publication*]
TRANSCR ... Transcribed
Transcr A ... Transcript Appeals [*New York*] [*A publication*]　(DLA)
TRANSCRON ... Transcription　(ROG)
Trans C S Peirce Soc ... Transactions. C. S. Peirce Society [*A publication*]
Transcult Psychiat Res ... Transcultural Psychiatric Research Review [*A publication*]
Trans Cumberland Westmorland Antiq Archaeol Soc N Ser ... Transactions. Cumberland and Westmorland Antiquarian and Archaeological Society. New Series [*A publication*]
TRANSDEC ... SONAR Transducer Test and Evaluation Center, Naval Electronics Laboratory [*San Diego, CA*] [*Navy*]
TRANSDEF ... Transducer Evaluation Facility
Trans Denbighshire Hist Soc ... Transactions. Denbighshire Historical Society [*A publication*]
TRANS/DEP ... Transportation of Dependents [*Navy*]　(DNAB)
Trans Desert Bighorn Counc ... Transactions. Desert Bighorn Council [*A publication*]
TRANSDIV ... Transport Division [*Navy*]
Transducer Technol ... Transducer Technology [*A publication*]
Trans Dumfries Galloway Nat Hist Antiq Soc ... Transactions. Dumfriesshire and Galloway Natural History and Antiquarian Society [*A publication*]
Trans Dumfries and Galloway NH and AS ... Transactions. Dumfriesshire and Galloway Natural History and Antiquarian Society [*A publication*]
Trans Dumfriesshire Galloway Natur Hist Antiq Soc ... Transactions. Dumfriesshire and Galloway Natural History and Antiquarian Society [*A publication*]
Trans Dumfriesshire Galloway Natur Hist Ant Soc ... Transactions. Dumfriesshire and Galloway Natural History and Antiquarian Society [*A publication*]
Trans Dynam Dev ... Transactions. Dynamics of Development [*A publication*]
Trans East Lothian Antiq Field Nat Soc ... Transactions. East Lothian Antiquarian and Field Naturalists' Society [*A publication*]
TRANSEC ... Transmission Security [*Communications*]
Trans Econ & Oper Anal ... Transport Economics and Operational Analysis [*A publication*]　(APTA)
TRANSED ... Transition Education
Trans Edinb Geol Soc ... Transactions. Edinburgh Geological Society [*A publication*]

Trans Edinburgh Geol Soc ... Transactions. Edinburgh Geological Society [*A publication*]
Trans Electrochem Soc ... Transactions. Electrochemical Society [*A publication*]
Trans Electr Supply Auth Eng Inst NZ ... Transactions. Electric Supply Authority Engineers' Institute of New Zealand, Inc. [*A publication*]
Trans Electr Supply Eng Inst ... Transactions. Annual Conference. Electric Supply Authority Engineers' Institute of New Zealand, Inc.
Trans E Lothian Antiq Fld Natur Soc ... Transactions. East Lothian Antiquarian and Field Naturalists' Society [*A publication*]
Trans Eng Inst Can ... Transactions. Engineering Institute of Canada [*A publication*]
Trans Engl Ceram Circle ... Transactions. English Ceramic Circle [*A publication*]
Trans Engl Ceram Soc ... Transactions. English Ceramic Society [*A publication*]
Trans Essex Arch Soc ... Transactions. Essex Archaeological Society [*A publication*]
Trans Est Agric Acad ... Transactions. Estonian Agricultural Academy [*A publication*]
Trans Eur Orthod Soc ... Transactions. European Orthodontic Society [*A publication*]
TRANSF ... Transferred
TRANSF ... Transformer　(AAG)
Trans Fac Hortic Chiba Univ ... Transactions. Faculty of Horticulture. Chiba University [*A publication*]
Trans Farady Soc ... Transactions. Faraday Society [*A publication*]
TRANSFAX ... Facsimile Transmission [*Telecommunications*]
TRANSFD ... Transferred　(ROG)
Trans Fed-Prov Wildl Conf ... Transactions. Federal-Provincial Wildlife Conference [*A publication*]
TRANSFER ... Transportation Simulation for Estimating Requirements　(DNAB)
TRANSFIG ... Transfiguration
TRANSFLTNG ... Transitional Flight Training　(NVT)
TRANSFORM ... Trade-Off Analysis - Systems/Force Mix Analysis [*Military*]
Transform (Papeterie) ... Transformation (Supplement to La Papeterie) [*A publication*]
Trans Geol Soc Glasg ... Transactions. Geological Society of Glasgow [*A publication*]
Trans Geol Soc S Afr ... Transactions. Geological Society of South Africa [*A publication*]
Trans Geotherm Resour Counc ... Transactions. Geothermal Resources Council [*United States*] [*A publication*]
Trans Glasgow Univ Orient Soc ... Transactions. Glasgow University Oriental Society [*A publication*]
Trans Greenwich Lewisham Antiq Soc ... Transactions. Greenwich and Lewisham Antiquarian Society [*A publication*]
TRANSGRPPHIBFOR ... Transportation Group Amphibious Forces [*Navy*]
TRANSGRPSOPAC ... Transport Group, South Pacific Force [*Navy*]
Trans Gulf Coast Ass Geol Soc ... Transactions. Gulf Coast Association of Geological Societies [*A publication*]
Trans Gulf Coast Assoc Geol Soc ... Transactions. Gulf Coast Association of Geological Societies [*A publication*]
Trans Gulf Coast Mol Biol Conf ... Transactions. Gulf Coast Molecular Biology Conference [*A publication*]
Trans Halifax Antiq Society ... Transactions. Halifax Antiquarian Society [*A publication*]
Trans Hawick Archaeol Soc ... Transactions. Hawick Archaeological Society [*A publication*]
Trans Hertfordshire Nat Hist Field Club ... Transactions. Hertfordshire Natural History Society and Field Club [*A publication*]
Trans Hertfordshire Nat Hist Soc Field Club ... Transactions. Hertfordshire Natural History Society and Field Club [*A publication*]
Trans Highl Agric Soc Scotl ... Transactions. Highland and Agricultural Society of Scotland [*A publication*]
Trans Hist Soc Ghana ... Transactions. Historical Society of Ghana [*A publication*]
Trans Hist Soc Lancashire Cheshire ... Transactions. Historic Society of Lancashire and Cheshire [*A publication*]
Trans Hunter Archaeol Soc ... Transactions. Hunter Archaeological Society [*A publication*]
Trans Hunter Soc ... Transactions. Hunterian Society [*A publication*]
Trans ILA ... Transactions. International Law Association [*1873-1924*] [*A publication*]　(DLA)
Trans Illinois State Acad Sci ... Illinois State Academy of Science. Transactions [*A publication*]
Trans Ill St Acad Sci ... Transactions. Illinois State Academy of Science [*A publication*]
Trans Ill State Acad Sci ... Transactions. Illinois State Academy of Science [*A publication*]
Trans Ill State Hortic Soc ... Transactions. Illinois State Horticultural Society [*A publication*]
Trans Ill State Hortic Soc Ill Fruit Counc ... Transactions. Illinois State Horticultural Society and the Illinois Fruit Council [*A publication*]
Trans Ill St Hort Soc ... Transactions. Illinois State Horticultural Society [*A publication*]

Trans Illum Eng Soc ... Transactions. Illuminating Engineering Society [*A publication*]

TRANSIM ... Transit Simplified Receiver [*Satellite navigation system*]

TRANSIM ... Transportation Simulator (DNAB)

Trans I Mar E ... Transactions. Institute of Marine Engineers [*A publication*]

Trans Indiana Acad Ophthalmol Otolaryngol ... Transactions. Indiana Academy of Ophthalmology and Otolaryngology [*A publication*]

Trans Indian Ceram Soc ... Transactions. Indian Ceramic Society [*A publication*]

Trans Indian Inst Chem Eng ... Transactions. Indian Institute of Chemical Engineers [*A publication*]

Trans Indian Inst Met ... Transactions. Indian Institute of Metals [*A publication*]

Trans Indian Inst Metals ... Transactions. Indian Institute of Metals [*A publication*]

Trans Indian Soc Desert Technol Univ Cent Desert Stud ... Transactions. Indian Society of Desert Technology and University Centre of Desert Studies [*A publication*]

Trans Ind Inst Chem Eng ... Transactions. Indian Institute of Chemical Engineers [*A publication*]

Trans Inf Process Soc Jpn ... Transactions. Information Processing Society of Japan [*A publication*]

Trans Inst Act Aust & NZ ... Transactions. Institute of Actuaries of Australia and New Zealand [*A publication*] (APTA)

Trans Inst Br Geogr New Ser ... Transactions. Institute of British Geographers. New Series [*A publication*]

Trans Inst Brit Geogr ... Transactions. Institute of British Geographers [*A publication*]

Trans Inst Chem Eng ... Transactions. Institution of Chemical Engineers [*A publication*]

Trans Inst Chem Eng (London) ... Transactions. Institution of Chemical Engineers (London) [*A publication*]

Trans Inst Chem Engrs ... Transactions. Institution of Chemical Engineers [*A publication*]

Trans Inst Civ Eng Ir ... Transactions. Institution of Civil Engineers of Ireland [*A publication*]

Trans Inst Electr Eng Jap ... Transactions. Institute of Electrical Engineers of Japan [*A publication*]

Trans Inst Electr Eng Jap Overseas Ed ... Transactions. Institute of Electrical Engineers of Japan. Overseas Edition [*A publication*]

Trans Inst Electr Eng Jpn ... Transactions. Institute of Electrical Engineers of Japan [*A publication*]

Trans Inst Electr Eng Jpn B ... Transactions. Institute of Electrical Engineers of Japan. Part B [*A publication*]

Trans Inst Electr Eng Jpn C ... Transactions. Institute of Electrical Engineers of Japan. Part C [*A publication*]

Trans Inst Electr Eng Jpn Part A ... Transactions. Institute of Electrical Engineers of Japan. Part A [*A publication*]

Trans Inst Electr Eng Jpn Part B ... Transactions. Institute of Electrical Engineers of Japan. Part B [*A publication*]

Trans Inst Electr Eng Jpn Part C ... Transactions. Institute of Electrical Engineers of Japan. Part C [*A publication*]

Trans Inst Electr Eng Jpn Sect E ... Transactions. Institute of Electrical Engineers of Japan. Section E [*A publication*]

Trans Inst Electron & Commun Eng Jap A ... Transactions. Institute of Electronics and Communication Engineers of Japan. Part A [*A publication*]

Trans Inst Electron & Commun Eng Jap B ... Transactions. Institute of Electronics and Communication Engineers of Japan. Part B [*A publication*]

Trans Inst Electron & Commun Eng Jap C ... Transactions. Institute of Electronics and Communication Engineers of Japan. Part C [*A publication*]

Trans Inst Electron & Commun Eng Jap D ... Transactions. Institute of Electronics and Communication Engineers of Japan. Part D [*A publication*]

Trans Inst Electron Commun Eng Jap Sect J Part A ... Transactions. Institute of Electronics and Communication Engineers of Japan. Section J. Part A [*A publication*]

Trans Inst Electron Commun Eng Jap Sect J Part C ... Transactions. Institute of Electronics and Communication Engineers of Japan. Section J. Part C [*A publication*]

Trans Inst Electron Commun Eng Jap Sect J Part D ... Transactions. Institute of Electronics and Communication Engineers of Japan. Section J [*Japanese*] Part D [*A publication*]

Trans Inst Electron and Commun Eng Jpn Part A ... Transactions. Institute of Electronics and Communication Engineers of Japan. Part A [*A publication*]

Trans Inst Electron Commun Eng Jpn Part B ... Transactions. Institute of Electronics and Communication Engineers of Japan. Part B [*A publication*]

Trans Inst Electron and Commun Eng Jpn Part C ... Transactions. Institute of Electronics and Communication Engineers of Japan. Part C [*A publication*]

Trans Inst Electron and Commun Eng Jpn Part D ... Transactions. Institute of Electronics and Communication Engineers of Japan. Part D [*A publication*]

Trans Inst Electron and Commun Eng Jpn Sect E ... Transactions. Institute of Electronics and Communication Engineers of Japan. Section E [*A publication*]

Trans Inst Electron Commun Eng Jpn Sect E (Engl) ... Transactions. Institute of Electronics and Communication Engineers of Japan. Section E (English) [*A publication*]

Trans Inst Eng Aust ... Transactions. Institution of Engineers of Australia [*A publication*]

Trans Inst Eng Aust Civ Eng ... Transactions. Institution of Engineers of Australia. Civil Engineering [*A publication*]

Trans Inst Eng Aust Electr Eng ... Transactions. Institution of Engineers of Australia. Electrical Engineering [*A publication*]

Trans Inst Eng Aust Mech Eng ... Transactions. Institution of Engineers of Australia. Mechanical Engineering [*A publication*]

Trans Inst Engrs Aust Civ Engng ... Transactions. Institution of Engineers of Australia. Civil Engineering [*A publication*]

Trans Inst Engrs Aust Mech Engng ... Transactions. Institution of Engineers of Australia. Mechanical Engineering [*A publication*]

Trans Inst Eng Shipbuilders Scot ... Transactions. Institution of Engineers and Shipbuilders in Scotland [*A publication*]

Trans Inst Gas Eng ... Transactions. Institution of Gas Engineers [*England*] [*A publication*]

Trans Inst Mar Eng ... Transactions. Institute of Marine Engineers [*A publication*]

Trans Inst Mar Eng Conf Pap ... Transactions. Institute of Marine Engineers. Conference Papers [*A publication*]

Trans Inst Mar Engrs ... Transactions. Institute of Marine Engineers [*A publication*]

Trans Inst Mar Eng Ser C ... Transactions. Institute of Marine Engineers. Series C [*A publication*]

Trans Inst Mar Eng Tech Meet Pap ... Transactions. Institute of Marine Engineers. Technical Meeting Papers [*A publication*]

Trans Inst Marine Eng ... Transactions. Institute of Marine Engineers [*A publication*]

Trans Inst Meas Control ... Transactions. Institute of Measurement and Control [*A publication*]

Trans Inst Measmt Control ... Transactions. Institute of Measurement and Control [*A publication*]

Trans Inst Met Finish ... Transactions. Institute of Metal Finishing [*A publication*]

Trans Inst Min Eng ... Transactions. Institution of Mining Engineers [*A publication*]

Trans Inst Mining Met Sect A ... Transactions. Institution of Mining and Metallurgy. Section A. Mining Industry [*A publication*]

Trans Inst Mining Met Sect B ... Transactions. Institution of Mining and Metallurgy. Section B. Applied Earth Science [*A publication*]

Trans Inst Mining Met Sect C ... Transactions. Institution of Mining and Metallurgy. Section C [*A publication*]

Trans Inst Min Metall ... Transactions. Institution of Mining and Metallurgy [*A publication*]

Trans Inst Min Metall (Ostrava) Min Geol Ser ... Transactions. Institute of Mining and Metallurgy (Ostrava). Mining and Geological Series [*A publication*]

Trans Inst Min Metall Sec A ... Transactions. Institution of Mining and Metallurgy. Section A. Mining Industry [*A publication*]

Trans Inst Min Metall Sec B ... Transactions. Institution of Mining and Metallurgy. Section B. Applied Earth Science [*A publication*]

Trans Inst Min Metall Sec C ... Transactions. Institution of Mining and Metallurgy. Section C [*United Kingdom*] [*A publication*]

Trans Inst Min Metall Sect A Min Ind ... Transactions. Institution of Mining and Metallurgy. Section A. Mining Industry [*A publication*]

Trans Inst Min Metall Sect B Appl Earth Sci ... Transactions. Institution of Mining and Metallurgy. Section B. Applied Earth Science [*United Kingdom*] [*A publication*]

Trans Instn Chem Engrs ... Transactions. Institution of Chemical Engineers [*A publication*]

Trans Instn Eng Aust ... Transactions. Institution of Engineers of Australia [*A publication*]

Trans Instn E Shipb Scot ... Transactions. Institution of Engineers and Shipbuilders in Scotland [*A publication*]

Trans Instn Min Metall ... Transactions. Institution of Mining and Metallurgy [*A publication*]

Trans Inst Plast Ind ... Transactions. Institute of the Plastics Industry [*A publication*]

Trans Inst Prof Eng ... Transactions. Institution of Professional Engineers of New Zealand [*A publication*]

Trans Inst Prof Eng NZ ... Transactions. Institution of Professional Engineers. New Zealand Civil Engineering Section [*A publication*]

Trans Inst Prof Eng NZ Civ Eng Sect ... Transactions. Institution of Professional Engineers of New Zealand. Civil Engineering Section [*A publication*]

Trans Inst Prof Eng NZ Electr Mech Chem Eng Sect ... Transactions. Institution of Professional Engineers of New Zealand. Electrical/Mechanical/Chemical Engineering Section [*A publication*]

Trans Inst Prof Eng NZ EMCh ... Transactions. Institution of Professional Engineers of New Zealand. Electrical/Mechanical/Chemical Engineering Section [*A publication*]

Trans Inst Pure Chem Reagents (Moscow) ... Transactions. Institute of Pure Chemical Reagents (Moscow) [*A publication*]

Trans Inst Rubber Ind ... Transactions. Institution of the Rubber Industry [*A publication*]

Trans Inst Water Eng ... Transactions. Institution of Water Engineers [*A publication*]
Trans Inst Weld (London) ... Transactions. Institute of Welding (London) [*A publication*]
Trans Int Assoc Math and Comput Simulation ... Transactions. International Association for Mathematics and Computers in Simulation [*A publication*]
Trans Int Astron Union ... Transactions. International Astronomical Union [*A publication*]
Trans Int Ceram Congr ... Transactions. International Ceramic Congress [*A publication*]
Trans Int Conf Endod ... Transactions. International Conference on Endodontics [*A publication*]
Trans Int Conf Oral Surg ... Transactions. International Conference on Oral Surgery [*A publication*]
Trans Int Conf Or Ja ... Transactions. International Conference of Orientalists in Japan [*A publication*]
Trans Int Conf Soil Sci ... Transactions. International Conference of Soil Science [*A publication*]
Trans Int Congr Agr Eng ... Transactions. International Congress of Agricultural Engineering [*A publication*]
Trans Int Congr Agric Engng ... Transactions. International Congress for Agricultural Engineering [*A publication*]
Trans Int Congr Entomol ... Transactions. International Congress of Entomology [*A publication*]
Trans Int Congr Soil Sci ... Transactions. International Congress of Soil Science [*A publication*]
Trans Intl... Journal pour le Transport International [*A publication*]
Trans Int Soc Geotherm Eng ... Transactions. International Society for Geothermal Engineering [*A publication*]
Trans Iowa State Hortic Soc ... Transactions. Iowa State Horticultural Society [*A publication*]
Trans Iowa St Hort Soc ... Transactions. Iowa State Horticultural Society [*A publication*]
Trans Iron Steel Inst Jap ... Transactions. Iron and Steel Institute of Japan [*A publication*]
Trans Iron Steel Inst Jpn ... Transactions. Iron and Steel Institute of Japan [*A publication*]
TRANSIS ... Transportation Safety Information System [*Department of Transportation*] (IID)
TRANSISTOR ... Transfer Resistor
TRANSITEX ... Transit Exercise (NVT)
Transition Met Chem ... Transition Metal Chemistry [*A publication*]
Transit J .... Transit Journal [*A publication*]
Transit L Rev ... Transit Law Review [*A publication*]
Transit Met Chem (Weinheim Ger) ... Transition Metal Chemistry (Weinheim, Germany) [*A publication*]
Transit Packag ... Transit Packaging [*A publication*]
Trans Japan Soc Civ Engrs ... Transactions. Japan Society of Civil Engineers [*A publication*]
Trans Japan Soc Compos Mater ... Transactions. Japan Society for Composite Materials [*A publication*]
Trans Japan Soc Mech Engrs Ser B ... Transactions. Japan Society of Mechanical Engineers. Series B [*A publication*]
Trans Japan Soc Mech Engrs Ser C ... Transactions. Japan Society of Mechanical Engineers. Series C [*A publication*]
Trans Jap Inst Met ... Transactions. Japan Institute of Metals [*A publication*]
Trans Jap Inst Metals ... Transactions. Japan Institute of Metals [*A publication*]
Trans Jap Soc Aeronaut Space Sci ... Transactions. Japan Society for Aeronautical and Space Sciences [*A publication*]
Trans Jap Soc Mech Eng ... Transactions. Japan Society of Mechanical Engineers [*A publication*]
Trans Jap Weld Soc ... Transactions. Japan Welding Society [*A publication*]
Trans J Br Ceram Soc ... Transactions and Journal. British Ceramic Society [*A publication*]
Trans J Brit Ceram Soc ... Transactions and Journal. British Ceramic Society [*A publication*]
Trans J Plast Inst ... Transactions and Journal. Plastics Institute [*England*] [*A publication*]
Trans Jpn Inst Met ... Transactions. Japan Institute of Metals [*A publication*]
Trans Jpn Inst Met Suppl ... Transactions. Japan Institute of Metals. Supplement [*A publication*]
Trans Jpn Pathol Soc ... Transactions. Japanese Pathological Society [*A publication*]
Trans Jpn Soc Aeronaut Space Sci ... Transactions. Japan Society for Aeronautical and Space Sciences [*A publication*]
Trans Jpn Soc Civ Eng ... Transactions. Japan Society of Civil Engineers [*A publication*]
Trans Jpn Soc Irrig Drain Reclam Eng ... Transactions. Japanese Society of Irrigation Drainage and Reclamation Engineering [*A publication*]
Trans Jpn Soc Mech Eng Ser B ... Transactions. Japan Society of Mechanical Engineers. Series B [*A publication*]
Trans Jpn Weld Soc ... Transactions. Japan Welding Society [*A publication*]
Trans Jt Mtg Comm Int Soc Soil Sci ... Transactions. Joint Meeting of Commissions. International Society of Soil Science [*A publication*]
Trans JWRI ... Transactions. JWRI [*Japanese Welding Research Institute*] [*A publication*]

Trans K Acad Sci ... Transactions. Kentucky Academy of Science [*A publication*]
Trans Kans Acad Sci ... Transactions. Kansas Academy of Science [*A publication*]
Trans Kansai Ent Soc ... Transactions. Kansai Entomological Society [*A publication*]
Transkei Dev Rev ... Transkei Development Review [*A publication*]
Trans Koll Geneeskd S-Afr ... Transaksies. Kollege van Geneeskunde van Suid-Afrika [*A publication*]
Trans Korean Inst Electr Eng ... Transactions. Korean Institute of Electrical Engineers [*A publication*]
Trans Korean Soc Mech Eng ... Transactions. Korean Society of Mechanical Engineers [*Republic of Korea*] [*A publication*]
Trans KY Acad Sci ... Transactions. Kentucky Academy of Science [*A publication*]
TRANSL ... Translation (AAG)
Trans Lancashire Cheshire Antiq Soc ... Transactions. Lancashire and Cheshire Antiquarian Society [*A publication*]
Trans Lancs and Chesh Antiq Soc ... Transactions. Lancashire and Cheshire Antiquarian Society [*A publication*]
TRANSLANG ... Translator Language [*Data processing*]
TRANSLANT ... Transports, Atlantic Fleet [*Navy*]
TRANSLANTEX ... Transatlantic Training Exercise (MCD)
Translat ..... Translation (BJA)
Trans Latv Branch All Union Soc Soil Sci ... Transactions. Latvian Branch. All-Union Society of Soil Science [*A publication*]
Transl Beltone Inst Hear Res ... Translations. Beltone Institute for Hearing Research [*A publication*]
Transl Commonw Sci Industr Res Organ (Aust) ... Translation. Commonwealth Scientific and Industrial Research Organisation (CSIRO) (Australia) [*A publication*]
Transld Contents Lists Russ Period ... Translated Contents Lists of Russian Periodicals [*A publication*]
Transl Dep Fish For (Can) ... Translation. Department of Fisheries and Forestry (Ottawa, Canada) [*A publication*]
Trans Leeds Geol Assoc ... Transactions. Leeds Geological Association [*A publication*]
Trans Leicestershire Archaeol Hist Soc ... Transactions. Leicestershire Archaeological and Historical Society [*A publication*]
Transl Fac For Univ BC ... Translation. Faculty of Forestry. University of British Columbia [*A publication*]
Transl For Comm (Lond) ... Translation. Forestry Commission (London) [*A publication*]
Trans Lich S Staffs Arch Hist Soc ... Transactions. Lichfield and South Staffordshire Archaeological and Historical Society [*A publication*]
Trans Linn Soc Lond ... Transactions. Linnean Society of London [*A publication*]
Trans Linn Soc NY ... Transactions. Linnaean Society of New York [*A publication*]
TRANSLIT ... Transliteration
Trans Liverpool Eng Soc ... Transactions. Liverpool Engineering Society [*A publication*]
Trans LJ .... Transportation Law Journal [*A publication*]
TRANSLOC ... Trade-Off Analysis Systems/Force Mix (MCD)
TRANSLOC ... Transportable LORAN-C (MCD)
Trans Lond Middx Archaeol Soc ... Transactions. London and Middlesex Archaeological Society [*A publication*]
Trans London Middlesex Archaeol Soc ... Transactions. London and Middlesex Archaeological Society [*A publication*]
Trans London M'sex Arch ... Transactions. London and Middlesex Archaeological Society [*A publication*]
Trans London Msex Arch Soc ... Transactions. London and Middlesex Archaeological Society [*A publication*]
Transl Reg-Index ... Translations Register-Index [*A publication*]
Transl Rev ... Translation Review [*A publication*]
Transl Russ Game Rep ... Translations of Russian Game Reports [*A publication*]
Transl Soviet Agr US Joint Publ Res Serv ... Translations on Soviet Agriculture. United States Joint Publications Research Service [*A publication*]
Transl US For Prod Lab (Madison) ... Translation. United States Forest Products Laboratory (Madison) [*A publication*]
Transm....... Transamerica Corp. [*Associated Press abbreviation*] (APAG)
TRANSM ... Transmission (AFM)
TRANSMAN ... Enlisted Transfer Manual [*Military*]
Trans Manchester Assoc Eng ... Transactions. Manchester Association of Engineers [*A publication*]
Trans Mass Hort Soc ... Transactions. Massachusetts Horticultural Society [*A publication*]
Trans Math Monographs ... Translations of Mathematical Monographs. American Mathematical Society [*A publication*]
Transm Distrib ... Transmission and Distribution [*A publication*]
Trans Med Soc Lond ... Transactions. Medical Society of London [*A publication*]
Trans Med Soc London ... Transactions. Medical Society of London [*A publication*]
Trans Meet Commns II & IV Int Soc Soil Sci ... Transactions. Meeting of Commissions II and IV. International Society of Soil Science [*A publication*]

Trans Metall Soc AIME ... Transactions. Metallurgical Society of AIME [*American Institute of Mining, Metallurgical, and Petroleum Engineers*] [*A publication*]
Trans Metall Soc AIME (Am Inst Min Metall Pet Eng) ... Transactions. Metallurgical Society of AIME (American Institute of Mining, Metallurgical, and Petroleum Engineers) [*A publication*]
Trans Met Heat Treat ... Transactions of Metal Heat Treatment [*China*] [*A publication*]
TRANSMGTSCOL ... Transportation Management School [*Navy*]   (DNAB)
Trans Min Geol Metall Inst India ... Transactions. Mining, Geological, and Metallurgical Institute of India [*A publication*]
Trans Mining Geol Met Inst India ... Transactions. Mining, Geological, and Metallurgical Institute of India [*A publication*]
Trans Min Metall Alumni Assoc ... Transactions. Mining and Metallurgical Alumni Association [*Japan*] [*A publication*]
Trans Min Metall Assoc (Kyoto) ... Transactions. Mining and Metallurgical Association (Kyoto) [*A publication*]
TRANSMO ... Transportation Model [*Military*]
Trans MO Acad Sci ... Transactions. Missouri Academy of Science [*A publication*]
Trans MO Acad Scie ... Transactions. Missouri Academy of Science [*A publication*]
TRANSMON ... Transmission   (ROG)
Trans Monumental Brass Soc ... Transactions. Monumental Brass Society [*A publication*]
TRANSMONUNIT ... Transient Monitoring Unit   (DNAB)
Trans Morris C Res Counc ... Transactions. Morris County Research Council [*A publication*]
Trans Mosc Math Soc ... Transactions. Moscow Mathematical Society [*A publication*]
Trans Moscow Math Soc ... Transactions. Moscow Mathematical Society [*A publication*]
TRANSMTG ... Transmitting
Trans Mycol Soc Jap ... Transactions. Mycological Society of Japan [*A publication*]
Trans Mycol Soc Japan ... Transactions. Mycological Society of Japan [*A publication*]
Trans Mycol Soc Jpn ... Transactions. Mycological Society of Japan [*A publication*]
Transn........ Transition [*A publication*]
Trans N Amer Wildlife Conf ... Transactions. North American Wildlife and Natural Resources Conference [*A publication*]
Trans N Am Wildl Nat Resour Conf ... Transactions. North American Wildlife and Natural Resources Conference [*A publication*]
Trans Nat Hist Northumberl Durham Newcastle Upon Tyne ... Transactions. Natural History Society of Northumberland, Durham, and Newcastle-Upon-Tyne [*A publication*]
Trans Nat Hist Soc Formosa ... Transactions. Natural History Society of Formosa [*A publication*]
Trans Nat Hist Soc Northumberl Durham Newcastle-Upon-Tyne ... Transactions. Natural History Society of Northumberland, Durham, and Newcastle-Upon-Tyne [*Later, Natural History Society of Northumbria. Transactions*] [*A publication*]
Trans Nat Hist Soc Northumbria ... Transactions. Natural History Society of Northumbria [*A publication*]
Transnational Data Rep ... Transnational Data Report [*A publication*]
Transnatl ... Transnational   (DLA)
Transnatl Data Rep ... Transnational Data Report [*A publication*]
Trans Natl Inst Sci India ... Transactions. National Institute of Sciences. India [*A publication*]
Transnat'l Rep ... Transnational Reporter [*A publication*]   (DLA)
Trans Natl Res Inst Met ... Transactions. National Research Institute for Metals [*Japan*] [*A publication*]
Trans Natl Res Inst Met (Tokyo) ... Transactions. National Research Institute for Metals (Tokyo) [*A publication*]
Trans Natl Saf Congr ... Transactions. National Safety Congress [*United States*] [*A publication*]
Trans Nat Res Inst Metals (Tokyo) ... Transactions. National Research Institute for Metals (Tokyo) [*A publication*]
Trans Nat Vac Symp ... Transactions. National Vacuum Symposium [*A publication*]
Trans Nebr Acad Sci ... Transactions. Nebraska Academy of Sciences [*A publication*]
Trans NEC Instn E Ship ... Transactions. North East Coast Institution of Engineers and Shipbuilders [*British*] [*A publication*]
Trans NE Cst Instn Engrs Shipbldrs ... Transactions. North East Coast Institution of Engineers and Shipbuilders [*British*] [*A publication*]
Trans Newbury Dist Fld Club ... Transactions. Newbury District Field Club [*A publication*]
Trans Newcomen Soc Study His Eng Technol ... Transactions. Newcomen Society for the Study of the History of Engineering and Technology [*A publication*]
Trans New Engl Obstet Gynecol Soc ... Transactions. New England Obstetrical and Gynecological Society [*United States*] [*A publication*]
Trans New Orleans Acad Ophthalmol ... Transactions. New Orleans Academy of Ophthalmology [*A publication*]
Trans News ... Transport News [*New Zealand*] [*A publication*]

Trans New York Acad Sci Ser II ... Transactions. New York Academy of Sciences. Series II [*A publication*]
Trans NJ Obstet Gynecol Soc ... Transactions. New Jersey Obstetrical and Gynecological Society [*A publication*]
Trans North Am Wildl Conf ... Transactions. North American Wildlife Conference [*A publication*]
Trans North Am Wildl Nat Res Conf ... Transactions. North American Wildlife and Natural Resources Conference [*A publication*]
Trans North Am Wildl Nat Resour Conf ... Transactions. North American Wildlife and Natural Resources Conference [*A publication*]
Trans North East Coast Inst Eng Shipbuild ... Transactions. North East Coast Institution of Engineers and Shipbuilders [*British*] [*A publication*]
Trans Northeast Sect Wildl Soc ... Transactions of the Northeast Section. Wildlife Society [*A publication*]
Trans NY Acad Sci ... Transactions. New York Academy of Sciences [*A publication*]
Trans NZ Inst Eng ... Transactions. New Zealand Institution of Engineers, Inc. [*A publication*]
Trans NZ Inst Eng CE ... Transactions. New Zealand Institution of Engineers, Incorporated. Civil Engineering Section [*A publication*]
Trans NZ Inst Eng EMCh ... Transactions. New Zealand Institution of Engineers, Incorporated. Electrical/Mechanical/Chemical Engineering Section [*A publication*]
Trans NZ Inst Eng Inc Civ Eng Sect ... Transactions. New Zealand Institution of Engineers, Incorporated. Civil Engineering Section [*A publication*]
Trans NZ Inst Eng Inc Electr Mech Chem Eng Sect ... Transactions. New Zealand Institution of Engineers, Incorporated. Electrical/Mechanical/Chemical Engineering Section [*A publication*]
Trans Ophthalmol Soc Aust ... Transactions. Ophthalmological Society of Australia [*A publication*]
Trans Ophthalmol Soc NZ ... Transactions. Ophthalmological Society of New Zealand [*A publication*]
Trans Ophthalmol Soc UK ... Transactions. Ophthalmological Societies of the United Kingdom [*A publication*]
Trans Ophthal Soc Aust ... Transactions. Ophthalmological Society of Australia [*A publication*]   (APTA)
Trans Opt Soc ... Transactions. Optical Society [*A publication*]
TRANSP ... Transparency   (AAG)
TRANSP ... Transportation
Transp........ Transporter [*A publication*]   (APTA)
Trans PA Acad Ophthalmol Otolaryngol ... Transactions. Pennsylvania Academy of Ophthalmology and Otolaryngology [*A publication*]
TRANSPAC ... Thermal Structure Monitoring Program in the Pacific [*Marine science*]   (MSC)
Trans-Pac .. Trans-Pacific [*A publication*]
TRANSPAC ... Transpacific
Trans Pac Coast Obstet Gynecol Soc ... Transactions. Pacific Coast Obstetrical and Gynecological Society [*United States*] [*A publication*]
Trans Pac Coast Oto-Ophthalmol Soc ... Transactions. Pacific Coast Oto-Ophthalmological Society [*A publication*]
Trans Pac Coast Oto-Ophthalmol Soc Annu Meet ... Transactions. Pacific Coast Oto-Ophthalmological Society. Annual Meeting [*United States*] [*A publication*]
TRANSPACMAG ... Trans-Pacific Magnetic Anomaly Study [*National Oceanic and Atmospheric Administration*]   (NOAA)
Trans Papers (L) Brit G ... Institute of British Geographers (Liverpool). Transactions and Papers [*A publication*]
Transp Aust ... Transport Australia [*A publication*]   (APTA)
Transp Commun Rev ... Transport and Communication Review [*A publication*]
Trans Peirce Soc ... Transactions. Charles S. Peirce Society [*A publication*]
Transp Eng ... Transportation Engineering [*A publication*]
Transp Eng J ASCE ... Transportation Engineering Journal. ASCE [*American Society of Civil Engineers*] [*A publication*]
Transp Engng ... Transportation Engineering [*Formerly, Traffic Engineering*] [*A publication*]
Transp Engng J Proc ASCE ... Transportation Engineering Journal. Proceedings of the American Society of Civil Engineers [*A publication*]
Transp Engr ... Transport Engineer [*A publication*]
Trans Peninsula Hortic Soc ... Transactions. Peninsula Horticultural Society [*A publication*]
Transp En J ... Transportation Engineering Journal. ASCE [*American Society of Civil Engineers*] [*A publication*]
TRANSPHIBLANT ... Transports, Amphibious Force, Atlantic Fleet [*Navy*]
TRANSPHIBPAC ... Transports, Amphibious Force, Pacific Fleet [*Navy*]
Trans Phil Inst Vic ... Transactions. Philosophical Institute of Victoria [*Australia*] [*A publication*]
Trans Philol Soc ... Transactions. Philological Society [*A publication*]
Trans Phil Soc ... Transactions. Philological Society [*A publication*]
Trans Phil Soc NSW ... Transactions. Philosophical Society of New South Wales [*Australia*] [*A publication*]
Transp His ... Transportation History [*A publication*]
Transp Hist ... Transport History [*A publication*]
TRANSPIRE ... Transpiration-Cooled Stacked Platelet Injection   (MCD)
Transp J..... Transport Journal [*A publication*]
Transp J..... Transportation Journal [*A publication*]
Transp J of Aust ... Transport Journal of Australia [*A publication*]   (APTA)

Transp Khranenie Nefti Nefteprod ... Transport i Khranenie Nefti i Nefteproduktov [*Former USSR*] [*A publication*]
transpl........ Transplant
TRANSPLAN ... Transaction Network Service Planning Model [*Telecommunications*]　(TEL)
Transplan P ... Transplantation Proceedings [*A publication*]
Transplan R ... Transplantation Reviews [*A publication*]
Transplant ... Transplantation [*A publication*]
Transplant Bull ... Transplantation Bulletin [*A publication*]
Transplant Clin Immunol ... Transplantation and Clinical Immunology [*A publication*]
Transplant Immunol Clin ... Transplantation et Immunologie Clinique [*A publication*]
Transplantn Proc ... Transplantation Proceedings [*A publication*]
Transplant Proc ... Transplantation Proceedings [*A publication*]
Transplant Proc Suppl ... Transplantation Proceedings. Supplement [*A publication*]
Transplant Rev ... Transplantation Reviews [*A publication*]
Transplant Soc Int Cong Proc ... Transplantation Society. International Congress. Proceedings [*A publication*]
Transp L J ... Transportation Law Journal [*A publication*]
Transp Manage ... Transport Management [*A publication*]
Transp-Med Vesti ... Transportno-Meditsinski Vesti [*A publication*]
Transp News ... Transport News of New Zealand [*A publication*]
Transp News Dig ... Transport News Digest [*A publication*]
Transportat ... Transportation [*A publication*]
Transportation J ... Transportation Journal [*A publication*]
Transportation Plann Tech ... Transportation Planning and Technology [*London*] [*A publication*]
Transportation Q ... Transportation Quarterly [*A publication*]
Transportation Res ... Transportation Research [*A publication*]
Transportation Res Part A ... Transportation Research. Part A. General [*A publication*]
Transportation Res Part B ... Transportation Research. Part B. Methodological [*A publication*]
Transportation Sci ... Operations Research Society of America. Transportation Science Section. Transportation Science [*A publication*]
Transport and Communications Bul Asia and Pacific ... Transport and Communications Bulletin for Asia and the Pacific [*A publication*]
Transport D ... Transport Digest [*A publication*]　(APTA)
Transport Theory Statist Phys ... Transport Theory and Statistical Physics [*A publication*]
Trans Powder Metall Assoc India ... Transactions. Powder Metallurgy Association of India [*A publication*]
Transp Plann Tech ... Transportation Planning and Technology [*A publication*]
Transp Plann Technol ... Transportation Planning and Technology [*A publication*]
Transp Plan and Technol ... Transport Planning and Technology [*A publication*]
Transp Policy Decision Making ... Transport Policy and Decision Making [*A publication*]
Transp Porous Media ... Transport in Porous Media [*A publication*]
Transp Q.... Transportation Quarterly [*A publication*]
Transp Res ... Transportation Research [*A publication*]
Transp Res Abstr ... Transportation Research Abstracts [*A publication*]
Transp Res Board Spec Rep ... Transportation Research Board. Special Report [*A publication*]
Transp Res Board Transp Res Rec ... Transportation Research Board. Transportation Research Record [*A publication*]
Transp Res News ... Transportation Research News [*A publication*]
Transp Res Part A ... Transportation Research. Part A. General [*A publication*]
Transp Res Part A Gen ... Transportation Research. Part A. General [*England*] [*A publication*]
Transp Res Part B ... Transportation Research. Part B. Methodological [*A publication*]
Transp Res Rec ... Transportation Research Record [*United States*] [*A publication*]
Transp Revs ... Transport Reviews [*A publication*]
Trans Princeton Conf Cerebrovasc Dis ... Transactions. Princeton Conference on Cerebrovascular Diseases [*A publication*]
Transp Road Res Lab (GB) TRRL Rep ... Transport and Road Research Laboratory (Great Britain). TRRL Report [*A publication*]
Trans Proc Birmingham Arch Soc ... Transactions and Proceedings. Birmingham Archaeological Society [*A publication*]
Trans Proc Bot Soc Edinb ... Transactions and Proceedings. Botanical Society of Edinburgh [*A publication*]
Trans Proc Geol Soc S Afr ... Transactions and Proceedings. Geological Society of South Africa [*A publication*]
Trans Proc Palaeontol Soc Jap ... Transactions and Proceedings. Palaeontological Society of Japan [*A publication*]
Trans Proc Palaeontol Soc Japan New Ser ... Transactions and Proceedings. Palaeontological Society of Japan. New Series [*A publication*]
Trans Proc Palaeontol Soc Jpn New Ser ... Transactions and Proceedings. Palaeontological Society of Japan. New Series [*A publication*]

Trans Proc Perthshire Soc Natur Sci ... Transactions and Proceedings. Perthshire Society of Natural Science [*A publication*]
Trans & Proc Roy Soc SA ... Transactions and Proceedings. Royal Society of South Australia [*A publication*]
Trans & Proc Roy Soc Vic ... Transactions and Proceedings. Royal Society of Victoria [*Australia*] [*A publication*]
Trans Proc R Soc South Aust ... Transactions and Proceedings. Royal Society of South Australia [*A publication*]
Trans Proc Torquay Natur Hist Soc ... Transactions and Proceedings. Torquay Natural History Society [*A publication*]
Transp Sci ... Transportation Science [*A publication*]
Transp Stroit ... Transportnoe Stroitel'stvo [*Former USSR*] [*A publication*]
Transp Theo ... Transport Theory and Statistical Physics [*A publication*]
Transp Theory Stat Phys ... Transport Theory and Statistical Physics [*A publication*]
Transp Th St P ... Transport Theory and Statistical Physics [*A publication*]
Transp Traffic ... Transport and Traffic [*A publication*]
Trans Q Am Soc Met ... Transactions Quarterly. American Society for Metals [*A publication*]
Trans Qld Phil Soc ... Transactions. Queensland Philosophical Society [*Australia*] [*A publication*]
Trans R...... Transatlantic Review [*A publication*]
Trans Radnorshire Soc ... Transactions. Radnorshire Society [*A publication*]
Trans R Can Inst ... Transactions. Royal Canadian Institute [*A publication*]
Trans R Entomol Soc Lond ... Transactions. Royal Entomological Society of London [*A publication*]
Trans R Ent Soc Lond ... Transactions. Royal Entomological Society of London [*A publication*]
Trans Res A ... Transportation Research. Part A. General [*A publication*]
Trans Res Abstr ... Transportation Research Abstracts [*A publication*]
Trans Res B ... Transportation Research. Part B. Methodological [*A publication*]
Trans R Geol Soc (Corn) ... Transactions. Royal Geological Society (Cornwall) [*A publication*]
Trans R Highl Agric Soc Scotl ... Transactions. Royal Highland and Agricultural Society of Scotland [*A publication*]
Trans Rhod Sci Assoc ... Transactions. Rhodesia Scientific Association [*A publication*]
Trans RINA ... Transactions. Royal Institutions of Naval Architects [*London*] [*A publication*]
Trans R Instn Naval Archit ... Quarterly Transactions. Royal Institution of Naval Architects [*London*] [*A publication*]
TRANSRON ... Transport Squadron [*Navy*]
Trans Royal Soc Can Sect 1 Sect 2 and Sect 3 ... Transactions. Royal Society of Canada. Section 1, Section 2, and Section 3 [*A publication*]
Trans Roy Inst Technol (Stockholm) ... Transactions. Royal Institute of Technology (Stockholm) [*A publication*]
Trans Roy Inst Tech (Stockholm) ... Transactions. Royal Institute of Technology (Stockholm) [*A publication*]
Trans Roy Soc Canada ... Transactions. Royal Society of Canada [*A publication*]
Trans Roy Soc Canada 4 ... Transactions. Royal Society of Canada. Chemical, Mathematical, and Physical Sciences. Fourth Series [*A publication*]
Trans Roy Soc NSW ... Transactions. Royal Society of New South Wales [*Australia*] [*A publication*]
Trans Roy Soc NZ Bot ... Transactions. Royal Society of New Zealand. Botany [*A publication*]
Trans Roy Soc SA ... Transactions. Royal Society of South Australia [*A publication*]
Trans Roy Soc S Aust ... Royal Society of South Australia. Transactions [*A publication*]　(APTA)
Trans Roy Soc South Africa ... Transactions. Royal Society of South Africa [*A publication*]
Trans R Sch Dent (Stockh Umea) ... Transactions. Royal Schools of Dentistry (Stockholm and Umea) [*A publication*]
Trans R Soc Arts ... Transactions. Royal Society of Arts [*A publication*]
Trans R Soc Can ... Transactions. Royal Society of Canada [*A publication*]
Trans R Soc Can Sect 3 ... Transactions. Royal Society of Canada. Section 3. Chemical, Mathematical, and Physical Sciences [*A publication*]
Trans R Soc Can Sect 4 ... Transaction. Royal Society of Canada. Section 4. Geological Sciences Including Mineralogy [*A publication*]
Trans R Soc Can Sect 5 ... Transactions. Royal Society of Canada. Section 5. Biological Sciences [*A publication*]
Trans R Soc Can Sect 1 2 3 ... Transactions. Royal Society of Canada. Section 1, Section 2, and Section 3 [*A publication*]
Trans R Soc Edinb ... Transactions. Royal Society of Edinburgh [*A publication*]
Trans R Soc Edinb Earth Sci ... Transactions. Royal Society of Edinburgh. Earth Sciences [*A publication*]
Trans R Soc Edinburgh ... Transactions. Royal Society of Edinburgh [*A publication*]
Trans R Soc Edinburgh Earth Sci ... Transactions. Royal Society of Edinburgh. Earth Sciences [*A publication*]
Trans R Soc NZ ... Transactions. Royal Society of New Zealand [*A publication*]
Trans R Soc NZ Biol Sci ... Transactions. Royal Society of New Zealand. Biological Science [*A publication*]

Trans R Soc NZ Bot ... Transactions. Royal Society of New Zealand. Botany [*A publication*]

Trans R Soc NZ Earth Sci ... Transactions. Royal Society of New Zealand. Earth Science [*A publication*]

Trans R Soc NZ Gen ... Transactions. Royal Society of New Zealand. General [*A publication*]

Trans R Soc NZ Geol ... Transactions. Royal Society of New Zealand. Geology [*A publication*]

Trans R Soc NZ Zool ... Transactions. Royal Society of New Zealand. Zoology [*A publication*]

Trans R Soc S Afr ... Transactions. Royal Society of South Africa [*A publication*]

Trans R Soc S Aust ... Transactions. Royal Society of South Australia [*A publication*]   (APTA)

Trans R Soc South Aust ... Transactions. Royal Society of South Australia [*A publication*]   (APTA)

Trans R Soc Trop Med Hyg ... Transactions. Royal Society of Tropical Medicine and Hygiene [*A publication*]

Trans Russ Inst Appl Chem ... Transactions. Russian Institute of Applied Chemistry [*A publication*]

Trans SAEST ... Transactions. SAEST [*Society for Advancement of Electrochemical Science and Technology*] [*A publication*]

Trans S Afr Inst Civ Eng ... Transactions. South African Institution of Civil Engineers [*A publication*]

Trans S Afr Inst Elec Eng ... Transactions. South African Institute of Electrical Engineers [*A publication*]

Trans S Afr Inst Electr Eng ... Transactions. South African Institute of Electrical Engineers [*A publication*]

Trans San Diego Soc Nat Hist ... Transactions. San Diego Society of Natural History [*A publication*]

TransSBA ... Transactions. Society of Biblical Archaeology [*London*] [*A publication*]   (BJA)

Trans Sci .... Transportation Science [*A publication*]

Trans Sci Soc China ... Transactions. Science Society of China [*A publication*]

Trans Sect ... Transverse Section [*Medicine*]   (AAMN)

Trans SHASE ... Transactions. Society of Heating, Air Conditioning, and Sanitary Engineers [*Japan*] [*A publication*]

Trans SHASE Japan ... Transactions. SHASE [*Society of Heating, Air Conditioning, and Sanitary Engineers*] (Japan) [*A publication*]

Trans Shikoku Entomol Soc ... Transactions. Shikoku Entomological Society [*A publication*]

Trans Shikoku Ent Soc ... Transactions. Shikoku Entomological Society [*A publication*]

Trans Shropshire Archaeol Soc ... Transactions. Shropshire Archaeological Society [*A publication*]

Trans SMPE ... Transactions. Society of Motion Picture Engineers [*A publication*]

Trans Soc Adv Electrochem Sci Technol ... Transactions. Society for Advancement of Electrochemical Science and Technology [*A publication*]

Trans Soc Bibl Arch ... Transactions. Society of Biblical Archaeology [*A publication*]

Trans Soc Br Ent ... Transactions. Society for British Entomology [*A publication*]

Trans Soc Br Entomol ... Transactions. Society for British Entomology [*A publication*]

Trans Soc Heat Air Cond Sanit Eng Jpn ... Transactions. Society of Heating, Air Conditioning, and Sanitary Engineers of Japan [*A publication*]

Trans Soc Ill Eng ... Transactions. Illuminating Engineering Society [*A publication*]

Trans Soc Instr Control Eng ... Transactions. Society of Instrument and Control Engineers [*Japan*] [*A publication*]

Trans Soc Instrum Control Eng ... Transactions. Society of Instrument and Control Engineers [*Japan*] [*A publication*]

Trans Soc Instrum & Control Engrs (Japan) ... Transactions. Society of Instrument and Control Engineers (Japan) [*A publication*]

Trans Soc Instrum Technol ... Transactions. Society of Instrument Technology [*England*] [*A publication*]

Trans Soc Min Eng AIME ... Transactions. Society of Mining Engineers. AIME [*American Institute of Mining, Metallurgical, and Petroleum Engineers*] [*A publication*]

Trans Soc Min Engrs AIME ... Transactions. Society of Mining Engineers. AIME [*American Institute of Mining, Metallurgical, and Petroleum Engineers*] [*A publication*]

Trans Soc Motion Pict Eng ... Transactions. Society of Motion Picture Engineers [*A publication*]

Trans Soc Mot Pict Eng ... Transactions. Society of Motion Picture Engineers [*A publication*]

Trans Soc NAME ... Transactions. Society of Naval Architects and Marine Engineers [*A publication*]

Trans Soc Naval Architects Mar Eng ... Transactions. Society of Naval Architects and Marine Engineers [*A publication*]

Trans Soc Occup Med ... Transactions. Society of Occupational Medicine [*A publication*]

Trans Soc Pathol Jpn ... Transactiones Societatis Pathologicae Japonicae [*Japan*] [*A publication*]

Trans Soc Pet Eng AIME ... Transactions. Society of Petroleum Engineers of AIME [*American Institute of Mining, Metallurgical, and Petroleum Engineers*] [*A publication*]

Trans Soc Rheol ... Transactions. Society of Rheology [*A publication*]

Trans Southwest Fed Geol Soc ... Transactions. Southwestern Federation of Geological Societies [*A publication*]

Trans SPWLA Annu Log Symp ... Transactions. SPWLA [*Society of Professional Well Log Analysts*] Annual Logging Symposium [*A publication*]

Trans S Staffordshire Archaeol Hist Soc ... Transactions. South Staffordshire Archaeological and Historical Society [*A publication*]

Trans S Staffs Archaeol Hist Soc ... Transactions. South Staffordshire Archaeological and Historical Society [*A publication*]

Trans S Staffs Arch Hist Soc ... Transactions. South Staffordshire Archaeological and Historical Society [*A publication*]

Trans State Inst Appl Chem ... Transactions. State Institute of Applied Chemistry [*A publication*]

Trans St John's Hosp Dermatol Soc ... Transactions. St. John's Hospital Dermatological Society [*A publication*]

Trans Stud Coll Physicians Phila ... Transactions and Studies. College of Physicians of Philadelphia [*A publication*]

Trans Suffolk Natur Soc ... Transactions. Suffolk Naturalists' Society [*A publication*]

Trans Symp Carl Neuberg Soc ... Carl Neuberg Society for International Scientific Relations. Transactions of the Symposium [*A publication*]

Trans Tech Sect Can Pulp Pap Assoc ... Transactions. Technical Section. Canadian Pulp and Paper Association [*A publication*]

Trans 8th Int Congr Soil Sci ... Transactions. 8th International Congress of Soil Science [*A publication*]

Trans Thoroton Soc Nottinghamshire ... Transaction. Thoroton Society of Nottinghamshire [*A publication*]

Trans Thoroton Soc Notts ... Transactions. Thoroton Society of Nottinghamshire [*A publication*]

Transtl .... Transitional   (DLA)

Trans Tokyo Univ Fish ... Transactions. Tokyo University of Fisheries [*A publication*]

Trans Tottori Soc Agric Sci ... Transactions. Tottori Society of Agricultural Sciences [*A publication*]

Trans Tottori Soc Agr Sci ... Transactions. Tottori Society of Agricultural Science [*A publication*]

Trans Tuberc Soc Scotl ... Transactions. Tuberculosis Society of Scotland [*A publication*]

Trans Udgivet Dan Ing ... Transactions. Udgivet af Dansk Ingenioeren [*Denmark*] [*A publication*]

Trans Univ Cent Desert Stud (Jodhpur India) ... Transactions. University Centre of Desert Studies (Jodhpur, India) [*A publication*]

Trans Utah Acad Sci ... Transactions. Utah Academy of Sciences [*A publication*]

TRANSV ... Transvaal [*South Africa*]   (ROG)

TRANSV ... Transverse   (AAG)

Transvaal Agric J ... Transvaal Agricultural Journal [*A publication*]

Transvaal Mus Bull ... Transvaal Museum. Bulletin [*A publication*]

Transvaal Mus Mem ... Transvaal Museum. Memoirs [*A publication*]

Transvaal Mus Monogr ... Transvaal Museum. Monograph [*A publication*]

Transvaal Mus Rep ... Transvaal Museum. Report [*A publication*]

Transvaal Nat Conserv Div Annu Rep ... Transvaal Nature Conservation Division. Annual Report [*A publication*]

Trans Vac Symp ... Transactions. Vacuum Symposium [*A publication*]

Trans Wagner Free Inst Sci Philadelphia ... Transactions. Wagner Free Institute of Science of Philadelphia [*A publication*]

Trans West Sect Am Urol Assoc ... Transactions. Western Section of the American Urological Association [*A publication*]

Trans West Surg Ass ... Transactions. Western Surgical Association [*A publication*]

Trans Wis Acad Sci ... Transactions. Wisconsin Academy of Sciences, Arts, and Letters [*A publication*]

Trans Wis Acad Sci Arts Lett ... Transactions. Wisconsin Academy of Sciences, Arts, and Letters [*A publication*]

Trans Wisc Acad Sci ... Transactions. Wisconsin Academy of Sciences, Arts, and Letters [*A publication*]

Trans & Wit ... Transvaal and Witswatersrand Reports [*A publication*]   (DLA)

Trans Woolhope Naturalists ... Transactions. Woolhope Naturalists' Field Club [*A publication*]

Trans Woolhope Natur Fld Club ... Transactions. Woolhope Naturalists' Field Club [*Herefordshire*] [*A publication*]

Trans Worc Arch Soc ... Transactions. Worcestershire Archaeological Society [*A publication*]

Trans Worc Arc Soc ... Transactions. Worcestershire Archaeological Society [*A publication*]

Trans Worcestershire Archaeol Soc 3 Ser ... Transactions. Worcestershire Archaeological Society. Series 3 [*A publication*]

Trans Worcs Arch Soc ... Transaction. Worcestershire Archaeological Society [*A publication*]

Trans Worcs Arc Soc ... Transactions. Worcestershire Archaeological Society [*A publication*]

Trans World Energy Conf ... Transactions. World Energy Conference [*A publication*]

Transylvania J Med ... Transylvania Journal of Medicine [*A publication*]

Trans Zimbabwe Sci Assoc ... Transactions. Zimbabwe Scientific Association [*A publication*]

Trans Zimb Sci Assoc ... Transactions. Zimbabwe Scientific Association [*A publication*]

Trans Zool Soc Lond ... Transactions. Zoological Society of London [*A publication*]
Tran USA .. Transportation USA [*A publication*]
TRAP........ Tactical Recovery of Aircraft and Personnel
TRAP........ Tandem Recursive Algorithm Process   (HGAA)
TRAP........ Tank, Racks, Adapters, Pylons [*Military*]
TRAP........ Tape Recorder Action Plan [*Committee*] [*NASA/Air Force*]
TRAP........ Tartrate Resistant Acid Phosphatase [*An enzyme*]
TRAP........ Terminal Radiation Airborne Program [*Air Force*]
TRAP........ Tetra-N-Propylammonium Perruthenate [*Organic chemistry*]
TRAP........ Thioguanine, Rubidomycin [*Daunorubicin*], Cytosine arabinoside [*ara-C*], Prednisone [*Antineoplastic drug regimen*]
TRAP........ Thrombospondin-Related Anonymous Protein [*Biochemistry*]
TRAP........ Time Response Approximation
TRAP........ Tracker Analysis Program   (MCD)
TRAP........ Transmission Reliability Analysis Program
TRAP........ Trapezoid   (MSA)
TRAP........ Treasury Relief Aid Project
TRAP........ Tyrosine-Rich Amelogenin Polypeptide [*Biochemistry of dental enamel*]
TRAPAC ... Fleet Training Command, Pacific [*Navy*]
TRAPATT ... Trapped Plasma Avalanche Triggered Transit [*Bell Laboratories*]
TRAPCON ... Transportable RADAR Approach Control [*Army*]
Tr A Ph A .. Transactions and Proceedings. American Philological Association [*A publication*]
TRAPP ...... Training and Retention as Permanent Party [*Army*]   (AABC)
Tr App .... Transcript Appeals [*New York*] [*1867-68*] [*A publication*]   (DLA)
TRAPS ...... Tactical Rapid Access Processing System   (KSC)
TRAPS ...... Training Requirements and Planning Subsystem [*Military*]
TRAPS ...... Transportable Reliable Acoustic Path SONAR   (MCD)
TRAPS ...... Troop Reaction and Posture Sequence   (MCD)
TRAPV ...... Trap on Overflow BIT [*Binary Digit*] Set [*Data processing*]
TRAQA ..... Traffic Quarterly [*A publication*]
TRAR........ Total Radiation Absolute Radiometer [*NASA*]
TRARON .. Training Squadron
TRAS........ Training Requirements Analysis System [*Army*]
TRASA ...... Traktory i Sel'khozmashiny [*A publication*]
TRASANA ... TRADOC [*Training and Doctrine Command*] Systems Analysis Activity [*White Sands Missile Range, NM*] [*Army*]
TRASANA ... TRADOC [*Training and Doctrine Command*] Systems Analysis Agency [*Army*]
Trasfus Sangue ... Trasfusione del Sangue [*A publication*]
TRASH...... Trash Remover and Satellite Hauler [*Proposed device to remove orbiting space debris*]
TRASH...... Tsunami Research Advisory System of Hawaii
TRASOP ... Tax Reduction Act Stock Ownership Plan
Trasp Pubbl ... Trasporti Pubblici [*A publication*]
TRASSO ... TRADOC Systems Staff Officer [*or Office*] [*Army*]
TRASTA ... Training Station [*Navy*]
TRAT........ Torpedo Readiness Assistance Team
TRAT........ Trade Aptitude Test [*Vocational guidance test*]
TRAT........ Travelers REIT [*Boston, MA*] [*NASDAQ symbol*]   (NQ)
TRAT........ Triacetylhexahydrotriazine [*Organic chemistry*]
TRATE..... Trace Test and Evaluation
TRATEL ... Tracking through Telemetry [*Air Force*]
Tratt.......... Trattenuto [*Music*]
Tratt Met ... Trattamenti dei Metalli [*A publication*]
TRAU .... Tanganyika Railway African Union
TrAu .... Triangulum Australe [*Constellation*]
TRAV .... Training Availability [*Navy*]   (NVT)
TRAV .... Travancore [*India*]   (ROG)
Trav........... Travel [*A publication*]
Trav........... Travel/Holiday [*A publication*]
Trav........... Travelling [*A publication*]
TRAV .... Travels [*or Traveler*]
TRAV .... Traverse   (AABC)
Travailleur Can ... Travailleur Canadien [*A publication*]
Trav Alphabet ... Travail de l'Alphabetisation [*A publication*]
Trav Assoc H Capitant ... Travaux. Association Henri Capitant [*A publication*]
Travaux Sem Anal Convexe ... Travaux. Seminaire d'Analyse Convexe [*A publication*]
TRAVC...... Travail Canada [*Labour Canada - LC*]
Trav Cent Rech Etudes Oceanogr ... Travaux. Centre de Recherches et d'Etudes Oceanographiques [*A publication*]
TRAVCHAR ... Cost Travel Chargeable
Trav-Cochin ... Indian Law Reports, Kerala Series [*A publication*]   (DLA)
Trav Com Int Etude Bauxites Alumine Alum ... Travaux. Comite International pour l'Etude des Bauxites, de l'Alumine, et de l'Aluminium [*A publication*]
Trav Com Int Etude Bauxites Oxydes Hydroxydes Alum ... Travaux. Comite International pour l'Etude des Bauxites, des Oxydes, et des Hydroxydes d'Aluminium [*A publication*]
TRAVEL ... Transportable Vertical Erectable Launcher
Trav/Holiday ... Travail/Holiday [*A publication*]
Trav Hum .. Travail Humain [*A publication*]
Trav Humain ... Travail Humain [*A publication*]

Trav Inst Franc Et And ... Travaux. Institut Francais d'Etudes Andines [*A publication*]
Trav Inst Franc Et Andines ... Travaux. Institut Francais d'Etudes Andines [*A publication*]
Trav Inst Geol Anthropol Prehist Fac Sci Poitiers ... Travaux. Institut de Geologie et d'Anthropologie Prehistorique. Faculte des Sciences de Poitiers [*A publication*]
Trav Inst L ... Travaux. Institut de Linguistique de Lund [*A publication*]
Trav Inst Med Super ... Travaux. Institut Medical Superieur [*A publication*]
Trav Inst Rech Sahar ... Travaux. Institut de Recherches Sahariennes [*A publication*]
Trav Inst Sci Cherifien Fac Sci Rabat Ser Gen ... Travaux. Institut Scientifique Cherifien et Faculte des Sciences de Rabat. Serie Generale [*A publication*]
Trav Inst Sci Cherifien Fac Sci Ser Sci Phys ... Travaux. Institut Scientifique Cherifien et Faculte des Sciences. Serie: Sciences Physiques [*A publication*]
Trav Inst Sci Cherifien Fac Sci Ser Zool ... Travaux. Institut Scientifique Cherifien et Faculte des Sciences. Serie Zoologie [*A publication*]
Trav Inst Sci Cherifien Ser Bot ... Travaux. Institut Scientifique Cherifien. Serie Botanique [*A publication*]
Trav Inst Sci Cherifien Ser Bot Biol Veg ... Travaux. Institut Scientifique Cherifien. Serie Botanique et Biologique Vegetale [*A publication*]
Trav Inst Sci Cherifien Ser Geol Geogr Phys ... Travaux. Institut Scientifique Cherifien. Serie Geologie et Geographie Physique [*A publication*]
Trav Inst Sci Cherifien Ser Sci Phys ... Travaux. Institut Scientifique Cherifien. Serie Sciences Physiques [*A publication*]
Trav Inst Sci Cherifien Ser Zool ... Travaux. Institut Scientifique Cherifien. Serie Zoologique [*A publication*]
Trav Inst Speleo "Emile Racovitza" ... Travaux. Institut de Speleologie "Emile Racovitza" [*A publication*]
TRAVIS..... Traffic Retrieval Analysis Validation and Information System [*Telecommunications*]   (TEL)
Travl .... [*The*] Travelers Corp. [*Associated Press abbreviation*]   (APAG)
Trav Lab Anthropol Prehist Ethnol Pays Mediterr Occid ... Travaux. Laboratoire d'Anthropologie de Prehistoire et d'Ethnologie des Pays de la Mediterranee Occidentale [*A publication*]
Trav Lab For Toulouse ... Travaux. Laboratoire Forestier de Toulouse [*A publication*]
Trav Lab For Toulouse Tome I Artic Divers ... Travaux. Laboratoire Forestier de Toulouse. Tome I. Articles Divers [*A publication*]
Trav Lab For Toulouse Tome II Etud Dendrol ... Travaux. Laboratoire Forestier de Toulouse. Tome II. Etudes Dendrologiques [*A publication*]
Trav Lab For Toulouse Tome V Geogr For Monde ... Travaux. Laboratoire Forestier de Toulouse. Tome V. Geographie Forestier du Monde [*A publication*]
Trav Lab For Univ Toulouse ... Travaux. Laboratoire Forestier. Universite de Toulouse [*A publication*]
Trav Lab Geol Ec Norm Super (Paris) ... Travaux. Laboratoire de Geologie. Ecole Normale Superieure (Paris) [*A publication*]
Trav Lab Geol Fac Sci Grenoble ... Travaux. Laboratoire de Geologie. Faculte des Sciences de Grenoble [*A publication*]
Trav Lab Geol Fac Sci Grenoble Mem ... Travaux. Laboratoire de Geologie. Faculte des Sciences de Grenoble. Memoires [*A publication*]
Trav Lab Geol Fac Sci Lyon ... Travaux. Laboratoire de Geologie. Faculte des Sciences de Lyon [*A publication*]
Trav Lab Geol Fac Sci Univ Bordeaux ... Travaux. Laboratoire de Geologie. Faculte des Sciences. Universite de Bordeaux [*A publication*]
Trav Lab Geol Hist Paleontol Cent St Charles Univ Provence ... Travaux. Laboratoire de Geologie Historique et de Paleontologie. Centre Saint Charles. Universite de Provence [*A publication*]
Trav Lab Hydrobiol Piscic Univ Grenoble ... Travaux. Laboratoire d'Hydrobiologie et de Pisciculture. Universite de Grenoble [*A publication*]
Trav Lab Hydrogeol Geochim Fac Sci Univ Bordeaux ... Travaux. Laboratoire d'Hydrogeologie Geochimie. Faculte des Sciences Universite de Bordeaux [*A publication*]
Trav Lab Matiere Med Pharm Galenique Fac Pharm (Paris) ... Travaux. Laboratoires de Matiere Medicale et de Pharmacie Galenique. Faculte de Pharmacie (Paris) [*A publication*]
Trav Lab Microbiol Fac Pharm Nancy ... Travaux. Laboratoire de Microbiologie. Faculte de Pharmacie de Nancy [*A publication*]
Travler .... [*The*] Travelers Corp. [*Associated Press abbreviation*]   (APAG)
Trav LJ ...... Travancore Law Journal [*India*] [*A publication*]   (DLA)
Trav LR ...... Travancore Law Reports [*India*] [*A publication*]   (DLA)
Trav LT ...... Travancore Law Times [*India*] [*A publication*]   (DLA)
Travl Wkly ... Travel Weekly [*A publication*]
Trav Met Deform ... Travail des Metaux par Deformation [*A publication*]
Trav et Meth ... Travail et Methodes [*A publication*]
Trav Mus Hist Nat "Gr Antipa" ... Travaux. Museum d'Histoire Naturelle "Grigore Antipa" [*A publication*]
Trav Mus Hist Nat "Grigore Antipa" ... Travaux. Museum d'Histoire Naturelle "Grigore Antipa" [*A publication*]

TRAVNEC ... Subject Travel Was Necessary at This Time and Time Consumed in Administrative Channels Prevented Written Orders Being Issue

Trav Quebec ... Travail Quebec [*A publication*]

Trav Sect Scient Tech Inst Fr Pondichery ... Travaux. Section Scientifique et Technique. Institut Francais de Pondichery [*A publication*]

Trav Sect Sci Tech Inst Franc Pondichery ... Travaux. Section Scientifique et Technique. Institut Francais de Pondichery [*A publication*]

Trav Sect Sci Tech Inst Fr Pondichery ... Travaux. Section Scientifique et Technique. Institut Francais de Pondichery [*A publication*]

Trav Secur ... Travail et Securite [*A publication*]

Trav Sta Rech Groenendaal ... Travaux. Station de Recherches des Eaux et Forets. Groenendaal-Hoeilaart [*A publication*]

Trav-Syndicalisme Bibl ... Travail-Syndicalisme. Bibliographie [*A publication*]

Trav & Tw L of N ... Travers and Twiss on Law of Nations [*A publication*] (DLA)

TRAWL ..... Tape Read and Write Library

T Ray .... [*Sir Thomas*] Raymond's English King's Bench Reports [*83 English Reprint*] [*1660-84*] [*A publication*] (DLA)

Tray Lat Max ... Trayner's Latin Maxims and Phrases, Etc. [*A publication*] (DLA)

Tray Leg Max ... Trayner's Latin Maxims and Phrases [*A publication*] (ILCA)

T Raym ...... [*Sir Thomas*] Raymond's English King's Bench Reports [*83 English Reprint*] [*A publication*] (DLA)

T Raym (Eng) ... [*Sir Thomas*] Raymond's English King's Bench Reports [*83 English Reprint*] [*A publication*] (DLA)

TRB .... Signature for Washington correspondent's column in "New Republic" magazine [*Said to have been derived by reversing the initialism for Brooklyn Rapid Transit: BRT*]

TRB .... Tactical Review Board [*Military*] (CAAL)

TRB .... Tapered Roller Bearing

TRB .... Tax Review Board [*Canada*]

TRB .... Technical Reference Branch [*Department of Transportation*] (IID)

TRB .... Technical Review Board [*NASA*] (KSC)

TRB .... Tennyson Research Bulletin [*A publication*]

TRB .... Test Requirement Bulletins [*NASA*] (KSC)

TRB .... Test Review Board [*NASA*] (NASA)

TRB .... Tom Robinson Band

TRB .... Topical Reference Books [*A publication*]

TRB .... Torpedo Recovery Boat

TRB .... Trabaccolo [*Small coasting vessel of the Adriatic*] (DS)

TRB .... Transportation Research Board (EA)

TRB .... Trapped Radiation Belt

TRB .... Treble

TRB .... [*The*] Tribune Co. [*NYSE symbol*] (SPSG)

Trb .... Tribunus [*Tribune*] [*Latin*]

TRB .... Trombone [*Music*]

TRB .... Troop Basis (MUGU)

TRB .... Turbo [*Colombia*] [*Airport symbol*] (OAG)

TRB .... United States Army TRADOC, Engineering School Library and Learning Resource Center, Fort Belvoir, VA [*OCLC symbol*] (OCLC)

TRBF .... Total Renal Blood Flow [*Medicine*]

TRBIDM... Trends in Biotechnology [*A publication*]

TRBK .... Trustbank Savings FSB [*NASDAQ symbol*] (NQ)

Trbl .... Tractatenblad [*A publication*]

TRBL .... Trouble (FAAC)

TRBL .... Troubleshooting (NASA)

TRBMA ..... Texas Reports on Biology and Medicine [*A publication*]

TRBN .... Trombone [*Music*]

TRBP .... Trainable Retractable Bow Propeller

TRBR .... Transportation Branch [*Navy*] (DNAB)

TRBU .... Treasury Bulletin

TRC .... [*The*] Radiochemical Centre [*British*]

TRC .... [*The*] Ranchero Club (EA)

TRC .... [*The*] Revitalization Corps (EA)

TRC .... Tanned Red Cell [*Clinical chemistry*]

TRC .... Tape Reader Calibrator

TRC .... Tape Reader Control

TRC .... Tape Record Coordinator [*Data processing*]

TRC .... Tape Relay Center (NATG)

TRC .... Taylor Ranch [*California*] [*Seismograph station code, US Geological Survey*] (SEIS)

TrC .... Tayloreed Corporation, Rochester, NY [*Library symbol*] [*Library of Congress*] (LCLS)

TRC .... Technical Repair Center [*Air Force*] (AFIT)

TRC .... Technical Research Center (MCD)

TRC .... Technical Resources Center [*Syracuse University*] [*Research center*]

TRC .... Technical Review Committee [*Environmental Protection Agency*] (GFGA)

TRC .... Technical Review Committee [*International Atomic Energy Agency*] (NRCH)

TRC .... Technology Reports Centre [*British*]

TRC .... Technology Resource Center [*Information service or system*] [*Phillipines*] (IID)

TRC .... Tejon Ranch Co. [*AMEX symbol*] (SPSG)

TRC .... Telemetry and Remote Control (IEEE)

TRC .... Telephone Relay Coupler (HGAA)

TRC .... Temperature Recording Controller

TRC .... Teryl Resources Corp. [*Vancouver Stock Exchange symbol*]

TRC .... Test Readiness Certificate (AAG)

TRC .... Textile Research Council [*British*]

TRC .... Thames Rowing Club [*British*] (DI)

TRC .... Thermal Regenerative Cracking [*Hydrocarbon pyrolysis process*]

TRC .... Thermodynamics Research Center [*College Station, TX*] [*Department of Commerce*] (GRD)

TRC .... Thoroughbred Racing Communications [*An association*] (EA)

TRC .... Thrombosis Research Center [*Temple University*] [*Research center*] (RCD)

TRC .... Tierce [*Unit of measurement*]

TRC .... Tithe Rent-Charge

TRC .... Token Ring Controller

TRC .... Topic [*Record label*] [*Great Britain*]

TRC .... Toroidal Propellant Container

TRC .... Torreon [*Mexico*] [*Airport symbol*] (OAG)

TRC .... Total Relevant Cost

TRC .... Total Residual Chlorine [*Environmental chemistry*]

TRC .... Total-Response Chromatogram

TRC .... Total Ridge Count [*Anthropology*]

TRC .... Tough Rubber-Sheathed Cable

TRC .... Toyon Research Corp.

TRC .... Tracking, RADAR-Input, and Correlation

TRC .... Trade Relations Council of the United States (EA)

TRC .... Traffic Records Committee (EA)

TRC .... Training Readiness Condition

TRC .... Transcaribbean (MCD)

TRC .... Transmission Release Code (DNAB)

TRC .... Transmit/Receive Control Unit

TRC .... Transportation Research Center [*Ohio*]

TRC .... Transverse Redundancy Check [*Data processing*] (IBMDP)

TRC .... Travelers Research Center [*Oceanography*]

TRC .... TRC Cos., Inc. [*Associated Press abbreviation*] (APAG)

trc .... Treble Crochet

TRC .... Tricon International Airlines [*Dallas, TX*] [*FAA designator*] (FAAC)

TRC .... Triumph Roadster Club (EA)

TRC .... Trona Railway Co. [*AAR code*]

TRC .... Type Requisition Code [*Military*]

TRC .... United States Army TRADOC, Fort Leavenworth Post Library, Commander, General Staff, Fort Leavenworth, KS [*OCLC symbol*] (OCLC)

TRCA .... Tricycle Racing Club of America

TRC-AS ..... Transmit/Receive Control Unit-Asynchronous Start/Stop

TRCC .... T-Carrier Restoration Control Center [*Bell System*]

TRCC .... Theodore Roosevelt Centennial Commission [*Government agency*] [*Terminated, 1959*]

TRCC .... Tripartite Research Coordination Committee (SAA)

TR8CCA .... TR8 Car Club of America (EA)

TRCCC ..... Tracking RADAR Central Control Console [*BMEWS*]

TrCda .... TransCanada Pipeline Ltd. [*Associated Press abbreviation*] (APAG)

TRCE .... Tactical Radio Communications Equipment

TRCE .... Terrace [*Classified advertising*] (ADA)

TRCE .... Thermionic Reactor Critical Experiment [*NASA*]

TRCE .... Trace

TRCE .... Trace Products [*NASDAQ symbol*] (NQ)

TRCH .... Tanned Red Cell Hemagglutination [*Immunology*] (MAE)

Trch .... Torchmark Corp. [*Associated Press abbreviation*] (APAG)

Tr Ch .... Transactions of the High Court of Chancery (Tothill's Reports) [*A publication*] (DLA)

Tr Chernomorsk Biol Stan Varna ... Trudove na Chernomorskata Biologichna Stantsiya v Varna [*A publication*]

TRCHI .... Tanned Red Cell Hemagglutination Inhibition Test [*Immunology*]

Trchmk ...... Torchmark Corp. [*Associated Press abbreviation*] (APAG)

TRCI .... Technology Research Corp. [*Clearwater, FL*] [*NASDAQ symbol*] (NQ)

TRCO .... Technical Representative of the Contracting Officer (MCD)

TRCO .... Trade and Commerce [*A publication*]

TRCO .... Transportation Research Command [*Army*] (KSC)

TRCO .... Trico Products Corp. [*NASDAQ symbol*] (NQ)

Tr Coll Physicians Phila ... Transactions and Studies. College of Physicians of Philadelphia [*A publication*]

TRCONS... Theater Rate Consolidation Data File [*Military*]

Tr Consist J ... Tristram's Consistory Judgments [*1872-90*] [*England*] [*A publication*] (DLA)

TRCP .... Tape Recorder Control Panel (MCD)

TRCR .... Tracer (MSA)

TRCR .... Tractor

TRCR .... Trail Riders of the Canadian Rockies (EA)

TRCRA ...... Tobacco Research Council. Research Paper [*A publication*]

TRCS .... Tactical Radio Communications System

TRCS .... Techniques for Determining RADAR Cross Section [*Air Force*]

TRC-SC ..... Transmit/Receive Control Unit-Synchronous Character

TRC-SF ..... Transmit/Receive Control Unit-Synchronous Framing

TRCVR ..... Transceiver (CET)

TRD .... Registry of Tissue Reactions to Drugs [*Later, DETP*] (EA)

TRD .... Target-Recognizing Domain [*Genetics*]
TRD .... Taxa Referencial Diaria [*Brazil*] (ECON)
TRD .... Technical Resource Document
TRD .... Test Requirements Document [*NASA*] (AAG)
TRD .... Thread (AAG)
TRD .... Three-Axis Rotational Control-Direct (SAA)
TRD .... Tongue-Retaining Device [*Medicine*]
TRD .... Toyota Racing Development [*Toyota Motor Corp.*]
TRD .... Transferred (ROG)
TRD .... Transmission Ratio Distortion [*Genetics*]
TRD .... Trapped Radiation Detector
TRD .... Tread
TRD .... Trivandrum [*India*] [*Seismograph station code, US Geological Survey*] (SEIS)
TRD .... Trivandrum [*India*] [*Geomagnetic observatory code*]
TRD .... Trondheim [*Norway*] [*Airport symbol*] (OAG)
TRD .... Trouble Reporting Desk [*NASA*] (KSC)
TRD .... Troudor Resources, Inc. [*Vancouver Stock Exchange symbol*]
TRD .... Try Repeating Dose [*Medicine*]
TRD .... Turbine Reduction Drive
TRD .... United States Army TRADOC, Fort Dix Post Library, Fort Dix, NJ [*OCLC symbol*] (OCLC)
TRDC .... Transport Research and Development Command [*Army*] (MCD)
TRDCBC ... Datum Collection. Tokai Regional Fisheries Research Laboratory [*A publication*]
TRDCR...... Tandem-Rocket Dual-Combustion Ramjet (MCD)
TRDE .... Transparent Rotating Disk Electrode [*Electrochemistry*]
TRDG .... Trading (DCTA)
TRDI......... Trim Die (AAG)
TRDIA....... Transmission and Distribution [*A publication*]
TRDJSDOPII ... [*The*] Reverend Doctor Jonathan Swift, Dean of Patrick's in Ireland [*Pseudonym used by Jonathan Swift*]
TRDL......... Tactical Reconnaissance Data Link (MCD)
TR & DL.... Tung Research and Development League [*Defunct*] (EA)
TRDM .... Tactical Reconnaissance Data Marking
TRDMRK .. Trademark
TRDR .... Test Readiness Design Review
TRDS........ Towards (ROG)
TRDT .... Trim and Drill Template (MCD)
TRDT .... Triple Rotating Directional Transmission [*Military*] (CAAL)
TRDTO ..... Tracking RADAR Data Takeoff
TRDx......... Texas Red-Labeled Dextran
TRDY .... Trudy Corp. [*NASDAQ symbol*] (NQ)
TRE .... Telecommunications Research Establishment [*British military*] (DMA)
TRE .... Temperature-Resistant Element (DNAB)
TRE .... Tempore Regis Edwardi [*In the Time of King Edward*] [*Latin*] (DLA)
TRE .... Terratech Resources, Inc. [*Toronto Stock Exchange symbol*]
TRE .... Theologische Realenzyklopaedie [*A publication*]
TRE .... Thyroid Hormone Response Element [*Endocrinology*]
TRE .... Thyroid-Responsive Element [*Genetics*]
TRE .... Tidal Regenerator Engine
TRE .... Timing Read Error
TRE .... Tiree Island [*Scotland*] [*Airport symbol*] (OAG)
TRE .... Total Rare Earths (NRCH)
TRE .... Total Resource Effectiveness Index [*Environmental Protection Agency*]
TRE .... Toxicity Reduction Evaluation
TRE .... Training Equipment (KSC)
TRE .... Training Readiness Evaluation (MCD)
TRE .... Training-Related Expenses [*Work Incentive Program*]
TRE .... Transient Radiation Effects
TRE .... Treasury
TRE .... Tremont Corp. [*NYSE symbol*] (SPSG)
TRE .... Trent University [*UTLAS symbol*]
TRE .... Trente [*Italy*] [*Seismograph station code, US Geological Survey*] [*Closed*] (SEIS)
TRE .... True Radiation Emittance
TRE .... Trusts and Estates [*A publication*]
TRE .... United States Army TRADOC, Fort Eustis Post Library and Translation School Library, Fort Eustis, VA [*OCLC symbol*] (OCLC)
TREA......... [*The*] Retired Enlisted Association (EA)
TREA & A ... [*The*] Real Estate Appraiser and Analyst [*Society of Real Estate Appraisers*] [*A publication*]
Tread.......... Treadway's South Carolina Constitutional Reports [*A publication*] (DLA)
Tread.......... Treadway's South Carolina Law Reports [*1812-16*] [*A publication*] (DLA)
TREAD...... Troop Recognition and Detection (MCD)
Tread Const ... Treadway's South Carolina Constitutional Reports [*A publication*] (DLA)
Treadway Const (SC) ... Treadway's South Carolina Constitutional Reports [*A publication*] (DLA)
TREAS ...... Treasurer (EY)
TREAS ...... Treasury (ROG)
Treas Dec... Treasury Decisions under Customs and Other Laws [*United States*] [*A publication*] (DLA)

Treas Dec Int Rev ... Treasury Decisions under Internal Revenue Laws [*A publication*] (DLA)
Treas Dept Cir ... Treasury Department Circular [*A publication*] (DLA)
Treas Regs ... United States Treasury Regulations [*A publication*] (DLA)
TREAT...... Transient Radiation Effects Automated Tabulation
TREAT...... Transient Reactor Test Facility
TREAT...... Treatment (AAG)
TREAT...... Trouble Report Evaluation and Analysis Tool (MCD)
Treatise Anal Chem ... Treatise on Analytical Chemistry [*A publication*]
Treatise Mater Sci Technol ... Treatise on Materials Science and Technology [*A publication*]
Treatises Sect Med Sci Pol Acad Sci ... Treatises of the Section of Medical Sciences. Polish Academy of Sciences [*A publication*]
Treat Tro.... Treatise on Trover and Conversion [*A publication*] (DLA)
TREB........ Treble (ROG)
Treballs Inst Bot Barc ... Treballs. Institut Botanic de Barcelona [*A publication*]
TREC........ Tracking RADAR Electronic Component (AFM)
TREC........ Transistor Radiation Effects Compilation [*Program*] (MCD)
TREC........ Treco [*NASDAQ symbol*] (NQ)
Tr Ecol Evo ... Trends in Ecology and Evolution [*A publication*]
TRECOM ... Transportation Research Command [*Fort Eustis, VA*] [*Army*]
TRECOM ... Transportation Research and Engineering Command (MUGU)
TRED .... TDA [*Taxpayer Delinquent Account*] Report Edit Data [*IRS*]
TRED .... Technology-Based Regional Economic Development
TRED .... Transmitting and Receiving Equipment Development (MCD)
TRED .... Treadco, Inc. [*NASDAQ symbol*] (SPSG)
Tred.......... Tredgold's Cape Colony Reports [*A publication*] (DLA)
TREDAT... Tree Crops Database
Tredgar ...... Tredegar Industries, Inc. [*Associated Press abbreviation*] (APAG)
TREDS ...... TRADOC Educational Data System
TREDS-NRI ... TRADOC [*Training and Doctrine Command*] Educational Data System - Nonresident Instruction [*Army*]
TREE........ Aspen Leaf, Inc. [*NASDAQ symbol*] (NQ)
TREE........ Transient Radiation Effects on Electronics [*Military*]
TREE........ Trustee
Tree Crops J ... Tree Crops Journal [*A publication*]
Tree Farm Proc ... Trees on Farms. Proceedings of a Seminar on Economic and Technical Aspects of Commercial Plantations. Agro-Forestry and Shelter Belts on Farms [*A publication*]
TREELS .... Time-Resolved Electron Energy-Loss Spectroscopy
Tree Plant Notes ... Tree Planters' Notes [*A publication*]
Tree Plant Notes US For Serv ... Tree Planter's Notes. United States Forest Service [*A publication*]
Tree-Ring Bull ... Tree-Ring Bulletin [*A publication*]
TREES ...... Time-Resolved Europium Excitation Spectroscopy
TREES ...... Transient Radiation Effects on Electronic Systems [*Air Force*] (MCD)
Trees Mag ... Trees Magazine [*A publication*]
Trees Nat Resour ... Trees and Natural Resources [*A publication*]
TREESS .... Tactical Reflected and Emitted Energy Suppression System
Trees S Afr ... Trees in South Africa [*A publication*]
Trees Victoria's Resour ... Trees and Victoria's Resources [*A publication*]
TREET ...... [*A*] Programming Language (CSR)
T Regswet .. Tydskrif vir Regswetenskap [*A publication*]
Trehern ...... British and Colonial Prize Cases [*A publication*] (DLA)
TREKA ...... Technical Reports. Engineering Research Institute. Kyoto University [*A publication*]
TREKZINE ... Trek Magazine [*Generic term for a publication of interest to fans of the television program "Star Trek"*]
TREL........ Transitron Electronic Corp. [*NASDAQ symbol*] (NQ)
Tr Elem Med ... Trace Elements in Medicine [*A publication*]
TREM........ Tape Reader Emulator Module
TREM........ TRADOC Research Center [*Monterey, CA*] [*Army*] (GRD)
Trem.......... Tremaine's Pleas of the Crown [*England*] [*A publication*] (DLA)
trem........... Tremolo [*Tremulous*] [*Music*] (WGA)
TREM........ Tropical Rainfall Explorer Mission (MCD)
Tremnt ...... Tremont Corp. [*Associated Press abbreviation*] (APAG)
Trem PC .... Tremaine's Pleas of the Crown [*England*] [*A publication*] (DLA)
TREN .... Trenwick Group, Inc. [*NASDAQ symbol*] (NQ)
tren............ Tris(aminoethyl)amine [*Organic chemistry*]
TRENA...... Tokyo Toritsu Eisei Kenkyusho Kenkyu Nempo [*A publication*]
TREND ..... Trade-Offs for Lifting Reentry Vehicle Evaluation and Nominal Design
TREND ..... Transportation Research News [*A publication*]
TREND ..... Tropical Environmental Data
Trend Card ... Trends in Cardiovascular Medicine [*A publication*]
Trend Eng ... Trends in Engineering [*A publication*]
Trend Eng Univ Wash ... Trends in Engineering. University of Washington [*A publication*]
Trend Prognosticke Inf ... Trend Prognosticke Informace [*A publication*]
Trends Anal Chem ... Trends in Analytical Chemistry [*A publication*]
Trends Analyt Chem ... Trends in Analytical Chemistry [*A publication*]
Trends Auton Pharmacol ... Trends in Autonomic Pharmacology [*A publication*]
Trends Biochem Sci ... Trends in Biochemical Sciences [*A publication*]

Trends Biochem Sci (Pers Ed) ... Trends in Biochemical Sciences (Personal Edition) [*Netherlands*] [*A publication*]
Trends Biochem Sci (Ref Ed) ... Trends in Biochemical Sciences (Reference Edition) [*Netherlands*] [*A publication*]
Trends Biot ... Trends in Biotechnology [*A publication*]
Trends Biotechnol ... Trends in Biotechnology [*A publication*]
Trends Ed .. Trends in Education [*A publication*]
Trends Educ ... Trends in Education [*A publication*]
Trends Endocrinol Metab ... Trends in Endocrinology and Metabolism [*A publication*]
Trends Fluoresc ... Trends in Fluorescence [*A publication*]
Trends Gen ... Trends in Genetics [*A publication*]
Trends Genet ... Trends in Genetics [*A publication*]
Trends Haematol ... Trends in Haematology [*A publication*]
Trends Neurosci ... Trends in Neurosciences [*Netherlands*] [*A publication*]
Trends Perspect Parasitol ... Trends and Perspectives in Parasitology [*A publication*]
Trends and Perspect Signal Process ... Trends and Perspectives in Signal Processing [*A publication*]
Trends Pharmacol Sci ... Trends in Pharmacological Sciences [*A publication*]
Trends Tech Contemp Dent Lab ... Trends and Techniques in the Contemporary Dental Laboratory [*A publication*]
TR (Eng) .... Term Reports [*99-101 English Reprint*] [*A publication*]   (DLA)
TRENS ..... Transcutaneous Random Electrical Nerve Stimulator [*Medicine*]
Trent LJ ..... Trent Law Journal [*A publication*]
Tr Entom Soc London ... Transactions. Entomological Society of London [*A publication*]
Trep .... Treponema [*Microbiology*]
Tr Eq .... Fonblanque's Treatise of Equity [*A publication*]   (DLA)
TRER .... Transient Radiation Effect on Radiation   (SAA)
TRES .... Tayside Rehabilitation Engineering Services [*British*]   (IRUK)
TRES .... Terminal Retrieval and Enquiry Services [*Department of Employment*] [*British*]
TRES .... Thermally Regenerative Electrochemical System [*Power source*]
TRES .... Time-Resolved Emission Spectra
TRES .... Trestle   (WGA)
TRESI .... Target Resolution Extraction of Statistical Invariances
TRESNET ... Trent Interlibrary Loan and Communication Network [*Canada*] [*Information service or system*]   (IID)
TRESNET ... Trent Resource Sharing Network [*Ontario Library Service Trent*] [*Richmond Hill, ON*] [*Telecommunications*]   (TSSD)
Tr and Est ... Trusts and Estates [*A publication*]
T Rev .... Translation Review [*A publication*]
TREVI .... Terrorisme, Radicalisme, Extremisme, Violence Internationale [*International anti-terrorist group*] [*Belgium*]
Trev Tax Suc ... Trevor's Taxes on Succession [*4th ed.*] [*1881*] [*A publication*]   (DLA)
TREX .... Intrex Financial Services, Inc. [*NASDAQ symbol*]   (NQ)
Trex .... Tyrannosaurus Rex [*A dinosaur*]
TRF .... T-Cell Replacing Factor [*Biochemistry*]
TRF .... Tank Range-Finder
TRF .... Tariff
TRF .... Technical Reference File
TRF .... Technical Replacement Factor
TRF .... Tele-Radio Systems Ltd. [*Toronto Stock Exchange symbol*]
TRF .... Terminal Renal Failure [*Medicine*]
TRF .... Test Tube and Ring-Shaped Forms [*AIDS cytology*]
TRF .... Thermal Radiation at Microwave Frequencies
TRF .... Thymus Cell Replacing Factor [*Immunology*]
TRF .... Thyrotrophin-Releasing Factor [*Later, TRH*] [*Endocrinology*]
TRF .... Tragicorum Romanorum Fragmenta [*A publication*]   (OCD)
TRF .... Transducer Repair Facility
TRF .... Transfer   (AABC)
TRF .... Transferrin [*Also, T, TF*] [*Biochemistry*]
TRF .... Transportation Research Forum   (EA)
TRF .... Transportation Research Foundation
TRF .... Tuna Research Foundation   (EA)
TRF .... Tuned Radio Frequency
TRF .... Turf Research Foundation [*Defunct*]   (EA)
TRF .... United States Army TRADOC, Fort McClellan, Fort McClellan, AL [*OCLC symbol*]   (OCLC)
TRFA .... Triple Revolving Fund Account   (AABC)
TRFA .... Trustees for Alaska. Newsletter [*A publication*]
TRFAD ...... Thomas Roderick Fraser and Andrew Dewar [*Pseudonym*]
TRFB .... Tariff Board [*Canada*]
TRFC .... Tanya Roberts Fan Club   (EA)
TRFC .... Tex Ritter Fan Club   (EA)
TRFC .... Traffic   (MSA)
TRFC .... Tristan Rogers Fan Club   (EA)
TRFCA ...... Tea Research Foundation (Central Africa) [*Malawi*]   (EAIO)
TRFCS .... Temperature Rate Flight Control System
Trfd .... Transferred [*Army*]
TRFI .... Trans Financial Bancorp, Inc. [*Bowling Green, KY*] [*NASDAQ symbol*]   (NQ)
Tr (Fifteenth) Internat Cong Hyg and Demog ... Transactions. Fifteenth International Congress on Hygiene and Demography [*A publication*]
TR/FLRES ... Transferred to Fleet Reserve   (DNAB)

TRFS .... Trace Fuselage Station   (MCD)
TRG .... [*The*] Record Group [*Funded by N. V. Philips*]
TRG .... T-Cell Rearranging Gene [*Genetics*]
TRG .... Tactical Reconnaissance Group
TRG .... Tauranga [*New Zealand*] [*Airport symbol*]   (OAG)
TRG .... Technical Research Group, Inc.   (MCD)
TRG .... Telecommunications Research Group [*Culver City, CA*] [*Telecommunications*]   (TSSD)
TRG .... Tertiary Research Group [*British*]
TRG .... Track-Rich Grains[*s*] [*Cosmic-ray path in meteorites*]
TRG .... Trailing   (AAG)
TRG .... Training
T/R & G ..... Transmit, Receive, and Guard   (MSA)
TRG .... [*The*] Triangle Corp. [*AMEX symbol*]   (SPSG)
TRG .... Trilogy Resource Corp. [*Toronto Stock Exchange symbol*]
TRG .... Triton Research Group   (EA)
TRG .... Trudeau, R. G., Bloomfield Hills MI [*STAC*]
TRG .... Tuned Rotor Gyro   (MCD)
TRG .... United States Army TRADOC, Fort Benning Post and Infantry School Library, Fort Benning, GA [*OCLC symbol*]   (OCLC)
TRGA .... Trust Co. of Georgia [*NASDAQ symbol*]   (NQ)
TRGC .... Theta Rho Girls' Club   (EA)
TRGEE2 .... Trends in Genetics [*A publication*]
Tr Geol Bulg Ser Geokhm Mineral Petrogr ... Trudove Vurkhu Geologiyata na Bulgariya. Seriya Geokhimaya Mineralogiya i Petrografiya [*A publication*]
Tr Geol Bulg Ser Inzh Geol Khidrogeol ... Trudove Vurkhu Geologiyata na Bulgariya. Seriya Inzhenerna Geologiya i Khidrogeologiya [*A publication*]
Tr Geol Bulg Ser Paleonto ... Trudove Vurkhu Geologiyata na Bulgariya. Seriya Paleontologiya [*A publication*]
Tr Geol Zavod Soc Repub Makedonija ... Trudovei na Geoloskiot Zavod na Socijalisticka Republika Makedonija [*A publication*]
TrgGpRM ... Training Group, Royal Marines [*British*]
TRGH .... Trough [*Freight*]
TRGL .... Toreador Royalty Corp. [*NASDAQ symbol*]   (NQ)
TRGLA ...... Triangle [*English Edition*] [*A publication*]
TrGlasgUOrS ... Transactions. Glasgow University Oriental Society [*Hertford, England*] [*A publication*]
TRGLB ...... Triangle [*A publication*]
TRGP .... Tactical Reconnaissance Group [*Air Force*]
TrGP .... Transcontinental Gas Pipe Line Corp. [*Associated Press abbreviation*]   (APAG)
TRGT .... Target   (AAG)
TRH .... Technical Reference Handbook
TRH .... Test Requirements Handbook   (MUGU)
TRH .... Their Royal Highnesses
TRH .... Thyrotrophin-Releasing Hormone [*Formerly, TRF*] [*Endocrinology*]
TRH .... Transatlantic Holdings [*NYSE symbol*]   (SPSG)
TRH .... Truss Head [*Engineering*]
TRH .... United States Army TRADOC, Fort Benjamin Harrison Library System, Fort Benjamin Harrison, IN [*OCLC symbol*]   (OCLC)
TRHADS ... Topical Reviews in Haematology [*A publication*]
TRHAZCON ... Training Hazardous Condition   (MCD)
Tr & H Pr .. Troubat and Haly's Pennsylvania Practice [*A publication*]   (DLA)
Tr & H Prec Ind ... Train and Heard's Precedents of Indictment [*A publication*]   (DLA)
TRH-R .... Thyrotrophin-Releasing Hormone Receptor [*Endocrinology*]
TRHS .... Transactions. Royal Historical Society [*A publication*]
TRHUA ..... Travail Humain [*A publication*]
TRI .... Bristol, TN [*Location identifier*] [*FAA*]   (FAAL)
TRI .... [*The*] Refractories Institute   (EA)
TRI .... Tactical Reconnaissance/Intelligence [*Air Force*]   (AFM)
TRI .... Technical Report Instruction   (AAG)
TRI .... Technical Research Institute [*Japan*]
TRI .... Telecomputer Research, Inc. [*Bala Cynwyd, PA*] [*Information service or system*] [*Telecommunications*]   (TSSD)
TRI .... Telemanagement Resources International, Inc.   (TSSD)
TRI .... Test Requirement Identification   (DNAB)
TRI .... Tetrazolium Reduction Inhibition   (MAE)
TRI .... Textile Research Institute   (EA)
TRI .... Time-Reversal Invariance [*Physics*]
TRI .... Tin Research Institute   (EA)
TRI .... Tire Retreading Institute   (EA)
TRI .... Torsion Reaction Integrating
TRI .... Total Response Index [*Psychology*]
TRI .... Toxic Chemical Release Inventory [*National Library of Medicine*] [*Information service or system*]   (CRD)
TRI .... Toxic Release Inventory [*Environmental Protection Agency*]
TRI .... Toxics Release Inventory [*Environmental Protection Agency*]
TRI .... Transaction Routing Index
TRI .... Translation Research Institute   (EA)
TR-I .... Translations Register - Index   (MCD)
TRI .... Transpacific Resources, Inc. [*Toronto Stock Exchange symbol*]
TRI .... Transponder Receiver Isolation
TRI .... Transportation Research Institute [*Oregon State University*] [*Research center*]   (RCD)

TRI............ Transportation Research Institute [*Carnegie-Mellon University*]
TRI............. Tri-City Airport [*Tennessee*] [*Airport symbol*]   (OAG)
TRI............ Tri-College Library, Moorhead, MN [*OCLC symbol*]   (OCLC)
TRI............ Tri-State Airlines, Inc. [*White Lake, NY*] [*FAA designator*]   (FAAC)
TRI............. Triangle Industries, Inc. [*NYSE symbol*]   (SPSG)
Tri............ Triangulation
Tri .... Triangulum [*Constellation*]
TRI........... Triassic [*Period, era, or system*] [*Geology*]
Tri .... Tribuna [*A publication*]
TRI............. Trichloroethylene [*Anesthesiology*]
TRI............ Tricycle   (AAG)
TRI............ Trieste [*Grotta Gigante*] [*Italy*] [*Seismograph station code, US Geological Survey*]   (SEIS)
TRI............. Triode   (AAG)
TRI............ Tropical Research Institute [*Smithsonian Institution*]
TRI............ Trucking Research Institute [*Research center*]   (RCD)
TRI............ Tuboreticular Inclusions [*Hematology*]
TRIA......... Target Radiant Intensity, Aerobee   (SAA)
TRIA......... Telemetry Range Instrumentation Aircraft
TRIA......... Temperature Removable Instrument Assembly [*Nuclear energy*]   (NRCH)
TRIA......... Triacontanol [*Plant growth regulator*]
TRIA......... Triangle Industries, Inc. [*NASDAQ symbol*]   (NQ)
Tria .... Triangulum [*Constellation*]
TRIAC....... Test Resources Improvement Advisory Council [*Military*]
TRIAC....... Triiodothyroacetic Acid [*Endocrinology*]
TRIAC....... Triode Alternating Current Semiconductor Switch
TRIACP..... [*The*] Triangle Corp. [*Associated Press abbreviation*]   (APAG)
TRIAD...... Target Resolving Information Augmentation Device   (MCD)
TRIAL....... Technique to Retrieve Information from Abstracts of Literature [*Data processing*]
Trial Advoc Q ... Trial Advocate Quarterly [*A publication*]   (DLA)
Trial Diplomacy J ... Trial Diplomacy Journal [*A publication*]
Trial Dpl J ... Trial Diplomacy Journal [*A publication*]
Trial Law Forum ... Trial Lawyers Forum [*A publication*]   (DLA)
Trial Law G ... Trial Lawyer's Guide [*A publication*]
Trial Law Guide ... Trial Lawyer's Guide [*A publication*]
Trial Law Q ... Trial Lawyers Quarterly [*A publication*]
TRIB......... Tire Retread Information Bureau   (EA)
TRIB......... Transfer Rate of Information BITs [*Binary Digits*] [*Dial telephone network*] [*American National Standards Institute*]
TRIB......... Tri-Basin Resources Ltd. [*NASDAQ symbol*]   (NQ)
TRIB......... Tribal
TRIB......... Tribulation   (DSUE)
Trib .... Tribunal
Trib .... Tribunale [*Ordinary Court of First Instance*] [*Italian*]   (DLA)
TRIB......... Tribunus [*Tribune*] [*Latin*]   (OCD)
trib.............. Tribus [*Tribe*] [*Latin*]
TRIB......... Tributary
TRIB......... Tribute   (ADA)
Trib CEBEDEAU ... Tribune. CEBEDEAU [*Centre Belge d'Etude et de Documentation des Eaux et de l'Air*] [*A publication*]
TRIBE .... Teaching and Research in Bicultural Education [*Indian organization in Maine*]
TriBeCa ..... Triangle Below Canal Street [*Artists' colony in New York City*] [*See also NoHo, SoHo, SoSo*]
Trib Farm (Curitiba) ... Tribuna Farmaceutica (Curitiba) [*A publication*]
Tri Bish...... Trial of the Seven Bishops [*A publication*]   (DLA)
Trib Mus.... Tribune Musical [*A publication*]
Trib Odontol ... Tribuna Odontologica [*A publication*]
Tribol Int ... Tribology International [*A publication*]
Tribol Lubrificazione ... Tribologia e Lubrificazione [*A publication*]
Tribologia & Lubr ... Tribologia e Lubrificazione [*A publication*]
Tribology ... Tribology International [*A publication*]
Tribology Int ... Tribology International [*A publication*]
TRIB POT ... Tribunicia Potestas [*Latin*]   (OCD)
Tribuna Postale ... Tribuna Postale e delle Telecomunicazioni [*A publication*]
Tribune ...... [*The*] Tribune Co. [*Associated Press abbreviation*]   (APAG)
TRIC......... Trachoma-Inclusion Conjunctivitis [*Ophthalmology*]
TRIC......... Tracking RADAR Input and Correlation   (MSA)
TRIC......... Transaction Identification Code [*Military*]   (AFIT)
TRIC......... Transit Research Information Center [*Department of Transportation*] [*Washington, DC*]   (GRD)
TRIC......... Transition Radiation and Ionization Calorimeter   (SSD)
TRIC......... Tri-Chem, Inc. [*NASDAQ symbol*]   (NQ)
TRIC......... Tricks for Research in Cancer
TRIC......... Triclinic [*Crystallography*]
TRICAP..... Triple Capability [*Army*]
TRICC....... Tariff Rules of the Interstate Commerce Commission
TRICCSMA ... Trident Command and Control Systems Maintenance Facility   (DNAB)
TRICE .... Transistorized Realtime Incremental Computer
Trich .... Trichomonas [*A protozoan*] [*Medicine*]
Trich .... Trichoptera [*Entomology*]
TRICI .... Trichinopoli Cigar   (DSUE)
TRICINE.... Tris(hydroxymethyl)methylglycine [*Biochemical analysis*]
TRICL .... Triclinic
TriCn .... Tri-Continental Corp. [*Associated Press abbreviation*]   (APAG)

TriCon........ Tri-Continental Corp. [*Associated Press abbreviation*]   (APAG)
TRICS .... Threat Reactive Integrated Combat System
TRICS .... Trajectory Incremental Correction System   (MCD)
TRID......... Track Identity
TRID......... Triduum [*Three Days*] [*Latin*]   (ADA)
TRIDAC.... Three-Dimensional Analog Computer [*British*]   (MCD)
TRIDENT ... South Atlantic Cooperative Investigation Phase [*Marine science*]   (MSC)
TRIDEX .... Tridex Corp. [*Associated Press abbreviation*]   (APAG)
TRIDO ...... Table Ronde Internationale pour le Developpement de l'Orientation [*International Round Table for the Advancement of Counselling - IRTAC*]   (EAIO)
TRIDOP.... Tridoppler
Tri E of Cov ... Trial of the Earl of Coventry [*A publication*]   (DLA)
Trier Archiv ... Trierisches Archiv [*A publication*]
TRI-FED ... Triathlon Federation/USA   (EA)
TRIFED/USA ... Triathlon Federation/USA [*Later, TRI-FED*]   (EA)
TRIFLATE ... Trifluoromethanesulfonate [*Organic chemistry*]
TRIFLIC ... Trifluoromethanesulfonic [*Organic chemistry*]
triFMA ...... Time-Resolved Immunofluorometric Assay [*Clinical chemistry*]
TRIG......... Triangulation   (AABC)
TRIG......... Trigger   (AAG)
trig.............. Triglycerides [*Clinical chemistry*]
TRIG......... Trigonal [*Crystallography*]
TRIG......... Trigonometry
TRIGA....... Training Reactor, Isotopes General Atomic [*Nuclear energy*]
TRIGA....... Traitement Industrial des Gadoues [*French company*]
TRIGAT .... Third Generation Antitank [*Army*]
TRIGLYME ... Triethylene Glycol Dimethyl Ether [*Organic chemistry*]
TRIGON ... Trigonometry   (ROG)
TRII .... Travelers Realty Income Investors [*Boston, MA*] [*NASDAQ symbol*]   (NQ)
TRIL......... Tailored Requirements Items List   (MCD)
TRIL......... Trilogy Ltd. [*NASDAQ symbol*]   (NQ)
TRIM......... Inertia Dynamics Corp. [*Chandler, AZ*] [*NASDAQ symbol*]   (NQ)
TRIM........ Tailored Reliable Integrated Modular
TRIM........ Tailored Retrieval and Information Management
TRIM........ Target Radiant Intensity Measurement   (MCD)
TRIM........ Targets, Receivers, Impacts, and Methods
TRIM........ Tax Reform Immediately   (EA)
TRIM........ Tax Reform Information Materials
TRIM........ Technical Requirements Identification Matrix   (MCD)
TRIM........ Technique for Report and Index Management [*Information service or system*] [*No longer available*]   (IID)
TRIM........ Tele-Research Item Movement, Inc. [*Commercial firm*]   (WDMC)
TRIM........ Test Rules for Inventory Management
TRIM........ Thin Region Integral Method
TRIM........ Throw Away/Repair Implications on Maintenance
TRIM........ Timely Responsive Integrated Multiuse System   (MCD)
TRIM........ Trails, Roads, and Interdiction Missions [*or Multisensor*] [*Navy*]
TRIM........ Training Relation and Instruction Mission [*Military*] [*Vietnam, France, United States*]
TRIM........ Training Requirements and Information Management System [*Navy*]
TRIM........ Transfer Income Model [*Department of Health and Human Services*]   (GFGA)
TRIM........ Transformation of Imagery [*Data processing*] [*NASA*]
TRI-M .... Tri-M Music Honor Society [*Acronym is based on former name, Modern Music Masters Society*]   (EA)
TRIM........ Trimmer [*Mining engineering*]
Trimas........ TriMas Corp. [*Associated Press abbreviation*]   (APAG)
Trim Econ .. Trimestre Economico [*A publication*]
Trimes Econ ... Trimestre Economico [*A publication*]
TRIMET ... Trimethylolethane [*Organic chemistry*]
TRIMIS..... Tri-Service Medical Information Systems [*Military*]
TRIMM..... Triple Missile Mount   (MCD)
TRIMMS .. Telecom Canada Remote Interface Monitoring and Management System
TRIMMS .. Total Refinement and Integration of Maintenance Management Systems [*Army*]
Trim Pol..... Trimestre Politico [*A publication*]
TRIMS ...... Trade-Related Investment Measures [*International finance*]   (ECON)
TRIMS ...... Training Requirements and Information Management System   (MCD)
TRIMS ...... Transportation Integrated Management System [*Air Force*]
TRIN .... Trans-Industries, Inc. [*NASDAQ symbol*]   (NQ)
TRIN .... Trans International Airlines
Trin .... Trinidad
TRIN .... Trinity
Trin .... Trinity Term [*British*] [*Legal term*]   (DLA)
TRINCO.... Trincomalee [*Sri Lanka port city*]   (DSUE)
Tr Indiana Med Soc ... Transactions. Indiana State Medical Society [*A publication*]
TRI Newsl ... Textile Research Institute. Newletter [*A publication*]
Trinidad LR ... Trinidad Law Reports [*A publication*]   (DLA)

Trinidad Tobago Min Petrol Mines Mon Bull ... Trinidad and Tobago. Ministry of Petroleum and Mines. Monthly Bulletin [*A publication*]
Trinity J ..... Trinity Journal [*A publication*]
Trinity Sem R ... Trinity Seminary Review [*A publication*]
Trinkwasser-Verord ... Trinkwasser-Verordnung [*A publication*]
Trinova .... Trinova Corp. [*Associated Press abbreviation*]   (APAG)
Tr Inst Khig Okhr Tr Prof Zabol ... Trudove na Instituta po Khigiena. Okhrana na Truda i Profesionalni Zabolyavaniya [*A publication*]
Trin Tob For ... Trinidad and Tobago Forester [*A publication*]
Trint T .... Trinity Term [*British*] [*Legal term*]   (DLA)
Trinty .... Trinity Industries, Inc. [*Associated Press abbreviation*]   (APAG)
TRIOS .... Thermionic Reactor for Installed Oceanic Service   (KSC)
Trip .... All India Reporter, Tripura [*A publication*]   (DLA)
TRIP .... [*The*] Road Information Program   (EA)
TRIP .... Tartar Reliability Improvement Plan [*Military*]
TRIP .... Technical Reports Indexing Project   (KSC)
TRIP .... Terrier/Tartar Reliability Improvement Program   (SAA)
TRIP .... Test Requirement Implementation Plan   (CAAL)
TRIP .... Thunderstorm Research International Project [*Meteorology*]
TRIP .... Transformation and Identification Program [*Commercial & Industrial Development Bureau*] [*Software package*]   (NCC)
TRIP .... Transformation-Induced Plasticity [*Steel*]
Tri per P ..... Trials per Pais [*A publication*]   (DLA)
TRIP .... Triplicate   (AABC)
Trip .... Tripoli
Trip .... Tripolitania [*Libya*]   (BJA)
TRIPER ..... Trident Planned Equipment Replacement   (DNAB)
TRIPI .... Tactical Reconnaissance Information Processing and Interpretation   (SAA)
Tripl .... Triplicate   (WGA)
TRipLH ..... Lauderdale County Hospital, Ripley, TN [*Library symbol*] [*Library of Congress*]   (LCLS)
TRIPLTEE ... True Temperature Tunnel [*Acronym pronounced, "Triple T"*]
TRIPOD .... Transit Injector Polaris Derived   (AAG)
TRIPOLD ... Transit Injector Polaris Derived
Tripp .... Tripp's Reports [*5, 6 Dakota*] [*A publication*]   (DLA)
TRIPREC ... Triplet Recall [*Neuropsychology test*]
TRIPS .... Transformation-Induced Plasticity (Steel)
TRIPS .... Transportation Planning Suite [*MVA Systematica*] [*Software package*]   (NCC)
TRIPS .... Triplets [*Slang*]   (DSUE)
TriQ .... Tri-Quarterly [*A publication*]
Tri-Quar .... Tri-Quarterly [*A publication*]
TriQuart .... Tri-Quarterly [*A publication*]
TRIREFFAC ... Trident Refit Facility   (DNAB)
TRIS .... Target Radiant Spectral Intensity Measurements from a Spin-Stabilized Vehicle   (SAA)
TRIS .... Tracking RADAR Instrumentation Ship   (SAA)
TRIS .... Transmit-Receive Image System   (DNAB)
TRIS .... Transportation Research Information Services [*National Academy of Sciences*] [*Washington, DC*] [*Bibliographic database*]
Tris .... Tris(2,3-dibromopropyl)phosphate [*Also, TDBP, TDBPP, Tris-BP*] [*Flame retardant, mutagen*]
TRIS .... Tris(hydroxymethyl)aminomethane [*Also, THAM*] [*Biochemical analysis*]
TrIs .... Trito-Isaiah   (BJA)
TRISAFE .. Triple Redundancy Incorporating Self-Adaptive Failure Exclusion   (MCD)
TRISAT ..... Target Recognition through Integral Spectrum Analysis Techniques   (MCD)
Tris-BP ...... Tris(2,3-dibromopropyl)phosphate [*Also, TDBP, TDBPP, Tris*] [*Flame retardant, mutagen*]
TRISECT .. Total Reconnaissance Intelligence System Evaluation and Comparison Technique   (MCD)
TRISNET ... Transportation Research Information Services Network [*Department of Transportation*] [*Library network*]
Tris Pr Pr ... Tristram's Probate Practice [*25th ed.*] [*1978*] [*A publication*]   (DLA)
TRISS .... Tactical Reconnaissance Intelligence Support Squadron
Trist .... Supplement to 4 Swabey and Tristram's Probate and Divorce Reports [*England*] [*A publication*]   (DLA)
TRIST .... Traveling Image Storage Tube   (MCD)
Trist .... Tristram's Consistory Judgments [*England*] [*A publication*]   (DLA)
Tri State Med J (Greensburo NC) ... Tri-State Medical Journal (Greensburo, North Carolina) [*A publication*]
Tri State Med J (Shreveport LA) ... Tri-State Medical Journal (Shreveport, Louisiana) [*A publication*]
Tristram ..... Tristram's Consistory Judgments [*1872-90*] [*A publication*]   (DLA)
Tristram ..... Tristram's Probate Practice [*25th ed.*] [*1978*] [*A publication*]   (DLA)
Tristram ..... Tristram's Supplement to 4 Swabey and Tristram [*A publication*]   (DLA)
TRISYLL .. Trisyllable   (ROG)
TRIT .... Triiodothyronine [*Endocrinology*]   (MAE)

TRIT .... Tritura [*Triturate*] [*Pharmacy*]
TRITAC ... DIFAR Triangular Tactic   (NVT)
TRITAC ... Tri-Service Tactical Communications System [*DoD*]
TRITAC ... Triservice Tactical Switch
TRITC .... Tetramethyl Rhodamine Isothiocyanate [*Organic chemistry*]
TritEng ...... Triton Energy Corp. [*Associated Press abbreviation*]   (APAG)
TRITRAFAC ... Trident Training Facility   (DNAB)
TRIUMF ... Tri-University-Meson Facility [*Nuclear research facility at the University of British Columbia*]
TRIUN ...... Department of Trusteeship and Information from Non-Self-Governing Territories of the United Nations
TRIX .... Total Rate Imaging with X-Rays
TRIYA ...... Trade and Industry [*A publication*]
TRJ .... Tarija [*Bolivia*] [*Seismograph station code, US Geological Survey*]   (SEIS)
TRJ .... Thermocouple Reference Junction
TRJ .... Towards Racial Justice [*British*]
TRJ .... United States Army TRADOC, Fort Jackson, Fort Jackson, SC [*OCLC symbol*]   (OCLC)
Tr Japan Path Soc ... Transactions. Japanese Pathological Society [*A publication*]
Tr Judge J ... Trial Judges' Journal [*A publication*]   (DLA)
TRJWD ..... Transactions. JWRI [*Japanese Welding Research Institute*] [*A publication*]
TRK .... Roche Products Ltd. [*Great Britain*] [*Research code symbol*]
TRK .... Tank Range-Finder Kit
TRK .... Tarakan [*Indonesia*] [*Airport symbol*]   (OAG)
TRK .... Track   (AAG)
TRK .... Transketolase [*An enzyme*]   (MAE)
TRK .... Truck   (AAG)
TRK .... Truckee, CA [*Location identifier*] [*FAA*]   (FAAL)
TRK .... Trunk   (AAG)
TRK .... United States Army TRADOC, Fort Knox, Library Service Center, RSL Section, Fort Knox, KY [*OCLC symbol*]   (OCLC)
TRKA .... Trak Auto Corp. [*NASDAQ symbol*]   (NQ)
Tr Kansas Acad Sc ... Transactions. Kansas Academy of Science [*A publication*]
TRKD .... Tracked
TRKDR ...... Truck-Drawn
TRKG .... Tracking   (AAG)
TrKH .... Die Transkriptionen des Hieronymus in Seinem Kommentarwerken [*A publication*]   (BJA)
TRKHD ..... Truck Head
TRKMTD ... Truck-Mounted   (AABC)
TRKR .... Tracker
TRKUA ...... Technology Reports. Kansai University [*A publication*]
TRKWHL ... Trick Wheel
TRL .... Tariff Reform League [*British*]   (ROG)
TRL .... Terrell, TX [*Location identifier*] [*FAA*]   (FAAL)
TRL .... Test Readiness List [*NASA*]   (NASA)
TRL .... Thermodynamics Research Laboratory [*National Institute of Standards and Technology*]   (MCD)
TRL .... Time Recovery Loop [*Navy Navigation Satellite System*]   (DNAB)
TRL .... Tool Room Lathe
TRL .... Trading Law [*British*]
TRL .... Trail   (MCD)
TRL .... Training Research Laboratory [*Army Research Institute for the Behavioral and Social Sciences*]   (RDA)
TRL .... Transistor Resistor Logic
trl .... Translator [*MARC relator code*] [*Library of Congress*]   (LCCP)
TrL .... Transmitted Light [*Microscopy*]
TRL .... Transuranium Research Laboratory [*AEC*]
TRL .... Trax Petroleums [*Vancouver Stock Exchange symbol*]
TRL .... Trial   (ROG)
TRL .... Trillo [*Trill*] [*Music*]   (ROG)
TRL .... Trunk Register Link [*Telecommunications*]   (TEL)
TRL .... United States Department of Transportation, Library, Washington, DC [*OCLC symbol*]   (OCLC)
TRLA .... Trans Louisiana Gas [*NASDAQ symbol*]   (NQ)
Trla .... Triola [*Record label*] [*Finland*]
TRLA .... Truck Renting and Leasing Association   (EA)
Tr Law Guide ... Trial Lawyer's Guide [*A publication*]
Tr Law Q ... Trial Lawyers Quarterly [*A publication*]
TRLB .... Temporarily Replaced by Lighted Buoy Showing Same Characteristic [*Maps and charts*]
TRLFSW ... Tactical Range Landing Force Support Weapon
TRLGA ...... Translog [*A publication*]
TRLP .... Transport Landplane [*Navy*]
TRLR .... Trailer
Tr LR .... Trinidad Law Reports [*A publication*]   (DLA)
TRLS .... Thousand Trails, Inc. [*NASDAQ symbol*]   (NQ)
TRLSC .... Time-Resolved Liquid Scintillation Counting [*Analytical procedure*]
TRLU .... TISEO RADAR Logic Unit [*Air Force*]   (MCD)
TRLY .... Trolley
TRM .... Task Response Module [*Office furniture*]
TRM .... Tay River Petroleum [*Vancouver Stock Exchange symbol*]
TRM .... TCW/DW Term Trust 2002 [*NYSE symbol*]   (SPSG)
TRM .... Telecommunications Regulatory Monitor [*A publication*]

TRM .... Terminal Response Monitor
TRM .... Test Request Message [*Data processing*]
TRM .... Test Requirements Manual
TRM .... Test Responsibility Matrix   (MCD)
TRM .... Theater Rates Model [*Military*]
TRM .... Thermal, CA [*Location identifier*] [*FAA*]   (FAAL)
TRM .... Thermal Remanent Magnetization [*Geophysics*]   (IEEE)
TRM .... Thermal Resistance Measurement
TRM .... Thermoremanence
TRM .... Thermoremanent Magnetism [*or Magnetization*]
TRM .... Thickness Readout Module
TRM .... Time Ratio Modulation
TRM .... Time Release Mechanism [*Martin-Baker seat system*] [*Aviation*]   (NG)
TRM .... Topics in Health Record Management [*A publication*]
TRM .... Totally Reflective Mirror
Tr M........... Traditional Music [*A publication*]
TRM .... TRADOC Resources Management   (MCD)
TRM .... TRADOC [*Training and Doctrine Command*] Review of Manpower
TRM .... Trial Run Model   (SAA)
TRM .... Turner [*Maine*] [*Seismograph station code, US Geological Survey*]   (SEIS)
TRM .... United States Army TRADOC, Fort Monroe Post Library and Headquarters Technical Library, Fort Monroe, VA [*OCLC symbol*]   (OCLC)
TRMAP..... Theater Rate Mapping Data File [*Military*]
TRMC .... Time-Resolved Microwave Conductivity [*Physical chemistry*]
TRMCA...... Transition Metal Chemistry [*New York*] [*A publication*]
TRMD....... Trimmed
TRME........ Theater Readiness Monitoring Equipment   (MCD)
TRMEA...... Trattamenti dei Metalli [*A publication*]
Tr Med and Phys Soc Bombay ... Transactions. Medical and Physical Society of Bombay [*A publication*]
TRMF........ Test Report Management Forms   (MCD)
TRMF........ Theater Readiness Monitoring Facility [*Missile testing*]
TRMF........ Theodore Roethke Memorial Foundation   (EA)
TRMG .... Tread Rubber Manufacturers Group   (EA)
TRMG .... Trimming
TRMI........ Tubular Rivet and Machine Institute   (EA)
Tr Minniya Nauchnoizsled Proekto Konstr Inst ... Trudove na Minniya Nauchnoizsledovatelski i Proektno Konstruktorski Institut [*A publication*]
TRMK .... Trustmark Corp. [*NASDAQ symbol*]   (SPSG)
TRML........ Target Reference Material List [*Air Force*]
TRML........ Terminal   (AFM)
TRML........ Tropical Research Medical Laboratory [*Army*]
TRMM ...... TRM Copy Centers [*NASDAQ symbol*]   (SPSG)
TRMM ...... Tropical Rainfall Measuring Mission [*Proposed satellite*]
TrMMx ..... Transportacion Maritima Mexicana [*Associated Press abbreviation*]   (APAG)
Tr Morsk Biol Stn Stalin ... Trudove na Morskata Biologichna Stantsiya v Stalin [*A publication*]
Tr Mosk Tekhnol Inst Pishch Promsti ... Trudy. Moskovskii Tekhnologicheskii Institut Pishchevoi Promyshlennosti [*A publication*]
TRMPDU ... University of Maryland. Sea Grant Program. Technical Report [*A publication*]
TRMR .... Trimmer [*Mining engineering*]
TRMS........ Technical Requirements Management System
TRMS........ Test Resource Management System [*TECOM*]   (RDA)
TRMT........ Terminate   (FAAC)
TRMT........ Treatment   (AFM)
TRMW ...... Triangle Microwave, Inc. [*NASDAQ symbol*]   (NQ)
TRN........... OCLC [*Online Computer Library Center*] Training Symbol, Columbus, OH [*OCLC symbol*]   (OCLC)
TRN........... Technical Research Note   (IEEE)
TRN........... Tectoreticular Neuron [*Neurology*]
TRN........... Temporary Record Number
TRN........... Teriton Resources Ltd. [*Vancouver Stock Exchange symbol*]
TRN........... Thomson Regional Newspapers [*The Thomson Corp.*] [*Publishing*]
TRN........... Three-Axis Rotational Control-Normal   (SAA)
TRN........... Trade Name   (MSA)
TRN........... Train   (FAAC)
TRN........... Transfer   (DEN)
TRN........... Transformation Research Network [*Canada*] [*Research center*]   (RCD)
TRN........... Transmit   (BUR)
TRN........... Trinidad [*Trinidad-Tobago*] [*Seismograph station code, US Geological Survey*]   (SEIS)
TRN........... Trinity Industries, Inc. [*NYSE symbol*]   (SPSG)
TRN........... Trunnion   (NASA)
TRN........... Turin [*Italy*] [*Airport symbol*]   (OAG)
tRNA......... Ribonucleic Acid, Transfer [*Replaces sRNA*] [*Biochemistry, genetics*]
TRNA .... Topolino Register of North America   (EA)
TrnatH....... Transatlantic Holdings [*Associated Press abbreviation*]   (APAG)

Tr Nauchnoizsled Inst Cherna Metal ... Trudove na Nauchnoizsledovatelskiya Institut po Cherna Metallurgiya [*A publication*]
Tr Nauchnoizsled Inst Epidemio Mikrobiol ... Trudove na Nauchnoizsledovatelskiya Instituta po Epidemiologiya i Mikrobiologiya [*A publication*]
Tr Nauchnoizsled Inst Farm ... Trudove na Nauchnoizsledovatelskiya Instituta po Farmatsiya [*A publication*]
Tr Nauchnoizsled Inst Okhr Tr Prof Zabol ... Trudove na Nauchnoizsledovatelskiya Instituta po Okhrana na Truda i Profesionalnite Zabolyavaniya [*A publication*]
Tr Nauchnoizsled Inst Stroit Mater (Sofia) ... Trudove na Nauchnoizsledovatelskiya Instituta po Stroitelni Materiali (Sofia) [*A publication*]
Tr Nauchnoizsled Inst Tekst Promst (Sofia) ... Trudove na Nauchnoizsledovatelskiya Instituta po Tekstilna Promishlenost (Sofia) [*A publication*]
Tr Nauchnoizsled Inst Vodosnabdyavane Kanaliz Sanit Tekh ... Trudove na Nauchnoizsledovatelskiya Institut po Vodosnabdyavane. Kanalizatsiya i Sanitarna Tekhnika [*Bulgaria*] [*A publication*]
Tr Nauchnoizsled Khim Farm Inst ... Trudove na Nauchnoizsledovatelskiya Khimiko-Farmatsevtichen Institut [*A publication*]
Tr Nauchnoizsled Proektokonstr Tekhnol Inst Tekst Promst ... Trudove na Nauchnoizsledovatelskiya. Proektokonstruktorski i Tekhnologicheski Institut po Tekstilna Promishlenost [*A publication*]
TRNBKL ... Turnbuckle [*Aerospace*]   (AAG)
TRNCAP ... Training Capability [*Military*]
TRN CRD ... Turn Coordination   (MSA)
TRND .... Turned   (MSA)
TRNE .... Trainee   (AABC)
Tr New York Acad Sc ... Transactions. New York Academy of Sciences [*A publication*]
TRNF......... Theologische Rundschau. Neue Folge [*A publication*]
TRNFR...... Transfer   (KSC)
TRNG .... Training
TRNGA ..... Traffic Engineering [*United States*] [*A publication*]
TRNGL...... Triangle   (MSA)
TrNGL........ Trident NGL, Inc. [*Associated Press abbreviation*]   (APAG)
TRNGR ...... Turning Gear
TRNGRS... Training Readiness Squadron
TRNI .... Trans-Industries, Inc. [*NASDAQ symbol*]   (NQ)
TRNJA .... Transportation Journal [*A publication*]
TRNO........ Terrano Corp. [*NASDAQ symbol*]   (NQ)
T & RNP.... Transportation and Recruiting Naval Personnel [*Budget appropriation title*]
TRNPS ...... Transpose   (MSA)
TRNR .... Touche Remnant Natural Resources [*Investment fund*] [*British*]
TRNR .... Trainer   (AAG)
TRNS........ Terrain-Referenced Navigation System [*Navy*]
TRNS........ Transition   (AABC)
TRNS........ Transmation, Inc. [*NASDAQ symbol*]   (NQ)
Trnsc......... Transco Energy Co. [*Associated Press abbreviation*]   (APAG)
TRNSLX ... Trans-Lux Corp. [*Associated Press abbreviation*]   (APAG)
Trnsm........ Transamerica Corp. [*Associated Press abbreviation*]   (APAG)
TRNSMT .. Transmitter
TRNSN....... Transition   (MSA)
TRNSP ...... Transport [*or Transportation*]   (AFM)
TRNSPF.... Transportation Flight [*Military*]
TRNSPLF .. Transportation Liaison Flight [*Military*]
TRNSPN ... Transportation   (KSC)
TRNSPOPS ... Transportation Operations Squadron
TRNSPR ... Transporter   (KSC)
TRNSPS... Transportation Squadron
TrnsRty...... Transcontinental Realty Investors [*Associated Press abbreviation*]   (APAG)
TrnsTec...... TransTechnology Corp. [*Associated Press abbreviation*]   (APAG)
TRNT .... TransNet Corp. [*NASDAQ symbol*]   (NQ)
TRNTBL ... Turntable   (MSA)
TR (NY).... Caines' Term Reports [*New York*] [*A publication*]   (DLA)
TRNZ .... Trinzic Corp. [*NASDAQ symbol*]   (SPSG)
TRNZN .... Tranzonic Cos. [*Associated Press abbreviation*]   (APAG)
TRO .... Taree [*Australia*] [*Airport symbol*]   (OAG)
TRO .... Tarron Industry [*Vancouver Stock Exchange symbol*]
TRO .... Tax Reduction Option
TRO .... Technical Records Office [*or Officer*] [*British*]
TRO .... Technical Reviewing Office   (AFM)
TRO .... Temporary Restraining Order
TRO .... Terminal Release Order [*Military*]   (AFIT)
TRO .... Test Requirements Outline
TRO .... Transportation Officer
TRO .... Trico Industries, Inc. [*NYSE symbol*]   (SPSG)
Tro .... Troades [*of Euripides*] [*Classical studies*]   (OCD)
Tro .... Troilus and Cressida [*Shakespearean work*]
TRO .... Tromsoe [*Norway*] [*Geomagnetic observatory code*]
TRO .... Tromsoe [*Norway*] [*Seismograph station code, US Geological Survey*]   (SEIS)
TRO .... Tropical [*Broadcasting antenna*]

TRO.......... Truck Route Order [*Army*] (AABC)
TRO.......... United States Army TRADOC, Fort Sill Post Library, Fort Sill, OK [*OCLC symbol*] (OCLC)
TROA........ [*The*] Retired Officers Association (EA)
TROANO ... [*Don Juan*] De Tro y Ortolano [*Acronym identifies manuscript discovered in library of Don Juan De Tro y Ortolano in 1866*]
TROB........ Twenty-First Century Robotics [*NASDAQ symbol*] (NQ)
TROC........ Tritium Removal with Organic Compound [*Nuclear energy*]
TROC........ Trocadero [*London*] (DSUE)
TROC........ Trochiscus [*Lozenge*] [*Pharmacy*] (ROG)
TROC........ Trouble Reporting Operations Center [*Federal Telecommunications System*] (GFGA)
TROCA..... Tangible Reinforcement Operant Conditioning Audiometry
TROCH..... Trochiscus [*Lozenge*] [*Pharmacy*]
TRODI...... Touchdown Rate of Descent Indicator [*Aviation*]
TROEA..... Tekko Rodo Eisei [*Japan*] [*A publication*]
TROF........ Trough [*Meteorology*] (FAAC)
TROL........ Tapeless Rotorless On-Line Cryptographic Equipment (NATG)
Trol........... Troland [*Unit of light intensity at the retina*]
TROLAMINE ... Triethanolamine [*Organic chemistry*] [*USAN*]
TROLL...... [*A*] Programming Language [*1966*] (CSR)
TRom........ Tribuna Romaniei [*A publication*]
TROM....... Trombone
TROMB ... Tromba [*Trumpet*] [*Music*] (ROG)
TROMB ... Trombone
TROMEX ... Tropical Oceanographic and Meteorological Experiment [*National Science Foundation*]
TROMP .... Trompette [*Trumpets*] [*Music*]
Tromso Mus Skr ... Tromsoe Museum. Skrifter [*A publication*]
TRON........ [*The*] Real-Time Operating System Nucleus [*Data processing*] (PCM)
TRON........ Trion, Inc. [*NASDAQ symbol*] (NQ)
TROO....... Transponder On-Off
TROP .... Tropical
Trop .... Tropical Agriculture [*A publication*]
TROP .... Tropopause [*Meteorology*] (FAAC)
Trop Abstr ... Tropical Abstracts [*A publication*]
TROPAG... Tropical Agriculture [*Royal Tropical Institute*] [*Bibliographic database*] [*Netherlands*]
Trop Agr .... Tropical Agriculture [*A publication*]
Trop Agr (Ceylon) ... Tropical Agriculturist (Ceylon) [*A publication*]
Trop Agric ... Tropical Agriculture [*A publication*]
Trop Agric (Colombo) ... Tropical Agriculturist (Colombo) [*A publication*]
Trop Agri (Ceylon) ... Tropical Agriculturist (Ceylon) [*A publication*]
Trop Agric Res Ser ... Tropical Agriculture Research Series [*A publication*]
Trop Agric Res Ser (Japan) ... Tropical Agriculture Research Series (Japan) [*A publication*]
Trop Agricst Mag Ceylon Agric Soc ... Tropical Agriculturist and Magazine. Ceylon Agricultural Society [*A publication*]
Trop Agri (Trinidad) ... Tropical Agriculturist (Trinidad) [*A publication*]
Trop Agron Tech Memo Aust CSIRO Div Trop Crops Pastures ... Australia. Commonwealth Scientific and Industrial Research Organisation. Division of Tropical Crops and Pastures. Tropical Agronomy. Technical Memorandum [*A publication*] (APTA)
Trop Anim Health Prod ... Tropical Animal Health and Production [*A publication*]
Trop Anim Prod ... Tropical Animal Production [*Dominican Republic*] [*A publication*]
TROPARC ... Center for Tropical and Subtropical Architecture Planning and Construction [*University of Florida*] [*Research center*] (RCD)
TROPB...... Tropenlandwirt [*A publication*]
Trop Build Res Notes Div Build Res CSIRO ... Tropical Building Research Notes. Division of Building Research. Commonwealth Scientific and Industrial Research Organisation [*A publication*] (APTA)
Trop Dent J ... Tropical Dental Journal [*A publication*]
Trop Dis Bull ... Tropical Diseases Bulletin [*A publication*]
Trop Doct... Tropical Doctor [*A publication*]
Trop Ecol ... Tropical Ecology [*A publication*]
Tropenlandwirt (Germany FR) ... Tropenlandwirtschaft (Germany, Federal Republic) [*A publication*]
Tropenmed P ... Tropenmedizin und Parasitologie [*A publication*]
Tropenmed Parasitol ... Tropenmedizin und Parasitologie [*A publication*]
TROPEX ... Tropical Experiment [*Proposed by BOMEX*]
Trop For Notes ... Tropical Forest Notes [*A publication*]
Trop Gastroenterol ... Tropical Gastroenterology [*A publication*]
Trop Geogr Med ... Tropical and Geographical Medicine [*A publication*]
Trop Geo Me ... Tropical and Geographical Medicine [*A publication*]
Trop Grain Legume Bull ... Tropical Grain Legume Bulletin [*A publication*]
Trop Grassl ... Tropical Grasslands [*A publication*]
Trop Grasslands ... Tropical Grasslands [*A publication*]
Trop Grasslds ... Tropical Grasslands [*A publication*] (APTA)
Trophoblast Res ... Trophoblast Research [*A publication*]
Tropical Ag ... Tropical Agriculturist [*A publication*]
TROPICS ... Tour Operators Integrated Computer System [*Airline ticket system*]
TROPM .... Tropical Man [*Leiden*] [*A publication*]
Trop Man... Tropical Man [*Leiden*] [*A publication*]

TROPMED ... Regional Project for Tropical Medicine and Public Health [*SEAMEO*] [*Research center*] [*Thailand*] (IRC)
Trop Med... Tropical Medicine [*A publication*]
Trop Med Hyg News ... Tropical Medicine and Hygiene News [*A publication*]
Trop Med Parasitol ... Tropical Medicine and Parasitology [*A publication*]
Trop Med Res Stud Ser ... Tropical Medicine Research Studies Series [*A publication*]
TROPO ..... Tropospheric
Trop Pest Bull ... Tropical Pest Bulletin [*A publication*]
Trop Pestic Res Inst Annu Rep ... Tropical Pesticides Research Institute. Annual Report [*A publication*]
Trop Pestic Res Inst Misc Rep ... Tropical Pesticides Research Institute. Miscellaneous Report [*A publication*]
Trop Pest Manage ... Tropical Pest Management [*A publication*]
Trop Prod Inst Crop Prod Dig ... Tropical Products Institute. Crop and Product Digest [*A publication*]
Trop Prod Inst Rep ... Tropical Products Institute. Report [*A publication*]
TROPRAN ... Tropical Regional Analysis [*National Weather Service*]
Trop Sci ..... Tropical Science [*A publication*]
Trop Sci Cent Occas Pap (San Jose Costa Rica) ... Tropical Science Center. Occasional Paper (San Jose, Costa Rica) [*A publication*]
Trop Stored Prod Inf ... Tropical Stored Products Information [*A publication*]
Trop Stored Prod Inform ... Tropical Stored Products Information [*A publication*]
Trop Subtrop Pflwelt ... Tropische und Subtropische Pflanzenwelt [*A publication*]
Trop Vet..... Tropical Veterinarian [*A publication*]
Trop Vet Bull ... Tropical Veterinary Bulletin [*A publication*]
Trop Woods ... Tropical Woods [*A publication*]
Trop Woods Yale Univ Sch For ... Tropical Woods. Yale University School of Forestry [*A publication*]
Trop Zool... Tropical Zoology [*A publication*]
TROS........ Tape Resident Operating System [*Data processing*] (IEEE)
TROS........ Transformer Read Only Storage
TROSA...... Tropical Science [*A publication*]
TROSCOM ... Troop Support Command [*Formerly, MECOM*] [*Army*] [*St. Louis, MO*]
TROTTS ... Theater Realignment of Traffic Transportation Support (MCD)
TROU........ Tround International, Inc. [*NASDAQ symbol*] (NQ)
Troub & H Prac ... Troubat and Haly's Pennsylvania Practice [*A publication*] (DLA)
Troub Lim Partn ... Troubat on Limited Partnership [*A publication*] (DLA)
Trouser....... Trouser Press [*A publication*]
TROV .... Tethered Remotely Operational Vehicle [*Marine science*] (MSC)
TROV .... Turnip Rosette Virus [*Plant pathology*]
TROW....... T. Rowe Price Associates, Inc. [*Baltimore, MD*] [*NASDAQ symbol*] (NQ)
Trow D & Cr ... Trower's Debtor and Creditor [*1860*] [*A publication*] (DLA)
Trow Eq ..... Trower's Manual of the Prevalance of Equity [*1876*] [*A publication*] (DLA)
T Roy Ent S ... Transactions. Royal Entomological Society of London [*A publication*]
T Roy Soc C ... Transactions. Royal Society of Canada [*A publication*]
TRP........... Maryland State Police [*Pikesville, MD*] [*FAA designator*] (FAAC)
TRP........... Table of Replaceable Parts
TRP........... Tamper Resistant Packaging [*Food and Drug Administration*]
TRP........... Tangible Research Property [*Business*]
TRP........... Target Reference Point (AABC)
TRP........... Target Reporting Parameters (MCD)
TRP........... Technical Report
TRP......... Technical Requirements Package (MCD)
TRP........... Television Remote Pickup
TRP........... Terminal Rendezvous Phase
TRP........... Threat Recognition Processor [*Navy*] (MCD)
TRP........... Threat Recognizer Programmer
TRP........... Thunderstorm Research Project [*Environmental Science Services Administration*]
TRP........... Timber Rights Purchase
TRP........... Time to Repair Part
TRP........... Timing Release Pin
TRP........... Total Refractory Period (MAE)
TRP........... Trade Pattern (MSA)
TRP........... Traffic Regulation Point [*Military*]
TRP........... Trainable Retractable Propeller
TRP........... Training Review Panel (CAAL)
TRP........... TransCanada Pipelines Ltd. [*NYSE symbol*] [*Toronto Stock Exchange symbol*] [*Vancouver Stock Exchange symbol*] (SPSG)
TrP............. Transpatent [*German*] (DLA)
TRP........... Transportation Proceedings [*A publication*]
TRP........... Tree Point, AK [*Location identifier*] [*FAA*] (FAAL)
TRP........... Trefpunt [*A publication*]
TRP........... Tricommand Review Panel [*Military*] (AFIT)
TRP........... Tripped
TRP........... Troop (AFM)
TRP........... Tropical (WGA)
TRP........... Trujillo [*Peru*] [*Seismograph station code, US Geological Survey*] (SEIS)
Trp............. Tryptophan [*Also, W*] [*An amino acid*]

TRP............ Tubular Reabsorption [*or Resorption*] of Phosphate
TRPA......... Tryptophan-Rich Prealbumin [*Biochemistry*]
Tr Pacific Coast Oto-Ophth Soc ... Transactions. Pacific Coast Oto-Ophthalmological Society [*A publication*]
Tr Path Soc London ... Transactions. Pathological Society of London [*A publication*]
TRPB......... Thoroughbred Racing Protective Bureau   (EA)
TRPCAR ... Troop Carrier [*Military*]   (CINC)
TRPCAR(M) ... Troop Carrier (Medium)   (CINC)
TRPCL...... Tropical   (FAAC)
TRPCO....... Tropical Continental [*American air mass*]   (FAAC)
TRPCSq...... Troop Carrier Squadron [*Air Force*]
TRPF......... Tax Resisters' Penalty Fund   (EA)
TRPGDA...... Tripropylene Glycol Diacrylate [*Organic chemistry*]
TRPH........ Total Recoverable Petroleum Hydrocarbon
TRPH .... Triumph Capital, Inc. [*NASDAQ symbol*]   (NQ)
TRPI.......... Training Requirement Priority Index
TRPL......... Terneplate [*Materials*]
TRPLA ...... Transplantation [*A publication*]
TRPLYR.... Trapping Layer   (FAAC)
TRPM........ Plymouth/Blackburne [*Montserrat Island*] [*ICAO location identifier*]   (ICLI)
Trp-mRNA ... Ribonucleic Acid, Messenger - Tryptophan Constitutive [*Biochemistry, genetics*]
TRPN .... Transportation
TRPO .... Track Reference Printout
TRPPA ...... Transplantation Proceedings [*A publication*]
TRPRB ...... Transplantation Reviews [*A publication*]
TRPS .... Temperature Regulating Power Supply
TRPS .... Troops
TRPSC...... Triple Screw
TRPT......... Theoretical Renal Phosphorus Threshold [*Medicine*]   (MAE)
TRPT .... Time to Reach Peak Tension
TRPX......... TRP Energy Sensors [*NASDAQ symbol*]   (NQ)
TRQ........... Task Ready Queue
TRQ.......... Torque   (AAG)
TRQ.......... Total Requirements   (AAG)
TRQ........... United States Army TRADOC, Fort Ord, CDEC Library, Fort Ord, CA [*OCLC symbol*]   (OCLC)
TRQUD ..... Transportation Quarterly [*A publication*]
TRR .... [*The*] Research Ranch [*An association*]   (EA)
TRR .... [*The*] Rohmer Review [*A publication*]
TRR .... Tactical Range Recorder [*Navy*]
TRR .... Tactical Reaction Reconnaissance
TRR .... Tape Read Register
TRR .... Target Ranging RADAR
TRR .... Tarraleah [*Tasmania*] [*Seismograph station code, US Geological Survey*]   (SEIS)
TRR .... Teaching and Research Reactor
TRR .... Technical Requirements Review   (MCD)
TRR .... Test Readiness Review [*NASA*]   (NASA)
TRR .... Test and Research Reactor [*Nuclear energy*]   (NRCH)
TRR .... Tethered RADAR Reflector
TRR .... Thailand Research Reactor
TRR .... Theoretical Research Report
TRR .... Topical Report Request [*or Review*] [*Nuclear energy*]   (NRCH)
TRR .... Trade Regulation Reporter [*A publication*]   (DLA)
TRR .... Trader Resource Corp. [*Toronto Stock Exchange symbol*]
TRR .... Transfer Relay Rack   (CAAL)
TRR .... TRC Cos., Inc. [*NYSE symbol*]   (SPSG)
TRR .... True Rate of Return [*Finance*]   (ADA)
TRR .... United States Army TRADOC, Fort Rucker Post Library and Aviation School Library, Fort Rucker, AL [*OCLC symbol*]   (OCLC)
TRRA........ Tera Corp. [*NASDAQ symbol*]   (NQ)
TRRA........ Terminal Railroad Association of St. Louis [*AAR code*]
TRRA........ Tilt Rotor Research Aircraft
TRRAPS.... Transportable Reliable Acoustic Path Sonobuoy   (NVT)
TRRB......... Test Readiness Review Board [*NASA*]
TRRB......... Transportation Research Board. Special Report [*United States*] [*A publication*]
TRRC......... Test Resources Review Committee [*DoD*]
TRRC......... Textile Resource and Research Center   (EA)
TRRE......... H & S Treat & Release, Inc. [*Brooklyn, NY*] [*NASDAQ symbol*]   (NQ)
TRRE......... Transportation Research Record [*A publication*]
TRREB...... Transportation Research [*A publication*]
TRRED...... Transportation Research Record [*A publication*]
Tr Resp Inst Epidemiol Mikrobiol ... Trudove na Respublikanskiya Instituta po Epidemiologiya i Mikrobiologiya [*A publication*]
TRRF......... [*The*] Refrigeration Research Foundation   (EA)
TRRF......... Training Review File [*IRS*]
TRRFDP ... Israel. Agricultural Research Organization. Division of Forestry. Triennial Report of Research [*A publication*]
TRRG .... Tax Reform Research Group   (EA)
TRRIA ...... Translations Register-Index [*A publication*]
TRRL......... Tooling Rejection and Rework Laboratory
TRRL......... Transport and Road Research Laboratory [*Departments of the Environment and Transport*] [*Information service or system*]   (IID)

TRRL Lab Rep ... TRRL [*Transport and Road Research Laboratory*] Laboratory Report [*A publication*]
TRRL Rep ... TRRL [*Transport and Road Research Laboratory*] Report [*A publication*]
TRRL Suppl Rep ... TRRL [*Transport and Road Research Laboratory*] Supplementary Report [*A publication*]
TRRN .... Terrain   (FAAC)
Tr Roy Soc Edinb ... Transactions. Royal Society of Edinburgh [*A publication*]
Tr Roy Soc Trop Med Hyg ... Transactions. Royal Society of Tropical Medicine and Hygiene [*A publication*]
TRRR........ Trilateral Range and Range Rate System
TRRS......... Transport and Road Research Laboratory. Supplementary Report [*A publication*]
TRR of ST L ... Terminal Railroad Association of St. Louis
TRRT........ Test Results Review Team [*Nuclear energy*]   (NRCH)
TRRT......... Tooling Rejection and Rework Tag
TRS............ Tactical RADAR System
TRS............ Tactical Radio Set
TRS............ Tactical Reconnaissance Squadron [*Air Force*]
TRS............ Tactical Reconnaissance System
TRS............ Tape Recorder Subsystem
TRS............ Target Range Servo
TRS............ Technical Repair Standards
TRS............ Technical Requirements Specification   (MCD)
TRS............ Technical Research Ship
TRS............ Teleoperator Retrieval System [*NASA*]
TRS............ Terrestrial Radio System
TRS............ Test Reference System
TRS............ Test Requirement Specification   (MCD)
TRS............ Test Requirements Summary   (MUGU)
TRS............ Test Research Service [*Defunct*]   (EA)
TRS............ Test Research Station
TRS............ Test Response Spectrum   (IEEE)
TRS............ Tetrahedral Research Satellite
TRS............ Textes Religieux Sumeriens du Louvre [*A publication*]   (BJA)
TRS............ Theatre Recording Society   (EA)
TRS............ Theologische Rundschau [*A publication*]
TRS............ Thermal Radiation Simulator
TRS............ Thermal Reactor Safety [*Nuclear energy*]   (NRCH)
TRS............ Thermal Residue Stress   (MCD)
TRS............ Third Readiness State   (AAG)
TRS............ Thorson Aviation, Inc. [*Aberdeen, SD*] [*FAA designator*]   (FAAC)
TRS............ Threat Reaction System
TRS............ Ticket Reservation Systems, Inc.
TRS............ Time Reference System   (MCD)
TRS............ Time-Resolved Spectrometry
TRS............ Toll Room Switch [*Telecommunications*]   (TEL)
TRS............ Top Right Side   (MCD)
TRS............ Torry Research Station [*British*]
TRS............ Total Reduced Sulfur [*Environmental chemistry*]
TRS............ Total Reducing Sugars [*Food science*]
TRS............ Tough Rubber-Sheathed [*Cable*]   (DEN)
TRS............ Traceability and Reporting System
TRS............ Training Reservation System   (MCD)
TRS............ Transfer   (ADA)
TRS............ Transportable Relay Station
TRS............ Transportation Research [*A publication*]
TRS............ Transpose   (ROG)
TRS............ Transverse Rupture Strength [*Metallurgy*]
TRS............ Traumatic Surgery [*Medical specialty*]   (DHSM)
TRS............ Travel Related Services Co., Inc.
TRS............ Treasure Island Resources [*Vancouver Stock Exchange symbol*]
TRS............ Tree-Ring Society   (EA)
TRS............ Trieste [*Campo Marzio*] [*Italy*] [*Seismograph station code, US Geological Survey*] [*Closed*]   (SEIS)
TRS............ Trieste [*Italy*] [*Airport symbol*]   (OAG)
TRS............ Tropical Revolving Storm [*Meteorology*]
TRS............ Troubleshooting Record Sheet [*NASA*]   (NASA)
TRS............ Truss [*Shipping*]
TRS............ Trust America Services [*AMEX symbol*]   (SPSG)
TRS............ Trustees
TRS............ Tuboreticular Structure [*Cytology*]
TRS............ Tug Rotational System [*NASA*]   (NASA)
TRS............ United States Department of Transportation, Transportation System Center, Cambridge, MA [*OCLC symbol*]   (OCLC)
TRSA......... Tax Reduction and Simplification Act of 1977
TRSA......... Terminal RADAR Service Area   (FAAC)
TRSA......... Textile Rental Services Association of America   (EA)
TRSAA ...... Transaction. Royal Society of South Africa [*A publication*]
TRSB......... Time Reference Scanning Beam [*Aviation*]
TRSBG....... Transcribing   (MSA)
TRSBMLS ... Time Reference Scanning Beam Microwave Landing System [*Aviation*]   (OA)
TRSBR....... Transcriber   (MSA)
TR/SBS ..... Teleoperator Retrieval/Skylab Boost System [*Aerospace*]   (MCD)
TRSC......... Transactions. Royal Society of Canada [*A publication*]
TRSC......... Triad Systems Corp. [*NASDAQ symbol*]   (NQ)
TRSCA ...... Transactions. Royal Society of Canada [*A publication*]
TRSCB ...... Transcribe   (MSA)

TRSCB ...... Transportation Science [*A publication*]
TRSD .... Test Requirements/Specification Document [*NASA*] (MCD)
TRSD .... Total Radiance Spectral Distribution
TRSD .... Total Rated Service Date [*Air Force*] (AFM)
TRSD .... Transferred
TRSD .... Transposed
Tr Ser .... Treaty Series [*A publication*] (DLA)
Tr Sev Zapadn Zaochn Politekh Inst ... Trudy. Severo-Zapadnyi Zaochnyi
　　　　　　Politekhnicheskii Institut [*A publication*]
TRSF .... Torque-Regulated Speed Follower
TRSG .... Third Reich Study Group (EA)
TRSG .... Track RADAR Simulation Group [*Military*] (CAAL)
TRSH .... Trim Shell
TRSI .... Test of Retail Sales Insight
TRSL .... Toms River Signal Laboratory [*Army*] (MCD)
TRSL .... Transactions. Royal Society of Literature [*A publication*]
TRSL .... Transnational Industries, Inc. [*NASDAQ symbol*] (NQ)
TRSLA ...... TRW Space Log [*A publication*]
TRSN .... Torsion (MSA)
TRSN .... Transition (FAAC)
TRSN .... Transition [*Indian and Northern Affairs, Canada*] [*A
　　　　　　publication*]
TRSOC ...... Trademark Society, Inc.
Tr Soc Trop Med and Hyg (London) ... Transactions. Society of Tropical
　　　　　　Medicine and Hygiene (London) [*A publication*]
TRSP .... Total Radiance Spectral Polarization
TRSP .... Transport Seaplane [*Navy*]
TRSP .... Tri-Star Pictures, Inc. [*New York, NY*] [*NASDAQ
　　　　　　symbol*] (NQ)
TRSq .... Tactical Reconnaissance Squadron [*Air Force*] (AFM)
TRSR .... Taxi and Runway Surveillance RADAR
TRSS .... Tactical Remote Sensor System (DWSG)
TRSS .... Teleoperator and Robotic System Simulation (MCD)
TRSS .... Triple Screw Ship
T Rs S Afr ... Transactions. Royal Society of South Africa [*A publication*]
TRSSCOMM ... Technical Research Ship Special Communications [*System*]
　　　　　　[*Pronounced "triss-com"*] [*Navy*]
TRSSGM .. Tactical Range Surface-to-Surface Guided Missile
TRSSM ...... Tactical Range Surface-to-Surface Missile
TRST .... Throttle Reset
TRST .... TrustCo Bank Corp. NY [*NASDAQ symbol*] (NQ)
TRSTA ...... Transactions. Royal Society of Tropical Medicine and Hygiene
　　　　　　[*A publication*]
T Rs Trop M ... Transactions. Royal Society of Tropical Medicine and
　　　　　　Hygiene [*A publication*]
TRSV .... Tobacco Ring Spot Virus
TRSY .... Treasury (AABC)
TRT .... San Antonio, TX [*Location identifier*] [*FAA*] (FAAL)
TRT .... TACFIRE Remote Terminal (MCD)
TRT .... Technical Review Team [*Nuclear energy*] (NRCH)
TRT .... Television Resource Teachers [*Canada*]
TRT .... Tempo di Restituzione Termica [*Thermal Restitution Test*]
　　　　　　[*Italian*] [*Medicine*]
TRT .... TEREC [*Tactical Electronic Reconnaissance*] Remote
　　　　　　Terminal (DWSG)
TRT .... Torpedo Rocket Thrown
TRT .... Total Relaxation Time [*Cardiology*]
TRT .... Total Running Time [*Broadcasting*] (WDMC)
TRT .... Trademark Registration Treaty
TRT .... Traffic Route Testing [*Telecommunications*] (TEL)
TRUK .... Transonic Research Tunnel (MCD)
trt .... Treatment [*Medicine*]
TRT .... Treherbert [*Cardiff*] [*Welsh depot code*]
TRT .... Trent Regional Library System [*UTLAS symbol*]
TRT .... Tretes [*Java*] [*Seismograph station code, US Geological
　　　　　　Survey*] (SEIS)
TRT .... Trim Template (MCD)
TRT .... Trinity Resources Ltd. [*Toronto Stock Exchange symbol*]
Trt .... Trityl [*Biochemistry*]
TRT .... Tuned Receiver Tuner
TRT .... Turkish Radio & Television Corp.
TRT .... Turret (AABC)
TRT .... Twisted Racetrack
TRT .... United States Army TRADOC, Fort Bliss, Fort Bliss, TX
　　　　　　[*OCLC symbol*] (OCLC)
TrT₃ .... Total Reverse Triiodothyronine
TRTC .... Tactical Record Traffic Center (MCD)
TRTC .... Trio-Tech International [*NASDAQ symbol*] (NQ)
TRTD .... Treated (MSA)
TR/TEA .... Transportability Report/Transportability Engineering Analysis
　　　　　　[*Army*]
TRTF .... Tactical Reconnaissance Task Force (CINC)
TRTF .... Tactical Record Traffic Facsimile (MCD)
TRTF .... Tasking Requirements and Tasking File (MCD)
TRTG .... Tactical RADAR Threat Generator (MCD)
TRTG .... Treating
TRTHB ...... Traitement Thermique [*A publication*]
TRTI .... Transtech Industries, Inc. [*NASDAQ symbol*] (NQ)
TRTL .... Transistor-Resistor-Transistor Logic (IEEE)
TRTMT ...... Treatment (MSA)

TRTP .... Toxicology Research and Testing Program [*National Institutes
　　　　　　of Health*]
TRTR .... [*National Organization of*] Test, Research, and Training
　　　　　　Reactors (EA)
TRTS .... Tactical Reconnaissance Training Squadron
TRTS .... Tactical Record Traffic System (MCD)
TRTS .... Track RADAR Test Set (MCD)
TRTS .... Triple Redundant Timing Systems (MCD)
Tr Tsentr Nauchnoizsled Inst Ribovud Varna Bulg Akad Nauk ... Trudove na
　　　　　　Tsentralniya Nauchnoizsledovatelski Institut po
　　　　　　Ribovudstvo i Ribolov. Varna. Bulgarska Akademiya na
　　　　　　Naukite [*A publication*]
TRTT .... Tactical Record Traffic Terminal [*Army*] (MCD)
Tr & TT .... Trial and Tort Trends [*A publication*] (DLA)
TRTTF ...... Trinity Resources Ltd. [*NASDAQ symbol*] (NQ)
TRU .... Taurus Resources [*Vancouver Stock Exchange symbol*]
TRU .... Test Replaceable Unit
TRu .... Theologische Rundschau [*Tuebingen*] [*A publication*]
TRU .... Thermal Receiver Unit [*Army*]
TRU .... Time Release Unit (MCD)
TRU .... Total Recycle Unit (OA)
TRU .... Transformer-Rectifier Unit (MCD)
TRU .... Transmit-Receive Unit
TRU .... Transportable Radio Unit [*Military*]
TRU .... Transuranic [*or Transuranium*] [*Chemistry*]
TRU .... Transuranium Processing Plant (NRCH)
TRU .... Trouw [*A publication*]
TRU .... Truancy [*FBI standardized term*]
Tru .... Trueman's New Brunswick Equity Cases [*1876-93*] [*A
　　　　　　publication*] (DLA)
TRU .... Trujillo [*Peru*] [*Airport symbol*] (OAG)
TRU .... Truk [*Caroline Islands*] [*Seismograph station code, US
　　　　　　Geological Survey*] [*Closed*] (SEIS)
TRU .... Truncated Variant [*Genetics*]
TRU .... Trustee (WGA)
TRU .... Turbidity Reducing Unit (AAMN)
TRU .... United States Army TRADOC, Fort Hood, Fort Hood, TX
　　　　　　[*OCLC symbol*] (OCLC)
T₃RU .... Triiodothyronine Resin Uptake [*Endocrinology*] (MAE)
TRUB .... Temporarily Replaced by Unlighted Buoy [*Maps and charts*]
Trubn Proizvod Urala ... Trubnoe Proizvodstvo Urala [*A publication*]
Truck & Bus Trans ... Truck and Bus Transportation [*A publication*] (APTA)
Truck & Bus Transp ... Truck and Bus Transportation [*A
　　　　　　publication*] (APTA)
Truck Bus Transpn ... Truck and Bus Transportation [*A publication*] (APTA)
Truck Off-Highw Ind ... Truck and Off-Highway Industries [*United States*] [*A
　　　　　　publication*]
TRUD .... Time Remaining until Dive [*Air Force*]
Trud Viss Ikonom Inst Karl Marks-Sofia ... Trudove. Vissija Ikonomiceski
　　　　　　Institut Karl Marks-Sofija [*A publication*]
TRUE .... Teacher Resources for Urban Education (AEBS)
True .... Trueman's New Brunswick Reports [*A publication*] (DLA)
Trueman Eq Cas ... Trueman's New Brunswick Equity Cases [*A
　　　　　　publication*] (DLA)
Truem Eq Cas ... Trueman's New Brunswick Equity Cases [*A
　　　　　　publication*] (DLA)
Tru Est .... Trusts and Estates [*A publication*]
TRUF .... Transferable Revolving Underwriting Facility
　　　　　　[*Finance*] (ADA)
TRUFOS ... True Unidentified Flying Objects
TRUK .... Builders Transport, Inc. [*NASDAQ symbol*] (NQ)
TRUMP ..... Target Radiation Ultraviolet Measurement Program (AAG)
TRUMP ..... Technical Review Updated Manuals and Publications (MCD)
TRUMP ..... Teller Register Unit Monitoring Program (IEEE)
TRUMP ..... Threat Reaction Upgrade Modernization (MCD)
TRUMP ..... Total Revision and Upgrading of Maintenance Procedures
　　　　　　[*Marine Corps*]
TRUMP ..... Transportable Understanding Mechanism Package [*Software
　　　　　　system*] (IT)
TRUMP ..... Tribal Class Update and Modernization Project [*Canadian
　　　　　　Navy*]
TRUN .... Trunnion [*Pivot*] (KSC)
TRUNANG ... Trunnion Angle (MCD)
Truppie ...... Trucker with Upscale Living Quarters in His or Her Vehicle
　　　　　　[*Lifestyle classification*]
Tru Railw Rep ... Truman's American Railway Reports [*A
　　　　　　publication*] (DLA)
TRURON .. Truronensis [*Signature of the Bishop of Truro*] [*Latin*] (ROG)
TRUST ...... Television Relay Using Small Terminals (MCD)
TRUST ...... Toluidine Red Unheated Serum Test
TRUST ...... Transportable Units and Self-Sufficient Teams (MCD)
TRUST ...... Trieste United States Troops
Trust Bull ... Trust Bulletin [*A publication*]
Trust Co Mag ... Trust Companies Magazine [*1904-38*] [*A
　　　　　　publication*] (DLA)
Trust Lett ... Trust Letter. American Bankers Association [*A
　　　　　　publication*] (DLA)
Trust Newsl ... Trust Newsletter [*National Trust of Australia*] [*A
　　　　　　publication*] (APTA)
Trust Nletter ... Trust Newsletter [*National Trust of Australia*] [*A
　　　　　　publication*] (APTA)

Trusts & Es ... Trusts and Estates [*A publication*]
Trusts & Est ... Trusts and Estates [*A publication*]
Trust Terr .. Trust Territory Reports [*A publication*]   (DLA)
TRUT .... Time Remaining until Transition [*Air Force*]
TRV .... Tank Recovery Vehicle [*Army*]   (AABC)
TRV .... Thrust Reduction Valve
TRV .... Timing Relay Valve
TRV .... Tobacco Rattle Virus
TRV .... Torpedo-Recovery Vessel [*Navy*] [*British*]
TRV .... Transient Recovery Voltage   (IEEE)
TRV .... Traverse
TRV .... Treviso [*Italy*] [*Seismograph station code, US Geological Survey*] [*Closed*]   (SEIS)
TRV .... Trivandrum [*India*] [*Airport symbol*]   (OAG)
TRV .... Trove Resources [*Vancouver Stock Exchange symbol*]
TRV .... United States Army TRADOC, Fort Lee Post, Logistic Center, Logistic, Quartermaster, Fort Lee, VA [*OCLC symbol*]   (OCLC)
TRVA .... Thermally Released Volatile Aromatics [*i.e., odors*] [*Slang*]
TRVB .... Tables of Redemption Values for US Savings Bonds
TRVED8 ..... Theory of Science Development [*A publication*]
TRVEH ..... Tracked Vehicle   (AABC)
Tr Vissh Inst Nar Stop (Varna Bulg) ... Trudove na Visshiya Institut za Narodno Stopanstvo "D. Blagoev" (Varna Bulgaria) [*A publication*]
Tr Vissh Pedagog Inst (Plovdiv) Mat Fiz Khim Biol ... Trudove na Visshiya Pedagogicheski Institut (Plovdiv). Matematika, Fizika, Khimiya, Biologiya [*A publication*]
TRVL .... Truvel Corp. [*NASDAQ symbol*]   (NQ)
TRVLG ..... Traveling   (MSA)
TRVLMT .. Travel Limit
TRVLR ..... Traveler   (MSA)
TRVM ...... Transistorized Voltmeter
TRVM ...... TRV Minerals Corp. [*NASDAQ symbol*]   (NQ)
TRVSA ..... Travail et Securite [*A publication*]
TRVTDJ .... Tropical Veterinarian [*A publication*]
TRVV ..... Time Radius and Velocity Vector
TRW .... Tactical Reconnaissance Wing [*Air Force*]   (MCD)
TRW .... Tarawa [*Kiribati*] [*Airport symbol*]   (OAG)
TRW .... Trade Winds Resources [*Vancouver Stock Exchange symbol*]
TRW .... Trail Riders of the Wilderness [*Later, AFA*]   (EA)
TRW .... Trans Western Airlines of Utah [*Logan, UT*] [*FAA designator*]   (FAAC)
TRW .... TRW, Inc. [*Formerly, Thompson Ramo Wooldridge, Inc.*] [*NYSE symbol*]   (SPSG)
TRW .... TRW, Inc. [*Formerly, Thompson Ramo Wooldridge, Inc.*] [*Associated Press abbreviation*]   (APAG)
TRW .... United States Army TRADOC, Fort Leonard Wood Post Library, Fort Leonard Wood, MO [*OCLC symbol*]   (OCLC)
TRWA ...... Trackway
TRWC ...... Threat Responsive Weapon Control [*Military*]   (CAAL)
TRWG ...... Tactical Reconnaissance Wing [*Air Force*]
TRW IND ... TRW Information Networks Division [*TRW, Inc.*] [*Torrance, CA*]   (TSSD)
TRWOA .... Traffic World [*A publication*]
TRWOV .... Transit Without Visa
Trx .... Thioredoxin [*Also, TD, TR*] [*Biochemistry*]
TRX .... Transaction
TRX .... Trenton, MO [*Location identifier*] [*FAA*]   (FAAL)
TRX .... Tri-State Resources Ltd. [*Vancouver Stock Exchange symbol*]
TRX .... Triplex
TRX .... Two-Region Physics Critical Experiment   (NRCH)
TRX .... United States Army TRADOC, Ordnance and Chemical School Library, Aberdeen Proving Ground, MD [*OCLC symbol*]   (OCLC)
TRXRD ...... Time-Resolved X-Ray Diffraction
TRY .... Teens for Retarded Youth [*Program in Fairfax County, Virginia*]
TRY .... Toronto Railway
TRY .... Tororo [*Uganda*] [*Airport symbol*]   (OAG)
TRY .... Tri-Arc Energy Ltd. [*Vancouver Stock Exchange symbol*]
TRY .... Troy [*New York*] [*Seismograph station code, US Geological Survey*]   (SEIS)
TRY .... Truly   (ROG)
Try .... Tryptophan [*An amino acid*]   (MAE)
TRY .... United States Army TRADOC, TRADOC System Analysis [*TRASANA*], White Sands Range, NM [*OCLC symbol*]   (OCLC)
Tryb Spold ... Trybuna Spoldzielcza [*A publication*]
Trye Jus Filiz ... Trye's Jus Filizarii [*A publication*]   (ILCA)
TRZ .... Taradale [*New Zealand*] [*Seismograph station code, US Geological Survey*]   (SEIS)
TRZ .... Thioridazine [*Tranquilizer*]
TRZ .... Tiruchirappalli [*India*] [*Airport symbol*]   (OAG)
TRZ .... United States Army Intelligence Center and School Library, Fort Huachuca, AZ [*OCLC symbol*]   (OCLC)
TRZO .... Terrazzo [*Classified advertising*]   (ADA)
TS .... Air Benin [*Benin*] [*ICAO designator*]   (FAAC)
TS .... Iraq [*Later, BZ*] [*License plate code assigned to foreign diplomats in the US*]

Ts .... Skin Temperature [*Medicine*]
TS .... [*The*] Steamboaters   (EA)
Ts .... T Suppressor [*Cell*] [*Immunology*]
TS .... Tab Set [*Typography*]   (WDMC)
TS .... Tailshaft Survey
TS .... Tall Salicornia Zone [*Ecology*]
TS .... Tangent to Spiral
TS .... Tank Scope   (DNAB)
TS .... Tank Steamer
TS .... Taoist Sanctuary [*Later, DS*]   (EA)
TS .... Tape Status [*Data processing*]   (OA)
TS .... Taper Shank [*Screw*]
TS .... Taper Sided
T/S .... Target Seeker
TS .... Target Strength
TS .... Task Statement   (MCD)
TS .... Task-Switched [*Data processing*]   (BYTE)
TS .... Tasto Solo [*Bass without Accompaniment*] [*Music*]
TS .... Tax Shelter
TS .... Taxpayers' Society [*British*]
TS .... Taylor-Schechter Collection. University Library [*Cambridge, England*]   (BJA)
TS .... Teacher Survey
TS .... Teachers Section [*Library Education Division*] [*American Library Association*]
TS .... Team Supervisor   (FAAC)
ts .... Teaspoon [*Measure*]   (WGA)
TS .... Technical School   (ADA)
T and S .... Technical and Scientific Information [*United Nations Development Program*]
TS .... Technical Secretariat   (NATG)
TS .... Technical Services Co.
TS .... Technical Specification   (MCD)
TS .... Technical Support   (NASA)
TS .... Ted Smith Aircraft [*ICAO aircraft manufacturer identifier*]   (ICAO)
TS .... Telecommunications System
TS .... Telegraph System   (MSA)
TS .... Television, Sound Channel
TS .... Telophase Society [*Commercial firm*]   (EA)
T-S .... Temperature-Salinity [*Oceanography*]
TS .... Temperature Sensitive
TS .... Temperature Switch
TS .... Template Set-Up   (MCD)
TS .... Temporal Stem [*Brain anatomy*]
TS .... Ten Silhouettes [*Psychological testing*]
TS .... Tennyson Society   (EA)
TS .... Tensile Strength
TS .... Tensile Stress
TS .... Tentative Specification
TS .... Teratology Society   (EA)
TS .... Terminal [*or Greater*] Sensation
TS .... Terminal Service
TS .... Terminal Strip   (DEN)
TS .... Terminal Student   (OICC)
TS .... Terra Santa [*Jerusalem*] [*A publication*]   (BJA)
TS .... Test
TS .... Test Items [*JETDS nomenclature*] [*Military*]   (CET)
TS .... Test Set   (KSC)
TS .... Test Site [*NASA*]   (NASA)
TS .... Test Solution [*of a chemical*] [*Medicine*]
TS .... Test Specification   (MSA)
T/S .... Test Stand   (AAG)
TS .... Test Station [*NASA*]   (MCD)
TS .... Test Stimulus
TS .... Test Summary
TS .... Test System
TS .... Text Setting [*Data processing*]   (PCM)
TS .... Textes Sogdiens. Edites. Traduits et Commentes [*A publication*]   (BJA)
TS .... Texts and Studies [*Cambridge*] [*A publication*]   (BJA)
TS .... Texts and Studies. Contributions to Biblical and Patristic Literature [*A publication*]
TS .... Theatre Studies [*A publication*]
TS .... Theatre Survey [*A publication*]
TS .... Theological Studies [*A publication*]
TS .... Theologische Studien [*Utrecht*] [*A publication*]   (BJA)
TS .... Theosophical Society
TS .... Thermal Microscope Stage
TS .... Thermal Spray [*Also, THSP*] [*Coating technology*]
TS .... Thermal Stethoscope [*Medical instrumentation*]
TS .... Thermal Synchrotron [*High-energy physics*]
TS .... Thermosetting [*Plastics technology*]
TS .... Thermospray [*Also, TSP*] [*Ionization*] [*Physics*]
T/S .... Third Stage [*Aerospace*]   (AAG)
T & S .... Thomson and Steger's Tennessee Statutes [*A publication*]   (ILCA)
TS .... Thoracic Surgery [*Medicine*]
TS .... Thoreau Society   (EA)
TS .... Threaded Stud
TS .... Three Stooges Club   (EA)

TS	Thunderstorm [*Meteorology*]	(FAAC)
TS	Thymidylate Synthase [*Also, ThS*] [*An enzyme*]	
TS	Thymostimulin [*Endocrinology*]	
T/S	Thyroid:Serum [*Radioiodide ratio*]	
TS	Tibet Society	(EA)
TS	Tide Surveyor [*British*]	(ROG)
TS	Tidewater Southern Railway Co. [*AAR code*]	
TS	Till Sale	
TS	Time Scheduled	(NASA)
TS	Time Shack [*NAS operations desk*]	
TS	Time Sharing [*Data processing*]	
TS	Time Slot [*Telecommunications*]	(TEL)
TS	Time Switch	(MSA)
TS	Timing Selector	
TS	Timing System	(MCD)
TS	Tinting Strength [*Dye chemistry*]	
ts	Tip Speed	
TS	Tippers [*Shipping*]	(DCTA)
TS	Titan Society	(EA)
TS	Titration System Software [*Metter Instruments*]	
TS	Today Show [*Television program*]	
TS	Today's Speech [*A publication*]	
TS	Tolkien Society [*Hove, East Sussex, England*]	(EAIO)
TS	Toll Switching [*Trunk*] [*Telecommunications*]	(TEL)
TS	Too Short [*Symbol stamped in shoes which are not actually of the size marked*]	
TS	Tool Sharpness	
TS	Tool Shed	(IIA)
TS	Tool Steel	
TS	Tool Storage	
TS	Tool Strength	(ADA)
TS	Top Secret	
TS	Top Spare	
TS	Topic Statement	(WGA)
TS	Torch Soldering	
TS	Torpedo Station	(MCD)
TS	Torstar Corp. [*Toronto Stock Exchange symbol*]	
Ts	Tosyl [*Also, Tos*] [*Organic chemistry*]	
TS	Total Solids [*Medicine*]	
TS	Totally Smutted [*Plant pathology*]	
T and S	Touch and Stay	
TS	Tough Situation [*Bowdlerized version*]	
TS	Tough Stuff	
TS	Tourette Syndrome [*Neurology*]	
TS	Touring Sedan [*As in Olds 98 TS*]	
TS	Tower Station	
TS	Toxic Substance	(MAE)
TS	Tracheal Sound [*Medicine*]	(AAMN)
ts	Tracheosyringeal [*Neuroanatomy of birds*]	
TS	Tracking Scope	
TS	Tracking Supervisor	(SAA)
TS	Tracking System	(AAG)
TS	Trade Study	(MCD)
TS	Trademark Society	(EA)
TS	Traffic Superintendent [*British*]	(DCTA)
TS	Trained Soldier [*British military*]	(DMA)
TS	Training Ship	
TS	Training Squadron [*British military*]	(DMA)
TS	Transaction Services	(MCD)
TS	Transfer Set	
TS	Transient Source	
TS	Transient State	(AAG)
TS	Transient Synovitis [*Medicine*]	
TS	Transit Storage	
TS	Translator Synthesizer	(DWSG)
TS	Transmission Service [*Telecommunications*]	
TS	Transmission Set	
TS	Transmittal Sheet [*Military*]	
TS	Transmitted Shock	
TS	Transmitter Station	
TS	Transplantation Society	(EA)
TS	Transport Service	(ROG)
TS	Transport Ship	(ROG)
TS	Transport and Supply	
TS	Transsexual [*Medicine*]	
T/S	Transtage [*Upper stage for Titan III C rocket*]	
TS	Transvaal Supreme Court Reports [*South Africa*] [*A publication*]	(DLA)
TS	Transverse Section [*Medicine*]	
TS	Transverse System [*Cytology*]	
TS	Travel Supplement [*Publishing*]	
TS	Travelling Showmen [*Public-performance tariff class*] [*British*]	
TS	Treasury Solicitor [*British*]	
TS	Treasury Stock	
TS	Treatment System [*Nuclear energy*]	(NRCH)
TS	Treaty Series [*A publication*]	(ILCA)
TS	Treaty. US State Department Series [*A publication*]	
TS	Tree Sparrow [*Ornithology*]	
TS	Tres Sage [*Wisest*] [*Presiding officer in the French rite*] [*Freemasonry*]	
TS	Tribology Series [*Elsevier Book Series*] [*A publication*]	

TS	Tricuspid Stenosis [*Cardiology*]	
TS	Trinidad Sector [*World War II*]	
TS	Triple Strength	
TS	Tropical Sprue [*Medicine*]	(MAE)
TS	Troubleshoot	(MCD)
ts	Trucial States [*United Arab Emirates*] [*MARC country of publication code*] [*Library of Congress*]	(LCCP)
TS	Trumann Southern Railroad	(IIA)
TS	Trust Secretary	
TS	Tub-Sized [*Paper*]	
TS	Tube Sheet	(MSA)
TS	Tuberous Sclerosis [*Medicine*]	
TS	Tubular [*Tracheal*] Sound	
TS	Tumor Specific [*Medicine*]	
TS	Tuning Stability	
TS	Tunisia [*Aircraft nationality and registration mark*]	(FAAC)
ts	Turboshaft Engine	(IEEE)
T/S	Turn-In Slip [*Military*]	
TS	Turner Society [*British*]	(EAIO)
T-S	Turonian-Santonian [*Paleontology*]	
TS	Tutto Solo [*All by Itself*] [*Music*]	
TS	Twin Screw	(ADA)
TS	Two-Stage Least Squares [*Statistics*]	
TS	Tyneside Scottish [*British military*]	(DMA)
T & S	Type and Screen	
TS	Type Specification	
TS	Typescript	
TS	United States Treaty Series [*A publication*]	(DLA)
T2S	Technology Transfer Society	(EA)
T2S2	Total Tank System Study [*Army*]	
TSA	Aloha Airlines, Inc. [*Air carrier designation symbol*]	
TSA	[*The*] Securities Association [*British*]	
TSA	Tablettes Sumeriennes Archaiques [*A publication*]	(BJA)
TSA	Taipei-Sung Shan [*Taiwan*] [*Airport symbol*]	(OAG)
TSA	Tamworth Swine Association	(EA)
TSA	Target Signature Analysis	
TSA	Target System Alternatives	(MCD)
TSA	Targhee Sheep Association	(EA)
TSA	Tariff Schedules of the United States, Annotated	
T & SA	Task and Skill Analysis	(AAG)
TSA	Tax-Sheltered Annuity	
TSA	Teater SA. Quarterly for South African Theater [*A publication*]	
TSA	Technical Supplemental Allowance [*Military*]	
TSA	Technical Support Activity [*Army*]	(RDA)
TSA	Technical Support Agent	(MCD)
TSA	Technical Support Alliance [*Data processing*]	(PCM)
TSA	Technical Support Asset	
TSA	Technical Surgical Assistance [*Medicine*]	(MAE)
TSA	Technology Student Association	(EA)
TSA	Tele-Systems Associates, Inc. [*Bloomington, MN*] [*Telecommunications service*]	(TSSD)
TSA	Telegraph System Analyzer	
TSA	Test Site Activation [*NASA*]	(KSC)
TSA	Test Start Approval [*NASA*]	(NASA)
TSA	Test Support Agent	(MCD)
TSA	Texas Shrimp Association	(EA)
TSA	Textile Salesmen's Association [*Defunct*]	(EA)
TSA	Theater Service Area	(MCD)
TS in A	Theosophical Society in America	(EA)
TSA	Thermal Swing Adsorption [*Chemical engineering*]	
TSA	Time Series Analysis	
TSA	Time-Shared Amplifier	
TSA	Time Slot Access	
TSA	Time Study Analysis	
TSA	Tolkien Society of America	
TSA	Toluenesulfonic Acid [*Organic chemistry*]	
TSA	Tom Skinner Associates	(EA)
TSA	Total Scan Area	(OA)
TSA	Total Surface Area [*Chemistry*]	
TSA	Total Survey Area	(WDMC)
TSA	Tourette Syndrome Association	(EA)
TSA	Track Subsystem Analyst	(MUGU)
TSA	Track Supply Association	
TSA	Training Services Agency [*Department of Employment*] [*British*]	
TSA	Training Situation Analysis [*Navy*]	
TSA	Training Support Agency [*Army*]	
TSA	Trans America Industries [*Vancouver Stock Exchange symbol*]	
TSA	Trans Sierra Airline [*Cupertino, CA*] [*FAA designator*]	(FAAC)
TSA	Transition State Analog	
TSA	Transportation Service, Army	
TSA	Transportation Standardization Agency [*DoD*]	
TSA	Transportation Stores Assignment [*British*]	
TSA	Tripoli Science Association	(EA)
TSA	Troop Support Agency [*Army*]	(AABC)
TSA	Troubleshooting Aid	(MCD)
TSA	Trypticase Soy Agar [*Cell growth medium*]	
TSA	Tube Support Assembly [*Nuclear energy*]	(NRCH)
TSA	Tuberous Sclerosis Association of Great Britain	
TSA	Tumor-Specific Antigens [*Immunology*]	
TSA	Turkish Studies Association	(EA)

TSA............ Two-Step Antenna
TSA............ Type-Specific Antibody [Immunology]
TSA............ University of Texas, Health Science Center at San Antonio, San
     Antonio, TX [OCLC symbol]   (OCLC)
T₄SA .... Thyroxine-Specific Activity [Medicine]   (MAE)
TSAA........ Tobacco Salesmen's Association of America   (EA)
TSAA........ Tuberous Sclerosis Association of America [Also known as
     American Tuberous Sclerosis Association and Asociacion
     de Esclerosis Tuberosa de America]   (EA)
TSaab........ Thyroid-Stimulating Autoantibody [Endocrinology]
TSAB........ Theatre-Screen Advertising Bureau [Defunct]
TSAb.......... Thyroid-Stimulating Antibodies [Endocrinology]
TSABF....... Troop Support Agency Bagger Fund   (MCD)
TSAC........ Target Signature Analysis Center   (MCD)
TSAC........ Testing Accessories   (AAG)
TSAC........ Time Slot Assignment Circuit [Telecommunications]   (TEL)
TSAC........ Title, Subtitle, and Caption
TSAC........ Topographic Scientific Advisory Committee [Terminated,
     1973] [Army]   (EGAO)
TSAC........ Tracking System Analytical Calibration
TSACA ...... Transactions. South African Institution of Civil Engineers [A
     publication]
TSAD........ Test System Analysis Directorate [Army]   (MCD)
TSAD........ Trajectory-Sensitive Arming Device   (SAA)
TSAE........ Training Support Activity - Europe   (MCD)
TSAEA ...... Transactions. South African Institute of Electrical Engineers [A
     publication]
TSAF .... Transportation Service for the Army in the Field   (MCD)
TSAF .... Typical System Acquisition Flow
TSAFA ...... Traffic Safety [A publication]
TSAG........ Tracking System Analysis Group [NASA]
TSAG........ Trivalent Sodium Antimony Gluconate [Pharmacology]
TsAGI....... Tsentralyni Aero-Gidrodinamichescky Institute [Institute of
     Aeronautical Research] [Former USSR]
TSAK........ Test Stand Adapter Kit
TSAK........ Training Support Activity - Korea   (MCD)
TSAM....... [The] Skill Alignment Module [Army]   (INF)
TSAM....... Time Series Analysis and Modeling [Software]
TSAM....... Training Surface-to-Air Missile
TSAP .... Time Series Analysis Package
TSAPG ...... Telecommunications Systems Architecture Planning
     Group   (DNAB)
TSAR........ Telemetry System Application Requirements
TSAR........ Throttleable Solid Augmented Rocket   (MCD)
TSAR........ Time Sows and Reaps [Acronym used in name of Tsar
     Publishing Co.]
TSAR........ Timed Scanned Array RADAR
TSAR........ TransAmerica Solar Auto Run [In name of solar-powered car
     TSAR Phoenix]
TSAR........ Transmission Security Analysis Report   (AFM)
TSARC...... Test Schedule and Review Committee [Army]   (AABC)
TSARCOM ... Troop Support and Aviation Materiel Readiness Command
     [Army]
TSAT .... Tube-Slide Agglutination Test [Clinical chemistry]
TSAU........ Time Slot Access Unit [Telecommunications]   (TEL)
TSAZ........ Target Seeker-Azimuth
TSB............ [The] School Brigade [Army]   (INF)
TSB............ Technical Service Bulletin
TSB............ Temporary Stowage Bag [NASA]   (KSC)
TSB............ Terminal Status Block [Data processing]   (IBMDP)
TSB............ Test Support Building
TSB............ Textiles Surveillance Body [Textile trade agreement]
TSB............ Theological Studies (Baltimore) [A publication]
TSB............ Thermally Stabilized Burner [Engineering]
TSB............ Thoreau Society. Bulletin [A publication]
TSB............ Thrust Section Blower   (AAG)
TSB............ Towed SONAR Body
TSB............ Toxic Substances Bulletin [A publication]
TSB............ Trade Show Bureau   (EA)
TSB............ Transportation Services Branch [Air Force]
TSB............ Trustee Savings Bank [British]
TSB............ Trypticase Soy Broth [Cell growth medium]
TSB............ Tsumeb [Namibia] [Airport symbol]   (OAG)
TSB............ Twin Sideband
TSB............ Two Complete Science Adventure Books [A publication]
TSBA .... Transactions of the Society of Biblical Archaeology [London] [A
     publication]   (BJA)
TSBB .... Transtracheal Selective Bronchial Brushing
     [Medicine]   (AAMN)
TSB(CI).... Trustee Savings Bank (Channel Islands) [British]
TSBD........ Tracking Servobridge Detector   (MCD)
TSBFA....... Traditional Siamese Breeders and Fanciers Association   (EA)
TS-3 Bibliograf Informacija ... TS-3 Bibliografija Informacija [A publication]
TSBK .... Taunton Savings Bank [Taunton, MA] [NASDAQ
     symbol]   (NQ)
TSBMD..... Tellus. Series B. Chemical and Physical Meteorology [A
     publication]
T S Booklet ... Thoreau Society. Booklet [A publication]
TSBUD...... Tennessee Survey of Business [A publication]
TSBY .... Tuscola & Saginaw Bay Railway Co., Inc. [AAR code]
TSC............ Passed a Territorial Army Course in Staff Duties [British]

TSC............ Tactical Support Center
TSC............ Tanker Service Committee
TSC............ Tape Station Conversion   (CET)
TSC............ Target Selection Console   (MCD)
TSC............ Targeted Selection Criteria   (GFGA)
TSC............ Tarleton State College [Later, TSU] [Texas]
TSC............ Technetium Sulfur Colloid [Medicine]   (MAE)
TSC............ Technical Subcommittee
TSC............ Technical Support Center [Nuclear energy]   (NRCH)
TSC............ Techniscope Development [Vancouver Stock Exchange
     symbol]
TSC............ Teleconferencing Systems Canada Ltd. [Etobicoke, ON]
     [Telecommunications service]   (TSSD)
TSC............ Teledyne Systems Corp.
TSC............ Telephone Software Connection, Inc.
TSC............ Television Scan Converter
TSC............ Terminal Sterilization Chamber
TSC............ Terrestrial Science Center   (MCD)
tsc............. Territorial Staff Course [British military]   (DMA)
TSC............ Test Acquisition Module Self Check   (CAAL)
TSC............ Test Set Computer
TSC............ Test Set Connection
TSC............ Test Setup Complete [NASA]   (NASA)
TSC............ Test Shipping Cask [Nuclear energy]   (NRCH)
TSC............ Test Steering Committee [Military]
TSC............ Test Support Controller [or Coordinator] [NASA]   (KSC)
TSC............ Texas Southmost College
TSC............ Thermal Shape Control   (SSD)
TSC............ Thermal Stress Crack [Plastics]
TSC............ Thermal Surface Coating
TSC............ Thermally Stimulated Conductivity [or Currents]
TSC............ Thiosemicarbazide [Organic chemistry]
TSC............ Three-State Control [Data processing]
TSC............ Time-Sharing Control Task [Data processing]   (BUR)
TSC............ Tonic Sol-Fa College [London]
TS-C .... Tooling Supplement to Contract   (SAA)
TSC............ Top Secret Control   (MCD)
TSC............ Total System Control [Architecture]
TSC............ Total System Cost [Aviation]
TSC............ Totally Self-Checking
TSC............ Towson State University, Towson, MD [OCLC
     symbol]   (OCLC)
TSC............ Toxic Substances Coordinator [Environmental Protection
     Agency]   (GFGA)
TSC............ Training Support Center [Army]   (MCD)
TSC............ Transfer Source C   (SAA)
TSC............ Transit Switching Center [Telecommunications]   (TEL)
TSC............ Transmitter Start Code [Bell System]
TSC............ Transportation Systems Center [Department of Transportation]
     [Cambridge, MA]
TSC............ Tri-Service Support Center [Military]   (MCD)
TSC............ Troop Support Command [Formerly, MECOM] [Army]
TSC............ Trouble-Shooting Checklist [Test for academic institutions]
TSC............ Tuscaloosa Oil & Gas [Vancouver Stock Exchange symbol]
TSC............ Two-Stage Command [NASA]   (GFGA)
TSCA .... Target Satellite Controlled Approach   (MUGU)
TSCA .... Textile Supplies and Credit Association   (EA)
TSCA .... TIGA Sailboard Class Association [Defunct]   (EA)
TSCA .... Timing Single-Channel Analyzer
TSCA .... Tool Subcontract Authorization   (AAG)
TSCA .... Top Secret Control Agency   (MCD)
TSCA .... Toxic Substances Control Act [1976]
TSCA .... Traditional Small Craft Association   (EA)
TSCAP ...... Thermally Stimulated Capacitance [Photovoltaic energy
     systems]
TSCAPP.... Toxic Substances Control Act Plant and Production Data
     [Chemical Information Systems, Inc.] [Information service
     or system]
TSCATS.... Toxic Substances Control Act Test Submissions
     [Environmental Protection Agency] [Database]
TSCC......... Technology Solutions [NASDAQ symbol]   (SPSG)
TSCC......... Telemetry Standards Coordination Committee
TSCC......... Test Support Control Center [NASA]   (KSC)
TSCC......... Top Secret Control Channels [Military]
TSCC......... Toxic Substances Coordinating Committee [Environmental
     Protection Agency]   (GFGA)
TSCC......... TSC Corp. [NASDAQ symbol]   (NQ)
TSCD......... Test Specification and Criteria Document   (MCD)
TSCD......... Tool Specification Control Drawing   (MCD)
TSCDP ...... Technical Service Career Development Program [Military]
TSCF .... Task Schedule Change Form [Nuclear energy]   (NRCH)
TSCF .... Template Set-Up Check Fixture   (MCD)
TSCF .... Top Secret Cover Folder   (AAG)
TSCGD...... GRS [Gesellschaft fuer Reaktorsicherheit] Translations. Safety
     Codes and Guides [A publication]
Tschermaks Mineralog u Petrog Mitt ... Tschermaks Mineralogische und
     Petrographische Mitteilungen [A publication]
Tschermaks Mineral Petrogr Mitt ... Tschermaks Mineralogische und
     Petrographische Mitteilungen [A publication]
TSCHLT ... Test Support Center High-Level Terminal   (CAAL)

Tsch Min Pe ... Tschermaks Mineralogische und Petrographische Mitteilungen [*A publication*]
TSCI .... Techscience Industries [*NASDAQ symbol*]   (NQ)
TSCIXS ..... Tactical Support Center Information Exchange Subsystem
TSCLT .... Transportable Satellite Communications Link Terminal
TSCM .... Taylor Series Correction Method
TSCM .... Technical Surveillance Countermeasures [*Program*] [*Air Force*]
TSCM .... Test Station Configuration Model   (MCD)
TSCN .... Trainer Specification Change Notice   (MCD)
TSCO .... Test Support Coordination Office [*NASA*]   (MCD)
TSCO .... Test Support Coordinator   (NASA)
TSCO .... Top Secret Control Officer [*Military*]
TSCOM ..... TS Communications [*Springfield, IL*] [*Telecommunications*]   (TSSD)
TSCP .... Tactical Satellite Communications Program   (SAA)
TSCP .... Top Secret Control Proceeding [*Navy*]
TSCP .... Training Simulator Control Panel [*NASA*]   (MCD)
TSCPA ...... Transactions and Studies. College of Physicians of Philadelphia [*A publication*]
TSCPAM .. Tentative Summary CPAM [*Military*]   (CAAL)
TSCR .... Telecom Securitor Cellular Radio Ltd. [*British*]
TSCRA ...... Texas and Southwestern Cattle Raisers Association   (EA)
TSCRS .... Teacher's Self-Control Rating Scale
TSCS .... Tactical Satellite Communications System [*Air Force*]   (CET)
TSCS .... Tactical Software Control Site [*Missile system evaluation*]   (RDA)
TSCS .... Tennessee Self-Concept Scale [*Psychology*]
TSCS .... Top Secret Control Section [*Navy*]
TSCT .... Transportable Satellite Communications Terminal
TSCVT ...... TACSATCOM Single Channel Vehicular Terminal System   (MCD)
TSCVT ...... Thomas Self-Concept Values Test [*Psychology*]
TSCW .... Top Secret Codeword   (MCD)
TSD .... Tactical Situation Display
TSD .... Tactical and Staff Duties [*British military*]   (DMA)
TSD .... TARAN [*Tactical Attack RADAR and Navigation*] System Data
TSD .... Target Skin Distance
TSD .... Tay-Sachs Disease [*Medicine*]
TSD .... Technical Support Division [*Environmental Protection Agency*]   (GFGA)
TSD .... Technical Support Document
TSD .... Temperature-Dependent Sex Determination
TSD .... Temperature-Salinity-Density-Depth [*Oceanography*]
TSD .... Tertiary of the Order of St. Dominic [*Roman Catholic religious order*]
TSD .... Test Sequence Document   (SAA)
TSD .... Test Start Date [*NASA*]   (NASA)
TSD .... Theater Shipping Document [*Military*]
TSD .... Theory of Signal Detection
TSD .... Thermally Stimulated Depolarization [*Chemistry*]
TSD .... Thermionic Specific Detector [*Analytical instrumentation*]
TSD .... Third-Degree Stochastic Dominance [*Agricultural statistics*]
TSD .... Time-Speed-Distance [*Driving skills*]
TSD .... Time Synchronization Device
TSD .... Torque Screwdriver
TSD .... Total Spectral Density
TSD .... Touch Sensitive Digitizer [*Electronics*]   (OA)
TSD .... Toured Sea Duty   (DNAB)
TSD .... Track Situation Display
TSD .... Traffic Situation [*Status*] Display
TSD .... Transient Signal Detector
TSD .... Transportation Stores Depot [*British military*]   (DMA)
TSD .... Treatment, Storage, or Disposal [*Hazardous waste management*]
TSD .... Triple-Sequence Diffusion
TSD .... Tubeless Steel Disc [*Wheel*] [*Automotive engineering*]
TSD .... United States Army TRADOC, Fort Devens, USAISD, Fort Devens, MA [*OCLC symbol*]   (OCLC)
TSDA .... Theory of Signal Detection Analysis
TSDB .... SCB [*Statistika Centralbyran*] Time Series Data Base [*Sweden*] [*Information service or system*]   (CRD)
TSDC .... Tennessee State Data Center [*Tennessee State Planning Office*] [*Nashville*] [*Information service or system*]   (IID)
TSDC .... Thermally Stimulated Discharge Current [*Voltage-induced polarization*]
TSDD .... Temperature-Salinity-Density-Depth   (IEEE)
TSDF .... Tactical Software Development Facility
TSDF .... Target System Data File
TSDF .... Treatment, Storage, and Disposal Facility [*Hazardous waste*]
TSDG .... Toxic Substances Dialogue Group [*Environmental Protection Agency*]   (GFGA)
TS-DHFR ... Thymidylate Synthetase Dihydrofolate Reductase [*Biochemistry*]
TSDI .... Tactical Situation Display Indicator
TSDK .... Torque Screwdriver Kit
TSDL .... Tuebingen Studien zur Deutschen Literatur [*A publication*]
TSDM .... Time-Shared Data Management [*System*] [*Data processing*]   (IEEE)
TS/DMS ... Time-Shared/Data Management System
TSDOS ...... Time-Shared Disk Operating System [*Data processing*]   (IEEE)

T/SDPS ..... Tube/Sea Differential Pressure Subsystem
TSDR .... Treatment, Storage, Disposal, or Recycling [*Hazardous waste management*]
TSDS .... Technological Services Delivery System [*UNIDO*]
TSDS .... Two-Speed Destroyer Sweeper [*Military*]
TSDTA ...... Tenside-Detergents [*A publication*]
TSDU .... Target System Data Update
TS D/W .... Tons Deadweight   (DS)
TSE .... Memphis, TN [*Location identifier*] [*FAA*]   (FAAL)
TSE .... Tactical Support Element   (AFM)
TSE .... Tactical Support Equipment [*Military*]   (MCD)
TSE .... Taipei Stock Exchange [*Taiwan*]
TSE .... Target State Estimator   (MCD)
TSE .... Target Support Element   (MCD)
TSE .... Technical Support Effort
TSE .... Technical Support Equipment
TSE .... Tender Support Equipment
TSE .... Terminal Source Editor
TSE .... Test Scoring Equipment
TSE .... Test Set Electrical
TSE .... Test of Spoken English
TSE .... Test Support Equipment [*NASA*]
TSE .... Testicular Self-Examination
TSE .... Texas South-Eastern Railroad Co. [*AAR code*]
TSE .... Texas Studies in English [*A publication*]
TSE .... Time Slice End [*Data processing*]   (OA)
TSE .... Tokyo Stock Exchange [*Japan*]
TSE .... Toronto Stock Exchange [*Toronto, ON*]
TSE .... Total Subsystem Evaluation
TSE .... Transmission Secondary Emission [*Physics*]
TSE .... Transportation Support Equipment   (NASA)
TSE .... Trisodium Edetate [*Inorganic chemistry*]   (MAE)
TSE .... Tulane Studies in English [*A publication*]
TSE .... Turboshaft Engine
TSE1 .... Tissue-Specific Extinguisher 1 [*Genetics*]
TSEA .... Training Subsystem Effectiveness Analysis
TSEC .... Taft Sanitary Engineering Center
TSEC .... Telecommunications Security [*Army*]   (AABC)
TSEC .... Terminal Secondary RADAR Beacon [*Aviation*]   (FAAC)
TSEC .... Top Secret   (MCD)
TSEC .... Transierra Explorations Corp. [*NASDAQ symbol*]   (NQ)
TSED .... Training Simulators Engineering Department
TSEE .... Test Support Equipment Evaluation   (MCD)
TSEE .... Thermally Stimulated Exoelectron Emission [*Dosimetry*]
TSEG .... Tactical Satellite Communications Executive Steering Group
TSEG .... Toronto Stock Exchange - Gold
TS-EI .... Thermospray-Electron Ionization [*Chemistry*]
TSEI .... Toronto Stock Exchange - Industrials
TSEI .... Transportation Safety Equipment Institute   (EA)
T/S-EL ...... Target Selector-Elevation   (SAA)
Tselliul Bum Karton ... Tselliuloza, Bumaga, i Karton [*Former USSR*] [*A publication*]
TSEM .... Toronto Stock Exchange - Mines
TSEM .... Transmission Secondary Emission Multiplier [*Physics*]
Tsem Rastvory Krepleniya Glubokikh Skvazhin ... Tsementnye Rastvory dlya Krepleniya Glubokikh Skvazhin [*A publication*]
Tsentr Ref Med Zh Ser B ... Tsentral'nyi Referativnyi Meditsinskii Zhurnal. Seriya B. Vnutrennye Bolezni [*A publication*]
Tsentr Ref Med Zh Ser G ... Tsentral'nyi Referativnyi Meditsinskii Zhurnal. Seriya G. Mikrobiologiya, Gigiena, i Sanitariya [*A publication*]
Tsentr Ref Med Zh Ser V ... Tsentral'nyi Referativnyi Meditsinskii Zhurnal. Seriya V. Khirurgiya [*A publication*]
TSEO .... Toronto Stock Exchange - Oils
TSEQ .... Time Sequenced [*NASA*]   (KSC)
T & SER .... Tilbury & Southend Railway [*British*]   (ROG)
TSERR ...... Type of Leaf Serration [*Botany*]
TSES .... Technical Simulation and Evaluation System
TSES .... Transportable Satellite Earth Station
TSESG .... Tactical Satellite Executive Steering Group
TSewU ...... University of the South, Sewanee, TN [*Library symbol*] [*Library of Congress*]   (LCLS)
TSewU-T ... University of the South, School of Theology, Sewanee, TN [*Library symbol*] [*Library of Congress*]   (LCLS)
TSF .... T/SF Communications Corp. [*Associated Press abbreviation*]   (APAG)
TSF .... Tab Sequence Format
TSF .... Tactical Strike Fighter   (MCD)
TSF .... Telephone Service Fitting
TSF .... Ten-Statement FORTRAN [*Data processing*]   (IEEE)
TSF .... Ten Story Fantasy [*A publication*]
TSF .... Terminal Sterilization Facility
TSF .... Test Aankoop [*A publication*]
TSF .... Tetraselenofulvalene [*Organic chemistry*]
TSF .... Textured Soy Flour
TSF .... Thai Support Foundation   (EA)
TSF .... Theological Students Fellowship   (EA)
TSF .... Theological Students Fellowship. Bulletin [*A publication*]
TSF .... Thermally Stable Fuel   (MCD)
TSF .... Thermoplastic Structural Foam   (MCD)
TSF .... Thin Solid Films   (IEEE)

TSF	Thrombopoietic Stimulating Factor [*Medicine*]
TSF	Tissue-Coding Factor [*Clinical chemistry*] (MAE)
TSF	Tower Shielding Facility [*Nuclear energy*]
TSF	Track Synthesis Frequency
TSF	Transverse Shear Force
TSF	Treasury Security Force [*Department of the Treasury*]
TSF	Tri-State Flite Services, Inc. [*Dubuque, IA*] [*FAA designator*] (FAAC)
TSF	Triceps Skinfold [*Medicine*]
TSF	Truncation Safety Factor [*In biological systems*]
TSF	Two-Seater Fighter [*Air Force*] [*British*]
TSFA	Two-Step Formal Advertising (MCD)
TSF Bul	TSF [*Theological Students Fellowship*] Bulletin [*A publication*]
TSFC	Tactical Support Functional Components (NVT)
TSFC	Thrust Specific Fuel Consumption
TSFC	Tom Sneva Fan Club (EA)
TSFC	Tribune/Swab-Fox Companies, Inc. [*Tulsa, OK*] [*NASDAQ symbol*] (NQ)
TSFC	Twisted Sister Fan Club (EA)
TSFET	Theater Service Forces, European Theater [*World War II*]
TSFMES ...	Thomas Say Foundation. Monographs [*A publication*]
TSFO	Training Set, Fire Observation (MCD)
TSFO	Training Set, Forward Observer [*Army*]
TSFO	Transportation Support Field Office [*Federal disaster planning*]
TSFR	Transfer (AFM)
TSFS	Trunk Servicing Forecasting System [*Telecommunications*] (TEL)
TSFSOILITU ...	[*The*] Search for Signs of Intelligent Life in the Universe [*Lily Tomlin one-woman show written by Jane Wagner*]
TSFSR	Transcaucasian Soviet Federation Socialist Republic
TSG	[*The*] Stelle Group (EA)
TSG	[*The*] Surgeon General [*Army*]
TSG	Tanacross, AK [*Location identifier*] [*FAA*] (FAAL)
TSG	Technical Specialty Group [*AIAA*]
TSG	Technical Steering Group (OICC)
TSG	Technical Subgroup (NATG)
TSG	Technology Support Group
TSG	Territorial Support Group [*Scotland Yard*] [*British*]
TSG	Test Signal Generator
TSG	Test and Switching Gear [*NASA*] (KSC)
TSG	Time Signal Generator
TSG	Timeslot Generator [*Telecommunications*] (TEL)
TSG	Timing Systems Group [*NASA*]
TSG	Tracking Signal Generator
TSG	Transglobe Resources [*Vancouver Stock Exchange symbol*]
TSG	Transport Supplement Grant [*British*]
TSG	Transversely Adjusted Gap (IEEE)
TSG	Travel Security Guide [*Control Risks Information Services - CRIS*] [*British*] [*Information service or system*] (IID)
TSG	Tri-Service Group [*NATO*]
TSG	Troubleshooting Guide (MCD)
TSG	Truebner's Simplified Grammars [*A publication*]
TSG	United States Army TRADOC, Fort Gordon, United States Army Signal School and Fort Gordon, Fort Gordon, GA [*OCLC symbol*] (OCLC)
TSGA	Three-Conductor, Shipboard, General Use, Armor Cable
TSGAD	Tri-Service Group on Air Defense [*NATO*] (NATG)
TSGB	Tensor Society of Great Britain
TSGCEE	Tri-Service Group on Communications and Electronic Equipment [*NATO*] (NATG)
TSGF	T-Suppressor-Cell Growth Factor [*Immunology*]
TSGMS	Test Set Guided Missile Set [*or System*]
TSGP	Test Sequence Generator Program [*European Space Research and Technology Center*] (NASA)
TSGR	Thunderstorm with Hail [*Meteorology*]
TSGS	Time Series Generation System
TSGT	Technical Sergeant [*Military*]
TSGT	Throgmorton Secured Growth Trust [*Commercial firm*] [*British*]
TSGT(C)....	Technical Sergeant (Commissary) [*Marine Corps*]
TsGw	Tydskrif vir Geesteswetenskappe [*A publication*]
TSH	Temperature Switch, High [*Nuclear energy*] (NRCH)
TSH	Tensor Surface Harmonic [*Physics*]
TSH	Their Serene Highnesses
TSH	Thermodynamic Suppression Head
TSH	Thyroid-Stimulating Hormone [*Thyrotrophin*] [*Also, TTH*] [*Endocrinology*]
TSH	Toluenesulfonyl Hydrazide [*Organic chemistry*]
TSh	Torah Shelemah [*A publication*] (BJA)
TSH	TSC Shannock Corp. [*Toronto Stock Exchange symbol*] [*Vancouver Stock Exchange symbol*]
TSH	Tshikapa [*Zaire*] [*Airport symbol*] (OAG)
TSHC	Two-Stage Hydrocracker [*Chemical engineering*]
TSHIDP	Tsurumi University Dental Journal [*A publication*]
TSHIRTS ...	TSHIRTS: the Society Handling the Interchange of Remarkable T-Shirts (EA)
TSHR	Thyrotropin-Stimmulating Hormone Receptor [*Endocrinology*]
TSH-RF	Thyroid-Stimulating Hormone-Releasing Factor [*Endocrinology*] (MAE)
TSHWR	Thundershower [*Meteorology*] (FAAC)
TSI	Target Signature Investigation

TSI	Task Status Index [*Data processing*] (OA)
TSI	Tax Shelter Insider [*Newsletter Management Corp.*] [*Defunct*] [*Information service or system*] (CRD)
TSI	Tayson Systems, Inc. [*Telecommunications service*] (TSSD)
TSI	Technical Standardization Inspection [*Military*]
TSI	Technology and Science of Informatics [*A publication*]
TSI	Telebase Systems, Inc. [*Information service or system*] (IID)
TSI	Teleconferencing Systems International, Inc. [*Elk Grove Village, IL*] (TSSD)
TSI	Teleguard System International [*Vancouver Stock Exchange symbol*]
TSI	Television Services International [*British*]
TSI	[*Degangi-Berk*] Test of Sensory Integration
TSI	Test of Social Insight [*Psychology*]
TSI	Test Support Instructions [*NASA*] (KSC)
TSI	Tests of Social Intelligence [*Psychology*]
TSI	Theological School Inventory [*Psychology*]
TSI	Threshold Signal-to-Interference Ratio (IEEE)
TSI	Threshold Soot Index
TSI	Thyroid-Stimulating Immunoglobulin [*Endocrinology*]
TSI	Time-Significant Item (MCD)
TSI	Time Slot Interchange [*Telecommunications*] (TEL)
TSI	Time Sterile Indicator
TSI	Tons per Square Inch (MCD)
TSI	Total Sum Insured (AIA)
TSI	Trans-Service Inc., Bala-Cynwyd PA [*STAC*]
TSI	Transmitting Subscriber Information [*Data processing*]
TSI	Transport Studies and Inquiries [*British*]
TSI	Transportation Safety Institute [*Department of Transportation*]
TSI	Triad Systems Integration Corp.
TSI	Triple Sugar-Iron [*Agar*] [*Microbiology*]
tsi	Tsimshian [*MARC language code*] [*Library of Congress*] (LCCP)
TSI	Turbo Sport Intercooler [*Automotive engineering*]
TSI	Turkish Standards Institution
TSIA	Trading Stamp Institute of America (EA)
TSIA	Triple Sugar-Iron Agar [*Microbiology*]
TSIAJ	This Scherzo Is a Joke [*Used by American composer Charles Edward Ives*]
TSIC	Transducer Systems, Inc. [*NASDAQ symbol*] (NQ)
TSID	Track Sector Identification
TSIE	Transformed Special Index of the External Standard [*Scintillation analysis*]
TSIFL	Trade Society of Iron Foundry Labourers [*A union*] [*British*]
T/SIG	Turn Signal [*Automotive engineering*]
TSII	TSI, Inc. [*NASDAQ symbol*] (NQ)
TSIL	Time-Significant Item List (AAG)
TSIM	(Trimethylsilyl)imidazole [*Also, TMSIM*] [*Organic chemistry*]
TSIMS	Telemetry Simulation Submodule
TSIN	Total Soluble Inorganic Nitrogen [*Analytical chemistry*]
TSIN	Transgenic Sciences, Inc. [*NASDAQ symbol*] (NQ)
TSIO	Time-Shared Input/Output [*Data processing*]
TSI-OH	Tube Sheet Inlet and Outlet Head (MSA)
TSIP	Technical Study Implementation Plan (SSD)
TSIR	Total System Integration Responsibility
Tsirk Shemakh Astrofiz Obs ...	Tsirkulyar Shemakhinskoi Astrofizicheskoi Observatorii [*Azerbaidzhan SSR*] [*A publication*]
TSIS	Total Specifications Information System
TSIT	Technical Service Intelligence Team [*Military*]
TSITA	Tsitologiya [*A publication*]
Tsititiksiny Sovrem Med ...	Tsititiksiny e Sovremennoi Meditsine [*A publication*]
Tsitol	Tsitologiya [*A publication*]
Tsitol Genet ...	Tsitologiya i Genetika [*A publication*]
Tsitol Genet Akad Nauk Ukr SSR ...	Tsitologiya i Genetika. Akademiya Nauk Ukrainsoi SSR [*A publication*]
Tsitologiya Genet ...	Tsitologiya i Genetika [*A publication*]
TSIU	Telephone System Interface Unit
TSJ	Toxic Substances Journal [*A publication*]
TSJ	Tsushima [*Japan*] [*Airport symbol*] (OAG)
TSJC	Trinidad State Junior College [*Colorado*]
TSJSN	Transactions. Samuel Johnson Society of the Northwest [*A publication*]
TSJSNW ...	Transactions. Samuel Johnson Society of the Northwest [*A publication*]
Ts Jur Foer Finland ...	Tidskrift Utgiven av Juridiska Foereningen i Finland [*A publication*]
TSK...........	Computer Task Group, Inc. [*NYSE symbol*] (SPSG)
TSK...........	Fort Hamilton Post Library, Morale Support Activities, Brooklyn, NY [*OCLC symbol*] (OCLC)
TSK...........	Task
TSK...........	Theologische Studien und Kritiken [*A publication*]
TSK...........	Time Shift Keying
TSK...........	Torque Screwdriver Kit
TSK...........	Tsukuba - Telemeter [*Japan*] [*Seismograph station code, US Geological Survey*] (SEIS)
TSKHAY...	Bulletin. Freshwater Fisheries Research Laboratory [*Tokyo*] [*A publication*]
TSKT	Test Kit (AAG)
TSKTA	Toyo Shokuhin Kogyo Tanki Daigaku. Toyo Shokuhin Kenkyusho Kenkyu Hokokusho [*A publication*]

TSKZA	Tekhnika v Sel'skom Khozyaistve [*A publication*]
TSL...........	Chicago, IL [*Location identifier*] [*FAA*] (FAAL)
TSL...........	[*The*] Software Link, Inc. [*Software manufacturer*]
TSL...........	Temporary Storage Location
TSL...........	Tennessee Studies in Literature [*A publication*]
TSL...........	Test Set Logic
TSL...........	Test Source Library
TSL...........	Test Stand Level (AAG)
TSL...........	Test Support List (CAAL)
TSL...........	Texas Short Line Railway [*AAR code*]
TSL...........	Thin Shock Layer
TSL...........	Time Spent Listening (WDMC)
TSL...........	Top of Slab [*Technical drawings*]
TSL...........	Torsatron/Stellarator Laboratory [*University of Wisconsin - Madison*] [*Research center*] (RCD)
TSL...........	Total Service Life [*Telecommunications*] (TEL)
TSL...........	Trans Siberian Landbridge (DS)
TSL...........	Triservice LASER
TSL...........	Tristate Logic [*Electronics*]
TSL...........	Troop Safety Line
TSL...........	Troubleshooting Loop
TSL...........	Tsaile [*Navajo Community College*] [*Arizona*] [*Seismograph station code, US Geological Survey*] (SEIS)
TSL...........	Two-Stage Liquefaction [*Chemical engineering*]
TSL...........	Typesetting Lead (MSA)
TSL...........	United States Army TRADOC, Defense Language Institute, Presidio of Monterey, CA [*OCLC symbol*] (OCLC)
TSLAET....	Technician of the Society of Licensed Aircraft Engineers and Technologists [*British*] (DBQ)
TS Lang	Typological Studies in Language [*A publication*]
TSLCC-E...	Total System Life Cycle Cost-Effectiveness
TSLCN	Texas State Library Communication Network [*Library network*]
TSLD........	Troubleshooting Logic Diagram (NASA)
TSLH........	TSL Holding [*Formerly, Tandon Corp.*] [*NASDAQ symbol*] (SPSG)
TSLI	Time Since Last Inspection (MCD)
TSLI	TSL, Inc. [*NASDAQ symbol*] (NQ)
TS Lit	Trierer Studien zur Literatur [*A publication*]
Ts LJ.........	Tulsa Law Journal [*A publication*]
TSLL	Texas Studies in Literature and Language [*A publication*]
TSLS.........	Toxic Shock-Like Syndrome [*Medicine*]
TSLS.........	Triservice LASER Seeker [*DoD*]
TSLS.........	Two-Stage Least Squares [*Statistics*]
TSM..........	Methodist Theological School in Ohio, Delaware, OH [*OCLC symbol*] (OCLC)
TSM..........	Tactical Survey Meter
TSM..........	Tail Service Mast [*NASA*] (KSC)
TSM..........	Tandem Scanning Microscope
TSM..........	Target Signature Model
TSM..........	Target-to-Surface-to-Missile Path
TSM..........	Tentative Standard Method [*of analysis*]
TSM..........	Terminal Support Module
TSM..........	Tesoro Sacro-Musical [*A publication*]
TSM..........	Test Site Manager [*Army*]
TSM..........	Test Standards Module
TSM..........	Test Support Manager [*NASA*] (KSC)
TSM..........	Texte des Spaeten Mittelalters [*A publication*]
TSM..........	Thermal Scale Model (MCD)
TSM..........	Thickness-Shear-Mode [*Instrumentation*]
TSM..........	Time Scheduled Maintenance
TSM..........	Time-Shared Monitor System [*Data processing*] (IEEE)
TSM..........	Ton Statute Mile (AAG)
TSM..........	Total Scheduled Maintenance [*Army*]
TSM..........	Total Suspended Matter [*Environmental science*]
TSM..........	Total System Management Concept (MCD)
TSM..........	Trade Study Management (NASA)
TSM..........	TRADOC System Manager [*Army*]
TSM..........	Training and Doctrine Command System Manager [*Army*] (MCD)
TSM..........	Training Site Manager (MCD)
TSM..........	Training System Manager (MCD)
TSM..........	Transportation Systems Management
TSM..........	Trends. Financieel Economisch Magazine [*A publication*]
TSM..........	Tri-State Motor Transit Co. of Delaware [*AMEX symbol*] (SPSG)
TSM..........	Troop Sergeant-Major [*British military*] (DMA)
TSM..........	Type, Series, and Model (MCD)
TSM..........	Type-Specific M (Protein) [*Immunology*]
TSMC........	Taiwan Semiconductor Manufacturing Co.
TSMC........	Technical Supply Management Code
TSMC........	Transportation Supply and Maintenance Command
TSMDA.....	Test-Section Melt-Down Accident [*Nuclear energy*] (NRCH)
TSMFM	Tunneling Stabilized Magnetic Force Microscopy [*Physics*]
TSMG.......	Thompson Submachine Gun
TSMNO	Transmitting Capability Out of Service (FAAC)
TSMO	TACSATCOM Management Office
TSMO	TRADOC Systems Management Office [*Military*] (RDA)
TSMOK.....	Transmitting Capability Returned to Service (FAAC)

TSMRD9...	Canada. Fisheries and Marine Service. Resource Development Branch. Maritimes Region Technical Report. Series Mar-T [*A publication*]
TSMS........	Tobacco Strippers Mutual Society [*A union*] [*British*]
TSMT........	Transmit
TSMT........	Trident SONAR Maintenance Trainer (DWSG)
TSMTS......	Tri-State Motor Tariff Service
TSMYDU ...	Thailheimer's Synthetic Methods of Organic Chemistry. Yearbook [*A publication*]
TSN	[*The*] Sierra Network [*Data processing*]
TSN	[*The*] Sports Network [*Cable-television system*] [*Information service or system*] (IID)
TSN	Tailshaft Renewed
TSN	Tan Son Nhut [*Air base*] [*Vietnam*]
TSN	Tape Serial Number [*Data processing*]
TSN	Tecsyn International, Inc. [*Toronto Stock Exchange symbol*]
TSN	Temporary Sort Number [*Data processing*]
TSN	Test Sequence Network (CAAL)
TSN	Thymosin [*A thymus hormone*]
TSN	Tianjin [*China*] [*Airport symbol*] (OAG)
TSN	Time since New [*Navy*] (NG)
TSN	Traffic Safety Now (EA)
TSN	Trimethoprim, Sulfamethoxazole, Nystatin [*Medicine*]
TSN	Tryptone Sulfite Neomycin (OA)
TSN	Tryptophan Peptone Sulfide Neomycin [*Agar*] (MAE)
TSN	Tsingtau [*Republic of China*] [*Seismograph station code, US Geological Survey*] (SEIS)
TSN	United States Army TRADOC, Fort Wadsworth, Chaplains Center Library, Fort Wadsworth, NY [*OCLC symbol*] (OCLC)
TSNA........	Tobacco-Specific Nitrosamine [*Biochemistry*]
TsNAG	Tijdschrift. Koninklijk Nederlandsch Aardrijkskundig Genootschap [*A publication*]
TSNG	Tseng Labs, Inc. [*Newtown, PA*] [*NASDAQ symbol*] (NQ)
TSNGA......	Trudy. Sredneaziatskii Nauchno-Issledovatel'skii Institut Geologii i Mineral'nogo Syr'ya [*A publication*]
TSNI.........	(Toluenesulfonyl)nitroimidazole [*Organic chemistry*]
TSNL Index Series ...	Texas System of Natural Laboratories. Index Series [*A publication*]
TSNSDH...	US National Oceanic and Atmospheric Administration. Northeast Fisheries Center Sandy Hook Laboratory. Technical Series Report [*A publication*]
TSNT........	(Toluenesulfonyl)nitrotriazole [*Organic chemistry*]
TSNT........	Transient (FAAC)
TSO	Carrollton, OH [*Location identifier*] [*FAA*] (FAAL)
TSo...........	Fayette County Free Library, Somerville, TN [*Library symbol*] [*Library of Congress*] (LCLS)
TSO	Information Society [*A publication*]
TSO	Isles Of Scilly-Tresco [*Airport symbol*] (OAG)
TSO	Table Structure Overview [*NASA*]
TSO	Tactical Surveillance Officer (MCD)
TSO	Target Systems Office [*Army Materiel Command*] (RDA)
TSO	Technical Service Organization [*A generic term*]
TSO	Technical Specification Order
TSO	Technical Staff Officer
TSO	Technical Standard Order [*FAA*]
TSO	Technical Standing Order (KSC)
TSO	Technical Support Organization [*AEC*]
TSO	Telecommunications Service Order [*Telecommunications*] (TEL)
TSO	Telephone Service Observation [*Telecommunications*] (TEL)
TSO	Terminator Sensor Output
TSO	Tesoro Petroleum Corp. [*NYSE symbol*] (SPSG)
TSO	Test Site Office [*NASA*]
TSO	Test Support Operations [*NASA*] (KSC)
TSO	Thrust Section Observer (AAG)
TSO	Time-Sharing Option [*Data processing*]
TSO	Time Since Overhaul [*of engine, or other equipment*]
TSO	Toronto Symphony Orchestra (CDAI)
TSO	Town Suboffice
TSO	Trans Southern Airways [*Florence, SC*] [*FAA designator*] (FAAC)
TSO	Transportation Supply Officer [*Military*]
TSO	Tulsa [*Oklahoma*] [*Seismograph station code, US Geological Survey*] [*Closed*] (SEIS)
TSOA	Technical Standard Order Authorization (MCD)
TSOA	Triumph Sports Owners Association (EA)
T Soc Rheol ...	Transactions. Society of Rheology [*A publication*]
TSODB......	Time Series Oriented Database
TSO/E.......	Time-Sharing Option Extensions (HGAA)
TSOET	Tests of Elementary Training [*Military*] [*British*]
TSOF........	TSO Financial Corp. [*Wilmington, DE*] [*NASDAQ symbol*] (NQ)
TSOL........	[*The*] Sound of London [*Record label*]
TSOL........	True Sounds of Liberty [*Musical group*]
TSOP........	[*The*] Sound of Philadelphia [*Song*]
TSOP........	Tactical Standing Operating Procedure [*Army*]
TSOP........	Technical Standard Operating Procedure [*NASA*] (KSC)
TSOP........	Thin Small-Outline Package [*Data processing*]
TSOR........	Tentative Specific Operational Requirement [*Military*]

TSORT......	Transmission System Optimum Relief Tool [*Telecommunications*] (TEL)
TSOS........	Time-Sharing Operating System [*Data processing*] (IEEE)
TSOSC......	Test Set Operational Signal Converter (AAG)
TSP...........	[*The*] Sentencing Project (EA)
TSP...........	Teaspoonful (GPO)
TSP...........	Technical Specification
TSP...........	Technical Support Package [*NASA*]
TSP...........	Tehachapi, CA [*Location identifier*] [*FAA*] (FAAL)
TSP...........	Telemetry Simulation Program
TSP...........	Telephone Switching Planning (ADA)
TSP...........	Teleprocessing Services Program [*General Service Administration*]
TSP...........	Telesphere Communications, Inc. [*AMEX symbol*] (SPSG)
TSP...........	Temperature-Sensitive Period
TSP...........	Temporary Standard Practice [*or Procedure*] (AAG)
TSP...........	Test Site Position [*NASA*] (KSC)
TSP...........	Test Software Program [*NASA*] (NASA)
TSP...........	Test Status Panel (MCD)
TSP...........	Test Support Package
TSP...........	Test Support Plan [*Army*]
TSP...........	Test Support Position
TSP...........	Test Support Program
TSP...........	Tesuque Peak [*New Mexico*] [*Seismograph station code, US Geological Survey*] (SEIS)
TSP...........	Textured Soy Protein [*Food industry*]
TSP...........	Thermospray [*Also, TS*] [*Ionization*] [*Physics*]
TSP...........	Theta Sigma Phi [*Later, Women in Communications*]
TSP...........	Threat Support Package [*DoD*]
TSP...........	Threat Support Plan (MCD)
TSP...........	Thrift Savings Plan [*Office of Personnel Management*] (GFGA)
TSP...........	Thrombospondin [*or Thrombin-Sensitive Protein*] [*Hematology*]
TSP...........	Thyroid-Stimulating Hormone of the Prepituitary Gland [*Endocrinology*]
TSP...........	Time Series Processor Software [*Bureau of the Census*] (GFGA)
TSP...........	Time Sorting Program
TSP...........	Time and Space Processing (MCD)
TSP...........	Titanium Sublimation Pump (OA)
TSP...........	Toronto Sun Publishing Corp. [*Toronto Stock Exchange symbol*]
TSP...........	Torpedo Seaplane [*Navy*]
TSP...........	Torpedo Setting Panel [*Military*] (CAAL)
TSP...........	Total Serum Protein [*Medicine*]
TSP...........	Total Suspended Particulates
TSP...........	Total Systems Performance [*MODCOMP*]
TSP...........	Traffic Service Position [*Telephone*]
TSP...........	Trans Penn Airlines [*Reedsville, PA*] [*FAA designator*] (FAAC)
TSP...........	Transponder
TSP...........	Transshipment Point (AFM)
TSP...........	Traveling Salesman Problem [*Mathematics*]
TSP...........	Traveling Scholar Program (EA)
TSP...........	Trial Shot Point
TSP...........	Tribal Sovereignty Program [*Later, SGFID*] (EA)
TSP...........	Trimethylsilyl Propionate [*Organic chemistry*]
TSP...........	Triple-Super Phosphates
TSP...........	Triservice Program [*Military*]
TSP...........	Trisodium Phosphate [*Inorganic chemistry*]
TSP...........	Tropical Spastic Paraparesis [*Neurology*]
TSP...........	Tube Support Plate [*Nuclear energy*] (NRCH)
TSP...........	Tulane Studies in Philosophy [*A publication*]
TSP...........	Twisted Shielded Pairs [*Cables*] (NASA)
TSP...........	United States Army TRADOC, Carlisle Barracks, Carlisle Barracks, PA [*OCLC symbol*] (OCLC)
TSPA........	Triethylenethiophosphoramide [*Also, THioTEPA*] [*Antineoplastic drug*]
TSPAC......	Transpacific (FAAC)
TSPAK......	Time Series Package [*Bell System*]
TSPAP......	Total Serum Prostatic Acid Phosphatase [*Medicine*] (MAE)
TSPC........	Thermal Sciences and Propulsion Center [*Purdue University*] [*Research center*] (RCD)
TSPC........	Toxic Substances Priority Committee [*Terminated, 1984*] [*Environmental Protection Agency*] (EGAO)
TSPC........	Tropical Stored Products Centre [*Tropical Products Institute*] [*Overseas Development Administration*] [*British*] (DS)
TSPEC......	Test Specification (MSA)
TSPED......	Trade Shows and Professional Exhibits Directory [*Formerly, TPED*] [*Later, TSW*] [*A publication*]
TSPI.........	Time-Space-Position-Information (MCD)
TSPIRS.....	Timber Sales Program Information Reporting System [*Department of the Interior*]
TSPLIB.....	Traveling Salesman Problem Library [*Electronic mail*]
TSPM........	Total Suspended Particulate Matter
TSpMH.....	South Pittsburg Municipal Hospital, South Pittsburg, TN [*Library symbol*] [*Library of Congress*] (LCLS)
tspn...........	Teaspoon [*Measure*] (WGA)
TSPO........	Threat Simulator Project Office [*Army Intelligence Agency*] (RDA)
TS & POP ...	Testing and Popping (SAA)
TSPP........	Tanker Safety and Pollution Prevention
TSPP........	Technetium Stannous Pyrophosphate [*Radiochemistry*]
TSPP........	Tetrasodium Pyrophosphate [*Inorganic chemistry*]
TSPP........	Training System Procurement Package
T & S Pr....	Tillinghast and Shearman's New York Practice [*A publication*] (DLA)
TSPR........	Total Systems Performance Reliability [*or Responsibility*] (MCD)
TSPR........	Training System Program Requirements (MCD)
TSPS........	Time-Sharing Programming System [*Data processing*] (IEEE)
TSPS........	Traffic Service Position System [*Telecommunications*]
TSPSCAP ...	Traffic Service Position System Real-Time Capacity Program [*Telecommunications*] (TEL)
TSPT.........	Transport (WGA)
TSP-Z........	Trisodium Phosphate - Zephiran [*Clinical chemistry*]
TSQ	T2 Medical, Inc. [*AMEX symbol*] [*NYSE symbol*] (SPSG)
TSQ	Technical Services Quarterly [*A publication*]
TSQ	Time and Super Quick
TSQ	Trade Specialty Qualification (MCD)
TSQ	Triple Stage Quadrupole [*Instrumentation*]
TSQLS.......	Thundersqualls [*Meteorology*] (FAAC)
TSR..........	[*The*] Shopper Report [*A publication*]
TSR..........	Tactical SONAR Range (NVT)
TSR..........	Tactical Strike and Reconnaissance
TSR..........	Tactical Studies Rules [*In corporation name TSR, Inc.*]
TSR..........	Technical Sales Representative
TSR..........	Technical Services Report [*A publication*] (EAAP)
TSR..........	Technical Services Representative (MCD)
TSR..........	Technical Status Review [*NASA*] (NASA)
TSR..........	Technical Study Report
TSR..........	Technical Summary Report
TSR..........	Technical Support Review (SSD)
TSR..........	Technically Specified Natural Rubber
TSR..........	Telecommunications Service Request (CET)
TSR..........	Telemarketing Sales Representative
TSR..........	Telephone Sales Representative (WDMC)
TSR..........	Telephone Support Request
TSR..........	Temporary Storage Register
TSR..........	Tensile Strength Retention [*Textile technology*]
TSR..........	Terminate and Stay Resident [*Data processing*]
TSR..........	Test Schedule Request
TSR..........	Test Status Report [*NASA*] (NASA)
TSR..........	Test Support Requirements (KSC)
TSR..........	Testosterone Sterilized Rat
TSR..........	Texas Star Airlines [*Ft. Worth, TX*] [*FAA designator*] (FAAC)
TSR..........	Thermal Shock Rig [*Nuclear energy*] (NRCH)
TSR..........	Thermally Stable Resin
TSR..........	Thermochemical Sulfate Reduction [*Chemistry*]
TSR..........	Thyroid Hormone Secretion Rate (OA)
TSR..........	Thyroid-to-Serum Ratio [*Medicine*] (MAE)
TSR..........	Tile-Shingle Roof [*Technical drawings*]
TSR..........	Time Sharing Resources, Inc. [*Information service or system*] (IID)
TSR..........	Time Status Register
TSR..........	Time to Sustained Respirations [*Obstetrics*]
TSR..........	Timisoara [*Romania*] [*Airport symbol*] (OAG)
TSR..........	Tokyo Shoko Research Ltd. [*Database producer*] [*Japan*]
TSR..........	Torpedo-Spotter Reconnaissance [*Obsolete*] [*Military*] [*British*]
TSR..........	Total Shoulder Replacement [*Medicine*]
TSR..........	Total Solar Radiation [*Botany*]
TSR..........	Total Stress Range [*Nuclear energy*] (NRCH)
TSR..........	Total System Responsibility
TSR..........	Towed SONAR Response
TSR..........	Tower Shielding Reactor [*Nuclear energy*]
TSR..........	Trade Study Report
TSR..........	Trans-Siberian Railway
TSR..........	Transistor Saturable Reactor
TSR..........	Transportable Surveillance RADAR (MCD)
TSR..........	Traveling Stock Reserve
TSR..........	Tri-Star Resources [*Vancouver Stock Exchange symbol*]
TSR...........	Tsuruga [*Japan*] [*Seismograph station code, US Geological Survey*] (SEIS)
TSR...........	Turbine Shaft Rate [*Military*] (CAAL)
TSR...........	Turnover Summary Report [*Military*]
TSR...........	United States Army TRADOC, Redstone Arsenal, USAMMCS [*United States Army Missile and Munitions Center School*] Technical Library, Redstone Arsenal, AL [*OCLC symbol*] (OCLC)
TSRA........	Total System Requirements Analysis (NASA)
TSRA........	Training Support Requirements Analysis (MCD)
TSRB........	Top Salaries Review Board [*British*]
TSRC........	Theta-Sensitive Regulatory Cell [*Hypothetical*] [*Hematology*]
TSRC........	Tubular and Split Rivet Council [*Later, TRMI*] (EA)
TSRE........	Tropospheric Scatter Radio Equipment (AAG)
TSRI.........	Technical Skill Reenlistment Incentive
TSRI.........	TSR, Inc. [*Hauppauge, NY*] [*NASDAQ symbol*] (NQ)
TSRL........	[*The*] Special Relief League (EA)
TSRL........	Total Support Requirements List (AAG)
TSRLD......	TRRL [*Transport and Road Research Laboratory*] Supplementary Report [*A publication*]

TSRLL....... Tulane Studies in Romance Languages and Literature [*A publication*]
TSRLM ..... Tandem Scanning Reflected Light Microscopy
TSRMP ..... Training System Resource Management Plan [*Army*]
TSRO........ Two-Stage Reverse Osmosis [*Chemical engineering*]
TSRP .... Technical Support Real Property
TSRP .... Toll Service Results Plan [*Bell System*]
TSRS .... Training Site Requirements Study [*DoD*]
TSRT .... Teacher Situation Reaction Test
TSRTAMAA ... Tactical Surveillance, Reconnaissance, and Target Acquisition Mission Area Analysis (MCD)
TSRU........ Tuberculosis Surveillance Research Unit [*Netherlands*] (EAIO)
TSRV........ Torpedo Ship Ranging Vessel [*Canadian Navy*]
TSRVA ...... Times Science Review [*A publication*]
TSS .... New York [*New York*] E. 34th Street [*Airport symbol*] (OAG)
TSS .... [*The*] Safety Society (EA)
TSS .... St. Andrews School, St. Andrews, TN [*Library symbol*] [*Library of Congress*] (LCLS)
TSS .... [*The*] Super Show (ITD)
TSS .... TACFIRE Software Specialist (MCD)
TSS .... Tactical Strike System
TSS .... Tactical Surveillance Sonobuoy (MCD)
TSS .... Tangential Signal Sensitivity
TSS .... Tank Surveillance Service [*Military Traffic Management Command*]
TSS .... Tape Search System
TSS .... Target Selector Switch
TSS .... Target Sensing Switch
TSS .... Task-State Segment [*Operating system data structure*] [*Data processing*]
TSS .... Technical Sales Seminars [*Department of Commerce*]
TSS .... Technical School Squadron [*Army*]
TSS .... Technical Services Staff [*Environmental Protection Agency*] (GFGA)
TSS .... Technical Specification Sheet
TSS .... Technical Support Services
TSS .... Technical Support Staff [*Environmental Protection Agency*] (GFGA)
TSS .... Telecommunication Switching System
TSS .... Telecommunications Security System (MCD)
TS/S .... Telemeter Set/Synthesized (DWSG)
TSS .... Teletype Switching System [*or Subsystem*]
TSS .... Temporary Storage Site [*DoD*]
TSS .... Tensile Shear Specimen [*Plastics technology*]
TSS .... Terminal Security System [*Data processing*]
TSS .... Terminal Send Side
TSS .... Terminal Support System
TSS .... Test Set Simulator
TSS .... Tethered Satellite System (MCD)
TSS .... Thrust Stand System
TSS .... Time-Sharing System [*Data processing*]
TSS .... Toll Switching System [*Telecommunications*] (TEL)
TSS .... Topographic Support System [*Army*] (RDA)
TSS .... Toroidal Space Station
TSS .... Toroidal Support Submarine
TSS .... Total Soluble Sulfur [*Analytical chemistry*]
TSS .... Total Subscriber Satisfaction [*HBO (Home Box Office) rating system*]
TSS .... Total Suspended Solids [*Environmental chemistry*]
TSS .... Total System Services, Inc. [*NYSE symbol*] (SPSG)
TSS .... TOW [*Tube-Launched, Optically Tracked, Wire-Guided (Weapon)*] Subsystem [*Army*]
TSS .... Toxic Shock Syndrome [*Medicine*]
TSS .... Tradeoff Study Suggestion (SSD)
TSS .... Trainer System Software
TSS .... Training Services [*Job Training and Partnership Act*] (OICC)
TSS .... Training Subsystem (MCD)
TSS .... Training Support Service [*ILO*] [*United Nations*] (DUND)
TSS .... Transistor Servo Simulator
TSS .... Transition State Spectroscopy [*Physics*]
TSS .... Transmission Surveillance System [*Bell System*]
TSS .... Transparent Semiconductor Shutter
TSS .... Trend-Set Industry [*Vancouver Stock Exchange symbol*]
TSS .... Tropical Splenomegaly Syndrome [*Medicine*] (MAE)
TSS .... Tropospheric Scatter System
TSS .... Trunk Servicing System [*Bell System*]
TSS .... Tsurugisan [*Anabuki*] [*Japan*] [*Seismograph station code, US Geological Survey*] (SEIS)
TSS .... Tug Structural Support [*NASA*] (NASA)
TSS .... Turbine Steam Ship
TSS .... Turner's Syndrome Society of the US (EA)
TSS .... Twin-Screw Steamer [*Nautical*]
TSS .... Typographic Support System (MCD)
TSS .... United States Army TRADOC, Fort Story, Fort Story, VA [*OCLC symbol*] (OCLC)
TSSA .... Tackle and Shooting Sports Agents Association (EA)
TSSA .... Telecommunications Sales Superintendents' Association [*A union*] [*British*]
TSSA .... Telemetry Subcarrier Spectrum Analyzer
TSSA .... Test Scorer and Statistical Analyzer [*Data processing*]
TSSA .... Test Site Support Activity [*NASA*]

TSSA .... Thunderstorm with Sandstorm [*Meteorology*]
TSSA .... Trade Show Services Association [*Defunct*] (EA)
TSSA .... Transport Salaried Staff's Association [*A union*] [*British*] (DCTA)
TSSA .... Tumor-Specific Surface Antigen [*Immunology*]
TSSAA ...... Tackle and Shooting Sports Agents Association (EA)
TSSC .... Target Selection and Seeking Console
TSSC .... Target System Service Charge (NG)
TSSC .... Toxic Substances Strategy Committee [*Nuclear energy*] (NRCH)
TSS-C .... Transmission Surveillance System - Cable [*Telecommunications*] (TEL)
TS & SCP .. Task, Schedule, and Status Control Plan (AAG)
TSSCS ...... Tactical Synchronous Satellite Communication System
TSSD .... Telecommunications Systems and Services Directory [*A publication*]
TSSDT ...... Thrust Subsystem Design Team [*NASA*]
TSSE .... Tactical Security Support Equipment [*Military*]
TSSE .... Toxic Shock Syndrome Exotoxin
T/SSI........ Technology/Scientific Services, Inc.
TSSI .... Telephone Support Systems, Inc. [*NASDAQ symbol*] (NQ)
TSSIC........ Tool and Stainless Steel Industry Committee (EA)
TSSL........ TSS Ltd. [*NASDAQ symbol*] (NQ)
TSSLS ...... Titan Standardized Space Launch System (SAA)
TSSM .... Thruster Subsystem Module [*NASA*]
TSSM .... Total Ship Simulation Model
TSSMS..... Time Sharing Services Management System (GFGA)
TSSNM ..... Technologist Section of the Society of Nuclear Medicine (EA)
TSSP........ Tactical Satellite Signal Processor (RDA)
TSSP......... Thickness-Sensitive Solar Paint [*Coating technology*]
TSSP......... Two Stripper in Series Permeater [*Chemical engineering*]
TSSPS .... Tsentralniya Suvet na Profesionalnite Suyuzi [*Central Council of Trade Unions*] [*Bulgaria*]
TSSR .... Theater Stock Status Report [*Military*]
TSSSP .... Tennessee Study of State Science Policy [*National Science Foundation*] (EA)
TSSST .... Time-Space-Space-Space-Time [*Telecommunications*] (TEL)
TSST .... Toxic Shock Syndrome Toxin [*Medicine*]
TSSU .... Test Signal Switching Unit (MCD)
TST............ Media Logic, Inc. [*AMEX symbol*] (SPSG)
TST............ [*The*] Science Teacher [*A publication*]
TST............ Tail Stop and Turning [*Automotive engineering*]
TST............ Technical and Scholastic Test [*Vocational guidance test*]
TST............ Telemetry Simulation Terminal
TST............ Television Signal Tracer (DEN)
TST............ Temperature Sensing Transducer
TST............ Test (AAG)
TST............ Test Support Table
TST............ Textile Science and Technology [*Elsevier Book Series*] [*A publication*]
TSt .... Texts and Studies [*A publication*] (BJA)
TST............ Thermistor Sterilization Test
TST............ Threshold Setting Tracer
TST............ Time-Sharing Terminals, Inc.
TST............ Time-Space-Time [*Digital switching*] [*Telecommunications*] (TEL)
TST............ Total Story Time [*Broadcasting*] (WDMC)
TST............ Total Surface Tested
TST............ Toxic Shock Toxin [*Biochemistry*]
TST............ Trang [*Thailand*] [*Airport symbol*] (OAG)
TST............ Transaction Step Task
TST............ Transition State Theory [*Physical chemistry*]
TST............ Transmission Scheme Translator (MCD)
TST............ Transmission System Test (MCD)
TST............ Treadmill Stress Testing [*Physiology*]
TST............ Triceps Skinfold Thickness [*Medicine*]
TST............ Trilogy Screening Technique
TST............ Troubleshooting Time (SAA)
TST............ Trust
TST............ Tumor Skin Test [*Medicine*] (MAE)
TST............ Twenty Statements Test
TST............ Two-Station Training
TST............ United States Army TRALINET, Systems Center, ATPL-AOT, Fort Monroe, VA [*OCLC symbol*] (OCLC)
TSTA .... Technology Security Technical Assessment [*DoD*]
TSTA .... Transmission, Signaling, and Test Access
TSTA .... Tritium Systems Test Assembly (MCD)
TSTA .... Tumor-Specific Transplantation Antigen [*Immunology*]
TSTC .... Target Selection and Tracking Console
TSTC .... Testamatic Corp. [*Albany, NY*] [*NASDAQ symbol*] (NQ)
TSTD .... Total Ship Test Director [*Navy*] (CAAL)
TSTE .... Training System Test and Evaluation (MCD)
TSTEE ...... Trustee
TSTEQ ...... Test Equipment
TSTFLT .... Test Set Fault (AAG)
TSTG........ Testing (MSA)
TsTK .... Tidsskrift for Teologi og Kirke [*Oslo*] [*A publication*]
TSTKA ...... Tsuchi To Kiso [*A publication*]
TStL & KC ... Toledo, St. Louis & Kansas City Railroad
TSTM........ Media Logic, Inc. [*NASDAQ symbol*] (NQ)
TSTM........ Thunderstorm [*Meteorology*] (FAAC)

TSTN.........	Triple Supertwist Nematic [*Video technology*] (PCM)
TSTNG......	Testing
TSTO........	Test Site Tool Order [*NASA*] (AAG)
TSTO	Testing Tool (AAG)
TSTP	Test of Selected Topics in Physics
TSTP	Thermistor Sterilization Test Program
TSTP	Total Ship Test Program [*Navy*] (CAAL)
TSTP	Traffic Safety Training Program
TSTPAC....	Transmission and Signaling Test Plan and Analysis Concept [*Telecommunications*] (TEL)
TSTP/AFS ...	Total Ship Test Program/Active Fleet Surface Ships [*Navy*] (CAAL)
TSTPI........	Tapered Steel Transmission Pole Institute [*Inactive*] (EA)
TSTP/SP...	Total Ship Test Program/Ship Production [*Navy*] (CAAL)
TSTR	Telstar Corp. [*NASDAQ symbol*] (NQ)
TSTR	Tester (MSA)
TSTR	Transistor (AAG)
TSTRZ	Transistorized (MSA)
TSTS	Tail Section Test Stand (AAG)
TSTS	Thermal Sight Test Set [*Army*]
TSTS	Third Stage Test Set [*Aerospace*] (MCD)
TSTS	Thrust Structure Test Stand (AAG)
TSTS	Tomahawk System Test Set
TSTS	Tracking System Test Set (AAG)
TSU	Tabiteuea South [*Kiribati*] [*Airport symbol*] (OAG)
TSU	Tandem Signal Unit [*Telecommunications*] (TEL)
TSU	Tape Search Unit (CET)
TSU	Tariff Selection Unit (OA)
TSU	Tarleton State University [*Formerly, TSC*] [*Texas*]
TSU	Task-Specific Utility
TSU	Technical Service Unit
TSU	Telecommunications Study Unit [*American Topical Association*] (EA)
TSU	Telephone Signal Unit [*Telecommunications*] (TEL)
TSU	Telescope Sight Unit (MCD)
TSU	Tennessee State University, Nashville, TN [*Library symbol*] [*Library of Congress*] [*OCLC symbol*] (LCLS)
TSU	Test Signal Unit [*Telecommunications*] (TEL)
TSU	Texas Southern University
TSU	Thermal Systems Unit (KSC)
TSU	This Side Up
TSU	Time Standard Unit
TSU	Trans-Species Unlimited [*Later, ARM*] (EA)
TSU	Transfer Switch Unit (AAG)
TSU	Transportation System Utilization Program [*Department of Energy*]
TSU	Triple Sugar-Urea Base [*Agar*] [*Microbiology*]
TSU	Tsu [*Japan*] [*Seismograph station code, US Geological Survey*] (SEIS)
TSU	Tsumeb [*South-West Africa*] [*Geomagnetic observatory code*]
TSU	Tulsa-Sapulpa Union Railway Co. [*AAR code*]
TSU	Twin and Subtract (SAA)
Tsukuba-Daigaku Shakaigaku J ...	Tsukuba-Daigaku Shakaigaku Journal [*A publication*]
Tsukuba J Math ...	Tsukuba Journal of Mathematics [*A publication*]
Tsukuba Univ Inst Geosci Annu Rep ...	Tsukuba University. Institute of Geoscience. Annual Report [*A publication*]
Tsukumo Earth Sci ...	Tsukumo Earth Science [*A publication*]
Tsurumi Univ Dent J ...	Tsurumi University. Dental Journal [*A publication*]
TSUS	Tariff Schedules of the United States [*Later, HTSUS*]
TSUSA	Tariff Schedules of the United States, Annotated
TSV...........	Terminal Stage Vehicle
TSV...........	Thru-Sight Video [*Army training device*] (INF)
TSV...........	Tobacco Streak Virus
TSV...........	Townsville [*Australia*] [*Airport symbol*] (OAG)
TSV...........	Turbine Stop Valve [*Nuclear energy*] (NRCH)
TSV..........	Twin Springs [*Nevada*] [*Seismograph station code, US Geological Survey*] [*Closed*] (SEIS)
Tsvet Metal ...	Tsvetnye Metally [*A publication*]
Tsvetn Met ...	Tsvetnye Metally [*A publication*]
Tsvetn Metall ...	Tsvetnaya Metallurgiya [*A publication*]
Tsvetn Metall (Ordzhonikidze, USSR) ...	Tsvetnaya Metallurgiya (Ordzhonikidze, USSR) [*A publication*]
TSVP	Tournez s'il Vous Plait [*Please Turn Over*] [*See also PTO*] [*French*]
TSVR........	Total Systemic Vascular Resistance
TSVS	Time Sharing - Virtual System [*Data processing*] (MCD)
Tsvtn Metall Nauchno Tekh Byull ...	Tsvetnaya Metallurgiya-Nauchno-Tekhnicheskii Byulleten [*A publication*]
TsVV.........	Tydskrif vir Volkskunde en Volkstaal [*A publication*]
TSW..........	Southwestern Baptist Theological Seminary, Fort Worth, TX [*OCLC symbol*] (OCLC)
TSW..........	T Switch Cell [*Immunology*]
TSW..........	Technical Scope of Work
T & SW......	Temperance and Social Welfare [*Free Church*] [*British*]
TSW..........	Temperature Switch (MSA)
TSW..........	Test Software (MCD)
TSW..........	Test Switch
TSW..........	Three Banks Review [*A publication*]
TSW..........	Time Switch [*Telecommunications*] (TEL)
TSW..........	Trade Shows Worldwide [*Formerly, TSPED*] [*A publication*]
TSW..........	Transfer Switch
TSW..........	Transmitting Slide Wire
TSW..........	Trau, Schau, Wem [*Trust, but Be Careful Whom*] [*German*] [*Motto of Christian I, Elector of Saxony (1560-91)*]
TSW..........	Tropical Summer Winter [*Vessel load line mark*]
tsw.............	Tswana [*MARC language code*] [*Library of Congress*] (LCCP)
TSW..........	Turbine-Building Service Water [*Nuclear energy*] (NRCH)
TSWE........	Test of Standard Written English
TSWG.......	Training Support Working Group [*Army*]
TsWK	Tydskrif vir Wetenskap en Kuns [*A publication*]
TSWL........	Tulsa Studies in Women's Literature [*A publication*]
TSWTT	Test Switch Thrust Termination
TSWV	Tomato Spotted Wilt Virus
TSX...........	Telephone Satellite, Experimental
TSX...........	Texscan Corp. [*AMEX symbol*] (SPSG)
TSX...........	Time-Sharing Executive [*Modular Computer Systems*] [*Data processing*]
TSX...........	Transfer and Set Index (SAA)
TSX...........	True Seed Exchange [*Later, SSE*] (EA)
TSX-4	Touring Sport Extra-4WD [*In automotive name Ghia Vignale TSX-4*]
TSY...........	Tech-Sym Corp. [*NYSE symbol*] (SPSG)
TSY...........	Trypticase Soy Yeast [*Cell growth medium*] (MAE)
TSYKDE ...	Annual Report. Tobacco Research Institute. Taiwan Tobacco and Wine Monopoly Bureau [*A publication*]
TT	Chad [*Aircraft nationality and registration mark*] (FAAC)
TT	Taal en Tongval [*Antwerpen*] [*A publication*]
TT	TABA [*Transportes Aereos da Bacia Amazonica SA*] [*Brazil*] [*ICAO designator*] (FAAC)
TT	Tablet Triturate [*Pharmacy*]
TT	Tactical Training [*Followed by location*] [*Military*]
TT	Tactile Tension [*Ophthalmology*]
TT	Taiga Times '71 [*A publication*]
TT	Tail-to-Tail [*Polymer structure*]
TT	Talar Tilt [*Angle of ankle joint*]
TT	Talith and Tefillin (BJA)
TT	Talmud Torah (BJA)
TT	Tanganyika Territory
TT	Tank Top (DS)
TT	Tank Truck [*Freight*]
T & T.........	Tanqueray [*Gin*] and Tonic
TT	Tantato Resources, Inc. [*Vancouver Stock Exchange symbol*]
TT	Target Towing Aircraft [*Navy*]
T & T.........	Tax and Tip
TT	Teacher Training
TT	Technical Team
TT	Technical Test
TT	Technical Training (OICC)
TT	Technical Translation [*A publication*] [*Obsolete*]
T & T.........	Technicals and Turnovers [*Basketball*]
TT	Technology Transfer (DS)
TT	Teetotaler [*Slang*]
TT	Telecommunications Technician [*British military*] (DMA)
TT	Telegraphic Transfer [*of funds*] [*Banking*]
TT	Teletype
TT	Teletypewriter [*Telecommunications*]
TT	Teletypewriter and Facsimile Apparatus [*JETDS nomenclature*] [*Military*] (CET)
TT	Tell Taanach (BJA)
TT	Tempelurkunden aus Tello [*A publication*] (BJA)
TT	Temperature Transmitter [*Nuclear energy*] (NRCH)
TT	Temporarily Transferred [*Telecommunications*] (TEL)
TT	Tendon Transfer [*Surgery*]
TT	Teologisk Tidsskrift [*A publication*]
T/T.............	Terminal Timing (KSC)
tt................	Terminus Technicus (BJA)
TT	Test Temperature [*Nuclear energy*] (NRCH)
TT	Testamentary Trust [*Legal term*]
TT	Tetanus Toxoid [*Medicine*]
TT	Tetrathionate [*Nutrient broth*] [*Microbiology*]
TT	Tetrazol (MAE)
TT	Texas Tower (SAA)
TT	Theology Today [*A publication*]
TT	Theorie en Techniek [*A publication*]
TT	Thermal-Tow
TT	Thermometric Titrimetry
TT	Think Time [*Computer order entry*]
TT	Thomas Thorpe [*Publisher of a 1609 edition of Shakespeare's sonnets*]
TT	Thrombin Time [*Hematology*]
TT	Thrust Termination
TT	Thymol Turbidity [*Clinical chemistry*]
TT	Tibial Tubercle [*Anatomy*]
TT	Ticarcillin and Tobramycin [*Antibacterial mixture*]
TT	Tidningarnas Telegrambyra [*Press agency*] [*Sweden*]
TT	Tight Torso [*Women's fashions*]
T & T.........	Tijuana & Tecate Railway Co. (IIA)
TT	Tile Threshold (MSA)
TT	Tilt Trailers (DCTA)
T & T.........	Time and Temperature
TT	Time and Tide [*A publication*]

TT	Times [*London*] [*A publication*]
TT	Timetable (DS)
T/T............	Timing and Telemetry
Tt................	Titus [*New Testament book*] (BJA)
TT................	Tobacco Tax Ruling Term (DLA)
TT	Tobramycin-Ticarcillin [*Antibiotic combination*]
TT	[*The*] Toledo Terminal Railroad Co. [*AAR code*]
TT	Tolytriazole [*Organic chemistry*]
TT	Tooling Tag (SAA)
TT	Tooling Template (MCD)
T & T.........	Tools and Tillage [*A publication*]
TT	Torpedo Tube
TT	Total Run Time [*Robotic assay*]
TT	Total Task Chaining [*Psychology*]
TT	Total Temperature (MCD)
TT	Total Thyroxine [*Endocrinology*]
TT	Total Time (MSA)
TT	Totus Tuus [*All Yours*] [*Latin*]
TT	Tourist Trophy [*Motorcycle racing*] [*British*]
TT	Tow Truck
TT	Townsend Thoreson [*Company running English Channel ferries*]
TT	Tracking Technician (SAA)
TT	Tracking Telescope
TT	Traffic Tester [*Telecommunications*] (TEL)
TT	Training Text
TT	Trans-Texas Airways
TT	Transaction Terminal (BUR)
TT	Transformation Toughened (MCD)
TT	Transit Time [*of blood through heart and lungs*]
TT	Transmitting Tract [*Botany*]
TT	Transonic Tunnel [*NASA*]
TT	Transport [*A publication*]
T & T.........	Transportation and Transportability
TT	TransTechnology Corp. [*NYSE symbol*] (SPSG)
TT	Transthoracic [*Medicine*]
T/T............	Travel/Tourism
TT	Travel and Tourism Program [*Association of Independent Colleges and Schools specialization code*]
TT	Tree Test [*Psychology*]
TT	Tree Tops
TT	Trees for Tomorrow (EA)
TT	Tributary Team [*Military*]
TT	Tricycle and Tail Skid [*Aerospace*] (AAG)
T/T............	Trienoic/Tetraenoic [*Ratio of unsaturated chemicals*]
TT	Trigesimo-Secundo [*Book from 10 to 12-1/2 centimeters in height*] [*Bibliography*]
TT	Trinidad and Tobago [*ANSI two-letter standard code*] (CNC)
TT	Trinity Term
TT	Triple Thermoplastic (SAA)
TT	Troop Test
TT	Trust Termination
TT	Trust Territories
tt................	Trust Territory of the Pacific Islands [*MARC country of publication code*] [*Library of Congress*] (LCCP)
TT	Trust Territory of the Pacific Islands [*Postal code*]
TT	Tuberculin Tested [*Milk*]
TT	Tufted Titmouse [*Ornithology*]
TT	Turbine Tanker
TT	Turbine Trip (IEEE)
TT	Turntable (ADA)
TT	Turret Trainer [*British military*] (DMA)
TT	Tyne and Tees [*50th Northumbrian Division*] [*British military*] (DMA)
TT₃.............	Total Triiodothyronine [*Endocrinology*]
TT4............	Total Thyroxine [*Endocrinology*]
TT's...........	Tripoli Trots [*Term used by entertainers in World War II*]
TTA	Tan Tan [*Morocco*] [*Airport symbol*] (OAG)
TTA	Tatalina [*Alaska*] [*Seismograph station code, US Geological Survey*] (SEIS)
TTA	Telecommunications and Telephone Association [*Arlington, VA*] [*Telecommunications service*] (TSSD)
TTA	Test Target Array (AFM)
TTA	Theatre Television Authority (EA)
TTA	Thenoyltrifluoroacetone [*Also, TTB*] [*Organic chemistry*]
TTA	Thermomechanical Test Area [*NASA*] (NASA)
TTA	Throughput Time Average [*Compression algorithm*] (MCD)
TTA	Throughput Transmitted Algorithm
TTA	Thrust Termination Assembly
TTA	Time to Apogee [*Aerospace*] (MCD)
TTA	Tolytriazole [*Organic chemistry*]
TTA	Total Tangible Assets [*Business term*] (ADA)
TTA	Total Titratable Acidity [*Analytical chemistry*]
TTA	Tourism Training Australia
TTA	Trade and Tourism Alliance [*Defunct*] (EA)
TTA	Traffic Trunk Administration [*Telecommunications*] (TEL)
T & TA.......	Training and Technical Assistance (OICC)
TTA	Trans-Texas Airways
TTA	Transformation Toughened Alumina (MCD)
TTA	Transit Time Accelerometer
TTA	Transtracheal Aspiration [*Medicine*]
TTA	Travel Time Authorized
TTA	Travel and Tourism Association (EA)
TTA	Triplet-Triplet Annihilation [*Spectroscopy*]
TTA	Tritolylamine [*Organic chemistry*]
TTA	Turbine-Alternator Assembly (MCD)
TTAB........	Tetradecyltrimethylammonium Bromide [*Organic chemistry*]
TTAB........	Trademark Trial and Appeal Board [*of Patent Office*]
TTAD........	Temporary Tour of Active Duty [*Military*]
TTADB.....	Tactical Terrain Analysis Database [*Army*]
TTAE........	Turk Tarih. Arkeologya ve Etnografya Dergisi [*A publication*]
TTAF........	Technical Training Air Force
TTAP........	Telemetry Technical Analysis Position (MCD)
TTAPS	[*R. P.*] Turco, [*O. B.*] Toon, [*T. P.*] Ackerman, [*J. B.*] Pollack, and [*Carl*] Sagan [*Authors of a paper on the biological and climatological effects of nuclear war*]
TTAT........	TACFIRE Training Assistance Team (MCD)
TTAT........	Torpedo Tube Acceptance Trials [*Navy*] (NG)
TTAV........	TTAV [*Technical Teachers Association of Victoria*] News [*A publication*] (APTA)
TTAWA.....	Typewriter Trade and Allied Workers' Association [*A union*] [*British*]
TTB...........	Tanker, Transport, Bomber [*Requirements*] [*Air Force*]
TTB...........	Target Triggered Burst
TTB...........	Tatuoca [*Brazil*] [*Geomagnetic observatory code*]
TTB...........	Technical Test Battery [*Aptitude test*]
TTB...........	Teletypewriter Buffer (CET)
TTB...........	Tetragonal Tungsten Bronze
TTB...........	Time to Blackout
TTB...........	Toll Testboard [*Telecommunications*] (TEL)
TTB...........	Trifluoro(thienyl)butanedione [*Also, TTA*] [*Organic chemistry*]
TTB...........	Typing Test for Business
TTBB........	First Tenor, Second Tenor, First Bass, and Second Bass [*in all-male choral groups*]
TTBOY.....	To the Best of You [*An association*] (EA)
TTBT.......	Threshold Test Ban Treaty [*1974*]
TTBWR....	Twisted Tape Boiling Water Reactor (IEEE)
TTC...........	Tape to Card
TTC...........	Target Track Central
TTC...........	Target Tracking Console (MCD)
TTC...........	Tatung [*Republic of China*] [*Seismograph station code, US Geological Survey*] (SEIS)
TTC...........	Teacher Training College
TTC...........	Technical Training Center [*Air Force*]
TTC...........	Technical Training Command [*Army Air Forces*] [*World War II*]
TTC...........	Telecommunication Training Centre [*Fiji*] [*Telecommunications*]
TTC...........	Telecommunications Techniques Corp.
TTC...........	Telemetry, Tracking, and Command (NASA)
TTC...........	Telemetry Traffic Control (SSD)
TTC...........	Telephone Terminal Cables (KSC)
TTC...........	Teletypewriter Center [*Military*]
TTC...........	Television Training Centre Ltd. [*British*] (CB)
TTC...........	Temperature Test Chamber
TTC...........	Tender to Contract Policy [*Export Credits Guarantee Department*] [*British*]
TTC...........	Terminating Toll Center (DEN)
TTC...........	Test Transfer Cask [*Nuclear energy*] (NRCH)
TTC...........	[*The*] Thomson Corp.
TTC...........	Tight Tape Contact
TTC...........	Time to Circularize Orbit (MCD)
TTC...........	Time to Control
TTC...........	Tin Telluride Crystal
TTC...........	Tobacco Tax Council (EA)
TTC...........	Tobramycin, Ticarcillin, and Cephalothin
TTC...........	Toro Co. [*NYSE symbol*] (SPSG)
TTC...........	Tow Target Cable
TT & C......	Tracking, Telemetry, and Command
TTC...........	Tracking, Telemetry, and Command
TTC...........	Tracking, Telemetry, and Control [*NASA*] (NASA)
TT & C......	Tracking, Telemetry, and Control [*NASA*] (MCD)
TTC...........	Training Technology Centers [*Army*]
TTC...........	Transient Temperature Control
TTC...........	Translation Thrust Control
TTC...........	Transportation Test Center [*Department of Transportation*] [*Pueblo, CO*] (GRD)
TTC...........	Travel for Tomorrow Council (EA)
TTC...........	Travelmaster Travel Club (EA)
TTC...........	Treasure Trove Club (EA)
TTC...........	Triphenyltetrazolium Chloride [*Also, RT, TPTZ*] [*Chemical indicator*]
TTC...........	Tropic Test Center [*Army*] (MCD)
TTC...........	Tube Temperature Control
TTC...........	Tubulinyl Tyrosine Carboxypeptidase
TTC...........	Tunnel Thermal Control (NASA)
TTCA........	T-Ten Class Association (EA)
TTCA........	Thiothiazolidinecarboxylic Acid [*Organic chemistry*]
T/TCA.......	Thrust/Translation Control Assembly [*NASA*] (KSC)
TTCA........	Tibetan Terrier Club of America (EA)
TTCC........	[*The*] Technical Cooperation Committee [*Army*] (AABC)
TTCE........	Tooth-to-Tooth Composite Error

TTC/FES .. Tender to Contract and Forward Exchange Supplement [*Export Credits Guarantee Department*] [*British*]   (DS)
TTCI......... Transient Temperature Control Instrument
TTC & M... Telemetry, Tracking, Command, and Monitoring
TTCMA..... Turk Tip Cemiyeti Mecmuasi [*A publication*]
TTCMSC .. Tonga and Tin Can Mail Study Circle   (EA)
TTCO .... Trustcorp, Inc. [*Formerly, Toledo Trustcorp*] [*NASDAQ symbol*]   (NQ)
TTCP .... Scarborough/Crown Point, Tobago [*Trinidad and Tobago*] [*ICAO location identifier*]   (ICLI)
TTCP .... [*The*] Technical Cooperation Program [*US, UK, Canada, Australia*] [*Research*]
TTCP .... Tripartite Technical Cooperation Program [*Military*]   (NG)
TTCQF ...... Technology Transfer Component Qualification Facility   (SSD)
TTCS .... Target Tracking and Control System   (MCD)
TTCS .... Toy Train Collectors Society   (EA)
TTCS .... Truck Transportable Communications Station
TTCT .... Torrance Tests of Creative Thinking [*Educational test*]
TTCU .... Teletypewriter Control Unit   (AABC)
TTCV .... Tracking, Telemetry, Command, and Voice [*Aerospace*]
TTD .... Tactical Terrain Data [*Army*]
TTD .... Tank Training Devices   (MCD)
TTD .... Teachers Training Diploma
TTD .... Technical Test Director
TTD .... Technical Training Detachment
TTD .... Temporary Text Delay
TTD .... Temporary Total Disablement [*Insurance*]   (AIA)
TTD .... Temporary Travel Document   (NATG)
TTD .... Tetraethylthiuram Disulfide [*Also, TETD*] [*Organic chemistry*]
TTD .... Textile Technology Digest [*A publication*]
TTD .... Things to Do
TTD .... [*The*] Third Degree [*A publication*]   (EAAP)
TTD .... Tissue Tolerance Dose   (MAE)
TTD .... Total Time to Doctorate
TTD .... Totals to Date   (MCD)
TTD .... Transponder Transmitter Detector
TTD .... Transportation Technical Data [*Army*]
TTD .... Triazolo-Thiadiazine [*Organic chemistry*]
TTD .... Troutdale, OR [*Location identifier*] [*FAA*]   (FAAL)
TTDI........ Teacher Training in Developing Institutions
TTDR .... Tracking Telemetry Data Receiver   (AAG)
TTDT........ Tactical Test Data Translator   (MUGU)
TTE .... Talks to Teachers of English [*A publication*]
TTE........... Task Training Exercise
TT & E ...... Technical Test and Evaluation
TTE........... Technical Training Engineer
TTE........... Technical Training Equipment   (MCD)
TTE........... Telephone Terminal Equipment
TTE........... Temporary Test Equipment   (AAG)
TTE........... Tentative Tables of Equipment
TTE........... Ternate [*Indonesia*] [*Airport symbol*]   (OAG)
TTE........... Texpress. Economisch en Technisch Weekblad voor de Textiel en Kledingindustrie en Handel in de Benelux [*A publication*]
TTE........... Thermal Transient Equipment [*Nuclear energy*]   (NRCH)
TTE........... Time to End
TTE........... Time to Event [*NASA*]   (KSC)
TTE........... Tool and Test Equipment [*DoD*]
T & TE ...... Tool and Test Equipment [*DoD*]   (AFIT)
TTE........... Total Tax Expenditures [*Economics*]
TTE........... Total Transportation Expenditure [*Department of Transportation*]
TTE........... Trailer Test Equipment   (AAG)
TTE........... Trigon Tech, Inc. [*Vancouver Stock Exchange symbol*]
TTEB........ Transfert de la Technologie de l'Energie dans les Batiments [*Buildings Energy Technology Transfer Program*] [*Canada*]
TTEC........ Teletypewriter Technician
TTEC......... Transpirator Technologies, Inc. [*NASDAQ symbol*]   (NQ)
T & TEC .... Trinidad & Tobago Electricity Commission
T Tech....... Track Technique Annual [*A publication*]
TTEE........ Trustee
TTeF .... Tetratellurafulvalene [*Organic chemistry*]
TTEGDA... Tetraethylene Glycol Diacrylate [*Organic chemistry*]
TTEK........ Taunton Technologies, Inc. [*NASDAQ symbol*]   (CTT)
TTEKA...... Tokyo Toritsu Eisei Kenkyusho Kenkyu Hokoku [*A publication*]
TTEL......... Tool and Test Equipment List [*NASA*]   (NASA)
TTele......... Tatar Tele Hem Adebijaty [*A publication*]
TTEM....... Tooling Test Equipment Team   (AAG)
TTEP .... Tactical Torpedo Evaluation Program [*Navy*]
TTEP .... Training and Training Equipment   (MCD)
TTET .... Turbine Transport Evaluation Team [*FAA*]   (MUGU)
TTF .... Tactical Task Force   (AFM)
TTF .... Tactical Training Flight [*Military*]
TTF .... Tanker Task Force   (AFM)
TTF .... Target Towing Flight [*British military*]   (DMA)
TTF .... Test to Failure   (NATG)
TTF .... Tetrathiofulvalene [*Organic chemistry*]
TTF .... Thai Fund [*NYSE symbol*]   (SPSG)
TTF........... Thoriated-Tungsten Filament   (SAA)

TTF........... Thyroid Transcription Factor [*Genetics*]
TTF........... Timber Trades Federation   (DAS)
TTF........... Time to Failure
TTF........... Time to Fire [*Military*]   (CAAL)
TTF........... Tone Telegraph Filter
TTF........... Training Task Force
TTF........... Transcription Termination Factor [*Genetics*]
TTF........... Transient Time Flowmeter [*Nuclear energy*]   (NRCH)
TTF........... Transistor Test Fixture
TTF........... Trend Type Forecast   (ADA)
TTF........... Two/Ten Foundation   (EA)
TTFA .... Target Transformation Factor Analysis [*Environmental Protection Agency*]   (GFGA)
TTFA .... Thallium Trifluoroacetate [*Organic chemistry*]
TTFA .... Training Technology Field Activity [*Army*]
TTFB .... Tetrachlorotrifluoromethylbenzimidazole [*Organic chemistry*]
TTFC .... Tactical and Technical Fire Control   (MCD)
TTFC .... Tanya Tucker Fan Club   (EA)
TTFD .... Thiamine Tetrahydrofurfuryl Disulfide [*Pharmacology*]
TTFF .... Time to First Fix [*Quality control*]
TTFN........ Ta Ta for Now
TTF & T.... Technology Transfer, Fabrication, and Test   (RDA)
TTFT .... Tetra(trifluoromethyl)thiophene [*Organic chemistry*]
TTF-TCNQ ... Tetrathiafulvene-Tetracyanoquinodimethane [*Organic chemistry*]
TTFTT .... Terminal Tax Filing Time Trauma
TTFW .... Too Tacky for Words [*Slang*]
TTG .... General Trustco of Canada [*Toronto Stock Exchange symbol*]
TTG .... Gibson General Hospital, Trenton, TN [*Library symbol*] [*Library of Congress*]   (LCLS)
TTG .... Tactical Training Group [*Military*]
TTG .... Technical Translation Group   (IEEE)
TTG .... Test Target Generator
TTG .... Time to Go [*Air Force*]
TTG .... Titograd [*Yugoslavia*] [*Seismograph station code, US Geological Survey*]   (SEIS)
TTG .... Tobacco Tax Guide [*Internal Revenue Service*]
TTG .... Travel Trade Gazette UK [*A publication*]
TTG .... Travel with Troops Going
TTGA .... Tellurite-Taurocholate-Gelatin Agar [*Microbiology*]
TTGAC ...... Travel and Tourism Government Affairs Council   (EA)
TTGD .... Time-to-Go Dial
TTGIC .... Thunder Group [*Formerly, Hemodynamics, Inc.*] [*NASDAQ symbol*]   (SPSG)
TTH .... Thyrotrophic Hormone [*Also, TSH*] [*Endocrinology*]
TTH.......... Title Tech, Inc. [*Vancouver Stock Exchange symbol*]
TTH.......... Tritiated Thymidine   (MAE)
TTHA .... Triethylenetetraminehexaacetic Acid [*Organic chemistry*]
TTHE .... Thermal Transient Histogram Equivalent [*Nuclear energy*]   (NRCH)
TTHFC...... Tom T. Hall Fan Club   (EA)
TTHM....... Total Trihalomethane [*Analytical chemistry*]
TTI........... Tactical Target Illustration   (AFM)
TTI............ [*Robert A.*] Taft Institute of Government   (EA)
TTI............ [*The*] Teachers, Inc.   (EA)
TTI............ Technical Tape, Inc. [*AMEX symbol*]   (SPSG)
TTI............ Technology Transfer Institute [*Santa Monica, CA*] [*Telecommunications*]   (TSSD)
TTI........... Teletype Test Instruction   (KSC)
TTI........... Tension Time Index   (AAMN)
TTI........... Texas Transportation Institute [*Texas A & M University*] [*Research center*]
TTI............ TIE/Telecommunications Canada Ltd. [*Toronto Stock Exchange symbol*]
TTI............ Time to Intercept [*Missiles*]   (NG)
TTI............ Time-Temperature Index
TTI............ Time Temperature Indicator   (IEEE)
TTI............ Time Template Indicator
TTI............ Training-Testing Intervals
TTI............ Transthoracic Impedance [*Medicine*]
TTI............ Travel Trends International [*Commercial firm*] [*British*]
TTI............ Traveling Ticket Inspector   (DCTA)
TTI............ True Total Ion
TTI............ Tuck Tummy In [*Slang*]
TTI............ Tulane Tax Institute [*A publication*]
TTI............ Turner Teleport, Inc. [*Atlanta, GA*] [*Telecommunications service*]   (TSSD)
TTI............ Tyco Toys, Inc. [*NYSE symbol*]   (SPSG)
TTIA .... Tube Temperature Indication and Alarm
TTIC .... Test Technology Information Center   (MCD)
TTIC .... Tropical Timber Information Center [*College of Environmental Science and Forestry at Syracuse*] [*Research center*]   (RCD)
TTIDA....... Teknisk Tidskrift [*Sweden*] [*A publication*]
TTIF .... Training Taxpayer Information File [*IRS*]
TTIG .... Training Task Indentification Guide
TTII .... Therapeutic Technologies, Inc. [*AMEX symbol*]   (NQ)
T Times...... These Times [*A publication*]
TT/IOTE... Technical Testing/Initial Operator Test and Evaluation [*Army*]
TTIPS........ Ticker Tape Information Processing System [*Online stock information service*]

TTIS .... Traveling Trickle Irrigation System
TTIS Publ ... TTIS [*Translation and Technical Information Service*] Publication [*A publication*]
TTITS....... Thrust Termination Initiator Test Set
TTJ .... Thermo Technology International [*Vancouver Stock Exchange symbol*]
TTJ .... Timber Trades Journal and Wood Processing [*A publication*]
TTJ .... Tottori [*Japan*] [*Airport symbol*]   (OAG)
TTK .... Terminate Task Key
TTK .... Tie Trunk [*Telecommunications*]
TTK .... Tokyo Tsushin Kogyo [*Tokyo Telecommunications Engineering Co.*]
TTK .... Turk Tarih Kurumu [*A publication*]
TTK .... Two-Tone Keying
TTK "Belleten" ... Turk Tarih Kurumu "Belleten" [*A publication*]
TTKi .... Tidsskrift for Teologi og Kirke [*Oslo*] [*A publication*]
TTKSA ...... Tokyo-Toritsu Kogyo Shoreikan Hokoku [*A publication*]
TTL........... Tatalina [*Alaska*] [*Seismograph station code, US Geological Survey*] [*Closed*]   (SEIS)
TTL........... Teletype Telling
TTL........... Texas Tech University, School of Law Library, Lubbock, TX [*OCLC symbol*]   (OCLC)
TTL........... Theological Translation Library [*A publication*]
TTL........... Thomson T-Line [*Commercial firm*] [*British*]
TTL........... Through the Lens [*Trademark of Spiratone, Inc.*]
TTL........... Title [*Online database field identifier*] [*Data processing*]
TTL........... To Take Leave
TTL........... Torotel, Inc. [*AMEX symbol*]   (SPSG)
TTL........... Torrent Resources Ltd. [*Vancouver Stock Exchange symbol*]
TTL........... Total Time to Launch [*NASA*]   (KSC)
TTL........... TRADOC Troop List   (MCD)
TTL........... Trail Termination Line   (MCD)
TTL........... Transistor-Transistor Logic [*Also, T²L*]
TTL........... Transit-Time LIDAR   (MCD)
TT & L .... Treasury Tax and Loan Account [*Banking*]
TTL........... Tribal Trust Land [*Zimbabwe*]
TTL........... Tribothermoluminescence
TTL........... Tubulinyl Tyrosine Ligase
TTL........... Turtle Island [*Fiji*] [*Airport symbol*]   (OAG)
TTL........... Twin Trapezoidal Links [*Mazda*] [*Automotive engineering*]
TTLC........ Themes and Topics of Literature Criticism [*A publication*]
TTLC........ Total Threshold Limit Concentration [*Environmental chemistry*]
TTLM....... Through-the-Lens Light Metering   (MCD)
TTLPA ...... Tekstil'naya Promyshlennost [*A publication*]
TTLR........ Tanganyika Territory Law Reports [*1921-47*] [*A publication*]   (DLA)
TTLS .... Team Training Launch Station   (AAG)
TTL-S .... Transistor-Transistor Logic - Schottky
TTM .... Tactical Target Materials
TTM .... Tactical Telemetry
TTM .... Taiwan Trade Monthly [*A publication*]
TTM .... Temperature Test Model
T/TM........ Test and Training Monitor   (AAG)
TTM .... Thermal Test Model
TTM .... Torpedo Tube Missile   (MCD)
TTM .... Transit Time Modulation   (DEN)
TTM .... Turtle Mountains [*California*] [*Seismograph station code, US Geological Survey*]   (SEIS)
TTM .... Two-Tone Modulation
TTMA ...... Truck Trailer Manufacturers Association   (EA)
TTMA ...... Tufted Textile Manufacturers Association [*Later, CRI*]   (EA)
TTMAD .... Testing-Teaching Module of Auditory Discrimination [*Child development test*]
TTMC....... Tactical Target Materials Catalogue   (MCD)
T/TMC..... Traffic/Traffic Management and Control [*British*]
TTMCFC .. Theater-Type Mobilization Corps Force Capabilities [*Military*]
TTMCFO.. Theater-Type Mobilization Corps Force Objective [*Military*]
TTME........ Tech:Time, Inc. [*Nokomis, FL*] [*NASDAQ symbol*]   (NQ)
TTMF........ Touch-Tone Multifrequency   (CET)
TTMM ...... Tergotrochanteral Muscle Motoneuron [*Zoology*]
TTMM ...... True Tape Motion Monitor
TTMP....... Tactical Targets Materials Program   (AFM)
TTMP....... Transit Time Magnetic Pumping
TTMS .... Telephoto Transmission Measuring Set
TTMTA..... Tungsram Technische Mitteilungen [*A publication*]
TTN .... Taitung [*Taito*] [*Republic of China*] [*Seismograph station code, US Geological Survey*]   (SEIS)
TTN .... Technology Transfer Network [*Michigan State Department of Commerce*] [*Lansing, MI*] [*Information service or system*]   (IID)
TT/N .... Test Tone to Noise Ratio [*Telecommunications*]   (TEL)
TTN .... [*The*] Titan Corp. [*NYSE symbol*]   (SPSG)
TTN .... Transient Tachypnea of Newborn [*Gynecology*]
TTN .... Trenton [*New Jersey*] [*Airport symbol*]   (OAG)
TTN .... Trenton, NJ [*Location identifier*] [*FAA*]   (FAAL)
TTN .... Trevecca Nazarene College, Nashville, TN [*OCLC symbol*]   (OCLC)
TTN .... Triton Canada Resources Ltd. [*Toronto Stock Exchange symbol*]
TTN .... Tumor Site, T-Stage, N-Stage [*Oncology*]

TTNA .... Trinidad and Tobago National Alliance [*Political party*]   (PPW)
TTNF........ Two/Ten National Foundation [*Later, TTF*]   (EA)
TTNG .... Tightening   (MSA)
TTNN .... (Tetrahydrotetramethylnaphthyl) Naphthoic Acid [*Antineoplastic drug*]
TTNP........ Tactical Telephone Numbering Plan   (MCD)
TTNPB..... ((Tetrahydrotetramethylnaphthalenyl)propenyl)benzoic Acid [*Antineoplastic drug*]
TTNS........ TOW [*Tube-Launched, Optically Tracked, Wire-Guided (Weapon)*] Thermal Night Sight [*Night vision device*] [*Army*]   (RDA)
TTNV .... Tomato Top Necrosis Virus [*Plant pathology*]
TTO .... Tactical Technology Office [*Arlington, VA*] [*DoD*]   (GRD)
TTO .... Telecommunications Technical Officer [*British*]
TTO .... Terminal Training Objective [*Army*]   (INF)
TTO .... To Take Out [*Medicine*]
TTO .... Total Toxic Organics [*Environmental chemistry*]
TTO .... Traffic Trunk Order [*Telecommunications*]   (TEL)
TTO .... Transit Tracers in the Ocean [*Oceanography*]
TTO .... Transmitter Turn-Off
TTO .... Travel and Transportation Order
TTO .... Trinidad and Tobago [*ANSI three-letter standard code*]   (CNC)
T Today..... Theology Today [*A publication*]
TTOE .... Tentative Tables of Organization and Equipment [*Army*]
TTOI......... TEMPEST Technologies, Inc. [*NASDAQ symbol*]   (NQ)
T Tokyo U F ... Transactions. Tokyo University of Fisheries [*A publication*]
TTOMT .... Tank Turret Organizational Maintenance Trainer [*Army*]
TTOR .... Transtector Systems, Inc. [*Hayden Lake, ID*] [*NASDAQ symbol*]   (NQ)
TTOS........ Toy Train Operating Society   (EA)
TT/OTE .... Technical Testing/Operational Testing Evaluation [*Army*]
TTP........... Tactical Targeting Program   (AFM)
TTP........... Tactics, Techniques, and Procedures
TTP........... Tamarind Technical Papers [*A publication*]
TTP........... Tape-to-Print
T & TP .... Terry and the Pirates [*Pop music group*]
TTP........... Test Transfer Port [*Nuclear energy*]   (GFGA)
TTP........... Tetilla Peak [*New Mexico*] [*Seismograph station code, US Geological Survey*]   (SEIS)
TTP........... Thermistor Test Program
TTP........... Thrombotic Thrombocytopenic Purpura [*Medicine*]
TTP........... Thymidine Triphosphate [*Biochemistry*]
TTP........... Time to Perigee   (MCD)
TTP........... Total Taxable Pay
TTP........... Total Temperature Probe   (MCD)
TTP........... Trailer Transfer Point
TTP........... Trainer Test Procedure [*Army*]
TT & P .... Training, Transient and Patient
TTP........... Transverse Thrust Propeller
TTP........... Trick-Taking Potential [*Statistics*]
TTP........... Tu-Tahl Petroleum, Inc. [*Vancouver Stock Exchange symbol*]
TTP........... Turn toward Peace [*Later, WWWC*] [*An association*]   (EA)
TTPA........ Triethylenethiophosphoramide [*Antineoplastic drug*]   (MAE)
TTPC........ Titanium Toroidal Propellant Container
TTPC........ Tripartite Technical Procedures Committee   (SAA)
TTPE........ Total Taxable Pay Earned
TTPES....... Torpedo Tube Pump Ejection System [*Navy*]   (CAAL)
TTPFC....... Terry and the Pirates Fan Club   (EA)
TTPG........ (Thenoylthio)propionylglycine [*Biochemistry*]
TTPH .... Team Trainer, Pearl Harbor
TTPI......... Trust Territory of the Pacific Islands
TTPP .... Port-Of-Spain/Piarco, Trinidad [*Trinidad and Tobago*] [*ICAO location identifier*]   (ICLI)
TTPR........ Trainer Test Procedures and Results [*Army*]
TTPRR....... Trainer Test Procedures and Results Report [*DoD*]
TTPS........ Port-Of-Spain/Port-Of-Spain, Trinidad [*Trinidad and Tobago*] [*ICAO location identifier*]   (ICLI)
TTP & S..... Trainees, Transients, Patients, and Students Program [*Military*]
TTQ .... Murphy, NC [*Location identifier*] [*FAA*]   (FAAL)
TTQ .... Tourism Training Queensland [*Australia*]
TTQ .... Tryptophan Tryptophylquinone [*Biochemistry*]
TTQ .... Tuebinger Theologische Quartalschrift [*A publication*]
TTQAP...... Teletherapy Treatment Quality Assurance Program [*Nuclear energy*]   (NRCH)
TTQS........ Tuebinger Theologische Quartalschrift (Stuttgart) [*A publication*]
TTR .... 2002 Target Term Trust [*NYSE symbol*]   (SPSG)
TTR .... Tab-Tronic Recorder   (DIT)
TTR .... Tactical Technical Requirements   (RDA)
TTR .... Tall Timbers [*An association*]   (EA)
TTR .... Tana Toraja [*Indonesia*] [*Airport symbol*]   (OAG)
TTR .... Tape-Reading Tripping Relay
TTR .... Target Track [*or Tracking*] RADAR [*Air Force*]
TTR .... Target Tracking Receiver [*Military*]   (CAAL)
TTR .... Tarl Town Reports [*New South Wales*] [*A publication*]   (DLA)
TTR .... Teletypewriter Translator   (CET)
TTR .... Thermal Test Reactor [*Nuclear energy*]   (AAG)
TTR .... Thermal Timing Relay
TTR .... Thermal Transpiration Ratio
TTR .... Thermotolerance Ratio [*Roentgenology*]
TTR .... Tijuana & Tecate Railway Co. [*AAR code*]

TTR	Time to Repair [*Military*] (CAAL)
TTR	Time-Temperature Recorder
TTR	Tonopah Test Range
TTR	Toshiba Training Reactor [*Japan*] (NRCH)
TTR	Total Tank Requirement
TTR	Transient Thermal Radiation
TTR	Transthyretin [*Biochemistry*]
TTR	Travel with Troops Returning
TTR	Triplet-Triplet Resonance [*Physics*]
TTR	Trust Territory Reports of Pacific Island [*A publication*] (DLA)
TTR	Type-Token Ratio [*Education of the hearing-impaired*]
TTRA........	Tetra Systems, Inc. [*NASDAQ symbol*] (NQ)
TTrA.........	Textes et Traitement Automatique [*A publication*]
TTRA........	Tongass [*National Forest*] Timber Reform Act
TTRA........	Travel and Tourism Research Association (EA)
TTRB........	Timken Tapered Roller Bearing
TTRC........	Transistorized Thyratron Ring Counter
TTRE........	Task Training Remedial Exercise [*Army*]
TTRI.........	Time-Temperature Recorder and Integrator (MCD)
TTRIF.......	Trident Resources [*NASDAQ symbol*] (NQ)
TTRR........	Technical Test Readiness Review [*Army*]
TTRSA	Twisted Telephone Radio, Shielded, Armored
TTRT........	Target Token Rotation Time [*Data processing*]
TTS...........	TACFIRE Training System (MCD)
TTS...........	Tactical Test Set (MCD)
TTS...........	Tactical Training Squadron
TTS...........	Tank Thermal Site
TTS...........	Target Trajectory Sensor
TTS...........	Tarleton State University, Dick Smith Library, Stephenville, TX [*OCLC symbol*] (OCLC)
TTS...........	Technical Training Squadron (MCD)
TTS...........	Tele-Tech Services [*McAfee, NJ*] [*Information service or system*] [*Telecommunications*] (TSSD)
TTS...........	Telecom Technology Showcase [*British*]
TTS...........	Telecommunications Terminal Systems
TTS...........	Telemetry Transmission System
TTS...........	Teletype Switching Facilities (FAAC)
TTS...........	Teletypesetter
TTS...........	Teletypewriter System
TTS...........	Temperature Test Set
TTS...........	Temporary Threshold Shift
TTS...........	Terminal Testing Section [*Social Security Administration*]
TTS...........	Terrain Trend System (MCD)
TTS...........	Test and Training Satellite [*Also, TATS, TETR*] [*NASA*]
TTS...........	Thanks to Scandinavia (EA)
TTS...........	[*The*] Theban Tombs Series [*London*] [*A publication*] (BJA)
TTS...........	Thermal Transfer Standard
TTS...........	Thomas Tallis Society [*British*]
TTS...........	Thule Tracking Station (MCD)
TTS...........	Thurstone Temperament Schedule [*Psychology*]
TTS...........	Tintina Mines Ltd. [*Toronto Stock Exchange symbol*]
TTS...........	Tissue Type Specific [*Antigen*]
TTS...........	Total Tectonic Subsidence
TTS...........	Tracker Test Set [*Dragon*] (MCD)
TTS...........	[*The*] Training School at Vineland [*An association*] (EA)
TTS...........	Transaction Tracking System (PCM)
TTS...........	Transactions. Thoroton Society [*A publication*]
TTS...........	Transdermal Therapeutic System [*Medicine*]
TTS...........	Transducer Tubing System
TTS...........	Transistor-Transistor Logic Schottky Barrier (IEEE)
TTS...........	Transmission Test Set (IEEE)
TTS...........	Transponder Test Set
TTS...........	Transportable Telemetry Set
TTS...........	True to Scale
TTS...........	Tsaratanana [*Madagascar*] [*Airport symbol*] (OAG)
TTSA........	Tactical Traffic and System Analysis (MCD)
TTSA........	Tandem Truck Safety Act [*1984*] (GFGA)
TTSA........	Transition Training Squadron, Atlantic [*Navy*]
TTSC........	TSC, Inc. of California [*NASDAQ symbol*] (NQ)
TTSD........	Telephone Tracking System Directory (MCD)
TTSF	Test and Timesharing Facility [*Social Security Administration*]
TTSF	Time to Subsequent Fix [*Quality control*]
TTSF	Tongass [*National Forest*] Timber Supply Fund [*Department of the Interior*]
TTSI	TTS, Inc. [*NASDAQ symbol*] (NQ)
TTSP	Training Test Support Package [*Army*]
TTSP	Transition Training Squadron, Pacific [*Navy*]
TTSPB.......	Transport Theory and Statistical Physics [*A publication*]
TTSPN.......	Two Terminal Series Parallel Networks
TTSR	Temporary Threshold Shift Reduction (SAA)
TTSS	[*The*] Trumpeter Swan Society (EA)
TTSt..........	Trierer Theologische Studien [*Trier*] [*A publication*] (BJA)
TTSU........	Tracker Test Set Supplemental Unit (MCD)
T & T Sup ..	Trinidad and Tobago Supreme Court Judgments [*A publication*] (ILCA)
TTT...........	Tactical Training Team [*Military*] (CAAL)
TTT...........	Taitung [*Taiwan*] [*Airport symbol*] (OAG)
TTT...........	Tallulah, LA [*Location identifier*] [*FAA*] (FAAL)

TTT...........	Tatiko-Tekhnicheskye-Trebovaniya [*Tactical Technical Requirement*] [*for military materiel*] [*Former USSR*] (RDA)
TTT...........	Telecom USA, Inc. [*NYSE symbol*] (CTT)
TTT...........	Tetrathiotetracene [*Organic chemistry*]
TTT...........	Texas College, Tyler, TX [*OCLC symbol*] (OCLC)
TTT...........	Thymol Turbidity Test [*Clinical chemistry*]
TTT...........	Time to Target (AAG)
TTT...........	Time Temperature Transformation
TTT...........	Time, Temperature, Turbulence [*Fuel technology*]
TTT...........	Time to Turn [*Ship or aircraft*]
TTT...........	Tolbutamide Tolerance Test [*Clinical chemistry*]
TTT...........	Trade Token Topics [*A publication*]
TTT...........	Training of Teacher Trainers
TTT...........	Transamerican Trailer Transport
TTT...........	Trilateral Tracking Technique
TTT...........	Trinidad & Tobago Television Co.
TTT...........	True Temperature Tunnel
TTT...........	Tyne Tees Television [*British*] (DI)
TTTA........	Teletypewriter Terminal Assembly
TTTAP	Territorial Teacher Training Assistance Program [*Department of Education*] (GFGA)
TTTE........	Tri-National Tornado Training Establishment [*British military*] (DMA)
TTTL	Transistor-to-Transistor-to-Transistor Logic (HGAA)
TTTS	Tanker-Transport Trailer System (MCD)
TTTS	Tanker Transport Training System [*Air Force*]
TTTT	Tartar-Talos-Terrier-Typhon [*Military*] (DNAB)
TTU	Tantalus Resources Ltd. [*Vancouver Stock Exchange symbol*]
TTU	Target Transfer Unit (MCD)
TTU	Tartu [*Dorpat, Jurjeio*] [*Former USSR*] [*Seismograph station code, US Geological Survey*] [*Closed*] (SEIS)
TTU	Tennessee Technical University, Cookville, TN [*OCLC symbol*] (OCLC)
TTU	Terminal Timing Unit [*NASA*] (KSC)
TTU	Terminal Transportation Unit [*Military*] (GFGA)
TTU	Tetuan [*Morocco*] [*Airport symbol*] (OAG)
TTU	Thrust Termination Unit (MSA)
TTU	Timing Terminal Unit (NASA)
TTU	Transportable Treatment Unit
TTU	Transportation Terminal Unit [*Army*]
TTuGS.......	Church of Jesus Christ of Latter-Day Saints, Genealogical Society Library, Tennessee South District Branch, Tullahoma, TN [*Library symbol*] [*Library of Congress*] (LCLS)
TTUSA	Trireme Trust USA [*An association*] (EA)
TTUV News ...	TTUV (Technical Teachers Union of Victoria) News [*A publication*]
TTV	Taiwan Television Enterprise (EY)
TTV	Teletape Video
TTV	Tenth Thickness Value [*Nuclear energy*] (NRCH)
TTV	Termination, Test, and Verification (NASA)
TTV	Territorial Petroleum [*Vancouver Stock Exchange symbol*]
TTV	Thermal Test Vehicle
TTV	Tow Test Vehicle [*Aerospace*]
TTVM	Thermal Transfer Voltmeter
TTVP........	Trentiner Tiroler Volkspartei [*Trentino Tirol People's Party*] [*Italy*] [*Political party*] (PPE)
TTW	Tactical Training Wing [*Air Force*]
TTW	Teletypewriter [*Telecommunications*]
TTW	Test [*A publication*]
TTW	Total Temperature and Weight
TTWB........	Turbine Trip with Bypass [*Nuclear energy*] (NRCH)
TTWL........	Twin Tandem Wheel Loading [*Aviation*]
TTWS	Terminal Threat Warning System
TTX	Teletex [*Telecommunications*]
TTX	Tetrodotoxin [*A poison*] [*Biochemistry*]
TTX	Thiothixene [*Tranquilizer*]
TTX	Tultex Corp. [*NYSE symbol*] (SPSG)
TTX	Tut Enterprises, Inc. [*Toronto Stock Exchange symbol*]
TTY	Teletype (CAAL)
TTY	Teletypewriter [*Telecommunications*]
TTY	Telex-Type [*Terminal*]
TTY	Torque-to-Yield [*Automotive engineering*]
TTYA........	Teletypewriter Assembly
TTYD	Tele-Typewriters for the Deaf [*An association*]
TTYQ/RSS ...	Teletypewriter Query-Reply Subsystem (CET)
TTZ...........	Tactical-Technical Assignment [*Army*] (RDA)
TTZ...........	Titizima [*Bonin Islands*] [*Seismograph station code, US Geological Survey*] [*Closed*] (SEIS)
TTZ...........	Transformation Toughened Zirconia [*Metallurgy*]
TTZ...........	Treats, Inc. [*Toronto Stock Exchange symbol*]
TTZED......	TIZ. Tonindustrie-Zeitung [*A publication*]
TTZP........	Piarco, Trinidad [*Trinidad and Tobago*] [*ICAO location identifier*] (ICLI)
TU.............	Ivory Coast [*Aircraft nationality and registration mark*] (FAAC)
TU.............	Societe Tunisienne de l'Air [*Tunisia*] [*ICAO designator*]
TU.............	Tanking Unit (AAG)
TU.............	Tanners' Union [*British*]
TU.............	Tape Unit

TU.............. Task Unit [*Military*]
TU.............. Taxicrinic Unit [*Data processing*]
TU.............. Technical Service Unit [*Military*]
TU.............. Technische Ueberwachung [*Technological Supervising*] [*A publication*]
TU.............. Technische Universitat [*Technical University*] [*German*]
TU.............. Technology Utilization
TU.............. Tenebrio Unit [*Endocrinology*]
TU.............. Terminal Unit
TU.............. Test Unit
TU.............. Testo Unico [*Consolidated Statutes*] [*Italian*]   (ILCA)
TU.............. Texte und Untersuchungen zur Geschichte der Altchristlichen Literatur [*Berlin*] [*A publication*]
TU.............. Thank You [*Communications operator's procedural remark*]
TU.............. Thermal Unit
TU.............. Thiouracil [*Biochemistry*]   (MAE)
TU.............. Thulium [*Chemical element*] [*Symbol is Tm*]   (ROG)
TU.............. Time-of-Update
TU.............. Timing Unit
TU.............. Todd Unit [*Medicine*]   (MAE)
TU.............. Torah Umesorah - National Society for Hebrew Day Schools   (EA)
TU.............. Toxic Unit [*Medicine*]
TU.............. Trade Union
TU.............. Traffic Unit
TU.............. Training Unit [*Army*]
TU.............. Transfer Unconditionally
TU.............. Transfer Unit   (AAG)
TU.............. Transmission Unit [*Telecommunications*]
TU.............. Transport Unit   (MCD)
TU.............. Transuranium [*Chemistry*]
TU.............. Tritium Unit [*Nuclear energy*]
TU.............. Trophic Unit [*Analytical biochemistry*]
TU.............. Trout Unlimited   (EA)
TU.............. Tuba
TU.............. Tube
Tu.............. Tubercle [*Anatomy*] [*Medicine*]
TU.............. Tuberculin Unit
TU.............. Tudor   (ROG)
TU.............. Tuesday
TU.............. Tugboatmen's Union [*British*]
TU.............. Tuition
TU.............. Tulane University [*New Orleans, LA*]
TU.............. Tundra Times [*A publication*]
TU.............. Tunis Airline   (DS)
TU.............. Tupolev [*Former USSR*] [*ICAO aircraft manufacturer identifier*]   (ICAO)
TU.............. Turbidity Unit
tu.............. Turkey [*MARC country of publication code*] [*Library of Congress*]   (LCCP)
TU.............. Turkey [*NATO*]
TU.............. Type Unique [*French standard troop train, World War I*]
TU.............. University of Tennessee, Knoxville, TN [*Library symbol*] [*Library of Congress*]   (LCLS)
T₃U .... Triiodothyronine Uptake [*Endocrinology*]
TUA.......... AT & T, Americus [*NYSE symbol*]   (SPSG)
TUA.......... Syndicat International des Travailleurs Unis de l'Automobile, de l'Aerospatiale, et de l'Outillage Agricole d'Amerique [*International Union, United Automobile, Aerospace, and Agricultural Implement Workers of America - UAW*] [*Canada*]
TUA.......... Teichuronic Acid [*Biochemistry*]
TUA.......... Telecommunications Users' Association   (TSSD)
TUA.......... Telephone Users Association   (EA)
TUA.......... Test Unit Adapter [*Aviation*]
TuA.......... Texte und Arbeiten [*Beuron*] [*A publication*]   (BJA)
TUA.......... Time Use Analysis [*Test*]
TUA.......... Tuai [*New Zealand*] [*Seismograph station code, US Geological Survey*]   (SEIS)
TUA.......... Tulcan [*Ecuador*] [*Airport symbol*]   (OAG)
TUAC........ Trade Union Advisory Committee [*British*]   (DAS)
TUAC........ Union Internationale des Travailleurs Unis de l'Alimentation et du Commerce [*United Food and Commercial Workers Union*] [*Canada*]
TUAC OECD ... Trade Union Advisory Committee to the Organization for Economic Cooperation and Development [*Paris, France*]   (EAIO)
TuAF......... Turkish Air Force
T/U/Ag...... Trustee under Agreement [*Legal term*]   (DLA)
TUAL........ Tentative Unit Allowance List [*Air Force*]   (AFM)
TUAR........ Turning Arbor
TUAS........ Temple University Aegean Symposium [*A publication*]
TUB.......... Temporary Unlighted Buoy [*Maps and charts*]
TUB.......... Troop Unit Basis [*Military*]
TUB.......... Tubing   (AAG)
TUB.......... Tubingen [*Federal Republic of Germany*] [*Seismograph station code, US Geological Survey*]   (SEIS)
TUB.......... Tubuai Island [*Austral Islands*] [*Airport symbol*]   (OAG)
TUB.......... Tubular [*Automotive engineering*]
TUB.......... Tulane University. Bulletin [*A publication*]
TUB.......... [*The*] Unborn Book [*A publication*]

TUBA .... John Phillip Tuba Corp. [*NASDAQ symbol*]   (NQ)
TUBA .... Tubists Universal Brotherhood Association   (EA)
TUBE......... Terminating Unfair Broadcasting Excesses [*Student legal action organization*]   (EA)
TUBE........ Trans-Urban Bicentennial Exposition
TUBEA........ Tubercle [*A publication*]
tuberc .... Tuberculosis [*Medicine*]
Tuberc Res ... Tuberculosis Research [*A publication*]
Tuberc Respir Dis ... Tuberculosis and Respiratory Diseases [*A publication*]
Tuberculol Thorac Dis ... Tuberculology and Thoracic Diseases [*A publication*]
Tuberk Forschungsinst Borstel Jahresber ... Tuberkulose Forschungsinstitut Borstel. Jahresbericht [*A publication*]
Tuberk Grenzgeb Einzeldarst ... Tuberkulose und Ihre Grenzgebiete in Einzeldarstellungen [*A publication*]
Tuberk Ihre Grenzgeb Einzeldarst ... Tuberkulose und Ihre Grenzgebiete in Einzeldarstellungen [*A publication*]
TUBITAK ... Scientific and Technical Research Council of Turkey [*Ankara*] [*Information service or system*]   (IID)
TUBLR...... Tubular [*Freight*]
TUBMEX ... Tubos De Acero De Mexico [*Associated Press abbreviation*]   (APAG)
TUBS........ Tubular Tires [*Cyclist term*] [*British*]   (DSUE)
Tubular Struct ... Tubular Structures [*A publication*]
TUBWPL.. Technische Universitaet Berlin. Arbeitspapiere zur Linguistik/ Working Papers in Linguistics [*A publication*]
TUC.......... Teaching Usefulness Classification [*of a hospital patient*]
TUC.......... Technology Utilization Center
TUC.......... Telecommunications Users Coalition   (EA)
TUC.......... Teleordering Users' Council [*British*]
TUC.......... Temporary Unemployment Compensation [*Labor*]
TUC.......... Terminal Usage Charge [*Data processing*]   (HGAA)
TUC.......... Time of Useful Consciousness [*Medicine*]
TUC.......... Tracer Resources [*Vancouver Stock Exchange symbol*]
TUC.......... Trade [*or Trades*] Union Council
TUC.......... Trades Union Congress [*British*]
TUC.......... Transportation, Utilities, Communications
Tuc.......... Tucana [*Constellation*]
TUC.......... Tucson [*Arizona*] [*Seismograph station code, US Geological Survey*]   (SEIS)
TUC.......... Tucson [*Arizona*] [*Geomagnetic observatory code*]
TUC.......... Tucuman [*Argentina*] [*Airport symbol*]   (OAG)
TUC.......... Type Unit Code   (CINC)
TUC.......... University of Tennessee at Chattanooga, Chattanooga, TN [*OCLC symbol*]   (OCLC)
TUCA .... Tilt-Up Concrete Association   (EA)
TUCA .... Transient Undercooling Accident [*Nuclear energy*]
TUCA .... Turning Cam [*Tool*]   (AAG)
TUCC .... Transport Users' Consultative Council [*British*]   (ILCA)
TUCC .... Triangle Universities Computation Center [*Durham, NC*]
TUCE .... Test of Understanding of College Economics
TUCHA ..... Type Unit Characteristics
Tu Civ LF... Tulane Civil Law Forum [*A publication*]   (DLA)
Tuck .... Tucker and Clephane's Reports [*21 District of Columbia*] [*1892-93*] [*A publication*]   (DLA)
TUCK .... Tucker Drilling Co., Inc. [*NASDAQ symbol*]   (NQ)
Tuck .... Tucker's New York Surrogate's Court Reports [*A publication*]   (DLA)
Tuck .... Tucker's Reports [*District of Columbia*] [*A publication*]   (DLA)
Tuck .... Tucker's Reports [*156-175 Massachusetts*] [*A publication*]   (DLA)
Tuck .... Tucker's Select Cases [*Newfoundland*] [*A publication*]   (DLA)
Tuck Bl Com ... Tucker's Blackstone's Commentaries [*A publication*]   (DLA)
Tuck & C.... Tucker and Clephane's Reports [*21 District of Columbia*] [*A publication*]   (DLA)
Tuck & Cl... Tucker and Clephane's Reports [*21 District of Columbia*] [*1892-93*] [*A publication*]   (DLA)
Tuck Dist of Col ... Tucker's District of Columbia Appeals [*A publication*]   (DLA)
Tucker........ Tucker [*F.A.*] Group, Inc. [*Associated Press abbreviation*]   (APAG)
Tucker........ Tucker's New York Surrogate's Court Reports [*A publication*]   (DLA)
Tucker's Blackstone ... Tucker's Blackstone's Commentaries [*A publication*]   (DLA)
Tuck Lect... Tucker's Lectures [*A publication*]   (DLA)
Tuck Pl ... Tucker's Pleadings [*A publication*]   (DLA)
Tuck Sel Cas ... Tucker's Select Cases [*1817-28*] [*Newfoundland*] [*A publication*]   (DLA)
Tuck Sur .... Tucker's Surrogate Reports, City of New York [*A publication*]   (DLA)
Tuck Surr... Tucker's Surrogate Reports, City of New York [*A publication*]   (DLA)
TUCN .... Trades Union Congress of Nigeria
Tucn .... Tucana [*Constellation*]
TUCOPS... [*The*] Universal Coterie of Pipe Smokers   (EA)
TUCOSP... Tehran Union Catalogue of Scientific Periodicals [*A publication*]
TUCR .... Troop Unit Change Request
TUCSA...... Trade Union Council of South Africa

TucsEP ...... Tucson Electric Power Co. [*Associated Press abbreviation*] (APAG)
TUD .... Tambacounda [*Senegal*] [*Airport symbol*] (OAG)
TUD .... Technology Utilization Division [*NASA*] (IEEE)
TUD .... Total Urethral Discharge [*Medicine*]
TUD .... Tugold Resources, Inc. [*Vancouver Stock Exchange symbol*]
TUDC .... Tauroursodeoxycholate [*Biochemistry*]
TUDCA ..... Tauroursodeoxycholic Acid [*Biochemistry*]
Tud Cas Merc Law ... Tudor's Leading Cases on Mercantile Law [*3 eds.*] [*1860-84*] [*A publication*] (DLA)
Tud Cas RP ... Tudor's Leading Cases on Real Property [*4 eds.*] [*1856-98*] [*A publication*] (DLA)
Tud Char Tr ... Tudor's Charitable Trusts [*2nd ed.*] [*1871*] [*A publication*] (DLA)
Tud Char Trusts ... Tudor's Charitable Trusts [*2nd ed.*] [*1871*] [*A publication*] (DLA)
Tud Ert Agrartud Egy Godollo ... Tudomanyos Ertesito-Agrartudomanyi Egyetem Godollo [*A publication*]
Tud Ert Agrartud Egy Godollo (Hung) ... Tudumanyos Ertesito-Agrartudomanyi Egyetem Godollo (Hungary) [*A publication*]
Tud Mezogazd ... Tudomany es Mezogazdasag [*A publication*]
Tud & Musz Tajek ... Tudomanyos es Muszaki Tajekoztatas [*A publication*]
Tudom Musz Tajek ... Tudomanyos es Muszaki Tajekoztatas [*A publication*]
Tudor Lead Cas Real Prop ... Tudor's Leading Cases on Real Property [*A publication*] (DLA)
Tudor's LCML ... Tudor's Leading Cases on Mercantile Law [*A publication*] (DLA)
Tudor's LCRP ... Tudor's Leading Cases on Real Property [*A publication*] (DLA)
TUDRIP .... Tube Plate Drilling Program [*Kongsberg Vaapenfabrikk*] [*Software package*] (NCC)
TUDS .... Tunnel Detection System (MCD)
Tud-Szerv Tajekoz ... Tudomanyszervezesi Tajekoztato [*A publication*]
TUE .... Tolerance of Unrealistic Experience [*Psychometrics*]
TUE .... Trainer Unique Equipment [*Navy*]
TUE .... Tuesday (AFM)
TUE .... Tupile [*Panama*] [*Airport symbol*] (OAG)
TUE .... University of Tokyo (EDUCATSS) [*UTLAS symbol*]
TUEL .... Trade Union Educational League
TUES .... Tuesday (EY)
TUES .... Tuesday Morning, Inc. [*Dallas, TX*] [*NASDAQ symbol*] (NQ)
TUeV Mitt Mitglieder Tech Ueberwach-Ver Bayern ... TUeV [*Technischer Ueberwachungs-Verein*] Mitteilungen fuer die Mitglieder. Technischer Ueberwachungs-Verein Bayern [*German Federal Republic*] [*A publication*]
TUF .... Tactical Undercover Function [*Chicago police operation*]
TUF .... Thermal Utilization Factor (MCD)
TUF .... Tours [*France*] [*Airport symbol*] (OAG)
TUF .... Trade Union Federation [*British*] (EY)
TUF .... Transmitter Underflow
TUF .... Umweltmagazin. Fachzeitschrift fuer Umwelttechnik in Industrie und Kommune [*A publication*]
TUFA .... Total Unsaturated Fatty Acid [*of foodstuffs*]
TUFA .... Trans Unsaturated Fatty Acids
TUFCDF .. Thorium-Uranium Fuel Cycle Development Facility [*Nuclear energy*]
TUFEC ...... Thailand-UNESCO Fundamental Education Centre
TUFF-TUG ... Tape Update of Formatted Files-Format Table Tape Updater and Generator [*Data processing*]
TUFI .... This Umbrella Folds Itself [*Trademark for type of umbrella*]
TUFL .... Trade Unionists for Labour [*British*]
TU-FM ...... University of Tennessee Center for the Health Sciences/ Memphis Department of Family Medicine, Memphis, TN [*Library symbol*] [*Library of Congress*] (LCLS)
TUFMIS ... Tactical Unit Financial Management Information System
TUFPB ...... Proceedings. Faculty of Science. Tokai University [*A publication*]
Tufs Folia Med ... Tufs Folia Medica [*A publication*]
Tufts Coll Studies ... Tufts College Studies [*A publication*]
Tufts Dent Outlook ... Tufts Dental Outlook [*A publication*]
Tufts Health Sci Rev ... Tufts Health Science Review [*A publication*]
TUFX .... Turning Fixture
TUG .... Maritrans Partners LP [*NYSE symbol*] (SPSG)
TUG .... Tape Unit Group [*Telecommunications*] (TEL)
TUG .... Telecommunications Users Group [*Montclair, NJ*] [*Telecommunications service*] (TSSD)
TUG .... Teleram Users Group (EA)
TUG .... Tire Uniformity Grading [*Automotive engineering*]
TUG .... Total Urinary Gonadotropin [*Clinical chemistry*]
TUG .... Towed Universal Glider
TUG .... TRANSAC [*Transistorized Automatic Computer*] Users Group
TUG .... Transtex Universal Gateway [*Data processing*]
TUG .... Tuguegarao [*Philippines*] [*Airport symbol*] (OAG)
TUG .... Tunable Ultraviolet Generation
TUGAL ..... Texte und Untersuchungen zur Geschichte der Altchristlichen Literatur [*A publication*]
TU Gazette ... University of Tasmania. Gazette [*A publication*] (APTA)
TUGEA ..... Teknisk Ukeblad [*A publication*]
TUGRA ..... Report of Investigations. University of Texas at Austin. Bureau of Economic Geology [*A publication*]

TUH .... Review of Economic Conditions [*Ankara*] [*A publication*]
TUH .... Tullahoma, TN [*Location identifier*] [*FAA*] (FAAL)
TU-H .... University of Tennessee Center for the Health Sciences/ Knoxville, Preston Medical Library, Knoxville, TN [*Library symbol*] [*Library of Congress*] (LCLS)
TUHC .... Tucker Holding Co., Inc. [*NASDAQ symbol*] (NQ)
TUHTKP... Time Urgent Hard Target Kill Potential (MCD)
TUI .... Green Bay, WI [*Location identifier*] [*FAA*] (FAAL)
TUI .... Tool Usage Instructions (MCD)
TUI .... Trade Union Immunities [*British*]
TUI .... Trade Union International
TUI .... Trade Unions International of Transport Workers (EAIO)
TUI .... Trypsin Units Inhibited [*Food technology*]
TUI .... Tuinderij. Vakblad voor de Intensieve Groenteteelt [*A publication*]
TUI .... Tuition (DSUE)
TUI .... Turaif [*Saudi Arabia*] [*Airport symbol*] (OAG)
TUIAFPW ... Trade Unions International of Agriculture, Forestry, and Plantation Workers [*See also UISTAFP*] [*Prague, Czechoslovakia*] (EAIO)
TUIFU .... [*The*] Ultimate in Foul Ups [*Military slang*] [*Bowdlerized version*]
TUII .... TU International, Inc. [*NASDAQ symbol*] (NQ)
TUIMWE ... Trade Unions International of Miners and Workers in Energy [*See also UISMTE*] (EAIO)
TUIPAE .... Trade Unions International of Public and Allied Employees [*Berlin, Federal Republic of Germany*] (EAIO)
TUIR .... Time until in Range
TUIREC .... Trade Union International Research and Education Group [*England*] (EAIO)
TUITW ...... Trade Unions International of Transport Workers (EAIO)
TUIWC ...... Trade Unions International of Workers in Commerce [*Prague, Czechoslovakia*] (EAIO)
TUJ .... Tubouterine Junction [*Anatomy*]
TUJ .... Tum [*Ethiopia*] [*Airport symbol*] (OAG)
TUK .... Nantucket, MA [*Location identifier*] [*FAA*] (FAAL)
TuK .... Text und Kritik [*A publication*]
TUK .... Tuckahoe Financial Corp. [*Toronto Stock Exchange symbol*]
TUK .... Turbat [*Pakistan*] [*Airport symbol*] (OAG)
tuk .... Turkmen [*MARC language code*] [*Library of Congress*] (LCCP)
TuL .... Tod und Leben nach der Vorstellungen der Babylonier [*A publication*] (BJA)
TUL .... Tula Peak, New Mexico [*Spaceflight Tracking and Data Network*] [*NASA*]
Tu L .... Tulane Law Review [*A publication*]
TUL .... Tulsa [*Oklahoma*] [*Geomagnetic observatory code*]
TUL .... Tulsa [*Oklahoma*] [*Seismograph station code, US Geological Survey*] (SEIS)
TUL .... Tulsa [*Oklahoma*] [*Airport symbol*] (OAG)
TUL .... Tulsa City-County Library System, Tulsa, OK [*OCLC symbol*] (OCLC)
TU-L .... University of Tennessee, Law Library, Knoxville, TN [*Library symbol*] [*Library of Congress*] (LCLS)
TULACS ... Tactical Unit Location and Communication System (MCD)
Tulane Law R ... Tulane Law Review [*A publication*]
Tulane L Rev ... Tulane Law Review [*A publication*]
Tulane St ... Tulane Studies in English [*A publication*]
Tulane Stud Eng ... Tulane Studies in English [*A publication*]
Tulane Stud Geol ... Tulane Studies in Geology [*A publication*]
Tulane Stud Geol Paleontol ... Tulane Studies in Geology and Paleontology [*A publication*]
Tulane Stud Phil ... Tulane Studies in Philosophy [*A publication*]
Tulane Stud Zool ... Tulane Studies in Zoology [*A publication*]
Tulane Stud Zool Bot ... Tulane Studies in Zoology and Botany [*A publication*]
Tulane U Stud Eng ... Tulane University. Studies in English [*A publication*]
TU Law R .. University of Tasmania. Law Review [*A publication*] (APTA)
TULC........ Trade Union Leadership Council (EA)
TULCC ...... Triangle University Library Cooperative Committee [*Library network*]
Tul Civ LF ... Tulane Civil Law Forum [*A publication*] (DLA)
TULE .... Transistorized Universal Logic Elements
TULF .... Tamil United Liberation Front [*Sri Lanka*] (PD)
Tul LR .... Tulane Law Review [*A publication*]
Tul L Rev ... Tulane Law Review [*A publication*]
Tu LR .... Tulane Law Review [*A publication*]
TULRA...... Trade Union and Labour Relations Act [*1974 and 1976*] [*British*] (DCTA)
TULS .... TRON [*The Real-Time Operating System Nucleus*] Universal Language System [*Data processing*]
TULS .... Tulsa World [*A publication*]
TULSA ...... Petroleum Abstracts [*Online*]
Tulsa Bs C ... Tulsa Business Chronicle [*A publication*]
Tulsa Geol Soc Dig ... Tulsa Geological Society. Digest [*A publication*]
Tulsa Geol Soc Digest ... Tulsa Geological Society. Digest [*A publication*]
Tulsa L J ... Tulsa Law Journal [*A publication*]
Tulsa Med ... Tulsa Medicine [*A publication*]
Tul Tax Inst ... Tulane Tax Institute [*A publication*]
Tultex........ Tultex Corp. [*Associated Press abbreviation*] (APAG)

Tul Tidelands Inst ... Tulane Mineral and Tidelands Law Institute [*A publication*]
TUM.......... Technical University in Munich [*Germany*]
TUM.......... Terminal User's Manual
TuM........... Texte und Materialien der Frau Professor Hilprecht Collection of Babylonian Antiquities im Eigentum der Univerisitaet Jena [*A publication*] (BJA)
TuM........... Torah Umesorah - National Society for Hebrew Day Schools
TUM.......... Total Unscheduled Maintenance Time
TUM.......... Trades Union Movement
TUM.......... Tumut [*Australia*] [*Airport symbol*] (OAG)
TUM.......... Tumwater [*Washington*] [*Seismograph station code, US Geological Survey*] (SEIS)
TUM.......... Tuning Unit Member (IEEE)
TUM.......... University of Tennessee, Center for the Health Sciences, Memphis, TN [*OCLC symbol*] (OCLC)
TU-M........ University of Tennessee Medical Units, Memphis, TN [*Library symbol*] [*Library of Congress*] (LCLS)
TUM.......... [*The*] Unsatisfied Man [*A publication*]
TUMA...... Tumacacori National Monument
TU-MDC... University of Tennessee, Downtown Memphis Center, Memphis, TN [*Library symbol*] [*Library of Congress*] (LCLS)
TUME....... [*The*] Ultimate Musical Experience [*Rock music group*]
TUMEA .... Tunisie Medicale [*A publication*]
Tumor Diagn ... Tumor Diagnostik [*A publication*]
Tumor Diagn Ther ... Tumor Diagnostik und Therapie [*A publication*]
Tumor Res ... Tumor Research [*A publication*]
Tumour Biol ... Tumour Biology [*A publication*]
TU-MS...... University of Tennessee Center for the Health Sciences Library, Stollerman Library, Memphis, TN [*Library symbol*] [*Library of Congress*] (LCLS)
TuMV .... Turnip Mosaic Virus
TUN........... Flint, MI [*Location identifier*] [*FAA*] (FAAL)
TUN........... Technical University of Nova Scotia [*UTLAS symbol*]
TUN........... Tennessee State University, Downtown Campus, Nashville, TN [*OCLC symbol*] (OCLC)
TUN........... Transfer Unconditionally
TUN........... Tuning (AAG)
TUN........... Tunis [*Tunisia*] [*Seismograph station code, US Geological Survey*] [*Closed*] (SEIS)
TUN........... Tunis [*Tunisia*] [*Airport symbol*] (OAG)
TUN........ Tunisia [*ANSI three-letter standard code*] (CNC)
TUN........... Turner Energy & Resources [*Vancouver Stock Exchange symbol*]
TUNA........ Tunable Attribute Display Subsystem (CAAL)
Tuners JL .. Tuners' Journal [*A publication*]
TUNG........ Tungsten (AAG)
Tungsram Tech Mitt ... Tungsram Technische Mitteilungen [*A publication*]
TUNICAT ... Tunicatae [*Coated*] [*Pharmacy*]
Tunis Agric ... Tunisie Agricole [*A publication*]
TUNISAIR ... Societe Tunisienne de l'Air [*Airline*] [*Tunisia*]
Tunisie Agr ... Tunisie Agricole [*A publication*]
Tunisie Econ ... Tunisie Economique [*A publication*]
Tunis Med ... Tunisie Medicale [*A publication*]
TUNL........ Triangle Universities Nuclear Laboratory [*Research center*] (RCD)
TUNL........ Tunnel
Tunnels Ouvrages Souterr ... Tunnels et Ouvrages Souterrains [*A publication*]
Tunnels Tunnell ... Tunnels and Tunnelling [*A publication*]
Tunnlg Technol Newsl ... Tunneling Technology Newsletter [*A publication*]
Tunn Technol Newsl ... Tunneling Technology Newsletter [*United States*] [*A publication*]
Tunn Tunn ... Tunnels and Tunnelling [*A publication*]
Tunn Tunnlg ... Tunnels and Tunnelling [*A publication*]
TUNX........ Tunex International, Inc. [*NASDAQ symbol*] (NQ)
TUO.......... Taupo [*New Zealand*] [*Airport symbol*] (OAG)
TUO.......... Technology Utilization Office [*NASA*]
TUO.......... Teuton Resources Corp. [*Vancouver Stock Exchange symbol*]
TUO........... Tucson Observatory [*Arizona*] [*Seismograph station code, US Geological Survey*] (SEIS)
TUOC........ Tactical Unit Operations Center (AFM)
TUP .... Technology Utilization Program [*Defunct*]
TUP .... Telephony User Part [*Telecommunications*] (TEL)
TUP .... Temple University Press
TUP .... Torres United Party [*Australia*] [*Political party*]
TUP .... Tovarystvo Ukrainskykh Progresystiv [*Ukrainian Progressive Association*] [*Russian*] [*Political party*] (PPE)
TUP .... Trickle Up Program (EA)
TUP .... Tupelo [*Mississippi*] [*Airport symbol*] (OAG)
TUP .... Tupik [*Former USSR*] [*Seismograph station code, US Geological Survey*] (SEIS)
TUP .... Twin Unit Pack [*for vehicles*]
Tup App.... Tupper's Appeal Reports [*Ontario*] [*A publication*] (DLA)
TUPC........ T. U. P. Charlton's Georgia Reports [*A publication*] (DLA)
TUPC........ Transfer Underwater Pressure Chamber (DNAB)
T U P Charlt ... T. U. P. Charlton's Georgia Reports [*A publication*] (DLA)
TUPE........ Tanganyika Union of Public Employees
TUPE........ Tupelo National Battlefield
TUPJ......... Roadtown/Beef Island [*Virgin Islands*] [*ICAO location identifier*] (ICLI)

TUPONA .. [*The*] United Provinces of North America [*See also EFISGA*] [*Suggested early name for Canada*]
Tupp........... Tupper's Appeal Reports [*Ontario*] [*A publication*] (DLA)
Tupp........... Tupper's Upper Canada Practice Reports [*A publication*] (DLA)
Tupp App... Tupper's Appeal Reports [*Ontario*] [*A publication*] (DLA)
Tupper ...... Tupper's Appeal Reports [*Ontario*] [*A publication*] (DLA)
Tupper .... Tupper's Upper Canada Practice Reports [*A publication*] (DLA)
TUPS........ Technical User Performance Specifications [*US Independent Telephone Association*] [*Telecommunications*] (TEL)
TUPW .... Virgin Gorda [*Virgin Islands*] [*ICAO location identifier*] (ICLI)
TUR........... American Turners [*An association*]
TUR........... Temporary Unattached Register [*Employment*] [*British*]
TUR........... Total Unemployment Rate
TUR........... Traffic Usage Recorder [*Telecommunications*]
TUR........... Transurethral Resection [*of prostate gland*]
TUR........... Tucurui [*Brazil*] [*Airport symbol*] (OAG)
TUR........... Turbat [*Former USSR*] [*Seismograph station code, US Geological Survey*] [*Closed*] (SEIS)
TUR........... Turbine
TUR........... Turkey [*ANSI three-letter standard code*] (CNC)
tur.............. Turkish [*MARC language code*] [*Library of Congress*] (LCCP)
TUR........... Turkish Economy [*A publication*]
TUR........... Turner Corp. [*AMEX symbol*] (SPSG)
Tur .... Turner's Reports [*99-101 Kentucky*] [*A publication*] (DLA)
Tur .... Turner's Reports [*35-48 Arkansas*] [*A publication*] (DLA)
Tur .... Turner's Select Pleas of the Forest [*Selden Society Publication, Vol. 13*] [*A publication*] (DLA)
TUR........... Turret (MSA)
TURB .... Transurethral Resection of the Bladder [*Medicine*] (AAMN)
TURB .... Turbidity (AAMN)
TURB .... Turbine (AAG)
TURB .... Turbulence
TURBC....... Turbulence (FAAC)
TURBO ..... Turbocharger [*Automotive engineering*]
TURBOALT ... Turboalternator (AAG)
TURBOCAT ... Turbine-Powered Catapult
TURBOGEN ... Turbogenerator (AAG)
Turbomachinery Int ... Turbomachinery International [*A publication*]
Turbomach Int ... Turbomachinery International [*A publication*]
TURBT..... Turbulent (FAAC)
Turbul Meas Liq Proc Symp ... Turbulence Measurements in Liquids. Proceedings of Symposium [*A publication*]
TURCO ..... Turnaround Control [*Navy*]
TUREA..... Tumor Research [*A publication*]
TURF........ Thorium-Uranium Recycle Facility [*Oak Ridge National Laboratory*]
TURF........ Turf Paradise, Inc. [*NASDAQ symbol*] (NQ)
Turf Bull ... Turf Bulletin [*A publication*]
Turf Cult .... Turf Culture [*A publication*]
TURK .... Turkey
Turk AD .... Turk Arkeoloji Dergisi [*A publication*]
Turk AEC Ankara Nucl Res Cent Tech J ... Turkish Atomic Energy Commission. Ankara Nuclear Research Center. Technical Journal [*A publication*]
Turk Ark Derg ... Turk Arkeoloji Dergisi [*A publication*]
Turk Biol Derg ... Turk Biologi Dergisi [*A publication*]
Turk Bitki Koruma Derg ... Turkiye Bitki Koruma Dergisi [*A publication*]
Turk Bull Hyg Exp Biol ... Turkish Bulletin of Hygiene and Experimental Biology [*A publication*]
Turk Cerrahi Cemiy Mecm ... Turk Cerrahi Cemiyeti Mecmuasi [*A publication*]
Turkest ...... Turkestan
Turkey Prod ... Turkey Producer [*A publication*]
Turk Fiz Dernegi Bul ... Turk Fizik Dernegi Bulteni [*A publication*]
Turk For Pol Rep ... Turkish Foreign Policy Report [*A publication*]
Turk Gen Kim Kurumu Derg B ... Turkiye Genel Kimyagerler Kurumu Dergisi-B [*A publication*]
Turk Hemsire Derg ... Turk Hemsireler Dergisi [*A publication*]
Turk Hifzissihha Tecr Biol Mecm ... Turk Hifzissihha ve Tecrubi Biologi Mecmuasi [*A publication*]
Turk Hij Deney Biyol Derg ... Turk Hijiyen ve Deneysel Biyoloji Dergisi [*A publication*]
Turk Hij Deneysel Biyol Derg ... Turk Hijiyen ve Deneysel Biyoloji Dergisi [*A publication*]
Turk Hij Tecr Biyol Derg ... Turk Hijiyen ve Tecruby Biyoloji Dergisi [*A publication*]
Turk J Biol ... Turkish Journal of Biology [*A publication*]
Turk Jeol Kurumu Bul ... Turkiye Jeoloji Kurumu Bulteni [*A publication*]
Turk Jeomorfologlar Dernegi Yayini ... Turkiye Jeomorfologlar Dernegi. Yayini [*A publication*]
Turk J Nucl Sci ... Turkish Journal of Nuclear Sciences [*A publication*]
Turk J Pediatr ... Turkish Journal of Pediatrics [*A publication*]
Turk Ljiyen Tecruebi Biyol Dergisi ... Turk Ljiyen ve Tecruebi Biyoloji Dergisi [*A publication*]
Turk Mikrobiyol Cemiy Derg ... Turk Mikrobiyoloji Cemiyeti Dergisi [*A publication*]
Turk Miner Res Explor Bull ... Turkey. Mineral Research and Exploration Institute. Bulletin [*A publication*]

Turkm Iskra ... Turkmenskaya Iskra [*Former USSR*] [*A publication*]
TurkmSSR ... Turkmen Soviet Socialist Republic
Turk Publ Adm Annu ... Turkish Public Administration Annual [*A publication*]
Turksh .... Turkish Investment Fund [*Associated Press abbreviation*] (APAG)
Turk Ship... Turkish Shipping [*A publication*]
Turk Tar Derg ... Turk Tarih. Arkeologya ve Etnografya Dergisi [*A publication*]
Turk Tip Akad Mecm ... Turkiye Tip Akademisi Mecmuasi [*A publication*]
Turk Tip Cemiy Mecm ... Turkiye Tip Cemiyeti Mecmuasi [*A publication*]
Turk Tip Cem Mecm ... Turkiye Tip Cemiyeti Mecmuasi [*Turkey*] [*A publication*]
Turk Tip Dern Derg ... Turk Tip Dernegi Dergisi [*A publication*]
Turk Tip Encumeni Ars ... Turkiye Tip Encumeni Arsivi [*A publication*]
Turn .... Turner's Reports [*35-48 Arkansas*] [*A publication*] (DLA)
Turn .... Turner's Reports [*99-101 Kentucky*] [*A publication*] (DLA)
Turn .... Turner's Select Pleas of the Forest [*Selden Society Publication, Vol. 13*] [*A publication*] (DLA)
Turn Anglo Sax ... Turner's History of the Anglo Saxon [*A publication*] (DLA)
TurnB........ Turner Broadcasting System, Inc. [*Associated Press abbreviation*] (APAG)
TURNBKLE ... Turnbuckle[s] [*Freight*]
Turnbull Libr Rec ... Turnbull Library Record [*A publication*]
Turn Ch Pr ... Turner's Practice of the Court of Chancery [*4th ed.*] [*1821*] [*A publication*] (DLA)
Turn Cop.... Turner on Copyright in Designs [*1849*] [*A publication*] (DLA)
Turn & P .... Turner and Phillips' English Chancery Reports [*A publication*] (DLA)
Turn Pat..... Turner on Patents [*1851*] [*A publication*] (DLA)
Turn & Ph ... Turner and Phillips' English Chancery Reports [*A publication*] (DLA)
Turn Pr ...... Turnbull's Practice [*New York*] [*A publication*] (DLA)
Turn Qui Tit ... Turner on Quieting Titles [*A publication*] (DLA)
Turn & R.... Turner and Russell's English Chancery Reports [*37 English Reprint*] [*A publication*] (DLA)
TURNRC .. Turner Corp. [*Associated Press abbreviation*] (APAG)
Turn Rec ..... Turnbull Library Record [*New Zealand*] [*A publication*]
Turn & R (Eng) ... Turner and Russell's English Chancery Reports [*37 English Reprint*] [*A publication*] (DLA)
Turn & Rus ... Turner and Russell's English Chancery Reports [*37 English Reprint*] [*A publication*] (DLA)
Turn & Russ ... Turner and Russell's English Chancery Reports [*37 English Reprint*] [*A publication*] (DLA)
Turon Yliopiston Julk Sar A-II ... Turon Yliopiston Julkaisuja. Sarja A-II [*A publication*]
TURP........ Transurethral Resection of the Prostate [*Medicine*]
TURPS...... Terrestrial Unattended Reactor Power System
TURQ....... Turquoise (ROG)
Tur & R...... Turner and Russell's English Chancery Reports [*37 English Reprint*] [*1822-24*] [*A publication*] (DLA)
TURRA ..... Turrialba [*Costa Rica*] [*A publication*]
Tur & Ru.... Turner and Russell's English Chancery Reports [*37 English Reprint*] [*1822-24*] [*A publication*] (DLA)
Tur & Rus .. Turner and Russell's English Chancery Reports [*37 English Reprint*] [*1822-24*] [*A publication*] (DLA)
TURS........ Terminal Usage Reporting System [*Data processing*]
Tu & Rus.... Turner and Russell's English Chancery Reports [*1822-24*] [*A publication*] (DLA)
TUS .... Tailored Upper Stage (MCD)
TUS .... Treasurer of the United States (AFM)
TUS .... Tucson [*Arizona*] [*Airport symbol*] (OAG)
TUS .... Tugboat Underwriting Syndicate [*Defunct*] (EA)
TUS .... Tuscarora [*New York*] [*Seismograph station code, US Geological Survey*] [*Closed*] (SEIS)
TUS .... Tushaun Resources, Inc. [*Vancouver Stock Exchange symbol*]
TUS .... Tuskegee Institute, Tuskegee, AL [*OCLC symbol*] (OCLC)
TUS .... Tussis [*Cough*] [*Pharmacy*]
TUSA........ Third United States Army [*Terminated, 1973*]
TUSA........ Trekville USA (EA)
TUSAB...... [*The*] United States Army Band (AABC)
TUSAC...... [*The*] United States Army Chorus (AABC)
TUSAFG ... [*The*] United States Air Force Group, American Mission for Aid to Turkey
TUSAS ...... Twayne's United States Authors Series [*A publication*]
TUSC .... Technology Use Studies Center [*Southeastern State College*]
TUSC........ Tuscarora, Inc. [*NASDAQ symbol*] (NQ)
Tusc.......... Tusculanae Disputationes [*of Cicero*] [*Classical studies*] (OCD)
TU-SI........ University of Tennessee, Space Institute Library, Tullahoma, TN [*Library symbol*] [*Library of Congress*] (LCLS)
TUSIDBAD ... Tomb of the Unknown Soldier Identification Badge [*Military decoration*] (GFGA)
Tuskegee Exp ... Tuskegee Normal and Industrial Institute. Experiment Station. Publications [*A publication*]
TUSLOG..... Turkish-United States Logistic Group
TUSLOG... [*The*] United States Logistics Group [*Military*] (AABC)
TUSLOGDET ... Turkish-United States Logistics Group Detachment (DNAB)

TUSQA ..... Quarterly Bulletin. Faculty of Science. Tehran University [*A publication*]
TUSSI .... Temple University Short Syntax Inventory [*Educational test*]
TUSSIL..... Tussilago [*Coltsfoot*] [*Pharmacology*] (ROG)
TUSS MOL ... Tussi Molesta [*When the Cough Is Troublesome*] [*Pharmacy*]
Tussock Grassl Mt Lands Inst Annu Rep ... Tussock Grasslands and Mountain Lands Institute. Annual Report [*A publication*]
TUSS URG ... Tussi Urgente [*When the Cough Is Troublesome*] [*Pharmacy*]
TUST........ Texarkana Union Station Trust [*AAR code*]
TUT .... Tafuna, AS [*Location identifier*] [*FAA*] (FAAL)
TUT .... Transistor under Test (IEEE)
TUT .... Travailleurs Unis du Telegraphe [*United Telegraph Workers - UTW*] [*Canada*]
TUT .... Travailleurs Unis des Transports [*United Transportation Union - UTU*] [*Canada*]
TUT .... Tube Template (MCD)
TUT .... Tube under Test (MSA)
TUT .... Tucson - Telemeter [*Arizona*] [*Seismograph station code, US Geological Survey*] [*Closed*] (SEIS)
tut .... Turko-Tataric [*MARC language code*] [*Library of Congress*] (LCCP)
TUT .... University of Saint Thomas, Houston, TX [*OCLC symbol*] (OCLC)
TUT's .... Totally Unified Theories [*Cosmology*]
TUTase...... Terminal Uridylyl Transferase [*An enzyme*]
Tutkimuksia Res Rep ... Tutkimuksia Research Reports [*A publication*]
Tutkimus Tek ... Tutkimus ja Tekniikka [*A publication*]
TUTNB ..... Tunneling Technology Newsletter [*A publication*]
TUTOR ...... [*A*] Programming Language (CSR)
TUTS........ True Ultimate Tensile Strength (MCD)
TUTT........ Tropical Upper Tropospheric Trough [*Meteorology*]
Tutt & C ..... Tuttle and Carpenter's Reports [*52 California*] [*A publication*] (DLA)
Tutt & Carp ... Tuttle and Carpenter's Reports [*52 California*] [*A publication*] (DLA)
Tuttle .... Tuttle and Carpenter's Reports [*52 California*] [*A publication*] (DLA)
Tuttle & Carpenter ... Tuttle and Carpenter's Reports [*52 California*] [*A publication*] (DLA)
TUTUB ..... Tunnels and Tunnelling [*A publication*]
TUU.......... Huntington, WV [*Location identifier*] [*FAA*] (FAAL)
TUU.......... Tabuk [*Saudi Arabia*] [*Airport symbol*] (OAG)
TUUL .... Trade Union Unity League
TUUL........ Transurethral Ultrasonic Uterolithotripsy [*Urology*]
TUV .... Tucupita [*Venezuela*] [*Airport symbol*] (OAG)
TUV .... Tuvalu [*ANSI three-letter standard code*] (CNC)
TUVX .... Tulip Virus X [*Plant pathology*]
TUW .... Trustee under Will [*Legal term*] (DLA)
TUW .... Tubala [*Panama*] [*Airport symbol*] (OAG)
TUWAH... Trade Union Women of African Heritage (EA)
TUWC....... Tactical Utilization Working Committee [*Navy*] (MCD)
TUWR .... Turning Wrench [*Tool*] (AAG)
TUX .... Tuxedo (DSUE)
TUX .... Tuxpeno [*Race of maize*]
TUXX .... Al's Formal Wear, Inc. [*NASDAQ symbol*] (NQ)
TUY .... Tulum [*Mexico*] [*Airport symbol*] [*Obsolete*] (OAG)
TuZ .... Texte und Zeichen [*A publication*]
TUZI........ Tuzigoot National Monument
TV .... Taff Vale Railway [*Wales*]
TV .... Target Valve (MCD)
T/V .... Target Vehicle [*Air Force*] (AAG)
TV .... Target Velocity
TV .... Target Vulnerability (MCD)
TV .... Telefunken Variable Microgroove [*Record label*] [*Germany*]
TV .... Television
TV .... Television [*A publication*]
TV .... Television, Vision Channel
TV .... Terminal Velocity [*Navy*]
TV .... Test Vehicle
T & V .... Test and Verify Programs [*Data processing*] (MDG)
TV .... Tetrazolium Violet [*Also, TZV*]
TV .... Thames Valley [*England*]
TV .... Thermal Vacuum
TV .... Throttle Valve
TV .... Thrust Vector [*Aerospace*] (NASA)
TV .... Tidal Volume [*Amount of air that moves in and out of lungs under given conditions*] [*Physiology*]
TV .... Time Variation of Gain
TV .... Title Verso [*Publishing*] (WDMC)
TV .... Total Value
TV .... Total Volume
TV .... Trans America Airlines, Inc. [*ICAO designator*] (FAAC)
TV .... Transfer Vector
TV .... Transfer and Void (MCD)
TV .... Transfer Voucher (AFM)
TV .... Transport Vehicle [*Military*]
TV .... Transversion [*Molecular biology*]
TV .... Transvestite [*Medicine*]
TV .... Travel Voucher (GFGA)
TV .... Traverse (IEEE)
TV .... Treji Varti [*A publication*]

TV .... Trial Visit (AAMN)
TV .... Trichomonas vaginalis [*A protozoan*] [*Medicine*]
TV .... Tricuspid Valve [*Anatomy*]
TV .... Trinidad Volunteers [*British military*] (DMA)
TV .... Trip Valve [*Railroad term*]
TV .... Tube Tester [*JETDS nomenclature*] [*Military*] (CET)
TV .... Tuberculin Volutin [*Medicine*] (MAE)
TV .... Tunica Vaginalis [*Anatomy*]
TV .... Turbo Vision [*Borland International*] [*Data processing*] (PCM)
tv .... Tuvalu [*gn (Gilbert and Ellice Islands) used in records cataloged before October 1978*] [*MARC country of publication code*] [*Library of Congress*] (LCCP)
TV .... Tuvalu [*ANSI two-letter standard code*] (CNC)
TV .... Tzertovnyia Viedomosti [*A publication*]
Tv .... Ventral Touch Neurons [*of a leech*]
TV .... [*The*] Voluntaryists (EA)
TV5 .... Television Francophone par Satellite [*France*] (EAIO)
TVA .... 369th Veterans' Association (EA)
TVA .... Morafenobe [*Madagascar*] [*Airport symbol*] (OAG)
TVA .... Tax on Value Added [*European manufacturing tax*]
TVA .... Taxe a la Valeur Ajoutee [*Value-Added Tax*] [*French*] [*Business term*]
TVA .... Television Age [*A publication*]
TvA .... Television Associates Network [*Canada*]
TVA .... Television Australia Ltd.
TVA .... Temporary Variance Authority [*or Authorization*] [*NASA*] (AAG)
TVA .... Temporary Volume Allowance
TVA .... Temporary Voluntary Allowance
TVA .... Tennessee Valley Authority [*Also, an information service or system*]
TVA .... Tennessee Valley Authority, Technical Library, Knoxville, TN [*OCLC symbol*] (OCLC)
TVA .... Textile Veterans Association (EA)
TVA .... Thrust Vector Actuator
TVA .... Thrust Vector Alignment [*Aerospace*] (MCD)
TVA .... Torah Va'Avodah (BJA)
TVA .... Tuned Vertical Array (CAAL)
TVA Bibliogr Tenn Val Auth Tech Libr ... TVA Bibliography. Tennessee Valley Authority. Technical Library [*A publication*]
TVAC........ Thrust Vector Activation Control [*Aerospace*]
TVAC........ Time-Varying Adaptive Correlation
TVA Chem Eng Rept ... Tennessee Valley Authority. Chemical Engineering Report [*A publication*]
Tvaett Ind .. Tvaett Industrin [*A publication*]
TVAHVF... Textile Veterans Association Hospitalized Veterans Fund [*Defunct*] (EA)
TVAR .... Test Variance (NASA)
TV-ARBS .. Television Angle Rate Bombing System (MCD)
Tvarinnictvo Ukr ... Tvarinnictvo Ukraini [*A publication*]
Tvarynnytstvo Ukr ... Tvarynnytstvo Ukrainy [*A publication*]
TVAT........ Television Air Trainer
TVA Tech Rept ... Tennessee Valley Authority. Technical Report [*A publication*]
TVB .... Caboot, MO [*Location identifier*] [*FAA*] (FAAL)
TvB .... Television Bureau of Advertising [*New York, NY*] (EA)
TVB .... Total Volatile Bases [*Chemistry*]
TVB .... Treu und Bestaendig [*Faithful and Steadfast*] [*German*] [*Motto of Johann Georg, Margrave of Brandenburg (1577-1624)*]
TVBN .... Total Volatile Basic Nitrogen [*Food analysis*]
TVBS .... Television Broadcast Satellite [*NASA*]
TVC .... Televideo Consultants, Inc. [*Evanston, IL*] [*Telecommunications*] (TSSD)
TVC .... Temperature Valve Control
TVC .... Thermal Vacuum Chamber (NASA)
TVC .... Thermal Voltage Converter
TVC .... Thoracic Vena Cava [*Medicine*]
TVC .... Throttle Valve Control
TVC .... Thrust Vector Control [*Aerospace*]
TVC .... Tientsin Volunteer Corps [*British military*] (DMA)
TVC .... Time-Varying Coefficient
TVC .... Timed Vital Capacity
TVC .... Torsional Vibration Characteristics
TVC .... Total Annual Variable Cost
TVC .... Total Variable Cost Curve [*Economics*]
TVC .... Total Viable Cells [*Microbiology*]
TVC .... Total Volume Capacity [*Physiology*]
TVC .... Transvaginal Cone [*Medicine*] (MAE)
TVC .... Traverse City [*Michigan*] [*Airport symbol*] (OAG)
TVC .... Triple Voiding Cystogram [*Medicine*]
TVCA........ Thrust Vector Control Actuator [*Aerospace*] (NASA)
TVCA........ Thrust Vector Control Assembly [*Aerospace*]
TVCAM..... Television Camera and Control Equipment
TVCD .... Thrust Vector Control Driver [*Aerospace*] (NASA)
TVC/JIC ... Thrust Vector Control/Jet Interaction Control
TVCL........ Toxic Victims Compensation Legislation
TV Commun ... TV Communications [*A publication*]
TVCS .... Television Communications Subsystem
TVCS .... Thrust Vector Control System [*Aerospace*] (KSC)
TVCS .... Tyler Vocational Card Sort [*Guidance*]

TVD........... Teatr Voennykh Deistvii [*Theater of Military Operations*] [*Former USSR*]
TVD........... Television Digest [*A publication*]
TVD........... Television Display (MCD)
TVD........... Thermal Voltaic Detection [*Analytical chemistry*]
TVD........... Toxic Vapor Detector
TVD........... Toxic Vapor Disposal [*NASA*] (KSC)
TVD........... Transmissable Virus Dementia [*Psychiatry*]
TVD........... True Vertical Depth [*Diamonds*]
TVD........... Tuned Viscoelastic Damper
TVDALV... Triple Vessel Disease with Abnormal Left Ventricle [*Cardiology*]
TVDC .... Test Volts, Direct Current
TVDC .... Tidewater Virginia Development Council
TVDP........ Terminal Vector Display Unit
TVDR .... Tag Vector Display Register
TVDS........ Toxic Vapor Detection System (SAA)
TVDT........ Tumor Volume Doubling Time [*Cytology*]
TVDY .... Television Deflection Yoke
TVE .... Technology Validation Experiment (SDI)
TVE .... Television Espanola [*Television network*] [*Spain*]
TVE .... Test Vehicle Engine (AAG)
TVE .... Thermal Vacuum Environment
TVE .... Tricuspid Valve Echophonocardiogram [*Cardiology*]
TVED .... Tuned Viscoelastic Damper
TVEI......... Technical and Vocational Education Initiative [*Manpower Services Commission*] [*British*]
TVEL........ Target Velocity
TVEL........ Track Velocity
TVER........ Tumor Virus Epidemiology Repository [*National Institutes of Health*]
TVERS ...... Television Evaluation and Renewal Standards [*Student legal action organization*]
TVEXPIS .. Television Experiment Interconnecting Station [*NASA*] (NASA)
TVF........... Tactile Vocal Fremitus [*Medicine*]
TVF........... Tape Velocity Fluctuation
TVF........... Templeton Value Fund [*NYSE symbol*] (SPSG)
TVF........... Thief River Falls [*Minnesota*] [*Airport symbol*] (OAG)
TVF........... Tidskrift foer Teknisk-Vettenskaplig Forskning [*A publication*]
TVF........... Total Variable Factor Curve [*Economics*]
TVFA........ Total Volatile Fatty Acid [*of foodstuffs*]
TVFS .... Tactical Vehicle Fleet Simulation (MCD)
TVFT........ Television Flyback Transformer
TVF Tek Vetensk Forsk ... TVF. Teknisk Vetenskaplig Forskning [*A publication*]
TVG .... Tavares & Gulf R. R. [*AAR code*]
TVG .... Temperature-Voltage-Gases (DNAB)
TVG .... Test Vector Generator
TVG .... Threshold Voltage Generator
TVG .... Time Variation of Gain
TVG .... Triggered Vacuum Gap
TVG .... TV Guide [*A publication*]
TvG .... Tydskrif vir Geesteswetenskappe [*A publication*]
TVGDHS .. Television Ground Data Handling System [*NASA*]
TVH.......... Total Vaginal Hysterectomy [*Gynecology*]
TVI............ Television Interference [*Communications*]
TVI............ Temperament and Values Inventory [*Interpersonal skills and attitudes test*]
TVI............ Thomasville, GA [*Location identifier*] [*FAA*] (FAAL)
TVI............ Total Vision, Inc. [*Houston, TX*] (TSSD)
TVI............ Transcript/Video Index [*A publication*]
TVI............ Transient Voltage Indicator
TVI............ Turbo Vapor Injector
TVI............ Tutored Videotape Instruction
TVIC......... Television Input Converter
TVIC......... Television Interference Committee
TVID......... Television Frame Identification Data [*NASA*]
TVID......... Television Sight Unit Identification (MCD)
TVIE......... TVI Corp. [*NASDAQ symbol*] (NQ)
TVIG......... Television and Inertial Guidance
TV Int ...... Television International [*A publication*]
TVIS .... Time Video Information Services, Inc. (IID)
T-VIS........ Toyota's Variable Induction System [*Automotive engineering*]
TVIS .... Tropical Vegetable Information Service [*Asian Vegetable Research and Development Center*] [*Information service or system*] (IID)
TVIS .... Turbine Vibration Indication System (NG)
TVIST....... Television Information Storage Tube
TVIV......... Taco Viva, Inc. [*NASDAQ symbol*] (NQ)
TVJ........... Thomas Jefferson University, Philadelphia, PA [*OCLC symbol*] (OCLC)
TV/JI........ Thrust Vector/Jet Interaction
TVK .... Target Value Kills (MCD)
TVK .... Toimihenkilo - ja Virkamiesjarjestojen Keskusliitto [*Confederation of Intellectual and Government Workers*] [*Finland*]
TVKMF..... Theodore Von Karman Memorial Foundation (EA)
TVL........... Lake Tahoe [*California*] [*Airport symbol*] (OAG)
TVL........... Tenth Value Layer

TVL............	Thermo Voltek [*Formerly, Universal Voltronics*] [*AMEX symbol*] (SPSG)
TVL............	Townsville [*Australia*] [*Seismograph station code, US Geological Survey*] [*Closed*] (SEIS)
Tvl..............	Transvaal [*South Africa*]
TVL............	Transverse Vertical Longitudinal
TVL............	Travel (AABC)
TvL............	Tydskrif vir Letterkunde [*A publication*]
TVLA........	Taco Villa, Inc. [*NASDAQ symbol*] (NQ)
TVLADVP ...	Travel Advance Payment [*TDY*]
TVLALWADV ...	Travel Allowance Advance [*in PCS*]
TVLALWS ...	Travel Allowance on Separation [*Army*]
Tvl Educ News ...	Transvaal Educational News [*A publication*]
TVLF..........	Transportable Very-Low-Frequency [*Transmitter*]
TVLRO......	Television Licensing and Records Office [*Post Office*] [*British*]
TVM..........	Tachometer Voltmeter
TVM..........	Target Via Missile [*Aviation*]
TVM..........	Techno Venture Management [*Germany*]
TVM..........	Television Malta
TVM..........	Television Monitor [*Video only*]
TVM..........	Thrust Vectoring Motor [*Aerospace*] (MUGU)
TVM..........	TOW [*Tube-Launched, Optically Tracked, Wire-Guided (Weapon)*] Visual Module [*Army*]
TVM..........	Track-Via-Missile
TVM..........	Trailer Van Mount
TVM..........	Transistorized Voltmeter
TVM..........	TRV Minerals Corp. [*Vancouver Stock Exchange symbol*]
TVMS.......	Test of Visual-Motor Skills [*Sensorimotor skills test*]
TVMV.......	Tobacco Vein Mottling Virus
TVN..........	Target Velocity, North
TVN..........	Television News, Inc.
TVN..........	Televisora Nacional [*Television network*] [*Venezuela*]
TVN..........	Test Verification Network [*NASA*] (NASA)
TVN..........	Total Volatile Nitrogen [*Analytical chemistry*]
TVO..........	Taravao [*Society Islands*] [*Seismograph station code, US Geological Survey*] (SEIS)
TVO..........	Tractor Vaporizing Oil [*Automotive engineering*]
TVOC.......	Television Operations Center [*NASA*] (KSC)
T Volkskd Volkstaal ...	Tydskrif vir Volkskunde en Volkstaal [*A publication*]
TVOP.......	Television Observation Post (CET)
TVOP........	[*The*] Vista Organization Partnership LP [*NASDAQ symbol*] (NQ)
TVOR.......	Terminal VHF [*Very-High Frequency*] Omnidirectional Range
TVOR.......	Terminal Visual Omnirange
TVOR.......	Translational Vestibulo-Ocular Reflex [*Ophthalmology*]
TVP..........	Tamil Vimukhti Peramena [*Sri Lanka*] [*Political party*] (PPW)
TVP..........	Television and Video Production [*A publication*]
TVP..........	Test Verification Program [*NASA*] (NASA)
TVP..........	Textured Vegetable Protein [*Trademark of Archer Daniels Midland Co. for soybean product*]
TVP..........	Thermo-Photo-Voltaic
TVP..........	Tricuspid Valve Prolapse [*Cardiology*]
TVP..........	True Vapor Pressure
TVP..........	Victoria Public Library, Victoria, TX [*OCLC symbol*] (OCLC)
TVPC........	TOW [*Tube-Launched, Optically Tracked, Wire-Guided (Weapon)*] Vehicle Power Conditioner (MCD)
TVPED......	Tennessee Valley Perspective [*A publication*]
TVPPA......	Tennessee Valley Public Power Association (EA)
TVPRA......	Teoriya Veroyatnostei i Ee Primeneniya [*A publication*]
TVPS........	Test of Visual-Perceptual Skills
TV Q.........	Television Quarterly [*A publication*]
TVQ..........	Top Visual Quality
TVR	Tadcaster Volunteer Rifles [*British military*] (DMA)
TVR	Television Recording (WDMC)
TVR	Temperature Variation of Resistance [*Electricity*]
TVR	Tennessee Valley Region
TVR	Thermal Vapor Recompressors [*For evaporators*]
TVR	Time Variable Reflectivity (MCD)
TVR	Tonic Vibration Reflex [*or Response*] [*Medicine*]
TVR	Trajectory Velocity RADAR (MCD)
TVR	Trevor (Wilkinson) [*Sports car named for its designer*] [*British*]
TVR	Tricuspid Valve Replacement [*Cardiology*]
TV Radio A ...	Television/Radio Age [*A publication*]
TV/Radio Age ...	Television/Radio Age [*A publication*]
TV/Radio Age Int ...	Television/Radio Age International [*A publication*]
TVRB........	Tactical Vehicle Review Board [*Army*] (AABC)
TVRCC......	TVR Car Club [*Later, TVRCCNA*] (EA)
TVRI........	Televisi Republik Indonesia [*Indonesian television network*] (FEA)
TVRM	Television Receiver/Monitor
TVRN	Tavern
TVRO	Television Receive Only [*Telecommunications*]
TVRP........	Television Reading Program
TVRS........	Television and Radio Suppression [*Electronics*]
TVRS........	Television Video Recording System (MCD)
TVS...........	Stedebouw en Volkshuisvesting [*A publication*]
TVS...........	Tactical Vocoder System
TVS...........	Telemetry Video Spectrum
TVS...........	Telephone Video System [*NEC America, Inc.*] [*Wood Dale, IL*] [*Telecommunications*] (TSSD)
TVS...........	Television Subsystem [*Spacecraft*]
TVS...........	Thermal [*or Thermostatic*] Vacuum Switch [*Automotive engineering*]
TVS...........	Thrust Vector System [*Aerospace*]
TVS...........	Total Volatile Solids [*Analytical chemistry*]
TVS...........	Toxic Vapor Suit [*NASA*] (NASA)
TVS...........	Transient Voltage Suppressor
TVS...........	Tube-Vehicle System (MCD)
TVS...........	Volunteer State Community College, Gallatin, TN [*OCLC symbol*] (OCLC)
TVSA........	Thrust Vector Position Servo Amplifier [*Aerospace*]
TV-SAT.....	Satellite Television [*Germany*]
TVSC........	Television Videotape Satellite Communications [*Group W Productions*] [*Pittsburgh, PA*] (TSSD)
TVSD........	Time-Varying Spectral Display
TVSG........	Television Signal Generator
TVSM........	Television System Monitor
TVSM........	Time-Varying Sequential Measuring [*Device*]
TVSO........	Television Space Observatory
TV SPOTTS ...	Tuneful Viewer's Society for the Preservation of Television Theme Songs
TVSS	Television Systems Section
TVSS	Television and Video Switching Subsystem (MCD)
TVSSIS	Television Subsystem Interconnecting Station [*NASA*] (NASA)
TVSU........	Television Sight Unit
TVSV........	Kingstown/Arnos Vale [*St. Vincent*] [*ICAO location identifier*] (ICLI)
TVSV........	Thermostatic Vacuum Switching Valve [*Automotive engineering*]
TVT	Target Verification Test [*Military*] (CAAL)
TVT	Television Terminal (CMD)
TVT	Television of Thailand (FEA)
TVT	Television Trainer/Tapes (MCD)
TVT	Television Typewriter
TVT	Thermal Vacuum Test
TVT	Tiverton, OH [*Location identifier*] [*FAA*] (FAAL)
TVT	Tunica Vaginalis Testis [*Anatomy*]
TVTA........	Thermal Vacuum Test Article (NASA)
TVTK........	Television Technology Corp. [*NASDAQ symbol*] (NQ)
TV TR.......	Television Tower [*Mast*]
TVTV........	Thermostatic Vacuum Transmitting Valve [*Automotive engineering*]
TVTV........	Top Value Television [*Group of 26 young people who photographed the 1972 Democratic convention and presented it on TV*]
TVU	Taveuni [*Fiji*] [*Airport symbol*] (OAG)
TVU	Total Volume Urine [*in 24 hours*]
TVV	Thermal Vacuum Valve [*Automotive engineering*]
TVV	Thermal Vent Valve [*Automotive engineering*]
TVW	Total Ventricular Weight [*Cardiology*]
TVW	Towed Vehicle Weight [*Automotive engineering*]
TVX	Target Vehicle Experimental [*Air Force*]
TVX	Tulip Virus X
TVX	TVX Mining Corp. [*Formerly, Treasure Valley Explorations Ltd.*] [*Toronto Stock Exchange symbol*]
TVXG........	TVX Broadcast Group, Inc. [*Virginia Beach, VA*] [*NASDAQ symbol*] (NQ)
TVY	Tavoy [*Myanmar*] [*Airport symbol*] (OAG)
TVYTA.....	Teplofizika Vysokikh Temperatur [*A publication*]
TW............	Journal of Technical Writing and Communication [*A publication*]
TW............	Tactical Warning (MCD)
TW............	Tail Warning [*RADAR*] (NATG)
TW............	Tail Wind
TW............	Tailwater
TW............	Taiwan [*ANSI two-letter standard code*] (CNC)
TW............	Tankwagon
TW............	Tap Water [*Medicine*]
TW............	Tapes and Recording Wires [*JETDS nomenclature*] [*Military*] (CET)
TW............	Tapwe [*A publication*]
TW............	Taxiway [*Aviation*]
TW............	Teamwork (MSA)
TW............	Technical Works [*Air Force*] (MCD)
TW............	Temperature Well (MSA)
TW............	Tempered Water
TW............	Temporary Warrant
TW............	Terawatt
TW............	Terre Wallonne [*A publication*]
TW............	Test Weight
TW............	Textil-Wirtschaft [*Textile Industry*] [*Deutscher Fachverlag GmbH*] [*Information service or system*] (IID)
TW............	Thermal Wire (KSC)
TW............	Thermit Welding
TW............	Thermoplastic Wire
TW............	Third World [*A publication*]
T-W...........	Three-Wheeler [*Type of motorcycle*]
TW............	Thrilling Wonder Stories [*A publication*]
T/W...........	Thrust-to-Weight
TW............	Thumbwheel (MCD)
TW............	Tight Wrapped (MSA)
TW............	Tile Wainscot [*Technical drawings*]

TW............	Time Word
TW.............	Tools and Weapons Illustrated by the Egyptian Collection University College. London [*A publication*]
TW.............	Top of Wall [*Technical drawings*]
TW.............	Torpedo Water
TW.............	Total Body Water
TW.............	Total Weight
TW.............	Total Woman [*Title of a 1973 book by Marabel Morgan and of TV seminars based on this book*]
TW.............	Total Work
TW.............	Trail Watcher (CINC)
TW.............	Trans World Airlines, Inc. [*ICAO designator*]
TW.............	Transit Working [*Telecommunications*] (TEL)
TW.............	Travel Warrant
TW.............	Travel Writer [*A publication*] (EAAP)
TW.............	Traveling Wave
TW......	Trow [*Ship's rigging*] (ROG)
TW.............	Tru-Wall Group Ltd. [*Toronto Stock Exchange symbol*]
TW.............	True Watt (MSA)
TW.............	Trustee under Will [*Legal term*] (DLA)
TW.............	TW Services [*NYSE symbol*] (SPSG)
TW.............	Twaddell [*Specific gravity scale*] [*Physics*]
TW.............	Twentieth Century Industries [*NYSE symbol*] (SPSG)
TW.............	Twin Screw (DS)
TW.............	Twister (AAG)
Tw..............	Tworczosc [*A publication*]
TW.............	Typewriter (AAG)
TW3............	That Was The Week That Was [*Also, TWTWTW*] [*Television program of English origin*]
TWA..........	Tap Water Agar [*Microbiology*]
TWA..........	Textile Waste Association [*Later, Textile Fibers and By-Products Association*] (EA)
TWA..........	Thames Water Authority [*British*]
TWA..........	Time Weighted Average [*Data sampling*]
TWA..........	Tooling Work Authorization
TWA..........	Toy Wholesalers Association of America (EA)
TWA..........	Trailing Wire Antenna [*on aircraft*]
TWA..........	Trans World Airlines, Inc. [*NYSE symbol*] [*Air carrier designation symbol*] [*Humorously interpreted as "Try Walking Across" and "Teeny Weeny Airlines"*] (SPSG)
TWA..........	Transaction Work Area
TWA..........	Transactions. Wisconsin Academy of Sciences, Arts, and Letters [*A publication*]
TWA..........	Transcontinental & Western Airlines [*Later, Trans World Airlines, Inc.*]
TWA..........	Traveling-Wave Amplifier
TWA..........	Trelew [*Argentina*] [*Geomagnetic observatory code*]
TWA..........	[*The*] Waferboard Association [*Later, SBA*] (EA)
TWA..........	[*The*] Woman Activist (EA)
TW/AA......	Tactical Warning/Attack Assessment
TWAB	Textile Work Assignment Boards [*Terminated, 1935*]
TWAC	Tactical Weather Analysis Center (MCD)
Twad	Twaddell [*Physics*]
TWADL......	Two-Way Air Data Link [*Tactical Air Command*]
TWAES......	Tactical Warfare Analysis and Evaluation System (MCD)
TWAH......	This Week at Headquarters [*Military publication*] (DNAB)
TWALNDG ...	Turnaway Landing [*Navy*] (NVT)
TWAP.......	Thin Wire Analysis Program [*Air Force*]
TWAR	Taiwan Acute Respiratory Disease [*Pneumonia-causing chlamydia strain named after the ailment that results from it*]
TWAS.......	Third World Academy of Sciences [*Trieste, Italy*] (EAIO)
TWAS.......	Twayne's World Authors Series [*A publication*]
TWASPIT ...	Therapeutic Work Aid Station for Physically Inactive Thinkers (MCD)
TWAT	Traveling-Wave Amplifier Tube
TWB	Toowoomba [*Australia*] [*Airport symbol*] (OAG)
TWB	Total Water Burden [*Environmental science*]
TWB	Traveling-Wave Beam [*LASER*]
TWB	Typewriter Buffer
TWB	Wayland Baptist College, Plainview, TX [*OCLC symbol*] (OCLC)
TWBC.......	Total White Blood Cells [*Medicine*]
TWBC.......	Transworld Bancorp [*NASDAQ symbol*] (NQ)
TWBFA.....	Treeing Walker Breeders and Fanciers Association (EA)
TWBNT.....	Theologisches Woerterbuch zum Neuen Testament [*A publication*] (BJA)
TWBS.......	Traditional Wooden Boat Society [*Defunct*] (EA)
TWC	Suao [*Republic of China*] [*Seismograph station code, US Geological Survey*] (SEIS)
TWC	Tennessee Wesleyan College
TWC	Texas Wesleyan College
TWC	Texas Wesleyan College, Fort Worth, TX [*OCLC symbol*] (OCLC)
TWC	Texas Western College [*Later, UTEP*]
TWC	Theater Weather Central [*Military*]
TWC	Three-Way Catalyst [*Vehicle exhaust control*]
TWC	Truncated Whitworth Coarse [*Thread*] (MSA)
TwC	Twentieth Century [*A publication*]
TWC	[*The*] Weather Channel [*Cable TV programming service*]
TWC	[*The*] Wordsworth Circle [*A publication*]
TWCA	T. W. Cape and Associates [*Atlanta, GA*] [*Telecommunications service*] (TSSD)
TWCRT....	Traveling-Wave Cathode-Ray Tube (IEEE)
TWCS.......	Test of Work Competency and Stability [*Psychology*]
TWCS.......	Through-Water Communications System [*Navy*] (CAAL)
TWD.........	Hualien [*Republic of China*] [*Seismograph station code, US Geological Survey*] (SEIS)
TWD.........	Tactical Weapons Delivery
TWD.........	Tail Wags Dog [*Airspace effects*]
TWD.........	Thermal Warning Device (MCD)
TWD.........	Torpedo Wire Dispenser
TWD.........	Total White and Differential Count [*Hematology*]
TWD.........	Toward
TWD.........	Tween Deck [*on a ship*] (DS)
TWD.........	Twisted Double Shielded (MCD)
TWDC.......	Tyne and Wear Development Corp. [*British*] (ECON)
TWDD......	Two-Way/Delay Dial [*Telecommunications*] (TEL)
TWDRA	Report. Texas Water Development Board [*A publication*]
TWDS.......	Tactical Water Distribution System (MCD)
TWE........	Tap Water Enema [*Medicine*]
TWE........	Test of Written English [*Educational test*]
TWE........	Textile Waste Exchange [*Later, Textile Fibers and By-Products Association*]
TWE	Thumb Wheel Encoder
TWE	Time Warner Entertainment (ECON)
TWE	Trans-Western Exploration, Inc. [*Toronto Stock Exchange symbol*]
TWE	[*The*] Washington Establishment
TWEA	Trading with the Enemy Act
TWEB.......	Transcribed Weather Broadcast
TWEC.......	[*Isaac N.*] Thut World Education Center [*University of Connecticut*] [*Research center*] (RCD)
TWEC.......	Twenty-First Century Envelope Co., Inc. [*NASDAQ symbol*] (NQ)
Tweener	Between Two Outfielders [*Baseball*] [*Also, a lifestyle classification*]
TWEN	20th Century Industries [*NASDAQ symbol*] (NQ)
Twen Cen ...	Twentieth Century [*A publication*] (APTA)
Twen Ct Lit ...	Twentieth Century Literature [*A publication*]
Twent Cent ...	Twentieth Century [*A publication*] (APTA)
Twent Century Lit ...	Twentieth Century Literature [*A publication*]
Twent Cen V ...	Twentieth Century Views [*A publication*]
TWEP.......	Terminate with Extreme Prejudice [*To kill*] [*Counterintelligence*]
TWERL.....	Tropical Wind, Energy Conversion, and Reference Level [*National Science Foundation*]
TWERLE ..	Tropical Wind, Energy Conversion, and Reference Level Experiment [*National Science Foundation*]
TWEX.......	Trans-Western Exploration, Inc. [*NASDAQ symbol*] (NQ)
TWF..........	Third World Forum [*Cairo, Egypt*] (EAIO)
TWF..........	Third World Foundation [*British*] (EAIO)
TWF..........	Transylvanian World Federation (EAIO)
TWF..........	Trasco Wind-Force [*Vancouver Stock Exchange symbol*]
TWF..........	Truncated Whitworth Fine [*Thread*] (MSA)
TWF..........	Twin Falls [*Idaho*] [*Airport symbol*] (OAG)
TWF..........	Yuli [*Republic of China*] [*Seismograph station code, US Geological Survey*] [*Closed*] (SEIS)
TWF1........	Yuli [*Republic of China*] [*Seismograph station code, US Geological Survey*] (SEIS)
TWFC.......	21st Century Communications, Inc. [*NASDAQ symbol*]
TWFC.......	Tom Wopat Fan Club (EA)
TWFS.......	TW Holdings, Inc. [*NASDAQ symbol*] (NQ)
TWG	Taitung [*Republic of China*] [*Seismograph station code, US Geological Survey*] (SEIS)
TWG	Technical Working Group [*of the Conference on the Discontinuance of Nuclear Weapon Tests*]
TWG	Telemetry Working Group
TWG	Test Working Group [*in various federal government agencies*] (KSC)
TWG	Transfer Working Group (MCD)
TWGC.......	Treatment of War Gas Casualties (MCD)
TWGI	[*The*] Westwood Group, Inc. [*Boston, MA*] [*NASDAQ symbol*] (NQ)
TWGSS	Tank Weapons Gunnery Simulation System (MCD)
TWH.........	Catalina Island [*California*] [*Airport symbol*] [*Obsolete*] (OAG)
TWH.........	Houston Baptist University, Houston, TX [*OCLC symbol*] (OCLC)
TWh..........	Terawatt Hour (ADA)
TWH.........	Toronto Western Hospital [*UTLAS symbol*]
TWHBEA ...	Tennessee Walking Horse Breeders' and Exhibitors' Association (EA)
TWHBEAA ...	Tennessee Walking Horse Breeders' and Exhibitors' Association of America [*Later, TWHBEA*] (EA)
TWHD......	Tons per Workable Hatch per Day [*Shipping*]
TWHF	Technoserve's World Harvest Fund (EA)
TWHL.......	Tail Wheel [*Aviation*]
TWHO	[*The*] White House Office
TWHTA	Tennessee Walking Horse Trainers' Association [*Later, Walking Horse Trainers Association*]
TW(I)........	Tail Warning (Indicator) [*RADAR*] (DEN)

TWI .... Threat Warning Information [*Air Force*]
TWI .... Toxic Waste Incinerator
TWI .... Trade-Weighted Index (ADA)
TWI .... Training with Industry Program [*Army*] (RDA)
twi............... Twi [*MARC language code*] [*Library of Congress*] (LCCP)
TWI .... Twilight (FAAC)
TWI .... [*The*] Way International [*An association*] (EA)
TWI .... [*The*] Welding Institute [*Information service or system*] (IID)
TWI .... Wichita, KS [*Location identifier*] [*FAA*] (FAAL)
TWI .... [*The*] Women's Institute (EA)
TWIB........ This Week in Baseball [*Television program*]
TWIC........ Theater Watch Intelligence Condition (NATG)
TWICE..... This Week in Consumer Electronics [*A publication*]
TWID .... Two-Way/Immediate Dial [*Telecommunications*] (TEL)
TWIDS..... Threat Warning Information Display System (MCD)
TWIF......... Tug-of-War International Federation [*Zevenhuizen, Netherlands*] (EAIO)
TWIFC ...... Tammy Wynette International Fan Club (EA)
TWIG .... Tandem Wing in Sound Effect (MCD)
TWIMC.. To Whom It May Concern
TWIN .... Third World Information Network [*British*] (EAIO)
TWIN .... Together Women in Neighborhoods
TWI-N ...... Twi-Night [*or Twilight-Night*] [*Doubleheader in baseball*]
TwinDs .... Twin Disc, Inc. [*Associated Press abbreviation*] (APAG)
TWIRP ...... [*The*] Woman Is Requested to Pay [*Some claim that this acronym, originally a designation for certain school dances, evolved into a slang term denoting any male unable to afford a date*]
TWIS......... Technical Writing Improvement Society
TWIS......... Technically Workable Ideal System [*Industrial engineering*]
T Wisc Ac .. Transactions. Wisconsin Academy of Sciences, Arts, and Letters [*A publication*]
TWITAS.... Third World Institute of Theatre Arts Studies
TWITW..... [*The*] Wind in the Willows [*Book by Kenneth Grahame*]
TWIU .... Tobacco Workers International Union [*Later, BCTWIU*] (EA)
TWIX........ Teletypewriter Message
TWIZN...... Twilight Zone [*Aviation*]
TWJ........... Tack Welded Joint
TWK .... Hsinying [*Republic of China*] [*Seismograph station code, US Geological Survey*] (SEIS)
TWK .... Too Well Known
TWK .... Tool Welders Kit
TWK .... Traveling-Wave Klystron
TWK .... Typewriter Keyboard
TWL .... Leased Teletypewriter Service
TWL .... Telex World Letter [*MCI International, Inc.*] [*Rye Brook, NY*] (TSSD)
TWL .... Top Water Level
TWL .... Total Weight Loss (MCD)
TWL .... Transepidermal Water Loss [*Physiology*] (MAE)
TWL .... Traveling-Wave LASER
TWL .... Tuberculosis Welfare League [*Defunct*] (EA)
TWL .... Twin Lakes [*California*] [*Seismograph station code, US Geological Survey*] (SEIS)
TWL .... Twin Wheel Loading [*Aviation*]
TWLA........ Turkish Women's League of America (EA)
TWLOA ... Technik Wlokienniczy [*A publication*]
TWLS........ Twayne's World Leaders Series [*A publication*]
TWLT........ Twilight
TWM .... Kaohsiung [*Republic of China*] [*Seismograph station code, US Geological Survey*] [*Closed*] (SEIS)
TWM .... Tape Wrapping Machine
TWM .... Traveling-Wave MASER
TWM .... Two-Way Mirror
TWM1 .... Kaohsiung [*Republic of China*] [*Seismograph station code, US Geological Survey*] (SEIS)
TW-MAE-W ... Third World Movement Against the Exploitation of Women [*Quezon City, Philippines*] (EAIO)
TWMAS.... Tobacco Workers' Mutual Assistance Society [*A union*] [*British*]
TWMBK.... Traveling-Wave Multiple-Beam Klystron (MSA)
TWMC ...... Trans World Music Corp. [*Albany, NY*] [*NASDAQ symbol*] (NQ)
TWMC ...... Transport, Wages, Maintenance, and Care
TWMD...... Toxics and Waste Management Division [*Environmental Protection Agency*] (GFGA)
TWMIP..... Third World Moving Images Project (EA)
TWMP ...... Track Width Mine Plow (MCD)
TWMR ...... Tungsten Water Moderated Reactor (KSC)
TWN......... Taiwan [*ANSI three-letter standard code*] (CNC)
TWN......... Taiwan Fund, Inc. [*NYSE symbol*] (SPSG)
TWN......... Thomas Wolfe Newsletter [*A publication*]
TWN......... Town (MCD)
TWN......... Twin Eagles Resources, Inc. [*Vancouver Stock Exchange symbol*]
TWN......... Twin Peaks [*California*] [*Seismograph station code, US Geological Survey*] (SEIS)
Tw Nat P.... Twiss. Law of Nations in Time of Peace [*2nd ed.*] [*1884*] [*A publication*] (DLA)
Tw Nat W .. Twiss. Law of Nations in Time of War [*2nd ed.*] [*1875*] [*A publication*] (DLA)

TWNG....... Towing
TWNP....... Tape-Wound Nylon Phenolic (SAA)
TWNT .... Theologisches Woerterbuch zum Neuen Testament [*A publication*] (BJA)
TWO.......... Financial World [*A publication*]
TWO.......... Meishan [*Republic of China*] [*Seismograph station code, US Geological Survey*] (SEIS)
TWO.......... Neoucom Processing Center, Rootstown, OH [*OCLC symbol*] (OCLC)
TWO.......... Ontario, CA [*Location identifier*] [*FAA*] (FAAL)
TWO.......... This Week Only (ADA)
TWO.......... Tooling Work Order (MCD)
TWO.......... Travelling Wave Oscillator
TWOATAF ... Second Allied Tactical Air Force Central Europe
TWOC ...... Taken Without Owner's Consent
TWODS .... [*The*] World of Dark Shadows (EA)
T Wolfe New ... Thomas Wolfe Newsletter [*A publication*]
T Wolfe Rev ... Thomas Wolfe Review [*A publication*]
TWOM...... Traveling-Wave Optical MASER
Tworzywa Sztuczne Med ... Tworzywa Sztuczne'w Medycynie [*A publication*]
TWOS ...... Total Warrant Officer System [*Army*]
TWOS ...... Tropical Wind Observing Ships [*Marine science*] (MSC)
TW/OT ..... Travel without Troops
Two-Year College Math J ... Two-Year College Mathematics Journal [*A publication*]
Two-Yr Coll Math J ... Two-Year College Mathematics Journal [*A publication*]
TWP .... Task Work Package (KSC)
TWP .... Technological War Plan
TWP .... Torwood [*Australia*] [*Airport symbol*] [*Obsolete*] (OAG)
TWP .... Total Wave Pressure
TWP .... Township
TWP .... Traveling-Wave Phototube
TWP .... Trawler Petroleum Explorations Ltd. [*Vancouver Stock Exchange symbol*]
TWP .... Trial Work Period [*Social Security Administration*] (OICC)
TWP .... Trondheim Workingpapers [*A publication*]
TWP......... True Whig Party [*Liberia*] (AF)
TWP .... Twisted Wire Pair
TWP .... Two Pesos, Inc. [*AMEX symbol*] (SPSG)
TWP .... [*The*] Washington Post [*A publication*]
TWPA....... Traveling-Wave Parametric Amplifier
TWPB....... Total Work Package Budget (MCD)
TWPESO .. Two Pesos, Inc. [*Associated Press abbreviation*] (APAG)
TWPL....... Teletypewriter, Private Line
TWPLA ..... Turkish Workers' and Peasants' Liberation Army
TWPP....... Truncated Whitworth, British Standard Pipe (Parallel) [*Thread*]
TWPS....... Traveling-Wave Phase Sifter
TWQ......... Third World Quarterly [*A publication*]
TWQ......... Tungshih [*Republic of China*] [*Seismograph station code, US Geological Survey*] (SEIS)
TWQM...... Tailwater Quality Numerical Model [*Army Corps of Engineers*]
TWR .... Tactical Weather RADAR
TWR .... Tape Write Register
TWR .... Test Work Release (MCD)
TWR .... Theater War Reserves [*Army*]
TWR .... Thomas Wolfe Review [*A publication*]
TWR .... Threat Warning RADAR
TWR .... Threat Warning Receiver
TWR .... Tom Walkinshaw Racing [*Auto racing*]
TWR .... Tool Wear Rate
TWR .... Torpedo Weapons Receiver
TWR .... Total Wrist Replacement [*Medicine*]
TWR .... Tower (AAG)
TWR .... Trans World Radio Pacific [*Guam*] (FEA)
TWR .... TransWorld Radio (EA)
TWR .... Traveling-Wave Resonator
TWR .... Twin Richfield Oils Ltd. [*Toronto Stock Exchange symbol*]
TWRA ...... Transpacific Westbound Rate Agreement (DS)
TWRG ...... Towering (FAAC)
TWRI........ Texas Water Resources Institute [*Department of the Interior*] [*Texas A & M University*] [*Research center*] (RCD)
TWRL....... Taylor Woodrow Research Laboratories [*Research center*] [*British*] (IRUK)
TWRS....... Towers
TWRX ...... [*The*] Software Toolworks, Inc. [*NASDAQ symbol*] (NQ)
TWS.......... Southwestern at Memphis, Memphis, TN [*OCLC symbol*] (OCLC)
TWS.......... Tactical Warning System (AAG)
TWS.......... Tactical Weapon System (NG)
TWS.......... Tactical Weather Station [*Military*]
TWS.......... Tail Warning Set [*or System*] [*Aerospace*] (MCD)
TWS.......... Tartar Weapons System
TWS.......... Teletypewriter Exchange Service
TWS.......... Terrier Weapons System
TWS.......... Test of Written Spelling [*Education*]
TWS.......... Texas World Speedway [*Auto racing*]
TWS.......... Thermal Weapon Sight [*Army*] (INF)
TWS.......... Thermal Wire Stripper
TWS.......... Thomas Wolfe Society (EA)
TWS.......... Thrilling Wonder Stories [*A publication*]

TWS.......... Track-while-Scan [*Communications*]
TWS.......... Truncated Whitworth Special [*Thread*]   (MSA)
TWS.......... Tsunami Warning System [*National Oceanic and Atmospheric Administration*]
TWS.......... Twin-Wheel Stripper
TWS.......... [*The*] Wildlife Society   (EA)
TWSB..... Twin Sideband
TWSC..... Twin Screw
TWSEAS... Tactical Warfare Simulation, Evaluation, and Analysis System [*Marine Corps*]   (MCD)
TWSO ...... Tactical Weapon Systems Operation
TWSP ...... Tactical Warfare Simulation Program
TWSR....... Track-while-Scan RADAR
TWSRO..... Track-while-Scan on Receive Only   (NG)
TWSRS ..... Track-while-Scan RADAR Simulator
TWST....... Torus Water Storage Tank   (IEEE)
TWST....... Twistee Treat Corp. [*NASDAQ symbol*]   (NQ)
TWSUA..... Taiwan Sugar [*A publication*]
TWT .... Ingenieursblad [*A publication*]
TWT .... Sturgis, KY [*Location identifier*] [*FAA*]   (FAAL)
TWT .... Tawi-Tawi [*Philippines*] [*Airport symbol*]   (OAG)
TWT .... Torpedo Water Tube
TWT .... Toy World Test [*Psychology*]
TWT .... Transonic Wind Tunnel [*NASA*]   (AAG)
TWT .... Transworld Corp. [*NYSE symbol*]   (SPSG)
TWT .... Travel with Troops
TWT .... Traveling-Wave Tube [*Radio*]
TWT .... Tri-West Resources Ltd. [*Vancouver Stock Exchange symbol*]
TWTM ...... Tritiated Waste Treatment [*Subsystem*]   (MCD)
TWT .... Two-Way Time [*Seismology*]
TWT .... Two-Way-Traffic-in-Ideas Conference [*of Labor Party*] [*British*]
TWT .... West Texas State University, Canyon, TX [*OCLC symbol*]   (OCLC)
TWT .... [*The*] Write Thing [*An association*]   (EA)
TWTA ...... Traveling-Wave Tube Amplifier [*Radio*]
TWTHF..... Twentieth Century Energy [*NASDAQ symbol*]   (NQ)
TWTWTW ... That Was The Week That Was [*Also, TW3*] [*Television program of English origin*]
TWU .... Tactical Weapons Unit [*British military*]   (DMA)
TWU .... Tata Workers' Union [*India*]
TWU .... Tawau [*Malaysia*] [*Airport symbol*]   (OAG)
TWU .... Technical Writing Unit [*NASA*]
TWU .... Telecommunications Workers Union [*Canada*]
TWU .... Texas Woman's University
TWU .... Tobacco Workers' Union [*British*]   (DCTA)
TWU .... Transport Workers' Union [*British*]
TWU .... Transport Workers Union of America   (EA)
TWU .... University of the South, Sewanee, TN [*OCLC symbol*]   (OCLC)
TWUA ...... Textile Workers Union of America [*Later, ACTWU*]
TWV .... Two-Wire Vertical [*Grape culture*]
TWVMP.... Tactical Wheeled Vehicle Modernization Program [*Army*]
TWW .... Independent Television for Wales and the West of England
TWWP ...... Third World Women's Project   (EA)
TWWS...... Two-Way/Wink Start [*Telecommunications*]   (TEL)
TWX .... Telegraphic Message   (MSA)
TWX .... Teletypewriter Exchange Service [*Western Union*] [*Term also used generically for teletypewriter message*]
TWX .... Teletypewriter Wire Transmission
TWX .... Time Warner, Inc. [*NYSE symbol*]   (SPSG)
TWX .... Time Wire Transmission
TWX .... Transport en Opslag. Maandblad voor Managers en Medewerkers op het Gebied van Intern Transport, Opslag, Magazijntechniek, en Distributietechniek [*A publication*]
TWXIL ...... TWX Interlibrary Loan Network [*Library network*]
TWY .... Taxiway [*Aviation*]   (AAG)
TWY .... Twenty   (ADA)
TWYL......... Taxiway-Link [*Aviation*]
TWZ .... Neifu [*Republic of China*] [*Seismograph station code, US Geological Survey*]   (SEIS)
TWZO .... Trade Wind Zone Oceanography
TX .... Nondramatic Literary Works [*US Copyright Office class*]
TX .... Tax
TX .... TELEX
TX .... Terminating Toll Operator [*Telecommunications*]   (TEL)
TX .... Tested Extra   (MCD)
TX .... Texaco, Inc. [*NYSE symbol*]   (SPSG)
TX .... Texas [*Postal code*]
TX .... Texas Reports [*A publication*]   (DLA)
Tx .... Texas State Library and Historical Commission, Austin, TX [*Library symbol*] [*Library of Congress*]   (LCLS)
TX .... Text Editor
Tx .... Therapy [*Medicine*]
TX .... Thromboxane [*Also, T, TA, Tx*] [*Biochemistry*]
Tx .... Thyroidectomy [*Medicine*]
TX .... Time to Equipment Reset [*Data processing*]   (MDG)
TX .... Toilet Exhaust   (OA)
TX .... Torque Transmitter
TX .... Traction [*Medicine*]
TX .... Transformer
TX .... Translation Hand Controller X-Axis Direction   (MCD)
TX .... Transmitter

Tx .... Transplant [*or Transplantation*] [*Medicine*]
TX .... Transportes Aereos Nacionales, SA [*Honduras*] [*ICAO designator*]   (FAAC)
TX .... Treatment
TX .... Treble Cash Ruling [*Business term*]
T & X .... Type and Crossmatch [*Clinical chemistry*]
TXA .... Texas A & M University, College Station, TX [*OCLC symbol*]   (OCLC)
TXA .... Texas American Bancshares, Inc. [*NYSE symbol*]   (SPSG)
TXA .... Thromboxane A [*Also, TA, TxA*] [*Biochemistry*]
TxAb.......... Abilene Public Library, Abilene, TX [*Library symbol*] [*Library of Congress*]   (LCLS)
TxAbC .... Abilene Christian University, Abilene, TX [*Library symbol*] [*Library of Congress*]   (LCLS)
TxAbH....... Hardin-Simmons University, Abilene, TX [*Library symbol*] [*Library of Congress*]   (LCLS)
TxAbM ..... McMurry College, Abilene, TX [*Library symbol*] [*Library of Congress*]   (LCLS)
TxAl.......... Stella Hill Memorial Library, Alto, TX [*Library symbol*] [*Library of Congress*]   (LCLS)
TxAlpS ...... Sul Ross State University, Alpine, TX [*Library symbol*] [*Library of Congress*]   (LCLS)
TxAlvC ...... Alvin Junior College, Alvin, TX [*Library symbol*] [*Library of Congress*]   (LCLS)
TxAm........ Amarillo Public Library, Amarillo, TX [*Library symbol*] [*Library of Congress*]   (LCLS)
TxAmC ...... Amarillo College, Amarillo, TX [*Library symbol*] [*Library of Congress*]   (LCLS)
TxAmM ..... Mason & Hanger-Silas Mason Co., Inc., Pantex Plant Library, Amarillo, TX [*Library symbol*] [*Library of Congress*]   (LCLS)
TxAmSP .... Southwestern Public Service Co., Amarillo, TX [*Library symbol*] [*Library of Congress*]   (LCLS)
TxAmV ...... United States Veterans Administration Hospital, Amarillo, TX [*Library symbol*] [*Library of Congress*]   (LCLS)
TxAng....... Brazoria County Library, Angleton, TX [*Library symbol*] [*Library of Congress*]   (LCLS)
TXAPA..... Toxicology and Applied Pharmacology [*A publication*]
TxArB........ Arlington Baptist Junior College, Arlington, TX [*Library symbol*] [*Library of Congress*]   (LCLS)
TxAr-G ...... Arlington Public Library, Genealogy Department, Arlington, TX [*Library symbol*] [*Library of Congress*]   (LCLS)
TxArJ .... Jet Research Center, Inc., Arlington, TX [*Library symbol*] [*Library of Congress*]   (LCLS)
TxArU .... University of Texas at Arlington, Arlington, TX [*Library symbol*] [*Library of Congress*]   (LCLS)
TxAtH .... Henderson County Junior College, Athens, TX [*Library symbol*] [*Library of Congress*]   (LCLS)
TxAu.......... Austin Public Library, Austin, TX [*Library symbol*] [*Library of Congress*]   (LCLS)
TxAuA ...... Charles E. Stevens American Atheist Library and Archives, Inc., Austin, TX [*Library symbol*] [*Library of Congress*]   (LCLS)
TxAu-AT ... Austin Public Library, Austin-Travis County Collection, Austin, TX [*Library symbol*] [*Library of Congress*]   (LCLS)
TxAuC .... Concordia Lutheran College, Austin, TX [*Library symbol*] [*Library of Congress*]   (LCLS)
TxAuCC..... Austin Community College, Austin, TX [*Library symbol*] [*Library of Congress*]   (LCLS)
TxAuCH .... Church Historical Society, Austin, TX [*Library symbol*] [*Library of Congress*]   (LCLS)
TxAuDR .... Daughters of the Republic of Texas Museum, Austin, TX [*Library symbol*] [*Library of Congress*]   (LCLS)
TxAuE .... Episcopal Theological Seminary of the Southwest, Austin, TX [*Library symbol*] [*Library of Congress*]   (LCLS)
TxAuEd ..... Texas Education Agency, Austin, TX [*Library symbol*] [*Library of Congress*]   (LCLS)
TxAuGS..... Church of Jesus Christ of Latter-Day Saints, Genealogical Society Library, Austin Branch, Austin, TX [*Library symbol*] [*Library of Congress*]   (LCLS)
TxAuHi...... Texas State Department of Highways and Public Transportation, Materials and Tests Research Library, Austin, TX [*Library symbol*] [*Library of Congress*]   (LCLS)
TxAuHT .... Huston-Tillotson College, Austin, TX [*Library symbol*] [*Library of Congress*]   (LCLS)
TxAuL .... Legislative Library Board, Legislative Reference Library, Austin, TX [*Library symbol*] [*Library of Congress*]   (LCLS)
TxAuLBJ... Lyndon B. Johnson School of Public Affairs, Lyndon Baines Johnson Library, Austin, TX [*Library symbol*] [*Library of Congress*]   (LCLS)
TxAuM ...... Texas Medical Association, Austin, TX [*Library symbol*] [*Library of Congress*]   (LCLS)
TxAuMH... Texas Department of Mental Health and Mental Retardation, Austin, TX [*Library symbol*] [*Library of Congress*]   (LCLS)
TxAuP .... Austin Presbyterian Theological Seminary, Austin, TX [*Library symbol*] [*Library of Congress*]   (LCLS)
TxAuPW ... Texas Department of Parks and Wildlife, Austin, TX [*Library symbol*] [*Library of Congress*]   (LCLS)

TxAuR .... Radian Corp., Austin, TX [*Library symbol*] [*Library of Congress*] (LCLS)

TxAuSE..... Saint Edward's University, Austin, TX [*Library symbol*] [*Library of Congress*] (LCLS)

TxAuSHos ... Austin State Hospital, Austin, TX [*Library symbol*] [*Library of Congress*] (LCLS)

TxAuT .... Tracor, Inc., Technical Library, Austin, TX [*Library symbol*] [*Library of Congress*] (LCLS)

TxAuW ...... Texas Water Development Board, Austin, TX [*Library symbol*] [*Library of Congress*] (LCLS)

TXB .... Abilene Public Library, Abilene, TX [*OCLC symbol*] (OCLC)

TXB .... TextielVisie. Vakblad voor de Textielbranche [*A publication*]

TXB .... Thromboxane B [*Also, TB, TxB*] [*Biochemistry*]

TxBea .... Tyrrell Public Library, Beaumont, TX [*Library symbol*] [*Library of Congress*] (LCLS)

TxBeaAM ... Beaumont Art Museum, Beaumont, TX [*Library symbol*] [*Library of Congress*] (LCLS)

TxBeaE...... Beaumont Enterprise & Journal, Beaumont, TX [*Library symbol*] [*Library of Congress*] (LCLS)

TxBeaG...... Gulf States Utilities Co., Beaumont, TX [*Library symbol*] [*Library of Congress*] (LCLS)

TxBeaL...... Lamar University, Beaumont, TX [*Library symbol*] [*Library of Congress*] (LCLS)

TxBeaMC ... Mobil Chemical Co., Research and Development Laboratory, Beaumont, TX [*Library symbol*] [*Library of Congress*] (LCLS)

TxBeaSE ... Saint Elizabeth Hospital, Health Science Library, Beaumont, TX [*Library symbol*] [*Library of Congress*] (LCLS)

TxBee......... Bee County Public Library, Beeville, TX [*Library symbol*] [*Library of Congress*] (LCLS)

TxBeeC...... Bee County College, Beeville, TX [*Library symbol*] [*Library of Congress*] (LCLS)

TxBelM ..... Mary Hardin-Baylor College, Belton, TX [*Library symbol*] [*Library of Congress*] (LCLS)

TxBHi........ Brownsville Historical Association, Brownsville, TX [*Library symbol*] [*Library of Congress*] (LCLS)

TxBl........... Bellaire City Library, Bellaire, TX [*Library symbol*] [*Library of Congress*] (LCLS)

TXBL......... Taxable

TxBlT .... Texaco, Inc., Bellaire, TX [*Library symbol*] [*Library of Congress*] (LCLS)

TxBor......... Hutchinson County Library, Borger, TX [*Library symbol*] [*Library of Congress*] (LCLS)

TxBorF ...... Frank Phillips College, Borger, TX [*Library symbol*] [*Library of Congress*] (LCLS)

Tx-BPH ..... Texas Regional Library, Division for the Blind and Physically Handicapped, Austin, TX [*Library symbol*] [*Library of Congress*] (LCLS)

TXBRA...... Texas Business Review [*A publication*]

TxBrd........ Brownwood Public Library, Brownwood, TX [*Library symbol*] [*Library of Congress*] (LCLS)

TxBrdH ..... Howard Payne College, Brownwood, TX [*Library symbol*] [*Library of Congress*] (LCLS)

TxBreB ...... Blinn College, Brenham, TX [*Library symbol*] [*Library of Congress*] (LCLS)

TxBry......... Bryan Public Library, Bryan, TX [*Library symbol*] [*Library of Congress*] (LCLS)

TxBryA...... Allen Academy, Bryan, TX [*Library symbol*] [*Library of Congress*] (LCLS)

TxBs .... Howard County Library, Big Spring, TX [*Library symbol*] [*Library of Congress*] (LCLS)

TxBS.......... Texas Southmost College, Brownsville, TX [*Library symbol*] [*Library of Congress*] (LCLS)

TxBsaA...... Ambassador College, Big Sandy, TX [*Library symbol*] [*Library of Congress*] (LCLS)

TxBsH .... Howard County Junior College, Big Spring, TX [*Library symbol*] [*Library of Congress*] (LCLS)

TxBsV........ United States Veterans Administration Hospital, Big Spring, TX [*Library symbol*] [*Library of Congress*] (LCLS)

TxBUC ...... Union Carbide Corp., Chemicals and Plastics Library, Brownsville, TX [*Library symbol*] [*Library of Congress*] (LCLS)

TX Bus Rev ... Texas Business Review [*A publication*]

TxBy .... Sterling Municipal Library, Baytown, TX [*Library symbol*] [*Library of Congress*] (LCLS)

TxByH .... Humble Oil & Refining Co., Technical Library, Baytown, TX [*Library symbol*] [*Library of Congress*] (LCLS)

TxByH-E... Humble Oil & Refining Co., Engineering Division Library, Baytown, TX [*Library symbol*] [*Library of Congress*] (LCLS)

TxByL........ Lee College, Baytown, TX [*Library symbol*] [*Library of Congress*] (LCLS)

TXC .... Abilene Christian University, Abilene, TX [*OCLC symbol*] (OCLC)

TXC .... Texaco Canada, Inc. [*AMEX symbol*] [*Toronto Stock Exchange symbol*] [*Vancouver Stock Exchange symbol*] (SPSG)

Txc .... Texaco, Inc. [*Associated Press abbreviation*] (APAG)

TXC .... Thurman, CO [*Location identifier*] [*FAA*] (FAAL)

TxCarP ...... Panola College, Carthage, TX [*Library symbol*] [*Library of Congress*] (LCLS)

TxCaW ...... West Texas State University, Canyon, TX [*Library symbol*] [*Library of Congress*] (LCLS)

TxCc .... La Retama Public Library, Corpus Cristi, TX [*Library symbol*] [*Library of Congress*] (LCLS)

TxCcD .... Del Mar College, Corpus Christi, TX [*Library symbol*] [*Library of Congress*] (LCLS)

TxCcGS ..... Church of Jesus Christ of Latter-Day Saints, Genealogical Society Library, Corpus Christi Branch, Corpus Christi, TX [*Library symbol*] [*Library of Congress*] (LCLS)

TxCcMST ... Art Museum of South Texas, Corpus Christi, TX [*Library symbol*] [*Library of Congress*] (LCLS)

TxCcNHi... Nueces County Historical Society, La Retama Public Library, Corpus Christi, TX [*Library symbol*] [*Library of Congress*] (LCLS)

TxCcT........ Texas A & I University at Corpus Christi, Corpus Christi, TX [*Library symbol*] [*Library of Congress*] (LCLS)

TxCcU .... University of Corpus Christi, Corpus Christi, TX [*Library symbol*] [*Library of Congress*] [*Obsolete*] (LCLS)

TxCeN .... Northwood Institute of Texas, Cedar Hill, TX [*Library symbol*] [*Library of Congress*] (LCLS)

TX Ci .... Texas Civil Appeals Reports [*A publication*] (DLA)

TxCiC .... Cisco Junior College, Cisco, TX [*Library symbol*] [*Library of Congress*] (LCLS)

TxClaC ...... Clarendon College, Clarendon, TX [*Library symbol*] [*Library of Congress*] (LCLS)

TxClcU ...... University of Houston at Clear Lake City, Houston, TX [*Library symbol*] [*Library of Congress*] (LCLS)

TxCle .... Cleburne Public Library, Cleburne, TX [*Library symbol*] [*Library of Congress*] (LCLS)

TxCli......... Nellie Pederson Civic Library, Clifton, TX [*Library symbol*] [*Library of Congress*] (LCLS)

TxClv .... Cleveland Public [*Charles O. Austin Memorial*] Library, Cleveland, TX [*Library symbol*] [*Library of Congress*] (LCLS)

TxClwC...... Celanese Corp., Clarkwood, TX [*Library symbol*] [*Library of Congress*] (LCLS)

TxCM .... Texas A & M University, College Station, TX [*Library symbol*] [*Library of Congress*] (LCLS)

TxCM-M... Texas A & M University, Medical Sciences Library, College Station, TX [*Library symbol*] [*Library of Congress*] (LCLS)

TXCO .... [*The*] Exploration Co. [*NASDAQ symbol*] (NQ)

TxComf...... Comfort Public Library, Comfort, TX [*Library symbol*] [*Library of Congress*] (LCLS)

TxComS..... East Texas State University, Commerce, TX [*Library symbol*] [*Library of Congress*] (LCLS)

TxComS-M ... East Texas State University, Museum, Commerce, TX [*Library symbol*] [*Library of Congress*] (LCLS)

TxCoN .... Navarro Junior College, Corsicana, TX [*Library symbol*] [*Library of Congress*] (LCLS)

TxConM .... Montgomery County Memorial Library, Conroe, TX [*Library symbol*] [*Library of Congress*] (LCLS)

TxCr........... Crockett Public Library, Crockett, TX [*Library symbol*] [*Library of Congress*] (LCLS)

TX Cr .... Texas Criminal Appeals Reports [*A publication*] (DLA)

TxCrMA.... Mary Allen Junior College, Crockett, TX [*Library symbol*] [*Library of Congress*] (LCLS)

TxCvS........ ARCO Chemical Co., Channelview, TX [*Library symbol*] [*Library of Congress*] (LCLS)

TxCvT........ Texas Butadine & Chemical Corp., Channelview, TX [*Library symbol*] [*Library of Congress*] (LCLS)

TXCYA...... Toxicology [*A publication*]

TXD.......... McMurry College, Abilene, TX [*OCLC symbol*] (OCLC)

TXD.......... Telephone Exchange (Digital) [*Telecommunications*] (TEL)

TXD.......... Transmit Data [*Data processing*]

TxDa.......... Dallas Public Library, Dallas, TX [*Library symbol*] [*Library of Congress*] (LCLS)

TxDaABC ... AMIGOS [*Access Method for Indexed Data Generalized for Operating System*] Bibliographic Council, Dallas, TX [*Library symbol*] [*Library of Congress*] (LCLS)

TxDaAC .... Anderson, Clayton & Co., Foods Division Technical Library, Dallas, TX [*Library symbol*] [*Library of Congress*] (LCLS)

TxDaAR-G ... Atlantic Richfield Co., Geoscience Library, Dallas, TX [*Library symbol*] [*Library of Congress*] (LCLS)

TxDaAR-R ... Atlantic Richfield Co., R and D Library, Dallas, TX [*Library symbol*] [*Library of Congress*] (LCLS)

TxDaAR-T ... Atlantic Richfield Co., Technical Library, Dallas, TX [*Library symbol*] [*Library of Congress*] (LCLS)

TxDaB .... Dallas Baptist College, Dallas, TX [*Library symbol*] [*Library of Congress*] (LCLS)

TxDaBC..... Bishop College, Dallas, TX [*Library symbol*] [*Library of Congress*] (LCLS)

TxDaBM ... Burgess-Manning Co., Dallas, TX [*Library symbol*] [*Library of Congress*] (LCLS)

TxDaBU .... Baylor University in Dallas, Dallas, TX [*Library symbol*] [*Library of Congress*] (LCLS)

TxDaCC .... Christian College of the Southwest, Dallas, TX [*Library symbol*] [*Library of Congress*] (LCLS)

TxDaCCD ... Callier Center for Communication Disorders, Dallas, TX [*Library symbol*] [*Library of Congress*] (LCLS)

TxDaCiA ... Court of Civil Appeals, Dallas, TX [*Library symbol*] [*Library of Congress*] (LCLS)

TxDaCL ..... Core Laboratories, Inc., Dallas, TX [*Library symbol*] [*Library of Congress*] (LCLS)

TxDaCR .... Collins Radio Co., Dallas, TX [*Library symbol*] [*Library of Congress*] (LCLS)

TxDaCS ..... Dallas County Community College System, Dallas, TX [*Library symbol*] [*Library of Congress*] (LCLS)

TxDaDC .... Dallas Christian College, Dallas, TX [*Library symbol*] [*Library of Congress*] (LCLS)

TxDaDF .... DeGoyler Foundation, Dallas, TX [*Library symbol*] [*Library of Congress*] (LCLS)

TxDaDL .... Dallas County Law Library, Dallas, TX [*Library symbol*] [*Library of Congress*] (LCLS)

TxDaDM ... DeGoyler and MacNaughton Library, Dallas, TX [*Library symbol*] [*Library of Congress*] (LCLS)

TxDaE .... El Centro College, Dallas, TX [*Library symbol*] [*Library of Congress*] (LCLS)

TxDaET ..... East Texas State University, Metroplex Center, Dallas, TX [*Library symbol*] [*Library of Congress*] (LCLS)

TxDaFR ..... Federal Reserve Bank of Dallas, Dallas, TX [*Library symbol*] [*Library of Congress*] (LCLS)

TxDaGS ..... Church of Jesus Christ of Latter-Day Saints, Genealogical Society Library, Dallas Branch, Dallas, TX [*Library symbol*] [*Library of Congress*] (LCLS)

TxDaHi ..... Dallas Historical Society, Dallas, TX [*Library symbol*] [*Library of Congress*] (LCLS)

TxDaJS ..... Johnson and Swanson, Law Library, Dallas, TX [*Library symbol*] [*Library of Congress*] (LCLS)

TxDaL .... Lone Star Gas Co., Dallas, TX [*Library symbol*] [*Library of Congress*] (LCLS)

TxDaM ...... Southern Methodist University, Dallas, TX [*Library symbol*] [*Library of Congress*] (LCLS)

TxDaME ... Mobil Exploration & Producing Services, Inc., Dallas, TX [*Library symbol*] [*Library of Congress*] (LCLS)

TxDaMF ... Dallas Museum of Fine Arts, Dallas, TX [*Library symbol*] [*Library of Congress*] (LCLS)

TxDaM-L .. Southern Methodist University, Law Library, Dallas, TX [*Library symbol*] [*Library of Congress*] (LCLS)

TxDaM-P .. Southern Methodist University, Perkins School of Theology, Dallas, TX [*Library symbol*] [*Library of Congress*] (LCLS)

TxDaM-SE ... Southern Methodist University, Science/Engineering Library, Dallas, TX [*Library symbol*] [*Library of Congress*] (LCLS)

TxDaMV ... Mountain View College, Dallas, TX [*Library symbol*] [*Library of Congress*] (LCLS)

TxDaP .... Dallas Power & Light Co., Dallas, TX [*Library symbol*] [*Library of Congress*] (LCLS)

TxDaPO .... Placid Oil Co. Exploration Library, Dallas, TX [*Library symbol*] [*Library of Congress*] (LCLS)

TxDaPP ..... Planned Parenthood of Northeast Texas, Dallas, TX [*Library symbol*] [*Library of Congress*] (LCLS)

TxDaR .... Richland College, Dallas, TX [*Library symbol*] [*Library of Congress*] (LCLS)

TxDaRI ...... Rockwell International, Collins Radio Group, Technical Information Center, Dallas, TX [*Library symbol*] [*Library of Congress*] (LCLS)

TxDaS .... University of Texas, Health Science Center at Dallas, Dallas, TX [*Library symbol*] [*Library of Congress*] (LCLS)

TxDaSM .... Mobil Research & Development Corp., Dallas, TX [*Library symbol*] [*Library of Congress*] (LCLS)

TxDaTI-A ... Texas Instruments, Inc., Apparatus Division Library, Dallas, TX [*Library symbol*] [*Library of Congress*] (LCLS)

TxDaTI-C ... Texas Instruments, Inc., Central Research and Engineering Library, Dallas, TX [*Library symbol*] [*Library of Congress*] (LCLS)

TxDaTI-IS ... Texas Instruments, Inc., IS & S Library, Dallas, TX [*Library symbol*] [*Library of Congress*] (LCLS)

TxDaTI-S .. Texas Instruments, Inc., Semiconductor Division, Dallas, TX [*Library symbol*] [*Library of Congress*] (LCLS)

TxDaTI-SS ... Texas Instruments, Inc., Science Services Division, Dallas, TX [*Library symbol*] [*Library of Congress*] (LCLS)

TxDaTS ..... Dallas Theological Seminary and Graduate School, Dallas, TX [*Library symbol*] [*Library of Congress*] (LCLS)

TxDaU .... University of Dallas, Irving, TX [*Library symbol*] [*Library of Congress*] (LCLS)

TxDaUSAF ... United States Army and Air Force Exchange Service, Dallas, TX [*Library symbol*] [*Library of Congress*] (LCLS)

TxDaUSFD ... United States Food and Drug Administration, Dallas, TX [*Library symbol*] [*Library of Congress*] (LCLS)

TxDaVA .... United States Veterans Administration Hospital, Dallas, TX [*Library symbol*] [*Library of Congress*] (LCLS)

TXDE .... Toluene-Xylene-Dioxane-Ethanol [*Scintillation solvent*]

TxDeni .... Denison Public Library, Denison, TX [*Library symbol*] [*Library of Congress*] (LCLS)

TxDeniG .... Grayson County College, Denison, TX [*Library symbol*] [*Library of Congress*] (LCLS)

TxDib .... T. L. L. Temple Memorial Library, Diboll, TX [*Library symbol*] [*Library of Congress*] (LCLS)

TxDN .... North Texas State University, Denton, TX [*Library symbol*] [*Library of Congress*] (LCLS)

TxDN-Hi ... North Texas State University, State Historical Collection, Denton, TX [*Library symbol*] [*Library of Congress*] (LCLS)

TxDpS .... Shell Oil Co., Deer Park, TX [*Library symbol*] [*Library of Congress*] (LCLS)

TxDpSC .... Shell Chemical Co., Deer Park, TX [*Library symbol*] [*Library of Congress*] (LCLS)

TxDunv ...... Duncanville Public Library, Duncanville, TX [*Library symbol*] [*Library of Congress*] (LCLS)

TxDW .... Texas Woman's University, Denton, TX [*Library symbol*] [*Library of Congress*] (LCLS)

TXE .... El Paso Community College, El Paso, TX [*OCLC symbol*] (OCLC)

TxE .... El Paso Public Library, El Paso, TX [*Library symbol*] [*Library of Congress*] (LCLS)

TXE .... Tax Executive [*A publication*]

TXE .... Telephone Exchange (Electronics) [*Telecommunications*] (IEEE)

TXE .... Telephone Exchange (Equipment) [*Telecommunications*]

TxEC .... El Paso Community College, El Paso, TX [*Library symbol*] [*Library of Congress*] (LCLS)

TXECB ...... Toxicological and Environmental Chemistry Reviews [*A publication*]

TxEdP .... Pan American University, Edinburg, TX [*Library symbol*] [*Library of Congress*] (LCLS)

TxEGS .... Church of Jesus Christ of Latter-Day Saints, Genealogical Society Library, El Paso Branch, El Paso, TX [*Library symbol*] [*Library of Congress*] (LCLS)

TxEHD ...... Hotel-Dieu Medical-Nursing Educational Media Center, El Paso, TX [*Library symbol*] [*Library of Congress*] (LCLS)

TXEL .... Texcel International, Inc. [*NASDAQ symbol*] (NQ)

TXEN .... Texas Energies, Inc. [*NASDAQ symbol*] (NQ)

TxENG ...... El Paso Natural Gas Co., Technical Information Center, El Paso, TX [*Library symbol*] [*Library of Congress*] (LCLS)

TxEU .... University of Texas at El Paso, El Paso, TX [*Library symbol*] [*Library of Congress*] (LCLS)

TxEWB ...... United States Army, William Beaumont General Hospital, Medical and Technical Library, El Paso, TX [*Library symbol*] [*Library of Congress*] (LCLS)

TXF .... Corpus Christi State University, Corpus Christi, TX [*OCLC symbol*] (OCLC)

TxF .... Fort Worth Public Library, Fort Worth, TX [*Library symbol*] [*Library of Congress*] (LCLS)

TXF .... Tax Exchange Format [*Data processing*] (PCM)

TXF .... Texfi Industries, Inc. [*NYSE symbol*] (SPSG)

TxFACM ... Amon Carter Museum of Western Art, Fort Worth, TX [*Library symbol*] [*Library of Congress*] (LCLS)

TxFAl .... Alcon Laboratories, Inc., Fort Worth, TX [*Library symbol*] [*Library of Congress*] (LCLS)

TxFbAD .... United States Army, Air Defense School, Fort Bliss, TX [*Library symbol*] [*Library of Congress*] (LCLS)

TxFBH ...... Bell Helicopter Co., Fort Worth, TX [*Library symbol*] [*Library of Congress*] (LCLS)

TxFCB .... Carter & Burgess, Inc., Fort Worth, TX [*Library symbol*] [*Library of Congress*] (LCLS)

TxFCC .... Fort Worth Christian College, Fort Worth, TX [*Library symbol*] [*Library of Congress*] (LCLS)

TxFCO .... Texas College of Osteopathic Medicine, Fort Worth, TX [*Library symbol*] [*Library of Congress*] (LCLS)

TxFF .... Fort Worth Art Museum, Fort Worth, TX [*Library symbol*] [*Library of Congress*] (LCLS)

TxFFAA .... United States Federal Aviation Administration, Fort Worth, TX [*Library symbol*] [*Library of Congress*] (LCLS)

TxFG .... General Dynamics/Convair Aerospace Division, Fort Worth, TX [*Library symbol*] [*Library of Congress*] (LCLS)

TxFGS .... Church of Jesus Christ of Latter-Day Saints, Genealogical Society Library, Fort Worth Branch, North Richland Hills, Fort Worth, TX [*Library symbol*] [*Library of Congress*] (LCLS)

TxFhH .... Darnell Army Hospital, Medical Library, Fort Hood, TX [*Library symbol*] [*Library of Congress*] (LCLS)

TxFJPS ...... John Peter Smith Hospital, Fort Worth, TX [*Library symbol*] [*Library of Congress*] (LCLS)

TxFK .... Kimbell Art Museum, Fort Worth, TX [*Library symbol*] [*Library of Congress*] (LCLS)

TxFM .... Fort Worth Museum of Science and History, Fort Worth, TX [*Library symbol*] [*Library of Congress*] (LCLS)

TxFNA ...... United States National Archives and Record Center, Fort Worth, TX [*Library symbol*] [*Library of Congress*] (LCLS)

TxFNIMH ... National Institute of Mental Health, Clinical Research Center Medical Library, Fort Worth, TX [*Library symbol*] [*Library of Congress*] (LCLS)

TxFrB .... Brazosport Junior College, Freeport, TX [*Library symbol*] [*Library of Congress*] (LCLS)

TxFrD .... Dow Chemical Co., Texas Division, Freeport, TX [*Library symbol*] [*Library of Congress*] (LCLS)

TxFS .... Southwestern Baptist Theological Seminary, Fort Worth, TX [*Library symbol*] [*Library of Congress*] (LCLS)

TxFshBH ... Brooke General Hospital, Medical Library, Fort Sam Houston, TX [*Library symbol*] [*Library of Congress*] (LCLS)

TxFshM..... Medical Field Service School, Fort Sam Houston, TX [*Library symbol*] [*Library of Congress*] (LCLS)

TxFSJ........ Saint Joseph Hospital, Medical and Nursing Library, Fort Worth, TX [*Library symbol*] [*Library of Congress*] (LCLS)

TxFT.......... Tarrant County Junior College, Fort Worth, TX [*Library symbol*] [*Library of Congress*] (LCLS)

TxFTC....... Texas Christian University, Fort Worth, TX [*Library symbol*] [*Library of Congress*] (LCLS)

TxFTE ...... Texas Electric Service Co., Fort Worth, TX [*Library symbol*] [*Library of Congress*] (LCLS)

TxFTM...... Terrell's Laboratories Medical Library, Fort Worth, TX [*Library symbol*] [*Library of Congress*] (LCLS)

TxFT-NE... Tarrant County Junior College, Northeast Campus, Hurst, TX [*Library symbol*] [*Library of Congress*] (LCLS)

TxFT-S...... Tarrant County Junior College, South Campus, Fort Worth, TX [*Library symbol*] [*Library of Congress*] (LCLS)

TxFTW...... Texas Wesleyan College, Fort Worth, TX [*Library symbol*] [*Library of Congress*] (LCLS)

TXG .... Austin Public Library, Austin, TX [*OCLC symbol*] (OCLC)

TXG .... Taxiing [*Aviation*] (FAAC)

TxGA......... United States Army, Army Engineering District, Office of Administrative Services, Galveston, TX [*Library symbol*] [*Library of Congress*] (LCLS)

TxGaiC ...... Cooke County Junior College, Gainsville, TX [*Library symbol*] [*Library of Congress*] (LCLS)

TxGar .... Nicholson Memorial Library, Garland, TX [*Library symbol*] [*Library of Congress*] (LCLS)

TxGarD ..... Dresser Industries, Inc., Garland, TX [*Library symbol*] [*Library of Congress*] (LCLS)

TxGarV...... Varo, Inc., Texas Division, Garland, TX [*Library symbol*] [*Library of Congress*] (LCLS)

TxGat......... Gatesville Public Library, Gatesville, TX [*Library symbol*] [*Library of Congress*] (LCLS)

TxGC .... Galveston Community College, Galveston, TX [*Library symbol*] [*Library of Congress*] (LCLS)

TxGeoS...... Southwestern University, Georgetown, TX [*Library symbol*] [*Library of Congress*] (LCLS)

TxGilGS .... Church of Jesus Christ of Latter-Day Saints, Genealogical Society Library, Longview Branch, Gilmer, TX [*Library symbol*] [*Library of Congress*] (LCLS)

TxGML ..... Texas A & M University, Moody College of Marine Sciences and Maritime Resources, Galveston, TX [*Library symbol*] [*Library of Congress*] (LCLS)

TxGoS........ Spanish Texas Microfilm Center, Goliad, TX [*Library symbol*] [*Library of Congress*] (LCLS)

TxGR .... Rosenberg Library, Galveston, TX [*Library symbol*] [*Library of Congress*] (LCLS)

TxGrp .... Grand Prairie Memorial Library, Grand Prairie, TX [*Library symbol*] [*Library of Congress*] (LCLS)

TxGUSFW ... United States National Marine Fisheries Service, Biological Laboratory, Galveston, TX [*Library symbol*] [*Library of Congress*] (LCLS)

TxH .... Houston Public Library, Houston, TX [*Library symbol*] [*Library of Congress*] (LCLS)

TXH.......... Transfer on Index High

TXH.......... University of Houston, Houston, TX [*OCLC symbol*] (OCLC)

TxHaJ .... Jarvis Christian College, Hawkins, TX [*Library symbol*] [*Library of Congress*] (LCLS)

TxHAM..... Houston Academy of Medicine for Texas Medical Center, Houston, TX [*Library symbol*] [*Library of Congress*] (LCLS)

TxHAWD ... Arnold, White & Durkee, Houston, TX [*Library symbol*] [*Library of Congress*] (LCLS)

TxHBa....... National Lead Industries, Inc., Baroid Division, Houston, TX [*Library symbol*] [*Library of Congress*] (LCLS)

TxHBB ...... Baker, Botts, Shepherd & Coates, Houston, TX [*Library symbol*] [*Library of Congress*] (LCLS)

TxHBC...... Houston Baptist University, Houston, TX [*Library symbol*] [*Library of Congress*] (LCLS)

TxHBec ..... Bechtel Group, Inc., Technical Library, Houston, TX [*Library symbol*] [*Library of Congress*] (LCLS)

TxHBR...... Brown & Root, Inc., Technical Library, Houston, TX [*Library symbol*] [*Library of Congress*] (LCLS)

TxHC......... Houston Community College System, Houston, TX [*Library symbol*] [*Library of Congress*] (LCLS)

TxHCC...... Continental Carbon Co., Houston, TX [*Library symbol*] [*Library of Congress*] (LCLS)

TxHCG...... Columbia Gulf Transmission Co., Houston, TX [*Library symbol*] [*Library of Congress*] (LCLS)

TxHCI .... Cameron Iron Works, Inc., Houston, TX [*Library symbol*] [*Library of Congress*] (LCLS)

TxHCS ...... Community Welfare Planning Association, Social Research Library, Houston, TX [*Library symbol*] [*Library of Congress*] (LCLS)

TxHDC...... Dow Chemical Co., E and CS Information Center, Houston, TX [*Library symbol*] [*Library of Congress*] (LCLS)

TxHDE...... Dresser Industries, Inc., Lane-Wells Co., Houston, TX [*Library symbol*] [*Library of Congress*] (LCLS)

TxHDom.... Dominican College, Houston, TX [*Library symbol*] [*Library of Congress*] (LCLS)

TxHe.......... Edwards Public Library, Henrietta, TX [*Library symbol*] [*Library of Congress*] (LCLS)

TxHE........ United States Air Force, Base Library, Ellington AFB, Houston, TX [*Library symbol*] [*Library of Congress*] (LCLS)

TxHebO..... Our Lady of Guadalupe Parish Library, Hebbronville, TX [*Library symbol*] [*Library of Congress*] (LCLS)

TxHE-NA ... United States Air Force, National Aerospace Education Library, Ellington AFB, Houston, TX [*Library symbol*] [*Library of Congress*] (LCLS)

TxHF......... Captain Theodore C. Freeman Memorial Library, Houston, TX [*Library symbol*] [*Library of Congress*] (LCLS)

TxHFE ...... Fluor Engineers & Constructors, Fluor Houston Library, Houston, TX [*Library symbol*] [*Library of Congress*] (LCLS)

TxHFO...... Fluor Ocean Services, Engineering Library, Houston, TX [*Library symbol*] [*Library of Congress*] (LCLS)

TxHFR ...... Freelance Research Service, Houston, TX [*Library of Congress*] (LCLS)

TxHG........ Gulf Coast Bible College, Houston, TX [*Library symbol*] [*Library of Congress*] (LCLS)

TxHGO ..... Gulf Oil Co.-US, Central Reference Library, Houston, TX [*Library symbol*] [*Library of Congress*] (LCLS)

TxHGP...... Gulf Publishing Co., Houston, TX [*Library symbol*] [*Library of Congress*] (LCLS)

TxHGS...... Church of Jesus Christ of Latter-Day Saints, Genealogical Society Library, Houston Branch, Houston, TX [*Library symbol*] [*Library of Congress*] (LCLS)

TxHGS-E.. Church of Jesus Christ of Latter-Day Saints, Genealogical Society Library, Houston East Branch, Houston, TX [*Library symbol*] [*Library of Congress*] (LCLS)

TxHH .... Black, Syvalls & Bryson, Inc., HOMCO Division, Houston, TX [*Library symbol*] [*Library of Congress*] (LCLS)

TxHHC ..... Houston Chronicle, Houston, TX [*Library symbol*] [*Library of Congress*] (LCLS)

TxHHG...... Houston-Galveston Area Council Library, Houston, TX [*Library symbol*] [*Library of Congress*] (LCLS)

TxHHH..... Herman Hospital, Houston, TX [*Library symbol*] [*Library of Congress*] (LCLS)

TxHHL...... Houston Lighting & Power Co., Houston, TX [*Library symbol*] [*Library of Congress*] (LCLS)

TxHHO ..... Humble Oil & Refining Co., General Services Library, Houston, TX [*Library symbol*] [*Library of Congress*] (LCLS)

TxHHO-E ... Humble Oil & Refining Co., Marketing Research Library, Houston, TX [*Library symbol*] [*Library of Congress*] (LCLS)

TxHHOM ... Houston Oil and Mineral Corp., Corporate Library, Houston, TX [*Library symbol*] [*Library of Congress*] (LCLS)

TxHHP...... Houston Post, Houston, TX [*Library symbol*] [*Library of Congress*] (LCLS)

TxHHT...... Hughes Tool Co., Houston, TX [*Library symbol*] [*Library of Congress*] (LCLS)

TxHI......... International Business Machines Corporation, Corporation Library, Houston, TX [*Library symbol*] [*Library of Congress*] (LCLS)

TXHI .... THT, Inc. [*Formerly, Texas Hitech, Inc.*] [*NASDAQ symbol*] (NQ)

TxHiC........ Hill Junior College, Hillsboro, TX [*Library symbol*] [*Library of Congress*] (LCLS)

TxHIR ...... Institute of Religion, Texas Medical Center, Houston, TX [*Library symbol*] [*Library of Congress*] (LCLS)

TXHL .... Texas Health Letter [*A publication*]

TxHLD...... City of Houston Legal Department, Houston, TX [*Library symbol*] [*Library of Congress*] (LCLS)

TxHLJ....... Memorial Baptist Hospital, Lillie Jolly School of Nursing, Houston, TX [*Library symbol*] [*Library of Congress*] (LCLS)

TxHLS...... Lunar Science Institute, Houston, TX [*Library symbol*] [*Library of Congress*] (LCLS)

TxHLT ...... Layne Texas Co., Houston, TX [*Library symbol*] [*Library of Congress*] (LCLS)

TxHM........ Museum of Fine Arts, Houston, TX [*Library symbol*] [*Library of Congress*] (LCLS)

TxHMa...... Magcobar Corp., Houston, TX [*Library symbol*] [*Library of Congress*] (LCLS)

TxHMC..... Houston Academy of Medicine, Houston, TX [*Library symbol*] [*Library of Congress*] (LCLS)

TxHMc..... McClelland Engineers, Inc., Houston, TX [*Library symbol*] [*Library of Congress*] (LCLS)

TxHMM.... Milwhite Co., Houston, TX [*Library symbol*] [*Library of Congress*] (LCLS)

TxHMon.... Monsanto Co., Houston, TX [*Library symbol*] [*Library of Congress*] (LCLS)

TxHN .... National Association of Corrosion Engineers, Houston, TX [*Library symbol*] [*Library of Congress*] (LCLS)

TxHNASA ... National Aeronautics and Space Administration, Manned Spacecraft Center, Technical Library, Houston, TX [*Library symbol*] [*Library of Congress*] (LCLS)

TxHNH ..... North Harris County College, Houston, TX [*Library symbol*] [*Library of Congress*] (LCLS)

TxHP......... Texas Research Institute of Mental Sciences, Houston, TX [*Library symbol*] [*Library of Congress*] (LCLS)

TxHPC ...... Pace Co., Houston, TX [*Library symbol*] [*Library of Congress*] (LCLS)

TxHPen ..... Pennzoil Exploration Library, Houston, TX [*Library symbol*] [*Library of Congress*] (LCLS)

TxHPH ...... Port of Houston World Trade Center, Houston, TX [*Library symbol*] [*Library of Congress*] (LCLS)

TxHPI .... Prudential Insurance Co. of America, Houston, TX [*Library symbol*] [*Library of Congress*] (LCLS)

TxHPT ...... Petro-Tex Chemical Corp., Research Library, Houston, TX [*Library symbol*] [*Library of Congress*] (LCLS)

TxHR .... Rice University, Houston, TX [*Library symbol*] [*Library of Congress*] (LCLS)

TxHRa .... Raymond International, Inc., Houston, TX [*Library symbol*] [*Library of Congress*] (LCLS)

TxHRH ..... Roy M. Huffington, Inc., Library, Houston, TX [*Library symbol*] [*Library of Congress*] (LCLS)

TxHRI .... Houston Research Institute, Houston, TX [*Library symbol*] [*Library of Congress*] (LCLS)

TxHSB ...... Southern Bible College, Houston, TX [*Library symbol*] [*Library of Congress*] (LCLS)

TxHSD ...... Shell Development Co., Bellaire Research Center, Houston, TX [*Library symbol*] [*Library of Congress*] (LCLS)

TxHSDW .. Shell Oil Development Co., Westhollow Research Center Library, Houston, TX [*Library symbol*] [*Library of Congress*] (LCLS)

TxHSJM ... San Jacinto Museum of History Association, Deer Park, TX [*Library symbol*] [*Library of Congress*] (LCLS)

TxHSOC ... Standard Oil Co. of Texas, Houston, TX [*Library symbol*] [*Library of Congress*] (LCLS)

TxHSOF .... Shell Oil Co., Information and Library Services Library, Houston, TX [*Library symbol*] [*Library of Congress*] (LCLS)

TxHSOIC ... Shell Oil Co., Information and Computing Services Center Library, Houston, TX [*Library symbol*] [*Library of Congress*] (LCLS)

TxHSP .... Shell Pipe Line Corp., R and D Library, Houston, TX [*Library symbol*] [*Library of Congress*] [*Obsolete*] (LCLS)

TxHSR ...... Southwestern Research Institute, Houston, TX [*Library symbol*] [*Library of Congress*] (LCLS)

TxHST ...... University of Saint Thomas, Houston, TX [*Library symbol*] [*Library of Congress*] (LCLS)

TxHSTC .... South Texas Junior College, Houston, TX [*Library symbol*] [*Library of Congress*] (LCLS)

TxHSTL .... South Texas College of Law, Houston, TX [*Library symbol*] [*Library of Congress*] (LCLS)

TxHSU ...... Superior Oil Exploration Library, Houston, TX [*Library symbol*] [*Library of Congress*] (LCLS)

TxHSW ..... Schlumberger Well Services, Houston, TX [*Library symbol*] [*Library of Congress*] (LCLS)

TxHTC ...... Transcontinental Gas Pipe Line Corp., Houston, TX [*Library symbol*] [*Library of Congress*] (LCLS)

TxHTE ...... Texas Eastern Transmission Corp., Houston, TX [*Library symbol*] [*Library of Congress*] (LCLS)

TxHTen ..... Tennessee Gas Transmission Co., Houston, TX [*Library symbol*] [*Library of Congress*] (LCLS)

TxHTexG .. Texas Gas Exploration Co., Houston, TX [*Library symbol*] [*Library of Congress*] (LCLS)

TxHTexO ... Texasgulf Oil & Gas Co., Houston, TX [*Library symbol*] [*Library of Congress*] (LCLS)

TxHTG ...... Trunkline Gas Co., Houston, TX [*Library symbol*] [*Library of Congress*] (LCLS)

TxHTGP ... Tennessee Gas Pipeline Co., Houston, TX [*Library symbol*] [*Library of Congress*] (LCLS)

TxHTGS .... Texas Gulf Sulphur Co., Inc., Houston, TX [*Library symbol*] [*Library of Congress*] (LCLS)

TxHTI .... Texas Instruments, Inc., Houston, TX [*Library symbol*] [*Library of Congress*] (LCLS)

TxHTide .... Getty Oil Co., Houston, TX [*Library symbol*] [*Library of Congress*] (LCLS)

TxHTide(Res) ... Getty Oil Co., Exploration and Production Research Library, Houston, TX [*Library symbol*] [*Library of Congress*] (LCLS)

TxHTI-I .... Texas Instruments, Inc., Industrial Products Division, Houston, TX [*Library symbol*] [*Library of Congress*] (LCLS)

TxHTM ..... Texas Manufacturers Association, Houston, TX [*Library symbol*] [*Library of Congress*] (LCLS)

TxHTO ...... Tenneco Oil Co., Exploration Research Library, Houston, TX [*Library symbol*] [*Library of Congress*] (LCLS)

TxHTRW .. TRW Systems Group, Houston, TX [*Library symbol*] [*Library of Congress*] (LCLS)

TxHTSU ... Texas Southern University, Houston, TX [*Library symbol*] [*Library of Congress*] (LCLS)

TxHTu .... Turner, Collie & Braden, Inc., Houston, TX [*Library symbol*] [*Library of Congress*] (LCLS)

TxHU .... University of Houston, Houston, TX [*Library symbol*] [*Library of Congress*] (LCLS)

TxHUC ...... Union Carbide Corp., Houston, TX [*Library symbol*] [*Library of Congress*] (LCLS)

TxHU-D .... University of Houston, Downtown College, Houston, TX [*Library symbol*] [*Library of Congress*] (LCLS)

TxHU-L ..... University of Houston, Law School, Houston, TX [*Library symbol*] [*Library of Congress*] (LCLS)

TxHurT ..... Tarrant County Junior College District, Hurst, TX [*Library symbol*] [*Library of Congress*] (LCLS)

TxHUSC ... United States Department of Commerce, Houston Field Office Library, Houston, TX [*Library symbol*] [*Library of Congress*] (LCLS)

TxHuT .... Sam Houston State University, Huntsville, TX [*Library symbol*] [*Library of Congress*] (LCLS)

TxHUTP ... Union Texas Petroleum Co., Houston, TX [*Library symbol*] [*Library of Congress*] (LCLS)

TxHVA ...... United States Veterans Administration Hospital, Houston, TX [*Library symbol*] [*Library of Congress*] (LCLS)

TxHVE ...... Vinson, Elkins, Searls, Connally & Smith, Law Library, Houston, TX [*Library symbol*] [*Library of Congress*] (LCLS)

TxHW .... Welex Division, Haliburton Co., Houston, TX [*Library symbol*] [*Library of Congress*] (LCLS)

TxHWB .... World Book Encyclopaedia Science Service, Inc., Houston, TX [*Library symbol*] [*Library of Congress*] (LCLS)

TxHWG .... Western Geophysical Co., Houston, TX [*Library symbol*] [*Library of Congress*] (LCLS)

TxHWH .... Westbury Senior High School, Houston, TX [*Library symbol*] [*Library of Congress*] (LCLS)

TxHWN .... Western Natural Gas Co., Houston, TX [*Library symbol*] [*Library of Congress*] (LCLS)

TXI .... Southwest Texas State University, San Marcos, TX [*OCLC symbol*] (OCLC)

TXI .... Texas Industries, Inc. [*NYSE symbol*] (SPSG)

TXI .... Texas International Airlines, Inc. [*Air carrier designation symbol*]

TXI .... Torex Minerals Ltd. [*Vancouver Stock Exchange symbol*]

TXI .... Transfer with Index Incremented

TxIr .... Irving Municipal Library, Irving, TX [*Library symbol*] [*Library of Congress*] (LCLS)

TxIrS .... Irving Independent School District, Irving, TX [*Library symbol*] [*Library of Congress*] (LCLS)

TXJ .... University of Texas at San Antonio, San Antonio, TX [*OCLC symbol*] (OCLC)

TxJaB .... Baptist Missionary Association Theological Seminary, Jacksonville, TX [*Library symbol*] [*Library of Congress*] (LCLS)

TxJaC .... Jacksonville College, Jacksonville, TX [*Library symbol*] [*Library of Congress*] (LCLS)

TxJaL .... Lon Morris College, Jacksonville, TX [*Library symbol*] [*Library of Congress*] (LCLS)

TXK .... Stephen F. Austin University, Nacogdoches, TX [*OCLC symbol*] (OCLC)

TXK .... Telephone Exchange (Crossbar) [*Telecommunications*] (TEL)

TXK .... Texarkana [*Arkansas*] [*Airport symbol*] (OAG)

TxKeeS ...... Southwestern Union College, Keene, TX [*Library symbol*] [*Library of Congress*] (LCLS)

TxKerS ...... Schreiner Institute, Kerrville, TX [*Library symbol*] [*Library of Congress*] (LCLS)

TXKF .... Bermuda Naval Air Station [*Bermuda*] [*ICAO location identifier*] (ICLI)

TxKiC .... Central Texas College, Killeen, TX [*Library symbol*] [*Library of Congress*] (LCLS)

TxKilC .... Kilgore College, Kilgore, TX [*Library symbol*] [*Library of Congress*] (LCLS)

TxKT .... Texas A & I University, Kingsville, TX [*Library symbol*] [*Library of Congress*] (LCLS)

TXL .... Berlin [*Germany*] [*Airport symbol*] (OAG)

TXL .... Lubbock City-County Libraries, Lubbock, TX [*OCLC symbol*] (OCLC)

TxL .... Lubbock City-County Libraries, Lubbock, TX [*Library symbol*] [*Library of Congress*] (LCLS)

TX L .... Texas Law Review [*A publication*]

TXL .... Transfer on Index Low

TxLaH .... United States Air Force, Base Library, Lackland Air Force Base, TX [*Library symbol*] [*Library of Congress*] (LCLS)

TxLaM ...... United States Air Force, Wilford Hall Medical Center, Lackland AFB, TX [*Library symbol*] [*Library of Congress*] (LCLS)

TxLapU ...... Upjohn Co., Polymer Chemicals Division Library, La Porte, TX [*Library symbol*] [*Library of Congress*] (LCLS)

TxLar .... Laredo Public Library, Laredo, TX [*Library symbol*] [*Library of Congress*] (LCLS)

TxLarC ...... Laredo Junior College, Laredo, TX [*Library symbol*] [*Library of Congress*] (LCLS)

TxLarU ...... Laredo State University, Laredo, TX [*Library symbol*] [*Library of Congress*] (LCLS)

TxLC .... Lubbock Christian College, Lubbock, TX [*Library symbol*] [*Library of Congress*] (LCLS)

TxLcD .... Soil and Water Conservation Districts Foundation, Davis Conservation Library, League City, TX [*Library symbol*] [*Library of Congress*] (LCLS)

TxLeS .... South Plains College, Levelland, TX [*Library symbol*] [*Library of Congress*] (LCLS)

TxLib .... Liberty City Library, Liberty, TX [*Library symbol*] [*Library of Congress*] (LCLS)

TxLivP....... Polk County Enterprise, Livingston, TX [*Library symbol*] [*Library of Congress*] (LCLS)
TX LJ........ Texas Law Journal [*A publication*] (DLA)
TxLjB......... Brazosport College, Lake Jackson, TX [*Library symbol*] [*Library of Congress*] (LCLS)
TxLMH...... Methodist Hospital, Lubbock, TX [*Library symbol*] [*Library of Congress*] (LCLS)
TxLoL........ LeTourneau College, Longview, TX [*Library symbol*] [*Library of Congress*] (LCLS)
TX LR....... Texas Law Review [*A publication*]
TXLRA...... Texas Law Review [*A publication*]
TxLT......... Texas Tech University, Lubbock, TX [*Library symbol*] [*Library of Congress*] (LCLS)
TxLTM...... Texas Tech University, School of Medicine at Lubbock, Lubbock, TX [*Library symbol*] [*Library of Congress*] (LCLS)
TxLufA...... Angelina College, Lufkin, TX [*Library symbol*] [*Library of Congress*] (LCLS)
TxLufFS .... Texas Forest Service, Forest Products Laboratory Library, Lufkin, TX [*Library symbol*] [*Library of Congress*] (LCLS)
TxLufK...... Kurth Memorial Library, Lufkin, TX [*Library symbol*] [*Library of Congress*] (LCLS)
TXM......... Middle Tennessee State University, Murfreesboro, TN [*OCLC symbol*] (OCLC)
TXM......... Tank Exchange Model
Tx-M......... Texas State Medical Library, Austin, TX [*Library symbol*] [*Library of Congress*] (LCLS)
TXM......... Trimel Corp. [*Toronto Stock Exchange symbol*]
TxMaIC..... ICI America, Inc., Darco Experimental Laboratory Library, Marshall, TX [*Library symbol*] [*Library of Congress*] (LCLS)
TxMaW..... Wiley College, Marshall, TX [*Library symbol*] [*Library of Congress*] (LCLS)
TxMCa...... McAllen Memorial Library, McAllen, TX [*Library symbol*] [*Library of Congress*] (LCLS)
TxMcaH.... Hidelgo County Library System, McAllen, TX [*Library symbol*] [*Library of Congress*] (LCLS)
TxMcgR.... North American Rockwell Corp., Solid Rocket Division, McGregor, TX [*Library symbol*] [*Library of Congress*] (LCLS)
TxMck....... McKinney Memorial Public Library, McKinney, TX [*Library symbol*] [*Library of Congress*] (LCLS)
TXMDA.... Texas Medicine [*A publication*]
TxMe......... Mesquite Public Library, Mesquite, TX [*Library symbol*] [*Library of Congress*] (LCLS)
TxMeE....... Eastfield College, Mesquite, TX [*Library symbol*] [*Library of Congress*] (LCLS)
TxMM....... Midland County Public Library, Midland, TX [*Library symbol*] [*Library of Congress*] (LCLS)
TXMX....... Southwest Cafes, Inc. [*Later, El Chico Restaurants*] [*NASDAQ symbol*] (SPSG)
TXN.......... Houston Public Library, Houston, TX [*OCLC symbol*] (OCLC)
TXN.......... Taxation
TXN.......... Texas Instruments, Inc. [*NYSE symbol*] (SPSG)
TXN.......... Texas Northern Oil & Gas [*Vancouver Stock Exchange symbol*]
TXN.......... Texas Satellite Network [*Telecommunications service*] (TSSD)
TXN.......... Tunxi [*China*] [*Airport symbol*] (OAG)
TxNacS...... Stephen F. Austin State University, Nacogdoches, TX [*Library symbol*] [*Library of Congress*] (LCLS)
TXNO....... Technogenetics, Inc. [*New York, NY*] [*NASDAQ symbol*] (NQ)
TXO......... Texico, NM [*Location identifier*] [*FAA*] (FAAL)
TXO......... University of Texas of the Permian Basin, Odessa, TX [*OCLC symbol*] (OCLC)
TxOC........ Odessa College, Odessa, TX [*Library symbol*] [*Library of Congress*] (LCLS)
TxOE........ Ector County Public Library, Odessa, TX [*Library symbol*] [*Library of Congress*] (LCLS)
TxOEP...... El Paso Products Co., Odessa, TX [*Library symbol*] [*Library of Congress*] (LCLS)
TxOGS...... Church of Jesus Christ of Latter-Day Saints, Genealogical Society Library, Odessa Stake Branch, Odessa, TX [*Library symbol*] [*Library of Congress*] (LCLS)
TXOL........ Texoil, Inc. [*NASDAQ symbol*] (NQ)
TXON....... Texon Energy Corp. [*NASDAQ symbol*] (NQ)
TxOr......... Orange Public Library, Orange, TX [*Library symbol*] [*Library of Congress*] (LCLS)
TXOrD...... E. I. Du Pont de Nemours & Co., Sabine River Works, Orange, TX [*Library symbol*] [*Library of Congress*] (LCLS)
TXP........... El Paso Public Library, El Paso, TX [*OCLC symbol*] (OCLC)
TxP........... Pasadena Public Library, Pasadena, TX [*Library symbol*] [*Library of Congress*] (LCLS)
TxPac........ Texas Pacific Land Trust [*Associated Press abbreviation*] (APAG)
TxPaIMS .. Institute of Marine Science, University of Texas, Port Aransas, TX [*Library symbol*] [*Library of Congress*] (LCLS)
TxParC...... Paris Junior College, Paris, TX [*Library symbol*] [*Library of Congress*] (LCLS)

TxPC......... Champion Papers, Inc., Pasadena, TX [*Library symbol*] [*Library of Congress*] (LCLS)
TxPE......... Ethyl Corp., Pasadena, TX [*Library symbol*] [*Library of Congress*] (LCLS)
TxPlao....... Plano Public Library, Plano, TX [*Library symbol*] [*Library of Congress*] (LCLS)
TxPlW....... Wayland Baptist College, Plainview, TX [*Library symbol*] [*Library of Congress*] (LCLS)
TxPnT....... Texas-United States Chemical Co., Process Engineering Section, R and D Library, Port Neches, TX [*Library symbol*] [*Library of Congress*] (LCLS)
TxPo .... Gates Memorial Library, Port Arthur, TX [*Library symbol*] [*Library of Congress*] (LCLS)
TXPRD...... Tax Period
TxPS......... San Jacinto College, Pasadena, TX [*Library symbol*] [*Library of Congress*] (LCLS)
TxPT......... Tenneco Chemicals, Inc., Pasadena, TX [*Library symbol*] [*Library of Congress*] (LCLS)
TxPvC....... Prairie View Agricultural and Mechanical College, Prairie View, TX [*Library symbol*] [*Library of Congress*] (LCLS)
TXPYR...... Taxpayer
TXQ.......... University of Texas, Austin, Law Library, Austin, TX [*OCLC symbol*] (OCLC)
TXR .... Lamar University, Beaumont, TX [*OCLC symbol*] (OCLC)
TXR .... Susitna Valley, AK [*Location identifier*] [*FAA*] (FAAL)
TXR .... Tank Exchange Ratio (MCD)
TXR .... Triex Resources Ltd. [*Vancouver Stock Exchange symbol*]
TxRaC .... Ranger Junior College, Ranger, TX [*Library symbol*] [*Library of Congress*] (LCLS)
TXRC........ Texas Export [*AAR code*]
TXReTR..... Texas Research Foundation, Renner, TX [*Library symbol*] [*Library of Congress*] (LCLS)
TXRF........ Total-Reflection X-Ray Fluorescence [*Analytical chemistry*]
TxRi.......... Richardson Public Library, Richardson, TX [*Library symbol*] [*Library of Congress*] (LCLS)
TxRiA .... Anderson Clayton Foods [*of Anderson, Clayton & Co.*], Richardson, TX [*Library symbol*] [*Library of Congress*] (LCLS)
TxRiS........ Sun Oil Co., Richardson, TX [*Library symbol*] [*Library of Congress*] (LCLS)
TXRX........ Transmitter-Receiver
TXS........... Hardin-Simmons University, Abilene, TX [*OCLC symbol*] (OCLC)
TXS........... Taxpayer Service [*IRS*]
TXS........... Telephone Exchange (Strowger) [*Telecommunications*] (TEL)
TXS........... Texas Star Resources Corp. [*Vancouver Stock Exchange symbol*]
TxSa .... San Antonio Public Library, San Antonio, TX [*Library symbol*] [*Library of Congress*] (LCLS)
TxSaBAM ... United States Air Force, School of Aerospace Medicine, Brooks Air Force Base, San Antonio, TX [*Library symbol*] [*Library of Congress*] (LCLS)
TxSaBHR ... United States Air Force, Human Resources Laboratory Library, Brooks Air Force Base, San Antonio, TX [*Library symbol*] [*Library of Congress*] (LCLS)
TxSaBM.... Bexar County Medical Library Association, San Antonio, TX [*Library symbol*] [*Library of Congress*] (LCLS)
TxSaC........ San Antonio College, San Antonio, TX [*Library symbol*] [*Library of Congress*] (LCLS)
TxSaGH .... Robert B. Green Memorial Hospital, San Antonio, TX [*Library symbol*] [*Library of Congress*] (LCLS)
TxSaGS ..... Church of Jesus Christ of Latter-Day Saints, Genealogical Society Library, San Antonio Branch, San Antonio, TX [*Library symbol*] [*Library of Congress*] (LCLS)
TxSaI........ Incarnate Word College, San Antonio, TX [*Library symbol*] [*Library of Congress*] (LCLS)
TxSal .... Tom Green County Library, San Angelo, TX [*Library symbol*] [*Library of Congress*] (LCLS)
TxSalA ...... Angelo State University, San Angelo, TX [*Library symbol*] [*Library of Congress*] (LCLS)
TxSaO .... Our Lady of the Lake College, San Antonio, TX [*Library symbol*] [*Library of Congress*] (LCLS)
TxSaOC..... Oblate College of the Southwest, San Antonio, TX [*Library symbol*] [*Library of Congress*] (LCLS)
TxSaSFRE ... Southwest Foundation for Research and Education, San Antonio, TX [*Library symbol*] [*Library of Congress*] (LCLS)
TxSaSM.... Saint Mary's University, San Antonio, TX [*Library symbol*] [*Library of Congress*] (LCLS)
TxSaSM-L ... Saint Mary's University, Law Library, San Antonio, TX [*Library symbol*] [*Library of Congress*] (LCLS)
TxSaSP...... St. Philip's College, San Antonio, TX [*Library symbol*] [*Library of Congress*] (LCLS)
TxSaSR ..... Southwest Research Institute, San Antonio, TX [*Library symbol*] [*Library of Congress*] (LCLS)
TxSaStJ..... Saint John's Seminary, San Antonio, TX [*Library symbol*] [*Library of Congress*] (LCLS)
TxSaT........ Trinity University, San Antonio, TX [*Library symbol*] [*Library of Congress*] (LCLS)
TxSaT-W... Trinity University, Whitsett Library Museum, San Antonio, TX [*Library symbol*] [*Library of Congress*] (LCLS)

TxSaU .... University of Texas at San Antonio, San Antonio, TX [*Library symbol*] [*Library of Congress*]   (LCLS)

TxSaUS ..... United Services Automobile Association, San Antonio, TX [*Library symbol*] [*Library of Congress*]   (LCLS)

TxSaV .... United States Veterans Administration Hospital, San Antonio, TX [*Library symbol*] [*Library of Congress*]   (LCLS)

Tx-SC .... Texas State Law Library, Austin, TX [*Library symbol*] [*Library of Congress*]   (LCLS)

TxSE .... Texas Studies in English [*A publication*]

TxSeTL ...... Texas Lutheran College, Seguin, TX [*Library symbol*] [*Library of Congress*]   (LCLS)

TxShA .... Austin College, Sherman, TX [*Library symbol*] [*Library of Congress*]   (LCLS)

TxShpM .... United States Air Force, Regional Hospital, Medical Library, Sheppard AFB, TX [*Library symbol*] [*Library of Congress*]   (LCLS)

TxSiW .... Rob and Bessie Welder Wildlife Foundation, Sinton, TX [*Library symbol*] [*Library of Congress*]   (LCLS)

TxSjM .... San Jacinto Museum of History Association, San Jacinto Monument, TX [*Library symbol*] [*Library of Congress*]   (LCLS)

TxSmS .... Southwest Texas State University, San Marcos, TX [*Library symbol*] [*Library of Congress*]   (LCLS)

TxSn .... Scurry County Library, Snyder, TX [*Library symbol*] [*Library of Congress*]   (LCLS)

TxSvT .... Tarleton State University, Stephenville, TX [*Library symbol*] [*Library of Congress*]   (LCLS)

TxSw .... Sweetwater City-County Library, Sweetwater, TX [*Library symbol*] [*Library of Congress*]   (LCLS)

TXT .... Texas Southern University, Houston, TX [*OCLC symbol*]   (OCLC)

TXT .... Text

TXT .... Textron, Inc. [*NYSE symbol*]   (SPSG)

TxTA .... American Oil Co. [*Later, Amoco Oil Co.*], Texas City, TX [*Library symbol*] [*Library of Congress*]   (LCLS)

TxTCM ..... College of the Mainland, Texas City, TX [*Library symbol*] [*Library of Congress*]   (LCLS)

TxTe .... Texarkana Public Library, Texarkana, TX [*Library symbol*] [*Library of Congress*]   (LCLS)

TxTeC .... Texarkana College, Texarkana, TX [*Library symbol*] [*Library of Congress*]   (LCLS)

TxTeET ..... East Texas State University, Texarkana, TX [*Library symbol*] [*Library of Congress*]   (LCLS)

TxTehW .... Westminster College, Tehuacana, TX [*Library symbol*] [*Library of Congress*]   (LCLS)

TxTemC ..... Temple Junior College, Temple, TX [*Library symbol*] [*Library of Congress*]   (LCLS)

TxTemH .... Scott and White Memorial Hospital, Temple, TX [*Library symbol*] [*Library of Congress*]   (LCLS)

TxTerS .... Southwestern Christian College, Terrell, TX [*Library symbol*] [*Library of Congress*]   (LCLS)

TxTeS .... East Texas State University at Texarkana, Texarkana, TX [*Library symbol*] [*Library of Congress*]   (LCLS)

TXTL .... Textile   (MSA)

TXTLE ...... Textile

TxTMC ..... Monsanto Co., Texas City, TX [*Library symbol*] [*Library of Congress*]   (LCLS)

TXTN .... Textone, Inc. [*NASDAQ symbol*]   (NQ)

TxTUC ...... Union Carbide Corp., Chemicals and Plastics Division, Texas City, TX [*Library symbol*] [*Library of Congress*]   (LCLS)

TxTy .... Tyler Carnegie Public Library, Tyler, TX [*Library symbol*] [*Library of Congress*]   (LCLS)

TxTyB .... Butler College, Tyler, TX [*Library symbol*] [*Library of Congress*]   (LCLS)

TxTyC .... Texas Eastern University, Tyler, TX [*Library symbol*] [*Library of Congress*]   (LCLS)

TxTyT .... Texas College, Tyler, TX [*Library symbol*] [*Library of Congress*]   (LCLS)

TXU .... Tabou [*Ivory Coast*] [*Airport symbol*]   (OAG)

txu .... Texas [*MARC country of publication code*] [*Library of Congress*]   (LCCP)

TXU .... Texas Utilities Co. [*NYSE symbol*]   (SPSG)

TXU .... Texoro Resources Ltd. [*Vancouver Stock Exchange symbol*]

TxU .... University of Texas, Austin, TX [*Library symbol*] [*Library of Congress*]   (LCLS)

TXU .... University of Texas at El Paso, El Paso, TX [*OCLC symbol*]   (OCLC)

TxU-A .... University of Texas, M. D. Anderson Hospital and Tumor Institute, Houston, TX [*Library symbol*] [*Library of Congress*]   (LCLS)

TxU-B .... University of Texas, Business Administration and Economics Library, Austin, TX [*Library symbol*] [*Library of Congress*]   (LCLS)

TxU-D .... University of Texas, School of Dentistry, Houston, TX [*Library symbol*] [*Library of Congress*]   (LCLS)

TxU-Da ..... University of Texas at Dallas, Richardson, TX [*Library symbol*] [*Library of Congress*]   (LCLS)

TxU-Hu ..... Humanities Research Center, University of Texas, Austin, TX [*Library symbol*] [*Library of Congress*]   (LCLS)

TxU-J .... University of Texas, Lyndon Baines Johnson Presidential Library, Austin, TX [*Library symbol*] [*Library of Congress*]   (LCLS)

TxU-L .... University of Texas, Law Library, Austin, TX [*Library symbol*] [*Library of Congress*]   (LCLS)

TxU-M ...... University of Texas, Medical School, Galveston, TX [*Library symbol*] [*Library of Congress*]   (LCLS)

TxU-O .... University of Texas of the Permian Basin, Odessa, TX [*Library symbol*] [*Library of Congress*]   (LCLS)

TxU-PH ..... University of Texas, School of Public Health, Houston, TX [*Library symbol*] [*Library of Congress*]   (LCLS)

TxU-STM ... University of Texas Medical School at San Antonio, San Antonio, TX [*Library symbol*] [*Library of Congress*]   (LCLS)

TxUvS .... Southwest Texas Junior College, Uvalde, TX [*Library symbol*] [*Library of Congress*]   (LCLS)

TXV .... Fairfield, CA [*Location identifier*] [*FAA*]   (FAAL)

TXV .... Texas Business Review [*A publication*]

TXV .... Textil Revue. Fachblatt fuer Textilhandel, Konfektionsindustrie, und Textilindustrie [*A publication*]

TXV .... University of Houston, Victoria Center, Victoria, TX [*OCLC symbol*]   (OCLC)

TxVeC .... Vernon Regional Junior College, Vernon, TX [*Library symbol*] [*Library of Congress*]   (LCLS)

TxVi .... Victoria Public Library, Victoria, TX [*Library symbol*] [*Library of Congress*]   (LCLS)

TxViC .... Victoria College, Victoria, TX [*Library symbol*] [*Library of Congress*]   (LCLS)

TxVidGS .... Church of Jesus Christ of Latter-Day Saints, Genealogical Society Library, Beaumont Branch, Vidor, TX [*Library symbol*] [*Library of Congress*]   (LCLS)

TxViHU ...... University of Houston, Victoria Center, Victoria, TX [*Library symbol*] [*Library of Congress*]   (LCLS)

TxW .... Waco-McLennan County Library, Waco, TX [*Library symbol*] [*Library of Congress*]   (LCLS)

TXW .... Waco-McLennan County Library, Waco, TX [*OCLC symbol*]   (OCLC)

TxWaS .... Southwestern Assemblies of God College, Waxahachie, TX [*Library symbol*] [*Library of Congress*]   (LCLS)

TxWB .... Baylor University, Waco, TX [*Library symbol*] [*Library of Congress*]   (LCLS)

TxWB-B .... Baylor University, Armstrong Browning Library, Waco, TX [*Library symbol*] [*Library of Congress*]   (LCLS)

TxWB-L .... Baylor University, Law School Library, Waco, TX [*Library symbol*] [*Library of Congress*]   (LCLS)

TxWB-Mus ... Baylor University, Museum Collection, Waco, TX [*Library symbol*] [*Library of Congress*]   (LCLS)

TxWeaC ..... Weatherford College, Weatherford, TX [*Library symbol*] [*Library of Congress*]   (LCLS)

TxWeiM .... Weimar Mercury, Weimar, TX [*Library symbol*] [*Library of Congress*]   (LCLS)

TxWFM .... Masonic Grand Lodge of Texas, Waco, TX [*Library symbol*] [*Library of Congress*]   (LCLS)

TxWhaC ..... Wharton County Junior College, Wharton, TX [*Library symbol*] [*Library of Congress*]   (LCLS)

TxWhaW .... Wharton County Library, Wharton, TX [*Library symbol*] [*Library of Congress*]   (LCLS)

TxWic .... Kemp Public Library, Wichita Falls, TX [*Library symbol*] [*Library of Congress*]   (LCLS)

TxWicM .... Midwestern State University, Wichita Falls, TX [*Library symbol*] [*Library of Congress*]   (LCLS)

TxWM ...... McClennan Community College, Waco, TX [*Library symbol*] [*Library of Congress*]   (LCLS)

TxWPQ ..... Paul Quinn College, Waco, TX [*Library symbol*] [*Library of Congress*]   (LCLS)

TxWV .... United States Veterans Administration Hospital, Waco, TX [*Library symbol*] [*Library of Congress*]   (LCLS)

TXX .... Southwestern University, Georgetown, TX [*OCLC symbol*]   (OCLC)

TY .... Air Caledonie [*France*] [*ICAO designator*]   (FAAC)

TY .... Dahomey [*Aircraft nationality and registration mark*]   (FAAC)

TY .... Talmud Yerushalmi   (BJA)

TY .... Tax Year

TY .... Tebul [*or Tevul*] Yom   (BJA)

Ty .... Temporary

TY .... Territorial Yeomanry [*British military*]   (DMA)

TY .... Territory

TY .... Thank You

Ty .... Thyroxine [*Also, T4, Thx*] [*An amino acid*] [*Endocrinology*]

TY .... Total Yield   (AABC)

TY .... Translation Hand Controller Y-Axis Direction   (MCD)

TY .... Transposon Yeast [*Genetics*]

TY .... Tri-Continental Corp. [*NYSE symbol*]   (SPSG)

TY .... Truly

TY .... Tyler's Quarterly Historical and Genealogical Magazine [*A publication*]

Ty .... Tyndale New Testament Commentaries [*A publication*]   (BJA)

TY .... Type

TY .... Typhoid Fever   (DSUE)

TYA .... Steele Aviation [*Fresno, CA*] [*FAA designator*]   (FAAC)

TYA .... Tygas Resources Corp. [*Vancouver Stock Exchange symbol*]

TYAA .... Textured Yarn Association of America (EA)
Tyazh Mashinostr ... Tyazhelie Mashinostroenie [*A publication*]
TYC .... Thames Yacht Club [*Later, RTYC*] [*British*] (DI)
TYC .... Toby Creek Resources Ltd. [*Vancouver Stock Exchange symbol*]
TYC .... Trinity College, Hartford, CT [*OCLC symbol*] (OCLC)
TYC .... Two-Year[-*Old*] Course [*Horse racing*]
TYC .... Tyco Laboratories, Inc. [*NYSE symbol*] (SPSG)
TYC .... Tylerdale Connecting [*AAR code*]
T-YCDT .... Ten-Year Chinese Dong Tang [*Turmoil*] Cycle [*Reference to the Kuomintang's defeat in 1946-48, Mao's Great Leap Forward in 1956, the Cultural Revolution in 1966, and the Gang of Four's fall in 1976*] [*Term coined by William Safire*]
TYCO .... Tylenol and Codeine [*Pharmacy*]
TycoLb....... Tyco Laboratories, Inc. [*Associated Press abbreviation*] (APAG)
TYCOM .... Type Commander
TYCOMSLANT ... Type Commands, Atlantic (DNAB)
TYCOMSPAC ... Type Commands, Pacific (DNAB)
TycoTy....... Tyco Toys, Inc. [*Associated Press abbreviation*] (APAG)
TYD .... Temporary Duty (MCD)
TyD .... Trabajos y Dias [*A publication*]
tyd .... Type Designer [*MARC relator code*] [*Library of Congress*] (LCCP)
TYDAC..... Typical Digital Automatic Computer
TYDE .... Type Designators (MSA)
TYDNAP... Annual Report. Tokyo College of Pharmacy [*A publication*]
TYDS........ Transactions. Yorkshire Dialect Society [*A publication*]
Tydskr Dieetkd Huishoudkd ... Tydskrif vir Dieetkunde en Huishoudkunde [*South Africa*] [*A publication*]
Tydskr Natuurwet ... Tydskrif vir Natuurwetenskappe [*A publication*]
Tydskr Natuurwetenskap ... Tydskrif vir Natuurwetenskappe. Suid-Afrikaanse Akademie vir Wetenskap en Kuns [*A publication*]
Tydskr S-Afr Ver Spraak Gehoorheelkd ... Tydskrif van die Suid-Afrikaanse Vereniging vir Spraaken Gehoorheelkunde [*A publication*]
Tydskr S-Afr Vet Ver ... Tydskrif. Suid-Afrikaanse Veterinere Vereniging [*A publication*]
Tydskr Skoon Lug ... Tydskrif vir Skoon Lug [*A publication*]
Tydskr Tandheelkd Ver S-Afr ... Tydskrif. Tandheelkundige Vereniging van Suid-Afrika [*A publication*]
Tydskr Wet Kuns ... Tydskrif vir Wetenskap en Kuns [*A publication*]
TYDV .... Tobacco Yellow Dwarf Virus [*Plant pathology*]
TYE .... Tye Explorations, Inc. [*Vancouver Stock Exchange symbol*]
TYE .... Tyonek, AK [*Location identifier*] [*FAA*] (FAAL)
TYF........... Panama City, FL [*Location identifier*] [*FAA*] (FAAL)
TYF........... Tung Yeun Feng [*Republic of China*] [*Seismograph station code, US Geological Survey*] (SEIS)
TYFSOK ... Thank You for Shopping Our K-Mart [*or Kresge's*] [*Slogan of K-Mart Corp.*]
TYG .... Temple Youth Group [*Local groups of National Federation of Temple Youth, sometimes called TYG-ers, pronounced "tigers"*]
TYG .... Trypticase, Yeast-Extract, Glucose [*Cell growth medium*]
tyg .... Typographer [*MARC relator code*] [*Library of Congress*] (LCCP)
TygP .... Tygodnik Powszechny [*A publication*]
TYGR .... Tigera Group, Inc. [*NASDAQ symbol*] (NQ)
TYH........... Tihany [*Hungary*] [*Geomagnetic observatory code*]
TYI............ Rocky Mount, NC [*Location identifier*] [*FAA*] (FAAL)
TYK .... Toyooka [*Japan*] [*Seismograph station code, US Geological Survey*] (SEIS)
TYKNAQ .. Annual Report. Tohoku College of Pharmacy [*A publication*]
TYL........... Talara [*Peru*] [*Airport symbol*] (OAG)
TYL........... TANU [*Tanganyika African National Union*] Youth League [*Tanganyika*]
TYL........... Tyler Corp. [*NYSE symbol*] (SPSG)
Tyl............. Tyler's Vermont Supreme Court Reports [*1800-03*] [*A publication*] (DLA)
Tyl Boun ... Tyler on Boundaries, Fences, Etc. [*A publication*] (DLA)
TYLC........ Tomato Yellow Leaf Curl [*Plant pathology*]
TYLCV ..... Tomato Yellow Leaf Curl Virus
Tyl Eccl L .. Tyler's American Ecclesiastical Law [*A publication*] (DLA)
Tyl Eject..... Tyler on Ejectment and Adverse Enjoyment [*A publication*] (DLA)
Tyler.......... Tyler Corp. [*Associated Press abbreviation*] (APAG)
Tyler.......... Tyler's Vermont Reports [*1800-03*] [*A publication*] (DLA)
Tyler Ej...... Tyler on Ejectment and Adverse Enjoyment [*A publication*] (DLA)
Tyler's........ Tyler's Quarterly Historical and Genealogical Magazine [*A publication*]
Tyler's Quar ... Tyler's Quarterly Historical and Genealogical Magazine [*A publication*]
Tyler Steph Pl ... Tyler's Edition of Stephen on Principles of Pleading [*A publication*] (DLA)
Tyl Fix .... Tyler on Fixtures [*A publication*] (DLA)
Tyl Inf........ Tyler on Infancy and Coverture [*A publication*] (DLA)
TYLN .... Tylan Corp. [*NASDAQ symbol*] (NQ)
Tyl Part...... Tyler on Partnership [*A publication*] (DLA)

Tyl St Pl..... Tyler's Edition of Stephen on the Principles of Pleading [*A publication*] (DLA)
Tyl Us .... Tyler on Usury, Pawns, and Loans [*A publication*] (DLA)
TYLX........ Tylox Resources Corp. [*NASDAQ symbol*] (NQ)
TYMNET ... Timeshare, Inc. Network [*Telecommunications*] (TEL)
tymp.......... Tympany
TYMV .... Turnip Yellow Mosaic Virus
TYN.......... Taiyuan [*China*] [*Seismograph station code, US Geological Survey*] (SEIS)
TYN.......... Taiyuan [*China*] [*Airport symbol*] (OAG)
TYN.......... Taywin Resources Ltd. [*Vancouver Stock Exchange symbol*]
TYNAA ..... Tydskrif vir Natuurwetenskappe [*A publication*]
Tyndale Bul ... Tyndale Bulletin [*A publication*]
TyndHB.... Tyndale House Bulletin [*Cambridge*] [*A publication*] (BJA)
Tyng.......... Tyng's Reports [*2-17 Massachusetts*] [*A publication*] (DLA)
TYO.......... Tokyo [*Japan*] [*Airport symbol*] (OAG)
TYO.......... Tokyo Newsletter [*A publication*]
TYO.......... Two-Year-Old [*Horse racing*] (ROG)
Tyoevaeen Taloudell Tutkimus Katsaus ... Tyoevaeen Taloudellinen Tutkimuslaitos Katsaus [*A publication*]
TYOG .... Take Your Own Gadgets
TYP........... Transitional Year Program [*Brandeis University*] (EA)
TY-P .... Trial Y-Plane
Typ............ Typed (BJA)
TYP........... Typical (AAG)
TYP........... Typography [*or Typographer*] (AAG)
TYP........... [*The*] Youth Project (EA)
typ cons..... Typus Conservandus [*Conserved Type*] [*Latin*]
TYPER ...... Typographical Error (AAG)
TYPH .... Typhoon
TYPL .... Type-Plate
Typ News ... Typewriting News [*A publication*]
TYPNO ..... Teletypewriter Communications Interrupted (FAAC)
Typo.......... Typographed [*Philately*]
TYPO .... Typographical
TYPOE...... Ten Year Plan for Ocean Exploration [*National Council on Marine Resources and Engineering Development*] (MSC)
TYPOG ..... Typographer [*or Typography*]
Typographical J ... Typographical Journal [*A publication*]
Typogr Monatsbl ... Typographische Monatsblaetter [*A publication*]
TYPOK...... Teletypewriter Communications Resumed (FAAC)
TYPOUT... Typewriter Output
TYPSTG.... Typesetting (MSA)
TYPW........ Typewriter (ADA)
TYPWRT .. Typewriter
TYPWRTR ... Typewriter
TYQ .... Indianapolis, IN [*Location identifier*] [*FAA*] (FAAL)
TYR .... Tyler [*Texas*] [*Airport symbol*] (OAG)
TYR .... Tyrone [*County in Ireland*] (ROG)
Tyr .... Tyrosine [*Also, Y*] [*An amino acid*]
Tyr .... Tyrwhitt and Granger's English Exchequer Reports [*1830-35*] [*A publication*] (DLA)
TYRE......... Export Tyre Holding Co. [*NASDAQ symbol*] (NQ)
Tyres & Access ... Tyres and Accessories [*A publication*]
Tyr & Gr .... Tyrwhitt and Granger's English Exchequer Reports [*1830-35*] [*A publication*] (DLA)
TyrRS .... Tyrosyl-tRNA [*Transfer Ribonucleic Acid*] Synthetase
Tyr Trig ..... Tyranni Triginta [*of Scriptores Historiae Augustae*] [*Classical studies*] (OCD)
Tyrw.......... Tyrwhitt and Granger's English Exchequer Reports [*1830-35*] [*A publication*] (DLA)
Tyrw & G ... Tyrwhitt and Granger's English Exchequer Reports [*1835-36*] [*A publication*] (DLA)
Tyrw & G (Eng) ... Tyrwhitt and Granger's English Exchequer Reports [*1835-36*] [*A publication*] (DLA)
TYRX........ Tyrex Oil Co. [*NASDAQ symbol*] (NQ)
TYS........... Knoxville [*Tennessee*] [*Airport symbol*] (OAG)
TYS........... Overzicht van de Economische Ontwikkeling [*A publication*]
TYS........... Tensile Yield Strength
TYS........... Tyler Resources, Inc. [*Toronto Stock Exchange symbol*]
TYS........... Tyseley [*British depot code*]
TYS........... Tyson Valley [*Missouri*] [*Seismograph station code, US Geological Survey*] (SEIS)
TYSD........ Total Years Service Date
TYSN........ Tyson Foods, Inc. [*NASDAQ symbol*] (NQ)
TYSP .... Tibetan Youth Sponsorship Programs (EA)
TYT .... Nantucket, MA [*Location identifier*] [*FAA*] (FAAL)
TYT .... Type Training [*Navy*] (NVT)
TYTIPT..... Type Training in Port [*Navy*] (NVT)
Tytler Mil Law ... Tytler on Military Law and Courts-Martial [*A publication*] (DLA)
Tyt Mil L ... Tytler on Military Law and Courts-Martial [*3rd ed.*] [*1812*] [*A publication*] (DLA)
TYTV......... Tomato Yellow Top Virus
TYU .... Tyuratam [*Satellite launch complex*] [*Former USSR*]
TYV .... Little Rock, AR [*Location identifier*] [*FAA*] (FAAL)
TYV .... Turnip Yellows Virus [*Plant pathology*]
TYVM .... Thank You Very Much
TYX .... Tylox Resources Corp. [*Vancouver Stock Exchange symbol*]
TYY .... Abilene, TX [*Location identifier*] [*FAA*] (FAAL)
TYZ .... Taylor [*Arizona*] [*Airport symbol*] [*Obsolete*] (OAG)

TZ.............. American Trans Air, Inc. [*ICAO designator*]   (FAAC)
TZ.............. Der Treue Zionswaechter [*Altona*] [*A publication*]   (BJA)
TZ.............. Mali [*Aircraft nationality and registration mark*]   (FAAC)
TZ.............. Tactical Zone [*Military*]   (AABC)
tz................ Tanzania [*MARC country of publication code*] [*Library of Congress*]   (LCCP)
TZ.............. Terrazo [*Technical drawings*]
TZ.............. Tidal Zone
TZ.............. Time Zero
TZ.............. Times of Zambia [*A publication*]
TZ.............. Transition Zone [*in plant growth*] [*Botany*]
TZ.............. Translation Hand Controller Z-Axis Direction   (NASA)
TZ.............. Transmitter Zone [*Telecommunications*]   (TEL)
TZ.............. Transportation Zone [*Department of Transportation*]
TZ.............. Trennzahl Values [*For carrier gas flow rates*] [*Chromatography*]
TZ.............. Tropical Zodiac
TZ.............. Tuberculin Zymoplastiche [*Medicine*]   (MAE)
TZ.............. [*The*] Twilight Zone [*Television program created by Rod Serling*]
TZ.............. Twilight-Zoner [*Undecided voter*] [*Political slang*]
TZ.............. United Republic of Tanzania [*ANSI two-letter standard code*]   (CNC)
TZA .... Finanzierung, Leasing, Factoring [*A publication*]
TZA .... United Republic of Tanzania [*ANSI three-letter standard code*]   (CNC)
TZC .... Tetrazolium Chloride Agar [*Biological stain*]
TZC .... Trizec Corp. Ltd. [*Toronto Stock Exchange symbol*]
TZD .... True Zenith Distance [*Navigation*]
TZE........... Topaz Exploration Ltd. [*Vancouver Stock Exchange symbol*]
TZE........... Transfer on Zero
TZG .... Thermofit Zap Gun
TZJ .... Tubular Zippered Jacket
TZKRA...... Tonindustrie-Zeitung und Keramische Rundschau [*A publication*]
TZM .... Titanium-Zirconium-Molybdenum [*Alloy*]
TZN .... South Andros [*Bahamas*] [*Airport symbol*]   (OAG)
TZN .... Tchaikazan Enterprises, Inc. [*Vancouver Stock Exchange symbol*]
TZNSDW ... Topographie und Zytologie Neurosekretorischer Systeme [*A publication*]
TZO .... Thorne-Zytkow Object [*Astronomy*]
TZP........... Temperate Zone Phase
TZP........... Time Zero Pulse
TZP........... Triazolopyridazine [*Potential antianxiety drug*]
TZ Prakt Metallbearb ... TZ fuer Praktische Metallbearbeitung [*A publication*]
TZR .... Tanzania-Zambia Railway   (PDAA)
TZR .... Torrez Resources Ltd. [*Vancouver Stock Exchange symbol*]
TZS........... Terzake Subsidies [*A publication*]
TZTh .... Tuebinger Zeitschrift fuer Theologie [*A publication*]   (BJA)
TZV .... Tetrazolium Violet [*Also, TV*]
TZX .... Trabzon [*Turkey*] [*Airport symbol*]   (OAG)
TZY .... Warsaw, IN [*Location identifier*] [*FAA*]   (FAAL)
TZZ........... Tabubil [*Papua New Guinea*] [*Seismograph station code, US Geological Survey*]   (SEIS)

U

U .... Audio and Power Connectors [*JETDS nomenclature*] [*Military*] (CET)
u------.......... Australasia [*MARC geographic area code*] [*Library of Congress*] (LCCP)
U .... Benzon [*Denmark*] [*Research code symbol*]
U .... Eased Up [*Horse racing*]
U .... Eaton Laboratories, Inc. [*Research code symbol*]
U .... Electric Tension [*Symbol*] [*IUPAC*]
u .... Group Velocity [*Symbol*] (DEN)
U .... Intensity Unknown [*Meteorology*] (FAAC)
U .... Internal Energy [*Symbol*] [*Thermodynamics*]
U .... Intrinsic Energy [*Symbol*] [*Physics*]
U .... Kosher Certification [*Union of Orthodox Jewish Congregations of America*] (WGA)
U .... Quartermon Versor [*Symbol of a function*] [*Mathematics*] (ROG)
U .... Shape Descriptor [*U-turn, for example. The shape resembles the letter for which it is named*]
U .... Thermal Transmittance per Unit of Area [*Heat transmission symbol*]
U .... Uafhaengige Parti [*Independent Party*] [*Denmark*] [*Political party*] (PPE)
U .... Ubiquinone [*Coenzyme Q*] [*Also, CoQ, Q, UQ*] [*Biochemistry*]
u .... Uebersetzen [*Translate*] [*German*]
U .... Ugly Sky [*Navigation*]
U .... Ugly Threatening Weather [*Meteorology*]
U .... Ugutio [*Huguccio*] [*Deceased, 1210*] [*Authority cited in pre-1607 legal work*] (DSA)
U .... Uhr [*Clock*] [*German*]
U .... Uitgelezen [*A publication*]
U .... Ullage (AAG)
U .... Ultraphon & Supraphon [*Record label*] [*Former Czechoslovakia*]
U .... Umpire [*Baseball*]
U .... Unbalanced
U .... Unburned [*Ecology*]
U .... Uncirculated
U .... Unclassified
U .... Uncle
U .... Uncle [*Phonetic alphabet*] [*Royal Navy*] [*World War I*] [*Pre-World War II*] [*World War II*] (DSUE)
U .... Uncommon Species
U .... Und [*And*] [*German*]
U .... Under
U .... Underfloor (NASA)
U .... Underwater [*Missile launch environment symbol*]
U .... Unemployed Parent [*Aid to Families with Dependent Children*] (OICC)
U .... Unemployment
U .... Unerupted (MAE)
U .... Unified
U .... Uniform
U .... Uniform [*Phonetic alphabet*] [*International*] (DSUE)
U .... Uniformly Labeled [*Also, UL*] [*Compound, with radioisotope*]
U .... Union [*or Unionist*]
U .... Union Association [*Major league in baseball, 1884*]
U .... Unionist Party [*Northern Ireland*] [*Political party*]
U .... Unit
U .... United
U .... Universal
U .... Universal/Unrestricted [*Film certificate*] [*British*]
U .... Universitas [*A publication*]
U .... University
U .... Unknown
U .... Unlimited [*Aviation*] (FAAC)
U .... Unlimited Time [*Broadcasting term*]
U .... Unoccupied
U .... Unpleasant
U .... Unrestricted [*Aviation*] (FAAC)
U .... Unseated Rider [*Horse racing*]
U .... Unsymmetrical

U .... Unter [*Among*] [*German*]
U .... Untreated [*Medicine*]
U .... Unwatched [*With reference to a light*] [*Maps and charts*]
U .... Up [*or Upper*]
u .... Up (quark) [*Atomic physics*]
U .... Update [*Data processing*]
U .... Upjohn Co. [*Research code symbol*]
U .... Upper (ROG)
U .... Upper Bow [*Music*] (ROG)
U .... Upper-Class Speech [*"Non-U" designates the opposite*]
U .... Upper School [*British*]
U .... Uracil [*Biochemistry*] (MAE)
U .... Uranium [*Chemical element*]
U .... Urban [*District Council*] [*British*]
U .... Urban Association [*Baseball*]
U .... Urgent
U .... Uridine [*One-letter symbol; see Urd*]
U .... Urinal (ROG)
U .... Urinate [*or Urine*] [*Medicine*]
U .... Urological Surgery [*Medical specialty*] (DHSM)
U .... Urology [*Medical Officer designation*] [*British*]
U .... Urschrift [*Original, as of a document*] [*German military*]
U .... Uruguay [*IYRU nationality code*]
U .... USAIR Group [*NYSE symbol*] (SPSG)
U .... Use
U .... Utah
U .... Utah Reports [*A publication*] (DLA)
U .... Utah State Library, Salt Lake City, UT [*Library symbol*] [*Library of Congress*] (LCLS)
U .... Utendus [*To Be Used*] [*Pharmacy*]
U .... Utility [*Economics*]
U .... Utility [*Designation for all US military aircraft*]
U .... UTVA Aircraft Factory [*Former Yugoslavia*] [*ICAO aircraft manufacturer identifier*] (ICAO)
U .... You [*Communications*] (FAAC)
U2 .... Popular music group
U² .... Unclassified, Unlimited [*DoD*]
5U .... Niger [*Aircraft nationality and registration mark*] (FAAC)
U (Bomb) ... [*A*] theoretical uranium-encased atomic or hydrogen bomb, the shell of which would be transformed into deadly radioactive dust upon detonation (MUGU)
UA............. Ukrainian Soviet Socialist Republic [*ISO two-letter standard code*] (CNC)
UA............. Ultra-Audible
UA............. Umbilical Artery [*Anatomy*]
UA............. Unable to Approve Arrival for the Time Specified [*Aviation*] (FAAC)
UA............. Unaggregated (MAE)
UA............. Unanesthetized [*Physiology*]
UA............. Unauthorized Absence (MUGU)
UA............. Unavailable
UA............. Unburned plus Ash [*Ecology*]
UA............. Und Andere [*And Others*] [*German*]
UA............. Under Age [*i.e., entitled neither to a daily rum ration nor money instead*] [*See also G, T*] [*Obsolete*] [*Navy*] [*British*]
U/A............ Under Agreement [*Legal term*] (DLA)
UA............. Understanding Aging (EA)
UA............. Underwater Actuator
UA............. Underwater Association for Scientific Research [*Margate, Kent, England*] (EAIO)
U/A............ Underwriting Account [*Insurance*]
UA............. Unidad Alavesa [*Spain*] [*Political party*] (EY)
UA............. Uniform Allowance [*Military*]
UA............. Union des Artistes [*Union of Artists*] [*Canada*]
UA............. Union Association [*Major league in baseball, 1884*]
U/A............ Unit of Account [*European Monetary Agreement*] (EY)
UA............. Unit Assets [*Army*]
UA............. Unit First Appearance (SAA)
UA............. United Air Lines, Inc. [*ICAO designator*]
ua.............. United Arab Republic [*Egypt*] [*MARC country of publication code*] [*Library of Congress*] (LCCP)

UA............. United Artists Communications, Inc.
UA............. United Asia [*A publication*]
UA............. United Association of Journeymen and Apprentices of the Plumbing and Pipe Fitting Industry of the United States and Canada (OICC)
U/A........... Units per Application (DNAB)
UA............. University of Alaska [*Anchorage, AK*]
U of A........ University of Alaska [*Anchorage, AK*]
UA............. University of Arizona [*Tucson, AZ*]
U of A........ University of Arkansas [*Fayetteville, AR*]
UA............. Unnumbered Acknowledge [*or Acknowledgment*] [*Telecommunications*] (IEEE)
UA............. Unstable Angina [*Medicine*]
UA............. Upper Arm
UA............. Ural-Altaische Jahrbuecher [*A publication*]
UA............. Uranyl Ammonium Phosphate [*Inorganic chemistry*] (SAA)
UA............. Urban Anthropology [*A publication*]
UA............. Urbanized Area (OICC)
UA............. Uric Acid
UA............. Urinalysis [*Medicine*] (KSC)
UA............. Urocanic Acid [*Organic chemistry*] (AAMN)
UA............. User Agent [*Telecommunications*] (PÇM)
UA............. User Area [*Information storage*]
UA............. Usque Ad [*As Far As*] [*Latin*] (ADA)
UA............. Uterine Aspiration [*Medicine*]
UAA.......... Undergarment Accessories Association (EA)
UAA.......... Union des Avocats Arabes [*Arab Lawyers Union - ALU*] (EAIO)
UAA.......... United Action for Animals (EA)
UAA.......... United African Appeal (EA)
UAA.......... United American and Australasian Film Productions
UAA.......... United Arab Airlines
UAA.......... Universitet i Bergen. Arbok. Historisk-Antikvarisk Rekke [*A publication*]
UAA.......... University of Alaska, Anchorage
UAA.......... University Athletic Association (EA)
UAA.......... University Aviation Association (EA)
UAA.......... Uracil Adenine Adenine [*Genetics*]
UAA.......... Urban Affairs Association (EA)
UAA.......... User Action Analyzer
UAA.......... Utility Arborist Association (EA)
UAAA....... Alma-Ata [*Former USSR*] [*ICAO location identifier*] (ICLI)
UAAF....... United Action Armed Forces [*A publication*]
UAAN....... Uzunagach [*Former USSR*] [*ICAO location identifier*] (ICLI)
UAAR....... United Activists for Animal Rights (EA)
UAAS....... Ukrainian Academy of Arts and Sciences in the US (EA)
UAAS....... Union Africaine des Artistes de Spectacle [*Union of African Performing Artists - UAPA*] (EAIO)
UAAUSA .. Ukrainian Artists Association in USA (EA)
UAB.......... Unemployment Assistance Board
UAB.......... University of Alabama in Birmingham
UAB.......... University of Alberta Biotron [*University of Alberta*] [*Research center*] (RCD)
UAB.......... University Appointments Board [*British*] (DAS)
UAB.......... Until Advised By [*Aviation*] (FAAC)
u-ac---........ Ashmore and Cartier Islands [*MARC geographic area code*] [*Library of Congress*] (LCCP)
UAC.......... Unicorp American Corp. [*AMEX symbol*] (SPSG)
UAC.......... Unified Arab Command (BJA)
UAC.......... Uniform Annual Cost
UAC.......... Uninterrupted Automatic Control
UAC.......... Union Army of Commemoration
UAC.......... United African Co.
UAC.......... United Aircraft Corp. [*Later, United Technologies Corp.*]
UAC.......... United American Croats
UAC.......... United Association of Coremakers [*A union*] [*British*]
UAC.......... Universal Airline Codes
UAC.......... Universal Area Code [*Bureau of Census*]
UAC.......... Universities Advisory Council
UAC.......... University of Alberta, Faculty of Library Science, Edmonton, AL, Canada [*OCLC symbol*] (OCLC)
UAC.......... University Analytical Center [*University of Arizona*] [*Research center*] (RCD)
UAC.......... Unusual Appearing Child [*Medicine*]
UAC.......... Upper Area Control Center [*Aviation*]
UAC.......... User Advisory Committee [*Environmental Protection Agency*] (GFGA)
UAC.......... Utility Airplane Council [*Defunct*] (EA)
UAC.......... Utility Assemble Compool
UACA....... United American Contractors Association (EA)
UACC....... Universal Autograph Collectors Club (EA)
UACC....... Upper Area Control Center [*Aviation*]
UACCDD .. University Affiliated Cincinnati Center for Developmental Disorders [*University of Cincinnati*] [*Research center*] (RCD)
UACCI...... United Association of Christian Counselors International (EA)
UACES...... University Association for Contemporary European Studies [*British*]
UACL .... United Aircraft of Canada Ltd.

UACMC .... Union Arabe de Ciment et des Materiaux de Construction [*Arab Union for Cement and Building Materials - AUCBM*] (EAIO)
UACN....... Unified Automated Communication Network
UACN....... University of Alaska Computer Network [*Research center*] (RCD)
UACNPM ... United American and Captive Nations Patriotic Movement (EA)
UACRL...... United Aircraft Corp. Research Laboratory (KSC)
UACSC...... United Aircraft Corporate Systems Center (KSC)
UACTA ..... United Against Cruelty to Animals [*British*] (DI)
UACTE...... Universal Automatic Control and Test Equipment
UAD.......... Salinas, CA [*Location identifier*] [*FAA*] (FAAL)
UAD.......... Underwater Acoustic Decoupler
UAD.......... Undetermined Aerodynamic Disturbance (MCD)
UAD.......... Unit Assembly Drawing
UADBU..... Unattended Automatic Dial Back Up [*Telecommunications*]
UADC....... Universal Air Data Computer
UADP........ Uniform Automated [*or Automatic*] Data Processing
UADPS...... Uniform Automated [*or Automatic*] Data Processing System
UADPS-ICP ... Uniform Automated [*or Automatic*] Data Processing System for Inventory Control Points [*Navy*]
UADPS/INAS ... Uniform Automated [*or Automatic*] Data Processing System/Industrial Naval Air Station
UADPS-SP ... Uniform Automated [*or Automatic*] Data Processing System for Stock Points [*Navy*]
UADS........ User Attribute Data Set [*Data processing*] (MDG)
UADV....... University of Alberta Devonian Botanic Garden [*Canada*]
UADW....... Universal Alliance of Diamond Workers [*See also AUOD*] [*Antwerp, Belgium*] (EAIO)
UAE.......... Unilateral Absence of Excretion [*Medicine*]
UAE.......... United Arab Emirates
UAE.......... Unrecoverable Application Error [*Data processing*] (PCM)
UAEC .... United Artists Entertainment Co. [*NASDAQ symbol*] (NQ)
UAEDE ..... Union des Associations Europeennes des Distributeurs d'Eau [*Union of European Associations of Water Suppliers*] [*Belgium*] (EAIO)
UAEE .... Union des Associations Europeennes d'Etudiants [*Union of European Student Associations*]
UAegAl..... Urkunden die Aegyptischen Altertums [*A publication*]
UAEI .... United American Energy, Inc. [*NASDAQ symbol*] (NQ)
UAEM....... Union of Associations of European Meat Meal Producers [*See also UAPEFV*] [*Later, Eurpoean Renderers Association - EURA*] (EAIO)
UA/EM ..... University Association for Emergency Medicine (EA)
UAERA ..... United States. Air Force. School of Aerospace Medicine. Technical Report [*A publication*]
UAES........ Utah Agricultural Experiment Station [*Utah State University*] [*Research center*] (RCD)
UAF .... Uganda Air Force (PDAA)
UAF .... Ultimate Asbestos Fibril
UAF .... Unit Authorization File
UAF .... University-Affiliated Facility
UAF .... University of Alaska, Fairbanks
UAF .... Upper Atmospheric Facilities Program [*Washington, DC*] [*National Science Foundation*] (GRD)
UAFA .... Union of Arab Football Associations (EAIO)
UAFC .... Universal Air Freight Corp.
UAFF........ Frunze [*Former USSR*] [*ICAO location identifier*] (ICLI)
UAFMMEEC ... Union of Associations of Fish Meal Manufacturers in the EEC (EAIO)
UAF-MR ... University-Affiliated Facility for the Mentally Retarded
UAFRA...... Uniform Aircraft Financial Responsibility Act [*National Conference of Commissioners on Uniform State Laws*]
UAFSC...... Utilization Air Force Specialty Code
UAFS/T .... Universal Aircraft Flight Simulator/Trainer
UAFUR ..... Urgent Amplified Failure of Unsatisfactory Report
UAFZAG... Contributions. Faculty of Science. University College of Addis Ababa (Ethiopia). Series C. Zoology [*A publication*]
UAG.......... Underwater Acoustic Group [*British*]
UAG.......... Union of Anarchist Groups [*British*]
UAG.......... Untersuchungen zur Altorientalischen Geschichte [*H. Winckler*] [*A publication*] (BJA)
UAG.......... Upper Atmosphere Geophysics (KSC)
UAG.......... Uracil Adenine Guanine [*Genetics*]
UAG.......... USSR. Academy of Science. Proceedings. Geographical Series [*A publication*]
UAGA........ Uniform Anatomical Gift Act [*For organ donation*]
UAH .... Ua Huka [*Marquesas Islands*] [*Airport symbol*] (OAG)
UAH .... Union of Arab Historians (EA)
UAH .... United American Healthcare Corp. [*NYSE symbol*] (SPSG)
UAH .... University of Alabama in Huntsville
UAHC........ Union of American Hebrew Congregations (EA)
UAHRI...... University of Alabama in Huntsville Research Institute
UAHS........ Ulster Architectural Heritage Society
UAI........... Union Academique Internationale [*International Academic Union - IAU*] (EAIO)
UAI........... Union des Associations Internationales [*Union of International Associations - UIA*] (EAIO)
UAI........... Union Astronomique Internationale [*International Astronomical Union - IAU*]

UAI .... Universal Azimuth Indicator
UAI .... Urban Affairs Institute (EA)
UAI .... Uterine Activity Interval [*Obstetrics*]
UAICC .... Underwater Acoustic Interference Coordinating Committee [*Military*]
UAIDE ...... Users of Automatic Information Display Equipment (EA)
UAII .... Chimkent [*Former USSR*] [*ICAO location identifier*] (ICLI)
UAIM .... United Andean Indian Mission [*Superseded by Ecuador Concerns Committee*]
UAIMS ...... United Aircraft Information Management System
UAIRA ...... US Aircraft Cl A [*NASDAQ symbol*] (NQ)
UAJ .... Union of Arab Jurists [*Baghdad, Iraq*] (EAIO)
UAJ .... Ural-Altaische Jahrbuecher [*A publication*]
UAJb .... Ural-Altaische Jahrbuecher [*A publication*]
UAJG .... Union d'Action des Jeunes de Guinee [*Guinean Union of Youth Action*]
UAK .... Narssarssuaq [*Greenland*] [*Airport symbol*] (OAG)
UAL .... UAL Corp. [*NYSE symbol*] (SPSG)
UAL .... Ukrainian American League (EA)
UAL .... Unit Allowance List (SAA)
UAL .... Unit Area Loading (AAG)
UAL .... Unit Authorization List
UAL .... Unite, Action, Liberation [*Guadeloupe*] [*Political party*] (EY)
UAL .... Unite Arithmetique et Logique [*Arithmetic and Logic Unit - ALU*] [*French*]
UAL .... United Air Lines, Inc. [*Air carrier designation symbol*]
UAL .... Universal Airline Codes (MCD)
UAL .... Upper Acceptance Limit
UAL .... Urea-Ammonia Liquor
UAL .... User Adaptive Language
UAL Cp .... UAL Corp. [*Associated Press abbreviation*] (APAG)
UALE .... Universala Artista Ligo de Esperantistoj [*Universal Artist League of Esperantists*] (EAIO)
UALI .... Unit Authorization List Item
UALI .... Universal Automatic LASER Interferometer (DNAB)
UALR LJ... University of Arkansas at Little Rock. Law Journal [*A publication*]
UAM .... Ultrasonically Assisted Machining [*Manufacturing term*]
UAM .... Und Anderes Mehr [*And So Forth*] [*German*]
UAM .... Underwater-to-Air Missile [*Air Force*]
UAM .... Union Africaine et Malagache [*African and Malagasy Union*] [*Later, Common Afro-Malagasy Organization*]
UAM .... United American Mechanics (EA)
UAM .... United Asset Management Corp. [*NYSE symbol*] (SPSG)
UAM .... United Asset Management Corp. [*Associated Press abbreviation*] (APAG)
UAM .... United States Medical Intelligence and Information Agency, Frederick, MD [*OCLC symbol*] (OCLC)
UAM .... Unnormalized Aid Magnitude (SAA)
UAM .... Urban Airshed Model [*Environmental Protection Agency*] (GFGA)
UAMBD .... Union Africaine de Management de Banques pour le Developpement [*African Union of Development Bank Management*] [*Benin*] (EAIO)
UAMBD .... Union Africaine et Mauricienne de Banques pour le Developpement [*African and Mauritian Union of Banks for Development*] [*Benin*] (AF)
UAMC .... Utility Assemble Master Compool
UAMCMDS ... Uniform Ambulatory Medical Case Minimum Data Set [*Department of Health and Human Services*] (GFGA)
UAMCT .... Union of Automobile, Motorcycle, and Cycle Technology
UAMH ...... University of Alberta Microfungus Collection and Herbarium [*Canada*]
UAMR .... United Association of Manufacturers' Representatives (EA)
UAMS .... Ukrainian Academy of Medical Sciences (EA)
UAMS .... Upper Atmosphere Mass Spectrometer
UAN .... Arcadian Partners Ltd. [*NYSE symbol*] (SPSG)
UAN .... Unidentified Atmospheric Noise (DNAB)
UAN .... Unified Automatic Network [*Telecommunications*] (OA)
UAN .... United Arab Nations (EAIO)
UAN .... Urea-Ammonium Nitrate [*Fertilizer*]
UAN .... Uric Acid Nitrogen
UANAS ..... Urea-Ammonium Nitrate Ammonium Sulfate [*Fertilizer*]
UANC .... United African National Congress
UANC....... United African National Council [*Zimbabwe*] [*Political party*] (PPW)
UANM ...... United African Nationalist Movement (EA)
UANM ...... Universal African Nationalist Movement (EA)
UAO .... Unconventional Aerial Object
UAO .... Und Andere Orte [*And Elsewhere*] [*German*]
UAO .... Unexplained Aerial Object
UAO .... Upper-Air Observation (SAA)
UAOD .... United Ancient Order of Druids [*Freemasonry*] (ROG)
UAOO .... Kzyl-Orda [*Former USSR*] [*ICAO location identifier*] (ICLI)
UAP .... Ua Pou [*Marquesas Islands*] [*Airport symbol*] (OAG)
UAP .... UAP, Inc. [*Toronto Stock Exchange symbol*]
UAP .... Unabhaengige Arbeiterpartei [*Independent Labor Party*] [*Germany*] [*Political party*] (PPE)
UAP .... Unidentified Atmospheric Phenomena
UAP .... Union Africaine de Physique [*African Union of Physics - AUP*] (EAIO)

UAP .... Union of American Physicians [*Later, UAPD*] (EA)
UAP .... United Amateur Press (EA)
UAP .... United Australia Party [*Political party*]
UAP .... Universal Availability of Publications [*International Federation of Library Associations*]
UAP .... University-Affiliated Program
UAP .... Unmanned Airborne Position (MCD)
UAP .... Upper Air Project
UAP .... Upper Arlington Public Library, Upper Arlington, OH [*OCLC symbol*] (OCLC)
UAP .... Urea-Ammonium Phosphate [*Organic chemistry*]
UAP .... User Area Profile
UAP .... Utility Amphibian Plane [*Navy*]
UAPA ...... Union of African Performing Artists [*See also UAAS*] (EAIO)
UAPA ...... United Amateur Press Association [*Later, UAP*] (EA)
UAPA .... United American Progress Association (EA)
UAPD .... Union of American Physicians and Dentists (EA)
UAPEFV ... Union des Associations des Producteurs Europeens de Farine de Viande [*Union of Associations of European Meat Meal Producers - UAEM*] [*Later, European Renderers Association - EURA*] (EAIO)
UAPPA ...... Union of Air Pollution Prevention Associations (EAIO)
UAPT ...... United Association for the Protection of Trade [*British*]
UAQ .... San Juan [*Argentina*] [*Airport symbol*] (OAG)
UAQI........ Uniform Air Quality Index [*Environmental Protection Agency*] (GFGA)
UAQUA..... Urban Affairs Quarterly [*A publication*]
UAR.......... Underwater Acoustic Resistance
UAR.......... Underwater Angle Receptacle
UAR.......... Uniform Airman Record
UAR.......... Unit Address Register
UAR.......... United Arab Republic [*Egypt and Syria*] [*Obsolete*]
UAR.......... Upper Air Route
UAR.......... Upper Atmosphere Research
UAR.......... Use as Required (MSA)
UARCEE... Union des Associations des Riziers de la CEE [*Union of Rice Associations of the EEC*] (ECED)
UARCO ..... UARCO, Inc. [*Formerly, United Autographic Register Co.*]
UAREP...... Universities Associated for Research and Education in Pathology (EA)
UARG .... Utility Air Regulatory Group [*Environmental Protection Agency*] (GFGA)
UAR Geol Surv Miner Res Dep Pap ... United Arab Republic. Geological Survey and Mineral Research Department. Papers [*A publication*]
UARI .... University of Alabama Research Institute (KSC)
UAR Inst Oceanogr Fish Bull ... United Arab Republic. Institute of Oceanography and Fisheries. Bulletin [*A publication*]
UARJ Anim Prod ... United Arab Republic. Journal of Animal Production [*A publication*]
UARJ Bot ... United Arab Republic. Journal of Botany [*A publication*]
UARJ Chem ... United Arab Republic. Journal of Chemistry [*A publication*]
UARJ Geol ... United Arab Republic. Journal of Geology [*A publication*]
UAR J Microbiol ... United Arab Republic. Journal of Microbiology [*A publication*]
UARJ Pharm Sci ... United Arab Republic. Journal of Pharmaceutical Sciences [*A publication*]
UAR J Phys ... United Arab Republic. Journal of Physics [*A publication*]
UARJ Soil Sci ... United Arab Republic. Journal of Soil Science [*A publication*]
UARJ Vet Sci ... United Arab Republic. Journal of Veterinary Science [*A publication*]
U Ark Little Rock LJ ... University of Arkansas at Little Rock. Law Journal [*A publication*]
UARL .... United Aircraft Research Laboratories
UAR Minist Agric Agrar Reform Tech Bull ... United Arab Republic. Ministry of Agriculture and Agrarian Reform. Technical Bulletin [*A publication*]
UAR Minist Agric Tech Bull ... United Arab Republic. Ministry of Agriculture. Technical Bulletin [*A publication*]
UARR .... Uralsk [*Former USSR*] [*ICAO location identifier*] (ICLI)
UARRSI .... Universal Aerial Refueling Receptacle Slipaway Installation (MCD)
UARS .... Underwater Acoustic Receiving System [*Navy*] (MCD)
UARS .... Unmanned Arctic Research Submersible
UARS .... Upper Atmosphere Research Satellite (MCD)
UAR (South Reg) Minist Agric Hydrobiol Dep Notes Mem ... United Arab Republic (Southern Region). Ministry of Agriculture. Hydrobiological Department. Notes and Memoirs [*A publication*]
UART .... Universal Asynchronous Receiver/Transmitter
UARZ/COM ... University of Arizona College of Medicine [*Tucson*]
UAS .... Ulster Archaeological Society
UAS .... Uniform Accounting System (OICC)
UAS .... Union of African States
UAS .... Unit Approval System [*for approval of aircraft materials, parts, and appliances*] [*FAA*]
UAS .... Unit Assets by State [*Army*]
UAS .... United Arab States
UAS........... University Air Squadrons
UAS .... University of Alabama. Studies [*A publication*]

UAS .... Unmanned Aerial [or Aerospace] Surveillance
UAS .... Unusual Aerial Sighting (ADA)
UAS .... Upper Atmospheric Sounder
UAS .... Upstream Activating Sequence [Genetics]
UAS .... Upstream Activation Site [Genetics]
UAS .... Uralic and Altaic Series. Indiana University. Publications [A publication]
UAS .... Urea-Ammonium Sulfate [Fertilizer]
UAS .... Urgent Action Service International [British Library]
UASE .... Union of Arab Stock Exchanges
UAS (Hebbal) Monogr Ser ... UAS (Hebbal) Monograph Series [A publication]
UASI .... UAS Automation Systems, Inc. [Bristol, CT] [NASDAQ symbol] (NQ)
UASS .... Unmanned Aerial Surveillance System (MCD)
UASSS ...... Underwater Acoustic Sound Source System
UAST .... Universal Association for Speech Tracing [See also TPA] (EAIO)
u-at--- .... Australia [MARC geographic area code] [Library of Congress] (LCCP)
UAT .... Ultraviolet Acquisition Technique
UAT .... Under Armor Tow (MCD)
UAT .... Underway Acceptance Trials (MCD)
UAT .... Union Aeromaritime de Transport [Privately-owned French airline]
UAT .... Until Advised by the Tower [Aviation] (FAAC)
UAT .... Urban Arts Theatre (EA)
UAT .... User Acceptance Test (MCD)
UATA .... Aralsk [Former USSR] [ICAO location identifier] (ICLI)
UATC .... United Artists Theatre Circuit, Inc.
UATE .... Universal Automatic Test Equipment
UATI .... Union de Asociaciones Tecnicas Internacionales [Union of International Engineering Organizations - UIEO] [Spanish] (ASF)
UATI .... Union des Associations Techniques Internationales [Union of International Technical Associations - UITA] (EAIO)
u-at-ne .... New South Wales [MARC geographic area code] [Library of Congress] (LCCP)
u-at-no .... Northern Territory [Australia] [MARC geographic area code] [Library of Congress] (LCCP)
UATP .... Universal Air Travel Plan [Commercial airlines credit system]
u-at-qn .... Queensland [MARC geographic area code] [Library of Congress] (LCCP)
UATR .... Chelkar [Former USSR] [ICAO location identifier] (ICLI)
u-at-sa .... South Australia [MARC geographic area code] [Library of Congress] (LCCP)
UATT .... Aktyubinsk [Former USSR] [ICAO location identifier] (ICLI)
u-at-tm .... Tasmania [MARC geographic area code] [Library of Congress] (LCCP)
UATV .... United Australian Television
u-at-vi .... Victoria [MARC geographic area code] [Library of Congress] (LCCP)
u-at-we .... Western Australia [MARC geographic area code] [Library of Congress] (LCCP)
UAU .... Universities Athletics Union [British]
UAUM .... Underwater-to-Air-to-Underwater Missile [Air Force]
UAUOC ..... United American Ukrainian Organizations Committee (EA)
UA/USA .... UNESCO Association/USA (EA)
UAV .... Ukrainian American Veterans (EA)
UAV .... University of the Andes [Merida] [Venezuela] [Seismograph station code, US Geological Survey] (SEIS)
UAV .... Unmanned Aerial [or Air] Vehicle (RDA)
UAVA .... Untersuchungen zur Assyriologie und Vorderasiatischen Archaologie [A publication]
UAV-SR .... Unmanned Aerial Vehicle - Short Range (DWSG)
UAW .... International Union, United Automobile, Aerospace, and Agricultural Implement Workers of America [Also known as United Auto Workers] (EA)
UAWB .... Universal Air Waybill [Shipping] (DS)
UAW-CAP ... United Auto Workers Community Action Program (EA)
UAWFA .... United Auto Workers, Family Auxiliary (EA)
UAWIU ..... United Allied Workers International Union (EA)
UAX .... Unit Automatic Exchange
UAZ .... East Hartford, CT [Location identifier] [FAA] (FAAL)
UB .... Burma Airways Corp. [Myanmar] [ICAO designator] (ICDA)
Ub .... Ubertus de Bobio [Flourished, 1214-37] [Authority cited in pre-1607 legal work] (DSA)
UB .... Ultimobranchial [Bodies] [Medicine]
UB .... Umno Baru [New Umno] [Malaysia] [Political party]
UB .... Unaccompanied Baggage (MCD)
UB .... Underwater Battery [Navy]
UB .... Undistributed Budget (MCD)
UB .... Unemployment Benefits [Unemployment insurance] (OICC)
UB .... Unicbank [Unique Bank] [Hungary]
UB .... Uniform Billing
UB .... Union Bank [British] (ROG)
UB .... Union of Burma Airways [ICAO designator] (FAAC)
UB .... Unit Bond (SAA)
UB .... United Benefice
UB .... United Biscuits [Commercial firm] [British]
UB .... United Brethren in Christ

UB .... United Brotherhood [Also written VC for secrecy] [Fenianism] (ROG)
UB .... University Bookman [A publication]
UB .... Upper Bench [Legal] [British] (ROG)
UB .... Upper Bound
UB .... Upper Brace (MCD)
UB .... Urban Buecher [A publication]
UB .... Urea Briquettes [Agronomy]
UB .... Usage Block (MSA)
UB .... Utica-Bend (SAA)
UB .... Utility Bridge (NASA)
UB .... Uttara Bharati [A publication]
UB1 .... University of Connecticut, Stamford Branch, Stamford, CT [OCLC symbol] (OCLC)
UB2 .... University of Connecticut, Hartford Branch, West Hartford, CT [OCLC symbol] (OCLC)
UB3 .... University of Connecticut, Southeastern Branch, Groton, CT [OCLC symbol] (OCLC)
UB4 .... University of Connecticut, MBA Library, Hartford, CT [OCLC symbol] (OCLC)
UB40 .... Name of British band, derived from code number on a British unemployment form
UBA .... Uberaba [Brazil] [Airport symbol] (OAG)
UBA .... Ulan Bator [Mongolia] [Geomagnetic observatory code]
UBA .... Ulusal Basin Ajansi [News agency] [Turkey] (MENA)
UBA .... Unblocking Acknowledge [Telecommunications] (TEL)
UBA .... Undenatured Bacterial Antigen
UBA .... Underwater Breathing Apparatus [Navy] (CAAL)
UBA .... Union of Burma Airways
UBA .... United Baltic Appeal (EA)
UBA .... United Bank for Africa Ltd.
UBA .... United Breweries of America (EA)
UBA .... Universal Beer Agar [Brewery bacteria culture medium]
UBA .... Universitet i Bergen. Arbok. Historisk-Antikvarisk Rekke [A publication]
UBAEC..... Union of Burma Atomic Energy Centre
UBAF........ Union des Banques Arabes et Francaises [Union of Arab and French Banks] [France]
UBAK .... United Bancorp of Alaska, Inc. [NASDAQ symbol] (NQ)
Ubal .... Ubaldus [Authority cited in pre-1607 legal work] (DSA)
U Baltimore L Rev ... University of Baltimore. Law Review [A publication]
U Balt LR .. University of Baltimore. Law Review [A publication]
U Balt L Rev ... University of Baltimore. Law Review [A publication]
UBAN........ Union Bancorp, Inc. [NASDAQ symbol] (NQ)
UBARI...... Union of Burma Applied Research Institute
UBAT .... Ultrasonic Bioassay Tank [Aerospace]
UBATS..... Ultrasonic Bioassay Tank System [Aerospace]
UBAZ .... United Bancorp of Arizona [NASDAQ symbol] (NQ)
UBB .... Union Bank of Bavaria
UBB .... Union of Burma Bank (DS)
UBB .... Universal Building Block
UBBA .... United Boys' Brigades of America [Later, BGBA] (EA)
UBBC .... Unsaturated (Vitamin) B_{12} Binding Capacity
Ub Bo........ Ubertus de Bobio [Flourished, 1214-37] (DSA)
Ub de Bo .... Ubertus de Bobio [Flourished, 1214-37] [Authority cited in pre-1607 legal work] (DSA)
UBBR .... University Bureaus of Business Research
UBC .... Unburned Carbon [Fuel technology]
UBC .... Uniform Broadband Channel [Telecommunications]
UBC .... Uniform Building Code (NRCH)
UBC .... United Black Christians (EA)
UBC .... United Brotherhood of Carpenters and Joiners of America (EA)
UBC .... United Business Communications, Inc. [Atlanta, GA] [Telecommunications] (TSSD)
UBC .... Universal Bibliographic Control
UBC .... Universal Block Channel
UBC .... Universal Buffer Controller
UBC .... University of British Columbia [Vancouver, BC]
UBC .... University of British Columbia Library [UTLAS symbol]
UBC .... Used Beverage Can
UBCA .... United Black Church Appeal (EA)
UBC Alumni Chronicle ... Alumni Association. University of British Columbia. Chronicle [A publication]
UBcGS....... Church of Jesus Christ of Latter-Day Saints, Genealogical Society Library, Brigham City South Branch, Brigham City, UT [Library symbol] [Library of Congress] (LCLS)
UBCHEA .. United Board for Christian Higher Education in Asia (EA)
UBcI.......... National Indian Training Center, Brigham City, UT [Library symbol] [Library of Congress] (LCLS)
UBCIO ...... University of British Columbia Institute of Oceanography [Canada] (MSC)
UBCJ......... United Brotherhood of Carpenters and Joiners of America
UBCL........ Union of Black Clergy and Laity of the Episcopal Church [Later, UBE] (EA)
UBC Legal N ... University of British Columbia. Legal Notes [A publication]
UBC Legal Notes ... University of British Columbia. Legal Notes [A publication]
UBCLN ..... University of British Columbia. Legal News [A publication] (DLA)
UBC LR..... University of British Columbia. Law Review [A publication]

UBC L Rev ... University of British Columbia. Law Review [*A publication*]
UBC Notes ... University of British Columbia. Legal Notes [*A publication*] (DLA)
UBCNREP ... University of British Columbia. Programme in Natural Resource Economics. Resources Paper [*A publication*]
UBCP........ Unibancorp, Inc. [*Chicago, IL*] [*NASDAQ symbol*] (NQ)
UBcT .... Thiokol Chemical Corp., Utah Division, Brigham City, UT [*Library symbol*] [*Library of Congress*] (LCLS)
UBCW .... United Brick and Clay Workers of America [*Later, ABCWIU*] (EA)
UBD.......... Bureau of Land Management, Billings, MT [*OCLC symbol*] (OCLC)
UBD.......... Union for Liberation and Democracy [*Suriname*] [*Political party*] (EY)
UBD.......... Universal Business Directory for the Pacific Islands [*A publication*]
UBD.......... Utility Binary Dump [*Data processing*]
UBDA........ Uniform Brain Death Act [*National Conference of Commissioners on Uniform State Laws*]
UBDC........ Urban Bikeway Design Collaborative (EA)
UBDd........ You Be Darned [*Bowdlerized version*] (DSUE)
UBDI .... Underwater Battery Director Indicator
UBDMA .... United Better Dress Manufacturers Association (EA)
UBE .... Union of Black Episcopalians (EA)
UBE .... Union Bouddhique d'Europe [*Buddhist Union of Europe - BUE*] (EAIO)
UBE .... Universal Bus Exercisor (NASA)
UBEA .... United Business Education Association [*Later, NBEA*]
UBEA Forum ... United Business Education Association. Forum [*A publication*]
UBeGS....... Church of Jesus Christ of Latter-Day Saints, Genealogical Society Library, Beaver Branch, Beaver, UT [*Library symbol*] [*Library of Congress*] (LCLS)
UBF .... Union Bank of Finland
UBF .... Universal Boss Fitting
UBF .... Universal Buddhist Fellowship (EA)
UBF .... Upstream Binding Factor [*Genetics*]
UBF .... Uterine Blood Flow [*Medicine*] (MAE)
UBFA........ United Black Fund of America (EA)
UBFC........ Underwater Battery Fire Control [*Navy*]
UBFCS ...... Underwater Battery Fire Control System [*Navy*]
UBG.......... Newberg, OR [*Location identifier*] [*FAA*] (FAAL)
UBG.......... Ultimobranchial Glands [*Endocrinology*]
UBG.......... Underground Building [*National Security Agency*]
UBG.......... Urobilinogen [*Medicine*] (MAE)
UBHC........ Unburned Hydrocarbon [*Also, UHC*] [*Fuel technology*]
UBHJ .... University of Birmingham. Historical Journal [*A publication*]
UBHR....... User Block Handling Routine [*Data processing*] (IBMDP)
UBI .... Buin [*Papua New Guinea*] [*Airport symbol*] (OAG)
UBI .... Ultraviolet Blood Irradiation
UBI .... Universal Battlefield Identification
UBIC......... Universal Bus Interface Controller (NASA)
UBIP......... Ubiquitous Immunopoietic Polypeptide [*Immunochemistry*]
U Birmingham Hist J ... University of Birmingham. Historical Journal [*A publication*]
UBIT......... Unrelated Business Income Tax
UBITRON ... Undulating Beam Interaction Electron Tube
UBJ........... Ube [*Japan*] [*Airport symbol*] (OAG)
UBJ........... Upper Ball Joint Suspension [*Automotive engineering*]
UBJSA ...... Union of Burma. Journal of Science and Technology [*A publication*]
UBK .... Unbleached Kraft [*Pulp and paper processing*]
UBK .... US Banknote Corp. [*NYSE symbol*] (SPSG)
UBKA .... Universitaetsbibliothek Karlsruhe [*Karlsruhe University Library*] [*Information retrieval*]
UBKHA..... Uspekhi Biologicheskoi Khimii [*A publication*]
UBKR........ United Bankers, Inc. [*NASDAQ symbol*] (NQ)
UBKS........ United Banks of Colorado, Inc. [*NASDAQ symbol*] (NQ)
UBL .... Unbleached (MSA)
UBL .... Unblocking [*Telecommunications*] (TEL)
UBL .... Undifferentiated B-Cell Lymphoma [*Medicine*]
UBL .... United Beverages [*Vancouver Stock Exchange symbol*]
UBLDP...... Union Belge et Luxembourgeoise de Droit Penal [*Belgian and Luxembourg Association of Penal Law*] (EAIO)
UBLR........ University of Baltimore. Law Review [*A publication*]
UBLSLJ .... University of Botswana, Lesotho, and Swaziland Law Journal [*A publication*] (DLA)
UBLU .... United Building Labourers' Union [*British*]
UBM......... Ultrasonic Bonding Machine
UBM.......... University of Bridgeport, Bridgeport, CT [*OCLC symbol*] (OCLC)
UBMT .... United Savings Bank FA [*Great Falls, MT*] [*NASDAQ symbol*] (NQ)
UBN.......... United Business Network [*United Business Communications, Inc.*] [*Atlanta, GA*] [*Telecommunications*] [*Defunct*] (TSSD)
UBN.......... Universal Broadband Network [*Telecommunications*]
UBN.......... University Bank NA [*AMEX symbol*] (SPSG)
UBNK........ Union Bank [*NASDAQ symbol*] (SPSG)
UBO.......... Uinta Basin Array [*Utah*] [*Seismograph station code, US Geological Survey*] [*Closed*] (SEIS)

UBO.......... Uinta Basin Observatory
UBO.......... Unemployment Benefit Office [*British*]
UBO.......... Unidentified Bright Object
UBOA....... United Bus Owners of America (EA)
U-BOOT.... Unterseeboot [*Submarine*] [*German*]
UBP .... Ubon Ratchathani [*Thailand*] [*Airport symbol*] (OAG)
UBP .... Ulusal Birlik Partisi [*National Unity Party*] [*Turkish Cyprus*] [*Political party*] (EY)
UBP ·········· Underwater Battery Plot [*Antisubmarine warfare*]
UBP .... Unit Beat Policing
UBP .... United Bahamian Party [*Political party*] (PPW)
UBP .... United Bermuda Party [*Political party*] (PPW)
UBP .... Upward Bound Programs [*Department of Labor*]
UBP .... Ureteral Back Pressure [*Medicine*] (MAE)
U-BPH....... Utah State Library Commission, Division of the Blind and Physically Handicapped, Salt Lake City, UT [*Library symbol*] [*Library of Congress*] (LCLS)
UBPLOT... Underwater Battery Plotting Room [*Navy*] (NVT)
UBPR........ Uniform Bank Performance Report [*Federal Financial Institutions Examination Council*]
UB Pr........ Upper Bench Precedents Tempore Car. I [*A publication*] (DLA)
UBPVLS.... Uniform Boiler and Pressure Vessel Laws Society (EA)
UBR.......... Uniform Business Rate [*Taxation*] [*British*]
UBR.......... United Bison Resources [*Vancouver Stock Exchange symbol*]
UBR.......... University of British Columbia Retrospective Conversion [*UTLAS symbol*]
UBR.......... Upper Burma Rulings [*India*] [*A publication*] (DLA)
U Brdgprt LR ... University of Bridgeport. Law Review [*A publication*]
UBRF........ Upper Branchial Filament
U Bridgeport L Rev ... University of Bridgeport. Law Review [*A publication*]
U Brit Col L Rev ... University of British Columbia. Law Review [*A publication*]
U Brit Colum L Rev ... University of British Columbia. Law Review [*A publication*]
UBS .... Columbus, MS [*Location identifier*] [*FAA*] (FAAL)
UBS .... Uniform Bearing Stress
UBS .... Union Bank of Switzerland
UBS .... Union Broadcasting System [*Fictitious broadcasting organization in film "Network"*]
UBS .... Unit Backspace Character [*Data processing*]
UBS .... United Bible Societies [*Stuttgart, Federal Republic of Germany*] (EA)
UBS .... United Broadcasting System [*Network in TV series "America 2-Night"*]
UBS .... Universal Builders Supply Co.
UBS .... University of British Columbia, School of Librarianship, Vancouver, BC, Canada [*OCLC symbol*] (OCLC)
UBS .... University of Buffalo. Studies [*A publication*]
UBS .... US Bioscience, Inc. [*AMEX symbol*] (SPSG)
UBSA........ United Business Schools Association [*Later, AICS*] (EA)
UBSB........ United Bible Societies. Bulletin [*London*] [*A publication*]
UBSC........ United Building Services Corp. of Delaware [*NASDAQ symbol*] (NQ)
UBSF........ United Bank FSB [*NASDAQ symbol*] (NQ)
UBSI........ United Bankshares, Inc. [*NASDAQ symbol*] (NQ)
UBSO........ Uinta Basin Seismological Observatory
UBST........ Unbonded Spool Type (DNAB)
UBT.......... Ubatuba [*Brazil*] [*Airport symbol*] [*Obsolete*] (OAG)
UBT.......... Universal Boattail Thor [*NASA*]
UBT.......... Universal Book Tester [*Measures performance of binding*]
UBTA .... Union Bank & Trust [*NASDAQ symbol*] (NQ)
UBTC .... University Bank & Trust Co. [*Newton, MA*] [*NASDAQ symbol*] (NQ)
UB/TIB ..... Universitatsbibliothek Hannover und Technische Informationsbibliothek [*University Library of Hannover and Technical Information Library*] [*Information service or system*] (IID)
UBTM .... United Bellows Tankage Module
UBU.......... UNESCO [*United Nations Educational, Scientific, and Cultural Organization*] Journal of Information Science, Librarianship, and Archives Administration [*A publication*]
UBV.......... Ultraviolet-Blue-Visual [*Photometric system*]
UBW......... Kuparuk, AK [*Location identifier*] [*FAA*] (FAAL)
UBW......... Unbewusste [*Unconscious Mind*] [*Psychology*]
UBW......... University of Connecticut, Waterbury Branch, Waterbury, CT [*OCLC symbol*] (OCLC)
UBWPS...... United Bargemen and Watermen's Protective Society [*A union*] [*British*]
UBX.......... Cuba, MO [*Location identifier*] [*FAA*] (FAAL)
UBZ.......... Upper Border Zone [*Geology*]
UBZC .... UBZ Corp. [*NASDAQ symbol*] (NQ)
UC............ Linea Aerea del Cobre Ltda. [*Chile*] [*ICAO designator*] (FAAC)
UC............ National Union Catalogue [*A publication*]
UC............ Ulcerative Colitis [*Medicine*]
UC............ Ultimate Collider [*Particle accelerator*]
UC............ Ultracentrifugal [*Biochemistry*] (MAE)
UC............ Umbilical Cable [*or Connector*]
UC............ Umbilical Cable Unit Cooler [*Aerospace*] (AAG)
UC............ Umbilical Connector

UC.............	Una Corda [*With one string or with the soft pedal*] [*Music*]
UC.............	Unaccompanied Child [*Airline notation*]
Uc.............	Uncanny Stories [*A publication*]
UC.............	Unchanged (MAE)
UC.............	Uncirculated Coins [*Numismatics*]
U/C............	Unclassified
UC.............	Unclipping [*Medicine*]
UC.............	Uncut Edges [*Bookbinding*]
UC.............	Undeducted Contributions
U/C............	Under Carriage (MCD)
UC.............	Under Charge
UC.............	Under Construction
U/C............	Under Conversion (NATG)
U/C............	Under Cover (ADA)
U/C............	Under Current (NASA)
UC.............	Undercut [*Technical drawings*]
UC.............	Underfashion Club (EA)
UC.............	Underwater Communications (MCD)
UC.............	Undifferentiated Carcinoma [*Oncology*]
UC.............	Unemployment Compensation
UC.............	UNESCO [*United Nations Educational, Scientific, and Cultural Organization*] Chronicle [*A publication*]
UC.............	Unichannel
Uc.............	Uniform, Coarse-Grained [*Soil*]
UC.............	Union Caledonienne [*Caledonian Union*] [*Political party*] (PPW)
UC.............	Union Camerounaise [*Cameroonese Union*] [*Political party*]
UC.............	Union Constitutionelle [*Constitutional Union*] [*Morocco*] [*Political party*] (PPW)
UC.............	Unit Call [*Also known as CCS*] [*Telecommunications*]
UC.............	Unit Chairman
UC.............	Unit Clerk
UC.............	Unit Cooler
UC.............	Unit Cost
UC.............	Unit Count (AFIT)
UC.............	United Canada Insurance Co.
UC.............	United Christian Party [*Australia*] [*Political party*]
uc.............	United States Miscellaneous Caribbean Islands [*MARC country of publication code*] [*Library of Congress*] (LCCP)
UC.............	Unity College [*London, England*]
UC.............	University of California
UC.............	University of Cincinnati [*Ohio*]
UC.............	University College
UC.............	University Colleges [*Public-performance tariff class*] [*British*]
UC.............	Unoperated Control
UC.............	Unsatisfactory Condition (NASA)
UC.............	Untreated Controls [*Medicine*]
UC.............	Up Converter
UC.............	Uplink Command
UC.............	Upper Canada
UC.............	Upper Cylinder
UC.............	Uppercase [*Typography*] (ADA)
UC.............	Uranium Canada Ltd.
UC.............	Uranium Carbide [*Inorganic chemistry*] (OA)
UC.............	Urbis Conditae [*From the Foundation of the City; that is, of Rome*] [*Latin*]
UC.............	Urea Clearance [*Clinical chemistry*]
UC.............	Urethral Catheterization [*Medicine*] (MAE)
U & C.........	Urethral and Cervical [*Medicine*]
UC.............	Urinary Catheter [*Medicine*]
U/C............	Urine Culture [*Clinical chemistry*] (MAE)
UC.............	Usable Control
UC.............	Using Command
U & C.........	Usual and Customary
UC.............	Usual Health-Care [*Medicine*]
UC.............	Uterine Contraction [*Obstetrics*] (AAMN)
UC.............	Utility Car [*British*]
UC.............	Utility Cargo
UC.............	Utility Corridor
UC.............	Utilization Control
UC1............	Underwater Control Rating 1st Class [*British military*] (DMA)
UC2............	Underwater Control Rating 2nd Class [*British military*] (DMA)
UCA..........	Under Color Addition [*Printing technology*]
UCA..........	Uniform Chart of Accounts [*DoD*]
UCA..........	Uniform Companies Act [*A publication*] (APTA)
UCA..........	United Carters' Association [*A union*] [*British*]
UCA..........	United Collision [*Vancouver Stock Exchange symbol*]
UCA..........	United Congressional Appeal (EA)
UCA..........	United States Court of Appeals for the District of Columbia, Judges Library, Washington, DC [*OCLC symbol*] (OCLC)
UCA..........	Unitized Component Assembly [*Aerospace*]
UCA..........	Units Consistency Analyzer [*Data processing*]
UCA..........	Universal Calibration Adapter
UCA..........	Upper Control Area (NATG)
UCA..........	User Computed Address [*Data processing*] (HGAA)
UCA..........	Utah Code, Annotated [*A publication*] (DLA)
UCA..........	Utica [*New York*] [*Airport symbol*] (OAG)
UCACEP...	United Council of Associations of Civil Employees of Pakistan
UCAE.......	United Carters' Association of England [*A union*]
UCAE.......	Universities Council for Adult Education [*British*]
UCAM.......	Camera Enterprises, Inc. [*NASDAQ symbol*] (NQ)
UCAM.......	United Campuses to Prevent Nuclear War (EA)
UCAN.......	Union of Catholic Asian News [*Kwun Tong, Hong Kong*] (EAIO)
UCAN.......	Utilities Conservation Action Now [*Federal Energy Administration*]
UCANF.....	United Canso Oil & Gas Ltd. [*NASDAQ symbol*] (NQ)
UC App......	Upper Canada Appeal Reports [*A publication*] (DLA)
UC App (Can) ...	Upper Canada Appeal Reports [*A publication*] (DLA)
UC App Rep ...	Upper Canada Appeal Reports [*A publication*] (DLA)
UCAR.......	United Carolina Bancshares Corp. [*NASDAQ symbol*] (NQ)
UCAR.......	University Corp. for Atmospheric Research (EA)
UCarb.......	Union Carbide Corp. [*Associated Press abbreviation*] (APAG)
UCARCIDE ...	Union Carbide Biocide [*Trademark*] [*Union Carbide Corp.*]
UCARS.....	Uniform Cost Accounting and Reporting System
UCAS.......	Uniform Cost Accounting Standards (MCD)
UCAS.......	Union of Central African States (EY)
UCASBJ....	Agro Sur [*A publication*]
UCATA.....	Uniform Contribution Among Tortfeasors Act [*National Conference of Commissioners on Uniform State Laws*]
UCATT.....	Union of Construction, Allied Trades, and Technicians [*British*]
UCAVJ.....	Union Continentale Africaine des Villes Jumelees [*Continental African Union of Twin Cities*]
UCB..........	Canadian Union Catalogue of Books [*National Library of Canada*] [*Information service or system*] (IID)
UCB..........	UCB [*Belgium*] [*Research code symbol*]
UCB..........	UCB Chemie [*Germany*] [*Research code symbol*]
UCB..........	Unconjugated Bilirubin
UCB..........	Union Chimique Belge [*Belgium*]
UCB..........	Unit Control Block (MCD)
UCB..........	United California Bank [*Los Angeles*] (IIA)
UCB..........	United Cambridge Mines [*Vancouver Stock Exchange symbol*]
UCB..........	United Commercial Bank Ltd. [*Bangladesh*]
UCB..........	Universal Character Buffer
UCB..........	University of California, Berkeley
UCB..........	University of California, Berkeley School of Library and Information Science, Berkeley, CA [*OCLC symbol*] (OCLC)
UCBC........	Parti de l'Unite et de la Communaute Belgo-Congolaise [*Political party*]
UCBEU	Uniao Cultural Brasil-Estados Unidos [*Brazil-United States Cultural Union*] [*Brazil*] (EAIO)
UCBI.........	United Central Bancshares [*NASDAQ symbol*] (NQ)
UCBLL......	Language Laboratory [*Research center*] (RCD)
UCBR........	Unconjugated Bilirubin (MAE)
UCBSRP ...	University of California, Berkeley, Sulfur Recovery Process
UCBT	Union pour le Commerce des Bois Tropicaux dans la CEE [*Association for Trade in Tropical Woods in the EEC*] (ECED)
UCBT	Universal Circuit Board Tester
UCBWM ...	United Church Board for World Ministries (EA)
UCC..........	Computing Center [*University of Rochester*] [*Research center*] (RCD)
UCC..........	Uccle [*Belgium*] [*Later, DOU*] [*Geomagnetic observatory code*]
UCC..........	Uccle [*Belgium*] [*Seismograph station code, US Geological Survey*] (SEIS)
UCC..........	Umbilical Checkout Cable
UCC..........	Unadjusted Contractual Changes
UCC..........	Uniform Classification Committee [*Later, NRFC*] (EA)
UCC..........	Uniform Code Council (EA)
UCC..........	Uniform Commercial Code [*National Conference of Commissioners on Uniform State Laws*]
UCC..........	Uniform Commercial Code Law Journal [*A publication*]
UCC..........	Uniform Credit Code
UCC..........	Union Camp Corp. [*NYSE symbol*] (SPSG)
UCC..........	Union Carbide Canada Ltd. [*Toronto Stock Exchange symbol*]
UCC..........	Union Carbide Corp. (KSC)
UCC..........	United Cancer Council (EA)
UCC..........	United Church of Christ
UCC..........	Universal Checkout Console (NASA)
UCC..........	Universal Copyright Convention
UCC..........	University of California. Chronicle [*A publication*]
UCC..........	University College, Cardiff [*Wales*]
UCC..........	University College Computer [*London, England*] (DEN)
UCC..........	University College, Cork [*Ireland*]
UCC..........	University Computer Center [*San Diego State University*] [*Research center*] (RCD)
UCC..........	University Computer Center [*Oklahoma State University*] [*Research center*] (RCD)
UCC..........	University Computer Center [*New Mexico State University*] [*Research center*] (RCD)
UCC..........	University Computer Center [*North Dakota State University*] [*Research center*] (RCD)
UCC..........	University Computer Center [*University of Minnesota*] [*Research center*] (RCD)
UCC..........	University Computing Co. [*International computer bureau*]
UCC..........	University of Corpus Christi [*Texas*] [*Closed, 1973*]
UCC..........	Upper Canada College
UCC..........	Upper Control Center (NATG)
UCC..........	Urgent Care Center [*Medicine*]
UCC..........	Uruguay Collectors Club (EA)
UCC..........	Utility Control Console

UCC.......... Yucca Flat, NV [*Location identifier*] [*FAA*]   (FAAL)
UC/CA ...... Current Anthropology. University of Chicago [*A publication*]
UCCA .... Ukrainian Congress Committee of America   (EA)
UCCA .... Universities Central Council on Admission [*British*]
UCCC .... Computing Center [*University of Cincinnati*] [*Research center*]   (RCD)
UCCC .... Uniform Consumer Credit Code [*National Conference of Commissioners on Uniform State Laws*]
UCCC .... Unmarried-Catholics Correspondence Club   (EA)
UCCCCWCS ... United Church of Christ Coordinating Center for Women in Church and Society   (EA)
UCCCRJ ... United Church of Christ Commission for Racial Justice   (EA)
UCCE .... Union des Capitales de la Communaute Europeenne [*Union of Capitals of the European Community*]
UCCE .... Universal Craftsmen Council of Engineers   (EA)
UCC/EMC ... Union Carbide and Carbon/Electric Metallurgical Co.   (AAG)
UCCEW .... University of Cape Coast. English Department. Workpapers [*A publication*]
UCCF........ United Campus Christian Fellowship [*Defunct*]
UC Ch........ Upper Canada Chancery Reports [*1849-82*] [*A publication*]   (DLA)
UC Cham... Upper Canada Chambers Reports [*A publication*]   (DLA)
UC Chamb ... Upper Canada Chambers Reports [*1846-52*] [*A publication*]   (DLA)
UC Cham (Can) ... Upper Canada Chambers Reports [*1846-52*] [*A publication*]   (DLA)
UC Chan.... Upper Canada Chancery Reports [*A publication*]   (DLA)
UC Ch (Can) ... Upper Canada Chancery Reports [*A publication*]   (DLA)
UC Ch Rep ... Upper Canada Chancery Reports [*1849-82*] [*A publication*]   (DLA)
UCC Law Letter ... Uniform Commercial Code Law Letter [*A publication*]
UCCL/GC ... United Church Coalition for Lesbian/Gay Concerns   (EA)
UCCLJ ...... Uniform Commercial Code Law Journal [*A publication*]
UCC-ND.... Union Carbide Corp. - Nuclear Division   (MCD)
UCCP .... Upper Canada Common Pleas Reports [*A publication*]   (DLA)
UCCP (Can) ... Upper Canada Common Pleas Reports [*A publication*]   (DLA)
UCCPD ..... Upper Canada Common Pleas Division Reports [*Ontario*] [*A publication*]   (DLA)
UCCPL...... United Citizens Coastal Protection League   (EA)
UCCR .... Upper Canada Court Records [*Report of Ontario Bureau of Archives*] [*A publication*]   (DLA)
UCCRC...... University of Chicago Cancer Research Center [*Research center*]   (RCD)
UCC Rep Serv ... Uniform Commercial Code Reporting Service [*A publication*]
UCCRL...... Union Carbide and Carbon Research Laboratories   (AAG)
UCCRP...... Union College Character Research Project   (EA)
UCCRS...... Underwater Coded Command Release System
UCCS........ Ultrasonic Chemical Cleaning System
UCCS........ United Cabinet and Chairmakers' Society [*A union*] [*British*]
UCCS........ Universal Camera Control System
UCCS........ University Classification and Compensation System
UCD.......... Unchanged Charge Distribution [*Fission*]
UCD.......... Uniform Call Distribution [*Telephone system*]
UCD.......... Union de Centro Democratico [*Union of the Democratic Center*] [*Spain*] [*Political party*]   (PPE)
UCD.......... United Canadian Shares Ltd. [*Toronto Stock Exchange symbol*]
UCD.......... University of California, Davis
UCD.......... University of California (Davis). Law Review [*A publication*]
UCD.......... University College, Dublin [*Ireland*]
UCd........... Urine Cadmium Level
UCD.......... Urine Collection Device [*NASA*]   (MCD)
UCD.......... Usual Childhood Diseases [*Medicine*]
UCDA .... University and College Designers Association   (EA)
UC Davis L Rev ... University of California (Davis). Law Review [*A publication*]   (DLA)
UCDC........ Ulster Constitution Defence Committee [*Northern Ireland*]
UCDC........ Uniado do Centro Democrata Cristao [*Union of the Christian Democratic Center*] [*Portugal*] [*Political party*]   (PPE)
UCDCC ..... Union Centro y Democratica Cristiana de Catalunya [*Union of the Center and Christian Democrats of Catalonia*] [*Spain*] [*Political party*]   (PPE)
UCdE .... Emery County Library, Castle Dale, UT [*Library symbol*] [*Library of Congress*]   (LCLS)
UCDEC ..... Union Chretienne Democrate d'Europe Centrale [*Christian Democratic Union of Central Europe - CDUCE*]   (EAIO)
UCdH .... Emery County High School, Castle Dale, UT [*Library symbol*] [*Library of Congress*]   (LCLS)
UCDL .... Union Chretienne Democrate Libanaise [*Lebanese Christian Democratic Union*] [*Political party*]   (PPW)
UCD LR..... University of California (Davis). Law Review [*A publication*]
UCD L Rev ... UCD [*University of California, Davis*] Law Review [*A publication*]
UCDP .... Uncorrected Data Processor
UCDPE...... University of California (Davis). Publications in English [*A publication*]
UCDS .... Unit Chemical Defense Study   (MCD)
UCDWN.... Until Cleared Down [*Aviation*]   (FAAC)
UCDWR .... University of California Division of War Research

UCE .... UCCEL Corp. [*NYSE symbol*]   (SPSG)
UCE .... Union Canadienne des Etudiants
UCE .... Unit Checkout Equipment
UCE .... Unit Correction Entry
UCE .... Upstream Control Element [*Genetics*]
UCE .... Ural Commodity Exchange [*Russian Federation*]   (EY)
UCEA .... Uniform Conservation Easement Act [*National Conference of Commissioners on Uniform State Laws*]
UCEA .... Uniform Criminal Extradition Act [*National Conference of Commissioners on Uniform State Laws*]
UCEA .... Union Chimique Elf-Aquitaine [*France*]
UCEA .... University Council for Educational Administration   (EA)
UCE & A.... Upper Canada Error and Appeal Reports [*1846-66*] [*A publication*]   (DLA)
UCEA .... Used Clothing Exporters Association of America   (EA)
UCEC .... Utility Commission Engineers Conference
UC/EDCC ... Economic Development and Cultural Change. University of Chicago [*A publication*]
UCeDe .... Union del Centro Democratico [*Union of the Democratic Center*] [*Argentina*] [*Political party*]   (EY)
UCEMT .... University Consortium in Educational Media and Technology [*Later, UCIDT*]
Ucenyje Zapiski Belorusskogo Gosud Univ ... Ucenyje Zapiski Belorusskogo Gosudarstvennogo Universiteta [*A publication*]
Ucenyje Zapiski Jaroslav ... Ucenyje Zapiski Jaroslavskogo Universiteta [*A publication*]
Ucenyje Zapiski Leningrad ... Ucenyje Zapiski Leningradskogo Gosudarstvennogo Universiteta [*A publication*]
Ucenyje Zapiski Leningrad Pedag Inst ... Ucenyje Zapiski Leningradskogo Gosudarstvennogo Pedagogiceskogo Instituta [*A publication*]
Ucenyje Zapiski Moskov Gosud Pedag Inst ... Ucenyje Zapiski Moskovskogo Gosudarstvennogo Pedagogiceskogo Instituta Inostraunych Jazykov [*A publication*]
Ucenyje Zapiski Moskva ... Ucenyje Zapiski Moskovskogo Gosudarstvennogo Universiteta Imeni Lononosova [*A publication*]
Ucenyje Zapiski (Tomsk) ... Ucenyje Zapiski Tomskogo Gosudarstvennogo Universiteta Imeni Kujbyseva (Tomsk) [*A publication*]
Ucen Zap CAGI ... Ucenyi Zapiski Central'nogo Aero-Gidrodinamiceskogo Instituta [*A publication*]
Ucen Zap Statist ... Ucenyi Zapiski po Statistike Akademija Nauk SSSR Central'nyi Ekonomiko-Matematiceskii Institut [*A publication*]
UCEP........ Upper Critical End Points [*Supercritical extraction*]
UCEPCEE ... Union du Commerce des Engrais des Pays de la Communaute Economique Europeenne [*Union of the Fertilizer Trade of Countries of the EEC*] [*Hasselt, Belgium*]   (EAIO)
UCER .... Unit Cost Exception Report [*Army*]
UCER .... University Center for Energy Research [*Oklahoma State University*] [*Research center*]   (RCD)
UC Err & App ... Upper Canada Error and Appeal Reports [*1846-66*] [*A publication*]   (DLA)
UC Err & App (Can) ... Upper Canada Error and Appeal Reports [*1846-66*] [*A publication*]   (DLA)
UCES......... University Center for Environmental Studies [*Virginia Polytechnic Institute and State University*] [*Research center*]   (RCD)
U Ceylon LR ... University of Ceylon. Law Review [*A publication*]   (DLA)
UCF .... Uniform Contract Format
UCF .... Union Culturelle Francais [*French Cultural Union*]
UCF .... Unit Control File [*Air Force*]
UCF .... United Cat Federation   (EA)
UCF .... United Companies Financial Corp. [*AMEX symbol*]   (SPSG)
UCF .... United Cooperative Farmers, Inc.
UCF .... University of Central Florida [*Orlando, FL*]
UCF .... Utility Control Facility
UCFA .... Uniform Comparative Fault Act [*National Conference of Commissioners on Uniform State Laws*]
UCFA .... Union pour la Communaute Franco-Africaine [*Union for the Franco-African Community*] [*Niger*]
UCFAC...... United Council of Filipino Associations in Canada
UCFC........ United Community Funds and Councils of America [*Later, UWA*]   (EA)
UCFCMHPH ... Union Centrafricaine de la Fraternite Chretienne des Malades et Handicapes   (EAIO)
UCFE........ Unemployment Compensation, Federal Employees
UCFML..... Union des Communistes de France Marxiste-Leniniste [*Marxist-Leninist Union of Communists of France*] [*Political party*]   (PPW)
UCFRU ..... Utah Cooperative Fishery Research Unit [*Utah State University*] [*Research center*]   (RCD)
UCG.......... Underground Coal Gasification
UCG.......... Unidirectional Categorical Grammar
UCG.......... University College Galway [*Ireland*]
UCG.......... Urinary Chorionic Gonadotrophin [*Endocrinology*]
UCGA .... University Center in Georgia, Inc. [*Library network*]
UCGF .... Undergraduate Computer Graphics Facility [*Stevens Institute of Technology*] [*Research center*]   (RCD)
UCH .... China Business Review [*A publication*]
UCH .... University College Hospital [*British*]   (DI)

UCH .... University of Connecticut, Health Center Library, Farmington, CT [*OCLC symbol*]   (OCLC)
UCHD .... Usual Childhood Diseases [*Medicine*]
Uchet Finan Kolkhoz Sovkhoz ... Uchet i Finansy v Kolkhozakh i Sovkhozakh [*A publication*]
UCHF .... Uncoupled Hartree-Fock [*Physical chemistry*]
U Chicago L Rev ... University of Chicago. Law Review [*A publication*]
U Chi L Rec ... University of Chicago. Law School. Record [*A publication*]
U Chi L Rev ... University of Chicago. Law Review [*A publication*]
UCHILS.... University of Chicago Law School   (DLA)
U Chi L Sch Rec ... University of Chicago. Law School. Record [*A publication*]
U Chi LS Conf Series ... University of Chicago. Law School. Conference Series [*A publication*]
U Chi L S Rec ... University of Chicago. Law School. Record [*A publication*]
UCHSC ..... University of Colorado Health Sciences Center [*Denver*]
Uch Zap Imp Yur'ev Univ ... Uchenyya Zapiskik Imperatorskogo Yur'evskago Universiteta [*A publication*]
UCI .... Imperial Chemical Industries [*British*]
UCI .... Union Cycliste Internationale [*International Cycling Union*] [*Switzerland*]   (EA)
UCI .... Unit Construction Index
UCI .... United Charity Institutions of Jerusalem   (EA)
UCI .... Universite Cooperative Internationale [*International Cooperative University*]
UCI .... University of California at Irvine
UCI .... Urinary Catheter In [*or Input*] [*Medicine*]
UCI .... User-Communication Interface [*Telecommunications*]
UCI .... Utility Card Input
UCI .... Utility Communicators International   (EA)
UCIB......... USAFE Command Intelligence Brief   (MCD)
UCID .... Independent Democratic Union of Cape Verde [*Political party*]   (PD)
UCIDT....... University Consortium for Instructional Development and Technology   (EA)
UCIIM....... Unione Cattolica Italiana Insegnanti Medi
UCIM .... UCI Medical Affiliates, Inc. [*Fort Lauderdale, FL*] [*NASDAQ symbol*]   (NQ)
UCIMHPLD ... Union of Catholic Institutions for the Mentally Handicapped and Persons with Learning Disabilities [*Germany*]   (EAIO)
UCIMT...... University Center for Instructional Media and Technology [*University of Connecticut*] [*Research center*]   (RCD)
U Cin LR.... University of Cincinnati. Law Review [*A publication*]
U Cin L Rev ... University of Cincinnati. Law Review [*A publication*]
UCIP.......... Union Catholique Internationale de la Presse [*International Catholic Union of the Press*]   (EAIO)
UCIR .... University Center for International Rehabilitation [*Michigan State University*] [*Research center*]   (RCD)
UCIS......... Unemployment Compensation Interpretation Service   (DLA)
UCIS......... University Center for International Studies [*University of Pittsburgh*] [*Research center*]   (IID)
UCIS......... University Computing and Information Services [*Villanova University*] [*Research center*]   (RCD)
UCIS......... Uprange Computer Input System
UCISS .... Union Catholique Internationale de Service Social [*Catholic International Union for Social Service*] [*Brussels, Belgium*]   (EAIO)
UCIT......... United Cities Gas Co. [*NASDAQ symbol*]   (NQ)
UCITS....... Undertakings for Collective Investment in Transferable Securities [*European Community*]
UCJ........... Unsatisfied Claim and Judgment [*State driver insurance*]
UCJG........ Alliance Universelle des Unions Chretiennes de Jeunes Gens [*World Alliance of Young Men's Christian Associations*]
UC Jur .... Upper Canada Jurist [*A publication*]   (DLA)
UC Jur (Can) ... Upper Canada Jurist [*A publication*]   (DLA)
UCK.......... Union Culturelle Katangaise [*Katangan Cultural Union*]
UCKB .... Upper Canada King's Bench Reports, Old Series [*1831-44*] [*A publication*]   (DLA)
UCKB (Can) ... Upper Canada King's Bench Reports, Old Series [*1831-44*] [*A publication*]   (DLA)
UCL .... Ulnar Collateral Ligament [*Anatomy*]
UCL .... Uncomfortable Loudness [*Audiometry*]
UCL .... Universal Consolidated Ltd. [*British*]
UCL .... University of Calgary Library [*UTLAS symbol*]
UCL .... University of Chicago. Law Review [*A publication*]
UCL .... University College of London   (KSC)
UCL .... University of Connecticut, Law Library, West Hartford, CT [*OCLC symbol*]   (OCLC)
UCL .... Unocal Corp. [*NYSE symbol*]   (SPSG)
UCL .... Update Control List
UCL .... Upper Confidence Level [*Industrial engineering*]   (IEEE)
UCL .... Upper Confidence Limit [*Statistics*]
UCL .... Upper Control Limit [*Nuclear energy*]
UCL .... Urea Clearance [*Test*] [*Medicine*]
UCL .... User Control List [*Data processing*]   (HGAA)
UCLA .... University of California, Los Angeles [*Databank originator*]
UCLA .... University at the Corner of Lenox Avenue [*Nickname for "The Tree of Life," a Harlem bookstore*]
UCLA-Alaska L Rev ... UCLA [*University of California, Los Angeles*]-Alaska Law Review [*A publication*]   (DLA)

UCLA Forum Med Sci ... UCLA [*University of California, Los Angeles*] Forum in Medical Sciences [*A publication*]
UCLA Intra L Rev ... UCLA [*University of California, Los Angeles*] Intramural Law Review [*A publication*]   (DLA)
UCLA J Envt'l L & Pol'y ... UCLA [*University of California, Los Angeles*] Journal of Environmental Law and Policy [*A publication*]   (DLA)
UCLA/JLAL ... Journal of Latin American Lore. University of California. Latin American Center [*A publication*]
UCLA Law R ... UCLA [*University of California, Los Angeles*] Law Review
UCLA Law Rev ... University of California at Los Angeles. Law Review [*A publication*]   (DLA)
UCLA L Rev ... University of California at Los Angeles. Law Review [*A publication*]   (DLA)
UCLA Pac Basin LJ ... UCLA [*University of California at Los Angeles*] Pacific Basin Law Journal [*A publication*]   (DLA)
UCLA Slav S ... UCLA [*University of California at Los Angeles*] Slavic Studies [*A publication*]
UCLA Symp Mol Cell Biol ... UCLA [*University of California, Los Angeles*] Symposia on Molecular and Cellular Biology [*A publication*]
UCLA (Univ Calif Los Ang) Symp Mol Cell Biol New Ser ... UCLA (University of California at Los Angeles) Symposia on Molecular and Cellular Biology. New Series [*A publication*]
UCLA (Univ Cal Los Angeles)-Alaska Law R ... UCLA (University of California, Los Angeles)-Alaska Law Review [*A publication*]
UCLA (Univ Cal Los Angeles) J Environmental Law and Policy ... UCLA (University of California, Los Angeles) Journal of Environmental Law and Policy [*A publication*]
UCLA (Univ Cal Los Angeles) Pacific Basin Law J ... UCLA (University of California, Los Angeles) Pacific Basin Law Journal [*A publication*]
UCLC .... Utah College Library Council [*Library network*]
UCLEA..... University and College Labor Education Association   (EA)
UCLG .... United Cement, Lime, Gypsum, and Allied Workers International Union [*Formerly, CLGW*]   (EA)
UCLJ .... University of California, La Jolla
UCLJ .... Upper Canada Law Journal [*1855-1922*] [*A publication*]   (DLA)
UCLJ (Can) ... Upper Canada Law Journal [*A publication*]   (DLA)
UCLJ NS... Upper Canada Law Journal, New Series [*A publication*]   (DLA)
UCLJ NS (Can) ... Upper Canada Law Journal, New Series [*A publication*]   (DLA)
UCLJ OS... Canada Law Journal, Old Series [*A publication*]   (DLA)
UCLM .... Unity of Czech Ladies and Men [*Later, CSA*]   (EA)
UCLR .... University of Ceylon. Law Review [*A publication*]   (DLA)
UCLR .... University of Chicago. Law Review [*A publication*]
UCLR .... University of Cincinnati. Law Review [*A publication*]
UCLR .... University of Colorado. Law Review [*A publication*]
UCLRL....... University of California Lawrence Radiation Laboratory
UCLS........ Underwater Crash Locator System   (MCD)
UCLT........ Until Cleared to Land by the Tower [*Aviation*]   (FAAC)
UCM......... Can You Come and See Me?
UCM......... Union of Catholic Mothers [*British*]   (DI)
UCM......... Union des Croyants Malagaches [*Malagasy Christian Union*]
UCM......... Universal Christian Movement   (EA)
UCM......... Universal Church of the Master   (IIA)
UCM......... Universal Communications Monitor
UCM......... University Christian Movement [*Formerly, NSCF*] [*Defunct*]
UCM......... Unresolved Complex Mixture
UCM......... User Command [*Data processing*]   (PCM)
UCMAE .... United Carters' and Motormen's Association of England [*A union*]
UCMJ....... Uniform Code of Military Justice
UCML .... Unit Committed Munitions List
UCMP .... UniComp, Inc. [*NASDAQ symbol*]   (NQ)
UCMP ...... Union Catalog of Medical Periodicals [*A publication*]
UCMS ...... Unit Capability Measurement System   (AFM)
UCMS ...... United Christian Missionary Society   (EA)
UCMSA..... UCLA [*University of California, Los Angeles*] Forum in Medical Sciences [*A publication*]
UCMSU ... United Chain Makers' and Strikers' Union [*British*]
UCMT ...... Unglazed Ceramic Mosaic Tile [*Technical drawings*]
UCN.......... Ultracold Neutron
UCN.......... Unemployment Compensation News [*James E. Frick, Inc.*] [*Information service or system*]   (CRD)
UCN.......... Uniform Control Number   (NASA)
UCN.......... Union del Centro Nacional [*Union of the National Center*] [*Guatemala*] [*Political party*]
UCN.......... Union Civica Nacional [*National Civic Union*] [*Dominican Republic*] [*Political party*]   (PPW)
UCNC....... Union Carbide Nuclear Corp.
UCNI........ Unclassified Controlled Nuclear Information [*Department of Energy*]
UCNI........ Unified Communications Navigation Identification
UCNS .... Universities Committee for Non-Teaching Staff [*British*]
UCNT .... Undifferentiated Carcinoma of Nasopharyngeal Type [*Oncology*]
UCNW....... University College of North Wales
UCNY........ Underfashion Club of New York [*Formerly, CBWC*]   (EA)

UCO.......... Union Corp. [*NYSE symbol*] (SPSG)
UCO.......... United Commercial Bank [*India*] (EY)
UCO.......... Universal Code [*Used for giving transport aircraft meteorological information in wartime*] (NATG)
UCO.......... Universal Communications Object (PCM)
UCO.......... Universal Weather Landing Code
UCO.......... Urethral Catheter Out [*Medicine*] (MAE)
UCO.......... Urinary Catheter Out [*or Output*] [*Medicine*]
UCO.......... Utility Compiler
UCOA.......... United Coasts Corp. [*NASDAQ symbol*] (NQ)
UCOD.......... University Clearing Office for Developing Countries
UCOFT...... Unit Combat Fire Trainer [*Army*]
U-COFT .... Unit Conduct of Fire Trainer [*Army*]
UCOIP ...... University of Chicago. Oriental Institute. Publications [*A publication*]
UCOL........ Union des Colons du Katanga [*Settlers' Union of Katanga*]
U Colo LR ... University of Colorado. Law Review [*A publication*]
U Colo L Rev ... University of Colorado. Law Review [*A publication*]
U Color L Rev ... University of Colorado. Law Review [*A publication*]
U Colo Stud ... University of Colorado. Studies [*A publication*]
UCOM....... Unified Command [*DoD*]
UCOM....... Union Catalog of Medical Monographs and Multimedia [*Medical Library Center of New York*] [*No longer available online*] [*Information service or system*] (CRD)
UCON .... Utility Control
UCONN .... University of Connecticut
UCOP....... University of Cambridge. Oriental Publications [*A publication*]
UCOPOM ... Union Europeenne du Commerce de Gros des Pommes de Terre [*European Union of the Wholesale Potato Trade*] [*Common Market*]
UCORC..... University of California/Operations Research Center
UCOS........ Upper Canada King's Bench Reports, Old Series [*1831-44*] [*A publication*] (DLA)
UCOS........ Uprange Computer Output System
UCOSDDEEC ... Union of Cafe Owners and Soft Drink Dealers of the European Economic Community [*Paris, France*] (EAIO)
UCOSL...... University of Colorado School of Law (DLA)
UCOWR.... Universities Council on Water Resources (EA)
UCP .... New Castle, PA [*Location identifier*] [*FAA*] (FAAL)
UCP .... Ubiquitous Crystallization Process [*Photovoltaic energy systems*]
UCP .... Unified Command Plan [*Military*] (AFM)
UCP .... Uniform Customs and Practice for Documentary Credits [*International Chamber of Commerce*] [*A publication*]
UC & P....... Uniform Customs and Practice for Documentary Credits [*International Chamber of Commerce*] [*A publication*] (DS)
UCP .... Uninterruptable Computer Power
UCP .... Union of Coffee Planters [*Madagascar*] (EAIO)
UCP .... Union Comorienne pour le Progres [*Comorian Union for Progress*] (PD)
UCP .... United Christian Party [*Australia*] [*Political party*] (ADA)
UCP .... United Country Party [*Australia*] [*Political party*]
UCP .... Universal Commercial Paper [*Investment term*]
UCP .... University of California. Publications in Classical Philology [*A publication*]
UCP .... University of Connecticut, Health Center Library, Processing Center, Farmington, CT [*OCLC symbol*] (OCLC)
UCP .... Update Control Process [*Telecommunications*] (TEL)
UCP .... Urinary C-Peptide [*Urology*]
UCP .... Urinary Coproporphyrin [*Urology*]
UCP .... Utilities Conservation Program [*Navy*] (NG)
UCP .... Utility Control Program
UCPA .... United Cerebral Palsy Associations (EA)
UCPA .... University of California. Publications in Classical Archaeology [*A publication*]
UCPA .... University Counseling and Placement Association (AEBS)
UCPC .... University of Connecticut Paleobotanical Collection
UCPCP...... University of California Publications in Classical Philology [*Berkeley and Los Angeles*] [*A publication*]
UCPE........ Unit of Comparative Plant Ecology [*Natural Environment Research Council*] [*British*] (IRUK)
UCPES ..... University of California. Publications in English Studies [*A publication*]
UCPF........ United Church Peace Fellowship [*Defunct*] (EA)
UCPFS ..... University of California. Publications in Folklore Studies [*A publication*]
UCPh........ Universitas Carolina: Philologica [*A publication*]
UCPL........ University of California. Publications in Linguistics [*A publication*]
UCPM ...... University of California. Publications in Music [*A publication*]
UCPMP..... University of California. Publications in Modern Philology [*A publication*]
UCPMPh... University of California. Publications in Modern Philology [*A publication*]
UCPN .... Union des Chefs et des Populations du Nord [*Union of Chiefs and Peoples of the North*] [*Togo*]
UCPN .... United Communist Party of Nepal [*Political party*] (EY)
UCPP........ Urban Crime Prevention Program [*Federal government*]
UCPPh ...... University of California. Publications in Classical Philology [*A publication*]

UCPR .... Upper Canada Practice Reports [*A publication*] (DLA)
UC Pract.... Upper Canada Practice Reports [*1850-1900*] [*A publication*] (DLA)
UC Pr (Can) ... Upper Canada Practice Reports [*A publication*] (DLA)
UCPREF ... United Cerebral Palsy Research and Educational Foundation (EA)
UC Pr R ..... Upper Canada Practice Reports [*A publication*] (DLA)
UCPSP ...... University of California. Publications in Semitic Philology [*A publication*]
UCPSPh.... University of California. Publications in Semitic Philology [*A publication*]
UCPT........ Urinary Coproporphyrin Test [*Urology*]
UCPTE...... Union pour la Coordination de la Production et du Transport de l'Electricite [*Union for the Coordination of the Production and Transport of Electric Power - UCPTE*] (EAIO)
UCPU .... Universal Central Processor Unit [*Computer hardware*]
UCPU .... Urine Collection and Pretreatment Unit (NASA)
UCQ........ University College Quarterly [*A publication*]
UCQB .... Upper Canada Queen's Bench Reports [*A publication*] (DLA)
UC QB OS ... Upper Canada Queen's Bench Reports, Old Series [*A publication*] (DLA)
UC QB OS (Can) ... Upper Canada Queen's Bench Reports, Old Series [*A publication*] (DLA)
UCR.......... Committee on Uniform Crime Records (EA)
UCR.......... Unconditioned Reflex [*or Response*] [*Psychometrics*]
UCR.......... Under-Color Removal [*Printing technology*]
UCR.......... Uniform Crime Reports [*FBI*]
UCR.......... Union Centriste et Radicale [*France*] [*Political party*] (EY)
UCR.......... Union Civica Radical [*Radical Civic Union*] [*Argentina*] (PD)
UCR.......... Unit Card Reader
UCR.......... Unit Cost Report [*Military*] (RDA)
UCR.......... University of California, Riverside (IID)
UCR.......... University of Ceylon. Review [*A publication*]
UCR.......... University of Cincinnati. Law Review [*A publication*]
UCR.......... Unsatisfactory Condition Report [*NASA*]
UCR.......... Upper Canada Reports [*A publication*] (DLA)
UCR.......... Upper Circulating Reflux [*Chemical engineering*]
UCR.......... User Control Routine (MCD)
UCR.......... Usual, Customary, and Reasonable Charges [*Medicine*]
UCR.......... Utah Coal Route [*AAR code*]
UCRC .... Underground Construction Research Council
UCRC .... Union Canadienne des Religieuses Contemplatives
UCRC .... United Civil Rights Committee
UC Rep ..... Upper Canada Reports [*A publication*] (DLA)
UC Rep FM Univ Calif Berkeley Dep Mech Eng ... UC. Report FM. University of California, Berkeley. Department of Mechanical Engineering [*A publication*]
UCRG .... Union des Clubs pour le Renouveau de la Gauche [*Union of Clubs for the Renovation of the Left*] [*France*] [*Political party*] (PPE)
UCRI .... Union Carbide Research Institute (KSC)
UCRI .... Union Civica Radical Intransigente [*Left-wing radical political party*] [*Argentina*]
U-CRIS...... Utah Computer Retrieval Information Service [*Utah State Office of Education*] (OLDSS)
UCRL .... University of California Radiation Laboratory (MCD)
UCRL .... University of California Research Laboratory (KSC)
UCrow....... Upstart Crow [*A publication*]
UCRP .... Uniform Crime Reporting Program [*FBI*]
UCRP .... Union Civica Radical del Pueblo [*Moderate radical political party*] [*Argentina*]
UCS .... Canadian Union Catalogue of Serials [*National Library of Canada*] [*Information service or system*] (IID)
UC/S......... Signs. University of Chicago Press [*A publication*]
UCS .... Southern Utah State College, Cedar City, UT [*Library symbol*] [*Library of Congress*] (LCLS)
UCS .... Unbalanced Current Sensing (MCD)
UCS .... Unclosed Contract Status [*Military*] (AFIT)
UCS .... Unconditioned Stimulus [*Psychometrics*]
UCS .... Unconscious [*Medicine*]
UCS .... Uncontrolled Stimulus (HGAA)
UCS .... Underwater Cable System
UCS .... Underwater Communications System
UCS .... Underwater Conservation Society [*British*] (DI)
UCS .... Unican Security Systems Ltd. [*Toronto Stock Exchange symbol*]
UCS .... Uniform Chromaticity Scale [*Illuminant*]
UCS .... Uniform Communications System
UCS .... Union de Campesinos Salvadorcenos [*Peasant Union*] [*El Salvador*]
UCS .... Union of Catholic Students [*British*] (AEBS)
UCS .... Union of Concerned Scientists (EA)
UCS .... Unit of Coastal Sedimentation [*NERC*] [*British*]
UCS .... Unit Cost of Sales
UCS .... Unit-Count System
UCS .... United Community Services
UCS .... United Computing Systems, Inc.
UCS .... United Concerned Students (EA)
UCS .... United States Army Corps of Engineers, Sacramento, Sacramento, CA [*OCLC symbol*] (OCLC)

UCS	Universal Call Sequence
UCS	Universal Camera Site (KSC)
UCS	Universal Card Scanner [*Data processing*] (DIT)
UCS	Universal Cargo Sling
UCS	Universal Character Set [*Data processing*]
UCS	Universal Classification System
UCS	Universal Clothing System [*Software package*] (NCC)
UCS	Universal Command System (KSC)
UCS	Universal Connector Strip
UCS	Universal Control System (NASA)
UCS	University Computer Services [*Ball State University*] [*Research center*] (RCD)
UCS	University Computing Services [*State University of New York at Buffalo*] [*Research center*] (RCD)
UCS	University Computing Services [*University of Southern California*] [*Research center*] (RCD)
UCS	Urine Collection System [*NASA*] (KSC)
UCS	User Control Store
UCS	Utilities Control System [*NASA*] (KSC)
UCS	Utility Consulting Services [*Petroleum Information Corp.*] [*Information service or system*] (IID)
UCSA	Ukrainian Canadian Servicemen's Association
UCSA	Uniform Controlled Substances Act [*National Conference of Commissioners on Uniform State Laws*]
UCSA	Union des Confederations Sportives Africaines [*Association of African Sports Confederations - AASC*] [*Yaounde, Cameroon*] (EAIO)
UCSA	United Chian Societies of America [*Later, CSA*] (EA)
UCSB	University of California, Santa Barbara
UCSBS	Ukrainian Catholic Soyuz of Brotherhoods and Sisterhoods (EA)
UCSC........	University of California, Santa Cruz
UCSC........	University City Science Center [*Research center*] (RCD)
UCSD	Universal Communications Switching Device
UCSD	University of California, San Diego
UC-SDRL ...	University of Cincinnati Structural Dynamics Research Laboratory
UCSEL......	University of California Structural Engineering Laboratory (KSC)
UCSF........	University of California, San Francisco
UCSGS.....	University of Colorado. Studies. General Series [*A publication*]
UCSJ	Union of Councils for Soviet Jews (EA)
UCSL........	Union Congolaise des Syndicats Libres [*Congolese Union of Free Syndicates*] [*Leopoldville*]
UCSL........	University of California. Studies in Linguistics [*A publication*]
UCSLL......	University of Colorado. Studies. Series in Language and Literature [*A publication*]
UCSM	Utility Control Strategy Model [*Developed at Carnegie Mellon University for acid rain analysis*]
UCSMP.....	University of California. Studies in Modern Philology [*A publication*]
UCSR........	Ukrainian Center for Social Research (EA)
UCSR........	Unionist Committee for Social Reform [*British*]
UCSS........	Universal Communications Switching System (MCD)
UC/SSL.....	University of California/Space Sciences Laboratory (KSC)
UCSSLL....	University of Colorado. Studies. Series in Language and Literature [*A publication*]
UCST........	Upper Critical-Solution-Temperature
UCSTR	Universal Code Synchronous Transmitter Receiver
UCSU	United Carters' and Storemen's Union [*British*]
UCSUR......	University Center for Social and Urban Research [*University of Pittsburgh*] [*Research center*] (RCD)
UCSUS......	Ukrainian Catholic Students of the United States [*Defunct*] (EA)
UCT	Order of United Commercial Travelers of America [*Columbus, OH*] (EA)
UCT	Ultrasonic Computed Tomography [*For examining interiors of solids*]
UCT	Unchanged Conventional Treatment [*Medicine*]
UCT	Underwater Construction Team [*Navy*] (NVT)
UCT	Union Carbide Canada Equipment Trust Units [*Toronto Stock Exchange symbol*]
UCT	Unite Centrale de Traitement [*Central Processing Unit - CPU*] [*French*]
UCT	United Cable Television Corp. [*NYSE symbol*] (SPSG)
UCT	Units Compatibility Test
UCT	Universal Coordinated Time
UCT	University of Cape Town [*South Africa*]
UCT	University of Connecticut [*Storrs*] [*Seismograph station code, US Geological Survey*] (SEIS)
UCT	Urine Culture Tube [*Clinical chemistry*]
UCTA	University and College Theatre Association (EA)
UCTA	Urine Collection/Transfer Assembly [*Apollo*] [*NASA*]
UCTC	Union Camerounaise des Travailleurs Croyants [*Cameroonese Union of Believing Workers*]
UCTC	United Counties Bancorporation [*NASDAQ symbol*] (NQ)
UCTF........	Union Culturelle et Technique de Langue Francaise [*French-Language Cultural and Technical Union*] [*Paris, France*] (EA)
UCTL........	Up Control [*Aerospace*] (AAG)
UCTPA......	United Coppersmiths Trade Protection Association [*A union*] [*British*]
UCTS........	United Chairmakers' Trade Society [*A union*] [*British*]
UCTS........	United Church Training School
UCTSE......	University of Cape Town. Studies in English [*A publication*]
UCU..........	University of California Union List, Berkeley, CA [*OCLC symbol*] (OCLC)
UCU..........	Utilicorp United, Inc. [*NYSE symbol*] [*Toronto Stock Exchange symbol*] (SPSG)
UCUE........	Udmurt Commodity Universal Exchange [*Russian Federation*] (EY)
UCV..........	Uncontrolled Variable
UCV..........	Unimproved Capital Value [*Business term*] (ADA)
UCV..........	United Confederate Veterans
UCW..........	Union of Communications Workers [*British*] (ECON)
UCW..........	Unit Control Word [*Data processing*] (BUR)
UCW..........	United Church Women of the National Council of Churches (EA)
UCW..........	University College of Wales
UCW..........	University of Connecticut, Storrs, CT [*OCLC symbol*] (OCLC)
UCWA........	United Construction Workers Association (OICC)
UCWE.......	Underwater Countermeasures and Weapons Establishment [*British*]
UCWR.......	Universities Council on Water Resources (MCD)
UCWR.......	Upon Completion Thereof Will Return To [*Air Force*]
UCWRE	Underwater Countermeasures and Weapons Research Establishment [*British militar y*] (DMA)
UCX..........	UC Corp. [*Formerly, Universal Communication Systems, Inc.*] [*AMEX symbol*] (SPSG)
UCX..........	Unemployment Compensation, Ex-Servicemen
UCX..........	Utility Jet Transport [*Air Force*]
UCY..........	Union City, TN [*Location identifier*] [*FAA*] (FAAL)
UCY..........	United Caribbean Youth
UCYM.......	United Christian Youth Movement [*Defunct*] (EA)
UD	Fast Air Ltda. [*Chile*] [*ICAO designator*] (FAAC)
UD	Ulnar Deviation [*Medicine*]
UD	Ultimate Dependability [*Automotive designation*]
UD	Unable to Approve Departure for the Time Specified [*Aviation*] (FAAC)
UD	Unavoidable Delay
UD	Undated
U/D............	Under Deck (ADA)
UD	Underdrive [*Automotive engineering*]
UD	Underground Distribution (MSA)
UD	Underwater Demolition [*Navy*] (NVT)
UD	Undesirable Discharge [*Military*]
UD	Undetected Defect
UD	Undifferentiated (BJA)
UD	Undiluted
UD	Unidentifiable (BJA)
UD	Unidirectional
UD	Uniflow Diesel [*Nissan-designed engine*]
UD	Union Democratique [*New Caledonia*] [*Political party*] (EY)
UD	Unit Designation
UD	Unit Diary
UD	Unit Director
UD	Unit Dose [*Medicine*]
UD	Unity-and-Diversity World Council (EA)
UD	Universal Dipole (DEN)
UD	University of Denver [*Colorado*]
U of D........	University of Detroit [*Michigan*]
U of D........	University of Dublin [*Ireland*]
UD	Unlawful Detainer [*Legal term for an eviction proceeding*]
UD	Unlisted Drugs [*A publication*]
UD	Unplanned Derating [*Electronics*] (IEEE)
U/D............	Up/Down (KSC)
UD	Update [*Data processing*] (NASA)
UD	Upper Deck [*Naval*]
UD	Urban District
UD	Urethral Discharge [*Medicine*]
UD	Uridine Diphosphate [*Biochemistry*] (AAMN)
UD	Uroporphyrinogen Decarboxylase [*Also, UDase*] [*An enzyme*]
UD	Usable Depth (MCD)
UD	Usage Data
UD	Ut Dictum [*As Directed*] [*Latin*]
UD	Utility Dog [*Dog show term*]
UDA..........	Ulster Defence Association
UDA..........	Ultrasonic Detergent Action
UDA..........	Union for Democratic Action
UDA..........	United States Department of the Interior, Alaska Resources, Anchorage, AK [*OCLC symbol*] (OCLC)
UDA..........	Universal Detective Association [*Defunct*] (EA)
UDA..........	Urban Development Agency [*British*]
UDA..........	Urtica Dioica Agglutinin [*Biochemistry*]
UDAA........	Unlawfully Driving Away Auto
UDAC........	User Digital Analog Controller
UDAG........	Urban Development Action Grant [*HUD*]
Udal..........	Udal's Fiji Law Reports [*A publication*] (DLA)
UDAM......	Universal Digital Avionics Module (MCD)
UDAP.......	Universal Digital Autopilot
UDAR.......	Universal Digital Adaptive Recognizer (IEEE)

UDAS .... Unified Direct Access System   (BUR)

UDAS .... Universal Data Acquisition System

UDAS .... Universal Database Access Service
[*Telecommunications*]   (TSSD)

UDase .... Uroporphyrinogen Decarboxylase [*Also, UD*] [*An enzyme*]

UDAT .... Unidata Systems, Inc. [*NASDAQ symbol*]   (NQ)

UDATS ..... Underwater Damage Assessment Television System   (DNAB)

U Day LR... University of Dayton. Law Review [*A publication*]

U Dayton L Rev ... University of Dayton. Law Review [*A publication*]

UDB .... Unified Data Base

UDB .... Union Democratique Bretonne - Unvaniezh Demokratel Breizh
[*Breton Democratic Union*] [*France*] [*Political
party*]   (PPW)

UDB .... Up-Data Buffer [*Data processing*]

UDC .... National Park Service, National Capital Region, Washington,
DC [*OCLC symbol*]   (OCLC)

UDC .... UDC Homes [*NYSE symbol*]   (SPSG)

UDC .... UDC Homes, Inc. [*Associated Press abbreviation*]   (APAG)

UDC .... UDC - Universal Development Ltd. [*Associated Press
abbreviation*]   (APAG)

UDC .... Ultrasonic Doppler Cardioscope [*Heartbeat monitor*]

UDC .... Underdeveloped Countries

UDC .... Underwater Decompression Computer [*Navy*]   (CAAL)

UDC .... Uniao Democratica de Cabo Verde [*Democratic Union of Cape
Verde*]

UDC .... Unidirectional Composite   (MCD)

UDC .... Union du Centre [*Mayotte*] [*Political party*]   (EY)

UDC .... Union of the Democratic Centre [*Sahara*] [*Political
party*]   (PPW)

UDC .... Union for Democratic Communications   (EA)

UDC .... Union of Democratic Control [*British*]

UDC .... Union Democratica Cristiana [*Christian Democratic Union*]
[*Bolivia*] [*Political party*]   (PPW)

UDC .... Union pour la Democratie Congolaise [*Political party*]   (EY)

UDC .... Union Democratique du Cameroun [*Political party*]   (EY)

UDC .... Union Democratique Centrafricaine [*Central African
Democratic Union*] [*Political party*]   (PPW)

UDC .... Union Democratique du Centre [*Democratic Union of the
Center*] [*Switzerland*] [*Political party*]   (PPE)

UDC .... Unit Deployment of Containers   (MCD)

UDC .... United Daughters of the Confederacy   (EA)

UDC .... Unity-and-Diversity Council [*Later, UD*]   (EA)

UDC .... Universal Decimal Classification [*Online database field
identifier*]

UDC .... Universal Digital Control

UDC .... Universal Disk Controller [*Central Point Software*]

UDC .... University of the District of Columbia

UDC .... Up-Down Counter

UDC .... Upper Dead Center

UDC .... Urban Development Corp. [*New York State agency*]

UDC .... Urban District Council [*British*]

UDC .... Ursodeoxycholate [*Biochemistry*]

UDC .... Ursodeoxycholic Acid

UDC .... User Designation Codes [*Navy*]   (NG)

UDC .... User Dissemination Circuit [*Air Force Weather Center*]

UDC .... Usual Diseases of Childhood [*Medicine*]

UDCA .... Undesirable Discharge, Trial by Civil Authorities [*Navy*]

UDCA .... Union pour la Defense des Commercants et des Artisans [*Union
for the Defense of Traders and Artisans*] [*France*] [*Political
party*]   (PPE)

UDCA .... Ursodeoxycholic Acid [*Pharmacology*]

UDCCS....... Uniform Data Classification Code Structure [*Navy*]   (NG)

UDCS .... United Data Collection System   (MCD)

UDCV .... Uniao Democratica de Cabo Verde [*Democratic Union of Cape
Verde*]

UDD .... Bermuda Dunes, CA [*Location identifier*] [*FAA*]   (FAAL)

UDD .... Bureau of Land Management, Denver, Denver, CO [*OCLC
symbol*]   (OCLC)

UDD .... Uddeholm [*Sweden*] [*Seismograph station code, US Geological
Survey*]   (SEIS)

UDD .... Ulster Diploma in Dairying

UDD .... Union pour la Democratie et le Developpement [*Mali*]
[*Political party*]   (EY)

UDD .... Union pour la Democratie et le Developpement Mayumba
[*Gabon*] [*Political party*]   (EY)

UDD .... Union Democratique Dahomeenne [*Benin*] [*Political party*]

UDDA....... Uniform Determination of Death Act [*National Conference of
Commissioners on Uniform State Laws*]

UDDE .... Undesirable Discharge, Desertion without Trial [*Navy*]

UDDF .... Up and Down Drafts [*Meteorology*]   (FAAC)

UDDIA ...... Union Democratique pour la Defense des Interets Africains
[*Democratic Union to Defend African Interests*]

UDDL .... Ultrasonic Dispersive Delay Line

UDDS .... Union para la Democracia y el Desarrollo Social [*Equatorial
Guinea*] [*Political party*]   (EY)

UDDS .... Urban Dynamometer Driving Schedule [*EPA engine test*]

UDE .... Underwater Detection Establishment [*British*]   (MCD)

UDE .... Undetermined Etiology

UDE .... Union Douaniere Equatoriale [*Equatorial Customs Union*]

UDE .... United States Fish and Wildlife Service, Region 2, Albuquerque,
NM [*OCLC symbol*]   (OCLC)

UDE .... Universal Data Entry

UDE .... Universal Data Exchange [*Data processing*]   (PCM)

UDEAC ..... Union Douaniere et Economique de l'Afrique Centrale [*Central
African Customs and Economic Union*]   (EAIO)

UDEAO..... Union Douaniere des Etats de l'Afrique et l'Ouest [*Customs
Union of West African States*] [*Later, CEAO*]

UDEC .... Unitized Digital Electronic Calculator   (MCD)

UDECMA-KMPT ... Parti Democratique Chretien Malgache [*Malagasy
Christian Democratic Party*] [*Political party*]   (PPW)

UDEFEC ... Union Democratique des Femmes Camerounaises
[*Cameroonese Democratic Women's Union*]

UDENAMO ... Uniao Democratica Nacional de Mocambique [*Mozambican
National Democratic Union*] [*Later, FRELIMO*] [*Political
party*]

Udenrigspolit Skr Ser 15 ... Udenrigspolitiske Skrifter. Serie 15 [*A
publication*]

UDET .... Universal Digital Element Tester   (MCD)

UDETA ..... Unsymmetric Diethyltrianine   (MCD)

U Det J Urb L ... University of Detroit. Journal of Urban Law [*A publication*]

U Det L J ... University of Detroit. Law Journal [*A publication*]

U Det L Rev ... University of Detroit. Law Review [*A publication*]   (DLA)

UDETO ...... Union Democratique Togolaise [*Togolese Democratic Union*]

U Detroit LJ ... University of Detroit. Law Journal [*A publication*]

UDF .... Boise Interagency Fire Center, Boise, ID [*OCLC
symbol*]   (OCLC)

UDF .... Federation Guadeloupeenne de l'Union pour la Democratie
Francaise [*Guadeloupe Federation of the Union for French
Democracy*] [*Political party*]   (PPW)

UDF .... UHF [*Ultrahigh Frequency*] Direction Finder   (FAAC)

UDF .... Ulster Defence Force

UDF .... Unducted Fan [*Type of prop engine developed by General
Electric Co.*]

UDF .... Union Defence Force [*British*]

UDF .... Union Democrata Foral [*Spain*] [*Political party*]   (EY)

UDF .... Union of Democratic Forces [*Bulgaria*] [*Political party*]

UDF .... Union of Democratic Forces [*Mauritania*] [*Political
party*]   (EY)

UDF .... Union pour la Democratie Francaise [*Union for French
Democracy*] [*Wallis and Futuna Islands*] [*Political
party*]   (EY)

UDF .... Union pour la Democratie Francaise [*Union for French
Democracy*] [*Mayotte*] [*Political party*]   (EY)

UDF .... Union pour la Democratie Francaise [*Union for French
Democracy*] [*France*] [*Political party*]   (PPW)

UDF .... Union pour la Democratie Francaise [*Union for French
Democracy*] [*New Caledonia*] [*Political party*]   (PPW)

UDF .... Union pour la Democratie Francaise [*Union for French
Democracy*] [*Reunion*] [*Political party*]   (PPW)

UDF .... Union pour la Democratie Francaise [*Union for French
Democracy*] [*French Guiana*] [*Political party*]   (PPW)

UDF .... Uniroyal, Dunlop, and Firestone [*Alternative translation of
South Africa's UDF, United Democratic Front.
Translation refers to method of execution consisting of
forcing a tire around the victim's body and setting it on
fire*]

UDF .... Unit Derating Factor [*Electronics*]   (IEEE)

UDF .... Unit Development Folder   (MCD)

UDF .... Unit Dining Facilities

UDF .... United Democratic Front [*India*] [*Political party*]   (PPW)

UDF .... United Democratic Front [*South Africa*] [*Political
party*]   (PPW)

UDF .... Upside-Down Flipper

UDF .... User-Defined Function [*Data processing*]   (PCM)

UDF .... Utility and Data Flow   (NASA)

UDFAA ..... Upholstery and Decorative Fabrics Association of America
[*Defunct*]   (EA)

UDFAM .... User-Defined File Access Method [*Data processing*]   (IT)

UDFE .... Undesirable Discharge, Fraudulent Enlistment [*Navy*]

UDFMA .... Upholstery and Drapery Fabric Manufacturers Association
[*Later, UFMA*]

UDFP .... Union Democratique des Forces du Progres [*Benin*] [*Political
party*]   (EY)

UDFT .... Union Democratique des Femmes Tunisiennes [*Democratic
Union of Tunisian Women*]

UDG .... National Fisheries Center, Kearneysville, WV [*OCLC
symbol*]   (OCLC)

UDG .... Unit Derated Generation [*Electronics*]   (IEEE)

UD(G)....... United Distillers (Guiness) [*Commercial firm*]

UDH .... National Park Service, Harpers Ferry Center, Harpers Ferry,
WV [*OCLC symbol*]   (OCLC)

UDH .... Universal Die Holder

UDH .... Unplanned Derated Hours [*Electronics*]   (IEEE)

UDHS .... Unit Demand History Summary [*Military*]   (AABC)

UDI .... Uberlandia [*Brazil*] [*Airport symbol*]   (OAG)

UDI .... Udine [*Italy*] [*Seismograph station code, US Geological
Survey*]   (SEIS)

UDI .... Unilateral Declaration of Independence [*of Southern Rhodesia*]

UDI .... Union Democratica Independiente [*Independent Democratic
Union*] [*Chile*] [*Political party*]   (PPW)

UDI .... Union Democratique des Independants [*Democratic Union of
Independents*] [*France*] [*Political party*]   (PPE)

UDI............ Unique Data Item　(MCD)
UDI............ United Dominion Industries Ltd. [*NYSE symbol*]　(SPSG)
UDI............ United States Department of the Interior, Natural Resources Library, Washington, DC [*OCLC symbol*]　(OCLC)
UDI............ Utility Data Institute [*Information service or system*]　(IID)
UDIA......... United Dairy Industry Association　(EA)
UDID......... Unique Data Item Description　(MCD)
U-Dink....... Upper Class - Double [*or Dual*] Income, No Kids [*Lifestyle classification*]
UDIR......... USAREUR Daily Intelligence Report　(MCD)
UDIRL...... University of Durham Industrial Research Laboratories [*British*]
UDIT .... Union pour la Defense des Interets du Tchad [*Union for the Defense of Chadian Interests*]
UDITPA.... Uniform Division of Income for Tax Purposes Act
UDITS....... Universal Digital Test Set
UDJ .... Northern Prairie Wildlife Research Center, Jamestown, ND [*OCLC symbol*]　(OCLC)
UDJM .... Union Democratique de la Jeunesse Marocaine [*Democratic Union of Moroccan Youth*]
UDJV .... Union Democratique de la Jeunesse Voltaique [*Voltaic Democratic Youth Union*]
UDK.......... United States Fish and Wildlife Service, Alaska Area Office, Anchorage, AK [*OCLC symbol*]　(OCLC)
UDK.......... Upper Deck
UDK.......... User Defined Key [*Data processing*]　(HGAA)
UDKKB ..... Utsunomiya Daigaku Kyoikugakubu Kiyo, Dai-2-Bu [*A publication*]
UDL.......... Bureau of Land Management, Boise District Office, Boise, ID [*OCLC symbol*]　(OCLC)
UDL.......... Ultrasonic Delay Line
UDL.......... Underwater Data Link　(MCD)
UDL.......... Uniform Data Language
UDL.......... Uniform Data Link
UDL.......... Unit Detail Listings [*Air Force*]
UDL.......... Unit Document Listing　(MCD)
UDL.......... Universal Development Laboratory [*Computer debugger*] [*Orion Instruments*]
UDL.......... Untersuchungen zur Deutschen Literaturgeschichte [*A publication*]
UDL.......... Up-Data Link [*Data processing*]
UDL.......... Urine Disposal Lock　(DNAB)
UDLP .... United Democratic Labour Party [*Trinidad and Tobago*] [*Political party*]　(PPW)
UDLP .... United Dominica Labour Party [*Political party*]　(PPW)
UDM .... National Mine Health and Safety Academy, Beckley, WV [*OCLC symbol*]　(OCLC)
UDM .... Unassigned Direct Material [*Navy*]　(DNAB)
UDM .... Unidimensional Drafting Manual
UDM .... Union of Democratic Mineworkers [*British*]
UDM .... Union Democratique Mauritanienne [*Mauritanian Democratic Union*] [*Political party*]　(PD)
UDM .... Universal Drafting Machine Corp.
UDM .... Upright Drilling Machine
UDMA...... United Dance Merchants of America　(EA)
UDMH ...... Unsymmetrical Dimethylhydrazine [*Rocket fuel base, convulsant poison*]
UDMH/H ... Unsymmetrical Dimethylhydrazine Hydrazine Blend　(NASA)
UDMU ...... Universal Decoder Memory Unit　(DNAB)
UDN .... National Park Service, National Register Division, Washington, DC [*OCLC symbol*]　(OCLC)
UDN .... Ulcerative Dermal Necrosis [*Medicine*]
UDN .... Underwater Doppler Navigation
UDN .... Uniao Democratica Nacional [*National Democratic Union*] [*Brazil*]
UDN .... Union Democrata Nacional [*National Democratic Union*] [*El Salvador*] [*Political party*]　(PPW)
UDN .... Union Democratica Nicaraguense [*Nicaraguan Democratic Union*] [*Political party*]　(PD)
UDNGA .... Utsonomiya Daigaku Nogakubu Gakujutsu Hokoku [*A publication*]
UDO .... Undetermined Origin [*Medicine*]　(AAMN)
UDO .... United States Fish and Wildlife Service, Billings, MT [*OCLC symbol*]　(OCLC)
Udobr Urozhai ... Udobrenie i Urozhai [*A publication*]
Udobr Urozhai Kom Khim Nar Khaz SSSR ... Udobrenie i Urozhai. Komitet po Khimaisatsii Narodnogo Khozyaistva SSSR [*A publication*]
Udobr Urozhai Minist Sel'sk Khoz SSSR ... Udobrenie i Urozhai. Ministerstvo Sel'skogo Khozyaistva SSSR [*A publication*]
UDOFT ..... Universal Digital Operational Flight Trainer [*Navy*]
UDomIn..... United Dominion Industries Ltd. [*Associated Press abbreviation*]　(APAG)
UDomR...... United Dominion Realty Trust, Inc. [*Associated Press abbreviation*]　(APAG)
UDOP....... UHF [*Ultrahigh Frequency*] Doppler System
UDOP....... Ultrahigh Doppler　(NASA)
UDP.......... National Park Service, Denver, Denver, CO [*OCLC symbol*]　(OCLC)
UDP.......... Ulster Diploma in Poultry Husbandry

UDP.......... Uniao Democratica Popular [*Popular Democratic Unity*] [*Portugal*] [*Political party*]
UDP.......... Unidad Democratica Popular [*Popular Democratic Unity*] [*Peru*] [*Political party*]　(PPW)
UDP.......... Unidad Democratica Popular [*Popular Democratic Unity*] [*Bolivia*] [*Political party*]
UDP.......... Unification du Droit Prive
UDP.......... Union pour la Democratie Populaire [*Union for People's Democracy*] [*Senegal*] [*Political party*]　(PPW)
UDP.......... United Data Processing　(BUR)
UDP.......... United Democratic Party [*Basotho*] [*Political party*]　(PPW)
UDP.......... United Democratic Party [*Belize*] [*Political party*]　(PD)
UDP.......... Uridine Diphosphate [*Biochemistry*]
UDP.......... User Datagram Protocol　(BYTE)
UDPAG .... Uridine(diphospho)acetylglucosamine [*Biochemistry*]
UDPB .... Union des Democrates et Patriotes Burkinabe [*Burkino Faso*] [*Political party*]　(EY)
UDPC....... UNIVAC Data Processing Center　(HGAA)
UDPG....... Uridine Diphosphate Glucose [*Biochemistry*]
UDPGA..... Uridine Diphosphate Glucuronic Acid [*Biochemistry*]
UDPGDH ... Uridinediphosphoglucose Dehydrogenase [*An enzyme*]
UDPGT ..... Uridine Diphosphate Glucuronosyltransferase [*An enzyme*] [*Biochemistry*]
UDPIA ...... Uniform Disclaimer of Property Interests Act [*National Conference of Commissioners on Uniform State Laws*]
UDP/IP ..... User Datagram Protocol/Internet Protocol [*Data processing*]
UDPK .... United Democratic Party of Kurdistan [*Political party*]　(BJA)
UDPL .... United Dated Parts List [*Configuration listing*]　(MCD)
UDPM....... Union Democratique du Peuple Malien [*Mali People's Democratic Union*] [*Political party*]　(PPW)
UDPS........ Union pour la Democratie et le Progres Social [*Democratic Union of Social Progress*] [*Political party*] [*Zaire*]
UDPS........ Union pour le Developpement et le Progres Social [*The Congo*] [*Political party*]　(EY)
UDPT .... Union Democratique des Populations Togolaises [*Democratic Union of Togolese People*]
UDQ .... Bureau of Land Management, Library, New Orleans, New Orleans, LA [*OCLC symbol*]　(OCLC)
UDQ .... University of Denver. Quarterly [*A publication*]
UDR.......... Udaipur [*India*] [*Airport symbol*]　(OAG)
UDR.......... Ulster Defence Regiment [*Military unit*] [*British*]
UDR.......... Undersampling Ratio
UDR.......... Union pour la Defense de la Republique [*Union for the Defense of the Republic*] [*France*] [*Political party*]　(PPE)
UDR.......... Union pour la Democratie Francaise [*Union for French Democracy*] [*Martinique*] [*Political party*]　(PPW)
UDR.......... United Dominion Realty Trust, Inc. [*NYSE symbol*]　(SPSG)
UDR.......... United States Department of the Interior, Bureau of Reclamation, Denver, CO [*OCLC symbol*]　(OCLC)
UDR.......... Universal Digital Readout
UDR.......... Universal Document Reader　(BUR)
UDR.......... University of Dayton. Review [*A publication*]
UDR.......... Urgent Data Request [*GIDEP*]
UDR.......... Usage Data Report
UDR.......... Utility Data Reduction
UDRA....... Uniform Divorce Recognition Act [*National Conference of Commissioners on Uniform State Laws*]
UDRA....... United Drag Racers Association　(EA)
UDRC....... Utility Data Retrieval Control
UDRI........ University of Dayton Research Institute [*Ohio*]
UDRN....... Union pour la Democratie et la Reconstruction Nationale [*Benin*] [*Political party*]　(EY)
UDRO....... Utility Data Retrieval Output
UDRP........ Uridine Diribose Phosphate [*Biochemistry*]
UDRPS..... Ultrasonic Data Recording and Processing System　(NRCH)
UDRS .... Union Democratique pour le Renouveau Social [*Benin*] [*Political party*]　(EY)
UDRS .... Universal Driver Rating System [*Harness racing*]
UDRT/RAD ... Union Democratique pour le Respect du Travail - Respect voor Arbeid en Democratie [*Democratic Union for the Respect of Labor*] [*Belgium*] [*Political party*]　(PPW)
U/DRV ...... Underdrive [*Automotive engineering*]
UDS........... Office of Surface Mining Reclamation and Enforcement, Region V, Denver, CO [*OCLC symbol*]　(OCLC)
UDS........... Ultraviolet Detector System
UDS........... Unified Data System [*Data processing*]
UDS........... Union pour la Democratie et la Solidarite Nationale [*Benin*] [*Political party*]　(EY)
UDS........... Union Democratique Senegalaise [*Senegalese Democratic Union*]
UDS........... Unit Data System [*Military*]
UDS........... Universal Data Set　(CMD)
UDS........... Universal Data System [*Army*]
UDS........... Universal Data Systems [*Hardware manufacturer*]
UDS........... Universal Digital Switch　(MCD)
UDS........... Universal Distributed System [*UNIVAC*]
UDS........... Universal Documentation System [*NASA*]
UDS........... Unscheduled DNA Synthesis [*Genetics*]
UDS........... Urban Data Service [*International City Management Association*]　(IID)

UDS...........	Urban Decision Systems, Inc. [*Information service or system*] (IID)
UDS...........	Utility Data Systems [*Information service or system*] (IID)
UDS...........	Utilization and Disposal Service [*Functions transferred to Property Management and Disposal Service*] [*General Services Administration*]
UDSG........	Union Democratique et Sociale Gabonaise [*Gabonese Democratic and Social Union*]
UDSKD.....	Udenrigspolitiske Skrifter. Serie 15 [*A publication*]
UDSL........	Union of Scientific Leisure Clubs [*France*] (EAIO)
UDSM.......	Union des Democrates Sociaux de Madagascar [*Union of Social Democrats of Madagascar*]
UDSM.......	Union Departementale de Syndicats du Mungo [*Departmental Union of the Trade Unions of Mungo*] [*Cameroon*]
UDSR........	Union Democratique et Socialiste de la Resistance [*Democratic and Socialist Union of the Resistance*] [*France*] [*Political party*] (PPE)
UDSR........	United Duroc Swine Registry (EA)
UDT..........	Underdeck Tonnage
UDT..........	Underwater Demolition Team [*Navy*]
UDT..........	Union of Democratic Thais in the US (EA)
UDT..........	United Detector Technology
UDT..........	United States Fish and Wildlife Service, Science Reference Library, Twin Cities, MN [*OCLC symbol*] (OCLC)
UDT...........	United Tire & Rubber Co. Ltd. [*Toronto Stock Exchange symbol*]
UDT..........	Universal Data Transcriber [*Navy*]
UDT..........	Universal Document Transport [*Data processing*] (OA)
UDT..........	Upgraded Data Terminal (MCD)
UDT..........	User Display Terminal
UDT.........	Utility Dog Tracker [*Degree of obedience training*]
UDTC........	User-Dependent-Type Code
UDTD.......	Updated (MSA)
UDTDET...	Underwater Demolition Team Detachment [*Navy*] (NVT)
UDT/EOD ...	Underwater Demolition Team/Explosive Ordnance Proposal [*Navy*] (MCD)
UDTI........	Universal Digital Transducer Indicator
UDTPHIBSPAC ...	Underwater Demolition Teams, Amphibious Forces, Pacific Fleet [*Navy*]
UDTS	Universal Data Transfer Service [*ITT World Communications, Inc.*] [*Secaucus, NJ*] [*Telecommunications*] (TSSD)
UDTS	Universal Data Transmission System [*For international access*]
UDTUNIA ...	Uniform Disclaimer of Transfers under Nontestamentary Instruments Act [*National Conference of Commissioners on Uniform State Laws*]
UDTX........	Utility Dog and Tracking Excellent [*Degree of obedience training*]
UDU	National Maritime Museum, San Francisco, CA [*OCLC symbol*] (OCLC)
UDU	Unabhaengige Demokratische Union [*Independent Democratic Union*] [*Austria*] [*Political party*] (PPE)
UDU	Underwater Demolition Unit
UDU	Union Democratique Unioniste [*Tunisia*] [*Political party*] (EY)
UDUAL.....	Union de Universidades de America Latina [*Union of Latin American Universities*] [*Mexico*]
UDucGS	Church of Jesus Christ of Latter-Day Saints, Genealogical Society Library, Duchesne Branch, Stake Center, Duchesne, UT [*Library symbol*] [*Library of Congress*] (LCLS)
UDUF........	Undesirable Discharge, Unfitness [*Navy*]
UDUPA.....	Uniform Distribution of Unclaimed Property Act [*National Conference of Commissioners on Uniform State Laws*]
UDURA.....	Udobrenie i Urozhai [*Ministerstvo Sel'skogo Khozyaistva SSSR*] [*A publication*]
UDV..........	Union Democratique Voltaique [*Voltaic Democratic Union*] [*Banned, 1974*]
UD-Ve........	Union Democratique pour la Cinquieme Republique [*Democratic Union for the Fifth Republic*] [*France*] [*Political party*] (PPE)
UDW	Ultradeep Water
UDW	Western Energy and Land Use Team, Fort Collins, CO [*OCLC symbol*] (OCLC)
UDX..........	Office of Surface Mining Reclamation and Enforcement, Washington, DC [*OCLC symbol*] (OCLC)
UDX..........	Utility Dog Excellent [*Dog show term*] [*Canada*]
UDY..........	USGS [*United States Geological Survey*] Water Resources Division, New York District, Albany, NY [*OCLC symbol*] (OCLC)
UDZ..........	United States Department of the Interior, Western Archeological Center, Tucson, AZ [*OCLC symbol*] (OCLC)
UE..............	Ultrasonic Engineering (MCD)
UE..............	Unemployment (GFGA)
UE..............	Unexpired (ADA)
UE..............	Unit Entry
UE..............	Unit Equipment [*as authorized to an Air Force unit*]
UE..............	Unit Establishment
UE..............	Unit Exception (CMD)
UE..............	Unit Exhausted [*Military*] (GFGA)
UE..............	United Air Services [*South Africa*] [*ICAO designator*] (FAAC)

UE..............	United Electrical, Radio, and Machine Workers of America (EA)
UE..............	United Electrical, Radio, and Machine Workers of Canada [*See also OUE*]
UE..............	United Electrodynamics (AAG)
UE..............	United Empire [*Canada*]
UE..............	Unity of Empire [*Award*] [*British*]
UE..............	Universale Economica [*A publication*]
UE..............	University Extension
UE..............	Until Exhausted
UE..............	Update and Ephemeria (MUGU)
UE..............	Upper Entrance [*Theater*]
UE..............	Upper Epidermis [*Botany*]
UE..............	Upper Extremity [*Medicine*]
UE..............	Urinary Energy [*Nutrition*]
UE..............	Use of English [*A publication*]
UE..............	User Equipment
UE..............	Uterine Epithelium [*Medicine*]
UEA..........	Graphic Arts Union Employers of America (EA)
UEA..........	Ulex europeus Agglutinin [*Immunology*]
UEA..........	Unattended Equipment Area
UEA..........	Union of European Abattoirs [*Belgium*] (EAIO)
UEA..........	Union Europeenne de l'Ameublement [*European Furniture Manufacturers Federation*] (EAIO)
UEA..........	Union Europeenne des Aveugles [*European Blind Union - EBU*] (EAIO)
UEA..........	United Egg Association (EA)
UEA..........	United Epilepsy Association [*Later, EFA*] (EA)
UEA..........	United Evangelical Action [*A publication*]
UEA..........	Universala Esperanto Asocio [*Universal Esperanto Association*] (EAIO)
UEA..........	University of East Anglia [*England*]
UEA..........	Uranium Enrichment Associates [*Bechtel Corp., Union Carbide Corp., Westinghouse Electric Corp.*]
UEAC.......	Union of Central African States
UEAC.......	Unit Equipment Aircraft
UEAC.......	United European American Club
UEAES......	Union Europeenne des Alcools, Eaux de Vie et Spiritueux [*European Union of Alcohol, Brandies and Spirits*] [*EC*] (ECED)
UEAI	Ulex Europaeus Agglutinin I
UEAI	Union Europeenne des Arabisants et des Islamisants [*European Union of Arab and Islamic Studies - EUAIS*] [*Spain*] (EAIO)
UEAPME ...	Union Europeenne de l'Artisanat et des Petites et Moyennes Entreprises [*European Association of Craft, Small and Medium-Sized Enterprises*] [*EC*] (ECED)
U East LJ ..	University of the East. Law Journal [*Manila, Philippines*] [*A publication*] (DLA)
UEAtc........	Union Europeenne pour l'Agrement Technique dans la Construction [*European Union of Agrement*] (EAIO)
UEAWS.....	Union of European Associations of Water Suppliers [*Belgium*] (EAIO)
Ueb............	Uebereinkommen [*Agreement*] [*German*] (ILCA)
UEB	Ultrasonic Epoxy Bonder
UEB	Unexploded Bomb
UEB	Union Economique BENELUX
UEB	Union of Evangelical Baptists (EAIO)
UEB	Upper Equipment Bay [*NASA*] (KSC)
UEBC	Union Espanola Benefica de California (EA)
Ueberr Tb ..	Ueberreuter Taschenbuecher [*A publication*]
Uebersee Rdsch ...	Uebersee Rundschau [*A publication*]
UEC..........	Union Electric Co.
UEC..........	Union des Etudiants Communistes [*France*]
UEC..........	Union Europeenne de la Carrosserie [*European Union of Coachbuilders - EUC*] [*Belgium*]
UEC..........	Union Europeenne des Experts Comptables Economiques et Financiers [*European Union of Public Accountants*]
UEC..........	Unit Endurance Chamber (MCD)
UEC..........	United Engineering Center
UEC..........	Unmanned Equipment Cabinet
UEC..........	Upper Epidermal Cell [*Botany*]
UEC..........	Urban Elderly Coalition (EA)
UEC..........	Urban Environment Conference (EA)
UEC..........	USS Engineers & Consultants, Inc. [*Information service or system*] (IID)
UECA........	Underground Engineering Contractors Association [*Later, ECA*] (EA)
UECA	Union Europeenne du Commerce Ambulant [*European Union of Door-to-Door Trade*] [*EC*] (ECED)
UECB	Union Europeenne des Commerces du Betail
UECBV......	Union Europeenne du Commerce du Betail et de la Viande [*European Livestock and Meat Trading Union*] (EAIO)
UECL.........	Union Europeenne des Constructeurs de Logements [*European Union of Independent Building Contractors*]
UECS.........	Unified Electronic Computer System [*Air Force*]
UECU	Union for Experimenting Colleges and Universities [*Later, UI*] (EA)
UED..........	Uranian Electrostatic Discharge [*Planetary science*]
UEDC........	Union Europeenne Democrate Chretienne [*European Christian Democratic Union*]

UEDS .... Uniao de Esquerda para a Democracia Socialista [*Left Union for Social Democracy*] [*Portugal*] [*Political party*]   (PPE)
UEE .... Queenstown [*Australia*] [*Airport symbol*]   (OAG)
UEE .... Unit Essential Equipment [*Military*]   (NATG)
UEE .... US Commercial Newsletter [*The Hague*] [*A publication*]
UEEA .... Union Europeenne des Exploitants d'Abbatoirs [*European Abbatoirs Union*] [*EC*]   (ECED)
UEEB........ Union des Exploitations Electriques en Belgique
UEEBA...... Bulletin. Utah Engineering Experiment Station [*A publication*]
U/EECM... Unattended/Expendable Electronic Countermeasure
UEEJ .... Union Europeenne des Etudiants Juifs [*European Union of Jewish Students - EUJS*]   (EA)
UEES Report ... Utah. Engineering Experiment Station. Report [*A publication*]
UEF .... Uniform Electric Field
UEF .... Union Europaeischer Forstberufsverbaende [*Union of European Foresters*] [*Teningen-Heimbach, Federal Republic of Germany*]   (EAIO)
UEF .... Union Europeenne des Federalistes
UEF .... Union Europeenne Feminine [*European Union of Women*]
UEF .... Upper End Fitting [*Nuclear energy*]   (NRCH)
UEFA........ Union of European Football Associations [*Switzerland*]   (EAIO)
UEFJA ...... Uniform Enforcement of Foreign Judgments Act [*National Conference of Commissioners on Uniform State Laws*]
UEFJM ..... Union of European Fashion Jewellery Manufacturers [*Italy*]   (EAIO)
UEFS .... United Enginemen's Friendly Society [*A union*] [*British*]
UEI .... Union of Educational Institutions [*British*]
UEI .... Union Energy [*Toronto Stock Exchange symbol*]   (SPSG)
UEIC......... United East India Co.
UEIES .... Uppsala English Institute. Essays and Studies [*A publication*]
UEIL.......... Union Europeenne des Independants en Lubrifiants [*European Union of Independent Lubricant Manufacturers*] [*EC*]   (ECED)
UEIS......... United Engineering Information System
UEITP .... Union Europeenne des Industries de Transformation de Pomme de Terre [*European Union of the Potato Processing Industries*]
UEJ........... Unattended Expendable Jammer   (MCD)
UEJ........... University of Edinburgh. Journal [*A publication*]
UEJDC...... Union Europeenne des Jeunes Democrates-Chretiens [*European Union of Young Christian Democrats*]
UEK .... Elmira, NY [*Location identifier*] [*FAA*]   (FAAL)
UEL .... Quelimane [*Mozambique*] [*Airport symbol*]   (OAG)
UEL .... Underwater Environmental Laboratory [*General Electric Co.*]
UEL .... United Empire Loyalist
UEL .... Uomini e Libri [*A publication*]
UEL .... Upper Electrical Limit [*Nuclear energy*]   (NRCH)
UEL .... Upper Explosive Limit
UEL .... Usage Exception List   (MCD)
UE Law J ... University of the East. Law Journal [*Manila, Philippines*] [*A publication*]   (DLA)
UELF .... Union des Editeurs de Langue Francaise   (EAIO)
UELJ .... UE [*University of the East*] Law Journal [*Manila*] [*A publication*]
UELL......... Chulman [*Former USSR*] [*ICAO location identifier*]   (ICLI)
UEM.......... Union Electrica Madrilena [*Spain*]
UEM.......... Union Europeenne de Malacologie [*European Malacological Union*]
UEM.......... Union Evangelique Mondiale [*World Evangelical Fellowship*]
UEM.......... Unite Electromagnetique [*Electromagnetic Unit*]
UEM.......... Universal Electron Microscope
UEM........ University Extension Manuals [*A publication*]
UEMC .... Unidentified Endosteal Marrow Cell [*Hematology*]
UEMN....... Union des Ecrivains du Monde Noir [*World Union of Black Writers - WUBW*]   (EAIO)
UEMO...... Europaische Vereinigung der Allgemeinartze [*European Union of General Practitioners*] [*Denmark*]   (EAIO)
UEMO...... Union Europeenne des Medecins Omnipraticiens [*European Union of General Practitioners*]   (EA)
UEMS .... Union Europeenne des Medecins Specialistes [*European Society of Medical Specialists*] [*Belgium*]   (SLS)
UEMS .... Unione Europea di Medicina Sociale [*European Union of Social Medicine - EUSM*]   (EAIO)
UEMTA .... European Union for the Prevention of Cruelty to Animals   (EAIO)
UEN.......... Unisave Energy Ltd. [*Vancouver Stock Exchange symbol*]
UENCPB... Union Europeenne des Negociants en Cuirs et Peaux Bruts [*European Association of Traders in Leather and Raw Hides*] [*EC*]   (ECED)
UENDC..... Union Europeenne des Negociants Detaillants en Combustibles [*European Union of Merchant Dealers in Combustibles*] [*Switzerland*]
UEO.......... Kume Jima [*Japan*] [*Airport symbol*]   (OAG)
UEO.......... Union of Electrical Operatives [*British*]
UEO.......... Union de l'Europe Occidentale [*Western European Union - WEU*]   (EAIO)
UEO.......... Unit Emplaning Officer [*Military*] [*British*]
UEOA........ Union des Etudiants Ouest Africains [*Union of West African Students*]

UEP .... Underwater Electric Potential
UEP .... Unequal Error Protection   (IEEE)
UEP .... Uniform External Pressure
UEP .... Union Electric Co. [*NYSE symbol*]   (SPSG)
UEP .... Union Europeenne de Pedopsychiatres [*European Union for Child Psychiatry*]
UEP .... Unit Evolutionary Period
UEP .... United Egg Producers   (EA)
UEP .... Unplanned Event Pickup [*NASA*]   (KSC)
UEP .... Unusual End of Program [*Data processing*]
UEPC......... Union Europeenne des Promoteurs Constructeurs [*European Union of Developers and House Builders*] [*Belgium*]   (EAIO)
UEPEDY... US Environmental Protection Agency. Office of Air and Waste Management. EPA-450 [*A publication*]
UEPH........ Unaccompanied Enlisted Personnel Housing [*Navy*]   (DNAB)
UEPMD .... Union Europeenne des Practiciens en Medecine Dentaire [*European Union of Dental Medicine Practitioners*]   (EAIO)
UEPR........ Unsatisfactory Equipment Performance Report [*Military*]   (AABC)
UEPS........ Union Europeenne des Pharmacies Sociales [*European Union of the Social Pharmacies*] [*EC*]   (ECED)
UEPS........ Union Europeenne de la Presse Sportive [*European Sports Press Union*]   (EAIO)
UEPS........ United Elvis Presley Society   (EAIO)
UER.......... Union Europeenne de Radiodiffusion [*European Broadcasting Union - EBU*]   (EAIO)
UER.......... Unique Equipment Register   (NASA)
UER.......... Unite d'Enseignement et de Recherche [*Units of Teaching and Research*] [*University of Paris*]
UER.......... Uniunea Evreilor Romani   (BJA)
UER.......... University Entrance Requirement [*British*]   (DI)
UER.......... Unplanned Event Record [*NASA*]   (KSC)
UER.......... Unsatisfactory Equipment Report
UER.......... Ust-Elegest [*Former USSR*] [*Seismograph station code, US Geological Survey*]   (SEIS)
UERA .... Umbilical Ejection Relay Assembly   (AAG)
UERA .... Uniform Extradition and Rendition Act [*National Conference of Commissioners on Uniform State Laws*]
UERD........ Underwater Explosives Research Division [*Navy*]
UERDC ..... Underwater Explosion Research and Development Center [*Navy*]   (CAAL)
UERE .... Ultrasonic Echo Ranging Equipment
UERE .... User Equivalent Range Error
UERG .... Universitywide Energy Research Group [*University of California*] [*Research center*]   (RCD)
UERL........ Underwater Explosives Research Laboratory
UERL........ Unplanned Event Record Log [*NASA*]   (KSC)
UERMWA ... United Electrical, Radio, and Machine Workers of America
UERP......... Unione Europea di Relazioni Pubbliche [*European Union of Public Relations - International Service Organization - EURPISO*]   (EAIO)
UERPS...... Uniform Excess Reporting Procedures [*DoD*]
UERS........ Unusual Event Recording System [*Jet transport*]
UERT .... Union Explosivos-Rio Tinto [*Spain*]
UERT .... Universal Engineer Tractor, Rubber-Tired [*Army*]
UES .... Snow College, Ephraim, UT [*Library symbol*] [*Library of Congress*]   (LCLS)
UES .... Uniform Emission Standard   (DCTA)
UES .... UNISA [*University of South Africa*] English Studies [*A publication*]
UES .... United Engineering Steels [*Commercial firm*] [*British*]
UES .... Universal Environmental Shelter   (KSC)
UES .... University Extension Series [*A publication*]
UES .... Upper Esophageal Sphincter [*Anatomy*]
UES .... Upstream Expression Sequence [*Genetics*]
UES .... Waukesha, WI [*Location identifier*] [*FAA*]   (FAAL)
UESA........ Ukrainian Engineers' Society of America   (EA)
UESC........ Union Electric Steel Corp. [*NASDAQ symbol*]   (NQ)
UESD .... Uniao da Esquerda Socialista Democratica [*Union of the Socialist and Democratic Left*] [*Portugal*] [*Political party*]   (PPW)
UESEG...... United Earth Sciences Exploration Group [*British*]
UESK........ Unit Emergency Supply Kit
UESK........ Unit Essential Spares Kit [*Military*]   (AFM)
UESPDE ... University of Tasmania. Environmental Studies Working Paper [*A publication*]
UESS .... United Education & Software, Inc. [*NASDAQ symbol*]   (NQ)
UEST........ Institute of Urban and Environmental Studies [*Brock University*] [*Canada*] [*Research center*]   (RCD)
UET .... Quetta [*Pakistan*] [*Airport symbol*]   (OAG)
UET .... Unattended Earth Terminal
UET .... Unit Equipment Table [*Military*]
UET .... United Engineering Trustees   (EA)
UET .... Universal Emulating Terminal
UET .... Universal Engineer Tractor [*Later, BEST*] [*Army*]
UET .... Universal Expenditure Tax [*British*]   (DI)
UET .... Ur Excavations: Texts [*London*] [*A publication*]   (BJA)
UETA .... Universal Engineer Tractor, Armored [*Army*]
UETRT...... Universal Engineer Tractor, Rubber-Tired [*Army*]

UEVP .... Union Europeenne des Veterinaires Practiciens [*European Union of Practising Veterinary Surgeons*]   (EAIO)
UEW .... United Electrical Workers
UEWS .... Ultimate Elastic Wall Stress [*Mechanical engineering*]
UEX .... Underexposed [*Photography*]
UEX .... Ur Excavations [*A publication*]   (BJA)
UF .... All Cargo Airlines Ltd. [*Great Britain*] [*ICAO designator*]   (FAAC)
UF .... Ugarit-Forschungen [*A publication*]
UF .... Ulster Folklife [*Belfast*] [*A publication*]
UF .... Ultrafilter [*or Ultrafiltration*]
UF .... Ultrafine
UF .... Ultrasonic Frequency   (MSA)
UF .... Unavailability Factor [*Electronics*]   (IEEE)
UF .... Under Frequency   (DNAB)
UF .... Underground Feeder
UF .... Unemployed Father   (OICC)
UF .... Uni Air International [*France*] [*ICAO designator*]   (ICDA)
UF .... Unified Forces [*Military*]
UF .... Union Fidelity Corp. [*NYSE symbol*]   (SPSG)
UF .... Union de Fribourg: Institut International des Sciences Sociales et Politiques [*Union de Fribourg: International Institute of Social and Political Sciences*] [*Fribourg/Pensier, Switzerland*]   (EAIO)
UF .... Unit of Fire [*Military*]   (MUGU)
UF .... United Focus [*Later, Omni Learning Institute*]   (EA)
UF .... United Force [*Guyana*]   (PD)
UF .... United Foundation
UF .... United Front [*Sri Lanka*] [*Political party*]   (FEA)
UF .... Uniterra Foundation   (EA)
UF .... Universities Funding Council [*British*]
UF .... University of Florida [*Gainesville*]
UF .... Unknown Factor
UF .... Unofficial Funds [*British*]
U & F .... Unterricht und Forschung [*A publication*]
UF .... Upper Air Fallout [*Civil Defense*]
UF .... Urea Formaldehyde
UF .... Used For
UF .... Utility File
UF .... Utilization Factor
UFA .... Ukrainian Fraternal Association   (EA)
UFA .... Unesterified Fatty Acid [*Biochemistry*]
UFA .... Uniform Firearms Act
UFA .... Uniformed Firefighters Association
UFA .... Union des Femmes d'Algerie [*Union of Algerian Women*]
UFA .... Union of Flight Attendants   (EA)
UFA .... United Families of America   (EA)
UFA .... United Fathers of America   (EA)
UFA .... University Film Association [*Later, UFVA*]   (EA)
UFA .... Universum-Film Aktien-Gesellschaft [*German motion picture company*]
UFA .... Unsaturated Fatty Acid [*Organic chemistry*]
UFA .... Until Further Advised
UFA .... Usable Floor Area [*Classified advertising*]   (ADA)
UFA .... Use Frequency Analysis
UFAA .... United Food Animal Association   (EA)
UFAC .... Unlawful Flight to Avoid Custody
UFAC .... Upholstered Furniture Action Council   (EA)
UFAED ...... Unit Forecast Authorization Equipment Data   (AFM)
UFAJ .... University Film Association. Journal [*A publication*]
UFAM .... Universal File Access Method
UFAP .... Ultrafine Ammonium Perchlorate   (MCD)
UFAP .... Union Francaise des Annuaires Professionels [*French Union for Professional Yearbooks*] [*Trappes*] [*Information service or system*]   (IID)
UFAP .... Universal-Fine Ammonium Perchlorate [*Organic chemistry*]   (MCD)
UFAP .... Unlawful Flight to Avoid Prosecution
UFA Rev Union Fed Coop Agric Suisse ... UFA Revue. Union des Federations Cooperatives Agricoles de la Suisse [*A publication*]
UFAS .... Unified Flight Analysis System [*NASA*]
UFAS .... Uniform Federal Accessibility Standards [*Department of Housing and Urban Development*]   (GFGA)
UFAT .... Unlawful Flight to Avoid Testimony
UFAW .... Universities Federation for Animal Welfare [*British*]
UFAW Courr ... UFAW [*Universities Federation for Animal Welfare*] Courrier [*A publication*]
UFAWU .... United Fishermen and Allied Workers' Union [*Canada*]
UFB .... Unfit for Broadcast   (WDMC)
UFBC .... United Financial Banking Companies, Inc. [*NASDAQ symbol*]   (NQ)
UFBK .... United Federal Bancorp, Inc. [*NASDAQ symbol*]   (NQ)
UFBS .... Union des Francais de Bon Sens [*Union of Frenchmen of Good Sense*] [*Political party*]   (PPW)
UFBS .... United Friendly Boilermakers' Society [*A union*] [*British*]
UFC .... Unidirectional Filamentary Composite
UFC .... Unified Fire Control   (MCD)
UFC .... Uniform Freight Classification
UFC .... Union des Facteurs du Canada [*Letter Carriers' Union of Canada - LCUC*]
UFC .... Unit Funded Costs   (MCD)

UFC .... United Flight Classification
UFC .... United Flowers-by-Wire Canada
UFC .... United Free Church [*Scotland*]
UFC .... Universal Flight Computer
UFC .... Universal Foods Corp. [*NYSE symbol*]   (SPSG)
UFC .... Universal Frequency Counter
UFC .... Universities Funding Council [*British*]   (ECON)
UFC .... Urinary Free Cortisol
UFCA .... Uniform Fraudulent Conveyance Act [*National Conference of Commissioners on Uniform State Laws*]
UFCA .... United Film Carriers Association [*Defunct*]   (EA)
UFCA .... Urethane Foam Contractors Association   (EA)
UFCC .... Underwater Fire Control Computer [*Navy*]   (CAAL)
UFCC .... Uniform Freight Classification Committee
UFCE .... Union Federaliste des Communautes Ethniques Europeennes [*Federal Union of European Nationalities*]
UFCG .... Underwater Fire Control Group
UFCP .... Up-Front Control Panel   (MCD)
UFCS .... UF-6 Chemical Feed Station [*Nuclear energy*]   (NRCH)
UFCS .... Underwater Fire Control System
UFCS .... United Fellowship for Christian Service [*Later, BMMFI*]   (EA)
UFCS .... United Fire & Casualty Co. [*NASDAQ symbol*]   (NQ)
UFCS .... United Free Church of Scotland   (DI)
UFCS .... Universal Fire Control System
UFCS .... Up-Front Control Set   (MCD)
UFCT .... United Federation of College Teachers [*AFL-CIO*]
UFCW .... United Food and Commercial Workers International Union   (EA)
UFCWIU... United Food and Commercial Workers International Union   (EA)
UFD .... Davis County Library, Farmington, UT [*Library symbol*] [*Library of Congress*]   (LCLS)
UFD .... Ultrafast Detection
UFD .... Union des Forces Democratiques [*Union of Democratic Forces*] [*France*] [*Political party*]   (PPE)
UFD .... Union des Forces Democratiques [*Union of Democratic Forces*] [*Mali*] [*Political party*]   (EY)
UFD .... United Foods, Inc. [*AMEX symbol*]   (SPSG)
UFD .... Universal Firing Device [*Military*]   (AABC)
UFD .... User File Directory   (NASA)
UFDC .... Union des Femmes Democratiques du Canada
UFDC .... Union des Forces Democratiques du Cameroun [*Union of Democratic Forces of Cameron*] [*Political party*]   (EY)
UFDC .... United Federation of Doll Clubs   (EA)
UFDC .... Universal Flight Director Computer
UFE .... Union des Feculeries de Pommes de Terre de la CE [*EC*]   (ECED)
UFE .... Union of the Finance-Personnel in Europe [*EC*]   (ECED)
UFE .... Union des Francais a l'Etranger [*Union of French Citizens Abroad*] [*Political party*]   (PPW)
UFE .... Union des Groupements Professionnels de l'Industrie de le Feculerie de Pommes de Terre [*Union of Professional Groups of the Potato Starch Industry*]
UFE .... Universal Field Element   (MCD)
UFEBB ...... Bulletin. Faculty of Education. Utsunomiya University [*A publication*]
UFEMAT ... Federation Europeenne des Associations Nationales des Negociants en Materiaux de Construction [*European Association of National Builders Merchants Associations*]   (EAIO)
UFEMTO ... Union des Femmes du Togo [*Togolese Women's Union*]
UFER .... Mouvement International pour l'Union Fraternelle entre les Races et les Peuples [*International Movement for Fraternal Union among Races and Peoples*]
UFERI .... Union des Federalistes et Republicains Independants [*Zaire*] [*Political party*]   (EY)
UFESA ...... United Fire Equipment Service Association   (EA)
UFF .... U-Landshjaelp fra Folk til Folk [*Development Aid From People to People*] [*Denmark*]   (EAIO)
UFF .... Ufficiale [*Official, Officer*]   (EY)
UFF .... Ulster Freedom Fighters
UFF .... Union et Fraternite Francaise [*French Union and Fraternity*] [*Political party*]   (PPE)
UFF .... UnionFed Financial [*NYSE symbol*]   (SPSG)
UFF .... United Freedom Front
UF-F .... Universal Flip-Flop [*Data processing*]
UFF .... University Film Foundation   (EA)
UFFCS .... IEEE Ultrasonics, Ferroelectrics, and Frequency Control Society   (EA)
UFFI .... Urea-Formaldehyde Foam Insulation
UFFT .... Upplands Fornminnesfoerenings Tidskrift [*A publication*]
UFFVA ..... United Fresh Fruit and Vegetable Association   (EA)
UFG .... Underwriters Financial Group [*Formerly, Chippewa Resources*] [*AMEX symbol*]   (SPSG)
UFGCC ...... Ultrafine Ground Calcium Carbonate [*Inorganic chemistry*]
UFGI .... United Financial Group, Inc. [*NASDAQ symbol*]   (NQ)
UFH .... Ultra-Light Field Howitzer [*British*]
UFH .... Upper Facial Height [*Medicine*]
UFi .... Fillmore City Library, Fillmore, UT [*Library symbol*] [*Library of Congress*]   (LCLS)
UFI .... Unifi, Inc. [*NYSE symbol*]   (SPSG)

UFI .... Union des Foires Internationales [*Union of International Fairs*] (EAIO)
UFI .... Unit Fault Isolation (MCD)
UFI .... Universal Fermi Interaction
UFI .... Usage Frequency Indicator
UFI .... User Friendly Interface
UFIB .... Union Federazioni Italiane Bocce [*Italian lawn bowling, or boccie, organization*]
UFIDA ...... Union Financiere Internationale pour le Developpement de l'Afrique [*International Financial Union for the Development of Africa*]
UFIPTE ..... Union Franco-Iberique pour la Coordination de la Production et du Transport de l'Electricite [*Franco-Iberian Union for Coordinating the Production and Transmission of Electricity*] (EAIO)
UFIRS .... Uniform Fire Incident Reporting System [*National Fire Protection Association*]
UFIRS .... Universal Far Infrared Sensor (MCD)
UFJC .... United Fund for Jewish Culture [*Defunct*] (EA)
UFKT .... Universitetsforlagets Kronikktjeneste [*A publication*]
UFL .... Underfull Employment [*Economics*]
UFL .... Upper Flammable Limit
U Fla LR ... University of Florida. Law Review [*A publication*]
U Fla L Rev ... University of Florida. Law Review [*A publication*]
UFLC .... Union Internationale des Femmes Liberales Chretiennes [*International Union of Liberal Christian Women*]
U Florida L Rev ... University of Florida. Law Review [*A publication*]
UFLT .... Uniflite, Inc. [*NASDAQ symbol*] (NQ)
UFM .... Uganda Freedom Movement (PD)
UFM .... Union Fleuve de Mano [*Mano River Union - MRU*] (EAIO)
UFM .... United Financial Management Ltd. [*Toronto Stock Exchange symbol*]
UFM .... University for Man [*Manhattan, KS*]
UFM .... Unnormalized Floating Multiply (SAA)
UFM .... Upper Figure of Merit
UFM .... User to File Manager
UFMA ...... United Fur Manufacturers Association (EA)
UFMA ...... Upholstered Furniture Manufacturers Association (EA)
UFMA ...... Upholstery Fabric Manufacturers Association [*Defunct*] (EA)
UFMCC ..... Universal Fellowship of Metropolitan Community Churches (EA)
UFMH .... University of Florida. Monographs. Humanities Series [*A publication*]
UFMOP .... Unintentional Frequency Modulation on Pulse (MCD)
UFMT .... Urban Federation for Music Therapists [*Later, AAMT*] (EA)
UFN .... UniCARE Financial Corp. [*AMEX symbol*] (SPSG)
UFN .... Union Franco-Nigerienne [*French-Nigerian Union*]
UFN .... Until Further Notice
UFN .... Uspechi Fiziceskich Nauk [*A publication*]
UFNAA ..... Uspekhi Fizicheskikh Nauk [*A publication*]
UFNSHD .. Unfinished
UFO .... Ultralight Flight Organization (EA)
UFO .... Unidentified Flying Object ["*Flying saucers*"] [*Facetious translation: "Undue Fuss Over"*]
UFO .... Uniform Field Organization [*DoD*]
UFO .... Unit Families Officer [*Military*] [*British*]
UFO .... United 510 Owners (EA)
UFO .... Universal Fiber Optic (MCD)
UFO .... Unlimited Freak-Out [*Slang*] (DSUE)
UFO .... Unwanted Falling Objects (MCD)
UFO .... User Friendly Operating System [*UFO Systems, Inc.*]
UFOA .... Union des Femmes de l'Ouest Africain [*West African Women's Union*]
UFOCAT ... UFO [*Unidentified Flying Object*] Catalog [*Center for Unidentified Flying Object Studies*]
UFOIN ...... UFO Investigators Network [*British*]
UFOIRC .... Unidentified Flying Object Information Retrieval Center, Inc. (EA)
UFood .... United Foods, Inc. [*Associated Press abbreviation*] (APAG)
UFOP .... Ultrafast-Opening Parachute (NG)
UFORDAT ... Umweltforschungsdatenbank [*Data Bank for Environmental Research Projects*] [*Deutsches Umweltbundesamt*] [*Germany*] [*Information service or system*] (CRD)
UFOS .... Unacceptable Face of Socialism (DSUE)
UFOs .... United Flying Octogenarians (EA)
UFP .... Ultrafine Powder [*Materials processing*]
UFP .... Under Frequency Protector (MCD)
UFP .... Unemployed Full Pay [*Military*] [*British*]
UFP .... Union Frontier Police [*European Economic Community*] (ECON)
UFP .... United Federal Party [*Northern Rhodesia*]
UFP .... United Federation of Planets (EA)
UFP .... Universal Folded Plate [*Structural system*] (RDA)
UFP .... Utility Facilities Program [*Data processing*] (IBMDP)
UFPA .... University Film Producers Association [*Later, UFVA*] (EA)
UFPC .... United Federation of Postal Clerks [*Formerly, NFPOC*] [*Later, APWU*] (EA)
UFPDP ...... Union des Forces Populaires pour la Democratie et le Progres [*Niger*] [*Political party*] (EY)
UFP-ICP ... Ultrafine Particle Inductively Coupled Plasma [*Spectrometry*]
UFPO .... Underground Facilities Protective Organization (EA)

UFR .... UF-6 Recovery Room [*Nuclear energy*] (NRCH)
UFR .... Under Frequency Relay
UFR .... Unfinanced Requirement [*Army*]
UFR .... Urine Flow Rate
UFRCC ...... Uniform Federal Regional Council City
UFRM .... United Federal Savings & Loan of Rocky Mount [*NASDAQ symbol*] (NQ)
UFRWO .... United Federation of Russian Workers' Organizations of USA and Canada (EA)
UFS .... Ulster Folklife Society (EA)
UFS .... Ultimate Factor of Safety
UFS .... Under Frequency Sensing (MCD)
UFS .... United Features Syndicate [*Commercial firm*]
UFS .... Unnormalized Floating Subtract
UFSA .... Ukrainian Free Society of America (EA)
UFSB .... University Savings Bank [*NASDAQ symbol*] (NQ)
UFSI-IWA ... Universities Field Staff International - Institute of World Affairs (EA)
UFSJ .... Unitarian Fellowship for Social Justice
UFSL .... Union Federal Savings & Loan Association [*Los Angeles, CA*] [*NASDAQ symbol*] (NQ)
UFSS .... Unified Flexible Spacecraft Simulation
UFSS .... Unmanned Free Swimming Submersibles (DNAB)
UFST .... Unifast Industries, Inc. [*NASDAQ symbol*] (NQ)
UFST .... United Federation of Canadian Star Trekkers
UFT .... Finance and Trade Review [*A publication*]
UFT .... Ultrasonic Frequency Transformer [*or Translator*]
UFT .... United Federation of Teachers [*New York*]
UFT .... United Fly Tyers (EA)
UFTA .... Uniform Fraudulent Transfer Act [*National Conference of Commissioners on Uniform State Laws*]
UFTAA ...... Universal Federation of Travel Agents' Associations [*Formed by a merger of International Federation of Travel Agencies and Universal Organization of Travel Agents' Associations*] [*Australia*] (EAIO)
UFTR .... University of Florida Teaching Reactor
UFTS .... United Furnishing Trades Society [*A union*] [*British*]
UFU .... United Fishermen Union [*British*]
UFU .... Utility Flight Unit [*Navy*]
UFUR .... Universal Furniture Ltd. [*NASDAQ symbol*] (NQ)
UFV .... Unsymmetrical Free Vibration
UFVA .... University Film and Video Association (EA)
UFVF .... University Film and Video Foundation (EA)
UFW .... United Farm Workers of America (EA)
UFW .... United Furniture Workers of America (EA)
UFW .... Urban Fighting Weapon (MCD)
UFWA .... United Farm Workers of America
UFWA .... United Furniture Workers of America
UFWDA .... United Four-Wheel Drive Associations (EA)
UFWOC .... United Farm Workers Organizing Committee [*Later, UFW*]
UFWU .... United Farm Workers Union
UG .... Norfolk Island Airlines [*Australia*] [*ICAO designator*] (ICDA)
UG .... Radio Frequency Connectors [*JETDS nomenclature*] [*Military*] (CET)
ug .... Uganda [*MARC country of publication code*] [*Library of Congress*] (LCCP)
UG .... Uganda [*ANSI two-letter standard code*] (CNC)
UG .... Uganda Airlines Corp. [*ICAO designator*] (FAAC)
Ug .... Ugaritica [*Paris*] [*A publication*]
Ug .... Ugutio [*Huguccio*] [*Deceased, 1210*] [*Authority cited in pre-1607 legal work*] (DSA)
UG .... Uncertain Glory: Folklore and the American Revolution [*A publication*]
UG .... Undergarment
UG .... Undergoing (DNAB)
UG .... Undergraduate
UG .... Underground [*Technical drawings*]
Ug .... Uniform, Fine-Grained [*Soil*]
UG .... Unite Guyanaise [*Guyana Unity*] [*Political party*] (PPW)
UG .... Universal Generalization [*Rule of quantification*] [*Logic*]
UG .... Universal Government
UG .... Upgrading Training [*Job Training and Partnership Act*] (OICC)
UG .... Urban Gorillas (EA)
UG .... Urogenital [*Medicine*]
UG .... US-North Africa (Gibraltar) Convoy [*World War II*]
UG .... User Group [*Data processing*]
UG .... Uteroglobin [*Physiology*]
UGA .... Uganda [*ANSI three-letter standard code*] (CNC)
uga .... Ugaritic [*MARC language code*] [*Library of Congress*] (LCCP)
UGA .... Ugashik [*Alaska*] [*Airport symbol*] (OAG)
UGA .... Ugashik, AK [*Location identifier*] [*FAA*] (FAAL)
UGA .... Underwriters Grain Association (EA)
UGA .... United Golfers' Association (EA)
UGA .... Unity Gain Amplifier
UGA .... Unscreened Granulated Aluminate [*Inorganic chemistry*]
UGA .... Untersuchungen zur Geschichte und Altertumskunde Agyptens [*A publication*]
UGA .... Uracil Guanine Adenine [*Genetics*]
UGA .... Urgeschichtlicher Anzeiger [*A publication*]

UGAA....... Untersuchungen zur Geschichte und Altertumskunde Aegyptens [*K. Sethe*] [*A publication*]   (BJA)
UGAL........ Union des Groupements d'Achat Cooperatifs de Detaillants de l'Europe [*Association of Cooperative Retailer-Owned Wholesalers of Europe - ACROWE*]   (EAIO)
UGAM...... United Gaming, Inc. [*NASDAQ symbol*]   (SPSG)
UGAN .... Uganda
Uganda Dep Agric Annu Rep ... Uganda. Department of Agriculture. Annual Report [*A publication*]
Uganda Dep Agric Mem Res Div Ser II Veg ... Uganda. Department of Agriculture. Memoirs of the Research Division. Series II. Vegetation [*A publication*]
Uganda For Dep Tech Note ... Uganda. Forest Department. Technical Note [*A publication*]
UgandaJ .... Uganda Journal [*A publication*]
Uganda Leg Focus ... Uganda Legal Focus [*A publication*]   (DLA)
Uganda LF ... Uganda Law Focus [*A publication*]   (DLA)
Uganda LR ... Uganda Protectorate Law Reports [*1904-51*] [*A publication*]   (DLA)
Uganda Natl Parks Dir Rep ... Uganda National Parks Director's Report [*A publication*]
UGAPB ..... Publication. Utah Geological Association [*A publication*]
Ugarit F ..... Ugarit-Forschungen. Internationales Jahrbuch fuer die Altertumskunde Syrien-Palaestinas [*A publication*]
UGAS .... Union Gas Systems [*NASDAQ symbol*]   (NQ)
UGB........... Pilot Point, AK [*Location identifier*] [*FAA*]   (FAAL)
UGB........... Union Giovantu Benadir [*Benadir Youth Union*] [*Somalia*]
UGB........... Union de Guerreros Blancos [*White Warriors' Union*] [*El Salvador*] [*Political party*]   (PD)
UGB........... United Gulf Bank [*Middle East*]
UGB........... Unity Gain Bandwidth
UGBW....... Unity Gain Bandwidth
UGC........... Ukrainian Gold Cross   (EA)
UGC........... Ultrasonic Grating Constant
UGC........... United Gold Corp. [*Vancouver Stock Exchange symbol*]
UGC........... United Nations Food and Agriculture Organization Intergovernmental Committee [*World Food Program*]
UGC........... Unity Gain Crossover
UGC........... Universal Guided Column
UGC........... University Grants Commission [*India*]
UGC........... University Grants Committee [*British*]
UGC........... Urgench [*Former USSR*] [*Airport symbol*]   (OAG)
UGCAA ..... Union Generale des Cooperatives Agricoles d'Approvisionnement
UGCW....... United Glass and Ceramic Workers of North America
UGD .... United Greenwood [*Vancouver Stock Exchange symbol*]
UGDP........ University Group Diabetes Program [*Study group involving 12 medical schools*] [*Defunct*]
UGE........... Undergraduate Engineering Program [*Air Force*]
UGEAO ..... Union Generale des Etudiants d'Afrique Occidentale [*General Union of West African Students*]
UGEC .... Union Generale des Etudiants Congolais [*General Union of Congolese Students*]
UGEE .... Yerevan/Zvartnots [*Former USSR*] [*ICAO location identifier*]   (ICLI)
UGEED ...... Union Generale des Etudiants et Eleves Dahomeens
U Gefl AWG ... Um Gefaellige Antwort Wird Gebeten [*The Favor of an Answer Is Requested*] [*German*] [*Correspondence*]
UGEG .... Union Generale des Etudiants Guineens [*General Union of Guinean Students*]
UGEM....... Union Generale des Etudiants du Maroc [*General Union of Moroccan Students*]
UGEMA .... Union Generale des Etudiants Musulmans d'Algerie [*General Union of Moslem Students of Algeria*]
UGEN........ University Genetics Co. [*NASDAQ symbol*]   (NQ)
Ugeskr Agron Hortonomer ... Ugeskrift foer Agronomer og Hortonomer [*A publication*]
Ugeskr Jordbrug ... Ugeskrift foer Jordbrug [*A publication*]
Ugeskr Laeg ... Ugeskrift foer Laeger [*A publication*]
Ugeskr Landm ... Ugeskrift foer Landmaend [*A publication*]
Ugeskr Landmaend ... Ugeskrift foer Landmaend [*A publication*]
UGESP...... Uniform Guidelines on Employee Selection Procedures [*Equal Employment Opportunity Commission*]   (GFGA)
UGET .... Union Generale des Etudiants Tunisiens [*General Union of Tunisian Students*]
Ug F .... Ugarit-Forschungen [*A publication*]
UGF........... Unidentified Growth Factor
UGF........... United Givers Fund
UGF........... Unserviceable Generation Factor [*Military*]
UGF........... US-North Africa (Gibraltar) Convoy-Fast [*World War II*]
UGFNAB .. Ultrasound-Guided Fine-Needle Aspiration Biopsy [*Medicine*]
UGGG........ Tbilisi/Novoalexeyevka [*Former USSR*] [*ICAO location identifier*]   (ICLI)
UGGI........ Union Geodesique et Geophysique Internationale [*International Union of Geodesy and Geophysics*]
UGGI Chron ... UGGI [*Union Geodesique et Geophysique Internationale*] Chronicle [*A publication*]
UGGSC ..... Uggscombe [*England*]
UGH .... Uveitis-Glaucoma-Hyphema [*Ophthalmology*]
UGHA .... United in Group Harmony Association   (EA)
UGHP........ Undergraduate Helicopter Pilot Training [*Army*]

UGI........... Uganik [*Alaska*] [*Airport symbol*]   (OAG)
UGI........... UGI Corp. [*Formerly, United Gas Improvement Co.*] [*NYSE symbol*]   (SPSG)
UGI........... UGI Corp. [*Formerly, United Gas Improvement Co.*] [*Associated Press abbreviation*]   (APAG)
UGI........... Union Geographique Internationale [*International Geographical Union*]
UGI........... Upper Gastrointestinal [*Medicine*]
UGIB......... Upper Gastrointestinal Bleeding [*Medicine*]
UGI Bull .... UGI [*Union Geographique Internationale*] Bulletin [*A publication*]
UGIH........ Upper Gastrointestinal Tract Hemorrhage [*Medicine*]
UgJ........... Uganda Journal [*A publication*]
UGJA .... United Galician Jews of America [*Defunct*]   (EA)
UGL........... Uglegorsk [*Former USSR*] [*Seismograph station code, US Geological Survey*]   (SEIS)
UGL........... Uitgelezen. Documentatieoverzicht Bibliotheek en Documentatiedienst Ministerie van Sociale Zaken [*A publication*]
UGL........... Utility General
UGLAA ..... Ugeskrift foer Laeger [*A publication*]
UGLAS...... Uniform General Ledger Accounting Structure   (NVT)
UGLE........ United Grand Lodge of England [*Masonry*]
UGLE........ Universal Graphics Language Executive   (MCD)
Ugleobogat Oborudovanie ... Ugleobogatitel'noe Oborudovanie [*A publication*]
Ug LF......... Uganda Law Focus [*A publication*]   (DLA)
UGLI .... Universal Gate for Logic Implementation [*Data processing*]   (MCD)
UGLIAC.... United Gas Laboratories Internally Programmed Automatic Computer
UGLJ........ University of Ghana. Law Journal [*A publication*]
Ug LR .... Uganda Law Reports [*Africa*] [*A publication*]   (DLA)
UGLRC ..... Upper Great Lakes Regional Commission [*Department of Commerce*]
UgM.......... Ugaritic Manual [*A publication*]   (BJA)
UG/M........ Umdrehungen je Minute [*Revolutions per Minute*] [*German*]
UGM .... Underwater Guided Missile [*DoD*]   (MCD)
UGM .... University of Georgia. Monographs [*A publication*]
UGM .... Urogenital Mesenchyme [*Medicine*]
UGMA....... Uniform Gifts to Minors Act [*National Conference of Commissioners on Uniform State Laws*]
Ug Man ...... Ugaritic Manual [*A publication*]
UGML....... Universal Guided Missile Launcher [*Navy*]   (MCD)
UGMM....... Mukhrani [*Former USSR*] [*ICAO location identifier*]   (ICLI)
UGN .... Waukegan, IL [*Location identifier*] [*FAA*]   (FAAL)
UGNCO ..... Unit Gas Noncommissioned Officer [*Army*] [*World War II*]
UGND .... Underground   (AABC)
UGNE......... Unigene Laboratories, Inc. [*NASDAQ symbol*]   (NQ)
UGO .... Uige [*Angola*] [*Airport symbol*] [*Obsolete*]   (OAG)
UGO .... Unigesco, Inc. [*Toronto Stock Exchange symbol*]
UGO .... Unit Gas Offices [*Army*] [*World War II*]
UGO .... Unmanned Geophysical Observatory [*National Science Foundation*]
UGOC........ United Greek Orthodox Charities [*Defunct*]   (EA)
Ugol' Ukr... Ugol' Ukrainy [*A publication*]
UGOT........ Urine Glutamic-Oxaloacetic Transaminase [*An enzyme*]
UGOUA .... Ugol' Ukrainy [*A publication*]
UGP........... Union des Gaullistes de Progres [*Union of Progressive Gaullists*] [*France*] [*Political party*]   (PPE)
UGP........... United Global Petroleum, Inc. [*Vancouver Stock Exchange symbol*]
UGPA .... Undergraduate Grade-Point Average [*Higher education*]
UGPCC...... Uniform Grocery Product Code Council [*Later, UPCC*]   (EA)
UGPP........ Uridine Diphosphoglucose Pyrophosphorylase [*An enzyme*]
Ug Pr LR ... Uganda Protectorate Law Reports [*Africa*] [*A publication*]   (DLA)
UGR........... Ultrasonic Grain Refinement
UGR........... United Gunn Resources [*Vancouver Stock Exchange symbol*]
UGR........... Universal Graphic Recorder [*Raytheon Co.*]
UGRDN...... United-Guardian, Inc. [*Associated Press abbreviation*]   (APAG)
UGRE .... Undergraduate Record Examination [*Education*]
UGRR .... Underground Railroad [*A smuggling system*] [*Criminal slang*]
UGS........... Unattended Ground Sensors
UGS........... Uniaxial Gyrostabilizer
UGS........... Union de la Gauche Socialiste
UGS........... Union Graduate School [*Yellow Springs, Ohio*]
UGS........... Union des Guineens au Senegal [*Union of Guineans in Senegal*] [*Political party*]   (PD)
UGS........... United Grounders' Society [*A union*] [*British*]
UGS........... Upper Group Stop [*Nuclear energy*]   (NRCH)
UGS........... Upper Guide Structure [*Nuclear energy*]   (NRCH)
UGS........... Urogenital Sinus [*Anatomy*]
UGS........... Urogenital System [*Medicine*]
UGS........... US-North Africa (Gibraltar) Convoy-Slow [*World War II*]
UGSA .... Union Generale des Syndicats Algeriens [*General Federation of Algerian Trade Unions*]
UGSP........ United Galaxy Sanitation Patrol [*In TV series "Quark"*]
UGSS......... Sukhumi [*Former USSR*] [*ICAO location identifier*]   (ICLI)
UgT........... Ugaritic Textbook [*A publication*]   (BJA)
UGT........... Underground Test   (MCD)

UGT.......... Union General de Trabajadores de Espana [*General Union of Spanish Workers*] [*In exile*]
UGT.......... United Bible Societies' Greek New Testament [*A publication*] (BJA)
UGT.......... Upgrade Training [*Military*] (AFM)
UGT.......... Upgraded Third-Generation Enroute Software Program [*Data processing*] (MCD)
UGT.......... Urgent
UGT.......... Urogenital Tract [*Medicine*]
UGTA........ Union Generale des Travailleurs Algeriens [*General Union of Algerian Workers*]
UGTAN..... Union Generale des Travailleurs d'Afrique Noire [*General Union of Workers of Black Africa*]
UGTC........ Union Generale des Travailleurs du Cameroun [*General Union of Workers of Cameroon*]
UGTC........ Union Generale des Travailleurs Centrafricains [*General Union of Central African Workers*]
UGTCI...... Union Generale des Travailleurs de la Cote D'Ivoire [*General Union of Workers of the Ivory Coast*]
UGTD....... Uniform Geometrical Theory of Diffraction (MCD)
UGTD....... Union Generale des Travailleurs du Dahomey [*General Union of Workers of Dahomey*]
UGTK....... Union Generale des Travailleurs du Kamerun [*General Union of Workers of the Cameroon*]
UGTM...... Union Generale des Travailleurs du Maroc [*General Union of Workers of Morocco*]
UGTM...... Union Generale des Travailleurs de Mauritanie [*General Union of Workers of Mauritania*]
UGTS .... Union Generale des Travailleurs du Senegal [*General Union of Workers of Senegal*]
UGTT .... Union Generale de Travailleurs Tunisiens [*General Federation of Tunisian Workers*]
UGV.......... Unmanned Ground Vehicle [*Military robotics*]
UGW......... United Garment Workers of America (EA)
UH .... Air-Cushion Vehicle built by Universal Hovercraft [*US*] [*Usually used in combination with numerals*]
UH .... Bristow Helicopters Group Ltd. [*Great Britain*] [*ICAO designator*] (FAAC)
UH .... Ugaritic Handbook [*C. H. Gordon*] [*A publication*] (BJA)
UH .... Ukrainian Herald [*A publication*]
UH .... Unavailable Hours [*Electronics*] (IEEE)
UH .... Underhatch
UH .... Unit Head
UH .... Unit Heater [*Technical drawings*]
UH .... United Humanitarians (EA)
UH .... University of Hawaii [*Honolulu, HI*]
UH .... Upper Half
UH .... Upper Hemispherical (MCD)
UH .... US Home Corp. [*NYSE symbol*] (SPSG)
UH .... Utah [*Obsolete*] (ROG)
UH .... Utility Helicopter [*Military*] (AABC)
UHA .... Ukrains'ka Halyts'ka Armiia
UHA .... Ultrahigh Altitude
UHA .... Unexpected Home Attack [*Medicine*]
UHA .... Union House of Assembly [*South Africa*] (DAS)
UHA .... Universitets- och Hogskoleambetet [*National Board of Universities and Colleges*] [*Ministry of Education and Cultural Affairs*] [*Information service or system*] [*Sweden*] (IID)
UHA .... Upper Half Assembly
UHAA .... United Horological Association of America [*Later, AWI*]
UHAB....... Urban Homesteading Assistance Board (EA)
UHAC....... United Hellenic American Congress (EA)
U Hart St L ... University of Hartford. Studies in Literature [*A publication*]
U Hawaii L Rev ... University of Hawaii. Law Review [*A publication*]
U Haw LR ... University of Hawaii. Law Review [*A publication*]
UHBP....... Ekimcham [*Former USSR*] [*ICAO location identifier*] (ICLI)
UHC .... Ultimate Holding Company
UHC .... Unburned Hydrocarbon [*Also, UBHC*] [*Fuel technology*]
UHC .... Under Honorable Conditions [*Military*]
UHC .... Unit Hardware Cost (MCD)
UHC .... University of Houston at Clear Lake City, Houston, TX [*OCLC symbol*] (OCLC)
UHCC....... University of Houston Coastal Center [*Research center*] (RCD)
UHCMWIU ... United Hatters, Cap, and Millinery Workers International Union
UHCO ...... Universal Holding Corp. [*NASDAQ symbol*] (NQ)
UHCP....... United Heritage Corp. [*NASDAQ symbol*] (NQ)
UHCS .... Ultrahigh Capacity Storage
UHDDS..... Uniform Hospital Discharge Data Set [*National Center for Health Statistics*]
UHE .... Uherske Hradiste [*Former Czechoslovakia*] [*Airport symbol*] [*Obsolete*] (OAG)
UHE .... Ultimate Hour Estimate (MCD)
UHE .... Ultrahigh Efficiency [*Arc lamp*]
UHE .... Ultrahigh Energy
UHE .... Usual Home Elsewhere [*Bureau of the Census*] (GFGA)
UHELP...... [*A*] Programming Language (CSR)
UHF......... Ulster Historical Foundation (EA)
UHF......... Ultrahigh-Frequency [*Electricity of radio waves*]
UHF......... Uniform Heat Flux [*Engineering*]

UHF......... United Health Foundations [*Defunct*]
UHF......... Unrestricted Hartree-Fock [*Wave-Function*]
UHFDF ..... Ultrahigh-Frequency Direction Finder
UHFF .... Ultrahigh-Frequency Filter
UHFG....... Ultrahigh-Frequency Generator
UHF/HF ... Ultrahigh-Frequency/High-Frequency (MCD)
UHFJ....... Ultrahigh-Frequency Jammer
UHFO....... Ultrahigh-Frequency Oscillator
UHFR....... Ultrahigh-Frequency Receiver
UHFRU ..... Ultrahigh Frequency Radio Unit (MCD)
UHFS .... Unsteady Heat Flux Sensor
UHG .... Urban History Group [*Defunct*] (EA)
UHHH...... Khabarovsk/Novy [*Former USSR*] [*ICAO location identifier*] (ICLI)
UHHO...... Troitskoye [*Former USSR*] [*ICAO location identifier*] (ICLI)
UHI.......... Upper Head Injection [*Nuclear energy*] (NRCH)
UHi.......... Utah State Historical Society, Salt Lake City, UT [*Library symbol*] [*Library of Congress*] (LCLS)
UHJA .... United Hungarian Jews of America (EA)
UHK .... University of Hard Knocks [*West Virginia*] [*"University" founded by Jim Comstock and based on the expression "school of hard knocks"*]
UHL.......... Unge Hoyres Landsforbund [*Norway*] [*Political party*] (EAIO)
UHL.......... Universal Hypertrichosis Lanuginosa [*Medicine*] (MAE)
UHL.......... User Header Label (CMD)
UHLCADS ... Ultra-High-Level Container Airdrop System [*Military*] (MCD)
UHLI .... United Home Life Insurance Co. [*Greenwood, IN*] [*NASDAQ symbol*] (NQ)
UHltCr ...... United Healthcare Corp. [*Associated Press abbreviation*] (APAG)
UHLVFD .. Ultra High Luminance Vacuum Fluorescent Display [*Automotive engineering*]
UHML....... Lavrentiya [*Former USSR*] [*ICAO location identifier*] (ICLI)
UHMR ...... Beringovsky [*Former USSR*] [*ICAO location identifier*] (ICLI)
UHMS....... Ultrasonic Helmet Mounted Sight [*Army*] (MCD)
UHMS...... Undersea and Hyperbaric Medical Society (EA)
UHMW ..... Ultrahigh Molecular Weight
UHMW-PE ... Ultrahigh Molecular Weight Polyethylene [*Organic chemistry*]
UHN .... Uranyl Hexahydrate Nitrate (GFGA)
UHP.......... Ugaritic-Hebrew Philology [*Rome*] [*M. Dahood*] [*A publication*] (BJA)
UHP.......... Ultra-High Performance [*in UHP Imposer, a product of Opti-Copy, Inc.*]
UHP.......... Ultrahigh Power
UHP.......... Ultrahigh Purity
UHP.......... Undergraduate Helicopter Pilot Training [*Army*]
UHP.......... University of Hawaii Press
UHPFB..... Untreated Hard Pressed Fiberboard
UHPMIS... Urban Homesteading Program Management Information System [*Department of Housing and Urban Development*] (GFGA)
UHPS .... Underground Hydro-Pumped Storage [*Room*]
UHPT .... Undergraduate Helicopter Pilot Training (MCD)
UHQ .... Utah Historical Quarterly [*A publication*]
UHR .... Ultrahigh Resistance
UHR .... Ultrahigh Resolution
UHR .... United Hearne Resources Ltd. [*Vancouver Stock Exchange symbol*]
UHR .... Upper Hybrid Resonance [*Spectroscopy*]
UHRA....... United Hunts Racing Association [*Later, NSHA*]
UHR-ESCA ... Ultrahigh-Resolution Electron Spectrometer for Chemical Analysis
UHRN ...... United Hearne Resources Ltd. [*NASDAQ symbol*] (NQ)
UHS......... Ultimate Heat Sink [*Nuclear energy*] (NRCH)
UHS.......... Ultrahigh Speed
UHS.......... Unit Handling System
UHS......... Unitarian Historical Society [*Later, UUHS*] (EA)
UHS......... United HIAS Service (EA)
UHS.......... Universalist Historical Society [*Later, UUHS*] (EA)
UHS......... University of Health Sciences - Chicago Medical School
UHSA....... United Halsingian Society of America [*Defunct*] (EA)
UHS-CMS ... University of Health Sciences - Chicago Medical School
UHSI........ Universal Health Services, Inc. [*NYSE symbol*] (NQ)
UHT .... Ultraheat Tested [*Milk*] (CDAI)
UHT .... Ultraheat Treated
UHT .... Ultrahigh Temperature
UHT .... Ultrasonic Hardness Tester
UHT .... Underheat
UHT .... Unit Horizontal Tail
UHT .... United Hebrew Trades of the State of New York (EA)
UHT .... Universal Hand Tool
UHT .... Universal Health Realty [*NYSE symbol*] (SPSG)
UHT .... Universal Horizontal Tail [*Aviation*] (NG)
UHTPB ..... Unsaturated Hydroxyl-Terminated Polybutadiene [*Organic chemistry*]
UHTREX .. Ultrahigh-Temperature Reactor Experiment [*Nuclear energy*]
UHTV...... Unmanned Hypersonic Test Vehicle (MCD)
UHV .... Ultrahigh Vacuum
UHV .... Ultrahigh Voltage
UHV .... Under Hatch Valve

UHVA .... United Hellenic Voters of America (EA)
UHVC .... Ultrahigh Vacuum Chamber
UHV/CVD ... Ultrahigh Vacuum Chemical Vapor Deposition [*Coating technology*] [*Semiconductor technology*]
UHVS .... Ultrahigh Vacuum System
UI .... Societe de Transport Aerien du Rwanda [*ICAO designator*] (FAAC)
UI .... Uj Iras [*A publication*]
U/I .... Under Instructions (ADA)
UI .... Underground Injection [*of wastes*]
UI .... Underwear Institute [*Later, NKMA*] (EA)
UI .... Undifferentiated Infiltrating [*Tumor*] [*Oncology*]
UI .... Unemployment Insurance
UI .... Unexplained Infertility
U/I .... Unidentified
UI .... Union Institute (EA)
UI .... Union Interparlementaire [*Inter-Parliamentary Union*] (EAIO)
UI .... Union-Intersection [*Statistics*]
UI .... Unit of Issue (KSC)
UI .... United Inches
UI .... United Inns, Inc. [*NYSE symbol*] (SPSG)
ui .... United Kingdom Miscellaneous Islands [*MARC country of publication code*] [*Library of Congress*] (LCCP)
UI .... Universal Instantiation [*Rule of quantification*] [*Logic*]
UI .... Universal-International Studios (IIA)
U of I .... University of Illinois [*Urbana, IL*]
U of I .... University of Iowa [*Iowa City, IA*] (OICC)
UI .... Unreported Income [*IRS*]
UI .... Unsigned Integer [*Data processing*]
UI .... Uranium Institute [*British*] (EAIO)
UI .... Urban Initiatives (EA)
UI .... Urban Institute (EA)
UI .... Urinary Infection [*Medicine*]
UI .... Uroporphyrin Isomerase [*An enzyme*] (AAMN)
UI .... USE, Inc. [*Acronym is now organization's official name*] (EA)
UI .... User Interface
UI .... Ut Infra [*As Below*] [*Latin*]
UIA .... Ukrainian Institute of America (EA)
UIA .... Ultrasonic Industry Association (EA)
UIA .... Unemployment Insurance Act [*Canada*]
UIA .... Union of International Associations [*See also UAI*] [*Brussels, Belgium*] (EAIO)
UIA .... Union of International Associations. Documents [*A publication*]
UIA .... Union Internationale des Architectes [*International Union of Architects*] (EAIO)
UIA .... Union Internationale des Avocats [*International Union of Lawyers*]
UIA .... Union Internationale Contre l'Alcoolisme
UIA .... Union Internationale des Syndicats des Industries Alimentaires
UIA .... Unit Identifier Applications (MCD)
UIA .... United Israel Appeal (EA)
UIA .... Universidad Iberoamericana, Mexico, DF, Mexico [*OCLC symbol*] (OCLC)
UIA .... Uranium Institute of America (EA)
UIA .... Urban Impact Analysis (EG)
UIA .... Usable Inside Area (MCD)
UIAA .... Chita/Kadala [*Former USSR*] [*ICAO location identifier*] (ICLI)
UIAA .... Union Internationale des Associations d'Alpinisme [*International Union of Alpine Associations*] [*Switzerland*]
UIAA .... Union Internationale des Associations d'Annonceurs [*International Union of Advertisers Associations*]
UIAA .... Union Internationale des Assureurs Aeronautiques
UIACM ..... Union Internationale des Automobile-Clubs Medicaux [*International Union of Associations of Doctor-Motorists*]
UIAL .... United Italian American League (EA)
UIALC .... United Italian American Labor Council (EA)
UIAMS ...... Union Internationale d'Action Morale et Sociale [*International Union for Moral and Social Action*]
UIAPME... Union Internationale de l'Artisanat et des Petites et Moyennes Entreprises [*International Association of Crafts and Small and Medium-Sized Enterprises*]
UIAPPA .... Union Internationale des Associations de Prevention de la Pollution Atmospherique [*International Union of Air Pollution Prevention Associations*] (EAIO)
UIARVEP ... Unione Italiana Agenti Rappresentati Viaggiatori e Piazzisti [*Italian Union of Agents and Travelers*]
UIASPPA ... Uniform Individual Accident and Sickness Policy Provisions Act [*National Association of Insurance Commissioners*]
UIAT .... Union Internationale des Syndicats des Industries de l'Alimentation et des Tabacs
UIATF .... United Indians of All Tribes Foundation (EA)
UIB .... Quibdo [*Colombia*] [*Airport symbol*] (OAG)
UIB .... Unidentified Infrared Band [*Astrophysics*]
UIB .... Union Internationale des Maitres Boulangers [*International Union of Master Bakers*]
UIB .... Unione Italiana Bancari [*Italian Union of Bank Employees*]
UIBB......... Bratsk [*Former USSR*] [*ICAO location identifier*] (ICLI)
UIBC......... Unsaturated Iron-Binding Capacity [*Clinical chemistry*]

UIBG .... Union Internationale de Banque en Guinee (EY)
UIBPIP...... United International Bureau for the Protection of Intellectual Property [*Superseded by WIPO*]
UIBWM .... Trade Unions International of Workers of Building, Wood, and Building Materials Industries
UIC .... Ultraviolet Image Converter
UIC .... Underground Injection Control [*Environmental Protection Agency*]
UIC .... Unemployment Insurance Code (OICC)
UIC .... Unemployment Insurance Commission [*Canada*]
UIC .... Unidad de Izquierda Comunista [*Unity of the Communist Left*] [*Mexico*] [*Political party*] (PPW)
UIC .... Union of International Conventions
UIC .... Union Internationale des Chemins de Fer [*International Union of Railways*] (EAIO)
UIC .... Union Internationale de Cristallographie [*International Union of Crystallography*] (EAIO)
UIC .... Unit Identification Code [*Army*] (AABC)
UIC .... United Industrial Corp. [*NYSE symbol*] (SPSG)
UIC .... Upper Information Center [*Aviation*]
UIC .... Urban Information Center [*Milwaukee Urban Observatory*] [*Information service or system*] [*Ceased operations*] (IID)
UIC .... Urinary Immune Complex
UIC .... User Identification Code
UICA .... Union of Independent Colleges of Art (EA)
UICA .... Union Internationale des Constructeurs d'Ascenseurs [*International Union of Elevator Constructors - IUEC*]
UICANY ... United Irish Counties Association of New York (EA)
UICB......... Union Internationale des Centres du Batiment [*International Union of Building Centers*] [*British*]
UICC .... Union Internationale Contre le Cancer [*International Union Against Cancer*] [*Switzerland*]
UICC .... University of Illinois at Chicago Circle
UICC Monogr Ser ... UICC [*Union Internationale Contre le Cancer*] Monograph Series [*A publication*]
UICC Tech Rep Ser ... UICC [*Union Internationale Contre le Cancer*] Technical Report Series [*A publication*]
UICGF....... Union Internationale du Commerce en Gros de la Fleur [*International Union for the Wholesale Flower Trade*]
UICI.......... United Insurance Companies, Inc. [*NASDAQ symbol*] (NQ)
UICIO .... Unit Identification Code Information Officer [*Military*] (AABC)
UICM .... Union Internationale Catholique des Classes Moyennes [*International Catholic Union of the Middle Classes*]
UICN .... Union Internationale pour la Conservation de la Nature et de Ses Ressources [*International Union for Conservation of Nature and Natural Resources*]
UICO .... UNICO, Inc. [*NASDAQ symbol*] (NQ)
UICP......... Uniform Inventory Control Point
UICP......... Uniform Inventory Control Points System [*Military*]
UICP......... Union Internationale de la Couverture et Plomberie (EA)
UICPA....... Union Internationale de Chimie Pure et Appliquee [*International Union of Pure and Applied Chemistry*]
UICR .... Union Internationale des Chauffeurs Routiers [*International Union of Lorry Drivers - IULD*] (EAIO)
UICSM...... University of Illinois Committee on School Mathematics
UICT......... Union Internationale Contre la Tuberculose [*International Union Against Tuberculosis - IUAT*] (EAIO)
UICTMR... Union Internationale Contre la Tuberculose et les Maladies Respiratoires [*International Union Against Tuberculosis and Lung Disease - IUATLD*] (EAIO)
UICWA ..... United Infants' and Children's Wear Association (EA)
UID........... Selected Decisions by Umpire for Northern Ireland, Respecting Claims to Benefit [*A publication*] (DLA)
UID........... Unemployment Insurance Department
UID........... Usable Inside Depth (MCD)
UIDA .... Union Internationale des Organisations de Detaillants de la Branche Alimentaire [*International Federation of Grocers' Associations*]
UIDA .... United Indian Development Association (EA)
UIDAC ...... Unione Italiana Dipendenti Aziende Commerciali ed Affini [*Italian Union of Commerical and Allied Workers*]
UIE .... UNESCO Institute for Education
UIE .... Union Internationale d'Editeurs [*International Publishers Association - IPA*] (EAIO)
UIE .... Union Internationale d'Electrothermie [*International Union for Electroheat*] (EAIO)
UIE .... Union Internationale des Etudiants [*International Union of Students - IUS*] (EAIO)
UIEA .... Union Internationale des Etudiants en Architecture [*International Union of Students in Architecture*]
UIEC.......... Union Internationale de l'Exploitation Cinematographique [*International Union of Cinematographic Exhibitors*] (EAIO)
UIEIS .... Union Internationale pour l'Etude des Insectes Sociaux [*International Union for the Study of Social Insects - IUSSI*] [*Netherlands*]
UIEO .... Union of International Engineering Organizations
UIEP......... Union Internationale des Entrepreneurs de Peinture

UIES......... Union Internationale d'Education pour la Sante [*International Union of Health Education - IUHE*] [*Paris, France*]   (EAIO)

UIES......... Union Internationale d'Etudes Sociales [*International Union for Social Studies*]

UIEUA ...... Upravlenie Yadernymi Energeticheskimi Ustanovkami [*A publication*]

UIEV .... Universal Imagery Exploitation Viewer   (DNAB)

UIF .... Ultraviolet Interference Filter

UIF .... Undegraded Insulin Factor [*Medicine*]   (MAE)

UIF .... Unfavorable Information File [*Military*]

UIF .... Union Internationale de Ferrecarriles [*International Union of Railways*]

UIF .... Universal Intermolecular Force

UIF .... Unserviceable Items File

UIF .... USLIFE Income Fund, Inc. [*NYSE symbol*]   (SPSG)

UIFA........ Union Internationale des Femmes Architectes [*International Union of Women Architects - IUWA*]   (EAIO)

UIFI........ Union Internationale des Fabricants d'Impermeables

UIFL........ Union Internationale des Federations de Detaillants en Produits Laitiers

uig .... Uigur [*MARC language code*] [*Library of Congress*]   (LCCP)

UIG........... Uniglobe International Energy Corp. [*Vancouver Stock Exchange symbol*]

UIG........... User Instruction Group

UIGDC...... Unione Internazionale des Giovani Democratici Cristiana [*International Union of Young Christian Democrats*]

UIGSE....... Union Internationale des Guides et Scouts d'Europe [*International Union of European Guides and Scouts - IUEGS*] [*Chateau Landon, France*]   (EAIO)

UIH........... Urban and Industrial Health   (KSC)

UIHE........ Union Internationale de l'Humanisme et de l'Ethique

UIHMSU .. Union Internationale d'Hygiene et de Medecine Scolaires et Universitaires [*International Union of School and University Health and Medicine - IUSUHM*] [*Brussels, Belgium*]   (EAIO)

UIHPS....... Union Internationale d'Histoire et de Philosophie des Sciences

UII .... Unified Industries, Inc.

UII .... Universal Identification Interface [*Allen-Bradley Co.*]

UII .... Utila Island [*Honduras*] [*Airport symbol*] [*Obsolete*]   (OAG)

UIIG .... Union Internationale de l'Industrie du Gaz [*International Gas Union - IGU*] [*Paris, France*]   (EAIO)

UIII........... Irkutsk [*Former USSR*] [*ICAO location identifier*]   (ICLI)

UIII........... Urban Information Interpreters, Inc.   (IID)

UIIO .... Ust-Ordynsky [*Former USSR*] [*ICAO location identifier*]   (ICLI)

UIJA......... Union Internationale des Journalistes Agricoles [*International Union of Agricultural Journalists*]

UIJDC....... Union Internationale de Jeunesse Democrate Chretienne [*International Union of Young Christian Democrats*]

UIJPLF ..... Union Internationale des Journalistes et de la Presse de Langue Francaise [*International Union of French-Language Journalists and Press - IUFLJP*]   (EAIO)

UIJS .... Union Internationale de la Jeunesse Socialiste [*International Union of Socialist Youth*]

UIKB .... Bodaybo [*Former USSR*] [*ICAO location identifier*]   (ICLI)

UIKK .... Kirensk [*Former USSR*] [*ICAO location identifier*]   (ICLI)

UIKW .... Vitim [*Former USSR*] [*ICAO location identifier*]   (ICLI)

UIL .... Quillayute, WA [*Location identifier*] [*FAA*]   (FAAL)

UIL .... Unione Italiana del Lavoro [*Italian Union of Labor*]

UIL .... United Illuminating Co. [*NYSE symbol*]   (SPSG)

UIL .... UNIVAC Interactive Language [*Data processing*]   (IEEE)

UIL .... University of Iowa, School of Library Science, Iowa City, IA [*OCLC symbol*]   (OCLC)

UIL .... User Interface Language   (SSD)

UILA .... Unione Italiana Lavoratori Assicurazioni [*Italian Union of Insurance Workers*]

UILAM...... Unione Italiana Lavoratori Albergo e Mensa [*Italian Union of Hotel and Restaurant Workers*]

UILE........ Union Internationale pour la Liberte d'Enseignement [*International Union for the Liberty of Education*]

UIL-GAS... Unione Italiana Lavoratori Aziende Gas [*Italian Union of Gas Workers*]

UILI.......... Union Internationale des Laboratoires Independents [*International Union of Independent Laboratories*] [*Elstree, Hertfordshire, England*]   (EAIO)

UILL......... University of Illinois. Studies in Language and Literature [*A publication*]

U Ill LB...... University of Illinois. Law Bulletin [*A publication*]   (DLA)

U Ill L Bull ... University of Illinois. Law Bulletin [*A publication*]   (DLA)

U Ill L F ... University of Illinois. Law Forum [*A publication*]

U Ill L Forum ... University of Illinois. Law Forum [*A publication*]

U Ill LR...... University of Illinois. Law Review [*A publication*]

U Ill L Rev ... University of Illinois. Law Review [*A publication*]

UIllu......... United Illuminating Co. [*Associated Press abbreviation*]   (APAG)

UIllum .... United Illuminating Co. [*Associated Press abbreviation*]   (APAG)

UILU .... University of Illinois, Urbana

UIM........... Quitman, TX [*Location identifier*] [*FAA*]   (FAAL)

UIM .... Ufficio Informazioni Militare [*Office of Military Information*] [*Italian*]

UIM .... Ultra-Intelligent Machine

UIM .... Ultrasonic Interferometer Manometer [*Instrumentation*]

UIM .... Union of International Motorboating   (EA)

UIM .... Union Internationale des Magistrats [*International Association of Judges - IAJ*]   (EAIO)

UIM .... Union Internationale des Metis [*International Union of Individuals of Mixed Parentage*]

UIM .... Union Internationale Monarchiste [*Weinsberg, Federal Republic of Germany*]   (EAIO)

UIM .... Union Internationale Motonautique [*Union of International Motorboating*]   (EAIO)

UIMC .... Union Internationale des Services Medicaux des Chemins de Fer [*International Union of Railway Medical Services*]

UIMI .... United Indian Missions, International   (EA)

UIMJ......... Union Internationale des Maisons de Jeunesse [*Service de la FIJC*]

UIMP .... Union Internationale pour le Protection de la Moralite Publique [*International Union for the Protection of Public Morale*] [*France*]

UIMS........ User Interface Management System [*Data processing*]

UIMVT ..... Union Internationale Contre les Maladies Veneriennes et les Treponematoses [*International Union Against the Venereal Diseases and the Treponematoses - IUVDT*]

UIN........... Quincy [*Illinois*] [*Airport symbol*]   (OAG)

UIN........... USR Industries, Inc. [*AMEX symbol*]   (SPSG)

UINA........ Uintah Energy Corp. [*NASDAQ symbol*]   (NQ)

UIND........ USR Industries, Inc. [*NASDAQ symbol*]   (NQ)

UINF .... Union Internationale de la Navigation Fluviale [*International Union for Inland Navigation - IUIN*]   (EAIO)

UINL .... Union Internationale du Notariat Latin [*International Union of Latin Notaries*]

UINN........ Nizhneudinsk [*Former USSR*] [*ICAO location identifier*]   (ICLI)

UINP .... Unit of Insect Neurophysiology and Pharmacology [*University of Cambridge*] [*British*]   (IRUK)

UIO........... Quito [*Ecuador*] [*Airport symbol*]   (OAG)

UIO........... Union Internationale des Orientalistes [*International Union of Orientalists*]

UIO........... United Infertility Organization   (EA)

UIO........... Units in Operation [*Business term*]

UIO........... Utility Iterative Operation

UIOD .... User Input/Output Devices [*Data processing*]   (RDA)

UIOF .... Union Internationale des Organismes Familiaux [*International Union of Family Organizations - IUFO*] [*France*]

UIOOT ...... Union Internationale des Organismes Officiels de Tourisme [*International Union of Official Travel Organizations*]

UIOVD...... Union Internationale des Ouvriers du Vetement pour Dames [*International Ladies' Garment Workers' Union - ILGW*]

U Iowa L Rev ... University of Iowa. Law Review [*A publication*]   (DLA)

UIP .... Quimper [*France*] [*Airport symbol*]   (OAG)

UIP .... Unallowable Items Program [*IRS*]

UIP .... Unfair Industrial Practice

UIP .... Union Internationale d'Associations de Proprietaires de Wagons Particuliers [*International Union of Private Railway Truck Owners' Associations*]   (EAIO)

UIP .... Union Internationale de Patinage [*International Skating Union - ISU*] [*Davos-Platz, Switzerland*]   (EAIO)

UIP .... Union Internationale de Physique Pure et Appliquee [*International Union of Pure and Applied Physics*]

UIP .... Union Internationale des Publicitaires

UIP .... Union Interparlementaire

UIP .... Unione Italiana Pescatori [*Italian Union of Fishermen*]

UIP .... United Ireland Party

UIP .... University of Illinois Press

UIP .... Usable in Place   (MCD)

UIP .... Usual Interstitial Pneumonia [*Medicine*]

UIPA .... United Indian Planners Association [*Defunct*]   (EA)

UIPC........ Underground Injection Practices Council   (EA)

UIPC......... Union Internationale de la Press Catholique [*International Union of the Catholic Press*] [*France*]

UIPC........ Union Internationale de la Presse Catholique [*International Catholic Press Union*]

UIPCG....... Union Internationale de la Patisserie, Confiserie, Glacerie [*International Union of Bakers and Confectioners*]

UIPD .... Ulrich's International Periodicals Directory [*A publication*]

UIPE......... Union Internationale de Protection de l'Enfance [*International Union for Child Welfare - IUCW*] [*Geneva, Switzerland*]   (EA)

UIPFB ...... Union Internationale de la Propriete Fonciere Batie [*International Union of Landed Property Owners*]

UIPI .... Union Internacional de Proteccion a la Infancia [*International Union for Child Welfare*]

UIPI.......... Union Internationale de la Propriete Immobiliere [*International Union of Property Owners*] [*Paris, France*]   (EAIO)

UIPM .... Union Internationale de la Presse Medicale [*International Union of the Medical Press*]

UIPMB...... Union Internationale de Pentathlon Moderne et Biathlon [*International Union for Modern Pentathlon and Biathlon*]   (EAIO)

UIPN .... Union Internationale pour la Protection de la Nature [*International Union for the Protection of Nature - IUPN*] [*Later, IUCN*]

UIPPA .... Union Internationale de Physique Pure et Appliquee [*International Union of Pure and Applied Physics*]

UIPPI .... Union Internationale pour la Protection de la Propriete Industrielle [*International Union for the Protection of Industrial Property*]

UIPRE .... Union Internationale de la Presse Radiotechnique et Electronique [*Freiburg, Federal Republic of Germany*] (EAIO)

UIPVT .... Union Internationale Contre le Peril Venerien et la Treponematose [*International Union Against the Venereal Diseases and the Treponematoses*]

UIQ .... Upper Inner Quadrant [*Anatomy*]

UIR .... Quirindi [*Australia*] [*Airport symbol*] [*Obsolete*] (OAG)

UIR .... Union Internationale des Radioecologistes [*International Union of Radioecologists - IUR*] (EAIO)

UIR .... Union Internationale des Rembourreurs de l'Amerique du Nord [*Upholsterers' International Union of North America - UIU*] [*Canada*]

UIR .... Unit Initial Range (MCD)

UIR .... Unitary Irreducible Representation

UIR .... United International Research, Inc.

UIR .... University-Industry Research Program [*University of Wisconsin-Madison*] [*Information service or system*] (IID)

UIR .... Upper Flight Information Region [*Aviation*] (FAAC)

UIR .... Upper Information Region (NATG)

UIR .... Urban Intelligence Reports (CINC)

UIR .... User Instruction Register

UIR .... User Interface Requirement

UIRC .... Universal Interline Reservations Code

UIRD .... Union Internationale de la Resistance et de la Deportation [*International Union of Resistance and Deportee Movements*]

UIRR .... University-Industry Research Relationship

UIR/Res Newsl ... UIR [*University-Industry Research Program*]/Research Newsletter [*A publication*]

UIS .... Ulster-Irish Society (EA)

UIS .... Unemployment Insurance Service [*Department of Labor*]

UIS .... Union Internationale de Secours [*International Relief Union*]

UIS .... Union Internationale de Speleologie [*International Union of Speleology - IUS*] (EAIO)

UIS .... Union Internationale des Syndicats des Travailleurs des Transports [*Trade Unions International of Transport Workers*] (EAIO)

UIS .... Unisys Corp. [*NYSE symbol*] (SPSG)

UIS .... Unit Identification System

UIS .... United Information Services, Inc. (IID)

UIS .... Universal Isolation Switch

UIS .... Unlimited Intermediate Storage [*Industrial engineering*]

UIS .... Upper Internals Structure [*Nuclear energy*] (NRCH)

UISA .... United Inventors and Scientists of America (EA)

UISAE .... Union Internationale des Sciences Anthropologiques et Ethnologiques [*International Union of Anthropological and Ethnological Sciences - IUAES*] (EAIO)

UISB .... Union Internationale des Sciences Biologiques [*International Union of Biological Sciences*]

UISC .... Unreported Interstate Shipment of Cigarettes

UISDC .... Unemployment Insurance Service Design Center [*Department of Labor*]

UISE .... Union Internationale de Secours aux Enfants

UISG .... Union Internationale des Superieures Majeures [*International Union of Superiors General*] [*Rome, Italy*] (EAIO)

UISIF .... Union Internationale des Societies d'Ingenieurs Forestiers [*International Union of Societies of Foresters - IUSF*] [*Ottawa, ON*] (EAIO)

UISJM ...... Upper Internals Structure Jacking Mechanism [*Nuclear energy*] (NRCH)

UISM .... Union Internationale des Syndicats des Mineurs [*Miners' Trade Unions International*]

UISMM ..... Union Internationale des Syndicats des Industries Metallurgiques et Mecaniques

UISMTE ... Union Internationale des Syndicats des Mineurs et des Travailleurs de l'Energie [*Trade Unions International of Miners and Workers in Energy - TUIMWE*] (EAIO)

UISN .... Union Internationale des Sciences de la Nutrition [*International Union of Nutritional Sciences - IUNS*] [*Wageningen, Netherlands*] (EA)

UISP .... Union Internationale des Societes de la Paix [*International Union of Peace Societies*]

UISP .... Union Internationale des Syndicats de Police [*International Union of Police Syndicates*] (EAIO)

UISPI .... Urethane Institute, Society of the Plastics Industry (EA)

UISPP .... Union Internationale des Sciences Prehistoriques et Protohistoriques [*International Union of Prehistoric and Protohistoric Sciences*]

UISPTT ..... Union Internationale Sportive des Postes, des Telephones, et des Telecommunications [*International Sports Union of Post, Telephone, and Telecommunications Services - ISUPTTS*] [*Switzerland*]

UISTABP ... Union Internacional de Sindicatos de Trabajadores de la Agricultura, de los Bosques, y de las Plantaciones [*Trade Unions International of Agricultural, Forestry, and Plantation Workers*]

UISTAF..... Union Internationale des Syndicats des Travailleurs Agricoles et Forestiers et des Organisations des Paysans Travailleurs

UISTAFP.. Union Internationale des Syndicats des Travailleurs de l'Agriculture, des Forets, et des Plantations [*Trade Unions International of Agriculture, Forestry, and Plantation Workers - TUIAFPW*] [*Prague, Czechoslovakia*] (EAIO)

UISTAV .... Union Internationale pour la Science, la Technique, et les Applications du Vide [*International Union for Vacuum Science, Technique, and Applications - IUVSTA*] (EAIO)

UISTC .... Union Internationale des Syndicats des Travailleurs du Commerce [*Trade Unions International of Workers in Commerce*]

UISTICPS ... Union Internationale des Syndicats des Travailleurs des Industries Chimiques du Petrole et Similaires

UIS Transport ... Union Internationale des Syndicats des Travailleurs des Transports [*Trade Unions International of Transport Workers*] [*Hungary*] (EAIO)

UIT .... Jaluit [*Marshall Islands*] [*Airport symbol*] (OAG)

UIT .... Ultraviolet Imaging Telescope

UIT .... Union des Independants de Tananarive [*Union of Independents of Tananarive*]

UIT .... Union Internationale des Telecommunications [*International Telecommunication Union*] [*French*] [*United Nations*] (DUND)

UIT .... Union Internationale de Tir [*International Shooting Union*] [*Germany*] [*See also IS*] (EAIO)

UIT .... Union Internationale des Typographes [*International Typographical Union - ITU*]

UIT .... Unit Impulse Train

UIT .... Unit Investment Trusts [*Standard and Poor's Corp.*] [*Information service or system*]

UIT .... Utility Interim Tape (SAA)

UITA .... Union of International Technical Associations [*See also UATI*] [*ICSU*] [*Paris, France*] (EAIO)

UITA .... Union Internationale des Travailleurs de l'Alimentation et des Branches Connexes [*International Union of Food and Allied Workers Associations*]

UITAM ..... Union Internationale de Mecanique Theorique et Appliquee [*International Union of Theoretical and Applied Mechanics*]

UITBB .... Union Internationale des Syndicats des Travailleurs du Batiment, du Bois, et des Materiaux de Construction [*Trade Unions International of Workers of the Building, Wood, and Building Materials Industries*]

UITCA .... International Union of Co-operative and Associated Tourism (EAIO)

Uitg .... Uitgave [*Edition*] [*Netherlands*] (ILCA)

Uitgaben Natuurwet Stud Suriname Ned Antillen ... Uitgaben Natuurwetenschappelijke Studichring voor Suriname en de Nederlandse Antillen [*A publication*]

Uitg Natuurwet Studiekring Suriname Ned Antillen ... Uitgaven Natuurwetenschappelijke Studiekring voor Suriname en de Nederlandse Antillen [*A publication*]

Uitg Natuurwet Werkgroep Ned Antillen (Curacao) ... Uitgaven. Natuurwetenschappelijke Werkgroep Nederlandse Antillen (Curacao) [*A publication*]

UITP......... Union Internationale des Transports Publics [*International Union of Public Transport*] (EAIO)

UIT Rep..... UIT [*Ulsan Institute of Technology*] Report [*A publication*]

Uitvoerige Versl Sticht Bosbouwproefstn De Dorschkamp ... Uitvoerige Verslagen van de Stichting Bosbouwproefstation "De Dorschkamp" [*A publication*]

Uitvoer Versl Bosbouwproefsta ... Uitvoerige Verslagen van de Stichting Bosbouwproefstation "De Dorschkamp" [*A publication*]

UIU........... Universal Interactive Unit [*Telecommunications*]

UIU........... University of Illinois, Urbana, IL [*OCLC symbol*] (OCLC)

UIU........... Upholsterers' International Union of North America [*Absorbed by USWA*]

UIU........... Upper Iowa University [*Fayette*]

UIUC........ University of Illinois, Urbana-Champaign

UIUH........ Khorinsk [*Former USSR*] [*ICAO location identifier*] (ICLI)

UIUSD ...... Union Internationale Universitaire Socialiste et Democratique [*International Union of Social Democratic Teachers*]

UIUU......... Ulan-Ude/Mukhino [*Former USSR*] [*ICAO location identifier*] (ICLI)

UIV .... Union Internationale des Villes et Pouvoirs Locaux [*International Union of Local Authorities*]

UIW .... United Iron Workers

UIW .... Usable Inside Width (MCD)

UIWU........ United Israel World Union (EA)

UIWV .... United Indian War Veterans, USA (EA)

UIZ .... Utica, MI [*Location identifier*] [*FAA*] (FAAL)

UJ .... Air Lanka [*Sri Lanka*] [*ICAO designator*] (FAAC)

UJ .... Uganda Journal [*A publication*]
UJ .... Ungarische Jahrbuecher [*A publication*]
UJ .... Union Jack
UJ .... Union Joint   (MSA)
UJ .... Unique Jargon
UJ .... Uniwersytet Jagiellonski [*A publication*]
U de J .... Ursulines of Jesus [*Roman Catholic women's religious order*]
UJ .... Uyoku Jiten [*A publication*]
UJA .... Ulster Journal of Archaeology [*A publication*]
UJA .... United Jewish Appeal   (EA)
UJAFJP .... United Jewish Appeal - Federation of Jewish Philanthropies of
         New York   (EA)
UJASU ...... Universal Jet Air Start Unit   (DWSG)
UJB .... UJB Financial Corp. [*Formerly, United Jersey Banks*]
         [*Associated Press abbreviation*]   (APAG)
UJB .... UJB Financial Corp. [*Formerly, United Jersey Banks*] [*NYSE
         symbol*]   (SPSG)
UJB .... Umbilical Junction Box
U Jb .... Ungarische Jahrbuecher [*A publication*]
U Jb .... Ural-Altaische Jahrbuecher [*A publication*]
UJB Fn ...... UJB Financial Corp. [*Formerly, United Jersey Banks*]
         [*Associated Press abbreviation*]   (APAG)
UJC .... Union Jack Club [*British military*]   (DMA)
UJC .... Union de la Jeunesse Congolaise [*Congolese Youth Union*]
UJC .... Union Junior College [*New Jersey*]
UJC .... Universal Japanese Coupe [*Automotive engineering*]
UJC .... Urbana Junior College [*Ohio*]
UJC .... Urgency Justification Code [*Military*]   (AFIT)
UJCC(M-L) ... Union de la Jeunesse Communiste du Canada (Marxiste-
         Leniniste)
UJCD .... Union de la Jeunesse de la Cote d'Ivoire [*Ivory Coast Youth
         Union*]
UJCD Union Jeunes Chir Dent ... UJCD. Union des Jeunes Chirurgiens-
         Dentistes [*A publication*]
UJCL .... Universal Job Control Language
UJCML ..... Union des Jeunesses Communistes Marxistes-Leninistes
         [*Union of Young Marxist-Leninist Communists*] [*France*]
         [*Political party*]   (PPE)
UJCT Rep ... UJCT [*Ulsan Junior College of Technology*] Report [*Republic
         of Korea*] [*A publication*]
UJD .... Ultriusque Juris Doctor [*Doctor of Either Law; i.e., Canon Law
         or Civil Law*]
UJDG .... Union de la Jeunesse Democratique Gabonaise [*Union of
         Democratic Youth of Gabon*]
UJDK .... Union de la Jeunesse Democratique du Kongo [*Union of
         Democratic Youth of the Congo*]
UJDS .... Universitetsjubilaeets Danske Samfund [*A publication*]
UJE .... Universal Jewish Encyclopedia [*New York*] [*1939-1943*] [*A
         publication*]   (BJA)
UJEKO ...... Union de la Jeunesse Congolaise [*Congolese Youth Union*]
UJF .... Unsatisfied Judgment Fund [*Insurance*]
UJH .... International Union of Journeymen Horseshoers of the United
         States and Canada
UJISLAA .. UNESCO [*United Nations Educational, Scientific, and Cultural
         Organization*] Journal of Information Science,
         Librarianship, and Archives Administration [*A
         publication*]
UJJ .... Ujjain [*India*] [*Geomagnetic observatory code*]
UJL .... Uninet Japan Ltd. [*Telecommunications*]
UJNR .... United States-Japan Cooperative Program on Natural
         Resources
U/JNT .... Universal Joint [*Automotive engineering*]
UJS .... Universal Jamming System
UJ (SC) ..... Unreported Judgments (Supreme Court) [*India*] [*A publication*]
UJSC/EA .. ECA [*Estudios Centroamericanos*]. Universidade
         Centroamericana Jose Simeon Canas [*San Salvador*] [*A
         publication*]
UJSP .... United States-Japan Science Program   (MSC)
UJT .... Ultrasonic Journal Tester
UJT .... Unijunction Transistor
UJTS .... United Jewish Teachers Seminary [*Montreal*] [*A
         publication*]   (BJA)
UJW .... Union of Jewish Women [*Zimbabwe*]   (EAIO)
UJWF .... United Jewish Welfare Fund   (IIA)
UK .... Air UK Ltd. [*Great Britain*] [*ICAO designator*]   (FAAC)
Uk .... British Library, London, United Kingdom [*Library symbol*]
         [*Library of Congress*]   (LCLS)
UK .... Pfizer Ltd. [*Great Britain*] [*Research code symbol*]
'Uk .... 'Ukzin   (BJA)
UK .... Unabkoemmlich [*Indispensable, irreplaceable*] [*German
         military - World War II*]
UK .... Union Carbide Corp. [*NYSE symbol*] [*Wall Street slang name:
         "Ukelele"*]   (SPSG)
UK .... Union Katangaise [*Katanga Union*]
UK .... Unit Check
UK .... United Kingdom
uk .... United Kingdom [*MARC country of publication code*] [*Library
         of Congress*]   (LCCP)
UK .... University of Kansas [*Lawrence, KS*]
U d K .... Universum der Kunst [*A publication*]
UK .... Unknown [*A publication*]

UK.............. Unknown
UK.............. Unknown Worlds [*A publication*]
UK.............. Urokinase [*An enzyme*]
UKA........... Ulster King-at-Arms
UKA........... United Kingdom Alliance
UkAc......... Accrington Public Library, Accrington, United Kingdom
         [*Library symbol*] [*Library of Congress*]   (LCLS)
UKAC .... United Kingdom Automation Council [*London, England*]
UKADGE .. United Kingdom Air Defense Ground Environment
UKADR ..... United Kingdom NATO Air Defense Region   (NATG)
UKAEA ..... United Kingdom Atomic Energy Authority [*Research center*]
         [*London, England*] [*Databank originator and operator*]
UKAEL..... United Kingdom Association for European Law [*British*]
UKaGS ...... Church of Jesus Christ of Latter-Day Saints, Genealogical
         Society Library, Kanab Branch, Stake Center, Kanab, UT
         [*Library symbol*] [*Library of Congress*]   (LCLS)
UKAIRCCIS ... United Kingdom Air Forces Command, Control, and
         Information System
U Kan City L Rev ... University of Kansas City. Law Review [*A publication*]
U Kan LR... University of Kansas. Law Review [*A publication*]
U Kan L Rev ... University of Kansas. Law Review [*A publication*]
U of Kansas City L Rev ... University of Kansas City. Law Review [*A
         publication*]
U of Kansas L Rev ... University of Kansas. Law Review [*A
         publication*]   (DLA)
U Kans Publ ... University of Kansas. Publications. Library Series [*A
         publication*]
UKAPC...... United Kingdom Agricultural Production Committee
UKAPE...... United Kingdom Association of Professional Engineers [*A
         union*]
UKARC ..... United Kingdom Agricultural Research Council
UKASE...... University of Kansas Automated Serials
UKASS...... United Kingdom Amalgamated Society of Shipwrights [*A
         union*]
UKASTA ... United Kingdom Agricultural Supply Trade Association   (DS)
UK At Energy Auth At Weapons Res Establ Lib Bibliogr ... United Kingdom.
         Atomic Energy Authority. Atomic Weapons Research
         Establishment. Library Bibliography [*A publication*]
UK At Energy Auth At Weapons Res Establ Rep Ser NR ... United Kingdom.
         Atomic Energy Authority. Atomic Weapons Research
         Establishment. Report. Series NR [*A publication*]
UK At Energy Auth At Weapons Res Establ Rep Ser O ... United Kingdom.
         Atomic Energy Authority. Atomic Weapons Research
         Establishment. Report. Series O [*A publication*]
UK At Energy Auth At Weapons Res Establ Rep Ser R ... United Kingdom.
         Atomic Energy Authority. Atomic Weapons Research
         Establishment. Report. Series R [*A publication*]
UK At Energy Auth Auth Health Saf Branch Mem ... United Kingdom.
         Atomic Energy Authority. Authority Health and Safety
         Branch. Memorandum [*A publication*]
UK At Energy Auth Auth Health Saf Branch Rep ... United Kingdom. Atomic
         Energy Authority. Authority Health and Safety Branch.
         Report [*A publication*]
UK At Energy Auth Dev Eng Group DEG Rep ... United Kingdom. Atomic
         Energy Authority. Development and Engineering Group.
         DEG Report [*A publication*]
UK At Energy Auth Harwell Lab Mem ... United Kingdom Atomic Energy
         Authority. Harwell Laboratory. Memorandum [*A
         publication*]
UK At Energy Auth Harwell Lab Rep ... United Kingdom Atomic Energy
         Authority. Harwell Laboratory. Report [*A publication*]
UK At Energy Auth Health Saf Code Auth Code ... United Kingdom. Atomic
         Energy Authority. Health and Safety Code. Authority Code
         [*A publication*]
UK At Energy Auth Ind Group IG Rep ... United Kingdom. Atomic Energy
         Authority. Industrial Group. IG Report [*A publication*]
UK At Energy Auth Prod Group PG Rep ... United Kingdom. Atomic Energy
         Authority. Production Group. PG Report [*A publication*]
UK At Energy Auth Radiochem Cent Mem ... United Kingdom. Atomic
         Energy Authority. Radiochemical Centre. Memorandum [*A
         publication*]
UK At Energy Auth Radiochem Cent Rep ... United Kingdom. Atomic Energy
         Authority. Radiochemical Centre. Report [*A publication*]
UK At Energy Auth React Group Rep ... United Kingdom. Atomic Energy
         Authority. Reactor Group. Report [*A publication*]
UK At Energy Auth React Group TRG Rep ... United Kingdom. Atomic
         Energy Authority. Reactor Group. TRG Report [*A
         publication*]
UK At Energy Auth Res Group Culham Lab Rep ... United Kingdom. Atomic
         Energy Authority. Research Group. Culham Laboratory.
         Report [*A publication*]
UK At Energy Auth Res Group Culham Lab Transl ... United Kingdom.
         Atomic Energy Authority. Research Group. Culham
         Laboratory. Translation [*A publication*]
UK At Energy Auth Saf Reliab Dir SRD Rep ... United Kingdom. Atomic
         Energy Authority. Safety and Reliability Directorate. SRD
         Report [*A publication*]
UK At Energy Res Establ Anal Method ... United Kingdom. Atomic Energy
         Research Establishment. Analytical Method [*A
         publication*]

UK At Energy Res Establ Bibliogr ... United Kingdom. Atomic Energy Research Establishment. Bibliography [*A publication*]
UK At Energy Res Establ Health Phys Med Div Res Prog Rep ... United Kingdom. Atomic Energy Research Establishment. Health Physics and Medical Division. Research Progress Report [*A publication*]
UK At Energy Res Establ Lect ... United Kingdom. Atomic Energy Research Establishment. Lectures [*A publication*]
UK At Energy Res Establ Memo ... United Kingdom. Atomic Energy Research Establishment. Memorandum [*A publication*]
UK At Energy Res Establ Rep ... United Kingdom. Atomic Energy Research Establishment. Report [*A publication*]
UK At Energy Res Establ Transl ... United Kingdom. Atomic Energy Research Establishment. Translation [*A publication*]
UkAul .... Ashton-Under-Lyne Public Library, Ashton-Under-Lyne, United Kingdom [*Library symbol*] [*Library of Congress*] (LCLS)
UKAWG .... United Kingdom Asian Women's Conference [*British*]
UKAWPCM ... United Kingdom Association of Wood Packing Case Makers [*A union*]
UkB .... Birmingham Public Libraries, Birmingham, United Kingdom [*Library symbol*] [*Library of Congress*] (LCLS)
UKB .... United Kingdom Base [*World War II*]
UKB .... Universal Keyboard [*Data processing*] (AABC)
UKB .... Unvaniezh Kevredel Breizh [*Federalist Union of Brittany - FUB*] [*France*] (EAIO)
UKBB .... Kiev/Borispol [*Former USSR*] [*ICAO location identifier*] (ICLI)
UKBC .... United Kingdom Bomber Command (NATG)
UKBelQU ... Queen's University of Belfast, Belfast, United Kingdom [*Library symbol*] [*Library of Congress*] (LCLS)
UKBHU ..... United Kingdom Band of Hope Union (EAIO)
UkBl .... Blackpool Central Library, Blackpool, United Kingdom [*Library symbol*] [*Library of Congress*] (LCLS)
UkBlG .... Blackpool Gazette & Herald Ltd., Blackpool, United Kingdom [*Library symbol*] [*Library of Congress*] (LCLS)
UkBoN ...... Bolton Evening News, Bolton, United Kingdom [*Library symbol*] [*Library of Congress*] (LCLS)
UkBot .... Burton-On-Trent Public Library, Burton-On-Trent, United Kingdom [*Library symbol*] [*Library of Congress*] (LCLS)
UkBP .... Birmingham Post & Mail Ltd., Birmingham, United Kingdom [*Library symbol*] [*Library of Congress*] (LCLS)
UkBrP .... Bristol Evening Post, Bristol, United Kingdom [*Library symbol*] [*Library of Congress*] (LCLS)
UKBS .... United Kingdom Base Section [*World War II*]
UkBU .... Birmingham University, Birmingham, United Kingdom [*Library symbol*] [*Library of Congress*] (LCLS)
UKC .... Ukrainian Gold Cross (EA)
UKC .... Unit Kind Code [*Military*] (AFIT)
UKC .... United Kennel Club (EA)
UKC .... University of Kansas City [*Later, University of Missouri at Kansas City*]
UKC .... University of Kansas City. Review [*A publication*]
UKCC .... United Kingdom Central Council [*for Nursing, Midwifery, and Health Visiting*]
UKCC .... United Kingdom Commercial Corp.
UkCh .... Chelmsford Library, Chelmsford, United Kingdom [*Library symbol*] [*Library of Congress*] (LCLS)
UKCHH .... United Kingdom or Continent (Havre to Hamburg) (ROG)
UKCICC .... United Kingdom Commanders-in-Chiefs' Committee
UKCIS .... United Kingdom Chemical Information Service [*University of Nottingham*] [*Nottingham, England*] [*Information broker, databank originator, and host*]
UKCMET ... United Kingdom Council for Music Education and Training (EAIO)
UkCoE .... Essex County Newspapers Ltd., Colchester, United Kingdom [*Library symbol*] [*Library of Congress*] (LCLS)
UK/Cont (BH) ... United Kingdom or Continent (Bordeaux-Hamburg) [*Shipping*] (DS)
UK/Cont (GH) ... United Kingdom or Continent (Gibraltar-Hamburg) [*Shipping*] (DS)
UK/Cont (HH) ... United Kingdom or Continent (Havre-Hamburg) [*Shipping*] (DS)
UKCOSA ... United Kingdom Council for Overseas Student Affairs (DS)
UkCov .... Coventry Corp., Coventry, United Kingdom [*Library symbol*] [*Library of Congress*] (LCLS)
UkCr .... Croydon Library, Croydon, United Kingdom [*Library symbol*] [*Library of Congress*] (LCLS)
UKCR .... United Kingdom Communication Region [*Air Force*] (MCD)
UKCR .... University of Kansas City. Review [*A publication*]
UkCrA .... Croydon Advertiser, Croydon, United Kingdom [*Library symbol*] [*Library of Congress*] (LCLS)
UkCraT ...... Cranfield Institute of Technology, Cranfield, Bedfordshire, United Kingdom [*Library symbol*] [*Library of Congress*] (LCLS)
UkCrC .... Coulsdon Library, Croydon, United Kingdom [*Library symbol*] [*Library of Congress*] (LCLS)
UkCrP .... Purley Library, Croydon, United Kingdom [*Library symbol*] [*Library of Congress*] (LCLS)
UKCRv ..... University of Kansas City. Review [*A publication*]
UKCS .... United Kingdom Continental Shelf

UKCSB ...... United Kingdom Combat Support Boat
UKCTA ..... United Kingdom Commercial Travellers Association (DI)
UkCU .... Cambridge University, Cambridge, United Kingdom [*Library symbol*] [*Library of Congress*] (LCLS)
UkCwN ...... North Wales Weekly News, Conway, United Kingdom [*Library symbol*] [*Library of Congress*] (LCLS)
UKD .... Unusual Killing Device [*Counterintelligence*]
UkDo .... Doncaster Public Library, Doncaster, United Kingdom [*Library symbol*] [*Library of Congress*] (LCLS)
UkDw .... Dewsbury Central Library, Dewsbury, United Kingdom [*Library symbol*] [*Library of Congress*] (LCLS)
UkE .... Edinburgh Public Library, Edinburgh, United Kingdom [*Library symbol*] [*Library of Congress*] (LCLS)
UKE .... Uke Resources [*Vancouver Stock Exchange symbol*]
UKE .... Ukelele (DSUE)
UKEA .... United Kingdom Energy Authority (DI)
UkEc .... Eccles Public Library, Central Library, Eccles, United Kingdom [*Library symbol*] [*Library of Congress*] (LCLS)
UKEMS ..... United Kingdom Environmental Mutagen Society (EAIO)
UkENL ...... National Library of Scotland, Edinburgh, United Kingdom [*Library symbol*] [*Library of Congress*] (LCLS)
UkEPh .... Pharmaceutical Society of Great Britain, Scottish Department, Edinburgh, United Kingdom [*Library symbol*] [*Library of Congress*] (LCLS)
UkERCP .... Royal College of Physicians, Edinburgh, United Kingdom [*Library symbol*] [*Library of Congress*] (LCLS)
UkERCS .... Royal College of Surgeons, Edinburgh, United Kingdom [*Library symbol*] [*Library of Congress*] (LCLS)
UkES .... Scottish Central Library, Edinburgh, United Kingdom [*Library symbol*] [*Library of Congress*] (LCLS)
UkEU .... University of Edinburgh, Edinburgh, United Kingdom [*Library symbol*] [*Library of Congress*] (LCLS)
UKF .... United Karate Federation (EA)
UKFBPW .. United Kingdom Federation of Business and Professional Women (DI)
UKFF .... Simferopol [*Former USSR*] [*ICAO location identifier*] (ICLI)
UKFO .... United Kingdom for Orders [*Shipping*]
UkGM .... Mitchell Library, Glasgow, United Kingdom [*Library symbol*] [*Library of Congress*] (LCLS)
UkGO .... George Outram & Co. Ltd., Glasgow, United Kingdom [*Library symbol*] [*Library of Congress*] (LCLS)
UkGP .... Royal Faculty of Procurators in Glasgow, Glasgow, United Kingdom [*Library symbol*] [*Library of Congress*] (LCLS)
UkGU .... University of Glasgow, Glasgow, United Kingdom [*Library symbol*] [*Library of Congress*] (LCLS)
UKH .... United Keno Hill Mines Ltd. [*Toronto Stock Exchange symbol*]
UkHA .... Atomic Energy Research Establishment, Didcot, Oxfordshire, United Kingdom [*Library symbol*] [*Library of Congress*] (LCLS)
UKHAD .... United Kingdom and Havre, Antwerp, and Dunkirk [*Shipping*] (DS)
UkHe .... Heywood Public Library, Heywood, Lancashire, United Kingdom [*Library symbol*] [*Library of Congress*] (LCLS)
UKHE .... Petrovskoye [*Former USSR*] [*ICAO location identifier*] (ICLI)
UKHEF ..... United Kingdom Home Economics Federation [*British*]
UKHH .... United Kingdom and Havre-Hamburg [*Shipping*] (DS)
UKHT .... United Kingdom Housing Trust
UkHu .... Huddersfield Public Libraries, Huddersfield, United Kingdom [*Library symbol*] [*Library of Congress*] (LCLS)
UKI .... Ukiah [*California*] [*Seismograph station code, US Geological Survey*] (SEIS)
UKI .... Ukiah, CA [*Location identifier*] [*FAA*] (FAAL)
UKIAS ...... United Kingdom Immigrants Advisory Service
UKIBEK .... United Kingdom Insurance Brokers European Committee
UKII .... Kishinev [*Former USSR*] [*ICAO location identifier*] (ICLI)
UKing .... United Kingdom Fund [*Associated Press abbreviation*] (APAG)
UKIP .... United Kingdom Import Plan
UKIRT ...... United Kingdom Infrared Telescope
UKITO ...... United Kingdom Information Technology Organization
UKJATFOR ... United Kingdom Joint Airborne Task Force [*British military*] (DMA)
UK Jt Fire Res Organ Fire Res Tech Pap ... United Kingdom. Joint Fire Research Organization. Fire Research Technical Paper [*A publication*]
UkK .... Keighley Central Library, Keighley, United Kingdom [*Library symbol*] [*Library of Congress*] (LCLS)
UKK .... Urho Kekkonen [*President of Finland*]
UkKi .... Kilmarnock Public Library, Central Library, Dick Institute, Kilmarnock, United Kingdom [*Library symbol*] [*Library of Congress*] (LCLS)
UKKK .... Kiev/Zhulyany [*Former USSR*] [*ICAO location identifier*] (ICLI)
UKKS .... Semyenovka [*Former USSR*] [*ICAO location identifier*] (ICLI)
UkKuK .... Knapp, Drewett & Sons Ltd., Kingston-Upon-Thames, United Kingdom [*Library symbol*] [*Library of Congress*] (LCLS)
UKL .... Utashik Lake [*Alaska*] [*Seismograph station code, US Geological Survey*] (SEIS)
UkLA .... Associated Newspapers Ltd., London, United Kingdom [*Library symbol*] [*Library of Congress*] (LCLS)
UKLA .... Ukalaha [*Quzinkie High School, Alaska*] [*A publication*]

UkLB .... Beaverbrook Newspapers Ltd., London, United Kingdom [*Library symbol*] [*Library of Congress*] (LCLS)
UkLBOA ... British Optical Association, London, United Kingdom [*Library symbol*] [*Library of Congress*] (LCLS)
UkLC .... Chemical Society, London, United Kingdom [*Library symbol*] [*Library of Congress*] (LCLS)
UkLCS .... Institute of Commonwealth Studies, London, United Kingdom [*Library symbol*] [*Library of Congress*] (LCLS)
UkLe .... Leeds City Library, Leeds, United Kingdom [*Library symbol*] [*Library of Congress*] (LCLS)
UKLF .... United Kingdom Land Forces [*Military*]
UkLG .... Guildhall Library, Aldermanbury, London, United Kingdom [*Library symbol*] [*Library of Congress*] (LCLS)
UkLH .... Hampstead Public Libraries, Central Library, London, United Kingdom [*Library symbol*] [*Library of Congress*] (LCLS)
UkLHu ...... A. J. Hurley Ltd., London, United Kingdom [*Library symbol*] [*Library of Congress*] (LCLS)
UkLi .... Liverpool Public Libraries, Liverpool, United Kingdom [*Library symbol*] [*Library of Congress*] (LCLS)
UkLin .... City of Lincoln Public Library, Lincoln, United Kingdom [*Library symbol*] [*Library of Congress*] (LCLS)
UkLIO .... India Office Library and Records, Foreign and Commonwealth Office, London, United Kingdom [*Library symbol*] [*Library of Congress*] (LCLS)
UkLIP .... IPC Newspapers Ltd., London, United Kingdom [*Library symbol*] [*Library of Congress*] (LCLS)
UkLiP .... Liverpool Daily Post & Echo Ltd., Liverpool, United Kingdom [*Library symbol*] [*Library of Congress*] (LCLS)
UkLiU .... University of Liverpool, Liverpool, United Kingdom [*Library symbol*] [*Library of Congress*] (LCLS)
UkLJ .... Jews' College, London, United Kingdom [*Library symbol*] [*Library of Congress*] (LCLS)
UKLL .... Lvov [*Former USSR*] [*ICAO location identifier*] (ICLI)
UkLLA ...... Library Association, London, United Kingdom [*Library symbol*] [*Library of Congress*] (LCLS)
UkLLT .... Lambeth Public Libraries, Tate Central Library, London, United Kingdom [*Library symbol*] [*Library of Congress*] (LCLS)
UkLMS ..... Morning Star Co-Operative Society, London, United Kingdom [*Library symbol*] [*Library of Congress*] (LCLS)
UkLNw ...... North West London Press Ltd., London, United Kingdom [*Library symbol*] [*Library of Congress*] (LCLS)
UkLPh .... Pharmaceutical Society of Great Britain, London, United Kingdom [*Library symbol*] [*Library of Congress*] (LCLS)
UkLPo .... H. Pordes, Publisher and Bookseller, London, United Kingdom [*Library symbol*] [*Library of Congress*] (LCLS)
UkLPR ...... Public Record Office, London, United Kingdom [*Library symbol*] [*Library of Congress*] (LCLS)
UkLQ .... Friends Reference Library, London, United Kingdom [*Library symbol*] [*Library of Congress*] (LCLS)
UKLR .... University of Kansas. Law Review [*A publication*] (DLA)
UkLRCP .... Royal College of Physicians, London, United Kingdom [*Library symbol*] [*Library of Congress*] (LCLS)
UkLRCS .... Royal College of Surgeons of England, London, United Kingdom [*Library symbol*] [*Library of Congress*] (LCLS)
UkLRSM ... Royal Society of Medicine, London, United Kingdom [*Library symbol*] [*Library of Congress*] (LCLS)
UkLS .... Science Museum, London, United Kingdom [*Library symbol*] [*Library of Congress*] (LCLS)
UkLTh .... Thomasons Ltd., London, United Kingdom [*Library symbol*] [*Library of Congress*] (LCLS)
UkLU .... University of London, London, United Kingdom [*Library symbol*] [*Library of Congress*] (LCLS)
UkLuH ...... Home Counties Newspapers Ltd., Luton, United Kingdom [*Library symbol*] [*Library of Congress*] (LCLS)
UkLU-K ..... University of London, Kings College, London, United Kingdom [*Library symbol*] [*Library of Congress*] (LCLS)
UkLW .... Wellcome Historical Medical Library, London, United Kingdom [*Library symbol*] [*Library of Congress*] (LCLS)
UkLWa ...... Wandsworth Borough News Co. Ltd., London, United Kingdom [*Library symbol*] [*Library of Congress*] (LCLS)
UKM .... UK MARC [*United Kingdom Machine-Readable Cataloging*] [*Source file*] [*UTLAS symbol*]
UKM .... United Kingdom Fund [*NYSE symbol*] (SPSG)
UkMa .... Manchester Public Libraries, Central Library, Manchester, United Kingdom [*Library symbol*] [*Library of Congress*] (LCLS)
UkMaG ..... Guardian Newspapers Ltd., Manchester, United Kingdom [*Library symbol*] [*Library of Congress*] (LCLS)
UK MARC ... UK [*British Library*] Machine Readable Catalogue [*Bibliographic database*]
UKMC .... University of Kentucky Medical Center [*Lexington, KY*]
UkMe .... Public Libraries, Central Library, Merthyr-Tydfil, United Kingdom [*Library symbol*] [*Library of Congress*] (LCLS)
UKMF .... United Kingdom Mobile Force
UKMF(A) ... United Kingdom Mobile Force (Air) [*British military*] (DMA)
UKMF(L) .. United Kingdom Mobile Force (Land) [*British military*] (DMA)
UkMg .... Margate Public Library, Margate, United Kingdom [*Library symbol*] [*Library of Congress*] (LCLS)
UK Miner Stat ... United Kingdom Mineral Statistics [*A publication*]

UKMJB ..... Ukrainian Mathematical Journal [*English Translation*] [*A publication*]
UKML .... United Knitwear Manufacturers League (EA)
UKMO .... United Kingdom Meteorological Office
UKMOSS ... United Kingdom Ministry of Supply Staff
UKMRC .... United Kingdom Medical Research Council
UKN .... Unknown (KSC)
UKN .... Waukon, IA [*Location identifier*] [*FAA*] (FAAL)
UKNCIAWPRC ... International Water Quality Association [*British*] (EAIO)
UKNCIAWPRC ... United Kingdom National Committee of the International Association on Water Pollution Research and Control (EAIO)
UK/NL ...... United Kingdom/Netherlands (MCD)
UKNND .... United Kingdom National Nutrient Databank [*Ministry of Agriculture and Royal Society of Chemistry*]
UkNr .... Norwich Public Libraries, Norwich, United Kingdom [*Library symbol*] [*Library of Congress*] (LCLS)
UKNR .... University of Kansas Nuclear Reactor
UkNrE .... Eastern Counties Newspapers Ltd., Norwich, United Kingdom [*Library symbol*] [*Library of Congress*] (LCLS)
UKNSDC .. United Kingdom National Serials Data Centre [*Information service or system*] (IID)
UKO .... Unverhofft Kommt Oft [*The Unexpected Often Happens*] [*Motto of Franz, Duke of Pomerania (1577-1620)*]
UKOA .... United Kingdom Offshore Operators' Association
UKOLUG ... United Kingdom On-Line User Group [*Information service or system*] (IID)
UKOO .... Odessa/Tsentralny [*Former USSR*] [*ICAO location identifier*] (ICLI)
UKOOA .... United Kingdom Offshore Operators' Association (DS)
UKOP .... United Kingdom Official Publications [*Information service or system*] (IID)
UkOxU ...... Oxford University, Bodleian Library, Oxford, United Kingdom [*Library symbol*] [*Library of Congress*] (LCLS)
UkOxU-AS ... Oxford University, All Souls College, Oxford, United Kingdom [*Library symbol*] [*Library of Congress*] (LCLS)
UkOxU-N ... Oxford University, Nuffield College, Oxford, United Kingdom [*Library symbol*] [*Library of Congress*] (LCLS)
UkOxU-Rh ... Oxford University, Bodleian Library, Rhodes House, Oxford, United Kingdom [*Library symbol*] [*Library of Congress*] (LCLS)
UKPA .... United Kingdom Patternmakers' Association [*A union*]
UKPA .... United Kingdom Pilots Association (DS)
UKPCA ..... United Kingdom Postal Clerks' Association [*A union*]
UkPe .... Sandeman Public Library, Perth, United Kingdom [*Library symbol*] [*Library of Congress*] (LCLS)
UKPG .... United Kingdom Press Gazette [*A publication*]
UKPHS ..... University of Kansas. Publications. Humanistic Studies [*A publication*]
UKPI .... United Kingdom Provident Institute [*Commercial firm*]
UKPIA .... United Kingdom Petroleum Industry Association
UKPJA ...... Ukrainian Physics Journal [*A publication*]
UKPO .... United Kingdom Post Office [*Telecommunications*] (TEL)
UKPPD ...... United Kingdom Paper and Packaging Directory [*A publication*]
UkPS .... Portsmouth & Sunderland Newspapers Ltd., Portsmouth, Hants, United Kingdom [*Library symbol*] [*Library of Congress*] (LCLS)
UKR .... Ukraine
ukr .... Ukrainian [*MARC language code*] [*Library of Congress*] (LCCP)
UKR .... Ukrainian Soviet Socialist Republic [*ISO three-letter standard code*] (CNC)
UKR .... Uranian Kilometric Radiation [*Planetary science*]
UKRA .... United Kingdom Reading Association [*British*]
Ukrainian Math J ... Ukrainian Mathematical Journal [*A publication*]
Ukrainian Q ... Ukrainian Quarterly [*A publication*]
Ukrain Mat Zh ... Akademiya Nauk Ukrainskoi SSR. Institut Matematiki. Ukrainskii Matematicheskii Zhurnal [*A publication*]
Ukrain Phys J ... Ukrainian Physics Journal [*A publication*]
Ukr Biochim Z ... Ukrains'kyj Biochimicnyj Zurnal [*A publication*]
Ukr Bot Z ... Ukrains'kyj Botanicnyj Zurnal [*A publication*]
Ukr Chim Z ... Ukrainskij Chimiceskij Zurnal [*A publication*]
UKREP ...... United Kingdom Permanent Representative [*EEC*] (DS)
UK Report ... Economic Progress Report (United Kingdom) [*A publication*]
Ukr Fiz Z ... Ukrains'kyj Fizycnyj Zurnal [*A publication*]
UkrI .... Ukrajins'kyj Istoryk [*A publication*]
UkRiH .... Richmond Herald Ltd., Richmond, Surrey, United Kingdom [*Library symbol*] [*Library of Congress*] (LCLS)
Ukr J Biochem ... Ukrainian Journal of Biochemistry [*A publication*]
Ukr J Chem ... Ukrainian Journal of Chemistry [*A publication*]
UKRK .... Ukrains'ka Kooperativna Rada Kanadi
UkrK .... Ukrajins'ka Knyha [*A publication*]
UkrM .... Ukrajins'ka Mova i Literatura v Skoli [*A publication*]
Ukr Math J ... Ukrainian Mathematical Journal [*A publication*]
Ukr Mov .... Ukrajins'ke Movnoznavstvo [*A publication*]
Ukr Nauchno Issled Inst Fiziol Rast Nauchn Tr ... Ukrainskii Nauchno-Issledovatel'skii Institut Fiziologii Rastenii Nauchnye Trudy [*A publication*]

Ukr Nauchno Issled Inst Pishch Promsti Sb Tr ... Ukrainskii Nauchno-Issledovatel'skii Institut Pishchevoi Promyshlennosti Sbornik Trudov [*A publication*]
UkRoS .... G. & A. N. Scott Ltd., Rochdale, United Kingdom [*Library symbol*] [*Library of Congress*] (LCLS)
Ukr Phys J ... Ukrainian Physics Journal [*A publication*]
Ukr Poligr Inst Nauchn Zap ... Ukrainskii Poligraficheskii Institut Nauchnye Zapiski [*A publication*]
Ukr Q .... Ukrainian Quarterly [*A publication*]
Ukr Quart .. Ukrainian Quarterly [*A publication*]
UkrR .... Ukrainian Review [*A publication*]
UkrS .... Ukrajins'kyj Samostijnyk [*A publication*]
UkrSSR ..... Ukranian Soviet Socialist Republic
UKS .... United Kingdom Subsatellite
UKSA .... United Kingdom Shipmakers' Association [*A union*]
UKSASS .... United Kingdom Society of Amalgamated Smiths and Strikers [*A union*]
UKSATA ... United Kingdom-South Africa Trade Association
UKSC .... United Kingdom Society of Coachmakers [*A union*]
UKSG .... United Kingdom Serials Group
UkSh .... Sheffield City Libraries, Central Library, Sheffield, United Kingdom [*Library symbol*] [*Library of Congress*] (LCLS)
UkShU .... University of Sheffield, Sheffield, United Kingdom [*Library symbol*] [*Library of Congress*] (LCLS)
UkSlO .... Slough Observer Ltd., Slough, United Kingdom [*Library symbol*] [*Library of Congress*] (LCLS)
UkSsB .... John H. Burrows & Sons Ltd., Southend-On-Sea, United Kingdom [*Library symbol*] [*Library of Congress*] (LCLS)
UKST .... United Kingdom Schmidt Telescope
UkSta .... Stamford Public Library and Museum, Stamford, United Kingdom [*Library symbol*] [*Library of Congress*] (LCLS)
UKSTC ...... United Kingdom Strike Command (NATG)
UKSTU ...... United Kingdom Schmidt Telescope Unit
UkSw .... Swansea Public Library, Swansea, United Kingdom [*Library symbol*] [*Library of Congress*] (LCLS)
UKT .... Quakertown, PA [*Location identifier*] [*FAA*] (FAAL)
UKT .... United Kingdom Tariff (DS)
UKTA .... United Kingdom Trade Agency
UKTD .... United Kingdom Treasury Delegation
UKTM ...... UK [*United Kingdom*] Trade Marks [*The Patent Office*] [*British*] [*Information service or system*] (IID)
UKTOTC ... United Kingdom Tariff and Overseas Trade Classification (DS)
UK Trends ... Economic Trends (United Kingdom) [*A publication*]
UKTS .... United Kingdom Treaty Series [*A publication*]
UKTTSMA ... United Kingdom Timber Trade Shipowners Mutual Association Ltd. (DS)
UKU .... Nuku [*Papua New Guinea*] [*Airport symbol*] (OAG)
UKUSA ..... United Kingdom-United States Agreement [*Intelligence*] [*1947*]
UKV .... Underground Keybox Vault (NATG)
UKVA .... Uitgaven der Koninklijke Vlaamse Academie voor Taal- en Letterkunde [*A publication*]
UKW .... Ultrakurzwelle [*Ultrashort wave*] [*German*]
UkWE .... Eton College, Windsor, Berks, United Kingdom [*Library symbol*] [*Library of Congress*] (LCLS)
UKWE ...... Ultrakurzwellenempfaenger [*Very-High-Frequency Receiver*] [*German*]
UkWg .... County Borough of Wigan Public Libraries, Central Library, Wigan, United Kingdom [*Library symbol*] [*Library of Congress*] (LCLS)
UkWoE ...... Express & Star Ltd., Wolverhampton, United Kingdom [*Library symbol*] [*Library of Congress*] (LCLS)
UkWr .... Wrexham Public Library, Wrexham, United Kingdom [*Library symbol*] [*Library of Congress*] (LCLS)
UKY .... United Kingdom Energy [*Vancouver Stock Exchange symbol*]
'Ukz .... 'Ukzin (BJA)
UL .... Lansa, SRL [*Honduras*] [*ICAO designator*] (ICDA)
UL .... Ugaritic Literature [*C. H. Gordon*] [*A publication*] (BJA)
Ul .... Uldericus de Bamberg [*Flourished, 12th century*] [*Authority cited in pre-1607 legal work*] (DSA)
Ul .... Ulisse [*A publication*]
UL .... Ulitsa [*Street*] (EY)
UL .... Ultralinear
UL .... Ultralow
UL .... Unauthorized Launch
UL .... Underlay
UL .... Underload (NASA)
UL .... Underwriters Laboratories (EA)
UL .... Undifferentiated Lymphoma [*Medicine*] (MAE)
UL .... Uniformly Labeled [*Compound, with radioisotope*] [*Also, U*]
UL .... Unilever ADR [*NYSE symbol*] (SPSG)
UL .... Union Liberal [*Liberal Union*] [*Spain*] [*Political party*] (PPW)
UL .... Union List
UL .... Unionist Liberal [*British*] (ROG)
U/L .... Unit Linked
UL .... United Left [*Political party*] [*Peru*]
UL .... Universal League (EAIO)
UL .... Universal Life [*Insurance*]
UL .... Universala Ligo [*Defunct*] (EA)
u/l .... Unlimited [*Water depth*]

UL .... Unterlafette [*Bottom carriage*] [*German military - World War II*]
U e L .... Uomini e Libri [*A publication*]
UL .... Up Left [*The rear left portion of a stage*] [*A stage direction*]
UL .... Up Link [*Data processing*]
U/L .... UpLink
UL .... Upper Laterals [*Botany*]
UL .... Upper Left [*S-band antenna*] (NASA)
UL .... Upper Leg
UL .... Upper Level [*Nuclear energy*] (NRCH)
UL .... Upper Limb [*Upper edge of sun, moon, etc.*] [*Navigation*]
UL .... Upper Limit
UL .... Upper Lobe [*Anatomy*]
U & L .... Upper and Lower (MSA)
UL .... Urban League (MCD)
UL .... Usage List (MSA)
UL .... Useful Life (SAA)
UL .... User Language [*Data processing*] (DIT)
UL .... Utility Lead [*Telecommunications*] (TEL)
ULA .... San Julian [*Argentina*] [*Airport symbol*] (OAG)
ULA .... UCLA [*University of California, Los Angeles*] Law Review [*A publication*]
ULA .... Ulamona Field Station [*New Britain*] [*Seismograph station code, US Geological Survey*] (SEIS)
ULA .... Uncommitted Logic Array [*Semiconductor technology*]
ULA .... Uniform Laws, Annotated [*A publication*] (DLA)
ULA .... Utah State University, Logan, UT [*Library symbol*] [*Library of Congress*] (LCLS)
ULAA .... Ukrainian Library Association of America (EA)
ULAA .... United Latin Americans of America (EA)
ULAB .... Unilab Corp. [*NASDAQ symbol*] (NQ)
ULAC .... Union Latinoamericana de Ciegos [*Latin American Blind Union - LABU*] [*Montevideo, Uruguay*] (EAIO)
ULAE .... Universal Limited Art Editions
ULAEY ...... Union of Latin American Ecumenical Youth (EA)
ULAIDS ..... Universal Locator Airborne Integrated Data System (MCD)
ULAJE ...... Union Latino-Americaine des Jeunesses Evangeliques [*Union of Latin American Evangelical Youth*]
ULAJE ...... Union Latinoamericana de Juventudes Ecumenicas [*Union of Latin American Ecumenical Youth - ULAEY*] (EAIO)
ULAK .... Kotlas [*Former USSR*] [*ICAO location identifier*] (ICLI)
ULANG ..... User Language [*Data processing*]
ULAPC ...... Union Latino-Americaine de la Presse Catholique
ULAS .... University of Louisville Archaeological Survey [*Research center*] (RCD)
ULASM ..... Undersea Multichannel Large-Scale Scattering Meter [*NASA*] (MCD)
ULAST ...... Union Latino Americana de Sociedades de Tisiologia [*Latin American Union of Societies of Phthisiology*]
ULB .... Underwater Locator Beacon (MCD)
ULB .... Universal Logic Block (IEEE)
ULBA .... Universal Love and Brotherhood Association [*Kyoto, Japan*] (EAIO)
ULBM .... Underlay Battle Manager
UlbR .... Ulbandus Review [*A publication*]
ULB-VUB Inter-Univ High Energ Rep ... ULB-VUB [*Universite Libre de Bruxelles - Vrije Universiteit Brussel*] Inter-University Institute for High Energies. Report [*A publication*]
ULC .... Cache County Public Library, Logan, UT [*Library symbol*] [*Library of Congress*] (LCLS)
ULC .... Philippines Civil Liberties Union (PD)
ULC .... Underwriters' Laboratories of Canada
ULC .... Uniform Loop Clock
ULC .... Union Library Catalogue
ULC .... Union de la Lutte Communiste [*Burkina Faso*] [*Political party*] (EY)
ULC .... Unit Ledger Card [*Data processing*]
ULC .... Unit Level Code (AFM)
ULC .... Unit Level Computers [*Army*]
ULC .... Unitary Launch Concept [*or Control*] (AAG)
ULC .... United Labor Congress [*Nigeria*]
ULC .... Universal Life Church
ULC .... Universal Load Cell
ULC .... Universal Logic Circuit
ULC .... Upper Left Center [*The rear left center portion of a stage*] [*A stage direction*]
U & LC ...... Uppercase and Lowercase [*i.e., capital and small letters*] [*Typography*]
ULC .... Urban Libraries Council (EA)
ULC .... Utah State Library, Salt Lake City, UT [*OCLC symbol*] (OCLC)
ULCA .... Ukrainian Life Cooperative Association (EA)
ULCC .... Ulster Loyalist Central Coordinating Committee [*Ireland*]
ULCC .... Ultralarge Crude Carrier [*Oil tanker*]
ULCE .... Unified Life Cycle Engineering (MCD)
ULCER ...... Underwater Launch Control Energy Requirements
ULCER ...... Underwater Launch Current and Energy Recorder
ULCHi .... Cache Valley Historical Society, Logan, UT [*Library symbol*] [*Library of Congress*] (LCLS)
ULCJ .... University Law College. Journal. Rajputana University [*India*] [*A publication*] (DLA)

ULCM .... United Lutheran Church Men [*Defunct*] (EA)
ULCP........ University Laboratory Cooperative Program
ULCS........ Unit Level Circuit Switch (CAAL)
ULCS........ Unit Level Computer Logistics System [*Army*]
ULD.......... Ultrasonic Leak Detector
ULD.......... Ultrasonic Light Diffraction
ULD.......... Union pour la Liberte et le Developpement [*Benin*] [*Political party*] (EY)
ULD.......... Unit Load Demand [*Nuclear energy*] (NRCH)
ULD.......... Unit Load Device [*Shipping containers*]
ULD.......... Unit Logic Device
ULD.......... Upper Level Deck [*Cargo containers*]
ULD.......... Upper-Limb Disorder [*Medicine*] (ECON)
ULDB........ Ultra-Light Displacement Boat (PS)
ULDEST .... Ultimate Destination [*Army*] (AABC)
ULDF .... United Left Democratic Front [*India*] [*Political party*] (PPW)
ULDMI ..... Ultraprecise LASER Distance Measuring Instrument
ULDP .... Ulster Loyalist Democratic Party [*Northern Ireland*] [*Political party*] (PPW)
ULDS........ Union Liberale-Democratique Suisse [*Liberal Democratic Union of Switzerland*] [*Political party*] (PPE)
ULE .... Sule [*Papua New Guinea*] [*Airport symbol*] (OAG)
ULE .... Ultralow Expansion [*Trademark, Corning Glass Works*]
ULE .... Unit Location Equipment (MCD)
ULEA .... University Labor Education Association [*Later, UCLEA*]
ULECA...... Ultralow Energy Charge Analyzer [*Instrumentation*]
ULES........ University of Lancaster Engineering Services [*Research center*] [*British*] (IRUK)
ULew........ Lewiston Public Library, Lewiston, UT [*Library symbol*] [*Library of Congress*] (LCLS)
ULEWAT ... Ultralow-Energy Wide-Angle Telescope
ULF .... Ultralow Frequency
ULF .... United Labour Front [*Trinidad and Tobago*] (PD)
ULF .... United Left Front [*Nepal*] [*Political party*] (EY)
ULF .... University Labour Federation [*British*]
ULF .... Upper Limiting Frequency (ADA)
ULFA........ United Liberation Front of Assam [*India*] [*Political party*] (ECON)
ULFJ .... Ultralow-Frequency Jammer
ULFO .... Ultralow-Frequency Oscillator
ULG.......... Upholstery Leather Group [*Later, AG*] (EA)
ULGCS...... United Lesbian and Gay Christian Scientists (EA)
ULGLAM ... Eugenics Laboratory. Memoirs [*A publication*]
ULGS........ Church of Jesus Christ of Latter-Day Saints, Genealogical Society Library, Cache Branch, Logan, UT [*Library symbol*] [*Library of Congress*] (LCLS)
ULH.......... Ukrains'ka Literaturna Hazeta [*A publication*]
ULI .... ULI - the Urban Land Institute (EA)
ULI .... Underwriters Laboratories, Inc. [*Also, UL*]
ULI .... Union pour la Langue Internationale Ido [*Union for the International Language Ido*]
ULI .... Uniono por la Linguo Internaciona Ido [*International Language Union*] (EA)
ULI .... Universal Logic Implementer
ULI .... Unsigned Long Integer [*Data processing*]
ULI .... [*The*] Urban Land Institute [*An association*] (EAAP)
ULI .... Urban Law Institute of Antioch School of Law (EA)
ULIA .... Unattached List, Indian Army
ULIB......... Utility Library [*National Center for Atmospheric Research*]
ULIDAT.... Umweltliteraturedatenbank [*Data Bank for Environmental Literature*] [*Deutsches Umweltbundesamt*] [*Germany*] [*Information service or system*] (CRD)
ULI Lm Rep ... Urban Land Institute. Landmark Report [*A publication*]
ULI Res Rep ... Urban Land Institute. Research Report [*A publication*]
ULIS.......... Uniform Law on the International Sale of Goods
ULI Spe Rep ... Urban Land Institute. Special Report [*A publication*]
ULJ........... Bedford, MA [*Location identifier*] [*FAA*] (FAAL)
Ul'janovsk Gos Ped Inst Ucen Zap ... Ul'janovskii Gosudarstvennyi Pedagogiceskii Institut Imeni I. N. Ul'janova. Ucennyi Zapiski [*A publication*]
ULL .... Savoonga, AK [*Location identifier*] [*FAA*] (FAAL)
ULL .... Ullage [*NASA*] (KSC)
ULL .... Unit Local Loading (AAG)
ULL .... Unitarian Laymen's League
ULL .... United States Department of Labor, Washington, DC [*OCLC symbol*] (OCLC)
ULL .... Upper Lip Length [*Medicine*]
ULLA........ Ultra-Low-Level Air-Drop [*British military*] (DMA)
ULLC........ Unit Level Learning Center
ULLDPE ... Ultra Linear Low-Density Polyethylene [*Plastics technology*]
ULLL........ Leningrad/Pulkovo [*Former USSR*] [*ICAO location identifier*] (ICLI)
UL-LL........ Upper-Limit, Lower-Limit (SAA)
UL-LLC...... Upper-Limit, Lower-Limit Comparator (SAA)
ULLOS...... University of London. London Oriental Series [*A publication*]
ULLS........ Ultrasonic Liquid Level Sensor
ULLS........ Unit Level Logistics System [*Army*]
Ullst DG .... Ullstein Deutsche Geschichte [*A publication*]
Ullst Kr...... Ullstein-Buecher. Kriminalromane [*A publication*]
Ullst Kunst ... Ullstein-Kunstgeschichte [*A publication*]
ULLV........ Unmanned Lunar Logistics Vehicle [*OMSF*]

ULM.......... Meiji University, Maruzen Co. Ltd. [*UTLAS symbol*]
ULM.......... Mine Safety and Health Administration, Denver, Denver, CO [*OCLC symbol*] (OCLC)
ULM.......... New Ulm [*Minnesota*] [*Airport symbol*] [*Obsolete*] (OAG)
ULM.......... New Ulm Flight Service, Inc. [*New Ulm, MN*] [*FAA designator*] (FAAC)
ULM.......... Ultramar Capital Corp. [*Toronto Stock Exchange symbol*]
ULM.......... Ultrasonic Light Modulator
ULM.......... Undersea [*or Underwater*] Long-Range Missile [*Navy*]
ULM.......... Union List of Manuscripts [*Canada*] [*A publication*]
ULM.......... Universal Line Multiplexer
ULM.......... Universal Logic Module
ULMA .... University Laboratory Managers Association [*Later, ALMA*] (EA)
Ulm L Rec ... Ulman's Law Record [*New York*] [*A publication*] (DLA)
ULMS....... Undersea [*or Underwater*] Long-Range Missile System [*Redesignated "Trident"*] [*Navy*]
ULMS....... Union List of Montana Serials [*Library network*]
ULMS....... Unit Level Message Switch
ULN.......... Ulan Bator [*Mongolia*] [*Airport symbol*] (OAG)
ULN.......... United Lincoln Resources, Inc. [*Vancouver Stock Exchange symbol*]
ULN.......... University of Lowell, North Campus, Lowell, MA [*OCLC symbol*] (OCLC)
ULN.......... Upper Limits of Normal [*Medicine*]
ULNN........ United Lincoln Resources, Inc. [*NASDAQ symbol*] (NQ)
ULO.......... Occupational Safety and Health Administration, Technical Data Center, Washington, DC [*OCLC symbol*] (OCLC)
ULO.......... Unilateral Ovariectomy [*Gynecology*]
ULO.......... United Labour Organization [*Burma*]
ULO.......... Unmanned Launch Operations [*NASA*] (KSC)
ULO.......... Unmanned Lunar Orbiter [*NASA*] (MCD)
ULO.......... Unrestricted Line Officer [*Navy*] (DNAB)
ULOL .... Velikiye Luki [*Former USSR*] [*ICAO location identifier*] (ICLI)
U Lond I Cl ... University of London. Institute of Classical Studies. Bulletin [*A publication*]
ULOS .... Unliquidated Obligations (MCD)
ULOSSOM ... Union List of Selected Serials of Michigan [*Wayne State University Libraries*] [*Information service or system*] [*Ceased*] (IID)
ULOTC ..... University of London Officer Training Corps [*British military*] (DMA)
ULOW....... Unmanned Launch Operations - Western Test Range [*NASA*] (KSC)
ULP .... Quilpie [*Australia*] [*Airport symbol*] (OAG)
Ulp .... [*Domitius*] Ulpianus [*Deceased, 228*] [*Authority cited in pre-1607 legal work*] (DSA)
ULP .... Ulster Petroleums Ltd. [*Toronto Stock Exchange symbol*]
ULP .... Ultralow Chamber Pressure (MCD)
ULP .... Unfair Labor Practice [*Department of Labor*]
ULP .... Uniform Latex Particles
ULP .... Unleaded Petrol [*British*] (ADA)
ULP .... Utilitaire Logique Processor [*Programming language*] [*Data processing*] [*French*]
ULP .... Utility Landplane [*Navy*]
ULPA........ Uniform Limited Partnership Act [*National Conference of Commissioners on Uniform State Laws*]
ULPA........ United Lightning Protection Association (EA)
Ulpia .... [*Domitius*] Ulpianus [*Deceased, 228*] [*Authority cited in pre-1607 legal work*] (DSA)
ULPOD ..... Urban Law and Policy [*A publication*]
ULPR........ Ultralow-Pressure Rocket
ULQ.......... Tulua [*Colombia*] [*Airport symbol*] (OAG)
ULQ.......... Upper Left Quadrant (AAMN)
ULQ.......... Utah Foreign Language Quarterly [*A publication*]
ULR .... Uganda Law Reports [*A publication*] (DLA)
ULR .... Uganda Protectorate Law Reports [*1904-51*] [*A publication*] (DLA)
ULR .... Ultralinear Rectifier
ULR .... Ultramar Corp. [*NYSE symbol*] (SPSG)
ULR .... Underwater Locator Beacon
ULR .... Uniform Law Review [*A publication*] (DLA)
ULR .... Union Labor Report [*Bureau of National Affairs*] [*Information service or system*] (CRD)
ULR .... Union Law Review [*South Africa*] [*A publication*] (DLA)
ULR .... United Liberty Resources Ltd. [*Vancouver Stock Exchange symbol*]
ULR .... University Law Review [*United States*] [*A publication*] (DLA)
ULR .... University of Leeds. Review [*A publication*]
ULR .... Utah Law Review [*A publication*]
ULR .... Utilities Law Reporter [*A publication*] (DLA)
ULRA .... United Lithuanian Relief Fund of America (EA)
ULRED...... UCLA [*University of California, Los Angeles*] Law Review [*A publication*]
ULRF........ Urban Land Research Foundation (EA)
Ulrich's Q .. Ulrich's Quarterly [*A publication*]
Ulrich's Qtly ... Ulrich's Quarterly [*A publication*]
ULRSA...... Union and League of Romanian Societies of America (EA)
ULS........... ULS Capital Corp. [*Toronto Stock Exchange symbol*]
ULS........... Ultimatist Life Society (EA)

ULS.......... Ultrasystems, Inc. [*AMEX symbol*]   (SPSG)
ULS.......... Ultraviolet Light Stabilizer
ULS.......... Ulysses, KS [*Location identifier*] [*FAA*]
ULS.......... Unit Level Switchboard   (MCD)
ULS.......... United Leukodystrophy Foundation   (EA)
ULS.......... United Limited Sprints [*Auto racing*]
ULS.......... United Lutheran Society   (EA)
ULS.......... University Libraries Section [*Association of College and Research Libraries*]
ULS.......... University of Lowell, South Campus, Lowell, MA [*OCLC symbol*]   (OCLC)
ULS.......... Unsecured Loan Stock   (DCTA)
ULS.......... Upward-Looking SONAR
ULSA........ Ultralow Sidelobe Antenna [*Air Force*]   (MCD)
UL Sci Mag ... UL [*University of Liberia*] Science Magazine [*A publication*]
ULSI......... Ultralarge-Scale Integration [*of circuits*] [*Semiconductor technology*]
ULSIA .... Uniform Land Security Interest Act [*National Conference of Commissioners on Uniform State Laws*]
ULSP........ Unified Legal Services Program
ULSPD...... Ultrasonics Symposium. Proceedings [*A publication*]
ULSS .... Underwater LASER Surveying System   (MCD)
ULSSCL.... Union List of Scientific Serials in Canadian Libraries [*A publication*]
ULSSSHCL ... Union List of Serials in the Social Sciences and Humanities Held by Canadian Libraries [*National Library of Canada*] [*Information service or system*]   (CRD)
ULSTD...... Union Label and Service Trades Department (of AFL-CIO) [*American Federation of Labor and Congress of Industrial Organizations*]   (EA)
Ulster Folk ... Ulster Folklife [*A publication*]
Ulster J Arch ... Ulster Journal of Archaeology [*A publication*]
Ulster J Archaeol 3 Ser ... Ulster Journal of Archaeology. Series 3 [*A publication*]
Ulster Journal Arch ... Ulster Journal of Archaeology [*A publication*]
Ulster Med J ... Ulster Medical Journal [*A publication*]
ULSV........ Unmanned Launch Space Vehicles [*NASA*]   (KSC)
ULT .... Ultimate   (AAG)
ULT .... Ultimate Corp. [*NYSE symbol*]   (SPSG)
ULT .... Ultime [*Lastly*] [*Pharmacy*]
ult.............. Ultimo [*In the Month Preceding the Present*] [*Latin*]   (WGA)
ULT .... Ultrahigh Temperature   (MAE)
ULT .... Ultralow Tar [*Cigarettes*] [*Tobacco industry*]
ULT .... Ultralow Temperature
ULT .... Ultramar Ltd. [*Toronto Stock Exchange symbol*]
ULT .... Ultramarine [*Philately*]   (ROG)
ULT .... Uniform Low-Frequency Technique
ULT .... Unione per la Lotta alla Tubercolosi [*Union of Anti-Tuberculosis Association Workers*] [*Italy*]
ULT .... United Lodge of Theosophists   (EA)
ULT .... Upper Layer Thickness [*Of ocean waters*] [*Oceanography*]
ULTA .... Uniform Land Transactions Act [*National Conference of Commissioners on Uniform State Laws*]
ULTB........ Ultra Bancorporation [*NASDAQ symbol*]   (NQ)
ULTC........ Urban Library Trustees Council [*Later, ULC*]   (EA)
ULTI........ Ultralow-Temperature Isotropic [*Carbon*]
Ultim Real Mean ... Ultimate Reality and Meaning [*A publication*]
ULTK .... Ultrak, Inc. [*NASDAQ symbol*]   (NQ)
Ultmte....... Ultimate Corp. [*Associated Press abbreviation*]   (APAG)
ULTO....... Ultimo [*In the Month Preceding the Present*] [*Latin*]
ULT PRAESCR ... Ultimo Praescriptus [*The Last Ordered*] [*Pharmacy*]   (ROG)
ULTRA...... Ultramarine [*Philately*]   (ROG)
ULTRA...... Ultrasonics [*A publication*]
ULTRACOM ... Ultraviolet Communications
ULTRAJ ... Ultrajectum [*Utrecht*] [*Imprint*] [*Latin*]   (ROG)
Ultram .... Ultramar Capital Corp. [*Associated Press abbreviation*]   (APAG)
Ultramicrosc ... Ultramicroscopy [*A publication*]
Ultraschall Med ... Ultraschall in der Medizin [*A publication*]
Ultrason..... Ultrasonics [*A publication*]
Ultrason Imaging ... Ultrasonic Imaging [*A publication*]
Ultrason Symp Proc ... Ultrasonics Symposium. Proceedings [*A publication*]
Ultrasound Annu ... Ultrasound Annual [*A publication*]
Ultrasound Med Biol ... Ultrasound in Medicine and Biology [*A publication*]
Ultrasound Teach Cases ... Ultrasound Teaching Cases [*A publication*]
Ultrastruct Pathol ... Ultrastructural Pathology [*A publication*]
ULTRA-X ... Universal Language for Typographic Reproduction Applications
ULTRD...... Ultramicroscopy [*A publication*]
Ult Real...... Ultimate Reality and Meaning [*A publication*]
ULTSIGN ... Ultimate Assignment
ULTT......... Tallin [*Former USSR*] [*ICAO location identifier*]   (ICLI)
ULU.......... Gulu [*Uganda*] [*Airport symbol*]   (OAG)
ULV .... Ultralow Volume
ULVA .... USS [*United States Ship*] Liberty Veterans Association   (EA)
ULW.......... Unsafe Landing Warning
ULWA .... Union of Latin Writers and Artists [*Paris, France*]   (EAIO)
ULWB ...... Belozyorsk [*Former USSR*] [*ICAO location identifier*]   (ICLI)
ULWC ...... Ultra-Lightweight Coated [*Paper*]
ULWT ...... Totma [*Former USSR*] [*ICAO location identifier*]   (ICLI)
ULWW ...... Vologda [*Former USSR*] [*ICAO location identifier*]   (ICLI)

ULY .... Ulyanovsk [*Former USSR*] [*Airport symbol*]   (OAG)
ULz .... Ukrajins'ke Literaturoznavstvo [*A publication*]
ULZP........ United Labor Zionist Party [*Later, LZA*]   (EA)
UM .... Air Manila, Inc. [*Philippines*] [*ICAO designator*]   (FAAC)
UM .... Salt Lake County Library System, Midvale, UT [*Library symbol*] [*Library of Congress*]   (LCLS)
UM .... Ugaritic Manual [*C. H. Gordon*] [*A publication*]   (BJA)
UM .... Umbilical Mast [*NASA*]   (KSC)
UM .... Umot Me'uhadot [*United Nations*] [*Hebrew*]
Um .... Umschau [*A publication*]
UM .... Unable to Maintain [*Aviation*]   (FAAC)
UM .... Unaccompanied Minor [*Airline passenger*]
UM .... Under-Mentioned [*i.e., mentioned later in a document*]
UM .... Underwater Mechanic
Um .... Uniform, Medium-Grained [*Soil*]
UM .... Uninsured Motorists [*Insurance*]
UM .... Unio Mallorquina [*Majorcan Union*] [*Political party*]   (PPW)
UM .... Union Movement Party [*British*]
UM .... Unione Maniferro [*Somalia*]
UM .... Unit of Measure   (MCD)
UM .... Unitas Malacologica [*An association*] [*Netherlands*]   (EAIO)
UM .... United Medical Corp. [*AMEX symbol*]   (SPSG)
UM .... United States Minor Outlying Islands [*ANSI two-letter standard code*]   (CNC)
UM .... Universal Machine Gun   (MCD)
UM .... Universal Measuring Microscope
UM .... Universal Monitor   (MCD)
UM .... University of Manitoba [*Canada*]
UM .... University of Massachusetts [*Amherst, MA*]
UM .... University of Miami [*Florida*]
U of M....... University of Michigan [*Ann Arbor, MI*]
UM .... University Microfilms [*A publication*]
UM .... University of Missouri Press
U/M.......... Unmanned   (NASA)
UM .... Unmarried
UM .... Unpopular Magnetic Fields
UM .... Unpriced Material
UM .... Unscheduled Maintenance
UM .... Upper Magazine [*Typography*]
UM .... Upper Motor [*Neurons*] [*Medicine*]
UM .... Uracil Mustard [*Antineoplastic drug*]   (AAMN)
UM .... Uromodulin
UM .... Use of Materials Bulletin [*Department of Housing and Urban Development*] [*A publication*]   (GFGA)
UM .... Useful Method
UM .... User Manual   (MCD)
U & M....... Utilization/Reutilization and Marketing [*DoD*]
UMA........ Ultrasonic Manufacturers Association [*Later, UIA*]   (EA)
UMA........ Uniform - Memory - Access [*Data processing*]
UMA........ Union Mathematique Africaine [*African Mathematical Union - AMU*]   (EA)
UMA........ Union Medicale Arabe [*Arab Medical Union*]   (EAIO)
UMA........ Union Membership Agreement   (DCTA)
UMA........ Union Mondiale des Aveugles [*World Blind Union - WBU*]   (EA)
UMA........ Union de Mujeres Americanas [*United Women of the Americas*]
UMA........ United Maritime Administration
UMA........ United Maritime Authority
UMA........ United Methodist Association of Health and Welfare Ministries   (EA)
UMA........ Universal Measurement Assembly   (MCD)
UMA........ Universal Measuring Amplifier   (KSC)
UMA........ University of Mid-America [*Consortium of six midwestern universities*]
UMA........ Unmanned Aircraft [*Aviation*]
UMA........ Unscheduled Maintenance Action [*Military*]   (AABC)
UMA........ Upper Memory Area [*Data processing*]
UMa.......... Ursa Major [*Constellation*]
UMAA....... United Martial Arts Association   (EA)
UMAB ...... University of Maryland at Baltimore
UMAC...... UMI [*University Microfilms International*] Article Clearinghouse [*Information service or system*]   (IID)
UMAD...... Umatilla Army Depot [*Oregon*]   (AABC)
UMAH ...... Union Mondiale d'Avancee Humaine [*World Union for Human Progress*]
U Maine L Rev ... University of Maine. Law Review [*A publication*]   (DLA)
UMaj .... Ursa Major [*Constellation*]
U of Malaya L Rev ... University of Malaya. Law Review [*A publication*]
UMan .... Manti City Library, Manti, UT [*Library symbol*] [*Library of Congress*]   (LCLS)
UMANA.... Ukrainian Medical Association of North America   (EA)
UMANA.... Uspekhi Matematicheskikh Nauk [*A publication*]
UMAP ...... ULTIMAP International Corp. [*NASDAQ symbol*]   (NQ)
UMAP ...... University of Michigan Assembly Program
UMARK .... Unit Maintenance Aircraft Recovery Kit   (MCD)
U Mary L Forum ... University of Maryland Law Forum [*A publication*]   (DLA)
UMASS..... University of Massachusetts [*Amherst, MA*]
UMASS..... Unlimited Machine Access from Scattered Sites [*Data processing*]

UMB......... Ultramicrobacteria
Umb .... Umbelliferyl [*Biochemistry*]
UMB......... Umberatana [*Australia*] [*Seismograph station code, US Geological Survey*] (SEIS)
UMB......... Umberto's Pasta Enterprises, Inc. [*Vancouver Stock Exchange symbol*]
UMB......... Umbilical (MCD)
umb .... Umbundu [*MARC language code*] [*Library of Congress*] (LCCP)
UMB......... Umnak, AK [*Location identifier*] [*FAA*] (FAAL)
UMB......... Union Medicale Balkanique [*Balkan Medical Union*] (EAIO)
UMB......... Union Mondiale de Billard [*World Billiards Union - WBU*] [*Switzerland*]
UMB......... United Merchant Bar [*Commercial firm*] [*British*]
UMB......... Universal Masonic Brotherhood (EA)
UMB......... Universal Medical Buildings, Inc. [*NYSE symbol*] (SPSG)
UMB......... Universal Missile Building (MCD)
UMB......... University Museum Bulletin. University of Pennsylvania [*A publication*]
UMB......... University of Pennsylvania. Museum Bulletin [*A publication*]
UMB......... Upper Memory Block [*Data processing*] (PCM)
UMBA...... United Mortgage Bankers of America [*Philadelphia, PA*] (EA)
UMBC...... Umbilical Cord [*Aerospace engineering*]
UMBC...... United Malayan Banking Corp.
UMBC...... University of Maryland, Baltimore County
UMBC Econ R ... UMBC Economic Review [*Kuala Lumpur*] [*A publication*]
UMBE....... UMB Equities, Inc. [*Milwaukee, WI*] [*NASDAQ symbol*] (NQ)
UMBL....... Umbilical (AAG)
UMBP .... University Museum. Bulletin (Philadelphia) [*A publication*]
Umbr......... Umbrian [*Language, culture, etc.*]
UMBR...... Unclad-Metal Breeder Reactor
UMBR...... Universal Multiple Bomb Rack (NG)
UMBS .... University of Michigan Biological Station [*Research center*] (RCD)
UMBS .... University Museum. Babylonian Section. University of Pennsylvania. Publications
UMBS .... University of Pennsylvania. University Museum. Publications of the Babylonian Section [*A publication*]
UMB V ...... Umbilical Vein [*Anatomy*]
UMC......... Ukrainian Museum of Canada [*UTLAS symbol*]
UMC......... Underwater Manifold Centre [*Shell Oil Co.*] [*British*]
UMC......... Unibus Microchannel
UMC......... Unidirectional Molding Compound (MCD)
UMC......... Unified Management Corp. Database [*Information service or system*] (CRD)
UMC......... Uniform Motion Coupling
UMC......... Uniform Moving Charge
UMC......... Uninsured Motorists Coverage [*Insurance*]
UMC......... Union du Moyen-Congo [*Union of the Middle Congo*]
UMC......... Unit Mail Clerk
UMC......... Unit Mobility Center [*Military*] (AFIT)
UMC......... United Maritime Council
UMC......... United Methodist Church
UMC......... United Mining Corp. [*Vancouver Stock Exchange symbol*]
UMC......... United Motor Courts
UMC......... Universal Match Corp.
UmC......... Universal Microfilming Corporation, Salt Lake City, UT [*Library symbol*] [*Library of Congress*] [*Obsolete*] (LCLS)
UMC......... University of Maryland, College Park, MD [*OCLC symbol*] (OCLC)
UMC......... Unspecified Minor Construction Program [*Navy*] (DNAB)
UMCA...... Ultra Marathon Cycling Association (EA)
UMCA...... United Mining Councils of America (EA)
UMCA...... Universities Mission to Central Africa [*Later, USPG*] [*British*]
UMCA...... Uraba, Medellin & Central Airways, Inc.
UMCAA ... Union Medicale du Canada [*A publication*]
UMCC....... United Maritime Consultative Committee
UMCE....... UMC Electronics [*NASDAQ symbol*] (NQ)
UMCEES.. University of Maryland Center for Environmental and Estuarine Studies
UMCI .... Universal Money Centers, Inc. [*NASDAQ symbol*] (NQ)
UMCJA..... University of Michigan. Medical Center. Journal [*A publication*]
UMCMP ... University of Michigan. Contributions in Modern Philology [*A publication*]
UMCO...... United Michigan Corp. [*NASDAQ symbol*] (NQ)
UMCOM... United Methodist Communications [*Information service or system*] (IID)
UMCOR.... United Methodist Committee on Relief (EA)
UMCP .... Unit Maintenance Collection Point [*Army*] (INF)
UMCP .... University of Maryland, College Park
UM/CR ..... Unsatisfactory Material/Condition Report (MCD)
UMCS .... Uniwersytet Marii Curie-Sklodowskiej [*A publication*]
UMD .... Ultrasonic Material Dispersion
UMD .... Union de Mouvements Democratiques [*Djibouti*] [*Political party*] (EY)
UMD .... Unit Manning Document [*DoD*]
UMD .... Unit Movement Data [*Military*]
UMD .... Unitized Microwave Devices

UMd .... Universal Medical Buildings Ltd. [*Associated Press abbreviation*] (APAG)
UMD .... University of Maryland [*College Park, MD*]
UMD .... University of Medicine and Dentistry of New Jersey
UMDA...... Umatilla Depot Activity [*Army*]
UMDA...... Uniform Marriage and Divorce Act [*National Conference of Commissioners on Uniform State Laws*]
UMDA...... United Micronesia Development Association
UMDC...... Union Mondiale Democrate Chretienne [*Christian Democratic World Union*]
UMDK...... United Movement for Democracy in Korea [*Later, UMDUK*] (EA)
U Md LF.... University of Maryland Law Forum [*A publication*] (DLA)
UMDNJ .... University of Medicine and Dentistry of New Jersey [*Newark*]
UMDUK.... United Movement for Democracy and Unification in Korea (EA)
UME......... Ultramicroelectrode [*Electrochemical microscopy*]
UME......... Umea [*Sweden*] [*Seismograph station code, US Geological Survey*] (SEIS)
UME......... Umea [*Sweden*] [*Airport symbol*] (OAG)
UME......... Uniform Manufacturers Exchange (EA)
UME......... Unit Mission Equipment (AAG)
UME......... Unit Mobility Equipment
UME......... Unit Monthly Equipment (MSA)
UME......... United Ministries in Education [*Later, HEMT/UMHE*] (EA)
UME......... University of Maryland, Eastern Shore, Princess Anne, MD [*OCLC symbol*] (OCLC)
UmE......... University Music Editions, New York, NY [*Library symbol*] [*Library of Congress*] (LCLS)
UME......... Unpredictable Main Event
UME......... Urethane Mixing Equipment
UMEA...... Universala Medicina Esperanto Asocio [*Universal Medical Esperanto Association*] (EAIO)
UMEA Psychol Rep ... UMEA Psychological Reports [*A publication*]
UMEA Psychol Reports ... UMEA Psychological Reports [*A publication*]
UMEB .... United Maritime Executive Board
UMEC...... Union Mondiale des Enseignants Catholiques [*World Union of Catholic Teachers*] [*Rome, Italy*]
UMED...... Unimed, Inc. [*NASDAQ symbol*] (NQ)
UMEJ........ Union Mondiale des Etudiants Juifs [*World Union of Jewish Students - WUJS*] (EAIO)
UMEMPA ... Union of Middle Eastern and Mediterranean Pediatric Societies [*Greece*] (EAIO)
UMEMPS ... Union of Middle Eastern and Mediterranean Pediatric Societies [*See also USPMOM*] [*Athens, Greece*] (EAIO)
UMES .... United Mechanical Engineers' Society [*A union*] [*British*]
UMES .... University of Maryland, Eastern Shore
UmF.......... National Cash Register Co., New York, NY [*Library symbol*] [*Library of Congress*] (LCLS)
UMF .... Ultramicrofiche
UMF .... Uniform Magnetic Field
UMF .... University of Maine at Farmington, Farmington, ME [*OCLC symbol*] (OCLC)
UMF .... User Message Format
UMFC....... United Methodist Free Churches
UMFCBMA ... United Male and Female Cardboard Box Makers' Association [*A union*] [*British*]
UMFDC .... Union Mundial de Mujeres Democrata Cristianas [*World Union of Christian Democratic Women*] [*Venezuela*] [*Political party*] (EAIO)
Umform Tech ... Umform Technik [*A publication*]
UMFP........ Unit Materiel Fielding Point [*Army*] (RDA)
Umfrev Off Cor ... Umfreville's Office of Coroner [*A publication*] (DLA)
UMFS........ United Mutual Fund Selector [*United Business Service Co.*]
UMG .... Universal Machine Gun (MCD)
UMG .... Universal Matchbox Group Ltd. [*NYSE symbol*] (SPSG)
UMG .... Universal Mercator Grid (NVT)
UMHE...... United Ministries in Higher Education [*Later, HEMT/UMHE*]
UMHI....... United Mobile Homes, Inc. [*Eatontown, NJ*] [*NASDAQ symbol*] (NQ)
UMHK ...... Union Miniere du Haut Katanga [*Mining Company of Upper Katanga*]
UMHP....... Union Mondiale des Societes d'Histoire Pharmaceutique [*World Organization of Societies of Pharmaceutical History*]
UMHS....... University of Miami. Hispanic Studies [*A publication*]
UMI.......... Udruzena Metalna Industrija [*Belgrade, Yugoslavia*]
UMI.......... Ukrainian Music Institute in America
UMI.......... Underway Material Inspection [*Navy*] (NVT)
UMI.......... Union Mathematique Internationale [*International Mathematical Union - IMU*] (EAIO)
UMI.......... Union de Melillenses Independientes [*Spanish North Africa*] [*Political party*] (MENA)
UMI.......... Union Mundial pro Interlingua (EA)
UMI.......... Unit Movement Identifier [*Army*] (AABC)
UMI.......... United Methodist Information [*Database*] [*United Methodist Communications*] [*Information service or system*] (CRD)
UMI.......... United States Minor Outlying Islands [*ANSI three-letter standard code*] (CNC)
UMI.......... University Microfilms International [*Database producer*] (IID)

UMi .... Ursa Minor [*Constellation*]
U Miami LR ... University of Miami. Law Review [*A publication*]
U Miami L Rev ... University of Miami. Law Review [*A publication*]
UMICH..... University of Michigan [*Ann Arbor, MI*]
U Mich Bus R ... University of Michigan. Business Review [*A publication*]
U Mich J Law Reform ... University of Michigan. Journal of Law Reform [*A publication*]
U Mich J L Ref ... University of Michigan. Journal of Law Reform [*A publication*]
UMIFA...... Uniform Management of Institutional Funds Act [*National Conference of Commissioners on Uniform State Laws*]
UMII .... Vitebsk [*Former USSR*] [*ICAO location identifier*] (ICLI)
UMIN........ United Mining Corp. [*Reno, NV*] [*NASDAQ symbol*] (NQ)
UMin......... Ursa Minor [*Constellation*]
UMINF ...... United Movement of Iranian National Forces (EA)
UMIP .... Uniform Material Issue Priority [*Navy*]
UMIPS..... Uniform Material Issue Priority System [*Navy*] (NG)
UMIS......... Urban Management Information System
U Missouri at KCL Rev ... University of Missouri at Kansas City. Law Review [*A publication*]
UMIST...... University of Manchester Institute of Science and Technology [*British*] [*Databank originator and research institute*]
UMIX .... User-Manufacturer Information Exchange
UMJ .... Ukrainian Mathematical Journal [*A publication*]
Umjet Rij ... Umjetnost Rijeci [*A publication*]
UMJL......... Union Mondiale pour un Judaisme Liberal
UMJOA .... Ulster Medical Journal [*A publication*]
UMK.......... University of Missouri at Kansas City, Kansas City, MO [*OCLC symbol*] (OCLC)
UMKC....... University of Missouri at Kansas City
UMKCLR ... University of Missouri at Kansas City. Law Review [*A publication*]
UMKC L Rev ... University of Missouri at Kansas City. Law Review [*A publication*]
UML.......... Universal Mission Load [*Military*] (AABC)
UML.......... University of Missouri, Columbia School of Library and Information Science, Columbia, MO [*OCLC symbol*] (OCLC)
U of MLB .. University of Missouri. Law Bulletin [*A publication*] (DLA)
UMLC .... Institute of Estate Planning, University of Miami Law Center (DLA)
UMLC .... Universal Multiline Controller
UMLC .... University of Miami Law Center (DLA)
UMLER..... Universal Machine Language Equipment Register [*Association of American Railroads*] [*Information service or system*] (CRD)
UMLR .... University of Malaya. Law Review [*A publication*]
UMLR .... University of Miami. Law Review [*A publication*]
UMLRB..... University of Miami. Law Review [*A publication*]
UMLS........ Ukrajins'ka Mova i Literatura v Skoli [*A publication*]
UMM .... Summit, AK [*Location identifier*] [*FAA*] (FAAL)
UMM .... Union Mondiale du Mapam [*World Union of Mapam - WUM*] (EAIO)
UMM .... United Merchants & Manufacturers, Inc. [*NYSE symbol*] (SPSG)
UMM .... Universal Measuring Machine
UMM .... University of Manitoba Medical Library [*UTLAS symbol*]
UM-MaP... University of Maryland Mathematics Project
UMMC....... Union Metal Manufacturing [*NASDAQ symbol*] (NQ)
UMMH..... Unscheduled Maintenance Manhours (MCD)
UMMIPS.. Uniform Materiel Movement and Issue Priority System [*Military*] (AFM)
UMMIPS.. Uniform Military Material Issue Priority System (DNAB)
UMMJ ...... University of Manitoba. Medical Journal [*A publication*]
UMML...... Unione Medicale Mediterranea Latina [*Latin Mediterranean Medical Union - LMMU*] [*Mantua, Italy*] (EAIO)
UMML ...... University of Miami Marine Laboratory [*Florida*]
UMMM..... Minsk/Loshitsa [*Former USSR*] [*ICAO location identifier*] (ICLI)
UMMMIPS ... Uniform Military Material Movement and Issue Priority System (DNAB)
UMMPA3 ... Contributions. Museum of Paleontology. University of Michigan [*A publication*]
UMMR...... Minnesota Review [*A publication*]
UMMS..... Unit Maintenance Management System
UMMZ...... University of Michigan Museum of Zoology
UMN .... Monett, MO [*Location identifier*] [*FAA*] (FAAL)
UMN .... Union pour la Majorite Nouvelle [*Union for the New Majority*] [*France*] [*Political party*] (PPE)
UMN .... Union des Musiciens Nordiques [*Nordic Musicians' Union - NMU*] (EAIO)
UMN .... Unsatisfactory Material Notice (MSA)
UMN .... Upper Motor Neuron [*Medicine*]
UMN .... Uspechi Matematiceskich Nauk [*A publication*]
UMNCF ... United Merchant Navy Christian Fellowship [*British*]
UMNL .... Upper Motor Neuron Lesion [*Neurology*]
UMNO...... United Malays National Organization [*Malaysia*] [*Political party*]
UMO .... Umbertino's Restaurant [*Vancouver Stock Exchange symbol*]
UMO .... Unconventional Military Operations (MCD)
UMO .... University of Maine, Orono

UMO .... Unmanned Orbital [*NASA*] (NASA)
U MO B Law Ser ... University of Missouri. Bulletin. Law Series [*A publication*] (DLA)
U MO Bull L Ser ... University of Missouri. Bulletin. Law Series [*A publication*] (DLA)
UMOC....... Ugly Man on Campus [*Contest*]
UMOES .... Universal Masonic Order of the Eastern Star (EA)
UMOFC .... Union Mondiale des Organisations Feminines Catholiques [*World Union of Catholic Women's Organizations - WUCWO*] [*Canada*]
U MO-Kansas City L Rev ... University of Missouri at Kansas City. Law Review [*A publication*]
U MO KCL Rev ... University of Missouri at Kansas City. Law Review [*A publication*]
UMOL....... Unmanned Orbital Laboratory
U MO L Bull ... University of Missouri. Law Bulletin [*A publication*] (DLA)
UMOS....... U-Grooved Metal Oxide Semiconductors (MCD)
UMoS .... University of Missouri. Studies [*A publication*]
UMOSBESL ... Union Mondiale des Organisations Syndicales sur Base Economique et Sociale Liberale [*World Union of Liberal Trade Union Organizations*]
UMOSEA ... Union Mondiale pour la Sauvegarde de l'Enfance et de l'Adolescence [*World Union for the Safeguard of Youth*]
UMP......... Umpire (DSUE)
UMP......... Uniformly Most Powerful Test [*Statistics*]
UMP......... Uninflated Movement Party [*Australia*] [*Political party*] (ADA)
UMP......... Union of Moderate Parties [*Vanuatua*] [*Political party*] (PPW)
UMP......... Upper Mantle Project
UMP......... Upper Merion & Plymouth Railroad Co. [*AAR code*]
UMP......... Upward Mobility Program
UMP......... Uracil Monophosphate [*Biochemistry*] (AAMN)
UMP......... Uridine Monophosphate [*Biochemistry*]
UMPAL..... University of Minnesota. Pamphlets on American Literature [*A publication*]
UMPAR..... Unit Mobilization Personnel Assignment Report [*Navy*] (DNAB)
UMPAW ... University of Minnesota. Pamphlets on American Writers [*A publication*]
UMPEAL ... University of Miami. Publications in English and American Literature [*A publication*]
UMPG....... University of Maine at Portland/Gorham
UMpGS ..... Church of Jesus Christ of Latter-Day Saints, Genealogical Society Library, Mount Pleasant Branch, Stake Center, Mount Pleasant, UT [*Library symbol*] [*Library of Congress*] (LCLS)
UMPLIS ... Informations- und Dokumentationssystem Umwelt [*Environmental Information and Documentation System*] [*Berlin*] [*Information retrieval*]
UMPLL..... University of Michigan. Publications in Language and Literature [*A publication*]
UMPR .... Uniform Military Personnel Record (AFM)
UMPS........ Union Mondiale des Pioniers de Stockholm [*World Union of Stockholm Pioneers*] (EAIO)
UMPT .... Ultrahigh-Frequency Multi-Platform Transceiver [*Navy*] (MCD)
UMpW ...... Wasatch Academy, Mount Pleasant, UT [*Library symbol*] [*Library of Congress*] (LCLS)
UMR.......... Ultraviolet Mitogenic Radiation
UMR.......... Unimar Indonesian Participating Units [*AMEX symbol*] (SPSG)
UMR.......... Unipolar Magnetic Regions
UMR.......... Unit Mail Room [*Air Force*] (AFM)
UMR.......... University of Missouri at Rolla
UMR.......... University of Missouri at Rolla, Library, Rolla, MO [*OCLC symbol*] (OCLC)
UMR.......... Unsatisfactory Material Report [*Military*] (AABC)
UMR.......... Upper Maximum Range
UMR.......... Usual Marketing Requirement [*Business term*]
UMR.......... Woomera [*Australia*] [*Airport symbol*] (OAG)
UMRAL .... University of Minnesota Rosemont Aeronautical Laboratories (SAA)
UMRB .... Upper Mississippi River Basin
UMRCC .... Upper Mississippi River Conservation Committee (EA)
UMREL..... Upper Midwest Regional Educational Laboratory, Inc.
UMREMP ... Upper Mississippi River Environmental Management Program [*Federal government*]
UMRG....... Ergli [*Former USSR*] [*ICAO location identifier*] (ICLI)
UMRI Ne .. UMRI [*University of Michigan Research Institute*] News [*A publication*]
UMRL .... Union Mondiale des Romains Libres [*World Union of Free Romanians - WUFR*] [*Creteil, France*] (EAIO)
UMR-MEC Conf Energy Resour Proc ... UMR-MEC [*University of Missouri, Rolla - Missouri Energy Council*] Conference on Energy Resources. Proceedings [*A publication*]
UMRR .... Riga/Spilve [*Former USSR*] [*ICAO location identifier*] (ICLI)
UMRR .... University of Missouri Research Reactor
UMRW...... Ventspils [*Former USSR*] [*ICAO location identifier*] (ICLI)
UMS.......... Ukrajins'ka Mova v Skoli [*A publication*]
UMS.......... Ultrasonic Motion Sensor (MCD)
UMS.......... Unattended Machinery Spaces (DS)

UMS	Undersea Medical Society, Inc.
UMS	Unfederated Malay States
UMS	Unit Manning System [*Army*]　(RDA)
UMS	United Missionary Society
UMS	Unity Management System [*Bytex Corp.*]
UMS	Universal Maintenance Standards
UMS	Universal Memory System [*Intel Corp.*]
UMS	Universal Military Service
UMS	Universal MODEM [*Modulate/Demodulate*] System　(DWSG)
UMS	University of Maine. Studies [*A publication*]
UMS	University of Michigan. Studies [*A publication*]
UMS	University of Missouri at St. Louis, St. Louis, MO [*OCLC symbol*]　(OCLC)
UMS	University of Missouri. Studies [*A publication*]
UMS	Unmanned Multifunction Satellite
UMS	Upstream Modulation Sequence [*Genetics*]
UMSA	United States Marine Safety Association　(EA)
UMSA	Utah-Manhattan-Sundt & Associates　(AAG)
UMSB	United Missouri Bancshares, Inc. [*NASDAQ symbol*]　(NQ)
Umsch........	Umschau [*A publication*]
Umschau....	Umschau in Wissenschaft und Technik [*A publication*]
Umsch Fortschr Wiss Tech ... Umschau ueber die Fortschritte in Wissenschaft und Technik [*A publication*]
UMSDC	Unscheduled Maintenance Sample Data Collection　(MCD)
UMSE	Unconditional Mean Square Error [*Statistics*]
UMSE	Unit Maintenance Support Equipment [*Army*]
UMSE	University of Mississippi. Studies in English [*A publication*]
UMSE	Unmanned Surveillance Equipment
UMSHS	University of Michigan. Studies. Humanistic Series [*A publication*]
UMSN	Union Mondiale de Ski Nautique [*World Water Ski Union - WWSU*] [*Montreaux, Switzerland*]　(EAIO)
UMSOA	Umi To Sora [*A publication*]
UMSP........	Universal Microscope Spectro-Photometer
UMSP........	User Maintenance Support Plan　(MCD)
UMSPA.....	Uniform Metric System Procedure Act [*National Conference of Commissioners on Uniform State Laws*]
UMSR	Universal Movement for Scientific Responsibility [*See also MURS*]　(EAIO)
UMSSS	UDAM [*Universal Digital Avionics Module*] Microprocessor Software Support System　(MCD)
Ums St G ...	Umsatzsteuergesetz [*A publication*]
Umst G.......	Umstellungsgesetz [*A publication*]
UMT..........	Ultrasonic Material Testing
UMT..........	Umiat, AK [*Location identifier*] [*FAA*]　(FAAL)
UMT..........	Union Marocaine du Travail [*Moroccan Labor Union*]
UMT..........	Unit of Medical Time [*Each 4-hour period after 40-hour work week*] [*British*]
UMT..........	Unit Ministry Team [*Military*]　(INF)
UMT..........	United Methodist Today [*A publication*]
UMT..........	Universal Microwave Trainer
UMT..........	Universal Military Training [*Participants known as Umtees*] [*Army*] [*Post World War II*]
UMTA	Urban Mass Transportation Act [*1964*]
UMTA	Urban Mass Transportation Administration [*Department of Transportation*]
UMTD.......	Using Mails to Defraud
UMTE	Unmanned Threat Emitter　(DWSG)
UMTR	Universal Movement Theater Repertory [*Defunct*]
UMTR	University of Maryland Teaching Reactor　(NRCH)
UMTRAP ...	Uranium Mill Trailings Remedial Action Program [*Department of Energy*]
UMTRCA ...	Uranium Mill Tailings Radiation Control Act　(GFGA)
UMTRI......	University of Michigan Transportation Research Institute [*Research center*]　(RCD)
UMTRIS ...	Urban Mass Transportation Research Information Service [*National Academy of Sciences*] [*Database*]　(IID)
UMTRI (Univ Mich Transportation Research Inst) ... UMTRI (University Michigan Transportation Research Institute) Research Review [*A publication*]
UMTS	Universal Military Training Service [*or System*]　(GPO)
UMTS	Universal Mobile Telecommunications Services
UMTSA....	Universal Military Training and Service Act
UMu	Murray Public Library, Murray, UT [*Library symbol*] [*Library of Congress*]　(LCLS)
UMU	Uplink Multiplexer Unit　(MCD)
UMUKY......	Universal Money Centers Ltd. ADR [*NASDAQ symbol*]　(NQ)
UMUS	Unbleached Muslin
UMVBA6 ..	Contributions. Laboratory of Vertebrate Biology. University of Michigan [*A publication*]
UMVF	Union Mondiale des Voix Francaises [*World Union of French-Speakers - WUFS*]　(EAIO)
UMVF	Unmanned Vertical Flight [*NASA*]　(NASA)
UMW.........	Ultramicrowaves
UMW.........	Umwelt [*A publication*]
UMW.........	United Mine Workers [*Also, UMWA*]　(CDAI)
UMW.........	Upper Midwest
UMWA......	International Union, United Mine Workers of America [*Also known as UMW*]　(EA)
UMWA......	United Machine Workers' Association [*A union*] [*British*]

Umwelt Inf Bundesminist Innern ... Umwelt. Informationen des Bundesministers des Innern zur Umweltplanung und zum Umweltschutz [*A publication*]
Umweltpolit Umweltplanung ... Umweltpolitik und Umweltplanung [*A publication*]
Umwelt-Rep ... Umwelt-Report [*A publication*]
Umweltschutz Gesundheitstech ... Umweltschutz. Gesundheitstechnik [*A publication*]
Umweltschutz - Staedtereinig ... Umweltschutz - Staedtereinigung [*A publication*]
UMW J	United Mine Workers. Journal [*A publication*]
Umw Planungsrecht ... Umwelt- und Planungsrecht [*A publication*]
UMWSF....	United Methodist Women in Switzerland and in France　(EAIO)
Umw St G ..	Umwandlungssteuergesetz [*A publication*]
UMWTA ...	Umwelt [*A publication*]
UMWW.....	Vilnius [*Former USSR*] [*ICAO location identifier*]　(ICLI)
UMx	University of Mexico [*A publication*]
UN	Nephi Public Library, Nephi, UT [*Library symbol*] [*Library of Congress*]　(LCLS)
UN	Unable　(FAAC)
UN	Unassigned [*Telecommunications*]　(TEL)
UN	Underworld Nobility [*Used by Walter Winchell to refer to mobsters in television series "The Untouchables"*]
UN	Unico National　(EA)
UN	Unified　(AAG)
UN	Unilever NV [*NYSE symbol*]　(SPSG)
UN	Union　(MSA)
UN	Union Flag [*Navy*] [*British*]
UN	Union Nacional [*National Union*] [*Spain*] [*Political party*]　(PPE)
UN	Union Nationale [*National Union*] [*Canada*] [*Political party*]
UN	Unit　(AAG)
UN	United
UN	United Nations　(EA)
UN	University
UN	Unknown [*Telecommunications*]　(TEL)
UN	Untreated [*Medicine*]
UN	Urea-Nitrogen [*Medicine*]
UNA	Ukrainian National Association　(EA)
UNA	Unalaska [*Alaska*] [*Seismograph station code, US Geological Survey*] [*Closed*]　(SEIS)
UNA	Underwear-Negligee Associates　(EA)
UNA	Unione Nazionale dell'Avicoltura [*Aviculture Union*] [*Italy*]　(EY)
UNA	United Nations Association
UNA	United Native Americans　(EA)
UNA	United States Naval Academy, Annapolis, MD [*OCLC symbol*]　(OCLC)
UNA	Universal Network Achitecture [*Telecommunications*]
UNA	Universal Night Answering [*Telecommunications*]　(TEL)
UNA	Use No Abbreviations　(DNAB)
UNAAA.....	Ukrainian National Aid Association of America　(EA)
UNAAF	Unified Action Armed Forces [*Military*]
UNAB.......	Unabridged　(ADA)
Unabashed Libn ... Unabashed Librarian [*A publication*]
UNABR.....	Unabridged
UNAC.......	United Nations Africa Council
UNAC.......	United Nations Appeal for Children
UNAC.......	United Nations Association in Canada　(EAIO)
UNAC.......	United Nations Association of the Congo　(EAIO)
UNACC......	Unaccompanied
UNACOM ...	Universal Army Communication System
UNA Commun ... UNA [*Utah Nurses Association*] Communique [*A publication*]
UNADE.....	Union Nacional Democratica [*National Democratic Union*] [*Ecuador*] [*Political party*]　(PPW)
UNADS.....	UNIVAC Automated Documentation System [*Data processing*]
UNAEC.....	United Nations Atomic Energy Commission [*Superseded by Disarmament Commission, 1952*]
UNAECC ...	United Nations Atomic Energy Control Commission
UNAF.......	Universities National Antiwar Fund
UNAFEI...	United Nations Asia and Far East Institute for the Prevention of Crime and Treatment of Offenders
UNAFPA...	Union des Associations des Fabricants de Pates Alimentaires de la Communaute Economique Europeenne [*Union of Organizations of Manufacturers of Pasta Products in the European Economic Community*]
UNAGA.....	Union Agriculture [*A publication*]
UNA-H......	United Nations Association of Hungary　(EAIO)
UNAH.......	Universidad Nacional Autonoma, Tegucigalpa [*Honduras*]
UNAIS.......	United Nations Association International Service [*British*]
UNAKI......	Union des Colons Agricoles du Kivu [*Union of Agricultural Settlers of Kivu*] [*Congo - Leopoldville*]
UNALC.....	User Network Access Link Control
UNALOT ..	Unallotted　(AABC)
UNALTD ..	Unaltered　(ROG)
UNAM	Unico American Corp. [*NASDAQ symbol*]　(NQ)
UNAMACE ...	Universal Automatic Map Compilation Equipment

UNAMAP ... Users Network for Applied Modeling of Air Pollution [*Set of computer simulation models being developed by Battelle for EPA*]
UNA-MEX ... United Nations Association of Mexico (EAIO)
UNAMI..... Uniao Nacional Africana de Mocambique Independente [*Mozambique*] [*Political party*]
UNAMIC.. United Nations Advance Mission in Cambodia (ECON)
UNAN ...... Unanimous
UNANSD ... Unanswered (ROG)
UNA Nursing J ... UNA Nursing Journal [*Royal Victorian College of Nursing*] [*A publication*] (APTA)
UNA Nurs J ... UNA [*Utah Nurses Association*] Nursing Journal [*A publication*]
UNAP........ Union Nationale Progressite [*National Progressive Union*] [*Burundi*]
UNAP....... United Nations Association of Poland (EAIO)
UNAPEC... United Nations Action Program for Economic Cooperation
UNAPEI.... Union Nationale des Associations de Parents et Amis de Personnes Handicapees Mentales [*Formerly, Union Nationale des Associations de Parents d'Enfants Inadeptes*] [*France*] (EAIO)
Un Apic...... Union Apicole [*A publication*]
UNAPOC.. United National Association of Post Office Craftsmen [*Later, APWU*]
UNAPPD .. Unappointed (ROG)
UNAPV ..... Unable to Approve (FAAC)
UNAR....... Association for the United Nations in Russia (EAIO)
UNAR....... Unable to Approve Altitude Requested [*Aviation*] (FAAC)
UNAR....... Union Nationale Ruandaise [*Ruanda National Union*]
UNARU..... Union Nationale Africaine du Ruanda-Urundi [*African National Union of Ruanda-Urundi*]
UNAS .... United Nations Association of Sweden (EAIO)
UNASA ..... Unasylva [*A publication*]
UNASABEC ... Union Nationale des Syndicats Agricoles Forestiers, des Bois, de l'Elevage, et de la Peche du Cameroun [*National Union of Farmers, Fishermen, Forest Guards, and Timber Workers of Cameroon*]
UNASGD.. Unassigned (AABC)
UNASGN.. Unassigned [*Navy*] (NVT)
UNASL...... United Nations Association of Sri Lanka (EAIO)
UNASSAD ... Union Nationale des Associations de Soins et Service a Domicile [*Also, National Organisation for Home Care*] [*France*] (EAIO)
UNASSD... Unassembled
UNAT........ Union Nationale des Agriculteurs Tunisiens [*National Union of Tunisian Farmers*]
UNAT....... United Nations Administrative Tribunal (EY)
UNAT....... United Nations Association of Turkey (EAIO)
UNATAC .. Union d'Assistance Technique pour l'Automobile et la Circulation Routiere [*Union of Technical Assistance for Motor Vehicle and Road Traffic*] [*Geneva, Switzerland*] (EAIO)
UNATRACAM ... Union des Associations Traditionelles du Cameroun [*Union of Traditional Associations of Cameroon*]
UNATRACO ... Union Nationale des Travailleurs du Congo [*National Union of Workers of the Congo*]
UNATT ..... Unattached (ROG)
UNATT ..... Unattended (ADA)
UNATTRIB ... Unattributed
UNA-UK ... United Nations Association of Great Britain and Northern Ireland (EAIO)
UNAUS..... United Nations Association of the United States of America (AEBS)
UNA-USA ... United Nations Association of the United States of America (EA)
Unauth....... Unauthorized (DLA)
UNAUTHD ... Unauthorized (AABC)
Unauth Prac News ... Unauthorized Practice News [*A publication*]
UNAVBL... Unavailable (FAAC)
UNAVEM ... United Nations Angola Verification Mission
UNAVIC ... United Nations Audiovisual Information Center
UNB.......... Fredericton [*New Brunswick*] [*Seismograph station code, US Geological Survey*] (SEIS)
UNB.......... Kanab, UT [*Location identifier*] [*FAA*] (FAAL)
UNB.......... Unbound (ROG)
UNB.......... Unexploded Booklet [*Philately*]
UNB.......... United Nations Beacon
UNB.......... Universal Navigation Beacon
UNB.......... University of New Brunswick [*Canada*]
UNB.......... University of New Brunswick Library [*UTLAS symbol*]
UNBAL..... Unbalanced [*Telecommunications*] (TEL)
UNBB....... Barnaul [*Former USSR*] [*ICAO location identifier*] (ICLI)
UNBC....... Union National Corp. [*NASDAQ symbol*] (NQ)
UnBCh...... United Board Chaplain [*British military*]
UNBCL..... University of Nebraska College of Law [*Lincoln, NE*] (DLA)
Un Bd Ch ... United Board Chaplain [*British military*] (DMA)
UNBIS....... United Nations Bibliographic Information System [*United Nations Headquarters*] (IID)
Un Bi Soc Bull ... United Bible Societies. Bulletin [*A publication*]
UNBJ .... United National Bancorp [*NASDAQ symbol*] (NQ)

UNB Law Journal ... University of New Brunswick. Law Journal [*A publication*]
UNB L J .... University of New Brunswick. Law Journal [*A publication*]
UNBLK ..... Unblanking (MSA)
UNBLSJ.... University of New Brunswick. Law School. Journal [*A publication*] (DLA)
UNBRO..... United Nations Border Relief Operation
UNBS .... United Buying Service International, Inc. [*NASDAQ symbol*] (NQ)
UNBSA ..... United Nations Bureau of Social Affairs
UNBT........ United Nations "Blue Top" [*A publication*]
UNBTAO.. United Nations Bureau of Technical Assistance Operations
UN Bul...... United Nations Bulletin [*A publication*]
UN Bull..... United Nations Bulletin [*A publication*]
UNC.......... UNC, Inc. [*Formerly, United Nuclear Corporation*] [*NYSE symbol*] (SPSG)
Unc........... Uncanny Stories [*A publication*]
UNC.......... Uncertain (ADA)
UNC.......... Uncirculated [*Numismatics*]
UNC.......... Unclassified (KSC)
UNC.......... Uncle (DSUE)
UNC.......... Unified Coarse [*Thread*]
UNC.......... Union Nationale Camerounaise [*Cameroon National Union*]
UNC.......... Union Nouvelle Caledonienne [*Political party*] [*New Caledonia*] (FEA)
UNC.......... United Corporations Ltd. [*Toronto Stock Exchange symbol*]
UNC.......... United National Convention [*Ghana*] [*Political party*] (PPW)
UNC.......... United Nations Command
UNC.......... United Network Co. [*TV broadcasting network*]
UNC.......... United New Conservationists (EA)
UNC.......... Universal Navigation Computer
UNC.......... University of North Carolina [*Chapel Hill, NC*]
UNC.......... University of Northern Colorado [*Formerly, Colorado State College*] [*Greeley*]
UNC.......... Uranyl Nitrate Concentrate [*Nuclear energy*]
UNCA........ United Nations Correspondents Association (EA)
UNCA....... United Neighborhood Centers of America (EA)
UNCAA..... United Nations Centre Against Apartheid (EA)
UNCACK .. United Nations Civil Assistance Command, Korea
UNCAFE... United Nations Commission for Asia and the Far East
UNCAH .... Union Nacional de Campesinas Autenticos de Honduras [*National Union of Authentic Peasants of Honduras*] (PD)
UNCAP ..... United Capital Corp. [*Associated Press abbreviation*] (APAG)
UNCAST... United Nations Conference on Applications of Science and Technology [*1963*]
UNCASTD ... United Nations Advisory Committee on the Application of Science and Technology to Development (ASF)
UNCAT ..... Uncatalogued (ADA)
UNCC........ Unable to Contact Company Radio (FAAC)
UNCC........ Union Nationale des Cheminots du Cameroun [*National Union of Railway Workers of Cameroon*]
UNCC........ University of North Carolina at Charlotte
UNC-CH ... University of North Carolina at Chapel Hill
UN CCOP Newslett ... United Nations Committee for Coordination of Joint Prospecting. Newsletter [*A publication*]
UNCCP ..... United Nations Conciliation Commission for Palestine
UNCDF ..... United Nations Capital Development Fund
UNCE........ Novokuznetsk [*Former USSR*] [*ICAO location identifier*] (ICLI)
UNCE........ United Nations Commission for Europe
UNCED..... United Nations Conference on Environment and Development
UNCERT... Uncertainty [*Standard deviation*] [*Data processing*]
UNCF .... United Companies Financial Corp. [*NASDAQ symbol*] (NQ)
UNCF .... United Negro College Fund (EA)
UNCG........ Uncage
UNCG........ University of North Carolina, Greensboro
UNCHBP.. Center for Housing, Building, and Planning [*United Nations*]
UNCHE..... United Nations Conference on the Human Environment (MSC)
UNCHR..... United Nations Centre for Human Rights [*Switzerland*] (EAIO)
UNCHR..... United Nations High Commissioner for Refugees (DLA)
UN Chron .. United Nations Chronicle [*A publication*]
UNCHS..... United Nations Center for Human Settlement [*Research center*] [*Kenya*] (IRC)
UNCI .... United Nations Committee on Information (EA)
UNCID...... Uniform Rules of Conduct for Interchange of Trade Data by Teletransmission [*ICC Publishing Co.*] [*A publication*]
UNCInc ..... UNC, Inc. [*Formerly, United Nuclear Corp.*] [*Associated Press abbreviation*] (APAG)
UNCIO...... Documents. United Nations Conference on International Organization [*A publication*]
UNCIO...... United Nations Conference on International Organization [*San Francisco, 1945*]
UNCIP....... United Nations Commission for India and Pakistan
UNCITRAL ... United Nations Commission on International Trade Law
UNCIVPOL ... United Nations Civilian Police [*Peace-keeping force in Cyprus*]
UNCIWC .. United Nations Commission for Investigation of War Criminals
UNCL........ Kolpashevo [*Former USSR*] [*ICAO location identifier*] (ICLI)

UNCLAS... Unclassified (AABC)
UNCLE ..... United Network Command for Law and Enforcement
 [*Fictitious intelligence organization in various television series*]
UNCLOS... United Nations Conference on the Law of the Sea
UNCLP...... Unclamp
UNCM....... User Network Control Machine
UNCMAC ... United Nations Command Military Armistice Commission
UNCMD.... United Nations Command
UnCmp ...... Union Camp Corp. [*Associated Press abbreviation*] (APAG)
UNCN .... United Nations Censorship Network
UNCOA..... UNESCO [*United Nations Educational, Scientific, and Cultural Organization*] Courier [*A publication*]
UNCOD .... United Nations Conference on Desertification
UNCOK.... United Nations Committee on Korea
UNCOL..... Universal Computer Oriented Language [*Programming language*] [*Data processing*]
UN Comm Int'l Trade LYB ... United Nations Commission on International Trade Law. Yearbook [*A publication*] (DLA)
uncomp....... Uncomplicated
uncon.......... Unconscious
UNCON .... Uncontainerable Goods [*Shipping*] (DS)
uncond........ Unconditioned
UNCONDL ... Unconditional (ROG)
UNCOND REF ... Unconditioned Reflex [*Psychometrics*] (AAMN)
UNCONFD ... Unconfirmed (ROG)
Unconsol Laws ... Unconsolidated Laws [*A publication*] (DLA)
UNCOPUOS ... United Nations Committee on the Peaceful Uses of Outer Space
UNCOR .... Uncorrected (WGA)
uncorr......... Uncorrected
Uncov......... Uncover
UNCP .... United Nations Conference of Plenipotentiaries
UNCR .... United Nations Command (Rear)
UNCR....... University of North Carolina. Record. Research in Progress [*A publication*]
UNCRD..... United Nations Center for Regional Development
unCS .... Unconditioned Stimulus [*Psychometrics*] (AAMN)
UNCSCL... University of North Carolina. Studies in Comparative Literature [*A publication*]
UNCSF...... United Nations Command Security Force [*Military*] (INF)
UNCSGL... University of North Carolina. Studies in Germanic Languages and Literatures [*A publication*]
UNCSGLL ... University of North Carolina. Studies in Germanic Languages and Literatures [*A publication*]
UNCSRL... University of North Carolina. Studies in the Romance Languages and Literatures [*A publication*]
UNCSRLL ... University of North Carolina. Studies in the Romance Languages and Literatures [*A publication*]
UNCSTD... United Nations Center for Science and Technology for Development [*Later, CSTD*] (EAIO)
UNCSTD... United Nations Centre for Science and Technology for Development (EA)
UNCT....... Unctus [*Smeared*] [*Pharmacy*]
UNCT....... Uncut (ROG)
UNCTAD .. United Nations Conference on Trade and Development
UNCTAD TDB ... United Nations Conference on Trade and Development, Trade and Development Board
UNCTC ..... United Nations Centre on Transnational Corporations (ECON)
UNCTD ..... Uncoated
UNCURK.. United Nations Commission for the Unification and Rehabilitation of Korea
UNCW....... Novy Vasyugan [*Former USSR*] [*ICAO location identifier*] (ICLI)
UND .... Kunduz [*Afghanistan*] [*Airport symbol*] [*Obsolete*] (OAG)
UND .... Undecaprenol [*Organic chemistry*]
UND .... Under (AAG)
und .... Undetermined [*MARC language code*] [*Library of Congress*] (LCCP)
Und .... Undivided (DLA)
UND .... Union Nacional Democratica [*El Salvador*] [*Political party*] (EY)
UND .... Union Nationale et Democratique [*National Democratic Union*] [*Monaco*] [*Political party*] (PPW)
UND .... Union Nigerienne Democratique [*Political party*] (EY)
UND .... Unit Derating [*Electronics*] (IEEE)
UND .... University of National Defense [*Formerly, Industrial College of the Armed Forces and National War College*]
UND .... University of North Dakota, Grand Forks, ND [*OCLC symbol*] (OCLC)
UND .... University of Notre Dame [*Indiana*] (KSC)
UND .... Urgency of Need Designator [*Military*] (AFM)
UND .... User Need Date (KSC)
UNDA .... International Catholic Association for Radio, Television and Audiovisuals [*Belgium*] (EAIO)
UNDA .... Uniform Narcotic Drug Act [*National Conference of Commissioners on Uniform State Laws*]
Und Art Cop ... Underwood on Art Copyright [*A publication*] (DLA)
UNDAT..... United Nations Development Advisory Team
UNDBK..... Undivided Back [*Deltiology*]
UNDC........ Undercurrent

UNDC........ Union Nationale pour la Democratie aux Comoros [*Political party*] (EY)
UNDC........ United Nations Disarmament Commission [*Also, DC, DC(UN)*]
UNDCC...... United Nations Development Cooperation Cycle
Und Child .. Understanding the Child [*A publication*]
Und Ch Pr ... Underhill's Chancery Procedure [*1881*] [*A publication*] (DLA)
Und Conv... Underhill on New Conveyancing [*1925*] [*A publication*] (DLA)
UNDD .... Union Nationale pour la Democratie et le Developpement [*Madagascar*] [*Political party*] (EY)
UNDED..... Undercurrents [*A publication*]
UNDED..... Undereducated
UNDEF ..... Undefined
UNDELORDCAN ... Undelivered Orders Cancelled [*Military*]
UNDERC .. University of North Dakota Energy Research Center [*Grand Forks, ND*] [*Department of Energy*] (GRD)
Undercur.... Undercurrents [*A publication*]
Underground Eng ... Underground Engineering [*A publication*]
Underground Min Symp ... Underground Mining Symposia [*A publication*]
Underground Water Conf Aust Newsl ... Underground Water Conference of Australia. Newsletter [*A publication*] (APTA)
Undergr Wat Supply Pap (Tasm) ... Underground Water Supply Papers (Tasmania) [*A publication*] (APTA)
Underhill Ev ... Underhill on Evidence [*A publication*] (DLA)
Under Lttr ... Underwater Letter [*A publication*]
UNDERSD ... Undersigned (ROG)
Undersea Biomed Res ... Undersea Biomedical Research [*A publication*]
Undersea Technol ... Undersea Technology [*A publication*]
UNDERSECNAV ... Under Secretary of the Navy
Under Sign ... Under the Sign of Pisces/Anais Nin and Her Circle [*A publication*]
UNDERSTG ... Understanding (ROG)
UNDERTG ... Undertaking (ROG)
Underwater Inf Bull ... Underwater Information Bulletin [*A publication*]
Underwater J ... Underwater Journal [*A publication*]
Underwater J Inf Bull ... Underwater Journal and Information Bulletin [*A publication*]
Underwater Nat ... Underwater Naturalist [*A publication*]
Underwater Sci Technol J ... Underwater Science and Technology Journal [*A publication*]
Underw J Inf Bull ... Underwater Journal and Information Bulletin [*A publication*]
Underwriters Lab Stand ... Underwriters Laboratories. Standards [*A publication*]
Underwrit Lab Bull Res ... Underwriters Laboratories. Bulletin of Research [*A publication*]
UNDET ..... Undetermined
UNDETD.. Undetermined (WGA)
UNDETM ... Undetermined (AABC)
UNDEX..... Underwater Explosion [*Navy*]
UNDEX..... United Nations Index [*A publication*]
UNDF........ Underfrequency
UNDG....... Undergoing (AABC)
UNDH....... Unit Derated Hours [*Electronics*] (IEEE)
UNDHR.... United Nations Declaration of Human Rights (BJA)
UNDI........ United Nations Document Index
Un Dk ...... Under Deck Tank [*on a ship*] (DS)
UNDK....... Undock [*NASA*] (KSC)
UNDLD..... Undelivered (FAAC)
UNDLD..... Underload
UNDO....... Ukrainian National Democratic Organization
UNDO .... Union for National Draft Opposition
UN Doc...... United Nations Documents [*A publication*]
UN Doc E .. United Nations Documents. Economic and Social Council [*A publication*]
UNDOF..... United Nations Disengagement Observer Force [*Damascus, Syria*]
UNDP........ Union Nationale pour la Democratie et le Progres [*Benin*] [*Political party*] (EY)
UNDP........ Union Nationale pour la Democratie et le Progres [*The Congo*] [*Political party*] (EY)
UNDP........ Union Nationale pour la Democratie et le Progres [*Cameroon*] [*Political party*] (EY)
UNDP........ Union Nationals Democracy Party [*Myanmar*] [*Political party*] (EY)
UNDP........ United Nations Development Programme (EA)
UNDP........ University of Notre Dame Press
Und Part .... Underhill on Parternship [*10th ed.*] [*1975*] [*A publication*] (DLA)
UNDP/FAO Pakistan Nat For Res Train Proj Rep ... UNDP [*United Nations Development Programme*]/FAO [*Food and Agriculture Organization of the United Nations*] Pakistan National Forestry Research and Training Project Report [*A publication*]
UNDRC...... United Nations Disaster Relief Coordination
UndrFn ...... Underwriters Financial Group [*Associated Press abbreviation*] (APAG)
UNDRO .... United Nations Disaster Relief Office (EAIO)
UND SHER ... Under Sheriff (DLA)
UNDTKR.. Undertaker (WGA)
Und Torts .. Underhill on Torts [*A publication*] (DLA)

Und Tr .... Underhill on Trusts and Trustees [*A publication*] (DLA)
UNDV........ Undervoltage
UNDW ...... Underwater (KSC)
UNDWC.... Ultrasonically Nebulized Distilled Water Challenge
UNE........... Qacha's Nek [*Lesotho*] [*Airport symbol*] (OAG)
UNE........... Umweltschutzdienst. Informationsdienst fuer Umweltfragen [*A publication*]
UNE........... Underground Nuclear Explosion
UNE........... United Nations European Headquarters [*Geneva, Switzerland*]
UNE........... Universal Nonlinear Element
UNE........... University of North Dakota, Law Library, Grand Forks, ND [*OCLC symbol*] (OCLC)
UNEA........ Unearth [*A publication*]
UNEASICO ... Union des Etudiants et Anciens des Instituts Sociaux de Congo [*Congolese Union of Students and Former Students of Social Institutes*]
UNEBIF .... Union Europeenne des Fabricants de Bijouterie Fantaisie [*Union of European Fashion Jewelry Manufacturers*] [*Italy*] (EAIO)
UNEC........ Union Nationale des Etudiants Camerounais [*National Union of Cameroonese Students*]
UNEC........ United Nations Education Conference
UNEC........ Unnecessary (FAAC)
UNECA ...... United Nations Economic Commission for Africa (EA)
UNECE ...... United Nations Economic Commission for Europe
UNECO..... Union Economique du Congo [*Economic Union of the Congo*] [*Usumbura*]
UNECOLAIT ... Union Europeenne du Commerce Laitier [*European Milk Trade Union*] [*Common Market*]
UN Econ Comm Asia Far East Water Resour Ser ... United Nations Economic Commission for Asia and the Far East. Water Resources Series [*A publication*]
UN Econ Comm Eur Comm Agr Prob Work Party Mech Agr AGRI/WP ... United Nations Economic Commission for Europe. Committee on Agricultural Problems. Working Party on Mechanization of Agriculture AGRI/WP [*A publication*]
UN Econo Comm Asia Far East Miner Resour Develop Ser ... United Nations Economic Commission for Asia and the Far East. Mineral Resources Development Series [*A publication*]
UNECOSOC ... United Nations Economic and Social Council. Official Record [*A publication*] (DLA)
UNECTES ... Union Europeenne des Conseillers Techniques et Scientifiques [*European Union of Technical and Scientific Advisers*] [*EC*] (ECED)
UNEDA..... United Nations Economic Development Administration
UN/EDIFACT ... United Nations Rules for Electronic Data Interchange for Administration, Commerce, and Transport
UN (Educ Sci Cult Organ) Cour ... UNESCO (United Nations Educational, Scientific, and Cultural Organization) Courier [*A publication*]
UNEEG ..... Union Nationale des Eleves et Etudiants de la Guadeloupe [*National Union of Pupils and Students of Guadeloupe*] (PD)
UNEEM .... Union Nationale des Eleves et Etudiants du Mali [*National Union of Pupils and Students of Mali*] (PD)
UNEF .... Unified Extra Fine [*Thread*]
UNEF .... United Nations Emergency Force [*to separate hostile forces of Israel and Egypt*]
UNEF .... United Nations Environment Fund
UNEGA..... Union Europeenne des Fondeurs et Fabricants de Corps Gras Animaux [*European Union of Animal Fat Producers*] (EA)
UnEl........... Union Electric Co. [*Associated Press abbreviation*] (APAG)
UnElec .... Union Electric Co. [*Associated Press abbreviation*] (APAG)
UNEM .... Union Nationale des Etudiants du Maroc [*National Union of Moroccan Students*] (PD)
Unempl Ins Rep ... Unemployment Insurance Reports [*Commerce Clearing House*] [*A publication*] (DLA)
Unempl Ins Rep (CCH) ... Unemployment Insurance Reports (Commerce Clearing House) [*A publication*] (DLA)
Unemployment Ins Statis ... Unemployment Insurance Statistics [*A publication*]
Unempl Unit Bull Briefing ... Unemployment Unit Bulletin and Briefing [*A publication*]
UNEO........ United Nations Emergency Operation (PDAA)
UNEP........ United Nations Environment Programme [*Kenya*] [*Database originator*] (EAIO)
UNEP........ University of New England Press [*Australia*] (ADA)
UNEP/IRS ... United Nations Environment Programme/International Referral System
UNEPPA... United Nations Environment Programme Participation Act of 1973
UNEPTA... United Nations Expanded Program of Technical Assistance
UNERG..... United Nations Conference on New and Renewable Sources of Energy [*1981*]
UNESCAP ... United Nations Economic and Social Commission for Asia and the Pacific
UNESCO .. United Nations Educational, Scientific, and Cultural Organization [*France*] [*Database originator and operator*] [*Research center*]

UNESCO B Li ... UNESCO [*United Nations Educational, Scientific, and Cultural Organization*] Bulletin for Libraries [*A publication*]
UNESCO Bul Lib ... UNESCO [*United Nations Educational, Scientific, and Cultural Organization*] Bulletin for Libraries [*A publication*]
UNESCO Bull Lib ... UNESCO [*United Nations Educational, Scientific, and Cultural Organization*] Bulletin for Libraries [*A publication*]
UNESCO Bull Libr ... UNESCO [*United Nations Educational, Scientific, and Cultural Organization*] Bulletin for Libraries [*A publication*]
UNESCO Cour ... UNESCO [*United Nations Educational, Scientific, and Cultural Organization*] Courier [*A publication*]
UNESCO Inf Circ ... Australian National Advisory Committee for UNESCO [*United Nations Scientific, Educational, and Cultural Organization*]. Information Circular [*A publication*] (APTA)
UNESCO/IRE ... International Review of Education. United Nations Educational, Scientific, and Cultural Organization. Institute for Education [*A publication*]
UNESCO J Inf Sci Librarianship and Arch Adm ... UNESCO [*United Nations Educational, Scientific, and Cultural Organization*] Journal of Information Science, Librarianship, and Archives Administration [*A publication*]
UNESCO Nat Resour Res ... United Nations Educational, Scientific, and Cultural Organization. Natural Resources Research [*A publication*]
UNESCOR ... United Nations Economic and Social Council Official Record [*A publication*] (DLA)
UNESCO Tech Pap Mar Sci ... UNESCO [*United Nations Educational, Scientific, and Cultural Organization*] Technical Papers in Marine Science [*A publication*]
UNESDA .. Union of EEC Soft Drinks Associations (EAIO)
UNESEM ... Union Europeenne des Sources d'Eaux Minerales du Marche Commun [*European Union of Natural Mineral Water Sources of the Common Market*] (EAIO)
UNESOB... United Nations Economic and Social Office in Beirut
UNET .... United Energy Technology [*NASDAQ symbol*] (NQ)
UNETAS... United Nations Emergency Technical Aid Service
UNETPSA ... United Nations Educational and Training Program for Southern Africa
UNEV .... Unevaluated (MCD)
unev........... Uneven [*Quality of the bottom*] [*Nautical charts*]
UNEW ...... United Newspapers Ltd. [*NASDAQ symbol*] (NQ)
U Newark L Rev ... University of Newark. Law Review [*A publication*] (DLA)
U New Brunswick LJ ... University of New Brunswick. Law Journal [*A publication*]
U New South Wales LJ ... University of New South Wales. Law Journal [*A publication*]
U New S Wales LJ ... University of New South Wales. Law Journal [*A publication*]
UNEX........ Unexecuted
UNEXPL... Unexplained
UNEXPL... Unexploded
UNEXPL... Unexplored
UNEXSO .. Underwater Explorers Society (EA)
UNF........... Unfinished [*Technical drawings*]
UNF........... Unfused (KSC)
UNF........... Unified Fine [*Thread*]
UNF........... Unifirst Corp. [*NYSE symbol*] (SPSG)
UNF........... Union Flights [*Sacramento, CA*] [*FAA designator*] (FAAC)
UNF........... Union Freight R. R. [*AAR code*]
UNF........... United National Front [*Lebanon*] (BJA)
UNF........... Universal National Fine (MCD)
UNF........... University of North Dakota, Medical Library, Grand Forks, ND [*OCLC symbol*] (OCLC)
UNFA........ Union Nationale des Femmes Algeriennes [*Algeria*] [*Political party*] (EY)
UNFAO..... United Nations Food and Agriculture Organization
UNFAO (Organ) World Soil Resour Rep ... United Nations. FAO (Food and Agriculture Organization) World Soil Resources Reports [*A publication*]
UNFAV ..... Unfavorable
UNFB .... United Nations Film Board
UNFC......... Universal Fuels Co. [*NASDAQ symbol*] (NQ)
UNFDAC .. United Nations Fund for Drug Abuse Control
UnfedF .... UnionFed Financial [*Associated Press abbreviation*] (APAG)
UNFF .... United First Federal Savings & Loan [*NASDAQ symbol*] (NQ)
UNFGA...... Unternehmensforschung [*A publication*]
UNFI .... Unfinished
UNFICYP ... United Nations Forces in Cyprus (DMA)
UNFIN ...... Unfinished
UNFKA ...... Uspekhi Nauchnoi Fotografii [*A publication*]
UNFO....... Unidentified Nonflying Objects
UNFP .... Union Nationale des Forces Populaires [*National Union of Popular Forces*] [*Political party*] [*Morocco*]
UNFP .... United National Federal Party [*Zimbabwe*] [*Political party*] (PPW)
UNFPA...... United Nations Fund for Population Activities

UNFR .... Uniforce Temporary Personnel, Inc. [*New Hyde Park, NY*] [*NASDAQ symbol*] (NQ)
UNFSSTD ... United Nations Financing System for Science and Technology for Development (EY)
UNFT .... Union Nationale des Femmes de Tunisie [*National Union of Tunisian Women*]
UNFTP...... Unified Navy Field Test Program (MCD)
UNFURNOTE ... Until Further Notice [*Military*]
UNG .... Kiunga [*Papua New Guinea*] [*Airport symbol*] (OAG)
UNG .... Ungava [*Canada*]
UNG .... Unguentum [*Ointment*] [*Pharmacy*]
UNG .... Union Gas Ltd. [*AMEX symbol*] [*Delisted*] [*Toronto Stock Exchange symbol*] (SPSG)
UNGA .... United Nations General Assembly (MCD)
UNGAOR ... United Nations General Assembly Official Record [*A publication*] (DLA)
Ungar Fil L ... Ungar Film Library [*A publication*]
Ungarische Rundschau ... Ungarische Rundschau fuer Historische und Sociale Wissenschaften [*A publication*]
UNGEGN ... United Nations Group of Experts on Geographical Names
Ungerer's Bull ... Ungerer's Bulletin [*A publication*]
Ung Forstwiss Rundsch ... Ungarische Forstwissenschaftliche Rundschau [*A publication*]
Un of Gh LJ ... University of Ghana. Law Journal [*A publication*] (DLA)
Ung Jhb ..... Ungarische Jahrbuecher [*A publication*]
UNGOMAP ... United Nations Good Offices Mission in Afghanistan and Pakistan [*Later, OSGAP*]
UNGR....... Ungermann-Bass, Inc. [*NASDAQ symbol*] (NQ)
UNGT....... Unguentum [*Ointment*] [*Pharmacy*]
UN-GTDI ... United Nations Guidelines for Trade Data Interchange
UNH .... United Healthcare Corp. [*Minnetonka, MN*] [*NYSE symbol*] (NQ)
UNH .... United Homes, Inc. [*Vancouver Stock Exchange symbol*]
UNH .... Uranyl Nitrate Hexahydrate [*Inorganic chemistry*]
UNHC ...... United Nations High Commission (BJA)
UNHCC ...... University of New Haven Computer Center [*Research center*] (RCD)
UNHCR..... United Nations High Commission [*or Commissioner*] for Refugees
UNHJ .... University of Newcastle. Historical Journal [*A publication*] (APTA)
UNHNOCY ... United Nations Headquarters Nongovernmental Organizations Committee on Youth (EA)
UNHQ....... United Nations Headquarters (DLA)
UNHRC..... United Nations Human Rights Commission (BJA)
UNHRD .... Unheard (FAAC)
UNI........... Athens/Albany, OH [*Location identifier*] [*FAA*] (FAAL)
UNI........... Undistributed Net Income [*Banking*]
UNI........... Uni-Marts, Inc. [*AMEX symbol*] (SPSG)
Uni .... Unicorn [*Record label*]
UNI........... Unicorp Canada Corp. [*Toronto Stock Exchange symbol*]
UNI........... Uniform (DSUE)
UNI........... Union Island [*Windward Islands*] [*Airport symbol*] (OAG)
UNI........... Union Nationale pour l'Independence [*National Union for Independence*] [*Djibouti*] (PPW)
UNI........... Union Nationale des Independants [*National Union of Independents*] [*Monaco*] (PPE)
UNI........... United News of India Ltd. [*News agency*] (FEA)
UNI........... United States International Airways
UNI........... Unity Railways Co. [*AAR code*]
Uni .... Universe Science Fiction [*A publication*]
UNI........... University (ADA)
UNI........... University of Northern Iowa [*Cedar Falls, IA*] (OICC)
UNI........... User Network Interface [*Data processing*]
UNIA........ Universal Negro Improvement Association [*Organization led by Marcus Aurelius Garvey*]
UNIA & ACLW ... Universal Negro Improvement Association and African Communities League of the World (EA)
UNIADUSEC ... Union Internationale des Associations de Diplomes Universitaires en Sciences Economiques et Commerciales
UNIATEC ... Union Internationale des Associations Techniques Cinematographiques [*International Union of Technical Cinematograph Associations - IUTCA*] (EAIO)
UNIBANK ... United City Bank [*Indonesia*] (EY)
UNIBID..... UNISIST International Centre for Bibliographic Descriptions [*UNESCO*] [*Information service or system*] (IID)
UNIBUS.... Universal Bus [*Digital Equipment Corp.*]
UNIC........ Union Internationale des Cinemas [*International Union of Cinemas*] (EAIO)
UNIC........ United International Club, Inc.
UNIC........ United Nations Information Centre
UNICA ...... Asociacion de Universidades del Caribe [*Association of Caribbean Universities and Research Institutes*] (EA)
UNICA ...... Union Internationale du Cinema Non Professionnel [*International Union of Amateur Cinema*] (EAIO)
UNICAP.... Universidade Catolica de Pernambuco [*Brazil*]
UniCare ..... UniCare Financial Corp. [*Associated Press abbreviation*] (APAG)
UNICCAP ... Universal Cable Circuit Analysis Program [*Bell System*]
UNICE ...... Union of Industrial and Employers' Confederations of Europe (EAIO)

UNICE ...... Union des Industries de la Communaute Europeenne [*Union of Industries of the European Community*]
UNICEF .... United Nations Children's Fund [*Acronym is based on former name, United Nations International Children's Emergency Fund*] (EA)
UNICEF-NZ ... New Zealand National Committee for UNICEF (EAIO)
UNICHAL ... Union Internationale des Distributeurs de Chaleur [*International Union of Heat Distributors*] (EAIO)
UNICIS ..... Unit Concept Indexing System
UNICIV Rep ... UNICIV [*School of Civil Engineering, University of New South Wales*] Report [*A publication*] (APTA)
UNICLO ... United Nations Information Centre and Liaison Office (PDAA)
UNICO...... Union pour les Interets du Peuple Congolais [*Union for the Interests of the Congolese People*]
UNICO...... Universal Cooperatives (EA)
UNICOCYM ... Union Internationale du Commerce et de la Reparation du Cycle et du Motocycle [*International Union of Cycle and Motocycle Trade and Repair*] [*Germany*]
UNICODE ... Unique Injector Concepts Development (MCD)
UNICOL ... Union des Colons de la Province Orientale [*Union of Settlers in Orientale Province*]
UNICOM ... Underwater Integration Communication
UNICOM ... Unidad Informativa Computable [*Computerized Information Unit*] [*Mexico*] [*Information service or system*] (IID)
UNICOM ... Unified Communications [*Radio station*]
UNICOM ... Universal Components [*Construction*]
UNICOM ... Universal Integrated Communication System [*Military*]
UNICOMP ... Universal Compiler (IEEE)
UNICON... Unidensity Coherent Light Recording (IEEE)
UNICORN ... Unilateral Arms Control
Unicorn J ... Unicorn Journal [*A publication*]
UNICYP... United Nations International Force, Cyprus
UNID........ Unidentified (FAAC)
UNIDA...... Unidia [*A publication*]
UNIDAHO ... Union des Independants du Dahomey [*Independents Union of Dahomey*]
UNIDENT ... Unidentified
UNIDF ...... United Nations Industrial Development Fund
UNIDIR .... United Nations Institute for Disarmament Research [*Research center*] [*Switzerland*] (IRC)
UNIDO...... United Nations Industrial Development Organization [*Austria*] [*Also, an information service or system*] (IID)
UNIDROIT ... Institut International pour l'Unification du Droit Prive [*International Institute for the Unification of Private Law*] (EAIO)
Unidroit Yb ... International Institute for the Unification of Private Law. Yearbook [*Rome, Italy*] [*A publication*] (DLA)
UNIEF...... USEUCOM [*United States European Command*] Nuclear Interface Element Fastbreak (MCD)
UNIEP...... Union Internationale des Entrepreneurs de Peinture [*International Union of Master Painters - IUMP*] (EAIO)
Unif........... Unified (DLA)
UNIF .... Uniflex, Inc. [*NASDAQ symbol*] (NQ)
UNIF .... Uniform (AFM)
UNIF .... Uniformity
UNIFAC.... Universal Functional Activity Coefficient [*Chemical engineering*]
Unif C Code ... Uniform Commercial Code Law Journal [*A publication*]
UNIFE...... Union des Industries Ferroviaires Europeennes [*Union of European Railway Industries*] (EA)
UNIFEM... United Nations Development Fund for Women (EA)
UNIFET .... Unipolar Field-Effect Transistor
Unifi.......... Unifi, Inc. [*Associated Press abbreviation*] (APAG)
Unific LYB ... Unification of Law Yearbook [*A publication*] (DLA)
UNIFIL.... United Nations Interim Force in Lebanon
Unif L Conf ... Proceedings, Uniform Law Conference of Canada [*A publication*] (DLA)
Unif L Conf ... Uniform Law Conference [*A publication*] (DLA)
Unif L Conf Can ... Uniform Law Conference of Canada [*A publication*] (DLA)
UNIFOM .. United Front of Political Movements [*Sierra Leone*] [*Political party*] (EY)
UNIFOR ... Unified Forces [*Military*]
UNIFORCE ... United Defense Force [*Established by the Brussels Treaty*] (NATG)
Uniform City Ct Act ... New York Uniform City Court Act [*A publication*]
Uniform City Ct Act ... Uniform City Court Act [*A publication*] (DLA)
Uniform Dist Ct Act ... New York Uniform District Court Act [*A publication*]
Uniform Dist Ct Act ... Uniform District Court Act [*A publication*] (DLA)
Uniform Just Ct Act ... New York Uniform Justice Court Act [*A publication*]
Uniform L Rev ... Uniform Law Review [*A publication*] (DLA)
UNI-FREDI ... Universal Flight Range and Endurance Data Indicator
UniFst........ Unifirst Corp. [*Associated Press abbreviation*] (APAG)
Unif Sys Citation ... Uniform System of Citation [*Legal term*] (DLA)
UNIG....... University Graphics, Inc. [*Atlantic Highlands, NJ*] [*NASDAQ symbol*] (NQ)
UNIGABON ... Union Interprofessionnelle du Gabon [*Inter-Trade Union of Gabon*]
UNIHI....... University of Hawaii [*Honolulu, HI*] (NOAA)
UNII .... Yeniseysk [*Former USSR*] [*ICAO location identifier*] (ICLI)
UNIIMOG ... United Nations Iran-Iraq Military Observer Group

UNIKOM ... United Nations Iraq/Kuwait Observer Mission
Unilab .... United Laboratories Inc. [*Philippines*]
UNILAC.... Universal Linear Accelerator
unilat.......... Unilateral
Unilevr ...... Unilever PLC [*Associated Press abbreviation*]   (APAG)
Uni Ljubljai Teh Fak Acta Tech Ser Chim ... Univerza v Ljubljani. Tehniska
              Fakulteta. Acta Technica. Series Chimica [*A publication*]
UNIMA..... Union Internationale de Grands Magasins [*International Union
              of Department Stores*]
UNIMA..... Union Internationale de la Marionnette [*International
              Puppeteers Union*] [*France*]
UNIMA..... Unione Nazionale Imprese di Meccanizzazione Agricola
              [*Agricultural Mechanization Enterprises Union*]
              [*Italy*]   (EY)
UNIMAR .. Unimar Co. [*Associated Press abbreviation*]   (APAG)
UNIMARC ... Universal Machine Readable Cataloging   (ADA)
UNIMA-USA ... American Center of the Union Internationale de la
              Marionette   (EA)
UNIMERC ... Universal Numeric Coding System [*Distilling industry*]
UNIMOD ... Unified Modular Plant [*Nuclear energy*]
UniMrt ...... Uni-Marts, Inc. [*State College, PA*] [*Associated Press
              abbreviation*]   (APAG)
UNIN......... Unilife Corp. [*NASDAQ symbol*]   (NQ)
Un Ins Co... Unemployment Insurance Code [*A publication*]   (DLA)
UN Int Mtg Oilfield Dev Techniques ... United Nations International Meeting
              on Oilfield Development Techniques [*A publication*]
UNIO......... United Nations Information Organization
Union Agric ... Union Agriculture [*A publication*]
Union Burma J Life Sci ... Union of Burma. Journal of Life Sciences [*A
              publication*]
Union Burma J Sci Technol ... Union of Burma. Journal of Science and
              Technology [*A publication*]
UnionC....... Union Corp. [*Associated Press abbreviation*]   (APAG)
Union Carbide Met Rev ... Union Carbide Metals Review [*A publication*]
UNION FLEURS ... Union Internationale du Commerce de Gros en Fleurs
              [*International Union of the Wholesale Flower Trade*]
Union Int Sci Biol Ser A Gen ... Union Internationale des Sciences
              Biologiques. Serie A. Generale [*A publication*]
Union Int Sci Biol Ser B Colloq ... Union Internationale des Sciences
              Biologiques. Serie B. Colloques [*A publication*]
Union Lab Rep BNA ... Union Labor Report. Bureau of National Affairs [*A
              publication*]
Union Med Can ... Union Medicale du Canada [*A publication*]
Union Med Mexico ... Union Medica de Mexico [*A publication*]
Union Med (Paris) ... Union Medicale (Paris) [*A publication*]
Union Oceanogr Fr ... Union des Oceanographes de France [*France*] [*A
              publication*]
Union Pac LDB ... Union Pacific Law Department. Bulletin [*A
              publication*]   (DLA)
Union Pharm ... Union Pharmaceutique [*A publication*]
Union Rec ... Union Recorder [*A publication*]   (APTA)
Union S Afr Dep Commer Ind Div Fish Invest Rep ... Union of South Africa.
              Department of Commerce and Industries. Division of
              Fisheries. Investigational Report [*A publication*]
Union Soc Fr Hist Nat Bull Trimest ... Union des Societes Francaises
              d'Histoire Naturelle. Bulletin Trimestriel [*A publication*]
Union S Q R ... Union Seminary. Quarterly Review [*A publication*]
Union Tank Car Co Graver Water Cond Div Tech Repr ... Union Tank Car
              Co. Graver Water Conditioning Division. Technical
              Reprint [*A publication*]
Union Univ Q ... Union University. Quarterly [*A publication*]
UNIP .... United National Independence Party [*Trinidad and Tobago*]
              [*Political party*]   (PPW)
UNIP .... United National Independence Party [*Zambia*] [*Political
              party*]   (PD)
UNIP .... United National Independence Party [*Nigeria*] [*Political party*]
UNIPAC.... Unified Prediction and Analysis Code   (MCD)
UNIPAC.... Unit Packaging
UNIPAC.... Universal Payload Accommodation Capsule
UNIPAL.... Universities Educational Fund for Palestinian Refugees
              [*British*]
UNIPEDE ... Union Internationale de Producteurs et Distributeurs d'Energie
              Electrique [*International Union of Producers and
              Distributors of Electrical Energy*] [*France*]
UNIPOCONGO ... Union des Populations Rurales du Congo [*Union of
              Rural People of the Congo*]
UNIPOL.... Universal Problem-Oriented Language [*Data
              processing*]   (MCD)
UNIPOL.... Universal Procedure-Oriented Language
UNIPRO ... Unite et Progres du Burundi [*Unity and Progress of Burundi*]
UNIPRO ... Universal Processor [*Data processing*]
UNIPZ....... United National Independence Party of Zambia
Uni of Q LR ... University of Queensland. Law Review [*A
              publication*]   (APTA)
UniqMbl .... Unique Mobility, Inc. [*Associated Press abbreviation*]   (APAG)
UNIQUAC ... Universal Quasichemical [*Chemical engineering*]
UNIQUE... Uniform Inquiry Update Element
UNIR .... Unemployment Insurance Review [*A publication*]
UNIR .... Union de Izquierda Revolucionaria [*Union of the
              Revolutionary Left*] [*Peru*] [*Political party*]   (PPW)

UNIR........ Union Nationale pour l'Initiative et la Responsabilite [*National
              Union for Initiative and Responsibility*] [*France*] [*Political
              party*]   (PPW)
UNIR .... United-Guardian, Inc. [*NASDAQ symbol*]   (NQ)
UNIRAC ... Union Involved Racketeering [*FBI undercover investigation*]
UNIRAR ... Universal Radio Relay
UNIS .... Ukrainian National Information Service   (EA)
UNIS .... Underwater Television and Inspection System
UNIS .... Unison
UNIS .... United Nations Information Service
UNIS .... United Nations International School
UNISA....... University of South Africa
UNISA Engl Stud ... UNISA [*University of South Africa*] English Studies [*A
              publication*]
UNISAP.... UNIVAC Share Assembly Program [*Sperry UNIVAC*] [*Data
              processing*]   (IEEE)
UNISA Psychol ... UNISA [*University of South Africa*] Psychologia [*A
              publication*]
UNISCAMTA ... Union Territoriale des Syndicats de Cadres, Agents de
              Maitrise, Techniciens, et Assimiles du Senegal [*Territorial
              Union of Leaders, Supervising Personnel, and Related
              Workers of Senegal*]
UNISCAN ... United Kingdom and Scandinavia   (NATG)
UNISCO.... Union des Interets Sociaux Congolais [*Congolese Union of
              Social Interests*]
UNISIST... United Nations Ingergovernmental System of Information in
              Science and Technology [*UNESCO*] [*Zagreb, Yugoslavia*]
UNISOMI ... Universal Symphony Orchestra and Music Institute   (AEBS)
UNISOR ... University Isotope Separator at Oak Ridge
UNISPACE ... United Nations Conference on the Exploration and Peaceful
              Uses of Outer Space
UNISPEC ... Universal Spectroscopy [*Trademark*] [*Kevex Corp.*]
UNISTAR ... UNIVAC Storage and Retrieval System [*Sperry UNIVAC*]
              [*Data processing*]
UNISTAR ... User Network for Information Storage, Transfer Acquisition,
              and Retrieval   (MCD)
UNISTAT ... University Science Statistics Project [*Information service or
              system*]   (IID)
UNISTOCK ... Union Professionnelle des Stockeurs de Cereales dans la CEE
              [*Organization of Cereal Storage Firms in the European
              Economic Community*]
UNISURV G Rep ... UNISURV G Report. School of Surveying. University of
              New South Wales [*A publication*]   (APTA)
UNISURV Rep ... UNISURV Report. School of Surveying. University of
              New South Wales [*A publication*]   (APTA)
UNISWEP ... Unified Switching Equipment Practice   (MCD)
Unisy......... Unisys Corp. [*Associated Press abbreviation*]   (APAG)
Unisys....... Unisys Corp. [*Associated Press abbreviation*]   (APAG)
UNISYS .... United Information Systems [*Formed by a merger of Burroughs
              Corp. and Sperry UNIVAC*]
Unit............ Unit Corp. [*Associated Press abbreviation*]   (APAG)
UNIT .... Unitarian
UNIT .... United Nations Information for Teachers [*Information service
              or system*]   (AEBS)
UNIT .... Universal Numerical Interchange Terminal
UNITA ...... Uniao Nacional para a Independencia Total de Angola
              [*National Union for the Complete Independence of
              Angola*]   (AF)
UNITA ...... Union for the Total Liberation of Angola
Unit Aborig Messenger ... United Aborigines' Messenger [*A
              publication*]   (APTA)
Unita R ...... Unitarian Review [*A publication*]
UNITAR.... United Nations Institute for Training and Research [*Research
              center*] [*New York*] [*ICSU*]
UNITAR Prepr or Proc ... UNITAR [*United Nations Institute for Training
              and Research*] Preprints or Proceedings [*A publication*]
Unitar Univ Wld ... Unitarian Universalist World [*A publication*]
UNITAS.... United International Antisubmarine Warfare
Uni-Taschenb ... Uni-Taschenbuecher [*A publication*]
Uni of Tas LR ... University of Tasmania. Law Review [*A
              publication*]   (APTA)
Uni-TB....... Uni-Taschenbuecher [*A publication*]
United Dent Hosp Syd Inst Dent Res Annu Rep ... United Dental Hospital of
              Sydney. Institute of Dental Research. Annual Report [*A
              publication*]
United Dent Hosp Sydney Inst Dent Res Annu Rep ... United Dental Hospital
              of Sydney. Institute of Dental Research. Annual Report [*A
              publication*]
United Fresh Fruit Veg Assoc Yearb ... United Fresh Fruit and Vegetable
              Association. Yearbook [*A publication*]
United Methodist Period Index ... United Methodist Periodical Index [*A
              publication*]
United Plant Assoc South India Sci Dep Bull ... United Planters' Association
              of Southern India. Scientific Department. Bulletin [*A
              publication*]
United Service Q ... United Service Quarterly [*A publication*]   (APTA)
United Serv Rev ... United Services Review [*A publication*]
UNITEL.... Universal Teleservice [*Satellite information service*]
UNITEL.... University Information Technology Corp. [*MIT-Harvard*]
UNITELV ... Unitel Video, Inc. [*Associated Press abbreviation*]   (APAG)
UNITIL.... UNITIL Corp. [*Associated Press abbreviation*]   (APAG)

UnitInd ...... United Industrial Corp. [*Associated Press abbreviation*] (APAG)
UnitInn ...... United Inns, Inc. [*Associated Press abbreviation*] (APAG)
UNITNG ... Unit Training (NVT)
UNITOPOS ... Unit to Which Ordered Will Operate in an Overseas Area a Contemplated Continuous Period of One Year or More [*Military*]
UNITOR ... United Nations International TOKAMAK Reactor [*Proposed experimental fusion power plant*]
UNITRAC ... Universal Trajector Compiler (IEEE)
Unitrde .... Unitrode Corp. [*Associated Press abbreviation*] (APAG)
UNITREP ... Unit Status and Identity Report [*DoD*]
Unit Univ Chr ... Unitarian Universalist Christian [*A publication*]
UNIUM ..... Union Nationale des Intellectuels et Universitaires Malgaches [*National Union of Intellectuals and University People of Madagascar*]
UNIV .... Univation, Inc. [*Milpitas, CA*] [*NASDAQ symbol*] (NQ)
UNIV .... Universal (AFM)
UNIV .... Universal International [*NASDAQ symbol*] (SPSG)
UNIV .... Universalist
Univ .... Universitas [*A publication*]
UNIV .... University (AFM)
Univ .... Universo [*A publication*]
UNIVA ...... Universitas [*A publication*]
Univ Abidjan Dep Geol Ser Doc ... Universite d'Abidjan. Departement de Geologie. Serie Documentation [*A publication*]
UNIVAC ... Universal Automatic Computer [*Remington Rand Corp.*] [*Early computer*]
Univ Adelaide Cent Precambrian Res Spec Pap ... University of Adelaide. Centre for Precambrian Research. Special Paper [*A publication*]
Univ Aff/Aff Univ ... University Affairs/Affaires Universitaires [*A publication*]
Univ Agric Sci (Bangalore) Curr Res ... University of Agricultural Sciences (Bangalore). Current Research [*A publication*]
Univ Agric Sci (Bangalore) Misc Ser ... University of Agricultural Sciences (Bangalore). Miscellaneous Series [*A publication*]
Univ Agric Sci (Bangalore) Res Ser ... University of Agricultural Sciences (Bangalore). Research Series [*A publication*]
Univ Agric Sci (Hebbal Bangalore) Annu Rep ... University of Agricultural Sciences (Hebbal, Bangalore). Annual Report [*A publication*]
Univ Agric Sci (Hebbal Bangalore) Ext Ser ... University of Agricultural Sciences (Hebbal, Bangalore). Extension Series [*A publication*]
Univ Agric Sci (Hebbal Bangalore) Stn Ser ... University of Agricultural Sciences (Hebbal, Bangalore). Station Series [*A publication*]
Univ Agric Sci (Hebbal Bangalore) Tech Ser ... University of Agricultural Sciences (Hebbal, Bangalore). Technical Series [*A publication*]
Univ Alaska Agric Stn Bull ... University of Alaska. Agricultural Experiment Station. Bulletin [*A publication*]
Univ Alaska Inst Mar Sci Rep ... University of Alaska. Institute of Marine Science. Report [*A publication*]
Univ Alaska IWR (Inst Water Resour) Ser ... University of Alaska. IWR (Institute of Water Resources) Series [*A publication*]
Univ Alberta Agric Bull ... University of Alberta. Agriculture Bulletin [*A publication*]
Univ Alberta Agric For Bull ... University of Alberta. Agriculture and Forestry Bulletin [*A publication*]
Univ Alberta Dep Civ Eng Struct Eng Rep ... University of Alberta. Department of Civil Engineering. Structural Engineering Report [*A publication*]
Univ Alberta Fac Agric Bull ... University of Alberta. Faculty of Agriculture. Bulletins [*A publication*]
Univ Alexandria Fac Eng Bull Chem Eng ... University of Alexandria. Faculty of Engineering. Bulletin. Chemical Engineering [*A publication*]
Univ Alger Trav Inst Rech Sahariennes ... Universite d'Alger. Travaux. Institut de Recherches Sahariennes [*A publication*]
Univ Allahabad Stud ... University of Allahabad. Studies [*A publication*]
Univ Allahabad Stud Biol Sect ... University of Allahabad. Studies. Biology Section [*A publication*]
Univ Allahabad Stud Bot Sect ... University of Allahabad. Studies. Botany Section [*A publication*]
Univ Allahabad Stud Chem Sect ... University of Allahabad. Studies. Chemistry Section [*A publication*]
Univ Allahabad Stud Math Sect ... University of Allahabad. Studies. Mathematics Section [*A publication*]
Univ Allahabad Stud New Ser ... University of Allahabad. Studies. New Series [*A publication*]
Univ Allahabad Stud Phys Sect ... University of Allahabad. Studies. Physics Section [*A publication*]
Univ Allahabad Stud Zool Sect ... University of Allahabad. Studies. Zoology Section [*A publication*]
Univ Ankara Fac Agri Publ ... Universite d'Ankara. Faculte de l'Agriculture. Publications [*A publication*]
Univ Ankara Fac Sci Commun Ser A ... Universite d'Ankara. Faculte des Sciences. Communications. Serie A. Mathematiques, Physique, et Astronomie [*A publication*]

Univ Ankara Fac Sci Commun Ser A2 ... Universite d'Ankara. Faculte des Sciences. Communications. Serie A2. Physique [*A publication*]
Univ Ankara Fac Sci Commun Ser C ... Universite d'Ankara. Faculte des Sciences. Communications. Serie C. Sciences Naturelles [*A publication*]
Univ Ankara Yearb Fac Agric ... University of Ankara. Yearbook. Faculty of Agriculture [*A publication*]
Univar .... Univar Corp. [*Formerly, VWR United Corp.*] [*Associated Press abbreviation*] (APAG)
UNIVAR ... Universal Valve Action Recorder
Univ Ariz Coop Ext Serv Bull ... University of Arizona. Cooperative Extension Service. Bulletin [*A publication*]
Univ Ariz Coop Ext Serv Circ ... University of Arizona. Cooperative Extension Service. Circular [*A publication*]
Univ Ariz Coop Ext Serv Ser P ... University of Arizona. Cooperative Extension Service. Series P [*A publication*]
Univ Arkansas Eng Exp Stn Res Rep Ser ... University of Arkansas. Engineering Experiment Station. Research Report Series [*A publication*]
Univ Arkansas Lecture Notes in Math ... University of Arkansas. Lecture Notes in Mathematics [*A publication*]
Univ Baghdad Nat Hist Res Cent Annu Rep ... University of Baghdad. Natural History Research Center. Annual Report [*A publication*]
Univ Baghdad Nat Hist Res Cent Publ ... University of Baghdad. Natural History Research Center. Publication [*A publication*]
Univ Bahia Esc Geol Publ Avulsa ... Universidade de Bahia. Escola de Geologia. Publicacao Avulsa [*A publication*]
Univ BC Bot Gard Tech Bull ... University of British Columbia. Botanical Garden. Technical Bulletin [*A publication*]
Univ BC Res For Annu Rep ... University of British Columbia. Research Forest. Annual Report [*A publication*]
Univ Beograd Publ Elektrotehn Fak Ser Mat Fiz ... Univerzitet u Beogradu. Publikacije Elektrotehnickog Fakulteta. Serija Matematika i Fizika [*A publication*]
Univ Beograd Tehn Fiz ... Univerzitet u Beogradu. Tehnicka Fizika [*A publication*]
Univ Bergen Arb Naturv R ... Universitetet i Bergen Arbok. Naturvitenskapelig Rekke [*A publication*]
Univ Bergen Arbok Med Rekke ... Universitetet i Bergen Arbok Medisinsk Rekke [*A publication*]
Univ Bergen Arbok Naturvitensk Rekke ... Universitetet i Bergen Arbok. Naturvitenskapelig Rekke [*A publication*]
Univ Bergen Arsmeld ... Universitetet i Bergen Arsmelding [*A publication*]
Univ Bergen Med Avh ... Universitetet i Bergen Medisinske Avhandlinger [*A publication*]
Univ Bergen Skr ... Universitetet i Bergen Skrifter [*A publication*]
Univ Botswana Swazil Agric Res Div Annu Rep ... University of Botswana and Swaziland. Agricultural Research Division. Annual Report [*A publication*]
Univ Botswana Swaziland Agric Res Div Annu Rep ... University of Botswana, Swaziland. Agricultural Research Division. Annual Report [*A publication*]
Univ Bras Cent Estud Zool Avulso ... Universidade do Brasil. Centro de Estudos Zoologicos Avulso [*A publication*]
Univ Brasov Lucrari Stiint ... Universitatea din Brasov. Lucrari Stiintifice [*A publication*]
Univ of Brit Columbia L Rev ... University of British Columbia. Law Review [*A publication*]
Univ British Columbia Law R ... University of British Columbia. Law Review [*A publication*]
Univ Bruxelles Inst Phys Bull ... Universite de Bruxelles. Institut de Physique. Bulletin [*A publication*]
UNIVC ...... Universal Energy Corp. [*NASDAQ symbol*] (NQ)
Univ Calicut Zool Monogr ... University of Calicut. Zoological Monograph [*A publication*]
Univ Calif Agric Ext Serv ... University of California. Agricultural Extension Service [*A publication*]
Univ Calif (Berkeley) Publ Agric Sci ... University of California (Berkeley). Publications in Agricultural Sciences [*A publication*]
Univ Calif (Berkeley) Publ Bot ... University of California (Berkeley). Publications in Botany [*A publication*]
Univ Calif (Berkeley) Publ Eng ... University of California (Berkeley). Publications in Engineering [*A publication*]
Univ Calif (Berkeley) Publ Entomol ... University of California (Berkeley). Publications in Entomology [*A publication*]
Univ Calif (Berkeley) Publ Health ... University of California (Berkeley). Publications in Public Health [*A publication*]
Univ Calif (Berkeley) Publ Pharmacol ... University of California (Berkeley). Publications in Pharmacology [*A publication*]
Univ Calif (Berkeley) Publ Zool ... University of California (Berkeley). Publications in Zoology [*A publication*]
Univ Calif (Berkeley) Sanit Eng Res Lab Rep ... University of California (Berkeley). Sanitary Engineering Research Laboratory. Report [*A publication*]
Univ Calif (Berkely) Publ Pathol ... University of California (Berkeley). Publications in Pathology [*A publication*]
Univ Calif Bull ... University of California. Bulletin [*A publication*]
Univ of Calif Davis L Rev ... University of California at Davis. Law Review [*Davis, California*] [*A publication*] (DLA)

Univ Calif Div Agric Sci Bull ... University of California. Division of Agricultural Sciences. Bulletin [*A publication*]
Univ Calif Div Agric Sci Leafl ... University of California. Division of Agricultural Sciences. Leaflet [*A publication*]
Univ Calif Lawrence Livermore Lab Rep ... University of California. Lawrence Livermore Laboratory. Report [*A publication*]
Univ Calif (Los Angeles) Symp Mol Cell Biol ... University of California (Los Angeles). Symposia on Molecular and Cellular Biology [*A publication*]
Univ California Los Angeles L Rev ... University of California at Los Angeles. Law Review [*Los Angeles, California*] [*A publication*]   (DLA)
Univ Calif Publ Am Archaeol Ethnol ... University of California. Publications in American Archaeology and Ethnology [*A publication*]
Univ Calif Publ Bot ... University of California. Publications in Botany [*A publication*]
Univ of Calif Publ in English Ling M Ph ... University of California. Publications in English, Linguistics, Modern Philology [*A publication*]
Univ Calif Publ Ent ... University of California. Publications in Entomology [*A publication*]
Univ Calif Publ Entomol ... University of California. Publications in Entomology [*A publication*]
Univ Calif Publ Geol Sci ... University of California. Publications in Geological Sciences [*A publication*]
Univ Calif Publications Zool ... University of California. Publications in Zoology [*A publication*]
Univ Calif Publ Physiol ... University of California. Publications in Physiology [*A publication*]
Univ Calif Publ Psychol ... University of California. Publications in Psychology [*A publication*]
Univ Calif Publs Ent ... University of California. Publications in Entomology [*A publication*]
Univ Calif Publ Zool ... University of California. Publications in Zoology [*A publication*]
Univ Calif Sea Water Convers Lab Rep ... University of California. Sea Water Conversion Laboratory. Report [*A publication*]
Univ Calif Univ Los Angeles Publ Biol Sci ... University of California. University at Los Angeles. Publications in Biological Sciences [*A publication*]
Univ Calif Univ Los Angeles Publ Math Phys Sci ... University of California. University at Los Angeles. Publications in Mathematical and Physical Sciences [*A publication*]
Univ Calif Water Resour Cent Contrib ... University of California. Water Resources Center. Contribution [*A publication*]
Univ Camb Dep Appl Biol Mem Rev Ser ... University of Cambridge. Department of Applied Biology. Memoirs. Review Series [*A publication*]
Univ Cambridge Dep Eng Rep CUDE/A-Aerodyn ... University of Cambridge. Department of Engineering. Report. CUDE [*Cambridge University Department of Engineering*]/A-Aerodynamics [*A publication*]
Univ Cambridge Dep Eng Rep CUDE/A-Thermo ... University of Cambridge. Department of Engineering. Report. CUDE [*Cambridge University Department of Engineering*]/A-Thermo [*A publication*]
Univ Cambridge Dep Eng Rep CUDE/A-Turbo ... University of Cambridge. Department of Engineering. Report. CUDE [*Cambridge University Department of Engineering*]/A-Turbo [*A publication*]
Univ Cambridge Inst Anim Pathol Rep Dir ... University of Cambridge. Institute of Animal Pathology. Report of the Director [*A publication*]
Univ Canterbury Publ ... University of Canterbury. Publications [*A publication*]
Univ Cathol Louvain Fac Sci Agron Lab Biochim Nutr Publ ... Universite Catholique de Louvain. Faculte des Sciences Agronomiques. Laboratoire de Biochimie de la Nutrition. Publication [*A publication*]
Univ Cathol Louv Inst Agron Mem ... Universite Catholique de Louvain. Institut Agronomique. Memoires [*A publication*]
Univ Cent Desert Stud Trans (Jodhpur India) ... University Centre of Desert Studies. Transactions (Jodhpur, India) [*A publication*]
Univ Chic ... Library of the University of Chicago [*A publication*]
Univ of Chicago L Rev ... University of Chicago. Law Review [*A publication*]
Univ Chicago Publ ... University of Chicago. Publications [*A publication*]
Univ Chicago Rep ... University of Chicago. Reports [*A publication*]
Univ Chic L ... University of Chicago. Law Review [*A publication*]
Univ Chic M ... University of Chicago. Magazine [*A publication*]
Univ Chic Rec ... University of Chicago. Record [*A publication*]
Univ of Chi Law Rev ... University of Chicago. Law Review [*A publication*]
Univ of Cincinnati L Rev ... University of Cincinnati. Law Review [*A publication*]
Univ Cincin Stud ... University of Cincinnati. Studies [*A publication*]
Univ of Cinc Law Rev ... University of Cincinnati. Law Review [*A publication*]
Univ Cluj-Napoca Gradina Bot Contrib Bot ... Universitatea din Cluj-Napoca. Gradina Botanica Contributii Botanice [*A publication*]
Univ Col Eng Exp Stn Bull ... University of Colorado. Engineering Experiment Station. Bulletin [*A publication*]

Univ Coll Dublin Agric Fac Rep ... University College of Dublin. Agricultural Faculty. Report [*A publication*]
Univ Coll Dublin Fac Gen Agric Res Rep ... University College of Dublin. Faculty of General Agriculture. Research Report [*A publication*]
Univ Coll Wales (Aberystwyth) Memorandum ... University College of Wales (Aberystwyth). Memorandum [*A publication*]
Univ of Colorado L Rev ... University of Colorado. Law Review [*A publication*]
Univ Color Stud Ser A ... University of Colorado. Studies. Series A. General Series [*A publication*]
Univ Color Stud Ser B ... University of Colorado. Studies. Series B. Studies in the Humanities [*A publication*]
Univ of Colo Studies ... University of Colorado. Studies [*A publication*]
Univ Colo Stud Ser Anthropol ... University of Colorado. Studies. Series in Anthropology [*A publication*]
Univ Colo Stud Ser Biol ... University of Colorado. Studies. Series in Biology [*A publication*]
Univ Colo Stud Ser Chem Pharm ... University of Colorado. Studies. Series in Chemistry and Pharmacy [*A publication*]
Univ Colo Stud Ser D ... University of Colorado. Studies. Series D. Physical and Biological Sciences [*A publication*]
Univ Colo Stud Ser Earth Sci ... University of Colorado. Studies. Series in Earth Sciences [*A publication*]
Univ Col Stud ... University of Colorado. Studies [*A publication*]
Univ Col Stud Ser C ... University of Colorado. Studies. Series C. Studies in the Social Sciences [*A publication*]
Univ Conn Occas Pap Biol Sci Ser ... University of Connecticut. Occasional Papers. Biological Science Series [*A publication*]
Univ Craiova An Ser 3 ... Universitatea din Craiova. Analele. Seria a/3. Stiinte Agricole [*A publication*]
Univ Craiova An Ser Biol Med Stiinte Agric ... Universitatea din Craiova. Analele. Seria. Biologie, Medicina, Stiinte Agricole [*A publication*]
Univ Craiova An Ser Mat Fiz Chim Electroteh ... Universitatea din Craiova. Analele. Seria. Matematica, Fizica, Chimie, Electrotehnica [*A publication*]
Univ D .... Doctor of the University
Univ Debaters Annual ... University Debaters' Annual [*A publication*]
Univ Del Mar Lab Inf Ser Publ ... University of Delaware. Marine Laboratories. Information Series Publication [*A publication*]
Univ Durban-Westville J ... University of Durban-Westville. Journal [*A publication*]
Univ Durban-Westville Tydskr ... Universiteit van Durban-Westville. Tydskrif [*A publication*]
Univ Durham King's Coll Dep Civ Eng Bull ... University of Durham. King's College. Department of Civil Engineering. Bulletin [*A publication*]
Univ Edinb Pfizer Med Monogr ... University of Edinburgh. Pfizer Medical Monographs [*A publication*]
Univ Edinburgh J ... University of Edinburgh. Journal [*A publication*]
UNIVER .... Universal Inverter and Register   (MCD)
Universe Nat Hist Ser ... Universe Natural History Series [*A publication*]
Univers Farm ... Universal Farmacia [*A publication*]
Universities Q ... Universities Quarterly [*A publication*]
University of Singapore School of Archre Jnl ... University of Singapore. School of Architecture. Journal [*A publication*]
University of Southern Calif School of Archre Yearbook ... University of Southern California. School of Architecture. Yearbook [*A publication*]
Univ Fed Pernambuco Esc Quim Dep Technol Publ Avulsa ... Universidade Federal de Pernambuco. Escola de Quimica. Departamento de Technologia. Publicacao Avulsa [*A publication*]
Univ Fed Pernambuco Inst Biocienc Publ Avulsa ... Universidade Federal de Pernambuco. Instituto de Biociencias. Publicacao Avulsa [*A publication*]
Univ Fed Pernambuco Inst Micol Publ ... Universidade Federal de Pernambuco. Instituto de Micologia. Publicacao [*A publication*]
Univ Fed Pernambuco Mem Inst Biocienc ... Universidade Federal de Pernambuco. Memorias do Instituto de Biociencias [*A publication*]
Univ Fed Rio De Janeiro Inst Geocienc Geol Bol ... Universidade Federal do Rio De Janeiro. Instituto de Geociencias. Geologia. Boletim [*A publication*]
Univ Fed Rio De J Inst Geocienc Bol Geol ... Universidade Federal do Rio De Janeiro. Instituto de Geociencias. Boletim Geologia [*A publication*]
Univ Fed Rio De J Inst Geocienc Dep Geol Contrib Dida ... Universidade Federal do Rio De Janeiro. Instituto de Geociencias. Departamento de Geologia. Contribuicao Didatica [*A publication*]
Univ Fed Rural Rio Grande Do Sul Dep Zootec Bol Tec ... Universidade Federal Rural do Rio Grande Do Sul. Departamento do Zootecnia. Boletin Tecnico [*A publication*]
Univ Fed Vicosa Bibl Centr Ser Bibliogr Espec ... Universidade Federal de Vicosa. Biblioteca Central. Serie Bibliografias Especializadas [*A publication*]
Univ Fed Vicosa Ser Tec Bol ... Universidade Federal de Vicosa. Serie Tecnica. Boletin [*A publication*]

Univ Ferrara Ann Sez 6 ... Universita di Ferrara. Annali. Sezione 6. Fisiologia e Chimica Biologica [*A publication*]
Univ Ferrara Mem Geopaleontol ... Universita di Ferrara. Memorie Geopaleontologiche [*A publication*]
Univ Fla Agric Ext Serv Circ ... University of Florida. Agricultural Extension Service. Circular [*A publication*]
Univ Fla Coastal Oceanogr Eng Lab Rep UFL COEL TR ... University of Florida. Coastal and Oceanographic Engineering Laboratory. Report. UFL/COEL/TR [*A publication*]
Univ Fla Coop Ext Serv Bull ... University of Florida. Cooperative Extension Service. Bulletin [*A publication*]
Univ Fla Inst Food Agric Sci Annu Res Rep ... University of Florida. Institute of Food and Agricultural Sciences. Annual Research Report [*A publication*]
Univ Fla Inst Food Agri Sci Publ ... University of Florida. Institute of Food and Agricultural Sciences. Publication [*A publication*]
Univ Fla Inst Gerontol Ser ... University of Florida. Institute of Gerontology Series [*A publication*]
Univ Fla Publ Biol Sci Ser ... University of Florida. Publications. Biological Science Series [*A publication*]
Univ Fla Water Resour Res Cent Publ ... University of Florida. Water Resources Research Center. Publication [*A publication*]
Univ of Florida L Rev ... University of Florida. Law Review [*A publication*]
Univ Fl SSM ... University of Florida. Social Sciences Monograph [*A publication*]
Univ For..... University Forum [*A publication*]
Univ For Bois (Sopron) Publ Sci ... Universite Forestiere et du Bois (Sopron). Publications Scientifiques [*A publication*]
Univ For Timber Ind (Sopron) Sci Publ ... University of Forestry and Timber Industry (Sopron). Scientific Publications [*A publication*]
Univ F Study ... University Film Study Center. Newsletter [*A publication*]
Univ GA Mar Sci Cent Tech Rep Ser ... University of Georgia. Marine Science Center. Technical Report Series [*A publication*]
Univ Gaz.... University Gazette [*University of Melbourne*] [*A publication*] (APTA)
Univ Genova Pubbl Ist Mat ... Universita di Genova. Pubblicazioni dell'Istituto di Matematica [*A publication*]
Univ Geograd Radovi Zavoda za Fiz ... Univerzitet u Geogradu Radovi. Zavoda za Ziziku [*A publication*]
Univ Ghana Agric Irrig Res Stn (Kpong) Annu Rep ... University of Ghana. Agricultural Irrigation Research Station (Kpong). Annual Report [*A publication*]
Univ Ghana Agric Res Stn (Kpong) Annu Rep ... University of Ghana. Agricultural Research Station (Kpong). Annual Report [*A publication*]
Univ of Ghana LJ ... University of Ghana. Law Journal [*London, England*] [*A publication*] (DLA)
Univ de Grenoble Annales n s Sci ... Universite de Grenoble. Sciences-Medecine. Annales [*A publication*]
Univ Hawaii Coll Trop Agric Dep Pap ... University of Hawaii. College of Tropical Agriculture. Departmental Paper [*A publication*]
Univ Hawaii Coop Ext Ser Misc Publ ... University of Hawaii. Cooperative Extension Service. Miscellaneous Publication [*A publication*]
Univ Hawaii Hawaii Inst Geophys Bienn Rep ... University of Hawaii. Hawaii Institute of Geophysics. Biennial Report [*A publication*]
Univ Hawaii Hawaii Inst Geophys Rep HIG ... University of Hawaii. Hawaii Institute of Geophysics. Report HIG [*A publication*]
Univ Hawaii Occas Pap ... University of Hawaii. Occasional Papers [*A publication*]
Univ Hawaii Res Publ ... University of Hawaii. Research Publications [*A publication*]
Univ H Sch J ... University High School. Journal [*A publication*]
Univ Human Rights ... Universal Human Rights [*A publication*]
Univ Hum Rts ... Universal Human Rights [*A publication*]
Univ IL Law ... University of Illinois. Law Forum [*A publication*]
Univ Ill Grad Sc Libr Sci Occas Pap ... University of Illinois. Graduate School of Library Science. Occasional Papers [*A publication*]
Univ of Illinois L Forum ... University of Illinois. Law Forum [*A publication*]
Univ Ill L Forum ... University of Illinois. Law Forum [*A publication*]
Univ Ill St Lang Lit ... University of Illinois. Studies in Language and Literature [*A publication*]
Univ Ill Urbana-Champaign Water Resour Cent Res Rep ... University of Illinois at Urbana-Champaign. Water Resources Center. Research Report [*A publication*]
Univ Ill Urbana-Champaign Water Resour Cent Spec Rep ... University of Illinois at Urbana-Champaign. Water Resources Center. Special Report [*A publication*]
Univ Indore Res J Sci ... University of Indore. Research Journal. Science [*A publication*]
Univ Iowa Monogr Studies in Med ... University of Iowa. Monographs. Studies in Medicine [*A publication*]
Univ Iowa Stud Nat Hist ... University of Iowa. Studies in Natural History [*A publication*]
Univ J Busan Natl Univ ... University Journal. Busan National University [*South Korea*] [*A publication*]
Univ J Busan Sanup Univ ... University Journal. Busan Sanup University [*A publication*]
Univ J of Business ... University Journal of Business [*A publication*]
Univ J Nat Sci Ser ... University Journal. Natural Sciences Series. Busan National University [*Republic of Korea*] [*A publication*]

Univ Joensuu Publ Sci ... University of Joensuu. Publications in Sciences [*A publication*]
Univ Jyvaskyla Stud Sport Phys Educ Health ... University of Jyvaskyla. Studies in Sport, Physical Education, and Health [*A publication*]
Univ Kansas Sci Bull ... University of Kansas. Science Bulletin [*A publication*]
Univ Kans Mus Nat Hist Misc Publ ... University of Kansas. Museum of Natural History. Miscellaneous Publication [*A publication*]
Univ Kans Mus Nat Hist Monogr ... University of Kansas. Museum of Natural History. Monograph [*A publication*]
Univ Kans Paleontol Contrib Artic ... University of Kansas. Paleontological Contributions. Article [*A publication*]
Univ Kans Paleontol Contrib Monogr ... University of Kansas. Paleontological Contributions. Monograph [*A publication*]
Univ Kans Paleontol Contrib Pap ... University of Kansas. Paleontological Contributions. Paper [*A publication*]
Univ Kans Primary Rec Psychol Publ ... University of Kansas. Primary Records in Psychology. Publication [*A publication*]
Univ Kans Publ Mus Nat Hist ... University of Kansas. Publications. Museum of Natural History [*A publication*]
Univ Kans Sci Bull ... University of Kansas. Science Bulletin [*A publication*]
Univ Kans Sci Bull Suppl ... University of Kansas. Science Bulletin. Supplement [*A publication*]
Univ KC R ... University of Kansas City. Review [*A publication*]
Univ K Inst Min Miner Res Tech Rep ... University of Kentucky. Institute for Mining and Minerals Research. Technical Report [*A publication*]
Univ Kiril Metodij-Skopje Fac Math ... Universite Kiril et Metodij-Skopje. Faculte des Mathematiques [*A publication*]
Univ KY Coll Agric Coop Ext Ser Rep ... University of Kentucky. College of Agriculture. Cooperative Extension Service. Report [*A publication*]
Univ KY Coop Ext Serv Circ ... University of Kentucky. Cooperative Extension Service. Circular [*A publication*]
Univ KY Coop Ext Serv 4-H ... University of Kentucky. Cooperative Extension Service. 4-H [*A publication*]
Univ KY Coop Ext Serv Leafl ... University of Kentucky. Cooperative Extension Service. Leaflet [*A publication*]
Univ KY Coop Ext Serv Misc ... University of Kentucky. Cooperative Extension Service. Miscellaneous [*A publication*]
Univ KY Eng Exp Stn Bull ... University of Kentucky. Engineering Experiment Station. Bulletin [*A publication*]
Univ KY Inst Min Miner Res Rep IMMR ... University of Kentucky. Institute for Mining and Minerals Research. Report IMMR [*A publication*]
Univ KY Inst Min Miner Res Tech Rep IMMR ... University of Kentucky. Institute for Mining and Minerals Research. Technical Report. IMMR [*A publication*]
Univ KY Off Res Eng Ser Bull ... University of Kentucky. Office of Research and Engineering Services. Bulletin [*A publication*]
Univ KY Publ Anthropol Archaeol ... University of Kentucky. Publications in Anthropology and Archaeology [*A publication*]
Univ Laval Dep Exploit Util Bois Note Rech ... Universite Laval. Departement d'Exploitation et Utilisation des Bois. Note de Recherches [*A publication*]
Univ Laval Dep Exploit Util Bois Note Tech ... Universite Laval. Departement d'Exploitation et Utilisation des Bois. Note Technique [*A publication*]
Univ L Coll J ... University Law College. Journal. Rajputana University [*India*] [*A publication*] (DLA)
Univ Leeds Med J ... University of Leeds. Medical Journal [*A publication*]
Univ Lesn Khoz Derevoobrab Prom-Sti (Sopron) Nauchn Publ ... Universitet Lesnogo Khozyaistva i Derevoobrabatyvaoushchei Promyshlennosti (Sopron) Nauchnye Publikatsii [*A publication*]
Univ Libre Bruxelles Inter-Univ Inst High Energ Rep ... Universite Libre de Bruxelles. Inter-University Institute for High Energies. Report [*A publication*]
Univ Liege Fac Sci Appl Coll Publ ... Universite de Liege. Faculte des Sciences Appliques. Collection des Publications [*Belgium*] [*A publication*]
Univ Lisboa Fac Farm Bol ... Universidade de Lisboa. Faculdade de Farmacia. Boletim [*A publication*]
Univ Liverp Rec ... University of Liverpool. Recorder [*A publication*]
Univ London Galton Lab Univ Coll Eugen Lab Mem ... University of London. Galton Laboratory. University College Eugenics Laboratory. Memoirs [*A publication*]
Univ Lond Univ Coll Galton Lab Eugen Lab Mem ... University of London. University College. Galton Laboratory. Eugenics Laboratory. Memoirs [*A publication*]
Univ LR ... University Law Review [*A publication*] (DLA)
Univ L Rev ... University Law Review [*A publication*] (DLA)
Univ Lund Dep Anat Commun ... University of Lund. Department of Anatomy. Communications [*A publication*]
Univ M....... University Magazine [*Montreal*] [*A publication*]
Univ Maine Orono Life Sci Agric Exp Stn Annu Rep ... University of Maine at Orono. Life Sciences and Agriculture Experiment Station. Annual Report [*A publication*]

Univ Maine Orono Life Sci Agric Exp Stn Tech Bull ... University of Maine at Orono. Life Sciences and Agriculture Experiment Station. Technical Bulletin [*A publication*]

Univ Maine Orono Maine Agric Exp Stn Ann Rep ... University of Maine at Orono. Maine Agricultural Experiment Station. Annual Report [*A publication*]

Univ of Maine Studies ... University of Maine. Studies [*A publication*]

Univ of Manila L Gaz ... University of Manila. Law Gazette [*Manila, Philippines*] [*A publication*]   (DLA)

Univ Maria Curie-Sklodowsk Ann Sect B ... Universitas Maria Curie-Sklodowsk. Annales. Sectio B [*A publication*]

Univ Mass Dep Geol Contrib ... University of Massachusetts. Department of Geology. Contribution [*A publication*]

Univ MD Nat Resour Inst Contrib ... University of Maryland. Natural Resources Institute. Contribution [*A publication*]

Univ MD Sea Grant Program Tech Rep ... University of Maryland. Sea Grant Program. Technical Report [*A publication*]

Univ MD Water Resour Res Cent Tech Rep ... University of Maryland. Water Resources Research Center. Technical Report [*A publication*]

Univ MD Water Resour Res Cent WRRC Spec Rep ... University of Maryland. Water Resources Research Center. WRRC Special Report [*A publication*]

Univ Med Rec (London) ... Universal Medical Record (London) [*A publication*]

Univ Melb Gaz ... University of Melbourne. Gazette [*A publication*]   (APTA)

Univ Melb Sch For Bull ... University of Melbourne. School of Forestry. Bulletin [*A publication*]   (APTA)

Univ Miami Law R ... University of Miami. Law Review [*A publication*]

Univ Miami Law Rev ... University of Miami. Law Review [*A publication*]

Univ of Miami L Rev ... University of Miami. Law Review [*A publication*]

Univ Miami Rosenstiel Sch Mar Atmos Sci Annu Rep ... University of Miami. Rosenstiel School of Marine and Atmospheric Science. Annual Report [*A publication*]

Univ Miami Rosenstiel Sch Mar Atmos Sci Res Rev ... University of Miami. Rosenstiel School of Marine and Atmospheric Science. Research Review [*A publication*]

Univ Miami Sea Grant Program Sea Grant Field Guide Ser ... University of Miami. Sea Grant Program. Sea Grant Field Guide Series [*A publication*]

Univ Miami Sea Grant Program Sea Grant Tech Bull ... University of Miami. Sea Grant Program. Sea Grant Technical Bulletin [*A publication*]

Univ Mich (Ann Arbor) Off Res Adm Res News ... University of Michigan (Ann Arbor). Office of Research Administration. Research News [*A publication*]

Univ Mich Bus R ... University of Michigan. Business Review [*A publication*]

Univ Mich Bus Rev ... University of Michigan. Business Review [*A publication*]

Univ Mich Dep Nav Archit Mar Eng Rep ... University of Michigan. Department of Naval Architecture and Marine Engineering. Report [*A publication*]

Univ of Michigan J of Law Reform ... University of Michigan. Journal of Law Reform [*A publication*]

Univ Mich Inst Sci Tech Rep ... University of Michigan. Institute of Science and Technology. Report [*A publication*]

Univ Mich J Law Reform ... University of Michigan. Journal of Law Reform [*A publication*]

Univ Mich Med Bull ... University of Michigan. Medical Bulletin [*A publication*]

Univ Mich Med Cent J ... University of Michigan. Medical Center. Journal [*A publication*]

Univ Mich Mus Anthropol Tech Rep ... University of Michigan. Museum of Anthropology. Technical Reports [*A publication*]

Univ Mich Mus Zool Circ ... University of Michigan. Museum of Zoology. Circular [*A publication*]

Univ Mich Pap Ling ... University of Michigan. Papers in Linguistics [*A publication*]

Univ Minn Agric Ext Serv Ext Bull ... University of Minnesota. Agricultural Extension Service. Extension Bulletin [*A publication*]

Univ Minn Agric Ext Serv Ext Folder ... University of Minnesota. Agricultural Extension Service. Extension Folder [*A publication*]

Univ Minn Agric Ext Serv Ext Pam ... University of Minnesota. Agricultural Extension Service. Extension Pamphlet [*A publication*]

Univ Minn Agric Ext Serv Misc ... University of Minnesota. Agricultural Extension Service. Miscellaneous Publications [*A publication*]

Univ Minn Agric Ext Serv Misc Publ ... University of Minnesota. Agricultural Extension Service. Miscellaneous Publications [*A publication*]

Univ Minn Agric Ext Serv Spec Rep ... University of Minnesota. Agricultural Extension Service. Special Report [*A publication*]

Univ Minn Contin Med Educ ... University of Minnesota. Continuing Medical Education [*A publication*]

Univ Minn Med Bull ... University of Minnesota. Medical Bulletin [*A publication*]

Univ Mississippi Stud Engl ... University of Mississippi. Studies in English [*A publication*]

Univ of Missouri at Kansas City L Rev ... University of Missouri at Kansas City. Law Review [*A publication*]

Univ Missouri Stud ... University of Missouri. Studies [*A publication*]

Univ MO Bull Eng Exp Stn Ser ... University of Missouri. Bulletin. Engineering Experiment Station Series [*A publication*]

Univ MO Eng Exp Sta Eng Ser Bull ... University of Missouri. Engineering Experiment Station. Engineering Series. Bulletin [*A publication*]

Univ Montreal Chercheurs ... Universite de Montreal. Chercheurs [*A publication*]

Univ MO Sch Mines Metall Bull Tech Ser ... University of Missouri. School of Mines and Metallurgy. Bulletin. Technical Series [*A publication*]

Univ MO Stud ... University of Missouri. Studies [*A publication*]

Univ of MO Studies ... University of Missouri. Studies [*A publication*]

Univ Mus Bull Univ PA ... University Museum. Bulletin. University of Pennsylvania [*A publication*]

Univ de Nancy Fac d Lettres Annales de l'Est ... Universite de Nancy. Faculte des Lettres. Annales de l'Est [*A publication*]

Univ Natal Wattle Res Inst Rep ... University of Natal. Wattle Research Institute. Report [*A publication*]

Univ Nebr Coll Agric Home Econ Q ... University of Nebraska. College of Agriculture and Home Economics. Quarterly [*A publication*]

Univ NE Bul ... University of New England. Bulletin [*A publication*]   (APTA)

Univ N Engl Annu Rep ... University of New England. Annual Report [*A publication*]

Univ N Engl Explor Soc Aust Rep ... University of New England. Exploration Society of Australia. Report [*A publication*]

Univ Nev Mackay Sch Mines Geol Min Ser Bull ... University of Nevada. Mackay School of Mines. Geological and Mining Series. Bulletin [*A publication*]

Univ Nev Max C Fleischmann Coll Agric R ... University of Nevada. Max C. Fleischmann College of Agriculture. R Series [*A publication*]

Univ Nev Max C Fleischmann Coll Agric Rep ... University of Nevada. Max C. Fleischmann College of Agriculture. Report [*A publication*]

Univ Nev Max C Fleischmann Coll Agric Ser B ... University of Nevada. Max C. Fleischmann College of Agriculture. B Series [*A publication*]

Univ Nev Max C Fleischmann Coll Agric T Ser ... University of Nevada. Max C. Fleischmann College of Agriculture. T Series [*A publication*]

Univ of New Brunswick LJ ... University of New Brunswick. Law Journal [*A publication*]

Univ Newcastle Tyne Med Gaz ... University of Newcastle Upon Tyne. Medical Gazette [*A publication*]

Univ Newcastle Upon Tyne Rep Dove Mar Lab Third Ser ... University of Newcastle Upon Tyne. Report of the Dove Marine Laboratory. Third Series [*A publication*]

Univ New Eng Bull ... University of New England. Bulletin [*A publication*]   (APTA)

Univ New South Wales Occas Pap ... University of New South Wales. Occasional Papers [*Australia*] [*A publication*]

Univ NM Bull Biol Ser ... University of New Mexico. Bulletin. Biological Series [*A publication*]

Univ NM Bull Geol Ser ... University of New Mexico. Bulletin. Geological Series [*A publication*]

Univ NM Inst Meteorit Spec Publ ... University of New Mexico. Institute of Meteoritics. Special Publication [*A publication*]

Univ NM Publ Anthropol ... University of New Mexico. Publications in Anthropology [*A publication*]

Univ NM Publ Biol ... University of New Mexico. Publications in Biology [*A publication*]

Univ NM Publ Geol ... University of New Mexico. Publications in Geology [*A publication*]

Univ NM Publ Meteorit ... University of New Mexico. Publications in Meteoritics [*A publication*]

Univ Nottingham Dep Agric Hortic Misc Publ ... University of Nottingham. Department of Agriculture and Horticulture. Miscellaneous Publication [*A publication*]

Univ NSW Law J ... University of New South Wales. Law Journal [*A publication*]

Univ NSW LJ ... University of New South Wales. Law Journal [*A publication*]   (APTA)

Univ NSW Occas Pap ... University of New South Wales. Occasional Papers [*A publication*]   (APTA)

Univ NSW Q ... University of New South Wales. Quarterly [*A publication*]   (APTA)

Univ Orange Free State Publ Ser C ... University of the Orange Free State. Publication. Series C [*A publication*]

Univ Oxford Dept Eng Sci Rep ... University of Oxford. Department of Engineering. Science Reports [*A publication*]

Univ PA Bull Vet Ext Q ... University of Pennsylvania. Bulletin. Veterinary Extension Quarterly [*A publication*]

Univ PA Libr Chron ... University of Pennsylvania. Library Chronicle [*A publication*]

Univ PA Med Bull ... University of Pennsylvania. Medical Bulletin [*A publication*]

Univ of PA Pub Pol Econ ... University of Pennsylvania. Publications in Political Economy [*A publication*]

Univ Paris Conf Palais Decouverte Ser A ... Universite de Paris. Conferences du Palais de la Decouverte. Serie A [*A publication*]

Univ Penn Law Rev ... University of Pennsylvania. Law Review [*A publication*]
Univ of Pennsylvania L Rev ... University of Pennsylvania. Law Review [*A publication*]
Univ Perspect ... University Perspectives [*A publication*]
Univ Peshawar J ... University of Peshawar. Journal [*A publication*]
Univ of Pittsburgh L Rev ... University of Pittsburgh. Law Review [*A publication*]
Univ Pretoria Publ Ser 2 ... University of Pretoria. Publications. Series 2. Natural Sciences [*A publication*]
Univ Q........ Universalist Quarterly Review [*Boston*] [*A publication*]
Univ Q........ Universities Quarterly [*London*] [*A publication*]
Univ Qd Agric Dep Pap ... University of Queensland. Agriculture Department. Papers [*A publication*]   (APTA)
Univ Qd Bot Dep Pap ... University of Queensland. Botany Department. Papers [*A publication*]   (APTA)
Univ Qd Ent Dep Pap ... University of Queensland. Entomology Department. Papers [*A publication*]   (APTA)
Univ Q Gaz ... University of Queensland. Gazette [*A publication*]   (APTA)
Univ Q Law J ... University of Queensland. Law Journal [*A publication*]   (APTA)
Univ Qld Gaz ... University of Queensland. Gazette [*A publication*]   (APTA)
Univ Qld Law J ... University of Queensland. Law Journal [*A publication*]   (APTA)
Univ Q LJ ... University of Queensland. Law Journal [*A publication*]   (APTA)
Univ Quart ... Universities Quarterly [*A publication*]
Univ of Queensland LJ ... University of Queensland. Law Journal [*A publication*]
Univ Queensl Comput Cent Pap ... University of Queensland. Computer Centre. Papers [*A publication*]
Univ Queensl Great Barrier Reef Comm Heron Isl Res Stn ... University of Queensland. Great Barrier Reef Committee. Heron Island Research Station [*A publication*]
Univ Queensl Pap Dep Bot ... University of Queensland. Papers. Department of Botany [*A publication*]
Univ Queensl Pap Dep Chem ... University of Queensland. Papers. Department of Chemistry [*A publication*]
Univ Queensl Pap Dep Entomol ... University of Queensland. Papers. Department of Entomology [*A publication*]
Univ Queensl Pap Dep Geol ... University of Queensland. Papers. Department of Geology [*A publication*]
Univ Queensl Pap Dep Zool ... University of Queensland. Papers. Department of Zoology [*A publication*]
Univ Queensl Pap Fac Vet Sci ... University of Queensland. Papers. Faculty of Veterinary Science [*A publication*]
Univ R........ Universal Review [*A publication*]
Univ R........ University Review [*A publication*]
Univ Reading Natl Inst Res Dairy Bienn Rev ... University of Reading. National Institute for Research in Dairying. Biennial Reviews [*A publication*]
Univ Reading Natl Inst Res Dairy Rep ... University of Reading. National Institute for Research in Dairying. Report [*A publication*]
Univ Rec .... University Record [*A publication*]
Univ Res N ... University Research News [*A publication*]
Univ Rhod Fac Med Res Lect Ser ... University of Rhodesia. Faculty of Medicine. Research Lecture Series [*A publication*]
Univ of Richmond L Not ... University of Richmond. Law Notes [*Richmond, Virginia*] [*A publication*]   (DLA)
Univ of Richmond L Rev ... University of Richmond. Law Review [*A publication*]
Univ RI Mar Publ Ser ... University of Rhode Island. Marine Publication Series [*A publication*]
Univ Rio Grande Do Sul Esc Geol Avulso ... Universidade do Rio Grande Do Sul. Escola de Geologia. Avulso [*A publication*]
Univ Rio Grande Do Sul Esc Geol Bol ... Universidade do Rio Grande Do Sul. Escola de Geologia. Boletim [*A publication*]
Univ Rochester Lib Bull ... University of Rochester. Library Bulletin [*A publication*]
Univ Rochester Libr Bull ... University of Rochester. Library Bulletin [*A publication*]
Univ Roma Ist Autom Not ... Universita di Roma. Istituto di Automatica. Notiziario [*A publication*]
Univ Roorkee Res J ... University of Roorkee. Research Journal [*A publication*]
Univ Rural Pernambuco Comun Tec ... Universidade Rural de Pernambuco. Comunicado Tecnico [*A publication*]
Univ of San Fernando Valley L Rev ... University of San Fernando Valley. Law Review [*Sepulveda, California*] [*A publication*]   (DLA)
Univ of San Francisco L Rev ... University of San Francisco. Law Review [*A publication*]
Univ Sao Paulo Esc Politec Geol Metal Bol ... Universidade de Sao Paulo. Escola Politecnica, Geologia, e Metalurgia. Boletim [*A publication*]
Univ Sao Paulo Esc Super Agric Luiz De Queiroz Bol Tec Cient ... Universidade de Sao Paulo. Escola Superior de Agricultura Luiz De Queiroz. Boletim Tecnico Cientifico [*A publication*]
Univ Sao Paulo Fac Filos Cienc Let Bol Bot ... Universidade de Sao Paulo. Faculdade de Filosofia, Ciencias, e Letras. Boletim. Botanica [*A publication*]

Univ Sao Paulo Fac Filos Cienc Let Bol Geol ... Universidade de Sao Paulo. Faculdade de Filosofia, Ciencias, e Letras. Boletim. Geologia [*A publication*]
Univ Sao Paulo Fac Filos Cienc Let Bol Mineral ... Universidade de Sao Paulo. Faculdade de Filosofia, Ciencias, e Letras. Boletim. Mineralogia [*A publication*]
Univ Sao Paulo Fac Filos Cienc Let Bol Quim ... Universidade de Sao Paulo. Faculdade de Filosofia, Ciencias, e Letras. Boletim. Quimica [*A publication*]
Univ Sao Paulo Inst Geocienc Astron Bol ... Universidade de Sao Paulo. Instituto de Geociencias e Astronomia. Boletim [*A publication*]
Univ Sao Paulo Inst Geocienc Bol IG ... Universidade de Sao Paulo. Instituto de Geociencias. Boletim IG [*Instituto de Geociencias*] [*A publication*]
Univ SC Governmental R ... University of South Carolina. Governmental Review [*A publication*]
Univ South Calif Allan Hancock Found ... University of Southern California. Allan Hancock Foundation [*A publication*]
Univs Q...... Universities Quarterly [*A publication*]
Univ Strathclyde Annu Rep ... University of Strathclyde. Annual Report [*A publication*]
Univ Strathclyde Res Rep ... University of Strathclyde. Research Report [*A publication*]
Univ Stud ... University Studies in History and Economics [*A publication*]   (APTA)
Univ Stud Hist ... University Studies in History [*A publication*]   (APTA)
Univ Stud Hist Ec ... University Studies in History and Economics [*A publication*]   (APTA)
Univ Stud Hist Econ ... University Studies in History and Economics [*A publication*]
Univ Studies ... University Studies in History and Economics [*A publication*]   (APTA)
Univ Studies ... University Studies in Western Australian History [*A publication*]   (APTA)
Univ Studies Math ... University Studies in Mathematics [*A publication*]
Univ Stud Math (Jaipur) ... University Studies in Mathematics (Jaipur) [*A publication*]
Univ Stud Univ Neb ... University Studies. University of Nebraska [*A publication*]
Univ Stud W Aust Hist ... University Studies in Western Australian History [*A publication*]
Univ Sydney Med J ... University of Sydney. Medical Journal [*A publication*]
Univ Syd Post Grad Ctee Med Bull ... University of Sydney. Postgraduate Committee in Medicine. Bulletin [*A publication*]   (APTA)
Univ Tas Gaz ... University of Tasmania. Gazette [*A publication*]   (APTA)
Univ Tas LR ... University of Tasmania. Law Review [*A publication*]   (APTA)
Univ Tasmania Environ Stud Occas Pap ... University of Tasmania. Environmental Studies. Occasional Paper [*A publication*]
Univ Tasmania Environ Stud Work Pap ... University of Tasmania. Environmental Studies. Working Paper [*A publication*]
Univ of Tasmania L Rev ... University of Tasmania. Law Review [*A publication*]
Univ Tas News ... University of Tasmania. News [*A publication*]
Univ Teheran Fac Agron Bull ... Universite de Teheran. Faculte d'Agronomie. Bulletin [*A publication*]
Univ Tenn Rec ... University of Tennessee. Record [*A publication*]
Univ Tenn Surv Bus ... University of Tennessee. Survey of Business [*A publication*]
Univ Tex Austin Bur Econ Geol Handb ... University of Texas at Austin. Bureau of Economic Geology. Handbook [*A publication*]
Univ Tex Austin Bur Econ Geol Miner Resour Circ ... University of Texas at Austin. Bureau of Economic Geology. Mineral Resource Circular [*A publication*]
Univ Tex Austin Bur Econ Geol Res Note ... University of Texas at Austin. Bureau of Economic Geology. Research Note [*A publication*]
Univ Tex Austin Cent Highw Res Res Rep ... University of Texas at Austin. Center for Highway Research. Research Report [*A publication*]
Univ Tex Austin Cent Res Water Resour Tech Rep ... University of Texas at Austin. Center for Research in Water Resources. Technical Report [*A publication*]
Univ Tex Bull ... University of Texas. Bulletin [*A publication*]
Univ Tex Bur Econ Geol Publ ... University of Texas. Bureau of Economic Geology. Publication [*A publication*]
Univ Tex Bur Econ Geol Rep Invest ... University of Texas. Bureau of Economic Geology. Report of Investigations [*A publication*]
Univ Tex MD Anderson Symp Fundam Cancer Res ... University of Texas. M. D. Anderson Symposium on Fundamental Cancer Research [*A publication*]
Univ Timisoara An Stiinte Fiz Chim ... Universitatea din Timisoara. Analele. Stiinte Fizice-Chimice [*A publication*]
Univ TLR... University of Tasmania. Law Review [*A publication*]
Univ Toledo Law R ... University of Toledo. Law Review [*A publication*]
Univ of Toledo L Rev ... University of Toledo. Law Review [*A publication*]
Univ Toronto Biol Ser ... University of Toronto. Biological Series [*A publication*]

Univ Toronto Fac For Tech Rep ... University of Toronto. Faculty of Forestry. Technical Report [*A publication*]
Univ Toronto Inst Environ Sci Eng Publ EH ... University of Toronto. Institute of Environmental Sciences and Engineering. Publication EH [*A publication*]
Univ Toronto Inst Environ Stud Publ EH ... University of Toronto. Institute for Environmental Studies. Publication EH [*A publication*]
Univ Toronto Law J ... University of Toronto. Law Journal [*A publication*]
Univ of Toronto LJ ... University of Toronto. Law Journal [*A publication*]
Univ Toronto Med J ... University of Toronto. Medical Journal [*A publication*]
Univ Toronto Q ... University of Toronto. Quarterly [*A publication*]
Univ Toronto Stud Biol Ser ... University of Toronto. Studies. Biological Series [*A publication*]
Univ Toronto Stud Geol Ser ... University of Toronto. Studies. Geological Series [*A publication*]
Univ Toronto Stud Pap Chem Lab ... University of Toronto. Studies. Papers from the Chemical Laboratories [*A publication*]
Univ Toronto Stud Pathol Ser ... University of Toronto. Studies. Pathological Series [*A publication*]
Univ Toronto Stud Physiol Ser .., University of Toronto. Studies. Physiological Series [*A publication*]
Univ Toronto Stud Phys Ser ... University of Toronto. Studies. Physics Series [*A publication*]
Univ Toronto Undergrad Dent J ... University of Toronto Undergraduate Dental Journal [*A publication*]
Univ Tor Q ... University of Toronto. Quarterly [*A publication*]
Univ Tripoli Bull Fac Eng ... University of Tripoli. Bulletin. Faculty of Engineering [*A publication*]
Univ of Tulsa LJ ... University of Tulsa. Law Journal [*Tulsa, Oklahoma*] [*A publication*] (DLA)
Univ Udaipur Res J ... University of Udaipur. Research Journal [*A publication*]
Univ Udaipur Res Stud ... University of Udaipur. Research Studies [*A publication*]
Univ Umea Commun Res Unit Proj Rep ... University of Umea. Communication Research Unit. Project Report [*A publication*]
Univ Utah Anthropol Pap ... University of Utah. Anthropological Papers [*A publication*]
Univ Utah Biol Ser ... University of Utah. Biological Series [*A publication*]
Univ V .... University Vision [*A publication*]
Univ VA News Letter ... University of Virginia. News Letter [*A publication*]
Univ WA Ann L Rev ... University of Western Australia. Annual Law Review [*A publication*]
Univ WA Law Rev ... University of Western Australia. Law Review [*A publication*] (APTA)
Univ WA L Rev ... University of Western Australia. Law Review [*A publication*] (APTA)
Univ Warsaw Dep Radiochem Publ ... University of Warsaw. Department of Radiochemistry. Publication [*A publication*]
Univ Wash Coll Fish Tech Rep ... University of Washington. College of Fisheries. Technical Report [*A publication*]
Univ Wash Eng Exp Stn Bull ... University of Washington. Engineering Experiment Station. Bulletin [*A publication*]
Univ Wash Eng Exp Stn Rep ... University of Washington. Engineering Experiment Station. Report [*A publication*]
Univ Wash Eng Exp Stn Tech Note ... University of Washington. Engineering Experiment Station. Technical Note [*A publication*]
Univ Wash Inst For Prod Contrib ... University of Washington. Institute of Forest Products. Contributions [*A publication*]
Univ Wash Publ Biol ... University of Washington. Publications in Biology [*A publication*]
Univ Wash Publ Fish ... University of Washington. Publications in Fisheries [*A publication*]
Univ Wash Publ Fish New Ser ... University of Washington. Publications in Fisheries. New Series [*A publication*]
Univ Wash Publ Geol ... University of Washington. Publications in Geology [*A publication*]
Univ Wash Publ Oceanogr ... University of Washington. Publications in Oceanography [*A publication*]
Univ Waterloo Biol Ser ... University of Waterloo. Biology Series [*A publication*]
Univ Waterloo Fac Environ Stud Occas Pap ... University of Waterloo. Faculty of Environmental Studies. Occasional Paper [*A publication*]
Univ of West Australia L Rev ... University of Western Australia. Law Review [*A publication*]
Univ Western Australia Law R ... University of Western Australia. Law Review [*A publication*]
Univ Western Ontario Series in Philos Sci ... University of Western Ontario. Series in Philosophy of Science [*A publication*]
Univ West Indies Reg Res Cent Soil Land Use Surv ... University of the West Indies. Regional Research Centre. Soil and Land Use Surveys [*A publication*]
Univ West Ont Med J ... University of Western Ontario. Medical Journal [*A publication*]
Univ West Ont Ser Philos Sci ... University of Western Ontario. Series in Philosophy in Science [*A publication*]
Univ Windsor R ... University of Windsor. Review [*A publication*]

Univ Wis Coll Agric Life Sci Res Div Bull ... University of Wisconsin. College of Agricultural and Life Sciences. Research Division. Bulletin [*A publication*]
Univ Wis Coll Agric Life Sci Res Div Res Rep ... University of Wisconsin. College of Agricultural and Life Sciences. Research Division. Research Report [*A publication*]
Univ Wis Eng Exp Stn Rep ... University of Wisconsin. Engineering Experiment Station. Report [*A publication*]
Univ Wis-Madison Coll Agric Life Sci Res Div Res Bull ... University of Wisconsin-Madison. College of Agricultural and Life Sciences. Research Division. Research Bulletin [*A publication*]
Univ Wis Milw Field Stn Bull ... University of Wisconsin-Milwaukee. Field Stations Bulletin [*A publication*]
Univ Wis Sea Grant Coll Tech Rep ... University of Wisconsin. Sea Grant College. Technical Report [*A publication*]
Univ Wis Sea Grant Program Tech Rep ... University of Wisconsin. Sea Grant Program. Technical Report [*A publication*]
Univ Wis Water Resour Cent Eutrophication Inf Prog Lit Rev ... University of Wisconsin. Water Resources Center. Eutrophication Information Program. Literature Review [*A publication*]
Univ Witwatersrand Dep Geogr Environ Stud Occas Pap ... University of the Witwatersrand. Department of Geography and Environmental Studies. Occasional Paper [*A publication*]
Univ of Wyoming Publ ... University of Wyoming. Publications [*A publication*]
Univ Wyo Publ ... University of Wyoming. Publications [*A publication*]
Univ Yaounde Fac Sci Ann Ser 3 ... Universite de Yaounde. Faculte des Sciences. Annales. Serie 3. Biologie-Biochimie [*A publication*]
Uniw Adama Mickiewicza Poznaniu Inst Chem Ser Chem ... Uniwersytet Imienia Adama Mickiewicza w Poznaniu. Instytut Chemii. Seria Chemia [*A publication*]
Uniw Adama Mickiewicza Poznaniu Ser Astron ... Uniwersytet Imienia Adama Mickiewicza w Poznaniu. Seria Astronomia [*A publication*]
Uniw Adama Mickiewicza Poznaniu Ser Biol ... Uniwersytet Imienia Adama Mickiewicza w Poznaniu. Seria Biologia [*A publication*]
Uniw Adama Mickiewicza Poznaniu Ser Chem ... Uniwersytet Imienia Adama Mickiewicza w Poznaniu. Seria Chemia [*A publication*]
Uniw Adama Mickiewicza w Poznaniu Ser Fiz ... Uniwersytet Imienia Adama Mickiewicza w Poznaniu. Seria Fizyka [*A publication*]
Uniw Lodz Acta Univ Lodz Ser 2 ... Uniwersytet Lodzki. Acta Universitatis Lodziensis. Seria 2 [*A publication*]
Uniw Marii Curie-Sklodowskiej Ann Sect AA ... Uniwersytet Marii Curie-Sklodowskiej. Annales. Sectio AA. Physica et Chemia [*A publication*]
Unix .... [*An*] operating system developed by Bell Laboratories [*Software*]
UNJA .... Union Nationale de la Jeunesse Algerienne [*Algeria*] [*Political party*] (EY)
UNJBS ...... United Nations Joint Board of Strategy
UNJC .... Unified National J Series Coarse [*Thread*]
UNJEF ...... Unified National J Series Extra Fine [*Thread*]
UNJF .... Unified National J Series Fine [*Thread*]
UNJS .... Unified National J Series Special [*Thread*]
UN Juridical YB ... United Nations Juridical Year Book [*A publication*] (DLA)
UN Jur YB ... United Nations Juridical Year Book [*A publication*] (DLA)
UNK .... Unalakleet [*Alaska*] [*Airport symbol*] (OAG)
UNK .... Unknown (AFM)
Unk .... Unknown Worlds [*A publication*]
UNKA .... Abakan [*Former USSR*] [*ICAO location identifier*] (ICLI)
UNKI .... Vanavara [*Former USSR*] [*ICAO location identifier*] (ICLI)
UNKK .... Krasnoyarsk [*Former USSR*] [*ICAO location identifier*] (ICLI)
UNKN .... Unknown
UNKO .... Sovetsky Rudnik [*Former USSR*] [*ICAO location identifier*] (ICLI)
UNKRA ..... United Nations Korean Reconstruction Agency
UNKT .... Podkamennaya Tunguska [*Former USSR*] [*ICAO location identifier*] (ICLI)
UNK UNK ... Unknown Unknowns [*Design engineering*]
UNKW .... Baykit [*Former USSR*] [*ICAO location identifier*] (ICLI)
UNKWN ... Unknown
UNL .... Umwelt. Forschung, Gestaltung, Schutz [*A publication*]
UNL .... United Leader Resources, Inc. [*Vancouver Stock Exchange symbol*]
UNL .... University of Nebraska - Lincoln
UNL .... University of New Brunswick Law Library [*UTLAS symbol*]
UNL .... Unleaded Fuel [*Automotive engineering*]
UNL .... Unlimited
UNL .... Unloading
UNLA .... Uganda National Liberation Army [*Political party*] (AF)
UNLCH ..... Unlatch (MCD)
UNLF .... Ugandan National Liberation Front [*Political party*] (PD)
UNLGTD .. Unlighted (FAAC)
UNLIM ..... Unlimited
UNLIQ ...... Unliquidated
UNLIS .... United National Life Insurance Society (EA)
UNLK .... Unlock
UNLKG ..... Unlocking

UNLL .... United Nations League of Lawyers
UnlNV .... Unilever NV [*Associated Press abbreviation*] (APAG)
UNLOS ..... United Nations Law of the Sea [*Conference*]
UNLR .... United Nations Law Reports [*A publication*] (DLA)
UNLTD ..... Unlighted (DNAB)
UNLV .... University of Nevada, Las Vegas
UNM .... National University of Mexico [*Mexico*] [*Seismograph station code, US Geological Survey*] [*Closed*] (SEIS)
UNM .... Unified Miniature
UNM .... United National Movement [*Saint Christopher and Nevis*] [*Political party*] (EY)
UNM .... United Nations Medal [*Military decoration*]
UnM .... University Microfilms International, Ann Arbor, MI [*Library symbol*] [*Library of Congress*] (LCLS)
UNM .... University of Nebraska, Medical Center, Omaha, NE [*OCLC symbol*] (OCLC)
UNM .... Unmarried
UNM .... UNUM Corp. [*NYSE symbol*] (SPSG)
UNMA ...... Uni-Marts, Inc. [*State College, PA*] [*NASDAQ symbol*] (NQ)
UNMA ...... Unified Network Management Architecture [*Data processing*]
UNMAC.... United Nations Mixed Armistice Commission
Unman Syst ... Unmanned Systems [*A publication*]
UNMC....... United Nations Mediterranean Command (BJA)
UNMC....... United Nations Mediterranean Commission
UNMC....... University of Nebraska Medical Center [*Omaha, NB*]
UNMCB.... Unscheduled Not Mission Capable Both [*Maintenance and supply*] (MCD)
UNMCM... Unscheduled Not Mission Capable Maintenance (MCD)
UnMd .... Universal Medical Buildings Ltd. [*Associated Press abbreviation*] (APAG)
UNMD ...... Unmanned (KSC)
Un Med Can ... Union Medicale du Canada [*A publication*]
UNMEM ... United Nations Middle East Mission (EY)
UNM/JAR ... Journal of Anthropological Research. University of New Mexico. Department of Anthropology [*A publication*]
UNMKD.... Unmarked
UnM-L....... University Microfilms Ltd., Penn, Buckinghamshire, United Kingdom [*Library symbol*] [*Library of Congress*] (LCLS)
UNMO's... United Nations Military Observers (BJA)
UN Mo Bul ... Monthly Bulletin of Statistics. United Nations [*A publication*]
UN Mo Chron ... UN Monthly Chronicle [*A publication*]
UNMOGIP ... United Nations Military Observer Group for India and Pakistan (AABC)
UNMON... Unable to Monitor (FAAC)
Unm Ox ..... Unmuzzled Ox [*A publication*]
UNMSC .... United Nations Military Staff Committee (AABC)
UNMT....... United Nations Multilateral Treaties [*A publication*] (DLA)
UNMTD.... Unmounted
UNNB........ University National Bank & Trust Co. [*NASDAQ symbol*] (NQ)
UNNE........ Universidad Nacional del Nordeste [*Argentina*]
UNNECY .. Unnecessary (ROG)
UNNEFO.. United Nations of the New Emerging Forces [*Indonesia*]
UNNN .... Novosibirsk/Tolmachevo [*Former USSR*] [*ICAO location identifier*] (ICLI)
Unnumbered Rep US Dep Agric Econ Stat Coop Serv Stat Res Div ... Unnumbered Report. United States Department of Agriculture. Economics, Statistics, and Cooperatives Service. Statistical Research Division [*A publication*]
UNNUS..... Uralic News and Notes from the United States [*A publication*]
UNO .... Unicorn Resources [*Vancouver Stock Exchange symbol*]
UNO .... Unified Nimbus Observatory (MCD)
UNO .... Union Nacional Odriista [*Peruvian political party*]
UNO .... Union Nacional Opositora [*Electoral alliance*] [*Nicaragua*] (EY)
UNO .... United Nations Observer Corps (BJA)
UNO .... United Nations Organization [*ICSU*]
UNO .... United Nicaraguan Opposition
UNO .... University of Nebraska at Omaha
UNO .... University of New Orleans [*Louisiana*]
UNO .... Uno Restaurant Corp. [*AMEX symbol*] (SPSG)
UNO .... Utility Night Observer
UNOBSD .. Unobserved (ROG)
UNOC .... Union Nationale des Ouvriers Congolais [*National Union of Congolese Workers*]
UNOC .... United Nations Operation in the Congo
UNOCA..... United Nations Office Coordinating Humanitarian and Economic Aid to Afghanistan (ECON)
Unocal........ Unocal Corp. [*Associated Press abbreviation*] (APAG)
UNO-CARA-PEN ... Union Internationale pour la Cooperation Culturelle [*International Union for Cultural Co-operation*]
UNODIR... Unless Otherwise Directed
UNOEOA ... United Nations Office for Emergency Operations in Africa (EA)
Unof .... Unofficial Reports [*A publication*] (DLA)
UNOFFL... Unofficial (FAAC)
UNOG .... United Nations Organization - Geneva
UNOGIL ... United Nations Observer Group in Lebanon
UNOINDC ... Unless Otherwise Indicated
UNOLS ..... University National Oceanographic Laboratory System [*National Science Foundation*]

UNOO .... United Nations Oceanographic Organization
UNOP........ Unopened (ADA)
UNOP........ Unopposed
UNOPAR .. Universal Operator Performance Analyzer and Recorder
UNORDCAN ... Unexecuted Portion of Orders Cancelled
UNOREQ ... Unless Otherwise Requested (NVT)
UNORST .. Uno Restaurant Corp. [*Associated Press abbreviation*] (APAG)
UNOS........ United Network for Organ Sharing [*Database*] (EA)
U Notr D St ... University of Notre Dame. Studies in the Philosophy of Religion [*A publication*]
UNP .... Unification National Party [*South Korea*] [*Political party*] (EY)
UNP.......... Union Nacional Paraguaya [*Paraguayan political party*]
UNP.......... Union Pacific Corp. [*NYSE symbol*] (SPSG)
UNP.......... United National Party [*Sri Lanka*] [*Political party*] (PPW)
UNP.......... United Nations Philatelists (EA)
UNP.......... United Northern Petroleum Corp. [*Vancouver Stock Exchange symbol*]
Unp .... Unnilpentium [*Chemical element*] (CDAI)
UNP.......... Unpaged
UNP.......... Unpostable [*Data processing*]
UNPA........ Unione Nazionale Protezione Antiaere [*Italy*]
UNPA........ United Nations Participation Act of 1945
UNPA........ United Nations Postal Administration
UN-PAAERD ... United Nations Programme of Action for African Economic Recovery and Development [*1986-1990*]
UnPac .... Union Pacific Corp. [*Associated Press abbreviation*] (APAG)
UNPAC..... Union Pacific Railroad Co.
UNPAD..... Universitas Negeri Padjadjaran [*Indonesia*]
Unpartizan R ... Unpartizan Review [*A publication*]
UNPC........ United Nations Palestine Commission
UNPCC.... United Nations Palestine Conciliation Commission (BJA)
UNPD........ Unpaid (AABC)
UNPD-MSTR ... Unpaid Master
UNPERF... Unperformed [*Music*]
UNPERFD ... Unperformed (ROG)
UNPIK ..... United Nations Partisan Infantry Korea
UNPOC..... United Nations Peace Observation Commission
Unpop R..... Unpopular Review [*A publication*]
Un Prac News ... Unauthorized Practice News [*A publication*]
UNPROFOR ... United Nations Protection Force [*Former Yugoslavia*] (ECON)
UNPS .... Unified Network Planning Study
UNPS .... United Nations Philatelic Society (EA)
UNPS .... Universal Power Supply
UNPUB..... Unpublished
UNPUBD.. Unpublished
UNQ .... Providence, RI [*Location identifier*] [*FAA*] (FAAL)
UNQ .... Unique Resources Ltd. [*Vancouver Stock Exchange symbol*]
Unq .... Unnilquadium [*Chemical element*] (CDAI)
UNQTE..... Unquote
UNQUAL ... Unqualified (AABC)
unr............. Ukrainian Soviet Socialist Republic [*MARC country of publication code*] [*Library of Congress*] (LCCP)
UNR.......... Ukrains'ka Natsional'na Rada
UNR.......... Uniao Nacional Republicana [*National Republican Union*] [*Portugal*] [*Political party*] (PPE)
UNR.......... Unicorp Resources Ltd. [*Toronto Stock Exchange symbol*]
UN R......... United Nations Review [*A publication*]
UNRCCFE ... United Nations Regional Cartographic Conferences on Asia and the Far East
UNRDBL .. Unreadable (FAAC)
UNREF..... United Nations Refugee Fund
UNREF...... Unreformed (ROG)
UNREL ..... Unreliable
UNREP ..... Underway Replenishment [*Military*]
Unrep Cr C ... Bombay Unreported Criminal Cases [*1862-98*] [*India*] [*A publication*] (DLA)
Unrep NY Est TC ... Unreported New York Estate Tax Cases [*Prentice-Hall, Inc.*] [*A publication*] (DLA)
Unrep Wills Cas ... Unreported Wills Cases [*Prentice-Hall, Inc.*] [*A publication*] (DLA)
UN Res ...... United Nations Resolutions [*A publication*] (DLA)
UN Rev ...... United Nations Review [*A publication*]
UNRF........ Uganda National Rescue Front (PD)
UNRGLTD ... Unregulated
UNRHCE ... United Nations Regional Housing Center for ESCAP [*Economic and Social Commission for Asia and the Pacific*] [*India*] (EAIO)
UNRI .... UNR Industries, Inc. [*NASDAQ symbol*] (NQ)
UNRIAA ... United Nations Reports of International Arbitral Awards [*A publication*] (DLA)
UNRIPS.... United Nations Regional Institute for Population Studies [*Legon, Ghana*] (EAIO)
UNRISD.... United Nations Research Institute for Social Development (EA)
UNROD .... United Nations Relief Operation in Dacca
UNRP........ University of Nottingham. Research Publications [*A publication*]
UNRPR ..... United Nations Relief for Palestine Refugees
UNRR........ Unable to Approve Route Requested [*Aviation*] (FAAC)

UNRRA ..... United Nations Relief and Rehabilitation Administration
   [*"United Nations" in this body's name derives from the
   wartime alliance of this name, not from any affiliation with
   the postwar international organization*]
UNRRC ..... United Nations Relief and Rehabilitation Conference
UNRS .... Union pour la Nouvelle Republique Senegalaise [*Union for the
   New Senegalese Republic*] [*Political party*]
UNRSTD... Unrestricted (FAAC)
UNRTD..... United Nations Resources and Transport Division
UNRWA.... United Nations Relief and Works Agency for Palestine Refugees
   in the Near East [*Austria*] (PD)
UNRWAPR ... United Nations Relief and Works Agency for Palestine
   Refugees in the Near East [*Austria*] (DLA)
UNRWAPRNE ... United Nations Relief and Works Agency for Palestine
   Refugees in the Near East [*Pronounced: "Unwrap me"*]
   [*Austria*]
UNS .... Umnak, AK [*Location identifier*] [*FAA*] (FAAL)
UnS .... Unconditioned Stimulus [*Psychometrics*] (AAMN)
UNS .... Unified Numbering Systems [*for metals*] (MCD)
UNS .... Unified Special [*Thread*]
UNS .... United News Shops [*British*]
UNS .... Universal News Service [*British*]
UNS .... Universal Night Sight
UNS .... University of Nebraska. Studies [*A publication*]
uns .... Unsatisfactory (MAE)
UNS .... Unsymmetrical
UNSA .... United Financial Corp. of South Carolina, Inc. [*NASDAQ
   symbol*] (NQ)
UNSAC ..... United Nations Scientific Advisory Committee [*ICSU*]
UNSAT ...... Unsatisfactory (AABC)
unsat.......... Unsaturated [*Chemistry*]
UNSATFY ... Unsatisfactory
UNSB .... United Bank, A Savings Bank [*NASDAQ symbol*] (NQ)
UNSBL...... Unseasonable (FAAC)
UNSC .... United Nations Security Council
UNSC .... United Nations Social Commission
UNSCC...... United Nations Standards Co-Ordinating Committee
UNSCC...... University of Nevada System Computing Center [*Research
   center*] (RCD)
UNSCCUR ... United Nations Scientific Conference on the Conservation and
   Utilization of Resources
UNSCEAR ... United Nations Scientific Committee on the Effects of Atomic
   Radiation
UNSCOB .. United Nations Special Committee on the Balkans [*Greece*]
UNSCOP... United Nations Special Committee on Palestine
UNSD .... Unsweetened (ROG)
UNSDD..... United Nations Social Development Division
UNSDRI.... United Nations Social Defense Research Institute [*UN/Italy*]
UNSE .... United Security Financial Corp. of Illinois [*NASDAQ
   symbol*] (NQ)
UN Sec Bur Soc Aff Ser K ... United Nations Secretariat. Bureau of Social
   Affairs. Series K [*A publication*]
UNSECNAV ... Under Secretary of the Navy
UnSemQR ... Union Seminary. Quarterly Review [*New York*] [*A publication*]
Unser Sozial Dorf ... Unser Sozialistisches Dorf [*A publication*]
Un Serv M ... United Service Magazine [*A publication*]
Un Serv (Phila) ... United Service (Philadelphia) [*A publication*]
UNSF........ United Nations Special Fund
UNSFH ..... United Nations Security Forces, Hollandia (AABC)
UNSG........ United Nations Secretary General
UNSGD ..... Unsigned (WGA)
UNSI .... United Service Source, Inc. [*NASDAQ symbol*] (NQ)
UNSIS .... United Nations Statistical Information System (DUND)
UNSKED.... Unscheduled (FAAC)
UNSL .... UNSL Financial Corp. [*Formerly, United Saving & Loan
   Association*] [*NASDAQ symbol*] (NQ)
UNSM .... United Nations Service Medal [*Military decoration*]
UNSO........ United Nations Sudano-Sahelian Office
UNSP .... Union Nationale pour la Solidarite et le Progres [*Benin*]
   [*Political party*] (EY)
UNSPD ..... Underground Space [*A publication*]
UNSPDPM ... United Nations Subcommission on the Prevention of
   Discrimination and the Protection of Minorities [*Geneva,
   Switzerland*] (EAIO)
UNSS........ United Nations Sales Section [*for UN documents*]
UNSSOD .. United Nations Special Session on Disarmament (PDAA)
UNST .... Union Nordique pour la Sante et le Travail [*Nordic Union for
   Health and Work*] (EAIO)
UNSTBL... Unstable
UNSTD ..... Union Nationale des Syndicats des Travailleurs du Dahomey
   [*National Federation of Workers' Unions of Dahomey*]
UNSTDY... Unsteady
UNSTHV.. Union Nationale des Syndicats des Travailleurs de la Haute
   Volta [*National Federation of Workers' Unions of the
   Upper Volta*]
UNSTL...... Unsettle (FAAC)
UNSU........ United Nations Staff Union (EA)
UNSU........ United Nations Study Unit [*Philatelic organization*] (EA)
UNSUB ..... Unknown Subject [*FBI*] [*Acronym also used as title of
   television series*]
UNSUPPR ... Unsuppressed (MSA)

UNSV .... United Savings Association [*Miami Lakes, FL*] [*NASDAQ
   symbol*] (NQ)
UNSVC ..... Unserviceable (AABC)
UNSVC-RT-R ... Unserviceable Return Rate
UNSVM ..... United Nations Service Medal
UNSWLJ .. University of New South Wales. Law Journal [*A
   publication*] (APTA)
UNSYM .... Unsymmetrical
UN Symp Dev Use Geotherm Resour Abstr ... United Nations Symposium on
   the Development and Use of Geothermal Resources.
   Abstracts [*A publication*]
UN Symp Dev Use Geotherm Resour Proc ... United Nations Symposium on
   the Development and Use of Geothermal Resources.
   Proceedings [*A publication*]
UnT............ Uncanny Tales [*A publication*]
UNT .... Undergraduate Navigator Training [*Air Force*] (AFM)
UNT .... Underground Nuclear Test
UNT .... Unit Corp. [*NYSE symbol*] (SPSG)
UNT .... Unitas [*Finland*] [*A publication*]
UNT .... United Tariff Bureau, Inc., New York NY [*STAC*]
UNT .... Unst [*Scotland*] [*Airport symbol*] (OAG)
UNT .... Untersuchungen zum Neuen Testament [*A publication*]
UNT .... Uppsala Nya Tidning [*A publication*]
UNTA .... Union Nationale des Travailleurs Angolais [*National Union of
   Angolan Workers*]
UNTA .... United Nations Technical Assistance
UNTAA ..... United Nations Technical Assistance Administration
UNTAC ..... United Nations Transitional Authority in Cambodia (ECON)
UNTAF ..... United Nations Technical Assistance Fellowship
UNTAG...... United Nations Transition Assistance Group
UNTC .... Unable to Establish Contact (FAAC)
UNTC .... Union Nationale des Travailleurs Congolais [*National Union of
   Congolese Workers*]
UNTCI ...... Union Nationale des Travailleurs de Cote d'Ivoire [*National
   Union of Ivory Coast Workers*]
UNTCOK.. United Nations Temporary Committee on Korea
UNTCOR.. United Nations Trusteeship Council Official Record [*A
   publication*] (DLA)
UNTD........ First United Bancshares, Inc. [*El Dorado, AR*] [*NASDAQ
   symbol*] (NQ)
UNTD........ University Naval Training Division [*Canada*]
UNTDED.. United Nations Data Elements Directory [*A publication*]
UNTE........ Unit Corp. [*NASDAQ symbol*] (NQ)
UNTEA ..... Undersea Technology [*A publication*]
UNTEA ..... United Nations Temporary Executive Authority [*Supervised
   transfer of Netherlands New Guinea to Indonesia*]
UnTech ...... United Technologies Corp. [*Associated Press
   abbreviation*] (APAG)
Unternehmungsfuehrung im Gewerbe ... Unternehmungsfuehrung im
   Gewerbe und Gewerbliche [*A publication*]
Unters Angebot Nachfrage Miner Rohst ... Untersuchungen ueber Angebot
   und Nachfrage Mineralischer Rohstoffe [*A publication*]
UnTex........ Union Texas Exploration [*Associated Press
   abbreviation*] (APAG)
UNTFDPP ... United Nations Trust Fund for Development Planning and
   Projections
UNTFSD... United Nations Trust Fund for Social Development
UNTG........ United Nations Theatre Group (EA)
UNTHD .... Unthreaded
UNTIS .... United Nations Treaty Information System (DUND)
UNTM....... Union Nationale des Travailleurs du Mali [*National Union of
   Malian Workers*]
UNTN........ Union Nationale des Travailleurs Nigeriens [*National Union of
   Nigerian Workers*]
Un Trav Dec ... Unreported Travancore Decisions [*A publication*] (DLA)
UNTS .... Undergraduate Navigator Training System [*Air Force*]
UNTS .... Union Nationale des Travailleurs du Senegal [*National Union
   of Workers of Senegal*]
UNTS .... United Nations Treaty Series [*Project*] [*University of
   Washington*]
UNTSO ..... United Nations Truce Supervision Organization
UNTT .... Union Nationale des Travailleurs du Togo [*National Union of
   Togolese Workers*]
UNTT .... United Nations Trust Territory
UNTW....... Untwist
UNTY........ Unity Healthcare Holding Co., Inc. [*NASDAQ symbol*] (NQ)
UNU .... Juneau, WI [*Location identifier*] [*FAA*] (FAAL)
UNU .... United Nations University [*Tokyo*]
UNU .... Universidad de las Naciones Unidas [*United Nations
   University*] [*Spanish*] (DUND)
UNU .... Universite des Nations Unies [*United Nations University*]
   [*French*] (DUND)
UNUIIST .. United Nations University International Institute for Software
UNUM ...... UNUM Corp. [*Associated Press abbreviation*] (APAG)
UNUMO ... Universal Underwater Mobile [*Robot*]
UNUSBL... Unusable
UNUSL ..... Unusual (ROG)
UNU/WIDER ... United Nations University / World Institute for
   Development Economics Research (DUND)
UNV........... State College, PA [*Location identifier*] [*FAA*] (FAAL)
UNV.......... United Nations Volunteers (EAIO)

UNV............	Unitel Video, Inc. [*AMEX symbol*] (SPSG)
Unverd	Unverified
UnvFd	Universal Foods Corp. [*Associated Press abbreviation*] (APAG)
UnvHlt.......	Universal Health Services, Inc. [*Associated Press abbreviation*] (APAG)
UnvHR.......	Universal Health Realty Income Trust [*Associated Press abbreviation*] (APAG)
UnvMed.....	Universal Medical Buildings, Inc. [*Associated Press abbreviation*] (APAG)
UNVPAT...	University Patents, Inc. [*Associated Press abbreviation*] (APAG)
UNVS-A	Universo [*Italy*] [*A publication*]
UnvslCp.....	Universal Corp. [*Associated Press abbreviation*] (APAG)
UNVX........	Universal Trading Exchange, Inc. [*NASDAQ symbol*] (NQ)
UNWAL Rev ...	University of Western Australia. Law Review [*A publication*] (APTA)
UN W Bul ...	United Nations Weekly Bulletin [*A publication*]
UNWCC....	Unions' Nation-Wide Coordinating Council for Oil and Allied Industries (EA)
UNWCC....	United Nations War Crimes Commission [*"United Nations" in this body's name derives from the wartime alliance of this name, not from any affiliation with the postwar international organization*]
UNWG	United Nations Women's Guild (EA)
UNWLA	Ukrainian National Women's League of America (EA)
UNWMG ..	Utility Nuclear Waste Management Group (EA)
UnwmK......	Unwatermarked [*Philately*]
UNWMKD ...	Unwatermarked (WGA)
UN World ...	United Nations World [*A publication*]
UNWR.......	Unwritten (ROG)
UNWRAP ...	United We Resist Additional Packaging [*Student legal action organization*]
UNWRF	United Westland Resources [*NASDAQ symbol*] (NQ)
UNWS.......	Uniwest Financial Corp. [*NASDAQ symbol*] (NQ)
UNWSA	Unterrichtswissenschaft [*A publication*]
UNX..........	Underground Nuclear Explosion
UNX..........	Univex Mining Corp. [*Vancouver Stock Exchange symbol*]
UNY..........	San Antonio, TX [*Location identifier*] [*FAA*] (FAAL)
UNY..........	United Nations of Yoga [*Stockholm, Sweden*] (EAIO)
UNY..........	University of New York (ROG)
UNYB.......	United Nations Year Book [*A publication*] (DLA)
UNYFA	Ukrainian National Youth Federation of America [*Later, Ukrainian Youth Association of America*] (EA)
UNYOM ...	United Nations Yemen Observation Mission
u-nz---........	New Zealand [*MARC geographic area code*] [*Library of Congress*] (LCCP)
UNZ..........	Unzendake [*Japan*] [*Seismograph station code, US Geological Survey*] (SEIS)
UO	Empresa Aero Uruguay SA [*ICAO designator*] (FAAC)
UO	Trans-Union [*France*] [*ICAO designator*] [*Obsolete*] (FAAC)
UO	Ukrainica Occidentalia [*Winnipeg*] [*A publication*]
UO	Ulm-Oberschwaben [*A publication*]
UO	Und Oefters [*And Often*] [*German*]
UO	Undelivered Orders [*Army*] (AABC)
UO	Union Office (ROG)
UO	Union Railroad of Oregon [*AAR code*]
UO	Unit Operator (NRCH)
UO	University of Oxford (ROG)
UO	Ureteral Orifice [*Anatomy*] (MAE)
UO	Urinary Output [*Medicine*]
U & O........	Use and Occupancy [*Real estate*]
U/O............	Used On (MSA)
UO	Weber County Library, Ogden, UT [*Library symbol*] [*Library of Congress*] (LCLS)
UOA	Unattached Officers' Association [*A union*] [*British*]
UOA	United Ostomy Association (EA)
UOA	University of Arizona [*Seismograph station code, US Geological Survey*] [*Closed*] (SEIS)
UOA	Use of Other Automobiles [*Insurance*]
UOA	Used on Assembly
UOBI........	United Oklahoma Bankshares, Inc. [*NASDAQ symbol*] (NQ)
UOBTPS ...	United Operative Bricklayers' Trade Protection Society [*A union*] [*British*]
UOC..........	Ultimate Operating Capability
UOC..........	Ultimate Operational Configuration (AAG)
UOC..........	Unequilibrated Ordinary Chondrites
UOC..........	Unilens Optical [*Vancouver Stock Exchange symbol*]
UOC..........	Union de l'Ouest Cameroun [*Union of West Cameroon*]
UOC..........	Unit of Choice
UOC..........	United Orpington Club (EA)
UOC..........	Universal Output Computer
UOC..........	Unusual Occurrence Control
UOC..........	Uranium Ore Concentrate
UOC..........	Useable on Code (MCD)
UOCA........	United Orpington Club of America [*Later, UOC*] (EA)
UOCB........	Uncrossed Olivocochlear Bundle [*Otology*]
UOCC........	Unilens Optical Corp. [*NASDAQ symbol*] (NQ)
UOCMWD ...	Union of Operative Card Makers and Wire Drawers [*British*]
UOCO	Union Oil Co.
UODDL......	User-Oriented Data Display Language [*Data processing*]

UODG	Underwater Ordnance Development Group
UOE...........	Unit of Error (MCD)
UOEF	Union de Obreros Estivadores de Filipinos [*Union of Longshoremen of the Philippines*]
UOF...........	Unplanned Outage Factor [*Electronics*] (IEEE)
UOFS	United States Forest Service, Intermountain Range and Experiment Station Library, Ogden, UT [*Library symbol*] [*Library of Congress*] (LCLS)
UOGC........	United Order of the Golden Cross [*Defunct*] (EA)
UOGF........	Uranium Off-Gas Filter [*Nuclear energy*] (NRCH)
UOGS........	Church of Jesus Christ of Latter-Day Saints, Genealogical Society Library, Ogden Branch, Ogden, UT [*Library symbol*] [*Library of Congress*] (LCLS)
UOH	Unplanned Outage Hours [*Electronics*] (IEEE)
UOHC	Under Other than Honorable Conditions [*Discharge*] [*Military*]
UOI...........	Unit of Instruction
UOI...........	University of Illinois [*Record label*]
UOI...........	User On-Line Interaction [*Data processing*]
UOIL........	Unioil [*NASDAQ symbol*] (NQ)
UOIW........	United Optical and Instrument Workers of America
UOJC	Union of Orthodox Jewish Congregations of America (EA)
UOJCA.....	Union of Orthodox Jewish Congregations of America (EA)
UOK	University of Oklahoma [*Record label*]
UOL	Underwater Object Locator
UOL	Utility Octal Load
UOL	Utility-Oriented Language (MCD)
UOLS	Underwater Object Location and Search Operations [*Navy*] (NVT)
U of Omaha Bull ...	Night Law School Bulletin. University of Omaha [*A publication*] (DLA)
UOMCA....	United Orthodox Ministers and Cantors Association of America and Canada (EA)
UOME.......	Union des Opposants Malgaches Exterieurs [*Madagascar*] [*Political party*] (EY)
UOMGCU ...	United Operative Masons' and Granite Cutters' Union [*British*]
UOMS.......	Union des Originaires de Mauritanie du Sud [*Union of Natives of South Mauritania*]
UOMS.......	Unmanned Orbital Multifunction Satellite
UON	Unless Otherwise Noted (OA)
UON	Urgency of Need (MCD)
UOO	Undelivered Orders Outstanding [*Military*] (AFM)
UOP..........	Understanding of the Problem (MCD)
UOP..........	Unit Operating Procedure (NRCH)
UOP..........	University of the Pacific [*Stockton, CA*]
UOP..........	Urine Output [*Physiology*]
UOP..........	User Operations Panel (SSD)
UOPA........	Uranium Ore Processing Association
UOPDP	Union Ouvriere et Paysanne pour la Democratie Proletarienne [*Peasant and Worker Union for Proletarian Democracy*] [*France*] [*Political party*] (PPE)
UOPH	Unaccompanied Officer Personnel Housing [*Navy*]
UOPLF......	United Oromo People's Liberation Front [*Ethiopia*] [*Political party*] (EY)
UOQ	Upper Outer Quadrant [*Anatomy*]
UOr...........	Orem City Library, Orem, UT [*Library symbol*] [*Library of Congress*] (LCLS)
UOR..........	Uniform Officer Record
UOR..........	Unplanned Outage Rate [*Electronics*] (IEEE)
UOR..........	Urgent Operation Requirement
UORUSC ..	Union of Orthodox Rabbis of the US and Canada (EA)
UOS..........	Sewanee, TN [*Location identifier*] [*FAA*] (FAAL)
UOS..........	Ultraviolet Ozone Spectrometer (MCD)
UOS..........	Undelivered Orders Schedule [*Army*]
UOS..........	Underwater Ordnance Station [*Navy*]
UOS..........	United Order of Smiths [*A union*] [*British*]
UOS..........	University of the South [*Record label*]
UOS..........	Unless Otherwise Specified (MSA)
UOS..........	Unmanned Orbital Satellite
UOS..........	User Operations Support (SSD)
UOSAT	University of Surrey Satellite
UOSG	User Operations Support Group (SSD)
UOSM.......	Urinary Osmolarity [*Medicine*]
UOT..........	Uncontrollable Overtime
UOT..........	Union, SC [*Location identifier*] [*FAA*] (FAAL)
UOT..........	Unit of Trading
UOT..........	Upper Outer Tube
UOTASP...	United Order of the Total Abstaining Sons of the Phoenix (ROG)
UOTC.......	University Officers Training Corps [*British military*] (DMA)
UOTHC....	Under Other than Honorable Conditions [*Discharge*] [*Military*]
UOTS	United Order True Sisters (EA)
UOV	Union Ouvriere du Viet-Nam [*Vietnam Labor Union*] [*South Vietnam*]
UOV	Units of Variance
UOW	Weber State College, Ogden, UT [*Library symbol*] [*Library of Congress*] (LCLS)
UOX..........	Oxford, MS [*Location identifier*] [*FAA*] (FAAL)
UOX..........	University [*Mississippi*] [*Airport symbol*] (OAG)
UP............	Air Foyle Ltd. [*Great Britain*] [*ICAO designator*] (FAAC)
UP.............	Journal of Urban Planning and Development [*A publication*]

UP.............. Lab. UPSA [*France*] [*Research code symbol*]
UP.............. Oregon Short Line R. R. [*of Union Pacific Railroad Co.*] [*AAR code*]
UP.............. Oregon-Washington R. R. & Navigation [*of Union Pacific Railroad Co.*] [*AAR code*]
UP.............. Provo Public Library, Provo, UT [*Library symbol*] [*Library of Congress*] (LCLS)
UP.............. Ulster Parliament (DAS)
UP.............. Ultra Presse [*Press agency*] [*Colombia*]
UP.............. Umbilical Pin
UP.............. Uncertainty Principle [*Quantum mechanics*]
UP.............. Uncertified Patient [*British*]
UP.............. Under-Proof [*Of spirituous liquors*] [*Distilling*]
UP.............. Under Provisions Of [*Military*]
UP.............. Undergraduate Program [*Subject area tests*]
UP.............. Unearned Premium [*Insurance*]
UP.............. Unemployed Parent [*Department of Health and Human Services*]
UP.............. Union Pacific Corp.
UP.............. Union Patriotica [*Patriotic Union*] [*Spain*] [*Political party*] (PPE)
UP.............. Union Patriotica [*Patriotic Union*] [*Colombia*] [*Political party*]
UP.............. Union Popular [*Popular Union*] [*Uruguay*] (PD)
UP.............. Union del Pueblo [*Union of the People*] [*Mexico*] (PD)
UP.............. Uniprocessor
UP.............. Unit Pack
UP.............. Unit Price
UP.............. United Party [*Papua New Guinea*] [*Political party*] (PPW)
UP.............. United Party [*Gambia*] [*Political party*] (PPW)
UP.............. United Presbyterian
UP.............. United Press [*Merged with International News Service to form UPI*]
UP.............. United Provinces [*India*]
up .... United States Miscellaneous Pacific Islands [*MARC country of publication code*] [*Library of Congress*] (LCCP)
UP.............. Unity Party [*Sierra Leone*] [*Political party*] (EY)
UP.............. Unity Party [*Liberia*] [*Political party*] (EY)
UP.............. Universal Processor [*TRW, Inc.-Motorola, Inc.*] [*Data processing*]
UP.............. University Presses [*General term applied to presses of various universities*]
UP.............. Uniwersytet Imienia Adama Mickiewicza w Poznaniu [*A publication*]
UP.............. Unpostable [*Data processing*]
UP.............. Unrealized Profit
UP.............. Unrotated Projectile [*Rocket*]
UP.............. Unsaturated Thermoset Polyester [*Organic chemistry*]
UP.............. Unsolicited Proposal (MCD)
UP.............. Unstained Pollen [*Botany*]
UP.............. Unterrichtspraxis [*A publication*]
UP.............. Update [*Online database field identifier*] [*Data processing*]
UP.............. Upper (ADA)
UP.............. Upper Peninsula [*Michigan*]
UP.............. Upper Proof (ROG)
UP.............. Upright Posture (MAE)
UP.............. Urea Phosphate (OA)
UP.............. Ureteropelvic [*Anatomy*]
UP.............. Uridine Phosphorylase [*An enzyme*]
U/P .... Urine-Plasma Ratio [*Clinical chemistry*]
UP.............. Uroporphyrin [*Biochemistry*]
UP.............. Urticaria Pigmentosa [*Dermatology*]
UP.............. User Program (MCD)
UP.............. Utility Path (IEEE)
UP.............. Utility Program (MCD)
U & P .... Uttering and Publishing [*Legal term*]
UPA .... Ukrains'ka Povstans'ka Armiia
UPA .... Ultimate Players Association (EA)
UPA .... Uncooled Parametric Amplifier
UPA .... Uniao das Populacoes de Angola [*Angolan People's Union*] [*Later, NFLA*]
UPA .... Uniform Partnership Act
UPA .... Union Panamericana [*Pan-American Union*] [*Washington, DC*]
UPA .... Union of Poles in America (EA)
UPA .... Union Postale Arabe [*Arab Postal Union*]
UPA .... Unique Product Advantage [*Advertising*]
UPA .... Unitary Pole Approximation
UPA .... United Patternmakers Association
UPA .... United Producers of America [*Motion picture company*]
UPA .... University Photographers Association of America
UPA .... University Press of America
UPA .... Unwed Parents Anonymous (EA)
UPA .... Urokinase Plasminogen Activator [*An enzyme*]
UPAA .... University Photographers Association of America (EA)
UPAC .... Unemployed and Poverty Action Council (EA)
UPAC .... Unificacion y Progreso [*Unification and Progress*] [*Mexico*] [*Political party*] (PPW)
UPAC .... United Parents of Absconded Children [*Defunct*] (EA)
UPACS ...... Universal Performance Assessment and Control System

UPADI ...... Union Pan-Americana de Asociaciones de Igenieros [*Pan American Federation of Engineering Societies*] [*Uruguay*] (EAIO)
UPAE .... Union Postal de las Americas y Espana [*Postal Union of the Americas and Spain - PUAS*] (EAIO)
UPAEP ...... Union Postal de las Americas, Espana, y Portugal [*Postal Union of the Americas, Spain, and Portugal*] [*Uruguay*] (EAIO)
UPAJ .... Union Panafricaine des Journalistes
UPAL .... Utrechtse Publikaties voor Algemene Literatuurwetenschap [*A publication*]
U PA Law Rev ... University of Pennsylvania. Law Review and American Law Register [*A publication*]
U PA LR .... University of Pennsylvania. Law Review [*A publication*]
U PA L Rev ... University of Pennsylvania. Law Review [*A publication*]
UPAM .... United People's Association of Matabeleland [*Zimbabwe*] [*Political party*] (PPW)
UPAO .... University Professors for Academic Order (EA)
UPAP........ Union Pan Africaine des Postes [*Pan African Postal Union - PAPU*] (EAIO)
UPAP........ Urban Planning Assistance Program
U-PARC .... University of Pittsburgh Applied Research Center [*Research center*] (RCD)
UPARR...... Urban Park and Recreation Recovery
UPAS........ Uniform Performance Assessment System [*Education*]
UPAT .... Union Panafricaine des Telecommunications [*Pan African Telecommunications Union - PATU*] (EAIO)
UPB .... Brigham Young University, Provo, UT [*Library symbol*] [*Library of Congress*] (LCLS)
UPB .... Union Patriotica Bonairiana [*Bonaire Patriotic Union*] [*Netherlands Antilles*] [*Political party*] (PPW)
UPB .... United Press of Bangladesh
UPB .... Universal Patents Bureau [*British*] (ROG)
UPB .... Upper Bound
UP/BA....... Unitary Payroll Benefit Accounting (MCD)
Up Ben Pr .. Upper Bench Precedents Tempore Car. I [*England*] [*A publication*] (DLA)
Up Ben Pre ... Upper Bench Precedents Tempore Car. I [*A publication*] (DLA)
UPB-L .... Brigham Young University, J. Reuben Clark Law Library, Provo, UT [*Library symbol*] [*Library of Congress*] (LCLS)
UPC .... Pennsylvania State University, Commonwealth Campuses, University Park, PA [*OCLC symbol*] (OCLC)
UPC .... Uganda People's Congress [*Suspended*]
UPC .... Underwater Pipe Cutter
UPC .... Uniform Practice Code
UPC .... Uniform Probate Code
UPC .... Union of the Corsican People [*France*]
UPC .... Union Planters Corp. [*NYSE symbol*] (CTT)
UPC .... Union des Populations Camerounaises [*Union of Cameroonian Peoples*] (PD)
UPC .... Union pour le Progres Comorien [*Union for Comorian Progress*] [*Political party*] (PPW)
UPC .... Union Progressiste Congolaise [*Congolese Progressive Union*]
UPC .... Union del Pueblo Canario [*Union of the Canarian People*] [*Spain*] [*Political party*] (PPE)
UPC .... Unione di u Populu Corsu [*Union of the Corsican People*] [*France*] [*Political party*] (PPE)
UPC .... Unit of Packed Cells
UPC .... Unit of Processing Capacity
UPC .... Unit Processing Code (AFM)
UPC .... Unit Production Cost
UPC .... United Power Co. [*British*]
UPC .... United Presbyterian Church
UPC .... Universal Peripheral Controller
UPC .... Universal Product Code [*Inventory control*]
UPC .... Unpostable Code [*Data processing*]
UPC .... USPCI, Inc. [*NYSE symbol*] (SPSG)
UPCA .... Uniform Planned Community Act [*National Conference of Commissioners on Uniform State Laws*]
UPCC .... Uniform Product Code Council [*Formerly, UGPCC*] (EA)
UPCHUK.. University Program for the Comprehensive Handling and Utilization of Knowledge [*Humorous*]
UPCI.......... Union pour Construire l'Independence [*New Caledonia*] [*Political party*] (EY)
UPCO .... Union Progressiste Congolaise [*Congolese Progressive Union*]
UPCO .... United Presidential Corp. [*NASDAQ symbol*] (NQ)
UPCON ..... Upgraded Constellation (MCD)
UPCS........ Universal Philatelic Cover Society
UP/CSEC ... Cuban Studies/Estudios Cubanos. University of Pittsburg. University Center for International Studies. Center for Latin American Studies [*A publication*]
UPD.......... Underpotential Deposition [*Electrochemistry*]
UPD.......... Union des Patriotes Democratiques [*Haiti*] [*Political party*] (EY)
UPD.......... Unit Power Density [*Lighting*]
UPD.......... Unpaid (ADA)
UPD.......... Update
UPD.......... Urban Planning Directorate [*British*]
UPDA........ United Plastics Distributors Association [*Later, NAPD*] (EA)

UPDATE...   Universal Prefabricated Depot Automatic Test Equipment   (DNAB)

UPDATE...   Unlimited Potential Data through Automation Technology in Education   (IEEE)

Update ....   Update on Law-Related Education [*A publication*]

UPDEA .....   Union des Producteurs, Transporteurs, et Distributeurs d'Energie Electrique d'Afrique [*Union of Producers, Conveyors, and Distributors of Electric Power in Africa - UPDEA*]   (EAIO)

UPDFT......   Updraft   (MSA)

UPDFTS ...   Updrafts   (FAAC)

UPDMA ....   United Popular Dress Manufacturers Association [*Later, LACA*]   (EA)

UPDP ....   Union des Patriotes Democrates et Progressistes [*Niger*] [*Political party*]   (EY)

UPDRS......   Unified Parkinson's Disease Rating Scale

UP/E..........   Ethnology. University of Pittsburgh [*A publication*]

UPE ....   Union Panafricaine des Etudiants [*All Africa Students Union - AASU*]   (EAIO)

UPE ....   Union de Patriotas Espanoles [*Union of Patriots*] [*Spanish*]

UPE ....   Unit Proficiency Exercise

UPE ....   Unitary Pole Expansion

UPE ....   Upstream Promoter Element [*Genetics*]

UPEB........   Union de Paises Exportadores de Banano [*Union of Banana-Exporting Countries - UBEC*]   (EAIO)

UPEBR......   Uncured Propellant End Burning Rocket   (MCD)

UPECO .....   Union Progressiste Congolaise [*Congolese Progressive Union*]

UPEI.........   Union Petroliere Europeenne Independante [*Independent European Petroleum Union*]   (EAIO)

UPEI.........   University of Prince Edward Island [*Canada*]

UPEN ....   Upper Peninsula Energy Corp. [*NASDAQ symbol*]   (NQ)

UPEP........   Undergraduate Preparation of Educational Personnel [*Office of Education*]

UPEPI ....   Union of European Practitioners in Industrial Property [*EC*]   (ECED)

UPEQUA ..   Union Progressiste de l'Equateur [*Progressive Union of Equateur Province*] [*Congo - Leopoldville*]

UPES........   Ultraviolet Photoelectron Spectroscopy

UPET........   Urokinase Pulmonary Embolism Trial

UPEU ....   Uganda Public Employees' Union

UPF ....   Uganda Popular Front [*Political party*]   (PD)

UPF ....   Union pour la France [*France*] [*Political party*]

UPF ....   United Parkinson Foundation   (EA)

UPF ....   United Patriotic Front   (EA)

UPF ....   United People's Front [*Singapore*] [*Political party*]   (PPW)

UPF ....   United People's Front [*Nepal*] [*Political party*]   (EY)

UPF ....   Unofficial Personnel Folder

UPFAW.....   United Packinghouse Food and Allied Workers [*Later, UFCWIU*]   (EA)

UPFD ....   United Pesticide Formulators and Distributors Association   (EA)

UPFDA......   United Pesticide Formulators and Distributors Association

UPFF ....   Universal Proutist Farmers Federation   (EA)

UPFM........   Union Progressive des Femmes Marocaines [*Progressive Union of Moroccan Women*]

UPG ....   Ujung Pandang [*Indonesia*] [*Airport symbol*]   (OAG)

UPG ....   Union du Peuple Gabonais [*Political party*]   (EY)

UPG ....   Union des Populations de Guinee [*Guinea People's Union*]   (PD)

UPG ....   Union Progressiste Guineenne [*Guinean Progressive Union*]

UPG ....   United Pacific Gold [*Vancouver Stock Exchange symbol*]

UPG ....   United Parents under God   (EA)

UPG ....   Unpaying Guest [*In a rooming or boarding house*]

UPG ....   Upgrade [*Data processing*]

UPG ....   Uroporphyrinogen [*Biochemistry*]   (MAE)

UPGMA ....   Unweighted Pair-Group Method with Arithmetic Means [*Phylogenetic analysis*]

UPGRADE ...   University of Pittsburgh Generalized Recording and Dissemination Experiment

UPGRADE ...   User-Prompted Graphic Data Evaluation [*US Council on Environmental Quality*]

UPGS.........   Church of Jesus Christ of Latter-Day Saints, Genealogical Society Library, Utah Valley Branch, Provo, UT [*Library symbol*] [*Library of Congress*]   (LCLS)

UPGS.........   Unione Progressista della Gioventu Somala [*Progressive Union of Somali Youth*]

UPGWA ....   International Union, United Plant Guard Workers of America   (EA)

UPH...........   Unaccompanied Personnel Housing [*Military*]

UPH...........   Underground Pumped Hydro [*Energy storage*]

UPH...........   Union Patriotique Haitienne [*Haitian Patriotic Union*]   (EA)

UPH...........   Union of Platers Helpers [*British*]

UPHA........   United Professional Horsemen's Association   (EA)

UPHC........   United Party of Haitian Communists

UPHCI ......   Undistributed Personal Holding Company Income

UPHD.......   Uphold [*Law*]   (ROG)

UPHD.......   Upholstered

UPHEWA ...   United Presbyterian Health, Education, and Welfare Association [*Later, PHEWA*]   (EA)

UPHG........   Upholstering

UPHLSTG ...   Upholstering   (WGA)

UPHOL.....   Upholstery   (WGA)

UPHPISEC ...   Union for the Protection of the Human Person by International, Social, and Economic Cooperation [*Defunct*]   (EA)

UPHR........   Up Here [*A publication*]

UPHSTR...   Upholster

UPHTDE ..   Annual Research Reviews. Ultrastructural Pathology of Human Tumors [*A publication*]

UPI ....   Fayetteville/Fort Bragg, NC [*Location identifier*] [*FAA*]   (FAAL)

UPI ....   United Press International   (EA)

UPI ....   Universal Presentation Interface [*Uniface Corp.*]

UPI ....   Upper Plenum Injection [*Nuclear energy*]   (NRCH)

UPI ....   Uteroplacental Insufficiency [*Medicine*]

UPIA ....   Underwater Photography Instruction Association [*Defunct*]   (EA)

UPIA ....   Uniform Principal and Income Act [*National Conference of Commissioners on Uniform State Laws*]

UPICV.......   Uniao dos Povos das Ilhas do Cabo Verde [*Union of the Peoples of the Cape Verde Islands*]

UPICV-R...   Uniao do Povo para Independencia de Cabo Verde-Ressusitacao [*Cape Verde*] [*Political party*]   (EY)

UPIF.........   Universal Proutist Intellectual Federation   (EA)

UPIGO ......   Union Professionnelle Internationale des Gynecologues et Obstetriciens [*International Union of Professional Gynecologists and Obstetricians*]

UPIINS .....   Uniform Procurement Instrument Identification Numbering System   (MCD)

UPIN ....   United Press International Newspictures

UPIR.........   Uniform Photographic Interpretation Report [*Military*]   (AFM)

U Pit Law...   University of Pittsburgh. Law Review [*A publication*]

UPITN.......   United Press International Television News

U Pitt L R ..   University of Pittsburgh. Law Review [*A publication*]

U Pitt L Rev ...   University of Pittsburgh. Law Review [*A publication*]

UPIU ....   United Paperworkers International Union   (EA)

UPJ..........   Underwater Pump Jet

UPJ..........   Upjohn Co. [*NYSE symbol*]   (SPSG)

UPJ..........   Ureteropelvic Junction [*Anatomy*]

Upjohn ......   Upjohn Co. [*Associated Press abbreviation*]   (APAG)

UPK ....   United Park City Mines Co. [*NYSE symbol*]   (SPSG)

UPK ....   Unpopped Kernel [*Popcorn*]

UPK ....   Upkeep Period [*Navy*]   (NVT)

UPkMn......   United Park City Mines Co. [*Associated Press abbreviation*]   (APAG)

UPL ....   Unidentified Process Loss

UPL ....   Union Populaire Locale [*Political party*] [*Wallis and Futuna Islands*]   (FEA)

UPL ....   Unit Personnel List [*Army*]

UPL ....   Universal Programming Language [*Data processing*]   (BUR)

UPL ....   Universal Publications, London [*British*]

UPL ....   Upala [*Costa Rica*] [*Airport symbol*] [*Obsolete*]   (OAG)

UPL ....   Uplink

UPL ....   Uranium Product Loadout [*Nuclear energy*]   (NRCH)

UPL ....   User Programming Language [*Burroughs Corp.*] [*Data processing*]   (IEEE)

UPLAC......   Union des Producteurs de Levure-Aliment de la CEE [*Union of Dried Yeast Producers of the Common Market*]

UP/LAIL...   Latin American Indian Literatures. University of Pittsburgh. Department of Hispanic Languages and Literatures [*A publication*]

UPLD ....   Upland [*Plateau, highland*] [*Board on Geographic Names*]

UPLF ....   Universal Payload Fairing [*NASA*]   (KSC)

UPLF ....   Universal Proutist Labour Federation   (EA)

UPLG ....   Union Populaire pour la Liberation de la Guadeloupe [*Popular Union for the Liberation of Guadeloupe*]   (PD)

UPLI ....   United Poets Laureate International   (EA)

UPLK........   Uplink   (NASA)

UPlntr........   Union Planters Corp. [*Associated Press abbreviation*]   (APAG)

UPLR........   Uganda Protectorate Law Reports [*1904-51*] [*A publication*]   (DLA)

UPLR........   United Provinces Law Reports [*India*] [*A publication*]   (DLA)

U of PLR....   University of Pennsylvania. Law Review [*A publication*]

UPLR........   Unplanned Loss Report [*Navy*]   (DNAB)

U of PL Rev ...   University of Pennsylvania. Law Review [*A publication*]

UPLT........   United Provinces Law Times [*India*] [*A publication*]   (DLA)

UPLV........   Upper Leg Vein [*Anatomy*]

UPM..........   Pennsylvania State University, University Park, PA [*OCLC symbol*]   (OCLC)

UPM..........   Uganda Patriotic Movement   (PD)

UPM..........   Ultrapure Metal

UPM..........   Umdrehung per Minuten [*Revolutions per Minute*] [*German*]

UPM..........   Union du Peuple Malgache [*Malagasy People's Union*]

UPM..........   Union Pontificale Missionnaire [*Pontifical Missionary Union - PMU*] [*Later, PMUPR*]

UPM.........   Union Progressiste Mauritanienne [*Mauritanian Progressive Union*]

UPM.........   Union Progressiste Melanesienne [*New Caledonia*] [*Political party*]   (FEA)

UPM.........   Union del Pueblo de Melilla [*Spanish North Africa*] [*Political party*]   (MENA)

UPM......... Unione Politica Maltese [*Maltese Political Union*] [*Political party*]   (PPE)
UPM......... Unit Production Manager [*Filmmaking*]
UPM......... United People's Movement [*Antigua*] [*Political party*]   (PPW)
UPM......... United People's Movement [*St. Vincent*] [*Political party*]   (PPW)
UPM......... Universal Permissive Module [*Nuclear energy*]   (IEEE)
UPM......... Unreached Peoples Mission   (EA)
UPMB....... University of Pennsylvania. Museum Bulletin [*A publication*]
UPMFF..... University of Pennsylvania. Monographs in Folklore and Folklife [*A publication*]
UPMI........ Union Progressiste Melanesienne [*Progressive Melanesian Union*] [*New Caledonia*] [*Political party*]   (PPW)
UPMR....... Unit Personnel Management Roster
UPN......... Union del Pueblo Navarrese [*Union of the Navarrese People*] [*Spain*] [*Political party*]   (PPW)
UPN.......... Unique Project Number   (SSD)
UPN.......... United Party of Nigeria
UPN.......... Uruapan [*Mexico*] [*Airport symbol*]   (OAG)
UPNCA ..... United Pants and Novelties Contractors Association [*Defunct*]   (EA)
UPNE....... University Press of New England
U P News ... Unauthorized Practice News [*A publication*]
UPNI .... Unionist Party of Northern Ireland [*Political party*]   (PPW)
UP (Noth) ... Ueberlieferungsgeschichte des Pentateuch (M. Noth) [*A publication*]   (BJA)
UPNS .... Ukrainian Philatelic and Numismatic Society   (EA)
UPO.......... Undistorted Power Output
UPO.......... Unidentified Paleontological Object
UPO.......... Unit Personnel Office [*or Officer*] [*Military*]
UPOR....... Usual Place of Residence   (MAE)
UPortR ..... University of Portland. Review [*A publication*]
UPOS .... Utility Program Operating System   (IEEE)
UPOV .... Union Internationale pour la Protection des Obtentions Vegetales [*International Union for the Protection of New Varieties of Plants*]   (EAIO)
UPP .... Hawi, HI [*Location identifier*] [*FAA*]   (FAAL)
UPP .... Ultraprecision Parachute   (NG)
UPP .... Undeducted Purchase Price
UPP .... UNESCO Publications and Periodicals
UPP .... Union del Pueblo Patriotico [*Ecuador*] [*Political party*]   (EY)
UPP .... Unionist Progressive Party [*Egypt*] [*Political party*]
UPP .... United Papermakers and Paperworkers [*Later, UPIU*]   (EA)
UPP .... United Peasants' Party [*Poland*] [*Political party*]   (PD)
UPP .... United People's Party [*Grenada*] [*Political party*]   (PPW)
UPP .... United People's Party [*Sierra Leone*] [*Political party*]
UPP .... United Press of Pakistan
UPP .... United Progressive Party [*Trinidad and Tobago*] [*Political party*]   (PPW)
UPP .... United Progressive Party [*Zambia*] [*Political party*]
UPP .... Universal PROM Programmer
UPP .... Upolu Point [*Hawaii*] [*Airport symbol*]   (OAG)
UPP .... Uppsala [*Sweden*] [*Seismograph station code, US Geological Survey*]   (SEIS)
UPP .... Urea (Prilled) in Paper Packets [*Agronomy*]
UPP .... User Parameter Processing   (NASA)
UPP .... Utility Print Punch
UPPA........ United People's Party of Arunachal [*India*] [*Political party*]   (PPW)
UPPC........ Universal Pin Pack Connector
UPPE......... Ultraviolet Photometric and Polarimetric Explorer
UPPF .... United Presbyterian Peace Fellowship   (EA)
UPPN .... Union Postale des Pays du Nord [*Nordic Postal Union - NPU*]   (EAIO)
UPPN .... United People's Party of Nigeria
UPPOE...... University of Pittsburgh Production Organization Exercise [*Simulation game*]
UPPP........ Uvulo-Palato-Pharyngoplasty [*Surgical procedure*] [*Initials are derived from the name of the problem the procedure cures*]
UPPS........ Ultimate Plant Protection System [*Nuclear energy*]   (NRCH)
UPPS......... Unified Pilot Publication System [*American Chemical Society*]
Uppsala Univ G Inst B ... Uppsala University. Geological Institution. Bulletin [*A publication*]
Upps Arsskr ... Uppsala Universitets Arsskrift [*A publication*]
Upps Univ Geol Inst Bull ... Uppsala University. Geological Institution. Bulletin [*A publication*]
UPr .... Ucilisten Pregled [*A publication*]
UPR .... Ultraportable RADAR   (MCD)
UPR .... Ultrasonic Parametric Resonance   (IEEE)
UPR .... Ultraviolet Proton Radiation
UPR .... Uniform Parole Reports [*Law Enforcement Assistance Administration*]
UPR .... Union des Populations Rurales [*Union of Rural People*] [*Lomela-Kasai*]
UPR .... University of Puerto Rico [*Mayaguez, PR*]
UPR .... Upper   (AAG)
UPR .... Uranium Production Reactor [*Nuclear energy*]
UPR .... Urethral Profile at Rest [*Medicine*]
Upravlenie Slozn Sistemami ... Upravlenie Sloznymi Sistemami. Rizskii Politehniceskii Institut [*A publication*]

Upravlyaemye Sistemy ... Upravlyaemye Sistemy Institut Matematiki Institut Kataliza Sibirskogo Otdeleniya Akademii Nauk SSSR [*A publication*]
Uprawa Rosl Nawozenie ... Uprawa Roslin i Nawozenie [*A publication*]
UPR Co...... Union Pacific Railroad Co. [*A publication*]
UPR/CS .... Caribbean Studies. University of Puerto Rico. Institute of Caribbean Studies [*A publication*]
UPrE.......... College of Eastern Utah, Price, UT [*Library symbol*] [*Library of Congress*]   (LCLS)
UPREAL ... Unit Property Record and Equipment Authorization List
UPREC ... Upon Receipt
UPREL...... Unit Property Record and Equipment List
UP Res Dig ... UP [*University of the Philippines*] Research Digest [*A publication*]
UPRG .... Unit Personnel Records Group [*Air Force*]   (AFM)
UPRGp...... Unit Personnel Records Group [*Air Force*]   (AFM)
UPrGS....... Church of Jesus Christ of Latter-Day Saints, Genealogical Society Library, Price Branch, Price, UT [*Library symbol*] [*Library of Congress*]   (LCLS)
UPRI.......... Up-Right, Inc. [*NASDAQ symbol*]   (NQ)
UPRI.......... Uteroplacental Respiratory Insufficiency [*Gynecology*]
UPRICO.... University of Puerto Rico [*Mayaguez, PR*]
Uprochnyayushchaya Term Termomekh Obrab Prokata ... Uprochnyayushchaya Termicheskaya i Termomekhanicheskaya Obrabotka Prokata [*A publication*]
UPROCO .. Union Progressiste du Congo [*Progressive Union of the Congo*] [*Niangara*]
UPRONA .. Union pour le Progres National [*Union for National Progress*] [*Burundi*] [*Political party*]   (PPW)
UPRP........ Union des Paysans Ruraux et Progressistes [*Union of Rural and Progressive Farmers*] [*Congo-Kasai*]
UPRR .... Union Pacific Railroad Co.
Upr Sist Mash ... Upravlyayushchie Sistemy i Mashiny [*Ukrainian SSR*] [*A publication*]
Upr Yad Energ Ustanovkami ... Upravlenie Yadernymi Energeticheskimi Ustanovkami [*A publication*]
UPS........... Ultraviolet Photoemission Spectroscopy
UPS........... Uncontested Physical Searches [*CIA term for break-ins*]
UPS........... Under Provisions of Section [*Military*]
UPS........... Underground Press Syndicate [*Later, APS*]   (EA)
UPS........... Underwater Photographic Society   (EA)
UP & S ...... Uniform Printing and Supply
UPS........... Uniform Procurement System
UPS........... Uninterruptible Power Supply [*or System*]
UPS........... Union Progressiste Senegalaise [*Senegalese Progressive Union*] [*Political party*]   (AF)
UPS........... Unit Personnel Section [*Military*]
UPS........... Unit Price Standards   (MCD)
UPS........... Unit Proficiency System   (AAG)
UPS........... United Parcel Service
UPS........... United Peregrine Society   (EA)
UPS........... Universal Polar Stereographic Grid
UPS........... Universal Press Syndicate Co.
UPS........... Universal Processing System
UPS........... Universities and Public Schools Battalions [*Military units*] [*British*] [*World War I*]
UPS........... Upright Perigee Stage [*Aerospace*]   (MCD)
UPS........... Urethral Profile under Stress [*Medicine*]
UPS........... Uterine Progesterone System [*Contraceptive device*]
UPSA......... Ukrainian Political Science Association in the United States   (EA)
UPSA......... Ukrainian Professional Society of America   (EA)
UPSA......... Uniform Program Salary Administration   (MCD)
Upsala J Med Sci ... Upsala Journal of Medical Sciences [*A publication*]
Upsala J Med Sci Suppl ... Upsala Journal of Medical Sciences. Supplement [*A publication*]
UPSD......... Union pour le Progres Social et le Democratie [*The Congo*] [*Political party*]   (EY)
UPSEELL ... University of Pennsylvania. Studies in East European Languages and Literatures [*A publication*]
UPSF .... Universal Proutist Student Federation   (EA)
UPSI.......... User Program Sense Indicator
UPSI.......... User Program Switch Indicator [*Data processing*]
UPSIS....... United States Political Science Information Service [*University of Pittsburgh*]   (IID)
Ups J Med Sci ... Upsala Journal of Medical Sciences [*A publication*]
Ups J Med Sci Suppl ... Upsala Journal of Medical Sciences. Supplement [*A publication*]
UPSLP ...... Upslope   (FAAC)
UPSN .... University Peace Studies Network   (EA)
UPSNET ... United Postal Service Network [*National mobile data network*] [*Proposed*]   (ECON)
UPSR........ Unit Procurement System Requirements   (AAG)
UPSS .... Ukrainska Partiia Samostiinykiv-Sotsialistiv [*Ukrainian Party of Socialist-Independentists*] [*Russian*] [*Political party*]   (PPE)
UPSS .... United Postal Stationery Society   (EA)
UPSSL....... University of Puget Sound School of Law   (DLA)
Ups Sto ...... Upshur's Review of Story on the Constitution [*A publication*]   (DLA)

UPSTAGE ... Upper-Stage Guidance Experiment
UPSTARS ... Universal Propulsion Stabilization, Retardation, and Separation [*Air Force*]
UPSTART ... Universal Parachute Support Tactical and Research Target (NG)
UPSTEP .... Undergraduated Pre-Service Teacher Education Program [*National Science Foundation*] (EA)
UPSUB ..... Submit Draft to a Superior for Approval [*From George Orwell's novel, "1984"*]
UPT .... Undergraduate Pilot Training [*Air Force*]
UP & T .... Unit Personnel and Tonnage Table [*Military*]
UPT .... University Patents, Inc. [*AMEX symbol*] (SPSG)
UPT .... Upgrade Pilot Training
UPT .... Urgent Postal Telegram
UPT .... US Platinum [*Vancouver Stock Exchange symbol*]
UPT .... User Process Table
UPTA .... Uniform Perpetuation of Testimony Act [*National Conference of Commissioners on Uniform State Laws*]
UPTA .... United Parent-Teachers Association of Jewish Schools (EA)
UPTAS ..... Utility Practical Transport Aircraft System [*Army*]
UPTC .... Union Panafricaine des Travailleurs Croyants [*Pan-African Union of Believing Workers*]
UPTD .... Unit Pulmonary Toxicity Dose [*Deep-sea diving*]
UPTF .... Upper Plenum Test Facility [*Nuclear energy*] (NRCH)
UPT-H ...... Undergraduate Pilot Training - Helicopter [*Air Force*]
UPTLM ..... Up-Link Telemetry [*NASA*] (NASA)
UP/TM ...... Tiers Monde. Universite de Paris. Institut d'Etude du Developpement Economique et Social [*Paris*] [*A publication*]
Upt Mar W ... Upton on Maritime Warfare and Prize [*A publication*] (DLA)
UPTP .... Universal Package Test Panel
UPTT .... Unit Personnel and Tonnage Table [*Military*] (AABC)
Upt Tr Mar ... Upton on Trade-Marks [*A publication*] (DLA)
UPU .... Union Postale Universelle [*Universal Postal Union*] [*French*]
UPU .... Union Postale Universelle [*Universal Postal Union*] [*Switzerland*] [*Also, an information service or system*] (IID)
UPU .... Universal Postal Union [*United Nations*] (MENA)
UPUC .... Unauthorized Publication or Use of Communications
UPUC .... Universal Postal Union Collectors (EA)
UPUC .... Universal Postal Union Convention
U Puget Sound L Rev ... University of Puget Sound. Law Review [*A publication*]
UPUP .... Ulster Popular Unionist Party [*Northern Ireland*] [*Political party*] (PPW)
UPUP .... Ulster Progressive Unionist Party [*Northern Ireland*] [*Political party*] (PPW)
UPUS .... United Public Utility Systems
UPUSA ...... UPU [*Universal Postal Union*] Staff Association (EAIO)
UPV .... Unfired Pressure Vessel
UPV .... Universal Pre-Vent, Inc. [*Vancouver Stock Exchange symbol*]
UPVC .... Unfired Pressure Vessel Code (AAG)
UPVC .... Unplasticized Polyvinyl Chloride
UP Vet ...... UP [*University of the Philippines*] Veterinarian [*A publication*]
UPW .... Union of Post Office Workers [*British*] (DCTA)
UPW .... United Port Workers' Union [*Ceylon*]
UPW .... United Presbyterian Women (EA)
UPW .... United Public Workers of America
UPWA ...... Union of Palestinian Women's Association in North America (EA)
UPWA ...... Union of Polish Women in America (EA)
UPWA ...... United Packinghouse Workers of America [*Later, UFCWIU*]
UPWA ...... United Polish Women of America (EA)
UPWARD ... Understanding Personal and Racial Dignity [*Navy program*]
UPWBA ..... Uniwersytet Imienia Adama Mickiewicza w Poznaniu. Wydzial Biologii i Nauk o Ziemi. Prace. Seria Geologia [*A publication*]
UPWD .... Upward (MSA)
UPWF .... Ukrainian Patriarchal World Federation (EA)
UPWT .... Unitary Plan Wind Tunnel (KSC)
UPY .... Union of People's Youth [*Bulgaria*]
UPYF .... Universal Proutist Youth Federation (EA)
UPz .... Urkunden der Ptolemaerzeit [*U. Wilcken*] [*A publication*] (BJA)
UQ .... Fronte dell'Uomo Qualunque; Uomo Qualunque [*Common Man Front*] [*Italy*] [*Political party*] (PPE)
UQ .... Ubiquinone [*Also, CoQ, Q, U*] [*Biochemistry*]
UQ .... Ukrainian Quarterly [*A publication*]
UQ .... Ultraquick [*Flashing*] Light [*Navigation signal*]
UQ .... United African Airline [*Libya*] [*ICAO designator*] (ICDA)
UQ .... Universities Quarterly [*A publication*]
UQ .... Upper Quadrant [*Anatomy*]
UQ .... Upper Quadrille
UQAC .... Universite du Quebec a Chicoutimi [*Canada*]
UQAH .... Universite du Quebec a Hull [*Canada*]
UQAM .... Universite du Quebec a Montreal [*Canada*]
UQAR .... Universite du Quebec a Rimouski [*Canada*]
UQB .... Universite de Quebec [*UTLAS symbol*]
UQC .... Underwater Telephone [*Navy*] (CAAL)
UQCP .... Uniform Quality Control Program
UQE .... Queen [*Alaska*] [*Airport symbol*] [*Obsolete*] (OAG)

UQGS .... Uniform Quality Grading System [*Tires*]
UQL .... Unacceptable Quality Level
UQLJ .... University of Queensland. Law Journal [*A publication*] (APTA)
UQOT .... Unquote (FAAC)
UQP .... Universities and the Quest for Peace [*An association*]
UQP .... University of Queensland. Papers [*A publication*]
UQP .... University of Queensland Press [*Australia*]
UQS .... Nuiqsut Village, AK [*Location identifier*] [*FAA*] (FAAL)
Uqs .... 'Uqsin (BJA)
U Qsld P SS ... University of Queensland. Papers. Social Sciences [*A publication*]
UQT .... User Queue Table
U Queens L J ... University of Queensland. Law Journal [*A publication*]
U Queensl LJ ... University of Queensland. Law Journal [*A publication*]
U Queens LR ... University of Queensland. Law Review [*A publication*]
UQY .... Kansas City, MO [*Location identifier*] [*FAA*] (FAAL)
UR .... AeroSun International, Inc. [*ICAO designator*] (FAAC)
UR .... [*The*] Item Requested Is Under Revision By the Proponent. Copies of Edition Presently in Use Are Not Available [*Advice of supply action code*] [*Army*]
UR .... Lab. J. Uriach & Cia. SA [*Spain*] [*Research code symbol*]
UR .... Lloyd's Universal Register of Shipping [*British*] (ROG)
UR .... Red Carpet Airlines, Inc. [*ICAO designator*] (ICDA)
UR .... Uganda Rifles [*British military*] (DMA)
UR .... Ukrainian Review [*London*] [*A publication*]
UR .... Ullage Rocket (KSC)
UR .... Umjetnost Rijeci [*A publication*]
UR .... Unattended Repeater [*Telecommunications*] (OA)
UR .... Unconditioned Response [*Psychometrics*]
UR .... Under the Rule [*Business term*]
U/R .... Underrange (IEEE)
UR .... Underreporter [*IRS*]
UR .... Undulator Radiation [*High-energy physics*]
UR .... Unfinanced Requirement [*Army*] (AABC)
UR .... Unfractionated Reservoir [*Geology*]
UR .... Unfunded Requirement [*Military*] (AFIT)
UR .... Uniao Republicana [*Republican Union*] [*Portugal*] [*Political party*] (PPE)
UR .... Unidentified Remittance [*IRS*]
UR .... Uniform Regulations
UR .... Unit Record [*Data processing*]
UR .... Unit Register
UR .... Unitatis Redintegratio [*Decree on Ecumenism*] [*Vatican II document*]
UR .... University Relations
UR .... University Review [*A publication*]
UR .... University of Rochester [*New York*] (KSC)
UR .... Unprogrammed Requirements (MCD)
UR .... Unrelated (AAMN)
UR .... Unreleasable (MCD)
UR .... Unreliable
UR .... Unsatisfactory Report
U/R .... Up Range [*NASA*] (KSC)
UR .... Up Right [*The rear right portion of a stage*] [*A stage direction*]
UR .... Upper Rail
UR .... Upper Respiratory [*Medicine*]
UR .... Upper Right (MCD)
UR .... Uranium (ROG)
UR .... Urban Rat [*Virus*]
UR .... Urgent Requirement (MCD)
UR .... Urinal (MSA)
UR .... Urine
UR .... Urology
Ur .... Uruguay
UR .... User Requirements [*Nuclear energy*] (NRCH)
ur .... USSR [*Union of Soviet Socialist Republics*] [*MARC country of publication code*] [*Library of Congress*] (LCCP)
UR .... Uti Rogas [*Be It as You Desire*] [*Used by Romans to express assent to a proposition*] [*Latin*]
UR .... Utility Room (MSA)
UR .... Utilization Review [*Preferred provider organization*] [*Medicine*]
URA .... Uniformly Redundant Array
URA .... United Red Army [*Japan*] (PD)
URA .... United Republicans of America
URA .... Universities Research Association (EA)
URA .... Upper Respiratory Allergy [*Medicine*]
Ura .... Uracil [*Biochemistry*]
URA .... Urakawa [*Japan*] [*Seismograph station code, US Geological Survey*] (SEIS)
Ura .... Urania [*Record label*] [*USA, Europe, etc.*]
URA .... Uranium Recycle Acid [*Nuclear energy*] (NRCH)
URA .... Urban Redevelopment Authority
URA .... Urban Renewal Administration [*of HHFA*] [*Terminated*]
URA .... Urine Receptacle Assembly [*NASA*] (MCD)
URA .... User Range Accuracy (SSD)
URA .... User Requirements Analysis
URA .... Utilization Review Agency [*Insurance*]
URAAA ..... Urania [*Poland*] [*A publication*]

URAC .... Union des Republiques de l'Afrique Centrale [*Union of Central African Republics*]
URACTY... Your Activity
URAD .... Unit for Research on Addictive Drugs [*University of Aberdeen*] [*British*] (IRUK)
URAD .... [*Reference*] Your Radio [*Message*] [*Military*]
URAEP ...... University of Rochester Atomic Energy Project
URAF .... Unidentified Remittance Amount File [*IRS*]
URAI .... Universities Research Association, Inc.
Ural Gos Univ Mat Zap ... Ural'skii Gosudarstvennyi Universitet Imeni A. M. Gor'kogo Ural'skoe Matematiceskoe Obscestvo Matematiceskie Zapiski [*A publication*]
Ural Metall ... Ural'skaya Metallurgiya [*A publication*]
URAM ...... Unrelated Adult Man
Uranium Abstr ... Uranium Abstracts [*A publication*]
Uranium Min Metall ... Uranium Mining and Metallurgy [*A publication*]
Uran Supply ... Uranium Supply and Demand. Perspectives to 1995 [*A publication*]
URAPA ..... Uniform Rendition of Accused Persons Act [*National Conference of Commissioners on Uniform State Laws*]
URARPAA ... Uniform Relocation Assistance and Real Property Acquisition Act [*1970*] (OICC)
URARPAPA ... Uniform Relocation Assistance and Real Property Acquisition Policies Act of 1970
URARRED ... US Army Readiness Command (MCD)
URAS .... Union des Republicains d'Action Sociale [*Union of Republicans of Social Action*] [*France*] [*Political party*] (PPE)
URAUZ ..... You Are Authorized (FAAC)
URAW ...... Unrelated Adult Woman
URB .... Union Regionale de Bamileke [*Regional Union of Bamileke*] [*Cameroon*]
URB .... University of Riyad. Bulletin. Faculty of Arts [*Saudi Arabia*] [*A publication*]
URB .... Unridable Bicycle
URB .... Urban
URB .... Urbana College, Urbana, OH [*OCLC symbol*] (OCLC)
URB .... Urubupunga [*Brazil*] [*Airport symbol*] (OAG)
Urb Aff Abstr ... Urban Affairs Abstracts [*A publication*]
Urb Aff Ann R ... Urban Affairs Annual Review [*A publication*]
Urb Aff Q ... Urban Affairs Quarterly [*A publication*]
Urb Aff Quart ... Urban Affairs Quarterly [*A publication*]
Urb Aff Rep ... Urban Affairs Reporter [*Commerce Clearing House*] [*A publication*] (DLA)
URBAMET ... Urbanisme, Amenagement, Equipments, et Transports [*Reseau URBAMET*] [*France*] [*Information service or system*] (CRD)
Urban Abs ... Urban Abstracts [*A publication*]
Urban Aff Abs ... Urban Affairs Abstracts [*A publication*]
Urban Affairs Q ... Urban Affairs Quarterly [*A publication*]
Urban Anthr ... Urban Anthropology [*A publication*]
Urban Can ... Urban Canada [*A publication*]
Urban Data Service Rept ... Urban Data Service Report [*A publication*]
Urban Des ... Urban Design [*A publication*]
Urban Design Intl ... Urban Design International [*A publication*]
Urban Des Int ... Urban Design International [*A publication*]
Urban Des Q ... Urban Design Quarterly [*A publication*]
Urban Ecol ... Urban Ecology [*A publication*]
Urban Ed ... Urban Education [*A publication*]
Urban Educ ... Urban Education [*A publication*]
Urban For .. Urban Forum [*A publication*]
Urban Hist R ... Urban History Review [*A publication*]
Urban Hist Yearb ... Urban History Yearbook [*A publication*]
Urban Hlth ... Urban Health [*A publication*]
URBANICOM ... Association Internationale Urbanisme et Commerce [*International Association for Town Planning and Distribution*] (EAIO)
Urban Innov Abroad ... Urban Innovation Abroad [*A publication*]
Urban Inst Policy Res Rep ... Urban Institute. Policy and Research Report [*A publication*]
URBANK .. Urban Development Bank
Urban L Ann ... Urban Law Annual [*A publication*]
Urban Law ... Urban Lawyer [*A publication*]
Urban Law An ... Urban Law Annual [*A publication*]
Urban Law Ann ... Urban Law Annual [*A publication*] (ILCA)
Urban Lif C ... Urban Life and Culture [*Later, Urban Life*] [*A publication*]
Urban LJ ... University of Detroit. Journal of Urban Law [*A publication*] (DLA)
Urban L Rev ... Urban Law Review [*A publication*] (DLA)
Urban R ..... Urban Review [*A publication*]
Urban Rev ... Urban Review [*A publication*]
Urban Soc C ... Urban and Social Change Review [*A publication*]
Urban Stud ... Urban Studies [*A publication*]
Urban Syst ... Urban Systems [*A publication*]
Urb Anthrop ... Urban Anthropology [*A publication*]
Urban Transp Abroad ... Urban Transportation Abroad [*A publication*]
URBC .... Uninfected Red Blood Cells [*Hematology*]
URBCOM ... [*The*] Urban Communications Game
URBE .... Urban Ecology [*Netherlands*] [*A publication*]
URBH .... Urban Health [*A publication*]
URBK .... Union Rheinische Braunkohlen Kraftstoff [*West Germany*]

Urb L Ann ... Urban Law Annual [*A publication*]
Urblaw .... Urban Law and Policy [*A publication*] (ILCA)
Urb Law ...... Urban Lawyer [*A publication*]
Urb Law Pol ... Urban Law and Policy [*A publication*]
Urb Life ..... Urban Life [*A publication*]
Urb Life & Cult ... Urban Life and Culture [*Later, Urban Life*] [*A publication*]
Urb L and P ... Urban Law and Policy [*A publication*]
Urb L and Poly ... Urban Law and Policy [*A publication*]
Urb L Rev .. Urban Law Review [*A publication*]
URBM .... Ultimate Range Ballistic Missile [*Air Force*]
URBN-A ..... Urbanisme [*France*] [*A publication*]
URBOE ..... Ultimatist Religious Bodies on Earth (EA)
URBPOP .... Urban Population File (MCD)
URBS-A ...... Urban Studies [*United Kingdom*] [*A publication*]
Urb Soc Change R ... Urban and Social Change Review [*A publication*]
Urb Stud .... Urban Studies [*A publication*]
URC .... Uganda Railways Corp. (DCTA)
URC .... Ultrasonic Resin Cleaner [*Nuclear energy*] (NRCH)
URC .... Undersea Research Corp.
URC .... Uniform Rules for Collections
URC .... Union du Rassemblement du Centre [*Mayotte*] [*Political party*] (EY)
URC .... Union de Rassemblement et du Centre [*France*] [*Political party*] (ECON)
URC .... Union des Republicains du Cameroun [*Political party*] (EY)
URC .... Unit Record Card
URC .... Unit Record Control
URC .... United Racing Club [*Auto racing*]
URC .... United Reform Church in England and Wales
URC .... University Research Centre [*British*]
URC .... Upper Rib Cage [*Anatomy*]
URC .... Upper Right Center (WGA)
URC .... Ursuline College Library, Pepper Pike, OH [*OCLC symbol*] (OCLC)
URC .... Urumqi [*China*] [*Airport symbol*] (OAG)
URC .... Utility Radio Communication
URCC .... University of Rochester Cancer Center [*Research center*] (RCD)
URCE .... Union Restaurants Collectifs Europeens [*European Catering Association*] [*Germany*] (EAIO)
URCF .... Unidentified Remittance Control File [*IRS*]
URCG .... Uniform Rules for Contract Guarantees
URCLK .... Universal Receiver Clock
URCO .... Union des Ressortissants du Congo pour la Defense et la Promotion du Congo [*Union of Congolese for the Defense and Promotion of the Congo*]
URCS .... Uniform Ration Cost System (MCD)
URD .... New York, NY [*Location identifier*] [*FAA*] (FAAL)
URD .... Underground Residential Distribution [*Cable*]
URD .... Union Republicana Democratica [*Democratic Republican Union*] [*Puerto Rico, Venezuela*]
URD .... Upper Respiratory Disease [*Medicine*]
urd .... Urdu [*MARC language code*] [*Library of Congress*] (LCCP)
Urd .... Uridine [*Also, U*] [*A nucleoside*]
URD .... User Requirements Document (MCD)
URDA .... Uniform Retirement Date Act [*National Conference of Commissioners on Uniform State Laws*]
URDA .... Urban Resources Development Agency (OICC)
URDIS ...... Your Dispatch [*Military*]
URDP .... Ukrains'ka Revoliutsiino-Demokratychna Partiia
URE .... Undergraduate Record Examination [*Education*]
URE .... Unintentional Radiation Exploitation (AFM)
URE .... User Range Error
UREBA ...... Union Revolutionnaire des Banques [*Burkina Faso*] (EY)
URECD ..... Urban Ecology [*A publication*]
UREHE ..... Union for Research and Experimentation in Higher Education [*Later, UECU*]
UREKA ..... Unlimited Resources Ensure Keen Answers
Uremia Invest ... Uremia Investigation [*A publication*]
UREP .... Unit Representative [*Military*] (INF)
UREP .... University Research Expeditions Programs
URES .... University Residence Environment Scale [*Student attitudes test*]
URESA ...... Uniform Reciprocal Enforcement of Support Act
U-REST ..... Universal Range, Endurance, Speed, and Time (NG)
ureth .... Urethra [*Anatomy*]
Urethane .... Urethane Plastics and Products [*A publication*]
Urethane Plast Prod ... Urethane Plastics and Products [*A publication*]
URETS ...... University Real Estate Trust [*NASDAQ symbol*] (NQ)
URev .... University Review [*Dublin*] [*A publication*]
URF .... Ukrainian Research Foundation [*Defunct*] (EA)
URF .... Unassigned Reading Frame [*Genetics*]
URF .... Unidentified Reading Frame [*Genetics*]
URF .... Unidentified Remittance File [*IRS*]
URF .... Union des Services Routiers des Chemins de Fer Europeens [*Union of European Railways Road Services*]
URF .... United Religious Front [*Israel*] (BJA)
URF .... United Republican Fund
URF .... Uterine-Relaxing Factor [*Endocrinology*]
URFDA-NYC ... United Retail Fish Dealers Association of New York City (EA)

URG.......... Underway Replenishment Group [*Military*]
URG.......... Unit Review Group [*Nuclear energy*]   (NRCH)
URG.......... United Rayore Gas [*Vancouver Stock Exchange symbol*]
URG.......... Universal Radio Group
URG.......... Urban Regeneration Grant [*British*]
URG.......... Urgent   (AFM)
URG.......... Urheberrechtsgesetz [*German Copyright Act*]   (DLA)
URG.......... Uruguaiana [*Brazil*] [*Airport symbol*]   (OAG)
URGAB .... Urologe. Ausgabe A [*A publication*]
URGE........ Urgent Care Centers of America [*NASDAQ symbol*]   (NQ)
URGENT .. Universal Relevance Group Enterprise in a National Theater [*Theater workshop*]
URGR........ Underway Replenishment Group [*Military*]
URGYA ..... Urology [*Ridgewood, NJ*] [*A publication*]
URHB....... Urban Renewal Handbook
URi............ Richmond City Library, Richmond, UT [*Library symbol*] [*Library of Congress*]   (LCLS)
URI .... Unexpected Real Incapacitation   (DNAB)
URI .... Union Research Institute, Kowloon, Hong Kong [*Library symbol*] [*Library of Congress*]   (LCLS)
URI .... United Research, Inc.
URI .... University Research Initiative [*DoD*]   (RDA)
URI .... University of Rhode Island
URI .... Unpublished Research Information [*Conducted by National Science Foundation*]
URI .... Upper Respiratory Infection [*Medicine*]
URI .... Uranium Resources, Inc. [*Vancouver Stock Exchange symbol*]
URI .... Uribe [*Colombia*] [*Airport symbol*] [*Obsolete*]   (OAG)
URIA........ Universal Real-Time Information and Administration
URICA...... Universal Real-Time Information Control and Administration   (MCD)
URICA...... University of Rhode Island Computer Access [*University of Rhode Island Library*]   (OLDSS)
URICA....... Using Reading in Creative Activities
U Rich LN ... University of Richmond. Law Notes [*A publication*]   (DLA)
U Rich LR ... University of Richmond. Law Review [*A publication*]
U Rich L Rev ... University of Richmond. Law Review [*A publication*]
U Richmond L Rev ... University of Richmond. Law Review [*A publication*]
URifGS...... Church of Jesus Christ of Latter-Day Saints, Genealogical Society Library, Richfield Branch, Richfield, UT [*Library symbol*] [*Library of Congress*]   (LCLS)
URII.......... Ukrainian Research and Information Institute [*Defunct*]   (EA)
URIMA ..... University Risk and Insurance Managers Association [*Later, URMIA*]   (EA)
URINA ...... Urologia Internationalis [*A publication*]
URINT ...... Unintentional Radiation Intelligence   (MCD)
URIPS ...... Undersea Radioisotope Power Supply
URIR .... Unified Radioactive Isodromic Regulator
URIS......... Urban and Regional Information System
URISA ...... Urban and Regional Information Systems Association   (EA)
URIX .... Uranium Resources, Inc. [*NASDAQ symbol*]   (NQ)
URIZR....... Your Recommendation Is Requested   (FAAC)
URJA........ United Roumanian Jews of America   (EA)
Urk............ Urkunde [*Document, Deed, Instrument*] [*German*]   (ILCA)
Urk............ Urkunden des Aegyptischen Altertums [*G. Steindorff*] [*Leipzig*] [*A publication*]   (BJA)
URKK .... Krasnodar [*Former USSR*] [*ICAO location identifier*]   (ICLI)
URL .... University of Regina Library [*UTLAS symbol*]
URL .... Unrequited Love [*Slang*]
URL .... Unrestricted Line Officer [*Navy*]
URL .... Upper Reference Limit [*Analytical chemistry*]
URL .... User Requirements Language [*Data processing*]
URLA .... Uniform Reciprocal Licensing Act [*State law*] [*Insurance*]
URLAA ..... Urban Land [*A publication*]
URLB......... University of Rochester. Library Bulletin [*A publication*]
URLBB ...... Urologe. Ausgabe B [*A publication*]
Url Cl........ Urling's Legal Guide for the Clergy [*A publication*]   (DLA)
Url For Pat ... Urling on Foreign Patents [*A publication*]   (DLA)
URLGA ...... Urologe [*A publication*]
URLH........ Urban Renewal and Low Income Housing [*A publication*]
URLTR...... [*Reference*] Your Letter [*Military*]
Url Trust.... Urling on the Office of a Trustee [*A publication*]   (DLA)
URM.......... Uncle Remus Museum   (EA)
URM.......... University Reform Movement [*in Latin America*]
URM.......... Unlimited Register Machine
URM.......... Urban Renewal Manual
URM.......... Uriman [*Venezuela*] [*Airport symbol*]   (OAG)
URMGM... [*Reference*] Your Mailgram [*Military*]
URMIA ..... University Risk Management and Insurance Association [*Madison, WI*]   (EA)
URMIS...... Uniform Retail Meat Identity Standard [*Pronounced "er-miss"*]
URMK....... Kislovodsk [*Former USSR*] [*ICAO location identifier*]   (ICLI)
UR M-L..... Uniao Revolucionaria, Marxista-Leninista [*Marxist-Leninist Revolutionary Union*] [*Portugal*] [*Political party*]   (PPE)
URMM...... Mineralnye Vody [*Former USSR*] [*ICAO location identifier*]   (ICLI)
URMSG .... [*Reference*] Your Message [*Military*]
URN.......... Covington/Cincinnati, OH [*Location identifier*] [*FAA*]   (FAAL)
URN.......... Ultrahigh Radio Navigation   (NATG)
URN.......... Uniform Random Numerator [*Data processing*]

URN.......... Union pour la Reconciliation Nationale [*Haiti*] [*Political party*]   (EY)
URN.......... Unique Record Number [*Data processing*]   (ADA)
URN.......... Unique Reference Number [*Customs*]   (DS)
URN.......... Urine   (NASA)
URNEA ..... Urologiya i Nefrologiya [*A publication*]
Urner Miner Freund ... Urner Mineralien Freund [*A publication*]
URNF .... Unidentified Remittance Name File [*IRS*]
URNG........ Unidad Revolucionaria Nacional Guatemalteca [*Guatemalan National Revolutionary Unity*] [*Political party*]   (PD)
URO.......... United Restitution Organization
URO.......... United Rink Operators [*Defunct*]   (EA)
URO.......... Urology
URO.......... Uroporphyrin [*Biochemistry*]
URO.......... Uroporphyrinogen [*Biochemistry*]
URO.......... User Readout   (MCD)
URO.......... Ustredni Rada Odboru [*Central Council of Trade Unions*] [*Czechoslovakia*]
UROBA .... United Russian Orthodox Brotherhood of America   (EA)
UROC....... United Railroad Operating Crafts [*Defunct*]
UROEA ..... UNESCO Regional Office for Education in Asia and Oceania [*Thailand*]   (DLA)
UROGEN ... Uroporphyrinogen [*Biochemistry*]
UROL........ Urology
UROLA ..... UNEP [*United Nations Environmental Programme*] Regional Office for Latin America   (EAIO)
Urol Ausg A ... Urologe. Ausgabe A [*A publication*]
Urol Clin North Am ... Urologic Clinics of North America [*A publication*]
Urol Cutaneous Rev ... Urologic and Cutaneous Review [*A publication*]
Urol Int ..... Urologia Internationalis [*A publication*]
Urol Intern ... Urologia Internationalis [*A publication*]
Urol Internat ... Urologia Internationalis [*A publication*]
Urol i Nefrol ... Urologiya i Nefrologiya [*A publication*]
Urol Nefrol (Mosk) ... Urologiia i Nefrologiia (Moskva) [*A publication*]
Urol Nephrol Sz ... Urologiai es Nephrologiai Szemle [*Hungary*] [*A publication*]
Uroloqe ...... Urologe. Ausgabe A [*A publication*]
Urologe B... Urologe. Ausgabe B. Organ des Berufverbandes der Deutschen Urologen [*A publication*]
Urol Panam ... Urologia Panamericana [*A publication*]
Urol Pol ..... Urologia Polska [*A publication*]
Urol Radiol ... Urologic Radiology [*A publication*]
Urol Res..... Urological Research [*A publication*]
Urol Suppl (Treviso) ... Urologia. Supplemento (Treviso) [*A publication*]
Urol Surv ... Urological Survey [*A publication*]
UROP........ Undergraduate Research Opportunities Program [*Pronounced "your-op"*] [*Massachusetts Institute of Technology*]
UROS........ Uroporphyrinogen I Synthase [*An enzyme*]
URP .... Undergraduate Research Participation [*National Science Foundation project*] [*Defunct*]   (EA)
URP .... Underreporter Program [*IRS*]
URP .... Union Republicaine du Peuple [*Benin*] [*Political party*]   (EY)
URP .... Unique Radiolytic Product [*Food technology*]
URP .... Unit Record Processor
URP .... United Reef Petroleums Ltd. [*Toronto Stock Exchange symbol*]
URP .... University of Rochester, Department of Physics
URP .... Unmanned Recovery Platform [*Navy*]   (NVT)
URP .... Untersuchungen zur Romanischen Philologie [*A publication*]
URP .... Upper-Stage Reusable Payload
URP .... Urban Renewal Project [*HUD*]   (OICC)
URPC .... User Level Remote Procedure Call [*Data processing*]
URPE........ Union for Radical Political Economics   (EA)
URPE........ Union des Resistants pour une Europe Unie [*Union of Resistance Veterans for a United Europe*]
URPE........ Union Revolucionaria Popular Ecuatoriana [*Ecuadorean Popular Revolutionary Union*] [*Political party*]   (PPW)
URPG .... President's Urban and Regional Policy Group [*Terminated, 1978*]   (EGAO)
URPP........ Undergraduate Research Participation Program [*Formerly, URP*]   (EA)
URPT-A .... Urban and Rural Planning Thought [*India*] [*A publication*]
URQ.......... Unsatisfactory Report Questionnaire
URQ.......... Upper Right Quadrant [*Medicine*]
URR .... Ultra-Rapid Reader [*Data processing*]
URR .... Ultrareliable RADAR   (MCD)
URR .... Union Railroad Co. [*Pittsburgh, PA*] [*AAR code*]
URR .... Unit Readiness Report [*Army*]   (AABC)
URR .... United Redford Resources, Inc. [*Vancouver Stock Exchange symbol*]
URR .... Universities Research Reactor [*British*]
URR .... Upstream Regulatory Region [*Genetics*]
URR .... Urrao [*Colombia*] [*Airport symbol*]   (OAG)
URR .... Utilization Research Report
URRC .... Urological Rehabilitation and Research Center [*University of Alabama in Birmingham*] [*Research center*]   (RCD)
URRM...... Morozovsk [*Former USSR*] [*ICAO location identifier*]   (ICLI)
URRR .... Rostov-Na-Donu [*Former USSR*] [*ICAO location identifier*]   (ICLI)
URS .... Ugurusu [*Japan*] [*Seismograph station code, US Geological Survey*]   (SEIS)
URS .... Unate Ringe Sum [*Logic expression*]   (IEEE)

Urs	Underwriters [*Insurance*]
URS	UNESCO Relations Staff
URS	Uniform Reporting System
URS	Union of Railway Signalmen [*British*]
URS	Unit Readiness System
URS	Unit Reference Sheet [*Military*] (AABC)
URS	United Research Service (MCD)
URS	Universal Reference System
URS	Universal Regulating System
URS	University Research Support [*Department of Energy*]
URS	Unmanned Repeater Station [*Telecommunications*] (OA)
URS	Update Report System (TEL)
URS	Urban Resource Systems (EA)
URS	URS Corp. [*NYSE symbol*] (SPSG)
URS	URS Corp. [*Associated Press abbreviation*] (APAG)
URS	Ursinus College, Collegeville, PA [*OCLC symbol*] (OCLC)
URS	User Readout Simulator [*Army*]
URS	Utilization Reporting System (MCD)
URSA	Unit Replacement System Analysis [*Military*]
URSA	United Russia Societies Association [*London*]
URSA	Urban and Rural Systems Associates
URSER	[*Reference*] Your Serial [*Military*]
URSI	Union Radio Scientifique Internationale [*International Union of Radio Science*] [*Also, ISRU*] [*Belgium*]
URSNSC	Union Regionale des Syndicats du Nyong-et-Sanaga
URSP	Universal RADAR Signal Processor
URSR	Ukrains'ka Radjans'ka Socialistyczna Respublika [*A publication*]
URSS	Sochi [*Former USSR*] [*ICAO location identifier*] (ICLI)
URSS	Union des Republiques Socialistes Sovietiques [*Union of Socialist Soviet Republics; USSR*]
URSTM	Unite de Recherche et de Service en Technologie Minerale de l'Abitibi-Temiscamingue [*University of Quebec at Abitibi-Temiscamingue*] [*Canada*] [*Research center*] (RCD)
URSUA	Urological Survey [*A publication*]
URSW	Union Regionale des Syndicats du Wouri [*Regional Union of Wouri Unions*]
URT	Surat Thani [*Thailand*] [*Airport symbol*] (OAG)
URT	Unit Recruit Training [*Army*] (AABC)
URT	Universal RADAR Tracker
URT	University Research and Training [*Programs*]
URT	Upper Respiratory Tract [*Medicine*]
URT	Upright (MSA)
Urt	Urteil [*Judgment, Decision*] [*German*] (ILCA)
URT	Utility Radio Transmitter
URTA	University Resident Theatre Association (EA)
URTEL	[*Reference*] Your Telegram [*Military*]
URTH	Unreasonable Risk to Health [*Drinking water standards*] [*Environmental Protection Agency*]
URTI	Universite Radiophonique et Televisuelle Internationale [*International Radio-Television University*]
URTI	Upper Respiratory Tract Infection [*Medicine*]
URTIA	Uniform Rights of the Terminally Ill Act [*National Conference of Commissioners on Uniform State Laws*]
URTNA	Union des Radio-Televisions Nationales Africaines [*African National Radio-Television Union*] (AF)
URTRO	Unloaded Radial Tire Run-Out
URTU	United Road Transport Union [*British*] (DCTA)
URTWAE	United Road Transport Workers' Association of England [*A union*]
URTX	URI Therm-X, Inc. [*NASDAQ symbol*] (NQ)
URU	Uruguay
URUC	UNCTAD [*United Nations Conference on Trade and Development*] Reference Unit Catalogue [*Information service or system*] (DUND)
URV	Undersea Research Vehicle [*or Vessel*]
URW	Ultrasonic Ring Welder
URW	United Racquetsports for Women (EA)
URW	United Rubber, Cork, Linoleum, and Plastic Workers of America (EA)
URWA	United Railroad Workers of America
URWC	Urinal Water Closet (MSA)
URWRO	Unloaded Radial Wheel Run-Out
URX	Ubersee Rundschau [*A publication*]
URY	Gurayat [*Saudi Arabia*] [*Airport symbol*] (OAG)
URY	Union Railway of Memphis [*AAR code*]
URY	Uruguay [*ANSI three-letter standard code*] (CNC)
URZ	Uroozgan [*Afghanistan*] [*Airport symbol*] [*Obsolete*] (OAG)
US	Military Airlift Command [*Air Force*] [*ICAO designator*] (FAAC)
US	Ubi Supra [*In the Place Mentioned Above*] [*Latin*]
US	Ultrasonic (AAMN)
US	Ultrasonic Spectroscopy
US	Ultrasound
U/S	Unassorted (ROG)
US	Uncle Sam
US	Unconditional Selection
US	Unconditional Surrender
US	Unconditioned Stimulus [*Psychometrics*]
US	Under Secretary
US	Underlying Stock [*Finance*]

U/S	Underside
US	Undersize (AAG)
US	Underspeed (MSA)
US	Underwriters' Special Request
U/S	Unhelpful, Helpless, Useless Persons [*From abbreviation for "unserviceable"*]
U & S	Unified and Specified [*or Strategic*] Command (MCD)
US	Uniform System
US	Union Settlement Association (EA)
US	Unit Separator [*Control character*] [*Data processing*]
US	Unitary Symmetry (MCD)
US	United Serpents (EA)
US	United Service
US	United Sisters (EA)
US	United States [*ANSI two-letter standard code*]
us	United States [*MARC country of publication code*] [*Library of Congress*] (LCCP)
US	United States Supreme Court Reports [*A publication*] (DLA)
US	Unites States of America [*IYRU nationality code*] (IYR)
US	Universal Service [*News agency*]
US	Universale Studium [*A publication*]
US	Unknown Significance
US	Unlike-Sexed
US	Unregistered Stock [*Finance*]
US	Unserviceable
U/S	Unsorted
US	Up Stage [*Away from audience*] [*A stage direction*]
US	Update State [*Online database field identifier*]
US	Upper Stage (MCD)
US	Uprighting Subsystem [*NASA*] (KSC)
US	US Ammunition Co. [*Vancouver Stock Exchange symbol*]
US	US Supreme Court Reports (GPO)
US	Useless
US	User Segment (SSD)
us	Ut Supra [*As Above*] [*Latin*] (WGA)
US	Uterine Stroma
US	Uusi Suomi [*A publication*]
US1	United States 1 Worksheets [*A publication*]
US3	Unit Self-Sufficiency System (MCD)
USA	INFO-DOC [*ACCORD*] [*UTLAS symbol*]
USA	Liberty All-Star Equity [*NYSE symbol*] (SPSG)
USA	Ukiyo-E Society of America (EA)
USA	Ullage Simulation Assembly (MCD)
USA	Ultrasonic Agitation
USA	Ultrastable Arc Lamp
USA	Ultraviolet Spectral Analysis
US of A	Under Secretary of the Army
USA	Underwater Society of America (EA)
USA	Unicycling Society of America [*Later, USA, Inc.*] (EA)
USA	Union of South Africa
USA	Union Syndicale de l'Agriculture [*Union of Agricultural Workers*] [*Morocco*]
USA	United Scenic Artists (EA)
USA	United Secularists of America (EA)
USA	United Shareholders Association (EA)
USA	United Shareowners of America (EA)
USA	United Shoppers Association
USA	United Sidecar Association [*Later, USCA*] (EA)
USA	United Soccer Association [*Later, NASL*]
USA	United Socialist Alliance [*Sri Lanka*] [*Political party*]
USA	United Spoilers of America [*Later, MERCPAC*] (EA)
USA	United Sprint Association (EA)
USA	United States [*ANSI three-letter standard code*]
USA	United States of ACORN [*Publication of the Association of Community Organizations for Reform Now*]
USA	United States of America
USA	United States Army
USA	United States Attorney (EPA)
USA	United States Automobile Association, San Antonio, TX [*OCLC symbol*] (OCLC)
USA	United Steelworkers of America
USA	United Stockcar Alliance [*Auto racing*]
USA	United Student Aid Funds (EA)
USA	United Students for America [*Defunct*] (EA)
USA	United Support of Artists [*In USA for Africa, the chorus of American pop stars who recorded "We Are the World" to benefit famine victims in Africa*]
USA	United Synagogue of America (EA)
USA	Unity for Safe Airtravel [*Program of Air Line Pilots Association*]
USA	Universal Subject Access [*Librarianship*]
USA	Unix Systems Association (EA)
USA	Unsegmented Storage Analyzer [*Instrumentation*]
USA	Urban Sanitary Authority [*British*]
USA	Utility Shareholders Association (EA)
USAA	United Specialty Agents Alliance [*Also known as USA Alliance*] (EA)
USAA	United States Academy of Arms (EA)
USAA	United States Arbitration Act [*A publication*] (DLA)
USAA	United States Armor Association (EA)
USAA	United States Athletes Association (EA)

USAA .... US Albacore Association (EA)
USAA .... US Armbrust Association (EA)
USAA .... US Armor Association (EA)
USAAA ..... United States Army Audit Agency
USAAA ..... US Amputee Athletic Association (EA)
USAAAVS ... United States Army Agency for Aviation Safety [*Formerly,* *USABAAR*] (AABC)
USAAAWR ... United States Army Audit Agency, Washington Region
USAAB...... United States Army Aviation Board
USAABELCTBD ... United States Army Airborne and Electronics Board [*Later, USAAESWBD*]
USA/ABF ... USA Amateur Boxing Federation (EA)
USAABMDA ... United States Army Advanced Ballistic Missile Defense Agency (AABC)
USAABMU ... United States Army Aircraft Base Maintenance Unit (AABC)
USAABNSOTBD ... United States Army Airborne and Special Operations Test Board (GFGA)
USAAC...... United States Army Administration Center [*Obsolete*] (AABC)
USAAC...... United States Army Air Corps
USAAC...... United States Army Aviation Center [*Fort Rucker*]
USAACDA ... United States Army Aviation Combat Developments Agency [*CDC*]
USAACEBD ... United States Army Airborne Communications and Electronics Board
USAADASCH ... United States Army Air Defense Artillery School
USAADAT ... United States Army Alcohol and Drug Abuse Team Training (MCD)
USAADB... United States Army Air Defense Board
USAADCEN ... United States Army Air Defense Center
USAADCENFB ... United States Army Air Defense Center and Fort Bliss (AABC)
USAADCS ... United States Army Air Defense Center and School
USAADEA ... United States Army Air Defense Engineering Agency [*Formerly, USASADEA*] [*AEC*]
USAADMAC ... United States Army Aeronautical Depot Maintenance Center
USAADS... United States Army Air Defense School (AABC)
USAADTA ... United States Army Aircraft Development Test Activity
USAADTC ... United States Army Armor and Desert Training Center
USAADVCOM ... United States Army Advance Command
USAAEFA ... United States Army Aviation Engineering Flight Activity [*Edwards Air Force Base, CA*]
USAAESWBD ... United States Army Airborne, Electronics, and Special Warfare Board (AABC)
USAAF...... United States Army Air Forces
USAAFIME ... United States Army Air Forces in the Middle East
USAAFINO ... United States Army Aviation Flight Information and Nav-Aids Office (AABC)
USAAFIO ... United States Army Aviation Flight Information Office
USAAFO... United States Army Avionics Field Office [*Formerly, USASAFO*]
USAAFUK ... United States Army Air Forces in the United Kingdom
USAAGAR ... United States Army Advisor Group O - Army Reserve (AABC)
USAAGCDA ... United States Army Adjutant General Combat Developments Agency (SAA)
USAAGDPSC ... United States Army Adjutant General Data Processing Service Center (AABC)
USAAGNG ... United States Army Advisory Group (National Guard) (AABC)
USAAGPC ... United States Army Adjutant General Publications Center
USAAGS... United States Army Adjutant General's School (AABC)
USAALS ... United States Army Aviation Logistics School (INF)
USAAMA ... United States Army Advent Management Agency (MUGU)
USAAMC ... United States Army Aeromedical Center
USAAMC ... United States Army Artillery and Missile Center
USAAMCCOM ... United States Army Armament, Munitions, and Chemical Command
USAAML ... United States Army Aviation Materiel Laboratories
USAAMRDC ... United States Army Air Mobility Research and Development Center
USAAMR & DL ... United States Army Air Mobility Research and Development Laboratory [*Also, AMR & DL, USAAMRDL*]
USAAMRDL ... United States Army Air Mobility Research and Development Laboratory [*Also, AMR & DL, USAAMR & DL*]
USAAMS.. United States Army Artillery and Missile School [*Later, Field Artillery School*]
USAAPDT ... United States Army Aviation Precision Demonstration Team (AABC)
USAAPSA ... United States Army Ammunition Procurement and Supply Agency
USAARC... United States Army Antiaircraft Replacement Center
USAARCOM ... United States Army Armament Command
USAARDC ... United States Army Aberdeen Research and Development Center
USAARENBD ... United States Army Armor and Engineer Board (AABC)
USAARL... United States Army Aeromedical Research Laboratory [*Ft. Rucker, AL*] (AABC)
USAARMA ... United States Assistant Army Attache

USAARMBD ... United States Army Armor Board
USAARMC ... United States Army Armor Center [*Fort Knox, KY*]
USAARMHRU ... United States Army Armor Human Research Unit [*Fort Knox, KY*] (AABC)
USAARMS ... United States Army Armor School
USAARTYBD ... United States Army Artillery Board
USAARTYCDA ... United States Army Artillery Combat Developments (SAA)
USAARU... United States Army Aeromedical Research Unit
USAAS...... United States Army Air Services [*World War II*]
USAASC ... United States Army Air Service Command
USAASCFBH ... United States Army Administrative School Center and Fort Benjamin Harrison (AABC)
USAASD... United States Army Aeronautical Services Detachment
USAASD-E ... United States Army Aeronautical Services Detachment, Europe (AABC)
USAASD-LA ... United States Army Aeronautical Services Detachment, Latin America (AABC)
USAASD-PAC ... United States Army Aeronautical Services Detachment, Pacific (AABC)
USAASL ... United States Army Atmospheric Sciences Laboratory (RDA)
USAASO... United States Army Aeronautical Services Office (AABC)
USAASTA ... United States Army Aviation Systems Test Activity [*Also, AASTA*]
USAATBD ... United States Army Arctic Test Board
USAATC... United States Army Arctic Test Center
USAATCO ... United States Army Air Traffic Coordinating Officer
USAATMS ... United States Army Air Traffic Management System
USAAVA... United States Army Audio-Visual Agency (AABC)
USAAVCOM ... United States Army Aviation Materiel Command (AABC)
USAAVLABS ... United States Army Aviation Materiel Laboratories (AABC)
USAAVNBD ... United States Army Aviation Board
USAAVNC ... United States Army Aviation Center [*CONARC*]
USAAVNDTA ... US Army Aviation Development Test Activity [*Fort Rucker, AL*] (GRD)
USAAVNHRU ... United States Army Aviation Human Research Unit [*Ft. Rucker, AL*] (AABC)
USAAVNS ... United States Army Aviation School [*CONARC*]
USAAVNSC ... United States Army Aviation Systems Command
USAAVNTA ... United States Army Aviation Test Activity (AABC)
USAAVNTBD ... United States Army Aviation Test Board
USAAVRADCOM ... United States Army Aviation Research and Development Command
USAAVS ... United States Agency for Aviation Safety (MCD)
USAAVSCOM ... United States Army Aviation Systems Command [*Obsolete*] (AABC)
USAB........ United States Air Base (AAG)
USAB........ United States Army, Berlin (AABC)
USAB........ US Animal Bank (EA)
USAB........ USA Bancorp, Inc. [*NASDAQ symbol*] (NQ)
USABA...... US Association for Blind Athletes (EA)
USABAAR ... United States Army Board for Aviation Accident Research [*Later, USAAAVS*]
USABC...... United States Advanced Battery Consortium
USABDA... United States Amateur Ballroom Dancers Association (EA)
USABESRL ... United States Behavioral Science Research Laboratory [*Obsolete*] (IEEE)
USABF...... United States Amateur Baseball Federation
USA-BIAC ... USA - Business and Industry Advisory Committee to the OECD [*Organization for Economic Cooperation and Development*] (EA)
USABIOLABS ... United States Army Biological Laboratories (AABC)
USABRDL ... United States Army Biomedical Research and Development Laboratory [*Fort Detrick, MD*]
USABRL... United States Army Ballistic Research Laboratories (AABC)
USABVAPAC ... United States Army Broadcasting and Visual Activities, Pacific
USAC .... Union des Syndicats Autonomes Camerounais [*Federation of Cameroonese Autonomous Unions*]
USAC .... United States Air Corps
USAC .... United States Alpine Club [*Defunct*]
USAC .... United States of America Confederation [*Later, USAC/RS*] (EA)
USAC .... United States Apparel Council [*Defunct*] (EA)
USAC .... United States Archery Congress (EA)
USAC .... United States Army Corps (AABC)
USAC .... United States Auto Club (EA)
USAC .... Urban Information Systems Inter-Agency Committee [*HUD*] [*Terminated*] (EGAO)
USAC .... US Antimony Corp. [*NASDAQ symbol*] (NQ)
USAC .... US Aquaculture Council [*Defunct*] (EA)
USAC .... User Services Advisory Committee [*NERComP*]
USAC .... Utah State Agricultural College
USACA...... United States Advanced Ceramics Association
USACA...... United States Allied Commission Austria
USACA...... United States Army Civil Affairs [*World War II*]
USACA...... United States Army Communications Agency
USACA...... US A-Division Catamaran Association (EA)
USACAA... United States Army Concepts Analysis Agency (AABC)
USACAC... United States Army Combined Arms Center (AABC)

USACAC... United States Army Continental Army Command [*CONARC*] [*Superseded by FORSCOM*]

USACACDA ... United States Army Civil Affairs Combat Developments Agency (SAA)

USACAF ... United States Army Construction Agency, France

USACAG... United States Army Combined Arms Group (SAA)

USACAK... United States Army Construction Agency, Korea

US-ACAN ... United States Advisory Committee on Antarctic Names [*1947*-]

USACARA ... United States Army Civilian Appellate Review Agency (GFGA)

USACARMSCDA ... United States Army Combined Arms Combat Developments Agency

USACAS ... United States Army Civil Affairs School

USACATB ... United States Army Combat Arms Training Board (AABC)

USACBRWOC ... United States Army Chemical, Biological, and Radiological Weapons Orientation Course (AABC)

USACBRWOCAAB ... United States Army Chemical, Biological, and Radiological Weapons Orientation Course Academic Advisory Board (AABC)

USACC...... United States Army Communications Command (AABC)

USACC...... US-Arab Chamber of Commerce (EA)

USACC...... USA Convertible Club (EA)

USACC-A ... United States Army Communications Command - Alaska (AABC)

USACCA... United States Army Congressional Correspondence Agency (AABC)

USACC-AMC ... United States Army Communications Command - Army Materiel Command (AABC)

USACC COMMAGCY-HSC ... United States Army Communications Command Communications Agency - Health Services Command (AABC)

USACC COMMAGCY-MTMC ... United States Army Communications Command Communications Agency - Military Traffic Management Command (AABC)

USACC COMMAGCY-USACIDC ... United States Army Communications Command Communications Agency - United States Army Criminal Investigation Command (AABC)

USACC COMMAGCY-USAINTC ... United States Army Communications Command Communications Agency - United States Army Intelligence Center

USACC-CONUS ... United States Army Communications Command - Continental United States (AABC)

USACC-EUR ... United States Army Communications Command - Europe (AABC)

USACC-FORCES ... United States Army Communications Command - Forces (AABC)

USACCIA ... United States Army Chemical Corps Intelligence Agency

USACCL ... United States Army Coating and Chemical Laboratory (AABC)

USACCO... United States Army Commercial Communications Office

USACC-PAC ... United States Army Communications Command - Pacific (AABC)

USACC-R/FMD ... United States Army Communications Command Radio and Frequency Management Division

USACCSA ... United States Army Command and Control Support Agency

USACC-SAFCA ... United States Army Communications Command Safeguard Communications Agency

USACCSD ... United States Army Command and Control Support Detachment (AABC)

USACC SIG GP (AD) ... United States Army Communications Command Signal Group (AD)

USACC-SO ... United States Army Communications Command - South (AABC)

USACC-T ... United States Army Communications Command - Thailand (AABC)

USACCTC ... United States Army Chemical Corps Technical Committee

USACC-TRADOC ... United States Army Communications Command - Training and Doctrine Command (AABC)

USACDA... United States Arms Control and Disarmament Agency

USACDA... United States Army Catalog Data Agency (AABC)

USACDC... United States Army Combat Developments Command

USACDCADA ... United States Army Combat Developments Command Air Defense Agency [*Fort Bliss, TX*] (AABC)

USACDCAGA ... United States Army Combat Developments Command Adjutant General Agency

USACDCARMA ... United States Army Combat Developments Command Armor Agency [*Fort Knox, KY*] (AABC)

USACDCARTYA ... United States Army Combat Developments Command Artillery Agency (AABC)

USACDCAVNA ... United States Army Combat Developments Command Aviation Agency [*Fort Rucker, AL*] (AABC)

USACDCCA ... United States Army Combat Developments Command Combined Arms Agency [*Fort Leavenworth, KS*]

USACDCCAA ... United States Army Combat Developments Command Civil Affairs Agency [*Fort Gordon, GA*] (AABC)

USACDCCAG ... United States Army Combat Developments Command Combat Army Group [*Obsolete*] [*Fort Leavenworth, KS*] (AABC)

USACDCCARMSA ... United States Army Combat Developments Command Combat Arms Agency

USACDCCBRA ... United States Army Combat Developments Command Chemical-Biological-Radiological Agency [*Fort McClellan, AL*] (AABC)

USACDCCEA ... United States Army Combat Developments Command Communications-Electronics Agency [*Fort Monmouth, NJ*] (AABC)

USACDCCHA ... United States Army Combat Developments Command Chaplain Agency [*Fort Lee, VA*] (AABC)

USACDCCOMSG ... United States Army Combat Developments Command Combat Systems Group (AABC)

USACDCCONFG ... United States Army Combat Developments Command Concept and Force Design Group (AABC)

USACDCCSG ... United States Army Combat Developments Command Combat Support Group [*Obsolete*] [*Fort Belvoir, VA*] (AABC)

USACDCCSSG ... United States Army Combat Developments Command Combat Service Support Group [*Obsolete*] [*Fort Lee, VA*] (AABC)

USACDCDPFO ... United States Army Combat Developments Command Data Processing Field Office (AABC)

USACDCEA ... United States Army Combat Developments Command Engineer Agency [*Later, USACDCENA*] [*Fort Belvoir, VA*] (AABC)

USACDCEC ... United States Army Combat Developments Command Experimentation Center [*or Command*] [*Fort Ord, CA*]

USACDCENA ... United States Army Combat Developments Command Engineer Agency [*Formerly, USACDCEA*] (AABC)

USACDCFAA ... United States Army Combat Developments Command Field Artillery Agency [*Fort Sill, OK*] (AABC)

USACDCFINA ... United States Army Combat Developments Command Finance Agency (AABC)

USACDCIA ... United States Army Combat Developments Command Infantry Agency [*Later, USACDCINA*] [*Fort Benning, GA*] (AABC)

USACDCIAS ... United States Army Combat Developments Command Institute of Advanced Studies [*Obsolete*] [*Carlisle Barracks, PA*] (AABC)

USACDCICAS ... United States Army Combat Developments Command Institute of Combined Arms and Support [*Obsolete*] [*Fort Leavenworth, KS*] (AABC)

USACDCIDDFO ... United States Army Combat Developments Command Internal Defense and Development Field Office (AABC)

USACDCILC ... United States Army Combat Developments Command Institute of Land Combat [*Obsolete*] [*Alexandria, VA*] (AABC)

USACDCINA ... United States Army Combat Developments Command Infantry Agency [*Formerly, USACDCIA*] (AABC)

USACDCINCSG ... United States Army Combat Developments Command Intelligence and Control Systems Group (AABC)

USACDCINS ... United States Army Combat Developments Command Institute of Nuclear Studies [*Obsolete*] [*Fort Bliss, TX*] (AABC)

USACDCINTA ... United States Army Combat Developments Command Intelligence Agency [*Fort Holabird, MD*] (MCD)

USACDCISA ... United States Army Combat Developments Command Institute of Systems Analysis [*Obsolete*] [*Fort Belvoir, VA*] (AABC)

USACDCISS ... United States Army Combat Developments Command Institute of Special Studies [*Obsolete*] [*Fort Belvoir, VA*] (AABC)

USACDCISSO ... United States Army Combat Developments Command Institute of Strategic and Stability Operations [*Obsolete*] (AABC)

USACDCJAA ... United States Army Combat Developments Command Judge Advocate Agency [*Charlottesville, VA*] (AABC)

USACDCMA ... United States Army Combat Developments Command Maintenance Agency [*Aberdeen Proving Ground, MD*] (AABC)

USACDCMPA ... United States Combat Developments Command Military Police Agency [*Fort Gordon, GA*] (AABC)

USACDCMSA ... United States Army Combat Developments Command Medical Service Agency [*Fort Sam Houston, TX*] (AABC)

USACDCNG ... United States Army Combat Developments Command Nuclear Group [*Fort Bliss, TX*]

USACDCNUA ... United States Army Combat Developments Command Nuclear Agency (AABC)

USACDCOA ... United States Army Combat Developments Command Ordnance Agency [*Aberdeen Proving Ground, MD*]

USACDCPALSG ... United States Army Combat Developments Command Personnel and Logistics Systems Group (AABC)

USACDCPASA ... United States Army Combat Developments Command Personnel and Administrative Services Agency [*Fort Benjamin Harrison, IN*] (AABC)

USACDCQA ... United States Army Combat Developments Command Quartermaster Agency [*Fort Lee, VA*]

USACDCSA ... United States Army Combat Developments Command Supply Agency [*Later, USACDCSUA*] [*Fort Lee, VA*] (AABC)

USACDCSAG ... United States Army Combat Developments Command Systems Analysis Group [*Fort Belvoir, VA*] (AABC)

USACDCSOA ... United States Army Combat Developments Command Special Operations Agency (AABC)
USACDCSSI ... United States Army Combat Developments Command Strategic Studies Institute (AABC)
USACDCSUA ... United States Army Combat Developments Command Supply Agency [*Formerly, USACDCSA*] (AABC)
USACDCSWA ... United States Army Combat Developments Command Special Warfare Agency [*Fort Bragg, NC*] (AABC)
USACDCSWCAG ... United States Army Combat Developments Command Special Warfare and Civil Affairs Group [*Fort Belvoir, VA*]
USACDCSWG ... United States Army Combat Developments Command Special Warfare Group
USACDCTA ... United States Army Combat Developments Command Transportation Agency [*Fort Eustis, VA*] (AABC)
USACDEC ... United States Army Combat Developments Experimentation Command (GFGA)
USACE ...... United States Army Corps of Engineers [*Merged with General Equipment Command*]
USACEBD ... United States Army Airborne Communications and Electronics Board (AABC)
USACECDA ... United States Army Communications-Electronics Combat Developments Agency [*Fort Huachuca, AZ*]
USACECOM ... United States Army Communications and Electronics Command
USACEEIA ... United States Army Communications-Electronics Engineering Installation Agency [*Fort Huachuca, AZ*] (AABC)
USACEEIA-PAC ... United States Army Communications-Electronics Engineering Installation Agency-Pacific (RDA)
USACEEIA-WH ... United States Army Communications-Electronics Engineering Installation Agency - Western Hemisphere (AABC)
USACEIBN ... United States Army Communications-Electronics Installation Battalion (AABC)
USACENCDCSA ... United States Army Corps of Engineers National Civil Defense Computer Support Agency (AABC)
USACERL ... US Army Construction Engineering Research Laboratory (RDA)
USACESSEC ... United States Army Computer Systems Support and Evaluation Command
USACGSC ... United States Army Command and General Staff College
USACHB... United States Army Chaplain Board
USACHS... United States Army Chaplain School
USACI ...... United States Army Advisory Commission on Information
USACICD ... United States Army Criminal Investigation Command [*Formerly, USACIDA*] (AABC)
USACIDA ... United States Army Criminal Investigation Division Agency [*Later, USACICD*] (AABC)
USACIECA ... United States Advisory Commission on International Educational and Cultural Affairs
USACII ..... United States of America Standard Code for Information Interchange (NOAA)
USACIL .... United States Army Criminal Investigation Laboratory (AABC)
USACIR .... United States Army Criminal Investigation Repository
USACISO ... United States Army Counterinsurgency Support Office, Okinawa [*Obsolete*] (AABC)
USACIU .... United States Army Command Information Unit (AABC)
USACJE.... United Synagogue of America Commission on Jewish Education (EA)
USACM..... US Association for Computational Mechanics (EA)
USACMA ... United States Army Club Management Agency (AABC)
USACMLC ... United States Army Chemical Center [*Later, United States Army Ordnance and Chemical Center and School*]
USACMLCB ... United States Army Chemical Corps Board
USACMLCS ... United States Army Chemical Center and School [*Later, United States Army Ordnance and Chemical Center and School*] (AABC)
USACMLCSCH ... United States Army Chemical Corps School
USACMLRDL ... United States Army Chemical Research and Development Laboratories
USACMLS ... United States Army Chemical School (AABC)
USACMR ... United States Army Court of Military Review (AABC)
USACMS.. United States Army Command Management School
USACOJE ... United Synagogue of America Commission on Jewish Education (EA)
USACOMISA ... United States Army Communications Management Information Systems Activity
USACOMZEUR ... United States Army Communications Zone, Europe
USACOR... US Association for the Club of Rome (EA)
USACPEB ... United States Army Central Physical Evaluation Board (AABC)
USACRAPAC ... United States Army Command Reconnaissance Activities, Pacific Command
USACRC... United States Army Crime Records Center (AABC)
USACRF ... United States Army Counterintelligence Records Facility (MCD)
USACRREL ... United States Army Cold Regions Research and Engineering Laboratory (AABC)
USAC/RS ... United States Amateur Confederation of Roller Skating (EA)
USACRTC ... United States Army Cold Regions Test Center (INF)
USACS ...... United States Army Combat Surveillance Agency (AAG)
USACS ...... United States Army Courier Service (AABC)

USACSA ... United States Army Combat Surveillance Agency
USACSA ... United States Army Communications Systems Agency (AABC)
USACSC ... United States Army Computer Systems Command [*Fort Belvoir, VA*]
USACSG ... United States Army CINPAC Support Group
USACSLA ... United States Army Communications Security Logistics Agency (AABC)
USACSR ... United States Air Corps Specialist Reserve
USACSS.... United States Army Chief of Support Services
USACSS.... United States Army Combat Surveillance School (AABC)
USACSSAA ... United States Army Computer Systems Selection and Acquisition Agency (AABC)
USACSSC ... United States Army Computer Systems Support and Evaluation Command (IEEE)
USACSSEA ... United States Army Computer Systems Support and Evaluation Agency (AABC)
USACSSEC ... United States Army Computer Systems Support and Evaluation Command
USACSTA ... United States Army Combat Systems Test Activity [*Aberdeen Proving Ground, MD*]
USACSTA ... United States Army Courier Station (AABC)
USACSTATC ... United States Army Combat Surveillance and Target Acquisition Training Command
USACT ...... United States Accident Containment Team [*Government agency in 1985 movie "Warning Sign"*]
USACTA ... US Army Central TMDE [*Test, Measurement, and Diagnostic Equipment*] Activity (RDA)
USACTC ... United States Army Clothing and Textile Center
USACTMC ... United States Army Clothing and Textile Materiel Center
USACWL.. United States Army Chemical Warfare Laboratory
USAD .... United States Army Dispensary (AABC)
USADA ..... United States Amateur Dancers Association (EA)
USADAC ... United States Army Davison Aviation Command (GFGA)
USADACS ... United States Army Defense Ammunition Center and School (AABC)
USADAOA ... United States Army Drug and Alcohol Operations Agency
USADATCOM ... United States Army Data Support Command
USADC ..... United States Army Data Support Command
USADC ..... United States Army Dental Clinic
USADCJ ... United States Army Depot Command, Japan (AABC)
USADEG... United States Army Dependents' Education Group (AABC)
USADESCOM ... United States Army Depot Support Command
USADIP.... United States Army Deserter Information Point (AABC)
USADJ...... United States Army Depot, Japan (AABC)
USADOFL ... United States Army Diamond Ordnance Fuze Laboratory [*Later, HDL*]
USADP...... Uniform Shipboard Automatic Data Processing
USADPC... United States Army Data Processing Center
USADPS ... Uniform Automatic Data Processing System [*Navy*]
USADRB... United States Army Discharge Review Board (AABC)
USADSC... United States Army Data Services and Administrative Systems Command
USADTC... United States Army Armor and Desert Training Center (AABC)
USAE......... United States Army Engineer (AABC)
USAEAGSC ... United States Army, Europe, Adjutant General Support Center (AABC)
USAEARA ... United States Army Equipment Authorization Review Activity (AABC)
USAEARC ... United States Army Equipment Authorizations Review Center (AABC)
USAEB...... United States Army Engineer Board
USAEC...... United States Army Electronics Command [*Obsolete*]
USAEC...... United States Atomic Energy Commission
USAECA... United States Army Electronics Command Computation Agency [*Obsolete*] (AABC)
USAECAV ... United States Army Engineer Construction Agency, Vietnam
USAECBDE ... United States Army Engineer Center Brigade (AABC)
USAECDA ... United States Army Engineer Combat Developments Agency (SAA)
USAECFB ... United States Army Engineer Center and Fort Belvoir (AABC)
USAECOM ... United States Army Electronics Command [*Obsolete*]
USAECR... United States Army Engineer Center Regiment (AABC)
USAEC Rep CONF ... US Atomic Energy Commission. Report. CONF [*A publication*]
USAEC Rep GJO ... United States. Atomic Energy Commission. Report GJO [*A publication*]
USAEC Res Dev Rep AEC-TR ... US Atomic Energy Commission. Research and Development Report. AEC-TR [*A publication*]
USAEC Res Dev Rep ANL ... US Atomic Energy Commission. Research and Development Report. ANL [*A publication*]
USAEC Res Dev Rep BNL ... US Atomic Energy Commission. Research and Development Report. BNL [*A publication*]
USAEC Res Dev Rep COO ... US Atomic Energy Commission. Research and Development Report. COO [*A publication*]
USAEC Res Dev Rep HASL ... US Atomic Energy Commission. Research and Development Report. HASL [*A publication*]
USAEC Res Dev Rep HW ... US Atomic Energy Commission. Research and Development Report. HW [*A publication*]

USAEC Res Dev Rep LAMS (LA) ... US Atomic Energy Commission. Research and Development Report. LAMS (LA) [*A publication*]
USAEC Res Dev Rep LF ... US Atomic Energy Commission. Research and Development Report. LF [*A publication*]
USAEC Res Dev Rep NYO ... US Atomic Energy Commission. Research and Development Report. NYO [*A publication*]
USAEC Res Dev Rep ORINS ... US Atomic Energy Commission. Research and Development Report. ORINS [*A publication*]
USAEC Res Dev Rep ORNL ... US Atomic Energy Commission. Research and Development Report. ORNL [*A publication*]
USAEC Res Dev Rep ORO ... US Atomic Energy Commission. Research and Development Report. ORO [*A publication*]
USAEC Res Dev Rep RLO ... US Atomic Energy Commission. Research and Development Report. RLO [*A publication*]
USAEC Res Dev Rep SCR ... US Atomic Energy Commission. Research and Development Report. SCR [*A publication*]
USAEC Res Dev Rep TID ... US Atomic Energy Commission. Research and Development Report. TID [*A publication*]
USAEC Res Dev Rep UCD ... US Atomic Energy Commission. Research and Development Report. UCD [*A publication*]
USAEC Res Dev Rep UCLA ... US Atomic Energy Commission. Research and Development Report. UCLA [*A publication*]
USAEC Res Dev Rep UCRL ... US Atomic Energy Commission. Research and Development Report. UCRL [*A publication*]
USAEC Res Dev Rep UCSF ... US Atomic Energy Commission. Research and Development Report. UCSF [*A publication*]
USAEC Res Dev Rep UH ... US Atomic Energy Commission. Research and Development Report. UH [*A publication*]
USAEC Res Dev Rep UR ... US Atomic Energy Commission. Research and Development Report. UR [*A publication*]
USAEC Res Dev Rep WT ... US Atomic Energy Commission. Research and Development Report. WT [*A publication*]
USAEC Symp Ser ... US Atomic Energy Commission. Symposium Series [*A publication*]
USAECV(P) ... United States Army Engineer Command, Vietnam (Provisional)
USAED ...... United States Army Engineer District
USAEDE ... United States Army Engineer Division, Europe (AABC)
USAEDH .. United States Army Engineer Division, Huntsville (AABC)
USAEDLMV ... United States Army Engineer Division, Lower Mississippi Valley (AABC)
USAEDM ... United States Army Engineer Division, Mediterranean (AABC)
USAEDMR ... United States Army Engineer Division, Missouri River (AABC)
USAEDNA ... United States Army Engineer Division, North Atlantic (AABC)
USAEDNC ... United States Army Engineer Division, North Central (AABC)
USAEDNE ... United States Army Engineer Division, New England (AABC)
USAEDNP ... United States Army Engineer Division, North Pacific (AABC)
USAEDOR ... United States Army Engineer Division, Ohio River (AABC)
USAEDPO ... United States Army Engineer Division, Pacific Ocean (AABC)
USAEDSA ... United States Army Engineer Division, South Atlantic (AABC)
USAEDSP ... United States Army Engineer Division, South Pacific (AABC)
USAEDSW ... United States Army Engineer Division, Southwestern (AABC)
USAEEA ... United States Army Enlistment Eligibility Activity (AABC)
USAEFMA ... United States Army Electronics Command Financial Management Agency [*Obsolete*] (AABC)
USAEGD ... United States Army Engineer, Gulf District
USAEGIMRADA ... US Army Engineer, Geodesy, Intelligence, and Mapping Research and Development Agency (NOAA)
USAEHA .. United States Army Environmental Hygiene Agency [*Aberdeen Proving Ground, MD*] (AABC)
USAEHL ... United States Army Environmental Health Laboratory
USAEIGHT ... Eighth United States Army (CINC)
USAEIS ..... United States Army Electronic Intelligence and Security (AABC)
USAELRO ... United States Army Electronics Logistics Research Office
USAELRU ... United States Army Electronics Research Unit
USAEMA ... United States Army Electronics Materiel Agency [*Formerly, USASSA*]
USAEMAFHPO ... United States Army Electronics Materiel Agency, Fort Huachuca Procurement Office
USAEMAFMPO ... United States Army Electronics Materiel Agency, Fort Monmouth Procurement Office
USAEMAPICO ... United States Army Electronics Materiel Agency, Plant Inventory Control Office
USAEMAWPO ... United States Army Electronics Materiel Agency, Washington Procurement Office
USAEMC ... United States Army Engineer Maintenance Center (SAA)
USAEMCA ... United States Army Engineer Mathematical Computation Agency (AABC)
USAEMSA ... United States Army Electronics Materiel Support Agency [*Formerly, USASMSA*]
USAENGCOMEUR ... United States Army Engineer Command, Europe (AABC)
USAENPG ... United States Army Engineer Power Group (RDA)
USAENPG-ED ... United States Army Engineer Power Group Engineering Division [*Fort Belvoir, VA*]
USAEPA ... United States Army Electronics Command Patent Agency [*Obsolete*] (AABC)

USAEPG ... United States Army Electronic Proving Ground [*Fort Huachuca, AZ*]
USAEPMARA ... United States Army, Europe, Personnel Management and Replacement Activity (AABC)
USAEPOC ... United States Army Engineer Procurement Office, Chicago
USAERA ... United States Army Electronics Command Logistics Research Agency [*Obsolete*] (AABC)
USAERADCOM ... United States Army Electronics Research and Development Command (RDA)
USAERDA ... United States Army Electronic Research and Development Agency
USAERDAW ... United States Army Electronics Research and Development Activity, White Sands [*New Mexico*] (AABC)
USAERDL ... United States Army Electronics Research and Development Laboratory [*Formerly, USASRDL*] (MCD)
USAEREC ... United States Army Enlisted Records and Evaluation Center (MCD)
USAERG ... United States Army Engineer Reactor Group (AABC)
USAERLO ... United States Army Electronics Regional Labor Office
US Aeros P ... United States Aerospace Industry Profile [*A publication*]
US Aerosp Med Res Lab Tech Rep AMRL-TR ... United States. Aerospace Medical Research Laboratory. Technical Report. AMRL-TR [*A publication*]
US Aerosp Res Lab Rep ... United States. Aerospace Research Laboratories. Reports [*A publication*]
USAES ...... United States Army Engineer School
USAES ...... United States Association of Evening Students (EA)
USAESC ... United States Army Electronics Support Command (AABC)
USAESC ... United States Army Engineer Studies Center [*Fort Belvoir, VA*]
USAESEIA ... United States Army Electronic Systems Engineering Installation Agency (GFGA)
USAET & DL (ECOM) ... United States Army Electronics Technology and Devices Laboratory (Electronics Command) (AABC)
USAETL ... United States Army Engineer Topographic Laboratories [*Fort Belvoir, VA*]
USAEU ..... United States Army Exhibit Unit (AABC)
USAEUR ... United States Army, Europe (MCD)
USAEWES ... United States Army Engineer Waterways Experiment Station
US of AF .... Under Secretary of the Air Force
USAF .... United States Aikido Federation (EA)
USAF .... United States Air Force [*Washington, DC*]
USAF .... United States Army Forces
USAF .... United Student Aid Fund
USAF .... United Students of America Foundation (EA)
USAF .... US Aquaculture Federation (EA)
USAF .... USA Foundation (EA)
USAFA ...... United States Air Force Academy [*Colorado*]
USAFA ...... US-Albania Friendship Association (EA)
USAFA ...... USA Finn Association (EA)
USAFABD ... United States Army Field Artillery Board [*Fort Sill, OK*] (AABC)
USAFAC ... United States Army Finance and Accounting Center (AABC)
USAFACFS ... United States Army Field Artillery Center and Fort Sill (AABC)
USAFACP ... United States Air Force Ammunition Control Point
USAFACS ... United States Air Force Air Crew School
USAFADS ... United States Air Force Air Demonstration Squadron
USAFADWC ... United States Air Force Air Defense Weapons Center (MCD)
USAF AFHRL ... United States. Air Force. Human Resources Laboratory [*A publication*]
USAFAG ... United States Air Force Auditor General
USAFAGOS ... United States Air Force's Air-Ground Operations School
USAFALCENT ... United States Air Force Airlift Center
USAFAPC ... United States Air Force Airframe Production Contract
USAFAPS ... United States Air Force Air Police School
USAFAS .... United States Army Field Artillery School [*Fort Sill, OK*] (AABC)
USAFAS/MSL ... United States Army Field Artillery School Morris Swett Technical Library Division [*Fort Sill, OK*]
USAFAVLO ... United States Air Force Audiovisual Liaison Office
USAFB ...... United States Army Field Band (AABC)
USAFBI ..... United States Army Forces in the British Isles
USAFBMD ... United States Air Force Ballistic Missile Division
USAFBMS ... United States Air Force Basic Military School
USAFBS .... United States Air Force Bandsman School (AFM)
USAFBS .... United States Air Force Bombardment School
USAFCBI ... United States Forces, China, Burma, India [*World War II*]
USAFCBIT ... United States Forces, China, Burma, India Theater [*World War II*]
USAFCC ... United States Army Forces in Central Canada [*World War II*]
USAF CMR ... United States Air Force Court of Military Review (AFM)
USAFCO ... United States Air Force, Southern Command (MCD)
USAFCRL ... United States Air Force Cambridge Research Laboratories
USAFD ..... United States Air Force Dictionary [*A publication*]
USAFE ...... United States Air Force in Europe
USAFEC ... United States Army Forces in Eastern Canada [*World War II*]
USAFECI ... United States Air Force Extension Course Institute
USAF/EDA ... Society of United States Air Force Flight Surgeons (EA)
USAFEHL ... United States Air Force Environmental Health Laboratory

USAFEISC ... United States Air Forces in Europe Inspection and Safety Center
USAFEL .... United States Air Force Epidemiological Laboratory   (AFM)
USAFEPC ... United States Air Forces in Europe Personnel Center
USAFESA ... United States Army Facilities Engineering Support Agency   (AABC)
USAFESA-ED ... United States Army Facilities Engineering Support Agency Engineering Division
USAFESA-RT ... United States Army Facilities Engineering Support Agency Research and Technology Division
USAFESA-RTD ... United States Army Facilities Engineering Support Agency Research and Technology Division
USAFESA-T ... United States Army Facilities Engineering Support Agency Technology Support Division [*Fort Belvoir, VA*]
USAFESA-TS ... United States Army Facilities Engineering Support Agency - Technology Support Division
USAFESA-TSD ... United States Army Facilities Engineering Support Agency - Technology Support Division
USAFE-T .. United States Air Forces in Europe - Turkey
USAFETAC ... United States Air Force Environmental Technical Applications Center [*Scott Air Force Base, IL*]   (AFM)
USAFETC ... United States Air Force Environmental Technical Application Center [*Scott Air Force Base, IL*]
USAFETO ... United States Army Forces, European Theater of Operations [*World War II*]
USAFETPS ... United States Air Force Experimental Test Pilot School
USAFEURPCR ... United States Air Force European Postal and Courier Region   (AFM)
USAFEUSA ... United States Army Forces (Korea), Eighth United States Army
USAFF ...... USA Film Festival   (EA)
USAFFACG ... United States Air Force Field Activity Group
USAFFACS ... United States Air Force Field Activity Squadron
USAFFE .... United States Army Forces, Far East [*World War II*]
USAFFGS ... United States Air Force Flexible Gunnery School
USAFFSR ... United States Air Force Flight Safety Research
USAFH ..... United States Air Force Hospital
USAFHA ... USA Field Hockey Association   (EA)
USAFHD .. United States Air Force Historical Division
USAFHG ... United States Air Force Honor Guard
USAFHRC ... United States Air Force Historical Research Center
USAFI .... United States Armed Forces Institute
USAFIA .... United States Army Forces in Australia
USAFIB ..... United States Army Aviation Flight Information Bulletin   (FAAC)
USAFIC ..... United States Association of Firearm Instructors and Coaches   (EA)
USAFICA ... United States Army Forces in Central Africa [*World War II*]
USAFICPA ... United States Army Forces in Central Pacific Area
USAFIFC .. United States Air Force Instrument Flight Center   (AFM)
USAFIGED ... United States Armed Forces Institute Test of General Educational Development   (AEBS)
USAFIK .... United States Army Forces in Korea
USAFIL ..... United States Army Forces in Liberia [*World War II*]
USAFIME ... United States Armed Forces in Middle East
USAFINCISCOM ... United States Army Finance and Comptroller Information Systems Command   (AABC)
USAFINTEL ... United States Air Force Intelligence Publication
USAFINZ ... United States Army Forces in New Zealand
USAFIP(NL) ... United States Army Forces in the Philippines (Northern Luzon) [*World War II*]
USAFISPA ... United States Army Forces in the South Pacific Area
USAFIT ..... United States Air Force Institute of Technology
USAFIWS ... United States Air Force Interceptor Weapons School
USAFLANT ... United States Air Forces, Atlantic   (AABC)
USAFMC .. United States Association of Former Members of Congress   (EA)
USAFMD ... United States Army Frequency Management Directorate   (MCD)
USAFMEPCR ... United States Air Force Mideast Postal and Courier Region   (AFM)
USAFMEPCS ... United States Air Force Mideast Postal and Courier Service   (AFM)
USAFMIDPAC ... United States Army Forces, Middle Pacific [*World War II*] [*See AFMIDPAC*]
USAFMPC ... United States Air Force Military Personnel Center
USAFMTC ... United States Air Force Marksmanship Training Center
USAFMTO ... United States Army Forces, Mediterranean Theater of Operations [*World War II*]
USAF NR .. United States. Air Force. News Release [*A publication*]
USAF/NRD ... United States Air Force, National Range Division
USAFNS ... United States Air Force Navigation School
USAF Nucl Saf ... USAF [*United States Air Force*] Nuclear Safety [*A publication*]
USAFO ...... United States Army Field Office   (RDA)
USAFOB ... USA Federation of Bocce   (EA)
USAFOCA ... United States Army Field Operating Cost Agency   (AABC)
USAFOCS ... United States Air Force Officer Candidate School
USAFOEHL ... United States Air Force Occupational and Environmental Health Laboratory [*Brooks Air Force Base, TX*]
USAFOF ... United States Army Flight Operations Facility   (AABC)

USAFOMC ... US Air Force Occupational Measurement Center [*Randolph Air Force Base, TX*]   (GRD)
USAFOSR ... United States Air Force Office of Scientific Research
USAFP ...... Uniformed Services Academy of Family Physicians   (EA)
USAFPAC ... United States Air Forces, Pacific
USAFPACPCR ... United States Air Force Pacific Postal and Courier Region
USAFPCS ... United States Air Force Postal and Courier Service
USAFPCS Eur-Me Rgn ... United States Air Force Postal and Courier Service, Europe-Mideast Region   (AFM)
USAFPCS LA Rgn ... United States Air Force Postal and Courier Service, Latin American Region   (AFM)
USAFPCS Pac Rgn ... United States Air Force Postal and Courier Service, Pacific Region   (AFM)
USAFPCS US Rgn ... United States Air Force Postal and Courier Service, United States Region   (AFM)
USAFPDC ... United States Air Force Personnel Development Center
USAFPEB ... United States Air Force Physical Evaluation Board   (AFM)
USAFPLREP ... United States Air Force Plant Representative Office
USAFPOA ... United States Army Forces, Pacific Ocean Areas [*World War II*]
USAFPRO ... United States Air Force Plant Representative Office
USAFPS .... United States Air Force Pilot School
USAFR ...... Union of South Africa
USAFR ...... United States Air Force Representative   (AFM)
USAFR ...... United States Air Force Reserve
USAFRD ... United States Air Force Recruiting Detachment
USAFRED ... United States Air Force Forces, Readiness Command
USAFRG ... United States Air Force Recruiting Group
USAFRHL ... United States Air Force Radiological Health Laboratory
USAFRO ... United States Air Force Recruiting Office
USAFROTC ... United States Air Force Reserve Officer Training Corps
USAFRR ... United States Air Force Resident Representative   (MCD)
USAFRS .... United States Air Force Recruiting Service
USAFRSQ ... United States Air Force Recruiting Squadron
USAFS ...... United States Army Finance School   (AABC)
USAFSA .... United States Army Forces in South America
USAFSA .... United States Army Forces, South Atlantic [*World War II*]
USAFSAAS ... United States Air Force School of Applied Aerospace Sciences   (AFM)
USAFSACS ... United States Air Force School of Applied Cryptologic Sciences   (AFM)
USAFSAG ... United States Air Force Special Activities Group
USAFSAM ... United States Air Force School of Aerospace Medicine
USAFSAM/ED ... Society of United States Air Force Flight Surgeons   (EA)
USAFSAS ... United States Air Force Special Activities Squadron
USAFSAWC ... United States Air Force Special Air Warfare Center   (AFM)
USAFSBSS ... United States Air Force Standard Base Supply System
USAFSC .... United States Army Food Service Center   (AABC)
USAFSCHCS ... United States Air Force School of Health Care Science
USAFSE .... United States Air Force Supervisory Examination   (AFM)
USAFSG ... United States Army Field Support Group   (AABC)
USAFSO ... United States Air Force Southern Air Division
USAFSO ... United States Air Forces Southern Command   (AABC)
USAFSOC ... United States Air Force Special Operations Center   (AFM)
USAFSOF ... United States Air Force Special Operations Force   (AFM)
USAFSOS ... United States Air Force Special Operations School   (AFM)
USAFSPA ... United States Air Force Security Policy Academy
USAFSRA ... United States Air Force Special Reporting Agency
USAFSS .... United States Air Force Security Service [*Later, AFESC*]
USAFSTC ... United States Air Force Special Treatment Center   (AFM)
USAFSTC ... United States Army Foreign Science and Technology Center   (AABC)
USAFSTRIKE ... United States Air Forces Strike Command   (AABC)
USAFTAC ... United States Air Force Technical Applications Center   (MCD)
USAFTALC ... United States Air Force Tactical Airlift Center   (AFM)
USAFTARC ... United States Air Force Tactical Air Reconnaissance Center   (AFM)
USAFTAWC ... United States Air Force Tactical Air Warfare Center   (AFM)
USAF TESTPLTSCH ... United States Air Force Test Pilot School
USAFTFWC ... United States Air Force Tactical Fighter Weapons Center   (AFM)
USAFTMCP ... United States Air Force Tactical Missile Control Point
USAFTPS ... United States Air Force Test Pilot School   (MCD)
USAFTS .... United States Air Force Technical School
USAFTTS ... United States Air Force Technical Training School
USAF-USPCR ... United States Air Force - United States Postal Courier Region   (AFM)
USAFWPLO ... United States Air Force Water Port Logistics Office
USAFWPO ... United States Air Force Water Port Liaison Office [*or Officer*]   (AFM)
USAG .... Underwater Sound Advisory Group [*Navy*]
USAG .... United States Army Garrison   (AABC)
USAG .... United States Army in Greece
USAGEM ... US Atlantic and Gulf Ports/Eastern Mediterranean and North African Freight Conference [*New York, NY*]   (EA)
USAGETA ... United States Army General Equipment Test Activity   (AABC)
USAGF ...... United States Army Ground Forces   (MUGU)
USAGG ..... United States Army Group, American Mission for Aid to Greece
USAGIMRADA ... United States Army Geodesy Intelligence and Mapping Research and Development Agency   (AABC)

USAGMPA ... United States Army General Materiel and Petroleum Activity

USAGMPC ... United States Army General Materiel and Parts Center (AABC)

USAGPC... United States Army Adjutant General Publications Center

US Agric .... United States. Department of Agriculture. Publications [*A publication*]

US Agric Mark Serv AMS Series ... United States. Agriculture Marketing Service. AMS Series [*A publication*]

US Agric Res Serv ARS-NC ... US Agricultural Research Service. ARS-NC [*A publication*]

US Agric Res Serv ARS-NE ... US Agricultural Research Service. ARS-NE [*A publication*]

US Agric Res Serv ARS-S ... US Agricultural Research Service. ARS-S [*A publication*]

US Agric Res Serv ARS-W ... US Agricultural Research Service. ARS-W [*A publication*]

US Agric Res Serv CA ... US Agricultural Research Service. CA [*A publication*]

US Agric Res Serv East Reg Res Lab Publ ... United States. Agricultural Research Service. Eastern Regional Research Laboratory. Publication [*A publication*]

US Agric Res Serv Mark Res Rep ... US Agricultural Research Service. Marketing Research Report [*A publication*]

US Agric Res Serv North Cent Reg Rep ... United States. Agricultural Research Service. North Central Region. Report [*A publication*]

US Agric Res Serv Northeast Reg Rep ARS NE ... US Agricultural Research Service. Northeastern Region Report. ARS-NE [*A publication*]

US Agric Res Serv South Reg Rep ... US Agricultural Research Service. Southern Region Report [*A publication*]

USAGSC ... United States Army General Supplies Commodity Center

USAH .... United States Army Hospital

USAH .... USA Harvest [*An association*] (EA)

USAHA ..... United States Animal Health Association (EA)

USAHAC .. United States Army Headquarters Area Command

USAHC .... United States Army Health Clinic (AABC)

USAHEL... United States Army Human Engineering Laboratories (AABC)

USAHOME ... United States Army Homes [*Prefabricated houses, shipped overseas*]

USAHS...... United States Army Hospital Ship

USAHSC... United States Army Health Service Command

USAHSDSA ... United States Army Health Services Data Systems Agency (AABC)

USAHTN .. United States Army Hometown News Center (AABC)

USAI......... US-Asia Institute (EA)

USAIA .... United States Army Institute of Administration (AABC)

USAIA .... United States Army Intelligence Agency (GFGA)

USAIAS .... United States Army Institute of Advanced Studies (SAA)

USAIB .... United States Army Infantry Board

USAIC....... United States Army Infantry Center [*Fort Benning, GA*]

USAIC....... United States Army Intelligence Command

USAICA .... United States Army Interagency Communications Agency (AABC)

USAICS..... United States Army Intelligence Center and School [*Fort Huachuca, AZ*] (AABC)

USAID....... United States Agency for International Development [*Also, AID*]

USAIDR.... United States Army Institute of Dental Research (AABC)

USAIDSC ... United States Army Information and Data Systems Command

USAIDSCOM ... United States Army Information and Data Systems Command (AABC)

USAIG....... United States Aircraft Insurance Group

USAIGC.... United States Association of Independent Gymnastic Clubs (EA)

USAIIA ..... United States Army Imagery Interpretation Agency (AABC)

USAIIC ..... United States Army Imagery Interpretation Center (AABC)

USAILC .... United States Army International Logistics Center

USAILCOM ... United States Army International Logistics Command (AABC)

USAILG .... United States Army International Logistics Group (AABC)

USAIMA... United States Army Institute for Military Assistance [*Fort Bragg, NC*] (AABC)

USAIMC... United States Army Inventory Management Center (AABC)

USAIMS ... United States Army Institute for Military Systems (AABC)

USAIN...... United States Agricultural Information Network

USA Inc..... Unicycling Society of America, Inc. (EA)

USAINFHRU ... United States Army Infantry Human Research Unit [*Ft. Benning, GA*] (AABC)

USAINSB ... United States Army Intelligence Security Board

USAINSBD ... United States Army Intelligence and Security Board (MCD)

USAINSCOM ... United States Army Intelligence and Security Command

USAINTA ... United States Army Intelligence Agency (AABC)

USAINTB ... United States Army Intelligence Board

USAINTC ... United States Army Intelligence Center

USAINTCA ... United States Army Intelligence Corps Agency

USAINTCDA ... United States Army Intelligence Combat Developments (SAA)

USAINTELMDA ... United States Army Intelligence Materiel Developments Agency (AABC)

USAINTS ... United States Army Intelligence School

USAIPSG ... United States Army Industrial and Personnel Security Group

USAIRA .... United States Air Attache

USAIRC .... United States Army Ionizing Radiation Center

US Air Force Acad Tech Rep ... US Air Force Academy. Technical Report [*A publication*]

US Air Force Aeronaut Syst Div Tech Note ... United States. Air Force. Aeronautical Systems. Division Technical Note [*A publication*]

US Air Force Aeronaut Syst Div Tech Rep ... US Air Force. Aeronautical Systems. Division Technical Report [*A publication*]

US Air Force Cambridge Res Lab Instrum Pap ... United States. Air Force. Cambridge Research Laboratories. Instrumentation Papers [*A publication*]

US Air Force Cambridge Res Lab Phy Sci Res Pap ... United States. Air Force. Cambridge Research Laboratories. Physical Sciences Research Papers [*A publication*]

US Air Force Hum Resour Lab Tech Rep AFHRL-TR ... US Air Force. Human Resources Laboratory. Technical Report AFHRL-TR

US Air Force Syst Command Air Force Flight Dyn Lab Tech Rep ... United States. Air Force. Systems Command Air Force Flight Dynamics Laboratory. Technical Report [*A publication*]

US Air Force Syst Command Air Force Mater Lab Tech Rep AFML ... United States. Air Force. Systems Command Air Force Materials Laboratory. Technical Report AFML [*A publication*]

US Air Force Syst Command Res Technol Div Tech Doc Rep ASD ... United States. Air Force. Systems Command Research and Technology Division. Technical Documentary Report. ASD [*A publication*]

US Air Force Tech Doc Rep ... United States. Air Force. Technical Documentary Report [*A publication*]

US Air Force Tech Doc Rep AFSWC-TDR ... US Air Force. Technical Documentary Report. AFSWC-TDR [*A publication*]

US Air Force Tech Doc Rep AMRL-TDR ... US Air Force. Technical Documentary Report. AMRL-TDR [*A publication*]

US Air Force Tech Doc Rep ARL-TDR ... US Air Force. Technical Documentary Report. ARL-TDR [*A publication*]

US Air Force Tech Doc Rep ASD-TDR ... US Air Force. Technical Documentary Report. ASD-TDR [*A publication*]

US Air Force Tech Doc Rep RTD-TDR ... US Air Force. Technical Documentary Report. RTD-TDR [*A publication*]

US Air Force Tech Doc Rep SAM-TDR ... US Air Force. Technical Documentary Report. SAM-TDR [*A publication*]

US Air Force Tech Doc Rep SEG-TDR ... US Air Force. Technical Documentary Report. SEG-TDR [*A publication*]

US Air Force WADC Tech Rep ... United States. Air Force. Wright Air Development Center. Technical Report [*A publication*]

US Air Force Weapons Lab Tech Rep AFWL-TR ... United States. Air Force. Weapons Laboratory Technical Report AFWL-TR [*A publication*]

US Air Force Wright Air Dev Cent Tech Notes ... US Air Force. Wright Air Development Center. Technical Notes [*A publication*]

US Air Force Wright Air Dev Cent Tech Rep ... US Air Force. Wright Air Development Center. Technical Report [*A publication*]

UsairG .... USAir Group, Inc. [*Associated Press abbreviation*] (APAG)

USAIRLO ... United States Air Liaison Officer (CINC)

USAIRMILCOMUN ... United States Air Force Representative, UN Military Staff Committee

USAIRO.... United States Army Inventory Research Office [*Philadelphia, PA*]

USAIRR.... United States Army Investigative Records Repository (AABC)

USAIS .... United States Army Infantry School

USAISC..... United States Army Information Systems Command [*Fort Huachuca, AZ*]

USAISC-A ... United States Army Information Systems Command - Alaska (GFGA)

USAISC-AMC ... United States Army Information Systems Command - Army Materiel Command (GFGA)

USAISC-FORSCOM ... United States Army Information Systems Command - Forces Command (GFGA)

USAISC-HSC ... United States Army Information Systems Command - Health Services Command (GFGA)

USAISC-INSCOM ... United States Army Information Systems Command - Intelligence and Security Command (GFGA)

USAISC-MTMC ... United States Army Information Systems Command - Military Traffic Management Command (GFGA)

USAISC-SO ... United States Army Information Systems Command - South (GFGA)

USAISC-5th Sig Cmd ... United States Army Information Systems Command - 5th Signal Command (GFGA)

USAISC-7th Sig Cmd ... United States Army Information Systems Command - 7th Signal Command (GFGA)

USAISC-TRADOC ... United States Army Information Systems Command - Training and Doctrine Command (GFGA)

USAISC-WESTCOM ... United States Army Information Systems Command - Western Command (GFGA)

USAISD .... United States Army Intelligence School, Fort Devens (GFGA)

USAISESA ... United States Army Information Systems Engineering Support Activity [*Fort Huachuca, AZ*]

USAISMA ... United States Army Information Systems Management Activity (GFGA)

USAISR..... United States Army Institute of Surgical Research [*Ft. Sam Houston, TX*] (AABC)

USAISSAA ... United States Army Information Systems Selection and Acquisition Activity (GFGA)

USAISSSC ... United States Army Information Systems Software Support Command (GFGA)

USA-ITA... United States Association of Importers of Textiles and Apparel (EA)

USAITAC ... United States Army Intelligence and Threat Analysis Center (AABC)

USAITAD ... United States Army Intelligence Threat Analysis Detachment

USAITAG ... United States Army Intelligence Threat Analysis Group

USAITC .... United States Army Intelligence Training Center

USAITFG ... United States Army Intelligence Threats and Forecasts Group (AABC)

USAJAPA ... United States Amateur Jai Alai Players Association (EA)

USAJFKCENMA ... United States Army John Fitzgerald Kennedy Center for Military Assistance (AABC)

USAJFKCENSPWAR ... United States Army John Fitzgerald Kennedy Center for Special Warfare [*Airborne*] (AABC)

USAJFKSWCS ... US Army John F. Kennedy Special Warfare Center and School (RDA)

USAJHGSOWA ... United States Army Joint Household Goods Shipping Office of the Armed Forces

USAJSC ..... United States Army Joint Support Command (AABC)

USAKF...... USA Karate Federation (EA)

USA-KKA ... USA-Korean Karate Association (EA)

USAKORSCOM ... United States Army Korea Support Command (AABC)

US des AL ... Union Syndicale des Artistes Lyriques [*French*] (ROG)

US Al .... US Alcohol Testing of America, Inc. [*Associated Press abbreviation*] (APAG)

USALA...... United States Amateur Lacrosse Association

USALAPA ... United States Army Los Angeles Procurement Agency (AABC)

USALC ..... United States Army Logistics Center

US ALC..... US Alcohol Testing of America, Inc. [*Associated Press abbreviation*] (APAG)

USALCA ... United States Army Logistic Control Activity (AABC)

USALCJ.... United States Army Logistics Center, Japan (AABC)

USALDC... United States Army Logistics Data Center

USALDJ ... United States Army Logistics Depot, Japan

USALDRHRU ... United States Army Leadership Human Research Unit [*Presidio of Monterey, CA*] (AABC)

USALDSRA ... United States Army Logistics Doctrine, Systems and Readiness Agency [*New Cumberland Army Depot, Harrisburg, PA*] (AABC)

USALEA ... United States Army Logistics Evaluation Agency (AABC)

USALGPM ... United States Army Liaison Group, Project Michigan

USALMC.. United States Army Logistics Management Center [*Fort Lee, VA*]

USALOGC ... United States Army Logistics Center (AABC)

USALS...... United States Army Language School

USALSA ... United States Army Legal Services Agency (AABC)

USALWL.. United States Army Limited War Laboratory (AABC)

USAM .... Unified Space Applications Mission (MCD)

USAM .... Union des Syndicats Autonomes de Madagascar [*Federation of Malagasy Autonomous Unions*]

USAM .... Unique Sequential Access Method

USAM .... United States Army Mothers Organization, National (EA)

USAM .... United States Army Automated Mail Service [*Telecommunications*] (TSSD)

USAM .... US Attorney's Manual [*A publication*] (DLA)

USAMAA ... United States Army Memorial Affairs Agency (AABC)

USAMANRRDC ... United States Army Manpower Resources Research and Development Center (AABC)

USAMAPLA ... United States Army Military Assistance Program Logistics Agency

USAMAPS ... United States Army Military Academy Preparatory School

USAMARDA ... US Army Manpower Requirements and Documentation Agency

USAMB..... United States Army Maintenance Board (AABC)

USAMBRDL ... United States Army Medical Bioengineering Research and Development Laboratory [*Fort Detrick, MD*] [*Later, USABRDL*] (AABC)

USAMBRL ... United States Army Medical Biomechanical Research Laboratory [*Walter Reed Army Medical Center*] (AABC)

USAMC..... United States Army Materiel Command [*Alexandria, VA*]

USAMC..... United States Army Medical Corps

USAMC..... United States Army Missile Command [*Obsolete*]

USAMC..... United States Army Mobility Command [*Later, Troop Support Command*]

USAMC..... United States Army Munitions Command [*Later, Armaments Command*]

USAMCALMSA ... United States Army Materiel Command Automated Logistics Management Systems Agency (AABC)

USAMCC ... United States Army Metrology and Calibration Center (AABC)

USAMCFG ... United States Army Medical Center, Fort Gordon (AABC)

USAMCFO ... United States Army Materiel Command Field Office (RDA)

USAMCFSA ... United States Army Materiel Command Field Safety Agency (AABC)

USAMC-IRO ... United States Army Materiel Command Inventory Research Office

USAMCI & SA ... United States Army Materiel Command Installations and Service Agency (AABC)

USAMC-ITC ... United States Army Materiel Command Intern Training Center

USAMCLDC ... United States Army Materiel Command Logistics Data Center

USAMCLSSA ... United States Army Materiel Command Logistic Systems Support Agency (AABC)

USAMCSFO ... United States Army Materiel Command Surety Field Office

USAMD .... United States Army Missile Detachment (AABC)

USAMDAR ... United States Army Medical Depot Activity, Ryukyu Islands (AABC)

USAMDPC ... United States Army Maintenance Data Processing Center

USAMEAF ... United States Army Middle East Air Forces [*World War II*]

USAMEC ... United States Army Mobility Equipment Command [*Obsolete*]

USAMECOM ... United States Army Mobility Equipment Command [*Obsolete*] (AABC)

USAMEDCOMEUR ... United States Army Medical Command, Europe (AABC)

USAMEDDBD ... United States Army Medical Department Board (RDA)

USAMEDLAB ... United States Army Medical Laboratory

USAMEDS ... United States Army Medical Service

USAMEDSVS ... United States Army Medical Service Veterinary School (AABC)

USAMEDTC ... United States Army Medical Training Center [*Ft. Sam Houston, TX*] (AABC)

USAMEERU ... United States Army Medical Environmental Engineering Research Unit

USAMEOS ... United States Army Medical Equipment and Optical School (AABC)

USAMERCC ... United States Army Middle East Regional Communications Command

USAMERDC ... United States Army Mobility Equipment Research and Development Center (AABC)

USAMERDL ... United States Army Medical Equipment Research and Development Laboratory (AABC)

USAMETA ... United States Army Management Engineering Training Activity [*Rock Island, IL*] (AABC)

USAMFSS ... United States Army Medical Field Service School (AABC)

USAMGIK ... United States Army Military Government in Korea

USAMHRC ... United States Army Military History Research Collection (AABC)

USAMICOM ... United States Army Missile Command [*Obsolete*] (AABC)

USAMIDA ... United States Army Major Item Data Agency (AABC)

USAMIIA ... United States Army Medical Intelligence and Information Agency (AABC)

USAML..... United States Army Medical Laboratory (AABC)

USAMMA ... United States Army Medical Materiel Agency (AABC)

USAMMAE ... United States Army Materiel Management Agency, Europe

USAMMAPAC ... United States Army Medical Materiel Agency, Pacific (AABC)

USAMMC ... United States Army Maintenance Management Center (AABC)

USAMMCS ... United States Army Missile and Munitions Center School (AABC)

USA-MMDA ... US Army Medical Materiel Development Activity (RDA)

USAMMT ... United States Army Military Mail Terminal

USAMN .... United States Army Mothers, National (EA)

USAMOAMA ... United States Army Medical Optical and Maintenance Activity

USAMOCOM ... United States Army Mobility Command [*Later, Troop Support Command*]

USAMOMA ... United States Army Medical Optical and Maintenance Agency (AABC)

USAMP..... United States Army Maintenance Plant

USAMP..... United States Army Mine Planter

USAMP & CS/TCTFM ... United States Army Military Police and Chemical Schools/Training Center and Fort McClellan

USAMPHIBFOR ... United States Amphibious Forces (AABC)

USAMPS .. United States Army Military Police School (AABC)

USAMPTAO ... United States Army Military Personnel and Transportation Assistance Office (AABC)

USAMRAA ... United States Army Medical Research Acquisition Agency

USAMRDC ... United States Army Medical Research and Development Command [*Fort Detrick, MD*]

USAMRICD ... United States Army Medical Research Institute for Chemical Defense [*Aberdeen Proving Ground, MD*] (RDA)

USAMRIID ... United States Army Medical Research Institute of Infectious Diseases [*Fort Detrick, MD*] (AABC)

USAMRL ... United States Army Medical Research Laboratory [*Fort Knox, KY*] (AABC)

USAMRN ... United States Army Medical Research and Nutrition (MCD)

USAMRNL ... United States Army Medical Research and Nutrition Laboratory [*Denver, CO*] (AABC)

USAMRSA ... United States Army Material Readiness Support Activity

USAMRU ... United States Army Medical Research Unit [*Malaysia, Panama*] (AABC)

USAMRU-E ... United States Army Medical Research Unit - Europe (INF)

USAMS..... United States Army Management School

USAMSAA ... United States Army Materiel Systems Analysis Agency

USAMSMADHS ... United States Army Medical Service Meat and Dairy Hygiene School

USAMSSA ... United States Army Management Systems Support Agency
USAM & TTC ... United States Army Mechanical and Technical Training Center [*Also called MECHTECH*]
USAMTU ... United States Army Marksmanship Training Unit
USAMU .... United States Army Marksmanship Unit [*Fort Benning, GA*]
USAMU .... United States Army Medical Unit [*Frederick, MD*]
USAMUCOM ... United States Army Munitions Command [*Later, Armaments Command*]
USAMUFD ... United States Army Medical Unit, Fort Detrick [*Maryland*] (AABC)
USAMV .... United States Association of Museum Volunteers [*Later, AAMV*] (EA)
USAN .... United States Adopted Name
USANA ..... United States Army Nuclear Agency (AABC)
USANAFBA ... United States Army, Navy, and Air Force Bandsmen's Association [*Defunct*]
USANAVEUR ... United States Navy, Europe
USANC ..... United States Army Nurse Corps
USANCA... US Army Nuclear and Chemical Agency (RDA)
USANCG .. United States Army Nuclear Cratering Group (AABC)
USANCSG ... United States Army Nuclear and Chemical Surety Group [*Formerly, USANWSG*] (AABC)
USANDL... United States Army Nuclear Defense Laboratory (AABC)
USANF...... United States Auxiliary Naval Force
U San Fernando Valley L Rev ... University of San Fernando Valley. Law Review [*A publication*] (DLA)
U San Fernando VL Rev ... University of San Fernando Valley. Law Review [*A publication*] (DLA)
U San Francisco L Rev ... University of San Francisco. Law Review [*A publication*]
U San Fran LR ... University of San Francisco. Law Review [*A publication*]
U San Fran L Rev ... University of San Francisco. Law Review [*A publication*]
USANG ..... United States Army National Guard
USanGS..... Church of Jesus Christ of Latter-Day Saints, Genealogical Society Library, Santaquin Stake Branch, Santaquin, UT [*Library symbol*] [*Library of Congress*] (LCLS)
USANIBC ... United States Army Northern Ireland Base Command [*World War II*]
USANIF .... United States Army Northern Ireland Force [*World War II*]
USA-NLABS ... United States Army Natick Laboratories
USANP...... United South African National Party
USANWCG ... United States Army Nuclear Weapon Coordination Group
USANWSG ... United States Army Nuclear Weapon Surety Group [*Later, USANCSG*]
USANWTC ... United States Army Northern Warfare Training Center (AABC)
USAOAC .. United States Army Ordnance Ammunition Command [*Merged with Munitions Command, which later became Armaments Command*]
USAOCBRL ... United States Army Ordnance Corps Ballistic Research Laboratory
USAOCCCL ... United States Army Ordnance Corps Coating and Chemical Laboratory
USAOCCS ... United States Army Ordnance-Chemical Center and School
USAOCDPS ... United States Army Ordnance Corps Development and Proof Services
USAOC & S ... United States Army Ordnance Center and School [*Later, United States Army Ordnance and Chemical Center and School*] (AABC)
USAOD ..... United States Army Ordnance District
USAOEC... United States Army Officer Evaluation Center
USAOGMS ... United States Army Ordnance Guided Missile School
USAOMC ... United States Army Ordnance Missile Command [*Later, Missile Command*]
USAOMMCS ... United States Army Ordnance Missile and Munitions Center and School
USAOMSA ... United States Army Ordnance Missile Support Agency (AAG)
USAORDCORPS ... United States Army Ordnance Corps
USAORP... United States Army Oversea Research Program
USAORRF ... United States Army Ordnance Rocket Research Facility
USAOSA... United States Army Overseas Supply Agency (CINC)
USAOSANO ... United States Army Overseas Supply Agency, New Orleans
USAOSANY ... United States Army Overseas Supply Agency, New York
USAOSASF ... United States Army Overseas Supply Agency, San Francisco
USAOSREPLSTA ... United States Army Oversea Replacement Station
USAOSWAC ... United States Army Ordnance Special Weapons-Ammunition Command
USAOWC ... United States Army Ordnance Weapons Command [*Merged with Missile Command*]
USAP......... United States Antarctic Program [*National Science Foundation*]
US Ap .... United States Appeals Reports [*A publication*] (DLA)
USAP......... USA Petites [*An association*] (EA)
USAPA...... United States Army Photographic Agency [*Obsolete*]
USAPACDA ... United States Army Personnel and Administration Combat Developments Activity (AABC)
USAPAE ... United States Army Procurement Agency, Europe (AABC)
USAPATACE ... United States Army Publications and Training Aids Center, Europe
USAPAV ... United States Army Procurement Agency, Vietnam
USAPC...... United States Army Petroleum Center

USAPC...... United States Army Pictorial Center
USAPCC ... United States Army Personnel Coordination Center
USAPDA... United States Army Physical Disability Agency
USAPDC... United States Army Property Disposal Center [*Merged with Defense Logistics Services Center*]
USAPDCE ... United States Army Petroleum Distribution Command, Europe (AABC)
USAPDSC ... United States Army Personnel Data Support Center (AABC)
USAPDSK ... United States Army Petroleum Distribution System, Korea (AABC)
USAPEB ... United States Army Physical Evaluation Board (AABC)
USAPEQUA ... United States Army Productions Equipment Agency
USAPERSCEN ... United States Army Personnel Center
USAPG...... United States Army Participation Group (AABC)
USAPHC... United States Army Primary Helicopter Center (AABC)
USAPHS... United States Army Primary Helicopter School
USAPIA .... United States Army Personnel Information Activity (AABC)
USAPIC ... United States Army Photointerpretation Center
USAPO...... United States Antarctic Projects Office
USAPO...... USA Plowing Organization (EA)
USAPOP... United States Army Port Operations, Pusan (AABC)
US App ..... United States Appeals Reports [*A publication*] (DLA)
US App (DC) ... United States Court of Appeals Reports (District of Columbia) [*A publication*]
USAPRC ... United States Army Physical Review Council (AABC)
USAPRDC ... United States Army Polar Research and Development Center
USAPRO... United States Army Personnel Research Office
USAPSG ... United States Army Personnel Security Group (AABC)
USAPT ...... United States Army Parachute Team
USAPWA ... United Stone and Allied Products Workers of America [*Later, USWA*] (EA)
USAQMC ... United States Army Quartermaster Corps [*Merged with Supply and Maintenance Command*]
USAQMCDA ... United States Army Quartermaster Combat Developments Agency (SAA)
USAQMCENFL ... United States Army Quartermaster Center and Fort Lee (AABC)
USAQMS ... United States Army Quartermaster School
USAQMTC ... United States Army Quartermaster Training Command
USAR .... Uniform Systems of Accounts and Reports for Certified Air Carriers [*Civil Aeronautics Board*]
USAR .... United States Aeronautical Reserve
USAR .... United States Army Reserve
USARA ..... United States Air Racing Association [*Formerly, PRPA*] (EA)
USARA...... US Army Ranger Association (EA)
US-Arab Commer ... US-Arab Commerce [*A publication*]
USARACS ... United States Army Alaska Communications Center
USARADABD ... United States Army Air Defense Artillery Board [*Fort Bliss, TX*]
USARADBD ... United States Army Air Defense Board
USARADCOM ... United States Army Air Defense Command
USARADSCH ... United States Army Air Defense School
USARADSCH ... United States Army Research and Development School (AAG)
USARAE... United States Army Reserve Affairs, Europe (AABC)
USARAL... United States Army, Alaska
USARB...... United States Army Retraining Brigade (AABC)
USARBCO ... United States Army Base Command, Okinawa (AABC)
USARC...... United States Army Reserve Center (AABC)
USARCARIB ... United States Army, Caribbean
USARCC ... US Association of Roller Canary Culturists (EA)
USA-RCEC ... USA-Republic of China Economic Council (EA)
USARCEN ... United States Army Records Center
USARCENT ... United States Army Forces, Central Command
USARCPC ... United States Army Reserve Components Personnel Center (AABC)
USARCS ... United States Army Claims Service (AABC)
USARCSWIS ... United States Army Claims Service Worldwide Information System (GFGA)
USARctBad ... United States Army Recruiter Badge [*Military decoration*] (AABC)
USARDA... United States Army Regional Dental Activity (AABC)
USARDAISA ... United States Army Research, Development, and Acquisition Information Systems Agency (AABC)
USARDL... United States Army Research and Development Laboratories
USARDORAG ... United States Army Research and Development Operational Research Advisory Group (AABC)
USARDSG-GE ... United States Army Research, Development, and Standardization Group - Germany (RDA)
USARDSG-UK ... US Army Research, Development, and Standardization Group - United Kingdom (RDA)
USAREC... United States Army Recruiting Command (AABC)
USARECSTA ... United States Army Reception Station
USARENBD ... United States Army Armor and Engineer Board (RDA)
USAREPG ... United States Army Electronic Proving Ground
USAREREC ... United States Army Enlisted Records and Evaluation Center
USARET-RSGSTA ... United States Army Returnee - Reassignment Station
USAREUR ... United States Army, Europe
USAREURAGLO ... United States Army, Europe, Adjutant General Liaison Office (AABC)

USAREURCSTC ... United States Army, Europe, Combat Support Training Center (AABC)
USAREURORDCOM ... United States Army European Ordnance Command
USARF ...... United States Army Reserve Forces
USARFA ... United States of America Rugby Fives Association (EA)
USARFANT ... United States Army Forces, Antilles
USARFEO ... United States Army Frequency Engineering Office (MCD)
USARFT ... United States Army Forces, Taiwan
USARFU ... United States of America Rugby Football Union (EA)
US Argonne Nat Lab Biol Med Res Div Semiannu Rep ... United States. Argonne National Laboratory. Biological and Medical Research Division. Semiannual Report [*A publication*]
US Argonne Natl Lab Rep ... US Argonne National Laboratory. Report [*A publication*]
USARHAW ... United States Army, Hawaii
USARIA .... United States Army Rock Island Arsenal
USARIBSS ... United States Army Research Institute for the Behavioral and Social Sciences (AABC)
USARIEM ... United States Army Research Institute of Environmental Medicine [*Natick, MA*] (AABC)
USARIOS ... Association of Maritime Transport Users in the Central American Isthmus [*Guatemala*] (EAIO)
USARIS ..... United States Army Information School [*Fort Slocum, New Rochelle, NY*]
USARJ ...... United States Army, Japan
USARK ...... United States Army, Korea (MCD)
USARLANT ... United States Army Forces, Atlantic (AABC)
USARLT ... United States Army Reserve Losses Tally
USARMA ... United States Army Attache
USARMCOM ... United States Army Armament Command
US Armed Forces Food Container Inst Libr Bull ... United States. Armed Forces Food and Container Institute. Library Bulletin [*A publication*]
US Armed Forces Med J ... US Armed Forces. Medical Journal [*A publication*]
US Armed Forc Med J ... United States. Armed Forces Medical Journal [*A publication*]
USARMIS ... United States Army Mission
USARMLO ... United States Army Liaison Officer
USARMY ... Uncle Sam Ain't Released Me Yet
US Army Armament Res Dev Command Tech Rep ... US Army. Armament Research and Development Command. Technical Report [*A publication*]
US Army Behav Sci Res Lab Tech Res Note ... US Army. Behavioral Science Research Laboratory. Technical Research Note [*A publication*]
US Army Behav Syst Res Lab Tech Res Note ... United States. Army. Behavior and Systems Research Laboratory. Technical Research Note [*A publication*]
US Army Behav Syst Res Lab Tech Res Rep ... United States. Army. Behavior and Systems Research Laboratory. Technical Research Report [*A publication*]
US Army Coastal Eng Res Cent Misc Pap ... United States. Army. Coastal Engineering Research Center. Miscellaneous Paper [*A publication*]
US Army Coastal Eng Res Cent Tech Memo ... US Army. Coastal Engineering Research Center. Technical Memorandum [*A publication*]
US Army Corps Eng Cold Reg Res Eng Lab Res Rep ... United States. Army Corps of Engineers. Cold Regions Research and Engineering Laboratory [*Hanover, New Hampshire*]. Research Report [*A publication*]
US Army Corps Eng Cold Reg Res Eng Lab Tech Rep ... United States. Army Corps of Engineers. Cold Regions Research and Engineering Laboratory [*Hanover, New Hampshire*]. Technical Report [*A publication*]
US Army Corps of Engineers Comm Tidal Hydraulics Rept ... United States. Army Corps of Engineers. Committee on Tidal Hydraulics. Report [*A publication*]
US Army Corps Engineers Waterways Expt Sta Misc Paper ... United States. Army Corps of Engineers. Waterways Experiment Station. Miscellaneous Paper [*A publication*]
US Army Corps Engineers Waterways Expt Sta Tech Rept ... United States. Army Corps of Engineers. Waterways Experiment Station. Technical Report [*A publication*]
US Army Diamond Ord Fuze Lab Tech Rep ... US Army. Diamond Ordnance Fuze Laboratories. Technical Report [*A publication*]
US Army Diamond Ordnance Fuze Lab Tech Rep ... United States. Army. Diamond Ordnance Fuze Laboratories. Technical Report [*A publication*]
US Army Eng Waterw Exp Stn Tech Rep ... US Army Engineers. Waterways Experiment Station. Technical Report [*A publication*]
US Army Med Res Lab Rep ... United States. Army. Medical Research Laboratory. Report [*A publication*]
US Army Natick Lab Tech Rep Microbiol Ser ... US Army. Natick Laboratories. Technical Report. Microbiology Series [*A publication*]
USARO ..... United States Army Research Office
USA-ROCEC ... USA-Republic of China Economic Council [*Crystal Lake, IL*] (EA)
USAROD .. United States Army Research Office (Durham)
USAROTC ... United States Army Reserve Officer Training Corps

USAROTCR ... United States Army Reserve Officers' Training Corps Region (AABC)
USARP ...... US Antarctic Research Program (EA)
USARPA ... United States Army Publications Agency (GFGA)
USARPA ... United States Army Radio Propagation Agency (AABC)
USARPAC ... United States Army, Pacific
USARPACINTS ... United States Army Pacific Intelligence School (AABC)
USARPERCEN ... United States Army Reserve Personnel Center
USARR ...... United States Army Readiness Regions (AABC)
USARRACL ... United States Army Reserve Report Activity Control List
USARRADCOM ... United States Army Armament Research and Development Command (RDA)
USARRED ... United States Army Forces, Readiness Command
USARS ...... US Army Regimental System (INF)
USARS ...... User Selected and Required Schedule (SAA)
USARSA ... United States Amateur Roller Skating Association [*Later, USAC/RS*] (EA)
USARSA ... United States Army School of the Americas [*Fort Benning, AR*] (INF)
USARSCV ... United States Army Support Command, Vietnam [*Obsolete*]
USARSG ... United States Army Standardization Group
USARSO ... United States Army Forces, Southern Command
USARSO-PR ... United States Army Forces, Southern Command - Puerto Rico (AABC)
USARSOUTHCOM ... United States Army Forces, Southern Command
USARSSO ... United States Army Safeguard Systems Office
USARSTRIKE ... United States Army Forces Strike Command (AABC)
USARSUPTHAI ... United States Army Support, Thailand (AABC)
USART ...... Universal Synchronous/Asynchronous Receiver and Transmitter [*Data processing*]
USARTL ... United States Army Research and Technical Labs (MCD)
USARTLS ... United States Army Reserve Troop List by State
USARUCU ... United States Army Reserve Unit Commander Unit
USARV ...... United States Army, Vehicle (SAA)
USARV ...... United States Army Vietnam [*Obsolete*]
USARYIS ... United States Army, Ryukyu Islands
USAS .... United States Air Service
USAS .... United States Airspace System (NOAA)
USAS .... United States of America Standard (IEEE)
USAS .... United States Antarctic Service [*1939-41*] [*Navy*]
USAS .... UNIVAC Standard Airline System (HGAA)
USAS .... US Aquatic Sports (EA)
USAS .... USA Waste Services, Inc. [*NASDAQ symbol*] (NQ)
USASA ... United States Army Security Agency
USASAALA ... United States Army Security Assistance Agency, Latin America (AABC)
USASAC ... United States Army Security Assistance Center
USASAC ... US Army Security Affairs Command (RDA)
USASACDA ... United States Army Security Agency Combat Development Activity (AABC)
USASACDSA ... United States Army Security Agency Command Data Systems Activity (AABC)
USASADEA ... United States Army Signal Air Defense Engineering Agency [*Later, USAADEA*]
USASAE ... United States Army Security Agency, Europe (AABC)
USASAFLOG ... United States Army Safeguard Logistics Command
USASAFO ... United States Army Signal Avionics Field Office [*Later, USAAFO*]
USASAFS ... United States Army Security Agency Field Station
USASAFSCOM ... United States Army Safeguard System Command (AABC)
USASAPAC ... United States Army Security Agency, Pacific (AABC)
USASASA ... United States Army Security Agency Systems Activity (AABC)
USASASA ... United States Army Small Arms Systems Agency
USASASSA ... United States Army Security Agency Signal Security Activity (AABC)
USASATCOMA ... United States Army Satellite Communications Agency (AABC)
USASATC & S ... United States Army Security Agency Training Center and School (AABC)
USASATEC ... United States Army Security Agency Test and Evaluation Center (AABC)
USASATSA ... United States Army Signal Aviation Test Support Activity
USASC ...... United States Army Safety Center
USASC ...... United States Army Signal Corps [*Merged with Communications and Electronics Command*]
USASC ...... United States Army Subsistence Center
USASC ...... United States Army Support Center
USASCA ... United States Army Safeguard Communications Agency (RDA)
USASCAF ... United States Army Service Center for the Armed Forces (AABC)
USASCC ... United States Army Strategic Communications Command
USASC & FG ... United States Army Signal Center and Fort Gordon (AABC)
USASCH ... United States Army Support Command, Hawaii (AABC)
USASCHEUR ... United States Army School, Europe [*Obsolete*] (AABC)
USASCII ... United States of America Standard Code for Information Interchange
USASCOCR ... United States of America Standard Character Set for Optical Character Recognition [*Data processing*]
USASCR ... United States Army Support Center, Richmond (AABC)

USASCS.... United States Army Signal Center and School
USASCSA ... United States Army Signal Communications Security Agency
USASCSOCR ... United States of America Standard Character Set for Optical Character Recognition [*Data processing*]
USASCV ... United States Army Support Command, Vietnam [*Obsolete*]
USASD...... United States Army Student Detachment (AABC)
USASDC... United States Army Strategic Defense Command
USASEA ... United States Army Signal Engineering Agency
USASESA ... United States Army Signal Equipment Support Agency (MCD)
USASESS ... United States Army Southeastern Signal School (AABC)
USASETAF ... United States Army Southern European Task Force
USASEUR ... United States Army School, Europe [*Obsolete*]
USASEW .. US Department of Agriculture. Soil Conservation Service. SCS-TP [*A publication*]
USASEXC ... United States Armed Services Exploitation Center (AABC)
USASF ...... United States Army Special Forces (CINC)
USASFG ... United States Army Special Forces Group
USASFGV ... United States Army Special Forces Group, Vietnam
USASFV.... United States Army Special Forces, Vietnam [*Obsolete*]
USASG(Aus) ... United States Army Standardization Group (Australia)
USASG(Ca) ... United States Army Standardization Group (Canada) (AABC)
USASG(UK) ... United States Army Standardization Group (United Kingdom) (AABC)
USASGV ... United States Army Support Group, Vietnam [*Obsolete*]
USASI .... United States of America Standards Institute [*Formerly, ASA*] [*Later, ANSI*]
USASIGC ... United States Army Signal Corps [*Merged with Communications and Electronics Command*]
USASIGS ... United States Army Signal School (AABC)
USASIMSA ... United States Army Signal Materiel Support Agency [*Later, USAEMSA*]
USASIS..... United States Army Strategic Intelligence School
USASLE.... Uniform Securities Agent State Law Examination [*Investment term*]
USASMA .. United States Army Sergeant Major Academy (AABC)
USASMC .. United States Army Supply and Maintenance Command
USASMC .. US Army Sergeants Major Course (INF)
USASMCOM ... United States Army Supply and Maintenance Command (MUGU)
USASMSA ... United States Army Signal Materiel Support Agency [*Later, USAEMSA*]
USASMSG ... United States Army Signal Missile Support Group
USASOC... US Army Special Operations Command (INF)
USASOPAC ... United States Army Support Office, Pacific (AABC)
USASOS ... United States Army Services of Supply
USASPSAE ... United States Army Special Services Agency, Europe (AABC)
USASPTAP ... United States Army Support Activity, Philadelphia (AABC)
USASPTC ... United States Army Support Center (AABC)
USASPTCC ... United States Army Support Command, Chicago
USASPTCM ... United States Army Support Center, Memphis (AABC)
USASPTCP ... United States Army Support Center, Philadelphia (AABC)
USASPTCR ... United States Army Support Center, Richmond (AABC)
USASRDL ... United States Army Signal Research and Development Laboratory [*Later, USAERDL*]
USASRU... United States Army Surgical Research Unit (AABC)
USASSA.... United States Army Signal Supply Agency [*Later, USAEC*]
USASSAFMPO ... United States Army Signal Supply Agency, Fort Monmouth Procurement Office
USASSAMRO ... United States Army Signal Supply Agency, Midwestern Regional Office
USASSAUSAEPGPO ... United States Army Signal Supply Agency, United States Army Electronic Proving Ground Procurement Office
USASSAWPO ... United States Army Signal Supply Agency, Washington Procurement Office
USASSAWRO ... United States Army Signal Supply Agency, Western Regional Office
USASSC.... United States Army Signal School and Center
USASSC & FBH ... United States Army Soldier Support Center and Fort Benjamin Harrison (AABC)
USASSD ... United States Army Special Security Detachment
USASSG ... United States Army Special Security Group (AABC)
USASTAF ... United States Army Southern European Task Force
USASTAF ... United States Army Strategic Air Forces in the Pacific
USASTC ... United States Army Signal Training Center [*Fort Gordon, GA*]
USASTCFM ... United States Army Signal Training Command and Fort Monmouth
USASTRATCOM ... United States Army Strategic Communications Command [*Later, USACC*] (AABC)
USASTRATCOM-A ... United States Army Strategic Communications Command - Alaska (AABC)
USASTRATCOM-CONUS ... United States Army Strategic Communications Command - Continental United States (AABC)
USASTRATCOM-EUR ... United States Army Strategic Communications Command - Europe (AABC)
USASTRATCOM-PAC ... United States Army Strategic Communications Command - Pacific (AABC)
USASTRATCOM-SIGGP-T ... United States Army Strategic Communications Command Signal Group - Thailand (AABC)

USASTRATCOM-SO ... United States Army Strategic Communications Command - South (AABC)
USASTRATCOM-V ... United States Army Strategic Communications Command - Vietnam [*Obsolete*] (AABC)
USASUPCOM-CRB ... United States Army Support Command - Cam Ranh Bay [*Obsolete*] (AABC)
USASUPCOM-QN ... United States Army Support Command - Qui Nhon [*Obsolete*] (AABC)
USASUPCOM-SGN ... United States Army Support Command - Saigon [*Obsolete*] (AABC)
USASWCDA ... United States Army Special Warfare Combat Developments Agency (SAA)
USASWL .. United States Army Signals Warfare Laboratory
USASWS... United States Army Special Warfare School
USAT........ United States Army Transport
USATAC... United States Army Terrain Analysis Center (MCD)
USATAC... United States Army Training Center, Engineer [*Fort Leonard Wood, MO*]
USATACOM ... United States Army Tank-Automotive Command [*Obsolete*]
USATAFO ... United States Army Transportation Aviation Field Office
USATALS ... United States Army Transportation and Aviation Logistics Schools (GFGA)
USATATSA ... United States Army Transportation Aircraft Test and Support Activity
USATA(WH) ... United States Army Transportation Agency (White House) (AABC)
USATB...... United States Army Training Board
USATC...... United States Army Air Target Chart
USATC...... United States Army Topographic Command
USATC...... United States Army Training Center
USATC...... United States Army Transportation Center and School
USATC...... United States Assault Training Center [*World War II*]
USATCA ... United States Army Terminal Command, Atlantic
USATCAD ... United States Army Training Center, Air Defense
USATCARMOR ... United States Army Training Center, Armor [*Fort Knox, KY*]
USATCBASIC ... United States Army Training Center, Basic
USATCD... United States Army Training Center, Air Defense
USATCEFLW ... United States Army Training Center, Engineer, Fort Leonard Wood [*Missouri*] (AABC)
USATCENGR ... United States Army Training Center, Engineer
USATCEUR ... United States Army Terminal Command, Europe (AABC)
USATC FA ... United States Army Training Center, Field Artillery [*Fort Sill, OK*] (AABC)
USATCFE ... United States Army Transportation Center and Fort Eustis (AABC)
USATCFLW ... United States Army Training Center and Fort Leonard Wood (AABC)
USATCG... United States Army Terminal Command, Gulf (AABC)
USATCINF ... United States Army Training Center, Infantry
USATCO... Universal Satellite Corp. [*New York, NY*] [*Telecommunications*] (TSSD)
USATCO... US Air Traffic Controllers Organization [*Defunct*] (EA)
USATCP... United States Army Terminal Command, Pacific
USATCRTSA ... United States Army Transportation Corps Road Test Support Activity
USATDA... United States Army Training Device Agency
USATDGL ... United States Army Terminal Detachment, Great Lakes (AABC)
USATEA ... United States Army Transportation Engineering Agency (AABC)
USATEC ... United States Army Test and Evaluation Command [*Obsolete*]
USATECOM ... United States Army Test and Evaluation Command [*Obsolete*]
USATHAMA ... United States Army Toxic and Hazardous Materials Agency (RDA)
USATIA .... United States Army Transportation Intelligence Agency
USATL...... United States Army Technical Library (DIT)
USATLA ... USA Toy Library Association (EA)
USATMACE ... United States Army Traffic Management Agency, Central Europe (AABC)
USATMC ... United States Army Transportation Materiel Command
USATMC ... United States Army Troop Medical Clinic (AABC)
US Atom Energy Commn Pub ... US Atomic Energy Commission. Publication [*A publication*]
US Atomic Energy Comm Map Prelim Map ... United States. Atomic Energy Commission. Map. Preliminary Map [*A publication*]
US Atomic Energy Comm Rept ... US Atomic Energy Commission. Report [*A publication*]
USATOPOCOM ... United States Army Topographic Command (AABC)
USATOWA ... United States Army Amateur Tug of War Association (EA)
USATRADOC ... United States Army Training and Doctrine Command
USATRASANA ... United States Army TRADOC Systems Analysis Activity (AABC)
USATRC... United States Army Transportation Research Command
USATRECOM ... United States Army Transportation Research and Engineering Command
USATREOG ... United States Army Transportation Environmental Operations Group (AABC)
USATRFSTA ... United States Army Transfer Station

USATRML ... United States Army Tropical Research Medical Laboratory
USATROSCOM ... United States Army Troop Support Command
USATSA ... United States Army Technical Support Activity (AABC)
USATSARCOM ... United States Army Troop Support and Aviation Materiel Readiness Command [*St. Louis, MO*]
USATSC ... United States Army Terrestrial Sciences Center (AABC)
USATSC ... United States Army Training Support Center
USATSCH ... United States Army Transportation School
USATSG ... United States Army, the Surgeon General
USATSG ... United States Army TMDE [*Test, Measurement, and Diagnostic Equipment*] Support Group
USATT ... Union des Syndicats Autonomes des Travailleurs Tchadiens [*Federation of Autonomous Workers Unions of Chad*]
USATTAY ... United States Army Transportation Test Activity, Yuma [*Arizona*] (AABC)
USATTB ... United States Army Transportation Terminal, Brooklyn
USATTC ... United States Army Transportation Training Command
USATTC ... United States Army Tropic Test Center (AABC)
USATTCA ... United States Army Transportation Terminal Command, Atlantic
USATTCARC ... United States Army Transportation Terminal Command, Arctic
USATTCG ... United States Army Transportation Terminal Command, Gulf
USATTCP ... United States Army Transportation Terminal Command, Pacific
USATTU ... United States Army Transportation Terminal Unit (AABC)
USATUC ... United States Army Terminal Unit, Canaveral (AABC)
USAUD3 ... US Air Force Academy. Technical Report [*A publication*]
US Auto Ind ... Structural Change in the United States Automobile Industry [*A publication*]
USAV ... United Savings Life Insurance [*NASDAQ symbol*] (NQ)
US Av ... United States Aviation Reports [*A publication*] (DLA)
USAVA ... USA Victory Alliance (EA)
USAVETS ... United States Army Veterinary School
US Aviation Rep ... United States Aviation Reports [*A publication*] (DLA)
US Avi Rep ... United States Aviation Reports [*A publication*] (DLA)
US Av R ... United States Aviation Reports [*A publication*] (DLA)
USAW ... Underwater Security Advance Warnings [*Navy*]
USAWC ... United States Army War College
USAWC ... United States Army Weapons Command [*Later, Armaments Command*]
USAWECOM ... United States Army Weapons Command [*Later, Armaments Command*] (AABC)
USAWES ... United States Army Waterways Experiment Station (AABC)
USAWF ... United States Amateur Wrestling Foundation (EA)
USAWOA ... United States Army Warrant Officers Association (EA)
USB ... Unified S-Band (MCD)
USB ... United Society of Brushmakers [*A union*] [*British*]
USB ... United States Banker [*A publication*]
USB ... United States Bases [*British*] [*World War II*]
USB ... Universal Serials and Book Exchange, Inc. [*ACCORD*] [*UTLAS symbol*]
USB ... Upflow Sludge Blanket [*Reactor, wastewater treatment*]
USB ... Upper Sideband
USB ... Upper Surface Blown [*Jet flap*] [*Aviation*]
USB ... US Bass (EA)
USB ... Uspechi Sovremennoj Biologii [*A publication*]
USBA ... Union Syndicale des Bases Americaines [*Union of American Base Workers*] [*Morocco*]
USBA ... United Savings Bank [*Salem, OR*] [*NASDAQ symbol*] (NQ)
USBA ... United States Badminton Association (EA)
USBA ... United States Bartenders Association (EA)
USBA ... United States Boardsailing Association (EA)
USBA ... United States Brewers Association [*Defunct*] (EA)
USBA ... US Base Association (EA)
USBA ... US Biathlon Association (EA)
USBA ... US Boomerang Association (EA)
US Banker ... United States Banker [*A publication*]
USBATU ... United States - Brazil Aviation Training Unit
USBBC ... United States Beef Breeds Council (EA)
USBBS ... United States Bureau of Biological Survey [*Terminated, 1940; later, Fish and Wildlife Service*]
USBBY ... US Board on Books for Young People (EA)
USBC ... United States Bureau of the Census (OICC)
USBC ... US Bancorp [*NASDAQ symbol*] (NQ)
USBCA ... United States Braille Chess Association (EA)
USBCC ... United States Border Collie Club (EA)
USBCJ ... US Business Committee on Jamaica [*New York, NY*] (EA)
USBE ... Unified S-Band Equipment
USBE ... United States Book Exchange (SAA)
USBE ... Universal Serials and Book Exchange, Inc. [*Acronym now used as official name of association*] (EA)
US Beach Erosion Board Bull Tech Memo Tech Rept ... United States. Beach Erosion Board. Bulletin. Technical Memorandum. Technical Report [*A publication*]
USBEP ... United States Bureau of Engraving and Printing
USBER ... United States Mission, Berlin
USBF ... United States Baseball Federation (EA)
USBF ... United States Bocce Federation (EA)
USBF ... United States Brewers Foundation [*Later, USBA*]
USBF ... United States Bureau of Fisheries [*Terminated*]

USBF ... US Bobsled and Skeleton Federation (EA)
USBFA ... US Bass Fishing Association [*Later, USB*] (EA)
USBFDC ... United States Bureau of Foreign and Domestic Commerce
USBG ... United States Bartenders Guild [*Later, USBA*] (EA)
USBG ... United States Botanic Garden
USBGA ... United States Blind Golfer's Association (EA)
USBGN ... United States Bureau on Geographical Names [*Terminated, 1947; later, Board on Geographical Names*]
USBIA ... United States Bowling Instructors Association (EA)
USBIA ... United States Bureau of Insular Affairs
USBIA ... Uspekhi Sovremennoi Biologii [*A publication*]
USBIC ... United States Business and Industrial Council [*Washington, DC*] (EA)
US BIOSCI ... US Bioscience, Inc. [*Associated Press abbreviation*] (APAG)
USBISS ... United Society of Boilermakers and Iron and Steel Shipbuilders [*A union*] [*British*]
USBJA ... United States Barrel Jumping Association (EA)
USBK ... United Savings Bank [*Vienna, VA*] [*NASDAQ symbol*] (NQ)
US BKNT ... US Banknote Corp. [*Associated Press abbreviation*] (APAG)
USBL ... United States Bureau of Lighthouses
USBL ... Usable (FAAC)
USBLM ... United States Bureau of Land Management [*Department of the Interior*]
USBLS ... United States Bureau of Labor Statistics
USBM ... United States Bureau of Mines [*Department of the Interior*]
USBMG ... United States Berlin Mission in Germany
USBN ... United States Bureau of Navigation
USBNP ... United States Bureau of Navy Personnel [*Terminated*]
USBP ... United States Border Patrol [*Department of the Treasury*]
USBP ... USBANCORP, Inc. [*NASDAQ symbol*] (NQ)
USBPA ... United States Bicycle Polo Association (EA)
USBPR ... United States Bureau of Public Roads
USBR ... United States Bureau of Reclamation [*Department of the Interior*] [*See also BOR*]
USBRO ... United States Base Requirements Overseas [*Military*] (AABC)
USBS ... Unified S-Band System [*Radio*]
USBS ... United States Bureau of Standards
USBSA ... United States Beet Sugar Association (EA)
USBSA ... United States Boardsailing Association (EA)
USBSF ... US Bobsled and Skeleton Federation (EA)
USBSSW ... United Society of Boilermakers, Shipbuilders, and Structural Workers [*A union*] [*British*]
USBTA ... United States Board of Tax Appeals [*Later, the Tax Court of the United States*]
USBTC ... University-Small Business Technology Consortium (EA)
USBTC ... US Battery Trade Council
US Bur Am Ethnology Bull ... US Bureau of American Ethnology. Bulletin [*A publication*]
US Bur Commer Fish Rep Cal Year ... US Bureau of Commercial Fisheries. Report for the Calendar Year [*A publication*]
US Bureau Sport Fish Wildl Invest Fish Control ... US Bureau of Sport Fisheries and Wildlife. Investigations in Fish Control [*A publication*]
USBurEducBul ... United States. Bureau of Education. Bulletins [*A publication*]
USBurEducCirc ... United States. Bureau of Education. Circulars [*A publication*]
US Bur Mines Bull ... United States. Bureau of Mines. Bulletin [*A publication*]
US Bur Mines Inf Circ ... US Bureau of Mines. Information Circular [*A publication*]
US Bur Mines Inform Circ ... United States. Bureau of Mines. Information Circular [*A publication*]
US Bur Mines Miner Yearb ... United States. Bureau of Mines. Minerals Yearbook [*A publication*]
US Bur Mines New Publ ... United States. Bureau of Mines. New Publications Monthly List [*A publication*]
US Bur Mines Rep Invest ... United States. Bureau of Mines. Report of Investigations [*A publication*]
US Bur Mines Rept Inv ... US Bureau of Mines. Report of Investigations [*A publication*]
US Bur Mines Tech Pa ... United States. Bureau of Mines. Technical Paper [*A publication*]
US Bur Mines Tech Prog Rep ... United States. Bureau of Mines. Technical Progress Report [*A publication*]
US Bur Reclam Div Des Dams Br Rep ... United States. Department of the Interior. Bureau of Reclamation. Division of Design [*Denver, Colorado*]. Dams Branch Report [*A publication*]
US Bur Reclam Eng Monogr ... United States. Department of the Interior. Bureau of Reclamation. Engineering Monographs [*A publication*]
US Bur Reclam Res Rep ... United States. Department of the Interior. Bureau of Reclamation. Research Report [*A publication*]
US Bur Reclam Tech Rec Des Constr ... United States. Department of the Interior. Bureau of Reclamation. Technical Record of Design and Construction. Dams and Powerplants [*A publication*]
US Bur Soils B ... US Bureau of Soils. Bulletin [*A publication*]
US Bur Sport Fish Wildl Invest Fish Control ... United States. Bureau of Sport Fisheries and Wildlife. Investigations in Fish Control [*A publication*]

US Bur Sport Fish Wildl Resour Publ ... United States. Bureau of Sport Fisheries and Wildlife. Resource Publication [*A publication*]
US Bur Sport Fish Wildl Res Rep ... US Bureau of Sport Fisheries and Wildlife. Research Report [*A publication*]
US Bur Sport Fish Wildl Tech Pap ... US Bureau of Sport Fisheries and Wildlife. Technical Papers [*A publication*]
USBWA ..... United States Basketball Writers Association   (EA)
USC .... Ultrasonic Storage Cell
USC .... Under Secretaries Committee
USC .... Under Separate Cover
USC .... Union of Sephardic Congregations   (EA)
USC .... Union Sociale Camerounaise [*Cameroonese Social Union*]
USC .... Unitarian Service Committee [*Later, UUSC*] [*Post-World War II*]
USC .... United Satellite Communications [*Cable TV programming service*]
USC .... United Service Club [*Charter jet service to Europe for servicemen and dependents*]
USC .... United Sisters of Charity   (EA)
USC .... United Somali Congress [*Political party*]   (EY)
USC .... United States Catalog [*A bibliographic publication*]
USC .... United States Citizen
USC .... United States Code [*Legal term*]
USC .... United States of Colombia
USC .... United States Congress
USC .... United States Custom Service, Washington, DC [*OCLC symbol*]   (OCLC)
USC .... United States Customs
USC .... United Strasser Club
USC .... United Survival Clubs   (EA)
USC .... Universal Specimen Chamber
USC .... University of Santa Clara [*California*]
USC .... University Scholarships of Canada
USC .... University of South Carolina [*Columbia, SC*]
USC ... University of Southern California [*Los Angeles*] [*Seismograph station code, US Geological Survey*]   (SEIS)
USC .... University of Southern California [*Los Angeles, CA*]
USC .... University Statistics Center [*New Mexico State University*] [*Research center*]   (RCD)
USC .... Up Stage Center [*Away from audience*] [*A stage direction*]
USC .... User Service Center   (MCD)
USC .... User Support Center   (MCD)
USC .... USLICO Corp. [*NYSE symbol*]   (SPSG)
USCA .... Under Secretary for Civil Aviation
USCA .... Uniformed Services Contingency Act
USCA .... United Sidecar Association   (EA)
USCA .... United States Canoe Association   (EA)
USCA .... United States Code Annotated [*Law*] [*Based on official USC*]
USCA .... United States Copper Association [*Later, American Bureau of Metal Statistics*]   (EA)
USCA .... United States Courts of Appeals
USCA .... United States Croquet Association   (EA)
USCA .... United States Curling Association   (EA)
USCA .... US Canola Association   (EA)
USCAA ...... United States Corporate Athletics Association   (EA)
USCA App ... United States Code, Annotated, Appendix [*A publication*]   (DLA)
USCAB ...... United States Congressional Advisory Board   (EA)
USCAC ...... United States Continental Army Command [*Superseded by FORSCOM*]
USCAD ..... University of Southern California. Abstracts of Dissertations [*A publication*]
USCAL ...... University of Southern California, Aeronautical Laboratory   (MCD)
US Cal Sch L Tax Inst ... University of Southern California School of Law Tax Institute   (DLA)
USCAM ..... United States Civil Aviation Mission   (AFM)
US & Can Av ... United States and Canadian Aviation Reports [*A publication*]
USCANS ... Unified S-Band Communication and Navigation System [*NASA*]
USCANW ... US Committee Against Nuclear War   (EA)
USCAPP ... Advanced Professional Programs, University of Southern California Law Center   (DLA)
USC App ... United States Code Appendix [*A publication*]   (DLA)
USCAR ..... United States Civil Administration, Ryukyu Islands
USCAR ...... United States Council for Automotive Research [*General Motors, Ford, and Chrysler*]   (ECON)
US Cath ..... United States Catholic [*A publication*]
US Cath Hist Rec ... US Catholic Historical Society. Historical Records and Studies [*A publication*]
US Cath M ... United States Catholic Magazine [*A publication*]
US Cath S ... United States Catholic Historical Society. Historical Records and Studies [*A publication*]
US & C Avi Rep ... United States and Canadian Aviation Reports [*A publication*]
US & C Av R ... United States and Canadian Aviation Reports [*A publication*]
USCB .... United Saudi Commercial Bank
USCB .... United States Customs Bonded
USCBC ...... US-China Business Council   (EA)

USCBRA ... United States CB Radio Association   (EA)
USCC .... Union des Syndicats Croyants du Cameroun [*Federation of Cameroonese Believers' Unions*]
USCC .... United Society of Cork Cutters [*A union*] [*British*]
USCC .... United States Calorimetry Conference
USCC .... United States Camaro Club   (EA)
USCC .... United States Catholic Conference   (EA)
USCC .... United States Cellular Corp. [*Park Ridge, IL*] [*Telecommunications*]   (TSSD)
USCC ...... United States Chamber of Commerce
USCC .... United States Circuit Court
USCC .... United States Citizens' Congress [*Defunct*]
USCC .... United States Commerical Co. [*World War II*]
USCC .... United States Cotton Commission
USCC .... United States Court of Claims [*Abolished, 1982*]
USCC .... United States Criminal Code
USCC .... United States Criminal Court
USCC .... United States Customs Court [*Later, United States Court of International Trade*]
USCC .... United Student Christian Council in United States
USCC .... US Cancellation Club   (EA)
USCC .... US Capital Corp. [*NASDAQ symbol*]   (NQ)
USCCA ...... United States Circuit Court of Appeals
USCCA ...... United States Circuit Court of Appeals Reports [*A publication*]   (DLA)
USCCCA ... United States Cross Country Coaches Association   (EA)
USCCEC ... United States Committee for Care of European Children [*Post-World War II*]
USCCHO .. United States Conference of City Health Officers   (EA)
USCCHSO ... United States Conference of City Human Service Officials   (EA)
USCCPA ... United States Court of Customs and Patent Appeals [*Abolished, 1982*]
USCCSA ... US Corporate Council on South Africa   (EA)
USCDC ...... United States Civil Defense Council   (EA)
USCEA ...... US Council for Energy Awareness   (EA)
USCEC ...... University of Southern California, Engineering Center   (MCD)
USCEF ...... US-China Education Foundation   (EA)
USCEFI ..... United Social, Cultural, and Educational Foundation of India
USCEI .... United States - China Educational Institute   (EA)
US CELL ... US Cellular Corp. [*Associated Press abbreviation*]   (APAG)
US Cem Frct ... United States Cement Consumption Forecast 1981-86. Market and Economic Research [*A publication*]
USCE/NPD ... United States Army, Corps of Engineers, North Pacific Division   (NOAA)
USCENTAF ... United States Central Command - Air Forces
USCENTCOM ... United States Central Command
US Cert Den ... Certiorari Denied by United States Supreme Court [*Legal term*]   (DLA)
US Cert Dis ... Certiorari Dismissed by United States Supreme Court [*Legal term*]   (DLA)
USCESS .... US Cultural Exchange and Sports Society   (EA)
USCF .... United States Chess Federation   (EA)
USCF .... United States Churchill Foundation [*Later, WCF*]
USCF .... United States Cycling Federation   (EA)
USCFSTI AD Rep ... United States. Clearinghouse for Federal Scientific and Technical Information. AD Reports [*A publication*]
USCFSTI PB Rep ... United States. Clearinghouse for Federal Scientific and Technical Information. PB Report [*A publication*]
USC & G .... United States Coast and Geodetic Survey [*Later, National Ocean Survey*]   (MUGU)
USCG .... United States Coast Guard
USCG .... United States Consul General
USCGA ...... United States Coast Guard Academy [*New London, CT*]
USCGA ...... United States Coast Guard Auxiliary
USCGAD .... United States Coast Guard Air Detachment
USC-GARP ... United States Committee for the Global Atmospheric Research Program [*Defunct*]   (EA)
USCGAS ... United States Coast Guard Air Station
USCGASB ... United States Coast Guard Aircraft and Supply Base
USCGAUX ... United States Coast Guard Auxiliary   (EA)
USCGB ...... United States Coast Guard Base
USCG-B .... United States Coast Guard Office of Boating Safety
USCGB ...... Uphill Ski Club of Great Britain   (EAIO)
USCGC ...... United States Coast Guard Cutter
USCG-C .... United States Coast Guard Office of Chief of Staff
USCGD ...... United States Coast Guard Depot
USCG-E .... United States Coast Guard Naval Engineering Division
USCG-M ... United States Coast Guard Office of Merchant Marine Safety
USCG-MFSRS ... United States Coast Guard Marine Fire and Safety Research Staff [*Groton, CT*]
USCG-N .... United States Coast Guard Office of Navigation
USC Govt'l Rev ... University of South Carolina. Governmental Review [*A publication*]   (DLA)
USCGR ...... United States Coast Guard Reserve
USCGRC ... United States Coast Guard Receiving Center
USCGR(T) ... United States Coast Guard, Reserve (Temporary)
USCGR(W) ... United States Coast Guard, Reserve (Women)
USC & GS ... United States Coast and Geodetic Survey [*Later, National Ocean Survey*]

USCGS...... United States Coast and Geodetic Survey [*Later, National Ocean Survey*]
USCGSCF ... United States Coast Guard Shore Communication Facilities
USCGTS ... United States Coast Guard Training Station
USCH........ University of South Carolina Herbarium
US Chil Bur Pub ... United States. Children's Bureau. Publications [*A publication*]
US China Bus R ... US-China Business Review [*Washington, DC*] [*A publication*]
USCHRB... US Council for Human Rights in the Balkans   (EA)
USCHS...... United States Capitol Historical Society   (EA)
USCHS...... US Catholic Historical Society   (EA)
USCI.......... United Satellite Communications Inc.
USCIA....... United States Customs Inspectors' Association Port of New York   (EA)
USCIAA .... United States Committee of the International Association of Art   (EA)
USCIB....... United States Communications Intelligence Board [*Later, National Security Agency*]
USCIB....... United States Council on International Banking   (EA)
USCIB....... United States Council for International Business   (EA)
USCIB/IC ... United States Communications Intelligence Board Intelligence Committee [*Obsolete*]
USCICC .... United States Council of the International Chamber of Commerce [*Later, USCIB*]   (EA)
USCICSW ... United States Committee of the International Council on Social Welfare   (EA)
USCID....... US Committee on Irrigation and Drainage   (EA)
USCIDFC ... US Committee on Irrigation, Drainage, and Flood Control [*Later, USCID*]   (EA)
USCIIC...... United States Civilian Internee Information Center [*Army*]   (AABC)
USCIIC(Br) ... United States Civilian Internee Information Center (Branch) [*Army*]   (AABC)
USCINCAFRED ... United States Commander-in-Chief, Air Force Forces, Readiness Command
USCINCARRED ... United States Commander-in-Chief, Army Forces, Readiness Command
USCINCCENT ... Commander-in-Chief, United States Central Command
USCINCEUR ... United States Commander-in-Chief, Europe
USCINCLANT ... Commander-in-Chief, United States Atlantic Command
USCINCMEAFSA ... United States Commander-in-Chief Middle East, Africa South of the Sahara, and Southern Asia   (GFGA)
USCINCPAC ... Commander-in-Chief, United States Pacific Command
USCINCRED ... United States Commander-in-Chief, Readiness Command
USCINCREDCOM ... Commander-in-Chief, US Readiness Command   (MCD)
USCINCSO ... United States Commander-in-Chief, Southern Command   (AFM)
USCINCSOUTH ... United States Commander-in-Chief, Southern Command
US Cir Ct Rep DC ... Hayward and Hazelton's United States Circuit Court Reports [*District of Columbia*] [*A publication*]   (DLA)
USCISCO ... United States Counterinsurgency Support Office
USCJ .... United Society of Carpenters and Joiners [*A union*] [*British*]
USCJE....... United Synagogue Commission on Jewish Education [*Later, USACJE*]   (EA)
USCL........ United Society for Christian Literature [*British*]
USCL........ United States Coalition for Life   (EA)
USCLA...... United States Club Lacrosse Association   (EA)
USCLHO .. United States Conference of Local Health Officers   (EA)
USCM .... Unit Simulated Combat Mission   (AAG)
USCM .... United States Conference of Mayors   (EA)
USCM .... Usibelli Coal Miner [*Usibelli, AK*] [*A publication*]
USCMA..... United States Catholic Mission Association   (EA)
USCMA..... United States Cheese Makers Association   (EA)
USCMA..... United States Court of Military Appeals   (EA)
USCMA..... United States Crutch Manufacturers Association   (EA)
USCMA Adv Op ... United States Court of Military Appeals, Advance Opinions [*A publication*]   (DLA)
USCMC..... United States Catholic Mission Council   (EA)
USCMH.... United States Commission of Maritime History   (MSC)
USCMI...... United States Commission on Mathematical Instruction
USCO .... United States Committee for the Oceans   (EA)
USCO .... US Commercial Office [*Department of Commerce, Department of State*]   (IMH)
USCOA ..... Uniformed Services Contingency Option Act
US Coast and Geod Survey Pub ... US Coast and Geodetic Survey. Publication [*A publication*]
US Coast Geod Surv Magnetograms Hourly Values MHV ... US Department of Commerce. Coast and Geodetic Survey. Magnetograms and Hourly Values MHV [*A publication*]
USCOB...... United States Commander, Berlin
US Code Cong & Ad News ... United States Code Congressional and Administrative News [*A publication*]   (DLA)
USCOLD... United States Committee on Large Dams of the International Commission on Large Dams   (EA)
USCOMEAST ... United States Commander, Eastern Atlantic   (MCD)
USCOMEASTLANT ... United States Commander, Naval Forces, Eastern Atlantic   (NATG)
US Comp St ... United States Compiled Statutes [*A publication*]   (DLA)

USCOMSUBGRUEASTLANT ... United States Commander, Submarines Group, Eastern Atlantic   (NATG)
USCONARC ... United States Continental Army Command [*Superseded by FORSCOM*]
US Cond Rep ... Peters' Condensed United States Reports [*A publication*]   (DLA)
US Const.... United States Constitution [*A publication*]   (DLA)
US Consum Marketing Serv C & MS ... US Consumer and Marketing Service. C & MS [*A publication*]
USCP........ United States Capitol Police
USCPAA ... United States Cerebral Palsy Athletic Association   (EA)
USCPFA.... US-China Peoples Friendship Association   (EA)
USCPSHHM ... United States Committee to Promote Studies of the History of the Habsburg Monarchy [*Later, SAHH*]   (EA)
USCR........ United States Committee for Refugees   (EA)
USCR........ US Census Report [*Database*] [*Business Publishers, Inc.*] [*Information service or system*]   (CRD)
USCRA...... United States Citizens' Rights Association   (EA)
USCS........ United States Coast Survey
USCS........ United States Code Service [*A publication*]   (DLA)
USCS........ United States Commercial Standard
USCS........ United States Conciliation Service [*Functions transferred to Federal Mediation and Conciliation Service, 1947*]
USCS........ United States Customary System [*System of units used in the US*]
USCS........ United States Customs Service   (MCD)
USCS........ Universal Ship Cancellation Society   (EA)
USCS........ Urine Sampling and Collection System [*NASA*]
USCS........ US Commercial Service [*International Trade Administration*]
USCSB ..... United States Communications Security Board
USCSC...... United States Chefs Ski Club   (EA)
USCSC...... United States Civil Service Commission [*Later, MSPB*]
USCSC...... United States Collegiate Sports Council   (EA)
USCSC...... United States Cuban Sugar Council [*Defunct*]   (EA)
USC/SCC ... Studies in Comparative Communism. University of Southern California [*A publication*]
USCSCV ... US Committee for Scientific Cooperation with Vietnam   (EA)
USCSE ...... United States Civil Service Examination
USC-SFI... United States Committee-Sports for Israel   (EA)
USCSRA ... United States Cane Sugar Refiners' Association   (EA)
USCSSB.... United States Cap Screw Service Bureau [*Later, Cap Screw and Special Threaded Products Bureau*]   (EA)
USCT........ Union des Syndicats Confederes du Togo [*Federation of Confederated Unions of Togo*]
USCT........ United States Colored Troops [*Civil War*]
USCTA...... United States Combined Training Association   (EA)
US Ct Cl ... United States Court of Claims   (DLA)
US-CUES ... US Campaign for the University of El Salvador   (EA)
USCUN ..... United States Committee for the United Nations [*Later, UNA-USA*]
USCV........ Union Scientifique Continentale de Verre [*European Union for the Scientific Study of Glass - EUSSG*]   (EAIO)
USCWC..... United States Chemical Warfare Committee
USCWCC.. United States Conference for the World Council of Churches   (EA)
USCWF..... US Council for World Freedom   (EA)
USC-WHO ... United States Committee for the World Health Organization   (EA)
USD .... Ultimate Strength Design   (IEEE)
USD .... Ultrasonic Separation Detector
USD .... Under Seas Defense Exposition   (ITD)
USD .... Uniao Social Democratico [*Social Democratic Union*] [*Portugal*] [*Political party*]   (PPE)
USD .... Unified School District
USD .... Union Social-Democrate [*Social Democratic Union*] [*The Ivory Coast*] [*Political party*]   (EY)
USD .... Union Sociale Democratique [*Cameroon*] [*Political party*]   (EY)
USD .... Union des Sociaux-Democrates [*Burkina Faso*] [*Political party*]   (EY)
USD .... United Society of Drillers [*A union*] [*British*]
USD .... United States Dispensatory [*Pharmacology*]
USD .... United States Diving, Inc.   (EA)
USD .... United States Dollars
USD .... United States Drone   (SAA)
USD .... Universal Standard Data
USD .... University of San Diego
USD .... University Science Development [*National Science Foundation*]
USD .... University of South Dakota, Vermillion, SD [*OCLC symbol*]   (OCLC)
USD .... Uranium Series Dating
USD .... Urban Sanitary District [*British*]
USD .... User-Supplied Data
USDA .... Uniform Simultaneous Death Act [*National Conference of Commissioners on Uniform State Laws*]
USDA .... United Square Dancers of America   (EA)
USDA .... United States Department of Agriculture [*Washington, DC*] [*Database originator*]
USDA .... United States Disarmament Administration [*Transferred to US Arms Control and Disarmament Agency, 1961*]

USDA .... United States Duffers' Association (EA)
USDA .... US Darting Association (EA)
USDA .... US Disc Sports Association (EA)
USDA Agr Econ Rep ... US Department of Agriculture. Agricultural Economic Report [*A publication*]
USDA Agr Handb ... United States. Department of Agriculture. Agricultural Handbook [*A publication*]
USDA Bur Biol Surv Bull ... US Department of Agriculture. Bureau of Biological Survey. Bulletin [*A publication*]
USDA Fert ... US Department of Agriculture. Fertilizer Supply [*A publication*]
USDA For Ser Res Bull PNW US Pac Northwest For Range Exp Stn ... USDA [*United States Department of Agriculture*]. Forest Service. Resource Bulletin PNW-United States. Pacific Northwest Forest and Range Experiment Station [*A publication*]
USDA For Ser Res Pap PSW US Pac Southwest For Range Exp Stn ... USDA [*United States Department of Agriculture*]. Forest Service. Research Paper PSW-United States. Pacific Southwest Forest and Range Experiment Station [*A publication*]
USDA For Serv Gen Tech Rep INT For Range Exp Stn ... USDA [*United States Department of Agriculture*]. Forest Service. General Technical Report INT-United States. Intermountain Forest and Range Experiment Station [*A publication*]
USDA For Serv Gen Tech Rep NC US North Cent For Exp Stn ... USDA [*United States Department of Agriculture*]. Forest Service. General Technical Report NC-United States. North Central Forest Experiment Station [*A publication*]
USDA For Serv Gen Tech Rep NE NE For Exp Stn ... USDA [*United States Department of Agriculture*]. Forest Service. General Technical Report NE-United States. Northeastern Forest Experiment Station [*A publication*]
USDA For Serv Gen Tech Rep PSW US Pac Southwest For Exp Stn ... USDA [*United States Department of Agriculture*]. Forest Service. General Technical Report PSW-United States. Pacific Southwest Forest and Range Experiment Station [*A publication*]
USDA For Serv Gen Tech Rep SE US Southeast For Exp Stn ... USDA [*United States Department of Agriculture*]. Forest Service. General Technical Report SE-United States. Southeastern Forest Experiment Station [*A publication*]
USDA For Serv Res Note FPL US For Prod Lab ... USDA [*United States Department of Agriculture*]. Forest Service. Research Note FPL-United States. Forest Products Laboratory [*A publication*]
USDA For Serv Res Note ITF Inst Trop For ... USDA [*United States Department of Agriculture*]. Forest Service. Research Note ITF-United States. Institute of Tropical Forestry [*A publication*]
USDA For Serv Res Note (PNW) ... USDA [*United States Department of Agriculture*]. Forest Service. Research Note (Pacific Northwest) [*A publication*]
USDA For Serv Res Note PSW US Pac Southwest For Range Exp St ... USDA [*United States Department of Agriculture*]. Forest Service. Research Note PSW-United States. Pacific Southwest Forest and Range Experiment Station [*A publication*]
USDA For Serv Res Note RM US Rocky Mt For Range Exp Stn ... USDA [*United States Department of Agriculture*]. Forest Service. Research Note RM-United States. Rocky Mountain Forest and Range Experiment Station [*A publication*]
USDA For Serv Res Note SE US Southeast For Exp Stn ... USDA [*United States Department of Agriculture*]. Forest Service. Research Note SE-United States. Southeastern Forest Experiment Station [*A publication*]
USDA For Serv Resour Bull NC US North Cent For Exp Stn ... USDA [*United States Department of Agriculture*]. Forest Service. Resource Bulletin NC-United States. North Central Forest Experiment Station [*A publication*]
USDA For Serv Res Pap INT US Intermt For Range Exp Stn ... USDA [*United States Department of Agriculture*]. Forest Service. Research Paper INT-United States. Intermountain Forest and Range Experiment Station [*A publication*]
USDA For Serv Res Pap NC US North Cent For Exp Stn ... USDA [*United States Department of Agriculture*]. Forest Service. Research Paper NC-United States. North Central Forest Experiment Station [*A publication*]
USDA For Serv Res Pap NE US Northeast For Exp Stn ... USDA [*United States Department of Agriculture*]. Forest Service. Research Paper NE-United States. Northeastern Forest Experiment Station [*A publication*]
USDA For Serv Res Pap (PNW) ... USDA [*United States Department of Agriculture*]. Forest Service. Research Paper (Pacific Northwest) [*A publication*]
USDA For Serv Res Pap RM US Rocky Mt For Range Exp Stn ... USDA [*United States Department of Agriculture*]. Forest Service. Research Paper RM-United States. Rocky Mountain Forest and Range Experiment Station [*A publication*]

USDA For Serv Res Pap SO ... USDA [*United States Department of Agriculture*]. Forest Service. Research Paper SO [*A publication*]
USDA-FSVP ... USDA-Forest Service Volunteers Program (EA)
USDAO ..... United States Defense Attache Office [*or Officer*] (AABC)
USDA PA ... United States. Department of Agriculture. PA [*Program Aid*] [*A publication*]
USDA Prod Res Rep ... United States. Department of Agriculture. Production Research Report [*A publication*]
USDA RDD ... USDA [*United States Department of Agriculture*] Regional Document Delivery [*Library network*]
USDASL ... USDA [*United States Department of Agriculture*] Sedimentation Laboratory [*Research center*] (RCD)
USDAW .... Union of Ship Distributive and Allied Workers [*British*] (DCTA)
USDB .... United States Disciplinary Barracks [*Military*]
USDC .... Underwater Search, Detection, Classification (AAG)
USDC .... United States Defense Committee (EA)
USDC .... United States Department of Commerce
USDC .... United States District of Columbia (DLA)
USDC .... United States District Court
USDC .... US Design Corp. [*NASDAQ symbol*] (NQ)
USDCFO... United States Defense Communication Field Office (NATG)
USDC Haw ... United States District Court, District of Hawaii (DLA)
USDC Haw ... United States District Court, District of Hawaii, Reports [*A publication*] (DLA)
USDC Hawaii ... United States District Court, District of Hawaii (DLA)
USDC Hawaii ... United States District Court, District of Hawaii, Reports [*A publication*] (DLA)
USDD .... United States Department of Defense
USDE .... United States Department of Education
USDE .... United States Department of Energy (MCD)
USDEL...... United States Delegate (NOAA)
USDELIADB ... United States Delegation, Inter-American Defense Board (AABC)
US Dep Agric Agric Handb ... US Department of Agriculture. Agriculture Handbook [*A publication*]
US Dep Agric Agric Inf Bull ... US Department of Agriculture. Agriculture Information Bulletin [*A publication*]
US Dep Agric Agric Monogr ... United States. Department of Agriculture. Agriculture Monograph [*A publication*]
US Dep Agric Agric Res Serv ARS Ser ... United States. Department of Agriculture. Agricultural Research Service. ARS Series [*A publication*]
US Dep Agric Agric Res Serv Rep ... United States. Department of Agriculture. Agricultural Research Service. Report [*A publication*]
US Dep Agric Agric Res Serv Stat Bull ... United States. Department of Agriculture. Agricultural Research Service. Statistical Bulletin [*A publication*]
US Dep Agric Bull ... United States. Department of Agriculture. Bulletin [*A publication*]
US Dep Agric Circ ... US Department of Agriculture. Circular [*A publication*]
US Dep Agric Conserv Res Rep ... US Department of Agriculture. Conservation Research Report [*A publication*]
US Dep Agric Farmers' Bull ... US Department of Agriculture. Farmers' Bulletin [*A publication*]
US Dep Agric For Serv For Prod Lab Rep ... United States. Department of Agriculture. Forest Service. Forest Products Laboratory. Report [*A publication*]
US Dep Agric For Serv Res Note (PNW) ... United States. Department of Agriculture. Forest Service. Research Note (Pacific Northwest) [*A publication*]
US Dep Agric For Serv Res Pap NC ... United States. Department of Agriculture. Forest Service. Research Paper NC [*A publication*]
US Dep Agric For Serv Res Pap (PNW) ... US Department of Agriculture. Forest Service. Research Paper (Pacific Northwest) [*A publication*]
US Dep Agric Home Econ Res Rep ... United States. Department of Agriculture. Home Economics Research Report [*A publication*]
US Dep Agric Home Gard Bull ... US Department of Agriculture. Home and Garden Bulletin [*A publication*]
US Dep Agric Index-Cat Med Vet Zool Spec Publ ... United States. Department of Agriculture. Index-Catalogue of Medical and Veterinary Zoology. Special Publication [*A publication*]
US Dep Agric Index-Cat Med Vet Zool Suppl ... United States. Department of Agriculture. Index-Catalogue of Medical and Veterinary Zoology. Supplement [*A publication*]
US Dep Agric Leafl ... US Department of Agriculture. Leaflet [*A publication*]
US Dep Agric Mark Res Rep ... United States. Department of Agriculture. Marketing Research Report [*A publication*]
US Dep Agric Misc Publ ... US Department of Agriculture. Miscellaneous Publications [*A publication*]
US Dep Agric Northeast For Exp Stn Stn Pap ... United States. Department of Agriculture. Northeastern Forest Experiment Station. Station Paper [*A publication*]
US Dep Agric Plant Inventory ... US Department of Agriculture. Plant Inventory [*A publication*]

US Dep Agric Prod Res Rep ... US Department of Agriculture. Production Research Report [*A publication*]
US Dep Agric Res Serv Mark Res Rep ... United States. Department of Agriculture. Agricultural Research Service. Marketing Research Report [*A publication*]
US Dep Agric Sci Educ Adm Agric Res Man ... US Department of Agriculture. Science and Education Administration. Agricultural Research Manual [*A publication*]
US Dep Agric Sci Educ Adm Agric Res Results ARR-S ... US Department of Agriculture. Science and Education Administration. Agricultural Research Results. ARR-S [*A publication*]
US Dep Agric Sci Educ Adm Agric Res Results ARR-W ... US Department of Agriculture. Science and Education Administration. Agricultural Research Results. ARR-W [*A publication*]
US Dep Agric Sci Educ Adm Bibliogr Lit Agric ... US Department of Agriculture. Science and Education Administration. Bibliographies and Literature of Agriculture [*A publication*]
US Dep Agric Soil Conserv Ser Soil Surv ... United States. Department of Agriculture. Soil Conservation Service. Soil Survey [*A publication*]
US Dep Agric Soil Conserv Serv SCS-TP ... US Department of Agriculture. Soil Conservation Service. SCS-TP [*A publication*]
US Dep Agric Soil Conserv Serv Soil Surv Invest Rep ... US Department of Agriculture. Soil Conservation Service. Soil Survey Investigation Report [*A publication*]
US Dep Agric Soil Surv ... United States. Department of Agriculture. Soil Survey [*A publication*]
US Dep Agric Stat Bull ... US Department of Agriculture. Statistical Bulletin [*A publication*]
US Dep Agric Tech Bull ... US Department of Agriculture. Technical Bulletin [*A publication*]
US Dep Agric Util Res Rep ... United States. Department of Agriculture. Utilization Research Report [*A publication*]
US Dep Agric Yearb Agric ... US Department of Agriculture. Yearbook of Agriculture [*A publication*]
US Dep Commer Natl Bur Stand Tech Note ... US Department of Commerce. National Bureau of Standards. Technical Note [*A publication*]
US Dep Commer Natl Mar Fish Serv Circ ... US Department of Commerce. National Marine Fisheries Service. Circular [*A publication*]
US Dep Commer Natl Mar Fish Serv Spec Sci Rep Fish ... US Department of Commerce. National Marine Fisheries Service. Special Scientific Report. Fisheries [*A publication*]
US Dep Commer Off Tech Serv PB Rep ... United States. Department of Commerce. Office of Technical Services. PB Report [*A publication*]
US Dep Energy Bartlesville Energy Technol Cent Pet Prod Surv ... US Department of Energy. Bartlesville Energy Technology Center. Petroleum Product Surveys [*A publication*]
US Dep Energy Bartlesville Energy Technol Cent Publ ... US Department of Energy. Bartlesville Energy Technology Center. Publications [*A publication*]
US Dep Energy Environ Meas Lab Environ Rep ... US Department of Energy. Environmental Measurements Laboratory. Environmental Report [*A publication*]
US Dep Health Educ Welfare Annu Rep ... US Department of Health, Education, and Welfare [*Later, US Department of Health and Human Services*] Annual Report [*A publication*]
US Dep Health Educ Welfare DHEW Publ (FDA) ... United States. Department of Health, Education, and Welfare. DHEW [*Department of Health, Education, and Welfare*] Publication. (FDA) [*Food and Drug Administration*] [*A publication*]
US Dep Health Educ Welfare DHEW Publ (NIH) ... US Department of Health, Education, and Welfare [*Later, US Department of Health and Human Services*] DHEW Publication (NIH) [*A publication*]
US Dep Health Educ Welfare Health Serv Adm Publ HSA ... United States. Department of Health, Education, and Welfare. Health Services Administration. Publication HSA [*Health Services Administration*] [*A publication*]
US Dep Health Educ Welfare Natl Inst Ment Health Sci Monogr ... US Department of Health, Education, and Welfare. National Institute of Mental Health. Science Monographs [*A publication*]
US Dep Health Hum Serv Natl Inst Ment Health Sci Monogr ... US Department of Health and Human Services. National Institute of Mental Health. Science Monographs [*A publication*]
US Dep Inter Bur Mines New Publ ... United States. Department of the Interior. Bureau of Mines. New Publications [*A publication*]
US Dep Inter Conserv Yearb ... US Department of the Interior. Conservation Yearbook [*A publication*]
US Dep Inter Fish Wildl Res Rep ... United States. Department of the Interior. Fish and Wildlife Service. Research Report [*A publication*]
US Dep Inter MESA Inf Rep ... US Department of the Interior. Mining Enforcement and Safety Administration. Informational Report [*A publication*]

US Dep Inter Off Libr Serv Bibliogr Ser ... United States. Department of the Interior. Office of Library Services. Bibliography Series [*A publication*]
US Dep State Bur Public Aff Backgr Notes ... United States. Department of State. Bureau of Public Affairs. Background Notes [*A publication*]
US Dept Agriculture Tech Bull Yearbook ... United States. Department of Agriculture. Technical Bulletin. Yearbook [*A publication*]
US Dept HEW Publ ... US Department of Health, Education, and Welfare [*Later, US Department of Health and Human Services*] Publications [*A publication*]
US Dept HHS Publ ... US Department of Health and Human Services. Publications [*A publication*]
US Dept Int ... United States Department of the Interior (DLA)
US Dep Transp (Rep) DOT/TST ... US Department of Transportation (Report). DOT/TST [*A publication*]
USDESEA ... United States Dependent Schools, European Area [*Army*]
USDF........ United States Dressage Federation (EA)
USDFRC ... US Dairy Forage Research Center [*Research center*] (RCD)
USDGA ..... United States Durum Growers Association (EA)
USDH........ United States Direct Hire [*Military*]
USDHE & W ... United States Department of Health, Education, and Welfare
USDHUD ... United States Department of Housing and Urban Development
USDI .... United States Department of the Interior
US Dig....... United States Digest [*A publication*] (DLA)
USDISBad ... United States Distinguished International Shooter Badge [*Military decoration*] (AABC)
US Dist Ct Haw ... United States District Court District of Hawaii (DLA)
USDJ......... United States Department of Justice
USDJ......... United States District Judge
USDL........ United States Department of Labor
USDLGI .... United States Defense Liaison Group, Indonesia [*Army*] (AABC)
USDNDR .. US Decade for Natural Disaster Reduction [*1990's*]
USDO........ United States Disbursing Officer
USDOC ..... United States Department of Commerce
USDOCO .. United States Documents Officer (AFM)
USDOCOLANDSOUTHEAST ... United States Document Office, Allied Land Forces, Southeastern Europe (AABC)
USDOD..... United States Department of Defense
USDOE ..... United States Department of Energy [*Also, an information service or system*]
USDOI ...... United States Department of the Interior (MCD)
USDOT ..... United States Department of Transportation (MCD)
USD(P)...... Undersecretary of Defense for Policy (MCD)
US Dp Agr B ... US Department of Agriculture. Bulletin [*A publication*]
US Dp Int .. US Department of the Interior. Publication [*A publication*]
USDR .... United States Divorce Reform (EA)
USDRE...... Office of the Under Secretary of Defense for Research and Engineering
USDRP...... Unia Socjaldemokratyczna Rzeczypospolitej Polskiej [*Social Democratic Union of the Republic of Poland*] [*Political party*]
USDS........ United States Department of State
USDS........ US Disc Sports Association (EA)
USDSA...... United States Deaf Skiers Association (EA)
USDSEA ... United States Dependent Schools, European Area [*Army*] (AABC)
USDT .... United States Department of Transportation
USDT .... United States Department of the Treasury
USDTA...... United States Dental Tennis Association (EA)
USDTP...... Ukrainska Sotsial Demokraticheskaia Truda Partiia [*Ukrainian Social Democratic Labor Party*] [*Russian*] [*Political party*] (PPE)
USDW .... Underground Sources of Drinking Water
USE .... Encyclopedia of United States Reports [*A publication*] (DLA)
USE .... Underground Service Entrance
USE .... Undersea Scientific Expedition
USE .... Unified S-Band Equipment
USE .... Unit Support Equipment
USE .... United States Economic Problems [*British*] [*World War II*]
USE .... United States Embassy
USE .... United States Envelope Co.
USE .... UNIVAC Scientific Exchange [*Later, UI, USE, Inc.*]
USE .... University of South Dakota, Law Library, Vermillion, SD [*OCLC symbol*] (OCLC)
USE .... University Space Experiments
USE .... Unmanned Surveillance Equipment
USE .... US English [*An association*] (EA)
USE .... User Support Environment (SSD)
USE .... Wauseon, OH [*Location identifier*] [*FAA*] (FAAL)
USEA........ Undersea (AABC)
USEASA ... United States Eastern Amateur Ski Association [*Later, ESA*]
USEC........ United States Endurance Cup [*Car racing*]
USEC........ United States Mission to European Communities [*Department of State*]
USEC........ United System of Electronic Computers (IEEE)
USEC........ Universal Security Instruments, Inc. [*NASDAQ symbol*] (NQ)
USECC ...... United States Employees' Compensation Commission [*Functions transferred to Federal Security Agency, 1946*]
USECOM ... United States Army Electronics Command [*Obsolete*]

US Econ P ... United States Economic Policies Affecting Industrial Trade [*A publication*]
US Econ Res Serv Foreign Agric Econ Rep ... US Economic Research Service. Foreign Agricultural Economic Report [*A publication*]
US Ec Outlk ... US Economic Outlook [*A publication*]
USecWar ... Under Secretary of War [*Obsolete*]
USED .... Underwater Sound Explosive Devices Branch [*Naval Weapons Station*] [*Yorktown, VA*]
USEE......... United States Exploring Expedition [*1838-42*] [*Navy*]
USEEM..... United States Establishment and Enterprise Microdata Base [*Brookings Institution*]
USEES ...... United States Naval Engineering Experiment Station [*Annapolis, MD*]
USEFP ...... United States Educational Foundation in Pakistan
USEG .... US Energy Corp. [*NASDAQ symbol*] (NQ)
US Egg....... United States Egg and Poultry Magazine [*A publication*]
USEI......... United States Society of Esperanto Instructors [*Later, AATE*]
USELMCENTO ... United States Element Central Treaty Organization (AFM)
USEM .... United States Egg Marketers (EA)
USEMA..... [*The*] United States Electronic Mail Association
USEMB..... United States Embassy (MCD)
USEMS ..... United Steam Engine Makers' Society [*A union*] [*British*]
USEN........ USENCO, Inc. [*Midland, TX*] [*NASDAQ symbol*] (NQ)
US Energy Res Dev Adm Rep CONF ... United States. Energy Research and Development Administration. Report CONF [*A publication*]
US Energy Res Dev Adm (Rep) GJO ... US Energy Research and Development Administration (Report) GJO [*Grand Junction Office*] [*A publication*]
USENET ... User Network (SSD)
US Environ Prot Agency Munic Constr Div Rep ... United States. Environmental Protection Agency. Municipal Construction Division. Report [*A publication*]
US Environ Prot Agency Natl Environ Res Cent Ecol Res Ser ... US Environmental Protection Agency. National Environmental Research Center. Ecological Research Series [*A publication*]
US Environ Prot Agency Off Air Qual Plann Stand Tech Rep ... US Environmental Protection Agency. Office of Air Quality Planning and Standards. Technical Report [*A publication*]
US Environ Prot Agency Off Air Waste Manage EPA-450 ... US Environmental Protection Agency. Office of Air and Waste Management. EPA-450 [*A publication*]
US Environ Prot Agency Off Pestic Programs Rep ... United States. Environmental Protection Agency. Office of Pesticide Programs. Report [*A publication*]
US Environ Prot Agency Off Radiat Programs EPA ... US Environmental Protection Agency. Office of Radiation Programs. EPA [*A publication*]
US Environ Prot Agency Off Radiat Programs EPA-ORP ... US Environmental Protection Agency. Office of Radiation Programs. EPA-ORP [*A publication*]
US Environ Prot Agency Off Radiat Programs Tech Rep ... United States. Environmental Protection Agency. Office of Radiation Programs. Technical Report [*A publication*]
US Environ Prot Agency Off Radiat Programs Tech Rep ORP-SID ... US Environmental Protection Agency. Office of Radiation Programs. Technical Reports ORP-SID [*A publication*]
US Environ Prot Agency Off Res Dev Rep EPA ... United States. Environmental Protection Agency. Office of Research and Development. Report EPA [*A publication*]
US Environ Prot Agency Off Res Dev Res Rep Ecol Res Ser ... US Environmental Protection Agency. Office of Research and Development. Research Reports. Ecological Research Series [*A publication*]
US Environ Prot Agency Publ AP Ser ... US Environmental Protection Agency. Publication. AP Series [*A publication*]
USEO .... United States Employment Opportunities
USEO .... United States Engineer Office
USEORD... Use Order [*Navy*] (NVT)
USEP......... United States Escapee Program
USEPA...... United States Environmental Protection Agency
US EPA Ecol Res ... US Environmental Protection Agency. Ecological Research [*A publication*]
US EPA Envir Health Res ... US Environmental Protection Agency. Environmental Health Effects Research [*A publication*]
US EPA Envir Monit ... United States. Environmental Protection Agency. Environmental Monitoring [*A publication*]
US EPA Envir Prot Technol ... US Environmental Protection Agency. Environmental Protection Technology [*A publication*]
US EPA Socioecon Studies ... United States. Environmental Protection Agency. Socioeconomic Environmental Studies [*A publication*]
US Eq Dig ... United States Equity Digest [*A publication*] (DLA)
USER......... Ultra-Small Electronics Research [*DoD*]
USER......... Unique-to-Site Equipment Review (SAA)
USERC...... US Environment and Resources Council (EA)
USERDA... United States Energy Research and Development Administration [*Superseded by Department of Energy, 1977*]

USERIA .... Ultrasensitive Enzymatic Radioimmunoassay [*Clinical chemistry*]
USERID.... User Identification [*Data processing*]
USER INC ... Urban Scientific and Educational Research, Inc. (EA)
USERS ...... Uniform Socio-Economic Reporting System [*Financial reporting system for voluntary health and welfare organizations*]
U Serv M ... United Service Magazine [*A publication*]
USES........ United States Employment Service [*Department of Labor*]
USES .... US Energy Search [*NASDAQ symbol*] (NQ)
USESF...... United States Exchange Stabilization Fund
US-ESRIC ... US-El Salvador Research and Information Center (EA)
USESSA.... United States Environmental Science Services Administration (AABC)
USET........ United South and Eastern Tribes (EA)
USET........ United States Equestrian Team (EA)
USEUCOM ... United States European Command
USEUCOM ... United States European Communications (SAA)
USEX........ US Exploration Corp. [*NASDAQ symbol*] (NQ)
USF........... Lommen Health Science Library, University of South Dakota, Vermillion, SD [*OCLC symbol*] (OCLC)
USF........... Und So Fort [*And So Forth*] [*German*]
USF........... Uniaxial Stress Field
USF........... United Scleroderma Foundation (EA)
USF........... United Socialist Front [*Thailand*] [*Political party*] (PD)
USF........... United Somali Front [*Political party*] (EY)
USF........... United States Filter Corp. [*AMEX symbol*] (SPSG)
USF........... United States Fleet
USF........... United States Forces (CINC)
USF........... University of San Francisco [*California*]
USF........... University of Santa Fe [*A publication*]
USF........... Upstream Stimualtory Factor [*Genetics*]
USFA........ United Sports Fans of America (EA)
USFA........ United States Fencing Association (EA)
USFA........ United States Fire Administration [*Federal Emergency Management Agency*] (GFGA)
USFA........ United States Forces in Austria
USFA........ United States Fuel Administration [*Terminated*]
USFA........ US Farmers Association (EA)
US Fachbuch ... U & S [*Urban & Schwarzenberg*] Fachbuch [*A publication*]
USFADTC ... United States Fleet Air Defense Training Center
USFAIRWINGMED ... United States Fleet Air Wing, Mediterranean (NATG)
US Farm .... US Farm News [*A publication*]
USFARS.... United States Federation of Amateur Roller Skaters [*Later, USAC-RS*] (EA)
USFBI .... United States Forces, British Isles [*World War II*]
USFC......... United States Foil Co.
USFCA ...... United States Fencing Coaches Association (EA)
USFCC ...... United States Fire Companies Conference [*Defunct*] (EA)
USFCC ...... US Federation for Culture Collections (EA)
USFCF....... USF Constellation Foundation (EA)
USFCT ...... United States Forces, China Theater
US Fed Railroad Adm Rep ... US Federal Railroad Administration. Report [*A publication*]
USFET ...... United States Forces, European Theater [*American headquarters for occupation of Germany after SHAEF was dissolved*] [*World War II*]
USFF .... United States Flag Foundation (EA)
USFFL....... United States Flag Football League (EA)
USF & G .... United States Fidelity & Guaranty Co.
USFG......... USF & G Corp. [*Associated Press abbreviation*] (APAG)
USFGC...... US Feed Grains Council (EA)
USFGP...... USF & G Pacholder Fund, Inc. [*Associated Press abbreviation*] (APAG)
USFHA ...... USA Field Hockey Association (EA)
USFI .... Unione Sindacale Ferrovieri Italiani [*National Union of Italian Railway Workers*]
USFIA .... United States Forces in Australia
US FILT .... United States Filter Corp. [*Associated Press abbreviation*] (APAG)
USFIP........ United States Forces in the Philippines
USFIS .... United States Foundation for International Scouting (EA)
USFISC..... United States Foreign Intelligence Surveillance Court
US Fish and Wildlife Service Fishery Bull ... US Fish and Wildlife Service. Fishery Bulletin [*A publication*]
US Fish Wildl Serv Biol Rep ... US Fish and Wildlife Service. Biological Report [*A publication*]
US Fish Wildl Serv Biol Serv Program FWS-OBS ... US Fish and Wildlife Service. Biological Services Program. FWS-OBS [*A publication*]
US Fish Wildl Serv Bur Commer Fish Fish Leafl ... US Fish and Wildlife Service. Bureau of Commercial Fisheries. Fishery Leaflet [*A publication*]
US Fish Wildl Serv Bur Commer Fish Stat Dig ... US Fish and Wildlife Service. Bureau of Commercial Fisheries. Statistical Digest [*A publication*]
US Fish Wildl Serv Bur Sport Fish Wildl EGL ... US Fish and Wildlife Service. Bureau of Sport Fisheries and Wildlife. EGL [*A publication*]

US Fish Wildl Serv Circ ... US Fish and Wildlife Service. Circular [*A publication*]

US Fish Wildl Serv Fish Bull ... US Fish and Wildlife Service. Fishery Bulletin [*A publication*]

US Fish Wildl Serv Fish Distrib Rep ... US Fish and Wildlife Service. Fish Distribution Report [*A publication*]

US Fish Wildl Serv Fish Wildl Leafl ... US Fish and Wildlife Service. Fish and Wildlife Leaflet [*A publication*]

US Fish Wildl Serv FWS-OBS ... US Fish and Wildlife Service. Biological Services Program. FWS-OBS [*A publication*]

US Fish Wildl Serv Invest Fish Control ... US Fish and Wildlife Service. Investigations in Fish Control [*A publication*]

US Fish Wildl Serv N Am Fauna ... US Fish and Wildlife Service. North American Fauna [*A publication*]

US Fish Wildl Serv Resour Publ ... US Fish and Wildlife Service. Resource Publication [*A publication*]

US Fish Wildl Serv Res Rep ... US Fish and Wildlife Service. Research Report [*A publication*]

US Fish Wildl Serv Spec Sci Rep Fish ... US Fish and Wildlife Service. Special Scientific Report. Fisheries [*A publication*]

US Fish Wildl Serv Spec Sci Rep Wildl ... US Fish and Wildlife Service. Special Scientific Report. Wildlife [*A publication*]

US Fish Wildl Serv Tech Pap ... US Fish and Wildlife Service. Technical Papers [*A publication*]

US Fish Wildl Serv Wildl Leafl ... US Fish and Wildlife Service. Wildlife Leaflet [*A publication*]

US Fish Wildl Serv Wildl Res Rep ... US Fish and Wildlife Service. Wildlife Research Report [*A publication*]

US Fish Wild Serv Fish Bull ... US Fish and Wildlife Service. Fishery Bulletin [*A publication*]

USFJ .... United States Forces, Japan (CINC)

USFK .... United States Forces, Korea

USFL .... US Football League (EA)

USFLQ ...... USF Language Quarterly [*A publication*]

USFLR ...... University of San Francisco. Law Review [*A publication*]

USF L Rev ... University of San Francisco. Law Review [*A publication*]

USFMG ..... United States Fastener Manufacturing Group (EA)

USFMG ..... United States Foreign Medical Graduate (DHSM)

USFMIA ... United States Fishmeal Importers Association [*Defunct*] (EA)

USFOA ...... United States Forces, Occupation Austria [*World War II*]

USFOA ...... Uspekhi Fotoniki [*A publication*]

USFODA ... US Fish and Wildlife Service. Biological Services Program. FWS-OBS [*A publication*]

USFODA ... US Fish and Wildlife Service. FWS-OBS [*A publication*]

US Food Drug Adm DHEW Publ ... United States. Food and Drug Administration. DHEW [*Department of Health, Education, and Welfare*] Publication

USFOR ...... United States Forces

USFORAZ ... United States Forces in Azores

US Forest Serv Agr Hdb ... United States. Forest Service. Agriculture Handbooks [*A publication*]

US Forest Serv Res Note ... US Forest Service. Research Notes [*A publication*]

US Forest Serv Res Paper ... US Forest Service. Research Papers [*A publication*]

US For Prod Lab Rep ... United States. Forest Products Laboratory. Reports [*A publication*]

US For Prod Lab Res Note FPL ... United States. Forest Products Laboratory. Research Note FPL [*A publication*]

US For Prod Lab Tech Notes ... United States. Forest Products Laboratory. Technical Notes [*A publication*]

US For Serv AIB ... US Forest Service. AIB [*A publication*]

US For Serv Cent States For Exp Stn Misc Release ... United States. Forest Service. Central States Forest Experiment Station. Miscellaneous Release [*A publication*]

US For Serv Div State Priv For North Reg Rep ... US Forest Service. Division of State and Private Forestry. Northern Region Report [*A publication*]

US For Serv For Insect & Dis Leafl ... US Forest Service. Forest Insect and Disease Leaflet [*A publication*]

US For Serv For Insect & Dis Manage North Reg Rep ... US Forest Service. Forest Insect and Disease Management. Northern Region Report [*A publication*]

US For Serv For Pest Leafl ... US Forest Service. Forest Pest Leaflet [*A publication*]

US For Serv For Pest Manage North Reg Rep ... US Forest Service. Forest Pest Management. Northern Region Report [*A publication*]

US For Serv For Prod Lab Annu Rep ... US Forest Service. Forest Products Laboratory. Annual Report [*A publication*]

US For Serv For Prod Lab Gen Tech Rep FPL ... United States. Forest Service. Forest Products Laboratory. General Technical Report FPL [*A publication*]

US For Serv For Resour Rep ... United States. Forest Service. Forest Resource Report [*A publication*]

US For Serv For Res What's New West ... US Forest Service. Forestry Research. What's New in the West [*A publication*]

US For Serv Gen Tech Rep INT ... US Forest Service. General Technical Report. INT [*A publication*]

US For Serv Gen Tech Rep NC ... US Forest Service. General Technical Report. NC [*A publication*]

US For Serv Gen Tech Rep NE ... US Forest Service. General Technical Report. NE [*A publication*]

US For Serv Gen Tech Rep PNW ... US Forest Service. General Technical Report. PNW [*A publication*]

US For Serv Gen Tech Rep PSW ... US Forest Service. General Technical Report. PSW [*A publication*]

US For Serv Gen Tech Rep RM ... US Forest Service. General Technical Report. RM [*A publication*]

US For Serv Gen Tech Rep SE ... US Forest Service. General Technical Report. SE [*A publication*]

US For Serv Gen Tech Rep SO ... US Forest Service. General Technical Report. SO [*A publication*]

US For Serv Gen Tech Rep WO ... US Forest Service. General Technical Report. WO [*A publication*]

US For Serv Northeast For Exp Stn Ann Rep ... United States. Forest Service. Northeastern Forest Experiment Station. Annual Report [*A publication*]

US For Serv Northeast For Exp Stn Annu Rep ... US Forest Service. Northeastern Forest Experiment Station. Annual Report [*A publication*]

US For Serv Northeast For Exp Stn Stn Pap ... United States. Forest Service. Northeastern Forest Experiment Station. Station Paper [*A publication*]

US For Serv North Reg Coop For Pest Manage Rep ... US Forest Service. Northern Region. Cooperative Forestry and Pest Management Report [*A publication*]

US For Serv North Reg For Environ Prot ... US Forest Service. Northern Region. Forest Environmental Protection [*A publication*]

US For Serv Pac Northwest For Range Experiment Stn Res Notes ... United States. Forest Service. Pacific Northwest Forest and Range Experiment Station. Research Notes [*A publication*]

US For Serv Pac Northwest For Range Exp Stn Ann Rep ... United States. Forest Service. Pacific Northwest Forest and Range Experiment Station. Annual Report [*A publication*]

US For Serv Pac Northwest For Range Exp Stn Annu Rep ... US Forest Service. Pacific Northwest Forest and Range Experiment Station. Annual Report [*A publication*]

US For Serv Pac Northwest For Range Exp Stn Res Pap ... United States. Forest Service. Pacific Northwest Forest and Range Experiment Station. Research Paper [*A publication*]

US For Serv Pac Northwest For Range Exp Stn Res Pap PNW ... US Forest Service. Pacific Northwest Forest and Range Experiment Station. Research Paper PNW [*A publication*]

US For Serv Pac Northwest For Range Exp Stn Res Prog ... US Forest Service. Pacific Northwest Forest and Range Experiment Station. Research Progress [*A publication*]

US For Serv Pac Southwest For Range Exp Stn Misc Pap ... United States. Forest Service. Pacific Southwest Forest and Range Experiment Station. Miscellaneous Paper [*A publication*]

US For Serv Res Note FPL ... US Forest Service. Research Note. FPL [*A publication*]

US For Serv Res Note Inst Trop For ... United States. Forest Service. Research Note. Institute of Tropical Forestry [*A publication*]

US For Serv Res Note INT ... US Forest Service. Research Note. INT [*A publication*]

US For Serv Res Note Intermt For Range Exp Sta ... United States. Forest Service. Research Note. Intermountain Forest and Range Experiment Station [*A publication*]

US For Serv Res Note ITF ... US Forest Service. Research Note. ITF [*A publication*]

US For Serv Res Note NC ... US Forest Service. Research Note. NC [*A publication*]

US For Serv Res Note NE ... US Forest Service. Research Note. NE [*A publication*]

US For Serv Res Note Nth Cent For Exp Sta ... United States. Forest Service. Research Note. North Central Forest Experiment Station [*A publication*]

US For Serv Res Note Ntheast For Exp Sta ... United States. Forest Service. Research Note. Northeastern Forest Experiment Station [*A publication*]

US For Serv Res Note Nth For Exp Sta ... United States. Forest Service. Research Note. Northern Forest Experiment Station [*A publication*]

US For Serv Res Note Pacif Nthwest For Range Exp Sta ... United States. Forest Service. Research Note. Pacific Northwest Forest and Range Experiment Station [*A publication*]

US For Serv Res Note Pacif Sthwest For Range Exp Sta ... US Forest Service. Research Note. Pacific Southwest Forest and Range Experiment Station [*A publication*]

US For Serv Res Note PNW ... US Forest Service. Research Note. PNW [*A publication*]

US For Serv Res Note PSW ... US Forest Service. Research Note. PSW [*A publication*]

US For Serv Res Note RM ... US Forest Service. Research Note. RM [*A publication*]

US For Serv Res Note Rocky Mt For Range Exp Sta ... US Forest Service. Research Note. Rocky Mountain Forest and Range Experiment Station [*A publication*]

US For Serv Res Note SE ... US Forest Service. Research Note. SE [*A publication*]

US For Serv Res Note SO ... US Forest Service. Research Note. SO [*A publication*]
US For Serv Res Note Stheast For Exp Sta ... US Forest Service. Research Note. Southeastern Forest Experiment Station [*A publication*]
US For Serv Res Note Sth For Exp Sta ... United States. Forest Service. Research Note. Southern Forest Experiment Station [*A publication*]
US For Serv Res Note US For Prod Lab (Madison) ... US Forest Service. Research Note. US Forest Products Laboratory (Madison, Wisconsin) [*A publication*]
US For Serv Resour Bull INT ... US Forest Service. Resource Bulletin. INT [*A publication*]
US For Serv Resour Bull NC ... US Forest Service. Resource Bulletin. NC [*A publication*]
US For Serv Resour Bull NE ... US Forest Service. Resource Bulletin. NE [*A publication*]
US For Serv Resour Bull PNW ... US Forest Service. Resource Bulletin. PNW [*A publication*]
US For Serv Resour Bull PSW ... US Forest Service. Resource Bulletin. PSW [*A publication*]
US For Serv Resour Bull SE ... US Forest Service. Resource Bulletin. SE [*A publication*]
US For Serv Resour Bull SO ... US Forest Service. Resource Bulletin. SO [*A publication*]
US For Serv Resource Bull Intermt For Range Exp Sta ... United States. Forest Service. Resource Bulletin. Intermountain Forest and Range Experiment Station [*A publication*]
US For Serv Resource Bull Nth Cent For Exp Sta ... US Forest Service. Resource Bulletin. North Central Forest Experiment Station [*A publication*]
US For Serv Resource Bull Ntheast For Exp Sta ... US Forest Service. Resource Bulletin. Northeastern Forest Experiment Station [*A publication*]
US For Serv Resource Bull Nth For Exp Sta ... US Forest Service. Resource Bulletin. Northern Forest Experiment Station [*A publication*]
US For Serv Resource Bull Pacif Nthwest For Range Exp Sta ... United States. Forest Service. Pacific Northwest Forest and Range Experiment Station. Resource Bulletin [*A publication*]
US For Serv Resource Bull Pacif Sthwest For Range Exp Sta ... US Forest Service. Resource Bulletin. Pacific Southwest Forest and Range Experiment Station [*A publication*]
US For Serv Resource Bull Stheast For Exp Sta ... US Forest Service. Resource Bulletin. Southeastern Forest Experiment Station [*A publication*]
US For Serv Resource Bull Sth For Exp Sta ... US Forest Service. Resource Bulletin. Southern Forest Experiment Station [*A publication*]
US For Serv Res Pap FPL ... US Forest Service. Research Paper. FPL [*A publication*]
US For Serv Res Pap Inst Trop For ... US Forest Service. Research Paper. Institute of Tropical Forestry [*A publication*]
US For Serv Res Pap INT ... US Forest Service. Research Paper. INT [*A publication*]
US For Serv Res Pap Intermt For Range Exp Sta ... US Forest Service. Research Paper. Intermountain Forest and Range Experiment Station [*A publication*]
US For Serv Res Pap ITF ... US Forest Service. Research Paper. ITF [*A publication*]
US For Serv Res Pap NC ... US Forest Service. Research Paper. NC [*A publication*]
US For Serv Res Pap NE ... US Forest Service. Research Paper. NE [*A publication*]
US For Serv Res Pap Nth Cent For Exp Sta ... US Forest Service. Research Paper. North Central Forest Experiment Station [*A publication*]
US For Serv Res Pap Ntheast For Exp Sta ... US Forest Service. Research Paper. Northeastern Forest Experiment Station [*A publication*]
US For Serv Res Pap Nth For Exp Sta ... United States. Forest Service. Research Paper. Northern Forest Experiment Station [*A publication*]
US For Serv Res Pap Pacif Nthwest For Range Exp Sta ... US Forest Service. Research Paper. Pacific Northwest Forest and Range Experiment Station [*A publication*]
US For Serv Res Pap Pacif Sthwest For Range Exp Sta ... US Forest Service. Research Paper. Pacific Southwest Forest and Range Experiment Station [*A publication*]
US For Serv Res Pap PNW ... US Forest Service. Research Paper. PNW [*A publication*]
US For Serv Res Pap PSW ... US Forest Service. Research Paper. PSW [*A publication*]
US For Serv Res Pap RM ... US Forest Service. Research Paper. RM [*A publication*]
US For Serv Res Pap Rocky Mt For Range Exp Sta ... United States. Forest Service. Research Paper. Rocky Mountain Forest and Range Experiment Station [*A publication*]
US For Serv Res Pap SE ... US Forest Service. Research Paper. SE [*A publication*]

US For Serv Res Pap SO ... US Forest Service. Research Paper. SO [*A publication*]
US For Serv Res Pap Stheast For Exp Sta ... US Forest Service. Research Paper. Southeastern Forest Experiment Station [*A publication*]
US For Serv Res Pap Sth For Exp Sta ... US Forest Service. Research Paper. Southern Forest Experiment Station [*A publication*]
US For Serv Res Pap US For Prod Lab (Madison) ... United States. Forest Service. Research Paper. United States Forest Products Laboratory (Madison, Wisconsin) [*A publication*]
US For Serv Res Pap WO ... US Forest Service. Research Paper. WO [*A publication*]
US For Serv Rocky Mount For Range Exp Stn For Sur Release ... United States. Forest Service. Rocky Mountain Forest and Range Experiment Station. Forest Survey Release [*A publication*]
US For Serv Rocky Mount For Range Exp Stn Res Notes ... United States. Forest Service. Rocky Mountain Forest and Range Experiment Station. Research Notes [*A publication*]
US For Serv Rocky Mount For Range Exp Stn Stn Pap ... United States. Forest Service. Rocky Mountain Forest and Range Experiment Station. Station Paper [*A publication*]
US For Serv Southeast For Exp Stn For Surv Release ... United States. Forest Service. Southeastern Forest Experiment Station. Forest Survey Release [*A publication*]
US For Serv Southeast For Exp Stn Res Notes ... United States. Forest Service. Southeastern Forest Experiment Station. Research Notes [*A publication*]
US For Serv Southeast For Exp Stn Stn Pap ... United States. Forest Service. Southeastern Forest Experiment Station. Station Paper [*A publication*]
US For Serv South For Exp Stn Annu Rep ... US Forest Service. Southern Forest Experiment Station. Annual Report [*A publication*]
US For Serv South For Exp Stn For Surv Release ... United States. Forest Service. Southern Forest Experiment Station. Forest Survey Release [*A publication*]
US For Serv Tech Bull ... US Forest Service. Technical Bulletin [*A publication*]
US For Serv Tree Plant Notes ... US Forest Service. Tree Planters' Notes [*A publication*]
USFP .... Union Socialiste des Forces Populaires [*Socialist Union of Popular Forces*] [*Morocco*] [*Political party*] (PPW)
USFP .... United States Federation of Pelota (EA)
USFP .... United States Forces, Police
USFPS .... United States Forces, Police Squadron
USFR .... United States Fleet Reserve
USFS .... United Society of Fitters and Smiths [*A union*] [*British*]
USFS .... United States Foreign Service [*Department of State*]
USFS .... United States Forest Service
USFS .... United States Frequency Standard
USFS .... US Flywheel Systems [*Research center*] (ECON)
USFSA ...... United States Figure Skating Association (EA)
USFSPA .... Uniformed Services Former Spouse Protection Act [*Military*]
USFSS .... United States Fleet SONAR School
USFSS .... US Federation of Scholars and Scientists (EA)
USFTA ...... United States Floor Tennis Association [*Defunct*] (EA)
USFU .... Unglazed Structural Facing Units [*Technical drawings*]
USFV .... United States Forces, Vietnam
USFVL Rev ... University of San Fernando Valley. Law Review [*A publication*] (DLA)
USFWS ..... United States Fish and Wildlife Service [*Department of the Interior*]
USFWSWRR ... United States. Fish and Wildlife Service. Wildlife Research Report [*A publication*]
USG .... Ultrasonic Space Grating
USG .... Ultrasonography
USG .... Ulysses Simpson Grant [*US general and president, 1822-1885*]
USG .... Underwater Systems Group [*Range Commanders Council*] [*White Sands Missile Range, NM*]
USG .... Union of Superiors General (EA)
USG .... United States Gauge
USG .... United States Government
USG .... US Grant Mining [*Vancouver Stock Exchange symbol*]
USG .... USG Corp. [*NYSE symbol*] (SPSG)
USG .... USG Corp. [*Associated Press abbreviation*] (APAG)
USGA .... Ulysses S. Grant Association (EA)
USGA .... United States Golf Association (EA)
USGA .... US Green Alliance (EA)
USGA Green Sect Rec US Golf Assoc ... USGA Green Section Record. US Golf Association [*A publication*]
USGC .... US Geodynamics Committee (EA)
USGCC/A ... United States Group Control Council/Austria [*World War II*]
USGCC/G ... United States Group Control Council/Germany [*World War II*]
USGCLR ... United States-German Committee on Learning and Remembrance (EA)
USGCM .... United States Government Correspondence Manual
US Geog G S Rocky Mtn Reg (Powell) ... United States Geographical and Geological Survey of the Rocky Mountain Region (Powell) [*A publication*]
US Geol S Bul ... United States. Geological Survey. Bulletin [*A publication*]
US Geol S Professional Pa ... United States. Geological Survey. Professional Paper [*A publication*]

US Geol Surv Annu Rep ... United States. Geological Survey. Annual Report [*A publication*]
US Geol Surv Bull ... United States. Geological Survey. Bulletin [*A publication*]
US Geol Surv Circ ... United States. Geological Survey. Circular [*A publication*]
US Geol Surv Coal Invest Map ... US Geological Survey. Coal Investigations Map [*A publication*]
US Geol Survey Bull ... United States. Geological Survey. Bulletin [*A publication*]
US Geol Survey Circ ... US Geological Survey. Circular [*A publication*]
US Geol Survey Coal Inv Map ... US Geological Survey. Coal Investigations Map [*A publication*]
US Geol Survey Geol Quad Map ... United States. Geological Survey. Geological Quadrangle Map [*A publication*]
US Geol Survey Geol Quadrangle Map ... US Geological Survey. Geologic Quadrangle Map [*A publication*]
US Geol Survey Geophys Inv Map ... US Geological Survey. Geophysical Investigations Map [*A publication*]
US Geol Survey Hydrol Inv Atlas ... US Geological Survey. Hydrologic Investigations Atlas [*A publication*]
US Geol Survey Index Geol Mapping US ... US Geological Survey. Index to Geologic Mapping in the United States [*A publication*]
US Geol Survey Mineral Inv Field Studies Map ... US Geological Survey. Mineral Investigations Field Studies Map [*A publication*]
US Geol Survey Mineral Inv Res Map ... US Geological Survey. Mineral Investigations Resource Map [*A publication*]
US Geol Survey Misc Geol Inv Map ... United States. Geological Survey. Miscellaneous Geologic Investigations Map [*A publication*]
US Geol Survey Oil and Gas Inv Chart ... US Geological Survey. Oil and Gas Investigations Chart [*A publication*]
US Geol Survey Oil and Gas Inv Map ... United States. Geological Survey. Oil and Gas Investigations Map [*A publication*]
US Geol Survey Prof Paper ... US Geological Survey. Professional Paper [*A publication*]
US Geol Survey Water-Supply Paper ... United States. Geological Survey. Water-Supply Paper [*A publication*]
US Geol Surv Geol Quadrangle Map ... US Geological Survey. Geologic Quadrangle Map [*A publication*]
US Geol Surv Geophys Invest Map ... United States. Geological Survey. Geophysical Investigations Map [*A publication*]
US Geol Surv Hydrol Invest Atlas ... US Geological Survey. Hydrologic Investigations Atlas [*A publication*]
US Geol Surv Miner Invest Field Stud Map ... United States. Department of the Interior. Geological Survey. Mineral Investigations Field Studies Map [*A publication*]
US Geol Surv Misc Field Stud Map ... US Geological Survey. Miscellaneous Field Studies Map [*A publication*]
US Geol Surv Misc Geol Invest Map ... United States. Geological Survey. Miscellaneous Geologic Investigations Map [*A publication*]
US Geol Surv Oil Gas Invest Chart ... US Geological Survey. Oil and Gas Investigations Chart [*A publication*]
US Geol Surv Oil Gas Invest Map ... US Geological Survey. Oil and Gas Investigations Map [*A publication*]
US Geol Surv Open-File Rep ... US Geological Survey. Open-File Report [*A publication*]
US Geol Surv Prof Pap ... United States. Geological Survey. Professional Paper [*A publication*]
US Geol Surv Trace Elem Memo Rep ... United States. Geological Survey. Trace Elements Memorandum Report [*A publication*]
US Geol Surv Water-Resour Invest ... US Geological Survey. Water-Resources Investigations [*A publication*]
US Geol Surv Water-Supply Pap ... US Geological Survey. Water-Supply Paper [*A publication*]
USGF .... United States Gymnastics Federation (EA)
US G Geog S Terr (Hayden) ... United States Geological and Geographies Survey of the Territories (Hayden) [*A publication*]
USGIPU .... United States Group of the Inter-Parliamentary Union (EA)
USGL .... US Gold Corp. [*NASDAQ symbol*] (SPSG)
USGLI .... United States Government Life Insurance
USGLW ..... Union of Saddlers and General Leather Workers [*British*]
USGM .... United States Government Manual [*A publication*] (OICC)
US Gov Res Dev Rep ... US Government Research and Development Reports [*A publication*]
US Gov Res Rep ... US Government Research Reports [*A publication*]
US Govt Paper Spec Std ... US Government Paper. Specification Standards [*A publication*]
US Govt Res Develop Rept ... United States Government Research and Development Reports [*A publication*]
US Govt Res Dev Reports ... US Government Research and Development Reports [*A publication*]
US Govt Res Rept ... United States Government Research Report [*A publication*]
USGP .... United States Grand Prix [*Auto racing*]
USGPM ..... United States Government Purchasing Mission [*World War II*]
USGPO ..... United States Government Printing Office
USGR .... United States Government Report (IEEE)
USGRA ..... United States Government Report Announcements (IID)
USGRDR ... United States Government Research and Development Reports [*Later, GRA*]

USGRDR-I ... United States Government Research and Development Reports Index [*Later, GRI*]
USGRR ...... United States Government Research Reports [*National Bureau of Standards publication*]
USGS .... United States Geological Survey [*Reston, VA*] [*Databank originator*]
USGSA ...... United States Grain Standards Act (GFGA)
USGSA ...... United States Grass Ski Association (EA)
USGSA ...... United States Gymnastic Safety Association
USGS An Rp PPB W-S P Mon Min Res G Atlas Top Atlas ... United States. Geological Survey. Annual Report. Professional Paper. Bulletin. Water-Supply Paper Monograph. Mineral Resources Geology Atlas [*A publication*]
USGSB ...... United States. Geological Survey. Bulletin [*A publication*]
USGSC ...... United States. Geological Survey. Circular [*A publication*]
USGSC ...... United States Global Strategy Council (EA)
USGSPP .... United States. Geological Survey. Professional Paper [*A publication*]
USGS Terr ... United States Geological Survey of the Territories [*A publication*]
USGW .... Underwater-to-Surface Guided Weapon (MCD)
US Gym Fed Gym News ... United States Gymnastic Federation. Gymnastic News [*A publication*]
U SH .... Shilling [*Monetary unit in Uganda*]
USH .... United Scientific Holdings [*Defense equipment manufacturer*] [*British*]
USH .... Ushuaia [*Argentina*] [*Airport symbol*] (OAG)
USH .... USLIFE Corp. [*NYSE symbol*] (SPSG)
USHA .... United States Handball Association (EA)
USHA .... United States Housing Authority [*Functions transferred to Public Housing Commissioner, 1947*]
USHB .... Uniformed Services Health Benefits
USHBP ...... Uniformed Services Health Benefits Program
USHC .... United States Housing Corp. [*Terminated, 1952*]
USHC .... US Healthcare, Inc. [*NASDAQ symbol*] (NQ)
USHCA ...... US Horse Cavalry Association (EA)
USHCC ...... US Hispanic Chamber of Commerce (EA)
USHDA ..... United States Highland Dancing Association (EA)
USHDI ...... United States Historical Documents Institute
USHE .... Upstream Heat Exchanger (AAG)
USHG .... United States Home Guard
USHGA ..... United States Hop Growers Association
USHGA ..... US Hang Gliding Association (EA)
USHH .... Khanty-Mansiysk [*Former USSR*] [*ICAO location identifier*] (ICLI)
USHI .... US Health, Inc. [*NASDAQ symbol*] (NQ)
USHIGEO ... United States National Committee for the History of Geology (EA)
USHL .... United States Hockey League
USHL .... United States Hydrograph Laboratory
USHL .... United States Hygienic Laboratory
USHMAC ... United States Health Manpower Advisory Council
USHMC .... US Holocaust Memorial Council (EA)
USHO .... United States Hydrographic Office [*Later, Naval Oceanographic Office*]
USHO .... US HomeCare [*NASDAQ symbol*] (SPSG)
USHP .... United States Helium Plant [*Amarillo, TX*]
USHRA ..... United States Hot Rod Association [*Auto racing*]
USHSLA ..... US Hide, Skin, and Leather Association (EA)
USHTA ..... United States Handicap Tennis Association (EA)
USHWA .... United States Harness Writers' Association (EA)
USHWC .... US Helsinki Watch Committee (EA)
US Hydrog Office Pub ... US Hydrographic Office. Publication [*A publication*]
USI .... Mabaruma [*Guyana*] [*Airport symbol*] (OAG)
USI .... Ultrasonic System [*Vancouver Stock Exchange symbol*]
USI .... Ultraviolet Spectroheliographic Instrument
USI .... United Schools International [*New Delhi, India*] (EAIO)
USI .... United Sons of Israel (EA)
USI .... United States Information Agency, Washington, DC [*OCLC symbol*] (OCLC)
USI .... United States Investor [*A publication*]
USI .... Universal Software Interface [*MRI Systems Corp.*]
USI .... Unlawful Sexual Intercourse
USI .... Unresolved Safety Issue [*Nuclear energy*] (NRCH)
USI .... Unsigned Short Integer [*Data processing*]
USI .... Update Software Identity (MCD)
USI .... Uranium Supply - Import Model [*Department of Energy*] (GFGA)
USI .... US, Inc. (EA)
USI .... US Intec, Inc. [*AMEX symbol*] (SPSG)
USI .... User Software Integration Subsystem [*Space Flight Operations Facility, NASA*]
USI .... User/System Interface
USI .... Usine Nouvelle [*A publication*]
USIA .... United States Information Agency [*Formerly called BECA, it later became known as ICA or USICA, then again as USIA*]
USIAC ...... United States Inter-American Council [*Later, COA*] (EA)
USIAEA .... United States Mission to the International Atomic Energy Agency

USIA/PC... Problems of Communism. United States Information Agency [*A publication*]
USIB......... United States Intelligence Board [*Later, NFIB*] [*National Security Council*]
US-IBP Anal Ecosyst Program Interbiome Abstr ... US-IBP [*International Biological Program*] Analyses of Ecosystems Program. Interbiome Abstracts [*A publication*]
US-IBP Ecosyst Anal Stud Abstr ... US-IBP [*International Biological Program*] Ecosystem Analysis Studies Abstracts [*A publication*]
US-IBP Synth Ser ... US-IBP [*International Biological Program*] Synthesis Series [*A publication*]
USIC......... Undersea Instrument Chamber [*Marine science*]   (MSC)
USIC......... Union Sportive Interuniversitaire Canadienne
USIC......... United States Industrial Council   (EA)
USIC......... United States Information Center [*Department of State*]   (MCD)
USICA....... United States International Communication Agency [*Also, ICA*] [*Formerly called BECA and USIA, it later became known again as USIA*]
USICC...... United States Industrial Chemical Co.   (KSC)
USICC Rep ... United States Interstate Commerce Commission Reports [*A publication*]   (DLA)
USICCVR ... United States Interstate Commerce Commission Valuation Reports [*A publication*]   (DLA)
US ICDBL ... US Branch of the International Committee for the Defense of the Breton Language   (EA)
USICF .... Union Sportive Interuniversitaire Canadienne Feminine
USICID ..... United States National Committee, International Commission on Irrigation and Drainage
US/ICID.... US Committee on Irrigation and Drainage [*Formerly, USCIDFC*]   (EA)
US/ICOMOS ... United States Committee of the International Council on Monuments and Sites   (EA)
USIDF....... United States Icelandic Defense Forces   (MCD)
USIFA .... US International Fireball Association   (EA)
USIHR ...... US Institute of Human Rights   (EA)
USIITA ..... United States Indian International Travel Agency, Inc.
USILA .... United States Intercollegiate Lacrosse Association   (EA)
USIMC...... United States International Marketing Center [*American Embassy, London*]   (CB)
USIMCA.... United States International Moth Class Association   (EA)
USINCC..... United States International Narcotics Control Commission
US Ind Outlk ... United States Industrial Outlook [*A publication*]
Usine Nouv ... Usine Nouvelle [*A publication*]
Usine Nouv Ed Suppl ... Usine Nouvelle. Edition Supplementaire [*France*] [*A publication*]
Usine Nouv M ... Usine Nouvelle. Monthly Edition [*A publication*]
Usine Nouv Suppl ... Usine Nouvelle. Edition Supplementaire [*A publication*]
Using Govt P ... Using Government Publications. Volume 2. Finding Statistics and Using Special Techniques [*A publication*]
USINOA ... US Immigration and Naturalization Officers' Association   (EA)
US Inst Text Res Bull ... United States Institute for Textile Research. Bulletin [*A publication*]
USINT....... United States Interests Section [*Foreign Service*]
US INTC ... US Intec, Inc. [*Associated Press abbreviation*]   (APAG)
US Interdep Comm Atmos Sci Rep ... US Interdepartmental Committee for Atmospheric Sciences. Report [*A publication*]
USIO .... Unidentified Submerged Illuminated Object   (DNAB)
USIO .... United States Industrial Outlook [*A publication*]
USIO .... United States Institute of Oceanography   (DNAB)
USIO .... Unlimited Sequential Input/Output
USIP......... United Solomon Islands Party   (PPW)
USIP......... University of Stockholm Institute of Physics
USIP......... US Institute of Peace   (EA)
USIPC....... Uniformed Services Identification and Privilege Card   (AFM)
USIPU...... United States Inter-Parliamentary Union   (EA)
USIRB....... United States Internal Revenue Bonded
USIS......... Ultraviolet Stratospheric Imaging Spectrometer   (MCD)
USIS......... United States Information Service [*Name used abroad for USIA offices*]
USISA .... United States International Sailing Association   (EA)
USISA .... United States International Skating Association
USISCA..... US Islands 17 Class Association [*Defunct*]   (EA)
USISL....... United States Information Service Library   (DIT)
USISSA..... United States International Speed Skating Association   (EA)
US-ISY ...... US International Space Year Association   (EA)
USIT......... Unit Share Investment Trust
USITA ...... United States Independent Telephone Association   (EA)
USITA ...... United States International Tempest Association   (EA)
USITC....... United States International Trade Commission
USITC Pub ... United States International Trade Commission. Publication [*A publication*]   (DLA)
USITT....... United States Institute for Theatre Technology   (EA)
USIU .... United States International University [*San Diego, CA*]
USJ........... United States Jaycees   (EA)
USJ........... United States Judo   (EA)
USJA .... United States Judo Association   (EA)
USJAC...... US-Japan Culture Center   (EA)
US JAYCEE ... United States Junior Chamber of Commerce [*Later, United States Jaycees*]   (EA)

USJB .... Union Saint-Jean-Baptiste   (EA)
USJBC....... US-Japan Business Council   (EA)
USJCA ...... United States Joint Communication Agency   (NATG)
USJCC ...... United States Junior Chamber of Commerce [*Later, United States Jaycees*]   (EA)
USJCC ...... US-Japan Culture Center   (EA)
USJCIRPTE ... United States-Japan Committee on Industry Related Policies and Their Trade Effects [*Acronym pronounced "use-jay-krip-tee"*]
USJCS....... United States Joint Chiefs of Staff   (NATG)
US-JCSC.... United States-Japan Committee on Scientific Cooperation [*Department of State*]
USJF .... United States Judo Federation   (EA)
USJF .... United States Justice Foundation   (EA)
USJNRP .... United States/Japan Natural Resources Panel
US Joint Publ Res Serv Transl E Eur Agr Forest Food Ind ... United States. Joint Publication Research Service. Translations on East European Agriculture, Forestry, and Food Industries [*A publication*]
USJPRS .... United States Joint Publications Research Service
US-JTC .... United States-Japan Trade Council   (EA)
USJTF....... United States Joint Task Force   (AABC)
US Jur .... United States Jurist [*A publication*]   (DLA)
USJUWTF ... United States Joint Unconventional Warfare Task Force   (AABC)
USK .... Ultrasonic Kit
USK .... United States Forces, Korea
USKA .... United States Kart Association [*Defunct*]   (EA)
USKBA...... United Strictly Kosher Butchers Association
USKBTC .... United States Kerry Blue Terrier Club   (EA)
USKEC...... US-Korea Economic Council [*Later, KS*]   (EA)
USKF....... United States Korfball Federation   (EA)
USKHA ..... Uspekhi Khimii [*A publication*]
USKOREA ... United States Forces Korea
USKOS...... US-Korea Society [*Later, KS*]   (EA)
USl............. Salt Lake City Public Library, Salt Lake City, UT [*Library symbol*] [*Library of Congress*]   (LCLS)
USL.......... Underwater Sound Laboratory [*New London, CT*] [*Navy*]
USL.......... Unemployed Supernumerary List [*Military*] [*British*]
USL.......... Unique Suppliers List
USL.......... Unit Spares List
USL.......... United Satellites Ltd. [*London, England*] [*Telecommunications*]   (TSSD)
USL.......... United Soccer League   (EA)
USL.......... United States Laws   (DLA)
USL.......... United States Legation
USL.......... Unix Systems Laboratory [*Data processing*]
USL.......... Up Stage Left [*Away from audience*] [*A stage direction*]
USL.......... Upper Specified Limit
USL.......... US Leasing International, Inc. [*NYSE symbol*]   (SPSG)
USL.......... US Long Distance [*Vancouver Stock Exchange symbol*]
USL.......... Useless Loop [*Australia*] [*Airport symbol*]   (OAG)
USL.......... Usual   (ROG)
USLA........ United States Committee for Justice to Latin American Political Prisoners [*Defunct*]   (EA)
USLA........ United States Lifesaving Association   (EA)
USLA........ United States Luge Association   (EA)
USLANT.... United States Atlantic Subarea [*NATO*]
US Law Ed ... United States Supreme Court Reports, Lawyers' Edition [*A publication*]   (DLA)
US Law Int ... United States Law Intelligencer and Review [*Providence and Philadelphia*] [*A publication*]   (DLA)
US Law Jour ... United States Law Journal [*A publication*]   (DLA)
US Law Mag ... United States Law Magazine [*A publication*]   (DLA)
US Law R... United States Law Review [*A publication*]
USlC .... Church of Jesus Christ of Latter-Day Saints, Historian's Office, Salt Lake City, UT [*Library symbol*] [*Library of Congress*]   (LCLS)
USLC......... United States Locals Collectors   (EA)
USLCA...... United States Lacrosse Coaches' Association   (EA)
USLCMBA ... US Letter Carriers Mutual Benefit Association [*Washington, DC*]   (EA)
USlD......... Daughters of Utah Pioneers Museum Library, Salt Lake City, UT [*Library symbol*] [*Library of Congress*]   (LCLS)
USLD........ Ultrasonic Link Detector
USLD........ Union des Syndicats Libres du Dahomey [*Federation of Free Unions of Dahomey*]
USLDMA ... United States Lanolin and Derivative Manufacturers Association   (EA)
USLE......... Universal Soil Loss Equation [*Agricultural engineering*]
USL Ed ...... Lawyers' Edition, United States Supreme Court Reports [*A publication*]   (DLA)
USL Ed 2d ... Lawyers' Edition, United States Supreme Court Reports, Second Series [*A publication*]   (DLA)
UslfeF .... USLIFE Income Fund, Inc. [*Associated Press abbreviation*]   (APAG)
USlGS........ Church of Jesus Christ of Latter-Day Saints, Genealogical Society Library, Salt Lake City, UT [*Library symbol*] [*Library of Congress*]   (LCLS)
USL & H.... United States Longshoremen and Harborworkers Act
USLH .... University of Southwestern Louisiana Herbarium

USLHS...... United States Lighthouse Society (EA)
USLICO .... USLICO Corp. [Associated Press abbreviation] (APAG)
USLIFE..... USLIFE Corp. [Associated Press abbreviation] (APAG)
US Lit Gaz ... United States Literary Gazette [A publication]
USLJ .... United States Law Journal [New Haven and New York] [A publication] (DLA)
USlL .... Latter-Day Saints Museum, Salt Lake City, UT [Library symbol] [Library of Congress] (LCLS)
USLL......... Utah Studies in Literature and Linguistics [A publication]
USL Mag.... United States Law Magazine [A publication] (DLA)
USLO .... United States Liaison Office [or Officer]
USLO .... University Students for Law and Order
US Long Term ... United States Long-Term Review [A publication]
USlOr .... Oregon Short Line Law Department, Salt Lake City, UT [Library symbol] [Library of Congress] [Obsolete] (LCLS)
USLO SACA ... United States Liaison Officer to Supreme Allied Commander, Atlantic (MUGU)
USlP .... Pioneer Memorial Museum, Salt Lake City, UT [Library symbol] [Library of Congress] (LCLS)
USLP......... United States Labor Party
USLR......... United States Law Review [A publication]
USL Rev .... United States Law Review [A publication]
USLS .... United States Lake Survey [Marine science] (MSC)
USLS .... United States Lighthouse Society (EA)
USLSA ...... United States League of Savings Associations [Later, USLSI]
USLSA ...... United States Livestock Sanitary Association [Later, United States Animal Health Association] (EA)
USLSI....... United States League of Savings Institutions [Chicago, IL] (EA)
USLSO ...... United States Logistics Support Office (AFM)
USIStM ..... College of Saint Mary-of-the-Wasatch, Salt Lake City, UT [Library symbol] [Library of Congress] [Obsolete] (LCLS)
USlT .... Utah Technical College at Salt Lake, Salt Lake City, UT [Library symbol] [Library of Congress] (LCLS)
USLTA...... United States Lawn Tennis Association [Later, USTA] (EA)
USLTC...... United States Lakeland Terrier Club (EA)
US Lthr...... United States Leather Holdings [Associated Press abbreviation] (APAG)
USLW........ United States Law Week [Bureau of National Affairs] [A publication] (DLA)
USlW .... Westminster College, Salt Lake City, UT [Library symbol] [Library of Congress] (LCLS)
USLW BNA ... United States Law Week. Bureau of National Affairs [A publication]
USM .... Underwater-to-Surface Missile [Air Force]
USM .... Uniform Staffing Methodologies [DoD]
USM .... United Securities Market [British] (CDAI)
USM .... United Service Magazine [A publication]
USM .... United States Mail
USM .... United States Marine
USM .... United States Mint
USM .... United States Minutemen [Defunct] (EA)
USM .... United States Representative to the Military Committee Memorandum [NATO]
USM .... University of Southern Mississippi
USM .... Unlisted Securities Market [London Stock Exchange]
USM .... Unsaponifiable Matter [Organic analytical chemistry]
USM .... Unscheduled Maintenance
USM .... US Cellular Corp.[AMEX symbol] (SPSG)
UsM........... US Microfilm Corp., Jacksonville, FL [Library symbol] [Library of Congress] (LCLS)
USM .... Usine Nouvelle [A publication]
USMA .... Union Special Corp. [NASDAQ symbol] (NQ)
USMA .... United States Maritime Administration
USMA .... United States Military Academy [West Point, NY]
USMA .... United States Military Attache
USMA .... United States Monopoly Association (EA)
USMA .... US Metric Association (EA)
USMAC..... United States Marine Air Corps
USMAC..... United States Military Assistance Command
USMACSV ... United States Military Assistance Command, South Vietnam [Obsolete]
USMACTHAI ... United States Military Assistance Command, Thailand [Obsolete] (AFM)
USMACV ... United States Military Assistance Command, Vietnam [Obsolete]
USMA/ESGS ... United States Military Academy Department of Earth, Space, and Graphic Sciences [West Point, NY]
USMAG .... United States Military Advisory Group
USMAPS .. United States Military Academy Preparatory School
USMAPU ... United States Military Academy Preparatory Unit
USMARC ... Advisory Committee for the US Meat Animal Research Center [Terminated, 1977] (EGAO)
USMATS .. United States Military Air Transport Service [Later, Military Airlift Command]
USMB .... United States Marine Barracks
USMB .... United States Metric Board [Terminated]
USMBHA .. US-Mexico Border Health Association (EA)
USMBP..... US-Mexico Border Program (EA)
USMC .... United States Marine Corps

USMC .... United States Maritime Commission [Functions transferred to Department of Commerce, 1950]
USMCA..... United States Men's Curling Association [Later, USCA] (EA)
USMCA..... US Mariner Class Association (EA)
USMCA..... US Mirror Class Association (EA)
USMCAM .. United States Military Community Activity, Mannheim
USMCAS.. United States Marine Corps Air Station
USMCB..... United States Marine Corps Base (MCD)
USMCC..... United States Marine Corps Mint - Carson City (ROG)
USMCCCA ... US Marine Corps Combat Correspondents Association (EA)
USMCDIA ... United States Marine Corps Drill Instructors Association (EA)
USMCEB.. United States Military Communications Electronics Board (NVT)
USMCOC ... United States-Mexico Chamber of Commerce [See also CCMEU] (EA)
USMCP..... United States Military Construction Program (CINC)
USMCR..... United States Marine Corps Reserve
USMCR(AF) ... United States Marine Corps Reserve (Aviation Fleet)
USMCR(AO) ... United States Marine Corps Reserve (Aviation, Organized)
USMCR(AV) ... United States Marine Corps Reserve (Aviation, Volunteer)
USMCR(F) ... United States Marine Corps Reserve (Fleet)
USMCR(LS) ... United States Marine Corps Reserve (Limited Service)
USMCR(NAV) ... United States Marine Corps Reserve (Naval Aviators)
USMCR(NAVO) ... United States Marine Corps Reserve (Graduate Aviation Cadets, Volunteer)
USMCR(NAVT) ... United States Marine Corps Reserve (Aviation Specialist Transport Pilot, Volunteer)
USMCR(O) ... United States Marine Corps Reserve (Organized)
USMCRTC ... United States Marine Corps Reserve Training Center
USMCR(V) ... United States Marine Corps Reserve (Volunteer)
USMCR(VS) ... United States Marine Corps Reserve (Volunteer Specialists)
USMCR(W) ... United States Marine Corps Reserve (Women)
USMCSS... United States Marine Corps Selective Service Selectee
USMCSSV ... United States Marine Corps Selective Service Volunteer
USMC(W) ... United States Marine Corps (Women)
USMCWR ... United States Marine Corps Women's Reserve
USMD .... US Medical Enterprises, Inc. [Santa Monica, CA] [NASDAQ symbol] (NQ)
USMECBL .. United States Mission to the European Communities in Belgium and Luxembourg
US Med ..... US Medicine [A publication]
USMEF..... United States Meat Export Federation (EA)
USMEMILCOMUN ... United States Members, United Nations Military Staff Committee
USMEOUN ... United States Mission to the European Office of the United Nations
USMEPC.. United States Military Enlistment Processing Command
USMEPCOM ... United States Military Entrance Processing Command
USMES ..... Unified Science and Mathematics for Elementary Schools [National Science Foundation]
USMF........ United States Sports Massage Federation (EA)
USMG .... United States Medical Graduate
USMH....... United States Marine Hospital
USMHS .... United States Marine Hospital Service
USMI........ Universal Software Market Identifier [Technique Learning] [Information service or system] (IID)
USMI........ US Mineral & Royalty Corp. [NASDAQ symbol] (NQ)
USMIAEAA ... United States Mission to the International Atomic Energy Agency in Austria
USMICC ... United States Military Information Control Committee (AFM)
USMID...... Ultrasensitive Microwave Infrared Detector
USMILADREP ... United States Military Advisor's Representative (CINC)
USMILADREPSMPO ... United States Military Advisor's Representative, Southeast Asia Treaty Organization, Military Planning Office (CINC)
USMILATTACHE ... United States Military Attache
USMILCOMUN ... United States Delegation, United Nations Military Staff Committee
USMILLIAS ... United States Military Liaison Office
USMILTAG ... United States Military Technical Advisory Group (AFM)
USMITT ... United States Masters International Track Team [Defunct] (EA)
USMKA .... Uspekhi Mikrobiologii [A publication]
USML....... United States Microgravity Laboratory [NASA]
USMLM.... United States Military Liaison Mission (MCD)
USML Mag ... United States Monthly Law Magazine [A publication] (DLA)
USMLMCINCGSFG ... United States Military Liaison Mission to Commander-in-Chief, Group Soviet Forces, Germany (AABC)
USMLO .... United States Military Liaison Office
USMLS..... United States Museum Librarian Society (EA)
USMM ...... Union Socialiste des Musulmans Mauritaniens [Socialist Union of Mauritanian Moslems]
USMM ...... United States Merchant Marine
USMMA ... United States Merchant Marine Academy [Kings Point, NY]
USMMCC ... United States Merchant Marine Cadet Corps
USMMVETS WW2 ... US Merchant Marine Veterans of World War II (EA)
USMNAM ... United States Military North African Mission [World War II]
US Month Law Mag ... United States Monthly Law Magazine [A publication] (DLA)
USMP........ United States Mallard Project [Army]

USMPA.....	United States Modern Pentathlon Association (EA)
USMPBA..	United States Modern Pentathlon and Biathlon Association [*Later, USMPA*] (EA)
USMPTC..	United States Modern Pentathlon Training Center [*Military*] (AABC)
USMR	US Mutual Financial Corp. [*NASDAQ symbol*] (NQ)
USMS........	Unattended Sensor Monitoring System
USMS........	United States Maritime Service
USMS........	United States Marshall Service [*Department of Justice*]
USMS........	United States Masters Swimming (EA)
USMS........	United States Mint - San Francisco (ROG)
USMSA.....	United States Marine Safety Association (EA)
USMSGS ..	United States Maritime Service Graduate Station
USMSMI..	United States Military Supply Mission to India (AFM)
USMSOS ..	United States Maritime Service Officers School
USMSR.....	United States Military Specification Requirements (MCD)
USMSSB...	United States Machine Screw Service Bureau [*Defunct*] (EA)
USMSTS...	United States Maritime Service Training School
USMSTS...	United States Maritime Service Training Ship
USMSTS...	United States Maritime Service Training Station
USMT	United States Military Transport
USMTF	United States Message Text Formating
USMTM ...	United States Military Training Mission (MCD)
USMTMSA ...	United States Military Training Mission to Saudi Arabia
USMWR ...	United States Mission Weekly Report [*Military*]
USMWW ..	United Society of Mechanical Wood Workers [*A union*] [*British*]
USMX	USMX, Inc. [*Formerly, US Minerals & Explorations Co.*] [*NASDAQ symbol*] (NQ)
USN	Ultrasonic Nebulizer
USN	Under Secretary of the Navy
USN	Union des Scolaires Nigeriens [*Union of Nigerian Scholars*]
USN	United States Navy
USNA	United States National Army
USNA	United States Naval Academy [*Annapolis, MD*]
USNA	United States Naval Aircraft
USNA	United States Naval Attache (GFGA)
USNAAA ..	United States Naval Academy Alumni Association
USNAAA ..	United States Naval Academy Athletic Association
USNA ANNA ...	United States Naval Academy, Annapolis [*Maryland*]
USNAAS...	United States Naval Auxiliary Air Station
USNAB ...	United States Naval Advanced Base [*World War II*]
USNAB	United States Naval Amphibious Base
USNAC	United States of America National Committee of the International Dairy Federation (EA)
USNAC	United States Naval Administrative Command
USNAC	United States Naval Air Corps
USNACC...	United States Naval Member of the Allied Control Commission [*Germany*]
USNADC ..	United States Naval Air Development Center
USNA-EPRD ...	United States Naval Academy Energy-Environment Study Group and Development Team
USNA-EW ...	United States Naval Academy Division of Engineering and Weapons
USNAF......	United States Naval Avionics Facility
USNAG	United States Navy Astronautics Group (SAA)
USNAHALO ...	United States NATO Hawk Liaison Office [*Missiles*] (NATG)
USNAMTC ...	United States Naval Air Missile Test Center
USNARS...	United States National Archives and Records Service (DIT)
USNAS......	United States Naval Air Service
USNAS......	United States Naval Air Station
USNASA Conf Publ ...	United States. National Aeronautics and Space Administration. Conference Publication [*A publication*]
USNATC...	United States Naval Air Training Center
US Natl Aeronaut Space Admin Spec Publ ...	US National Aeronautics and Space Administration. Special Publication [*A publication*]
US Natl Bur Stand Handb ...	US National Bureau of Standards. Handbook [*A publication*]
US Natl Bur Stand J Res ...	United States. National Bureau of Standards. Journal of Research [*A publication*]
US Natl Bur Stand J Res Sec A ...	US National Bureau of Standards. Journal of Research. Section A [*A publication*]
US Natl Cancer Inst Carcinog Tech Rep Ser ...	US National Cancer Institute. Carcinogenesis Technical Report Series [*A publication*]
US Natl Clgh Drug Abuse Inf Rep Ser ...	US National Clearinghouse for Drug Abuse. Information Report Series [*A publication*]
US Natl Fert Dev Cent Bull Y ...	United States National Fertilizer Development Center. Bulletin Y [*A publication*]
US Natl Ind Pollut Control Counc Publ ...	US National Industrial Pollution Control Council. Publications [*A publication*]
US Natl Inst Drug Abuse Res Issues ...	US National Institute on Drug Abuse. Research Issues [*A publication*]
US Natl Inst Health Natl Toxicol Program Tech Rep Ser ...	US National Institutes of Health. National Toxicology Program Technical Report Series
US Natl Inst Health Publ ...	US National Institutes of Health. Publication [*A publication*]
US Natl Lab (Oak Ridge Tenn) Rev ...	United States National Laboratory (Oak Ridge, Tennessee). Review [*A publication*]

US Natl Mar Fish Serv Curr Fish Stat ...	US National Marine Fisheries Service. Current Fisheries Statistics [*A publication*]
US Natl Mar Fish Serv Fish Bull ...	US National Marine Fisheries Service. Fishery Bulletin [*A publication*]
US Natl Mar Fish Serv Fish Facts ...	US National Marine Fisheries Service. Fishery Facts [*A publication*]
US Natl Mar Fish Serv Mar Fish Rev ...	US National Marine Fisheries Service. Marine Fisheries Review [*A publication*]
US Natl Mar Fish Serv Rep Natl Mar Fish Serv ...	US National Marine Fisheries Service. Report of the National Marine Fisheries Service [*A publication*]
US Natl Mar Fish Serv Stat Dig ...	US National Marine Fisheries Service. Statistical Digest [*A publication*]
US Natl Mus Bull ...	US National Museum. Bulletin [*A publication*]
US Natl Mus Bull Proc ...	United States National Museum. Bulletin. Proceedings [*A publication*]
US Natl Oceanic Atmos Adm Environ Data Serv Tech Memo ...	United States. National Oceanic and Atmospheric Administration. Environmental Data Service. Technical Memorandum [*A publication*]
US Natl Oceanic Atmos Adm Key Oceanogr Rec Doc ...	US National Oceanic and Atmospheric Administration. Key to Oceanographic Records Documentation [*A publication*]
US Natl Oceanog Data Center Pub ...	US National Oceanographic Data Center. Publication [*A publication*]
US Natl Park Serv Ecol Serv Bull ...	US National Park Service. Ecological Services Bulletin [*A publication*]
US Natl Park Serv Fauna Natl Parks US Fauna Ser ...	US National Park Service. Fauna of the National Parks of the United States. Fauna Series [*A publication*]
US Natl Park Service Nat History Handb Ser ...	US National Park Service. Natural History Handbook Series [*A publication*]
US Natl Park Serv Natl Cap Reg Sci Rep ...	US National Park Service. National Capitol Region Scientific Report [*A publication*]
US Natl Park Serv Nat Resour Rep ...	US National Park Service. Natural Resources Report [*A publication*]
US Natl Park Serv Occas Pap ...	US National Park Service. Occasional Paper [*A publication*]
US Natl Park Serv Sci Monogr Ser ...	US National Park Service. Scientific Monograph Series [*A publication*]
US Natl Sci Found Res Appl Natl Needs Rep ...	United States. National Science Foundation. Research Applied to National Needs Report [*A publication*]
US Nat Mus Bull ...	United States National Museum. Bulletin [*A publication*]
US Nat Mus Rept ...	United States National Museum. Reports [*A publication*]
USNATO ..	United States Mission to the North Atlantic Treaty Organization [*Department of State*] (NATG)
USNATRA ...	United States Naval Training
US Nav Aerosp Med Inst (Pensacola) Monogr ...	US Naval Aerospace Medical Institute (Pensacola). Monograph [*A publication*]
US Nav Aerosp Med Inst (Pensacola) NAMI ...	US Naval Aerospace Medical Institute (Pensacola). NAMI [*A publication*]
US Nav Aerosp Med Res Lab (Pensacola) NAMRL ...	US Naval Aerospace Medical Research Laboratory (Pensacola). NAMRL [*A publication*]
US Nav Aerosp Med Res Lab (Pensacola) Spec Rep ...	US Naval Aerospace Medical Research Laboratory (Pensacola). Special Report [*A publication*]
US Nav Air Dev Cent NADC ...	US Naval Air Development Center. NADC [*A publication*]
US Naval Aerospace Med Inst ...	US Naval Aerospace Medical Institute [*A publication*]
US Naval Med Bull ...	United States Naval Medical Bulletin [*A publication*]
US Naval Ordnance Test Sta NAVORD Report ...	United States. Naval Ordnance Test Station. NAVORD Report [*A publication*]
US Naval Res Lab Shock Vib Bull ...	United States. Naval Research Laboratories. Shock and Vibration Bulletin [*A publication*]
US Naval Submar Med Cent Rep ...	US Naval Submarine Medical Center. Report [*A publication*]
US Nav Civ Eng Lab Tech Rep ...	United States. Department of the Navy. Naval Civil Engineering Laboratory [*Port Hueneme, California*]. Technical Report [*A publication*]
USNAVEUR ...	United States Naval Forces Europe (MCD)
USNAVFORCONAD ...	United States Naval Forces, Continental Air Defense Command (DNAB)
US Nav Inst Proc ...	US Naval Institute. Proceedings [*A publication*]
US Nav Med Bull ...	United States Naval Medical Bulletin [*A publication*]
US Nav Med Res Lab Rep ...	US Naval Medical Research Laboratory. Report [*A publication*]
USNAVMILCOMUN ...	United States Navy Representative, Military Staff Committee, United Nations (DNAB)
US Nav Oceanogr Off Spec Publ ...	US Naval Oceanographic Office. Special Publication [*A publication*]
US Nav Postgrad Sch Tech Rep/Res Paper ...	United States. Naval Postgraduate School. Technical Report/Research Paper [*A publication*]
USNAVPRO ...	United States Navy Plan Representative Office
USNAVREGDENCEN ...	United States Naval Regional Dental Center (DNAB)

USNAVREGMEDCEN ... United States Naval Regional Medical Center (DNAB)
US Nav Sch Aviat Med Monogr ... US Naval School of Aviation Medicine. Monograph [*A publication*]
US Nav Sch Aviat Med Res Rep ... US Naval School of Aviation Medicine. Research Report [*A publication*]
US Nav Ship Eng Cent Ship Struct Com Rep ... United States. Department of the Navy. Naval Ship Engineering Center. Ship Structure Committee. Report [*A publication*]
US Nav Ship Res Dev Cent Rep ... United States. Naval Ship Research and Development Center. Report [*A publication*]
USNAVSO ... United States Navy Forces Southern Command (AFM)
USNAVSOUTHC ... United States Navy Southern Command
USNAVSOUTHCOM ... United States Navy Southern Command
US Nav Submar Med Cent Memo Rep ... US Naval Submarine Medical Center. Memorandum Report [*A publication*]
US Nav Submar Med Cent Rep ... United States. Naval Submarine Medical Center. Report [*A publication*]
US Nav Submar Med Res Lab Memo Rep ... United States. Naval Submarine Medical Research Laboratory. Memorandum Report [*A publication*]
US Nav Submar Med Res Lab Rep ... US Naval Submarine Medical Research Laboratory. Report [*A publication*]
USNAVSUPACT ... United States Naval Supply Activity (CINC)
USNAVWEASERV ... United States Navy Weather Service
US Navy Electronics Lab Rept ... United States. Navy Electronics Laboratory. Report [*A publication*]
US Navy Med ... US Navy Medicine [*A publication*]
USNAVYMILCOMUN ... United States Naval Representative, United Nations Military Staff Committee
USNB .... United States Naval Base (MUGU)
USNC .... United States National Commission for UNESCO [*of the Department of State*]
USNC .... United States National Committee [*IEC*]
USNCB...... United States National Central Bureau
USNCB...... United States Naval Construction Battalion [*SEABEES*] [*BUDOCKS; later, FEC, NFEC*]
USNCBS ... US National Committee for Byzantine Studies (EA)
USNC/CIE ... US National Committee of the Commission Internationale de l'Eclairage [*International Commission on Illumination*] (EA)
USNC/DNDR ... United States National Committee for the Decade for Natural Disaster Reduction
USNCEL... United States Naval Civil Engineering Laboratory [*Port Hueneme, CA*] (SAA)
USNCEREL ... United States Naval Civil Engineering Research and Evaluation Laboratory
USNCFID ... United States National Committee for Federation Internationale de Documentation
USNC/IBP ... United States National Committee for the International Biological Program [*Defunct*] (EA)
USNCIEC ... United States National Committee of the International Electrotechnical Commission
USNC-IGY ... United States National Committee for the International Geophysical Year
USNCIPS ... United States National Committee of the International Peat Society (EA)
USNCPNM ... United States National Committee for the Preservation of Nubian Monuments [*Defunct*] (EA)
USNCSCOR ... US National Committee for the Scientific Committee on Oceanic Research (EA)
USNCSM & FE ... United States National Council on Soil Mechanics and Foundation Engineering
USNC-STR ... United States National Committee for Solar-Terrestrial Research (MCD)
USNC/TAM ... US National Committee on Theoretical and Applied Mechanics (EA)
USNC/UPSI ... United States National Committee/International Union of Radio Science (MCD)
USNC-URSI ... United States National Committee for the Union Radio Scientifique Internationale [*International Union of Radio Science*] (EA)
USNCWEC ... United States National Committee of the World Energy Conference (EA)
USNCWFD ... US National Committee for World Food Day (EA)
USNDC ..... United States Nuclear Data Committee [*Nuclear Regulatory Commission*]
USNDD ..... United States Naval Drydocks
USNEDS... United States Navy Experimental Diving Station
USNEES ... United States Naval Engineering Experiment Station [*Annapolis, MD*] (SAA)
USNEL...... United States Naval Electronics Laboratory
USNELM ... United States Naval Forces, Eastern Atlantic and Mediterranean (MCD)
US News .... US News and World Report [*A publication*]
US News World Rep ... US News and World Report [*A publication*]
USNFCLC ... US National Federation of Christian Life Communities (EA)
USNFEC ... US National Fruit Export Council [*Defunct*] (EA)
USNFP...... US Nicaragua Friendship Project (EA)
USNFPN... US Nuclear Free Pacific Network (EA)
USNFR...... United States Naval Fleet Reserve

USNG .... United States National Guard
USNH....... United States Naval Hospital
USNH....... United States, North of Cape Hatteras [*Shipping*]
USNHO .... United States Navy Hydrographic Office [*Later, NOO*] (NATG)
USNI .... United States Naval Institute (EA)
USN-I .... United States Regular Navy - Inductee
USN-I-CB ... United States Regular Navy - Inductee - Construction Battalion
USNID ...... United States National Institute of Dance (EA)
US N Inst Proc ... United States. Naval Institute. Proceedings [*A publication*]
USNIP .... United States. Naval Institute. Proceedings [*A publication*]
USN(I)(SA) ... United States Navy (Inductee) (Special Assignment)
USNL .... United States Navy League
USNLO ...... United States Naval Liaison Officer
USNM....... United States National Museum [*Smithsonian Institution*]
USNMATOEROF ... United States Mission to the North Atlantic Treaty Organization and European Regional Organizations in France
USNMDL ... United States Navy Mine Defense Laboratory (MUGU)
USNMF..... United States Naval Missile Facility
USNMF..... United States Navy Memorial Foundation (EA)
USNMPS.. United States Naval Motion Picture Service (DNAB)
USNMR ... United States National Military Representative
USNMRC ... United States Naval Manpower Center (DNAB)
USNMSC ... United States Navy Medical Service Corps
USNMTC ... United States Naval Missile Test Center [*Point Mugu, CA*] (AAG)
USNO........ United Sabah National Organization [*Malaysia*] [*Political party*] (PPW)
USNO........ United States Naval Observatory
USNOA ..... United States Norton Owners' Association (EA)
USNOADS ... United States Naval Observatory Automated Data Service [*Database*] [*Information service or system*] (CRD)
USNOBSY ... United States Naval Operating Bases System
USNOBSYSUBSTA ... United States Naval Observatory, Time Service Sub-Station (DNAB)
USNOF ..... United States NOTAM Office (FAAC)
USNOO..... United States Naval Oceanographic Office [*Marine science*] (MSC)
US North Cent For Exp Res Pap NC ... US North Central Forest Experiment Station. Research Paper NC [*A publication*]
US (Noth).. Ueberlieferungsgeschichtliche Studien (M. Noth) [*A publication*] (BJA)
USNO-TS ... United States Naval Observatory Time Service Division [*Washington, DC*]
USNOTS... United States Naval Ordnance Test Station
USNOWSP ... United States National Ocean-Wide Survey Program (NOAA)
USNP .... United States Naval Prison
USNP .... United States Newspaper Program [*National Foundation on the Arts and the Humanities*] [*Information service or system*] (IID)
USNPACMISTESCEN ... US Navy Pacific Missile Test Center
USNPG ..... United States Naval Proving Ground
USNPGS... United States Naval Postgraduate School (MUGU)
USNPS...... United States Naval Postgraduate School
USNR .... United States Naval Reserve
USNR .... United States Navy Regulations
USN-R....... United States Navy - Retired (DNAB)
USNRB...... United States Naval Repair Base
USNRC ..... United States Nuclear Regulatory Commission (NRCH)
USNRDL.... United States Naval Radiological Defense Laboratory
USNRDL.... United States Navy Research and Development Laboratory
USN(Ret)... United States Navy (Retired)
USNRF...... United States Naval Reserve Force
USNRL...... United States Naval Research Laboratory
USNRM .... United States Merchant Marine Reserve
USNRM1 .. United States Merchant Marine Reserve Seagoing
USNRM2 .. United States Merchant Marine Reserve Coastal Defense
USNRO..... United States Organized Naval Reserve
USNRO1... United States Organized Naval Reserve Seagoing
USNRO2... United States Organized Naval Reserve Aviation
USN-ROTC ... United States Navy - Reserve Officers Training Corps
USNRP...... United States National Reference Preparation [*Centers for Disease Control*]
USNR-R..... United States Naval Reserve - Retired (DNAB)
USNR-S..... United States Naval Reserve - Standby (DNAB)
USNRS...... United States Navy Recruiting Station
USNR & SL ... United States Navy Radio and Sound Laboratory [*San Diego, CA*]
USNRSV.... United States Naval Reserve, Selective Volunteer
USNRTC.... United States Naval Reserve Training Center
USNRV ..... United States Naval Reserve, Volunteer
USNR(W) ... United States Naval Reserve (Women's Reserve)
USNS......... United States Naval Ship [*Civilian manned*]
USNS......... United States Naval Station
USNS......... Universal Stabilized Night Sight
USNSA...... United States National Student Association [*Later, USSA*]
USNSC ..... United States Navy Safety Code
USNSCF ... United States Naval Shore Communication Facilities
USNSISSMFE ... US National Society for the International Society of Soil Mechanics and Foundation Engineering (EA)

USNSMC ...   United States Naval Submarine Medical Center
USNSMSES ...   United States Navy Ship Missile System Engineering Station
USNSO .....   United States Navy Southern Command
USNSPO...   United States Navy Special Projects Office   (DNAB)
USNSPS....   United States National Stockpile Purchase Specification [*for metals*]
USN-SV ....   United States Regular Navy Selective Volunteer
USNTC......   United States Naval Training Center
USNTDC...   United States Naval Training Device Center
USNTI......   United States Navy Travel Instructions
US NTIS AD Rep ...   United States. National Technical Information Service. AD Report [*A publication*]
USNTIS PB Rep ...   United States. National Technical Information Service. PB Report [*A publication*]
USNTPS ..   United States Naval Test Pilot School
USNTS......   United States Naval Training School
USNUSL...   United States Navy Underwater Sound Laboratory [*BUSHIPS; later, ESC, NESC*]
USN & USMCRC ...   United States Navy and United States Marine Corps Reserve Center   (DNAB)
USNWC ....   United States Naval War College
USNWR ....   US News and World Report [*A publication*]
USNZC......   United States-New Zealand Council   (EA)
USO..........   Under Secretary of the Navy's Office
USO..........   Unidentified Submarine Object
USO..........   Unilateral Salpingo-Oophorectomy [*Gynecology*]   (MAE)
USO..........   Unit Security Officer   (AAG)
USO..........   United Service Organizations, Inc.   (EA)
USO..........   United Siscoe Mines, Inc. [*Toronto Stock Exchange symbol*]
USO..........   Universal Service Order [*Bell System*]   (TEL)
USO..........   Unmanned Seismological Observatory
USO..........   US Office - UTLAS Corp. [*UTLAS symbol*]
USOA ....   Uniform System of Accounts [*Telecommunications*]   (TEL)
USOA ....   United Shoppers of America, Inc. [*NASDAQ symbol*]   (NQ)
USOA ....   United States Olympic Association [*Later, USOC*]
USOA ....   United States Othello Association   (EA)
USOA ....   United States Overseas Airlines
US Oak Ridge Natl Lab Radiat Shield Inf Cent Rep ...   United States. Oak Ridge National Laboratory. Radiation Shielding Information Center. Report [*A publication*]
USOAS......   United States Mission to the Organization of American States [*Department of State*]
USO-ASPCC ...   USO [*United Service Organizations*]-All Service Postal Chess Club [*Later, ASPCC*]   (EA)
USOC ....   Uniform Service Order Code [*Bell System*]   (TEL)
USOC ....   United States Olympic Committee   (EA)
USOCA .....   United States Office of Consumer Affairs
USOCA .....   US 1 Class Association   (EA)
USOCA .....   US Out of Central America   (EA)
U So Cal Tax Inst ...   University of Southern California Tax Institute   (DLA)
U So Carol ...   University of South Carolina. Business and Economic Review [*A publication*]
USOCDC ..   US Overseas Cooperative Development Committee   (EA)
USO-CLAT ...   US Relations Office of CLAT [*Central Latinoamericana de Trabajadores*]   (EA)
USOE ....   United States Office of Education [*Later, USDE*]
USOECD...   United States Mission to the Organization for Economic Cooperation and Development [*Department of State*]
USOF ....   United States Orienteering Federation   (EA)
USOFA......   Under Secretary of the Army
USOFAF ...   Under Secretary of the Air Force
US Office Ed Bul ...   United States. Office of Education. Bulletin [*A publication*]
US Office Ed Circ ...   United States. Office of Education. Circulars [*A publication*]
US Office Ed Pub ...   United States. Office of Education. Publications [*A publication*]
US Office Ed Voc Div Bul ...   United States. Office of Education. Vocational Division. Bulletin [*A publication*]
US Office Saline Water Research and Devel Progress Rept ...   United States. Office of Saline Water Research and Development. Progress Report [*A publication*]
US Off Libr Serv Bibliogr Ser ...   US Office of Library Service. Bibliography Series [*A publication*]
US Off Nav Res Rep ACR ...   United States. Office of Naval Research. Report ACR [*A publication*]
US Off Pub Roads B ...   US Office of Public Roads. Bulletin [*A publication*]
US Off Saline Water Res Dev Prog Rep ...   United States. Office of Saline Water Research and Development. Progress Report [*A publication*]
USOID ......   United States Oversea Internal Defense [*Army*]   (AABC)
USOL ....   US Oil Co. [*NASDAQ symbol*]   (NQ)
USOLTA...   Uniform Simplification of Land Transfers Act [*National Conference of Commissioners on Uniform State Laws*]
USOM.......   United States Operations Mission [*Military*]
USOMC ....   United States Ordnance Missile Command
USONIA ...   United States of North America [*Name of a cooperative community in Pleasantville, NY designed by Frank Lloyd Wright*]
USONR.....   United States Office of Naval Research
USOPA......   United States Ordnance Producers Association [*Inactive*]   (EA)

USOSP......   United States Ocean Survey Plan   (NOAA)
US Outlook ...   United States Industrial Outlook [*A publication*]
USOVA .....   United States Outdoor Volleyball Association   (EA)
USp...........   Springville City Library, Springville, UT [*Library symbol*] [*Library of Congress*]   (LCLS)
USP...........   Ultrasensitive Position   (AFM)
USP...........   Under the Sign of Pisces [*A publication*]
USP...........   Underwater Sound Projection
USP...........   Uniform Specification Program   (AAG)
USP...........   Unique Selling Point
USP...........   Unique Selling Proposition [*Advertising*]
USP...........   Unit Stream Power [*Hydrology*]
USP...........   Unit Support Plan   (MCD)
USP...........   United Socialist Party [*South Korea*] [*Political party*]   (PPW)
USP...........   United States Patent
USP...........   United States Penitentiary
USP...........   United States Pharmacopeia [*Following name of a substance, signifies substance meets standards set by USP*]
USP...........   United States Pharmacopeial Convention [*Database producer*]   (EA)
USP...........   United States Postal Service Library, Washington, DC [*OCLC symbol*]   (OCLC)
USP...........   United States Property
USP...........   Universal Signal Processor
USP...........   Universal Systems Patching [*Mod-Tap System, Inc.*]
USP...........   Upper Sequential Permissive [*Nuclear energy*]   (NRCH)
USP...........   Upper Solution Point
USP...........   Urban Studies Project
USP...........   US Precious Metals, Inc. [*Toronto Stock Exchange symbol*] [*Vancouver Stock Exchange symbol*]
USP...........   Usage Sensitive Pricing [*Telecommunications*]
USP...........   Utility Seaplane [*Navy, Coast Guard*]
USP...........   Utility Storage Print   (SAA)
USP...........   Utility Summary Program
USPA.........   Uniform Single Publication Act [*National Conference of Commissioners on Uniform State Laws*]
USPA.........   Uniformed Services Pay Act
USPA.........   United States Parachute Association   (EA)
USPA.........   United States Passport Agency [*Department of State*]
USPA.........   United States Pilots Association   (EA)
USPA.........   United States Polo Association   (EA)
USPA.........   United States Potters' Association   (EA)
USPA.........   US Patents Alert [*Derwent, Inc.*] [*Database*]
USPA.........   US Psychotronics Association   (EA)
USPAACC ...   United States PanAsian American Chamber of Commerce   (EAIO)
US Pacific RR Expl ...   US War Department. Pacific Railroad Explorations [*A publication*]
US Pac Northwest For Range Exp Stn Res Note PNW ...   US Pacific Northwest Forest and Range Experiment Station. Research Note PNW [*A publication*]
USPACOM ...   United States Pacific Command [*Military*]
USPAK......   US-Pakistan Economic Council   (EA)
US Pap Maker ...   United States Paper Maker [*A publication*]
US Pat Off Off Gaz US Pat Off Pat ...   US Patent Office. Official Gazette of the United States Patent Office. Patents [*A publication*]
US Pat Q....   United States Patent Quarterly [*A publication*]   (DLA)
US Pat Quar ...   United States Patent Quarterly [*A publication*]   (DLA)
US Pat Quart ...   United States Patent Quarterly [*A publication*]   (DLA)
US Pat Trademark Off Off Gaz US Pat Trademark Off Pat ...   US Patent and Trademark Office. Official Gazette of the United States Patent and Trademark Office. Patents [*A publication*]
Usp Biol Chim ...   Uspechi Biologiceskoj Chimii [*A publication*]
Usp Biol Khim ...   Uspekhi Biologicheskoi Khimii [*Former USSR*] [*A publication*]
USPC.........   Union des Syndicats Professionels du Cameroun [*Federation of Professional Trade Unions of Cameroon*]
USPC.........   United States Parole Commission [*Formerly, United States Parole Board*]
USPC.........   United States Peace Corps   (EA)
USPC.........   United States Pony Clubs   (EA)
USPC.........   United States Procurement Committee
USPC.........   United States Purchasing Commission
USPC.........   US Peace Council   (EA)
USPC.........   US Playing Card Corp. [*NASDAQ symbol*]   (NQ)
USPCA......   United States Police Canine Association   (EA)
USPCC......   Utility and Support Programming Control Committee   (SAA)
USPCF......   US Professional Cycling Federation [*Later, USPRO*]   (EA)
Usp Chim...   Uspechi Chimii [*A publication*]
USPCS ......   US Philatelic Classics Society   (EA)
USPCU......   US Postal Chess Union   (EA)
USPD.........   Unabhaengige Sozialdemokratische Partei Deutschlands [*Independent Social Democratic Party of Germany*] [*Political party*]   (PPE)
USPD.........   US Publicity Director [*A publication*]
USPDCA....   United States Professional Diving Coaches Association   (EA)
USPDI.......   United States Pharmacopeia Dispensing Information
USPDI.......   United States Professional Development Institute [*Silver Spring, MD*]
USPDLTR ...   [*Reference*] Your Speedletter [*Military*]
USPDO .....   United States Property and Disbursing Officer

USP & DO ... United States Property and Disbursing Officer
USPE .... United States Purchasing Exchange
USPEC ...... United States Paper Exporters Council   (EA)
Uspehi Fiz Nauk ... Akademija Nauk SSSR. Uspehi Fiziceskih Nauk [*A publication*]
Uspehi Mat Nauk ... Akademija Nauk SSSR i Moskovskoe Matematiceskoe Obscestvo. Uspehi Matematiceskih Nauk [*A publication*]
Uspekhi Fiz Nauk ... Uspekhi Fizicheskikh Nauk [*A publication*]
Uspekhi Mat Nauk ... Uspekhi Matematicheskikh Nauk [*A publication*]
USPEPA .... United States Poultry and Egg Producers Association   (EA)
USPF .... US Powerlifting Federation   (EA)
Usp Fizic N ... Uspechi Fizicesickh Nauk [*A publication*]
Usp Fiziol Nauk ... Uspekhi Fiziologicheskikh Nauk [*A publication*]
Usp Fiz Nau ... Uspekhi Fizicheskikh Nauk [*A publication*]
Usp Fiz Nauk ... Uspekhi Fizicheskii Nauk [*A publication*]
USPFO ...... United States Property and Fiscal Officer [*Military*]
Usp Foton .. Uspekhi Fotoniki [*A publication*]
Usp Fotoniki ... Uspekhi Fotoniki [*A publication*]
US/PFUN ... United States People for the United Nations [*Defunct*]   (EA)
USPG .... Uniform System of Accounts Prescribed for Natural Gas Companies
USPG .... United Society for the Propagation of the Gospel [*Formed by a merger of Society for the Propagation of the Gospel in Foreign Parts and UMCA*]   (EAIO)
USpGS ...... Church of Jesus Christ of Latter-Day Saints, Genealogical Society Library, Springville Branch, Springville, UT [*Library symbol*] [*Library of Congress*]   (LCLS)
USPh .... United States Pharmacopoeia
US Pharm ... US Pharmacist [*A publication*]
USPHD5 ... US Pharmacist [*A publication*]
USPHS ...... United States Postal History Society [*Defunct*]   (EA)
USPHS ...... United States Public Health Service
USPHSR .... United States Public Health Service Reserve
USPHT ...... United States Precision Helicopter Team
USPI .... Unione Stampa Periodica Italiana [*Press association*]   (EY)
USPI .... University Science Partners, Inc. [*NASDAQ symbol*]   (NQ)
USPIN ...... United States Pacific Issues Network   (EA)
USPIRG .... US Public Interest Research Group   (EA)
Usp Kh ...... Uspekhi Khimii [*A publication*]
Usp Khim ... Uspekhi Khimii [*A publication*]
Usp Khim Fosfororg Seraorg Soedin ... Uspekhi Khimii Fosfororganicheskikh i Seraorganicheskikh Soedinenii [*A publication*]
Usp Khim Tekhnol Polim ... Uspekhi Khimii i Tekhnologii Polimerov [*A publication*]
USPL .... Uniform System of Accounts, Public Utilities, and Licensees [*Federal Power Commission*]
USPL .... Unpriced Spare Parts List
USPLS ...... United States Public-Land Surveys
USPLTA .... United States Professional Lawn Tennis Association [*Later, USPTA*]   (EA)
USPM .... United Society of Pattern Makers [*A union*] [*British*]
USPM .... US Precious Metals, Inc. [*Vancouver, BC*] [*NASDAQ symbol*]   (NQ)
Usp Mat Nauk ... Uspekhi Matematicheskikh Nauk [*A publication*]
USPMF ..... US Patent Model Foundation   (EA)
Usp Mikrobiol ... Uspekhi Mikrobiologii [*A publication*]
Usp Mol Biol ... Uspekhi na Molekulyarnata Biologiya [*A publication*]
USPMOM ... Union des Societes de Pediatrie du Moyen-Orient et de la Mediterranee [*Union of Middle Eastern and Mediterranean Pediatric Societies - UMEMPS*] [*Athens, Greece*]   (EAIO)
USPN .... US Pawn, Inc. [*NASDAQ symbol*]   (NQ)
Usp Nauchn Fotogr ... Uspekhi Nauchnoi Fotografii [*A publication*]
USPO .... United Sabah People's Organization [*Pertubuhan Rakyat Sabah Bersatu*] [*Malaysia*] [*Political party*]   (PPW)
USPO .... United States Patent Office [*Department of Commerce*]
USPO .... United States Post Office [*Later, United States Postal Service*]
US Polit Sci Doc ... United States Political Science Documents [*A publication*]
US Posture ... United States Military Posture [*A publication*]
USPP .... United States Pacifist Party [*Political party*]   (EA)
USPP .... United States Park Police [*Department of the Interior*]
USPP .... University Science Policy Planning [*Program*] [*National Science Foundation*]
USPPA ...... United States Pulp Producers Association [*Later, API*]   (EA)
USPPI .... United States Producer Price Index [*Database*] [*Department of Labor*] [*Information service or system*]   (CRD)
USPPS ...... US Possessions Philatelic Society   (EA)
USPQ .... United States Patents Quarterly
USPQ BNA ... United States Patents Quarterly. Bureau of National Affairs [*A publication*]
USPRO ...... US Professional Cycling Federation   (EA)
USPS .... United States Postal Service
USPS .... United States Power Squadrons   (EA)
USPSA ...... US Practical Shooting Association   (EA)
USPSD ...... United States Political Science Documents [*Information service or system*] [*A publication*]
USPSDA ... United States Private Security and Detective Association   (EA)
USPSF .... United States Pigeon Shooting Federation [*Defunct*]   (EA)
Usp Sovrem Biol ... Uspekhi Sovremennoi Biologii [*A publication*]
Usp Sovrem Genet ... Uspekhi Sovremennoi Genetiki [*A publication*]
USPT .... United Societies of Physiotherapists   (EA)

USPTA ...... United States Physical Therapy Association   (EA)
USPTA ...... United States Pony Trotting Association   (EA)
USPTA ...... United States Professional Tennis Association   (EA)
USPTA ...... US Paddle Tennis Association   (EA)
USPTO ...... United States Patent and Trademark Office
USPTR ...... United States Professional Tennis Registry   (EA)
USPTS .... USP Real Estate Investment Trust SBI [*NASDAQ symbol*]   (SPSG)
US Publ H Rep ... US Public Health Report [*A publication*]
US Public Health Serv Public Health Monogr ... United States. Public Health Service. Public Health Monograph [*A publication*]
US Public Health Serv Radiol Health Data Rep ... US Public Health Service. Radiological Health Data and Reports [*A publication*]
USPWIC ... United States Prisoner of War Information Center [*Army*]   (AABC)
USPWIC(Br) ... United States Prisoner of War Information Center (Branch) [*Army*]   (AABC)
USQ .... United States Quarterly Book Review [*A publication*]
US Q Bk R ... United States Quarterly Book Review [*A publication*]
USQBL ...... United States Quarterly Book List [*A publication*]
USQBR ...... United States Quarterly Book Review [*A publication*]
USQMC ..... United States Quartermaster Corps
USQR .... Union Seminary. Quarterly Review [*A publication*]
US Quartermaster Food Container Inst Armed Forces Libr Bull ... US Quartermaster Food and Container Institute for the Armed Forces. Library Bulletin [*A publication*]
USR .... Ukrainska Partiia Sotsialistov Revolyutsionerov [*Ukrainian Socialist Revolutionary Party*] [*Russian*] [*Political party*]   (PPE)
USR .... Ultrasonic Radiation
USR .... Under Speed Relay   (MCD)
USR .... Unheated Serum Reagin (Test) [*Clinical chemistry*]   (AAMN)
USR .... Union Seminary. Review [*A publication*]
USR .... Unit Site Representative [*Army*]
USR .... Unit Status Report [*Army*]
USR .... United States [*Supreme Court*] Reports
USR .... United States Reserves
USR .... Up Stage Right [*Away from audience*] [*A stage direction*]
USR .... US Shoe Corp. [*NYSE symbol*]   (SPSG)
USR .... User Service Request
USR .... User Service Routine [*Digital Equipment Corp.*]
USR .... User Status Reporting   (MCD)
USR .... Usher of the Scarlet Rod   (ROG)
USRA .... United Sportsman Racers Association   (EA)
USRA .... United States Racquetball Association   (EA)
USRA .... United States Railway Association [*In 1974, superseded United States Railroad Administration, which had been absorbed by the Department of Transportation in 1939*] [*Terminated in 1987*]
USRA .... United States Revolver Association   (EA)
USRA .... United States Rowing Association   (EA)
USRA .... United Street Rod Association   (EA)
USRA .... Universities Space Research Association   (EA)
USRAC ...... US Repeating Arms Company
USRAD ...... United States Fleet Shore Radio Station
USR-Borotbists ... Ukrainska Partiia Sotsialistov Revolyutsionerov-Borotbists [*Ukrainian Socialist Revolutionary Party-Fighters*] [*Russian*] [*Political party*]   (PPE)
USRCMM ... US Region of Congregation of Mariannhill Missionaries [*Later, CMM*]   (EA)
USRCPAC ... United States Reserve Components and Personnel Administration Center
USRCS ...... United States Revenue Cutter Service
USRCSI ..... United States Red Cedar Shingle Industry
USRD .... Underwater Sound Reference Detachment [*Navy*] [*Orlando, FL*]
US-RDA .... Union Soudanaise - Rassemblement Democratique Africain [*Mali*] [*Political party*]   (EY)
USRDA ..... US Recommended Daily Allowance [*Nutrition*]
USRD/NRL ... Underwater Sound Reference Division, Naval Research Laboratory
USRE .... US Facilities Corp. [*Costa Mesa, CA*] [*NASDAQ symbol*]   (NQ)
USREC ...... United States Environment and Resources Council [*Marine science*]   (MSC)
USREDA ... United States Rice Export Development Association [*Later, RCMD*]
USREDCOM ... United States Readiness Command
US Reg .... United States Register [*Philadelphia*] [*A publication*]   (DLA)
US Reh Den ... Rehearing Denied by United States Supreme Court [*Legal term*]   (DLA)
US Reh Dis ... Rehearing Dismissed by United States Supreme Court [*Legal term*]   (DLA)
US Rep .... United States Reports [*A publication*]   (DLA)
US Rep (L Ed) ... United States Supreme Court Reports, Lawyers' Edition [*A publication*]   (DLA)
USREPMC ... United States Representative to the Military Committee [*NATO*]
USREPMILCOMLO ... United States Representative to the Military Committee Liaison Office [*NATO*]

USREPMILCOMUN ... United States Representative, Military Staff Committee, United Nations
USREPOF ... United States Navy Reporting Office [*or Officer*]
US Res Developm Rep ... United States Government Research and Development Reports [*A publication*]
US Rev St .. United States Revised Statutes [*A publication*]   (DLA)
USRFP ...... US Requests for Proposals [*Washington Representative Service*] [*Information service or system*] [*Defunct*]   (CRD)
USRI.......... US Resources, Inc. [*Columbus, OH*] [*NASDAQ symbol*]   (NQ)
USRL.......... Laryak [*Former USSR*] [*ICAO location identifier*]   (ICLI)
USRL........ Underwater Sound Reference Laboratory [*Navy*]
USRL.......... US Realty Partners Ltd. [*Greenville, SC*] [*NASDAQ symbol*]   (NQ)
USRM .... United States Revenue Marine
USRN .... Nizhnevartovsk [*Former USSR*] [*ICAO location identifier*]   (ICLI)
USRNMC ... United States Representative to NATO Military Committee   (AABC)
USRO .... Ultrasmall Structures Research Office [*University of Michigan*] [*Research center*]   (RCD)
USRO .... United States Mission to NATO and European Regional Organizations
USRO .... United States Navy Routing Office
USRP .... United States Refugee Program
USRPA....... United States Racing Pigeon Association [*Defunct*]   (EA)
USRPHC... US Real Property Holding Co.
USRR.......... Surgut [*Former USSR*] [*ICAO location identifier*]   (ICLI)
USRRC ...... United States Road Racing Championship
USRR Lab Bd Dec ... Decisions of the United States Railroad Labor Board [*A publication*]   (DLA)
USRS......... United States Reclamation Service
USRS......... United States Revised Statutes
USRS......... United States Robotics Society   (CSR)
USRS......... United States Rocket Society   (EA)
USRS......... United States Rowing Society   (EA)
USRSA....... United States Racquet Stringers Association   (EA)
USRSG...... United States Representative, Standing Group [*Military*]   (AABC)
USRT......... Universal Synchronous Receiver/Transmitter
USRTA...... United States Recreational Tennis Association   (EA)
USRX........ US Robotics [*NASDAQ symbol*]   (SPSG)
USS........... Ultrasound Scanning
USS........... Ultraviolet Scanning Spectrometer
US of S....... Under Secretary of State
USS........... Underwater Sound Source
USS........... Unified S-Band System [*Radio*]
USS........... Union Syndicale Suisse [*Swiss Federation of Trade Unions*]
USS........... Unique Signal Switch
USS........... United Scholarship Service [*Later, NCAIAE, NCAIE*]
USS........... United Seamen's Service   (EA)
USS........... United States Naval Vessel
USS........... United States Sellers [*Standard threads*]   (DEN)
USS........... United States Senate
USS........... United States Ship
USS........... United States Standard
USS........... United States Steamer
USS........... United States Surgical Corp. [*NYSE symbol*]   (SPSG)
USS........... United States Swimming, Inc.   (EA)
USS........... United Swedish Societies   (EA)
USS........... Universities Superannuation Scheme
USS........... US Steel Canada, Inc. [*Toronto Stock Exchange symbol*]
USS........... US Steel Corp. [*Also, USSC*] [*Later, USX Corp.*]
USS........... USAF [*United States Air Force*] Security Service
USSA......... Usage Sensitive Service [*Telecommunications*]
USS........... USAREUR [*United States Army, Europe*] Support System
USS........... User Services Support   (SSD)
USS........... User Support System   (MCD)
USS........... Utility Support Structure   (MCD)
USSA .... Underground Security Storage Association [*Defunct*]
USSA......... Uniaxial Split-Sphere Apparatus [*Mineralogy*]
USSA......... Union Suisse des Syndicats Autonomes [*Swiss Association of Autonomous Unions*]
USSA......... United Saw Service Association   (EA)
USSA......... United States Salvage Association   (EA)
USSA......... United States Security Authority [*for NATO affairs*]
USSA......... United States Ski Association   (EA)
USSA......... United States Snowshoe Association   (EA)
USSA......... United States Sports Academy   (EA)
USSA......... United States Standard Atmosphere   (KSC)
USSA......... United States Student Association   (EA)
USSA......... United States Swimming Association   (EA)
USSL......... United Sugar Samplers' Association [*Defunct*]
USSA......... US Sidewinder Association   (EA)
USSA......... US Soling Association   (EA)
USSAC ...... United States Army Ambulance Service Association [*Defunct*]   (EA)
USSAC....... United States Security Authority for CENTO Affairs   (AABC)
USSAF ...... United States Strategic Air Force [*Later, Strategic Air Command*]
USSAF ...... US Sports Acrobatic Federation   (EA)

USSAFE.... United States Strategic Air Forces in Europe
USSAG...... United States Support Activities Group [*Military*]
USSAH...... United States Soldiers' and Airmen's Home   (AABC)
USSALEP ... US-South Africa Leader Exchange Program   (EA)
USSAN...... United States Security Authority, NATO
USSAS ...... United States Security Authority for SEATO Affairs   (AABC)
USSB .... United States Satellite Broadcasting Co., Inc. [*Minneapolis, MN*] [*Telecommunications*]   (TSSD)
USSB .... United States Shipping Board [*Terminated, 1933*]
USSB .... United States Shipping Board Decisions [*A publication*]   (DLA)
USSBA ...... United States Seniors Bowling Association [*Later, Seniors Division of the American Bowling Congress*]   (EA)
USSBB ...... United States Shipping Board Bureau Decisions [*A publication*]   (DLA)
USSBD ...... United States Savings Bonds Division [*Department of the Treasury*]
USSBF .... United States Skibob Federation   (EA)
USSBIA ..... United States Stone and Bead Importers Association   (EA)
USSBL....... United States Stickball League   (EA)
USSBS....... United States Strategic Bombing Survey [*Disbanded, 1946*]
USSC .... United States Servas Committee   (EA)
USSC .... United States Strike Command [*Military combined Tactical Air Command and Strategic Army Command Force*]
USSC........ United States Supreme Court
USSC......... US Steel Corp. [*Also, USS*] [*Later, USX Corp.*]   (MCD)
USSC......... US Systems Corp.   (EA)
USSCA ...... US Ski Coaches Association   (EA)
US-SCAN ... United States Special Committee on Antarctic Names [*1943-47*]
US Sci Educ Adm Agric Res Man ... US Science and Education Administration. Agricultural Research Manual [*A publication*]
USSC Rep ... United States Supreme Court Reports [*A publication*]   (DLA)
USSCT ...... United States Supreme Court
USSDP ...... Uniformed Services Savings Deposits Program   (AABC)
USSE .... Severouralsk [*Former USSR*] [*ICAO location identifier*]   (ICLI)
USSE .... Ultrasonic Soldering Equipment
USSE .... University of Saga. Studies in English [*A publication*]
USSEA ...... United States Scientific Export Association
USSEA ...... United States Society for Education through Art   (EA)
USSEA ...... United States Space Education Association   (EA)
USSECMILCOMUN ... [*The*] Secretary, United States Delegation United Nations Military Staff Committee
US Seed Rep ... United States Seed Reporter [*A publication*]
USSEF .... United States Ski Educational Foundation   (EA)
USSEI .... United States Society of Esperanto Instructors [*Later, AATE*]   (AEBS)
US Serv M ... United States Service Magazine [*A publication*]
USSES....... US Sheep Experiment Station [*University of Idaho*] [*Research center*]   (RCD)
USSF .... Ulster Special Service Force [*British military*]   (DMA)
USSF .... United States Soccer Federation   (EA)
USSF .... United States Softball Federation
USSF .... United States Space Foundation   (EA)
USSF .... United States Special Forces
USSF .... United States Steel Foundation
USSF .... United States Surfing Federation   (EA)
USSF .... United States Swimming Foundation   (EA)
USSFA ...... United States Soccer Football Association [*Later, USSF*]   (EA)
USSFFA .... United Soft Serve and Fast Food Association [*Later, NSSFFA*]   (EA)
USSF(P) ..... United States Special Forces (Provisional)   (CINC)
USSFR....... US Scottish Fiddling Revival   (EA)
USSG........ United States Standard Gauge
USSGA...... United States Seniors Golf Association [*Defunct*]   (EA)
USSGA...... Uspekhi Sovremennoi Genetiki [*A publication*]
USSGREP... United States Standing Group Representative [*NATO*]
USSH .... United States Soldiers' Home
US Ship Struct Com Rep ... United States. Ship Structure Committee. Report [*A publication*]
USSHN ..... Usher Syndrome Self-Help Network   (EA)
USShoe...... US Shoe Corp. [*Associated Press abbreviation*]   (APAG)
USSI .... Ivdel [*Former USSR*] [*ICAO location identifier*]   (ICLI)
USSI .... Ultrasonic Soldering Iron
USSI .... United Software Security, Inc. [*Vienna, VA*] [*NASDAQ symbol*]   (NQ)
USSI .... United States Strategic Institute   (EA)
USSI .... USS Interphase   (EA)
USSIA .... United States Shellac Importers Association   (EA)
USSIAFCM ... USS Intrepid Association of Former Crew Members   (EA)
USSID .... United States Signal Intelligence Directive   (AABC)
US-SIOP ... United States Single Integrated Operational Plan   (NATG)
USSIS........ United States Signals Intelligence System   (MCD)
USSLL....... United States Savings and Loan League [*Later, USLSL*]   (EA)
USSMA ...... US Spanish Merchants Association   (EA)
USSNBA ... USS [*United States Ship*] Natoma Bay Association   (EA)
USSOA...... USS [*United States Ship*] Oklahoma Association   (EA)
USSOC....... United States Special Operations Command [*DoD*]
USSOCOM ... United States Special Operations Command [*DoD*]
US Soil Conserv Service Sedimentation Bull (TP) ... United States. Soil Conservation Service. Sedimentation Bulletin (Technical Publication) [*A publication*]

US Soil Conserv Serv Soil Surv ... US Soil Conservation Service. Soil Survey [*A publication*]
USSOUTHCOM ... United States Southern Command [*Air Force*]
USSP .... User Systems Support Plan
USSPA ...... Uniformed Services Special Pay Act (DNAB)
USSPA ...... United States Student Press Association [*Superseded by CPS*]
USSPACECOM ... United States Space Command
USSPC ...... US Student Pugwash Committee (EA)
USSPEI ..... Union des Syndicats des Services Publics Europeens et Internationaux [*European and International Public Services Union*] [*Later, EUROFEDOP*] (EAIO)
USSPG ...... United States Senate Press Photographers Gallery (EA)
USSPG ...... US Sweetener Producers Group [*Later, ASA*] (EA)
USSPL ...... United Ship Scrapers' Protection League [*A union*] [*British*]
USSPPG .... United States Senate Press Photographers Gallery (EA)
USSR .... State Music Trust [*Record label*] [*Former USSR*]
USSR .... Uninterrupted Sustained Silent Reading
USSR .... Union of Soviet Socialist Republics [*See also SSSR, CCCP*]
U d SSR ..... Union der Sozialistischen Sowjetrepubliken [*A publication*]
USSRA ...... United States Squash Racquets Association (EA)
USSRCFT ... USSR State Committee for Foreign Tourism (EAIO)
USSR Comp Info B ... USSR. Union of Composers. Information Bulletin [*A publication*]
USSR Computational Math and Math Phys ... USSR Computational Mathematics and Mathematical Physics [*A publication*]
USSR Comput Math Math Phys ... USSR Computational Mathematics and Mathematical Physics [*A publication*]
USSRM ..... State Music Trust [*78 RPM*] [*Record label*] [*Former USSR*]
USSRN ...... Under Secretary of State for the Royal Navy [*British*]
USSR Rep Earth Sci ... USSR Report. Earth Sciences [*Arlington*] [*A publication*]
USSR Rep Eng Equip ... USSR Report. Engineering Equipment [*A publication*]
USSS .... Sverdlovsk [*Former USSR*] [*ICAO location identifier*] (ICLI)
USSS .... Undersea Surveillance System (MCD)
USSS .... United States Secret Service [*Department of the Treasury*]
USSS .... United States Signals Intelligence System (MCD)
USSS .... United States Steamship
USSS .... Unmanned Sensing Satellite System
USSS .... US Shelter Corp. [*NASDAQ symbol*] (NQ)
USSSA ...... United States Slo-Pitch Softball Association (EA)
USSSA ...... United States Snowshoe Association (EA)
USSSI .... United Stamp Society for Shut-Ins (EA)
USSSI .... United States Satellite Systems, Inc. [*Defunct*] (TSSD)
USSSI .... United States Synchronized Swimming, Inc. (EA)
USSSMA .. US Shake and Shingle Manufacturers Association (EA)
USSSO ...... United States Sending State Office [*Navy*]
USSST ...... United States Sellers Standard Thread
USSS/UD ... United States Secret Service Uniformed Division
USSTAF .... United States Strategic Air Force [*Later, Strategic Air Command*]
USSTAFE ... United States Strategic Tactical Air Force, Europe
US Stat ...... United States Statutes at Large [*A publication*] (DLA)
US Steel News ... United States Steel News [*A publication*]
US St at L ... United States Statutes at Large [*A publication*] (DLA)
USSTRICOM ... United States Strike Command [*Military combined Tactical Air Command and Strategic Army Command Force*]
USSTS ...... US Student Travel Service (EA)
US St Tr ..... United States State Trials [*Wharton*] [*A publication*] (DLA)
US Sup Ct ... United States Supreme Court Reporter [*A publication*] (DLA)
US Sup Ct (L Ed) ... United States Supreme Court Reports, Lawyers' Edition [*A publication*] (DLA)
US Sup Ct R ... United States Supreme Court Reporter [*A publication*] (DLA)
US Sup Ct Rep ... United States Supreme Court Reporter [*A publication*] (DLA)
US Sup Ct Reps ... Supreme Court Reporter [*A publication*] (DLA)
US Surg ..... United States Surgical Corp. [*Associated Press abbreviation*] (APAG)
USSWA ...... United States Ski Writers Association [*Later, NASJA*] (EA)
UST .... Ultrasonic Test
UST .... Ultrasonic Transducer [*Crystal*] [*Used in measuring human cardiac output*]
UST .... Unblocked Serial Telemetry (MCD)
UST .... Underground Storage Tank [*Environmental Protection Agency*]
UST .... Undersea Technology
UST .... Uniform Specification Tree
UST .... Union Senegalaise du Travail [*Senegalese Labor Union*]
UST .... Union Socialiste Tchadienne [*Chadian Socialist Union*]
UST .... Unit Security Technician
UST .... United States Testing Co., Inc. (NASA)
UST .... United States Time
UST .... United States Treaties and Other International Agreements [*A publication*] (DLA)
UST .... Universal Servicing Tool (NASA)
UST .... Universal Subscriber Terminal (DNAB)
UST .... University of Saint Thomas [*Texas*]
UST .... UST, Inc. [*Formerly, US Tobacco*] [*NYSE symbol*] (SPSG)
UST .... UST, Inc. [*Associated Press abbreviation*] (APAG)
UST .... Ustilago [*A fungus*]
UST .... Ustus [*Burnt*] [*Pharmacy*]

USTA .... Union des Syndicats des Travailleurs Algeriens [*Federation of Unions of Algerian Workers*]
USTA .... United States Telephone Association (EA)
USTA .... United States Tennis Association, Inc. (EA)
USTA .... United States Trademark Association (EA)
USTA .... United States Trotting Association (EA)
USTA .... United States Twirling Association (EA)
USTA .... Unlisted Securities Trading Act [*1936*]
USTA .... US Tornado Association (EA)
USTA .... US Triathlon Association [*Later, TRI-FED*] (EA)
USTA .... US Trivia Association (EA)
U-Stadtbibliothek ... Universitaets- und Stadtbibliothek [*A publication*]
USTAF ...... United States/Thai Forces
USTA/NJTL ... USTA [*United States Tennis Association*] National Junior Tennis League (EA)
US Tariff Comm Rep ... United States. Tariff Commission. Reports [*A publication*]
US Tariff Comm TC Publ ... United States. Tariff Commission. TC Publication [*A publication*]
Ustav Jad Fyz Cesk Akad Ved Rep ... Ustav Jaderne Fyziky Ceskoslovenska Akademia Ved. Report [*A publication*]
Ustav Vedeckotech Inf Zemed ... Ustav Vedeckotechnickych Informaci pro Zemedelstvi [*A publication*]
Ustav Vedeckotech Inf Zemed Stud Inf Ochr Rostl ... Ustav Vedeckotechnickych Informaci pro Zemedelstvi Studijni Informace Ochrana Rostlin [*A publication*]
Ustav Vyzk Vyuziti Paliv Monogr ... Ustav pro Vyzkum a Vyuziti Paliv Monografie [*A publication*]
US Tax Cas ... United States Tax Cases [*Commerce Clearing House*] [*A publication*] (DLA)
US Tax Cas CCH ... US Tax Cases. Commerce Clearing House [*A publication*]
US Tax Rpt ... United States Tax Report [*A publication*]
US Tb .... U & S [*Urban & Schwarzenberg*] Taschenbuecher [*A publication*]
USTB .... United States Travel Bureau
USTB .... UST Corp. [*NASDAQ symbol*] (NQ)
USTC .... Union Syndicale de Travail Centrafricaine [*Union of Central African Workers*] (EY)
USTC .... United States Tariff Commission [*Later, ITC*]
USTC .... United States Tax Cases [*Commerce Clearing House*] [*A publication*] (DLA)
USTC .... United States Testing Co., Inc.
USTC .... United States Tourist Council (EA)
USTC .... United States Transportation Commission [*Proposed commission to consolidate CAB, ICC, and FMC*]
USTC .... Universal Systems Technologies Corp.
USTC .... US-Tibet Committee (EA)
USTC .... US Trade Center [*Mexico*] (IMH)
USTC .... US Trust Corp. [*NASDAQ symbol*] (NQ)
USTCA ...... United States Track Coaches Association [*Later, TFA/USA*]
USTC Jl BG ... United States Tobacco and Candy Journal Buyer's Guide [*A publication*]
USTC Jrl ...... United States Tobacco and Candy Journal [*A publication*]
USTC & TBA ... US Tennis Court and Track Builders Association (EA)
USTD .... Union des Syndicats des Travailleurs du Dahomey [*Federation of Workers' Unions of Dahomey*]
USTD .... United States Treasury Department
USTD .... United States Treaty Development [*A publication*] (DLA)
USTDA ...... United States Truck Drivers Association
USTDC ...... United States Forces, Taiwan Defense Command (CINC)
USTDC ...... US Travel Data Center (EA)
US TEL ..... US Telephone, Inc. [*Dallas, TX*] [*Telecommunications*] (TSSD)
USTES ...... United States Training and Employment Service [*Abolished, 1971*] [*Department of Labor*]
USTF .... Uniformed Services Treatment Facility [*DoD*]
USTF .... United States Tuna Foundation (EA)
USTFA ...... United States Trout Farmers Association (EA)
USTFF .... United States Track and Field Federation [*Later, TFA/USA*]
USTFFA .... United States Touch and Flag Football Association (EA)
U St G .... Umsatzsteuergesetz [*A publication*]
USTG .... Union Syndicale des Travailleurs de Guinee [*Guinean Federation of Workers*]
UStgD .... Dixie College, St. George, UT [*Library symbol*] [*Library of Congress*] (LCLS)
UStgGS ...... Church of Jesus Christ of Latter-Day Saints, Genealogical Society Library, St. George Branch, St. George, UT [*Library symbol*] [*Library of Congress*] (LCLS)
UStgW .... Washington County Library, St. George, UT [*Library symbol*] [*Library of Congress*] (LCLS)
USTHF ...... US Team Handball Federation (EA)
USTI .... United Systems Technology, Inc. [*NASDAQ symbol*] (NQ)
USTIIC ...... United States Technical Industrial Intelligence Committee (MCD)
USTJ .... United States Tobacco Journal [*A publication*]
USTL .... US Telephone, Inc. [*NASDAQ symbol*] (NQ)
USTOA ...... United States Tour Operators Association (EA)
USTOL ...... Ultrashort Takeoff and Landing [*Aviation*] (MCD)
USTOPS ... United States Travelers' Overseas Personalized Service [*Also known as TOPS*]

USTR......... United States Trade Representative [*Formerly, SRTN*] [*Executive Office of the President*]
USTR......... United Stationers, Inc. [*NASDAQ symbol*]   (NQ)
USTRA...... United States Touring Riders Association   (EA)
USTRANSCOM ... United States Transportation Command
USTRC....... United States Transportation Research Command [*Army*]
U St Rd ... Umsatzsteuer-Rundschau [*A publication*]
US Treas Dept ... United States Treasury Department   (DLA)
US Treas Reg ... United States Treasury Regulations [*A publication*]   (DLA)
US Treaty Ser ... United States Treaty Series [*A publication*]   (DLA)
USTS......... Ultrahigh Frequency Satellite Terminal System   (MCD)
USTS......... Union Syndicale des Travailleurs du Soudan [*Federation of Sudanese Workers*] [*Mali*]
USTS......... United States Time Standard [*National Institute of Standards and Technology*]
USTS......... United States Transmission Systems, Inc. [*Secaucus, NJ*]   (TSSD)
USTS......... United States Travel Service [*Replaced by United States Travel and Tourism Administration*] [*Department of Commerce*]
USTSA...... US Targhee Sheep Association   (EA)
USTSA...... US Telecommunications Suppliers Association [*Later, TIA*]   (EA)
USTTA...... United States Table Tennis Association   (EA)
USTTA...... United States Travel and Tourism Administration [*Formerly, US Travel Service*] [*Department of Commerce*]
USTTI....... US Telecommunications Training Institute [*Washington, DC*] [*Telecommunications*]   (TSSD)
USTU .... Ultrasonic Test Unit
USTU .... US Taekwondo Union   (EA)
USTU .... US Taxpayers Union   (EA)
USTV........ Universal Subscription Television
USTV........ Unmanned Supersonic Test Vehicle   (MCD)
USTVA...... United States Tennessee Valley Authority
Ust Ved Inf MZLVH Rostl Vyroba ... Ustav Vedeckotechnickych Informaci. Ministerstva Zemedelstvi. Lesnlho a Vodnlho Hospodarstvi. Rostlinna Vyroba [*A publication*]
Ust Ved Inf MZLVH Stud Inf Pudoz ... Ustav Vedeckotechnickych Informaci. MZLVH [*Ministerstva Zemedelstvi. Lesniho a Vodnlho Hospodarstvi*] Studijni Informace Pudoznalstvi a Meliorace [*A publication*]
Ust Ved Inf MZ Rostl Vyroba ... Ustav Vedeckotechnickych Informaci. Ministerstva Zemedelstvi. Rostlinna Vyroba [*A publication*]
Ust Ved Inf MZVZ Rostl Vyroba ... Ustav Vedeckotechnickych Informaci. Ministerstva Zemedelstvi a Vyzivy. Rostlinna Vyroba [*A publication*]
USTW .... Sovetsky [*Former USSR*] [*ICAO location identifier*]   (ICLI)
USTWA..... US Tennis Writers Association   (EA)
USTZD...... Unsensitized
USU .... Ultimate Sampling Unit   (GFGA)
USU .... Unbundled Stock Unit [*Investment term*] [*Obsolete*]
USU .... Uniformed Services University of the Health Sciences Library, Bethesda, MD [*OCLC symbol*]   (OCLC)
USU .... United Stevedores' Union [*British*]
USU .... Usually
USUA .... United States Ultralight Association   (EA)
USUARIOI ... Association of Maritime Transport Users in the Central American Isthmus [*Guatemala, Guatemala*]   (EAIO)
USUB .... Unglazed Structural Unit Base [*Technical drawings*]
USUCA ..... United Steel Workers' Union of Central Africa [*Rhodesia and Nyasaland*]
USUG........ US Sugar Corp. [*NASDAQ symbol*]   (NQ)
USUHS ..... Uniformed Services University of the Health Sciences [*DoD*] [*Bethesda, MD*]   (EGAO)
US/UK....... United States/United Kingdom
USUMS...... Utah State University. Monograph Series [*A publication*]
USUN........ United States United Nations Delegation   (CINC)
USUNEP... United States Committee for the United Nations Environment Program   (EA)
USURP...... Usurpandus [*To Be Used*] [*Pharmacy*]
USUSA...... United Societies of the United States of America [*McKeesport, PA*]   (EA)
USV .... U-Save Foods Ltd. [*Vancouver Stock Exchange symbol*]
USV .... United States Volunteers [*Civil War*]
USV .... Unmanned Strike Vehicle
USVAAD... United States Veteran's Administration Administrator's Decisions [*A publication*]   (DLA)
USVAC..... United States Veterans' Assistance Center   (OICC)
USVB........ United States Veterans Bureau
USVBA..... United States Volleyball Association   (EA)
USVBA...... US Venetian Blind Association   (EA)
USVBDD... United States Veterans Bureau Director's Decisions [*A publication*]   (DLA)
USVC........ US LICO Corp. [*Formerly, United Services Life Insurance*] [*NASDAQ symbol*]   (NQ)
US Veterans Adm (W) Dep Med Surg Bull Prosthet Res ... United States. Veterans Administration (Washington, DC). Department of Medicine and Surgery. Bulletin of Prosthetics Research [*A publication*]
US Veterans Bureau Med Bull ... United States. Veterans Bureau. Medical Bulletin [*A publication*]

USVH .... United States Veterans Hospital
USVIP .... Uniformed Services Voluntary Insurance Program
USVMD .... Urine Specimen Volume Measuring Device
USVMS..... Urine Sample Volume Measurement System   (MCD)
USVR........ US Vacation Resorts [*NASDAQ symbol*]   (NQ)
USVS......... United Services Advisors, Inc. [*San Antonio, TX*] [*NASDAQ symbol*]   (NQ)
USVT........ Universal Stray Voltage Tester
USW .... Ultrashort Wave
USW .... Ultrasonic Welding
USW .... Under Secretary of War [*Obsolete*]
USW .... Undersea Warfare
USW .... United Steelworkers [*Also, USWA*]   (CDAI)
USW .... United Steelworkers [*Trade union*] [*British*]
USW .... Universitaets-Seminar fuer Wirtschaft [*Wiesbaden*] [*A publication*]
USW .... US West, Inc. [*NYSE symbol*]   (SPSG)
USW .... US Wheat Associates   (EA)
USWA .... American Association for Study of the United States in World Affairs   (EA)
USWA .... United Shoe Workers of America [*Later, ACTWU*]   (EA)
USWA .... United States Wayfarer Association   (EA)
USWA .... United Steelworkers of America [*Also known as USW*]   (EA)
USWAB.... United States Warehouse Act Bonded
USWACC ... United States Women's Army Corps Center
USWACS .. United States Women's Army Corps School
USWAP..... United South West Africa Party [*Namibia*] [*Political party*]
USWAP..... United Steel Workers' Association of the Philippines
US War Dp Chief Eng An Rp ... United States. War Department. Chief of Engineers. Annual Report [*A publication*]
US Waterw Exp Stn Contract Rep ... United States. Waterways Experiment Station. Contract Report [*A publication*]
US Waterw Exp Stn Misc Pap ... United States. Waterways Experiment Station. Miscellaneous Paper [*A publication*]
US Waterw Exp Stn Res Rep ... United States. Waterways Experiment Station. Research Report [*A publication*]
US Waterw Exp Stn Tech Rep ... United States. Waterways Experiment Station. Technical Report [*A publication*]
US Waterw Exp Stn (Vicksburg Miss) Misc Pap ... United States. Waterways Experiment Station (Vicksburg, Mississippi). Miscellaneous Paper [*A publication*]
US Waterw Exp Stn (Vicksburg Miss) Res Rep ... United States. Waterways Experiment Station (Vicksburg, Mississippi). Research Report [*A publication*]
US Waterw Exp Stn (Vicksburg Miss) Tech Rep ... United States. Waterways Experiment Station (Vicksburg, Mississippi). Technical Report [*A publication*]
USWB .... United States Weather Bureau [*Later, National Weather Service*]
USWBC..... United States War Ballot Commission [*World War II*]
USWCA..... United States Women's Curling Association   (EA)
USWDIV.... Undersea Warfare Division [*Navy*]   (DNAB)
USWF....... United States Weightlifting Federation   (EA)
USWF....... United States Wrestling Federation   (EA)
USWFA..... United States Water Fitness Association   (EA)
USWGA .... United States Wholesale Grocers' Association [*Later, NAWGA*]   (EA)
USWI........ United States West Indies
USWISOMWAGMOHOTM ... United Single Women in Search of Men Who Aren't Gay, Married, or Hung-Up on Their Mothers [*Fictitious association*]
USWLA..... United States Women's Lacrosse Association   (EA)
USWN....... US WEST NewVector Group, Inc. [*NASDAQ symbol*]   (NQ)
US Women's Bur Bul ... United States. Women's Bureau. Bulletin [*A publication*]
USWP........ United States Water Polo   (EA)
USWSRA .. United States Women's Squash Racquets Association   (EA)
USWSSB... United States Wood Screw Service Bureau [*Defunct*]   (EA)
USWst....... US West, Inc. [*Associated Press abbreviation*]   (APAG)
USWTCA ... United States Women's Track Coaches Association   (EA)
USWV .... United Spanish War Veterans   (EA)
USX .... Ultrasoft X-Ray
USX .... US Steel Corp. [*Formerly, USS, USSC*]
USX .... USX-Marathon Group [*Associated Press abbreviation*]   (APAG)
USXDel ..... USX Delhi Group [*Associated Press abbreviation*]   (APAG)
USXFS....... Ultrasoft X-Ray Fluorescence [*Spectroscopy*]
USXMar.... USX-Marathon Group [*Associated Press abbreviation*]   (APAG)
USXRS ...... Ultrasoft X-Ray Spectroscopy
USXUSS ... USX Corp. [*Formerly, US Steel Corp.*] [*Associated Press abbreviation*]   (APAG)
USXX......... US Technologies, Inc. [*NASDAQ symbol*]   (NQ)
USY .... United Synagogue Youth
USY .... US Pay-Tel, Inc. [*Vancouver Stock Exchange symbol*]
USYC........ United States Youth Council   (EA)
USYEC...... US Yugoslav Economic Council   (EA)
USYRU ..... US Yacht Racing Union   (EA)
USYSA ..... United States Youth Soccer Association   (EA)
USZI......... United States Zone of the Interior

UT............. Conference Internationale pour l'Unite Technique des Chemins de Fer
UT............. Tooele Public Library, Tooele, UT [*Library symbol*] [*Library of Congress*]   (LCLS)
UT............. Ugaritic Text [*A publication*]
UT............. Ultrasonic Test
UT............. Ultrathin
UT............. Umbilical Tower [*Aerospace*]
UT............. Uncontrolled Term [*Online database field identifier*]
UT............. Under the Tongue [*Pharmacy*]
U/T........... Under Training [*British military*]   (DMA)
U/T........... Under Trust [*Legal term*]   (DLA)
UT............. Underway Trials [*Shipbuilding*]
UT............. Unemployed Time [*Military*] [*British*]
UT............. Unexpired Term [*Real estate*] [*British*]   (ROG)
UT............. Union Terminal Railway Co. [*AAR code*]
UT............. Union de Transports Aeriens [*France*] [*ICAO designator*]   (FAAC)
UT............. Unit   (MCD)
UT............. Unit Tester   (NASA)
UT............. Unit Trust   (ILCA)
UT............. United Technologies Corp.
UT............. United Telecommunications, Inc. [*NYSE symbol*]   (SPSG)
UT............. United Territory
UT............. United Together   (EA)
UT............. Universal Time [*Astronomy*]
UT............. Universal Torpedo   (MCD)
UT............. Universal Trainer
UT............. Universal Turret   (MCD)
UT............. University of Tennessee
UT............. University of Texas
UT............. University of Toronto [*Ontario*]
U of T........ University of Toronto [*Ontario*]
UT............. University of Tulsa [*Oklahoma*]
UT............. Unser Tsait/Unzer Tsayt [*A publication*]
UT............. Unspecified Temperature
UT............. Untested
U/T........... Untrained
UT............. Up Through [*Parapsychology*]
UT............. Up Time
UT............. Upper Torso
UT............. Urinary Tract [*Medicine*]
UT............. User Test
UT............. User's Terminal   (MCD)
UT............. Utah [*Postal code*]
UT............. Utah Music Educator [*A publication*]
UT............. Utah Reports [*A publication*]   (DLA)
UT............. Utah Territory [*Prior to statehood*]
UT............. Utendum [*To Be Used*] [*Pharmacy*]   (ROG)
UT............. Utilitiesman [*Navy rating*]
UT............. Utility   (BUR)
UT............. Utility Boat
UT............. Utility Player
UT1........... Utilitiesman, First Class [*Navy rating*]
UT2........... Utilitiesman, Second Class [*Navy rating*]
UT3........... Utilitiesman, Third Class [*Navy rating*]
UTA........... Ultrasonic Thermal Action
UTA........... Union de Transports Aeriens [*Air Transport Union*] [*Private airline*] [*France*]   (EY)
UTA........... Unit Training Assembly [*Military*]   (AABC)
UTA........... Unit Trust Association [*British*]
UTA........... United Technologies Automotive
UTA........... United Typothetae of America [*Later, Printing Industries of America*]
UTA........... University of Texas at Arlington
UTA........... Upper Terminal Area   (NATG)
UTA........... Urban Transportation Administration [*HUD*]
UTA........... User Transfer Address
UTAC........ Union Tunisienne de l'Artisanat et du Commerce [*Tunisian Union of Artisans and Merchants*]
UTACV ..... Urban Tracked Air-Cushion Vehicle [*Transit*] [*Department of Transportation*]
UTAD........ Utah Army Depot   (AABC)
UTAEC...... University of Tennessee, Atomic Energy Commission   (SAA)
UTAH........ Utah Railway Co. [*AAR code*]
Utah........... Utah Reports [*A publication*]
Utah........... Utah Supreme Court Reports [*A publication*]   (DLA)
Utah Acad Sci Proc ... Utah Academy of Sciences, Arts, and Letters. Proceedings [*A publication*]
Utah Ac Sc Tr ... Utah Academy of Sciences. Transactions [*A publication*]
Utah Admin Bull ... State of Utah Bulletin [*A publication*]   (DLA)
Utah Admin R ... Administrative Rules of the State of Utah [*A publication*]
Utah Admin R ... Administrative Rules of Utah [*A publication*]   (DLA)
Utah Ag Exp ... Utah. Agricultural Experiment Station. Publications [*A publication*]
Utah Agric Exp Stn Bull ... Utah. Agricultural Experiment Station. Bulletin [*A publication*]
Utah Agric Exp Stn Circ ... Utah. Agricultural Experiment Station. Circular [*A publication*]
Utah Agric Exp Stn Res Rep ... Utah. Agricultural Experiment Station. Research Report [*A publication*]

Utah Agric Exp Stn Spec Rep ... Utah. Agricultural Experiment Station. Special Report [*A publication*]
Utah Agric Exp Stn Utah Resour Ser ... Utah. Agricultural Experiment Station. Utah Resources Series [*A publication*]
Utah Bar Bull ... Utah Bar Bulletin [*A publication*]
Utah B Bull ... Utah Bar Bulletin [*A publication*]
Utah BJ ..... Utah Bar Journal [*A publication*]
Utah Bull ... State of Utah Bulletin [*A publication*]
Utah Code Ann ... Utah Code, Annotated [*A publication*]   (DLA)
Utah 2d ...... Utah Reports, Second Series [*A publication*]   (DLA)
Utah Dep Nat Resour Tech Publ ... Utah. Department of Natural Resources. Technical Publication [*A publication*]
Utah Dep Nat Resour Water Cir ... Utah. Department of Natural Resources. Water Circular [*A publication*]
Utah Dept Nat Resources Tech Pub ... Utah. Department of Natural Resources. Division of Water Rights. Technical Publication [*A publication*]
Utah Div Water Resources Coop Inv Rept ... Utah. Division of Water Resources. Cooperative Investigations Report [*A publication*]
Utah Econ and Bus R ... Utah Economic and Business Review [*A publication*]
Utah Eng Exp Stn Bull ... Utah. Engineering Experiment Station. Bulletin [*A publication*]
Utah Farm Home Sci ... Utah Farm and Home Science [*A publication*]
Utah Geol .. Utah Geology [*A publication*]
Utah Geol Assoc Publ ... Utah Geological Association. Publication [*A publication*]
Utah Geol and Mineralog Survey Bull ... Utah. Geological and Mineralogical Survey. Bulletin [*A publication*]
Utah Geol and Mineralog Survey Circ ... Utah. Geological and Mineralogical Survey. Circular [*A publication*]
Utah Geol and Mineralog Survey Quart Rev ... Utah. Geological and Mineralogical Survey. Quarterly Review [*A publication*]
Utah Geol and Mineralog Survey Spec Studies ... Utah. Geological and Mineralogical Survey. Special Studies [*A publication*]
Utah Geol and Mineralog Survey Water Resources Bull ... Utah. Geological and Mineralogical Survey. Water Resources Bulletin [*A publication*]
Utah Geol Mineral Surv Bull ... Utah. Geological and Mineralogical Survey. Bulletin [*A publication*]
Utah Geol Mineral Surv Circ ... Utah. Geological and Mineralogical Survey. Circular [*A publication*]
Utah Geol Mineral Surv Spec Stud ... Utah. Geological and Mineralogical Survey. Special Studies [*A publication*]
Utah Geol Mineral Surv Water Resour Bull ... Utah. Geological and Mineralogical Survey. Water Resources Bulletin [*A publication*]
Utah Geol Miner Surv Circ ... Utah. Geological and Mineralogical Survey. Circular [*A publication*]
Utah Geol Miner Surv Q Rev ... Utah. Geological and Mineralogical Survey. Quarterly Review [*A publication*]
Utah Geol Miner Surv Surv Notes ... Utah. Geological and Mineralogical Survey. Survey Notes [*A publication*]
Utah Geol Soc Guidebook to Geology of Utah ... Utah Geological Society. Guidebook to the Geology of Utah [*A publication*]
Utah Hist Q ... Utah Historical Quarterly [*A publication*]
Utah Hist Quar ... Utah Historical Quarterly [*A publication*]
Utah Hist Quart ... Utah Historical Quarterly [*A publication*]
Utah IC Bull ... Utah Industrial Commission. Bulletin [*A publication*]   (DLA)
Utah Laws ... Laws of Utah [*A publication*]
Utah Lib...... Utah Libraries [*A publication*]
Utah Lib Assn Newsl ... Utah Library Association. Newsletter [*A publication*]
Utah Libr... Utah Libraries [*A publication*]
Utah LR..... Utah Law Review [*A publication*]
Utah L Rev ... Utah Law Review [*A publication*]
Utah M ...... Utah Genealogical and Historical Magazine [*A publication*]
Utah Med Bull ... Utah Medical Bulletin [*A publication*]
Utah PUC ... Utah Public Utilities Commission Report [*A publication*]   (DLA)
Utah R .... Utah Reports [*A publication*]   (DLA)
Utah Resour Ser Utah Agr Exp Sta ... Utah Resources Series. Utah Agricultural Experiment Station [*A publication*]
Utah Sci..... Utah Science [*A publication*]
Utah Sci Utah Agric Exp Stn ... Utah Science. Utah Agricultural Experiment Station [*A publication*]
Utah State Engineer Bienn Rept Tech Pub ... Utah State Engineer. Biennial Report. Technical Publications [*A publication*]
Utah State Engineer Inf Bull ... Utah State Engineer. Information Bulletin [*A publication*]
Utah State Eng Off Basic Data Rep ... Utah. State Engineer's Office. Basic Data Report [*A publication*]
Utah State Eng Tech Publ ... Utah State Engineer. Technical Publication [*A publication*]
Utah State Med J ... Utah State Medical Journal [*A publication*]
Utah State Univ Agric Exp Stn Bull ... Utah State University. Agricultural Experiment Station. Bulletin [*A publication*]
Utah Univ Anthropol Papers Bull ... Utah University. Anthropological Papers. Bulletin [*A publication*]
Utah Univ Eng Exp Stn Tech Pap ... Utah University. Engineering Experiment Station. Technical Paper [*A publication*]

Utah Univ Eng Expt Sta Bull ... Utah University. Engineering Experiment Station. Bulletin [*A publication*]
UTAL .... Upper Transition Altitude (SAA)
UTAP .... Unified Transportation Assistance Program [*Proposed*]
UTAP .... Urban Transportation Assistance Program [*Canada*]
UTAS........ Underwater Target-Activated Sensor (MCD)
U Tas LR ... University of Tasmania. Law Review [*A publication*]
U Tasmania L Rev ... University of Tasmania. Law Review [*A publication*]
U Tasm L Rev ... University of Tasmania. Law Review [*A publication*]
UTASN ...... University of Texas at Austin School of Nursing
UT/AT....... Underway Trial/Acceptance Trial [*Navy*] (NVT)
UTATA ..... Uniform Testamentary Additions to Trusts Act [*National Conference of Commissioners on Uniform State Laws*]
UTB .... Muttaburra [*Australia*] [*Airport symbol*] (OAG)
UTB .... Uni Taschenbuecher GmbH [*German publishers cooperative*]
UTB .... United Tariff Bureau
UTB .... Universitaets-Taschenbuecher [*A publication*]
UTB .... University of Toronto Library, Brieflisted Records [*UTLAS symbol*]
UTB .... Utilitiesman, Boilerman [*Navy rating*]
UTBC .... Union Trust Bancorp [*NASDAQ symbol*] (NQ)
UTBG .... Unbound Thyroxine Binding Globulin [*Endocrinology*] (AAMN)
UT BJ .... Utah Bar Journal [*A publication*]
UTBK .... United Bancorp, Inc. [*Salt Lake City, UT*] [*NASDAQ symbol*] (NQ)
UTBN .... Utah Bancorp [*NASDAQ symbol*] (NQ)
UTBU .... Unhealthy to be Unpleasant [*Theatrical play*] (IIA)
UTC .... Uncle Tom's Cabin [*Title of book by Harriet Beecher Stowe*]
UTC .... Underwater Training Centre [*British*]
UTC .... Unit Test Cases (NASA)
UTC .... Unit Time Coding
UTC .... Unit Total Cost
UTC .... Unit Training Center [*Military*]
UTC .... Unit Type Code (AFM)
UTC .... United Canso Oil & Gas Ltd. [*Toronto Stock Exchange symbol*]
UTC .... United States Tax Court, Library, Washington, DC [*OCLC symbol*] (OCLC)
UTC .... United Technologies Corp. [*Information service or system*] (IID)
UTC .... United Trust & Credit [*Finance group*] [*British*]
UTC .... Universal Test Console (KSC)
UTC .... Universal Time Code
UTC .... Universal Time Coordinated [*The universal time emitted by coordinated radio stations*]
UTC .... Universal Time Corrected (MCD)
UTC .... University Teachers Certificate
UTC .... University of Tennessee at Chattanooga
UTC .... University Training Corps [*British*]
UTC .... Urban Technology Conference
UTC .... Urban Training Center
UTC .... Utilities Telecommunications Council (EA)
UTC .... Utilities, Transportation, Communication
UTC .... Utilitiesman, Chief [*Navy rating*]
UTC .... Utility Tape Copy (SAA)
UTCA .... Constructionman Apprentice, Utilitiesman, Striker [*Navy rating*]
UTCA .... Utica Bankshares Corp. [*NASDAQ symbol*] (NQ)
UTCAA ..... Uncle Tom Cobley and All [*Refers to everyone*] [*Slang*] [*British*] (DSUE)
UTCC .... University of Tennessee at Knoxville Computer Center [*Research center*] (RCD)
UTCL........ Union des Travailleurs Communistes Libertaires [*Union of Libertarian Communist Workers*] [*France*] [*Political party*] (PPW)
UTCLK...... Universal Transmitter Clock
UTCM .... Utilitiesman, Master Chief [*Navy rating*]
UTCN .... Constructionman, Utilitiesman, Striker [*Navy rating*]
UTCPTT ... Union Internationale des Organismes Touristiques et Culturels des Postes et des Telecommunications [*International Union of Tourist and Cultural Associations in the Postal and Telecommunications Services*]
UTCS........ Urasenke Tea Ceremony Society (EA)
UTCS........ Urban Traffic Control System
UTCS........ Utilitiesman, Senior Chief [*Navy rating*]
UTCT .... Undermanned Tank Crew Test [*Military*] (MCD)
UTD .... Kermisgids [*A publication*]
UTD .... Undetermined
UTD .... United
UTD .... United Investors Management Co. Non-Voting [*NYSE symbol*] (SPSG)
UTD .... Universal Transfer Device
UTD .... University of Texas at Dallas (MCD)
UTD .... Up to Date (MAE)
UTD .... Uranium-Thorium Dating
UTD .... User Terminal and Display Subsystem [*Space Flight Operations Facility, NASA*]
UtdAmHlt ... United American Healthcare Corp. [*Associated Press abbreviation*] (APAG)
UTDC .... Urban Transportation Development Corp. [*Canada*]
UTDD........ Dushanbe [*Former USSR*] [*ICAO location identifier*] (ICLI)

UTDEMS ... University of Tulsa. Department of English. Monograph Series [*A publication*]
UTDF .... Universal Tracking Data Format (SSD)
UT DICT ... Ut Dictum [*As Directed*] [*Latin*]
UtdInv........ United Investors Management Co. [*Associated Press abbreviation*] (APAG)
UtdMM ..... United Merchants & Manufacturers, Inc. [*Associated Press abbreviation*] (APAG)
UTDO........ Oktyabrsky [*Former USSR*] [*ICAO location identifier*] (ICLI)
UTE .... Chandler, AZ [*Location identifier*] [*FAA*] (FAAL)
UTE .... Underwater Tracking Equipment (MCD)
UTE .... Union Technique de l'Electricite [*France*]
UTE .... Universal Test Equipment
UTE .... Utilization of Theoretical Energy
UTEC .... Universal Test Equipment Compiler (KSC)
UTEC .... Utah University Engineering College
U Tech Umweltmag ... U das Technische Umweltmagazin [*West Germany*] [*A publication*]
UTED .... Dzhizak [*Former USSR*] [*ICAO location identifier*] (ICLI)
UTEELRAD ... Utilization of Enemy Electromagnetic Radiation (MSA)
UTEL........ United Telecontrol Electronics, Inc. [*NASDAQ symbol*] (NQ)
UTEND..... Utendus [*To Be Used*] [*Pharmacy*]
utend mor sol ... Utendus More Solito [*To be Used in the Usual Manner*] [*Latin*] [*Pharmacy*] (MAE)
UTEP........ University of Texas at El Paso
UTEPDF ... University of Tasmania. Environmental Studies Occasional Paper [*A publication*]
UTES........ Unit Training Equipment Site [*Military*] (AABC)
UTET........ Unione Tipografico-Editrice Torinese [*Publisher*] [*Italy*]
UTET Boll Ed ... UTET [*Unione Tipigrafico-Editrice Torinese*] Bollettino Editoriale [*A publication*]
UTF .... Underwater Tank Facility
UTF .... Underwater Test Facility [*GE*]
UTF .... Unsuccessful Tenderers Fees
UTF .... Valparaiso [*Chile*] [*Seismograph station code, US Geological Survey*] (SEIS)
U T Fac L Rev ... University of Toronto. Faculty of Law. Review [*A publication*]
UT Faculty LR ... Faculty of Law Review. University of Toronto [*A publication*]
UTFO .... Untouchable Force Organization [*Rap recording group*]
UTFS......... University of Toronto. French Series [*A publication*]
UTG.......... United Tasmania Group [*Political party*] [*Australia*]
UTG.......... University of Toronto Library, Government Documents [*UTLAS symbol*]
UTGA....... United Tobacco Growers Association (EA)
UT & GS.... Uplink Text and Graphics System (NASA)
UTGT .... Under Thirty Group for Transit [*Defunct*] (EA)
UTH .... Udon Thani [*Thailand*] [*Airport symbol*] (OAG)
UTH .... Union Texas Petroleum Holdings, Inc. [*NYSE symbol*] (SPSG)
UTH .... Upper Turret Half
UTHE........ Union des Associations des Etablissements Thermaux de la CE [*Union of Associations of Thermal Baths Establishments in the EC*] (ECED)
UTHS .... University of Texas. Hispanic Studies [*A publication*]
UTHSCSA ... University of Texas Health Science Center at San Antonio
UTI .... International Universal Time [*Telecommunications*] (TEL)
UTI .... Union Telegraphique Internationale (MSC)
UTI .... United Transport International [*Bennett's Transport*] [*British*]
UTI .... Universal Text Interchange [*Data processing*] (PCM)
UTI .... Universal Trident Industries Ltd. [*Vancouver Stock Exchange symbol*]
UTI .... Urinary Tract Infection [*Medicine*]
UTI .... User Test Instrumentation [*Army*]
UTIA .... University of Toronto, Institute of Aerophysics (MCD)
UTIAS .... University of Toronto, Institute for Aerospace Studies [*Research center*] (MCD)
UTIC........ USAREUR Tactical Intelligence Center (MCD)
UTICI .... Union Technique des Ingenieurs Conseils [*French*]
UT-IG........ University of Texas at Austin Institute for Geophysics [*Research center*] (RCD)
UTIL......... Utility [*or Utilization*] (AFM)
Utilc .... Utilicorp United, Inc. [*Associated Press abbreviation*] (APAG)
UtiliC......... Utilicorp United, Inc. [*Associated Press abbreviation*] (APAG)
UtiliCo .... Utilicorp United, Inc. [*Associated Press abbreviation*] (APAG)
UTILIDOR ... Utility Corridor (SAA)
Utilitas Math ... Utilitas Mathematica [*A publication*]
Util L Rep .. Utilities Law Reporter [*Commerce Clearing House*] [*A publication*] (DLA)
Util L Rep CCH ... Utilities Law Reports. Commerce Clearing House [*A publication*]
UTILN....... Utilitarian (AAG)
Util Sect Newl ... Utility Section Newsletter [*A publication*] (DLA)
UT INF ...... Ut Infra [*As Below*] [*Latin*] (ADA)
UTIPS .... Upgraded Tactical Information Processing System [*Data processing*]
UTIRS .... United Tiberias Institutions Relief Society (EA)
UTJ........... Uterotubal Junction [*Medicine*]
UTK.......... University of Tennessee, at Knoxville
UTK .... Utirik [*Marshall Islands*] [*Airport symbol*] (OAG)

UTK/PSL ... University of Tennessee at Knoxville Plasma Science Laboratory
UTL .... Unit Transmission Loss
UTL .... Unit Transmittal Letter [*Army*]
UTL .... UNITIL Corp. [*AMEX symbol*] (SPSG)
UTL .... UnivEd Technologies Ltd. [*British*] (IRUK)
UTL .... Universal Transporter Loader (MCD)
UTL .... University of Toledo, College of Law, Toledo, OH [*OCLC symbol*] (OCLC)
UTL .... University of Toronto Library [*UTLAS symbol*]
UTL .... Up Telecommunications Switch
UTL .... User Trailer Label (CMD)
UTLAS ..... UTLAS International Canada [*Formerly, University of Toronto Library Automation System*] [*Library network*]
UTLC........ University of Tennessee College of Law (DLA)
UTLC........ UTL Corp. [*NASDAQ symbol*] (NQ)
UTLD .... Utah Test of Language Development [*Education*]
UTLJ .... University of Toronto. Law Journal [*A publication*]
UTLL........ Utilitech, Inc. [*NASDAQ symbol*] (NQ)
UTLM .... Up Telemetry (MCD)
UT LR .... Utah Law Review [*A publication*]
UTLX........ UTILX Corp. [*NASDAQ symbol*] (SPSG)
UTLY........ Utility (BUR)
UTM .... Union des Travailleurs de Mauritanie [*Union of Workers of Mauritania*]
UTM .... Union des Travailleurs de Mayotte [*Comoros*] (PD)
UTM .... Universal Test Message
UTM .... Universal Testing Machine
UTM .... Universal Transverse Mercator [*Cartography*]
UTM .... Universal Turing Machine [*Mathematical model*] [*Data processing*] (BYTE)
UTM .... University of Tennessee at Martin
UTMA .... Uniform Transfers to Minors Act [*National Conference of Commissioners on Uniform State Laws*]
UTMA .... United Tank Makers' Association [*A union*] [*British*]
UTMAWTU ... United Turners', Machinists', and Athletic Woodworkers' Trade Union [*British*]
UTMB .... University of Texas Medical Branch [*Galveston*]
UTMCI...... Union des Travailleurs de la Moyenne Cote d'Ivoire [*Union of Middle Ivory Coast Workers*]
UTMC/K... University of Tennessee Medical Center/Knoxville
UTMD...... Utah Medical Products, Inc. [*NASDAQ symbol*] (NQ)
UTMDAH ... University of Texas, M. D. Anderson Hospital
UTMED ... United Medical Corp. [*Associated Press abbreviation*] (APAG)
UT/MI...... Underway Trials and Material Inspection (MCD)
UTML .... Utility Motor Launch
UTN.......... University of Tennessee at Nashville
UTN.......... Upington [*South Africa*] [*Airport symbol*] (OAG)
UTN.......... Urban Telephone Network (OA)
UTN.......... Utensil (MSA)
UTNOTREQ ... Utilization of Government Facilities Not Required as It Is Considered Such Utilization Would Adversely Affect Performance of Assigned Temporary Duty
UTNRS...... Underwater Terrain Navigation and Reconnaissance Simulator (MCD)
UTO.......... Indian Mountain, AK [*Location identifier*] [*FAA*] (FAAL)
UTO.......... United Telephone Organizations
UTO.......... United Towns Organisation [*See also FMVJ*] [*Paris, France*] (EAIO)
UTO.......... Utopia Creek [*Alaska*] [*Airport symbol*] (OAG)
UTOA........ United Truck Owners of America (EA)
UTOA........ United TVRO [*Television Receive Only*] Owners Association (EA)
UTOC........ United Technologies Online Catalog [*United Technologies Corp.*] [*Information service or system*] (IID)
UTOCO...... Utah Oil Co.
UTOG........ Unitog Co. [*NASDAQ symbol*] (NQ)
UTOL........ Universal Translator Oriented Language
UTOLCL... University of Toledo College of Law (DLA)
U Toledo Intra LR ... University of Toledo. Intramural Law Review [*A publication*] (DLA)
U Toledo L Rev ... University of Toledo. Law Review [*A publication*]
U Tol Law ... University of Toledo. Law Review [*A publication*]
U Tol LR.... University of Toledo. Law Review [*A publication*]
U Tol L Rev ... University of Toledo. Law Review [*A publication*]
UTOPIA.... Universal Terminalized Online Printing and Investigative Aid [*Bancroft-Parkman, Inc.*] [*Information service or system*]
Utopian E... Utopian Eyes [*A publication*]
U Tor Fac LR ... University of Toronto. Faculty of Law. Review [*A publication*]
U Tor Law J ... University of Toronto. Law Journal [*A publication*]
U Tor LJ.... University of Toronto. Law Journal [*A publication*]
U Tor L Rev ... University of Toronto. School of Law. Review [*A publication*] (DLA)
U Toronto Fac L Rev ... University of Toronto. Faculty of Law. Review [*A publication*]
U Toronto Faculty L Rev ... University of Toronto. Faculty of Law. Review [*A publication*]
U Toronto L J ... University of Toronto. Law Journal [*A publication*]
U Toronto Q ... University of Toronto. Quarterly [*A publication*]

U Toronto Sch L Rev ... University of Toronto. School of Law. Review [*A publication*] (DLA)
UTP .... Unified Test Plan
UTP .... Unit Territory Plan
UTP .... Unit Test Plan
UTP .... United Teaching Profession (MCD)
UTP .... United Trade Press (Holdings) Ltd. [*Commercial firm*] [*British*]
UTP .... Universal Tape Processor
UTP .... Universal Test Point (CAAL)
UTP .... Unlisted Trading Privileges
UTP .... Unshielded Twisted-Pair [*Data processing*] (PCM)
UTP .... Upper Thames Patrol [*British military*] (DMA)
UTP .... Upper Trip Point
UTP .... Upper Turning Point
UTP .... Urban Transportation Planning [*Department of Transportation*] (GFGA)
UTP .... Uridine Triphosphatase [*An enzyme*]
UTP .... Uridine Triphosphate [*Biochemistry*]
UTP .... User Test Program [*Army*]
UTP .... Utah Power & Light Co. [*NYSE symbol*] (SPSG)
UTP .... Utapao [*Thailand*] [*Airport symbol*] [*Obsolete*] (OAG)
UTP .... Utility Tape Processor
UTPA .... Uniform Trustees' Powers Act [*National Conference of Commissioners on Uniform State Laws*]
UTPase...... Uridine Triphosphatase [*An enzyme*]
UTPL........ Urban Transportation Planning Laboratory [*University of Pennsylvania*] [*Research center*] (RCD)
UTPLF ...... Universita di Torino. Pubblicazioni della Facolta di Lettere e Filosofia [*A publication*]
UTPMS..... Unit Trust Portfolio Management Service [*Investment term*] [*British*]
UTPP........ Urban Transportation Planning Package [*Bureau of the Census*] (GFGA)
UTPS........ UMTA [*Urban Mass Transit Administration*] Transportation Planning System
UTQ.......... Hinesville, GA [*Location identifier*] [*FAA*] (FAAL)
UTQ.......... University of Toronto. Quarterly [*A publication*]
UTQA........ Uutuqtwa. Bristol Bay High School [*A publication*]
UTQG........ Uniform Tire Quality Grade
UTQGS ..... Uniform Tire Quality Grading Standards [*Department of Transportation*] (GFGA)
UTR .... Underwater Tracking Range
UTR .... Union Transportation [*AAR code*]
UTR.......... Unitrode Corp. [*NYSE symbol*] (SPSG)
UTR.......... Universal Torah Registry (EA)
UTR.......... Universal Training Reactor [*Nuclear energy*] (GFGA)
UT R .... University of Tampa. Review [*A publication*]
UTR .... University of Toronto, Thomas Fisher Rare Book Library [*UTLAS symbol*]
UTR .... University Training Reactor
UTR .... Unprogrammed Transfer Register
UTR .... Untranslated Region [*Genetics*]
UTR .... Up Time Ratio
UTR .... Urticarial Transfusion Reaction [*Medicine*]
UTRA .... Upper Torso Restraint Assembly
UTRANSRON ... Utility Transport Squadron (DNAB)
UTRAO..... Radio Astronomy Observatory [*University of Texas at Austin*] [*Research center*] (RCD)
UTRC .... United Techniques Research Center [*Navy*] (DNAB)
UTRC .... United Technologies Research Centre
Utredn Norsk Tretekn Inst ... Utredning. Norsk Treteknisk Institutt [*A publication*]
UTREP...... University of Tennessee Rehabilitation Engineering Program
UTRF........ Update Training File [*IRS*]
UTRK .... US Truck Lines, Inc. of Delaware [*NASDAQ symbol*] (NQ)
Utr Micropaleontol Bull ... Utrecht Micropaleontological Bulletins [*A publication*]
Utr Micropaleontol Bull Spec Publ ... Utrecht Micropaleontological Bulletins. Special Publication [*A publication*]
UTROAA .. Units to Round Out the Active Army
UTRON..... Utility Squadron [*Navy*]
UTRONFWDAREA ... Utility Squadron, Forward Area [*Navy*]
UTRP........ Underwater Tactical Range, Pacific
UTRR .... University of Teheran Research Reactor
UTRTD ..... Untreated
UTRX........ Unitronix Corp. [*NASDAQ symbol*] (CTT)
UTS .... Huntsville, TX [*Location identifier*] [*FAA*] (FAAL)
UTS .... Ullrich-Turner Syndrome [*Genetics*]
UTS .... Ultimate Tensile Strength [*or Stress*]
UTS .... Umbilical Test Set
UTS .... Underwater Telephone System
UTS .... Unified Transfer System [*Computer to translate Russian to English*]
UTS .... Union Theological Seminary
UTS .... Union des Travailleurs du Senegal [*Senegalese Workers Union*]
UTS .... Unit Training Standard
UTS .... Unit Trouble Shooting
UTS .... United Tanners' Society [*A union*] [*British*]
UTS .... United Theological Seminary, Dayton, OH [*OCLC symbol*] (OCLC)

UTS .... United Tri-Star Resources Ltd. [*Toronto Stock Exchange symbol*]
UTS .... Universal Terminal System [*Sperry UNIVAC*] [*Data processing*]
UTS .... Universal Test Station
UTS .... Universal Thrust Stand
UTS .... Universal Time Sharing [*Data processing*]   (IEEE)
UTS .... Universal Time Standards   (NG)
UTS .... University Tutorial Series [*A publication*]
UTS .... Unmanned Teleoperator Spacecraft   (MCD)
UTS .... Update Transaction System   (TEL)
UTS .... Urine-Transfer System [*Apollo*] [*NASA*]
UTS .... Utility Interim Table Simulation   (SAA)
UTS .... Utility Tactical Support   (SAA)
UTS .... Utsunomiya [*Japan*] [*Seismograph station code, US Geological Survey*]   (SEIS)
UTSCB ...... Utah Science [*A publication*]
UTSCC ...... University of Texas System Cancer Center [*Houston, TX*] [*Research center*]
U of T School of LR ... School of Law. Review. Toronto University [*Canada*] [*A publication*]   (DLA)
UTSE .... United Transport Service Employees [*Later, BRAC*]   (EA)
UTSE .... University of Texas. Studies in English [*A publication*]
UTS-FO ..... Union Territoriale des Syndicats - Force Ouvrieres [*Territorial Federation of Trade Unions - Workers' Force*] [*French Somaliland*]
UTSH .... University of Tennessee. Studies in the Humanities [*A publication*]
UTSI .... University of Tennessee Space Institute
UTSL .... University of Texas School of Law   (DLA)
UTSM .... Tamdy-Bulak [*Former USSR*] [*ICAO location identifier*]   (ICLI)
UTS-M .... Universal Timesharing System for Mainframes   (HGAA)
UTSMS .... University of Texas Southwestern Medical School
UTSN .... Used Truck Sales Network   (EA)
UTSS .... Samarkand [*Former USSR*] [*ICAO location identifier*]   (ICLI)
UTS-S .... Universal Timesharing System for Superminis   (HGAA)
UTST .... Termez [*Former USSR*] [*ICAO location identifier*]   (ICLI)
UT SUP ..... Ut Supra [*As Above*] [*Latin*]
UT SUPR .. Ut Supra [*As Above*] [*Latin*]
UTSV .... Union Theological Seminary in Virginia
UTT .... Umtata [*South Africa*] [*Airport symbol*]   (OAG)
UTT .... UT Technologies [*Vancouver Stock Exchange symbol*]
UTT .... Utility Tactical Transport   (MCD)
UTT .... Uttering [*FBI standardized term*]
UTTA .... United Thoroughbred Trainers of America   (EA)
Uttar Pradesh Dir Geol Min Monogr ... Uttar Pradesh. Directorate of Geology and Mining. Monograph [*A publication*]
Uttar Pradesh J Zool ... Uttar Pradesh Journal of Zoology [*A publication*]
Uttar Pradesh State Dent J ... Uttar Pradesh State Dental Journal [*A publication*]
UTTAS ...... Utility Tactical Transport Aircraft System [*Helicopter*] [*Military*]
UTTBA ...... Bulletin. International Union Against Tuberculosis [*A publication*]
UTTC .... Universal Tape-to-Tape Converter
UTTL .... Uttlesford [*England*]
UTTR .... Utah Test and Training Range [*Air Force*]
UTTS .... Union Territoriale du Senegal des Travailleurs [*Senegalese Workers Union*]
UTTS .... Universal Target Tracking Station   (MCD)
UTTT .... Tashkent/Yuzhny [*Former USSR*] [*ICAO location identifier*]   (ICLI)
UTU .... Ultrasonic Test Unit
UTU .... Underway Training Unit
UTU .... United Transportation Union   (EA)
UTU .... Ustupo [*Panama*] [*Airport symbol*]   (OAG)
utu .... Utah [*MARC country of publication code*] [*Library of Congress*]   (LCCP)
UTUC .... Uganda Trades' Union Congress
UTUC .... United Trades Union Congress [*India*]
UTV .... Ulster Television [*Ireland*]   (DI)
UTV .... Uncompensated Temperature Variation   (TEL)
UTV .... Underwater Television
UTV .... Universal Test Vehicle [*Military*]
UTVI .... United Television, Inc. [*NASDAQ symbol*]   (NQ)
UTVS .... Ucebni Texty Vysokych Skol [*A publication*]
UTW .... Ultrathin Window [*Spectroscopy*]
UTW .... Under the Wing [*Aircraft*]
UTW .... United Telegraph Workers [*Later, C/UBC*]   (EA)
UTW .... Utilitiesman, Water and Sanitation [*Navy rating*]
UTWA .... United Textile Workers of America   (EA)
UTWG ...... Utility Wing [*Navy*]   (MUGU)
UTWING .. Utility Wing [*Navy*]
UTWINGSERVLANT ... Utility Wing, Service Force, Atlantic [*Navy*]
UTWINGSERVPAC ... Utility Wing, Service Force, Pacific [*Navy*]
UTX .... Jupiter, FL [*Location identifier*] [*FAA*]   (FAAL)
UTX .... United Technologies Corp. [*NYSE symbol*]   (SPSG)
UTY .... Utility Air, Inc. [*Moberly, MO*] [*FAA designator*]   (FAAC)
UU .... Reunion Air Service [*France*] [*ICAO designator*]   (FAAC)
UU .... Uglies Unlimited   (EA)

UU .... Ulster Unionist Party
UU .... Ultimate User [*Nuclear energy*]
UU .... Unemployment Unit [*An association*] [*British*]
UU .... Unicorns Unanimous [*An association*]   (EA)
UU .... Union University [*Tennessee*]
UU .... University of Utah, Salt Lake City, UT [*Library symbol*] [*Library of Congress*]   (LCLS)
UU .... Urine Urobilinogen [*Clinical chemistry*]
UU .... User Unit   (MCD)
UUA .... Southern Utah State College, Cedar City, UT [*OCLC symbol*]   (OCLC)
UUA .... Unitarian Universalist Society for Alcohol and Drug Education
UUA .... UNIVAC Users Association [*Later, AUUA*]
UUA .... Uppsala Universitets Arsskrift [*A publication*]
UUABCWG ... Unitarian Universalist Association Black Concerns Working Group   (EA)
UUAC........ United Unionist Action Council [*Northern Ireland*]
UUARC ..... United Ukrainian American Relief Committee   (EA)
UUA/WO ... Unitarian Universalist Association of Congregations-Washington Office   (EA)
UUA/WOSC ... Unitarian Universalist Association-Washington Office for Social Concern [*Later, UUA/WOSJ*]   (EA)
UUA/WOSJ ... Unitarian Universalist Association of Congregations-Washington Office for Social Justice   (EA)
UUB........... Brigham Young University, School of Library and Information Science, Provo, UT [*OCLC symbol*]   (OCLC)
UUBCWG ... Unitarian Universalist Black Concerns Working Group   (EA)
UUBP .... Bryansk [*Former USSR*] [*ICAO location identifier*]   (ICLI)
UUC........... Salt Lake County Library System, Salt Lake City, UT [*OCLC symbol*]   (OCLC)
UUC........... United University Club [*British*]
UUCA........ United Underwear Contractors Association [*Defunct*]   (EA)
UUCD........ USA-USSR Citizens' Dialogue [*Inactive*]   (EA)
UUCF .... Unitarian Universalist Christian Fellowship   (EA)
UUCP .... Unix-to-Unix Copy Program [*Data processing*]
UUD .... Logan Public Library, Logan, UT [*OCLC symbol*]   (OCLC)
UUE.......... University of Utah, Eccles Health Science Library, Salt Lake City, UT [*OCLC symbol*]   (OCLC)
UUE.......... Use until Exhausted
UUEE........ Moskva/Sheremetyevo [*Former USSR*] [*ICAO location identifier*]   (ICLI)
UUEM....... Kalini/Migalovo [*Former USSR*] [*ICAO location identifier*]   (ICLI)
UUEW....... United Unions for Employees and Workers [*Lebanon*]
UUFSJ ...... Unitarian Universalist Fellowship for Social Justice   (EA)
UUGS........ Unitarian and Universalist Genealogical Society [*Defunct*]   (EA)
UUHS........ Unitarian Universalist Historical Society   (EA)
UUID........ Universally Unique Identifier [*Data processing*]
UUIP .... Uppsala University Institute of Physics [*Sweden*]
UUK......... Kuparuk, AK [*Location identifier*] [*FAA*]   (FAAL)
UU-L.......... University of Utah, Law Library, Salt Lake City, UT [*Library symbol*] [*Library of Congress*]   (LCLS)
UULGC ..... Unitarian Universalist Lesbian Gay Caucus   (EA)
UUM .... Underwater-to-Underwater Missile [*Air Force*]
UU-M .... University of Utah, Library of Medical Sciences, Salt Lake City, UT [*Library symbol*] [*Library of Congress*]   (LCLS)
UUM .... University of Utah, Salt Lake City, UT [*OCLC symbol*]   (OCLC)
UUMA....... Unitarian Universalist Ministers Association   (EA)
UUMN ..... Unitarian Universalist Musicians' Network   (EA)
UUMPS .... Unitarian Universalist Ministers' Partners Society   (EA)
UUN .... Urinary Urea Nitrogen [*Clinical medicine*]
UUO .... Weber State College, Ogden, UT [*OCLC symbol*]   (OCLC)
UUOO .... Voronezh [*Former USSR*] [*ICAO location identifier*]   (ICLI)
UUP........... Salt Lake City Public Library, Salt Lake City, UT [*OCLC symbol*]   (OCLC)
UUP........... Ulster Unionist Party [*British*] [*Political party*]
UUP........... Urine Uroporphyrin [*Medicine*]   (MAE)
UUPP .... Unused Undeducted Purchase Price
UU/PS....... Peasant Studies. University of Utah. Department of History [*A publication*]
UUR.......... Under Usual Reserves
UURWAW ... United Union of Roofers, Waterproofers, and Allied Workers   (EA)
UUS.......... Utah State University, Logan, UT [*OCLC symbol*]   (OCLC)
UUSAE ..... Unitarian Universalist Society for Alcohol Education [*Later, UUA*]   (EA)
UUSC .... Unitarian Universalist Service Committee   (EA)
UUSS........ University of Utah Seismograph Stations [*Research center*]   (RCD)
UUT........... Unit under Test
UUU .... Manumu [*Papua New Guinea*] [*Airport symbol*]   (OAG)
UUUC....... United Ulster Unionist Coalition [*Northern Ireland*]
UUUM ...... Moskva [*Former USSR*] [*ICAO location identifier*]   (ICLI)
UUUM ...... United Ulster Unionist Movement [*Northern Ireland*]
UUUP....... United Ulster Unionist Party [*Northern Ireland*] [*Political party*]   (PPW)
UUUU ...... Moskva [*Former USSR*] [*ICAO location identifier*]   (ICLI)
UUV.......... Unmanned Undersea Vehicle [*Military robotics*]
UUW .... Unitarian Universalist World [*A publication*]

UUW .... Westminster College, Salt Lake City, UT [*OCLC symbol*]   (OCLC)
UUWF ...... Unitarian Universalist Women's Federation   (EA)
UU/WPQ .. Western Political Quarterly. University of Utah [*A publication*]
UUWW ..... Moskva/Vnukovo [*Former USSR*] [*ICAO location identifier*]   (ICLI)
UUYEP ..... US-USSR Youth Exchange Program   (EA)
UUYT........ Ust-Kulom [*Former USSR*] [*ICAO location identifier*]   (ICLI)
UUYY .... Syktyvkar [*Former USSR*] [*ICAO location identifier*]   (ICLI)
UUZ........... Utah State Library, Processing Center, Salt Lake City, UT [*OCLC symbol*]   (OCLC)
UV.............. Ultra Vans   (EA)
UV.............. Ultraviolet [*Electromagnetic spectrum range*]
UV.............. Ultravisible
UV.............. Umbilical Vein [*Medicine*]
UV.............. Unabhaengige Volkspartei [*Independent People's Party*] [*Political party*] [*Germany*]   (EAIO)
UV.............. Unadilla Valley Railroad   (IIA)
UV.............. Under Voltage
UV.............. Underwater Vehicle
UV.............. Union Valdotaine [*Valdotaine Union*] [*Italy*] [*Political party*]   (EAIO)
UV.............. Union Valenciana [*Spain*] [*Political party*]   (EY)
UV.............. Universal Aviation, Inc. [*ICAO designator*]   (FAAC)
uv.............. Upper Volta [*MARC country of publication code*] [*Library of Congress*]   (LCCP)
Uv.............. Uppsala Virus [*Medicine*]   (MAE)
UV.............. Urinary Volume [*Physiology*]
UV.............. Uterine Vein [*Anatomy*]
UV.............. Uterine Volume
UV.............. Utility Value [*Psychology*]
UVA........... Ultraviolet Absorption
UVA........... Ultraviolet Light, Long Wave
UVA........... University of Virginia
UVA........... Uvalde Aero Service [*Uvalde, TX*] [*FAA designator*]   (FAAC)
UVA........... Uvalde, TX [*Location identifier*] [*FAA*]   (FAAL)
UVAL .... Ultraviolet Argon LASER
UVAN....... Ukrainian Academy of Arts and Sciences of Canada
UVAR .... University of Virginia Reactor
UVAS .... Unmanned Vehicle for Aerial Surveillance   (MCD)
UVASER ... Ultraviolet Amplification by Stimulated Emission of Radiation
UVASERS ... Ultraviolet Amplification by Stimulated Emission of Radiation System
UV-B......... Ultraviolet Band
UVBF........ Umbilical Vein Blood Flow
UVC........... Pennsylvania State University, Capitol Campus, Middletown, PA [*OCLC symbol*]   (OCLC)
UVC........... Ullucus Virus C [*Plant pathology*]
UVC........... Ultrahigh Vacuum Chamber
UVC........... Ultraviolet Communications System
UVC........... Uniform Vehicle Code
UVC........... Union Valley Corp. [*AMEX symbol*]   (SPSG)
UVCA .... Uniform Vehicle Code Annotated
UVCB .... Unknown or Variable Composition, Complex Reaction Products, and Biological Materials [*Chemical Abstracts Services*]
UVCE .... Unconfined Vapor Cloud Explosion
UVD.......... Ultrasonic Vapor Degresser
UVD.......... Ultraviolet Detector
UVD.......... Undervoltage Device
UVD.......... Unintegrated Viral DNA [*Deoxyribonucleic Acid*] [*Pathology*]
UVD.......... Upper Vas Deferens [*Anatomy*]
UVDB .... Union des Verts pour le Developpement du Burkina [*Burkina Faso*] [*Political party*]   (EY)
UVDC....... Urban Vehicle Design Competition
UVD-SV .... Upper Vas Deferens-Seminal Vesicle Complex [*Anatomy*]
UVE.......... Ouvea [*Loyalty Islands*] [*Airport symbol*]   (OAG)
UV-EPROMS ... Ultraviolet-Erasable Programmable Read-Only Memories [*Data processing*]
UVF .... St. Lucia [*West Indies*] Hewanorra Airport [*Airport symbol*]   (OAG)
UVF .... Ulster Volunteer Force
UVF .... Ultraviolet Filter
UVF .... Ultraviolet Floodlight   (AAG)
UVF .... Unmanned Vertical Flight [*NASA*]   (NASA)
UVFLT ...... Ultraviolet Floodlight
UVFO .... Ultraviolet Fiber Optics
UVG.......... UV [*Ultraviolet*] Spectrometry Group [*British*]
UVGS .... Church of Jesus Christ of Latter-Day Saints, Genealogical Society Library, Uintah Basin Branch, Vernal, UT [*Library symbol*] [*Library of Congress*]   (LCLS)
UVH .... Univentricular Heart [*Cardiology*]
UVHFDS... Ultraviolet Hydrogen Fire Detection System   (DNAB)
UVI .... Ultraviolet Irradiation
UVI .... Uvira [*Zaire*] [*Seismograph station code, US Geological Survey*] [*Closed*]   (SEIS)
UVIC .... University of Victoria [*British Columbia*]
UVICON ... Ultraviolet Image Converter   (WGA)
UVIL......... Ultraviolet Inspection Light
UVIL......... Ultraviolet Ion LASER
UVIRSG .... Ultraviolet Infrared Scene Generator

UVJ .... Ureterovesical Junction [*Anatomy*]   (MAE)
UVL .... New Valley [*Egypt*] [*Airport symbol*]   (OAG)
UVL.......... Ultraviolet Lamp
UVL.......... Ultraviolet LASER
UVL.......... Ultraviolet Light
UVL.......... Universal Voltronics Corp. [*Later, Thermo Voltek*] [*AMEX symbol*]   (SPSG)
UVL.......... Untersuchungen zur Vergleichenden Literatur [*Hamburg*] [*A publication*]
UVLI......... Ustav Vedeckych Lekarskych Informaci [*Institute for Medical Information*] [*Former Czechoslovakia*] [*Database operator*] [*Information service or system*]   (IID)
UVLS........ Ultraviolet Light Stabilizer
UVM.......... Ultraviolet Meter
UVM.......... Universal Vendor Marking   (WGA)
UVM.......... Universitas Viridis Montis [*University of the Green Mountains; i.e., University of Vermont*]
UVM.......... University of Virginia. Magazine [*A publication*]
UVMag...... University of Virginia. Magazine [*A publication*]
UVMC...... United Voluntary Motor Corps   (EA)
UVN.......... Unionville [*Nevada*] [*Seismograph station code, US Geological Survey*] [*Closed*]   (SEIS)
UVNO ...... Ultraviolet Nitric-Oxide Experiment
UVO .... Uvol [*Papua New Guinea*] [*Airport symbol*]   (OAG)
UVP.......... Ultrahigh Vacuum Pump
UVP.......... Ultraviolet Photometry
UVP.......... Unified Vocational Preparation [*Manpower Services Commission*] [*British*]
UVPES...... Ultraviolet Photoelectron Spectroscopy
UVPJU...... Uganda Vernacular, Primary and Junior Secondary Teachers' Union
UVPROM ... Ultraviolet Programmable Read Only Memory
UVPS........ Ultrahigh Vacuum Pumping Station
UV-PSdA... Unione Valdostana-Partito Sardo d'Azione [*Italy*] [*Political party*]   (ECED)
UVR.......... Uitenhage Volunteer Rifles [*British military*]   (DMA)
UVR.......... Ultraviolet Radiation
UVR.......... Ultraviolet Radiometer   (MCD)
UVR.......... Ultraviolet Receiver
UVR.......... Ultraviolet Rocket
UVR.......... Under Voltage Relay
UVR.......... University of Virginia Reactor
UVR.......... User Visible Resources
UVS.......... Ultraviolet Spectrometer
UVS.......... Under Voltage Sensing   (MCD)
UVS.......... United Voluntary Services   (EA)
UVS.......... Unmanned Vehicle System
UVSC........ Ultraviolet Solar Constant
UVSC........ Uranium Ventilation Scrubber Cell [*Nuclear energy*]   (NRCH)
UVSP........ Ultraviolet Spectral Photometer
UV Spectrom Group Bull ... UV Spectrometry Group. Bulletin [*A publication*]
UVT.......... Ultraviolet Transmission
UVT.......... Ultraviolet Tube
UVT.......... Universal Voltage Tester
UVT.......... Usable Vector Table
UVTB .... United Vermont Bancorp. [*Rutland, VT*] [*NASDAQ symbol*]   (NQ)
UVTEI....... Ustredi Vedeckych, Technickych, a Ekonomickych Informaci [*Former Czechoslovakia*] [*Information service or system*]   (IID)
UVV.......... Universal Corp. [*NYSE symbol*]   (SPSG)
UVV.......... Upward Vertical Velocity [*Meteorology*]   (FAAC)
UV-VIS...... Ultraviolet/Visible [*Spectroscopy*]
UVVO....... United Vietnam Veterans Organization   (EA)
UVX.......... Univar Corp. [*Formerly, VWR United Corp.*] [*NYSE symbol*]   (SPSG)
UW .... Air Rwanda [*Rwanda*] [*ICAO designator*]   (ICDA)
UW .... Service des Transports Publics Aeriens [*Portugal*] [*ICAO designator*]   (FAAC)
UW .... Ultimate Weapon   (AAG)
UW .... Ultrasonic Wave
UW .... Unburned, Warmed [*Ecology*]
UW .... Unconventional Warfare [*Army*]
U/W.......... Under Will [*Legal term*]   (DLA)
UW .... Underwater
UW .... Underwater Weapons [*British*]
U/W.......... Underway   (NVT)
U/W.......... Underwriter [*Insurance*]
UW .... United Way   (OICC)
UW .... United Weldors International Union
U of W...... University of Washington [*Seattle, WA*]
UW .... University of Washington [*Seattle, WA*]
U of W...... University of Windsor [*Ontario*]
UW .... University of Wisconsin [*Madison, WI*]   (MCD)
UW .... Untere Winkelgruppe [*Angles up to 45*] [*German military - World War II*]
UW .... Uppity Women [*An association*]   (EA)
UW .... Upset Welding
UW .... Us Wurk [*A publication*]
UW .... Usable Width   (MCD)
U/W.......... Used With

UW .... Utility Water (AAG)
UWA......... Ukrainian Workingmen's Association [*Later, UFA*] (EA)
UWA......... United Way of America (EA)
UWA......... United Weighers Association (EA)
UWA......... United Women of the Americas (EA)
UWA......... United World Atheists (EA)
UWA......... User Working Area
UWA......... Uwajima [*Japan*] [*Seismograph station code, US Geological Survey*] (SEIS)
UWA......... Ware, MA [*Location identifier*] [*FAA*] (FAAL)
UWAC...... Ukrainian Women's Association of Canada
UWAGE.... Union Women's Alliance to Gain Equality [*Defunct*] (EA)
UWAL....... Underwater Wide-Angle Lens
UWAL....... University of Washington Aeronautical Laboratory (MCD)
UWALR .... University of Western Australia. Law Review [*A publication*] (APTA)
UWAL Rev ... University of Western Australia. Law Review [*A publication*]
UWARC .... United Whiteruthenian [*Byelorussian*] American Relief Committee (EA)
UWARS..... Universal Water-Activated Release System (DWSG)
U Wash L Rev ... University of Washington. Law Review [*A publication*] (DLA)
UWASIS ... United Way of America Services Identification System
UWAT .... User Written Application Test [*Data processing*]
UWATS..... Universal Weapons Assembly Test Standard (MCD)
UWATU... Underway Training Unit
UW Austl L Rev ... University of Western Australia. Law Review [*A publication*]
UWAVM... Underwater Antivehicle Mine (MCD)
UWAVWA ... Union of West African Voluntary Workcamps Associations [*Ghana*] (EAIO)
UWAYTUNORVA ... Underway Training Unit, Norfolk, Virginia (DNAB)
UWB......... Universal White Brotherhood [*An association*] [*France*] (EAIO)
UWBBR .... University of Wisconsin - Madison Bureau of Business Research [*Research center*] (RCD)
UWBS .... Uniform Work Breakdown Structure
UWC......... Ulster Workers' Council
UWC......... Underwater Communications [*Navy*] (CAAL)
UWC......... Universal Water Charts [*Air Force*]
UWC......... Universal Winding Co. (MCD)
UWC......... Widener College, Chester, PA [*OCLC symbol*] (OCLC)
UWCCARG ... University of Washington. Contributions. Cloud and Aerosol Research Group [*A publication*]
UWCCCM ... Union of Watch, Clock, and Clock Case Makers [*British*]
UWCCPGR ... University of Washington. Contributions. Cloud Physics Group. Collections from Reprints [*A publication*]
UWCETG ... University of Washington. Contributions. Energy Transfer Group. Collections from Reprints [*A publication*]
UWCS .... Underwater Weapons Control System
UWCSS.... Universal Weapon Control Stabilization System
UWD .... Underwater Weapons Department [*British military*] (DMA)
UWD .... UWD [*Umweltschutz-Dienst*] Informationsdienst fuer Umweltfragen [*A publication*]
UWDD ...... Undersea Warfare Development Division [*Navy*] (MCD)
UWE......... University Women of Europe (EA)
UWE......... Uwekahuna [*Hawaii*] [*Seismograph station code, US Geological Survey*] (SEIS)
UWEN....... United Western Energy [*NASDAQ symbol*] (NQ)
UWERT .... United World Education and Research Trust (EAIO)
U West Aust Ann L Rev ... University of Western Australia. Annual Law Review [*A publication*]
U of West Aust L Rev ... University of Western Australia. Law Review [*A publication*]
U Western Aust Ann L Rev ... University of Western Australia. Annual Law Review [*A publication*]
U Western Aust L Rev ... University of Western Australia. Law Review [*A publication*]
U Western Ont L Rev ... University of Western Ontario. Law Review [*A publication*]
U West LA L Rev ... University of West Los Angeles. Law Review [*A publication*]
U West Los Angeles L Rev ... University of West Los Angeles. Law Review [*A publication*]
UWF .... United World Federalists [*Later, World Federalists Association*] (EA)
UWF .... University of West Florida [*Pensacola*]
UWFC .... Underwater Fire Control [*Navy*] (CAAL)
UWFCS..... Underwater Fire Control System
UWFPC..... Union Wallisienne et Futunienne pour la Caledonie [*Wallisian and Futunian Union for Caledonia*] [*Political party*] (PPW)
UWG......... Gesetz Gegen den Unlauteren Wettbewerb [*Law Against Unfair Competition*] [*German*] (DLA)
UWGB...... University of Wisconsin at Green Bay
UWH .... Underwater Habitat
UWH .... Underwater Welding Habitat [*Deep-sea diving*]
UW-HF ..... Upset Welding-High Frequency
UWI .... Dalton, GA [*Location identifier*] [*FAA*] (FAAL)
UWI .... United Way International (EA)

UWI.......... United Westburne Industries Ltd. [*Toronto Stock Exchange symbol*]
UWI.......... University of the West Indies [*Jamaica*]
UW-I......... Upset Welding-Induction
UWI/CQ ... Caribbean Quarterly. University of the West Indies [*A publication*]
UWI/JCH ... Journal of Caribbean History. University of the West Indies. Department of History and Caribbean Universities Press [*A publication*]
UWINDS .. Upper Winds (FAAC)
U Windsor L Rev ... University of Windsor. Law Review [*A publication*] (DLA)
UWI/SES ... Social and Economic Studies. University of the West Indies. Institute of Social and Economic Research [*A publication*]
UWIST...... University of Wales Institute of Science and Technology [*British*]
UWKD...... Kazan [*Former USSR*] [*ICAO location identifier*] (ICLI)
UWL......... New Castle, IN [*Location identifier*] [*FAA*] (FAAL)
UWL......... Underwater Launch
UWL......... University of Winnipeg Library [*UTLAS symbol*]
UWL......... Utowana Lake [*New York*] [*Seismograph station code, US Geological Survey*] (SEIS)
UWLA LR ... University of West Los Angeles. Law Review [*A publication*]
UWLA L Rev ... University of West Los Angeles. Law Review [*A publication*]
UWLA Rev ... University of West Los Angeles. School of Law. Law Review [*A publication*] (DLA)
UWM........ Uniform Wave Motion
UWM........ United World Mission (EA)
UWM........ University of Wisconsin at Milwaukee [*Seismograph station code, US Geological Survey*] (SEIS)
UWM........ University of Wisconsin at Milwaukee
UWMAK... University of Wisconsin TOKAMAK
UWNE...... Brotherhood of Utility Workers of New England (EA)
UWNR...... University of Wisconsin - Madison Nuclear Reactor Laboratory [*Research center*] (RCD)
UWO .... University of Western Ontario (MCD)
UWO .... University of Western Ontario Library [*UTLAS symbol*]
UWO .... University of Western Ontario, School of Library and Information Science, London, ON, Canada [*OCLC symbol*] (OCLC)
UWOA ...... Unclassified without Attachment
UWOA ...... Unconventional Warfare Operations Area [*Army*] (AABC)
UWOL Rev ... University of Western Ontario. Law Review [*A publication*]
UWOMA6 ... University of Western Ontario. Medical Journal [*A publication*]
UWO Med J ... UWO [*University of Western Ontario*] Medical Journal [*A publication*]
UW Ont L Rev ... University of Western Ontario. Law Review [*A publication*]
UWOPGS ... University of Warwick. Occasional Papers in German Studies [*A publication*]
UWORDTECH ... Underwater Ordnance Technician [*Navy*] (DNAB)
UWO (Univ West Ont) Med J ... UWO (University of Western Ontario) Medical Journal [*A publication*]
UWP......... Dominica United Workers' Party [*Political party*] (EY)
UWP......... United Workers' Party [*Hungary*] [*Political party*] (PPW)
UWP......... United Workers' Party [*Guyana*] [*Political party*] (EY)
UWP......... United Workers' Party [*St. Lucia*] [*Political party*] (PPW)
UWP......... Up with People (EA)
UWPC .... United World Press Cooperative [*Later, The Peoples Media Cooperative*] (EA)
UWPFAO ... University of Washington. Publications in Fisheries. New Series [*A publication*]
UWPLL..... University of Washington. Publications in Language and Literature [*A publication*]
UWPP .... Penza [*Former USSR*] [*ICAO location identifier*] (ICLI)
UWR......... Underwater Range (MUGU)
U/Wr .... Underwriter [*Insurance*] (DLA)
UWR......... Unexpected Wildlife Refuge (EA)
UWR......... United Water Resources, Inc. [*NYSE symbol*] (SPSG)
UWR......... United Water Resources, Inc. [*Associated Press abbreviation*] (APAG)
UWR......... University of Windsor. Review [*A publication*]
UWRC....... Urban Wildlife Research Center (EA)
UW-RF...... University of Wisconsin-River Falls
UWRFAY ... Research in Fisheries. Annual Report. School of Fisheries. University of Washington [*A publication*]
UWRR ...... University of Wyoming Research Reactor
UWS .... Undersea Weapon System
UWS .... Unmanned Weather Station
UWS .... User Work Station (NASA)
UWSAMBS ... United Women's Societies of the Adoration of the Most Blessed Sacrament [*Later, NUWSAMBS*] (EA)
UWSB .... Union Warren Savings Bank [*Boston, MA*] [*NASDAQ symbol*] (NQ)
UWSDDMS ... Underwater Weapons System Design Disclosure Management Systems (KSC)
UWSEC..... Underwater Weapons Systems Engineering Center [*Navy*] (DNAB)
UWSI........ United Wisconsin Services, Inc. [*NASDAQ symbol*] (SPSG)
UWSRD .... Underwater Weapons Systems Reliability Data (KSC)
UWST .... United Western Corp. [*NASDAQ symbol*] (NQ)

UWT.......... Underwater Telephone
UWT.......... Uniform Wave Train
UWT.......... Union of Women Teachers [*British*] (DI)
UWT.......... Unit Weight (MSA)
UWT.......... United World Education and Research Trust [*British*] (EAIO)
UWTCA .... Umschau in Wissenschaft und Technik [*A publication*]
UWTM...... Underwater Team (MSA)
UWTR...... Underwater (AABC)
UWTR...... University of Washington Training Reactor
UWU .... Los Angeles, CA [*Location identifier*] [*FAA*] (FAAL)
UWU .... Utility Workers Union of America
UWUA...... Utility Workers Union of America (EA)
UWW........ University without Walls [*Twenty-one-university consortium*]
UWWR..... Unpublished Scholarly Writings on World Religions (BJA)
UWWW..... Kuybyshev/Kurumoch [*Former USSR*] [*ICAO location identifier*] (ICLI)
UX............. Lotus Airways [*Egypt*] [*ICAO designator*] (FAAC)
ux .... Uxor [*Wife*] [*Latin*] (WGA)
UXAA....... Unexploded Antiaircraft [*Shell*]
UXAPB..... Unexploded Antipersonnel Bomb
UXB.......... Unexploded Bomb
UXC.......... Unocal Exploration Corp. [*NYSE symbol*] (SPSG)
UXGB....... Unexploded Gas Bomb
UXIB .... Unexploded Incendiary Bomb
UXM......... Universal Extension Mechanism (KSC)
UXO.......... Unexploded Ordnance
UXOI........ Unexploded Ordnance Incident
UXPLD..... Unexploded Bomb (SAA)
UXPM...... Unexploded Parachuted Mine
UXS .... Unexploded Shell [*British military*] (DMA)
UXTGM .... Unexploded Type G Mine
UXW......... South Bend, IN [*Location identifier*] [*FAA*] (FAAL)
UY............. Cameroon Airlines [*ICAO designator*] (FAAC)
UY............. Unit Years [*Electronics*] (IEEE)
UY............. Universal Youth
uy............... Uruguay [*MARC country of publication code*] [*Library of Congress*] (LCCP)
UY............. Uruguay [*ANSI two-letter standard code*] (CNC)
UYA.......... University Year for ACTION [*Refers to federal program, ACTION, which is not an acronym*]
UYC.......... Uxbridge Yeomanry Cavalry [*British military*] (DMA)
UYF.......... London, OH [*Location identifier*] [*FAA*] (FAAL)
UYL.......... Nyala [*Sudan*] [*Airport symbol*] (OAG)
UYLNA ..... Ukrainian Youth League of North America [*Defunct*] (EA)
UYN.......... Yulin [*China*] [*Airport symbol*] (OAG)
UZ............. Uhrzuender [*Clockwork fuze*] [*German military - World War II*]
UZ............. United Aviation Services SA [*Great Britain*] [*ICAO designator*] (FAAC)
UZ............. Upper Zone [*Geology*]
UZ............. Ustredna Zidov [*Slovakia*] [*A publication*]
U Zambia LB ... University of Zambia. Law Bulletin [*A publication*] (DLA)
uzb............. Uzbek [*MARC language code*] [*Library of Congress*] (LCCP)
Uzbek Iztim Fanlar ... Uzbekiztonda Iztimoii Fanlar [*A publication*]
UZH .... Uzhgorod [*Unuar*] [*Former USSR*] [*Seismograph station code, US Geological Survey*] (SEIS)
UZK.......... Indianapolis, IN [*Location identifier*] [*FAA*] (FAAL)
uzr .... Uzbek Soviet Socialist Republic [*MARC country of publication code*] [*Library of Congress*] (LCCP)
UZRA .... United Zionist Revisionists of America [*Later, Herut - USA*] (EA)
UZU.......... Curuzu Cuatia [*Argentina*] [*Airport symbol*] (OAG)
UZW......... Und Zwar [*That Is*] [*German*]

V

V..............	Abstracted Valuation Decisions [*A publication*] (DLA)
V..............	Deflection of the Vertical
V..............	Digestum Vetus [*A publication*] (DSA)
V..............	Electric Potential [*Symbol*] [*IUPAC*]
V..............	Electromotive Force [*Symbol*] [*See also E, EMF*] [*Electrochemistry*] (DEN)
V..............	Five [*Roman numeral*]
V..............	Five Dollars [*Slang*]
V..............	Five-Year Sentence [*Criminal slang*]
V..............	Fixed-Wing Aircraft [*Navy symbol*]
V..............	Frequency [*Spectroscopy*]
V..............	Potential Difference [*Symbol*]
V..............	Potential Energy [*Symbol*] [*IUPAC*]
V..............	Promotional Fare [*Also, K, L, Q*] [*Airline fare code*]
V..............	Ranger-Parachutist [*Army skill qualification identifier*] (INF)
V..............	[*A*] Safe [*Criminal slang*]
V..............	Sanol Arzneimittel Dr. Schwarz [*Germany*] [*Research code symbol*]
V..............	Shape Descriptor [*V-sign, for example. The shape resembles the letter for which it is named.*]
v..............	Specific Volume [*Symbol*] [*IUPAC*]
V..............	Staff Transport [*When V is the first of two letters in a military aircraft designation*]
V..............	Swiss Volksbank [*Bank*]
V..............	Unusual Visibility
V..............	V3 London Gun [*British military*] (DMA)
V..............	Vacated [*Same case vacated*] [*Used in Shepard's Citations*] [*Legal term*] (DLA)
V..............	Vaccella [*Flourished, 12th century*] [*Authority cited in pre-1607 legal work*] (DSA)
V..............	Vaccinated [*Medicine*]
V..............	Vacuole
V..............	Vacuum (AAG)
V..............	Vagabond
V..............	Vale (ROG)
V..............	Valencia [*A publication*]
V..............	Valine [*One-letter symbol; see Val*]
V..............	Valley (ROG)
V..............	Value
V..............	Valve
V..............	Van
V..............	Van Container [*Shipping*] (DS)
V..............	Vanadium [*Chemical element*]
V..............	Vancouver Stock Exchange [*Canada*]
V..............	Vapor
V..............	Variable
V..............	Variable Region [*Immunochemistry*]
V..............	Variant [*Genetics*]
V..............	Variation
V..............	Variety [*A publication*]
V..............	Variety Theatres and Shows [*Public-performance tariff class*] [*British*]
V..............	Varnish (AAG)
V..............	Varnish-Treated [*Insulation*] (MSA)
V..............	Varsity
V..............	Vascular Tissue [*Botany*]
V..............	Vatican City
V..............	Vector [*Mathematics*]
V..............	Veen, Publishers [*Holland*]
V..............	Vehicles (MCD)
V..............	Vein
V..............	Vel [*Or*] [*Pharmacy*]
V..............	Velocity
V..............	Vendor (AAG)
V..............	Venerable
V..............	Venereology [*Medical Officer designation*] [*British*]
V..............	Venezuela [*IYRU nationality code*] (IYR)
V..............	Venous [*Medicine*]
V..............	Venstre [*Liberal Party*] [*Norway*] [*Political party*] (PPE)
V..............	Venstre (Liberale Parti) [*Liberal Party*] [*Denmark*] [*Political party*] (PPE)
V..............	Vent
V..............	Ventilator
V..............	Ventral
V..............	Ventur [*Quality of carburetor barrel*] [*Automotive engineering*]
V..............	Venturi [*Automotive engineering*]
V..............	Venue
V..............	Verapamil [*A coronary vasodilator*]
V..............	Verb
V..............	Verbal
V..............	Verbo [*A publication*]
V..............	Verfassung [*Constitution*] [*German*] (ILCA)
V..............	Verfuegung [*Order, Decree*] [*German*] (ILCA)
V..............	Vergeltung [*Retaliation*] [*German*]
V..............	Vermessung [*Survey*] [*German military*]
V..............	Vermiculite
V..............	Vermont Reports [*A publication*] (DLA)
V..............	Verordnung [*Decree, Regulation, Ordinance*] [*German*] (ILCA)
V..............	Verse
V..............	Versicle
V..............	Versiculo [*In Such a Way*] [*Latin*] (ROG)
V..............	Version
V..............	Verso
V..............	Versus [*Against*]
V..............	Vert [*Heraldry*]
V..............	Verte [*Turn Over*]
V..............	Vertex
V..............	Vertical [*RADAR*]
V..............	Vertical in Line [*Aircraft engine*]
V..............	Verticillium Wilt [*Plant pathology*]
V..............	Very
V..............	Vespers
V..............	Veto (OICC)
V..............	Via [*By Way Of*] [*Latin*] (ADA)
V..............	Vibrio [*Microbiology*]
V..............	Vic [*Phonetic alphabet*] [*Pre-World War II*] (DSUE)
V..............	Vicar [*or Vicarage*]
V..............	Vice [*In a position or title*]
v..............	Vicinal [*Also, vic*] [*Chemistry*]
V..............	Victor [*Phonetic alphabet*] [*World War II*] [*International*] (DSUE)
V..............	Victoria
V..............	Victory [*As in "the V campaign" in Europe, during World War II*]
V..............	Victualling [*British military*] (DMA)
v..............	Vide [*See*] [*Latin*] (WGA)
V..............	Video (SAA)
V..............	Village
V..............	Vinblastine [*See VBL*]
V..............	Vincentius Hispanus [*Deceased, 1248*] [*Authority cited in pre-1607 legal work*] (DSA)
V..............	Vincristine [*Also, LCR, O, V, VC, VCR*] [*Antineoplastic drug*]
V..............	Vinegar [*Phonetic alphabet*] [*Royal Navy*] [*World War I*] (DSUE)
V..............	Vinyl
V..............	Violet
V..............	Violin [*Music*]
V..............	Virgin
V..............	Virginia Reports [*A publication*] (DLA)
V..............	Virtual (HGAA)
V..............	Virulent
V..............	Virus
V..............	Viscosity
V..............	Viscount [*or Viscountess*]
V..............	Vise Break Distance [*Stress test for steel*]
V..............	Visibility
V..............	Vision [*A publication*]
V..............	Vision
V..............	Visit
V..............	Visiting Practice Only [*Chiropody*] [*British*]
V..............	Visual

V................. Visual Acuity [*Also, VA*] [*Ophthalmology*]
V................. Visual Capacity   (AAMN)
V................. Visual Magnitude [*When followed by a two-digit number*]
v................. Vitamin   (MAE)
V................. Vivra, Inc. [*NYSE symbol*]   (SPSG)
V................. Vixisti [*You Lived*] [*Latin*]
V................. Vixit [*He Lived*] [*Latin*]
V................. VMS Hotel   (SPSG)
V................. Vocative
V................. Voce [*Voice*] [*Latin*]
V................. Voice
V................. Voice Data [*NASA*]
V................. Void [*Decision or finding held invalid for reasons given*] [*Used in Shepard's Citations*] [*Legal term*]   (DLA)
V................. Volcano   (ROG)
V................. Volt [*Symbol*] [*SI unit of electric potential difference*]
V................. Voltage
V................. Voltare [*Turn Over*] [*Latin*]   (ROG)
V................. Volti [*Turn Over*] [*Music*]
V................. Voltmeter
V................. Volts
V................. Volume [*Symbol*] [*IUPAC*]
V................. Volume [*Bibliography*]
V................. Voluntary Aided School [*British*]
V................. Volunteer [*US Naval Reserve*]
V................. Vomiting [*Medicine*]
V................. Von [*Of, From*] [*German*]
V................. VOR [*Very-High-Frequency Omnidirectional Range*] Federal Airway [*Followed by identification*]
V................. Vous [*You*] [*French*]   (ROG)
V................. Vowel
V................. VTOL [*Vertical Takeoff and Landing*] [*or STOL - Short Takeoff and Landing*] [*when V is the second or only letter in a military aircraft designation*]
V................. Vulgate [*Latin translation of the Bible*] [*A publication*]   (BJA)
V................. Wrong Verb Form [*Used in correcting manuscripts, etc.*]
V₁................. Takeoff Decision Speed [*Aviation*]
V-1 .... Vergeltungswaffe 1 [*Pilotless flying bomb employed by the Germans*] [*World War II*]
V₂................. Takeoff Safety Speed [*Aviation*]
V-2 .... Vergeltungswaffe 2 [*Rocket bomb employed by the Germans*] [*World War II*]
V3 .... Takeoff Speed Over Screen [*Aviation code*]   (AIA)
V4 .... Steady Initial Climb Speed [*Aviation code*]   (AIA)
5V .... Togo [*Aircraft nationality and registration mark*]   (FAAC)
V (Bomb).... Vergeltungswaffe Bomb [*German "vengeance weapon"*]
VA............. Alveolar Ventilation
VA............. Alveolar Volume [*Clinical chemistry*]   (AAMN)
VA............. Attack Squadron [*Symbol*]   (MCD)
VA............. Avian Aircraft Ltd. [*Canada*] [*ICAO aircraft manufacturer identifier*]   (ICAO)
VA............. End of Work [*Morse telephony*]   (FAAC)
VA............. Gilmer's Virginia Reports [*A publication*]   (DLA)
VA............. University of Virginia, Charlottesville, VA [*OCLC symbol*]   (OCLC)
Va............. Vacarius [*Flourished, 1144-70*] [*Authority cited in pre-1607 legal work*]   (DSA)
Va............. Vaccella [*Flourished, 12th century*] [*Authority cited in pre-1607 legal work*]   (DSA)
VA............. Vacuum Aspiration [*Medicine*]
VA............. Valentine   (WGA)
Va............. Valid [*Decision or finding held valid for reasons given*] [*Used in Shepard's Citations*] [*Legal term*]   (DLA)
VA............. Valium Anonymous   (EA)
VA............. Valproic Acid [*Anticonvulsant compound*]
V and A ...... Valuable and Attractive [*A marking used by RAF on such supplies as watches and cameras*] [*British*]
VA............. Value Added   (ADA)
VA............. Value Analysis
VA............. Variable Annuity
Va............. Variance   (WGA)
Va............. Vasari [*A publication*]
VA............. Vatican City [*ANSI two-letter standard code*]   (CNC)
VA............. Vehicle Analyst   (MCD)
VA............. Vehicular Accident [*British police*]
VA............. Velocity at Apogee   (MCD)
VA............. Venezolana Internacional de Aviacion Sociedad Anonima (VIASA) [*Venezuela*] [*ICAO designator*]   (ICDA)
VA............. Ventral Area [*Anatomy*]
VA............. Ventricular Aneurysm [*Cardiology*]
VA............. Ventricular Arrhythmia [*Cardiology*]
VA............. Ventriculoatrial [*Cardiology*]   (WGA)
VA............. Verb Active
VA............. Verbal Adjective
VA............. VERLORT [*Very-Long-Range Tracking*] Azimuth [*NASA*]
VA............. Vermiculite Association   (EA)
VA............. Verpflegungsausgabestelle [*Rations distributing point*] [*German military - World War II*]
VA............. Vertebral Artery [*Anatomy*]
VA............. Vesicular-Arbuscular [*Mycorrhiza*] [*Botany*]

VA............. [*Department of*] Veterans Affairs [*Formerly, Veterans Administration*]
V-A............. Vibroacoustic   (NASA)
VA............. Vibroacoustic Test   (NASA)
VA............. Vicar Apostolic
VA............. Vice Admiral [*Also, VADM, VADML*]
V-A............. Vickers-Armstrong Gun
V-A............. Vickers-Armstrong Ltd.
VA............. Victims Anonymous   (EA)
V & A .... Victoria and Albert Museum [*London, England*]
VA............. Victoria and Albert Order [*British*]
VA............. Victualling Allowance [*British military*]   (DMA)
VA............. Video Amplifier
V/A............. Video/Analog   (NASA)
V/A............. Video/Audio [*Telecommunications*]
VA............. Vincent's Angina [*Medicine*]
VA............. Viola [*Music*]
V-A............. Viper-Arrow   (SAA)
VA............. Virginia [*Postal code*]
VA............. Virginia Reports [*A publication*]   (DLA)
VA............. Virginia Supreme Court Reports [*A publication*]   (DLA)
VA............. Virtual Address
VA............. Virus-Antibody [*Immunology*]
VA............. Visual Acuity [*Also, V*] [*Ophthalmology*]
VA............. Visual Aid
VA............. Visual Approach [*Aviation*]   (FAAC)
VA............. Visual Arts [*US Copyright Office class*]
VA............. Visual Training Aid Specialist [*Navy*]
VA............. Vita Apollonii [*of Philostratus*] [*Classical studies*]   (OCD)
VA............. Vital Area   (NRCH)
VA............. Voice Actuation   (MCD)
VA............. Voice of America
V-A............. Volt-Ampere   (AAG)
VA............. Voltaire Alternative
VA............. Voluntary Aid   (ADA)
VA............. Volunteer Artillery [*Military*] [*British*]   (ROG)
V of A .... Volunteers of America   (EA)
VA............. Vorausabteilung [*Advance detachment*] [*German military - World War II*]
VA............. Vorderasiatische Abteilung der Staatlichen Museen zu Berlin [*A publication*]
VA............. Vorderasien   (BJA)
VA............. Vote America   (EA)
VA............. Votre Altesse [*Your Highness*] [*French*]
V/A............. Voucher Attached [*Banking*]
VA............. Voyage Alliance [*Later, IVA*]   (EA)
VA............. Vulnerability Assessment
VA............. Vulnerable Area   (NATG)
VAA........... Vaasa [*Finland*] [*Airport symbol*]   (OAG)
VAA........... Vegetarian Association of America   (EA)
VAA........... Vehicle Assembly Area [*NASA*]   (MCD)
VAA........... Venezuelan American Association of the United States   (EA)
VAA........... Verhandelingen. Koninklijke Akademie van Wetenschappen te Amsterdam [*A publication*]
VAA........... Verticilliuum albo-atrium [*A fungus*]
VAA........... Vietnamese American Association
VAA........... Viewpoint Adapter Assembly   (NASA)
VAA........... Voice Access Arrangement
VAAC......... Vanadyl Acetylacetonate [*Organic chemistry*]
VA Acts...... Acts of the General Assembly, Commonwealth of Virginia [*A publication*]   (DLA)
VA Ag Dept ... Virginia. Department of Agriculture and Immigration. Publications [*A publication*]
VA Ag Exp ... Virginia Polytechnic Institute. Agricultural Experiment Station. Publications [*A publication*]
VA Agric Exp Stn Bull ... Virginia. Agricultural Experiment Station. Bulletin [*A publication*]
VA Agric Exp Stn Tech Bull ... Virginia. Agricultural Experiment Station. Technical Bulletin [*A publication*]
VAAH........ Ahmadabad [*India*] [*ICAO location identifier*]   (ICLI)
VAAHDJ... Virchows Archiv. A. Pathological Anatomy and Histopathology [*A publication*]
VAAK........ Akola [*India*] [*ICAO location identifier*]   (ICLI)
VAAL .... Vaal Reefs Exploration and Mining Co. Ltd. [*NASDAQ symbol*]   (NQ)
VAAP......... Volunteer Army Ammunition Plant   (AABC)
VA App...... Virginia Appeals [*A publication*]   (DLA)
Va App....... Virginia Court of Appeals Reports [*A publication*]
VAAR .... Vinyl Alcohol Acetate Resin [*NASA*]   (KSC)
VAAS........ Vermont Academy of Arts and Sciences
VAAU........ Aurangabad [*India*] [*ICAO location identifier*]   (ICLI)
VAAUS...... Venezuelan American Association of the United States   (EA)
VAB .... Van Allen Belts
VAB .... Variable Action Button   (NVT)
VAB .... Vehicle Assembly Building [*NASA*]   (AFM)
VAB .... Vertical Assembly Building [*NASA*]
VAB .... Vertical Axis Bearing
VAB .... Vinblastine, Actinomycin D, Bleomycin [*Antineoplastic drug regimen*]
VAB .... Voice Answer Back

VAB .... Vorderasiatische Bibliothek [*H. Winckler and A. Jeremias*] [*Leipzig*] [*A publication*] (BJA)
VABA .... Value Added by Advertising
VA BAJ ..... Virginia Bar Association. Journal [*A publication*]
VA Bar News ... Virginia Bar News [*A publication*] (DLA)
VABB......... Bombay [*India*] [*ICAO location identifier*] (ICLI)
VABBA...... Vestsi Akademii Navuk BSSR. Seryya Biyalagichnykh Navuk [*A publication*]
VABCD...... Vinblastine, Adriamycin, Bleomycin, CCNU [*Lomustine*], Dacarbazine [*Antineoplastic drug regimen*]
VABD .... Van Allen Belt Dosimeter
VABF......... Bombay [*India*] [*ICAO location identifier*] (ICLI)
VABF......... Variety Artistes' Benevolent Fund [*British*] (ROG)
VABF......... Virginia Beach Federal Savings Bank [*NASDAQ symbol*] (NQ)
VABFA...... Vestsi Akademii Navuk BSSR. Seryya Fizika-Tekhnichnykh Navuk [*A publication*]
VABI......... Bilaspur [*India*] [*ICAO location identifier*] (ICLI)
VAB-I .... Vinblastine, Actinomycin D [*Dactinomycin*], Bleomycin [*Antineoplastic drug regimen*]
VAB-II ...... Vinblastine, Actinomycin D [*Dactinomycin*], Bleomycin, Cisplatin [*Antineoplastic drug regimen*]
VAB-III ..... Vinblastine, Actinomycin D [*Dactinomycin*], Bleomycin, Cisplatin, Chlorambucil, Cyclophosphamide [*Antineoplastic drug regimen*]
VABJ .... Bhuj [*India*] [*ICAO location identifier*] (ICLI)
VABM .... Belgaum [*India*] [*ICAO location identifier*] (ICLI)
VABM .... Vertical Angle Bench Mark
VABO .... Baroda/Vadodara [*India*] [*ICAO location identifier*] (ICLI)
VABP......... Bhopal [*India*] [*ICAO location identifier*] (ICLI)
VABPDE ... Virchows Archiv. B. Cell Pathology Including Molecular Pathology [*A publication*]
VABPF ...... Vice Admiral British Pacific Fleet
VABR .... Vehicle Assembly Building Repeater [*NASA*] (KSC)
VABV .... Bhaunagar [*India*] [*ICAO location identifier*] (ICLI)
VAC .... Alternating Current Volts
VAC .... Fifth Amphibious Corps
VAC .... Vacancy [*Real estate*] (ADA)
VAC .... Vacant (AFM)
VAC .... Vacate
VAC .... Vacation
Vac .... Vaccella [*Flourished, 12th century*] [*Authority cited in pre-1607 legal work*] (DSA)
VAC .... Vaccination [*or Vaccine*] [*Medicine*]
VAC .... Vacuolar Apical Compartment [*Cytology*]
VAC .... Vacuum (AABC)
VAC .... Value-Added Carrier [*Telecommunications*]
VAC .... Variable Air Capacitor
VAC .... Variance at Completion (MCD)
VAC .... Vector Analog Computer
VAC .... Vehicle Assembly and Checkout [*NASA*] (NASA)
VAC .... Verified Audit Circulation [*Newspaper auditing firm*] [*Advertising*]
VAC .... Vermont American Corp. [*AMEX symbol*] (SPSG)
VAC .... Vertical Air Current
VAC .... Veterans Administration Center
VAC .... Veterans Affairs Canada [*See also AACC*]
VAC .... Vice-Admiralty Court [*British*]
VAC .... Victor Analog Computer [*Data processing*]
VAC .... Video Amplifier Chain
VAC .... Vidicon Alignment Coil
VAC .... Vincristine, Actinomycin D, Cyclophosphamide [*Antineoplastic drug regimen*]
VAC .... Vincristine, Adriamycin, Cyclophosphamide [*Also, VACY*] [*Antineoplastic drug regimen*]
VAC .... Visual Aid Console
VAC .... Vital Area Center (CAAL)
VAC .... Volt-Ampere Characteristics [*Microwave emission*]
VAC .... Volts Alternating Current
VAC .... Voluntary Action Center
VAC .... Volunteer Adviser Corps (EA)
VACAB...... Veterans Administration Contract Appeals Board
VACAPES ... Virginia Capes [*Navy*] (CAAL)
VA Cas....... Virginia Cases (Brockenbrough and Holmes) [*A publication*] (DLA)
VA Cas....... Virginia Criminal Cases [*3-4 Virginia*] [*1789-1826*] [*A publication*] (DLA)
VA Cavalcade ... Virginia Cavalcade [*A publication*]
Vacc .... Vaccella [*Flourished, 12th century*] [*Authority cited in pre-1607 legal work*] (DSA)
vacc .... Vaccinate
VACC .... Value-Added Common Carrier [*Telecommunications*]
VAcC .... Visual Acuity with Spectacle Correction
VACCI....... Vaccine [*Medicine*]
VACCJ ...... VACC [*Victorian Automobile Chamber of Commerce*] Journal [*A publication*] (APTA)
VAcCL....... Visual Acuity with Contact Lens Correction
VACE......... Verification and Checkout Equipment
VACF......... Vietnamese-American Children's Fund [*Defunct*] (EA)
VACHA ..... Virginias Automated Clearing House Association
VA Ch Dec ... Wythe's Virginia Chancery Reports [*1788-99*] [*A publication*] (DLA)

VA Cir....... Virginia Circuit Court Opinions [*A publication*] (DLA)
VACM .... Vector Averaging Current Meter [*Marine science*] (MSC)
VACM .... Vincristine, Adriamycin, Cyclophosphamide, Methotrexate [*Antineoplastic drug regimen*]
Vac Microbalance Tech ... Vacuum Microbalance Techniques [*A publication*]
Va Code Ann ... Code of Virginia Annotated [*A publication*]
VA Col Dec ... Virginia Colonial Decisions (Randolph and Barrandall) [*A publication*] (DLA)
VACP......... Vacation Publications, Inc. [*NASDAQ symbol*] (NQ)
VACR .... Variable Amplitude Correction Rack [*Telecommunications*] (OA)
VACR .... Visual Aircraft Recognition (MCD)
VACRS...... Vocational Assistance Commission for Retired Servicemen (CINC)
VACSAT ... Vaccine Satellite Program (MCD)
VACT........ Alternating Current Test Volts (MSA)
VACTERL ... Vertebral, Anal, Cardiac, Tracheosophageal, Renal, and Limb [*Defects*]
VACTL...... Vertical Assembly Component Test Laboratory
VACU .... Virtual Access Control Unit
VACUA ..... Vacuum [*A publication*]
VACURG .. Veterans Administration Cooperative Urological Research Group
Vacuum Chem ... Vacuum Chemistry [*Japan*] [*A publication*]
Vacuum R .. Vacuum Review [*A publication*] (APTA)
VACVVD... Vacuum and Vent Control Valve Distributor [*Automotive engineering*]
VACVVT... Vacuum and Vent Control Valve Thermactor [*Automotive engineering*]
VACW .... Alternating Current Working Volts (MSA)
VACY .... Vincristine, Adriamycin, Cyclophosphamide [*Also, VAC*] [*Antineoplastic drug regimen*]
VAD........... Vacuum Arc Degassing [*Metal technology*]
VAD........... Val d'Or Explorations [*Vancouver Stock Exchange symbol*]
VAD........... Valdosta, GA [*Location identifier*] [*FAA*] (FAAL)
VAD........... Value Added and Data [*Communications network*]
VAD........... Value-Added Dealer [*Business term*]
VAD........... Value-Added Distributor
VAD........... Value-Added Driver [*Data processing*] (PCM)
VAD........... Vandenberg Addendum Document [*Air Force*] (NASA)
VAD........... Vapor Axial Deposition [*Optical fiber technology*]
VAD........... Velocity-Azimuth Display
VAD........... Ventricle-Assist Device [*Cardiology*]
VAD........... Vereinigte Arbeitnehmerpartei Deutschland [*United Employees' Party of Germany*] [*Germany*] [*Political party*] (PPW)
VAD .... Veterans' Affairs Decisions, Appealed Pension and Civil Service Retirement Cases [*United States*] [*A publication*] (DLA)
VAD........... Veterans Against Drugs
VAD........... Voltmeter Analog-to-Digital Converter
VAD........... Voluntary Aid Detachment [*British World War I nursing unit*]
VAD........... Vought Aeronautics Division [*Ling-Temco-Vought*]
VAD........... Vulcan Air Defense (MCD)
VADA .... Versatile Automatic Data Exchange
VADA .... VFR [*Visual Flight Rules*] Arrival Delay Advisory [*Aviation*] (FAAC)
VADAC ..... Voice Analyzer Data Converter
VADC .... Video Analog to Digital Converter
VADC .... Voice Analyzer and Data Converter (MCD)
VADE .... Vandenberg Automatic Data Equipment [*Air Force*]
VADE .... Vandenberg Automatic Data Evaluation [*Air Force*]
VADE .... Versatile Automatic Data Exchange (MCD)
VADE .... Voice Analog to Digital Encoder
VA Dec....... Virginia Decisions [*A publication*] (DLA)
VA Dent J ... Virginia Dental Journal [*A publication*]
VA Dept Highways Div Tests Geol Yearbook ... Virginia. Department of Highways. Division of Tests. Geological Yearbook [*A publication*]
VA Dept Labor and Industry Ann Rept ... Virginia. Department of Labor and Industry. Annual Report [*A publication*]
VADER ...... Vacuum Arc Double-Electrode Remelting [*Metallurgy*]
VADER ..... Vader Group, Inc. [*Associated Press abbreviation*] (APAG)
VADF .... Vietnamese Air Defense Force (MCD)
VADIC....... Vincristine, Adriamycin, DIC [*Dacarbazine*] [*Antineoplastic drug regimen*]
VADIS....... Voice and Data Integrated System [*Telecommunications*] (TEL)
VA Div Geol Bull ... Virginia. Division of Geology. Bulletin [*A publication*]
VA Div Geology Bull Reprint Ser ... Virginia. Division of Geology. Bulletin. Reprint Series [*A publication*]
VA Div Mineral Res Bull Inf Circ Mineral Res Circ ... Virginia. Division of Mineral Resources. Bulletin. Information Circular. Mineral Resources Circular [*A publication*]
VA Div Miner Resour Bull ... Virginia. Division of Mineral Resources. Bulletin [*A publication*]
VA Div Miner Resour Inf Cir ... Virginia. Division of Mineral Resources. Information Circular [*A publication*]
VA Div Miner Resour Miner Resour Rep ... Virginia. Division of Mineral Resources. Mineral Resources Report [*A publication*]
VA Div Miner Resour Rep Invest ... Virginia. Division of Mineral Resources. Report of Investigations [*A publication*]

VADM....... Vice Admiral [*Also, VA, VADML*]
VADM....... Virtual Axial Dipole Moment [*Geophysics*]
VADML .... Vice Admiral [*Also, VA, VADM*] (FAAC)
VADMS.... Voice-Analog-Digital Manual Switch (MCD)
VADS .... Value Added and Data Services
VADS .... Velocity-Aligned Doppler Spectroscopy
VADS .... Vendor Automated Data System (MCD)
VADS .... Veterans Assistance Discharge System (MCD)
VADS .... Visual-Aural Digit Span Test [*Educational test*]
VADS .... Vulcan Air Defense Systems (MCD)
VAE .... Vinta Exploration Ltd. [*Vancouver Stock Exchange symbol*]
VAE .... Vinyl Acetate - Ethylene [*Organic chemistry*]
VAE .... Votre Altesse Electorale [*Your Electoral Highness*] [*French*]
VAEBAI .... Agricultural Experiment Station. University of Vermont. Bulletin [*A publication*]
VAEP........ Variable, Attributes, Error Propagation (IEEE)
VaEP.......... Virginia Electric & Power Co. [*Associated Press abbreviation*] (APAG)
Vaerml Bergsmannafoeren Ann ... Vaermlaendska Bergsmannafoereningens Annaler [*A publication*]
VAES........ Voice-Activated Encoding System
VAE VA Agric Econ VA Polytech Inst State Univ Coop Ext Serv ... VAE. Virginia Agricultural Economics. Virginia Polytechnic Institute and State University. Cooperative Extension Service [*A publication*]
VAEVC...... Vinyl Acetate - Ethylene - Vinyl Chloride [*Organic chemistry*]
Vaextskyddsanst-Notiser ... Vaextskyddsanstalt-Notiser [*A publication*]
VAF .... Valence [*France*] [*Airport symbol*] (OAG)
VAF .... Vane Airflow [*Automotive engineering*]
VAF .... Vendor Approval Form
VAF .... Vernacular Architecture Forum (EA)
VAF .... Vietnamese Air Force (MCD)
VAF .... Viral Antibody-Free [*Environment*]
VAF .... Volume Air Flow [*Automotive engineering*]
VAF .... Voluntary Application Fill (DNAB)
VAFAC...... Vincristine, Amethopterin [*Methotrexate*], Fluorouracil, Adriamycin, Cyclophosphamide [*Antineoplastic drug regimen*]
VA Farm Econ VA Polytech Inst Agr Ext Serv ... Virginia Farm Economics. Virginia Polytechnic Institute. Agricultural Extension Service [*A publication*]
VAFB........ Valley Federal Savings Bank [*NASDAQ symbol*] (NQ)
VAFB........ Vandenberg Air Force Base [*California*]
VAFD .... Valley Federal Savings Bank [*NASDAQ symbol*] (NQ)
VAFF........ Variable Aperture Far Field
VA Fish Lab Educ Ser ... Virginia Fisheries Laboratory. Educational Series [*A publication*]
VA Fruit..... Virginia Fruit [*A publication*]
VAG .... Vagabond (DSUE)
VAG .... Vaginal [*Medicine*]
VAG .... Vaginitis [*Medicine*]
VAG .... Vagrancy [*FBI standardized term*]
VAG .... Vananda Gold [*Vancouver Stock Exchange symbol*]
VAG .... Vancouver Art Gallery [*Canada*]
VAG .... Varginha [*Brazil*] [*Airport symbol*] (OAG)
VAG .... Vastgoed [*A publication*]
VAG .... Vernacular Architecture Group [*British*]
VAG .... Volkswagen Audi Group
Vaga .... Vagabond [*A publication*]
VAGA .... Vagabond Hotels [*NASDAQ symbol*] (NQ)
VAGA .... Visual Artists and Galleries Association (EA)
VA Geol Surv Circ ... Virginia. Geological Survey. Circular [*A publication*]
VA Geol Survey Bull ... Virginia. Geological Survey. Bulletin [*A publication*]
VA Geol Surv Repr Ser ... Virginia. Geological Survey. Reprint Series [*A publication*]
VAGO........ Goa [*India*] [*ICAO location identifier*] (ICLI)
VAGO........ Vanderbilt Gold Corp. [*NASDAQ symbol*] (NQ)
VA GSB..... Virginia. Geological Survey. Bulletin [*A publication*]
VAH.......... Heavy Attack Squadron [*Symbol*] (MCD)
VAH.......... Vaihoa [*Tuamotu Archipelago*] [*Seismograph station code, US Geological Survey*] (SEIS)
VAH.......... Vertical Array Hydrophone
VAH.......... Veterans Administration Hospital [*Later, VAMC*]
VAH.......... Virilizing Adrenal Hyperplasia [*Medicine*]
VAH.......... Vitiated Air Heater
VA Hist Soc Coll ... Virginia Historical Society. Collections [*A publication*]
VA Horse Ind Yearb ... Virginia Horse Industry Yearbook [*A publication*]
VAHR........ Veterans Administration Hospital Representative [*Red Cross*]
VAHS........ Virus-Associated Hemophagocytic Syndrome [*Medicine*]
VAHT........ Vertical Axis Hydropower Turbine
VAI .... Vanimo [*Papua New Guinea*] [*Airport symbol*] (OAG)
VAI .... Vassar Attitude Inventory [*Education*]
VAI .... Ventilation Air Intake [*Hovercraft*]
VA & I........ Verb Active and Intransitive (ROG)
VAI .... Video Arts International, Inc.
VAI .... Video-Assisted Instruction
VAI .... Visual Alignment Indicators [*Tire maintenance*]
VAI .... Voluntary Action Indicated [*FDA*]
VAI .... Vorticity Area Index [*Meteorology*]
VA IC Ops ... Virginia Industrial Commission Opinions [*A publication*] (DLA)

VAID .... Indore [*India*] [*ICAO location identifier*] (ICLI)
VAIL......... Vail Associates [*NASDAQ symbol*] (NQ)
VA Inst Mar Sci Spec Sci Rep ... Virginia Institute of Marine Science. Special Scientific Report [*A publication*]
Vaizey .... Vaizey's Law of Settlements [*1887*] [*A publication*] (DLA)
VAJ........... Vajont [*Belluno*] [*Italy*] [*Seismograph station code, US Geological Survey*] (SEIS)
VAJB......... Jabalpur [*India*] [*ICAO location identifier*] (ICLI)
VA J Ed ..... Virginia Journal of Education [*A publication*]
VA J Educ ... Virginia Journal of Education [*A publication*]
VA J Int L ... Virginia Journal of International Law [*A publication*]
VA J Intl L ... Virginia Journal of International Law [*A publication*]
VAJJ .... Bombay/Juhu [*India*] [*ICAO location identifier*] (ICLI)
VAJM........ Jamnagar [*India*] [*ICAO location identifier*] (ICLI)
VA J Nat Resources L ... Virginia Journal of Natural Resources Law [*A publication*]
VA J Nat Resour Law ... Virginia Journal of Natural Resources Law [*A publication*]
VAJODH .. Lantbrukshogskolan Vaxtskyddsrapporter Jordbruk [*A publication*]
VA Jour Sci ... Virginia Journal of Science [*A publication*]
VA J Sci..... Virginia Journal of Science [*A publication*]
VAK.......... Aerial Refueling Squadron [*Navy symbol*] (DNAB)
VAK .... Chevak [*Alaska*] [*Airport symbol*] (OAG)
VAK .... Vertical Access Kit (NASA)
VAK .... Vertical Assembly Kit (NASA)
Vakbl Biol ... Vakblad voor Biologen [*A publication*]
VAKD .... Khandwa [*India*] [*ICAO location identifier*] (ICLI)
VAKE .... Kandla [*India*] [*ICAO location identifier*] (ICLI)
Vak Inf...... Vakuum Information [*A publication*]
VAKP........ Kolhapur [*India*] [*ICAO location identifier*] (ICLI)
VAKS........ Keshod [*India*] [*ICAO location identifier*] (ICLI)
Vakstudie... Fiscale Encyclopedie de Vakstudie [*A publication*]
VAKT .... Visual, Association, Kinesthetic, Tactile [*With reference to reading*]
VAKT .... Visual-Auditory-Kinesthetic-Tactual
VAKTA...... Vakuum-Technik [*A publication*]
Vak-Tech ... Vakuum-Technik [*A publication*]
Vak-Technik ... Vakuum-Technik [*A publication*]
VAL .... Light Attack Aircraft [*Symbol*] (MCD)
VAL .... Plattsburgh, NY [*Location identifier*] [*FAA*] (FAAL)
VAL .... University of Virginia, Law Library, Charlottesville, VA [*OCLC symbol*] (OCLC)
Val............ Valcausus [*Gualcosius*] [*Flourished, 11th-12th century*] [*Authority cited in pre-1607 legal work*] (DSA)
VAL .... Valentia [*Ireland*] [*Seismograph station code, US Geological Survey*] (SEIS)
VAL .... Valentia [*Ireland*] [*Geomagnetic observatory code*]
VAL .... Valid [*or Validation*] (KSC)
Val............ Valine [*Also, V*] [*An amino acid*]
VAL .... Valley (MSA)
Val............ Valley Girl [*Lifestyle classification*]
VAL .... Valspar Corp. [*AMEX symbol*] (SPSG)
VAL .... Valuation
VAL .... Valuation [*A publication*]
VAL .... Value
VAL .... Value Investment Corp. [*Toronto Stock Exchange symbol*]
VAL .... Valve
VAL .... Variable Angle Launcher
VAL .... Vehicle Authorization List [*Military*] (AFM)
VAL .... Vertical Assault Lift
VAL .... Vicarm Arm Language
VAL .... Vieques Air Link [*Caribbean airline*]
VA L .... Virginia Law Review [*A publication*]
VAL .... Visual Approach and Landing Chart [*Aviation*]
VAL .... Vortex Arc LASER
VAL .... Vulnerability Assessment Laboratory [*White Sands Missile Range, NM*] [*Military*] (RDA)
Valasis .... Valassis Communications [*Associated Press abbreviation*] (APAG)
VA Law J... Virginia Law Journal [*Richmond*] [*A publication*] (DLA)
VA Law R .. Virginia Law Review [*A publication*]
VA Law Rev ... Virginia Law Review [*A publication*]
VALB........ Veterans of the Abraham Lincoln Brigade (EA)
VALCO ..... Volta Aluminum Co. Ltd.
Val Com ..... Valen's Commentaries [*A publication*] (DLA)
VALD .... Valued (ROG)
VA L Dig..... Virginia Law Digest [*A publication*] (DLA)
VALDN ..... Validation
VALE........ [*The*] Valley Railroad Co. [*AAR code*]
VALE........ Visual Acuity, Left Eye [*Ophthalmology*] (MAE)
Vale Evesham Hist Soc Res Pap ... Vale of Evesham Historical Society. Research Papers [*A publication*]
Valero .... Valero Energy Corp. [*Associated Press abbreviation*] (APAG)
VALFRG ... Valley Forge Corp. [*Associated Press abbreviation*] (APAG)
Valhi .... Valhi, Inc. [*Associated Press abbreviation*] (APAG)
ValHlth...... Value Health, Inc. [*Associated Press abbreviation*] (APAG)
VALI.......... Validate (AABC)
VA Lib Bul ... Virginia Library Bulletin [*A publication*]
VA Libn ..... Virginia Librarian [*A publication*]
VALID....... Validation (NASA)

VALIPR..... Validation In-Process Review [DoD]
VA LJ .... Virginia Law Journal [A publication] (DLA)
VALL....... Vortex Arc LASER Light
Vallalatvez -Szerv ... Vallalatvezetes-Vallalatszervezes [A publication]
VALLYRS ... Valley Resources, Inc. [Associated Press abbreviation] (APAG)
VALM ...... Valmont Industries, Inc. [NASDAQ symbol] (NQ)
ValMer...... Value Merchants, Inc. [Associated Press abbreviation] (APAG)
VALN .... Vallen Corp. [NASDAQ symbol] (NQ)
VALN .... Valuation
VALN .... Victorian Adult Literacy News [A publication] (APTA)
VALNET ... Veterans Administration Library Network [Veterans Administration] [Washington, DC]
ValNG........ Valero Natural Gas Partners Ltd. [Associated Press abbreviation] (APAG)
VALOR ..... Veterans Administration Libraries Online Resources
VALP......... Valex Petroleum, Inc. [NASDAQ symbol] (NQ)
VALP......... Vortex Arc LASER Pump
Valparaiso Univ Law R ... Valparaiso University. Law Review [A publication]
Valparaiso Univ L Rev ... Valparaiso University. Law Review [A publication]
VALPO...... Valparaiso (DSUE)
VA LR........ Virginia Law Review [A publication]
VALRA...... Variable-Area Light-Reflecting Assembly [Invented by T. C. Howard of Synergetics, Inc.]
VA L Reg ... Virginia Law Register [A publication] (DLA)
VA L Reg NS ... Virginia Law Register, New Series [A publication] (DLA)
Val Rep ...... Valuation Reports, Interstate Commerce Commission [A publication] (DLA)
Val Rep ICC ... Valuation Reports, Interstate Commerce Commission [A publication] (DLA)
VA L Rev ... Virginia Law Review [A publication]
VALS......... Value and Lifestyle [Classifications] [Marketing]
Valsa......... Valsalva [A publication]
VALSAS.... Variable Length Word Symbolic Assembly System (IEEE)
VALSPR.... Valspar Corp. [Associated Press abbreviation] (APAG)
VALT........ Valtek, Inc. [NASDAQ symbol] (NQ)
VALT........ VTOL [Vertical Takeoff and Landing] Approach and Landing Technology [Program]
Valt Maatalouskoetoiminnan Julk ... Valtion Maatalouskoetoiminnan Julkaisuja [A publication]
VALT(S).... Vulnerability and Lethality Test (System) (MCD)
Valt Tek Tutkimuskeskus Reaktorilab Tied ... Valtion Teknillinen Tutkimuskeskus. Reaktorilaboratorio. Tiedonanto [A publication]
Valt Tek Tutkimuslaitos Julk ... Valtion Teknillinen Tutkimuslaitos. Julkaisu [A publication]
Valt Tek Tutkimuslaitos Tiedotus Sar 2 ... Valtion Teknillinen Tutkimuslaitos. Tiedotus. Sarja 2. Metalli [A publication]
Valt Tek Tutkimuslaitos Tiedotus Sar 4 ... Valtion Teknillinen Tutkimuslaitos. Tiedotus. Sarja 4. Kemia [A publication]
Valt Tek Tutkimuslaitos Tiedotus Sar 1 Puu ... Valtion Teknillinen Tutkimuslaitos. Tiedotus. Sarja 1. Puu [A publication]
Valt Tek Tutkimuslaitos Tied Sar 2 ... Valtion Teknillinen Tutkimuslaitos. Tiedotus. Sarja 2. Metalli [A publication]
Valt Tek Tutkimuslaitos Tied Sar 3 ... Valtion Teknillinen Tutkimuslaitos. Tiedotus. Sarja 3. Rakennus [A publication]
Valt Tek Tutkimuslaitos Tied Sar I PUU ... Valtion Teknillinen Tutkimuslaitos Tiedotus. Sarja I. PUU [A publication]
VALU .... Value Line, Inc. [NASDAQ symbol] (NQ)
VALUE....... Validated Aircraft Logistics Utilization Evaluation [Navy]
VALUE...... Visible Achievement Liberates Unemployment [DoD project for disadvantaged youth]
ValueCty .... Value City Department Stores [Associated Press abbreviation] (APAG)
Value Eng .. Value Engineering [A publication]
Value Line ... Value Line Investment Survey [A publication]
Val U LR.... Valparaiso University. Law Review [A publication]
Val U L Rev ... Valparaiso University. Law Review [A publication]
VALUON.. Valuation
Valvo Tech Inf Ind ... Valvo Technische Informationen fuer die Industrie [A publication]
VA L Wk Dicta Comp ... Virginia Law Weekly Dicta Compilation [A publication] (DLA)
VALY........ Vallicorp Holdings, Inc. [NASDAQ symbol] (NQ)
VAM......... Medium Attack Aircraft [Navy symbol] (NVT)
VAM......... University of Virginia, C. Moore Health Sciences Library, Charlottesville, VA [OCLC symbol] (OCLC)
VAM......... Vacuum-Assisted Molding [Automotive technology]
VAM......... Value Aluminizing Machine
VAM......... Vamos [Greece] [Seismograph station code, US Geological Survey] (SEIS)
VAM......... Vector Airborne Magnetometer (IEEE)
VAM......... Vehiculos Automotores Mexicanos [Commercial firm]
VAM......... Vending and Affixing Machine
VAM......... Vesicular Arbuscular Mycorrhizae [Botany]
VAM......... Veterans Administration Matters [FBI standardized term]
VAM......... Vinyl Acetate Monomer [Organic chemistry]
VA M .... Virginia Magazine of History and Biography [A publication]
VAM......... Virtual Access Method
VAM......... Vista Mines, Inc. [Toronto Stock Exchange symbol]
VAM......... Visual Approach Monitor [Aviation]
VAM......... Vogel's Approximation Method

VAM......... Voltammeter
VAM......... VP-16-213 [Etoposide], Adriamycin, Methotrexate [Antineoplastic drug regimen]
VA Mag Hist ... Virginia Magazine of History and Biography [A publication]
VA Mag Hist Biog ... Virginia Magazine of History and Biography [A publication]
VA Mag Hist Biogr ... Virginia Magazine of History and Biography [A publication]
VAMC ...... Veterans Administration Medical Center [Formerly, VAH]
VAMCO..... Village & Marketing Corp. [Jamaica]
VAMD...... Virginia & Maryland Railroad [AAR code]
VA Med ..... Virginia Medical [A publication]
VA Med Mon ... Virginia Medical Monthly [Later, Virginia Medical] [A publication]
VAMFO .... Variable Angle Monochromatic Fringe Observation [Film thickness determination]
VA Miner... Virginia Minerals [A publication]
VAMIS...... Versatile Automated Maintenance Information System (MCD)
VAMIS...... Virginia Medical Information System [Library network]
VAMOS .... Verified Additional Military Occupational Specialty
VAMOSC ... Visibility and Management of Operating and Support Costs [Army]
VAMP ...... Value Analysis of Management Practices (MCD)
VAMP ...... Vandenberg Atlas Modification Program [Air Force] (MCD)
VAMP ...... Variable [or Visual] Anamorphic Motion Picture [Training device to provide realistic environment during simulated flight training] (MCD)
VAMP ...... Vector Arithmetic Multiprocessor [Data processing] (IEEE)
VAMP ...... Vietnam Ammunition Program (AFM)
VAMP ...... Vincristine, Actinomycin, Methotrexate, Prednisone [Antineoplastic drug regimen]
VAMP ...... Vincristine Amethopterin [Antitumor agent]
VAMP ...... Vincristine, Amethopterin [Methotrexate], Mercaptopurine, Prednisone [Antineoplastic drug regimen]
VAMP ...... Visual-Acoustic-Magnetic Pressure (IEEE)
VAMP ...... Visual-Acoustic-Magnetic Program [NOO]
VAMP ...... Visual Anamorphic Motion Picture (AIA)
VAMP ...... Vulnerability Assessment Modeling Program [Air Force]
VAMR ...... Vernon's Annotated Missouri Rule [A publication] (DLA)
VAMROC ... [Department of] Veterans Affairs Medical and Regional Office Center
VAMS....... Vernon's Annotated Missouri Statutes [A publication] (DLA)
VAMS....... Victor Airspeed Measuring System (MCD)
VAMS....... Visual Analog Mood Scale
VAMSI...... Visual Approach Multiple Slope Indicator [Aviation]
VAMT ...... Vertical Assault Medium Transport (MCD)
VAN.......... Northern Virginia Community College, Springfield, VA [OCLC symbol] (OCLC)
VAN.......... Value-Added Network [Data processing] [Telecommunications]
VAN.......... Van [Turkey] [Airport symbol] (OAG)
VAN.......... Vance, SC [Location identifier] [FAA] (FAAL)
VAN.......... Vandeno [Race of maize]
VAN.......... Vanderbilt Law Review [A publication]
Van.......... Vanguard [Record label]
Van.......... Vanguard Science Fiction [A publication]
VAN.......... Vanguard Tracking Station [NASA] (NASA)
VAN.......... Vanier College [UTLAS symbol]
VAN.......... Vannovskaya [Former USSR] [Seismograph station code, US Geological Survey] (SEIS)
VAN.......... Vanwin Resources Corp. [Vancouver Stock Exchange symbol]
VAN.......... Variable Area Nozzle
VAN.......... Vehicle Area Network [Automotive engineering]
VAN.......... Voluntary Action News [A publication]
VAN.......... Vorlaeufige Arbeitsnormen
VANB......... Vesci Akademii Navuk BSSR [A publication]
Vancoram Rev ... Vancoram Review [A publication]
Vancouver Op Jnl ... Vancouver Opera Journal [A publication]
Vand.......... De Bello Vandalico [of Procopius] [Classical studies] (OCD)
VAND....... Nanded [India] [ICAO location identifier] (ICLI)
VAND....... Vacuum-Air-Nitrogen Distribution
VAND....... Van Den Bergh [Liver function test]
VAND....... Van Dusen Air, Inc. [NASDAQ symbol] (NQ)
Vanderbilt J Transnat'l L ... Vanderbilt Journal of Transnational Law [A publication]
Vanderbilt LR ... Vanderbilt Law Review [A publication] (DLA)
Vanderbilt Univ Abs Theses Bull ... Vanderbilt University. Abstracts of Theses. Bulletin [A publication]
Vander L.... Vanderlinden's Laws of Holland [A publication] (DLA)
Vander Law ... Vanderbilt Law Review [A publication]
Vanderstr... Vanderstraaten's Reports [1869-71] [Ceylon] [A publication] (DLA)
Vanderstraaten ... Vanderstraaten's Decisions in Appeal, Supreme Court [1869-71] [Sri L.] [A publication] (DLA)
Vand Int ... Vanderbilt International [A publication]
Vand J Trans L ... Vanderbilt Journal of Transnational Law [A publication]
Vand J Transnatl L ... Vanderbilt Journal of Transnational Law [A publication]
Vand LR..... Vanderbilt Law Review [A publication]
Vand L Rev ... Vanderbilt Law Review [A publication]
VanDrn....... Van Dorn Co. [Associated Press abbreviation] (APAG)

VAND UNIV Q ... Vanderbilt University Quarterly [*Tennessee*] [*A publication*]

VANF .... VanFed Bancorp [*NASDAQ symbol*] (CTT)

VANFIS .... Visible and Near-Visible Frequency Intercept System [*Navy*]

Van Fleet Coll Attack ... Van Fleet on Collateral Attack [*A publication*] (DLA)

VANGI ...... Variable-Area Nozzle by Gas Injection (SAA)

VANHC ..... Veterans Administration Nursing Home Care Program (GFGA)

Van Hey Eq ... Van Heythuysen's Equity Draftsman [*2nd ed.*] [*1828*] [*A publication*] (DLA)

Van Hey Mar Ev ... Van Heythuysen on Maritime Evidence [*A publication*] (DLA)

Van Hey Rud ... Van Heythuysen's Rudiments of English Law [*A publication*] (DLA)

VANHP ..... Virginia Natural Heritage Program [*Virginia State Department of Conservation and Historic Resources*] [*Information service or system*] (IID)

VANIS .... Volume Analysis Information System Software

Van K .... Van Koughnet's Reports [*15-21 Upper Canada Common Pleas*] [*1864-71*] [*A publication*] (DLA)

Van K & H ... Upper Canada Common Pleas Reports [*1864-71*] [*A publication*] (DLA)

Van L .... Vander Linden's Practice [*Cape Colony*] [*A publication*] (DLA)

Van N .... Van Ness' Prize Cases, United States District Court, District of New York [*A publication*] (DLA)

VAN N .... Van Norden Magazine [*New York*] [*A publication*] (ROG)

Van Ness Prize Cas ... Van Ness' Prize Cases, United States District Court, District of New York [*A publication*] (DLA)

VANP .... Nagpur [*India*] [*ICAO location identifier*] (ICLI)

VANR .... Nasik Road [*India*] [*ICAO location identifier*] (ICLI)

VANS .... Value-Added Network Service [*Data processing*] [*Telecommunications*]

VANS .... Van Schaack & Co. [*NASDAQ symbol*] (NQ)

VANS .... Vans, Inc. [*NASDAQ symbol*] (SPSG)

VANS .... Vehicle Austere Night Sight [*Army*] (MCD)

Van Sant Ch J ... Van Santvoord's Lives of the Chief Justices of the United States [*A publication*] (DLA)

Van Sant Eq Pr ... Van Santvoord's Equity Practice [*A publication*] (DLA)

Van Sant Pl ... Van Santvoord's Pleadings [*A publication*] (DLA)

Van Sant Prec ... Van Santvoord's Precedents [*A publication*] (DLA)

Vant .... [*Sebastianus*] Vantius [*Flourished, 16th century*] [*Authority cited in pre-1607 legal work*] (DSA)

VANT .... Vibration and Noise Tester (SAA)

VA Num ..... Virginia Numismatist [*A publication*]

VA Nurse ... Virginia Nurse [*A publication*]

VA Nurse Q ... Virginia Nurse Quarterly [*Later, Virginia Nurse*] [*A publication*]

VANUSL ... Vanderbilt University School of Law (DLA)

VANWACE ... Vulnerability Analysis of Nuclear Weapons in Allied Command, Europe [*Army*] (AABC)

VANZ .... Vanzetti Systems, Inc. [*NASDAQ symbol*] (NQ)

Van Zee Ld ... Van Zee tot Land [*A publication*]

VAO .... Veterans Administration Office

VAO .... Voting Assistance Officer

VAOKN ..... Visual Acuity by Optokinetic Nystagmus

VAOR .... VHF [*Very-High-Frequency*] Aural Omnirange

VAP .... Photographic Squadron (Heavy) [*Navy symbol*] (NVT)

VAP .... Vaginal Acid Phosphatase [*An enzyme*]

VAP .... Valence-Alternation Pair [*Solid-state physics*]

VAP .... Value-Added Process [*Data processing*] (PCM)

VAP .... Van Kampen Merritt Advanced Pennsylvania Municipal [*NYSE symbol*] (SPSG)

VAP .... Vaporization [*or Vaporizer*] (KSC)

VAP .... Vehicle Antenna Position [*NASA*]

VAP .... Velocity Analysis Program

VAP .... Vertical Axis Pivots

VAP .... Veteran Air Pilots

VAP .... Vibrationally Adiabatic Potential [*Chemical physics*]

VAP .... Video/Audio Participative [*Education*] (OA)

VAP .... Videotex Access Point [*Data processing*] (IT)

VAP .... Vinblastine, Actinomycin D [*Dactinomycin*], Platinol [*Cisplatin*] [*Antineoplastic drug regimen*]

VAP .... Vincristine, Adriamycin, Prednisone [*Antineoplastic drug regimen*]

VAP .... Vincristine, Adriamycin, Procarbazine [*Antineoplastic drug regimen*]

VAP .... Voluntary Assistance Program

VAP .... Voting Age Population

VAPA .... Video Alliance for the Performing Arts (EA)

VAPC .... Vector Adaptive Predictive Coding [*Telecommunications*]

VAPC .... Veterans Administration Prosthetics Center [*Later, VAREC*]

VAP-Cyclo ... Vincristine, Adriamycin, Prednisolone, Cyclophosphamide [*Antineoplastic drug regimen*]

VAPH .... Visual Acuity with Pin Hole

VAPHD ..... Virchows Archiv. A. Pathological Anatomy and Histology [*A publication*]

VAPI .... Visual Approach Path Indicator [*Aviation*]

VAPO .... Pune [*India*] [*ICAO location identifier*] (ICLI)

VAPO .... Vaporizing Oil

VA Polytech Inst Bull Eng Expt Sta Ser ... Virginia Polytechnic Institute. Bulletin. Engineering Experiment Station Series [*A publication*]

VA Polytech Inst Eng Ext Ser Cir ... Virginia Polytechnic Institute. Engineering Extension Series. Circular [*A publication*]

VA Polytech Inst Res Div Bull ... Virginia Polytechnic Institute. Research Division. Bulletin [*A publication*]

VA Polytech Inst Res Div Wood Res Wood Constr Lab Bull ... Virginia Polytechnic Institute. Research Division. Wood Research and Wood Construction Laboratory [*Blacksburg*]. Bulletin [*A publication*]

VA Polytech Inst State Univ Res Div Bull ... Virginia Polytechnic Institute and State University. Research Division. Bulletin [*A publication*]

VA Polytech Inst State Univ Res Div Monogr ... Virginia Polytechnic Institute and State University. Research Division. Monograph [*A publication*]

VA Polytech Inst State Univ Res Div Rep ... Virginia Polytechnic Institute and State University. Research Division. Report [*A publication*]

VA Polytech Inst State Univ Sch For Wildl Resour Publ FWS ... Virginia Polytechnic Institute and State University. School of Forestry and Wildlife Resources. Publication FWS [*A publication*]

VA Polytech Inst State Univ VA Water Resour Res Cent Bull ... Virginia Polytechnic Institute and State University. Virginia Water Resources Research Center. Bulletin [*A publication*]

VA Polytech Inst State Univ Water Resour Res Cent Bull ... Virginia Polytechnic Institute and State University. Water Resources Research Center. Bulletin [*A publication*]

VAPR .... Porbandar [*India*] [*ICAO location identifier*] (ICLI)

VAPR .... Veterans Administration Procurement [*or Purchase*] Regulations

VAPS .... V/STOL Approach System (MCD)

VAPS .... Virtual Avionics Prototyping System [*Virtual Prototypes, Inc.*]

VAPS .... Volume, Article [*or Chapter*], Paragraph, Sentence [*Numbers*] [*Indexing*]

VAQ .... Tactical Electronic Warfare Squadron [*Navy symbol*] (DNAB)

VAQ .... Visiting Airmen's Quarters [*Air Force*]

VAQ .... Visual Air Quality

Va/Qc .... Ventilation/Perfusion Quotient [*Medicine*] (MAE)

VA Q R ...... Virginia Quarterly Review [*A publication*]

VA Q Rev ... Virginia Quarterly Review [*A publication*]

VAR .... Corps of Volunteers Artillery Regiment [*British military*] (DMA)

VA R .... Gilmer's Virginia Reports [*A publication*] (DLA)

VAR .... Reactive Volt-Ampere

VAR .... Vacuum Arc Remelting [*Steel alloy*]

VAR .... Validation Analysis Report [*Social Security Administration*]

VAR .... Value-Added Remarketer [*or Reseller or Retailer*] [*Business term*]

VAR .... VANAIR, Inc. [*Gasport, NY*] [*FAA designator*] (FAAC)

VAR .... Varanasi [*India*] [*Seismograph station code, US Geological Survey*] (SEIS)

VAR .... Variable (AFM)

Var .... Variae [*of Cassiodorus*] [*Classical studies*] (OCD)

VAR .... Varian Associates [*NYSE symbol*] (SPSG)

VAR .... Variance Analysis Report (MCD)

VAR .... Variant [*Numismatics*]

VAR .... Variation

VAR .... Variegated

var .... Varietas [*Variety*] [*Biology*]

VAR .... Variety

VAR .... Variety [*A publication*]

VAR .... Variometer (WGA)

VAR .... Various

VAR .... Varitech Resources [*Vancouver Stock Exchange symbol*]

VAR .... Varna [*Bulgaria*] [*Airport symbol*] (OAG)

VAR .... Varnish [*Technical drawings*]

Var .... Varsity [*Record label*]

VAR .... Vector Autoregressive Model [*Mathematics*]

VAR .... Velocity Acceleration Relationship

VAR .... Vendor Approval Request (AAG)

VAR .... Verification Analysis Report (NASA)

VAR .... Vertical Acceleration Ramp

VAR .... Vertical Air Rocket (NATG)

VAR .... Veterans Administration Regulations

VAR .... Victorian Administrative Reports [*Australia*] [*A publication*]

VAR .... Video-Audio Range [*Radio*]

VAR .... Vintage Austin Register [*Ashover, Derbyshire, England*] (EAIO)

VAR .... Visual-Aural Range [*Radio*]

VAR .... Volt-Ampere Reactive

VAR .... Voltage in Acceptable Range (MCD)

VAR .... Voltage Adjusting Rheostat

VAR .... Voluntary Auto Restraints [*Import quotas on automobiles*]

VAR .... Volunteer Air Reserve [*Air Force*]

VAR .... Votre Altesse Royale [*Your Royal Highness*] [*French*]

VAR .... Vrij Anti-Revolutionaire Partij [*Free Anti-Revolutionary Party*] [*Netherlands*] [*Political party*] (PPE)

VARA .... Vereinigung van Arbeiders Radio Amateurs

VARAD ..... Varying Radiation (IEEE)
VA R Ann .. Virginia Reports, Annotated [*A publication*] (DLA)
Vara Palsd ... Vara Palsdjur [*A publication*]
VARBLK ... Variable Block [*Data processing*]
VARC .... Variable Axis Rotor Control System
     [*Telecommunications*] (TEL)
VARC .... Virginia Associated Research Campus [*Later, Continuous*
     Electron Beam Accelerator Facility] [*Research*
     center] (RCD)
Varco.......... Varco International, Inc. [*Associated Press*
     abbreviation] (APAG)
Var Cond.... Variable Condenser [*Radio*]
vard .... Varied [*Quality of the bottom*] [*Nautical charts*]
VARE .... Visual Acuity, Right Eye [*Ophthalmology*] (MAE)
VAREC...... Veterans Administration Rehabilitation Engineering Center
     [*Formerly, VAPC*]
Va Regs Reg ... Virginia Register of Regulations [*A publication*]
VA Rep Anno ... Virginia Reports, Annotated [*A publication*] (DLA)
VARES ...... Vega Aircraft RADAR Enhancing System [*FAA*]
VARG .... Ratnagiri [*India*] [*ICAO location identifier*] (ICLI)
VARGUS... Variable Generator of Unfamiliar Stimuli [*Computer program*]
VARHM.... Var-Hour Meter [*Electricity*]
Vari .... Variegation [*A publication*]
VARI.......... Varityper
VARIA....... Variamento [*In a Varied Style*] [*Music*] (ROG)
Varian .... Varian Associates [*Associated Press abbreviation*] (APAG)
Varian Instrum Appl ... Varian Instrument Applications [*A publication*]
VARICAP ... Variable Capacitor
VARIG....... Viacao Aerea Rio-Grandense [*Airline*] [*Brazil*] (FAAC)
Varilna Teh ... Varilna Tehnika [*A publication*]
VARION ... Variation (ROG)
Various Publ Ser ... Various Publications Series [*Aarhus*] [*A publication*]
VARISTOR ... Variable Resistor
VARITRAN ... Variable-Voltage Transformer (IEEE)
Varity .... Varity Corp. [*Associated Press abbreviation*] (APAG)
VARK .... Rajkot [*India*] [*ICAO location identifier*] (ICLI)
VAR LECT ... Varia Lectio [*Variant Reading*] [*Latin*] (ROG)
VARM .... Varmeter [*Engineering*]
Varme- o Sanit-Tek ... Vearme- och Sanitetsteknikern [*A publication*]
VARN .... Variation (FAAC)
VARN .... Varnish
var nov....... Varietas Nova [*New Variety*] [*Biology*]
VARO......... Veterans Administration Regional Office (AFM)
VARP........ Raipur [*India*] [*ICAO location identifier*] (ICLI)
VARP........ Vietnam Asset Reconciliation Procedure [*Military*] (AABC)
VARPC..... Veterans Administration Records Processing Center
VARR .... Variable Range Reflector (IEEE)
VARR .... Visual-Aural Radio Range (MSA)
VARS........ Various (ROG)
VARS........ Vertical Azimuth Reference System (NATG)
VARS........ Vocational Adaptation Rating Scales [*Test*]
Var Sci Inst Rebois Tunis ... Varietes Scientifiques. Institut de Reboisement
     de Tunis [*A publication*]
VARSITY ... University [*British*] (ROG)
Var Spom .. Varstvo Spomenikov [*A publication*]
VART .... Volunteer Air Reserve Training [*Air Force*]
VARTA Spez Rep ... VARTA Spezial Report [*West Germany*] [*A*
     publication]
VARTU ..... Volunteer Air Reserve Training Unit [*Air Force*]
VARVS...... Variable Acuity Remote Viewing System (MCD)
VAS .... Sivas [*Turkey*] [*Airport symbol*] (OAG)
VAS .... Validation System (SSD)
VAS .... Value-Added Service [*Telecommunications*] (TEL)
VAS .... Value-Added Statement (ADA)
VAS .... Variable Angle Scatterometer (MCD)
VAS .... Vassijaure [*Sweden*] [*Seismograph station code, US Geological*
     Survey] [*Closed*] (SEIS)
VAS .... Vector Addition System
VAS .... Venomological Artifact Society (EA)
VAS .... Vesicle Attachment Sites [*Neurology*]
VAS .... Veterinary Assistant Surgeon [*British military*] (DMA)
VAS .... Vibration Analysis System
VAS .... Visible Atmospheric Sounder (MCD)
VAS .... VISSR [*Visible-Infrared Spin Scan Radiometer*] Atmospheric
     Sounder [*NASA*]
VAS .... Visual Analog [*Pain*] Scale
VAS .... Visual Analysis System [*Military*]
VAS .... Visual Attack System
VAS .... Visual Audit Sheet (DNAB)
VAS .... Visual Augmentation System
VAS .... Vorderasiatische Schriftdenkmaeler der Koeniglichen [*or*
     Staatlichen] Museen zu Berlin [*A publication*]
VAS .... Vortex Advisory System [*FAA*]
VASA........ Sihora [*India*] [*ICAO location identifier*] (ICLI)
VASA........ Viola d'Amore Society of America (EA)
Vasa Suppl ... Vasa Supplementum [*A publication*]
VA SBA ..... Virginia State Bar Association, Reports [*A publication*] (DLA)
VASC........ Vascular
VASC........ Verbal Auditory Screen for Children
VASC......... Vision and Autonomous Systems Laboratory, Carnegie Mellon
     University [*Research center*] (RCD)

VAsC .... Visual Acuity without Spectacle Correction [*Unaided*]
VASCA ...... Vacation and Senior Citizens Association (EA)
VASCAR ... Visual Average Speed Computer and Recorder [*Speed trap*]
Vasc Dis..... Vascular Diseases [*A publication*]
Vasc Surg... Vascular Surgery [*A publication*]
VASD .... Value-Added System Distributor (HGAA)
VASD .... Veroeffentlichungen. Deutsche Akademie fuer Sprache und
     Dichtung [*A publication*]
VaSd .... Vorderasiatische Schriftdenkmaeler der Koeniglichen [*or*
     Staatlichen] Museen zu Berlin [*A publication*]
VASE........ Variable Angle Spectroscopic Ellipsometer
Vasenlisten ... Vasenlisten zur Griechischen Heldensage [*A*
     publication] (OCD)
VASG........ Songadh [*India*] [*ICAO location identifier*] (ICLI)
VAS of GB ... Vasectomy Advancement Society of Great Britain
VASI .... Vertical Approach Slope Indicator
VASI .... Visual Approach Slope Indicator [*Aviation*]
VASI .... Volunteer Ambulance School of Instruction [*Military*]
     [*British*] (ROG)
VASIM ...... Voltage and Synchro Interface Module
VASIS ...... Visual Approach Slope Indicator System [*Aviation*]
VASL......... Sholapur [*India*] [*ICAO location identifier*] (ICLI)
VA Social Science J ... Virginia Social Science Journal [*A publication*]
VASODIL ... Vasodilatation [*Physiology*] (AAMN)
VASOG ..... Veterans Administration Surgical Oncology Group
VASP .... Value-Added Service Provider [*Agreement*] (IT)
VASP........ Variable Automatic Synthesis Program [*NASA*]
VASP........ Viacao Aerea Sao Paulo SA [*Airline*] [*Brazil*]
Vasq......... [*Ferdinand*] Vasquez Menchaca [*Deceased, 1566*] [*Authority*
     cited in pre-1607 legal work] (DSA)
VASRD...... Veterans Administration Schedule for Rating
     Disabilities (AABC)
VASS .... Van Allen Simplified Scoring [*Tennis*] (IIA)
VASS .... Variable Angle Sample Spinning [*Physics*]
VASS .... VAX Applicant Search System [*Science Applications*
     International Corp.]
VASS .... Visual Analysis Subsystem [*Military*]
VASS .... Visually Activated Switch System (MCD)
Vassar Bros Inst Tr ... Vassar Brothers Institute. Transactions [*A publication*]
VASSEL.... Validation of ASW [*Antisubmarine Warfare*] Subsystem
     Effectiveness Levels [*Navy*] (CAAL)
VASSS...... Van Alen Simplified Scoring System [*Tennis*]
VAST........ Versatile Automatic Specification Tester
VAST........ Versatile Avionics Shop Test System (SAA)
VAST........ Versatile Avionics System Tester (GFGA)
VAST........ Virtual Archival Storage Technology [*Data processing*]
VA State Lib Bull ... Virginia State Library. Bulletin [*A publication*]
Vasterbotten ... Vasterbottens Lans Hambygdsforenings Arsbok [*A*
     publication]
Vastergotlands Fornminnesforen Tidskr ... Vastergotlands
     Fornminnesforenings Tidskrift [*A publication*]
Vastmanlands Fornminnesforen Arsskr ... Vastmanlands
     Fornminnesforenings Arsskrift [*A publication*]
VASTT ...... Versatile Aerial Simulation TOW [*Tube-Launched, Optically*
     Tracked, Wire-Guided (Weapon)] Target (MCD)
VASU .... Surat [*India*] [*ICAO location identifier*] (ICLI)
Vasuti Tud Kut Intez Evk ... Vasuti Tudomanyos Kutato Intezet Evkoenyve
     [*Hungary*] [*A publication*]
vas vit......... Vas Vitreum [*A Glass Vessel*] [*Latin*] [*Pharmacy*] (MAE)
VAS VITR ... Vas Vitreum [*A Glass Vessel*] [*Pharmacy*]
VAT .... Vacuum Arc Thrustor Program (MCD)
VAT .... Value-Added Tax
VAT .... Vane Air Temperature [*Automotive engineering*]
VAT .... Variable Area Turbine
VAT .... Variant Antigenic Type [*Genetics, immunology*]
VAT .... Varity Corp. [*NYSE symbol*] [*Toronto Stock Exchange symbol*]
     [*Vancouver Stock Exchange symbol*] (SPSG)
VAT .... Vatican
VAT .... Vatican City [*ANSI three-letter standard code*] (CNC)
VAT .... Vatomandry [*Madagascar*] [*Airport symbol*] (OAG)
VAT .... Ventricular Activation Time [*Cardiology*]
VAT .... Veterinary Aptitude Test
VAT .... Vibration Acceptance Test
VAT .... Vibroacoustic Test (NASA)
VAT .... Village Assistance Team (DNAB)
VAT .... Vinyl Asbestos Tile [*Technical drawings*]
VAT .... Virtual Address Translation
VAT .... Visual Acquisition Technique
VAT .... Visual Action Time
VAT .... Visual Apperception Test [*Psychology*]
VAT .... Vitro Assistance Team
VAT .... Vocational Apperception Test [*Psychology*]
VAT .... Voice-Activated Typewriter
VAT .... Volt-Ampere Tester
VAT .... Voltage Amplifier Tube
VAT .... Vulnerability Analysis Team (MCD)
VATA .... Vertical Assembly and Test Area (SSD)
VATA .... Vibroacoustic Test Article (NASA)
VA Tax R... Virginia Tax Review [*A publication*]
Va Tax Rev ... Virginia Tax Review [*A publication*] (DLA)

VatBA .... Biblioteca Apostolica Vaticana, Vatican City, Vatican City [*Library symbol*] [*Library of Congress*] (LCLS)
VATD .... Vincristine, ara-C [*Cytarabine*], Thioguanine, Daunorubicin [*Antineoplastic drug regimen*]
VATE .... Vandenberg Automatic Test Equipment [*Air Force*]
VATE .... Versatile Automatic Test Equipment [*Computers*]
V-ATE ...... Vertical Anisotropic Etch [*Raytheon Co.*]
VA Teach ... Virginia Teacher [*A publication*]
VATEJ ...... Victorian Association for the Teaching of English. Journal [*A publication*] (APTA)
VATER ...... Vascular Tracheoesophageal-Limb-Reduction [*Endocrinology*]
VATER ...... Vertebral, Anal, Tracheal, Esophageal, Renal
VATF .... Vibration and Acoustic Test Facility (NASA)
VAtf .... Visual Acuity with Trial Frame
VATH .... Vinblastine, Adriamycin, Thiotepa [*Antineoplastic drug regimen*]
VATH .... Vinblastine, Adriamycin, Thiotepa, Halotestin [*Fluoxymesterone*] [*Antineoplastic drug regimen*]
VATISJ ..... VATIS [*Victorian Association of Teachers in Independent Schools*] Journal [*A publication*] (APTA)
VATLIT .... Very Advanced Technology Light Twin (MCD)
VATLS ...... Visual Airborne Target Locator System [*Military*]
VATR .... Variable Aperture Target Recognition (MCD)
VATRD8 ... Lantbrukshogskolan Vaxtskyddsrapporter Tradgard [*A publication*]
VATRD8 ... Sveriges Landbruksuniversitet Vaxtskyddsrapporter Tradgard [*A publication*]
VA Truck Exp ... Virginia Truck Experiment Station. Publications [*A publication*]
VATS .... Vehicle Acquisition and Tracking System (SAA)
VATS .... Vehicle Anti-Theft System [*General Motors Corp.*]
VATS .... Vehicle Automatic Test System
VATS .... Vernon's Annotated Texas Statutes [*A publication*] (DLA)
VATS .... Versatile Avionics Test [*or Tester*] Shop [*NASA*] (DNAB)
VATS .... Vertical-Lift Airfield for Tactical Support (NVT)
VATS .... Vibration Analysis Test Set (DWSG)
VATS .... Video-Augmented Tracking System (MCD)
VATS/SNAP ... Video-Augmented Tracking System/Single Seat Night Attack Program (MCD)
Vatt .... Vattel's Law of Nations [*A publication*] (DLA)
Vattel .... Vattel's Law of Nations [*A publication*] (DLA)
Vattel Law Nat ... Vattel's Law of Nations [*A publication*] (DLA)
VATTR ...... Value Added Tax Tribunal Reports [*A publication*]
VA/TVTA ... Vibroacoustic/Thermal/Vacuum Test Article (NASA)
VATW .... Varity Corp. [*NASDAQ symbol*] (NQ)
VAU .... Vertical Accelerometer Unit
VAU .... Vertical Arithmetic Unit
vau .... Virginia [*MARC country of publication code*] [*Library of Congress*] (LCCP)
VAU .... Volume Accumulator Unit
VAU .... Volunteer Air Units
VAUB .... Vehicle Authorization Utilization Board [*Military*]
VAUD .... Vaudeville
Vaug .... Vaughan's English Common Pleas Reports [*124 English Reprint*] [*A publication*] (DLA)
Vaugh .... Vaughan's English Common Pleas Reports [*124 English Reprint*] [*A publication*] (DLA)
Vaughan ..... Vaughan's English Common Pleas Reports [*124 English Reprint*] [*A publication*] (DLA)
Vaughan (Eng) ... Vaughan's English Common Pleas Reports [*124 English Reprint*] [*A publication*] (DLA)
VA Univ Ph Soc B Sc S ... Virginia University. Philosophical Society. Bulletin. Scientific Series [*A publication*]
VAUSSI .... Veteran's Association of the USS [*United States Ship*] Iowa (EA)
VAUX .... Vauxhall [*Automobile*] (DSUE)
Vaux .... Vaux's Recorder's Decisions [*1841-45*] [*Philadelphia, PA*] [*A publication*] (DLA)
Vaux (PA) ... Vaux's Recorder's Decisions [*1841-45*] [*Philadelphia, PA*] [*A publication*] (DLA)
Vaux Rec Dec ... Vaux's Recorder's Decisions [*1841-45*] [*Philadelphia, PA*] [*A publication*] (DLA)
VAV .... Variable Air Volume
VAV .... Vava'u [*Tonga Island*] [*Airport symbol*] (OAG)
VAV .... Visicalc Advanced Version (HGAA)
VAV .... VP-16-213 [*Etoposide*], Adriamycin, Vincristine [*Antineoplastic drug regimen*]
VAVP .... Variable Angle, Variable Pitch
VAVS .... Veterans Administration Voluntary Service
VAW .... Carrier Airborne Early Warning Squadron [*Navy symbol*] (NVT)
VAW .... Valley Airways, Inc. [*McAllen, TX*] [*FAA designator*] (FAAC)
VAW .... Vertical Arc Welder
VA Water Resour Res Cent Bull ... Virginia Water Resources Research Center. Bulletin [*A publication*]
VA Wildl .... Virginia Wildlife [*A publication*]
VAWM ...... Washim [*India*] [*ICAO location identifier*] (ICLI)
VAWP .... Voice-Activated Word Processor [*Data processing*]
VAWT .... Vertical Axis Wind Turbine [*Power generator*] [*See also VAWTG*]
VAWTG ..... Vertical Axis Wind Turbine Generator [*Also, VAWT*]

VAX .... Alexandria Public Library, Alexandria, VA [*OCLC symbol*] (OCLC)
VAX .... Heavy Attack Aircraft, Experimental
VAX .... Trademark of Digital Equipment Corp.
VAX .... Virtual Address Extension [*Data processing*]
VAX-L .... Aircraft Attack, Experimental-Light [*Navy*]
Vaxtekol Stud ... Vaxtekologiska Studier [*A publication*]
Vaxt-Nar-Nytt ... Vaxt-Narings-Nytt [*A publication*]
Vaxtodling Inst Vaxtodlingslara Lantbrukshogsk ... Vaextodling. Institutionen foer Vaextodlingslara. Lantbrukshoegskolan [*A publication*]
Vaxtskyddsnotiser Sver Lantbruksuniver ... Vaxtskyddsnotiser. Sveriges Lantbruksuniversitet [*A publication*]
VAY .... Valandovo [*Yugoslavia*] [*Seismograph station code, US Geological Survey*] (SEIS)
Vayr .... Vayikra Rabba (BJA)
Vazduhoplovni Glas ... Vazduhoplovni Glasnik [*Yugoslavia*] [*A publication*]
VB .... Bombing Plane [*Navy symbol*]
VB .... Bretagne Air Services [*France*] [*ICAO designator*] (FAAC)
VB .... Dive Bomber Squadron [*Navy symbol*]
VB .... Valence Bond (DEN)
VB .... Valve Box
VB .... Vanity Bar [*Classified advertising*] (ADA)
VB .... Vapor Barrier [*Boots*] [*Army*] (INF)
VB .... Vascular Bundle [*Botany*]
VB .... Ventrobasal Complex [*Brain anatomy*]
VB .... Verb
Vb. .... Verordeningenblad [*A publication*]
VB .... Vertical Beam [*of light*]
VB .... Vertical Bomb [*Air Force*]
VB .... Vertical Main Boiler [*on a ship*] (DS)
V & B .... Vesey and Beames' English Chancery Reports [*35 English Reprint*] [*A publication*] (DLA)
VB .... Veterinary Bulletin [*Database*] [*Commonwealth Bureau of Animal Health*] [*Information service or system*] (CRD)
VB .... Viable Birth [*Medicine*]
VB .... Vibration (AAG)
VB .... Vinblastine, Bleomycin [*Antineoplastic drug regimen*]
VB .... Vir Bonus [*A Good Man*] [*Latin*]
vb. .... Virgin Islands, British [*MARC country of publication code*] [*Library of Congress*] (LCCP)
VB .... Visbreaker [*Petroleum technology*]
VB .... Visual Basic [*Data processing*] (PCM)
VB .... Viven and Bassiere [*Rifle grenade*]
VB .... Voelkischer Beobachter [*A publication*]
VB .... Voice Band [*Telecommunications*]
VB .... Voice Bank [*Telecommunications*] (TEL)
VB .... Voks Bulletin [*A publication*]
VB .... Volunteer Battalion [*Military*]
VB .... Vorgeschobener Beobachter [*Forward Observer*] [*German military*]
VB .... Vulgate Bible
VBA .... NIMO [*Nederlands Instituut voor Maatschappelijke Opbouw*] Kroniek. Nieuwsbulletin [*A publication*]
VBA .... Vegetarian Brotherhood of America [*Defunct*] (EA)
VBA .... Veterans Benefits Administration [*Department of Veterans Affairs*]
VBA .... Vibrating Beam Accelerometer [*Inertial sensor*] (IEEE)
VBA .... Vincristine, BCNU [*Carmustine*], Adriamycin [*Antineoplastic drug regimen*]
VBAA .... Vanilla Bean Association of America (EA)
VBAC .... Vaginal Birth After Caesarean [*Obstetrics*]
VBAN .... Ann [*Myanmar*] [*ICAO location identifier*] (ICLI)
VBAN .... V Band Corp. [*NASDAQ symbol*] (NQ)
VBAP .... Vincristine, BCNU [*Carmustine*], Adriamycin, Prednisone [*Antineoplastic drug regimen*]
VBAS .... Anisakan [*Myanmar*] [*ICAO location identifier*] (ICLI)
VBAS .... Von Braun Astronomical Society (EA)
VBAT .... Battery Voltage [*Automotive engineering*]
VB (B) .... Voelkischer Beobachter (Berlin) [*A publication*]
vbb .... Volgens Bygaande Brief [*According to Accompanying Letter*] [*Afrikaans*] [*Correspondence*]
VBBM ...... Bhamo [*Myanmar*] [*ICAO location identifier*] (ICLI)
Vb Bo .... Verordeningenblad Bedrijfsorganisatie [*A publication*]
VBBP .... Bokepyin [*Myanmar*] [*ICAO location identifier*] (ICLI)
VBBS .... Bassein [*Myanmar*] [*ICAO location identifier*] (ICLI)
VBC .... Bridgewater College, Bridgewater, VA [*OCLC symbol*] (OCLC)
VBC .... Variable Boost Control [*System*] [*Automotive engineering*]
VBC .... Venetian Blind Council [*Formerly, VBI*]
VBC .... Veterans Benefit Counselor [*Veterans Administration*] (GFGA)
VBC .... Vinylbenzyl Chloride [*Organic chemistry*]
VBC .... Vogel-Bonner Citrate [*Growth medium*]
VBCI .... Coco Island [*Myanmar*] [*ICAO location identifier*] (ICLI)
VBD .... Vector-Borne Disease
VBD .... Veronal-Buffered Diluent
VBD .... Vertebrobasilar Dolichoectasia [*Medicine*]
VBD .... Vinblastine, Bleomycin, Diamminedichloroplatinum [*Cisplatin*] [*Antineoplastic drug regimen*]
VBD .... Voice Band Data (KSC)
VBDMA .... Vinylbenzyldimethylamine [*Organic chemistry*]

VBE	Vernacular Black English (WGA)
VBE	Vibrating Plate Extractor [*Chemical engineering*]
VBE	Video BIOS [*Basic Input-Output System*] Extension [*Data processing*] (PCM)
VBelGrN....	Vesci Akademii Navuk Belaruskaj SSR. Seryja Gramadskich Navuk [*A publication*]
VBF	Bomber-Fighter Squadron [*Navy symbol*]
VBF	Bombing-Fighting Aircraft [*Navy symbol*]
VBF	Variable Bandwidth Filter
VBF	Vibrated Fluid Bed [*Chemical engineering*]
VBF	Vibratory Bowl Feeder
VBG	Lompoc, CA [*Location identifier*] [*FAA*] (FAAL)
VBG	Vein Aortocoronary Artery Bypass Graft [*Cardiology*] (AAMN)
VBGG	Gangaw [*Myanmar*] [*ICAO location identifier*] (ICLI)
VBGH	Volunteer Battalion Gordon Highlanders [*British military*] (DMA)
VBGQ	Vacuum Brazed - Gas Quenched
VBGW	Gwa [*Myanmar*] [*ICAO location identifier*] (ICLI)
VBHB	Hmawbi [*Myanmar*] [*ICAO location identifier*] (ICLI)
VBHH	Hebo [*Myanmar*] [*ICAO location identifier*] (ICLI)
VBHL	Homalin [*Myanmar*] [*ICAO location identifier*] (ICLI)
VBHN	Htilin [*Myanmar*] [*ICAO location identifier*] (ICLI)
VBI	Venetian Blind Institute [*Later, VBC*] (EA)
VBI	Vertical Blanking Interval [*Telecommunications*]
VBI	Video Bible Institute [*Defunct*] (EA)
VBI	Vital Bus Inverter [*Data processing*] (IEEE)
V-BIG	Ventricular Bigeminy [*Medicine*]
VBJ	Vacuum Bell Jar
VBKG	Kengtung [*Myanmar*] [*ICAO location identifier*] (ICLI)
VBKK	Kutkai [*Myanmar*] [*ICAO location identifier*] (ICLI)
VBKM	Kalemyo [*Myanmar*] [*ICAO location identifier*] (ICLI)
VBKP	Kyaukpyu [*Myanmar*] [*ICAO location identifier*] (ICLI)
VBKTPS....	Vierteljahrschrift fuer Bibelkunde, Talmudische, und Patristische Studien [*A publication*]
VBKU	Kyauktu [*Myanmar*] [*ICAO location identifier*] (ICLI)
VBL..........	BOCES [*Boards of Cooperative Educational Services*], Monroe 1, Penfield, NY [*OCLC symbol*] (OCLC)
Vbl...........	Vakblad [*A publication*]
VBL..........	Vakblad voor de Bloemisterij [*A publication*]
VBL..........	Vector Biology Laboratory [*University of Notre Dame*] [*Research center*] (RCD)
VBL..........	Verbal
VBl...........	Verordnungsblatt [*Official Gazette*] [*German*] (ILCA)
VBL..........	Vertical-Blank [*Data processing*] (BYTE)
VBL..........	Vinblastine [*Velban, Vincaleukoblastine*] [*Also, V, Ve, VLB*] [*Antineoplastic drug*]
VBL..........	Voyager Biological Laboratory [*NASA*]
VBLK	Loikaw [*Myanmar*] [*ICAO location identifier*] (ICLI)
VBLN	Lonekin [*Myanmar*] [*ICAO location identifier*] (ICLI)
VBLO	Langkho [*Myanmar*] [*ICAO location identifier*] (ICLI)
VBLS	Lashio [*Myanmar*] [*ICAO location identifier*] (ICLI)
V BLT	Vee Built [*Ship classification term*] (DS)
VBLY	Lanywa [*Myanmar*] [*ICAO location identifier*] (ICLI)
VBM	BOCES [*Boards of Cooperative Educational Services*], Monroe 2, Orleans, Spencerport, NY [*OCLC symbol*] (OCLC)
VBM	Valence Bond Maximum [*Physics*]
VBM	Vincristine, Bleomycin, Methotrexate [*Antineoplastic drug regimen*]
VBMA	Vacuum Bag Manufacturers Association (EA)
VBMH	Mong-Hpayak [*Myanmar*] [*ICAO location identifier*] (ICLI)
VBMI	Mongyai [*Myanmar*] [*ICAO location identifier*] (ICLI)
VBMK	Myitkyina [*Myanmar*] [*ICAO location identifier*] (ICLI)
VBML	Meiktila [*Myanmar*] [*ICAO location identifier*] (ICLI)
VBMM	Moulmein [*Myanmar*] [*ICAO location identifier*] (ICLI)
VBMN	Manaung [*Myanmar*] [*ICAO location identifier*] (ICLI)
VBMO	Momeik [*Myanmar*] [*ICAO location identifier*] (ICLI)
VBMP	Mong Pyin [*Myanmar*] [*ICAO location identifier*] (ICLI)
VBMR	Ventilation Barrier Machine Room [*Nuclear energy*] (NRCH)
VBMS	Mong-Hsat [*Myanmar*] [*ICAO location identifier*] (ICLI)
VBMT	Mong Tong [*Myanmar*] [*ICAO location identifier*] (ICLI)
VBMU	Myauk U [*Myanmar*] [*ICAO location identifier*] (ICLI)
VB (Mu).....	Voelkischer Beobachter (Muenich) [*A publication*]
VBMW	Magwe [*Myanmar*] [*ICAO location identifier*] (ICLI)
VBMWMO ...	Vintage BMW Motorcycle Owners (EA)
VBN	Verbal Noun
VBN	Veterans Bedside Network (EA)
VBN	Victorian Bar News [*A publication*] (APTA)
VBND	VeloBind, Inc. [*NASDAQ symbol*] (NQ)
VBNIDQ ..	Vogelkundliche Berichte aus Niedersachsen [*A publication*]
VBNM	Naungmon [*Myanmar*] [*ICAO location identifier*] (ICLI)
VBNP	Nampong [*Myanmar*] [*ICAO location identifier*] (ICLI)
VBNS	Namsang [*Myanmar*] [*ICAO location identifier*] (ICLI)
VBNT	Namtu [*Myanmar*] [*ICAO location identifier*] (ICLI)
VBNU	Nyaung U [*Myanmar*] [*ICAO location identifier*] (ICLI)
VBO	Bouwwereld. Universeel Veertiendaags Vaktijdschrift voor de Bouwnijverheid [*A publication*]
VBO	Oswego County BOCES [*Boards of Cooperative Educational Services*], Mexico, NY [*OCLC symbol*] (OCLC)
VBo	Verordeningenblad Bedrijfsorganisatie [*A publication*]
VBO	Veterans Benefits Office
VBOB	Veterans of the Battle of the Bulge (EA)
VBOMP	Virtual Base Organization and Maintenance Processor
VBOS........	Veronal-Buffered Oxalated Saline
VBot..........	Verstreute Boghazkoei-Texte [*A. Goetze*] [*A publication*] (BJA)
VBP...........	Vacuum Backing Pump
VBP...........	Vinblastine, Bleomycin, and Platinol [*Antineoplastic drug regimen*] (MAE)
VBP...........	Virtual Block Processor
VBP...........	Vortex Breakdown Position
VBPA........	Pa-An [*Myanmar*] [*ICAO location identifier*] (ICLI)
VBPB	Phaungbyin [*Myanmar*] [*ICAO location identifier*] (ICLI)
VBPE	Paletwa [*Myanmar*] [*ICAO location identifier*] (ICLI)
VBPF	Variable Bandpass Filter
VBPG........	Pegu [*Myanmar*] [*ICAO location identifier*] (ICLI)
VBPI........	Pearl Island [*Myanmar*] [*ICAO location identifier*] (ICLI)
VBPK	Pauk [*Myanmar*] [*ICAO location identifier*] (ICLI)
VBPL........	Pinlebu [*Myanmar*] [*ICAO location identifier*] (ICLI)
VBPP	Papun [*Myanmar*] [*ICAO location identifier*] (ICLI)
VBPR	Prome [*Myanmar*] [*ICAO location identifier*] (ICLI)
VBPT	Putao [*Myanmar*] [*ICAO location identifier*] (ICLI)
VBPU	Pakokku [*Myanmar*] [*ICAO location identifier*] (ICLI)
VBPW	Palaw [*Myanmar*] [*ICAO location identifier*] (ICLI)
VBQ	Visvabharati Quarterly [*A publication*]
VBR	Vacuum Bottoms Recycle [*Petroleum refining*]
VBR	Variable BIT [*Binary Digit*] Rate [*Telecommunications*]
VBR	Ventricle Brain Ratio [*Medicine*]
VBR	Vinyl Bromide [*Organic chemistry*]
VBR	Virginia Blue Ridge Railway [*AAR code*]
VBRA	Sittwe [*Myanmar*] [*ICAO location identifier*] (ICLI)
VBRM	Mandalay [*Myanmar*] [*ICAO location identifier*] (ICLI)
VBRN	Mergui [*Myanmar*] [*ICAO location identifier*] (ICLI)
VBRR........	Rangoon/Mingaladon [*Myanmar*] [*ICAO location identifier*] (ICLI)
VBS..........	Vacation Bible Schools (EA)
VBS..........	Variable Ballast System
VBS..........	Veronal-Buffered Saline
VBS..........	Virtual Bragg Scattering [*Physics*]
VBSA	Saw [*Myanmar*] [*ICAO location identifier*] (ICLI)
VBSFA	Vestsi Akademii Navuk BSSR. Seryya Fizika-Matematychnykh Navuk [*A publication*]
VBS:FBS ...	Veronal-Buffered Saline-Fetal Bovine Serum (MAE)
VBSK	Sinkaling Khamti [*Myanmar*] [*ICAO location identifier*] (ICLI)
VBSKA	Vestsi Akademii Navuk BSSR. Seryya Khimichnykh Navuk [*A publication*]
VBSL	Salingyi [*Myanmar*] [*ICAO location identifier*] (ICLI)
VBSO........	Sidoktaya [*Myanmar*] [*ICAO location identifier*] (ICLI)
VBST	Shante [*Myanmar*] [*ICAO location identifier*] (ICLI)
VBSW	Shinbweyang [*Myanmar*] [*ICAO location identifier*] (ICLI)
VBSY	Sandoway [*Myanmar*] [*ICAO location identifier*] (ICLI)
VBT	Bombing, Torpedo Plane [*Navy symbol*]
VBT	Tabak Plus [*A publication*]
VBT	Valence-Bond Theory [*Physical chemistry*]
VBT	Videos for Business and Training [*A publication*]
VBTL	Tachilek [*Myanmar*] [*ICAO location identifier*] (ICLI)
VBTN	Tanai [*Myanmar*] [*ICAO location identifier*] (ICLI)
VBTPS......	Vierteljahrschrift fuer Bibelkunde, Talmudische, und Patristische Studien [*A publication*]
VBTV	Tavoy [*Myanmar*] [*ICAO location identifier*] (ICLI)
VBTY	Tanyang [*Myanmar*] [*ICAO location identifier*] (ICLI)
VBU	Vibrating Bag Unloader
VBULE	Vestibule [*Classified advertising*] (ADA)
VBV	Documentatieblad voor Onderwijs en Wetenschappen [*A publication*]
VBV	Vanuabalavu [*Fiji*] [*Airport symbol*] (OAG)
VBVP	Kawthaung [*Myanmar*] [*ICAO location identifier*] (ICLI)
VBVT	Valley Bank [*NASDAQ symbol*] (NQ)
VBW	Bridgewater, VA [*Location identifier*] [*FAA*] (FAAL)
VBW	Vakbondskrant van Nederland [*A publication*]
VBW	Video Bandwidth
VBW	Vortraege der Bibliothek Warburg [*A publication*]
VBWR	Vallecitos Boiling Water Reactor
VBX	Visual Basic Extension [*Data processing*]
VBY	Visby [*Sweden*] [*Airport symbol*] (OAG)
VBYE........	Ye [*Myanmar*] [*ICAO location identifier*] (ICLI)
VC	British Aircraft Corp. Ltd. [*ICAO aircraft manufacturer identifier*] (ICAO)
VC	Capillary Volume [*Clinical chemistry*] (AAMN)
VC	Circular Velocity
VC	Color Vision [*Ophthalmology*]
VC	Composite Aircraft Squadron [*Navy symbol*]
VC	Creditreform Databank [*Verband der Vereine Creditreform eV*] [*Information service or system*] (IID)
VC	Cruise Speed [*Aviation*]
VC	St. Vincent and the Grenadines [*ANSI two-letter standard code*] (CNC)
VC	Vacuolated Cell
VC	Valuable Cargo
VC	Valuation Clause
VC	Vaporizer Concentrate [*Nuclear energy*] (NRCH)
VC	Variable Capacitor (DEN)

VC .... Variable Charge (DCTA)
VC .... [*Total*] Variable Costs
VC .... Varnished Cambric [*Insulation*]
VC .... Vasoconstrictor [*Medicine*]
VC .... Vatel Club (EA)
vc .... Vatican City [*MARC country of publication code*] [*Library of Congress*] (LCCP)
VC .... Vector Character (NASA)
V/C .... Vector Control (KSC)
Vc .... Vecuronium [*A muscle relaxant*]
VC .... Vegetative Capability [*Biology*]
VC .... Vehicular Communications (MCD)
VC .... Velocity Character (MCD)
VC .... Velocity, Closing
VC .... Velocity Compounded
VC .... Velocity Counter (KSC)
VC .... Vena Cava [*Anatomy*]
VC .... Vendor Call (MCD)
VC .... Vendor Code (MCD)
VC .... Vendor Contact
VC .... Venereal Case [*Medical slang*]
VC .... Venice Committee (EA)
VC .... Venous Capacitance [*Clinical chemistry*] (AAMN)
VC .... Ventilated Containers [*Shipping*] (DCTA)
V/C .... Ventilation/Circulation Ratio [*Medicine*] (MAE)
VC .... Ventilatory Capacity [*Physiology*]
VC .... Ventricular Complex [*Cardiology*]
VC .... Ventricular Coupling [*Cardiology*]
VC .... Venture Capital [*or Capitalist*] [*Finance*]
VC .... Verb-Consonant [*Education of the hearing-impaired*]
VC .... Verbi Causa [*For Example*] [*Latin*]
VC .... Verification Condition
VC .... Vernair Flying Services [*British*] [*ICAO designator*] (ICDA)
VC .... Vernal Conjunctivitis [*Ophthalmology*]
VC .... Versatility Code
VC .... Vertical Center (SAA)
VC .... Vertical Curve
VC .... Veterinary Corps [*Military*]
VC .... Vicar Choral
VC .... Vice Chairman [*or Chairperson or Chairwoman*]
VC .... Vice Chancellor
VC .... Vice-Chancellor's Courts [*England*] (DLA)
VC .... Vice Commodore [*Navy*] (NVT)
VC .... Vice Consul
VC .... Victoria Cross [*British*]
VC .... Video Channel [*Auckland, NZ*]
VC .... Video Correlator
VC .... Videodisc Controller
VC .... Vietcong [*Vietnamese Communists*]
VC .... Vigilance Committee
VC .... Vigiliae Christianae [*A publication*]
VC .... Village of Childhelp (EA)
VC .... Vincristine [*Also, LCR, O, V, VCR*] [*Antineoplastic drug*] (AAMN)
VC .... Vinyl Chloride [*Organic chemistry*]
VC .... Violoncello [*Music*]
VC .... Vir Clarissimus [*A Most Illustrious Man*] [*Latin*]
VC .... Virginia Cavalcade [*A publication*]
VC .... Virginia Central Railway [*AAR code*]
VC .... Virtual Circuit
VC .... Viscous Coupling [*Automotive engineering*]
VC .... Viscous Criterion
VC .... Visicalc (HGAA)
VC .... Vision Controllor [*Printer technology*]
V/C .... Visiting Committee [*British*]
VC .... Vista Chemical [*NYSE symbol*] (SPSG)
VC .... Visual Capacity [*Acuity*]
VC .... Visual Coincidence (SAA)
VC .... Visual Cortex
VC .... Visum Cultum [*Seen Cultivated*] [*Botany*] (ROG)
VC .... Vital Capacity
VC .... Vitreous Carbon
VC .... Vitrified Clay [*Technical drawings*]
VC .... Vocal Cord
VC .... Voice Ciphony (CET)
VC .... Voice Circuit (SSD)
VC .... Voice Coil
VC .... Volt-Coulomb (DEN)
VC .... Voltage Comparator [*or Compensator*] (DEN)
VC .... Volume of Compartment [*Technical drawings*]
VC .... Volume Control (DEN)
VC .... Voluntary Closing [*Prosthesis*] [*Medicine*]
VC .... Volunteer Consultant [*Red Cross*]
VC .... Volunteer Corps
VC .... Voters for Choice [*Later, VFC*] (EA)
VC .... Voyage Charter
VC .... Vuelta de Correo [*Return Mail*] [*Spanish*]
VC's .... Vocal Chords [*Musical slang*]
VCA .... Vacant Code Announcement (DNAB)
VCA .... Valve Control Amplifier (MDG)

VCA .... Vancomycin-Colistin-Anisomycin [*Growth-inhibiting mixture*] [*Microbiology*]
VCA .... Vanished Children's Alliance (EA)
VCA .... Vehicle Checkout Area
VCA .... Venture Clubs of the Americas (EA)
VCA .... Veteran Corps of Artillery, State of New York, Constituting the Military Society of the War of 1812 (EA)
VCA .... Victims of Crime Assistance Act
VCA .... Video Capture Adapter (PCM)
VCA .... Viewdata Corp. of America, Inc. [*Miami Beach, FL*] [*Telecommunications*] (TSSD)
VCA .... Vinchina [*Argentina*] [*Seismograph station code, US Geological Survey*] (SEIS)
VCA .... Viral Capsid Antibody [*Hematology*]
VCA .... Viral Capsular Antigen [*Immunology*]
VCA .... Virtual City Associates Ltd. [*London, England*] [*Telecommunications*] (TSSD)
VCA .... Visual Course Adapter (MUGU)
VCA .... Vitrified China Association [*Defunct*]
VC of A ...... Vizsla Club of America (EA)
VCA .... Voice Connecting Arrangement [*Telecommunications*] (TEL)
VCA .... Voltage Control of Amplification
VCAD .... Vertical Contact Analog Display
VC Adm ..... Victoria Reports, Admiralty [*A publication*] (DLA)
VCAM .... Vascular Cell Adhesion Molecule [*Cytology*]
VCAM .... Volunteer Committees of Art Museums (EA)
VCAMCUS ... Volunteer Committees of Art Museums of Canada and the United States (EA)
VCAP .... Vehicle Charging and Potential Experiment (NASA)
VCAP .... Vincristine, Cyclophosphamide, Adriamycin, Prednisone [*Antineoplastic drug regimen*]
V-CAP III ... VP-16-213 [*Etoposide*], Cyclophosphamide, Adriamycin, Platinol [*Cisplatin*] [*Antineoplastic drug regimen*]
VCAR .... Vector Aeromotive Corp. [*NASDAQ symbol*] (NQ)
VCARE ...... Veterans Council for American Rights and Equality (EA)
VCAS .... Vice-Chief of the Air Staff [*British*]
VCASS .... Visually Coupled Airborne Systems Simulator (IEEE)
VCB .... CBNU Learning Resources Center, Virginia Beach, VA [*OCLC symbol*] (OCLC)
VCB .... Construction Battalion [*USNR classification*]
VCB .... Vertical Location of the Center of Buoyancy
VCB .... Visual Control Board
VCBA .... Variable Control Block Area [*Data processing*]
VCBFE ...... Vauxhall College of Building and Further Education [*London, England*]
VCBI .... Colombo/Katunayake [*Sri Lanka*] [*ICAO location identifier*] (ICLI)
VCC .... Vancouver Community College Library [*UTLAS symbol*]
VCC .... Variable Ceramic Capacitor
VCC .... Variable Characteristic Car (ADA)
VCC .... Variable Command Count (MCD)
VCC .... Vasoconstrictor Center [*Physiology*]
VCC .... Vehicle Crew Chief [*NASA*] (KSC)
VCC .... Verification Code Counter (MCD)
VCC .... Vermilion Community College, Ely, MN [*OCLC symbol*] (OCLC)
VCC .... Versatile Corp. [*Toronto Stock Exchange symbol*]
VCC .... Vertical Centering Control
VCC .... Vertical Channel Computer (SAA)
VCC .... Vice-Chancellor's Courts (DLA)
VCC .... Video Coaxial Connector
VCC .... Video Compact Cassette [*Video recorder*] [*Philips*]
VCC .... Vietcong Captured
VCC .... Virginia Community College System
VCC .... Viscous-Damped Converter Clutch [*Automotive engineering*]
VCC .... Visual Communications Congress
VCC .... Vogelback Computing Center [*Northwestern University*] [*Research center*] (RCD)
VCC .... Voice Control Center [*NASA*] (KSC)
VCC .... Voltage Coefficient of Capacitance
VCC .... Voltage-Controlled Capacitor
VCC .... Voluntary Census Committee (EA)
VCC .... Volunteer Cadet Corps [*British*]
VCC .... Volunteer Capital Corp. [*NYSE symbol*] (SPSG)
VCC .... Vuilleumier Cycle Cooler
VCCA .... Anuradhapura [*Sri Lanka*] [*ICAO location identifier*] (ICLI)
VCCA .... Vintage Chevrolet Club of America (EA)
VCCB........ Batticaloa [*Sri Lanka*] [*ICAO location identifier*] (ICLI)
VCCC........ Colombo/Ratmalana [*Sri Lanka*] [*ICAO location identifier*] (ICLI)
VCCC........ Vuilleumier Cycle Cryogenic Cooler
VCCG .... Galoya/Amparai [*Sri Lanka*] [*ICAO location identifier*] (ICLI)
VCCJ .... Jaffna/Kankesanturai [*Sri Lanka*] [*ICAO location identifier*] (ICLI)
VCCN .... Valley Capital Corp. [*NASDAQ symbol*] (NQ)
VCCS .... Visually Coupled Control System (MCD)
VCCS........ Voltage-Controlled Current Source [*Electronics*]
VCCT........ Trincomalee/China Bay [*Sri Lanka*] [*ICAO location identifier*] (ICLI)
VCCUS...... Venezuelan Chamber of Commerce of the United States
VCCW .... Wirawila [*Sri Lanka*] [*ICAO location identifier*] (ICLI)

VCD	Value City Department Stores [*NYSE symbol*] (SPSG)
VCD	Vapor Compression Distillation
VCD	Variable-Capacitance Diode
VCD	Variable Center Distance [*Data processing*] (OA)
VCD	Verification Control Document (NASA)
VCD	Vernier Engine Cutoff [*Aerospace*]
VCD	Vibrational Circular Dichroism [*Spectrometry*]
VCD	Victoria Diego Resource Corp. [*Vancouver Stock Exchange symbol*]
VCD	Visiting Card (BJA)
VCD	Voltage Crossing Detector
VCDS	Vapor Compression Distillation Subsystem (NASA)
VCDS	Vice-Chief of Defence Staff [*British*]
VCDS(P & L) ...	Vice Chief of Defence Staff Personnel and Logistics [*British*] (RDA)
VCE	Vapor Compression Evaporation
VCE	Variable Cycle Engine (MCD)
VCE	Vehicle Condition Evaluation (MCD)
VCE	Venice [*Italy*] [*Airport symbol*] (OAG)
VCE	Vertical Centrifugal
VCE	Vice
VCE	Vinyl Chloride Ethylene [*Organic chemistry*]
VCE	Voice (NASA)
VCEL	Vanguard Cellular Systems, Inc. [*NASDAQ symbol*] (NQ)
Vcela Morav ...	Vcela Moravska [*A publication*]
VCEMA	Vinyl Chloride Ethylene Methyl Acrylate [*Organic chemistry*]
VC Eq	Victoria Reports, Equity [*A publication*] (DLA)
VCF	Vapor Chamber Fin
VCF	Vapor Crystal Facility [*Materal processing center*] (SSD)
VCF	Variable Crystal Filter (DEN)
Vcf	Velocity of Circumferential Fiber Shortening [*Cardiology*]
VCF	Venture Capital Fund [*Finance*]
VCF	Verified Circulation Figure [*Advertising*]
VCF	Vietnam-Canada Foundation
VCF	Vincristine, Cyclophosphamide, Fluorouracil [*Antineoplastic drug regimen*]
VCF	Visual Comfort Factor
VCF	Voltage-Controlled Filter
VCF	Voltage-Controlled Frequency (IEEE)
VCFC	Vik Chandler Fan Club (EA)
VCFUSA ...	Vietnamese Catholic Federation in the USA (EA)
VCG	Calcutta Volunteer Guards [*British military*] (DMA)
VCG	Vapor Crystal Growth [*Materials processing*]
VCG	Vectorcardiogram [*Medicine*]
VCG	Vehicle Control Group
VCG	Verification Condition Generator
VCG	Vertical Location of the Center of Gravity
VCG	Vice-Consul General [*British*] (ROG)
VCG	Video Command Generator (MCD)
VCG	Voltage-Controlled Generator
VCGS	Vapor Crystal Growth System [*Materials processing*]
VCGS	Vice Chief of the General Staff [*in the field*] [*Military*] [*British*] (RDA)
VCH	Veterinary Convalescent Hospital
VCH	Vichadero [*Uruguay*] [*Airport symbol*] [*Obsolete*] (OAG)
VCH	Victoria County History [*Classical studies*] (OCD)
VCH	Video Concert Hall
VCH	Vinylcyclohexene [*Organic chemistry*]
VCHO	Vicar Choral
VCHP	Variable Conductance Heat Pipe
VCHP	Vegas Chips, Inc. [*NASDAQ symbol*] (NQ)
VChr	Vigiliae Christianae [*A publication*]
V Christ	Vetera Christianorum [*A publication*]
VCI	Valassis Communications, Inc. [*NYSE symbol*] (SPSG)
VCI	Variety Clubs International (EA)
VCI	Vegetation Condition Index [*for detecting and tracking droughts*] [*National Oceanic and Atmospheric Administration*]
VCI	Vehicle Cone Index [*Engineering*] (OA)
VCI	Velocity Change Indicator (NASA)
VCI	Vibration Control Index
VCI	Videtics International Corp. [*Vancouver Stock Exchange symbol*]
VCI	Vietcong Infrastructure
VCI	Virtual Circuit Identifier [*Data processing*]
VCI	Visual Comfort Index
VCI	Volatile Corrosion Inhibitor [*See also VPI*] [*Metallurgy*]
VCID	Very Close in Defense
VCIGS	Vice-Chief of the Imperial General Staff [*British*]
VCIM	Varnished Cambric Insulation Material
VCINS	Vietcong Infrastructure Neutralization System
VCIP	Veterans Cost-of-Instruction Program [*Higher Education Act*]
VCIS	Voluntary Cooperative Information System [*American Public Welfare Association*] (EGAO)
V-CITE	Vertical-Cargo Integration Test Equipment [*NASA*] (MCD)
VC-K	Eli Lilly & Co. [*Canada*] [*Research code symbol*]
VCK	Veckans Affarer [*A publication*]
VCK	Video Camera Kit
VCK	Vietcong Killed
VC KIA(BC) ...	Vietcong Killed in Action (Body Count)
VC KIA(POSS) ...	Vietcong Killed in Action (Possible)

VCKV	Vacuum Control Check Valve [*Automotive engineering*]
VCL	Vehicle Checkout Laboratory
VCL	Vertical Center Line
VCL	Violincello [*Music*]
VCL	Voice Communications Laboratory
VCL	Voluntary College Letter [*British*]
VCLE	Versicle
VCLF	Vertical Cask-Lifting Fixture [*Nuclear energy*] (NRCH)
VCLK	Video Clock [*Data processing*]
VCLLO	Violoncello [*Music*]
VCLO	Voltage-Controlled Local Oscillator
VCM	Vacuum (AAG)
VCM	Vacuum Condensible Material [*Astronomy*] (OA)
VCM	Vehicle Condition Monitor [*Automotive engineering*]
VCM	Vehicle Control Module [*Automotive engineering*]
VCM	Ventilation Control Module [*NASA*]
VCM	Veracruz [*Mexico*] [*Seismograph station code, US Geological Survey*] (SEIS)
VCM	Vertical Current Meter
VCM	Vertical Cutter Motion
VCM	Vibrating Coil Magnetometer
VCM	Victoria College of Music [*London*] (ROG)
VCM	Viking Continuation Mission [*NASA*]
VCM	Vinyl Chloride Monomer [*Organic chemistry*]
VCM	Visual Countermeasure
VCM	Volatile Combustible Material
VCM	Volatile Condensable Material
VCM	Voltage-Controlled Multivibrator
VCM	Voorhees College, Denmark, SC [*OCLC symbol*] (OCLC)
VCMA	Vacuum Cleaner Manufacturers Association (EA)
VCMA	Vinyl Chloride Methyl Acrylate [*Organic chemistry*]
VCmax	Maximum Viscous Response [*Medicine*]
VCMP	Vincristine, Cyclophosphamide, Melphalan, Prednisone [*Antineoplastic drug regimen*]
VCN	Christopher Newport College, Newport News, VA [*OCLC symbol*] (OCLC)
VCN	Millville, NJ [*Location identifier*] [*FAA*] (FAAL)
VCN	Vancomycin-Colistin-Nystatin [*Growth-inhibiting mixture*] [*Microbiology*]
VCN	Vendor Contract Notice
VCN	Verification Completion Notice (NASA)
VCN	Vibrio cholerae Neuraminidase [*An enzyme*]
VCN	Vinyl Cyanide [*Organic chemistry*]
VCN	Visual Communications Network, Inc. [*Cambridge, MA*]
VCN	Vulcan Resources [*Vancouver Stock Exchange symbol*]
VCNM	Vice Chief of Naval Material Command
VCNO	Vice Chief of Naval Operations
VCNS........	Vice-Chief of the Naval Staff [*British*]
VCNTY	Vicinity (AFM)
VC/NVA....	Vietcong/North Vietnamese Army
VCO	Glendale, AZ [*Location identifier*] [*FAA*] (FAAL)
VCO	Variable Cycle Operation
VCO	Vehicle Control Officer [*Air Force*] (AFM)
VCO	Verbal Concrete Object
VCO	Verbit & Co., Consultants to Management [*Bala Cynwyd, PA*] [*Telecommunications*] (TSSD)
VCO	Vertical Control Operator [*Military*]
VCO	Viceroy's Commissioned Officer [*British military*] (DMA)
VCO	Voice-Controlled Oscillator [*Telecommunications*] (TEL)
VCO	Voltage-Controlled Oscillator
VCOA	Volkswagen Convertible Owners of America (EA)
VCoA	Volvo Club of America (EA)
VCOD........	Vertical Carrier Onboard Delivery
VCOFGWBS ...	Vietnamese Cross of Gallantry with Bronze Star [*Military decoration*] (AABC)
VCOFGWGS ...	Vietnamese Cross of Gallantry with Gold Star [*Military decoration*] (AABC)
VCOFGWP ...	Vietnamese Cross of Gallantry with Palm [*Military decoration*] (AABC)
VCOFGWSS ...	Vietnamese Cross of Gallantry with Silver Star [*Military decoration*] (AABC)
VCOI	Veterans Cost-of-Instruction
V Conv R....	Victorian Conveyancing Cases [*Australia*] [*A publication*]
VCOP	Variable Control Oil Pressure (MSA)
VCOR	Vencor, Inc. [*NASDAQ symbol*] (NQ)
VCOS	Vehicle Control and Operating System [*Army*]
VCOS	Vice-Chiefs of Staff [*British*]
VCOS	Visible Caching Operating System [*AT & T*]
VCOT	VFR [*Visual Flight Rules*] Conditions on Top [*Aviation*] (FAAC)
VCOV	Volunteer Consultant for Office of Volunteers [*Red Cross*]
VCP	Sao Paulo [*Brazil*] Viracopos Airport [*Airport symbol*] (OAG)
VCP	Valosin-Containing Protein [*Biochemistry*]
VCP	Variable Cam Phasing [*Automotive engineering*]
VCP	Vector Correction Program (SAA)
VCP	Vehicle Check Point [*Military*]
VCP	Vehicle Collecting Point
VCP	Velocity Control Programmer
VCP	VERDAN [*Versatile Differential Analyzer*] Checkout Panel
VCP	Veterinary Collecting Post [*British military*] (DMA)
VCP	Veterinary Creolin-Pearson

VCP .... Video Cassette Player
VCP .... Vincristine, Cyclophosphamide, Prednisone [*Antineoplastic drug regimen*]
VCP .... Virtual Channel Processor [*Data processing*]
VCP .... Virtual Counterpoise Procedure [*Physical chemistry*]
VCP .... Virus Cancer Program [*National Cancer Institute*]
VCP .... Voluntary Cooperation Program [*World Meteorological Organization*] [*United Nations*]
VCPA .... Virginia-Carolina Peanut Association   (EA)
VCPA .... Virginia Crab Packers Association [*Defunct*]   (EA)
VCPI .... Virtual Control Program Interface [*Data processing*]   (PCM)
VCPM .... Video-Enhanced Contrast Polarization Microscopy
VCPOR ..... Vanguardia Comunista del Partido Obrero Revolucionario [*Bolivia*] [*Political party*]   (PPW)
VCPP .... Virginia-Carolina Peanut Promotions [*An association*]   (EA)
VCPS .... Velocity Control Propulsion Subsystem [*NASA*]
VCPS .... Video Copyright Protection Society [*British*]
VC PW .... Vietcong Prisoner of War
VCR .... Go-Video, Inc. [*AMEX symbol*]   (SPSG)
VCR .... Vacuum Contact Relay
VCR .... Valclair Resources Ltd. [*Vancouver Stock Exchange symbol*]
VCR .... Valuation by Components Rule   (ADA)
VCR .... Variable Compression Ratio
VCR .... Vasoconstrictive [*Physiology*]
VCR .... Vertical Crater Retreat [*Mining technology*]
VCR .... Video Cassette Recorder
VCR .... Vincristine [*Also, LCR, O, V, VC*] [*Antineoplastic drug*]
VCR .... Visual Control Room
VCR .... Viva Cristo Rey [*Long Live Christ the King*] [*Spanish*]
VCR .... Vocal Character Recognition
VCR .... Voltage Coefficient of Resistance
VCRAS ..... Office of Vice Chancellor for Research and Advanced Study [*University of Alaska*] [*Research center*]   (RCD)
VCRC........ Vector Control Research Centre [*India*]
VCRC........ Voice Circuit Reconfiguration Confirmation   (SSD)
VCRE......... Vari-Care, Inc. [*NASDAQ symbol*]   (NQ)
VC Rep...... Vice-Chancellor's Reports [*English, Canadian*] [*A publication*]   (DLA)
VCRI......... Verification Cross Reference Index
VCRI......... Video Communications & Radio, Inc. [*NASDAQ symbol*]   (NQ)
VCRT........ Variable Contrast Resolution Test [*Optics*]
VCS........... Cruiser-Scouting Aircraft Squadron [*Navy symbol*]
VCS........... Vacuum Control Switch
VCS........... Validation Control System
VCS........... Vane Control System   (MCD)
VCS........... Vapor Coating System
VCS........... Vapor Cooling System
VCS........... Variable Correlation Synchronization
VCS........... Vasoconstrictor Substance [*Physiology*]
VCS........... Vehicular Communications System
VCS........... Velocity Cutoff System   (KSC)
VCS........... Ventilation Control System [*NASA*]   (KSC)
VCS........... Verbal Communication Scales [*Educational testing*]
VCS........... Verification Control Sheet   (NASA)
VCS........... Vernier Control System
VCS........... Veterans Canteen Service [*Veterans Administration*]
VCS........... Veterinary Cancer Society   (EA)
VCS........... Vice Chief of Staff
VC of S....... Vice Chief of Staff
VCS........... Video Cassette System
VCS........... Video Clutter Suppression   (CAAL)
VCS........... Video Communications System
VCS........... Video Computer System [*Atari, Inc.*]
VCS........... Video Contrast Seeker
VCS........... Vietcong Suspect
VCS........... View Control System   (HGAA)
VCS........... Viking Change Status [*NASA*]
VCS........... Virginia & Carolina Southern R. R. [*AAR code*]
VCS........... Visual Call Sign [*Communications*]
VCS........... Visually Coupled System   (IEEE)
VCS........... Vocabulary Comprehension Scale [*Educational test*]
VCS........... Voice Command System [*Ground Communications Facility, NASA*]
VCS........... Voice Communication System
VCS........... Voice Control Switch [*NASA*]
VCS........... Voltage Calibration Set
VCS........... Voltage-Current-Sequence   (MCD)
VCSA........ Vice Chief of Staff, Army [*Formerly, VC of SA*]
VC of SA.... Vice Chief of Staff, Army [*Later, VCSA*]   (AABC)
VC/SAF..... Vice Chief of Staff, Air Force
VCS Bul..... VCS [*Victorian Computer Society*] Bulletin [*A publication*]   (APTA)
VCSCT ...... Vacuum Control Switch - Cold Temperature [*Automotive engineering*]
VCSDI .... Vacuum Control Switch - Deceleration Idle [*Automotive engineering*]
VCSEL ...... Vertical-Cavity Surface Emitting LASER
VCSFO ...... Veterans Canteen Service Field Office [*Veterans Administration*]
VCSI .... VCS, Inc. [*NASDAQ symbol*]   (NQ)

VCSL .... Voice Call Signs List
VCSP .... Voice Call Signs Plan
VCSR .... Voltage-Controlled Shift Register
VCSS .... Value Creation Study Society   (CINC)
VCSS .... Voice Communications Security System
VCT .... St. Vincent and the Grenadines [*ANSI three-letter standard code*]   (CNC)
VCT .... Variable Cycle Technology
VCT .... Vector [*A publication*]
VCT .... Venous Clotting Time [*Clinical chemistry*]
VCT .... Victor   (WGA)
VCT .... Victoria [*Texas*] [*Airport symbol*]   (OAG)
VCT .... Vidicon Camera Tube
VCT .... Vinyl Composition Tile
VCT .... Vitrified Clay Tile [*Technical drawings*]
VCT .... Voice Code Translation   (BUR)
VCT .... Voltage Control Transfer
VCT .... Voltage Curve Tracer
VCT .... Volume Control Tank [*Nuclear energy*]   (NRCH)
VCTA General J ... Victorian Commercial Teachers' Association. General Journal [*A publication*]   (APTA)
VCTCA ..... Virtual Channel to Channel Adapter
VCTD .... Vendor Contract Technical Data
VCTR........ Vector   (NASA)
VCTR........ Vector Graphic, Inc. [*NASDAQ symbol*]   (NQ)
VCTS .... Vacuum Control Temperature Switch [*Automotive engineering*]
VCTS........ Variable Cockpit Training System   (MCD)
VCTY........ Vicinity   (NVT)
VCU .... Video Control Unit   (MCD)
VCU .... Videocystourethrography [*Medicine*]
VCU .... Virginia Commonwealth University
VCU .... Viscous Coupling Unit [*Automotive engineering*]
VCU .... Voiding Cystourethrogram [*Medicine*]
VCU .... Voltage Control Unit
VCUG .... Vesicoureterogram [*Urology*]
VCUG .... Voiding Cystourethrogram [*Medicine*]
VCV .... Clinch Valley College of the University of Virginia, Wise, VA [*OCLC symbol*]   (OCLC)
VCV .... Vacuum Check Valve
VCV .... Vacuum Control Valve [*Automotive engineering*]
VCV .... Vicia Cryptic Virus [*Plant pathology*]
VCV .... Victorville, CA [*Location identifier*] [*FAA*]   (FAAL)
VCV .... Vietnam Combat Veterans   (EA)
VCVAC..... Vinyl Chloride Vinyl Acetate [*Organic chemistry*]
VCVDC...... Vinyl Chloride Vinylidene Chloride [*Organic chemistry*]
VCVS........ Vehicle Component Verification System [*Automotive engineering*]
VCVS........ Voltage-Controlled Voltage Source
VCXO .... Voltage-Controlled Crystal Oscillator
VCY .... Valley City, ND [*Location identifier*] [*FAA*]   (FAAL)
VCY .... Ventura County Railway Co. [*Army*]
VCZ .... Vinylcarbazole [*Organic chemistry*]
VD............. Double Vibrations [*Cycles*]
VD............. Leo Pharm. Products [*Denmark*] [*Research code symbol*]
VD............. Photographic Squadron [*Navy symbol*]
VD............. RTZ Services Ltd. [*British*] [*ICAO designator*]   (ICDA)
VD............. Valuation Decisions [*A publication*]   (DLA)
VD............. Vandyke [*Graphics*]
VD............. Vapor Density
VD............. Various Dates [*Bibliography*]
VD............. Vault Door   (AAG)
VD............. Venereal Disease
VD............. Ventilating Deadlight [*Technical drawings*]
VD............. Ventricular Dilator [*Neuron*] [*Medicine*]
VD............. Verbal Discrimination [*Psychology*]
VD............. Verbum Domini [*Rome*] [*A publication*]   (BJA)
VD............. Vertical Drive
VD............. Viceroy-Designate [*British*]
VD............. Victoria Docks [*British*]   (ROG)
VD............. Victorian Decoration [*British*]
VD............. Video Decoder
VD............. Video Disk   (BUR)
VD............. Violent Defectives [*British*]
VD............. Viral Diarrhea   (MAE)
VD............. Virtual Data
VD............. Visiting Dignitary
V/D............ Voice/Data   (BUR)
VD............. Void   (AAG)
VD............. Voltage Detector
VD............. Voltage Drop   (MSA)
Vd............. Volume Dead Air Space   (MAE)
VD............. Volume Deleted [*Finance*]
VD............. Volume Discount [*Investment term*]
VD............. Volume of Distribution
VD............. Volunteer Decoration [*British*]
VDA.......... Valve Drive Amplifier
VDA.......... Valve Driver Assembly   (NASA)
VDA.......... Variable Data Area   (NASA)
VDA.......... Variable Depth ASDIC   (NATG)
VDA.......... Vehicle Dynamics Area

VDA...........	Vendor Data Article
VDA...........	Versatile Drone Autopilot (MCD)
VDA...........	Vertical Danger Angle [*Navigation*]
V & DA	Video and Data Acquisition (MCD)
V & DA	Video and Data Processing Assembly (NASA)
VDA	Video Dimension Analysis [*Sports medicine*]
VDA...........	Video Distribution Amplifier
VDA...........	Viola d'Amore [*Music*]
VDA...........	Visual Discriminatory Acuity
VDA...........	Volksbund fuer das Deutschtum im Ausland [*NAZI Germany*]
VDAC.......	Vaginal Delivery after Caesarean [*Obstetrics*]
VDAC.......	Vendor Data Article Control
VDAC........	Voltage-Dependent, Anion-Selective Channels [*In the membrane of a mitochondrion*]
VDA/D	Video Display Adapter with Digital Enhancement [*AT & T*]
VDAM......	Virtual Data Access Method (IEEE)
VDAS	Vehicle Data and Acquisition System [*Automotive engineering*]
VDAS	Vibration Data Acquisition System (KSC)
VDAS	Video Data Acquisition System
VDAS	Voltage-Dependent, Anion-Selective [*Proteins*] [*Biochemistry*]
VDASD	Veroeffentlichungen. Deutsche Akademie fuer Sprache und Dichtung [*A publication*]
VDB...........	Brooklyn College, Brooklyn, NY [*OCLC symbol*] (OCLC)
VdB...........	Van Den Bergh [*Liver function test*]
VDB...........	Vector Data Buffer
VDB...........	Vehicle Data Bus [*Automotive engineering*]
VDB...........	Very Dear Brother [*Freemasonry*]
VDB...........	Victor D. Brenner [*Designer's mark, when appearing on US coins*]
VDB...........	Video Display Board
VDB...........	Vrijzinnige-Democratische Bond [*Radical Democratic League*] [*Netherlands*] [*Political party*] (PPE)
VDBG.......	Battambang [*Cambodia*] [*ICAO location identifier*] (ICLI)
VDBR	Volume of Distribution of Bilirubin [*Medicine*] (MAE)
VDC........	Van Dorn Co. [*NYSE symbol*] (SPSG)
VDC...........	Vanadocene Dichloride [*Antineoplastic drug*]
VDC...........	Variable Diode Circuit
VDC...........	Variable Displacement Compressor [*Automotive engineering*]
VDC...........	Vasodilator Center [*Physiology*]
VDC...........	Vendor Data Control (MCD)
VDC...........	Ventilation Duct Chase [*Nuclear energy*] (NRCH)
VDC...........	Venture Development Corp. [*Natick, MA*] [*Telecommunications*] (TSSD)
VDC...........	Video-Documentary Clearinghouse (EA)
VDC...........	Voltage to Digital Converter
VDC...........	Voltage Doubler Circuit
VDC...........	Volts Direct Current
VDC...........	Volunteer Defense Corps
VDC...........	Volunteer Development Corps (EA)
VDCC.......	Voltage-Dependent Calcium Channel [*Neurobiology*]
VDCP	Video Data Collection Program
VDCT	Direct-Current Test Volts
VDCU	Videograph Display Control Unit
VDCW.......	Direct-Current Working Volts
VDD...........	Verification Description Document (NASA)
VDD...........	Version Description Document (KSC)
VDD...........	Video Detector Diode
VDD...........	Visual Display Data
VDD...........	Voice Digital Display
VDDI	Voyager Data Detailed Index [*NASA*] (KSC)
VDDL	Voyager Data Distribution List [*NASA*] (KSC)
VDDP	Video Digital Data Processing
VDDR	Vitamin D-Dependent Rickets [*Medicine*]
VDDS	Voice/Document Delivery System [*Data processing*]
VDDS	Voyager Data Description Standards [*NASA*] (KSC)
VDE	Vacuum Deposition Equipment
VDE...........	Valverde [*Canary Islands*] [*Airport symbol*] (OAG)
VDE...........	Variable Displacement Engine
VDE...........	Variable Display Equipment
VDE...........	Verband Deutscher Elektrotechniker [*Association of German Electrical Engineers*] (EG)
VDE...........	Visual Development Environment [*Data processing*] (PCM)
VDECS......	Vehicle Detector and Cueing System
VDEF........	Vie de France Corp. [*McLean, VA*] [*NASDAQ symbol*] (NQ)
VDEFA......	VDE [*Verband Deutscher Elektrotechniker*] Fachberichte [*A publication*]
VDE Fachber ...	VDE [*Verband Deutscher Elektrotechniker*] Fachberichte [*A publication*]
VDEh.........	Verein Deutscher Eisenhuttenleute [*German Iron and Steel Engineers Association*] (IID)
VDEL........	Variable Delivery
VDEL........	Venereal Disease Experimental Laboratory
VDEM.......	Vasodepressor Material [*Physiology*] (MAE)
VDEO........	Video Station, Inc. [*NASDAQ symbol*] (NQ)
VDET	Voltage Detector (IEEE)
VDETS......	Voice Data Entry Terminal System
VDEV	"V" Device [*Military decoration*] (AABC)
VDEW (Ver Dtsch Elektrizitaetswerke) Informationsdienst ... VDEW (Vereinigung Deutscher Elektrizitaetswerke) Informationsdienst (German Federal Republic) [*A publication*]	

VDF	Very-High-Frequency Direction-Finding
VDF	Vibration Damping Fastener
VDF	Video Frequency
VDF	Vinylidene Fluoride [*Organic chemistry*]
VDF	Voice Data Fax [*Telecommunications*]
VDF	Vorkaempfer Deutscher Freiheit. Series [*Munich*] [*A publication*]
VDFG.........	Variable Diode Function Generator
VDG..........	Royal Inniskilling Dragoon Guards [*Military unit*] [*British*]
VDG..........	Vehicle Data Guide
VDG..........	Venereal Disease Gonorrhea
VDG..........	Vertical and Direction Gyro
VDG..........	Vertical Display Generator (NG)
VDG..........	Video Display Generator
vdg............	Voiding (MAE)
VdgB.........	Vereinigung der Gegenseitigen Bauernhilfe [*Mutual Farmers' Aid Society*] [*Germany*]
VDGIA	Verhandlungen. Deutsche Gesellschaft fuer Innere Medizin [*A publication*]
VDGKA	Verhandlungen. Deutsche Gesellschaft fuer Kreislaufforschung [*A publication*]
VDGPA	Verhandlungen. Deutsche Gesellschaft fuer Pathologie [*A publication*]
VDGRA	Verhandlungen. Deutsche Gesellschaft fuer Rheumatologie [*A publication*]
VdGSA	Viola da Gamba Society of America (EA)
VdGSA	Viola da Gamba Society of America. Journal [*A publication*]
VDH	Valvular Disease of the Heart [*Medicine*]
VDH	Van Der Hout Associates Ltd. [*Toronto Stock Exchange symbol*]
VDH	Variable Length Divide or Halt (SAA)
VDI	Vat Dye Institute [*Later, American Dye Manufacturers Institute*] (EA)
VDI	Vendor Documentation Inventory (NASA)
VDI	Verein Deutscher Ingenieure [*Society of German Engineers*]
VDI	Vertical Direction Indicator (CAAL)
VDI	Vertical Display Indicator (NG)
VDI	Vidalia, GA [*Location identifier*] [*FAA*] (FAAL)
VDI	Video Data Interrogator (SAA)
VDI	Video Display Input
VDI	Video Display Interface
VDI	Virtual Device Interface [*Computer technology*]
VDI	Visual Display Input
VDI	Voluntary Data Inquiry
VDI Ber	VDI [*Verein Deutscher Ingenieure*] Berichte [*A publication*]
VDICAPP ...	Verein Deutscher Ingenieure-Commission on Air Pollution Prevention (EAIO)
VDIEO.......	Vendor Data Information Engineering Order (MCD)
VDIFA.......	VDI [*Verein Deutscher Ingenieure*] Forschungsheft [*A publication*]
VDI Forschungsh ...	VDI [*Verein Deutscher Ingenieure*] Forschungsheft [*A publication*]
VDIG	Vertical Display Indicator Group
VDIKRL	Verein Deutscher Ingenieure-Kommission Reinhaltung der Luft [*VDI - Commis sion on Air Pollution Prevention*] (EAIO)
VDI-N........	VDI-Nachrichten [*VDI-Verlag GmbH*] [*Database*]
VDI Nachr ...	Verein Deutscher Ingenieure. Nachrichten [*A publication*]
VDISK	Virtual Disk [*Data processing*]
VDI Z Fortschr Ber Reihe 5 ...	VDI [*Verein Deutscher Ingenieure*] Zeitschriften. Fortschritt-Berichte. Reihe 5. Grund- und Werkstoffe [*A publication*]
VDJ...........	Variable-Diversity-Joining [*Genetics*]
VDK...........	Vicinal Diketone [*Organic chemistry*]
VDKC.......	Kompong Cham [*Cambodia*] [*ICAO location identifier*] (ICLI)
VDKH.......	Kompong Chnang [*Cambodia*] [*ICAO location identifier*] (ICLI)
VDKT	Kratie [*Cambodia*] [*ICAO location identifier*] (ICLI)
VDL...........	Van Diemen's Land [*Former name of Tasmania*]
VDL...........	Variable Delay Line
VDL...........	Vasodepressor Lipid [*Physiology*]
VDL...........	Ventilating Deadlight
VDL...........	Video Data Link (NVT)
VDL...........	Vienna Definition Language [*1960*] [*Data processing*] (CSR)
VDL...........	Visual Detection Level (MAE)
VDL...........	Voice Direct Line
VDLF........	Variable Depth Launch Facility (AAG)
VDM..........	Variable Direction Microphone
VDM..........	Varian Data Machines
VDM..........	Vasodepressor Material [*Physiology*]
VDM..........	Vector Dominance Model [*Physics*]
VDM..........	Vector Drawn Map
VDM..........	Vehicle Deadlined for Maintenance (AFM)
VDM..........	Verbi Dei Minister [*Minister, or Preacher, of the Word of God*] [*Latin*]
VDM..........	Vibration Damping Mount
VDM..........	Video Delta Modulation
VDM..........	Viedma [*Argentina*] [*Airport symbol*] (OAG)
VDM..........	Vienna Development Method [*Data processing*]
VDM..........	Virtual Dipole Moment [*Geodesy*]
VDM..........	Virtual DOS [*Disk Operating System*] Machine [*Data processing*] (PCM)

VDME .... Vibrating Dropping Mercury Electrode [*Electrochemistry*]
VDMIE ...... Verbum Domini Manet in Eternum [*The Word of the Lord Endureth Forever*] [*Latin*]
VDMK .... Democratic Community of Vojvodina Hungarians [*Former Yugoslavia*] [*Political party*]
VDMOS .... Vertical Double Diffused Metal Oxide Semiconductor   (MCD)
VDMS .... Video Delta Modulation System
VDMS .... Vocal Data Management System
VDMSC .... Volunteer Durham Medical Staff Corps [*British military*]   (DMA)
VDN .... Varudeklarationsnamnden [*Labeling system*] [*Sweden*]
VDN .... Vedron Ltd. [*Toronto Stock Exchange symbol*]
VdN .... Voix des Notres [*Record label*] [*France*]
VDNAA ..... VDI [*Verein Deutscher Ingenieure*] Nachrichten [*A publication*]
VDNCOA ... Veterans Division of the Non-Commissioned Officers Association of the USA   (EA)
VDNH .... VD [*Venereal Disease*] National Hotline [*Later, NSTDH*]   (EA)
VDO .... Videotron Groupe Ltee. SV [*Toronto Stock Exchange symbol*]
VDOP .... Vertical Dilution of Precision
VD/OS .... Vacuum Distillation/Overflow Sampler [*Nuclear energy*]   (NRCH)
VDP .... Vacuum Diffusion Pump
VDP .... Variable Length Divide or Proceed   (SAA)
VDP .... Vehicle Deadlined for Parts
VDP .... Venture Database Publisher [*Data processing*]
VDP .... Verenigde Democratische Partijen [*United Democratic Parties*] [*Surinam*] [*Political party*]   (PPW)
VDP .... Vertical Data Processing
VDP .... Vertical Dipole   (MCD)
VDP .... Vertical Director Pointer   (SAA)
VDP .... Vibration Diagnostic Program
VDP .... Vibration-Dissociation Process
VDP .... Video Data Processor
VDP .... Videodisc Player [*RCA Corp.*]
VDP .... Vincristine, Daunorubicin, Prednisone [*Antineoplastic drug regimen*]
VDP .... Visual Descent Point [*Aviation*]   (FAAC)
VDP .... Volunteer Reservists in Drill Pay Status [*Navy*]
VDP .... Von Deutscher Poeterey [*A publication*]
VDPh .... Verhandlung. Versammlung Deutscher Philologen [*A publication*]
VDPI .... Vehicle Direction and Position Indicator
VDPI .... Voyager Data Processing Instructions [*NASA*]   (KSC)
VDPP .... Phnom-Penh [*Cambodia*] [*ICAO location identifier*]   (ICLI)
VDPS .... Voice Data Processor System
VDPT .... Pongtuk [*Cambodia*] [*ICAO location identifier*]   (ICLI)
VDQ .... Visual Display of Quality
VDQS .... Vins Delimites de Qualite Superieure [*Designation on French wine labels*]
VDR .... Vader Group, Inc. [*AMEX symbol*]   (SPSG)
VDR .... Validated Data Record
VDR .... Variable Deposit Requirement [*Business term*]   (ADA)
VDR .... Variable Diameter Rotor
VDR .... Vehicle Deselect Request [*NASA*]   (KSC)
VDR .... Vendor Data Request
VDR .... Venous Diameter Ratio [*Cancer detection*]
VDR .... Video Disc Recorder
VDR .... Vitamin D Receptor [*Genetics*]
VDR .... Voice & Data Resources, Inc. [*Ashbury Park, NJ*] [*Information service or system*] [*Telecommunications*]   (TSSD)
VDR .... Voice Digitization Rate
VDR .... Voltage-Dependent Resistor   (DEN)
VDR .... Voyage Data Recorder
VDRA .... Voice and Data Recording Auxiliary [*NASA*]   (KSC)
VDRE .... Vitamin D-Responsive Element [*Biochemistry*]
VDRG .... Vendor Data Release Group   (MCD)
VDRL .... Venereal Disease Research Laboratory
VDRS .... Verdun Depression Rating Scale [*Medicine*]   (MAE)
VDRT .... Venereal Disease Reference Test [*of Harris*]
VDRY .... Vacu-Dry Co. [*NASDAQ symbol*]   (NQ)
VDS .... Vadso [*Norway*] [*Airport symbol*]   (OAG)
VDS .... Vapor Deposited Silica [*Optical fiber technology*]
VDS .... Vapor Detection System
VDS .... Variable Depth SONAR
VDS .... Vasodilator Substance [*Physiology*]
VDS .... Vehicle Description Summary [*General Motors Corp.*]
VDS .... Vehicle Descriptor Section
VDS .... Vehicle Dynamics Simulator [*NASA*]   (NASA)
VDS .... Vendor Data Service
VDS .... Vendor Direct Shipment
VDS .... Venereal Disease Syphilis
VDS .... Veroeffentlichungen. Deutsche Schillergesellschaft [*A publication*]
VDS .... Vertical Display System [*Navy*]
VDS .... Video Digitizer System   (MCD)
VDS .... Vindesine [*Also, E*] [*Antineoplastic drug*]
VDS .... Viola d'Amore Society   (EA)
VDS .... Visual Display System
VDS .... Visual Docking Simulator

VDS .... Voice Data Switch
VDS .... Volatile Dissolved Solids   (MCD)
VDSA .... Veut Dieu Saint Amour [*Knights Templar*] [*Freemasonry*]
VDSA .... Video Superstores of America, Inc. [*NASDAQ symbol*]   (NQ)
VDSM .... Internationaler Verband der Stadt-, Sport-, und Mehrzweckhallen [*International Federation of City, Sport, and Multi-Purpose Halls*]   (EAIO)
VDSP .... Videospection, Inc. [*NASDAQ symbol*]   (NQ)
VDSR .... Siem-Reap [*Cambodia*] [*ICAO location identifier*]   (ICLI)
VDSS .... Variable Depth SONAR System
VDSS .... Volume of Distribution at Steady State
VDST .... Stung Treng [*Cambodia*] [*ICAO location identifier*]   (ICLI)
VDSV .... Sihanouk [*Cambodia*] [*ICAO location identifier*]   (ICLI)
VDT .... Van Doorne's Transmissie BV [*Netherlands*] [*Automotive engineering*]
VDT .... Varactor Diode Test
VDT .... Variable Deflection Thruster [*Helicopter*]
VDT .... Variable Density Tunnel
VDT .... Variable Depth Transducer [*Navy*]   (NVT)
VDT .... Variable Differential Transformer
VDT .... Vehicle Data Table [*NASA*]   (MCD)
VDT .... Video Data Terminal [*Data processing*]
VDT .... Video [*or Visual*] Display Terminal [*Data processing*]
VDT .... Videotex World [*A publication*]
VDTA .... Vacuum Dealers Trade Association   (EA)
VDTIAX .... Flemish Veterinary Journal [*A publication*]
VDTS .... Variable Display Training System
VDTS .... Vehicle Data Transmission System
VDTT .... Very Difficult to Test [*Audiology*]
VDU .... Refugio, TX [*Location identifier*] [*FAA*]   (FAAL)
VDU .... Vacuum Distillation Unit [*Petroleum technology*]
VdU .... Verband der Unabhaengigen [*League of Independents*] [*Dissolved, 1956*] [*Austria*]   (PPE)
VDU .... Video [*or Visual*] Display Unit [*Data processing*]
VDU .... Visual Display Unit   (OA)
VDV .... Vacuum Differential Valve [*Automotive engineering*]
VDV .... Ventricular End-Diastolic Volume [*Medicine*]   (MAE)
VDV .... Vojski Drzavne Varnosti [*Yugoslavia*]
VDV .... Vozdushno-Desantnye Voiska [*Airborne Troops*] [*An autonomous command*] [*Former USSR*]
VD-VF .... Vacuum Distillation - Vapor Filtration
VDVS .... Voeune Sai [*Cambodia*] [*ICAO location identifier*]   (ICLI)
VDW .... Venus Departure Window [*NASA*]
VDW .... Very Deep Water
VDX .... Vandorex Energy [*Vancouver Stock Exchange symbol*]
VDYK .... Van Dyk Research Corp. [*NASDAQ symbol*]   (NQ)
VDZ .... Valdez [*Alaska*] [*Airport symbol*]   (OAG)
VE .... AVENSA Aerovias Venezolanas SA [*Venezuela*] [*ICAO designator*]   (FAAC)
Ve .... Biblioteca Nacional, Caracas, Venezuela [*Library symbol*] [*Library of Congress*]   (LCLS)
VE .... Vaginal Epithelium [*Endocrinology*]
VE .... Vaginal Examination [*Medicine*]
VE .... Value Effectiveness
VE .... Value Engineering [*Military*]
VE .... Varicose Eczema [*Medicine*]
VE .... Vehicle Experimental   (MCD)
Ve .... Velban [*See VBL*]
VE .... Velocity Equipment   (MCD)
VE .... Velocity, Equivalent
VE .... Velocity Error
ve .... Venezuela [*MARC country of publication code*] [*Library of Congress*]   (LCCP)
VE .... Venezuela [*ANSI two-letter standard code*]   (CNC)
VE .... Ventilating Equipment   (MSA)
VE .... Verbal Emotional (Stimuli) [*Psychology*]
V-E .... VERLORT [*Very-Long-Range Tracking*] Elevation [*NASA*]
VE .... Vermont Music Educators News [*A publication*]
VE .... Vernal Equinox
VE .... Vernier Engine [*as a modifier*]   (AAG)
VE .... Vertical Exaggeration [*Geology*]
Ve .... Vesey, Senior's, English Chancery Reports [*27, 28 English Reprint*] [*A publication*]   (ILCA)
VE .... Vesicular Exanthema [*Virus*]
VE .... Veuve [*Widow*] [*French*]   (ROG)
VE .... Vibration Eliminator   (OA)
VE .... Victory in Europe [*as in VE-Day*]
VE .... Vidatron Enterprise Ltd. [*Vancouver Stock Exchange symbol*]
V & E .... Vinethene and Ether
VE .... Visalia Electric Railroad Co. [*AAR code*]
VE .... Visual Efficiency
VE .... Visual Emissions [*Environmental Protection Agency*]   (GFGA)
VE .... Vocational Education   (OICC)
VE .... Voltage Efficiency [*Electrochemistry*]
VE .... Volume Ejection [*Medicine*]
VE .... Voluntary Effort [*A cost containment program established by AHA, AMA, and FAH*]
VE .... Votre Eminence [*Your Eminence*] [*French*]
VE .... Vox Evangelica [*A publication*]
V-E (Day) .. Victory in Europe Day [*World War II*]
VEA .... Value Engineering Audit

VEA .... Variable Energy Absorber (MCD)
VEA .... Vehicle Engineering Analysis
VEA .... Veliger Escape Aperture
VEA .... Ventricular Ectopic Activity [*Cardiology*] (MAE)
VEA .... Ventricular Ectopic Arrhythmia [*Cardiology*] (AAMN)
VEA .... Veterans Educational Assistance [*Act*]
VEA .... Viral Envelope Antigens [*Immunology*]
VEA .... Vocational Education Act [*1963*]
VEAB Ert .. VEAB Ertesitoe [*Hungary*] [*A publication*]
VEAMCOP ... Viking Error Analysis Monte Carlo Program [*Data processing*]
VEAN........ Along [*India*] [*ICAO location identifier*] (ICLI)
VEAP........ Veterans Educational Assistance Program [*DoD*]
VEAT........ Agartala [*India*] [*ICAO location identifier*] (ICLI)
VEAZ........ Aizwal [*India*] [*ICAO location identifier*] (ICLI)
Veazey...... Veazey's Reports [*36-44 Vermont*] [*A publication*] (DLA)
VEB .... Financieel Ekonomische Tijd [*A publication*]
VEB .... Variable Elevation Beam [*RADAR*]
VE & B .... Vehicle Energy and Biotechnology (MCD)
VEB .... Vehicle Equipment Bay (MCD)
VEB .... Ventricular Ectopic Beats [*Cardiology*]
VEB .... Venus Entry Body [*NASA*]
Ve & B .... Vesey and Beames' English Chancery Reports [*35 English Reprint*] [*A publication*] (DLA)
VEB .... Vneshekonombank [*State Bank for Foreign Economic Affairs*] [*Former USSR*]
VEB .... Vocational Education Board (OICC)
VEBA........ Calcutta (Behala) [*India*] [*ICAO location identifier*] (ICLI)
VEBA........ Vereinigte Elektrizitaets und Bergwerks, AG [*Holding company*] [*Germany*]
VEBA........ Voluntary Employee Benefit Association [*Type of trust established by a company, a union, or both to provide members with various insurance benefits*]
VEBC........ Berachampa [*India*] [*ICAO location identifier*] (ICLI)
VEBD .... Baghdogra [*India*] [*ICAO location identifier*] (ICLI)
VEBG .... Balurghat [*India*] [*ICAO location identifier*] (ICLI)
VEBK........ Bokaro [*India*] [*ICAO location identifier*] (ICLI)
VEBL........ Barbil [*India*] [*ICAO location identifier*] (ICLI)
VEBR........ Visual Evoked Brain Response
VEBS .... Bhubaneswar [*India*] [*ICAO location identifier*] (ICLI)
VEB Verlag Tech Mon Tech Rev ... VEB [*Volkseigener Betrieb*] Verlag Technik. Monthly Technical Review [*A publication*]
VEBW........ Vacuum Electron Beam Welder
VEC .... Vacation Exchange Club (EA)
VEC .... Value Engineering Change
VEC .... Variable Energy Cyclotron (IEEE)
VEC .... Vector (KSC)
VEC .... Vector Control (MUGU)
VEC .... Vertical Electrical Chase [*Nuclear energy*] (NRCH)
VeC .... Vertice (Coimbra) [*A publication*]
VEC .... Vibration Exciter Control
VEC .... Video-Enhanced Contrast Technique [*Microscopy*]
VEC .... Visual Education Consultants, Inc. (AEBS)
VEC .... Voice Equivalent Channel (MCD)
VeCAL....... Archivo del Libertador, Caracas, Venezuela [*Library symbol*] [*Library of Congress*] (LCLS)
VECAS...... Vertical Escape Collision Avoidance System [*Aviation*]
VECC........ Calcutta [*India*] [*ICAO location identifier*] (ICLI)
VECC........ Value Engineering Control Committee [*Military*]
VECC........ Variable Energy Content Curves (NOAA)
VECF........ Calcutta [*India*] [*ICAO location identifier*] (ICLI)
VECHCC.... Voluntary Effort to Contain Health Care Costs (EA)
VECI.......... Vehicle Emission Control Information [*Automotive engineering*]
VECI.......... Vehicular Equipment Complement Index (IEEE)
VECIB .... Vehicle Engineering Change Implementation Board (NASA)
VECK........ Chakulia [*India*] [*ICAO location identifier*] (ICLI)
VECM .... Vocational Education Curriculum Materials Database [*University of California, Berkeley*] [*Information service or system*] (CRD)
VECO .... Cooch-Behar [*India*] [*ICAO location identifier*] (ICLI)
VECO .... Vernier Engine Cutoff [*Aerospace*]
VECOS...... Vehicle Checkout Set
VECP........ Value Engineering Change Proposal [*Military*]
VECP........ Visually Evoked Cortical Potential [*Neurophysiology*]
VECR........ Vendor Engineering Change Request [*DoD*]
VECS .... Vocational Education Curriculum Specialists (OICC)
Vect.......... De Vectigalibus [*of Xenophon*] [*Classical studies*] (OCD)
V-ECT .... Ventricular Ectopy
VECTAC ... Vectored Attack [*Navy*] (NVT)
VECTAR ... Value, Expertise, Client, Time, Attorney, Result [*Lawyer evaluation method*]
VECTRAN ... [*A*] Programming Language (CSR)
VECX........ Car Nicobar [*India*] [*ICAO location identifier*] (ICLI)
VED .... Vacuum Energy Diverter
VED .... Vacuum Erection Device [*Medicine*]
VED .... Ventricular Ectopic Depolarization
VED .... Viscoelastic Damper
VED .... Volumetric Energy Density [*of fuels*]
VEDA .... Vestibular Disorders Association (EA)
VEDAR ..... Visible Energy Detection and Ranging

Veda Tech Mladezi ... Veda a Technika Mladezi [*Czechoslovakia*] [*A publication*]
Veda Tech SSSR ... Veda a Technika v SSSR [*A publication*]
Veda Vyzk Potravin Prum ... Veda a Vyzkum v Potravinarskem Prumyslu [*A publication*]
Veda Vyzk Prum Sklarskem ... Veda a Vyzkum v Prumyslu Sklarskem [*A publication*]
Veda Vyzk Prum Text ... Veda a Vyzkum v Prumyslu Textilnim [*A publication*]
VEDB .... Dhanbad [*India*] [*ICAO location identifier*] (ICLI)
VEDC .... Vitreous Enamel Development Council [*British*] (DI)
VEDIC....... Video-Enhanced Differential Interference Contrast [*Microscopy*]
Ved Kes ..... Vedanta Kesari [*Madras*] [*A publication*]
VeDo .... Verbum Domino [*A publication*]
VEDR .... Value Engineering Design Review
VEDS........ Vehicle Emergency Detection System [*NASA*] (KSC)
VEDS........ Vocational Education Data System
Ved Svet .... Vedecky Svet [*A publication*]
VEDZ .... Deparizo [*India*] [*ICAO location identifier*] (ICLI)
VEE .... Vagina, Ectocervix, and Endocervix [*Cytopathology*]
VEE .... Veeco Instruments, Inc. [*NYSE symbol*] (SPSG)
VEE .... Venetie [*Alaska*] [*Airport symbol*] (OAG)
VEE .... Venezuelan Equine Encephalomyelitis [*Virus*]
Veeartsenijk Blad Nederl-Indie ... Veeartsenijkundige Bladen voor Nederlandsch-Indie [*A publication*]
VEECO...... Vacuum Electronics Engineering Co. (MCD)
VEED .... Veeco Instruments, Inc. [*NASDAQ symbol*] (NQ)
VEEG .... Vector Electroencephalograph
VEEGA ..... Venus-Earth-Earth-Gravity-Assist [*Spacecraft trajectory*]
VEEI.......... Vehicle Electrical Engine Interface [*NASA*] (NASA)
VEEI.......... Vehicle Electronics Engineering Institute
VEEP........ Vice President
VEER........ Variable Emergence Electronically Rotated (MCD)
VEESS...... Vehicle Engine Exhaust Smoke System [*Army*] (RDA)
Veeteelt Zuivelber ... Veeteelt- en Zuivelberichten [*A publication*]
VEF........... Variable Electronic Filter
VEF........... Viscoelastic Fiber
VEF........... Viscoelastic Flow
VEF........... Vision Educational Foundation (EA)
VEF........... Visually Evoked Field [*Neurophysiology*]
VEFCA ..... Value Engineering Functional Cost Analysis
VEFCO...... Vertical Function Checkout
VEF Inf Bul ... VEF [*Victorian Employers' Federation*] Information Bulletin [*A publication*] (APTA)
VEG .... Maikwak [*Guyana*] [*Airport symbol*] (OAG)
VEG .... Value Engineering Guideline
Veg .... Vega [*Record label*] [*France*]
VEG .... Vegetable [*or Vegetation*] (KSC)
VEGA .... Vega Biotechnologies, Inc. [*NASDAQ symbol*] (NQ)
VEGA .... Venera [*Venus*] and Gallei [*Halley*] [*Russian spacecraft*]
VEGANET ... Vegetarian Awareness Network (EA)
Veg Crops Ser Calif Univ Dept Veg Crops ... Vegetable Crops Series. California University. Department of Vegetable Crops [*A publication*]
Vegetarian Mo ... Vegetarian Monthly [*A publication*] (APTA)
Veg Ex .... Vegetable Exchange [*Dietetics*]
VEGG .... Ventura Entertainment Group, Ltd. [*NASDAQ symbol*] (NQ)
Veg Grower ... Vegetable Grower [*A publication*] (APTA)
Veg Grow News ... Vegetable Growers News [*A publication*]
VEGIL....... Vehicle Equipment and Government-Furnished Infrared Locator
VEGK .... Gorakhpur [*India*] [*ICAO location identifier*] (ICLI)
VEGL........ Value Engineering Guideline
Veg Situat TVS US Dep Agric Econ Res Serv ... Vegetable Situation. United States Department of Agriculture. Economic Research [*A publication*]
VEGT .... Gauhati [*India*] [*ICAO location identifier*] (ICLI)
Veg Times ... Vegetarian Times [*A publication*]
VEGY .... Gaya [*India*] [*ICAO location identifier*] (ICLI)
Vegyip Kut Intez Kozl ... Vegyipari Kutato Intezetek Kozlemenyei [*A publication*]
VEH.......... Emory and Henry College, Emory, VA [*OCLC symbol*] (OCLC)
VEH.......... Valence Effective Hamiltonian [*Physical chemistry*]
VEH.......... Vehicle (AFM)
VEH.......... Veterinary Evacuation Hospital
vehic .... Vehiculum [*Vehicle*] [*Latin*] (MAE)
VEHID ...... Vehicle Identification [*NASA*] (MCD)
VEHK .... Hirakud [*India*] [*ICAO location identifier*] (ICLI)
Veh News Ltr ... Experimental Vehicle Newsletter [*A publication*]
Veh Syst Dyn ... Vehicle System Dynamics [*A publication*]
VEI........... Value Engineered Indicator (NG)
VEI........... Value Engineering Incentive [*Office of Federal Procurement Policy*]
VEI........... Vehicle End Item (NASA)
VEI........... Volcanic Explosivity Index [*Measure of amounts of gas and ash that reach the atmosphere*]
VEIM........ Imphal [*India*] [*ICAO location identifier*] (ICLI)
VEIS .... Vocational Education Information System
VEITA .... Vietnam Era Veterans Inter-Tribal Association (EA)

VEJ............ DHZ Markt. Vakblad voor de Doe het Zelf Ondernemer [*A publication*]
VEJH........ Jharsuguda [*India*] [*ICAO location identifier*] (ICLI)
VEJP........ Jeypore [*India*] [*ICAO location identifier*] (ICLI)
VEJS........ Jamshedpur [*India*] [*ICAO location identifier*] (ICLI)
VEJT .... Jorhat [*India*] [*ICAO location identifier*] (ICLI)
VEK .... Veterana Esperantista Klubo [*Esperantist Club of Veterans - ECV*] (EAIO)
VEKH .... Katihar [*India*] [*ICAO location identifier*] (ICLI)
VEKJ .... Keonjhar [*India*] [*ICAO location identifier*] (ICLI)
VEKM .... Kamalpur [*India*] [*ICAO location identifier*] (ICLI)
VEKN .... Konark [*India*] [*ICAO location identifier*] (ICLI)
VEKR........ Kailashahar [*India*] [*ICAO location identifier*] (ICLI)
VEKU .... Silchar/Kumbhirgram [*India*] [*ICAO location identifier*] (ICLI)
VEKW .... Khowai [*India*] [*ICAO location identifier*] (ICLI)
VEL........... Vehicle Emissions and Fuel Economy Laboratory [*Texas A & M University*] [*Research center*] (RCD)
VEL........... Vehicular Electronics Laboratory
Vel............. Vela [*Constellation*]
VEL........... Vellum
VEL........... Velocity (AFM)
Vel............. Veltro' [*A publication*]
VEL........... Vernal [*Utah*] [*Airport symbol*] (OAG)
VEL........... Virginia Electric & Power Co. [*NYSE symbol*] (SPSG)
VELARC ... Vertical Ejection Launch Aero-Reaction Control (MCD)
VELC........ Velcro Industries NV [*NASDAQ symbol*] (NQ)
VELCOR... Velocity Correction
VELCRO ... Velour and Crochet [*Interlocking nylon tapes - one with tiny loops, the other with tiny hooks - invented as a reusable fastener by George de Mestral*]
VELES....... Vibrational Energy Loss Electron Spectroscopy
VELF .... Velocity Filter (IEEE)
VELG........ Velocity Gain (AAG)
Vell Pat ...... Velleius Paterculus [*First century AD*] [*Classical studies*] (OCD)
Vel Lt Trap ... Velvet Light Trap [*A publication*]
VELOC...... Velocity
VELR........ Lilabari/North Lakhimpur [*India*] [*ICAO location identifier*] (ICLI)
vel sim .... Vel Similis [*Or Similar*] [*Latin*] (WGA)
VELXF ...... Velvet Exploration Co. Ltd. [*NASDAQ symbol*] (NQ)
VEM .... Eastern Mennonite College, Harrisonburg, VA [*OCLC symbol*] (OCLC)
VEM .... Value Engineering Model (NG)
VEM .... Vasoexcitor Material [*Physiology*]
VEM .... Vendor Engineering Memorandum (MCD)
VEM .... Versatile Exercise Mine [*Navy*] [*British*]
VEM .... Vertical Extent of Mortality [*Intertidal organisms*]
VEM .... Virtual Electrode Model (OA)
Vema Res Ser ... Vema Research Series [*A publication*]
VEMASID ... Vehicle Magnetic Signature Duplicator (MCD)
VEMH .... Malda [*India*] [*ICAO location identifier*] (ICLI)
VEMN .... Mohanbari [*India*] [*ICAO location identifier*] (ICLI)
VEMS........ Vehicle and Equipment Maintenance System [*Software*]
VEMZ .... Mazuffarpur [*India*] [*ICAO location identifier*] (ICLI)
VEN .... Hawaiian Sky Tours [*Honolulu, HI*] [*FAA designator*] (FAAC)
VEN .... Variable Exhaust Nozzle
Ven............. Vendome [*Record label*] [*France*]
VEN .... Venerable
VEN .... Venetian
VEN .... Venezuela [*ANSI three-letter standard code*] (CNC)
VEN .... Venice [*Italy*] [*Seismograph station code, US Geological Survey*] [*Closed*] (SEIS)
VEN .... Venite [*95th Psalm*]
VEN .... Venture [*A publication*]
VEN .... Venture Gold Corp. [*Vancouver Stock Exchange symbol*]
VEN .... Venture Science Fiction [*A publication*]
VEN .... Venture Stores, Inc. [*NYSE symbol*] (SPSG)
Ven............. Venus and Adonis [*Shakespearean work*]
VenAmCham ... Venezuelan-American Chamber of Commerce and Industry (EA)
Vencor........ Vencor, Inc. [*Associated Press abbreviation*] (APAG)
Vend.......... Vending Times [*A publication*]
Vend .... Vending Times International Buyers Guide and Directory [*A publication*]
VEND....... Vendor (KSC)
VEND....... Venerated
VENDAC .. Vendor Data Control
Vend Intnl ... Vending International [*A publication*]
VENET...... Venetian (ROG)
VEN EX..... Venditione Exponas [*Writ of Execution for Sheriff to Sell Goods*] [*Latin*] (ROG)
VENEZ...... Venezuela
Venez Dir Geol Bol Geol ... Venezuela. Direccion de Geologia. Boletin de Geologia [*A publication*]
Venez Dir Geol Bol Geol Publ Esp ... Venezuela. Direccion de Geologia. Boletin de Geologia. Publicacion Especial [*A publication*]
Venez Inst Nac Nutr Publ ... Venezuela. Instituto Nacional de Nutricion. Publicacion [*A publication*]

Venez Min Minas Hidrocarburos Dir Geol Bol Geol ... Venezuela. Ministerio de Minas e Hidrocarburos. Direccion de Geologia. Boletin de Geologia [*A publication*]
Venez Odontol ... Venezuela Odontologica [*A publication*]
Venez UTD ... Venezuela Up-to-Date [*A publication*]
VEN FA..... Venire Facias [*Writ to Sheriff to Summon Jury*] [*Latin*] (ROG)
Vengarskaya Farmakoter ... Vengarskaya Farmakoterapiya [*A publication*]
VENP .... Nawapara [*India*] [*ICAO location identifier*] (ICLI)
VENP .... Vincristine, Endoxan [*Cyclophosphamide*], Natulan [*Procarbazine*], Prednisone [*Antineoplastic drug regimen*]
VenPK........ Venizelikon Phileleftheron Komma [*Venizelist Liberal Party*] [*Greek*] [*Political party*] (PPE)
VENR .... Veneer
VenSt .... Venture Stores, Inc. [*Associated Press abbreviation*] (APAG)
VENT .... Ventilation (AFM)
VENT .... Ventilator
VENT .... Ventricular [*Cardiology*]
VENT .... Ventriloquist
Vent........... Ventris' English Common Pleas Reports [*86 English Reprint*] [*A publication*] (DLA)
Vent........... Ventris' English King's Bench Reports [*A publication*] (DLA)
VENT .... Venturian Corp. [*NASDAQ symbol*] (NQ)
Vent Cap Invest ... Venture Capital Investment [*A publication*]
Vent (Eng) ... Ventris' English Common Pleas Reports [*86 English Reprint*] [*A publication*] (DLA)
Vent (Eng) ... Ventris' English King's Bench Reports [*A publication*] (DLA)
VENT FIB ... Ventricular Fibrillation [*Also, VF, VFIB*] [*Cardiology*] (AAMN)
Vent Forth ... Venture Forth [*A publication*]
Vent Kond Vozdukha Zdanii ... Ventilyatsiya i Konditsionirovanie Vozdukha Zdanii [*A publication*]
Vent Kond Vozdukha Zdanii Sooruzh ... Ventilyatsiya i Konditsionirovanie Vozdukha Zdanii Sooruzhenii [*A publication*]
Vent Ochistka Vozdukha ... Ventilyatsiya i Ochistka Vozdukha [*A publication*]
ventr .... Ventral
Ventr .... Ventris' English Common Pleas Reports [*86 English Reprint*] [*A publication*] (DLA)
Ventr Dev... News from Venture Development Corp. [*A publication*]
ventric .... Ventricular
Vent Shakht Rudn ... Ventilyatsiya Shakht i Rudnikov [*A publication*]
VentSt .... Venture Stores, Inc. [*Associated Press abbreviation*] (APAG)
Venul.......... Venuleius Saturninus [*Flourished, 2nd century*] [*Authority cited in pre-1607 legal work*] (DSA)
VENUS...... Valuable and Effective Network Utility Services (BUR)
VENUS...... Video-Enhanced User System [*Video conferencing*]
VENUS...... Vulcain Experimental Nuclear Study [*Nuclear reactor*] [*Belgium*]
Venus Jpn J Malacol ... Venus: The Japanese Journal of Malacology [*A publication*]
VEO .... Value Engineering Organization
VEO .... Veronex Resources Ltd. [*Vancouver Stock Exchange symbol*]
VEO .... Visual Emission Observation [*Environmental Protection Agency*] (GFGA)
VEOP .... Veterans Education Outreach Program [*Department of Education*] (GFGA)
VEOS........ Versatile Electro-Optical System (MCD)
VEP........... Value Engineering Program
VEP........... Value Engineering Proposal [*Army*] (RDA)
VEP........... Vector Equilibrium Principle [*Crystallography*]
VEP........... Verpakken. Het Vakblad voor de Verpakkende Industrie en Verpakkingsindustrie [*A publication*]
VEP........... Vertical Extrusion Press
VEP........... Veterans Education Project (EA)
VEP........... Visual Evoked Potential [*Electrophysiology*]
VEP........... Visually Evoked Potential [*Neurophysiology*]
VEP........... Vocational Exploration Program [*Office of Youth Programs*]
VEP........... Voter Education Project (EA)
VEPA......... Vincristine, Endoxan [*Cyclophosphamide*], Prednisone, Adriamycin [*Antineoplastic drug regimen*]
VEPA......... Vocational Education Planning Areas (OICC)
VEPB........ Port Blair [*India*] [*ICAO location identifier*] (ICLI)
VEPCO...... Virginia Electric & Power Co.
VEPG........ Pasighat [*India*] [*ICAO location identifier*] (ICLI)
VEPG........ Value Engineering Program Guideline
VEPH .... Panagarh [*India*] [*ICAO location identifier*] (ICLI)
VEPIS........ Vocational Education Program Information System
VEPL......... Vendor Engineering Procurement Liaison (MCD)
VEPM........ Value Engineering Program Manager [*Military*] (AABC)
VEPN .... Phulbani [*India*] [*ICAO location identifier*] (ICLI)
VEPOL...... Vehicular Planimetric Dead Reckoning Computer Operating Language
VEPP .... Padampur [*India*] [*ICAO location identifier*] (ICLI)
VEPR........ Value Engineering Program Requirement [*Office of Federal Procurement Policy*] (NG)
VEPT .... Patna [*India*] [*ICAO location identifier*] (ICLI)
VEQ .... Visiting Enlisted Quarters [*Army*] (AABC)
VEQUD..... Veterinary Quarterly [*A publication*]
VER .... Boonville, MO [*Location identifier*] [*FAA*] (FAAL)
VER .... Veracruz [*Mexico*] [*Airport symbol*] (OAG)
VER .... Verandah [*Classified advertising*] (ADA)

VER .... Verapamil [*A coronary vasodilator*]
VeR .... Verbum (Rio De Janeiro) [*A publication*]
VER .... Verein [*Association*] [*German*]
Ver .... Vereniging [*Association*] [*Dutch*]   (ILCA)
VER .... Verfkroniek [*A publication*]
VER .... Verge   (ROG)
VER .... Verify   (AFM)
VER .... Verit Industries [*AMEX symbol*]   (SPSG)
Ver .... Veritas [*A publication*]
VER .... Vermifuge [*Destroying Worms*] [*Pharmacy*]   (ROG)
VER .... Vermilion   (ROG)
VER .... Vermillion Resources [*Vancouver Stock Exchange symbol*]
VER .... Vermont   (ROG)
Ver .... Vermont Reports [*A publication*]   (DLA)
VER .... Vernier [*Engine*]   (AAG)
Ver .... Verri [*A publication*]
VER .... Verse
VER .... Version   (ROG)
Ver .... Versty [*A publication*]
VER .... Vert [*Heraldry*]
VER .... Vertex   (WGA)
VER .... Vertical   (KSC)
VER .... Vertical Earth Rate
VER .... Vertical Ejector Rack   (MCD)
VER .... Verwaltungsfuehrung Organisation Personalwesen [*A publication*]
VER .... Veterans Employment Representative [*Department of Labor*]
VER .... Visual Evoked Response
VER .... Voluntary Export Restraints
VERA .... Ranuna [*India*] [*ICAO location identifier*]   (ICLI)
VERA .... Variable Eddington Radiation Approximation   (MCD)
VERA .... Versatile Experimental Reactor Assembly   (DEN)
VERA .... Veterans' Employment and Readjustment Act of 1972
VERA .... Vision Electric Recording Apparatus [*BBC*]
VERAD9 ... Veterinary Radiology [*A publication*]
VERAS ...... Vehicule Experimental de Recherches Aerothermodynamique et Structurale [*Glider*] [*France*]
VERB........ Verbatim   (MSA)
VERB........ Verbessert [*Improved*] [*German*]
VERB........ Victor Electrowriter Remote Blackboard [*Educational device of Victor Comptometer Corp.*]
Verb C........ Verbum Caro [*A publication*]
VERB ET LIT ... Verbatim et Literatim [*Word for Word, An Exact Copy*] [*Latin*]   (ROG)
Ver Bibl Landes NRW Mitt ... Verband der Bibliotheken des Landes Nordrhein-Westfalen. Mitteilungsblatt [*A publication*]
Ver Bl......... Verordeningblad voor het Bezette Nederlandse Gebied [*A publication*]
Verb Sap .... Verbum Sapienti Sat Est [*A Word to the Wise Is Sufficient*] [*Latin*]
VERC......... Ranchi [*India*] [*ICAO location identifier*]   (ICLI)
VERC......... Vacation Eligibility and Request Card [*Military*]
VERC......... Vehicle Effectiveness Remaining Converter
VERDAN .. Versatile Differential Analyzer
Ver Destill Ztg ... Vereinigte Destillateur-Zeitungen [*A publication*]
VERDIN.... Antijam MODEM [*Modulate, Demodulate*], Very-Low Frequency   (CAAL)
Verdi Newsl ... Verdi Newsletter [*A publication*]
VERDT...... Verdict   (ROG)
Ver Dtsch Ing Z Fortschr Ber Reihe 5 ... Verein Deutscher Ingenieure. Zeitschriften. Fortschritt-Berichte. Reihe 5. Grund- und Werkstoffe [*A publication*]
VERDUP... Verify Duplication   (DNAB)
Vereinigung Schweizer Petroleum-Geologen u Ingenieure Bull ... Vereinigung Schweizerischer Petroleum-Geologen und Ingenieure. Bulletin [*A publication*]
Ver Erdk Dresden Mitt ... Verein fuer Erdkunde zu Dresden. Mitteilungen [*A publication*]
Ver Erdk Leipzig Mitt ... Verein fuer Erdkunde zu Leipzig. Mitteilungen [*A publication*]
Ver Exploit Proefzuivelboerderij Hoorn Versl ... Vereniging tot Exploitatie eener Proefzuivelboerderij te Hoorn. Verslag [*A publication*]
Verfahrenstech ... Verfahrenstechnik International [*A publication*]
Verfass Recht Uebersee ... Verfassung und Recht in Uebersee [*A publication*]
Verfassung u -Wirklichkeit ... Verfassung und Verfassungswirklichkeit [*A publication*]
Verfinst TNO Circ ... Verfinstituut TNO [*Nederlands Centrale Organisatie voor Toegepast - Natuurwetenschappelijk Onderzoek*] Circulaire [*A publication*]
Ver Freunde Naturg Mecklenberg Arch ... Verein der Freunde der Naturgeschichte in Mecklenberg. Archiv [*A publication*]
Ver Freunden Erdk Leipzig Jber ... Verein von Freunden der Erdkunde zu Leipzig. Jahresbericht [*A publication*]
VERG .... Rayaguda [*India*] [*ICAO location identifier*]   (ICLI)
Verg............ Vergil [*First century BC*] [*Classical studies*]   (OCD)
Ver f d Gesch Berlins Schr ... Verein fuer die Geschichte Berlins. Schriften [*A publication*]
Ver f Gesch Dresdens Mitt ... Verein fuer Geschichte Dresdens. Mitteilungen [*A publication*]
VERGL....... Vergleische [*Compare*] [*German*]   (ROG)

Verh Anat Ges ... Verhandlungen. Anatomische Gesellschaft [*A publication*]
Verhandl Deutsch Path Gesellsch ... Verhandlungen. Deutsche Pathologische Gesellschaft [*A publication*]
Verhandl Deutsch Zool Gesellsch ... Verhandlungen. Deutsche Zoologische Gesellschaft [*A publication*]
Verhandl DPG ... Verhandlungen. Deutsche Physikalische Gesellschaft [*Stuttgart*] [*A publication*]
Verhandl Geol Bundesanstalt ... Verhandlungen. Geologische Bundesanstalt [*A publication*]
Verhandl Gesellsch Deutsch Naturf u Aerzte ... Verhandlungen. Gesellschaft Deutscher Naturforscher und Aerzte [*A publication*]
Verhandl Naturw Ver Hamburg ... Verhandlungen. Naturwissenschaftlicher Verein in Hamburg [*A publication*]
Verhandl Naturw Ver Karlsruhe ... Verhandlungen. Naturwissenschaftlicher Verein in Karlsruhe [*A publication*]
Verhandlungsber Kolloid-Ges ... Verhandlungsberichte. Kolloid-Gesellschaft [*A publication*]
VerhBer Dt Zool Ges ... Verhandlungsbericht. Deutsche Zoologische Gesellschaft [*A publication*]
Verh Bot Ver Prov Brandenb ... Verhandlungen. Botanischer Verein der Provinz Brandenburg [*A publication*]
Verh Dt Ges Angew Ent ... Verhandlungen. Deutsche Gesellschaft fuer Angewandte Entomologie [*A publication*]
Verh Dtsch Ges Angew Entomol ... Verhandlungen. Deutsche Gesellschaft fuer Angewandte Entomologie [*A publication*]
Verh Dtsch Ges Exp Med ... Verhandlungen. Deutsche Gesellschaft fuer Experimentelle Medizin [*A publication*]
Verh Dtsch Ges Inn Med ... Verhandlungen. Deutsche Gesellschaft fuer Innere Medizin [*A publication*]
Verh Dtsch Ges Kreislaufforsch ... Verhandlungen. Deutsche Gesellschaft fuer Kreislaufforschung [*A publication*]
Verh Dtsch Ges Pathol ... Verhandlungen. Deutsche Gesellschaft fuer Pathologie [*A publication*]
Verh Dtsch Ges Rheumatol ... Verhandlungen. Deutsche Gesellschaft fuer Rheumatologie [*A publication*]
Verh Dtsch Phys Ges ... Verhandlungen. Deutsche Physikalische Gesellschaft [*A publication*]
Verh Dtsch Zool Ges ... Verhandlungen. Deutsche Zoologische Gesellschaft [*A publication*]
Verh Dt Zool Ges Bonn ... Verhandlungen. Deutsche Zoologische Gesellschaft in Bonn [*Rhein*] [*A publication*]
Verh Dt Zool Ges Erlangen ... Verhandlungen. Deutsche Zoologische Gesellschaft in Erlangen [*A publication*]
Verh Dt Zool Ges Frankfurt ... Verhandlungen. Deutsche Zoologische Gesellschaft in Frankfurt [*A publication*]
Verh Dt Zool Ges Goett ... Verhandlungen. Deutsche Zoologische Gesellschaft in Goettingen [*A publication*]
Verh Dt Zool Ges Graz ... Verhandlungen. Deutsche Zoologische Gesellschaft in Graz [*A publication*]
Verh Dt Zool Ges Hamburg ... Verhandlungen. Deutsche Zoologische Gesellschaft in Hamburg [*A publication*]
Verh Dt Zool Ges Jena ... Verhandlungen. Deutsche Zoologische Gesellschaft in Jena [*A publication*]
Verh Dt Zool Ges (Kiel) ... Verhandlungen. Deutsche Zoologische Gesellschaft (Kiel) [*A publication*]
Verh Dt Zool Ges (Tuebingen) ... Verhandlungen. Deutsche Zoologische Gesellschaft (Tuebingen) [*A publication*]
Verh Dt Zool Ges (Wien) ... Verhandlungen. Deutsche Zoologische Gesellschaft (Wien) [*A publication*]
Verh Dt Zool Ges (Wilhelmshaven) ... Verhandlungen. Deutsche Zoologische Gesellschaft (Wilhelmshaven) [*A publication*]
Verh Geol Bundesanst ... Verhandlungen. Geologische Bundesanstalt [*A publication*]
Verh Geol Bundesanst Bundeslaenderser ... Verhandlungen. Geologische Bundesanstalt. Bundeslaenderserie [*A publication*]
Verh Ges Dsch Naturfrsch Aerzte ... Verhandlungen. Gesellschaft Deutscher Naturforscher und Aerzte [*A publication*]
Verh Hist Nied Bay ... Verhandlungen. Historischer Vereine von Niederbayern [*A publication*]
Verh Hist Oberpfalz ... Verhandlungen. Historischer Vereine von Oberpfalz und Regensburg [*A publication*]
Verh Inst Praev Geneeskd ... Verhandelingen. Instituut voor Praeventieve Geneeskunde [*A publication*]
Verh Int Psychother Kongr ... Verhandlungen. Internationaler Psychotherapie Kongress [*A publication*]
Ver Hist ..... Verae Historiae [*of Lucian*] [*Classical studies*]   (OCD)
Verh K Acad Geneeskd Belg ... Verhandelingen. Koninklijke Academie voor Geneeskunde van Belgie [*A publication*]
Verh K Acad Wet Lett & Schone Kunsten Belg ... Verhandelingen. Koninklijke Academie voor Wetenschappen. Letteren en Schone Kunsten van Belgie [*A publication*]
Verh K Acad Wet Lett Schone Kunsten Belg Kl Wet ... Verhandelingen. Koninklijke Academie voor Wetenschappen. Letteren en Schone Kunsten van Belgie. Klasse der Wetenschappen [*A publication*]
Verh K Akad Wet Amsterdam Afd Natuurkd ... Verhandelingen. Koninklijke Akademie van Wetenschappen te Amsterdam. Afdeeling Natuurkunde [*A publication*]
Verh K Ned Akad Wet Afd Natuurkd Reeks 1 ... Verhandelingen. Koninklijke Nederlandse Akademie van Wetenschappen. Afdeling Natuurkunde. Reeks 1 [*A publication*]

Verh K Ned Akad Wet Afd Natuurkd Reeks 2 ... Verhandelingen. Koninklijke Nederlandse Akademie van Wetenschappen. Afdeling Natuurkunde. Reeks 2 [*A publication*]
Verh K Ned Akad Wet Afd Natuurkd Tweede Reeks ... Verhandelingen. Koninklijke Nederlandse Akademie van Wetenschappen. Afdeling Natuurkunde. Tweede Reeks [*A publication*]
Verh K Ned Akad Wetensch Afd Natuurk Reeks 1 ... Verhandelingen. Koninklijke Nederlandse Akademie van Wetenschappen. Afdeling Natuurkunde. Reeks 1 [*Netherlands*] [*A publication*]
Verh K Ned Akad Wetensch Afd Natuurk Reeks 2 ... Verhandelingen. Koninklijke Nederlandse Akademie van Wetenschappen. Afdeling Natuurkunde. Reeks 2 [*Netherlands*] [*A publication*]
Verh K Ned Geol Mijnbouwkd Genoot ... Verhandelingen. Koninklijke Nederlands Geologisch Mijnbouwkundig Genootschap [*A publication*]
Verh K Ned Geol Mijnbouwkd Genoot Geol Ser ... Verhandelingen. Koninklijke Nederlandse Geologisch Mijnbouwkundig Genootschap. Geologische Serie [*A publication*]
Verh K Ned Geol Mijnbouwkd Genoot Mijnbouwkd Ser ... Verhandelingen. Koninklijke Nederlandse Geologisch Mijnbouwkundig Genootschap. Mijnbouwkundige Serie [*A publication*]
Verh Konink Acad Wetensch Belgie ... Verhandelingen. Koninklijke Academie voor Wetenschappen. Letteren en Schone Kunsten van Belgie [*A publication*]
Verh Kon Nederl Ak Wetensch Afd Lett ... Verhandelingen. Koninklijke Nederlandse Akademie van Wetenschappen. Afdeling Letterkunde [*A publication*]
Verh K Vlaam Acad Geneesk Belg ... Verhandelingen. Koninklijke Vlaamse Academie voor Geneeskunde van Belgie [*Belgium*] [*A publication*]
Verh K Vlaam Acad Geneeskd Belg ... Verhandelingen. Koninklijke Vlaamse Academie voor Geneeskunde van Belgie [*A publication*]
Verh K Vlaam Acad Wetensch Belg Kl Wetensch ... Verhandelingen. Koninklijke Vlaamse Academie voor Wetenschappen, Letteren, en Schone Kunsten van Belgie. Klasse der Wetenschappen [*Belgium*] [*A publication*]
Verh K Vlaam Acad Wet Lett Schone Kunsten Belg Kl Wet ... Verhandelingen. Koninklijke Vlaamse Academie voor Wetenschappen, Letteren, en Schone Kunsten van Belgie. Klasse der Wetenschappen [*A publication*]
Verh Naturforsch Ges Basel ... Verhandlungen. Naturforschende Gesellschaft in Basel [*A publication*]
Verh Naturforsch Ver Bruenn ... Verhandlungen. Naturforschender Verein in Bruenn [*A publication*]
Verh Natur-Med Ver Heidelb ... Verhandlungen. Naturhistorisch-Medizinischer Verein zu Heidelberg [*A publication*]
Verh Ornithol Ges Bayern ... Verhandlungen. Ornithologische Gesellschaft in Bayern [*A publication*]
Verh Phys-Med Ges Wuerzb ... Verhandlungen. Physikalisch-Medizinische Gesellschaft in Wuerzburg [*A publication*]
Verh Phys-Med Ges Wuerzburg ... Verhandlungen. Physikalisch-Medizinische Gesellschaft in Wuerzburg [*A publication*]
Verh Rijksinst Natuurbeheer ... Verhandelingen. Rijksinstituut voor Natuurbeheer [*A publication*]
Verh Ver Schweiz Physiol ... Verhandlungen. Verein der Schweizer Physiologen [*A publication*]
Verh Zool-Bot Ges Wien ... Verhandlungen. Zoologisch-Botanische Gesellschaft in Wien [*A publication*]
VERI .... Veritec, Inc. [*Calabasas Park, CA*] [*NASDAQ symbol*]   (NQ)
VERI .... Vineyard Environmental Research Institute [*Research center*]   (RCD)
VERIC .... Vocational Education Resources Information Center
VERIF .... Verification   (MSA)
VERIS .... Vitamin E Research and Information Service   (EA)
VeritCarit... Veritatem in Caritate. Orgaan van de Protestanse Theologische Faculteit te Brussel [*A publication*]   (BJA)
VERK .... Rourkela [*India*] [*ICAO location identifier*]   (ICLI)
Verkehrsmed Grenzgeb ... Verkehrsmedizin und Ihre Grenzgebiete [*A publication*]
Verkehrsmed Ihre Grenzgeb ... Verkehrsmedizin und Ihre Grenzgebiete [*German Democratic Republic*] [*A publication*]
VerkF .... Verkuendigung und Forschung [*Munich*] [*A publication*]
Verksamheten Stift Rasforadl Skogstrad ... Verksamheten. Stiftelsen foer Rasforadling av Skogstrad [*A publication*]
VERL .... Raxaul [*India*] [*ICAO location identifier*]   (ICLI)
VERLORT ... Very-Long-Range Tracking [*NASA*]
VERLOT ... Very-Long-Range Tracking [*NASA*]   (DNAB)
Ver LR .... Vermont Law Review [*A publication*]
VERM .... Vermilion   (ROG)
VERM .... Vermont
Verm .... Vermont Reports [*A publication*]   (DLA)
Vermess-Inf ... Vermessungs-Informationen [*A publication*]
Verm Nox Weeds Destr Board Leafl ... Leaflet. Vermin and Noxious Weeds Destruction Board [*Victoria*] [*A publication*]   (APTA)
Verm Nox Weeds Destrn Bd (Melb) Surv ... Vermin and Noxious Weeds Destruction Board (Melbourne). Survey [*A publication*]   (APTA)
Vermont Bs ... Vermont Business [*A publication*]

Vermont Geol Survey Bull ... Vermont. Geological Survey. Bulletin [*A publication*]
Vermont Lib ... Vermont Libraries [*A publication*]
Vermont L Rev ... Vermont Law Review [*A publication*]
Vermont R ... Vermont Reports [*A publication*]   (DLA)
Vermont Regist Nurse ... Vermont Registered Nurse [*A publication*]
Vermont Rep ... Vermont Reports [*A publication*]   (DLA)
Vermt .... Vermont Reports [*A publication*]   (DLA)
VERN .... Rangeilunda [*India*] [*ICAO location identifier*]   (ICLI)
VERN .... Vernacular   (ADA)
VERN .... Vernier [*Engineering*]
Vern .... Vernon's English Chancery Reports [*23 English Reprint*] [*A publication*]   (DLA)
Vernacular Architect ... Vernacular Architecture [*A publication*]
Vernacular Archre ... Vernacular Architecture [*A publication*]
Vernacular Bldg ... Vernacular Building [*A publication*]
VERNAV... Vertical Navigation System
Vern (Eng) ... Vernon's English Chancery Reports [*23 English Reprint*] [*A publication*]   (DLA)
Verniciature Decor ... Verniciature e Decorazioni [*A publication*]
VERNITRAC ... Vernier Tracking by Automatic Correlation [*Aerospace*]
Vernon's Ann CCP ... Vernon's Annotated Texas Code of Criminal Procedure [*A publication*]   (DLA)
Vernon's Ann Civ St ... Vernon's Annotated Texas Civil Statutes [*A publication*]   (DLA)
Vernon's Ann PC ... Vernon's Annotated Texas Penal Code [*A publication*]   (DLA)
Vern & S .... Vernon and Scriven's Irish King's Bench Reports [*1786-88*] [*A publication*]   (DLA)
Vern & Sc... Vernon and Scriven's Irish King's Bench Reports [*1786-88*] [*A publication*]   (DLA)
Vern & Scr ... Vernon and Scriven's Irish King's Bench Reports [*1786-88*] [*A publication*]   (DLA)
Vern & Scriv ... Vernon and Scriven's Irish King's Bench Reports [*1786-88*] [*A publication*]   (DLA)
Vern & S (Ir) ... Vernon and Scriven's Irish King's Bench Reports [*1786-88*] [*A publication*]   (DLA)
Veroeff Bundesanst Alp Landwirtsch Admont ... Veroeffentlichungen. Bundesanstalt fuer Alpine Landwirtschaft in Admont [*A publication*]
Veroeff Dtsch Geod Komm Reihe A ... Veroeffentlichungen. Deutsche Geodaetiske Kommission. Bayerische Akademie der Wissenschaften. Reihe A [*West Germany*] [*A publication*]
Veroeffentl Leibniz-Archivs ... Veroeffentlichungen. Leibniz-Archiv [*A publication*]
Veroeff Geobot Inst Eidg Tech Hochsch Stift Ruebel Zuer ... Veroeffentlichungen. Geobotanisches Institut. Eidgenoessische Technische Hochschule Stiftung Ruebel in Zuerich [*A publication*]
Veroeff Geobot Inst Eidg Tech Hochsch Stift Ruebel Zuerich ... Veroeffentlichungen. Geobotanisches Institut. Eidgenoessische Technische Hochschule Stiftung Ruebel in Zuerich [*A publication*]
Veroeff Geobot Inst Ruebel ... Veroeffentlichungen. Geobotanisches Institut Ruebel [*A publication*]
Veroeff Inst Meeresforsch Bremerhaven ... Veroeffentlichungen. Institut fuer Meeresforschung in Bremerhaven [*A publication*]
Veroeff Inst Meeresforsch Bremerhaven Suppl ... Veroeffentlichungen. Institut fuer Meeresforschung in Bremerhaven. Supplement [*A publication*]
Veroeff Kaiser Wilhelm Inst Silikatforsch Berlin Dahlem ... Veroeffentlichungen. Kaiser-Wilhelm-Institut fuer Silikatforschung in Berlin-Dahlem [*A publication*]
Veroeff Landwirtsch Chem Bundesversuchsanst (Linz) ... Veroeffentlichungen. Landwirtschaftlich-Chemische Bundesversuchsanstalt (Linz) [*A publication*]
Veroeff Meteorol Dienstes DDR ... Veroeffentlichungen. Meteorologischer Dienst. Deutsche Demokratische Republik [*A publication*]
Veroeff Meterol Hydrol Dienstes DDR ... Veroeffentlichungen. Meteorologischer und Hydrologischer Dienst. Deutsche Demokratische Republik [*A publication*]
Veroeff Naturhist Mus (Basel) ... Veroeffentlichungen. Naturhistorischer Museum (Basel) [*A publication*]
Veroeff Naturh Mus (Wien) ... Veroeffentlichungen. Naturhistorischer Museum (Wien) [*A publication*]
Veroeff Reichsgesundheitsamts ... Veroeffentlichungen. Reichsgesundheitsamt [*A publication*]
Veroeff Ueberseemus (Bremen) Reihe A ... Veroeffentlichungen. Ueberseemuseum (Bremen). Reihe A [*A publication*]
Veroeff Wiss Zent Lab Photogr Abt AGFA ... Veroeffentlichungen. Wissenschaftliches Zentral Laboratorium. Photographische Abteilung AGFA [*A publication*]
Veroeff Zentralinst Phys Erde ... Veroeffentlichungen. Zentralinstitut Physik der Erde [*Czechoslovakia*] [*A publication*]
Veroeff Zool Staatssamml (Muench) ... Veroeffentlichungen. Zoologische Staatssammlung (Muenchen) [*A publication*]
Veroeff Zool StSamml (Muench) ... Veroeffentlichungen. Zoologische Staatssammlung (Muenchen) [*A publication*]

Veroff Inst Agrarmet Univ (Leipzig) ... Veroeffentlichungen. Institut fuer Agrarmeteorologie und des Agrarmeteorologischen Observatoriums. Karl Marx-Universitaet (Leipzig) [*A publication*]
Veroff Land-Hauswirtsch Auswertungs-Informationsdienst ... Veroeffentlichungen. Land- und Hauswirtschaftlicher Auswertungs- und Informationsdienst [*A publication*]
VERP .... Vertical Effective Radiated Power (MCD)
Verpack Chemiebetr ... Verpackung im Chemiebetrich [*A publication*]
Verpack Mag ... Verpackungs-Magazin [*A publication*]
Verpack-Rundsch ... Verpackungs-Rundschau [*A publication*]
Verpl Cont ... Verplanck on Contracts [*A publication*] (DLA)
Verpl Ev ..... Verplanck on Evidence [*A publication*] (DLA)
Verr .... In Verrem [*of Cicero*] [*Classical studies*] (OCD)
Ver Rep ...... Vermont Reports [*A publication*] (DLA)
Verre Silic Ind ... Verre et Silicates Industriels [*A publication*]
Verres Refract ... Verres et Refractaires [*A publication*]
Verres Refract Part 1 ... Verres et Refractaires. Part 1. Articles Originaux [*A publication*]
Verres Refract Part 2 ... Verres et Refractaires. Part 2. Documentation [*A publication*]
Verre Text Plast Renf ... Verre Textile, Plastiques Renforces [*France*] [*A publication*]
Verrigtinge Kongr S-Afr Genet Ver ... Verrigtinge van die Kongres van die Suid-Afrikaanse Genetiese Vereniging [*A publication*]
VERS .... Versed Sine [*Engineering*] (KSC)
VERS .... Versicherung [*Insurance*] [*German*] [*Business term*]
VERS .... Version (ROG)
VERSACOMM ... Versatile Contour Measuring Machine (MCD)
VERSAR ... Versar, Inc. [*Associated Press abbreviation*] (APAG)
Ver Schweizer Petroleum-Geologen u Ingenieure Bull ... Vereinigung Schweizerischer Petroleum-Geologen und Ingenieure. Bulletin [*A publication*]
Ver Schweiz Pet-Geol Ing Bull ... Vereinigung Schweizerischer Petroleum-Geologen und Ingenieure. Bulletin [*A publication*]
Vers Landbouwkd Onderz ... Verslagen van Landbouwkundige Onderzoekingen [*A publication*]
Versl Interprov Proeven Proefstn Akkerbouw Lelystad (Neth) ... Verslagen van Interprovinciale Proeven. Proefstation voor de Akkerbouw Lelystad (Netherlands) [*A publication*]
Versl Interprov Proeven Proefstn Akkerbouw (Wageningen) ... Verslagen van Interprovinciale Proeven. Proefstation voor de Akkerbouw (Wageningen) [*A publication*]
Versl Landbouwkd Onderz A ... Verslagen van Landbouwkundige Onderzoekingen A. Rijkslandbouwproefstation en Bodemkundig Instituut te Groningen [*A publication*]
Versl Landbouwkd Onderz (Agric Res Rep) ... Verslagen van Landbouwkundige Onderzoekingen (Agricultural Research Reports) [*A publication*]
Versl Landbouwkd Onderz B ... Verslagen van Landbouwkundige Onderzoekingen B. Bodemikundig Instituut te Groningen [*A publication*]
Versl Landbouwkd Onderz C ... Verslagen van Landbouwkundige Onderzoekingen C. Rijkslandbouwproefstation te Hoorn [*A publication*]
Versl Landbouwkd Onderz E ... Verslagen van Landbouwkundige Onderzoekingen E. Rijkslandbouwproefstation voor Veevoederonderzoek te Wageningen [*A publication*]
Versl Landbouwkd Onderz G ... Verslagen van Landbouwkundige Onderzoekingen G. Onderzoekingen Uitgevoerd in Opdracht van den Algemeenen Nederlandschen Zuivelbond [*A publication*]
Versl Landbouwkd Onderz Rijkslandbouwproefstn ... Verslagen van Landbouwkundige Onderzoekingen der Rijkslandbouwproefstations [*A publication*]
Versl Landbouwk Onderz ... Verslagen van Landbouwkundige Onderzoekingen [*A publication*]
Versl Landbouwk Onderz Cent Lanbouwpubl Landbouwdoc ... Verslagen van Landbouwkundige Onderzoekingen. Centrum voor Landbouwpublikatien en Landbouwdocumentatie [*A publication*]
Versl Landbouwk Onderz Ned ... Verslagen van het Landbouwkundig Onderzoek in Nederland [*A publication*]
Versl Meded Kon Vl Ak Taal & Letterk ... Verslagen en Mededeelingen. Koninklijke Vlaamse Akademie voor Taal- en Letterkunde [*A publication*]
Versl Meded K Vlaam Acad Taal Lett ... Verslagen en Mededeelingen. Koninklijke Vlaamse Academie voor Taal- en Letterkunde [*A publication*]
Versl Meded Rijkslandbouwconsul Westelijk Drenthe ... Verslagen en Mededelingen van het Rijkslandbouwconsulentschap Westelijk Drenthe [*A publication*]
Versl Tien-Jarenplan Graanonderzoek Sticht Nederl Graan-Cent ... Verslagen. Tien-Jarenplan voor Graanonderzoek. Stichting Nederlands Graan-Centrum [*A publication*]
Versl Ver Chem Tech Landbouwkd Advis ... Verslagen der Vereniging van Chemisch-Technischen. Landbouwkundig Adviseurs [*A publication*]
VERSO ...... Reverso [*Left-Hand Page of Open Book*] (ROG)
VERST ...... Versatile
Verstaendliche Wiss ... Verstaendliche Wissenschaft [*A publication*]

Versuchsergeb Bundesanst Pflanzenbau Samenpruefung Wien ... Versuchsergebnisse der Bundesanstalt fuer Pflanzenbau und Samenpruefung in Wien [*A publication*]
Versuchsgrubenges Quartalsh ... Versuchsgrubengesellschaft Quartalshefte [*West Germany*] [*A publication*]
VERT .... Venture Evaluation and Review Technique
Vert .... Vermont Reports [*A publication*] (DLA)
VERT .... Vertebrate
VERT .... Vertical (MCD)
Vert .... Vertical Lights [*Navigation signal*]
VERT .... Vertical Polarization (AFM)
VERT .... Verticom, Inc. [*Sunnyvale, CA*] [*NASDAQ symbol*] (NQ)
VERTAR ... Versatile Test Analysis RADAR (MCD)
VERTCL ... Vertical Clearance (DNAB)
VERTEB ... Vertebrate
Vertebr Hung ... Vertebrata Hungarica [*A publication*]
Vertebr Palasiat ... Vertebrata Palasiatica [*A publication*]
Vertebr Palasiatica ... Vertebrata Palasiatica [*A publication*]
VERTEX ... Vertical Transport and Exchange [*Oceanographic research program*]
VERT-2-EXP ... Vertical Double-Expansion [*Engine*] (DNAB)
VERT-3-EXP ... Vertical Triple-Expansion [*Engine*] (DNAB)
VERT-4-EXP ... Vertical Quadruple-Expansion [*Engine*] (DNAB)
Vert File Ind ... Vertical File Index [*A publication*]
Vert File Index ... Vertical File Index [*A publication*]
VERTIC .... Verification Technology Information Centre [*British*] (CB)
VERTIJET ... Vertical Takeoff and Landing Jet [*Aircraft*]
VERTOL ... Vertical Takeoff and Landing [*Also, VTOL*]
VERTREP ... Vertical Replenishment [*Navy*] (NVT)
VERU .... Rupsi [*India*] [*ICAO location identifier*] (ICLI)
Ver Vaterl Naturk Wuerttemberg Jahresh ... Verein fuer Vaterlaendische Naturkunde in Wuerttemberg. Jahreshefte [*A publication*]
Ver Verbr Naturwiss Kenntnisse Wien Schr ... Verein zur Verbreitung Naturwissenschaftlicher Kenntnisse in Wien. Schriften [*A publication*]
Verwarm Vent ... Verwarming en Ventilatie [*A publication*]
VerwG .... Verwaltungsgericht [*Administrative Court or Tribunal*] [*German*] (ILCA)
VERY .... Vanderbilt Energy Corp. [*NASDAQ symbol*] (NQ)
Verzam Overdruk Plantenziektenk Dienst (Wageningen) ... Verzamelde Overdrukken. Plantenziektenkundige Dienst (Wageningen) [*A publication*]
Verzekerings-Arch ... Verzekerings-Archief [*A publication*]
VES .... Vacuum Evaporator System
VES .... Vapor Extraction System [*Engineering*]
VES .... Variable Elasticity of Substitution [*Industrial production*]
VES .... Variable Explanation Sheet [*Army*]
VES .... Vehicle Ecological System (AAG)
VES .... Vehicle Engagement Simulator (MCD)
VES .... Versailles, OH [*Location identifier*] [*FAA*] (FAAL)
Ves .... Vesey, Senior's, English Chancery Reports [*27, 28 English Reprint*] [*A publication*] (DLA)
VES .... Vesica [*Bladder*] [*Latin*] (ADA)
VES .... Vesicula [*Blister*] [*Latin*] (ADA)
VES .... Vesicular (AAMN)
VES .... Vespere [*In the Evening*] [*Latin*] (ADA)
VES .... Vessel (AABC)
VES .... Vestaur Securities, Inc. [*NYSE symbol*] (SPSG)
VES .... Vestry [*Ecclesiastical*] (WGA)
VES .... Veterans Employment Service [*Later, VETS*] [*of USES*]
VES .... Veterinary Evacuating Station [*British military*] (DMA)
VES .... Victorian Era Series [*A publication*]
VES .... Vieques Air Link, Inc. [*Vieques, PR*] [*FAA designator*] (FAAC)
VES .... Visual Effects Simulator (MCD)
VES .... Visual Efficiency Scale
VES .... Vulcan Engagement Simulator (MCD)
VESA .... Video Electronics Standards Association
VESADE ... Elektronmikroskopievereniging van Suidelike Afrika. Verrigtings [*Electron Microscopy Society of Southern Africa. Proceedings*] [*A publication*]
Ves & B ...... Vesey and Beames' English Chancery Reports [*35 English Reprint*] [*A publication*] (DLA)
Ves & Bea .. Vesey and Beames' English Chancery Reports [*35 English Reprint*] [*A publication*] (DLA)
Ves & Beam ... Vesey and Beames' English Chancery Reports [*35 English Reprint*] [*A publication*] (DLA)
Ves & B (Eng) ... Vesey and Beames' English Chancery Reports [*35 English Reprint*] [*A publication*] (DLA)
VESC .... Vehicle Equipment Safety Commission
VESCA(S) ... Vessels and Cargo
VESCF .... Variable Eletronegativity Self-Consistent Field [*Physics*]
Vesci Akad Navuk BSSR Ser Fiz-Mat Navuk ... Vesci Akademii Navuk BSSR. Seryja Fizika-Matematycnyh Navuk [*A publication*]
Vesci Ak BSSR ... Vesci Akademii Navuk BSSR [*A publication*]
VESDA ...... Very Early Smoke Detection Alarm
VESE .... Value Engineering Staff Engineer
VESG .... Vocational Education Services Grant (OICC)
VESI .... Victor Educational Services Institute [*Educational division of Victor Comptometer Corp.*]
VESIAC ..... Vela Seismic Information Analysis Center (SAA)
Vesic .... Vesicula [*Blister*] [*Latin*]

vesic........... Vesicular
Vesientutkimuslaitoksen Julk ... Vesientutkimuslaitoksen Julkaisuja [*A publication*]
Ves Jr......... Vesey, Junior's, English Chancery Reports [*30-34 English Reprint*] [*A publication*]   (DLA)
Ves Jr (Eng) ... Vesey, Junior's, English Chancery Reports [*30-34 English Reprint*] [*A publication*]   (DLA)
Ves Jr Suppl ... Supplement to Vesey, Junior's, English Chancery Reports, by Hovenden [*34 English Reprint*] [*A publication*]   (DLA)
Ves Jun...... Vesey, Junior's, English Chancery Reports [*30-34 English Reprint*] [*A publication*]   (DLA)
Ves Jun Supp ... Supplement to Vesey, Junior's, English Chancery Reports, by Hovenden [*34 English Reprint*] [*A publication*]   (DLA)
Ves Jun Supp (Eng) ... Supplement to Vesey, Junior's, English Chancery Reports, by Hovenden [*34 English Reprint*] [*A publication*]   (DLA)
Vesn Zavod Geol Geofiz Istraz NR Srb ... Vesnik Zavod za Geoloska i Geofizicka Istrazivanja NR Srbije [*A publication*]
Vesn Zavod Geol Geofiz Istraz Ser A ... Vesnik Zavod za Geoloska i Geofizicka Istrazivanja. Serija A. Geologija [*A publication*]
Vesn Zavod Geol Geofiz Istraz Ser C ... Vesnik Zavod za Geoloska i Geofizicka Istrazivanja. Serija C. Priminjena Geofizika [*A publication*]
VESO........ Vocalization of the Egyptian Syllabic Orthography [*W. F. Albright*] [*A publication*]   (BJA)
VESP........ Value Engineering Supplier Program
Vesp.......... Vespae [*Wasps*] [*of Aristophanes*] [*Classical studies*]   (OCD)
VESP........ Vesper [*Evening*] [*Pharmacy*]
VESP........ Vesper Corp. [*NASDAQ symbol*]   (NQ)
VESPER.... Vehicle Sizing and Performance   (MCD)
VESR........ Vallecitos Experimental Superheat Reactor
VESR........ Value Engineering Study Request   (MCD)
VESS........ Vehicle Exhaust Smoke System   (MCD)
VESS........ Visual Environment Simulation System   (MCD)
Ves Sen...... Vesey, Senior's, English Chancery Reports [*27, 28 English Reprint*] [*A publication*]   (DLA)
Ves Sen Supp ... Supplement to Vesey, Senior's, English Chancery Reports [*28 English Reprint*] [*A publication*]   (DLA)
Ves Sr........ Vesey, Senior's, English Chancery Reports [*27, 28 English Reprint*] [*A publication*]   (DLA)
Ves Sr (Eng) ... Vesey, Senior's, English Chancery Reports [*27, 28 English Reprint*] [*A publication*]   (DLA)
Ves Sr Supp ... Supplement to Vesey, Senior's, English Chancery Reports [*28 English Reprint*] [*1747-56*] [*A publication*]   (DLA)
Ves Sr Supp (Eng) ... Supplement to Vesey, Senior's, English Chancery Reports [*28 English Reprint*] [*A publication*]   (DLA)
Ves Supp.... Supplement to Vesey, Junior's, English Chancery Reports, by Hovenden [*34 English Reprint*] [*1789-1817*] [*A publication*]   (DLA)
VEST........ Vertical Earth Scanning Test   (SAA)
VEST........ Vestibule   (MSA)
VEST........ Vestro Foods, Inc. [*NASDAQ symbol*]   (NQ)
VEST........ Vestry [*Ecclesiastical*]   (ROG)
VEST........ Volunteer Engineers, Scientists, and Technicians [*An association*]
Vest Latv PSR Akad ... Vestis Latvijas Pasomju Socialistikas Republikas Zinatu Akademija [*Riga, USSR*] [*A publication*]
Vestn USSR Acad Med Sci ... Vestnik. USSR Academy of Medical Science [*A publication*]
VestSe........ Vestaur Securities, Inc. [*Associated Press abbreviation*]   (APAG)
Vestsi Akad Navuk BSSR Khim Navuk ... Vestsi Akademii Navuk Belaruskai SSR. Khimichnykh Navuk [*A publication*]
Vestsi Akad Navuk BSSR Ser ... Vestsi Akademii Navuk Belaruskai SSR. Seriya [*A publication*]
Vestsi Akad Navuk BSSR Ser Biyal Navuk ... Vestsi Akademii Navuk Belaruskai SSR. Seryya Biyalagichnykh Navuk [*A publication*]
Vestsi Akad Navuk BSSR Ser Fiz-Ehnerg Navuk ... Vestsi Akademii Navuk BSSR. Seryya Fizika-Ehnergetychnykh Navuk [*A publication*]
Vestsi Akad Navuk BSSR Ser Fiz-Mat ... Vestsi Akademii Navuk BSSR. Seriya Fizika-Matematicheskikh [*A publication*]
Vestsi Akad Navuk BSSR Ser Fiz-Mat Navuk ... Vestsi Akademii Navuk BSSR. Seryya Fizika-Matematychnykh Navuk [*A publication*]
Vestsi Akad Navuk BSSR Ser Fiz-Tekh Navuk ... Vestsi Akademii Navuk BSSR. Seryya Fizika-Tekhnichnykh Navuk [*A publication*]
Vestsi Akad Navuk BSSR Ser Gramadskikh Navuk ... Vestsi Akademii Navuk BSSR. Seryya Gramadskikh Navuk [*Belorussian SSR*] [*A publication*]
Vestsi Akad Navuk BSSR Ser Khim ... Vestsi Akademii Navuk BSSR. Seriya Khimicheskikh [*Former USSR*] [*A publication*]
Vestsi Akad Navuk BSSR Ser Khim Navuk ... Vestsi Akademii Navuk Belaruskai SSR. Seryya Khimichnykh Navuk [*A publication*]
Vestsi Akad Navuk BSSR Ser Sel'skagas Navuk ... Vestsi Akademii Navuk Belaruskai SSR. Seryya Sel'skagaspadar Navuk [*A publication*]

Vestsi Belarus Akad Navuk Ser Biyal Navuk ... Vestsi Belaruskaya Akademiya Navuk. Seryya Biyalagichnykh Navuk [*A publication*]
Vestsyi Akad Navuk BSSR Ser Fyiz-Ehnerg Navuk ... Vestsyi Akademhyiyi Navuk BSSR. Seryya Fyizyika-Ehnergetychnykh Navuk [*A publication*]
Vestsyi Akad Navuk BSSR Ser Fyiz-Mat Navuk ... Vestsyi Akademhyiyi Navuk BSSR. Seryya Fyizyika-Matehmatychnykh Navuk [*A publication*]
Vestsyi Akad Navuk BSSR Ser Fyiz-Tehkh Navuk ... Vestsyi Akademhyiyi Navuk BSSR. Seryya Fyizyika-Tehkhnyichnykh Navuk [*A publication*]
Vestsyi Akad Navuk BSSR Ser Khyim Navuk ... Vestsyi Akademhyiyi Navuk BSSR. Seryya Khyimyichnykh Navuk [*A publication*]
VES UR..... Vesica Urinaria [*Urinary Bladder*]
VESV........ Vesicular Exanthema Swine Virus
Veszpremi Vegyip Egy Tud Ulesszakanak Eloadasai ... Veszpremi Vegyipari Egyetem Tudomanyos Ulesszakanak Eloadasai [*Hungary*] [*A publication*]
Veszprem Koezl ... Veszprem Megyei Muzeumok Koezlemenyei [*A publication*]
Veszprem Megyei Muz ... Veszprem Megyei Muzeumok Koezlemenyei [*A publication*]
Veszprem Megyei Muz Koezlem ... Veszprem Megyei Muzeumok Koezlemenyei [*A publication*]
Veszprmi Vegyip Egy Kozl ... Veszpremi Vegyipari Egyetem Kozlemenyei [*A publication*]
VET .... Care Vet Pharmacy [*Vancouver Stock Exchange symbol*]
VET .... Value Engineering Training
VET .... Vehicle Elapsed Time   (MCD)
VeT .... Ventilatory Threshold [*Cardiology*]
VET .... Verbal Test
V & ET....... Verification and Evaluation Tests   (MCD)
VET .... Versatile Engine Tester
VET .... Vertical Test   (SAA)
VET .... Vestigial Testes [*Anatomy*]
VET .... Veteran   (AFM)
VET .... Veterans Administration, Somerville, NJ [*OCLC symbol*]   (OCLC)
Vet .... Veterinaria [*A publication*]
VET .... Veterinary   (AFM)
VET .... Veterinary Centers of America [*AMEX symbol*]   (SPSG)
VET .... Vibrational Energy Transfer [*LASER*]   (MCD)
v et.............. Vide Etiam [*See Also*] [*Latin*]   (MAE)
VET .... Video Editing Terminal [*Data processing*]
VET .... Vidicon Electron Tube
Vet Anesth ... Veterinary Anesthesia [*A publication*]
Vet Annu..... Veterinary Annual [*A publication*]
Vet Arh ...... Veterinarski Arhiv [*A publication*]
Vet Bull...... Veterinary Bulletin [*A publication*]
Vet Bull (London) ... Veterinary Bulletin (London) [*A publication*]
Vet Bull (Weybridge Eng) ... Veterinary Bulletin (Weybridge, England) [*A publication*]
Vet Cas....... Veterinarsky Casopis [*A publication*]
Vet Cas (Kosice) ... Veterinarsky Casopis (Kosice) [*A publication*]
VetChr .... Vetera Christianorum [*A publication*]
Vet Clin North Am ... Veterinary Clinics of North America [*A publication*]
Vet Clin North Am Equine Pract ... Veterinary Clinics of North America. Equine Practice [*A publication*]
Vet Clin North Am Food Anim Pract ... Veterinary Clinics of North America. Food Animal Practice [*A publication*]
Vet Clin North Am (Large Anim Pract) ... Veterinary Clinics of North America (Large Animal Practice) [*A publication*]
Vet Clin North Am (Small Anim Pract) ... Veterinary Clinics of North America (Small Animal Practice) [*A publication*]
Vet Clin Pathol ... Veterinary Clinical Pathology [*A publication*]
VETDOC... Veterinary Literature Documentation [*Derwent Publications Ltd.*] [*Bibliographic database*] [*London, England*]
Vet Econ..... Veterinary Economics [*A publication*]
Vetensk Publ Tek Hoegsk Helsingfors ... Vetenskapliga Publikationer. Tekniska Hoegskolan i Helsingfors [*A publication*]
Vetensk Soc i Lund Arsbok ... Vetenskaps-Societeten i Lund. Aarsbok [*A publication*]
Vetera Chr ... Vetera Christianorum [*A publication*]
Ve Tes .... Vetus Testamentum [*A publication*]
Vet Espan .. Veterinaria Espanola [*A publication*]
VETF .... Value Engineering Task Force
Vet Glas ...... Veterinarski Glasnik [*A publication*]
Vet Glasn ... Veterinarski Glasnik [*A publication*]
Vet Hist...... Veterinary History Bulletin. Veterinary History Society [*A publication*]
Vet Hum Toxicol ... Veterinary and Human Toxicology [*A publication*]
Vet Immunol Immunopathol ... Veterinary Immunology and Immunopathology [*A publication*]
Vet Insp Annu Inst Vet Insp NSW ... Veterinary Inspector Annual. Institute of Veterinary Inspectors of New South Wales [*A publication*]
Vet Int........ Veteres Intrationes [*A publication*]   (DLA)
Vet Ital........ Veterinaria Italiana [*A publication*]
VETJ .... Tezu [*India*] [*ICAO location identifier*]   (ICLI)
Vet J.......... Veterinary Journal [*A publication*]

Vet J and Ann Comp Path ... Veterinary Journal and Annals of Comparative Pathology [*A publication*]
Vet J (Bratislava) ... Veterinary Journal (Bratislava) [*A publication*]
VETK .... Tarakeshwar [*India*] [*ICAO location identifier*] (ICLI)
Vet Mag ..... Veterinary Magazine [*A publication*]
Vet MB ...... Bachelor of Veterinary Medicine
Vet Med ..... Veterinarni Medicina [*A publication*]
Vet Med ..... Veterinary Medicine [*A publication*]
Vet Med ..... Veterinary Medicine and Small Animal Clinician [*A publication*]
Vet Med Nauki ... Veterinarno Meditsinski Nauki [*A publication*]
Vet Med Nauki (Sofia) ... Veterinarno Meditsinski Nauki (Sofia) [*A publication*]
Vet Med (Prague) ... Veterinarni Medicina (Prague) [*A publication*]
Vet Med (Praha) ... Veterinarni Medicina (Praha) [*A publication*]
Vet Med Rev ... Veterinary Medical Review [*A publication*]
Vet Med/SAC ... Veterinary Medicine and Small Animal Clinician [*A publication*]
Vet Med Sci ... Veterinary Medical Science [*A publication*]
Vet Med Small Anim Clin ... Veterinary Medicine and Small Animal Clinician [*A publication*]
Vet Microbiol ... Veterinary Microbiology [*Netherlands*] [*A publication*]
VETMIS .... Vehicle Technical Management Information System
VETMIS .... Vertical Technical Management Information System (MCD)
Vet Na B ..... Old Natura Brevium [*A publication*] (DLA)
VETNAL ... Veterinariya [*Moscow*] [*A publication*]
Vet N B ...... Vetus Natura Brevium [*A publication*] (DSA)
Vet N Br ..... Old Natura Brevium [*A publication*] (ILCA)
Vet News .... Veterinary News [*A publication*]
Vet Obozr ... Veterinarnoe Obozrienie [*A publication*]
VETP .... Vandenberg Engineering Test Program (SAA)
Vet Parasitol ... Veterinary Parasitology [*A publication*]
Vet Path ..... Veterinary Pathology [*A publication*]
Vet Pathol ... Veterinary Pathology [*A publication*]
Vet Pathol (Suppl) ... Veterinary Pathology. Supplement [*A publication*]
Vet Q .... Veterinary Quarterly [*A publication*]
Vet QQJ Vet Sci ... Veterinary Quarterly. Quarterly Journal of Veterinary Science [*A publication*]
Vet Radiol ... Veterinary Radiology [*A publication*]
Vet Rec .... Veterinary Record [*A publication*]
Vet Res Commun ... Veterinary Research Communications [*A publication*]
Vet Resp Mizhvid Temat Nauk Zb ... Veterinariya Respublikanskyu Mizhvidomchyi Tematychnyi Naukovyi Zbirnyk [*A publication*]
Vet Rev .... Veterinary Review [*A publication*]
VETRONICS ... Vehicle Electronics [*Program*] [*Army*]
Vetro Silic .. Vetro e Silicati [*A publication*]
VETS .... Animed, Inc. [*Roslyn, NY*] [*NASDAQ symbol*] (NQ)
VETS .... Tusra [*India*] [*ICAO location identifier*] (ICLI)
VETS .... Vehicle Electrical Test System (ADA)
VETS .... Vertical Engine Test Stand
VETS .... Veterans' Employment and Training Service [*Department of Labor*]
Vet Sbirka ... Veterinarna Sbirka [*A publication*]
Vet Sbir (Sof) ... Veterinarna Sbirka (Sofia) [*A publication*]
Vet Sb (Sofia) ... Veterinarna Sbirka (Sofia) [*A publication*]
VetSci .... Veterinary Science
Vet Sci Commun ... Veterinary Science Communications [*A publication*]
Vet Stars .... Vets Stars and Stripes for Peace [*A publication*]
Vet Surg ..... Veterinary Surgery [*A publication*]
Vet Surgery ... Veterinary Surgery [*A publication*]
Vett Cens ... De Veterum Censura [*of Dionysius Halicarnassensis*] [*Classical studies*] (OCD)
Vet Test ...... Vetus Testamentum [*A publication*]
Vet Toxicol ... Veterinary Toxicology [*A publication*]
Vet Urug .... Veterinaria Uruguay [*A publication*]
Vetus Test ... Vetus Testamentum [*A publication*]
Vet World .. Veterinary World [*A publication*]
VETX .... Vertex Industries, Inc. [*Clifton, NJ*] [*NASDAQ symbol*] (NQ)
VEU .... Very Extreme Ultraviolet (MCD)
VEUK .... Utkela [*India*] [*ICAO location identifier*] (ICLI)
VEUV .... Very Extreme Ultraviolet (MCD)
VEV .... Barakoma [*Solomon Islands*] [*Airport symbol*] (OAG)
VEV .... Vernier Engine Vibration [*Aerospace*]
VEV .... Verre Oosten. Orgaan van de Landenkamers Verre Oosten [*A publication*]
VEV .... Vietnam Era Veterans (OICC)
VEV .... Vlaams Economisch Verbond
VEV .... Voice-Excited VOCODER
VEVA .... Vereingung der Europaischen Verbande des Automatenwirtschaft [*Federation of European Coin-Machine Associations*] (EAIO)
VEV Ber ..... VEV [*Vlaams Economisch Verband*] Berichten [*A publication*]
VEVERP ... Vietnam Era Veteran Recruitment Program
VEVITA .... Vietnam Era Veterans Inter-Tribal Association (EA)
VEVZ .... Vishakhapatnam [*India*] [*ICAO location identifier*] (ICLI)
VEWAA .... Vocational Evaluation and Work Adjustment Association (EA)
VEWS .... Very Early Warning System
VEWU .... Vietnam Educational Workers' Union [*North Vietnam*]
VEX .... Tioga, ND [*Location identifier*] [*FAA*] (FAAL)
VEXP .... Virtual Machine Experience

VEY .... Vestmannaeyjar [*Iceland*] [*Airport symbol*] (OAG)
Vez .... Vezey's [*or Vesey's*] English Chancery Reports [*A publication*] (DLA)
Vezelinst TNO Delft VI Pam ... Vezelinstituut TNO [*Nederlands Centrale Organisatie voor Toegepast-Natuurwetenschappelijk Onderzoek*] Delft VI Pamflet [*A publication*]
Vezetestud ... Vezetestudomany [*A publication*]
VEZO .... Zero [*India*] [*ICAO location identifier*] (ICLI)
VF .... British Air Ferries Ltd. (FAAC)
VF .... De Vrije Fries [*A publication*]
VF .... Fighter Plane [*Navy symbol*]
VF .... Fighter Squadron [*Navy symbol*]
VF .... Flaps-Down Speed [*Aviation*]
VF .... Valley Forge Corp. [*AMEX symbol*] (SPSG)
VF .... Value Foundation (EA)
VF .... Vaporizer Feed [*Nuclear energy*] (NRCH)
VF .... Variable Factor [*Economics*]
VF .... Variable Frequency [*Electricity*] (MSA)
VF .... Variant Frequency [*Biology*]
VF .... Vector Field
VF .... Velocity Failure
VF .... Ventral Funiculus [*Anatomy*]
VF .... Ventricular Fibrillation [*Also, vent fib, VFIB*] [*Cardiology*]
VF .... Ventricular Fluid [*Cardiology*] (MAE)
VF .... Ventricular Flutter [*Cardiology*] (AAMN)
VF .... Verification of Function
VF .... Verkuendigung und Forschung [*Munich*] [*A publication*]
VF .... Vertical File
VF .... Vertical Flight (NASA)
VF .... Very Fair
VF .... Very Fine [*Condition*] [*Antiquarian book trade, numismatics, etc.*]
VF .... Very Fine Soil [*Agronomy*]
VF .... VFW [*Vereinigte Flugtechnische Werke*]-Fokker [*Germany*] [*ICAO aircraft manufacturer identifier*] (ICAO)
VF .... Vicarius Foraneus [*Vicar-Forane*] [*Latin*]
VF .... Video Frequency
VF .... View Factor
VF .... Viewfinder [*Photography*]
VF .... Vilagirodalmi Figyelo [*A publication*]
VF .... Villers Foundation [*Later, Families USA Foundation*] (EA)
VF .... Vinyl Fabric [*Technical drawings*]
VF .... Vinylferrocene [*Organic chemistry*]
VF .... Virile Female Project [*RJ Reynolds Tobacco Co. marketing strategy for proposed Dakota brand*]
VF .... Vision Foundation (EA)
VF .... Vision Frequency
VF .... Visiting Friends [*An association*] (EA)
VF .... Visual Field
VF .... Visual Flight [*Aviation*] (FAAC)
VF .... Vocal Fremitus
VF .... Voice Foundation (EA)
VF .... Voice Frequency [*Communications*]
V/F .... Voltage to Frequency [*Converter*] [*Data processing*]
VF .... Volunteer Fireman
VF .... Vulcanized Fiber
VFA .... Variation Flow Analysis
VFA .... Victoria Falls [*Zimbabwe*] [*Airport symbol*] (OAG)
VFA .... Video Free America (EA)
VFA .... Video Frequency Amplifier
VFA .... Videotape Facilities Association (EA)
VFA .... Visual Flight Attachment [*Aviation*] (RDA)
VFA .... Volatile Fatty Acid [*Organic chemistry*]
VFA .... Volunteer Fire Alarm (TEL)
VFAS .... Vertical Force Accounting System
VFAS/TL .. Vertical Force Accounting System/Troop List (MCD)
VFAT .... Visual Functioning Assessment Tool [*Educational test*]
VF AW ...... Fighter Squadron - All Weather [*Navy symbol*] (MCD)
VFAX .... Heavier-than-Air Fighter/Attack/Experimental [*Aircraft*]
VFB .... Fighter Bombing Plane [*Navy symbol*]
VFB .... Vertical Format Buffer
VFB .... Vierteljahrschrift fuer Bibelkunde, Talmudische, und Patristische Studien [*A publication*]
VFBK .... Eastern Bancorp, Inc. [*Formerly, Vermont Federal Bank FSB*] [*NASDAQ symbol*] (NQ)
VFC .... Ferrum College, Ferrum, VA [*OCLC symbol*] (OCLC)
VFC .... V Fan Club (EA)
VFC .... Variable File Channel
VFC .... Variable Frequency Control
VFC .... Ventricular Function Curve [*Cardiology*] (AAMN)
VFC .... Vertical Format Control
VFC .... Very Fine Cognac
VFC .... VF Corp. [*NYSE symbol*] (SPSG)
VFC .... Video Film Converter (OA)
VFC .... Video Frequency Carrier [*or Channel*] (CET)
VFC .... Visual Field Control [*Aviation*]
VFC .... Voice Frequency Carrier [*or Channel*]
VFC .... Volatile Flavor Compound
VFC .... Voltage to Frequency Converter
VFC .... Volunteer Field Consultant [*Red Cross*]
VFC .... Vortex Flow Control

VFC............	Voters for Choice/Friends of Family Planning (EA)
VFCBA9	Forests Commission Victoria. Bulletin [*A publication*]
VFC/FFP...	Voters for Choice/Friends of Family Planning [*Later, VFC*] (EA)
VF Cp........	VF Corp. [*Associated Press abbreviation*] (APAG)
VFCS........	Vehicle Flight Control System
VFCT........	Voice Frequency Carrier [*or Channel*] Telegraph [*or Teletype*]
VFCTT	Voice Frequency Carrier Teletype (MSA)
VFD	Vacuum Fluorescent Display [*Data processing*]
VFD	Value for Duty [*Business term*]
VFD	Variable Frequency Drive [*Instrumentation*]
VFD	Verified Free Distribution [*British*]
VFD	Vocal Feedback Device [*Aid for stutterers developed at the University of Pittsburgh by Dr. George Shames*]
VFD	Volunteer Fire Department
VFDF........	Very Fast Death Factor
VFDM	Vsemirnaia Federatsiia Demokraticheskoi Molodezhi [*World Federation of Democratic Youth*]
VFDMIS ...	Vertical Force Development Management Information Systems
VFDR........	Variable-Flow Directed Rocket
VFE...........	Vendor-Furnished Equipment (NASA)
VFED........	Valley Federal Savings & Loan Association [*NASDAQ symbol*] (NQ)
VFER	Veterans Federal Employment Representative [*Civil Service Commission*]
VFF...........	Valence Force Field
VFF...........	Voice Frequency Filter
VFFDR	Variable Fuel Flow Ducted Rocket (MCD)
VFFM........	Vestlandets Forstlige Forsoksstasjon. Meddelelse [*A publication*]
VFFT	Voice Frequency Facility Terminal [*Telecommunications*] (TEL)
VFG	Valley Fig Growers (EA)
VFG	Visual Flight Guide [*A publication*] (APTA)
VFH..........	Vacuum Film Handling
VFH..........	Vertical Flow Horizontal
VFHG	Versammlungen der Freunde des Humanistischen Gymnasiums [*A publication*]
VFHS........	Valley Forge Historical Society (EA)
VFHT........	Vacuum Film Handling Technique
VFI...........	Verification Flight Instrumentation (NASA)
VFI...........	VF RADAR Intercept Officer (DNAB)
VFI...........	Vinyl Fabrics Institute [*Later, Chemical Fabrics and Film Association*] (EA)
VFI...........	Visual Field Information [*Aviation*]
VFI...........	Vocational Foundation, Inc. (EA)
VFI...........	Volunteers for Israel (EA)
VFIB.........	Ventricular Fibrillation [*Also, vent fib, VF*] [*Cardiology*]
VFL..........	LeMoyne College, Syracuse, NY [*OCLC symbol*] (OCLC)
VFL..........	Variable Field Length (MCD)
VFL..........	Variable Focal Length
VFL..........	Victorian Football League [*Australia*] [*Receives television coverage in the US through the Entertainment and Sports Programming Network*]
VFL..........	Voice Frequency Line [*Telecommunications*] (TEL)
VFLA........	Volume Folding and Limiting Amplifier
VFLC........	Video Fluorometric Detection Liquid Chromatograph
VFLT........	Visual Flight [*Aviation*] (FAAC)
VF(M)........	Fighter Plane (Two-Engine) [*Navy symbol*]
VFM	Jahresberichte ueber die Veraenderungen und Fortschritte im Militaerwesen [*A publication*]
VFM	Vacuum Forming Machine
VFM	Value for Money [*Accounting*]
VFM	Van Kampen Merritt Florida Quality Municipal [*NYSE symbol*] (SPSG)
VFM	Variable Frequency Monitor [*Sony Corp.*]
VFM	Vendor-Furnished Material (MCD)
VFM	Vertical Flight Maneuver
VFM	Volt Frequency Monitor (DNAB)
VFMED.....	Variable Format Message Entry Device [*Data processing*] (MCD)
VF(N)........	Night Fighter Squadrons [*Navy symbol*]
VFN	Verticillium Wilt, Fusarium Wilt, Nematode Resistance [*Tomato culture*]
VFO	Vandenberg Field Office [*Air Force*] (MCD)
VFO	Vaporized Fuel Oil [*Process*]
VFO	Variable Frequency Oscillator
VFO	Viking Flight Operations [*NASA*]
VFON........	Volunteer Flight Officers Network
VFOX	Vicon Fiber Optics Corp. [*NASDAQ symbol*] (NQ)
VFP...........	Fighter Squadron, Photo [*Navy symbol*] (MCD)
VFP...........	Vacuum Flash Pyrolysis
VFP...........	Vacuum Fore Pump
VFP...........	Variable-Factor Programming
VFP...........	Variance Frequency Processor (MCD)
VFP...........	Ventricular Fluid Pressure [*Cardiology*] (MAE)
VFP...........	Vereenigde Feministiche Partij [*Belgium*] [*Political party*] (EY)
VFP...........	Veterans for Peace (EA)
VFP...........	Volunteers for Peace (EA)
VFP.........	Vsemirnaja Federacija Profsojuzov [*World Federation of Trade Unions*]
VFPC........	Vertical Flight Performance Criteria
VFPR........	Via Flight Planned Route [*Aviation*] (FAAC)
VFR.........	Vehicle Flight Readiness (KSC)
VFR.........	Vehicle Force Ratio (MCD)
VFR.........	Verein fuer Raumschiffahrt [*Society for Space Travel*] [*Germany*]
VFR...........	Victorian Fiction Research Guides [*A publication*]
VFR...........	Visiting Friends and Relatives [*Airlines*]
VFR...........	Visual Flight Rules [*Aviation*]
VFR...........	Volunteer Field Representative [*Red Cross*]
VFRA........	Volume Footwear Retailers of America [*Later, FDRA*]
VFRC........	Valley Forge Research Center [*University of Pennsylvania*] [*Research center*] (RCD)
VFRCTS....	Visual Flight Rules Control Tower Simulator [*Aviation*] (MCD)
VFRSA	VFR [*Visual Flight Rules*] Restrictions Still Apply [*Aviation*] (FAAC)
VFS...........	Vapor Feed System
VFS...........	Variable Frequency Synthesizer [*Ariel Corp.*] [*Data processing*]
VFS...........	Ventilated Flight Suit
VFS...........	Visual Flight Simulator
VFS...........	Voice from the Silence [*An association*] (EA)
VFS...........	Volume Fraction of Solids in a Slurry
VFSB	Verein der Freunde Schloss Blutenburg [*Association of Friends of Schloss Blutenburg-AFSB*] [*Germany*] (EAIO)
VFSB	Virginia First Savings Bank FSB [*NASDAQ symbol*] (NQ)
VFSC........	Vermont Financial Services Corp. [*NASDAQ symbol*] (NQ)
Vf Sch G...	Verfassungsschutzgesetz [*A publication*]
VFSL	Valdosta Federal Savings & Loan Association [*NASDAQ symbol*] (NQ)
VFSS.........	Voice Frequency Signaling System
VFSSMCQ ...	Victorian Federation of State Schools Mothers Clubs. Quarterly Review [*A publication*] (APTA)
VFSW	Variable Frequency Sine Wave
VFSW	Vierteljahrsschrift fuer Sozial- und Wirtschaftsgeschichte [*A publication*]
VFT...........	Vacuum Form Tool (MCD)
VFT...........	Vacuum Friction Test
VFT...........	Velocity False Target [*Military*] (CAAL)
VFT...........	Ventricular Fibrillation Threshold [*Cardiology*]
VFT...........	Verification Flight Test (MCD)
VFT...........	Vertical Flight Test (MCD)
VFT...........	Viking Flight Team [*NASA*]
VFT...........	Voice Frequency Telegraphy (NATG)
VFT...........	Voice Frequency Terminal
VFTG.........	Voice Frequency Telegraphy
VFTTA	Visa for Travel to Australia (ADA)
VFU	Van Wert, OH [*Location identifier*] [*FAA*] (FAAL)
VFU	Vertical Format Unit (BUR)
VFU	Vocabulary File Utility
VFUNDW ...	Voluntary Fund for the United Nations Decade for Women (EA)
VFV...........	Variable Fuel Vehicle [*General Motors Corp.*] [*Automotive engineering*]
VFV...........	Venus Flyby Vehicle [*NASA*]
VFVC........	Vacuum Freezing, Vapor Compression [*Desalination*]
VFW	Variable/Fixed Wavelength [*Electronics*]
VFW	Verwaltungsamt fuer Wirtschaft [*Executive Committee for Economics*] [*Germany*]
VFW	Veterans of Foreign Wars of the USA (EA)
VFW	Veterans of Future Wars [*Facetious organization formed by Princeton students in 1930's*]
VFY...........	Verify (AFM)
VG.............	British Virgin Islands [*ANSI two-letter standard code*] (CNC)
VG.............	Central Caraibes SA [*Haiti*] [*ICAO designator*] (FAAC)
VG.............	Grundriss der Vergleichenden Grammatik der Semitischen Sprachen [*A publication*] (BJA)
VG.............	Light Transport Plane [*Single-engine*] [*Navy symbol*]
VG.............	Validity Generalization Testing (OICC)
VG.............	Varga Aircraft Corp. [*ICAO aircraft manufacturer identifier*] (ICAO)
VG.............	Variable Geometry [*Refers to an aircraft that is capable of altering the sweep of the wings while in flight*] (NATG)
VG.............	Vector Generator [*Computer graphics*]
VG.............	Velocity Gravity
VG.............	Ventricular Gallop [*Cardiology*]
VG.............	Verbi Gratia [*For Example*] [*Latin*]
V & G	Vergangenheit und Gegenwart [*A publication*]
VG.............	Vertical Grain
V-G	Vertical Gust (MCD)
VG	Vertical Gyro (MCD)
VG.............	Very Good [*Condition*] [*Antiquarian book trade, numismatics, etc.*]
VG.............	Vibration Greatness
VG.............	Vicarius Generalis [*Vicar-General*] [*Latin*]
VG.............	Vice Grand [*Freemasonry*] (ROG)
VG.............	Vinylguaiacol [*Biochemistry*]
VG.............	Viscosity Grade [*Automotive engineering*]
VG.............	Vocational Guidance (ADA)

VG............. Voice Grade [*Telecommunications*]   (TEL)
VG............. Volksgrenadier [*Title given to infantry divisions with distinguished combat records*] [*Germany*] [*World War II*]
VG............. Voltage Gain
VG............. Volunteer Guards [*British military*]   (DMA)
VG............. Votre Grace [*Your Grace*] [*French*]
VG............. Votre Grandeur [*Your Highness*] [*French*]
Vg............... Vulgate [*Latin translation of the Bible*]   (BJA)
VGA........... Vapor Generation Accessory [*Instrumentation*]
VGA........... Variable Gain Amplifier
VGA........... Vertical Gyro Alignment
VGA........... Very General Algorithm   (KSC)
VGA........... Victorian Green Alliance [*Political party*] [*Australia*]
VGA........... Video Graphics Array [*Computer technology*]
VGA........... Vijayawada [*India*] [*Airport symbol*]   (OAG)
VGA........... Virginia Air Cargo, Inc. [*Charlottesville, VA*] [*FAA designator*]   (FAAC)
VGAA....... Vegetable Growers Association of America [*Defunct*]   (EA)
VGAM....... Vector Graphics Access Method
VGAT........ Visual General Aviation Trainer
VGB........... British Virgin Islands [*ANSI three-letter standard code*]   (CNC)
VGBD....... Virtual Grain Boundary Dislocation
Vgbl........... Bayerische Vorgeschichtsblaetter [*A publication*]
VGC........... Variable Gas Capacitor
VGC........... Velocity Gate Capture [*Military*]   (CAAL)
VGC........... Verdstone Gold Corp. [*Vancouver Stock Exchange symbol*]
VGC........... Very Good Condition [*Doll collecting*]
VGC........... Vesterheim Genealogical Center   (EA)
VGC........... Video Graphics Controller [*Apple Computer, Inc.*]
VGC........... Viscosity Gravity Constant
VGCA....... Voice Gate Circuit Adaptors [*Data processing*]   (MCD)
VGCB....... Cox's Bazar [*Bangladesh*] [*ICAO location identifier*]   (ICLI)
VGCF....... Vapor-Phase-Grown Carbon Fiber
VGCH....... Vent Gas Collection Header [*Nuclear energy*]   (NRCH)
VGCI........ Veta Grande Companies [*NASDAQ symbol*]   (NQ)
VGCL....... Vietnam General Confederation of Labor
VGCM....... Comilla [*Bangladesh*] [*ICAO location identifier*]   (ICLI)
VGD.......... Valentine Gold [*Vancouver Stock Exchange symbol*]
VGDIP....... Very God-Damned Important Person
VGE.......... Valery Giscard d'Estaing [*Former French President*]
VGE.......... Video-Game Epilepsy [*Neurology*]
VGE.......... Visual Gross Error
VGEBA...... Verhandlungen. Geologische Bundesanstalt (Austria) [*A publication*]
VGEG .... Chittagong [*Bangladesh*] [*ICAO location identifier*]   (ICLI)
VGF.......... Escort Fighter Squadron [*Navy symbol*]
VGF.......... Vaccinia Growth Factor [*Biochemistry*]
VGF.......... Virus Growth Factor [*Biochemistry*]
VGFR........ Dhaka [*Bangladesh*] [*ICAO location identifier*]   (ICLI)
VGFTU...... Vietnam General Federation of Trade Unions [*North Vietnam*]
VGG.......... Valhalla Gold Group [*Vancouver Stock Exchange symbol*]
VGH .... Vancouver General Hospital
VGH .... Velocity, Normal Gravity, and Height
VGH .... Verwaltungsgerichtshof [*A publication*]
VGH .... Very Good Health [*Medicine*]
VGH .... Veterinary General Hospital
VGHN........ Vaughn Communications, Inc. [*NASDAQ symbol*]   (NQ)
VGHQ........ Dhaka [*Bangladesh*] [*ICAO location identifier*]   (ICLI)
VGI .... Variable Geometry Inlet
VGI .... Vertical Gyro Indicator
VGIEMTP ... Veroeffentlichungen. Grabmann Institut zur Erforschung der Mittelalterlichen Theologie und Philosophie [*A publication*]
VGIMU ..... Velocity to Be Gained Related to IMU Orientation   (MCD)
VGIN .... Virgin Group Ltd. [*NASDAQ symbol*]   (NQ)
VGIS .... Ishurdi [*Bangladesh*] [*ICAO location identifier*]   (ICLI)
VGJ........... Vorgeschichtliches Jahrbuch [*A publication*]
VGJR.......... Jessore [*Bangladesh*] [*ICAO location identifier*]   (ICLI)
VGLI.......... Veterans Group Life Insurance
VGLIS........ Video Guidance, Landing, and Imaging System [*NASA*]
VGLKV...... Vierteljahrsschrift fuer Geschichte und Landeskunde Vorarlbergs [*A publication*]
VGLL........ Valstybine Grozines Literaturos Leidykla [*A publication*]
V/GLLD.... Vehicular/Ground LASER Locator Designator   (MCD)
VGLM .... Lalmonirhat [*Bangladesh*] [*ICAO location identifier*]   (ICLI)
VGM.......... George Mason University, Fairfax, VA [*OCLC symbol*]   (OCLC)
VGM.......... Ventriculogram [*A roentgenogram*]
VGM.......... VGM Capital Corp. [*Formerly, Vestgron Mines Ltd.*] [*Toronto Stock Exchange symbol*]
VGM.......... Vice Grand Master   (BJA)
VGM.......... Villa Grajales [*Mexico*] [*Seismograph station code, US Geological Survey*] [*Closed*]   (SEIS)
VGML........ Vegetarian Meal [*Airline notation*]
VGMU........ Vulcan Gunner Monitor Unit   (MCD)
VGN........... Variable Geometry Nozzle
VGN........... Virginian Railway Co. [*AAR code*]
VGO.......... Vacuum Gas Oil [*Petroleum technology*]
VGO.......... Vereinigte Gruenen Oesterreich [*United Green Party of Austria*] [*Political party*]   (EY)
VGO........... Vicar General's Office [*British*]   (ROG)

VGO.......... Vickers Gas Operated [*British military*]   (DMA)
VGO.......... Vigo [*Spain*] [*Airport symbol*]   (OAG)
VGOR........ Vandenberg Ground Operations Requirement [*Air Force*]   (NASA)
VGOR........ Vehicle Ground Operation Requirements [*NASA*]   (NASA)
VGP .... Vehicle Ground Point [*NASA*]   (NASA)
VGP .... Victorian Government Publications [*A publication*]   (APTA)
VGP .... Virtual Geomagnetic Pole [*Geophysics*]
VGPI........ Visual Glide Path Indicator
VGPI........ Visual Ground Position Indicator   (NATG)
VGPO .... Velocity Gate Pulloff [*Military*]   (CAAL)
VGQ.......... Vocational Guidance Quarterly [*A publication*]
VGR .... Variable Geometry Rotor
VGR .... Vigoro Corp. [*NYSE symbol*]   (SPSG)
VGRJ........ Rajshahi [*Bangladesh*] [*ICAO location identifier*]   (ICLI)
VGS .... Escort-Scouting Squadron [*Navy symbol*]
VGS .... Variable Geometry Structure
VGS .... Variable-Grade Gravity Sewer
VGS .... Vehicle Generating System
VGS .... Velocity Gate Stealer [*Military*]   (CAAL)
VGS .... Visual Guidance System [*Aviation*]   (FAAC)
VGS .... Volunteer Gliding Schools [*British*]
VGSD .... Saidpur [*Bangladesh*] [*ICAO location identifier*]   (ICLI)
VGSG .... Thakuragaon [*Bangladesh*] [*ICAO location identifier*]   (ICLI)
VGSH .... Shamshernagar [*Bangladesh*] [*ICAO location identifier*]   (ICLI)
VGSI........ Visual Glide Slope Indicator
VGSY........ Sylhet Osmani [*Bangladesh*] [*ICAO location identifier*]   (ICLI)
VGT .... Las Vegas [*Nevada*] North Terminal [*Airport symbol*]   (OAG)
VGT .... Las Vegas, NV [*Location identifier*] [*FAA*]   (FAAL)
VGT .... National Victoria & Grey Trustco Ltd. [*Toronto Stock Exchange symbol*]
VGT .... Variable Geometry Turbocharger [*Automotive engineering*]
VGT .... Vehicle Ground Test [*NASA*]   (NASA)
VGT .... Videographic Terminal
VGTE .... Vulcan Gunner Tracking Evaluation   (MCD)
VGTJ .... Dhaka/Tejgaon [*Bangladesh*] [*ICAO location identifier*]   (ICLI)
VGU .... Des Moines, IA [*Location identifier*] [*FAA*]   (FAAL)
VGV .... Vacuum Gate Valve
VG & VF .... Vicar General and Vicar Foreign [*British*]   (ROG)
VGVT .... Vertical Ground Vibration Test   (MCD)
VGW .... Variable Geometry Wing [*Aircraft*]
VGWA ...... Variable Geometry Wing Aircraft   (AAG)
VGWO...... Velocity Gate Walkoff [*Military*]   (CAAL)
VGX .... Velocity to Be Gained [*Body X-Axis*] [*NASA*]   (NASA)
VGY .... Velocity to Be Gained [*Body Y-Axis*] [*NASA*]   (NASA)
VGZ .... Velocity to Be Gained [*Body Z-Axis*] [*NASA*]   (NASA)
VGZR .... Dhaka/Zia International [*Bangladesh*] [*ICAO location identifier*]   (ICLI)
VH .... Air Volta [*Upper Volta*] [*ICAO designator*]   (FAAC)
VH .... Ambulance Plane [*Navy symbol*]
VH .... Australia [*Aircraft nationality and registration mark*]   (FAAC)
Vh................ Heater Voltage [*Electronics*]   (OA)
VH .... Rescue Squadrons [*Navy symbol*]
VH .... Vacuum Housing
VH .... Vaginal Hysterectomy [*Gynecology*]
VH .... Value Health, Inc. [*AMEX symbol*]   (SPSG)
VH .... Varia Historia [*of Aelianus*] [*Classical studies*]   (OCD)
VH .... Variable Heavy
V/H............. Velocity/Height
VH .... Venice Hospital [*Venice, FL*]
VH .... Venous Hematocrit [*Medicine*]   (MAE)
VH .... Vent Hole [*Technical drawings*]
VH .... Vermont History [*A publication*]
V & H....... Vertical and Horizontal [*Telecommunications*]   (TSSD)
VH .... Very Heavy [*Cosmic ray nuclei*]
VH .... Very High
VH .... Veterans Hospital
VH .... Vickers Hardness Number [*Also, HV, VHN*]   (AAG)
VH .... Vir Honestus [*A Worthy Man*] [*Latin*]
VH .... Viral Hepatitis [*Medicine*]
V/H............. Vulnerability/Hardness [*Refers to a weapon system's weakness and capabilities in withstanding adverse operating environments*]
VH-1 .... Video Hits One [*Cable-television system*] [*Companion to MTV*]
VHA........... Van Houten Associates [*Information service or system*]   (IID)
VHA........... Variable Housing Allowance   (MCD)
VHA........... Very High Altitude
VHA........... Very High Aluminum [*Rock composition*]
VHA........... Voluntary Hospitals of America   (EA)
VHAA .... Very High Altitude Abort [*NASA*]   (KSC)
VHAAH .... Vitterhets, Historie- och Antikvitets-Akademiens Handlingar [*A publication*]
VHAP........ Volatile Hazardous Air Pollutant   (EG)
VHB........... Buffalo and Erie County Public Library, Buffalo, NY [*OCLC symbol*]   (OCLC)
VHB........... Very Heavy Bombardment [*Air Force*]
VHB........... Very High Bond Tape [*3M Co.*]
Vh BAG ..... Verhandlungen. Berliner Gesellschaft fuer Anthropologie, Ethnologie, und Urgeschichte [*A publication*]
VHBR .... Very High Burning Rate   (MCD)

VHBW	Very-High-Speed Black and White [*Photography*]
VHC	Hollins College, Hollins College, VA [*OCLC symbol*] (OCLC)
VHC	Saurimo [*Angola*] [*Airport symbol*] (OAG)
VHC	Ventech Healthcare Corp., Inc. [*Toronto Stock Exchange symbol*]
VHC	Vertical Hold Control
VHC	Very High Contrast [*Liquid crystal display*]
VHC	Very Highly Commended
VHCH	Cheung Chau [*Hong Kong*] [*ICAO location identifier*] (ICLI)
VHCL	VHC Ltd. [*New York, NY*] [*NASDAQ symbol*] (NQ)
VHD	Valvular Heart Disease
VHD	Video High Density [*Television*]
VHD	Viral Hematodepressive Disease (MAE)
VHDL	Very-High Density Lipoprotein [*Biochemistry*]
VHDL	VHSIC [*Very-High-Speed Integrated Circuit*] Hardware Description Language [*Data processing*]
VHDV	Very High Dollar Value
VHE	Very-High Energy
VHE	Volatile Human Effluents
VHEDD8	Vogelkundliche Hefte Edertal [*A publication*]
VH Eq Dr	Van Heythuysen's Equity Draftsman [*2nd ed.*] [*1828*] [*A publication*] (DLA)
VHF	Vacuum Hydrogen Furnace
VHF	Very-High-Frequency [*Electronics*]
VHF	Visual Half-Field
VHF/AM	Very-High-Frequency, Amplitude Modulated (NASA)
VHFC	Van Halen Fan Club (EA)
VHF/DF	Very-High-Frequency Direction-Finding
VHFF	Very-High-Frequency Filter
VHF-FM	Very-High-Frequency, Frequency Modulated (NOAA)
VHFG	Very-High-Frequency Generator
VHFI	Very-High-Frequency Indeed [*Ultrahigh frequency*] [*British*]
VHFJ	Very-High-Frequency Jammer
VHFO	Very-High-Frequency Oscillator
VHFOR	Very-High-Frequency Omnirange (AFM)
VHFR	Very-High-Frequency Receiver
VHFS	Videnskabernes Selskabs Historisk-Filologiske Skrifter [*A publication*]
VHFS	Vint Hill Farms Station [*Army*]
VHFT	Very-High-Frequency Termination
VHG	Vertragshilfegesetz [*A publication*]
VHHH	Hong Kong/International [*Hong Kong*] [*ICAO location identifier*] (ICLI)
VHHK	Hong Kong [*Hong Kong*] [*ICAO location identifier*] (ICLI)
VHI	Banyan Hotel Investment Fund [*AMEX symbol*] [*Formerly, VMS Hotel Investment Fund*] (SPSG)
VHI	Valhi, Inc. [*NYSE symbol*] (SPSG)
VHIP	Vehicle Hit Indicator, Pyrotechnic
VHis	Vida Hispanica [*A publication*]
VHIS	Vietnam Head Injury Study
VHJ	Victorian Historical Journal [*A publication*] (APTA)
VHKT	Kai Tak [*Hong Kong*] [*ICAO location identifier*] (ICLI)
VHL	Viceroy Homes Ltd. [*Toronto Stock Exchange symbol*]
VHL	Von Hippel-Lindau Disease
VHLH	Very Heavy Lift Helicopter
VHLL	Very-High-Level Language
VHM	Victorian Historical Magazine [*Australia*] [*A publication*]
VHM	Virtual Hardware Monitor [*Data processing*] (IEEE)
VHM	Visitation Nuns [*Roman Catholic religious order*]
VHM	Vista Hermosa [*Mexico*] [*Seismograph station code, US Geological Survey*] [*Closed*] (SEIS)
VHMCP	Voluntary Home Mortgage Credit Program [*of HHFA*] [*Terminated*]
VHN	Van Horn, TX [*Location identifier*] [*FAA*] (FAAL)
VHN	Verhandlungen. Historischer Vereine von Niederbayern [*A publication*]
VHN	Vickers Hardness Number [*Also, HV, VH*]
VHO	Very High Output
VHO	Vila Coutinho [*Mozambique*] [*Airport symbol*] [*Obsolete*] (OAG)
VHO	Vista Hermosa [*Mexico*] [*Seismograph station code, US Geological Survey*] (SEIS)
VHO	Volatile Halogenated Organic [*Analytical chemistry*]
VHOC	Volatile Halogenated Organic Compound [*Environmental chemistry*]
VHOL	Very-High-Order Language
VHP	County of Henrico Public Library, Richmond, VA [*OCLC symbol*] (OCLC)
VHP	Variable Horsepower
VHP	Very High Performance
VHP	Very High Polarization [*Raw sugar grade*]
VHP	Very High Pressure
VHP	Vooruitstrevende Hervormings Partij [*Progressive Reform Party*] [*Surinam*] [*Political party*] (PPW)
VHPA	Vietnam Helicopter Pilots Association (EA)
VHR	Very-Highly Repeated [*Genetics*]
VHR	Video-to-Hardcopy Recorder
VHRR	Very High Resolution Radiometer [*NASA*]
VHRTG	Veterans' Hospital Radio and Television Guild (EA)
VHS	Hampden-Sydney College, Hampden-Sydney, VA [*OCLC symbol*] (OCLC)
VHS	Honorary Surgeon to the Viceroy of India
vHs	Van Hove Singularities [*Physics*]
VHS	Versatile High Speed [*Copier*]
VHS	Vertical and Horizontal Spread [*Landfills*] (EG)
VHS	Very High Speed [*Copier*]
VHS	Victorian House of Studies
VHS	Video Home System
VHS	Viral Hemorrhagic Septicemia [*Medicine*]
VHS-C	Video Home System - Compact
VHSI	Very-High-Speed Integrated [*Electronics*]
VHSIC	Very-High-Speed Integrated Circuit [*Electronics*]
VHSK	Sek Kong [*Hong Kong*] [*ICAO location identifier*] (ICLI)
VHSKA	Vital and Health Statistics. Series 11 [*United States*] [*A publication*]
VHSOC	Very-High-Speed Optic Cable
VHS & RA	Veterans Health Services and Research Administration [*Department of Veterans Affairs*]
VHST	Very-High-Speed Transit
VHTR	Very-High-Temperature Reactor [*Nuclear energy*]
V/HUD	Vertical/Heads-Up Display [*Aviation*] (MCD)
VHUP	Veterinary Hospital of the University of Pennsylvania
VHVNB	Verhandlungen. Historischer Verein von Niederbayern [*A publication*]
VHVOR	Verhandlungen. Historischer Verein von Oberpfalz und Regensburg [*A publication*]
VHW	Verband Hannoverscher Warmblutzuchter [*Germany*] (EAIO)
VHWG	Vulnerability and Hardening Working Group
VHY	Vess, Henry, Kansas City MO [*STAC*]
VI	Congregation of the Incarnate Word and the Blessed Sacrament [*Roman Catholic women's religious order*]
VI	Inertial Velocity
VI	Internal Velocity (SSD)
VI	Societe de Travail Aerien [*Algeria*] [*ICAO designator*] (FAAC)
VI	Vaginal Irrigation [*Medicine*]
VI	Valley Industries, Inc. [*NYSE symbol*] (SPSG)
VI	Value Included Entry [*Business term*]
VI	Values Inventory [*Management test*]
VI	Vancouver Island
VI	Variable Interval [*Reinforcement schedule*]
VI	Vasoinhibitory [*Medicine*]
VI	Vector International (EA)
VI	Vegetation Index
VI	Velocity, Internal
VI	Vendor Item [*Sales*] (AAG)
VI	Vent Isolation [*Nuclear energy*] (NRCH)
VI	Verb Intransitive
VI	Vereniging Intercoop [*International Agricultural Society Intercoop*] [*Switzerland*] (EAIO)
VI	Vermiculite Institute [*Defunct*]
VI	Vertical Interval [*Mapmaking*]
VI	Veterinary Inspector (ADA)
VI	Vial
Vi	Viator [*A publication*]
VI	Vibration Institute (EA)
VI	Victoria Institute [*British*] (DAS)
vi	Vide Infra [*See Below*] [*Latin*] (WGA)
VI	Video Integrator
Vi	Vincentius Hispanus [*Deceased, 1248*] [*Authority cited in pre-1607 legal work*] (DSA)
VI	Vinegar Institute (EA)
VI	Viol [*A publication*]
VI	Violet
VI	Virgin Island Reports [*A publication*]
VI	Virgin Islands Reports [*A publication*] (DLA)
vi	Virgin Islands of the US [*MARC country of publication code*] [*Library of Congress*] [*IYRU nationality code*] (LCCP)
VI	Virgin Islands of the US [*Postal code*]
VI	Virgin Islands of the US [*ANSI two-letter standard code*] (CNC)
Vi	Virginia State Library, Richmond, VA [*Library symbol*] [*Library of Congress*] (LCLS)
Vi	Virginium (MAE)
VI	Virgo Intacta [*Medicine*]
Vi	Virulence [*Antigen*] [*Immunology*]
VI	Viscosity Improver [*Element in multigrade engine oil*]
VI	Viscosity Index
VI	Visual Identification
VI	Visual Impairment
VI	Visual Information
VI	Visual Inspection
Vi	Vivianus Tuscus [*Flourished, 13th century*] [*Authority cited in pre-1607 legal work*] (DSA)
V & I	Voix et Images. Etudes Quebecoises [*A publication*]
VI	Volume Index [*Medicine*] (DHSM)
VI	Volume Indicator [*Radio equipment*]
VI	Volume Investigation [*Three-dimensional imaging technology developed at The Toronto Hospital in Canada*]
VI	Voluntary Indefinite [*Status*] [*Army*] (INF)
VI	Voluntary Interceptor [*World War II*] [*British*]
VI	Volunteers for Israel (EA)

VIA .... Arlington County Department of Libraries, Arlington, VA
            [*OCLC symbol*]   (OCLC)
VIA .... Variable Income Annuity
VIA .... Viacom, Inc. [*AMEX symbol*]   (SPSG)
VIA .... Viaduct
V & IA .... Victorian and Interstate Airways [*Australia*]
VIA .... Video Image Analysis
VIA .... Videotex Industry Association   (EA)
VIA .... Viral Interval Antigen [*Virology*]
VIA .... Virus Inactivating Agency [*Medicine*]
VIA .... Virus Infection Associated Antigen [*Immunology*]
VIA .... Vision Institute of America [*Later, VSP*]   (EA)
VIA .... Vocational Interests and Vocational Aptitudes [*Psychology*]
VIA .... Voice Interactive Avionics [*Army*]
VIA .... Volunteers in Asia   (EA)
ViAb .... Washington County Public Library, Abingdon, VA [*Library
            symbol*] [*Library of Congress*]   (LCLS)
VIABLE ..... Vertical Installation Automated Baseline [*Army*]
ViAc .... Eastern Shore Public Library, Accomac, VA [*Library symbol*]
            [*Library of Congress*]   (LCLS)
Viac .... Viacom, Inc. [*Associated Press abbreviation*]   (APAG)
VIAC.......... Vienna Allied Command [*British military*]   (DMA)
VIACOM .. Viacom, Inc. [*Associated Press abbreviation*]   (APAG)
VIAFF .... Vancouver International Amateur Film Festival [*Canada*]
VIAG .... Agra [*India*] [*ICAO location identifier*]   (ICLI)
VIAH .... Aligarh [*India*] [*ICAO location identifier*]   (ICLI)
ViAl........... Alexandria Library, Alexandria, VA [*Library symbol*] [*Library
            of Congress*]   (LCLS)
VIAL.......... Allahabad [*India*] [*ICAO location identifier*]   (ICLI)
ViAlA........ United States Army Material Command Headquarters,
            Technical Library, Alexandria, VA [*Library symbol*]
            [*Library of Congress*]   (LCLS)
ViAlbS .... Southside Virginia Community College, Christanna Campus,
            Alberta, VA [*Library symbol*] [*Library of
            Congress*]   (LCLS)
ViAlD........ Defense Technical Information Center, Cameron Station,
            Alexandria, VA [*Library symbol*] [*Library of
            Congress*]   (LCLS)
ViAlDL...... Defense Logistics Agency, Cameron Station, Alexandria, VA
            [*Library symbol*] [*Library of Congress*]   (LCLS)
ViAlP .... Jacob Simpson Payton Library, Alexandria, VA [*Library
            symbol*] [*Library of Congress*]   (LCLS)
ViAlTh....... Protestant Episcopal Theological Seminary in Virginia,
            Alexandria, VA [*Library symbol*] [*Library of
            Congress*]   (LCLS)
ViAnGS ..... Church of Jesus Christ of Latter-Day Saints, Genealogical
            Society Library, Annandale Branch, Annandale, VA
            [*Library symbol*] [*Library of Congress*]   (LCLS)
ViAnN....... Northern Virginia Community College, Annandale, VA
            [*Library symbol*] [*Library of Congress*]   (LCLS)
Viansa .... Vicky and Sam [*Sebastiani*] [*Brand name of wines made by the
            Sebastianis*]
VIAP.......... Vanuatu Independent Alliance Party [*Political party*]   (PPW)
VIAR.......... Amritsar [*India*] [*ICAO location identifier*]   (ICLI)
ViAr .... Arlington County Department of Libraries, Arlington, VA
            [*Library symbol*] [*Library of Congress*]   (LCLS)
ViAr-A .... Arlington County Department of Libraries, Aurora Hills
            Branch, Arlington, VA [*Library symbol*] [*Library of
            Congress*]   (LCLS)
ViArAL...... Center for Applied Linguistics, Arlington, VA [*Library symbol*]
            [*Library of Congress*]   (LCLS)
ViAr-Ch ..... Arlington County Department of Libraries, Cherrydale Branch,
            Arlington, VA [*Library symbol*] [*Library of
            Congress*]   (LCLS)
ViAr-Cl ...... Arlington County Department of Libraries, Clarendon Branch,
            Arlington, VA [*Library symbol*] [*Library of
            Congress*]   (LCLS)
ViAr-F........ Arlington County Department of Libraries, Fairlington Branch,
            Arlington, VA [*Library symbol*] [*Library of
            Congress*]   (LCLS)
ViAr-G .... Arlington County Department of Libraries, Glencarlyn Branch,
            Arlington, VA [*Library symbol*] [*Library of
            Congress*]   (LCLS)
ViArHD..... United States Historical Documents Institute, Inc., Arlington,
            VA [*Library symbol*] [*Library of Congress*]   (LCLS)
ViArM .... Marymount College, Arlington, VA [*Library symbol*] [*Library
            of Congress*]   (LCLS)
ViArNG ..... National Graduate University, Arlington, VA [*Library symbol*]
            [*Library of Congress*]   (LCLS)
ViAr-W ...... Arlington County Department of Libraries, Westover Branch,
            Arlington, VA [*Library symbol*] [*Library of
            Congress*]   (LCLS)
VIAS.......... Voice Interference Analysis Set
VIASA .... Venezolana Internacional de Aviacion Sociedad Anonima
            [*Airline*] [*Venezuela*]
ViAsM .... Mobil Chemical Co., Industrial Chemicals Division, Ashland,
            VA [*Library symbol*] [*Library of Congress*]   (LCLS)
ViAsR .... Randolph-Macon College, Ashland, VA [*Library symbol*]
            [*Library of Congress*]   (LCLS)
Viata Med (Buchar) ... Viata Medicala (Bucharest) [*A publication*]
Viator Med ... Viator. Medieval and Renaissance Studies [*A publication*]

VIB............ Vanilla Information Bureau   (EA)
VIB............ Veal Infusion Broth [*Immunology*]
VIB............ Vertical Integration Building [*NASA*]
VIB............ Vibraphone [*Music*]
VIB............ Vibrate   (AAG)
VIB............ Vitamin Information Bureau [*Commercial firm*]   (EA)
VIB............ Volunteer Infantry Brigade [*British military*]   (DMA)
VIBG......... Vibrating   (AAG)
VIBGYOR ... Violet, Indigo, Blue, Green, Yellow, Orange, Red [*Mnemonic
            for the colors of the spectrum*]
VIBH .... Banihal [*India*] [*ICAO location identifier*]   (ICLI)
VIBI.......... Virgini Immaculatae Bavaria Immaculata [*To the Immaculate
            Virgin Immaculate Bavaria*] [*Latin*] [*Motto of the Order of
            St. George of Bavaria*]
VIBJ .... Virgin Islands Bar Journal [*A publication*]
VIBK......... Bikaner [*India*] [*ICAO location identifier*]   (ICLI)
VIBL.......... Bakshi Ka Talab [*India*] [*ICAO location identifier*]   (ICLI)
ViBlbV .... Virginia Polytechnic Institute and State University, Blacksburg,
            VA [*Library symbol*] [*Library of Congress*]   (LCLS)
ViBluC .... Bluefield College, Bluefield, VA [*Library symbol*] [*Library of
            Congress*]   (LCLS)
VIBN .... Varanasi [*India*] [*ICAO location identifier*]   (ICLI)
VIBN .... Vibration   (AAG)
Vi-BPH..... Virginia State Library for the Visually and Physically
            Handicapped, Richmond, VA [*Library symbol*] [*Library of
            Congress*]   (LCLS)
VIBR......... Kulu/Bhuntar [*India*] [*ICAO location identifier*]   (ICLI)
VIBR......... Vibration
VIBRA .... Vehicle Inelastic Bending Response Analysis [*Computer
            program*]
VIBRAM ... Vitale Bramani [*Inventor of rubber soles for boots used in
            mountain climbing*]
ViBrC .... Bridgewater College, Bridgewater, VA [*Library symbol*]
            [*Library of Congress*]   (LCLS)
VIBRECON ... Vibration-Recording Console   (SAA)
VIBROT .... Vibrational-Rotational [*Spectra*] [*Data processing*]
ViBS.......... Sullins College, Bristol, VA [*Library symbol*] [*Library of
            Congress*]   (LCLS)
VIBS .... Vocabulatory, Information, Block Design, Similarities
            [*Psychology*]
Vib Spectr .. Vibrational Spectroscopy [*A publication*]
Vib Spectra Struct ... Vibrational Spectra and Structure [*A publication*]
VIBT......... Bhatinda [*India*] [*ICAO location identifier*]   (ICLI)
ViBV .... Virginia Intermont College, Bristol, VA [*Library symbol*]
            [*Library of Congress*]   (LCLS)
VIBW........ Bhiwani [*India*] [*ICAO location identifier*]   (ICLI)
VIBY......... Bareilly [*India*] [*ICAO location identifier*]   (ICLI)
ViC .... McIntire Public Library, Charlottesville, VA [*Library symbol*]
            [*Library of Congress*]   (LCLS)
VIC .... University of Victoria Library [*UTLAS symbol*]
VIC .... Value Incentive Clause [*General Services Administration*]
VIC .... Values Inventory for Children [*Attitude test*]
VIC .... Van Kampen Merritt Investment Grade California Municipal
            [*NYSE symbol*]   (SPSG)
VIC .... Vapor Injection Curing [*Plastics technology*]
VIC .... Variable Instruction Computer
VIC .... Varnish Insulating Compound
VIC .... Vasoinhibitory Center [*Physiology*]
VIC .... Vehicle Identification Code   (SSD)
VIC .... Vehicle Intercommunications System   (MCD)
VIC .... Very Important Cargo [*Shipping*]
VIC .... Very Important Contributors [*Political*]
VIC .... Very Important Customer
VIC .... Veterinary Investigation Centre [*Ministry of Agriculture,
            Fisheries, and Food*] [*British*]
VIC .... Vicar [*or Vicarage*]
VIC .... Vices [*Times*] [*Pharmacy*]
vic.............. Vicinal [*Also, v*] [*Chemistry*]
VIC .... Vicinity   (AABC)
Vic .... Victor [*Record label*]
VIC .... Victoria [*British Columbia*] [*Geomagnetic observatory code*]
VIC .... Victoria [*British Columbia*] [*Seismograph station code, US
            Geological Survey*]   (SEIS)
VIC .... Vienna International Centre [*United Nations*]
VIC .... Viking Integrated Change [*NASA*]
VIC .... Virgin Islands Code [*A publication*]   (DLA)
VIC .... Virgin Islands Corp. [*Intended to promote VI economic
            development, dissolv ed 1966*] [*Department of the
            Interior*]
VIC .... Virginia Intermont College
VIC .... Virginia State Library, Richmond, VA [*OCLC
            symbol*]   (OCLC)
VIC .... Virtual Interaction Controller
VIC .... Visibility of Intransit Cargo [*Shipping*]
VIC .... Visitor Information Center [*Kennedy Space Center*]
VIC .... Visual Information Center [*Oldsmobile*] [*Automotive
            engineering*]
VIC .... Vortex in Cell [*Fluid Mechanics*]
VIC .... VSC Tech, Inc. [*Vancouver Stock Exchange symbol*]
VICA.......... Video Corp. of America [*NASDAQ symbol*]   (NQ)
VICA.......... Vision Industry Council of America   (EA)

VICA......... Vocational Industrial Clubs of America (EA)
Vic ACR..... Victorian Accident Compensation Reports [*Australia*] [*A publication*]
ViCAF........ United States Army, Foreign Science and Technical Center, Charlottesville, VA [*Library symbol*] [*Library of Congress*] (LCLS)
ViCAHi...... Abermarle County Historical Society, Charlottesville, VA [*Library symbol*] [*Library of Congress*] (LCLS)
VIC and ALB ... Victoria and Albert Museum [*London*] (DSUE)
VICAM...... Virtual Integrated Communications Access Method [*Sperry UNIVAC*]
VICANA.... Vietnamese Cultural Association of North America (EA)
VICAP....... Violent Criminal Apprehension Program [*Quantico, VA*] [*National Center for the Analysis of Violent Crime*] [*Department of Justice*]
VICAR....... Video Image Communication and Retrieval
Vic Assn Teach Eng J ... Victorian Association for the Teaching of English. Journal [*A publication*] (APTA)
Vic Bar News ... Victorian Bar News [*A publication*] (APTA)
VIC C......... Victoria Cross (DSUE)
Vic CC........ County Court Reports (Victoria) [*A publication*] (APTA)
Vic Chamber of Manufactures Econ Serv ... Victorian Chamber of Manufactures. Economic Service [*A publication*] (APTA)
Vic Chap News ... Victorian Chapter Newsletter [*Australian College of Education*] [*A publication*] (APTA)
Vic Comm Teach Assn General J ... Victorian Commercial Teachers' Association. General Journal [*A publication*] (APTA)
Vic Comput ... Vic Computing [*A publication*]
Vic Conf Soc Welfare Proc ... Victorian Conference of Social Welfare. Proceedings [*A publication*] (APTA)
Vic Creditman ... Victorian Creditman [*A publication*] (APTA)
Vic Dairyfarmer ... Victorian Dairyfarmer [*A publication*] (APTA)
Vic Dep Agric Tech Bull ... Victoria. Department of Agriculture. Technical Bulletin [*A publication*] (APTA)
VICE......... Vast Integrated Communications Environment [*Carnegie Mellon University*] [*Pittsburgh, PA*]
VICE......... Vilnius Commodity Exchange [*Lithuania*] (EY)
Vic Ed Gaz ... Education Gazette and Teachers Aid (Victoria) [*A publication*] (APTA)
Vic Elec Contractor ... Victorian Electrical Contractor [*A publication*] (APTA)
Vic Employers' Federation AR ... Victorian Employers' Federation. Annual Report [*A publication*] (APTA)
Vicenza Econ ... Vicenza Economica [*A publication*]
VICF......... Victoria Financial Corp. [*NASDAQ symbol*] (NQ)
Vic Fam Alm ... Victorian Family Almanac [*A publication*]
Vic For Comm Bull ... Victoria. Forests Commission. Bulletin [*A publication*] (APTA)
VICG......... Chandigarh [*India*] [*ICAO location identifier*] (ICLI)
VICGEN... Vicar General's Office [*British*]
Vic Geogr J ... Victorian Geographical Journal [*A publication*] (APTA)
Vic Govt Gaz ... Victorian Government Gazette [*A publication*] (APTA)
Vic His J .... Victorian Historical Journal [*A publication*]
Vic Hist J... Victorian Historical Journal [*A publication*]
Vic Hist Mag ... Victorian Historical Magazine [*A publication*] (APTA)
Vic Hortic Dig ... Victorian Horticultural Digest [*A publication*] (APTA)
ViChT........ John Tyler Community College, Chester, VA [*Library symbol*] [*Library of Congress*] (LCLS)
VICI.......... Vantage Information Consultants, Inc. [*Information service or system*] (IID)
VICI.......... Velocity Indicating Coherent Integrator
VICI.......... Video Console Indexing
VICI.......... Video Isolation Channel Identifier (MCD)
VICI.......... Voice Input Child Identicant [*Pronounced "Vicki"*] [*Young robot in television show "Small Wonder"*]
VICI.......... Voice Input Code Identifier (MCD)
Vic Inst Coll News ... Victoria Institute of Colleges. Newsletter [*A publication*] (APTA)
Vic Inst Ed Res Bull ... Victorian Institute of Educational Research. Bulletin [*A publication*]
VICK......... Vicksburg National Military Park
VICL......... Vienna International Centre Library [*Information service or system*] (IID)
Vic Legal Exec ... Victorian Legal Executive [*A publication*] (APTA)
ViClR........ Robbins Mills, Inc., Clarksville, VA [*Library symbol*] [*Library of Congress*] (LCLS)
Vic LSAJ ... Victorian LSA [*Limbless Soldiers' Association*] Journal [*A publication*] (APTA)
VICM .... VICOM, Inc. [*Eden Prairie, MN*] [*NASDAQ symbol*] (NQ)
VicN.......... Victorian Naturalist [*A publication*]
Vic Nat....... Victorian Naturalist [*A publication*] (APTA)
Vic Naturalist ... Victorian Naturalist [*A publication*] (APTA)
VIC News .. Victoria Institute of Colleges. Newsletter [*A publication*]
VICO .... Virginia International Co.
VICO .... Volkswagen Insurance Co.
ViCoC .... Castle Hill Museum, Cobham, VA [*Library symbol*] [*Library of Congress*] (LCLS)
VI Code Ann ... Virgin Islands Code Annotated [*A publication*]
VICOED.... Visual Communications Education
VICOM ..... Visual Communications Management

VICON ...... Vicon Industries, Inc. [*Associated Press abbreviation*] (APAG)
VICON ...... Visual Confirmation [*of voice takeoff clearing system*] [*Aviation*]
VICORE.... Visual Conceptual Reading
ViCou .... Walter Cecil Rawls Library and Museum, Courtland, VA [*Library symbol*] [*Library of Congress*] (LCLS)
ViCovI....... Industrial Rayon Corp., Covington, VA [*Library symbol*] [*Library of Congress*] (LCLS)
ViCovW ..... West Virginia Pulp & Paper Co., Covington, VA [*Library symbol*] [*Library of Congress*] (LCLS)
ViCP .... Piedmont Virginia Community College, Learning Resources Center, Charlottesville, VA [*Library symbol*] [*Library of Congress*] (LCLS)
VICP .... VINES [*Virtual Networking Software*] Interprocess Communications Protocol [*Data processing*] (PCM)
Vic Parl Deb ... Victorian Parliamentary Debates [*A publication*] (APTA)
Vic Parl Parl Deb ... Victoria. Parliament. Parliamentary Debates [*A publication*] (APTA)
Vic Poultry J ... Victorian Poultry Journal [*A publication*] (APTA)
VICR......... Vicor Corp. [*NASDAQ symbol*] (SPSG)
VICR......... Victor Technologies [*NASDAQ symbol*] (NQ)
ViCRA ...... National Radio Astronomy Observatory, Charlottesville, VA [*Library symbol*] [*Library of Congress*] (LCLS)
Vic Railways Newsletter ... Victorian Railways Newsletter [*A publication*] (APTA)
Vic Resour ... Victoria's Resources [*A publication*] (APTA)
Vic Resources ... Victoria's Resources [*A publication*] (APTA)
Vic Rev....... Victorian Review [*A publication*] (APTA)
VICS......... Variable Inertia Charging System [*Mazda Motor Co.*] [*Automotive engineering*]
VICS......... Verbal Interaction Category System [*Student teacher test*]
VICS......... Vocational Information through Computer Systems [*Philadelphia School District*] [*Pennsylvania*] [*Information service or system*] (IID)
Vic's Res .... Victoria's Resources [*A publication*]
Vic Stat Pub ... Victorian Statistics Publications [*A publication*] (APTA)
ViCT .... Institute of Textile Technology, Charlottesville, VA [*Library symbol*] [*Library of Congress*] (LCLS)
VICT......... Victoria Bankshares, Inc. [*NASDAQ symbol*] (NQ)
Vict............ Victorian Reports [*A publication*]
VICTA....... Valett Inventory of Critical Thinking Abilities [*Child development test*]
Vict Acts .... Victoria Acts of Parliament [*A publication*] (DLA)
Vict Cancer News ... Victorian Cancer News [*A publication*] (APTA)
Vict Co Hist ... Victoria History of the Counties of England [*A publication*]
Vict CS........ Victorian Consolidated Statutes [*A publication*] (ILCA)
Vict Dairyfmr ... Victorian Dairyfarmer [*A publication*] (APTA)
Vic Teachers J ... Victorian Teachers Journal [*A publication*] (APTA)
Vic Teach J ... Victorian Teachers Journal [*A publication*] (APTA)
Vict For Comm Bull ... Victoria. Forests Commission. Bulletin [*A publication*] (APTA)
Vict For Comm For Tech Pap ... Victoria. Forests Commission. Forestry Technical Paper [*A publication*] (APTA)
Vict For Comm Misc Publ ... Victoria. Forests Commission. Miscellaneous Publication [*A publication*] (APTA)
Vict Geogr J ... Victorian Geographical Journal [*A publication*] (APTA)
Vict Geol Surv Bull ... Victoria. Geological Survey. Bulletin [*A publication*] (APTA)
Vict Geol Surv Mem ... Victoria. Geological Survey. Memoirs [*A publication*] (APTA)
Vict Hist Mag ... Victorian Historical Magazine [*A publication*] (APTA)
Vict Hort Dig ... Victorian Horticultural Digest [*A publication*] (APTA)
Vict L .... Victorian Law Journal [*A publication*] (DLA)
Vict L (Austr) ... Victorian Reports (Law)(Australia) [*A publication*] (ILCA)
Vict LJ....... Victorian Law Journal [*A publication*] (APTA)
Vict LR....... Victorian Law Reports [*A publication*]
Vict LT....... Victorian Law Times [*A publication*] (APTA)
Vict Nat...... Victorian Naturalist [*A publication*]
Vict Naturalist ... Victorian Naturalist [*A publication*] (APTA)
Vict Newsl ... Victorian Newsletter [*A publication*]
Victoria Country Roads Board Eng Note ... Victoria. Country Roads Board. Engineering Note [*A publication*] (APTA)
Victoria Country Roads Board Tech Bull ... Victoria. Country Roads Board. Technical Bulletin [*A publication*] (APTA)
Victoria Dep Agric Res Proj Ser ... Victoria. Department of Agriculture. Research Project Series [*A publication*] (APTA)
Victoria Dep Agric Tech Bull ... Victoria. Department of Agriculture. Technical Bulletin [*A publication*] (APTA)
Victoria Dep Agric Tech Rep Ser ... Victoria. Department of Agriculture. Technical Report Series [*A publication*] (APTA)
Victoria Fish Wildl Dep Fish Contrib ... Victoria. Fisheries and Wildlife Department. Fisheries Contribution [*Australia*] [*A publication*]
Victoria Fish Wildl Dep Wildl Contrib ... Victoria. Fisheries and Wildlife Department. Wildlife Contribution [*A publication*]
Victoria Geol Bull ... Victoria. Geological Survey. Bulletin [*A publication*] (APTA)
Victoria Geol Surv Mem ... Victoria. Geological Survey. Memoirs [*A publication*]
Victoria Inst Tr ... Victoria Institute or Philosophical Society of Great Britain. Journal of the Transactions [*A publication*]

Victoria Inst (Trinidad) Pr ... Victoria Institute (Trinidad). Proceedings [*A publication*]
Victoria Mines Dep Annu Rep ... Victoria. Mines Department. Annual Report [*A publication*]
Victoria Mines Dep Groundwater Invest Program Rep ... Victoria. Mines Department. Groundwater Investigation Program. Report [*Australia*] [*A publication*]
Victoria Minist Conserv Environ Stud Program Proj Rep ... Victoria. Ministry for Conservation. Environmental Studies Program. Project Report [*A publication*]   (APTA)
Victorian Entomol ... Victorian Entomologist [*A publication*]
Victorian Hist J ... Victorian Historical Journal [*A publication*]
Victorian Hist Mag ... Victorian Historical Magazine [*A publication*]
Victorian Nat ... Victorian Naturalist [*A publication*]
Victorian Natl Parks Assoc J ... Victorian National Parks Association. Journal [*A publication*]   (APTA)
Victorian Railw ... Victorian Railways [*A publication*]   (APTA)
Victorian Stud ... Victorian Studies [*A publication*]
Victorian Vet Proc ... Victorian Veterinary Proceedings [*A publication*]
Victoria's Resour ... Victoria's Resources [*A publication*]
Victoria State Rivers Water Supply Comm Annu Rep ... Victoria. State Rivers and Water Supply Commission. Annual Report [*A publication*]
Victoria Univ Antarct Data Ser ... Victoria University of Wellington. Antarctic Data Series [*New Zealand*] [*A publication*]
Vict Poet .... Victorian Poetry [*A publication*]
Vict Poetry ... Victorian Poetry [*A publication*]
Vict R .... Victorian Reports (Australian) [*A publication*]   (DLA)
Vict Rep ..... Victorian Reports [*A publication*]
Vict Rep (Adm) ... Victorian Reports (Admiralty) [*A publication*]   (DLA)
Vict Rep (Austr) ... Victorian Reports (Australian) [*A publication*]
Vict Rep (Eq) ... Victorian Reports (Equity) [*A publication*]
Vict Rep (Law) ... Victorian Reports (Law) [*A publication*]
Vict Res ...... Victoria's Resources [*A publication*]   (APTA)
Vict Resour ... Victoria's Resources [*A publication*]   (APTA)
Vict Rev ...... Victorian Review [*A publication*]
Vict Soil Conserv Auth TC ... Victoria. Soil Conservation Authority. TC Report [*A publication*]   (APTA)
Vict Soil Conserv Auth TC Rep ... Victoria. Soil Conservation Authority. TC Report [*A publication*]   (APTA)
Vict Stud .... Victorian Studies [*A publication*]
Vict U C L Rev ... Victoria University. College Law Review [*A publication*]
Vict UL Rev ... Victoria University. Law Review [*A publication*]   (DLA)
Vict U of Wellington L Rev ... Victoria University of Wellington. Law Review [*A publication*]
Vict U Well L Rev ... Victoria University of Wellington. Law Review [*A publication*]
Vict Vet Proc ... Australian Veterinary Association. Victorian Division. Annual General Meeting. Proceedings [*A publication*]   (APTA)
Vict Vet Proc ... Australian Veterinary Association. Victorian Division. Victorian Veterinary Proceedings [*A publication*]   (APTA)
Vic Veg Grower ... Victorian Vegetable Grower [*A publication*]   (APTA)
Vic Vet Proc ... Victorian Veterinary Proceedings [*A publication*]   (APTA)
ViCVH .... Virginia Highway Research Council, Charlottesville, VA [*Library symbol*] [*Library of Congress*]   (LCLS)
VICX .... Kanpur/Chakeri [*India*] [*ICAO location identifier*]   (ICLI)
Vic Yrbk ..... Victoria Yearbook [*A publication*]   (APTA)
ViD .... Danville Public Library, Danville, VA [*Library symbol*] [*Library of Congress*]   (LCLS)
VID .... Vide [*or Videte*] [*See*] [*Latin*]
VID .... Video   (AAG)
VID .... Video-Data [*Computer graphics*]   (BYTE)
VID .... Video Image Display Assembly [*Space Flight Operations Facility, NASA*]
Vid .... Vidian's Exact Pleader [*1684*] [*A publication*]   (DLA)
VID .... Vidin [*Bulgaria*] [*Airport symbol*]   (OAG)
VID .... Vidipress Nieuwsbrief [*A publication*]
vid .... Vidua [*Widow*] [*Latin*]   (WGA)
VID .... Vienna Institute for Development   (EAIO)
VID .... Virtual Image Display   (MCD)
VID .... Visual Identification   (CAAL)
VID .... Volunteers for International Development [*Later, Peaceworkers*]   (EA)
VID .... Vspomogatel'nye Istoricheskie Distsipliny [*A publication*]
ViDA .... Averette College, Danville, VA [*Library symbol*] [*Library of Congress*]   (LCLS)
VIDA .... Ventricular Impulse Detector and Alarm [*Cardiology*]
Vida Agr .... Vida Agricola [*A publication*]
Vida Agric ... Vida Agricola [*A publication*]
VIDAC .... Virtual Data Acquisition and Control [*Data processing*]   (HGAA)
VIDAC .... Visual Information Display and Control
VidaL .... Vida Literaria [*A publication*]
Vida Med ... Vida Medica [*A publication*]
VIDAMP ... Video Amplifier
Vida Odontol ... Vida Odontologica [*A publication*]
VIDAP .... Vibration Data Accuracy Program
VIDAR .... Velocity Integration, Detection, and Ranging   (NG)
VIDAS .... Video Image Digitiser and Storage System [*Sirton Computer*] [*London, England*]

VIDAS .... Vitek ImmunoDiagnostic Assay System
VIDAT .... Visual Data Acquisition
ViDC .... Danville Community College, Danville, VA [*Library symbol*] [*Library of Congress*]   (LCLS)
VIDC .... Video Connection of America [*NASDAQ symbol*]   (NQ)
VIDC .... Virgin Islands Department of Commerce   (EA)
VIDD .... Delhi/Safdarjung [*India*] [*ICAO location identifier*]   (ICLI)
VIDD .... Vehicle Intrusion Detection Device
VIDD .... Vertical Interval Data Detector   (NASA)
VIDE .... Video Display Corp. [*NASDAQ symbol*]   (NQ)
VIDEC .... Vibration Analysis and Detection Concept   (DNAB)
VIDEM ...... Vietnam Demonstration [*FBI security file*]
Videnskabs-Selsk Christiana Forh ... Videnskabs-Selskabet i Christiania. Forhandlingar [*A publication*]
Vidensk Medd Dan Naturhist Foren ... Videnskabelige Meddelelser fra Dansk Naturhistorisk Forening [*A publication*]
Vidensk Medd Dan Naturhist Foren Khobenhavn ... Videnskabelige Meddelelser fra Dansk Naturhistorisk Forening i Khobenhavn [*A publication*]
Video .... Video-Tronics [*A publication*]   (APTA)
VIDEO ...... Visual Data Entry On-Line [*Data processing*]
Videodical .. [*Special-Interest*] Video Cassette Issued Periodically
Video Mktg ... Video Marketing Newsletter [*A publication*]
Video Syst ... Video Systems [*A publication*]
Vide Tech-Appl ... Vide. Technique-Applications [*France*] [*A publication*]
VIDF .... Delhi [*India*] [*ICAO location identifier*]   (ICLI)
VIDF .... Vertical Side of Intermediate Distribution Frame [*Telecommunications*]   (TEL)
VIDF .... Video Frequency   (IEEE)
Vid Game T ... Video Games Today [*A publication*]
VIDI .... Visual Input Detection Instrumentation   (MCD)
VIDICODER ... Video Interphone Communications System   (SAA)
VIDN .... Dehra Dun [*India*] [*ICAO location identifier*]   (ICLI)
VIDO .... Paralax Video Enterprises, Inc. [*New York, NY*] [*NASDAQ symbol*]   (NQ)
VIDO .... Veterinary Infectious Disease Organization [*University of Saskatchewan*] [*Canada*] [*Research center*]   (RCD)
VIDP .... Delhi/Indira Gandhi International [*India*] [*ICAO location identifier*]   (ICLI)
VIDPI .... Visually Impaired Data Processors International   (EA)
VIDR .... Dadri [*India*] [*ICAO location identifier*]   (ICLI)
ViDR .... Dan River Mills Co., Danville, VA [*Library symbol*] [*Library of Congress*]   (LCLS)
ViDS .... Stratford College, Danville, VA [*Library symbol*] [*Library of Congress*]   (LCLS)
VIDS .... Vertical Instruments Display System   (MCD)
VIDS .... Video Science Technology, Inc. [*Dallas, TX*] [*NASDAQ symbol*]   (NQ)
VIDS .... Virtual Image Display System
VIDS .... Visual Information Display System   (MCD)
VIDSL .... Veroeffentlichungen. Institut fuer Deutsche Sprache und Literatur. Deutsche Akademie der Wissenschaften zu Berlin [*A publication*]
VIDS/MAF ... Visual Information Display System/Maintenance Action Form   (NVT)
VIDV .... Veroeffentlichungen. Institut fuer Deutsche Volkskunde. Deutsche Akademie der Wissenschaften zu Berlin [*A publication*]
Vidya B ...... Vidya. Section B. Sciences [*A publication*]
Vidya Bhar ... Vidya Bharati [*Bangalore*] [*A publication*]
VIE .... Vampire Information Exchange   (EA)
VIE .... Vibration Isolation Equipment   (RDA)
VIE .... Vienna [*Austria*] [*Seismograph station code, US Geological Survey*]   (SEIS)
VIE .... Vienna [*Austria*] [*Airport symbol*]   (OAG)
vie .... Vietnamese [*MARC language code*] [*Library of Congress*]   (LCCP)
VIE .... Viewpoint [*A publication*]
VIE .... Vigilance, Initiative, Excellence [*Aerospace Defense Command's acronym for the Zero Defects Program*]
VIE .... Villeneuve Resources [*Vancouver Stock Exchange symbol*]
VIE .... Voluntary Import Expansion [*International trade*]   (ECON)
VIE .... Volunteers in Education
Vie Acad Acad Sci (Paris) ... Vie Academique. Academie des Sciences (Paris) [*A publication*]
Vie Agric Meuse ... Vie Agricole de la Meuse [*A publication*]
Vie Agric et Rurale ... Vie Agricole et Rurale [*A publication*]
Vie Camp ... Vie a la Campagne [*A publication*]
Vie Econ (Berne) ... Vie Economique (Berne) [*A publication*]
ViElM .... Merck & Co., Inc., Stonewall Process Development Library, Elkton, VA [*Library symbol*] [*Library of Congress*]   (LCLS)
Vie Med ..... Vie Medicale [*A publication*]
Vie Med Can Fr ... Vie Medicale au Canada Francais [*A publication*]
Vie Milie A ... Vie et Milieu. Serie A. Biologie Marine [*A publication*]
Vie Milie B ... Vie et Milieu. Serie B. Oceanographie [*A publication*]
Vie Milie C ... Vie et Milieu. Serie C. Biologie Terrestre [*A publication*]
Vie Milieu Ser A ... Vie et Milieu. Serie A. Biologie Marine [*France*] [*A publication*]
Vie Milieu Ser A Biol Mar ... Vie et Milieu. Serie A. Biologie Marine [*A publication*]

Vie Milieu Ser B Oceanogr ... Vie et Milieu. Serie B. Oceanographie [*A publication*]
Vie Milieu Ser C Biol Terr ... Vie et Milieu. Serie C. Biologie Terrestre [*A publication*]
ViEmoE ..... Emory and Henry College, Emory, VA [*Library symbol*] [*Library of Congress*] (LCLS)
ViEmP .... Greenville County Library, Emporia, VA [*Library symbol*] [*Library of Congress*] (LCLS)
Vie Mus ..... Vie Musicale [*A publication*]
Vie Mus Belge ... Vie Musicale Belge [*A publication*]
Vien .... Viennola [*Record label*] [*Austria*]
Vienna Circle Coll ... Vienna Circle Collection [*A publication*]
VIEO .... Vendor's Item Engineering Order
Vie Ped ...... Vie Pedagogique [*A publication*]
VIER Bul ... Victorian Institute of Educational Research. Bulletin [*A publication*] (APTA)
VIER Bull ... Victorian Institute of Educational Research. Bulletin [*A publication*] (APTA)
VIERS .... Virgin Islands Ecological Research Station
Vierteljahreschr Gerichtl Med Oeff Sanitaetswes ... Vierteljahrschrift fuer Gerichtliche Medizin und Oeffentliches Sanitaetswesen [*A publication*]
Vierteljahressch Wirtschaftsforsch ... Vierteljahresschrift Wirtschaftsforschung [*West Germany*] [*A publication*]
Vierteljahrschr Prakt Pharm ... Vierteljahrschrift fuer Praktische Pharmazie [*A publication*]
Vierteljahrsh Zeitgesch ... Vierteljahrshefte fuer Zeitgeschichte [*A publication*]
Vierteljahrsschr Naturforsch Ges (Zuer) ... Vierteljahrsschrift. Naturforschende Gesellschaft (Zuerich) [*A publication*]
Vierteljahrsschr Naturforsch Ges (Zuerich) ... Vierteljahrsschrift. Naturforschende Gesellschaft (Zuerich) [*A publication*]
Vierteljahrsschr Soz Wirtschgesch ... Vierteljahrsschrift fuer Sozial- und Wirtschaftsgeschichte [*A publication*]
Viert Naturf Ges Zuerich ... Vierteljahrschrift der Naturforschenden Gesellschaft in Zuerich [*A publication*]
Vier Zeitg... Vierteljahrshefte fuer Zeitgeschichte [*A publication*]
VIESA .... Vocational Interest, Experience, and Skill Assessment [*Vocational guidance test*]
Vie Sci Econ ... Vie et Sciences Economiques [*A publication*]
Vie et Sciences Econs ... Vie et Sciences Economiques [*A publication*]
Vie Soc .... Vie Sociale [*A publication*]
Vietnam Chim Acta ... Vietnamica Chimica Acta [*A publication*]
Viet Stud .... Vietnamese Studies [*Hanoi*] [*A publication*]
VIEW .... Viewlogic Systems [*NASDAQ symbol*] (SPSG)
VIEW .... Virtual Interface Environment Workstation
VIEW .... Visible, Informative, Emotionally Appealing, Workable [*Package evaluation in marketing*]
VIEW .... Vital Information for Education and Work (OICC)
VIEW .... Vocational Information for Education and Work (AEBS)
View Bot ... View from the Bottom [*A publication*]
Viewdata .... Viewdata and Television User [*A publication*]
Vieweg Stud Aufbaukurs Math ... Vieweg Studium. Aufbaukurs Mathematik [*A publication*]
Vieweg Tracts Pure Appl Phys ... Vieweg Tracts in Pure and Applied Physics [*A publication*]
Viewpoints Biol ... Viewpoints in Biology [*A publication*]
Viewpoint Ser Aust Conserv Fdn ... Viewpoint Series. Australian Conservation Foundation [*A publication*] (APTA)
Viewpoints Teach & Learn ... Viewpoints in Teaching and Learning [*A publication*]
VIEWS ...... VAST/IMA [*Versatile Avionics System Tester/Intermediate Maintenance Activity*] Effectiveness by Workload Simulation
VIEWS ...... Vibration Indicator Early Warning System (MCD)
VIEWS ...... Virtual Interactive Environment Workstation [*NASA*] (BYTE)
VIEWS ...... Vocational Information and Evaluation Work Samples [*Vocational guidance test*]
Views & R .. Views and Reviews [*A publication*]
ViF .... Fairfax County Public Library, Fairfax, VA [*Library symbol*] [*Library of Congress*] (LCLS)
VIF .... Vale International Airlines, Inc. [*Nashville, TN*] [*FAA designator*] (FAAC)
VIF .... Vanier Institute of the Family [*Canada*]
VIF .... Variance Inflation Factor [*Statistics*]
VIF .... Vertical Infrared Fuze (CAAL)
VIF .... Video Information [*Winslow Associates*] [*Information service or system*] [*No longer available*] (IID)
VIF .... Virion Infectivity Factor [*Genetics*]
VIF .... Virus-Induced Interferon [*Cell biology*]
VIF .... Visual Image Formula [*of psychotherapist Joseph Bird's self-help theory*]
ViFarL .... Longwood College, Farmville, VA [*Library symbol*] [*Library of Congress*] (LCLS)
VIFB .... Farrukhabad [*India*] [*ICAO location identifier*] (ICLI)
ViFbE......... United States Army Engineer School, Fort Belvoir, VA [*Library symbol*] [*Library of Congress*] (LCLS)
ViFbEM..... United States Army, Engineer Museum, Fort Belvoir, VA [*Library symbol*] [*Library of Congress*] (LCLS)

ViF-BPH ... Fairfax County Public Library, Services for the Blind and Physically Handicapped, Alexandria, VA [*Library symbol*] [*Library of Congress*] (LCLS)
VIFC .... VTOL [*Vertical Takeoff and Landing*] Integrated Flight Control
VIFD........... Faridkot [*India*] [*ICAO location identifier*] (ICLI)
ViFeAM...... United States Army, Air Mobility Research and Development Laboratory, Fort Eustis, VA [*Library symbol*] [*Library of Congress*] (LCLS)
ViFeAT...... United States Army Transportation School, Fort Eustis, VA [*Library symbol*] [*Library of Congress*] (LCLS)
ViFerF....... Ferrum College, Ferrum, VA [*Library symbol*] [*Library of Congress*] (LCLS)
VIFF .... Vectoring in Forward Flight (MCD)
ViFGM ...... George Mason College [*Later, George Mason University*], Fairfax, VA [*Library symbol*] [*Library of Congress*] (LCLS)
VIFI .... Voyager Information Flow Instructions [*NASA*] (KSC)
ViFIL.......... United States Army Logistics Management Center, Fort Lee, VA [*Library symbol*] [*Library of Congress*] (LCLS)
ViFlQ.......... Quartermaster Technical Library, Fort Lee, VA [*Library symbol*] [*Library of Congress*] (LCLS)
ViFmTD .... United States Army, Training and Doctrine Command Library, Fort Monroe, VA [*Library symbol*] [*Library of Congress*] (LCLS)
ViFmTS ..... United States Army Tralinet Systems Center, Fort Monroe, VA [*Library symbol*] [*Library of Congress*] (LCLS)
ViFmUS..... United States Army Field Forces Library, Fort Monroe, VA [*Library symbol*] [*Library of Congress*] (LCLS)
ViFmyA ..... United States Army, Fort Meyer Post Library, Fort Meyer, VA [*Library symbol*] [*Library of Congress*] (LCLS)
ViFraC....... Camp Manufacturing Co., Franklin, VA [*Library symbol*] [*Library of Congress*] (LCLS)
ViFraPC..... Paul D. Camp Community College, Franklin, VA [*Library symbol*] [*Library of Congress*] (LCLS)
ViFre.......... Central Rappahannock Regional Library, Fredericksburg, VA [*Library symbol*] [*Library of Congress*] (LCLS)
ViFreJM.... James Monroe Memorial Foundation, Fredericksburg, VA [*Library symbol*] [*Library of Congress*] (LCLS)
ViFreM...... Mary Washington College of the University of Virginia, Fredericksburg, VA [*Library symbol*] [*Library of Congress*] (LCLS)
ViFroA....... American Viscose Co., Front Royal, VA [*Library symbol*] [*Library of Congress*] (LCLS)
VIFS .... Village Financial Services Ltd. [*NASDAQ symbol*] (NQ)
VIFSC........ VTOL [*Vertical Takeoff and Landing*] Integrated Flight System Control
VIFZ.......... Ferojpur [*India*] [*ICAO location identifier*] (ICLI)
VIG .... Vaccinia Immune Globulin [*Medicine*]
VIG .... Van Kampen Merritt Investment Grade [*NYSE symbol*] (SPSG)
VIG .... Video Image Generator
VIG .... Video Integrating Group
Vig............. Vigente [*In Force*] [*Italian*] (ILCA)
VIG .... Vigil (ROG)
VIG .... Vigilant Identification (MCD)
VIG .... Vignette (ADA)
VIG .... Vigoroso [*With Vigor*] [*Music*] (ROG)
VIG .... Visible Gold, Inc. [*Vancouver Stock Exchange symbol*]
VIGB.......... Variable Inlet Guide Blades (MCD)
Vig C .... Vigiliae Christianae [*A publication*]
Vig Chr ...... Vigiliae Christianae [*A publication*]
ViGcS........ Scott County Library, Gate City, VA [*Library symbol*] [*Library of Congress*] (LCLS)
VIGIL........ Vertical Indicating Gyro Internally Lighted (MCD)
Vigil Chris ... Vigiliae Christianae [*A publication*]
Vigl............ Viglius ab Ayta Zuichemus [*Deceased, 1577*] [*Authority cited in pre-1607 legal work*] (DSA)
VIGN .... Guna [*India*] [*ICAO location identifier*] (ICLI)
VIGORN.... Vigorniensis [*Signature of the Bishops of Worcester*] [*Latin*] (ROG)
Vigoro .... Vigoro Corp. [*Associated Press abbreviation*] (APAG)
ViGpD........ Deepsea Ventures, Inc., Gloucester Point, VA [*Library symbol*] [*Library of Congress*] (LCLS)
ViGpM....... Virginia Institute of Marine Science, Gloucester Point, VA [*Library symbol*] [*Library of Congress*] (LCLS)
VIGR .... Gwalior [*India*] [*ICAO location identifier*] (ICLI)
VIGS.......... Vertical Impact Guidance System [*Army*] (MCD)
VIGS.......... Video Disc Gunnery Simulator [*Army*] (INF)
VIGS.......... Video Interactive Gunnery System [*Military*] (INF)
VIGS.......... Visual Glide Slope
VIH............ Rolla/Vichy, MO [*Location identifier*] [*FAA*] (FAAL)
VIH............ Velocity Impact Hardening
ViHa .... Charles H. Taylor Memorial Library, Hampton, VA [*Library symbol*] [*Library of Congress*] (LCLS)
ViHaI........ Hampton Institute, Hampton, VA [*Library symbol*] [*Library of Congress*] (LCLS)
ViHal......... Halifax County-South Boston Regional Library, Halifax, VA [*Library symbol*] [*Library of Congress*] (LCLS)
ViHaNASA ... National Aeronautics and Space Administration, Langley Research Center, Hampton, VA [*Library symbol*] [*Library of Congress*] (LCLS)

ViHar........ Rockingham Public Library, Harrisonburg, VA [*Library symbol*] [*Library of Congress*]   (LCLS)
ViHarEM .. Eastern Mennonite College, Harrisonburg, VA [*Library symbol*] [*Library of Congress*]   (LCLS)
ViHarT ...... James Madison University, Harrisonburg, VA [*Library symbol*] [*Library of Congress*]   (LCLS)
ViHaT........ Thomas Nelson Community College, Hampton, VA [*Library symbol*] [*Library of Congress*]   (LCLS)
ViHaV........ United States Veterans Administration Center, Medical Library, Hampton, VA [*Library symbol*] [*Library of Congress*]   (LCLS)
ViHdsC...... Hampden-Sydney College, Hampden-Sydney, VA [*Library symbol*] [*Library of Congress*]   (LCLS)
ViHi .... Virginia Historical Society, Richmond, VA [*Library symbol*] [*Library of Congress*]   (LCLS)
ViHo .... Hollins College, Hollins College, VA [*Library symbol*] [*Library of Congress*]   (LCLS)
ViHop .... Appomattox Regional Library, Hopewell, VA [*Library symbol*] [*Library of Congress*]   (LCLS)
ViHopA ..... Allied Corp., Hopewell, VA [*Library symbol*] [*Library of Congress*]   (LCLS)
ViHopAT ... American Tobacco Co., Department of Research and Development, Hopewell, VA [*Library symbol*] [*Library of Congress*]   (LCLS)
ViHopHC .. Hercules Powder Co. [*Later, Hercules, Inc.*], Cellulose Products Division, Hopewell, VA [*Library symbol*] [*Library of Congress*]   (LCLS)
ViHopHV .. Hercules Powder Co. [*Later, Hercules, Inc.*], Virginia Cellulose Division, Hopewell, VA [*Library symbol*] [*Library of Congress*]   (LCLS)
VIHR .... Hissar [*India*] [*ICAO location identifier*]   (ICLI)
VII.............. Vacuum-Impregnated Inductor
VII.............. Vicon Industries, Inc. [*AMEX symbol*]   (SPSG)
VII.............. Viscosity Index Improver [*for motor oil*]
VII.............. Vocational Interest Inventory [*Vocational guidance test*]
VIIS .... Virgin Islands National Park
Viitor Soc ... Viitorul Social [*A publication*]   (EA)
VIJ .... Vera Institute of Justice
VIJ .... Virgin Gorda [*British Virgin Islands*] [*Airport symbol*]   (OAG)
VIJ .... Vishveshvaranand Indological Journal [*A publication*]
Vijes (Zagreb) ... Vijesti Muzealaca i Konservatora (Zagreb) [*A publication*]
VIJN.......... Jhansi [*India*] [*ICAO location identifier*]   (ICLI)
VIJO .... Jodhpur [*India*] [*ICAO location identifier*]   (ICLI)
VIJP .... Jaipur [*India*] [*ICAO location identifier*]   (ICLI)
VIJR .... Jaiselmer [*India*] [*ICAO location identifier*]   (ICLI)
VIJU .... Jammu [*India*] [*ICAO location identifier*]   (ICLI)
VIK .... Kavik River, AK [*Location identifier*] [*FAA*]   (FAAL)
VIK .... Vik [*Iceland*] [*Seismograph station code, US Geological Survey*] [*Closed*]   (SEIS)
VIK .... Viking International Air Freight, Inc. [*Minneapolis, MN*] [*FAA designator*]   (FAAC)
Vik .... Viking. Norsk Arkeologisk Selskap [*A publication*]
VIKA.......... Kanpur [*India*] [*ICAO location identifier*]   (ICLI)
VIKA.......... Viking Air Lines
VIKD .... Kud [*India*] [*ICAO location identifier*]   (ICLI)
ViKeS........ Southside Virginia Community College, John H. Daniel Campus, Keysville, VA [*Library symbol*] [*Library of Congress*]   (LCLS)
VIKG .... Viking Freight, Inc. [*NASDAQ symbol*]   (NQ)
Viking Fund Publ Anthropol ... Viking Fund Publication in Anthropology [*A publication*]
VIKJ .... Khajuraho [*India*] [*ICAO location identifier*]   (ICLI)
VIK Mitt.... VIK [*Vereinigung Industrielle Kraftwirtschaft*] Mitteilungen [*A publication*]
VIKO .... Kota [*India*] [*ICAO location identifier*]   (ICLI)
Vikram Quart Res J Vikram University ... Vikram. Quarterly Research Journal of Vikram University [*A publication*]
VIL............. Dakhla [*Mauritania*] [*Airport symbol*]   (OAG)
ViL............. Jones Memorial Library, Lynchburg, VA [*Library symbol*] [*Library of Congress*]   (LCLS)
VIL............. University of Victoria Law Library [*UTLAS symbol*]
VIL............. Vendor Item List [*Sales*]   (AAG)
VIL............. Vertical Injection Logic [*Data processing*]
VIL............. Very Important Ladies
VIL............. Very Important Launch   (MUGU)
VIL............. Villa Mercy [*Maryland*] [*Seismograph station code, US Geological Survey*] [*Closed*]   (SEIS)
VIL............. Village
Vi-L............. Virginia State Law Library, Richmond, VA [*Library symbol*] [*Library of Congress*]   (LCLS)
VIL............. Vivisection Investigation League   (EA)
VIL............. VTI Industries, Inc. [*Vancouver Stock Exchange symbol*]
ViLanAF.... United States Air Force, Langley Air Force Base Library, Langley AFB, VA [*Library symbol*] [*Library of Congress*]   (LCLS)
Vilas........... Vilas' Criminal Reports [*1-5 New York*] [*A publication*]   (DLA)
ViLaw........ Brunswick-Greensville Regional Library, Lawrenceville, VA [*Library symbol*] [*Library of Congress*]   (LCLS)
ViLawS ...... Saint Paul's College, Lawrenceville, VA [*Library symbol*] [*Library of Congress*]   (LCLS)

Vil & Br...... Vilas and Bryant's Edition of the Wisconsin Reports [*A publication*]   (DLA)
ViLBW....... Babcock & Wilcox Co., Lynchburg, VA [*Library symbol*] [*Library of Congress*]   (LCLS)
ViLC .... Lynchburg College, Lynchburg, VA [*Library symbol*] [*Library of Congress*]   (LCLS)
ViLCV........ Central Virginia Community College, Lynchburg, VA [*Library symbol*] [*Library of Congress*]   (LCLS)
VILD.......... Ludhaiha [*India*] [*ICAO location identifier*]   (ICLI)
V I Lenin Sakharth Politekh Inst Samecn Srom ... V. I. Leninis Sahelobis Sromis Citheli Drosis Ordenosani Sakharthvelos Politekhnikuri Instituti. Samecniero Sromebi [*A publication*]
VILIOR ..... Vladimir Ilyich Lenin, Initiator of the October Revolution [*Given name popular in Russia after the Bolshevik Revolution*]
VILK.......... Lucknow [*India*] [*ICAO location identifier*]   (ICLI)
VILL.......... Village
Vill .... Villandry Festival [*Record label*] [*France*]
Villanova L Rev ... Villanova Law Review [*A publication*]
Vill L Rev... Villanova Law Review [*A publication*]
Vilniaus Valstybinis Univ Mokslo Darb ... Vilniaus Valstybinis Universitetas Mokslo Darbai [*A publication*]
ViLoGH..... Gunston Hall Plantation Library, Lorton, VA [*Library symbol*] [*Library of Congress*]   (LCLS)
VILP .... Lalitpur [*India*] [*ICAO location identifier*]   (ICLI)
VILP .... Vector Impedance Locus Plotter
ViLRM ...... Randolph-Macon Woman's College, Lynchburg, VA [*Library symbol*] [*Library of Congress*]   (LCLS)
VILTAR .... Viltrevy [*Stockholm*] [*A publication*]
VILTCH.... Verapamil, Imipramine, Lidocaine, Tamoxifen, Chlorpromazine, Haloperidol [*Antineoplastic drug regimen*]
ViLuV .... Virginia Oak Tannery, Luray, VA [*Library symbol*] [*Library of Congress*]   (LCLS)
Vil V .... Village Voice [*A publication*]
ViLx .... Botetourt-Rockbridge Regional Library, Lexington, VA [*Library symbol*] [*Library of Congress*]   (LCLS)
ViLxV .... Virginia Military Institute, Lexington, VA [*Library symbol*] [*Library of Congress*]   (LCLS)
ViLxW .... Washington and Lee University, Lexington, VA [*Library symbol*] [*Library of Congress*]   (LCLS)
ViLxW-L ... Washington and Lee University, Law Library, Lexington, VA [*Library symbol*] [*Library of Congress*]   (LCLS)
VIM .... Vacuum Induction Melting [*Metallurgy*]
VIM .... Vendor Independent Messaging [*Data processing*]   (PCM)
VIM .... Vendor Initial Measurement [*Sales*]
VIM .... Ventral Intersegmental Muscles [*Anatomy*]
VIM .... Vertical Improved Mail [*Mail-delivery system for large buildings in which all tenants pick up their mail from lockboxes in a central mailroom*]
VIM .... Vibration Isolation Module
VIM .... Vibrational Microlamination   (MCD)
VIM .... Video Intensified Microscopy
VIM .... Vinyl Insulation Material
VIM .... Vision Intensified Microscopy
VIM .... Vocational Instructional Materials Section   (EA)
VIM .... Voice Input Module [*Cascade Graphics Development Ltd.*] [*Software package*]   (NCC)
ViMan........ Ruffner-Carnegie Public Library, Manassas, VA [*Library symbol*] [*Library of Congress*] [*Obsolete*]   (LCLS)
ViManCo ... Prince William County Public Library, Manassas, VA [*Library symbol*] [*Library of Congress*]   (LCLS)
ViMarC ..... Marion Junior College, Marion, VA [*Library symbol*] [*Library of Congress*]   (LCLS)
ViMat .... Mathews Memorial Library, Mathews, VA [*Library symbol*] [*Library of Congress*]   (LCLS)
VIMBA...... Veroeffentlichungen. Institut fuer Meeresforschung in Bremerhaven [*A publication*]
ViMcC .... Central Intelligence Agency, McLean, VA [*Library symbol*] [*Library of Congress*]   (LCLS)
ViMelE ...... Eastern Shore Community College, Learning Resources Center, Melfa, VA [*Library symbol*] [*Library of Congress*]   (LCLS)
VIMEX...... Visit Mexico [*Airline fares*]
VIMG .... Moga [*India*] [*ICAO location identifier*]   (ICLI)
VIMHEX... Venezuela International Meteorological and Hydrological Experiment [*Colorado State University project*]
ViMidL...... Lord Fairfax Community College, Learning Resources Center, Middletown, VA [*Library symbol*] [*Library of Congress*]   (LCLS)
ViMiN .... Notre Dame Institute, Middleburg, VA [*Library symbol*] [*Library of Congress*]   (LCLS)
ViMiNS ..... National Sporting Library, Inc., Middleburg, VA [*Library symbol*] [*Library of Congress*]   (LCLS)
VIMP......... Vertical Impulse
VIMS........ Mandasor [*India*] [*ICAO location identifier*]   (ICLI)
VIMS........ Variable Integration Management System
VIMS........ Vehicle Integrated Management System
VIMS........ Verification Information Management System   (DNAB)
VIMS........ Virginia Institute of Marine Science [*College of William and Mary*] [*Research center*]

VIMS......... Visual Infrared Mapping Spectrometer
VIMTPG ... Virtual Interactive Machine Test Program Generator
ViMtvL...... Mount Vernon Ladies' Association of the Union, Mount Vernon, VA [*Library symbol*] [*Library of Congress*] (LCLS)
VIMVAR... Vacuum Induction Melt, Vacuum Arc Remelt
ViMvD...... E. I. Du Pont de Nemours & Co., Martinsville, VA [*Library symbol*] [*Library of Congress*] (LCLS)
VIN .... Miami, FL [*Location identifier*] [*FAA*] (FAAL)
ViN .... Norfolk Public Library, Norfolk, VA [*Library symbol*] [*Library of Congress*] (LCLS)
VIN .... Vehicle Identification Number
VIN .... Vendor Identification Number [*Sales*] (MCD)
VIN .... Victorian Industrial Notes [*A publication*]
Vin.............. Vincentius Hispanus [*Deceased, 1248*] [*Authority cited in pre-1607 legal work*] (DSA)
Vin.............. Vinduet [*A publication*]
VIN .... Vineyard [*California*] [*Seismograph station code, US Geological Survey*] [*Closed*] (SEIS)
VIN .... Vintage Enterprises, Inc. [*AMEX symbol*] (SPSG)
VIN .... Vinum [*Wine*] [*Pharmacy*] (ROG)
VIN .... Vinyl [*Technical drawings*]
VIN .... Voltage Input (TEL)
Vin Abr ...... Supplement to Viner's Abridgment of Law and Equity [*England*] [*A publication*] (DLA)
Vin Abr (Eng) ... Viner's Abridgment of Law and Equity [*1741-53*] [*A publication*] (DLA)
Vina Q........ Vina Quarterly [*A publication*]
ViNarC ...... Celanese Corp., Narrows, VA [*Library symbol*] [*Library of Congress*] (LCLS)
Vinar Obz .. Vinarsky Obzor [*A publication*]
ViNC......... Chrysler Art Museum, Jean Outland Chrysler Library, Norfolk, VA [*Library symbol*] [*Library of Congress*] (LCLS)
Vinc........... Vincentius Hispanus [*Deceased, 1248*] [*Authority cited in pre-1607 legal work*] (DSA)
Vinc Cr L ... Vincent's Manual of Criminal Law [*A publication*] (DLA)
Vinc Cr & Lib ... Vincent on Criticism and Libel [*A publication*] (DLA)
Vincent de Franch ... Vincentius de Franchis [*Deceased, 1601*] [*Authority cited in pre-1607 legal work*] (DSA)
Vin Comm ... Viner's Abridgment [*or Commentaries*] [*A publication*] (DLA)
VIND .... Vicarious Interpolations Not Desired
VIND .... Vindication (ROG)
VIndJ .... Vishveshvaranand Indological Journal [*A publication*]
ViNE......... Eastern Virginia Medical School, Norfolk, VA [*Library symbol*] [*Library of Congress*] (LCLS)
ViNe.......... Newport News Public Library, Newport News, VA [*Library symbol*] [*Library of Congress*] (LCLS)
ViNeC .... Christopher Newport College, Newport News, VA [*Library symbol*] [*Library of Congress*] (LCLS)
ViNeM....... Mariners' Museum, Newport News, VA [*Library symbol*] [*Library of Congress*] (LCLS)
ViNeN....... Newport News Shipbuilding & Dry Dock Co., Newport News, VA [*Library symbol*] [*Library of Congress*] (LCLS)
Viner Abr ... Viner's Abridgment of Law and Equity [*1741-53*] [*A publication*] (DLA)
VINES ...... Virtual Networking Software [*Banyan Systems*]
ViNeV .... Virginia Associated Research Center, Newport News, VA [*Library symbol*] [*Library of Congress*] (LCLS)
VINFA...... Volunteers in the National Forests Act [*1972*]
Vingt Siecle Feder ... Vingtieme Siecle Federaliste [*A publication*]
VINH........ Nuh [*India*] [*ICAO location identifier*] (ICLI)
Vinifera Wine Grow J ... Vinifera Wine Growers Journal [*A publication*]
Vini Ital...... Vini d'Italia [*A publication*]
VINITI ...... Vsesoyuznyy Institut Nauchnoy i Tekhnicheskoy Informatsii [*All-Union Institute of Scientific and Technical Information*] [*Former USSR*]
VINL......... Naranaup [*India*] [*ICAO location identifier*] (ICLI)
ViNM........ Norfolk County Medical Society, Inc., Norfolk, VA [*Library symbol*] [*Library of Congress*] (LCLS)
ViNMoN.... Monsanto Chemical Co., Norfolk, VA [*Library symbol*] [*Library of Congress*] (LCLS)
Vinn ad Inst ... Vinnius' Commentary on the Institutes of Justinian [*A publication*] (DLA)
ViNO .... Old Dominion University, Norfolk, VA [*Library symbol*] [*Library of Congress*] (LCLS)
VINO........ WINE, Inc. [*NASDAQ symbol*] (NQ)
Vinodel Vinograd SSSR ... Vinodelie i Vinogradarstvo SSSR [*A publication*]
Vinograd Plodovod (Budapest) ... Vinogradarstvo i Plodovodstvo (Budapest) [*A publication*]
Vinograd Vinar (Budapest) ... Vinogradarstvo i Vinarstvo (Budapest) [*A publication*]
Vinograd Vinorobstvo ... Vinogradarstvo i Vinorobstvo [*A publication*]
ViNott........ Nottoway County Library, Nottoway, VA [*Library symbol*] [*Library of Congress*] (LCLS)
Vin Palaeot ... Vincentius Palaeotus [*Deceased, 1498*] [*Authority cited in pre-1607 legal work*] (DSA)
ViNR......... F. S. Royster Guano Co., Norfolk, VA [*Library symbol*] [*Library of Congress*] (LCLS)
ViNS .... Norfolk State College, Norfolk, VA [*Library symbol*] [*Library of Congress*] (LCLS)
VINS......... Velocity Inertia Navigation System

VINS......... Very Intense Neutron Source [*Nuclear science*] (OA)
ViNSC .... United States Armed Forces Staff College, Norfolk, VA [*Library symbol*] [*Library of Congress*] (LCLS)
Vin Supp .... Supplement to Viner's Abridgment of Law and Equity [*A publication*] (DLA)
ViNT .... Norfolk Testing Laboratories, Norfolk, VA [*Library symbol*] [*Library of Congress*] (LCLS)
VINT .... Video Integrate (NVT)
VInt.......... Vie Intellectuelle [*A publication*] (BJA)
VINT .... Vintage Group, Inc. [*NASDAQ symbol*] (NQ)
VINT² .... Vehicle Integrated Intelligence [*Army*]
Vint Can Law ... Vinton's American Canon Law [*A publication*] (DLA)
VintgPt....... Vintage Petroleum [*Associated Press abbreviation*] (APAG)
ViNWe....... Virginia Wesleyan College, Norfolk, VA [*Library symbol*] [*Library of Congress*] (LCLS)
Vinyls Polym ... Vinyls and Polymers [*Japan*] [*A publication*]
VIO .... Heavy [*Used to qualify interference or static reports*] [*Telecommunications*] (FAAC)
VIO .... Veroeffentlichungen. Institut fuer Orientforschung. Deutsche Akademie der Wissenschaften zu Berlin [*A publication*]
VIO .... Very Important Object (DCTA)
VIO .... Veterinary Investigation Officer [*Ministry of Agriculture, Fisheries, and Food*] [*British*]
VIO .... Video Input/Output
VIO .... Violet (AAG)
VIO .... Violino [*Violin*] [*Music*] (ROG)
VIO .... Vior Miniere d'Exploration Societe, Inc. [*Toronto Stock Exchange symbol*]
VIO .... Virtual Input/Output [*Data processing*] (IBMDP)
VIO .... Visual Intercept Officer [*Navy*]
VIOC .... Variable Input-Output Code
VIOL .... Viola [*Music*] (ROG)
viol............. Violaceus [*Purple*] [*Latin*] (WGA)
VIOLE....... Violone [*Double Bass*] [*Music*] (ROG)
VIOLENT ... Viewers Intent on Listing Violent Episodes on Nationwide Television [*Student legal action organization*]
VIOLO ...... Violino [*Violin*] [*Music*] (ROG)
ViOr........... Orange County Public Library, Orange, VA [*Library symbol*] [*Library of Congress*] (LCLS)
VIP............ Value Improving Products
VIP............ Value in Performance
VIP............ Variable Incentive Pay [*Military*] (NVT)
VIP............ Variable Individual Protection [*Insurance*]
VIP............ Variable Inductance Pickup
VIP............ Variable Information Processing [*Naval Ordnance Laboratory*] [*Information retrieval*]
VIP............ Variable Input Phototypesetter
VIP............ Variable Interest Plus [*Banking*]
VIP............ Vasoactive Inhibitory Principle [*Biochemistry*]
VIP............ Vasoactive Intestinal Peptide [*or Polypeptide*] [*Biochemistry*]
VIP............ Vasoinhibitory Peptide [*Medicine*] (MAE)
VIP............ Vector Instruction Processor
VIP............ Ventilated Improved Pit [*Latrine*]
VIP............ Verification Integration Plan (SSD)
VIP............ Verifying the Installation of Products [*Military*] (SAA)
VIP............ Vermont Information Processes, Inc. [*Information service or system*] (IID)
VIP............ Versatile Information Processor [*Data processing*]
VIP............ Very Important Passenger
VIP............ Very Important Patient (MAE)
VIP............ Very Important Person
VIP............ Very Important Poor
VIP............ Very Important Pregnancy [*In book title, "VIP Program"*]
VIP............ Vice President (AAG)
VIP............ Video Inertial Pointing [*System*] [*NASA*]
VIP............ Video Integrator and Processor
VIP............ Viewers in Profile [*A. C. Nielsen Co. reports for television industry*]
VIP............ Virgil Partch [*Cartoonist*]
VIP............ Virtual Image Processing [*Optics*]
VIP............ Viscosity-Index Improver [*for motor oil*]
VIP............ Visible Ink Press [*Publisher*]
VIP............ Vision Information Program (IID)
VIP............ Visit-Investigate-Purchase [*Department of Commerce program*]
VIP............ Visitor Information Publications (EA)
VIP............ Visual Identification Point (AFM)
VIP............ Visual Image Projection
VIP............ Visual Information Processing
VIP............ Visual Information Projection
VIP............ Visual Input [*System*] [*AT & T*]
VIP............ Visual Integrated Presentation [*Aviation*] (FAAC)
VIP............ Vocational Interviewing and Placement (DNAB)
VIP............ Voice Information Processor
VIP............ Voice Integrated Presentations [*Telecommunications*] (RDA)
VIP............ Voix et Images du Pays [*University of Quebec*] [*A publication*]
VIP............ Volume Inverse Pricing [*Business term*]
VIP............ Voluntary Interruption of Pregnancy [*Obstetrics*] (MAE)
VIP............ Volunteer Informant Program [*Navy*] (DNAB)
VIP............ Vulcan Packaging, Inc. [*Toronto Stock Exchange symbol*]
VIP............ Vulcanized Interlinked Polyethylene [*Union Carbide Corp.*]
VIPA......... Volunteers in the Parks Act [*1969*]

ViPe .... Vita e Pensiero [*Milan*] [*A publication*]
VIPER .... Verifiable Integrated Processor for Enhanced Reliability [*Data processing*] (BYTE)
VIPER .... Video Processing and Electronic Reduction (IEEE)
VIPERSCAN ... Viper Rocket with Scanner (SAA)
ViPet .... Petersburg Public Library, Petersburg, VA [*Library symbol*] [*Library of Congress*] (LCLS)
ViPetA .... Allied Chemical Corp., Fibers Division, Technical Center Library, Petersburg, VA [*Library symbol*] [*Library of Congress*] (LCLS)
ViPetS .... Virginia State College, Petersburg, VA [*Library symbol*] [*Library of Congress*] (LCLS)
VIPI .... Very Important Person Indeed
VIPI .... Volunteers in Probation, Inc. [*Later, VIP Division of National Council on Crime and Delinquency*] (EA)
VIPID .... Visual Information Processing Interface Device (MCD)
VIPK .... Pathankot [*India*] [*ICAO location identifier*] (ICLI)
VIPL .... Patiala [*India*] [*ICAO location identifier*] (ICLI)
VIPL .... Vulcan Packaging Ltd. [*Formerly, Vulcan Industrial Packaging Ltd.*] [*NASDAQ symbol*] (NQ)
ViPo .... Portsmouth Public Library, Portsmouth, VA [*Library symbol*] [*Library of Congress*] (LCLS)
ViPoN .... Norfolk Naval Hospital, Portsmouth, VA [*Library symbol*] [*Library of Congress*] (LCLS)
ViPoVC ...... Virginia Chemicals, Inc., Portsmouth, VA [*Library symbol*] [*Library of Congress*] (LCLS)
ViPoVS ...... Virginia Smelting Co., Portsmouth, VA [*Library symbol*] [*Library of Congress*] (LCLS)
VIPP .... Variable Information Processing Package
VIPP .... Venda Independent People's Party [*Political party*] (PPW)
ViPrA .... American Cyanamid Co., Pigments Division, Piney River, VA [*Library symbol*] [*Library of Congress*] (LCLS)
VIPRA .... Vest Individual Protective Reflective Adjustable [*System*] [*Military*] (INF)
VIPRE FIRE ... Visual Precision Fire Control [*Navy*] (DNAB)
VIPS .... Variable Induction Port System [*Automotive engineering*]
VIPS .... Variable Item Processing System
VIPS .... Verbal Instruction Programmed System
VIPS .... Versatile Isotope Power System (MCD)
VIPS .... Veterans in Public Service Act
VIPS .... Video Image Processing System
VIPS .... Video Interactive Processing System
VIPS .... Voice Information Processing System [*UNISYS Corp.*] [*Blue Bell, PA*] [*Telecommunications service*] (TSSD)
VIPS .... Voice Interruption Priority System
VIPT .... Nainital (Pantnagar) [*India*] [*ICAO location identifier*] (ICLI)
VIPT .... Vinland Property Trust [*NASDAQ symbol*] (NQ)
VIPTI .... Visually Impaired Piano Tuners International (EA)
ViPur .... Purcellville Library, Purcellville, VA [*Library symbol*] [*Library of Congress*] (LCLS)
VIQ .... Neillsville, WI [*Location identifier*] [*FAA*] (FAAL)
VIQG .... Qazigund [*India*] [*ICAO location identifier*] (ICLI)
ViQM .... United States Marine Corps Schools, Quantico, VA [*Library symbol*] [*Library of Congress*] (LCLS)
ViQM-E ..... United States Marine Corps Schools, Educational Center, Quantico, VA [*Library symbol*] [*Library of Congress*] (LCLS)
VIR .... A. H. Robins Co., Richmond, VA [*OCLC symbol*] (OCLC)
VIR .... Point Barrow, AK [*Location identifier*] [*FAA*] (FAAL)
ViR .... Richmond Public Library, Richmond, VA [*Library symbol*] [*Library of Congress*] (LCLS)
VIR .... Si Vires Permittant [*If the Strength Will Bear It*] [*Pharmacy*] (ROG)
VIR .... Variable Interest Rate
VIR .... Vendor Information Request [*Sales*]
VIR .... Vendor Item Release [*Sales*]
VIR .... Vertical Interval Reference [*Automatic color adjustment*] [*Television*]
ViR .... Viata Romaneasca [*Bucharest*] [*A publication*]
VIR .... Victoria Imperatrix Regina [*Victoria Empress and Queen*] (ILCA)
VIR .... Victorian Industrial Reports [*A publication*]
VIR .... Virco Manufacturing Corp. [*AMEX symbol*] (SPSG)
VIR .... Virgin Islands of the US [*ANSI three-letter standard code*] (CNC)
Vir .... Virginia Cases (Brockenbrough and Holmes) [*A publication*] (DLA)
Vir .... Virgin's Reports [*52-60 Maine*] [*A publication*] (DLA)
Vir .... Virgo [*Constellation*]
Vir .... Viridis [*Green*] [*Pharmacy*]
Vir .... Virittaja [*A publication*]
VIR .... Virology
VIR .... Virtuoso [*A publication*]
VIR .... Virulent
VIR .... Visible [*or Visual*] and Infrared Radiometer [*NASA*]
VIR .... Vulcanized India Rubber
ViRa .... Radford College, Radford, VA [*Library symbol*] [*Library of Congress*] (LCLS)
ViRA .... Richmond Academy of Medicine, Richmond, VA [*Library symbol*] [*Library of Congress*] (LCLS)
VIRA .... Vehicular Infrared Alarm (MCD)

VIRA .... Venus International Reference Atmosphere [*Meteorology*]
VIRA .... Video Review Award
Vira-A .... Vidarabine [*Also, ara-A*] [*Biochemistry*]
VIRAD ...... Virtual RADAR Defense [*Army*] (MCD)
ViralTst ..... Viral Testing [*Associated Press abbreviation*] (APAG)
ViRaP .... Radford Public Library, Radford, VA [*Library symbol*] [*Library of Congress*] (LCLS)
Viratek .... Viratek, Inc. [*Associated Press abbreviation*] (APAG)
ViRAV .... Atlantic Varnish & Paint Co., Richmond, VA [*Library symbol*] [*Library of Congress*] (LCLS)
VIRB .... Raibarelli/Fursatganj [*India*] [*ICAO location identifier*] (ICLI)
ViRC .... Museum of the Confederacy, Richmond, VA [*Library symbol*] [*Library of Congress*] (LCLS)
Virc Arch A ... Virchows Archiv. A. Pathological Anatomy and Histology [*A publication*]
Virc Arch B ... Virchows Archiv. B. Cell Pathology [*A publication*]
ViRCC .... [*The*] Computer Co., Richmond, VA [*Library symbol*] [*Library of Congress*] (LCLS)
Virchows Arch Abt A ... Virchows Archiv. Abteilung A. Pathologische Anatomie [*A publication*]
Virchows Arch Abt A Pathol Anat ... Virchows Archiv. Abteilung A. Pathologische Anatomie [*A publication*]
Virchows Arch Abt B ... Virchows Archiv. Abteilung B. Zellpathologie [*A publication*]
Virchows Arch Abt B Zellpathol ... Virchows Archiv. Abteilung B. Zellpathologie [*A publication*]
Virchows Arch A Pathol Anat Histol ... Virchows Archiv. A. Pathological Anatomy and Histology [*A publication*]
Virchows Arch A Pathol Anat Histopathol ... Virchows Archiv. A. Pathological Anatomy and Histopathology [*A publication*]
Virchows Arch B Cell Pathol ... Virchows Archiv. B. Cell Pathology [*A publication*]
Virchows Arch B Cell Pathol Incl Mol Pathol ... Virchows Archiv. B. Cell Pathology Including Molecular Pathology [*A publication*]
Virchows Arch Path Anat ... Virchows Archiv fuer Pathologische Anatomie [*A publication*]
Virchows Arch Pathol Anat Physiol Klin Med ... Virchows Archiv fuer Pathologische Anatomie und Physiologie und fuer Klinische Medizin [*A publication*]
Virch PM ... Virchow on Post Mortem Examinations [*A publication*] (DLA)
VIRCO .... Virco Manufacturing Corp. [*Associated Press abbreviation*] (APAG)
ViRCU .... Virginia Commonwealth University, Richmond, VA [*Library symbol*] [*Library of Congress*] (LCLS)
ViRCU-A ... Virginia Commonwealth University, Academic Division, Richmond, VA [*Library symbol*] [*Library of Congress*] (LCLS)
ViRCU-H .. Virginia Commonwealth University, Health Sciences Division, Richmond, VA [*Library symbol*] [*Library of Congress*] (LCLS)
VIREDF .... Virus Research [*A publication*]
ViREP .... Virginia Electric & Power Co., Richmond, VA [*Library symbol*] [*Library of Congress*] (LCLS)
ViREx .... Experiment, Inc., Richmond, VA [*Library symbol*] [*Library of Congress*] (LCLS)
ViRFR .... Federal Reserve Bank of Richmond, Richmond, VA [*Library symbol*] [*Library of Congress*] (LCLS)
VIRG .... Reengus [*India*] [*ICAO location identifier*] (ICLI)
ViRG .... Richmond Guano Co., Richmond, VA [*Library symbol*] [*Library of Congress*] (LCLS)
VIRG .... Virgin
Virg .... Virgin's Reports [*52-60 Maine*] [*A publication*] (DLA)
Virg .... Virgo [*Constellation*]
Virg Cas ..... Virginia Cases (Brockenbrough and Holmes) [*A publication*] (DLA)
Virgin .... Virgin's Reports [*52-60 Maine*] [*A publication*] (DLA)
Virginia Div Mineral Rsources Rept Inv ... Virginia. Division of Mineral Resources. Report of Investigations [*A publication*]
Virginia Jour Sci ... Virginia Journal of Science [*A publication*]
Virginia J Sci ... Virginia Journal of Science [*A publication*]
Virginia Med Month ... Virginia Medical Monthly [*Later, Virginia Medical*] [*A publication*]
Virginia Miner ... Virginia Minerals [*Charlottesville*] [*A publication*]
Virginia M Month ... Virginia Medical Monthly [*A publication*]
Virginia Polytech Inst Research Div Bull ... Virginia Polytechnic Institute. Research Division. Bulletin [*A publication*]
Virginia Polytech Inst Research Div Mon ... Virginia Polytechnic Institute. Research Division. Monograph [*A publication*]
Virginia Q R ... Virginia Quarterly Review [*A publication*]
Virgin Pilo ... Virginian-Pilot [*A publication*]
Virg J Int'l L ... Virginia Journal of International Law [*A publication*]
Virg LJ .... Virginia Law Journal [*Richmond*] [*A publication*] (DLA)
ViRGS .... Church of Jesus Christ of Latter-Day Saints, Genealogical Society Library, Richmond Stake Branch, Richmond, VA [*Library symbol*] [*Library of Congress*] (LCLS)
VIRGS .... VISSR [*Visible-Infrared Spin Scan Radiometer*] Image Registration and Gridding System (MCD)
Virg & Star L ... Virginian-Pilot and Ledger-Star [*A publication*]
ViRHC .... Henrico County Public Library, Richmond, VA [*Library symbol*] [*Library of Congress*] (LCLS)
VIRIS .... Visible/Infrared Intelligent Spectrometer

Vir LJ......... Virginia Law Journal [*A publication*]   (DLA)
VIRM .... Variable-Interest-Rate Mortgage [*Real estate*]
ViRMu....... Virginia Museum of Fine Arts, Richmond, VA [*Library symbol*] [*Library of Congress*]   (LCLS)
VIRNS...... Velocity Inertia RADAR Navigation System
ViRo........... Roanoke Public Library, Roanoke, VA [*Library symbol*] [*Library of Congress*]   (LCLS)
ViRoA .... American Viscose Co., Roanoke, VA [*Library symbol*] [*Library of Congress*]   (LCLS)
Virol.......... Virology [*A publication*]
Virol Abstr ... Virology Abstracts [*A publication*]
Virol Monogr ... Virology Monographs [*A publication*]
ViRoNW .... Norfolk & Western Railway Co., Roanoke, VA [*Library symbol*] [*Library of Congress*]   (LCLS)
ViRoV .... Virginia Western Community College, Brown Library, Roanoke, VA [*Library symbol*] [*Library of Congress*]   (LCLS)
ViRPM ...... Philip Morris Research Center, Richmond, VA [*Library symbol*] [*Library of Congress*]   (LCLS) .
ViRPol .... W. P. Poythress Co., Richmond, VA [*Library symbol*] [*Library of Congress*]   (LCLS)
Vir Q R...... Virginia Quarterly Review [*A publication*]
ViRR .... Reynolds Metals Co., Richmond, VA [*Library symbol*] [*Library of Congress*]   (LCLS)
VIRR.......... Visible [*or Visual*] and Infrared Radiometer [*NASA*]
ViRRC .... J. Sargeant Reynolds Community College, Downtown Campus, Richmond, VA [*Library symbol*] [*Library of Congress*]   (LCLS)
ViRR-E ...... Reynolds Metals Co., Executive Office Library, Richmond, VA [*Library symbol*] [*Library of Congress*]   (LCLS)
VIR & Regs ... Virgin Islands Rules and Regulations [*A publication*]   (DLA)
ViRRob ...... A. H. Robins Co., Richmond, VA [*Library symbol*] [*Library of Congress*]   (LCLS)
ViRR-P ...... Reynolds Metals Co., Packaging Research Division, Richmond, VA [*Library symbol*] [*Library of Congress*]   (LCLS)
ViRR-T ...... Reynolds Metals Co., Technical Information Services Library, Richmond, VA [*Library symbol*] [*Library of Congress*]   (LCLS)
VIRS .... Veroeffentlichungen. Institut fuer Romanische Sprachwissenschaft. Deutsche Akademie der Wissenschaften zu Berlin [*A publication*]
VIRS .... Visual Technology Research Simulator   (MCD)
Virt............. De Virtutibus [*of Philo*]   (BJA)
Virt............. Virtually   (ILCA)
Virtk.......... Viratek, Inc. [*Associated Press abbreviation*]   (APAG)
ViRU.......... University of Richmond, Richmond, VA [*Library symbol*] [*Library of Congress*]   (LCLS)
ViRUCA .... United States Circuit Court of Appeals, Fourth Circuit, Richmond, VA [*Library symbol*] [*Library of Congress*]   (LCLS)
Viruly's Tech Maandbl Wasind ... Viruly's Technisch Maandblad voor de Wasindustrie [*A publication*]
Virus Res ... Virus Research [*A publication*]
Virus Res Suppl ... Virus Research. Supplement [*A publication*]
ViRUT .... Union Theological Seminary, Richmond, VA [*Library symbol*] [*Library of Congress*]   (LCLS)
ViRUV .... United Virginia Bankshares, Inc., Richmond, VA [*Library symbol*] [*Library of Congress*]   (LCLS)
ViRV .... United States Veterans Administration Hospital, Richmond, VA [*Library symbol*] [*Library of Congress*]   (LCLS)
ViRVal .... Valentine Museum, Richmond, VA [*Library symbol*] [*Library of Congress*]   (LCLS)
ViRVB .... Virginia Baptist Historical Society, University of Richmond, Richmond, VA [*Library symbol*] [*Library of Congress*]   (LCLS)
ViRVI........ Virginia Institute for Scientific Research, Richmond, VA [*Library symbol*] [*Library of Congress*]   (LCLS)
ViRVM ...... Valentine Meat Juice Co., Richmond, VA [*Library symbol*] [*Library of Congress*]   (LCLS)
ViRVU .... Virginia Union University, Richmond, VA [*Library symbol*] [*Library of Congress*]   (LCLS)
VIS............. Minority Vendor Information Service [*National Minority Supplier Development Council, Inc.*]   (IID)
VIS............. Vaginal Irrigation Smear [*Medicine*]   (MAE)
VIS............. Variable Induction System [*Automotive engineering*]
VIS............. Variance Index Score [*Statistics*]
VIS............. Vector Instruction Set [*Data processing*]
VIS............. Vegetarian Information Service   (EA)
VIS............. Vehicle Indicator Section
VIS............. Vehicle Information System [*Automotive engineering*]
VIS............. Vehicular Intercommunications System
VIS............. Verification Information System   (NASA)
VIS............. Veroeffentlichungen. Institut fuer Slawistik. Deutsche Akademie zu Berlin [*A publication*]
VIS............. Veterinary Investigation Service [*Ministry of Agriculture, Fisheries, and Food*] [*British*]
VIS............. Vibration Isolation System
VIS............. Victim Impact Statement
VIS............. Videotex Information System [*Radio Shack*] [*Information service or system*]   (IID)
VIS............. Vietnamese Information Service

VIS............. Virtual Information Storage   (BUR)
VIS............. Visalia [*California*] [*Airport symbol*]   (OAG)
VIS............. Viscosity
VIS............. Viscount [*or Viscountess*]
VIS............. Viscount Resources Ltd. [*Vancouver Stock Exchange symbol*]
VIS............. Vishakhapatnam [*Andhra, Waltair*] [*India*] [*Seismograph station code, US Geological Survey*]   (SEIS)
VIS............. Visible [*or Visibility*]   (AFM)
VIS............. Vision   (AAMN)
VIS............. Visit [*or Visitor*]
VIS............. Vista
VIS............. Visual
VIS............. Visual Imagery System [*NASA*]
VIS............. Visual Information Storage
VIS............. Visual Information System
VIS............. Visual Instrumentation Subsystem
VIS............. Visual Spectrophotometry
VIS............. VNR [*Van Nostrand Reinhold*] Information Services   (IID)
VIS............. Voice Information Service [*Telecommunications*]
VIS............. Voice Interactive Subsystem   (MCD)
VIS............. Voice Intercom Subsystem   (MCD)
ViSa .... Salem Public Library, Salem, VA [*Library symbol*] [*Library of Congress*]   (LCLS)
VISA .... Ventricular Inhibiting Synchronous with Atrium [*Cardiac pacemaker*] [*Trademark*]
VISA .... [*The*] Vista Organization Ltd. [*New York, NY*] [*NASDAQ symbol*]   (NQ)
VISA .... Vocational Interest and Sophistication Assessment [*Vocational guidance test*]
Vis Aids News ... Visual Aids News [*A publication*]   (APTA)
Vis Aids Rev ... Visual Aids Review [*A publication*]   (APTA)
VISAR .... Velocity Interferometer System for Any Reflector   (MCD)
ViSaRC...... Roanoke College, Salem, VA [*Library symbol*] [*Library of Congress*]   (LCLS)
Vis Arts...... Visual Arts [*A publication*]
Vis Arts Bul ... Visual Arts Bulletin [*A publication*]
ViSaV......... United States Veterans Administration Hospital, Salem, VA [*Library symbol*] [*Library of Congress*]   (LCLS)
VISB .... Sikandrabad [*India*] [*ICAO location identifier*]   (ICLI)
Visbl Lang ... Visible Language [*A publication*]
VISC .... Video Disc
visc .... Visceral
VISC .... Viscosity   (AAG)
VISC .... Viscount [*or Viscountess*]
VISC .... Visual Industries, Inc. [*NASDAQ symbol*]   (NQ)
VISC .... Vitreous Infusion Suction Cutter [*Ophthalmology*]
VISCA Rev Visayas State Coll Agric ... VISCA Review. Visayas State College of Agriculture [*A publication*]
VISCO....... Visual Systems Corp.
VISCOM... Visual Communications
VIS-COM-UK ... Visual Communications Exhibition and Conference, United Kingdom   (ITD)
VISCT .... Viscount [*or Viscountess*]
Vis Educ..... Visual Education [*A publication*]
VI Sess Laws ... Virgin Islands Session Laws [*A publication*]
Vishay........ Vishay Intertechnology, Inc. [*Associated Press abbreviation*]   (APAG)
Vish Indo J ... Vishveshvaranand Indological Journal [*Hoshiarpur*] [*A publication*]
VISI .... VisionTech, Inc. [*Roswell, GA*] [*NASDAQ symbol*]   (NQ)
VISI .... Volar Intercalated Segment Instability [*Orthopedics*]
Visible Lang ... Visible Language [*A publication*]
VISID .... Visual Identification   (MSA)
Vis Ind .... Vision Index [*A publication*]
Visindafelag Isl Greinar ... Visindafelag Islendinga. Greinar [*A publication*]
Visindafelag Isl Rit ... Visindafelag Islendinga. Rit [*A publication*]
Vis Index.... Vision Index [*A publication*]
VISION...... Volunteers in Service to India's Oppressed and Neglected   (EA)
Vision Res ... Vision Research [*A publication*]
Vision Res Suppl ... Vision Research. Supplement [*A publication*]
VISIT........ Project VISIT - Vehicle Internal Systems Investigative Team   (EA)
VISIT........ Visual Information Systems for Image Transformation [*Air Force*]
VISITS ...... Very Important Small Institution Travel Support
VISITT ...... Vendor Information System for Innovative Treatment Technology [*Environmental Protection Agency*] [*Database*]
VISI............ Veroeffentlichungen. Institut fuer Slawistik. Deutsche Akademie der Wissenschaften zu Berlin [*A publication*]
VisL .... Visible Language [*A publication*]
VIS LAB... Visibility Laboratory [*Research center*]   (RCD)
VISM......... Simla [*India*] [*ICAO location identifier*]   (ICLI)
VISMEM .. Visual Memory Task [*Neuropsychology test*]
VISMOD... Visual Modifications [*Program*] [*Army*]   (RDA)
VISMR .... Viscometer [*Engineering*]
VISN.......... Vision Interfaith Satellite Network
Visn Akad Nauk Ukr RSR ... Visnyk Akademiyi Nauk Ukrayins'koyi RSR [*A publication*]
Visnik Kiiv Univ Ser Mat Meh ... Visnik Kiivs'kogo Universitetu. Serija Matematiki ta Mehaniki [*A publication*]

Visnik Kiiv Univ Ser Mat Mekh ... Visnik Kiivs'kogo Universitetu. Seriya Matematiki ta Mekhaniki [*A publication*]
Visnik L'viv Derz Univ Ser Meh-Mat ... Visnik L'vivs'kogo Ordena Lenina Derzavogo Universitetu Imeni Ivana Franka. Serija Mehaniko-Matematicnu [*A publication*]
Visnik L'viv Politehn Inst ... Visnik L'vivs'kogo Politehnicnogo Institutu [*A publication*]
VIS/NIR.... Visible and Near-Visible Infrared   (MCD)
Visn Kharkiv Univ Astron ... Visnik Kharkivs'kogo Universitetu. Astronomiya [*Ukrainian SSR*] [*A publication*]
Visn Kharkiv Univ Radiofiz ... Visnik Kharkivs'kogo Universitetu. Radiofizika [*Ukrainian SSR*] [*A publication*]
Visn Kharkiv Univ Radiofiz Elektron ... Visnik Kharkivs'kogo Universitetu. Radiofizika i Elektronika [*Ukrainian SSR*] [*A publication*]
Visn Kiiv Politekh Inst Ser Khim Mashinobuduv Tekhnol ... Visnik Kiivs'kogo Politekhnichnogo Institutu. Seriya Khimichnogo Mashinobuduvannya ta Tekhnologii [*Ukrainian SSR*] [*A publication*]
Visn Kiiv Univ Ser Astron ... Visnik Kiivs'kogo Universitetu. Seriya Astronomii [*Ukrainian SSR*] [*A publication*]
Visn Kiiv Univ Ser Astron Fiz Khim ... Visnik Kiivs'kogo Universitetu. Seriya Astronomii, Fiziki, ta Khimii [*A publication*]
Visn Kiiv Univ Ser Biol ... Visnik Kiivs'kogo Universitetu. Seriya Biologii [*Ukrainian SSR*] [*A publication*]
Visn Kiiv Univ Ser Fiz ... Visnik Kiivs'kogo Universitetu. Seriya Fiziki [*A publication*]
Visn Kiiv Univ Ser Fiz Khim ... Visnik Kiivs'kogo Universitetu. Seriya Fiziki ta Khimii [*Ukrainian SSR*] [*A publication*]
Visn Kiiv Univ Ser Geol Geogr ... Visnik Kiivs'kogo Universitetu. Seriya Geologii ta Geografii [*A publication*]
Visn Kiiv Univ Ser Khim ... Visnik Kiivs'kogo Universitetu. Seriya Khimii [*Ukrainian SSR*] [*A publication*]
Visn Kiyiv Univ Ser Fiz ... Visnik Kiyivs'kogo Universitetu. Seriya Fizika [*Ukrainian SSR*] [*A publication*]
Visn Kyyiv Univ Ser Biol ... Visnyk Kyyivs'koho Universitetu. Seriya Biolohiyi [*A publication*]
Visn L'viv Derzh Univ Ser Biol ... Visnik L'vivs'kogo Derzhavnogo Universitetu. Seriya Biologichna [*A publication*]
Visn L'viv Derzh Univ Ser Fiz ... Visnik L'vivs'kii Derzhavnii Universitet Imeni Ivana Franka. Seriya Fizichna [*Ukrainian SSR*] [*A publication*]
Visn L'viv Derzh Univ Ser Geol ... Visnik L'vivs'kogo Derzhavnogo Universitetu. Seriya Geologichna [*A publication*]
Visn L'viv Derzh Univ Ser Khim ... Visnik L'vivs'kogo Derzhavnogo Universitetu Imeni Ivana Franka. Seriya Khimichna [*Ukrainian SSR*] [*A publication*]
Visn L'viv Univ Ser Biol Heohr ... Visnyk L'vivs'koho Universytetu. Seriya Biolohiyi, Heohrafiyi, ta Heolohiyi [*A publication*]
Visn L'viv Univ Ser Biol Heohr Heol ... Visnyk L'vivs'koho Universytetu. Seriya Biolohiyi, Heohrafiyi, ta Heolohiyi [*A publication*]
Visn Sil-Hospod Nauky ... Visnyk Sil's'kohospodars'koyi Nauky [*A publication*]
Visn Sil's'kohospod Nauki ... Visnyk Sil's'kohospodars'koy Nauki [*A publication*]
Visn Tsentr Resp Bot Sad Akad Nauk Ukr RSR ... Visnik Tsentral'nii Respublikans'kii Botanichnii Sad Akademiya Nauk Ukrains'koi RSR [*A publication*]
Visnyk Akad Nauk Ukr RSR ... Visnyk Akademiyi Nauk Ukrayins'koyi RSR [*A publication*]
VISP .... Saharanpur/Sarsawa [*India*] [*ICAO location identifier*]   (ICLI)
VISPAC..... Videotex Information Service Providers Association of Canada [*Defunct*]   (IID)
ViSpN .... National Technical Information Service, Springfield, VA [*Library symbol*] [*Library of Congress*]   (LCLS)
VISR .... Srinagar [*India*] [*ICAO location identifier*]   (ICLI)
VISR .... Virginia Institute for Scientific Research [*University of Richmond*] [*Research center*]   (MCD)
VISR .... Viscount Resources Ltd. [*NASDAQ symbol*]   (NQ)
Vissh Inst Arkhit Stroit Sofiya God ... Vissh Institut po Arkhitektura i Stroitelstvo-Sofiya. Godishnik [*A publication*]
VISSI .... Visindafelag Islendinga. Societas Scientiarum Islandica [*A publication*]
VISSR....... Visible-Infrared Spin Scan Radiometer [*NASA*]
VIST .... Satna [*India*] [*ICAO location identifier*]   (ICLI)
ViSt .... Staunton Public Library, Staunton, VA [*Library symbol*] [*Library of Congress*]   (LCLS)
VISTA .... Variable Interlace System for Television Applications
VISTA .... Variable (Stability) In-Flight Simulator Test Aircraft
VISTA .... Varied Intelligent System Target Acquisition
VISTA .... Verbal Information Storage and Text Analysis [*in FORTRAN computer language*]
VISTA .... Very Intelligent Surveillance and Target Acquisition [*Army*]   (RDA)
VISTA .... Videodisc Interpersonal Skills Training and Assessment   (INF)
VISTA .... Viewing Instantly Security Transactions Automatically [*Wall Street*]
VISTA .... Visual Information for Satellite Telemetry Analysis
VISTA .... Visually Impaired Secretarial/Transcribers Association [*Indianapolis, IN*]   (EA)
VISTA .... Volunteers in Service to America   (EA)
VistaRs ...... Vista Resources, Inc. [*Associated Press abbreviation*]   (APAG)

Vistas Astron ... Vistas in Astronomy [*A publication*]
Vistas Astronaut ... Vistas in Astronautics [*A publication*]
Vistas Bot .. Vistas in Botany [*A publication*]
Vistas Volunt ... Vistas for Volunteers [*A publication*]
ViSte .... Sterling Public Library, Sterling, VA [*Library symbol*] [*Library of Congress*]   (LCLS)
Visti Akad Nauk Ukr RSR ... Visti Akademii Nauk Ukrains'koi RSR [*A publication*]
Visti Inst Fiz Khim Akad Nauk Ukr RSR ... Visti Institutu Fizichnoi Khimii Akademiya Nauk Ukrains'koi RSR [*A publication*]
Visti Ukr Nauk Dosl Inst Fiz Khim ... Visti Ukrains'kogo Naukovo Doslidchogo Institutu Fizichnoi Khimii [*A publication*]
ViStM .... Mary Baldwin College, Staunton, VA [*Library symbol*] [*Library of Congress*]   (LCLS)
VISTRAC ... Visual Target Reconnaissance and Acquisition   (MCD)
ViStrR........ Robert E. Lee Memorial Association, Stratford Hall, Stratford, VA [*Library symbol*] [*Library of Congress*]   (LCLS)
VISTTA..... Visibility Impairment for Sulfur Transformation and Transport in the Atmosphere [*Environmental Protection Agency*]   (GFGA)
Visual Aids R ... Visual Aids Review [*A publication*]   (APTA)
Visual Com ... Studies in Visual Communication [*A publication*]
Visual Ed ... Visual Education [*A publication*]
Visual Med ... Visual Medicine [*A publication*]
Visual Sonic Med ... Visual Sonic Medicine [*A publication*]
VIS-UV...... Visible Ultraviolet Spectrometer   (MCD)
VIS/UV ..... Visual/Ultraviolet   (SSD)
ViSwC........ Sweet Briar College, Sweet Briar, VA [*Library symbol*] [*Library of Congress*]   (LCLS)
VISX .... VISX, Inc. [*Associated Press abbreviation*]   (APAG)
VISX .... VISX, Inc. [*NASDAQ symbol*]   (NQ)
VIT............. Roanoke, VA [*Location identifier*] [*FAA*]   (FAAL)
VIT............. Van Kampen Merritt Intermediate Term High Income Trust [*NYSE symbol*]   (SPSG)
VIT............. Variable Impedance Tube
VIT............. Variable Inductive Transducer [*Automotive engineering*]
VIT............. Vertically Integrated Team [*Engineering*]
VIT............. Very Important Traveler
VIT............. Vibration Isolation Table
VIT............. Victoria Resources [*Vancouver Stock Exchange symbol*]
VIT............. Vineyard Telemeter [*California*] [*Seismograph station code, US Geological Survey*] [*Closed*]   (SEIS)
Vit .... Vita [*of Josephus*] [*Classical studies*]   (OCD)
Vit .... Vitae Parallelae [*of Plutarch*] [*Classical studies*]   (OCD)
VIT............. Vital
VIT............. Vital Speeches of the Day [*A publication*]
VIT............. Vitamin
Vit .... Vitellius [*of Suetonius*] [*Classical studies*]   (OCD)
vit .... Vitellus [*Yolk*] [*Latin*] [*Pharmacy*]   (MAE)
VIT............. Vitoria [*Spain*] [*Airport symbol*]   (OAG)
VIT............. Vitreous   (AAG)
VIT............. Voice Interactive Technology
VITA.......... Vitalink Communications Corp. [*NASDAQ symbol*]   (NQ)
VITA.......... VMEbus International Trade Association   (EA)
VITA.......... Volunteer Income Tax Assistance Program [*Internal Revenue Service*]
VITA.......... Volunteers in Technical Assistance   (EA)
VITAE........ Video Imaging Technique for Assessing Exposure [*to pesticides*]
Vita Hum ... Vita Humana [*A publication*]
Vita Int....... Vita International [*A publication*]
Vita Ital....... Vita Italiana [*A publication*]
VITAL .... Variably Initialized Translator for Algorithmic Languages [*Data processing*]
VITAL .... VAST [*Versatile Avionics Shop Test*] Interface Test Application Language
VITAL .... Verification of Interceptor Tactics Logic   (SAA)
VITAL .... Virtual Image Takeoff and Landing [*Simulator*]   (MCD)
Vital C........ Vital Christianity [*A publication*]
Vital Health Stat 1 ... Vital and Health Statistics. Series 1. Programs and Collection Procedures [*Unied States*] [*A publication*]
Vital Health Stat 2 ... Vital and Health Statistics. Series 2. Data Evaluation and Methods Research [*United States*] [*A publication*]
Vital Health Stat 3 ... Vital and Health Statistics. Series 3. Analytical Studies [*United States*] [*A publication*]
Vital Health Stat 4 ... Vital and Health Statistics. Series 4. Documents and Committee Reports [*United States*] [*A publication*]
Vital Health Stat 10 ... Vital and Health Statistics. Series 10. Data from the National Health Survey [*United States*] [*A publication*]
Vital Health Stat 11 ... Vital and Health Statistics. Series 11. Data from the National Health Survey [*United States*] [*A publication*]
Vital Health Stat 13 ... Vital and Health Statistics. Series 13. Data from the National Health Survey [*United States*] [*A publication*]
Vital Health Stat 14 ... Vital and Health Statistics. Series 14. Data on National Health Resources [*United States*] [*A publication*]
Vital Health Stat 20 ... Vital and Health Statistics. Series 20. Data from the National Vital Statistics System [*United States*] [*A publication*]
Vital Health Stat 21 ... Vital and Health Statistics. Series 21. Data from the National Vital Statistics System [*United States*] [*A publication*]

Vital Health Stat 23 ... Vital and Health Statistics. Series 23. Data from the National Survey of Family Growth [*United States*] [*A publication*]
Vital Health Statist Ser 2 Data Evaluation Methods Res ... Vital and Health Statistics. Series 2. Data Evaluation and Methods Research [*A publication*]
Vital S HD ... Monthly Vital Statistics Report. Hospital Discharge Survey Data [*US*] [*A publication*]
Vital S HI .. Monthly Vital Statistics Report. Health Interview Survey [*US*] [*A publication*]
Vital S HS ... Monthly Vital Statistics Report. Health Statistics [*US*] [*A publication*]
Vital S MS ... Monthly Vital Statistics Report. Advance Report of Final Mortality Statistics. 1981 [*US*] [*A publication*]
Vital Speeches ... Vital Speeches of the Day [*A publication*]
Vital Speeches Day ... Vital Speeches of the Day [*A publication*]
Vital St A ... Monthly Vital Statistics Report. Annual Summary of Births, Deaths, Marriages, and Divorces. 1983 [*US*] [*A publication*]
Vital Stat .... Monthly Vital Statistics Report. Births, Marriages, Divorces, and Deaths [*US*] [*A publication*]
Vital St N ... Monthly Vital Statistics Report. Advance Report of Final Natality Statistics. 1981 [*US*] [*A publication*]
Vitalstoffe .. Vitalstoffe Zivilisationskrankheiten [*A publication*]
Vitalst Zivilisationskr ... Vitalstoffe Zivilisationskrankheiten [*A publication*]
Vita Luc ..... Vita Lucani [*of Suetonius*] [*Classical studies*]   (OCD)
Vitam D Dig ... Vitamin D Digest [*A publication*]
Vitam Eksp Klin ... Vitaminy v Eksperimente i Klinike [*A publication*]
Vitam Horm ... Vitamins and Hormones [*A publication*]
Vita Mon .... Vita Monastica [*A publication*]
Vitam Resur Ikh Ispol'z ... Vitaminnye Resursy i Ikh Ispol'zovanie [*A publication*]
Vitams Horm ... Vitamins and Hormones [*A publication*]
VITAP .... Viking Targeting Analysis Program [*NASA*]
VITAS ...... Visual Target Acquisition System [*Navy*]   (MCD)
VITAS ...... Vocational Interest, Temperament, and Aptitude System [*Aptitude test*]
Vit Auct ...... Vitarum Auctio [*of Lucian*] [*Classical studies*]   (OCD)
VITC .... Vertical Internal Time Code [*Electronic musical instruments*]
VITC .... Victoria Creations, Inc. [*Warwick, RI*] [*NASDAQ symbol*]   (NQ)
vit cap .... Vital Capacity   (MAE)
VITEK .... Life Technology   (MCD)
Vitel .... Vitellus [*Yolk*] [*Pharmacy*]
VITIC .... Viticulture
Vitic Arboric ... Viticulture, Arboriculture [*A publication*]
Vitic Enol (Budapest) ... Viticulture and Enology (Budapest) [*A publication*]
VITIS-VEA ... VITIS-Viticulture and Enology Abstracts [*International Food Information Service*] [*Information service or system*]   (IID)
Viti-Vinic (Budapest) ... Viti-Viniculture (Budapest) [*A publication*]
VITL .... Vitality Unlimited [*NASDAQ symbol*]   (NQ)
Vit Ov Sol .. Vitello Ovi Solutus [*Dissolved in the Yolk of an Egg*] [*Pharmacy*]
VITR .... Vitramon, Inc. [*NASDAQ symbol*]   (NQ)
VITR .... Vitreum [*Glass*] [*Latin*]   (ADA)
Vitr .... Vitruvius [*First century BC*] [*Classical studies*]   (OCD)
VITRAN .... Vibration Transient Analysis   (MCD)
Vitro .... Vitro, Sociedad Anonima [*Associated Press abbreviation*]   (APAG)
VITRONIC ... Vitronics Corp. [*Associated Press abbreviation*]   (APAG)
VITS .... Vertical Interval Test Signal   (IEEE)
VITT .... Vehicle Integration Test Team [*NASA*]   (MCD)
ViU .... University of Virginia, Charlottesville, VA [*Library symbol*] [*Library of Congress*]   (LCLS)
VIU .... Vehicle in Use
VIU .... Video Interface Unit   (MCD)
VIU .... Voice Intercommunications Unit
VIU .... Voice Interface Unit [*Telecommunications*]   (TEL)
VIUD .... Udaipur [*India*] [*ICAO location identifier*]   (ICLI)
ViU-ES ...... University of Virginia, School of General Studies, Eastern Shore Branch, Wallops Island, VA [*Library symbol*] [*Library of Congress*]   (LCLS)
ViU-H .... University of Virginia Medical Center, Health Sciences Library, Charlottesville, VA [*Library symbol*] [*Library of Congress*]   (LCLS)
ViU-L .... University of Virginia, Law Library, Charlottesville, VA [*Library symbol*] [*Library of Congress*]   (LCLS)
ViU-Mu ..... University of Virginia, Music Library, Charlottesville, VA [*Library symbol*] [*Library of Congress*]   (LCLS)
VIURAM ... Video Interface Unit Random Access Memory
ViU-ST ...... University of Virginia, Science/Technology Information Center, Charlottesville, VA [*Library symbol*] [*Library of Congress*]   (LCLS)
VIV .... Variable Inlet Vane [*Nuclear energy*]   (NRCH)
VIV .... Vivace [*Lively*] [*Music*]
Viv .... Vivarium [*A publication*]
VIV .... Vivian, LA [*Location identifier*] [*FAA*]   (FAAL)
VIV .... Vivid-Inventive-Vital [*Spring fashions*]
VIV .... Vivigani [*Papua New Guinea*] [*Airport symbol*]   (OAG)
VIV .... Vivigen, Inc. [*AMEX symbol*]   (NQ)

VIV :.......... Vlaamse Ingenieurs-Vereinigung
VIVA .... Victory in Vietnam Association
VIVA .... Virgin Islands Visitors Association
VIVA .... Visually Impaired Veterans of America   (EA)
VIVA .... Voices in Vital America
Vivar .... Vivarium. A Journal for Mediaeval Philosophy and the Intellectual Life of the Middle Ages [*A publication*]
ViVb .... Department of Public Libraries and Information, City of Virginia Beach, Reference Department, Virginia Beach, VA [*Library symbol*] [*Library of Congress*]   (LCLS)
ViVbGS ..... Church of Jesus Christ of Latter-Day Saints, Genealogical Society Library, Norfolk Virginia Stake Branch, Virginia Beach, VA [*Library symbol*] [*Library of Congress*]   (LCLS)
ViVbRE ..... Association for Research and Enlightenment, Virginia Beach, VA [*Library symbol*] [*Library of Congress*]   (LCLS)
VIVED .... Virtual Visual Environment Display [*Helmet equipped with liquid crystal display screens viewed through wide-angle lenses*] [*NASA*]
Vivi .... Vivianus Tuscus [*Flourished, 13th century*] [*Authority cited in pre-1607 legal work*]   (DSA)
VIVI .... Vivienda [*Mexico*] [*A publication*]
Vivia .... Vivianus Tuscus [*Flourished, 13th century*] [*Authority cited in pre-1607 legal work*]   (DSA)
Vivra .... Vivra, Inc. [*Associated Press abbreviation*]   (APAG)
ViW .... College of William and Mary, Williamsburg, VA [*Library symbol*] [*Library of Congress*]   (LCLS)
ViWaR .... Rappahannock Community College, North Campus, Warsaw, VA [*Library symbol*] [*Library of Congress*]   (LCLS)
ViWarUS ... United States Army, Post Library, Vint Hill Farms Station, Warrenton, VA [*Library symbol*] [*Library of Congress*]   (LCLS)
ViWb .... Waynesboro Public Library, Waynesboro, VA [*Library symbol*] [*Library of Congress*]   (LCLS)
ViWbD .... E. I. Du Pont de Nemours & Co., Benger Laboratory, Waynesboro, VA [*Library symbol*] [*Library of Congress*]   (LCLS)
ViWbF .... Fairfax Hall Junior College, Waynesboro, VA [*Library symbol*] [*Library of Congress*]   (LCLS)
ViWC .... Colonial Williamsburg, Inc., Williamsburg, VA [*Library symbol*] [*Library of Congress*]   (LCLS)
ViWI .... Institute of Early American History and Culture, Williamsburg, VA [*Library symbol*] [*Library of Congress*]   (LCLS)
ViWiN .... United States National Aeronautics and Space Administration, Technical Library, Wallops Island, VA [*Library symbol*] [*Library of Congress*]   (LCLS)
ViWisC ...... Clinch Valley College of the University of Virginia, Wise, VA [*Library symbol*] [*Library of Congress*]   (LCLS)
ViW-L .... College of William and Mary, Law School, Williamsburg, VA [*Library symbol*] [*Library of Congress*]   (LCLS)
ViWn .... Handley Library, Winchester, VA [*Library symbol*] [*Library of Congress*]   (LCLS)
ViWnS .... Shenandoah College and Conservatory of Music, Winchester, VA [*Library symbol*] [*Library of Congress*]   (LCLS)
ViWyC .... Wytheville Community College, Wytheville, VA [*Library symbol*] [*Library of Congress*]   (LCLS)
VIX .... Vitoria [*Brazil*] [*Airport symbol*]   (OAG)
VIX .... Vixit [*He Lived*] [*Latin*]
VIY .... Nashville, TN [*Location identifier*] [*FAA*]   (FAAL)
VIY .... Visserij. Voorlichtingsblad voor de Nederlandse Visserij [*A publication*]
ViYNW ...... United States Naval Weapons Station, Yorktown, VA [*Library symbol*] [*Library of Congress*]   (LCLS)
VIZ .... Videlicet [*Namely*] [*Latin*]
Viz .... Vizardinus [*Guizzardinus*] [*Deceased, 1222*] [*Authority cited in pre-1607 legal work*]   (DSA)
VIZ .... Vizianagram [*India*] [*Seismograph station code, US Geological Survey*]   (SEIS)
Vizar .... Vizardinus [*Guizzardinus*] [*Deceased, 1222*] [*Authority cited in pre-1607 legal work*]   (DSA)
Vizgazdalkodasi Tud Kut Intez Tanulmanyok Kut Eredmenyek ... Vizgazdalkodasi Tudomanyos Kutato Intezet Tanulmanyok es Kutatasi Eredmenyek [*A publication*]
Viz Koezl .... Vizuegyi Koezlemenyek [*A publication*]
Viz Pr .... Vizard's Practice of the Court in Banc [*A publication*]   (DLA)
Vizugyi Kozl ... Vizugyi Kozlemenyek [*A publication*]
Vizugyi Kozlem ... Vizugyi Kozlemenyek [*A publication*]
VizV .... Vizantiiskii Vremenik [*A publication*]
Viz Vrem .... Vizantijskij Vremennik [*A publication*]
VJ .... Sempati Air Transport P.T. [*Indonesia*] [*ICAO designator*]   (FAAC)
VJ .... Utility Plane [*Navy symbol*]
VJ .... V-Joint [*Technical drawings*]
VJ .... Vacuum-Jacketed   (KSC)
VJ .... Variable Joining [*Genetics*]
VJ .... Vassar Journal of Undergraduate Studies [*A publication*]
VJ .... Ventriculojugular [*Medicine*]
VJ .... Video Jockey [*Television version of disc jockey; originated on all-rock-music cable station MTV*]
VJ .... Visiting Judges [*British*]
V-J (Day) ... Victory over Japan [*Japanese surrender, World War II, 14 August 1945*]

VJA........... Adelphi University, Garden City, NY [*OCLC symbol*] (OCLC)
VJA........... V-8 Juice Agar [*Microbiology*]
VJB........... Verdan Junction Box
VJB........... Victorian Judgements Bulletin [*Australia*] [*A publication*]
Vjber......... Vierteljahresberichte [*A publication*]
VJC........... Vallejo Junior College [*California*]
VJC........... Vermont Junior College
VJC........... Virginia Junior College [*Minnesota*] [*Later, Mesabi Community College*]
Vjes A Muz Zagreb ... Vjesnik Arheoloskog Muzeja u Zagrebu [*A publication*]
Vjes Dal ..... Vjesnik za Arheologiju i Historiju Dalmatinsku [*Bulletin d'Archeologie et d'Histoire Dalmates*] [*A publication*]
Vjesn Bibliot Hrv ... Vjesnik Bibliotekara Hrvatske [*A publication*]
VJH........... Victorian Journal of History [*A publication*]
Vjhber Probl Entwickllaend ... Vierteljahresberichte Probleme der Entwicklungslaender [*A publication*]
Vjhefte Zeitgesch ... Vierteljahreshefte fuer Zeitgeschichte [*A publication*]
Vjh WF ...... Vierteljahreshefte fuer Wirtschaftsforschung [*A publication*]
Vjh Wirtsch-Forsch ... Vierteljahreshefte fuer Wirtschaftsforschung [*A publication*]
V Jh f Z...... Vierteljahrshefte fuer Zeitgeschichte [*A publication*]
Vjh Zeitg.... Vierteljahrshefte fuer Zeitgeschichte [*A publication*]
Vjh Zeitgesch ... Vierteljahreshefte fuer Zeitgeschichte [*A publication*]
V Jh ZG ..... Vierteljahrshefte fuer Zeitgeschichte [*A publication*]
VJJ .... Johnson & Johnson Dental Products Co., Science Information Center, East Windsor, NJ [*OCLC symbol*] (OCLC)
VJLB .... Veterans Jewish Legion. Bulletin [*A publication*]
VJ Lit........ Deutsche Vierteljahrsschrift fuer Literaturwissenschaft und Geistesgeschichte [*A publication*]
VJMC....... Vintage Japanese Motorcycle Club (EA)
Vj Nat Ges (Zuer) ... Vierteljahresschrift der Naturforschenden Gesellschaft (Zuerich) [*A publication*]
Vj NGZ...... Vierteljahresschrift. Naturforschende Gesellschaft [*Zuerich*] [*A publication*]
VJNRL...... Virginia Journal of Natural Resources Law [*A publication*] (DLA)
Vjschr Naturf Ges (Zuerich) ... Vierteljahrsschrift. Naturforschende Gesellschaft (Zuerich) [*A publication*]
Vjschr Soz- und Wirtschaftsgesch ... Vierteljahrschrift fuer Sozial- und Wirtschaftsgeschichte [*A publication*]
Vj SR........ Vierteljahresschrift fuer Sozialrecht [*A publication*]
VJSW .... Voice Jamming Simulator, Weapons (SAA)
VJTA .... Veterans' Job Training Act
VJWI .... Velcro-Jumping while Intoxicated
VK........... Airbus Industrie [*France*] [*ICAO designator*] (FAAC)
VK........... Vedanta Kesari [*Mylapore*] [*A publication*]
VK........... Ventral Wall, Kidney [*Anatomy*]
VK........... Verbundkatalog Maschinenlesbarer Katalogdaten Deutscher Bibliotheken [*Deutsches Bibliotheksinstitut*] [*Germany*] [*Information service or system*] (CRD)
VK........... Vertical Keel
VK........... Voelkische Kultur [*A publication*]
VK........... Volkskrant [*A publication*]
VKA .... Van Kampen Merritt Advanced Municipal Income Trust [*NYSE symbol*] (SPSG)
VKA .... Vienna-Kobenzl [*Austria*] [*Seismograph station code, US Geological Survey*] (SEIS)
VKA .... Volatile Keying Assembly (AFM)
VKAW .... Verhandelingen. Koninklijke Akademie van Wetenschappen [*A publication*]
VKC .... Canisius College, Buffalo, NY [*OCLC symbol*] (OCLC)
VKC .... Van Kampen Merritt California Municipal Trust [*AMEX symbol*] (CTT)
VKCAL...... Van Kampen Merritt California Municipal Trust [*Associated Press abbreviation*] (APAG)
VKE .... Von Karman Equation
VKF.......... Von Karman Gas Dynamics Facility [*Air Force*] [*Arnold Air Force Base, TN*]
VKH.......... Vogt-Koyanagi-Harada [*Syndrome*] [*Ophthalmology*]
VKI .... Von Karman Institute (NATG)
VKIFD ...... Von Karman Institute for Fluid Dynamics [*Belgium*]
VKL .... Verhandelingen. Koninklijke Akademie van Wetenschappen. Letterkunde [*Elsevier Book Series*] [*A publication*]
VKM......... Van Kampen Merritt California Quality Municipal [*NYSE symbol*] (SPSG)
VKMAd ..... Van Kampen Merritt Advanced Municipal Income Trust [*Associated Press abbreviation*] (APAG)
VKMCA .... Van Kampen Merritt California Quality Municipal [*Associated Press abbreviation*] (APAG)
VKMFL..... Van Kampen Merritt Florida Quality Municipal [*Associated Press abbreviation*] (APAG)
VKMI .... Van Kampen Merritt Investment Grade Municipal Trust [*Associated Press abbreviation*] (APAG)
VKMIG ..... Van Kampen Merritt Trust for Investment Grade Municipals [*Associated Press abbreviation*] (APAG)
VKMIM .... Van Kampen Merritt Trust for Insured Municipals [*Associated Press abbreviation*] (APAG)
VKML .... Van Kampen Merritt Ltd. [*Associated Press abbreviation*] (APAG)
VKMMT ... Van Kampen Merritt Municipal Trust [*Associated Press abbreviation*] (APAG)

VKMNY .... Van Kampen Merritt New York Quality Municipal [*Associated Press abbreviation*] (APAG)
VKMO....... Van Kampen Merritt Municipal Opportunity Trust [*Associated Press abbreviation*] (APAG)
VKMOH.... Van Kampen Merritt Ohio Quality Municipal [*Associated Press abbreviation*] (APAG)
VKMPA..... Van Kampen Merritt Advantage Municipal [*Associated Press abbreviation*] (APAG)
VKMPA..... Van Kampen Merritt Pennsylvania Quality Municipal [*Associated Press abbreviation*] (APAG)
VKmpM..... Van Kampen Merritt Municipal Income Trust [*Associated Press abbreviation*] (APAG)
VKMSS ..... Van Kampen Merritt Strategic Sector Municipal Trust [*Associated Press abbreviation*] (APAG)
VKMT .... Van Kampen Merritt Intermediate Term High Income Trust [*Associated Press abbreviation*] (APAG)
VKN.......... Barre-Montpelier, VT [*Location identifier*] [*FAA*] (FAAL)
VKN.......... Verhandelingen. Koninklijke Akademie van Wetenschappen. Natuurkunde [*Elsevier Book Series*] [*A publication*]
VKNA .... Verhandelingen. Koninklijke Nederlandse Akademie van Wetenschappen. Afdeling Letterkunde [*A publication*]
VKNAL ..... Verhandelingen. Koninklijke Nederlandse Akademie van Wetenschappen. Afdeling Letterkunde [*A publication*]
VKNAW .... Verhandelingen. Koninklijke Nederlandse Akademie van Wetenschappen [*A publication*]
VKO......... Moscow [*Former USSR*] Vnukovo Airport [*Airport symbol*] (OAG)
VKQ.......... Van Kampen Merritt Municipal [*NYSE symbol*] (SPSG)
VKR .... Volkstum und Kultur der Romanen [*A publication*]
VKS........... Van Kampen Merritt Strategic Securities Municipal [*NYSE symbol*] (SPSG)
VKS........... Vicksburg, MS [*Location identifier*] [*FAA*] (FAAL)
VKS........... Vlees en Vleeswaren [*A publication*]
VKSI .... Vikonics, Inc. [*NASDAQ symbol*] (NQ)
VKT .... Vane Kindergarten Test [*Child development test*]
VKT .... Vehicle Kilometers Traveled (GFGA)
VKT .... Vehicle Kit Test
VKTCA...... Van Kampen Merritt Trust Investment California [*Associated Press abbreviation*] (APAG)
VKTFL ...... Van Kampen Merritt Trust Florida [*Associated Press abbreviation*] (APAG)
VKTNJ ...... Van Kampen Merritt Trust New Jersey [*Associated Press abbreviation*] (APAG)
VKTNY ..... Van Kampen Merritt Trust New York [*Associated Press abbreviation*] (APAG)
VKTPA...... Van Kampen Merritt Trust Pennsylvania [*Associated Press abbreviation*] (APAG)
VKyjU....... Visnyk Kyjivs'koho Universytetu [*A publication*]
VL............. Deutsche Vierteljahrsschrift fuer Literaturwissenschaft und Geistesgeschichte [*A publication*]
VL............. Eagleair Ltd. [*Arnarflug hf*] [*Iceland*] [*ICAO designator*] (FAAC)
VL............. Valmet OY [*Finland*] [*ICAO aircraft manufacturer identifier*] (ICAO)
VL............. Value Line Investment Survey [*Finance*]
V-L........... Van Langenhoven [*Rifle*]
VL............. Vandalia Line [*Railroad*]
V/L........... Vapor-to-Liquid
VL............. Vapor Return Line
VL............. Varia Lectio [*Variant Reading*] [*Latin*]
VL............. Variable Length
VL............. Variable Light [*Immunology*]
VL............. Vario-Losser [*Electronics*]
VL............. Velar Lobe
VL............. Velocity Limit
VL............. Ventralis Lateralis [*Brain anatomy*]
VL............. Ventrolateral [*Anatomy*]
VL............. Vereinigte Linke [*United Left*] [*Germany*] [*Political party*] (PPW)
VL............. Vereniging Lucht [*Clean Air Society in the Netherlands-CLAN*] (EAIO)
VL............. Vertical Ladder [*Technical drawings*]
VL............. Vertical Landing (MCD)
VL............. Vestre Landsret [*Western Court of Appeal*] [*Denmark*] (ILCA)
VL............. Vetenskaps-Societeten i Lund [*A publication*]
VL............. Vice Lieutenant [*British*]
VL............. Vide Locum [*See the Place Indicated*] [*Latin*]
VL............. Videlicet [*Namely*] [*Latin*]
VL............. Video Logic (IEEE)
V & L....... Vie et Langage [*A publication*]
VL............. View Loss
VL............. Viking Lander [*NASA*]
VL............. Ville
VL............. Violation of Lawful [*Order*] [*Military*]
VL............. Violin [*Music*] (ROG)
VL............. Vision, Left Eye
VL............. Visual Laydown
VL............. Vraie Lumiere [*True Light*] [*French*] [*Freemasonry*] (ROG)
VL............. Vulgar Latin
VLA .... Vachel Lindsay Association (EA)
VLA .... Valhalla Energy Corp. [*Vancouver Stock Exchange symbol*]

VLA .... Vandalia, IL [*Location identifier*] [*FAA*] (FAAL)
VLA .... Vertical Landing Aid [*Military*] (CAAL)
VLA .... Vertical Launch ASROC [*Antisubmarine Rocket*]
VLA .... Vertical-Launched Antisubmarine Rocket (MCD)
VLA .... Vertical Line Array
VLA .... Very Large Array [*Radioscope*]
VLA .... Very Late Activation Antigen [*Immunology*]
VLA .... Very Low Altitude
VLA .... Veterans' Land Act [*Canada*]
VLA .... Video Logarithmic Amplifier
VLa .... Vie et Langage [*A publication*]
VLA .... Viola [*Music*]
VLA .... Visual Landing Aid
VLA .... Vladivostok [*Former USSR*] [*Geomagnetic observatory code*]
VLA .... Vladivostok [*Former USSR*] [*Seismograph station code, US Geological Survey*] (SEIS)
VLA .... Voice of Liberty Association (EA)
VLA .... Volume Limiting Amplifier
VLA .... Volunteer Lawyers for the Arts (EA)
VLAB .... Vipont Pharmaceutical, Inc. [*Formerly, Vipont Laboratories*] [*NASDAQ symbol*] (SPSG)
VLAC .... Vertical Lift Aircraft Council (EA)
VLAD .... Vertical Line Array DIFAR (MCD)
VLAD .... Vertical Line Array Directional
VLADD ..... Visual Low-Angle Drogue Delivery (AFM)
Vladimir Gos Ped Inst Ucen Zap ... Vladimirskii Gosudarstvennyi Pedagogiceskii Institut Imeni P. I. Lebedeva-Poljanskogo. Ucenyi Zapiski [*A publication*]
VLAM ...... Variable Level Access Method [*Data processing*]
VLAM ...... Vlamertinghe [*City in Flanders*] [*Army*] [*World War I*] (DSUE)
VLAN ...... VMS Strategic Land Trust [*NASDAQ symbol*] (NQ)
V Lang ...... Visible Language [*A publication*]
VLAO .... Vientiane [*Laos*] [*ICAO location identifier*] (ICLI)
VLAP .... Attopeu [*Laos*] [*ICAO location identifier*] (ICLI)
VLAP .... Vietnam Laboratory Assistance Program [*Naval Oceanographic Office*]
VLAPA ..... Vietnam Laboratory Assistance Program, Army (RDA)
VLAR .... VFR [*Visual Flight Rules*] Low-Altitude High-Speed Routes [*Aviation*] (FAAC)
VLAT .... Very Large Array Telescope [*NASA*]
VLATME .. Very-Lighweight Air Traffic Management Equipment (MCD)
VLB .... Glider [*Special*] [*Navy symbol*]
VLB .... Vacuum Lens Blank
VLB .... Very Long Baseline
VLB .... Verzeichnis Lieferbarer Buecher [*List of Deliverable Books, i.e., books in print*] [*Germany*]
VLB .... Vincaleukoblastine [*Also, V, VBL, Ve*] [*Antineoplastic drug*]
VLB .... Visual LASER Beam
VLBA .... Very Long Baseline Array
VLBI .... Very Long Baseline Interferometer [*or Interferometry*]
VLBI .... Viking Lander Biological Instrument [*NASA*]
VLBR .... Very Low Birth Rate
VLBTI .... Very Long-Burning Target Indicator [*British military*] (DMA)
VLBW .... Very Low Birth Weight [*Medicine*]
VLC .... Longwood College, Farmville, VA [*OCLC symbol*] (OCLC)
VLC .... Nortankers, Inc. [*AMEX symbol*] (SPSG)
VLC .... Valencia [*Spain*] [*Airport symbol*] (OAG)
VLC .... Variable-Length Coding [*Data processing*]
VLC .... Viking Lander Capsule [*NASA*]
VLC .... Violoncello [*Music*]
VLC .... Vital Load Center (MSA)
VLCC .... Very Large Cargo [*or Crude*] Carrier [*Oil tanker*]
VLCD .... Very-Low-Calorie Diet
VLCE .... Visible LASER Communication Experiment
VLCF .... Vectored Lift Cannon Fighter [*Air Force*] (MCD)
VLCF .... Victoria League for Commonwealth Fellowship [*British*]
VLCFA ...... Very-Long-Chain Saturated Fatty Acid [*Organic chemistry*]
VLCHV ..... Very-Low-Cost Harassment Vehicle (MCD)
VLCM .... ValCom, Inc. [*NASDAQ symbol*] (NQ)
VLCR .... Variable Length Cavity Resonance
VLCS .... Voltage-Logic-Current-Switching [*Electronics*]
VLCTY ...... Velocity (FAAC)
VLD .... Vacuum Leak Detector
VLD .... Valdez [*Alaska*] [*Seismograph station code, US Geological Survey*] [*Closed*] (SEIS)
VLD .... Valdosta [*Georgia*] [*Airport symbol*] (OAG)
VLD .... Vendor List of Drawings
VLD .... Victorian Licensing Decisions [*A publication*] (APTA)
VLD .... Village and Local Development
VLD .... Visual Laydown Delivery (AFM)
VLD .... Vulnerability/Lethality Division [*Ballistic Research Laboratory*] (RDA)
VLDB .... Very-Large Data Base (ADA)
VLDBS ...... Very-Large Data Base System
VLDF .... Very-Long Delay Fuze [*Military*] (CAAL)
VLDL .... Very-Low-Density Lipoprotein [*Biochemistry*]
VLDTA8.... Veldtrust [*Johannesburg*] [*A publication*]
VLD-TG .... Very-Low-Density Lipoprotein Triglyceride [*Biochemistry*] (AAMN)
VLDTN ..... Validation (AAG)

VLE........... Landing-Gear-Extended Speed [*Aviation*]
VLE........... V & L Enterprises [*ACCORD*] [*UTLAS symbol*]
VLE........... Valle, AZ [*Location identifier*] [*FAA*] (FAAL)
VLE........... Vapor-Liquid Equilibrium
VLE........... Victorian Legal Executive [*A publication*] (APTA)
VLE........... Violone [*Violins*] [*Music*]
VLE........... Visible Light Emission
VLEASS.... Very Long Endurance Acoustic Submarine Simulator
VLED........ Visible Light-Emitting Diodes
VLF........... Installatie [*A publication*]
VLF........... Variable Length Field
VLF........... Vectored Lift Fighter (MCD)
VLF........... Vertical Launch Facility
VLF........... Very-Low Fluence [*Physics*]
VLF........... Very-Low-Frequency [*Electronics*]
VLFG........ Valley Forge Scientific Corp. [*NASDAQ symbol*] (NQ)
VLFJ........ Very-Low-Frequency Jammer [*Electronics*]
VLFR........ Very-Low-Frequency Receiver [*Electronics*]
VLFS........ Variable Low-Frequency Standard
VLFS........ Very Large Floating Structure [*Oceanography*]
VLG .... Maximum Landing Gear Operating Speed [*Aviation code*] (AIA)
VLG .... Valerie Gold Resources [*Vancouver Stock Exchange symbol*]
VLG .... Vertical Load Gun
VLG .... Villa Gesell [*Argentina*] [*Airport symbol*] (OAG)
VLG .... Village (MCD)
VLG .... Visible Light Generator
VLG .... Vlaamse Gids [*A publication*]
VLGE........ Village Super Market, Inc. [*NASDAQ symbol*] (NQ)
VLGM .... Vertical Loading Gun Mount (MCD)
VLH........... Very Large Herbivores
VLH........... Very Lightly Hinged [*Philately*]
VLH........... Volatile Liquid Hydrocarbon
VLHS........ Bane Houei Say [*Laos*] [*ICAO location identifier*] (ICLI)
VLI............ Port Vila [*Vanuata*] [*Airport symbol*] (OAG)
VLI............ Variable Life Insurance
VLI............ Very-Low Inertia
VLI............ Video Load Impedance
VLIA......... Virus-Like Infectious Agent [*Medicine*]
VLIB......... Valodas un Literaturas Instituta Biletens [*A publication*]
VLID......... Valid Logic Systems, Inc. [*NASDAQ symbol*] (NQ)
VLIR......... Valodas un Literaturas Instituta Raksti [*A publication*]
VLIS......... Viking Lander Imaging System [*NASA*]
VLIS......... Viking Library System [*Library network*]
VLIS .... VLI Corp. [*NASDAQ symbol*] (NQ)
VLIW........ Very Long Instruction Word [*Computer architecture*] [*Multiflow Computer, Inc.*]
Vliyanie Rab Sred Svoistva Mater ... Vliyanie Rabochikh Sred na Svoistva Materialov [*A publication*]
VLJ .... Val Joyeux [*France*] [*Later, CLF*] [*Geomagnetic observatory code*]
VLKG .... Khong Island [*Laos*] [*ICAO location identifier*] (ICLI)
VLKT........ Kene Thao [*Laos*] [*ICAO location identifier*] (ICLI)
VLL........... Amigo Airways [*Harlingen, TX*] [*FAA designator*] (FAAC)
VLL........... Valladolid [*Spain*] [*Airport symbol*] (OAG)
VLLB........ Luang Prabang [*Laos*] [*ICAO location identifier*] (ICLI)
VLLC........ Very Long Linear Collider [*Former USSR*] [*Proposed*]
VLLD........ Vehicular LASER Locator Designator
VLLN........ Luong Nam Tha [*Laos*] [*ICAO location identifier*] (ICLI)
VLLO........ Violoncello [*Music*]
VLM .... Variable Length Multiply
VLM .... Visceral Larval Migrans [*Medicine*]
VLM .... Vortex Lattice Method
VLMB....... Vertical Launch Modular Booster (MCD)
VLMR....... Value Merchants, Inc. [*NASDAQ symbol*] (SPSG)
VLMS........ Villa-Lobos Music Society (EA)
VLMS........ Vintage Light Music Society [*British*]
VLMTRC .. Volumetric
VLN .... Training Glider [*Navy symbol*]
VLN .... Valencia [*Venezuela*] [*Airport symbol*] (OAG)
VLN .... Vanua-Lava [*Sola*] [*New Hebrides*] [*Seismograph station code, US Geological Survey*] (SEIS)
VLN .... Very Low Nitrogen [*Fuel technology*]
VLN .... Villebon Resources Ltd. [*Vancouver Stock Exchange symbol*]
VLN .... Violin [*Music*]
VLNT........ Violent (FAAC)
VLO .... Maximum Speed to Extend or Retract Landing Gear [*Aviation code*] (AIA)
VLO .... Valero Energy Corp. [*NYSE symbol*] (SPSG)
VLO .... Vereniging van Luguaart Onderhoudbedrywe [*Association of Aviation Maintenance Organizations*] (EAIO)
VLO .... Vertical Lockout
VLOL........ Violating Local Option Law (WGA)
VLON........ Verwaltungslexikon [*Administration Dictionary*] [*NOMOS Datapool*] [*Information service or system*]
VLONAB .. Agricultural Research Reports [*Wageningen*] [*A publication*]
VLOS........ Oudomsay [*Laos*] [*ICAO location identifier*] (ICLI)
VLP........... Valero Natural Gas Partners LP [*NYSE symbol*] (SPSG)
VLP........... Valpar Resources [*Vancouver Stock Exchange symbol*]
VLP........... Valparaiso [*Chile*] [*Seismograph station code, US Geological Survey*] (SEIS)

VLP............	Vaporizing Liquid Plenum
VLP............	Vasopressin-Like Peptide [*Biochemistry*]
VLP............	Vertical Landing Point (AFM)
VLP............	Vertical Long Period
VLP............	Video Long Player [*Video disk system*] [*Philips/MCA*]
VLP............	Vincristine, L-Asparaginase, Prednisone [*Antineoplastic drug regimen*]
VLP............	Virus-Like Particle
VLPE........	Very Long Period Experiment [*Geophysics*]
VLPK........	Paksane [*Laos*] [*ICAO location identifier*] (ICLI)
VLPP........	Very Low Pressure Pyrolysis
VLPS........	Pakse [*Laos*] [*ICAO location identifier*] (ICLI)
VLPS........	Vandenberg Launch Processing System [*Aerospace*] (MCD)
VLPV........	Phong Savanh [*Laos*] [*ICAO location identifier*] (ICLI)
VLR..........	Randolph-Macon Woman's College, Lynchburg, VA [*OCLC symbol*] (OCLC)
VLR..........	Transport Glider [*Navy symbol*]
VLR..........	Valar Resources Ltd. [*Vancouver Stock Exchange symbol*]
VLR..........	Vanderbilt Law Review [*A publication*]
VLR..........	Variable Loan Rate [*Business term*]
VLR..........	Vertical-Looking RADAR
VLR..........	Very Long Range
VLR..........	Very Low Range
VLR..........	Victorian Law Reports [*A publication*] (APTA)
VLR..........	Violation of Law of Road [*Traffic offense charge*]
VLR..........	Virginia Law Review [*A publication*]
VLR..........	Voice Logging Recorder (DWSG)
VLR..........	Voluntary Loss Rate [*of Air Force officers resigning before retirement*]
VLR (Adm) ...	Victorian Law Reports (Admiralty) [*A publication*] (APTA)
VLR (E)	Victorian Law Reports (Equity) [*A publication*] (APTA)
VLR (Eq) ...	Victorian Law Reports (Equity) [*A publication*]
VLR (IP & M) ...	Victorian Law Reports (Insolvency, Probate, and Matrimonial) [*A publication*] (APTA)
VLR (L)	Victorian Law Reports (Law) [*A publication*] (APTA)
VLR (M)....	Victorian Law Reports (Mining) [*A publication*] (APTA)
VLR (P & M) ...	Victorian Law Reports (Probate and Matrimonial) [*A publication*] (APTA)
VLRSN......	Violation of Lawful Regulation Issued by the Secretary of the Navy
VLS............	Vacuum Loading System
VLS............	Valesdir [*Vanuata*] [*Airport symbol*] (OAG)
VLS............	Valsamata [*Kephallenia*] [*Greece*] [*Seismograph station code, US Geological Survey*] (SEIS)
VLS............	Valstieciu Liaudininku Sajunga [*Peasant Populist Union*] [*Lithuania*] [*Political party*] (PPE)
VLS............	Vandenberg Launch Site [*Air Force*]
VLS............	Vandenberg Launch Site [*Aerospace*] (MCD)
VLS............	Vapor-Liquid-Solid
VLS............	Vertical Launch System [*Military*]
VLS............	Vertical Liquid Spring
VLS............	Very Long Shot [*A photograph or motion picture sequence taken from a considerable distance*]
VLS............	Very Low Speed
VLS............	Viking Lander System [*NASA*] (KSC)
VLS............	Village Voice. Literary Supplement [*A publication*]
VLS............	Virtual Linkage System [*or Subsystem*]
VLS............	Visible Light Sensors (MCD)
VLS............	Visual Lunacy Society (EA)
VLS............	Volume Loadability Speed (IEEE)
VLS............	Vry Langs Skip [*Free Alongside Ship*] [*Afrikaans*]
VLSB........	Sayaboury [*Laos*] [*ICAO location identifier*] (ICLI)
VLSB........	Very Low Surface Brightness [*Optics*]
VLSI.........	Very-Large-Scale Integration [*of circuits*] [*Electronics*]
VLSI.........	VLSI Technology, Inc. [*NASDAQ symbol*] (NQ)
VLSIC......	Very-Large-Scale Integrated Circuit [*Electronics*]
VLSID......	Very Large Scale Integrated Device (SSD)
VLSIIC......	VLSI Implementation Centre [*Research center*] [*Queen's University, Kingston*] [*Canada*]
VLSIPS	Very-Large-Scale Immobilized Polymer Synthesis [*Affymax Research Institute*] [*Organic chemistry*]
VLSK........	Savannakhet [*Laos*] [*ICAO location identifier*] (ICLI)
VLSM.......	Vertical Launched Standard Missile (MCD)
VLSN.......	Sam Neua [*Laos*] [*ICAO location identifier*] (ICLI)
VLSV.......	Saravane [*Laos*] [*ICAO location identifier*] (ICLI)
VLSW.......	Vertical Launch SEAWOLF [*Military*] [*British*]
VLSW.......	Virtual Line Switch
VLT...........	Van Kampen Merritt Ltd. [*NYSE symbol*] (SPSG)
VLT...........	Vault Explorations, Inc. [*Vancouver Stock Exchange symbol*]
VLT...........	Vehicle Licensing and Traffic [*British*]
VLT...........	Very Large Telescope [*Proposed*] [*European Southern Observatory*]
VLT...........	Very Low Titanium [*Geology*]
VLT...........	Victorian Law Times [*A publication*] (APTA)
VLT...........	Video Layout Terminal [*Data processing*]
VLT...........	Video Lottery Terminal (ECON)
VLT...........	Volute
VLTG........	Voltage (AAG)
VLTK........	Thakhek [*Laos*] [*ICAO location identifier*] (ICLI)
VLTS........	Video Lottery Technologies [*NASDAQ symbol*] (SPSG)
VLTSV	Virusoid Lucerne Transient Streak Virus

VLTT........	Vehicular Leger Toot Terrain [*Light All-Terrain Vehicle*] [*French*] (MCD)
VLU..........	Vacuum Lifting Unit
VLU..........	Video Logic Unit (MCD)
VLU..........	Worldwide Value Fund [*NYSE symbol*] (SPSG)
VLV..........	Valdivia [*Chile*] [*Seismograph station code, US Geological Survey*] (SEIS)
VLV..........	Valera [*Venezuela*] [*Airport symbol*] (OAG)
VLV..........	Valve (AAG)
VLV..........	Vanguard Launch Vehicle (SAA)
VLV..........	Velvet Exploration Co. Ltd. [*Vancouver Stock Exchange symbol*]
VLV..........	Very-Low Volume
VLV..........	Visna Lentivirus
VLvivU	Visnyk L'vivs'koho Derzavnoho Universytetu [*A publication*]
VLVL........	Video Library, Inc. [*San Diego, CA*] [*NASDAQ symbol*] (NQ)
v-LVN.......	Ventral Lateral Ventricular Nerve [*Anatomy*]
VLVS........	Voltage-Logic-Voltage-Switching [*Electronics*]
VLVT.......	Vientiane/Wattay [*Laos*] [*ICAO location identifier*] (ICLI)
VLW..........	Village Level Workers [*India*]
VLW..........	Washington and Lee University, Lexington, VA [*OCLC symbol*] (OCLC)
VLXG.......	Xieng Khouang [*Laos*] [*ICAO location identifier*] (ICLI)
VLXK.......	Xieng Khouang (Plaine Des Jarres) [*Laos*] [*ICAO location identifier*] (ICLI)
VLY..........	Valley (MCD)
VLY..........	Valley Oil & Gas [*Vancouver Stock Exchange symbol*]
VLZ...........	Valdez [*Alaska*] [*Seismograph station code, US Geological Survey*] (SEIS)
VM............	Abacus Air [*West Germany*] [*ICAO designator*] (FAAC)
VM............	V-Mail Specialists [*Navy*]
VM............	Validation Material [*Social Security Administration*]
VM............	Valles Marineris [*A filamentary mark on Mars*]
VM............	Value Management
VM............	Vane Meter [*Automotive engineering*]
VM............	Vasomotor [*Physiology*]
VM............	Vastus Medialis [*A muscle*]
VM............	Vector Message
VM............	Velocity Meter
VM............	Velocity Modulation
VM............	Ventilation Management
VM............	Ventricular Muscle [*Cardiology*] (MAE)
VM............	Verslagen en Mededeelingen [*A publication*]
VM............	Vertical Magnet
VM............	Vertical Meridian [*Optics, Eye anatomy*]
VM............	Vestibular Membrane [*Medicine*]
VM............	Victory Medal [*British*]
VM............	Vietminh (CINC)
vm..............	Vietnam [*MARC country of publication code*] [*Library of Congress*] (LCCP)
VM............	Viomycin [*Antibiotic compound*] (AAMN)
VM............	Vir Magnificus [*A Great Man*] [*Latin*]
VM............	Viral Myocarditis [*Medicine*]
VM............	Virgin and Martyr [*Church calendars*]
V & M........	Virgin and Martyr [*Church calendars*]
VM............	Virtual Machine [*Data processing*]
VM............	Virtual Memory [*Data processing*] (MCD)
VM............	VM Software, Inc. [*NYSE symbol*] [*Later, SMX*] (CTT)
VM............	Voice Modulation
VM............	Volatile Matter
VM............	Volksmarine
VM............	Voltmeter
V/m...........	Volts per Meter [*Also, VPM*]
V/M..........	Volts per Mil (DEN)
VM............	Vorigen Monats [*Of Last Month*] [*German*]
VM............	Votre Majeste [*Your Majesty*] [*French*]
VM............	Voyager Mars [*NASA*]
VMA.........	Marine Attack Squadron [*Navy symbol*] (NVT)
VMA.........	Valid Memory Address [*Data processing*]
VMA.........	Valve Manufacturers Association of America (EA)
VMA.........	Vanillylmandelic Acid [*Also, HMMA*] [*Biochemistry*]
VMA.........	Vehicle Maintenance Area
VMA.........	Vero Monmouth Airlines [*Vero Beach, FL*] [*FAA designator*] (FAAC)
VMA.........	Virtual Machine Assist [*IBM Corp.*]
VMA.........	Virtual Memory Allocation
VMA.........	Visual Maneuverability Aids (MCD)
VMAAI......	Violin Makers Association of Arizona International (EA)
VMA(AW) ...	Marine Attack Squadron (All-Weather) [*Navy symbol*] (NVT)
VMAD.......	Vincristine, Methotrexate, Adriamycin, Actinomycin D [*Antineoplastic drug regimen*]
VMAP	Video Map Equipment
VMAPS.....	Virtual Memory Array Processing System
VMAQ.......	Marine Tactical Electronic Warfare Squadron [*Navy symbol*] (DNAB)
VMAT	Marine Attack Training Squadron [*Navy symbol*] (DNAB)
VMAT(AW) ...	Marine All-Weather Attack Training Squadron [*Navy symbol*] (DNAB)
VMAVA	Verdun-Meuse-Argonne Veterans Association (EA)
VMAW......	Verslagen en Mededeelingen. Koninklijke Akademie van Wetenschappen [*A publication*]

VMAX.......	Maximum Velocity
VMB..........	Marine Medium and Heavy Patrol Bomber Squadron [*Land-based and seaplane*] [*Navy symbol*]
VMB..........	Mary Baldwin College, Staunton, VA [*OCLC symbol*] (OCLC)
VMB..........	Vandringar Med Boeker [*A publication*]
VMB..........	Vermont Motor Rate Bureau Inc., Barre VT [*STAC*]
VMBC........	Vintage Motor Bike Club (EA)
VMBF........	Marine Fighter Bomber Squadron [*Navy symbol*]
VMBLOK ...	Virtual Machine Control Block [*Data processing*] (IBMDP)
VMBR........	Visual Motor Behavior Rehearsal [*Psychology*]
VMC..........	James Madison University, Harrisonburg, VA [*OCLC symbol*] (OCLC)
VMC..........	Variable Message Cycle
VMC..........	Variable Mica Capacitor
VMC..........	Vasomotor Center [*Physiology*]
VMC..........	Velocity Minimum Control (AAG)
VMC..........	Veritable Master of Crewelwork
VMC..........	Vertical Motion Compensation (CAAL)
VMC..........	Viet Montagnard Cong
VMC..........	Villa Madonna College [*Kentucky*]
VMC..........	Villa Maria College [*Erie, PA*]
VMC..........	Ville Marie [*Quebec*] [*Seismograph station code, US Geological Survey*] [*Closed*] (SEIS)
VMC..........	Virginia Medical College
VMC..........	Visual Meteorological Conditions [*Aviation*]
VMC..........	Void Metallic Composite
VMC..........	Vulcan Materials Co. [*NYSE symbol*] (SPSG)
Vmca..........	Minimum Control Speed in Air [*Aviation code*] (AIA)
VMCB........	Virtual Machine Control Block
VMCCA......	Veteran Motor Car Club of America (EA)
VMCF........	Virtual Machine Communication Facility
Vmcg..........	Minimum Control Speed on the Ground [*Aviation code*] (AIA)
VMCJ........	Marine Composite Reconnaissance [*Photo*] Squadron [*Navy symbol*]
Vmcl..........	Minimum Control Speed for the Landing Approach [*Aviation code*] (AIA)
VMCM......	Vector-Measuring Current Meter [*Instrumentation*]
VM/CMS..	Virtual Machine/Conversational Monitor System [*Data processing*]
VMCP........	Vincristine, Melphalan, Cyclophosphamide, Prednisone [*Antineoplastic drug regimen*]
VMCR........	Volunteer Marine Corps Reserve
VMD..........	Doctor of Veterinary Medicine
VMD..........	Marine Photographic Squadron [*Navy symbol*]
VMD..........	Vector Meson Dominance [*Particle physics*] (OA)
VMD..........	Vertical Magnetic Dipole (IEEE)
VMD..........	Volume Median Diameter [*Particle size*]
VMDF........	Vertical Side of Main Distribution Frame [*Telecommunications*] (TEL)
VMDI........	Vector Miss Distance Indicator
VMDP........	Veterinary Medical Data Program [*Association of Veterinary Medical Data Program Participants*] [*Information service or system*] (IID)
VME..........	British Columbia Ministry of Education [*UTLAS symbol*]
VME..........	Villa Mercedes [*Argentina*] [*Airport symbol*] (OAG)
VME..........	Vinyl Methyl Ether [*Organic chemistry*]
VME..........	Virtual Machine Environment [*International Computers Ltd.*]
VME..........	Volvo, Michigan, Euclid [*In company name VME Americas, Inc.*]
VMEC........	Vehicle Mounted Explosive Container (MCD)
VMF..........	Marine Fighter Squadron [*Navy symbol*]
VMF..........	Vacuum Melting Furnace
VMF..........	Vertical Maintenance Facility (NASA)
VMFA........	Marine Fighter Attack Squadron [*Navy symbol*] (NVT)
VMFAT.....	Marine Fighter Attack Training Squadron [*Navy symbol*] (NVT)
VMF(AW) ...	Marine Fighter Squadron (All-Weather) [*Navy symbol*] (NVT)
VMFI........	Voltage Monitor and Fault Indicating
VMF(N).....	Marine Night Fighter Squadron [*Navy symbol*]
VMFP........	Marine Tactical Reconnaissance Squadron [*Navy symbol*] (DNAB)
VMFPDET ...	Marine Tactical Reconnaissance Squadron Detachment [*Navy symbol*] (DNAB)
VMG..........	Banyan Mortgage Investment Fund [*NYSE symbol*] [*Formerly, VMS Mortgate Investment Fund*] (SPSG)
Vmg..........	Velocity Made Good (WGA)
VMG..........	Vickers Machine Gun [*British military*] (DMA)
VMG..........	Video Mapping Group
VMG..........	Video Mixer Group
VMG..........	Voluntary Movement Group (EAIO)
VMGR.......	Marine Aerial Refueler/Transport Squadron [*Navy symbol*] (NVT)
VMGSE.....	Vehicle Measuring Ground Support Equipment (KSC)
VMH.........	Misericordia Hospital, Medical Library, Bronx, NY [*OCLC symbol*] (OCLC)
VMH	Ventral Medial Hypothalamus [*Anatomy*]
VMH	Victoria Medal of Honour
VMHB.......	Virginia Magazine of History and Biography [*A publication*]
VMHI.......	Victorian Military History Institute [*Defunct*] (EA)
VMI..........	Developmental Test of Visual-Motor Integration [*Beery & Buktenica*]
VMI..........	Meubel. Weekblad voor de Meubelindustrie, Meubelhandel, Woninginrichting, en Toeleveringsbedrijven [*A publication*]
VMI..........	Variable Moment of Inertia [*Nuclear physics*]
VMI..........	Vertical Markets Information Database [*Amidon/Litman Associates*] [*Information service or system*] (CRD)
VMI.........	Vertical Motion Index (PCM)
VMI.........	Vibration Measurement Integrator
VMI.........	Video Mosaic Imaging [*Computer technology*]
VMI.........	Videodisc-Mouse Interface
VMI..........	Virginia Military Institute, Lexington, VA [*OCLC symbol*] (OCLC)
VMI..........	Visual Maneuvering Indicator (MCD)
VMI..........	Voicemail International, Inc. [*Cupertina, CA*] [*Telecommunications*] (TSSD)
VMIA.......	Vinyl Metal Industry Association [*Defunct*] (EA)
VMIC........	Vermont Maple Industry Council (EA)
VMID.......	Virtual Machine Identifier
VMIF........	Veterans' Mortgage Indemnity Fund [*Department of Veterans Affairs*]
VMIG	View-Master Ideal Group, Inc. [*NASDAQ symbol*] (NQ)
VMII 1986 ...	Vertical Markets Information Index 1986 [*Amidon/Litman Associates*] [*A publication*]
V/mil.........	Volts per Mil
VMIRL......	VMI [*Virginia Military Institute*] Research Laboratories [*Research center*] (RCD)
VMJ.........	Marine Utility Squadron [*Navy symbol*]
VMJ..........	Vertical Multijunction [*Solar cell*]
VMJ/BIV ..	Boletin Indigenista Venezolano. Organo de la Comision Indigenista. Ministerio de Justicia [*A publication*]
VMK........	Vita-Metall-Keramik [*German dental material for crowns and bridgework*]
VMKA	Verslagen en Mededeelingen. Koninklijke Akademie voor Nederlandse Taal- en Letterkunde [*A publication*]
VMKey	Voice Master Key
VMKT	Victory Markets [*NASDAQ symbol*] (NQ)
VMKVA	Verslagen en Mededeelingen. Koninklijke Vlaamse Akademie voor Taal- en Letterkunde [*A publication*]
VML.........	Marine Glider Squadron [*Navy symbol*]
VML	Mohawk Valley Library Association, Schenectady County Public Library, Schenectady, NY [*OCLC symbol*] (OCLC)
VML.........	Valley Migrant League (EA)
VML.........	Virtual Memory Linking [*Data processing*]
VMLB.......	Vertical Medium-Lead Burst [*Neuron*]
VMLH.......	Ventromedial and Lateral Hypothalami [*Neuroanatomy*]
VMLI.......	Veterans Mortgage Life Insurance
VMLP........	VMS Mortgage Investors LP [*Chicago, IL*] [*NASDAQ symbol*] (NQ)
VMLS/MLA ...	Veterinary Medical Libraries Section/Medical Library Association (EA)
VMM........	Vacuum Melting Module
V & MM	Vandalism and Malicious Mischief [*Insurance*]
VMM........	Vehicle Maintenance Monitor [*Automotive engineering*]
VMM........	Vehicle Model Movement
VMM........	Vertical Milling Machine
VMM........	Video Map Module
VMM........	Virtual Machine Monitor [*Data processing*] (IEEE)
VMM........	Virtual Memory Manager [*Data processing*] (BYTE)
VMM........	Volunteer Missionary Movement [*London Colney, Hertfordshire, England*] (EAIO)
VMMC......	Macau [*Macau*] [*ICAO location identifier*] (ICLI)
VMMC......	Veterans Memorial Medical Center
VMMOA...	Virginia Medical Monthly [*Later, Virginia Medical*] [*A publication*]
VMMPS....	Vehicle Management and Mission Planning System [*NASA*]
VMN.........	Ventromedial Nucleus [*Brain anatomy*]
VMN.........	Voyageur Minnesota Municipal Income Fund, Inc. [*AMEX symbol*] (SPSG)
VMO.........	Marine Observation Squadron [*Navy symbol*]
VMO.........	Maximum Operating Speed (MCD)
VMO.........	Van Kampen Merritt Municipal Opportunities [*NYSE symbol*] (SPSG)
VMO.........	Vastus Medialis Obliquus [*Muscle*]
VMO.........	Velocity-Modulated Oscillator
VMO.........	Very Massive Object [*Astronomy*]
VMO.........	Visiting Medical Officer (ADA)
VMO(AS) ...	Marine Observation Squadron (Artillery Spotting) [*Navy symbol*]
VMOR.......	VMS Mortgage Investors LP III [*NASDAQ symbol*] (NQ)
VMOS.......	V-Groove Metal-Oxide Semiconductor (MCD)
VMOS.......	Virtual Memory Operating System [*Sperry UNIVAC*] [*Data processing*] (IEEE)
VMOW......	Vice Minister of War (MCD)
VMP..........	Value as Marine Policy [*Insurance*] (DS)
VMP..........	Variable Major Protein [*Genetics*]
VM & P....	Varnish Makers' and Painters' Naphtha
vMP........	Ventral Midline Precursor [*Neuroanatomy*]
VMP..........	Vertically Moored Platform [*Offshore drilling*]
VMP..........	Visiting Medical Practitioner
VMPA.......	Vancouver Museums and Planetarium Association [*Canada*]

VMPP........ Vincristine, Melphalan, Prednisone, Procarbazine [*Antineoplastic drug regimen*]
VM-26PP .. VM-26 [*Teniposide*], Procarbazine, Prednisone [*Antineoplastic drug regimen*]
VM/Prolog ... Virtual Machine/Programming in Logic [*Data processing*] (HGAA)
VMR .... Marine Transport Squadron [*Navy symbol*]
VMR .... Variance to Mean Rate
VMR .... Vasomotor Rhinitis [*Medicine*]
VMR .... Victoria Mounted Rifles [*British military*] (DMA)
VMR .... Violation Monitor and Remover [*Bell System*]
VMR .... Volumetric Mixing Ratio
VMR .... Volunteer Military Rejectee (DNAB)
VMRB .... Vereinigte Metallwerke Ranshofen-Berndorf [*AG*]
VMRC .... Virginia Mason Research Center [*Virginia Mason Hospital and Mason Clinic*] [*Research center*] (RCD)
VMRI .... Veterinary Medical Research Institute [*Iowa State University*] [*Research center*] (RCD)
VMRMDS ... Vehicle-Mounted Road Mine Detector System
VMRO .... Vnatresna Makedonska Revolucionerna Organizacija [*Internal Macedonian Revolutionary Organization (Known popularly among English-speaking nations as the IMRO)*] [*Former Yugoslavia*] [*Political party*] (PPE)
VMRO .... Vutreshna Makidoniski Revoliutsionna Organizatsiia [*Internal Macedonian Revolutionary Organization*] [*Bulgaria*] [*Political party*] (PPE)
VMRO-DPMNE ... Internal Macedonian Revolutionary Organization - Democratic Party for Macedonian National Unity [*Political party*]
VMRO(U) ... Vnatresna Makedonska Revolucionerna Organizacija (Udruzena) [*Internal Macedonian Revolutionary Organization (United)*] [*Former Yugoslavia*] [*Political party*] (PPE)
VMRR .... Vendor Material Review Report [*NASA*] (KSC)
VMRS........ Vehicle Maintenance Reporting Standard [*American Trucking Association*]
VMRS........ Vessel Movement Reporting System
VMS .... Valve Mounting System
VMS .... Variable Mass System
VMS .... Variable Message Sign
VMS .... Vehicle Management System
VMS .... Vehicle Monitoring System (RDA)
VMS .... Velocity Measurement System
VMS .... Vertical Motion Simulator [*NASA*]
VMS .... Vibration Measuring System
VMS .... Vicinity Map Series [*Bureau of the Census*] (GFGA)
VMS .... Victorian Military Society (EAIO)
VMS .... Video Modulation System
VMS .... Video Movie System [*For video recording tapes*]
VMS .... Videofile Microwave System
VMS .... Viewfinder-Metering System (KSC)
VMS .... Virtual Memory Operating System [*Data processing*]
VMS .... Visual Memory Scale [*Educational test*]
VMS .... Visual Motion Simulator (MCD)
VMS .... Voice Messaging System [*Telecommunications*]
VMSB........ Marine Scout Bombing Squadron [*Navy symbol*]
VMSDA..... Vysokomolekulyarnye Soedineniya [*A publication*]
VMSEA..... Vehicle Monitoring System Electronics Assembly (RDA)
VMSFRJ ... Variable-Mode Solid-Fueled Ramjet (MCD)
Vmsl......... Minimum Speed in a Stall [*Aviation code*] (AIA)
Vmso......... Minimum Speed in a Stall, Flaps Down [*Aviation code*] (AIA)
VMSODA ... Vie et Milieu. Serie AB. Biologie Marine et Oceanographie [*A publication*]
VMSP........ Volunteer Management Support Program [*ACTION*]
VMT .... Validate Master Tape
VMT .... Van Kampen Merritt Municipal Income Trust [*NYSE symbol*] (CTT)
VMT .... Variable Microcycle Timing
VMT .... Variable Mu Tube [*Electronics*]
VMT .... Vehicle-Miles Traveled
VMT .... Velocity-Modulated Transistor [*Solid-state physics*]
VMT .... Velocity-Modulated Tube
VMT .... Very Many Thanks
VMT .... Video Matrix Terminal
VMT .... Virtual Memory Technique [*Data processing*] (MDG)
VMT .... Virtual Method Table [*Data processing*] (PCM)
VMT .... Voltage-Modulated Transmission [*Electronics*]
VMT .... Von Mises Theory
VMTB .... Marine Torpedo Bomber Squadron [*Navy symbol*]
VMTG .... VMS Mortgage Investors LP II [*Chicago, IL*] [*NASDAQ symbol*] (NQ)
VMTH....... Veterinary Medical Teaching Hospital [*University of California, Davis*]
VMTOL .... Very Many Takeoffs and Landings (MCD)
VMTP........ Versatile Message Transaction Protocol [*Data processing*]
VMTSS ..... Virtual Machine Time-Sharing System [*Data processing*] (IEEE)
VMU .... Baimuru [*Papua New Guinea*] [*Airport symbol*] (OAG)
Vmu.......... Minimum Unstick Speed [*Aviation code*] (AIA)
VMU......... Velocity Measuring Unit (MCD)
VMV......... Viola Mottle Virus

VMVBORG ... Verslagen en Mededeelingen van de Vereeniging tot Beoefening van Overijsselsch Recht en Geschiedenis [*A publication*]
VMVOVR ... Verslagen en Mededeelingen van de Vereeniging tot Uitgaaf van der Bronnen van het Oud-Vaderlandsche Recht [*A publication*]
VMW......... Mary Washington College, Fredericksburg, VA [*OCLC symbol*] (OCLC)
VMW......... Vierteljahrschrift fuer Musikwissenschaft [*A publication*]
V Mw .... Vierteljahrsschrift fuer Musikwissenschaft [*A publication*]
VMWWI ... Victory Medal World War I [*British*]
VMWWII ... Victory Medal World War II [*British*]
VMXI .... VMX, Inc. [*NASDAQ symbol*] (NQ)
VMY .... York College of the City University of New York, Jamaica, NY [*OCLC symbol*] (OCLC)
VN .... Hang Khong Vietnam [*Vietnam*] [*ICAO designator*] (FAAC)
VN............. Training Plane [*Navy symbol*]
VN............. Vakstudie-Nieuws [*A publication*]
VN............. Van Ness' Prize Cases [*United States*] [*A publication*] (DLA)
VN............. Vangold Resources, Inc. [*Vancouver Stock Exchange symbol*]
VN............. (Vanillyl)nonanamide [*Biochemistry*]
VN............. Vegetative Nucleus [*Botany*]
VN............. Ventral Nerve [*Neuroanatomy*]
VN............. Ventral Nozzle
VN............. Verb Neuter
VN............. Verbal Noun
VN............. Verify Number If No Answer [*Telecommunications*] (TEL)
VN............. Victorian Newsletter [*A publication*]
VN............. Vietnam [*ANSI two-letter standard code*] (CNC)
vn.............. Vietnam, North [*vm (Vietnam) used in records cataloged after January 1978*] [*MARC country of publication code*] [*Library of Congress*] (LCCP)
VN............. VietNow (EA)
VN............. Violin [*Music*]
VN............. Virus Neutralization
VN............. Visiting Nurse
VN............. Vladimir Nabokov [*In book title, "VN: The Life and Art of Vladimir Nabokov"*]
VN............. Vocational Nurse
VN............. Volatile Nitrogen (OA)
VN............. Vomeronasal [*Anatomy*]
VN............. Von Neumann [*Procedure*] [*Statistics*]
VN............. Vulnerability Number
VNA.......... Air Viet-Nam
VNA.......... Jetstream International Airlines [*Latrobe, PA*] [*FAA designator*] (FAAC)
VNA.......... Mercy Hospital, Library, Watertown, NY [*OCLC symbol*] (OCLC)
VNA.......... Vienna, GA [*Location identifier*] [*FAA*] (FAAL)
VNA.......... Vietnam News Agency
VNA.......... Vietnamese National Army
VNA.......... Virtual Network Application [*Data processing*]
VNA.......... Visiting Nurse Association
VNAA....... Visiting Nurse Associations of America (EA)
VNAF .... Vietnam Air Force
VNAF .... Vietnam Armed Forces
VNAF I & M ... Vietnam Air Force Improvement and Modernization Program
VNAGA2... Archives Geologiques du Vietnam [*A publication*]
VNAS .... Vehicle Navigation Aid System
VNAV .... Vertical Navigation Mode (IEEE)
VNAWAG ... Koninklijke Nederlandse Akademie van Wetenschappen. Verhandelingen. Afdeling Natuurkunde. Tweede Reeks [*A publication*]
V N B .... Vetus Natura Brevium [*A publication*] (DSA)
VNB.......... Wadhams Hall Seminary College, Library, Ogdensburg, NY [*OCLC symbol*] (OCLC)
VNBG........ Bajhang [*Nepal*] [*ICAO location identifier*] (ICLI)
VNBJ........ Bhojpur [*Nepal*] [*ICAO location identifier*] (ICLI)
VNBL........ Baglung [*Nepal*] [*ICAO location identifier*] (ICLI)
VNBP........ Bharatpur [*Nepal*] [*ICAO location identifier*] (ICLI)
VNBP .... Valley National Bancorp [*Formerly, Valley National Bancorp of Passaic*] [*NASDAQ symbol*] (NQ)
VNBR .... Bajura [*Nepal*] [*ICAO location identifier*] (ICLI)
VNBT .... Baitadi [*Nepal*] [*ICAO location identifier*] (ICLI)
VNBW....... Bhairawa [*Nepal*] [*ICAO location identifier*] (ICLI)
VNC.......... North Country Reference and Research Resources Council, Union List of Serials, Canton, NY [*OCLC symbol*] (OCLC)
VNC.......... Variable Neutralizing Capacitor
VNC.......... Venice, FL [*Location identifier*] [*FAA*] (FAAL)
VNC.......... Ventral Nerve Cord [*Neuroanatomy*]
VNC.......... VNC Video Network [*Vancouver Stock Exchange symbol*]
VNC.......... Voice Numerical Control
VNC.......... Votes National Committee (EA)
VNCCI...... Volunteer - The National Center [*Later, NVC*] (EA)
VNCF .... Vietnam-Canada Foundation
VNCG........ Chandragarhi [*Nepal*] [*ICAO location identifier*] (ICLI)
VNCP........ Valley National Corp. [*NASDAQ symbol*] (NQ)
VNCS......... Vietnam Christian Service [*Defunct*] (EA)

VND.......... Jefferson Community College, Library, Watertown, NY [*OCLC symbol*] (OCLC)
VND.......... Vanda [*Antarctica*] [*Seismograph station code, US Geological Survey*] (SEIS)
VND.......... Vprasanja Nasih Dni [*A publication*]
VNDG....... Dang [*Nepal*] [*ICAO location identifier*] (ICLI)
VNDH....... Dhangarhi [*Nepal*] [*ICAO location identifier*] (ICLI)
VNDP....... Dolpa [*Nepal*] [*ICAO location identifier*] (ICLI)
VNDR....... Dhorpatan [*Nepal*] [*ICAO location identifier*] (ICLI)
VNDT....... Doti [*Nepal*] [*ICAO location identifier*] (ICLI)
VNE.......... Ogdensburg Public Library, Ogdensburg, NY [*OCLC symbol*] (OCLC)
VNE.......... Velocity Never to Exceed
VNE.......... Verbal Nonemotional (Stimuli) [*Psychology*]
VNESE...... Vietnamese
Vnesn Torg ... Vnesnjaja Torgovlja [*A publication*]
VNET .... Virtual Networks [*Data processing*] (HGAA)
VNETF...... Vietnam Expediting Task Force [*Military*]
VNF .... Paul Smiths College, Library, Paul Smiths, NY [*OCLC symbol*] (OCLC)
VNF .... Vietnam Foundation (EA)
VNFH........ Vjesnik Narodnog Fronta Hrvatske [*A publication*]
VNG.......... Ventral Surface, Nephridial Gland [*Anatomy*]
VNG.......... W. Alton Jones Cell Science Center Library, Lake Placid, NY [*OCLC symbol*] (OCLC)
VNGGA..... Verhandelingen. Koninklijke Nederlands Geologisch Mijnbouwkundig Genootschap. Geologische Serie [*A publication*]
VNGK....... Gorkha [*Nepal*] [*ICAO location identifier*] (ICLI)
VNHP....... Vermont Natural Heritage Program [*Information service or system*] (IID)
VNI .... Violini [*Violins*] [*Music*]
VNIC .... Voltage Negative Immittance Converter
VNIIMP .... Vsesoiuznyi Nauchno-Issledovatel'skii Institut Miasnoi Promyshlennosti [*All-Union Scientific Research Institute of the Meat Industry*]
VNIR .... Visible and Near-Visible Infrared (MCD)
VNIS......... Vehicle Navigation Information System [*Automotive engineering*]
Vnitr Lek ... Vnitrni Lekarstvi [*A publication*]
VNJI.......... Jiri [*Nepal*] [*ICAO location identifier*] (ICLI)
VNJL......... Jumla [*Nepal*] [*ICAO location identifier*] (ICLI)
VNJP........ Janakpur [*Nepal*] [*ICAO location identifier*] (ICLI)
VNJS........ Jomsom [*Nepal*] [*ICAO location identifier*] (ICLI)
VNKT .... Kathmandu/International [*Nepal*] [*ICAO location identifier*] (ICLI)
VNL.......... Bogalusa, LA [*Location identifier*] [*FAA*] (FAAL)
VNL.......... Variable Neodymium LASER
VNL.......... Via Net Loss [*Telecommunications*]
VNL.......... Victorian Newsletter [*A publication*]
VNL.......... Vrij Nederland [*A publication*]
VNLD........ Lamidada [*Nepal*] [*ICAO location identifier*] (ICLI)
VNLF........ Via Net Loss Factor (TEL)
VNLK........ Lukla [*Nepal*] [*ICAO location identifier*] (ICLI)
VNLT........ Langtang [*Nepal*] [*ICAO location identifier*] (ICLI)
VNM.......... Van Kampen Merritt New York Quality Municipal [*NYSE symbol*] (SPSG)
VNM.......... Vietnam [*ANSI three-letter standard code*] (CNC)
VNMA....... Manang [*Nepal*] [*ICAO location identifier*] (ICLI)
VNMC....... Vietnam Marine Corps
VNMG....... Meghauli [*Nepal*] [*ICAO location identifier*] (ICLI)
VNMN....... Mahendranagar [*Nepal*] [*ICAO location identifier*] (ICLI)
VNN .... Eastern Virginia Medical Authority, Norfolk, VA [*OCLC symbol*] (OCLC)
VNN .... Mount Vernon, IL [*Location identifier*] [*FAA*] (FAAL)
VNN .... Vacant National Number [*Telecommunications*] (TEL)
VNN .... Vietnam Navy
VNNG....... Nepalgung [*Nepal*] [*ICAO location identifier*] (ICLI)
VNO .... Cruising Speed [*Aviation code*] (AIA)
VNO .... Value Not Obtained
VNO .... Vilnius [*Former USSR*] [*Airport symbol*] (OAG)
VNO .... Vital National Objective (AAG)
VNO .... Vomeronasal Organ [*Anatomy*]
VNO .... Vornado, Inc. [*NYSE symbol*] (SPSG)
VNP .... Vehicle Network Protocol [*Automotive engineering*]
VNP .... Venda National Party [*Political party*] (PPW)
VNPK........ Pokhara [*Nepal*] [*ICAO location identifier*] (ICLI)
VNPL........ Phaplu [*Nepal*] [*ICAO location identifier*] (ICLI)
VNR.......... Van Nostrand Reinhold Co., Inc. [*Publisher*]
VNR.......... Variable Navigation Ratio
VNR.......... Veneer [*Technical drawings*]
VNR.......... VFR [*Visual Flight Rules*] Not Recommended [*Pilot brief*] [*Aviation*] (FAAC)
VNR.......... Video News Release [*A news release in the form of video tape*]
VNR.......... Vietnam Reactor
VNRB........ Rajbiraj [*Nepal*] [*ICAO location identifier*] (ICLI)
VNRK........ Rukumkot (Chaurjhari) [*Nepal*] [*ICAO location identifier*] (ICLI)
VNRN........ Vladimir Nabokov Research Newletter [*A publication*]
VNRP .... Rolpa [*Nepal*] [*ICAO location identifier*] (ICLI)
VNRS .... Vietnamese National Railway System (CINC)

VNRT .... Rumjatar [*Nepal*] [*ICAO location identifier*] (ICLI)
VNS .... Bondsspaarbanken [*A publication*]
VNS .... Norfolk State College, Norfolk, VA [*OCLC symbol*] (OCLC)
VNS .... Vagus Nerve Stimulation [*Physiology*]
VNS .... Varanasi [*India*] [*Airport symbol*] (OAG)
VNS .... Vasomotor Nervous System [*Physiology*]
VNS .... Ventral Nervous System [*Neuroanatomy*]
VNS .... Very North Shore [*Women's Wear Daily*]
VNS .... Visiting Nurse Service
VNS .... Vladimir Nabokov Society (EA)
VNSB........ Syanboche [*Nepal*] [*ICAO location identifier*] (ICLI)
VnSc......... Florence Williams Public Library, Christiansted, St. Croix, VI [*Library symbol*] [*Library of Congress*] (LCLS)
VNSF........ Vietnamese Special Forces (CINC)
VNSI......... Simara [*Nepal*] [*ICAO location identifier*] (ICLI)
VNSK........ Surkhet [*Nepal*] [*ICAO location identifier*] (ICLI)
VNSL........ Variable Nozzle Slow Landing (MCD)
VNSM....... Kathmandu [*Nepal*] [*ICAO location identifier*] (ICLI)
VNSP........ Vacant Nozzle Shield Plug [*Nuclear energy*] (NRCH)
VNSR........ Safebagar [*Nepal*] [*ICAO location identifier*] (ICLI)
VnSt......... Saint Thomas Public Library, Charlotte Amalie, VI [*Library symbol*] [*Library of Congress*] (LCLS)
VNST........ Simikot [*Nepal*] [*ICAO location identifier*] (ICLI)
VnStC .... College of the Virgin Islands, St. Thomas, VI [*Library symbol*] [*Library of Congress*] (LCLS)
VNT .... Variable-Nozzle Turbocharger [*Automotive engineering*]
VNT .... Ventora Resources Ltd. [*Vancouver Stock Exchange symbol*]
VNTJ........ Taplejung [*Nepal*] [*ICAO location identifier*] (ICLI)
VNTP........ Tikapur [*Nepal*] [*ICAO location identifier*] (ICLI)
VNTR .... Tumlingtar [*Nepal*] [*ICAO location identifier*] (ICLI)
VNTR .... Variable Number of Tandem Repeats [*Genetics*]
VNTRF...... Ventora Resources Ltd. [*NASDAQ symbol*] (NQ)
VNTS........ Vertical Nutrient-Solution Transport System [*i.e., plant stem*] [*Slang*]
VNTX .... Ventritex, Inc. [*NASDAQ symbol*] (SPSG)
VNU.......... Verenigde Nederlandse Uitgeversbedrijven [*Publishing group*] [*Netherlands*]
VNV.......... Vlaamsch Nationaal Verbond [*Flemish National League*] [*Dissolved*] [*Belgium*] [*Political party*] (PPE)
VNVO....... Verbal-Nonverbal Operation [*Psychometrics*]
VNVT .... Biratnagar [*Nepal*] [*ICAO location identifier*] (ICLI)
VNW......... Van Wert, OH [*Location identifier*] [*FAA*] (FAAL)
VNX.......... Oceanographic Development Squadron [*Navy symbol*] (DNAB)
VNXL........ Vane Axial
VNY.......... Van Nuys, CA [*Location identifier*] [*FAA*] (FAAL)
VO............. Battleship Observation Squadron [*Navy symbol*]
VO............. De Verborum Obligationibus [*A publication*] (DLA)
Vo............. Initial Velocity
VO............. Observation Plane [*Navy symbol*]
VO............. [*The*] Seagram Co. Ltd. [*NYSE symbol*] [*Toronto Stock Exchange symbol*] [*Vancouver Stock Exchange symbol*]
VO............. Valve Oscillator (DEN)
VO............. Varying Order [*British*]
VO............. Vehicle Operations [*NASA*] (NASA)
VO............. Verb-Object [*Education of the hearing-impaired*]
VO............. Verbal Orders
VO............. Verbindungsoffizier [*Liaison Officer*] [*German military - World War II*]
VO............. Vernehmungsoffizier [*Interrogation Officer*] [*German military - World War II*]
VO............. Verpflegungsoffizier [*Mess Officer*] [*German military - World War II*]
VO............. Verso
VO............. Vertical Oculus
VO............. Very Old [*Wines and spirits*]
VO............. Vesnjani Orbriji [*Kyjiv*] [*A publication*]
VO............. Veterinary Officer [*British*]
VO............. Victorian Order [*British*] (ROG)
VO............. Viking Orbiter [*NASA*]
VO............. Violation of [*Local*] Ordinance
VO............. Violino [*Violin*] [*Music*] (ROG)
VO............. Visa Office [*Department of State*]
VO............. Vocal (AAG)
VO............. Voice [*A publication*]
VO............. Voice (AAG)
VO............. Voice Over [*Commentary read over a program*] [*Television*]
Vo............. Voices [*A publication*]
VO............. Volatile Oil
VO............. Volcanic Origin (AAG)
VO............. Volt (ROG)
VO............. Volume
VO............. Voluntary Opening [*Prosthesis*] [*Medicine*]
VO............. Von Oben [*From the Top*] [*German*]
VO............. VOTEC, Servicos Aereos Regionais SA [*Brazil*] [*ICAO designator*] (ICDA)
VO............. Voucher (MCD)
VOA.......... Vibrational Optical Activity [*Spectroscopy*]
VOA.......... Voice of America [*United States Information Agency*]
VOA.......... Volkswagen of America
VOA.......... Volunteers of America (EA)

VOA..........	Voorlichter [*A publication*]
VO-AG	Vocational Agriculture [*Education*]
VOAPA	Vultee Owners and Pilots Association (EA)
VOARS......	Velocity over Altitude Ratio Sensor (MCD)
VOB..........	Vacuum Optical Bench
VOB..........	Volume over Bark [*Forestry*]
VOBANC..	Voice Band Compression (CET)
VOBG........	Bangalore [*India*] [*ICAO location identifier*] (ICLI)
VOBI	Bellary [*India*] [*ICAO location identifier*] (ICLI)
VOBL BZ ..	Verordnungsblatt fuer die Britische Zone [*Official Gazette of the Former British Zone of Occupation*] [*German*] (ILCA)
VOBR	Bidar [*India*] [*ICAO location identifier*] (ICLI)
VOBZ	Vijayawada [*India*] [*ICAO location identifier*] (ICLI)
VOC..........	Observation Spotter Squadron [*Navy symbol*]
VOC..........	Onondaga Community College, Syracuse, NY [*OCLC symbol*] (OCLC)
VOC..........	Variable Oil Capacitor
VOC..........	Variable Output Circuit (DEN)
VOC..........	Vehicle Observer Corps [*Road Haulage Association*] [*British*] (DCTA)
VOC..........	Vehicle Out of Commission [*Army*] (AFIT)
VOC..........	Verbal Orders of the Commander
VOC..........	Vincent Owners Club (EA)
VOC..........	Virago Owners Club (EA)
VOC..........	VM. Voorlichtingsblad van het Ministerie van Volksgezondheid en Milieuhygiene [*A publication*]
VOC..........	Vocabulary [*Linguistics*]
VOC..........	Vocal (ADA)
VOC..........	Vocational
VOC..........	Vocative
VOC..........	Voice of Calvary [*An association*]
VOC..........	Voice-Operated Coder
VOC..........	Voice Order Circuit (CET)
VOC..........	Volatile Organic Chemical
VOC..........	Volatile Organic Compound [*Environmental chemistry*]
VOC..........	Volunteer Officer Candidate [*Army*]
VOCA	Victims of Crime Act of 1984
VOCA	Visiting Orchestra Consultative Association [*British*] (DI)
VOCA	Voice of China and Asia Missionary Society (EA)
VOCA	Voice Communications Assembly [*Ground Communications Facility, NASA*]
VOCA	Voice Output Communications Aid
VOCA	Voltmeter Calibrator
VOCA	Volunteers in Overseas Cooperative Assistance (EA)
VOCAB	Vocabulary
VOCAL	Vessel Ordnance Allowance List
VOCAL	Victims of Child Abuse Laws (EA)
VOCAL	Victims of Crime and Leniency (EA)
VOCAP	VP-16-213 [*Etoposide*], Oncovin [*Vincristine*], Cyclophosphamide, Adriamycin, Platinol [*Cisplatin*] [*Antineoplastic drug regimen*]
Voc Aspect Ed ...	Vocational Aspect of Education [*A publication*]
VOCAT	Vocational
VOCAT	Vocative [*Grammar*] (ROG)
Vocat Asp Educ ...	Vocational Aspect of Education [*A publication*]
Vocat Guid ...	Vocational Guidance Quarterly [*A publication*]
Vocational Aspect ...	Vocational Aspect of Education [*A publication*]
Vocat Train Bull ...	Vocational Training. Bulletin [*A publication*]
Vocat Training ...	Vocational Training [*A publication*]
VOCB	Coimbatore [*India*] [*ICAO location identifier*] (ICLI)
VOCC	Cochin [*India*] [*ICAO location identifier*] (ICLI)
VOC-ED	Vocational Education (OICC)
VocEd Insider ...	VocEd Business and Office Insider. Journal of the American Vocational Association [*A publication*]
Voc Educ....	Vocational Education [*A publication*]
Voc Educ M ...	Vocational Education Magazine [*A publication*]
VOCG........	Verbal Orders of Commanding General
Voc Guid Q ...	Vocational Guidance Quarterly [*A publication*]
VOCL	Calicut [*India*] [*ICAO location identifier*] (ICLI)
VOCM.......	St. John's, NF [*AM radio station call letters*]
VOCM.......	Vehicle Out of Commission for Maintenance [*Military*]
VOCM-FM ...	St. John's, NF [*FM radio station call letters*]
VOCNA.....	Velocette Owners Club of North America (EA)
VOCO........	Verbal Orders of Commanding Officer
VOCODER ...	Voice Coder
VOCOM....	Voice Communications
VOCP	Cuddapah [*India*] [*ICAO location identifier*] (ICLI)
VOCP	Vehicle Out of Commission for Parts [*Military*]
VocRehab...	Vocational Rehabilitation (OICC)
VOCS	Verbal Orders of the Chief of Staff
VOCX	Carnicobar [*India*] [*ICAO location identifier*] (ICLI)
VOD..........	Old Dominion University, Norfolk, VA [*OCLC symbol*] (OCLC)
VOD..........	Vacuum Oxygen Decarburization [*Stainless-steel processing*]
VOD..........	Vehicle On-Board Delivery
VOD..........	Velocity of Detonation (IEEE)
VOD..........	Veno-Occlusive Disease [*of the liver*]
VOD..........	Vertical On-Board Delivery [*Navy*] (NVT)
VOD..........	Via Omnidirect (FAAC)
VOD..........	Vision, Right Eye

VOD..........	Vodafone Group [*NYSE symbol*] (SPSG)
VODACOM ...	Voice Data Communications
VODARO ...	Vertical Ozone Distribution from the Absorption and Radiation of Ozone (AAG)
VODAS	Voice-Operated Device Antising (CET)
VODAT	Voice-Operated Device for Automatic Transmission
VODC........	Viking Orbiter Design Change [*NASA*]
VODER	Voice Coder
VODER	Voice-Operated Demonstrator
Vodfne.......	Vodafone Group [*Associated Press abbreviation*] (APAG)
VODG........	Dundigul [*India*] [*ICAO location identifier*] (ICLI)
VODK........	Donakonda [*India*] [*ICAO location identifier*] (ICLI)
VODK........	[*The*] Voice of Democratic Kampuchea [*Radio station of the Red Khmers*] (PD)
Vodn Hospod ...	Vodni Hospodarstvi [*A publication*]
Vodn Hospod Rada B ...	Vodni Hospodarstvi. Rada B [*A publication*]
Vodni Hospod ...	Vodni Hospodarstvi [*A publication*]
Vodni Hospod A ...	Vodni Hospodarstvi. Rada A [*Czechoslovakia*] [*A publication*]
Vodni Hospod Rada B ...	Vodni Hospodarstvi. Rada B [*A publication*]
Vodn Resur ...	Vodnye Resursy [*Former USSR*] [*A publication*]
Vodohospod Cas ...	Vodohospodarsky Casopis [*A publication*]
Vodopodgot Ochistka Prom Stokov ...	Vodopodgotovka i Ochistka Promyshlennykh Stokov [*A publication*]
Vodorosli Griby Sib Dal'nego Vostoka ...	Vodorosli i Griby Sibiri i Dal'nego Vostoka [*A publication*]
Vodosnabzh Kanaliz Gidrotekh Sooruzh ...	Vodosnabzhenie Kanalizatsiya Gidrotekhnicheskie Sooruzheniya [*A publication*]
Vodosnabzh Sanit Tekh ...	Vodosnabzhenie i Sanitarnaya Tekhnika [*A publication*]
Vodos Sanit Tekhn ...	Vodosnabzhenie i Sanitarnaya Tekhnika [*A publication*]
VODP........	Verbal-Orders by Direction of the President
VODS........	Video Operator Distress Syndrome (HGAA)
VOE..........	Venus Orbit Ejection [*NASA*] (MCD)
VOE..........	Visual Order Error
VOE..........	Vocational Office Education [*NASA employment program*]
VOEC	Vegetable Oil Export Corp. (EA)
VOECRN ..	Vietnamese Organization to Exterminate Communists and Restore the Nation (EA)
Voedingsmiddelen Technol ...	Voedingsmiddelen Technologie [*A publication*]
Voegel Rheinl ...	Voegel des Rheinlandes [*A publication*]
VOEI	Veroeffentlichungen. Osteuropa-Institut [*A publication*]
Voen Khim ...	Voennaya Khimiya [*A publication*]
Voen Med Delo ...	Voenno Meditsinsko Delo [*A publication*]
Voenna Tekh ...	Voenna Tekhnika [*Bulgaria*] [*A publication*]
Voen Sanit Delo ...	Voenno-Sanitarnoe Delo [*A publication*]
Voen Znaniya ...	Voennye Znaniya [*Former USSR*] [*A publication*]
VOF..........	Covington, GA [*Location identifier*] [*FAA*] (FAAL)
VOF..........	Observation Fighter Squadron [*Navy symbol*]
VOF..........	Variable Operating Frequency (NATG)
VOF..........	Vennootschap Onder Firma [*Limited Partnership*] [*Dutch*] (ILCA)
VOF..........	Vsesoiuznoe Obshchestvo Filatelistov [*or Fizioterapistov*]
v1of...........	Lift-Off Speed [*Aviation code*] (AIA)
VOG..........	Observation Plane Squadron [*Navy symbol*]
VOG..........	Vanguard Operations Group
VOG..........	Vectoroculogram
VOG..........	Vessel Off-Gas [*Nuclear energy*] (NRCH)
Vog...........	Vogue [*Record label*] [*France*]
VOG..........	Volgograd [*Former USSR*] [*Airport symbol*] (OAG)
VOGAA	Voice-Operated Gain-Adjusting Amplifier [*NASA*]
VOGAD	Voice-Operated Gain-Adjusting Device [*NASA*]
VOGB........	Gulbarga [*India*] [*ICAO location identifier*] (ICLI)
Vogelkd Hefte Edertal ...	Vogelkundliche Hefte Edertal [*A publication*]
VOGIN......	Nederlandse Vereniging van Gebruikers van Online Informatie-Systemen [*Netherlands Association of Users of Online Information Systems*] (EAIO)
Vog Liv.......	Vogue Living [*A publication*] (APTA)
VOGOV......	Verbal Orders of the Governor
VOGT........	Vogart Crafts Corp. [*NASDAQ symbol*] (NQ)
VOH	Grootkeuken. Voedingsblad voor Instellingen en Bedrijven [*A publication*]
VOH	Vohemar [*Madagascar*] [*Airport symbol*] (OAG)
VOHCA.....	Veterans Omnibus Health Care Act of 1976
VOHY.......	Hyderabad [*India*] [*ICAO location identifier*] (ICLI)
VOI...........	Vehicle Ordnance Installation
VOI...........	Video Output Impedance
VOI...........	Vocational Opinion Index (OICC)
VOI...........	Voinjama [*Liberia*] [*Airport symbol*] (OAG)
VOIB	Veroeffentlichungen. Abteilung fuer Slavische Sprachen und Literaturen. Osteuropa-Institut [*Slavisches Seminar*]. Freie Universitaet Berlin [*A publication*]
VOIC	Voicemail International, Inc. [*NASDAQ symbol*] (NQ)
VOICE.......	Victims of Incest Can Emerge (EA)
Voice	Village Voice [*A publication*]
VOICE.......	Vocabulary of Intelligence Concept Expressions
VOICE.......	Vocal Output and Input-Controlled Environment
VOICE.......	Voice of Informed Community Expression
VOICE.......	Volunteer Oil Industry Communications Effort [*Program*] [*Phillips Petroleum Co.*]

VOICECON ... Voice Telephone Conference
VOIR .... Venus Orbiting and Imaging RADAR [*NASA*]
VOIS .... Visual Observation Instrumentation Subsystem [*Lunar space program*]
VOIS .... Visual Observation Integration Subsystem (AAG)
VOIS .... Voice-Operated Inspection System [*Software*]
VOISC .... Variable Orifice Idle Spark Control [*Automotive engineering*]
VOIT .... Voit Corp. [*NASDAQ symbol*] (NQ)
Voith Forsch Konstr ... Voith Forschung und Konstruktion [*A publication*]
Voith Res & Constr ... Voith Research and Construction [*A publication*]
VOIZD ...... Voice of Z-39 [*Later, Information Standards Quarterly*] [*A publication*]
Vojenskozdrav Knih ... Vojenskozdravotnicka Knihovna [*A publication*]
Vojen Zdrav Listy ... Vojenske Zdravotnicke Listy [*A publication*]
Vojnoekon Pregl ... Vojnoekonomski Pregled [*Yugoslavia*] [*A publication*]
Vojnosanit Pregl ... Vojnosanitetski Pregled [*A publication*]
VOK .... Camp Douglas, WI [*Location identifier*] [*FAA*] (FAAL)
VOK .... Volkskrant [*A publication*]
VOK .... Vry op Kaai [*Free on Quay*] [*Afrikaans*]
VOKM .... Khamampet [*India*] [*ICAO location identifier*] (ICLI)
VOKS .... Soviet Union Society for Cultural Relations with Foreign Countries. Weekly News Bulletin [*A publication*]
VOKS .... Vsesoiuznoe Obshchestvo Kul'turnoi Sviazi s Zagranitsei [*All-Union Society for Cultural Relations with Foreign Countries*] [*Former USSR*]
VOL .... Variable Orientation Launcher (AAG)
Vol .... Volans [*Constellation*]
VOL .... Volante [*Lightly and Rapidly*] [*Music*] (ROG)
Vol .... Volar [*Anatomy*] (WGA)
VOL .... Volatilis [*Volatile*] [*Pharmacy*]
Vol .... Volcanic [*Quality of the bottom*] [*Nautical charts*]
VOL .... Volcano [*Maps and charts*]
VOL .... Volume (EY)
VOL .... Voluntary [*or Volunteer*] (AFM)
VOLA .... Volume, American Stock Exchange [*Selection symbol*]
VOLAD ..... Voice of the Lakes [*A publication*]
VOLAG ..... Voluntary Agency [*Generic term for a charitable organization*]
VOLAR ..... Volunteer Army [*Project, absorbed by MVA, 1972*]
Vol Ash ...... Volcanic Ash [*Quality of the bottom*] [*Nautical charts*]
VOLB .... Volunteer Bancshares, Inc. [*Jackson, TN*] [*NASDAQ symbol*] (NQ)
VOLC .... Volcanics [*Lithology*]
VOLC .... Volcano
Volcani Inst Agric Res Div For Ilanot Leafl ... Volcani Institute of Agricultural Research. Division of Forestry. Ilanot Leaflet [*A publication*]
Volcani Inst Agric Res Div Sci Publ Pam ... Volcani Institute of Agricultural Research. Division of Scientific Publications. Pamphlet [*A publication*]
Volcanol Bull Jpn Meterol Agency ... Volcanological Meteorological Bulletin. Japan Meteorological Agency [*A publication*]
Volcanol Soc Jap Bull ... Volcanological Society of Japan. Bulletin [*A publication*]
VOLCAS ... Voice-Operated Loss Control and Suppressor
VolCC .... Volunteer Capital Corp. [*Associated Press abbreviation*] (APAG)
VOLCOM ... Value of Life Committee (EA)
VOLCUF ... Voluntary Organisations' Liaison Council for Under-Fives [*British*] (DI)
Vol Effort Q ... Voluntary Effort Quarterly [*A publication*]
VOLERE ... Voluntary/Legal/Regulatory (IEEE)
Vol Feeding Mgt ... Volume Feeding Management [*A publication*]
VOLIR .... Volumetric Indicating RADAR
VOLKS ...... Volkswagen [*Automobile*] (DSUE)
Volksm .... Volksmusik [*A publication*]
Volkstum Landschaft ... Volkstum und Landschaft. Heimatblaetter der Muensterlaendische Tageszeitung [*A publication*]
Volleyball Mag ... Volleyball Magazine [*A publication*]
Volleyball Tech J ... Volleyball Technical Journal [*A publication*]
VOLMET ... Meteorological Information for Aircraft in Flight [*Aviation code*] (FAAC)
Voln .... Volans [*Constellation*]
VOLN .... Volume, New York Stock Exchange [*Selection symbol*]
Vo LR .... Villanova Law Review [*A publication*]
Volr .... Volunteer [*British military*] (DMA)
VOLRA ..... Volta Review [*A publication*]
Vol Ret Merch ... Volume Retail Merchandising [*A publication*]
VOLRY ...... Voluntary
VOLS .... Voluntary Overseas Libraries Service
VOLSCAN ... Volumetric Scanning RADAR
VOLSER ... Volume/Serial
VOLT .... Volt Information Sciences, Inc. [*NASDAQ symbol*] (NQ)
VOLT .... Volume, Toronto Stock Exchange [*Selection symbol*]
VOLTAN .. Voltage Amperage Normalizer
Volta R .... Volta Review [*A publication*]
Volt Electr Trade Mon ... Volt. Electrical Trade Monthly [*Japan*] [*A publication*]
Volunt Action ... Voluntary Action [*A publication*]
Volunt Action Leadersh ... Voluntary Action Leadership [*A publication*]
Volunt Adm ... Volunteer Administration [*A publication*]
Volunt Forum Abs ... Voluntary Forum Abstracts [*A publication*]

Volunt Housing ... Voluntary Housing [*A publication*]
Volunt Leader ... Volunteer Leader [*A publication*]
VOLV .... Volvendus [*To Be Rolled*] [*Pharmacy*] (ADA)
VOLV .... Volvo AB [*Sweden*] [*NASDAQ symbol*]
VOLVEND ... Volvendus [*To Be Rolled*] [*Pharmacy*]
VOLY .... Voluntary (ROG)
VOM .... Nux Vomica Strychnia [*Strychnine-producing plant*] [*Pharmacy*] (ROG)
VOM .... Voice of the Mediterranean [*Broadcasting service jointly owned by Maltese and Libyan Governments*] (EY)
VOM .... Volcano Resources Corp. [*Vancouver Stock Exchange symbol*]
VOM .... Volt-Ohm Meter
VOM .... Volt-Ohm-Milliammeter
VOMD .... Madurai [*India*] [*ICAO location identifier*] (ICLI)
VOMD .... VAFB [*Vandenberg Air Force Base*] Operations and Maintenance Documentation (NASA)
VOMF ...... Madras [*India*] [*ICAO location identifier*] (ICLI)
VOMG ...... Magadi [*India*] [*ICAO location identifier*] (ICLI)
VOMH ...... Mahad [*India*] [*ICAO location identifier*] (ICLI)
VOMI .... Volksdeutsche Mittelstelle [*NAZI Germany*]
VOML .... Mangalore [*India*] [*ICAO location identifier*] (ICLI)
VOMM ...... Madras [*India*] [*ICAO location identifier*] (ICLI)
VOM URG ... Vomitione Urgente [*The Vomiting Being Troublesome*] [*Pharmacy*] (ROG)
VOMY .... Mysore [*India*] [*ICAO location identifier*] (ICLI)
VON .... Avon, CO [*Location identifier*] [*FAA*] (FAAL)
VON .... Victorian Order of Nurses
VON .... Vons Companies [*NYSE symbol*] (SPSG)
Von H Const Hist ... Von Holst's Constitutional History of the United States [*A publication*] (DLA)
Von Ihr Str for L ... Von Ihring's Struggle for Law [*A publication*] (DLA)
VONJY ...... Elan Populaire pour l'Unite Nationale [*Popular Impulse for National Unity*] [*Malagascar*] [*Political party*] (PPW)
Von Roll Mitt ... Von Roll Mitteilungen [*A publication*]
VONS .... Committee for the Defense of Persons Unjustly Persecuted [*Former Czechoslovakia*] [*Political party*] (PD)
VONS .... Nagarjunsagar [*India*] [*ICAO location identifier*] (ICLI)
Vons .... Vons Companies [*Associated Press abbreviation*] (APAG)
VOofA .... Vasa Order of America [*Cranston, RI*] (EA)
Voorh Code ... Voorhies' Code [*New York*] [*A publication*] (DLA)
Voorh Cr Jur ... Voorhies' Criminal Jurisprudence of Louisiana [*A publication*] (DLA)
Voorh St ..... Voorhies' Louisiana Revised Statutes [*A publication*] (DLA)
Voorlichting Onderz ... Voorlichting en Onderzoek [*A publication*]
VOP .... Valued as in Original Policy [*Insurance*]
VOP .... Vertical Ozone Profile
VOP .... Very Old Pale [*Designation on brandy labels*]
VOP .... Viral Oncology Program [*National Cancer Institute*]
VOPA .... Verbal Order Purchase Agreement [*Sales*]
VOPAN ..... Voice Pitch Analysis [*Consumer Response Corp.*]
VOPB .... Port Blair [*India*] [*ICAO location identifier*] (ICLI)
VOPB .... Voice of the People of Burma [*Radio station of the Burma Communist Party*] (PD)
VOPLEX ... Voplex Corp. [*Associated Press abbreviation*] (APAG)
VOPNAV .. Vice Chief of Naval Operations
VOPO .... Volkspolizei [*Also, VP*]
VOPP .... Veterinary Medicine, Optometry, Podiatry, and Pharmacy [*HEW program*]
VOPR .... Voice-Operated Relay
VOPT .... Voice of the People of Thailand [*Radio station of the Communist Party of Thailand*] (PD)
VOQ .... Van Kampen Merritt Ohio Quality Municipal [*NYSE symbol*] (SPSG)
VOQ .... Visiting Officers' Quarters [*Military*]
VOR .... Vehicle off the Road [*British*]
VOR .... Vertical Omnidirectional Radio
VOR .... Very-High-Frequency Omnidirectional Range
VOR .... Vestibulo-Ocular Reflex [*Neurology*]
VOR .... Visual Omnidirectional Range (DNAB)
VOR .... Visual Omnirange [*Directional Beacon*] [*Aviation*] (NG)
VOR .... Voice-Operated Relay
VOR .... Vortex Science Fiction [*A publication*]
VORAD ..... Vehicular On-Board RADAR [*Automotive engineering*] (PS)
VOR/ATCS ... VHF [*Very-High-Frequency*] Omnidirectional Radio Beacon and Air Traffic Communications Station (SAA)
VORDAC .. VHF [*Very-High-Frequency*] Omnidirectional Range/Distance-Measuring for Air Coverage
VORDME ... VHF [*Very-High-Frequency*] Omnidirectional Range/Distance-Measuring Equipment (CET)
VOR/DMET ... VHF [*Very-High-Frequency*] Omnidirectional Range/Distance-Measuring Equipment Compatible with TACAN
VOR-FIX ... Vestibuloocular Reflex with Fixation Light [*Ophthalmology*]
VORG .... Ramagundam [*India*] [*ICAO location identifier*] (ICLI)
VORHDW ... Voegel des Rheinlandes [*A publication*]
Vorlesungen Fachbereich Math Univ Essen ... Vorlesungen aus dem Fachbereich Mathematik. Universitaet Essen [*A publication*]
Vorlesungen Math Inst Giessen ... Vorlesungen. Mathematisches Institut Giessen [*A publication*]
VORLOC .. VHF [*Very-High-Frequency*] Omnirange Localizer (CET)
VORM .... Ramnad [*India*] [*ICAO location identifier*] (ICLI)

VORM.......	Vormittags [*In the Morning*] [*German*]
Vornad	Vornado, Inc. [*Associated Press abbreviation*] (APAG)
VORR	Raichur [*India*] [*ICAO location identifier*] (ICLI)
VORS	Vestibulo-Ocular Reflex Suppression [*Ophthalmology*]
Vorsokr	Fragmente der Vorsokratiker [*A publication*] (OCD)
VORT	Vorticity (FAAC)
VORTAC...	Variable Omnirange Tactical (NASA)
VORTAC...	VHF [*Very-High-Frequency*] Omnirange TACAN
VORTAN ..	Visual Omnirange/Tactical Air Navigation (MCD)
VORTEX...	Venus Orbiter Radiometric Temperature Experiment [*NASA*]
Vortr Gesamtgeb Bot ...	Vortraege aus dem Gesamtgebiet der Botanik [*A publication*]
Vortr Pflanzenz Deut Landwirt Ges Pflanzenzuchtabt ...	Vortraege fuer Pflanzenzuchter. Deutsche Landwirtschaftliche Gesellschaft Pflanzenzuchtabteilung [*A publication*]
VORY	Rajahmundry [*India*] [*ICAO location identifier*] (ICLI)
VOS	Observation Scout Plane [*Navy symbol*]
VOS	Vehicle Origin Survey [*R. L. Polk & Co.*] [*Information service or system*] (IID)
VOS	Vehicle on Stand (MCD)
VOS	Veterans of Safety (EA)
VOS	Veterinary Orthopaedic Society (EA)
VOS	Viking Orbiter System [*NASA*]
VOS	Virtual Operating System
VOS	Visicoder Oscillograph System
VOS	Vision, Left Eye
VOS	Vitello Ovi Solutus [*Dissolved in the Yolk of an Egg*] [*Pharmacy*] (ROG)
VOS	Voice-Operated Switch [*or System*]
VOS	Voluntary Observing Ships [*Marine science*] (MSC)
Vos	Voskhod (BJA)
VOS	Vostok [*Former USSR*] [*Geomagnetic observatory code*]
VOSA	Variable Orifice Sound Attenuator [*System*] (DNAB)
VOSA	Verbal Orders of the Secretary of the Army
VOSAA	Vox Sanguinis [*A publication*]
VOSAF......	Verbal Orders of the Secretary of the Air Force
VOSC	VAST [*Versatile Avionics Shop Test*] Operating System Code
VOSH.......	Volunteer Optometric Services to Humanity/International (EA)
VOSL........	Variable Operating and Safety Level (DNAB)
VOST........	Volatile Organic Sampling Train [*For air analysis*]
V Ost Geschichtsv ...	Veroeffentlichungen. Verband Oesterreichischer Geschichts- Vereine [*A publication*]
Vost Neft....	Vostochnaya Neft [*A publication*]
VOSW	Very Old Scotch Whisky
VOT..........	Valve Opening Time [*Nuclear energy*] (NRCH)
VOT..........	Very Old Tawny [*Wines and spirits*]
VOT..........	VHF [*Very-High-Frequency*] Omnitest
VOT..........	Vision of Tomorrow [*A publication*]
VOT..........	Vocational Office Trainee
VOT..........	Voice Onset Time
VOT..........	Voplex Corp. [*AMEX symbol*] (SPSG)
VOT..........	VOR [*Very-High-Frequency Omnidirectional Range*] Test Signal (CET)
VOT..........	Vorticity (FAAC)
vot.............	Votic [*MARC language code*] [*Library of Congress*] (LCCP)
VOTA	Vibration Open Test Assembly [*Nuclear energy*] (NRCH)
VOTACT...	Validation of Theoretical Automatic Checkout Techniques (MCD)
VOTAG	Verbal Orders of the Adjutant General
VOTC	Volume Table of Contents [*Data processing*]
VOTCA	Victims of Terrorism Compensation Act
VO-TECH ...	Vocational-Technical
VOTJ........	Tanjore [*India*] [*ICAO location identifier*] (ICLI)
VOTM.......	Vacuum-Operated Throttle Modulator [*Automotive engineering*]
VOTP	Tirupeti [*India*] [*ICAO location identifier*] (ICLI)
VOTR	Tiruchchirappalli [*India*] [*ICAO location identifier*] (ICLI)
VOTV	Trivandrum [*India*] [*ICAO location identifier*] (ICLI)
VOTX	Tambaram [*India*] [*ICAO location identifier*] (ICLI)
VOTX	Votrax International, Inc. [*NASDAQ symbol*] (NQ)
VOU	Visio Oculus Uterque [*Vision, Each Eye*] [*Latin*] [*Ophthalmology*] (MAE)
VOU	Voucher (AFM)
VOU	Vouglans [*France*] [*Seismograph station code, US Geological Survey*] (SEIS)
VOU DED ...	Voucher Deduction [*Military*] (DNAB)
VOV..........	Very Old Version
VOV..........	Video Output Voltage
VOVB........	Vikarabad [*India*] [*ICAO location identifier*] (ICLI)
VOVR........	Vellore [*India*] [*ICAO location identifier*] (ICLI)
VOW..........	Voice Order Wire
VOW..........	Voice of Women
VOWA.......	Warangal [*India*] [*ICAO location identifier*] (ICLI)
VOWF.......	Value-Operated Water Flash (DNAB)
VOWR.......	St. John's, NF [*AM radio station call letters*]
VOX..........	Audiovox Corp. Class A [*AMEX symbol*] (SPSG)
VOX..........	Voice Controlled Relay
VOX..........	Voice-Operated Keying [*Data processing*]
VOX..........	Voice-Operated Transmission
VOX..........	Voice Output Exchange

voxel...........	Volume Element (MAE)
VOX POP ...	Vox Populi [*Voice of the People*] [*Latin*]
Vox Sang...	Vox Sanguinis [*A publication*]
Vox Sanguin ...	Vox Sanguinis [*A publication*]
VoxTh........	Vox Theologica [*Assen*] [*A publication*]
VoxTheol ...	Vox Theologica [*Assen*] [*A publication*]
VOY..........	Viceroy Resources Corp. [*Toronto Stock Exchange symbol*] [*Vancouver Stock Exchange symbol*]
voy.............	Voyage (DS)
VOYA	Voice of Youth Advocates [*A publication*]
VoyAZ	Voyageur Arizona Municipal Income Fund [*Associated Press abbreviation*] (APAG)
VoyFla	Voyageur Florida Insured Municipal Income [*Associated Press abbreviation*] (APAG)
VoyMN......	Voyageur Minnesota Municipal Income Fund [*Associated Press abbreviation*] (APAG)
VoyMO......	Voyageur Missouri Municipal Income Fund [*Associated Press abbreviation*] (APAG)
Voz Farm (Lima) ...	Voz Farmaceutica (Lima) [*A publication*]
VOZNA.....	Voennye Znaniya [*A publication*]
Vozr...........	Vozrozdenie [*A publication*]
VP	All India Reporter, Vindhya Pradesh [*1951-57*] [*A publication*] (DLA)
VP	Patrol Plane [*Navy symbol*]
VP	Patrol Squadron [*Navy symbol*]
VP	Shore Based [*Navy symbol*]
VP	United Kingdom Colonies and Protectorates [*Aircraft nationality and registration mark*] (FAAC)
VP	Vacant Property (ADA)
VP	Vacuum Packaged
VP	Vacuum Pickup
VP	Vacuum Pump
V & P........	Vagotomy and Pyloroplasty [*Medicine*]
VP	Validation Plan [*Social Security Administration*]
VP	Valve Pit (AAG)
VP	Valve Positioner
VP	Vanishing Point [*Term in art/drawing*]
VP	Vanuaaku Pati [*New Hebrides*] [*Political party*] (PD)
VP	Vanuatu Pati (PD)
VP	Vapor Pressure
VP	Variable Pitch [*as, an aircraft propeller*]
VP	Variable Procedure (AAG)
VP	Variable Property
VP	Variant Pinocytic [*Cell*] [*Medicine*]
VP	Variegate Porphyria [*Medicine*]
VP	Various Paging [*Bibliography*]
vp...............	Various Places [*MARC country of publication code*] [*Library of Congress*] (LCCP)
VP	Various Publishers [*Bibliography*]
VP	Vasopressin [*Endocrinology*]
VP	Vector Processor
VP	Velocity Pressure
V & P........	Vendor and Purchaser [*Sales*] (ROG)
VP	Venereal Pamphlet [*Navy*]
VP	Venipuncture [*Medicine*] (MAE)
VP	Venous Pressure [*Medicine*]
VP	Vent-Clearing Pressure [*Nuclear energy*] (NRCH)
VP	Vent Pipe [*Technical drawings*]
V-P...........	Ventilation-Perfusion Scintigraphy
VP	Ventral Pioneer [*Neuron*]
VP	Ventral Posterior [*Anatomy*]
VP	Ventriculoperitoneal [*Medicine*]
VP	Verb Passive
VP	Verb Phrase
VP	Verification Polarization (NASA)
VP	Verifying Punch (CMD)
VP	Verstell Propeller (MCD)
VP	Vertex Processor
VP	Vertical Planning (NG)
VP	Vertical Polarization
VP	Vest Pocket
VP	Viacao Aerea Sao Paulo, SA [*Brazil*] [*ICAO designator*] (FAAC)
VP	Vice President
VP	Vice-Principal [*British*]
VP	Victorian Poetry [*A publication*]
VP	Video Processor (NVT)
VP	Videoplayer
VP	Vietnam Press
VP	Viewpoint (NASA)
VP	Vincristine and Prednisone [*Antineoplastic drug regimen*]
VP	Vinylphenol [*Biochemistry*]
VP	Vinylpyrrolidinone [*Organic chemistry*]
VP	Viral Particle [*Medicine*]
VP	Viral Protein [*Biochemistry, genetics*]
VP	Virtual Pitch [*Neurophysiology*]
VP	Virtual Processor
VP	Visa Petition
VP	Visitor's Passport [*British*]
VP	Vivre et Penser [*A publication*] (BJA)
VP	Voce del Passato [*A publication*]

VP .... Voges-Proskauer [*Bacteriology*]
VP .... Void in Part [*Decision or finding held invalid in part for reasons given*] [*Used in Shepard's Citations*] [*Legal term*] (DLA)
VP .... Volkspartie [*People's Party*] [*Liechtenstein*] [*Political party*] (PPE)
VP .... Volkspolizei [*Also, VOPO*]
VP .... Volume-Pressure (MAE)
VP .... Voluntary Patient [*British*]
VP .... Vorposten [*Outpost*] [*German military*]
VP .... Vossa Paternidade [*Yours Paternally*] [*Portuguese*]
V & P .... Votes and Proceedings [*A publication*] (APTA)
VP .... Voting Pool [*Said of disposition of stocks*]
VP .... Vulnerable Period [*Physiology*]
VP .... Vulnerable Point
VP-16-213 ... Vepeside [*Etoposide*] [*Antineoplastic drug*]
VPA .... Valproic Acid [*Anticonvulsant compound*]
VPA .... Value Purchase Agreement (HGAA)
VPA .... Vascular Permeability Assay [*Clinical chemistry*]
VPA .... Vehicle Power Adapter
VPA .... Vibration Pickup Amplifier
VPA .... Victorian Planning Appeal Decisions [*A publication*] (APTA)
VPA .... Videotape Production Association (EA)
VPA .... Virtual Population Analysis
VPA .... Visual Packaging Association (EA)
VPA .... Volatile Profile Analysis [*Food chemistry*]
VPA .... Volume Purchase Agreement [*Sales*]
VPA .... Vote Profile Analysis
VPAM .... Virtual Partitioned Access Method
VPAP .... Voluntary Petroleum Allocation Program [*Presidential*]
VPARD ...... Veterinary Parasitology [*A publication*]
VPB........... Medium and Heavy Patrol Bomber Squadron [*Land based and seaplane*] [*Navy symbol*]
VPB........... Patrol-Bombing Plane [*Navy symbol*]
VPB........... Vendors per Block [*Sales*]
VPB........... Ventricular Premature Beat [*Cardiology*]
VPB........... Vertical Plot Board [*Navy*]
VPB........... Vinblastine, Platinol [*Cisplatin*], Bleomycin [*Antineoplastic drug regimen*]
VPBA........ Varipolarization Beacon Antenna
VPBA........ Virginia Poultry Breeders Association (EA)
VPBC........ Virginia Poultry Breeders Club [*Later, VPBA*] (EA)
VPB(HL) ... Patrol Bomber, Four-Engine, Landplane [*Navy symbol*]
VPB(HS) ... Patrol Bomber, Four-Engine, Seaplane [*Navy symbol*]
VPB(ML) .. Patrol Bomber, Two-Engine, Landplane [*Navy symbol*]
VPB(MS)... Patrol Bomber, Two-Engine, Seaplane [*Navy symbol*]
VPC .... La Vente par Correspondance [*Mail Order*] [*Business term*] [*French*]
VPC .... Vacuum Pump Chamber
VPC .... Vapor Permeation Curing [*Plastics technology*]
VPC .... Vapor-Phase Chromatography
VPC .... Variable Padder Capacitor
VPC .... Ventricular Premature Contraction [*Cardiology*]
VPC .... Verpackungsberater [*A publication*]
VPC .... Veterinary Products Committee [*British*]
VPC .... Video Processor Control (MCD)
VPC .... Visual Punch Card
VPC .... Voltage Phasing Control (DEN)
VPC .... Voltage to Pulse Converter
VPC .... Volume Packed Cells
VPC .... Volume Percent (MAE)
VPC .... Volume-Pulse-Charge
VPC .... Volunteer Program Consultant [*Red Cross*]
VPC .... Volunteers for Peaceful Change (EA)
VPC .... Vulval Precursor Cell [*Genetics*]
VPCA........ Video Prelaunch Command Amplifier
VPCDS ..... Video Prelaunch Command Data System [*Air Force*]
VPCE .... Vapor-Phase Catalytic Exchange (MCD)
VPCMF ..... Vincristine, Prednisone, Cyclophosphamide, Methotrexate, Fluorouracil [*Antineoplastic drug regimen*]
VPCPr .... Vincristine, Prednisone, Vinblastine, Chlorambucil, Procarbazine [*Antineoplastic drug regimen*]
VPD .... Vapor-Phase Deacidification [*of books and documents*]
VPD .... Vapor Pressure Deficit [*Meteorology*]
VPD .... Variation per Day [*Navigation*]
VPD .... Vehicle Performance Data
VPD .... Vehicles per Day [*Military*] (AFM)
VPD .... Ventricular Premature Depolarization [*Cardiology*]
VPD .... Vertically Polarized Dipole (MCD)
VPD .... Victorian Parliamentary Debates [*A publication*]
VPD .... Vierte Partei Deutschlands [*Fourth Party of Germany*] [*Political party*] (PPW)
VPD .... Villa Park Dam [*California*] [*Seismograph station code, US Geological Survey*] (SEIS)
VPD .... Vremennik Puskinskogo Doma [*A publication*]
VPDF .... Vacuum Pump Discharge Filter
VPE........... Vapor-Phase Epitaxy
VPE........... Vehicle Positioning Equipment (MCD)
VPE........... Video Processing Equipment
VPen .... Vita e Pensiero [*A publication*]
VPF........... Vacuum Pump Filter
VPF........... Variable Parts Feeder

VPF............ Variable Phase Filter
VPF............ Vascular-Permeability Factor [*Medicine*]
VPF............ Vertical Processing Facility [*NASA*] (MCD)
VPF............ Vibratory Pan Feeder
VPF............ Viscoplastic Flow
VPFAS...... Vice President of the Faculty of Architects and Surveyors [*British*] (DBQ)
VPFG .... Variable Phase Function Generator
VPG .... Vallentine Peace Group [*Political party*] [*Australia*]
VPG .... Variable-Rate Pulse Generator
VPG .... Vehicle Product Group
VPGS........ Venous Pressure Gradient Support Stocking
VPGS........ Vice-President of the Geological Society [*British*]
VPH .... Variation per Hour [*Navigation*]
VPH .... Vehicles per Hour [*Traffic*] (AFM)
VPH .... Veterans of Pearl Harbor (EA)
VPH .... Volkspolizeihelfer
VPHD........ Vertical Payload Handling Device [*NASA*] (MCD)
VPI........... Vacuum Pressure Impregnation (IEEE)
VPI........... Valve Position Indicator (KSC)
VPI........... Vapor-Phase Inhibitor [*See also VCI*] [*Chemical technology*]
VPI........... Vendor Parts Index [*Sales*]
VPI........... Vertical Point of Intersection [*Transportation*]
VPI........... Very Promotable Item (WDMC)
VPI........... Vessel Patentcy Index [*Medicine*]
VPI........... Vintage Petroleum [*NYSE symbol*] (SPSG)
VPI........... VIP Dynasty International Marketing Corp. [*Vancouver Stock Exchange symbol*]
VPI........... Virginia Polytechnic Institute and State University [*Blacksburg*]
VPI........... Virginia Polytechnic Institute and State University, Blacksburg, VA [*OCLC symbol*] (OCLC)
VPI........... Vocational Preference Inventory [*Psychology*]
VPII.......... Vita Plus Industries, Inc. [*NASDAQ symbol*] (NQ)
VPIMD..... Vilniaus Pedagoginio Instituto Mokslo Darbai [*A publication*]
VPJT .... Vertical Power Jump Test
VPK .... Valley Airpark, Inc. [*Fort Collins, CO*] [*FAA designator*] (FAAC)
VPK .... Vehicle per Kilometer (AABC)
VPK .... Verdi Peak [*California*] [*Seismograph station code, US Geological Survey*] (SEIS)
VPK .... Vest Pocket Kodak [*Camera*]
VPK .... Volts Peak (NASA)
VPKA........ Volkspolizeikreisamt
VP(L)........ US Navy Patrol Squadron (Land) (CINC)
VPL........... Variable Pulse LASER
VPL........... Vendor Parts List (AAG)
VPL........... Ventral Posterolateral [*Anatomy*]
VPL........... Virginia Beach Public Library System, Virginia Beach, VA [*OCLC symbol*] (OCLC)
VPL........... Visible Panty Line [*In reference to clothing*]
VPL........... Volunteer Prison League [*Defunct*] (EA)
VPL........... Vulcano Piano [*Lipari Islands*] [*Seismograph station code, US Geological Survey*] (SEIS)
VPLCC ...... Vehicle Propellant Loading Control Center
VPLR........ Vacuum Pack Life Raft (DWSG)
VPLS .... Vice-President of the Linnaean Society [*British*]
VPLX........ Videoplex, Inc. [*Somerset, NJ*] [*NASDAQ symbol*] (NQ)
VPM .... Vacuum Pumping Module
VPM .... Variation per Minute [*Navigation*]
VPM .... Vascular Permeability Mediator [*Hematology*]
VPM .... Vehicle Project Manager [*NASA*] (NASA)
VPM .... Vehicles per Mile
VPM .... Velocity Preset Module (MCD)
VPM .... Vendor Part Modification (AAG)
VPM .... Versatile Packaging Machine
VPM .... Vertical Panel Mount
VPM .... Vertical Polarization Mode
VPM .... Vibrations per Minute
VPM .... Voix du Peuple Murundi [*Voice of the Murundi People*]
VPM .... Volts per Meter [*Also, V/m*]
VPM .... Volts per Mil
VPM .... Volumes per Million [*Measure of gas contamination*]
VPMA .... Vegetable Parchment Manufacturers Association [*Later, API*] (EA)
VPMLL ..... Valstybine Politines ir Mokslines Literatu [*A publication*]
VPMOS..... Verified Primary Military Occupational Specialty
VPMR .... Vanguard Party of the Malagasy Revolution
VPMS .... Virchow-Pirquet Medical Society (EA)
VPN .... Vendor Parts Number
VPN .... Vickers Pyramid Number [*Hardness test*]
VPN .... Victorian Periodicals Newsletter [*A publication*]
VPN .... Virtual Page Number
VPN .... Virtual Private Network [*US Sprint Communications Co.*] [*Atlanta, GA*] (TSSD)
VPN .... Vopnafjordur [*Iceland*] [*Airport symbol*] (OAG)
VPNL........ Variable Pulse Neodymium LASER
VPO .... Vapor-Phase Oxidation [*Chemical processing*]
VPO .... Vapor Pressure Osmometer [*or Osmometry*] [*Analytical chemistry*]
VPO .... Vienna Philharmonic Orchestra
VPO .... Viking Project Office [*NASA*] (KSC)

VPOF........	Vacuum-Processed Oxide Free
VPOP.........	Vice Directorate for Production Office Procedure [*Defense Intelligence Agency*] (MCD)
VPP...........	Vacuum Pickup Pencil
VPP...........	Value Payable by Post
VPP...........	Variable Pitch Propeller
VPP...........	Vegetable Protein Products [*Food technology*]
VPP...........	Velocity per Performance
VPP...........	Velocity Prediction Program
VPP...........	Vertical Pinpoint (AFM)
VPP...........	Vertical Pouch Packager
VPP...........	Very Public Person
VPP...........	Viral Porcine Pneumonia [*Veterinary medicine*]
VPP...........	Viscous Plastic Processing [*Materials science and technology*]
V P-P.........	Volt Peak-to-Peak (NASA)
VPP...........	Voluntary Projects Programme [*British*]
VPP....	Voluntary Protection Program [*OSHA*]
VPP...........	Volunteer Political Party [*Northern Ireland*]
VPPB.........	Vendor Provisioning Parts Breakdown (AAG)
VPPD........	Vice Presidential Protective Division [*US Secret Service*]
VPPN........	Vampire Pen Pal Network (EA)
VPPS.........	Vehicle Parking Protection Services [*British*]
VPQ.........	Van Kampen Merritt Pennsylvania Quality Municipal [*NYSE symbol*] (SPSG)
VPR...........	Valveless Pulse Rocket
VPR...........	Vaporize (MSA)
VPR...........	Variable Parameter Regression [*Statistics*]
VPR...........	Ventricle Pressure Response [*Cardiology*]
VPR...........	Verpackungs-Rundschau [*A publication*]
VPR...........	Virtual PPI [*Plan-Position Indicator*] Reflectoscope [*RADAR*]
VPR...........	Virtual Processor Ratio [*Data processing*]
VPR...........	Vital Pacific Resources Ltd. [*Vancouver Stock Exchange symbol*]
VPR...........	Voluntary Price Reduction (AABC)
VPRC........	Volume of Packed Red Cells [*Hematology*]
VPRES......	Vice-President
VPRF........	Variable Pulse Repetition Frequency (IEEE)
VPRGS.....	Vice-President of the Royal Geographical Society [*British*]
VPRI.........	Vice-President of the Royal Institute [*British*]
VPR-NMP ...	Virtual PPI [*Plan-Position Indicator*] Reflectoscope with Navigational Microfilm Projector [*RADAR*]
VPRON	US Navy Patrol Squadron (CINC)
VPRS........	Vice-President of the Royal Society [*British*]
VPRT........	Vector Pressure Ratio Transducer
VPS...........	Fort Walton Beach [*Florida*] [*Airport symbol*] (OAG)
VP(S)........	US Navy Patrol Squadron (Sea-Based) (CINC)
VPS...........	Vacuum Pickup System
VPS...........	Vacuum Pipe Still [*Chemical engineering*]
VPS...........	Vacuum Pump System
VPS...........	Valparaiso, FL [*Location identifier*] [*FAA*] (FAAL)
VPS...........	Vanguard Planning Summary [*Air Force*]
VPS...........	Variable Parameter System
VPS...........	Variable Power Supply (MCD)
VPS...........	Vatican Philatelic Society (EA)
VPS...........	Vehicle Power Supply [*Automotive engineering*]
VPS...........	Vernier Propulsion System [*Aerospace*]
VPS...........	Versatile Pacific Shipyards [*Shipbuilder*] [*Vancouver, Canada*]
VPS...........	Vibrations per Second
VPS...........	Vibrator Power Supply
VPS...........	Video-Pac Systems Ltd. [*Hollywood, CA*] [*Telecommunications service*] (TSSD)
VPS...........	Viewers-per-Set [*Television ratings*] (WDMC)
VPS...........	Vinylpolysilane [*Organic chemistry*]
VPS...........	Visitor Program Service of Meridian House International (EA)
VPS...........	Visual Programs Systems
VPS...........	Voice Processing System [*Data processing*] (IT)
VPS...........	Volcan Poas [*Costa Rica*] [*Seismograph station code, US Geological Survey*] (SEIS)
VPS...........	Voluntary Product Standard [*National Bureau of Standards*]
VPSA........	Vice-President of the Society of Antiquaries [*British*]
VPSB........	Veterans Placement Service Board [*Post-World War II*]
VPSS........	Vector Processing Subsystem
VPSS/VF...	Vector Processing Subsystem/Vector Facility [*Data processing*] (HGAA)
VPSW.......	Virtual Program Status Word
VPT...........	Patrol Torpedo Plane [*Navy symbol*]
VPT...........	Ventral Posterior Thalamic [*Electrode for stimulation*]
VPT...........	Vibratron Pressure Transducer
VPT...........	Video Pulse Termination
VPT...........	Voice plus Telegraph [*Telecommunications*] (TEL)
VPT...........	Volume-Price Trend [*Finance*]
VPTAR......	Variable Parameter Terrain-Avoidance RADAR
VPTRM.....	Viscous Partial Thermoremanent Magnetization [*Geophysics*]
VPU	Pace University Library, Union List of Serials, New York, NY [*OCLC symbol*] (OCLC)
VPU	Vacuum Penetration Unit
VPU	Vibrator Power Unit (MSA)
VPUA.......	Vibration Pickup Amplifier
VPUG	Ventura Publisher User's Group (EA)
VPVCPr...	Vincristine, Prednisone, Vinblastine, Chlorambucil, Procarbazine [*Antineoplastic drug regimen*]

VPVLBZ....	Scientific Works. Forest Research Institute in Zvolen [*A publication*]
VPVZB9	Scientific Works. Research Institute of Animal Production at Nitra [*A publication*]
VPW	Variable Pulse Width [*Automotive engineering*]
VPW	Ventral Prostate Weight [*Medicine*]
VPW	Vertically Polarized Wave
VPW	Vorarbeiten zum Pommerschen Woerterbuch [*A publication*]
VPX	Pineville, WV [*Location identifier*] [*FAA*] (FAAL)
VPY	Vinylpyridine [*Organic chemistry*]
VPZ...........	Valparaiso [*Indiana*] [*Airport symbol*] (OAG)
VPZ...........	Valparaiso, IN [*Location identifier*] [*FAA*] (FAAL)
VPZ...........	Virtual Processing Zero
VPZS.........	Vice-President of the Zoological Society [*British*]
VQ............	Aermediterranea Linee Aeree Mediterranee SpA [*Italy*] [*ICAO designator*] (FAAC)
VQ............	Fleet Air Reconnaissance Squadron [*Navy symbol*] (CINC)
VQ............	United Kingdom Colonies and Protectorates [*Aircraft nationality and registration mark*] (FAAC)
VQ............	Vector Quantizer [*Data processing*]
V/Q...........	Ventilation/Perfusion [*Quotient*] [*Medicine*]
VQ............	Vermont Quarterly [*A publication*]
VQ............	Very Quick [*Flashing*] Light [*Navigation signal*]
VQ............	Virtual Quantum
VQ............	Visvabharati Quarterly [*A publication*]
VQ............	Voluntary Quit [*Unemployment insurance*] [*Bureau of Labor Statistics*] (OICC)
VQA..........	Al Sigl Center Library, Rochester, NY [*OCLC symbol*] (OCLC)
VQA..........	Vendor Quality Assurance
VQAR........	Vendor Quality Assurance Representative [*Nuclear energy*] (NRCH)
VQB	Bausch & Lomb, Inc., Library, Rochester, NY [*OCLC symbol*] (OCLC)
VQC..........	Canandaigua Veterans Administration Medical Center Library, Canandaigua, NY [*OCLC symbol*] (OCLC)
VQC..........	Variable Quartz Capacitor
VQC..........	Vendor Quality Certification
VQD..........	Center for Governmental Research Library, Rochester, NY [*OCLC symbol*] (OCLC)
VQD..........	Vendor Quality Defect
VQE..........	Colgate-Rochester Divinity School, Library, Rochester, NY [*OCLC symbol*] (OCLC)
VQE..........	San Antonio, TX [*Location identifier*] [*FAA*] (FAAL)
VQF..........	Convalescent Hospital for Children, Library, Rochester, NY [*OCLC symbol*] (OCLC)
VQG..........	Eastman Dental Center, Basil G. Bibby Library, Rochester, NY [*OCLC symbol*] (OCLC)
VQH	Eastman Kodak Co., KAD Library, Rochester, NY [*OCLC symbol*] (OCLC)
VQI...........	Eastman Kodak Co., Business Library, Rochester, NY [*OCLC symbol*] (OCLC)
VQJ	Eastman Kodak Co., Engineering Division, Library, Rochester, NY [*OCLC symbol*] (OCLC)
VQK..........	Eastman Kodak Co., Health and Safety Laboratory, Library, Rochester, NY [*OCLC symbol*] (OCLC)
V Qk Fl	Very-Quick Flashing Light
VQL..........	Eastman Kodak Co., Photographic Technology Library, Rochester, NY [*OCLC symbol*] (OCLC)
VQL	Variable Quantization Level [*Algorithm developed by Aydin Monitor Corp.*] [*Telecommunications*]
VQM.........	Detroit, MI [*Location identifier*] [*FAA*] (FAAL)
VQM.........	Eastman Kodak Co., Research Laboratories, Library, Rochester, NY [*OCLC symbol*] (OCLC)
VQMG.......	Vice-Quartermaster-General
VQN..........	General Railway Signal Co., Library, Rochester, NY [*OCLC symbol*] (OCLC)
VQO	Genesee Hospital, Stabins Health Science Library, Rochester, NY [*OCLC symbol*] (OCLC)
VQO	Provincetown, MA [*Location identifier*] [*FAA*] (FAAL)
VQP..........	Highland Hospital, Williams Health Science Library, Rochester, NY [*OCLC symbol*] (OCLC)
VQQ..........	Mixing Equipment Co., Library, Rochester, NY [*OCLC symbol*] (OCLC)
VQR..........	Virginia Quarterly Review [*A publication*]
VQS	Isla De Vieques, PR [*Location identifier*] [*FAA*] (FAAL)
VQS	Mobil Chemical Co., Plastics Division, Research Library, Macedon, NY [*OCLC symbol*] (OCLC)
VQS	Valve Qualification Study
VQS	Vieques [*Puerto Rico*] [*Later, SJG*] [*Geomagnetic observatory code*]
VQS	Vieques [*Puerto Rico*] [*Seismograph station code, US Geological Survey*] [*Closed*] (SEIS)
VQS	Vieques [*Puerto Rico*] [*Airport symbol*] (OAG)
VQT..........	Monroe Community College, L. V. Good Library, Rochester, NY [*OCLC symbol*] (OCLC)
VQT..........	Viewers for Quality Television (EA)
VQU..........	Monroe Community Hospital, Medical-Nursing Library, Rochester, NY [*OCLC symbol*] (OCLC)
VQV..........	Monroe County Department of Health, Library, Rochester, NY [*OCLC symbol*] (OCLC)
VQV..........	Vacaville, CA [*Location identifier*] [*FAA*] (FAAL)

VQW.......... Monroe Development Center, Library, Rochester, NY [*OCLC symbol*]   (OCLC)
VQX.......... Park Ridge Hospital, Medical Library, Rochester, NY [*OCLC symbol*]   (OCLC)
VQY.......... Pennwalt Corp., Pharmaceutical Division, Library, Rochester, NY [*OCLC symbol*]   (OCLC)
VQZ.......... R. T. French Co., Library, Rochester, NY [*OCLC symbol*]   (OCLC)
VQZD....... Vendor Quality Zero Defects
VR............. Fleet Tactical Support [*Navy symbol*]   (NVT)
VR............. Relative Voltage
VR............. Transport Plane [*Multiengine*] [*Navy symbol*]
VR............. Transport Squadron [*Navy symbol*]
VR............. Transportes Aereos de Cabo Verde [*Portugal*] [*ICAO designator*]   (FAAC)
VR............. United Kingdom Colonies and Protectorates [*Aircraft nationality and registration mark*]   (FAAC)
VR............. Vagabonds Removed [*Prison van nickname used during reign of VR, Victoria Regina*] [*British*]   (DSUE)
VR............. Vale of Rheidol Light Railway [*Wales*]
V of R........ Vale of Rheidol Light Railway [*Wales*]
VR............. Validation and Recovery
VR............. Validation Report [*Army*]
VR............. Valley Resources, Inc. [*AMEX symbol*]   (SPSG)
VR............. Valtionrautatiet [*Finnish State Railways*]
VR............. Valuation Reports, Interstate Commerce Commission [*A publication*]   (DLA)
VR............. Valve Replacement [*Cardiology*]
VR............. Vanguardia Revolucionaria [*Revolutionary Vanguard*] [*Peru*] [*Political party*]   (PPW)
VR............. Variable Ratio [*Reinforcement*]
VR............. Variable Reluctance
VR............. Variant Reading
VR............. Vascular Resistance [*Medicine*]   (MAE)
VR............. Veer [*Aviation*]   (FAAC)
VR............. Vehicle Recovery
VR............. Velocity, Relative   (MCD)
VR............. Vendor Rating [*Sales*]
VR............. Venous Return [*Medicine*]
VR............. Ventilation Rate
VR............. Ventral Root [*of a spinal nerve*] [*Anatomy*]
VR............. Ventricular Rate [*Cardiology*]
VR............. Verb Reflexive
VR............. Verification Receiver
V-R............ VERLORT [*Very-Long-Range Tracking*] Range [*NASA*]
VR............. Vermont Reports [*A publication*]   (DLA)
VR............. Vertical Resistance
VR............. Vertical Retort
VR............. Very High Speed Radial Tire [*Automotive engineering*]
VR............. Very Respectfully [*Letter closing*]
VR............. Vested Right
VR............. Veterinary and Remount Service [*British military*]
VR............. VFR [*Visual Flight Rules*] Military Training Routes [*Aviation*]   (FAAC)
VR............. Viata Romaneasca [*Bucharest*] [*A publication*]
V-R............ Vibrational-Rotational [*Chemical kinetics*]
VR............. Vicar Rural
VR............. Victoria Regina [*Queen Victoria*]
VR............. Victorian Reports [*A publication*]   (APTA)
VR............. Video Recorder   (NASA)
VR............. Viera i Razum [*A publication*]
VR............. Villanova Law Review [*A publication*]
VR............. Virtual Reality
VR............. Virtual-Reality Machine [*Video technology*]   (ECON)
VR............. Virtual Route [*Data processing*]
VR............. Viscous Response [*Medicine*]
VR............. Vision, Right Eye
VR............. Visit Request   (AAG)
VR............. Visor
VR............. Visual Reconnaissance
VR............. Visual Resources [*A publication*]
VR............. Vital Records [*Genealogy*]
VR............. Vocal Resonance
VR............. Vocational Rehabilitation
VR............. Voice of Reason [*Later, Americans for Religious Liberty*]   (EA)
VR............. Volja Rossii [*A publication*]
VR............. Voltage Reference   (DEN)
VR............. Voltage Regulator
VR............. Voltage Relay
VR............. Voltage Repair
VR............. Volume Reduction [*Nuclear energy*]   (NRCH)
VR............. Voluntary Returnees [*Immigration Service*]
VR............. Volunteer Regiment [*British military*]   (DMA)
VR............. Volunteer Reserve   (BJA)
VR............. Vox Reformata: Australasian Journal for Christian Scholarship [*A publication*]   (APTA)
VR............. Vox Romanica [*A publication*]
VR............. Voyage Repairs [*Navy*]   (NVT)
Vr.............. Vroom's Law Reports [*30-85 New Jersey*] [*A publication*]   (DLA)
VR............. Vulcanized Rubber

VR............. Vulnerability Reduction [*Military*]   (RDA)
VRA......... Radford College, Radford, VA [*OCLC symbol*]   (OCLC)
VRA......... Rough-Air [*or Turbulence*] Speed [*Aviation*]
VRA......... Varadero [*Cuba*] [*Airport symbol*]   (OAG)
VRA......... Vertical Reference Attitude
VRA......... Vertical Rising Aircraft
VRA......... Veterans Readjustment Appointment
VRA......... Veterans Readjustment Authority
VRA......... [*The*] Victorian Railways of Australia   (DCTA)
VRA......... Viking RADAR Altimeter [*NASA*]
VRA......... Viratek, Inc. [*AMEX symbol*]   (SPSG)
VRA......... Vocational Rehabilitation Act [*1973*]
VRA......... Vocational Rehabilitation Administration [*Later, Social and Rehabilitation Service*] [*HEW*]
VRA......... Vocational Rehabilitation Association
VRA......... Voltage Reference Amplifier
VRA......... Voltage Regulator Alarm
VRA......... Voluntary Restraint Arrangement [*Import quotas*]
VRA......... Voluntary Restriction Agreement [*Pact between the US and Japan on automotive imports*]
VRA......... Voting Rights Act [*1965, 1970, 1975*]
VRA......... Vraag en Aanbod voor Techniek, Nijverheid, Bouwvak, en Handel [*A publication*]
Vrach Delo ... Vrachebnoe Delo [*A publication*]
Vrach Gaz ... Vrachebnaia Gazeta [*A publication*]
VRAD....... Vertically Referenced Attitude Display
VR (Adm).. Victorian Reports (Admiralty) [*A publication*]   (DLA)
VRAH....... Vertical Receiving Array Hydrophone
VRAM...... Variable Random Access Memory [*Data processing*]
VRAM...... Variable Rate Adaptive Multiplexing [*Telecommunications*]   (TEL)
VRAM...... Video Random Access Memory
VRAM...... Virtual Random Access Memory [*Data processing*]
Vrashchenie i Prilivnye Deform Zemli ... Vrashchenie i Prilivnye Deformatsii Zemli [*A publication*]
VRASS...... Voice Recognition and Synthesis System [*Aviation*] [*Navy*]
VRB........... Variable
VRB........... Variable Reenlistment Bonus [*Military*]   (AABC)
VRB........... Vehicle Retaining Board
VRB........... Vero Beach [*Florida*] [*Airport symbol*]   (OAG)
VRB........... Vero Beach, FL [*Location identifier*] [*FAA*]   (FAAL)
VRB........... Verordeningenblad Bedrijfsorganisatie [*A publication*]
VRB........... VHF [*Very-High-Frequency*] Recovery Beacon [*NASA*]   (KSC)
VRB........... Violet Red Bile [*Microorganism growth medium*]
VRB........... Voice Rotating Beacon
VRB........... Volunteer Reenlistment Bonus
VRBA....... Violet Red Bile Agar [*Microorganism growth medium*]
VRBB....... VR Business Brokers, Inc. [*Boston, MA*] [*NASDAQ symbol*]   (NQ)
VRBC........ Volume, Red Blood Cell [*Hematology*]   (MAE)
VRBG........ Viceroy's Bodyguard [*British military*]   (DMA)
VRBL........ Variable   (FAAC)
VRBM...... Variable Range Ballistic Missile [*DoD*]   (MCD)
VRC.......... Fleet Tactical Support Squadron Carrier [*Navy symbol*]   (CINC)
VRC.......... Vampire Research Center   (EA)
VRC.......... Varco International, Inc. [*NYSE symbol*]   (SPSG)
VRC.......... Variable Reluctance Cartridge
VRC.......... Vehicle Research Corp.
VRC.......... Vertical Redundancy Check [*Telecommunications*]   (BUR)
VRC.......... Vertical Ride Control   (OA)
VRC.......... Vibrating Reed Capacitor
VRC.......... Victoria Rifles of Canada   (DMA)
VRC.......... Virac [*Philippines*] [*Airport symbol*]   (OAG)
VRC.......... Virginia Commonwealth University, Richmond, VA [*OCLC symbol*]   (OCLC)
VRC.......... Virtual Redundancy Check [*Data processing*]
VRC.......... Viscometer Recorder-Controller
VRC.......... Visual Record Computer
VR & C...... Vocational Rehabilitation and Counseling Service [*Veterans Administration*]
VRC.......... Voice Recognition Control   (MCD)
VRC.......... Volunteer Rifle Corps [*Military*] [*British*]   (ROG)
VRCA........ Voice Recording Assembly [*Ground Communications Facility, NASA*]
VRCAMS.. Vehicle-Road Compatibility Analysis and Modification System   (RDA)
VRCCC...... Vandenberg Range Communications Control Center [*Air Force*]   (MCD)
VRCI........ Variable Resistive Components Institute   (EA)
VRCODX .. Veterinary Research Communications [*A publication*]
VRCS........ Vector Reaction Control System   (SSD)
VRCS........ Vernier [*Engine*] Reaction Control System [*Aerospace*]   (NASA)
VRCS........ Veterinary and Remount Conducting Section [*British military*]   (DMA)
VRCTR...... Varactor   (MSA)
VRD.......... Vacuum-Tube Relay Driver
VRD.......... Vehicle Reception Depot [*British military*]   (DMA)
VRD.......... Virtual Resource Unit, Deferred
VRD.......... Voltage Regulating Diode

VRD...........	Volunteer Reserve Decoration [*British*]
VRDDO.....	Variable Retention of Diatomic Differential [*Physics*]
VRDEA	Vrachebnoe Delo [*A publication*]
VRDS........	Vacuum Residuum Desulfurization [*Petroleum refining*]
VRDV	Vacuum Retard Delay Valve [*Automotive engineering*]
VRDX	Verdix Corp. [*NASDAQ symbol*] (NQ)
VRE	Venezuelan Economic Review [*A publication*]
VRE	Vermont Research Corp. [*AMEX symbol*] (SPSG)
VRE	Vibrating Reed Electrometer
VR (E)........	Victorian Reports (Equity) [*A publication*] (APTA)
VR & E.......	Vocational Rehabilitation and Education (MAE)
VRE	Voltage Regulator-Exciter
VRE	Volume Review Exercise (DNAB)
Vrednaya Polezn Fauna Bespozvon Mold ...	Vrednaya i Poleznaya Fauna Bespozvonochnykh Moldavii [*A publication*]
VREF........	Reference Voltage [*Automotive engineering*]
VREF........	Vanguard Real Estate Fund [*Associated Press abbreviation*] (APAG)
V/REG.......	Voltage Regulator [*Automotive engineering*]
VREL........	Velocity, Relative (GFGA)
Vremennik Gl Palaty Mer Vesov ...	Vremennik Glavnoi Palaty Mer i Vesov [*A publication*]
VR (Eq)......	Victorian Reports (Equity) [*A publication*]
VRES........	Vacuum Reservoir [*Automotive engineering*]
VRES........	VICORP Restaurants, Inc. [*NASDAQ symbol*] (NQ)
VREST	Vacuum Restrictor [*Automotive engineering*]
V Rev.........	Very Reverend
VRF...........	Aircraft Ferry Squadron [*Navy*]
VRF...........	Ferry Squadron [*Navy symbol*] (NVT)
VRF...........	Vascular Research Foundation
VRF...........	Versatile Repair Facility
VRF...........	Vertical Removal Fixture (NASA)
VRF...........	Vietnam Refugee Fund (EA)
VRF...........	Visual Recording Facility (MCD)
VRFI........	Voice Reporting Fault Indicator
VRFWS.....	Vehicle Rapid-Fire Weapon System [*Army*]
VRFWSS...	Vehicle Rapid-Fire Weapons System Successor (IEEE)
VRFY........	Verify (MSA)
VRG	Veering (WGA)
VRG	Vegetarian Resource Group (EA)
VRG	Visual Reference Gate [*Aviation*] (FAAC)
VRG	Vocationally Related Annual Goal
VRGC	Voucher Register and General Control [*Military*] (AABC)
VRGN.......	Gan [*Maldives*] [*ICAO location identifier*] (ICLI)
VRGN........	Viragen, Inc. [*NASDAQ symbol*] (NQ)
VRH..........	Var-Hour Meter [*Electricity*]
VRH..........	Vertical Receiving Hydrophone
VR(HL)......	Transport, Four-Engine, Landplane [*Navy symbol*]
VRHMU....	Visor Rectical Helmet Mounted Unit [*Navy*] (MCD)
VR(HS)......	Transport, Four-Engine, Seaplane [*Navy symbol*]
VRHU........	Hanimaadhoo [*Maldives*] [*ICAO location identifier*] (ICLI)
VRI	Varistor [*Telecommunications*] (TEL)
VRI	Varitech Investors Corp. [*Toronto Stock Exchange symbol*]
VRI	Vehicle Research Institute [*Society of Automotive Engineers*]
VRI	Verbal Response Inventory
VRI	Veterans Reopened Insurance
VR et I.......	Victoria Regina et Imperatrix [*Victoria, Queen and Empress*]
VRI	Victoria Regina et Imperatrix [*Victoria, Queen and Empress*]
VRI	Viral Respiratory Infection [*Medicine*]
VRI	Visual Rule Instrument Landing (AAG)
VRI	Vrincioaia [*Romania*] [*Seismograph station code, US Geological Survey*] (SEIS)
VRI	Vulcanized Rubber Installation
VR (IE & M) ...	Victorian Reports (Insolvency, Ecclesiastical, and Matrimonial) [*A publication*] (APTA)
VRIFS........	Vector Recurrent Iterated Function System [*Iterated Systems, Inc.*] [*Digital imaging*]
Vrije Univ Brussel Inter-Univ Inst High Energ Rep ...	Vrije Universiteit Brussel. Inter-University Institute for High Energies. Report [*A publication*]
VRIL..........	Vendor Repairable Items List
VRIS	Varistor [*Electronics*]
VRIS	Vietnam Refugee and Information Services
VRISL........	Vancouver Island, BC, Canada (FAAC)
VRK..........	Varkaus [*Finland*] [*Airport symbol*] (OAG)
VRK	Video Recorder Kit
VRK	Viral Respiratory Kit [*Medicine*]
VRKD	Kadhdhoo [*Maldives*] [*ICAO location identifier*] (ICLI)
VRL	Validation Reject Listing (MCD)
VRL	Vanterra Resources Ltd. [*Vancouver Stock Exchange symbol*]
VRL	Vertical Recovery Line [*NASA*] (NASA)
VRL	Vertical Reference Line [*Technical drawings*]
VRL	Veterinary Research Laboratory [*Montana State University*] [*Research center*]
VRL	Vibration Research Laboratory [*Stanford University*] (MCD)
VR (L)........	Victorian Reports (Law) [*A publication*] (APTA)
VRL	Vila Real [*Portugal*] [*Airport symbol*] (OAG)
VRL	Virus Reference Laboratory
VRL	Virus Reference Library (MAE)
VR (Law) ...	Victorian Law Reports (Law) [*A publication*]
VRLN	Varlen Corp. [*NASDAQ symbol*] (NQ)
VRLTRY ...	Vale of Rheidol Light Railway [*Wales*]
VRLY.........	Voltage Relay
VRM	Randolph-Macon College, Ashland, VA [*OCLC symbol*] (OCLC)
VRM	Van Riebeeck Medal [*British military*] (DMA)
VRM	Variable Range Marker [*RADAR technology*]
VRM	Variable-Rate Mortgage [*Real estate*]
VRM	Variable Reluctance Microphone
VRM	Vendor Receiving Memorandum [*Sales*]
VRM	Venus RADAR Mapper [*Planetary exploration*]
VRM	Vermiculite [*Technical drawings*]
VRM	Viscous Remanant Magnetization
VRM	Voice Recognition Module [*Data processing*]
VRM	Voltage Regulator Module
VRM	Volumetric Redox Measurement [*Analytical chemistry*]
VR(ML)....	Transport, Two-Engine, Landplane [*Navy symbol*]
VRMM	Male/International [*Maldives*] [*ICAO location identifier*] (ICLI)
VR(MS)....	Transport, Two-Engine, Seaplane [*Navy symbol*]
VRMS.......	Voltage Root Mean Square
VRN..........	Vernier [*Engine*] (AAG)
VRN..........	Vernitron Corp. [*AMEX symbol*] (SPSG)
VRN..........	Verona [*Italy*] [*Airport symbol*] (OAG)
VRN..........	Vessel Radiated Noise
VR Newsletter ...	Victorian Railways Newsletter [*A publication*] (APTA)
VRNF	Von Recklinghausen Neurofibromatosis [*Medicine*]
VRNR	Vernier [*Engine*] (NASA)
VRO..........	Roanoke College, Salem, VA [*OCLC symbol*] (OCLC)
VRO...........	Vanguard Real Estate Fund I [*AMEX symbol*] (SPSG)
VRO...........	Variable Ratio Oiling
VRO...........	Varo, Inc. [*NYSE symbol*] (SPSG)
VRO...........	Verified Record Output [*Data processing*]
VRO...........	Veterinary Research Officer [*British*]
VRo	Viata Romaneasca [*A publication*]
VROA	Verslagen Omtrent's Rijks Oude Archieven [*A publication*]
VROC	Vertical Rate of Climb [*Aviation*]
VROM	Vocabulary Read-Only Memory [*Data processing*]
VROOM....	Vintage Racers of Old Motorcycles (EA)
Vroom	Vroom's Law Reports [*30-85 New Jersey*] [*A publication*] (DLA)
Vroom (G D W) ...	[*G. D. W.*] Vroom's Law Reports [*36-63 New Jersey*] [*A publication*] (DLA)
VROOMM ...	Virtual Real-Time Object-Oriented Memory Manager [*Data processing*]
Vroom (NJ) ...	Vroom's Law Reports [*30-85 New Jersey*] [*A publication*] (DLA)
Vroom (P D) ...	[*P. D.*] Vroom's Law Reports [*30-35 New Jersey*] [*A publication*] (DLA)
VROT	Velocity, Rotation (MCD)
VRP	Richmond Public Library, Richmond, VA [*OCLC symbol*] (OCLC)
VRP	Vapor Reheat Process
VRP	Variable Reluctance Pickup
VRP	Vector-to-Raster Processor [*Computer graphics terminology*]
VRP	Ventral Root Potential [*Neurophysiology*]
VRP	Very Reliable Product (AAMN)
VRP	Vestra Reverendissima Paternitas [*Your Very Reverend Paternity*] [*Latin*]
VRP	Visual Record Printer
VRP	Visual Reporting Post (MCD)
VRP	Visual Routine Processor [*Data processing*]
VR-PC	Vanguardia Revolucionaria - Proletario Comunista [*Revolutionary Vanguard - Proletarian Communist*] [*Peru*] [*Political party*] (PPW)
VRPF........	Voltage-Regulated Plate Filament
VRPS........	Vintage Radio and Phonograph Society (EA)
VRPS........	Voltage-Regulated Power Supply
VRR	Rochester Regional Research Library Council, Rochester, NY [*OCLC symbol*] (OCLC)
VRR	Validity, Repeatability, and Reliability [*Examination*]
VRR	Valley Railroad
VRR	Verification Readiness Review (NASA)
VRR	Vero Aero [*Vero Beach, FL*] [*FAA designator*] (FAAC)
VRR	Veterans Reemployment Rights
VRR	Vibrating Reed Relay
VRR	Visual Radio Range
VRR	Visual Rapid Reorder (MCD)
VRRC........	Vehicle Radio Remote Control
VRRI..........	Vocational and Rehabilitation Research Institute [*University of Calgary*] [*Research center*] (RCD)
VRRTFL....	Variable Reach Rough Terrain Forklift [*Military*]
VRS...........	Rochester 3R's Union List of Serials, Rochester, NY [*OCLC symbol*] (OCLC)
VRS...........	Vacuum Regulator Solenoid [*Automotive engineering*]
VRS...........	Vacuum Relief System [*Nuclear energy*] (NRCH)
VRS...........	Vehicle Registration System [*Army*]
VRS...........	Vehicular RADIAC [*Radioactivity Detection, Indication, and Computation*] System
VRS...........	Velocity Response Shape (CET)
VRS...........	Veterinary and Remount Service [*British military*] (DMA)
VRS...........	Vibration Reducing Stiffener [*Automotive engineering*]

VRS............	Video Reception System
VRS............	Video Relay System
VRS............	Visual Reference System
VRS............	Visual Response System
VRS............	Vocational Rehabilitation Services
VRS............	Voice Recognition System
VRS............	Voice Recording Subsystem
VRS............	Volatile Reducing Substance (OA)
VRS............	Volume Reduction and Solidification [*Hazardous waste disposal*]
VRS............	Volunteer Reserve Section
VRS............	Vortex Rate Sensor
VRS............	Voter Research & Surveys [*Commercial firm*]
VRSA........	Versa Technologies, Inc. [*NASDAQ symbol*] (NQ)
VRSA........	Voice Reporting Signal Assembly
VRSI..........	Viral Response Systems, Inc. [*Greenwich, CT*] [*NASDAQ symbol*] (NQ)
VRSP..........	Voltage Regulator Supervisory Panel (MCD)
VRSS........	Voice Reporting Signal System
VRSY........	Varitronic Systems, Inc. [*NASDAQ symbol*] (NQ)
VRT..........	Vacuum Rectifying Tube
VRT..........	Vanguard Real Estate Fund II [*AMEX symbol*] (SPSG)
VRT..........	Variable Reluctance Transducer
VRT..........	Vernon, TX [*Location identifier*] [*FAA*] (FAAL)
VRT..........	Visual Recognition Threshold
VRT..........	Vocational Rehabilitation Therapist
VRT..........	Voltage Reference Tube
VRT..........	Voltage Regulator Tube
VRT..........	Volume-Rendering Technique [*Computer graphics*] (BYTE)
VRT..........	Voluntary Reserve Training [*British military*] (DMA)
VRTC........	Vehicle Research and Test Center [*National Highway Traffic Safety Administration*] (GRD)
V-RTIF......	Vandenberg Real Time Interface (MCD)
VRTMOTN ...	Vertical Motion (FAAC)
VRTX........	Vertex Pharmaceuticals [*NASDAQ symbol*] (SPSG)
VRTX........	Virtual Real-Time Executive
VRTX........	Vortec Corp. [*NASDAQ symbol*] (NQ)
VRTY........	Variety (MSA)
VRU..........	University of Richmond, Richmond, VA [*OCLC symbol*] (OCLC)
VRU..........	Velocity Reference Unit
VRU..........	Vertical Reference Unit (MCD)
VRU..........	Virtual Resource Unit (MCD)
VRU..........	Voice Recognition Unit
VRU..........	Voice Response Unit
VRU..........	Voltage Readout Unit
VRU..........	Vryburg [*South Africa*] [*Airport symbol*] (OAG)
VRV..........	Vacuum Regulator Valve [*Automotive engineering*]
VRV..........	Ventricular Residual Volume [*Cardiology*] (MAE)
VRV..........	Viper Retrovirus
VRV..........	Visual Range Visibility [*Aviation*] (MCD)
VRX..........	Vestor Exploration [*Vancouver Stock Exchange symbol*]
VRX..........	Virtual Resource Executive [*Software*] [*NCR Corp.*]
VRY..........	Fayetteville/Fort Bragg, NC [*Location identifier*] [*FAA*] (FAAL)
VRY..........	Vaeroy [*Norway*] [*Airport symbol*] (OAG)
VRYG........	Varying
VS..............	Air Antisubmarine Squadron [*Navy*]
VS..............	Intercontinental Airlines Ltd. [*Nigeria*] [*ICAO designator*] (FAAC)
VS..............	La Vie Spirituelle [*Paris*] [*A publication*]
VS..............	Search Plane [*Navy symbol*]
VS..............	Shore-Based Search Squadron [*Navy symbol*]
VS..............	Single Vibrations [*Half cycles*]
VS..............	Staging Velocity [*NASA*] (NASA)
VS..............	Vaccination Scar [*Medicine*]
VS..............	Vacuum Switch
VS..............	Vaginal Stroma
VS..............	Valley & Siletz Railroad Co. [*AAR code*]
VS..............	Vapor Seal [*Technical drawings*]
VS..............	Vapor Suppression [*Nuclear energy*] (NRCH)
VS..............	Variable Speed (IEEE)
VS..............	Variable Sweep (IEEE)
VS..............	Variance Score [*Statistics*]
VS..............	Vascular Strand [*Botany*]
VS..............	Vascular System (SAA)
VS..............	Vectoring Service
VS..............	Vegan Society [*Oxford, England*] (EAIO)
VS..............	Vehicle Station [*NASA*] (KSC)
VS..............	Velocity Search (MCD)
VS..............	Velocity, Staging
Vs..............	Venae Sectio [*Venesection*] [*Latin*] [*Medicine*] (MAE)
V/S..............	Vendor Supplier [*Sales*] (MCD)
VS..............	Venerable Sage [*Freemasonry*] (ROG)
VS..............	Venesection [*Medicine*]
VS..............	Venstresocialisterne [*Left Socialists Party*] [*Denmark*] [*Political party*] (PPE)
VS..............	Vent Stack [*Technical drawings*]
VS..............	Ventilation System [*NASA*]
VS..............	Ventral Subiculum [*Brain anatomy*]
VS..............	Venture Capital/Special Situations [*Business term*]

VS	Verbal Scale
VS	Verbum Salutis [*Paris*] [*A publication*]
VS	Vergilian Society (EA)
VS	Vermont Statutes [*A publication*] (DLA)
VS	Vernacular Society (EA)
V & S........	Vernon and Scriven's Irish King's Bench Reports [*1786-88*] [*A publication*] (DLA)
VS	Verse
VS	Versus [*Against*] [*Latin*]
VS	Vertical [*Activity*] Sensor [*Physiology*]
VS	Vertical Software [*AI Software*] [*Data processing*]
VS	Vertical Sounding [*Telecommunications*] (OA)
VS	Vertical Speed [*Aviation*]
VS	Vertical Stereoscopic [*Photograph*]
VS	Vertical Stripes [*Navigation markers*]
VS	Vertical System [*Government arrangement*] (OICC)
VS	Very Small Inclusions [*Diamond clarity grade*]
VS	Very Soluble
VS	Very Strong [*Spectral*]
VS	Very Superior
VS	Very Susceptible [*Plant pathology*]
VS	Vesicular Sound [*in auscultation of chest*] [*Medicine*]
VS	Vesicular Stomatitis [*Also, VSV*] [*Virus*]
V of S........	Veterans of Safety (EA)
VS	Veterinary Surgeon
VS	Vibration Seconds
VS	Victorian Society (EA)
VS	Victorian Studies [*A publication*]
VS	Vida Sobrenatural [*A publication*]
VS	Vide Supra [*See Above*] [*Latin*]
VS	Videnskabs Selskapet Skrifter [*A publication*]
VS	Video Selection
vs..............	Vietnam, South [*vm (Vietnam) used in records cataloged after January 1978*] [*MARC country of publication code*] [*Library of Congress*] (LCCP)
VS	Vieux Style [*Old Style*] [*French*]
VS	Villas
VS	Villonodular Synovitis [*Medicine*] (MAE)
VS	Violoncello Society (EA)
VS	Virgil Society (EA)
VS	Virtual Storage [*Data processing*]
VS	Virtual System
VS	Visceral Sinus
VS	Visible Supply
VS	Vista Resources, Inc. [*NYSE symbol*] (SPSG)
VS	Visual Signaling [*Military*]
VS	Visual Storage [*Data processing*]
VS	Visum Siccum [*Seen in a Dried State*] [*Botany*] (ROG)
VS	Vitae Sophistarum [*of Philostratus*] [*Classical studies*] (OCD)
VS	Vital Signs [*Medicine*]
VS	Vivisection
VS	Vocal Students Practice Aid Records [*Record label*]
VS	Vocal Synthesis
VS	Voicespondence Club (EA)
vs................	Voids [*Medicine*] (MAE)
VS	Volatile Solids [*Environmental science*]
VS	Voltaire Society (EA)
VS	Volti Subito [*Turn Over Quickly*] [*Music*]
VS	Voltmeter Switch (MSA)
VS	Volumetric Solution
VS	Voluntary Sterilization
VS	Voorschrift [*Rule, Order*] [*Dutch*] (ILCA)
VS	Votre Seigneurie [*Your Lordship*] [*French*]
VS	Vulcan Society (EA)
VS1	Virtual Storage One [*Data processing*] (HGAA)
V2S	V-Groove on Two Sides [*Lumber*]
VSA	By Visual Reference to the Ground [*Aviation*] (FAAC)
VSA	Mitteilungsblatt. Vereinigung Schweizerischer Angestelltenverbaende [*A publication*]
VSA	Vacuum Swing Adsorption [*Chemical engineering*]
VSA	Vancouver School of Art
VSA	Variable Stability Aircraft (NASA)
VSA	Variant-Specific Surface Antigen [*Genetics, immunology*]
VSA	Variation Simulation Analysis [*Automotive engineering*]
VSA	Vehicle Security Association (EA)
VSA	Velocity Sensor Antenna
VSA	Verification Site Approval [*NASA*] (MCD)
VSA	Vermont Statutes, Annotated [*A publication*] (DLA)
VSA	Vernier Solo Accumulator [*Aerospace*] (AAG)
VS & A.......	Veronis, Suhler & Associates, Inc. [*Telecommunications service*] (TSSD)
VSA	Vertical Sensor Assembly
VSA	Very Special Arts (EA)
VSA	Vibrating String Accelerometer
VSA	Victorian Society in America (EA)
VSA	Victualling Store Allowance [*British military*] (DMA)
VSA	Videocom Satellite Associates [*Dedham, MA*] [*Telecommunications*] (TSSD)
VSA	Videographic Systems of America, Inc. [*Information service or system*] [*Ceased operation*] (IID)
VSA	Villahermosa [*Mexico*] [*Airport symbol*] (OAG)

VSA .... Vintage Sailplane Association (EA)
VSA .... Violin Society of America (EA)
VSA .... Violin Society of America. Journal [*A publication*]
VSA .... Viscoelastic Stress Analysis
VSA .... Visual Skills Appraisal [*Child development test*]
VSA .... Voltage-Sensitive Amplifier
VSA/1800 ... Volvo Sports America 1800 (EA)
vSAA .... Very Severe Aplastic Anemia [*Hematology*]
V-SAC .... Vehicle Speed Activated Converter [*Automotive engineering*]
VSAD .... Vacuum Spark Advance Disconnect [*Auto air pollution control device*]
V/SAF .... Vulnerability and Survivability of the Armed Forces (MCD)
VSAG .... Viral Superantigen [*Immunochemistry*]
VSAL .... Visual Technology [*NASDAQ symbol*] (NQ)
VSALS .... Vision Approach and Landing System [*Aviation*]
VSAM .... Virtual Sequential Access Method
VSAM .... Virtual Storage Access Method [*Data processing*]
VSAM .... Virtual System Access Method
VSAT .... Very Small Aperture Terminal [*Telecommunications*] (TSSD)
VSAV .... Vydavtel'stvo Slovenskej Akademie Vied [*A publication*]
VSB .... Scout-Bombing Plane [*Navy symbol*]
VSB .... Sweet Briar College Library, Sweet Briar, VA [*OCLC symbol*] (OCLC)
VSB .... Venae Sectio Brachii [*Bleeding in the Arm*] [*Pharmacy*] (ROG)
VSB .... Vent and Supply Bay
VSB .... Vestigial Sideband [*Radio*]
VSB .... Victorian Studies Bulletin [*A publication*]
VSB .... Video Source Book [*A publication*]
VSB .... Visible (FAAC)
VSB .... Vision. The European Business Magazine [*A publication*]
VSB .... Volunteer Services for the Blind [*Later, ASB*] (EA)
VSB-AM.... Vestigial Sideband - Amplitude Modulation
VSBC .... VSB Bancorp, Inc. [*NASDAQ symbol*] (CTT)
VSBF .... Vestigial Sideband Filter
VSBL .... Visible (MSA)
VSBS .... Very Small Business System
VSBY .... Visibility [*Aviation*] (FAAC)
VSBYDR .. Visibility Decreasing Rapidly [*Aviation*] (FAAC)
VSBYIR..... Visibility Increasing Rapidly [*Aviation*] (FAAC)
VSC .... Valdosta State College [*Georgia*]
VSC .... Variable Speech Control [*Device that permits distortion-free rapid playback of speech recorded on tape*]
VSC .... Variable Speed Chopper
VSC .... Varnville [*South Carolina*] [*Seismograph station code, US Geological Survey*] (SEIS)
VSC .... Vehicle Sectoring Code
VSC .... Vehicle System Control
VSC .... Vela Seismological Center [*Alexandria, VA*]
VSC .... Vendor Shipping Configuration (AAG)
VSC .... Ventral Spinal Cord [*Anatomy*]
VSC .... Vermont State College
VSC .... Vibration Safety Cutoff [*NASA*] (KSC)
VSC .... Vidicon Camera System (MCD)
V-S/C........ Viking Spacecraft [*NASA*]
VSC .... Vincentian Sisters of Charity [*Roman Catholic religious order*]
VSC .... Virginia State College [*Petersburg*]
VSC .... Virginia State College, Petersburg, VA [*OCLC symbol*] (OCLC)
VSC .... Virtual Subscriber Computer
VSC .... Vocations for Social Change [*Employment clearinghouse*] [*Defunct*] (EA)
VSC .... Volatile Sulfur Compound [*Chemistry*]
VSC .... Voltage-Saturated Capacitor
VSC .... Volunteer Staff Corps [*British*] (ROG)
VSCA .... Vacation and Senior Citizens Association (EA)
VSCA .... Vietnamese Senior Citizens Association (EA)
VSCAN...... Vendor Scan
VSCAN...... Visual Scan
VSCC .... Voltage-Sensitive Calcium Channel [*Physiology*]
VSCCA ...... Vintage Sports Car Club of America (EA)
VSCDF ...... Vatican's Sacred Congregation for the Doctrine of the Faith
VSCE .... Variable Stream Control Engine [*NASA*] (MCD)
VSCF .... Variable Speed Constant Frequency
V Sch G...... Verfassungsschutzgesetz [*A publication*]
VSCNY...... Vedanta Society of the City of New York (EA)
VSCP .... Vital Statistics Cooperative Program [*Department of Health and Human Services*] (GFGA)
VSCS .... Voice Switch and Control System [*FAA*]
VSD .... Valve Solenoid Driver
VSD .... Variable Slope Delta
VSD .... Variable Speed Drive
VSD .... Vendor's Shipping Document
VSD .... Vendredi, Samedi, Dimanche [*A publication*]
VSD .... Ventricular Septal Defect [*Cardiology*]
VSD .... Versatile Signal Device
VSD .... Vertical Situation Display
VSD .... Video Subcarrier Detector
VSD .... Village Self-Development
VSD .... Virtually Safe Dose [*Toxicology*]
VSDA .... Video Software Dealers Association (EA)
VSD/ADI .. Vertical Situation Display/Attitude Director Indicator (MCD)
VSDI........ Voluntary Short-Term Disability Insurance

VSDM .... Variable Slope Delta Modulation
VSDR........ Vierteljahrsheft zur Statistik des Deutschen Reichs [*Germany*]
VSE........... Steam Explosion in Vessel [*Nuclear energy*] (NRCH)
VSE........... Vancouver Stock Exchange [*Canada*]
VSE........... Vehicle Systems Engineer (SAA)
VSE........... Vessel (Reactor) Steam Explosion [*Nuclear energy*] (IEEE)
VSE........... Virtual Storage Extension [*IBM Corp.*] [*Data processing*]
Vse .... Vsesvit [*Kiev*] [*A publication*]
VSEC......... VSE Corp. [*NASDAQ symbol*] (NQ)
VSEGEI.... Vsesojuznyj Naucno-Issledovatel'skij Geologiceskij Institut [*Moskau*] [*A publication*]
VSEL .... Vickers Shipbuilding and Engineering Ltd. [*British*]
VSEP .... Very Superior Extra Pale [*Designation on brandy labels*] (WGA)
VSEPR ...... Valence-Shell Electron Pair Repulsion [*Theory of molecular structure*]
Vses Geogr O-Vo Izv ... Vsesoyuznoye Geograficheskoye Obshchestvo. Izvestiya [*A publication*]
Vses Nauchno Issled Geol Inst Inf Sb ... Vsesoyuznyi Nauchno-Issledovatel'skii Geologicheskii Institut. Informatsionnyi Sbornik [*A publication*]
Vses Nauchno-Issled Geologorazved Neft Inst Tr ... Vsesoyuznyy Nauchno-Issledovatel'skiy Geologorazvedochnyi Neftyanoy Institut. Trudy [*A publication*]
Vses Nauchno Issled Inst Eksp Vet Im Ya R Kovalenko Byull ... Vsesoyuznyi Nauchno-Issledovatel'skii Institut Eksperimental'noi Veterinarii Imeni Ya. R. Kovalenko. Byulleten [*A publication*]
Vses Nauchno Issled Inst Konditer Promsti Tr ... Vsesoyuznyi Nauchno-Issledovatel'skii Institut Konditerskoi Promyshlennosti. Trudy [*A publication*]
Vses Nauchno Issled Khim Farm Inst Khim Med ... Vsesoyuznyi Nauchno-Issledovatel'skii Khimiko-Farmatsevticheskii Institut. Khimiya i Meditsina [*A publication*]
Vses Nauchn O-Vo Neirokhir ... Vsesoyuznoe Nauchnoe Obshchestvo Neirokhirurgii [*A publication*]
Vses Neft Nauchno Issled Geologorazved Inst Tr ... Vsesoyuznyi Neftyanoi Nauchno-Issledovatel'skii Geologorazvedochnyi Institut. Trudy [*A publication*]
Vsesoyunaya Nauchno Metod Konf Vet Patologoanat ... Vsesoyuznaya Nauchno-Metod Konferentsiya Veterinarnykh Patologoanatomov [*A publication*]
Vsesoyuznoe Paleont Obshch Ezhegodnik ... Vsesoyuznoe Paleontologicheskoe Obshchestvo Ezhegodnik [*A publication*]
VSF .... Antisubmarine Fighter Squadron [*Navy*]
VSF .... Springfield [*Vermont*] [*Airport symbol*] (OAG)
VSF .... Springfield, VT [*Location identifier*] [*FAA*] (FAAL)
VSF .... Vestigial Sideband Filter
VSF .... Vitreous Silica Fabric
VSF .... Voice Store and Forward [*Voice messaging*]
VSFC .... Vince Smith Fan Club (EA)
VSFP .... Venous Stop-Flow Pressure [*Medicine*]
VSFR .... Vertical Seismic Floor Response (IEEE)
VSFR .... Visibility Forecast (SAA)
VSG .... Variable Speed Gear (DEN)
VSG .... Variable [*or Variant*] Surface Glycoprotein [*Biochemistry*]
VSG .... Variant Surface Glycoprotein [*Immunology*]
VSG .... Vernier Step Gauge [*Aerospace*]
VSG .... Versatile Signal [*or Symbol*] Generator
VSG .... Vertical Sweep Generator [*Telecommunications*] (OA)
VSG .... Vierteljahrsschrift fuer Sozial- und Wirtschaftsgeschichte [*A publication*]
VSG .... Vulture Study Group [*South Africa*] (EAIO)
VSH .... Vie Economique. Rapports Economiques et de Statistique Sociale [*A publication*]
VSH .... Village Self-Help
VSH .... Vishay Intertechnology, Inc. [*NYSE symbol*] (SPSG)
VSH .... Vishnu Resources [*Vancouver Stock Exchange symbol*]
VSHPS ...... Vernier Solo Hydraulic Power System [*Aerospace*] (AAG)
VSI............ College of Staten Island, St. George Campus Library, Staten Island, NY [*OCLC symbol*] (OCLC)
VSI............ Velocity and Steering Indicator (MCD)
VSI............ Vendor Shipping Instruction
VSI............ Vertical Signal [*or Situation*] Indicator [*Helicopters*]
VSI............ Vertical Speed Indicator [*Aviation*]
VSI............ Very Seriously Ill [*Army*] (AABC)
VSI............ Video Simulation Interface (NASA)
VSI............ Video Sweep Integrator
VSI............ Videoconferencing Systems, Inc. [*Norcross, GA*] [*Telecommunications service*] (TSSD)
VSI............ Vinyl Siding Institute (EA)
VSI............ Virtual Screen Interface [*Data processing*] (HGAA)
VSI............ Voluntary Service International [*British*] (EAIO)
VSI............ Vsemirnaja Istorija [*A publication*]
VSI............ Vuesenoria Ilustrisima [*Your Illustrious Ladyship (or Lordship)*] [*Spanish*]
VS Ilma...... Vossa Senhoria Ilustrissima [*Your Illustrious Lordship*] [*Portuguese*]
VSIP .... Valence State Ionization Potentials [*of atoms*]
VSJW .... Vise Jaw [*Tool*] (AAG)

VSL............ Metaal en Kunststof [*A publication*]
VSL............ Special Libraries Cataloguing, Inc. [*UTLAS symbol*]
VSL............ Value of a Statistical Life [*Mortality rating*]
VSL............ Valve Signal Light
VSL............ Variable Safety Level
VSL............ Variable Specification List
VSL............ Ventilation Sampling Line (IEEE)
VSL............ Vermont State Department of Libraries, Montpelier, VT [*OCLC symbol*] (OCLC)
VSL............ Vessel (FAAC)
VSL............ Vetenskaps-Societeten i Lund [*A publication*]
VSL............ Viscous Shock Layer
VSL............ Volume of the Sacred Law [*Freemasonry*]
VSL............ VS Services Ltd. [*Toronto Stock Exchange symbol*]
VSLA........ Vetenskaps-Societeten i Lund. Aarsbok [*A publication*]
VSL Bibs.... Research Service Bibliographies. State Library of Victoria [*A publication*] (APTA)
VSLE .... Very Small Local Exchange [*Telecommunications*] (TEL)
VSLE .... Voiceband Subscriber Loop Emulator [*Telecom Analysis Systems, Inc.*]
VSLF .... VMS Strategic Land Fund II [*NASDAQ symbol*] (CTT)
VSLI .... Veterans Special Life Insurance [*Veterans Administration*]
VSLS .... Very Slightly Soluble
VSM .... Vascular Smooth Muscle [*Anatomy*]
VSM .... Vehicle State Monitor
VSM .... Vestigial Sideband Modulation
VSM .... Vibrating Sample Magnetometer
VSM .... Video Switching Matrix (KSC)
VSM .... Vietnam Service Medal [*Military decoration*] (AFM)
VSM .... Virtual Storage Manager (BUR)
VSM .... Virtual Storage Memory [*Data processing*] (MCD)
VSM .... Voice Switch Monitor (MCD)
VSMA........ Vibrating Screen Manufacturers Association (EA)
VSMC........ Vascular Smooth Muscle Cell [*Cytology*]
VSMF........ Vendor Specification Microfilm File (DNAB)
VSMF........ Visual Search Microfilm File [*Trademark*] [*Data processing*]
VSMOS..... Verified Secondary Military Occupational Specialty
VSMS........ Video Switching Matrix System
VSMS........ Vineland Social Maturity Scale [*Psychology*]
VSN .... Scout-Training Plane [*Navy symbol*]
VSN .... Video Switching Network (MCD)
VSN .... Vision
VSN .... Volume-Sequence-Number [*Data processing*]
VSNL........ Videsh Sanchar Nigam Ltd. [*India*] [*Telecommunications service*] (TSSD)
VSN(M)..... Training Plane, 2-Engine [*Navy symbol*]
VSNP........ Viking Society for Northern Research [*British*]
VSNS........ Virgil C. Summer Nuclear Station (NRCH)
VSNY .... Vegetarian Society of New York (EA)
VSO .... Scout Observation Plane [*Navy symbol*]
VSO .... Valdosta Southern Railroad [*AAR code*]
VSO .... Verso (BJA)
VSO .... Very Special Old
VSO .... Very Stable Oscillator
VSO .... Very Superior Old [*Designation on brandy labels*]
VSO .... Victualling Stores Officer [*British military*] (DMA)
VSO .... Voluntary Service Overseas [*Military*]
VSOE........ Venice Simplon Orient-Express [*London-to-Venice train*]
VSOK .... Vital Signs Normal [*Medicine*] (MAE)
VSOM .... Velocity Sensor, Oscillator, Multiplier (DNAB)
VSOP........ Very Superior Old Pale [*Designation on brandy labels. Facetious French translation is "Versez sans Oublier Personne," or "Pour without Forgetting Anyone"*]
V Soz WG .. Vierteljahrsschrift fuer Sozial- und Wirtschaftsgeschichte [*A publication*]
VSP............ Variable Size Parameter [*Thermodynamics*]
VSP............ Vectored Slipstream Principle
VSP............ Vehicle Scheduling Program [*Data processing*]
VSP............ Vehicle Synthesis Program [*Aerospace*]
VSP............ Vertical Seismic Profile [*Geology*]
VSP............ Vertical Speed [*Aviation*] (FAAC)
VSP............ Victorian Socialist Party [*Australia*] [*Political party*]
VSP............ Video Signal Processor
VSP............ Video System Processor [*Telecommunications*] (TSSD)
VSP............ Vikki's Special People (EA)
VSP............ Virtual Switching Point [*Telecommunications*] (TEL)
VSP............ Vision Service Plan National (EA)
VSP............ Visitor Services Project [*National Park Service*]
V SP.......... Visum Sponanteum [*Seen Wild*] [*Botany*] (ROG)
V SP.......... Visum Sporadicum [*Seen Wild*] [*Botany*] (ROG)
VSP............ Vital Speeches of the Day [*A publication*]
VSPA........ Vacation Spa Resorts, Inc. [*NASDAQ symbol*] (NQ)
VSPC........ Virtual Storage Personal Computing [*IBM Corp.*] [*Data processing*]
V/SPD .... Variable Speed
VSPEP....... Vehicle Sizing and Performance Evaluation Program (MCD)
VSPG........ Vehicle Speed Pulse Generator [*Automotive engineering*]
VSPP .... Vangiya Sahitya Parisat Patrika [*A publication*]
VSPRITES ... Virtual Sprites [*Amiga computer hardware*]
VSPS .... Vernier Solo Power Supply [*Aerospace*] (AAG)
VSPX .... Vehicle Scheduling Program Extended [*Data processing*]

VSQ .... St. Vladimir's Seminary. Quarterly [*A publication*]
VSQ .... Very Special Quality
VSR .... Vacuum Short Resid [*Petroleum technology*]
VSR............ Validation Summary Report
VSR............ Vallecitos Experimental Superheat Reactor (NRCH)
VSR............ Versar, Inc. [*AMEX symbol*] (SPSG)
VSR............ Vertical Storage and Retrieval Systems
VSR............ Very Short Range
VSR............ Very Short Run [*Printing technology*]
VSR............ Very Special Reserve (ADA)
VSR............ Vibration Sensitive Relay
VSR............ Vietnam Supply Rate [*Military*] (MCD)
VSR............ Vincit Sapientia Robur [*Wisdom Overcomes Strength*] [*Latin*] [*Motto of Johann Ernst, Duke of Saxony-Eisenach (1566-1638)*]
VSR............ Visual Security Range (NATG)
VSR............ Voltage-Sensing Relay
VSRADS ... Very-Short-Range Air Defense Weapon System (MCD)
VSRADWS ... Very-Short-Range Air Defense Weapon System (NATG)
VSRBM ..... Very-Short-Range Ballistic Missile
VSRC........ Vehicle Safety Recall Campaign
VSRGSR.... Very-Short-Range Ground Surveillance RADAR (MCD)
VSS .... V/STOL Support Ship
VSS .... Vampire Studies Society [*Defunct*] (EA)
VSS............ Vapor Saver System [*Automobile*]
VSS............ Variable Slit Set
VSS............ Variable SONAR System
VSS............ Variable Stability System [*Aviation*]
VSS............ Vascular Surgical Society [*British*]
VSS............ Vassouras [*Brazil*] [*Geomagnetic observatory code*]
VSS............ Vector Scoring System [*Navy*] (MCD)
VSS............ Vehicle Speed Sensor [*Automotive engineering*]
VSS............ Vehicle Stability System [*Truck engineering*]
VSS............ Vehicle Surveillance System
VSS............ Vehicle System Simulator
VSS............ Velocity Sensor System
VSS............ Versions (ROG)
VSS............ Vertical Sounding System
VSS............ Vertical Spike Soderberg [*Pot*] [*Aluminum processing*]
VSS............ Vertical Support Structure
VSS............ Vessel Support System (MCD)
VSS............ Victim Support Scheme [*British*] (DI)
VSS............ Victor Scoring System
VSS............ Videnskabs Selskapet Skrifter [*A publication*]
VSS............ Video Select Switch (MCD)
VSS............ Video Signal Simulator (NATG)
VSS............ Video Storage System [*or Subsystem*]
VSS............ Video Supervisory Signal
VSS............ Virtual Storage System [*SEMIS*]
VSS............ Visual Sensor Set
VSS............ Visual Systems Simulator [*FAA*]
VSS............ Vital Signs Stable [*Medicine*]
VSS............ Vocabulary Switching System [*Data processing*]
VSS............ Voice Signaling System
VSS............ Voice Storage System [*AT & T*]
VSS............ VoiceStation System [*Sydis, Inc.*] [*San Jose, CA*] (TSSD)
VSS............ Volatile Suspended Solids [*Environmental science*]
VSS............ Voltage-Sensing Switch
VSS............ Voltage to Substrate and Sources [*Microelectronics*]
VSSC........ Voyager Spacecraft Subsystem [*NASA*]
VSSC........ Vedanta Society of Southern California (EA)
VSSF........ Videnskabs Selskapet Skrifter. Forhandlingar [*A publication*]
VSSM........ Video Scanner Switch Matrix
VSSP........ Vendor Standard Settlement Program (AAG)
VSSR........ Vierteljahresschrift fuer Sozialrecht [*A publication*]
VSSSN ..... Verification Status Social Security Number (AABC)
VS Suppl.... Vie Spirituelle. Supplement [*A publication*]
VST............ Banyan Short Term Inc. Trust [*AMEX symbol*] [*Formerly, VMS Short Term Inc. Trust*] (SPSG)
VST .... St. Thomas [*Virgin Islands*] [*Seismograph station code, US Geological Survey*] (SEIS)
VST............ Valve Seat (MSA)
VST............ Valve Setpoint Tolerance [*Nuclear energy*] (NRCH)
VST............ Vancouver School of Theology [*University of British Columbia*]
VST............ Vanstates Resources Ltd. [*Vancouver Stock Exchange symbol*]
VST............ Variable Stability Trainer [*Aviation*]
VST............ Vasteras [*Sweden*] [*Airport symbol*] (OAG)
VST............ Venom Skin Test [*Immunology*]
VST............ Video Scroller Terminal [*Data processing*]
VST............ Video System Test
VST............ Visit (NVT)
VST............ Vocational Skills Training [*Funds*] [*Job Corps*]
VST............ Volume Sensitive Tariff [*Telecommunications*] (TEL)
VSTA........ Victoria Station [*NASDAQ symbol*] (NQ)
VSTA........ Virus-Serum-Toxin Act
VSTAG..... Vandenberg Shuttle Turnaround Analysis Group [*NASA*] (NASA)
VSTAR..... Variable Search and Track Air Defense RADAR
VSTC........ Vermont State Teachers College
VSTC........ Very Short Time Constant (MCD)

VSTCB ...... Vuoto, Scienza, e Tecnologia [*A publication*]
V St DV...... Vermoegensteuer- Durchfuehrungsverordnung [*A publication*]
V St G .... Vermoegensteuergesetz [*A publication*]
VSTI .... Versus Tech, Inc. [*NASDAQ symbol*]   (NQ)
VSTKJ....... Vesientutkimuslaitoksen Julkaisuja [*Publications. Finnish Water Research Institute*] [*A publication*]
VSTM....... Valve Stem   (MSA)
VSTO........ Vertical/Short Takeoff [*and Landing*]   (MCD)
V/STOL .... Vertical/Short Takeoff and Landing [*Aircraft*]
VSTP .... Visual Satellite Tracking Program
VSTPT....... Vulcan-Stinger Troop Proficiency Trainer [*Army*]
VSTR .... Ventral Striatum [*Neurology*]
VSTR .... Vestar, Inc. [*NASDAQ symbol*]   (NQ)
VSTR .... Volt Second Transfer Ratio
VSTSP....... Visit Ship in Port [*Navy*]   (NVT)
VSTT .... Variable Speed Tactical Trainer [*Air Force*]   (MCD)
VSTT .... Variable Speed Training Target
VSUH........ Virginia State University Herbarium
VSULA ...... Vaccination Scar Upper Left Arm [*Medicine*]   (MAE)
VSV........... Vacuum Switching Valve [*Automotive engineering*]
VSV........... Vesicular Stomatitis Virus [*Also, VS*]
VSv........... Vokrug Sveta [*Moscow*] [*A publication*]
VSVG........ Vesicular Stomatitis Virus Glycoprotein [*Biochemistry*]
VSVVS ...... Vereinigung Schweizerischer Versuchs und Vermittlungstellen fuer Saatkartoffeln [*Solothurn*] [*A publication*]
VSW .... Variable Sweep Wing
VSW .... Ventricular Stroke Work [*Cardiology*]   (MAE)
VSW .... Vertrau Schau Wem [*Trust, but Be Careful Whom*] [*German*] [*Motto of Johann Georg, Duke of Wohlau (1552-92)*]
VSW .... Very Short Wave
VSW .... Vierteljahrsschrift fuer Sozial- und Wirtschaftsgeschichte [*A publication*]
VSW .... Visual Studies Workshop   (EA)
VSW .... Vitrified Stoneware
VSW .... Voltage Standing Wave
VSWF .... Voltage Standing-Wave Frequency   (DNAB)
VSWR........ Variable Standing Wave Ratio   (MCD)
VSWR........ Visual Standing Wave Ratio   (NASA)
VSWR........ Voltage Standing-Wave Ratio
VSX........... Navy Submarine Attack Airplane - Experimental   (MCD)
VSYNC....... Vertical Synchronous [*Data processing*]
VSystems ... Video Systems [*A publication*]
VT .... Air-Cushion Vehicle built by Vosper Thorneycroft [*England*] [*Usually used in combination with numerals*]
VT .... Air Polynesie [*France*] [*ICAO designator*]   (FAAC)
VT .... India [*Aircraft nationality and registration mark*]   (FAAC)
Vt .... State of Vermont, Department of Libraries, Montpelier, VT [*Library symbol*] [*Library of Congress*]   (LCLS)
VT .... Target-on-Threshold Speed [*Aviation*]
VT .... Torpedo Plane [*Navy symbol*]
VT .... Training Squadron [*Navy symbol*]   (NVT)
VT .... Vacuum Tube [*Electronics*]
VT .... Vacuum Tuberculin [*Medicine*]   (MAE)
VT .... Validation Testing   (MCD)
VT .... Valitocin [*Endocrinology*]
VT .... Vaportight   (MSA)
VT .... Variable Thrust
VT .... Variable Time [*Fuse*] [*Also known as a "proximity fuse"*]
VT .... Variable Transformer
VT .... Variable Transmission   (ADA)
VT .... Vascular Time
VT .... Vasotocin
VT .... Vat Petroleum [*Vancouver Stock Exchange symbol*]
VT .... Vaulted Tombs of the Mesara [*A publication*]
VT .... Vehicle Theft
VT .... Vehicular Technology   (MCD)
VT .... Velocity, Target
V-T .... Velocity Time   (MUGU)
VT .... Vent   (NASA)
VT .... Ventricular Tachycardia [*Cardiology*]
VT .... Verb Transitive
VT .... Verfuegungstruppen   (BJA)
VT .... Vermont [*Postal code*]
VT .... Vermont Reports [*A publication*]   (DLA)
VT .... Verotoxin [*Biochemistry*]
VT .... Vertical Tabulation [*Data processing*]
VT .... Vertical Tail
VT .... Vesalius Trust   (EA)
VT .... Vetus Testamentum [*A publication*]
VT .... Vetus Testamentum [*Old Testament*] [*of the Bible*] [*Latin*]
VT .... Vibration Testing
V-T .... Vibrational-to-Translational [*Energy transfer*]
VT .... Victa Ltd. [*Aviation Division*] [*Australia*] [*ICAO aircraft manufacturer identifier*]   (ICAO)
VT .... Video Terminal
VT .... Video Times [*A publication*]
VT .... Videotape
VT .... Viere i Tzerkov [*A publication*]
VT .... Vinyl Tile [*Technical drawings*]
VT .... Violet Tetrazolium   (MAE)
VT .... Virtual Terminal   (BYTE)

VT .... Viscous Transmission [*Automotive engineering*]
VT .... Vision Test [*Ophthalmology*]
VT .... Visual Telegraphy
VT .... Visual Toss
VT .... Vocational-Technical
V & T .... Vodka and Tonic
VT .... Voice Tube [*Technical drawings*]
V & T .... Volume and Tension [*of pulse*]
VT .... Voting Trust [*Investment term*]
VTA .... Vacuum-Tube Amplifier
VTA .... Variable Transfer Address
VTA .... Varnished Tube Association
VTA .... Ventral Tegmental Area [*Anatomy*]
VTA .... Verkeerskunde [*A publication*]
VTA .... Vertical Tracking Angle [*of a phonograph cartridge*]
VTA .... Vision Test Apparatus [*Ophthalmology*]
VTAADS ... Vertical the Army Authorization Document System
VTAB........ Vertical Tabulation Character [*Data processing*]
VTAC........ Video Timing and Control
VTAC........ VOR [*Very-High-Frequency Omnidirectional Range*] Collocated with TACAN   (FAAC)
V-TACH .... Ventricular Tachycardia [*Cardiology*]
VT Admin Comp ... Vermont Administrative Procedure Compilation [*A publication*]   (DLA)
VT Admin Proc Bull ... Vermont Administrative Procedures Bulletin [*A publication*]
VT Admin Proc Comp ... Vermont Administrative Procedures Compilation [*A publication*]
VT Ag Exp ... Vermont. Agricultural Experiment Station. Publications [*A publication*]
VT Agric Exp Stn Bull ... Vermont. Agricultural Experiment Station. Bulletin [*A publication*]
VTAJX ...... Navy Trainer Advanced Jet - Experimental   (MCD)
VTAM .... Virtual Telecommunications [*or Teleprocessing*] Access Method [*IBM Corp.*] [*Data processing*]
VTAM .... Virtual Terminal Access Method
VTAM .... VORTEX [*Varian Omnitask Real-Time Executive*] Telecommunications Access Method
VTAME..... Virtual Telecommunications Access Method Entry
V-TAS....... Vericom Test Application System [*Vericom Ltd.*] [*Software package*]   (NCC)
VTAS........ Visual Target Acquisition System [*Navy*]
VtB............. Fletcher Free Library, Burlington, VT [*Library symbol*] [*Library of Congress*]   (LCLS)
VTB .... Torpedo-Bombing Plane [*Navy symbol*]
VTB .... Velocity Test Barrel
VtB............. Verkehrswasserbaubibliothek [*Bundesanstalt fuer Wasserbau*] [*Database*]
VTB .... Vinyl T-Butylstyrene [*Organic chemistry*]
VTB .... Vlaamsche Toeristenbond
VTB .... Voltage Time to Breakdown   (DEN)
VTB .... Volunteer Talent Bank [*American Association of Retired Persons*]
VTBA........ Bangkok [*Thailand*] [*ICAO location identifier*]   (ICLI)
VT BA....... Vermont Bar Association Reports [*A publication*]   (DLA)
VTBB........ Bangkok [*Thailand*] [*ICAO location identifier*]   (ICLI)
VtBC.......... Champlain College, Burlington, VT [*Library symbol*] [*Library of Congress*]   (LCLS)
VTBC........ Chanthaburi [*Thailand*] [*ICAO location identifier*]   (ICLI)
VTBD .... Bangkok/International [*Thailand*] [*ICAO location identifier*]   (ICLI)
VTBE........ Saraburi [*Thailand*] [*ICAO location identifier*]   (ICLI)
VtBef.......... Rockingham Free Public Library, Bellows Falls, VT [*Library symbol*] [*Library of Congress*]   (LCLS)
VtBenn....... Bennington Free Library, Bennington, VT [*Library symbol*] [*Library of Congress*]   (LCLS)
VtBennC .... Bennington College, Bennington, VT [*Library symbol*] [*Library of Congress*]   (LCLS)
VtBennM ... Bennington Museum, Inc., Bennington, VT [*Library symbol*] [*Library of Congress*]   (LCLS)
VtBennP .... Putnam Memorial Hospital, Medical Library, Bennington, VT [*Library symbol*] [*Library of Congress*]   (LCLS)
VTBF .... Chachoengsao/Phanom Sarakhan [*Thailand*] [*ICAO location identifier*]   (ICLI)
VtBFB....... Grand Lodge of Vermont, F & AM Library, Burlington, VT [*Library symbol*] [*Library of Congress*]   (LCLS)
VTBG .... Kanchanaburi [*Thailand*] [*ICAO location identifier*]   (ICLI)
VTBH........ Lop Buri/Sa Pran Nak [*Thailand*] [*ICAO location identifier*]   (ICLI)
VTBHA .... Vuoriteollisuus/Bergshanteringen [*A publication*]
VTBI.......... Prachin Buri [*Thailand*] [*ICAO location identifier*]   (ICLI)
VTBJ .... Phetchaburi/Tha Yang [*Thailand*] [*ICAO location identifier*]   (ICLI)
VTBK........ Nakhon Pathom/Kamphaeng Saen [*Thailand*] [*ICAO location identifier*]   (ICLI)
VTBL........ Lop Buri [*Thailand*] [*ICAO location identifier*]   (ICLI)
VTBM .... Phetchaburi/Maruk [*Thailand*] [*ICAO location identifier*]   (ICLI)
VTBN .... Prachuap Khiri Khan/Pran Buri [*Thailand*] [*ICAO location identifier*]   (ICLI)

VTBP......... Prachuap Khiri Khan [*Thailand*] [*ICAO location identifier*]   (ICLI)
VTBR........ Ratchaburi [*Thailand*] [*ICAO location identifier*]   (ICLI)
VtBran .... Brandon Free Public Library, Brandon, VT [*Library symbol*] [*Library of Congress*]   (LCLS)
VTBR Case ... Victorian Taxation Board of Review Case [*Australia*] [*A publication*]
VtBrt.......... Brooks Memorial Library, Brattleboro, VT [*Library symbol*] [*Library of Congress*]   (LCLS)
VtBrtS........ School for International Training, Brattleboro, VT [*Library symbol*] [*Library of Congress*]   (LCLS)
VTBS......... Chon Buri/Sattahip [*Thailand*] [*ICAO location identifier*]   (ICLI)
VTBT......... Chon Buri/Bang Phra [*Thailand*] [*ICAO location identifier*]   (ICLI)
VtBT .... Trinity College, Burlington, VT [*Library symbol*] [*Library of Congress*]   (LCLS)
VTBU .... Rayong/Utapao [*Thailand*] [*ICAO location identifier*]   (ICLI)
VT Bul .... Vermont. Free Public Library Commission and State Library. Bulletin [*A publication*]
VTBW........ Prachin Buri/Watthana Nakhon [*Thailand*] [*ICAO location identifier*]   (ICLI)
VTC .... Vandenberg Test Center [*Air Force*]
VTC .... Variable Trimmer Capacitor
VTC .... Vehicular Traffic Control
VTC .... Veractor Tuned Microwave Cavity
VTC .... Vertical Trash Compactor   (DWSG)
VTC .... Viable Titanium Composite
VTC .... Video Tape Center [*Commercial firm*] [*British*]
VTC .... Video Teleconferencing
VTC .... Vidicon Television Camera
VTC .... Vitronics Corp. [*AMEX symbol*]   (SPSG)
VTC .... Volunteer Training Corps [*An organization for home defense*] [*British*] [*World War I*]
VTC .... Voting Trust Certificate [*or Company*] [*Investment term*]
VTCA........ Chiang Rai/Chiang Khong [*Thailand*] [*ICAO location identifier*]   (ICLI)
VTCA........ Vernon's Texas Codes, Annotated [*A publication*]   (DLA)
VTCA........ Vintage Thunderbird Club of America [*Later, VTCI*]   (EA)
VtCasT....... Castleton State College, Castleton, VT [*Library symbol*] [*Library of Congress*]   (LCLS)
VTCB........ Chiang Rai/Ban Chiang Kham [*Thailand*] [*ICAO location identifier*]   (ICLI)
VTCC........ Chiang Mai [*Thailand*] [*ICAO location identifier*]   (ICLI)
VTCC........ Variable Temperature Compensation Capacitor
VTCCHE... Tidewater Consortium, Librarians' Networking Committee [*Library network*]
VTCD .... Nan/Chiang Klang [*Thailand*] [*ICAO location identifier*]   (ICLI)
VTCE........ Nan/Ban Pua [*Thailand*] [*ICAO location identifier*]   (ICLI)
VTCE........ Vehicle Team Combat Exercise [*Army*]   (INF)
VTCF........ Uttaradit (West) [*Thailand*] [*ICAO location identifier*]   (ICLI)
VTCH........ Mae Hong Son [*Thailand*] [*ICAO location identifier*]   (ICLI)
VTCI.......... Mae Hong Son/Pai [*Thailand*] [*ICAO location identifier*]   (ICLI)
VTCI.......... Vintage Thunderbird Club International   (EA)
VTCK........ Mae Hong Son/Khun Yuam [*Thailand*] [*ICAO location identifier*]   (ICLI)
VTCL.......... Lampang [*Thailand*] [*ICAO location identifier*]   (ICLI)
VTCN .... Nan [*Thailand*] [*ICAO location identifier*]   (ICLI)
VTC News ... Vocational Training Council. Newsletter [*New Zealand*] [*A publication*]
VTCP......... Phrae [*Thailand*] [*ICAO location identifier*]   (ICLI)
VTCR........ Chiang Rai [*Thailand*] [*ICAO location identifier*]   (ICLI)
VTCS........ Mae Hong Son/Mae Sariang [*Thailand*] [*ICAO location identifier*]   (ICLI)
VTCS........ Variable Thermal Control Surface
VTCS......... Vega Target Control System [*Computer flight control of test vehicles*]
VTCS........ Vehicular Traffic Control System   (IEEE)
VTCS........ Video Telemetering Camera Systems   (AAG)
VTD .... Aircraft (Training) [*Navy symbol*]
VTD .... Variable Time Delay
VTD .... Variable Torque Distribution [*Automotive engineering*]
VTD .... Vertical Tape Display   (KSC)
VTD .... Vision Testing Device [*Ophthalmology*]
VTDC......... Vacuum Tube Development Committee [*Columbia University*]   (MCD)
VTDI.......... Variable Threshold Digital Input
VTE .... Variable Thrust Engine
VTE .... Vertical Tube Effects [*Desalination*]
VTE .... Vertical Tube Evaporation [*Desalination*]
VTE .... Vibration Test Equipment
VTE .... Vicarious Trial and Error [*Psychology*]
VTE .... Vientiane [*Laos*] [*Airport symbol*]   (OAG)
VTE .... Viscous Transonic Equation
VTEC........ Valve Timing and Lift Electronically Controlled [*Automotive engineering*]
VTEC........ Verotoxin-Producing Escherichia Coli
VTEC-E..... Variable Valve-Timing and Lift Electronic Control System - Economy [*Automotive technology*]

V-TECS ..... Vocational Technical Education Consortium of States   (OICC)
VTEK........ Vodavi Technology Corp. [*NASDAQ symbol*]   (NQ)
VTEL........ Vitel Fiber Optics Corp. [*NASDAQ symbol*]   (NQ)
VTEN .... Vision Ten [*NASDAQ symbol*]   (SPSG)
VTERL...... Veterinary Toxicology and Entomology Research Laboratory [*Department of Agriculture*] [*College Station, TX*]   (GRD)
VTERM..... Variable Temperature Electrical Resistivity Measurement [*Physics*]
VTES .... Variable Thrust Engine System
VTES .... Vinyltriethoxysilane [*Organic chemistry*]
VTEX........ Vertex Communications Corp. [*Kilgore, TX*] [*NASDAQ symbol*]   (NQ)
VTF........... Vacuum Test Furnace
VTF........... Van Kampen Merritt Investment Grade Florida Municipal [*NYSE symbol*]   (SPSG)
VTF........... Variable Time, Fragmentation [*Military*]   (CAAL)
VTF........... Venezuelan Trust Fund [*Inter-American Development Bank*]
VTF........... Vertical Test Facility [*NASA*]
VTF........... Vertical Test Fixture
VTF........... Vertical Test Flight   (MCD)
VTF........... Vertical Tracking Force [*of a phonograph cartridge*]
VTF........... Voltage Transfer Function
VT Farm Home Sci ... Vermont Farm and Home Science [*A publication*]
VTFDA...... Ankara Universitesi. Veteriner Fakultesi. Dergisi [*A publication*]
VTFE........ Vertical Tube Foam Evaporation [*Chemical engineering*]
VTFS .... Visual Technology Flight Simulator   (MCD)
VTFT .... Value Task Force Team
VTG .... Vantage [*Washington*] [*Seismograph station code, US Geological Survey*]   (SEIS)
VTG .... Vitellogenin [*Biochemistry*]
VTG .... Volume Thoracic Gas [*Medicine*]
VTG .... Voting [*Business term*]
VT Geol Sur Econ Geol ... Vermont. Geological Survey. Economic Geology [*A publication*]
VT Geol Surv Bull ... Vermont. Geological Survey. Bulletin [*A publication*]
VT Geol Surv Water Resour Dep Environ Geol ... Vermont. Geological Survey. Water Resources Department. Environmental Geology [*A publication*]
VTGO .... Vacations to Go, Inc. [*Houston, TX*] [*NASDAQ symbol*]   (NQ)
VThB .... Vocabulaire de Theologie Biblique [*A publication*]   (BJA)
VtHi.......... Vermont Historical Society, Montpelier, VT [*Library symbol*] [*Library of Congress*]   (LCLS)
VT His S .... Vermont Historical Society. Proceedings [*A publication*]
VT Hist...... Vermont History [*A publication*]
VtHS......... Vermont Historical Society. Proceedings [*A publication*]
VTI............ Statens Vag- och Trafikinstitut [*Swedish Road and Traffic Research Institute*] [*Linkoping*] [*Information service or system*]   (IID)
VTI............ Valparaiso Technical Institute [*Indiana*]
VTI............ Vanguard Technologies International, Inc. [*AMEX symbol*]   (SPSG)
VTI............ Vermont Telecommunications, Inc. [*Winooski, VT*] [*Telecommunications*]   (TSSD)
VTI............ Video Terminal Interface
VTI............ Vinton, IA [*Location identifier*] [*FAA*]   (FAAL)
VTI............ Volume Thickness Index
VTI............ Voluntary Termination Incentive [*Business term*]
VTIP.......... Visual Target Identification Point   (AFM)
VTJ........... Johnson State College, Johnson, VT [*OCLC symbol*]   (OCLC)
VTJ........... Van Kampen Merritt Investment Grade New Jersey Municipal [*NYSE symbol*]   (SPSG)
VtJoT........ Johnson State College, Johnson, VT [*Library symbol*] [*Library of Congress*]   (LCLS)
VTK .... Viatech, Inc. [*AMEX symbol*]   (SPSG)
VTL........... Vacuum-Tube Launcher
VTL........... Variable Threshold Logic
VTL........... Vertical Turret Lathe
VTL........... Video Tape Lecture
VTL........... Virtual Tape Library
Vt Laws..... Laws of Vermont [*A publication*]
VT Lib....... Vermont Libraries [*A publication*]
VTLM....... Vitalmetrics, Inc. [*NASDAQ symbol*]   (NQ)
Vt-LR .... Vermont Legislative Council, Montpelier, VT [*Library symbol*] [*Library of Congress*]   (LCLS)
VT L Rev ... Vermont Law Review [*A publication*]
VTLS .... Virginia Technical Library System [*Virginia Polytechnic Institute and State University Center for Library Automation*] [*Information service or system*]
VtLyL .... Lyndon State College, Lyndonville, VT [*Library symbol*] [*Library of Congress*]   (LCLS)
VTM .... Vacuum-Tube Module
VTM .... Vehicle Test Meter [*TACOM*] [*Army*]   (RDA)
VTM .... Vehicles to the Mile [*Military*]
VTM .... Verification Test Matrix
VTM .... Verification Traceability Matrix
VTM .... Versatile Tracking Mount   (MCD)
VTM .... Vibration Test Module   (MCD)
VTM .... Voltage Tunable Magnetron
VTM .... Volume Tidal Mechanical   (MAE)

VtMan .... Mark Skinner Public Library, Manchester, VT [*Library symbol*] [*Library of Congress*] (LCLS)
VtMarC ..... Marlboro College, Marlboro, VT [*Library symbol*] [*Library of Congress*] (LCLS)
VTMC .... Viable Titanium Matrix Composite
VTMDA .... Veterinarni Medicina [*A publication*]
VTMIDB... Annual Research Reviews. Vitamin-Trace Mineral-Protein Interactions [*A publication*]
VtMiM ...... Middlebury College, Middlebury, VT [*Library symbol*] [*Library of Congress*] (LCLS)
VtMiS .... Sheldon Art Museum, Middlebury, VT [*Library symbol*] [*Library of Congress*] (LCLS)
VTMO .... Voltage Tunable Microwave Oscillator
VtMor .... Morristown Centennial Library, Morrisville, VT [*Library symbol*] [*Library of Congress*] (LCLS)
VTMoV ..... Velvet Tobacco Mottle Virus
VtMS .... Office of the Secretary of State, State Papers Division, Montpelier, VT [*Library symbol*] [*Library of Congress*] (LCLS)
VTMS .... Vessel Traffic Management System (DS)
VTMS .... Vinyltrimethysilane [*Organic chemistry*]
VtN .... Brown Public Library, Northfield, VT [*Library symbol*] [*Library of Congress*] (LCLS)
VT(N) .... Night Torpedo Bomber Squadron [*Navy symbol*]
VTN .... Valentine, NE [*Location identifier*] [*FAA*] (FAAL)
VTN .... Van Kampen Merritt Investment Grade New York Municipal [*NYSE symbol*] (SPSG)
VTN .... Ventral Tegmental Nuclei [*Neuroanatomy*]
VTN .... Verification Test Network [*NASA*] (MCD)
VTN .... Video Tape Network (EA)
VTN .... Vitran Corp., Inc. [*Toronto Stock Exchange symbol*]
VTNA .... VTAM Telecommunications Network Architecture
VTNC .... VTN Corp. [*NASDAQ symbol*] (NQ)
VTNF .... Variable Time Non-Fragmenting [*Military*] (CAAL)
VtNN .... Norwich University, Northfield, VT [*Library symbol*] [*Library of Congress*] (LCLS)
VTNS .... Voltage Tunable Noise Source
VTO .... Vertical Takeoff
VTO .... Viable Terrestrial Organism
VTO .... Visual Training Officer [*Navy*]
VTO .... Vitro, Sociedad Anonima ADS [*NYSE symbol*] (SPSG)
VTO .... Vocational Training Officer [*Navy*]
VTO .... Voltage Tunable Oscillator
VTOC .... Volume Table of Contents [*Data processing*]
VTOGW .... Vertical Takeoff Gross Weight
VTOHL ..... Vertical Takeoff and Horizontal Landing
VTOL .... Vertical Takeoff and Landing [*Also, VERTOL*] [*Acronym used for a type of aircraft*]
VTOVL ...... Vertical Takeoff Vertical Landing
VTP .... Valid Target Presentation [*Military*] (CAAL)
VTP .... Van Kampen Merritt Investment Grade Pennsylvania Municipal [*NYSE symbol*] (SPSG)
VTP .... Vandenberg Test Program [*Air Force*]
VTP .... Vehicle Test Plan [*NASA*] (NASA)
VTP .... Vendor Test Procedure
VTP .... Verification Test Plan [*or Program*] (NASA)
VTP .... VIEWDATA Terminal Program
VTP .... Virtual Terminal Protocol
VTP .... Visual Transmitter Power
VTP .... Voluntary Termination of Pregnancy [*Medicine*]
VTPA .... Vertical Turbine Pump Association [*Defunct*]
VTPA .... (Vinylthiazolidinylidene)phenylamine [*Organic chemistry*]
VTPAI .... Victorian Town Planning Appeals Tribunal. Index of Appeals Decisions [*A publication*] (APTA)
VTPH .... Prachuap Khiri Khan/Hua Hin [*Thailand*] [*ICAO location identifier*] (ICLI)
VTPI .... Nakhon Sawan/Takhli [*Thailand*] [*ICAO location identifier*] (ICLI)
VtPifi .... Free Library, Pittsfield, VT [*Library symbol*] [*Library of Congress*] (LCLS)
VTPL .... Pretchabun/Lom Sak [*Thailand*] [*ICAO location identifier*] (ICLI)
VtPlaG .... Goddard College, Plainfield, VT [*Library symbol*] [*Library of Congress*] (LCLS)
VTPM .... Tak/Mae Sot [*Thailand*] [*ICAO location identifier*] (ICLI)
VTPN .... Nakhon Sawan [*Thailand*] [*ICAO location identifier*] (ICLI)
VtPom .... Abbott Memorial Library, Pomfret, VT [*Library symbol*] [*Library of Congress*] (LCLS)
VtPouG ...... Green Mountain College, Poultney, VT [*Library symbol*] [*Library of Congress*] (LCLS)
VTPP .... Phitsanulok [*Thailand*] [*ICAO location identifier*] (ICLI)
Vt-PR .... Vermont Public Records Library, Montpelier, VT [*Library symbol*] [*Library of Congress*] (LCLS)
VTPR .... Vertical Temperature Profile [*or Profiling*] Radiometer
VTPS .... Phitsanulok/Sarit Sena [*Thailand*] [*ICAO location identifier*] (ICLI)
VTPS .... Vibration Test Plotting System
VTPT .... Tak [*Thailand*] [*ICAO location identifier*] (ICLI)
VTPU .... Uttaradit [*Thailand*] [*ICAO location identifier*] (ICLI)
VtPuW .... Windham College, Putney, VT [*Library symbol*] [*Library of Congress*] (LCLS)

VTPY .... Tak/Sam Ngao [*Thailand*] [*ICAO location identifier*] (ICLI)
VtQ .... Vermont Quarterly [*A publication*]
VTR .... McGrath, AK [*Location identifier*] [*FAA*] (FAAL)
VTR .... Value of Time Research [*British*]
VTR .... Variable Tandem Repetition [*Genetics*]
VTR .... Vector (FAAC)
VTR .... Vehicle Track Recovery [*Military*]
VTR .... Vehicle Tracking Receiver
VTR .... Vendor Trouble Report
VTR .... Verification Test Report (NASA)
VTR .... Vermont Railway, Inc. [*AAR code*]
VT R .... Vermont Reports [*A publication*] (DLA)
VTR .... Vertical Radial (MSA)
VTR .... Vertical Test Range
VTR .... Veto Resources Ltd. [*Vancouver Stock Exchange symbol*]
VTR .... Videotape Recorder [*or Recording*]
VTR .... Vintage Triumph Register (EA)
VTR .... Virginia Tax Review [*A publication*]
VTR .... Voltage Transformation Ratio [*Physics*]
VTRAN ..... Vast Translator (KSC)
VtRaStM ... Saint Mary's Seminary, Randolph, VT [*Library symbol*] [*Library of Congress*] (LCLS)
VTRB .... Variable Trim Reentry Body (MCD)
VT Regist Nurse ... Vermont Registered Nurse [*A publication*]
VT Rep .... Vermont Reports [*A publication*] (DLA)
VTRO .... Vitro Diagnostics [*NASDAQ symbol*] (CTT)
VtRoc .... Rochester Public Library, Rochester, VT [*Library symbol*] [*Library of Congress*] (LCLS)
VTRR .... Visual Target RADAR Ranging
VTRS .... Videotape Recording System
VTRS .... Videotape Response System
VTRS .... Visual Technology Research Simulator (CAAL)
VTRSH .... Vermont Research Corp. [*Associated Press abbreviation*] (APAG)
VTRX .... Ventrex Laboratories, Inc. [*NASDAQ symbol*] (NQ)
VTS .... IEEE Vehicular Technology Society (EA)
VTS .... Vacuum Thermal Stability Test (MCD)
VTS .... Vandenberg Tracking Station [*Air Force*]
VTS .... Vanillin Thiosemicarbazone (IIA)
VTS .... Variable Time Step
VTS .... Variable Tracking Strategy (MCD)
VTS .... Vehicle Time Reproducer (SAA)
VTS .... Venture Touring Society (EA)
VTS .... Versatile Training Systems (MCD)
VTS .... Vertical Test Site [*NASA*] (MCD)
VTS .... Vertical Test Stand [*NASA*] (KSC)
VTS .... Vertical Test System (NASA)
VTS .... Vertical Thrust Stand
VTS .... Vessel Traffic Service [*Harbor RADAR system*] [*Coast Guard*]
VTS .... Vetus Testamentum. Supplementum [*Leiden*] [*A publication*]
VTS .... Vibration Test Specification
VTS .... Vibration Test System
VTS .... Viewfinder Tracking System
VTS .... Viral Testing Systems [*AMEX symbol*] (SPSG)
VTS .... Virginia Theological Seminary, Alexandria, VA [*OCLC symbol*] (OCLC)
VTS .... Virology Testing Systems [*Formerly, TeleConcepts Corp.*] [*AMEX symbol*] (SPSG)
VTS .... Visual Typing System (MCD)
VTS .... Vitosha [*Bulgaria*] [*Seismograph station code, US Geological Survey*] (SEIS)
VTS .... Vocational Training Scheme [*British*]
VTS .... Vocational Training Service
VTS .... Vote Tally System
VTS .... Vulcan Training System (MCD)
VTSA .... Satun [*Thailand*] [*ICAO location identifier*] (ICLI)
VTSB .... Surat Thani [*Thailand*] [*ICAO location identifier*] (ICLI)
VTSC .... Narathiwat [*Thailand*] [*ICAO location identifier*] (ICLI)
VTSD .... Chumpon [*Thailand*] [*ICAO location identifier*] (ICLI)
VTSD .... Variable-Temperature Stepwise Desorption [*Chemical engineering*]
VTSE .... Vehicle Team Subcaliber Exercise [*Army*] (INF)
VTSH .... Songkhla [*Thailand*] [*ICAO location identifier*] (ICLI)
VtShelM .... Shelburne Museum, Inc., Research Library, Shelburne, VT [*Library symbol*] [*Library of Congress*] (LCLS)
VTSI .... Vac-Tec Systems, Inc. [*NASDAQ symbol*] (NQ)
VTSK .... Pattani [*Thailand*] [*ICAO location identifier*] (ICLI)
VTS/MA ... Virtual Terminal Session/Multiple Access [*Data processing*] (HGAA)
VTSN .... Nakhon Si Thammarat [*Thailand*] [*ICAO location identifier*] (ICLI)
VTSO .... Surat Thani/Don Nok [*Thailand*] [*ICAO location identifier*] (ICLI)
VTSP .... Phuket [*Thailand*] [*ICAO location identifier*] (ICLI)
VTSPS .... Vsesoyuznyy Tsentral'nyy Sovet Professional'nykh Soyuzov [*All-Union Central Council of Trade Unions*] [*Former USSR*]
VTSR .... Ranong [*Thailand*] [*ICAO location identifier*] (ICLI)
VTSRS .... Verdun Target Symptom Rating Scale (MAE)
VTSS .... Songkhla/Hat Yai [*Thailand*] [*ICAO location identifier*] (ICLI)
VTSS .... Vitesse Semiconductor [*NASDAQ symbol*] (SPSG)

VTST	Trang [*Thailand*] [*ICAO location identifier*] (ICLI)
VTST	Variant Transition State Theory [*Chemical physics*]
VTST	Variational Transition State Theory [*Physical chemistry*]
VT Stat Ann ...	Vermont Statutes, Annotated [*A publication*] (DLA)
VT St G Rp ...	Vermont State Geologist. Report [*A publication*]
VtStjA	St. Johnsbury Atheneum, St. Johnsbury, VT [*Library symbol*] [*Library of Congress*] (LCLS)
VtStjF	Fairbanks Museum of Natural Science, St. Johnsbury, VT [*Library symbol*] [*Library of Congress*] (LCLS)
VTSuppl	Vetus Testamentum. Supplementum [*Leiden*] [*A publication*]
Vt-SWRL...	Vermont Department of Libraries, Southwest Regional Library, Rutland, VT [*Library symbol*] [*Library of Congress*] (LCLS)
VTSY	Ya La [*Thailand*] [*ICAO location identifier*] (ICLI)
VTT	Vacuum Thermal Testing
VTT	Vacuum-Tube Transmitter
VTT	Valtion Teknillinen Tutkimuskeskus [*Technical Research Center of Finland*] [*Espoo*] [*Information service or system*] (IID)
VTT	Variable Threshold Transistor
VTTJA	Valtion Teknillinen Tutkimuslaitos. Julkaisu [*A publication*]
VTU	Las Tunas [*Cuba*] [*Airport symbol*] (OAG)
VTU	Oxnard, CA [*Location identifier*] [*FAA*] (FAAL)
VTU	University of Vermont, Bailey Library, Burlington, VT [*OCLC symbol*] (OCLC)
VtU	University of Vermont, Burlington, VT [*Library symbol*] [*Library of Congress*] (LCLS)
vtu	Vermont [*MARC country of publication code*] [*Library of Congress*] (LCCP)
V + TU......	Voice plus Teleprinter Unit
VTU	Volunteer Reserve Training Unit [*Coast Guard*]
VTU	Volunteer Training Unit
VTUA	Kalasin/Ban Na Khu [*Thailand*] [*ICAO location identifier*] (ICLI)
VTUB	Bakhon Phanom/Mukdahan [*Thailand*] [*ICAO location identifier*] (ICLI)
VTUC	Chaiyaphum [*Thailand*] [*ICAO location identifier*] (ICLI)
VTUD	Udon Thani [*Thailand*] [*ICAO location identifier*] (ICLI)
VTUE	Sakon Nakhon/Nam Phung Dam (North) [*Thailand*] [*ICAO location identifier*] (ICLI)
VTUF........	Sakon Nakhon/Nam Phung Dam (South) [*Thailand*] [*ICAO location identifier*] (ICLI)
VTUG	Chaiyaphum/Phu Khieo [*Thailand*] [*ICAO location identifier*] (ICLI)
VTUH.......	Nakhon Ratchasima/Pak Chong [*Thailand*] [*ICAO location identifier*] (ICLI)
VTUI	Sakon Nakhon/Bankhai [*Thailand*] [*ICAO location identifier*] (ICLI)
VTUK	Khon Kaen [*Thailand*] [*ICAO location identifier*] (ICLI)
VTUL	Loei [*Thailand*] [*ICAO location identifier*] (ICLI)
VTUM	Nongkhai [*Thailand*] [*ICAO location identifier*] (ICLI)
VtU-Med ...	University of Vermont, College of Medicine, Burlington, VT [*Library symbol*] [*Library of Congress*] (LCLS)
VTU(MMS) ...	Volunteer Training Unit (Merchant Marine Safety)
VTUN........	Nakhon Ratchasima [*Thailand*] [*ICAO location identifier*] (ICLI)
VTUP	Nakhon Phanom [*Thailand*] [*ICAO location identifier*] (ICLI)
VTUR	Roi Et [*Thailand*] [*ICAO location identifier*] (ICLI)
VTUS........	Sakon Nakhon [*Thailand*] [*ICAO location identifier*] (ICLI)
VTUT	Ubon Ratchathani/Loeng Nok Tha [*Thailand*] [*ICAO location identifier*] (ICLI)
VTUU........	Ubon Ratchathani [*Thailand*] [*ICAO location identifier*] (ICLI)
VTUW	Nakhon Phanom (West) [*Thailand*] [*ICAO location identifier*] (ICLI)
VtU-W	University of Vermont and State Agricultural College, Wilbur Collection, Burlington, VT [*Library symbol*] [*Library of Congress*] (LCLS)
VTUZ	Khon Kaen/Nam Phung Dam [*Thailand*] [*ICAO location identifier*] (ICLI)
VTV	Vacuum Transmitting Valve [*Automotive engineering*]
VT(V)........	Vacuum-Tube (Voltmeter) (DEN)
VTV	Value Television [*Television program*]
VTV	Verification Test Vehicle [*Military*] (CAAL)
VtVe..........	Bixby Memorial Free Library, Vergennes, VT [*Library symbol*] [*Library of Congress*] (LCLS)
VT Verfahrenstech ...	VT. Verfahrenstechnik [*A publication*]
VTVM	Vacuum-Tube Voltmeter
VTW	Variable Transmission Window
VtWeo........	Wilder Memorial Library, Weston, VT [*Library symbol*] [*Library of Congress*] (LCLS)
VtWinoS	Saint Michael's College, Winooski, VT [*Library symbol*] [*Library of Congress*] (LCLS)
VTX	Vacuum-Tube Transmitter
VTX	Ventex Energy [*Vancouver Stock Exchange symbol*]
VTX	Vertex [*A publication*]
VTX	Vertex
VTX	Videotex [*Telecommunications*]
VTX	Vortex (AAG)
VTX	VTX Electronics [*Associated Press abbreviation*] (APAG)
VTX	VTX Electronics [*AMEX symbol*] (SPSG)

VTXTS	Navy Jet Trainer (MCD)
VTXX........	Vertz Corp. [*NASDAQ symbol*] (NQ)
VTY	Vatovaky [*Madagascar*] [*Seismograph station code, US Geological Survey*] (SEIS)
VTZ	Vishakhapatnam [*India*] [*Airport symbol*] (OAG)
VU............	Societe Air Ivoire [*Ivory Coast*] [*ICAO designator*] (FAAC)
VU............	Utility Squadron [*Navy symbol*] (MCD)
VU............	Validation Unit (AAG)
VU............	Vanity Unit [*Classified advertising*] (ADA)
VU............	Varicose Ulcer [*Medicine*]
VU............	Vaterlaendische Union [*Patriotic Union*] [*Liechtenstein*] [*Political party*] (PPE)
VU............	Vehicle Unit (KSC)
VU............	Vehicle Utility (MCD)
VU............	Velvet Underground [*Musical group*]
VU............	Very Urgent
VU............	Voice of Uganda [*A publication*]
VU............	Voice Unit [*Signal amplitude measurement*]
VU............	Volksunie [*People's Union*] [*Belgium*] [*Political party*]
VU............	Volksunite [*United People's Party*] [*Belgium*] [*Political party*]
VU............	Volume Unit [*Signal amplitude measurement*]
VU............	Von Unten [*From the Bottom*] [*German*]
VUA...........	Valorous Unit Award [*Military decoration*]
VUA...........	Verbal Underachievers [*Education*]
VUA...........	Virtual Unit Address (BUR)
VUB...........	Variational Upper Bound
VUB...........	Vrije Universiteit Brussel [*Free University of Brussels*] [*Belgium*] [*Information service or system*] (IID)
VUBN........	Valley Utah Bancorporation [*Salt Lake City, UT*] [*NASDAQ symbol*] (NQ)
VUBT........	Vuebotics Corp. [*NASDAQ symbol*] (NQ)
VUCC	Computer Center [*Vanderbilt University*] [*Research center*] (RCD)
VUCDT	Ventilation Unit Condensate Drain Tank (IEEE)
VUCLR.....	Victoria University. College Law Review [*A publication*]
VUCS........	Ventilation Umbilical Connector System
VUE...........	Upper Hudson Library Federation, Albany, NY [*OCLC symbol*] (OCLC)
VUE...........	Visible/Ultraviolet Experiment
Vues Econ Aquitaine ...	Vues sur l'Economie d'Aquitaine [*A publication*]
VU-EVA	Volksunie-Europese Vrije Alliante [*Belgium*] [*Political party*] (ECED)
VuF...........	Verkuendigung und Forschung [*A publication*]
VUF...........	Vertical Upward Force
VuG...........	Vergangenheit und Gegenwart [*A publication*]
VUHZ........	Vyzkumny Ustav Hutnictvi Zeleza, Dobra [*Dobra Iron and Steel Research Institute*] [*Information service or system*] (IID)
VUL..........	Vulcan [*Taviliu*] [*New Britain*] [*Seismograph station code, US Geological Survey*] (SEIS)
VUL..........	Vulcan International Corp. [*AMEX symbol*] (SPSG)
VUL..........	Vulcanize (AAG)
VUL..........	Vulnerary [*Medicine to heal wounds*] (ROG)
Vul...........	Vulpecula [*Constellation*]
VULBS	Virginia Union List of Biomedical Serials [*Library network*]
VULC	Vanguard Unionist Loyalist Coalition [*Northern Ireland*] [*Political party*]
VULC	Vulcanize
VULCAN ..	[*A*] programming language (CSR)
VULCCP ...	Vulcan International Corp. [*Associated Press abbreviation*] (APAG)
VulcM........	Vulcan Materials Co. [*Associated Press abbreviation*] (APAG)
VULG	Vulgar
VULG	Vulgate [*Version of the Bible*]
Vulkanol Seismol ...	Vulkanologiya i Seismologiya [*A publication*]
Vulp..........	Vulpecula [*Constellation*]
VULR	Valparaiso University. Law Review [*A publication*]
VULREP ...	Vulnerability Report [*Navy*] (NVT)
Vultei	[*Hermannus*] Vulteius [*Deceased, 1634*] [*Authority cited in pre-1607 legal work*] (DSA)
VUMD.......	Vilniaus Valstybinio V. Kapsuko Vardo Universiteto Mokslo Darbai [*A publication*]
VUMS........	Vyzkumny Ustav pro Matematickych Stroju [*Research Institute for Mathematical Machines*] [*Czechoslovakia*]
VUN..........	Vunikawai [*Fiji*] [*Seismograph station code, US Geological Survey*] (SEIS)
VUNC........	Voice of United Nations Command
Vuorit Bergshant ...	Vuoriteollisuus/Bergshanteringen [*A publication*]
Vuoto........	Vuoto, Scienza, e Tecnologia [*A publication*]
Vuoto Sci Tecnol ...	Vuoto, Scienza, e Tecnologia [*A publication*]
VUP	Valledupar [*Colombia*] [*Airport symbol*] (OAG)
VUP	Vela Uniform Platform
VUPP........	Vanguard Unionist Progressive Party [*Northern Ireland*] [*Political party*]
VUQ..........	Dayton, OH [*Location identifier*] [*FAA*] (FAAL)
VUR..........	Vesicoureteral Reflex [*Nephrology*]
VURB-A ...	Vie Urbaine [*France*] [*A publication*]
VUS..........	Versatile Upper Stage [*NASA*]
VUSA	Visit USA [*Airline fare*]
VUSH........	Vanderbilt University. Studies in the Humanities [*A publication*]

VUT.......... Union Theological Seminary Library, Richmond, VA [*OCLC symbol*]   (OCLC)

Vutr Boles ... Vutreshni Bolesti [*A publication*]

VUTS......... Verification Unit Test Set   (AFM)

VUU........... Virginia Union University [*Richmond*]

VUU........... Virginia Union University, Richmond, VA [*OCLC symbol*]   (OCLC)

VUV........... Vacuum Ultraviolet

VUV........... Very Ultraviolet   (SSD)

VUW......... Eugene Isle, LA [*Location identifier*] [*FAA*]   (FAAL)

VUWLR .... Victoria University of Wellington. Law Review [*A publication*]

VUWL Rev ... Victoria University of Wellington. Law Review [*A publication*]

VUZ........... Birmingham, AL [*Location identifier*] [*FAA*]   (FAAL)

VV............. First and Second Violins [*Music*]   (ROG)

VV............. Nile Valley Aviation Co. [*Egypt*] [*ICAO designator*]   (FAAC)

VV............. Vaccinia Virus

VV............. Vacuum Valve

V/V........... Validation/Verification   (CAAL)

VV............. Vanguard Ventures [*Vancouver Stock Exchange symbol*]

VV............. Variable Venturi [*Automotive engineering*]

VV............. Varicose Vein   (MAE)

VV............. Veins [*Medicine*]

VV............. Velocity Vector   (AAG)

VV............. Velocity-Volume

vv............. Venerabiles [*Venerables*] [*Latin*]   (WGA)

VV............. Vent Valve

VV............. Verbs   (ADA)

V & V .... Verification and Validation [*Data processing*]

VV............. Verses

VV............. Vertebral Vein [*Anatomy*]

V/V........... Vertical Velocity

VV............. Vestron, Inc. [*NYSE symbol*]   (SPSG)

V-V........... Vibrational-to-Vibrational [*Energy transfer*]

VV............. Vibrio Vulnificus [*A microorganism*]

VV............. Vice Versa

VV............. Victims for Victims   (EA)

VV............. Vietnam Veterans   (OICC)

VV............. Village Voice [*A publication*]

VV............. Violini [*Violins*] [*Music*]

VV............. Viper Venom   (MAE)

VV............. Visna Virus

VV............. Vista Ventures [*Commercial firm*] [*British*]

VV............. Visum Vivum [*Seen Alive*] [*Botany*]   (ROG)

VV............. Viva Voce [*Spoken Aloud*] [*Latin*]   (ADA)

VV............. Vizantiiskii Vremenik [*A publication*]

VV............. Voices [*Music*]

VV............. Volk und Volkstum [*A publication*]

V/V........... Volume/Volume

V for V .... Volunteers for Vision [*Defunct*]   (EA)

VV............. Vulva and Vagina [*Physiology*]

VVA .... Southern Adirondack Library System, Saratoga Springs, NY [*OCLC symbol*]   (OCLC)

VVA .... Variable Valve Actuation [*Automotive engineering*]

VVA .... Venturi Vacuum Amplifier [*Automotive engineering*]

VVa........... Vida Vasca [*A publication*]

VVA .... Vietnam Veterans of America   (EA)

VVAA .... Vietnam Veterans Association of Australia

VVAG .... Vietnam Veterans Arts Group [*Later, CTVWA*]   (EA)

VVAOVI.... Vietnam Veterans Agent Orange Victims   (EA)

VVAP......... Mouvement Socialiste Occitan - Volem Viure al Pais [*Occitanian Socialist Movement*] [*France*] [*Political party*]   (PPW)

VVAW .... Vietnam Veterans Against the War   (EA)

VVB .... Baruch College, New York, NY [*OCLC symbol*]   (OCLC)

VVB .... Mahanoro [*Madagascar*] [*Airport symbol*]   (OAG)

VVBAA..... Venetian and Vertical Blind Association of America [*Defunct*]

VVBM .... Buonmethuot/Chung Duc [*Viet Nam*] [*ICAO location identifier*]   (ICLI)

VVC .... Colgate University, Hamilton, NY [*OCLC symbol*]   (OCLC)

VVC .... Variable Vacuum Capacitor

VVC .... Vertical Velocity Console

VVC .... Villavicencio [*Colombia*] [*Airport symbol*]   (OAG)

VVC .... Voltage Variable Capacitor

VVCB........ Caobang [*Viet Nam*] [*ICAO location identifier*]   (ICLI)

VVCC........ Viri Clarissimi [*Most Illustrious Men*] [*Latin*]

VVCD .... Voltage Variable Capacitance Diode

VVCEC...... Voice and Video Control and Editing Components   (MCD)

VVCO .... US Video Vending Corp. [*Iselin, NJ*] [*NASDAQ symbol*]   (NQ)

VVCS........ Conson [*Viet Nam*] [*ICAO location identifier*]   (ICLI)

VVCS........ Vernier Velocity Correction System [*Aerospace*]   (KSC)

VVCT........ Cantho [*Viet Nam*] [*ICAO location identifier*]   (ICLI)

VVCUS...... Veteran Vespa Club, US   (EA)

VVD........... Downstate Medical Center, SUNY [*State University of New York*], Brooklyn, NY [*OCLC symbol*]   (OCLC)

VVD........... Valid Verifiable Defense [*Stamped on dismissed traffic tickets*]

VVD........... Valverde [*Canary Islands*] [*Seismograph station code, US Geological Survey*]   (SEIS)

VVD........... Volkspartij voor Vrijheid en Democratie [*People's Party for Freedom and Democracy*] [*Netherlands*] [*Political party*]   (EAIO)

VVD........... Voltage Variable Diode

VVDB .... Dienbienphu [*Viet Nam*] [*ICAO location identifier*]   (ICLI)

VVDL .... Dalat/Lienkhuong [*Viet Nam*] [*ICAO location identifier*]   (ICLI)

VVDN....... Danang [*Viet Nam*] [*ICAO location identifier*]   (ICLI)

VVDS........ Video Verter Decision Storage

VVE .... Erie Community College-North, Buffalo, NY [*OCLC symbol*]   (OCLC)

VVE .... Vertical Vertex Error   (OA)

VVF.......... New York Medical College, New York, NY [*OCLC symbol*]   (OCLC)

VVF.......... Veseco Vaginal Fistula [*Medicine*]

VVG.......... New York State Institute for Research in Mental Retardation, Staten Island, NY [*OCLC symbol*]   (OCLC)

VVGF....... Vincent Van Gogh Foundation   (EA)

VVGL .... Hanoi/Gialam [*Viet Nam*] [*ICAO location identifier*]   (ICLI)

VVH.......... Daemen College, Buffalo, NY [*OCLC symbol*]   (OCLC)

VVH.......... Very Very Heavy [*Cosmic ray nuclei*]

VVH.......... Veterans Vigil of Honor   (EA)

VVHR....... Vibration Velocity per Hour

VVI .... Beth Israel Medical Center, New York, NY [*OCLC symbol*]   (OCLC)

VVI .... Vertical Velocity Indicator   (MCD)

VVI .... Vice Viewers International   (EA)

VVI .... Vietnam Veterans, Inc.   (EA)

VVI .... Vietnam Veterans Institute [*Research center*]   (RCD)

VVI .... Vocational Values Inventory [*Guidance in education*]

VVI .... Voltage Variation Indicator

VVIC......... Vietnam Era Veterans in Congress   (EA)

VVIP......... Very, Very Important Person

VVIR........ Voice and Vision of the Iranian Revolution [*Iranian television*]

VVIRA...... Vietnam Veterans Institute for Research and Advocacy   (EA)

VVIS......... Vision Communication Corp. [*Formerly, Videovision, Inc.*] [*NASDAQ symbol*]   (NQ)

VVITA...... Vietnam Veterans Inter-Tribal Association   (EA)

VVJ........... John Jay College of Criminal Justice, New York, NY [*OCLC symbol*]   (OCLC)

VVK .... New York Academy of Medicine, New York, NY [*OCLC symbol*]   (OCLC)

VVK .... Van Vleck [*Quantum mechanics*]

VVK .... Vastervik [*Sweden*] [*Airport symbol*]   (OAG)

VVKP........ Kep [*Viet Nam*] [*ICAO location identifier*]   (ICLI)

VVL .... Mount Sinai School of Medicine of the City University of New York, New York, NY [*OCLC symbol*]   (OCLC)

VVL .... Vee en Vlees. Het Vakblad voor Handelaar en Producent [*A publication*]

VVLK........ Laokay [*Viet Nam*] [*ICAO location identifier*]   (ICLI)

VV LL .... Variae Lectiones [*Variant Readings*] [*Latin*]

VVLP........ Vietnam Veterans Leadership Program [*ACTION*]

VVM.......... Memorial Sloan-Kettering Cancer Center, New York, NY [*OCLC symbol*]   (OCLC)

VVM.......... Vector Voltmeter

VVM.......... Velocity Vector Measurement

VVMC ...... Voice and Video Monitoring Component   (MCD)

VVMF....... Vietnam Veterans Memorial Fund   (EA)

VVMS....... Velocity Vector Measurement System

VVN.......... Niagara University, Niagara University, NY [*OCLC symbol*]   (OCLC)

VVNB....... Hanoi/Noibai [*Viet Nam*] [*ICAO location identifier*]   (ICLI)

VVNS .... Nasan [*Viet Nam*] [*ICAO location identifier*]   (ICLI)

VVNT .... Nhatrang [*Viet Nam*] [*ICAO location identifier*]   (ICLI)

VVnW....... Veterans of the Vietnam War   (EA)

VVO.......... New York Medical College, Westchester Medical Center, Valhalla, NY [*OCLC symbol*]   (OCLC)

VVO.......... Very Very Old [*Designation on brandy labels*]

VVOH ...... Vacuum Valve Operating Handle

VVP .... Bard College, Annandale-On-Hudson, NY [*OCLC symbol*]   (OCLC)

VVPB........ Hue/Phubai [*Viet Nam*] [*ICAO location identifier*]   (ICLI)

VVPK........ Pleiku/Cu-Hanh [*Viet Nam*] [*ICAO location identifier*]   (ICLI)

VVPP........ Variable Volume Piston Pump

VVPQ .... Phuquoc [*Viet Nam*] [*ICAO location identifier*]   (ICLI)

VVQ.......... Roosevelt Hospital, Medical Library, New York, NY [*OCLC symbol*]   (OCLC)

VVQN....... Quinhon [*Viet Nam*] [*ICAO location identifier*]   (ICLI)

VVR .... Rockland Community College, Suffern, NY [*OCLC symbol*]   (OCLC)

VVR .... Vancouver Ventures [*Vancouver Stock Exchange symbol*]

VVR .... Variable Voltage Rectifier

VVR .... Vehicle Vapor Recovery [*Automobile*]

VVR .... Viewdata/Videotex Report [*Link Resources Corp.*] [*Information service or system*]   (CRD)

VVRG .... Rachgia [*Viet Nam*] [*ICAO location identifier*]   (ICLI)

VVRI........ Veterinary Virus Research Institute [*New York State Veterinary College*]

VVRM .... Vortex Valve Rocket Motor   (MCD)

VVRS........ Viscous Vortex Rate Sensor

VVS........... Connellsville, PA [*Location identifier*] [*FAA*]   (FAAL)

VVS........... Sarah Lawrence College, Bronxville, NY [*OCLC symbol*]   (OCLC)

VVS........... Vein Ventures Ltd. [*Vancouver Stock Exchange symbol*]

VVS............ Very Very Slightly Flawed [*Gems*]
VVS............ Very, Very Small Inclusions [*Diamond clarity grade*]
VVS............ Very Very Superior
VVS............ Voenno-Vozdushnye Sily [*Army Air Forces*] [*Part of the MO*] [*Former USSR*]
VVS............ Voice Verification System
VVSA........ Velocity Vector Sensor Assembly
VVSO .... Very, Very Superior Old [*Designation on brandy labels*]
VVSOP...... Very, Very Superior Old Pale [*Designation on brandy labels*]
VVSS .... Vertical Volute Spring Suspension [*Technical drawings*]
VVS Tidsk Energ VVS-Tek ... VVS. Tidskrift foer Energi- och VVS [*Vaerme, Ventilation, Sanitet*]-Teknik [*A publication*]
VVS Tidskr Vaerme Vent Sanit Kyltetek ... VVS. Tidskrift foer Vaerme, Ventilation, Sanitet, och Kylteteknik [*A publication*]
VVS Tidskr Varme Vent Sanit ... VVS. Tidskrift foer Vaerme, Ventilation, Sanitet [*Sweden*] [*A publication*]
VVS-VMF ... Voenno-Vozdushnye Sily - Voenno-Morskogo Flota [*Naval Air Force*] [*Former USSR*]
VVT .... Teachers College, Columbia University, New York, NY [*OCLC symbol*] (OCLC)
VVT .... Velocity Variation Tube
VVT .... Venturi Vacuum Transducer [*Engineering*]
VVT .... Visual-Verbal Test [*Psychology*]
VVTBA .... Vaeg- och Vattenbyggaren [*A publication*]
VVTC........ Vendor-Vendee Technical Committee
VVTS........ Hochiminh/Tansonnhat [*Viet Nam*] [*ICAO location identifier*] (ICLI)
VVU .... New York University, Medical Center, New York, NY [*OCLC symbol*] (OCLC)
VVUU Zpr ... VVUU [*Vedeckovyzkumny Uhelny Ustav*] Ostrava-Radvanice Zprava [*A publication*]
VVV .... Ortonville, MN [*Location identifier*] [*FAA*] (FAAL)
VVV .... Utica College of Syracuse University, Utica, NY [*OCLC symbol*] (OCLC)
VVV .... Vacuum Vent Valve [*Automotive engineering*]
VVVH........ Vinh [*Viet Nam*] [*ICAO location identifier*] (ICLI)
VVVT........ Vungtau [*Viet Nam*] [*ICAO location identifier*] (ICLI)
VVVV .... Hanoi [*Viet Nam*] [*ICAO location identifier*] (ICLI)
VVW .... Westchester Library System, Yonkers, NY [*OCLC symbol*] (OCLC)
VVWCA .... Vintage Volkswagen Club of America (EA)
VV:WT ...... Vaccinia Virus: Wild Type [*Virology*]
VVX .... Nassau Community College, Garden City, NY [*OCLC symbol*] (OCLC)
VVY .... St. Luke's Hospital, Bolling Medical Library, New York, NY [*OCLC symbol*] (OCLC)
VVZ .... Medical Library Center of New York, New York, NY [*OCLC symbol*] (OCLC)
VW............. Air Concept [*Germany*] [*ICAO aircraft manufacturer identifier*] (ICAO)
VW............. Early Warning Squadron [*Symbol*] (MCD)
Vw .... Maximum Winch Launching Speed [*Gliders*] (AIA)
VW............. Transportes Aereos Trafe SA [*ICAO designator*] (FAAC)
VW............. Very Weak [*Spectral*]
VW............. Very Worshipful
VW............. Vessel Wall
VW............. Vie Wallonne [*A publication*]
VW............. View (MCD)
VW............. Volkswagen [*German automobile*]
VWA.......... Vacuum Window Assembly
VWA.......... Vendor Working Authority
VWA.......... Verband der Weiblichen Angestellten [*Association of Female Employees*] [*West Germany*]
VWA.......... Vintage Wireless Association [*British*]
VWA.......... Volume-Weighted Average [*Statistics*]
VWB .... Bronx Community College Library, Bronx, NY [*OCLC symbol*] (OCLC)
VWBN....... Valley West Bancorp [*Springfield, OR*] [*NASDAQ symbol*] (NQ)
VWC......... Villa Walsh College [*New Jersey*]
VWC......... Vulcan Wheeled Carrier
VWCA ...... Volkswagen Club of America (EA)
VWCL....... Volkswagen Caminhoes Limitada [*Brazil*]
VWD......... Vereinigte Wirtschaftsdienste [*Press agency*] [*West Germany*]
VWD......... Video-West Distributors Ltd. [*Vancouver Stock Exchange symbol*]
VWD......... Vinyl Window and Door Institute (EA)
vWD.......... Von Willebrand's Disease [*Medicine*]
VWDU....... Viewing Window Deicing Unit
VWE .... Vanadium Wire Equilibration [*Nuclear energy*] (NRCH)
VWED....... Vanadium Wire Equilibration Device [*Nuclear energy*] (NRCH)
VWF .... Vehicle Work Flow
VWF .... Vibration-Induced White Finger [*Medicine*]
vWf........... Von Willebrand factor [*Also, vWF, VWF*] [*Hematology*]
VWFC....... Very-Wide-Field Camera
VWG .... Vital Wheat Gluten [*Vegetable protein*]
VWGA ...... Vinifera Wine Growers Association (EA)
VWH .... Vale of White Horse [*Hounds*]
VWH .... Vertical Weld Head
VWHA....... Vertical Weld Head Assembly

VWL .... College of William and Mary, Law School, Williamsburg, VA [*OCLC symbol*] (OCLC)
VWL .... Variable Word Length
VWM......... College of William and Mary, Williamsburg, VA [*OCLC symbol*] (OCLC)
VWM......... Virginia Woolf Miscellany [*A publication*]
VWM......... Volume-Weighted Mean [*Statistical technique*]
VWMP ...... Vietnam Women's Memorial Project (EA)
VWN......... Virginia Woolf Newsletter [*A publication*]
VWO......... Valves Wide Open [*Nuclear energy*] (NRCH)
VWO......... Woolsey, GA [*Location identifier*] [*FAA*] (FAAL)
VWOA...... Veteran Wireless Operators Association (EA)
VWOA...... Volkswagen of America
VWP .... Variable Width Pulse
VWP .... Vietnam Workers' Party [*Political party*] (PPW)
VWPI........ Vacuum Wood Preservers Institute (EA)
VWQ......... Virginia Woolf Quarterly [*A publication*]
VWR......... North Country Reference and Research Resources Council, Canton, NY [*OCLC symbol*] (OCLC)
VWR......... Volkswirtschaftsrat [*Political Economy Bureau*] [*German*]
VWRRC..... Virginia Water Resources Research Center [*Virginia Polytechnic Institute and State University*] [*Research center*] (RCD)
VWRS........ Vibrating Wire Rate Sensor
VWRX .... VWR Corp. [*Seattle, WA*] [*NASDAQ symbol*] (NQ)
VWS .... Valdez, AK [*Location identifier*] [*FAA*] (FAAL)
VWS .... Variable Word Size
VWS .... Ventilated Wet Suit (DNAB)
VWS .... Virginia Woolf Society (EA)
VWS .... Voice Warning System
VWSS .... Vertical Wire Sky Screen (KSC)
VWSWCA .. Volkswagen Split Window Club of America (EA)
VWTA .... Vintage White Truck Association (EA)
VW-TCA ... Volkswagen Toy Collectors of America (EA)
VWU.......... Chincoteague Island, VA [*Location identifier*] [*FAA*] (FAAL)
VWV .... Waterville, OH [*Location identifier*] [*FAA*] (FAAL)
VWW........ Velocity of Wireless Waves
VWWI ...... Veterans of World War I of USA (EA)
VWY .... Visway Transport, Inc. [*Toronto Stock Exchange symbol*]
VX............. Air Development Squadron [*Navy*]
VX............. Experimental Squadron [*Symbol*] (MCD)
VX............. International Veronex Resources Ltd. [*AMEX symbol*] (SPSG)
VX............. Nerve Gas [*US Chemical Corps symbol*]
VX............. Transvalair [*Switzerland*] [*ICAO designator*] (FAAC)
VX............. Vanex Resources Ltd. [*Vancouver Stock Exchange symbol*]
VX............. Vauxhall [*Automobile*] [*British*]
VX............. Velocity along the X-Axis (NASA)
VX............. Vertex [*Medicine*]
VX............. Vivas, Care [*May You Live, Dear One*] [*Latin*]
VX............. Voice
VX............. Volume Unknown [*Medicine*]
VX-1.......... OPTEVFOR [*Operational Test and Evaluation Force*] Air Test and Evaluation Squadron One, Naval Air Station, Patuxent River, MD (CAAL)
VX-4.......... OPTEVFOR [*Operational Test and Evaluation Force*] Air Test and Evaluation Squadron Four, Naval Air Station, Pt. Mugu, CA (CAAL)
VX-5.......... OPTEVFOR [*Operational Test and Evaluation Force*] Air Test and Evaluation Squadron Five, Naval Weapons Center, China Lake, CA (CAAL)
VXA .... Harlem Hospital Center, Health Sciences Library, New York, NY [*OCLC symbol*] (OCLC)
VXC .... Lichinga [*Mozambique*] [*Airport symbol*] (OAG)
VXD.......... New York University, College of Dentistry Library, New York, NY [*OCLC symbol*] (OCLC)
VxD.......... Virtual Device Driver [*Data processing*] (PCM)
VXE .... Elmira College, Elmira, NY [*OCLC symbol*] (OCLC)
VXE .... Sao Vicente [*Cape Verde Islands*] [*Airport symbol*] (OAG)
VXF........... State University of New York, College of Environmental Science and Forestry, Syracuse, NY [*OCLC symbol*] (OCLC)
VXG .... New York Botanical Garden Library, Bronx, NY [*OCLC symbol*] (OCLC)
VXH.......... Herkimer County Community College, Herkimer, NY [*OCLC symbol*] (OCLC)
VXI .... Iona College, New Rochelle, NY [*OCLC symbol*] (OCLC)
VXJ........... Jewish Theological Seminary of America, New York, NY [*OCLC symbol*] (OCLC)
VXL .... Albany Medical College, Schaffer Library of Health Sciences, Albany, NY [*OCLC symbol*] (OCLC)
VXLB........ Verex Laboratories, Inc. [*NASDAQ symbol*] (NQ)
VXM.......... General Theological Seminary, St. Mark's Library, New York, NY [*OCLC symbol*] (OCLC)
VXN.......... New York State Department of Health, Albany, NY [*OCLC symbol*] (OCLC)
VXO.......... Houghton College, Houghton, NY [*OCLC symbol*] (OCLC)
VXO.......... Variable Crystal Oscillator
VXO.......... Vaxjo [*Sweden*] [*Airport symbol*] (OAG)
VXP .... State University of New York, College of Optometry, New York, NY [*OCLC symbol*] (OCLC)

VXR .... Rochester Museum and Science Center, Rochester, NY [*OCLC symbol*]   (OCLC)
VXR .... Vertex Resources Ltd. [*Vancouver Stock Exchange symbol*]
VXT .... Tompkins-Cortland Community College, Dryden, NY [*OCLC symbol*]   (OCLC)
VXU .... Chautauqua-Cattaraugus Library System, Jamestown, NY [*OCLC symbol*]   (OCLC)
VXV .... Hudson Valley Community College, Troy, NY [*OCLC symbol*]   (OCLC)
VXW .... Vassar College, Poughkeepsie, NY [*OCLC symbol*]   (OCLC)
VXX .... Long Island University, C. W. Post Center, Greenvale, NY [*OCLC symbol*]   (OCLC)
VXX .... Venturex Resources [*Vancouver Stock Exchange symbol*]
VXY .... Centro de Estudios Puertorriquenos, New York, NY [*OCLC symbol*]   (OCLC)
VXZ .... Dowling College, Oakdale, NY [*OCLC symbol*]   (OCLC)
VY .... Abelag Airways [*Belgium*] [*ICAO designator*]   (ICDA)
VY .... Air Belgium [*Belgium*] [*ICAO designator*]   (FAAC)
VY .... Valley   (ADA)
VY .... Various Years [*Bibliography*]
VY .... Velocity along the Y-Axis   (NASA)
VY .... Very   (ROG)
VY .... Victualling Yard [*Obsolete*] [*Navy*] [*British*]   (ROG)
VY .... Vyquest, Inc. [*AMEX symbol*]   (SPSG)
VYA .... Molloy College, Rockville Centre, NY [*OCLC symbol*]   (OCLC)
VYB .... St. Barnabas Medical Staff Library, Livingston, NJ [*OCLC symbol*]   (OCLC)
VYB .... Vivian, Younger & Bond Ltd.
VYB .... Vyborg [*Former USSR*] [*Seismograph station code, US Geological Survey*] [*Closed*]   (SEIS)
Vyber Inf Organ Vypocetni Tech ... Vyber Informaci z Organizacni a Vypocetni Techniky [*A publication*]
VYBN .... Valley Bancorporation [*NASDAQ symbol*]   (NQ)
VYC .... Cornell University, Medical College, New York, NY [*OCLC symbol*]   (OCLC)
Vychisl Metody Progam ... Vychislitel'nye Metody i Programmirovanie [*A publication*]
Vychisl Metody & Program ... Vychislitel'nye Metody i Programmirovanie [*A publication*]
Vychisl Seismol ... Vychislitel'naya Seismologiya [*Former USSR*] [*A publication*]
Vychisl Sist ... Vychislitel'nye Sistemy [*A publication*]
Vychisl Tekhn i Voprosy Kibernet ... Leningradskii Gosudarstvennyi Universitet Vychislitel'nyi Tsentr Moskovskii Gosudarstvennyi Universitet Vychislitel'nyi Tsentr Vychislitel'naya Tekhnika i Voprosy Kibernetiki [*A publication*]
Vycisl Mat i Vycisl Tehn (Kharkov) ... Vycislitel'naja Matematika i Vycislitel'naja Tehnika (Kharkov) [*A publication*]
Vycisl Prikl Mat (Kiev) ... Vycislitel'naja i Prikladnaja Matematika (Kiev) [*A publication*]
Vycisl Tehn v Masinostroen ... Vycislitel'naja Tehnika v Masinostroenii [*A publication*]
VYD .... Capital District Library Council, Troy, NY [*OCLC symbol*]   (OCLC)
VYD .... Vryheid [*South Africa*] [*Airport symbol*]   (OAG)
VYE .... Manhattanville College, Purchase, NY [*OCLC symbol*]   (OCLC)
Vyestsi Akad Navuk BSSR Syer Biyal Navuk ... Vyestsi Akademii Navuk BSSR. Syeryya Biyalagichnykh Navuk [*A publication*]
Vyestsi Akad Navuk BSSR Syer Syel' Skahaspad Navuk ... Vyestsi Akademii Navuk BSSR. Syeryya Syel' Skahaspadarchukh Navuk [*A publication*]
VYF .... Fordham University, Bronx, NY [*OCLC symbol*]   (OCLC)
VYG .... Finger Lakes Library System, Ithaca, NY [*OCLC symbol*]   (OCLC)
VYGS........ Vermont Yankee Generating Station [*Nuclear energy*]   (NRCH)
VYI .... Kahului, HI [*Location identifier*] [*FAA*]   (FAAL)
Vyisn Akad Nauk Ukr RSR ... Vyisnik Akademyiyi Nauk Ukrayins'koyi RSR [*A publication*]
Vyisn Kiyiv Unyiv Ser Astron ... Vyisnik Kiyivs'kogo Unyiversitetu. Seryiya Astronomii [*A publication*]
Vyisn Kiyiv Unyiv Ser Fyiz ... Vyisnik Kiyivs'kogo Unyiversitetu. Seryiya Fyizika [*Former USSR*] [*A publication*]
Vyisn L'vyiv Derzh Unyiv Ser Fyiz ... Vyisnik L'vyivs'kij Derzhavnij Unyiversitet Imeni I. Franka. Seryiya Fyizichna [*A publication*]
Vyisn Syil'skogospod Nauki ... Vyisnik Syil'skogospodars'koyi Nauki [*A publication*]
VYJ .... Martinsburg, WV [*Location identifier*] [*FAA*]   (FAAL)
VYK .... Christ the King Seminary, East Aurora, NY [*OCLC symbol*]   (OCLC)
VYK .... Colombia, SC [*Location identifier*] [*FAA*]   (FAAL)
VYL .... Lehman College, Bronx, NY [*OCLC symbol*]   (OCLC)
VYM .... United States Merchant Marine Academy, Kings Point, NY [*OCLC symbol*]   (OCLC)
VYN .... Dallas-Fort Worth, TX [*Location identifier*] [*FAA*]   (FAAL)
VYN .... Union Theological Seminary, New York, NY [*OCLC symbol*]   (OCLC)
VYNAA ..... Vynalezy [*A publication*]
Vynohrad Vynorobstvo ... Vynohradarstvo i Vynorobstvo [*A publication*]

VYNP .... Vermont Yankee Nuclear Plant   (NRCH)
VYNPS....... Vermont Yankee Nuclear Power Station   (NRCH)
VYQ .... Upstate Medical Center, Syracuse, NY [*OCLC symbol*]   (OCLC)
VYR .... Rome Air Development Center, Griffiss AFB, NY [*OCLC symbol*]   (OCLC)
VYS........... St. Bonaventure University, St. Bonaventure, NY [*OCLC symbol*]   (OCLC)
VYS........... Visceral Yolk Sac [*Embryology*]
Vysk Ustav Lesn Hospod Zvolene Lesn Stud ... Vyskumny Ustav Lesneho Hospodarstvavo Zvolene Lesnicke Studie [*A publication*]
Vysokomol Soed ... Vysokomolekulyarnye Soedineniya [*A publication*]
Vysokomol Soedin ... Vysokomolekulyarnye Soedineniya [*A publication*]
Vysokomol Soedin Geterotsepnye Vysokomol Soedin ... Vysokomolekulyarnye Soedineniya Geterotsepnye Vysokomolekulyarnye Soedineniya [*Former USSR*] [*A publication*]
Vysokomol Soedin Ser A ... Vysokomolekulyarnye Soedineniya. Seriya A [*A publication*]
Vysokomol Soedin Ser B ... Vysokomolekulyarnye Soedineniya. Seriya B [*A publication*]
Vysokomol Soedin Vses Khim Ovo ... Vysokomolekulyarnye Soedineniya Vsesoyuznoe Khimicheskoe Obshchestvo [*A publication*]
Vyso Soed A ... Vysokomolekulyarnye Soedineniya. Seriya A [*A publication*]
Vyso Soed B ... Vysokomolekulyarnye Soedineniya. Seriya B [*A publication*]
Vyssh Nervn Deyat Norme Patol ... Vysshaya Nervnaya Deyatel'nost v Norme i Patologii [*A publication*]
Vyssh Uchebn Zaved Izv Geol Razved ... Vysshoye Uchebnoye Zavedeniye. Izvestiya Geologiya i Razvedka [*A publication*]
Vys Sk Chem-Technol Praze Sb Oddil Chem Inz ... Vysoka Skola Chemicko-Technologicka v Praze. Sbornik. Oddil. Chemicke Inzenyrstvi [*A publication*]
Vys Soed B ... Vysokomolekulyarnye Soedineniya. Seriya B [*A publication*]
VYT .... Clarkson College of Technology, Potsdam, NY [*OCLC symbol*]   (OCLC)
Vytr Boles .. Vytreshni Bolesti [*A publication*]
VyV .... Verdad y Vida [*Milan*] [*A publication*]
VYV .... Wegvervoer [*A publication*]
Vyz Lidu..... Vyziva Lidu [*A publication*]
Vyznach Prisnovod Vodor Ukr RSR ... Vyznachnyk Prisnovodnykh Vodorostei Ukrains'koi RSR
Vyz Rodine ... Vyziva v Rodine [*A publication*]
VyzS........... Vyzvol'nyj Sljax [*A publication*]
Vyz Zdravie ... Vyzica a Zdravie [*A publication*]
VZ.............. Nefertiti Aviation [*Egypt*] [*ICAO designator*]   (FAAC)
VZ.............. Varicella-Zoster [*Also, VZV*] [*A virus*]
VZ.............. Velocity along the Z-Axis   (NASA)
V f Z.......... Vierteljahrshefte fuer Zeitgeschichte [*A publication*]
VZ.............. Virtual Zero
Vz.............. Vizardinus [*Guizzardinus*] [*Deceased, 1222*] [*Authority cited in pre-1607 legal work*]   (DSA)
VZ.............. Vostocnye Zapiski [*A publication*]
Vz.............. Zener Voltage [*Electronics*]   (OA)
Vzar........... Vizardinus [*Guizzardinus*] [*Deceased, 1222*] [*Authority cited in pre-1607 legal work*]   (DSA)
V Zashch Mira ... V Zashchitu Mira [*A publication*]
VZB .... State University of New York at Stony Brook, Health Sciences Library, Stony Brook, NY [*OCLC symbol*]   (OCLC)
VZC .... Clinton-Essex-Franklin Library, Plattsburgh, NY [*OCLC symbol*]   (OCLC)
VZD .... Vendor Zero Defect
VZE .... Mercy College, Dobbs Ferry, NY [*OCLC symbol*]   (OCLC)
VZF........... St. Francis College, Brooklyn, NY [*OCLC symbol*]   (OCLC)
VZG .... St. Joseph's College Library, Suffolk Campus, Patchogue, NY [*OCLC symbol*]   (OCLC)
V f ZG .... Vierteljahreshefte fuer Zeitgeschichte [*A publication*]
VZH........... Hartwick College, Oneonta, NY [*OCLC symbol*]   (OCLC)
VZI .... Stony Brook Institute for Advanced Studies of World Religions, Stony Brook, NY [*OCLC symbol*]   (OCLC)
VZIG........ Varicella-Zoster Immune Globulin
VZJ .... St. John Fisher College, Rochester, NY [*OCLC symbol*]   (OCLC)
VZK .... King's College, Briarcliff Manor, NY [*OCLC symbol*]   (OCLC)
VZL........... Pace University, Law Library, White Plains, NY [*OCLC symbol*]   (OCLC)
VZL........... Vinzolidine [*Antineoplastic drug*]
VZM .... Margaret Woodbury Strong Museum, Rochester, NY [*OCLC symbol*]   (OCLC)
VZM .... Von Zeipel Method
VZN........... College of New Rochelle, New Rochelle, NY [*OCLC symbol*]   (OCLC)
Vznik Pocatky Slov ... Vznik a Pocatky Slovanu [*Origine et Debuts des Slaves*] [*A publication*]
VZO........... Coatesville, PA [*Location identifier*] [*FAA*]   (FAAL)
VZP........... Pace University, New York, NY [*OCLC symbol*]   (OCLC)
VZP........... Verenigde Verzekeringspers. Wekelijks Verschijnend Vakblad voor het Verzekeringswezen in Binnenland en Buitenland [*A publication*]
VZQ .... Pratt Institute, Brooklyn, NY [*OCLC symbol*]   (OCLC)
VZR .... Roswell Park Memorial Institute, Buffalo, NY [*OCLC symbol*]   (OCLC)

VZS............ Skidmore College, Saratoga Springs, NY [*OCLC symbol*]   (OCLC)
VZS............ Valdez South [*Alaska*] [*Seismograph station code, US Geological Survey*]   (SEIS)
VZT .... St. Joseph's College, Brooklyn, NY [*OCLC symbol*]   (OCLC)
VZU........... Pace University, Pleasantville, Pleasantville, NY [*OCLC symbol*]   (OCLC)
VZV .... College of Mount Saint Vincent, New York, NY [*OCLC symbol*]   (OCLC)
VZV .... Varicella-Zoster Virus [*Also, VZ*]
VZW .... College of White Plains, White Plains, NY [*OCLC symbol*]   (OCLC)
VZW .... Valdez West [*Alaska*] [*Seismograph station code, US Geological Survey*]   (SEIS)
VZX .... Western New York Library Resources Council, Buffalo, NY [*OCLC symbol*]   (OCLC)
VZY .... Montefiore Hospital, Bronx, NY [*OCLC symbol*]   (OCLC)
VZZ .... International Museum of Photography, Eastman House, Rochester, NY [*OCLC symbol*]   (OCLC)

W

W .... Climatic Data for the World [*A publication*]
W .... Coast Guard Ship [*When precedes vessel classification*] [*Navy symbol*]
W .... Diameter of Driving-Wheel in Inches [*Railroad term*]
W .... Electrical Energy [*Symbol*] (DEN)
w .... Flow Rate [*Heat transmission symbol*]
W .... Indefinite Ceiling [*Meteorology*] (FAAC)
w .... Load per Unit of Length
W .... Requires an Engineer [*Search and rescue symbol that can be stamped in sand or snow*]
W .... Total Load
w------ .... Tropics [*MARC geographic area code*] [*Library of Congress*] (LCCP)
W .... Tryptophan [*One-letter symbol; see Trp*]
W .... Underwater [*JETDS nomenclature*]
W .... Waffle [*Used in correcting manuscripts, etc.*]
W .... Wages [*Economics*]
W .... Waist (ADA)
W .... Wait Time [*Data processing*]
W .... Wales
W .... Walk [*Baseball*]
W .... Wall
W .... Wallace Laboratories [*Research code symbol*]
W .... Waltz [*Music*]
W .... Wander AG [*Switzerland*] [*Research code symbol*]
W .... Wanderer Books [*Publisher's imprint*]
W .... Wanting
W .... War
W .... Warden
W .... Wardroom [*Aerospace*]
W .... Warehouse
W .... Warhead [*Nuclear*] (NG)
W .... Warm
W .... Warner-Lambert Pharmaceutical Co. [*Research code symbol*]
W .... Warning [*Railroad signal arm*] [*British*]
W .... Warning Area [*Followed by identification*]
W .... Warrant [*A document entitling holder to purchase a given issue of stock*] [*Investment term*]
W .... Washington Reports [*1890-1939*] [*A publication*] (DLA)
W .... Waste
W .... Watch Time
W .... Water
W .... Water Point [*British Waterways Board sign*]
W .... Water Vapor Content
W .... Waterloo [*Army*] [*British*] (ROG)
W .... Watermeyer's Cape Of Good Hope Supreme Court Reports [*A publication*] (DLA)
W .... Watt [*Symbol*] [*SI unit of power*] (GPO)
W .... Wattle [*Ornithology*]
W .... Watt's Pennsylvania Reports [*A publication*] (DLA)
W .... Wave Height Correction
W .... Waveguide (SAA)
W .... Weak [*Spectral*]
W .... Weather
W .... Weather Aircraft Equipped with Meteorological Gear [*Designation for all US military aircraft*]
W .... Weather Review [*A publication*]
W .... Web
W .... Weber [*Hearing test*] (MAE)
W .... Weber Fraction [*Psychology*]
W .... Wednesday
W .... Week
W .... Weekblad van het Recht [*A publication*]
W .... Weekend Travel [*Also, Z*] [*Airline fare code*]
w .... Weekly
W .... Weekly Dose [*Medicine*]
W .... Weeping [*Shrub*]
W .... Wehnelt [*A unit of roentgen ray hardness*] (AAMN)
W .... Weight
W .... Weld (DAS)

W .... Welding Program [*Association of Independent Colleges and Schools specialization code*]
W .... Welsh [*or Welch*]
W .... Wendell's Reports [*1826-41*] [*New York*] [*A publication*] (DLA)
W .... Wesleyan
W .... West [*or Western*]
W .... West Point, NY [*Mint mark when appearing on US coins*]
W .... Westcoast Energy, Inc. [*Toronto Stock Exchange symbol*]
W .... Westcoast Energy, Inc. [*Vancouver Stock Exchange symbol*]
W .... Westerhout [*Astronomy*]
W .... Westinghouse [*as in "Group W"*]
W .... Westvaco Corp. [*NYSE symbol*] (SPSG)
W .... Wet
W .... Wet Dew
W .... Wheaton's Reports [*14-25 United States*] [*A publication*] (DLA)
W .... Wheeled [*Vehicles*] (NATG)
W .... Whip
W .... Whiskey [*Phonetic alphabet*] [*International*] (DSUE)
W .... White [*Light, buoy, beacon*]
W .... White Cell [*Medicine*] (AAMN)
W .... White Return [*Round trip fare for specified period*] [*British*]
W .... Whitehorse Star [*A publication*]
W .... Whole [*Response*] [*Medicine*]
W .... Whole Word Designator [*Data processing*]
W .... Whorls and Compounds [*Fingerprint description*]
W .... Wicked (DAS)
W .... Wicket
W .... Wide
W .... Widow [*or Widower*]
W .... Width
W .... Wife
W .... Will Advise [*Business term*]
w .... Will Factor [*Psychology*]
W .... Wille [*Will Factor*] [*Psychology*]
W .... William [*Phonetic alphabet*] [*Royal Navy*] [*World War I*] [*Pre-World War II*] [*World War II*] (DSUE)
W .... William (King of England) (DLA)
W .... Wilson's [*or Willson's*] Reports [*Texas Civil Cases, Court of Appeals*] [*A publication*] (DLA)
W .... Winch (DS)
W .... Wind [*In reference to wind velocity*]
W .... Window (NASA)
W .... Windward [*Botany*]
W .... Wins [*Sports*]
W .... Winter [*Vessel load line mark*]
W .... Winter [*A publication*]
W .... Wire
W .... Wisconsin Reports [*A publication*] (DLA)
W .... With
W .... Withdrawal
W .... Within (WGA)
W .... Without Voice Facilities on Range or Radiobeacon Frequency
W .... Witwatersrand Local Division Reports [*South Africa*] [*A publication*] (DLA)
W .... Wolfram [*Tungsten*] [*Chemical element*]
W .... Woman (ADA)
W .... Women's Reserve, Unlimited Service [*USNR officer designation*]
W .... Won [*Sports statistics*]
W .... Won [*Monetary unit*] [*South Korea*]
W .... Wood
W .... Wooden [*Shipping*] (ROG)
W .... Woody Plant [*Botany*]
W .... Word
W .... Work [*or w*] [*Symbol*] [*IUPAC*]
W .... Workmen's Compensation [*Insurance*]
W .... World
w .... WORLDSCALE [*Worldwide Tanker Nominal Freight Scale*] (DS)

W................ Worshipful [*Freemasonry*]
W................ Wortkunst [*A publication*]
W................ [*Alfred*] Wotquenne [*When used in identifying C. P. E. Bach's compositions, refers to cataloging of his works by musicologist Wotquenne*]
W................ Wright's Ohio Reports [*1831-34*] [*A publication*]   (DLA)
W................ Write
W................ Writer Officer [*British military*]
W................ Wrong
W................ Wyoming Reports [*A publication*]   (DLA)
1/W............ One-Way
1-W .... Selective Service Class [*for Conscientious Objector Performing Alternate Service Contributing to Maintenance of National Health, Safety, or Interest*]
W2.............. Second Statute of Westminster [*A publication*]   (DSA)
W-2 .... Wage and Tax Statement [*IRS*]
W2.............. William II [*German emperor and king of Prussia, 1888-1918*]   (DSUE)
3W.............. Three-Wire   (MSA)
W3.............. World-Wide Web [*Information service*] [*European Organization for Nuclear Research*]   (ECON)
W-4 .... Employee's Withholding Allowance Certificate [*IRS*]
4W.............. Four-Wire
4-W .... Selective Service Class [*for Conscientious Objector Who Has Completed Alternate Service Contributing to National Health, Safety, or Interest*]
5W.............. Western Samoa [*Aircraft nationality and registration mark*]   (FAAC)
3W1............ Third World First [*An association*] [*British*]
3W's........... [*The*] Who, What, or Where Game [*Also, WWW*] [*Television show*]
3W's........... Worry, Want, and Wickedness [*Causes of insanity, according to Victorian medical theory*]
5W's .... Who, What, When, Where, Why [*Journalism*]
W (Colds)... Whole Colds [*Medicine*]
WA.............. Appleton Public Library, Appleton, WI [*Library symbol*] [*Library of Congress*]   (LCLS)
WA.............. Independent Watchmen's Association
WA.............. Voice of Washington Music [*A publication*]
WA.............. Wabash Railroad Co. [*NYSE symbol*]   (SPSG)
WA.............. Wadsworth Athneneum [*Hartford, CT*]
WA.............. Wage Record [*Social Security Administration*]   (OICC)
WA.............. Wainscot
WA.............. Waiver
WA.............. Walking Association   (EA)
WA.............. War Aims [*British*]
WA.............. Warbirds of America [*Later, WB*] [*An association*]   (EA)
WA.............. Warm Air
W/A .... Warrant of Arrest
Wa.............. Warsaw [*A publication*]
WA.............. Washer
WA.............. Washington [*State*] [*Postal code*]
Wa.............. Washington Reports [*A publication*]   (DLA)
Wa.............. Washington State Library, Olympia, WA [*Library symbol*] [*Library of Congress*]   (LCLS)
WA.............. Wassmer Aviation [*France*] [*ICAO aircraft manufacturer identifier*]   (ICAO)
WA.............. Water Agar [*Microbiology*]
WA.............. Water Authority [*British*]   (DCTA)
WA.............. Watertown Arsenal [*Massachusetts*] [*Army*]
Wa.............. Watts' Reports [*1890-1939*] [*A publication*]   (DLA)
WA.............. Waveform Analyzer
WA.............. Weapon Armourer [*British military*]   (DMA)
WA.............. Weapons Analyst [*British military*]   (DMA)
WA.............. Weapons Assignment   (NVT)
WA.............. Weather Almanac [*A publication*]
WA.............. Weather Atlas of the United States [*A publication*]
WA.............. Wedge Action [*British military*]   (DMA)
WA.............. Weekly Announcements
WA.............. Weighted Average [*Accounting*]
WA.............. Weizmann Israel Archives [*Rehovoth*]   (BJA)
WA.............. Welfare Administration [*Became Social and Rehabilitation Service*] [*HEW*]
WA.............. Wellness Associates   (EA)
Wa.............. Wellsiania [*An association*]   (EA)
WA.............. Weltwirtschaftliches Archiv [*A publication*]
WA.............. West Africa
WA.............. West Africa [*A publication*]
WA.............. Western Airlines, Inc. [*ICAO designator*]
WA.............. Western Allegheny Railroad   (IIA)
WA.............. Western Approaches [*to Great Britain and Ireland*] [*Obsolete*]
WA.............. Western Area
W of A........ [*The*] Western Railway of Alabama
WA.............. [*The*] Western Railway of Alabama [*AAR code*]
WA.............. Westminster Abbey [*London*]
WA.............. When Awake
WA.............. Wide Angle [*Photography*]
WA.............. Will Adjust   (AABC)
wa.............. Will Advise   (HGAA)
WA.............. Williams Act [*1968*]
WA.............. Wire Armored [*Cables*]

WA............. Wire Assembly   (MSA)
WA............. Wire Association [*Later, WAI*]
WA............. With Answers
WA............. With Average [*Insurance*]
WA............. Withholding Agent   (DLA)
WA............. Wohl Associates [*Bala Cynwyd, PA*] [*Telecommunications*]   (TSSD)
WA............. Women's Reserve, Aviation Nonflying Duties [*USNR officer designation*]
WA............. Womenwealth Ambika [*British*]   (EAIO)
WA............. Woolknit Associates   (EA)
WA............. Woolwich Armstrong Gun
WA............. Word Add
WA............. Word After [*Message handling*]
WA............. Work Assignment   (MCD)
WA............. Work Authorization   (MCD)
WA............. Workers Anonymous [*Mythical organization devoted to helping human beings overcome their desire to lead productive lives; created by columnist Arthur Hoppe in satirizing short work week and early retirement schemes*]
WA............. Workmanship Assurance
WA............. Workshop Assembly [*Torpedo*]
WA............. World Archaeology [*A publication*]
WA............. Wright Aeronautical Corp.   (KSC)
WA............. Writing Ability
WA............. Writing Academy   (EA)
WA1.......... Wongan Hills [*Australia*] [*Seismograph station code, US Geological Survey*]   (SEIS)
WA2.......... Wagin [*Australia*] [*Seismograph station code, US Geological Survey*]   (SEIS)
WA3.......... Talbot Brook [*Australia*] [*Seismograph station code, US Geological Survey*]   (SEIS)
W-4A .... Wage Withholding Form [*Revised version*] [*IRS*]
WaA.......... Aberdeen Public Library, Aberdeen, WA [*Library symbol*] [*Library of Congress*]   (LCLS)
WAA......... Wabash Motor Freight Tariff Association, Springfield IL [*STAC*]
WAA......... Wales [*Alaska*] [*Airport symbol*]   (OAG)
WAA......... Wales, AK [*Location identifier*] [*FAA*]   (FAAL)
WAA......... War Assets Administration [*For disposal of US surplus war property*] [*Post-World War II*]
WAA......... Warden's Association of America [*Later, NAAWS*]   (EA)
WAA......... Waris [*Papua New Guinea*] [*Seismograph station code, US Geological Survey*]   (SEIS)
WAA......... Wartime Aircraft Activity   (AFM)
Wa A .... Washington Appellate Reports [*A publication*]   (DLA)
WAA......... Water-Augmented Air Jet
WAA......... Water Authorities Association [*British*]   (ECON)
WAA......... Watermark Association of Artisans   (EA)
WAA......... Welded Aluminum Alloy
WAA......... West Australian Airways   (ADA)
WAA......... Western Amateur Astronomers   (EA)
WAA......... Western Awning Association [*Later, NPEA*]   (EA)
WAA......... Wide-Aperture Array   (MCD)
WAA......... Wien Air Alaska [*Air carrier designation symbol*]
WAA......... Women's Action Alliance   (EA)
WAA......... Worker Adjustment Assistance
WAA......... World Aluminum Abstracts [*Aluminum Association*] [*Information service or system*] [*A publication*]   (IID)
WAA......... World American Airlift   (FAAC)
WAA......... World Atlatl Association   (EA)
WAA......... Writing Assistants' Association [*A union*] [*British*]
WAAA....... Ujung Pandang/Hasanuddin [*Indonesia*] [*ICAO location identifier*]   (ICLI)
WAAA...... Walleye Anglers Association of America [*Defunct*]   (EA)
WAAA...... Western Armenian Athletic Association   (EA)
WAAA...... Winston-Salem, NC [*AM radio station call letters*]
WAAB....... Bau Bau/Betoambari [*Indonesia*] [*ICAO location identifier*]   (ICLI)
WAABI..... National Women's Association of Allied Beverage Industries   (EA)
WAAC...... Valdosta, GA [*FM radio station call letters*]
WAAC...... War Artists' Advisory Committee [*British military*]   (DMA)
WAAC...... West African Airways Corp.
WAAC...... Western Association for Art Conservation   (EA)
WAAC...... Women's Army Auxiliary Corps [*Name later changed to WAC*] [*World War II*]
WAAC...... World Academy of Arts and Culture   (EA)
WAACC's Motor Ind ... WAACC's [*Western Australian Automobile Chamber of Commerce*] Motor Industry [*A publication*]
WAACP...... Western Atlantic Airlift Command Post [*Navy*]   (DNAB)
WAAD...... Westinghouse Air Arm Division
WAADS .... Washington Air Defense Sector [*ADC*]
WAAE...... World Association for Adult Education
WAAF ...... Women's Auxiliary Air Force [*Functioned under direct command of RAF*] [*World War II*] [*British*]
WAAF ...... Worcester, MA [*FM radio station call letters*]
WAAFB...... Walker Air Force Base   (AAG)
WAAG...... Galesburg, IL [*FM radio station call letters*]
WaAG........ Grays Harbor College, Aberdeen, WA [*Library symbol*] [*Library of Congress*]   (LCLS)

WAAG....... Malimpung [*Indonesia*] [*ICAO location identifier*]   (ICLI)
WAAH...... Houghton, MI [*FM radio station call letters*]
WAAI....... Hurlock, MD [*FM radio station call letters*]
WAAI .... Malili [*Indonesia*] [*ICAO location identifier*]   (ICLI)
WAAIC...... Women's Association of the African Independent Churches
WAAJ....... Huntsville, AL [*AM radio station call letters*]
WAAJ........ Mamuju/Tampa Padang [*Indonesia*] [*ICAO location identifier*]   (ICLI)
WAAJ........ Water-Augmented Air Jet
WAAK .... Dallas, NC [*AM radio station call letters*]
WAAL ...... Binghamton, NY [*FM radio station call letters*]
WAAL ...... Ponggaluku [*Indonesia*] [*ICAO location identifier*]   (ICLI)
WaAlVA ... United States Veterans Administration Hospital, American Lake, WA [*Library symbol*] [*Library of Congress*]   (LCLS)
WAAM...... Ann Arbor, MI [*AM radio station call letters*]
WAAM...... Masamba/Andi Jemma [*Indonesia*] [*ICAO location identifier*]   (ICLI)
WAAM...... Wide-Area Antiarmor Munitions [*Military*]   (MCD)
WAAMA ... Woman's Auxiliary to the American Medical Association [*Later, AMAA*]   (EA)
WAAMAC ... Weight, Alignment, and Mass Center Determination Equipment   (AAG)
WAAMMS ... Women's Auxiliary of the American Merchant Marine [*World War II*]
WaAn......... Anacortes Public Library, Anacortes, WA [*Library symbol*] [*Library of Congress*]   (LCLS)
WAAN...... West African Archaeological Newsletter [*A publication*]
WAAN....... Wide-Area AppleTalk Network [*Telecommunications*]
WA Ann LR ... University of Western Australia. Annual Law Review [*A publication*]   (APTA)
WAAO...... Andalusia, AL [*FM radio station call letters*]
WAAP ...... Burlington, NC [*Television station call letters*]
WAAP ...... Kolaka/Pomalaa [*Indonesia*] [*ICAO location identifier*]   (ICLI)
WAAP ...... World Association for Animal Production [*Rome, Italy*]   (EAIO)
WAAPM ... Wide-Area Antipersonnel Mine [*Military*]
WAAQ...... Big Rapids, MI [*FM radio station call letters*]
WAAR ...... Raha/Sugi Manuru [*Indonesia*] [*ICAO location identifier*]   (ICLI)
WAAR ...... Wartime Aircraft Activity Reporting [*System*]
WAAR ...... Western Australian Arbitration Reports [*A publication*]   (APTA)
WA Arb R ... Western Australian Arbitration Reports [*A publication*]   (APTA)
WaArI........ Indian Ridge Treatment Center, Staff Library, Arlington, WA [*Library symbol*] [*Library of Congress*]   (LCLS)
WaArI-R.... Indian Ridge Treatment Center, Resident Library, Arlington, WA [*Library symbol*] [*Library of Congress*]   (LCLS)
WA Art Gall Bull ... Western Australian Art Gallery. Bulletin [*A publication*]   (APTA)
WAAS ...... Columbia, SC [*FM radio station call letters*]
WAAS ...... Soroako [*Indonesia*] [*ICAO location identifier*]   (ICLI)
WAAS ...... Warning and Attack Assessment   (MCD)
WAAS ...... Wide-Area Active Surveillance [*Military*]   (MCD)
WAAS ...... Women's Auxiliary Army Service [*British*]
WAAS ...... World Academy of Art and Science [*Solna, Sweden*]   (EA)
WAASC... Women's Auxiliary Army Service Corps [*British*]
WAAT ...... Makale/Pongtiku [*Indonesia*] [*ICAO location identifier*]   (ICLI)
WAATS...... Weights Analysis for Advanced Transportation Systems [*NASA*]
WaAu........ Auburn Public Library, Auburn, WA [*Library symbol*] [*Library of Congress*]   (LCLS)
WAAU....... Kendari/Wolter Monginsidi [*Indonesia*] [*ICAO location identifier*]   (ICLI)
WaAuG...... Green River Community College, Auburn, WA [*Library symbol*] [*Library of Congress*]   (LCLS)
WAAV ...... Leland, NC [*AM radio station call letters*]
WAAVP... World Association for the Advancement of Veterinary Parasitology [*Thessaloniki, Greece*]   (EAIO)
WAAW...... Williston, SC [*FM radio station call letters*]
WAAX ...... Gadsden, AL [*AM radio station call letters*]
WAAY ...... Huntsville, AL [*Television station call letters*]
WAAZ ...... Crestview, FL [*FM radio station call letters*]
WAAZ ...... Ujung Pandang [*Indonesia*] [*ICAO location identifier*]   (ICLI)
WAB .... Aero Industries, Inc. [*Richmond, VA*] [*FAA designator*]   (FAAC)
WAB .... Wabag [*Papua New Guinea*] [*Seismograph station code, US Geological Survey*]   (SEIS)
WAB .... Wabash Railroad System [*AAR code*] [*Obsolete*]
WAB .... Waffenabwurfbehaelter [*Parachute Weapons Container*] [*German military - World War II*]
WAB .... Wage Adjustment Board [*World War II*]
WAB .... Wage Appeals Board [*Department of Labor*]
WAB .... Water-Activated Battery
WAB .... Weapons Allocation Branch   (SAA)
WAB .... Westamerica Bancorporation [*AMEX symbol*]   (SPSG)
WAB .... Western Actuarial Bureau [*Later, ISO*]   (EA)
WAB .... Western Aphasia Battery [*Neuropsychology test*]
WAB .... When Authorized By
WAB .... Wine Advisory Board [*Later, WAG*]   (EA)

WAB .... Work Allotment Board [*New Deal*]
WAB .... World Association for Buiatrics [*Hanover, Federal Republic of Germany*]   (EAIO)
WABA ...... Aguadilla, PR [*AM radio station call letters*]
WABA ...... Women's American Basketball Association   (EA)
Waban...... Waban, Inc. [*Associated Press abbreviation*]   (APAG)
WABASH VLY ALSA ... Wabash Valley Area Library Services Authority [*Library network*]
WaBB .... Bellevue Community College, Bellevue, WA [*Library symbol*] [*Library of Congress*]   (LCLS)
WABB .... Biak/Frans Kaisiepo [*Indonesia*] [*ICAO location identifier*]   (ICLI)
WABB ...... Mobile, AL [*AM radio station call letters*]
WABB-FM ... Mobile, AL [*FM radio station call letters*]
WABC .... New York, NY [*AM radio station call letters*]
WABCO ... Westinghouse Air Brake Co.
WABC-TV ... New York, NY [*Television station call letters*]
WABD .... Fort Campbell, KY [*AM radio station call letters*]
WABD .... Moanamani [*Indonesia*] [*ICAO location identifier*]   (ICLI)
WABE .... Atlanta, GA [*FM radio station call letters*]
WaBe .... Bellingham Public Library, Bellingham, WA [*Library symbol*] [*Library of Congress*]   (LCLS)
WABE .... Western Allenbee Oil & Gas Co. Ltd. [*NASDAQ symbol*]   (NQ)
WABE .... Western Association of Broadcast Engineers [*Canada*]
WaBeCo..... Whatcom County Public Library, Bellingham, WA [*Library symbol*] [*Library of Congress*]   (LCLS)
WaBeSJ.... Saint Joseph Hospital, Bellingham, WA [*Library symbol*] [*Library of Congress*]   (LCLS)
WaBeSL .... Saint Luke's Hospital, Bellingham, WA [*Library symbol*] [*Library of Congress*]   (LCLS)
WaBeW ..... Western Washington State College [*Later, WWU*], Bellingham, WA [*Library symbol*] [*Library of Congress*]   (LCLS)
WABF........ Fairhope, AL [*AM radio station call letters*]
WABF........ Numfor/Jemburwo [*Indonesia*] [*ICAO location identifier*]   (ICLI)
WaBfM..... Mission Creek Youth Camp, Staff Library, Belfair, WA [*Library symbol*] [*Library of Congress*]   (LCLS)
WaBfM-R ... Mission Creek Youth Camp, Resident Library, Belfair, WA [*Library symbol*] [*Library of Congress*]   (LCLS)
WABG ...... Greenwood, MS [*AM radio station call letters*]
WABG .... Waghete [*Indonesia*] [*ICAO location identifier*]   (ICLI)
WaBGS...... Church of Jesus Christ of Latter-Day Saints, Genealogical Society Library, Bellevue Branch, Bellevue, WA [*Library symbol*] [*Library of Congress*]   (LCLS)
WABG-TV ... Greenwood, MS [*Television station call letters*]
WABH....... Bath, NY [*AM radio station call letters*]
WABI......... Bangor, ME [*AM radio station call letters*]
WABI......... Nabire [*Indonesia*] [*ICAO location identifier*]   (ICLI)
WABI........ Western Australian Biographical Index [*A publication*]   (APTA)
WABI-TV ... Bangor, ME [*Television station call letters*]
WABJ........ Adrian, MI [*AM radio station call letters*]
WABK .... Gardiner, ME [*AM radio station call letters*]
WABK-FM ... Gardiner, ME [*FM radio station call letters*]
WABL....... Amite, LA [*AM radio station call letters*]
WABL....... Ilaga [*Indonesia*] [*ICAO location identifier*]   (ICLI)
WABLC..... Wilmington Area Biomedical Libraries [*Library network*]
WABM....... Birmingham, AL [*Television station call letters*]
WABN....... Abingdon, VA [*FM radio station call letters*]
WABN....... Kokonau [*Indonesia*] [*ICAO location identifier*]   (ICLI)
WABO....... Serui/Sujarwo Condronegoro [*Indonesia*] [*ICAO location identifier*]   (ICLI)
WABO....... Waynesboro, MS [*AM radio station call letters*]
WABO-FM ... Waynesboro, MS [*FM radio station call letters*]
WaBOH..... Overlake Hospital, Medical Library, Bellevue, WA [*Library symbol*] [*Library of Congress*]   (LCLS)
WaBP .... Puget Sound Power and Light Co., Bellevue, WA [*Library symbol*] [*Library of Congress*]   (LCLS)
WABP........ Timika/Tembagapura [*Indonesia*] [*ICAO location identifier*]   (ICLI)
Wa-BPH.... Washington Regional Library for the Blind and Physically Handicapped, Seattle, WA [*Library symbol*] [*Library of Congress*]   (LCLS)
WABQ....... Cleveland, OH [*AM radio station call letters*]
WaBr .... Kitsap Regional Library, Bremerton, WA [*Library symbol*] [*Library of Congress*]   (LCLS)
WABR....... Tifton, GA [*FM radio station call letters*]
WabR........ Wabash Railroad Co. [*Associated Press abbreviation*]   (APAG)
WABR .... West Asia Blocking Ridge [*Meteorology*]
WaBrH ...... Harrison Memorial Hospital, Bremerton, WA [*Library symbol*] [*Library of Congress*]   (LCLS)
WaBrNP.... United States Navy, Puget Sound Naval Shipyard, Engineering Library, Bremerton, WA [*Library symbol*] [*Library of Congress*]   (LCLS)
WaBrNR.... United States Navy, Naval Regional Medical Center, Bremerton, WA [*Library symbol*] [*Library of Congress*]   (LCLS)
WaBrNS.... United States Navy, Naval Submarine Base, Bangor Library, Bremerton, WA [*Library symbol*] [*Library of Congress*]   (LCLS)
WaBrO ...... Olympic College, Bremerton, WA [*Library symbol*] [*Library of Congress*]   (LCLS)

WaBrOC.... Olympic Center, Bremerton, WA [*Library symbol*] [*Library of Congress*] (LCLS)

WABS........ Arlington, VA [*AM radio station call letters*]

WaBS......... Bellevue School District, Instructional Materials Center, Bellevue, WA [*Library symbol*] [*Library of Congress*] (LCLS)

Wabsh........ Wabash National Corp. [*Associated Press abbreviation*] (APAG)

WABSIH... Society for Italic Handwriting, Western American Branch [*Later, WASIH*] (EA)

WABT .... Dundee, IL [*FM radio station call letters*]

WABT .... Enarotali [*Indonesia*] [*ICAO location identifier*] (ICLI)

WABTOC ... When Authorized by the Oversea Commander [*Military*]

WABU .... Biak/Manuhua [*Indonesia*] [*ICAO location identifier*] (ICLI)

WaBucR..... Rainier School, Staff Library, Buckley, WA [*Library symbol*] [*Library of Congress*] (LCLS)

WaBucR-R ... Rainier School, Resident Library, Buckley, WA [*Library symbol*] [*Library of Congress*] (LCLS)

WABV .... Abbeville, SC [*AM radio station call letters*]

WABW ...... Pelham, GA [*Television station call letters*]

WABW ...... Waren [*Indonesia*] [*ICAO location identifier*] (ICLI)

W A'B & W ... Webb, A'Beckett, and Williams' Reports [*A publication*] (APTA)

W A'B & W Eq ... Webb, A'Beckett, and Williams' Equity Reports [*A publication*] (APTA)

W A'B & W IE & M ... Webb, A'Beckett, and Williams' Insolvency, Ecclesiastical, and Matrimonial Reports [*A publication*] (APTA)

W A'B & W Min ... Webb, A'Beckett, and Williams' Mining Cases [*A publication*] (APTA)

WABX .... Clare, MI [*AM radio station call letters*]

WABY .... Albany, NY [*AM radio station call letters*]

WABZ .... Albemarle, NC [*FM radio station call letters*]

WABZ .... Biak [*Indonesia*] [*ICAO location identifier*] (ICLI)

WAC......... Waca [*Ethiopia*] [*Airport symbol*] (OAG)

WAC......... Wake Analysis and Control (MCD)

WAC......... War Assets Corp. [*Post-World War II*] [*Succeeded by War Assets Administration*]

WAC......... Warnaco Group [*NYSE symbol*] (SPSG)

WAC......... Weapon Arming Computer (MCD)

WAC......... Weapons Assignment Console

WAC......... Weber Aircraft Co.

WAC......... Weighted Average Coupon [*Finance*]

WAC......... Wells American Corp. [*AMEX symbol*] (SPSG)

WAC......... Welsh Arts Council (EAIO)

WAC......... West Africa Command [*World War II*]

WAC......... West Africa Committee (EA)

WAC......... Western Archeological Center [*Department of the Interior*] (GRD)

WAC......... Western Athletic Conference (EA)

WAC......... Wide-Open Throttle Air-Conditioning Cut-Off Switch [*Automotive engineering*]

WAC......... Wolfe Angel Committee [*Defunct*] (EA)

WAC......... Women's Advisory Committee [*Trades Union Congress*] [*British*] (DCTA)

WAC......... Women's Aerobic Circuit [*Exercise regimen at some health spas*]

WAC......... Women's Army Corps [*Formerly, WAAC*] [*Abolished, 1978*] (GPO)

WAC......... Women's Auxiliary Corps [*British*] (DAS)

WAC......... Work Accomplishment Code [*Military*] (AFIT)

WAC......... Work Activities Center

WAC......... Work Assignment Card (MCD)

WAC......... Work and Occupations [*A publication*]

WAC......... Worked All Continents [*Contacted at least one station on all continents*] [*Amateur radio*]

WAC......... Working Alternating Current (DEN)

WAC......... World Aeronautical Chart [*Air Force*] [*A publication*] (APTA)

WAC......... World Affairs Center for the United States [*Later, FPA*]

WAC......... World Area Code (MCD)

WAC......... World Assistance Corps [*Paris, France*] (EAIO)

WAC......... Wright Aeronautical Corp. (MCD)

WAC......... Write Address Counter

WACA ...... Ithaca, NY [*Television station call letters*]

WACA ...... Walnut Canyon National Monument

WACA ...... West African Court of Appeal, Selected Judgments [*A publication*] (DLA)

WACA ...... Western Agricultural Chemicals Association (EA)

WACA ...... Winchester Arms Collectors Association (EA)

WACA ...... Women's Apparel Chains Associations (EA)

WACA ...... World Airlines Clubs Association [*Montreal, PQ*] (EAIO)

WACA ...... World Association of Center Associates (EA)

WACAAI... Women's Africa Committee of the African-American Institute (EA)

WACAS..... Wave and Current Advisory Service [*British*]

WACASC.. West African Consolidated Administrative Service Center [*Foreign Service*]

WACB ...... Kittanning, PA [*AM radio station call letters*]

WACB ...... Women's Army Classification Battery (AABC)

WACC ...... Warning and Caution Computer [*Aviation*] (MCD)

WACC ...... Washing Corrosion Control (MCD)

WACC .... Weighted Average Cost of Capital [*Accounting*] (ADA)

WACC .... World Africa Chamber of Commerce (EA)

WACC .... World Association for Christian Communication

WACCC..... Worldwide Air Cargo Commodity Classification (DS)

WACCM ... World Association for Chinese Church Music (EAIO)

WACD....... Alexander City, AL [*AM radio station call letters*]

WACE .... Chicopee, MA [*AM radio station call letters*]

WaCeC ...... Centralia College, Centralia, WA [*Library symbol*] [*Library of Congress*] (LCLS)

WaCeM ..... Maple Lane School, Staff Library, Centralia, WA [*Library symbol*] [*Library of Congress*] (LCLS)

WaCeW ..... Weyerhaeuser Co., Forestry Research Center, Centralia, WA [*Library symbol*] [*Library of Congress*] (LCLS)

WACF....... Paris, IL [*FM radio station call letters*]

WACG....... Augusta, GA [*FM radio station call letters*]

WACH....... Columbia, SC [*Television station call letters*]

WACH....... Wedge Adjustable Cushioned Heel [*Orthopedics*]

WACH....... West African Clearing House [*Sierra Leone*]

WACH....... Worship Arts Clearing House (EA)

WACHA...... Wisconsin Automated Clearing House Association

WaChehG ... Green Hill School, Staff Library, Chehalis, WA [*Library symbol*] [*Library of Congress*] (LCLS)

WaChehYS ... Washington State Twin City Center for Youth Services, Chehalis, WA [*Library symbol*] [*Library of Congress*] (LCLS)

WaChenE .. Eastern Washington State College, Cheney, WA [*Library symbol*] [*Library of Congress*] (LCLS)

Wachovia ... Wachovia Corp. [*Associated Press abbreviation*] (APAG)

WACI .... Atlantic City, NJ [*Television station call letters*]

WACI .... Western Approaches Convoy Instructions [*British military*] (DMA)

WACI .... Women's Army Corps of India [*British military*] (DMA)

WACIID.... Winter Advanced Course for Immunology and Infectious Diseases [*Japan International Friendship and Welfare Foundation*]

WACK .... Newark, NY [*AM radio station call letters*]

WACK .... Wait before Transmitting Positive Acknowledgment

Wackh....... Wackenhut Corp. [*Associated Press abbreviation*] (APAG)

WaCl......... Asotin County Library, Clarkston, WA [*Library symbol*] [*Library of Congress*] (LCLS)

WACL ...... Wacoal Corp. [*Japan*] [*NASDAQ symbol*]

WACL ...... Waycross, GA [*AM radio station call letters*]

WACL ...... Worcester Area Cooperating Libraries [*Worcester, MA*] [*Library network*]

WACL ...... World Anti-Communist League [*South Korea*] (EAIO)

WaClvSC... Spruce Canyon Correctional Center, Staff Library, Colville, WA [*Library symbol*] [*Library of Congress*] (LCLS)

WaClvSC-R ... Spruce Canyon Correctional Center, Resident Library, Colville, WA [*Library symbol*] [*Library of Congress*] (LCLS)

WACM ...... West Springfield, MA [*AM radio station call letters*]

WACM ...... Western Association of Circuit Manufacturers

WACO ...... Waco, TX [*AM radio station call letters*]

WACO ...... Waterman Marine [*NASDAQ symbol*] (NQ)

WACO ...... World Air Cargo Organisation (PDAA)

WACO ...... Written Advice of Contracting Officer [*Military*]

WACO-FM ... Waco, TX [*FM radio station call letters*]

WaCol........ Whitman County Library, Colfax, WA [*Library symbol*] [*Library of Congress*] (LCLS)

WACP .... Western Acceptance Corp. [*NASDAQ symbol*] (NQ)

WACPAC ... Whimsical Alternative Coalition Political Action Committee (EA)

WACQ...... Tallassee, AL [*AM radio station call letters*]

WACQ...... Tuskegee, AL [*FM radio station call letters*]

WACR...... Columbus, MS [*AM radio station call letters*]

WA Craftsman ... Western Australian Craftsman [*A publication*] (APTA)

WACRAL ... World Association of Christian Radio Amateurs and Listeners [*Hull, England*] (EAIO)

WACRAX ... Cocoa Research Institute. Council for Scientific and Industrial Research. Annual Report [*A publication*]

WACRES .. Women's Army Corps Reserve

WACR-FM ... Columbus, MS [*FM radio station call letters*]

WACRI ...... West African Cocoa Research Institution

WACS....... Dawson, GA [*Television station call letters*]

WACS....... Warning and Caution System [*Aviation*] (MCD)

WACS....... Weather Analysis Computer System [*Accu-Weather, Inc.*]

WACS....... West African College of Surgeons [*See also COAC*] [*Nigeria*] (EAIO)

WACS....... Whole Animal Cell Sorting

WACS....... Wire Automated Check System (MCD)

WACS....... Workshop Attitude Control System (MCD)

WACS....... World Association of Cooks Societies (EA)

WACSM..... Women's Army Corps Service Medal [*Military decoration*]

WACT .... Tuscaloosa, AL [*AM radio station call letters*]

WACT-FM ... Tuscaloosa, AL [*FM radio station call letters*]

WACU....... West African Customs Union

WACU....... Western Association of College and University Business Officers (AEBS)

WACV .... Montgomery, AL [*AM radio station call letters*]

WACVA...... Women's Army Corps Veterans Association (EA)

WACX .... Leesburg, FL [*Television station call letters*]

WACY .... Fenton, MI [*AM radio station call letters*]
WACY 2000 ... World Association for Celebrating the Year 2000 [*British*]
WACZ .... Dansville, NY [*FM radio station call letters*]
WAD .... Andriamena [*Madagascar*] [*Airport symbol*]   (OAG)
WAD .... Waddy Lake Resources, Inc. [*Toronto Stock Exchange symbol*]
   [*Vancouver Stock Exchange symbol*]
WAD .... Warta Ekonomi Maritim. Facts and Analysis in
   Communications, Commerce, and Finance [*A publication*]
WAD .... Washington Aqueduct Division [*Army*]
WAD .... Weapon Assignment Display [*Air Force*]
WAD .... Wide-Angle Optics Weapon Assignment Display [*DoD*]
WAD .... Wide-Area Display   (MCD)
WAD .... William Addison Dwiggins [*American type designer and
   illustrator, 1880-1956*]
WAD .... Work Authorization and Delegation
WAD .... Work Authorization Document [*NASA*]
WAD .... World Association of Detectives   (EA)
WAD .... World Aviation Directory [*A publication*]
WAD .... World Wide Military Command Control System Automated
   Data Processing
WAD .... Wright Aeronautical Division [*Curtiss-Wright Corp.*]
WAD .... WWMCCS [*Worldwide Military Command and Control
   System*] Architecture Division
Wa 2d .... Washington State Reports, Second Series [*A
   publication*]   (DLA)
WADA ...... Shelby, NC [*AM radio station call letters*]
WADAAA ... Washington District Army Audit Agency   (MUGU)
WADB .... Point Pleasant, NJ [*FM radio station call letters*]
WADB .... West African Development Bank [*Togo*]   (EA)
WADC ...... Parkersburg, WV [*AM radio station call letters*]
WADC ...... Western Air Defense Command
WADC ...... Wright Air Development Center [*Air Force*]
WADC Tech Rept ... Wright Air Development Center. Technical Report [*A
   publication*]
W ADD ...... With Added [*Freight*]
WADD ...... Wright Air Development Division [*Air Force*]
Wad Dig ..... Waddilove's Digest of Ecclesiastical Cases [*1849*] [*A
   publication*]   (DLA)
WADE .... Wadesboro, NC [*AM radio station call letters*]
WADE .... World Association of Document Examiners   (EA)
Wade Am Mining Law ... Wade on American Mining Law [*A
   publication*]   (DLA)
Wade Attachm ... Wade on Attachment and Garnishment [*A
   publication*]   (DLA)
WADEBR ... Wadebridge [*England*]
Wade Min ... Wade on American Mining Law [*A publication*]   (DLA)
WA Democrat ... West Australian Democrat [*A publication*]   (APTA)
Wade Not... Wade on the Law of Notice [*A publication*]   (DLA)
Wade Retro L ... Wade on Retroactive Laws [*A publication*]   (DLA)
WADEX .... Words and Authors Index [*Computer-produced index*]
WADF ...... Western Air Defense Force
WADFFU ... Women's Association for the Defense of Four Freedoms for
   Ukraine   (EA)
WADH ...... Wadham College [*Oxford University*]   (ROG)
WADI .... Corinth, MS [*FM radio station call letters*]
WADJ....... Somerset, PA [*AM radio station call letters*]
WADK ...... Newport, RI [*AM radio station call letters*]
WADL ...... Mount Clemens, MI [*Television station call letters*]
WADL ...... Wiener Arbeiten zur Deutschen Literatur [*A publication*]
WADL .... Windshear Air Data Loader [*Aviation*]
Wadley Med Bull ... Wadley Medical Bulletin [*A publication*]
WADM ...... Decatur, IN [*AM radio station call letters*]
WADM ...... Wide-Area Defense Missile   (MCD)
Wad Mar & Div ... Waddilove on Marriage and Divorce [*1864*] [*A
   publication*]   (DLA)
WADN...... Concord, MA [*AM radio station call letters*]
WADO...... New York, NY [*AM radio station call letters*]
WADP ...... World Association for Dynamic Psychiatry   (EAIO)
WADR ...... Remsen, NY [*AM radio station call letters*]
WADR ...... Weight Analysis Data Report
WADS ...... Ansonia, CT [*AM radio station call letters*]
WADS ...... Wide-Angle Display System
WADS ...... Wide-Area Data Service [*Data transmission service*]
WAD/SO... Work Authorization Document/Shop Order   (NASA)
Wadsworth Ath Bul ... Wadsworth Atheneum. Bulletin [*A publication*]
WADTF..... Western Atmospheric Deposition Task Force [*Environmental
   Protection Agency*]   (GFGA)
WADU....... Norco, LA [*AM radio station call letters*]
WADU....... Reserve, LA [*FM radio station call letters*]
WADV ...... Lebanon, PA [*AM radio station call letters*]
W Adv .... Wesleyan Advocate [*A publication*]
WADVBS ... World Association of Daily Vacation Bible Schools [*Later,
   VBS*]   (EA)
WADX ...... Trenton, GA [*AM radio station call letters*]
WaE .... Everett Public Library, Everett, WA [*Library symbol*] [*Library
   of Congress*]   (LCLS)
WAE .... Waterkampioen [*A publication*]
WAE .... Weapon Aiming Error
WAE .... When [*or While*] Actually Employed [*Government short jobs*]
WAE .... Wilfred American Educational Corp. [*NYSE symbol*]   (SPSG)
WAE .... Wills and Administration of Estates [*Law*]

WAEA ...... World Airline Entertainment Association
WaEawC.... Canyon View Group Home, East Wenatchee, WA [*Library
   symbol*] [*Library of Congress*]   (LCLS)
WAEB ...... Allentown, PA [*AM radio station call letters*]
WAEB-FM ... Allentown, PA [*FM radio station call letters*]
WAEC .... Atlanta, GA [*AM radio station call letters*]
WAEC .... War Agricultural Executive Committee [*British*]   (DAS)
Wa-Ec .... Washington State Library, Ecology Department, Olympia, WA
   [*Library symbol*] [*Library of Congress*]   (LCLS)
WAEC ...... West African Economic Community [*Ivory Coast, Mali,
   Mauritania, Niger, Senegal, Upper Volta*]   (ASF)
WAEC ...... Wheel at Each Corner [*Automotive engineering*]
WAED ...... Westinghouse Aerospace Electrical Division
WA Ed Circ ... Education Circular. Education Department of Western
   Australia [*A publication*]   (APTA)
WaEdE ...... Edmonds Community College, Edmonds, WA [*Library symbol*]
   [*Library of Congress*]   (LCLS)
WAEDM ... World Association for Emergency and Disaster Medicine
   [*Bristol, England*]   (EAIO)
WA Educ News ... WA Education News. Education Department of Western
   Australia [*A publication*]   (APTA)
WaEE .... Everett Community College, Everett, WA [*Library symbol*]
   [*Library of Congress*]   (LCLS)
WaEG .... Everett General Hospital, Medical Library, Everett, WA
   [*Library symbol*] [*Library of Congress*]   (LCLS)
WA Egg Marketing Board Nletter ... Western Australia. Egg Marketing Board.
   Newsletter [*A publication*]   (APTA)
WaEGS...... Church of Jesus Christ of Latter-Day Saints, Genealogical
   Society Library, Everett, Washington Stake Branch,
   Everett, WA [*Library symbol*] [*Library of
   Congress*]   (LCLS)
WAEJ........ World Association of Esperanto Journalists [*See also TEJA*]
   [*Cittadella, Italy*]   (EAIO)
WaEJP ...... Washington State Office of Juvenile Parole Services, Everett,
   WA [*Library symbol*] [*Library of Congress*]   (LCLS)
WaEl .... Ellensburg Public Library, Ellensburg, WA [*Library symbol*]
   [*Library of Congress*]   (LCLS)
WAEL....... Maricao, PR [*FM radio station call letters*]
WAEL....... Mayaguez, PR [*AM radio station call letters*]
WaElC .... Central Washington State College, Ellensburg, WA [*Library
   symbol*] [*Library of Congress*]   (LCLS)
WAELD..... Wave Electronics [*A publication*]
WA Electr Contract ... WA [*Western Australian*] Electrical Contractor [*A
   publication*]   (APTA)
WAEMA ... Western and English Manufacturers Association [*Denver,
   CO*]   (EA)
WaEp .... Ephrata Public Library, Ephrata, WA [*Library symbol*] [*Library
   of Congress*]   (LCLS)
WAEP....... World Association for Element Building and Prefabrication
   [*Hamburg, Federal Republic of Germany*]   (EAIO)
WAEPA ..... War Agencies Employees Protective Association
WAEPA ..... Worldwide Assurance for Employees of Public Agencies [*Falls
   Church, VA*]   (EA)
WaEPH ..... Providence Hospital, Everett, WA [*Library symbol*] [*Library of
   Congress*]   (LCLS)
WaEpS....... Sunrise Group Home, Ephrata, WA [*Library symbol*] [*Library
   of Congress*]   (LCLS)
WAER ...... Syracuse, NY [*FM radio station call letters*]
WAER .... World Association for Educational Research [*See also AMSE*]
   [*Ghent, Belgium*]   (EAIO)
Waerme Kaeltech ... Waerme- und Kaeltetechnik [*A publication*]
Waerme Stoffuebertrag/Thermo Fluid Dyn ... Waerme- und
   Stoffuebertragung/Thermo and Fluid Dynamics [*A
   publication*]
Waermetech ... Waermetechnik [*A publication*]
WAERSA .. World Agricultural Economics and Rural Sociology Abstracts
   [*A publication*]
WAES........ Workshop on Alternative Energy Strategies
WAEV ...... Savannah, GA [*FM radio station call letters*]
WAEW ...... Crossville, TN [*AM radio station call letters*]
WAEY ...... Princeton, WV [*AM radio station call letters*]
WAEY-FM ... Princeton, WV [*FM radio station call letters*]
WaEYS....... Washington State Center for Youth Services, Everett, WA
   [*Library symbol*] [*Library of Congress*]   (LCLS)
WAEZ .... Milton, WV [*FM radio station call letters*]
WAF .... Wafer   (AAG)
Wa-F.......... Washington State Film Library, Olympia, WA [*Library symbol*]
   [*Library of Congress*]   (LCLS)
WAF .... West Africa [*A publication*]
WAF .... West African Forces [*British military*]   (DMA)
WAF .... Width across Flats   (MSA)
WAF .... Wiring around Frame   (MSA)
WAF .... With All Faults [*i.e., to be sold as is*]
WAF .... Woman Activist Fund   (EA)
WAF .... Women in the Air Force
WAF .... Women's Aglow Fellowship   (EA)
WAF .... Women's Auxiliary Force [*British*] [*World War I*] [*Later,
   Victory Corps*]
WAF .... Word Address Format
WAF .... World Apostolate of Fatima [*The Blue Army*]   (EAIO)
WAF .... Wound Angiogensis Factor [*Biochemistry*]

WAF.......... WTC, Inc. [*AMEX symbol*]   (SPSG)
WAFAH .... West African Federation of Associations for the Advancement of Handicapped Persons [*See also FOAPH*] [*Bamako, Mali*]   (EAIO)
WAFB....... Baton Rouge, LA [*Television station call letters*]
WAFB....... Warren Air Force Base [*Wyoming*]   (AAG)
WAFB....... Whiteman Air Force Base   (SAA)
WAFC........ Clewiston, FL [*AM radio station call letters*]
WAFC........ Wendel Adkins Fan Club   (EA)
WAFC........ West African Fisheries Commission
WAFC........ Western Area Frequency Coordinator
WAFC-FM ... Clewiston, FL [*FM radio station call letters*]
WAF/CP ... Women and Foundations/Corporate Philanthropy   (EA)
WAFE........ Wives of the Armed Forces, Emeritus [*Defunct*]   (EA)
WAFF........ Huntsville, AL [*Television station call letters*]
WAFF........ Wartime Fuel Factors
WAFF........ West African Frontier Force
WAFF........ Wrap-Around Folding Fin   (MCD)
WAFFLE... Wide-Angle Fixed-Field Locating Equipment
WAFG ...... Fort Lauderdale, FL [*FM radio station call letters*]
WAFL........ Milford, DE [*FM radio station call letters*]
W Af LR .... West African Law Reports [*A publication*]   (DLA)
WAFLT Forum ... Washington Association of Foreign Language Teachers. Forum [*A publication*]
WAFM ...... Amory, MS [*FM radio station call letters*]
WaForC..... Clearwater Correctional Center, Staff Library, Forks, WA [*Library symbol*] [*Library of Congress*]   (LCLS)
WaForC-R ... Clearwater Correctional Center, Resident Library, Forks, WA [*Library symbol*] [*Library of Congress*]   (LCLS)
Wa For LR ... Wake Forest Law Review [*A publication*]
WAFP........ Woody Allen's Fall Picture [*Designation reflecting the filmmaker's reluctance to provide information about his movies in advance of their commercial release*] [*See also WASP*]
W Afr .... West Africa [*A publication*]
W AFR....... West Africa
WAFR....... Wrap-Around Fin Rocket   (MCD)
W Afr App ... West African Court of Appeal Reports [*A publication*]   (DLA)
W Africa .... West Africa [*A publication*]
W African Rel ... West African Religion [*A publication*]
W Afr J Arc ... West African Journal of Archaeology [*A publication*]
WA Fruitgrower ... Western Australian Fruitgrower [*A publication*]   (APTA)
WAFS........ Atlanta, GA [*AM radio station call letters*]
WAFS........ Women's Air Force Services [*British military*]   (DMA)
WAFS........ Women's Auxiliary Ferrying Squadron [*Part of Air Transport Command*] [*World War II*]
WAFS........ Women's Auxiliary Fire Service [*British*] [*World War II*]
WAFS........ World Area Forecast System [*Meteorology*]
WaFsWS ... Western State Hospital, Staff Library, Fort Steilacoom, WA [*Library symbol*] [*Library of Congress*]   (LCLS)
WAFT........ Valdosta, GA [*FM radio station call letters*]
WAFT........ Wichita Auditory Fusion Test
WaFtl........ United States Army, Fort Lewis Library System, Grandstaff Library, Fort Lewis, WA [*Library symbol*] [*Library of Congress*]   (LCLS)
WaFW ...... Whatcom Community College, Ferndale, WA [*Library symbol*] [*Library of Congress*]   (LCLS)
WAFWA.... Western Association of Fish and Wildlife Agencies   (EA)
WaFwS ...... Federal Way School District Central Library, Federal Way, WA [*Library symbol*] [*Library of Congress*]   (LCLS)
WAFX....... Suffolk, VA [*FM radio station call letters*]
WAFY....... Middletown, MD [*FM radio station call letters*]
WAG......... Wagon   (MSA)
WAG......... Walgreen Co. [*NYSE symbol*]   (SPSG)
WAG......... Wanganui [*New Zealand*] [*Airport symbol*]   (OAG)
WAG......... Warfare Analysis Group [*Navy*]
WAG......... Water-Alternating Gas [*Petroleum engineering*]
WAG......... Wellsville, Addison & Galeton Railroad Corp. [*AAR code*]
WAG......... Western Australian Green Party [*Political party*]
WAG......... Wiederaufbaugesellschaft fuer die Juedische Bevoelkerung der Bucovina [*A publication*]   (BJA)
WAG......... Wild Aim Guess [*Bowdlerized version*]
WAG......... Wine Appreciation Guild   (EA)
WAG......... Wireless Air Gunner [*British military*]   (DMA)
WAG......... World Agricultural Economics and Rural Sociology Abstracts [*A publication*]
WAG......... World Area Grid   (MCD)
WAG......... Writers' Action Group [*British*]
WAG......... WWMCCS [*Worldwide Military Command and Control System*] Action Group
WAGA...... Atlanta, GA [*Television station call letters*]
WaGaI ...... Intermediate School District 113, Instructional Materials Center, Galvin, WA [*Library symbol*] [*Library of Congress*]   (LCLS)
WAGB....... Wildfowlers' Association of Great Britain
WAGC ...... Centre, AL [*AM radio station call letters*]
WaGc......... Grand Coulee Public Library, Grand Coulee, WA [*Library symbol*] [*Library of Congress*]   (LCLS)
WAGC....... World Amateur Golf Council   (EA)
WAGCOM ... War Game Comparison   (MCD)
WAGE .... Leesburg, VA [*AM radio station call letters*]

WAGE .... Union Women's Alliance to Gain Equality [*Defunct*]   (EA)
WAGEA .... Waste Age [*A publication*]
Wage & Hour Cas BNA ... Wage and Hour Cases. Bureau of National Affairs [*A publication*]
Wage & Hour Rep ... Wage and Hour Reporter [*Bureau of National Affairs*] [*A publication*]   (DLA)
Wage-Price Law and Econ R ... Wage-Price Law and Economics Review [*A publication*]
Wage-Price L & Econ Rev ... Wage-Price Law and Economics Review [*A publication*]
Wage-Pr L ... Wage-Price Law and Economics Review [*A publication*]
WAGE$..... Women Achieving Greater Economic Status [*Commercial firm*]   (EA)
WAGF .... Dothan, AL [*AM radio station call letters*]
WAGFEI ... Women's Action Group on Excision and Infibulation [*British*]   (EAIO)
WAGG....... Birmingham, AL [*AM radio station call letters*]
WAGG....... Western Australia Government Gazette [*A publication*]   (APTA)
Wagga Hist Soc News ... Wagga Wagga and District Historical Society. Newsletter [*A publication*]   (APTA)
WAGGGS ... World Association of Girl Guides and Girl Scouts [*See also AMGE*] [*British*]   (EAIO)
WaGhP...... Purdy Treatment Center for Women, Gig Harbor, WA [*Library symbol*] [*Library of Congress*]   (LCLS)
WAGI .... Gaffney, SC [*FM radio station call letters*]
WAGL .... Lancaster, SC [*AM radio station call letters*]
WAGM....... Presque Isle, ME [*Television station call letters*]
WAGN....... Menominee, MI [*AM radio station call letters*]
Wagner Free Inst Sci Bull Cards ... Wagner Free Institute of Science. Bulletin. Cards [*A publication*]
Wagner Free I Sc Tr ... Wagner Free Institute of Science [*Philadelphia*]. Transactions [*A publication*]
WAGO....... Reading, PA [*AM radio station call letters*]
WA Govt Gaz ... Western Australia Government Gazette [*A publication*]   (APTA)
WAGP .... Beaufort, SC [*FM radio station call letters*]
WAGR....... Lexington, MS [*FM radio station call letters*]
WAGR....... Lumberton, NC [*AM radio station call letters*]
WAGR....... Wald, Arnold, Goldberg, Rushton [*Test*] [*Statistics*]
WAGR....... Western Australian Government Railways   (PDAA)
WAGR....... Wilms Tumor, Aniridia, Genitourinary Abnormalities, and Mental Retardation [*Syndrome*] [*Medicine*]
WAGR....... Windscale Advanced Gas-Cooled Reactor
WAGRO.... Warsaw Ghetto Resistance Organization   (EA)
WAGS .... Bishopville, SC [*AM radio station call letters*]
WAGS .... Weighted Agreement Scores
WAGS .... Wireless Air Gunners School [*British military*]   (DMA)
WAGS .... Worldwide Atmospheric Gravity Wave Study [*Ionospheric physics*]
WAGSO...... Wiener Archiv fuer Geschichte des Slawentums und Osteuropas [*A publication*]
Wag St .... Wagner's Missouri Statutes [*A publication*]   (DLA)
Wag Stat ..... Wagner's Missouri Statutes [*A publication*]   (DLA)
WAGT .... Augusta, GA [*Television station call letters*]
WAGW...... Waynesboro, GA [*FM radio station call letters*]
WAGX....... Manchester, OH [*FM radio station call letters*]
WAGY....... Forest City, NC [*AM radio station call letters*]
WAH .... Wahluke [*Washington*] [*Seismograph station code, US Geological Survey*]   (SEIS)
WAH .... Westair Holding, Inc. [*AMEX symbol*]   (CTT)
WAH .... Womack Army Hospital Medical Library, Fort Bragg, NC [*OCLC symbol*]   (OCLC)
WAH .... Writings on American History [*A publication*]
WAHA....... Wide-Angle High Aperture   (MCD)
WAHC....... West African Health Community   (EA)
WAHC....... World Airlines Hobby Club   (EA)
WAHD ..... Wilson, NC [*FM radio station call letters*]
WaHi .... Washington State Historical Society, Tacoma, WA [*Library symbol*] [*Library of Congress*]   (LCLS)
WA Hist Soc J ... Western Australian Historical Society. Journal and Proceedings [*A publication*]   (APTA)
WAHLC .... World Association for Hebrew Language and Culture   (EAIO)
Wahlco....... Wahlco Environment Systems, Inc. [*Associated Press abbreviation*]   (APAG)
WAHO ...... World Arabian Horse Organization [*Windermere, England*]   (EAIO)
WAHR....... Huntsville, AL [*FM radio station call letters*]
WAHS....... Auburn Hills, MI [*FM radio station call letters*]
WAHS....... World Airline Historical Society   (EA)
WAHT....... Annville-Cleona, PA [*AM radio station call letters*]
WAHVM... World Association for the History of Veterinary Medicine [*Hanover, Federal Republic of Germany*]   (EAIO)
WAI .... Antsohihy [*Madagascar*] [*Airport symbol*]   (OAG)
WAI .... Wairiri [*Glentunnel*] [*New Zealand*] [*Seismograph station code, US Geological Survey*] [*Closed*]   (SEIS)
WAI .... Walk Around Inspection
WAI .... Wall Street Journal. European Edition [*A publication*]
WAI .... Water Absorption Index [*Analytical chemistry*]
WAI .... Water Alcohol Injection   (MCD)
WAI .... Wire Association International   (EA)

WAI.......... Work in America Institute   (EA)
WAIA .... St. Mary's, GA [*FM radio station call letters*]
WAIC .... Springfield, MA [*FM radio station call letters*]
WAICA...... Women's Auxiliary of the ICA [*International Chiropractors Association*]   (EA)
WAID .... Clarksdale, MS [*FM radio station call letters*]
WAID .... Wage and Information Documents [*IRS*]
WAIF........ Cincinnati, OH [*FM radio station call letters*]
WAIF........ World Adoption International Fund
WAIG .... Western Australian Industrial Gazette [*A publication*]   (APTA)
WAIHA...... Warm Autoimmune Hemolytic Anemia [*Medicine*]
WAIJ .... Grantsville, MD [*FM radio station call letters*]
WAIK .... Galesburg, IL [*AM radio station call letters*]
Waikato Univ Antarct Res Unit Rep ... Waikato University. Antarctic Research Unit. Reports [*A publication*]
WAIL........ Key West, FL [*FM radio station call letters*]
WAIM .... Anderson, SC [*AM radio station call letters*]
WAIN .... Columbia, KY [*AM radio station call letters*]
WAIN .... Wainwright Bank & Trust Co. [*NASDAQ symbol*]   (CTT)
WA Ind Gaz ... Western Australian Industrial Gazette [*A publication*]   (APTA)
WA Indus Gaz ... Western Australian Industrial Gazette [*A publication*]   (APTA)
WAIN-FM ... Columbia, KY [*FM radio station call letters*]
Wainoc....... Wainoco Oil Corp. [*Associated Press abbreviation*]   (APAG)
WAIOP ..... Will Accept, If Offered, the Position of _____   (FAAC)
WAIP........ World Association for Infant Psychiatry [*Later, WAIPAD*]   (EA)
WAIPAD... World Association for Infant Psychiatry and Allied Disciplines   (EA)
WAIQ .... Montgomery, AL [*Television station call letters*]
WAIR .... Atlanta, MI [*FM radio station call letters*]
W Air Trans ... World Air Transport Statistics [*A publication*]
WAIS........ Buchtel, OH [*AM radio station call letters*]
WAIS........ Wechsler Adult Intelligence Scale [*Education*]
WAIS........ West Antarctic Ice Sheet [*Geology*]
WAIS-R..... Wechsler Adult Intelligence Scale-Revised [*Test*]
WAIT........ Crystal Lake, IL [*AM radio station call letters*]
WAIT........ Weighted Average Inlet Temperature [*Chemical engineering*]
WAIT........ Woodstock, IL [*FM radio station call letters*]
Wait Act & Def ... Wait's Actions and Defences [*A publication*]   (DLA)
Wait Co...... Wait's New York Annotated Code [*A publication*]   (DLA)
Wait Dig .... Wait's New York Digest [*A publication*]   (DLA)
Wait L & P ... Wait's Law and Practice in New York Justices' Courts [*A publication*]   (DLA)
Wait Pr ...... Wait's New York Practice [*A publication*]   (DLA)
WAITRO... World Association of Industrial and Technological Research Organizations [*Arhus, Denmark*]
WAITS...... Wide Area Information Transfer System [*Data processing*]   (PCM)
Waits Prac ... Wait's New York Practice [*A publication*]   (DLA)
Wait St Pap ... Wait's State Papers of the United States [*A publication*]   (DLA)
Wait Tab Ca ... Wait's New York Table of Cases [*A publication*]   (DLA)
WAIV .... Spring Valley, IL [*FM radio station call letters*]
WAJ.......... Wajima [*Japan*] [*Seismograph station code, US Geological Survey*]   (SEIS)
WAJ.......... Water-Augmented Jet
WAJ.......... World Association of Judges   (EA)
WAJA........ Arso [*Indonesia*] [*ICAO location identifier*]   (ICLI)
WAJA....... Franklin, NC [*AM radio station call letters*]
WAJA....... West African Journal of Archaeology [*A publication*]
WAJB....... Bokondini [*Indonesia*] [*ICAO location identifier*]   (ICLI)
WAJC....... Indianapolis, IN [*FM radio station call letters*]
WAJCSC... W. Alton Jones Cell Science Center, Inc. [*Research center*]   (RCD)
WAJD....... Gainesville, FL [*AM radio station call letters*]
WAJD....... Wak̃de [*Indonesia*] [*ICAO location identifier*]   (ICLI)
WAJE....... West African Journal of Education [*A publication*]
WAJF....... Decatur, AL [*AM radio station call letters*]
WAJI........ Fort Wayne, IN [*FM radio station call letters*]
WAJI........ Sarmi/Orai [*Indonesia*] [*ICAO location identifier*]   (ICLI)
WAJJ .... Jayapura/Sentani [*Indonesia*] [*ICAO location identifier*]   (ICLI)
WAJK....... Kiwirok [*Indonesia*] [*ICAO location identifier*]   (ICLI)
WAJK....... La Salle, IL [*FM radio station call letters*]
WAJL....... Lereh [*Indonesia*] [*ICAO location identifier*]   (ICLI)
WAJL....... Pine Castle-Sky Lake, FL [*AM radio station call letters*]
WAJM....... Mulia [*Indonesia*] [*ICAO location identifier*]   (ICLI)
WAJM...... Palatka, FL [*Television station call letters*]
WAJML...... West Africa Journal of Modern Language [*A publication*]
WAJO ...... Marion, AL [*AM radio station call letters*]
WAJO ...... Oksibil [*Indonesia*] [*ICAO location identifier*]   (ICLI)
WAJR....... Morgantown, WV [*AM radio station call letters*]
WAJR....... Waris [*Indonesia*] [*ICAO location identifier*]   (ICLI)
WAJS....... Senggeh [*Indonesia*] [*ICAO location identifier*]   (ICLI)
WAJU ...... Ubrub [*Indonesia*] [*ICAO location identifier*]   (ICLI)
WAJW...... Wamena [*Indonesia*] [*ICAO location identifier*]   (ICLI)
WAJY....... New Ellenton, SC [*FM radio station call letters*]
WAJZ....... Jayapura Sector [*Indonesia*] [*ICAO location identifier*]   (ICLI)
WAK.......... Ankazoabo [*Madagascar*] [*Airport symbol*]   (OAG)

WAK.......... Wackenhut Corp. [*NYSE symbol*]   (SPSG)
WAK.......... Wait Acknowledge
wak............ Wakashan [*MARC language code*] [*Library of Congress*]   (LCCP)
WAK.......... Wakkanai [*Japan*] [*Seismograph station code, US Geological Survey*]   (SEIS)
WAK.......... Water Analyzer Kit
WAK.......... Wearable Artificial Kidney
WAK.......... Write Access Key
WAKA ...... Akimuga [*Indonesia*] [*ICAO location identifier*]   (ICLI)
WAKA ...... Selma, AL [*Television station call letters*]
Wakayama Med Rep ... Wakayama Medical Reports [*A publication*]
WAKC .... Akron, OH [*Television station call letters*]
WAKD....... Mindiptana [*Indonesia*] [*ICAO location identifier*]   (ICLI)
WAKE .... Bade [*Indonesia*] [*ICAO location identifier*]   (ICLI)
WAKE .... Valparaiso, IN [*AM radio station call letters*]
Wake Forest Intra L Rev ... Wake Forest Intramural Law Review [*A publication*]   (DLA)
Wake Forest L Rev ... Wake Forest Law Review [*A publication*]
Wake For L Rev ... Wake Forest Law Review [*A publication*]
Wake For Univ Dev Nations Monogr Ser Ser II Med Behav Sci ... Wake Forest University. Developing Nations Monograph Series. Series II. Medical Behavioral Science [*A publication*]
Wake For Unive Dev Nations Monogr Ser Ser II Med Behav Sci ... Wake Forest University. Developing Nations Monograph Series. Series II. Medical Behavioral Science [*A publication*]
WaKel........ Kelso Public Library, Kelso, WA [*Library symbol*] [*Library of Congress*]   (LCLS)
WaKeM ..... Mid-Columbia Regional Library, Kennewick, WA [*Library symbol*] [*Library of Congress*]   (LCLS)
WaKenS..... Saint Thomas Seminary, Kenmore, WA [*Library symbol*] [*Library of Congress*]   (LCLS)
WAKG ...... Agats [*Indonesia*] [*ICAO location identifier*]   (ICLI)
WAKG ...... Danville, VA [*FM radio station call letters*]
WAKH....... Abohoy [*Indonesia*] [*ICAO location identifier*]   (ICLI)
WAKH....... McComb, MS [*FM radio station call letters*]
WAKI .... McMinnville, TN [*AM radio station call letters*]
WaKiN....... Northwest College, Kirkland, WA [*Library symbol*] [*Library of Congress*]   (LCLS)
WAKK ...... McComb, MS [*AM radio station call letters*]
WAKK ...... Merauke/Mopah [*Indonesia*] [*ICAO location identifier*]   (ICLI)
WAKM...... Franklin, TN [*AM radio station call letters*]
WAKN...... Primapun [*Indonesia*] [*ICAO location identifier*]   (ICLI)
WAKO...... Lawrenceville, IL [*AM radio station call letters*]
WAKO....... Okaba [*Indonesia*] [*ICAO location identifier*]   (ICLI)
WAKO-FM ... Lawrenceville, IL [*FM radio station call letters*]
WAKP ...... Kepi [*Indonesia*] [*ICAO location identifier*]   (ICLI)
WAKQ ...... Paris, TN [*FM radio station call letters*]
WAKR ...... Akron, OH [*AM radio station call letters*]
WAKS....... Cape Coral, FL [*FM radio station call letters*]
Waksman Inst Microbiol Rutgers Univ Annu Rep ... Waksman Institute of Microbiology. Rutgers University. Annual Report [*A publication*]
WAKT ...... Tanah Merah [*Indonesia*] [*ICAO location identifier*]   (ICLI)
WAKW...... Cincinnati, OH [*FM radio station call letters*]
WAKX...... Duluth, MN [*FM radio station call letters*]
WAKY ...... Greensburg, KY [*AM radio station call letters*]
WAL.......... Chincoteague, VA [*Location identifier*] [*FAA*]   (FAAL)
WAL.......... Lawrence University, Appleton, WI [*Library symbol*] [*Library of Congress*]   (LCLS)
WAL .... Wahlco Environment Systems [*NYSE symbol*]   (SPSG)
wal.............. Walamo [*MARC language code*] [*Library of Congress*]   (LCCP)
Wal .... Waldorf [*Record label*]
WAL .... Wallace [*Idaho*] [*Seismograph station code, US Geological Survey*]   (SEIS)
WAL .... Walloon   (ROG)
WAL .... Walnut   (WGA)
WAL .... Walsh College, Canton, OH [*OCLC symbol*]   (OCLC)
Wa-L.......... Washington State Law Library, Olympia, WA [*Library symbol*] [*Library of Congress*]   (LCLS)
WAL .... Waterloo Resources, Inc. [*Vancouver Stock Exchange symbol*]
WAL .... Watertown Arsenal Laboratory [*Massachusetts*] [*Army*]
WAL .... We Are Lost [*Army*]
WAL .... Weather Almanac [*A publication*]
WAL .... Western Airlines, Inc. [*Facetious translation: What an Airline*]
WAL .... Western Allegheny Railroad Co. [*AAR code*]
WAL .... Western American Literature [*A publication*]
W-AL.......... Westinghouse-Astronuclear Laboratories
WAL .... Wide-Angle Lens
WAL .... World Association of Lawyers   (EA)
WAL .... Wright Aeronautical Laboratories   (MCD)
WALA ...... Mobile, AL [*Television station call letters*]
WALA News ... West African Library Association. News [*A publication*]
WALB....... Albany, GA [*Television station call letters*]
WALB....... Walbro Corp. [*NASDAQ symbol*]   (NQ)
WALC .... West African Lands Committee. Report [*A publication*]   (ILCA)
WALC .... Worldwide Aviation Logistics Conference   (RDA)
Wal Ch....... Walker's Michigan Chancery Reports [*A publication*]   (DLA)
WalCS .... Wallace Computer Services, Inc. [*Associated Press abbreviation*]   (APAG)

WALD ...... Waldbaum, Inc. [*NASDAQ symbol*]   (NQ)
Wald .... Walden [*Record label*]
WALD ...... Walterboro, SC [*FM radio station call letters*]
WALDO .... Wichita Automatic Linear Data Output
WALDO .... Winona Tri College University Library Network [*Library network*]
WALE .... Providence, RI [*AM radio station call letters*]
WALF .... Alfred, NY [*FM radio station call letters*]
Walf Cust... Walford's Laws of the Customs [*1846*] [*A publication*]   (DLA)
Walford's Antiq ... Walford's Antiquarian and Bibliographer [*A publication*]
Walf Part ... Walford's Parties to Actions [*1842*] [*A publication*]   (DLA)
Walf Railw ... Walford on Railways [*2nd ed.*] [*1846*] [*A publication*]   (DLA)
WALG .... Albany, GA [*AM radio station call letters*]
Walgrn ...... Walgreen Co. [*Associated Press abbreviation*]   (APAG)
WALH .... Mountain City, GA [*AM radio station call letters*]
WALI .... Cumberland, MD [*AM radio station call letters*]
Wal Jr .... [*J. W.*] Wallace's United States Circuit Court Reports [*A publication*]   (DLA)
WALK .... Patchogue, NY [*AM radio station call letters*]
Walk .... Walker's Michigan Chancery Reports [*A publication*]   (DLA)
Walk .... Walker's Pennsylvania Reports [*1855-85*] [*A publication*]   (DLA)
Walk .... Walker's Reports [*96, 109 Alabama*] [*A publication*]   (DLA)
Walk .... Walker's Reports [*22-25, 38-51, 72-88 Texas*] [*1-10 Civil Appeals Texas*] [*A publication*]   (DLA)
Walk .... Walker's Reports [*1 Mississippi*] [*A publication*]   (DLA)
Walk Am Law ... Walker's American Law [*A publication*]   (DLA)
Walk Bank L ... Walker's Banking Law [*2nd ed.*] [*1885*] [*A publication*]   (DLA)
Walk Ch..... Walker's Michigan Chancery Reports [*A publication*]   (DLA)
Walk Chanc Rep ... Walker's Michigan Chancery Reports [*A publication*]   (DLA)
Walk Ch Cas ... Walker's Michigan Chancery Reports [*A publication*]   (DLA)
Walk Ch Mich ... Walker's Michigan Chancery Reports [*A publication*]   (DLA)
Walk Com L ... Walker's Theory of the Common Law [*A publication*]   (DLA)
Walk Eq Pl ... Walker's Equity Pleader's Assistant [*A publication*]   (DLA)
Walker ...... Walker's Michigan Chancery Reports [*A publication*]   (DLA)
Walker ...... Walker's Pennsylvania Reports [*1855-85*] [*A publication*]   (DLA)
Walker ...... Walker's Reports [*96, 109 Alabama*] [*A publication*]   (DLA)
Walker ...... Walker's Reports [*22-25, 38-51, 72-88 Texas*] [*1-10 Civil Appeals Texas*] [*A publication*]   (DLA)
Walker ...... Walker's Reports [*1 Mississippi*] [*A publication*]   (DLA)
Walker's Ch R ... Walker's Michigan Chancery Reports [*A publication*]   (DLA)
Walk Exec ... Walker and Elgood's Executors and Administrators [*6th ed.*] [*1926*] [*A publication*]   (DLA)
WALK-FM ... Patchogue, NY [*FM radio station call letters*]
Walk Int..... Walker's Introduction to American Law [*A publication*]   (DLA)
Walk LA Dig ... Walker's Louisiana Digest [*A publication*]   (DLA)
Walk (Mic) Ch ... Walker's Michigan Chancery Reports [*A publication*]   (DLA)
Walk Mich ... Walker's Michigan Chancery Reports [*A publication*]   (DLA)
Walk Michig Rep ... Walker's Michigan Chancery Reports [*A publication*]   (DLA)
Walk Miss ... Walker's Reports [*1 Mississippi*] [*A publication*]   (DLA)
Walk PA .... Walker's Pennsylvania Reports [*1855-85*] [*A publication*]   (DLA)
Walk Pat.... Walker on Patents [*A publication*]   (DLA)
Walk Tex ... Walker's Reports [*22-25, 38-51, 72-88 Texas*] [*1-10 Civil Appeals Texas*] [*A publication*]   (DLA)
Walk Wills ... Walker on Wills [*A publication*]   (DLA)
WALL .... Middletown, NY [*AM radio station call letters*]
Wall .... Wallace's Nova Scotia Reports [*A publication*]   (DLA)
Wall .... Wallace's Supreme Court Reports [*68-90 United States*] [*1863-74*] [*A publication*]   (DLA)
Wall .... Wallace's United States Circuit Court Reports [*A publication*]   (DLA)
WALL .... Wallachian   (ROG)
WALL .... Wallingford [*Municipal borough in England*]
Wall .... Wallis' Irish Chancery Reports [*A publication*]   (DLA)
Wal by L .... Wallis' Irish Chancery Reports, by Lyne [*A publication*]   (DLA)
Wall .... Wallis' Philadelphia Reports [*1855-85*] [*Pennsylvania*] [*A publication*]   (DLA)
WALL .... Walloon   (ROG)
Wallace Jr Rept ... [*J. W.*] Wallace, Junior's, United States Circuit Court Reports [*A publication*]   (DLA)
Wallaces F ... Wallaces Farmer [*A publication*]
Walla Walla Coll Publ ... Walla Walla College. Publications [*A publication*]
Wall CC ..... Wallace's United States Circuit Court Reports [*A publication*]   (DLA)
Wallerstein Lab Commun ... Wallerstein Laboratories. Communications [*A publication*]
Wallerstein Lab Commun Sci Pract Brew ... Wallerstein Laboratories. Communications on the Science and Practice of Brewing [*A publication*]
Wallis........ Wallis' Irish Chancery Reports [*A publication*]   (DLA)
Wallis (Ir).. Wallis' Irish Chancery Reports [*A publication*]   (DLA)
Wallis by L ... Wallis' Irish Chancery Reports, by Lyne [*1776-91*] [*A publication*]   (DLA)

Wallis by Lyne ... Wallis' Irish Chancery Reports, by Lyne [*1766-91*] [*A publication*]   (DLA)
Wall Jr....... [*J. W.*] Wallace's United States Circuit Court Reports [*A publication*]   (DLA)
Wall Jr CC ... [*J. W.*] Wallace's United States Circuit Court Reports [*A publication*]   (DLA)
Wall Lyn.... Wallis' Irish Chancery Reports, by Lyne [*1776-91*] [*A publication*]   (DLA)
Wall Pr ...... Wallace's Principles of the Laws of Scotland [*A publication*]   (DLA)
Wallraf-Richartz Jahr ... Wallraf-Richartz Jahrbuch [*A publication*]
Wall Rep.... Wallace's "The Reporters" [*A publication*]   (DLA)
Wall Rep.... Wallace's Supreme Court Reports [*68-90 United States*] [*A publication*]   (DLA)
Wall SC ..... Wallace's Supreme Court Reports [*68-90 United States*] [*A publication*]   (DLA)
Wall Sen .... [*J. B.*] Wallace's United States Circuit Court Reports [*A publication*]   (DLA)
Wall St J.... Wall Street Journal [*A publication*]
Wall St J East Ed ... Wall Street Journal. Eastern Edition [*A publication*]
Wall St J Midwest Ed ... Wall Street Journal. Midwest Edition [*A publication*]
Wall St Jnl ... Wall Street Journal [*A publication*]
Wall St J Three Star East Ed ... Wall Street Journal. Three Star Eastern Edition [*A publication*]
Wall St R Bk ... Wall Street Review of Books [*A publication*]
Wall Street J Index ... Wall Street Journal Index [*A publication*]
Wall Str J .. Wall Street Journal [*A publication*]
Wall St T ... Wall Street Transcript [*A publication*]
WALM ...... Albion, MI [*AM radio station call letters*]
WalMart ... Wal-Mart Stores, Inc. [*Associated Press abbreviation*]   (APAG)
WALMS.... West African Language Monograph Series [*A publication*]
WALO ...... Humacao, PR [*AM radio station call letters*]
WaLo .... Longview Public Library, Longview, WA [*Library symbol*] [*Library of Congress*]   (LCLS)
WaLoGS.... Church of Jesus Christ of Latter-Day Saints, Genealogical Society Library, Longview Stake Branch, Longview, WA [*Library symbol*] [*Library of Congress*]   (LCLS)
WaLoL....... Lower Columbia College, Longview, WA [*Library symbol*] [*Library of Congress*]   (LCLS)
WALOPT ... Weapons Allocation and Desired Ground-Zero Optimizer [*Military*]
WALP........ Weapons Assignment Linear Program
WALP....... World Association of Law Professors   (EA)
Wal Prin .... Wallace's Principles of the Laws of Scotland [*A publication*]   (DLA)
Walp Rub... Walpole's Rubric of Common Law [*A publication*]   (DLA)
WALR ...... Athens, GA [*FM radio station call letters*]
WALR ...... University of Western Australia. Law Review [*A publication*]
Wa LR....... Washington Law Review [*A publication*]
WALR ...... West African Law Reports [*Gambia, Ghana, and Sierra Leone*] [*A publication*]
WALR ...... Western Australian Law Reports [*A publication*]   (APTA)
WaLrC....... Cedar Creek Youth Camp, Littlerock, WA [*Library symbol*] [*Library of Congress*]   (LCLS)
WALRC Bull ... Western Australia Law Reform Commission. Bulletin [*A publication*]
WALRUS.. Water and Land Resources Use Simulation
WALS........ Walshire Assurance Co. [*NASDAQ symbol*]   (NQ)
WALS........ World Association of Law Students   (EA)
Walsh........ Walsh's Irish Registry Cases [*A publication*]   (DLA)
Walsh's R .. Walsh's American Review [*A publication*]
Wal Sr........ [*J. B.*] Wallace's United States Circuit Court Reports [*A publication*]   (DLA)
Wal Steve J ... Wallace Stevens Journal [*A publication*]
WALT....... Meridian, MS [*AM radio station call letters*]
WALT....... Warning Assessment Logic Terminal [*Air Force*]
WALT....... West's Automatic Law Terminal
Walter....... Walter's Reports [*14-16 New Mexico*] [*A publication*]   (DLA)
Walter Andree Nottbeck Found Sci Rep ... Walter and Andree de Nottbeck Foundation. Scientific Reports [*A publication*]
Walter C .... Walter's Code [*A publication*]   (DLA)
Walter Reed Army Med Cent Prog Notes ... Walter Reed Army Medical Center. Progress Notes [*A publication*]
Walter Reed Gen Hosp Dep Med Prog Notes ... Walter Reed General Hospital. Department of Medicine. Progress Notes [*A publication*]
Walters J ... Walters Art Gallery [*Baltimore*]. Journal [*A publication*]
Walt H & W ... Walton on Husband and Wife [*Scotland*] [*A publication*]   (DLA)
Walt Lim.... Walter's Statute of Limitations [*4th ed.*] [*A publication*]   (DLA)
WALTSTOW ... Walthamstow [*England*]
Walt Whit R ... Walt Whitman Review [*A publication*]
Wal US Rep ... Wallace's United States Reports [*A publication*]   (DLA)
WALV ...... Cleveland, TN [*FM radio station call letters*]
WALX ...... Selma, AL [*FM radio station call letters*]
WALY ...... Bellwood, PA [*FM radio station call letters*]
WALZ....... Machias, ME [*FM radio station call letters*]
WAM........ Ambatondrazaka [*Madagascar*] [*Airport symbol*]   (OAG)
WAM........ Appleton Memorial Hospital, Appleton, WI [*Library symbol*] [*Library of Congress*]   (LCLS)
WAM........ Emirates News Agency [*United Arab Emirates*]   (MENA)

WAM........ Waitress-Actress-Model [*Lifestyle classification*]
WAM........ Walleye Measurements Program
WAM........ Wambrook [*Australia*] [*Seismograph station code, US Geological Survey*] (SEIS)
WAM........ Warburton Minerals [*Vancouver Stock Exchange symbol*]
WAM........ Weapon Allocation Model
WAM........ Weight after Melt [*Metallurgy*]
WAM........ Weighted Average Maturity [*Finance*]
WAM........ Western Apparel Manufacturers Show (ITD)
WAM........ Western Associated Modelers (EA)
WAM........ Wide-Area Mine [*Military*] (MCD)
WAM........ Wiltshire Archaeological Magazine [*A publication*]
WAM........ Wiltshire Archaeological and Natural History Magazine [*A publication*]
WAM........ Women in Advertising and Marketing (EA)
WAM........ Women's Action Movement
WAM........ Words a Minute
WAM........ Working Association of Mothers [*British*] (DI)
WAM........ Worth Analysis Model (IEEE)
wam............ Writer of Accompanying Material [*MARC relator code*] [*Library of Congress*] (LCCP)
WAMA...... Galela/Gamarmalamo [*Indonesia*] [*ICAO location identifier*] (ICLI)
WAMA...... Tampa, FL [*AM radio station call letters*]
WAMA...... Weight after Mars Arrival [*NASA*]
WA Manuf ... West Australian Manufacturer [*A publication*] (APTA)
WA Manufacturer ... West Australian Manufacturer [*A publication*] (APTA)
WaMaS .... Sno-Isle Regional Library, Marysville, WA [*Library symbol*] [*Library of Congress*] (LCLS)
WAMB...... Donelson, TN [*AM radio station call letters*]
WAMB...... Kotamubagu/Mopait [*Indonesia*] [*ICAO location identifier*] (ICLI)
WAMBC ... Westamerica Bancorporation [*Associated Press abbreviation*] (APAG)
WAMB-FM ... Donelson, TN [*FM radio station call letters*]
WAMC...... Albany, NY [*FM radio station call letters*]
WAMC...... Tentena [*Indonesia*] [*ICAO location identifier*] (ICLI)
WAMD...... Hickory Hills, MD [*AM radio station call letters*]
WAMD...... Jailolo/Kuripasai [*Indonesia*] [*ICAO location identifier*] (ICLI)
WAMDII... Wide-Angle, Michelson-Doppler Imaging Interferometer (SSD)
WAME...... Statesville, NC [*AM radio station call letters*]
WaMeH...... Eastern State Hospital, Medical Lake, WA [*Library symbol*] [*Library of Congress*] (LCLS)
WaMeI ...... Interlake School, Staff Library, Medical Lake, WA [*Library symbol*] [*Library of Congress*] (LCLS)
WaMeL ..... Lakeland Village School, Medical Lake, WA [*Library symbol*] [*Library of Congress*] (LCLS)
WaMeP ..... Pine Lodge Correctional Center, Staff Library, Medical Lake, WA [*Library symbol*] [*Library of Congress*] (LCLS)
WaMeP-R ... Pine Lodge Correctional Center, Resident Library, Medical Lake, WA [*Library symbol*] [*Library of Congress*] (LCLS)
WAMF ...... Tallahassee, FL [*FM radio station call letters*]
WAMFLEX ... Wave Momentum Flux Experiment [*National Science Foundation*]
WAMG...... Gallatin, TN [*AM radio station call letters*]
WAMG...... Gorontalo/Jalaluddin [*Indonesia*] [*ICAO location identifier*] (ICLI)
WAMH ..... Amherst, MA [*FM radio station call letters*]
WAMH ..... Tahuna/Naha [*Indonesia*] [*ICAO location identifier*] (ICLI)
WAMI ...... Opp, AL [*AM radio station call letters*]
WAMI ...... Toli Toli/Lalos [*Indonesia*] [*ICAO location identifier*] (ICLI)
WAMI ...... Washington, Alaska, Montana, and Idaho [*Program for states without medical schools*]
WAMI-FM ... Opp, AL [*FM radio station call letters*]
WaMiH ..... Highline Community College, Midway, WA [*Library symbol*] [*Library of Congress*] (LCLS)
WA Mining & Commercial R ... West Australian Mining and Commercial Review [*A publication*] (APTA)
WAMIS..... Watershed Management Information System
WAMJ...... South Bend, IN [*AM radio station call letters*]
WAMK...... Kao/Kuabang [*Indonesia*] [*ICAO location identifier*] (ICLI)
WAMK...... Kingston, NY [*FM radio station call letters*]
WAML...... Laurel, MS [*AM radio station call letters*]
WaMl........ Moses Lake Public Library, Moses Lake, WA [*Library symbol*] [*Library of Congress*] (LCLS)
WAML...... Palu/Mutiara [*Indonesia*] [*ICAO location identifier*] (ICLI)
WAML...... Watertown Arsenal Medical Laboratory [*Massachusetts*] [*Army*]
WAML...... Western Association of Map Libraries (EA)
WAML...... Work Authorization Material List (DNAB)
WAML...... Wright Aero Medical Laboratory [*Air Force*]
WaMlB...... Big Bend Community College, Moses Lake, WA [*Library symbol*] [*Library of Congress*] (LCLS)
WaMlGS ... Church of Jesus Christ of Latter-Day Saints, Genealogical Society Library, Moses Lake Branch, Moses Lake, WA [*Library symbol*] [*Library of Congress*] (LCLS)
WAMM..... Manado/Sam Ratulangi [*Indonesia*] [*ICAO location identifier*] (ICLI)
WAMM..... Women Against Military Madness (EA)
WAMM..... Woodstock, VA [*AM radio station call letters*]

WAMN...... Green Valley, WV [*AM radio station call letters*]
WAMN...... Melangguane [*Indonesia*] [*ICAO location identifier*] (ICLI)
WAMO...... Pittsburgh, PA [*FM radio station call letters*]
WAMOC... Women's Auxiliary to the Military Order of the Cootie (EA)
WAMOD... Wave Motion [*A publication*]
WaMonR... Washington State Reformatory, Monroe, WA [*Library symbol*] [*Library of Congress*] (LCLS)
WaMonT... Twin Rivers Correctional Center, Monroe, WA [*Library symbol*] [*Library of Congress*] (LCLS)
WAMOSCOPE ... Wave-Modulated Oscilloscope
WAMP ...... Poso/Kasigunou [*Indonesia*] [*ICAO location identifier*] (ICLI)
WAMPUM ... Wage and Manpower Process Utilizing Machine [*Bureau of Indian Affairs*]
WAMPUM ... Wartime Availability of Medical Personnel upon Mobilization
WAMQ...... Bada [*Indonesia*] [*ICAO location identifier*] (ICLI)
WAMQ...... Loretto, PA [*AM radio station call letters*]
WAMR...... Morotai/Pitu [*Indonesia*] [*ICAO location identifier*] (ICLI)
WAMR...... Venice, FL [*AM radio station call letters*]
WAMRAC ... World Association of Methodist Radio Amateurs and Clubs
WAMS ..... Weapon Aiming and Mode Selector (MCD)
WAMS ...... Wilmington, DE [*AM radio station call letters*]
WAMS ...... Women's Automotive Maintenance Staff
WAMSTAS ... Wide-Area Mine Seismic Target Acquisition Sensor [*Military*] (MCD)
WAMT ...... Ternate/Babullah [*Indonesia*] [*ICAO location identifier*] (ICLI)
WaMtJF... John Fluke Manufacturing Co., Mountlake Terrace, WA [*Library symbol*] [*Library of Congress*] (LCLS)
WAMTMTS ... Western Area, Military Traffic Management and Terminal Service (AABC)
WaMtv....... Mount Vernon Public Library, Mount Vernon, WA [*Library symbol*] [*Library of Congress*] (LCLS)
WaMtvGS ... Church of Jesus Christ of Latter-Day Saints, Genealogical Society Library, Mount Vernon Branch, Mount Vernon, WA [*Library symbol*] [*Library of Congress*] (LCLS)
WaMtvS .... Skagit Valley College, Mount Vernon, WA [*Library symbol*] [*Library of Congress*] (LCLS)
WAMU...... Washington, DC [*FM radio station call letters*]
WAMU...... Washington Mutual Savings Bank [*NASDAQ symbol*] (NQ)
WAMU...... Wuasa [*Indonesia*] [*ICAO location identifier*] (ICLI)
WAMV...... Amherst, VA [*AM radio station call letters*]
WAMW..... Luwuk/Bubung [*Indonesia*] [*ICAO location identifier*] (ICLI)
WAMW..... Washington, IN [*AM radio station call letters*]
WAMW-FM ... Washington, IN [*FM radio station call letters*]
WAMX...... Ann Arbor, MI [*FM radio station call letters*]
WAMY...... Amory, MS [*AM radio station call letters*]
WAMY...... World Assembly of Muslim Youth [*Riyadh, Saudi Arabia*] (EAIO)
WAMZ...... Louisville, KY [*FM radio station call letters*]
WAMZ...... Menado Sector [*Indonesia*] [*ICAO location identifier*] (ICLI)
WAn.......... Antigo Public Library, Antigo, WI [*Library symbol*] [*Library of Congress*] (LCLS)
WAN......... Wang Laboratories, Inc. [*AMEX symbol*] (SPSG)
WAN......... Wanigan
WAN......... Wanliss Street [*New Britain*] [*Seismograph station code, US Geological Survey*] (SEIS)
WAN......... Western Air Navigation Ltd. [*Australia*]
WAN......... Wide Area Network [*Telecommunications*]
WAN......... Women's Aquatic Network (EA)
WAN......... Women's Royal Australian Naval Service [*World War II*] (DSUE)
WAN......... Work Authorization Number (NASA)
WANA....... Anniston, AL [*AM radio station call letters*]
WANA...... Woodworking Association of North America (EA)
WANAP...... Washington [*DC*] National Airport
WaNasY ... Naselle Youth Camp, Staff Library, Naselle, WA [*Library symbol*] [*Library of Congress*] (LCLS)
WaNasY-R ... Naselle Youth Camp, Resident Library, Naselle, WA [*Library symbol*] [*Library of Congress*] (LCLS)
WA Nat...... Western Australian Naturalist [*A publication*] (APTA)
WANATCA (West Aust Nut & Tree Crop Assoc) Yearb ... WANATCA (West Australian Nut and Tree Crop Association) Yearbook [*A publication*]
WA Naturalist ... Western Australian Naturalist [*A publication*] (APTA)
WANB...... Waynesburg, PA [*AM radio station call letters*]
WANB-FM ... Waynesburg, PA [*FM radio station call letters*]
WANC...... Ticonderoga, NY [*FM radio station call letters*]
WAND...... Decatur, IL [*Television station call letters*]
WAND...... Women and Development Unit (EA)
WAND...... Women's Action for Nuclear Disarmament (EA)
WAND EF ... WAND [*Women's Action for Nuclear Disarmament*] Education Fund (EA)
Wandell ..... Wandell's New York Reports [*A publication*] (DLA)
WANE...... Fort Wayne, IN [*Television station call letters*]
WA News... West Australian News [*A publication*] (APTA)
WANL....... Albany, GA [*AM radio station call letters*]
WANL....... Westinghouse-Astronuclear Laboratories
WANM...... Tallahassee, FL [*AM radio station call letters*]
WANN ..... Annapolis, MD [*AM radio station call letters*]
WANO ...... Pineville, KY [*AM radio station call letters*]
WANO ...... World Association of Nuclear Operators (ECON)

WANQ....... Delmar, NY [*AM radio station call letters*]
WANR....... Warren, OH [*AM radio station call letters*]
WANRDN ... Walter and Andree de Nottbeck Foundation. Scientific Reports [*A publication*]
WANS .... Anderson, SC [*AM radio station call letters*]
WANST..... Wanstead [*England*]
WANT....... Richmond, VA [*AM radio station call letters*]
WANT....... Wantage [*Urban district in England*]
WANT....... Warrant Apprehension Narcotics Team [*In US Marshal Service's "Operation WANT"*]
WANV....... Staunton, VA [*FM radio station call letters*]
WANV....... Waynesboro, VA [*AM radio station call letters*]
WANY....... Albany, KY [*AM radio station call letters*]
WANY-FM ... Albany, KY [*FM radio station call letters*]
WAO.......... Outagamie County Hospital, Appleton, WI [*Library symbol*] [*Library of Congress*] (LCLS)
WaO .... Timberland Regional Library, Olympia, WA [*Library symbol*] [*Library of Congress*] (LCLS)
WAO......... Weapons Assignment Officer [*Air Force*] (AFM)
WAO......... Women's American ORT (EA)
WAOA....... Melbourne, FL [*FM radio station call letters*]
WaOAP..... Washington State Office of Adult Probation and Parole, Olympia, WA [*Library symbol*] [*Library of Congress*] (LCLS)
WaOAr...... State of Washington Department of General Administration, Division of Archives and Records Management, Olympia, WA [*Library symbol*] [*Library of Congress*] (LCLS)
WaOB........ Washington State Department of Public Assistance, Ben Tidball Memorial Library, Olympia, WA [*Library symbol*] [*Library of Congress*] (LCLS)
WAOB....... Winamac, IN [*AM radio station call letters*]
WAOB....... World Agricultural Outlook Board [*Department of Agriculture*] (GFGA)
WAOC....... St. Augustine, FL [*AM radio station call letters*]
WaOE........ Evergreen State College, Olympia, WA [*Library symbol*] [*Library of Congress*] (LCLS)
WaOEd..... Washington State Department of Education, Olympia, WA [*Library symbol*] [*Library of Congress*] (LCLS)
WaOEng.... Washington State Energy Office, Olympia, WA [*Library symbol*] [*Library of Congress*] (LCLS)
WaOGS..... Church of Jesus Christ of Latter-Day Saints, Genealogical Society Library, Olympia Branch, Olympia, WA [*Library symbol*] [*Library of Congress*] (LCLS)
WAOK....... Atlanta, GA [*AM radio station call letters*]
WaOLI...... State of Washington Department of Labor and Industries Libraries, Olympia, WA [*Library symbol*] [*Library of Congress*] (LCLS)
WaOLN.... Washington Library Network, Olympia, WA [*Library symbol*] [*Library of Congress*] (LCLS)
WaONR..... Washington State Department of Natural Resources, Division of Geology and Earth Resources, Olympia, WA [*Library symbol*] [*Library of Congress*] (LCLS)
WAOR....... Niles, MI [*FM radio station call letters*]
WaOrtS ..... Washington Soldiers' Home, Staff Library, Orting, WA [*Library symbol*] [*Library of Congress*] (LCLS)
WaOrtS-R ... Washington Soldiers' Home, Resident Library, Orting, WA [*Library symbol*] [*Library of Congress*] (LCLS)
WAOS....... Austell, GA [*AM radio station call letters*]
WAOS .... Wide-Angle Optical System
WaOSM .... Saint Martin's College, Olympia, WA [*Library symbol*] [*Library of Congress*] (LCLS)
WaOSP...... Saint Peter's Hospital, Olympia, WA [*Library symbol*] [*Library of Congress*] (LCLS)
WaOT........ Washington State Department of Transportation, Olympia, WA [*Library symbol*] [*Library of Congress*] (LCLS)
WaOTC..... Olympia Technical Community College, Olympia, WA [*Library symbol*] [*Library of Congress*] (LCLS)
WAOV....... Vincennes, IN [*AM radio station call letters*]
WAOW....... Wausau, WI [*Television station call letters*]
WAP .... Institute of Paper Chemistry, Appleton, WI [*Library symbol*] [*Library of Congress*] (LCLS)
WAP .... Wandering Atrial Pacemaker [*Cardiology*]
WAP .... Wapentake [*Subdivision of some English shires*]
WAP .... Warner Audio Publishing
W Ap......... Washington Appellate Reports [*A publication*] (DLA)
WAP .... Waste Analysis Plan [*Environmental Protection Agency*] (GFGA)
WAP .... Wax Appearance Point [*Temperature at which waxy substances in fuel start to precipitate*]
WAP .... Weak Anthropic Principle [*Term coined by authors John Barrow and Frank Tipler in their book, "The Anthropic Cosmological Principle"*]
WAP .... Weekly Average Price
WAP .... Weight after Processing [*Metallurgy*]
WAP .... Whey Acidic Protein
WAP .... Wide-Angle Panorama [*Photography*] [*NASA*]
WAP .... Wideband Acoustical Processor (CAAL)
WAP .... Wire Adhesion Promoter
WAP .... Women Against Pornography (EA)
WAP .... Women's Action Program [*HEW*]
WAP .... Work Activity Program

WAP......... Work Analysis Program [*Data processing*] (BUR)
WAP......... Work Assignment Procedure
WAPA....... Amahai [*Indonesia*] [*ICAO location identifier*] (ICLI)
WaPa .... Pasco Public Library, Pasco, WA [*Library symbol*] [*Library of Congress*] (LCLS)
WAPA ...... San Juan, PR [*AM radio station call letters*]
WAPA ...... Western Area Power Administration [*Department of Energy*]
WAPA ...... White American Political Association (EA)
WAP (A).... Work and People (Australia) [*A publication*]
WaPaAp ... Washington State Office of Adult Probation and Parole, Pasco, WA [*Library symbol*] [*Library of Congress*] (LCLS)
WaPaC ...... Columbia Basin College, Pasco, WA [*Library symbol*] [*Library of Congress*] (LCLS)
WaPaGS.... Church of Jesus Christ of Latter-Day Saints, Genealogical Society Library, Pasco Branch, Pasco, WA [*Library symbol*] [*Library of Congress*] (LCLS)
WAPALS .. Workload and Productivity Analysis (MCD)
WA Parent & Cit ... Western Australian Parent and Citizen [*A publication*] (APTA)
WA Parent & Citizen ... Western Australian Parent and Citizen [*A publication*] (APTA)
WA Parl Deb ... Western Australia. Parliamentary Debates [*A publication*] (APTA)
WAPA-TV ... San Juan, PR [*Television station call letters*]
WAPB....... Bula [*Indonesia*] [*ICAO location identifier*] (ICLI)
WAPC....... Banda [*Indonesia*] [*ICAO location identifier*] (ICLI)
WAPC ...... Women's Auxiliary Police Corps [*British*] [*World War II*]
WAPCB.... West African Produce Control Board [*World War II*]
WAPCOS ... Water and Power Development Consultancy Services
WAPD ...... Dobo [*Indonesia*] [*ICAO location identifier*] (ICLI)
WAPD ...... Western Air Procurement District
WAPD ...... Western Australian Parliamentary Debates [*A publication*]
WAPE....... Jacksonville, FL [*FM radio station call letters*]
WAPE....... Mangole [*Indonesia*] [*ICAO location identifier*] (ICLI)
WAPF....... McComb, MS [*AM radio station call letters*]
WAPF....... West African Pharmaceutical Federation [*Lagos, Nigeria*] (EAIO)
WAPG ...... High-Endurance Coast Guard Cutter [*Later, WHEC*] (CINC)
WAPH....... Labuhu/Usman Sadik [*Indonesia*] [*ICAO location identifier*] (ICLI)
WAPI....... Birmingham, AL [*AM radio station call letters*]
WAPI........ Saumlaki [*Indonesia*] [*ICAO location identifier*] (ICLI)
WAPI........ World Aerial Photographic Index [*Meteorology*]
WAPI-FM ... Birmingham, AL [*FM radio station call letters*]
WAPL....... Appleton, WI [*FM radio station call letters*]
WAPL........ Langgur/Dumatubun [*Indonesia*] [*ICAO location identifier*] (ICLI)
WAPL....... Western Aerial Photography Laboratory [*Department of Agriculture*]
WAPLA..... Water, Air, and Soil Pollution [*A publication*]
WaPlP .... Pacific Lutheran University, Parkland, WA [*Library symbol*] [*Library of Congress*] (LCLS)
WAPME.... Writers and Artists for Peace in the Middle East (EA)
WAPN ...... Holly Hill, FL [*FM radio station call letters*]
WAPN ...... Sanana [*Indonesia*] [*ICAO location identifier*] (ICLI)
WAPO ...... Jasper, TN [*AM radio station call letters*]
WAPOA .... Water Power [*England*] [*A publication*]
WaPoN ...... North Olympic Library System, Port Angeles, WA [*Library symbol*] [*Library of Congress*] (LCLS)
WaPoP....... Peninsula College, Port Angeles, WA [*Library symbol*] [*Library of Congress*] (LCLS)
WAPOR .... World Association for Public Opinion Research (EA)
WAPP........ Ambon/Pattimura [*Indonesia*] [*ICAO location identifier*] (ICLI)
WAPP....... Berryville, VA [*FM radio station call letters*]
Wap Pr R ... Waples on Proceedings in Rem [*A publication*] (DLA)
WAPPS ..... Work Aptitude Profile and Practice Set [*Test*]
WAPQ ...... Crestline, OH [*FM radio station call letters*]
WAPR ...... Avon Park, FL [*AM radio station call letters*]
WAPR ...... Namlea [*Indonesia*] [*ICAO location identifier*] (ICLI)
WAPR ...... World Association for Psychosocial Rehabilitation (EAIO)
WAPR ...... World Association for Psychosocial Rehabilitation - US Branch (EA)
WA Primary Princ ... WA Primary Principal. West Australian Primary Principals Association [*A publication*] (APTA)
WA Primary Principal ... West Australian Primary Principals Association [*A publication*] (APTA)
WAPS....... Akron, OH [*FM radio station call letters*]
WAPS....... Selaru [*Indonesia*] [*ICAO location identifier*] (ICLI)
WaPS........ Washington State University, Pullman, WA [*Library symbol*] [*Library of Congress*] (LCLS)
WAPS....... Weighted Airman Promotion System [*Air Force*]
WAPS....... Women of the American Press Service [*Accredited American women war correspondents*] [*World War II*]
WAPS....... World Association of Pathology Societies
WA/PSF.... Work Authorization/Program Status Factor
WaPS-V..... Washington State University, Veterinary Medical Library, Pullman, WA [*Library symbol*] [*Library of Congress*] (LCLS)
WAPT....... Jackson, MS [*Television station call letters*]
WAPT........ Taliabu [*Indonesia*] [*ICAO location identifier*] (ICLI)

WAPT....... Wichita Auditory Processing Test [*Child development test*]
WAPT....... Wild Animal Propagation Trust [*Defunct*]
WAPT....... Work Area Pointer Table [*Data processing*]
WaPuS....... Washington State University, Western Washington Research
 and Extension Center, Puyallup, WA [*Library symbol*]
 [*Library of Congress*] (LCLS)
WAPW...... Atlanta, GA [*FM radio station call letters*]
WAPX...... Clarksville, TN [*FM radio station call letters*]
WAPY ...... Apalachicola, FL [*FM radio station call letters*]
WAPZ....... Ambon Sector [*Indonesia*] [*ICAO location identifier*] (ICLI)
WAPZ....... Wetumpka, AL [*AM radio station call letters*]
WAQ......... Antsalova [*Madagascar*] [*Airport symbol*] (OAG)
WAQE...... Rice Lake, WI [*FM radio station call letters*]
WaQGS ..... Church of Jesus Christ of Latter-Day Saints, Genealogical
 Society Library, Quincy Branch, Quincy, WA [*Library
 symbol*] [*Library of Congress*] (LCLS)
WAQI....... Miami, FL [*AM radio station call letters*]
WAQP...... Saginaw, MI [*Television station call letters*]
WAQQ...... Charlotte, NC [*FM radio station call letters*]
WAQS...... Charlotte, NC [*AM radio station call letters*]
WAQX...... Manlius, NY [*FM radio station call letters*]
WAQX...... Syracuse, NY [*AM radio station call letters*]
WAQY...... East Longmeadow, MA [*AM radio station call letters*]
WAQY...... Springfield, MA [*FM radio station call letters*]
WAQZ....... Milford, OH [*FM radio station call letters*]
WAR......... Warrant
WAR......... Warrenton Railroad Co. [*AAR code*]
WAR......... Warrior Industry Ltd. [*Vancouver Stock Exchange symbol*]
WAR......... Warsaw [*Poland*] [*Seismograph station code, US Geological
 Survey*] (SEIS)
WAR......... Warwickshire (ROG)
WAR......... Wassermann Antigen Reaction [*Test for syphilis*] [*Medicine*]
WAR......... We Are Ridiculous [*Antiwar slogan*]
WAR......... Weapon Accuracy and Results [*Model*] (MCD)
WAR......... West African Regiment [*Military unit*] [*British*]
WAR......... Western Australian Reports [*A publication*] (APTA)
WAR......... White Aryan Resistance (EA)
WAR......... Whiteruthenian American Relief (EA)
WAR......... Wisconsin Academy. Review [*A publication*]
WAR......... With All Risks [*Insurance*]
WAR......... Women Against Rape [*An association*] (EA)
WAR......... Work Acquisition Routine
WAR......... Work Authorization Report [*or Request*] [*NASA*] (MCD)
WAR......... World Administrative Radio Conference for Space
 Communication
WAR......... World Affairs Report [*Database*] [*California Institute of
 International Studies*] [*Information service or
 system*] (CRD)
WARA...... Attleboro, MA [*AM radio station call letters*]
War Adv Att ... Warren's Adventures of an Attorney in Search of Practice [*A
 publication*] (DLA)
WARAMS ... Wartime Alignment of Reserve and Active Medical Systems
WARB...... Covington, LA [*AM radio station call letters*]
WARBA ... Water Resources Bulletin [*A publication*]
War Bell..... Ward on Belligerent and Neutral Powers [*A
 publication*] (DLA)
Warburg & Courtauld Inst Jnl ... Warburg and Courtauld Institute. Journal [*A
 publication*]
WARC...... Meadville, PA [*FM radio station call letters*]
War C........ War Cry [*A publication*]
WARC...... Washington Archaeological Research Center [*Washington State
 University*] [*Research center*] (RCD)
WARC...... Wharton Applied Research Center [*University of Pennsylvania*]
 [*Research center*] (RCD)
WARC...... World Administrative Radio Conference [*Also known as
 IAARC*] [*Takes place every 20 years*] [*Held in 1979 in
 Geneva, Switzerland*] [*International Telecommunications
 Union*]
WARC...... World Alliance of Reformed Churches [*Formed by a merger of
 Alliance of the Reformed Churches throughout the World
 Holding the Presbyterian System and International
 Congregational Council*] (EAIO)
WARCAD ... War Department - Civil Affairs Division [*Obsolete*]
WARCAT ... Workload and Resources Correlation Analysis Technique
 [*Army*]
W Arch ...... Western Architect [*A publication*]
W Arch ...... World Archaeology [*A publication*]
WARC-MAR ... World Administrative Radio Conference for Maritime
 Mobile Telecommunications
WARCO .... War Correspondent (DSUE)
War Cr L.... Warren's Ohio Criminal Law [*A publication*] (DLA)
WARC-ST ... World Administrative Radio Conference for Space
 Telecommunications
WARD...... Pittston, PA [*AM radio station call letters*]
Ward .... Warden's State Reports [*2, 4 Ohio*] [*A publication*] (DLA)
WARD...... Wardship
WARDA .... West Africa Rice Development Association
Ward AW .. Ward's Auto World [*A publication*]
Warden ..... Warden's State Reports [*2, 4 Ohio*] [*A publication*] (DLA)
Warden's Law & Bk Bull ... Warden's Weekly Law and Bank Bulletin [*Ohio*]
 [*A publication*] (DLA)

Warden & Smith ... Warden and Smith's State Reports [*3 Ohio*] [*A
 publication*] (DLA)
War Dept BCA ... United States War Department, Decisions of Board of
 Contract Adjustment [*A publication*] (DLA)
Ward Just .. Ward's Justice of the Peace [*A publication*] (DLA)
Ward Leg... Ward on Legacies [*A publication*] (DLA)
Ward Nat... Ward's Law of Nations [*A publication*] (DLA)
WARDS..... Welfare of Animals Used for Research in Drugs and Therapy
Wards Auto ... Ward's Automotive Reports [*A publication*]
Ward's Bull ... Ward's Bulletin [*A publication*]
Ward & Sm ... Warden and Smith's State Reports [*3 Ohio*] [*A
 publication*] (DLA)
Wards Yrbk ... Ward's Automotive Yearbook [*A publication*]
WaRe......... Renton Public Library, Renton, WA [*Library symbol*] [*Library
 of Congress*] (LCLS)
WARE ...... Ware, MA [*AM radio station call letters*]
Ware .... Ware's United States District Court Reports [*A
 publication*] (DLA)
WARE ...... Water Research [*A publication*]
WAREH .... Wareham [*Municipal borough in England*]
Warehousing Superv Bull ... Warehousing Supervisor's Bulletin [*United
 States*] [*A publication*]
War Emerg Proc Inst Mech Eng ... War Emergency Proceedings. Institution of
 Mechanical Engineers [*A publication*]
WARES..... Workload and Resources Evaluation System [*Navy*]
Ware's CC Rep ... Ware's United States District Court Reports [*A
 publication*] (DLA)
Ware's Rep ... Ware's United States District Court Reports [*A
 publication*] (DLA)
WaRetV ..... Washington Veterans' Home, Medical Library, Retsil, WA
 [*Library symbol*] [*Library of Congress*] (LCLS)
WaRetV-R ... Washington Veterans' Home, Resident Library, Retsil, WA
 [*Library symbol*] [*Library of Congress*] (LCLS)
WaReVG .. Valley General Hospital, Renton, WA [*Library symbol*]
 [*Library of Congress*] (LCLS)
WAREX..... Warrant Issued for Extradite
WARF....... Jasper, AL [*AM radio station call letters*]
WARF....... Warfare (AFM)
WARF...... Wartime Active Replacement Factors (AABC)
WARF....... Wartime Replacement Factors [*DoD*]
WARF...... Weekly Audit Report File [*IRS*]
WARF....... Wide-Aperture Research Facility [*For hurricane detection*]
WARG...... Summit, IL [*FM radio station call letters*]
WARHD... Warhead (AAG)
WARHUD ... Wide-Angle Raster Head-Up Display (MCD)
War Hung ... War on Hunger [*A publication*]
WARI .... Abbeville, AL [*AM radio station call letters*]
WaRi......... Richland Public Library, Richland, WA [*Library symbol*]
 [*Library of Congress*] (LCLS)
WARI .... Wheezing Associated with Respiratory Injections
WaRiAR .... Atlantic Richfield Hanford Co., Richland, WA [*Library symbol*]
 [*Library of Congress*] (LCLS)
WaRiB .... Battelle Memorial Institute, Pacific Northwest Laboratory,
 Richland, WA [*Library symbol*] [*Library of
 Congress*] (LCLS)
WaRiBN .... Battelle-Northwest Hospital, Life Science Library, Richland,
 WA [*Library symbol*] [*Library of Congress*] (LCLS)
WaRiGS .... Church of Jesus Christ of Latter-Day Saints, Genealogical
 Society Library, Richland Branch, Richland, WA [*Library
 symbol*] [*Library of Congress*] (LCLS)
WaRiMC... Mid-Columbia Mental Health Center, Richland, WA [*Library
 symbol*] [*Library of Congress*] (LCLS)
WArI-R...... Indian Ridge Treatment Center, Resident Library, Arlington,
 WA [*Library symbol*] [*Library of Congress*] (LCLS)
WaRit........ Ritzville Public Library, Ritzville, WA [*Library symbol*]
 [*Library of Congress*] (LCLS)
WARK ...... Hagerstown, MD [*AM radio station call letters*]
WARKS..... Warwickshire [*County in England*]
WARLA.... Wide-Aperture Radio Location Array
WARLOCE ... Wartime Lines of Communication, Europe (AABC)
WARLOG ... Wartime Logistics (AABC)
War L St ... Warren's Law Studies [*A publication*] (DLA)
WARM...... Scranton, PA [*AM radio station call letters*]
WARM...... Warranty [*Cost Effectiveness*] Model
WARM...... Weapons Assignment Research Model [*Military*]
WARM...... Wood and Solid Fuel Association of Retailers and
 Manufacturers (EA)
WARM...... York, PA [*FM radio station call letters*]
WARMA ... Waerme [*A publication*]
WARMAPS ... Wartime Manpower Planning System
War Med... War Medicine [*A publication*]
WARMEDY ... Warm, Family Comedy [*Type of television show*]
WARN....... Warner Electric Brake & Clutch Co. [*NASDAQ symbol*] (NQ)
WARN....... Warning (NASA)
WARN....... Weather Amateur Radio Network (NOAA)
WARN....... Women of All Red Nations (EA)
WARN....... Worker Adjustment and Retraining Notification Act [*1988*]
WARNA .... Worker Adjustment and Retraining Notification Act [*1988*]
Warnac ...... Warnaco Group, Inc. [*Associated Press abbreviation*] (APAG)
WarnL........ Warner-Lambert Co. [*Associated Press abbreviation*] (APAG)
WARNORD ... Warning Order [*Military*] (INF)

WARO....... Claremont, VA [*AM radio station call letters*]
War Op...... Warwick's Opinions [*City Solicitor of Philadelphia, PA*] [*A publication*] (DLA)
WARP....... Worldwide Ammunition Reporting Program (NG)
WARP....... Worldwide AUTODIN [*Automatic Digital Information Network*] Restoral Plan (CET)
WARPAC ... Wartime Repair Parts Consumption (MCD)
WARPATH ... World Association to Remove Prejudice Against the Handicapped
War Prof Dut ... Warren. Moral, Social, and Professional Duties of Attorneys and Solicitors [*2nd ed.*] [*1851*] [*A publication*] (DLA)
Warr.......... Warrant [*A document entitling holder to purchase a given issue of stock*] [*Investment term*]
WARR....... Warranty (MSA)
WARR....... Warrenton, NC [*AM radio station call letters*]
WARR....... Water Resources Research [*A publication*]
WARRAMP ... Wartime Requirements for Ammunition, Materiel, and Personnel
WARRC..... Western Aerospace Rescue and Recovery Center [*Air Force*]
WARRF..... Warrior Research Ltd. [*NASDAQ symbol*] (NQ)
WARRT..... Warrant (ROG)
WARRTD ... Warranted (WGA)
Wars.......... [*The*] Jewish Wars [*of Josephus*] [*A publication*] (BJA)
WARS....... Warfare Analysis and Research System [*Navy*]
WARS....... Wide-Area Remote Sensors
WARS....... Worldwide Ammunition Reporting System [*Military*]
Warsaw Agric Univ SGGW-AR Ann Anim Sci ... Warsaw Agricultural University. SGGW-AR [*Szkola Glowna Gospodarstwa Wiejskiego - Akademia Rolnicza*] Annals. Animal Science [*A publication*]
WARSCAP ... Wartime Support Capability
WARSIC ... Water Resources Scientific Information Center [*US Geological Survey*] [*Reston, VA*] [*Database originator*] (IT)
WARSL..... War Reserve Stockage List (MCD)
WART....... Port Orange, FL [*AM radio station call letters*]
WART....... Weighted Average Remaining Term [*Finance*]
WART....... Wenceslaus Anxiety Representation Taxonomy [*Satirical psychology term*]
Warta Geol ... Warta Geologi [*A publication*]
Warta Geol (Kuala Lumpur) ... Warta Geologi (Kuala Lumpur) [*A publication*]
Warth Code ... West Virginia Code [*1899*] [*A publication*] (DLA)
WARU....... Peru, IN [*AM radio station call letters*]
WARU-FM ... Peru, IN [*FM radio station call letters*]
WARV....... Warwick, RI [*AM radio station call letters*]
Warv Abst ... Warvelle on Abstracts of Title [*A publication*] (DLA)
Warv El RP ... Warvelle's Elements of Real Property [*A publication*] (DLA)
Warv V & P ... Warvelle's Vendors and Purchasers of Real Property [*A publication*] (DLA)
WARW..... Cornwall, NY [*AM radio station call letters*]
WARW..... Warwickshire [*County in England*]
WARWICKS ... Warwickshire [*County in England*]
Warwick's Op ... Warwick's Opinions [*City Solicitor of Philadelphia, PA*] [*A publication*] (DLA)
WARWS.... Warwickshire [*County in England*]
WARX....... Hagerstown, MD [*FM radio station call letters*]
WARY....... Valhalla, NY [*FM radio station call letters*]
WaS........... Seattle Public Library, Seattle, WA [*Library symbol*] [*Library of Congress*] (LCLS)
WAs........... Vaughn Public Library, Ashland, WI [*Library symbol*] [*Library of Congress*] (LCLS)
WAS.......... Wadley Southern Railway Co. [*AAR code*] [*Obsolete*]
WAS.......... Wallops Station [*Later, WFC*] [*NASA*]
WAS.......... War at Sea (NVT)
WAS.......... Ward Atmosphere Scale [*Psychology*]
WAS.......... Ware Resources Ltd. [*Vancouver Stock Exchange symbol*]
WAS.......... Warner & Swasey Co., Solon, OH [*OCLC symbol*] (OCLC)
WAS.......... Washington [*District of Columbia*] [*Seismograph station code, US Geological Survey*] [*Closed*] (SEIS)
WAS.......... Washington [*District of Columbia*] [*Airport symbol*] (OAG)
was .... Washo [*MARC language code*] [*Library of Congress*] (LCCP)
WAS......... Waste-Activated Sludge
WAS.......... Waste International [*A publication*]
WAS......... Waynesburg Southern [*AAR code*]
WAS.......... Weapons Alert System [*NORAD*] (MCD)
WAS.......... Weapons Application Study (SAA)
WAS.......... Weekly Arrival Schedule [*Military*] (AFIT)
WAS.......... Wide Analysis Sheet
WAS.......... Wide-Angle Sensor
WAS.......... Wideband Antenna System
WAS.......... Wiskott-Aldrich Syndrome [*Immunology*]
WAS.......... Witchcraft and Sorcery [*A publication*]
WAS.......... Women's Addiction Service [*National Institute of Mental Health*]
WAS.......... Worcester Archaeological Society. Transactions [*A publication*]
WAS.......... Worked All States [*Contacted at least one station in all states*] [*Amateur radio*]
WAS.......... World Animal Science [*Elsevier Book Series*] [*A publication*]
WAS.......... World Aquaculture Society (EA)
WAS.......... World Archaeological Society (EA)
WAS.......... World Around Songs (EA)

WAS.......... World Artifex Society (EAIO)
WAS.......... World Association for Sexology (EA)
WASA....... Havre De Grace, MD [*AM radio station call letters*]
WaSA....... Seattle Art Museum, Seattle, WA [*Library symbol*] [*Library of Congress*] (LCLS)
WASA....... Women's All-Star Association (EA)
WaSAA..... Catholic Archdiocese of Seattle, Archives, Seattle, WA [*Library symbol*] [*Library of Congress*] (LCLS)
WaSAB..... Atomic Bomb Casualty Commission, Seattle, WA [*Library symbol*] [*Library of Congress*] (LCLS)
WASAC..... Working Group of the Army Study Advisory Committee (AABC)
WASAG.... Washington Special Action Group [*National Security Council*]
WASAL..... Wisconsin Academy of Sciences, Arts, and Letters
WASAR..... Wide Application System Adapter
WASB....... Brockport, NY [*AM radio station call letters*]
WaSB........ Pacific Northwest Bibliographic Center, Seattle, WA [*Library symbol*] [*Library of Congress*] (LCLS)
WASB....... Steenkol/Bintuni [*Indonesia*] [*ICAO location identifier*] (ICLI)
WaSBa...... Battelle Human Affairs Research Center, Seattle, WA [*Library symbol*] [*Library of Congress*] (LCLS)
WASBB.... Waerme- und Stoffuebertragung [*A publication*]
WaSBo....... [*The*] Boeing Co., Commercial Airplane Group, Technical Libraries, Seattle, WA [*Library symbol*] [*Library of Congress*] (LCLS)
WaSBo-A... [*The*] Boeing Co., Aerospace Division, Technical Library, Kent, WA [*Library symbol*] [*Library of Congress*] (LCLS)
WASC........ Ransiki/Abresso [*Indonesia*] [*ICAO location identifier*] (ICLI)
WaSC........ Seattle Central Community College, Seattle, WA [*Library symbol*] [*Library of Congress*] (LCLS)
WASC....... Spartanburg, SC [*AM radio station call letters*]
WASC....... West Africa Supply Centre [*World War II*]
WASC....... Western Association of Schools and Colleges (EA)
WASC....... White Anglo-Saxon Catholic
WASC....... Williams Awareness Sentence Completion [*Personality development test*] [*Psychology*]
WASCAL .. Wide-Angle Scanning Array Lens Antenna
WascanaR ... Wascana Review [*A publication*]
WaSC-N .... North Seattle Community College, Seattle, WA [*Library symbol*] [*Library of Congress*] (LCLS)
WaSCO ..... Children's Orthopedic Hospital and Medical Center, Seattle, WA [*Library symbol*] [*Library of Congress*] (LCLS)
WASCO ..... War Safety Council
WaSC-S..... South Seattle Community College, Seattle, WA [*Library symbol*] [*Library of Congress*] (LCLS)
WaSC-Sh... Shoreline Community College, Seattle, WA [*Library symbol*] [*Library of Congress*] [*Obsolete*] (LCLS)
WASD ...... Wide-Angle Self-Destruct (MCD)
WASE........ Fort Knox, KY [*FM radio station call letters*]
WASE........ Kebar [*Indonesia*] [*ICAO location identifier*] (ICLI)
WASE........ Saint Elizabeth Hospital, Appleton, WI [*Library symbol*] [*Library of Congress*] (LCLS)
WASEC..... Warner Amex Satellite Entertainment Co. [*Cable television*]
Waseda Polit Stud ... Waseda Political Studies [*A publication*]
Waseda Pol Studies ... Waseda Political Studies [*A publication*]
WaSelY...... Yakima Valley School, Selah, WA [*Library symbol*] [*Library of Congress*] (LCLS)
WASF........ Fak Fak/Torea [*Indonesia*] [*ICAO location identifier*] (ICLI)
WaSF........ Fircrest School, Staff Library, Seattle, WA [*Library symbol*] [*Library of Congress*] (LCLS)
WASF........ Water Authorities Superannuation Fund [*British*]
WaSFC ...... Firland Correctional Center, Staff Library, Seattle, WA [*Library symbol*] [*Library of Congress*] (LCLS)
WaSFC-R .. Firland Correctional Center, Resident Library, Seattle, WA [*Library symbol*] [*Library of Congress*] (LCLS)
WaSF-R..... Fircrest School, Resident Library, Seattle, WA [*Library symbol*] [*Library of Congress*] (LCLS)
WaSFRC ... Federal Records Center, Seattle, WA [*Library symbol*] [*Library of Congress*] (LCLS)
WASG ...... Atmore, AL [*AM radio station call letters*]
WaSG .... Seattle Genealogical Society, Seattle, WA [*Library symbol*] [*Library of Congress*] (LCLS)
WASGFC .. Western Association of State Game and Fish Commissioners [*Later, Western Association of Fish and Wildlife Agencies*] (EA)
WaSGH ..... Group Health Cooperative of Puget Sound, Medical Library, Seattle, WA [*Library symbol*] [*Library of Congress*] (LCLS)
WaSGS...... Church of Jesus Christ of Latter-Day Saints, Genealogical Society Library, Seattle North Branch, Seattle, WA [*Library symbol*] [*Library of Congress*] (LCLS)
WaSGS...... Good Samaritan Hospital, Seattle, WA [*Library symbol*] [*Library of Congress*] (LCLS)
WaSh .... Shelton Public Library, Shelton, WA [*Library symbol*] [*Library of Congress*] (LCLS)
WaSH........ Virginia Mason Hospital, Medical Library, Seattle, WA [*Library symbol*] [*Library of Congress*] (LCLS)
WASH ...... Washer (AAG)
WASH...... Washington (AAG)
WASH...... Washington, DC [*FM radio station call letters*]
Wash.......... Washington Reports [*A publication*] (DLA)

Wash.......... Washington State Reports [*A publication*]   (DLA)
Wash.......... Washington Territory Reports [*1854-88*] [*A publication*]   (DLA)
WASH....... Washington Trust Bancorp, Inc. [*NASDAQ symbol*]   (NQ)
Wash.......... Washington's Reports [*16-23 Vermont*] [*A publication*]   (DLA)
Wash.......... Washington's Reports [*1, 2 Virginia*] [*A publication*]   (DLA)
Wash.......... Washington's United States Circuit Court Reports [*A publication*]   (DLA)
Wash Actions Health ... Washington Actions on Health [*A publication*]
Wash Admin Code ... Washington Administrative Code [*A publication*]   (DLA)
Wash Admin Reg ... Washington State Register [*A publication*]   (DLA)
Wash Ag Exp ... Washington. Agricultural Experiment Station. Publications [*A publication*]
Wash Agric Exp Stn Bull ... Washington. Agricultural Experiment Station. Bulletin [*A publication*]
Wash Agric Exp Stn Cir ... Washington. Agricultural Experiment Station. Circular [*A publication*]
Wash Agric Exp Stn Stn Circ ... Washington. Agricultural Experiment Station. Station Circular [*A publication*]
Wash Agric Exp Stn Tech Bull ... Washington. Agricultural Experiment Station. Technical Bulletin [*A publication*]
Wash App ... Washington Appellate Reports [*A publication*]   (DLA)
Washb Easem ... Washburn on Easements and Servitudes [*A publication*]   (DLA)
Wash B News ... Washington Bar News [*A publication*]   (DLA)
Washb Real Prop ... Washburn on Real Property [*A publication*]   (DLA)
Wash Bsn J ... Washington Business Journal [*A publication*]
Washburn.. Washburn's Reports [*18-23 Vermont*] [*A publication*]   (DLA)
Washburn Coll Lab N H B ... Washburn College. Laboratory of Natural History. Bulletin [*A publication*]
Washburn L J ... Washburn Law Journal [*A publication*]
Wash Bus L Rpr ... Washington Business Law Reporter [*A publication*]
WaShC ...... Washington Correction Center, Staff Library, Shelton, WA [*Library symbol*] [*Library of Congress*]   (LCLS)
WASHCAP ... Washington Operations Capabilities System
Wash CC.... Washington's United States Circuit Court Reports [*A publication*]   (DLA)
Wash CCR ... Washington's United States Circuit Court Reports [*A publication*]   (DLA)
Wash Co .... Washington County Reports [*Pennsylvania*] [*A publication*]   (DLA)
Wash Co (PA) ... Washington County Reports [*Pennsylvania*] [*A publication*]   (DLA)
Wash Co R ... Washington County Reports [*Pennsylvania*] [*A publication*]   (DLA)
Wash Co Repr ... Washington County Reports [*Pennsylvania*] [*A publication*]   (DLA)
WaSHCR... Fred Hutchinson Cancer Research Center, Seattle, WA [*Library symbol*] [*Library of Congress*]   (LCLS)
WaShC-R .. Washington Correction Center, Resident Library, Shelton, WA [*Library symbol*] [*Library of Congress*]   (LCLS)
Wash Cr L ... Washburn on Criminal Law [*A publication*]   (DLA)
Wash 2d..... Washington Reports, Second Series [*A publication*]   (DLA)
Wash Dec... Washington Decisions [*A publication*]   (DLA)
Wash Dep Ecol State Water Program Bienn Rep ... Washington. Department of Ecology. State Water Program. Biennial Report [*A publication*]
Wash Dep Ecol Tech Rep ... Washington. Department of Ecology. Technical Report [*A publication*]
Wash Dep Ecol Water Supply Bull ... Washington. Department of Ecology. Water Supply Bulletin [*A publication*]
Wash Dep Fish Annu Rep ... Washington. Department of Fisheries. Annual Report [*A publication*]
Wash Dep Fish Fish Res Pap ... Washington. Department of Fisheries. Fisheries Research Papers [*A publication*]
Wash Dep Fish Res Bull ... Washington. Department of Fisheries. Research Bulletin [*A publication*]
Wash Dep Fish Tech Rep ... Washington. Department of Fisheries. Technical Report [*A publication*]
Wash Dep Water Resour Water Supply Bull ... Washington. Department of Water Resources. Water Supply Bulletin [*A publication*]
Wash Dig... Washburn's Vermont Digest [*A publication*]   (DLA)
Wash Div Geol Earth Resour Geol Map ... Washington. Division of Geology and Earth Resources. Geologic Map [*A publication*]
Wash Div Geol Earth Resour Inf Circ ... Washington. Division of Geology and Earth Resources. Information Circular [*A publication*]
Wash Div Mines Geol Bull ... Washington. Department of Natural Resources. Division of Mines and Geology. Bulletin [*A publication*]
Wash Div Mines Geol Inform Circ ... Washington. Department of Conservation. Division of Mines and Geology. Information Circular [*A publication*]
Wash Div Mines Geol Rep Invest ... Washington. Department of Conservation. Division of Mines and Geology. Report of Investigations [*A publication*]
Wash Div Mines Min Rep Invest ... Washington. Division of Mines and Mining. Report of Investigations [*A publication*]
Wash Drug Rev ... Washington Drug Review [*A publication*]
Wash Ease ... Washburn on Easements and Servitudes [*A publication*]   (DLA)

WashEn ..... Washington Energy Co. [*Associated Press abbreviation*]   (APAG)
Wash Fin Rep ... Washington Financial Reports [*A publication*]
Wash Fin Rep (BNA) ... Washington Financial Reports (Bureau of National Affairs) [*A publication*]   (DLA)
Wash Geol Earth Resour Div Bull ... Washington. Department of Natural Resources. Geology and Earth Resources Division. Bulletin [*A publication*]
WashGs ..... Washington Gas Light Co. [*Associated Press abbreviation*]   (APAG)
Wash GSB ... Washington. Geological Survey. Bulletin [*A publication*]
Wash & Haz PEI ... Washburton and Hazard's Reports [*Prince Edward Island, Canada*] [*A publication*]   (DLA)
Wash Health Costs Let ... Washington Health Costs Letter [*A publication*]
Wash His Q ... Washington Historical Quarterly [*A publication*]
Wash His S ... Washington State Historical Society. Publications [*A publication*]
Wash Hist Q ... Washington Historical Quarterly [*A publication*]
WaSHi....... Seattle Historical Society, Seattle, WA [*Library symbol*] [*Library of Congress*]   (LCLS)
Washington Acad Sci Jour ... Washington Academy of Sciences. Journal [*A publication*]
Washington Dept Water Resources Water Supply Bull ... Washington. Department of Water Resources. Water Supply Bulletin [*A publication*]
Washington Div Mines and Geology Bull ... Washington. Division of Mines and Geology. Bulletin [*A publication*]
Washington Div Mines and Geology Geol Map ... Washington. Division of Mines and Geology. Geologic Map [*A publication*]
Washington Div Mines and Geology Inf Circ ... Washington. Division of Mines and Geology. Information Circular [*A publication*]
Washington and Lee L Rev ... Washington and Lee Law Review [*A publication*]
Washington L Rev ... Washington Law Review [*A publication*]
Washington M ... Washington Monthly [*A publication*]
Washington Univ L Quart ... Washington University. Law Quarterly [*A publication*]
WaShIR..... ITT Rayonier, Inc., Olympic Research Center, Shelton, WA [*Library symbol*] [*Library of Congress*]   (LCLS)
Wash Journ Rev ... Washington Journalism Review [*A publication*]
Wash Jur ... Washington Jurist [*A publication*]   (DLA)
Wash Law Re ... Washington Law Review [*A publication*]
Wash Law Rep ... Washington Law Reporter [*District of Columbia*] [*A publication*]   (DLA)
Wash Laws ... Laws of Washington [*A publication*]
Wash and Lee LR ... Washington and Lee Law Review [*A publication*]
Wash & Lee L Rev ... Washington and Lee Law Review [*A publication*]
Wash Legis Serv ... Washington Legislative Service (West) [*A publication*]   (DLA)
Wash Legis Serv (West) ... Washington Legislative Service (West) [*A publication*]
Wash LR.... Washington Law Review [*A publication*]
Wash LR (Dist Col) ... Washington Law Reporter (District of Columbia) [*A publication*]   (DLA)
Wash L Rep ... Washington Law Reporter [*District of Columbia*] [*A publication*]   (DLA)
Wash L Rev ... Washington Law Review [*A publication*]
Wash M ..... Washington Monthly [*A publication*]
Wash Med Ann ... Washington Medical Annals [*A publication*]
WASHMIC ... Washington Military Industrial Complex
Wash Mon ... Washington Monthly [*A publication*]
Wash News Beat ... Washington News Beat [*A publication*]
Wash Nurse ... Washington Nurse [*A publication*]
WASHO.... Western Association of State Highway Officials
Wash Post ... Washington Post [*A publication*]
Wash Prop L Rpr ... Washington Property Law Reporter [*A publication*]
Wash Public Policy Notes ... Washington Public Policy Notes [*A publication*]
Wash PUR ... Washington Public Utility Commission Reports [*A publication*]   (DLA)
Wash Q...... Washington Quarterly [*A publication*]
Wash Rep .. Washington Report [*A publication*]
Wash Rep Med Health ... Washington Report on Medicine and Health [*A publication*]
Wash Rev Code ... Revised Code of Washington [*A publication*]   (DLA)
Wash Rev Code Ann ... Revised Code of Washington Annotated [*A publication*]
Wash Rev Code Ann ... Washington Revised Code, Annotated [*A publication*]   (DLA)
Wash RP.... Washburn on Real Property [*A publication*]   (DLA)
Wash SBA ... Washington State Bar Association. Proceedings [*A publication*]
Wash St ..... Washington State Reports [*A publication*]   (DLA)
Wash State Coll Agric Exp Stn Tech Bull ... Washington State College. Washington Agricultural Experiment Station. Institute of Agricultural Sciences. Technical Bulletin [*A publication*]
Wash State Coll Research Studies ... Washington State College. Research Studies [*A publication*]
Wash State Council Highway Research Eng Soils Manual ... Washington State. Council for Highway Research Engineering. Soils Manual [*A publication*]
Wash State Dent J ... Washington State Dental Journal [*A publication*]

Wash State For Prod Inst Bull New Wood Use Ser ... Washington State Forest Products Institute. Bulletins. New Wood-Use Series [*A publication*]
Wash State Hortic Assoc Proc ... Proceedings. Washington State Horticultural Association [*A publication*]
Wash State Inst Technol Circ ... Washington State Institute of Technology. Circular [*A publication*]
Wash State Inst Technology Bull ... Washington State Institute of Technology. Bulletin [*A publication*]
Wash State Inst Technol Tech Rep ... Washington State Institute of Technology. Technical Report [*A publication*]
Wash State J Nurs ... Washington State Journal of Nursing [*A publication*]
Wash State Univ Agric Exp Stn Tech Bull ... Washington State University. Agricultural Experiment Station. Institute of Agricultural Sciences. Technical Bulletin [*A publication*]
Wash State Univ Agric Res Cent Res Bull ... Washington State University. Agricultural Research Center. Research Bulletin [*A publication*]
Wash State Univ Coll Agric Res Cent Bull ... Washington State University. College of Agriculture. Research Center. Bulletin [*A publication*]
Wash State Univ Coll Agric Res Cent Tech Bull ... Washington State University. College of Agriculture. Research Center. Technical Bulletin [*A publication*]
Wash State Univ Coll Eng Bull ... Washington State University. College of Engineering. Bulletin [*A publication*]
Wash State Univ Coll Eng Circ ... Washington State University. College of Engineering. Circular [*A publication*]
Wash State Univ Coop Serv Ext Bull ... Washington State University. Cooperative Extension Service. Extension Bulletin [*A publication*]
Wash State Univ Ext Ser Ext Bull ... Washington State University. Extension Service. Extension Bulletin [*A publication*]
Wash State Univ Ext Serv EM ... Washington State University. Extension Service. EM [*A publication*]
Wash State Univ Int Symp Particleboard Proc ... Washington State University. International Symposium on Particleboard. Proceedings [*A publication*]
Wash State Univ Publ Geol Sci ... Washington State University. Publications in Geological Sciences [*A publication*]
Wash State Univ Symp Particleboard Proc ... Washington State University. Symposium on Particleboard. Proceedings [*A publication*]
Wash St G An Rp ... Washington State Geologist. Annual Report [*A publication*]
Wash St Reg ... Washington State Register [*A publication*]
WASH T.... Washington Territory (ROG)
Wash T ...... Washington Territory Opinions [*1854-64*] [*A publication*] (DLA)
Wash T ...... Washington Territory Reports [*1854-88*] [*A publication*] (DLA)
Wash Ter ... Washington Territory Opinions [*1854-64*] [*A publication*] (DLA)
Wash Ter ... Washington Territory Reports [*1854-88*] [*A publication*] (DLA)
Wash Ter NS ... Allen's Washington Territory Reports, New Series [*A publication*] (DLA)
Wash Terr ... Washington Territory Opinions [*1854-64*] [*A publication*] (DLA)
Wash Terr ... Washington Territory Reports [*1854-88*] [*A publication*] (DLA)
WASHTO ... Western Association of State Highway and Traffic Officials
Wash Ty .... Washington Territory Opinions [*1854-64*] [*A publication*] (DLA)
Wash Ty .... Washington Territory Reports [*1854-88*] [*A publication*] (DLA)
Wash UJ Urb & Contemp L ... Washington University. Journal of Urban and Contemporary Law [*A publication*] (DLA)
Wash U L Q ... Washington University. Law Quarterly [*A publication*]
Wash UL Rev ... Washington University. Law Review [*A publication*] (DLA)
Wash Univ Bull ... Washington University. Bulletin [*A publication*]
Wash Univ Dent J ... Washington University. Dental Journal [*A publication*]
Wash Univ Dep Geol Sci Abstr Res ... Washington University. Department of Geological Sciences. Abstracts of Research [*A publication*]
Wash Univ Pub G ... Washington University. Publications in Geology [*A publication*]
Wash Univ St Hum Ser ... Washington University. Studies. Humanistic Series [*A publication*]
Wash Univ St Sci Ser ... Washington University. Studies. Scientific Series [*A publication*]
Wash Univ Stud Lang & Lit ... Washington University. Studies. Language and Literature [*A publication*]
Wash Univ Stud Sci & Tech ... Washington University. Studies. Science and Technology [*A publication*]
Wash Univ Stud Sci & Tech NS ... Washington University. Studies. Science and Technology. New Series [*A publication*]
Wash Univ Stud Social & Philos Sci ... Washington University. Studies. Social and Philosophical Sciences [*A publication*]
Wash Univ Stud Social & Philos Sci NS ... Washington University. Studies. Social and Philosophical Sciences. New Series [*A publication*]
Wash VA ... Washington's Reports [*1, 2 Virginia*] [*A publication*] (DLA)

WASI........ Inanwatan [*Indonesia*] [*ICAO location identifier*] (ICLI)
WASI........ Whimbey Analytical Skills Inventory [*Educational test*]
WASIA...... Women's Armed Services Integration Act of 1948
WaSIF .... International Fisheries Commission, Seattle, WA [*Library symbol*] [*Library of Congress*] (LCLS)
WASIH ..... Western American Society for Italic Handwriting [*Formerly, WABSIH*] (EA)
WASK........ Kaimana (Utarom) [*Indonesia*] [*ICAO location identifier*] (ICLI)
WaSK .... King County Medical Society, Seattle, WA [*Library symbol*] [*Library of Congress*] (LCLS)
WASK........ Lafayette, IN [*AM radio station call letters*]
WaSKC...... King County Library System, Seattle, WA [*Library symbol*] [*Library of Congress*] (LCLS)
WASK-FM ... Lafayette, IN [*FM radio station call letters*]
WASL........ Dyersburg, TN [*FM radio station call letters*]
WAsM .... Memorial Medical Center, Health Sciences Library, Ashland, WI [*Library symbol*] [*Library of Congress*] (LCLS)
WASM .... Merdei [*Indonesia*] [*ICAO location identifier*] (ICLI)
WaSM .... Mountaineers, Inc., Seattle, WA [*Library symbol*] [*Library of Congress*] (LCLS)
WASM ...... White Anglo-Saxon Male
Wasmann J Biol ... Wasmann Journal of Biology [*A publication*]
WASME.... World Assembly of Small and Medium Enterprises [*See also AMPME*] [*India*] (EAIO)
WAsN........ Northland College, Ashland, WI [*Library symbol*] [*Library of Congress*] (LCLS)
WasN......... Washington National Corp. [*Associated Press abbreviation*] (APAG)
WASNA .... Western Apicultural Society of North America (EA)
WaSNH..... Northwest Hospital, Effie M. Storey Learning Center, Seattle, WA [*Library symbol*] [*Library of Congress*] (LCLS)
WaSnqE..... Echo Glen Children's Center, Staff Library, Snoqualmie, WA [*Library symbol*] [*Library of Congress*] (LCLS)
WaSnqE-R ... Echo Glen Children's Center, Resident Library, Snoqualmie, WA [*Library symbol*] [*Library of Congress*] (LCLS)
WASO .... Babo [*Indonesia*] [*ICAO location identifier*] (ICLI)
WASO .... Women's Association for Symphony Orchestras [*Later, AMSO*] (EA)
WASOG .... World Association on Sarcoidosis and Other Granulomatous Disorders (EAIO)
WASP........ Brownsville, PA [*AM radio station call letters*]
WASP........ MARINALG International, World Association of Seaweed Processors (EA)
WaSp .... Spokane Public Library, Spokane, WA [*Library symbol*] [*Library of Congress*] (LCLS)
WASP........ Wait-and-See Parsing [*Data processing*] (BYTE)
WASP........ War Air Service Program [*Department of Commerce*]
WASP........ Water, Air, and Soil Pollution [*A publication*]
WASP........ Water Spectrum [*A publication*]
WASP........ Water and Steam Program [*NASA*]
WASP........ Weather-Atmospheric Sounding Projectile [*Research rocket*]
WASP........ Weber Advanced Spatial Perception Test [*Vocational guidance test*]
WASP........ Weed-Activated Spray Process [*Agriculture*]
WASP........ Weightless Analysis Sounding Probe [*NASA*]
WASP........ Westinghouse Advanced Systems Planning Group
WASP........ White Anglo-Saxon Protestant
WASP........ White Appalachian Southern Protestant [*Chicago slang*]
WASP........ White Ashkenazi Sabra with Pull [*Israeli variation on White Anglo-Saxon Protestant*]
WASP........ Wide Antiarmor Minimissile (MCD)
WASP........ Williams Aerial Systems Platform [*One-man flying platform*]
WASP........ Wind-Assisted Ship Propulsion (DS)
WASP........ Window Atmosphere Sounding Projectile [*NASA*]
WASP........ Women's Airforce Service Pilots [*World War II*]
WASP........ Woody Allen's Spring Picture [*Designation reflecting the filmmaker's reluctance to provide information about his movies in advance of their commercial release*] [*See also WAFP*]
WASP........ Work Activity Sampling Plan
WASP........ Workshop Analysis and Scheduling Programming
WASP........ World Association of Societies of Pathology - Anatomic and Clinical (EA)
WASP........ World Associations for Social Psychiatry (EA)
WASP........ Wrap-Around Simulation Program [*Military*] (CAAL)
WASPA..... White Anglo-Saxon Protestant Ambulatory [*Extension of WASP; indicates the necessity of being able-bodied as an additional requirement for success*]
WASPB..... Water Spectrum [*A publication*]
WaSpBM... United States Bureau of Mines, Mining Research Center, Spokane, WA [*Library symbol*] [*Library of Congress*] (LCLS)
WaSpBMW ... United States Bureau of Mines, Western Field Operations Center, Spokane, WA [*Library symbol*] [*Library of Congress*] (LCLS)
WaSPC...... Seattle Pacific College, Seattle, WA [*Library symbol*] [*Library of Congress*] (LCLS)
WaSpCN ... Center for Nursing Education, Spokane, WA [*Library symbol*] [*Library of Congress*] (LCLS)

WaSpCo..... Spokane County Library, Spokane, WA [*Library symbol*] [*Library of Congress*] (LCLS)

WaSpD ...... Deaconess Hospital, School of Nursing, Spokane, WA [*Library symbol*] [*Library of Congress*] (LCLS)

WaSPe....... Perkins, Coie, Stone, Olsen & Williams, Seattle, WA [*Library symbol*] [*Library of Congress*] (LCLS)

WaSpG ...... Gonzaga University, Spokane, WA [*Library symbol*] [*Library of Congress*] (LCLS)

WaSpGL.... Church of Jesus Christ of Latter-Day Saints, Genealogical Society Library, Spokane Branch, Spokane, WA [*Library symbol*] [*Library of Congress*] (LCLS)

WaSpG-L .. Gonzaga University, Law Library, Spokane, WA [*Library symbol*] [*Library of Congress*] (LCLS)

WaSpGS.... United States Geological Survey, Spokane, WA [*Library symbol*] [*Library of Congress*] (LCLS)

WaSpH...... Holy Family Hospital, Spokane, WA [*Library symbol*] [*Library of Congress*] (LCLS)

WaSPH ..... United States Public Health Service Hospital, Medical Service Library, Seattle, WA [*Library symbol*] [*Library of Congress*] (LCLS)

WaSpHiE .. Eastern Washington State Historical Society, Museum Library, Spokane, WA [*Library symbol*] [*Library of Congress*] (LCLS)

WaSpIn...... Intermediate School District 101, Professional Materials Library, Spokane, WA [*Library symbol*] [*Library of Congress*] (LCLS)

WaSpJ .... Jesuit Archives of the Province of Oregon, Spokane, WA [*Library symbol*] [*Library of Congress*] (LCLS)

WaSpJP .... Washington State Office of Juvenile Parole Services, Spokane, WA [*Library symbol*] [*Library of Congress*] (LCLS)

WaSpJS..... Jesuit Scholastic Library, Spokane, WA [*Library symbol*] [*Library of Congress*] (LCLS)

WaSPM..... Providence Hospital, Medical Library and Learning Resource Center, Seattle, WA [*Library symbol*] [*Library of Congress*] (LCLS)

WaSpM ..... Spokane County Medical Library, Spokane, WA [*Library symbol*] [*Library of Congress*] (LCLS)

WaSpMF... Murphey Favre, Inc., Spokane, WA [*Library symbol*] [*Library of Congress*] (LCLS)

WaSpN ...... Fort Wright College, Spokane, WA [*Library symbol*] [*Library of Congress*] (LCLS)

WASP-NN ... White Anglo-Saxon Protestant Native Born of Native Parents

WaSPoD.... Population Dynamics, Seattle, WA [*Library symbol*] [*Library of Congress*] (LCLS)

Was Polit ... Waseda Political Studies [*A publication*]

WaSpPS .... Spokane Public Schools, Curriculum Library, Spokane, WA [*Library symbol*] [*Library of Congress*] (LCLS)

WASPRU.. West African Stored Products Research Unit

WaSPS ...... Seattle Public Schools, Library Technical Service, Seattle, WA [*Library symbol*] [*Library of Congress*] (LCLS)

WaSpS....... Spokane Community College, Spokane, WA [*Library symbol*] [*Library of Congress*] (LCLS)

WASPS ..... Women's Agricultural Security Production Service [*British military*] (DMA)

WASPS ..... Women's Auxiliary Service Platoon

WaSpSF .... Spokane Falls Community College, Spokane, WA [*Library symbol*] [*Library of Congress*] (LCLS)

WaSpSH.... Sacred Heart Medical Center, Spokane, WA [*Library symbol*] [*Library of Congress*] (LCLS)

WaSpSL .... Saint Luke's Hospital, Spokane, WA [*Library symbol*] [*Library of Congress*] (LCLS)

WaSpSL .... Spokane County Law Library, Spokane, WA [*Library symbol*] [*Library of Congress*] (LCLS)

WaSpStM ... Saint Michael's Institute, Spokane, WA [*Library symbol*] [*Library of Congress*] (LCLS)

WaSpVA.... United States Veterans Administration Hospital, Spokane, WA [*Library symbol*] [*Library of Congress*] (LCLS)

WaSpW ..... Whitworth College, Spokane, WA [*Library symbol*] [*Library of Congress*] (LCLS)

WASPWWII ... Women Airforce Service Pilots WWII (EA)

WaSpYS .... Washington State Center for Youth Services, Spokane, WA [*Library symbol*] [*Library of Congress*] (LCLS)

WASR....... Manokwari/Rendani [*Indonesia*] [*ICAO location identifier*] (ICLI)

WASR....... Wolfeboro, NH [*AM radio station call letters*]

WaSS......... Schick's Schadel Hospital, Medical Library, Seattle, WA [*Library symbol*] [*Library of Congress*] (LCLS)

WASS........ Sorong/Jefman [*Indonesia*] [*ICAO location identifier*] (ICLI)

Wass .... Wassermann [*Test for syphilis*]

WASS........ Wavefront Analysis of Spatial Sampling [*Aircraft landing approach*]

WASS........ Wide-Angle Sun Seekers (SAA)

WASS........ Wide-Area Active Surveillance System [*Military*] (MCD)

WaSSB ...... Washington State Office for the Services for the Blind, Seattle, WA [*Library symbol*] [*Library of Congress*] (LCLS)

Wasser- Energiewirt ... Wasser- und Energiewirtschaft [*A publication*]

Wasser Luft Betr ... Wasser, Luft, und Betrieb [*A publication*]

Wasserwirtsch-Wassertech ... Wasserwirtschaft-Wassertechnik [*A publication*]

Wasserwirt-Wassertech ... Wasserwirtschaft-Wassertechnik [*A publication*]

WaSSh....... Shoreline Community College, Seattle, WA [*Library symbol*] [*Library of Congress*] (LCLS)

WaSSH...... Swedish Hospital Medical Center, Seattle, WA [*Library symbol*] [*Library of Congress*] (LCLS)

WASSM .... WWMCCS [*Worldwide Military Command and Control System*] ADP [*Automatic Data Processing*] System Security Manager (MCD)

W Assn Map Lib Inf Bull ... Western Association of Map Libraries. Information Bulletin [*A publication*]

WASSO...... WWMCCS [*Worldwide Military Command and Control System*] ADP [*Automatic Data Processing*] System Security Officer (MCD)

WASSP ..... Wallingford Storm Sewer Package [*Hydraulics Research*] [*Software package*] (NCC)

WASSP ..... Wire Arc Seismic Section Profiler

WaSSW ..... Shannon & Wilson, Inc., Seattle, WA [*Library symbol*] [*Library of Congress*] (LCLS)

Wasswirt Wasstech ... Wasserwirtschaft-Wassertechnik [*A publication*]

WAST....... Teminabuan [*Indonesia*] [*ICAO location identifier*] (ICLI)

Waste......... Waste Management, Inc. [*Associated Press abbreviation*] (APAG)

WASTE ..... Wisdom, Acclaim, and Status through Expenditures [*Fictional government agency in book "Alice in Blunderland"*]

WASTE ..... World Association for Solid Waste Transfer and Exchange

Waste Disposal Water Manage Aust ... Waste Disposal and Water Management in Australia [*A publication*] (APTA)

Waste Dispos Water Manage Aust ... Waste Disposal and Water Management in Australia [*A publication*]

Waste Disp Recyc Bull ... Waste Disposal and Recycling Bulletin [*A publication*]

WaSteM .... McNeil Island Correction Center, Steilacoom, WA [*Library symbol*] [*Library of Congress*] (LCLS)

Waste Manage ... Waste Management [*A publication*]

Waste Manage Pap ... Waste Management Paper [*London*] [*A publication*]

Waste Mgmt Inf Bull ... Waste Management Information Bulletin [*A publication*]

Waste Mgmt Res ... Waste Management Research [*A publication*]

Wastes Eng ... Wastes Engineering [*A publication*]

Wastes Mgmt ... Wastes Management [*A publication*]

WastMI ..... Waste Management International [*Associated Press abbreviation*] (APAG)

WASU ...... Boone, NC [*FM radio station call letters*]

WaSU .... Seattle University, Seattle, WA [*Library symbol*] [*Library of Congress*] (LCLS)

WaSUN ..... United Nursing Homes, Seattle, WA [*Library symbol*] [*Library of Congress*] (LCLS)

WASV........ Asheville, NC [*Television station call letters*]

WaSVA..... United States Veterans Administration Hospital, Seattle, WA [*Library symbol*] [*Library of Congress*] (LCLS)

WASW ...... Wasior [*Indonesia*] [*ICAO location identifier*] (ICLI)

WASWC.... World Association of Soil and Water Conservation (EA)

WaSWG .... West Seattle General Hospital, Seattle, WA [*Library symbol*] [*Library of Congress*] (LCLS)

WASZ........ Ashland-Lineville, AL [*FM radio station call letters*]

WaT .... Tacoma Public Library, Tacoma, WA [*Library symbol*] [*Library of Congress*] (LCLS)

WAT........ University of Waterloo Library [*UTLAS symbol*]

WAT .... Water [*Automotive engineering*]

Wat .... Watermeyer's Cape Of Good Hope Supreme Court Reports [*1857*] [*South Africa*] [*A publication*] (DLA)

WAT .... Watertown Free Public Library, Watertown, MA [*OCLC symbol*] (OCLC)

WAT .... Watheroo [*Australia*] [*Seismograph station code, US Geological Survey*] [*Closed*] (SEIS)

WAT .... Watheroo [*Australia*] [*Later, GNA*] [*Geomagnetic observatory code*]

WAT .... Weapons Assignment Technician (AFM)

WAT......... Web Action Time (MCD)

WAT .... Weight, Altitude, and Temperature (IEEE)

WAT .... Weight Average Temperature [*Chemical engineering*]

WAT .... Wet Anode Tantalum

WAT .... What Acronym's That? [*A publication*] (APTA)

WAT .... White Adipose Tissue [*Physiology*]

WAT .... Wide-Angle Tail [*Galactic radio source*]

WAT .... Wideband Adapter Transformer

WAT .... Word Association Test [*Psychology*]

WAT's .... Wide-Angle [*Galilean*] Telescopes

WATA ...... Boone, NC [*AM radio station call letters*]

WATA ...... Wisconsin Automatic Test Apparatus

WATA ...... World Association of Travel Agencies (EAIO)

WaTAC .... Allenmore Community Hospital, Tacoma, WA [*Library symbol*] [*Library of Congress*] (LCLS)

WaTAH..... United States Army [*Madigan*] General Hospital, Tacoma, WA [*Library symbol*] [*Library of Congress*] (LCLS)

Wat Aust ... Water in Australia [*A publication*] (APTA)

WATB ...... South Yarmouth, MA [*FM radio station call letters*]

WATBOL ... Waterloo COBOL [*Common Business-Oriented Language*] [*University of Waterloo*] [*Canada*]

Wat Bull.... Water Bulletin [*A publication*]

WATC ...... Atlanta, GA [*Television station call letters*]

WATC .... [*The*] Washington Terminal Co. [*AAR code*]

WATC ....   Western Australian Tourism Commission
WATC ....   Women's Ambulance and Transportation Corps
WaTCC......   Tacoma Community College, Tacoma, WA [*Library symbol*] [*Library of Congress*]   (LCLS)
Wat CGH...   Watermeyer's Cape Of Good Hope Reports [*South Africa*] [*A publication*]   (DLA)
WaTCH .....   Mary Bridge Children's Health Center, Tacoma, WA [*Library symbol*] [*Library of Congress*]   (LCLS)
WATCH ....   Watchers Against Television Commercial Harrassment [*Student legal action organization*]
WATCH ....   Working Group on the Assessment of Toxic Chemicals [*British*]
WATCH ....   World Against Toys Causing Harm
WATCIM ...   Waterloo Centre for Integrated Manufacturing [*University of Waterloo*] [*Canada*] [*Research center*]   (RCD)
WaTCJ ......   Cascadia Juvenile Diagnostic Center, Tacoma, WA [*Library symbol*] [*Library of Congress*]   (LCLS)
Wat Con ...   Watkins on Conveyancing [*9th ed.*] [*1845*] [*A publication*]   (DLA)
Wat Cop.....   Watkins on Copyholds [*6th ed.*] [*1829*] [*A publication*]   (DLA)
Wat Cr Dig ...   Waterman's Criminal Digest [*United States*] [*A publication*]   (DLA)
Wat Cr Proc ...   Waterman's Criminal Procedure [*A publication*]   (DLA)
WaTD ....   Doctors Hospital, Tacoma, WA [*Library symbol*] [*Library of Congress*]   (LCLS)
WATD ....   Marshfield, MA [*FM radio station call letters*]
WATDOC ...   Water Resources Document Reference Centre [*Canadian Department of Fisheries and the Environment*] [*Database*]   (IID)
WATE ....   Knoxville, TN [*Television station call letters*]
WA Teachers J ...   Western Australian Teachers' Journal [*A publication*]   (APTA)
WA Teach J ...   Western Australian Teachers' Journal [*A publication*]   (APTA)
WATER.....   Women's Alliance for Theology, Ethics, and Ritual   (EA)
Water Air Soil Pollut ...   Water, Air, and Soil Pollution [*A publication*]
Water Am Inst Chem Eng ...   Water. American Institute of Chemical Engineers [*A publication*]
Water A S P ...   Water, Air, and Soil Pollution [*A publication*]
Water Biol Syst ...   Water in Biological Systems [*A publication*]
Water Electrolyte Metab Proc Symp ...   Water and Electrolyte Metabolism. Proceedings of the Symposium [*A publication*]
Water E & M ...   Water Engineering and Management [*A publication*]
Water Eng ...   Water and Wastes Engineering [*A publication*]
WATERF ..   Waterford [*County in Ireland*]   (ROG)
WATERFD ...   Waterford [*County in Ireland*]
Water Invest Mich Geol Surv Div ...   Water Investigation. Michigan Geological Survey Division [*A publication*]
Water Law Newsl ...   Water Law Newsletter [*United States*] [*A publication*]
Water Manage News ...   Water Management News [*A publication*]
Water Manage Techn Rep Colorado State Univ ...   Colorado State University. Water Management Technical Report [*A publication*]
Watermeyer ...   Watermeyer's Cape Of Good Hope Reports [*South Africa*] [*A publication*]   (DLA)
Water Poll Abstr ...   Water Pollution Abstracts [*A publication*]
Water Poll Cont Fed J ...   Water Pollution Control Federation. Journal [*A publication*]
Water Poll Control Fed J ...   Water Pollution Control Federation. Journal [*A publication*]
Water Pollut Abstr ...   Water Pollution Abstracts [*A publication*]
Water Pollut Contr Fed J ...   Water Pollution Control Federation. Journal [*A publication*]
Water Pollut Control ...   Water Pollution Control [*A publication*]
Water Pollut Control (Don Mills Can) ...   Water and Pollution Control (Don Mills, Canada) [*A publication*]
Water Pollut Control (London) ...   Water Pollution Control (London) [*A publication*]
Water Pollut Control Res Ser ...   Water Pollution Control Research Series [*A publication*]
Water Pollut Res Can ...   Water Pollution Research in Canada [*A publication*]
Water Pollut Res (Stevenage) ...   Water Pollution Research (Stevenage) [*A publication*]
Water Purif Liquid Wastes Treat ...   Water Purification and Liquid Wastes Treatment [*Japan*] [*A publication*]
Water Qual Instrum ...   Water Quality Instrumentation [*A publication*]
Water Res ..   Water Research [*A publication*]
Water Res Cent Notes Water Res ...   Water Research Centre. Notes on Water Research [*A publication*]
Water Res Found Aust Annu Rep Balance Sheet ...   Water Research Foundation of Australia Ltd. Annual Report and Balance Sheet [*A publication*]
Water Res Found Aust Bull ...   Water Research Foundation of Australia Ltd. Bulletin [*A publication*]
Water Res Found Aust Lted Ann Rep Balance Sheet ...   Water Research Foundation of Australia Ltd. Annual Report and Balance Sheet [*A publication*]
Water Res Found of Aust Newsl ...   Water Research Foundation of Australia Ltd. Newsletter [*A publication*]   (APTA)
Water Res Found Aust Rep ...   Water Research Foundation of Australia Ltd. Report [*A publication*]   (APTA)
Water Res Inst W Va Univ Inf Rep ...   Water Research Institute. West Virginia University. Information Report [*A publication*]

Water Res News ...   Water Research News [*A publication*]
Water Resour ...   Water Resources [*A publication*]
Water Resour Bull ...   Water Resources Bulletin [*A publication*]
Water Resour Bull Nev Div Water Resour ...   Water Resources Bulletin. Nevada Division of Water Resources [*A publication*]
Water Resour Bull (PR) ...   Water Resources Bulletin (Puerto Rico) [*A publication*]
Water Resources Res ...   Water Resources Research [*A publication*]
Water Resour Circ Arkansas Geol Comm ...   Water Resources Circular. Arkansas Geological Commission [*A publication*]
Water Resour (Engl Transl Vodnye Resursy) ...   Water Resources (English Translation of Vodnye Resursy) [*A publication*]
Water Resour Invest ...   Water Resources Investigations [*A publication*]
Water Resour Invest US Geol Surv ...   Water Resources Investigations. United States Geological Survey [*A publication*]
Water Resour J Econ Soc Comm Asia Pac ...   Water Resources Journal. Economic and Social Commission for Asia and the Pacific [*A publication*]
Water Resour Manag Ser ...   Water Resource Management Series [*A publication*]
Water Resour Newsl ...   Water Resources Newsletter [*A publication*]   (APTA)
Water Resour Reconnaissance Ser Nev Div Water Resour ...   Water Resources. Reconnaissance Series. Nevada Division of Water Resources [*A publication*]
Water Resour Rep Ariz State Land Dep ...   Water Resources Report. Arizona State Land Department [*A publication*]
Water Resour Rep Ont Minist Environ Water Resour Branch ...   Water Resources Report. Ontario Ministry of the Environment. Water Resources Branch [*A publication*]
Water Resour Res ...   Water Resources Research [*A publication*]
Water Resour Res Cent VA Polytech Inst State Univ Bull ...   Water Resources Research Center. Virginia Polytechnic Institute and State University. Bulletin [*A publication*]
Water Resour Rev Streamflow Ground-Water Cond ...   Water Resources Review for Streamflow and Ground-Water Conditions [*United States - Canada*] [*A publication*]
Water Resour Ser Tenn Div Water Resour ...   Water Resources Series. Tennessee Division of Water Resources [*A publication*]
Water Resour Symp ...   Water Resources Symposium [*A publication*]
Water Res R ...   Water Resources Research [*A publication*]
Water (S Afr) ...   Water (South Africa) [*A publication*]
Water and San ...   Water and Sanitation [*A publication*]
Water Sanit ...   Water and Sanitation [*A publication*]
Water Sanit Eng ...   Water and Sanitary Engineer [*A publication*]
Water Sci & Technol ...   Water Science and Technology [*A publication*]
Water Serv ...   Water Services [*A publication*]
Water Sewage Effl ...   Water, Sewage, and Effluent [*A publication*]
Water & Sewage Works ...   Water and Sewage Works [*A publication*]
Water Supply Manage ...   Water Supply and Management [*England*] [*A publication*]
Water Supply Pap Geol Surv GB Hydrogeol Rep ...   Water Supply Papers. Geological Survey of Great Britain. Hydrogeological Report [*A publication*]
Water Supply Pap US Geol Surv ...   Water Supply Paper. United States Geological Survey [*A publication*]
Water Treat Exam ...   Water Treatment and Examination [*A publication*]
Water Waste ...   Water and Wastes Engineering [*A publication*]
Water & Waste Engng ...   Water and Waste Engineering [*A publication*]
Water Wastes Dig ...   Water and Wastes Digest [*A publication*]
Water Wastes Eng ...   Water and Wastes Engineering [*A publication*]
Water Wastes Eng Ind ...   Water and Wastes Engineering/Industrial [*A publication*]
Water Waste Treat ...   Water and Waste Treatment [*A publication*]
Water Waste Treat J ...   Water Waste Treatment Journal [*A publication*]
Water Wastewater Treat Plants Oper Newsl ...   Water and Wastewater Treatment Plants Operators' Newsletter [*A publication*]
Water Water Eng ...   Water and Water Engineering [*A publication*]
Water (WC and IC Staff Journal) ...   Water (Water Conservation and Irrigation Commission Staff Journal) [*A publication*]   (APTA)
Water Well J ...   Water Well Journal [*A publication*]
Water Well Jour ...   Water Well Journal [*A publication*]
Water Works Eng ...   Water Works Engineering [*A publication*]
Water Works Wastes Eng ...   Water Works and Wastes Engineering [*A publication*]
WATF........   Waterford Wedgwood Ltd. [*NASDAQ symbol*]   (NQ)
WATFIV ...   Waterloo FORTRAN [*Formula Translating System*] IV [*University of Waterloo*] [*Canada*]   (HGAA)
WATFOR ...   Waterloo FORTRAN [*University of Waterloo*] [*Canada*]
WaTFS ......   Fort Steilacoom Community College, Tacoma, WA [*Library symbol*] [*Library of Congress*]   (LCLS)
WaTG ....   Tacoma Branch Genealogical Library, Tacoma, WA [*Library symbol*] [*Library of Congress*]   (LCLS)
WaTGH.....   Tacoma General Hospital, Pierce County Medical Library, Tacoma, WA [*Library symbol*] [*Library of Congress*]   (LCLS)
WaTGS......   Church of Jesus Christ of Latter-Day Saints, Genealogical Society Library, Tacoma Branch, Tacoma, WA [*Library symbol*] [*Library of Congress*]   (LCLS)
WATH.......   Athens, OH [*AM radio station call letters*]

WaTJP ...... Washington State Office of Juvenile Parole Services, Tacoma, WA [*Library symbol*] [*Library of Congress*] (LCLS)

Wat Just .... Waterman's Justices' Manual [*A publication*] (DLA)

WATK .... Antigo, WI [*AM radio station call letters*]

Watk Con... Watkins on Conveyancing [*A publication*] (DLA)

Watk Conv ... Watkins on Conveyancing [*A publication*] (DLA)

Watk Cop... Watkins on Copyholds [*A publication*] (DLA)

Watk Copyh ... Watkins on Copyholds [*A publication*] (DLA)

Watk Des... Watkins on Descents [*A publication*] (DLA)

WatkJn... Watkins-Johnson Co. [*Associated Press abbreviation*] (APAG)

WATL....... Atlanta, GA [*Television station call letters*]

WaTLG...... Lakewood General Hospital and Convalescent Center, Tacoma, WA [*Library symbol*] [*Library of Congress*] (LCLS)

WATM ...... Altoona, PA [*Television station call letters*]

WATN .... Watertown, NY [*AM radio station call letters*]

WATO .... Oak Ridge, TN [*AM radio station call letters*]

WaTO .... Oakridge Group Home, Tacoma, WA [*Library symbol*] [*Library of Congress*] (LCLS)

WaTP .... Pioneer Group Home, Tacoma, WA [*Library symbol*] [*Library of Congress*] (LCLS)

WaTPC...... Pierce County Library, Tacoma, WA [*Library symbol*] [*Library of Congress*] (LCLS)

WaTPG...... Puget Sound General Hospital, Tacoma, WA [*Library symbol*] [*Library of Congress*] (LCLS)

WATPL..... Wartime Traffic Priority List (NATG)

WaTPM..... Pierce County Medical Library, Tacoma, WA [*Library symbol*] [*Library of Congress*] (LCLS)

WatPolAb ... Water Pollution Abstracts [*A publication*]

Wat Pollut Control ... Water Pollution Control [*A publication*]

Wat Pollut Res J Can ... Water Pollution Research Journal of Canada [*A publication*]

WaTPS ...... Tacoma Public Schools, Professional and Curriculum Library, Tacoma, WA [*Library symbol*] [*Library of Congress*] (LCLS)

Wat Pwr..... Water Power [*A publication*]

WATQ .... New Martinsville, WV [*FM radio station call letters*]

WATR .... Tetra Tech [*NASDAQ symbol*] (SPSG)

WATR .... Water Attenuation by Tritium Relaxation [*Physics*]

WATR .... Waterbury, CT [*AM radio station call letters*]

WATR .... Waterville [*AAR code*]

WATRA .... Water Research [*A publication*]

WatResAb ... Water Resources Abstracts [*A publication*]

Wat Res Fdn Aust Bull ... Water Research Foundation of Australia Ltd. Bulletin [*A publication*] (APTA)

Wat Res Fdn Rep ... Water Research Foundation of Australia Ltd. Report [*A publication*] (APTA)

Wat Resour Res ... Water Resources Research [*A publication*]

Watrhse ..... Waterhouse Investor Services, Inc. [*Associated Press abbreviation*] (APAG)

WATS....... Sayre, PA [*AM radio station call letters*]

WATS....... Wide-Area Military Traffic Management and Terminal Service

WATS........ Wide-Area Telecommunications [*formerly, Telephone*] Service [*American Telephone & Telegraph Co. contract billing system*]

WATS....... Wide Area Transmission Service

WATS........ Women's Auxiliary Territorial Service [*British military*] (DMA)

WATS....... Women's Auxiliary Training Service

Wats Arb ... Watson on Arbitration [*A publication*] (DLA)

Watsc......... Watsco, Inc. [*Associated Press abbreviation*] (APAG)

Wats Cler Law ... Watson's Clergyman's Law [*A publication*] (DLA)

Wats Com Man ... Watson's United States Commissioners' Manual [*A publication*] (DLA)

Wats Comp Eq ... Watson's Compendium of Equity [*A publication*] (DLA)

Wats Const Hist ... Watson's Constitutional History of Canada [*A publication*] (DLA)

Wat Serv .... Water Services [*A publication*]

Wat Set-Off ... Waterman on Set-Off [*A publication*] (DLA)

WaTSJ ...... Saint Joseph Hospital, Tacoma, WA [*Library symbol*] [*Library of Congress*] (LCLS)

Wats Med Jur ... Watson's Medical Jurisprudence [*A publication*] (DLA)

Watson....... Watson's Compendium of Equity [*2 eds.*] [*1873, 1888*] [*A publication*] (DLA)

Watson Eq ... Watson's Compendium of Equity [*A publication*] (DLA)

Watson House Bull ... Watson House Bulletin [*A publication*]

Wats Part... Watson on Partnership [*2nd ed.*] [*1807*] [*A publication*] (DLA)

Wats Sher .. Watson's Office and Duty of Sheriff [*2nd ed.*] [*1848*] [*A publication*] (DLA)

WATSTORE ... National Water Data Storage and Retrieval System [*US Geological Survey*] [*Information service or system*] (CRD)

WATT .... Cadillac, MI [*AM radio station call letters*]

WATT .... Watts Industries, Inc. [*North Andover, MA*] [*NASDAQ symbol*] (NQ)

WATTec.... Welding and Testing Technology Energy Conference [*Acronym is used as name of association*]

Wattle Res Inst Univ Natal (S Afr) Rep ... Wattle Research Institute. University of Natal (South Africa). Report [*A publication*]

Wat Tres .... Waterman on the Law of Trespass [*A publication*] (DLA)

Watts .... Watts' Pennsylvania Reports [*1832-40*] [*A publication*] (DLA)

Watts .... Watts' Reports [*16-24 West Virginia*] [*A publication*] (DLA)

Watts (PA) ... Watts' Pennsylvania Reports [*1832-40*] [*A publication*] (DLA)

Watts & S .. Watts and Sergeant's Pennsylvania Reports [*1841-45*] [*A publication*] (DLA)

Watts & Serg ... Watts and Sergeant's Pennsylvania Reports [*1841-45*] [*A publication*] (DLA)

Watts & S (PA) ... Watts and Sergeant's Pennsylvania Reports [*1841-45*] [*A publication*] (DLA)

WaTU........ University of Puget Sound, Tacoma, WA [*Library symbol*] [*Library of Congress*] (LCLS)

WATU .... Western Approaches Tactical Unit [*Navy*]

WATV ...... Birmingham, AL [*AM radio station call letters*]

Wat Vict ...... Water in Victoria [*A publication*] (APTA)

WATW ...... Ashland, WI [*AM radio station call letters*]

WaTW .... Weyerhaeuser Co., Tacoma, WA [*Library symbol*] [*Library of Congress*] (LCLS)

WATW ...... Wood Awning Type Window

Wat Waste Treat ... Water and Waste Treatment [*A publication*]

Wat Wat Engng ... Water and Water Engineering [*A publication*]

WaTWH.... Western State Hospital, Staff Library, Tacoma, WA [*Library symbol*] [*Library of Congress*] (LCLS)

WaTWH-R ... Western State Hospital, Resident Library, Tacoma, WA [*Library symbol*] [*Library of Congress*] (LCLS)

WaTW-T ... Weyerhaeuser Co., Technical Center, Tacoma, WA [*Library symbol*] [*Library of Congress*] (LCLS)

WATX .... Algood, TN [*AM radio station call letters*]

WATZ .... Alpena, MI [*AM radio station call letters*]

WATZ-FM ... Alpena, MI [*FM radio station call letters*]

WAU......... University of Washington, Seattle, WA [*OCLC symbol*] (OCLC)

WaU.......... University of Washington, Seattle, WA [*Library symbol*] [*Library of Congress*] (LCLS)

wau .... Washington [*MARC country of publication code*] [*Library of Congress*] (LCCP)

WAU......... Weapon Assignment Unit [*Military*] (CAAL)

WAUB .... Auburn, NY [*AM radio station call letters*]

WAUC .... Wauchula, FL [*AM radio station call letters*]

WAUD .... Auburn, AL [*AM radio station call letters*]

WaU-D ...... University of Washington, Drama Library, Seattle, WA [*Library symbol*] [*Library of Congress*] (LCLS)

WaU-EA.... University of Washington, East Asia Library, Seattle, WA [*Library symbol*] [*Library of Congress*] (LCLS)

WaU-FE .... University of Washington, Far Eastern Library, Seattle, WA [*Library symbol*] [*Library of Congress*] [*Obsolete*] (LCLS)

WAUG....... New Hope, NC [*AM radio station call letters*]

WaU-HS.... University of Washington, Health Sciences Library, Seattle, WA [*Library symbol*] [*Library of Congress*] (LCLS)

WAUK .... Waukesha, WI [*AM radio station call letters*]

WaU-L....... University of Washington, Law Library, Seattle, WA [*Library symbol*] [*Library of Congress*] (LCLS)

WAU Law R ... University of Western Australia. Law Review [*A publication*] (APTA)

WAULR .... Western Australia University. Law Review [*A publication*] (APTA)

WaU-MC... University of Washington, Harborview Medical Center Library, Seattle, WA [*Library symbol*] [*Library of Congress*] (LCLS)

WAUN...... Kewaunee, WI [*FM radio station call letters*]

WA Univ Gaz ... University of Western Australia. Gazette [*A publication*]

WA Univ Geog Lab Res Rept ... University of Western Australia. Geography Laboratory. Research Report [*A publication*] (APTA)

WAUR ...... Sandwich, IL [*AM radio station call letters*]

WAUS .... Berrien Springs, MI [*FM radio station call letters*]

WAUS .... World Association of Upper Silesians (EA)

W Aust For Dep Bull ... Western Australia. Forests Department. Bulletin [*A publication*] (APTA)

W Aust Geol Surv Bull ... Western Australia. Geological Survey. Bulletin [*A publication*] (APTA)

W Aust Geol Surv 1:250000 Geol Ser ... Western Australia. Geological Survey. 1:250,000 Geological Series [*A publication*] (APTA)

W Aust Hist Soc ... Western Australian Historical Society. Journal [*A publication*]

W Austl...... Western Australian Reports [*A publication*] (DLA)

W Austl Ind Gaz ... Western Australian Industrial Gazette [*A publication*] (DLA)

W Austl LR ... Western Australian Law Reports [*A publication*] (DLA)

W Austl R .. Western Australia Law Reports [*A publication*] (DLA)

W Aust Nat ... Western Australian Naturalist [*A publication*] (APTA)

W Aust Repr Acts ... Reprinted Acts of Western Australia [*A publication*] (DLA)

WAUXCP ... West Auxiliary Airborne Command Post (MCD)

WaV .... Fort Vancouver Regional Library, Vancouver, WA [*Library symbol*] [*Library of Congress*] (LCLS)

WAV .... Williford Aviation, Inc. [*Atlanta, GA*] [*FAA designator*] (FAAC)

WAV .... Wirtschaftliche Aufbau Vereinigung [*Economic Reconstruction Union*] [*Germany*] [*Political party*] (PPE)

WAVA .... Arlington, VA [*FM radio station call letters*]

WAVA .... World Association of Veteran Athletes (EAIO)

WAVA .... World Association of Veterinary Anatomists (EA)

WAVAW ... Women Against Violence Against Women (EA)

WAVB .... LaJas, PR [*AM radio station call letters*]

WaVC .... Clark College, Vancouver, WA [*Library symbol*] [*Library of Congress*] (LCLS)
WAVC .... Duluth, MN [*FM radio station call letters*]
WAVD .... Decatur, AL [*AM radio station call letters*]
WAVE .... Louisville, KY [*Television station call letters*]
WAVE .... Water-Augmented Vehicle
WAVE .... Wavetech, Inc. [*NASDAQ symbol*] (NQ)
WAVE .... Weather Altimeter Voice Equipment
Wave Electron ... Wave Electronics [*A publication*]
Wave Part Dualism ... Wave. Particle Dualism [*A publication*]
WAVES ..... Weight and Value Engineering System [*Data processing*]
WAVES ..... Women Accepted for Volunteer Emergency Service [*US Navy Women's Reserve*] [*World War II and later*]
WAVES ..... Women Appointed Volunteer Emergency Services [*British*] [*World War II*]
WAVES ..... Worker and Visitor Entrance System [*Secret Service*] (GFGA)
WAVF .... Hanahan, SC [*FM radio station call letters*]
WAVFH .... World Association of Veterinary Food-Hygienists [*See also AMVHA*] [*Berlin, Federal Republic of Germany*] (EAIO)
WAVG .... Louisville, KY [*AM radio station call letters*]
WAVH .... Mobile, AL [*FM radio station call letters*]
WaVHS ..... United States Park Service, Fort Vancouver National Historical Site, Vancouver, WA [*Library symbol*] [*Library of Congress*] (LCLS)
WAVI .... Christiansted, VI [*FM radio station call letters*]
WAVJ .... Black Mountain, NC [*AM radio station call letters*]
WAVK .... Marathon, FL [*FM radio station call letters*]
WAVL .... Apollo, PA [*AM radio station call letters*]
WAVLD .... World Association of Veterinary Laboratory Diagnosticians (EAIO)
WAVM ...... Maynard, MA [*FM radio station call letters*]
WaVMH.... Vancouver Memorial Hospital, Vancouver, WA [*Library symbol*] [*Library of Congress*] (LCLS)
WAVMI .... World Association of Veterinary Microbiologists, Immunologists, and Specialists in Infectious Diseases [*See also AMVMI*] [*Maisons-Alfort, France*] (EAIO)
WAVN .... Southaven, MS [*AM radio station call letters*]
WAVO .... Decatur, GA [*AM radio station call letters*]
WAVP .... Western Australian. Votes and Proceedings [*A publication*]
WAVP .... World Association of Veterinary Pathologists (EAIO)
WAVPM ... Women Against Violence in Pornography and Media (EA)
WAVR .... Waverly, Inc. [*NASDAQ symbol*] (NQ)
WAVR .... Waverly, NY [*FM radio station call letters*]
WAVS .... Davie, FL [*AM radio station call letters*]
WAVS........ Wide Angle Visual System (MCD)
WaVSB ..... Washington State School for the Blind, Vancouver, WA [*Library symbol*] [*Library of Congress*] (LCLS)
WaVSD ..... Washington State School for the Deaf, Vancouver, WA [*Library symbol*] [*Library of Congress*] (LCLS)
WaVStJ ..... Saint Joseph Community Hospital, Vancouver, WA [*Library symbol*] [*Library of Congress*] (LCLS)
WAVT .... Pottsville, PA [*FM radio station call letters*]
WAVU .... Albertville, AL [*AM radio station call letters*]
WAVV .... Marco, FL [*FM radio station call letters*]
WaVVA ..... United States Veterans Administration Hospital, Vancouver, WA [*Library symbol*] [*Library of Congress*] (LCLS)
WAVW ...... Vero Beach, FL [*FM radio station call letters*]
WAVX .... Thomaston, ME [*FM radio station call letters*]
WAVY .... Portsmouth, VA [*Television station call letters*]
WAVZ .... New Haven, CT [*AM radio station call letters*]
WAW .... University of Washington, School of Librarianship, Seattle, WA [*OCLC symbol*] (OCLC)
WaW .... Walla Walla Public Library, Walla Walla, WA [*Library symbol*] [*Library of Congress*] (LCLS)
WAW .... Ward's Auto World [*A publication*]
WAW .... Warsaw [*Poland*] [*Airport symbol*] (OAG)
WAW .... Waynesburg & Washington Railroad Co. [*Absorbed into Consolidated Rail Corp.*] [*AAR code*]
WAW .... Wings Airways [*Blue Bell, PA*] [*FAA designator*] (FAAC)
WAWA ...... West Africa Wins Again [*A reminder that visitors to this region must exercise caution if they wish to avoid bureaucratic harrassment and overcharging*]
WAWA ...... Woolens and Worsteds of America [*Defunct*] (EA)
WaWC .... Walla Walla College, College Place, WA [*Library symbol*] [*Library of Congress*] (LCLS)
WAWC ...... West Africa War Council [*World War II*]
WAWD...... Fort Walton Beach, FL [*Television station call letters*]
WaWeC ..... Central Washington Hospital, Health Sciences Library, Wenatchee, WA [*Library symbol*] [*Library of Congress*] (LCLS)
WaWeN..... North Central Regional Library, Wenatche, WA [*Library symbol*] [*Library of Congress*] (LCLS)
WaWeW .... Wenatchee Valley College, Wenatchee, WA [*Library symbol*] [*Library of Congress*] (LCLS)
WaWeYS... Washington State Center for Youth Services, Wenatchee, WA [*Library symbol*] [*Library of Congress*] (LCLS)
WAWF ...... William Allen White Foundation (EA)
WAWF ...... World Arm Wrestling Federation (EA)
WAWF ...... World Association for World Federation [*Netherlands*]
WAWG...... Where Are We Going?

WaWiS ...... Wilbur Public Schools System, Wilbur, WA [*Library symbol*] [*Library of Congress*] (LCLS)
WAWK ..... Kendallville, IN [*AM radio station call letters*]
WAWL ...... Signal Mountain, TN [*FM radio station call letters*]
WaWnvGH ... Woodenville Group Home, Woodenville, WA [*Library symbol*] [*Library of Congress*] (LCLS)
WaWP .... Washington State Penitentiary, Walla Walla, WA [*Library symbol*] [*Library of Congress*] (LCLS)
WAWS ...... Jacksonville, FL [*Television station call letters*]
WAWV ...... Sylacauga, AL [*FM radio station call letters*]
WaWV .... United States Veterans Administration Hospital, Walla Walla, WA [*Library symbol*] [*Library of Congress*] (LCLS)
WaWW ...... Whitman College, Walla Walla, WA [*Library symbol*] [*Library of Congress*] (LCLS)
WaWWC... Walla Walla Community College, Walla Walla, WA [*Library symbol*] [*Library of Congress*] (LCLS)
WAWZ ...... Zarephath, NJ [*FM radio station call letters*]
WAX......... Waxman Industries, Inc. [*NYSE symbol*] (SPSG)
WAX......... Weak Anion Exchanger [*Chemistry*]
WAX......... Weapon Assignment and Target Extermination
WAXA ...... Anderson, SC [*Television station call letters*]
WAXD...... Wide-Angle X-Ray Diffraction
WAXE .... Vero Beach, FL [*AM radio station call letters*]
WAXF .... Sharpsville, PA [*FM radio station call letters*]
WAXI .... Rockville, IN [*FM radio station call letters*]
WAXM ...... Big Stone Gap, VA [*FM radio station call letters*]
Waxmn ...... Waxman Industries, Inc. [*Associated Press abbreviation*] (APAG)
WAXO....... Lewisburg, TN [*AM radio station call letters*]
WAXS........ Oak Hill, WV [*FM radio station call letters*]
WAXS........ Wide-Angle X-Ray Scattering
WAXT .... Alexandria, IN [*FM radio station call letters*]
WAXX .... Eau Claire, WI [*FM radio station call letters*]
WAXY .... Fort Lauderdale, FL [*FM radio station call letters*]
WAXZ .... Georgetown, OH [*FM radio station call letters*]
WAY.......... Wayne State College, Wayne, NE [*OCLC symbol*] (OCLC)
WAY.......... Waynesburg [*Pennsylvania*] [*Seismograph station code, US Geological Survey*] [*Closed*] (SEIS)
WAY.......... Waynesburg, PA [*Location identifier*] [*FAA*] (FAAL)
WAY.......... World Assembly of Youth [*Bronshoj, Denmark*] (EAIO)
WaY.......... Yakima Valley Regional Library, Yakima, WA [*Library symbol*] [*Library of Congress*] (LCLS)
WAYA ...... Spring City, TN [*FM radio station call letters*]
WaYacL..... Larch Mountain Correctional Center, Staff Library, Yacolt, WA [*Library symbol*] [*Library of Congress*] (LCLS)
WaYacL-R ... Larch Mountain Correctional Center, Resident Library, Yacolt, WA [*Library symbol*] [*Library of Congress*] (LCLS)
WAYB .... Graysville, TN [*FM radio station call letters*]
WAYC .... Bedford, PA [*AM radio station call letters*]
WAYC-FM ... Bedford, PA [*FM radio station call letters*]
WAYE .... Birmingham, AL [*AM radio station call letters*]
WAYED5 .. WANATCA [*West Australian Nut and Tree Crop Association*] Yearbook [*A publication*]
WAYF .... West Palm Beach, FL [*FM radio station call letters*]
WAYG .... Sarasota, FL [*FM radio station call letters*]
WaYGS...... Church of Jesus Christ of Latter-Day Saints, Genealogical Society Library, Yakima Branch, Yakima, WA [*Library symbol*] [*Library of Congress*] (LCLS)
WAYI .... Hudson Falls, NY [*FM radio station call letters*]
WAYJ........ Fort Myers, FL [*FM radio station call letters*]
WaYJP ...... Washington State Office of Juvenile Parole Services, Yakima, WA [*Library symbol*] [*Library of Congress*] (LCLS)
WAYK .... Melbourne, FL [*Television station call letters*]
WAYM ...... Columbia, TN [*FM radio station call letters*]
WaYM .... Yakima Valley Memorial Hospital, Yakima, WA [*Library symbol*] [*Library of Congress*] (LCLS)
WAYMCA ... World Alliance of Young Men's Christian Associations [*Geneva, Switzerland*] (EAIO)
WaYMHi... Yakima Valley Museum and Historical Association, Yakima, WA [*Library symbol*] [*Library of Congress*] (LCLS)
WAYN...... Rockingham, NC [*AM radio station call letters*]
Wayne LR ... Wayne Law Review [*A publication*]
Wayne L Rev ... Wayne Law Review [*A publication*]
WAYP .... Holmes Beach, FL [*FM radio station call letters*]
WAYQ....... Daytona Beach, FL [*Television station call letters*]
WAYR .... Orange Park, FL [*AM radio station call letters*]
WAYS........ Macon, GA [*FM radio station call letters*]
WaYSE...... Saint Elizabeth Hospital, Health Sciences Library, Yakima, WA [*Library symbol*] [*Library of Congress*] (LCLS)
Way Suppl ... Way. Supplement [*A publication*]
WAYT .... Wabash, IN [*AM radio station call letters*]
WAYV .... Atlantic City, NJ [*FM radio station call letters*]
WAYX .... Waycross, GA [*AM radio station call letters*]
WAYY .... Chippewa Falls, WI [*AM radio station call letters*]
WaYY .... Yakima Valley College, Yakima, WA [*Library symbol*] [*Library of Congress*] (LCLS)
WaYYS...... Washington State Center for Youth Services, Yakima, WA [*Library symbol*] [*Library of Congress*] (LCLS)
WAYZ .... Waynesboro, PA [*AM radio station call letters*]
WAYZ-FM ... Waynesboro, PA [*FM radio station call letters*]
WAZE .... Dawson, GA [*FM radio station call letters*]

WAZF....... Yazoo City, MS [*AM radio station call letters*]
WAZF-FM ... Yazoo City, MS [*FM radio station call letters*]
WAZL....... Hazleton, PA [*AM radio station call letters*]
WAZR .... Woodstock, VA [*FM radio station call letters*]
WAZS....... Summerville, SC [*AM radio station call letters*]
WAZU .... Springfield, OH [*FM radio station call letters*]
WAZX....... Alpharetta, GA [*AM radio station call letters*]
WAZY .... Lafayette, IN [*FM radio station call letters*]
WB............ Wachovia Corp. [*NYSE symbol*]   (SPSG)
WB............ Wage Board [*Civil Service classification*]
WB............ Wagon Box   (MSA)
W & B .... Walferstan and Bristowe's Election Cases [*1859-65*] [*A publication*]   (DLA)
WB............ Wall Box   (ROG)
WB............ Wallboard
WB............ Warbirds of America   (EA)
WB............ Warehouse Book
WB............ Wash Basin
WB............ Wash Bucket
WB............ Washable Base   (ADA)
WB............ Waste Book   (ROG)
WB............ Water Ballast [*Shipping*]
WB............ Water Board
W/B .... Water Boiler   (KSC)
WB............ Water Bottle
WB............ Water Box
WB............ Waterproof Breathable [*Textile technology*]
WB............ Wave-Band   (ADA)
WB............ Waybill [*Shipping*]
WB............ Weather Bomber [*Air Force*]
WB............ Weather Bureau [*Later, National Weather Service*]   (EA)
WB............ Weatherboard   (ADA)
Wb............ Weber [*Symbol*] [*SI unit of magnetic flux*]
WB............ Wechsler-Bellevue [*Psychological test*]
WB............ Wedge Biopsy [*Medicine*]
WB............ Weekly Boarding
WB............ Weekly Bulletin [*Army*]   (AABC)
W/B .... Weight and Balance
WB............ Weight Bearing
WB............ Weimarer Beitraege [*A publication*]
wb.............. West Berlin [*MARC country of publication code*] [*Library of Congress*]   (LCCP)
WB............ Westbound
WB............ Westbridge Computer Corp. [*Toronto Stock Exchange symbol*]
WB............ Western Blot [*Blood test*]
WB............ Westminster Biographies [*A publication*]
WB............ Wet Bulb [*Thermometer, of a psychrometer*] [*Meteorology*]
WB............ Whale Boat
WB............ Wheelbarrow   (MSA)
WB............ Wheelbase
WB............ Whole Blood
WB............ Whole Body [*Nuclear energy*]   (NRCH)
WB............ Whole Body [*Medicine*]
WB............ Whole Bow [*Music*]   (ROG)
WB............ Wideband [*Radio transmission*]
WB............ Widebeam   (NATG)
WB............ Wiener Blaetter fuer die Freunde der Antike [*A publication*]
WB............ Will Be   (AABC)
WB............ Willowbrook [*Virus*]   (MAE)
WB............ Winchester Word Book [*A publication*]
WB............ Wingback [*Football*]
WB............ Winner's Bitch [*Dog show term*]
W/B .... Wire Bundles   (MCD)
WB............ Wirebar [*Metal industry*]
WB............ Woerterbuch der Aegyptischen Sprache [*A publication*]   (BJA)
WB............ Women's Bureau [*Department of Labor*]
WB............ Wood Base [*Technical drawings*]
WB............ Wood Burning [*Fireplace*] [*Classified advertising*]
WB............ Wool Back [*Knitting*]
WB............ Wool Bureau   (EA)
WB............ Word Before [*Message handling*]
WB............ Work Book
WB............ Workbench   (AAG)
W & B .... Works and Building Services [*British military*]   (DMA)
WB............ World Bank
WB............ World Brotherhood
WB............ Worlds Beyond [*A publication*]
WB............ Worldways Canada Ltd. [*Canada*] [*ICAO designator*]   (FAAC)
WB............ Wort und Brauch [*A publication*]
WB............ Write Buffer
W/B .... Writing on Back [*Deltiology*]
WB2.......... Warramunga Array [*Australia*] [*Seismograph station code, US Geological Survey*]   (SEIS)
WB3.......... Warramunga Array [*Australia*] [*Seismograph station code, US Geological Survey*]   (SEIS)
WB & A ..... Washington, Baltimore & Annapolis Railroad [*Nickname: Wobble, Bump, and Amble*]
WBA .... Wax Bean Agglutinin [*Biochemistry*]
WBA .... Weekly Benefit Amount [*Unemployment insurance*]
WBA .... Weekly of Business Aviation [*McGraw-Hill Information Services Co.*] [*Information service or system*]   (CRD)

WBA .... Western Blot Assay [*Analytical biochemistry*]
WBA .... Wideband Amplifier
WBA .... Wire Bundle Assembly   (MCD)
WBA .... Woman's Benefit Association [*Later, NABA*]
WBA .... Works and Building, High Priority [*British*] [*World War II*]
WBA .... World Boxing Association [*Later, WBO*]   (EA)
WBA .... World Buffalo Association Ltd. Agricultural Association   (EA)
WBA .... Worn by Astronaut [*NASA*]   (KSC)
WBAA ...... West Lafayette, IN [*AM radio station call letters*]
WBAA-FM .. West Lafayette, IN [*FM radio station call letters*]
WBAB .... Babylon, NY [*FM radio station call letters*]
WBAC .... Cleveland, TN [*AM radio station call letters*]
WBAD .... Leland, MS [*FM radio station call letters*]
WBAEA..... Wholesale Beer Association Executives of America   (EA)
WBAF .... Barnesville, GA [*AM radio station call letters*]
WBAG .... Burlington-Graham, NC [*AM radio station call letters*]
WBAI .... New York, NY [*FM radio station call letters*]
WBAI........ Wesley Bull & Associates, Inc. [*Seattle, WA*] [*Telecommunications*]   (TSSD)
WBAIS ...... Walworth Barbour American International School in Israel   (BJA)
WBAJ .... Blythwood, SC [*AM radio station call letters*]
WBAK ...... Anduki/Seria [*Brunei*] [*ICAO location identifier*]   (ICLI)
WBAK ...... Terre Haute, IN [*Television station call letters*]
WBAL........ Baltimore, MD [*AM radio station call letters*]
WBAL-TV ... Baltimore, MD [*Television station call letters*]
WBAM ...... Montgomery, AL [*FM radio station call letters*]
WBAMC .. William Beaumont Army Medical Center   (AABC)
WBAN ...... Weather Bureau, Air Force, Navy [*Manuals*] [*Obsolete*]
WBANA .... Wild Blueberry Association of North America   (EA)
WBANK .... Bank of Canada Weekly Financial Statistics [*I. P. Sharp Associates*] [*Information service or system*]   (CRD)
WBAP........ Fort Worth, TX [*AM radio station call letters*]
WBAQ .... Greenville, MS [*FM radio station call letters*]
WBAR .... Bartow, FL [*AM radio station call letters*]
WBAR .... Lake Luzerne, NY [*FM radio station call letters*]
WBAR .... Wing Bar Lights [*Aviation*]
WBaraC..... Circus World Museum, Baraboo, WI [*Library symbol*] [*Library of Congress*]   (LCLS)
WBaraHi ... Sauk County Historical Society, Baraboo, WI [*Library symbol*] [*Library of Congress*]   (LCLS)
WBAS........ Weather Bureau Airport Station [*Obsolete*]
WBAS........ Woerterbuch der Aegyptischen Sprache [*A publication*]   (BJA)
WBasR....... Randall Consolidated School, Bassett, WI [*Library symbol*] [*Library of Congress*]   (LCLS)
WBAT .... Marion, IN [*AM radio station call letters*]
WBAT .... Westport Bancorp, Inc. [*Westport, CT*] [*NASDAQ symbol*]   (NQ)
WBAT .... Wideband Adapter Transformer
WBAU .... Garden City, NY [*FM radio station call letters*]
WBAW ...... Barnwell, SC [*AM radio station call letters*]
WBAW-FM ... Barnwell, SC [*FM radio station call letters*]
WBAWS.... Weather, Briefing, Advisory, and Warning Service   (AABC)
WBAX .... Wilkes-Barre, PA [*AM radio station call letters*]
WBAY .... Green Bay, WI [*Television station call letters*]
WBAZ .... Southold, NY [*FM radio station call letters*]
WBB .... Beloit College, Beloit, WI [*Library symbol*] [*Library of Congress*]   (LCLS)
WBB .... Stebbins [*Alaska*] [*Airport symbol*]   (OAG)
WBB .... Stebbins, AK [*Location identifier*] [*FAA*]   (FAAL)
WBB .... Webb [*Del E.*] Corp. [*NYSE symbol*]   (SPSG)
WBB .... Wide Band Beam [*Physics*]
WBBA .... Pittsfield, IL [*AM radio station call letters*]
WBBA .... Western Bird Banding Association   (EA)
WBBA-FM ... Pittsfield, IL [*FM radio station call letters*]
WBBB....... Burlington, NC [*AM radio station call letters*]
WBBC....... Blackstone, VA [*AM radio station call letters*]
WBBC....... [*The*] Webb Co. [*NASDAQ symbol*]   (NQ)
WBBC-FM ... Blackstone, VA [*FM radio station call letters*]
WBBD .... Wheeling, WV [*AM radio station call letters*]
WBBE .... Columbia City, IN [*FM radio station call letters*]
WBBF........ Rochester, NY [*AM radio station call letters*]
WBBG .... Youngstown, OH [*FM radio station call letters*]
WBBH........ Fort Myers, FL [*Television station call letters*]
WBBI........ Abingdon, VA [*AM radio station call letters*]
WBBJ........ Jackson, TN [*Television station call letters*]
WBBK........ Blakely, GA [*AM radio station call letters*]
WBBM ...... Chicago, IL [*AM radio station call letters*]
WBBM-FM ... Chicago, IL [*FM radio station call letters*]
WBBM-TV ... Chicago, IL [*Television station call letters*]
WBBN .... Taylorsville, MS [*FM radio station call letters*]
WBBO .... Forest City, NC [*FM radio station call letters*]
WBBP....... Memphis, TN [*AM radio station call letters*]
WBBQ .... Augusta, GA [*AM radio station call letters*]
WBBQ-FM ... Augusta, GA [*FM radio station call letters*]
WBBR........ Travelers Rest, SC [*AM radio station call letters*]
WBBS........ Great Barrington, MA [*FM radio station call letters*]
WBBT........ Lyons, GA [*AM radio station call letters*]
WBBV........ Vicksburg, MS [*FM radio station call letters*]
WBBW ...... Youngstown, OH [*AM radio station call letters*]
WBBX........ Kingston, TN [*AM radio station call letters*]

WBBY........ Westerville, OH [*FM radio station call letters*]
WBBZ........ Ponca City, OK [*AM radio station call letters*]
WBC .... Bloembollencultuur [*A publication*]
WBC .... Warm-Blood Cardioplegia [*Medicine*]
WBC .... Washington, DC [*Location identifier*] [*FAA*]　(FAAL)
WBC .... Water Binding Capacity [*Also, WHC*] [*Food industry*]
WBC .... Wayland Baptist College [*Texas*]
WBC .... Weather Bureau Central Office [*Obsolete*]
WBC .... Weather Bureau Communications [*Obsolete*]
WBC .... Welsh Books Council
WBC .... Westbridge Capital Corp. [*AMEX symbol*]　(SPSG)
WBC .... Western Boundary Current [*Marine science*]　(MSC)
WBC .... Westinghouse Broadcasting Co.
WBC .... White Blood Cell [*or Corpuscle*] [*Medicine*]
WBC .... White Blood Cell Count [*Medicine*]
WBC .... Wideband Coupler
WBC .... Wien Bridge Circuit [*Physics*]
WBC .... Wilkes-Barre Connecting Railroad [*AAR code*]
WBC .... Wilkes College Library, Wilkes-Barre, PA [*OCLC symbol*]　(OCLC)
WBC .... Wire Bridge Circuit
WBC .... Women's Broadcasting Corp.
WBC .... World Book Congress
WBC .... World Boxing Council [*Information service or system*]　(IID)
WBC .... World Business Council [*Washington, DC*]　(EA)
WBC .... Wycliffe Bible Commentary [*A publication*]　(BJA)
WBCA .... Bay Minette, AL [*AM radio station call letters*]
WBCA .... Welsh Black Cattle Association　(EA)
WBCA .... Women's Basketball Coaches Association　(EA)
WBCA .... Wyandotte Bantam Club of America　(EA)
WBCB........ Levittown-Fairless Hills, PA [*AM radio station call letters*]
WBCC........ Cocoa, FL [*Television station call letters*]
WBCCI .... Wally Byam Caravan Club International　(EA)
WBCD .... White Blood Cell Differential [*Hematology*]
WBCE........ Wickliffe, KY [*AM radio station call letters*]
WBCF........ Florence, AL [*AM radio station call letters*]
WBCG .... Murfreesboro, NC [*FM radio station call letters*]
WBCH .... Hastings, MI [*AM radio station call letters*]
WBCH-FM ... Hastings, MI [*FM radio station call letters*]
WBC/HPF ... White Blood Cells per High Power Field [*Hematology*]　(MAE)
WBCK .... Battle Creek, MI [*AM radio station call letters*]
WBCL........ Fort Wayne, IN [*FM radio station call letters*]
WBCN........ Boston, MA [*FM radio station call letters*]
WBCO........ Bucyrus, OH [*AM radio station call letters*]
WBCO....... Wallace Barnes Co.
WBCO....... Waveguide below Cutoff　(IEEE)
WBCP....... Urbana, IL [*AM radio station call letters*]
WBCQ....... Quakertown, PA [*AM radio station call letters*]
WBCR .... Beloit, WI [*FM radio station call letters*]
WBCS........ Wideband Communications Subsystem
WBCT........ Whole-Blood Clotting Time [*Hematology*]
WBCT........ Wideband Current Transformer
WBCU .... Union, SC [*AM radio station call letters*]
WBCV .... Bristol, TN [*AM radio station call letters*]
WBCV .... Wideband Coherent Video　(IEEE)
WBCW ..... Jeanette, PA [*AM radio station call letters*]
WBCX .... Gainesville, GA [*FM radio station call letters*]
WBCY .... Archbold, OH [*FM radio station call letters*]
WBD.......... Befandriana [*Madagascar*] [*Airport symbol*]　(OAG)
WBD.......... Wallboard
WBD.......... Ward's Business Directory [*A publication*]
WBD.......... Washboard [*Musical instrument used in some jazz bands*]
WBD.......... Watts Bar Dam [*TVA*]
WBD.......... Wideband Data
WBD.......... Wire Bound　(IEEE)
WBD.......... World Business Directory [*A publication*]
WBD.......... Worlds Beyond [*A publication*]
WBDA .... Wideband Data Assembly [*Ground Communications Facility, NASA*]
WBDC .... Huntingburg, IN [*FM radio station call letters*]
WBDDS.... Weapons Bay Door Drive Subsystem [*Military*]
WBDF........ Wideband Dicke-Fix　(CET)
WBDFX...... Wideband Dicke-Fix　(MSA)
WBDG .... Indianapolis, IN [*FM radio station call letters*]
WBDI .... Wideband Data Interleaver　(MCD)
W & B Dig ... Walter and Bates' Ohio Digest [*A publication*]　(DLA)
WBDL .... Wideband Data Line [*or Link*]
WBDNA .... Women Band Directors National Association　(EA)
WBdSJ ...... Saint Joseph's Hospital, Beaver Dam, WI [*Library symbol*] [*Library of Congress*]　(LCLS)
WBDX .... Trenton, GA [*FM radio station call letters*]
WBDX .... Wideband Data Switch
WBDY .... Bluefield, VA [*AM radio station call letters*]
WBDY-FM ... Bluefield, VA [*FM radio station call letters*]
WBE .... Bealanana [*Madagascar*] [*Airport symbol*]　(OAG)
WBE .... Waterloo County Board of Education, Professional Education Library [*UTLAS symbol*]
WBE .... Weekblad voor Fiscaal Recht [*A publication*]
WBE .... West Bromwich [*England*] [*Seismograph station code, US Geological Survey*] [*Closed*]　(SEIS)
WBE .... Whole-Body Extract [*Immunology*]

WBE .... Wideband Electronics
WBE .... Women's Business Enterprise
WBEA .... Western Business Education Association　(AEBS)
WBEB....... Athens, KY [*AM radio station call letters*]
WBEC....... Pittsfield, MA [*AM radio station call letters*]
WBEC-FM ... Pittsfield, MA [*FM radio station call letters*]
WBED .... Classic Corp. [*NASDAQ symbol*]　(NQ)
WBEE....... Harvey, IL [*AM radio station call letters*]
WBEE....... Rochester, NY [*FM radio station call letters*]
WB/EI .... West Britain/East Ireland
WBEJ....... Elizabethton, TN [*AM radio station call letters*]
WBEL........ South Beloit, IL [*AM radio station call letters*]
WBEL........ Western Bell Communications, Inc. [*Los Angeles, CA*] [*NASDAQ symbol*]　(NQ)
WBelH....... Holy Family Convent, Benet Lake, WI [*Library symbol*] [*Library of Congress*]　(LCLS)
WBelSB .... Saint Benedict's Abbey, Benet Library, Benet Lake, WI [*Library symbol*] [*Library of Congress*]　(LCLS)
WBEM ..... Windber, PA [*AM radio station call letters*]
WBEN ...... Buffalo, NY [*AM radio station call letters*]
WBEP....... Wiener Beitraege zur Englischen Philologie [*A publication*]
WBer.......... Berlin Public Library, Berlin, WI [*Library symbol*] [*Library of Congress*]　(LCLS)
WBER....... Rochester, NY [*FM radio station call letters*]
WBES....... Dunbar, WV [*FM radio station call letters*]
WBET....... Brockton, MA [*AM radio station call letters*]
WBEU ...... Beaufort, SC [*AM radio station call letters*]
WBEV ...... Beaver Dam, WI [*AM radio station call letters*]
WBEX....... Chillicothe, OH [*AM radio station call letters*]
WBEY....... California, MD [*FM radio station call letters*]
WBEZ....... Chicago, IL [*FM radio station call letters*]
WBF.......... Whole Blood Folate [*Hematology*]　(MAE)
WBF.......... Wood Block Floor [*Technical drawings*]
WBF.......... Wood-Burning Fireplace [*Classified advertising*]　(WGA)
WBF.......... Workmen's Benefit Fund of the USA [*Carle Place, NY*]　(EA)
WBF.......... World Bridge Federation
WBFA .... Western Bohemian Fraternal Association [*Later, WFLA*]　(EA)
WBFC........ Kota Kinabalu [*Malaysia*] [*ICAO location identifier*]　(ICLI)
WBFC........ Stanton, KY [*AM radio station call letters*]
WBFD........ Bedford, PA [*AM radio station call letters*]
WBFF........ Baltimore, MD [*Television station call letters*]
WBFG....... Effingham, IL [*FM radio station call letters*]
WBFH .... Bloomfield Hills, MI [*FM radio station call letters*]
WBFI .... McDaniels, KY [*FM radio station call letters*]
WBFI .... Wild Bird Feeding Institute　(EA)
WBFJ .... Winston-Salem, NC [*AM radio station call letters*]
WBFL .... Bellows Falls, VT [*FM radio station call letters*]
WBFM....... Seneca, SC [*FM radio station call letters*]
WBFM...... Wideband Frequency Modulation
WBFN ...... Quitman, MS [*AM radio station call letters*]
WBFO ...... Buffalo, NY [*FM radio station call letters*]
WBFP....... Wood-Burning Fireplace [*Classified advertising*]
WBFR....... Birmingham, AL [*FM radio station call letters*]
WBFS....... Miami, FL [*Television station call letters*]
WBFX....... Grand Marais, MN [*FM radio station call letters*]
WBG......... Webbing
WBGA ...... Long Atip [*Malaysia*] [*ICAO location identifier*]　(ICLI)
WBGA ...... Waycross, GA [*AM radio station call letters*]
WBGB ...... Bintulu [*Malaysia*] [*ICAO location identifier*]　(ICLI)
WBGB ...... Mount Dora, FL [*AM radio station call letters*]
WBGC ...... Belaga [*Malaysia*] [*ICAO location identifier*]　(ICLI)
WBGC ...... Chipley, FL [*AM radio station call letters*]
WBGD...... Brick Township, NJ [*FM radio station call letters*]
WBGD...... Long Semado [*Malaysia*] [*ICAO location identifier*]　(ICLI)
WBGE ...... Long Geng [*Malaysia*] [*ICAO location identifier*]　(ICLI)
WBGE ...... Peoria, IL [*FM radio station call letters*]
WBGF....... Belle Glade, FL [*FM radio station call letters*]
WBGF........ Wholesale Buyers' Gifts Fair [*British*]　(ITD)
WBGG ...... Kuching [*Malaysia*] [*ICAO location identifier*]　(ICLI)
WBGJ .... Limbang [*Malaysia*] [*ICAO location identifier*]　(ICLI)
WBGK ...... Mukah [*Malaysia*] [*ICAO location identifier*]　(ICLI)
WBGL ...... Champaign, IL [*FM radio station call letters*]
WBGL ...... Long Akah [*Malaysia*] [*ICAO location identifier*]　(ICLI)
WBGM ...... Marudi [*Indonesia*] [*ICAO location identifier*]　(ICLI)
WBGM ...... Tallahassee, FL [*FM radio station call letters*]
WBGN ...... Bowling Green, KY [*AM radio station call letters*]
WBGN ...... Sematan [*Indonesia*] [*ICAO location identifier*]　(ICLI)
WBGO ...... Lio Matu [*Malaysia*] [*ICAO location identifier*]　(ICLI)
WBGO ...... Newark, NJ [*FM radio station call letters*]
WBGP ...... Kapit [*Indonesia*] [*ICAO location identifier*]　(ICLI)
WBGP ...... Waterborne Guard Post　(NVT)
WBGQ ...... Bakelalan [*Malaysia*] [*ICAO location identifier*]　(ICLI)
WBGR ...... Baltimore, MD [*AM radio station call letters*]
WBGR ...... Miri [*Indonesia*] [*ICAO location identifier*]　(ICLI)
WBGS ...... Point Pleasant, WV [*AM radio station call letters*]
WBGS ...... Sibu [*Malaysia*] [*ICAO location identifier*]　(ICLI)
WBGT ...... Wet Bulb Globe Temperature
WBGT ...... Wet Bulb Globe Thermometer
WBGTI ...... Wet Bulb Globe Temperature Index　(RDA)
WBGU....... Bowling Green, OH [*FM radio station call letters*]
WBGU-TV ... Bowling Green, OH [*Television station call letters*]

WBGW	Fort Branch, IN [*FM radio station call letters*]
WBGW	Lawas [*Malaysia*] [*ICAO location identifier*] (ICLI)
WBGY	Simanggang [*Malaysia*] [*ICAO location identifier*] (ICLI)
WBGZ	Alton, IL [*AM radio station call letters*]
WBGZ	Bario [*Malaysia*] [*ICAO location identifier*] (ICLI)
WBH..........	Whole Blood Hematocrit [*Hematology*] (MAE)
WBHA........	Hot Springs, VA [*FM radio station call letters*]
WBHB	Fitzgerald, GA [*AM radio station call letters*]
WBHC.......	Hampton, SC [*AM radio station call letters*]
WBHC-FM ...	Hampton, SC [*FM radio station call letters*]
WBHF	Cartersville, GA [*AM radio station call letters*]
WBHI	Chicago, IL [*FM radio station call letters*]
WBHL	Florence, AL [*FM radio station call letters*]
WBHM.......	Birmingham, AL [*FM radio station call letters*]
WBHN	Bryson City, NC [*AM radio station call letters*]
WBHO	Weather Bureau Hurricane Forecast Office [*Obsolete*]
WBHP	Huntsville, AL [*AM radio station call letters*]
WBHQ.......	Bloomfield, IN [*AM radio station call letters*]
WBHR	Bellaire, OH [*FM radio station call letters*]
WBHS	Tampa, FL [*Television station call letters*]
WBHV	State College, PA [*FM radio station call letters*]
WBHY.......	Mobile, AL [*AM radio station call letters*]
WBHY-FM ...	Mobile, AL [*FM radio station call letters*]
WBI	Ward Behavior Inventory [*Psychology*]
WBI	Washington Beverage Insight [*Wells & Associates*] [*Information service or system*] (IID)
WBI	Westburne International Industries Ltd. [*AMEX symbol*] [*Toronto Stock Exchange symbol*] (SPSG)
WBI	Whiskey Butte [*Idaho*] [*Seismograph station code, US Geological Survey*] [*Closed*] (SEIS)
WBI	Will Be Issued
WBI	Wooden Box Institute [*Defunct*] (EA)
WBIB........	Centreville, AL [*AM radio station call letters*]
WBIC........	Royston, GA [*AM radio station call letters*]
WBIF	Wideband Intermediate Frequency (MCD)
WBIG	Aurora, IL [*AM radio station call letters*]
WBII..........	Washington Business Information, Inc. [*Information service or system*] (IID)
WBII..........	Whirley Ball International [*NASDAQ symbol*] (NQ)
WBIL........	Tuskegee, AL [*AM radio station call letters*]
WBIL-FM ...	Tuskegee, AL [*FM radio station call letters*]
WBIM	Bridgewater, MA [*FM radio station call letters*]
WBIN	Benton, TN [*AM radio station call letters*]
WBINVD ..	Write Back and Invalidate Data [*Cache*] [*Computer instruction*] (PCM)
WBIP........	Booneville, MS [*AM radio station call letters*]
WBIP........	Whitaker's Books in Print [*J. Whitaker & Sons Ltd.*] [*Information service or system*] (IID)
WBIP-FM ...	Booneville, MS [*FM radio station call letters*]
WBIQ	Birmingham, AL [*Television station call letters*]
WBIR........	Knoxville, TN [*Television station call letters*]
WBIS	Bristol, CT [*AM radio station call letters*]
WBIT........	Adel, GA [*AM radio station call letters*]
WBIU	Denham Springs, LA [*AM radio station call letters*]
WBIV	Natick, MA [*AM radio station call letters*]
WBIW	Bedford, IN [*AM radio station call letters*]
WBIZ.........	Eau Claire, WI [*AM radio station call letters*]
WBIZ-FM ...	Eau Claire, WI [*FM radio station call letters*]
WBJA........	Guayama, PR [*AM radio station call letters*]
WBJB	Lincroft, NJ [*FM radio station call letters*]
WBJC........	Baltimore, MD [*FM radio station call letters*]
WBK	Webb & Knapp (Canada) Ltd. [*Vancouver Stock Exchange symbol*]
WBK	Western Banker [*A publication*]
WBK	Westpac Banking ADS [*NYSE symbol*] (SPSG)
WBKA	Semporna [*Malaysia*] [*ICAO location identifier*] (ICLI)
WBKB........	Alpena, MI [*Television station call letters*]
WBKC.......	Painesville, OH [*AM radio station call letters*]
WBKD	Lahad Datu [*Malaysia*] [*ICAO location identifier*] (ICLI)
WBKE........	North Manchester, IN [*AM radio station call letters*]
WBKG	Keningau [*Malaysia*] [*ICAO location identifier*] (ICLI)
WBKH.......	Hattiesburg, MS [*AM radio station call letters*]
WBKI........	Bremen, GA [*AM radio station call letters*]
WBKJ	Kosciusko, MS [*FM radio station call letters*]
WBKK	Kota Kinabalu [*Malaysia*] [*ICAO location identifier*] (ICLI)
WBKL........	Labuan [*Malaysia*] [*ICAO location identifier*] (ICLI)
WBKL........	Wiener Beitraege zur Kulturgeschichte und Linguistik [*A publication*]
WBKN	Brookhaven, MS [*FM radio station call letters*]
WBKO	Bowling Green, KY [*Television station call letters*]
WBKP........	Pamol [*Malaysia*] [*ICAO location identifier*] (ICLI)
WBKQ	Van Buren, ME [*FM radio station call letters*]
WBKR	Owensboro, KY [*FM radio station call letters*]
WBKR	Ranau [*Malaysia*] [*ICAO location identifier*] (ICLI)
WBKS........	Sandakan [*Malaysia*] [*ICAO location identifier*] (ICLI)
WBKT........	Brockport, NY [*FM radio station call letters*]
WBKT........	Kudat [*Malaysia*] [*ICAO location identifier*] (ICLI)
WBKV	West Bend, WI [*AM radio station call letters*]
WBKW	Dublin, VA [*FM radio station call letters*]
WBKW	Tawau [*Malaysia*] [*ICAO location identifier*] (ICLI)
WBKZ	Jefferson, GA [*AM radio station call letters*]

W Bl..........	[*Sir William*] Blackstone's English King's Bench Reports [*1746-80*] [*A publication*] (DLA)
WBL	Weak Black Liquor [*Pulp and paper technology*]
WBL	Western Biological Laboratories
WBL	White Bluff [*Washington*] [*Seismograph station code, US Geological Survey*] (SEIS)
WBL	Wideband LASER
WBL	Wideband Limiting (IEEE)
WBL	Women's Basketball League [*Defunct*] (EA)
WBL	Wood Blocking
W Bla	[*Sir William*] Blackstone's English King's Bench Reports [*1746-80*] [*A publication*] (DLA)
WBLA.......	Elizabethtown, NC [*AM radio station call letters*]
W Black	[*Sir William*] Blackstone's English King's Bench Reports [*1746-80*] [*A publication*] (ILCA)
WBLB........	Pulaski, VA [*AM radio station call letters*]
WBLC........	Lenoir City, TN [*AM radio station call letters*]
WBLC........	Water-Borne Logistics Craft
WBLD	Orchard Lake, MI [*FM radio station call letters*]
WBLE........	Batesville, MS [*FM radio station call letters*]
W Bl (Eng) ...	[*Sir William*] Blackstone's English King's Bench Reports [*1746-80*] [*A publication*] (DLA)
WBLF	Bellefonte, PA [*AM radio station call letters*]
Wbl voor Fiscaal Recht ...	Weekblad voor Fiscaal Recht [*A publication*]
WBLG	Smiths Grove, KY [*FM radio station call letters*]
WBLI	Patchogue, NY [*FM radio station call letters*]
WBLJ	Dalton, GA [*AM radio station call letters*]
WBLK.......	Depew, NY [*FM radio station call letters*]
WBLL........	Bellefontaine, OH [*AM radio station call letters*]
WBLM	Portland, ME [*FM radio station call letters*]
WBLMC....	Worldwide Branch Locations of Multinational Companies [*A publication*]
WBLN	Murray, KY [*FM radio station call letters*]
WBLO	Weak Black Liquor Oxidation [*Pulp and paper technology*]
WBLQ	Block Island, RI [*FM radio station call letters*]
WBLR	Batesburg, SC [*AM radio station call letters*]
WBLS........	New York, NY [*FM radio station call letters*]
WBLT........	Bedford, VA [*AM radio station call letters*]
WBLU	Moneta, VA [*FM radio station call letters*]
WBLV	Twin Lake, MI [*FM radio station call letters*]
WBLX........	Fairhope, AL [*AM radio station call letters*]
WBLX........	Mobile, AL [*FM radio station call letters*]
WBLY	Springfield, OH [*AM radio station call letters*]
WBM	Beloit Memorial Hospital, Beloit, WI [*Library symbol*] [*Library of Congress*] (LCLS)
WBM	Wapenamanda [*Papua New Guinea*] [*Airport symbol*] (OAG)
W B M	Weber Meter
WBM	Wing Battle Manager [*Air Force*]
WBM	Woerterbuch der Mythologie [*A publication*] (BJA)
WBM	Women's Board of Missions
WBMA	Dedham, MA [*AM radio station call letters*]
WBMA	Western Building Material Association (EA)
WBMA	Whirlpool Bath Manufacturers Association [*Glen Ellyn, IL*] (EA)
WBMA	Wirebound Box Manufacturers Association (EA)
WBMB	West Branch, MI [*AM radio station call letters*]
WBMC	McMinnville, TN [*AM radio station call letters*]
WBMC	Weight before Mars Capture [*NASA*]
WBMCR....	Wideband Multichannel Receiver
WBMD	Baltimore, MD [*AM radio station call letters*]
WBMG	Birmingham, AL [*Television station call letters*]
WBMG	Walter Bernard and Milton Glaser [*Founders of the magazine-design firm that bears their initials*]
WBMH	Birmingham, AL [*FM radio station call letters*]
WBMI	West Branch, MI [*FM radio station call letters*]
WBMI	Women's Board of Missions of the Interior
WBMJ	San Juan, PR [*AM radio station call letters*]
WBML	Macon, GA [*AM radio station call letters*]
WBMO......	Weather Bureau Meteorological Observation Station [*Obsolete*]
WBMQ	Savannah, GA [*AM radio station call letters*]
WBMR	Telford, PA [*FM radio station call letters*]
WBMS.......	Wilmington, NC [*AM radio station call letters*]
WBMS.......	World Bureau of Metal Statistics [*British*] (EAIO)
WBMT	Boxford, MA [*FM radio station call letters*]
WBMW	Ledyard, CT [*FM radio station call letters*]
WBMX	Boston, MA [*FM radio station call letters*]
WbMyth	Woerterbuch der Mythologie [*A publication*] (BJA)
WBN..........	Waban, Inc. [*NYSE symbol*] (SPSG)
WBN..........	Weekly Book Newsletter [*A publication*]
WBN..........	Well Behaved Net
WBN..........	West by North
W Bn	White Beacon
WBN..........	Wolfenbuetteler Barock-Nachrichten [*A publication*]
WBNA	Louisville, KY [*Television station call letters*]
WBNB	Charlotte Amalie, VI [*Television station call letters*]
WBNC	Conway, NH [*AM radio station call letters*]
WBNC	Washington Bancorp, Inc. [*NASDAQ symbol*] (NQ)
WBND.......	Pensacola Beach, FL [*AM radio station call letters*]
WBND.......	Westbound (FAAC)
W BNDR ...	With Binder [*Freight*]
WBNG.......	Binghamton, NY [*Television station call letters*]

WBNH....... Pekin, IL [*FM radio station call letters*]
WBNI .... Fort Wayne, IN [*FM radio station call letters*]
WBNJ........ Cape May Court House, NJ [*FM radio station call letters*]
WBNK .... Binghamton, NY [*AM radio station call letters*]
WBNL .... Boonville, IN [*AM radio station call letters*]
WBNL .... Wideband Noise Limiting
WBNL-FM ... Boonville, IN [*FM radio station call letters*]
WBNM...... Gordon, GA [*AM radio station call letters*]
WBNN....... Union City, OH [*FM radio station call letters*]
WBNO .... Bryan, OH [*AM radio station call letters*]
WBNP .... Watts Bar Nuclear Plant   (NRCH)
WBNP .... Wood Buffalo National Park. Newsletter [*A publication*]
WBNQ .... Bloomington, IL [*FM radio station call letters*]
WBNR .... Beacon, NY [*AM radio station call letters*]
WBNS .... Columbus, OH [*AM radio station call letters*]
WBNS ...... Water Boiler Neutron Source Reactor [*Nuclear energy*]
WBNS-FM ... Columbus, OH [*FM radio station call letters*]
WBNS-TV ... Columbus, OH [*Television station call letters*]
WBNT....... Oneida, TN [*FM radio station call letters*]
WBNV....... Barnesville, OH [*FM radio station call letters*]
WBNV....... Wideband Noise Voltage
WB/NWRC ... Weather Bureau/National Weather Records Center
            [*Obsolete*]   (KSC)
WBNX....... Akron, OH [*Television station call letters*]
WBNY .... Buffalo, NY [*FM radio station call letters*]
WBNZ .... Frankfort, MI [*FM radio station call letters*]
WBO .... Beroroha [*Madagascar*] [*Airport symbol*]   (OAG)
WBO .... Weather Bureau Office [*Later, National Weather Service*]
WBO .... Wideband Oscilloscope
WBO .... Wideband Overlap
WBO .... Wien Bridge Oscillator [*Physics*]
W/BO .... With Blowout   (MSA)
WBO .... World Boxing Organization   (EA)
WBOB .... Galax, VA [*AM radio station call letters*]
WBOC .... Salisbury, MD [*Television station call letters*]
WBOD....... Waste Biochemical Oxygen Demand [*Oceanography*]
WBOK .... New Orleans, LA [*AM radio station call letters*]
WBOL .... Bolivar, TN [*AM radio station call letters*]
WBOLA .... Wasser, Boden, Luft [*A publication*]
WBOP .... Churchville, VA [*FM radio station call letters*]
WBOQ .... Gloucester, MA [*FM radio station call letters*]
WBOR .... Brunswick, ME [*FM radio station call letters*]
W/BOR ..... White Border [*Deltiology*]
WBOS .... Brookline, MA [*FM radio station call letters*]
WBOW ...... Terre Haute, IN [*AM radio station call letters*]
WBOX .... Bogalusa, LA [*AM radio station call letters*]
WBOX .... Varnado, LA [*FM radio station call letters*]
WBOY .... Clarksburg, WV [*Television station call letters*]
WBP .... Wartime Basic Plan
WBP .... Water Bank Program [*Department of Agriculture*]
WBP .... Water Binding Potential [*of protein*]
WBP .... Weather- and Boil-Proof   (IEEE)
WBP .... Woodwind World - Brass and Percussion [*A publication*]
WBPA....... Elkhorn City, KY [*AM radio station call letters*]
WBPH....... Bethlehem, PA [*Television station call letters*]
WBPK....... Flemingsburg, KY [*FM radio station call letters*]
WBPM ...... Kingston, NY [*FM radio station call letters*]
WBPR....... Georgetown, SC [*FM radio station call letters*]
W v B Pr.... Wetboek van Burgerlijk Procesrecht [*A publication*]
WBPS .... Winder, GA [*AM radio station call letters*]
WBPT....... Naples, FL [*FM radio station call letters*]
WBPTT ..... Whole Blood Partial Thromboplastin Time [*Hematology*]
WBPV....... Charlton, MA [*FM radio station call letters*]
WBPW ...... Presque Isle, ME [*FM radio station call letters*]
WBPZ .... Lock Haven, PA [*AM radio station call letters*]
WBQ .... Beaver [*Alaska*] [*Airport symbol*]   (OAG)
WBQ .... Beaver, AK [*Location identifier*] [*FAA*]   (FAAL)
WBQB .... Fredricksburg, VA [*FM radio station call letters*]
WBQN....... Barceloneta, PR [*AM radio station call letters*]
WBQQ....... Kennebunk, ME [*FM radio station call letters*]
WBQR .... Attica, IN [*FM radio station call letters*]
WBR .... Water Boiler Reactor
WBR .... Westbank Resources, Inc. [*Vancouver Stock Exchange symbol*]
WBR .... Wetboek van Burgerlijke Regtsvordering [*Code of Civil
            Procedure*] [*Dutch*]   (ILCA)
WBR .... Whole Body Radiation
WBR .... Wideband Data Recorder
WBR .... Wideband Receiver
WBR .... Word Buffer Register   (MSA)
WBR .... Workbench Rack   (MCD)
WBRA .... Roanoke, VA [*Television station call letters*]
WBRB....... Mount Clemens, MI [*AM radio station call letters*]
WBRBN .... Will Be Reported by NOTAM [*Notice to Airmen*]   (FAAC)
WBRC ...... Birmingham, AL [*Television station call letters*]
WBRC .... Walter Bagehot Research Council on National
            Sovereignty   (EA)
WBRD .... Palmetto, FL [*AM radio station call letters*]
WBRD .... Wallboard
WBrE........ Elmbrook Memorial Hospital, Brookfield, WI [*Library symbol*]
            [*Library of Congress*]   (LCLS)
WBRE........ Wilkes-Barre, PA [*Television station call letters*]

WBRF........ Galax, VA [*FM radio station call letters*]
WBRG .... Lynchburg, VA [*AM radio station call letters*]
W/BRG..... Wheel Bearing [*Automotive engineering*]
WBRH .... Baton Rouge, LA [*FM radio station call letters*]
WBRH .... Weather Bureau Regional Headquarters [*Obsolete*]   (FAAC)
WBRI........ Indianapolis, IN [*AM radio station call letters*]
WBrI........ International Foundation of Employee Benefit Plans,
            Information Center, Brookfield, WI [*Library symbol*]
            [*Library of Congress*]   (LCLS)
WBRJ .... Marietta, OH [*AM radio station call letters*]
WBRK .... Pittsfield, MA [*AM radio station call letters*]
WBRL....... Berlin, NH [*AM radio station call letters*]
WBRM ...... Marion, NC [*AM radio station call letters*]
WBRN ...... Big Rapids, MI [*AM radio station call letters*]
WBRN-FM ... Big Rapids, MI [*FM radio station call letters*]
WBro......... Brodhead Memorial Public Library, Brodhead, WI [*Library
            symbol*] [*Library of Congress*]   (LCLS)
WBRO ...... Waynesboro, GA [*AM radio station call letters*]
WBRO ...... Weather Bureau Regional Office [*Obsolete*]
W BRO ..... Worshipful Brother [*Freemasonry*]
WBRQ ...... Cidra, PR [*FM radio station call letters*]
WBRR .... Bradford, PA [*FM radio station call letters*]
WBRR .... Weather Bureau RADAR Remote [*Meteorology*]
WBRS........ Waltham, MA [*FM radio station call letters*]
WBRS........ Wideband Remote Switch   (IEEE)
WBRS........ Wrought Brass   (MSA)
WBRT....... Bardstown, KY [*AM radio station call letters*]
WBRT....... Weather Bureau Radiotheolite [*Meteorology*]
WBRT....... Whole-Blood Recalcification Time [*Hematology*]
WBRU .... Providence, RI [*FM radio station call letters*]
WBRV ...... Boonville, NY [*AM radio station call letters*]
WBRV-FM ... Boonville, NY [*FM radio station call letters*]
WBRW ...... Bridgewater, NJ [*AM radio station call letters*]
WBRX .... Patton, PA [*FM radio station call letters*]
WBRY .... Woodbury, TN [*AM radio station call letters*]
WBRZ....... Baton Rouge, LA [*Television station call letters*]
WBS......... Wage Board Staff
WB-S......... Wage Board, Supervisor [*Civil Service classification*]
WBS.......... Wallace Barnes Steel [*Wallace Barnes Co.*]
WBS.......... Washington Bibliographic Service [*Information service or
            system*]   (IID)
WBS.......... Waterloo County Board of Education [*UTLAS symbol*]
WBS.......... Weight and Balance System   (MCD)
WBS.......... Welsh Bibliographical Society [*British*]
WBS.......... West by South
WBS.......... Western Base Section [*England*] [*World War II*]
WBS.......... Western Conservative Baptist Theological Seminary, Portland,
            OR [*OCLC symbol*]   (OCLC)
WBS.......... Whole Blood Serotonin [*Biochemistry*]
WBS.......... Whole Body Shower
WBS.......... Wideband System [*Ground Communications Facility, NASA*]
WBS.......... Without Benefit of Salvage
WBS.......... Work Breakdown Sheets [*Army*]
WBS.......... Work Breakdown Structure [*Data processing*]
WBSA....... Boaz, AL [*AM radio station call letters*]
WBSA....... Weather Bureau Synoptic and Aviation Reporting Station
            [*Obsolete*]
WBSA....... Westlands Diversified Bancorp [*NASDAQ symbol*]   (NQ)
WBSB....... Baltimore, MD [*FM radio station call letters*]
WBSB....... Brunei/International [*Brunei*] [*ICAO location
            identifier*]   (ICLI)
WBSC....... Bennettsville, SC [*AM radio station call letters*]
WBSC....... Wideband Signal Conditioner   (NASA)
WBSC........ Work Breakdown Structure Code   (MCD)
WBSCB .... Work Breakdown Structure Control Board [*Army*]   (AABC)
WBSD....... Burlington, WI [*FM radio station call letters*]
WBSF........ Melbourne, FL [*Television station call letters*]
WBSG....... Brunswick, GA [*Television station call letters*]
WBSH ...... Heflin, AL [*AM radio station call letters*]
WBSI........ Western Behavioral Sciences Institute   (EA)
WBSIGSTA ... Weather Bureau Signal Station [*Obsolete*]
WBSK........ Portsmouth, VA [*AM radio station call letters*]
WBSL........ Bay St. Louis, MS [*AM radio station call letters*]
WBSL........ Sheffield, MA [*FM radio station call letters*]
WBSL........ Wide Beam Special LASER   (MCD)
WBSM...... New Bedford, MA [*AM radio station call letters*]
WBSN....... New Orleans, LA [*FM radio station call letters*]
WBSO .... Clinton, MA [*AM radio station call letters*]
WBSP........ Western Beet Sugar Producers [*Defunct*]
WBSR....... Pensacola, FL [*AM radio station call letters*]
WBSS .... Millville, NJ [*FM radio station call letters*]
WBST .... Muncie, IN [*FM radio station call letters*]
WBST........ Webster Financial Corp. [*Waterbury, CT*] [*NASDAQ
            symbol*]   (NQ)
WBSU ...... Brockport, NY [*FM radio station call letters*]
WBSV....... Venice, FL [*Television station call letters*]
WBSX....... Ann Arbor, MI [*Television station call letters*]
WBT .... Charlotte, NC [*AM radio station call letters*]
WBT .... Wet Bulb Temperature
WBT .... Wichita Board of Trade [*Defunct*]   (EA)
WBT .... Wideband Terminal   (MCD)

WBT .... Wideband Transformer [or Transmitter]
WBT .... Women in Broadcast Technology   (EA)
WBT .... Wycliffe Bible Translators   (EA)
WBTA ...... Batavia, NY [AM radio station call letters]
WBTA .... Wisconsin Board of Tax Appeals Decisions [A
                publication]   (DLA)
WBTA-CCH Tax Reporter ... Wisconsin Board of Tax Appeals Decisions
                (Commerce Clearing House) [A publication]   (DLA)
WBTB........ Beaufort, NC [AM radio station call letters]
WBTC........ Uhrichsville, OH [AM radio station call letters]
WBTC........ Waterways Bulk Transportation Council   (EA)
WBTE........ Weapon Battery Terminal Equipment [Air Force]
WBTE........ Windsor, NC [AM radio station call letters]
WBTF........ Attica, NY [FM radio station call letters]
WBTF........ Wrightsville Beach Test Facility [Department of the
                Interior]   (NOAA)
WBT-FM... Charlotte, NC [FM radio station call letters]
WBTG .... Sheffield, AL [AM radio station call letters]
WBTG-FM ... Sheffield, AL [FM radio station call letters]
WBTH....... Williamson, WV [AM radio station call letters]
WBTI........ Lexington, MI [FM radio station call letters]
WBTM ...... Danville, VA [AM radio station call letters]
WBTM HYDRO ... Weather Bureau Technical Memorandum: Hydrology
                [Office of Hydrology] [Washington, DC] [A publication]
WBTN .... Bennington, VT [AM radio station call letters]
WBTO .... Linton, IN [AM radio station call letters]
WBTQ ...... Buckhannon, WV [FM radio station call letters]
WBTR........ Carrollton, GA [FM radio station call letters]
WBTS........ Bridgeport, AL [AM radio station call letters]
WBTS........ Waco, Beaumont, Trinity & Sabine Railway Co. [AAR code]
WBTS........ Whereabouts   (FAAC)
WBTS........ Wideband Transmission System   (KSC)
WBTU .... Kendallville, IN [FM radio station call letters]
WBTV........ Charlotte, NC [Television station call letters]
WBTV........ Weather Briefing Television   (AFM)
WBTW ...... Florence, SC [Television station call letters]
WBTX........ Broadway-Timberville, VA [AM radio station call letters]
WBTY........ Homerville, GA [FM radio station call letters]
WBU.......... Boulder [Colorado] [Airport symbol]   (OAG)
WBU.......... Welsh Badminton Union   (EAIO)
WBU.......... Wilberforce University, Wilberforce, OH [OCLC
                symbol]   (OCLC)
WBU.......... World Billiards Union   (EAIO)
WBU.......... World Blind Union   (EA)
WBUB ...... St. George, SC [FM radio station call letters]
WBUC .... Buckhannon, WV [AM radio station call letters]
WBUC .... Western Boundary Undercurrent [Atlantic Ocean]
WBUC-FM ... Buckhannon, WV [FM radio station call letters]
WBUD....... Trenton, NJ [AM radio station call letters]
WBUF .... Buffalo, NY [FM radio station call letters]
WBUG....... Amsterdam, NY [AM radio station call letters]
WBUK .... Fort Shawnee, OH [FM radio station call letters]
WBUQ....... Bloomsburg, PA [FM radio station call letters]
WBUR .... Boston, MA [FM radio station call letters]
WBur .... Burlington Public Library, Burlington, WI [Library symbol]
                [Library of Congress]   (LCLS)
WBurSFC ... Saint Francis College, Burlington, WI [Library symbol] [Library
                of Congress] [Obsolete]   (LCLS)
WBURY .... Westbury [England]
WBUS .... Kankakee, IL [FM radio station call letters]
WBUT .... Butler, PA [AM radio station call letters]
WBUX .... Doylestown, PA [AM radio station call letters]
WBUY .... Holly Springs, MS [Television station call letters]
WBUZ .... Fredonia, NY [AM radio station call letters]
WBV .... Wideband Voltage
WBV .... Woningraad. Informatiekrant voor Woningcorporaties [A
                publication]
WBVCO .... Wideband Voltage-Controlled Oscillator
WBVCXO ... Wideband Voltage-Controlled Crystal Oscillator
WBVI......... Fostoria, OH [FM radio station call letters]
WBVM ...... Tampa, FL [FM radio station call letters]
WBVN .... Carrier Mills, IL [FM radio station call letters]
WBVP........ Beaver Falls, PA [AM radio station call letters]
WBVR .... Russellville, KY [FM radio station call letters]
WBVRC..... West Bromwich Volunteer Rifle Corps [British
                military]   (DMA)
WBVTR..... Wideband Video Tape Recorder
WBW .... Wilkes-Barre, PA [Location identifier] [FAA]   (FAAL)
WBW .... Wilson Butte [Washington] [Seismograph station code, US
                Geological Survey]   (SEIS)
WBW .... World Bowling Writers   (EA)
WBW .... World Business Weekly [A publication]
WBWB ...... Bloomington, IN [FM radio station call letters]
WBWC ...... Berea, OH [FM radio station call letters]
WBWI .... West Bend, WI [FM radio station call letters]
WBWT ...... Wright Brothers Memorial Wind Tunnel [Massachusetts
                Institute of Technology] [Research center]   (RCD)
WBX .... Wooden Box   (MSA)
WBXB........ Edenton, NC [FM radio station call letters]
WBXL........ Baldwinsville, NY [FM radio station call letters]
WBXQ .... Cresson, PA [FM radio station call letters]

WBXR .... Fayetteville, TN [AM radio station call letters]
WBXT........ Canton, OH [AM radio station call letters]
WBXX .... Battle Creek, MI [FM radio station call letters]
WBY .... Wimberly Resources [Vancouver Stock Exchange symbol]
WBYE........ Calera, AL [AM radio station call letters]
WBYG ...... Point Pleasant, WV [FM radio station call letters]
WBYO .... Sellersville, PA [FM radio station call letters]
WBYQ ...... Baltimore, MD [FM radio station call letters]
WBYR .... Van Wert, OH [FM radio station call letters]
WBYS........ Canton, IL [AM radio station call letters]
WBYS-FM ... Canton, IL [FM radio station call letters]
WBYU .... New Orleans, LA [AM radio station call letters]
WBYW ...... Grand Rapids, MI [FM radio station call letters]
WBYY .... Rockford, MI [FM radio station call letters]
WBYZ........ Baxley, GA [FM radio station call letters]
WBZ .... Boston, MA [AM radio station call letters]
WBZ .... Wadati-Benioff Zone [Geology]
WBZ .... Works and Building, Low Priority [British] [World War II]
WBZA ...... Glens Falls, NY [AM radio station call letters]
WBZB........ Selma, NC [AM radio station call letters]
WBZD ...... Cadiz, KY [FM radio station call letters]
WBZI........ Xenia, OH [AM radio station call letters]
WBZK .... York, SC [AM radio station call letters]
WBZL........ Brazil, IN [AM radio station call letters]
WBZR .... Destin, FL [AM radio station call letters]
WBZS........ Eatonville, FL [AM radio station call letters]
WBZ-TV.... Boston, MA [Television station call letters]
WBZW ...... Loudonville, OH [FM radio station call letters]
WBZY .... New Castle, PA [AM radio station call letters]
WBZZ........ Pittsburgh, PA [FM radio station call letters]
WC............ Cudahy Public Library, Cudahy, WI [Library symbol] [Library
                of Congress]   (LCLS)
WC............ Wage Change
WC............ Wages Council [British]   (DCTA)
W/C .... Waiver of Coinsurance [Fire contract clause]
WC............ Walkways Center   (EA)
WC............ Walnut Council   (EA)
WC............ War Cabinet [World War II]
WC............ War College
WC............ War Communications
WC............ Ward Clerk [Medicine]
WC............ Warning Computer [Aviation]
WC............ Watch Commanders
WC............ Watch Committee [British]   (ILCA)
WC............ Water Chiller   (DWSG)
WC............ Water Closet [A toilet] [Slang]
WC............ Water Cock   (ROG)
WC............ Water Column [Mechanical engineering]
WC............ Water Content
WC............ Water-Cooled   (DEN)
WC............ Waterfront Center   (EA)
W/C .... Watts per Candle [Electricity]
W/C .... Wave Change
WC............ WCN Investment [Vancouver Stock Exchange symbol]
WC............ We Care   (EA)
WC............ Weapon Carrier
WC............ Weapons Command [Later, Armaments Command] [Army]
WC............ Weapons Control [or Controller]   (NVT)
WC............ Weather Condition [Nuclear energy]   (NRCH)
W/C .... Week Commencing   (ADA)
WC............ Weiman Co., Inc. [AMEX symbol]   (SPSG)
WC............ Wesleyan Chapel   (ROG)
WC............ West Central [Refers especially to London postal district]
WC............ West Coast Airlines, Inc.
WC............ Westbeth Corp.   (EA)
WC............ Western Cedar [Utility pole] [Telecommunications]   (TEL)
WC............ Western Central
WC............ Western Classification
WC............ Western Command
WC............ Westminster College [London, England]
WC............ Westminster Commentaries [Oxford] [A publication]   (BJA)
W & C .... Westmorland and Cumberland Yeomanry [British
                military]   (DMA)
WC............ Whale Center   (EA)
WC............ Wheel Center   (MSA)
WC............ Wheelchair
WC............ White Cell [Medicine]
WC............ White Cell Cast [Hematology]   (MAE)
W/C .... White Clothing [British military]   (DMA)
W/C .... White Collar [Worker]   (DCTA)
WC............ White Confederacy   (EA)
WC............ White Count [Hematology]
WC............ Whole Complement   (MAE)
WC............ Whooping Cough [Medicine]
WC............ Width Codes   (AAG)
WC............ Will Call
WC............ Wills Club   (EA)
WC............ Willys Club   (EA)
WC............ Wilshire Club   (EA)
W & C .... Wilson and Courtenay's Scotch Appeal Cases [A
                publication]   (DLA)

WC............ Wing Commander [*British military*]
WC............ Wings Club   (EA)
WC............ Winston Cup
W & C .... Wire and Cable   (NASA)
WC............ Wire Chief [*Test clerk*] [*Telecommunications*]   (TEL)
WC............ With Corrections [*Publishing*]
WC............ Without Charge
WC............ Woden's Coven [*Germany*]   (EAIO)
W-C............ Women-Church: an Australian Journal of Feminist Studies in
                Religion [*A publication*]   (APTA)
WC............ Women in Communications   (EA)
WC............ Women's Reserve, Communications Duties [*USNR officer
                designation*]
WC............ Wood Casing
WC............ Wood Covers   (DS)
WC............ Woolwich College [*London, England*]
WC............ Word Count [*Data processing*]
WC............ Wordsworth Circle [*A publication*]
WC............ Work Capacity   (MAE)
WC............ Work Card   (AAG)
WC............ Work Center   (AFM)
WC............ Work Circle   (AAG)
WC............ Work Control   (AAG)
WC............ Working Capital
WC............ Working Circle [*Technical drawings*]
WC............ Workmen's Circle [*New York, NY*]   (EA)
WC............ Workmen's Compensation [*Department of Health and Human
                Services*]
WC............ World Christian [*A publication*]
WC............ World Concern   (EA)
WC............ World Coordinate
WC............ World's Classics [*A publication*]
WC............ Write and Compute
WC............ Written Component [*Qualification test*] [*Military*]
WC............ Wspolczesnosc [*A publication*]
3WC.......... Third Wave Civilization [*Title of record album by Ian Lloyd*]
WCA.......... Warrant Claims Action [*Army*]
WCA.......... Water Companies' Association [*British*]
WCA.......... Weapon Control Area [*Military*]   (CAAL)
WCA.......... Weimaraner Club of America   (EA)
WCA.......... West Coast of Africa   (ROG)
WCA.......... West Coast Airlines, Inc.
WCA.......... West Coast Airlines Ltd. [*Ghana*]
WCA.......... Westair Commuter Airlines [*Santa Rosa, CA*] [*FAA
                designator*]   (FAAC)
WCA.......... Western College Association   (EA)
WCA.......... Who Cares, Anyway?
WCA.......... Whole Core Accident [*Nuclear energy*]   (NRCH)
WCA.......... Wideband Cassegrain Antenna
WCA.......... Willys Club of America [*Later, WC*]   (EA)
WCA.......... Windmill Class Association   (EA)
WCA.......... Wine Conference of America   (EA)
WCA.......... Winston S. Churchill Association   (EA)
WCA.......... Wireless Cable Association   (TSSD)
WCA.......... Wisco of Canada Ltd. [*Vancouver Stock Exchange symbol*]
WCA.......... Women's Caucus for Art   (EA)
WCA.......... Women's Christian Association
WCA.......... Women's Cricket Association [*British*]
WCA.......... Workmen's Compensation Act
WCA.......... World Campus Afloat [*Cruise ship educational program*]   (EA)
WCA.......... World Citizens Assembly [*Later, AWC*]   (EA)
WCA.......... World Communication Association   (EA)
WCA.......... Worst Case Analysis
WCAA........ Window Coverings Association of America   (EA)
WCAB .... Rutherfordton, NC [*AM radio station call letters*]
WCAB .... Working Committee of the Aeronautical Board
WCAC .... Sebring, FL [*FM radio station call letters*]
WCACTC ... West Coast Air Corps Training Center
WCAD....... San Juan, PR [*FM radio station call letters*]
WCAE .... Nekoosa, WI [*AM radio station call letters*]
WCAFS ..... Wideband Cassegrain Antenna Feed System
WCAG....... Oviedo, FL [*AM radio station call letters*]
WCAI .... Water Conditioning Association International [*Later,
                WQA*]   (EA)
WCAL .... Northfield, MN [*AM radio station call letters*]
WCAL-FM ... Northfield, MN [*FM radio station call letters*]
WCAM ...... Camden, SC [*AM radio station call letters*]
WCAM ...... Wisconsin Center for Applied Microelectronics [*University of
                Wisconsin - Madison*] [*Research center*]   (RCD)
WCAN....... Canajoharie, NY [*FM radio station call letters*]
WCAN....... Worldwide Crisis Alerting Network   (MCD)
W Can J Ant ... West Canadian Journal of Anthropology [*A publication*]
WCAO....... Baltimore, MD [*AM radio station call letters*]
WCAP ...... Lowell, MA [*AM radio station call letters*]
WCAP ...... Westinghouse Commercial Atomic Power
WCAP ...... World Climate Applications Program [*WMO*] [*ICSU*]
WCAR ...... Livonia, MI [*AM radio station call letters*]
WCAR ...... West Coast Formula Atlantic (Racing)
WCAR ...... Western Carolina Savings & Loan Association, Inc. [*NASDAQ
                symbol*]   (NQ)
WCAS........ Tarboro, NC [*FM radio station call letters*]

WCAS........ Western Casualty & Surety [*NASDAQ symbol*]   (NQ)
WCASS ..... World Conference of Ashkenazi and Sephardi Synagogues
WCAT .... Athol, MA [*FM radio station call letters*]
WCAT .... Orange-Athol, MA [*AM radio station call letters*]
WCAT .... Weiss Comprehensive Articulation Test [*Education*]
WCAT .... WICAT Systems, Inc. [*NASDAQ symbol*]   (NQ)
WCAU .... Philadelphia, PA [*Television station call letters*]
WCAV .... Brockton, MA [*FM radio station call letters*]
WCAW ..... Charleston, WV [*AM radio station call letters*]
WCAX .... Burlington, VT [*Television station call letters*]
WCAZ .... Carthage, IL [*AM radio station call letters*]
WCAZ-FM ... Carthage, IL [*FM radio station call letters*]
WCB .... War Communications Board [*World War II*]
WCB .... Warramunga Array [*Australia*] [*Seismograph station code, US
                Geological Survey*]   (SEIS)
WCB .... Water Control Board
WCB .... Way Control Block
WCB .... Weekly Criminal Bulletin [*Canada Law Book, Inc.*]
                [*Information service or system*]
WCB .... Wellington County Board of Education [*UTLAS symbol*]
WCB .... Will Call Back
WCB .... William C. Brown Publishers
WCB .... Workmen's Compensation Board
WCBA .... Corning, NY [*AM radio station call letters*]
WCBA-FM ... Corning, NY [*FM radio station call letters*]
WCBB........ Augusta, ME [*Television station call letters*]
WCBC........ Cumberland, MD [*AM radio station call letters*]
WCBC........ West Coast Bancorp [*NASDAQ symbol*]   (NQ)
WCBC........ World Candlepin Bowling Council
WCBD .... Charleston, SC [*Television station call letters*]
WCBD (Vic) ... Workers Compensation Board Decisions (Victoria) [*A
                publication*]   (APTA)
WCBD (WA) ... Workers Compensation Board Decisions (Western Australia)
                [*A publication*]   (APTA)
WCBG .... Chambersburg, PA [*AM radio station call letters*]
WCBH........ Casey, IL [*FM radio station call letters*]
WCBI .... Columbus, MS [*Television station call letters*]
WCBK .... Martinsville, IN [*FM radio station call letters*]
WCBK .... Workingmens Corp. [*NASDAQ symbol*]   (NQ)
WCBL........ Benton, KY [*AM radio station call letters*]
WCBL........ World Council of Blind Lions [*Later, ACBL*]   (EA)
WCBL-FM ... Benton, KY [*FM radio station call letters*]
WCBM ..... Baltimore, MD [*AM radio station call letters*]
WCBN ...... Ann Arbor, MI [*FM radio station call letters*]
WCBQ ...... Oxford, NC [*AM radio station call letters*]
WCBR ...... Arlington Heights, IL [*FM radio station call letters*]
WCBR ...... Richmond, KY [*AM radio station call letters*]
WCBS .... New York, NY [*AM radio station call letters*]
WCBS........ World Confederation of Billiards Sports [*Malaysia*]   (EAIO)
WCBS-FM ... New York, NY [*FM radio station call letters*]
WCBS-TV ... New York, NY [*Television station call letters*]
WCBSU...... West Coast Base Service Unit [*Navy*]
WCBT........ Roanoke Rapids, NC [*AM radio station call letters*]
WCBU .... Peoria, IL [*FM radio station call letters*]
WCB (Vic) ... Workers Compensation Board Decisions (Victoria) [*A
                publication*]   (APTA)
WCBW ...... Columbia, IL [*FM radio station call letters*]
WCBX ...... Fieldale, VA [*AM radio station call letters*]
WCBY ...... Cheboygan, MI [*AM radio station call letters*]
WCBZ....... Bowling Green, KY [*FM radio station call letters*]
WCC .... Gerard P. Weeg Computing Center [*University of Iowa*]
                [*Research center*]   (RCD)
WCC .... Wallace Communications Consultants [*Tampa, FL*]
                [*Telecommunications*]   (TSSD)
WCC .... War Claims Commission [*Abolished, 1954*]
WCC .... War Cover Club   (EA)
WCC .... Washington's United States Circuit Court Reports [*A
                publication*]   (DLA)
WCC .... Waste Collection Containers
WCC .... Water-Cooled Copper
WCC .... Waters Computing Center [*Rose-Hulman Institute of
                Technology*] [*Research center*]   (RCD)
WCC .... Watson Collectors Club   (EA)
WCC .... Weapon Control Computer   (MCD)
WCC .... Weapon Control Console [*Military*]   (CAAL)
WCC .... Weapons Control Concept   (MCD)
WCC .... Welsh Consumer Council [*British*]   (ILCA)
WCC .... Westchester Community College [*Valhalla, NY*]
WCC .... Westchester Community College, Technical Services, Valhalla,
                NY [*OCLC symbol*]   (OCLC)
WCC .... Western Canada Concept [*Political party*]   (PPW)
WCC .... Western Carolina College [*Later, WCU*] [*North Carolina*]
WCC .... Westminster Choir College [*Princeton, NJ*]
WCC .... Whim Creek Consolidated [*Toronto Stock Exchange symbol*]
WCC .... White Cell Count [*Hematology*]   (MAE)
WCC .... Whitney Communications Corp. [*New York, NY*]
WCC .... Widows Consultation Center [*Defunct*]   (EA)
WCC .... Wildfire Coordinating Committee   (EA)
WCC .... Wilson Cloud Chamber [*Physics*]
WCC .... Wingate Computer Center   (HGAA)
WCC .... Women of the Church Coalition   (EA)

WCC .... Women's Classical Caucus (EA)
WCC .... Women's College Coalition (EA)
WCC .... Women's Consultative Committee [*Ministry of Labour*] [*British*] [*World War II*]
WCC .... Work Center Code
WCC .... Work Control Center (AAG)
WCC .... Workers' Compensation Cases [*A publication*] (APTA)
WCC .... Workmen's Circle Call [*A publication*]
WCC .... Workmen's Compensation Cases [*Legal*] [*British*]
WCC .... World Cheerleader Council (EA)
WCC .... World for Christ Crusade (EA)
WCC .... World Congress Centre [*Melbourne, Australia*]
WCC .... World Congress on Computing [*Trade show*]
WCC .... West Council of Christians (EA)
WCC .... World Council of Churches [*Geneva, Switzerland*]
WCC .... World Council of Clergy (EA)
WCC .... World Crafts Council (EA)
WCC .... Worldwide Collectors Club [*Later, ISWSC*] (EA)
WCCA ...... Shallotte, NC [*FM radio station call letters*]
WCCA ...... West Coast Crossarm Association [*Defunct*]
WCCA ...... Whiteruthenian [*Byelorussian*] Congress Committee of America [*Later, Byelorussian Congress Committee of America*] (EA)
WCCA ...... Whooping Crane Conservation Association (EA)
WCCA ...... World Court Clubs Association [*Defunct*] (EA)
WCCA ...... Worst Case Circuit Analysis
WCCB .... Charlotte, NC [*Television station call letters*]
WCCC ...... Hartford, CT [*AM radio station call letters*]
WCCC ...... Warwick China Collectors Club (EA)
WCCC ...... Wayne County Community College [*Detroit, MI*]
WCCC ...... Western Commercial [*Fresno, CA*] [*NASDAQ symbol*] (NQ)
WCCC ...... Wisconsin Clinical Cancer Center [*University of Wisconsin*] [*Research center*] (RCD)
WCCC ...... World Convention of Churches of Christ (EA)
WCCC-FM ... Hartford, CT [*FM radio station call letters*]
WCC&CRA ... World Championship Cutter and Chariot Racing Association (EA)
WCCD ...... Parma, OH [*AM radio station call letters*]
WCCE .... Buie's Creek, NC [*FM radio station call letters*]
WCCE ...... West Coast Commodity Exchange
WCCE .... World Council of Christian Education [*Later absorbed into Office of Education of World Council of Churches*]
WCCES ..... World Council of Comparative Education Societies (EA)
WCCESSA ... World Council of Christian Education and Sunday School Association [*Later, WCCE*] (EA)
WCCF .... Punta Gorda, FL [*AM radio station call letters*]
WCCG ...... Hope Mills, NC [*FM radio station call letters*]
WCCH ...... Holyoke, MA [*FM radio station call letters*]
WCCI .... Savanna, IL [*FM radio station call letters*]
WCCI .... World Council for Curriculum and Instruction (EA)
WCCK ...... Erie, PA [*FM radio station call letters*]
WCCK ...... Weapons Control Check (NVT)
WCCL .... Columbus, OH [*AM radio station call letters*]
WCCL .... New Orleans, LA [*Television station call letters*]
WCCLS ..... Washington County Cooperative Library Services [*Library network*]
WCCM ...... Lawrence, MA [*AM radio station call letters*]
WCCMORS ... West Coast Classified Military Operations Research Symposium
WCCN .... Neillsville, WI [*AM radio station call letters*]
WCCN-FM ... Neillsville, WI [*FM radio station call letters*]
WCC (NZ) ... Workers' Compensation Cases (New Zealand) [*A publication*] (DLA)
WCCO ...... Minneapolis, MN [*AM radio station call letters*]
WCCON ...... Whether Cleared Customs or Not [*Shipping*] (DS)
W & C Conv ... Wolstenholme and Cherry's Conveyancing Statutes [*13th ed.*] [*1972*] [*A publication*] (DLA)
WCCO-TV ... Minneapolis, MN [*Television station call letters*]
WCCP .... Clemson, SC [*AM radio station call letters*]
WCCP .... Woodward-Clyde Consultants, Pasadena [*California*]
WCCPPS... Waste Channel and Containment Pressurization and Penetration System (IEEE)
WCCQ ...... Crest Hill, IL [*FM radio station call letters*]
WCCR .... Clarion, PA [*FM radio station call letters*]
WCCR .... Washington's United States Circuit Court Reports [*A publication*] (DLA)
WCCRS ..... Western Catholic Charismatic Renewal Services [*A publication*]
WCCS .... Homer City, PA [*AM radio station call letters*]
WCCS .... Window Contamination Control Number
WCCS .... World Chamber of Commerce Service (EA)
WCCSIS.... Westchester County Community Services Information System [*Westchester Library System*] [*Information service or system*] (IID)
WCCT .... Harwich, MA [*FM radio station call letters*]
WCCU .... Urbana, IL [*Television station call letters*]
WCC/US... US Conference for the World Council of Churches (EA)
WCCV ...... Arecibo, PR [*Television station call letters*]
WCCV ...... Cartersville, GA [*FM radio station call letters*]
WCCW ...... Traverse City, MI [*AM radio station call letters*]
WCCW-FM ... Traverse City, MI [*FM radio station call letters*]
WCCX .... Waukesha, WI [*FM radio station call letters*]

WCCY .... Houghton, MI [*AM radio station call letters*]
WCCZ .... New Smyrna Beach, FL [*AM radio station call letters*]
WCCZ .... Spangler, PA [*FM radio station call letters*]
WCD .... We Can Do! [*An association*] (EA)
WCD........ Weapons Classification Defects [*Navy*] (NG)
WCD........ Western Canadian Mining [*Vancouver Stock Exchange symbol*]
WCD......... Work Center Description (AFM)
WCD......... Workshop for Cultural Democracy (EA)
WCDA ...... Vorheesville, NY [*FM radio station call letters*]
WCDB .... Albany, NY [*FM radio station call letters*]
WCDB .... Wing Control During Boost
WCDB .... Work Control Data Base (NASA)
WCDC ...... Adams, MA [*Television station call letters*]
WCDC ...... West Coast [*Naval Publications*] Distribution Center
WCDE ...... Elkins, WV [*FM radio station call letters*]
WCDF .... World Children's Day Foundation (EA)
WCDFMA ... Water Cooler and Drinking Fountain Manufacturers Association
WCDJ........ Boston, MA [*FM radio station call letters*]
WCDK ...... Virginia, MN [*FM radio station call letters*]
WCDL ...... Carbondale, PA [*AM radio station call letters*]
WCDN ...... Chardon, OH [*AM radio station call letters*]
WCDO...... Sidney, NY [*AM radio station call letters*]
WCDO...... War Consumable Distribution Objective (AFM)
WCDO-FM ... Sidney, NY [*FM radio station call letters*]
WCDP ...... Widows', Children's, and Dependents' Pension [*British*]
WCDP ...... World Climate Data Program [*WMO*] [*ICSU*]
WCDQ...... Sanford, ME [*FM radio station call letters*]
WCDR ...... Cedarville, OH [*FM radio station call letters*]
W/Cdr....... Wing Commander [*British military*]
WCDS .... Glasgow, KY [*AM radio station call letters*]
WCDS .... West Coast Naval Publications Distribution Center (DNAB)
WCDT .... Winchester, TN [*AM radio station call letters*]
WCDV ...... Covington, IN [*FM radio station call letters*]
WCDX ...... Mechanicsville, VA [*FM radio station call letters*]
WCE......... Weapon Control Equipment
WCE .... West Coast of England [*Shipping*]
WCE .... Western Corporate Enterprises, Inc. [*Toronto Stock Exchange symbol*]
WCE .... Wiener Canonical Expansion [*Mathematics*]
WCE .... World Christian Encyclopedia [*A publication*]
WCEB........ Corning, NY [*FM radio station call letters*]
WCED ...... Du Bois, PA [*AM radio station call letters*]
WCED ...... World Commission on Environment and Development (EA)
WCEE....... Mount Vernon, IL [*Television station call letters*]
WCEE........ Women's Council on Energy and the Environment (EA)
WCEF....... Ripley, WV [*FM radio station call letters*]
WCEG ...... Middleborough, MA [*AM radio station call letters*]
WCEH ...... Hawkinsville, GA [*AM radio station call letters*]
WCEH-FM ... Hawkinsville, GA [*FM radio station call letters*]
WCEI........ Easton, MD [*AM radio station call letters*]
WCEI-FM ... Easton, MD [*FM radio station call letters*]
WC & EL ... Workers' Compensation and Employers' Liability [*Insurance*]
WCEM ...... Cambridge, MD [*AM radio station call letters*]
WCEMA ... West Coast Electronic Manufacturers' Association [*Later, AEA*]
WCEM-FM ... Cambridge, MD [*FM radio station call letters*]
WCEN .... Mount Pleasant, MI [*AM radio station call letters*]
WCEN-FM ... Mount Pleasant, MI [*FM radio station call letters*]
WCEO ...... Birmingham, AL [*AM radio station call letters*]
WCER .... Wisconsin Center for Education Research [*Madison*]
WCES........ Wolfson Centre for Electrochemical Science [*British*] (CB)
WCES........ Women's Caucus of the Endocrine Society (EA)
WCES........ Wrens, GA [*Television station call letters*]
WCET........ Cincinnati, OH [*Television station call letters*]
WCEU ...... New Smyrna Beach, FL [*Television station call letters*]
WCEU ...... World's Christian Endeavor Union (EA)
WCEV ...... Cicero, IL [*AM radio station call letters*]
WCEZ........ Delaware, OH [*FM radio station call letters*]
WCf............ Chippewa Falls Public Library, Chippewa Falls, WI [*Library symbol*] [*Library of Congress*] (LCLS)
WCF .... Waste Calcination [*or Calcining*] Facility [*Nuclear energy*]
WCF .... Water Conditioning Foundation [*Later, WQA*] (EA)
WCF .... White Cathode Follower
WCF .... Winston Churchill Foundation (EA)
WCF .... Women's Campaign Fund (EA)
WCF .... Workload Control File
WCF .... World Congress of Faiths - The Inter-Faith Fellowship [*British*] (EAIO)
WCF .... World Congress of Flight
WCF .... World Curling Federation [*British*] (EAIO)
WCFA ...... Wholesale Commission Florists of America [*Later, WF & FSA*]
WCFA....... Wildlife Conservation Fund of America (EA)
WCFBA ..... World Catholic Federation for the Biblical Apostolate [*Stuttgart, Federal Republic of Germany*] (EAIO)
WCFC....... Chicago, IL [*Television station call letters*]
WCFC....... Washington Capitals Fan Club (EA)
WCFE........ Plattsburgh, NY [*FM radio station call letters*]
WCFE-TV ... Plattsburgh, NY [*Television station call letters*]
WCFI........ Lajas, PR [*FM radio station call letters*]
WCFJ........ Chicago Heights, IL [*AM radio station call letters*]
WCFL........ Morris, IL [*FM radio station call letters*]

WCFN .... Springfield, IL [*Television station call letters*]
WCfNC...... Northern Wisconsin Colony and Training School, Chippewa Falls, WI [*Library symbol*] [*Library of Congress*] (LCLS)
WCFPR ..... Washington Center of Foreign Policy Research (MCD)
WCFR........ Springfield, VT [*AM radio station call letters*]
WCFR........ Washington Citizens for Recycling (EA)
WCFRU..... Washington Cooperative Fishery Research Unit [*University of Washington*] [*Research center*] (RCD)
WCfSJ .... Saint Joseph's Hospital, Chippewa Falls, WI [*Library symbol*] [*Library of Congress*] (LCLS)
WCFT........ Tuscaloosa, AL [*Television station call letters*]
WCFTB ..... West Coast Freight Tariff Bureau
WCFW....... Chippewa Falls, WI [*FM radio station call letters*]
WCFX........ Clare, MI [*FM radio station call letters*]
WCFY........ Lafayette, IN [*AM radio station call letters*]
WCG......... War Crimes Group [*British*]
WCG......... Washington Calligraphers Guild (EA)
WCG......... Water-Cooled Garment
WCG......... Weapon Control Group [*Military*] (CAAL)
WCG......... Willis Corroon ADS [*NYSE symbol*] (SPSG)
WCG......... Women of the Church of God (EA)
WCG......... Worldwide Church of God
WCGA....... Woodbine, GA [*AM radio station call letters*]
WCGA....... World Computer Graphics Association (EA)
WCGB....... Juana Diaz, PR [*AM radio station call letters*]
WCGC....... Belmont, NC [*AM radio station call letters*]
WCGL .... Jacksonville, FL [*AM radio station call letters*]
WCGLJO.. World Congress of Gay and Lesbian Jewish Organizations (EA)
WCGM...... Maryville, TN [*AM radio station call letters*]
WCGM...... Writable Character Generation Module [*Data processing*] (BUR)
WCGO....... Chicago Heights, IL [*AM radio station call letters*]
WCGQ....... Columbus, GA [*FM radio station call letters*]
WCGR .... Canandaigua, NY [*AM radio station call letters*]
WCGS........ Western Collaborative Group Study [*University of California*] [*Psychology*]
WCGS........ Wolf Creek Generating Station [*Nuclear energy*] (NRCH)
WCGTC..... World Council for Gifted and Talented Children (EA)
WCGV .... Milwaukee, WI [*Television station call letters*]
WCGW....... Nicholasville, KY [*AM radio station call letters*]
WCGY .... Lawrence, MA [*FM radio station call letters*]
WCGZ .... World Confederation of General Zionists [*Later, WCUZ*] (EA)
WCh........... Chippewa Falls Public Library, Chippewa Falls, WI [*Library symbol*] [*Library of Congress*] [*Obsolete*] (LCLS)
WCH.......... Skyline Aviation, Inc. [*Winchester, VA*] [*FAA designator*] (FAAC)
WCH.......... Weekly Contact Hours
WCH.......... West Coast Handling
WCH.......... Working Class Hero (EA)
WCH.......... Workshop Conferences Hoechst [*Elsevier Book Series*] [*A publication*]
WCHA....... Chambersburg, PA [*AM radio station call letters*]
WCHA....... Western Collegiate Hockey Association (EA)
WCHA....... Wooden Canoe Heritage Association (EA)
WCHB....... Taylor, MI [*AM radio station call letters*]
WCHC....... Worcester, MA [*FM radio station call letters*]
WCHE....... West Chester, PA [*AM radio station call letters*]
WCHEN..... Western Council on Higher Education for Nursing
W'CHESTER ... Winchester [*Borough in South England*] (ROG)
WCHF .... Wet Crude Handling Facilities [*Petroleum engineering*]
WCHI .... Chillicothe, OH [*AM radio station call letters*]
WCHI .... Westworld Community Healthcare, Inc. [*Lake Forest, CA*] [*NASDAQ symbol*] (NQ)
WCHI .... Women's Council for the Histadrut in Israel (EA)
WCHJ .... Brookhaven, MS [*AM radio station call letters*]
WCHK....... Canton, GA [*AM radio station call letters*]
WCHK-FM ... Canton, GA [*FM radio station call letters*]
WCHL....... Chapel Hill, NC [*AM radio station call letters*]
WCHM...... Clarkesville, GA [*AM radio station call letters*]
WCHN....... Norwich, NY [*AM radio station call letters*]
Wchnbl K K Gesellsch Aerzte Wien ... Wochenblatt. K. K. Gesellschaft der Aerzte in Wien [*A publication*]
Wchnschr Ges Heilk ... Wochenschrift fuer die Gesamte Heilkunde [*A publication*]
Wchnschr Tierh u Viehzucht ... Wochenschrift fuer Tierheilkunde und Viehzucht [*A publication*]
WCHO ...... Washington Court House, OH [*FM radio station call letters*]
WCHODW ... Workshop Conferences Hoechst [*Elsevier Book Series*] [*A publication*]
WCHP....... Champlain, NY [*AM radio station call letters*]
WCHQ ...... Camuy, PR [*AM radio station call letters*]
WCHQ-FM ... Camuy, PR [*FM radio station call letters*]
WCHR....... Trenton, NJ [*FM radio station call letters*]
WCHR....... Water Chiller
WCHR....... Worldwide Creme Horse Registry (EA)
WCHS .... Charleston, WV [*AM radio station call letters*]
WCHS-TV ... Charleston, WV [*Television station call letters*]
WCHT........ Escanaba, MI [*AM radio station call letters*]
WCHV....... Charlottesville, VA [*AM radio station call letters*]
WCHW...... Bay City, MI [*FM radio station call letters*]
WCHX....... Lewistown, PA [*FM radio station call letters*]

WCHY....... Savannah, GA [*AM radio station call letters*]
WCHY-FM ... Savannah, GA [*FM radio station call letters*]
WCI .... Warner Communications, Inc. [*NYSE symbol*] (SPSG)
WCI .... Washington International College, Washington, DC [*OCLC symbol*] (OCLC)
WCI .... Weapon Control Index [*Military*] (CAAL)
WCI .... White Cast Iron
WCI .... Wildlife Conservation International (EA)
WCI .... Workshop Computer Interface
WCIA .... Champaign, IL [*Television station call letters*]
WCIA .... Welsh Centre for International Affairs [*British*] (CB)
WCIB........ Falmouth, MA [*FM radio station call letters*]
WCIC........ Pekin, IL [*FM radio station call letters*]
WCIC........ Watch Check Is Completed (FAAC)
WCID .... Friendship, NY [*FM radio station call letters*]
WCIE .... Lakeland, FL [*FM radio station call letters*]
WCIE .... Spring Lake, NC [*AM radio station call letters*]
WCIE .... World Center for Islamic Education (EA)
WCIF .... Melbourne, FL [*FM radio station call letters*]
WCIG .... Mullins, SC [*FM radio station call letters*]
WCIH .... Elmira, NY [*FM radio station call letters*]
WCII .... Spencer, NY [*FM radio station call letters*]
WCIK....... Bath, NY [*FM radio station call letters*]
WCIL........ Carbondale, IL [*AM radio station call letters*]
WCIL-FM ... Carbondale, IL [*FM radio station call letters*]
WCIN .... Cincinnati, OH [*AM radio station call letters*]
WC & Ins (Eng) ... Workmen's Compensation and Insurance Reports [*1912-33*] [*England*] [*A publication*] (DLA)
WC Ins Rep ... Workmen's Compensation and Insurance Reports [*1912-33*] [*A publication*] (DLA)
WC & Ins Rep ... Workmen's Compensation and Insurance Reports [*1912-33*] [*England*] [*A publication*] (DLA)
WCIP........ Weapon Control Indicator Panel [*Military*] (CAAL)
WCIP........ World Climate Impacts Program [*WMO*] [*ICSU*]
WCIP........ World Council of Indigenous Peoples [*Ottawa, ON*] (EAIO)
WCIQ .... Mount Cheaha State Park, AL [*Television station call letters*]
WCIR........ Beckley, WV [*FM radio station call letters*]
WC & IR ... Workmen's Compensation and Insurance Reports [*1912-33*] [*England*] [*A publication*] (DLA)
WC & I Rep ... Workmen's Compensation and Insurance Reports [*1912-33*] [*A publication*] (DLA)
WCIS........ Morganton, NC [*AM radio station call letters*]
WCIS........ Wisconsin Career Information System [*Information service or system*]
WC-ISA..... Women's Commission of the Iranian Students Association (EA)
WCIT........ Lima, OH [*AM radio station call letters*]
WCIU .... Chicago, IL [*Television station call letters*]
WCIU .... Workshop Computer Interface Unit (MCD)
WCIV........ Charleston, SC [*Television station call letters*]
WCIW ...... [*The*] World Community of Al-Islam in the West
WCIX........ Miami, FL [*Television station call letters*]
WCIY........ Canandaigua, NY [*FM radio station call letters*]
WCIY........ Westmorland and Cumberland Imperial Yeomanry [*British military*] (DMA)
WCIZ........ Watertown, NY [*FM radio station call letters*]
WCJ.......... White Cloud Journal of American Indian/Alaska Native Mental Health [*A publication*]
WCJA........ Western Canadian Journal of Anthropology [*A publication*]
WCJA........ World Council of Jewish Archives (EAIO)
WCJB........ Gainesville, FL [*Television station call letters*]
WCJC....... Van Buren, IN [*FM radio station call letters*]
WCJC........ Webster City Junior College [*Iowa*]
WCJC........ Wharton County Junior College [*Texas*]
WCJCC ..... World Confederation of Jewish Community Centers (EA)
WCJCS..... World Conference of Jewish Communal Service (EA)
WCJE .... World Council on Jewish Education
WCJL........ Marinette, WI [*AM radio station call letters*]
WCJL........ Menominee, MI [*FM radio station call letters*]
WCJM....... West Point, GA [*FM radio station call letters*]
WCJO....... Jackson, OH [*FM radio station call letters*]
WCJS .... World Congress of Jewish Studies [*A publication*]
WCJU....... Columbia, MS [*AM radio station call letters*]
WCJW...... Warsaw, NY [*AM radio station call letters*]
WCJX....... Five Points, FL [*FM radio station call letters*]
WCK......... Whiskey Creek Resources [*Vancouver Stock Exchange symbol*]
WCK......... Wilson Creek [*Kentucky*] [*Seismograph station code, US Geological Survey*] (SEIS)
WCKA ...... Sutton, WV [*FM radio station call letters*]
WCKB ...... Dunn, NC [*AM radio station call letters*]
WCKG ...... Elmwood Park, IL [*FM radio station call letters*]
WCKI .... Greer, SC [*AM radio station call letters*]
WCKL........ Catskill, NY [*AM radio station call letters*]
WCKO....... Carrollton, AL [*AM radio station call letters*]
WCKP....... Shelbyville, KY [*FM radio station call letters*]
WCKQ....... Campbellsville, KY [*FM radio station call letters*]
WCKR....... Hornell, NY [*FM radio station call letters*]
WCKS........ Fruithurst, AL [*FM radio station call letters*]
WCKT ...... Lehigh Acres, FL [*FM radio station call letters*]
WCKU ...... Nicholasville, KY [*FM radio station call letters*]
WCKW...... Garyville, LA [*AM radio station call letters*]

WCKW ...... La Place, LA [*FM radio station call letters*]
WCKX .... London, OH [*FM radio station call letters*]
WCKY .... Cincinnati, OH [*AM radio station call letters*]
WCKZ .... Gastonia, NC [*FM radio station call letters*]
WCL .... Washington College of Law, Washington, DC [*OCLC symbol*]　(OCLC)
WCL .... Water Coolant Line　(MCD)
WCL .... Water Coolant Loop　(MCD)
WCL .... WCI Canada Ltd. [*Toronto Stock Exchange symbol*]
WCL .... Weekly Cost Ledger　(MCD)
WCL .... Western Carolinas League [*Baseball*]
WCL .... White Clip Level [*Video technology*]
WCL .... White Cross League [*British*]
WCL .... Wholesale Commodity Line　(GFGA)
WCL .... Word Control Logic
WCL .... World Confederation of Labour [*See also CMT*] [*Brussels, Belgium*]　(EAIO)
WCL .... Wright Center of Laboratories
WCLA .... Claxton, GA [*AM radio station call letters*]
WCLA .... West Coast Lumbermen's Association [*Later, WWPA*]　(EA)
WCLA .... Workers' Compensation Legislation in Australia [*A publication*]
WCLA-FM ... Claxton, GA [*FM radio station call letters*]
WCL-ARS ... Agricultural Research Service Water Conservation Laboratory [*Tempe, AZ*]
WCLB........ Warehouse Club, Inc. [*Skokie, IL*] [*NASDAQ symbol*]　(NQ)
WCLC........ Jamestown, TN [*AM radio station call letters*]
WCLC........ Watch Check List Completed　(FAAC)
WCLC........ World Christian Life Community [*Italy*]　(EAIO)
WCLC-FM ... Jamestown, TN [*FM radio station call letters*]
WCLCV...... White Clover Large Cryptic Virus [*Plant pathology*]
WCLD .... Cleveland, MS [*AM radio station call letters*]
WCLD .... Water-Cooled　(AAG)
WCLD-FM ... Cleveland, MS [*FM radio station call letters*]
WCLE........ Cleveland, TN [*AM radio station call letters*]
WCLF........ Clearwater, FL [*Television station call letters*]
WCLG .... Morgantown, WV [*AM radio station call letters*]
WCLG-FM ... Morgantown, WV [*FM radio station call letters*]
WCLH........ Wilkes-Barre, PA [*FM radio station call letters*]
WCLI......... Corning, NY [*AM radio station call letters*]
WCII .... Lakeshore Technical Institute, Educational Resource Center, Cleveland, WI [*Library symbol*] [*Library of Congress*]　(LCLS)
WCLIB ...... West Coast Lumber Inspection Bureau　(EA)
WCLJ .... Bloomington, IN [*Television station call letters*]
WCLJ .... Workmen's Compensation Law Journal [*A publication*]　(DLA)
WCLK........ Atlanta, GA [*FM radio station call letters*]
WCLL........ Wesson, MS [*FM radio station call letters*]
WCLM ...... Highland Springs, VA [*AM radio station call letters*]
WCLMV.... White Clover Mosaic Virus [*Plant pathology*]
WCLN .... Clinton, NC [*AM radio station call letters*]
WCLN-FM ... Clinton, NC [*FM radio station call letters*]
WCLO .... Janesville, WI [*AM radio station call letters*]
WCLP........ Chatsworth, GA [*Television station call letters*]
WCLP....... Western Center on Law and Poverty　(EA)
WCLP....... Women's Computer Literacy Project [*Commercial firm*]　(EA)
WCLQ .... Wausau, WI [*FM radio station call letters*]
WCLR........ Piqua, OH [*FM radio station call letters*]
WCLR........ Workmen's Compensation Law Review [*A publication*]　(DLA)
WCLS........ Oscoda, MI [*FM radio station call letters*]
WCLT........ Newark, OH [*AM radio station call letters*]
WCLT-FM ... Newark, OH [*FM radio station call letters*]
WCLU .... Glasgow, KY [*AM radio station call letters*]
WCLV....... Cleveland, OH [*FM radio station call letters*]
WCLX........ Wisconsin Central Transportation [*NASDAQ symbol*]　(SPSG)
WCLY....... Raleigh, NC [*AM radio station call letters*]
WCLZ........ Brunswick, ME [*AM radio station call letters*]
WCLZ-FM ... Brunswick, ME [*FM radio station call letters*]
WCM .... Warland Creek [*Montana*] [*Seismograph station code, US Geological Survey*] [*Closed*]　(SEIS)
WCM .... Water Control Module　(KSC)
WCM .... Weapon Control Module　(MCD)
WCM .... Welded Cordwood Module
WCM .... Wesleyan Calvinistic Methodists　(ROG)
WCM .... Wheat Curl Mite [*Entomology*]
WCM .... Whole Cow's Milk
WCM .... Winchester City Museum [*British*]
WCM .... Winkelmann Countermeasures, Inc. [*Vancouver Stock Exchange symbol*]
WCM........ Wired-Core Matrix
WCM........ Wired-Core Memory
WCM........ Word Combine and Multiplexer
WCM........ Writable Control Memory [*Data processing*]　(BUR)
W/CM² ...... Watts per Square Centimeter　(CET)
WCMA ...... Corinth, MS [*AM radio station call letters*]
WCMA ...... West Coast Mineral Association　(EA)
WCMA ...... Wisconsin Cheese Makers' Association　(EA)
WCMA ...... Working Capital Management Account [*Merrill Lynch & Co.*]
WCMB ...... Harrisburg, PA [*AM radio station call letters*]
WCMC ...... Wildwood, NJ [*AM radio station call letters*]

WCMC ...... World Conservation Monitoring Centre [*Information service or system*]　(IID)
WCMD ...... Advanced Certificate of the Welsh College of Music and Drama [*British*]　(DBQ)
WCME ...... Boothbay Harbor-Bath, ME [*FM radio station call letters*]
WCMF ...... Rochester, NY [*FM radio station call letters*]
WCMF ...... World Congress on Metal Finishing　(PDAA)
WCMH...... Columbus, OH [*Television station call letters*]
WCMI ...... Ashland, KY [*AM radio station call letters*]
WCMI ...... Catlettsburg, KY [*FM radio station call letters*]
WCMIA ...... West Coast Metal Importers Association　(EA)
WCMJ ...... Cambridge, OH [*FM radio station call letters*]
WCML ...... Alpena, MI [*FM radio station call letters*]
WCML ...... Women's Caucus for the Modern Languages　(EA)
WCML-TV ... Alpena, MI [*Television station call letters*]
WCMN...... Arecibo, PR [*AM radio station call letters*]
WCMN-FM ... Arecibo, PR [*FM radio station call letters*]
WCMO ...... Marietta, OH [*FM radio station call letters*]
WCMP ...... Pine City, MN [*AM radio station call letters*]
WCMP-FM ... Pine City, MN [*FM radio station call letters*]
WCMQ ...... Hialeah, FL [*FM radio station call letters*]
WCMQ ...... Miami Springs, FL [*AM radio station call letters*]
WCMR ...... Elkhart, IN [*AM radio station call letters*]
WCMR ...... Western Contract Management Region [*Air Force*]
WCMS...... Norfolk, VA [*AM radio station call letters*]
WCMS-FM ... Norfolk, VA [*FM radio station call letters*]
WCMT ...... Martin, TN [*AM radio station call letters*]
WCMT-FM ... Martin, TN [*FM radio station call letters*]
WCMU ...... Mount Pleasant, MI [*FM radio station call letters*]
WCMU-TV ... Mount Pleasant, MI [*Television station call letters*]
WCMV ...... Cadillac, MI [*Television station call letters*]
WCMV ...... White Clover Mosaic Virus
WCMV ...... Wild Cucumber Mosaic Virus [*Plant pathology*]
WCMW ...... Manistee, MI [*Television station call letters*]
WCMW ...... Williamsburg, VA [*FM radio station call letters*]
WCMX ...... Leominster, MA [*AM radio station call letters*]
WCMY ...... Ottawa, IL [*AM radio station call letters*]
WCMZ ...... Sault Ste. Marie, MI [*FM radio station call letters*]
WCN.......... Walthard's Cell Nest [*Gynecology*]　(AAMN)
WCN.......... Washoe City [*Nevada*] [*Seismograph station code, US Geological Survey*]　(SEIS)
WCN.......... Wescan Energy Ltd. [*Vancouver Stock Exchange symbol*]
WCN.......... Workload Control Number　(MCD)
WCN.......... World Coin News [*A publication*]
WCNA .... Clearwater, SC [*FM radio station call letters*]
WCNA .... Western Co. of North America [*Associated Press abbreviation*]　(APAG)
WCNB .... Connersville, IN [*FM radio station call letters*]
WCNC....... Charlotte, NC [*Television station call letters*]
WCNC....... Elizabeth City, NC [*AM radio station call letters*]
WCND...... Shelbyville, KY [*AM radio station call letters*]
WCNDT...... World Conference on Non-Destructive Testing　(PDAA)
WCNDT...... World Conference on Nondestructive Testing
WCNE .... Batavia, OH [*FM radio station call letters*]
WCNG....... Murphy, NC [*FM radio station call letters*]
WCNH ...... Belmont, NH [*FM radio station call letters*]
WCNI .... New London, CT [*FM radio station call letters*]
WCNJ....... Hazlet, NJ [*FM radio station call letters*]
WCNL .... Carlinville, IL [*FM radio station call letters*]
WCNL .... Winter Cities Newsletter [*A publication*]
WCNN .... North Atlanta, GA [*AM radio station call letters*]
WCNO....... Palm City, FL [*FM radio station call letters*]
WCNR .... Bloomsburg, PA [*AM radio station call letters*]
WCNS .... Latrobe, PA [*AM radio station call letters*]
WCNT .... Charlotte, NC [*AM radio station call letters*]
WCNU....... Crestview, FL [*AM radio station call letters*]
WCNW ...... Fairfield, OH [*AM radio station call letters*]
WCNX ...... Middletown, CT [*AM radio station call letters*]
WCNY .... Syracuse, NY [*FM radio station call letters*]
WCNY-TV ... Syracuse, NY [*Television station call letters*]
WCO.......... Columbia Helicopters, Inc. [*Lake Charles, LA*] [*FAA designator*]　(FAAC)
WCO......... War Cabinet Office [*World War II*]
WCO......... Warrant Communication Officer [*British military*]　(DMA)
WCO......... Weapons Control Officer
WCO......... Weapons Control Order
WCO......... Western Coordination Office [*Later, WOO*] [*NASA*]
WCO......... Wet Chemical Oxidation [*Chemistry*]
WCO......... Wrather Corp. [*AMEX symbol*]　(SPSG)
WCOA .... Pensacola, FL [*AM radio station call letters*]
W Coach Clinic ... Women's Coaching Clinic [*A publication*]
W Coast Rep ... West Coast Reporter [*A publication*]　(DLA)
WCOAT .... Wolfe Computer Operator Aptitude Test
WCOBL..... Wolfe Programming Language Test: COBOL
WCOD...... Hyannis, MA [*FM radio station call letters*]
WCOD...... Western Canada Outdoors. Combining The Whooper and Defending All Outdoors [*A publication*]
WCOE .... La Porte, IN [*FM radio station call letters*]
WCOF .... Women's Catholic Order of Foresters [*Later, NCSF*]　(EA)
WCOG .... Ridgeland, SC [*AM radio station call letters*]
WCOH ...... Newnan, GA [*AM radio station call letters*]

WCoins ...... World Coins [*A publication*]
WCOJ .... Coatesville, PA [*AM radio station call letters*]
WCOK ...... Sparta, NC [*AM radio station call letters*]
WCOL ...... Walker Color, Inc. [*NASDAQ symbol*] (NQ)
WCOL-FM ... Columbus, OH [*FM radio station call letters*]
WCOM ...... Mansfield, OH [*Television station call letters*]
W Comm .... Wing Commander [*British military*] (DMA)
WCOMMRGN ... Western Communications Region [*Air Force*]
W Comp Pres Docs ... Weekly Compilation of Presidential Documents [*A publication*]
WCON .... Cornelia, GA [*AM radio station call letters*]
WCON-FM ... Cornelia, GA [*FM radio station call letters*]
WCOO ...... Immokalee, FL [*FM radio station call letters*]
WCOP .... Warner Robins, GA [*AM radio station call letters*]
WC Ops ..... Workmen's Compensation Opinions, United States Department of Commerce [*A publication*] (DLA)
WCOR ...... Lebanon, TN [*AM radio station call letters*]
WCOS .... Columbia, SC [*AM radio station call letters*]
WCOS-FM ... Columbia, SC [*FM radio station call letters*]
WCOT ...... Wall Coated Open Tubular [*Instrumentation*]
WCOTP ...... World Confederation of Organizations of the Teaching Profession [*Formed by a merger of International Federation of Secondary Teachers and IFTA*] (EAIO)
WCOU .... Wheelwrights and Coachmakers Operatives' Union [*British*]
WCOV .... Montgomery, AL [*Television station call letters*]
WCOW ...... Sparta, WI [*AM radio station call letters*]
WCOW-FM ... Sparta, WI [*FM radio station call letters*]
WCOX ...... Camden, AL [*AM radio station call letters*]
WCOZ .... Paris, KY [*FM radio station call letters*]
WCP .... War Control Planners (EA)
WCP .... Warner Insurance Services [*NYSE symbol*] (SPSG)
WCP .... Waste Collector Pump (IEEE)
WCP .... Wayne County Public Library, Wooster, OH [*OCLC symbol*] (OCLC)
WCP .... Weapon Control Panel [*Aviation*]
WCP .... Weapon Control Processor [*Military*] (CAAL)
WCP .... Welder Control Panel
WCP .... Western Canada Party [*Separatist political party*]
WCP .... White Combination Potentiometer
WCP .... Wing Chord Plane [*Aviation*]
WCP .... Wing Command Post (MCD)
WCP .... Woman CPA [*A publication*]
WCP .... Work Control Plan (AAG)
WCP .... World Climate Program [*WMO*] [*ICSU*]
WCP .... World Community Projects (EA)
WCP .... World Congress of Poets (EA)
WCP .... World Council of Peace (NATG)
WCPA ...... Clearfield, PA [*AM radio station call letters*]
WCPA ...... Western College Placement Association (AEBS)
WCPA ...... World Constitution and Parliament Association (EA)
WCPAB ...... War Contracts Price Adjustment Board [*All functions dispersed, 1951*]
WCPB .... Salisbury, MD [*Television station call letters*]
WCPC .... Houston, MS [*AM radio station call letters*]
WCPD .... Waterloo Centre for Process Development [*University of Waterloo*] [*Research center*] (RCD)
WCPDD5 .. World Crops Production Utilization Description [*A publication*]
WCPE .... Raleigh, NC [*FM radio station call letters*]
WCPH .... Etowah, TN [*AM radio station call letters*]
WCPH .... World Congress of Professional Hypnotists (EA)
WCPI .... White Collar Productivity Improvement (MCD)
WCPM ...... Cumberland, KY [*AM radio station call letters*]
WCPMEF ... Willa Cather Pioneer Memorial and Educational Foundation (EA)
WCPN ...... Cleveland, OH [*FM radio station call letters*]
WCPO ...... Cincinnati, OH [*Television station call letters*]
WCPP .... Women of Color Partnership Program (EA)
WCPQ ...... Havelock, NC [*AM radio station call letters*]
WCPR .... Coamo, PR [*AM radio station call letters*]
WCPR .... Weston, Clevedon & Portishead Railway [*British*]
WCPS .... Tarboro, NC [*AM radio station call letters*]
WCPS .... Women's Caucus for Political Science (EA)
WCPS .... World Confederation of Productivity Science (EAIO)
WCPSC ..... Western Conference of Public Services Commissioners
WCPT .... Alexandria, VA [*AM radio station call letters*]
WCPT .... World Confederation for Physical Therapy [*British*] (EA)
WCPX .... Orlando, FL [*Television station call letters*]
WCPZ .... Sandusky, OH [*FM radio station call letters*]
WCQA ...... Fredonia, NY [*FM radio station call letters*]
WCQL .... Portsmouth, NH [*AM radio station call letters*]
WCQL .... York Center, ME [*FM radio station call letters*]
WCQM ...... Park Falls, WI [*FM radio station call letters*]
WCQR ...... Fairlawn, VA [*AM radio station call letters*]
WCQS ...... Asheville, NC [*FM radio station call letters*]
WCR .... Chandalar [*Alaska*] [*Airport symbol*] (OAG)
WCR .... Chandalar Lake, AK [*Location identifier*] [*FAA*] (FAAL)
WCR .... Warm Core Ring [*Oceanography*]
WCR .... Water-Cooled Reactor
WCR .... Water-Cooled Rod
WCR .... Watercooler (AAG)

WCR .... Waterloo and City Railway (ROG)
WCR .... West Coast Review [*A publication*]
WCR .... Western Communications Region [*Air Force*] (MCD)
WCR .... Willcrest Resources Ltd. [*Vancouver Stock Exchange symbol*]
WCR .... Wire Contact Relay
WCR .... Women's Council of Realtors [*of the National Association of Realtors*] (EA)
WCR .... Word Control [*or Count*] Register
WCR .... Workers' Compensation Reports [*New South Wales*] [*A publication*] (APTA)
WCR .... World Communication Report [*Database*] [*UNESCO*] (DUND)
WCRA ...... Effingham, IL [*AM radio station call letters*]
WCRA ...... Weather Control Research Association [*Later, Weather Modification Association*]
WCRA ...... Western College Reading Association (EA)
WCRA ...... Wet Crease Recovery Angle [*Textile technology*]
WCRB ...... Waltham, MA [*AM radio station call letters*]
WCRB ...... West Coast Review of Books [*A publication*]
WCRC .... Effingham, IL [*FM radio station call letters*]
WCRC .... Water Conditioning Research Council [*Later, WQRC*] (EA)
WCRD ...... War Consumables Requirements Document [*Military*] (AFIT)
WCRE .... Cheraw, SC [*AM radio station call letters*]
WCRED .... WESCON [*Western Electronics Show and Convention*] Conference Record [*A publication*]
WC Rep .... Workmen's Compensation Reports [*A publication*] (DLA)
WCRF .... Cleveland, OH [*FM radio station call letters*]
WCRF .... Weekly Collection Report File [*IRS*]
WCRH ...... Williamsport, MD [*FM radio station call letters*]
WCRI .... Eureka, IL [*FM radio station call letters*]
WCRJ .... Jacksonville, FL [*FM radio station call letters*]
WCRK ...... Morristown, TN [*AM radio station call letters*]
WCRL ...... Oneonta, AL [*AM radio station call letters*]
WCRLA .... Western College Reading and Learning Association (EA)
WCRM ...... Fort Myers, FL [*AM radio station call letters*]
WCRN ...... Cherry Valley, MA [*AM radio station call letters*]
WCR (NSW) ... Workers' Compensation Reports (New South Wales) [*A publication*] (APTA)
WCRO ...... Johnstown, PA [*AM radio station call letters*]
WCROS ..... White Crossover Vote [*Political science*]
WCRP .... Guayama, PR [*FM radio station call letters*]
WCRP .... World Climate Research Programme [*WMO*] [*ICSU*]
WCRP .... World Conference on Religion and Peace (EAIO)
WCRP/USA ... World Conference on Religion and Peace, USA Section (EA)
WCRQ ...... Arab, AL [*FM radio station call letters*]
WCR (Q) .... Workers' Compensation Reports (Queensland) [*A publication*] (APTA)
WCR (Qld) ... Workers' Compensation Reports (Queensland) [*A publication*] (APTA)
WCR (Qn) ... Workers' Compensation Reports (Queensland) [*A publication*]
WCRR .... Rural Retreat, VA [*AM radio station call letters*]
WCRR-FM ... Rural Retreat, VA [*FM radio station call letters*]
WCRS .... Greenwood, SC [*AM radio station call letters*]
WCRS .... [*The*] WCRS Group Ltd. [*NASDAQ symbol*] (NQ)
WC:RS .... Women's Caucus: Religious Studies (EA)
WCRSI ...... Western Concrete Reinforcing Steel Institute [*Later, CRSI*] (EA)
WCRV ...... Collierville, TN [*AM radio station call letters*]
WCRW ...... Chicago, IL [*AM radio station call letters*]
WCR(WA) ... Workers' Compensation Reports (Western Australia) [*A publication*]
WCRX ...... Chicago, IL [*FM radio station call letters*]
WCRZ ...... Flint, MI [*FM radio station call letters*]
WCS .... Wallace Computer Services, Inc. [*NYSE symbol*] (SPSG)
WCS .... Wang Computer System
WCS .... Waste Collection System [*NASA*] (MCD)
WCS .... Waste Compaction Station [*Nuclear energy*] (NRCH)
WCS .... Waste Control System (SSD)
WCS .... Weak Calf Syndrome [*Veterinary medicine*]
WCS .... Weapon Control Station [*Military*] (CAAL)
WCS .... Weapon Control Status [*Military*] (INF)
WCS .... Weapons Control Status
WCS .... Weapons Control System
WCS .... Wedgwood Collectors Society [*Commercial firm*] (EA)
WCS .... Western Cover Society (EA)
WCS .... William Cobbett Society (EAIO)
WCS .... Woman Citizen Series [*A publication*]
WCS .... Work Control Station
WCS .... Work Control System (NASA)
WCS .... Work Core Storage
WCS .... World Congress on Superconductivity [*An association*]
WCS .... World Council of Synagogues (EA)
WCS .... Writable Control Storage [*Data processing*]
WCSA .... Ripley, MS [*AM radio station call letters*]
WCSA .... West Coast of South America
WCSB .... Cleveland, OH [*FM radio station call letters*]
WCSB .... Weapon Control Switchboard [*Military*] (CAAL)
WCSB(G) .. Weapon Control Switchboard (Gun)
WCSB(M) ... Weapon Control Switchboard (Missile)
WCSB(UB) ... Weapon Control Switchboard (Underwater Battery)
WCSC .... Charleston, SC [*Television station call letters*]

WCSC........ Weapon Control System Console
WCSC........ Weapons Control System Coordinator (NVT)
WCSC........ West Coast Switching Center [*Jet Propulsion Laboratory, NASA*]
WCSC........ World Correctional Service Center (EA)
WCSCV..... White Clover Small Cryptic Virus [*Plant pathology*]
WCSF....... Joliet, IL [*FM radio station call letters*]
WCSFMA ... Wisconsin Cheese and Specialty Food Merchants Association (EA)
WCSG........ Grand Rapids, MI [*FM radio station call letters*]
WCSG........ WWMCCS [*Worldwide Military Command and Control System*] Council Support Group (MCD)
WCSH ...... Portland, ME [*Television station call letters*]
WCSI......... Columbus, IN [*AM radio station call letters*]
WCSI........ World Centre for Scientific Information
WCSI......... Worldwide Computer Services, Inc. [*Wayne, NJ*] [*NASDAQ symbol*] (NQ)
WCSICEC ... Working Committee of the Scientific Institutes for Crafts in the EEC Countries [*Munich, Federal Republic of Germany*] (EAIO)
WCSJ .... Morris, IL [*AM radio station call letters*]
WCSK........ Kingsport, TN [*FM radio station call letters*]
WCSL........ Cherryville, NC [*AM radio station call letters*]
WCSM...... Celina, OH [*AM radio station call letters*]
WCSM....... World Congress of Sports Medicine
WCSM-FM ... Celina, OH [*FM radio station call letters*]
WCSMLL ... Western Canadian Studies in Modern Languages and Literature [*A publication*]
WCSP....... Crystal Springs, MS [*AM radio station call letters*]
WCSP....... Wisconsin Cheese and Sausage Promotions (EA)
WCSPA ..... West Coast Shrimp Producers Association (EA)
WCSQ .... Central Square, NY [*FM radio station call letters*]
WCSR........ Hillsdale, MI [*AM radio station call letters*]
WCSRC..... Wild Canid Survival and Research Center - Wolf Sanctuary (EA)
WCSR-FM ... Hillsdale, MI [*FM radio station call letters*]
WCSS .... Amsterdam, NY [*AM radio station call letters*]
WCSS .... Weapons Control Subsystem (MCD)
WCSS .... Weapons Control System Simulator
WCSS .... West Coast Sound School [*Navy*]
WCST........ Berkeley Springs, WV [*AM radio station call letters*]
WCST....... Wisconsin Card Sorting Test [*Neuropsychology test*]
WCST-FM ... Berkeley Springs, WV [*FM radio station call letters*]
WCSU .... Western Connecticut State University [*Danbury*]
WCSU .... Wilberforce, OH [*FM radio station call letters*]
WCSUICA ... Women's Coalition to Stop US Intervention in Central America [*Later, WCSUICAC*] (EA)
WCSUICAC ... Women's Coalition to Stop US Intervention in Central America and the Caribbean (EA)
WCSV........ Crossville, TN [*AM radio station call letters*]
WCSV........ Wheat Chlorotic Streak Virus [*Plant pathology*]
WCSW........ Shell Lake, WI [*AM radio station call letters*]
WCSX........ Birmingham, MI [*FM radio station call letters*]
WCSX........ WCS International [*NASDAQ symbol*] (NQ)
WCSY........ South Haven, MI [*AM radio station call letters*]
WCSY-FM ... South Haven, MI [*FM radio station call letters*]
WCT .... Trinity Memorial Hospital, Cudahy, WI [*Library symbol*] [*Library of Congress*] (LCLS)
WCT .... Waukesha County Institute, Pewaukee, WI [*OCLC symbol*] (OCLC)
WCT .... West Coast Travel [*Information service or system*] (IID)
WCT .... Westek Communications, Inc. [*Vancouver Stock Exchange symbol*]
WCT .... Wetlands Conservation Team
WCT .... World Championship Tennis, Inc.
WCT .... World Confederation of Teachers [*See also CSME*] [*Brussels, Belgium*] (EAIO)
WCT .... Worthy Chief Templar
WCTA ...... Alamo, TN [*AM radio station call letters*]
WCTA ...... Western Coal Transportation Association (EA)
WCTA ...... World Committee for Trade Action [*See also CMAP*] [*Brussels, Belgium*] (EAIO)
WCTB........ West Country Tourist Board [*British*] (DCTA)
WCTB........ Western Carriers Tariff Bureau
WCTC........ New Brunswick, NJ [*AM radio station call letters*]
WCTD ...... World Congress of Teachers of Dancing (EA)
WCTE....... Cookeville, TN [*Television station call letters*]
WCTEV...... White Clover Temperate Virus [*Plant pathology*]
WCTF...... Vernon, CT [*AM radio station call letters*]
WCTG ...... Columbia, SC [*AM radio station call letters*]
WCTG ...... Woodcutting (MSA)
WCTH...... Plantation Key, FL [*FM radio station call letters*]
WCTI........ New Bern, NC [*Television station call letters*]
WCTK....... New Bedford, MA [*FM radio station call letters*]
WCTL....... Union City, PA [*FM radio station call letters*]
WCTM ..... Eaton, OH [*AM radio station call letters*]
WCTN ...... Potomac-Cabin John, MD [*AM radio station call letters*]
WCTO ...... Smithtown, NY [*FM radio station call letters*]
WCTP....... Charleston, SC [*Television station call letters*]
WCTP........ Wire Chief Test Panel [*Telecommunications*] (TEL)
WCTQ .... Venice, FL [*FM radio station call letters*]

WCTR ...... Chestertown, MD [*AM radio station call letters*]
WCTR ...... WCTU Railway Co. [*AAR code*]
WCTS........ Minneapolis, MN [*FM radio station call letters*]
WCTS........ Weapon Cost Test Site [*Military*] (CAAL)
WCTS........ Weapons Controller Training Squadron
W Ct SA.... Union of South Africa Water Courts Decisions [*A publication*] (DLA)
WCTT........ Corbin, KY [*AM radio station call letters*]
WCTT........ Weapons Crew Training Test [*TCATA*] (RDA)
WCTT-FM ... Corbin, KY [*FM radio station call letters*]
WCTU .... National Woman's Christian Temperance Union (EA)
WCTU .... Women's Connubial Temperance Union [*Satirical*]
WCTV ...... Thomasville, GA [*Television station call letters*]
WCTV ...... Westcott Communications [*NASDAQ symbol*] (SPSG)
WCTX ...... Palmyra, PA [*FM radio station call letters*]
WCTY ...... Norwich, CT [*FM radio station call letters*]
WCTZ........ Clarksville, TN [*AM radio station call letters*]
WCu.......... Cumberland Public Library, Cumberland, WI [*Library symbol*] [*Library of Congress*] (LCLS)
WCU.......... Water Cooler Unit (AAG)
WCU.......... Weapons Control Unit (MCD)
WCU.......... West Coast University [*Los Angeles, CA*]
WCU.......... Western Carolina University [*Cullowhee, NC*]
WCU.......... Western Catholic Union (EA)
WCUB ...... Two Rivers, WI [*AM radio station call letters*]
WCUC ...... Clarion, PA [*FM radio station call letters*]
WCUE .... Cuyahoga Falls, OH [*AM radio station call letters*]
WCUG....... Cuthbert, GA [*AM radio station call letters*]
WCUH ...... Western Carolina University Herbarium
WCUK ...... West Coast of the United Kingdom
WCUL .... Culpeper, VA [*FM radio station call letters*]
WCUM....... Bridgeport, CT [*AM radio station call letters*]
WCUMBS ... Western Canadian Universities Marine Biological Society
WCUNDDP ... World Committee for the United Nations Decade of Disabled Persons (EA)
WCUW ...... Worcester, MA [*FM radio station call letters*]
WCUZ....... Grand Rapids, MI [*AM radio station call letters*]
WCUZ....... World Confederation of United Zionists (EA)
WCUZ-FM ... Grand Rapids, MI [*FM radio station call letters*]
WCV .... Water Check Valve
WCV .... Winant and Clayton Volunteers (EA)
WCVA ...... Culpeper, VA [*AM radio station call letters*]
WCVB ...... Boston, MA [*Television station call letters*]
WCVC ...... Tallahassee, FL [*AM radio station call letters*]
WCVE ...... Richmond, VA [*FM radio station call letters*]
WCVE-TV ... Richmond, VA [*Television station call letters*]
WCVF....... Fredonia, NY [*FM radio station call letters*]
WCVG ...... Covington, KY [*AM radio station call letters*]
WCVH....... Flemington, NJ [*FM radio station call letters*]
WCVI......... Connellsville, PA [*AM radio station call letters*]
WCVJ........ Jefferson, OH [*FM radio station call letters*]
WCVK....... Bowling Green, KY [*FM radio station call letters*]
WCVL........ Crawfordsville, IN [*AM radio station call letters*]
WCVM ..... Western College of Veterinary Medicine [*Canada*]
WCVN....... Covington, KY [*Television station call letters*]
WCVO....... Gahanna, OH [*FM radio station call letters*]
WCVP........ Murphy, NC [*AM radio station call letters*]
WCVP........ Robbinsville, NC [*FM radio station call letters*]
WCVQ ...... Fort Campbell, KY [*FM radio station call letters*]
WCVR ...... Randolph, VT [*FM radio station call letters*]
WCVS........ Springfield, IL [*AM radio station call letters*]
WCVU ...... Naples, FL [*FM radio station call letters*]
WCVV ...... Belpre, OH [*FM radio station call letters*]
WCVW ..... Richmond, VA [*Television station call letters*]
WCVX ...... Vineyard Haven, MA [*Television station call letters*]
WCVY ...... Coventry, RI [*FM radio station call letters*]
WCVZ....... Zanesville, OH [*FM radio station call letters*]
WCW.......... Western College for Women [*Ohio*]
WCW.......... Western College for Women, Oxford, OH [*OCLC symbol*] [*Inactive*] (OCLC)
WCW.......... Wood Casement Window [*Technical drawings*]
WCWA ..... Toledo, OH [*AM radio station call letters*]
WCWB ...... Trenton, FL [*FM radio station call letters*]
WCWB ...... World Council for the Welfare of the Blind [*Later, WBU*] (EAIO)
WCWC ...... Ripon, WI [*AM radio station call letters*]
WCWE ...... WCW Western Canada Water Enterprises, Inc. [*NASDAQ symbol*] (NQ)
WCWL ...... Stockbridge, MA [*FM radio station call letters*]
WCWN..... William Carlos Williams Newsletter [*A publication*]
WC/WO .... Working Committee on Weather Operations
WCWP ...... Brookville, NY [*FM radio station call letters*]
WCWR ...... William Carlos Williams Review [*A publication*]
WCWS....... Wooster, OH [*FM radio station call letters*]
WCWT ...... Centerville, OH [*FM radio station call letters*]
WCWV ...... Summersville, WV [*FM radio station call letters*]
WCX .... Weak Cation Exchanger [*Chemistry*]
WCX .... Westmoreland Coal Co. [*NYSE symbol*] (SPSG)
WCXI........ Detroit, MI [*AM radio station call letters*]
WCXJ........ Braddock, PA [*AM radio station call letters*]
WCXN .... Claremont, NC [*AM radio station call letters*]

WCXQ .... Moca, PR [*AM radio station call letters*]
WCXR ...... Woodbridge, VA [*FM radio station call letters*]
WCXT .... Hart, MI [*FM radio station call letters*]
WCXU ...... Caribou, ME [*FM radio station call letters*]
WCXX ...... Madawaska, ME [*FM radio station call letters*]
WCY .... Viking Express, Inc. [*West Chicago, IL*] [*FAA designator*]   (FAAC)
WCY .... World Communications Year [*1983*]
WCYB ...... Bristol, VA [*Television station call letters*]
WCYC ...... Chicago, IL [*FM radio station call letters*]
WCYC .... Westmorland and Cumberland Yeomanry Cavalry [*British military*]   (DMA)
WCYJ .... Waynesburg, PA [*FM radio station call letters*]
WCYK ...... Crozet, VA [*AM radio station call letters*]
WCYK-FM ... Crozet, VA [*FM radio station call letters*]
WCYN ...... Cynthiana, KY [*AM radio station call letters*]
WCYN-FM ... Cynthiana, KY [*FM radio station call letters*]
WCYO ...... Irvine, KY [*FM radio station call letters*]
WCYS .... Worcester County Institution for Savings [*Worcester, MA*] [*NASDAQ symbol*]   (NQ)
WCZI .... Washington, NC [*FM radio station call letters*]
WCZN .... Chester, PA [*AM radio station call letters*]
WCZQ .... Monticello, IL [*FM radio station call letters*]
WCZR ...... Charleston, WV [*AM radio station call letters*]
WCZX .... Hyde Park, NY [*FM radio station call letters*]
WCZY .... Mount Pleasant, MI [*FM radio station call letters*]
WD............ Decisions Won [*Boxing*]
WD............ [*Qualified for*] Deck Watch [*USNR officer classification*]
WD............ General Warranty Deed [*Real estate*]
Wd............ Seaweed [*Quality of the bottom*] [*Nautical charts*]
WD............ Two-Conductor Cables [*JETDS nomenclature*] [*Military*]   (CET)
WD............ Wallerian Degeneration [*Medicine*]
WD............ War Damage
WD............ War Department [*Created, 1789; became Department of the Army, 1947*]
WD............ Ward
WD............ Wardair Canada Ltd. [*ICAO designator*]   (FAAC)
WD............ Warehouse Distributor
WD............ Warranted
WD............ Washington Decisions [*A publication*]   (DLA)
WD............ Waste Disposal [*Nuclear energy*]   (NRCH)
WD............ Water Damage   (ADA)
WD............ Water Desurger
WD............ Water Division [*Environmental Protection Agency*]   (GFGA)
WD............ Watt Demand Meter   (MSA)
WD............ Wavelength Dispersive [*Spectrometry*]
WD............ Weapon Description   (MCD)
WD............ Weapon Director [*SAGE*]
WD............ Weapons Data [*Navy*]
WD............ Weather Division [*Air Force*]   (MCD)
WD............ Web Depth
WD............ [*The*] Weekly Dispatch [*A publication*]
WD............ Well Deck
W-D .... Well-Developed [*Medicine*]
WD............ Well Differentiated [*Medicine*]
WD............ Well-Drained [*Soil*]
WD............ West Division   (ROG)
WD............ Westminster Dragoons [*British military*]   (DMA)
WD............ Wet Dressing
WD............ Wheel Drive [*Engineering*]
WD............ When Directed
WD............ When Discovered
WD............ When Distributed [*Stock exchange term*]   (SPSG)
WD............ Whole Depth
WD............ Widow
WD............ Width   (MSA)
W/D.......... Width-to-Diameter [*Ratio*]   (KSC)
WD-.......... Wife's Divorce   (ROG)
WD............ Will Dated [*Genealogy*]   (ROG)
WD............ Wilson Dam [*TVA*]
WD............ Wilson's Disease [*Medicine*]
WD............ Wind   (MSA)
WD............ Wind Deflection [*Ballistics*]
WD............ Wind Direction
WD............ Window Detector
WD............ Window Dimension [*Technical drawings*]
WD............ [*Bob*] Winkelmann and [*Hugh*] Dibley, [*Automotive designers*] [*British*]
WD............ Winner's Dog [*Dog show term*]
WD............ Winter's Digest [*A publication*]
WD............ Wired Discrete   (NASA)
WD............ With Dependents   (MCD)
WD............ With Disease   (MAE)
W/D.......... Withdrawal   (DLA)
WD............ Withdrawn   (AFM)
WD............ Wittenberg Door [*A publication*]
W & D .... Wolferstan and Dew's English Election Cases [*1856-58*] [*A publication*]   (DLA)
WD............ Woman's Day [*A publication*]
WD............ Wood   (AAG)

WD............ Wood Door [*Technical drawings*]
Wd............ Word [*A publication*]
WD............ Word
WD............ Word Display
WD............ Work [*or Working*] Day   (AFM)
WD............ Work Description   (MCD)
WD............ Work Directive   (MCD)
WD............ Working Distance [*Microscopy*]
WD............ Works Department
Wd............ World [*A publication*]
WD............ World Development [*A publication*]
W & D........ Wort und Dienst [*A publication*]
WD............ Would
WD............ Wound   (AAMN)
WD............ Wrist Disarticulation [*Medicine*]
WD............ Write Data
WD............ Write Direct
WD............ Writers Digest [*A publication*]
WD............ Writer's Directory [*A publication*]
WD............ Wrongful Detention [*British*]
WD............ Wydmar Developmental Corp. [*Vancouver Stock Exchange symbol*]
2WD.......... Two-Wheel Drive [*Automotive engineering*]
W 2d.......... Washington State Reports, Second Series [*A publication*]   (DLA)
4WD.......... Four-Wheel Drive [*Vehicle*]
W4D.......... Worth Four-Dot Test [*Ophthalmology*]
WDA......... Aram Public Library, Delavan, WI [*Library symbol*] [*Library of Congress*]   (LCLS)
WDA......... Wallcovering Distributors Association   (EA)
WDA......... Warehouse Distributors Association for Leisure and Mobile Products   (EA)
WDA......... Waste Disposal Authority [*British*]
WDA......... Wave Data Analyzer [*Marine science*]   (MSC)
WDA......... Weapons Defended Area
WDA......... Welsh Development Agency [*British*]   (DS)
WDA......... Western District Area [*Air Force*]
WDA......... Wheel Drive Assembly
WDA......... Wholesale Distributors Association   (EA)
WDA......... Wildlife Disease Association   (EA)
WDA......... Wilson's Disease Association   (EA)
WDA......... Withdrawal of Availability [*Military*]   (AFM)
WDA......... Women's Diocesan Association [*British*]
WDA......... World Aquathemes Ltd. [*Vancouver Stock Exchange symbol*]
WDA......... World Development Action [*An association*] [*British*]
WDA......... World Dredging Association   (MSC)
WDAC....... Lancaster, PA [*FM radio station call letters*]
WDAD....... Indiana, PA [*AM radio station call letters*]
WDAE....... Tampa, FL [*AM radio station call letters*]
WDAF....... Kansas City, MO [*AM radio station call letters*]
WDAF....... Western Desert Air Force
WDAF-TV ... Kansas City, MO [*Television station call letters*]
WDAHAC ... National Society Women Descendants of the Ancient and Honorable Artillery Company   (EA)
WDAK...... Lafayette, AL [*AM radio station call letters*]
WDAL....... Linden, AL [*FM radio station call letters*]
WDALMP ... Warehouse Distributors Association for Leisure and Mobile Products   (EA)
WDAM...... Laurel, MS [*Television station call letters*]
WDAN...... Danville, IL [*AM radio station call letters*]
WDAO...... Dayton, OH [*AM radio station call letters*]
WDAP...... World Dictionary of Awards and Prizes [*A publication*]
WDAQ...... Danbury, CT [*FM radio station call letters*]
WDar .... Darien Public Library, Darien, WI [*Library symbol*] [*Library of Congress*]   (LCLS)
WDAR...... Darlington, SC [*AM radio station call letters*]
WDAR-FM ... Darlington, SC [*FM radio station call letters*]
WDAS....... Philadelphia, PA [*AM radio station call letters*]
WDAS-FM ... Philadelphia, PA [*FM radio station call letters*]
WDAU....... Ozark, AL [*Television station call letters*]
WDAV....... Davidson, NC [*FM radio station call letters*]
WDAX...... McRae, GA [*AM radio station call letters*]
WDAX-FM ... McRae, GA [*FM radio station call letters*]
WDAY...... Fargo, ND [*AM radio station call letters*]
WDAY-FM ... Fargo, ND [*FM radio station call letters*]
WDAY-TV ... Fargo, ND [*Television station call letters*]
WDAZ....... Devils Lake, ND [*Television station call letters*]
WdB.......... Weekblad der Belastingen [*A publication*]
WDB........ Weekblad der Directe Belastingen [*A publication*]
WDB........ Westminster Dictionary of the Bible [*A publication*]   (BJA)
WDB........ Wide Deadband [*NASA*]
WDB........ Wideband [*Radio*]   (MCD)
WDB........ Winkelmann-Dibley Formula B [*Race car*]
WDBA...... Du Bois, PA [*FM radio station call letters*]
WDBB ...... Tuscaloosa, AL [*Television station call letters*]
WDBC....... Escanaba, MI [*AM radio station call letters*]
WDBD...... Jackson, MS [*Television station call letters*]
WDBF....... Delray Beach, FL [*AM radio station call letters*]
WDBI........ Tawas City, MI [*FM radio station call letters*]
WDBJ........ Roanoke, VA [*Television station call letters*]
WDBK....... Blackwood, NJ [*FM radio station call letters*]

WDBK	Wordbook (ROG)
WDBL	Springfield, TN [*AM radio station call letters*]
WDBL-FM ...	Springfield, TN [*FM radio station call letters*]
WDBM	East Lansing, MI [*FM radio station call letters*]
WDBN	Woodbine Petroleum, Inc. [*NASDAQ symbol*] (NQ)
WDBO	Orlando, FL [*AM radio station call letters*]
WDBOR	Wood Boring
WDBQ	Dubuque, IA [*AM radio station call letters*]
WDBR	Springfield, IL [*FM radio station call letters*]
WDBY	Duxbury, MA [*FM radio station call letters*]
WDC	War Damage Commission [*British*]
WDC	War Damage Corp. [*World War II*]
WDC	War Department Constabulary [*British military*] (DMA)
WDC	Washington Document Center
WDC	Waste Disposal Cask [*Nuclear energy*] (NRCH)
WDC	Waste Disposal Code
WDC	Water Data Center [*Department of Agriculture*] [*Information service or system*] (IID)
WDC	Weapon Delivery Computer (MCD)
WDC	Weapon Direction Computer [*Military*] (CAAL)
WDC	Western Defense Command [*Army*]
WDC	Western Digital Corp. [*NYSE symbol*] (SPSG)
WDC	Westinghouse Defense Center
WDC	Whiskeytown Dam [*California*] [*Seismograph station code, US Geological Survey*] (SEIS)
WDC	Wideband Directional Coupler
WDC	Women's Distance Committee (EA)
WDC	Workers' Defence Committee [*Ghana*] [*Political party*] (PPW)
WDC	Workers' Defense Committee [*Poland*] (PD)
WDC	Working Direct Current (DEN)
WDC	World Data Center [*National Academy of Sciences*] [*Data collection and exchange center*]
WDC	World Development Corp.
WDC	World Disarmament Campaign (EAIO)
WDC	World Disarmament Conference (NATG)
WDC	World Druze Congress (EA)
WDC	Write Data Check (CMD)
WDCA	Washington, DC [*Television station call letters*]
WDC-A	World Data Center A [*National Academy of Sciences*]
WDCA	World Diving Coaches Association (EA)
WDCB	Glen Ellyn, IL [*FM radio station call letters*]
WDC-B	World Data Center B [*National Academy of Sciences*]
WDCC	Sanford, NC [*FM radio station call letters*]
WDCE	Richmond, VA [*FM radio station call letters*]
WDCF	Dade City, FL [*AM radio station call letters*]
WDCG	Durham, NC [*FM radio station call letters*]
WDCI	Bridgeport, WV [*FM radio station call letters*]
WDCK	Williamsburg, VA [*FM radio station call letters*]
WDCL	Somerset, KY [*FM radio station call letters*]
WDCM	Cruz Bay, VI [*FM radio station call letters*]
WDCMC ...	War Department Classified Message Center [*Obsolete*] [*World War II*]
WDCN	Nashville, TN [*Television station call letters*]
WDCO	Cochran, GA [*FM radio station call letters*]
WDCO	Western Energy Development Co., Inc. [*NASDAQ symbol*] (NQ)
WDCO-TV ...	Cochran, GA [*Television station call letters*]
WDCQ	Pine Island Centre, FL [*AM radio station call letters*]
WDCR	Hanover, NH [*AM radio station call letters*]
WDCS	Weapons Data Correlation System (MCD)
WDCS	Women's Division of Christian Service [*of the Board of Missions, The Methodist Church*]
WDCS	Writable Diagnostic Control Store
WDCSA	War Department Chief of Staff, US Army [*World War II*]
WDCSM....	Walt Disney Comic Strip Maker [*Apple computer software*]
WDCT	Fairfax, VA [*AM radio station call letters*]
WDCT	Woodcut (ROG)
WDCU	Washington, DC [*FM radio station call letters*]
WDCV	Carlisle, PA [*FM radio station call letters*]
WDCX	Buffalo, NY [*FM radio station call letters*]
WDCY	Douglasville, GA [*AM radio station call letters*]
WDD	Wave Dynamics Division [*US Army Corps of Engineers*]
WDD	Western Development Division [*ARDC*]
WDD	Word Description Drawing
WD (2d)	Washington Decisions, Second Series [*A publication*] (DLA)
WDDC	Portage, WI [*FM radio station call letters*]
WDDC	Well Deck Debarkation Control [*Navy*] (CAAL)
WDDD	Johnston City, IL [*AM radio station call letters*]
WDDD	Marion, IL [*FM radio station call letters*]
WDDJ	Paducah, KY [*FM radio station call letters*]
WDDK	Greensboro, GA [*FM radio station call letters*]
WDDO	Macon, GA [*AM radio station call letters*]
WDDQ	Adel, GA [*FM radio station call letters*]
WDDT	Greenville, MS [*AM radio station call letters*]
WDE	Weapons Directing Equipment (NVT)
WDE	Weapons Direction Evaluation (SAA)
wde	Wood-Engraver [*MARC relator code*] [*Library of Congress*] (LCCP)
WDEA	Ellsworth, ME [*AM radio station call letters*]
WDEB	Jamestown, TN [*AM radio station call letters*]
WDEB-FM ...	Jamestown, TN [*FM radio station call letters*]

WDEC	Americus, GA [*AM radio station call letters*]
WDEC-FM ...	Americus, GA [*FM radio station call letters*]
WDED	Wounded [*Military*]
WDEE	Reed City, MI [*AM radio station call letters*]
WDEF	Chattanooga, TN [*AM radio station call letters*]
WDEFA	Welding Design and Fabrication [*A publication*]
WDEF-FM ...	Chattanooga, TN [*FM radio station call letters*]
WDEF-TV ...	Chattanooga, TN [*Television station call letters*]
WDEH	Sweetwater, TN [*AM radio station call letters*]
WDEH-FM ...	Sweetwater, TN [*FM radio station call letters*]
WDEK	De Kalb, IL [*FM radio station call letters*]
WDEL	Weapons Development Effectiveness Laboratory (MCD)
WDEL	Wilmington, DE [*AM radio station call letters*]
WDEMCO ...	Walt Disney Educational Media Co.
WDEN	Macon, GA [*AM radio station call letters*]
WDEN-FM ...	Macon, GA [*FM radio station call letters*]
WDEOAT ...	Wolfe Data Entry Operator Aptitude Test
WDEP	Western Deep Levels Ltd. [*NASDAQ symbol*] (NQ)
WDEQ	De Graff, OH [*FM radio station call letters*]
WDER	Derry, NH [*AM radio station call letters*]
WDET	Detroit, MI [*FM radio station call letters*]
WDEV	Waterbury, VT [*AM radio station call letters*]
WDEX	Monroe, NC [*AM radio station call letters*]
WDEZ	Wausau, WI [*FM radio station call letters*]
WDF	Wall Distribution Frame (MUGU)
WDF	Weapon Defense Facility (AAG)
WDF	Weather Data Facility
WDF	Western Desert Force [*World War II*]
WDF	Winkelmann-Dibley Ford [*Race car*]
WDF	Wood Door and Frame [*Technical drawings*]
WDF	Woodruff
WDF	World Darts Federation (EAIO)
WDF	World Draughts (Checkers) Federation [*See also FMJD*] [*Dordrecht, Netherlands*] (EAIO)
WDFB	Junction City, KY [*AM radio station call letters*]
WDFC	WD-40 Co. [*NASDAQ symbol*] (NQ)
WD/FE	Water Dispenser/Fire Extinguisher [*Apollo*] [*NASA*]
WDFL	Cross City, FL [*AM radio station call letters*]
WDFL-FM ...	Cross City, FL [*FM radio station call letters*]
WDFM	Defiance, OH [*FM radio station call letters*]
WDFP	World Day for Peace (EA)
WDFX	Detroit, MI [*FM radio station call letters*]
WDFZ	Tullahoma, TN [*AM radio station call letters*]
WDG	Enid [*Oklahoma*] [*Airport symbol*] (OAG)
WDG	Enid, OK [*Location identifier*] [*FAA*] (FAAL)
WDG	Wallace Dam [*Georgia*] [*Seismograph station code, US Geological Survey*] (SEIS)
WDG	Weapons Display Generator (MCD)
WDG	Wedgestone Financial [*NYSE symbol*] (SPSG)
WDG	Winding (MSA)
WDG	Wording (WGA)
WDG	World Diplomatic Guide [*A publication*]
WDGB	Wuerzburger Diozesangeschichtsblaetter [*A publication*]
WDGC	Downers Grove, IL [*FM radio station call letters*]
WDGE	Saranac Lake, NY [*FM radio station call letters*]
WDGF	War Department Ground Forces [*Obsolete*]
WDGI	Wholesale Dry Goods Institute [*Later, NATAD*]
W Dgns	Westminster Dragoons [*British military*] (DMA)
WDGO	War Department General Order [*Obsolete*]
WDGR	Dahlonega, GA [*AM radio station call letters*]
WDGS	New Albany, IN [*AM radio station call letters*]
WDGS	War Department General Staff [*Obsolete*]
WDG TBA ...	Wording to Be Agreed [*Insurance*] (AIA)
WDH	Watery Diarrhea, Hypokalemia [*Syndrome*] [*Medicine*]
WDH	Winchell's Donut House [*NYSE symbol*] (SPSG)
WDH	Windhoek [*Namibia*] [*Airport symbol*] (OAG)
WDH	Winkelmann-Dibley Hillclimb [*Race car*]
WDH	Wiring Data Handbook
WDHA	Dover, NJ [*FM radio station call letters*]
WDHA	Watery Diarrhea, Hypokalemia, Achlorhydria [*Medicine*]
WDHCB	War Department Hardship Claims Board [*Obsolete*]
WDHD	Woodhead Industries, Inc. [*NASDAQ symbol*] (NQ)
WDHH	Watery Diarrhea, Hypokalemia, Hypochlorhydria [*Syndrome*] [*Medicine*]
WDHHA ...	Watery Diarrhea, Hypochlorhydria, Hypokalemia, and Alkalosis [*Medicine*]
WDHI	Delhi, NY [*FM radio station call letters*]
WDHM	Salem, IN [*FM radio station call letters*]
WDHN	Dothan, AL [*Television station call letters*]
WDHR	Pikeville, KY [*FM radio station call letters*]
WDHS	Worldwide Dental Health Service (EA)
WDHT	Brantley, AL [*FM radio station call letters*]
WDI	War Department Intelligence [*Obsolete*]
WDI	Wardair, Inc. [*Toronto Stock Exchange symbol*]
WDI	Warfarin Dose Index
WDI	Warhead Detection Indicator (AAG)
WDI	Weapon Data Index [*Navy*] (MCD)
WDI	Weapon Delivery Impairment (NVT)
WDI	Web Depth Index
WDI	Wind Direction Indicator [*Aviation*] (FAAC)
WDI	Wood and Iron [*Freight*]

WDIA .... Memphis, TN [*AM radio station call letters*]
WDIA .... Weekblad der Directe Belastingen, Invoerrechten en Accijnzen [*A publication*]
WDIC .... Clinchco, VA [*AM radio station call letters*]
WDICC ...... War Department Intelligence Collection Committee
WDIC-FM ... Clinchco, VA [*FM radio station call letters*]
WDICPC .... War Department Intelligence Collection Planning Committee
WDIF .... Marion, OH [*FM radio station call letters*]
WDIF .... Women's Democratic International Federation (NATG)
W Dig .... New York Weekly Digest [*A publication*] (DLA)
WDIG .... Steubenville, OH [*AM radio station call letters*]
WDigitl ..... Western Digital Corp. [*Associated Press abbreviation*] (APAG)
WDIH .... Salisbury, MD [*FM radio station call letters*]
WDIM .... With Design in Mind International [*NASDAQ symbol*] (NQ)
WDIO .... Duluth, MN [*Television station call letters*]
WDIP .... Weapon Data Insert Panel (MCD)
WDIQ .... Dozier, AL [*Television station call letters*]
WDIR .... Wind Direction
WDIRN ..... What Do I Read Next? [*A publication*]
WDIV .... Detroit, MI [*Television station call letters*]
WDIX .... Yadkinville, NC [*AM radio station call letters*]
WDIZ .... Orlando, FL [*FM radio station call letters*]
WdJ .... Wissenschaft des Judentums [*A publication*] (BJA)
WDJC .... Birmingham, AL [*FM radio station call letters*]
WDJK .... Xenia, OH [*FM radio station call letters*]
WDJM ...... Framingham, MA [*FM radio station call letters*]
WDJQ .... Alliance, OH [*FM radio station call letters*]
WDJR .... Enterprise, AL [*FM radio station call letters*]
WDJS .... Mount Olive, NC [*AM radio station call letters*]
WDJT .... Milwaukee, WI [*Television station call letters*]
WDJW ...... Somers, CT [*FM radio station call letters*]
WDJX .... Louisville, KY [*AM radio station call letters*]
WDJX-FM ... Louisville, KY [*FM radio station call letters*]
WDJZ .... Bridgeport, CT [*AM radio station call letters*]
W Dk .... Weather Deck [*of a ship*] (DS)
WDKA ...... Paducah, KY [*Television station call letters*]
WDKB ...... De Kalb, IL [*FM radio station call letters*]
WDKD ...... Kingstree, SC [*AM radio station call letters*]
WDKN ...... Dickson, TN [*AM radio station call letters*]
WDKT .... Madison, AL [*AM radio station call letters*]
WDKX .... Rochester, NY [*FM radio station call letters*]
WDKY .... Danville, KY [*Television station call letters*]
WD KY ...... United States District Court for the Western District of Kentucky (DLA)
WDKZ .... Blakely, GA [*FM radio station call letters*]
WDL .... Warren Library Association and County Division, Warren, PA [*OCLC symbol*] (OCLC)
WDL .... Waveguide Directional Localizer
WDL .... Weapon Data Link (MCD)
WDL .... Weapons Density List (AABC)
WDL .... Well-Differentiated Lymphocytic [*Lymphoma classification*]
WDL .... Westdeutsche Luftwerbung [*Airline*] [*Germany*]
WDL .... Western Development Laboratories
WDL .... Western d'Eldona Resources Ltd. [*Toronto Stock Exchange symbol*]
WDL .... Wien Displacement Law [*Physics*]
WDL .... Wireless Data Link
Wdl .... Wirkung der Literatur [*A publication*]
WDL .... Workers' Defense League (EA)
WD LA ...... United States District Court for the Western District of Louisiana (DLA)
WDLA .... Walton, NY [*AM radio station call letters*]
WDLA-FM ... Walton, NY [*FM radio station call letters*]
WDLB .... Marshfield, WI [*AM radio station call letters*]
WDLC .... Port Jervis, NY [*AM radio station call letters*]
WDLF .... Old Fort, NC [*FM radio station call letters*]
WDLI .... Canton, OH [*Television station call letters*]
WDLJ .... Indianola, MS [*FM radio station call letters*]
WDLK .... Dadeville, AL [*AM radio station call letters*]
WDLL .... Well-Differentiated Lymphatic [*or Lymphocytic*] Lymphoma [*Oncology*]
WDLM ...... East Moline, IL [*AM radio station call letters*]
WDLM-FM ... East Moline, IL [*FM radio station call letters*]
WDLR .... Delaware, OH [*AM radio station call letters*]
WDLS .... Dallas, PA [*FM radio station call letters*]
WDLT .... Chickasaw, AL [*FM radio station call letters*]
WDLX .... Washington, NC [*FM radio station call letters*]
WDLY .... Gatlinburg, TN [*FM radio station call letters*]
WDLY .... Widely (FAAC)
WDM .... Wavelength Division Multiplex [*Telecommunications*]
WDM .... Weight after Departure from Mars [*NASA*]
WDM .... World Development Movement [*British*]
WDMA ...... Wholesale Druggists Merchandising Association (EA)
WDMB ...... War Department Manpower Board [*Obsolete*]
WDMC ...... [*The*] Woodmoor Corp. [*NASDAQ symbol*] (NQ)
WDME ...... Dover-Foxcroft, ME [*AM radio station call letters*]
WDME-FM ... Dover-Foxcroft, ME [*FM radio station call letters*]
WDMET ... Wound Data Munitions Effectiveness Team (MCD)
WDMF ...... Knoxville, TN [*AM radio station call letters*]
WDMF ...... Weak Disordered Magnetic Field
WDMG ...... Douglas, GA [*AM radio station call letters*]

WDMG-FM ... Douglas, GA [*FM radio station call letters*]
WD Mich ... United States District Court for the Western District of Michigan (DLA)
WDMJ .... Marquette, MI [*AM radio station call letters*]
WDML ...... Wiring Diagram Maintenance List
WDML ...... Woodlawn, IL [*FM radio station call letters*]
WD MO ..... United States District Court for the Western District of Missouri (DLA)
WDMO ...... Weight before Departure from Mars Orbit [*NASA*]
WDMP ...... Dodgeville, WI [*AM radio station call letters*]
WDMP-FM ... Dodgeville, WI [*FM radio station call letters*]
WDMS ...... Greenville, MS [*FM radio station call letters*]
WDMT ...... Eufaula, AL [*FM radio station call letters*]
WDMV ...... Pocomoke City, MD [*AM radio station call letters*]
WDMX ...... Vienna, WV [*FM radio station call letters*]
WDN .... Wooden
WDNA ...... Miami, FL [*FM radio station call letters*]
WDNC ...... Durham, NC [*AM radio station call letters*]
WDNC ...... United States District Court for the Western District of North Carolina (DLA)
WDND ...... Wilmington, IL [*FM radio station call letters*]
WDNE ...... Elkins, WV [*AM radio station call letters*]
WDNE-FM ... Elkins, WV [*FM radio station call letters*]
WDNG ...... Anniston, AL [*AM radio station call letters*]
WDNH ...... Honesdale, PA [*FM radio station call letters*]
WDNL ...... Danville, IL [*FM radio station call letters*]
WDNO ...... Laurel, DE [*FM radio station call letters*]
WDNOWRE ... Wooden Ware [*Freight*]
WDNR ...... Chester, PA [*FM radio station call letters*]
WDNS ...... Bowling Green, KY [*FM radio station call letters*]
WDNT ...... Dayton, TN [*AM radio station call letters*]
WDNX ...... Olive Hill, TN [*FM radio station call letters*]
WDNY ...... Dansville, NY [*AM radio station call letters*]
WDNY ...... United States District Court for the Western District of New York (DLA)
WDO .... Web Depth Order
WDO .... Widespread Depression Orchestra
WDO .... Window (MSA)
WDOC ...... Prestonsburg, KY [*AM radio station call letters*]
WDOD ...... Chattanooga, TN [*AM radio station call letters*]
WDOD-FM ... Chattanooga, TN [*FM radio station call letters*]
WDOE ...... Dunkirk, NY [*AM radio station call letters*]
WDOG ...... Allendale, SC [*AM radio station call letters*]
WDOG-FM ... Allendale, SC [*FM radio station call letters*]
WDOH ...... Delphos, OH [*FM radio station call letters*]
WDOK ...... Cleveland, OH [*FM radio station call letters*]
WD Okla ... United States District Court for the Western District of Oklahoma (DLA)
WDOM ..... Providence, RI [*FM radio station call letters*]
WDON ...... Geneva, OH [*FM radio station call letters*]
WDOP ...... Weighted Dilution of Precision
WDOPD .... War Department, Operations Division, General Staff [*World War II*]
WDOR ...... Sturgeon Bay, WI [*AM radio station call letters*]
WDOR-FM ... Sturgeon Bay, WI [*FM radio station call letters*]
WDOS ...... Oneonta, NY [*AM radio station call letters*]
WDOS ...... Wooton Desk Owners Society (EA)
WDOT ...... Burlington, VT [*AM radio station call letters*]
WDOT ...... Warren, VT [*FM radio station call letters*]
WDOV ...... Dover, DE [*AM radio station call letters*]
WDOW ..... Dowagiac, MI [*AM radio station call letters*]
WDOW-FM ... Dowagiac, MI [*FM radio station call letters*]
WDOX ...... Wildwood Crest, NJ [*FM radio station call letters*]
WDOY ...... Fajardo, PR [*FM radio station call letters*]
WDP .... Weapons Direction Program
WDP .... Wenner Difference Potentiometer
WDP .... Women in Data Processing (EA)
WDP .... Wood Panel (AAG)
WDP .... Work Distribution Policy (AAG)
WD PA ...... United States District Court for the Western District of Pennsylvania (DLA)
WDPA ...... Wisconsin Dairy Products Association (EA)
WDPB ...... Seaford, DE [*Television station call letters*]
WDPC ...... Dallas, GA [*AM radio station call letters*]
WDPC ...... Western Data Processing Center [*University of California, Los Angeles*]
WDPMG-ID ... War Department Provost Marshal General, Investigation Division [*Obsolete*]
WDPN ...... Alliance, OH [*AM radio station call letters*]
WDPR ...... Dayton, OH [*FM radio station call letters*]
WDPS ...... Dayton, OH [*FM radio station call letters*]
WDPT ...... Water-Drop-Penetration Time [*Agriculture*]
WDQN ...... Du Quoin, IL [*AM radio station call letters*]
WDQN-FM ... Du Quoin, IL [*FM radio station call letters*]
WDR .... Wardair International Ltd. [*Toronto Stock Exchange symbol*] [*Vancouver Stock Exchange symbol*]
Wdr .... Wardmaster [*British military*] (DMA)
WDR .... Westdeutscher Rundfunk [*Radio network*] [*West Germany*]
WDR .... Wide Dynamic Range
WDR .... Wider (WGA)
WDR .... Winder, GA [*Location identifier*] [*FAA*] (FAAL)

WDR.........	Window Definition Record [*Data processing*]
WDR.........	Withdrawal
WDR.........	Women's Drug Research Project (EA)
WDR.........	Write Drum
WDRAA	Welding Research Abroad [*A publication*]
WDRB.......	Louisville, KY [*Television station call letters*]
WDRC.......	Hartford, CT [*AM radio station call letters*]
WDRC.......	Women's Defence Relief Corps [*British*] [*World War I*]
WDRC-FM ...	Hartford, CT [*FM radio station call letters*]
WDRE.......	Garden City, NY [*FM radio station call letters*]
WDRG.......	Women's Direct Response Group [*Garden City, NY*] (EA)
WDRKA	Waseda Daigaku Rikogaku Kenkyusho Hokoku [*A publication*]
WDRL.......	Cuthbert, GA [*FM radio station call letters*]
Wdr L.........	Wardmaster Lieutenant [*British military*] (DMA)
WDRM......	Decatur, AL [*FM radio station call letters*]
WDROP	Water Distribution Register of Organic Pollutants [*National Institutes of Health*]
WDRP	Windsor, NC [*FM radio station call letters*]
WDRSA.....	Wood Research [*A publication*]
WDRT.......	Water Detection Response Team [*DoD*]
WDRU.......	Bunnell, FL [*Television station call letters*]
WDRZ.......	Etowah, TN [*FM radio station call letters*]
WDS..........	Four Winds Aviation Ltd. [*Colorado Springs, CO*] [*FAA designator*] (FAAC)
WDS..........	Washington Document Service [*Information service or system*] (IID)
WD(S).......	Waste Disposal (System) [*Nuclear energy*] (NRCH)
WDS..........	Wavelength Dispersive Spectrometer
WDS..........	Weapon Delivery System
WDS..........	Weapons Directing System [*Navy*]
WDS.........	Wire Data Service
WDS.........	Wood Dye Stain
WDS..........	Woodside [*California*] [*Seismograph station code, US Geological Survey*] (SEIS)
WDS..........	Woodward's Ltd. [*Toronto Stock Exchange symbol*] [*Vancouver Stock Exchange symbol*]
WDS..........	Word Discrimination Score
WDS..........	World Deist Society (EA)
WDS..........	Wounds
WDSC.......	Dillon, SC [*AM radio station call letters*]
WDSD.......	Dover, DE [*FM radio station call letters*]
WDSD.......	Water Data Sources Directory [*US Geological Survey*] [*Information service or system*] (CRD)
WDSD.......	Wisconsin School for the Deaf, Delavan, WI [*Library symbol*] [*Library of Congress*] (LCLS)
WDSE.......	Duluth, MN [*Television station call letters*]
WDSG.......	Dyersburg, TN [*AM radio station call letters*]
WDSI........	Chattanooga, TN [*Television station call letters*]
WDSI........	Worlco Data Systems, Inc. [*NASDAQ symbol*] (NQ)
WDSL.......	Mocksville, NC [*AM radio station call letters*]
WdSL........	Welt der Slaven [*A publication*]
WDSM.......	Superior, WI [*AM radio station call letters*]
WDSN.......	Reynoldsville, PA [*FM radio station call letters*]
WDSO.......	Chesterton, IN [*FM radio station call letters*]
WDSPR.....	Widespread
WDSPRD ...	Widespread [*Meteorology*] (FAAC)
WDSR.......	Lake City, FL [*AM radio station call letters*]
WDSRF.....	Windsor Resources, Inc. [*NASDAQ symbol*] (NQ)
WDSS........	War Department Special Staff [*Obsolete*]
WDS SATSIM ...	Weapon Direction System Satellite Simulation [*Military*] (CAAL)
WDST.......	Woodstock, NY [*FM radio station call letters*]
WDST.......	Wordstar International, Inc. [*NASDAQ symbol*] (NQ)
WD STL	Wood or Steel [*Freight*]
WD STV ...	Wood Stove [*Freight*]
WDSU.......	New Orleans, LA [*Television station call letters*]
WDSY	Pittsburgh, PA [*FM radio station call letters*]
WDT.........	Warmth Detection Threshold
WDT.........	Watch Dog Timer
WDT.........	Wear Durability Trial
WDT.........	Wedtech Corp. [*AMEX symbol*] (SPSG)
WDT.........	Weight Distribution Table
WDT.........	Width
WDT.........	Wiedemann Developed Template (MCD)
WDT.........	World Cement Industries [*Vancouver Stock Exchange symbol*]
WDT.........	World Development [*A publication*]
WDTC......	Western Defense Tactical Command (AAG)
WD Tenn ...	United States District Court for the Western District of Tennessee (DLA)
WD Tex	United States District Court for the Western District of Texas (DLA)
WDTF.......	Wetting-Drying and Temperature Fluctuation [*Geochemistry*]
WDTL	Cleveland, MS [*AM radio station call letters*]
WDTL-FM ...	Cleveland, MS [*FM radio station call letters*]
WDTM......	Selmer, TN [*AM radio station call letters*]
WDTN.......	Dayton, OH [*Television station call letters*]
WDTR.......	Detroit, MI [*FM radio station call letters*]
WDTU.......	War Dog Training Unit [*British military*] (DMA)
WDTV	Weston, WV [*Television station call letters*]
WDu...........	Durand Free Library, Durand, WI [*Library symbol*] [*Library of Congress*] (LCLS)
WdU	Wahlpartei der Unabhaengigen [*Electoral Party of Independents*] [*Austria*] [*Political party*] (PPE)
WDU	Water Data Unit (DCTA)
WDU	Weapons Director Unit (MCD)
WDU	Window Deicing Unit
WDU	Wireless Development Unit
WDU	Workers' Defence Union [*British*]
WDUB......	Granville, OH [*FM radio station call letters*]
WDUF	Duffield, VA [*AM radio station call letters*]
WDUK.......	Havana, IL [*FM radio station call letters*]
WDUN.......	Gainesville, GA [*AM radio station call letters*]
WDUQ	Pittsburgh, PA [*FM radio station call letters*]
WDUR.......	Durham, NC [*AM radio station call letters*]
WDUV.......	Bradenton, FL [*FM radio station call letters*]
WDUX.......	Waupaca, WI [*AM radio station call letters*]
WDUX-FM ...	Waupaca, WI [*FM radio station call letters*]
WDUZ.......	Green Bay, WI [*AM radio station call letters*]
WDV..........	War Department Vehicle [*Obsolete*]
WDV..........	Western Diverging Volcanism [*Geology*]
WDV..........	Wheat Dwarf Virus [*Plant pathology*]
WDV..........	Winkelmann-Dibley Volkswagen [*Race car*]
WDV..........	Written Down Value [*Accounting*]
WDVA	Danville, VA [*AM radio station call letters*]
WD VA	United States District Court for the Western District of Virginia (DLA)
WDVE.......	Pittsburgh, PA [*FM radio station call letters*]
WDVI........	Dadeville, AL [*FM radio station call letters*]
WDVR.......	Delaware Township, NJ [*FM radio station call letters*]
WDW........	Wholesale Dealer in Wines
WDW........	Window
WDW........	Wood and Wire [*Freight*]
WD Wash ...	United States District Court for the Western District of Washington (DLA)
WD Wis	United States District Court for the Western District of Wisconsin (DLA)
WDWL......	Bayamon, PR [*Television station call letters*]
WDWN......	Auburn, NY [*FM radio station call letters*]
WDWN......	Well Developed - Well Nourished [*Medicine*]
WDWRA ...	Welding in the World [*A publication*]
WDWRK ..	Woodwork [*Freight*]
WDWS.......	Champaign, IL [*AM radio station call letters*]
WDX.........	Wavelength Dispersive X-Ray [*Spectrometer*]
WDXA	Wave-Length Dispersive X-Ray Analysis
WDXC.......	Pound, VA [*FM radio station call letters*]
WDXE.......	Lawrenceburg, TN [*AM radio station call letters*]
WDXE-FM ...	Lawrenceburg, TN [*FM radio station call letters*]
WDXI........	Jackson, TN [*AM radio station call letters*]
WDXL.......	Lexington, TN [*AM radio station call letters*]
WDXN......	Clarksville, TN [*AM radio station call letters*]
WDXR......	Golconda, IL [*FM radio station call letters*]
WDXR......	Paducah, KY [*AM radio station call letters*]
WDXRF....	Wavelength-Dispersive X-Ray Fluorescence
WDXRS....	Wavelength Dispersive X-Ray Spectrometry
WDXW......	L'Anse, MI [*AM radio station call letters*]
WDXX.......	Selma, AL [*FM radio station call letters*]
WDXY.......	Sumter, SC [*AM radio station call letters*]
WDXZ.......	Mount Pleasant, SC [*FM radio station call letters*]
WDY..........	Woody [*California*] [*Seismograph station code, US Geological Survey*] [*Closed*] (SEIS)
WDY..........	Wordy [*Used in correcting manuscripts, etc.*]
WDYL.......	Chester, VA [*FM radio station call letters*]
WDYN.......	Chattanooga, TN [*FM radio station call letters*]
WDYT.......	What Do You Think?
WDYTYCIWSS ...	Why Don't You Take Your Change In War Savings Stamps [*Cashier's sign*] [*World War II*]
WDZ.........	Decatur, IL [*AM radio station call letters*]
WDZ..........	Werner Dahnz Co. Ltd. [*Toronto Stock Exchange symbol*]
WDZD......	Shallotte, NC [*FM radio station call letters*]
WDZE	Carolina, PR [*Television station call letters*]
WDZK	Chester, SC [*FM radio station call letters*]
WDZL	Miami, FL [*Television station call letters*]
WDZQ......	Decatur, IL [*FM radio station call letters*]
WDZZ	Flint, MI [*FM radio station call letters*]
WE............	Eau Claire Public Library, Eau Claire, WI [*Library symbol*] [*Library of Congress*] (LCLS)
WE............	Staff Meteorologist [*AFSC*]
WE............	Wage Earner [*Social Security Administration*] (OICC)
WE............	War Establishment
WE............	Watch Error [*Navigation*]
WE............	Watchman-Examiner [*A publication*] (BJA)
WE............	Water Equivalent (MCD)
We............	Watt Electric
WE............	WDL Flugdienst GmbH [*Germany*] [*ICAO designator*] (ICDA)
WE............	Weapons Electrical [*Navy*] [*British*]
WE............	Weapons Engineering [*Navy*] [*British*]
WE............	Weather Emergency
WE............	Webbing Equipment [*British military*] (DMA)
We............	Weber Number [*IUPAC*]
WE............	Wednesday
W/E	Week Ending

WE............ Weekend (ADA)
WE............ Wescap Enterprises Ltd. [*Vancouver Stock Exchange symbol*]
WE............ Westcoast Energy, Inc. [*NYSE symbol*] (SPSG)
WE............ Western Electric Co. (AAG)
WE............ Western Encephalitis [*Medicine*] (MAE)
WE............ Western Encephalomyelitis [*Medicine*] (MAE)
We............. Western Tithe Cases [*England*] [*A publication*] (DLA)
We............. West's English Chancery Reports [*A publication*] (DLA)
We............. West's Reports, English House of Lords [*A publication*] (DLA)
WE............ White Edges (ADA)
WE............ Whole Economy [*Department of Employment*] [*British*]
W/e........... Width-to-Length [*Ratio*] (MDG)
WE............ Winesburg Eagle [*A publication*]
WE............ Wing Elevon (MCD)
WE............ With Equipment (AABC)
WE............ Withholding Exemptions [*Army*] (AABC)
WE............ Women Educators (EA)
WE............ Women Employed [*Chicago, IL*] (EA)
WE............ Women and Employment [*An association*] (EA)
WE............ Women in Energy (EA)
WE............ Women Entrepreneurs [*San Francisco, CA*] (EA)
WE............ Women Exploited (EA)
WE............ Women's Reserve, Engineering Duties [*USNR officer
       designation*]
WE............ Work Experience
WE............ World Ecologists Foundation [*Philippines*] (EAIO)
WE............ World Education, Inc.
WE............ World Evangelism (EA)
WE............ Write Enable (IEEE)
W/E........... Writer/Editor (MCD)
WEa........... East Troy Public Library, East Troy, WI [*Library symbol*]
       [*Library of Congress*] (LCLS)
WEA......... Eastern Washington State College, Cheney, WA [*OCLC
       symbol*] (OCLC)
WEA......... Royal West of England Academy
WEA......... Wall Effect Amplifier
WEA......... Warner-Eddison Associates, Inc. [*Information service or
       system*] (IID)
WEA......... Weak Equity Axiom
WEA......... Weather (AABC)
WEA......... Weatherford, TX [*Location identifier*] [*FAA*] (FAAL)
WEA......... Western Economic Association International (EA)
WEA......... Wilderness Education Association (EA)
WEA......... Women Employed Advocates (EA)
WEA......... Workers' Educational Association
WEAA....... Baltimore, MD [*FM radio station call letters*]
WEAAC.... Western European Airport Authorities Conference (MCD)
WEAAP.... Western European Association for Aviation Psychology (EA)
WEAB....... Adamsville, TN [*AM radio station call letters*]
WEA Bul ... WEA [*Workers Educational Association*] Bulletin [*A
       publication*] (APTA)
WEAC....... Gaffney, SC [*AM radio station call letters*]
WEAC....... Winchester Engineering and Analytical Center [*Food and Drug
       Administration*] [*Winchester, MA*] (GRD)
WEACAP.. Weapon Capability (SAA)
WEADES.. Western Electric Air Defense Engineering Service (SAA)
WEADSC.. World Esperantist Association for Education, Science, and
       Culture [*Germany*] (EAIO)
WEAG...... Starke, FL [*AM radio station call letters*]
WEAG-FM ... Starke, FL [*FM radio station call letters*]
WEAI........ Lynnville, IL [*FM radio station call letters*]
WEAI........ Western Economic Association International [*Later,
       WEA*] (EA)
WEAL....... Women's Equity Action League (EA)
WEAM..... Columbus, GA [*AM radio station call letters*]
Wean........ Wean United, Inc. [*Associated Press abbreviation*] (APAG)
WEA-N...... Westinghouse Engineers Association National (EA)
WeanU....... Wean United, Inc. [*Associated Press abbreviation*] (APAG)
WEAO....... Akron, OH [*Television station call letters*]
WEAPD..... Western Air Procurement District
WEAQ...... Eau Claire, WI [*AM radio station call letters*]
WEAR ...... Pensacola, FL [*Television station call letters*]
WEARCON ... Weather Observation and Forecasting Control System
WEARECONRON ... Weather Reconnaissance Squadron [*Air
       Force*] (DNAB)
WEARESFAC ... Weather Research Facility [*Navy*] (GFGA)
WEARSCHFAC ... [*Naval*] Weather Research Facility
WEAS....... Savannah, GA [*AM radio station call letters*]
WEASEL... Weapon Selection (SAA)
WEASERVCOMM ... Weather Service Command [*Navy*]
WEAS-FM ... Savannah, GA [*FM radio station call letters*]
WEAT ...... Weathertight
WEAT ...... West Palm Beach, FL [*AM radio station call letters*]
WEAT-FM ... West Palm Beach, FL [*FM radio station call letters*]
Weather and Clim ... Weather and Climate [*A publication*]
Weather C & M ... Weather, Crops, and Markets [*A publication*]
Weather Dev Res Bull ... Weather Development and Research Bulletin
       [*Australia, Commonwealth Bureau of Meteorology*] [*A
       publication*] (APTA)
Weather Research Bull ... Weather Research Bulletin [*A publication*]
WEAU....... Eau Claire, WI [*Television station call letters*]

WEAV .... Plattsburgh, NY [*AM radio station call letters*]
WEAX .... Angola, IN [*FM radio station call letters*]
WEAX .... En Route Weather Forecast [*Navy*] (NVT)
WEAZ .... Philadelphia, PA [*AM radio station call letters*]
WEAZ-FM ... Philadelphia, PA [*FM radio station call letters*]
WEB .... National Westminster Bank. Quarterly Review [*A publication*]
WEB .... Wagner Earth Bridge
WEB .... War Engineering Board
WEB .... Wealthbuilding [*A publication*]
WEB .... Webbing (AAG)
WEBA ...... Allendale, SC [*Television station call letters*]
WEBA ...... Women Exploited by Abortion (EA)
WEBB...... Baltimore, MD [*AM radio station call letters*]
Webb........ Webb's Reports [*6-20 Kansas*] [*A publication*] (DLA)
Webb........ Webb's Reports [*11-20 Texas Civil Appeals*] [*A
       publication*] (DLA)
WEBB....... Writer's Electronic Bulletin Board [*Information service or
       system*] (IID)
Webb A'B & W ... Webb, A'Beckett, and Williams' Reports [*A
       publication*] (APTA)
Webb A'B & W Eq ... Webb, A'Beckett, and Williams' Equity Reports [*A
       publication*] (APTA)
Webb A'B & W IE & M ... Webb, A'Beckett, and Williams' Insolvency,
       Ecclesiastical, and Matrimonial Reports [*A
       publication*] (APTA)
Webb A'B & W IP & M ... Webb, A'Beckett, and Williams' Insolvency,
       Probate, and Matrimonial Reports [*A publication*] (APTA)
Webb A'B & W Min ... Webb, A'Beckett, and Williams' Mining Cases [*A
       publication*] (APTA)
Webb Cr Dig ... Webb's Digest of Texas Criminal Cases [*A
       publication*] (DLA)
WebbD...... Webb [*Del E.*] Corp. [*Associated Press abbreviation*] (APAG)
Webb & D .. Webb and Duval's Reports [*1-3 Texas*] [*A publication*] (DLA)
Webb & Duval ... Webb and Duval's Reports [*1-3 Texas*] [*A
       publication*] (DLA)
Webbia Racc Scr Bot ... Webbia; Raccolta di Scritti Botanici [*A publication*]
Webb Jud Act ... Webb on the Judicature Act [*A publication*] (DLA)
Webb Pl & Pr ... Webb's Kansas Pleading and Practice [*A publication*] (DLA)
Webb RR ... Webb's Railroad Laws of Maine [*A publication*] (DLA)
Webb Supr Ct Pr ... Webb's English Supreme Court Practice [*A
       publication*] (DLA)
WEBC....... Duluth, MN [*AM radio station call letters*]
WEBE....... Western European Basic Encyclopedia (MCD)
WEBE....... Westport, CT [*FM radio station call letters*]
WEBELOS ... We'll Be Loyal Scouts [*Boy Scout slogan*]
Weber........ Descriptive Catalogue of the Collection of Greek Coins Formed
       by Sir Hermann Weber [*A publication*]
WEBJ....... Brewton, AL [*AM radio station call letters*]
WEBN....... Cincinnati, OH [*FM radio station call letters*]
WEBO....... Owego, NY [*AM radio station call letters*]
Web Pat ..... Webster's New Patent Law [*4th ed.*] [*1854*] [*A
       publication*] (DLA)
Web Pat Cas ... Webster's Patent Cases [*1601-1855*] [*A publication*] (DLA)
Web PC...... Webster's Patent Cases [*1601-1855*] [*A publication*] (DLA)
WEBQ...... Eldorado, IL [*FM radio station call letters*]
WEBQ...... Harrisburg, IL [*AM radio station call letters*]
WEBR....... Buffalo, NY [*AM radio station call letters*]
Web R .... Webster Review [*A publication*]
WEBROCK ... Weather Buoy Rocket
WEBS....... Calhoun, GA [*AM radio station call letters*]
WEBS....... Weapons Effectiveness Buoy System
WEBS....... Webster Clothes, Inc. [*Baltimore, MD*] [*NASDAQ
       symbol*] (NQ)
Webs .... Webster's Patent Cases [*England*] [*A publication*] (DLA)
WEBSEC... Western Beaufort Sea Ecological Cruise [*Coast Guard*]
Webs Pat Cas ... Webster's Patent Cases [*England*] [*A publication*] (DLA)
Webst Dict ... Webster's Dictionary [*A publication*] (DLA)
Webst Dict Unab ... Webster's Unabridged Dictionary [*A publication*] (DLA)
Webster Pat Cas ... Webster's Patent Cases [*1601-1855*] [*A
       publication*] (DLA)
Webster Pat Cas (Eng) ... Webster's Patent Cases [*England*] [*A
       publication*] (DLA)
Webster in Sen Doc ... Webster in Senate Documents [*A publication*] (DLA)
Webst Int Dict ... Webster's International Dictionary [*A publication*] (DLA)
Webst New Int D ... Webster's New International Dictionary [*A
       publication*] (DLA)
WEBT....... Langdale, AL [*FM radio station call letters*]
Web Tr....... Trial of Professor Webster for Murder [*A publication*] (DLA)
WEBY....... Milton, FL [*AM radio station call letters*]
WEBZ....... Mexico Beach, FL [*FM radio station call letters*]
WEC .... District One Technical Institute, Eau Claire, Eau Claire, WI
       [*OCLC symbol*] (OCLC)
WEC .... Eau Claire County Hospital, Eau Claire, WI [*Library symbol*]
       [*Library of Congress*] (LCLS)
WEC .... Walking with Eyes Closed [*Equilibrium test*]
WEC .... Warhead Electrical Connector
WEC .... Water Export Control
WEC .... Weapon Engagement Console [*Military*] (CAAL)
WEC .... Weapon Engagement Controller [*Military*] (CAAL)
WEC .... Wescal Resources, Inc. [*Vancouver Stock Exchange symbol*]
WEC .... West European Container Liners [*Shipping*]

WEC .... Westinghouse Electric Corp.
WEC .... Whole Earth Catalog [*A publication*]
WEC .... Wind Energy Conversion
WEC .... Wisconsin Energy Corp. [*NYSE symbol*]　(SPSG)
WEC .... Women's Emergency Corps [*British*] [*World War I*]
WEC .... World Endurance Championship [*Auto racing*]
WEC .... World Energy Conference [*See also CME*] [*London, England*]　(EAIO)
WEC .... World Environment Center　(EA)
WEC .... Worldwide Evangelization Crusade　(EA)
WECA .... Western Capital Investment Corp. [*Denver, CO*] [*NASDAQ symbol*]　(NQ)
WECAF ..... Western Central Atlantic Fisheries Commission [*Food and Agriculture Organization of the UN*]
WECAFC .. Western Central Atlantic Fisheries Commission [*Food and Agriculture Organization of the UN*]　(EAIO)
WECAF (West Cent Atl Fish Comm) Stud ... WECAF (Western Central Atlantic Fishery Commission) Studies [*A publication*]
WECB .... Weapons Evaluation and Control Bureau [*USACDA*]
WECB .... St. Mary's, GA [*AM radio station call letters*]
WECC .... White English Celtic Catholic
WECE .... Due West, SC [*FM radio station call letters*]
WECEN .... Weather Center [*Air Force*]
WECI .... Richmond, IN [*FM radio station call letters*]
WECI .... WEC International　(EA)
WECK .... Cheektowaga, NY [*AM radio station call letters*]
WECL .... Elk Mound, WI [*FM radio station call letters*]
WECM ...... Milton, FL [*AM radio station call letters*]
WECM ...... Warranted Existing Class Maintained　(DS)
WECN .... Naranjito, PR [*Television station call letters*]
WECO .... Wartburg, TN [*AM radio station call letters*]
WECO .... Western Electric Co.　(MCD)
WECO .... Westinghouse Electric Corp.
WECO-FM ... Wartburg, TN [*FM radio station call letters*]
WECOM .. Weapons Command [*Later, Armaments Command*] [*Army*]
WECON .... Weather Controlled Messages　(NVT)
W Econ J ... Western Economic Journal [*A publication*]
WECPNL .. Weighted Equivalent Continuous Perceived Noise Level
WECQ .... Geneva, NY [*FM radio station call letters*]
WECS .... Water-Glycol Evaporator Control System　(SAA)
WECS .... Willimantic, CT [*FM radio station call letters*]
WECS .... Wind Energy Conversion System
WECST ..... Waste Evaporator Condensate Storage Tank [*Nuclear energy*]　(NRCH)
WECT .... Wilmington, NC [*Television station call letters*]
WECU .... Peoria, IL [*FM radio station call letters*]
WECV .... Chippewa Valley Museum, Eau Claire, WI [*Library symbol*] [*Library of Congress*]　(LCLS)
WECW ...... Elmira, NY [*FM radio station call letters*]
WECY .... Seaford, DE [*AM radio station call letters*]
WECY-FM ... Seaford, DE [*FM radio station call letters*]
WECZ .... Punxsutawney, PA [*AM radio station call letters*]
WED .... Walter Elias Disney [*These initials also identify the theme park division of Walt Disney Enterprises*]
WED .... War Emergency Dose　(DEN)
WED .... Water Enforcement Division [*Environmental Protection Agency*]　(EPA)
WED .... Weak Exchange Degeneracy [*Particle physics*]　(OA)
WED .... Weapons Engineering Duty [*Navy*]　(NG)
WED .... Wedau [*Papua New Guinea*] [*Airport symbol*]　(OAG)
WED .... Wedco Technology, Inc. [*AMEX symbol*]　(SPSG)
WED .... Wednesday　(EY)
WED .... West Delta Resources Ltd. [*Vancouver Stock Exchange symbol*]
WED .... Work Force Effectiveness and Development Group [*Office of Personnel Management*]　(GRD)
WEDA .... Western Dredging Association　(EA)
WEDA .... Women's Enterprise Development Agency [*Established in 1987*] [*British*]
WEDAC .... Westinghouse Digital Airborne Computer
WEDC .... Chicago, IL [*AM radio station call letters*]
WEDCOM ... Weapon Effects on D-Region Communications [*Computer code*]
WEDE .... Eden, NC [*AM radio station call letters*]
WEDE .... Western Development Corp. [*NASDAQ symbol*]　(NQ)
WEDG .... Edgewater, FL [*FM radio station call letters*]
WEDGE .... Waterless Electrical Data Generating Effortless
WEDGE .... Weapon Development Glide Entry
WEDGE .... Western Education Development Group [*University of British Columbia*] [*Canada*] [*Research center*]
Wedg Gov & Laws ... Wedgwood on American Government and Laws [*A publication*]　(DLA)
Wedg & Hom ... Wedgwood and Homan's Manual for Notaries and Bankers [*A publication*]　(DLA)
Wedgw Dict Eng Etymology ... Wedgwood's Dictionary of English Etymology [*A publication*]　(DLA)
WEDH .... Hartford, CT [*Television station call letters*]
WEDM ...... Indianapolis, IN [*FM radio station call letters*]
WEDN .... Norwich, CT [*Television station call letters*]
WEDO .... McKeesport, PA [*AM radio station call letters*]
WEDO .... Womens' Environment and Development Organization
WEDR .... Miami, FL [*FM radio station call letters*]

WEDS .... Weapons Effect Display System [*AEC*]
WEDU ...... Tampa, FL [*Television station call letters*]
WEDW ...... Bridgeport, CT [*Television station call letters*]
WEDW ...... Stamford, CT [*FM radio station call letters*]
WEDY ...... New Haven, CT [*Television station call letters*]
WEE .... Weerberichten. Informatiebulletin over Windenergie en Zonne-Energie [*A publication*]
WEE .... Western Equine Encephalomyelitis [*Virus*]
WEE .... Work Experience Education　(DNAB)
WEEA .... Women's Educational Equity Act [*1974*]
WEEB .... Southern Pines, NC [*AM radio station call letters*]
WEEC .... Springfield, OH [*FM radio station call letters*]
WEECN .... Women's Educational Equity Communications Network [*Defunct*]
WEED .... Rocky Mount, NC [*AM radio station call letters*]
Weed Abstr ... Weed Abstracts [*A publication*]
Weed Res ... Weed Research [*A publication*]
Weed Sci .... Weed Science [*A publication*]
Weeds Weed Cont ... Weeds and Weed Control [*A publication*]
WEEE .... Cherry Hill, NJ [*FM radio station call letters*]
WEEF .... Highland Park, IL [*AM radio station call letters*]
WEEF .... Western Electric Educational Fund
WEEGA .... Welding Engineer [*A publication*]
WEEI .... Boston, MA [*AM radio station call letters*]
WEEJ .... Port Charlotte, FL [*FM radio station call letters*]
WEEK .... Peoria, IL [*Television station call letters*]
Week Cin LB ... Weekly Cincinnati Law Bulletin [*A publication*]　(DLA)
Week Dig ... New York Weekly Digest [*A publication*]　(DLA)
Week Dig (NY) ... New York Weekly Digest [*A publication*]　(DLA)
Week-End R ... Australian Week-End Review of Current Books, the Arts, and Entertainments [*A publication*]　(APTA)
Week Jur ... Weekly Jurist [*Bloomington, IL*] [*A publication*]　(DLA)
Week Law & Bk Bull ... Weekly Law and Bank Bulletin [*A publication*]　(DLA)
Week Law Bull ... Weekly Law Bulletin and Ohio Law Journal [*A publication*]　(DLA)
Week Law Gaz ... Weekly Law Gazette [*Ohio*] [*A publication*]　(DLA)
Week L Gaz ... Weekly Law Gazette [*Ohio*] [*A publication*]　(DLA)
Week L Mag ... Weekly Law Magazine [*1842-43*] [*A publication*]　(DLA)
Week LR .... Weekly Law Reports [*A publication*]　(DLA)
Week L Rec ... Weekly Law Record [*A publication*]　(DLA)
Week L Record ... Weekly Law Record [*A publication*]　(DLA)
Week LR (Eng) ... Weekly Law Reports (England) [*A publication*]　(DLA)
Week L Rev ... Weekly Law Review [*San Francisco*] [*A publication*]　(DLA)
Weekly Cin Law Bull ... Cincinnati Weekly Law Bulletin [*A publication*]　(DLA)
Weekly Compilation Presidential Docum ... Weekly Compilation of Presidential Documents [*A publication*]
Weekly Comp of Pres Doc ... Weekly Compilation of Presidential Documents [*A publication*]
Weekly Law B ... Weekly Law Bulletin [*Ohio*] [*A publication*]　(DLA)
Weekly L Bull ... Weekly Law Bulletin [*England*] [*A publication*]　(DLA)
Weekly LR ... Weekly Law Reports [*England*] [*A publication*]　(DLA)
Weekly NC ... Weekly Notes of Cases [*Pennsylvania*] [*A publication*]　(DLA)
Weekly N L ... Weekly News Letter. United States Department of Agriculture [*A publication*]
Weekly Underw ... Weekly Underwriter [*A publication*]
Week No .... New South Wales Weekly Notes [*A publication*]
Week No .... Weekly Notes of Cases [*Pennsylvania*] [*A publication*]　(DLA)
Week No .... Weekly Notes of Cases (Law Reports) [*England*] [*A publication*]　(DLA)
Week No Cas ... Weekly Notes of Cases [*Pennsylvania*] [*A publication*]　(DLA)
Week No Cas ... Weekly Notes of Cases (Law Reports) [*England*] [*A publication*]　(DLA)
Week Notes Cas ... Weekly Notes of Cases (Law Reports) [*England*] [*A publication*]　(DLA)
Week R ...... Weekly Reporter [*1853-1906*] [*A publication*]　(DLA)
Week R (Eng) ... Weekly Reporter (England) [*A publication*]　(DLA)
Week Rep ... Weekly Reporter [*England*] [*A publication*]　(DLA)
Week Reptr ... Weekly Reporter [*Bengal*] [*A publication*]　(DLA)
Week Reptr ... Weekly Reporter [*London*] [*A publication*]　(DLA)
Weeks Att at Law ... Weeks on Attorneys at Law [*A publication*]　(DLA)
Weeks DA Inj ... Weeks' Damnum Absque Injuria [*A publication*]　(DLA)
Weeks Dep ... Weeks on Depositions [*A publication*]　(DLA)
Weeks Min ... Weeks on Mines and Mineral Law [*A publication*]　(DLA)
Weeks Min Leg ... Weeks' Mining Legislation of Congress [*A publication*]　(DLA)
Week Trans Rep ... Weekly Transcript Reports [*New York*] [*A publication*]　(DLA)
Week Trans Repts ... Weekly Transcript Reports [*New York*] [*A publication*]　(DLA)
WEEL .... Shadyside, OH [*FM radio station call letters*]
WEEM ...... Pendleton, IN [*FM radio station call letters*]
WEEN ...... Lafayette, TN [*AM radio station call letters*]
WEEO .... Waynesboro, PA [*AM radio station call letters*]
WEEP .... Pittsburgh, PA [*AM radio station call letters*]
WEEP .... Women's Educational Equity Program　(EA)
WEEP .... Work Experience on Employer's Premises [*Manpower Services Commission*] [*British*]　(DI)

Weer........... Weerakoon's Appeal Court Reports [*Ceylon*] [*A publication*] (DLA)
WEER........ Welfare Entered Employment Rate [*Job Training and Partnership Act*] (OICC)
WEESA ..... Weed Science [*A publication*]
WEEU ...... Reading, PA [*AM radio station call letters*]
WEEX....... Easton, PA [*AM radio station call letters*]
WEEZ........ Heidelberg, MS [*FM radio station call letters*]
WEF........... Economic Inquiry [*A publication*]
WEF........... WAND [*Women's Action for Nuclear Disarmament*] Education Fund (EA)
WEF........... War Emergency Formula
WEF........... Water Emersion Facility
WEF........... With Effect From
WEF........... World Economic Forum (EAIO)
WEF........... World Education Fellowship (EA)
WEF........... World Evangelical Fellowship (EA)
WEF........... Write End of File (SAA)
WEFAX..... Weather Facsimile Experiment [*Environmental Science Services Administration*]
WEFC....... Roanoke, VA [*Television station call letters*]
WEFM...... Michigan City, IN [*FM radio station call letters*]
WEFR....... Erie, PA [*FM radio station call letters*]
WEFT........ Champaign, IL [*FM radio station call letters*]
WEFT........ Wings, Engines, Fuselage, Tail [*System for identifying aircraft*]
WEFX....... Norwalk, CT [*FM radio station call letters*]
WEG......... Washington Energy Co. [*NYSE symbol*] (SPSG)
WEG......... Weapons Evaluation Group [*Military*]
WEG......... Wegen [*A publication*]
WEG......... Wind Energy Generator
WEGA...... Vega Baja, PR [*AM radio station call letters*]
WEGC...... Leesburg, GA [*FM radio station call letters*]
WEGE....... Crossville, TN [*FM radio station call letters*]
Wege Soz Versicherung ... Wege zur Sozialversicherung [*A publication*]
WEGG...... Rose Hill, NC [*AM radio station call letters*]
WEGL...... Auburn, AL [*FM radio station call letters*]
WEGM...... Hormigueros, PR [*FM radio station call letters*]
WEGO...... Concord, NC [*AM radio station call letters*]
WEGR ...... Memphis, TN [*FM radio station call letters*]
WEGS....... Milton, FL [*FM radio station call letters*]
WEGW...... Wheeling, WV [*FM radio station call letters*]
WEGX...... Philadelphia, PA [*FM radio station call letters*]
WEGZ...... Washburn, WI [*FM radio station call letters*]
WEH......... Hungarian News Agency. Weekly Bulletin [*A publication*]
WE-H .... Weapons Employment Handbook [*DASA*] (MCD)
WEHH ...... Elmira Heights-Horseheads, NY [*AM radio station call letters*]
WEHN...... North East, PA [*AM radio station call letters*]
Wehrmed Monatsschr ... Wehrmedizinische Monatsschrift [*A publication*]
Wehrtech ... Wehrtechnik [*A publication*]
Wehr und Wirt ... Wehr und Wirtschaft [*A publication*]
WEHS ...... Aurora, IL [*Television station call letters*]
WEHSA .... Work-Environment-Health [*A publication*]
WEHT...... Evansville, IN [*Television station call letters*]
WEI .... Immanuel Lutheran College, Eau Claire, WI [*Library symbol*] [*Library of Congress*] (LCLS)
WEI .... Weapon Effectiveness Index (MCD)
WEI .... Weipa [*Australia*] [*Airport symbol*] (OAG)
WEI .... Western European Institute for Wood Preservation (EAIO)
WEI .... Wherehouse Entertainment, Inc. [*AMEX symbol*] (SPSG)
WEI .... Women Employed Institute (EA)
WEI .... Wood Energy Institute [*Later, WHA*] (EA)
WEI .... Work Experience Instructor (OICC)
WEI .... World Education (EA)
WEI .... World Energy Industry [*A publication*]
WEI .... World Environment Institute
WEI .... Wound Elastomeric Insulation (MCD)
WEIB........ Northampton, MA [*FM radio station call letters*]
Weibulls Arsb ... Weibulls Arsbok [*A publication*]
WEIC........ Charleston, IL [*AM radio station call letters*]
WEIC-FM .. Charleston, IL [*FM radio station call letters*]
WEIF........ Utica, NY [*FM radio station call letters*]
Weight Med Leg Gaz ... Weightman's Medico-Legal Gazette [*A publication*] (DLA)
Weight M & L ... Weightman's Marriage and Legitimacy [*1871*] [*A publication*] (DLA)
WEI/IEO .. Western European Institute for Wood Preservation/Institut de l'Europe Occidentale pour l'Impregnation du Bois (EAIO)
WEIM .... Fitchburg, MA [*AM radio station call letters*]
Weinbau Kellerwirtsch (Budapest) ... Weinbau und Kellerwirtschaft (Budapest) [*A publication*]
WeinRl....... Weingarten Realty, Inc. [*Associated Press abbreviation*] (APAG)
Wein-Wiss ... Wein-Wissenschaft [*A publication*]
WEIQ .... Mobile, AL [*Television station call letters*]
Weir .... Weir's Criminal Rulings [*India*] [*A publication*] (DLA)
WEIR........ Weirton, WV [*AM radio station call letters*]
Weirt........ Weirton Steel Corp. [*Associated Press abbreviation*] (APAG)
WEIS........ Centre, AL [*AM radio station call letters*]
WEIS........ Weisfields, Inc. [*NASDAQ symbol*] (NQ)
WEIS......... World Event/Interaction Survey (DNAB)
WeisMk..... Weis Markets, Inc. [*Associated Press abbreviation*] (APAG)

Weiterbildungszentrum Math Kybernet Rechentech ... Weiterbildungszentrum fuer Mathematische Kybernetik und Rechentechnik [*A publication*]
WEIU .... Charleston, IL [*FM radio station call letters*]
WEIU .... Women's Educational and Industrial Union (EA)
WEIU-TV ... Charleston, IL [*Television station call letters*]
WEI/WUV ... Weapons Effectiveness Indices/Weighted Unit Values [*Military*]
WEIZ......... Hogansville, GA [*FM radio station call letters*]
Weizmann Mem Lect ... Weizmann Memorial Lectures [*A publication*]
WEJ........... Western Economic Journal [*A publication*]
WEJC....... Lexington, NC [*Television station call letters*]
WEJL....... Scranton, PA [*AM radio station call letters*]
WEJT....... Shelbyville, IL [*FM radio station call letters*]
WEJUA..... Welding Journal [*Miami*] [*A publication*]
WEJY....... Monroe, MI [*FM radio station call letters*]
WEJZ....... Jacksonville, FL [*FM radio station call letters*]
WEK .... Werkgever [*A publication*]
WEK .... Wewak [*Papua New Guinea*] [*Seismograph station code, US Geological Survey*] (SEIS)
WEKC....... Williamsburg, KY [*AM radio station call letters*]
WEKG .... Jackson, KY [*AM radio station call letters*]
WEKH...... Hazard, KY [*FM radio station call letters*]
WEKLA..... Wiadomosci Ekologiczne [*A publication*]
WEKO ...... Cabo Rojo, PR [*AM radio station call letters*]
WEKR ...... Fayetteville, TN [*AM radio station call letters*]
WEKT....... Elkton, KY [*AM radio station call letters*]
WEKU ...... Richmond, KY [*FM radio station call letters*]
WEKW ...... Keene, NH [*Television station call letters*]
WEKY ...... Richmond, KY [*AM radio station call letters*]
WEKZ ...... Monroe, WI [*AM radio station call letters*]
WEKZ-FM ... Monroe, WI [*FM radio station call letters*]
WEL .... Luther Hospital, Eau Claire, WI [*Library symbol*] [*Library of Congress*] (LCLS)
WEl........... Matheson Memorial Library, Elkhorn, WI [*Library symbol*] [*Library of Congress*] (LCLS)
WEL .... Warren Explorations Ltd. [*Toronto Stock Exchange symbol*]
WEL .... Weapons Effects Laboratory [*Army*] (RDA)
WEL .... Weapons/Equipment List
WEL .... Welfare
WEL .... Welkom [*South Africa*] [*Airport symbol*] (OAG)
WEL .... Wellcome Plc [*NYSE symbol*] (SPSG)
WEL .... Wellesley College, Wellesley, MA [*OCLC symbol*] (OCLC)
WEL .... Wellesley Hospital, Toronto [*UTLAS symbol*]
WEL .... Wellington [*New Zealand*] [*Seismograph station code, US Geological Survey*] (SEIS)
wel .... Welsh [*MARC language code*] [*Library of Congress*] (LCCP)
Wel............ Welsh's Irish Registry Cases [*A publication*] (DLA)
WEL .... Welt-Eis-Lehre [*Cosmic Ice Theory*] [*German*]
WEL .... Weltwirtschaftliches Archiv [*A publication*]
WELA....... East Liverpool, OH [*FM radio station call letters*]
WELB....... Elba, AL [*AM radio station call letters*]
WELB....... Welbilt Corp. [*NASDAQ symbol*] (NQ)
WELC....... Welch, WV [*AM radio station call letters*]
WELC....... World Electrotechnical Congress (PDAA)
WELC-FM ... Welch, WV [*FM radio station call letters*]
WElCL....... Walworth County Law Library, Elkhorn, WI [*Library symbol*] [*Library of Congress*] (LCLS)
Welcom...... Wellcome Plc [*Associated Press abbreviation*] (APAG)
WELD .... Fisher, WV [*AM radio station call letters*]
WELD .... Petersburg, WV [*FM radio station call letters*]
Weld Des Fabr ... Welding Design and Fabrication [*A publication*]
Weld Dsgn ... Welding Design and Fabrication [*A publication*]
Weld Eng ... Welding Engineer [*A publication*]
Weld Fabr Des ... Welding Fabrication and Design [*A publication*]
Weld Fabrication Design ... Welding Fabrication and Design [*A publication*] (APTA)
Weld Fabric Design ... Welding Fabrication and Design [*A publication*] (APTA)
Weld Ind .... Welding Industry [*A publication*]
Welding J .. Welding Journal [*A publication*]
Welding Rev ... Welding Review [*A publication*]
Weld Int .... Welding International [*United Kingdom*] [*A publication*]
Weld J....... Welding Journal [*A publication*]
Weld J (London) ... Welding Journal (London) [*A publication*]
Weld J (Miami) ... Welding Journal (Miami) [*A publication*]
Weld J (NY) ... Welding Journal (New York) [*A publication*]
Weld J Res Suppl ... Welding Journal Research. Supplement [*A publication*]
Weld Jrl..... Welding Journal [*A publication*]
Weld Metal Fab ... Welding and Metal Fabrication [*A publication*]
Weld Metal Fabr ... Welding and Metal Fabrication [*A publication*]
Weld Met Fabr ... Welding and Metal Fabrication [*A publication*]
Weld News ... Welding News [*A publication*]
Weld Prod ... Welding Production [*A publication*]
Weld Prod (USSR) ... Welding Production (USSR) [*A publication*]
Weld Res Abroad ... Welding Research Abroad [*A publication*]
Weld Res C ... Welding Research Council. Bulletin [*A publication*]
Weld Res Counc Bull ... Welding Research Council. Bulletin [*A publication*]
Weld Res Counc Prog Rep ... Welding Research Council. Progress Reports [*A publication*]
Weld Res Int ... Welding Research International [*A publication*]

Weld Res (London) ... Welding Research (London) [*A publication*]
Weld Res (Miami) ... Welding Research (Miami) [*A publication*]
Weld Res (Miami Fla) ... Welding Research (Miami, Florida) [*A publication*]
Weld Res News ... Welding Research News [*A publication*]
Weld Rev.... Welding Review [*A publication*]
Weld Tech ... Welding Technique [*Japan*] [*A publication*]
WELDTRN ... Weldotron Corp. [*Associated Press abbreviation*] (APAG)
Weld Wld... Welding in the World/Le Soudage dans le Monde [*A publication*]
Weld World ... Welding in the World [*A publication*]
Weld World Soudage Monde ... Welding in the World/Le Soudage dans le Monde [*A publication*]
WELE........ Ormond Beach, FL [*AM radio station call letters*]
Weleda Korrespondenzbl Aerzte ... Weleda Korrespondenzblaetter fuer Aerzte [*A publication*]
WELF........ Dalton, GA [*Television station call letters*]
WelF .... Wells Fargo & Co. [*Associated Press abbreviation*] (APAG)
WELF .... Woman's Education and Leadership Forum (EA)
Welfare L Bull ... Welfare Law Bulletin [*A publication*] (DLA)
Welfare L News ... Welfare Law News [*A publication*] (DLA)
Welf Eq ..... Welford's Equity Pleadings [*1842*] [*A publication*] (DLA)
Welf Focus ... Welfare Focus [*A publication*]
Welf News ... Welfare News [*A publication*]
WELGRD ... Wells-Gardner Electronics Corp. [*Associated Press abbreviation*] (APAG)
WELI........ New Haven, CT [*AM radio station call letters*]
WELK....... Elkins, WV [*FM radio station call letters*]
WELL....... Battle Creek, MI [*AM radio station call letters*]
WElL .... Lakeland Hospital, Elkhorn, WI [*Library symbol*] [*Library of Congress*] (LCLS)
WELL....... LivingWell, Inc. [*Houston, TX*] [*NASDAQ symbol*] (NQ)
WELL....... Marshall, MI [*FM radio station call letters*]
WElLC....... Lakeland Counseling Center, Elkhorn, WI [*Library symbol*] [*Library of Congress*] (LCLS)
WELLCO.. Wellco Enterprises, Inc. [*Associated Press abbreviation*] (APAG)
Well High .. Wellbeloved on Highways [*1829*] [*A publication*] (DLA)
Well Inventory Ser (Metric Units) Inst Geol Sci ... Well Inventory Series (Metric Units). Institute of Geological Sciences [*A publication*]
Wellmn ...... Wellman, Inc. [*Associated Press abbreviation*] (APAG)
Well Serv ... Well Servicing [*A publication*]
WellsF .... Wells Fargo & Co. [*Associated Press abbreviation*] (APAG)
Wells Frgo ... Wells Fargo Bank. Business Review [*A publication*]
Wells Inst Juries ... Wells on Instruction to Juries and Bills of Exception [*A publication*] (DLA)
Wells Jur ... Wells on the Jurisdiction of Courts [*A publication*] (DLA)
Wells L & F ... Well's Questions of Law and Facts [*A publication*] (DLA)
Wells Mar Wom ... Wells on the Separate Property of Married Women [*A publication*] (DLA)
Wells Rep .. Wells on Replevin [*A publication*] (DLA)
Wells Repl ... Wells on Replevin [*A publication*] (DLA)
Wells' Res Ad ... Wells' Res Adjudicata and Stare Decisis [*A publication*] (DLA)
Wellw Abr ... Wellwood's Abridgment of Sea Laws [*A publication*] (DLA)
Wellworthy Top ... Wellworthy Topics [*A publication*]
WELM ...... Elmira, NY [*AM radio station call letters*]
WELO .... Tupelo, MS [*AM radio station call letters*]
WELP....... Easley, SC [*AM radio station call letters*]
WELP........ Wisconsin Electric Power Co. [*NASDAQ symbol*] (NQ)
WelptH ...... Wellpoint Health Networks [*Associated Press abbreviation*] (APAG)
WELR........ Roanoke, AL [*AM radio station call letters*]
WELR-FM ... Roanoke, AL [*FM radio station call letters*]
WELS .... Kinston, NC [*AM radio station call letters*]
WELS .... Wisconsin Evangelical Lutheran Synod
WELS .... World-Wide Engineering Logistics Support [*Military*]
Welsb H & G ... Welsby, Hurlstone, and Gordon's English Exchequer Reports [*1848-56*] [*A publication*]
Welsb Hurl & G ... Welsby, Hurlstone, and Gordon's English Exchequer Reports [*1848-56*] [*A publication*] (DLA)
Welsby H & G ... Welsby, Hurlstone, and Gordon's English Exchequer Reports [*1848-56*] [*A publication*] (DLA)
Welsby H & G (Eng) ... Welsby, Hurlstone, and Gordon's English Exchequer Reports [*1848-56*] [*A publication*] (DLA)
Welsfd........ Wellsford Residential Property [*Associated Press abbreviation*] (APAG)
Welsh........ Welsh's Irish Case of James Feighny [*1838*] [*A publication*] (DLA)
Welsh........ Welsh's Irish Case at Siligo [*1838*] [*A publication*] (DLA)
Welsh........ Welsh's Irish Registry Cases [*A publication*] (DLA)
Welsh Bee J ... Welsh Bee Journal [*A publication*]
Welsh Beekprs' Ass Q Bull ... Welsh Beekeepers' Association. Quarterly Bulletin [*A publication*]
Welsh Hist ... Welsh History Review [*A publication*]
Welsh Hist Rev ... Welsh History Review [*A publication*]
Welsh H R ... Welsh History Review [*A publication*]
Welsh J Agric ... Welsh Journal of Agriculture [*A publication*]
Welsh M.... Welsh Music [*A publication*]
Welsh Plant Breed Stn (Aberystwyth) Annu Rep ... Welsh Plant Breeding Station (Aberystwyth) Annual Report [*A publication*]

Welsh Plant Breed Stn (Aberystwyth) Rep ... Welsh Plant Breeding Station (Aberystwyth). Report [*A publication*]
Welsh Plant Breed Stn (Aberystwyth) Tech Bull ... Welsh Plant Breeding Station (Aberystwyth). Technical Bulletin [*A publication*]
Welsh Plant Breed Stn Bull Ser ... Welsh Plant Breeding Station. Bulletin Series [*A publication*]
Welsh Reg Cas ... Welsh's Irish Registry Cases [*A publication*] (DLA)
Welt Isl ...... Die Welt des Islam [*A publication*]
Weltlit Farbenchem ... Weltliteratur der Farbenchemie [*A publication*]
Weltraumfahrt Raketentech ... Weltraumfahrt und Raketentechnik [*A publication*]
Weltwir Arc ... Weltwirtschaftliches Archiv [*A publication*]
Weltwirt ..... Weltwirtschaft [*A publication*]
Weltwirtschaft Archiv ... Weltwirtschaftliches Archiv [*Kiel*] [*A publication*]
Weltwirtsch Archiv ... Weltwirtschaftliches Archiv [*A publication*]
WELU .... Aguadilla, PR [*Television station call letters*]
WELV........ Ellenville, NY [*AM radio station call letters*]
WELW ...... Willoughby-Eastlake, OH [*AM radio station call letters*]
WELX........ Callahan, FL [*AM radio station call letters*]
WELY........ Ely, MN [*AM radio station call letters*]
WELZ........ Belzoni, MS [*AM radio station call letters*]
WEM .... War Eagle Mining Co. [*Vancouver Stock Exchange symbol*]
WEM .... Welfare of Enlisted Men [*Air Force*]
WEM .... West Essex Militia [*British*]
WEM .... Western Energy Management [*AMEX symbol*] (SPSG)
WEM .... Western European Metal Trades Employers Organization [*Cologne, Federal Republic of Germany*] (EA)
WeM .... Western Microfilm Ltd., Edmonton, AB, Canada [*Library symbol*] [*Library of Congress*] (LCLS)
WEM .... Western Miner [*A publication*]
WEM .... Wireless and Electrical Mechanic [*British*] (DSUE)
WEM .... World's Epoch Makers [*A publication*]
WEM .... Woven Elastic Manufacturers Association [*Later, EFMCNTA*] (MSA)
WEMA ..... Western Electronic Manufacturers Association [*Later, AEA*] (EA)
WEMA ..... Woven Elastic Manufacturers Association [*Later, EFMCNTA*] (EA)
WEMB ..... Erwin, TN [*AM radio station call letters*]
WEMC...... Harrisonburg, VA [*FM radio station call letters*]
WEMD...... Western Electronics Maintenance Depot
WEMG ..... Knoxville, TN [*AM radio station call letters*]
WEMI ...... Neenah-Menasha, WI [*FM radio station call letters*]
WEMJ ...... Laconia, NH [*AM radio station call letters*]
WEMM ..... Huntington, WV [*FM radio station call letters*]
WEMOB ... Wehrmedizinische Monatsschrift [*A publication*]
WEMOS ... International Women's Network on Pharmaceuticals [*Amsterdam, Netherlands*] (EAIO)
WEMP ...... Milwaukee, WI [*AM radio station call letters*]
WEMQ ...... Knoxville, TN [*FM radio station call letters*]
WEMR ...... Tunkhannock, PA [*AM radio station call letters*]
WEMR ...... Welding Equipment Maintenance and Repair [*UAW job classification*]
WEMSB.... Western European Military Supply Board [*NATO*] (NATG)
WEMT ...... Greeneville, TN [*Television station call letters*]
WEMU...... Ypsilanti, MI [*FM radio station call letters*]
WEMX ...... McConnellsburg, PA [*FM radio station call letters*]
WEN .... Waive Exchange If Necessary
Wen.......... Wendell's Reports [*New York*] [*A publication*] (DLA)
wen .... Wendic [*MARC language code*] [*Library of Congress*] (LCCP)
WEN .... Wendy's International, Inc. [*NYSE symbol*] (SPSG)
WEN .... Wenkite [*A zeolite*]
WEN .... Wentworth Institute of Technology, Boston, MA [*OCLC symbol*] (OCLC)
WEN .... Wentworth Public Library [*UTLAS symbol*]
WENA ...... Penuelas, PR [*AM radio station call letters*]
WenBR ...... Wendt Bristol Health Service [*Associated Press abbreviation*] (APAG)
WENC...... Whiteville, NC [*AM radio station call letters*]
W/ENCL... With Enclosure (DNAB)
WEND....... Brandon, FL [*AM radio station call letters*]
Wend.......... Wendell's Reports [*1826-41*] [*New York*] [*A publication*] (DLA)
Wend Bl .... Wendell's Blackstone [*A publication*] (DLA)
Wendel...... Wendell's Reports [*New York*] [*A publication*] (DLA)
Wendell...... Wendell's Reports [*1826-41*] [*New York*] [*A publication*] (DLA)
Wendell Rep ... Wendell's Reports [*New York*] [*A publication*] (DLA)
Wendell's Rep ... Wendell's Reports [*New York*] [*A publication*] (DLA)
Wend (NY) ... Wendell's Reports [*1826-41*] [*New York*] [*A publication*] (DLA)
Wend R ...... Wendell's Reports [*New York*] [*A publication*] (DLA)
Wend Rep .. Wendell's Reports [*New York*] [*A publication*] (DLA)
WENDS .... World Energy Data System [*Department of Energy*] [*Information service or system*] (IID)
Wendt .... Wendt's Reports of Cases [*Ceylon*] [*A publication*] (DLA)
WendtBr .... Wendt Bristol Health Service [*Associated Press abbreviation*] (APAG)
Wendt Mar Leg ... Wendt's Maritime Legislation [*3rd ed.*] [*1888*] [*A publication*] (DLA)

Wendys	Wendys International, Inc. [*Associated Press abbreviation*] (APAG)
WENELA	Witwatersrand Native Labour Association [*Nyasaland*]
WENG	Englewood, FL [*AM radio station call letters*]
WENH	Durham, NH [*Television station call letters*]
WENK	Union City, TN [*AM radio station call letters*]
WENL	Gladstone, MI [*FM radio station call letters*]
WENMD	Water Engineering and Management [*A publication*]
WENN	Birmingham, AL [*FM radio station call letters*]
Wenner-Gren Cent Int Symp Ser	Wenner-Gren Center. International Symposium Series [*A publication*]
WENO	Nashville, TN [*AM radio station call letters*]
WENOA	Weekly Notice to Airmen [*FAA*]
WENR	Englewood, TN [*AM radio station call letters*]
WENS	Shelbyville, IN [*FM radio station call letters*]
WENS	World Electroless Nickel Society [*Defunct*] (EA)
WENT	Gloversville, NY [*AM radio station call letters*]
W Ent	Winch's Book of Entries [*A publication*] (DLA)
Wentworth Mag	Wentworth Magazine [*A publication*] (APTA)
WENU	Hudson Falls, NY [*FM radio station call letters*]
WENY	Elmira, NY [*AM radio station call letters*]
WENY-FM	Elmira, NY [*FM radio station call letters*]
WENY-TV	Elmira, NY [*Television station call letters*]
Wenz	Wenzell's Reports [*60 Minnesota*] [*A publication*] (DLA)
WEO	War Economic Operation [*World War II*]
WEO	Warehouse Economy Outlet [*A & P Co.*]
WEO	Weaco Resources Ltd. [*Vancouver Stock Exchange symbol*]
WEO	Weapons Engineer Officer [*British military*] (DMA)
WEO	West-Ost-Journal [*A publication*]
WEO	Western Europe and Others [*United Nations*]
WEO	Where Economy Originates [*A & P Co. marketing slogan, now obsolete*]
WEO	World Economic Outlook [*A publication*]
WEO	World Energy Outlook [*International Energy Agency*]
WEOG	Western European and Others Group [*United Nations*]
WEOK	Poughkeepsie, NY [*AM radio station call letters*]
WEOL	Elyria, OH [*AM radio station call letters*]
WEOS	Geneva, NY [*FM radio station call letters*]
WEOS	Water Extraction of Orange Solids [*Citrus processing*]
WEOW	Key West, FL [*FM radio station call letters*]
WEOW	Weapons Engineer Officer's Writer [*British military*] (DMA)
WEOZ	Saegertown, PA [*FM radio station call letters*]
WEP	War and Emergency Plan [*DoD*]
WEP	Waseda Economic Papers [*A publication*]
WEP	Water Electrolysis Plenum
WEP	Water Entry Point [*Navy*] (CAAL)
WEP	Water-Extended Polyester
WEP	Weak Equivalence Principle [*Gravity*]
WEP	Weam [*Papua New Guinea*] [*Airport symbol*] (OAG)
WEP	Weapon
WEP	Weather Processor (MCD)
WEP	Windfall Elimination Provision (GFGA)
WEP	Windows Entertainment Pack [*Data processing*]
WEP	Wisconsin Experiment Package [*NASA*] (MCD)
WEP	Women's Equity Program (EA)
WEP	Work Experience Program [*Department of Labor*]
WEP	World Employment Program [*of the International Labour Organization*] [*Geneva, Switzerland*] [*United Nations*]
WEP	Writing, Editing, and Publishing
WEPA	Eupora, MS [*AM radio station call letters*]
WEPA	Welded Electrical Packaging Association
WEPC	Weapons and Equipment Policy Committee [*British*] (RDA)
WEPC	West Chemical Products [*NASDAQ symbol*] (NQ)
WEPCOSE	Weapon Control Systems Engineering [*Navy*] (NG)
WEPEX	Weapons Exercise [*Navy*] (NVT)
WEPG	South Pittsburg, TN [*AM radio station call letters*]
WEPH	Weapon Phenomenology (RDA)
WEPM	Martinsburg, WV [*AM radio station call letters*]
WEPR	Greenville, SC [*FM radio station call letters*]
WEPR	Walker Energy Partners [*NASDAQ symbol*] (NQ)
WEPR	Women Executives in Public Relations [*New York, NY*] (EA)
WEPRA	Welding Production [*English Translation*] [*A publication*]
WEPREC	West Pakistan Research and Evaluation Center
WEPS	Elgin, IL [*FM radio station call letters*]
WEPS	Weapons System [*Navy*]
WEPSO	Naval Weapons Services Office [*Also known as NAVWPNSERVO, NWSO*]
WEPTA	War Excess Profits Tax Act [*1917*]
WEPTAC	Weapons and Tactics Analysis Center [*Navy*] (MCD)
WEPTRAEX	Weapons Training Exercise (NVT)
WEPTU	Weapons Reserve Training Units [*Navy*]
WEPZA	World Export Processing Zones Association [*Flagstaff, AZ*] (EA)
WEQ	Wind Erosion Equation
WEQR	Goldsboro, NC
WEQX	Manchester, VT [*FM radio station call letters*]
WER	Water Electrolysis Rocket
WER	Webcor Electronics, Inc. [*AMEX symbol*] (SPSG)
WER	Week End Review [*A publication*]
WER	Weight Estimating Relationship (KSC)
WER	Werombi [*Australia*] [*Seismograph station code, US Geological Survey*] (SEIS)
WERA	Plainfield, NJ [*AM radio station call letters*]
WERA	Western Eastern Roadracers Association (EA)
WERA	Western/English Retailers of America (EA)
WERA	World Energy Research Authority
WERB	Berlin, CT [*FM radio station call letters*]
WERC	Birmingham, AL [*AM radio station call letters*]
WERC	Warehousing Education and Research Council (EA)
WERC	Western Energy Resources, Inc. [*NASDAQ symbol*] (NQ)
WERC	Women's Education Resource Centre [*Women's Education Group*] [*British*] (CB)
WERC	World Environment and Resources Council [*Louvain, Belgium*] (EAIO)
WERE	Cleveland, OH [*AM radio station call letters*]
WERG	Erie, PA [*FM radio station call letters*]
WERH	Hamilton, AL [*AM radio station call letters*]
WERH-FM	Hamilton, AL [*FM radio station call letters*]
WERI	Water and Energy Research Institute of the Western Pacific [*University of Guam*] [*Guam*] [*Research center*] (RCD)
WERI	Westerly, RI [*AM radio station call letters*]
WERK	Muncie, IN [*AM radio station call letters*]
Werk	Werk/Archithese [*A publication*]
WERKA	Werkstattstechnik [*A publication*]
WERK-FM	Muncie, IN [*FM radio station call letters*]
Werkstatt und Betr	Werkstatt und Betrieb [*A publication*]
Werkstatt Betr	Werkstatt und Betrieb [*A publication*]
Werkst Korros	Werkstoffe und Korrosion [*A publication*]
Werkst u Korrosion	Werkstoffe und Korrossion (Wernheim) [*A publication*]
WERL	Eagle River, WI [*AM radio station call letters*]
WERL	Water Engineering Research Laboratory [*Cincinnati, OH*] [*Environmental Protection Agency*] (GRD)
WERM	World Encyclopedia of Recorded Music, 1925-55 [*A publication*]
WERN	Madison, WI [*FM radio station call letters*]
WERN	Werner Enterprises, Inc. [*Omaha, NE*] [*NASDAQ symbol*] (NQ)
Wernerian N H Soc Mem	Wernerian Natural History Society. Memoirs [*A publication*]
WERP	Women's Economic Rights Project (EA)
WERPG	Western European Regional Planning Group [*NATO*] (NATG)
WERQ	Baltimore, MD [*AM radio station call letters*]
WERQ-FM	Baltimore, MD [*FM radio station call letters*]
WERR	Utuado Rosa, PR [*FM radio station call letters*]
WERS	Boston, MA [*FM radio station call letters*]
WERS	War Emergency Radio Service
WERS	Weapons Effect Reporting Station [*Civil defense*]
WERS	Wing Equipment Repair Squadron
WERSI	Committee on Women's Employment and Related Social Issues (EA)
WERT	Van Wert, OH [*AM radio station call letters*]
WERT	Women's Economic Round Table (EA)
WERTS	Writers' Ever-Ready Textual Service [*Rent-A-Script*] [*Satirical*]
WERU	Blue Hill, ME [*FM radio station call letters*]
WERZ	Exeter, NH [*FM radio station call letters*]
WES	Sacred Heart Hospital, Eau Claire, WI [*Library symbol*] [*Library of Congress*] (LCLS)
WES	W. E. Schulz & Associates, Inc. [*Telecommunications service*] (TSSD)
WES	Warhead Electrical System
WES	Washington Ethical Society (EA)
WES	Water Electrolysis System
WES	Waterways Experiment Station [*Army Corps of Engineers*] [*Vicksburg, MS*]
WES	Weapon Electrical System
WES	Weapon Engineering Station (MCD)
WES	Weapons Effects Systems (MCD)
WES	Weather Editing Section [*FAA*] (FAAC)
WES	Wes-Martin Aviation [*Red Bluff, CA*] [*FAA designator*] (FAAC)
Wes	[*Mathaeus*] Wesenbeccius [*Deceased, 1586*] [*Authority cited in pre-1607 legal work*] (DSA)
WES	Wesleyan [*A publication*]
WES	Wesleyan [*Religion*] (ROG)
WES	West [*or Western*]
WES	Westbury [*British depot code*]
WES	Westcorp, Inc. [*AMEX symbol*] (SPSG)
WES	Westmills Carpets Ltd. [*Toronto Stock Exchange symbol*]
WES	Weston [*Massachusetts*] [*Seismograph station code, US Geological Survey*] (SEIS)
WES	Weston [*Massachusetts*] [*Geomagnetic observatory code*]
WES	Westport Public Library, Westport, CT [*OCLC symbol*] (OCLC)
WES	Wind Electric System [*Telecommunications*] (TEL)
WES	Wisdom of the East Series [*A publication*]
WES	Work Environment Scale [*Test*]
WES	World Economic Summit
WES	World-Wide Education Service [*Parents' National Educational Union*] [*British*]
WESA	Charleroi, PA [*AM radio station call letters*]

WESA........ White Sands National Monument [*New Mexico*]
WESA........ Wind Energy Society of America [*Inactive*]
WESA........ Wind Energy Systems Act of 1980
WESA-FM ... Charleroi, PA [*FM radio station call letters*]
Wes Aust.... West Australian [*A publication*]
WESB........ Bradford, PA [*AM radio station call letters*]
WESB........ Western Beef [*NASDAQ symbol*] (NQ)
WESC........ Greenville, SC [*AM radio station call letters*]
WESC........ Wasatch Education Systems Corp. [*NASDAQ symbol*] (NQ)
WESC........ Weapon Engagement Simulation Component (MCD)
WESC........ Whole Earth Software Catalog [*A publication*]
WESCAR .. Western Carolines [*Navy*]
WESCARSUBAREA ... Western Carolines Subarea [*Navy*]
WESC-FM ... Greenville, SC [*FM radio station call letters*]
Wes CLJ.... Westmoreland County Law Journal [*A publication*] (DLA)
WESCO..... Walnut Export Sales Co. (EA)
WESCO..... Wesco Financial Corp. [*Associated Press abbreviation*] (APAG)
WESCO..... Westinghouse Corp.
WESCOBASESERVUNIT ... West Coast Base Service Unit [*Navy*]
WESCOM ... Weapons System Cost Model
WESCOM ... Western Command [*Army*] (AABC)
WESCON ... Western Electronics Show and Convention [*IEEE*]
WESCON Tech Pap ... WESCON [*Western Electronics Show and Convention*] Technical Papers [*United States*] [*A publication*]
WESCOSOUNDSCOL ... West Coast Sound School [*Navy*]
W/ESDC ... Weapons/Equipment System Designator Code
WESDET .. Wing Engineer Squadron Detachment (DNAB)
WESE........ Baldwyn, MS [*FM radio station call letters*]
WESE........ Wills Eye Society of Ex-Residents (EA)
WESED..... Weapons System Evaluation Division [*DoD*]
WESEG..... Weapons System Evaluation Group [*DoD*]
Wesen .... [*Mathaeus*] Wesenbeccius [*Deceased, 1586*] [*Authority cited in pre-1607 legal work*] (DSA)
Wesenb ...... [*Mathaeus*] Wesenbeccius [*Deceased, 1586*] [*Authority cited in pre-1607 legal work*] (DSA)
WESF........ Waste Encapsulation Storage Facility [*Nuclear energy*] (NRCH)
WESG........ Women Executives in State Government (EA)
WESH .... Daytona Beach, FL [*Television station call letters*]
WESI......... Strasburg, VA [*FM radio station call letters*]
WESIAC ... Weapons Effectiveness Systems Industry Advisory Committee (MCD)
Weskett Ins ... Weskett's Complete Digest of the Theory, Laws, and Practice of Insurance [*A publication*] (DLA)
Wesk Ins.... Weskett's Complete Digest of the Theory, Laws, and Practice of Insurance [*A publication*] (DLA)
WESL........ East St. Louis, IL [*AM radio station call letters*]
Wesley Th J ... Wesleyan Theological Journal [*A publication*]
Wesley W Spink Lect Comp Med ... Wesley W. Spink Lectures on Comparative Medicine [*A publication*]
WESM....... Princess Anne, MD [*FM radio station call letters*]
WESN .... Bloomington, IL [*FM radio station call letters*]
WESO .... Southbridge, MA [*AM radio station call letters*]
WESO .... Weapons Engineering Service Office [*DoD*]
WESOS..... Water-Extracted Soluble Orange Solids [*Citrus processing*]
WESP........ Dothan, AL [*FM radio station call letters*]
WESP........ War and Emergency Support Plan [*DoD*]
WESP........ Wespac Investors Trust [*NASDAQ symbol*] (NQ)
W/E & SP ... With Equipment and Spare Parts
WESPAR .. Weapon Evaluation System Photographic Analog Recorder (MCD)
WESPEX... War and Emergency Support Plan Exercise [*DoD*]
WESQ .... Rocky Mount, NC [*FM radio station call letters*]
WESR........ Onley-Onancock, VA [*AM radio station call letters*]
WESRAC .. Western Research Application Center [*University of Southern California*]
WESREP.... Weapon Engineering Station Representative (MCD)
Wes Res Law Jo ... Western Reserve Law Journal [*A publication*] (DLA)
Wes Res Law Jrl ... Western Reserve Law Journal [*Ohio*] [*A publication*] (DLA)
WESR-FM ... Onley-Onancock, VA [*FM radio station call letters*]
WESS .... East Stroudsburg, PA [*FM radio station call letters*]
WESS .... Weapons Effect Signature Simulator
WESS .... Weapons Engagement Scoring System
WESS .... Weapons System Status
WESS .... Western European Specialists Section [*Association of College and Research Libraries*]
WESSEAFRON ... Western Sea Frontier [*Navy*]
WEST........ Easton, PA [*AM radio station call letters*]
WEST........ Weapons Effectiveness Simulated Threat (MCD)
WEST........ Weapons Exhaust Study [*Military*] (MCD)
West.......... West Co., Inc. [*Associated Press abbreviation*] (APAG)
WEST........ West One Bancorp [*NASDAQ symbol*] (NQ)
West.......... Westbury's European Arbitration (Reilly) [*A publication*] (DLA)
WEST........ Western Earth Sciences Technologies [*Research center*] (RCD)
WEST........ Western Educational Society for Telecommunications [*Defunct*] (EA)

WEST........ Western Energy Supply and Transmission Associates [*Utility antipollution group*]
WEST........ Western Transportation Co. [*Later, WTCO*] [*AAR code*]
West.......... Western's London Tithe Cases [*England*] [*A publication*] (DLA)
West.......... Westminster [*Record label*]
West.......... Westmoreland County Law Journal [*Pennsylvania*] [*A publication*] (DLA)
West.......... Weston's Reports [*11-14 Vermont*] [*A publication*] (DLA)
West.......... West's English Chancery Reports [*A publication*] (DLA)
West.......... West's Reports, English House of Lords [*A publication*] (DLA)
WEST........ Women's Enlistment Screening Test [*Military*]
WESTA ..... White Sands Electromagnetic Pulse Systems Test Array [*New Mexico*] (RDA)
WESTAF... Western Transport Air Force
West Afr .... West Africa [*London*] [*A publication*]
West Afr Cocoa Res Inst Tech Bull ... West African Cocoa Research Institute. Technical Bulletin [*A publication*]
West African Farm Food Proc ... West African Farming and Food Processing [*A publication*]
West African J of Ed ... West African Journal of Education [*A publication*]
West Afr Inst Oil Palm Res Annu Rep ... West African Institute for Oil Palm Research. Annual Report [*A publication*]
West Afr J Archaeol ... West African Journal of Archaeology [*A publication*]
West Afr J Biol Appl Chem ... West African Journal of Biological and Applied Chemistry [*A publication*]
West Afr J Biol Chem ... West African Journal of Biological Chemistry [*A publication*]
West Afr J Pharmacol Drug Res ... West African Journal of Pharmacology and Drug Research [*A publication*]
West Afr Med J ... West African Medical Journal [*A publication*]
West Afr Med J Nigerian Pract ... West African Medical Journal and Nigerian Practitioner [*A publication*]
West Afr Med J Niger Med Dent Pract ... West African Medical Journal and Nigerian Medical and Dental Practitioner [*A publication*]
West Afr Pharm ... West African Pharmacist [*A publication*]
West Am Lit ... Western American Literature [*A publication*]
West Am Sc ... West American Scientist [*A publication*]
WESTAR .. Waterways Experiment Station Terrain Analyzer RADAR
West Assn Map Libs Inf Bul ... Western Association of Map Libraries. Information Bulletin [*A publication*]
West AULR ... Western Australia University. Law Review [*A publication*]
West Aust Clin Rep ... Western Australian Clinical Reports [*A publication*] (APTA)
West Aust Conf Australas Inst Min Metall ... Western Australian Conference. Australasian Institute of Mining and Metallurgy [*A publication*] (APTA)
West Aust Dep Agric Annu Rep ... Western Australia. Department of Agriculture. Annual Report [*A publication*] (APTA)
West Aust Dep Fish Fauna Rep ... Western Australia. Department of Fisheries and Fauna. Report [*A publication*]
West Aust Dep Fish Wildl Rep ... Western Australia. Department of Fisheries and Wildlife. Report [*A publication*]
West Aust Dep Mines Annu Rep ... Western Australia. Department of Mines. Annual Report [*A publication*] (APTA)
West Aust Dep Mines Miner Resour West Aust Bull ... Western Australia. Department of Mines. Mineral Resources of Western Australia. Bulletin [*A publication*] (APTA)
West Aust Dep Mines Min Resour West Aust Bull ... Western Australia. Department of Mines. Mineral Resources of Western Australia. Bulletin [*A publication*] (APTA)
West Aust Dep Mines Rep Gov Mineral Anal Chem ... Western Australia. Department of Mines. Report of the Government Mineralogist, Analyst, and Chemist [*A publication*]
West Aust Fish ... Western Australia Fisheries [*A publication*]
West Aust Geol Surv Annu Prog Rep ... Western Australia. Geological Survey. Annual Progress Report [*A publication*] (APTA)
West Aust Geol Surv Annu Rep ... Western Australia. Geological Survey. Annual Report [*A publication*] (APTA)
West Aust Geol Surv Bull ... Western Australia. Geological Survey. Bulletin [*A publication*] (APTA)
West Aust Geol Surv 1:250000 Geol Ser ... Western Australia. Geological Survey. 1:250,000 Geological Series [*A publication*] (APTA)
West Aust Geol Surv Geol Ser Explan Notes ... Western Australia. Geological Survey. Geological Series. Explanatory Notes [*A publication*] (APTA)
West Aust Geol Surv Miner Resour Bull ... Western Australia. Geological Survey. Mineral Resources Bulletin [*A publication*] (APTA)
West Aust Geol Surv Rep ... Western Australia. Geological Survey. Report [*A publication*] (APTA)
West Aust Herb Res Notes ... Western Australian Herbarium. Research Notes [*A publication*]
West Aust Inst Technol Gaz ... Western Australian Institute of Technology. Gazette [*A publication*]
West Austl ... Western Australian Reports [*A publication*]
West Aust L Rev ... University of Western Australia. Law Review [*A publication*]

West Aust Mar Res Lab Fish Res Bull ... Western Australian Marine Research Laboratories. Fisheries Research Bulletin [*A publication*] (APTA)

West Aust Mus Spec Publ ... Western Australian Museum. Special Publication [*A publication*] (APTA)

West Aust Nat ... Western Australian Naturalist [*A publication*]

West Aust Nat Reserve Manage Plan ... Western Australian Nature Reserve Management Plan [*A publication*]

West Aust Naturalist ... Western Australian Naturalist [*A publication*] (APTA)

West Aust Nutgrow Soc Yearb ... Western Australian Nutgrowing Society. Yearbook [*A publication*]

West Aust Rep Gov Chem Lab ... Western Australia. Report. Government Chemical Laboratories [*A publication*]

West Austr L ... Western Australian Law Reports [*A publication*]

West Aust Sch Mines ... Western Australian School of Mines [*A publication*]

West Aust SWANS ... Western Australia SWANS [*State Wildlife Authority News Service*] [*A publication*]

West Aust SWANS (State Wildl Auth News Serv) ... Western Australia SWANS (State Wildlife Authority News Service) [*A publication*]

West Aust Wildl Res Cent Wildl Res Bull ... Western Australia Wildlife Research Centre. Wildlife Research Bulletin [*A publication*]

West Bird Bander ... Western Bird Bander [*A publication*]

West Birds ... Western Birds [*A publication*]

West Build ... Western Building [*United States*] [*A publication*]

West Bus.... Western Business [*A publication*]

West Canad J Anthropol ... Western Canadian Journal of Anthropology [*A publication*]

West Can Beekpr ... Western Canada Beekeeper [*A publication*]

West Can J Anthropol ... Western Canadian Journal of Anthropology [*A publication*]

West Canner Packer ... Western Canner and Packer [*A publication*]

West Can Water Sewage Conf Pap Annu Conv ... Western Canada Water and Sewage Conference. Papers Presented at the Annual Convention [*A publication*]

West Can Water and Sewage Conf Proc Annu Conv ... Western Canada Water and Sewage Conference. Proceedings of the Annual Convention [*A publication*]

West Ch ..... West's English Chancery Cases [*25 English Reprint*] [*A publication*] (DLA)

West Chapter Int Shade Tree Conf Proc ... Western Chapter. International Shade Tree Conference. Proceedings [*A publication*]

West Chem Metall ... Western Chemist and Metallurgist [*A publication*]

West Ch (Eng) ... West's English Chancery Cases [*25 English Reprint*] [*A publication*] (DLA)

Westchester Co Hist Soc Publ ... Westchester County Historical Society. Publications [*A publication*]

Westchester Med Bull ... Westchester Medical Bulletin [*New York*] [*A publication*]

West Chy ... West's English Chancery Cases [*25 English Reprint*] [*A publication*] (DLA)

West City ... Western City [*A publication*]

West Coast R ... West Coast Review [*A publication*]

West Coast Rep ... West Coast Reporter [*A publication*] (DLA)

WESTCOM ... Western Command [*Army*]

West Com .. Western's Commentaries on the Laws of England [*A publication*] (DLA)

WESTCOMMRGN ... Western Communications Region [*Air Force*] (AFM)

West Constr ... Western Construction [*A publication*]

West Contract ... Western Contractor [*A publication*]

West Co Rep ... West Coast Reporter [*A publication*] (DLA)

WESTCP... Westcorp, Inc. [*Associated Press abbreviation*] (APAG)

West Crop Farm Manage N Ed ... Western Crops and Farm Management. Northern Edition [*A publication*]

West Crop Farm Manage S Ed ... Western Crops and Farm Management. Southern Edition [*A publication*]

West Dent Soc Bull ... Western Dental Society. Bulletin [*A publication*]

WESTDIVNAVFACENGCOM ... Western Division, Naval Facilities Engineering Command (DNAB)

West Drug ... Western Druggist [*A publication*]

Westd Zeit ... Westdeutsche Zeitschrift fuer Geschichte und Kunst [*A publication*] (OCD)

WESTE ..... Weapons Effectiveness and System Test Environment [*Air Force*] (AFM)

WESTEC... Western Metal and Tool Exposition and Conference [*American Society for Metals*] (TSPED)

West Econ Jour ... Western Economic Journal [*A publication*]

West Elec E ... Western Electric Engineer [*A publication*]

West Electr Eng ... Western Electric Engineer [*A publication*]

Westerm M ... Westermanns Monatshefte [*A publication*]

Westerm Monatsh ... Westermanns Monatshefte [*A publication*]

Western Am Lit ... Western American Literature [*A publication*]

Western Australia Geol Survey Rept ... Western Australia. Geological Survey. Report. Government Printer [*A publication*]

Western Australia Main Roads Dep Tech Bull ... Western Australia. Main Roads Department. Technical Bulletin [*A publication*] (APTA)

Western Bs ... Western Business [*A publication*]

Western EE ... Western Electric Engineer [*A publication*]

Western Electric Eng ... Western Electric Engineer [*A publication*]

Western Eng ... Western Engineering [*A publication*]

Western Hist Q ... Western Historical Quarterly [*A publication*]

Western Hum R ... Western Humanities Review [*A publication*]

Western Hum Rev ... Western Humanities Review [*A publication*]

Western L Jour ... Western Law Journal (Reprint) [*A publication*]

Western L Rev ... Western Law Review [*Canada*] [*A publication*] (DLA)

Western Med ... Western Medicine [*A publication*]

Western Ont L Rev ... Western Ontario Law Review [*A publication*]

Western Pol Q ... Western Political Quarterly [*A publication*]

Western Res ... Western Reserve Business Review [*A publication*]

Western Reserve Hist Soc Tracts ... Western Reserve Historical Society. Tracts [*A publication*]

Western Reserve LN ... Western Reserve Law Notes [*A publication*] (DLA)

Western Res L Rev ... Western Reserve Law Review [*A publication*]

Western Rv Sc ... Western Review of Science and Industry [*A publication*]

Western Speleol Inst Bull ... Western Speleological Institute. Bulletin [*A publication*]

Western Wash Ag Exp B ... Western Washington Agricultural Experiment Station. Monthly Bulletin [*A publication*]

West Europe Ed ... Western European Education [*A publication*]

West Eur Politics ... West European Politics [*A publication*]

West-Eur Symp Clin Chem ... West-European Symposia on Clinical Chemistry [*A publication*]

West Ext .... West on Extents [*1817*] [*A publication*] (DLA)

Westfael Bienenztg ... Westfaelische Bienenzeitung [*A publication*]

West Farmer ... Western Farmer [*A publication*]

Westf Bienenztg ... Westfaelische Bienenzeitung [*A publication*]

West Feed ... Western Feed [*A publication*]

West Feed Seed ... Western Feed and Seed [*A publication*]

West Fire Jnl ... Western Fire Journal [*A publication*]

West Folk .. Western Folklore [*A publication*]

West Folkl ... Western Folklore [*A publication*]

WESTFORNET ... Western Forestry Information Network [*Forest service*] [*Library network*]

West Found Vertebr Zool Occas Pap ... Western Foundation of Vertebrate Zoology. Occasional Papers [*A publication*]

Westfriesch Jb ... Westfriesch Jaarboek [*A publication*]

West Frozen Foods ... Western Frozen Foods [*A publication*]

West Fruit Grow ... Western Fruit Grower [*A publication*]

West Gas ... Western Gas [*A publication*]

West Hist Q ... Western Historical Quarterly [*A publication*]

West HL .... West's Reports, English House of Lords [*A publication*] (DLA)

West Horse ... Western Horseman [*A publication*]

West HR ... Western Humanities Review [*A publication*]

West Humanities Rev ... Western Humanities Review [*A publication*]

West Hum R ... Western Humanities Review [*A publication*]

West Hum Rev ... Western Humanities Review [*A publication*]

West II .... Second Statute of Westminster [*A publication*] (DSA)

West Ind Bull ... West Indian Bulletin [*A publication*]

West Indian Med J ... West Indian Medical Journal [*A publication*]

Westinghouse Eng ... Westinghouse Engineer [*A publication*]

Westinghouse Engr ... Westinghouse Engineer [*A publication*]

West Int Law Bul ... West International Law Bulletin [*A publication*]

West J Agric Econ ... Western Journal of Agricultural Economics [*A publication*]

West J Med ... Western Journal of Medicine [*A publication*]

West J Nurs Res ... Western Journal of Nursing Research [*A publication*]

West J Surg ... Western Journal of Surgery, Obstetrics, and Gynecology [*A publication*]

West J Surg Obstet Gynecol ... Western Journal of Surgery. Obstetrics and Gynecology [*A publication*]

West Jur .... Western Jurist [*Des Moines, Iowa*] [*A publication*] (DLA)

Westlake Int Private Law ... Westlake's Private International Law [*A publication*] (DLA)

WESTLANT ... Western Atlantic Area

West Law J ... Western Law Journal [*A publication*]

West Law Jour ... Western Law Journal (Reprint) [*A publication*]

West Law M ... Western Law Monthly [*Ohio*] [*A publication*] (DLA)

West Law Mo ... Western Law Monthly (Reprint) [*Ohio*] [*A publication*] (DLA)

West Law Month ... Western Law Monthly [*Ohio*] [*A publication*] (DLA)

West Law Rev ... Western Law Review [*Canada*] [*A publication*] (DLA)

WestLB..... Westdeutsche Landesbank [*West German bank*]

Westl Confl ... Westlake's Conflict of Laws [*A publication*] (DLA)

West Legal Obser ... Western Legal Observer [*A publication*] (DLA)

West Leg Obs ... Western Legal Observer [*A publication*] (DLA)

West L Gaz ... Western Law Gazette [*Cincinnati, OH*] [*A publication*] (DLA)

West Lit J .. Western Literary Journal [*A publication*]

West Livestock J ... Western Livestock Journal [*A publication*]

West LJ ..... Western Law Journal [*A publication*]

West LJ (Ohio) ... Western Law Journal (Ohio) [*A publication*]

West LM... Western Law Monthly [*Ohio*] [*A publication*] (DLA)

West L Mo ... Western Law Monthly [*Ohio*] [*A publication*] (DLA)

West L Month ... Western Law Monthly [*Ohio*] [*A publication*] (DLA)

West Locker ... Western Locker [*A publication*]

Westl Priv Int Law ... Westlake's Private International Law [*A publication*] (DLA)

West LR..... Western Law Reporter [*Canada*] [*A publication*] (DLA)

West LR (Can) ... Western Law Reporter [*Canada*] [*A publication*] (DLA)

West L Rev ... Western Law Review [*A publication*] (DLA)

West LT ..... Western Law Times [*Canada*] [*A publication*] (DLA)
Westly .... Westerly [*A publication*]
West M ...... Western Monthly Magazine [*A publication*]
Westm .... Westmeath [*County in Ireland*] (WGA)
WESTM .... Westminster [*London*]
Westm .... Westminster Review [*A publication*]
Westm .... Westmoreland County Law Journal [*Pennsylvania*] [*A publication*] (DLA)
West Mach Steel World ... Western Machinery and Steel World [*A publication*]
West Malays Geol Surv Dist Mem ... West Malaysia. Geological Survey. District Memoir [*A publication*]
West Malays Geol Surv Econ Bull ... West Malaysia. Geological Survey. Economic Bulletin [*A publication*]
WESTMD ... Westmorland [*County in England*]
West Med .. Western Medicine [*A publication*]
West Med Med J West ... Western Medicine; the Medical Journal of the West [*A publication*]
West Met ... Western Metals [*A publication*]
West Metalwork ... Western Metalworking [*A publication*]
Westm Hall Chron ... Westminster Hall Chronicle and Legal Examiner [*1835-36*] [*A publication*] (DLA)
West Miner ... Western Miner [*A publication*]
Westminster Inst Rev ... Westminister Institute Review [*A publication*]
Westminster Stud Educ ... Westminster Studies in Education [*A publication*]
Westm LJ .. Westmoreland County Law Journal [*A publication*] (DLA)
West Mo R .. Western Monthly Review [*A publication*]
Westmore Co LJ (PA) ... Westmoreland County Law Journal [*Pennsylvania*] [*A publication*] (DLA)
Westmoreland ... Westmoreland County Law Journal [*Pennsylvania*] [*A publication*] (DLA)
Westmoreland Co LJ ... Westmoreland County Law Journal [*Pennsylvania*] [*A publication*] (DLA)
Westm Th J ... Westminster Theological Journal [*A publication*]
WESTN ..... Western
West Nat .... Western Naturalist [*A publication*]
WESTNAVELEX ... Naval Electronics Systems Command, Western Division, Mare Island, Vallejo, California
WESTNAVFACENGCOM ... Western Division, Naval Facilities Engineering Command
West New Engl L Rev ... Western New England Law Review [*A publication*]
West NY Mg ... Western New York Magazine [*A publication*]
West Oil Refin ... Western Oil Refining [*A publication*]
West Oil Rep ... Western Oil Reporter [*A publication*]
WESTOMP ... Western Ocean Meeting Point
Weston .... Weston's Reports [*11-14 Vermont*] [*A publication*] (DLA)
West Ont L Rev ... Western Ontario Law Review [*A publication*]
WESTPAC ... Western Pacific [*Military*] (CINC)
WESTPACBACOM ... Western Pacific Base Command [*Navy*]
WEST PACK ... Western Packaging Exposition (TSPED)
WESTPACNORTH ... Western Pacific North [*Navy*] (CINC)
WESTPACTRAMID ... Western Pacific Training Program for Midshipmen [*Navy*] (DNAB)
West PA Hist Mag ... Western Pennsylvania Historical Magazine [*A publication*]
West Paint Rev ... Western Paint Review [*A publication*]
West Pak J Agric Res ... West Pakistan Journal of Agricultural Research [*A publication*]
West Pat .... West on Patents [*A publication*] (DLA)
West Penn Hist Mag ... Western Pennsylvania Historical Magazine [*A publication*]
West Pet Refiners Assoc Tech Publ ... Western Petroleum Refiners Association. Technical Publication [*A publication*]
West Plast ... Western Plastics [*A publication*]
WESTPO .. Western Governors Policy Office
West Polit Q ... Western Political Quarterly [*A publication*]
West Polit Quart ... Western Political Quarterly [*A publication*]
West Pol Q ... Western Political Quarterly [*A publication*]
West Poult Dis Conf ... Western Poultry Disease Conference [*A publication*]
West Pr Int Law ... Westlake's Private International Law [*7th ed.*] [*1925*] [*A publication*] (DLA)
West Pulp Pap ... Western Pulp and Paper [*A publication*]
West R .... Western Reporter [*A publication*] (DLA)
West R .... Western Review [*A publication*]
West Reg Ext Publ Co-Op Ext US Dep Ag ... Western Region Extension Publication. Cooperative Extension. United States Department of Agriculture [*A publication*]
West Reg Pub Colo St Univ Exp Stn ... Western Regional Publication. Colorado State University. Experiment Station [*A publication*]
West Rep ... Western Reporter [*A publication*] (DLA)
West Res Coll ... Western Reserve College
West Reserve Law Rev ... Western Reserve Law Review [*A publication*]
West Res Law Rev ... Western Reserve Law Review [*A publication*]
West Res L Rev ... Western Reserve Law Review [*A publication*]
West Resour Conf ... Western Resources Conference [*A publication*]
West Rev .... Westminster Review [*A publication*]
West Roads ... Western Roads [*A publication*] (APTA)
West Sch Law Dig ... Western School Law Digest [*A publication*]
West School L Rev ... Western School Law Review [*A publication*] (DLA)

West Scot Agric Coll Res Bull ... West of Scotland Agricultural College. Research Bulletin [*A publication*]
West Scot Iron Steel Inst J ... West of Scotland Iron and Steel Institute. Journal [*A publication*]
West Scotl Agric Coll Res Bull ... West of Scotland Agricultural College. Research Bulletin [*A publication*]
WESTSEAFRON ... Western Sea Frontier [*Navy*] (MUGU)
West Shade Tree Conf Proc Annu Meet ... Western Shade Tree Conference. Proceedings of the Annual Meeting [*A publication*]
West Soc Eng J ... Western Society of Engineers. Journal [*A publication*]
West Soc Malacol Annu Rep ... Western Society of Malacologists. Annual Report [*A publication*]
West Soc Malacol Occas Pap ... Western Society of Malacologists. Occasional Paper [*A publication*]
West's Op .. West's Opinions [*City Solicitor of Philadelphia, PA*] [*A publication*] (DLA)
West's Symb ... West's Symboleographie [*Many eds.*] [*1590-1641*] [*A publication*] (DLA)
West States Jew Hist Q ... Western States Jewish Historical Quarterly [*A publication*]
West States Sect Combust Inst Pap ... Western States Section. Combustion Institute. Paper [*A publication*]
West State UL Rev ... Western State University. Law Review [*A publication*]
West St U LR ... Western State University. Law Review [*A publication*]
West St U L Rev ... Western State University. Law Review [*A publication*]
WESTT ..... Weapon System Tactical Tester
West Teach ... Western Teacher [*A publication*] (APTA)
West Tenn Hist Soc Pap ... West Tennessee Historical Society. Papers [*A publication*]
West Texas Geol Soc Pub ... West Texas Geological Society. Publication [*A publication*]
West Tex B ... West Texas Business Journal [*A publication*]
West Tex Today ... Western Texas Today [*A publication*]
West T H ... West's English Chancery Reports Tempore Hardwicke [*1736-39*] [*A publication*] (DLA)
West T Hard ... West's English Chancery Reports Tempore Hardwicke [*1736-39*] [*A publication*] (DLA)
West T Hardw ... West's English Chancery Reports Tempore Hardwicke [*1736-39*] [*A publication*] (DLA)
West Th J .. Westminster Theological Journal [*A publication*]
West Ti Cas ... Western's London Tithe Cases [*1535-1822*] [*A publication*] (DLA)
West Tithe Cas ... Western's London Tithe Cases [*England*] [*A publication*] (DLA)
WestTJ ...... Westminster Theological Journal [*Philadelphia*] [*A publication*]
West Union Tech Rev ... Western Union Technical Review [*A publication*]
West Va ..... West Virginia Reports [*A publication*] (DLA)
West Va Lib ... West Virginia Libraries [*A publication*]
West Va L Rev ... Western Virginia Law Review [*A publication*] (DLA)
West Va Rep ... West Virginia Reports [*A publication*] (DLA)
West Vet .... Western Veterinarian [*A publication*]
West Virginia Geol and Econ Survey Basic Data Rept ... West Virginia. Geological and Economic Survey. Basic Data Report [*A publication*]
West Virginia Geol and Econ Survey Circ ... West Virginia. Geological and Economic Survey. Circular [*A publication*]
West Virginia L Rev ... West Virginia Law Review [*A publication*]
West Week (Can) ... Western Weekly Notes (Canada) [*A publication*] (DLA)
West Week N ... Western Weekly Notes [*Canada*] [*A publication*] (DLA)
West Week N (Can) ... Western Weekly Notes (Canada) [*A publication*] (DLA)
West Week NS ... Western Weekly, New Series [*Canada*] [*A publication*] (DLA)
West Week Rep ... Western Weekly Reports [*Canada*] [*A publication*] (DLA)
West Wildlands ... Western Wildlands [*A publication*]
West Wkly ... Western Weekly Notes (Canada) [*A publication*] (DLA)
WESU .... Middletown, CT [*FM radio station call letters*]
WESV .... Richton, MS [*FM radio station call letters*]
WESX .... Salem, MA [*AM radio station call letters*]
WESY .... Leland, MS [*AM radio station call letters*]
WESYP ..... Weapons System Plan [*Navy*] (NG)
WESZ .... Lincoln, IL [*FM radio station call letters*]
WET .... Wagethe [*Indonesia*] [*Airport symbol*] (OAG)
WET .... Waste, Environment, and Technology [*Matrix*] [*Environmental Protection Agency*]
WET .... Waste Extraction Test
WET .... Water Exercise Technique [*In book title "The W.E.T. Workout"*]
WET .... Weapons Effectiveness Testing
WET .... Westfort Petroleums Ltd. [*Toronto Stock Exchange symbol*]
WET .... Westinghouse Electronic Tubeless
WET .... Wet Environment Trainer [*Navy*]
WET .... Wettzell [*Federal Republic of Germany*] [*Seismograph station code, US Geological Survey*] (SEIS)
WET .... Work Experience and Training
WETA .... War Estate Tax Act [*1917*]
WETA .... Washington, DC [*FM radio station call letters*]
WETAC ..... Westinghouse Electronic Tubeless Analog Computer
WETAF ..... Weather Task Force
WETARFAC ... Work Element Timer and Recorder for Automatic Computing

WETA-TV ... Washington, DC [*Television station call letters*]
WETB........ Johnson City, TN [*AM radio station call letters*]
Wet Bydraes PU CHO Reeks B Natuurwet ... Wetenskaplike Bydraes van die
    PU [*Potchefstroomse Universiteit*] vir CHO [*Christelike
    Hoere Onderwys*]. Reeks B: Natuurwetenskappe [*A
    publication*]
WETC........ Wendell-Zebulon, NC [*AM radio station call letters*]
WETD .... Alfred, NY [*FM radio station call letters*]
Wetenskap Studiereeks ... Wetenskaplike Studiereeks [*A publication*]
WETF........ Weightless Environment Training Facility (SSD)
WETG .... Erie, PA [*Television station call letters*]
Wet Ground Mica Assoc Inc Tech Bull ... Wet Ground Mica Association,
    Incorporated. Technical Bulletin [*A publication*]
WETH .... Wetherley [*England*]
Weth .... Wethey's Reports [*Canada*] [*A publication*] (DLA)
Wethey....... Wethey's Reports, Upper Canada Queen's Bench [*A
    publication*] (DLA)
Weth UC.... Wethey's Reports, Upper Canada Queen's Bench [*A
    publication*] (DLA)
WE TIP ..... We Turn in Pushers [*Organization combating drug traffic*]
WETK....... Burlington, VT [*Television station call letters*]
WETL........ South Bend, IN [*FM radio station call letters*]
WETM ...... Elmira, NY [*Television station call letters*]
WETM ...... Weather Team [*Air Force*] (AFM)
Wet Meded KNNV ... Wetenschappelijke Mededeling KNNV [*Koninklijke
    Nederlandse Natuurhistorische Vereniging*] [*A publication*]
WETN .... Wheaton, IL [*FM radio station call letters*]
WETNETNG ... Wet-Net Training [*Navy*] (NVT)
WETP........ Work Experience Training Program (OICC)
WETS........ Johnson City, TN [*FM radio station call letters*]
WETS........ Weapon Effects Training Simulator (MCD)
WETS........ Week-End Training Site [*Military*] (AABC)
Wet Samenleving ... Wetenschap en Samenleving [*A publication*]
WETSU .... We Eat This Stuff Up [*Army slang, bowdlerized*]
WETT........ Ocean City, MD [*AM radio station call letters*]
WETT........ Wetterau, Inc. [*NASDAQ symbol*] (NQ)
Wett .... Wettstein's Novum Testamentum Graecum [*A
    publication*] (BJA)
Wett Gesch Bl ... Wetterauer Geschichtsblaetter [*A publication*]
Wet Tijd..... Wetenschappelijke Tijdingen. Vereniging voor Wetenschapp de
    Gent [*A publication*]
Wett Leben ... Wetter und Leben [*A publication*]
WETV........ Key West, FL [*Television station call letters*]
WETZ........ New Martinsville, WV [*AM radio station call letters*]
WEU .... University of Wisconsin-Eau Claire, Eau Claire, WI [*Library
    symbol*] [*Library of Congress*] (LCLS)
WEU .... Ward's Engine Update [*A publication*]
WEU .... Western European Union [*Also, WU*] [*See also UEO*] (EAIO)
WEUC .... Ponce, PR [*AM radio station call letters*]
WEUC-FM ... Ponce, PR [*FM radio station call letters*]
WEUL .... Kingsford, MI [*FM radio station call letters*]
WEUP .... Huntsville, AL [*AM radio station call letters*]
W Europe Educ ... Western European Education [*A publication*]
W Eur Policies ... West European Policies [*A publication*]
W Eur Politics ... West European Politics [*A publication*]
WEUX .... Chippewa Falls, WI [*Television station call letters*]
WEV .... Western European Vision
WEV .... World Economy [*A publication*]
WEVA .... Emporia, VA [*AM radio station call letters*]
WEVA .... World Esperantist Vegetarian Association [*See also TEVA*]
    [*Dublin, Republic of Ireland*] (EAIO)
WEVA-FM ... Emporia, VA [*FM radio station call letters*]
WEVD .... New York, NY [*AM radio station call letters*]
WEVE........ Eveleth, MN [*AM radio station call letters*]
WEVE-FM ... Eveleth, MN [*FM radio station call letters*]
WEVL........ Memphis, TN [*FM radio station call letters*]
WEVO .... Concord, NH [*FM radio station call letters*]
WEVO ...... Waehrungsergaenzungsverordnung [*A publication*]
WEVR .... River Falls, WI [*AM radio station call letters*]
WEVR ...... Weaver Arms Corp. [*NASDAQ symbol*] (NQ)
WEVR-FM ... River Falls, WI [*FM radio station call letters*]
WEVS........ Saugatuck, MI [*FM radio station call letters*]
WEVU .... Naples, FL [*Television station call letters*]
WEVV .... Evansville, IN [*Television station call letters*]
WEW .... St. Louis, MO [*AM radio station call letters*]
WEW .... Wasser- und Energiewirtschaft [*A publication*]
WeW.......... Welt und Wort [*A publication*]
WEW .... Western Electronic Week
WEW .... Wewak [*Papua New Guinea*] [*Seismograph station code, US
    Geological Survey*] [*Closed*] (SEIS)
WEWAS.... Water Equipment Wholesalers and Suppliers [*Formerly,
    WEWSA*]
WEWS....... Cleveland, OH [*Television station call letters*]
WEWSA.... Water Equipment Wholesalers and Suppliers Association
    [*Later, WEWAS*] (EA)
WEWZ ...... Elwood, IN [*FM radio station call letters*]
WEX .... Business Science Experts [*NOMOS Datapool*] [*Germany*]
    [*Information service or system*] (CRD)
WEX .... Wexford [*County in Ireland*] (ROG)
WEX .... Win-Eldrich Mines Ltd. [*Toronto Stock Exchange symbol*]
WEX .... Wine Exchange [*Computer network*]

WEXC .... Greenville, PA [*FM radio station call letters*]
WEXC .... Wolverine Exploration Co. [*NASDAQ symbol*] (NQ)
WEXF........ Wexford [*County in Ireland*] (ROG)
WEXFD..... Wexford [*County in Ireland*]
WEXI........ Jupiter, FL [*AM radio station call letters*]
WEXITA ... Women Executives International Tourism Association (EA)
WEXL........ Royal Oak, MI [*AM radio station call letters*]
WEXR .... Mosinee, WI [*AM radio station call letters*]
WEXR .... Plymouth, WI [*FM radio station call letters*]
WEXS....... Patillas, PR [*AM radio station call letters*]
WEXT........ Wrist Extension [*Sports medicine*]
WEXY....... Wilton Manors, FL [*AM radio station call letters*]
WEY .... West Yellowstone, MT [*Location identifier*] [*FAA*] (FAAL)
WEYE....... Surgoinsville, TN [*FM radio station call letters*]
Weyerh....... Weyerhaeuser Co. [*Associated Press abbreviation*] (APAG)
Weyerhauser For Pap ... Weyerhauser Forestry Paper [*A publication*]
WEYI........ Saginaw, MI [*Television station call letters*]
WEYM ...... Weymouth [*Municipal borough in England*]
WEYQ .... Marietta, OH [*FM radio station call letters*]
WEYS....... Key West, FL [*Television station call letters*]
WEYS....... Weyenberg Shoe Manufacturing Co. [*NASDAQ symbol*] (NQ)
WEYY .... Talladega, AL [*FM radio station call letters*]
WEYZ .... Erie, PA [*AM radio station call letters*]
WEZB........ New Orleans, LA [*FM radio station call letters*]
WEZC........ Hickory, NC [*FM radio station call letters*]
WEZE........ Boston, MA [*AM radio station call letters*]
WEZF........ Burlington, VT [*FM radio station call letters*]
WEZG .... North Syracuse, NY [*FM radio station call letters*]
WEZJ .... Williamsburg, KY [*AM radio station call letters*]
WEZJ-FM ... Williamsburg, KY [*FM radio station call letters*]
WEZK .... Knoxville, TN [*FM radio station call letters*]
WEZL........ Charleston, SC [*FM radio station call letters*]
WEZN .... Bridgeport, CT [*FM radio station call letters*]
WEZO .... Fairfield, ME [*FM radio station call letters*]
WEZQ .... Wethersfield Township, NY [*FM radio station call letters*]
WEZR....... Brillion, WI [*FM radio station call letters*]
WEZU .... Witterungseinfluesse und Zeitunterschied [*Weather factors and
    time difference*] [*German military - World War II*]
WEZV .... Monticello, IN [*FM radio station call letters*]
WEZW ...... Wauwatosa-Milwaukee, WI [*FM radio station call letters*]
WEZX........ Scranton, PA [*FM radio station call letters*]
WEZY....... Lakeland, FL [*FM radio station call letters*]
WEZZ........ Clanton, AL [*FM radio station call letters*]
WF .... Four-Conductor Cables [*JETDS nomenclature*]
    [*Military*] (CET)
WF .... Wake Forest University [*North Carolina*]
wf................ Wallis and Futuna [*MARC country of publication code*]
    [*Library of Congress*] (LCCP)
WF .... Wallis and Futuna [*ANSI two-letter standard code*] (CNC)
WF .... Ward Foundation (EA)
WF .... Wash Fountain (AAG)
W & F........ Water and Feed
WF .... Water Filter
WF .... Water Finish [*Paper*]
WF .... Watershed Foundation (EA)
W + F........ Ways plus Filling [*Textile testing*]
WF .... Wehrforschung [*A publication*]
WF .... Weighting Factor (EG)
WF .... Weil-Felix Reaction [*Medicine*] (MAE)
WF .... Welch Fusiliers [*British military*] (DMA)
WF .... Weld Fixture
WF .... Welfare Appointment Full Time [*Chiropody*] [*British*]
WF .... West Feliciana Railroad (IIA)
WF .... Western Folklore [*A publication*]
WF .... Western Front [*World War I*]
WF .... Westfaelische Forschungen [*A publication*]
WF .... Westfair Foods Ltd. [*Toronto Stock Exchange symbol*]
WF .... White Falcon [*A publication*] (DNAB)
WF .... White Fathers [*Roman Catholic men's religious order*]
WF .... White Female
WF .... White Fir [*Botany*]
WF .... Wideroe's Flyveselskap A/S [*Norway*] [*ICAO
    designator*] (FAAC)
WF .... Wildfowl Foundation (EA)
WF .... Wind Force (WGA)
WF .... Window-Frame
WF .... Windstar Foundation (EA)
WF .... Wing Forward (WGA)
WF .... Wingfold
WF .... Winston Furniture [*AMEX symbol*] (SPSG)
WF .... Wire Foundation (EA)
WF .... Wistar-Furth [*Rat strain*]
WF .... Withdrawn Failing [*Education*] (WGA)
WF .... Won on Foul [*Boxing*]
WF .... Word Fluency [*Psychology*]
W & F........ Work and Flop [*Printing*] (WDMC)
WF .... Work Function [*Physics*]
W/F............ Wow and Flutter
WF .... Write Forward
W/F .... Writing on Face [*Deltiology*]
WF .... Wrong Font [*Typesetting*] [*Proofreader's mark*]

WFA .... War Food Administration [*Determined military, civilian, and foreign requirements for human and animal food, and for food used industrially*] [*World War II*] [*Terminated, 1945*]

WFA .... Weight-for-Age (ADA)

WFA .... Weightlifting Federation of Africa (EAIO)

WFA .... Western Fairs Association (EA)

WFA .... Western Falconry Association [*Defunct*] (EA)

WFA .... White Fish Authority [*MAFF*] [*British*]

WFA .... Wide-Frequency Antenna

WFA .... Wire Fabricators Association [*Naperville, IL*] (EA)

WFA .... World Federalist Association (EA)

WFA .... World Federation of Advertisers [*See also FMA*] [*Brussels, Belgium*] (EAIO)

WFA .... World Footbag Association (EA)

WFA .... World Friendship Association

WFA .... Worlds of Fantasy [*1968-*] [*A publication*]

WFAA .... Dallas, TX [*Television station call letters*]

WFAA .... World Federation of Americans Abroad [*France*] (EAIO)

WFAB .... Ceiba, PR [*AM radio station call letters*]

WFAC .... World Federal Authority Committee [*Dundas, ON*] (EAIO)

WFAD .... Middlebury, VT [*AM radio station call letters*]

WFAE .... Charlotte, NC [*FM radio station call letters*]

WFAFW .... World Federation of Agriculture and Food Workers (EA)

WFaH .... Hoard Historical Museum, Fort Atkinson, WI [*Library symbol*] [*Library of Congress*] (LCLS)

WFAI .... Fayetteville, NC [*AM radio station call letters*]

WFAL .... Falmouth, MA [*FM radio station call letters*]

WFALW .... Weltbund Freiheitlicher Arbeitnehmerverbande auf Liberaler Wirtschaftsgrundlage [*World Union of Liberal Trade Union Organisations - WULTUO*] [*Zurich, Switzerland*] (EAIO)

WFAM ...... Augusta, GA [*AM radio station call letters*]

WFAN .... New York, NY [*AM radio station call letters*]

WFAOS ..... World Federation of Associations of YMCA Secretaries [*Nigeria*] (EAIO)

WFAOSB .. World Food and Agricultural Outlook and Situation Board [*Department of Agriculture*]

WFAP .... Women's Funding Assistance Project (EA)

WFAPS ..... World Federation of Associations of Pediatric Surgeons [*Barcelona, Spain*] (EAIO)

WFAR .... Danbury, CT [*FM radio station call letters*]

WFAS .... White Plains, NY [*AM radio station call letters*]

WFAS-FM ... White Plains, NY [*FM radio station call letters*]

WFAU .... Augusta, ME [*AM radio station call letters*]

WFAV .... Cordele, GA [*FM radio station call letters*]

WFAW ...... Fort Atkinson, WI [*AM radio station call letters*]

WFAW ...... World Federation of Agricultural Workers [*See also FMTA*] (EAIO)

WFAX .... Falls Church, VA [*AM radio station call letters*]

WFB .... Waferboard Corp. Ltd. [*Toronto Stock Exchange symbol*]

WFB .... Waterways Freight Bureau [*Inactive*] (EA)

WFB .... Wide Flange Beam [*Metal industry*]

WFB .... World Fellowship of Buddhists [*Bangkok, Tahiland*] (EAIO)

WFBBA .... World Federation of Bergen-Belsen Associations (EA)

WFBC .... Greenville, SC [*AM radio station call letters*]

WFBC-FM ... Greenville, SC [*FM radio station call letters*]

WFBE .... Flint, MI [*FM radio station call letters*]

WFBF .... Buffalo, NY [*FM radio station call letters*]

WFBG .... Altoona, PA [*AM radio station call letters*]

WFBI .... Memphis, TN [*Television station call letters*]

WFBI .... Wood Fiber Blanket Institute [*Defunct*]

WFBL .... Syracuse, NY [*AM radio station call letters*]

WFBMA .... Woven Fabric Belting Manufacturers Association (EA)

WFBQ ...... Indianapolis, IN [*FM radio station call letters*]

WFBR .... Cambridge, MD [*FM radio station call letters*]

WFBSC ..... World Federation of Building Service Contractors (EA)

WFBTMA ... World Federation of Baton Twirling and Majorette Associations (EA)

WFBY .... World Fellowship of Buddhist Youth [*Bangkok, Thailand*]

WFC .... Committee on the World Food Crisis [*Defunct*] (EA)

WFC .... Wake Forest College [*Later, WFU*] [*North Carolina*]

WFC .... Wall Financial Co. [*Vancouver Stock Exchange symbol*]

WFC .... Wall Financial Corp. [*Toronto Stock Exchange symbol*]

WFC .... Walleye Filter Changer

WFC .... Wallops Flight Center [*Formerly, WS*] [*NASA*]

WFC .... War Finance Committee

WFC .... Water Facts Consortium [*Defunct*] (EA)

WFC .... Weld Flange Connection

WFC .... Wells Fargo & Co. [*NYSE symbol*] (SPSG)

WFC .... Wesleyan Free Church

WFC .... West Florida Coast

WFC .... Western Football Conference

WFC .... Western Forestry Center (EA)

WFC .... Wheat Foods Council (EA)

WFC .... Wide Field Camera

WFC .... Wolf First Class [*A philanderer*] [*Slang*]

WFC .... Women's Forage Corps [*British*] [*World War I*]

WFC .... World Food Council [*United Nations*] (EAIO)

WFC .... World Forestry Center (EA)

WFC .... World Friendship Centre (EA)

WFC .... Worldwide Fiero Club (EA)

WFCA .... Ackerman, MS [*FM radio station call letters*]

WFCA .... Western Forestry and Conservation Association (EA)

WFCB .... Chillicothe, OH [*FM radio station call letters*]

WFCC .... Chatham, MA [*FM radio station call letters*]

WFCC .... World Federation for Culture Collections (EAIO)

WFCE .... World Federation of Czechoslovak Exile (EA)

WFCG ...... Franklinton, LA [*AM radio station call letters*]

WFCH ...... Charleston, SC [*FM radio station call letters*]

WFCI .... Franklin, IN [*FM radio station call letters*]

WFCJ .... Miamisburg, OH [*FM radio station call letters*]

WFCL .... Clintonville, WI [*AM radio station call letters*]

WFCLC ..... World Federation of Christian Life Communities [*See also FMCVC*] [*Rome, Italy*] (EAIO)

WFCMV.... Wheeled Fuel-Consuming Motor Vehicle

WFCNLM ... World Federation of the Cossack National Liberation Movement [*Later, WFCNLMC*] (EA)

WFCNLMC ... World Federation of the Cossack National Liberation Movement of Cossackia (EA)

WFCO ...... Lancaster, OH [*FM radio station call letters*]

WFCR .... Amherst, MA [*FM radio station call letters*]

WFCS .... New Britain, CT [*FM radio station call letters*]

WFCS .... Warren Five Cents Savings Bank [*Peabody, MA*] [*NASDAQ symbol*] (NQ)

WFCS .... World's Fair Collectors Society (EA)

WFCT .... Fayetteville, NC [*Television station call letters*]

WFCV .... Fort Wayne, IN [*AM radio station call letters*]

WFCY .... World Federation of Catholic Youth

WFCYWG ... World Federation of Catholic Young Women and Girls [*Later, WFCY*]

WFD .... Waveform Distortion [*Telecommunications*] (TEL)

WFD .... Westfield Minerals Ltd. [*Toronto Stock Exchange symbol*] [*Vancouver Stock Exchange symbol*]

WFD .... Wool Forward [*Knitting*]

WFD .... World Fax Directory [*Information service or system*] (IID)

WFD .... World Federation of the Deaf [*Rome, Italy*]

WFD .... World Food Day [*October 16*]

WFD .... Worldwide Franchise Directory [*A publication*]

WFDA ...... World Fast-Draw Association (EA)

WFDD ...... Winston-Salem, NC [*FM radio station call letters*]

WFDF .... Flint, MI [*AM radio station call letters*]

WFDF .... World Flying Disc Federation (EAIO)

WFDFI ...... World Federation of Development Financing Institutions [*See also FEMIDE*] [*Madrid, Spain*] (EAIO)

WFDG ...... New Bedford, MA [*Television station call letters*]

WFDL .... Lomira, WI [*FM radio station call letters*]

WFDR ...... Manchester, GA [*AM radio station call letters*]

WFDRHL ... World Federation of Doctors Who Respect Human Life (United States Section) (EA)

WFDS .... Warm Fog Dispenser System (MCD)

WFDSA ..... World Federation of Direct Selling Associations [*Washington, DC*] (EA)

WFDSC ..... World Federation of Dark Shadows Clubs (EA)

WFDU ...... Teaneck, NJ [*FM radio station call letters*]

WFDW ...... World Federation of Democratic Women

WFDWRHL ... World Federation of Doctors Who Respect Human Life [*Ostend, Belgium*] (EAIO)

WFDY .... World Federation of Democratic Youth [*See also FMJD*] [*Budapest, Hungary*] (EAIO)

WFe .... Dwight T. Parker Public Library, Fennimore, WI [*Library symbol*] [*Library of Congress*] (LCLS)

WFE .... Wiped Film Evaporation

WFE .... With Food Element

WFE .... World Federation of Europeans (By Birth or Descent) (EA)

WFEA .... Manchester, NH [*AM radio station call letters*]

WFEA .... World Federation of Educational Associations [*Later, WCOTP*] (EA)

WFEB .... Sylacauga, AL [*AM radio station call letters*]

WFEB .... Worcester Foundation for Experimental Biology

WFEC .... San Juan, PR [*Television station call letters*]

WFEF .... Terre Haute, IN [*FM radio station call letters*]

WFEL .... Towson, MD [*AM radio station call letters*]

WFEN ...... Rockford, IL [*FM radio station call letters*]

WFEO ...... World Federation of Engineering Organizations [*Paris, France*]

WF & EQ... Wave Filters and Equalizers (MCD)

WFEWC.... World Federation of Estonian Women's Clubs (EA)

WFEX .... Western Fruit Express

WFEZ .... Williston, FL [*FM radio station call letters*]

WFF .... Wanderer Forum Foundation (EA)

WFF .... Well-Formed Formula [*Logic*]

WFF .... Western Frontier Force [*British military*] (DMA)

WFF .... Whiting Field [*Milton*] [*Florida*] [*Seismograph station code, US Geological Survey*] [*Closed*] (SEIS)

WFF .... William Faulkner Foundation [*Defunct*] (EA)

WFF .... Wold Farm Foods [*Commercial firm*] [*British*]

WFF .... World Friendship Federation

WFFA .... Women's Fashion Fabrics Association (EA)

WFFC .... Ferrum, VA [*FM radio station call letters*]

WFFF .... Columbia, MS [*AM radio station call letters*]

WFFF-FM ... Columbia, MS [*FM radio station call letters*]

WFFG .... Marathon, FL [*AM radio station call letters*]

WFFL........ World Federation of Free Latvians (EA)
WFFM....... Ashburn, GA [*FM radio station call letters*]
WFFM....... World Federation of Friends of Museums [*See also FMAM*]
       [*Paris, France*] (EAIO)
WFFN........ Cordova, AL [*FM radio station call letters*]
WF & FSA ... Wholesale Florists and Florist Suppliers of America (EA)
WFFT .... Fort Wayne, IN [*Television station call letters*]
WFFTH..... World Federation of Workers in Food, Tobacco, and Hotel
       Industries [*See also FMATH*] (EAIO)
WFFX........ Tuscaloosa, AL [*FM radio station call letters*]
WFG .... Water Fog
WFG .... Waveform Function Generator
WFG .... Waveform Generator
WFGB........ Kingston, NY [*FM radio station call letters*]
WFGH....... Fort Gay, WV [*FM radio station call letters*]
WFGI........ Germantown, TN [*FM radio station call letters*]
WFGM....... Fairmont, WV [*FM radio station call letters*]
WFGN .... Gaffney, SC [*AM radio station call letters*]
WFGW ...... Black Mountain, NC [*AM radio station call letters*]
WFGX .... Fort Walton Beach, FL [*Television station call letters*]
WFGY .... Altoona, PA [*FM radio station call letters*]
WFH .... World Federation of Hemophilia [*Montreal, PQ*] (EA)
WFHA .... World Federation of Hungarian Artists (EA)
WFHAAVSC ... World Federation of Health Agencies for the Advancement
       of Voluntary Surgical Contraception (EA)
WFHC .... Henderson, TN [*FM radio station call letters*]
WFHC .... Westside Federal Savings & Loan Association of Seattle
       [*NASDAQ symbol*] (NQ)
WFHFF ..... World Federation of Hungarian Freedom Fighters (EA)
WFHG....... Bristol, VA [*AM radio station call letters*]
WFHJ........ World Federation of Hungarian Jews (EA)
WFHK .... Pell City, AL [*AM radio station call letters*]
WFHL .... Decatur, IL [*Television station call letters*]
WFHN .... Fairhaven, MA [*FM radio station call letters*]
WFHR .... Wisconsin Rapids, WI [*AM radio station call letters*]
WFHSLPAC ... Water-Flooded Helical Screw Low-Pressure Air Compressor
       [*Navy*] (CAAL)
WFHT .... Quincy, FL [*FM radio station call letters*]
WFI........... Fianarantsoa [*Madagascar*] [*Airport symbol*] (OAG)
WFI........... Wait for It (DI)
WFI........... Water for Injection [*Pharmacy*]
WFI........... Wheat Flour Institute [*Absorbed by Miller's National
       Federation*] (EA)
WFI........... Wishes and Fears Inventory [*Psychology*]
WFI........... Wood Flooring Institute of America [*Later, WSFI*] (EA)
WFI........... Wood Foundation Institute (EA)
WFI........... World Faiths Insight [*A publication*]
WFI........... World Federation of Investors (EAIO)
WFI........... Worldwide Friendship International (EA)
WFIA........ Louisville, KY [*AM radio station call letters*]
WFIA........ Wells Fargo Investment Advisors (ECON)
WFIA........ Western Forest Industries Association (EA)
WFIC........ Collinsville, VA [*AM radio station call letters*]
WFICM..... World Federation of International Music Competitions
       [*Switzerland*] (EAIO)
WFID........ Rio Piedras, PR [*FM radio station call letters*]
WFIE......... Evansville, IN [*Television station call letters*]
WFIF .... Milford, CT [*AM radio station call letters*]
WFIL .... Florence, SC [*Television station call letters*]
WFIM........ World Federation of Islamic Missions [*Karachi,
       Pakistan*] (EAIO)
WFIMC..... World Federation of International Music Competitions [*See
       also FMCIM*] (EAIO)
WFIN .... Findlay, OH [*AM radio station call letters*]
WFIN .... Women and Food Information Network (EA)
WFIQ........ Florence, AL [*Television station call letters*]
WFIR........ Roanoke, VA [*AM radio station call letters*]
WFIS........ Fountain Inn, SC [*AM radio station call letters*]
WFIS........ World Federation of Iranian Students
WFIT .... Melbourne, FL [*FM radio station call letters*]
WFIU......... Bloomington, IN [*FM radio station call letters*]
WFIV......... Kissimmee, FL [*AM radio station call letters*]
WFIW....... Fairfield, IL [*AM radio station call letters*]
WFIW-FM ... Fairfield, IL [*FM radio station call letters*]
WFIX........ Huntsville, AL [*AM radio station call letters*]
WFIX........ Rogersville, AL [*FM radio station call letters*]
WFJA........ Sanford, NC [*FM radio station call letters*]
WFJJ........ World Federation of Jewish Journalists [*Tel Aviv,
       Israel*] (EAIO)
WFK .... Frenchville [*Maine*] [*Airport symbol*] (OAG)
WFKB....... Colonial Heights, TN [*AM radio station call letters*]
WFKJ .... Cashtown, PA [*AM radio station call letters*]
WFKN .... Franklin, KY [*AM radio station call letters*]
WFKX....... Henderson, TN [*FM radio station call letters*]
WFKY....... Frankfort, KY [*AM radio station call letters*]
WFKZ........ Plantation Key, FL [*FM radio station call letters*]
WFL.......... Windflower Mining Ltd. [*Vancouver Stock Exchange symbol*]
WFL.......... Woman's Freedom League
WFL.......... Work Flow Language [*Data processing*] (BUR)
WFL.......... World Football League [*Dissolved, 1975*]
WFL.......... Worshipful [*Freemasonry*] (ROG)

WFL........... Wredemann-Frang Law
WFLA........ Tampa, FL [*AM radio station call letters*]
WFLA........ Western Fraternal Life Association (EA)
WFLA-TV ... Tampa, FL [*Television station call letters*]
WFLB........ Fayetteville, NC [*AM radio station call letters*]
WFLC........ Miami, FL [*FM radio station call letters*]
WFLD........ Chicago, IL [*Television station call letters*]
WFLD........ Work/Family Life Database [*Database*]
WFLE........ Flemingsburg, KY [*AM radio station call letters*]
WFLI......... Cleveland, TN [*Television station call letters*]
WFLI......... Lookout Mountain, TN [*AM radio station call letters*]
WFLN....... Philadelphia, PA [*FM radio station call letters*]
WFLO........ Farmville, VA [*AM radio station call letters*]
WFLO-FM ... Farmville, VA [*FM radio station call letters*]
WFLQ....... French Lick, IN [*FM radio station call letters*]
WFLR....... Dundee, NY [*AM radio station call letters*]
WFLR-FM .. Dundee, NY [*FM radio station call letters*]
WFLRY ..... World Federation of Liberal and Radical Youth [*Later, IFLRY*]
WFLS .... Fredericksburg, VA [*AM radio station call letters*]
WFLS-FM ... Fredericksburg, VA [*FM radio station call letters*]
WFLT........ Flint, MI [*AM radio station call letters*]
WFLT........ Wellfleet Communications [*NASDAQ symbol*] (SPSG)
WFLU........ Florence, SC [*AM radio station call letters*]
WFLW....... Monticello, KY [*AM radio station call letters*]
WFLX........ West Palm Beach, FL [*Television station call letters*]
WFLY........ Troy, NY [*FM radio station call letters*]
WFLZ........ Tampa, FL [*FM radio station call letters*]
WFM .... Water Flow Meter
WFM .... Waveform Monitor
WFM .... Waveguide Frequency Meter
WFM .... Wells Fargo Mortgage & Equity Trust [*NYSE symbol*] (SPSG)
WFM .... Western Federation of Miners
WFM .... Westford [*Massachusetts*] [*Seismograph station code, US
       Geological Survey*] (SEIS)
WFM .... World Federalist Movement [*Netherlands*] (EAIO)
WFMA ...... World Folk Music Association (EA)
WFMB...... Springfield, IL [*FM radio station call letters*]
WFMC ...... Goldsboro, NC [*AM radio station call letters*]
WFMC ...... Welding Filler Material Control [*Nuclear energy*] (NRCH)
WFMD ...... Frederick, MD [*AM radio station call letters*]
WFME ...... Newark, NJ [*FM radio station call letters*]
WFME....... West Milford, NJ [*Television station call letters*]
WFME....... World Federation for Medical Education (EA)
WFMF ...... Baton Rouge, LA [*FM radio station call letters*]
WFMG ...... Richmond, IN [*FM radio station call letters*]
WFMH ...... Cullman, AL [*AM radio station call letters*]
WFMH ...... World Federation for Mental Health (EA)
WFMH-FM ... Cullman, AL [*FM radio station call letters*]
WFMI........ Bay Minette, AL [*FM radio station call letters*]
WFMJ ...... Youngstown, OH [*Television station call letters*]
WFMK ...... East Lansing, MI [*FM radio station call letters*]
WFML....... Vincennes, IN [*FM radio station call letters*]
WFMLTA ... World Federation of Modern Language Teachers'
       Association (EA)
WFMM ..... Harbor Beach, MI [*FM radio station call letters*]
WFMO ...... Fairmont, NC [*AM radio station call letters*]
WFMPT .... Wet-Fluorescence Magnetic Particle Technique [*Corrosion
       crack detection*]
WFMQ ...... Lebanon, TN [*FM radio station call letters*]
WFMR ...... Menomonee Falls, WI [*FM radio station call letters*]
WFMS...... Indianapolis, IN [*FM radio station call letters*]
WFMT....... Chicago, IL [*FM radio station call letters*]
WFMU ...... East Orange, NJ [*FM radio station call letters*]
WFMU ...... Weather and Fixed Map Unit [*FAA*]
WFMV ...... Blairstown, NJ [*FM radio station call letters*]
WFMW ..... Madisonville, KY [*AM radio station call letters*]
WFMW ..... World Federation of Methodist Women [*Seoul, Republic of
       Korea*] (EAIO)
WFMWNAA ... World Federation of Methodist Women, North America
       Area (EA)
WFMX ...... Statesville, NC [*FM radio station call letters*]
WFMY ...... Greensboro, NC [*Television station call letters*]
WFMZ........ Allentown, PA [*FM radio station call letters*]
WFMZ-TV ... Allentown, PA [*Television station call letters*]
WFN .... Weapons and Facilities, Navy (NG)
WFN .... Well-Formed Net
WFN .... Westminster College, New Wilmington, PA [*OCLC
       symbol*] (OCLC)
WFN .... World Federation of Neurology (EA)
WFNA ...... White Fuming Nitric Acid
WFNC....... Fayetteville, NC [*AM radio station call letters*]
WFNL........ Sturgeon Bay, WI [*FM radio station call letters*]
WFNM ...... Lancaster, PA [*FM radio station call letters*]
WFNMW .. World Federation of Trade Unions of Non-Manual Workers
       [*See also FMTNM*] [*Antwerp, Belguim*] (EAIO)
WFNP........ New Paltz, NY [*FM radio station call letters*]
WFNR ...... Blacksburg, VA [*AM radio station call letters*]
WFNR ...... Christiansburg, VA [*FM radio station call letters*]
WFNS....... Plant City, FL [*AM radio station call letters*]
WFNS........ Women's Forum on National Security [*Defunct*] (EA)

WFNS........	World Federation of Neurosurgical Societies [*Nijmegen, Netherlands*] (EA)
WFNW	Naugatuck, CT [*AM radio station call letters*]
WFNX	Lynn, MA [*FM radio station call letters*]
WFO..........	Wide Field Optics
WF/O	Wife Of [*Genealogy*]
WFOB	Fostoria, OH [*AM radio station call letters*]
WFOC	Western Field Operations Center [*Bureau of Mines*] [*Spokane, WA*] (GRD)
WFOF........	Covington, IN [*FM radio station call letters*]
WFOF........	Wide Field Optical Filter
WFOG	Suffolk, VA [*FM radio station call letters*]
WFOM	Marietta, GA [*AM radio station call letters*]
WFon	Fond Du Lac Public Library, Fond Du Lac, WI [*Library symbol*] [*Library of Congress*] (LCLS)
WFON	Fond du Lac, WI [*FM radio station call letters*]
WFonM	Marian College of Fond Du Lac, Fond Du Lac, WI [*Library symbol*] [*Library of Congress*] (LCLS)
WFonMM ...	Mercury Marine, Fond Du Lac, WI [*Library symbol*] [*Library of Congress*] (LCLS)
WFonSA	Saint Agnes Hospital, Fond Du Lac, WI [*Library symbol*] [*Library of Congress*] (LCLS)
WFont........	Fontana Public Library, Fontana, WI [*Library symbol*] [*Library of Congress*] (LCLS)
WFonU	University of Wisconsin-Fond Du Lac, Fond Du Lac, WI [*Library symbol*] [*Library of Congress*] (LCLS)
WFOR	Hattiesburg, MS [*AM radio station call letters*]
WFOR	Washington Federal Savings Bank [*NASDAQ symbol*] (NQ)
WFOS........	Cheasapeake, VA [*FM radio station call letters*]
WFOT	World Federation of Occupational Therapists [*London, ON*] (EAIO)
WFOV	Pittsfield, ME [*FM radio station call letters*]
WFOV	Wide Field of View
WFOX	Gainesville, GA [*FM radio station call letters*]
WFOY	St. Augustine, FL [*AM radio station call letters*]
WF & P	Wabash, Frisco, and Pacific Association (EA)
WFP..........	Warm Front [*or Frontal*] Passage [*Meteorology*] (FAAC)
WFP..........	Wearout Failure Period
WFP..........	Witness for Peace (EA)
WFP..........	World Federation of Parasitologists [*Bilthoven, Netherlands*] (EAIO)
WFP..........	World Food Programme [*Rome, Italy*] [*United Nations*]
WFP..........	Worldwide Fast for Peace [*An association*] [*Defunct*] (EA)
WFPA........	Fort Payne, AL [*AM radio station call letters*]
WFPA........	Washington Forest Protection Association (EA)
WFPA........	World Federation for the Protection of Animals [*Also known as FMPA, WTB*] [*Later, WSPA*]
WFPC........	Petersburg, IN [*FM radio station call letters*]
WFPC........	Wide Field/Planetary Camera
WFPFC......	Worldwide Fair Play for Frogs Committee (EA)
WFPG........	Atlantic City, NJ [*AM radio station call letters*]
WFPG-FM ...	Atlantic City, NJ [*FM radio station call letters*]
WFPHA	World Federation of Public Health Associations (EA)
WFPK........	Louisville, KY [*FM radio station call letters*]
WFPL........	Louisville, KY [*FM radio station call letters*]
WFPLCA	World Federation of Pipe Line Contractors Association (EA)
WFPMA....	World Federation of Personnel Management Associations [*Alexandria, VA*] (EA)
WFPMM....	World Federation of Proprietary Medicine Manufacturers
WFPR........	Hammond, LA [*AM radio station call letters*]
WFPR........	Western Federal Savings Bank [*Mayaguez, PR*] [*NASDAQ symbol*] (NQ)
WFPS	Freeport, IL [*FM radio station call letters*]
WFPS	Wild Flower Preservation Society (EA)
WFPT........	Frederick, MD [*Television station call letters*]
WFPT........	Welsh Figure Preference Test [*Psychology*]
WFPT........	World Federation for Physical Therapy
WFQS........	Franklin, NC [*FM radio station call letters*]
WFQX	Front Royal, VA [*FM radio station call letters*]
WFR	Wafer (MSA)
WFR	Weekblad voor Fiscaal Recht [*A publication*]
WFR	Weight Flow Rate (SAA)
WFR	Weil-Felix Reaction [*Medicine*] (MAE)
WFR	Wharf Resources Ltd. [*Toronto Stock Exchange symbol*]
WFR	Wheal and Flare Reaction [*Immunology*]
WFR	Wide-Finding RADAR (MCD)
WFR	Worcestershire and Sherwood Foresters Regiment [*Military unit*] [*British*]
WFRA........	Franklin, PA [*AM radio station call letters*]
WFRA........	Wharf Resources Ltd. [*NASDAQ symbol*] (NQ)
WFRA-FM ...	Franklin, PA [*FM radio station call letters*]
WFRB........	Frostburg, MD [*AM radio station call letters*]
WFRBC.....	Washed, Filtered Red Blood Cells [*Hematology*]
WFRB-FM ...	Frostburg, MD [*FM radio station call letters*]
WFRC........	Columbus, GA [*FM radio station call letters*]
WFRD	Hanover, NH [*FM radio station call letters*]
WFRE	Frederick, MD [*FM radio station call letters*]
WFRG	Rome, NY [*FM radio station call letters*]
WFRJ	Johnstown, PA [*FM radio station call letters*]
WFRK........	Coleman, FL [*AM radio station call letters*]
WFRL........	Freeport, IL [*AM radio station call letters*]

WFRM	Coudersport, PA [*AM radio station call letters*]
WFRM-FM ...	Coudersport, PA [*FM radio station call letters*]
WFRN	Elkhart, IN [*FM radio station call letters*]
WFRO	Fremont, OH [*AM radio station call letters*]
WFRO-FM ...	Fremont, OH [*FM radio station call letters*]
WFRS........	Smithtown, NY [*FM radio station call letters*]
WFRS........	World Federation of Rose Societies [*Hurlingham, Argentina*] (EAIO)
WFRV........	Green Bay, WI [*Television station call letters*]
WFRW	Webster, NY [*FM radio station call letters*]
WFRX........	West Frankfort, IL [*AM radio station call letters*]
WFRX-FM ...	West Frankfort, IL [*FM radio station call letters*]
WFS..........	Waterhouse-Friderichsen Syndrome [*Medicine*]
WFS..........	Weapon Fire Simulator (MCD)
WFS..........	Welfare Food Service [*British*]
WF & S	Wichita Falls & Southern Railroad (IIA)
WFS..........	Women in Fire Service (EA)
WFS..........	Women for Sobriety (EA)
WFS..........	Wood Furring Strips [*Technical drawings*]
WFS..........	Work Function Surface
WFS..........	World Fertility Survey [*Program*]
WFS..........	World Food Security [*FAO program*] [*United Nations*]
WFS..........	World Future Society (EA)
WFSA........	Wash Frock Salesmen's Association (EA)
WFSA........	Western Federal Savings & Loan Association [*Marina Del Rey, CA*] [*NASDAQ symbol*] (NQ)
WFSA........	Wilhelm Furtwangler Society of America (EA)
WFSA........	World Federation of Societies of Anaesthesiologists [*Bristol, England*] (EAIO)
WFSB........	Hartford, CT [*Television station call letters*]
WFSB........	Washington Federal Savings Bank [*NASDAQ symbol*] (NQ)
WFSBP......	World Federation of the Societies of Biological Psychiatry (EA)
WFSC........	Franklin, NC [*AM radio station call letters*]
WFSE........	Edinboro, PA [*FM radio station call letters*]
WFSEC	World Fellowship of Slavic Evangelical Christians (EA)
WFSF	Ozark, AL [*AM radio station call letters*]
WFSF	World Futures Studies Federation (EA)
WFSG........	Panama City, FL [*Television station call letters*]
WFSGI	World Federation of the Sporting Goods Industry (EAIO)
WFSH	Valparaiso-Niceville, FL [*AM radio station call letters*]
WFSI	Annapolis, MD [*FM radio station call letters*]
WFSICCM ...	World Federation of Societies of Intensive and Critical Care Medicine (EAIO)
WFSK........	Nashville, TN [*FM radio station call letters*]
WFSL	Washington Federal Savings & Loan Association [*NASDAQ symbol*] (NQ)
WFSM.......	Tazewell, TN [*FM radio station call letters*]
WFSP	Kingwood, WV [*AM radio station call letters*]
WFSP-FM ...	Kingwood, WV [*FM radio station call letters*]
WFSQ.......	Tallahassee, FL [*FM radio station call letters*]
WFSR	Harlan, KY [*AM radio station call letters*]
WFSS	Fayetteville, NC [*FM radio station call letters*]
WFSS	Welsh Folk Song Society [*British*]
WFST	Caribou, ME [*AM radio station call letters*]
WFSt..........	Wehrmachtfuehrungsstab [*Armed Forces Operations Staff*] [*German military - World War II*]
WFSU........	Tallahassee, FL [*FM radio station call letters*]
WFSUDO ...	World Fertility Survey. Country Reports [*A publication*]
WFSU-TV ...	Tallahassee, FL [*Television station call letters*]
WFSW.......	World Federation of Scientific Workers [*See also FMTS*] [*ICSU*] [*British*] (EAIO)
WFS (World Fertil Surv) Comp Stud ...	WFS (World Fertility Survey) Comparative Studies [*A publication*]
WFSY........	Panama City, FL [*FM radio station call letters*]
WFT..........	Warm Fluctuating Temperatures
WFT..........	West Fraser Timber Co. Ltd. [*Toronto Stock Exchange symbol*] [*Vancouver Stock Exchange symbol*]
WFT..........	Wildfowl Trust [*British*]
WFTA.......	Fulton, MS [*FM radio station call letters*]
WFTA.......	Winograd Fourier Transform Algorithm (MCD)
WFTA.......	World Federation of Taiwanese Associations (EA)
WFTC.......	Kinston, NC [*FM radio station call letters*]
WFTC.......	Western Flying Training Command [*AAFWFTC*]
WFTD.......	Marietta, GA [*AM radio station call letters*]
WFTD.......	Women's Flying Training Detachment [*World War II*]
WFTE.......	Salem, IN [*Television station call letters*]
WFTF	Rutland, VT [*FM radio station call letters*]
WFTG.......	London, KY [*AM radio station call letters*]
WFTH	Richmond, VA [*AM radio station call letters*]
WFTI	St. Petersburg, FL [*FM radio station call letters*]
WFTJW	World Federation of Travel Journalists and Writers (EA)
WFTK.......	Wake Forest, NC [*AM radio station call letters*]
WFTL	Fort Lauderdale, FL [*AM radio station call letters*]
WFTM.......	Maysville, KY [*AM radio station call letters*]
WFTM-FM ...	Maysville, KY [*FM radio station call letters*]
WFTN	Franklin, NH [*AM radio station call letters*]
WFTN-FM ...	Franklin, NH [*FM radio station call letters*]
WFTO	Fulton, MS [*AM radio station call letters*]
WFTP.......	Weapons Fly-To Point [*Military*] (CAAL)
WFTR.......	Front Royal, VA [*AM radio station call letters*]
WFTR-FM ...	Front Royal, VA [*FM radio station call letters*]

WFTS........	Tampa, FL [*Television station call letters*]
WFTS........	Western Fish Toxicology Station [*Environmental Protection Agency*]
W FTTNGS ...	With Fittings [*Freight*]
WFTU	World Federation of Trade Unions [*See also FSM*] [*Prague, Czechoslovakia*] (EAIO)
WFTUNMW ...	World Federation of Trade Unions of Non-Manual Workers [*Belgium*] (EY)
WFTV........	Orlando, FL [*Television station call letters*]
WFTVN.....	Women's Film, Television, and Video Network (EAIO)
WFTW.......	Fort Walton Beach, FL [*AM radio station call letters*]
WFTX........	Cape Coral, FL [*Television station call letters*]
WFTY........	Washington, DC [*Television station call letters*]
WFTZ........	Manchester, TN [*FM radio station call letters*]
WFU.........	Wake Forest University [*Winston-Salem, NC*]
WFU	War Frauds Unit
WFUCA.....	World Federation of UNESCO Clubs and Associations
WFUD.......	Honeoye Falls, NY [*FM radio station call letters*]
WFUL........	West Florida Union List [*Library network*]
WFUM	Flint, MI [*FM radio station call letters*]
WFUM-TV ...	Flint, MI [*Television station call letters*]
WFUN	Ashtabula, OH [*AM radio station call letters*]
WFUNA	World Federation of United Nations Associations (EA)
WFUPA.....	World Federation of Ukrainian Patriarchal Associations (EA)
WFUR	Grand Rapids, MI [*AM radio station call letters*]
WFUR-FM ...	Grand Rapids, MI [*FM radio station call letters*]
WFUV	New York, NY [*FM radio station call letters*]
WFUWO ...	World Federation of Ukrainian Women's Organizations [*Toronto, ON*] (EA)
WFVA........	Fredericksburg, VA [*AM radio station call letters*]
WFVR........	Valdosta, GA [*AM radio station call letters*]
WFW	Walden Forever Wild (EA)
WFWA	Fort Wayne, IN [*Television station call letters*]
WFWC......	Springville, NY [*AM radio station call letters*]
WFWC.......	Walden Forever Wild Committee (EA)
WFWI	Fort Wayne, IN [*FM radio station call letters*]
WFWL	Camden, TN [*AM radio station call letters*]
WFWM	Frostburg, MD [*FM radio station call letters*]
WFXA........	Augusta, GA [*AM radio station call letters*]
WFXA-FM ...	Augusta, GA [*FM radio station call letters*]
WFXB........	East St. Louis, IL [*FM radio station call letters*]
WFXC........	Durham, NC [*FM radio station call letters*]
WFXD	Marquette, MI [*FM radio station call letters*]
WFXE	Columbus, GA [*FM radio station call letters*]
WFXF........	Indianapolis, IN [*AM radio station call letters*]
WFXF-FM ...	Indianapolis, IN [*FM radio station call letters*]
WFXG	Augusta, GA [*Television station call letters*]
WFXH	Hilton Head Island, SC [*FM radio station call letters*]
WFXI	Morehead, NC [*Television station call letters*]
WFXL........	Albany, GA [*Television station call letters*]
WFXM	Forsyth, GA [*FM radio station call letters*]
WFXN	Goldsboro, NC [*AM radio station call letters*]
WFXO	Iuka, MS [*FM radio station call letters*]
WFXQ	Chase City, VA [*FM radio station call letters*]
WFXR........	Harwichport, MA [*FM radio station call letters*]
WFXS	Soddy-Daisy, TN [*FM radio station call letters*]
WFXT........	Boston, MA [*Television station call letters*]
WFXU	Live Oak, FL [*Television station call letters*]
WFXV	Utica, NY [*Television station call letters*]
WFXW	Geneva, IL [*AM radio station call letters*]
WFXX........	South Williamsport, PA [*AM radio station call letters*]
WFXX-FM ...	South Williamsport, PA [*FM radio station call letters*]
WFXY	Middlesboro, KY [*AM radio station call letters*]
WFY	World Federalist Youth [*Netherlands*]
WFYC........	Alma, MI [*AM radio station call letters*]
WFYC-FM ...	Alma, MI [*FM radio station call letters*]
WFYI........	Indianapolis, IN [*FM radio station call letters*]
WFYI-TV ..	Indianapolis, IN [*Television station call letters*]
WFY/NIO ...	World Federalist Youth - Youth Movement for a New International Order [*Amsterdam, Netherlands*] (EAIO)
WFYR........	Chicago, IL [*FM radio station call letters*]
WFY-USA ...	World Federalist Youth - United States of America [*Later, Action for World Community: World Federalist Youth in the USA*] (EA)
WFYV........	Atlantic Beach, FL [*FM radio station call letters*]
WFYV........	Jacksonville, FL [*AM radio station call letters*]
WFZ	Weapons Free Zone
WFZ	Wirtschaftswoche [*A publication*]
WG............	Air Ecosse Ltd. [*British*] [*ICAO designator*] (FAAC)
WG............	Riker Laboratories Ltd. [*British*] [*Research code symbol*]
WG............	Waehrungsgesetz [*A publication*]
WG............	Wage Grade [*Federal employee job classification*]
Wg............	Wandlung [*A publication*]
WG............	Wartime Guidance [*Air Force*] (AFM)
WG............	Waste Gas [*Nuclear energy*] (NRCH)
WG............	Water Gauge
W/G..........	Water Glycol (KSC)
WG............	Water Resources News-Clipping Service. General Issue. Water Management Service. Department of the Environment [*Ottawa*] [*A publication*]
WG............	Waveguide

WG............	Weather Group [*Air Force*]
WG............	Wedge (MSA)
WG............	Wegener's Granulomatosis [*Medicine*]
WG............	Weighing (ROG)
WG............	Weight Guaranteed
WG............	Welsh Guards [*Military unit*] [*British*]
WG............	West German
WG............	Willcox & Gibbs, Inc. [*NYSE symbol*] (SPSG)
WG............	Window Guard (AAG)
WG............	Wine Gallon
WG............	Wing
WG............	Wire Gauge
WG............	Wired Glass [*Technical drawings*]
W & G	Wissen und Glauben [*A publication*]
WG............	Wissenschaft und Gegenwart [*A publication*]
WG............	With Grain
WG............	Women for Guatemala (EA)
WG............	Working Group (FAAC)
WG............	World Goodwill (EA)
WG............	Wright-Giemsa [*A stain*] [*Cytology*]
WG............	Writing [*Law*] (ROG)
4WG..........	Weather Group (4th) [*Washington, DC*] [*Air Force*]
WGA.........	Wagga Wagga [*Australia*] [*Airport symbol*] (OAG)
WGA.........	Waveguide Assembly
WGA.........	Weekblad voor de Nederlandse Bond van Gemeenteambtenaren [*A publication*]
WGA.........	Weekly Government Abstracts [*National Technical Information Service*]
WGA.........	Weighted Guidelines Analysis [*Air Force*] (MCD)
WGA.........	Wells-Gardner Electronics Corp. [*AMEX symbol*] (SPSG)
WGA........	Western Golf Association (EA)
WGA........	Western Growers Association (EA)
WGA.........	Wheat Germ Agglutinin [*Biochemistry*]
WGA........	Wild Goose Association (EA)
WGA........	Women Grocers of America (EA)
WGA........	Writers Guild of America, West (EA)
WGAA	Cedartown, GA [*AM radio station call letters*]
WGAB	Newburgh, IN [*AM radio station call letters*]
WGAC......	Augusta, GA [*AM radio station call letters*]
WGAD.......	Gadsden, AL [*AM radio station call letters*]
WGAE	Writers Guild of America, East (EA)
WGAE-US ...	World Government of the Age of Enlightenment - US (EA)
WGAF	West Germany Air Force
WGAI	Elizabeth City, NC [*AM radio station call letters*]
WGAI	Working Group Agenda Item (SAA)
WGAJ........	Deerfield, MA [*FM radio station call letters*]
WGAL	Lancaster, PA [*Television station call letters*]
WGAM......	Greenfield, MA [*AM radio station call letters*]
WGAN......	Portland, ME [*AM radio station call letters*]
WGAO......	Franklin, MA [*FM radio station call letters*]
WGAO......	World Guide to Abbreviations of Organizations [*A publication*]
WGAP	Maryville, TN [*AM radio station call letters*]
WGAP-FM ...	Maryville, TN [*FM radio station call letters*]
WGAR......	Cleveland, OH [*FM radio station call letters*]
WGAS	South Gastonia, NC [*AM radio station call letters*]
WGAT	Gate City, VA [*AM radio station call letters*]
WGAU......	Athens, GA [*AM radio station call letters*]
WGAW......	Gardner, MA [*AM radio station call letters*]
WGAW	Writers Guild of America, West (EA)
WGAY	Washington, DC [*FM radio station call letters*]
WGB..........	Weekblad voor Gemeentebelangen. Orgaan van de Vereniging van Nederlandse Gemeenten [*A publication*]
WGB..........	Weltgewerkschaftsbund [*World Federation of Trade Unions*]
WGBA	Green Bay, WI [*Television station call letters*]
WGBC	Waveguide Operating below Cutoff (IEEE)
WGBE	Williamsport, PA [*FM radio station call letters*]
WGBF	Henderson, KY [*FM radio station call letters*]
WGBH......	Boston, MA [*FM radio station call letters*]
WGBH-TV ...	Boston, MA [*Television station call letters*]
WGBI	Scranton, PA [*AM radio station call letters*]
WGBI-FM ...	Scranton, PA [*FM radio station call letters*]
WGBO.......	Joliet, IL [*Television station call letters*]
WGBP	Green Bay, WI [*FM radio station call letters*]
WGBQ	Galesburg, IL [*FM radio station call letters*]
WGBR	Goldsboro, NC [*AM radio station call letters*]
WGBS.......	Philadelphia, PA [*Television station call letters*]
WGBV	Smyrna, GA [*AM radio station call letters*]
WGBW	Green Bay, WI [*FM radio station call letters*]
WGBX	Boston, MA [*Television station call letters*]
WGBY	Springfield, MA [*Television station call letters*]
WGc..........	Genoa City Public Library, Genoa City, WI [*Library symbol*] [*Library of Congress*] (LCLS)
WGC.........	Waste Gas Compressor [*Nuclear energy*] (NRCH)
WGC.........	Waveguide Shutter
WGC.........	West Georgia College [*Carollton*]
WGC.........	Western Gear Corp.
WGC.........	Western Governors Conference
WGC.........	Winslow Gold Corp. [*Vancouver Stock Exchange symbol*]
WGC.........	Wisconsin Gas Co. [*NYSE symbol*] (SPSG)
WGC.........	World Games Council (EAIO)
WGC.........	World Gospel Crusades (EA)

WGC......... Worthy Grand Chaplain [*Freemasonry*]
WGC......... Worthy Grand Conductor [*Freemasonry*]　(ROG)
WGCA...... Quincy, IL [*FM radio station call letters*]
WGCA...... Wisconsin Gift Cheese Association　(EA)
WGCB ...... Red Lion, PA [*AM radio station call letters*]
WGCB-FM ... Red Lion, PA [*FM radio station call letters*]
WGCB-TV ... Red Lion, PA [*Television station call letters*]
WGCC...... World Games Coordination Committee [*Karsruhe, Federal Republic of Germany*]　(EAIO)
WGCC-FM ... Batavia, NY [*FM radio station call letters*]
WGCD...... Chester, SC [*AM radio station call letters*]
WG/CDR .. Wing Commander [*British military*]　(NATG)
WGCDR .... Working Group for Community Development Reform　(EA)
WGCH...... Greenwich, CT [*AM radio station call letters*]
WGCI .... Chicago, IL [*AM radio station call letters*]
WGCI-FM ... Chicago, IL [*FM radio station call letters*]
WGCL ...... Bloomington, IN [*AM radio station call letters*]
WGCL ...... Window Glass Cutters League of America [*Later, GBBA*]　(EA)
WGCM...... Gulfport, MS [*AM radio station call letters*]
Wg Cmdr ... Wing Commander [*British military*]　(DMA)
WGCM-FM ... Gulfport, MS [*FM radio station call letters*]
WGCO...... Jesup, GA [*FM radio station call letters*]
WGCR ...... Brevard, NC [*AM radio station call letters*]
WGCR ...... West Georgia College. Review [*A publication*]
Wg Cr........ Wing Commander [*British military*]　(DMA)
WGCS........ Goshen, IN [*FM radio station call letters*]
WGCV ...... Petersburg, VA [*AM radio station call letters*]
WGCX ...... Atmore, AL [*FM radio station call letters*]
WGCY ...... Gibson City, IL [*FM radio station call letters*]
WGD......... Windshield Guidance Display
WGD......... Working Group Director
WGD......... Worldwide Government Directory [*A publication*]
WGDA...... Watermelon Growers and Distributors Association
WGDC....... Waveguide Directional Coupler
WGDC....... Working Group for Democracy in Chile　(EA)
WGDHP.... Working Group on Domestic Hunger and Poverty　(EA)
WGDL....... Lares, PR [*AM radio station call letters*]
WGDL....... Waveguide Delay Line
WGDN ...... Gladwin, MI [*AM radio station call letters*]
WGDN-FM ... Gladwin, MI [*FM radio station call letters*]
WGDR....... Plainfield, VT [*FM radio station call letters*]
WGDS .... Warm Gas Distribution System
WGDS .... Waste Gas Disposal System [*Nuclear energy*]　(NRCH)
WGDT....... Waste Gas Decay Tank [*Nuclear energy*]　(NRCH)
WGE......... Walgett [*Australia*] [*Airport symbol*]　(OAG)
WGE......... World's Great Explorers [*A publication*]
WGEA ...... Geneva, AL [*AM radio station call letters*]
WGEE .... Green Bay, WI [*AM radio station call letters*]
WGEEIA... Western Ground Electronics Engineering Installation Agency　(AAG)
WGEIO ..... World Guide to Environmental Issues [*A publication*]
WGEL .... Greenville, IL [*FM radio station call letters*]
WGEM...... Quincy, IL [*AM radio station call letters*]
WGEM-FM ... Quincy, IL [*FM radio station call letters*]
WGEM-TV ... Quincy, IL [*Television station call letters*]
WGEN ...... Geneseo, IL [*AM radio station call letters*]
WGEN....... Watson General Corp. [*NASDAQ symbol*]　(SPSG)
WGEN-FM ... Geneseo, IL [*FM radio station call letters*]
WGER .... Saginaw, MI [*FM radio station call letters*]
WGER .... Working Group on Extraterrestrial Resources [*Defunct*] [*NASA*]
WGES........ Oswego, NY [*FM radio station call letters*]
WGET .... Gettysburg, PA [*AM radio station call letters*]
WGETS...... Wayne George Encoder Test Set
WGEV .... Beaver Falls, PA [*FM radio station call letters*]
WGEZ .... Beloit, WI [*AM radio station call letters*]
WGF .... Waveguide Filter
WGF .... Western Goals Foundation　(EA)
WGF .... Wound Glass Fiber
WGFA .... Watseka, IL [*AM radio station call letters*]
WGFA-FM ... Watseka, IL [*FM radio station call letters*]
WGFAR..... Wenner-Gren Foundation for Anthropological Research　(EA)
WGFB........ Plattsburgh, NY [*FM radio station call letters*]
WGFC .... Floyd, VA [*AM radio station call letters*]
WGFL........ High Springs, FL [*Television station call letters*]
WGFM ...... Cheboygan, MI [*FM radio station call letters*]
WGFP........ Webster, MA [*AM radio station call letters*]
WGFR .... Glens Falls, NY [*FM radio station call letters*]
WGFS........ Covington, GA [*AM radio station call letters*]
WGFT........ Youngstown, OH [*AM radio station call letters*]
WGFX .... Gallatin, TN [*FM radio station call letters*]
WGG......... Warm Gas Generator
WGG......... Worthy Grand Guardian [*Freemasonry*]
WGG......... Worthy Grand Guide [*Freemasonry*]
WGGA....... Cleveland, GA [*FM radio station call letters*]
WGGA....... Gainesville, GA [*AM radio station call letters*]
WGGB........ Springfield, MA [*Television station call letters*]
WGGB........ Writers' Guild of Great Britain　(DCTA)
WGGD....... Melbourne, FL [*FM radio station call letters*]
WGGG....... Gainesville, FL [*AM radio station call letters*]
WGGH ...... Marion, IL [*AM radio station call letters*]

WGGL....... Houghton, MI [*FM radio station call letters*]
WGGM....... Chester, VA [*AM radio station call letters*]
WGGN ...... Castalia, OH [*FM radio station call letters*]
WGGN ...... Sandusky, OH [*Television station call letters*]
WGGO ...... Salamanca, NY [*AM radio station call letters*]
WGGO ...... Silver Springs, FL [*FM radio station call letters*]
WGGR ...... Greenwood, IN [*FM radio station call letters*]
WGGS ...... Greenville, SC [*Television station call letters*]
WGGT ...... Greensboro, NC [*Television station call letters*]
WGGY ...... State College, PA [*FM radio station call letters*]
WGGZ ...... Baton Rouge, LA [*FM radio station call letters*]
WGH .... Newport News, VA [*AM radio station call letters*]
WGH .... Warren Gamaliel Harding [*US president, 1865-1923*]
WGH .... Worthy Grand Herald [*Freemasonry*]
WGHB ...... Farmville, NC [*AM radio station call letters*]
WGHC....... Clayton, GA [*AM radio station call letters*]
WGH-FM ... Newport News, VA [*FM radio station call letters*]
WGHN ...... Grand Haven, MI [*AM radio station call letters*]
WGHN-FM ... Grand Haven, MI [*FM radio station call letters*]
WGHP-TV ... High Point, NC [*Television station call letters*]
WGHQ ...... Kingston, NY [*AM radio station call letters*]
WGHR ...... Marietta, GA [*FM radio station call letters*]
WGHT....... Weigh-Tronix, Inc. [*NASDAQ symbol*]　(NQ)
WGI .... Nieuwe West-Indische Gids [*A publication*]
WGI .... Waveguide Isolator
WGI .... Western Goldfields, Inc. [*Toronto Stock Exchange symbol*]
WGI .... Wirtschaftsgeographisches Institut [*A publication*]
WGI .... Within-Grade Increase
WGI .... Word of God Institute [*Later, NIWG*]　(EA)
WGI .... Work Glove Institute [*Later, WGMA*]　(EA)
WGI .... World Geophysical Interval
WGIA .... Blackshear, GA [*AM radio station call letters*]
WGIB .... Birmingham, AL [*FM radio station call letters*]
WGIC .... Wheat Gluten Industry Council　(EA)
WGIG .... Brunswick, GA [*AM radio station call letters*]
WGII .... Western Grain International, Inc. [*NASDAQ symbol*]　(NQ)
WGII .... Working Group on Internal Instrumentation [*NASA*]
WGIL .... Galesburg, IL [*AM radio station call letters*]
WGIQ....... Louisville, AL [*Television station call letters*]
WGIR .... Manchester, NH [*AM radio station call letters*]
WGIR-FM ... Manchester, NH [*FM radio station call letters*]
WGIV .... Charlotte, NC [*AM radio station call letters*]
WGIX .... Gouverneur, NY [*FM radio station call letters*]
WGJ .... Worm Gear Jack
WGJB .... World's Greatest Jazz Band
WGKA ...... Atlanta, GA [*AM radio station call letters*]
WGKI .... Cadillac, MI [*Television station call letters*]
WGKX ...... Memphis, TN [*FM radio station call letters*]
WGL .... Fort Wayne, IN [*AM radio station call letters*]
WGL .... Warangal [*India*] [*Seismograph station code, US Geological Survey*]　(SEIS)
WGL .... Warren, Gorham & Lamont, Inc. [*Publisher*]
WG & L .... Warren, Gorham & Lamont, Inc. [*Publisher*]
WGL .... Washington Gas Light Co. [*NYSE symbol*]　(SPSG)
WGL .... Waveguide Load
WGL .... Weapons Guidance Laboratory
WGL .... Weighted Guidelines [*DoD*]
WGL .... Westar Group Ltd. [*Toronto Stock Exchange symbol*] [*Vancouver Stock Exchange symbol*]
WGL .... Western Guidance Laboratory [*Wright Air Development Center*]　(MUGU)
WGL .... Westeuropaeische Gesellschaft fuer Luftfahrtpsychologie [*Western European Association for Aviation Psychology - WEAAP*]　(EA)
WGL .... Wire Glass　(AAG)
WGL .... Wire Grid Lens
WGL .... Wueste und Gelobtes Land [*A publication*]　(BJA)
W GLAM .. West Glamorgan [*County in Wales*]
WGLB .... Port Washington, WI [*AM radio station call letters*]
WGLB-FM ... Port Washington, WI [*FM radio station call letters*]
WGLC .... Mendota, IL [*AM radio station call letters*]
WGLC-FM ... Mendota, IL [*FM radio station call letters*]
WGLD ...... Greensboro, NC [*AM radio station call letters*]
WGLE .... Lima, OH [*FM radio station call letters*]
WGLF....... Tallahassee, FL [*FM radio station call letters*]
WGLI........ Babylon, NY [*AM radio station call letters*]
WGLI........ Warren, Gorham & Lamont, Inc.　(DLA)
WGLL........ Mercersburg, PA [*FM radio station call letters*]
WGLO........ Pekin, IL [*FM radio station call letters*]
WGLQ .... Escanaba, MI [*FM radio station call letters*]
WGLR .... Lancaster, WI [*AM radio station call letters*]
WGLR .... Wissenschaftliche Gesellschaft fuer Luft- und Raumfahrt [*Scientific Association for Air and Space Travel*] [*German*]
WGLR-FM ... Lancaster, WI [*FM radio station call letters*]
WGLS-FM ... Glassboro, NJ [*FM radio station call letters*]
WGLT .... Normal, IL [*FM radio station call letters*]
WGLU ...... Johnstown, PA [*FM radio station call letters*]
WGLV ...... Hartford, VT [*FM radio station call letters*]
WGLW ...... Welsh Grand Lodge of Wales [*Freemasonry*]
WGLX ...... Galion, OH [*AM radio station call letters*]
WGLY .... Waterbury, VT [*FM radio station call letters*]

WGLZ .... West Liberty, WV [*FM radio station call letters*]
WGM......... Waveguide Meter
WGM......... Weighted Guidelines Method [*Navy*]
WGM......... World Gospel Mission (EA)
WGM......... Worthy Grand Marshal [*or Master*] [*Freemasonry*]
WGMA...... Spindale, NC [*AM radio station call letters*]
WGMA...... Washington Gallery of Modern Art
WGMA...... West Gulf Maritime Association (EA)
WGMA...... Wet Ground Mica Association [*Inactive*] (EA)
WGMA...... Work Glove Manufacturers Association (EA)
WGMA...... Working Group on Multilateral Assistance [*Department of the Treasury*]
WGMB...... Baton Rouge, LA [*Television station call letters*]
WGMC...... Greece, NY [*FM radio station call letters*]
WGMC...... West Germanic [*Language, etc.*]
WGMD...... Rehoboth Beach, DE [*FM radio station call letters*]
WGME-TV ... Portland, ME [*Television station call letters*]
WGMF ...... Watkins Glen, NY [*AM radio station call letters*]
WGMG...... Crawford, GA [*FM radio station call letters*]
WGMK...... Donalsonville, GA [*FM radio station call letters*]
WGML...... Hinesville, GA [*AM radio station call letters*]
WGMM...... Big Flats, NY [*FM radio station call letters*]
WGMO...... Shell Lake, WI [*FM radio station call letters*]
WGMR...... Tyrone, PA [*FM radio station call letters*]
WGMS..... Bethesda, MD [*AM radio station call letters*]
WGMS..... Washington, DC [*FM radio station call letters*]
WGMS..... World Glacier Monitoring Service [*of the International Union of Geodesy and Geophysics*] (EA)
WGMT..... Lyndon, VT [*FM radio station call letters*]
WGMX..... Marathon, FL [*FM radio station call letters*]
WGMZ..... Tuscola, MI [*FM radio station call letters*]
WGN .... Chicago, IL [*AM radio station call letters*]
WGN .... Wagon
WGN .... World's Greatest Newspaper [*Sometimes used in reference to Chicago Tribune*]
WGNA...... Albany, NY [*AM radio station call letters*]
WGNA-FM ... Albany, NY [*FM radio station call letters*]
WGNB...... Zeeland, MI [*FM radio station call letters*]
WGNC...... Gastonia, NC [*AM radio station call letters*]
WGNE...... Panama City, FL [*AM radio station call letters*]
WGNE...... Titusville, FL [*FM radio station call letters*]
WGNG...... Western Gold 'n Gas Co. [*NASDAQ symbol*] (NQ)
WGNI....... Wilmington, NC [*FM radio station call letters*]
WGNJ .... Alberta, VA [*FM radio station call letters*]
WGNL....... Greenwood, MS [*FM radio station call letters*]
WGNL....... Waveguide Nitrogen Load
WGNM...... Macon, GA [*Television station call letters*]
WGNO...... New Orleans, LA [*Television station call letters*]
WGNP...... Albany, GA [*FM radio station call letters*]
WGNR...... Grand Rapids, MI [*FM radio station call letters*]
WGNR...... Wegener Corp. [*NASDAQ symbol*] (NQ)
WGNRR.... Women's Global Network on Reproductive Rights [*Formerly, International Contraception, Abortion, and Sterilisation Campaign*] (EA)
WGNS....... Murfreesboro, TN [*AM radio station call letters*]
WGNT....... Portsmouth, VA [*Television station call letters*]
WGN-TV... Chicago, IL [*Television station call letters*]
WGNU ...... Granite City, IL [*AM radio station call letters*]
WGNV...... Milladore, WI [*FM radio station call letters*]
WGNX...... Atlanta, GA [*Television station call letters*]
WGNY....... Newburgh, NY [*AM radio station call letters*]
WGNY-FM ... Newburgh, NY [*FM radio station call letters*]
WGO .... Wehrmacht Graeberoffizier [*Armed forces graves registration officer*] [*German military - World War II*]
Wg O......... Wing Officer [*British military*] (DMA)
WGO .... Winnebago Industries, Inc. [*NYSE symbol*] (SPSG)
WGOC...... Kingsport, TN [*AM radio station call letters*]
WGOC....... World Government Organization Coalition (EAIO)
WGOCC.... World Government Organization Coordinating Council [*Later, WGOC*]
WGOD ...... Charlotte Amalie, VI [*FM radio station call letters*]
Wg Offr...... Wing Officer [*British military*] (DMA)
WGOG ...... Walhalla, SC [*AM radio station call letters*]
WGOG-FM ... Walhalla, SC [*FM radio station call letters*]
WGOH ...... Grayson, KY [*AM radio station call letters*]
WGOJ .... Conneaut, OH [*FM radio station call letters*]
WGOK...... Mobile, AL [*AM radio station call letters*]
WGOL...... Lynchburg, VA [*FM radio station call letters*]
WGOM ..... Marion, IN [*AM radio station call letters*]
WGOS....... High Point, NC [*AM radio station call letters*]
WGOT....... Merrimack, NH [*Television station call letters*]
WGOT....... Williams Grove Old Timers [*An association*] (EA)
WGOV....... Valdosta, GA [*AM radio station call letters*]
WGOW...... Chattanooga, TN [*AM radio station call letters*]
WGOX...... Inverness, FL [*Television station call letters*]
WGP .... Waingapu [*Indonesia*] [*Airport symbol*] (OAG)
WGP .... Wattle Grove Press
WGp.......... Weather Group [*Air Force*] (AFM)
WGP .... Western Gas Processors [*NYSE symbol*] (SPSG)
WGP .... Westgrowth Petroleums Ltd. [*Toronto Stock Exchange symbol*]
WGP .... Wire Grid Polarizer

WGPA ...... Bethlehem, PA [*AM radio station call letters*]
WGPC .... Albany, GA [*AM radio station call letters*]
WGPC-FM ... Albany, GA [*FM radio station call letters*]
WGPH ...... Vidalia, GA [*FM radio station call letters*]
WGPMS.... Warehousing Gross Performance Measurement System (AFM)
WGPR ...... Detroit, MI [*FM radio station call letters*]
WGPR-TV ... Detroit, MI [*Television station call letters*]
WGPT ...... Oakland, MD [*Television station call letters*]
WGPTDR ... Danube Tourist Commission [*Formerly, Working Group for the Promotion of Tourism in the Danube Region*] [*Austria*] (EAIO)
WGQR...... Elizabethtown, NC [*FM radio station call letters*]
WGr .... Brown County Library, Green Bay, WI [*Library symbol*] [*Library of Congress*] (LCLS)
WGR......... Buffalo, NY [*AM radio station call letters*]
WGR......... War Guidance Requirements (AFM)
WGR......... Water Graphite Reactor Experiment [*Nuclear energy*]
WGR......... Westbridge Resources Ltd. [*Vancouver Stock Exchange symbol*]
WGR......... Western Gas Resources [*NYSE symbol*] (SPSG)
WGR......... Women in Government Relations (EA)
WGR......... Working Group Report
WGRA....... Cairo, GA [*AM radio station call letters*]
WGRA....... Worksheet Global Recalculation Automatic [*Data processing*]
WGrB .... Bellin Memorial Hospital, Green Bay, WI [*Library symbol*] [*Library of Congress*] (LCLS)
WGRB ...... Campbellsville, KY [*Television station call letters*]
WGrBC...... Brown County Hospital, Green Bay, WI [*Library symbol*] [*Library of Congress*] (LCLS)
WGRC ...... Lewisburg, PA [*FM radio station call letters*]
WGRD...... Grand Rapids, MI [*AM radio station call letters*]
WGRD-FM ... Grand Rapids, MI [*FM radio station call letters*]
WGRE .... Greencastle, IN [*FM radio station call letters*]
WGREPO ... Western Governors Regional Energy Policy Office
WGR-FM .. Buffalo, NY [*FM radio station call letters*]
WGRIDA .. World GRID Association (EA)
WGRK...... Greensburg, KY [*FM radio station call letters*]
WGRM...... Greenwood, MS [*AM radio station call letters*]
WGRM-FM ... Greenwood, MS [*FM radio station call letters*]
WGRN...... Greenville, IL [*FM radio station call letters*]
WGrN........ Northeastern Wisconsin Technical Institute, Green Bay, WI [*Library symbol*] [*Library of Congress*] (LCLS)
WGrNM .... Neville Public Museum, Green Bay, WI [*Library symbol*] [*Library of Congress*] (LCLS)
WGRO...... Lake City, FL [*AM radio station call letters*]
WGRP ...... Greenville, PA [*AM radio station call letters*]
WGRQ...... Colonial Beach, VA [*FM radio station call letters*]
WGRR ...... Hamilton, OH [*FM radio station call letters*]
WGRS ...... Guilford, CT [*FM radio station call letters*]
WGrSM..... Saint Mary's Hospital, Green Bay, WI [*Library symbol*] [*Library of Congress*] (LCLS)
WGrSV ...... Saint Vincent Hospital, Green Bay, WI [*Library symbol*] [*Library of Congress*] (LCLS)
WGrU .... University of Wisconsin-Green Bay, Green Bay, WI [*Library symbol*] [*Library of Congress*] (LCLS)
WGRV ...... Greeneville, TN [*AM radio station call letters*]
WGRX ...... Westminster, MD [*FM radio station call letters*]
WGRY .... Grayling, MI [*AM radio station call letters*]
WGRY-FM ... Roscommon, MI [*FM radio station call letters*]
WGRZ....... Buffalo, NY [*Television station call letters*]
WG(S)........ Waste Gas (System) [*Nuclear energy*] (NRCH)
WGS .... Water Gas Shift [*Chemical reaction*]
WGS .... Water Glycol Service Unit (MCD)
WGS .... Waterford Generating Station [*Nuclear energy*] (NRCH)
WGS......... Waveguide Glide Slope
WGS......... Web Guide System
WGS......... Work Group System [*Computer hardware*] (PCM)
WGS......... World Geodetic System (MUGU)
WGS......... World Government Sponsors
WGS .... Worthy Grand Sentinel [*Freemasonry*]
WGSA ...... Ephrata, PA [*AM radio station call letters*]
WGSB ...... Mebane, NC [*AM radio station call letters*]
WGSC....... War Gaming and Simulation Center [*National Defense University*]
WGSC....... Wide Gap Spark Chamber [*Electronics*] (OA)
WGSE....... Myrtle Beach, SC [*Television station call letters*]
WGSF....... Arlington, TN [*AM radio station call letters*]
WGSG ...... Mayo, FL [*FM radio station call letters*]
WGSI........ Russell, PA [*FM radio station call letters*]
WGSIM .... Working Group on Satellite Ionospheric Measurements [*NASA*]
WGSJ .... Worm Gear Screw Jack
WGSK .... South Kent, CT [*FM radio station call letters*]
WGSL .... Loves Park, IL [*FM radio station call letters*]
WGSM ...... Huntington, NY [*AM radio station call letters*]
WGSN ...... North Myrtle Beach, SC [*AM radio station call letters*]
WGSP....... Charlotte, NC [*AM radio station call letters*]
WGSPR..... Working Group for Space Physics Research
WGSQ .... Cookeville, TN [*FM radio station call letters*]
WGST....... Atlanta, GA [*AM radio station call letters*]
WGST....... Waste Gas Storage Tank [*Nuclear energy*] (IEEE)
WGSU .... Geneseo, NY [*FM radio station call letters*]

WGSV .... Guntersville, AL [*AM radio station call letters*]
WGSW ...... Greenwood, SC [*AM radio station call letters*]
WGSX ...... Bayamon, PR [*FM radio station call letters*]
WGSY .... Phenix City, AL [*FM radio station call letters*]
WGT .... Water-Glycol Cooling Unit Technician   (SAA)
WGT .... Wayne General and Technical College, Orrville, OH [*OCLC symbol*] [*Inactive*]   (OCLC)
WGT .... Weapons Guidance and Tracking   (SAA)
WGT .... Weight [*Shipping*]   (DS)
WGTA .... Summerville, GA [*AM radio station call letters*]
WGTA .... Wisconsin General Test Apparatus [*Psychology*]
WGTC .... New Carlisle, IN [*FM radio station call letters*]
WG-T-C... Waveguide-to-Coaxial [*Aerospace*]   (AAG)
WGTC .... Working Group on Tracking and Computation [*NASA*]
WGT/COMB ... Weighter/Combiner   (MCD)
WGTD .... Kenosha, WI [*FM radio station call letters*]
WGTE .... Toledo, OH [*FM radio station call letters*]
WGTE-TV ... Toledo, OH [*Television station call letters*]
WGTF........ Dothan, AL [*FM radio station call letters*]
WGTH....... Richlands, VA [*FM radio station call letters*]
WGTJ........ Greenville, NC [*Television station call letters*]
WGTK .... Middlebury, VT [*FM radio station call letters*]
WGTL .... Kannapolis, NC [*AM radio station call letters*]
WGTM....... Wilson, NC [*AM radio station call letters*]
WGTN .... Andrews, SC [*FM radio station call letters*]
WGTN .... Georgetown, SC [*AM radio station call letters*]
WGTO .... Pine Hills, FL [*AM radio station call letters*]
WGTQ .... Sault Ste. Marie, MI [*Television station call letters*]
WGTR .... Gallipolis, OH [*FM radio station call letters*]
WGTS........ Takoma Park, MD [*FM radio station call letters*]
WGTT .... Alabaster, AL [*AM radio station call letters*]
WGTU .... Traverse City, MI [*Television station call letters*]
WGTV .... Athens, GA [*Television station call letters*]
WGTW ...... Burlington, NJ [*Television station call letters*]
WGTX .... De Funiak Springs, FL [*AM radio station call letters*]
WGTY .... Gettysburg, PA [*FM radio station call letters*]
WGTZ .... Eaton, OH [*FM radio station call letters*]
WGU.......... Working Group on Untouchables   (EA)
WGUC....... Cincinnati, OH [*FM radio station call letters*]
WGUD....... Moss Point, MS [*AM radio station call letters*]
WGUD....... Pascagoula-Moss Point, MS [*FM radio station call letters*]
WGUF .... Marco, FL [*FM radio station call letters*]
WGUL .... Dunedin, FL [*AM radio station call letters*]
WGUL .... New Port Richey, FL [*FM radio station call letters*]
WGUN ...... Atlanta, GA [*AM radio station call letters*]
WGUS .... Augusta, GA [*FM radio station call letters*]
WGUS .... North Augusta, SC [*AM radio station call letters*]
WGUSEASA ... Working Group of US Overseas Educational Advisers in South America   (EA)
WGVA .... Geneva, NY [*AM radio station call letters*]
WGVE .... Gary, IN [*FM radio station call letters*]
WGVK .... Kalamazoo, MI [*Television station call letters*]
WGVM...... Greenville, MS [*AM radio station call letters*]
WGVU....... Allendale, MI [*FM radio station call letters*]
WGVU....... Grand Rapids, MI [*Television station call letters*]
WGW......... Wallila Gap [*Washington*] [*Seismograph station code, US Geological Survey*]   (SEIS)
WGW......... Waveguide Window
WGW......... Wedgewood Resources [*Vancouver Stock Exchange symbol*]
WGW......... Wheat Gluten World [*A publication*]   (EAAP)
WGWC...... Working Group on Weather Communications [*NATO*]   (NATG)
WGWC...... World Service Authority of the World Government of World Citizens   (EAIO)
WGWD...... Gretna, FL [*FM radio station call letters*]
WGWG...... Boiling Springs, NC [*FM radio station call letters*]
WGWP...... Working Group on Weather Plans [*NATO*]   (NATG)
WGXA .... Macon, GA [*Television station call letters*]
WGXM...... Dayton, OH [*FM radio station call letters*]
WGY .... Schenectady, NY [*AM radio station call letters*]
WGY-FM .. Schenectady, NY [*FM radio station call letters*]
WGYJ........ Atmore, AL [*AM radio station call letters*]
WGYL .... Vero Beach, FL [*FM radio station call letters*]
WGYV ...... Greenville, AL [*AM radio station call letters*]
WGZB .... Corydon, IN [*FM radio station call letters*]
WGZS........ Dothan, AL [*AM radio station call letters*]
WH .... City-Flug GmbH [*West Germany*] [*ICAO designator*]   (FAAC)
WH .... Henry Wriothesley, Earl of Southampton; or Sir William Harvey; or William Hathaway; or William Herbert, Earl of Pembroke [*Possible identities of the W. H. to whom Shakespeare's sonnets were supposedly dedicated by publisher Thomas Thorpe in 1609*]
Wh .... Interrogative [*Linguistics*]
WH .... Wage and Hour Cases [*Bureau of National Affairs*] [*A publication*]   (DLA)
W & H........ Wage and Hour Division [*Department of Labor*]   (OICC)
WH .... Wald und Holz [*A publication*]
WH .... Walking Hinge   (KSC)
WH .... Wall Hung [*Technical drawings*]
WH .... Wall Hydrant   (AAG)
W-H........... Walsh-Healey Act [*Labor*]

WH .... Warhead
W/H........... Warheading Building   (NATG)
WH .... Water Heater
WH .... Watt-Hour
WH .... We Have, Ready with Called Party [*Telecommunications*]   (TEL)
WH .... Wehrmacht-Heer [*Marking on Army vehicles*] [*German military - World War II*]
WH .... Well Healed [*Medicine*]   (AAMN)
WH .... Welsh Horse [*British military*]   (DMA)
WH .... Western Hemisphere
WH .... Western Hemlock [*Utility pole*] [*Telecommunications*]   (TEL)
WH .... Wharf
Wh .... Wharton's Pennsylvania Supreme Court Reports [*1835-41*] [*A publication*]   (DLA)
Wh .... Wheaton's International Law [*A publication*]   (DLA)
Wh .... Wheaton's Reports [*14-25 United States*] [*A publication*]   (DLA)
Wh .... Wheeler's New York Criminal Reports [*3 vols.*] [*A publication*]   (DLA)
WH .... Wheelhouse   (MSA)
WH .... Where   (AABC)
WH .... Which
Wh .... While   (AIA)
WH .... Whispered   (ADA)
WH .... White [*Thoroughbred racing*]
WH .... White
WH .... White Hornet [*Immunology*]
WH .... White House
WH .... Whitman Co. [*NYSE symbol*]   (SPSG)
WH .... Who
WH .... Whore   (DSUE)
WH .... Wildwood House [*Publisher*] [*British*]
WH .... William Heinemann [*Publisher*] [*British*]
WH .... Wings of Hope [*An association*]   (EA)
WH .... Withholding   (AFM)
WH .... Work Hour   (KSC)
WH .... Workable Hatch [*Shipping*]   (DS)
WH2 .... Whipple Mountains Number 2 [*California*] [*Seismograph station code, US Geological Survey*]   (SEIS)
WHA .... Madison, WI [*AM radio station call letters*]
WHA .... W. H. Allen [*Commercial firm*] [*British*]
WHA .... Wahaula [*Hawaii*] [*Seismograph station code, US Geological Survey*]   (SEIS)
WHA .... Walkaloosa Horse Association   (EA)
WHA .... Washington Headquarters Association   (EA)
WHA .... Weld Head Assembly
WHA .... Western Hardwood Association   (EA)
WHA .... Western History Association   (EA)
WHA .... Wood Heating Alliance   (EA)
WHA .... World Hockey Association
WHA .... Wounded by Hostile Action
WHAA...... Madison, ME [*FM radio station call letters*]
WHAB....... Acton, MA [*FM radio station call letters*]
WHAB....... Westminster Historical Atlas to the Bible [*A publication*]   (BJA)
WHAC....... World Hemophilia AIDS [*Acquired Immune Deficiency Syndrome*] Center   (EA)
WHACK... Warhead Attack Cruise Killer   (MCD)
WHAD....... Delafield, WI [*FM radio station call letters*]
WHAG....... Hagerstown, MD [*Television station call letters*]
WHAG ...... Halfway, MD [*AM radio station call letters*]
WHAI....... Bridgeport, CT [*Television station call letters*]
WHAI....... Greenfield, MA [*AM radio station call letters*]
WHAI....... Walter Hinchman Associates, Inc. [*Telecommunications*] [*Defunct*]   (TSSD)
WHAI-FM ... Greenfield, MA [*FM radio station call letters*]
WHAJ....... Bluefield, WV [*FM radio station call letters*]
WHAK....... Rogers City, MI [*AM radio station call letters*]
WHAL....... Shelbyville, TN [*AM radio station call letters*]
WHAL....... Wellington Hall Ltd. [*NASDAQ symbol*]   (NQ)
WHAM .... Rochester, NY [*AM radio station call letters*]
WHAM .... Water Hammer
WHAM .... Wayne Horizontal Acceleration Mechanism
WHAM .... Winning the Hearts and Minds [*of the people*] [*Vietnam pacification program*]
WHAM .... Work Handling and Maintenance [*Navy*]   (NG)
WHAN ...... Wellness and Health Activation Networks   (EA)
WHAP....... Hopewell, VA [*AM radio station call letters*]
WHAP....... When [*or Where*] Applicable
WHAP....... Women's Health and Abortion Project   (EA)
WHAR....... Clarksburg, WV [*AM radio station call letters*]
Whar......... Wharton's Pennsylvania Supreme Court Reports [*1835-41*] [*A publication*]   (DLA)
WHAR...... Whereafter [*Legal*] [*British*]   (ROG)
WHAR...... Wild Horses of America Registry   (EA)
Whar Ag .... Wharton on Agency [*A publication*]   (DLA)
Whar Am Cr L ... Wharton's American Criminal Law [*A publication*]   (DLA)
Whar Confl Law ... Wharton's Conflict of Laws [*A publication*]   (DLA)
Whar Con Law ... Wharton's Conflict of Laws [*A publication*]   (DLA)
Whar Conv ... Wharton on Principles of Conveyancing [*1851*] [*A publication*]   (DLA)

Whar Cr Ev ... Wharton on Criminal Evidence [*A publication*] (DLA)
Whar Cri Pl ... Wharton's Criminal Pleading and Practice [*A publication*] (DLA)
Whar Cr Law ... Wharton's American Criminal Law [*A publication*] (DLA)
Whar Cr Pl ... Wharton's Criminal Pleading and Practice [*A publication*] (DLA)
Whar Dig ... Wharton's Pennsylvania Digest [*A publication*] (DLA)
Whar Dom ... Wharton on the Law of Domicile [*A publication*] (DLA)
Whar Ev ..... Wharton on Evidence in Civil Issues [*A publication*] (DLA)
Whar Hom ... Wharton's Law of Homicide [*A publication*] (DLA)
Whar Ind ... Wharton's Precedents of Indictments and Pleas [*A publication*] (DLA)
Whar Innk ... Wharton on Innkeepers [*1876*] [*A publication*] (DLA)
Whar Law Dic ... Wharton's Law Lexicon [*14th ed.*] [*1938*] [*A publication*] (DLA)
Whar Leg Max ... Wharton's Legal Maxims [*3rd ed.*] [*1903*] [*A publication*] (DLA)
Whar Neg .. Wharton's Law of Negligence [*A publication*] (DLA)
Whar Prec Ind ... Wharton's Precedents of Indictments and Pleas [*A publication*] (DLA)
Whar & St Med Jur ... Wharton and Stille's Medical Jurisprudence [*A publication*] (DLA)
Whar St Tr ... Wharton's United States State Trials [*A publication*] (DLA)
Whart......... Legal Maxims with Observations by George Frederick Wharton [*A publication*] (DLA)
Whart......... Wharton's Pennsylvania Supreme Court Reports [*1835-41*] [*A publication*] (DLA)
Whart Ag ... Wharton on Agency [*A publication*] (DLA)
Whart Am Cr Law ... Wharton's American Criminal Law [*A publication*] (DLA)
Whart Confl Laws ... Wharton's Conflict of Laws [*A publication*] (DLA)
Whart Cr Ev ... Wharton on Criminal Evidence [*A publication*] (DLA)
Whart Crim Law ... Wharton's American Criminal Law [*A publication*] (DLA)
Whart Cr Law ... Wharton's American Criminal Law [*A publication*] (DLA)
Whart Cr Pl & Prac ... Wharton's Criminal Pleading and Practice [*A publication*] (DLA)
Whart Ev ... Wharton on Evidence in Civil Issues [*A publication*] (DLA)
Whart Hom ... Wharton's Law of Homicide [*A publication*] (DLA)
Whart Homicide ... Wharton's Law of Homicide [*A publication*] (DLA)
Whart Law Dict ... Wharton's Law Dictionary [*or Lexicon*] [*A publication*] (DLA)
Whart Law Lexicon ... Wharton's Law Lexicon [*A publication*] (DLA)
Whart Lex ... Wharton's Law Lexicon [*A publication*] (DLA)
Whartn Ann ... Wharton Annual [*A publication*]
Whart Neg ... Wharton on Negligence [*A publication*] (DLA)
Whartn Mag ... Wharton Magazine [*A publication*]
Wharton..... Wharton Magazine [*A publication*]
Wharton..... Wharton's American Criminal Law [*A publication*] (DLA)
Wharton..... Wharton's Law Lexicon [*A publication*] (DLA)
Wharton..... Wharton's Pennsylvania Supreme Court Reports [*1835-41*] [*A publication*] (DLA)
Wharton Crim Evidence ... Wharton's Criminal Evidence [*A publication*] (DLA)
Wharton Crim Proc ... Wharton's Criminal Law and Procedure [*A publication*] (DLA)
Wharton M ... Wharton Magazine [*A publication*]
Wharton Mag ... Wharton Magazine [*A publication*]
Wharton Q ... Wharton Quarterly [*A publication*]
Whart PA .. Wharton's Pennsylvania Supreme Court Reports [*1835-41*] [*A publication*] (DLA)
Whart & S Med Jur ... Wharton and Stille's Medical Jurisprudence [*A publication*] (DLA)
Whart State Tr ... Wharton's United States State Trials [*A publication*] (DLA)
Whart St Tr ... Wharton's United States State Trials [*A publication*] (DLA)
WHAS....... Louisville, KY [*AM radio station call letters*]
WHAS....... Whereas
WHASA ... White House Army Signal Agency
WHAS-TV ... Louisville, KY [*Television station call letters*]
WHAT....... Philadelphia, PA [*AM radio station call letters*]
WHAT....... What's Here and There [*Australia*] [*A publication*]
WHAT....... Winds, Heights, and Temperatures
Whats New ... What's New in Advertising and Marketing [*A publication*]
Whats New Bldg ... What's New in Building [*A publication*]
What's New Comput ... What's New in Computing [*A publication*]
Whats New in For Res ... What's New in Forest Research [*A publication*]
Whats New Home Econ ... What's New in Home Economics [*A publication*]
Whats New Plant Physiol ... What's New in Plant Physiology [*A publication*]
WHATSR ... Whatsoever
WHA-TV ... Madison, WI [*Television station call letters*]
WHAV....... Haverhill, MA [*AM radio station call letters*]
WHAV....... When Available (KSC)
WHAW....... Weston, WV [*AM radio station call letters*]
WHAY....... Whitley City, KY [*FM radio station call letters*]
WHAZ....... Troy, NY [*AM radio station call letters*]
WHB.......... Kansas City, MO [*AM radio station call letters*]
WHB.......... [*The*] Wandering Hand Brigade [*Men who are likely to take liberties with women*]
WHB.......... Waste Heat Boiler [*Nuclear energy*] (CAAL)
WHB.......... Wheel Bumpers [*Technical drawings*]

WHB.......... Which? [*A publication*]
WHB.......... Wiener Humanistische Blaetter [*A publication*]
WHB.......... Wire Harness Board (MCD)
WHBB....... Selma, AL [*AM radio station call letters*]
WHBC....... Canton, OH [*AM radio station call letters*]
WHBC-FM ... Canton, OH [*FM radio station call letters*]
WHBF....... Rock Island, IL [*Television station call letters*]
WHBFC..... Wayne Hann Band Fan Club (EA)
WHBG....... Harrisonburg, VA [*AM radio station call letters*]
WHBI....... Lake Worth, FL [*Television station call letters*]
WHBK....... Marshall, NC [*AM radio station call letters*]
WHBL....... Sheboygan, WI [*AM radio station call letters*]
WH Bl....... Wiener Humanistische Blaetter [*A publication*]
WHBL....... World Home Bible League [*Later, BL*] (EA)
WHBM...... Park Falls, WI [*FM radio station call letters*]
WHBMA... Wood Hat Block Manufacturers Association (EA)
WHBN....... Harrodsburg, KY [*AM radio station call letters*]
WHBN-FM ... Harrodsburg, KY [*FM radio station call letters*]
WHBQ....... Memphis, TN [*AM radio station call letters*]
WHBQ-TV ... Memphis, TN [*Television station call letters*]
WHBR....... Pensacola, FL [*Television station call letters*]
WHBS...... Waste Heat Boiler Survey (DS)
WHBT....... Tallahassee, FL
WHBU....... Anderson, IN [*AM radio station call letters*]
WHBY....... Appleton, WI [*AM radio station call letters*]
WHBY....... Whereby
WHC.......... Wages for Housework Committee (EA)
WHC.......... Washington Hospital Center, Washington, DC [*OCLC symbol*] (OCLC)
WHC.......... Water Holding Capacity [*Also, WBC*] [*Food industry*]
WHC.......... Watt-Hour Meter with Contact Device
WHC.......... Westinghouse Hanford Co. (NRCH)
WHC.......... White House Conference
WHC.......... Whitehorse [*Yukon Territory*] [*Seismograph station code, US Geological Survey*] (SEIS)
WHC.......... Winchester Capital [*Vancouver Stock Exchange symbol*]
WHC.......... World Hereford Council (EAIO)
WHC.......... World Heritage Committee [*See also CPM*] (EAIO)
WHCA....... War Hazards Compensation Act
WHCA....... White House Communications Agency (AABC)
WHCA....... White House Correspondents' Association (EA)
WHCA....... World Hobie Class Association [*Later, IHCA*] (EA)
WH Cas ..... Wage and Hour Cases [*Bureau of National Affairs*] [*A publication*] (DLA)
WHCB....... Bristol, TN [*FM radio station call letters*]
WHCC....... Waynesville, NC [*AM radio station call letters*]
WHCCY ... White House Conference on Children and Youth (EA)
WHCDHP ... Wainwright House Center for Development of Human Potential [*Later, WH*] (EA)
WHCDHR ... Wainwright House Center for Development of Human Resources [*Later, WH*] (EA)
WHCE....... Highland Springs, VA [*FM radio station call letters*]
WHCF....... Bangor, ME [*FM radio station call letters*]
WHCF....... White House Conference on Families [*June 5-July 3, 1980*] (EGAO)
WHcGS ..... Church of Jesus Christ of Latter-Day Saints, Genealogical Society Library, Milwaukee Branch, Hales Corners, WI [*Library symbol*] [*Library of Congress*] (LCLS)
WH Chron ... Westminster Hall Chronicle and Legal Examiner [*1835-36*] [*A publication*] (DLA)
WHCJ....... Savannah, GA [*FM radio station call letters*]
WHCL....... Clinton, NY [*FM radio station call letters*]
WHCLIS ... White House Conference on Library and Information Services [*Washington, DC, 1979*]
WHCLIST ... White House Conference on Library and Information Services Taskforce
WHCM...... Parkersburg, WV [*FM radio station call letters*]
WHCN ...... Hartford, CT [*FM radio station call letters*]
WHCO ...... Sparta, IL [*AM radio station call letters*]
WHCO ...... Wheeled Coach Industries [*NASDAQ symbol*] (NQ)
WHCOA.... White House Conference on Aging
WHCOLIS ... White House Conference on Library and Information Services
WHCR ...... New York, NY [*FM radio station call letters*]
Wh Cr Cas ... Wheeler's New York Criminal Cases [*3 vols.*] [*A publication*] (DLA)
Wh Crim Cas ... Wheeler's New York Criminal Cases [*A publication*] (DLA)
WHcS .... Sacred Heart School of Theology, Hales Corners, WI [*Library symbol*] [*Library of Congress*] (LCLS)
WHCS .... Well History Control System [*Later, Historical Well Data On-Line*] [*Petroleum Information Corp.*] [*Information service or system*] (IID)
WHCSA .... Welsh Health Common Services Authority
WHCT....... Hartford, CT [*Television station call letters*]
WHCU ...... Ithaca, NY [*AM radio station call letters*]
WHCU ...... Window Heat Control Unit
WHD .... Wage and Hour Division [*Department of Labor*]
WHD .... Warhead
WHD .... Western Hemisphere Defense
WHD .... Wheeler Dam [*TVA*]
WHD .... Wirlwind Resources Ltd. [*Vancouver Stock Exchange symbol*]
WHD .... Write Head Driver (SAA)

WHDB....... Woods Hole Database, Inc. [*Information service or system*] (IID)
W-HDCS... Wyeth Laboratories - Human Diploid Cell Strain [*Rabies vaccine*]
WHDH...... Boston, MA [*AM radio station call letters*]
WHDH-TV ... Boston, MA [*Television station call letters*]
WHDL....... Olean, NY [*AM radio station call letters*]
WHDM ..... McKenzie, TN [*AM radio station call letters*]
WHDM ..... Watt-Hour Demand Meter
WHDQ ...... Claremont, NH [*FM radio station call letters*]
WHDS....... Warhead Section [*Military*] (AABC)
WHE......... Water Hammer Eliminator
WHE......... Wheaton College, Norton, MA [*OCLC symbol*] (OCLC)
WHE......... Whole Human Embryo [*Type of cell line*]
Wheat .... Wheaton's Reports [*14-25 United States*] [*A publication*] (DLA)
Wheat Board Gaz ... Wheat Board Gazette [*A publication*]
Wheat Cap ... Wheaton on Maritime Captures and Prizes [*A publication*] (DLA)
Wheat El Int Law ... Wheaton's Elements of International Law [*A publication*] (DLA)
WHEATH ... Wheathampstead [*England*]
Wheat Hist Law Nat ... Wheaton's History of the Law of Nations [*A publication*] (DLA)
Wheat Inform Serv ... Wheat Information Service [*A publication*]
Wheat Inf Serv ... Wheat Information Service [*A publication*]
Wheat Int Law ... Wheaton's Elements of International Law [*7th ed.*] [*1944*] [*A publication*] (DLA)
Wheat Int Law ... Wheaton's International Law [*A publication*] (DLA)
Wheat Law of Nat ... Wheaton's History of the Law of Nations [*A publication*] (DLA)
Wheaton .... Wheaton's Reports [*14-25 United States*] [*A publication*] (DLA)
Wheat Situation Bur Agr Econ (Aust) ... Wheat Situation. Bureau of Agricultural Economics (Australia) [*A publication*]
Wheat Stud Food Res Inst ... Wheat Studies. Food Research Institute [*A publication*]
WHEB....... Portsmouth, NH [*FM radio station call letters*]
WHEC....... High-Endurance Coast Guard Cutter [*Formerly, WAPG*] (CINC)
WHEC....... Rochester, NY [*Television station call letters*]
WHEC....... Wildlife Habitat Enhancement Council (EA)
WHECON ... Wheel Control (MCD)
WHEE....... Martinsville, VA [*AM radio station call letters*]
WHEE....... Wheel Extended [*A publication*]
Wheel........ Wheeler's New York Criminal Cases [*A publication*] (DLA)
Wheel........ Wheelock's Reports [*32-37 Texas*] [*A publication*] (DLA)
Wheel Abr ... Wheeler's Abridgment of American Common Law Cases [*A publication*] (DLA)
Wheel Br Cas ... Wheeling Bridge Case [*A publication*] (DLA)
Wheel Cr C ... Wheeler's New York Criminal Cases [*A publication*] (DLA)
Wheel Cr Cas ... Wheeler's New York Criminal Cases [*A publication*] (DLA)
Wheel Cr Ch ... Wheeler's New York Criminal Cases [*A publication*] (DLA)
Wheel Cr Rec ... Wheeler's New York Criminal Recorder [*1 Wheeler's Criminal Cases*] [*A publication*] (DLA)
Wheeler Abr ... Wheeler's Abridgment [*A publication*] (DLA)
Wheeler Am Cr Law ... Wheeler's Abridgment of American Common Law Cases [*A publication*] (DLA)
Wheeler CC ... Wheeler's New York Criminal Cases [*A publication*] (DLA)
Wheeler Cr Cas ... Wheeler's New York Criminal Cases [*A publication*] (DLA)
Wheeler Cr Cases ... Wheeler's New York Criminal Cases [*A publication*] (DLA)
Wheeler Crim Cas ... Wheeler's New York Criminal Cases [*A publication*] (DLA)
Wheeler's Cr Cases ... Wheeler's New York Criminal Cases [*A publication*] (DLA)
Wheel Ext ... Wheel Extended [*A publication*]
Wheel Slav ... Wheeler on Slavery [*A publication*] (DLA)
Wheel (Tex) ... Wheelock's Reports [*32-37 Texas*] [*A publication*] (DLA)
WHEI....... Tiffin, OH [*FM radio station call letters*]
WHEL....... Roadmaster Industries, Inc. [*NASDAQ symbol*] (NQ)
WHEN....... Syracuse, NY [*AM radio station call letters*]
WHENCESR ... Whencesoever [*Legal*] [*British*] (ROG)
WHENR.... Whenever [*Legal*] [*British*] (ROG)
WHENSR ... Whensoever [*Legal*] [*British*] (ROG)
WHEO ...... Stuart, VA [*AM radio station call letters*]
WHEP ...... Foley, AL [*AM radio station call letters*]
WHEP .... Warhead Engagement Program [*Military*]
WHER....... Hattiesburg, MS [*FM radio station call letters*]
WHER....... Whether [*Legal*] [*British*] (ROG)
Where to Find Out More about Educ ... Where to Find Out More about Education [*A publication*]
WHERER ... Wherever [*Legal*] [*British*] (ROG)
WHERF .... Wood Heating Education and Research Foundation (EA)
WHES ...... World Hunger Education Service (EA)
WHET ...... Sturgeon Bay, WI [*FM radio station call letters*]
Whet......... Whetstone [*A publication*]
WHETS..... Washington Higher Education Telecommunications System [*Washington State University*] [*Pullman*] [*Telecommunications service*] (TSSD)

WHEV...... Garner, NC [*AM radio station call letters*]
WHEW...... Fort Myers, FL [*FM radio station call letters*]
WHEY ...... Harlem, GA [*FM radio station call letters*]
WHEZ ...... Portage, MI [*AM radio station call letters*]
WHF......... Waveguide Harmonic Filter
WHF......... Wharf
WHF......... Women in Housing and Finance (EA)
WHF......... Women's Hall of Fame [*Later, NWHF*] (EA)
WHF......... World Heritage Fund [*UNESCO*]
WHFA....... Western Hemisphere Friendship Association (EA)
WHFB....... Benton Harbor, MI [*AM radio station call letters*]
WHFB-FM ... Benton Harbor, MI [*FM radio station call letters*]
WHFC....... Bel Air, MD [*FM radio station call letters*]
WHFD....... Lawrenceville, VA [*FM radio station call letters*]
WHFE....... Lakeland, GA [*FM radio station call letters*]
WHFG....... Wharfage [*Shipping*]
WHFH...... Flossmoor, IL [*FM radio station call letters*]
WHFI....... Lindside, WV [*FM radio station call letters*]
WHFM...... Southampton, NY [*FM radio station call letters*]
WHFM...... Wherefrom [*Legal*] [*British*] (ROG)
WHFMS.... Woman's Home and Foreign Mission Society (EA)
WHFORE ... Wherefore [*Legal*] [*British*] (ROG)
WHFR....... Dearborn, MI [*FM radio station call letters*]
WHFR ...... Wharfinger [*Shipping*] [*British*] (ROG)
WHFS....... Annapolis, MD [*FM radio station call letters*]
WHFT....... Miami, FL [*Television station call letters*]
WHFTB..... Waste Heat Fire Tube Boiler (DS)
WHFTBS .. Waste Heat Fire Tube Boiler Survey (DS)
WHF-USA ... World Health Foundation, United States of America [*Inactive*] (EA)
WHFX...... Waycross, GA [*FM radio station call letters*]
WHG .... Wasserhaushaltsgesetz [*A publication*]
WH & G ... Welsby, Hurlstone, and Gordon's English Exchequer Reports [*1848-56*] [*A publication*] (DLA)
WHGC...... Bennington, VT [*FM radio station call letters*]
WHGDP.... World Hunger/Global Development Program (EA)
WHGE...... Wharfage [*Shipping*]
WHGG...... Knoxville, TN [*FM radio station call letters*]
WHGH...... Thomasville, GA [*AM radio station call letters*]
WHGL...... Canton, PA [*FM radio station call letters*]
WHGL...... Troy, PA [*AM radio station call letters*]
WHGR...... Houghton Lake, MI [*AM radio station call letters*]
WHH .... Hartford Memorial Hospital, Hartford, WI [*Library symbol*] [*Library of Congress*] (LCLS)
WHH .... Werthamar-Helfand-Hohenberg Theory [*Solid state physics*]
WHH .... William Henry Harrison [*US president, 1773-1841*]
WHHA ...... White House Historical Association (EA)
WHHB ...... Holliston, MA [*FM radio station call letters*]
WHHH...... Indianapolis, IN [*FM radio station call letters*]
WHHI ...... Highland, WI [*FM radio station call letters*]
WHHL...... Watanabe Hereditary Hyperlipidemic [*Rabbits*]
WHHM...... Henderson, TN [*FM radio station call letters*]
WHHO...... Hornell, NY [*AM radio station call letters*]
WHHR ...... Hilton Head Island, SC [*AM radio station call letters*]
WHHS...... Havertown, PA [*FM radio station call letters*]
WHHT ...... Cave City, KY [*FM radio station call letters*]
WHHV ...... Hillsville, VA [*AM radio station call letters*]
WHHY ...... Montgomery, AL [*AM radio station call letters*]
WHHY-FM ... Montgomery, AL [*FM radio station call letters*]
WHi .... State Historical Society of Wisconsin, Madison, WI [*Library symbol*] [*Library of Congress*] (LCLS)
WHI.......... Washington Homes, Inc. [*NYSE symbol*] (SPSG)
WHI.......... Wave Height Indicator [*Oceanography*]
WHI.......... Weekly Hospital Indemnity [*Insurance*]
WHI.......... Western Highway Institute (EA)
WHI.......... Whitney [*Hawaii*] [*Seismograph station code, US Geological Survey*] [*Closed*] (SEIS)
WHI.......... Wild Horse Industry [*Vancouver Stock Exchange symbol*]
WHI.......... Woman Health International (EA)
WHI.......... World Trade Information [*A publication*]
WHIA....... Dawson, GA [*AM radio station call letters*]
WHIA....... Woolen Hosiery Institute of America [*Defunct*] (EA)
WHIC....... Hardinsburg, KY [*AM radio station call letters*]
WHIC....... Women's Health Information Centre [*British*] (CB)
WHIC-FM ... Hardinsburg, KY [*FM radio station call letters*]
Which Comput ... Which Computer? [*A publication*]
Which Word Process ... Which Word Processor? [*A publication*]
Which Word Process and Off Syst ... Which Word Processor and Office System? [*A publication*]
WHIDDA ... Wideband High-Density Data Acquisition (MCD)
WHIE .... Griffin, GA [*AM radio station call letters*]
WHIG........ Ward Howell International Group [*British*]
WHIJ......... Ocala, FL [*FM radio station call letters*]
WHIL .... Mobile, AL [*FM radio station call letters*]
WHIL .... Raeford, NC [*AM radio station call letters*]
WHIM .... Providence, RI [*AM radio station call letters*]
WHIM....... Wet High-Intensity Magnet [*for mineral processing*]
WHIM....... Women Happy in Minis [*Boise, Idaho, group opposing below-the-knee fashions introduced in 1970*]
WHIMSY ... Western Humor and Irony Membership. Serial Yearbook [*Tempe, Arizona*] [*A publication*]

WHIN........ Gallatin, TN [*AM radio station call letters*]
WHIN........ Wherein [*Legal*] [*British*]   (ROG)
WHIO........ Dayton, OH [*AM radio station call letters*]
WHIO-TV .. Dayton, OH [*Television station call letters*]
WHIP........ Mooresville, NC [*AM radio station call letters*]
WHIP........ Walks plus Hits Divided by Innings Pitched [*Baseball*]
WHIP........ Wideband High Intercept Probability
WHIPS...... Widebeam High-Density Pulsed Source   (MCD)
WHIQ....... Huntsville, AL [*Television station call letters*]
WHIR....... Danville, KY [*AM radio station call letters*]
WHIS .... Bluefield, WV [*AM radio station call letters*]
WHIS .... Whiskeytown-Shasta-Trinity National Recreation Area
WHIS .... Whistle [*Navigation*]
Whishaw.... Whishaw's Law Dictionary [*A publication*]   (DLA)
Whish LD.. Whishaw's New Law Dictionary [*1829*] [*A publication*]   (DLA)
WHISP...... Woods Hole In-Situ Pump [*Marine biology*] [*Instrumentation*]
WHIST...... Worldwide Household Goods Information System for Traffic
             Management [*Army*]   (AABC)
W Hist Q ... Western Historical Quarterly [*A publication*]
WHIT .... Madison, WI [*AM radio station call letters*]
WHIT .... Whitman Medical Corp. [*NASDAQ symbol*]   (NQ)
Whitak Liens ... Whitaker on Liens [*A publication*]   (DLA)
WHITCH .. Whitchurch [*England*]
White .... White's Justiciary Court Reports [*3 vols.*] [*Scotland*] [*A
             publication*]   (DLA)
White .... White's Reports [*10-15 West Virginia*] [*A publication*]   (DLA)
White .... White's Reports [*31-44 Texas Appeals*] [*A publication*]   (DLA)
White Char ... Whiteford on Charities [*1878*] [*A publication*]   (DLA)
White & Civ Cas Ct App ... White and Willson's Civil Cases, Texas Court of
             Appeals [*A publication*]   (DLA)
White Coll ... White's New Collection of the Laws, Etc., of Great Britain,
             France, and Spain [*A publication*]   (DLA)
Whitehl...... Whitehall Corp. [*Associated Press abbreviation*]   (APAG)
White LL ... White's Land Law of California [*A publication*]   (DLA)
White Met News Lett ... White Metal News Letter [*A publication*]
White New Coll ... White's New Collection of the Laws; Etc. of Great Britain,
             France, and Spain [*A publication*]   (DLA)
Whit Eq Pr ... Whitworth. Equity Precedents [*A publication*]   (ILCA)
Whit Eq Pr ... Whitworth's Equity Precedents [*A publication*]   (DLA)
White's Ann Pen Code ... White's Annotated Penal Code [*Texas*] [*A
             publication*]   (DLA)
White's Rep ... White's Reports [*10-15 West Virginia*] [*A publication*]   (DLA)
White's Rep ... White's Reports [*31-44 Texas Appeals*] [*A
             publication*]   (DLA)
White Suppl ... White on Supplement and Revivor [*A publication*]   (DLA)
White & TL Cas ... White and Tudor's Leading Cases in Equity [*A
             publication*]   (DLA)
White & T Lead Cas Eq ... White and Tudor's Leading Cases in Equity
             [*England*] [*A publication*]   (DLA)
White & T Lead Cas in Eq (Eng) ... White and Tudor's Leading Cases in
             Equity [*England*] [*A publication*]   (DLA)
White & Tud LC ... White and Tudor's Leading Cases in Equity [*9th ed.*]
             [*1928*] [*A publication*]   (DLA)
White & Tudor ... White and Tudor's Leading Cases in Equity [*A
             publication*]   (DLA)
White & W ... White and Willson's Reports, Civil Cases, Texas Court of
             Appeals [*A publication*]   (DLA)
White & W Civ Cas Ct App ... White and Wilson's [*or Willson's*] Civil Cases,
             Texas Court of Appeals [*A publication*]   (DLA)
White & W Civil Cases Ct App ... Texas Civil Cases [*A publication*]   (DLA)
White & Willson ... Texas Civil Cases [*A publication*]   (DLA)
White W & M ... Whiteley's Weights, Measures, and Weighing Machines
             [*1879*] [*A publication*]   (DLA)
White & W (Tex) ... White and Willson's Reports, Civil Cases, Texas Court of
             Appeals [*A publication*]   (DLA)
Whit Lien... Whitaker's Rights of Lien and Stoppage in Transitu [*1812*] [*A
             publication*]   (DLA)
Whitm Adopt ... Whitemore on Adoption of Children [*A publication*]   (DLA)
Whitman Pat Cas (US) ... Whitman's Patent Cases [*United States*] [*A
             publication*]   (DLA)
Whitm BL ... Whitmarsh's Bankrupt Law [*2nd ed.*] [*1817*] [*A
             publication*]   (DLA)
Whitm Lib Cas ... Whitman's Massachusetts Libel Cases [*A
             publication*]   (DLA)
Whitmn...... Whitman Corp. [*Associated Press abbreviation*]   (APAG)
Whitm Pat Cas ... Whitman's Patent Cases [*United States*] [*A
             publication*]   (DLA)
Whitm Pat Law ... Whitman's Patent Laws of All Countries [*A
             publication*]   (DLA)
Whitm Pat Law Rev ... Whitman's Patent Law Review [*Washington, DC*] [*A
             publication*]   (DLA)
Whitney ..... Whitney's Land Laws [*Tennessee*] [*A publication*]   (DLA)
Whit Pat .... Whitman's Patent Laws of All Countries [*A
             publication*]   (DLA)
Whit Pat Cas ... Whitman's Patent Cases [*United States*] [*A
             publication*]   (DLA)
WHITS...... Whitstone [*England*]
Whit Schol ... Whitgift Scholar [*British*]
Whit St Tr ... Whitaker's Rights of Lien and Stoppage in Transitu [*1812*] [*A
             publication*]   (DLA)
Whitt......... Whittlesey's Reports [*32-41 Missouri*] [*A publication*]   (DLA)

Whittakr .... Whittaker Corp. [*Associated Press abbreviation*]   (APAG)
Whittier L Rev ... Whittier Law Review [*A publication*]
WHITTL... Whittlesey [*Urban district in England*]
Whittlesey ... Whittlesey's Reports [*32-41 Missouri*] [*A publication*]   (DLA)
Whitt L Rev ... Whittier Law Review [*A publication*]
WHIY .... Moulton, AL [*AM radio station call letters*]
WHIZ .... Zanesville, OH [*AM radio station call letters*]
WHIZ-FM ... Zanesville, OH [*FM radio station call letters*]
WHIZ-TV ... Zanesville, OH [*Television station call letters*]
WHJB ...... Greensburg, PA [*AM radio station call letters*]
WHJC ...... Matewan, WV [*AM radio station call letters*]
WHJE ...... Carmel, IN [*FM radio station call letters*]
WHJJ .... Providence, RI [*AM radio station call letters*]
WHJM ...... Knoxville, TN [*AM radio station call letters*]
WHJT .... Clinton, MS [*FM radio station call letters*]
WHJX ...... Brunswick, GA [*FM radio station call letters*]
WHJX-FM ... Brunswick, GA [*FM radio station call letters*]
WHJY .... Providence, RI [*FM radio station call letters*]
WHK .... Cleveland, OH [*AM radio station call letters*]
WHK .... Whakatane [*New Zealand*] [*Airport symbol*]   (OAG)
WHKE...... Kenosha, WI [*Television station call letters*]
WHKO...... Dayton, OH [*FM radio station call letters*]
WHKP...... Hendersonville, NC [*AM radio station call letters*]
WHKQ ..... Racine, WI [*FM radio station call letters*]
WHKR...... Rockledge, FL [*FM radio station call letters*]
WHKS...... Port Allegany, PA [*FM radio station call letters*]
WHKX...... Lafayette, FL [*FM radio station call letters*]
WHKY....... Hickory, NC [*AM radio station call letters*]
WHKY-TV ... Hickory, NC [*Television station call letters*]
WHKZ....... Cayce, SC [*FM radio station call letters*]
WHL......... Watt-Hour Meter with Loss Compensator   (MSA)
WHL......... Western Hockey League
WHL......... Westland Helicopters Ltd. [*British*]   (IRUK)
WHL......... Wheel   (AAG)
WHL......... World Heritage List [*UNESCO*]
WHLA...... La Crosse, WI [*FM radio station call letters*]
WHLA-TV ... La Crosse, WI [*Television station call letters*]
WHLB....... Virginia, MN [*AM radio station call letters*]
WHLD....... Niagara Falls, NY [*AM radio station call letters*]
WHLD....... Wheeled
WHLDY.... Western Holdings ADR [*NASDAQ symbol*]   (NQ)
WHLE ...... Byhalia, MS [*FM radio station call letters*]
WHLF .... South Boston, VA [*AM radio station call letters*]
WHLG....... Jensen Beach, FL [*FM radio station call letters*]
WHLI .... Hempstead, NY [*AM radio station call letters*]
WHLL .... Worcester, MA [*Television station call letters*]
WHLM...... Bloomsburg, PA [*FM radio station call letters*]
WHLN....... Harlan, KY [*AM radio station call letters*]
WHLO....... Akron, OH [*AM radio station call letters*]
WhlPit .... Wheeling-Pittsburgh Steel Corp. [*Associated Press
             abbreviation*]   (APAG)
WhlPitt ...... Wheeling-Pittsburgh Steel Corp. [*Associated Press
             abbreviation*]   (APAG)
WHLQ...... Louisburg, NC [*FM radio station call letters*]
WHLS ...... Port Huron, MI [*AM radio station call letters*]
WHLS ...... [*The*] Wholesale Club, Inc. [*Indianapolis, IN*] [*NASDAQ
             symbol*]   (NQ)
WHLT ...... Hattiesburg, MS [*Television station call letters*]
WhlTch...... Wheelabrator Technology, Inc. [*Associated Press
             abbreviation*]   (APAG)
WHLV....... Hattiesburg, MS [*AM radio station call letters*]
WHLX...... Bethlehem, WV [*FM radio station call letters*]
WHLZ....... Manning, SC [*FM radio station call letters*]
WHM .... Watt-Hour Meter
WHM .... Weighmaster   (WGA)
WHM .... Wickham [*Australia*] [*Airport symbol*]
WHM .... Wild Horse Parks [*Montana*] [*Seismograph station code, US
             Geological Survey*] [*Closed*]   (SEIS)
WHMA ..... Anniston, AL [*AM radio station call letters*]
WHMA ..... Women's Home Mission Association
WHMAA..... Wool Hat Manufacturers Association of America   (EA)
WHMA-FM ... Anniston, AL [*FM radio station call letters*]
WH Man ... Wage and Hour Reference Manual [*Bureau of National Affairs*]
             [*A publication*]   (DLA)
WHMB-TV ... Indianapolis, IN [*Television station call letters*]
WHMC...... Conway, SC [*FM radio station call letters*]
WHMC...... Wilford Hall United States Air Force Medical Center [*Lackland
             Air Force Base, TX*]   (GRD)
WHMC-TV ... Conway, SC [*Television station call letters*]
WHMD ..... Hammond, LA [*FM radio station call letters*]
WHME...... South Bend, IN [*FM radio station call letters*]
WHME-TV ... South Bend, IN [*Television station call letters*]
WHMH-FM ... Sauk Rapids, MN [*FM radio station call letters*]
WHMI....... Howell, MI [*AM radio station call letters*]
WHMI....... Whitman Mission National Historic Site
WHMI-FM ... Howell, MI [*FM radio station call letters*]
WHMIS .... Wage and Hour Management Information System [*Department
             of Labor*]   (GFGA)
WHMIS .... Workplace Hazardous Materials Information System [*Canada*]
WHMM .... Washington, DC [*Television station call letters*]
WHMP...... Northampton, MA [*AM radio station call letters*]

WHMP-FM ... Northampton, MA [*FM radio station call letters*]
WHMQ ..... North Baltimore, OH [*FM radio station call letters*]
WHMS-FM ... Champaign, IL [*FM radio station call letters*]
WHMT...... Humboldt, TN [*AM radio station call letters*]
WHMX...... Lincoln, ME [*FM radio station call letters*]
WHN .... Wharton & Northern Railroad Co. [*Absorbed into Consolidated Rail Corp.*] [*AAR code*]
WHN .... Whonnock Industries Ltd. [*Toronto Stock Exchange symbol*] [*Vancouver Stock Exchange symbol*]
WHN .... Women's History Network   (EA)
WHNC ...... Henderson, NC [*AM radio station call letters*]
WHND ..... Monroe, MI [*AM radio station call letters*]
WHNE....... Cumming, GA [*AM radio station call letters*]
WHNK ...... Madison, TN [*AM radio station call letters*]
WHNN ...... Bay City, MI [*FM radio station call letters*]
WHNPA.... White House News Photographers Association   (EA)
WHNR ...... Cypress Gardens, FL [*AM radio station call letters*]
WHNR ...... Whenever [*Legal*] [*British*]   (ROG)
WHNRC.... Western Human Nutrition Research Center [*Department of Agriculture*] [*Research center*]   (RCD)
WHNS...... Asheville, NC [*Television station call letters*]
WHNS...... Wartime Host Nation Support
WHNSR.... Whensoever [*Legal*] [*British*]   (ROG)
WHNT...... Huntsville, AL [*Television station call letters*]
WHNY ...... McComb, MS [*AM radio station call letters*]
WHO .... Des Moines, IA [*AM radio station call letters*]
WHO .... War on Hunger Office [*Department of State*]
WHO .... Waterhouse Investor Services [*NYSE symbol*]   (SPSG)
WHO .... Western Heraldry Organization   (EA)
WHO .... Westhill Resources [*Vancouver Stock Exchange symbol*]
WHO .... [*The*] White House Office
WHO .... World Health Organization [*The pronunciation "who" is not acceptable*] [*United Nations affiliate*] [*Switzerland*] [*Databank originator*]
WHO .... World Housing Organization
WHO .... Wrist-Hand Orthosis [*Medicine*]
WHOA ...... American Equine Products, Inc. [*South Norwalk, CT*] [*NASDAQ symbol*]   (NQ)
WHOA ...... Montgomery, AL [*Television station call letters*]
WHOA ...... Walking Horse Owner's Association of America   (EA)
WHOA ...... Why Have Overages Afterwards [*DoD*]
WHOA! ..... Wild Horse Organized Assistance   (EA)
WHOAA .... Walking Horse Owner's Association of America   (EA)
WHOB ...... Nashua, NH [*FM radio station call letters*]
WHOC ...... Philadelphia, MS [*AM radio station call letters*]
WHOCA.... World Health Organization. Chronicle [*A publication*]
WHO Chron ... WHO [*World Health Organization*] Chronicle [*A publication*]
WHO Chronicle ... World Health Organization. Chronicle [*A publication*]
WHOD ...... Jackson, AL [*AM radio station call letters*]
WHOD-FM ... Jackson, AL [*FM radio station call letters*]
WHO Environ Health ... WHO (World Health Organization) Environmental Health [*A publication*]
WHO/EPR ... World Health Organization/Panafrican Centre for Emergency Preparedness and Response [*United Nations*]
WHOER.... Whoever [*Legal*] [*British*]   (ROG)
WHOF....... Whereof [*Legal*] [*British*]   (ROG)
WHOF....... Wildwood, FL [*AM radio station call letters*]
WHO Food Addit Ser ... WHO [*World Health Organization*] Food Additives Series [*A publication*]
WHOG ...... Hobson City, AL [*AM radio station call letters*]
WHO Hist Int Public Health ... WHO (World Health Organization) History of International Public Health [*A publication*]
WHOI........ Peoria, IL [*Television station call letters*]
WHOI........ Woods Hole Oceanographic Institution [*Woods Hole, MA*] [*Research center*]
WHO Int Agency Res Cancer Annu Rep ... World Health Organization International Agency for Research on Cancer. Annual Report [*A publication*]
WHOI Technical Report ... Woods Hole Oceanographic Institution. Technical Report [*A publication*]
WHOK ...... Lancaster, OH [*FM radio station call letters*]
WHOL....... Allentown, PA [*AM radio station call letters*]
WHOL....... Wholesale   (WGA)
WHO Libr Ne ... WHO [*World Health Organization*] Library News [*A publication*]
WHOM ..... Mount Washington, NH [*FM radio station call letters*]
WHOMAP ... FAO [*Food and Agriculture Organization of the United Nations*] Nutritional Studies [*A publication*]
WHO Monogr Ser ... World Health Organization. Monograph Series [*A publication*]
WHON ...... Centerville, IN [*AM radio station call letters*]
WHON ...... Whereon [*Legal*] [*British*]   (ROG)
WHOO ...... Orlando, FL [*AM radio station call letters*]
WHOO ...... Waterhouse Investor Services, Inc. [*NASDAQ symbol*]   (NQ)
WHO Offset Publ ... WHO [*World Health Organization*] Offset Publication [*A publication*]
WHOP....... Hopkinsville, KY [*AM radio station call letters*]
WHOPAY ... World Health Organization. Public Health Papers [*A publication*]

WHO Pestic Residues Ser ... WHO [*World Health Organization*] Pesticide Residues Series [*A publication*]
WHOP-FM ... Hopkinsville, KY [*FM radio station call letters*]
WHO Publ ... WHO [*World Health Organization*] Publications [*A publication*]
WHO Publ Hlth Pap ... WHO [*World Health Organization*] Public Health Papers [*A publication*]
WHO Public Health Pap ... World Health Organization. Public Health Papers [*A publication*]
WHO Public Health Papers ... World Health Organization. Public Health Papers [*A publication*]
WHOS...... Decatur, AL [*AM radio station call letters*]
WHOSOR ... Whosoever [*Legal*] [*British*]   (ROG)
WHOT ...... Youngstown, OH [*AM radio station call letters*]
WHO Tech Rep Ser ... World Health Organization. Technical Report Series [*A publication*]
WHO Tech Rep Sers ... World Health Organization. Technical Report Series [*A publication*]
WHOT-FM ... Youngstown, OH [*FM radio station call letters*]
WHO-TV .. Des Moines, IA [*Television station call letters*]
WHOU ...... Houlton, ME [*AM radio station call letters*]
WHOU-FM ... Houlton, ME [*FM radio station call letters*]
Whous........ Warehouse
WHOV ...... Hampton, VA [*FM radio station call letters*]
WHOW ..... Clinton, IL [*AM radio station call letters*]
WHOW-FM ... Clinton, IL [*FM radio station call letters*]
WHOX ...... Charlestown, IN [*FM radio station call letters*]
WHOY ...... Salinas, PR [*AM radio station call letters*]
WHP......... Harrisburg, PA [*AM radio station call letters*]
WHP.......... Los Angeles, CA [*Location identifier*] [*FAA*]   (FAAL)
WHP.......... Water Horsepower
WHP.......... West Hartford Public Library, West Hartford, CT [*OCLC symbol*]   (OCLC)
WHP.......... Western Health Plans, Inc. [*AMEX symbol*]   (SPSG)
whp............ Whirlpool   (MAE)
WHP.......... White House Police [*Later, Executive Protective Service*]
WHPA....... Hollidaysburg, PA [*FM radio station call letters*]
WHPB .... Belton, SC [*AM radio station call letters*]
WHPC....... Garden City, NY [*FM radio station call letters*]
WHPC....... Wage and Hour and Public Contracts Division [*Obsolete*] [*Department of Labor*]
WHPCA .... Walsh-Healey Public Contracts Act [*1936*] [*Labor*]
WHPCD .... Wage and Hour and Public Contracts Division [*Obsolete*] [*Department of Labor*]
WHPE....... High Point, NC [*FM radio station call letters*]
WHP-FM .. Harrisburg, PA [*FM radio station call letters*]
WHPK-FM ... Chicago, IL [*FM radio station call letters*]
whpl .... Whirlpool
WHPO....... Hoopeston, IL [*FM radio station call letters*]
WHPO....... White House Personnel Office [*Terminated, 1974*]
WHPR....... Highland Park, MI [*FM radio station call letters*]
WHPS .... Baltimore, MD [*FM radio station call letters*]
WHP-TV ... Harrisburg, PA [*Television station call letters*]
WHPY....... Clayton, NC [*AM radio station call letters*]
WHQ .... War Headquarters   (NATG)
WHQ .... Western Historical Quarterly [*A publication*]
WHQO ...... Skowhegan, ME [*FM radio station call letters*]
WHQR ...... Wilmington, NC [*FM radio station call letters*]
WHQT ...... Coral Gables, FL [*FM radio station call letters*]
WHR......... Vail [*Colorado*] [*Airport symbol*]   (OAG)
WHR......... Wage and Hour Reporter [*Bureau of National Affairs*] [*A publication*]   (DLA)
WHR......... Waste Heat Removal
W-HR .... Watt-Hour   (AAG)
WHR......... Welsh History Review [*A publication*]
WHR......... Western Hemisphere Reserve
WHR......... Western Humanities Review [*A publication*]
WHR......... Whether
WHR......... Whirlpool Corp. [*NYSE symbol*]   (SPSG)
WHR......... William H. Rorer [*Research code symbol*]
WHR......... Women and Health Roundtable   (EA)
WHR......... Working Heart Rate [*Cardiology*]
WHRA...... Western Historical Research Associates [*Defunct*]   (EA)
WHRABTS ... Whereabouts [*Legal*] [*British*]   (ROG)
WHRAS .... Whereas [*Legal*] [*British*]   (ROG)
WHRAT .... Whereat [*Legal*] [*British*]   (ROG)
WHRB....... Cambridge, MA [*FM radio station call letters*]
WHRC....... Norwell, MA [*Television station call letters*]
WHRC....... Washington Home Rule Committee [*Later, SDDC*]   (EA)
WHRC....... World Health Research Center
WHRD....... Huntington, WV [*AM radio station call letters*]
WHRF .... Bel Air, MD [*AM radio station call letters*]
WHRH ...... Warner Robins, GA [*FM radio station call letters*]
WHRIN...... Wherein
WHRK...... Memphis, TN [*FM radio station call letters*]
WHRL....... Albany, NY [*FM radio station call letters*]
Whrlpl .... Whirlpool Corp. [*Associated Press abbreviation*]   (APAG)
WHRM...... Wausau, WI [*FM radio station call letters*]
WHR Man ... Wage and Hour Reference Manual [*Bureau of National Affairs*] [*A publication*]   (DLA)
WHRM-TV ... Wausau, WI [*Television station call letters*]

WHRO ...... Hampton-Norfolk, VA [*Television station call letters*]
WHRO ...... Norfolk, VA [*FM radio station call letters*]
WHRS .... Winchester, KY [*AM radio station call letters*]
WHRT .... Hartselle, AL [*AM radio station call letters*]
WHRU ...... Waste Heat Recovery Unit [*Chemical engineering*]
WHRV .... Norfolk, VA [*FM radio station call letters*]
WHRW ...... Binghamton, NY [*FM radio station call letters*]
WHRY .... Hurley, WI [*AM radio station call letters*]
WHRZ .... Providence, KY [*FM radio station call letters*]
WHS .... Warehouse   (AABC)
WHS .... Washington Headquarters Services [*Military*]
WHS .... Water Hydraulic Section
WHS .... Weekly Hansard - Senate [*A publication*]   (APTA)
WHS .... Wesleyan Historical Society [*British*]
WHS .... Western Harvest Sea [*Vancouver Stock Exchange symbol*]
WHS .... Whalsay [*Shetland Islands*] [*Airport symbol*]   (OAG)
WHS .... White Scale
WHS .... William Hunter Society   (EA)
WHS .... Wolf-Hirschorn Syndrome [*Medicine*]
WHS .... Works. Richard Hakluyt Society [*A publication*]
WHS .... World Health Statistics Data Base [*World Health Organization*]
              [*Information service or system*]   (IID)
WHSA .... Brule, WI [*FM radio station call letters*]
WHSB .... Alpena, MI [*FM radio station call letters*]
WHSC .... Hartsville, SC [*AM radio station call letters*]
WHSC .... White House Science Council
WHSCH .... Whitworth Scholar [*British*]
WHSD .... Hinsdale, IL [*FM radio station call letters*]
WHSD .... W. H. Smith Distributors [*British*]
WHSE .... Newark, NJ [*Television station call letters*]
WHSE .... Warehouse   (AAG)
W/HSE ...... Wheelhouse [*Automotive engineering*]
WHSG .... Monroe, GA [*Television station call letters*]
WHSH .... Marlborough, MA [*Television station call letters*]
WHSHS .... Wilbur Hot Springs Health Sanctuary   (EA)
WHSI .... Smithtown, NY [*Television station call letters*]
WHSK .... Kokomo, IN [*FM radio station call letters*]
WHSL .... East St. Louis, IL [*Television station call letters*]
WHSLE ..... Wholesale
WHSM ...... Hayward, WI [*AM radio station call letters*]
WHSM-FM ... Hayward, WI [*FM radio station call letters*]
WHSMN ... Warehouseman   (AABC)
WHSN .... Bangor, ME [*FM radio station call letters*]
WHSNA .... Welsh Harp Society of North America   (EA)
WHSNG .... Warehousing
WHSP .... Vineland, NJ [*Television station call letters*]
WHSR .... White House Situation Room   (MCD)
WHSR .... Winchester, MA [*FM radio station call letters*]
WHSS .... Hamilton, OH [*FM radio station call letters*]
WHSS .... White House Signal Support
WHSUPA ... Wharton School, University of Pennsylvania   (DLA)
WHSV ...... Harrisonburg, VA [*Television station call letters*]
WHSV .... Weight-Hourly Space Velocity [*Fuel technology*]
WHSW ...... Baltimore, MD [*Television station call letters*]
WHSY .... Hattiesburg, MS [*AM radio station call letters*]
WHSY-FM ... Hattiesburg, MS [*FM radio station call letters*]
WHT .... Watt-Hour Demand Meter, Thermal Type   (IEEE)
WHT .... White   (AAG)
WHT .... Whitehall Corp. [*NYSE symbol*]   (SPSG)
WHT .... William Herschel Telescope
WHT .... William Howard Taft [*US president, 1857-1930*]
WHT .... Women's Health Trial [*Department of Health and Human
              Services*]   (GFGA)
WHT .... Wometco Home Theatre [*Subscription television service*]
WHTA .... Walking Horse Trainers Association   (EA)
WHTB .... Fall River, MA [*AM radio station call letters*]
WHTC .... Holland, MI [*AM radio station call letters*]
WHTCA ..... Wehrtechnik [*A publication*]
WHTE .... Williamston, NC [*FM radio station call letters*]
WHTF .... Starview, PA [*FM radio station call letters*]
WHTG .... Eatontown, NJ [*AM radio station call letters*]
WHTG-FM ... Eatontown, NJ [*FM radio station call letters*]
WHTH .... Heath, OH [*AM radio station call letters*]
WHTJ .... Charlottesville, VA [*Television station call letters*]
WHTK .... Port Royal, SC [*FM radio station call letters*]
WHTL .... Whitehall, WI [*FM radio station call letters*]
Wh & TLC ... White and Tudor's Leading Cases in Equity [*9 eds.*] [*1849-
              1928*] [*A publication*]   (DLA)
WHTM ...... Harrisburg, PA [*Television station call letters*]
WHTM ...... Wisconsin Hydrologic Transport Model
WHTN ...... Murfreesboro, TN [*Television station call letters*]
WHTO ...... Muncy, PA [*FM radio station call letters*]
WHTO ...... Whereto [*Legal*] [*British*]   (ROG)
WHTQ ...... Orlando, FL [*FM radio station call letters*]
WHTS .... Western Hemisphere Transmission System
WHTT .... Buffalo, NY [*AM radio station call letters*]
WHTT-FM ... Buffalo, NY [*FM radio station call letters*]
Wh & Tud .. White and Tudor's Leading Cases in Equity [*9th ed.*] [*1928*] [*A
              publication*]   (DLA)
WHTV .... Jackson, MI [*Television station call letters*]
WHTZ .... Newark, NJ [*FM radio station call letters*]

WHU .... Well Head Unit
WHU .... Wild Horse [*Utah*] [*Seismograph station code, US Geological
              Survey*]   (SEIS)
WHUB ...... Cookeville, TN [*AM radio station call letters*]
WHUB-FM ... Cookeville, TN [*FM radio station call letters*]
WHUC ...... Hudson, NY [*AM radio station call letters*]
WHud .... Hudson Public Library, Hudson, WI [*Library symbol*] [*Library
              of Congress*]   (LCLS)
WHUD ...... Peekskill, NY [*FM radio station call letters*]
WHudSO... Hudson Star-Observer, Hudson, WI [*Library symbol*] [*Library
              of Congress*]   (LCLS)
WHUG ...... Jamestown, NY [*FM radio station call letters*]
WHUN ...... Huntingdon, PA [*AM radio station call letters*]
WHUR ...... Washington, DC [*FM radio station call letters*]
WHUS ...... Storrs, CT [*FM radio station call letters*]
WHUT ...... Anderson, IN [*AM radio station call letters*]
WHV .... Woodchuck Hepatitis Virus
WHVE ...... Sarasota, FL [*FM radio station call letters*]
WHVK ...... Tullahoma, TN [*FM radio station call letters*]
WHVN ...... Charlotte, NC [*AM radio station call letters*]
WHVP ...... Wedged Hepatic Venous Pressure
WHVR ...... Hanover, PA [*AM radio station call letters*]
WHVS ...... Wharves   (WGA)
WHVT ...... Clyde, OH [*FM radio station call letters*]
WHVW ...... Hyde Park, NY [*AM radio station call letters*]
WHVY ...... Grasonville, MD [*FM radio station call letters*]
WHW .... Women Helping Women   (EA)
WHWB ...... Rutland, VT [*AM radio station call letters*]
WHWC ...... Menomonie, WI [*FM radio station call letters*]
WHWC-TV ... Menomonie, WI [*Television station call letters*]
WHWE ...... Howe, IN [*FM radio station call letters*]
WHWH ...... Princeton, NJ [*AM radio station call letters*]
WHWK ...... Binghamton, NY [*FM radio station call letters*]
WHWL ...... Marquette, MI [*FM radio station call letters*]
WHWPNLA ... World Health Workers for Peace and NonIntervention in
              Latin America   (EAIO)
WHWTB ... Waste Heat Water Tube Boiler   (DS)
WHWTBS ... Waste Heat Water Tube Boiler Survey   (DS)
WHWTCA ... West Highland White Terrier Club of America   (EA)
WHWTH .. Wherewith [*Legal*] [*British*]   (ROG)
WHWY ...... Saint Augustine Beach, FL [*AM radio station call letters*]
WHX.......... Wheeling-Pittsburgh Steel Corp. [*NYSE symbol*]   (SPSG)
WHXT .... Easton, PA [*FM radio station call letters*]
WHY .... What Have You? [*British*]   (ADA)
WHY .... World Hunger Year   (EA)
WHYB ...... Peshtigo, WI [*FM radio station call letters*]
WHYC .... Swan Quarter, NC [*FM radio station call letters*]
WHYD ...... Columbus, GA [*AM radio station call letters*]
WHYDFTFT ... What Have You Done for the Fleet Today? [*Navy*]
WHYI .... Fort Lauderdale, FL [*FM radio station call letters*]
WHYL .... Carlisle, PA [*AM radio station call letters*]
WHYL-FM ... Carlisle, PA [*FM radio station call letters*]
WHYM...... Pensacola, FL [*AM radio station call letters*]
WHYN ...... Springfield, MA [*AM radio station call letters*]
WHYN-FM ... Springfield, MA [*FM radio station call letters*]
WHYR...... Saco, ME [*FM radio station call letters*]
WHYT .... Detroit, MI [*FM radio station call letters*]
WHYY ...... Philadelphia, PA [*FM radio station call letters*]
WHYY ...... Wilmington, DE [*Television station call letters*]
WHYZ ...... Greenville, SC [*AM radio station call letters*]
WHZR ...... Royal Center, IN [*FM radio station call letters*]
WHZT .... Mahomet, IL [*FM radio station call letters*]
WI .... Oak Harbor, Whidbey Island, WA [*Naval base*]
WI .... Walk In   (ADA)
WI .... Wallops Island [*Off coast of Virginia*]
WI .... Water Injection
W & I .... Weighing and Inspection
WI .... Welding Institute [*Database originator and operator*]   (EA)
WI .... Welt des Islams [*A publication*]
WI .... West Coast Airlines Ltd. [*Ghana*] [*ICAO designator*]   (FAAC)
WI .... West Indies [*Formerly, BWI*]
WI .... Westerners International   (EA)
WI .... Wexas International [*Commercial firm*] [*British*]   (EAIO)
WI .... When Issued [*Stock exchange term*]   (SPSG)
WI .... White Information [*Banking*] [*British*]
WI .... Wiadomosci [*A publication*]
Wi .... Wiez [*A publication*]
WI .... Wimpy International [*Commercial firm*] [*British*]
WI .... Wine Institute   (EA)
WI .... Winter [*Germany*] [*ICAO aircraft manufacturer
              identifier*]   (ICAO)
WI .... Wire
WI .... Wisconsin [*Postal code*]
WI .... Wisconsin School Musician [*A publication*]
WI .... Within
WI .... Wohnungswirtschaftliche Informationen [*A publication*]
WI .... Women's Institute [*British*]
WI .... Women's Reserve, Intelligence Duties [*USNR officer
              designation*]
WI .... Wood Industries [*A publication*]
WI .... Woprosy Istorii [*A publication*]

WI .... Word Intelligibility
WI .... World Impact (EA)
WI .... Worldwatch Institute (EA)
WI .... Wrought Iron
WIA .... Manitowoc Public Library, Manitowoc, WI [*OCLC symbol*] (OCLC)
WIA .... Waking Imagined Analgesia [*Medicine*]
WIA .... Watusi International Association (EA)
WIA .... Western Interpreters Association [*Later, NAI*] (EA)
WIA .... Wien-Auhof [*Austria*] [*Geomagnetic observatory code*]
WIA .... Winward Islands Airways International [*Netherlands Antilles*] (EY)
WIA .... Wirtschaftskonjunktur. Analysen, Perspektiven, Indikatoren [*A publication*]
WIA .... Women in Aerospace (EA)
WIA .... Women in Agribusiness [*An association*] (EA)
WIA .... Women in the Arts Foundation (EA)
WIA .... Wounded in Action [*Military*]
WIAA .... Interlochen, MI [*FM radio station call letters*]
WIAA .... Sabang [*Indonesia*] [*ICAO location identifier*] (ICLI)
WIAB......... Banda Aceh/Maimun Saleh [*Indonesia*] [*ICAO location identifier*] (ICLI)
WIAB......... Wilderness Alberta [*A publication*]
WIAC .... San Juan, PR [*AM radio station call letters*]
WIAC .... Women's International Art Club
WIAC-FM ... San Juan, PR [*FM radio station call letters*]
WIACLALS ... West Indian Association for Commonwealth Literature and Language Studies [*Jamaica*] (EAIO)
WIACO ..... World Insulation and Acoustic Congress Organization (EA)
Wiad A .... Wiadomosci Archeologiczne. Bulletin Archeologique Polonias [*A publication*]
Wiad Bot.... Wiadomosci Botaniczne [*A publication*]
Wiad Chem ... Wiadomosci Chemiczne [*A publication*]
Wiad Ekol ... Wiadomosci Ekologiczne [*A publication*]
Wiad Elektrotech ... Wiadomosci Elektrotechniczne [*A publication*]
Wiad Gorn ... Wiadomosci Gornicze [*Poland*] [*A publication*]
Wiad Hist .. Wiadomosci Historyczne [*A publication*]
Wiad Hutn ... Wiadomosci Hutnicze [*A publication*]
Wiad Inst Melior Uzytkow Zielon (Warsaw) ... Wiadomosci. Instytut Melioracji i Uzytkow Zielonych (Warsaw) [*A publication*]
Wiad Lek ... Wiadomosci Lekarskie [*A publication*]
Wiad Mat .. Wiadomosci Matematyczne [*A publication*]
Wiad Melior Lak ... Wiadomosci Melioracyjne i Lakarskie [*A publication*]
Wiad Melior Lakarsk ... Wiadomosci Melioracyjne i Lakarskie [*A publication*]
Wiad Meteorol Gospod Wodnej ... Wiadomosci Meteorologii i Gospodarki Wodnej [*A publication*]
Wiad Naft.. Wiadomosci Naftowe [*A publication*]
Wiad Num Arch ... Wiadomosci Numizmatyczno-Archeologiczne [*Later, Wiadomosci Numizmatyczne*] [*A publication*]
Wiadom Mat ... Wiadomosci Matematyczne [*A publication*]
Wiadom Statyst ... Wiadomosci Statystyczne [*A publication*]
Wiad Parazyt ... Wiadomosci Parazytologiczne [*A publication*]
Wiad Parazytol ... Wiadomosci Parazytologiczne [*A publication*]
Wiad Stat... Wiadomosci Statystyczne [*A publication*]
Wiad St Hydrol Met ... Wiadomosci Sluzby Hydrologicznej i Meteorologicznej [*A publication*]
Wiad Telekomun ... Wiadomosci Telekomunikacyjne [*A publication*]
Wiad Zielarskie ... Wiadomosci Zielarskie [*A publication*]
WIAG .... Menggala/Astrakestra [*Indonesia*] [*ICAO location identifier*] (ICLI)
WIAI......... Danville, IL [*FM radio station call letters*]
WIAJ......... Semplak/Atang Senjaya [*Indonesia*] [*ICAO location identifier*] (ICLI)
WIAK .... Margahayu/Sulaiman [*Indonesia*] [*ICAO location identifier*] (ICLI)
WIAL......... Eau Claire, WI [*FM radio station call letters*]
WIAM....... Tasikmalaya/Cibeureum [*Indonesia*] [*ICAO location identifier*] (ICLI)
WIAM....... Williamston, NC [*AM radio station call letters*]
WIAP........ Banyumas/Wirasaba [*Indonesia*] [*ICAO location identifier*] (ICLI)
WIAP........ Wartime Individual Augmentation Program [*Military*]
WIAP........ Westinghouse Industrial Atomic Power (MCD)
WIAR .... Madiun/Iswahyudi [*Indonesia*] [*ICAO location identifier*] (ICLI)
WIAS........ Malang/Abdul Rachman Saleh [*Indonesia*] [*ICAO location identifier*] (ICLI)
WIAS........ West Indies Associated State
WIAS........ Whiteruthenian Institute of Arts and Science [*Later, BIAS*] (EA)
WIB .... Lawrence University, Appleton, WI [*OCLC symbol*] (OCLC)
WIB .... Wallcovering Information Bureau (EA)
WIB .... Wartime Information Board [*World War II*] [*Canada*]
WIB .... Weather Information Branch [*Air Force*] (MCD)
WIB .... Wetboek van de Inkomstenbelastingen [*A publication*]
WIB .... Wetenschapsbeleid [*A publication*]
WIB .... When Interrupt Block (NASA)
WIB .... When-Issued-Basis [*Business term*]
WIB .... Women's Information Bank (EA)
WIBA......... Madison, WI [*AM radio station call letters*]

WIBA-FM ... Madison, WI [*FM radio station call letters*]
WIBB......... Macon, GA [*AM radio station call letters*]
WIBB......... Pekanbaru [*Indonesia*] [*ICAO location identifier*] (ICLI)
WIBC......... Indianapolis, IN [*AM radio station call letters*]
WIBC......... Women's International Bowling Congress (EA)
WIBC......... World Institute of Black Communications (EA)
WIBD......... Dumai/Pinangkampai [*Indonesia*] [*ICAO location identifier*] (ICLI)
WIBF......... Jenkintown, PA [*FM radio station call letters*]
WIBFD...... Will Be Forwarded (NOAA)
WIBG......... Ocean City, NJ [*AM radio station call letters*]
WIBI......... Carlinville, IL [*FM radio station call letters*]
WIBIS .... Will Be Issued (NOAA)
WI Bl......... Wirtschaftsrechtliche Informations-Blaetter [*A publication*]
WIBM .... Jackson, MI [*AM radio station call letters*]
WIBM-FM ... Jackson, MI [*FM radio station call letters*]
WIBN .... Earl Park, IN [*FM radio station call letters*]
WIBP........ Semilinang/Peranap [*Indonesia*] [*ICAO location identifier*] (ICLI)
WIBQ .... Remsen, NY [*FM radio station call letters*]
WIBR........ Baton Rouge, LA [*AM radio station call letters*]
WIBR........ Sipora/Rokot [*Indonesia*] [*ICAO location identifier*] (ICLI)
WIBS......... Bengkalis/Sungai Pakning [*Indonesia*] [*ICAO location identifier*] (ICLI)
WIBS......... Charlotte Amalie, VI [*AM radio station call letters*]
WIBS......... Wool Industry Bureau of Statistics [*British*] (CB)
WIBT........ Tanjung Balai/Sungai Bati [*Indonesia*] [*ICAO location identifier*] (ICLI)
WIBU........ Poynette, WI [*AM radio station call letters*]
WIBV......... Belleville, IL [*AM radio station call letters*]
WIBW .... Topeka, KS [*AM radio station call letters*]
WIBW-FM ... Topeka, KS [*FM radio station call letters*]
WIBW-TV ... Topeka, KS [*Television station call letters*]
WIBX........ Utica, NY [*AM radio station call letters*]
WIBZ........ Wedgefield, SC [*FM radio station call letters*]
WIC .... Medical College of Wisconsin, Milwaukee, WI [*OCLC symbol*] (OCLC)
WIC .... Warning Information Correlation (MCD)
WIC .... Washington International Center (EA)
WIC .... Water Infiltration Course [*Army*]
WIC .... Wax Insulating Compound
WIC .... Wayfarer International Committee [*Axminster, Devonshire, England*] (EAIO)
WIC .... Weighted Ion Concentration [*Air pollution measure*]
WIC .... Welding Institute of Canada (EAIO)
WIC .... West India Committee [*British*] (EAIO)
WIC .... Wheat Industry Council (EA)
WIC .... Whitbread Investment Co. [*British*]
WIC .... WIC Western International Communications Ltd. [*Toronto Stock Exchange symbol*] [*Vancouver Stock Exchange symbol*]
WIC .... Wick [*Scotland*] [*Airport symbol*] (OAG)
WIC .... WICOR, Inc. [*NYSE symbol*] (SPSG)
WIC .... Wildlife Information Center (EA)
WIC .... Windsor Institute of Complementology [*Later, ICS*] (EA)
WIC .... Women in Cable (EA)
WIC .... Women in Communications
WIC .... Women in Crisis (EA)
WIC .... Women, Infants, and Children [*Supplemental food program*] [*Department of Agriculture*]
WIC .... Women's Interart Center (EA)
WIC .... Worksheet Inspection Card
WIC .... World Institute Council (EA)
WICA .... Judgments of the West Indian Court of Appeal [*A publication*] (DLA)
WICA .... While in Control Area [*Aviation*] (FAAC)
WICA .... Wind Cave National Park
WICA .... Witches International Craft Association (EA)
WICB........ Ithaca, NY [*FM radio station call letters*]
WICB........ Women in Cell Biology (EA)
WICBC...... World Invitation Club Basketball Championships [*British*]
WICBE...... World Information Centre for Bilingual Education [*See also CMIEB*] [*Paris, France*] (EAIO)
WICC........ Bridgeport, CT [*AM radio station call letters*]
WICC........ Women's Inter-Church Council of Canada
WICD........ Champaign, IL [*Television station call letters*]
WICE........ Pawtucket, RI [*AM radio station call letters*]
WICEM..... World Industry Conference on Environmental Management
WICF........ Women's International Cultural Federation [*See also FICF*] (EAIO)
WICH .... Norwich, CT [*AM radio station call letters*]
Wi Ch........ Wirtschaftspolitische Chronik [*A publication*]
WICHE ..... Western Interstate Commission for Higher Education
WICHE Publ ... Western Interstate Commission for Higher Education. Publications [*A publication*]
Wichita Eag ... Wichita Eagle-Beacon [*A publication*]
WICHRO .. Wichita River Oil Corp. [*Associated Press abbreviation*] (APAG)
WICI......... Women in Communications, Inc. (EA)
WICK........ Scranton, PA [*AM radio station call letters*]
WICK........ Wicklow [*County in Ireland*] (ROG)

WICK......... Wicklund Petroleum Corp. [*NASDAQ symbol*] (NQ)
WICKF...... Wickford [*England*]
WICKL...... Wicklow [*County in Ireland*]
WICL......... Work Inspection Characteristics List
WICN........ Worcester, MA [*FM radio station call letters*]
WICO........ Salisbury, MD [*AM radio station call letters*]
WICO........ W. I. Carr Sons & Co. Overseas [*Stockbroker*] [*Hong Kong*]
WICO-FM ... Salisbury, MD [*FM radio station call letters*]
WICOMATIC ... Wiring and Connective Device, Semiautomatic (DNAB)
WICOR...... WICOR, Inc. [*Associated Press abbreviation*] (APAG)
WICR......... Indianapolis, IN [*FM radio station call letters*]
WICR......... Wilson's Creek Battlefield National Park
WICS......... Springfield, IL [*Television station call letters*]
WICS......... Women in Community Service (EA)
WICS......... Worldwide Intelligence Communications System (MCD)
WI & CTF ... Welsh Industry and Commerce Trade Fair (ITD)
WICU........ Erie, PA [*Television station call letters*]
WICY........ Malone, NY [*AM radio station call letters*]
WICZ......... Binghamton, NY [*Television station call letters*]
WICZ......... While in Control Zone [*Aviation*] (FAAC)
WID.......... University of Wisconsin, Madison Library School, Madison, WI [*OCLC symbol*] (OCLC)
WID.......... Wean, Inc. [*NYSE symbol*] (SPSG)
WID.......... Weekly Intelligence Digest [*Military*] (CINC)
WID.......... West India Dock
WID.......... Widow [*or Widower*]
WID.......... Width
WID.......... Wind River Resources [*Vancouver Stock Exchange symbol*]
WID.......... Window Identifier [*Data processing*]
WID.......... Women in Development [*Bureau of the Census*] [*A publication*] (GFGA)
WID.......... Women in Development [*Peace Corps*]
WID.......... World Institute on Disability (EA)
WIDA........ Carolina, PR [*AM radio station call letters*]
WIDA-FM ... Carolina, PR [*FM radio station call letters*]
WIDE........ Biddeford, ME [*AM radio station call letters*]
WIDE........ Wide-Angle Infinity Display Equipment
WIDE........ Widergren Communications [*NASDAQ symbol*] (NQ)
WIDE........ Wiring Integration Design (IEEE)
WIDETRACK ... Wideband Transmission Relay Acoustic Communications (MCD)
WIDF......... Women's International Democratic Federation [*See also FDIF*] [*Berlin, German Democratic Republic*] (EAIO)
WIDG........ St. Ignace, MI [*AM radio station call letters*]
Wi Di .... Wirtschaftsdienst [*A publication*]
WIDI .... Women in Design International [*Later, DI*] (EA)
WIDJET.... Waterloo Interactive Direct Job Entry Terminal System [*IBM Corp.*]
WIDL .... Caro, MI [*FM radio station call letters*]
WIDO........ Eutaw, AL [*FM radio station call letters*]
WIDOWAC ... Wing Design Optimization with Aerolastic Constraints [*Computer program*]
WIDP .... Guayama, PR [*Television station call letters*]
WIDR .... Kalamazoo, MI [*FM radio station call letters*]
WIDS........ Russell Springs, KY [*AM radio station call letters*]
WIDS........ Waterborne Intrusion Detection System (MCD)
WIDU........ Fayetteville, NC [*AM radio station call letters*]
WIDU........ Wireless Intelligence and Development Unit [*British military*] (DMA)
WIE .... University of Wisconsin-Superior, Jim Dan Hill Library, Superior, WI [*OCLC symbol*] (OCLC)
WIE .... With Immediate Effect (FAAC)
WIE .... Women in Engineering Centre (EAIO)
WIE .... Women in Entertainment [*British*]
WIE .... Women's Information Exchange (EA)
WIEB/WINB ... Western Interstate Energy Board/Western Interstate Nuclear Board (EA)
WIEC......... Ponce, PR [*Television station call letters*]
WIEC......... West Indian Institute of Ecology and Cancer [*See also IMEC*] (EAIO)
Wiederbeleb Organersatz Intensivmed ... Wiederbelebung. Organersatz. Intensivmedizin [*A publication*]
Wiederg G ... Gesetz zur Regelung der Wiedergutmachung Nationalsozialistischen Unrechts fuer Angehoerige des Oeffentlichen Dienstes [*A publication*]
Wiederherstellungschir Traumatol ... Wiederherstellungschirurgie und Traumatologie [*A publication*]
WIEL......... Elizabethtown, KY [*AM radio station call letters*]
Wien Arch Innere Med ... Wiener Archiv fuer Innere Medizin [*A publication*]
Wien Arch Psychol Psychiat Neurol ... Wiener Archiv fuer Psychologie, Psychiatrie, und Neurologie [*A publication*]
Wien Beitr ... Wiener Beitraege zur Englischen Philologie [*A publication*]
Wien Beitr Chir ... Wiener Beitraege zur Chirurgie [*A publication*]
Wien Beitr Gesch Med ... Wiener Beitraege zur Geschichte der Medizin [*A publication*]
Wien Chem Ztg ... Wiener Chemiker Zeitung [*A publication*]
Wien Entom Monatschr ... Wiener Entomologische Monatsschrift [*A publication*]
Wien Ent Rd ... Wiener Entomologische Rundschau [*A publication*]
Wiener Ethnohist Bl ... Wiener Ethnohistorische Blaetter [*A publication*]
Wiener Voelkerk Mitt ... Wiener Voelkerkundliche Mitteilungen [*A publication*]

Wien Geschichtsbl ... Wiener Geschichtsblaetter [*A publication*]
Wien Jahrb Kunstgesch ... Wiener Jahrbuch fuer Kunstgeschichte [*A publication*]
Wien Klin W ... Wiener Klinische Wochenschrift [*A publication*]
Wien Klin Wochenschr ... Wiener Klinische Wochenschrift [*A publication*]
Wien Klin Wochenschr Suppl ... Wiener Klinische Wochenschrift. Supplementum [*A publication*]
Wien Klin Ws ... Wiener Klinische Wochenschrift [*A publication*]
Wien Landwirtsch Ztg ... Wiener Landwirtschaftliche Zeitung [*A publication*]
Wien Med Presse ... Wiener Medizinische Presse [*A publication*]
Wien Med Wochenschr ... Wiener Medizinische Wochenschrift [*A publication*]
Wien Med Wochenschr (Beih) ... Wiener Medizinische Wochenschrift (Beihefte) [*A publication*]
Wien Med Wochenschr Suppl ... Wiener Medizinische Wochenschrift. Supplementum [*A publication*]
Wien Med Ws ... Wiener Medizinische Wochenschrift [*A publication*]
Wien Med Wschr ... Wiener Medizinische Wochenschrift [*A publication*]
Wien Mitt Photogr Inhalts ... Wiener Mitteilungen Photographischen Inhalts [*A publication*]
Wien Mitt Wasser Abwasser Gewaesser ... Wiener Mitteilungen. Wasser, Abwaesser, Gewaesser [*A publication*]
Wien Naturh Mus Annalen ... Wien Naturhistorischer Museum. Annalen [*A publication*]
Wien Pharm Wochenschr ... Wiener Pharmazeutische Wochenschrift [*A publication*]
Wien Stud .. Wiener Studien [*A publication*] (OCD)
Wien Tieraerztl Monatsschr ... Wiener Tieraerztliche Monatsschrift [*A publication*]
Wien Tieraerztl Mschr ... Wiener Tieraerztliche Monatsschrift [*A publication*]
Wien Voelkerk Mitt ... Wiener Voelkerkundliche Mitteilungen [*A publication*]
Wien Zt...... Wiener Zeitung [*A publication*]
WIERD...... Wind Energy Report [*A publication*]
WIEU .... Weekly Intelligence Estimate Update [*Vietnam*]
WIEZ......... Lewistown, PA [*AM radio station call letters*]
WIF........... Mid-Wisconsin Federated Library System, Fond Du Lac, WI [*OCLC symbol*] (OCLC)
WIF........... Water Immersion Facility [*NASA*] (KSC)
WIF........... Weapons Integration Facility (MCD)
WIF........... West India Fruit & Steamship [*AAR code*]
WIF........... West Indies Federation
WIF........... Wildfire Resources Ltd. [*Vancouver Stock Exchange symbol*]
WiF .... William Faulkner. Materials, Studies, and Criticism [*A publication*]
WIF........... Wilt-Inducing Factor [*Plant pathology*]
WIF........... Women in Film (EA)
WIF........... Worlds of If [*A publication*]
WIF........... Worldview International Foundation (EAIO)
WIFA......... Washington Institute of Foreign Affairs (EA)
WIFC......... Wausau, WI [*FM radio station call letters*]
WIFE......... Connersville, IN [*AM radio station call letters*]
WIFE......... Women Involved in Farm Economics (EA)
WIFE......... Women's Independent Film Exchange (EA)
WIFF......... Auburn, IN [*AM radio station call letters*]
WIFF......... Wang [*Laboratories, Inc.*] Image File Format [*Data processing*] (PCM)
WIFF-FM ... Auburn, IN [*FM radio station call letters*]
WIFM........ Elkin, NC [*FM radio station call letters*]
WIFNA...... White Inhibited Fuming Nitric Acid (SAA)
WIFO .... Jesup, GA [*FM radio station call letters*]
WIFO......... Wildfowl [*A publication*]
WIFP........ Women's Institute for Freedom of the Press (EA)
WIFR......... Freeport, IL [*Television station call letters*]
WIFS .... Work Injury Followback Survey [*Bureau of Labor Statistics and National Center for Health Statistics*] (GFGA)
WIFU........ Western Interprovincial Football Union [*Canada*]
WIFX........ Jenkins, KY [*FM radio station call letters*]
WIG .... Washington Information Group, Ltd. [*Research center*] (TSSD)
WIG .... West-Indische Gids [*A publication*]
WIG .... Wiggins Airways [*Norwood, MA*] [*FAA designator*] (FAAC)
Wig............ Wigram on Loills [*A publication*] (DLA)
WIG .... Wing in Ground
WIG .... Wisconsin State Library, Processing Center, Madison, WI [*OCLC symbol*] (OCLC)
WIG .... Wolfram Inert Gas (MCD)
Wig Disc .... Wigram on Discovery [*2nd ed.*] [*1840*] [*A publication*] (DLA)
WIGE .... Wax-Impregnated Graphite Electrode
Wig Ev .... Wigram on Extrinsic Evidence [*A publication*] (DLA)
WIGG .... Wiggins, MS [*AM radio station call letters*]
Wight .... Wightwick's English Exchequer Reports [*145 English Reprint*] [*A publication*] (DLA)
Wight El Cas ... Wight's Scottish Election Cases [*1784-96*] [*A publication*] (DLA)
Wightw ...... Wightwick's English Exchequer Reports [*145 English Reprint*] [*A publication*] (DLA)
Wightw (Eng) ... Wightwick's English Exchequer Reports [*145 English Reprint*] [*A publication*] (DLA)
WIGL......... Orangeburg, SC [*FM radio station call letters*]
WIGM .... Medford, WI [*AM radio station call letters*]

Wigm Ev .... Wigmore on Evidence [*A publication*]   (DLA)
WIGM-FM ... Medford, WI [*FM radio station call letters*]
WIGO........ Atlanta, GA [*AM radio station call letters*]
WIGO........ What Is Going On? [*Humorous definition of science*]
WIGORN.. Wigorniensis [*Signature of Bishop of Worcester*]
             [*British*]   (ROG)
WIGS......... Gouverneur, NY [*AM radio station call letters*]
Wig Wills... Wigmore on Wills [*A publication*]   (DLA)
WIH........... State Historical Society of Wisconsin, Madison, WI [*OCLC symbol*]   (OCLC)
WIH........... Work in Hand   (ILCA)
WIHN....... Normal, IL [*FM radio station call letters*]
WIHP .... Journal. Wisconsin Association for Health, Physical Education, and Recreation [*A publication*]
WIHS .... Middletown, CT [*FM radio station call letters*]
WIHS .... Western Institute for Health Studies   (EA)
WII .... Beloit College Library, Beloit, WI [*OCLC symbol*]   (OCLC)
WII .... Weatherford International, Inc. [*AMEX symbol*]   (SPSG)
WIIA......... Tangerang/Budiarto [*Indonesia*] [*ICAO location identifier*]   (ICLI)
WIIAD....... Winrock International Institute for Agricultural Development   (EA)
WIIB.......... Bandung/Husein Sastranegara [*Indonesia*] [*ICAO location identifier*]   (ICLI)
WIIB.......... Bloomington, IN [*Television station call letters*]
WIIC......... Cirebon/Panggung [*Indonesia*] [*ICAO location identifier*]   (ICLI)
WIID .... Jakarta/Kemayoran [*Indonesia*] [*ICAO location identifier*]   (ICLI)
WIIG .... Jakarta/Pulau Panjang [*Indonesia*] [*ICAO location identifier*]   (ICLI)
WIIH .... Jakarta/Halim Perdanakusuma [*Indonesia*] [*ICAO location identifier*]   (ICLI)
WIII........... Jakarta/Cengkareng [*Indonesia*] [*ICAO location identifier*]   (ICLI)
WIIJ .... Yogyakarta/Adi Sucipto [*Indonesia*] [*ICAO location identifier*]   (ICLI)
WIIK......... Kalijati [*Indonesia*] [*ICAO location identifier*]   (ICLI)
WIIL.......... Cilacap/Tunggul Wulung [*Indonesia*] [*ICAO location identifier*]   (ICLI)
WIIM .... Iron Mountain, MI [*Television station call letters*]
WIIN .... Vicksburg, MS [*FM radio station call letters*]
WIIP.......... Jakarta/Pondok Cabe [*Indonesia*] [*ICAO location identifier*]   (ICLI)
WIIP.......... Waters Intelligent Information Processor
WIIQ .... Demopolis, AL [*Television station call letters*]
WIIR.......... Pelabuhan Ratu [*Indonesia*] [*ICAO location identifier*]   (ICLI)
WIIS .... Key West, FL [*FM radio station call letters*]
WIIS .... Semarang/Achmad Yani [*Indonesia*] [*ICAO location identifier*]   (ICLI)
WIIS .... Wang Integrated Image System
WIIS .... Women in International Security   (EA)
WIIT.......... Tanjung Karang/Branti [*Indonesia*] [*ICAO location identifier*]   (ICLI)
WIIU .... Worker's International Industrial Union
WIIW........ Wiener Institut fuer Internationale Wirtschaftsvergleiche [*Vienna Institute for Comparative Economic Studies*] [*Information service or system*]   (IID)
WIIX......... Jakarta [*Indonesia*] [*ICAO location identifier*]   (ICLI)
WIIZ.......... Jakarta [*Indonesia*] [*ICAO location identifier*]   (ICLI)
WIJ .... Arrowhead Library System, Janesville Public Library, Janesville, WI [*OCLC symbol*]   (OCLC)
WIJ .... Warburg Institute. Journal [*A publication*]
WIJK........ Evergreen, AL [*AM radio station call letters*]
WIJK-FM ... Evergreen, AL [*FM radio station call letters*]
Wijsgerig Perspect Maatsch Wet ... Wijsgerig Perspectief op Maatschappij en Wetenschap [*A publication*]
Wijsig Perspect ... Wijsgerig Perspectief op Maatschappij en Wetenschap [*A publication*]
WIJY .... Hilton Head Island, SC [*FM radio station call letters*]
WIK .... Deutsches Institut fuer Wirtschaftsforschung. Wochenbericht [*A publication*]
WIK .... Kenosha Public Library, Kenosha, WI [*OCLC symbol*]   (OCLC)
WIK .... Wien-Kobenzl [*Austria*] [*Geomagnetic observatory code*]
WIKB........ Batam/Hang Nadim [*Indonesia*] [*ICAO location identifier*]   (ICLI)
WIKB........ Iron River, MI [*AM radio station call letters*]
WIKB-FM ... Iron River, MI [*FM radio station call letters*]
WIKC........ Bogalusa, LA [*AM radio station call letters*]
WIKD .... Tanjung Pandan/Bulu Tumbang [*Indonesia*] [*ICAO location identifier*]   (ICLI)
WIKE........ Newport, VT [*AM radio station call letters*]
WIKI......... Carrollton, KY [*FM radio station call letters*]
WIKK........ Newton, IL [*FM radio station call letters*]
WIKK .... Pangkal Pinang [*Indonesia*] [*ICAO location identifier*]   (ICLI)
WIKN .... Tanjung Pinang/Kijang [*Indonesia*] [*ICAO location identifier*]   (ICLI)
Wiko .... Wirtschaftskonjunktur [*A publication*]
WIKQ........ Greeneville, TN [*FM radio station call letters*]
WIKS........ New Bern, NC [*FM radio station call letters*]
WIKS........ Singkep/Dabo [*Indonesia*] [*ICAO location identifier*]   (ICLI)

WIKU .... Pikeville, TN [*FM radio station call letters*]
WIKY .... Evansville, IN [*AM radio station call letters*]
WIKY-FM ... Evansville, IN [*FM radio station call letters*]
WIKZ........ Chambersburg, PA [*FM radio station call letters*]
WIL .... Lakeland College, Sheboygan, WI [*OCLC symbol*]   (OCLC)
WIL .... Nairobi-Wilson [*Kenya*] [*Airport symbol*]   (OAG)
WIL .... St. Louis, MO [*FM radio station call letters*]
WIL .... Ward Indicator Light
WIL .... White Indicating Light
WIL .... Wilco Mining Co. Ltd. [*Toronto Stock Exchange symbol*]
WIL .... Wilkes [*Antarctica*] [*Seismograph station code, US Geological Survey*] [*Closed*]   (SEIS)
WIL .... Wirtschaftliche Lage in der Bundesrepublik Deutschland [*A publication*]
WIL .... Women in Leadership [*Project*]
WILA........ Danville, VA [*AM radio station call letters*]
WI Law Rev ... Wisconsin Law Review [*A publication*]
Wilberforce ... Wilberforce on Statute Law [*A publication*]   (DLA)
Wilb Stat.... Wilberforce on Construction and Operation of Statutes [*1881*] [*A publication*]   (DLA)
WILC........ Laurel, MD [*AM radio station call letters*]
WILC........ West Central Illinois Library Cooperative [*Library network*]
Wilc Cond .. Wilcox's Condensed Ohio Reports (Reprint) [*1-7 Ohio*] [*A publication*]   (DLA)
Wilc Cond Rep ... Wilcox's Condensed Ohio Reports (Reprint) [*1-7 Ohio*] [*A publication*]   (DLA)
Wilc Mun Corp ... Wilcox on Municipal Corporations [*Ohio*] [*A publication*]   (DLA)
WILCO...... Western Interstate Library Coordinating Organization
WILCO...... Will Comply [*Used after "Roger"*] [*Radio term*]
Wilcox....... Wilcox's Lackawanna Reports [*Pennsylvania*] [*A publication*]   (DLA)
Wilcox....... Wilcox's Reports [*10 Ohio*] [*A publication*]   (DLA)
Wilcox Cond ... Wilcox's Condensed Ohio Reports [*A publication*]   (DLA)
WilcxG...... Willcox & Gibbs, Inc. [*Associated Press abbreviation*]   (APAG)
WILD .... Boston, MA [*AM radio station call letters*]
WILD .... What I Like to Do [*Psychological testing*]
WILD .... Wildey, Inc. [*NASDAQ symbol*]   (NQ)
WILD .... Women's Independent Label Distribution Network   (EA)
Wild Barfield Heat-Treat J ... Wild Barfield Heat-Treatment Journal [*A publication*]
Wild Barfield J ... Wild Barfield Journal [*A publication*]
Wild Camp ... Wilderness Camping [*A publication*]
Wild Cat..... Wild Cat Monthly [*A publication*]   (APTA)
Wilde Conv ... Wilde's Supplement to Barton's Conveyancing [*A publication*]   (DLA)
Wildenowia Beih ... Wildenowia Beiheft [*A publication*]
Wilde Sup .. Wilde's Supplement to Barton's Conveyancing [*A publication*]   (DLA)
Wildfire Stat US Dep Agric For Serv ... Wildfire Statistics. United States Department of Agriculture. Forest Service [*A publication*]
Wildl A ...... Wildlife in Australia [*A publication*]
Wildl Aust ... Wildlife in Australia [*A publication*]   (APTA)
Wildl Dis ... Wildlife Diseases [*A publication*]
Wildl Dis Assoc Bull ... Wildlife Disease Association. Bulletin [*A publication*]
Wildlife...... Wildlife in Australia [*A publication*]   (APTA)
Wildlife A .. Wildlife in Australia [*A publication*]
Wildlife Aust ... Wildlife in Australia [*A publication*]   (APTA)
Wildlife R .. Wildlife Review [*A publication*]
Wild Life Rev ... Wild Life Review [*A publication*]
Wildlif Res ... Wildlife Research [*A publication*]
Wildl Manage Bull (Ottawa) Ser 1 ... Wildlife Management Bulletin (Ottawa). Series 1 [*A publication*]
Wildl Manage Bull (Ottawa) Ser 2 ... Wildlife Management Bulletin (Ottawa). Series 2 [*A publication*]
Wildl Monogr ... Wildlife Monographs [*A publication*]
Wildl Res Q ... Wildlife Research Quarterly [*A publication*]
Wildl Rev ... Wildlife Review [*A publication*]
Wildl Rev NZ Wildl Serv ... Wildlife Review. New Zealand Wildlife Service [*A publication*]
Wildl Soc Bull ... Wildlife Society. Bulletin [*A publication*]
Wildl Wildlands Inst Monogr ... Wildlife-Wildlands Institute. Monograph [*A publication*]
Wildm Int L ... Wildman's International Law [*A publication*]   (ILCA)
Wildm Int Law ... Wildman's International Law [*A publication*]   (DLA)
Wildm Search ... Wildman. Search, Capture, and Prize [*A publication*]   (ILCA)
WILE......... Cambridge, OH [*AM radio station call letters*]
Wiley Lib Newsl ... Wiley-Interscience Librarian's Newsletter [*A publication*]
Wiley Ser Curr Top Reprod Endocrinol ... Wiley Series on Current Topics in Reproductive Endocrinology [*A publication*]
WILF......... Williamsport, PA [*Television station call letters*]
WILF........ Wilson Foods Corp. [*NASDAQ symbol*]   (NQ)
Wilhelm Roux' Arch ... Wilhelm Roux' Archiv fuer Entwicklungsmechanik der Organismen [*Later, Roux' Archives of Developmental Biology*] [*A publication*]
Wilhelm Roux' Arch Dev Biol ... Wilhelm Roux' Archives of Developmental Biology [*A publication*]
Wilhelm Roux' Arch Entwicklungsmech Org ... Wilhelm Roux' Archiv fuer Entwicklungsmechanik der Organismen [*Later, Roux' Archives of Developmental Biology*] [*A publication*]

Wilhelm Roux Arch EntwMech Org ... Wilhelm Roux' Archiv fuer Entwicklungsmechanik der Organismen [*A publication*]
WILI .... Willimantic, CT [*AM radio station call letters*]
WILI-FM .. Willimantic, CT [*FM radio station call letters*]
WILJ .... West Indian Law Journal [*Jamaica*] [*A publication*]   (DLA)
WILK .... Wilkes-Barre, PA [*AM radio station call letters*]
Wilk .... Wilkinson, Owen, Paterson, and Murray's New South Wales Reports [*1862-65*] [*A publication*]   (DLA)
Wilk .... Wilkinson. Texas Court of Appeals and Civil Appeals [*A publication*]   (DLA)
Wilk Funds ... Wilkinson on Public Funds [*1839*] [*A publication*]   (DLA)
Wilk Leg Ang Sax ... Wilkins' Leges Anglo-Saxonicae Ecclesiasticae et Civiles [*A publication*]   (DLA)
Wilk Lim .... Wilkinson. Limitation of Actions [*A publication*]   (ILCA)
Wilk & Mur ... Wilkinson, Owen, Paterson, and Murray's New South Wales Reports [*1862-65*] [*A publication*]   (DLA)
Wilk & Ow ... Wilkinson, Owen, Paterson, and Murray's New South Wales Reports [*1862-65*] [*A publication*]   (DLA)
Wilk & Pat ... Wilkinson, Owen, Paterson, and Murray's New South Wales Reports [*1862-65*] [*A publication*]   (DLA)
Wilk P & M ... Wilkinson, Paterson, and Murray's New South Wales Reports [*1862-65*] [*A publication*]   (DLA)
Wilk Prec ... Wilkinson on Precedents in Conveyancing [*4th ed.*] [*1890*] [*A publication*]   (DLA)
Wilk Repl ... Wilkinson on Replevin [*1825*] [*A publication*]   (DLA)
Wilk Sh ..... Wilkinson's Office of Sheriff [*A publication*]   (DLA)
Wilk Ship .... Wilkinson on Shipping [*1843*] [*A publication*]   (DLA)
WILL .... Urbana, IL [*AM radio station call letters*]
WILL .... Wiley [*John*] & Sons, Inc. [*NASDAQ symbol*]   (NQ)
Will .... Willes' English Common Pleas Reports [*125 English Reprint*] [*A publication*]   (DLA)
Will .... William (King of England)   (DLA)
Will .... Williams' Massachusetts Reports [*1 Massachusetts*] [*1804-05*] [*A publication*]   (DLA)
Will .... Williams' Vermont Reports [*27-29 Vermont*] [*A publication*]   (DLA)
Will .... Willson's Reports [*29-30 Texas Appeals*] [*1, 2, Texas Civil Appeals*] [*A publication*]   (DLA)
WILL .... Workshop In Library Leadership [*Canada*]
WILL .... Workshop Institute for Living-Learning   (EA)
Will Abr ..... Williams' Abridgment of Cases [*1798-1803*] [*A publication*]   (DLA)
Willamette L J ... Willamette Law Journal [*A publication*]
Willamette L Rev ... Willamette Law Review [*A publication*]
Will Ann Reg ... Williams' Annual Register [*New York*] [*A publication*]   (DLA)
Will Auct .... Williams' Auctions [*5th ed.*] [*1829*] [*A publication*]   (DLA)
Will Bankt ... Williams' Law and Practice of Bankruptcy [*19th ed.*] [*1977*] [*A publication*]   (DLA)
Will-Bund St Tr ... Willis-Bund's Cases from State Trials [*A publication*]   (DLA)
Willc Const ... Willcock's The Office of Constable [*A publication*]   (DLA)
Willc Med Pr ... Willcock's Medical Profession [*1830*] [*A publication*]   (DLA)
Willc Mun Corp ... Willcock's Municipal Corp. [*A publication*]   (ILCA)
Willcock Mun Corp ... Willcock's Municipal Corp. [*A publication*]   (DLA)
Will Com .... Williams on Rights of Common [*A publication*]   (DLA)
Will Con Rep ... Texas Civil Cases [*A publication*]   (DLA)
WillCor ...... Willis Corroon Ltd. [*Associated Press abbreviation*]   (APAG)
Will Cr L .... Willan's Criminal Law of Canada [*A publication*]   (DLA)
Willdenowia Beih ... Willdenowia Beiheft [*A publication*]
Will Eq Jur ... Willard's Equity Jurisprudence [*A publication*]   (DLA)
Will Eq Pl .. Willis on Equity Pleading [*1820*] [*A publication*]   (DLA)
Willes .... Willes' English Common Pleas Reports [*125 English Reprint*] [*A publication*]   (DLA)
Willes (Eng) ... Willes' English Common Pleas Reports [*125 English Reprint*] [*A publication*]   (DLA)
Will Ex .... Williams on Executors [*15th ed.*] [*1970*] [*A publication*]   (DLA)
WILL-FM ... Urbana, IL [*FM radio station call letters*]
William Car ... William Carlos Williams Review [*A publication*]
William L Hutcheson Mem For Bull ... William L. Hutcheson Memorial Forest. Bulletin [*A publication*]
William and Mary Bus R ... William and Mary Business Review [*A publication*]
William and Mary Law R ... William and Mary Law Review [*A publication*]
William & Mary L Rev ... William and Mary Law Review [*A publication*]
William Mary Q ... William and Mary College Quarterly [*A publication*]
William Mitchell L Rev ... William Mitchell Law Review [*A publication*]
William M Q ... William and Mary Quarterly [*A publication*]
Williams .... Peere-Williams' English Chancery Reports [*A publication*]   (DLA)
Williams .... Williams Companies [*Associated Press abbreviation*]   (APAG)
Williams .... Williams' Reports [*10-12 Utah*] [*A publication*]   (DLA)
Williams .... Williams' Reports [*1 Massachusetts*] [*A publication*]   (DLA)
Williams .... Williams' Vermont Reports [*27-29 Vermont*] [*A publication*]   (DLA)
Williams & B Adm Jur ... Williams and Bruce's Admiralty Practice [*3 eds.*] [*1869-1902*] [*A publication*]   (DLA)
Williams B Pr ... Williams' Bankruptcy Practice [*17 eds.*] [*1870-1958*] [*A publication*]   (DLA)
Williams & Bruce Ad Pr ... Williams and Bruce's Admiralty Practice [*3 eds.*] [*1869-1902*] [*A publication*]   (DLA)

Williams Common ... Williams on Rights of Common [*A publication*]
Williams Ex'rs ... Williams on Executors [*A publication*]   (DLA)
Williams Ex'rs R & T Ed ... Williams on Executors, Randolph and Talcott Edition [*A publication*]   (DLA)
Williams P ... Peere-Williams' English Chancery Reports [*1695-1736*] [*A publication*]   (DLA)
Williams Pers Prop ... Williams on Personal Property [*A publication*]   (DLA)
Williams Real Prop ... Williams on Real Property [*A publication*]   (DLA)
Williams Saund ... Williams' Notes to Saunders' Reports [*A publication*]   (DLA)
Williams Seis ... Williams on Seisin [*A publication*]   (DLA)
William W Story's Rept ... William W. Story's United States Circuit Court Reports [*A publication*]   (DLA)
Willis Eq .... Willis on Equity Pleading [*1820*] [*A publication*]   (DLA)
Willis Int .... Willis on Interrogatories [*A publication*]   (DLA)
Williston .... Williston on Contracts [*A publication*]   (DLA)
Williston .... Williston on Sales [*A publication*]   (DLA)
Williston Basin Oil Rev ... Williston Basin Oil Review [*A publication*]
Willis Trust ... Willis on Trustees [*A publication*]   (DLA)
Will Just .... Williams' Justice [*A publication*]   (DLA)
Will LD ...... Williams' Law Dictionary [*A publication*]   (DLA)
Will LJ .... Willamette Law Journal [*A publication*]
Will LR ...... Willamette Law Review [*A publication*]
Willm .... [*The*] Williams Companies [*Associated Press abbreviation*]   (APAG)
Will Mass .. Williams' Reports [*1 Massachusetts*] [*A publication*]   (DLA)
Will Mass Cit ... Williams' Massachusetts Citations [*A publication*]   (DLA)
Willm W & D ... Willmore, Wollaston, and Davison's English Queen's Bench Reports [*1837*] [*A publication*]   (DLA)
Willm W & H ... Willmore, Wollaston, and Hodges' English Queen's Bench Reports [*1838-39*] [*A publication*]   (DLA)
Will P .... Peere-Williams' English Chancery Reports [*A publication*]   (DLA)
Will Per Pr ... [*J.*] Williams on Personal Property [*18th ed.*] [*1926*] [*A publication*]   (DLA)
Will Pet Ch ... Williams' Petitions in Chancery [*1880*] [*A publication*]   (DLA)
Will Real Ass ... Williams' Real Assets [*1861*] [*A publication*]   (DLA)
Will Real Est ... Willard on Real Estate and Conveyancing [*A publication*]   (DLA)
Will Real Pr ... Williams on Real Property [*A publication*]   (DLA)
Will Saund ... Williams' Notes to Saunders' Reports [*A publication*]   (DLA)
Wills Circ Ev ... Wills on Circumstantial Evidence [*A publication*]   (DLA)
Wills Cir Ev ... Wills on Circumstantial Evidence [*A publication*]   (DLA)
Will Seis .... Williams on Seisin of the Freehold [*1878*] [*A publication*]   (DLA)
Wills Est Tr ... Wills, Estates, Trusts [*Prentice-Hall, Inc.*] [*A publication*]   (DLA)
Wills Est & Tr (P-H) ... Wills, Estates, and Trusts (Prentice-Hall, Inc.) [*A publication*]   (DLA)
Wills Est & Tr Serv P-H ... Wills, Estates, and Trust Service. Prentice-Hall [*A publication*]
Will Sett ..... Williams on the Settlement of Real Estates [*A publication*]   (DLA)
Willson .... Willson's Reports, Civil Cases [*29-30 Texas Appeals*] [*1, 2 Texas Court of Appeals*] [*A publication*]   (DLA)
Willson Civ Cas Ct App ... White and Willson's Civil Cases, Texas Court of Appeals [*A publication*]   (DLA)
Willson's CC ... Texas Civil Cases [*A publication*]   (DLA)
Willson Tex Cr Law ... Willson's Revised Penal Code, Code of Criminal Procedure, and Penal Laws of Texas [*A publication*]   (DLA)
Will St L .... Williams on the Study of the Law [*A publication*]   (DLA)
WILL-TV .. Urbana, IL [*Television station call letters*]
Will VT ...... Williams' Vermont Reports [*27-29 Vermont*] [*A publication*]   (DLA)
Will Woll & D ... Willmore, Wollaston, and Davison's English Queen's Bench Reports [*1837*] [*A publication*]   (DLA)
Will Woll & Dav ... Willmore, Wollaston, and Davison's English Queen's Bench Reports [*1837*] [*A publication*]   (DLA)
Will Woll & H ... Willmore, Wollaston, and Hodges' English Queen's Bench Reports [*1838-39*] [*A publication*]   (DLA)
Will Woll & Hodg ... Willmore, Wollaston, and Hodges' English Queen's Bench Reports [*1838-39*] [*A publication*]   (DLA)
WILM .... Wildlife Monographs [*A publication*]
WILM .... Wilmington, DE [*AM radio station call letters*]
WILM .... Wilmington Trust Co. [*NASDAQ symbol*]   (NQ)
Wilm .... Wilmot's Notes and Opinions, King's Bench [*97 English Reprint*] [*A publication*]   (DLA)
Wilm Burg ... Wilmot's Digest of the Law of Burglary [*A publication*]   (DLA)
WilmCS ..... Williams Coal Seam Royalty Trust [*Associated Press abbreviation*]   (APAG)
Wilm Judg ... Wilmot's Notes and Opinions, King's Bench [*97 English Reprint*] [*A publication*]   (DLA)
Wilm Mort ... Wilmot on Mortgages [*A publication*]   (DLA)
Wilm Op .... Wilmot's Notes and Opinions, King's Bench [*97 English Reprint*] [*A publication*]   (DLA)
Wilmot's Notes ... Wilmot's Notes and Opinions, King's Bench [*97 English Reprint*] [*A publication*]   (DLA)
Wilmot's Notes (Eng) ... Wilmot's Notes and Opinions, King's Bench [*97 English Reprint*] [*A publication*]   (DLA)

Wilm W & D ... Willmore, Wollaston, and Davison's English Queen's Bench Reports [*A publication*] (DLA)
WILN .... Panama City, FL [*FM radio station call letters*]
WILN .... Wildlife News [*A publication*]
WILN .... Wilson [*H. J.*] Co. [*NASDAQ symbol*] (NQ)
WILO .... Frankfort, IN [*AM radio station call letters*]
WILPF ...... Women's International League for Peace and Freedom [*Switzerland*] (EAIO)
WILPFNSW Branch Monthly Bulletin ... WILPF [*Women's International League for Peace and Freedom*]. New South Wales Branch. Monthly Bulletin [*A publication*] (APTA)
WILPF-US ... Women's International League for Peace and Freedom, US Section (EA)
WILQ .... Williamsport, PA [*FM radio station call letters*]
Wil Q .... Wilson Quarterly [*A publication*]
WI LR .... Wisconsin Law Review [*A publication*]
WILS .... Lansing, MI [*AM radio station call letters*]
WILS .... Wang Interactive Learning System [*Data processing*] (HGAA)
WILS .... Western Illinois Library System [*Library network*]
Wils .... Wilson's English Chancery Reports [*37 English Reprint*] [*A publication*] (DLA)
Wils .... Wilson's English Common Pleas Reports, 3 [*95 English Reprint*] [*A publication*] (DLA)
Wils .... Wilson's English King's Bench Reports [*95 English Reprint*] [*1742-74*] [*A publication*] (DLA)
WILS .... Wisconsin Interlibrary Loan Service
Wils Arb .... Wilson on Arbitrations [*A publication*] (DLA)
Wils Ch ...... Wilson's English Chancery Reports [*37 English Reprint*] [*A publication*] (DLA)
Wils Ch (Eng) ... Wilson's English Chancery Reports [*37 English Reprint*] [*A publication*] (DLA)
Wils & Court ... Wilson and Courtenay's Scotch Appeal Cases [*A publication*] (DLA)
Wils CP ...... Wilson's English Common Pleas [*A publication*] (DLA)
Wils (Eng) ... Wilson's English Common Pleas Reports, 3 [*95 English Reprint*] [*A publication*] (DLA)
Wils Ent ..... Wilson's Entries and Pleading [*3 Lord Raymond's King's Bench and Common Pleas Reports*] [*England*] [*A publication*] (DLA)
Wils Ex ...... Wilson's English Exchequer Reports [*159 English Reprint*] [*1805-17*] [*A publication*] (DLA)
Wils Exch .. Wilson's English Exchequer Reports [*159 English Reprint*] [*A publication*] (DLA)
Wils Exch (Eng) ... Wilson's English Exchequer Reports [*159 English Reprint*] [*A publication*] (DLA)
Wils Fines ... Wilson on Fines and Recoveries [*A publication*] (DLA)
WilshrO ..... Wilshire Oil Co. of Texas [*Associated Press abbreviation*] (APAG)
Wils Ind ..... Wilson's Indiana Superior Court Reports [*A publication*] (DLA)
Wils Ind Gloss ... Wilson's Glossary of Indian Terms [*A publication*] (DLA)
Wils Jud Acts ... Wilson on the Judicature Acts, Etc. [*A publication*] (DLA)
Wils KB ..... Sergeant Wilson's English King's Bench Reports [*1724-74*] [*A publication*] (DLA)
Wils Minn ... Wilson's Reports [*48-59 Minnesota*] [*A publication*] (DLA)
Wils Mod Eng Law ... Wilson's History of Modern English Law [*A publication*] (DLA)
Wilson .... Wilson Quarterly [*A publication*]
Wilson .... Wilson's English Chancery Reports [*37 English Reprint*] [*A publication*] (DLA)
Wilson .... Wilson's English King's Bench and Common Pleas Reports [*A publication*] (DLA)
Wilson .... Wilson's Exchequer in Equity Reports [*England*] [*A publication*] (DLA)
Wilson .... Wilson's Indiana Superior Court Reports [*A publication*] (DLA)
Wilson .... Wilson's Reports [*1-3 Oregon*] [*A publication*] (DLA)
Wilson .... Wilson's Reports [*48-59 Minnesota*] [*A publication*] (DLA)
Wilson B .... Wilson Bulletin [*A publication*]
Wilson Bull ... Wilson Bulletin [*A publication*]
Wilson Lib Bul ... Wilson Library Bulletin [*A publication*]
Wilson Lib Bull ... Wilson Library Bulletin [*A publication*]
Wilson Librr Bull ... Wilson Library Bulletin [*A publication*]
Wilson Q ..... Wilson Quarterly [*A publication*]
Wilson & Shaw ... Wilson and Shaw's Scottish Appeal Cases [*1825-35*] [*A publication*] (DLA)
Wilson's R ... Wilson's Indiana Superior Court Reports [*A publication*] (DLA)
Wilson's Rev & Ann St ... Wilson's Revised and Annotated Statutes [*Oklahoma*] [*A publication*] (DLA)
Wilson Super Ct (Ind) ... Wilson's Indiana Superior Court Reports [*A publication*] (DLA)
Wils Oreg .. Wilson's Reports [*1-3 Oregon*] [*A publication*] (DLA)
Wils Parl L ... Wilson's Parliamentary Law [*A publication*] (DLA)
Wils PC ...... Wilson's English Privy Council Reports [*A publication*] (DLA)
Wils & S ..... Wilson and Shaw's Scottish Appeal Cases [*1825-35*] [*A publication*] (DLA)
Wils & Sh .. Wilson and Shaw's Scottish Appeal Cases [*1825-35*] [*A publication*] (DLA)
Wils & S (Scot) ... Wilson and Shaw's Scottish Appeal Cases [*1825-35*] [*A publication*] (DLA)

Wils Super (Ind) ... Wilson's Indiana Superior Court Reports [*A publication*] (DLA)
Wils Uses ... Wilson on Springing Uses [*A publication*] (DLA)
WILS/WLC ... Wisconsin Interlibrary Loan Service - Wisconsin Library Consortium [*Library network*]
Wilt A Nat Hist Mag ... Wiltshire Archaeological and Natural History Magazine [*A publication*]
WilTel .... Williams Telecommunications Co. [*Tulsa, OK*] [*Telecommunications service*] (TSSD)
WILTS ...... Wiltshire [*County in England*]
Wilts Arch Natur Hist Mag ... Wiltshire Archaeological and Natural History Magazine [*A publication*]
Wilts Beekprs Gaz ... Wiltshire Beekeepers' Gazette [*A publication*]
Wiltshire Archaeol Natur Hist Mag ... Wiltshire Archaeological and Natural History Magazine [*A publication*]
Wiltshire Arch Mag ... Wiltshire Archaeological Magazine [*Later, Wiltshire Archaeological and Natural History Magazine*] [*A publication*]
Wiltshire Arch Natur Hist Mag ... Wiltshire Archaeological and Natural History Magazine [*A publication*]
WILUCL ... Willamette University College of Law (DLA)
WILX .... Onondaga, MI [*Television station call letters*]
WILY .... Centralia, IL [*AM radio station call letters*]
WIM .... Madison Public Library, Madison, WI [*OCLC symbol*] (OCLC)
WIM .... Waksman Institute of Microbiology [*Rutgers University*] [*Research center*] (RCD)
WIM .... Warm Ionized Medium [*Astrophysics*]
WIM .... Washington, Idaho & Montana Railway Co. [*AAR code*]
WIM .... Weigh in Motion
WIM .... Women in Management [*Chicago, IL*] (EA)
WIM .... Women in Mining National (EA)
WIMA .... Labuhan Bilik/Ajamu [*Indonesia*] [*ICAO location identifier*] (ICLI)
WIMA .... Lima, OH [*AM radio station call letters*]
WIMA .... Women's International Motorcycle Association (EA)
WIMA .... World International Medical Association (EA)
WIMA .... Writing Instrument Manufacturers Association (EA)
WIMB .... Gunung Sitoli/Binaka [*Indonesia*] [*ICAO location identifier*] (ICLI)
WIMB .... Wimborne Minster [*Urban district in England*]
WIMC .... Crawfordsville, IN [*FM radio station call letters*]
WIMC .... Whom It May Concern
WIME .... Padang Sidempuan/Aek Godang [*Indonesia*] [*ICAO location identifier*] (ICLI)
WIMEA ..... Wiretap, Investigation Monitoring, and Eavesdrop Activities (MCD)
WIMG .... Padang/Tabing [*Indonesia*] [*ICAO location identifier*] (ICLI)
WIMG .... Trenton, NJ [*AM radio station call letters*]
WIMG .... Women in Municipal Government (EA)
WIMI .... Ironwood, MI [*FM radio station call letters*]
WIMI .... Warburg Investment Management International
WIMI .... Warwick Insurance Managers, Inc. [*NASDAQ symbol*] (NQ)
WIMI .... Watercraft Intensively Managed Items (AABC)
WIMIS ...... Walk-In Management Information System [*Data processing*]
WIMK .... Iron Mountain, MI [*FM radio station call letters*]
WIMK .... Kisaran/Tanah Gambus [*Indonesia*] [*ICAO location identifier*] (ICLI)
WIML .... Kisaran/Aek Loba [*Indonesia*] [*ICAO location identifier*] (ICLI)
WIML .... Wrightsville, GA [*FM radio station call letters*]
WIMM ...... Medan/Polonia [*Indonesia*] [*ICAO location identifier*] (ICLI)
WIMM ...... Weapons Integrated Materiel Manager [*Military*]
WIMN .... Waunakee, WI [*FM radio station call letters*]
WIMN .... Women in Mining National (EA)
WIMO .... Winder, GA [*AM radio station call letters*]
WIMP .... Prapat/Sibisa [*Indonesia*] [*ICAO location identifier*] (ICLI)
WIMP .... WARF [*Wartime Replacement Factors*] Intermediate Materiel Processor [*Military*]
WIMP .... Weakly Interacting Massive [*or Integrated Magnetic*] Particle [*Astrophysics*]
WIMP .... Windows/Icons/Mouse/Pull-Down-Menus [*Data processing*] (BYTE)
WIMR .... Pematang Siantar/Gunung Pamela [*Indonesia*] [*ICAO location identifier*] (ICLI)
WIMS .... Michigan City, IN [*AM radio station call letters*]
WIMS .... Sibolga/Pinang Sori [*Indonesia*] [*ICAO location identifier*] (ICLI)
WIMS .... Wartime Instruction Manual for Merchant Ships [*For deck officers of the United States Merchant Marine; popularly known as the "Convoy Bible"*] [*World War II*]
WIMS .... Waveguide Impedance Measuring Set
WIMS .... Works Information and Management System [*M & E White Consultants Ltd.*] [*Software package*] (NCC)
WIMS .... World Information Management System [*Air Force*] (GFGA)
WIMS .... Worldwide Integrated Management of Subsistence
WIMSA ..... Webster Institute for Mathematics, Science, and Arts [*Webster College*]
WIMT .... Lima, OH [*FM radio station call letters*]
WIMT .... Tebing Tingci/Pabatu [*Indonesia*] [*ICAO location identifier*] (ICLI)

WIMV .... Madison, FL [*FM radio station call letters*]
WIMX .... Harrisburg, PA [*FM radio station call letters*]
WIMZ .... Knoxville, TN [*AM radio station call letters*]
WIMZ .... Medan Sector [*Indonesia*] [*ICAO location identifier*]   (ICLI)
WIMZ-FM ... Knoxville, TN [*FM radio station call letters*]
WIN .... INELEC Library Project, Menomonie, WI [*OCLC symbol*]
              [*Inactive*]   (OCLC)
WIN .... Irwin, Australia [*Spaceflight Tracking and Data Network*]
              [*NASA*]
WIN .... Water-Insoluble Nitrogen [*Analytical chemistry*]
WIN .... Weapon Index Number [*Military*]   (CAAL)
WIN .... Weapons Interception [*Military electronics*]
WIN .... Well Information Network [*Database*]
WIN .... Western Information Network
WIN .... Whip Inflation Now [*Slogan of President Gerald R. Ford's anti-
              inflation program, 1974*] [*Program discontinued March,
              1975*]
WIN .... White-Indian-Negro
Win .... Win Magazine [*A publication*]
Win .... Winch's English Common Pleas Reports [*124 English Reprint*]
              [*A publication*]   (DLA)
WIN .... Windhoek [*Namibia*] [*Seismograph station code, US Geological
              Survey*]   (SEIS)
WIN .... Window [*Technical drawings*]
WIN .... Windsor Board of Education [*UTLAS symbol*]
Win .... Winer's Unreported Opinions, New York Supreme Court [*A
              publication*]   (DLA)
WIN .... Winn-Dixie Stores, Inc. [*NYSE symbol*]   (SPSG)
Win .... Winston's North Carolina Reports [*1863-64*] [*A
              publication*]   (DLA)
Win .... Winter [*A publication*]
WIN .... Winter
WIN .... Winthrop Laboratories [*Research code symbol*]
WIN .... Winton [*Australia*] [*Airport symbol*]   (OAG)
WIN .... Wireless In-Building Network [*Motorola, Inc.*] [*Data
              processing*]
WIN .... Wollongong Integrated Network   (HGAA)
WIN .... Women's International Network   (EA)
WIN .... Work Incentive Program [*Later, ETSC*]   (EA)
WIN .... Workshop in Nonviolence   (EA)
WIN .... World Information Network [*Information service or
              system*]   (IID)
WIN .... WWMCCS [*Worldwide Military Command and Control
              System*] Intercomputer Network [*DoD*]
W/IN² .... Watts per Square Inch
WINA .... Charlottesville, VA [*AM radio station call letters*]
WINA .... Webb Institute of Naval Architecture [*Glen Cove, NY*]
WINA .... Witton Network Analyzer
WINAP ..... Women's Information Network for Asia and the Pacific
              [*ESCAP*] [*United Nations*]   (DUND)
WINB .... Western Interstate Nuclear Board   (NRCH)
WINBA ..... World International Nail and Beauty Association   (EA)
WINBAN .. Windward Islands' Banana Association
WINC .... Western Interstate Nuclear Compact [*Later, WIEB/WINB*]
WINC .... White Incumbent
WINC .... Winchester, VA [*AM radio station call letters*]
WINC .... Worldwide Integrated Communications [*Mohawk Data
              Sciences Corp.*] [*Parsippany, NJ*]
              [*Telecommunications*]   (TSSD)
WINC-FM ... Winchester, VA [*FM radio station call letters*]
WINCH..... Winchcombe [*England*]
WINCH..... Winchester [*City in England*]   (ROG)
Winch........ Winch's English Common Pleas Reports [*124 English Reprint*]
              [*A publication*]   (DLA)
Winch (Eng) ... Winch's English Common Pleas Reports [*124 English
              Reprint*] [*A publication*]   (DLA)
WIND........ Chicago, IL [*AM radio station call letters*]
WIND........ Weather Information Network and Display
WIND........ Windsor [*Municipal borough in England*]
WIND........ Windsor Life Insurance Co. of America [*NASDAQ
              symbol*]   (NQ)
WIND....... Women in Distribution [*Commercial firm*]
WINDAV .. Wind Direction and Velocity Indicator [*Aviation*]
WINDEE... Wind Tunnel Data Encoding and Evaluation [*System*] [*Boeing
              Co.*]
Wind Energy Rep ... Wind Energy Report [*United States*] [*A publication*]
Wind Eng... Wind Engineering [*England*] [*A publication*]
Wind Engng ... Wind Engineering [*A publication*]
Wind En Rpt ... Wind Energy Report [*A publication*]
W Indian Dig ... West Indian Digest [*A publication*]
W Indian Med J ... West Indian Medical Journal [*A publication*]
W Indian World ... West Indian World [*A publication*]
WINDII..... Wind Imaging Interferometer
Wind Inst Melior Uzytkow Zielonych ... Windomosci Instytutu Melioracji i
              Uzytkow Zielonych [*A publication*]
WinDix ...... Winn-Dixie Stores, Inc. [*Associated Press
              abbreviation*]   (APAG)
W Ind Med J ... West Indian Medical Journal [*A publication*]
Windmr...... Windmere Corp. [*Associated Press abbreviation*]   (APAG)
Wind Muz Ziemi ... Windomosci Muzeum Ziemi [*A publication*]

WINDO..... Wide Information Network Data Online [*Government Printing
              Office*]
Wind O ...... Windless Orchard [*A publication*]
Window Inds ... Window Industries [*A publication*]
Wind Power Dig ... Wind Power Digest [*A publication*]
WINDS...... Weather Information Network and Display System [*NASA*]
Windsat ..... Wind Satellite
Windsor ..... Windsor Magazine [*A publication*]
Windsor R ... Windsor Report [*A publication*]
Windsor Yearb Access ... Windsor Yearbook of Access to Justice [*A
              publication*]
Wind Technol J ... Wind Technology Journal [*A publication*]
WINE .... Brookfield, CT [*AM radio station call letters*]
WINE .... Schagrins, Inc. [*NASDAQ symbol*]   (NQ)
WINE .... Warning and Indications in Europe   (MCD)
WINE .... Webb Institute of Naval Engineering
Wine Hdbk ... Wine Marketing Handbook [*A publication*]
Win Ent...... Winch's Book of Entries [*A publication*]   (DLA)
Win Eq ...... Winston's North Carolina Equity Reports [*A
              publication*]   (DLA)
Wine Rev.... Wine Review [*A publication*]
WINES...... World Integrated Nuclear Evaluation System [*Department of
              Energy*]   (GFGA)
Wine Vine .. Wines and Vines Statistical Issue [*A publication*]
WINF .... Winfrith [*England*]
Winfield Words & Phrases ... Winfield's Adjudged Words and Phrases, with
              Notes [*A publication*]   (DLA)
WING .... Dayton, OH [*AM radio station call letters*]
Wing .... Wing Newsletter [*A publication*]
Wing .... Wingate's Maxims [*A publication*]   (DLA)
WING .... Wings West Airlines, Inc. [*Santa Monica, CA*] [*NASDAQ
              symbol*]   (NQ)
Wing Max ... Wingate's Maxims [*A publication*]   (DLA)
WINGO..... Women's International Non-Government Organisation
              [*British*]   (DI)
Wings Afr .. Wings over Africa [*A publication*]
WINI .... Murphysboro, IL [*AM radio station call letters*]
WINJ .... Pulaski, TN [*FM radio station call letters*]
WINK .... Fort Myers, FL [*AM radio station call letters*]
WINK .... Warning in Korea   (MCD)
WINK .... Winkleigh [*England*]
WINK-FM ... Fort Myers, FL [*FM radio station call letters*]
WINKS...... Women in Numerous Kitchens [*World War II*]
WINK-TV ... Fort Myers, FL [*Television station call letters*]
WINM .... Angola, IN [*Television station call letters*]
WINN .... North Vernon, IN [*FM radio station call letters*]
WINN .... Wedding Information Network, Inc. [*NASDAQ symbol*]   (NQ)
Winnbg ..... Winnebago Industries, Inc. [*Associated Press
              abbreviation*]   (APAG)
Winnip Clin Q ... Winnipeg Clinic. Quarterly [*A publication*]
WINNS ...... Winn Enterprises [*NASDAQ symbol*]   (NQ)
WINP .... Water Insoluble Nonstarchy Polysaccharide [*Food
              composition*]
WINQ....... Winchendon, MA [*FM radio station call letters*]
WINR .... Binghamton, NY [*AM radio station call letters*]
WINRA ..... Women in the National Rifle Association
WINS........ New York, NY [*AM radio station call letters*]
WINS........ Weapons and Integrated Navigation System   (MCD)
WINS........ Wideband Information Network Services [*Data processing*]
WINS........ Winslow [*England*]
WINS........ Women in National Service [*Name given by Ladies' Home
              Journal to American housewives and their teen-age
              daughters, "the greatest reserve strength of America"*]
              [*World War II*]
WINS........ Women in Naval Service
WINS........ Women's Industrial and National Service Corps [*World War II*]
              [*British*]
WINSNAMS ... Wind Indicating Systems for Navigation Aircraft in Missile
              Support
Winst .... Winston's North Carolina Equity Reports [*A
              publication*]   (DLA)
Winst .... Winston's North Carolina Law Reports [*A publication*]   (DLA)
WINST...... Winstree [*England*]
WINSTAN ... Wings, Nonstraight-Taper Analysis   (MCD)
Winst Eq .... Winston's North Carolina Equity Reports [*A
              publication*]   (DLA)
Winst Eq (NC) ... Winston's North Carolina Equity Reports [*A
              publication*]   (DLA)
Winst L (NC) ... Winston's North Carolina Law Reports [*A
              publication*]   (DLA)
WINSTRS ... Winston Resources Ltd. [*Associated Press
              abbreviation*]   (APAG)
WINT .... Crossville, TN [*Television station call letters*]
WINT .... Walker International Industries, Inc. [*NASDAQ symbol*]   (NQ)
WINT .... Winter   (FAAC)
Wintertag... Wintertagung [*A publication*]
Winter Tb .. Winter's Naturwissenschaftliche Taschenbuecher [*A
              publication*]
Winterthur ... Winterthur Portfolio [*A publication*]
Winterthur Jb ... Winterthur Jahrbuch [*A publication*]
Winterthur Port ... Winterthur Portfolio [*A publication*]

WINTEX... Winter Exercise (MCD)
Winthr St M ... Winthrop Studies on Major Modern Writers [*A publication*]
WINTON .. [*Bishop of*] Winchester [*British*]
WINU .... Highland, IL [*AM radio station call letters*]
WINV .... Inverness, FL [*AM radio station call letters*]
WINW .... Canton, OH [*AM radio station call letters*]
WINX .... Rockville, MD [*AM radio station call letters*]
WINY .... Putnam, CT [*AM radio station call letters*]
WINZ .... Miami, FL [*AM radio station call letters*]
WIO .... Nashotah House, Nashotah, WI [*OCLC symbol*] (OCLC)
WIO .... Wilcannia [*Australia*] [*Airport symbol*] (OAG)
WIO .... Women's International ORT
WIOA .... San Juan, PR [*FM radio station call letters*]
WIOB .... Bengkayang [*Indonesia*] [*ICAO location identifier*] (ICLI)
WIOB .... Mayaguez, PR [*FM radio station call letters*]
WIOC .... Ponce, PR [*FM radio station call letters*]
WIOD .... Miami, FL [*AM radio station call letters*]
WIOF .... Waterbury, CT [*FM radio station call letters*]
WIOG .... Bay City, MI [*FM radio station call letters*]
WIOG .... Nangapinoh [*Indonesia*] [*ICAO location identifier*] (ICLI)
WIOH .... Paloh/Liku [*Indonesia*] [*ICAO location identifier*] (ICLI)
WIOI .... New Boston, OH [*AM radio station call letters*]
WIOI .... Singkawang II [*Indonesia*] [*ICAO location identifier*] (ICLI)
WIOK .... Falmouth, KY [*FM radio station call letters*]
WIOK .... Ketapang/Rahadi Usman [*Indonesia*] [*ICAO location identifier*] (ICLI)
WION .... Ionia, MI [*AM radio station call letters*]
WION .... Natuna/Ransi [*Indonesia*] [*ICAO location identifier*] (ICLI)
WIOO .... Carlisle, PA [*AM radio station call letters*]
WIOO .... Pontianak/Supadio [*Indonesia*] [*ICAO location identifier*] (ICLI)
WIOP .... Putusibau/Pangsuma [*Indonesia*] [*ICAO location identifier*] (ICLI)
WIOQ .... Philadelphia, PA [*FM radio station call letters*]
WIOS .... Sintang/Susilo [*Indonesia*] [*ICAO location identifier*] (ICLI)
WIOS .... Tawas City, MI [*AM radio station call letters*]
WIOT .... Toledo, OH [*FM radio station call letters*]
WIOU .... Kokomo, IN [*AM radio station call letters*]
WIOV .... Ephrata, PA [*FM radio station call letters*]
WIOZ .... Pontianak Sector [*Indonesia*] [*ICAO location identifier*] (ICLI)
WIOZ .... Southern Pines, NC [*FM radio station call letters*]
WIP .... Philadelphia, PA [*AM radio station call letters*]
WIP .... Ripon College Library, Ripon, WI [*OCLC symbol*] (OCLC)
WIP .... Wartime Intelligence Plan (NATG)
WIP .... Weapon Indicator Panel [*Military*] (CAAL)
WIP .... Weapons Installation Plan [*Navy*] (NG)
WIP .... Women in Information Processing (EA)
WIP .... Women in Production (EA)
WIP .... Work Incentive Program [*Department of Health, Education, and Welfare; Department of Labor*] (DLA)
WIP .... Work in Place (AABC)
WIP .... Work in Process
WIP .... Work in Progress [*A publication*]
WIP .... Work in Progress (AFM)
WIP .... Workgroup Indian Project [*Netherlands*]
WIP .... Working Group Indigenous Peoples [*Netherlands*] (EAIO)
WIPA .... Jambi/Sultan Taha [*Indonesia*] [*ICAO location identifier*] (ICLI)
WIPACE ... Wartime Intelligence Plan, Allied Command Europe (NATG)
WIPB .... Muncie, IN [*Television station call letters*]
WIPC .... Lake Wales, FL [*AM radio station call letters*]
WIPC .... Rimbo Bujang [*Indonesia*] [*ICAO location identifier*] (ICLI)
WIPC .... Writers in Prison Committee of International PEN [*British*] (EAIO)
WIPE .... Tanjung Enim/Bangko [*Indonesia*] [*ICAO location identifier*] (ICLI)
WIPF .... Kuala Tungkal [*Indonesia*] [*ICAO location identifier*] (ICLI)
WIPH .... Sungai Penuh/Depati Parbo [*Indonesia*] [*ICAO location identifier*] (ICLI)
WIPI .... Bungo Tebo/Pasir Mayang [*Indonesia*] [*ICAO location identifier*] (ICLI)
WIPI .... Word Intelligibility by Picture Identification [*Artificial intelligence*]
WIPIS .... Who Is Publishing in Science [*An Institute for Scientific Information publication*] [*Trademark*]
WIPJ .... Jambi/Dusun Aro [*Indonesia*] [*ICAO location identifier*] (ICLI)
WIPL .... Bengkulu/Padang Kemiling [*Indonesia*] [*ICAO location identifier*] (ICLI)
WIPM .... Mayaguez, PR [*Television station call letters*]
WIPM .... West Indian People's Movement [*Netherlands Antilles*] [*Political party*] (EY)
WIPM .... Work in Process Measurement (MCD)
WIPO .... World Intellectual Property Organization [*Switzerland*] (IID)
WIPP .... Palembang/Sultan Mahmud Badaruddin II [*Indonesia*] [*ICAO location identifier*] (ICLI)
WIPP .... Waste Isolation Pilot Plant [*Department of Energy*]
WIPP .... Work Isolation Pilot Project [*NASA*]
WIPPL ...... Women in Political and Public Life [*British*] (DI)
WIPQ .... Pendoro [*Indonesia*] [*ICAO location identifier*] (ICLI)
WIPR........ Rengat/Japura [*Indonesia*] [*ICAO location identifier*] (ICLI)

WIPR........ San Juan, PR [*AM radio station call letters*]
Wi Pr .... Wirtschafts-Praxis [*A publication*]
WIPR-FM ... San Juan, PR [*FM radio station call letters*]
WIPR-TV .. San Juan, PR [*Television station call letters*]
WIPS .... Ticonderoga, NY [*AM radio station call letters*]
WIPS .... Washington Intelligence Data Processing System (SAA)
WIPS .... Women in Production Service [*A voluntary, semimilitary organization of women employees, primarily at the E. I. du Pont de Nemours & Co., at Richmond, Va.*] [*World War II*]
WIPS .... Word Image Processing System [*Datacopy Corp.*]
WIPTC ...... Women's International Professional Tennis Council (EA)
WIPU .... Muko Muko [*Indonesia*] [*ICAO location identifier*] (ICLI)
WIPV .... Keluang [*Indonesia*] [*ICAO location identifier*] (ICLI)
WIPY .... Bentayan [*Indonesia*] [*ICAO location identifier*] (ICLI)
WIPZ .... Palembang Sector [*Indonesia*] [*ICAO location identifier*] (ICLI)
WIQ .... Appleton Public Library, Appleton, WI [*OCLC symbol*] (OCLC)
WIQB .... Ann Arbor, MI [*FM radio station call letters*]
WIQH........ Concord, MA [*FM radio station call letters*]
WIQO........ Covington, VA [*FM radio station call letters*]
WIQQ .... Leland, MS [*FM radio station call letters*]
WIQT .... Horseheads, NY [*AM radio station call letters*]
WIQUD..... Wilson Quarterly [*A publication*]
WIR .... Racine Public Library, Racine, WI [*OCLC symbol*] (OCLC)
WIR .... War Information Report [*British military*] (DMA)
WIR .... Weapons Inspection Report [*Navy*] (NG)
WIR .... Weekly Intelligence Review
WIR .... Welfare in Review [*A publication*]
WIR .... West India Regiment
WIR .... West Indian Reports [*A publication*] (DLA)
WIR .... Western Intelligence Report [*A publication*] (APTA)
WIR .... Western Investment Real Estate Trust SBI [*AMEX symbol*] (SPSG)
WIR .... Wildrose Petroleum Ltd. [*Vancouver Stock Exchange symbol*]
W & IR....... Work and Inspection Record (SAA)
WIR .... Wuerttemberg Israelitische Religionsgemeinschaft [*A publication*] (BJA)
WIRA .... Fort Pierce, FL [*AM radio station call letters*]
WIRA .... Wool Industry Research Association [*British*] (DI)
Wirbelsacule Forsch Prax ... Wirbelsacule in Forschung und Praxis [*A publication*]
WIRC........ Hickory, NC [*AM radio station call letters*]
WIRC........ Women's International Resource Centre [*British*] (EAIO)
WIRD .... Lake Placid, NY [*AM radio station call letters*]
WIRDS..... Weather Information Remoting and Display System
WIRE........ Lebanon, IN [*FM radio station call letters*]
WIRE........ Waseca Inter-Library Resource Exchange [*Library network*]
WIRE........ Weapons Interference Reduction Effort [*Navy*] (NG)
WIRE........ Wildlife Review. British Columbia Ministry of Environment [*A publication*]
WIRE........ Women's International Resource Exchange (EA)
Wire Ind..... Wire Industry [*A publication*]
Wire J .... Wire Journal [*A publication*]
Wire J Int .. Wire Journal International [*A publication*]
Wireless Eng ... Wireless Engineer [*A publication*]
Wirel Wld .. Wireless World [*A publication*]
Wirel World ... Wireless World [*A publication*]
Wire Prod ... Wire and Wire Products [*A publication*]
WIRES ...... Women in Radio and Electrical Service [*World War II*]
WIRET ...... Western Investment Real Estate Trust [*Associated Press abbreviation*] (APAG)
Wire Technol ... Wire Technology [*A publication*]
Wire and Wire Prod ... Wire and Wire Products [*A publication*]
Wire World Int ... Wire World International [*A publication*]
WIRF .... Women's International Religious Fellowship (EA)
WIRGA ..... West Indian Royal Garrison Artillery [*British military*] (DMA)
Wiring Install and Supplies ... Wiring Installations and Supplies [*A publication*]
WIRJ .... Humboldt, TN [*AM radio station call letters*]
WIRK .... West Palm Beach, FL [*FM radio station call letters*]
Wirkerei Strickerei Tech ... Wirkerei und Strickerei Technik [*A publication*]
WIRL........ Peoria, IL [*AM radio station call letters*]
WIRMIT ... Women in RMIT [*Royal Melbourne Institute of Technology*] Group [*Australia*]
WIRO .... Ironton, OH [*AM radio station call letters*]
WIRO .... Wyoming Infrared Observatory
WIRQ .... Rochester, NY [*FM radio station call letters*]
WIRR........ Virginia-Hibbing, MN [*FM radio station call letters*]
WIRS........ Wage Information Retrieval System [*IRS*]
WIRS........ Western Illinois Regional Studies [*A publication*]
WIRS........ Workplace Industrial Relations Survey [*British*]
WIRS........ Yauco, PR [*Television station call letters*]
WIRT........ Hibbing, MN [*Television station call letters*]
Wirt.......... Wirtschaftsdienst [*A publication*]
WirtBer Lateinam Laender sowie Spanien und Port ... Wirtschaftsbericht ueber die Lateinamerikanischen Laender sowie Spanien und Portugal [*A publication*]
Wirt Futter ... Wirtschaftseigene Futter [*A publication*]
Wirt und Ges ... Wirtschaft und Gesellschaft [*A publication*]

Wirt und Investment ... Wirtschaft und Investment [*A publication*]
Wirt Pol ..... Monatsblaetter fuer Freiheitliche Wirtschaftspolitik [*A publication*]
Wirt und Recht ... Wirtschaft und Recht [*A publication*]
Wirt Reihe ... Lange Reihen zur Wirtschaftsentwicklung [*A publication*]
WIRTSCH ... Wirtschaft [*Economy, Industry*] [*German*]
Wirtschaft ... Wirtschafts-Blaetter [*A publication*]
Wirtschaftspol Chron ... Wirtschaftspolitische Chronik [*A publication*]
Wirtschaftswiss ... Wirtschaftswissenschaft [*A publication*]
Wirtsch-Dienst ... Wirtschaftsdienst [*A publication*]
Wirtsch u Recht ... Wirtschaft und Recht [*A publication*]
Wirtschseig Futter ... Wirtschaftseigene Futter [*A publication*]
Wirtsch Stat ... Wirtschaft und Statistik [*A publication*]
Wirtsch Verwalt ... Wirtschaft und Verwaltung [*German Federal Republic*] [*A publication*]
Wirtsch Wettbewerb ... Wirtschaft und Wettbewerb [*West Germany*] [*A publication*]
Wirtsch-Wiss ... Wirtschaftswissenschaft [*A publication*]
Wirt und Sozwiss Inst Mitt ... Wirtschafts- und Sozialwissenschaftliches Institut. Mitteilungen [*A publication*]
Wirt und Statis ... Wirtschaft und Statistik [*A publication*]
Wirtswoche ... Wirtschaftswoche [*A publication*]
Wirt und Wettbewerb ... Wirtschaft und Wettbewerb [*A publication*]
Wirt u Wiss ... Wirtschaft und Wissen [*A publication*]
Wirt Wiss Inst Mitt ... Wirtschaftswissenschaftliches Institut Mitteilungen [*A publication*]
Wirt in Za .. Wirtschaft in Zahlen [*A publication*]
WIRV .... Irvine, KY [*AM radio station call letters*]
WIRX........ St. Joseph, MI [*FM radio station call letters*]
WIRY........ Plattsburgh, NY [*AM radio station call letters*]
WIS............ Columbia, SC [*Television station call letters*]
WIS............ University of Wisconsin, Stevens Point, Stevens Point, WI [*OCLC symbol*] (OCLC)
WIS............ Washington Inventory Service
WIS............ Washington Irving Society (EA)
WIS............ Wave Information Study [*US Army Corps of Engineers*]
WIS............ Weather Information Service [*Air Force*] (MCD)
WIS............ Wedgwood International Seminar (EA)
WIS............ Winchester Diversified [*Vancouver Stock Exchange symbol*]
WIS............ Wireless Interphone System (MCD)
WIS............ Wisconsin (AAG)
Wis............ Wisconsin Reports [*A publication*] (DLA)
Wis............ Wisconsin Reports [*A publication*]
Wis............ Wisdom [*Old Testament book*]
WIS............ Women in Sales Association (EA)
WIS............ Women in Soccer (EA)
WIS............ World Impact Services (EA)
WIS............ World of Islam [*A publication*]
WIS............ Worldwide Information System [*Navy*]
WIS............ Wright Investors' Service [*Information service or system*] (IID)
WIS............ WWMCCS [*Worldwide Military Command and Control System*] Information Systems
WISA........ Isabela, PR [*AM radio station call letters*]
WISA........ West Indian Students Association (EA)
WISA........ West Indies Sugar Association [*Later, SAC*]
WISA........ Wholesale Interservice Supply Agreement [*Military*] (NG)
WISA........ Wholesale Interservices Support Agreement [*DoD*]
WISA........ Women's International Surfing Association (EA)
Wis Acad Sci Arts Lett ... Wisconsin Academy of Sciences, Arts, and Letters [*A publication*]
Wis Acad Sciences Trans ... Wisconsin Academy of Sciences, Arts, and Letters. Transactions [*A publication*]
Wis Acad of Sci Trans ... Wisconsin Academy of Sciences, Arts, and Letters. Transactions [*A publication*]
Wis Admin Code ... Wisconsin Administrative Code [*A publication*] (DLA)
Wis Admin Reg ... Wisconsin Administrative Register [*A publication*]
Wis Ag Dept ... Wisconsin. Department of Agriculture. Publications [*A publication*]
Wis Ag Exp ... Wisconsin. Agricultural Experiment Station. Publications [*A publication*]
Wis Agric Exp Stn Bull ... Wisconsin. Agricultural Experiment Station. Bulletin [*A publication*]
Wis Agric Exp Stn Res Bull ... Wisconsin. Agricultural Experiment Station. Research Bulletin [*A publication*]
Wis Agric Exp Stn Res Rep ... Wisconsin. Agricultural Experiment Station. Research Report [*A publication*]
Wis Agric Exp Stn Spec Bull ... Wisconsin. Agricultural Experiment Station. Special Bulletin [*A publication*]
WISA Law Rep ... Western Indian States Agency Law Reports [*A publication*] (DLA)
WISALR.... Western Indian States Agency Law Reports [*A publication*] (DLA)
Wis Alum M ... Wisconsin Alumni Magazine [*A publication*]
WISAP .... Waste Isolation Safety Assessment Program
Wis Arch.... Wisconsin Archaeologist [*A publication*]
WISARD... Wideband System for Acquiring and Recording Data
Wisb........... Laws of Wisby [*Maritime law*] [*A publication*] (DLA)
WISB .... Wildlife Society. Bulletin [*A publication*]
WISB .... Wisbech [*Municipal borough in England*]
WiSB .... Women in Show Business (EA)

Wis BA Bull ... Wisconsin State Bar Association. Bulletin [*A publication*] (DLA)
Wis Badger Bee ... Wisconsin's Badger Bee [*A publication*]
Wis Bar Bull ... Wisconsin State Bar Association. Bulletin [*A publication*] (DLA)
Wis B Bulletin ... Wisconsin Bar Bulletin [*A publication*]
Wis Beekeep ... Wisconsin Beekeeping [*A publication*]
Wis BTA.... Wisconsin Board of Tax Appeals Reports [*A publication*] (DLA)
WISC........ Madison, WI [*Television station call letters*]
WISC........ Wang Information Services Corp. [*Telecommunications service*] (TSSD)
WISC........ Wechsler Intelligence Scale for Children [*Education*]
WISC........ Wisconsin (AFM)
Wisc.......... Wisconsin Reports [*A publication*] (DLA)
WISC........ Wisconsin Southern Gas Co., Inc. [*NASDAQ symbol*] (NQ)
WISC........ Women's Information and Study Centre
WISC........ Writable Instruction Set Computer [*Term coined by Phil Koopman, Jr.*] (BYTE)
Wisc Busn ... Wisconsin Business [*A publication*]
WiscE .... Wisconsin Energy Corp. [*Associated Press abbreviation*] (APAG)
WISCII...... Wang International Standard Code for Information Interchange [*Pronounced "whiskey"*] [*Canada*]
Wisc LB ..... Wisconsin Library Bulletin [*A publication*]
Wisc Lib Bull ... Wisconsin Library Bulletin [*A publication*]
Wisc LR ..... Wisconsin Law Review [*A publication*]
Wisc Med J ... Wisconsin Medical Journal [*A publication*]
Wis Coll Agric Life Sci Res Div Res Rep ... Wisconsin College of Agricultural and Life Sciences. Research Division. Research Report [*A publication*]
Wis Coll Agric Life Sci Res Div Sci Rep Bull ... Wisconsin College of Agricultural and Life Sciences. Research Division. Science Report Bulletin [*A publication*]
WISCOM ... Wisconsin Information Science and Communications Consortium [*University of Wisconsin - Madison*] [*Research center*] (RCD)
Wis Conserv Bull ... Wisconsin Conservation Bulletin [*A publication*]
Wis Conserv Dep Tech Bull ... Wisconsin Conservation Department. Technical Bulletin [*A publication*]
Wisconsin Acad Sci Arts and Letters Trans ... Wisconsin Academy of Sciences, Arts, and Letters. Transactions [*A publication*]
Wisconsin Acad Sci Arts Lett Trans ... Wisconsin Academy of Sciences, Arts, and Letters. Transactions [*A publication*]
Wisconsin Agric Exp Stn Bull ... Wisconsin. Agricultural Experiment Station. Bulletin [*A publication*]
Wisconsin L Rev ... Wisconsin Law Review [*A publication*]
Wisconsin Med J ... Wisconsin Medical Journal [*A publication*]
Wisconsin MJ ... Wisconsin Medical Journal [*A publication*]
WiscPS ...... Wisconsin Public Service Corp. [*Associated Press abbreviation*] (APAG)
WISC-R..... Wechsler Intelligence Scale for Children - Revised [*Education*]
Wisc Stud BJ ... Wisconsin Student Bar Journal [*A publication*] (DLA)
WISD........ Wisdom [*Old Testament book*]
Wis 2d........ Wisconsin Reports, Second Series [*A publication*] (DLA)
Wis Dent Assoc J ... Wisconsin Dental Association. Journal [*A publication*]
Wis Dep Nat Resour Publ ... Wisconsin. Department of Natural Resources. Publication [*A publication*]
Wis Dep Nat Resour Tech Bull ... Wisconsin. Department of Natural Resources. Technical Bulletin [*A publication*]
Wisd of Sol ... Wisdom of Solomon [*Old Testament book*]
WISE......... Asheville, NC [*AM radio station call letters*]
WISE......... Wang Intersystem Exchange
WISE......... Warning Indicators System Europe (MCD)
WISE......... Weapon Installation System Engineering
WISE......... Welsh Initiative for Specialised Employment
WISE......... Whirlwind I SAGE [*Semi-Automatic Ground Equipment*] Evaluation (SAA)
WISE......... Wholesalers Institutional Service Extension [*Division of National American Wholesale Grocers Association*]
WISE......... [*The*] Wiser Oil Co. [*NASDAQ symbol*] (NQ)
WISE......... Women into Science and Engineering [*1984 campaign sponsored by the Equal Opportunities Commission and the Engineering Council*] [*British*]
WISE......... Women in Space Earliest (SAA)
WISE......... Women's Information Service, Inc.
WISE......... Women's Issues, Status, and Education (EA)
WISE......... World Information Service on Energy (EA)
WISE......... World Information Synthesis and Encyclopaedia [*Project of American Association for the Advancement of Science and American Society for Information Science*]
WISE......... World Information Systems Exchange [*Defunct*] (EA)
WISE......... World-Wide Information Service [*Information service or system*] (IID)
Wis Energy Ext Serv Agric-Energy Transp Dig ... Wisconsin. Energy Extension Service. Agricultural-Energy Transportation Digest [*A publication*]
Wis Eng ..... Wisconsin Engineer [*A publication*]
Wis Eng Exp Stn Repr ... Wisconsin. Engineering Experiment Station. Reprint [*A publication*]
Wis Engineer ... Wisconsin Engineer [*A publication*]

WISER ...... Western Information System for Energy Resources [*Dataline, Inc.*] [*Canada*] [*Information service or system*]
WiseR .... Wiseman Review [*A publication*]
Wis Geol Nat Hist Surv Bull ... Wisconsin. Geological and Natural History Survey. Bulletin [*A publication*]
Wis Geol Survey Bull Inf Circ ... Wisconsin. Geological Survey. Bulletin. Information Circular [*A publication*]
Wis G S...... Wisconsin. Geological and Natural History Survey [*A publication*]
Wis G S G Wis B ... Wisconsin. Geological Survey. Geology of Wisconsin. Bulletin [*Later, Wisconsin Geological and Natural History Survey*] [*A publication*]
WISH .... Indianapolis, IN [*Television station call letters*]
WISH .... Women in the Senate and House [*Political fund-raising group*]
WISH .... World Institute for Scientific Humanism (EA)
Wis His Col ... Wisconsin State Historical Society. Collections [*A publication*]
Wis His Proc ... Wisconsin Historical Society. Proceedings [*A publication*]
Wis His S Domesday Bk ... Wisconsin State Historical Society. Domesday Book [*A publication*]
Wis Hist Soc Proc ... Wisconsin State Historical Society. Proceedings [*A publication*]
Wis Hort... Wisconsin Horticulture [*A publication*]
WISI .... World Index of Space Imagery [*Meteorology*]
Wis IC........ Wisconsin Industrial Commission Workmen's Compensation Reports [*A publication*] (DLA)
Wis Int'l LJ ... Wisconsin International Law Journal [*A publication*] (DLA)
Wis J Ed .... Wisconsin Journal of Education [*A publication*]
WISJMPO ... Worldwide Military Command and Control Information Systems, Joint Program Office
WISK........ Americus, GA [*AM radio station call letters*]
WISL........ Shamokin, PA [*AM radio station call letters*]
WISL......... Woven Integrated Structure Laminates [*Army*]
Wis Law R ... Wisconsin Law Review [*A publication*]
Wis Laws ... Laws of Wisconsin [*A publication*]
Wis Legis Serv ... Wisconsin Legislative Service [*A publication*]
Wis Legis Serv ... Wisconsin Legislative Service (West) [*A publication*] (DLA)
Wis Leg N ... Wisconsin Legal News [*Milwaukee*] [*A publication*] (DLA)
Wis Lib Bul ... Wisconsin Library Bulletin [*A publication*]
Wis LN ..... Wisconsin Legal News [*Milwaukee*] [*A publication*] (DLA)
Wis LR....... Wisconsin Law Review [*A publication*]
Wis L Rev .. Wisconsin Law Review [*A publication*]
WISM........ Altoona, WI [*FM radio station call letters*]
WISM........ Eau Claire, WI [*AM radio station call letters*]
Wis M........ Wisconsin Magazine of History [*A publication*]
Wis Mag Hist ... Wisconsin Magazine of History [*A publication*]
Wis Med J ... Wisconsin Medical Journal [*A publication*]
Wis M Hist ... Wisconsin Magazine of History [*A publication*]
WISN......... Milwaukee, WI [*AM radio station call letters*]
Wis Nat Resour Bull ... Wisconsin Natural Resources Bulletin [*A publication*]
Wis N H Soc B ... Wisconsin Natural History Society. Bulletin [*A publication*]
WISN-TV ... Milwaukee, WI [*Television station call letters*]
WISO .... Ponce, PR [*AM radio station call letters*]
WISP .... Warning Improvement Study Plan (MCD)
WISP .... Wartime Information Security Program (MCD)
WISP .... Waves in Space Plasma (SSD)
WISP .... Weaponization of Increased Speed Projectiles (MCD)
WISP .... Wide-Range Imaging Spectrophotometer [*Naval Oceanographic Office*]
WisP .... Wisconsin Power & Light Co. [*Associated Press abbreviation*] (APAG)
WISP .... Women in Scholarly Publishing (EA)
Wis Paper Ind Newsl ... Wisconsin Paper Industry. Information Service Newsletter [*A publication*]
Wis Pharm ... Wisconsin Pharmacist [*A publication*]
Wis Pharm Ext Bull ... Wisconsin. Pharmacy Extension Bulletin [*A publication*]
Wi Spieg .... Wirtschaftsspiegel [*A publication*]
Wis PSC .... Wisconsin Public Service Commission Reports [*A publication*] (DLA)
Wis PSC Ops ... Wisconsin Public Service Commission Opinions and Decisions [*A publication*] (DLA)
WISQ........ Niellsville, WI [*FM radio station call letters*]
WISR........ Butler, PA [*AM radio station call letters*]
Wis R........ Wisconsin Reports [*A publication*] (DLA)
Wis RC Ops ... Wisconsin Railroad Commission Opinions and Decisions [*A publication*] (DLA)
Wis RCR.... Wisconsin Railroad Commission Reports [*A publication*] (DLA)
Wis Rep ..... Wisconsin Reports [*A publication*] (DLA)
WISS .... Berlin, WI [*AM radio station call letters*]
WISS .... Weapon Impact Scoring System [*Navy*] (MCD)
WISS .... Weekly Induction Scheduling System [*Navy*] (NG)
WISS .... World Institute of Sephardic Studies (BJA)
WISSA ...... Wholesale Interservice Supply Support Agreements [*Military*]
Wiss Arch Landwirtsch Abt A ... Wissenschaftliches Archiv fuer Landwirtschaft. Abteilung A. Archiv fuer Pflanzenbau [*A publication*]
Wiss Arch Landwirtsch Abt B ... Wissenschaftliches Archiv fuer Landwirtschaft. Abteilung B. Archiv fuer Tierernaehrung und Teirzucht [*A publication*]

Wis SBA Bull ... Wisconsin State Bar Association. Bulletin [*A publication*] (DLA)
Wiss Dienst Ostmitteleur ... Wissenschaftlicher Dienst fuer Ostmitteleuropa [*A publication*]
Wiss Dienst Sudosteuropa ... Wissenschaftlicher Dienst Suedosteuropa [*A publication*]
Wiss Di Suedost Eur ... Wissenschaftlicher Dienst Suedosteuropa [*A publication*]
Wissenschaftstheorie- Wissenschaft Philos ... Wissenschaftstheorie- Wissenschaft und Philosophie [*A publication*]
Wissenschaftstheor Wiss Philos ... Wissenschaftstheorie- Wissenschaft und Philosophie [*A publication*]
WISS-FM ... Berlin, WI [*FM radio station call letters*]
Wiss Fortschr ... Wissenschaft und Fortschritt [*A publication*]
Wiss Fortschritt ... Wissenschaft und Fortschritt [*A publication*]
Wiss Geg.... Wissenschaft und Gegenwart [*A publication*]
Wiss Kult... Wissenschaft und Kultur [*A publication*]
WisSL........ Wisconsin Studies in Literature [*A publication*]
Wiss Prax Ki Ges ... Wissenschaft und Praxis in Kirche und Gesellschaft [*A publication*]
Wis Stat ..... Wisconsin Statutes [*A publication*] (DLA)
Wis Stat Ann (West) ... West's Wisconsin Statutes, Annotated [*A publication*] (DLA)
Wis State Cartogr Off Inf Circ ... Wisconsin State Cartographer's Office. Information Circular [*A publication*]
Wiss-Tech Fortschr Landw ... Wissenschaftlich-Technischer Fortschrift fuer die Landwirtschaft [*A publication*]
Wiss-Tech Inf VEB Kombinat Automatisierungsanlagenbau ... Wissenschaftlich-Technische Informationen des VEB Kombinat Automatisierungsanlagenbau [*A publication*]
Wis Stud Contemp Lit ... Wisconsin Studies in Contemporary Literature [*Later, Contemporary Literature*] [*A publication*]
Wiss Umwelt ISU ... Wissenschaft und Umwelt ISU [*Interdisziplinaerer Sonderbereich Umweltschutz*] [*German Federal Republic*] [*A publication*]
WissUnNT ... Wissenschaftliche Untersuchungen zum Neuen Testament [*Tuebingen*] [*A publication*] (BJA)
Wiss Wb .... Wissenschaft und Weltbild [*A publication*]
Wiss Weis ... Wissenschaft und Weisheit [*A publication*]
Wiss Welt .. Wissenschaft und Weltbild [*A publication*]
Wiss Weltb ... Wissenschaft und Weltbild [*A publication*]
Wiss Wirtsch Polit ... Wissenschaft, Wirtschaft, Politik [*A publication*]
WIST .... Lobelville, TN [*FM radio station call letters*]
WIST .... Whitaker Index of Schizophrenic Thinking
Wi St .... Wirtschaftswissenschaftliches Studium [*A publication*]
Wistar Inst Symp Monogr ... Wistar Institute. Symposium. Monograph [*A publication*]
Wis Tax App C ... Wisconsin Tax Appeals Commission Reports [*A publication*] (DLA)
Wi St G ...... Wirtschaftsstrafgesetz [*A publication*]
WISU........ Federation of Westinghouse Independent Salaried Unions
WISU......... Terre Haute, IN [*FM radio station call letters*]
Wis U Bul Eng S ... Bulletin. University of Wisconsin. Engineering Series [*A publication*]
Wis Univ Coll Eng Eng Exp Stn Rep ... Wisconsin University. College of Engineering. Engineering Experiment Station. Report [*A publication*]
Wis Univ Dept Meteorology Rept Lakes and Streams Inv Comm ... Wisconsin University. Department of Meteorology. Report to the Lakes and Streams Investigations Committee [*A publication*]
Wis Univ Eng Exp Stn Bull ... Wisconsin University. Engineering Experiment Station. Bulletin [*A publication*]
Wis Univ Geol Nat Hist Surv Spec Rep ... Wisconsin University. Geological and Natural History Survey. Special Report [*A publication*]
Wis Univ Geol Natur Hist Surv Inform Circ ... Wisconsin University. Geological and Natural History Survey. Information Circular [*A publication*]
WIT .... Washington Institute of Technology [*Washington, DC*]
WIT .... Whitbread Investment Trust [*British*]
WIT .... Winnebago International Travelers (EA)
WIT .... Wiring Interface Tester (MCD)
WIT .... Wisconsin Institute of Technology
WIT .... Witco Corp. [*NYSE symbol*] (SPSG)
WIT .... Witness (AABC)
WIT .... Wittenberg University, Springfield, OH [*OCLC symbol*] (OCLC)
WIT .... Witteveen [*Netherlands*] [*Seismograph station code, US Geological Survey*] (SEIS)
WIT .... Witteveen [*Netherlands*] [*Geomagnetic observatory code*]
WIT .... Women in Telecommunications [*Defunct*] (EA)
WIT .... Women in Transition (EA)
WIT .... World Ice Theory [*Hans Horbiger*]
WITA........ Knoxville, TN [*AM radio station call letters*]
WITA......... Tapak Tuan/Teuku Cut Ali [*Indonesia*] [*ICAO location identifier*] (ICLI)
WITA........ Women in the Army (MCD)
WITA........ Women in the Arts (EA)
WITA........ Women's International Tennis Association (EA)
WITAG...... West Indies Trade Advisory Group [*British Overseas Trade Board*] (DS)

WITAMIR ... Wisconsin Tandem Mirror
WITAN ..... Wind-Time Analyzer
WITB......... Salem, WV [*FM radio station call letters*]
WITC......... Cazenovia, NY [*FM radio station call letters*]
WITC......... Meulaboh/Cut Nyak Dien [*Indonesia*] [*ICAO location identifier*] (ICLI)
WITCH ..... Women Incensed over Traditional Coed Hoopla [*Feminist group*]
WITCH ..... Women's Independent Cinema House [*British*]
WITCH ..... Women's International Terrorist Conspiracy from Hell [*Feminist group*]
Witco......... Witco Corp. [*Associated Press abbreviation*] (APAG)
WITF......... Harrisburg, PA [*FM radio station call letters*]
WITF......... Women's International Tennis Federation
WITF-TV ... Harrisburg, PA [*Television station call letters*]
WITG .... Sinabang/Lasikin [*Indonesia*] [*ICAO location identifier*] (ICLI)
WITG .... Western International Trade Group (EA)
WITH........ Baltimore, MD [*AM radio station call letters*]
WITH........ Witheridge [*England*]
With Corp Cas ... Withrow's American Corporation Cases [*A publication*] (DLA)
WITHDRL ... Withdrawal (ROG)
Withrow..... Withrow's American Corporation Cases [*A publication*] (DLA)
Withrow..... Withrow's Reports [*9-21 Iowa*] [*A publication*] (DLA)
WITHT ...... Without (ROG)
WITI......... Milwaukee, WI [*Television station call letters*]
WITIS ...... Weather Integration with Tactical Intelligence System (MCD)
Witkin Cal Summary ... Witkin's Summary of California Law [*A publication*] (DLA)
WITL......... Lansing, MI [*AM radio station call letters*]
WITL......... Lhok Sukon [*Indonesia*] [*ICAO location identifier*] (ICLI)
WITL-FM ... Lansing, MI [*FM radio station call letters*]
WITM .... Elizabethton, TN [*AM radio station call letters*]
WITM .... Whok Seumawe/Malikus Saleh [*Indonesia*] [*ICAO location identifier*] (ICLI)
WITN .... Washington, NC [*Television station call letters*]
WITNED... Witnessed
WITNESS ... Wire Installation Tester for Negating Errors by Sequencing and Standardization
WITNETH ... Witnesseth [*Legal*] [*British*] (ROG)
WITNS..... Witness [*Legal*] [*British*] (ROG)
WITR......... Henrietta, NY [*FM radio station call letters*]
WITS .... Sebring, FL [*AM radio station call letters*]
WITS .... Seumayam [*Indonesia*] [*ICAO location identifier*] (ICLI)
WITS .... Wang Integrated Technology Show [*British*]
WITS .... Washington Interagency Telecommunications System [*GSA*]
WITS .... Weather Information Telemetry System [*Air Force*] (CET)
WITS .... West Integrated Test Stand [*NASA*]
WITS .... Women in Technical Service [*World War II*]
WITS .... Work Item Tracking System [*Nuclear energy*] (NRCH)
WITS .... Worldwide Information and Trade System
WITS .... Worldwide Interactive Trading System [*Information service or system*] (IT)
WITSEC.... Witness Security Program [*US government program for protection of witnesses whose lives are endangered by their testimony*]
WITSS...... Witnesses [*Legal*] [*British*] (ROG)
WITT......... Banda Aceh/Blangbintang [*Indonesia*] [*ICAO location identifier*] (ICLI)
WITT......... Tuscola, IL [*FM radio station call letters*]
Witthaus & Becker's Med Jur ... Witthaus and Becker's Medical Jurisprudence [*A publication*] (DLA)
Wittheit Bremen Jahrb ... Wittheit zu Bremen. Jahrbuch [*A publication*]
WITTL ...... Wittlesford [*England*]
Witt Schlesw-Holst ... Witterung in Schleswig-Holstein [*A publication*]
WITV........ Charleston, SC [*Television station call letters*]
WITW .... We Interrupt This Week [*Television program*]
WITX........ Beaver Falls, PA [*FM radio station call letters*]
WITY........ Danville, IL [*AM radio station call letters*]
WITZ........ Jasper, IN [*AM radio station call letters*]
WITZ-FM ... Jasper, IN [*FM radio station call letters*]
WIU........... Warhead Interface Unit (MCD)
WIU........... Water Injection Unit
WIU........... Weather Intelligence Unit [*Army*] (MCD)
WIU........... Western Illinois University [*Macomb*]
WIU........... Western International University, Phoenix, AZ [*OCLC symbol*] (OCLC)
wiu............. Wisconsin [*MARC country of publication code*] [*Library of Congress*] (LCCP)
WIU........... Witu [*Papua New Guinea*] [*Airport symbol*] (OAG)
WIUJ......... St. Thomas, VI [*FM radio station call letters*]
WIUM....... Macomb, IL [*FM radio station call letters*]
WIUP .... Indiana, PA [*FM radio station call letters*]
WIUS........ Macomb, IL [*FM radio station call letters*]
WIUV .... Castleton, VT [*FM radio station call letters*]
Wiv............. [*The*] Merry Wives of Windsor [*Shakespearean work*]
WIV .... Vakblad voor Textielreiniging [*A publication*]
WIV .... Waukesha Public Library, Waukesha, WI [*OCLC symbol*] (OCLC)

WIV .... WIC [*Women, Infants, and Children*] Income Verification Survey [*Food and Nutrition Service*] [*Department of Agriculture*]
WIVA .... Aguadilla, PR [*FM radio station call letters*]
WIVAB...... Women's Inter-Varsity Athletics Board [*British*] (DI)
WIVB........ Buffalo, NY [*Television station call letters*]
Wi Verw..... Wirtschaftsverwaltung [*A publication*]
WIVI......... Charlotte Amalie, VI [*FM radio station call letters*]
WIVK .... Knoxville, TN [*AM radio station call letters*]
WIVK-FM ... Knoxville, TN [*FM radio station call letters*]
WIVV .... Vieques, PR [*AM radio station call letters*]
WIVY .... Jacksonville, FL [*FM radio station call letters*]
WIW .... Marathon County Public Library, Wausau, WI [*OCLC symbol*] (OCLC)
WIW .... Wer Informiert Woruber [*Who Advises about What*] [*Gesellschaft fuer Informationsmarkt-Forschung - GIF*] [*Detmold, Federal Republic of Germany*] [*Information service or system*] (IID)
WIW? .... Who's Inventing What? [*A publication*]
WIW .... WI Wheels International [*Vancouver Stock Exchange symbol*]
WIW .... Wooded Island [*Washington*] [*Seismograph station code, US Geological Survey*] (SEIS)
WIWC .... Kokomo, IN [*FM radio station call letters*]
WIWHA .... Western International Walking Horse Association (EA)
Wi Wi........ Wirtschaftswissenschaft [*A publication*]
Wi Wiss ..... Wirtschaftswissenschaft [*A publication*]
WIWO........ Walk In, Walk Out (ADA)
WIWP........ World Institute for World Peace
WIWS........ Beckley, WV [*AM radio station call letters*]
WIX .... Steenbock Memorial Library, Madison, WI [*OCLC symbol*] (OCLC)
WIX .... Wait for Index (NASA)
WIX .... Wickes Companies, Inc. [*Later, Collins & Aikman Corp.*] [*AMEX symbol*] (SPSG)
WIX .... Winex Resources, Inc. [*Vancouver Stock Exchange symbol*]
WIXAMT ... Wixamtree [*England*]
WIXE........ Monroe, NC [*AM radio station call letters*]
WIXI......... Naples Park, FL [*FM radio station call letters*]
WIXK .... New Richmond, WI [*AM radio station call letters*]
WIXK-FM ... New Richmond, WI [*FM radio station call letters*]
WIXN .... Dixon, IL [*AM radio station call letters*]
WIXN-FM ... Dixon, IL [*FM radio station call letters*]
WIXQ .... Millersville, PA [*FM radio station call letters*]
WIXT........ Syracuse, NY [*Television station call letters*]
WIXV .... Savannah, GA [*FM radio station call letters*]
WIXX........ Green Bay, WI [*FM radio station call letters*]
WIXZ........ McKeesport, PA [*AM radio station call letters*]
WIY .... University of Wisconsin, Primate Research Center, Primate Library, Madison, WI [*OCLC symbol*] (OCLC)
WIYC........ Charlotte Amalie, VI [*FM radio station call letters*]
WIYD .... Palatka, FL [*AM radio station call letters*]
WIYN .... Deposit, NY [*FM radio station call letters*]
WIYQ .... Ebensburg, PA [*FM radio station call letters*]
WIYY .... Baltimore, MD [*FM radio station call letters*]
WiZ............ Wiedza i Zycie [*A publication*]
WiZ............ Wort in der Zeit [*A publication*]
WIZA .... Savannah, GA [*AM radio station call letters*]
WIZA .... Workgroup for Indians in South America [*Netherlands*]
WIZB .... Abbeville, AL [*FM radio station call letters*]
WIZD .... Rudolph, WI [*FM radio station call letters*]
WIZE .... Springfield, OH [*AM radio station call letters*]
WIZF........ Erlanger, KY [*FM radio station call letters*]
WIZK .... Bay Springs, MS [*AM radio station call letters*]
WIZK-FM ... Bay Springs, MS [*FM radio station call letters*]
WIZM .... La Crosse, WI [*AM radio station call letters*]
WIZM-FM ... La Crosse, WI [*FM radio station call letters*]
WIZN .... Vergennes, VT [*FM radio station call letters*]
WIZO .... Franklin, TN [*AM radio station call letters*]
WIZO .... Women's International Zionist Organization [*Tel Aviv, Israel*] (EA)
WIZR........ Johnstown, NY [*AM radio station call letters*]
WIZS........ Henderson, NC [*AM radio station call letters*]
WIZY........ East Jordan, MI [*FM radio station call letters*]
WIZZ........ Streator, IL [*AM radio station call letters*]
WJ .... Joule [*Unit of work*] (ROG)
WJ .... Nihon Kinkyori Airways [*ICAO designator*] (FAAC)
WJ .... Wars of the Jews [*of Josephus*] [*A publication*] (BJA)
W & J........ Washington and Jefferson College [*Pennsylvania*] (IIA)
WJ .... Water Jacket (MSA)
WJ .... Watkins-Johnson Co. [*NYSE symbol*] (SPSG)
wj.............. West Bank of the Jordan River [*MARC country of publication code*] [*Library of Congress*] (LCCP)
WJ .... Western Jurist [*United States*] [*A publication*] (DLA)
WJ .... Wiener Jahreshefte [*A publication*]
WJ .... Wolfram-Jahrbuch [*A publication*]
WJ .... Wood Jalousie
WJ .... World Justice [*A publication*]
WJa .... Janesville Public Library, Janesville, WI [*Library symbol*] [*Library of Congress*] (LCLS)
WJA.......... Women's Jewelry Association (EA)
WJA.......... Woolen Jobbers Association (EA)

WJA..........	World Jazz Association [*Defunct*] (EA)
WJA..........	World Jurist Association (EAIO)
WJA..........	Wuerzburger Jahrbuecher fuer die Altertumswissenschaft [*A publication*]
WJAA.......	Austin, IN [*FM radio station call letters*]
WJaB.........	Blackhawk Technical Institute, Janesville, WI [*Library symbol*] [*Library of Congress*] (LCLS)
WJAB.......	Huntsville, AL [*FM radio station call letters*]
WJAC.......	Johnstown, PA [*AM radio station call letters*]
WJAC-TV ...	Johnstown, PA [*Television station call letters*]
WJAD.......	Bainbridge, GA [*FM radio station call letters*]
WJAG.......	Norfolk, NE [*AM radio station call letters*]
WJAL.......	Hagerstown, MD [*Television station call letters*]
WJAM......	Marion, AL [*FM radio station call letters*]
WJaM	Mercy Hospital, Janesville, WI [*Library symbol*] [*Library of Congress*] (LCLS)
WJAN	Sunderland, VT [*FM radio station call letters*]
WJAQ	Marianna, FL [*FM radio station call letters*]
WJAR.......	Providence, RI [*Television station call letters*]
WJaRH	Rock County Health Care Center, Janesville, WI [*Library symbol*] [*Library of Congress*] (LCLS)
WJAS.......	Pittsburgh, PA [*AM radio station call letters*]
WJAT.......	Swainsboro, GA [*AM radio station call letters*]
WJAT-FM ...	Swainsboro, GA [*FM radio station call letters*]
WJAX.......	Jacksonville, FL [*AM radio station call letters*]
WJAY.......	Mullins, SC [*AM radio station call letters*]
WJAZ.......	Summerdale, PA [*FM radio station call letters*]
WJB.......	Wire Jig Board (MCD)
W Jb	Wolfram-Jahrbuch [*A publication*]
W J Barrow Res Lab Publ ...	W. J. Barrow Research Laboratory. Publication [*A publication*]
WJBB.......	Haleyville, AL [*AM radio station call letters*]
W Jbb Alt ..	Wuerzburger Jahrbuecher fuer die Altertumswissenschaft [*A publication*]
WJBB-FM ...	Haleyville, AL [*FM radio station call letters*]
WJBC.......	Bloomington, IL [*AM radio station call letters*]
WJBC.......	Winnipeg Jets Booster Club (EA)
WJBD.......	Salem, IL [*AM radio station call letters*]
WJBD-FM ...	Salem, IL [*FM radio station call letters*]
WJBF.......	Augusta, GA [*Television station call letters*]
WJBI........	Batesville, MS [*AM radio station call letters*]
WJBI	Winslow, ME [*FM radio station call letters*]
WJBK.......	Detroit, MI [*Television station call letters*]
W J Bl......	Wiener Juristische Blaetter [*A publication*]
WJBM......	Jerseyville, IL [*AM radio station call letters*]
WJBO.......	Baton Rouge, LA [*AM radio station call letters*]
WJBR.......	Wilmington, DE [*AM radio station call letters*]
WJBR-FM ...	Wilmington, DE [*FM radio station call letters*]
WJBS	Holly Hill, SC [*AM radio station call letters*]
WJBT.......	Green Cove Springs, FL [*FM radio station call letters*]
WJBU.......	William Jennings Bryan University [*Tennessee*]
WJBY.......	Rainbow City, AL [*AM radio station call letters*]
WJBZ.......	Seymour, TN [*FM radio station call letters*]
WJC..........	Washington and Jefferson College [*Pennsylvania*]
WJC..........	Washington Journalism Center (EA)
WJC..........	William Jewell College [*Liberty, MO*]
WJC..........	Wood Junior College [*Mathison, MS*]
WJC..........	Worcester Junior College [*Massachusetts*]
WJC..........	World Jewish Congress, American Section (EA)
WJC..........	Worthington Junior College [*Minnesota*] [*Later, Worthington Community College*]
WJCAR.....	World Jewish Congress. Annual Report [*New York*] [*A publication*]
WJCB.......	Norfolk, VA [*Television station call letters*]
WJCB.......	World Jersey Cattle Bureau [*Jersey, Channel Islands, England*]
WJCC.......	Norfolk, MA [*AM radio station call letters*]
WJCC.......	Western Joint Computer Conference
WJCC.......	Women's Joint Congressional Committee (EA)
WJCF.......	Nashua, NH [*FM radio station call letters*]
WJCH	Joliet, IL [*FM radio station call letters*]
WJCIB	World Jewish Congress. Information Bulletin [*New York*] [*A publication*]
WJCL.......	Savannah, GA [*FM radio station call letters*]
WJCL-TV ...	Savannah, GA [*Television station call letters*]
WJCM......	Sebring, FL [*AM radio station call letters*]
WJCO.......	Jackson, MI [*AM radio station call letters*]
WJCR.......	Millerstown, KY [*FM radio station call letters*]
WJCT.......	Jacksonville, FL [*Television station call letters*]
WJCT-FM ...	Jacksonville, FL [*FM radio station call letters*]
WJCV.......	Jacksonville, NC [*AM radio station call letters*]
WJCW......	Johnson City, TN [*AM radio station call letters*]
WJD	Welded Joint Design
WJDA.......	Quincy, MA [*AM radio station call letters*]
WJDB.......	Thomasville, AL [*AM radio station call letters*]
WJDB-FM ...	Thomasville, AL [*FM radio station call letters*]
WJDJ	Burnside, KY [*FM radio station call letters*]
WJDM	Elizabeth, NJ [*AM radio station call letters*]
WJDQ	Meridian, MS [*FM radio station call letters*]
WJDR.......	Prentiss, MS [*FM radio station call letters*]
WJDS.......	Jackson, MS [*AM radio station call letters*]
WJDT........	Rogersville, TN [*FM radio station call letters*]
WJDX........	Jackson, MS [*FM radio station call letters*]
WJDY........	Salisbury, MD [*AM radio station call letters*]
WJDZ........	Levittown, PR [*FM radio station call letters*]
WJE..........	Willis, Joyce, McMinnville OR [*STAC*]
WJEB	Jacksonville, FL [*Television station call letters*]
WJEC.......	Vernon, AL [*FM radio station call letters*]
WJEC.......	Welsh Joint Education Committee [*British*]
WJED.......	Dogwood Lakes Estate, FL [*FM radio station call letters*]
WJEF	Lafayette, IN [*FM radio station call letters*]
WJEH	Gallipolis, OH [*AM radio station call letters*]
WJEJ	Hagerstown, MD [*AM radio station call letters*]
WJEL	Indianapolis, IN [*FM radio station call letters*]
WJEM......	Valdosta, GA [*AM radio station call letters*]
WJEP.......	Ochlocknee, GA [*AM radio station call letters*]
WJEQ........	Macomb, IL [*FM radio station call letters*]
WJER........	Dover-New Philadelphia, OH [*AM radio station call letters*]
WJER........	Dover, OH [*FM radio station call letters*]
WJES........	Johnston, SC [*AM radio station call letters*]
WJET........	Erie, PA [*FM radio station call letters*]
WJET........	Wetjet International Ltd. [*NASDAQ symbol*] (NQ)
WJET-TV ...	Erie, PA [*Television station call letters*]
WJEZ........	Pontiac, IL [*FM radio station call letters*]
WJF..........	Lancaster, CA [*Location identifier*] [*FAA*] (FAAL)
WJF..........	Palmdale/Lancaster [*California*] Fox [*Airport symbol*] (OAG)
WJF..........	White Jewish Female [*Classified advertising*]
WJF..........	Widowed Jewish Female [*Classified advertising*]
WJFB.......	Lebanon, TN [*Television station call letters*]
WJFC.......	Jefferson City, TN [*AM radio station call letters*]
WJFC.......	Waylon Jennings Fan Club (EA)
WJFC-FM ...	Jefferson City, TN [*FM radio station call letters*]
WJFD.......	New Bedford, MA [*FM radio station call letters*]
WJFF.......	Jeffersonville, NY [*FM radio station call letters*]
WJFFC......	Worldwide John Fogerty Fanclub (EAIO)
WJFI	Women's Jazz Festival [*Defunct*] (EA)
WJFJ	Women Judges' Fund for Justice (EA)
WJFK	Baltimore, MD [*AM radio station call letters*]
WJFK	Manassas, VA [*FM radio station call letters*]
WJFM.......	Grand Rapids, MI [*FM radio station call letters*]
WJFR.......	Jacksonville, FL [*FM radio station call letters*]
WJFW.......	Rhinelander, WI [*Television station call letters*]
WJFX.......	New Haven, IN [*FM radio station call letters*]
WJGA.......	Jackson, GA [*FM radio station call letters*]
WJGC.......	Jacksonville, FL [*AM radio station call letters*]
WJGF.......	Romney, WV [*FM radio station call letters*]
WJGO	World Jewish Genealogy Organization (EA)
WJh	Wiener Jahreshefte [*A publication*]
WJHB	Fair Bluff, NC [*AM radio station call letters*]
WJHD	Portsmouth, RI [*FM radio station call letters*]
WJHG	Panama City, FL [*Television station call letters*]
WJHH	Soperton, GA [*AM radio station call letters*]
WJHL	Johnson City, TN [*Television station call letters*]
WJHM	Daytona Beach, FL [*FM radio station call letters*]
WJHO	Opelika, AL [*AM radio station call letters*]
WJHR	Flemington, NJ [*AM radio station call letters*]
WJHS	Columbia City, IN [*FM radio station call letters*]
WJHT	Cedar Bluff, VA [*FM radio station call letters*]
WJHU	Baltimore, MD [*FM radio station call letters*]
WJI	WinJak, Inc. [*NYSE symbol*] (SPSG)
WJI...........	Wire Journal International [*A publication*] (EAAP)
WJIC	Salem, NJ [*AM radio station call letters*]
WJIE	Okolona, KY [*FM radio station call letters*]
WJIF	Opp, AL [*FM radio station call letters*]
WJIL	Jacksonville, IL [*AM radio station call letters*]
WJIM........	Lansing, MI [*AM radio station call letters*]
WJIM-FM ...	Lansing, MI [*FM radio station call letters*]
WJIR	Key West, FL [*FM radio station call letters*]
WJIS	Bradenton, FL [*FM radio station call letters*]
WJIV	Cherry Valley, NY [*FM radio station call letters*]
WJIW........	Cazenovia, NY [*AM radio station call letters*]
WJIZ	Albany, GA [*FM radio station call letters*]
WJJA	Racine, WI [*Television station call letters*]
WJJB	Romney, WV [*FM radio station call letters*]
WJJC	Commerce, GA [*AM radio station call letters*]
WJJD	Chicago, IL [*AM radio station call letters*]
WJJF........	Hope Valley, RI [*AM radio station call letters*]
WJJH	Ashland, WI [*FM radio station call letters*]
WJJJ	Christiansburg, VA [*AM radio station call letters*]
WJJL	Niagara Falls, NY [*AM radio station call letters*]
WJJM	Lewisburg, TN [*AM radio station call letters*]
WJJM-FM ...	Lewisburg, TN [*FM radio station call letters*]
WJJN	Dothan, AL [*FM radio station call letters*]
WJJO	Watertown, WI [*FM radio station call letters*]
WJJQ	Tomahawk, WI [*AM radio station call letters*]
WJJQ-FM ...	Tomahawk, WI [*FM radio station call letters*]
WJJR	Rutland, VT [*FM radio station call letters*]
WJJS........	Lynchburg, VA [*AM radio station call letters*]
WJJT........	Jellico, TN [*AM radio station call letters*]
WJJW	North Adams, MA [*FM radio station call letters*]
WJJY	Baxter, MN [*AM radio station call letters*]
WJJY	Brainerd, MN [*FM radio station call letters*]
WJK..........	Wiener Jahrbuch fuer Kunstgeschichte [*A publication*]

WJKA........ Wilmington, NC [*Television station call letters*]
WJKC........ Christiansted, VI [*FM radio station call letters*]
WJ f Kg...... Wiener Jahrbuch fuer Kunstgeschichte [*A publication*]
WJKG...... Wiener Jahrbuch fuer Kunstgeschichte [*A publication*]
WJKI........ Woodruff, SC [*AM radio station call letters*]
WJKL........ Elgin, IL [*FM radio station call letters*]
WJKM....... Hartsville, TN [*AM radio station call letters*]
WJKS........ Jacksonville, FL [*Television station call letters*]
WJKX........ Ellisville, MS [*FM radio station call letters*]
WJKY........ Jamestown, KY [*AM radio station call letters*]
WJKZ........ White Bluff, TN [*AM radio station call letters*]
WJLA........ Washington, DC [*Television station call letters*]
WJLB........ Detroit, MI [*FM radio station call letters*]
WJLC........ Wye Junction Latching Circulator
WJLCER... Women's Joint Legislative Committee for Equal Rights
        [*Defunct*] (EA)
WJLD........ Fairfield, AL [*AM radio station call letters*]
WJLE........ Smithville, TN [*AM radio station call letters*]
WJLE-FM ... Smithville, TN [*FM radio station call letters*]
WJLF........ Gainesville, FL [*FM radio station call letters*]
WJLK........ Asbury Park, NJ [*AM radio station call letters*]
WJLK-FM ... Asbury Park, NJ [*FM radio station call letters*]
WJLM....... Salem, VA [*FM radio station call letters*]
WJLQ........ Pensacola, FL [*FM radio station call letters*]
WJLS .... Beckley, WV [*AM radio station call letters*]
WJLS-FM ... Beckley, WV [*FM radio station call letters*]
WJLT .... Fort Wayne, IN [*FM radio station call letters*]
WJLU........ New Smyrna Beach, FL [*FM radio station call letters*]
WJLW........ De Pere, WI [*FM radio station call letters*]
WJLY........ Ramsey, IL [*FM radio station call letters*]
WJM .... Widowed Jewish Male [*Classified advertising*]
WJMA........ Orange, VA [*AM radio station call letters*]
WJMA-FM ... Orange, VA [*FM radio station call letters*]
WJMB....... Brookhaven, MS [*AM radio station call letters*]
WJMC....... Rice Lake, WI [*AM radio station call letters*]
WJMC-FM ... Rice Lake, WI [*FM radio station call letters*]
WJMD ...... Hazard, KY [*FM radio station call letters*]
WJMDA.... Western Journal of Medicine [*United States*] [*A publication*]
WJMF........ Smithfield, RI [*FM radio station call letters*]
WJMG ...... Hattiesburg, MS [*FM radio station call letters*]
WJMH ...... Reidsville, NC [*FM radio station call letters*]
WJMI........ Jackson, MS [*FM radio station call letters*]
WJMJ........ Hartford, CT [*FM radio station call letters*]
WJMK....... Chicago, IL [*FM radio station call letters*]
WJML....... Petoskey, MI [*AM radio station call letters*]
WJML-FM ... Petoskey, MI [*FM radio station call letters*]
WJMM ...... Versailles, KY [*FM radio station call letters*]
WJMN....... Escanaba, MI [*Television station call letters*]
WJMO ...... Cleveland Heights, OH [*AM radio station call letters*]
WJMO-FM ... Cleveland Heights, OH [*FM radio station call letters*]
WJMP....... Kent, OH [*AM radio station call letters*]
WJMQ....... Clintonville, WI [*FM radio station call letters*]
WJMR....... Fredricktown, OH [*FM radio station call letters*]
WJMS........ Ironwood, MI [*AM radio station call letters*]
WJMT........ Merrill, WI [*AM radio station call letters*]
WJMU ...... Decatur, IL [*FM radio station call letters*]
WJMW ...... Bloomsburg, PA [*AM radio station call letters*]
WJMX....... Cheraw, SC [*FM radio station call letters*]
WJMX....... Florence, SC [*AM radio station call letters*]
WJMY....... Marquette, MI [*Television station call letters*]
WJNC .... Jacksonville, NC [*AM radio station call letters*]
WJNF........ Marianna, FL [*FM radio station call letters*]
WJNO .... West Palm Beach, FL [*AM radio station call letters*]
WJNR....... Iron Mountain, MI [*FM radio station call letters*]
WJNS........ Yazoo City, MS [*FM radio station call letters*]
WJNT........ Pearl, MS [*AM radio station call letters*]
WJNW ...... Janesville, WI [*Television station call letters*]
WJNX....... Fort Pierce, FL [*AM radio station call letters*]
WJNY....... Watertown, NY [*AM radio station call letters*]
WJNZ....... Greencastle, IN [*FM radio station call letters*]
W Jo........... [*Sir William*] Jones' English King's Bench Reports [*A
        publication*] (DLA)
WJOB....... Hammond, IN [*AM radio station call letters*]
WJOC....... Chattanooga, TN [*AM radio station call letters*]
WJOD ...... Galena, IL [*FM radio station call letters*]
WJOE........ Port St. Joe, FL [*AM radio station call letters*]
WJOI........ Detroit, MI [*FM radio station call letters*]
WJOL........ Joliet, IL [*AM radio station call letters*]
WJON .... St. Cloud, MN [*AM radio station call letters*]
W Jones ..... [*Sir William*] Jones' English King's Bench Reports [*A
        publication*] (DLA)
W Jones (Eng) ... [*Sir William*] Jones' English King's Bench Reports [*A
        publication*] (DLA)
WJOR .... St. Joseph, TN [*AM radio station call letters*]
WJOR-FM ... St. Joseph, TN [*FM radio station call letters*]
WJOS........ Elkin, NC [*AM radio station call letters*]
WJOY........ Burlington, VT [*AM radio station call letters*]
WJP........... Water Jet Pump
WJPA........ Washington, PA [*AM radio station call letters*]
WJPC .... Chicago, IL [*AM radio station call letters*]
WJPC .... Lansing, IL [*FM radio station call letters*]

WJPD........ Ishpeming, MI [*AM radio station call letters*]
WJPD-FM ... Ishpeming, MI [*FM radio station call letters*]
WJPEB...... Woodcock-Johnson Psychoeducational Battery [*Educational
        test*]
WJPF .... Herrin, IL [*AM radio station call letters*]
WJPH........ Monticello, FL [*FM radio station call letters*]
WJPJ........ Huntingdon, TN [*AM radio station call letters*]
WJPM....... Florence, SC [*Television station call letters*]
WJPR........ Lynchburg, VA [*Television station call letters*]
WJPZ........ Syracuse, NY [*FM radio station call letters*]
WJQI........ Chesapeake, VA [*AM radio station call letters*]
WJQI........ Virginia Beach, VA [*FM radio station call letters*]
WJQK........ Zeeland, MI [*FM radio station call letters*]
WJQY........ Fort Lauderdale, FL [*FM radio station call letters*]
WJQZ........ Wellsville, NY [*FM radio station call letters*]
WJR.......... Cypress Fund [*AMEX symbol*] (SPSG)
WJR.......... Detroit, MI [*AM radio station call letters*]
WJR.......... Wajir [*Kenya*] [*Airport symbol*] (OAG)
WJR.......... Washington Journalism Review [*A publication*]
WJR.......... World Jewish Register [*A publication*] (BJA)
WJRA........ Priceville, AL [*AM radio station call letters*]
WJRD........ Russellville, AL [*AM radio station call letters*]
WJRE........ Kewanee, IL [*FM radio station call letters*]
WJRH ...... Easton, PA [*FM radio station call letters*]
WJRI........ Lenoir, NC [*AM radio station call letters*]
WJRL........ Calhoun City, MS [*AM radio station call letters*]
WJRM....... Troy, NC [*AM radio station call letters*]
WJRO ...... Glen Burnie, MD [*AM radio station call letters*]
WJRQ....... Saluda, SC [*FM radio station call letters*]
WJRS .... Jamestown, KY [*FM radio station call letters*]
WJRT .... Flint, MI [*Television station call letters*]
WJRX....... East Ridge, TN [*FM radio station call letters*]
WJRZ........ Manahawkin, NJ [*FM radio station call letters*]
WJRZ........ Toms River, NJ [*AM radio station call letters*]
WJS.......... Watchmaker, Jeweller, and Silversmith [*A publication*]
WJS.......... Wife's Judicial Separation [*Legal*] [*British*] (ROG)
WJSA .... Jersey Shore, PA [*AM radio station call letters*]
WJSA-FM ... Jersey Shore, PA [*FM radio station call letters*]
WJSB .... Crestview, FL [*AM radio station call letters*]
WJSC........ Johnson, VT [*FM radio station call letters*]
WJSG........ Hamlet, NC [*FM radio station call letters*]
WJSH........ Terre Haute, IN [*AM radio station call letters*]
WJSJ .... Belzoni, MS [*FM radio station call letters*]
WJSK........ Lumberton, NC [*FM radio station call letters*]
WJSL .... Houghton, NY [*FM radio station call letters*]
WJSM...... Martinsburg, PA [*AM radio station call letters*]
WJSM-FM ... Martinsburg, PA [*FM radio station call letters*]
WJSN........ Jackson, KY [*FM radio station call letters*]
WJSO........ Pikeville, KY [*FM radio station call letters*]
WJSP .... Columbus, GA [*Television station call letters*]
WJSP .... Warm Springs, GA [*FM radio station call letters*]
WJSQ....... Athens, TN [*FM radio station call letters*]
WJSR .... Birmingham, AL [*FM radio station call letters*]
WJST .... Port St. Joe, FL [*FM radio station call letters*]
WJSU .... Anniston, AL [*Television station call letters*]
WJSU .... Jackson, MS [*FM radio station call letters*]
WJSUD..... World Journal of Surgery [*A publication*]
WJSV........ Morristown, NJ [*FM radio station call letters*]
WJT.......... World Journal Tribune [*Defunct New York City afternoon
        newspaper*]
WJTA........ Kosciusko, MS [*FM radio station call letters*]
WJTB........ North Ridgeville, OH [*AM radio station call letters*]
WJTC........ Pensacola, FL [*Television station call letters*]
WJTG........ Fort Valley, GA [*FM radio station call letters*]
WJTH........ Calhoun, GA [*AM radio station call letters*]
WJTL........ Lancaster, PA [*FM radio station call letters*]
WJTN........ Jamestown, NY [*AM radio station call letters*]
WJTO........ Bath, ME [*AM radio station call letters*]
WJTP........ Newland, NC [*AM radio station call letters*]
WJTR........ Jackson, TN [*FM radio station call letters*]
WJTT .... Red Bank, TN [*FM radio station call letters*]
WJTV........ Jackson, MS [*Television station call letters*]
WJTW........ Joliet, IL [*FM radio station call letters*]
WJTY........ Lancaster, WI [*FM radio station call letters*]
WJTZ........ Blountville, TN [*AM radio station call letters*]
WJu .... Juneau Public Library, Juneau, WI [*Library symbol*] [*Library of
        Congress*] (LCLS)
WJUE........ Battle Creek, MI [*Television station call letters*]
WJUL........ Lowell, MA [*FM radio station call letters*]
WJuMe...... Dodge County Mental Health Center, Juneau, WI [*Library
        symbol*] [*Library of Congress*] (LCLS)
WJUN .... Mexico, PA [*AM radio station call letters*]
WJUN-FM ... Mexico, PA [*FM radio station call letters*]
WJURDJ .. World Journal of Urology [*A publication*]
WJUS........ Fort Walton Beach, FL [*FM radio station call letters*]
WJVL........ Janesville, WI [*FM radio station call letters*]
WJVO........ South Jacksonville, IL [*FM radio station call letters*]
WJVS........ Cincinnati, OH [*FM radio station call letters*]
WJW .... Cleveland, OH [*Television station call letters*]
WJWF....... Artesia, MS [*FM radio station call letters*]
WJWF........ Columbus, MS [*AM radio station call letters*]

WJWJ .... Beaufort, SC [*FM radio station call letters*]
WJWJ-TV ... Beaufort, SC [*Television station call letters*]
WJWN ...... San Sebastian, PR [*Television station call letters*]
WJWS .... South Hill, VA [*AM radio station call letters*]
WJX........... Wajax Ltd. [*Toronto Stock Exchange symbol*]
WJXL .... Jacksonville, AL [*AM radio station call letters*]
WJXN .... Jackson, MS [*AM radio station call letters*]
WJXQ .... Jackson, MI [*FM radio station call letters*]
WJXR .... Macclenny, FL [*FM radio station call letters*]
WJXT .... Jacksonville, FL [*Television station call letters*]
WJXY .... Conway, SC [*AM radio station call letters*]
WJXY-FM ... Conway, SC [*FM radio station call letters*]
WJY........... Westmoreland County Community College, Youngwood, PA
              [*OCLC symbol*]   (OCLC)
WJYE .... Buffalo, NY [*FM radio station call letters*]
WJYF .... Nashville, GA [*FM radio station call letters*]
WJYJ .... Fredericksburg, VA [*FM radio station call letters*]
WJYM .... Bowling Green, OH [*AM radio station call letters*]
WJYP .... South Charleston, WV [*FM radio station call letters*]
WJYQ .... Moncks Corner, SC [*FM radio station call letters*]
WJYR .... Myrtle Beach, SC [*FM radio station call letters*]
WJYS .... Hammond, IN [*Television station call letters*]
WJYY .... Concord, NH [*FM radio station call letters*]
WJYZ .... Albany, GA [*AM radio station call letters*]
WJZ........... Baltimore, MD [*Television station call letters*]
WJZE .... Washington, DC [*FM radio station call letters*]
WJZK .... Dresden, TN [*FM radio station call letters*]
WJZM........ Clarksville, TN [*AM radio station call letters*]
WJZQ .... Kenosha, WI [*FM radio station call letters*]
WJZS .... Orangeburg, SC [*AM radio station call letters*]
WJZY .... Belmont, NC [*Television station call letters*]
WJZZ .... Detroit, MI [*FM radio station call letters*]
WK........... Ratioflug Luftfahrtunternehmen GmbH, Frankfurt Am Main
              [*West Germany*] [*ICAO designator*]   (FAAC)
wk.............. Wake Island [*MARC country of publication code*] [*Library of
              Congress*]   (LCCP)
WK........... Warburg-Keilin System [*Cytochrome-cytochrome oxidase
              system*] [*Named for Otto Warburg and D. Keilin*]
WK........... Warehouse Keeper [*British*]   (ROG)
WK........... Waylands Korongo [*Tanzania*]
WK........... Weak   (FAAC)
WK........... Week   (AFM)
WK........... Well-Known
WK........... Wernicke-Korsakoff [*Syndrome*] [*Medicine*]
WK........... Western Alaska [*Airlines*]   (OAG)
WK........... Wetboek van Koophandel [*Commercial Code*] [*Dutch*]   (ILCA)
WK........... Wilson-Kimmelstiel [*Disease*]   (MAE)
WK........... Wit Kommando [*White Commando*] [*South Africa*]
WK........... Work
WK........... Worksheet [*Data format*]
Wk .... Wreck [*Nautical charts*]
WKa .... Kaukauna Public Library, Kaukauna, WI [*Library symbol*]
              [*Library of Congress*]   (LCLS)
WKA .... Waffenkarren [*Weapons Cart*] [*German military - World War
              II*]
WKA .... Wkay Resources [*Vancouver Stock Exchange symbol*]
WKAA ...... Ocilla, GA [*FM radio station call letters*]
WKAC ...... Athens, AL [*AM radio station call letters*]
WKACC ..... Work Accomplishment Code [*Navy*]   (NG)
WKAI .... Macomb, IL [*FM radio station call letters*]
WKAJ........ Saratoga Springs, NY [*AM radio station call letters*]
WKAK ...... Albany, GA [*FM radio station call letters*]
WKAL .... Kalkaska, MI [*AM radio station call letters*]
WKAM...... Goshen, IN [*AM radio station call letters*]
WKAN ...... Kankakee, IL [*AM radio station call letters*]
WKAP .... Allentown, PA [*AM radio station call letters*]
WKAQ .... San Juan, PR [*AM radio station call letters*]
WKAQ-FM ... San Juan, PR [*FM radio station call letters*]
WKAQ-TV ... San Juan, PR [*Television station call letters*]
WKAR .... East Lansing, MI [*AM radio station call letters*]
WKAR-FM ... East Lansing, MI [*FM radio station call letters*]
WKAR-TV ... East Lansing, MI [*Television station call letters*]
WKAS........ Ashland, KY [*Television station call letters*]
WKAT .... North Miami, FL [*AM radio station call letters*]
Wk Aust..... Weekend Australian [*A publication*]
WKAV .... Charlottesville, VA [*AM radio station call letters*]
WKAX .... Russellville, AL [*AM radio station call letters*]
WKAY .... Kannapolis, NC [*Television station call letters*]
WKAZ .... St. Albans, WV [*AM radio station call letters*]
WKB .... Wentzel-Kramers-Brillouin Approximation [*Mathematics*]
WKBA .... Vinton, VA [*AM radio station call letters*]
WKBB........ West Point, MS [*FM radio station call letters*]
WKBC .... North Wilkesboro, NC [*AM radio station call letters*]
WKBC-FM ... North Wilkesboro, NC [*FM radio station call letters*]
WKBD .... Detroit, MI [*Television station call letters*]
WKBE........ Warrensburg, NY [*FM radio station call letters*]
WKBF .... Rock Island, IL [*AM radio station call letters*]
WKBH .... Holmen, WI [*AM radio station call letters*]
WKBH ...... Trempealeau, WI [*FM radio station call letters*]
WKBI........ St. Mary's, PA [*AM radio station call letters*]
WKBI-FM ... St. Mary's, PA [*FM radio station call letters*]

WKBJ .... Milan, TN [*AM radio station call letters*]
WKBJ .... Wentzel-Kramers-Brillouin-Jeffreys [*Approximation or
              Method*] [*Physics*]
WKBK .... Keene, NH [*AM radio station call letters*]
Wkb Krb .... Weekberichten van de Kredietbank [*A publication*]
WKBL........ Covington, TN [*AM radio station call letters*]
WKBL-FM ... Covington, TN [*FM radio station call letters*]
WKBM ...... Coal City, IL [*FM radio station call letters*]
WKBN ...... Youngstown, OH [*AM radio station call letters*]
WKBN-FM ... Youngstown, OH [*FM radio station call letters*]
WKBN-TV ... Youngstown, OH [*Television station call letters*]
WKBO .... Harrisburg, PA [*AM radio station call letters*]
WKBQ .... Granite City, IL [*FM radio station call letters*]
WKBR .... Manchester, NH [*AM radio station call letters*]
WKBS........ Altoona, PA [*Television station call letters*]
WKBT .... La Crosse, WI [*Television station call letters*]
WKBV .... Richmond, IN [*AM radio station call letters*]
WKBW .... Buffalo, NY [*Television station call letters*]
WKBX .... Kingsland, GA [*FM radio station call letters*]
WKBY ...... Chatham, VA [*AM radio station call letters*]
WKBZ .... Muskegon, MI [*AM radio station call letters*]
WKBZ .... Whitehall, MI [*FM radio station call letters*]
WKC.......... Walker Ridge [*California*] [*Seismograph station code, US
              Geological Survey*]   (SEIS)
WKC.......... Westminster Kennel Club   (EA)
WKCA ...... Owingsville, KY [*FM radio station call letters*]
WKCB ...... Hindman, KY [*AM radio station call letters*]
WKCB-FM ... Hindman, KY [*FM radio station call letters*]
WKCC .... Grayson, KY [*FM radio station call letters*]
WKCD .... Kittery, ME [*FM radio station call letters*]
WKCE .... Harriman, TN [*AM radio station call letters*]
WKCF........ Clermont, FL [*Television station call letters*]
WKCG .... Augusta, ME [*FM radio station call letters*]
WKCH...... Knoxville, TN [*Television station call letters*]
WKCI........ Hamden, CT [*FM radio station call letters*]
WKCJ .... Lewisburg, WV [*FM radio station call letters*]
WKCK ...... Orocavis, PR [*AM radio station call letters*]
WKCL........ Ladson, SC [*FM radio station call letters*]
WKCM ...... Cannelton, IN [*AM radio station call letters*]
WKCM ...... Hawesville, KY [*AM radio station call letters*]
WKCO .... Gambier, OH [*FM radio station call letters*]
WKCONSUPVR ... Work Control Supervisor [*Air Force*]
WKCQ .... Saginaw, MI [*FM radio station call letters*]
WKCR .... New York, NY [*FM radio station call letters*]
WKCS........ Knoxville, TN [*FM radio station call letters*]
WKCT .... Bowling Green, KY [*AM radio station call letters*]
WKCU .... Corinth, MS [*AM radio station call letters*]
WKCW ...... Warrenton, VA [*AM radio station call letters*]
WKCX .... Rome, GA [*FM radio station call letters*]
WKCY .... Harrisonburg, VA [*AM radio station call letters*]
WKCY-FM ... Harrisonburg, VA [*FM radio station call letters*]
WKD.......... Weekday
WKDA .... Nashville, TN [*AM radio station call letters*]
WKDAY ...... Weekday
WKDB .... Asheville, NC [*FM radio station call letters*]
WKDC .... Elmhurst, IL [*AM radio station call letters*]
WKDD .... Akron, OH [*FM radio station call letters*]
WKDE .... Altavista, VA [*AM radio station call letters*]
WKDE-FM ... Altavista, VA [*FM radio station call letters*]
WKDF .... Nashville, TN [*FM radio station call letters*]
WKDI .... Denton, MD [*AM radio station call letters*]
WKDJ......... Clarksdale, MS [*FM radio station call letters*]
WKDK .... Newberry, SC [*AM radio station call letters*]
WKDL .... Dwight, IL [*FM radio station call letters*]
WKDM ...... New York, NY [*AM radio station call letters*]
WKDN ...... Camden, NJ [*FM radio station call letters*]
WKDO ...... Liberty, KY [*AM radio station call letters*]
WKDO-FM ... Liberty, KY [*FM radio station call letters*]
WKDP .... Corbin, KY [*AM radio station call letters*]
WKDP-FM ... Corbin, KY [*FM radio station call letters*]
WKDQ....... Henderson, KY [*FM radio station call letters*]
WKDR .... Plattsburgh, NY [*AM radio station call letters*]
WKDS........ Kalamazoo, MI [*FM radio station call letters*]
WKDU....... Philadelphia, PA [*FM radio station call letters*]
WKDW....... Staunton, VA [*AM radio station call letters*]
WKDX .... Hamlet, NC [*AM radio station call letters*]
WKDZ .... Cadiz, KY [*AM radio station call letters*]
WKE .... Wake [*Wake Island*] [*Seismograph station code, US Geological
              Survey*] [*Closed*]   (SEIS)
WKEA .... Scottsboro, AL [*FM radio station call letters*]
WKEB .... Islamorada, FL [*Television station call letters*]
WKED .... Frankfort, KY [*AM radio station call letters*]
WKED-FM ... Frankfort, KY [*FM radio station call letters*]
WKEE........ Huntington, WV [*AM radio station call letters*]
WKEE-FM ... Huntington, WV [*FM radio station call letters*]
WKEF........ Dayton, OH [*Television station call letters*]
WKEG .... Washington, PA [*AM radio station call letters*]
WKEI .... Kewanee, IL [*AM radio station call letters*]
W Kel .... [*William*] Kelynge's English Chancery Reports [*A
              publication*]   (DLA)
WKEL........ Myrtle Beach, SC [*AM radio station call letters*]

W Kelynge (Eng) ... [*William*] Kelynge's English Chancery Reports [*A publication*]   (DLA)
WKEN .... Dover, DE [*AM radio station call letters*]
WKen .... Gilbert M. Simmons Public Library, Kenosha, WI [*Library symbol*] [*Library of Congress*]   (LCLS)
WKenA ...... Armitage Academy Library, Kenosha, WI [*Library symbol*] [*Library of Congress*]   (LCLS)
WKenC ...... Carthage College, Kenosha, WI [*Library symbol*] [*Library of Congress*]   (LCLS)
WKEND .... Weekend ..
WKenG ...... Gateway Technical Institute, Kenosha, WI [*Library symbol*] [*Library of Congress*]   (LCLS)
WKenG-E .. Gateway Technical Institute, Elkhorn Campus, Elkhorn, WI [*Library symbol*] [*Library of Congress*]   (LCLS)
WKenG-R ... Gateway Technical Institute, Racine Campus, Racine, WI [*Library symbol*] [*Library of Congress*]   (LCLS)
WKenHi ..... Kenosha County Historical Association, Kenosha, WI [*Library symbol*] [*Library of Congress*]   (LCLS)
WKenM ..... Kenosha Memorial Hospital, Kenosha, WI [*Library symbol*] [*Library of Congress*]   (LCLS)
WKenOS ... Old Songs Library, Kenosha, WI [*Library symbol*] [*Library of Congress*]   (LCLS)
WKenSC .... St. Catherine's Hospital, Kenosha, WI [*Library symbol*] [*Library of Congress*]   (LCLS)
WKenSD.... Unified School District Number One, Media Center, Kenosha, WI [*Library symbol*] [*Library of Congress*]   (LCLS)
WKenSD-B ... Unified School District Number One, Mary D. Bradford High School, Kenosha, WI [*Library symbol*] [*Library of Congress*]   (LCLS)
WKenSD-R ... Unified School District Number One, Walter Reuther High School, Kenosha, WI [*Library symbol*] [*Library of Congress*]   (LCLS)
WKenSD-T ... Unified School District Number One, Tremper High School, Kenosha, WI [*Library symbol*] [*Library of Congress*]   (LCLS)
WKenU ...... University of Wisconsin-Parkside, Kenosha, WI [*Library symbol*] [*Library of Congress*]   (LCLS)
WKenU-A ... University of Wisconsin-Parkside, Archives and Art Research Center, Kenosha, WI [*Library symbol*] [*Library of Congress*]   (LCLS)
WKEQ .... Burnside, KY [*AM radio station call letters*]
WKER .... Pompton Lakes, NJ [*AM radio station call letters*]
WKES........ St. Petersburg, FL [*FM radio station call letters*]
WKET........ Kettering, OH [*FM radio station call letters*]
WKEU .... Griffin, GA [*AM radio station call letters*]
WKEW .... Greensboro, NC [*AM radio station call letters*]
WKEX .... Blacksburg, VA [*AM radio station call letters*]
WKEY .... Covington, VA [*AM radio station call letters*]
WKF .... Well-Known Factor
WKFD .... Wickford, RI [*AM radio station call letters*]
WKFE .... Yauco, PR [*AM radio station call letters*]
WKFI........ Wilmington, OH [*AM radio station call letters*]
WKFL........ Bushnell, FL [*AM radio station call letters*]
WKFM .... Fulton, NY [*FM radio station call letters*]
WKFN .... Oxford, AL [*FM radio station call letters*]
WKFR........ Battle Creek, MI [*FM radio station call letters*]
WKFT........ Fayetteville, NC [*Television station call letters*]
WKFX........ Kaukauna, WI [*FM radio station call letters*]
WKG .... Working   (MSA)
WKGA .... Zion, IL [*AM radio station call letters*]
WKGB .... Bowling Green, KY [*Television station call letters*]
WKGB .... Susquehanna, PA [*FM radio station call letters*]
WKGC .... Panama City Beach, FL [*AM radio station call letters*]
WKGC .... Panama City, FL [*FM radio station call letters*]
WKGG .... Cape Vincent, NY [*FM radio station call letters*]
Wkg Girls Newsl ... Working with Girls Newsletter [*A publication*]
WKGH........ Allegan, MI [*FM radio station call letters*]
WKGK .... Kinston, NC [*FM radio station call letters*]
WKGM ...... Smithfield, VA [*AM radio station call letters*]
WKGN ...... Knoxville, TN [*AM radio station call letters*]
WKGO .... Cumberland, MD [*FM radio station call letters*]
WKGQ .... Milledgeville, GA [*AM radio station call letters*]
WKGR .... Fort Pierce, FL [*FM radio station call letters*]
WKGT .... Century, FL [*FM radio station call letters*]
WKGW .... Utica, NY [*FM radio station call letters*]
WKGX .... Lenoir, NC [*AM radio station call letters*]
WKHA .... Hazard, KY [*Television station call letters*]
WKHG........ Leitchfield, KY [*FM radio station call letters*]
WKHI......... Ocean City, MD [*FM radio station call letters*]
WKHJ .... Mountain Lake Park, MD [*FM radio station call letters*]
WKHK .... Colonial Heights, VA [*FM radio station call letters*]
WKHL....... Hughesville, PA [*AM radio station call letters*]
WKHL....... Salladasburg, PA [*FM radio station call letters*]
WKHM....... Jackson, MI [*AM radio station call letters*]
WKHO ...... Pinehurst, NC [*AM radio station call letters*]
WKHQ ...... Charlevoix, MI [*FM radio station call letters*]
WKHR....... Bainbridge, OH [*FM radio station call letters*]
WKHS....... Worton, MD [*FM radio station call letters*]
WKHX....... Atlanta, GA [*AM radio station call letters*]
WKHX....... Marietta, GA [*FM radio station call letters*]
WKHY....... Lafayette, IN [*FM radio station call letters*]

WKi........... Kiel Public Library, Kiel, WI [*Library symbol*] [*Library of Congress*]   (LCLS)
WKIC......... Hazard, KY [*AM radio station call letters*]
WKID .... Vevay, IN [*FM radio station call letters*]
WKIE........ Richmond, VA [*AM radio station call letters*]
WKIG .... Glennville, GA [*AM radio station call letters*]
WKIG-FM ... Glennville, GA [*FM radio station call letters*]
WKII......... Port Charlotte, FL [*AM radio station call letters*]
WKIJ .... Parrish, AL [*AM radio station call letters*]
WKIK .... Leonardtown, MD [*AM radio station call letters*]
WKIN .... Kingsport, TN [*AM radio station call letters*]
WKIO .... Urbana, IL [*FM radio station call letters*]
WKIP........ Arlington, NY [*FM radio station call letters*]
WKIP........ Poughkeepsie, NY [*AM radio station call letters*]
WKIQ .... Eustis, FL [*AM radio station call letters*]
WKIR .... Columbus, MS [*FM radio station call letters*]
WKIS........ Boca Raton, FL [*FM radio station call letters*]
WKIS........ Wilson Knight Interdiscipline Society   (EA)
WKISF ..... Wilson Knight Interdiscipline Society and Foundation   (EA)
WKIT........ Brewer, ME [*FM radio station call letters*]
WKIX .... Raleigh, NC [*AM radio station call letters*]
WKIY .... West Kent Imperial Yeomanry [*British military*]   (DMA)
WKIZ........ Key West, FL [*AM radio station call letters*]
WKJ .... Wakkanai [*Japan*] [*Airport symbol*]   (OAG)
WKJA .... Belhaven, NC [*FM radio station call letters*]
WKJB .... Mayaguez, PR [*AM radio station call letters*]
WKJB-FM ... Mayaguez, PR [*FM radio station call letters*]
WKJC........ Tawas City, MI [*FM radio station call letters*]
WKJE........ Hertford, NC [*FM radio station call letters*]
WKJF .... Cadillac, MI [*AM radio station call letters*]
WKJF-FM ... Cadillac, MI [*FM radio station call letters*]
WKJG........ Fort Wayne, IN [*Television station call letters*]
WKJG........ Nappanee, IN [*FM radio station call letters*]
WKJN ...... Hammond, LA [*FM radio station call letters*]
WKJQ....... Parsons, TN [*AM radio station call letters*]
WKJQ-FM ... Parsons, TN [*FM radio station call letters*]
WKJR........ Muskegon Heights, MI [*AM radio station call letters*]
WKJR........ Sullivan, IL [*FM radio station call letters*]
WKJX....... Elizabeth City, NC [*FM radio station call letters*]
WKJY........ Hempstead, NY [*FM radio station call letters*]
WKK .... Aleknagik [*Alaska*] [*Airport symbol*]   (OAG)
WKK .... Aleknagik, AK [*Location identifier*] [*FAA*]   (FAAL)
WKKB .... Key Colony Beach, FL [*FM radio station call letters*]
WKKC....... Chicago, IL [*FM radio station call letters*]
WKKD .... Aurora, IL [*AM radio station call letters*]
WKKD-FM ... Aurora, IL [*FM radio station call letters*]
WKKE .... St. Pauls, NC [*AM radio station call letters*]
WKKG .... Columbus, IN [*FM radio station call letters*]
WKKI .... Celina, OH [*FM radio station call letters*]
WKKJ .... Chillicothe, OH [*FM radio station call letters*]
WKKL .... West Barnstable, MA [*FM radio station call letters*]
WKKM ..... Harrison, MI [*FM radio station call letters*]
WKKN ...... Rockford, IL [*AM radio station call letters*]
WKKO ...... Toledo, OH [*FM radio station call letters*]
WKKQ ...... Nashwauk, MN [*AM radio station call letters*]
WKKR ...... Auburn, AL [*FM radio station call letters*]
WKKS....... Vanceburg, KY [*AM radio station call letters*]
WKKS-FM ... Vanceburg, KY [*FM radio station call letters*]
WKKT .... Hopkinsville, KY [*Television station call letters*]
WKKV ...... Racine, WI [*AM radio station call letters*]
WKKV-FM ... Racine, WI [*FM radio station call letters*]
WKKW ...... Clarksburg, WV [*FM radio station call letters*]
WKKX ...... Jerseyville, IL [*FM radio station call letters*]
WKKZ .... Dublin, GA [*FM radio station call letters*]
WKL .... Waikoloa [*Hawaii*] [*Airport symbol*]   (OAG)
WKLA .... Ludington, MI [*AM radio station call letters*]
WKLA-FM ... Ludington, MI [*FM radio station call letters*]
WKLB....... Manchester, KY [*AM radio station call letters*]
WKLC....... St. Albans, WV [*FM radio station call letters*]
WKLD .... Oneonta, AL [*FM radio station call letters*]
WKLE....... Lexington, KY [*Television station call letters*]
WKLEERI ... W. K. Lypynsky East European Research Institute   (EA)
WKLF....... Clanton, AL [*AM radio station call letters*]
WKLG....... Rock Harbor, FL [*FM radio station call letters*]
WKLH .... Milwaukee, WI [*FM radio station call letters*]
WKLI........ Albany, NY [*FM radio station call letters*]
W Klin Wschr ... Wiener Klinische Wochenschrift [*A publication*]
WKLJ .... Oxford, MS [*FM radio station call letters*]
WKLK .... Cloquet, MN [*AM radio station call letters*]
WKLL........ Frankfort, NY [*FM radio station call letters*]
WKLM ...... Millersburg, OH [*FM radio station call letters*]
WKLO .... Danville, KY [*AM radio station call letters*]
WKLP....... Keyser, WV [*AM radio station call letters*]
WKLQ....... Holland, MI [*FM radio station call letters*]
WKLR....... Indianapolis, IN [*FM radio station call letters*]
WKLS....... Atlanta, GA [*FM radio station call letters*]
WKLT....... Kalkaska, MI [*FM radio station call letters*]
WKLV....... Bradenton, FL [*AM radio station call letters*]
WKLW ...... Paintsville, KY [*AM radio station call letters*]
W KI Ws .... Wiener Klinische Wochenschrift [*A publication*]
WKLX......... Rochester, NY [*FM radio station call letters*]

WKLY........ Hartwell, GA [*AM radio station call letters*]
WKLY........ Weekly
Wkly Cin Law Bul ... Weekly Cincinnati Law Bulletin [*Ohio*] [*A publication*] (DLA)
Wkly Coal ... Weekly Coal Production [*A publication*]
Wkly Dig ... New York Weekly Digest [*A publication*] (DLA)
Wkly Energy Rep ... Weekly Energy Report [*United States*] [*A publication*]
Wkly Inf Bull ... Weekly Information Bulletin [*A publication*]
Wkly Law Bul ... Weekly Law Bulletin [*Ohio*] [*A publication*] (DLA)
Wkly Law Gaz ... Weekly Law Gazette [*Ohio*] [*A publication*] (DLA)
Wkly L Bul ... Weekly Law Bulletin [*Ohio*] [*A publication*] (DLA)
Wkly L Gaz ... Weekly Law Gazette [*Ohio*] [*A publication*] (DLA)
Wkly NC.... Weekly Notes of Cases [*Pennsylvania*] [*A publication*] (DLA)
Wkly Notes Cas ... Weekly Notes of Cases [*Pennsylvania*] [*A publication*] (DLA)
Wkly Notes Cas (PA) ... Weekly Notes of Cases [*Pennsylvania*] [*A publication*] (DLA)
Wkly Rec ... Weekly Record [*United States*] [*A publication*]
Wkly Rep... Weekly Reporter [*London*] [*A publication*] (DLA)
WKM......... Hwange National Park [*Zimbabwe*] [*Airport symbol*] (OAG)
WKM......... State University of New York, Agricultural and Technical College, Cobleskill, Cobleskill, NY [*OCLC symbol*] (OCLC)
WKMA...... Madisonville, KY [*Television station call letters*]
WKMB...... Stirling, NJ [*AM radio station call letters*]
WKMC...... Roaring Spring, PA [*AM radio station call letters*]
WKMD...... Loogootee, IN [*FM radio station call letters*]
WKMF...... Flint, MI [*AM radio station call letters*]
WKMG...... Newberry, SC [*AM radio station call letters*]
WKMI....... Kalamazoo, MI [*AM radio station call letters*]
WKMIA .... Wakayama Igaku [*A publication*]
WKMJ...... Louisville, KY [*Television station call letters*]
WKMK...... Sylvester, GA [*FM radio station call letters*]
WKML...... Lumberton, NC [*FM radio station call letters*]
WKMM...... Kingwood, WV [*FM radio station call letters*]
WKMO...... Hodgenville, KY [*FM radio station call letters*]
WKMP...... Rocky Mount, NC [*AM radio station call letters*]
WKMQ...... Winnebago, IL [*FM radio station call letters*]
WKMR...... Morehead, KY [*Television station call letters*]
WKMS...... Murray, KY [*FM radio station call letters*]
WKMT...... Kings Mountain, NC [*AM radio station call letters*]
WKMU...... Murray, KY [*Television station call letters*]
WKMX...... Enterprise, AL [*FM radio station call letters*]
WKMY...... Princeton, WV [*FM radio station call letters*]
WKMZ...... Martinsburg, WV [*FM radio station call letters*]
WKN......... Wakunai [*Papua New Guinea*] [*Airport symbol*] (OAG)
WKN......... Weaken
Wk N........ Weekly Notes of Cases [*Pennsylvania*] [*A publication*] (DLA)
WKNC...... Raleigh, NC [*FM radio station call letters*]
WKND...... Weekend
WKND...... Windsor, CT [*AM radio station call letters*]
WKNDDH ... Annual Report. Research Institute for Wakan-Yaku Toyama Medical and Pharmaceutical University [*A publication*]
WKNE....... Keene, NH [*AM radio station call letters*]
WKNE-FM ... Keene, NH [*FM radio station call letters*]
WKNF....... Oak Ridge, TN [*FM radio station call letters*]
WKNG....... Tallapoosa, GA [*AM radio station call letters*]
WKNH...... Keene, NH [*FM radio station call letters*]
WKNI........ Lexington, AL [*AM radio station call letters*]
WKNJ........ Lakeside, NJ [*AM radio station call letters*]
WKNJ .... Union Township, NJ [*FM radio station call letters*]
WKNK...... Edmonton, KY [*FM radio station call letters*]
WKNL....... Knoxville, TN [*AM radio station call letters*]
WKNL....... Walter Kidde Nuclear Laboratories, Inc. (MCD)
WKNN...... Pascagoula, MS [*FM radio station call letters*]
WKNO...... Memphis, TN [*FM radio station call letters*]
WKNO-TV ... Memphis, TN [*Television station call letters*]
WKNR....... Cleveland, OH [*AM radio station call letters*]
WKNS...... Kinston, NC [*FM radio station call letters*]
WKNU....... Brewton, AL [*FM radio station call letters*]
WKNV....... Dublin, VA [*AM radio station call letters*]
WKNW...... Canaan, VT [*FM radio station call letters*]
WKNW...... Sault Ste. Marie, MI [*AM radio station call letters*]
WKNX...... Frankenmuth, MI [*AM radio station call letters*]
WKNY...... Kingston, NY [*AM radio station call letters*]
WKNZ....... Collins, MS [*FM radio station call letters*]
WKOA....... Murrell's Inlet, SC [*FM radio station call letters*]
WKOC...... Elizabeth City, NC [*FM radio station call letters*]
WKOD...... Yorktown, VA [*FM radio station call letters*]
WKOH ...... Owensboro, KY [*Television station call letters*]
WKOI........ Richmond, IN [*Television station call letters*]
WKOJ....... Middletown, NY [*FM radio station call letters*]
WKOK...... Sunbury, PA [*AM radio station call letters*]
WKOL...... Amsterdam, NY [*FM radio station call letters*]
WKOM...... Columbia, TN [*FM radio station call letters*]
WKON...... Owenton, KY [*Television station call letters*]
WKOO ...... Jacksonville, NC [*FM radio station call letters*]
WKOP...... Knoxville, TN [*FM radio station call letters*]
WKOR...... Starkville, MS [*AM radio station call letters*]
WKOR-FM ... Starkville, MS [*FM radio station call letters*]
WKOS .... Kingsport, TN [*FM radio station call letters*]

WKOT....... Marseilles, IL [*FM radio station call letters*]
WKOV....... Wellston, OH [*FM radio station call letters*]
WKOW...... Madison, WI [*Television station call letters*]
WKOX...... Framingham, MA [*AM radio station call letters*]
WKOY....... Bluefield, WV [*AM radio station call letters*]
WKOZ...... Kosciusko, MS [*AM radio station call letters*]
WKP......... Wochenschrift fuer Klassische Philologie [*A publication*]
WKPA....... New Kensington, PA [*AM radio station call letters*]
WKPB........ Henderson, KY [*FM radio station call letters*]
WKPC...... Louisville, KY [*Television station call letters*]
WKPD...... Paducah, KY [*Television station call letters*]
WKPE....... Orleans, MA [*AM radio station call letters*]
WKPE-FM ... Orleans, MA [*FM radio station call letters*]
WKPG....... Port Gibson, MS
WKPI........ Pikeville, KY [*Television station call letters*]
WKPK ...... Gaylord, MI [*FM radio station call letters*]
WKPL....... Platteville, WI [*FM radio station call letters*]
WKPQ....... Hornell, NY [*FM radio station call letters*]
WKPR....... Kalamazoo, MI [*AM radio station call letters*]
WKPT....... Kingsport, TN [*AM radio station call letters*]
WKPT-TV ... Kingsport, TN [*Television station call letters*]
WKPV....... Ponce, PR [*Television station call letters*]
WKPX....... Sunrise, FL [*FM radio station call letters*]
WKQDR.... Work Queue Directory
WKQG...... Rochester, NY [*AM radio station call letters*]
WKQI....... Detroit, MI [*FM radio station call letters*]
WKQL....... Jacksonville, FL [*FM radio station call letters*]
WKQQ...... Lexington, KY [*FM radio station call letters*]
WKQR...... Citronelle, AL [*FM radio station call letters*]
WKQS....... Johnstown, PA [*FM radio station call letters*]
WKQT....... Newport, NC [*FM radio station call letters*]
WKQW...... Oil City, PA [*AM radio station call letters*]
WKQX...... Chicago, IL [*FM radio station call letters*]
WKQZ...... Midland, MI [*FM radio station call letters*]
WKR......... Walker's Cay [*Bahamas*] [*Airport symbol*] (OAG)
WKR......... Whittaker Corp. [*NYSE symbol*] (SPSG)
WKR......... Work Ranch [*California*] [*Seismograph station code, US Geological Survey*] (SEIS)
WKR......... Worker
WKR......... Wrecker (AAG)
WKRA...... Holly Springs, MS [*AM radio station call letters*]
WKRA-FM ... Holly Springs, MS [*FM radio station call letters*]
WKRB .... Brooklyn, NY [*FM radio station call letters*]
WKRC....... Cincinnati, OH [*AM radio station call letters*]
WKRC-TV ... Cincinnati, OH [*Television station call letters*]
WKRE....... Exmore, VA [*FM radio station call letters*]
WKRG ...... Mobile, AL [*AM radio station call letters*]
WKRG-FM ... Mobile, AL [*FM radio station call letters*]
WKRG-TV ... Mobile, AL [*Television station call letters*]
WKRH....... Bath, ME [*FM radio station call letters*]
WKRI .... West Warwick, RI [*AM radio station call letters*]
WKRK...... Murphy, NC [*AM radio station call letters*]
WKRM...... Columbia, TN [*AM radio station call letters*]
WKRN...... Nashville, TN [*Television station call letters*]
WKRO...... Cairo, IL [*AM radio station call letters*]
WKRP...... Charleston, WV [*Television station call letters*]
WKRP........ North Vernon, IN [*AM radio station call letters*]
WKRQ...... Cincinnati, OH [*FM radio station call letters*]
WKRR...... Asheboro, NC [*FM radio station call letters*]
WKRS...... Waukegan, IL [*AM radio station call letters*]
WKRT....... Cortland, NY [*AM radio station call letters*]
WKRU...... Burnettown, SC [*AM radio station call letters*]
WKRV...... Vandalia, IL [*FM radio station call letters*]
WKRX...... Roxboro, NC [*FM radio station call letters*]
WKRY ...... Key West, FL [*FM radio station call letters*]
WKRZ....... Wilkes-Barre, PA [*FM radio station call letters*]
WKS .... Works
WKS .... Worksheet File [*Data processing*]
WKS .... Workshop (AAG)
WKSA....... Isabela, PR [*FM radio station call letters*]
WKSA....... Wernicke-Korsakoff Syndrome Association (EA)
WKSB....... Williamsport, PA [*FM radio station call letters*]
WKSC...... Kershaw, SC [*AM radio station call letters*]
WKSC...... Western Kentucky State College [*Later, WKSU*]
WKSD ...... Paulding, OH [*FM radio station call letters*]
WKSE........ Niagara Falls, NY [*FM radio station call letters*]
Wks Engng ... Works Engineering [*A publication*]
Wks Engng Fact Serv ... Works Engineering and Factory Services [*A publication*]
WKSF....... Asheville, NC [*FM radio station call letters*]
WKSG...... Mount Clemens, MI [*FM radio station call letters*]
WKSH...... Sussex, WI [*AM radio station call letters*]
WKSI........ Greensboro, NC [*FM radio station call letters*]
WKSJ........ Mobile, AL [*FM radio station call letters*]
WKSJ........ Prichard, AL [*AM radio station call letters*]
WKSK...... West Jefferson, NC [*AM radio station call letters*]
WKSL........ Greencastle, PA [*FM radio station call letters*]
WKSM...... Fort Walton Beach, FL [*FM radio station call letters*]
Wks Mgmt ... Works Management [*A publication*]
WKSN...... Jamestown, NY [*AM radio station call letters*]
WKSO .... Orangeburg, SC [*FM radio station call letters*]

WKSO .... Somerset, KY [*Television station call letters*]
WKSP .... Workshop
WKSQ ...... Ellsworth, ME [*FM radio station call letters*]
WKSR .... Pulaski, TN [*AM radio station call letters*]
WKSS .... Hartford-Meriden, CT [*FM radio station call letters*]
WKST .... Ellwood City, PA [*FM radio station call letters*]
WKST .... New Castle, PA [*AM radio station call letters*]
Wk Study ... Work Study [*A publication*]
Wk Study Mgmt Serv ... Work Study and Management Services [*Later,
          Management Services*] [*A publication*]
WKSU ...... Kent, OH [*FM radio station call letters*]
WKSU ...... Western Kentucky State University [*Formerly, WKSC*]
WKSW ...... Urbana, OH [*FM radio station call letters*]
WKSX .... Johnston, SC [*FM radio station call letters*]
WKSY ...... Marion, SC [*FM radio station call letters*]
WKSZ .... Media, PA [*FM radio station call letters*]
WKT .... Wicket
WKTA ...... Evanston, IL [*AM radio station call letters*]
WKTC ...... Goldsboro, NC [*FM radio station call letters*]
WKTD ...... Wilmington, NC [*AM radio station call letters*]
WKTE ...... King, NC [*AM radio station call letters*]
WKTG ...... Madisonville, KY [*FM radio station call letters*]
WKTI .... Milwaukee, WI [*FM radio station call letters*]
WKTJ .... Farmington, ME [*AM radio station call letters*]
WKTJ-FM ... Farmington, ME [*FM radio station call letters*]
WKTK ...... Crystal River, FL [*FM radio station call letters*]
WKTL .... Struthers, OH [*FM radio station call letters*]
WKTM ...... Soperton, GA [*FM radio station call letters*]
WKTN ...... Kenton, OH [*FM radio station call letters*]
WKTP .... Jonesboro, TN [*AM radio station call letters*]
WKTQ ...... South Paris, ME [*AM radio station call letters*]
WKTR ...... Earlysville, VA [*FM radio station call letters*]
WKTS .... Sheboygan, WI [*AM radio station call letters*]
WKTT .... Cleveland, WI [*FM radio station call letters*]
WKTU ...... Ocean City, NJ [*FM radio station call letters*]
WKTV ...... Utica, NY [*Television station call letters*]
WKTX ...... Cortland, OH [*AM radio station call letters*]
WKTY ...... La Crosse, WI [*AM radio station call letters*]
WKTZ ...... Jacksonville, FL [*FM radio station call letters*]
WKU .... Wakaura [*Wakayama Eri*] [*Japan*] [*Seismograph station code,
          US Geological Survey*] (SEIS)
WKU .... Western Kentucky University [*Formerly, WKSC*] [*Bowling
          Green*]
WKUB ...... Blackshear, GA [*FM radio station call letters*]
WKUBA .... Werkstatt und Betrieb [*A publication*]
WKUE ...... Elizabethtown, KY [*FM radio station call letters*]
WKUL .... Cullman, AL [*FM radio station call letters*]
WKUN ...... Monroe, GA [*AM radio station call letters*]
WKUZ ...... Wabash, IN [*FM radio station call letters*]
WKVA ...... Lewistown, PA [*AM radio station call letters*]
WKVF ...... Kankakee, IL [*FM radio station call letters*]
WKVF ...... West Kent Volunteer Force [*British military*]   (DMA)
WKVG ...... Jenkins, KY [*AM radio station call letters*]
WKVI .... Knox, IN [*AM radio station call letters*]
WKVI-FM ... Knox, IN [*FM radio station call letters*]
WKVM ...... San Juan, PR [*AM radio station call letters*]
WKVQ ...... Eatonton, GA [*AM radio station call letters*]
WKVR ...... Huntingdon, PA [*FM radio station call letters*]
WKVT ...... Brattleboro, VT [*AM radio station call letters*]
WKVT-FM ... Brattleboro, VT [*FM radio station call letters*]
WKVX ...... Wooster, OH [*AM radio station call letters*]
WKW .... Working Woman [*A publication*]
WKWC ...... Owensboro, KY [*FM radio station call letters*]
WKWF ...... Key West, FL [*AM radio station call letters*]
WKWI ...... Kilmarnock, VA [*FM radio station call letters*]
WKWK ...... Wheeling, WV [*AM radio station call letters*]
WKWK-FM ... Wheeling, WV [*FM radio station call letters*]
WKWL ...... Florala, AL [*AM radio station call letters*]
WKWM ...... Kentwood, MI [*AM radio station call letters*]
WKWQ ...... Batesburg, SC [*FM radio station call letters*]
WKWSA .... Wiener Klinische Wochenschrift. Supplementum (Austria) [*A
          publication*]
WKWT ...... Union City, TN [*FM radio station call letters*]
WKWX ...... Savannah, TN [*FM radio station call letters*]
WKWZ ...... Syosset, NY [*FM radio station call letters*]
WKXA ...... Findlay, OH [*FM radio station call letters*]
WKXC .... Aiken, SC [*AM radio station call letters*]
WKXC-FM ... Aiken, SC [*FM radio station call letters*]
WKXE .... White River Junction, VT [*FM radio station call letters*]
WKXF ...... Eminence, KY [*FM radio station call letters*]
WKXG ...... Greenwood, MS [*AM radio station call letters*]
WKXH ...... Alma, GA [*FM radio station call letters*]
WKXI .... Jackson, MS [*AM radio station call letters*]
WKXI .... Magee, MS [*FM radio station call letters*]
WKXJ .... South Pittsburg, TN [*FM radio station call letters*]
WKXK ...... Fort Valley, GA [*FM radio station call letters*]
WKXL .... Concord, NH [*AM radio station call letters*]
WKXL-FM ... Concord, NH [*FM radio station call letters*]
WKXM ...... Winfield, AL [*AM radio station call letters*]
WKXM-FM ... Winfield, AL [*FM radio station call letters*]
WKXN .... Greenville, AL [*FM radio station call letters*]

WKXO .... Berea, KY [*AM radio station call letters*]
WKXO-FM ... Berea, KY [*FM radio station call letters*]
WKXQ ...... Rushville, IL [*FM radio station call letters*]
WKXR ...... Asheboro, NC [*AM radio station call letters*]
WKXS .... Marion, SC [*AM radio station call letters*]
WKXT ...... Knoxville, TN [*Television station call letters*]
WKXT ...... Sardis, MS [*AM radio station call letters*]
WKXU ...... Portage, PA [*FM radio station call letters*]
WKXV ...... Knoxville, TN [*AM radio station call letters*]
WKXW ...... Trenton, NJ [*FM radio station call letters*]
WKXX ...... Birmingham, AL [*FM radio station call letters*]
WKXY ...... Sarasota, FL [*AM radio station call letters*]
WKXZ ...... Norwich, NY [*FM radio station call letters*]
WKY .... Oklahoma City, OK [*AM radio station call letters*]
WKY .... Wakayama [*Japan*] [*Seismograph station code, US Geological
          Survey*]   (SEIS)
WKY .... Warwickshire Yeomanry [*British military*]   (DMA)
WKY .... West Kent Yeomanry [*British military*]   (DMA)
WKY .... Wistar-Kyoto [*Rat variety*]
WKYA ...... Central City, KY [*FM radio station call letters*]
WKYB ...... Hemingway, SC [*AM radio station call letters*]
WKYC ...... Cleveland, OH [*Television station call letters*]
WKYE ...... Johnstown, PA [*FM radio station call letters*]
WKYG ...... Parkersburg, WV [*AM radio station call letters*]
WKYK ...... Burnsville, NC [*AM radio station call letters*]
WKYM ...... Monticello, KY [*FM radio station call letters*]
WKYN ...... St. Mary's, PA [*FM radio station call letters*]
WKYO ...... Caro, MI [*AM radio station call letters*]
WKYQ ...... Paducah, KY [*FM radio station call letters*]
WKYR ...... Burkesville, KY [*AM radio station call letters*]
WKYR-FM ... Burkesville, KY [*FM radio station call letters*]
WKYS .... Washington, DC [*FM radio station call letters*]
WKYT ...... Lexington, KY [*Television station call letters*]
WKYU ...... Bowling Green, KY [*FM radio station call letters*]
WKYU-TV ... Bowling Green, KY [*Television station call letters*]
WKYW ...... Frankfort, KY [*FM radio station call letters*]
WKYX ...... Paducah, KY [*AM radio station call letters*]
WKYY ...... Lancaster, KY [*AM radio station call letters*]
WKYZ ...... Gray, KY [*AM radio station call letters*]
WKZA ...... Kane, PA [*AM radio station call letters*]
WKZB ...... Drew, MS [*FM radio station call letters*]
WKZC ...... Scottville, MI [*FM radio station call letters*]
WKZD ...... Murrayville, GA [*AM radio station call letters*]
WKZE ...... Salisbury, CT [*FM radio station call letters*]
WKZE ...... Sharon, CT [*AM radio station call letters*]
WKZF .... Bayboro, NC [*FM radio station call letters*]
WKZG ...... Keyser, WV [*FM radio station call letters*]
WKZI .... Casey, IL [*AM radio station call letters*]
WKZK ...... North Augusta, SC [*AM radio station call letters*]
WKZL .... Winston-Salem, NC [*FM radio station call letters*]
WKZM ...... Sarasota, FL [*FM radio station call letters*]
WKZN ...... Lewiston, ME [*AM radio station call letters*]
WKZO ...... Kalamazoo, MI [*AM radio station call letters*]
WKZQ ...... Myrtle Beach, SC [*AM radio station call letters*]
WKZQ-FM ... Myrtle Beach, SC [*FM radio station call letters*]
WKZR ...... Milledgeville, GA [*FM radio station call letters*]
WKZS .... Auburn, ME [*FM radio station call letters*]
WKZT ...... Elizabethtown, KY [*Television station call letters*]
WKZT ...... Fulton, KY [*AM radio station call letters*]
WKZW ...... Peoria, IL [*FM radio station call letters*]
WKZY ...... La Belle, FL [*FM radio station call letters*]
WL .... Compagnie Aerienne du Languedoc [*France*] [*ICAO
          designator*]   (FAAC)
WL .... Lao Air Lines [*Later, LS*] [*ICAO designator*]   (FAAC)
WL .... Wagons-Lits [*Railroad Sleeping or Pullman cars in Europe*]
          [*French*]
WL .... Waiting List
WL .... Walther League   (EA)
WL .... War Legislation [*British*] [*World War II*]
WL .... Warner-Lambert Pharmaceutical Co.
WL .... Warning Light   (SAA)
W & L .... Washington and Lee Law Review [*A publication*]
W & L .... Washington and Lee University [*Lexington, VA*]
WL .... Water Line
WL .... Waterload Test [*Clinical chemistry*]
WL .... Wavelength [*Electronics*]
W & L .... Weapon and/or Launcher
WL .... Weapons Laboratory   (MCD)
WL .... Wehrmacht-Luftwaffe [*Marking on Air Force vehicles*]
          [*German military - World War II*]
W & L .... Welshpool & Llanfair Light Railway [*Wales*]
WL .... West Longitude   (SSD)
WL .... Western Larch [*Utility pole*] [*Telecommunications*]   (TEL)
WL .... Western League [*Baseball*]
WL .... Westland Helicopters Ltd. [*British*] [*ICAO aircraft
          manufacturer identifier*]   (ICAO)
WL .... Westminster Library [*A publication*]
WL .... Wheel Locks
WL .... Wheeler Laboratories, Inc.   (MCD)
WL .... White Laboratories, Inc. [*Research code symbol*]
WL .... White Leghorn [*Poultry*]

WL............	White Light (MSA)
WL............	Wideband Limiter
WL............	Wiener Library [*London*] (BJA)
WL............	Will (FAAC)
WL............	Wind Load
WL............	Wiring List
W-L............	Wisconsin State Law Library [*Wisconsin State Library*], Madison, WI [*Library symbol*] [*Library of Congress*] (LCLS)
WL............	With Restrictive Language (MCD)
W & L........	Women and Literature [*A publication*]
WL............	Women's Legion [*British*] [*World War I*]
WL............	Women's Liberation (ADA)
WL............	Women's Lobby [*Defunct*] (EA)
WL............	Women's Reserve, Legal Specialist Duties [*USNR officer designation*]
WL............	Wool
WL............	Word in Life: Journal of Religious Education [*A publication*] (APTA)
WL............	Word Line
WL............	Work Light
WL............	Work Line (MSA)
WL............	Working Level
WL............	Workload (AABC)
WL............	World of Learning [*A publication*]
WL............	World List of Future International Meetings [*A publication*]
WL............	Worldloppet (EA)
WL............	Wydawnictwo Literackie [*A publication*]
WL............	Wydawnictwo Lodzkie [*A publication*]
WL............	Wyeth Laboratories [*Research code symbol*]
WL0............	Water Line Zero (KSC)
WLA..........	Warner-Lambert Co. [*NYSE symbol*] (SPSG)
WLA..........	Welsh Lacrosse Association (EAIO)
WLA..........	Wescosa Lumber Association [*Defunct*] (EA)
WLA..........	Western Lacrosse Association [*Canada*]
WLA..........	Western Literature Association (EA)
WLA........	White Lung Association (EA)
WLA..........	Wire Line Adapter (MCD)
WLA..........	Wire Line Antenna
WLA	Wissenschaftlicher Literaturanzeiger [*A publication*]
WLA..........	Wittsburg Lake [*Arkansas*] [*Seismograph station code, US Geological Survey*] [*Closed*] (SEIS)
WLA..........	Women's Land Army [*Part of the United States Crop Corps*] [*World War II*]
WLA..........	World Literary Academy (EAIO)
WLAB........	Fort Wayne, IN [*FM radio station call letters*]
WLac	La Crosse Public Library, La Crosse, WI [*Library symbol*] [*Library of Congress*] (LCLS)
WLAC	Nashville, TN [*AM radio station call letters*]
WLAC	Watson Laboratories Air Materiel Command (SAA)
WLAC	Western Labour Arbitration Cases [*A publication*] (DLA)
WLAC-FM ...	Nashville, TN [*FM radio station call letters*]
WLacFW ...	United States Fish and Wildlife Service, Fish Control Laboratory, La Crosse, WI [*Library symbol*] [*Library of Congress*] (LCLS)
WLacL........	La Crosse Lutheran Hospital, La Crosse, WI [*Library symbol*] [*Library of Congress*] (LCLS)
WLacSF.......	Saint Francis Hospital, La Crosse, WI [*Library symbol*] [*Library of Congress*] (LCLS)
WLacU	University of Wisconsin-La Crosse, La Crosse, WI [*Library symbol*] [*Library of Congress*] (LCLS)
WLacVC....	Viterbo College, La Crosse, WI [*Library symbol*] [*Library of Congress*] (LCLS)
WLAD	Danbury, CT [*AM radio station call letters*]
WLadM	Mount Senario College, Ladysmith, WI [*Library symbol*] [*Library of Congress*] (LCLS)
WLAE........	New Orleans, LA [*Television station call letters*]
WLAF........	La Follette, TN [*AM radio station call letters*]
WLAF........	World League of American Football [*1991*]
WLAG	La Grange, GA [*AM radio station call letters*]
WLag	Lake Geneva Public Library, Lake Geneva, WI [*Library symbol*] [*Library of Congress*] (LCLS)
WLagB.......	Badger Union High School District, Lake Geneva, WI [*Library symbol*] [*Library of Congress*] (LCLS)
WLagF.......	Franciscan Education Center, Lake Geneva, WI [*Library symbol*] [*Library of Congress*] (LCLS)
WLagSD....	Joint School District Number One, Lake Geneva, WI [*Library symbol*] [*Library of Congress*] (LCLS)
WLAJ	Lansing, MI [*Television station call letters*]
WLAK	Huntingdon, PA [*FM radio station call letters*]
WLAM	Gorham, ME [*AM radio station call letters*]
WLAM	Lewiston, ME [*AM radio station call letters*]
WLAN	Lancaster, PA [*AM radio station call letters*]
WLAN-FM ...	Lancaster, PA [*FM radio station call letters*]
WLAP........	Lexington, KY [*AM radio station call letters*]
WLAP-FM ...	Lexington, KY [*FM radio station call letters*]
WLAQ	Rome, GA [*AM radio station call letters*]
WLAR	Athens, TN [*AM radio station call letters*]
WLAS........	Jacksonville, NC [*AM radio station call letters*]
WLA/TMDL ...	Wasteload Allocation / Total Maximum Daily Load [*Environmental Protection Agency*] (EPA)

WLAU	Laurel, MS [*AM radio station call letters*]
WLAV	Grand Rapids, MI [*AM radio station call letters*]
WLAV	Will Advise (FAAC)
WLAV-FM ...	Grand Rapids, MI [*FM radio station call letters*]
WLAW	Fairhaven, MA [*AM radio station call letters*]
W Law Bul ...	Weekly Law Bulletin [*Ohio*] [*A publication*] (DLA)
WLAX	La Crosse, WI [*Television station call letters*]
WLAY	Muscle Shoals, AL [*AM radio station call letters*]
WLAY-FM ...	Muscle Shoals, AL [*FM radio station call letters*]
WLB	National War Labor Board [*World War II*]
WLB	Seagoing Buoy Tender [*Coast Guard*] (NVT)
WLB	Wallboard (AAG)
WLB	Weapons Logbook [*Military*] (AABC)
WLB	Weekly Law Bulletin [*Ohio*] [*A publication*] (DLA)
WLB	Wiener Library Bulletin [*London*] [*A publication*]
WLB	Wilson Library Bulletin [*A publication*]
WLB	Wisconsin Library Bulletin [*A publication*]
WLBA........	Gainesville, GA [*AM radio station call letters*]
WLBB........	Carrollton, GA [*AM radio station call letters*]
WLBC........	Muncie, IN [*AM radio station call letters*]
WLBC-FM ...	Muncie, IN [*FM radio station call letters*]
WLBE........	Leesburg, FL [*AM radio station call letters*]
WLBF........	Montgomery, AL [*FM radio station call letters*]
WLBG	Laurens, SC [*AM radio station call letters*]
WLBH	Mattoon, IL [*AM radio station call letters*]
WLBH-FM ...	Mattoon, IL [*FM radio station call letters*]
WLBJ	Bowling Green, KY [*AM radio station call letters*]
WLBK	De Kalb, IL [*AM radio station call letters*]
WLBK.......	[*The*] Waltham Corp. [*NASDAQ symbol*] (NQ)
WLBL.......	Auburndale, WI [*AM radio station call letters*]
WLBM	Wing-Level Bombing System (SAA)
WLBN	Lebanon, KY [*AM radio station call letters*]
WLBQ	Morgantown, KY [*AM radio station call letters*]
WLBR.......	Lebanon, PA [*AM radio station call letters*]
WLBS........	Wright Laboratories [*NASDAQ symbol*] (NQ)
WLBT........	Jackson, MS [*Television station call letters*]
WL Bull	Weekly Law Bulletin [*Ohio*] [*A publication*] (DLA)
WL Bull (Ohio) ...	Weekly Law Bulletin [*Ohio*] [*A publication*] (DLA)
WLBZ.......	Bangor, ME [*Television station call letters*]
WLC	Weapon-Launching Console (MCD)
WLC	Weapons Laboratory Civil Engineering Division [*Kirtland Air Force Base, NM*]
WLC	Well Logging Cable
WLC	Wellco Enterprises, Inc. [*AMEX symbol*] (SPSG)
WLC	West London College [*England*]
WLC	White Light Coronagraph (KSC)
WLC	Wildcat
WLC	Wine Label Circle (EA)
WLC	World Literacy of Canada (EAIO)
WLCA	Godfrey, IL [*FM radio station call letters*]
WLCAC.....	Watts Labor Community Action Committee [*Los Angeles, CA*]
WLCB.......	Leesburg, FL [*Television station call letters*]
WLCC.......	Luray, VA [*FM radio station call letters*]
WLCC.......	Walker-Lybarger Construction Co. [*Colorado*]
WLCE.......	White Light Coronagraph Experiment (KSC)
WLCH	Lancaster, PA [*FM radio station call letters*]
WLCK.......	Scottsville, KY [*AM radio station call letters*]
WLCL.......	Micanopy, FL [*FM radio station call letters*]
WL(CL)....	War Legislation, Civil Liabilities [*British*] [*World War II*]
WLCM	Lancaster, SC [*AM radio station call letters*]
WLCN	Madisonville, KY [*Television station call letters*]
WLCO	Clyde, OH [*FM radio station call letters*]
WLCQ	Clarksville, VA [*FM radio station call letters*]
WLCR	Lawrence Township, NJ [*FM radio station call letters*]
WLCS........	North Muskegon, MI [*FM radio station call letters*]
WLCS........	Workload and Cost Schedule [*Military*] (AABC)
WLCSS......	Weapon Launch Console Switching Section (MCD)
WLCX.......	Farmville, VA [*FM radio station call letters*]
WLCY.......	Blairsville, PA [*FM radio station call letters*]
WLD..........	South African Law Reports, Witwatersrand Local Division [*A publication*] (DLA)
WLD..........	Water and Land Division [*Environmental Protection Agency*] (GFGA)
WLD.........	Weapon Loading Director (NVT)
WLD.........	Welded (MSA)
WLD..........	Weldotron Corp. [*AMEX symbol*] (SPSG)
WLD.........	West Longitude Date (AABC)
WLD..........	Winfield/Arkansas City, KS [*Location identifier*] [*FAA*] (FAAL)
WLD..........	World Technology Industry [*Vancouver Stock Exchange symbol*]
Wld Aerospace Syst ...	World Aerospace System [*A publication*]
Wld Aff	World Affairs [*A publication*]
Wld Anim Rev ...	World Animal Review [*A publication*]
Wld Cem	World Cement [*A publication*]
Wld Cem Tech ...	World Cement Technology [*Later, World Cement*] [*A publication*]
Wld Chr Ed ...	World Christian Education [*A publication*]
Wld Conf Med Educ ...	World Conference on Medical Education [*A publication*]
Wld Conf Psych ...	World Conference of Psychiatry [*A publication*]

Wld Crops ... World Crops [*A publication*]
Wld Develop ... World Development [*A publication*]
Wld Dev Rpt ... World Development Report [*A publication*]
Wld Drink R ... World Drinks Report - World Food Report [*A publication*]
Wld En Out ... World Energy Outlook [*A publication*]
WLDF....... Women's Legal Defense Fund (EA)
Wld Fd & Drk ... World Food and Drink Report [*A publication*]
Wld Fd Probl ... World Food Problems [*A publication*]
Wld Fishg .. World Fishing [*A publication*]
Wld Food Rt ... World Food Report [*A publication*]
Wld For Congr ... World Forestry Congress. Proceedings [*A publication*]
Wld Gas Rpt ... World Gas Report [*A publication*]
Wld Gold ... World Mine Production of Gold [*A publication*]
Wld Grain Tr Stat ... World Grain Trade Statistics [*A publication*]
Wld Hlth.... World's Health [*A publication*]
Wld Hlth Org Publ Hlth Pap ... World Health Organization. Public Health
    Papers [*A publication*]
Wld Hlth Org Techn Rep Ser ... World Health Organization. Technical
    Report Series [*A publication*]
W & L Dig ... Wood and Long's Digest [*Illinois*] [*A publication*] (DLA)
WLDINC... World Income Fund, Inc. [*Associated Press
    abbreviation*] (APAG)
WLDLF ..... Wildlife
Wld Marx R ... World Marxist Review [*A publication*]
Wld Med.... World Medicine [*A publication*]
Wld Med Ass Bull ... World Medical Association. Bulletin [*A publication*]
Wld Med J ... World Medical Journal [*A publication*]
Wld Mil Ex ... World Military Expenditures and Arms Transfers [*A
    publication*]
Wld Mining ... World Mining Equipment [*A publication*]
Wld Min Reg ... World Mines Register [*A publication*]
Wld Money ... World Money Outlook [*A publication*]
WLDMT.... Weldment (MSA)
WLDND.... Wildland
Wld Orchid Conf ... World Orchid Conference [*A publication*]
Wld Pap Tr Rev ... World's Paper Trade Review [*A publication*]
Wld Pol...... World Politics. A Quarterly Journal of International Relations
    [*A publication*]
Wld Polit.... World Politics [*A publication*]
Wld Pollen Spore Flora ... World Pollen and Spore Flora [*A publication*]
Wld Poult Sci J ... World's Poultry Science Journal [*A publication*]
Wld P & PDem ... World Pulp and Paper Demand, Supply, and Trade [*A
    publication*]
Wld Pumps ... World Pumps [*A publication*]
WLDR .... Traverse City, MI [*FM radio station call letters*]
WLDR .... Welder (MSA)
WLDR .... Wilderness Experience, Inc. [*NASDAQ symbol*] (NQ)
WLDRA .... Welder [*England*] [*A publication*]
Wld Raw Mat ... World Demand for Raw Materials in 1985 and 2000 [*A
    publication*]
Wld Refrig Air Condit ... World Refrigeration and Air Conditioning [*A
    publication*]
Wld Rev Pest Control ... World Review of Pest Control [*A publication*]
WLDS........ Jacksonville, IL [*AM radio station call letters*]
WLDS........ Weldless
Wld Sci Rev ... World Science Reviews [*A publication*]
Wld Silver ... World Production of Silver [*A publication*]
Wld's Pap Trade Rev ... World's Paper Trade Review [*A publication*]
Wld Surv.... World Survey [*A publication*]
Wld Ten ... World Tennis [*A publication*]
Wldtex .... Worldtex, Inc. [*Associated Press abbreviation*] (APAG)
Wld Tobacco ... World Tobacco [*A publication*]
Wld Today ... World Today [*A publication*]
Wld Trade ... World Trade. Computer Age [*A publication*]
Wld Vet Abstr J ... World Veterinary Abstracting Journal [*A publication*]
Wld Wast... Management of World Waste [*A publication*]
Wld Wide Abstr Gen Med ... World-Wide Abstracts of General Medicine [*A
    publication*]
Wld Work Rep ... World of Work Report [*A publication*]
WLDX .... Fayette, AL [*AM radio station call letters*]
WLDY .... Ladysmith, WI [*AM radio station call letters*]
WLDY-FM ... Ladysmith, WI [*FM radio station call letters*]
Wld Yrbk Educ ... World Yearbook of Education [*A publication*]
WLE .... Ward Lock Educational [*Publisher*] [*British*]
WLE .... Wellore Energy, Inc. [*Toronto Stock Exchange symbol*]
WLE .... Wheeling & Lake Erie Railway Co. [*NYSE symbol*] [*AAR
    code*] (SPSG)
WLEA........ Hornell, NY [*AM radio station call letters*]
WLEC........ Sandusky, OH [*AM radio station call letters*]
WLED .... Littleton, NH [*Television station call letters*]
WLEE .... Richmond, VA [*AM radio station call letters*]
WLEF .... Park Falls, WI [*Television station call letters*]
WLEM ...... Emporium, PA [*AM radio station call letters*]
WLEN .... Adrian, MI [*FM radio station call letters*]
WLEO .... Ponce, PR [*AM radio station call letters*]
WLER........ Butler, PA [*FM radio station call letters*]
WLES........ Lawrenceville, VA [*AM radio station call letters*]
WLET........ Toccoa, GA [*AM radio station call letters*]
WLEV........ Easton, PA [*FM radio station call letters*]
WLEW ...... Bad Axe, MI [*AM radio station call letters*]
WLEW-FM ... Bad Axe, MI [*FM radio station call letters*]

WLEX........ Lexington, KY [*Television station call letters*]
WLEY........ Cayey, PR [*AM radio station call letters*]
WLF.......... Walferdange [*Belgium*] [*Seismograph station code, US
    Geological Survey*] (SEIS)
WLF.......... Wallis and Futuna [*ANSI three-letter standard code*] (CNC)
WLF.......... Washington Legal Foundation (EA)
WLF.......... Welfare (AABC)
WLF.......... Whole Lithosphere Failure [*Geology*]
WLF.......... Williams-Landel-Ferry [*Polymer physics*]
WLF.......... Wolf River Resources Ltd. [*Vancouver Stock Exchange symbol*]
W LF......... Women's Law Forum [*A publication*]
WLF.......... Women's Law Fund (EA)
WLF.......... Word of Life Fellowship (EA)
WLF.......... Worklife [*A publication*]
WLF.......... Workload Factor (AFM)
WLF.......... World Law Fund (EA)
WLFA........ West Lancashire Field Artillery [*Military unit*] [*British*]
WLFA........ Wildlife Legislative Fund of America (EA)
WLFB........ Bluefield, WV [*Television station call letters*]
WLFB........ Wolfeboro Railroad Co., Inc. [*AAR code*]
WLFC........ Findlay, OH [*FM radio station call letters*]
WLFC........ Washington Library Film Circuit [*Library network*]
WLFD........ World League for Freedom and Democracy [*South
    Korea*] (EAIO)
WLFE........ St. Albans, VT [*FM radio station call letters*]
WLFG........ Grundy, VA [*Television station call letters*]
WLFH ...... Little Falls, NY [*AM radio station call letters*]
WLFI......... Lafayette, IN [*Television station call letters*]
WLFJ .... Greenville, SC [*FM radio station call letters*]
WLFL........ Raleigh, NC [*Television station call letters*]
WLFM....... Appleton, WI [*FM radio station call letters*]
WLFMA.... Welding and Metal Fabrication [*A publication*]
WLFN....... La Crosse, WI [*AM radio station call letters*]
WLFPA .... World League for the Protection of Animals
WLFQ....... Bruce, MS [*FM radio station call letters*]
WLFR........ Pomona, NJ [*FM radio station call letters*]
WLFW....... Oregon, IL [*FM radio station call letters*]
WLFX........ Welding Fixture (AAG)
WLFX........ Winchester, KY [*FM radio station call letters*]
WLG .... Waldron Ledge [*Hawaii*] [*Seismograph station code, US
    Geological Survey*] (SEIS)
WLG .... Washington Liaison Group (AFM)
WLG .... Weekly Law Gazette [*Ohio*] [*A publication*] (ILCA)
WLG .... Wellington [*New Zealand*] [*Airport symbol*] (OAG)
WLG .... Wiener Linguistische Gazette [*A publication*]
WL Gaz...... Weekly Law Gazette (Reprint) [*Ohio*] [*A publication*] (DLA)
WL Gaz (Ohio) ... Weekly Law Gazette (Ohio) [*A publication*] (DLA)
WLGC ...... Greenup, KY [*FM radio station call letters*]
WLGI........ Hemingway, SC [*FM radio station call letters*]
WLGL........ Riverside, PA [*FM radio station call letters*]
WLGN ...... Logan, OH [*AM radio station call letters*]
WLGN-FM ... Logan, OH [*FM radio station call letters*]
WLGO....... Lexington, SC [*AM radio station call letters*]
WLGQ ...... Gaston, NC [*FM radio station call letters*]
WLGW ...... Lancaster, NH [*AM radio station call letters*]
WLGW-FM ... Lancaster, NH [*FM radio station call letters*]
WLH.......... Society for the Study of Women in Legal History (EA)
WLH.......... Walaha [*Vanuatu*] [*Airport symbol*] (OAG)
WLH.......... Wealth Resources Ltd. [*Vancouver Stock Exchange symbol*]
WLH.......... Wilhelmshaven [*Federal Republic of Germany*] [*Geomagnetic
    observatory code*]
WLHB ...... Women's League of Health and Beauty (EAIO)
WLHE .... Water LASER Heat Exchange
WLHFP.... Women's Labor History Film Project (EA)
WLHM...... Logansport, IN [*FM radio station call letters*]
WLHN....... Wolohan Lumber Co. [*NASDAQ symbol*] (NQ)
WLHPA ... Wu Li Hsueh Pao [*A publication*]
WLHQ....... Enterprise, AL [*AM radio station call letters*]
WLHS .... West Chester, OH [*FM radio station call letters*]
WLHT....... Grand Rapids, MI [*FM radio station call letters*]
WLI .... Water Landing Impact (SAA)
WLI .... Wellesley Island [*New York*] [*Seismograph station code, US
    Geological Survey*] [*Closed*] (SEIS)
WLI .... Wilderness Leadership International (EA)
WLI .... Women's League for Israel (EA)
WLIB........ New York, NY [*AM radio station call letters*]
WLIC........ Construction Tender [*Coast Guard symbol*] (DNAB)
WLIC........ Frostburg, MD [*FM radio station call letters*]
WLIF........ Baltimore, MD [*FM radio station call letters*]
WLIG........ Riverhead, NY [*Television station call letters*]
WLIH........ Whitneyville, PA [*FM radio station call letters*]
WLII........ Caguas, PR [*Television station call letters*]
WLIJ........ Shelbyville, TN [*AM radio station call letters*]
WLIK........ Newport, TN [*AM radio station call letters*]
WLIL........ Lenoir City, TN [*AM radio station call letters*]
WLIL-FM ... Lenoir City, TN [*FM radio station call letters*]
WLIM....... Patchogue, NY [*AM radio station call letters*]
WLIN .... Gluckstadt, MS [*FM radio station call letters*]
WLIO........ Lima, OH [*Television station call letters*]
WLIP........ Kenosha, WI [*AM radio station call letters*]
WLIQ .... Harriman, TN [*FM radio station call letters*]

WLIR........	Spring Valley, NY [*AM radio station call letters*]
WLIS.........	Old Saybrook, CT [*AM radio station call letters*]
WLIT........	Chicago, IL [*FM radio station call letters*]
W Lit..........	World Literature Written in English [*A publication*]
WLIU	Lincoln University, PA [*FM radio station call letters*]
WLIV........	Livingston, TN [*AM radio station call letters*]
WLIW.......	Garden City, NY [*Television station call letters*]
WLIX.........	Islip, NY [*AM radio station call letters*]
WLJ..........	Washburn Law Journal [*A publication*]
WLJ..........	Western Law Journal [*A publication*]
WLJ..........	Willamette Law Journal [*A publication*] (ILCA)
WLJ..........	Wyoming Law Journal [*A publication*]
WLJA.......	Ellijay, GA [*AM radio station call letters*]
WLJA-FM ...	Ellijay, GA [*FM radio station call letters*]
WLJC.......	Beattyville, KY [*FM radio station call letters*]
WLJC-TV ...	Beattyville, KY [*Television station call letters*]
WLJE.......	Valparaiso, IN [*FM radio station call letters*]
WLJK.......	Aiken, SC [*FM radio station call letters*]
WLJN.......	Elmwood Township, MI [*AM radio station call letters*]
WLJN.......	Traverse City, MI [*FM radio station call letters*]
WL Jour.....	Washburn Law Journal [*A publication*]
WL Jour.....	Western Law Journal [*A publication*]
WL Jour.....	Willamette Law Journal [*A publication*]
WL Jour.....	Wyoming Law Journal [*A publication*]
WLJP........	Monroe, NY [*FM radio station call letters*]
WLJS	Jacksonville, AL [*FM radio station call letters*]
WLJT........	Lexington, TN [*Television station call letters*]
WLJY........	Marshfield, WI [*FM radio station call letters*]
WLK	Selawik [*Alaska*] [*Airport symbol*] (OAG)
WLK	Selawik, AK [*Location identifier*] [*FAA*] (FAAL)
wlk............	Wales [*MARC country of publication code*] [*Library of Congress*] (LCCP)
WLK	Walk
WLK	Westlake Industry [*Vancouver Stock Exchange symbol*]
WLK	Wiest Lake [*California*] [*Seismograph station code, US Geological Survey*] (SEIS)
WLKA	Canandaigua, NY [*FM radio station call letters*]
WLKC.......	Henderson, NY [*FM radio station call letters*]
WLKE.......	Oshkosh, WI [*AM radio station call letters*]
WLKF.......	Lakeland, FL [*AM radio station call letters*]
WLKI........	Angola, IN [*FM radio station call letters*]
WLKK	Erie, PA [*AM radio station call letters*]
WLKL.......	Mattoon, IL [*FM radio station call letters*]
WLKM	Three Rivers, MI [*AM radio station call letters*]
WLKM	Welkom Gold Mining Co. Ltd. [*NASDAQ symbol*] (NQ)
WLKM-FM ...	Three Rivers, MI [*FM radio station call letters*]
WLKO.......	Fort Plain, NY [*FM radio station call letters*]
WLKQ.......	Buford, GA [*FM radio station call letters*]
WLKR.......	Norwalk, OH [*FM radio station call letters*]
WLKR.......	Walker [*B. B.*] Co. [*NASDAQ symbol*] (NQ)
WLKS.......	Walker-Scott Corp. [*NASDAQ symbol*] (NQ)
WLKS.......	West Liberty, KY [*AM radio station call letters*]
WLKW	Providence, RI [*AM radio station call letters*]
WLKX.......	Forest Lake, MN [*FM radio station call letters*]
WLKY.......	Louisville, KY [*Television station call letters*]
WLKZ.......	Wolfeboro, NH [*FM radio station call letters*]
WLL..........	Williamstown [*Massachusetts*] [*Seismograph station code, US Geological Survey*] [*Closed*] (SEIS)
WLLA.......	Kalamazoo, MI [*Television station call letters*]
WLLE.......	Raleigh, NC [*AM radio station call letters*]
WLLF	Mercer, PA [*FM radio station call letters*]
WLLG.......	Lowville, NY [*FM radio station call letters*]
WLLH.......	Lowell, MA [*AM radio station call letters*]
WLLI........	Joliet, IL [*FM radio station call letters*]
WLLJ	Cassopolis, MI [*AM radio station call letters*]
WLLK.......	Somerset, KY [*FM radio station call letters*]
WLLL.......	Lynchburg, VA [*AM radio station call letters*]
WLLN	Lillington, NC [*AM ràdio station call letters*]
WLLR.......	East Moline, IL [*FM radio station call letters*]
WLLR.......	Moline, IL [*AM radio station call letters*]
WLLR.......	Washington and Lee Law Review [*A publication*]
W & LLR ...	Welshpool & Llanfair Light Railway [*Wales*]
WLLS	Hartford, KY [*AM radio station call letters*]
WLLS-FM ...	Hartford, KY [*FM radio station call letters*]
WLLT.......	Polo, IL [*FM radio station call letters*]
WLLV.......	Louisville, KY [*AM radio station call letters*]
WLLX.......	Lawrenceburg, TN [*FM radio station call letters*]
WLLY.......	Wilson, NC [*AM radio station call letters*]
WLLZ.......	Detroit, MI [*FM radio station call letters*]
WLM	Coastal Buoy Tender [*Coast Guard symbol*] (DNAB)
WLM	Warning Light Monitor
WLM	Wellman, Inc. [*NYSE symbol*] (CTT)
WLM	Western Law Monthly [*Cleveland, OH*] [*A publication*] (DLA)
WLM	Western Lumber Manufacturers [*An association*] [*Later, Western Timber Association*] (EA)
WLM	Willow Mountain [*Alaska*] [*Seismograph station code, US Geological Survey*] [*Closed*] (SEIS)
WLM	Wire Line MODEMS
WLM	Working Level Month [*Nuclear energy*]
WLMB	Lima, OH [*FM radio station call letters*]
WLME	Hawesville, KY [*FM radio station call letters*]
WLMF.......	Webster, NY [*FM radio station call letters*]
WLMG	New Orleans, LA [*FM radio station call letters*]
WLMH.......	Morrow, OH [*FM radio station call letters*]
WLMI........	Kane, PA [*FM radio station call letters*]
WLMJ.......	Jackson, OH [*AM radio station call letters*]
WLMK	Horse Cave, KY [*FM radio station call letters*]
WLML.......	Montezuma, GA [*FM radio station call letters*]
WLMM	Woodbury, TN [*FM radio station call letters*]
WLMO.....	Worldwide Logistics Management Office [*Army*]
WLMT	Memphis, TN [*Television station call letters*]
WLMU	Harrogate, TN [*FM radio station call letters*]
WLMX	Rossville, GA [*AM radio station call letters*]
WLMX-FM ...	Rossville, GA [*FM radio station call letters*]
WLN..........	Washington Library Network [*Washington State Library*] [*Olympia, WA*] [*Library network*]
WLN..........	Welcome North Mines [*Vancouver Stock Exchange symbol*]
WLN..........	Wellington [*British depot code*]
WLN..........	Western Library Network [*Formerly, Washington Library Network*] [*Library of Congress*] [*Olympia, WA*] [*Database*]
WLN..........	Wired Librarian's Newsletter [*A publication*]
WLN..........	Wiswesser Line Notation [*Chemical structure*]
WLNA.......	Peekskill, NY [*AM radio station call letters*]
WLNB	Ligonier, IN [*FM radio station call letters*]
WLNC.......	Laurinburg, NC [*AM radio station call letters*]
WLNE.......	Montgomery, AL [*FM radio station call letters*]
WLNE.......	New Bedford, MA [*Television station call letters*]
WLNED	Water Law Newsletter [*A publication*]
WLNG.......	Sag Harbor, NY [*AM radio station call letters*]
WLNG-FM ...	Sag Harbor, NY [*FM radio station call letters*]
WLNH.......	Laconia, NH [*AM radio station call letters*]
WLNH-FM ...	Laconia, NH [*FM radio station call letters*]
WLNL	Horseheads, NY [*AM radio station call letters*]
WLNL	Wellness Newsletter [*A publication*]
WLNS.......	Lansing, MI [*Television station call letters*]
WLNX.......	Lincoln, IL [*FM radio station call letters*]
WLO.........	Waterloo Railroad Co. [*AAR code*]
WLO.........	Weapons Liaison Officer (NVT)
WLO.........	Wilson [*Oklahoma*] [*Seismograph station code, US Geological Survey*] (SEIS)
WLO.........	Working Layout (SAA)
WLOB	Portland, ME [*AM radio station call letters*]
WLOC	Munfordville, KY [*AM radio station call letters*]
WLOC-FM ...	Munfordville, KY [*FM radio station call letters*]
WLOD.......	Loudon, TN [*AM radio station call letters*]
WLOD-FM ...	Loudon, TN [*FM radio station call letters*]
WLOE.......	Eden, NC [*AM radio station call letters*]
WLOG.......	Logan, WV [*AM radio station call letters*]
WLOH.......	Lancaster, OH [*AM radio station call letters*]
WLOI	La Porte, IN [*AM radio station call letters*]
WLOJ........	New Bern, NC [*AM radio station call letters*]
WLOK.......	Memphis, TN [*AM radio station call letters*]
WLOL	Cambridge, MN [*FM radio station call letters*]
WLON......	Lincolnton, NC [*AM radio station call letters*]
W Lon	West Longitude
W Lond Med J ...	West London Medical Journal [*A publication*]
WLOP	Jesup, GA [*AM radio station call letters*]
WLOQ	Winter Park, FL [*FM radio station call letters*]
WLOS	Asheville, NC [*Television station call letters*]
WLOT	Trenton, TN [*FM radio station call letters*]
WLOU	Louisville, KY [*AM radio station call letters*]
WLOV	Washington, GA [*AM radio station call letters*]
WLOV	West Point, MS [*Television station call letters*]
WLOV-FM ...	Washington, GA [*FM radio station call letters*]
WLOW	Bluffton, SC [*FM radio station call letters*]
WLOW	Wicklow [*County in Ireland*] (ROG)
WLOX	Biloxi, MS [*Television station call letters*]
WLP..........	Wallops Island, NASA Center (MCD)
WLP..........	Ways of Looking at People Scale [*Psychology*] (AEBS)
WLP..........	Wellpoint Health Networks [*NYSE symbol*] (SPSG)
WLP..........	Western Legal Publications [*Database*] [*Western Legal Publications Ltd.*] [*Information service or system*] (CRD)
WLP..........	White Light Position
WLP..........	Women's Law Project (EA)
WLPA.......	Lancaster, PA [*AM radio station call letters*]
WLPB.......	Baton Rouge, LA [*Television station call letters*]
WLPB.......	Woodcock Language Proficiency Battery [*Achievement test*]
WL/PD......	Warner-Lambert/Parke-Davis [*Computer files of chemical and biological data*]
WLPE.......	Augusta, GA [*FM radio station call letters*]
WLPF	William L. Patterson Foundation (EA)
WLPH	Irondale, AL [*AM radio station call letters*]
WLPI........	Wellington Leisure Products, Inc. [*NASDAQ symbol*] (CTT)
WLPJ	New Port Richey, FL [*FM radio station call letters*]
WLPM.......	Suffolk, VA [*AM radio station call letters*]
WLPO	La Salle, IL [*AM radio station call letters*]
WLPR.......	Prichard, AL [*AM radio station call letters*]
WLPS	Watermen and Lightermen's Protective Society [*A union*] [*British*]
WLPT........	Jesup, GA [*FM radio station call letters*]
WLPW.......	Lake Placid, NY [*FM radio station call letters*]

WLPY........ Purcellville, VA [*AM radio station call letters*]
WLPZ........ Westbrook, ME [*AM radio station call letters*]
WLQ.......... Washington University. Law Quarterly [*A publication*]
WLQE........ Villas, NJ [*FM radio station call letters*]
WLQH....... Chiefland, FL [*AM radio station call letters*]
WLQH-FM ... Chiefland, FL [*FM radio station call letters*]
WLQI .... Rensselaer, IN [*FM radio station call letters*]
WLQM...... Franklin, VA [*AM radio station call letters*]
WLQM-FM ... Franklin, VA [*FM radio station call letters*]
WLQR .... Toledo, OH [*FM radio station call letters*]
WLQV........ Detroit, MI [*AM radio station call letters*]
WLQY .... Hollywood, FL [*AM radio station call letters*]
WLR .... River Buoy Tender, Large or Small [*Coast Guard symbol*]   (DNAB)
WLR .... Washington Law Reporter [*District of Columbia*] [*A publication*]   (DLA)
WLR .... Washington Law Review [*A publication*]
WLR .... Water Level Recorder
WLR .... Weapons Locating RADAR   (AABC)
WLR .... Weekly Law Reports [*British*]
WLR .... Weighted Linear Regression [*Mathematics*]
WLR .... West London Railway   (ROG)
WLR .... Western Law Reporter [*Canada*] [*A publication*]   (DLA)
WLR .... Wilanour Resources Ltd. [*Toronto Stock Exchange symbol*]
WLR .... Wisconsin Law Review [*A publication*]
WLR .... World Law Review [*A publication*]   (DLA)
WLR .... Wrong Length Record [*Data processing*]
WLRA .... Lockport, IL [*FM radio station call letters*]
WLRA .... Wagner Labor Relations Act   (OICC)
WLRA .... World Leisure and Recreation Association [*Formerly, IRA*]   (EA)
WLRB........ Macomb, IL [*AM radio station call letters*]
WLRC........ Walnut, MS [*AM radio station call letters*]
WLRD .... Warning Light Relay Driver
WLRF........ WLR Foods, Inc. [*NASDAQ symbol*]   (NQ)
WLRG .... Timmonsville, SC [*AM radio station call letters*]
WLRH .... Huntsville, AL [*FM radio station call letters*]
WLRI........ Warner-Lambert Research Institute [*New Jersey*]
WLRM .... Ridgeland, MS [*AM radio station call letters*]
WLRN .... Miami, FL [*FM radio station call letters*]
WLRN-TV ... Miami, FL [*Television station call letters*]
WLRP........ San Sebastian, PR [*AM radio station call letters*]
WLRP........ Wandsworth's Legal Resource Project [*A publication*]   (DLA)
WLRQ .... Cocoa, FL [*FM radio station call letters*]
WLRR .... Milledgeville, GA [*FM radio station call letters*]
WLRS........ Louisville, KY [*FM radio station call letters*]
WLRT........ Kankakee, IL [*FM radio station call letters*]
WLRV........ Lebanon, VA [*AM radio station call letters*]
WLRW ...... Champaign, IL [*FM radio station call letters*]
WLRX........ Nappanee, IN [*FM radio station call letters*]
WLRZ........ Peru, IL [*FM radio station call letters*]
WLS.......... Chicago, IL [*AM radio station call letters*]
WLS.......... Livingston-Steuben-Wyoming BOCES [*Boards of Cooperative Educational Services*], Educational Communications Center, Geneseo, NY [*OCLC symbol*]   (OCLC)
WLS.......... Wallis Island [*Wallis and Futuna Islands*] [*Airport symbol*]   (OAG)
WLS.......... Water Lily Society   (EA)
WLS.......... Weighted Least Squares [*Statistics*]
WLS.......... Wells
WLS.......... Welschbruch [*France*] [*Seismograph station code, US Geological Survey*]   (SEIS)
WLS.......... Welsh Language Society   (EA)
WLS.......... Westchester Library System [*Library network*]
WLS.......... Westchester Public Library [*UTLAS symbol*]
WLS.......... Western Launch Site [*Military*]
WLS.......... Williams Air, Inc. [*Medford Lakes, NJ*] [*FAA designator*]   (FAAC)
WLS.......... Winnefox Library System [*Library network*]
WLS.......... World Listening Service   (EA)
WLSA........ Louisa, VA [*FM radio station call letters*]
WLSA........ Wage and Labor Standards Administration   (OICC)
WLSB........ Copperhill, TN [*AM radio station call letters*]
WLSBA ...... Wildlife Society. Bulletin [*A publication*]
WLSC........ Loris, SC [*AM radio station call letters*]
WLSC........ West Liberty State College [*West Virginia*]
WLSD........ Big Stone Gap, VA [*AM radio station call letters*]
WLSE........ Wallace, NC [*AM radio station call letters*]
WLS-FM ... Chicago, IL [*FM radio station call letters*]
WLSH .... Lansford, PA [*AM radio station call letters*]
WLSH .... Wochenblatt der Landesbauernschaft Schleswig-Holstein [*A publication*]
WLSI .... Pikeville, KY [*AM radio station call letters*]
WLSK........ Lebanon, KY [*FM radio station call letters*]
WLSL........ Crisfield, MD [*FM radio station call letters*]
WLSL........ Walseal
WLSM....... Louisville, MS [*AM radio station call letters*]
WLSM-FM ... Louisville, MS [*FM radio station call letters*]
WLSN........ Greenville, OH [*FM radio station call letters*]
WLSP........ World List of Scientific Periodicals [*A publication*]   (DIT)
WLSQ........ Dalton, GA [*AM radio station call letters*]

WLSR........ Lima, OH [*FM radio station call letters*]
WLST........ Marinette, WI [*FM radio station call letters*]
WLS-TV ... Chicago, IL [*Television station call letters*]
WLSU....... La Crosse, WI [*FM radio station call letters*]
WLSV........ Wellsville, NY [*AM radio station call letters*]
WLSW....... Scottdale, PA [*FM radio station call letters*]
WLSY........ Jeffersontown, KY [*FM radio station call letters*]
WLSZ........ Humboldt, TN [*FM radio station call letters*]
WLT .... Weighing Less Than
WLT .... Western Law Times [*1890-95*] [*A publication*]   (DLA)
WLT .... Wire Line Timing
WLT .... World Literature Today [*A publication*]
WLTAS ..... Wingfoot Lighter-Than-Air Society [*Later, Lighter-Than-Air Society*]   (EA)
WLTBU..... Watermen, Lightermen, Tugmen, and Bargemen's Union [*British*]
WLTC........ Gastonia, NC [*AM radio station call letters*]
WLTC........ Wimbledon Lawn Tennis Championship [*British*]
WLTD .... Lexington, MS [*FM radio station call letters*]
WLTE........ Minneapolis, MN [*FM radio station call letters*]
WLTE........ Warrant Loss to Enlisted Status [*Revocation of appointment*] [*Navy*]
WLTF........ Cleveland, OH [*FM radio station call letters*]
WLTG .... Panama City, FL [*AM radio station call letters*]
WLTH .... Gary, IN [*AM radio station call letters*]
WLTI........ Detroit, MI [*FM radio station call letters*]
WLTJ .... Pittsburgh, PA [*FM radio station call letters*]
WLTK........ Broadway, VA [*FM radio station call letters*]
WLTK........ Wiltek, Inc. [*NASDAQ symbol*]   (NQ)
WLTL........ La Grange, IL [*FM radio station call letters*]
WLTM ...... Rantoul, IL [*FM radio station call letters*]
WLTN .... Lisbon, NH [*FM radio station call letters*]
WLTN .... Littleton, NH [*AM radio station call letters*]
WLTN .... Wilton Enterprises, Inc. [*Woodridge, IL*] [*NASDAQ symbol*]   (NQ)
WLTO ...... Harbor Springs, MI [*FM radio station call letters*]
WLTP....... Parkersburg, WV [*AM radio station call letters*]
WLTQ ...... Milwaukee, WI [*FM radio station call letters*]
WLTR........ Columbia, SC [*FM radio station call letters*]
WLTS........ Slidell, LA [*FM radio station call letters*]
WLTT........ Bethesda, MD [*FM radio station call letters*]
WLTU .... Manitowoc, WI [*FM radio station call letters*]
WLTV........ Miami, FL [*Television station call letters*]
WLTW....... New York, NY [*FM radio station call letters*]
WLTX........ Columbia, SC [*Television station call letters*]
WLTY........ Norfolk, VA [*FM radio station call letters*]
WLTZ........ Columbus, GA [*Television station call letters*]
WLU .... Washington and Lee University [*Virginia*]
WLU .... Wesleyan University, Middletown, CT [*OCLC symbol*]   (OCLC)
WLU .... Wilfrid Laurier University [*Canada*]
WLub........ Wydawnictwo Lubelskie [*A publication*]
WLUC .... Marquette, MI [*Television station call letters*]
WLUC ...... Women Life Underwriters Conference   (EA)
WLUJ .... Petersburg, IL [*FM radio station call letters*]
WLUK .... Green Bay, WI [*Television station call letters*]
WLUM...... Milwaukee, WI [*FM radio station call letters*]
WLUN .... Lumberton, MS [*FM radio station call letters*]
WLUP .... Chicago, IL [*AM radio station call letters*]
WLUP-FM ... Chicago, IL [*FM radio station call letters*]
WLUR .... Lexington, VA [*FM radio station call letters*]
WLUS .... Gainesville, FL [*AM radio station call letters*]
WLUV .... Loves Park, IL [*AM radio station call letters*]
WLUV-FM ... Loves Park, IL [*FM radio station call letters*]
WLUW ...... Chicago, IL [*FM radio station call letters*]
WLUX .... Baton Rouge, LA [*AM radio station call letters*]
WLUZ .... Bayamon, PR [*AM radio station call letters*]
WLV .... Lightship [*Coast Guard symbol*]   (DNAB)
WLVA........ Lynchburg, VA [*AM radio station call letters*]
WLVC........ Fort Kent, ME [*AM radio station call letters*]
WLVE........ Miami Beach, FL [*FM radio station call letters*]
WLVF....... Haines City, FL [*AM radio station call letters*]
WLVF-FM ... Haines City, FL [*FM radio station call letters*]
WLVH........ Manchester, CT [*AM radio station call letters*]
WLVI........ Cambridge, MA [*Television station call letters*]
WLVJ .... Royal Palm Beach, FL [*AM radio station call letters*]
WLVL....... Lockport, NY [*AM radio station call letters*]
WLVN ...... Luverne, AL [*AM radio station call letters*]
WLVQ ...... Columbus, OH [*FM radio station call letters*]
WLVR........ Bethlehem, PA [*FM radio station call letters*]
WLVS........ Lake Worth, FL [*AM radio station call letters*]
WLVT........ Allentown, PA [*Television station call letters*]
WLVU ...... Dunedin, FL [*AM radio station call letters*]
WLVU ...... Holiday, FL [*FM radio station call letters*]
WLVV ...... Mobile, AL [*AM radio station call letters*]
WLVW ...... Salisbury, MD [*AM radio station call letters*]
WLVW-FM ... Salisbury, MD [*FM radio station call letters*]
WLVX........ Bloomfield, CT [*AM radio station call letters*]
WLVY........ Elmira, NY [*FM radio station call letters*]
WLVZ........ Athens, OH [*AM radio station call letters*]
WLW .... Cincinnati, OH [*AM radio station call letters*]

WLW.........	Weldwood of Canada Ltd. [*Toronto Stock Exchange symbol*]
WLW.........	Willows, CA [*Location identifier*] [*FAA*] (FAAL)
WLW.........	Women Library Workers (EA)
WLWE......	World Literature Written in English [*A publication*]
WLWH......	Workshop Library on World Humour (EA)
WLWI.......	Montgomery, AL [*AM radio station call letters*]
WLWI-FM ...	Montgomery, AL [*FM radio station call letters*]
WLWL.......	Rockingham, NC [*AM radio station call letters*]
WLWN......	Kershaw, SC [*FM radio station call letters*]
WLWT	Cincinnati, OH [*Television station call letters*]
WLWZ......	Easley, SC [*FM radio station call letters*]
WLXI........	Greensboro, NC [*Television station call letters*]
WLXN	Lexington, NC [*AM radio station call letters*]
WLXR.......	La Crosse, WI [*FM radio station call letters*]
WLXY	Northport, AL [*FM radio station call letters*]
WLY	Westerly
WLYC.......	Williamsport, PA [*AM radio station call letters*]
WLYF........	Miami, FL [*FM radio station call letters*]
WLYH	Lancaster, PA [*Television station call letters*]
WLYJ	Clarksburg, WV [*Television station call letters*]
WLYK	Lynchburg, VA [*FM radio station call letters*]
WLYN	Lynn, MA [*AM radio station call letters*]
WLYT.......	Haverhill, MA [*FM radio station call letters*]
WLYU	Lyons, GA [*FM radio station call letters*]
WLYV.......	Fort Wayne, IN [*AM radio station call letters*]
WLYX.......	Memphis, TN [*FM radio station call letters*]
WLYY.......	Lansing, MI [*FM radio station call letters*]
WLZA.......	Starkville, MS [*FM radio station call letters*]
WLZQ	South Whitley, IN [*FM radio station call letters*]
WLZR.......	Milwaukee, WI [*AM radio station call letters*]
WLZR-FM ...	Milwaukee, WI [*FM radio station call letters*]
WLZT.......	Miami, WV [*FM radio station call letters*]
WLZW	Utica, NY [*FM radio station call letters*]
WLZZ.......	Montpelier, OH [*FM radio station call letters*]
WM...........	[*Qualified for*] Engineering Watch [*USNR officer classification*]
WM...........	Milwaukee Public Library, Milwaukee, WI [*Library symbol*] [*Library of Congress*] (LCLS)
WM...........	Multiple-Conductor Cables [*JETDS nomenclature*] [*Military*] (CET)
WM...........	Waldenstrom's Macroglobulinemia [*Medicine*]
W & M	War and Marine (DS)
WM...........	War Memorial
WM...........	Ward Manager [*Medicine*]
WM...........	Warming
WM...........	Warrant Mechanician [*British military*] (DMA)
W & M	Washburn and Moen [*Wire gauge*]
W/M..........	Washing Machine [*Classified advertising*] (ADA)
WM...........	Washington Monthly [*A publication*]
WM...........	Waste Management (NASA)
WM...........	Waste Minimization
WM...........	Water Meter
WM...........	Water Monitor (DS)
WM...........	Watermark
WM...........	Watt Meter
WM...........	Wave Meter
WM...........	Ways and Means (DLA)
WM...........	Weapon Mechanician [*British military*] (DMA)
WM...........	Wehrmacht-Marine [*Marking on Navy vehicles*] [*German military - World War II*]
W/M..........	Weight or Measurement
WM...........	Welding Memorandum
WM...........	Wertpapier-Mitteilungen [*A publication*]
WM...........	West Midlands [*Metropolitan county in England*]
WM...........	Westermanns Monatshefte [*A publication*]
WM...........	Western Maryland Railway Co. [*NYSE symbol*] [*AAR code*] [*Wall Street slang name: "Wet Mary"*] (SPSG)
WM...........	Wheel-Made (BJA)
WM...........	White Male
WM...........	White Metal
WM...........	Whitten's Medium [*for cell incubation*]
WM...........	Whole Milk (MAE)
WM...........	Whole Mount (AAMN)
Wm	William (King of England)
W & M	William and Mary [*King and Queen of England*] (ROG)
W & M	William and Mary Law Review [*A publication*]
W & M	Wilson & McLane, Inc. [*Information service or system*] (IID)
WM...........	Windward Islands Airways International NV [*Netherlands*] [*ICAO designator*] (ICDA)
W/M..........	Wing Main [*Airfield*] (NATG)
WM...........	Wire Mesh
WM...........	Without Margin
WM...........	Woman Marine (SAA)
WM...........	Women in the Mainstream (EA)
WM...........	Women Marines
W & M	Woodbury and Minot's United States Circuit Court Reports [*3 vols.*] [*A publication*] (DLA)
WM...........	Word Mark (BUR)
W/M..........	Words per Minute (KSC)
WM...........	Work of Mary [*An association*] (EAIO)
WM...........	Work Measurement [*Army*] (AABC)
WM...........	Working Memory [*Psychology*]
WM...........	Works Management [*A publication*]
WM...........	World Markets [*British investment firm*] [*Formerly, Wood Mackenzie*]
WM...........	World Meetings [*A publication*]
WM...........	World Monitor [*Television program*]
WM...........	World of Music [*London*] [*A publication*]
WM...........	Worshipful Master [*Freemasonry*]
WM...........	Wustite Magnetite [*Geology*]
W/M²..........	Watts per Square Meter
WMA........	Alverno College, Milwaukee, WI [*Library symbol*] [*Library of Congress*] (LCLS)
WMa.........	Madison Public Library, Madison, WI [*Library symbol*] [*Library of Congress*] (LCLS)
WMA........	Mandritsara [*Madagascar*] [*Airport symbol*] (OAG)
WMA........	Wallcovering Manufacturers Association (EA)
WMA........	War Measures Act
WMA........	Washington Metropolitan Area (AFM)
WMA........	Waste Management Area [*NASA*]
WMA........	Waterbed Manufacturers Association (EA)
WMA........	Weather Modification Association (EA)
WMA........	Welding Machine Arc
WMA........	Wentworth Military Academy [*Lexington, MO*]
WMA........	West Mesa [*New Mexico*] [*Seismograph station code, US Geological Survey*] (SEIS)
WMA........	Wheelchair Motorcycle Association (EA)
WMA........	Wikalat Al-Maghreb Al-Arabi [*News agency*] [*Morocco*] (MENA)
WMA........	Wing Main Airfield (NATG)
WMA........	Women Marines Association (EA)
WMA........	Workers' Music Association [*British*]
WMA........	World Manx Association
WMA........	World Medical Association [*Ferney-Voltaire, France*]
WMA........	World Modeling Association (EA)
WMAA......	Bahau [*Malaysia*] [*ICAO location identifier*] (ICLI)
WMAA......	Warrant Master-at-Arms [*British military*] (DMA)
WMAA......	Whitney Museum of American Art [*New York, NY*]
WMAA......	World Martial Arts Association
WMaAR ...	Wisconsin Alumni Research Foundation, Madison, WI [*Library symbol*] [*Library of Congress*] (LCLS)
WMAB	Batu Pahat [*Malaysia*] [*ICAO location identifier*] (ICLI)
WMAB	Mississippi State, MS [*FM radio station call letters*]
WMAB	Weather Modification Advisory Board
WMaBR	Wisconsin Department of Health and Social Services, Bureau of Research, Madison, WI [*Library symbol*] [*Library of Congress*] (LCLS)
WMAB-TV ...	Mississippi State, MS [*Television station call letters*]
WMAC......	Benta [*Malaysia*] [*ICAO location identifier*] (ICLI)
WMaC.......	Central Wisconsin Colony, Staff Library, Madison, WI [*Library symbol*] [*Library of Congress*] (LCLS)
WMAC......	Metter, GA [*AM radio station call letters*]
WMAC......	Waste Management Advisory Council [*British*] (DCTA)
WMaCH....	Wisconsin Department of Health and Social Services, Community Health Service, Madison, WI [*Library symbol*] [*Library of Congress*] (LCLS)
WMACS....	AC Spark Plug Co., Electronics Division, Milwaukee, WI [*Library symbol*] [*Library of Congress*] (LCLS)
WMaCT	Children's Treatment Center, Madison, WI [*Library symbol*] [*Library of Congress*] (LCLS)
WMAD......	Bentong [*Malaysia*] [*ICAO location identifier*] (ICLI)
WMAD......	Sun Prairie, WI [*AM radio station call letters*]
WMAD-FM ...	Sun Prairie, WI [*FM radio station call letters*]
WMAE......	Bidor [*Malaysia*] [*ICAO location identifier*] (ICLI)
WMAE......	Booneville, MS [*FM radio station call letters*]
WMAE-TV ...	Booneville, MS [*Television station call letters*]
WMAF	Madison, FL [*AM radio station call letters*]
WMaF	United States Forest Products Laboratory, Madison, WI [*Library symbol*] [*Library of Congress*] (LCLS)
WMAFPH ...	World Medical Association for Perfect Health [*Also known as United States Association of Physicians*] (EA)
WMAG......	Dungun [*Malaysia*] [*ICAO location identifier*] (ICLI)
WMAG......	High Point, NC [*FM radio station call letters*]
WMaG.......	Madison General Hospital, Madison, WI [*Library symbol*] [*Library of Congress*] (LCLS)
WMaG-N ..	Madison General Hospital, School of Nursing, Madison, WI [*Library symbol*] [*Library of Congress*] (LCLS)
WMAH	Biloxi, MS [*FM radio station call letters*]
WMAH	Grik [*Malaysia*] [*ICAO location identifier*] (ICLI)
WMaH	Wisconsin Division of Health Policy and Planning Library, Madison, WI [*Library symbol*] [*Library of Congress*] (LCLS)
WMAH-TV ...	Biloxi, MS [*Television station call letters*]
WMAI.......	Gua Musang [*Malaysia*] [*ICAO location identifier*] (ICLI)
W Mail......	Western Mail [*A publication*] (APTA)
W Mail Ann ...	Western Mail Annual [*A publication*] (APTA)
WMaJ	Jackson Clinic, Madison, WI [*Library symbol*] [*Library of Congress*] (LCLS)
WMAJ.......	Jendarata [*Malaysia*] [*ICAO location identifier*] (ICLI)
WMAJ.......	State College, PA [*AM radio station call letters*]
WMAK......	London, KY [*AM radio station call letters*]
WMAL	Kuala Krai [*Malaysia*] [*ICAO location identifier*] (ICLI)
WMAL	Washington, DC [*AM radio station call letters*]

WMaLS..... Wisconsin Division for Library Services, Bureau for Reference and Local Services, Madison, WI [*Library symbol*] [*Library of Congress*] (LCLS)
WMAM..... Langkawi [*Malaysia*] [*ICAO location identifier*] (ICLI)
WMAM..... Marinette, WI [*AM radio station call letters*]
WMaM...... Methodist Hospital School of Nursing, Madison, WI [*Library symbol*] [*Library of Congress*] (LCLS)
WMaMS ... Mendota Mental Health Institute, Madison, WI [*Library symbol*] [*Library of Congress*] (LCLS)
WMan....... Manawa Public Library, Manawa, WI [*Library symbol*] [*Library of Congress*] (LCLS)
WMAN...... Mansfield, OH [*AM radio station call letters*]
WMani ...... Manitowoc Public Library, Manitowoc, WI [*Library symbol*] [*Library of Congress*] (LCLS)
WManiH ... Holy Family Hospital, Manitowoc, WI [*Library symbol*] [*Library of Congress*] (LCLS)
WManiHN ... Holy Family School of Nursing, Manitowoc, WI [*Library symbol*] [*Library of Congress*] (LCLS)
WMANT ... Wissenschaftliche Monographien zum Alten und Neuen Testament [*A publication*] (BJA)
WMAO..... Greenwood, MS [*FM radio station call letters*]
WMAO..... Kong Kong [*Malaysia*] [*ICAO location identifier*] (ICLI)
WMAO-TV ... Greenwood, MS [*Television station call letters*]
WMAP ...... Kluang [*Malaysia*] [*ICAO location identifier*] (ICLI)
WMAP ...... Monroe, NC [*AM radio station call letters*]
WMAP ...... Pageland, SC [*FM radio station call letters*]
WMaPI...... Department of Public Instruction, Division for Library Services, Professional Library, Madison, WI [*Library symbol*] [*Library of Congress*] (LCLS)
WMaPI-CC ... Department of Public Instruction, Division for Library Services, Cooperative Children's Book Center, Madison, WI [*Library symbol*] [*Library of Congress*] (LCLS)
WMaPI-PL ... Department of Public Instruction, Division for Library Services, Public Library Services, Madison, WI [*Library symbol*] [*Library of Congress*] (LCLS)
WMaPI-RL ... Department of Public Instruction, Division for Library Services, Reference and Loan Library, Madison, WI [*Library symbol*] [*Library of Congress*] (LCLS)
WMaPR .... Wisconsin Regional Primate Research Center, Madison, WI [*Library symbol*] [*Library of Congress*] (LCLS)
WMAQ...... Chicago, IL [*AM radio station call letters*]
WMAQ...... Labis [*Malaysia*] [*ICAO location identifier*] (ICLI)
WMAQ-TV ... Chicago, IL [*Television station call letters*]
WMAR ...... Baltimore, MD [*Television station call letters*]
WMaR....... Raltech Scientific Services, Inc., Madison, WI [*Library symbol*] [*Library of Congress*] (LCLS)
WMAR ...... Western Marine Electronics Co. [*NASDAQ symbol*] (NQ)
WMaraS.... Saint Anthony Friary, Marathon, WI [*Library symbol*] [*Library of Congress*] (LCLS)
WMarC ..... Marshfield Clinic, Marshfield, WI [*Library symbol*] [*Library of Congress*] (LCLS)
WMARC ... World Maritime Administrative Radio Conference (DS)
WMarSJ.... Saint Joseph's Hospital, Marshfield, WI [*Library symbol*] [*Library of Congress*] (LCLS)
WMarW .... Wood County Hospital, Marshfield, WI [*Library symbol*] [*Library of Congress*] (LCLS)
WMAS ...... Springfield, MA [*AM radio station call letters*]
WMaS ...... Student Association for the Study of Hallucinogens, Madison, WI [*Library symbol*] [*Library of Congress*] (LCLS)
WMAS-FM ... Springfield, MA [*FM radio station call letters*]
WMaSM ... Saint Mary's Hospital, Doctors' Library, Madison, WI [*Library symbol*] [*Library of Congress*] (LCLS)
WMaSM-N ... Saint Mary's Hospital, School of Nursing, Madison, WI [*Library symbol*] [*Library of Congress*] (LCLS)
W Mass Bus ... Western Massachusetts Business Journal [*A publication*]
WMAT ...... Lima Blas [*Malaysia*] [*ICAO location identifier*] (ICLI)
WMAT ...... Wastemate Corp. [*NASDAQ symbol*] (NQ)
WMaTC .... Madison Area Technical College, Madison, WI [*Library symbol*] [*Library of Congress*] (LCLS)
WMAU...... Bude, MS [*FM radio station call letters*]
WMau........ Mauston Public Library, Mauston, WI [*Library symbol*] [*Library of Congress*] (LCLS)
WMAU...... Mersing [*Malaysia*] [*ICAO location identifier*] (ICLI)
WMAU...... Women's Martial Arts Union [*Defunct*] (EA)
WMaUCS ... University of Wisconsin-Center System, Madison, WI [*Library symbol*] [*Library of Congress*] (LCLS)
WMaUEx ... University of Wisconsin-Extension, Madison, WI [*Library symbol*] [*Library of Congress*] (LCLS)
WMAU-TV ... Bude, MS [*Television station call letters*]
WMAV ...... Muar [*Malaysia*] [*ICAO location identifier*] (ICLI)
WMAV ...... Oxford, MS [*FM radio station call letters*]
WMaVA .... United States Veterans Administration Hospital, Madison, WI [*Library symbol*] [*Library of Congress*] (LCLS)
WMAV-TV ... Oxford, MS [*Television station call letters*]
WMAW..... Meridian, MS [*FM radio station call letters*]
WMaW...... Wisconsin Alumni Research Foundation Institute, Inc., Madison, WI [*Library symbol*] [*Library of Congress*] (LCLS)
WMAW-TV ... Meridian, MS [*Television station call letters*]
WMAX...... Grand Rapids, MI [*AM radio station call letters*]
WMAY ...... Springfield, IL [*AM radio station call letters*]

WMAZ ...... Macon, GA [*AM radio station call letters*]
WMAZ ...... Segamat [*Malaysia*] [*ICAO location identifier*] (ICLI)
WMAZ-TV ... Macon, GA [*Television station call letters*]
WMB......... Walnut Marketing Board (EA)
WMB......... War Mobilization Board
WMB......... Warrnambool [*Australia*] [*Airport symbol*] (OAG)
WMB......... [*The*] Williams Companies [*NYSE symbol*] (SPSG)
WMB......... Williamsburg Technical College, Kingstree, SC [*OCLC symbol*] (OCLC)
WMB......... Women in Business [*A publication*]
WMBA ...... Ambridge, PA [*AM radio station call letters*]
WMBA ...... Sitiawan [*Malaysia*] [*ICAO location identifier*] (ICLI)
WMBA ...... Wire Machinery Builders Association [*Later, WISA*] (EA)
WMBB ...... Panama City, FL [*Television station call letters*]
WMBB ...... Sungei Patani [*Malaysia*] [*ICAO location identifier*] (ICLI)
WMBC ...... Columbus, MS [*FM radio station call letters*]
WMBC ...... Newton, NJ [*Television station call letters*]
WMBC ...... Wisconsin Baptist State Convention, Milwaukee, WI [*Library symbol*] [*Library of Congress*] (LCLS)
WMBD ...... Peoria, IL [*AM radio station call letters*]
WMBD-TV ... Peoria, IL [*Television station call letters*]
WMBE ...... Chilton, WI [*AM radio station call letters*]
WMBE ...... Temerloh [*Malaysia*] [*ICAO location identifier*] (ICLI)
WMBF....... Ulu Bernam [*Malaysia*] [*ICAO location identifier*] (ICLI)
WMBG ...... Williamsburg, VA [*AM radio station call letters*]
WMBH...... Joplin, MO [*AM radio station call letters*]
WMBH...... Kroh [*Malaysia*] [*ICAO location identifier*] (ICLI)
WMBI ...... Chicago, IL [*AM radio station call letters*]
WMBI ...... Taiping [*Malaysia*] [*ICAO location identifier*] (ICLI)
WMBI-FM ... Chicago, IL [*FM radio station call letters*]
Wm Bl........ [*Sir William*] Blackstone's English King's Bench Reports [*1746-80*] [*A publication*] (DLA)
WMBL ...... Morehead City, NC [*AM radio station call letters*]
WMBL ...... Wrightsville Marine Biomedical Laboratory
WMBM ..... Miami Beach, FL [*AM radio station call letters*]
WMBN...... Petoskey, MI [*FM radio station call letters*]
WMBO...... Auburn, NY [*AM radio station call letters*]
WMBP ...... Belpre, OH [*FM radio station call letters*]
WMBR ...... Cambridge, MA [*FM radio station call letters*]
WMBS....... Uniontown, PA [*AM radio station call letters*]
WMBS....... West Massachusetts Bankshares, Inc. [*Greenfield, MA*] [*NASDAQ symbol*] (NQ)
WMBT ...... Pulau Pioman [*Malaysia*] [*ICAO location identifier*] (ICLI)
WMBT ...... Shenandoah, PA [*AM radio station call letters*]
WMBTOPCITBWTNTALI ... We May Be the Only Phone Company in Town, but We Try Not to Act Like It [*Slogan*]
WMBV..... Dixonis Mills, AL [*FM radio station call letters*]
WMBW..... Chattanooga, TN [*FM radio station call letters*]
WMC......... Concordia College, Milwaukee, WI [*Library symbol*] [*Library of Congress*] (LCLS)
WMC......... Memphis, TN [*AM radio station call letters*]
WMC......... War Manpower Commission [*Within the Office of Emergency Management*] [*World War II*]
WMC......... Waste Management Compartment [*NASA*] (KSC)
WMC......... Weapons and Mobility Command [*Army*]
WMC......... Weapons Monitoring Center
WMC......... Weapons Monitoring Console
WMC......... Western Maryland College [*Westminster*]
WMC......... Western Mining Corp. Holdings ADS [*NYSE symbol*] (SPSG)
WMC......... White Male Candidate [*Politics*]
WMC......... Wilmington College, Wilmington, OH [*OCLC symbol*] (OCLC)
WmC......... Windsor Microfilming Co., Windsor, ON, Canada [*Library symbol*] [*Library of Congress*] (LCLS)
WMC......... Winnemucca, NV [*Location identifier*] [*FAA*] (FAAL)
WMC......... Wisconsin Motor Carriers Association Inc., Madison WI [*STAC*]
WMC......... Wool Manufacturers Council (EA)
WMC......... World Meteorological Center [*World Meteorological Organization*]
WMC......... World Methodist Council (EA)
WMC......... World Ministries Commission (EA)
WMC......... World Missions to Children [*Later, WMF*] (EA)
WMC......... World Muslim Congress (BJA)
WMCA ..... New York, NY [*AM radio station call letters*]
WMCB ...... Martinsville, IN [*AM radio station call letters*]
WMCC ...... Marion, IN [*Television station call letters*]
WMCCMEC ... Women's Missionary Council of the Christian Methodist Episcopal Church (EA)
WMCCS.... Worldwide Military Command and Control System [*DoD*] (MCD)
WMCCSA ... World Masters Cross-Country Ski Association (EA)
WMCD...... Statesboro, GA [*FM radio station call letters*]
WMCE ...... Erie, PA [*FM radio station call letters*]
WMCF ...... Montgomery, AL [*Television station call letters*]
WMC-FM ... Memphis, TN [*FM radio station call letters*]
WMCG...... Milan, GA [*FM radio station call letters*]
WMCG...... Milwaukee County General Hospital, Milwaukee, WI [*Library symbol*] [*Library of Congress*] (LCLS)
WMCH...... Church Hill, TN [*AM radio station call letters*]

WMCH...... Columbia Hospital School of Nursing, Milwaukee, WI [*Library symbol*] [*Library of Congress*] (LCLS)
WMCHi .... Milwaukee County Historical Society, Milwaukee, WI [*Library symbol*] [*Library of Congress*] (LCLS)
WMCI .... Mattoon, IL [*FM radio station call letters*]
WMCI .... World Mail Center, Inc. [*NASDAQ symbol*] (NQ)
WMCJ .... Moncks Corner, SC [*AM radio station call letters*]
WMcK .... William McKinley [*US president, 1843-1901*]
WMCL ...... McLeansboro, IL [*AM radio station call letters*]
WMCL ...... Wideband Communications Line
WMCL ...... William & Clarissa, Inc. [*NASDAQ symbol*] (NQ)
WMCL ...... William Mitchell College of Law [*St. Paul, MN*]
WMCM ..... Milwaukee County Institutions, Mental Health Centers Libraries, Milwaukee, WI [*Library symbol*] [*Library of Congress*] (LCLS)
WMCM ..... Rockland, ME [*FM radio station call letters*]
WMCN...... St. Paul, MN [*FM radio station call letters*]
WMCO...... New Concord, OH [*FM radio station call letters*]
WMCO...... Williams Controls, Inc. [*NASDAQ symbol*] (NQ)
WMCP ...... Columbia, TN [*AM radio station call letters*]
WMCP ...... Woman's Medical College of Pennsylvania
WMCQ...... Richmond, KY [*FM radio station call letters*]
WMCQ...... William and Mary College. Quarterly [*A publication*]
WMCR ...... Oneida, NY [*AM radio station call letters*]
WMCR-FM ... Oneida, NY [*FM radio station call letters*]
WMCS....... Machias, ME [*AM radio station call letters*]
WMCSC.... Cardinal Stritch College, Milwaukee, WI [*Library symbol*] [*Library of Congress*] (LCLS)
WMCT ...... Mountain City, TN [*AM radio station call letters*]
WMC-TV .. Memphis, TN [*Television station call letters*]
WMCU..... Miami, FL [*FM radio station call letters*]
WMCW..... Harvard, IL [*AM radio station call letters*]
WMCW..... World Movement of Christian Workers [*See also MMTC*] [*Brussels, Belgium*] (EAIO)
WMCX...... West Long Branch, NJ [*FM radio station call letters*]
WMD......... Digital Equipment Corp., Westminster, Westminster, MA [*OCLC symbol*] (OCLC)
WMD........ Doctors Hospital, Milwaukee, WI [*Library symbol*] [*Library of Congress*] (LCLS)
WMD........ Mandabe [*Madagascar*] [*Airport symbol*] (OAG)
WMD......... Mars Graphic Services, Inc. [*Later, Dimark, Inc.*] [*AMEX symbol*] (SPSG)
WMD......... Waste Management Division [*Environmental Protection Agency*] (GFGA)
WMD........ Water Management Division [*Environmental Protection Agency*] (GFGA)
WMD......... Water Mineral Development [*A publication*] (APTA)
WMD........ Weapon Mounted Display
WMD........ Wind Measuring Device
WMDA...... Woodworking Machinery Distributors Association (EA)
WMDAA... Watch Material Distributors Association of America [*Later, WMJDA*] (EA)
W M Day Studies ... Romance Studies Presented to William Morton Day [*A publication*]
WMDB...... Nashville, TN [*AM radio station call letters*]
WMDB...... Waste Management Database [*IAEA*] [*United Nations*] (DUND)
WMDC...... Hazlehurst, MS [*AM radio station call letters*]
WMDC-FM ... Hazlehurst, MS [*FM radio station call letters*]
WMDD...... Fajardo, PR [*AM radio station call letters*]
WMDe....... Deaconess Hospital, Milwaukee, WI [*Library symbol*] [*Library of Congress*] (LCLS)
WMDE...... Remerton, GA [*AM radio station call letters*]
WMDH ..... New Castle, IN [*AM radio station call letters*]
WMDH-FM ... New Castle, IN [*FM radio station call letters*]
WMDio...... Diocesan Library, Milwaukee, WI [*Library symbol*] [*Library of Congress*] [*Obsolete*] (LCLS)
WMDJ ...... Allen, KY [*FM radio station call letters*]
WMDJ ...... Martin, KY [*AM radio station call letters*]
WMDK...... Peterborough, NH [*FM radio station call letters*]
WMDM..... Lexington Park, MD [*FM radio station call letters*]
WMDO ..... Wheaton, MD [*AM radio station call letters*]
WMDR...... Alcoa, TN [*AM radio station call letters*]
WMDR...... DePaul Rehabilitation Hospital Medical Library, Milwaukee, WI [*Library symbol*] [*Library of Congress*] (LCLS)
WMDT ...... Salisbury, MD [*Television station call letters*]
WME......... Eaton Corp., Milwaukee, WI [*Library symbol*] [*Library of Congress*] (LCLS)
WMe.......... Elisha D. Smith Public Library, Menasha, WI [*Library symbol*] [*Library of Congress*] (LCLS)
WME......... Waste Management International Plc ADS [*NYSE symbol*] (SPSG)
WME......... Window Meteoroid Experiment [*NASA*] (KSC)
WME......... Women and Mathematics Education (EA)
WME......... Worldwide Marriage Encounter (EA)
WMEA ...... Biddeford, ME [*Television station call letters*]
WMEA ...... Portland, ME [*AM radio station call letters*]
WMEA ...... Welded Modules for Electronic Assemblies [*NASA*]
WMEB ...... Orono, ME [*FM radio station call letters*]
WMEB ...... West Midlands Enterprise Board [*British*] (ECON)
WMEB-TV ... Orono, ME [*Television station call letters*]

WMEC ...... Macomb, IL [*Television station call letters*]
WMEC ...... Medium Endurance Cutter [*Coast Guard*] (NVT)
WMEC ...... Western Military Electronics Center (KSC)
WMECO ... Western Massachusetts Electric Co.
WMED ...... Calais, ME [*FM radio station call letters*]
WMED ...... Waste Management and Economics Division [*Environmental Protection Agency*] (EPA)
WMED-TV ... Calais, ME [*Television station call letters*]
WMEE ...... Fort Wayne, IN [*FM radio station call letters*]
WMEG ...... Guayama, PR [*FM radio station call letters*]
WMEH...... Bangor, ME [*FM radio station call letters*]
WMEI .... Arecibo, PR [*Television station call letters*]
WMEJ .... Proctorville, OH [*FM radio station call letters*]
WMEK ...... Chase City, VA [*AM radio station call letters*]
WMEL ...... Melbourne, FL [*AM radio station call letters*]
WMEM ..... Presque Isle, ME [*FM radio station call letters*]
WMEM-TV ... Presque Isle, ME [*Television station call letters*]
WMen....... Mabel Tainter Memorial Free Library, Menomonie, WI [*Library symbol*] [*Library of Congress*] (LCLS)
WMenM.... Memorial Hospital and Nursing Home, Menomonie, WI [*Library symbol*] [*Library of Congress*] (LCLS)
WMenofH ... Community Memorial Hospital, Health Science Library, Menomonee Falls, WI [*Library symbol*] [*Library of Congress*] (LCLS)
WMenU..... University of Wisconsin-Stout, Menomonie, WI [*Library symbol*] [*Library of Congress*] (LCLS)
WMeq........ Frank L. Weyenberg Library, Mequon, WI [*Library symbol*] [*Library of Congress*] (LCLS)
WMEQ...... Menomonie, WI [*AM radio station call letters*]
WMEQ-FM ... Menomonie, WI [*FM radio station call letters*]
WMeqW.... Wisconsin Lutheran Seminary, Mequon, WI [*Library symbol*] [*Library of Congress*] (LCLS)
WMER ...... Meridian, MS [*AM radio station call letters*]
WMer .... T. B. Scott Free Library, Merril, WI [*Library symbol*] [*Library of Congress*] (LCLS)
WMET ...... Gaithersburg, MD [*AM radio station call letters*]
WMET ...... Valdosta, GA [*FM radio station call letters*]
WMeU....... University of Wisconsin-Green Bay, Fox Valley Campus, Menasha, WI [*Library symbol*] [*Library of Congress*] (LCLS)
WMEV ...... Marion, VA [*AM radio station call letters*]
WMEV-FM ... Marion, VA [*FM radio station call letters*]
WMEW ..... Waterville, ME [*FM radio station call letters*]
WMEX ...... Boston, MA [*AM radio station call letters*]
WMEZ ...... Pensacola, FL [*FM radio station call letters*]
WMF .... Maude Shunk Public Library, Menomonee Falls, WI [*OCLC symbol*] (OCLC)
WMF .... White Middle-Aged Female (MAE)
WMF .... Windows Metafile [*Vector file format*] [*Data processing*] (PCM)
WMF .... Wire Mattress Federation
WMF .... World Mercy Fund (EA)
WMF .... World Missions Fellowship (EA)
WMF .... World Monuments Fund (EA)
WMFC ...... Kuala Lumpur [*Malaysia*] [*ICAO location identifier*] (ICLI)
WMFC ...... Monroeville, AL [*AM radio station call letters*]
WMFC-FM ... Monroeville, AL [*FM radio station call letters*]
WMFD ...... Wilmington, NC [*AM radio station call letters*]
WMFE....... Orlando, FL [*FM radio station call letters*]
WMFE-TV ... Orlando, FL [*Television station call letters*]
WMFG ...... Hibbing, MN [*AM radio station call letters*]
WMFG-FM ... Hibbing, MN [*FM radio station call letters*]
WMFJ .... Daytona Beach, FL [*AM radio station call letters*]
WMFL....... Monticello, FL [*AM radio station call letters*]
WMFM ..... Petal, MS [*FM radio station call letters*]
WMFM ..... Wisconsin Scottish Rite Bodies AASR, Milwaukee, WI [*Library symbol*] [*Library of Congress*] (LCLS)
WMFO ...... Medford, MA [*FM radio station call letters*]
WMFP...... Lawrence, MA [*Television station call letters*]
WMFQ ...... Ocala, FL [*FM radio station call letters*]
WMFR ...... High Point, NC [*AM radio station call letters*]
WMFX ...... St. Andrews, SC [*FM radio station call letters*]
WMG......... Globe-Union, Inc., Milwaukee, WI [*Library symbol*] [*Library of Congress*] (LCLS)
WMG........ Wire Measure Gauge
WMG........ Wire Metallizing Gun
WMGA ...... Moultrie, GA [*AM radio station call letters*]
W & M GA ... Washburn and Moen Gauge (MSA)
WMGa....... Wisconsin Gas Co., Milwaukee, WI [*Library symbol*] [*Library of Congress*] (LCLS)
WMGC ...... Binghamton, NY [*Television station call letters*]
WMGE...... Danville, KY [*FM radio station call letters*]
WMGF ...... Mount Dora, FL [*FM radio station call letters*]
WMGG ...... Columbus, OH [*FM radio station call letters*]
WMGH...... Tamaqua, PA [*FM radio station call letters*]
WMGI .... Terre Haute, IN [*FM radio station call letters*]
WMGJ ...... Gadsden, AL [*AM radio station call letters*]
WMGK...... Philadelphia, PA [*FM radio station call letters*]
WMGL...... Ravenel, SC [*FM radio station call letters*]
WMGL...... Wilmington Marine Geological Laboratory [*North Carolina*] (NOAA)

WMGM......	Atlantic City, NJ [*FM radio station call letters*]
WMGM......	Wildwood, NJ [*Television station call letters*]
WMGN......	Madison, WI [*FM radio station call letters*]
WMGO	Canton, MS [*AM radio station call letters*]
WMGQ......	New Brunswick, NJ [*FM radio station call letters*]
WMGR......	Bainbridge, GA [*AM radio station call letters*]
WMGR......	Worm Gear [*Mechanical engineering*]
WMGS	Wilkes-Barre, PA [*FM radio station call letters*]
WMGT......	Macon, GA [*Television station call letters*]
WMGU......	Stevens Point, WI [*FM radio station call letters*]
WMGV......	Oshkosh, WI [*FM radio station call letters*]
WMGW.....	Meadville, PA [*AM radio station call letters*]
WMGX......	Portland, ME [*FM radio station call letters*]
WMGY......	Montgomery, AL [*AM radio station call letters*]
WMH	Mountain Home [*Arkansas*] [*Airport symbol*] (OAG)
WMH	Wine Marketing Handbook [*A publication*]
WMH	Wisconsin Magazine of History [*A publication*]
WMH	WM Helijet [*Vancouver Stock Exchange symbol*]
WMHB......	Waterville, ME [*FM radio station call letters*]
WMHC......	South Hadley, MA [*FM radio station call letters*]
WMHD......	Terre Haute, IN [*FM radio station call letters*]
WMHE......	Delta, OH [*FM radio station call letters*]
WMHE......	Women and Health [*A publication*]
WMHG......	Muskegon, MI [*FM radio station call letters*]
WMHI.......	Cape Vincent, NY [*FM radio station call letters*]
WMHK......	Columbia, SC [*FM radio station call letters*]
WMHN	Webster, NY [*FM radio station call letters*]
WMHR......	Syracuse, NY [*FM radio station call letters*]
WMHS......	Miamisburg, OH [*FM radio station call letters*]
WMHS......	Wall-Mounted Handling System [*AEC*]
WMHS......	World Methodist Historical Society (EA)
WMHT.......	Schenectady, NY [*FM radio station call letters*]
WMHT-TV ...	Schenectady, NY [*Television station call letters*]
WMHU	Renovo, PA [*FM radio station call letters*]
WMHW ...	Mount Pleasant, MI [*FM radio station call letters*]
WMHX......	Schenectady, NY [*Television station call letters*]
WMHY......	World Mental Health Year [*1960*]
WMI	War Materials, Inc.
WMI	Washington Music Institute
WMI	Waveguide Moisture Indicator
WMI	Westmin Resources Ltd. [*Toronto Stock Exchange symbol*] [*Vancouver Stock Exchange symbol*]
WMI	Wildlife Management Institute (EA)
WMI	Winthrop Insured Mortgage Investors II [*AMEX symbol*] (SPSG)
WMI	Woodlands Mountain Institute (EA)
WMI	Work Motivation Inventory [*Test*]
WMI	World Manufacturer Identifier
WMI	World Metal Index [*Sheffield City Libraries*] [*British*] [*Information service or system*] (IID)
WMI	World Meteorological Intervals
WMIA	Arecibo, PR [*AM radio station call letters*]
WMIA	Woodworking Machinery Importers Association of America (EA)
WMIB	Marco Island, FL [*AM radio station call letters*]
WMIB	Waste Management Information Bureau [*Atomic Energy Authority*] [*British*] [*Information service or system*] (IID)
WMIC	Sandusky, MI [*AM radio station call letters*]
WMIC	Western Microwave, Inc. [*NASDAQ symbol*] (NQ)
WMIC/CHCC ...	Welsh Music Information Centre - Canolfan Hysbysrwydd Cerddoriaeth Cymru [*University College*] (CB)
WMID.......	Atlantic City, NJ [*AM radio station call letters*]
WMID-FM ...	Pleasantville, NJ [*FM radio station call letters*]
WMIE	Cocoa, FL [*FM radio station call letters*]
WMII	Hendersonville, TN [*AM radio station call letters*]
WMIK	Middlesboro, KY [*AM radio station call letters*]
WMIK-FM ...	Middlesboro, KY [*FM radio station call letters*]
WMIL........	Waukesha, WI [*FM radio station call letters*]
WMiltM	Milton College, Milton, WI [*Library symbol*] [*Library of Congress*] (LCLS)
WMIM	Mount Carmel, PA [*AM radio station call letters*]
WMIN	Maplewood, MN [*AM radio station call letters*]
WMINST ...	Westminster [*England*]
WMIO.......	Cabo Rojo, PR [*FM radio station call letters*]
WMIP........	Weapons Management Improvement Program [*Military*] (AABC)
WMIQ.......	Iron Mountain, MI [*AM radio station call letters*]
WMIR	Lake Geneva, WI [*AM radio station call letters*]
WMIS.......	Natchez, MS [*AM radio station call letters*]
WMIT	Black Mountain, NC [*FM radio station call letters*]
WMIW	Atlantic Beach, SC [*AM radio station call letters*]
WMIX	Mount Vernon, IL [*AM radio station call letters*]
WMIX-FM ...	Mount Vernon, IL [*FM radio station call letters*]
WMIY	Fairview, NC [*AM radio station call letters*]
WMIZ	Vineland, NJ [*AM radio station call letters*]
WMJ	Johnson Controls, Corporate Information Center, Milwaukee, WI [*Library symbol*] [*Library of Congress*] (LCLS)
WMJ	World of Michael Jackson (EA)
WMJB.......	Evansville, WI [*FM radio station call letters*]
WMJC.......	Bremen, IN [*FM radio station call letters*]
WMJD	Grundy, VA [*FM radio station call letters*]

WMJDA....	Watch Material and Jewelry Distributors Association [*Formerly, WMDAA*] (EA)
WMJE.......	Clarkesville, GA [*FM radio station call letters*]
WMJI	Cleveland, OH [*FM radio station call letters*]
WMJJ	Birmingham, AL [*FM radio station call letters*]
WMJK.......	Kissimmee, FL [*AM radio station call letters*]
WMJL.......	Marion, KY [*AM radio station call letters*]
WMJL-FM ...	Marion, KY [*FM radio station call letters*]
WMJM	Cordele, GA [*AM radio station call letters*]
WMJQ	Buffalo, NY [*FM radio station call letters*]
WMJR.......	Warrenton, VA [*FM radio station call letters*]
WMJS	Prince Frederick, MD [*FM radio station call letters*]
WMJT.......	Pinconning, MI [*FM radio station call letters*]
WMJV.......	Patterson, NY [*FM radio station call letters*]
WMJW	Cleveland, MS [*FM radio station call letters*]
WMJX......	Boston, MA [*FM radio station call letters*]
WMJZ.......	Gaylord, MI [*FM radio station call letters*]
WMK........	Watermark
W/(M K)...	Watts per Meter Kelvin
WMK........	Weis Markets, Inc. [*NYSE symbol*] (SPSG)
W/(M² K)..	Watts per Square Meter Kelvin
WMKA	Alor Setar/Sultan Abdul Halim [*Malaysia*] [*ICAO location identifier*] (ICLI)
WMKB	Butterworth [*Malaysia*] [*ICAO location identifier*] (ICLI)
WMKB	Ridgebury, PA [*FM radio station call letters*]
WMKC......	Kota Bahru/Sultan Ismail Petra [*Malaysia*] [*ICAO location identifier*] (ICLI)
WMKC......	St. Ignace, MI [*FM radio station call letters*]
WMKD......	Kuantan [*Malaysia*] [*ICAO location identifier*] (ICLI)
WMKD......	Watermarked (WGA)
WMKE......	Kerteh [*Malaysia*] [*ICAO location identifier*] (ICLI)
WMKF......	Simpang [*Malaysia*] [*ICAO location identifier*] (ICLI)
WMKG......	Eden, NC [*FM radio station call letters*]
WMKI	Ipoh [*Malaysia*] [*ICAO location identifier*] (ICLI)
WMKJ......	Johore Bahru [*Malaysia*] [*ICAO location identifier*] (ICLI)
WMKJ......	Newnan, GA [*FM radio station call letters*]
WMKK......	Kuala Lumpur/International [*Malaysia*] [*ICAO location identifier*] (ICLI)
WMKM.....	Inkster, MI [*AM radio station call letters*]
WMKM.....	Malacca [*Malaysia*] [*ICAO location identifier*] (ICLI)
WMKN......	Kuala Trengganu/Sultan Mahmud [*Malaysia*] [*ICAO location identifier*] (ICLI)
WMKO......	Millen, GA [*FM radio station call letters*]
WMKP	Penang [*Malaysia*] [*ICAO location identifier*] (ICLI)
WMKS	Kuala Lumpur [*Malaysia*] [*ICAO location identifier*] (ICLI)
WMKS	Springfield, VT [*FM radio station call letters*]
WMKT......	Charlevoix, MI [*AM radio station call letters*]
WMKX......	Brookville, PA [*FM radio station call letters*]
WMKY......	Morehead, KY [*FM radio station call letters*]
WMKZ......	Monticello, KY [*FM radio station call letters*]
WML.........	Lakeside Laboratories, Milwaukee, WI [*Library symbol*] [*Library of Congress*] (LCLS)
WML.........	Malaimbandy [*Madagascar*] [*Airport symbol*] (OAG)
WML.........	Westar Mining Ltd. [*Toronto Stock Exchange symbol*] [*Vancouver Stock Exchange symbol*]
WML.........	Willamette Law Journal [*A publication*]
WMLB	Glen Arbor, MI [*FM radio station call letters*]
WMLC......	Monticello, MS [*AM radio station call letters*]
WMLC......	Way of Mountain Learning Center (EA)
WMLH......	Lutheran Hospital of Milwaukee, Milwaukee, WI [*Library symbol*] [*Library of Congress*] (LCLS)
WMLI........	Sauk City, WI [*FM radio station call letters*]
Wm LJ.......	Willamette Law Journal [*A publication*]
WMLM	St. Louis, MI [*AM radio station call letters*]
WMLN......	Milton, MA [*FM radio station call letters*]
WMLO......	Havana, FL [*FM radio station call letters*]
WMLP.......	Milton, PA [*AM radio station call letters*]
WMLQ......	Rogers City, MI [*FM radio station call letters*]
WMLR	Hohenwald, TN [*AM radio station call letters*]
WMLR	William and Mary Law Review [*A publication*]
W and M LR ...	William and Mary Law Review [*A publication*]
WMLR	William Mitchell Law Review [*A publication*]
W & M L Rev ...	William and Mary Law Review [*A publication*]
WMLT	Dublin, GA [*AM radio station call letters*]
WMLV	Ironton, OH [*FM radio station call letters*]
WMLX......	Florence, KY [*AM radio station call letters*]
WMLY	Conway, NH [*FM radio station call letters*]
WMM........	Marquette University, Milwaukee, WI [*Library symbol*] [*Library of Congress*] (LCLS)
WMM.......	Wall-Mounted Manipulator [*Nuclear energy*] (NRCH)
WMM.......	White Middle-Aged Male (MAE)
Wm & M ...	William and Mary (King and Queen of England) (DLA)
WMM.......	William Mitchell College of Law Library, St. Paul, MN [*OCLC symbol*] (OCLC)
WMM.......	Willow Mixed Media (EA)
WMM.......	Women Make Movies (EA)
WMM.......	World Medical Mission (EA)
WMM.......	World Movement of Mothers [*See also MMM*] [*Paris, France*] (EAIO)
WMMA.....	Wood Machinery Manufacturers of America (EA)
Wm Mar Q ...	William and Mary Quarterly [*A publication*]

Wm and Mary L Rev ... William and Mary Law Review [*A publication*]
Wm & Mary Q ... William and Mary Quarterly [*A publication*]
Wm & Mary Rev VA L ... William and Mary Review of Virginia Law [*A publication*]   (DLA)
WMMB ..... Melbourne, FL [*AM radio station call letters*]
WMMB ..... Milwaukee Blood Center, Inc., Milwaukee, WI [*Library symbol*] [*Library of Congress*]   (LCLS)
WMMBC .. Miller Brewing Co., Research Library, Milwaukee, WI [*Library symbol*] [*Library of Congress*]   (LCLS)
WMMC ..... Marshall, IL [*FM radio station call letters*]
WMMC ..... Milwaukee Children's Hospital, Milwaukee, WI [*Library symbol*] [*Library of Congress*]   (LCLS)
WMMCW ... Medical College of Wisconsin, Medical-Dental Library, Milwaukee, WI [*Library symbol*] [*Library of Congress*]   (LCLS)
WMME ..... Augusta, ME [*AM radio station call letters*]
WMME-FM ... Augusta, ME [*FM radio station call letters*]
WMMF ..... Fond du Lac, WI [*Television station call letters*]
WMMG ..... Brandenburg, KY [*AM radio station call letters*]
WMMG-FM ... Brandenburg, KY [*FM radio station call letters*]
WMMGIC ... MGIC Investment Corp., Milwaukee, WI [*Library symbol*] [*Library of Congress*]   (LCLS)
WMMH .... Misericordia Hospital, Milwaukee, WI [*Library symbol*] [*Library of Congress*]   (LCLS)
WMMI ...... Shepherd, MI [*AM radio station call letters*]
Wm Mitchell L Rev ... William Mitchell Law Review [*A publication*]
WMMJ ..... Bethesda, MD [*FM radio station call letters*]
WMMK .... Destin, FL [*FM radio station call letters*]
WMM-L .... Marquette University, School of Law, Milwaukee, WI [*Library symbol*] [*Library of Congress*]   (LCLS)
WMMM ... Westport, CT [*AM radio station call letters*]
WMMMM ... Verona, WI [*FM radio station call letters*]
WMM/MWS ... Western Material Management, Machinery, and Welding Show [*Canada*]   (ITD)
WMMN ..... Fairmont, WV [*AM radio station call letters*]
WMM-N ... Marquette University, College of Nursing, Milwaukee, WI [*Library symbol*] [*Library of Congress*]   (LCLS)
WMMO .... Orlando, FL [*FM radio station call letters*]
WMMP ..... Wood Moulding and Millwork Producers [*Later, WMMPA*]   (EA)
WMMPA .. Wood Moulding and Millwork Producers Association   (EA)
WMMQ ..... Charlotte, MI [*FM radio station call letters*]
WMMR .... Philadelphia, PA [*FM radio station call letters*]
WMMRRI ... Wyoming Mining and Mineral Resource Research Institute [*University of Wyoming*] [*Research center*]   (RCD)
WMMS ..... Cleveland, OH [*FM radio station call letters*]
WMMS ..... Mount Sinai Hospital, Milwaukee, WI [*Library symbol*] [*Library of Congress*]   (LCLS)
WMMt ...... Mount Mary College, Milwaukee, WI [*Library symbol*] [*Library of Congress*]   (LCLS)
WMMT ..... Whitesburg, KY [*FM radio station call letters*]
WMMTA .. World Minerals and Metals [*A publication*]
WMMus .... Milwaukee Public Museum, Reference Library, Milwaukee, WI [*Library symbol*] [*Library of Congress*]   (LCLS)
WMMV ..... Bay Minette, AL [*FM radio station call letters*]
WMMW .... Meriden, CT [*AM radio station call letters*]
WMMX ..... Fairborn, OH [*AM radio station call letters*]
WMMY ..... Solana, FL [*FM radio station call letters*]
WMMZ ..... Ocala, FL [*FM radio station call letters*]
WMN .... Maroantsetra [*Madagascar*] [*Airport symbol*]   (OAG)
WMN .... Western Morning News [*United Kingdom*] [*A publication*]
WMN .... Winnemucca [*Nevada*] [*Seismograph station code, US Geological Survey*] [*Closed*]   (SEIS)
WMNA ...... Gretna, VA [*AM radio station call letters*]
WMNA-FM ... Gretna, VA [*FM radio station call letters*]
WMNB ...... North Adams, MA [*FM radio station call letters*]
WMNC ...... Morganton, NC [*AM radio station call letters*]
WMNF ...... Tampa, FL [*FM radio station call letters*]
WMNG ...... Northwest General Hospital, Milwaukee, WI [*Library symbol*] [*Library of Congress*]   (LCLS)
WMNI ...... Columbus, OH [*AM radio station call letters*]
WMNI ...... Wildlife Management News (Iceland) [*A publication*]
WMNJ ...... Madison, NJ [*FM radio station call letters*]
WMNK ...... Montawk, NY [*FM radio station call letters*]
Wmn Lib .... Women's Liberation [*A publication*]
WMNM ...... Port Henry, NY [*FM radio station call letters*]
WMNR ...... Monroe, CT [*FM radio station call letters*]
WMNS ...... Olean, NY [*AM radio station call letters*]
WMNS ...... William B. McGuire Nuclear Station   (NRCH)
WMNT ...... Manati, PR [*AM radio station call letters*]
WMNV ...... Rupert, VT [*FM radio station call letters*]
WMNX ...... Wilmington, NC [*FM radio station call letters*]
WMNY ...... Elloree-Santee, SC [*AM radio station call letters*]
WMNZ ...... Montezuma, GA [*AM radio station call letters*]
WMO .... White Mountain [*Alaska*] [*Airport symbol*]   (OAG)
WMO .... White Mountain, AK [*Location identifier*] [*FAA*]   (FAAL)
WMO .... Wichita Mountains Array [*Oklahoma*] [*Seismograph station code, US Geological Survey*] [*Closed*]   (SEIS)
WMO .... Wing Maintenance Officer
WMO .... World Meteorological Organization [*See also OMM*] [*Geneva, Switzerland*] [*United Nations*]   (EAIO)

WMO .... World Monetary Organization
WMO .... World Monetary Organization
WMOA ...... Marietta, OH [*AM radio station call letters*]
WMOB ...... Mobile, AL [*AM radio station call letters*]
WMOBA ...... WMO [*World Meteorological Organization*] Bulletin [*A publication*]
WMO Bull ... WMO [*World Meteorological Organization*] Bulletin [*A publication*]
WMOC ...... Chattanooga, TN [*AM radio station call letters*]
WMOD ...... Bolivar, TN [*FM radio station call letters*]
WMOG ..... Brunswick, GA [*AM radio station call letters*]
WMOG ..... St. Simons Island, GA [*FM radio station call letters*]
WMOH ...... Hamilton, OH [*AM radio station call letters*]
WMOI ...... Monmouth, IL [*FM radio station call letters*]
WMOK ...... Metropolis, IL [*AM radio station call letters*]
WMOM ...... La Plata, MD [*AM radio station call letters*]
WMoM ...... Monroe Clinic, Monroe, WI [*Library symbol*] [*Library of Congress*]   (LCLS)
WMON ..... Montgomery, WV [*AM radio station call letters*]
WMOO ..... Derby Center, VT [*FM radio station call letters*]
WMOP ...... Ocala, FL [*AM radio station call letters*]
WMO Publ ... WMO [*World Meteorological Organization*] Publication [*A publication*]
WMOR ...... Morehead, KY [*AM radio station call letters*]
WmorC ...... Westmoreland Coal Co. [*Associated Press abbreviation*]   (APAG)
WMO Rep Mar Sci Aff ... World Meteorological Organization. Reports on Marine Science Affairs [*A publication*]
WMOR-FM ... Morehead, KY [*FM radio station call letters*]
WMoS .... Saint Clare Hospital, Monroe, WI [*Library symbol*] [*Library of Congress*]   (LCLS)
WMO Spec Environ Rep ... World Meteorological Organization. Special Environmental Report [*A publication*]
WMOT ...... Murfreesboro, TN [*FM radio station call letters*]
WMO Tech Note ... World Meteorological Organization. Technical Note [*A publication*]
WMOU ..... Berlin, NH [*AM radio station call letters*]
WMOV ...... Ravenswood, WV [*AM radio station call letters*]
WMOX ...... Meridian, MS [*AM radio station call letters*]
WMP .... War and Mobilization Plan [*Air Force documents*]
WMP .... Waste Management Paper [*British*]   (DCTA)
WMP .... Weapon Monitor Panel   (MCD)
WMP .... Weather Modification Program [*Department of Commerce*] [*Boulder, CO*]
WMP .... Wiener Mapping Procedure
WMP .... With Much Pleasure [*Meaning, "We accept the invitation"*]
WMP .... Women and the Military Project [*An association*]   (EA)
WmP .... World Microfilms Publications, London, United Kingdom [*Library symbol*] [*Library of Congress*]   (LCLS)
WMPA ..... Mansfield, PA [*FM radio station call letters*]
WMPA ...... Wet Maximum Power Available   (SAA)
WMPA ...... Women's Military Pilots Association   (EA)
WMPB ..... Baltimore, MD [*Television station call letters*]
WMPC ..... Lapeer, MI [*AM radio station call letters*]
WMPC ...... War Manpower Commission [*Within the Office of Emergency Management*] [*World War II*]
WMPC ...... War Materiel Procurement Capability   (AFIT)
WMPCE ...... World Meeting Planners Congress and Exposition [*Defunct*]   (EA)
WMPCES(P) ... War Manpower Commission Employment Stabilization (Plan) [*Terminated, 1945*]
WMPG ..... Gorham, ME [*FM radio station call letters*]
WMPH ...... Wilmington, DE [*FM radio station call letters*]
WM & PHF ... Waste Management and Personal Hygiene Facility [*NASA*]   (KSC)
WMPI .... Scottsburg, IN [*FM radio station call letters*]
WMPI .... Women of the Motion Picture Industry, International [*Dallas, TX*]
WMPL ...... Hancock, MI [*AM radio station call letters*]
WMPL .... Western Maryland Public Libraries Regional Resource Center [*Library network*]
WMPL .... World Mission Prayer League   (EA)
WMPM ..... Smithfield, NC [*AM radio station call letters*]
WMPN ...... Jackson, MS [*FM radio station call letters*]
WMPN-TV ... Jackson, MS [*Television station call letters*]
WMPO ...... Middleport-Pomeroy, OH [*AM radio station call letters*]
WMPO ...... Weather Modification Program Office [*Marine science*]   (MSC)
WMPO-FM ... Middleport-Pomeroy, OH [*FM radio station call letters*]
WMPR ...... Jackson, MS [*FM radio station call letters*]
WMPRT ...... Wartime Manpower and Personnel Readiness Team [*Military*]
WMPS ...... Millington, TN [*AM radio station call letters*]
WMPT ...... Annapolis, MD [*Television station call letters*]
WMPV ...... Mobile, AL [*Television station call letters*]
WMPX ...... Midland, MI [*AM radio station call letters*]
WMQ .... Quarles & Brady, Law Library, Milwaukee, WI [*Library symbol*] [*Library of Congress*]   (LCLS)
WMQ .... Westmount Public Library [*UTLAS symbol*]
W & M Q ... William and Mary Quarterly [*A publication*]
WMQ .... William and Mary Quarterly [*A publication*]
WMQ .... Wulumuchi [*Republic of China*] [*Seismograph station code, US Geological Survey*]   (SEIS)

WMQC...... Westover, WV [*FM radio station call letters*]
WMQQ ..... Springfield, KY [*FM radio station call letters*]
WMQT...... Ishpeming, MI [*FM radio station call letters*]
WMQX...... Winston-Salem, NC [*AM radio station call letters*]
WMQX-FM ... Winston-Salem, NC [*FM radio station call letters*]
WMR........ Mananara [*Madagascar*] [*Airport symbol*] (OAG)
WMR........ Reinhart, Boerner, Van Deuren, Norris and Rieselbach, Law Library, Milwaukee, WI [*Library symbol*] [*Library of Congress*] (LCLS)
WMR........ Wake Measurements RADAR [*Army*] (MCD)
WMR........ War Maintenance Reserve [*British*]
WMR........ War Materiel Requirement (AFIT)
WMR........ Water Meter
WMR........ Water-Moderated Reactor
WMR........ Wideband Multichannel Receiver
WMR........ William and Mary Review of Virginia Law [*A publication*]
WMR........ Wonder Marine Resources [*Vancouver Stock Exchange symbol*]
WMR........ Work Metabolic Rate (MAE)
WMR........ World Marxist Review [*A publication*]
WMR........ World Medical Relief (EA)
WMRA...... Harrisonburg, VA [*FM radio station call letters*]
WMRC...... Milford, MA [*AM radio station call letters*]
WMRC...... War Minerals Relief Commission [*Department of the Interior*] [*Abolished, 1940*] (EGAO)
WMREI..... Waste Management Research and Education Institute [*University of Tennessee*]
WMRF ...... Lewistown, PA [*FM radio station call letters*]
WMRH...... Waupun, WI [*AM radio station call letters*]
WMRI .... Marion, IN [*FM radio station call letters*]
WMRK...... Selma, AL [*AM radio station call letters*]
WMRK...... Westmark International, Inc. [*NASDAQ symbol*] (NQ)
WMRL...... Lexington, VA [*FM radio station call letters*]
WMRL ...... Water Management Research Laboratory [*Department of Agriculture*] [*Fresno, CA*] (GRD)
WMRN...... Marion, OH [*AM radio station call letters*]
WMRN-FM ... Marion, OH [*FM radio station call letters*]
Wm Rob..... William Robinson's English Admiralty Reports [*1838-52*] [*A publication*] (DLA)
Wm Rob Adm ... William Robinson's English Admiralty Reports [*1838-52*] [*A publication*] (DLA)
WMRS ...... Monticello, IN [*FM radio station call letters*]
WMRS ...... White Mountain Research Station [*Research center*] (RCD)
WMRT ...... Marietta, OH [*FM radio station call letters*]
WMRV...... Endicott, NY [*AM radio station call letters*]
WMRV-FM ... Endicott, NY [*FM radio station call letters*]
WMRW..... Gordon, GA [*FM radio station call letters*]
WMRX...... Beaverton, MI [*FM radio station call letters*]
WMRY...... Columbus, GA [*AM radio station call letters*]
WMRZ...... South Miami, FL [*AM radio station call letters*]
WMS .... Warehouse Material Stores (AAG)
WMS .... Waste Management System (MCD)
WMS .... Water Management Section [*Apollo*] [*NASA*]
WMS .... Weapons Monitoring System
WMS .... Weather Mapping System
WMS .... Wechsler Memory Scale [*Neuropsychological test*]
WMS .... Wesleyan Missionary Society
WMS .... West Middle School [*South Carolina*] [*Seismograph station code, US Geological Survey*] (SEIS)
W v M S..... Wetboek van Militair Strafrecht [*A publication*]
WMS .... Whaling Museum Society (EA)
WMS .... Wilderness Medical Society (EA)
WMS .... Willem Mengelberg Society (EA)
WMS .... William Morris Society [*Later, WMS/AB*] (EA)
WMS .... Wind Measuring System
WMS .... Wire Mesh Screen (OA)
WMS .... WMS Industries, Inc. [*Formerly, Williams Electronics*] [*NYSE symbol*] (SPSG)
WMS .... WMS Industries, Inc. [*Formerly, Williams Electronics*] [*Associated Press abbreviation*] (APAG)
WMS .... Women for a Meaningful Summit (EA)
WMS .... Women in the Medical Service [*Army*]
WMS .... Women's Medical Specialist
WMS .... Women's Missionary Society, AME [*African Methodist Episcopal*] Church (EA)
WMS .... [*Canada's International*] Woodworking Machinery and Supply Show (ITD)
WMS .... Work Measurement System [*Postal Service*]
WM & S..... Work Methods and Standards
WMS .... Workforce Management Staff [*Environmental Protection Agency*] (GFGA)
WMS .... World Magnetic Survey [*Defunct*]
WMS .... World Mariculture Society (EA)
WmS.......... World Microfilms Division, Oyez Equipment Ltd., London, United Kingdom [*Library symbol*] [*Library of Congress*] (LCLS)
WMSA ...... Massena, NY [*AM radio station call letters*]
WMSA ...... Saint Anthony Hospital, Milwaukee, WI [*Library symbol*] [*Library of Congress*] (LCLS)
WMS/AB .. William Morris Society, American Branch (EA)

Wms Ann Reg ... Williams' Annual Register [*New York*] [*A publication*] (DLA)
Wms Bank ... [*R. V.*] Williams on Bankruptcy [*17 eds.*] [*1870-1958*] [*A publication*] (DLA)
Wms & Bruce ... [*R. G.*] Williams and [*Sir G.*] Bruce's Admiralty Practice [*3 eds.*] [*1865-1902*] [*A publication*] (DLA)
WMSC...... Upper Montclair, NJ [*FM radio station call letters*]
WMSC...... Weather Message Switching Center
WMSC...... White Mountain Scenic Railroad [*AAR code*]
WMSC...... Women's Medical Specialists Corps
WMSCMC ... Women's Missionary and Service Commission of the Mennonite Church (EA)
WMSE...... Milwaukee School of Engineering, Walter Schroeder Library, Milwaukee, WI [*Library symbol*] [*Library of Congress*] (LCLS)
WMSE...... Milwaukee, WI [*FM radio station call letters*]
Wms Ex ..... Williams on Executors [*15th ed.*] [*1970*] [*A publication*] (DLA)
Wms Exors ... [*E. V.*] Williams on Executors [*13 eds.*] [*1832-1953*] [*A publication*] (DLA)
Wms Ex'rs ... [*E. V.*] Williams on Executors [*13 eds.*] [*1832-1953*] [*A publication*] (DLA)
Wms Exs.... [*E. V.*] Williams on Executors [*13 eds.*] [*1832-1953*] [*A publication*] (DLA)
WMSF...... Saint Francis Seminary, Milwaukee, WI [*Library symbol*] [*Library of Congress*] (LCLS)
WMSFH... Saint Francis Hospital, Milwaukee, WI [*Library symbol*] [*Library of Congress*] (LCLS)
WMSFT ... Wormshaft
WMSG ...... Oakland, MD [*AM radio station call letters*]
WMSH...... Sturgis, MI [*AM radio station call letters*]
WMSH-FM ... Sturgis, MI [*FM radio station call letters*]
WMSI....... Jackson, MS [*FM radio station call letters*]
WMSI....... Western Management Science Institute [*University of California*] (KSC)
WMSI....... Williams Industries, Inc. [*NASDAQ symbol*] (NQ)
WMSJ .... Harpswell, ME [*FM radio station call letters*]
WMSJ .... Saint Joseph's Hospital, Milwaukee, WI [*Library symbol*] [*Library of Congress*] (LCLS)
WMSJ .... William Morris Society. Journal [*A publication*]
WMSK ...... Morganfield, KY [*AM radio station call letters*]
WMSKF .... William Morris Society and Kelmscott Fellowship [*Formed by a merger of Kelmscott Fellowship and William Morris Society*] (EAIO)
WMSK-FM ... Morganfield, KY [*FM radio station call letters*]
WMSL....... Athens, GA [*FM radio station call letters*]
WMSL....... Saint Luke's Hospital, Milwaukee, WI [*Library symbol*] [*Library of Congress*] (LCLS)
WMSL....... Wet Mock Simulated Launch [*NASA*] (KSC)
WMSL....... Wichita Mountains Seismological Laboratory
WMSM ..... Saint Mary's Hospital, Milwaukee, WI [*Library symbol*] [*Library of Congress*] (LCLS)
Wms Mass ... Williams' Reports [*1 Massachusetts*] [*A publication*] (DLA)
WMSMi.... Saint Michael Hospital, Milwaukee, WI [*Library symbol*] [*Library of Congress*] (LCLS)
WMSMN .. Saint Mary's School of Nursing, Milwaukee, WI [*Library symbol*] [*Library of Congress*] (LCLS)
WMSN ...... Madison, WI [*Television station call letters*]
Wms Notes ... Williams' Notes to Saunders' Reports [*England*] [*A publication*] (DLA)
WMSO...... Wichita Mountains Seismological Observatory
WMSP....... Elk Hills, WV [*AM radio station call letters*]
Wms P .... Peere-Williams' English Chancery Reports [*1695-1736*] [*A publication*] (DLA)
Wms Peere ... Peere-Williams' English Chancery Reports [*A publication*] (DLA)
Wms PP..... [*J.*] Williams on Personal Property [*18 eds.*] [*1848-1926*] [*A publication*] (DLA)
WMSQ ...... Havelock, NC [*FM radio station call letters*]
WMSR ...... Manchester, TN [*AM radio station call letters*]
W/(M² SR) ... Watts per Square Meter Steradian
WMSRG.... Weather-Modification Statistical Research Groups
Wms RP..... [*J.*] Williams on Real Property [*24 eds.*] [*1824-1926*] [*A publication*] (DLA)
WMSS....... Middletown, PA [*FM radio station call letters*]
Wms Saund ... [*Sir Edmund*] Saunders' Reports, Edited by Williams [*85 English Reprint*] [*A publication*] (DLA)
Wms Saund (Eng) ... [*Sir Edmund*] Saunders' Reports, Edited by Williams [*85 English Reprint*] [*A publication*] (DLA)
WMST....... Mount Sterling, KY [*AM radio station call letters*]
WMST-FM ... Mount Sterling, KY [*FM radio station call letters*]
Wms VT..... Williams' Vermont Reports [*27-29 Vermont*] [*A publication*] (DLA)
WMSW ..... Hatillo, PR [*AM radio station call letters*]
WMSWH .. Southeastern Wisconsin Health Systems Agency, Health Science Library, Milwaukee, WI [*Library symbol*] [*Library of Congress*] (LCLS)
WMSX ...... Brockton, MA [*AM radio station call letters*]
WMSY ...... Marion, VA [*Television station call letters*]
WMT........ Auslandmerkte/Marches Etrangers [*Lausanne*] [*A publication*]
WMT........ Cedar Rapids, IA [*AM radio station call letters*]
WMT........ Wal-Mart Stores, Inc. [*NYSE symbol*] (SPSG)

WMT.........	Waste Monitor Tank (IEEE)
WMT.........	Weighing More Than
WMT.........	West Meridian Time
WMT.........	Western Motor Tariff Bureau, Los Angeles CA [*STAC*]
WMT.........	Wet Metric Ton [*Waste management*]
WMTB......	Emmitsburg, MD [*FM radio station call letters*]
WMTB......	Western Motor Tariff Bureau
WMTBF....	Warranty Mean Time Between Failures [*Army*]
WMTC......	Milwaukee Technical College, Milwaukee, WI [*Library symbol*] [*Library of Congress*] (LCLS)
WMTC......	Vancleve, KY [*AM radio station call letters*]
WMTC......	Waste Management Technology Center [*Oak Ridge National Laboratory*]
WMTC-FM ...	Vancleve, KY [*FM radio station call letters*]
WMTC-N ...	Milwaukee Area Technical College, North Campus Center Library, Mequon, WI [*Library symbol*] [*Library of Congress*] (LCLS)
WMTC-S...	Milwaukee Area Technical College, South Campus Center Library, Oak Creek, WI [*Library symbol*] [*Library of Congress*] (LCLS)
WMTC-W ...	Milwaukee Area Technical College, West Campus Center Library, West Allis, WI [*Library symbol*] [*Library of Congress*] (LCLS)
WMTD......	Hinton, WV [*AM radio station call letters*]
WMTD-FM ...	Hinton, WV [*FM radio station call letters*]
WMTE	Manistee, MI [*AM radio station call letters*]
WMT-FM ...	Cedar Rapids, IA [*FM radio station call letters*]
WMTG......	Dearborn, MI [*AM radio station call letters*]
WMTH......	Park Ridge, IL [*FM radio station call letters*]
WMTH......	Westmeath [*County in Ireland*] (ROG)
WMTI	Morovis, PR [*AM radio station call letters*]
WMTJ.......	Fajardo, PR [*Television station call letters*]
WMTK	Littleton, NH [*FM radio station call letters*]
WMTL	Leitchfield, KY [*AM radio station call letters*]
WMTM.....	Moultrie, GA [*AM radio station call letters*]
WMTM-FM ...	Moultrie, GA [*FM radio station call letters*]
WMTN......	Morristown, TN [*AM radio station call letters*]
WMTO......	Port St. Joe, FL [*FM radio station call letters*]
WMTR......	Archbold, OH [*FM radio station call letters*]
WMTR......	Morristown, NJ [*AM radio station call letters*]
WMTR......	Wheeled Mobility Test Rig [*Army*] (RDA)
WMTS......	Murfreesboro, TN [*AM radio station call letters*]
WMTS......	Western Manufacturing Technology Show and Conference (ITD)
WMTT	Cookeville, TN [*Television station call letters*]
WMTT	Willamette Industries, Inc. [*NASDAQ symbol*] (NQ)
WMTU......	Jackson, TN [*Television station call letters*]
WMTV	Madison, WI [*Television station call letters*]
WMTW.....	Poland Spring, ME [*Television station call letters*]
WMTX	Clearwater, FL [*FM radio station call letters*]
WMTX	Pinellas Park, FL [*AM radio station call letters*]
WMTY	Greenwood, SC [*AM radio station call letters*]
WMTY-FM ...	Greenwood, SC [*FM radio station call letters*]
WMTZ	Martinez, GA [*FM radio station call letters*]
WMU.........	West Mountain [*Utah*] [*Seismograph station code, US Geological Survey*] (SEIS)
WMU.........	Western Michigan University [*Kalamazoo*]
WMU.........	Woman's Missionary Union (EA)
WMU.........	World Maritime University [*Sweden*] (DCTA)
WMUA......	Amherst, MA [*FM radio station call letters*]
WMUB......	Oxford, OH [*FM radio station call letters*]
WMUC......	College Park, MD [*FM radio station call letters*]
WMUF......	Paris, TN [*AM radio station call letters*]
WMUF......	Universal Foods Corp., Technical Information Services, Milwaukee, WI [*Library symbol*] [*Library of Congress*] (LCLS)
WMUF-FM ...	Paris, TN [*FM radio station call letters*]
WMUH......	Allentown, PA [*FM radio station call letters*]
WMUK......	Kalamazoo, MI [*FM radio station call letters*]
WMUL......	Huntington, WV [*FM radio station call letters*]
WMUR......	Manchester, NH [*Television station call letters*]
WMUS......	Muskegon, MI [*AM radio station call letters*]
WMUSE....	World Markets for US Exports [*A publication*]
WMUS-FM ...	Muskegon, MI [*FM radio station call letters*]
WMUU	Greenville, SC [*AM radio station call letters*]
WMUU-FM ...	Greenville, SC [*FM radio station call letters*]
WMUW.....	Columbus, MS [*FM radio station call letters*]
WMUW.....	University of Wisconsin-Milwaukee, Milwaukee, WI [*Library symbol*] [*Library of Congress*] (LCLS)
WMUZ......	Detroit, MI [*FM radio station call letters*]
WMV.........	Valuation Research Corp., Milwaukee, WI [*Library symbol*] [*Library of Congress*] (LCLS)
WMV.........	War Munition Volunteers [*British*] [*World War I*]
WMV.........	Watermelon Mosaic Virus
WMVA......	Martinsville, VA [*AM radio station call letters*]
WMV-E.....	Watermelon Mosaic Virus E
WMVG......	Milledgeville, GA [*AM radio station call letters*]
WMVI.......	Mechanicville, NY [*AM radio station call letters*]
WMVN......	Ishpeming, MI [*AM radio station call letters*]
WMVO......	Mount Vernon, OH [*AM radio station call letters*]
WMVP	Greenfield, WI [*AM radio station call letters*]

WMVR......	Sidney, OH [*AM radio station call letters*]
WMVR-FM ...	Sidney, OH [*FM radio station call letters*]
WMVS......	Milwaukee, WI [*Television station call letters*]
WMVT......	Milwaukee, WI [*Television station call letters*]
WMVV......	McDonough, GA [*FM radio station call letters*]
WMVY......	Tisbury, MA [*FM radio station call letters*]
WMW........	Whyte & Hirschboeck, Law Library, Milwaukee, WI [*Library symbol*] [*Library of Congress*] (LCLS)
WMW........	Women's Media Workshop [*Defunct*] (EA)
WMWA......	Glenview, IL [*FM radio station call letters*]
WMWG......	Weichselland, Mitteilungen des Westpreussischen Geschichtsvereins [*A publication*]
WMWHL ...	Wormwheel
WMWK......	Milwaukee, WI [*FM radio station call letters*]
WMWM......	Salem, MA [*FM radio station call letters*]
WMWN......	[*The*] Weatherford, Mineral Wells & Northwestern Railway Co. [*AAR code*]
WMWOA ...	Wiener Medizinische Wochenschrift [*A publication*]
WMWV.....	Conway, NH [*FM radio station call letters*]
WMX........	Wamena [*Indonesia*] [*Airport symbol*] (OAG)
WMX........	Waste Management, Inc. [*NYSE symbol*] [*Toronto Stock Exchange symbol*] (SPSG)
WMX........	Whirlpool, Massage, Exercise [*Medicine*]
WMXA	Opelika, AL [*FM radio station call letters*]
WMXB	Richmond, VA [*FM radio station call letters*]
WMXC	Charlotte, NC [*FM radio station call letters*]
WMXD	Detroit, MI [*FM radio station call letters*]
WMXF	Laurinburg, NC [*AM radio station call letters*]
WMXF-FM ...	Laurinburg, NC [*FM radio station call letters*]
WMXG	Macon, MS [*FM radio station call letters*]
WMXH	South Bend, IN [*FM radio station call letters*]
WMXI	Laurel, MS [*FM radio station call letters*]
WMXJ.......	Pompano Beach, FL [*FM radio station call letters*]
WMXK	Morristown, TN [*FM radio station call letters*]
WMXL	Margate City, NJ [*FM radio station call letters*]
WMXM......	Lake Forest, IL [*FM radio station call letters*]
WMXN......	Norfolk, VA [*FM radio station call letters*]
WMXO......	Olean, NY [*FM radio station call letters*]
WMXP	New Kensington, PA [*FM radio station call letters*]
WMXR	Woodstock, VT [*FM radio station call letters*]
WMXT	Pamplico, SC [*FM radio station call letters*]
WMXU	Starkville, MS [*FM radio station call letters*]
WMXW.....	Vestal, NY [*FM radio station call letters*]
WMXX	Jackson, TN [*FM radio station call letters*]
WMXY	Hogansville, GA [*AM radio station call letters*]
WMXZ	New Orleans, LA [*FM radio station call letters*]
WMY........	Wakamiya [*Japan*] [*Seismograph station code, US Geological Survey*] [*Closed*] (SEIS)
WMY........	Weird Mystery [*A publication*]
WMYA	Cape Charles, VA [*FM radio station call letters*]
WMYB	Socastee, SC [*FM radio station call letters*]
WMYD......	Rice Lake, WI [*AM radio station call letters*]
WMYF	Exeter, NH [*AM radio station call letters*]
WMYG......	Braddock, PA [*FM radio station call letters*]
WMYI.......	Hendersonville, NC [*FM radio station call letters*]
WMYJ.......	Pocomoke City, MD [*FM radio station call letters*]
WMYM......	Minocqua, WI [*AM radio station call letters*]
WMYN......	Mayodan, NC [*AM radio station call letters*]
WMYQ......	Newton, MS [*AM radio station call letters*]
WMYQ-FM ...	Newton, MS [*FM radio station call letters*]
WMYR......	Fort Myers, FL [*AM radio station call letters*]
WMYT......	Carolina Beach, NC [*AM radio station call letters*]
WMYU......	Sevierville, TN [*FM radio station call letters*]
WMYX	Milwaukee, WI [*FM radio station call letters*]
WMYY	Schoharie, NY [*FM radio station call letters*]
WMZK	Merrill, WI [*FM radio station call letters*]
WMZQ	Arlington, VA [*AM radio station call letters*]
WMZQ......	Washington, DC [*FM radio station call letters*]
WMZX	Owosso, MI [*FM radio station call letters*]
WN	Calcutta Weekly Notes [*A publication*] (DLA)
WN	Neenah Public Library, Neenah, WI [*Library symbol*] [*Library of Congress*] (LCLS)
WN	Nor-Fly A/S [*Norway*] [*ICAO designator*] (FAAC)
WN	Wake Newsletter [*A publication*]
WN	Washington [*Obsolete*] (ROG)
Wn	Washington Reports [*A publication*] (DLA)
WN	WAVES [*Women Accepted for Volunteer Emergency Service*] National (EA)
WN	Wawatay News [*Sioux Lookout, Ontario*] [*A publication*]
WN	Weekblad voor het Notariaat [*A publication*]
WN	Weekly Notes of English Law Reports [*A publication*] (DLA)
W & N......	Weidenfeld & Nicolson [*Publisher*]
W/N...........	Weight Note [*Tea trade*] (ROG)
W-N...........	Well-Nourished [*Medicine*]
WN	Weston [*George*] Ltd. [*Toronto Stock Exchange symbol*] [*Vancouver Stock Exchange symbol*]
WN	White-Breasted Nuthatch [*Ornithology*]
WN	White Noise
WN	Wiadomosci Numizmatyczne [*A publication*]
WN	Will Not
WN	Winch (AAG)

WN .... Wisconsin [*Obsolete*] (ROG)
WN .... Within (ROG)
WN .... Work Notice (AAG)
WN .... World Neighbors (EA)
WN .... Wrong Number [*Telecommunications*] (TEL)
WN .... Wynn's International, Inc. [*NYSE symbol*] (SPSG)
WNA .... Napaskiak [*Alaska*] [*Airport symbol*] (OAG)
WNA .... Napaskiak, AK [*Location identifier*] [*FAA*] (FAAL)
WNa .... Nashotah House, Nashotah, WI [*Library symbol*] [*Library of Congress*] (LCLS)
WNA .... Wa National Army [*Myanmar*] [*Political party*] (EY)
WNA .... Washington [*DC*] National Airport [*FAA*]
WNA .... Wedge Nozzle Assembly
WNA .... Welcome to the North Atlantic [*A publication*]
WNA .... Winter, North Atlantic [*Vessel load line mark*]
WNA .... World Nature Association (EA)
WNAA .... Greensboro, NC [*FM radio station call letters*]
WNAAA .... Women of the National Agricultural Aviation Association (EA)
WNAB ...... Nashville, TN [*Television station call letters*]
WNAC .... Providence, RI [*Television station call letters*]
WNACFWB ... Woman's National Auxiliary Convention of Free Will Baptists (EA)
WNAE .... Warren, PA [*AM radio station call letters*]
WNAF ...... Women's National Aquatic Forum (EA)
WNAH ...... Nashville, TN [*AM radio station call letters*]
WNAI .... Word and Number Assessment Inventory [*Aptitude test*]
WNAK .... Nanticoke, PA [*AM radio station call letters*]
WNAL .... Gadsden, AL [*Television station call letters*]
WNAM .... Neenah-Menasha, WI [*AM radio station call letters*]
WNAP .... Norristown, PA [*AM radio station call letters*]
WNAP .... Washington [*DC*] National Airport
WNAR .... Biometric Society, Western North American Region (EA)
WNAS .... New Albany, IN [*FM radio station call letters*]
WNAT .... Natchez, MS [*AM radio station call letters*]
WNAU .... New Albany, MS [*AM radio station call letters*]
WNAV .... Annapolis, MD [*AM radio station call letters*]
WNAW .... North Adams, MA [*AM radio station call letters*]
WNAX .... Yankton, SD [*AM radio station call letters*]
WNAZ .... Nashville, TN [*FM radio station call letters*]
W v NB ...... Weekblad voor de Nederlandse Bond van Gemeenteambtenaren [*A publication*]
WNB .... Will Not Be
WNB .... Winter Navigation Board
WNBA .... Women's National Basketball Association [*Defunct*] (EA)
WNBA .... Women's National Book Association (EA)
WNBA .... World Ninepin Bowling Association [*Germany*] (EAIO)
WNBC .... New York, NY [*Television station call letters*]
WNBE .... Alamo, TN [*FM radio station call letters*]
WNBF .... Binghamton, NY [*AM radio station call letters*]
WNBH .... New Bedford, MA [*AM radio station call letters*]
WNbH .... New Berlin Memorial Hospital, New Berlin, WI [*Library symbol*] [*Library of Congress*] (LCLS)
WNBI .... Park Falls, WI [*AM radio station call letters*]
WNBN .... Meridian, MS [*AM radio station call letters*]
WNBP .... Newburyport, MA [*AM radio station call letters*]
WNBR .... Fuquay Varina, NC [*AM radio station call letters*]
WNBR .... Wind Baron Corp. [*NASDAQ symbol*] (NQ)
WNBS .... Murray, KY [*AM radio station call letters*]
WNBT .... Wellsboro, PA [*AM radio station call letters*]
WNBT-FM ... Wellsboro, PA [*FM radio station call letters*]
WNBY .... Newberry, MI [*AM radio station call letters*]
WNBY-FM ... Newberry, MI [*FM radio station call letters*]
WNBZ .... Saranac Lake, NY [*AM radio station call letters*]
WNC .... Naval War College, Newport, RI [*OCLC symbol*] (OCLC)
WNC .... Wabash National [*NYSE symbol*] (SPSG)
WNC .... WAVES National Corp. [*An association*] (EA)
WNC .... Weak Neutral Current [*Chemistry*]
WNC .... Weekly Notes of Cases [*Pennsylvania*] [*A publication*] (DLA)
WNC .... Wencarro Resources Ltd. [*Vancouver Stock Exchange symbol*]
WNC .... Wilmington [*North Carolina*] [*Seismograph station code, US Geological Survey*] (SEIS)
WNC .... Women's National Commission [*British*] (EAIO)
WNCA .... Siler City, NC [*AM radio station call letters*]
WN-CAELA ... Women's Network of the Council for Adult Education in Latin America [*See also RM-CEAAL*] [*Quito, Ecuador*] (EAIO)
WN (Calc) ... Calcutta Weekly Notes [*A publication*] (DLA)
WN Cas ..... Weekly Notes of Cases [*Pennsylvania*] [*A publication*] (DLA)
WN Cas (PA) ... Weekly Notes of Cases [*Pennsylvania*] [*A publication*] (DLA)
WNCB .... Duluth, MN [*FM radio station call letters*]
WNCC .... Barnesboro, PA [*AM radio station call letters*]
WNCCC .... Women's National Cancer Control Campaign [*British*]
WNCD .... Niles, OH [*FM radio station call letters*]
WNCE .... Lancaster, PA [*FM radio station call letters*]
WNCI .... Columbus, OH [*FM radio station call letters*]
WNCM ...... Jacksonville, FL [*FM radio station call letters*]
WNCN .... New York, NY [*FM radio station call letters*]
WNCO .... Ashland, OH [*AM radio station call letters*]
WNCO .... Winco Petroleum Corp. [*NASDAQ symbol*] (NQ)
WNCO-FM ... Ashland, OH [*FM radio station call letters*]

WN Covers (NSW) ... Weekly Notes Covers (New South Wales) [*A publication*] (APTA)
WNC (PA) ... Weekly Notes of Cases [*Pennsylvania*] [*A publication*] (DLA)
WNCQ ...... Watertown, NY [*AM radio station call letters*]
WNCS ...... Montpelier, VT [*FM radio station call letters*]
WNCT ...... Greenville, NC [*AM radio station call letters*]
WNCT-FM ... Greenville, NC [*FM radio station call letters*]
WNCT-TV ... Greenville, NC [*Television station call letters*]
WNCW ..... Spindale, NC [*FM radio station call letters*]
WNCX ...... Cleveland, OH [*FM radio station call letters*]
WND .... Wind (KSC)
WND .... Windham [*New York*] [*Seismograph station code, US Geological Survey*] (SEIS)
WND .... Windmere Corp. [*NYSE symbol*] (SPSG)
WND .... Wound (MSA)
Wn 2d........ Washington Reports, Second Series [*A publication*] (DLA)
WNDA ...... Huntsville, AL [*FM radio station call letters*]
WNDB ...... Daytona Beach, FL [*AM radio station call letters*]
WNDC ...... Baton Rouge, LA [*AM radio station call letters*]
WNDC ...... Woman's National Democratic Club (EA)
WNDE .... Indianapolis, IN [*AM radio station call letters*]
WNDH ...... Napoleon, OH [*FM radio station call letters*]
WNDI .... Sullivan, IN [*AM radio station call letters*]
WNDI-FM ... Sullivan, IN [*FM radio station call letters*]
WNDJ .... White Stone, VA [*FM radio station call letters*]
WNDLS..... Windlass
WNDO ...... Weather Network Duty Officer [*Air Force*] (AFM)
WNDR....... Syracuse, NY [*AM radio station call letters*]
WNDR....... Winder
WNDS ...... Derry, NH [*Television station call letters*]
WNDS ...... Windsor Industries [*NASDAQ symbol*] (NQ)
WNDT .... [*The*] Wendt-Bristol Co. [*Columbus, OH*] [*NASDAQ symbol*] (NQ)
WNDU ...... South Bend, IN [*AM radio station call letters*]
WNDU-FM ... South Bend, IN [*FM radio station call letters*]
WNDU-TV ... South Bend, IN [*Television station call letters*]
WNDY .... Crawfordsville, IN [*FM radio station call letters*]
WNDZ....... Portage, IN [*AM radio station call letters*]
WNE......... Welsh National Eisteddfod (DAS)
WNE.......... Western New England College, Springfield, MA [*OCLC symbol*] (OCLC)
WNEA ...... Newnan, GA [*AM radio station call letters*]
WNEB ...... Worcester, MA [*AM radio station call letters*]
WNEC ...... Henniker, NH [*FM radio station call letters*]
WNEC ...... Western New England College [*Springfield, MA*]
WNED...... Buffalo, NY [*FM radio station call letters*]
WNED-TV ... Buffalo, NY [*Television station call letters*]
WNEG...... Toccoa, GA [*AM radio station call letters*]
WNEG-TV ... Toccoa, GA [*Television station call letters*]
WNEH...... Greenwood, SC [*Television station call letters*]
WNEK ...... Springfield, MA [*FM radio station call letters*]
WNEL .... Caguas, PR [*AM radio station call letters*]
WNelH ...... New London Community Hospital, Health Science Library, New London, WI [*Library symbol*] [*Library of Congress*] (LCLS)
WNEM...... Bay City, MI [*Television station call letters*]
WN (Eng) .. Weekly Notes of English Law Reports [*A publication*] (DLA)
W N Eng LR ... Western New England Law Review [*A publication*]
WNEO....... Alliance, OH [*Television station call letters*]
WNEP .... Scranton, PA [*Television station call letters*]
WNEQ-TV ... Buffalo, NY [*Television station call letters*]
WNES .... Central City, KY [*AM radio station call letters*]
WNET .... Newark, NJ [*Television station call letters*]
WNEW...... New York, NY [*AM radio station call letters*]
W New Eng L Rev ... Western New England Law Review [*A publication*]
WNEW-FM ... New York, NY [*FM radio station call letters*]
WNEX .... Macon, GA [*AM radio station call letters*]
WNEZ....... New Britain, CT [*AM radio station call letters*]
WNF......... Well-Nourished Female [*Medicine*]
WNF......... [*The*] Winfield Railroad Co. [*AAR code*]
WNFA ...... Port Huron, MI [*FM radio station call letters*]
WNFB ...... Lake City, FL [*FM radio station call letters*]
WNFC ...... Willie Nelson Fan Club (EA)
WNFGA ..... Woman's National Farm and Garden Association (EA)
WNFI .... Palatka, FL [*FM radio station call letters*]
WNFK .... Perry, FL [*FM radio station call letters*]
WNFL........ Green Bay, WI [*AM radio station call letters*]
WNFM ...... Reedsburg, WI [*FM radio station call letters*]
WNFM ...... World Nuclear Fuel Market (NRCH)
WNFQ ...... Newberry, FL [*FM radio station call letters*]
WNFR .... Winifrede Railroad Co. [*AAR code*]
WNFT .... Jacksonville, FL [*Television station call letters*]
WNG .... Wang Laboratories, Inc., Lowell, MA [*OCLC symbol*] (OCLC)
WNG .... Warning (AFM)
WNG .... Weighing
WNG .... West New Guinea
WNG .... Williams Natural Gas Co. [*NYSE symbol*] (SPSG)
WNG .... Wing [*of a ship*] (DS)
WNG .... Wingst [*Federal Republic of Germany*] [*Geomagnetic observatory code*]
WNGA....... Nashville, GA [*AM radio station call letters*]

WNGA....... Wholesale Nursery Growers of America   (EA)
WNGC....... Athens, GA [FM radio station call letters]
WNGC....... Western Natural Gas Co. [NASDAQ symbol]   (NQ)
WNGGA.... Welsh National Gymanfa Ganu Association   (EA)
WNGM..... Athens, GA [Television station call letters]
WNGN ...... Hoosick Falls, NY [FM radio station call letters]
WNGO ...... Mayfield, KY [AM radio station call letters]
WNGS ...... West Palm Beach, FL [FM radio station call letters]
WNGZ....... Montour Falls, NY [FM radio station call letters]
WNH .... Whiteface [New Hampshire] [Seismograph station code, US
              Geological Survey]   (SEIS)
WNHA ...... Concord, NH [AM radio station call letters]
WNHC ...... New Haven, CT [AM radio station call letters]
WNHP....... Washington Natural Heritage Program [Washington State
              Department of Natural Resources] [Olympia]
              [Information service or system]   (IID)
WNHP....... Wyoming Natural Heritage Program [Wyoming State
              Department of Environmental Quality] [Cheyenne]
              [Information service or system]   (IID)
WNHT....... Concord, NH [Television station call letters]
WNHU ...... West Haven, CT [FM radio station call letters]
WNHV ...... White River Junction, VT [AM radio station call letters]
WNHW ...... Nags Head, NC [FM radio station call letters]
WNHX ...... Moultonborough, NH [FM radio station call letters]
WNI........... Wang Institute of Graduate Studies, Tyngsboro, MA [OCLC
              symbol]   (OCLC)
WNI........... Windkracht Nederland Information Centre [Netherlands Wind
              Energy Information Centre] [Nethergy Ltd.] [Database
              producer]   (IID)
WNI........... Women's National Institute [Defunct]   (EA)
WNIB .... Chicago, IL [FM radio station call letters]
WNIC........ Dearborn, MI [FM radio station call letters]
WNIC........ Wide Area Network Interface Co-Processor [Communications
              adapter]   (PCM)
WNIJ......... Rockford, IL [FM radio station call letters]
WNIK .... Arecibo, PR [AM radio station call letters]
WNIK-FM ... Arecibo, PR [FM radio station call letters]
WNIL .... Niles, MI [AM radio station call letters]
WNIM....... Wide-Area-Network Module [Telecommunications]
WNIN....... Evansville, IN [Television station call letters]
WNIN-FM ... Evansville, IN [FM radio station call letters]
WNINTEL ... Warning Notice: Sensitive Intelligence Sources and Methods
              Involved   (MCD)
WNIR .... Kent, OH [FM radio station call letters]
WNIS .... Norfolk, VA [AM radio station call letters]
WNIT .... South Bend, IN [Television station call letters]
WNIU........ De Kalb, IL [FM radio station call letters]
WNIV .... Atlanta, GA [AM radio station call letters]
WNIX .... Greenville, MS [AM radio station call letters]
WNIZ .... Zion, IL [FM radio station call letters]
WNJ .... Whitman Numismatic Journal [A publication]
WNJB........ New Brunswick, NJ [Television station call letters]
WNJC........ Senatobia, MS [FM radio station call letters]
WNJM ...... Montclair, NJ [Television station call letters]
WNJN .... Atlantic City, NJ [FM radio station call letters]
WNJR....... Newark, NJ [AM radio station call letters]
WNJS........ Berlin, NJ [FM radio station call letters]
WNJS........ Camden, NJ [Television station call letters]
WNJT........ Trenton, NJ [Television station call letters]
WNJT-FM ... Trenton, NJ [FM radio station call letters]
WNJU .... Linden, NJ [Television station call letters]
WNJX........ Mayaguez, PR [Television station call letters]
WNJY........ Delphi, IN [FM radio station call letters]
WNKC .... Kimberly-Clark Corp., Research and Engineering Library,
              Neenah, WI [Library symbol] [Library of
              Congress]   (LCLS)
WNKJ .... Hopkinsville, KY [FM radio station call letters]
WNKO....... Newark, OH [FM radio station call letters]
WNKU....... Highland Heights, KY [FM radio station call letters]
WNKV .... St. Johnsbury, VT [FM radio station call letters]
WNKX .... Centerville, TN [AM radio station call letters]
WNKX-FM ... Centerville, TN [FM radio station call letters]
WNKY....... Neon, KY [AM radio station call letters]
WNL.......... Nicolet College, Learning Resources Center, Rhinelander, WI
              [OCLC symbol]   (OCLC)
WNL.......... Waveguide Nitrogen Load
Wn L.......... Wayne Law Review [A publication]
WNL.......... Within Normal Limits [Medicine]
WNLA ...... Indianola, MS [AM radio station call letters]
WNLA ...... Witwatersrand Native Labour Association [Nyasaland]
WNLA-FM ... Indianola, MS [FM radio station call letters]
WNLB .... Rocky Mount, VA [AM radio station call letters]
WNLC .... New London, CT [AM radio station call letters]
WNLE .... Fernadina Beach, FL [FM radio station call letters]
WNLF....... Charlotte, MI [AM radio station call letters]
WNLK .... Norwalk, CT [AM radio station call letters]
WNLL .... Womens's National Loyal League [Established by Elizabeth
              Cady Stanton and Susan B. Anthony]
WNLN....... Western Nigeria Legal Notice [A publication]   (DLA)
WNLR .... Churchville, VA [AM radio station call letters]
Wn LR .... Washington Law Review [A publication]

Wn LR .... Wayne Law Review [A publication]
WNLR .... Weighted Nonlinear Regression [Mathematics]
WNLR .... Western Nigeria Law Reports [A publication]   (DLA)
WNLS........ Tallahassee, FL [AM radio station call letters]
WNLSC...... Women's National Land Service Corps [British] [World War I]
WNLT .... Harrison, OH [FM radio station call letters]
WNM .... Warm Neutral Medium [Astrophysics]
WNM .... Washington National Monument
WNM .... Well-Nourished Male [Medicine]
WNM .... White Noise Making [Psychology]
WNMA...... Washington National Monument Association   (EA)
WNMB....... North Myrtle Beach, SC [FM radio station call letters]
WNMC...... Traverse City, MI [FM radio station call letters]
WNMC...... Weather Network Management Center [Air Force]   (AFM)
WNMC...... Wincom Corp. [NASDAQ symbol]   (NQ)
WNMH ...... Northfield, MA [FM radio station call letters]
WN Misc ... Weekly Notes, Miscellaneous [A publication]   (DLA)
WNMT....... Garden City, GA [AM radio station call letters]
WNMU ..... Marquette, MI [FM radio station call letters]
WNMU-TV ... Marquette, MI [Television station call letters]
WNMX....... Newberry, SC [FM radio station call letters]
WNN .... World News Network [In Muriel Dobbin's novel "Going Live"]
WNNC....... Newton, NC [AM radio station call letters]
WNND....... Fuquay Varina, NC [FM radio station call letters]
WNNE....... Hartford, VT [Television station call letters]
WNNH ...... Henniker, NH [FM radio station call letters]
WNNJ .... Newton, NJ [AM radio station call letters]
WNNJ-FM ... Newton, NJ [FM radio station call letters]
WNNK....... Harrisburg, PA [AM radio station call letters]
WNNK-FM ... Harrisburg, PA [FM radio station call letters]
WNNN ..... Canton, NJ [FM radio station call letters]
WNNO ..... Wisconsin Dells, WI [AM radio station call letters]
WNNO-FM ... Wisconsin Dells, WI [FM radio station call letters]
WNNQ ..... Ashburn, GA [AM radio station call letters]
WNNR...... Sodus, NY [FM radio station call letters]
WNNR Spes Versl ... WNNR [Suid-Afrikaanse Wetenskaplike en
              Nywerheidnavorsingsraad] Spesiale Verslag [A
              publication]
WNNS....... Springfield, IL [FM radio station call letters]
WN (NSW) ... Weekly Notes (New South Wales) [A publication]   (APTA)
WNNT....... Warsaw, VA [AM radio station call letters]
WNNT-FM ... Warsaw, VA [FM radio station call letters]
WNNW ..... Salem, NH [AM radio station call letters]
WNNZ....... Westfield, MA [AM radio station call letters]
WNO .... Wa National Organization [Myanmar] [Political party]   (EY)
WNO .... Welsh National Opera
WNO .... Wharton & Northern Railroad Co. [Later, WHN] [AAR code]
WNO .... Wrong Number [Telecommunications]   (TEL)
WNOE....... New Orleans, LA [AM radio station call letters]
WNOE-FM ... New Orleans, LA [FM radio station call letters]
WNOG ...... Naples, FL [AM radio station call letters]
WNOI........ Flora, IL [FM radio station call letters]
WNOK....... Columbia, SC [FM radio station call letters]
WNOL....... New Orleans, LA [Television station call letters]
WNOO ..... Chattanooga, TN [AM radio station call letters]
WNOP....... Newport, KY [AM radio station call letters]
WNOR....... Norfolk, VA [AM radio station call letters]
WNOR-FM ... Norfolk, VA [FM radio station call letters]
WNOS ...... New Bern, NC [AM radio station call letters]
WNOV...... Milwaukee, WI [AM radio station call letters]
WNOW ..... Mint Hill, NC [AM radio station call letters]
WNOZ...... Aguadilla, PR [AM radio station call letters]
WNP......... Naga [Phillipines] [Airport symbol]   (OAG)
WNP......... Washington Nuclear Plant   (NRCH)
WNP......... Welsh Nationalist Party   (DI)
WNP......... Westland New Post [Terrorist organization] [Belgium]   (EY)
WNP......... Will Not Proceed
WNP......... Will Not Process
WNP......... Wire Nonpayment
WNPB ...... Morgantown, WV [Television station call letters]
WNPC .... Newport, TN [AM radio station call letters]
WNPC .... Women's National Press Club [Later, WPC]   (EA)
WNPE .... Watertown, NY [Television station call letters]
WNPI .... Norwood, NY [Television station call letters]
WNPL .... Naples, FL [Television station call letters]
WNPQ....... New Philadelphia, OH [FM radio station call letters]
WNPR .... Norwich, CT [FM radio station call letters]
WNPT .... Linden, AL [FM radio station call letters]
WNPT .... Tuscaloosa, AL [AM radio station call letters]
WNPV .... Lansdale, PA [AM radio station call letters]
WNPW ...... Wide, Notched P Wave [Cardiology]
WNQM ...... Nashville, TN [AM radio station call letters]
WNR......... Weapons Neutron Research Facility [Los Alamos]
WNR......... Weekblad voor Notaris-Ambt en Registratie [A publication]
WNR......... Western NORAD Region
WNR......... Windorah [Australia] [Airport symbol]   (OAG)
WNR......... Winners Corp. [NYSE symbol] [Later, VCC]   (SPSG)
WNR......... World New Religion [An association]   (EA)
WNRB .... Niles, OH [AM radio station call letters]
WNRC .... Dudley, MA [FM radio station call letters]
WNRC....... Washington National Records Center [GSA]   (AABC)

WNRC....... Women's National Republican Club (EA)
WNRCEN ... Washington National Records Center [*GSA*]
WNRE....... Whiteshell Nuclear Research Establishment [*Atomic Energy of Canada Ltd.*] [*Research center*]
WNRG...... Grundy, VA [*AM radio station call letters*]
WNRG....... WEPCo Energy Co. [*NASDAQ symbol*] [*NASDAQ symbol*] (NQ)
WNRI....... Woonsocket, RI [*AM radio station call letters*]
WNRJ....... Circleville, OH [*AM radio station call letters*]
WNRK...... Newark, DE [*AM radio station call letters*]
WNRR...... Bellevue, OH [*FM radio station call letters*]
WNRS...... Saline, MI [*AM radio station call letters*]
WNRT...... Manati, PR [*FM radio station call letters*]
WNRV...... Narrows, VA [*AM radio station call letters*]
WNRW...... Winston-Salem, NC [*Television station call letters*]
WNS........ Nawab Shah [*Pakistan*] [*Airport symbol*] (OAG)
WNS......... Technieuws Washington. Korte Berichten op Technisch Wetenschappelijk Gebied [*A publication*]
WNS........ Women's News Service
WNS........ Worldwide News Service. Jewish Telegraphic Agency (BJA)
WNS......... Wren Resources Ltd. [*Vancouver Stock Exchange symbol*]
WNSA....... Woman's National Sabbath Alliance [*Defunct*]
WNSB...... Norfolk, VA [*FM radio station call letters*]
WNSB ...... West Newton Savings Bank [*West Newton, MA*] [*NASDAQ symbol*] (NQ)
WNSC ...... Rock Hill, SC [*FM radio station call letters*]
WNSC-TV ... Rock Hill, SC [*Television station call letters*]
WNSEA..... Wood Naval Stores Export Association
WNSH...... Beverly, MA [*AM radio station call letters*]
WNSI........ WNS, Inc. [*Houston, TX*] [*NASDAQ symbol*] (NQ)
WNSL....... A. W. Wright Nuclear Structure Laboratory [*Yale University*] [*Research center*] (RCD)
WNSL....... Laurel, MS [*FM radio station call letters*]
WNSN...... South Bend, IN [*FM radio station call letters*]
WNSR...... New York, NY [*FM radio station call letters*]
WNSR ...... West Nova Scotia Regiment (DMA)
WNSS........ North Syracuse, NY [*AM radio station call letters*]
WNST...... Milton, WV [*AM radio station call letters*]
WNST ...... Winston Mills, Inc. [*NASDAQ symbol*] (NQ)
WNSW...... Brewer, ME [*AM radio station call letters*]
WNT......... Foreign Trade [*A publication*]
WNT......... Washington National Corp. [*NYSE symbol*] (SPSG)
Wn T......... Washington Territory Reports [*1854-88*] [*A publication*] (ILCA)
WNT......... Waste Neutralization Tank [*Nuclear energy*] (NRCH)
WNT......... What's New in Travel [*CompuServe Information Service*] [*Information service or system*] (CRD)
WNT......... World News Tonight [*Television program*]
WNTC ...... Theda Clark Memorial Hospital, Neenah, WI [*Library symbol*] [*Library of Congress*] (LCLS)
WNTE ...... Mansfield, PA [*FM radio station call letters*]
WNTF ...... Western Naval Task Force [*Navy*]
WNTH...... Winnetka, IL [*FM radio station call letters*]
WNTI....... Hackettstown, NJ [*FM radio station call letters*]
WNTJ....... Johnstown, PA [*AM radio station call letters*]
WNTK...... Lebanon, NH [*FM radio station call letters*]
WNTK...... Newport, NH [*AM radio station call letters*]
WNTL...... Indian Head, MD [*AM radio station call letters*]
WNTL ...... Winterhalter, Inc. [*NASDAQ symbol*] (NQ)
WNTN...... Newton, MA [*AM radio station call letters*]
WNTQ...... Syracuse, NY [*FM radio station call letters*]
WNTR...... Silver Spring, MD [*AM radio station call letters*]
Wntr Sldr... Winter Soldier [*A publication*]
WNTS ...... Indianapolis, IN [*AM radio station call letters*]
WNTT ...... Tazewell, TN [*AM radio station call letters*]
WNTV....... Greenville, SC [*Television station call letters*]
WNTX...... Nantucket, MA [*FM radio station call letters*]
WNTXD .... Wentex International, Inc. [*NASDAQ symbol*] (NQ)
WNTY...... Southington, CT [*AM radio station call letters*]
WNTZ...... Natchez, MS [*Television station call letters*]
WNU....... Western Newspaper Union
WNUA...... Chicago, IL [*FM radio station call letters*]
WNUB...... Northfield, VT [*FM radio station call letters*]
WNUE...... Fort Walton Beach, FL [*AM radio station call letters*]
WNUR...... Evanston, IL [*FM radio station call letters*]
WNUS...... Belpre, OH [*FM radio station call letters*]
WNUV...... Baltimore, MD [*Television station call letters*]
WNUY...... Bluffton, IN [*FM radio station call letters*]
WNUZ...... Talladega, AL [*AM radio station call letters*]
WNV......... Wehrmachtnachrichtenverbindungen [*Armed Forces Signal Communications*] [*German military - World War II*]
WNV......... West Nile Virus
WNVA....... Norton, VA [*AM radio station call letters*]
WNVA-FM ... Norton, VA [*FM radio station call letters*]
WNVC....... Fairfax, VA [*Television station call letters*]
WNVL....... Nicholasville, KY [*AM radio station call letters*]
WNVR....... Vernon Hills, IL [*AM radio station call letters*]
WNVT....... Goldvein, VA [*Television station call letters*]
WNVZ....... Norfolk, VA [*FM radio station call letters*]
WNW......... Superior Public Library, Superior, WI [*OCLC symbol*] (OCLC)

WNW......... Wenatchee [*Washington*] [*Seismograph station code, US Geological Survey*] (SEIS)
WNW......... West-Northwest
WNWC...... Madison, WI [*FM radio station call letters*]
WNWI...... Valparaiso, IN [*AM radio station call letters*]
WNWK...... Newark, NJ [*FM radio station call letters*]
WNWN...... Coldwater, MI [*FM radio station call letters*]
WNWO...... Toledo, OH [*Television station call letters*]
WNWRN... West-Northwestern [*Meteorology*] (FAAC)
WNWS...... Brownsville, TN [*AM radio station call letters*]
WnWste..... Western Waste Industries [*Associated Press abbreviation*] (APAG)
WNWV...... Elyria, OH [*FM radio station call letters*]
WNWWD ... West-Northwestward [*Meteorology*] (FAAC)
WNWZ...... Germantown, TN [*AM radio station call letters*]
WNXT ...... Portsmouth, OH [*AM radio station call letters*]
WNXT-FM ... Portsmouth, OH [*FM radio station call letters*]
WNY......... Washington [*DC*] Naval Yard
WNY......... Wilmington [*New York*] [*Seismograph station code, US Geological Survey*] (SEIS)
WNY......... Wynyard [*Australia*] [*Airport symbol*] (OAG)
WNYB...... Buffalo, NY [*Television station call letters*]
WNYC...... New York, NY [*AM radio station call letters*]
WNYC-FM ... New York, NY [*FM radio station call letters*]
WNYC-TV ... New York, NY [*Television station call letters*]
WNYE....... New York, NY [*FM radio station call letters*]
WNYE-TV ... New York, NY [*Television station call letters*]
WNYG....... Babylon, NY [*AM radio station call letters*]
WNYHSL... Western New York Health Science Librarians [*Library network*]
WNYK...... Nyack, NY [*FM radio station call letters*]
WNYLRC ... Western New York Library Resources Council [*Buffalo, NY*] [*Library network*]
WNYNRC ... Western New York Nuclear Research Center Reactor (NRCH)
WNYP ...... Cortland, NY [*FM radio station call letters*]
WNYR....... Waterloo, NY [*FM radio station call letters*]
WNYS...... Canton, NY [*AM radio station call letters*]
WNYT...... Albany, NY [*Television station call letters*]
WNYU...... New York, NY [*FM radio station call letters*]
WNYV...... Whitehall, NY [*FM radio station call letters*]
WNYW...... New York, NY [*Television station call letters*]
WNZ......... Wairakei [*New Zealand*] [*Seismograph station code, US Geological Survey*] (SEIS)
WNZE....... Plymouth, IN [*FM radio station call letters*]
WNZK...... Dearborn Heights-Detroit, MI [*AM radio station call letters*]
WNZN...... Lorain, OH [*FM radio station call letters*]
WNZQ...... St. Cloud, FL [*AM radio station call letters*]
WNZR...... Mount Vernon, OH [*FM radio station call letters*]
WNZS...... Jacksonville, FL [*AM radio station call letters*]
WNZT...... Columbia, PA [*AM radio station call letters*]
WO .... Wait Order
WO .... Walkover
WO .... Walter Owen Bentley [*Automotive engineer*] [*British*]
WO .... War Office [*British*]
WO .... War Orientation [*Navy*]
WO .... Warning Order
WO .... Warrant Officer [*Usually in combination with numbers to denote serviceman's grade*] [*Military*]
WO .... Wash Out [*Medicine*]
WO .... Washington Office [*FAA*] (FAAC)
W/O.......... Water-in-Oil
WO .... Water Outlet Gasket [*Automotive engineering*]
W/O.......... Weight Percent (SAA)
WO .... Welfare Officer [*British military*] (DMA)
WO .... Welsh Office (DCTA)
WO .... Welt des Orients [*A publication*]
WO .... Western Operation
WO .... White Oval [*on Jupiter*]
WO .... Wind Offset
WO .... Wipe Out (MSA)
WO .... Wireless Operator
WO .... Without (AFM)
wo .... Wollastonite [*CIPW classification*] [*Geology*]
WO .... Women
WO .... Women Outdoors (EA)
WO .... Women's Reserve, Ordnance Duties [*USNR officer designation*]
WO .... Work Order
WO .... Working Overseer (ADA)
WO .... World Airways, Inc. [*ICAO designator*] (FAAC)
WO .... World of Opera [*A publication*]
W/O.......... Write-Off [*Accounting*]
WO .... Write Only
WO .... Write Out
WO .... Writer Officer [*British military*] (DMA)
W/O.......... Written Order [*Medicine*]
WO1 .... Warrant Officer One [*Army*]
WOA........ Warrant Officers Association of the United States of America [*Defunct*] (EA)
WOA........ Washington Office on Africa (EA)
WOA........ Weapons Orientation Advanced (AFM)
WOA........ Web Offset Association (EA)

WOA	Work Order Authorization (MCD)
WOA	WorldCorp., Inc. [*NYSE symbol*] (SPSG)
WOAB	Ozark, AL [*FM radio station call letters*]
WOAC	Canton, OH [*Television station call letters*]
WOAD	Jackson, MS [*AM radio station call letters*]
WOAD	Utica, MS [*FM radio station call letters*]
WOAI	San Antonio, TX [*AM radio station call letters*]
WOAK	La Grange, GA [*FM radio station call letters*]
WOAL	Pippa Passes, KY [*FM radio station call letters*]
WOAP	Owosso, MI [*AM radio station call letters*]
WOAR	Women Organized Against Rape
WOAS	Ontonagon, MI [*FM radio station call letters*]
WOAS	Wave-Off Advisory System [*Aircraft carrier*] [*Navy*]
WOASH	Women Organised Against Sexual Harassment [*British*] (DI)
WOAY	Oak Hill, WV [*AM radio station call letters*]
WOAY-TV	Oak Hill, WV [*Television station call letters*]
WOB	Walter Owen Bentley [*Automotive engineer*] [*British*]
WOB	Washed Overboard [*Shipping*]
WOB	Weight on Bit [*Drilling technology*]
WOB	Without Optical Brightener [*Biochemistry*]
WOB	Woburn [*Parish in England*]
WOB	[*Survey of*] Women-Owned Businesses [*Bureau of the Census Survey*] (GFGA)
WOB	Work Order Bin (MCD)
WOB	World of Banking [*A publication*]
WOBC	Oberlin, OH [*FM radio station call letters*]
WOBC	Waveguide Operating below Cutoff
WOBG	Clarksburg, WV [*AM radio station call letters*]
WOBG	Salem, WV [*FM radio station call letters*]
WOBL	Oberlin, OH [*AM radio station call letters*]
WOBM	Lakewood, NJ [*AM radio station call letters*]
WOBM	Toms River, NJ [*FM radio station call letters*]
WOBN	Westerville, OH [*FM radio station call letters*]
W O BNDR	Without Binder [*Freight*]
WOBO	Batavia, OH [*FM radio station call letters*]
W/OBO	Without Blowout (MSA)
WOBO	World Organization of Building Officials (EA)
WOBR	Wanchese, NC [*AM radio station call letters*]
WOBR-FM	Wanchese, NC [*FM radio station call letters*]
WOBS	First Woburn Bancorp, Inc. [*NASDAQ symbol*] (NQ)
WOBS	New Albany, IN [*AM radio station call letters*]
WOBT	Rhinelander, WI [*AM radio station call letters*]
WOC	Davenport, IA [*AM radio station call letters*]
WOC	Waiting on Cement
WOC	Water-Oil Contact
WOC	Wilshire Oil Co. of Texas [*NYSE symbol*] (SPSG)
WOC	Win Over Communism [*A fund-raising subsidiary of the Unification Church*]
WOC	Wing Operations Center (CINC)
WOC	Without Compensation (ADA)
WOC	Women's Ordination Conference (EA)
WOC	Wood's Oriental Cases [*Malaya*] [*A publication*] (DLA)
WOC	Work and Occupations [*A publication*]
WOC	Work Order Control (MCD)
WOC	World Coal [*A publication*]
WOC	World Oceanographic Center (MSC)
WOCA	Ocala, FL [*AM radio station call letters*]
WOCA	World Outside Communist Areas
WOCAR	Aviation Warrant Officer Career Course [*Army*]
WOCC	Corydon, IN [*AM radio station call letters*]
WOCC	Worldwide Operations Control Center [*United States Information Agency*]
WOCCI	War Office Central Card Index [*British military*] (DMA)
WOccM	Memorial Hospital at Oconomowoc, Oconomowoc, WI [*Library symbol*] [*Library of Congress*] (LCLS)
WOccR	Redemptorist Seminary, Oconomowoc, WI [*Library symbol*] [*Library of Congress*] (LCLS)
WOCCU	World Council of Credit Unions [*Madison, WI*] (EA)
WOCD	Amsterdam, NY [*Television station call letters*]
WOCE	World Ocean Circulation Experiment [*World Climate Research Programme*]
WOCG	Huntsville, AL [*FM radio station call letters*]
Wochbl Papierfabr	Wochenblatt fuer Papierfabrikation [*A publication*]
Wochenschr Brau	Wochenschrift fuer Brauerei [*A publication*]
Woch Pap Fab	Wochenblatt fuer Papierfabrikation [*A publication*]
WOCIT	We Oppose Computers in Tournaments [*A chess players' group, formed in 1983*]
WOCL	De Land, FL [*FM radio station call letters*]
WOCL	War Office Casualty List [*British military*] (DMA)
WOCLS	World Ocean and Cruise Liner Society (EA)
WOCMDC	Warrant Officer Candidate Military Development Course
WOCN	Miami, FL [*AM radio station call letters*]
WOCO	Oconto, WI [*AM radio station call letters*]
WOCO	World of Computers [*NASDAQ symbol*] (NQ)
WOCO	World Council of Service Clubs [*New Zealand*] (EAIO)
WOCO	World Council of Young Men's Service Clubs (EA)
WOCOD	World Coal [*A publication*]
WOCO-FM	Oconto, WI [*FM radio station call letters*]
WOCP	World Organization of China Painters (EA)
WOCQ	Berlin, MD [*FM radio station call letters*]
WOCR	Olivet, MI [*FM radio station call letters*]
WOCS	Work Order Control System (MCD)
WOCT	WAC [*Women's Army Corps*] Officer Candidate Test (AABC)
WOCU	War on Community Ugliness [*Program*] [*Defunct*] (EA)
WOCV	Oneida, TN [*AM radio station call letters*]
WOCW	Parris Island, SC [*FM radio station call letters*]
WOD	Washington & Old Dominion R. R. [*AAR code*]
WOD	Wind over Deck (MCD)
WOD	Without Dependents [*Military*] (AFM)
WOD	Woodstream Corp. [*AMEX symbol*] (SPSG)
WODA	World Organization of Dredging Associations (EA)
WODADIBOF	Workshop on the Determination of Anti-Epileptic Drugs in Body Fluids
WODC	Virginia Beach, VA [*FM radio station call letters*]
WODC	Women's Olympic Distance Committee [*Later, WDC*] (EA)
WODCON	World Dredging Conference
WODCON	World Organization of Dredging Associations Proceedings of World Dredging Congress [*A publication*] (EAAP)
WODD	Wave-Off Decision Device (MCD)
WODD	World Oceanographic Data Display
WODDIN	Worldwide On-Line Data and Document Intelligence System
WODECO	Western Offshore Drilling & Exploration Co.
WODED	World Development [*A publication*]
WODI	Brookneal, VA [*AM radio station call letters*]
WODJ	Greenville, MI [*FM radio station call letters*]
WODS	Boston, MA [*FM radio station call letters*]
WODY	Bassett, VA [*AM radio station call letters*]
WODZ	Memphis, TN [*AM radio station call letters*]
WOE	Warhead Output Evaluation (MCD)
WOE	Watchdogs on Environment
WOE	Weapon Optical Effects
WOE	Withdrawal of Enthusiasm [*Airline pilots objection to "Welcome aboard" talks*]
WOE	Without Enclosure (MCD)
WOE	Without Equipment
WOE	World Economy [*A publication*]
WOE	Wound of Entry [*Medicine*]
WOEC	Warrant Officer Entry Course [*Military*] (INF)
WOEC-RC	Warrant Office Entry Course, Reserve Component [*Army*] (INF)
WOEL	Elkton, MD [*FM radio station call letters*]
Woelm Publ	Woelm Publication [*A publication*]
WOEQ	Royal Palm Beach, FL [*AM radio station call letters*]
Woerner Adm'n	Woerner's Treatise on the American Law of Administration [*A publication*] (DLA)
Woert Sach	Woerter und Sachen [*A publication*]
WOES	Ovid-Elsie, MI [*FM radio station call letters*]
WOES	Warrant Officer Education System
W/OE & SP	Without Equipment and Spare Parts
WOEZ	Milton, PA [*FM radio station call letters*]
WOF	Walk on Floor [*Ataxia*]
WOF	Warmed-Over Flavor [*Food technology*]
WOF	Widowed Oriental Female [*Classified advertising*]
WOF	Work of Fracture [*Ceramic property*]
WOF	Worlds of Fantasy [*1950-1954*] [*A publication*]
WOFA	Westinghouse Optimized Fuel Assembly [*Nuclear energy*] (NRCH)
WOFC	Western Ohio Film Circuit [*Library network*]
WOFE	Rockwood, TN [*AM radio station call letters*]
WOFE-FM	Rockwood, TN [*FM radio station call letters*]
WOFF	Weight of Fuel Flow (MCD)
WOFG	Wolf Financial Group, Inc. [*New York, NY*] [*NASDAQ symbol*] (NQ)
WOFI	Wood Office Furniture Institute (EA)
WOFIWU	World Federation of Industrial Workers' Unions
WOFL	Orlando, FL [*Television station call letters*]
WOFP	Wearout Failure Period
WOFR	Washington Court House, OH [*AM radio station call letters*]
WOFS	Weather Observing and Forecasting System [*Air Force*] (MCD)
WOFT	Warrant Officer Flight Training [*Army*] (INF)
W O FTTNGS	Without Fittings [*Freight*]
WOFX	Fairfield, OH [*FM radio station call letters*]
WOG	Water-Oil-Gas (AAG)
WOG	Weapon Order Generation [*Military*] (CAAL)
WOG	Werner Oil & Gas Co. [*Vancouver Stock Exchange symbol*]
WOG	Westernized Oriental Gentleman [*Singapore term for native following Western fashions*] [*Other translations include "Wily Oriental Gentleman" and "Wonderful Oriental Gentleman"*]
WOG	With Other Goods [*Business term*]
WOG	Work Order Generator [*Military*]
WOG	World Organization of Gastroenterology [*See also OMGE*] [*Edinburgh, Scotland*] (EAIO)
WOG	Wrath of God [*Israeli counterterrorist group*]
WOGA	Western Oil and Gas Association (EA)
WOGL	Philadelphia, PA [*AM radio station call letters*]
WOGL-FM	Philadelphia, PA [*FM radio station call letters*]
WOGO	Hallie, WI [*AM radio station call letters*]
WOGR	Charlotte, NC [*AM radio station call letters*]
WOGS	Wrath of God Syndrome
WOGSC	World Organisation of General Systems and Cybernetics [*Lytham St. Annes, Lancashire, England*] (EAIO)

WOGX....... Ocala, FL [*Television station call letters*]
WOH .... War on Hunger [*Program*]   (EA)
WOH .... Washington Office on Haiti   (EA)
WOH .... Western Oklahoma Herbarium [*Southwest Oklahoma State University*]
WOH .... Wings of Hope [*An association*]   (EA)
WOH .... Work on Hand [*Insurance*]
WOHC ...... Warrant Officer Hospital Corps
WOHE ...... World Health [*A publication*]
WOHELO ... Work, Health, Love [*Camp Fire Girls slogan*]
WOHH...... Women's Organization of Hapoel Hamizrachi [*Later, EWA*]   (EA)
WOHI....... East Liverpool, OH [*AM radio station call letters*]
WOHMA .. Waste Oil Heating Manufacturers Association   (EA)
WOHP...... Portsmouth, OH [*FM radio station call letters*]
WOHP...... World Organization for Human Potential   (EA)
WO & HPS ... Wall Oven and Hot Plates [*Classified advertising*]   (ADA)
WOHRC..... Women's Occupational Health Resource Center   (EA)
WOHS....... Shelby, NC [*AM radio station call letters*]
WOHT ...... Jackson, MS [*FM radio station call letters*]
WOI........... Ames, IA [*AM radio station call letters*]
WOI........... Wealth of India [*A publication*]
WOI........... World Income Fund, Inc. [*AMEX symbol*]   (CTT)
WOI........... World Opportunities International   (EA)
WOIC........ Columbia, SC [*AM radio station call letters*]
WOI-FM .. Ames, IA [*FM radio station call letters*]
WOIL .... Wright Brothers Energy, Inc. [*San Antonio, TX*] [*NASDAQ symbol*]   (NQ)
WOIO....... Shaker Heights, OH [*Television station call letters*]
WOIR .... Homestead, FL [*AM radio station call letters*]
WOIS .... Worn Out in Service [*Military*]
WOI-TV .... Ames, IA [*Television station call letters*]
WOIZ .... Guayanilla, PR [*AM radio station call letters*]
WOJAC..... World Organization for Jews from Arab Countries   (EA)
WOJB........ Reserve, WI [*FM radio station call letters*]
WOJC........ Willys Overland Jeepster Club   (EA)
WOJD .... World Organization of Jewish Deaf [*Tel Aviv, Israel*]   (EAIO)
WOJG .... Warrant Officer Junior Grade
WOJO .... Evanston, IL [*FM radio station call letters*]
Wojsk Przegl Tech ... Wojskowy Przeglad Techniczny [*Poland*] [*A publication*]
WOK......... Wiener Oeffentlicher Kueche [*Viennese Open Kitchen*] [*Nonprofit temperance restaurant chain*] [*Austria*]
WOK......... Wokingham [*Municipal borough in England*]
WOK......... Wonken [*Venezuela*] [*Airport symbol*]   (OAG)
WOKA...... Douglas, GA [*AM radio station call letters*]
WOKA-FM ... Douglas, GA [*FM radio station call letters*]
WOKC....... Okeechobee, FL [*AM radio station call letters*]
WOKC-FM ... Okeechobee, FL [*FM radio station call letters*]
WOKD...... Arcadia, FL [*AM radio station call letters*]
WOKD-FM ... Arcadia, FL [*FM radio station call letters*]
WOKE .... Charleston, SC [*AM radio station call letters*]
WOKF .... Folkston, GA [*FM radio station call letters*]
WOKH ...... Bardstown, KY [*FM radio station call letters*]
WOKI .... Oak Ridge, TN [*FM radio station call letters*]
WOKJ .... Jackson, MS [*AM radio station call letters*]
WOKK....... Meridian, MS [*FM radio station call letters*]
WOKO ...... Burlington, VT [*FM radio station call letters*]
WOKQ....... Dover, NH [*FM radio station call letters*]
WOKR....... Rochester, NY [*Television station call letters*]
WOKR....... Willys-Overland-Knight Registry   (EA)
WOKS ...... Columbus, GA [*AM radio station call letters*]
WOKT....... Cannonsburg, KY [*AM radio station call letters*]
WOKV ...... Brunswick, GA [*FM radio station call letters*]
WOKV ...... Jacksonville, FL [*AM radio station call letters*]
WOKW...... Curwensville, PA [*FM radio station call letters*]
WOKX....... High Point, NC [*AM radio station call letters*]
WOKY ...... Milwaukee, WI [*AM radio station call letters*]
WOL.......... Wainoco Oil Co. [*NYSE symbol*]   (SPSG)
WOL.......... War-Office Letter [*An order or an instruction*] [*British*]
WOL.......... Washington, DC [*AM radio station call letters*]
WOL.......... Wedge Opening Load
WOL.......... Weird and Occult Library [*A publication*]
WOL.......... Wharf Owner's Liability [*Insurance*]
Wol............. Wolcott's Chancery Reports [*7 Delaware*] [*A publication*]   (DLA)
Wol............. Wollaston's English Bail Court Reports [*A publication*]   (DLA)
WOL.......... Wollongong [*Australia*] [*Airport symbol*]
wol............. Wolof [*MARC language code*] [*Library of Congress*]   (LCCP)
WOL.......... Wolverton [*England*] [*Seismograph station code, US Geological Survey*]   (SEIS)
WOL.......... Worklife [*Canada*] [*A publication*]
WOLA....... Barranquitas, PR [*AM radio station call letters*]
WOLA ...... Washington Office on Latin America   (EA)
WOLC....... Princess Anne, MD [*FM radio station call letters*]
WOLD....... Marion, VA [*AM radio station call letters*]
WOLD-FM ... Marion, VA [*FM radio station call letters*]
WOLE .... Aguadilla, PR [*Television station call letters*]
WOLF ...... Committee for Wildlife on the Last Frontier
WOLF ...... Houghton, MI [*FM radio station call letters*]
WOLF .... Scranton, PA [*Television station call letters*]

WOLF .... Syracuse, NY [*AM radio station call letters*]
WOLF .... Wayne Oakland Library Federation [*Library network*]
WOLF .... Work Order Load Forecast   (MCD)
Wolf & B .... Wolferstan and Bristow's English Election Cases [*1859-65*] [*A publication*]   (DLA)
Wolf & D.... Wolferstan and Dew's English Election Cases [*1856-58*] [*A publication*]   (DLA)
Wolfen-Buetteler B ... Wolfenbuetteler Beitraege [*A publication*]
Wolfenbuetteler Forsch ... Wolfenbuetteler Forschungen [*A publication*]
WOLFHB ... Wolf [*Howard B.*], Inc. [*Associated Press abbreviation*]   (APAG)
WOLL .... Riviera Beach, FL [*FM radio station call letters*]
Woll .... Wollaston's English Bail Court Reports, Practice Cases [*1840-41*] [*A publication*]   (DLA)
Woll BC ..... Wollaston's English Bail Court Reports [*A publication*]   (DLA)
Wollen- Leinen-Ind ... Wollen- und Leinen-Industrie [*A publication*]
WOLM...... Wainoco Oil Corp. [*NASDAQ symbol*]   (NQ)
WOLO....... Columbia, SC [*Television station call letters*]
WOLR....... Branford, FL [*FM radio station call letters*]
WOLS....... Florence, SC [*AM radio station call letters*]
WOLV ...... Wolverton [*Urban district in England*]
WolvrW ..... Wolverine World Wide, Inc. [*Associated Press abbreviation*]   (APAG)
WOLW...... Cadillac, MI [*FM radio station call letters*]
Wolw .... Woolworth [*F.W.*] Corp. [*Wall Street slang name: "Five & Dime"*] [*Associated Press abbreviation*]   (APAG)
Wolwth ...... Woolworth [*F.W.*] Corp. [*Wall Street slang name: "Five & Dime"*] [*Associated Press abbreviation*]   (APAG)
WOLX....... Baraboo, WI [*FM radio station call letters*]
WOLY ...... Battle Creek, MI [*AM radio station call letters*]
WOLZ .... Fort Myers, FL [*FM radio station call letters*]
WOM .... Weapons Output Makeup
WOM .... Wideband Optical Modulation
WOM .... Widowed Oriental Male [*Classified advertising*]
WOM .... Wireless Operator Mechanic [*British*]   (DSUE)
WOM .... Wise Old Men [*Term used to refer to group of US statesmen including Dean Acheson, Charles Bohlen, Averell Harriman, George Kennan, Robert Lovett, and John McCloy*]
WOM .... Word-of-Mouth   (WDMC)
WOM .... Write-Only Memory [*Data processing*]
WOM .... Write Optional Memory   (IEEE)
WOMA...... Algoma, WI [*FM radio station call letters*]
WOMAA.. Works Management [*A publication*]
WOMAN .. World Organization of Mothers of All Nations
Woman Art J ... Woman's Art Journal [*A publication*]
Woman Cit ... Woman Citizen [*A publication*]
Woman Home C ... Woman's Home Companion [*A publication*]
Woman Offend Rep ... Woman Offender Report [*A publication*]   (DLA)
Woman's H C ... Woman's Home Companion [*A publication*]
Woman's J ... Woman's Journal [*A publication*]
WOMBAT ... Waves on Magnetized Beams and Turbulence [*Physics*]   (ADA)
WOMC...... Detroit, MI [*FM radio station call letters*]
Women....... Women/Poems [*A publication*]
Women Coach Clin ... Women's Coaching Clinic [*A publication*]
Women of Eur ... Women of Europe [*A publication*]
Women and Hist ... Women and History [*A publication*]
Women and L ... Women and Law [*A publication*]
Women Labour Conf Pap ... Women and Labour Conference. Papers [*A publication*]
Women Law J ... Women Lawyers Journal [*A publication*]
Women Lawyers J ... Women Lawyers Journal [*A publication*]
Women Lit ... Women and Literature [*A publication*]
Women & Lit ... Women and Literature [*A publication*]
Women L Jour ... Women Lawyers Journal [*A publication*]
Women L Jour ... Women's Law Journal [*A publication*]   (DLA)
Women Rev ... Women and Revolution [*A publication*]
Women Rights L Rep ... Women's Rights Law Reporter [*A publication*]
Women's Bur Bull ... Women's Bureau Bulletin [*A publication*]
Women's LJ ... Women's Law Journal [*A publication*]   (DLA)
Women's L Rptr ... Women's Law Reporter [*A publication*]   (DLA)
Women's Review ... Women's Review of Books [*A publication*]
Women's Rights L Rep ... Women's Rights Law Reporter [*A publication*]
Women's Rights L Reptr ... Women's Rights Law Reporter [*A publication*]   (ILCA)
Women's Rights L Rptr ... Women's Rights Law Reporter [*A publication*]
Women's Rts L Rep Rutgers Univ ... Women's Rights Law Reporter. Rutgers University [*A publication*]
Women's Stud Assoc Conf Pap ... Women's Studies Association. Conference Papers [*New Zealand*] [*A publication*]
Women's Studies ... Women's Studies: An Interdisciplinary Journal [*A publication*]
Womens Studs Newsl ... Women's Studies Newsletter [*A publication*]
Women Stud ... Women's Studies: An Interdisciplinary Journal [*A publication*]
Women Stud Abstr ... Women Studies Abstracts [*A publication*]
Women Stud Abstracts ... Women Studies Abstracts [*A publication*]
Women & Ther ... Women and Therapy [*A publication*]
Women Wear ... Women's Wear Daily [*A publication*]
Women Wkrs Bull ... Women Workers Bulletin [*A publication*]
WOMG ...... Columbia, SC [*AM radio station call letters*]

WOMG-FM ... Columbia, SC [*FM radio station call letters*]
WomHealth ... Women and Health [*A publication*]
WOMI....... Owensboro, KY [*AM radio station call letters*]
Wom March ... Women on the March [*New Delhi*] [*A publication*]
WOMN ..... Women's Health Centers of America, Inc. [*San Diego, CA*] [*NASDAQ symbol*] (NQ)
Womn Prss ... Women's Press [*A publication*]
Womn Rgts ... Women's Rights Law Reporter [*A publication*]
Womn Sprt ... Womanspirit [*A publication*]
WOMP...... Bellaire, OH [*AM radio station call letters*]
WOMP...... Western Ocean Meeting Point (DMA)
WOMP...... World Order Models Project
WOMP-FM ... Bellaire, OH [*FM radio station call letters*]
WOMPI .... Women of the Motion Picture Industry, International (EA)
WOMR...... Provincetown, MA [*FM radio station call letters*]
Womspk..... Womanspeak [*A publication*]
WOMT...... Manitowoc, WI [*AM radio station call letters*]
WOMUA... World of Music [*A publication*]
WOMX...... Orlando, FL [*AM radio station call letters*]
WOMX-FM ... Orlando, FL [*FM radio station call letters*]
WON .... Wool over Needle [*Knitting*]
WON .... Work Order Number (MCD)
WONA ...... Winona, MS [*AM radio station call letters*]
WONAAC ... Women's National Abortion Action Coalition [*Defunct*]
WONA-FM ... Winona, MS [*FM radio station call letters*]
WONARD ... Woman's Organization of the National Association of Retail Druggists (EA)
WONB....... Ada, OH [*FM radio station call letters*]
WONC....... Naperville, IL [*FM radio station call letters*]
WONCA.... World Organization of National Colleges, Academies, and Academic Associations of General Practitioners/Family Physicians [*Australia*] (EAIO)
WOND ...... Pleasantville, NJ [*AM radio station call letters*]
WONE....... Akron, OH [*FM radio station call letters*]
WONE....... Dayton, OH [*AM radio station call letters*]
WONE...... Westwood One, Inc. [*Culver City, CA*] [*NASDAQ symbol*] (NQ)
WONF....... With Other Natural Flavors [*Food science*]
WONF....... Wonford [*England*]
WONG ..... Canton, MS [*AM radio station call letters*]
WONG ...... Weight on Nose Gear [*Aviation*] (MCD)
WONN ..... Lakeland, FL [*AM radio station call letters*]
WONO...... Walterboro, SC [*FM radio station call letters*]
WONQ ...... Orlando, FL [*AM radio station call letters*]
Wont Land Reg ... Wontner's Land Registry Practice [*12th ed.*] [*1975*] [*A publication*] (DLA)
W Ont L Rev ... Western Ontario Law Review [*A publication*]
WONU ...... Kankakee, IL [*FM radio station call letters*]
WONW ...... Defiance, OH [*AM radio station call letters*]
WONX....... Evanston, IL [*AM radio station call letters*]
WONY....... Oneonta, NY [*FM radio station call letters*]
WONZ....... Hammonton, NJ [*AM radio station call letters*]
WOO .... College of Wooster, Wooster, OH [*OCLC symbol*] (OCLC)
WOO .... Waiting on Orders
WOO .... Warrant Ordnance Officer [*Navy*] [*British*]
WOO .... Werke ohne Opuszahl [*Works without Opus Number*] [*Music*]
WOO .... Western Operations Office [*Later, WSO*] [*NASA*]
WOO .... Woodchopper, AK [*Location identifier*] [*FAA*] (FAAL)
WOO .... Woodstock [*Maryland*] [*Seismograph station code, US Geological Survey*] [*Closed*] (SEIS)
WoO.......... Work without Opus Number (WGA)
WOO .... World Oceanographic Organization
WOO .... World of Outlaws [*Auto racing*]
WOOD ...... Grand Rapids, MI [*AM radio station call letters*]
Wood.......... Wood on Mercantile Agreements [*A publication*] (DLA)
Wood.......... Wood's English Tithe Cases, Exchequer [*4 vols.*] [*A publication*] (DLA)
Wood.......... Woods' United States Circuit Court Reports [*A publication*] (DLA)
WOOD ...... Woodward & Lothrop [*NASDAQ symbol*] (NQ)
Woodb & M ... Woodbury and Minot's United States Circuit Court Reports [*A publication*] (DLA)
Woodb & Min (CC) ... Woodbury and Minot's United States Circuit Court Reports, First Circuit [*A publication*] (DLA)
Wood Brass Perc ... Woodwind, Brass, and Percussion [*A publication*]
Wood Civ L ... Wood's Institutes of the Civil Law of England [*A publication*] (DLA)
Wood Com L ... Wood's Institutes of the Common Law [*A publication*] (DLA)
Wood Conv ... Wood on Conveyancing [*A publication*] (DLA)
Wood Decr ... Wood's Tithe Cases [*England*] [*A publication*] (DLA)
Wooddesson Lect ... Wooddesson's Lecture [*A publication*] (DLA)
Woodd Lect ... Wooddesson's Lectures on the Laws of England [*A publication*] (DLA)
Wood El Jur ... Wooddesson's Elements of Jurisprudence [*A publication*] (DLA)
Woodf .... Woodfall on Landlord and Tenant [*25 eds.*] [*1802-1958*] [*A publication*] (DLA)
WOODF.... Woodford [*England*]
Woodf Cel Tr ... Woodfall's Celebrated Trials [*A publication*] (DLA)

Woodf Landl & T ... Woodfall on Landlord and Tenant [*25 eds.*] [*1802-1958*] [*A publication*] (DLA)
Woodf Landl & Ten ... Woodfall on Landlord and Tenant [*25 eds.*] [*1802-1958*] [*A publication*] (DLA)
Woodf L & T ... Woodfall on Landlord and Tenant [*28th ed.*] [*1978*] [*A publication*] (DLA)
WOOD-FM ... Grand Rapids, MI [*FM radio station call letters*]
Woodf Parl Deb ... Woodfall's Parliamentary Debates [*A publication*] (DLA)
Wood H...... Hutton Wood's Decrees in Tithe Cases [*England*] [*A publication*] (DLA)
Wood Ind ... Wood Industry [*A publication*]
Wood Inst .. Wood's Institutes of English Law [*A publication*] (DLA)
Wood Inst Com Law ... Wood's Institutes of the Common Law [*A publication*] (DLA)
Wood Inst Eng L ... Wood's Institutes of English Law [*A publication*] (DLA)
WOODL.... Woodleigh [*England*]
Wood Landl & Ten ... Wood on Landlord and Tenant [*A publication*] (DLA)
Wood Land & T ... Wood on Landlord and Tenant [*A publication*] (DLA)
Woodlds Res Index ... Woodlands Research Index. Pulp and Paper Research Institute of Canada [*A publication*]
Wood Lect ... Wooddesson's Lectures on the Laws of England [*A publication*] (DLA)
Wood Lim .. Wood on Limitation of Actions [*A publication*] (DLA)
Woodl Pap Pulp Pap Res Inst Can ... Woodlands Papers. Pulp and Paper Research Institute of Canada [*A publication*]
Woodl Res Note Union Camp Corp ... Woodland Research Notes. Union Camp Corp. [*A publication*]
Woodl Sect Index Canad Pulp Pap Ass ... Woodlands Section Index. Canadian Pulp and Paper Association [*A publication*]
Wood & M ... Woodbury and Minot's United States Circuit Court Reports [*A publication*] (DLA)
Wood Mag ... Woodwind Magazine [*A publication*]
Wood Man ... Wood on Mandamus [*A publication*] (DLA)
Woodman Cr Cas ... Woodman's Reports of Thacher's Criminal Cases [*Massachusetts*] [*A publication*] (DLA)
Wood Mast & Serv ... Wood on Master and Servant [*A publication*] (DLA)
Wood Mayne Dam ... Wood's Mayne on Damages [*A publication*] (DLA)
WOODMEM ... Leonard Wood Memorial [*Later, LWM*] [*Also known as American Leprosy Foundation*] (EA)
Wood & Minot ... Woodbury and Minot's United States Circuit Court Reports [*A publication*] (DLA)
Woodm & T For Med ... Woodman and Tidy on Forensic Medicine [*A publication*] (DLA)
Wood Nuis ... Wood on Nuisances [*A publication*] (DLA)
Wood Preserv ... Wood Preserving [*A publication*]
Wood Preserv (Chicago) ... Wood Preserving (Chicago) [*A publication*]
Wood Preserv N ... Wood Preserving News [*A publication*]
Wood Preserv News ... Wood Preserving News [*A publication*]
Wood Pres Rep For Prod Res Ind Developm Comm (Philippines) ... Wood Preservation Report. Forest Products Research and Industries Development Commission College (Laguna, Philippines) [*A publication*]
Wood Prod ... Wood and Wood Products [*A publication*]
Wood Res... Wood Research [*A publication*]
Wood Ry Law ... Wood's Law of Railroads [*A publication*] (DLA)
Woods .... Woods' United States Circuit Court Reports [*A publication*] (DLA)
Woods CC ... Woods' United States Circuit Court Reports [*A publication*] (DLA)
Wood Sci.... Wood Science [*A publication*]
Wood Sci Te ... Wood Science and Technology [*A publication*]
Wood Sci Technol ... Wood Science and Technology [*A publication*]
Wood's Civ Law ... Wood's Institutes of the Civil Law of England [*A publication*] (DLA)
Wood's Dig ... Wood's Digest of Laws [*California*] [*A publication*] (DLA)
Woods Hole Oceanogr Inst Annu Rep ... Woods Hole Oceanographic Institution. Annual Report [*A publication*]
Woods Hole Oceanogr Inst Annu Sea Grant Rep ... Woods Hole Oceanographic Institution. Annual Sea Grant Report [*A publication*]
Woods Hole Oceanogr Inst Collect Reprints ... Woods Hole Oceanographic Institution. Collected Reprints [*A publication*]
Woods Hole Oceanogr Inst Tech Rep ... Woods Hole Oceanographic Institution. Technical Report [*A publication*]
Woods Ins ... Wood on Fire Insurance [*A publication*] (DLA)
Woods Ins ... Wood's Institutes of English Law [*A publication*] (DLA)
Wood's Inst Civ L ... Wood's Institutes of the Civil Law of England [*A publication*] (DLA)
Wood's Inst Com L ... Wood's Institutes of the Common Law [*A publication*] (DLA)
Wood South Afr ... Wood Southern Africa [*A publication*]
Wood's R ... Wood's Manitoba Reports [*1875-83*] [*A publication*] (DLA)
Woods St Frauds ... Wood's Treatise on the Statutes of Frauds [*A publication*] (DLA)
WOODST ... Wood Strength [*Botany*]
WOODSTEIN ... [*Bob*] Woodward and [*Carl*] Bernstein [*Washington Post reporters who uncovered the Watergate story*]
Wood Sthn Afr ... Wood Southern Africa [*A publication*]
Wood Tech ... Wood Technic [*A publication*]
Wood Ti Cas ... Wood's Tithe Cases [*1650-1798*] [*A publication*] (DLA)
Wood Tit Cas ... Wood's Tithe Cases [*1650-1798*] [*A publication*] (DLA)

Wood Tr M ... Wood on Trade Marks [*1876*] [*A publication*]   (DLA)
Woodw .... Woodward's Decisions [*Pennsylvania*] [*A publication*]   (DLA)
Woodw Dec ... Woodward's Decisions [*1861-74*] [*Pennsylvania*] [*A publication*]   (DLA)
Woodw Dec PA ... Woodward's Decisions [*1861-74*] [*Pennsylvania*] [*A publication*]   (DLA)
Woodwind B ... Woodwind, Brass, and Percussion [*A publication*]
Woodwkg Ind ... Woodworking Industry [*A publication*]
Wood Wood Prod ... Wood and Wood Products [*A publication*]
Wood & Wood Prod ... Wood and Wood Products [*A publication*]
Wood World ... Woodwind World [*Later, Woodwind World - Brass and Percussion*] [*A publication*]
Wood World-Brass ... Woodwind World - Brass and Percussion [*A publication*]
WOODWT ... Wood Weight [*Botany*]
WOOF .... Dothan, AL [*AM radio station call letters*]
Woof. .... Well-Off, Older Folks [*Lifestyle classification*]
Woof. .... Well-Off, Over Fifty [*Lifestyle classification*]
WOOF-FM ... Dothan, AL [*FM radio station call letters*]
WOOG ...... Kissimmee, FL [*FM radio station call letters*]
Wool. .... Woolworth's United States Circuit Court Reports [*A publication*]   (DLA)
Wool CC .... Woolworth's United States Circuit Court Reports (Miller's Decisions) [*A publication*]   (DLA)
Woolf Adult ... Woolf on Adulterations [*1874*] [*A publication*]   (DLA)
Wool Int ..... Woolsey's Introduction to Study of International Law [*6th ed.*] [*1888*] [*A publication*]   (DLA)
Woolr Cert ... Woolrych's Certificates [*1826*] [*A publication*]   (DLA)
Woolr Com ... Woolrych's Rights of Common [*2nd ed.*] [*1850*] [*A publication*]   (DLA)
Woolr Cr L ... Woolrych's Criminal Law [*1862*] [*A publication*]   (DLA)
Wool Rec. .... Wool Record [*A publication*]
Wool Rec. .... Wool Record and Textile World [*A publication*]
Wool Rec Text World ... Wool Record and Textile World [*A publication*]
Woolr LW ... Woolrych's Law of Waters [*2nd ed.*] [*1851*] [*A publication*]   (DLA)
Woolr PW ... Woolrych's Party Walls [*1845*] [*A publication*]   (DLA)
Woolr Sew ... Woolrych's Sewert [*3rd ed.*] [*1864*] [*A publication*]   (DLA)
Woolr Waters ... Woolrych's Law of Waters [*A publication*]   (DLA)
Woolr Ways ... Woolrych's Law of Ways [*2nd ed.*] [*1847*] [*A publication*]   (DLA)
Woolr Wind L ... Woolrych's Window Lights [*2nd ed.*] [*1864*] [*A publication*]   (DLA)
Wool Sci Rev ... Wool Science Review [*A publication*]
Woolsey Polit Science ... Woolsey's Political Science [*A publication*]   (DLA)
Wools Int L ... Woolsey's Introduction to Study of International Law [*6th ed.*] [*1888*] [*A publication*]   (DLA)
Wools Pol Science ... Woolsey's Political Science [*A publication*]   (DLA)
Wool Tech ... Wool Technology [*A publication*]
Wool Tech ... Wool Technology and Sheep Breeding [*A publication*]   (APTA)
Wool Technol ... Wool Technology [*A publication*]   (APTA)
Wool Technol ... Wool Technology and Sheep Breeding [*A publication*]   (APTA)
Wool Technol Sheep Breed ... Wool Technology and Sheep Breeding [*A publication*]
Wool Technol (Syd) ... Wool Technology (Sydney) [*A publication*]   (APTA)
Wool Tech & Sheep ... Wool Technology and Sheep Breeding [*A publication*]   (APTA)
Wool Tech & Sheep Breeding ... Wool Technology and Sheep Breeding [*A publication*]   (APTA)
Woolw .... Woolworth's Reports [*1 Nebraska*] [*A publication*]   (DLA)
Woolw .... Woolworth's United States Circuit Court Reports [*A publication*]   (DLA)
Woolwld ..... Woolworld [*New Zealand*] [*A publication*]
Woolworth ... Woolworth's United States Circuit Court Reports [*A publication*]   (DLA)
Woolworth's Cir Ct R ... Woolworth's United States Circuit Court Reports [*A publication*]   (DLA)
Woolw Rep ... Woolworth's Reports [*1 Nebraska*] [*A publication*]   (DLA)
Woolw Rep ... Woolworth's United States Circuit Court Reports [*A publication*]   (DLA)
WOOMB. ... World Organization of the Ovulation Method - Billings, USA [*Later, Families of the Americas Foundation*]
WOOO ...... Shelbyville, IN [*AM radio station call letters*]
Woopie .... Well-Off Older Person [*Lifestyle classification*]
Woo Sok Univ Med J ... Woo Sok University. Medical Journal [*A publication*]
WOOW ..... Greenville, NC [*AM radio station call letters*]
WOOZ-FM ... Harrisburg, IL [*FM radio station call letters*]
WOP .... War on Poverty   (OICC)
WOP .... Wing Outer Panel [*Aviation*]
WOP .... Wireless Operator [*RAF slang*] [*World War II*]
WOP .... Without Passport [*Stamped on papers of turn-of-the-century immigrants who were arriving to work in specific factories or on railroad gangs. A high percentage of these immigrants were Italian, and the designation eventually became a derogatory term for members of that nationality. Alternate theories hold that the term means "Works on Pavement" or that it derived from the Spanish "guapo" through the Sicilian "guappo," a tough, brave man*]
WOP .... Without Payment

W/O/P .... Without Penalty
WOP .... Without Personnel
WOP .... Without Preference [*Rating*]
WOP .... Without Priorities
WOP .... World Oil Project [*National Science Foundation*] [*Massachusetts Institute of Technology*]   (IID)
WOPA .... Chicago, IL [*AM radio station call letters*]
WOPA .... War Overtime Pay Act [*1943*]
W O PAR. .. Without Partition [*Freight*]
WOPC .... World Oceanographic Data Processing and Services Center   (MSC)
WOPD .... Warrant Officer Professional Development [*Military*]   (MCD)
WOPE .... Without Personnel and Equipment
Wo Peo. ...... Work and People [*A publication*]
WOPHA. .... Woman Physician [*A publication*]
WOPI .... Bristol, TN [*AM radio station call letters*]
WOPOP .... WOPOP: Working Papers on Photography [*A publication*]   (APTA)
WOPP .... Opp, AL [*AM radio station call letters*]
WOPR .... Oak Park, MI [*FM radio station call letters*]
WOPR .... War Operation Plan Response [*Pronounced "whopper"*] [*Name of NORAD computer in film "WarGames"*]
WOQ .... Wave Officers' Quarters
WOQI .... Ponce, PR [*FM radio station call letters*]
WOQT .... Warrant Officer Qualification Test [*Military*]
WOR. .... New York, NY [*AM radio station call letters*]
WOR. .... Water-Oil Ratio
WOR. .... Wearout Rate   (SAA)
WOR. .... White and Orange [*Buoy*]
WOR. .... White Owners Register   (EA)
WOR. .... Wool Record and Textile World [*A publication*]
WOR. .... Worcester [*Massachusetts*] [*Seismograph station code, US Geological Survey*] [*Closed*]   (SEIS)
WOR. .... Work Order Register   (MCD)
WOR. .... Work Order Release   (MCD)
WOR. .... Work Order Request
WOR. .... Work Outline Retrieval   (MCD)
WoR. .... World Review [*A publication*]
Wor .... Worldview [*A publication*]
WOR. .... Worshipful
WOR. .... Worthen Banking Corp. [*AMEX symbol*]   (SPSG)
WORA .... Mayaguez, PR [*AM radio station call letters*]
WORAM. ... Word-Oriented Random Access Memory [*Data processing*]   (MCD)
WORA-TV ... Mayaguez, PR [*Television station call letters*]
WORB .... Farmington Hills, MI [*FM radio station call letters*]
WORBAT ... Wartime Order of Battle   (NATG)
Wor Bib Leg ... Worrall's Bibliotheca Legum [*A publication*]   (DLA)
WORC .... Washington Operations Research Council   (MCD)
WORC .... Worcester, MA [*AM radio station call letters*]
WORC .... Worcestershire [*County in England*]
Worcest Dict ... Worcester's Dictionary [*A publication*]   (DLA)
Worcester... Worcester's Dictionary of the English Language [*A publication*]   (DLA)
Worcester Med News ... Worcester Medical News [*Massachusetts*] [*A publication*]
Worcester Mus Ann ... Worcester, Massachusetts. Worcester Art Museum. Annual [*A publication*]
Worcester Mus N Bul ... Worcester, Massachusetts. Worcester Art Museum. News Bulletin and Calendar [*A publication*]
Worc M ...... Worcester Magazine [*A publication*]
WORCS. .... Worcestershire [*County in England*]
WORCS. .... Work Ordering and Reporting Communication System [*Army*]
WORD. ...... Pittsburgh, PA [*FM radio station call letters*]
WORD. ...... Spartanburg, SC [*AM radio station call letters*]
WORD. ...... Wind Oriented Rapid [*or Rocket*] Deployment   (MCD)
Wor Dict .... Worcester's Dictionary [*A publication*]   (DLA)
Word and Inf Process ... Word and Information Processing [*A publication*]
Word Proc ... Word Processing and Information Systems [*A publication*]
Word Process Comput Inf Systems ... Word Processing Computer Information Systems [*A publication*]
Word Process and Inf Syst ... Word Processing and Information Systems [*A publication*]
Word Process Now ... Word Processing Now [*A publication*]
Word Process Syst ... Word Processing Systems [*A publication*]
Word Process World ... Word Processing World [*A publication*]
WordsC. ...... Wordsworth Circle [*A publication*]
Words Elect ... Wordsworth's Law of Elections [*6th ed.*] [*1868*] [*A publication*]   (DLA)
Words Elect Cas ... Wordsworth's Election Cases [*England*] [*A publication*]   (DLA)
Words JS. ... Wordsworth's Law of Joint-Stock Companies [*A publication*]   (DLA)
Words Min ... Wordsworth's Law of Mining [*A publication*]   (DLA)
Words Pat ... Wordsworth's Law of Patents [*A publication*]   (DLA)
Words Ry & C ... Wordsworth's Railway and Canal Companies [*A publication*]   (DLA)
Wordsworth ... Wordsworth Circle [*A publication*]
Word W ..... Word Watching [*A publication*]
WORG. ...... Elloree, SC [*FM radio station call letters*]
WORI .... World Order Research Institute

WORK....... Barre, VT [*FM radio station call letters*]
WORKD.... Worklife [*A publication*]
Work-Environ-Health ... Work-Environment-Health [*A publication*]
WORKHO ... Workhouse [*British*] (ROG)
Working Papers ... Working Papers for a New Society [*A publication*]
Workmen's Comp L Rep ... Workmen's Compensation Law Reporter [*Commerce Clearing House*] [*A publication*] (DLA)
Workmen's Comp L Rep CCH ... Workmen's Compensation Law Reports. Commerce Clearing House [*A publication*]
Workmen's Comp L Rev ... Workmen's Compensation Law Review [*A publication*] (DLA)
Work Pap Aust Arid Zone Res Conf ... Working Papers. Australian Arid Zone Research Conference [*A publication*] (APTA)
Work Pap Aust Cereal Pasture Plant Breed Conf ... Working Papers. Australian Cereal and Pasture Plant Breeding Conference [*A publication*] (APTA)
Work Pap Bur Meteorol ... Working Paper. Bureau of Meteorology [*A publication*] (APTA)
Work Papers ... Working Papers Magazine [*A publication*]
Work Pap Giannini Found Agric Econ Calif Agric Exp Stn ... Working Paper. Giannini Foundation of Agricultural Economics. California Agricultural Experiment Station [*A publication*]
Work Pap Lang Linguist ... Working Papers in Language and Linguistics [*A publication*] (APTA)
Work Pap Ling (H) ... Working Papers in Linguistics (Honolulu) [*A publication*]
Work Pap New Soc ... Working Papers for a New Society [*A publication*]
Work Plant Maint ... Work and Plant Maintenance [*A publication*]
Work Prog ... Work in Progress [*A publication*]
Work Rel Abstr ... Work Related Abstracts [*A publication*]
Work Relat Abstr ... Work Related Abstracts [*A publication*]
Works Courts ... Works on Courts and Their Jurisdiction [*A publication*] (DLA)
Works Eng ... Works Engineering [*England*] [*A publication*]
Works Eng Fact Serv ... Works Engineering and Factory Services [*A publication*]
Workshop Conf Hoechst ... Workshop Conferences Hoechst [*A publication*]
Workshop Ser Pharmacol Sect Nat Inst Ment Health ... Workshop Series. Pharmacology Section. National Institute of Mental Health [*A publication*]
Works Inst Higher Nerv Act Acad Sci USSR Pathophysiol Ser ... Works. Institute of Higher Nervous Activity. Academy of Sciences of the USSR. Pathophysiological Series [*A publication*]
Works Inst Higher Nerv Act Acad Sci USSR Physiol Ser ... Works. Institute of Higher Nervous Activity. Academy of Sciences of the USSR. Physiological Series [*A publication*]
Works Inst Higher Nerv Act Pathophysiol Ser ... Works. Institute of Higher Nervous Activity. Pathophysiological Series [*A publication*]
Works Inst Higher Nerv Act Physiol Ser ... Works. Institute of Higher Nervous Activity. Physiological Series [*A publication*]
Works Pavlov Inst Physiol Acad Sci USSR ... Works. Pavlov Institute of Physiology. Academy of Sciences of the USSR [*A publication*]
Works and Plant Maint ... Works and Plant Maintenance [*A publication*]
Works Pr ... Works' Practice, Pleading, and Forms [*A publication*] (DLA)
Work Stud Abstr ... Work Study and O and M Abstracts [*A publication*]
Work Study and Manage Serv ... Work Study and Management Services [*Later, Management Services*] [*A publication*]
Work Vang ... Workers Vanguard [*A publication*]
Work Wom ... Working Woman [*A publication*]
WORL....... Christmas, FL [*AM radio station call letters*]
WORL....... Worlco, Inc. [*NASDAQ symbol*] (NQ)
World........ National Geographic World [*A publication*]
World........ World Magazine [*A publication*]
World A ..... World Archaeology [*A publication*]
World Aff... World Affairs [*A publication*]
World Affairs J ... World Affairs. Journal [*A publication*]
World Aff Q ... World Affairs. Quarterly [*A publication*]
World Ag ... World Agriculture [*A publication*]
World Agr ... World Agriculture [*A publication*]
World Agric ... World Agriculture [*A publication*]
World Agric Econ ... World Agricultural Economics and Rural Sociology Abstracts [*A publication*]
World Agri Econ & Rural Sociol Abstr ... World Agricultural Economics and Rural Sociology Abstracts [*A publication*]
World Alum Abstr ... World Aluminum Abstracts [*A publication*]
World Anim Rev ... World Animal Review [*A publication*]
World Anthropol ... World Anthropology [*A publication*]
World Archa ... World Archaeology [*A publication*]
World Archaeol ... World Archaeology [*A publication*]
World Assn for Adult Ed B ... World Association for Adult Education. Bulletin [*A publication*]
World Bibl Social Security ... World Bibliography of Social Security [*A publication*]
World Bus W ... World Business Weekly [*A publication*]
World Cem ... World Cement [*London*] [*A publication*]
World Cem Technol ... World Cement Technology [*Later, World Cement*] [*A publication*]
World Commod Rep Met Ed ... World Commodity Report. Metals Edition [*A publication*]

World Conf Earthquake Eng Proc ... World Conference on Earthquake Engineering. Proceedings [*A publication*]
World Constr ... World Construction [*A publication*]
World Crops Prod Util Descr ... World Crops Production Utilization Description [*A publication*]
World Dev ... World Development [*Oxford*] [*A publication*]
World Devel ... World Development [*A publication*]
WORLDDIDAC ... World Association of Manufacturers and Distributors of Educational Materials (EAIO)
World Dist ... World Distribution [*A publication*]
World Dredging & Mar Const ... World Dredging and Marine Construction [*A publication*]
World Dredging Mar Constr ... World Dredging and Marine Construction [*A publication*]
World Econ ... World Economy [*England*] [*A publication*]
World Eco S ... World Economic Survey. Supplement [*A publication*]
World Educ Rep ... World Education Reports [*A publication*]
World Energy Conf Trans ... World Energy Conference. Transactions [*A publication*]
World Farm ... World Farming [*A publication*]
World Fertil Surv Ctry Rep ... World Fertility Survey. Country Reports [*A publication*]
World Fertil Surv Sci Rep ... World Fertility Survey. Scientific Reports [*A publication*]
World Fert Surv ... World Fertility Survey [*A publication*]
World Fish Abstr ... World Fisheries Abstracts [*A publication*]
World For Ser Bull ... World Forestry Series. Bulletin [*A publication*]
World Health Organ Chron ... World Health Organization. Chronicle [*A publication*]
World Health Organ Tech Rep Ser ... World Health Organization. Technical Report Series [*A publication*]
World Health Stat Q ... World Health Statistics. Quarterly [*A publication*]
World Health Stat Rep ... World Health Statistics. Report [*A publication*]
World Highw ... World Highways [*A publication*]
World Hosp ... World Hospitals [*A publication*]
World Ir Nurs ... World of Irish Nursing [*A publication*]
World Jnl Trib ... World Journal Tribune [*Defunct New York City afternoon newspaper*] [*A publication*]
World J Surg ... World Journal of Surgery [*A publication*]
World J Urol ... World Journal of Urology [*A publication*]
World Jus ... World Justice [*A publication*]
World List Pub Stds ... Worldwide List of Published Standards [*A publication*]
World Lit T ... World Literature Today [*A publication*]
World Lit Today ... World Literature Today [*A publication*]
World L Rev ... World Law Review [*A publication*] (DLA)
World M .... World of Music [*A publication*]
World Marxist R ... World Marxist Review [*A publication*]
World Marx R ... World Marxist Review [*A publication*]
World Med ... World Medicine [*A publication*]
World Med Electron ... World Medical Electronics [*England*] [*A publication*]
World Med Instrum ... World Medical Instrumentation [*England*] [*A publication*]
World Med J ... World Medical Journal [*A publication*]
World Meet Outside US Can ... World Meetings: Outside United States and Canada [*A publication*]
World Meet Outs US Can ... World Meetings: Outside United States and Canada [*A publication*]
World Meet US Can ... World Meetings: United States and Canada [*A publication*]
World Metal Statis ... World Metal Statistics [*A publication*]
World Meteorol Organ Bull ... World Meteorological Organization. Bulletin [*A publication*]
World Meteorol Organ Publ ... World Meteorological Organization. Publications [*A publication*]
World Min ... World Mining [*A publication*]
World Min Equip ... World Mining Equipment [*A publication*]
World Miner Met ... World Minerals and Metals [*A publication*]
World Miner Stat ... World Mineral Statistics [*A publication*]
World Min US Ed ... World Mining. United States Edition [*A publication*]
World Mus ... World of Music [*A publication*]
World Neurol ... World Neurology [*A publication*]
World O ..... World Order [*A publication*]
World Obstet Gynecol ... World of Obstetrics and Gynecology [*Japan*] [*A publication*]
World Oil... World Oil Forecast. Review Issue [*A publication*]
World Outl ... World Outlook [*A publication*]
World Patent Inf ... World Patent Information [*A publication*]
World Pet... World Petroleum [*A publication*]
World Pet Cong Prepr ... World Petroleum Congress. Preprints [*A publication*]
World Pet Congr Proc ... World Petroleum Congress. Proceedings [*A publication*]
World Petrol ... World Petroleum [*A publication*]
World Pol... World Policy [*A publication*]
World Pol... World Politics [*A publication*]
World Poult ... World's Poultry Science Journal [*A publication*]
World Poultry Sci J ... World's Poultry Science Journal [*A publication*]
World Press R ... World Press Review [*A publication*]
World R ..... World Review [*A publication*]
World Refrig ... World Refrigeration [*England*] [*A publication*]

World Rep ... World Report [*A publication*]
World Resour ... World Resources [*A publication*]
World Rev ... World Review [*A publication*]
World Rev Anim Prod ... World Review of Animal Production [*A publication*]
World Rev Nutr Diet ... World Review of Nutrition and Dietetics [*A publication*]
World Rev Pest Contr ... World Review of Pest Control [*A publication*]
World Rev Pest Control ... World Review of Pest Control [*A publication*]
World R Pest Control ... World Review of Pest Control [*A publication*]
WORLDS ... Western Ohio Regional Library Development System [*Library network*]
World's Butter Rev ... World's Butter Review [*A publication*]
World Sci News ... World Science News [*India*] [*A publication*]
World's Pap Trade Rev ... World's Paper Trade Review [*A publication*]
World's Poultry Cong Conf Papers Sect C ... World's Poultry Congress. Conference Papers. Section C [*A publication*]
World's Poultry Sci J ... World's Poultry Science Journal [*A publication*]
World's Poult Sci J ... World's Poultry Science Journal [*A publication*]
World Steel (Jpn) ... World of Steel (Japan) [*A publication*]
World Steel Metalwork Export Man ... World Steel and Metalworking Export Manual [*A publication*]
World Surface Coat Abs ... World Surface Coatings Abstracts [*A publication*]
World Surf Coat ... World Surface Coatings Abstracts [*A publication*]
World Surf Coat Abstr ... World Surface Coatings Abstracts [*A publication*]
World Surv ... World Survey [*A publication*]
World Text Abstr ... World Textile Abstracts [*A publication*]
World Textile Abs ... World Textile Abstracts [*A publication*]
World Textile Abstr ... World Textile Abstracts [*A publication*]
World Trade LJ ... World Trade Law Journal [*A publication*] (DLA)
Worldwatch Pap ... Worldwatch Paper [*A publication*]
WorldWIDE ... World Women in the Environment [*Formerly, World Women in Defense of the Environment*] (EA)
Worldwide Abstr ... Worldwide Abstracts [*A publication*]
Worldwide List Published Stand ... Worldwide List of Published Standards [*A publication*]
World-Wide MinAbs ... World-Wide Mining Abstracts [*A publication*]
Worldwide Nucl Power ... Worldwide Nuclear Power [*A publication*]
World Yr Bk Ed ... World Yearbook of Education [*A publication*]
WORM ...... Earthworm, Inc. [*NASDAQ symbol*] (NQ)
WORM ...... Savannah, TN [*AM radio station call letters*]
Worm .... White, Older Rich Man [*Lifestyle classification*]
WORM ...... Write Once, Read Mainly [*or Many Times, or Mostly*] [*Data processing*]
WORM ...... Write-One Read Memory
WORM-FM ... Savannah, TN [*FM radio station call letters*]
Worm R ..... Wormwood Review [*A publication*]
Worm Runner's Dig ... Worm Runner's Digest [*A publication*]
WORMS ... Warrant Officer Personnel Management System [*Army*]
WORMS ... World Organization to Restore Male Supremacy (EA)
WORN ...... Write Once, Read Never [*Data processing*]
WORO ...... Corozal, PR [*FM radio station call letters*]
WORO ...... Weapons Operations Research Office
WOROM ... Write-Only Read-Only Memory [*Data processing*] (MDG)
WORP ...... Word Processing [*Data processing*] (DCTA)
Wor Pol ...... World Politics [*A publication*]
WORQ ...... Green Bay, WI [*FM radio station call letters*]
WORR ...... Quebradillas, PR [*AM radio station call letters*]
Wor R .... World Review [*A publication*] (APTA)
WORSAMS ... Worldwide Organizational Structure for Army Medical Support (AABC)
WORSE9 ... World Resources [*A publication*]
WORT ...... Madison, WI [*FM radio station call letters*]
WORTAC ... Westinghouse Overall RADAR Tester and Calibrator
Worth Jur .. Worthington's Power of Juries [*1825*] [*A publication*] (DLA)
WORTHN ... Worthen Banking Corp. [*Associated Press abbreviation*] (APAG)
Worth Prec Wills ... Worthington's General Precedent for Wills [*5th ed.*] [*1852*] [*A publication*] (DLA)
Worth Star T ... Fort Worth Star-Telegram [*A publication*]
Wort Wahr ... Wort und Wahrheit [*A publication*]
WORV ...... Hattiesburg, MS [*AM radio station call letters*]
WORW ...... Port Huron, MI [*FM radio station call letters*]
WORX ...... Madison, IN [*AM radio station call letters*]
WORX-FM ... Madison, IN [*FM radio station call letters*]
WOS .... Web Offset Section [*Later, WOA*] (EA)
WOS .... Wilson Ornithological Society (EA)
WOS .... Winchester Financial [*Vancouver Stock Exchange symbol*]
WOS .... Wonders of the Spaceways [*A publication*]
WOS .... Worcester [*British depot code*]
WOSA ...... Windows Open Services Architecture [*Microsoft Corp.*] (PCM)
WOSA ...... Workers' Organization for Socialist Action [*South Africa*] [*Political party*] (EY)
WOSAC .... Worldwide Synchronization of Atomic Clocks
WOSB ...... Irondequoit, NY [*FM radio station call letters*]
WOSB ...... War Office Selection Board [*British*]
WOSB ...... Weather Observation Site Building (AABC)
WOSC ...... Western Oregon State College
WOSC ...... World Organisation of Systems and Cybernetics (EAIO)
WOSD ...... Weapons Operational Systems Development [*NORAD*]
WOSF .... Work Order Status File (MCD)

WOsh .... Oshkosh Public Library, Oshkosh, WI [*Library symbol*] [*Library of Congress*] (LCLS)
WOSH ...... Oshkosh, WI [*AM radio station call letters*]
WOshM ..... Mercy Hospital, Nursing Library, Oshkosh, WI [*Library symbol*] [*Library of Congress*] (LCLS)
WOshM-M ... Mercy Medical Center, Medical Library, Oshkosh, WI [*Library symbol*] [*Library of Congress*] (LCLS)
WOshU ..... University of Wisconsin-Oshkosh, Oshkosh, WI [*Library symbol*] [*Library of Congress*] (LCLS)
WOSIC ...... Watchmakers of Switzerland Information Center (EA)
WOSL ...... Women's Overseas Service League (EA)
WOSM ...... Ocean Springs, MS [*FM radio station call letters*]
WOSO ...... San Juan, PR [*AM radio station call letters*]
WOSS ...... Ossining, NY [*FM radio station call letters*]
WOSSU ..... Women on Stamps Study Unit [*American Topical Association*] (EA)
WOST ...... Block Island, RI [*Television station call letters*]
WOST ...... World's Oldest Socketed Tool [*A copper implement made around 2500BC and possibly used for digging or chopping. It was discovered in 1966 at Non Nok Tha, Thailand, by archeologist Donn Bayard*]
WOSU ...... Columbus, OH [*AM radio station call letters*]
WOSU-FM ... Columbus, OH [*FM radio station call letters*]
WOSUS ..... Wang Office Systems User Society (CSR)
WOSU-TV ... Columbus, OH [*Television station call letters*]
WOSV ...... Mansfield, OH [*FM radio station call letters*]
WOSX ...... Spencer, WI [*FM radio station call letters*]
WOT .... Wide-Open Throttle
WOT .... Worlds of Tomorrow [*A publication*]
WOTA ...... Vicksburg, MS [*AM radio station call letters*]
WOTB ...... Middletown, RI [*FM radio station call letters*]
WOTB ...... Welfare of the Blind (EA)
WOTCU ..... Wave-Off and Transition Control Unit
WOTD ...... Winamac, IN [*FM radio station call letters*]
WOTF ...... Writers of the Future [*Science fiction writing award*]
WOTHDJ ... Women and Therapy [*A publication*]
WOTJ .... Morehead City, NC [*FM radio station call letters*]
WOTL ...... Toledo, OH [*FM radio station call letters*]
WOTO ...... Women on Their Own [*An association*] (EA)
WOTP ...... World Organization of the Teaching Professions [*Switzerland*]
WOTP ...... World Organization of the Teaching Professions [*Switzerland*]
WOTR ...... Wolf Trap Farm Park [*National Park Service designation*]
WOTRAC ... Woods Hole Oceanographic Institution. Technical Report [*A publication*]
WOTS ...... Mitchell, IN [*FM radio station call letters*]
WOTS ...... Warrant Officer Training System [*Military*] (INF)
WOTS ...... Water Operations Technical Support [*US Army Corps of Engineers*]
WOTS ...... Wide-Open Throttle Switch [*Automotive engineering*]
WOTT ...... Wolves on the Track [*A group of philanderers looking for girls*] [*Slang*]
WOTTCS .. Warrant Officer Technical and Tactical Certification System [*Army*]
Wott Leg Wal ... Wotton. Leges Wallicae [*A publication*] (DLA)
WOTV ...... Grand Rapids, MI [*Television station call letters*]
WOU .... Women's Outpatient Unit (AAMN)
WOU .... Work Opportunities Unlimited
WOUB ...... Athens, OH [*AM radio station call letters*]
WOUB-FM ... Athens, OH [*FM radio station call letters*]
WOUB-TV ... Athens, OH [*Television station call letters*]
WOUC ...... Cambridge, OH [*FM radio station call letters*]
WOUC-TV ... Cambridge, OH [*Television station call letters*]
WOUI .... Chicago, IL [*FM radio station call letters*]
WOUL ...... Ironton, OH [*FM radio station call letters*]
WOUR ...... Utica, NY [*FM radio station call letters*]
WOV .... Warren & Ouachita Valley Railway Co. [*AAR code*]
WOV .... Wolverine Technologies, Inc. [*NYSE symbol*] (SPSG)
WOVI .... Novi, MI [*FM radio station call letters*]
WOVK ...... Wheeling, WV [*FM radio station call letters*]
WOVV ...... Fort Pierce, FL [*FM radio station call letters*]
WOW .... Omaha, NE [*AM radio station call letters*]
WOW .... Waiting on Weather [*Ocean storms*]
WOW .... War on Want [*An association*] (EAIO)
WOW .... War on Waste [*Navy*]
WOW .... War on Words
WOW .... Washington Opportunities for Women
WOW .... Weight-on-Wheels (NASA)
WOW .... Wereld in Ontwikkeling. Veertiendaags Overzicht van Tijdschriftartikelen en Rapporten over Problemen van de Ontwikkelingsgebieden [*A publication*]
WOW .... Wider Opportunities for Women (EA)
WOW .... Woman Ordnance Worker
WOW .... Women Our Wonders [*Antifeminist men's group*]
WOW .... Women on Wheels (EA)
WOW .... Women on Wine (EA)
WOW .... Woodmen of the World (EA)
WOW .... Word on the Way
WOW .... World of Winners [*A publication*]
WOW .... World of Winners [*A publication*]
WOW .... World of Work [*Career-oriented course of study*]
WOW .... Worlds of Wonder [*Electronic toy manufacturer*]

WOW	....	Worldwide Equities Ltd. [*Toronto Stock Exchange symbol*]
WOW	....	Worn-Out Wolf [*An aging philanderer*] [*Slang*]
WOW	....	Worst-on-Worst
Wow	....	Wort und Wahrheit [*A publication*]
WOW	....	Written Order of Withdrawal [*Banking*]
WO-WA	...	Work Order-Work Authorization (SSD)
WoWa	....	Wort und Wahrheit [*A publication*]
WOWAR	...	Work Order and Work Accomplishment Record
WOWATE	...	World War II Equivalent [*Three-year and eight-month unit of time measurement proposed by former Under Secretary of the Navy R. James Woolsey*]
WOWB	......	Little Falls, NY [*FM radio station call letters*]
WOWBDG	...	Instytut Zootechniki w Polsce Wyniki Oceny Wartosci Hodowlanej Buhajow [*A publication*]
WOWE	......	Vassar, MI [*FM radio station call letters*]
WOW-FM	...	Omaha, NE [*FM radio station call letters*]
WOWI	......	Norfolk, VA [*FM radio station call letters*]
WOWI	......	Women on Words and Images (EA)
WOWI	......	Worlds of Wonder, Inc. [*Fremont, CA*] [*NASDAQ symbol*] (NQ)
W & O Wills	...	Wilgram and O'Hara on Wills [*A publication*] (DLA)
WOWK	......	Huntington, WV [*Television station call letters*]
WOWL	......	Florence, AL [*Television station call letters*]
WOWLON	...	Weight-on-Wheels Lock-On [*NASA*] (NASA)
WOWN	.....	Shawano, WI [*FM radio station call letters*]
WOWN	.....	Without Winch
WOWO	.....	Fort Wayne, IN [*AM radio station call letters*]
WOWO	.....	Huntington, IN [*FM radio station call letters*]
WOWQ	.....	DuBois, PA [*FM radio station call letters*]
WOWS	.....	Wire Obstacle Warning System (IEEE)
WOWS	......	Women Ordnance Workers [*A national voluntary organization*] [*World War II*]
WOWT	......	Omaha, NE [*Television station call letters*]
WOWW	.....	Pensacola, FL [*FM radio station call letters*]
WOXD	......	Oxford, MS [*FM radio station call letters*]
WOXO	....	Norway, ME [*FM radio station call letters*]
WOXR	......	Oxford, AL [*AM radio station call letters*]
WOXY	......	Oxford, OH [*FM radio station call letters*]
WOYE	......	Mayaguez, PR [*FM radio station call letters*]
WOYK	......	York, PA [*AM radio station call letters*]
WOYL	......	Oil City, PA [*AM radio station call letters*]
WOYL	......	Women of the Year Luncheon [*British*] (DI)
WOYS	......	Apalachicola, FL [*FM radio station call letters*]
WOZI	......	Presque Isle, ME [*FM radio station call letters*]
WOZK	......	Ozark, AL [*AM radio station call letters*]
WOZN	......	Key West, FL [*FM radio station call letters*]
WOZQ	......	Northampton, MA [*FM radio station call letters*]
WOZZ	....	New London, WI [*FM radio station call letters*]
WP	....	Empresa de Aviacion Aeronaves del Peru [*ICAO designator*] (FAAC)
WP	....	Pakistan Law Reports, West Pakistan Series [*A publication*] (DLA)
WP	....	Portage Free Public Library, Portage, WI [*Library symbol*] [*Library of Congress*] (LCLS)
WP	....	Waiting Period (OICC)
WP	....	Waiver of Premium [*Insurance*]
WP	....	Waman Puma [*A publication*]
WP	....	War and Peace Foundation (EA)
WP	....	War Plans
WP	....	Warm Pipe [*Nuclear energy*] (NRCH)
WP	....	Warming Pan [*Refers to a clergyman holding a job under a bond of resignation*] [*Obsolete*] [*Slang*] [*British*] (DSUE)
WP	....	Warsaw Pact (NATG)
WP	....	Washington Post [*A publication*]
WP	....	Waste Pipe [*Technical drawings*]
WP	....	Wastepaper
WP	....	Water Packed
WP	....	Water Plane (MSA)
WP	....	Water Point
WP	....	Water Propeller (AAG)
WP	....	Water Pump (AAG)
WP	....	Waterproof
WP	....	Way-Point
WP	....	We the People [*Later, WPU*] (EA)
WP	....	Weakly Positive (MAE)
WP	....	Weapons Power
WP	....	Weather Permitting
WP	....	Weatherproof
WP	....	Weekly Premium [*Insurance*]
WP	....	Weight Penalty
WP	....	Welding Procedure [*Nuclear energy*] (NRCH)
WP	....	Wespercorp [*AMEX symbol*] (SPSG)
WP	....	West Point
WP	....	[*The*] Western Pacific Railroad Co. [*AAR code*]
WP	....	Western Pine [*Utility pole*] [*Telecommunications*] (TEL)
WP	....	Wet Pack [*Medicine*] (AAMN)
WP	....	Wet Process (MSA)
WP	....	Wettable Powder
WP	....	Wheel of Progress (EA)
WP	....	Whirlpool [*Medicine*]
WP	....	White Painted (BJA)

WP	....	White Paper (ADA)
WP	....	White Phosphorus [*Military*]
WP	....	Wide Pore [*Chromatography*]
WP	....	Wiedza Powszechna [*A publication*]
WP	....	Wild Pitch [*Baseball*]
WP	....	Will Proceed To
WP	....	Will Proved [*Legal*] [*British*] (ROG)
WP	....	Windfall Profit
WP	....	Winning Pitcher [*Baseball*]
WP	....	Wire Payment
WP	....	Withdrawn Passing [*Education*] (WGA)
WP	....	Without Prejudice
WP	....	Wolfe Pack (EA)
WP	....	Wolseley Pattern [*British military*] (DMA)
W and P	.....	Women and Performance [*A publication*]
WP	....	Wood Pattern (MSA)
WP	....	Woodstock Papers [*A publication*]
WP	....	Word Processing [*Movement to improve secretarial/clerical function through a managed system of people, procedures, and modern office equipment*]
WP	....	Word Processor (ADA)
WP	....	Word Punch
WP	....	Work Package (NASA)
W/P	....	Work Picture [*or Print*] [*Cinematography*]
WP	....	Work Procedure [*Nuclear energy*] (NRCH)
WP	....	Work Program (NATG)
WP	....	Work in Progress [*A publication*]
WP	....	Worker's Party [*Ireland*] [*Political party*]
WP	....	Working Paper
WP	....	Working Party
WP	....	Working Point
WP	....	Working Pressure
WP	....	World Peacemakers (EA)
WP	....	World Petroleum [*A publication*]
WP	....	World Politics [*A publication*]
WP	....	World Priorities (EA)
WP	....	Worship
WP	....	Worthy Patriarch
WP	....	Wrist Pitch (MCD)
WP	....	Write Protect
WP	....	Writers for Peace (EA)
WP3	....	Working Party Three [*Economic Policy Committee of the Organization for Economic Cooperation and Development*]
WPA	....	Wagner-Peyser Act [*1933*] (OICC)
WPA	....	Water Jet Propulsion Assembly (MCD)
WPA	....	Water Pump Assembly
WPA	....	Webb-Pomerene Act [*1918*]
WPA	....	Western Pine Association [*Later, WWPA*] (EA)
WPA	....	Western Pistachio Association (EA)
WPA	....	Western Provident Association [*British*] (DI)
WPA	....	Western Psychological Association (MCD)
WPA	....	Wet-Process Phosphoric Acid [*Fertilizer*]
WPA	....	Wheelchair Pilots Association (EA)
WPA	....	Whiskey Painters of America (EA)
WPA	....	William Penn Association [*Pittsburgh, PA*] (EA)
WPA	....	With Particular Average
WPA	....	Women's Prison Association (EA)
WPA	....	Woody Point [*Australia*] [*Seismograph station code, US Geological Survey*] [*Closed*] (SEIS)
WPA	....	Work Package Action (MCD)
WPA	....	Work Package Address (MCD)
WPA	....	Working People's Alliance [*Guyana*] (PD)
WPA	....	Works Progress Administration [*Created, 1935, to operate public works projects for unemployed persons; name changed to Work Projects Administration, 1939; later, absorbed by Federal Works Agency, which was terminated in 1942*]
WPA	....	Workshop of the Players Art [*New York City*]
WPA	....	World Parliament Association
WPA	....	World Pheasant Association [*Reading, Berkshire, England*] (EAIO)
WPA	....	World Presbyterian Alliance
WPA	....	World Press Archives [*A publication*]
WPA	....	World Psychiatric Association [*Copenhagen, Denmark*] (EAIO)
WPA	....	Worst Possible Accident [*Nuclear safety*]
WPAA	....	Andover, MA [*FM radio station call letters*]
WPAAS	.....	Word Processing and Administrative Support System [*Data processing*] (HGAA)
WPAB	....	Ponce, PR [*AM radio station call letters*]
WPAB	....	Word Processing Aptitude Battery [*Test*]
WPAB	....	Word Processor Assessment Battery [*Selection and placement test*]
WPAC	....	Ogdensburg, NY [*FM radio station call letters*]
WPAC	....	Walden Pond Advisory Committee (EA)
WPAC	....	Working Program Advisory Committee [*DoD*]
WPAD	....	Paducah, KY [*AM radio station call letters*]
WPAFB	.....	Wright-Patterson Air Force Base [*Ohio*]
W PA Hist Mag	...	Western Pennsylvania Historical Magazine [*A publication*]

WPAK .... Farmville, VA [*AM radio station call letters*]
W Pakistan J Agr Res ... West Pakistan Journal of Agricultural Research [*A publication*]
WPAL....... Charleston, SC [*AM radio station call letters*]
WPAM ...... Pottsville, PA [*AM radio station call letters*]
WPAN ...... Fort Walton Beach, FL [*Television station call letters*]
WPAP .... Panama City, FL [*FM radio station call letters*]
WPAQ .... Mount Airy, NC [*AM radio station call letters*]
WPAQ ...... Westra Preschool Assessment Questionnaire
WPAR .... Hickory, NC [*FM radio station call letters*]
W PAR....... With Partition [*Freight*]
WP/AS ...... Word Processing/Administrative Support [*Extension of Word Processing*]
WPAS....... Zephyrhills, FL [*AM radio station call letters*]
WPAT....... Atauro [*East Timor*] [*ICAO location identifier*] (ICLI)
WPAT....... Paterson, NJ [*AM radio station call letters*]
WPAT....... Wolfe Programming Aptitude Test
WPATC.... Western Pennsylvania Advanced Technology Center [*Research center*] (RCD)
WPAT-FM ... Paterson, NJ [*FM radio station call letters*]
WPA-USA ... World Pheasant Association of the USA (EA)
WPAW ...... Pawley's Island, SC [*FM radio station call letters*]
WPAWA ... World Professional Armwrestling Association (EA)
WPAX .... Thomasville, GA [*AM radio station call letters*]
WPAY .... Portsmouth, OH [*AM radio station call letters*]
WPAY-FM ... Portsmouth, OH [*FM radio station call letters*]
WPAZ....... Pottstown, PA [*AM radio station call letters*]
WPB .... Gunboat [*Coast Guard*] (NVT)
WPB .... Port Berge [*Madagascar*] [*Airport symbol*] (OAG)
WPB .... Wall Plate Box
WPB .... War Production Board [*World War II*]
WPB .... Waste Processing Building [*Nuclear energy*] (NRCH)
WPB .... Wastepaper Basket [*or Bin*]
WPB .... Whirlpool Bath [*Medicine*]
WPB .... Wide Pulse Blanking (MCD)
WPB .... Wiener Enterprises, Inc. [*AMEX symbol*] (SPSG)
WPB .... World Peace Brigade (EA)
WPB .... Write Printer Binary
WPBA....... Atlanta, GA [*Television station call letters*]
WPBA....... Women Professional Bowlers Association (EA)
WPBA....... Women's Professional Billiard Alliance (EA)
WPBC....... Bangor, ME [*FM radio station call letters*]
WPBC....... Western Pacific Base Command [*Marianas*] [*World War II*]
WPBCWS ... Waste Processing Building Chilled Water System [*Nuclear energy*] (NRCH)
WPBE....... Conyers, GA [*AM radio station call letters*]
WPBEF ..... West Pakistan Bank Employees' Federation
WPBF .... Tequesta, FL [*Television station call letters*]
WPBG .... West Palm Beach, FL [*AM radio station call letters*]
WPBI .... Martinsville, VA [*FM radio station call letters*]
WPBIC ...... Walker Problem Behavior Identification Checklist [*Education*]
WPBK....... Whitehall, MI [*AM radio station call letters*]
WPBK-FM ... Whitehall, MI [*FM radio station call letters*]
WPBL........ Women's Professional Basketball League [*Defunct*] (EA)
WPBN .... Traverse City, MI [*Television station call letters*]
WPBO ...... Portsmouth, OH [*Television station call letters*]
WPBR....... Palm Beach, FL [*AM radio station call letters*]
WPBRL ..... Warsaw Pact/Ballistic Research Laboratory (MCD)
WPBT .... Miami, FL [*Television station call letters*]
WPBX....... Southampton, NY [*FM radio station call letters*]
WPBY....... Huntington, WV [*Television station call letters*]
WPC .... Walter P. Chrysler Club (EA)
WPC .... War Pensions Committee [*British military*] (DMA)
WPC .... Warrior Preparation Center [*Kaiserslautern, Federal Republic of Germany*] [*USAREUR*]
WPC .... Warsaw Pact Countries (MCD)
WPC .... Washington Press Club [*Formerly, WNPC*]
WPC .... Waste Product Costs [*Solid waste management*]
WPC .... Water Pollution Control
WPC .... Watts per Candle [*Electricity*]
WPC .... Webster's Patent Cases [*1601-1855*] [*A publication*] (DLA)
WPC .... Wedge Power Clamp
WPC .... Weldable Printed Circuit
WPC .... Wheat Protein Concentrate [*Food technology*]
WPC .... Whey Protein Concentrate [*Food technology*]
WPC .... William Penn College [*Oskaloosa, IA*]
WPC .... William Peterson College of New Jersey
WPC .... Wired Program Computer
WPC .... Wollaston's English Bail Court Reports, Practice Cases [*A publication*] (DLA)
WPC .... Woman Police Constable [*Scotland Yard*]
WPC .... Women's Political Caucus
WPC .... Wood-Plastic Combination [*or Composite*]
WPC .... Word Processing Center
WPC .... Work Package Concept (MCD)
WP + C..... Work Planning and Control [*Data processing*]
WPC .... Workers Party of Canada
WPC .... World Peace Congress
WPC .... World Peace Council [*See also CMP*] (EAIO)
WPC .... World Petroleum Congresses - a Forum for Petroleum Science, Technology, Economics, and Management (EAIO)

WPC .... World Philatelic Congress of Holy Land, Israel, and Judaica Societies (EA)
WPC .... World Planning Chart [*Aviation*]
WPC .... World Pooling Committee (MCD)
WPC .... World Power Conference [*Later, WEC*]
WPC .... World Print Council (EA)
WPC .... World Pumpkin Confederation (EA)
WPCA ...... Water Pollution Control Administration [*Department of the Interior*]
WPCA ...... Wool Pullers Council of America (EA)
WPCAA..... White Park Cattle Association of America (EA)
WP Cas..... Webster's Patent Cases [*1601-1855*] [*A publication*] (DLA)
WP Cas...... Wollaston's English Bail Court Reports, Practice Cases [*A publication*] (DLA)
WPCB....... Greensburg, PA [*Television station call letters*]
WPCB........ Western Pennsylvania Christian Broadcasting Co. [*A cable TV station*]
WPCC....... Clinton, SC [*AM radio station call letters*]
WPCC....... Wilson Pharmaceutical & Chemical Corp.
WPCC....... World Paper Currency Collectors (EA)
WPCC....... WPC [*Walter P. Chrysler*] Club (EA)
WPCC....... Wright-Patterson Contracting Center [*Ohio*] [*Air Force*]
WPCD....... Champaign, IL [*FM radio station call letters*]
WPCE....... Portsmouth, VA [*AM radio station call letters*]
WPCF....... Panama City Beach, FL [*AM radio station call letters*]
WPCF....... Water Pollution Control Federation (EA)
WPCF....... Water Pollution Control Federation. Journal [*A publication*]
WPCF-FM ... Panama City Beach, FL [*FM radio station call letters*]
WPCF Highlights ... Water Pollution Control Federation. Highlights [*A publication*]
WPCFJ...... Water Pollution Control Federation. Journal [*A publication*]
WPCH .... Atlanta, GA [*FM radio station call letters*]
WPCHLIJS ... World Philatelic Congress of Holy Land, Israel, and Judaica Societies (EA)
WPCI........ Greenville, SC [*AM radio station call letters*]
WPCJ........ Pittsford, MI [*FM radio station call letters*]
WPCM....... Burlington, NC [*FM radio station call letters*]
WPCN .... Mount Pocono, PA [*AM radio station call letters*]
WPCND .... Women's Patriotic Conference on National Defense (EA)
WPCO .... Mount Vernon, IN [*AM radio station call letters*]
WPCO .... Whiting Petroleum Corp. [*Denver, CO*] [*NASDAQ symbol*] (NQ)
WPCR....... Plymouth, NH [*FM radio station call letters*]
WPCR....... Water Pollution Control Research [*Environmental Protection Agency*]
WPCS........ Pensacola, FL [*FM radio station call letters*]
WPCSA..... Welsh Pony and Cob Society of America (EA)
WPCT....... Danville, VA [*Television station call letters*]
WPCV....... Winter Haven, FL [*FM radio station call letters*]
WPCX....... Auburn, NY [*FM radio station call letters*]
WPD......... War Plan Division [*World War II*]
WPD......... Water Planning Division [*Environmental Protection Agency*] (EPA)
WPD......... Western Procurement Division [*Marine Corps*]
WPD......... Work Package Description [*NASA*] (NASA)
WPD......... World Pharmaceuticals Directory [*A publication*]
WPD......... Write Printer Decimal
WPDA....... Jeffersonville, NY [*FM radio station call letters*]
WPDA....... Writing Pushdown Acceptor
WPDB....... Suai [*East Timor*] [*ICAO location identifier*] (ICLI)
WPDC....... Elizabethtown, PA [*AM radio station call letters*]
W/PDC...... Workers'/People's Defence Committee [*Political party*] [*Ghana*]
WPDE .... Florence, SC [*Television station call letters*]
WPDES..... Waste Pollution Discharge Elimination System (IEEE)
WPDH....... Poughkeepsie, NY [*FM radio station call letters*]
WPDJ....... Huntington, IN [*AM radio station call letters*]
WPDL....... Dili [*East Timor*] [*ICAO location identifier*] (ICLI)
WPDM....... Potsdam, NY [*AM radio station call letters*]
WP/DP...... Word Processing/Data Processing System (HGAA)
WPDQ....... Jacksonville, FL [*AM radio station call letters*]
WPDR....... Portage, WI [*AM radio station call letters*]
WPDS....... Beverly Hills, FL [*FM radio station call letters*]
WPDX....... Clarksburg, WV [*AM radio station call letters*]
WPDX ...... Word Processing Document Exchange Program
WPDX-FM ... Clarksburg, WV [*FM radio station call letters*]
WPE .... West Pittston-Exeter Railroad Co. [*AAR code*]
WPE .... Western Pacific Energy [*Vancouver Stock Exchange symbol*]
WPE .... Western Plastics Exposition [*HBJ Expositions and Conferences*] (TSPED)
WPE .... Work and People [*A publication*]
WPEA....... Exeter, NH [*FM radio station call letters*]
WPEB....... Philadelphia, PA [*FM radio station call letters*]
WPEC....... Baucau [*East Timor*] [*ICAO location identifier*] (ICLI)
WPEC....... Weapons Production Engineering Center [*Navy*]
WPEC....... West Palm Beach, FL [*Television station call letters*]
WPEC....... World Plan Executive Council [*Later, WGAE-US*] (EA)
WPEG....... Concord, NC [*FM radio station call letters*]
WPEH....... Louisville, GA [*AM radio station call letters*]
WPEH-FM ... Louisville, GA [*FM radio station call letters*]
WPEL........ Montrose, PA [*AM radio station call letters*]

WPEL-FM ... Montrose, PA [*FM radio station call letters*]
WPEN .... Philadelphia, PA [*AM radio station call letters*]
WPen .... West Penn Power Co. [*Associated Press abbreviation*]   (APAG)
WPEO .... Peoria, IL [*AM radio station call letters*]
WPEP .... Taunton, MA [*AM radio station call letters*]
WPES .... Ashland, VA [*AM radio station call letters*]
WPET .... Greensboro, NC [*AM radio station call letters*]
WPET .... Western Petroleum Corp. [*NASDAQ symbol*]   (NQ)
W Petro 2000 ... World Petroleum Availability 1980-2000 [*A publication*]
WPeW .... Waukesha County Technical Institute, Pewaukee, WI [*Library symbol*] [*Library of Congress*]   (LCLS)
WPEX .... Hampton, VA [*AM radio station call letters*]
WPEZ .... Macon, GA [*FM radio station call letters*]
WPF .... War and Peace Foundation   (EA)
WPF .... War Production Fund [*World War II*]
WPF .... Watcor Purification Systems, Inc. [*Vancouver Stock Exchange symbol*]
WPF .... Weather Profile Facility
WPF .... Weight, Power, Fulcrum
WPF .... Whale Protection Fund   (EA)
WPF .... Wirtschaftspruefung [*A publication*]
WPF .... Work Process Flow [*NASA*]   (NASA)
WPF .... World Peace Foundation   (EA)
WPF .... World Prohibition Federation
WPF .... Worldwide Pen Friends   (EA)
WPFA .... William Penn Fraternal Association [*Later, WPA*]   (EA)
WPFB .... Middletown, OH [*AM radio station call letters*]
WPFB-FM ... Middletown, OH [*FM radio station call letters*]
WPFC .... Commission for Fisheries Research in the West Pacific
WPFC .... Waterproof Fan Cooled   (MSA)
WPFC .... Westbeth Playwrights Feminist Collective [*Defunct*]   (EA)
WPFC .... William Perry Fan Club   (EA)
WPFC .... World Press Freedom Committee   (EA)
WPFD .... Fairview, TN [*AM radio station call letters*]
WPFDM .... Working Papers. Fondazione Dalle Molle [*A publication*]
WPFE .... Ogdensburg, NY [*FM radio station call letters*]
WPFF .... Sturgeon Bay, WI [*FM radio station call letters*]
WPFILD.... West Point Fellowship in Leader Development [*US Military Academy*]   (INF)
WPFL .... Fuiloro [*East Timor*] [*ICAO location identifier*]   (ICLI)
WPFL .... West Pakistan Federation of Labor
WPFL .... Winter Park, FL [*FM radio station call letters*]
WPFL .... Worshipful   (ROG)
WPFM .... Panama City, FL [*FM radio station call letters*]
WPFM .... Wiping Form   (AAG)
WPFMC.... Western Pacific Fishery Management Council [*National Oceanic and Atmospheric Administration*]   (GFGA)
WPFR .... Terre Haute, IN [*FM radio station call letters*]
WPFTA ..... White Plate Flat Trackers Association   (EA)
WPFUL..... Worshipful
WPFW .... Washington, DC [*FM radio station call letters*]
WPG .... Waterproofing   (AAG)
WPG .... Weighted Pair Group
WPG .... West Point Graduate
WPG .... Wiping   (MSA)
WPG .... Worcester Polytechnic Institute, Worcester, MA [*OCLC symbol*]   (OCLC)
WPG .... Work Package Grouping [*NASA*]   (NASA)
WPGA .... Perry, GA [*AM radio station call letters*]
WPGA-FM ... Perry, GA [*FM radio station call letters*]
WPGA-TV ... Perry, GA [*Television station call letters*]
WPGB .... Blountville, TN [*FM radio station call letters*]
WPGC .... Morningside, MD [*AM radio station call letters*]
WPGC-FM ... Morningside, MD [*FM radio station call letters*]
WPGD .... Hendersonville, TN [*Television station call letters*]
WPGH .... Pittsburgh, PA [*Television station call letters*]
WPGI .... Western Publishing Group, Inc. [*New York, NY*] [*NASDAQ symbol*]   (NQ)
WPGM ...... Danville, PA [*AM radio station call letters*]
WPGM-FM ... Danville, PA [*FM radio station call letters*]
WPGR .... Philadelphia, PA [*AM radio station call letters*]
WPGS .... Mims, FL [*AM radio station call letters*]
WPGT .... Group Fore - Women's Pro Golf Tour   (EA)
WPGT .... Roanoke Rapids, NC [*FM radio station call letters*]
WPGU .... Urbana, IL [*FM radio station call letters*]
WPGW ...... Portland, IN [*AM radio station call letters*]
WPGW-FM ... Portland, IN [*FM radio station call letters*]
WPGX .... Panama City, FL [*Television station call letters*]
W & PH ..... Wage and Purchase Hire
WPH .... West Pit [*Hawaii*] [*Seismograph station code, US Geological Survey*] [*Closed*]   (SEIS)
WPH .... William Penn House   (EA)
WPH .... WPL Holdings [*NYSE symbol*]   (SPSG)
WPHB .... Philipsburg, PA [*AM radio station call letters*]
WPHB-FM ... Philipsburg, PA [*FM radio station call letters*]
WPHC .... Waverly, TN [*AM radio station call letters*]
WPHD .... Tioga, PA [*FM radio station call letters*]
WPHE .... Phoenixville, PA [*AM radio station call letters*]
WPHG .... Exmore, VA [*FM radio station call letters*]
WPHI .... Western Pennsylvania Horological Institute
WPHK .... Blountstown, FL [*FM radio station call letters*]

WPHL .... Philadelphia, PA [*Television station call letters*]
WPHM ...... Port Huron, MI [*AM radio station call letters*]
WPHM ...... Western Pennsylvania Historical Magazine [*A publication*]
WPHN ...... Gaylord, MI [*FM radio station call letters*]
WPHOA.... Women Public Health Officer's Association [*British*]
WPHP .... Wheeling, WV [*FM radio station call letters*]
WPHQ ...... Bloomer, WI [*FM radio station call letters*]
WPHR .... Cleveland, OH [*FM radio station call letters*]
WPHS .... Warren, MI [*FM radio station call letters*]
WPHUJ .... Working Papers. Hebrew University of Jerusalem [*A publication*]
WPI .... Wall Paper Institute [*Later, Wallcovering Manufacturers Association*]   (EA)
WPI .... Waxed Paper Institute [*Later, FPA*]   (EA)
WPI .... Wedding Photographers International   (EA)
WPI .... West Pride Industry [*Vancouver Stock Exchange symbol*]
WPI .... Western Personality Inventory [*Psychology*]
WPI .... Western Personnel Institute   (AEBS)
WPI .... Whey Products Institute [*Later, ADPI*]   (EA)
WPI .... Wholesale Price Index [*Economics*]
WPI .... Women and Priests Involved   (EA)
WPI .... Women's Peace Initiative   (EA)
WPI .... Worcester Polytechnic Institute [*Massachusetts*]
WPI .... Work Process Indicator   (NASA)
WPI .... Work Progress Indicator [*NASA*]   (NASA)
WPI .... World Patents Index [*Derwent Publications Ltd.*] [*Database*]
WPI .... World Peace One [*An association*]   (EA)
WPI .... World Policy Institute   (EA)
WPI .... World Press Institute   (EA)
WPIB .... Salem, VA [*FM radio station call letters*]
WPIC .... Sharon, PA [*AM radio station call letters*]
WPIC .... Water Port Identifier Code
WPIC .... Western Psychiatric Institute and Clinic [*University of Pittsburgh*] [*Research center*]   (RCD)
WPID .... Piedmont, AL [*AM radio station call letters*]
WPIE .... Trumansburg, NY [*AM radio station call letters*]
WPIG .... Olean, NY [*FM radio station call letters*]
WPIK .... Summerland Key, FL [*FM radio station call letters*]
WPINDEX ... Wholesale Price Index [*Data File*]
WPIO .... Titusville, FL [*FM radio station call letters*]
WPIP .... Winston-Salem, NC [*AM radio station call letters*]
WPIR .... Bluefield, WV [*FM radio station call letters*]
WP/IS .... Word Processing and Information Systems [*A publication*]
WPIT .... Pittsburgh, PA [*AM radio station call letters*]
WPIT-FM ... Pittsburgh, PA [*FM radio station call letters*]
WPIX .... New York, NY [*Television station call letters*]
WPJ .... Weakened Plane Joint
WPJ .... Workers' Party of Jamaica [*Political party*]   (EY)
WPJB .... Narragansett Pier, RI [*FM radio station call letters*]
WPJC .... Adjuntas, PR [*AM radio station call letters*]
WPJJ .... Jackson, MS [*Television station call letters*]
WPJK .... Orangeburg, SC [*AM radio station call letters*]
WPJL .... Raleigh, NC [*AM radio station call letters*]
WPJM ...... Greer, SC [*AM radio station call letters*]
WPJS .... Conway, SC [*AM radio station call letters*]
WPJV .... Willard, OH [*FM radio station call letters*]
WPK .... Air-Lift Associates, Inc. [*Morrisville, NC*] [*FAA designator*]   (FAAC)
WPK .... Winpak Ltd. [*Toronto Stock Exchange symbol*]
WPKE .... Pikeville, KY [*AM radio station call letters*]
WPKM ...... Scarborough, ME [*FM radio station call letters*]
WPKN ...... Bridgeport, CT [*FM radio station call letters*]
WPKO ...... Bellefontaine, OH [*FM radio station call letters*]
WPKR .... Waupun, WI [*FM radio station call letters*]
WPKT .... Meriden, CT [*FM radio station call letters*]
WPKX .... Enfield, CT [*FM radio station call letters*]
WPKY .... Princeton, KY [*AM radio station call letters*]
WPKY-FM ... Princeton, KY [*FM radio station call letters*]
WPKZ .... Elkton, VA [*FM radio station call letters*]
WPL .... War Plan, Long-Range   (CINC)
WPL .... Warren Public Library, Warren, OH [*OCLC symbol*]   (OCLC)
WPL .... Waste Pickle Liquor [*Industrial waste*]
WPL .... Wave Propagation Laboratory [*Boulder, CO*] [*National Oceanic and Atmospheric Administration*]
WPL .... Winnipeg Public Library [*UTLAS symbol*]
WPL .... Working Papers in Linguistics [*A publication*]
WPL .... Worshipful
WPL .... Worst Path Loss
WPlaU....... University of Wisconsin-Platteville, Platteville, WI [*Library symbol*] [*Library of Congress*]   (LCLS)
WPLB .... Greenville, MI [*AM radio station call letters*]
WPLC .... Spotsylvania, VA [*FM radio station call letters*]
WPLG .... Miami, FL [*Television station call letters*]
WPLH .... Tifton, GA [*AM radio station call letters*]
WPL H ...... WPL Holdings [*Associated Press abbreviation*]   (APAG)
WPLJ .... New York, NY [*FM radio station call letters*]
WPLJ .... White Port and Lemon Juice [*Title of both song and drink*]
WPLK .... Palatka, FL [*AM radio station call letters*]
WPLM....... Plymouth, MA [*AM radio station call letters*]
WPLM-FM ... Plymouth, MA [*FM radio station call letters*]
WPLN .... Nashville, TN [*FM radio station call letters*]

WPLO .... Grayson, GA [*AM radio station call letters*]
WPLO .... Water Port Liaison Office [*or Officer*] [*Air Force*]   (AFM)
WPLR .... New Haven, CT [*FM radio station call letters*]
WPLS .... Greenville, SC [*FM radio station call letters*]
WPLS .... Western Plains Library System [*Library network*]
WPLT .... Plattsburgh, NY [*FM radio station call letters*]
WPLTO ...... Western Plateau [*FAA*]   (FAAC)
WPLU .... Working Papers. Lund University. Department of Linguistics [*A publication*]
WPLUH .... Working Papers in Linguistics (University of Hawaii) [*A publication*]
WPLV .... West Point, GA [*AM radio station call letters*]
WPLW .... Carnegie, PA [*AM radio station call letters*]
WPLX .... Collierville, TN [*AM radio station call letters*]
WPLY .... Plymouth, WI [*AM radio station call letters*]
WPlyM ...... Mission House Theological Seminary, Plymouth, WI [*Library symbol*] [*Library of Congress*]   (LCLS)
WPLZ .... Petersburg, VA [*FM radio station call letters*]
WPM .... War Plan, Mid-Range
WPM .... War Planning Memorandum   (NATG)
WPM .... Waterproof Membrane
WPM .... West Point-Pepperell, Inc. [*NYSE symbol*]   (SPSG)
WPM .... Western Premium [*Vancouver Stock Exchange symbol*]
WPM .... White Pine [*Michigan*] [*Seismograph station code, US Geological Survey*]   (SEIS)
WPM .... Wipim [*Papua New Guinea*] [*Airport symbol*]   (OAG)
WPM .... Wire-Wound Porous Material
WPM .... Wood Plastic Material
WPM .... Words per Minute
WPM .... Work Package Management   (MCD)
WPM .... World Presbyterian Missions   (EA)
WPM .... Write Program Memory [*Data processing*]
WPM .... Write Protect Memory
WPMA ...... Waterproof Paper Manufacturers Association [*Later, API*]
WPMA ...... Windows/Presentation Manager Association   (EA)
WPMA ...... Wood Products Manufacturers Association   (EA)
WPMA ...... Writing Paper Manufacturers Association [*Later, API*]   (EA)
WPMB ...... Vandalia, IL [*AM radio station call letters*]
WPMC ...... Jellico, TN [*Television station call letters*]
WPMC ...... Waxed Paper Merchandising Council [*Defunct*]
WPMCP .... Work Package Manpower and Cost Plan [*NASA*]   (NASA)
WPME ...... Women for Peace in the Middle East   (EA)
WPMH ...... Portsmouth, VA [*AM radio station call letters*]
WPMI .... Mobile, AL [*Television station call letters*]
WPMN ...... Maliana [*East Timor*] [*ICAO location identifier*]   (ICLI)
WPMR ...... Tobyhanna, PA [*FM radio station call letters*]
WPMRR.... Work Package Milestone Progress Report   (MCD)
WPMT ...... York, PA [*Television station call letters*]
WPMW .... Mullens, WV [*FM radio station call letters*]
WPMX ...... Tupelo, MS [*AM radio station call letters*]
WPN .... Weapon   (AAG)
WPN .... Weapons Procurement, Navy   (NVT)
WPN .... Wolverhampton [*British depot code*]
WPN .... Write Punch [*Data processing*]   (MCD)
WPNA ...... Oak Park, IL [*AM radio station call letters*]
WPNA ...... World Proof Numismatic Association   (EA)
WPNC .... Plymouth, NC [*AM radio station call letters*]
WPNC-FM ... Plymouth, NC [*FM radio station call letters*]
WPNE ...... Green Bay, WI [*Television station call letters*]
WPNE-FM ... Green Bay, WI [*FM radio station call letters*]
WPNF........ Brevard, NC [*AM radio station call letters*]
WPNFPT .. Weapon Fly-to-Point   (NVT)
WPNGL .... Workpapers in Papua New Guinea Languages [*A publication*]
WPNH....... Plymouth, NH [*AM radio station call letters*]
WPNH-FM ... Plymouth, NH [*FM radio station call letters*]
WPNI .... Kentland, IN [*FM radio station call letters*]
WPNL .... Clinton, IN [*FM radio station call letters*]
WPNN....... Gorham, ME [*AM radio station call letters*]
WPNR ...... Utica, NY [*FM radio station call letters*]
WPNR .... Weekblad voor Privaatrecht, Notariaat, en Registratie [*A publication*]
WPNSTA.. Weapons Station
WPNT ...... Chicago, IL [*AM radio station call letters*]
WPNT-FM ... Chicago, IL [*FM radio station call letters*]
WPNTS..... War Plan Naval Transportation Service
WPNX ...... Phenix City, AL [*AM radio station call letters*]
WPO .... War Plan Orange [*World War II*]
WPO .... Warsaw Pact Organization   (MCD)
WPO .... Washington Post Co. Class B [*NYSE symbol*]   (SPSG)
WPO .... Water for Peace Office [*Department of State*]
WPO .... Water Programs Office [*Environmental Protection Agency*]
WPO .... West Pacific Ocean   (SAA)
WPO .... World Packaging Organization [*See also OME*] [*Paris, France*]   (EAIO)
WPO .... World Ploughing Organisation [*Carlisle, Cumbria, England*]   (EAIO)
WPOA ...... Western Pacific Orthopaedic Association   (EA)
WPOB-FM ... Plainview, NY [*FM radio station call letters*]
WPOC .... Baltimore, MD [*FM radio station call letters*]
WPOC .... Oecussi [*East Timor*] [*ICAO location identifier*]   (ICLI)
WPOC .... Water and Pollution Control [*A publication*]

WPOCA .... Water Pollution Control [*Maidstone, England*] [*A publication*]
WPoCC...... ICA [*International Co-Operative Alliance*] Working Party on Co-Operative Communications   (EAIO)
WPoCP ...... ICA [*International Co-Operative Alliance*] Working Party on Co-Operative Press [*Later, WPoCC*]   (EAIO)
WPOD...... Water Port of Debarkation   (AFM)
WPOE ...... Water Port of Embarkation   (AFM)
WPOG ...... Willard Pease Oil & Gas Co. [*NASDAQ symbol*]   (NQ)
WPOK ...... Pontiac, IL [*AM radio station call letters*]
W Pol Q ... Western Political Quarterly [*A publication*]
WPOM...... Riviera Beach, FL [*AM radio station call letters*]
WPON ...... Pontiac, MI [*AM radio station call letters*]
WPOP ...... Hartford, CT [*AM radio station call letters*]
WPOR ...... Portland, ME [*AM radio station call letters*]
WPOR-FM ... Portland, ME [*FM radio station call letters*]
WPOS....... Holland, OH [*FM radio station call letters*]
WP/OS...... Word Processing/Office Systems   (HGAA)
WPOW ...... Miami, FL [*FM radio station call letters*]
WPP.......... UCLA [*University of California at Los Angeles*] Working Papers in Phonetics [*A publication*]
WPP.......... Wage Pause Program [*Business term*]   (ADA)
WPP.......... Washington Promotion Plan [*FAA*]   (FAAC)
WPP.......... Water Pump Package   (NASA)
WPP.......... Waterproof Paper Packing
WPP.......... Weapon Position Preparation   (MCD)
WPP.......... Weapons Production Program
WPP.......... Web Printing Press
WPP.......... Weibull Probability Paper [*Statistics*]
WPP.......... Windward Passage Patrol [*Navy*]   (NVT)
WPP.......... Work Package Plan [*NASA*]   (NASA)
WPP.......... World Pen Pals   (EA)
WPP.......... Writing Proficiency Program [*Educational test*]
WPPA........ Pottsville, PA [*AM radio station call letters*]
WPPB........ Boca Raton, FL [*Television station call letters*]
WPPC....... Penuelas, PR [*AM radio station call letters*]
WPPC....... Warning Point Photocell
WPPC....... West Penn Power Co.
WPPC....... West Point Parents Club   (EA)
WPPD....... Whole-Powder-Pattern Decomposition [*Crystallography*]
WPPDA..... Welfare and Pension Plans Disclosure Act [*1958*] [*Department of Labor*]
WPPG........ WPP Group Ltd. [*NASDAQ symbol*]   (NQ)
WPPI .... Carrollton, GA [*AM radio station call letters*]
WPP/IS..... Writing Proficiency Program/Intermediate System [*Educational test*]
WPPL........ Blue Ridge, GA [*FM radio station call letters*]
WPPM....... Weight Part per Million
WPPO .... Wood Products Purchasing Office [*Defense Construction Supply Center*] [*Defense Supply Agency*]
WPPS........ Work Package Planning Sheet [*NASA*]   (NASA)
WPPSI....... Wechsler Preschool and Primary Scale of Intelligence [*Education*]
WPPSS...... Washington Public Power Supply System [*Nicknamed "Whoops"*]
WPPW....... Association of Western Pulp and Paper Workers
WPQ......... Western Political Quarterly [*A publication*]
WPQR .... Uniontown, PA [*FM radio station call letters*]
WPQR .... Welding Procedure Qualification Record [*Nuclear energy*]   (NRCH)
WPR .... Ward Pound Ridge [*New York*] [*Seismograph station code, US Geological Survey*]   (SEIS)
WPR .... Wartime Personnel Requirements   (NATG)
WPR .... Webster's Patent Reports [*England*] [*A publication*]   (DLA)
WPR .... Weekblad voor Privaatrecht, Notariaat, en Registratie [*A publication*]
WPR .... Weekly Pharmacy Reports: The Green Sheet [*A publication*]
WPR .... West Pakistan Railway
WPR .... White Puerto Rican
WPR .... Widescope Resources Ltd. [*Vancouver Stock Exchange symbol*]
WPR .... Witness Protection and Relocation [*Government agency in film "F/X"*]
WPR .... Woodpecker Repellent [*In company name, WPR Co.*]
WPR .... Working Party on Rationing [*Allied German Occupation Forces*]
WPR .... Working Pressure
WPRA ...... Mayaguez, PR [*AM radio station call letters*]
WPRA ...... Women's Professional Racquetball Association   (EA)
WPRA ...... Women's Professional Rodeo Association   (EA)
WPRB........ Princeton, NJ [*FM radio station call letters*]
WPRC........ Lincoln, IL [*AM radio station call letters*]
WPRCDZ ... International Conference on Water Pollution Research. Proceedings [*A publication*]
WPRD .... Winter Park, FL [*AM radio station call letters*]
WPRE........ Prairie du Chien, WI [*AM radio station call letters*]
WPRE-FM ... Prairie du Chien, WI [*FM radio station call letters*]
WPRG .... Bar Harbor, ME [*FM radio station call letters*]
WPRG .... Workers-Peasants Red Guards [*North Korea*]
WPRH....... Galax, VA [*FM radio station call letters*]
WPRI........ Providence, RI [*Television station call letters*]
WPRI........ Wartime Pacific Routing Instructions [*Navy*]
WPRK........ Winter Park, FL [*FM radio station call letters*]

WPRL........	Lorman, MS [*FM radio station call letters*]
WPRL........	Water Pollution Research Laboratory [*British*]
WPRM	San Juan, PR [*FM radio station call letters*]
WPRN	Butler, AL [*AM radio station call letters*]
WPRO	Providence, RI [*AM radio station call letters*]
WPRO-FM ...	Providence, RI [*FM radio station call letters*]
WPRP........	Ponce, PR [*AM radio station call letters*]
WPRR........	Altoona, PA [*FM radio station call letters*]
WPRS........	Paris, IL [*AM radio station call letters*]
WPRS........	War Powers Reporting System
WPRS........	Water and Power Resources Service [*Formerly, Bureau of Reclamation*] [*Department of the Interior*] [*Name changed back to Bureau of Reclamation, 1981*]
WPRS........	Wittenborn Psychiatric Rating Scale
WPRT........	Prestonsburg, KY [*AM radio station call letters*]
WPRV........	Fajardo, PR [*Television station call letters*]
WPRW	Manassas, VA [*AM radio station call letters*]
WPRY........	Perry, FL [*AM radio station call letters*]
WPRZ........	Warrenton, VA [*AM radio station call letters*]
WPS...........	International Association of Word Processing Specialists [*Formerly, NAWPS*] (EA)
WPS...........	War Plan, Short-Range
WPS...........	War Planning Slate (CINC)
WPS...........	Warner Publishing Services
WPS...........	Wartime Capability Play, Short Range (SAA)
WPS...........	Waste Processing System [*Nuclear energy*] (NRCH)
WPS...........	Water Phase Salt [*of smoked food*]
WPS...........	Water Pressure Switch
WPS...........	Water Purification System
WPS...........	Watermen's Protective Society [*A union*] [*British*]
WPS...........	Waterproof Shroud
WPS...........	Watts per Steradian
WPS...........	Wave Power Source
WPS...........	Waveform Processing System
WPS...........	Weapons Program Section
WPSL........	Welding Procedure Specification [*Nuclear energy*] (NRCH)
WPS...........	White Power Structure
WPS...........	Widowed Persons Service (EA)
WPS...........	Wind Power System
WPS...........	Windows Printing System [*Microsoft Corp.*] (PCM)
WPS...........	Wireless Preservation Society [*British*]
WPS...........	Wisconsin Physicians Service [*Army*]
WPS...........	Wisconsin Public Service Corp. [*NYSE symbol*] (SPSG)
WPS...........	With Prior Service
WPS...........	Women in Public Service (EA)
WPS...........	Word Processing System (BUR)
WPS...........	Words per Second
WPS...........	Workplace Shell [*IBM Corp.*] [*Data processing*] (PCM)
WPS...........	Workstation Publishing Software
WPS...........	World Photography Society (EA)
WPS...........	World Politics Simulation
WPS...........	World Population Society (EA)
WPS...........	Worldwide Plug and Socket [*Proposed standard electrical plug for international use*] [*Pronounced "whoops"*]
WPSA........	Paul Smith's, NY [*FM radio station call letters*]
WPSA........	Welsh Pony Society of America [*Later, WPCSA*] (EA)
WPSA........	World Professional Squash Association (EA)
WPSA........	World's Poultry Science Association [*See also AVI*] [*Celle, Federal Republic of Germany*] (EAIO)
WPSA........	World's Poultry Science Association, USA Branch (EA)
WPSC........	Pageland, SC [*AM radio station call letters*]
WPSC........	Shipping Control War Plan [*Navy*]
WPSC........	Wayne, NJ [*FM radio station call letters*]
WPSD........	Paducah, KY [*Television station call letters*]
WPSE........	Erie, PA [*AM radio station call letters*]
WPSI........	Word Processing Society, Inc. (EA)
WPSI........	World Poetry Society Intercontinental (EA)
WPSK........	Pulaski, VA [*FM radio station call letters*]
WPSL........	Port St. Lucie, FL [*AM radio station call letters*]
WPSL........	Western Primary Standard Laboratory
WPSM.......	Fort Walton Beach, FL [*FM radio station call letters*]
WPSM.......	Same [*East Timor*] [*ICAO location identifier*] (ICLI)
WPSO.......	New Port Richey, FL [*AM radio station call letters*]
WPSR........	Evansville, IN [*FM radio station call letters*]
WPSR........	Weekly Performance Status Report (MCD)
WPS-RA	World Pro Skiing-Racers Association [*Defunct*] (EA)
WPST........	Trenton, NJ [*FM radio station call letters*]
WPSU.......	State College, PA [*FM radio station call letters*]
WPSX.......	Clearfield, PA [*Television station call letters*]
WPT	Paper. European Journal for the Pulp, Paper, and Board Industries [*A publication*]
WP & T......	War Plans and Training
WPT	Waypoint (FAAC)
WPT	Western Personnel Tests [*General intelligence test*]
WPT	Windfall Profit Tax
WPT	With Promotion To (NOAA)
WPT	Wolfe Screening Test for Programming Aptitude
WPT	Word Processing Test
WPT	Workers' Party of Turkey
WPT	Working Point [*Technical drawings*]
WPTA........	Fort Wayne, IN [*Television station call letters*]

WPTA........	Wooden Pail and Tub Association
WPTB........	Statesboro, GA [*AM radio station call letters*]
WPTB........	Wartime Prices and Trade Board
WPTD........	Dayton, OH [*Television station call letters*]
WPTF	Durham, NC [*Television station call letters*]
WPTF	National Council for a World Peace Tax Fund (EA)
WPTF	Raleigh, NC [*AM radio station call letters*]
WPTG	West Point, VA [*FM radio station call letters*]
WPTH	Olney, IL [*FM radio station call letters*]
WPTI	Wildlife Preservation Trust International (EA)
WPTJ	Johnstown, PA [*Television station call letters*]
WPTL........	Canton, NC [*AM radio station call letters*]
WPTLC	World Peace through Law Center (EA)
WPTM	Roanoke Rapids, NC [*FM radio station call letters*]
WPTN	Cookeville, TN [*AM radio station call letters*]
WPTNG	Weapons Training (NVT)
WPTO	Oxford, OH [*Television station call letters*]
WPTR	Albany, NY [*AM radio station call letters*]
WPTR........	Wespac Investors Trust II [*NASDAQ symbol*] (NQ)
WPTS	Pittsburgh, PA [*FM radio station call letters*]
WPTT	Pittsburgh, PA [*Television station call letters*]
WPTV	West Palm Beach, FL [*Television station call letters*]
WPTW	Piqua, OH [*AM radio station call letters*]
WPTX........	Lexington Park, MD [*AM radio station call letters*]
WPTY	Memphis, TN [*Television station call letters*]
WPTZ........	North Pole, NY [*Television station call letters*]
WPU	We the People, United (EA)
WPU	With Power Unit (NATG)
WPU	Women's Protestant Union [*British*]
WPU	Write Punch [*Data processing*]
WPUB	Camden, SC [*FM radio station call letters*]
WPUC	Waste-Paper Utilization Council [*Defunct*]
W/PUG	Word Processing Users' Group
WPUL	South Daytona, FL [*AM radio station call letters*]
WPUM	Rensselaer, IN [*FM radio station call letters*]
WPUP	Royston, GA [*FM radio station call letters*]
WPUR	Americus, GA [*FM radio station call letters*]
WPUT	Brewster, NY [*AM radio station call letters*]
WPUV	Pulaski, VA [*AM radio station call letters*]
WPVA	Waynesboro, VA [*FM radio station call letters*]
WPVB.......	Culpeper, VA [*FM radio station call letters*]
WPVG	Funkstown, MD [*AM radio station call letters*]
WPVI........	Philadelphia, PA [*Television station call letters*]
WPVM	Howland, ME [*FM radio station call letters*]
WPVQ	Viqueque [*East Timor*] [*ICAO location identifier*] (ICLI)
WPVR.......	Roanoke, VA [*FM radio station call letters*]
WPW	Wolff-Parkinson-White [*Syndrome*] [*Cardiology*]
WPWB	Byron, GA [*FM radio station call letters*]
WPWC	Dumfries-Triangle, VA [*AM radio station call letters*]
WPWM	Wide Pulse Width Modulation
WPWOD...	Will Proceed Without Delay
WPWR	Gary, IN [*Television station call letters*]
WPWR	World-Wide Plantation Walker Registry (EA)
WPXC.......	Hyannis, MA [*FM radio station call letters*]
WPXI........	Pittsburgh, PA [*Television station call letters*]
WPXN	Paxton, IL [*FM radio station call letters*]
WPXR.......	Rock Island, IL [*FM radio station call letters*]
WPXT.......	Portland, ME [*Television station call letters*]
WPXY	Rochester, NY [*FM radio station call letters*]
WPXZ.......	Punxsutawney, PA [*FM radio station call letters*]
WPY	White Pass & Yukon Corp. Ltd. [*Toronto Stock Exchange symbol*] [*Vancouver Stock Exchange symbol*] [*AAR code*]
WPY	World Population Year [*1974*] [*United Nations*]
WPYB.......	Benson, NC [*AM radio station call letters*]
WPYEEJS ...	Working Papers in Yiddish and East European Jewish Studies [*A publication*]
WPYK.......	Dora, AL [*AM radio station call letters*]
WP&YR.....	White Pass & Yukon Railway [*Nickname: Wait Patiently and You'll Ride*]
WPYX.......	Albany, NY [*FM radio station call letters*]
WPZ	Waipapa Point [*New Zealand*] [*Seismograph station code, US Geological Survey*] [*Closed*] (SEIS)
WPZA.......	Ann Arbor, MI [*AM radio station call letters*]
WPZZ.......	Franklin, IN [*FM radio station call letters*]
WQ	Bahamas World Airlines Ltd. [*ICAO designator*] (FAAC)
WQ	Science Wonder Quarterly [*A publication*]
WQ	Water Quenching (OA)
WQ	Wilson Quarterly [*A publication*]
WQ	Wind Quarterly [*A publication*]
WQ	Wonder Stories Quarterly [*A publication*]
WQ	Wool Quarterly [*A publication*]
WQA.........	Water Quality Act (GFGA)
WQA.........	Water Quality Association (EA)
WQA.........	Weld Quality Assurance
WQAB	Philippi, WV [*FM radio station call letters*]
WQAD.......	Moline, IL [*Television station call letters*]
WQAI	Fernandina Beach, FL [*AM radio station call letters*]
WQAL.......	Cleveland, OH [*FM radio station call letters*]
WQAM......	Miami, FL [*AM radio station call letters*]
WQAQ.......	Hamden, CT [*FM radio station call letters*]
WQAU-P...	Water Quality Analysis Unit - Purification [*Army*]

WQB......... Water-Quality Biological [*Survey*] [*Army*]   (RDA)
WQBA....... Miami, FL [*AM radio station call letters*]
WQBA-FM ... Miami, FL [*FM radio station call letters*]
WQBB ...... Powell, TN [*AM radio station call letters*]
WQBC .... Vicksburg, MS [*AM radio station call letters*]
WQBE .... Charleston, WV [*AM radio station call letters*]
WQBE-FM ... Charleston, WV [*FM radio station call letters*]
WQBH...... Detroit, MI [*AM radio station call letters*]
WQBK....... Rensselaer, NY [*AM radio station call letters*]
WQBK-FM ... Rensselaer, NY [*FM radio station call letters*]
WQBN....... Temple Terrace, FL [*AM radio station call letters*]
WQBQ....... Leesburg, FL [*AM radio station call letters*]
WQBR .... Atlantic Beach, FL [*AM radio station call letters*]
WQBS .... San Juan, PR [*AM radio station call letters*]
WQBZ....... Fort Valley, GA [*FM radio station call letters*]
WQC.......... Quinsigamond Community College, Worcester, MA [*OCLC symbol*]   (OCLC)
WQC.......... Water Quality Certification [*Nuclear energy*]   (NRCH)
WQC.......... Wheat Quality Council   (EA)
WQCB .... Brewer, ME [*FM radio station call letters*]
WQCD .... New York, NY [*FM radio station call letters*]
WQCH ...... La Fayette, GA [*AM radio station call letters*]
WQCK .... Clinton, LA [*FM radio station call letters*]
WQCM...... Halfway, MD [*FM radio station call letters*]
WQCR .... Jackson, TN [*AM radio station call letters*]
WQCS .... Fort Pierce, FL [*FM radio station call letters*]
WQCT .... Bryan, OH [*AM radio station call letters*]
WQCY .... Quincy, IL [*FM radio station call letters*]
WQDK....... Ahoskie, NC [*FM radio station call letters*]
WQDQ ...... Lebanon, TN [*AM radio station call letters*]
WQDR....... Raleigh, NC [*FM radio station call letters*]
WQDW...... Kinston, NC [*AM radio station call letters*]
WQDY....... Calais, ME [*AM radio station call letters*]
WQDY-FM ... Calais, ME [*FM radio station call letters*]
WQEC....... Quincy, IL [*Television station call letters*]
WQEC/C... Weapons Quality Engineering Center, Crane [*Indiana*]
WQED....... Pittsburgh, PA [*Television station call letters*]
WQED-FM ... Pittsburgh, PA [*FM radio station call letters*]
WQEL....... Bucyrus, OH [*FM radio station call letters*]
WQEN....... Gadsden, AL [*FM radio station call letters*]
WQEQ....... Freeland, PA [*FM radio station call letters*]
WQEX .... Pittsburgh, PA [*Television station call letters*]
WQEZ....... Chillicothe, IL [*FM radio station call letters*]
WQF.......... Wider Quaker Fellowship   (EA)
WQFA .... Hudson, NY [*FM radio station call letters*]
WQFB .... Concord, NH [*FM radio station call letters*]
WQFE .... Brownsburg, IN [*FM radio station call letters*]
WQFL........ Rockford, IL [*FM radio station call letters*]
WQFM....... Milwaukee, WI [*FM radio station call letters*]
WQFS .... Greensboro, NC [*FM radio station call letters*]
WQFX .... Gulfport, MS [*AM radio station call letters*]
WQFX-FM ... Gulfport, MS [*FM radio station call letters*]
WQGL....... Butler, AL [*FM radio station call letters*]
WQGN ...... Groton, CT [*FM radio station call letters*]
WQHA ...... Aquada, PR [*Television station call letters*]
WQHC ...... Nashville, IL [*FM radio station call letters*]
WQHF....... Freehold Township, NJ [*FM radio station call letters*]
WQHG ...... Huntingdon, PA [*FM radio station call letters*]
WQHH...... De Witt, MI [*FM radio station call letters*]
WQHK ...... Fort Wayne, IN [*AM radio station call letters*]
WQHL........ Live Oak, FL [*AM radio station call letters*]
WQHL-FM ... Live Oak, FL [*FM radio station call letters*]
WQHM ..... McComb, MS [*Television station call letters*]
WQHN....... Spangler, PA [*FM radio station call letters*]
WQHQ ...... Ocean City-Salisbury, MD [*FM radio station call letters*]
WQHS....... Cleveland, OH [*Television station call letters*]
WQHT....... New York, NY [*FM radio station call letters*]
WQHY ...... Prestonsburg, KY [*FM radio station call letters*]
WQI.......... Water Quality Index
WQI.......... Water Quality Instrument
WQIC .... Meridian, MS [*AM radio station call letters*]
WQID....... Biloxi, MD [*AM radio station call letters*]
WQII .... San Juan, PR [*AM radio station call letters*]
WQIK .... Jacksonville, FL [*AM radio station call letters*]
WQIK-FM ... Jacksonville, FL [*FM radio station call letters*]
WQIN........ Lykens, PA [*AM radio station call letters*]
WQIO....... Mount Vernon, OH [*FM radio station call letters*]
WQIP .... Water Quality Incentive Program [*Department of Agriculture*]
WQIS........ Laurel, MS [*AM radio station call letters*]
WQIS........ Water Quality Indicator System [*Marine science*]   (GFGA)
WQIS........ Water Quality Insurance Syndicate   (EA)
WQIX .... Horseheads, NY [*FM radio station call letters*]
WQIZ .... St. George, SC [*AM radio station call letters*]
WQJU .... Mifflintown, PA [*FM radio station call letters*]
WQJY....... West Salem, WI [*FM radio station call letters*]
WQKC...... Seymour, IN [*AM radio station call letters*]
WQKI .... St. Matthews, SC [*AM radio station call letters*]
WQKK........ Metter, GA [*FM radio station call letters*]
WQKR ...... Portland, TN [*AM radio station call letters*]
WQKS ...... Hopkinsville, KY [*AM radio station call letters*]
WQKT .... Wooster, OH [*FM radio station call letters*]

WQKX....... Sunbury, PA [*FM radio station call letters*]
WQKY....... Emporium, PA [*FM radio station call letters*]
WQKZ....... Catskill, NY [*FM radio station call letters*]
WQLA .... La Follette, TN [*AM radio station call letters*]
WQLA-FM ... La Follette, TN [*FM radio station call letters*]
WQLC....... Watertown, FL [*FM radio station call letters*]
WQLH....... Green Bay, WI [*FM radio station call letters*]
WQLK .... Richmond, IN [*FM radio station call letters*]
WQLM....... Punta Gorda, FL [*FM radio station call letters*]
WQLN....... Erie, PA [*FM radio station call letters*]
WQLN-TV ... Erie, PA [*Television station call letters*]
WQLR....... Kalamazoo, MI [*FM radio station call letters*]
WQLS .... Ozark, AL [*FM radio station call letters*]
WQLT .... Florence, AL [*FM radio station call letters*]
WQLX .... Galion, OH [*FM radio station call letters*]
WQM........ University of Massachusetts, Medical Center, Worcester, MA [*OCLC symbol*]   (OCLC)
WQM........ Water Quality Management
WQMA....... Marks, MS [*AM radio station call letters*]
WQMC....... Sumter, SC [*AM radio station call letters*]
WQMD....... Water Quantity Measuring Device
WQME...... Anderson, IN [*FM radio station call letters*]
WQMF...... Jeffersonville, IN [*FM radio station call letters*]
WQMG...... Greensboro, NC [*AM radio station call letters*]
WQMG-FM ... Greensboro, NC [*FM radio station call letters*]
WQMP...... Water Quality Management Project
WQMR...... Federalsburg, MD [*FM radio station call letters*]
WQMT...... Chatsworth, GA [*FM radio station call letters*]
WQMU ..... Indiana, PA [*FM radio station call letters*]
WQMX...... Medina, OH [*FM radio station call letters*]
WQMZ....... Charlottesville, VA [*FM radio station call letters*]
WQNA....... Springfield, IL [*FM radio station call letters*]
WQNJ .... Ocean Acres, NJ [*FM radio station call letters*]
WQNS....... Waynesville, NC [*FM radio station call letters*]
WQNX....... Aberdeen, NC [*AM radio station call letters*]
WQNY....... Ithaca, NY [*FM radio station call letters*]
WQNZ....... Natchez, MS [*FM radio station call letters*]
WQO .... Water Quality Office [*Later, OWP*] [*Environmental Protection Agency*]
WQOK....... South Boston, VA [*FM radio station call letters*]
WQOL....... Vero Beach, FL [*FM radio station call letters*]
WQON....... Grayling, MI [*FM radio station call letters*]
WQOW..... Eau Claire, WI [*Television station call letters*]
WQOX....... Memphis, TN [*FM radio station call letters*]
WQPM...... Princeton, MN [*AM radio station call letters*]
WQPM-FM ... Princeton, MN [*FM radio station call letters*]
WQPO....... Harrisonburg, VA [*FM radio station call letters*]
WQPR....... Muscle Shoals, AL [*FM radio station call letters*]
WQPT-TV ... Moline, IL [*Television station call letters*]
WQPW...... Valdosta, GA [*FM radio station call letters*]
WQQB....... Bowling Green, KY [*Television station call letters*]
WQQK....... Hendersonville, TN [*FM radio station call letters*]
WQQQ ...... Stamford, CT [*FM radio station call letters*]
WQQT .... Springfield, GA [*FM radio station call letters*]
WQQW ..... Waterbury, CT [*AM radio station call letters*]
WQRA....... Warrenton, VA [*FM radio station call letters*]
WQRC....... Barnstable, MA [*FM radio station call letters*]
WQRC....... Water Quality Research Council   (EA)
WQRF .... Rockford, IL [*Television station call letters*]
WQRI .... Bristol, RI [*FM radio station call letters*]
WQRK....... Bedford, IN [*FM radio station call letters*]
WQRL....... Benton, IL [*FM radio station call letters*]
WQRM...... Smethport, PA [*FM radio station call letters*]
WQRP .... Water Quality Research Program [*US Army Corps of Engineers*]
WQRP .... West Carollton, OH [*FM radio station call letters*]
WQRS ...... Detroit, MI [*FM radio station call letters*]
WQRT .... Salamanca, NY [*FM radio station call letters*]
WQRX ...... Valley Head, AL [*AM radio station call letters*]
WQSA ...... Sarasota, FL [*AM radio station call letters*]
WQSB .... Albertville, AL [*FM radio station call letters*]
WQSI........ Frederick, MD [*AM radio station call letters*]
WQSM...... Fayetteville, NC [*FM radio station call letters*]
WQSN...... Kalamazoo, MI [*AM radio station call letters*]
WQSR....... Catonsville, MD [*FM radio station call letters*]
WQSS .... Camden, ME [*FM radio station call letters*]
WQST .... Forest, MS [*AM radio station call letters*]
WQST-FM ... Forest, MS [*FM radio station call letters*]
WQSU...... Selinsgrove, PA [*FM radio station call letters*]
WQSV....... Ashland City, TN [*AM radio station call letters*]
WQT.......... Water Quench Test
WQTC ...... Manitowoc, WI [*FM radio station call letters*]
WQTE ...... Adrian, MI [*FM radio station call letters*]
WQTL .... Ottawa, OH [*FM radio station call letters*]
WQTO...... Ponce, PR [*Television station call letters*]
WQTQ ...... Hartford, CT [*FM radio station call letters*]
WQTU...... Rome, GA [*FM radio station call letters*]
WQTV....... Boston, MA [*Television station call letters*]
WQTW...... Latrobe, PA [*AM radio station call letters*]
WQTX .... Roanoke, IN [*FM radio station call letters*]
WQTY .... Linton, IN [*FM radio station call letters*]

WQTZ .... Decatur, IN [*FM radio station call letters*]
WQUE....... New Orleans, LA [*AM radio station call letters*]
WQUE-FM ... New Orleans, LA [*FM radio station call letters*]
WQUH ...... De Funiak Springs, FL [*FM radio station call letters*]
WQUIS ..... Water Quality Indicator System [*Marine science*]   (MSC)
WQUL....... Griffin, GA [*FM radio station call letters*]
WQUT....... Johnson City, TN [*FM radio station call letters*]
WQVE....... Camilla, GA [*FM radio station call letters*]
WQVR...... Southbridge, MA [*FM radio station call letters*]
WQWK...... State College, PA [*FM radio station call letters*]
WQWM...... Kaukauna, WI [*AM radio station call letters*]
WQWQ ..... Muskegon Heights, MI [*AM radio station call letters*]
WQWQ-FM ... Muskegon Heights, MI [*FM radio station call letters*]
WQXA....... York, PA [*FM radio station call letters*]
WQXA-FM ... York, PA [*FM radio station call letters*]
WQXB .... Grenada, MS [*FM radio station call letters*]
WQXC....... Otsego, MI [*AM radio station call letters*]
WQXC-FM ... Otsego, MI [*FM radio station call letters*]
WQXE .... Elizabethtown, KY [*FM radio station call letters*]
WQXI .... Atlanta, GA [*AM radio station call letters*]
WQXJ........ Clayton, GA [*FM radio station call letters*]
WQXK ...... Salem, OH [*FM radio station call letters*]
WQXL .... Columbia, SC [*AM radio station call letters*]
WQXO...... Munising, MI [*AM radio station call letters*]
WQXO-FM ... Munising, MI [*FM radio station call letters*]
WQXR....... New York, NY [*AM radio station call letters*]
WQXR-FM ... New York, NY [*FM radio station call letters*]
WQXT .... Owego, NY [*FM radio station call letters*]
WQXX .... Morganton, NC [*FM radio station call letters*]
WQXY .... Hazard, KY [*AM radio station call letters*]
WQXZ .... Taylorsville, NC [*AM radio station call letters*]
WQYK .... Seffner, FL [*AM radio station call letters*]
WQYK-FM ... St. Petersburg, FL [*FM radio station call letters*]
WQYX .... Clearfield, PA [*FM radio station call letters*]
WQZK ...... Keyser, WV [*FM radio station call letters*]
WQZM ...... Mountaintop, PA [*FM radio station call letters*]
WQZQ...... Dickson, TN [*FM radio station call letters*]
WQZS .... Meyersdale, PA [*FM radio station call letters*]
WQZX ...... Greenville, AL [*FM radio station call letters*]
WQZY ...... Dublin, GA [*FM radio station call letters*]
WQZZ .... Lawrenceburg, TN [*AM radio station call letters*]
WR............ Journal of Water Resources Planning and Management [*A publication*]
WR............ Sutherland's Weekly Report [*India*] [*A publication*]   (DLA)
WR............ Wagons-Restaurants [*Railroad dining cars in Europe*] [*French*]
WR............ Wall Receptacle   (MUGU)
WR............ War Reserve   (AABC)
WR............ War Risk
WR............ War Risk Insurance Decisions [*United States*] [*A publication*]   (DLA)
WR............ Wardrobe
WR............ Wardroom [*Navy*]
WR............ Warehouse Receipt [*Often negotiable*]
WR............ Warner-Lambert Pharmaceutical Co. [*Research code symbol*]
WR............ Wartime Report   (MCD)
WR............ Wartime Requirements [*Air Force document*]   (AFM)
W/R .... Was Received
WR............ Washington Report. News and World Report Newsletter [*A publication*]
WR............ Washout Rate
WR............ Washroom
WR............ Wassermann Reaction [*Test for syphilis*] [*Medicine*]
W & R .... Water and Rail [*Transportation*]
WR............ Water and Rail [*Transportation*]
WR............ Water Repellant [*Technical drawings*]
W/R .... Water/Rock [*Ratio*] [*Geochemistry*]
WR............ Wave Retardation   (DEN)
WR............ Waveguide, Rectangular
WR............ Weakly Reactive   (MAE)
WR............ Weapon Radius   (NVT)
WR............ Weapon Range   (NATG)
WR............ Weapons Requirement [*DoD*]
WR............ Wear Resistant
WR............ Weather Reconnaissance
WR............ Weather Resistant   (MSA)
WR............ Weekly Record [*A publication*]
WR............ Weekly Reporter [*Bengal*] [*A publication*]   (DLA)
WR............ Weekly Reporter [*England*] [*A publication*]   (DLA)
WR............ Weekly Reporter, Cape Provincial Division [*South Africa*] [*A publication*]   (DLA)
WR............ Weekly Review [*A publication*]
WR............ Welfare Recipient   (OICC)
W & R .... Welfare and Recreation [*Navy*]
WR............ Wendell's Reports [*1826-41*] [*New York*] [*A publication*]   (DLA)
WR............ Western Resources, Inc. [*Formerly, Kansas Power & Light Co.*] [*NYSE symbol*]   (SPSG)
WR............ Western Review [*A publication*]
WR............ West's English Chancery Reports Tempore Hardwicke [*1736-39*] [*A publication*]   (DLA)
WR............ Wet Runway [*Aviation*]   (FAAC)

W/R .... White Room [*NASA*]   (KSC)
WR............ Whiteshell Reactor [*Canada*]
WR............ Whole Rock [*Geology*]
WR............ Wide Range [*Nuclear energy*]   (NRCH)
WR............ Wide Ratio [*Automotive engineering*]
WR............ Wide Receiver [*Football*]
WR............ Wild Rose Resources [*Vancouver Stock Exchange symbol*]
WR............ Willelmus Rex [*King William*]
WR............ Wilson Repeater   (IEEE)
WR............ Wiping Reflex [*Physiology*]
WR............ Wire Recorder   (DEN)
WR............ Wire Rope   (AAG)
WR............ Wirral Railway [*British*]   (ROG)
WR............ Wisconsin Reports [*A publication*]   (DLA)
WR............ Wiseman Review [*A publication*]
WR............ Wissenschaftsrat [*Science Council*] [*Germany*]
WR............ With Rights [*Securities*]
WR............ Wolf-Raye [*Star classification*]
WR............ Wolseley Register   (EA)
WR............ Women's Reserve [*Navy*]
WR............ Women's Review [*A publication*]
WR............ Women's Roundtable   (EA)
WR............ Woodmen Rangers   (EA)
WR............ Word Restoration
WR............ Work Rate   (AAMN)
WR............ Work Request   (MCD)
WR............ Work Requirement   (CAAL)
WR............ Working Register
WR............ World Reporter [*World Council of Credit Unions*] [*A publication*]
WR............ World River [*Geology*]
WR............ Worthington Register   (EA)
WR............ Wrap
WR............ Wreath   (WGA)
WR............ Wrench   (MSA)
Wr .... Wright [*Blood group*]
Wr .... Wright's Reports [*37-50 Pennsylvania*] [*A publication*]   (DLA)
WR............ Wrist [*Medicine*]
WR............ Wrist Roll   (NASA)
WR............ Write
WR............ Writer   (MSA)
wr .... Wrong
WR2........... Warramunga Array [*Australia*] [*Seismograph station code, US Geological Survey*]   (SEIS)
WRA .... Walter Reed Army Medical Center, Washington, DC [*OCLC symbol*]   (OCLC)
WRA .... War Relocation Authority [*Within Office of Emergency Management*] [*To provide for the relocation of persons whose removal seemed necessary for national security, and for their maintenance and supervision*] [*World War II*]
WRA .... War Reserve Allowance   (CINC)
WRA .... Ward Room Attendant [*British military*]   (DMA)
WRA .... Warramunga Array [*Australia*] [*Seismograph station code, US Geological Survey*]   (SEIS)
WRA .... Waste Regulation Authority [*British*]
WRA .... Water Research Association [*British*]   (DCTA)
WRA .... Water Resources Abstracts [*Database*] [*A publication*]
WRA .... Weapons Replaceable [*or Replacement*] Assembly
WRA .... Western Railroad Association   (EA)
WRA .... Western Range Association   (EA)
WRA .... Whiteware Research Association [*Defunct*]   (EA)
WRA .... Wind Restraint Area   (SAA)
WRA .... Windarra Minerals Ltd. [*Vancouver Stock Exchange symbol*] [*Toronto Stock Exchange symbol*]
WRA .... With the Rule Astigmatism [*Ophthalmology*]
WRA .... Women's Rabbinic Alliance [*Later, WSA*]   (EA)
WRA .... Work Related Abstracts [*A publication*]
WRA .... World Road Association [*Finland*]   (EAIO)
WRAA .... Luray, VA [*AM radio station call letters*]
WRAB .... Arab, AL [*AM radio station call letters*]
WRABD .... Wilhelm Roux' Archives of Developmental Biology [*A publication*]
WRABDT ... Roux's Archives of Developmental Biology [*A publication*]
WR/ABPR ... Weekly Record/American Book Publishing Record [*A publication*]
WRac .... Racine Public Library, Racine, WI [*Library symbol*] [*Library of Congress*]   (LCLS)
WRAC .... West Union, OH [*FM radio station call letters*]
WRAC .... Willow Run Aeronautical Center [*Michigan*]   (MCD)
WRAC .... Women's Royal Army Corps [*British*]
WRacC....... Racine County Institutions Medical Library, Racine, WI [*Library symbol*] [*Library of Congress*]   (LCLS)
WRacCL.... Racine County Law Library, Racine, WI [*Library symbol*] [*Library of Congress*]   (LCLS)
WRacD ...... DeKoven Foundation for Church Work, Racine, WI [*Library symbol*] [*Library of Congress*]   (LCLS)
WRACELD ... Wounds Received in Action [*Incurred in*] Combat with the Enemy or in Line of Duty [*Army*]   (AABC)
WRacGS.... Girl Scouts of Racine County, Racine, WI [*Library symbol*] [*Library of Congress*]   (LCLS)

WRacJ .... S. C. Johnson & Son, Inc., Racine, WI [*Library symbol*]
[*Library of Congress*] (LCLS)
WRacSD .... Racine Unified School District Number One, Racine, WI
[*Library symbol*] [*Library of Congress*] (LCLS)
WRacSL .... Saint Luke's Memorial Hospital, School of Nursing, Racine, WI
[*Library symbol*] [*Library of Congress*] (LCLS)
WRacSM ... Saint Mary's Hospital, Racine, WI [*Library symbol*] [*Library of
Congress*] (LCLS)
WRacWa ... Walker Manufacturing Co., Racine, WI [*Library symbol*]
[*Library of Congress*] (LCLS)
WRacWM ... Wustum Museum of Fine Arts, Racine, WI [*Library symbol*]
[*Library of Congress*] (LCLS)
WRacWP ... Western Publishing Co., Inc., Racine, WI [*Library symbol*]
[*Library of Congress*] (LCLS)
WRacY ...... Young Radiator Co., Racine, WI [*Library symbol*] [*Library of
Congress*] (LCLS)
WRAD .... Radford, VA [*AM radio station call letters*]
WRAF .... Toccoa Falls, GA [*FM radio station call letters*]
WRAF .... Women's Royal Air Force [*British*]
WRAFVR .. Women's Royal Air Force Volunteer Reserve [*British
military*] (DMA)
WRAG .... Carrollton, AL [*AM radio station call letters*]
WRAI .... San Juan, PR [*AM radio station call letters*]
WRAIN ..... Walter Reed Army Institute of Nursing (AABC)
WRAIR ...... Walter Reed Army Institute of Research [*Washington,
DC*] (MCD)
WRAIS ...... Wide Range Analog Input Subsystem
WRAJ .... Anna, IL [*AM radio station call letters*]
WRAJ-FM ... Anna, IL [*FM radio station call letters*]
WRAK .... Williamsport, PA [*AM radio station call letters*]
WRAL .... Raleigh, NC [*FM radio station call letters*]
WRALC ..... Warner Robins Air Logistics Center [*Formerly,
WRAMA*] (MCD)
WRAL-TV ... Raleigh, NC [*Television station call letters*]
WRAM ...... Monmouth, IL [*AM radio station call letters*]
WRAM ...... Water Resources Assessment Methodology [*Army Corps of
Engineers*]
WRAM ...... Wide-Range Recording and Monitoring [*System*] [*Radiation*]
WRAMA .... Warner Robins Air Materiel Area [*Later, WRALC*]
WRAMC ... Walter Reed Army Medical Center
WRAMC Prog Notes ... WRAMC [*Walter Reed Army Medical Center*]
Progress Notes [*A publication*]
WRANG .... Wrangler (ROG)
WRAP .... Waste Reduction Assessments Program [*Environmental
Protection Agency*]
WRAP .... Waste Reduction Audit Protocol
WRAP .... Water Reactor Analysis Program [*Nuclear energy*] (NRCH)
WRAP .... Weapons Readiness Achievement Program (MUGU)
WRAP .... Weapons Readiness Analysis Program [*Navy*]
WRAP .... Weapons Reliability Assurance Program [*Navy*] (DNAB)
WRAP .... Women's Radical Action Project [*Feminist group*]
WRAP .... Woodland Resource Analysis Program [*Tennessee Valley
Authority*]
WRAP .... Worker Readjustment Program [*Department of Labor*]
WRAP .... World Risk Analysis Package [*S. J. Rundt & Associates*]
[*Information service or system*] (IID)
WRAR .... Tappahannock, VA [*AM radio station call letters*]
WRAR-FM ... Tappahannock, VA [*FM radio station call letters*]
WRAS .... Atlanta, GA [*FM radio station call letters*]
WRAS .... Women's Reserve Ambulance Society [*British*] [*World War I*]
WRASPD .. World Rehabilitation Association for the Psycho-Socially
Disabled (EA)
WRAT .... Wide-Range Achievement Test
Wrat-R ...... Wide Range Achievement Test-Revised
WRAU .... Elkhorn City, KY [*FM radio station call letters*]
WRAV .... Ravena, NY [*FM radio station call letters*]
WRAW ...... Reading, PA [*AM radio station call letters*]
WRAX .... Bedford, PA [*FM radio station call letters*]
WRAY .... Princeton, IN [*AM radio station call letters*]
WRAY-FM ... Princeton, IN [*FM radio station call letters*]
WRB .... Macon/Warner Robins, GA [*Location identifier*]
[*FAA*] (FAAL)
WRB .... Walter Reed Army Medical Center, Post/Patient Library,
Washington, DC [*OCLC symbol*] (OCLC)
WRB .... War Refugee Board [*Terminated, 1945*]
WRB .... Wardrobe (MSA)
WRB .... Warramunga Array [*Australia*] [*Seismograph station code, US
Geological Survey*] (SEIS)
WRB .... Water Resources Board [*British*] (DCTA)
WRB .... Wide-Range Burner (DNAB)
WRBA .... Springfield, FL [*FM radio station call letters*]
WRBA .... World Robotic Boxing Association (EA)
WRBB .... Banjarmasin/Syamsuddin Noor [*Indonesia*] [*ICAO location
identifier*] (ICLI)
WRBB .... Boston, MA [*FM radio station call letters*]
WRBC .... Batu Licin [*Indonesia*] [*ICAO location identifier*] (ICLI)
WRBC .... Lewiston, ME [*FM radio station call letters*]
WRBC .... Weather Relay Broadcast Center
WRBD .... Pompano Beach, FL [*AM radio station call letters*]
WRBE .... Lucedale, MS [*AM radio station call letters*]
WRBE-FM ... Lucedale, MS [*FM radio station call letters*]

WRBH .... New Orleans, LA [*FM radio station call letters*]
WRBI .... Batesville, IN [*FM radio station call letters*]
WRBI .... Pangkalan Bun/Iskandar [*Indonesia*] [*ICAO location
identifier*] (ICLI)
WRBK ...... Flomaton, AL [*AM radio station call letters*]
WRBK ...... Kotabaru/Setagen [*Indonesia*] [*ICAO location
identifier*] (ICLI)
WRBL .... Columbus, GA [*Television station call letters*]
WRBM ...... Muaratewe/Beringin [*Indonesia*] [*ICAO location
identifier*] (ICLI)
WRBN .... Tanjung/Warukin [*Indonesia*] [*ICAO location
identifier*] (ICLI)
WRBND .... Wire Bound
WRBP .... Palangkaraya/Panarung [*Indonesia*] [*ICAO location
identifier*] (ICLI)
WRBQ .... St. Petersburg, FL [*AM radio station call letters*]
WRBQ .... Tampa, FL [*FM radio station call letters*]
WRBR .... Richland, MS [*AM radio station call letters*]
WRBR ...... South Bend, IN [*FM radio station call letters*]
WRBR ...... Wright Brothers National Memorial
WRBS .... Baltimore, MD [*FM radio station call letters*]
WRBS .... Sampit/H. Hasan [*Indonesia*] [*ICAO location
identifier*] (ICLI)
WRBT .... Mt. Carmel, IL [*FM radio station call letters*]
WRBT .... Teluk Kepayang [*Indonesia*] [*ICAO location identifier*] (ICLI)
WRBU .... Buntok/Sanggau [*Indonesia*] [*ICAO location identifier*] (ICLI)
WRBW ...... Orlando, FL [*Television station call letters*]
WRBX .... Reidsville, GA [*FM radio station call letters*]
WRBZ .... Banjarmasin Sector [*Indonesia*] [*ICAO location
identifier*] (ICLI)
WRC .... W. R. Carpenter Airlines [*Australia*]
WRC .... War Resources Council [*Terminated*]
WRC .... Washed Red Cells [*Medicine*]
WRC .... Washington, DC [*Television station call letters*]
WRC .... Washington Research Council [*Research center*] (RCD)
WRC .... Water Research Centre [*Research center*] [*British*] (IRC)
WRC .... Water Resources Center [*University of Illinois*]
WRC .... Water Resources Congress (EA)
WRC .... Water Resources Council [*Inactive*]
WRC .... Water-Retention Coefficient
WRC .... Watson Research Center [*IBM Corp.*]
WRC .... Weapons Release Computer [*or Controller*]
WRC .... Weather Relay Center
WRC .... Weekly Readiness Check
WRC .... Welding Research Council (EA)
WRC .... Well to Right of Course [*Aviation*] (FAAC)
WRC .... Werewolf Research Center (EA)
WRC .... Wildland Resources Center [*University of California*] [*Research
center*] (RCD)
WRC .... Wildlife Rehabilitation Council (EA)
WRC .... Williams Ranch [*California*] [*Seismograph station code, US
Geological Survey*] [*Closed*] (SEIS)
WRC .... Williams Research Corp.
WRC .... Women's Relief Corps
WRC .... Women's Rights Committee (EA)
WRC .... World Rally Championship
WRC .... World Relief Canada
WRC .... World Relief Corp. (EA)
WRC .... World Romani Congress
WRCA .... W. R. Carpenter Airlines [*Australia*]
WRCA .... Waltham, MA [*AM radio station call letters*]
WRCA .... Western Red Cedar Association (EA)
WR Calc ..... Sutherland's Weekly Reporter, Calcutta [*India*] [*A
publication*] (DLA)
WRCB ...... Chattanooga, TN [*Television station call letters*]
WRCB .... War Relief Control Board [*President's*]
WRCC .... Warner Robins, GA [*AM radio station call letters*]
WRCCC ..... Wheeler AFB Range Communications Control Center (MCD)
WRCC-FM ... Warner Robins, GA [*FM radio station call letters*]
WRCCHE ... Western Regional Consortium, Librarians' Networking
Committee [*Library network*]
WRCD .... Clyde, NY [*FM radio station call letters*]
WRCF .... Whale Research and Conservation Fund (EA)
WRCG .... Columbus, GA [*AM radio station call letters*]
WRCGR .... Women's Reserve of the Coast Guard Reserve
WRCH .... New Britain, CT [*FM radio station call letters*]
Wr Ch .... Wright's Ohio Reports [*1831-34*] [*A publication*] (DLA)
WRCI .... Hillsboro, NH [*FM radio station call letters*]
WRC Inf .... WRC [*Water Research Centre*] Information [*A publication*]
WRCK .... Utica, NY [*FM radio station call letters*]
WRCLA .... Western Red Cedar Lumber Association (EA)
WRCN .... Riverhead, NY [*FM radio station call letters*]
WRCNS .... Women's Royal Canadian Naval Service [*World War II*]
WRCO .... Richland Center, WI [*AM radio station call letters*]
WRCO-FM ... Richland Center, WI [*FM radio station call letters*]
WRCP .... Providence, RI [*AM radio station call letters*]
WRCPATT ... World Rabbinic Committee for the Preservation of Ancient
Tombs in Tiberias (EA)
WRCQ .... Dunn, NC [*FM radio station call letters*]
WRCR .... Rushville, IN [*FM radio station call letters*]

WRCR .... Wife's Restitution of Conjugal Rights [*Law suit*] [*British*] (ROG)

WRCR .... Wisconsin Railroad Commission Reports [*A publication*] (DLA)

WRCR .... Wyoming Resources Corp. [*NASDAQ symbol*] (NQ)

WRC Research Report ... Water Resources Center. Research Report [*A publication*]

WRCS........ Ahoskie, NC [*AM radio station call letters*]

WRCS........ Weapons Release Computer Set [*or System*] (MCD)

WRCS........ Work Ordering and Reporting Communications System [*Army*] (MCD)

WRCT .... Pittsburgh, PA [*FM radio station call letters*]

WRCU....... Hamilton, NY [*FM radio station call letters*]

WRCW....... Canton, OH [*AM radio station call letters*]

WRCZ .... Pittsfield, MA [*FM radio station call letters*]

WRD.......... Warden [*Washington*] [*Seismograph station code, US Geological Survey*] (SEIS)

WRD.......... Water Resources Division [*US Geological Survey*]

WRD.......... Whole Rumen Digesta [*Dairy science*] (OA)

WRD.......... Words [*A publication*]

WRD.......... World's Fair [*A publication*]

WRD.......... Worm Runner's Digest [*A satirical publication*]

WRDA .... Water Resources Development Act (GFGA)

WRDB .... Reedsburg, WI [*AM radio station call letters*]

WRDB .... Worldwide Water Resources Database

WRDC .... Western Rural Development Center [*Oregon State University*] [*Research center*] (RCD)

WRDC .... Westinghouse Research and Development Center (MCD)

WRDC .... Wright Research and Development Center [*Wright-Patterson Air Force Base*] (GRD)

WRDD....... Ebensburg, PA [*AM radio station call letters*]

WRDI .... We Remember Dean International (EA)

WRDIR...... Wrong Direction

WRDJ........ Bridgewater, VA [*FM radio station call letters*]

WRDJ........ Daleville, AL [*AM radio station call letters*]

WRDL .... Ashland, OH [*FM radio station call letters*]

WRDN....... Durand, WI [*AM radio station call letters*]

WRDN-FM ... Durand, WI [*FM radio station call letters*]

WRDO....... Fitzgerald, GA [*FM radio station call letters*]

WRDR .... Egg Harbor, NJ [*FM radio station call letters*]

WRDU....... Wilson, NC [*FM radio station call letters*]

WRDV .... Warminster, PA [*FM radio station call letters*]

WRDW....... Augusta, GA [*AM radio station call letters*]

WRDW....... Wrens, GA [*FM radio station call letters*]

WRDW-TV ... Augusta, GA [*Television station call letters*]

WRDX .... Salisbury, NC [*FM radio station call letters*]

WRDZ .... Cleveland, OH [*AM radio station call letters*]

WRE .... Tokyo Financial Review [*A publication*]

WRE .... Washington Real Estate Investment Trust [*AMEX symbol*] (SPSG)

WRE .... Weapon Research Establishment

WRE .... Whangarei [*New Zealand*] [*Airport symbol*] (OAG)

WRE .... Whole Ragweed Extract (MAE)

WRE .... Winston Resources Ltd. [*Vancouver Stock Exchange symbol*]

WREA .... Dayton, TN [*AM radio station call letters*]

WREAFS... Waste Reduction Evaluation at Federal Sites [*Environmental Protection Agency*]

WREB........ Holyoke, MA [*AM radio station call letters*]

WREC .... Memphis, TN [*AM radio station call letters*]

WRECISS ... Weapons Research Establishment Camera Interception Single Shot

WRECS..... Weapon Radiation Effects on Communications Systems (MCD)

WRED .... Gibsonville, OH [*FM radio station call letters*]

WREDAC ... Weapons Research Establishment Digital Automatic Computer

WREE........ Women for Racial and Economic Equality (EA)

WREF........ Ridgefield, CT [*AM radio station call letters*]

WREFC..... We Remember Elvis Fan Club (EA)

WREG .... Memphis, TN [*Television station call letters*]

W/REG...... Window Regulator [*Automotive engineering*]

W Reg R..... Wetboek van Registratierechten [*A publication*]

WREI........ Quebradillas, PR [*FM radio station call letters*]

WREI........ Wisconsin Real Estate Investment Trust [*NASDAQ symbol*] (NQ)

WREI........ Women's Research and Education Institute (EA)

WREK .... Atlanta, GA [*FM radio station call letters*]

WREL .... Buena Vista, VA [*FM radio station call letters*]

WREL........ Lexington, VA [*AM radio station call letters*]

WREM ...... Monticello, ME [*AM radio station call letters*]

WREN .... Women's Royal English Navy (IIA)

WRENACK ... WREN [*Women's Royal Naval Service*] Assistant Cook [*British military*] (DMA)

WRENAM ... WREN [*Women's Royal Naval Service*] Air Mechanic [*British military*] (DMA)

WRENCINE(AB) ... WREN [*Women's Royal Naval Service*] Cinema Operator (Able) [*British military*] (DMA)

WRENCINE(ORD) ... WREN [*Women's Royal Naval Service*] Cinema Operator (Ordinary) [*British military*] (DMA)

WRENCK ... WREN [*Women's Royal Naval Service*] Cook [*British military*] (DMA)

WRENDHYG ... WREN [*Women's Royal Naval Service*] Dental Hygienist [*British military*] (DMA)

WRENDSA ... WREN [*Women's Royal Naval Service*] Dental Surgery Assistant [*British military*] (DMA)

WRENEDUC ... WREN [*Women's Royal Naval Service*] Education Assistant [*British military*] (DMA)

WRENMET ... WREN [*Women's Royal Naval Service*] Meteorological Observer [*British military*] (DMA)

WRENMT ... WREN [*Women's Royal Naval Service*] Motor Transport Driver [*British military*] (DMA)

WRENPHOT ... WREN [*Women's Royal Naval Service*] Photographer [*British military*] (DMA)

WRENQA ... WREN [*Women's Royal Naval Service*] Quarters Assistant [*British military*] (DMA)

WREN(R) ... WREN [*Women's Royal Naval Service*] (RADAR) [*British military*] (DMA)

WRENREG ... WREN [*Women's Royal Naval Service*] Regulating [*British military*] (DMA)

WRENREM ... WREN [*Women's Royal Naval Service*] Radio Electrical Mechanic [*British military*] (DMA)

WRENRO(M)1 ... WREN [*Women's Royal Naval Service*] Radio Operator (Morse) 1st Class [*British military*] (DMA)

WRENRO(M)2 ... WREN [*Women's Royal Naval Service*] Radio Operator (Morse) 2nd Class [*British military*] (DMA)

WRENS..... Women's Royal Naval Service [*Acronym is a phonetic reference to members of this British service branch*] [*Also, WRNS*]

WRENSA ... WREN [*Women's Royal Naval Service*] Stores Accountant [*British military*] (DMA)

WRENS(C) ... WREN [*Women's Royal Naval Service*] Stores Assistant (Clothes) [*British military*] (DMA)

WRENS(S) ... WREN [*Women's Royal Naval Service*] Stores Assistant (Stores) [*British military*] (DMA)

WRENSTD ... WREN [*Women's Royal Naval Service*] Steward [*British military*] (DMA)

WRENS(V) ... WREN [*Women's Royal Naval Service*] Stores Assistant (Victualling) [*British military*] (DMA)

WRENTEL ... WREN [*Women's Royal Naval Service*] Telephonist [*British military*] (DMA)

WRENTSA ... WREN [*Women's Royal Naval Service*] Training Support Assistant [*British military*] (DMA)

WRENWA ... WREN [*Women's Royal Naval Service*] Weapon Analyst [*British military*] (DMA)

WRENWTR(G) ... WREN [*Women's Royal Naval Service*] Writer (General) [*British military*] (DMA)

WRENWTR(P) ... WREN [*Women's Royal Naval Service*] Writer (Pay) [*British military*] (DMA)

WRENWTR(S) ... WREN [*Women's Royal Naval Service*] Writer (Shorthand) [*British military*] (DMA)

WREO .... Ashtabula, OH [*FM radio station call letters*]

W Rep .... West's English Chancery Reports Tempore Hardwicke [*1736-39*] [*A publication*] (DLA)

WRERA..... Water Resources Research [*A publication*]

WRES........ Cocoa, FL [*Television station call letters*]

W Res L Rev ... Western Reserve Law Review [*A publication*]

WREST .... Washington Regional Engineers, Scientists, and Technicians

WREST ..... Wide Range Employability Sample Test

Wrest .... Wrestling USA [*A publication*]

WRET........ Spartanburg, SC [*Television station call letters*]

WRET .... Wespac Investors Trust III [*NASDAQ symbol*] (NQ)

WREU .... Western Railway Employees' Union [*India*]

WREV .... Reidsville, NC [*AM radio station call letters*]

WREX .... Rockford, IL [*Television station call letters*]

WREX .... Wrexham [*City in Wales*]

WREY .... Millville, NJ [*AM radio station call letters*]

WREZ........ Metropolis, IL [*FM radio station call letters*]

WRF .... University of Wisconsin, River Falls, River Falls, WI [*OCLC symbol*] (OCLC)

WRF .... Weak Radial Field

WRF .... Weibull Reliability Function [*Statistics*]

WRF .... Wheat Ridge Foundation (EA)

WRF .... World Rehabilitation Fund (EA)

WRF .... World Research Foundation (EA)

WRFA....... Largo, FL [*AM radio station call letters*]

W R Far East ... Weekly Review of the Far East [*A publication*]

WRFC........ Athens, GA [*AM radio station call letters*]

WRFCG..... War Reserve Functional Coordinating Group [*DoD*]

WRFD .... Columbus-Worthington, OH [*AM radio station call letters*]

WRFE .... Aguada, PR [*FM radio station call letters*]

WRFG .... Atlanta, GA [*FM radio station call letters*]

WRFG .... Wharfage [*Shipping*] (WGA)

WRFH .... Marietta, PA [*FM radio station call letters*]

WRFL........ Lexington, KY [*FM radio station call letters*]

WRFM....... Hialeah, FL [*AM radio station call letters*]

WRFR....... Franklin, NC [*FM radio station call letters*]

WRFS........ Garrisonville, VA [*AM radio station call letters*]

WRFT........ Indianapolis, IN [*FM radio station call letters*]

WRfU .... University of Wisconsin-River Falls, River Falls, WI [*Library symbol*] [*Library of Congress*] (LCLS)

WRFW ...... River Falls, WI [*FM radio station call letters*]

WRFX........ Kannapolis, NC [*FM radio station call letters*]

WRFY........ Reading, PA [*FM radio station call letters*]

WRG.........	Wearing (MSA)
WRG.........	Weather Reconnaissance Group [*Military*]
WRG.........	Westport Research Group [*Information service or system*] (IID)
WRG.........	White River [*Alaska*] [*Seismograph station code, US Geological Survey*] (SEIS)
WRG.........	Wire Routing Guide (MCD)
WRG.........	Wiring
WRG.........	Wrangell [*Alaska*] [*Airport symbol*] (OAG)
WRG.........	Wrangell, AK [*Location identifier*] [*FAA*] (FAAL)
WRG.........	Wrong [*Telecommunications*] (TEL)
WRGA......	Rome, GA [*AM radio station call letters*]
WRGA......	Western River Guides Association (EA)
WRGB......	Schenectady, NY [*Television station call letters*]
WRGC......	Sylva, NC [*AM radio station call letters*]
WRGH......	Walter Reed General Hospital (MCD)
WRGI......	Naples, FL [*FM radio station call letters*]
WRGM......	Ontario, OH [*AM radio station call letters*]
WRGN......	Sweet Valley, PA [*FM radio station call letters*]
WRGR......	Tupper Lake, NY [*FM radio station call letters*]
WRGR......	Wringer
WRGS......	Rogersville, TN [*AM radio station call letters*]
WRGT......	Dayton, OH [*Television station call letters*]
WRh..........	Rhinelander Public Library, Rhinelander, WI [*Library symbol*] [*Library of Congress*] (LCLS)
WRH.........	Warnkenhagen [*German Democratic Republic*] [*Geomagnetic observatory code*]
WRH.........	William Randolph Hearst [*American newspaper publisher, 1863-1951*]
WRH.........	World Radio Handbook
WRHA......	Johnsonville, SC [*FM radio station call letters*]
WRHB......	Barnesboro, PA [*FM radio station call letters*]
WRHC......	Coral Gables, FL [*AM radio station call letters*]
WRHD......	Riverhead, NY [*AM radio station call letters*]
WRHE......	Kingston, NY [*FM radio station call letters*]
WRHF......	Farmington, NH [*FM radio station call letters*]
WRHG......	Natchez, MS [*FM radio station call letters*]
WRHI......	Rock Hill, SC [*AM radio station call letters*]
WRHL......	Rochelle, IL [*AM radio station call letters*]
WRHL-FM ...	Rochelle, IL [*FM radio station call letters*]
WRHM......	Lancaster, SC [*FM radio station call letters*]
WRHN......	Rhinelander, WI [*FM radio station call letters*]
WRHO......	Oneonta, NY [*FM radio station call letters*]
WRHP......	Syracuse, NY [*FM radio station call letters*]
WRHQ......	Richmond Hill, GA [*FM radio station call letters*]
WRHT......	Morehead, NC [*FM radio station call letters*]
WRHU......	Hempstead, NY [*FM radio station call letters*]
WRHV......	Poughkeepsie, NY [*FM radio station call letters*]
WRHX......	Herndon, VA [*AM radio station call letters*]
WRI	International Water Resources Institute [*George Washington University*] [*Research center*] (RCD)
WRI	War Resisters International [*British*]
WRI	War Risks Insurance [*British*]
WRI	Water Research Institute [*West Virginia University*] [*Research center*] (RCD)
WRI	Water-Resources Investigation [*A publication*]
WRI	Waterloo Research Institute [*University of Waterloo*] [*Research center*] (RCD)
WRI	Weatherstrip Research Institute
WRI	Weingarten Realty, Inc. [*NYSE symbol*] (SPSG)
WRI	Welfare Research, Inc. (EA)
WRI	Western Research Institute [*Laramie, WY*] [*Department of Energy*] (GRD)
WRI	Winzen Research, Inc.
WRI	Wire Reinforcement Institute (EA)
WRI	Wire Rope Institute
WRI	World Research, Inc. [*San Diego, CA*] (EA)
WRI	World Resources Institute (EA)
WRI	Wrightstown, NJ [*Location identifier*] [*FAA*] (FAAL)
WRIB........	Providence, RI [*AM radio station call letters*]
WRIC........	Petersburg, VA [*Television station call letters*]
WRIC........	Richlands, VA [*AM radio station call letters*]
WRIC-FM ...	Richlands, VA [*FM radio station call letters*]
WRIE........	Erie, PA [*AM radio station call letters*]
WRIF........	Detroit, MI [*FM radio station call letters*]
WRIF........	Water Resources Information File [*Terrain Analysis Center*] [*Army*]
WRIG	Schofield, WI [*AM radio station call letters*]
Wright........	Wright's Ohio Reports [*1831-34*] [*A publication*] (DLA)
Wright........	Wright's Reports [*37-50 Pennsylvania*] [*A publication*] (DLA)
Wright Ch ...	Wright's Ohio Reports [*1831-34*] [*A publication*] (DLA)
Wright Cr Cons ...	Wright's Criminal Conspiracies [*1873*] [*A publication*] (DLA)
Wright NP ...	Wright's Ohio Nisi Prius Reports [*A publication*] (DLA)
Wright (Ohio C) ...	Wright's Ohio Reports [*A publication*] (DLA)
Wright R ...	Wright's Ohio Reports [*A publication*] (DLA)
Wright's Rep ...	Wright's Ohio Reports [*A publication*] (DLA)
Wright St L ...	Wright's Advice on the Study of the Law [*A publication*] (DLA)
Wright Ten ...	Wright on Tenures [*A publication*] (DLA)
Wrigley	Wrigley [*Wm.*] Jr. Co. [*Associated Press abbreviation*] (APAG)

WRII.........	Waste Recovery, Inc. [*Dallas, TX*] [*NASDAQ symbol*] (NQ)
WRIJ	Masontown, PA [*FM radio station call letters*]
WRIK	Brookport, IL [*AM radio station call letters*]
WRIK	Metropolis, IL [*FM radio station call letters*]
WRIN	Rensselaer, IN [*AM radio station call letters*]
WRINS	Women's Royal Indian Naval Service [*British military*] (DMA)
WRIO	Ponce, PR [*FM radio station call letters*]
WRIOT	Wide Range Interest and Opinion Test
WRIP.........	Versailles, IN [*FM radio station call letters*]
WRipC......	Ripon College, Ripon, WI [*Library symbol*] [*Library of Congress*] (LCLS)
WRIPT	Wide Range Intelligence-Personality Test [*Personality development test*] [*Psychology*]
WRIQ	Radford, VA [*FM radio station call letters*]
WRI Rep	WRI [*Wattle Research Institute*] Report [*A publication*]
WRIS........	Roanoke, VA [*AM radio station call letters*]
WRIS........	Water Resources Information System (NOAA)
WRISC	Western Regional Information Service Center [*University of California*] [*Information service or system*] [*Defunct*] (IID)
WRISE	Waste Reduction Institute for Scientists and Engineers [*Environmental Protection Agency*]
WRIS Technical Bulletin ...	Water Resources Information System. Technical Bulletin [*A publication*]
WRIT........	Walterboro, SC [*AM radio station call letters*]
WRIT........	Washington Real Estate Investment Trust [*Associated Press abbreviation*] (APAG)
WRIT........	Wright [*William E.*] Co. [*NASDAQ symbol*] (NQ)
Writ Am Hist ...	Writings on American History [*A publication*]
Writ Cent S ...	Writers of the 21st Century. Series [*A publication*]
WRITE......	Waste Reduction Innovative Technology Evaluation [*Environmental Protection Agency*]
WRITG......	Writing (ROG)
Writ Ring ...	Writers' Ring [*A publication*]
WRIU	Kingston, RI [*FM radio station call letters*]
WRIU	Weather RADAR Interface Unit (MCD)
WRIU	Write Interface Unit
WRIV	Riverhead, NY [*AM radio station call letters*]
WRIX........	Homeland Park, SC [*AM radio station call letters*]
WRIX........	Honea Path, SC [*FM radio station call letters*]
WRIZ........	Lakeview, MI [*FM radio station call letters*]
WRJ..........	Wallraz-Richartz-Jahrbuch [*A publication*]
WRJA........	Sumter, SC [*FM radio station call letters*]
WRJA-TV ...	Sumter, SC [*Television station call letters*]
WRJB	Camden, TN [*FM radio station call letters*]
WRJC........	Mauston, WI [*AM radio station call letters*]
WRJCD9 ..	Water Pollution Research Journal of Canada [*A publication*]
WRJC-FM ...	Mauston, WI [*FM radio station call letters*]
WRJH	Brandon, MS [*FM radio station call letters*]
WRJL	Hanceville, AL [*AM radio station call letters*]
WRJM	Geneva, AL [*FM radio station call letters*]
WRJM-TV ...	Troy, AL [*Television station call letters*]
WRJN	Racine, WI [*AM radio station call letters*]
WRJO	Eagle River, WI [*FM radio station call letters*]
WRJQ.......	Appleton, WI [*AM radio station call letters*]
WRJS	Oil City, PA [*FM radio station call letters*]
WRJW	Picayune, MS [*AM radio station call letters*]
WRJZ........	Knoxville, TN [*AM radio station call letters*]
WRK..........	Wall & Redekop Corp. [*Toronto Stock Exchange symbol*] [*Vancouver Stock Exchange symbol*]
WRK..........	Work (FAAC)
WRK..........	Wrecker
WRKA	Atambua/Haliwen [*Indonesia*] [*ICAO location identifier*] (ICLI)
WRKA	St. Matthews, KY [*FM radio station call letters*]
WRKB	Bajawa/Padhameleda [*Indonesia*] [*ICAO location identifier*] (ICLI)
WRKB	Kannapolis, NC [*AM radio station call letters*]
WRKC	Maumere/Wai Oti [*Indonesia*] [*ICAO location identifier*] (ICLI)
WRKC	Wilkes-Barre, PA [*FM radio station call letters*]
WRKD	Rockland, ME [*AM radio station call letters*]
WRKE	Ende/Ipi [*Indonesia*] [*ICAO location identifier*] (ICLI)
WRKE	Ocean View, DE [*FM radio station call letters*]
WRKF......	Baton Rouge, LA [*FM radio station call letters*]
WRKF........	Maskolen [*Indonesia*] [*ICAO location identifier*] (ICLI)
WRKG	Lorain, OH [*AM radio station call letters*]
WRKG	Ruteng/Satartacik [*Indonesia*] [*ICAO location identifier*] (ICLI)
WRKI	Brookfield, CT [*FM radio station call letters*]
WRKI	Mbai [*Indonesia*] [*ICAO location identifier*] (ICLI)
WRKJ........	Dothan, AL [*Television station call letters*]
WRKJ........	Mena [*Indonesia*] [*ICAO location identifier*] (ICLI)
WRKK	Jersey Shore, PA [*FM radio station call letters*]
WRKK	Kupang/Eltari [*Indonesia*] [*ICAO location identifier*] (ICLI)
WRKL........	Larantuka/Gewayentana [*Indonesia*] [*ICAO location identifier*] (ICLI)
WRKL........	New City, NY [*AM radio station call letters*]
WRKM......	Carthage, TN [*AM radio station call letters*]
WRKM......	Kalabahi/Mali [*Indonesia*] [*ICAO location identifier*] (ICLI)
WRKN........	Brandon, MS [*AM radio station call letters*]

WRKN....... Naikliu [*Indonesia*] [*ICAO location identifier*]   (ICLI)
WRKO....... Boston, MA [*AM radio station call letters*]
WRKP....... Moundsville, WV [*FM radio station call letters*]
Wrk Paper ... Working Papers for a New Society [*A publication*]
Wrk Power ... Workers Power [*A publication*]
WRKQ....... Madisonville, TN [*AM radio station call letters*]
WRKR....... Portage, MI [*FM radio station call letters*]
WRKR....... Rote/Lekunik [*Indonesia*] [*ICAO location identifier*]   (ICLI)
WRKS....... New York, NY [*FM radio station call letters*]
WRKS....... Sabu/Tardanu [*Indonesia*] [*ICAO location identifier*]   (ICLI)
WRKT....... North East, PA [*FM radio station call letters*]
WRKU....... Grove City, PA [*FM radio station call letters*]
Wrk World ... Workers' World [*A publication*]
WRKX....... Ottawa, IL [*FM radio station call letters*]
WRKY....... Steubenville, OH [*FM radio station call letters*]
WRKZ....... Hershey, PA [*FM radio station call letters*]
WRKZ....... Kupang Sector [*Indonesia*] [*ICAO location identifier*]   (ICLI)
WRl........... Rice Lake Public Library, Rice Lake, WI [*Library symbol*]
               [*Library of Congress*]   (LCLS)
WRL .... War Resisters League   (EA)
WRL .... Wellcome Research Laboratories [*Research center*]
               [*British*]   (IRC)
WRL .... Western Reserve Law Review [*A publication*]   (ILCA)
WRL .... Westinghouse Research Laboratories   (KSC)
WRL .... Wien Radiation Law [*Physics*]
WRL .... Willow Run Laboratory [*NASA*]   (KSC)
WRL .... Wing Reference Line [*Aviation*]
WRL .... Worland [*Wyoming*] [*Airport symbol*]   (OAG)
WRL .... Worland, WY [*Location identifier*] [*FAA*]   (FAAL)
WRLA .... Sangata [*Indonesia*] [*ICAO location identifier*]   (ICLI)
WRLB....... Florence, NJ [*AM radio station call letters*]
WRLB....... Long Bawan/Juvai Semaring [*Indonesia*] [*ICAO location
               identifier*]   (ICLI)
WRLC....... Bontang [*Indonesia*] [*ICAO location identifier*]   (ICLI)
WRLC....... Williamsport, PA [*FM radio station call letters*]
WRLD .... Batu Putih/Talisayam [*Indonesia*] [*ICAO location
               identifier*]   (ICLI)
WRLD ...... Lanett, AL [*AM radio station call letters*]
WRLD ...... World Acceptance [*NASDAQ symbol*]   (SPSG)
WrldCp ...... World Corp. [*Associated Press abbreviation*]   (APAG)
WrldVl....... Worldwide Value Fund [*Associated Press
               abbreviation*]   (APAG)
WRLF....... Fairmont, WV [*FM radio station call letters*]
WRLG .... Tanjung Selor/Tanjung Harapan [*Indonesia*] [*ICAO location
               identifier*]   (ICLI)
WRLH....... Tanah Grogot [*Indonesia*] [*ICAO location identifier*]   (ICLI)
WRLH-TV ... Richmond, VA [*Television station call letters*]
WRLI........ Tiong Chong [*Indonesia*] [*ICAO location identifier*]   (ICLI)
WRLK....... Tanjung Redep/Kalimarau [*Indonesia*] [*ICAO location
               identifier*]   (ICLI)
WRLK-TV ... Columbia, SC [*Television station call letters*]
WRLL........ Balikpapan/Sepinggan [*Indonesia*] [*ICAO location
               identifier*]   (ICLI)
WRLM ...... Malinau [*Indonesia*] [*ICAO location identifier*]   (ICLI)
WRLN .... Long Mawang [*Indonesia*] [*ICAO location identifier*]   (ICLI)
WRLO .... Antigo, WI [*FM radio station call letters*]
WRLO .... Ongko Asa [*Indonesia*] [*ICAO location identifier*]   (ICLI)
WRLR....... Taraken [*Indonesia*] [*ICAO location identifier*]   (ICLI)
W R LR..... Women's Rights Law Reporter [*A publication*]
WRLRAR ... University of Wisconsin. Water Resources Center.
               Eutrophication Information Program. Literature Review [*A
               publication*]
WRLS........ Hayward, WI [*FM radio station call letters*]
WRLS........ Samarinda/Temindung [*Indonesia*] [*ICAO location
               identifier*]   (ICLI)
WRLS........ Working Reference of Livestock Regulatory Establishments,
               Stations, and Officials [*A publication*]
WRLT....... Franklin, TN [*FM radio station call letters*]
WRLT........ Tanjung Santan [*Indonesia*] [*ICAO location identifier*]   (ICLI)
WRLU ...... Sangkulirang [*Indonesia*] [*ICAO location identifier*]   (ICLI)
WRLU .... Watermen and Riverside Labourers' Union [*British*]
WRLV....... Salyersville, KY [*AM radio station call letters*]
WRLV-FM ... Salyersville, KY [*FM radio station call letters*]
WRLW ...... Muara Wahau [*Indonesia*] [*ICAO location identifier*]   (ICLI)
WRLX....... Tuscaloosa, AL [*AM radio station call letters*]
WRLX....... World Airways, Inc. [*Air carrier designation symbol*]
WRM........ War Readiness Materiel [*Air Force*]
WRM........ War Reserve Mobilization   (CINC)
WRM........ War Reserve Munitions
WRM........ Wardroom   (WGA)
WRM........ Warm   (FAAC)
WRM......... Warmifontaine [*Belgium*] [*Seismograph station code, US
               Geological Survey*]   (SEIS)
WRM........ Water Removal Mechanism
WRM........ West Rim Resources, Inc. [*Vancouver Stock Exchange symbol*]
WRM........ What Really Matters
WR(M)...... Wide Range (Monitor) [*Nuclear energy*]   (NRCH)
WRM........ William Richard Morris [*Automobile industrialist*] [*British*]
WRM......... Worcester State College, Worcester, MA [*OCLC
               symbol*]   (OCLC)
WRM........ Working Reference Material [*Nuclear energy*]   (NRCH)

WRM........ World Rainforest Movement [*Penang, Malaysia*]   (EAIO)
WRMA ...... Welded Ring Manufacturers Association [*Defunct*]
WRMB ...... Boynton Beach, FL [*FM radio station call letters*]
WRMC...... Middlebury, VT [*FM radio station call letters*]
WRMD...... St. Petersburg, FL [*AM radio station call letters*]
WRMF ...... Palm Beach, FL [*FM radio station call letters*]
WRMF ...... World Radio Missionary Fellowship   (EA)
WRMFNT ... Warm Front [*Meteorology*]   (FAAC)
WRMG...... Red Bay, AL [*AM radio station call letters*]
WRMJ...... Aledo, IL [*FM radio station call letters*]
WRMM..... Rochester, NY [*AM radio station call letters*]
WRMM-FM ... Rochester, NY [*FM radio station call letters*]
WRMN...... Elgin, IL [*AM radio station call letters*]
WRMN...... Wireman   (AABC)
WRMR...... Cleveland, OH [*AM radio station call letters*]
WRMR ...... War Reserve Materiel Requirement   (AFIT)
WRMRATE ... War Readiness Materiel Rating [*Air Force*]
WRMRB .. War Reserve Materiel Requirement Balance   (AFIT)
WRMRP.... War Reserve Materiel Requirement Protectable   (AFIT)
WRMRS... War Reserve Materiel Rating System
WRMS ...... Beardstown, IL [*AM radio station call letters*]
WRMS ...... War Reserve Materiel Stocks
WRMS ...... Watts Root-Mean-Square
WRMS-FM ... Beardstown, IL [*FM radio station call letters*]
WRMSTAT ... War Readiness Materiel Status [*Air Force*]
WRMT ...... Rocky Mount, NC [*AM radio station call letters*]
WRMT ...... Woodcock Reading Mastery Tests [*Educational test*]
WRMU ...... Alliance, OH [*FM radio station call letters*]
WRMX ...... Murfreesboro, TN [*FM radio station call letters*]
WRMY ...... Rocky Mount, NC [*Television station call letters*]
WRN......... Blue Bell, Inc. [*Greensboro, NC*] [*FAA designator*]   (FAAC)
WRN......... War Relief for Nicaraguans   (EA)
WRN......... Warnaco of Canada Ltd. [*Toronto Stock Exchange symbol*]
WRN......... Warning   (MSA)
WRN......... Western
WRN......... Wool Round Needle [*Knitting*]
WRNA....... China Grove, NC [*AM radio station call letters*]
WRNB....... Warren Bancorp, Inc. [*NASDAQ symbol*]   (NQ)
WRNC...... Reidsville, NC [*AM radio station call letters*]
WRNE....... Pensacola, FL [*AM radio station call letters*]
WRNG...... Warning   (FAAC)
WRNI .... Wide-Range Neutron Indicator   (IEEE)
WRNI .... Wide-Range Nuclear Instrument   (IEEE)
WrnIns....... Warner Insurance Services [*Associated Press
               abbreviation*]   (APAG)
WRNJ....... Hackettstown, NJ [*AM radio station call letters*]
WRNL....... Richmond, VA [*AM radio station call letters*]
WRNLR .... Western Region of Nigeria Law Reports [*A publication*]   (DLA)
WRNO....... New Orleans, LA [*FM radio station call letters*]
WRNOA ... Washington Reef Net Owners Association   (EA)
WRNQ....... Poughkeepsie, NY [*FM radio station call letters*]
WRNR....... Martinsburg, WV [*AM radio station call letters*]
WRNR....... West Riding National Reserve [*British military*]   (DMA)
WRNR....... Women's Royal Naval Reserve [*British military*]   (DMA)
WRNS ...... Kinston, NC [*AM radio station call letters*]
WRNS ...... Women's Royal Naval Service [*Also, WRENS*] [*A member is
               familiarly called a "Wren"*] [*British*]
WRNS-FM ... Kinston, NC [*FM radio station call letters*]
WRNSR..... Women's Royal Naval Service Reserve [*British
               military*]   (DMA)
WRNT .... Warrant   (AABC)
WRNT .... Warrenton Railroad Co. [*Later, WAR*] [*AAR code*]
WRNVR .... Women's Royal Naval Volunteer Reserve [*British
               military*]   (DMA)
WRNWCA ... Western Red and Northern White Cedar Association [*Later,
               WRCA*]   (EA)
WRNWS ... Worldwide Radio Navigation Warning System
               [*Intergovernmental Maritime Consultative
               Organization*]   (GFGA)
WRNX....... Amherst, MA [*FM radio station call letters*]
WRNY .... Rome, NY [*AM radio station call letters*]
WRNZ....... Lancaster, KY [*FM radio station call letters*]
WRO.......... ARC [*Agricultural Research Council*] Weed Research
               Organization [*Research center*] [*British*]   (IRC)
WRO.......... Rotor-Aids, Inc. [*Abbeville, LA*] [*FAA designator*]   (FAAC)
WRO.......... War Records Office
WRO.......... War Risks Only
WRO.......... Water Rights Office [*Bureau of Indian Affairs*]
WRO.......... Western Regional Office
WRO.......... Wichita River Oil Corp. [*AMEX symbol*]   (SPSG)
WRO.......... Work Release Order   (MCD)
WRO.......... Worship Resources Office [*An association*]   (EA)
WRO.......... Wroclaw [*Poland*] [*Airport symbol*]   (OAG)
WROA....... Gulfport, MS [*AM radio station call letters*]
W Rob .... [*W.*] Robinson's English Admiralty Reports [*166 English
               Reprint*] [*A publication*]   (DLA)
WROB....... West Point, MS [*AM radio station call letters*]
W Rob Adm ... [*W.*] Robinson's English Admiralty Reports [*166 English
               Reprint*] [*A publication*]   (DLA)
W Rob Adm (Eng) ... [*W.*] Robinson's English Admiralty Reports [*166 English
               Reprint*] [*A publication*]   (DLA)

WROC....... Rochester, NY [*Television station call letters*]
Wrocl Zap Num ... Wroclawskie Zapiski Numizmatyczne [*A publication*]
WROD....... Daytona Beach, FL [*AM radio station call letters*]
WROE....... Neenah-Menasha, WI [*FM radio station call letters*]
WROG....... Cumberland, MD [*FM radio station call letters*]
Wr Ohio..... Wright's Ohio Reports [*A publication*]   (DLA)
WROI....... Rochester, IN [*FM radio station call letters*]
WROK....... Rockford, IL [*AM radio station call letters*]
WROL....... Boston, MA [*AM radio station call letters*]
WROM..... Rome, GA [*AM radio station call letters*]
WRON....... Ronceverte, WV [*AM radio station call letters*]
WRON-FM ... Ronceverte, WV [*FM radio station call letters*]
WROPA2 .. University of Wisconsin. Water Resources Center. Eutrophication Information Program. Occasional Paper [*A publication*]
WROQ....... Anderson, SC [*FM radio station call letters*]
WROR....... Zeeland, MI [*AM radio station call letters*]
WROS....... Jacksonville, FL [*AM radio station call letters*]
WROU....... West Carrollton, OH [*FM radio station call letters*]
W Roux A DB ... Wilhelm Roux' Archives of Developmental Biology [*A publication*]
WROV....... Roanoke, VA [*AM radio station call letters*]
WROV-FM ... Martinsville, VA [*FM radio station call letters*]
WROW....... Albany, NY [*AM radio station call letters*]
WROW-FM ... Albany, NY [*FM radio station call letters*]
WROX....... Clarksdale, MS [*AM radio station call letters*]
WROY....... Carmi, IL [*AM radio station call letters*]
WRP .... United States News and World Report [*A publication*]
WRP .... Water Resource Planning
WRP .... Water Resources Publications
WRP .... Weapons Release Programmer
WRP .... Weather Research Program [*Boulder, CO*] [*Department of Commerce*]   (GRD)
WRP .... Wellsford Residential Property Trust [*NYSE symbol*]   (SPSG)
WRP .... Wiener Random Process [*Mathematics*]
WRP .... Wildlife Research Project
WRP .... Wing Reference Plan [*Aviation*]
WRP .... Women's Rights Project   (EA)
WRP .... Workers' Revolutionary Party [*British*]   (PPW)
WRPA .... Water Resources Planning Act [*1965*]
Wr PA....... Wright's Reports [*37-50 Pennsylvania*] [*A publication*]   (DLA)
WRPC........ San German, PR [*FM radio station call letters*]
WRPC .... Weather Records Processing Centers
WRPG .... Warping
WRPI........ Troy, NY [*FM radio station call letters*]
WRPL....... Wadesboro, NC [*AM radio station call letters*]
WRPLS ..... Western Regional Public Library System [*Library network*]
WRPM ...... Poplarville, MS [*AM radio station call letters*]
WRPN .... Ripon, WI [*FM radio station call letters*]
WRPPD..... Wrapped
WRPQ .... Baraboo, WI [*AM radio station call letters*]
WRPR....... Mahwah, NJ [*FM radio station call letters*]
WRPR........ Wrapper
WRPS....... Rockland, MA [*FM radio station call letters*]
WRPS........ WearEver-Proctor Silex, Inc. [*Chillicothe, OH*] [*NASDAQ symbol*]   (NQ)
WRPSM.... War Reserve Publication Shipment Memorandum
WRPT........ Peterborough, NH [*AM radio station call letters*]
WRPX....... Hudson, WI [*AM radio station call letters*]
WRQ......... Westinghouse Resolver/Quantizer   (IEEE)
WRQK....... Canton, OH [*FM radio station call letters*]
WRQN....... Bowling Green, OH [*FM radio station call letters*]
WRQO....... Monticello, MS [*FM radio station call letters*]
WRQQ....... Farrell, PA [*AM radio station call letters*]
WRQR....... Farmville, NC [*FM radio station call letters*]
WRQT....... Bear Lake, MI [*FM radio station call letters*]
WRQX....... Washington, DC [*FM radio station call letters*]
WRR.......... Dallas, TX [*FM radio station call letters*]
WRR.......... Warm Run Record
WRR .... Warrington, Inc. [*Toronto Stock Exchange symbol*]
WRR .... Water Resource Region [*Water Resources Council*]
WRR .... Water Resources Research [*A publication*]   (NOAA)
WRR .... Woodmen Rangers and Rangerettes   (EA)
WRRA .... Frederiksted, VI [*AM radio station call letters*]
WRRA .... Mataram/Selaparang [*Indonesia*] [*ICAO location identifier*]   (ICLI)
WRRA .... Water Resources Research Act [*1964*]
WRRB .... Bima/Palibelo [*Indonesia*] [*ICAO location identifier*]   (ICLI)
WRRC .... Lawrenceville, NJ [*FM radio station call letters*]
WRRC .... Water Resources Research Center [*Indiana University*]   (RCD)
WRRC .... Water Resources Research Center [*University of Arizona*]   (RCD)
WRRC .... Water Resources Research Center [*University of Minnesota of Minneapolis Saint Paul*]   (RCD)
WRRC .... Water Resources Research Center [*Purdue University*]   (RCD)
WRRC .... Water Resources Research Center [*University of Massachusetts*]   (RCD)
WRRC .... Water Resources Research Center [*University of Hawaii*]   (RCD)
WRRC .... Western Rail Road Co. [*AAR code*]

WRRC .... Western Regional Research Center [*Department of Agriculture*] [*Albany, CA*]   (GRD)
WRRC .... Western Regional Resource Center [*University of Oregon*] [*Research center*]   (RCD)
WRRC .... Willow Run Research Center [*Air Force*]
WRRC .... Women's Research and Resources Centre   (EAIO)
WRRC .... Women's Research and Resources Centre Newsletter [*A publication*]
WRRC Report (Washington) ... Water Resources Research Center. Report (Washington) [*A publication*]
WRRC Spec Rep Univ MD ... WRRC [*Water Resources Research Center*] Special Report. University of Maryland [*A publication*]
WRRD .... Blennerhassett, WV [*AM radio station call letters*]
WRRE .... Juncos, PR [*AM radio station call letters*]
WRRF........ Washington, NC [*AM radio station call letters*]
WRRG ...... River Grove, IL [*FM radio station call letters*]
WRRH .... Franklin Lakes, NJ [*FM radio station call letters*]
WRRI .... Alabama Water Resources Research Institute [*Auburn, AL*] [*Department of the Interior*]   (GRD)
WRRI........ Water Resources Research Institute [*New Mexico State University*] [*Research center*]   (RCD)
WRRI........ Water Resources Research Institute [*Oregon State University*] [*Research center*]   (RCD)
WRRI........ Water Resources Research Institute [*Clemson University*] [*Research center*]
WRRI Auburn Univ Bull ... WRRI [*Water Resources Research Institute*]. Auburn University. Bulletin [*A publication*]
WRRK .... Manistee, MI [*FM radio station call letters*]
WRRL........ Rainelle, WV [*AM radio station call letters*]
WRRL-FM ... Rainelle, WV [*FM radio station call letters*]
WRRM ...... Cincinnati, OH [*FM radio station call letters*]
WRRN ...... Warren, PA [*FM radio station call letters*]
WRRO ...... Warren, OH [*AM radio station call letters*]
WRRR .... Bali International/Ngurah Rai [*Indonesia*] [*ICAO location identifier*]   (ICLI)
WRRR .... Rockford, IL [*AM radio station call letters*]
WRRR .... St. Mary's, WV [*FM radio station call letters*]
WRRR .... Walter Reed Research Reactor [*Military*]
WRRS........ Sumbawa/Sumbawa Besar [*Indonesia*] [*ICAO location identifier*]   (ICLI)
WRRS........ Wire Relay Radio System
WRRT .... Waikabubak/Tambolaka [*Indonesia*] [*ICAO location identifier*]   (ICLI)
WRRW ...... Waingapu/Mau Hau [*Indonesia*] [*ICAO location identifier*]   (ICLI)
WRRZ .... Bali [*Indonesia*] [*ICAO location identifier*]   (ICLI)
WRRZ .... Clinton, NC [*AM radio station call letters*]
WRS .... Walter Reed Society   (EA)
WRS .... War Reserve Stocks   (AABC)
WRS .... Warning and Report System   (CET)
WRS .... Warsak [*Pakistan*] [*Seismograph station code, US Geological Survey*]   (SEIS)
WRS .... Wasabi Resources Ltd. [*Toronto Stock Exchange symbol*] [*Vancouver Stock Exchange symbol*]
WRS .... Washington Representative Services, Inc. [*Information service or system*]   (IID)
WRS .... Water Recirculation System
WRS .... Water Recovery Subsystem [*NASA*]   (KSC)
WRS .... Wave Radiometer System
WRS .... Weapons Recommendation Sheet   (MCD)
WRS .... Weather RADAR Set [*or System*]
WRS .... Weather Reconnaissance Squadron [*Air Force*]   (CINC)
WRS .... Western Massachusetts Regional Library System, Springfield, MA [*OCLC symbol*]   (OCLC)
WRS .... Wide-Range Sensor
WRS .... Winston Resources Ltd. [*AMEX symbol*]   (SPSG)
WRS .... Word Recognition System
WRS .... Working Transmission Reference System [*Telecommunications*]   (TEL)
WRS .... Worse   (FAAC)
WRS .... Write Strobe
WRSA....... Decatur, AL [*FM radio station call letters*]
WRSA....... War Reserve Stocks for Allies   (MCD)
WRSA....... World Rabbit Science Association [*Cheltenham, Gloucestershire, England*]   (EAIO)
WRSC....... Cepu/Ngloram [*Indonesia*] [*ICAO location identifier*]   (ICLI)
WRSC....... State College, PA [*AM radio station call letters*]
WRSD .... Folsom, PA [*FM radio station call letters*]
WRSE........ Elmhurst, IL [*FM radio station call letters*]
WRSF........ Columbia, NC [*FM radio station call letters*]
WRSFA ..... Western Reinforcing Steel Fabricators Association
WRSG ...... Panama City, FL [*FM radio station call letters*]
WRSH ...... Rockingham, NC [*FM radio station call letters*]
WRSI .... Greenfield, MA [*FM radio station call letters*]
WRSIC...... Water Resources Scientific Information Center [*US Geological Survey*] [*Reston, VA*] [*Database originator*]
WRSJ .... Bayamon, PR [*AM radio station call letters*]
WRSJ .... Surabaya/Juanda [*Indonesia*] [*ICAO location identifier*]   (ICLI)
WRSK....... Slippery Rock, PA [*FM radio station call letters*]
WRSK........ War Readiness Spares Kit [*Air Force*]   (AFM)
WRSL........ Stanford, KY [*AM radio station call letters*]

WRSL-FM ... Stanford, KY [*FM radio station call letters*]
WRSM ...... Sumiton, AL [*AM radio station call letters*]
WRSP........ Springfield, IL [*Television station call letters*]
WRSP........ Surabaya/Perak [*Indonesia*] [*ICAO location identifier*]　(ICLI)
WRSP........ World Register of Scientific Periodicals
WRSQ .... Solo/Adi Sumarmo Wiryokusumo [*Indonesia*] [*ICAO location identifier*]　(ICLI)
WRSq .... Weather Reconnaissance Squadron [*Air Force*]　(AFM)
WRSR........ Two Harbors, MN [*FM radio station call letters*]
WRSR........ Water Reactor Safety Research [*Nuclear energy*]　(NRCH)
WRSS .... San Sebastian, PR [*AM radio station call letters*]
WRSS .... Surabaya/Gedangan [*Indonesia*] [*ICAO location identifier*]　(ICLI)
WRSSR ..... White Russian Soviet Socialist Republic　(IIA)
WRST........ Oshkosh, WI [*FM radio station call letters*]
WRST........ Sumenep/Trunojoyo [*Indonesia*] [*ICAO location identifier*]　(ICLI)
WRSU .... New Brunswick, NJ [*FM radio station call letters*]
WRSV........ Rocky Mount, NC [*FM radio station call letters*]
WRSV........ Wheat Rosette Stunt Virus [*Plant pathology*]
WRSW........ Warsaw, IN [*AM radio station call letters*]
WRSW-FM ... Warsaw, IN [*FM radio station call letters*]
WRT .... Warrior River Terminal Co. [*AAR code*]
WRT .... Water Round Torpedo　(MSA)
WRT .... Westerra Resources Ltd. [*Vancouver Stock Exchange symbol*]
WRT .... With Reference To
WRT .... With Respect To　(KSC)
WRT .... Wright Air Lines, Inc. [*Cleveland, OH*] [*FAA designator*]　(FAAC)
WRT .... Wright-Hargreaves Mines Ltd. [*Toronto Stock Exchange symbol*]　(SPSG)
WRT .... Wrought
WRTA .... Altoona, PA [*AM radio station call letters*]
WRTA .... Western Railroad Traffic Association　(EA)
WRTB........ Washington, IN [*FM radio station call letters*]
WRTB........ Wire Rope Technical Board　(EA)
WRTC .... Hartford, CT [*FM radio station call letters*]
WRTC .... Working Reference Telephone Circuit [*Telecommunications*]　(TEL)
WRTC .... [*The*] Writer Corp. [*NASDAQ symbol*]　(NQ)
WRTE........ Cahokia, IL [*FM radio station call letters*]
WRTH....... St. Louis, MO [*AM radio station call letters*]
WRTH....... World Radio TV Handbook [*A publication*]
WRTHG..... Worthing [*City in England*]
WRTI........ Philadelphia, PA [*FM radio station call letters*]
WRTN .... New Rochelle, NY [*FM radio station call letters*]
WRTO ...... Goulds, FL [*FM radio station call letters*]
WRTP .... Chapel Hill, NC [*AM radio station call letters*]
WRTQ .... Harrisburg, PA [*FM radio station call letters*]
WRTTM.... Warhead Replacement Tactical Telemetry System　(DWSG)
WRTU ...... San Juan, PR [*FM radio station call letters*]
WRTV .... Indianapolis, IN [*Television station call letters*]
WRTX .... Dover, DE [*FM radio station call letters*]
WRTY .... Jackson Township, PA [*FM radio station call letters*]
WRU.......... Watershed Research Unit [*Department of Agriculture*] [*Columbia, MO*]　(GRD)
WRU.......... Wave Run-Up
WRU.......... Western Reserve University [*Later, Case Western Reserve University*]
WRU.......... Western Reserve University. Bulletin [*A publication*]
WRU.......... Who Are You? [*Communication*]
WRUA....... Fajardo, PR [*Television station call letters*]
WRUB .... Pittsville, MD [*AM radio station call letters*]
WRUC .... Schenectady, NY [*FM radio station call letters*]
WRUF .... Gainesville, FL [*AM radio station call letters*]
WRUF-FM ... Gainesville, FL [*FM radio station call letters*]
WRUL .... Carmi, IL [*FM radio station call letters*]
WRUM...... Rumford, ME [*AM radio station call letters*]
WRUN....... Utica, NY [*AM radio station call letters*]
WRUR ...... Rochester, NY [*FM radio station call letters*]
WRUS ...... Russellville, KY [*AM radio station call letters*]
WRUSS.... Western Reserve University Relay Searching Selector　(SAA)
WRUT ...... West Rutland, VT [*FM radio station call letters*]
WRUV ...... Burlington, VT [*FM radio station call letters*]
WRUW...... Cleveland, OH [*FM radio station call letters*]
WRV .... Water Relief Valve
WRV .... Water-Retention Value
WRV .... West Riding Volunteers [*British military*]　(DMA)
WRVA....... Richmond, VA [*AM radio station call letters*]
WRVC .... Ashland, KY [*FM radio station call letters*]
WRVC .... Huntington, WV [*AM radio station call letters*]
WRVE .... Watertown, NY [*FM radio station call letters*]
WRVF........ Upper Arlington, OH [*FM radio station call letters*]
WRVG .... Georgetown, KY [*FM radio station call letters*]
WRVI .... Virden, IL [*FM radio station call letters*]
WRVK ...... Mount Vernon, KY [*AM radio station call letters*]
WRVL........ Lynchburg, VA [*FM radio station call letters*]
WRVM ...... Suring, WI [*FM radio station call letters*]
WRVN ...... Utica, NY [*FM radio station call letters*]
WRVO....... Oswego, NY [*FM radio station call letters*]
WRVP........ Wedged Renal Venous Pressure [*Medicine*]　(MAE)

WRVQ .... Richmond, VA [*FM radio station call letters*]
WRVR....... Memphis, TN [*FM radio station call letters*]
WRVS........ Elizabeth City, NC [*FM radio station call letters*]
WRVS........ Women's Royal Voluntary Service [*Formerly, WVS*] [*British*]
WRVT .... Rutland, VT [*FM radio station call letters*]
WRVU....... Nashville, TN [*FM radio station call letters*]
WRVW ...... Hudson, NY [*FM radio station call letters*]
WRVX .... Mt. Carmel, TN [*AM radio station call letters*]
WRVY .... Henry, IL [*FM radio station call letters*]
WR(W) ..... War Reserve (Weapon)
WRW .... Weather Reconnaissance Wing [*Military*]
WRW .... Will's Air [*Barnstable, MA*] [*FAA designator*]　(FAAC)
WRWA ..... Dothan, AL [*FM radio station call letters*]
WRWC ...... Rockton, IL [*FM radio station call letters*]
WRWD ..... Highland, NY [*FM radio station call letters*]
WRWg ...... Weather Reconnaissance Wing [*Air Force*]　(AFM)
WRWH..... Cleveland, GA [*AM radio station call letters*]
WRWK ..... Warwick Railway Co. [*AAR code*]
WRWR ..... San Juan, PR [*Television station call letters*]
WRWX ..... Sanibel, FL [*FM radio station call letters*]
WRX .... Western Refrigerator Line Co. [*AAR code*]
WRXB .... St. Petersburg Beach, FL [*AM radio station call letters*]
WRXC .... Shelton, CT [*FM radio station call letters*]
WRXK ...... Bonita Springs, FL [*FM radio station call letters*]
WRXL....... Richmond, VA [*FM radio station call letters*]
WRXO ...... Roxboro, NC [*AM radio station call letters*]
WRXR ...... Aiken, SC [*AM radio station call letters*]
WRXR-FM ... Aiken, SC [*FM radio station call letters*]
WRXX ...... Centralia, IL [*FM radio station call letters*]
WRXY ...... Tice, FL [*Television station call letters*]
WRXZ ...... Le Roy, IL [*FM radio station call letters*]
WRY .... Westray [*Scotland*] [*Airport symbol*]　(OAG)
WRY .... Wheeling Railway
WRY .... World Refugee Year
WRYM ..... New Britain, CT [*AM radio station call letters*]
WRYT ...... Edwardsville, IL [*AM radio station call letters*]
WRZ .... Western Rift Zone [*Geology*]
WRZAA ... Weltraumfahrt und Raketentechnik [*A publication*]
WRZI........ Buffalo, KY [*FM radio station call letters*]
WRZN ...... Hernando, FL [*AM radio station call letters*]
WRZQ ...... Greenburg, IN [*FM radio station call letters*]
WRZZ ...... Ravenswood, WV [*FM radio station call letters*]
WS .... Single Conductor Cable [*JETDS nomenclature*] [*Military*]　(CET)
WS .... Superior Public Library, Superior, WI [*Library symbol*] [*Library of Congress*]　(LCLS)
WS .... Waardenburg's Syndrome [*Medicine*]
WS .... Wagner's Missouri Statutes [*A publication*]　(DLA)
WS .... Wall Street
WS .... Wallops Station [*Later, WFC*] [*NASA*]
WS .... War Scale　(ADA)
WS .... War Service
WS .... War Substantive [*British military*]　(DMA)
WS .... Ware Shoals Railroad Co. [*AAR code*]
WS .... Warm Shop [*Nuclear energy*]　(NRCH)
WS .... Warthin-Starry [*Silver impregnation stain*]
WS .... Washine Chemical Corp. [*Research code symbol*]
WS .... Waste Stack [*Technical drawings*]
WS .... Waste System
WS .... Water Safety
WS .... Water Servicer　(NASA)
WS .... Water Soluble
WS .... Water-Storage Cell [*Botany*]
WS .... Water Supply
WS .... Water Surface [*Elevation*]
WS .... Water System
WS .... Watered Stock
W S .... Watt Second
w/s............ Watt-Seconds
W & S......... Watts and Sergeant's Pennsylvania Reports [*1841-1845*] [*A publication*]　(DLA)
W/S............ Watts per Steradian　(NG)
WS .... Wave Soldering
WS .... Weak Signals [*Radio*]
WS .... Weapon System
WS .... Weapons Specifications　(NG)
W/S............ Weapons System
WS .... Weather Service
W/S............ Weather Ship　(NATG)
WS .... Weather Squadron　(MCD)
WS .... Weather Station
WS .... Weatherstripping　(AAG)
WS .... Wedgwood Society　(EA)
WS .... Wee Scots
WS .... Weirton Steel Corp. [*NYSE symbol*]　(SPSG)
WS .... Welsh Society　(EA)
WS .... Welt der Slaven [*A publication*]
WS .... Werner's Syndrome [*Medicine*]
WS .... West Saxon [*Dialect of Old English*] [*Language, etc.*]
WS .... West Semitic　(BJA)

ws	Western Samoa [*MARC country of publication code*] [*Library of Congress*] (LCCP)
WS	Western Samoa [*ANSI two-letter standard code*] (CNC)
WS	Western Speech [*A publication*]
WS	Wet Smoothed (BJA)
W v S	Wetboek van Strafrecht [*A publication*]
WS	Wetted Surface
WS	Wheat Straw
W & S	Whiskey and Soda
WS	White Sisters [*Missionary Sisters of Our Lady of Africa*] [*Roman Catholic religious order*]
WS	White Sucker [*Ichthyology*]
WS	White-Throated Sparrow [*Ornithology*]
WS	Wide Shot [*Photography*]
WS	Wiener Studien [*A publication*]
W-S	Wigner-Seitz [*Construction cell*] [*Solid state physics*]
WS	Wilderness Society (EA)
WS	[*The*] Wildlife Society
WS	Will Ship (MCD)
WS	Williams Syndrome [*Medicine*]
WS	Willow Society (EA)
W & S	Wilson and Shaw's Scotch Appeal Cases, English House of Lords [*A publication*] (DLA)
WS	Wind Satellite (SSD)
WS	Wind Shield (NASA)
WS	Wind Speed
WS	Windsonde (KSC)
WS	Windspeaker [*A publication*]
WS	Wing Station [*Aviation*]
WS	Wingspread (WGA)
WS	Wire Send [*Telecommunications*] (TEL)
WS	Wire Sound
WS	Wireless Set (MCD)
WS	Wirtschaft und Statistik [*Germany*]
WS	Wirtschaftsflug Rhein Main GmbH & Co. KG [*West Germany*] [*ICAO designator*] (FAAC)
Ws	Wisdom [*Old Testament Book*] (BJA)
W/S	With Stock [*Business term*]
WS	Withholding Statement (AAG)
W & S	Woerter und Sachen [*A publication*]
W & S	Woerter und Sachen [*A publication*]
WS	Women's Services [*Military*] [*British*]
WS	Women's Size
WS	Women's Studies: An Interdisciplinary Journal [*A publication*]
WS	Women's Suffrage (ROG)
WS	Wonder Stories [*A publication*]
WS	Wood-Sheathed Deck [*of a ship*] (DS)
WS	Word Study [*A publication*]
WS	Word Sync
WS	WordStar [*Computer program*]
WS	Work Stand (MCD)
WS	Work Statement (AAG)
W/S	Work Station [*NASA*] (NASA)
WS	Work Stoppage (AAG)
WS	Working Space
WS	Working Storage [*Data processing*] (MDG)
WS	Worksheet (AAG)
WS	World Solidarity [*Belgium*] (EAIO)
WS	Worldscale
WS	Worldwide Searches (EA)
WS	Wort und Sinn [*A publication*]
WS	Worthy Sister (BJA)
WS	Writer to the Signet [*British*]
WS	Wrought Steel (MSA)
2WS	Two-Wheel Steering [*Automotive engineering*]
4WS	Four-Wheel Steering [*Automotive engineering*]
WSA	Intereconomics. Monthly Review of International Trade and Development [*A publication*]
WSA	Wagner Society of America (EA)
WSA	War Shipping Administration [*Within Office of Emergency Management*] [*World War II*]
WSA	War Supplies Agency (NATG)
WSA	Water-Soluble Adjuvant [*Immunology*]
WSA	Waveguide Slot Array
WSA	Weapons Systems Analysis [*Army*] (AABC)
WSA	Web Sling Association [*Later, WSTDA*] (EA)
WSA	Weed Society of America [*Later, WSSA*] (EA)
WSA	West Sea Development [*Vancouver Stock Exchange symbol*]
WSA	Western Slavonic Association [*Later, WSA Fraternal Life*] (EA)
WSA	Western Surfing Association (EA)
WSA	Western Surgical Association (EA)
WSA	Wholesale Stationers' Association (EA)
WSA	Wilderness Study Area [*Department of the Interior*]
WSA	Williams Syndrome Association (EA)
WSA	Winter Soldier Archive (EA)
WSA	Wisconsin Statutes Annotated [*A publication*] (DLA)
WSA	Wolfenbuetteler Studien zur Aufklarung [*A publication*]
WSA	Wolverine Society of America (EA)
WSA	Women Studies Abstracts [*A publication*]
WSA	Women's Student Association (EA)
WSA	Wonder Story Annual [*A publication*]
WSA	Workplace Standards Administration [*Department of Labor*]
WSA	World Service Authority, District 5: Orient-Mediterranean Sea Coast [*Israel*] (EAIO)
WSA	World Sign Associates (EA)
WSA	Writers' Sodality of America [*Defunct*]
WSAA	Warrenton, GA [*FM radio station call letters*]
WSAA	Waveguide Slot Array Antenna
WSAA	Western States Angus Association (EA)
WSAAA	Western States Advertising Agencies Association (EA)
WSAB	Pentwater, MI [*FM radio station call letters*]
WSAC	Louisa, KY [*FM radio station call letters*]
WSAC	Washington State Apple Commission (EA)
WSAC	Water Space Amenity Commission [*British*] (DCTA)
WSAC	West of Scotland Agricultural College [*British*] (IRUK)
WSAD	Vandalia, MI [*FM radio station call letters*]
WSAD	Weapon System Analysis Division [*Navy*]
WSAE	Spring Arbor, MI [*FM radio station call letters*]
WSAF	Trion, GA [*AM radio station call letters*]
WSAG	Poquonock, CT [*AM radio station call letters*]
WSAG	Sembawang [*Singapore*] [*ICAO location identifier*] (ICLI)
WSAG	Washington Special Action Group [*National Security Council*]
WSAH	World Smoking and Health [*A publication*]
WSAI	Cincinnati, OH [*AM radio station call letters*]
WSAI	[*The*] Wine Society of America, Inc. [*NASDAQ symbol*] (NQ)
WSAJ	Grove City, PA [*AM radio station call letters*]
WSAJ-FM	Grove City, PA [*FM radio station call letters*]
WSAL	Logansport, IN [*AM radio station call letters*]
WSAM	Saginaw, MI [*AM radio station call letters*]
WSAM	Weapon Systems Acquisition Management [*Navy*] (MCD)
WSAN	Vieques, PR [*FM radio station call letters*]
WSAO	Senatobia, MS [*AM radio station call letters*]
WSAO	Weapon System Analysis Office [*Navy*] (MCD)
WSAP	Paya Lebar [*Singapore*] [*ICAO location identifier*] (ICLI)
WSAP	Weapon Status and Approval Panel [*Military*] (CAAL)
WSAP	Weapon System Acquisition Process (MCD)
WSAP	Weighted Sensitivity Analysis Program [*Environmental Protection Agency*]
W & S App	Wilson and Shaw's Scotch Appeal Cases, English House of Lords [*A publication*] (DLA)
WSAQ	Port Huron, MI [*FM radio station call letters*]
WSAR	Fall River, MA [*AM radio station call letters*]
WSAR	Singapore [*Singapore*] [*ICAO location identifier*] (ICLI)
WSAR	Weekly Significant Action Report (AFIT)
WSAS	Weapon System Acceptance Schedule (AAG)
WSASSA	Wholesale School, Art, and Stationery Supplies Association [*Later, WSA*] (EA)
WSAT	Salisbury, NC [*AM radio station call letters*]
WSAT	Tengah [*Singapore*] [*ICAO location identifier*] (ICLI)
WSAT	Weapon Systems Accuracy [*formerly, Acceptance*] Trials [*Navy*] (NG)
WSATO	War Shipping Administration Training Organization [*Terminated*]
WSAU	Wausau Paper Mills Co. [*NASDAQ symbol*] (NQ)
WSAU	Wausau, WI [*AM radio station call letters*]
WSAV	Savannah, GA [*Television station call letters*]
WSAVA	World Small Animal Veterinary Association [*See also AMVPA*] [*Hatfield, Hertfordshire, England*] (EAIO)
WSAW	Wausau, WI [*Television station call letters*]
WSAWD	White Sands Air Weather Detachment [*New Mexico*]
WSA-WGWC	World Service Authority of the World Government of World Citizens (EA)
WSAX	West Saxon [*Dialect of Old English*] [*Language, etc.*]
WSAY	Rocky Mount, NC [*FM radio station call letters*]
WSAZ	Huntington, WV [*Television station call letters*]
WSB	Atlanta, GA [*AM radio station call letters*]
WSB	Steamboat Bay, AK [*Location identifier*] [*FAA*] (FAAL)
WSB	Wage Stabilization Board [*Terminated, 1953*]
Wsb	Washburn Law Journal [*A publication*]
WSB	Water-Soluble Base
WSB	Water Spray Boiler (NASA)
WSB	Weekly Statistical Bulletin [*Database*] [*American Petroleum Institute*] [*Information service or system*] (CRD)
WSB	Wheat-Soya Blend (EA)
WSB	Will Send Boat
WSB	World Scout Bureau [*Geneva, Switzerland*] (EA)
WSBA	York, PA [*AM radio station call letters*]
WSBB	New Smyrna Beach, FL [*AM radio station call letters*]
WSBC	Chicago, IL [*AM radio station call letters*]
WSBC	Wesbanco, Inc. [*NASDAQ symbol*] (NQ)
WSbD	Door County Library, Sturgeon Bay, WI [*Library symbol*] [*Library of Congress*] (LCLS)
WSBE	Providence, RI [*Television station call letters*]
WSBF	Clemson, SC [*FM radio station call letters*]
WSB-FM	Atlanta, GA [*FM radio station call letters*]
WSBG	Stroudsburg, PA [*FM radio station call letters*]
WSBI	Static, TN [*AM radio station call letters*]
WSBK	Boston, MA [*Television station call letters*]
WSBK	Western Bank [*Coos Bay, OR*] [*NASDAQ symbol*] (NQ)
WSBL	Selbyville, DE [*FM radio station call letters*]
WSBM	Florence, AL [*AM radio station call letters*]

WSBM.......	Wheat Soilborne Mosaic Virus
WSBMV....	Wheat Soilborne Mosaic Virus
WSBN	Norton, VA [*Television station call letters*]
WSBP.......	Western Society of Business Publications [*Defunct*] (EA)
WSBR.......	Boca Raton, FL [*AM radio station call letters*]
WSBS	Great Barrington, MA [*AM radio station call letters*]
WSBSA	Weapon System Base Supply Account [*Military*] (AFIT)
WSBT.......	South Bend, IN [*AM radio station call letters*]
WSBT-TV ...	South Bend, IN [*Television station call letters*]
WSB-TV....	Atlanta, GA [*Television station call letters*]
WSBU	St. Bonaventure, NY [*FM radio station call letters*]
WSBU	Wahlenbergia. Scripta Botanica Umensia [*A publication*]
WSBV.......	South Boston, VA [*AM radio station call letters*]
WSBW.......	Weddell Sea Bottom Water [*Oceanography*]
WSBX........	[*The*] Washington Savings Bank FSB [*NASDAQ symbol*] (NQ)
WSBY.......	Salisbury, MD [*FM radio station call letters*]
WSC	Ebareport. Weekly Special Survey of Turkish Business, Industrial Investment, and Contracts Markets [*A publication*]
WSC	Wall Street Computer Review [*A publication*]
WSC	Washington Science Center [*Maryland*] [*Seismograph station code, US Geological Survey*] [*Closed*] (SEIS)
WSC	Water Systems Council (EA)
WSC	Weapon System Computer (MCD)
WSC	Weapon System Console [*Military*] (CAAL)
WSC	Weapon System Contractor
WSC	Weapon System Costing [*Navy*]
WSC	Weapons System Code
WSC	Weber State College [*Ogden, UT*]
WSC	Wesco Financial Corp. [*AMEX symbol*] (SPSG)
WSC	Westair Commuter Airlines [*Santa Rosa, CA*] [*FAA designator*] (FAAC)
WSC	Westech Resources Ltd. [*Vancouver Stock Exchange symbol*]
WSC	Western Sahara Campaign for Human Rights and Humanitarian Relief (EA)
WSC	Western Simulation Council
WSC	Western Snow Conference (EA)
WSC	Western Snow Conference. Proceedings [*A publication*]
WSC	White Sisters of Charity of St. Vincent de Paul [*Roman Catholic religious order*]
WSC	Wideband Signal Conditioner (MCD)
WSC	Wildcat Service Corp. (EA)
WSC	Wilkinson Sword Company [*British military*] (DMA)
WSC	William Shatner Connection (EA)
WSC	Wind Sounding Capability
WSC	Wing Security Control [*Air Force*] (AFM)
WSC	Winona State College [*Later, Winona State University*] [*Minnesota*]
WSC	Winston Spencer Churchill [*1874-1965*] [*British statesman and prime minister*]
WSC	Wisconsin State College [*Later, University of Wisconsin*]
WSC	Working Security Committee [*Navy*]
WSC	World Series Cricket
WSC	World Spanish Congress (EA)
WSC	World Spiritual Council (EA)
WSC	World Sportscar Championship [*Auto racing*]
WSC	World Straw Conference
WSC	World Survey of Climatology [*Elsevier Book Series*] [*A publication*]
WSC	Wrap-Spring Clutch
WSC	Wright State, Celina Branch, Celina, OH [*OCLC symbol*] (OCLC)
WSC	Writing Services Center
WSCA.......	Weather Service Cooperating Agencies [*National Weather Service*] (NOAA)
WSCA.......	World Surface Coatings Abstracts [*Paint Research Association*] [*Information service or system*] [*A publication*]
WSCB.......	Springfield, MA [*FM radio station call letters*]
WSCC.......	Somerset, KY [*FM radio station call letters*]
WSCC.......	Weapon System Configuration Control [*Navy*] (AAG)
WSCC.......	Weather Service Communications Center [*National Weather Service*] (NOAA)
WSCC.......	Western State College of Colorado [*Gunnison*]
WSCC.......	Western Systems Coordinating Council [*Regional power council*]
WSCC.......	Work Station Control Center [*NASA*] (NASA)
WSCCM....	Weapon System Configuration Control Manual [*Navy*] (NG)
WSCD	Duluth, MN [*FM radio station call letters*]
WSCD	Welfare and Service Conditions Department [*British military*] (DMA)
WSCF.......	Vero Beach, FL [*FM radio station call letters*]
WSCF.......	World Student Christian Federation (EA)
WSCF Books ...	World Student Christian Federation Books [*A publication*]
WSCH	Aurora, IN [*FM radio station call letters*]
WSCH	Weather Service Communications Handbook [*National Weather Service*] (NOAA)
WSCHP.......	Wen Shih Che Hsueh-Pao [*Taiwan University*] [*A publication*]
WSCI.......	Charleston, SC [*FM radio station call letters*]
WSCI.........	Washington Scientific Industries, Inc. [*NASDAQ symbol*] (NQ)

WSCL........	Salisbury, MD [*FM radio station call letters*]
WSCL........	Wisconsin Studies in Contemporary Literature [*Later, Contemporary Literature*] [*A publication*]
WSCM......	Cobleskill, NY [*AM radio station call letters*]
WSCM......	Weapon System Compatible Munition [*Military*]
WSCMB ...	Weapon System Configuration Management Board (MCD)
WSCN	Cloquet, MN [*FM radio station call letters*]
WSCO	Suring, WI [*Television station call letters*]
WSCO	Weber State College [*Odgen, UT*]
WSCOC....	Wills Sainte Claire Owners Club (EA)
WSCP........	Sandy Creek-Pulaski, NY [*AM radio station call letters*]
WSCP........	Weapon System Stock Control Plan (SAA)
WSCP........	Weapons System Control Point
WSCPA	Western States Section. Combustion Institute. Paper [*United States*] [*A publication*]
WSCP-FM ...	Pulaski, NY [*FM radio station call letters*]
WSCQ	West Columbia, SC [*FM radio station call letters*]
WSCS	Washington State College. Studies [*A publication*]
WSCS	Waste Solidification and Compaction Station [*Nuclear energy*] (NRCH)
WSCS	Weapon System Communications System (AAG)
WSCS	Wide Sense Cyclo-Stationary [*Communication*]
WSCSR	Weapons System Contract Status Report [*Navy*] (NG)
WSCT........	Wainscot [*Technical drawings*]
WSCV.......	Fort Lauderdale, FL [*Television station call letters*]
WSCW.......	South Charleston, WV [*AM radio station call letters*]
WSCZ........	Greenwood, SC [*FM radio station call letters*]
WSD	Sheboygan County Federated Library System, Mead Public Library, Sheboygan, WI [*OCLC symbol*] (OCLC)
WSD	Warfare Systems Directorate (MCD)
WSD	Weapon Support Detachment (MCD)
WSD	Weapon System Designator
WSD	Weapon System Development [*Military*] (CAAL)
WSD	Weapon System Director
WSD	Weapons System Demonstration (MCD)
WSD	White Sands, NM [*Location identifier*] [*FAA*] (FAAL)
WSD	Wind Speed Detector
WSD	Wirtschaftsdienst. Wirtschaftspolitische Monatsschrift [*A publication*]
WSD	Working Stress Design [*Nuclear energy*] (NRCH)
WSD	World Space Directory [*A publication*]
WSD	World Systems Division [*of Communications Satellite Corp.*] [*Telecommunications*] (TEL)
WSDA	Water and Sewer Distributors of America (EA)
WSDB.......	World Studies Data Bank (IID)
WSDC	Weapon System Design Criteria (AAG)
WSDC	Weapons System Designator Code (NVT)
WSDC	Wisconsin State Data Center [*Wisconsin State Department of Administration*] [*Madison*] [*Information service or system*] (IID)
WSDD	Weapon Status Digital Display
WSDH	Sandwich, MA [*FM radio station call letters*]
WSDI........	Wall Street Deli [*Formerly, Sandwich Chef*] [*NASDAQ symbol*] (SPSG)
WSDL.......	Weapons System Development Laboratory
WSDL.......	Weapons Systems Data Link (MCD)
WSDM	Brazil, IN [*FM radio station call letters*]
WSDM	Weapon System Data Module
WSDP.......	Plymouth, MI [*FM radio station call letters*]
WSDP.......	Weapons System Development Plan
WSDQ	Dunlap, TN [*AM radio station call letters*]
WSDR	Sterling, IL [*AM radio station call letters*]
WSDS.......	Ypsilanti, MI [*AM radio station call letters*]
WSDT.......	Soddy-Daisy, TN [*AM radio station call letters*]
WSD/TD...	Weapon System Demonstration Test Directive (AAG)
WSE...........	National Weather Service Employees Organization
WSE...........	Weapon Support Equipment [*Navy*] (NG)
WSE...........	Weapon System Engineering [*Navy*] (NG)
WSE...........	Weapons System Evaluator (MCD)
WSE...........	Weapons Systems Effectiveness
WSE...........	West-Southeast (ROG)
WSE...........	Western Allenbee Oil & Gas Co. Ltd. [*Vancouver Stock Exchange symbol*]
WSE...........	Western Society of Engineers
WSE...........	Winnipeg Stock Exchange (HGAA)
WSE...........	Work Shop Equipment (SAA)
WSE...........	Wound, Skin, Enteric [*Isolation*] [*Medicine*]
WSE...........	WWMCCS [*Worldwide Military Command and Control System*] Systems Engineer (MCD)
WSEB.......	Englewood, FL [*FM radio station call letters*]
WSEC........	Jacksonville, IL [*Television station call letters*]
WSEC........	Washington State Electronics Council
WSEC........	Watt-Second (AAG)
WSECL.......	Weapon System Equipment Component List
WSED........	Weapon System Electrical Diagrams
WSEE........	Erie, PA [*Television station call letters*]
WSEES......	Weapon System Electromagnetic Environment Simulator (MCD)
WSEF	Weapons System Evaluation Facility (MCD)
WSEF	Weapons Systems Effectiveness Factors
WSEFGT...	Weapons System Evaluation Facility Group Test (MCD)

WSEG........	Weapon System Evaluation Group [*DoD and Air Force*] (MCD)
WSEH	Cumberland, KY [*FM radio station call letters*]
WSEI........	Olney, IL [*FM radio station call letters*]
WSEIAC ...	Weapon System Effectiveness Industry Advisory Committee
WSEJ	Marianna, FL [*FM radio station call letters*]
WSEK.......	Somerset, KY [*FM radio station call letters*]
WSEL.......	Pontotoc, MS [*AM radio station call letters*]
WSEL........	Weapon System Engineering Laboratory
WSEL-FM ...	Pontotoc, MS [*FM radio station call letters*]
WSEM.......	Donalsonville, GA [*AM radio station call letters*]
WSEM......	Weapon System Evaluation Missile [*Air Force*] (AFM)
WSem	West Semitic (BJA)
WSEN	Baldwinsville, NY [*AM radio station call letters*]
WSEN-FM ...	Baldwinsville, NY [*FM radio station call letters*]
WSEO	Nelsonville, OH [*FM radio station call letters*]
WSEO	Weather Service Evaluation Officer [*National Weather Service*]
WSEO	WWMCCS [*Worldwide Military Command and Control System*] System Engineering Office (MCD)
WSEP........	Waste Solidification Engineering Prototype Plant [*Nuclear energy*]
WSEP........	Weapon System Evaluation Program [*Air Force*]
WSEQ	Reidland, KY [*FM radio station call letters*]
WSER........	Elkton, MD [*AM radio station call letters*]
WSES	Waterford Steam Electric Station [*Nuclear energy*] (NRCH)
WSES	Weapons System Evaluation Squadron
WSESA	Weapon System and Equipment Support Analysis
WSET.......	Lynchburg, VA [*Television station call letters*]
WSET	Weapon System Evaluation Test [*Navy*] (NG)
WSET	Writers and Scholars Educational Trust [*British*] (EAIO)
WSEU	Hinesville, GA [*FM radio station call letters*]
WSEV	Sevierville, TN [*AM radio station call letters*]
WSEW.......	Sanford, ME [*FM radio station call letters*]
WSEZ........	Paoli, IN [*AM radio station call letters*]
WSF..........	Waste Shipping Facility [*Nuclear energy*] (NRCH)
WSF..........	Water/Sand Fillable
WSF..........	Water-Soluble Fraction
WSF..........	Water Supply Forecast (NOAA)
WSF..........	Wave Soldering Fixture (MCD)
WSF..........	Weapon System File (MCD)
WSF..........	Weather Support Force [*Military*] (AFM)
WSF..........	Week Second Feet
WSF..........	Well Spouse Foundation (EA)
WSF..........	Well-Springs Foundation (EA)
WSF..........	Western Sea Frontier [*Navy*]
WSF..........	William Shatner Fellowship (EA)
WSF..........	Women for a Secure Future (EA)
WSF..........	Women's Sports Foundation (EA)
WSF..........	Work Station Facility
WSF..........	World Salt Foundation (EA)
WSF..........	World Science Fiction [*France*] (EAIO)
WSF..........	World Scout Foundation [*Geneva, Switzerland*] (EAIO)
WSF..........	World Sephardi Federation [*See also FSM*] [*Geneva, Switzerland*] (EAIO)
WSF..........	World SF [*Science Fiction*] (EA)
WSF..........	World Space Foundation (EA)
WSF..........	World Strengthlifting Federation [*India*] (EAIO)
WSFA.......	Montgomery, AL [*Television station call letters*]
WSFB	Quitman, GA [*AM radio station call letters*]
WSFC........	Somerset, KY [*AM radio station call letters*]
WSFC........	Wall Street Financial Corp. [*NASDAQ symbol*] (NQ)
WSFC........	White Sands Field Center [*New Mexico*]
WSFC........	Women's Solid Fuel Council [*British*] (DI)
WSFI........	Wood and Synthetic Flooring Institute (EA)
WSFJ........	Newark, OH [*Television station call letters*]
WSFL.......	New Bern, NC [*AM radio station call letters*]
WSFL-FM ...	New Bern, NC [*FM radio station call letters*]
WSFM.......	Southport, NC [*FM radio station call letters*]
WSFO.......	Weather Service Forecast Office [*National Weather Service*]
WSFP	Fort Myers, FL [*FM radio station call letters*]
WSFP	World Showcase Fellowship Program [*Walt Disney World*]
WSFPF......	Westfort Petroleums Ltd. [*NASDAQ symbol*] (NQ)
WSFP-TV ...	Fort Myers, FL [*Television station call letters*]
WSFS	Wilmington Savings Fund Society FSB [*Wilmington, DE*] [*NASDAQ symbol*] (NQ)
WSFS	World Science Fiction Society (EA)
WSFT	Thomaston, GA [*AM radio station call letters*]
WSFU........	Union Springs, AL [*FM radio station call letters*]
WSFW.......	Seneca Falls, NY [*AM radio station call letters*]
WSFW-FM ...	Seneca Falls, NY [*FM radio station call letters*]
WSFX........	Nanticoke, PA [*FM radio station call letters*]
WSG	International Wool Study Group
WSG	Washington [*Pennsylvania*] [*Airport symbol*] (OAG)
WSG	Wehrsportegruppe Hoffman Truppe [*Hoffman Paramilitary Troop*] [*Germany*]
WSG	Wells Gold Ltd. [*Vancouver Stock Exchange symbol*]
WSG	Wesleyan Service Guild [*Defunct*] (EA)
WSG	Western Suburbs Greens [*Political party*] [*Australia*]
WSG	Winter Study Group
WSG	Wire Strain Gauge
WSG	Wired Shelf Group [*Telecommunications*] (TEL)

WSG	Worthiest Soldier in the Group
WSGA	Savannah, GA [*AM radio station call letters*]
WSGA	Water Soluble Gum Association (EA)
WSGA	Wine and Spirits Guild of America (EA)
WSGB.......	Sutton, WV [*AM radio station call letters*]
WSGC......	Ringgold, GA [*FM radio station call letters*]
WSGC......	Williams-Sonoma, Inc. [*NASDAQ symbol*] (NQ)
WSGD	Carbondale, PA [*FM radio station call letters*]
WSGE.......	Dallas, NC [*FM radio station call letters*]
WSGE.......	Western Society of Gear Engineers (MCD)
WSGH	Lewisville, NC [*AM radio station call letters*]
WSGI........	Springfield, TN [*AM radio station call letters*]
WSGL.......	Naples, FL [*FM radio station call letters*]
WSGM	Staunton, VA [*FM radio station call letters*]
WSGN	Gadsden, AL [*FM radio station call letters*]
WSGO	Oswego, NY [*AM radio station call letters*]
WSGR	Port Huron, MI [*FM radio station call letters*]
WSGS	Hazard, KY [*FM radio station call letters*]
WSGT.......	White Sands Ground Terminal [*NASA*] (MCD)
WSGU	Window Sash Glaziers' Union [*British*]
WSGW	Saginaw, MI [*AM radio station call letters*]
WSGY	Tifton, GA [*FM radio station call letters*]
Wsh..........	Washington State Reports [*A publication*] (DLA)
WSH..........	Weather Service Headquarters (NOAA)
WsH..........	William S. Hein & Co., Inc., Buffalo, NY [*Library symbol*] [*Library of Congress*] (LCLS)
WSH..........	Wilshire Energy Resources, Inc. [*Toronto Stock Exchange symbol*]
WS and H ..	World Smoking and Health [*A publication*]
WSha	Bringham Memorial Library, Sharon, WI [*Library symbol*] [*Library of Congress*] (LCLS)
WSHA	Raleigh, NC [*FM radio station call letters*]
WShawGS ...	Church of Jesus Christ of Latter-Day Saints, Genealogical Society Library, Wisconsin East District Branch, Shawano, WI [*Library symbol*] [*Library of Congress*] (LCLS)
WSHC	Shepherdstown, WV [*FM radio station call letters*]
WSHD	Eastport, ME [*FM radio station call letters*]
WSHE	Fort Lauderdale, FL [*FM radio station call letters*]
WShe	Mead Public Library, Sheboygan, WI [*Library symbol*] [*Library of Congress*] (LCLS)
WSheL.......	Lakeland College, Sheboygan, WI [*Library symbol*] [*Library of Congress*] (LCLS)
WSheM	Sheboygan Memorial Hospital, Sheboygan, WI [*Library symbol*] [*Library of Congress*] (LCLS)
WSheSN	Saint Nicholas Hospital, Sheboygan, WI [*Library symbol*] [*Library of Congress*] (LCLS)
WSheU	University of Wisconsin Center-Sheboygan, Sheboygan, WI [*Library symbol*] [*Library of Congress*] (LCLS)
WSHF	Wives Self-Help Foundation (EA)
WSHFT.....	Wind Shift (FAAC)
WSHG	Ridgeland, SC [*FM radio station call letters*]
WSHG	Washing (MSA)
WSHGA	Washington State Holly Growers Association [*Defunct*] (EA)
WSHH	Pittsburgh, PA [*FM radio station call letters*]
WSHI	Washington Homes, Inc. [*NASDAQ symbol*] (NQ)
WSHJ	Southfield, MI [*FM radio station call letters*]
WSHK	Russellville, AL [*FM radio station call letters*]
WSHL	Easton, MA [*FM radio station call letters*]
WSHLD	Windshield (AAG)
WSHN......	Fremont, MI [*AM radio station call letters*]
WshNat	Washington National Corp. [*Associated Press abbreviation*] (APAG)
WSHN-FM ...	Fremont, MI [*FM radio station call letters*]
WSHO.......	New Orleans, LA [*AM radio station call letters*]
WSHP	Shippensburg, PA [*AM radio station call letters*]
WSHPA8...	Acta Microbiologica Sinica [*A publication*]
WshPst	Washington Post Co. [*Associated Press abbreviation*] (APAG)
WSHQ	Cobleskill, NY [*FM radio station call letters*]
WSHR	Lake Ronkonkoma, NY [*FM radio station call letters*]
WSHR	Washer (MSA)
WSHS.......	Sheboygan, WI [*FM radio station call letters*]
WSHU.......	Fairfield, CT [*FM radio station call letters*]
WSHV	South Hill, VA [*FM radio station call letters*]
WSHW	Frankfort, IN [*FM radio station call letters*]
WshWt......	Washington Water Power Co. [*Associated Press abbreviation*] (APAG)
WSHY	Shelbyville, IL [*AM radio station call letters*]
WSI...........	Wafer-Scale Integration [*Microelectronics*]
WSI...........	WaferScale Integration, Inc.
WSI...........	Waingapu [*Sumba Island*] [*Seismograph station code, US Geological Survey*] (SEIS)
WSI...........	War Service Indefinite
WSI...........	War-Supporting Industry
WSI...........	Water Safety Instructor [*Red Cross*]
WSI...........	Water Ski Industry Association (EA)
WSI...........	Water Solubility Index [*Analytical chemistry*]
WSI...........	Water Stability Index [*Agronomy*]
WSI...........	Weapon System Integration (MCD)
WSI...........	Weather Services International Corp. [*Information service or system*] (IID)
WSI...........	Wind Speed Indicator

WSI..........	Women's Studies Index [*A publication*]
WSI..........	World Synoptic Interval
WSI..........	Writers and Scholars International [*British*] (EAIO)
WSIA........	Staten Island, NY [*FM radio station call letters*]
WSIA........	Water Ski Industry Association (EA)
WSIA........	Water Supply Improvement Association [*Later, IDA*] (EA)
WSIA........	Weapons Systems Integration Agent (MCD)
WSIA J......	WSIA [*Water Supply Improvement Association*] Journal [*United States*] [*A publication*]
WSIA Journal ...	Water Supply Improvement Association. Journal [*A publication*]
WSIB........	Selmer, TN [*FM radio station call letters*]
WSIC........	Statesville, NC [*AM radio station call letters*]
WSIC........	Watchmakers of Switzerland Information Center (EA)
WSIE........	Edwardsville, IL [*FM radio station call letters*]
WSIF........	Wilkesboro, NC [*FM radio station call letters*]
WSIG........	Mount Jackson, VA [*FM radio station call letters*]
WSIIP.......	Weapons Installation Interrupted for Parts (DNAB)
WSIL.........	Harrisburg, IL [*Television station call letters*]
WSI/L.......	War Supporting Industries and Logistics (MCD)
WSIM.......	Water Separation Index, Modified
WSI Mitt ...	WSI [*Wirtschafts- und Sozialwissenschaftliches Institut*] Mitteilungen [*German Federal Republic*] [*A publication*]
WSIP........	Paintsville, KY [*AM radio station call letters*]
WSIP........	Weapons System Improvement Program (DWSG)
WSIP-FM ...	Paintsville, KY [*FM radio station call letters*]
WSIR........	White Sands Integrated Range [*New Mexico*] (AAG)
WSIR........	Winter Haven, FL [*AM radio station call letters*]
WSIT........	Washington State Institute of Technology (KSC)
WSIT........	Water Safety Instructor Trainer [*Red Cross*]
WSITS......	Weapon System Interface Trade Study [*Military*]
WSIU........	Carbondale, IL [*FM radio station call letters*]
WSIU-TV ...	Carbondale, IL [*Television station call letters*]
WSIV........	East Syracuse, NY [*AM radio station call letters*]
WSIX........	Nashville, TN [*FM radio station call letters*]
WSIY........	West Somerset Imperial Yeomanry [*British military*] (DMA)
WSIZ........	Ocilla, GA [*AM radio station call letters*]
WSIZ-FM ...	Ocila, GA [*FM radio station call letters*]
WSJ..........	San Juan, AK [*Location identifier*] [*FAA*] (FAAL)
WSJ..........	Wall Street Journal [*A publication*]
WSJ..........	Wiener Slawistisches Jahrbuch [*A publication*]
WSJ..........	Worm Screw Jack
WSJ..........	WSFA [*Washington Science Fiction Association*] Journal [*A publication*]
WSJB.......	Standish, ME [*FM radio station call letters*]
WSJC.......	Magee, MS [*AM radio station call letters*]
WSJC.......	Singapore [*Singapore*] [*ICAO location identifier*] (ICLI)
WSJE.......	San Juan, PR [*FM radio station call letters*]
WSJ Europe ...	Wall Street Journal. European Edition [*A publication*]
WSJHQ.....	Western States Jewish Historical Quarterly [*A publication*]
WSJK.......	Sneedville, TN [*Television station call letters*]
WSJL.......	Cape May, NJ [*FM radio station call letters*]
WSJM.......	St. Joseph, MI [*AM radio station call letters*]
WSJN.......	San Juan, PR [*Television station call letters*]
WSJ NJ.....	Wall Street Journal 3 Star. Eastern (Princeton, NJ) Edition [*A publication*]
W S Jour....	Wallace Stevens Journal [*A publication*]
WSJP.......	Murray, KY [*AM radio station call letters*]
WSJR.......	Madawaska, ME [*AM radio station call letters*]
WSJS........	Winston-Salem, NC [*AM radio station call letters*]
WSJU.......	San Juan, PR [*Television station call letters*]
WSJV.......	Elkhart, IN [*Television station call letters*]
WSJY.......	Fort Atkinson, WI [*FM radio station call letters*]
WSK........	Waste Age [*A publication*]
WSKB.......	Westfield, MA [*FM radio station call letters*]
WSKE.......	Everett, PA [*AM radio station call letters*]
WSKE-FM ...	Everett, PA [*FM radio station call letters*]
WSKG	Binghamton, NY [*Television station call letters*]
WSKG-FM ...	Binghamton, NY [*FM radio station call letters*]
WSKI........	Montpelier, VT [*AM radio station call letters*]
WSKO.......	Buffalo Gap, VA [*FM radio station call letters*]
WSKQ	New York, NY [*FM radio station call letters*]
WSKQ	Newark, NJ [*AM radio station call letters*]
WSKR.......	Petersburg, NJ [*FM radio station call letters*]
WSKS.......	Sparta, GA [*FM radio station call letters*]
WSKT.......	Spencer, IN [*FM radio station call letters*]
WSKV.......	Stanton, KY [*FM radio station call letters*]
WSKW	Skowhegan, ME [*AM radio station call letters*]
WSKX.......	Hinesville, GA [*FM radio station call letters*]
WSKY.......	Asheville, NC [*AM radio station call letters*]
WSKZ.......	Chattanooga, TN [*FM radio station call letters*]
WSL..........	University of Wisconsin Studies in Language and Literature [*A publication*]
WSL..........	War Substantive Lieutenant [*British*]
WSL..........	Warren Spring Laboratory [*Research center*] [*British*] (DCTA)
Ws L........	Washington Law Review [*A publication*]
WSL..........	Weather Seal (AAG)
WSL..........	Welt der Slaven [*A publication*]
WSL..........	Western Savings & Loan Association [*NYSE symbol*] (SPSG)
WSL..........	Windscale
WSLA........	Slidell, LA [*AM radio station call letters*]
W Sl A	Wiener Slawistischer Almanach [*A publication*]
WSlav	Welt der Slaven [*A publication*]
WSLB.......	Ogdensburg, NY [*AM radio station call letters*]
WSLBA	Wasser, Luft, und Betrieb [*A publication*]
WSLC.......	Roanoke, VA [*AM radio station call letters*]
WSLC.......	World Shortwave Listeners Club (EA)
WSLD.......	Whitewater, WI [*FM radio station call letters*]
WSLE.......	Cairo, GA [*FM radio station call letters*]
WSLF	Western Somali Liberation Front
WSLG.......	Gonzales, LA [*AM radio station call letters*]
WSLI........	Jackson, MS [*AM radio station call letters*]
WSL-INT ..	Weltbund zum Schutze des Lebens [*World Union for the Protection of Life - WUPL-INT*] (EAIO)
WSLJb	Wiener Slawistisches Jahrbuch [*A publication*]
WSLL........	Saranac Lake, NY [*FM radio station call letters*]
WSLM.......	Salem, IN [*AM radio station call letters*]
WSLM-FM ...	Salem, IN [*FM radio station call letters*]
WSLN.......	Delaware, OH [*FM radio station call letters*]
WSLO.......	Malone, NY [*FM radio station call letters*]
WSLO.......	Weapon System Logistics Officer [*Air Force*] (AFM)
WSLQ.......	Roanoke, VA [*FM radio station call letters*]
WSLR.......	Akron, OH [*AM radio station call letters*]
WSLR.......	Weapon System Logistic Reviews [*Navy*] (NG)
WSLS	Roanoke, VA [*Television station call letters*]
WSLT.......	Ocean City, NJ [*FM radio station call letters*]
WSLU.......	Canton, NY [*FM radio station call letters*]
WSLV.......	Ardmore, TN [*AM radio station call letters*]
WSLW.......	White Sulphur Springs, WV [*AM radio station call letters*]
WSLX.......	New Canaan, CT [*FM radio station call letters*]
WSLY.......	York, AL [*FM radio station call letters*]
WSM	Nashville, TN [*AM radio station call letters*]
WSM	Weapon Support Manager [*Air Force*]
WSM	Weapon System Manager [*Air Force*] (AFM)
WSM	Weapon System Manual
WSM	West-Mar Resources Ltd. [*Vancouver Stock Exchange symbol*]
WSM	Western Samoa [*ANSI three-letter standard code*] (CNC)
WSM	Western Society of Malacologists (EA)
WSM	Wheat Streak Mosaic [*Plant pathology*]
WSM	White Single Male [*Classified advertising*]
WSM	Wigner-Seitz Method [*Solid state physics*]
WSM	Windowing System Manager [*Data processing*] (PCM)
WSM	Wiseman [*Alaska*] [*Airport symbol*] (OAG)
WSM	Wiseman, AK [*Location identifier*] [*FAA*] (FAAL)
WSM	Women's Suffrage Movement (ROG)
WSM	World Solar Markets [*A publication*]
WSM	Wright State University, Health Sciences Library, Dayton, OH [*OCLC symbol*] (OCLC)
WSMA	Marine City, MI [*AM radio station call letters*]
WSMA	Western States Meat Association (EA)
WSMA	Window Shade Manufacturers Association (EA)
WSMAC....	Weapon System Maintenance Action Center
WSMaT....	Weapon System Management Team [*Army*] (RDA)
WSMB.......	New Orleans, LA [*AM radio station call letters*]
WSMC.......	Collegedale, TN [*FM radio station call letters*]
WSMC.......	Weapons System Management Codes [*Navy*]
WSMC.......	Western Space and Missile Center [*Air Force*] [*Vandenberg Air Force Base, CA*]
WSMC......	Western States Movers Conference
WSMD	Mechanicsville, MD [*FM radio station call letters*]
WSME.......	Sanford, ME [*AM radio station call letters*]
WSM-FM ...	Nashville, TN [*FM radio station call letters*]
WSMG	Greeneville, TN [*AM radio station call letters*]
WSMH	Flint, MI [*Television station call letters*]
WSMI........	Litchfield, IL [*AM radio station call letters*]
WSMI-FM ...	Litchfield, IL [*FM radio station call letters*]
WSMIS	Weapon Systems Management Information System [*Air Force*] (GFGA)
WSMK	Buchanan, MI [*FM radio station call letters*]
WSML.......	Graham, NC [*AM radio station call letters*]
WSML.......	Saltfree Meal [*Airline notation*]
WSMN	Nashua, NH [*AM radio station call letters*]
WSMO	Weapon System Materiel Officer [*Air Force*] (AFM)
WSMO	Weather Service Meteorological Observatory [*or Observations*] [*National Weather Service*] (NOAA)
WSMP.......	WSMP, Inc. [*Formerly, Western Steer Mom 'n' Pop's, Inc.*] [*NASDAQ symbol*] (SPSG)
WSMPA....	Western States Meat Association (EA)
WSMQ.......	Bessemer, AL [*AM radio station call letters*]
WSMR.......	White Sands Missile Range [*Army*] [*New Mexico*]
WSMS.......	Memphis, TN [*FM radio station call letters*]
WSMT......	Sparta, TN [*AM radio station call letters*]
WSMT......	Weapons System Maintenance Test (MCD)
WSMTC....	White Sands Missile Test Center [*New Mexico*]
WSMT-FM ...	Sparta, TN [*FM radio station call letters*]
WSMTT......	White Star Mobile Training Teams [*Military*] (CINC)
WSMU......	North Dartmouth, MA [*FM radio station call letters*]
WSMV	Nashville, TN [*Television station call letters*]
WSMV	Wheat Streak Mosaic Virus
WSMX	Winston-Salem, NC [*AM radio station call letters*]
WSMY	Weldon, NC [*AM radio station call letters*]
WSMYA....	Washington Monthly [*A publication*]

WSMZ....... Coleman, MI [*FM radio station call letters*]
WSN .... South Naknek [*Alaska*] [*Airport symbol*] (OAG)
WSN .... South Naknek, AK [*Location identifier*] [*FAA*] (FAAL)
WSN .... Spokane County Library, Spokane, WA [*OCLC symbol*] [*Inactive*] (OCLC)
WSN .... Wallace Stevens Newsletter [*A publication*]
WSN .... Wang System Networking (HGAA)
WSN .... Warm Springs [*Nevada*] [*Seismograph station code, US Geological Survey*] [*Closed*] (SEIS)
WSN .... Water-Soluble Nitrogen [*Analytical chemistry*]
WSN .... Western Co. of North America [*NYSE symbol*] (SPSG)
WSN .... Western Resources Technology [*Vancouver Stock Exchange symbol*]
WSN .... Western Society of Naturalists (EA)
WSNA Mini J ... Washington State Nurses Association. Mini Journal [*A publication*]
WSNC .... Winston-Salem, NC [*FM radio station call letters*]
WSND .... Notre Dame, IN [*FM radio station call letters*]
WSNE .... Taunton, MA [*FM radio station call letters*]
WSNG .... Torrington, CT [*AM radio station call letters*]
WSNGT .... White Sands NASA Ground Terminal (MCD)
WSNI........ Thomasville, GA [*FM radio station call letters*]
WSNJ........ Bridgeton, NJ [*AM radio station call letters*]
WSNJ-FM ... Bridgeton, NJ [*FM radio station call letters*]
WSNN ...... Potsdam, NY [*FM radio station call letters*]
WSNO ...... Barre, VT [*AM radio station call letters*]
WSNP .... Water-Soluble Nonstarchy Polysaccharide [*Food composition*]
WSNQ .... Gaylord, MI [*AM radio station call letters*]
WSNR .... Syracuse, NY [*Television station call letters*]
WSNS........ Chicago, IL [*Television station call letters*]
WSNSCA.. Washable Suits, Novelties, and Sportswear Contractors Association (EA)
WSNT ...... Sandersville, GA [*AM radio station call letters*]
WSNT-FM ... Sandersville, GA [*FM radio station call letters*]
WSNU .... Lock Haven, PA [*FM radio station call letters*]
WSNW ...... Seneca, SC [*AM radio station call letters*]
WSNX .... Muskegon, MI [*AM radio station call letters*]
WSNX-FM ... Muskegon, MI [*FM radio station call letters*]
WSNY .... Columbus, OH [*FM radio station call letters*]
WSNY .... Wagner Society of New York (EA)
WSO .... Warrant Stores Officer [*Navy*] [*British*]
WSO .... Washabo [*Surinam*] [*Airport symbol*] (OAG)
WSO .... Washington Standardization Officers
WSO .... Water Service Operator (MCD)
WSO .... Watsco, Inc. [*AMEX symbol*] (SPSG)
WSO .... Weapon System Officer [*or Operator*] [*Air Force*] (AFM)
WSO .... Weapon System Operator
WSO .... Weather Service Office [*National Weather Service*] (NOAA)
WSO .... Western Support Office [*Formerly, WOO*] [*NASA*]
WSO .... White Sands Operations [*New Mexico*] [*Formerly, White Sands Missile Operations*] [*NASA*]
WSO .... Wilcox Solar Observatory
WSO .... [*The*] WorkSheet Optimizer [*Laptop tool*] [*Brubaker Software*] (PCM)
WSO .... World Safety Organization [*United Nations*]
WSO .... World Simulation Organization
WSO .... WRAF [*Women's Royal Naval Air Force*] Staff Officer [*British military*] (DMA)
WSO(AG) ... Weather Service Office for Agriculture [*National Weather Service*] (NOAA)
WSO(AV) ... Weather Service Office for Aviation [*National Weather Service*] (NOAA)
WSOC .... Charlotte, NC [*AM radio station call letters*]
WSOC .... Weapon System Operational Concept (AAG)
W Soc E J .. Western Society of Engineers. Journal [*A publication*]
WSOC-FM ... Charlotte, NC [*FM radio station call letters*]
WSOC-TV ... Charlotte, NC [*Television station call letters*]
WSOE .... Elon College, NC [*FM radio station call letters*]
WSOEA..... Wholesale Stationery and Office Equipment Association [*Later, WSA*] (EA)
WSOF........ Madisonville, KY [*FM radio station call letters*]
WSO(FW) ... Weather Service Office for Fire-Weather [*National Weather Service*] (NOAA)
WSOK .... Savannah, GA [*AM radio station call letters*]
WSOL........ San German, PR [*AM radio station call letters*]
WSOM ...... Salem, OH [*AM radio station call letters*]
WSOM ...... Weather Service Operations Manual [*National Weather Service*] (FAAC)
WSON .... Henderson, KY [*AM radio station call letters*]
WSON .... Worldwide Satellite Observing Network (MCD)
WSOO ...... Sault Ste. Marie, MI [*AM radio station call letters*]
WSOP....... White Supercalendered Offset Paper [*Publishing*]
WSOR .... Naples, FL [*FM radio station call letters*]
WSOS........ St. Augustine, FL [*FM radio station call letters*]
WSOT .... Weapon System Operability Test [*Military*] (CAAL)
WSOU .... South Orange, NJ [*FM radio station call letters*]
WSOY .... Decatur, IL [*AM radio station call letters*]
WSOY .... Werner Soederstroem Osakeyhtio [*Book printer*] [*Finland*]
WSOY-FM ... Decatur, IL [*FM radio station call letters*]
WSP........... Ward's Sales Prospector [*A publication*]
W/SP......... Warheads and Special Projects Laboratory [*Picatinny Arsenal*]

WSP........... Washington School of Psychiatry
WSP........... Washington Square Press [*Publisher's imprint*]
WSP........... Water Spray Protection [*Shipping*] (DS)
WSP........... Water Supply Papers
WSP........... Water Supply Point
WSP........... Weapon Support Processor [*Military*] (CAAL)
WSP........... Weapon System Program (SAA)
WSP........... Weapon Systems Pouch (AFM)
WSP........... Weibull Shape Parameter [*Statistics*]
WSP........... West Penn Power Co. [*NYSE symbol*] (SPSG)
WSP........... Wideband Signal Processor
WSP........... Winspear Resources [*Vancouver Stock Exchange symbol*]
WSP........... Women Strike for Peace (EA)
WSP........... Work Simplification Program [*Military*]
WSP........... Work Study Program (OICC)
WSP........... Working Steam Pressure
WSP........... Workshop (NATG)
WSP........... Wright State University, Piqua Branch Campus, Piqua, OH [*OCLC symbol*] (OCLC)
Wsp........... Wspolczesnosc [*Warsaw*] [*A publication*]
WSpa .... Sparta Free Library, Sparta, WI [*Library symbol*] [*Library of Congress*] (LCLS)
WSPA....... Spartanburg, SC [*AM radio station call letters*]
WSPA....... World Society for the Protection of Animals [*Formed by a merger of WFPA and ISPA*] (EA)
WSPACS... Weapon Systems Planning [*or Programming*] and Control System
WSPA-FM ... Spartanburg, SC [*FM radio station call letters*]
WSPAT ..... Wolfe-Spence Programming Aptitude Test
WSPA-TV ... Spartanburg, SC [*Television station call letters*]
WSPB....... Sarasota, FL [*AM radio station call letters*]
WSPC........ St. Paul, VA [*AM radio station call letters*]
WSPC....... Weapons System Partnerships Committee [*NATO*] (NATG)
WSPC....... Weapons System Program Code [*Defense Supply Agency*]
WSPC....... World Sports Prototype Championship [*Auto racing*]
WSPD....... Toledo, OH [*AM radio station call letters*]
WSPD....... Weapon System Planning Document (NVT)
WSPD....... Weapons System Planning Data [*Navy*]
WSPF .... Watergate Special Prosecution Force [*Terminated, 1977*] [*Department of Justice*]
WSPG....... Wall Street Planning Group (EA)
WSPG....... Weapon System Phasing Group
WSPG....... Weapon System Purchasing Group
WSPG....... White Sands Proving Ground [*New Mexico*] [*Obsolete*]
WSPGL ..... Weapon System Program Guide List
WSPH .... Murray, KY [*Television station call letters*]
WSPI .... Shamokin, PA [*FM radio station call letters*]
WSP-I........ World Socialist Party - Ireland [*Political party*] (EAIO)
WSPK .... Poughkeepsie, NY [*FM radio station call letters*]
WSPL........ La Crosse, WI [*FM radio station call letters*]
WSPN....... Saratoga Springs, NY [*FM radio station call letters*]
WSPNZ.... World Socialist Party of New Zealand [*Political party*] (EAIO)
WSPO....... Stevens Point, WI [*AM radio station call letters*]
WSPO....... Weapon System Project Office [*Air Force*]
WSPOP...... Weapon System Phase-Out Procedure [*Air Force*] (AFM)
W Sports.... Women's Sports [*A publication*]
WSPPD .... Weapons Systems Personnel Planning Data (MCD)
WSPR....... Springfield, MA [*AM radio station call letters*]
WSPR....... Weapon System Program Review [*Army*]
WSPRD .... Weapons Systems Progress Reporting Data
WSPS .... Concord, NH [*FM radio station call letters*]
WSpS......... Saint Michael's Hospital, Stevens Point, WI [*Library symbol*] [*Library of Congress*] (LCLS)
WSPS .... Wire Strike Protection System (MCD)
WSPT....... Stevens Point, WI [*FM radio station call letters*]
WSpU .... University of Wisconsin-Stevens Point, Stevens Point, WI [*Library symbol*] [*Library of Congress*] (LCLS)
WSPU....... Women's Social and Political Union [*British*]
WSPUS ..... World Socialist Party of the United States (EA)
WSPY .... Plano, IL [*FM radio station call letters*]
WSQ .... Wake Seeding and Quenching
WSq .... Weather Squadron [*Air Force*] (AFM)
WSQ .... Wonder Stories Quarterly [*A publication*]
WSQC .... Oneonta, NY [*FM radio station call letters*]
WSQG .... Ithaca, NY [*FM radio station call letters*]
WSQN ...... Scranton, SC [*FM radio station call letters*]
WSQR .... Sycamore, IL [*AM radio station call letters*]
WSQV .... Berwick, PA [*AM radio station call letters*]
WSR .... War Service Regulation
WSR .... Warm Springs Repeater [*Nevada*] [*Seismograph station code, US Geological Survey*] [*Closed*] (SEIS)
WSR .... Warren & Saline River Railroad Co. [*AAR code*]
WSR .... Waterschapsbelangen [*A publication*]
W/sr.......... Watts per Steradian
WSR .... Weak Signal Reception
WSR .... Weapon System Reliability [*Air Force*] (AFM)
WSR .... Weapon Systems Requirement (MCD)
WSR .... Weapons Spares Report [*Navy*]
WSR .... Weapons Status Report [*Navy*] (NG)
WSR .... Weapons System Review (NVT)
WSR .... Weather Search RADAR (MCD)

WSR	Weather Surveillance RADAR
WSR	Weekly Summary Report
WSR	Wet Snow on Runway [*Aviation*] (FAAC)
WSR	Wild and Scenic Rivers Act
WSR	Windsor Resources, Inc. [*Vancouver Stock Exchange symbol*]
WSR	Wire Shift Register
WSR	Wood-Shingle Roof [*Technical drawings*]
WSR	World Students Relief
WSRA	Wild and Scenic Rivers Act
WSRB	Wall Street Review of Books [*A publication*]
WSRB	Walpole, MA [*FM radio station call letters*]
WSRC	Durham, NC [*AM radio station call letters*]
WSRCC	War, Strikes, Riots, and Civil Commotions [*Insurance*] (AIA)
WSRD	Johnstown, NY [*FM radio station call letters*]
WSRE........	Pensacola, FL [*Television station call letters*]
WSRF........	Fort Lauderdale, FL [*AM radio station call letters*]
WSRH	Weather Service Regional Headquarters [*National Weather Service*] (NOAA)
WSRI........	World Safety Research Institute
WSRK........	Oneonta, NY [*FM radio station call letters*]
WSRL........	Water Supply Research Laboratory [*National Environmental Research Center*]
WSRL........	Wisconsin Survey Research Laboratory [*University of Wisconsin*] [*Research center*] (RCD)
WSRM	Weather Surveillance RADAR Manual (NOAA)
WSRN	Swarthmore, PA [*FM radio station call letters*]
WSRO	Marlboro, MA [*AM radio station call letters*]
WSRO	Weapon System Replacement Operations (MCD)
WSRO	Whole System Replacement Operation [*Army*] (INF)
WSRO	World Sugar Research Organisation (EAIO)
WSRP........	Weapons System Requisitioning Procedure [*Military*] (AABC)
WSRQ	Bushnell, IL [*FM radio station call letters*]
WSRR.......	West Shore Railroad
WSRS	Wildlife Sound Recording Society [*British*]
WSRS	Worcester, MA [*FM radio station call letters*]
WSRT	Weapon System Readiness Test
WSRT	Weapons System Reliability Test (CINC)
WSRT	Westerbork Synthesis Radio Telescope
WSRU	Slippery Rock, PA [*FM radio station call letters*]
WSRW.......	Hillsboro, OH [*AM radio station call letters*]
WSRW-FM ...	Hillsboro, OH [*FM radio station call letters*]
WSRX	Fort Meyers, FL [*FM radio station call letters*]
WSRZ........	Sarasota, FL [*FM radio station call letters*]
WSS...........	War Savings Staff
WSS...........	Warfare Systems School [*Air Force*] (AFM)
WSS...........	Washington Strategy Seminar (EA)
WSS...........	Weapon Support Systems
WSS...........	Weapon System Specification (AAG)
WSS...........	Weather Service Specialist [*National Weather Service*]
WSS...........	Weekend Stress Syndrome [*Psychiatry*]
WSS...........	Wheel Speed Sensor [*Automotive engineering*]
WSS...........	Wheelwrights' and Smiths' Society [*A union*] [*British*]
WSS...........	Wholesale Storage Site (DNAB)
WSS...........	Wind Shear Spike (SAA)
WSS...........	Winston-Salem Southbound Railway Co. [*AAR code*]
WSS...........	Women's Social Services [*Salvation Army*]
WSS...........	Women's Studies Section [*Association of College and Research Libraries*]
WSS...........	Work Summarization System (MCD)
WSS...........	Workpack Scheduling System [*Industrial engineering*]
WSS...........	World Ship Society [*Haywards Heath, West Sussex, England*]
WSS...........	WWMCCS [*Worldwide Military Command and Control System*] Systems Specification (MCD)
WSSA........	Morrow, GA [*AM radio station call letters*]
WSSA........	Weapon System Support Activities (AAG)
WSSA........	Weed Science Society of America (EA)
WSSA........	Welsh Secondary Schools Association [*British*]
WSSA........	Western Social Science Association (EA)
WSSA........	White Sands Signal Agency [*New Mexico*] [*Military*] (MCD)
WSSA........	Wine and Spirits Shippers Association (EA)
WSSA........	World Secret Service Association [*Later, WAD*] (EA)
WSSAB	Weller-Strawser Scales of Adaptive Behavior [*Educational test*]
WSSB	Orangeburg, SC [*FM radio station call letters*]
WSSBA	Western Single Side Band Association (EA)
WSSC	Sumter, SC [*AM radio station call letters*]
WSSC	Weapon System Support Center (AAG)
WSSC	Weapon System Support Code [*Navy*] (NG)
WSSCA	Welsh Springer Spaniel Club of America (EA)
WSSCA	White Sands Signal Corps Agency [*New Mexico*] [*Military*] (AAG)
WSSCL......	Weapon System Stock Control List (AAG)
WSSD.......	Chicago, IL [*FM radio station call letters*]
WSSD........	Weapon System Support Development (MCD)
WSSF	Weapons System Security Flight [*Military*]
WSSF	Weather Service Support Facility [*National Weather Service*] (FAAC)
WSSFN	World Society for Stereotactic and Functional Neurosurgery (EA)
WSSG........	Weapon System Support Group (MCD)
WSSH.......	Boston, MA [*AM radio station call letters*]
WSSH........	Lowell, MA [*FM radio station call letters*]

WSSI	Carthage, MS [*AM radio station call letters*]
WSSI	Women's Social Service for Israel (EA)
WSSIB......	WWMCCS [*Worldwide Military Command and Control System*] Standard System Information Base (MCD)
WSSI-FM ...	Carthage, MS [*FM radio station call letters*]
WSSJ........	Camden, NJ [*AM radio station call letters*]
WSSL	Gray Court, SC [*FM radio station call letters*]
WSSL	Greenville, SC [*AM radio station call letters*]
WSSL	Seletar [*Singapore*] [*ICAO location identifier*] (ICLI)
WSSL	Weapon System Stock List [*Army*]
WSSL	Weapon System Stock/Support List [*Air Force*] (AFIT)
WSSL	Western Secondary Standards Laboratory
WSSM.......	Weapon System Staff Manager [*Army*] (RDA)
WSSM.......	Weapon System Support Manager (AAG)
WSSMV	Wheat Spindle Streak Mosaic Virus
WSSN.......	Weston, WV [*FM radio station call letters*]
WSSO.......	Starkville, MS [*AM radio station call letters*]
WSSO.......	Weapon System Support Officer [*Army*] (RDA)
WSSP	Weapon Systems Support Program [*Defense Supply Agency*]
WSSPM	Weapons System Support Program Manager (AFIT)
WSSQ.......	Sterling, IL [*FM radio station call letters*]
WSSR	Georgetown, DE [*AM radio station call letters*]
WSSRS	Waksman Social Skills Rating Scale
WSSS	Singapore Changi [*Singapore*] [*ICAO location identifier*] (ICLI)
WSSS	Weapon System Storage Site
WSSSFAF ...	Wartime Standard Support System for Foreign Armed Forces (MCD)
WSSSP	Western States Small School Project
WSST	Cordele, GA [*Television station call letters*]
WSSU........	Springfield, IL [*FM radio station call letters*]
WSSU........	Weather Service Support Unit [*National Weather Service*] (FAAC)
WSSV	Stillwater, NY [*FM radio station call letters*]
WSSW.......	Mackinaw City, MI [*FM radio station call letters*]
WSSX	Charleston, SC [*FM radio station call letters*]
WSSX	Wessex Corp. [*Franklin, TN*] [*NASDAQ symbol*] (NQ)
WSSY	Talladega, AL [*FM radio station call letters*]
WSSZ	Greensburg, PA [*FM radio station call letters*]
WSt............	D. R. Moon Memorial Library, Stanley, WI [*Library symbol*] [*Library of Congress*] (LCLS)
WST..........	Watch Station Trainer [*Military*] (DWSG)
WST..........	Water Supply Tank
WST..........	Weapon Safety Trainer
WST..........	Weapon System Test
WST..........	Weapon System Trainer [*Navy*]
WST..........	Weightlessness Simulation Test
WST..........	West Co., Inc. [*NYSE symbol*] (SPSG)
WST..........	Westerly [*Rhode Island*] [*Airport symbol*] (OAG)
WST..........	Westerly, RI [*Location identifier*] [*FAA*] (FAAL)
WST..........	Western Air Express [*Houston, TX*] [*FAA designator*] (FAAC)
WST..........	Wholesale Sales Tax
W St	Wiener Studien [*A publication*]
WST..........	Wine and Spirit [*A publication*]
WSt............	Word Study [*A publication*]
WST..........	World Ship Trust [*Cambridge, England*]
WST..........	Write Symbol Table
WSTA........	Charlotte Amalie, VI [*AM radio station call letters*]
WSTA........	Weapon System Task Analysis (AAG)
WSTA........	White Slave Traffic Act
WSTB........	Streetsboro, OH [*FM radio station call letters*]
WSTBRC ..	Westbridge Capital Corp. [*Associated Press abbreviation*] (APAG)
WSTC........	Stamford, CT [*AM radio station call letters*]
WSTC........	Weapon System Total Complex
WSTC........	Weapons System Test Card (MCD)
WSTC........	Willimantic State Teachers College [*Connecticut*]
WSTCH.....	Wasatch Range [*National Weather Service*] (FAAC)
WstctE	Westcoast Energy, Inc. [*Associated Press abbreviation*] (APAG)
WSTD.......	Standish, MI [*FM radio station call letters*]
WSTDA.....	Web Sling and Tiedown Association (EA)
WSTE........	Ponce, PR [*Television station call letters*]
WSTEA	Weapon System Training Effectiveness Analysis
WSTED.....	Water Science and Technology [*A publication*]
WSTE MAT ...	Waste Material [*Freight*]
WSTEN.....	Western Energy Management, Inc. [*Associated Press abbreviation*] (APAG)
WSTENG ...	Western Energy Management, Inc. [*Associated Press abbreviation*] (APAG)
WSTF	Cocoa Beach, FL [*FM radio station call letters*]
WSTF	Western Financial Corp. [*NASDAQ symbol*] (NQ)
WSTF	White Sands Test Facility [*New Mexico*] [*Military*]
WSTG........	Biddeford, ME [*FM radio station call letters*]
WStG	Wehrstrafgesetz [*Military Criminal Law*] [*German*] (ILCA)
WstgE	Westinghouse Electric Corp. [*Associated Press abbreviation*] (APAG)
WstgEl.......	Westinghouse Electric Corp. [*Associated Press abbreviation*] (APAG)
WstGR	Western Gas Resources [*Associated Press abbreviation*] (APAG)

WSTH .... Alexander City, AL [*FM radio station call letters*]
WSTH .... Weapon System Tactical Handbook   (MCD)
WSTI .... Quitman, GA [*FM radio station call letters*]
WSTI .... Welded Steel Tube Institute [*Later, STINA*]   (EA)
WSTIB ...... Woolen and Silk Textiles Industries Board [*New Deal*]
WSTJ .... St. Johnsbury, VT [*AM radio station call letters*]
WSTK .... Colonial Heights, VA [*AM radio station call letters*]
WSTL .... South Glens Falls, NY [*AM radio station call letters*]
WSTL .... Weapon System Test Laboratory
WSTL .... Whistle   (MSA)
WStL & P .. Wabash, St. Louis & Pacific Railway
WSTM .... Syracuse, NY [*Television station call letters*]
WSTM .... Western Micro Technology, Inc. [*NASDAQ symbol*]   (NQ)
WSTM .... White Sands Missile Range Transverse Mercator
                      [*Army*]   (AABC)
WstMn .... Western Mining Corp. [*Associated Press abbreviation*]   (APAG)
WstmorC ... Westmoreland Coal Co. [*Associated Press
                      abbreviation*]   (APAG)
WSTN .... Somerville, TN [*AM radio station call letters*]
WSTN .... Western
WSTN .... Weston [*Roy F.*], Inc. [*West Chester, PA*] [*NASDAQ
                      symbol*]   (NQ)
WstnGR ..... Western Gas Resources [*Associated Press
                      abbreviation*]   (APAG)
WstnRes .... Western Resources, Inc. [*Associated Press
                      abbreviation*]   (APAG)
WSTO .... Owensboro, KY [*FM radio station call letters*]
WSTP .... Salisbury, NC [*AM radio station call letters*]
WSTP .... Weapon System Test Program
W & StP ... Winona & St. Peter Railroad
Wstpc .... Westpac Banking Corp. [*Associated Press
                      abbreviation*]   (APAG)
WSTPN ..... Wrist Pin
WSTQ .... Streator, IL [*FM radio station call letters*]
WSTR .... Cincinnati, OH [*Television station call letters*]
WSTR .... Smyrna, GA [*FM radio station call letters*]
WSTR .... Westar Corp. [*Las Vegas, NV*] [*NASDAQ symbol*]   (NQ)
W v Str ...... Wetboek van Strafrecht [*A publication*]
WSTS .... Fairmont, NC [*FM radio station call letters*]
WSTS .... Weapon System Training Set   (AFM)
WSTS .... Western States Life Insurance [*NASDAQ symbol*]   (NQ)
WSTS .... World Semiconductor Trade Statistics [*Semiconductor Industry
                      Association*] [*Information service or system*]   (IID)
WSTSA ..... Wall Street Transcript [*A publication*]
WSTSHD ... Watershed
WSTT .... Thomasville, GA [*AM radio station call letters*]
WSTU .... Stuart, FL [*AM radio station call letters*]
W St UL Rev ... Western State University. Law Review [*A publication*]
WSTV .... Steubenville, OH [*AM radio station call letters*]
WSTV .... World Service Television [*BBC*]   (ECON)
Wstvco .... Westvaco Corp. [*Associated Press abbreviation*]   (APAG)
WSTW .... Westworld Resources, Inc. [*NASDAQ symbol*]   (NQ)
WSTW .... Wilmington, DE [*FM radio station call letters*]
WSTX .... Christiansted, VI [*AM radio station call letters*]
WSTX .... Westronix, Inc. [*Midvale, UT*] [*NASDAQ symbol*]   (NQ)
WSTX-FM ... Christiansted, VI [*FM radio station call letters*]
WSTZ .... Vicksburg, MS [*FM radio station call letters*]
WSU .... University of Wisconsin-Superior, Superior, WI [*Library
                      symbol*] [*Library of Congress*]   (LCLS)
WSU .... Washington State University
WSU .... Wasu [*Papua New Guinea*] [*Airport symbol*]   (OAG)
WSU .... Water Servicing Unit   (NASA)
WSU .... Wayne State University [*Michigan*]
WSU .... Windmill Study Unit [*American Topical Association*]   (EA)
WSU .... Women on Stamps Unit [*American Topical Association*]   (EA)
WSU .... Work Station Utility
WSU .... Wright State University, Dayton, OH [*OCLC symbol*]   (OCLC)
WSUA .... Miami, FL [*AM radio station call letters*]
WSUB .... Groton, CT [*AM radio station call letters*]
WSUC .... Cortland, NY [*FM radio station call letters*]
W Succ R ... Wetboek van Successierechten [*A publication*]
WSUE .... Sault Ste. Marie, MI [*FM radio station call letters*]
WSUH .... Oxford, MS [*AM radio station call letters*]
WSU/HB... Human Biology. Official Publication. Human Biology Council.
                      Wayne State University. School of Medicine [*A
                      publication*]
WSUI......... Iowa City, IA [*AM radio station call letters*]
WSUL .... Monticello, NY [*FM radio station call letters*]
WSUN .... St. Petersburg, FL [*AM radio station call letters*]
WSUOPR ... Washington State University, Open Pool Reactor
WSUP .... Platteville, WI [*FM radio station call letters*]
WSUR .... Ponce, PR [*Television station call letters*]
WSUS....... Franklin, NJ [*FM radio station call letters*]
WSU-SDL ... Washington State University Shock Dynamics Laboratory
                      [*Pullman*]
WSUV .... Fort Myers Villas, FL [*FM radio station call letters*]
WSUW ...... Whitewater, WI [*FM radio station call letters*]
WSUY .... Charleston, SC [*FM radio station call letters*]
WSV .... Wall Street Ventures [*Vancouver Stock Exchange symbol*]
WSV .... Water Solenoid Valve
WSV .... Water-Soluble Vitamin

WSVA........ Harrisonburg, VA [*AM radio station call letters*]
WSVA........ Wang Software Vendors' Association [*Defunct*]   (EA)
WSVG .... Mount Jackson, VA [*AM radio station call letters*]
WSVH .... Savannah, GA [*FM radio station call letters*]
WSVI .... Christiansted, VI [*Television station call letters*]
WSVM ..... Valdese, NC [*AM radio station call letters*]
WSVN .... Miami, FL [*Television station call letters*]
WSVQ .... Harrogate, TN [*AM radio station call letters*]
WSVS........ Crewe, VA [*AM radio station call letters*]
WSVS........ Wiland Services, Inc. [*Boulder, CO*] [*NASDAQ symbol*]   (NQ)
WSVS-FM ... Crewe, VA [*FM radio station call letters*]
WSVV .... Petersburg, VA [*FM radio station call letters*]
WSW .... Southwest Wisconsin Library System, Fennimore, WI [*OCLC
                      symbol*]   (OCLC)
WSW .... Wall Street Week [*Television program*]
WSW .... West-Southwest
WSW .... Western Shelf Water [*Oceanography*]
WSW .... White Sidewall [*Tires*]
WSW .... Wirtschaftswissenschaft [*A publication*]
WSWA ...... Wine and Spirits Wholesalers of America   (EA)
WSWB...... Scranton, PA [*Television station call letters*]
WSWI........ Evansville, IN [*AM radio station call letters*]
WSWL .... Pensacola, FL [*AM radio station call letters*]
WSWL .... Warheads and Special Weapons Laboratory   (MCD)
WSWMA .. Water and Sewage Works Manufacturers Association [*Later,
                      WWEMA*]   (EA)
WSWMA .. Western States Weights and Measures Association
WSWN ...... Belle Glade, FL [*AM radio station call letters*]
WSWO .... Wilmington, OH [*FM radio station call letters*]
WSWOA ... Water and Sewage Works [*A publication*]
WSWP....... Grandview, WV [*Television station call letters*]
WSWR...... Shelby, OH [*FM radio station call letters*]
WSWRN ... West-Southwestern [*Meteorology*]   (FAAC)
WSWS....... Opelika, AL [*Television station call letters*]
WSWSA.... Wasserwirtschaft-Wassertechnik [*A publication*]
WSWT...... Peoria, IL [*FM radio station call letters*]
WSWTA.... Wasserwirtschaft [*A publication*]
WSWV ..... Pennington Gap, VA [*AM radio station call letters*]
WSWV-FM ... Pennington Gap, VA [*FM radio station call letters*]
WSWWD.. West-Southwestward [*Meteorology*]   (FAAC)
WSWZ....... Lancaster, OH [*FM radio station call letters*]
WSX .... Western Air Lines, Inc. [*Later, WAL*] [*NYSE symbol*]   (SPSG)
WSY .... Airlie Beach [*Australia*] [*Airport symbol*]
WSY .... West Somerset Yeomanry [*British military*]   (DMA)
WSYA .... Montgomery, AL [*AM radio station call letters*]
WSYA-FM ... Montgomery, AL [*FM radio station call letters*]
WSYB....... Rutland, VT [*AM radio station call letters*]
WSYC........ Shippensburg, PA [*FM radio station call letters*]
WSYC........ West Somerset Yeomanry Cavalry [*British military*]   (DMA)
WSYD .... Mount Airy, NC [*AM radio station call letters*]
WSYE .... Houston, MS [*FM radio station call letters*]
WSYL .... Sylvania, GA [*AM radio station call letters*]
WSYM ..... Lansing, MI [*Television station call letters*]
WSYN .... Georgetown, SC [*FM radio station call letters*]
WSYP .... White Sulphur Springs & Yellowstone Park Railway Co. [*AAR
                      code*]
WSYR........ Syracuse, NY [*AM radio station call letters*]
WSYT........ Syracuse, NY [*Television station call letters*]
WSYW .... Indianapolis, IN [*AM radio station call letters*]
WSYW-FM ... Danville, IN [*FM radio station call letters*]
WSYX........ Columbus, OH [*Television station call letters*]
WSYY........ Millinocket, ME [*AM radio station call letters*]
WSYY-FM ... Millinocket, ME [*FM radio station call letters*]
WSYZ........ Newburgh, IN [*FM radio station call letters*]
WSZ........... Vereniging Surinaams Bedrijfsleven. Weekbericht [*A
                      publication*]
WSZ........... Westport [*New Zealand*] [*Airport symbol*]   (OAG)
WSZ........... Wheat-Sheep Zone [*Agriculture*]
WSZ........... Wrong Signature Zero [*Nuclear science*]   (OA)
WSZE .... Saipan, CM [*Television station call letters*]
WT .... Three-Conductor Cables [*JETDS nomenclature*]
                      [*Military*]   (CET)
WT .... WAAC Ltd. - Nigeria Airways [*Nigeria*] [*ICAO
                      designator*]   (ICDA)
WT .... Waist Tether [*NASA*]   (KSC)
WT .... Wait Time [*Computer order entry*]
W/T .... Walkie-Talkie
WT .... Wall Thickness [*Nuclear energy*]   (NRCH)
WT .... War Tax
WT .... War Transport [*British military*]   (DMA)
WT .... Warm Tone [*Photography*]
WT .... Warning Tag   (AAG)
WT .... Warrant
WT .... Warrant Telegraphist [*British military*]   (DMA)
WT .... Wartime
WT .... Wash Trough
WT .... Washington Territory [*Prior to statehood*]
WT .... Washington Territory Reports [*1854-88*] [*A
                      publication*]   (DLA)
WT .... Waste Tank
WT .... Watch Time

WT.............	Watchdog Timer (MCD)	
WT.............	Watchdogs of the Treasury (EA)	
WT.............	Water Tank	
WT.............	Water Tanker [*British*]	
WT.............	Water Tender [*Navy*]	
WT.............	Water Thermometer	
WT.............	Water-Tube Boiler [*Naval*]	
WT.............	Watertight	
WT.............	Waveguide Transmission	
WT.............	Weapon Test	
WT.............	Weapon Training (MCD)	
WT.............	Weapons Technician [*Air Force*] (AFM)	
WT.............	Weapons Tight [*Weapons will engage only objects identified as hostile*]	
WT.............	Weight (AAG)	
WT.............	Weird Tales [*A publication*]	
WT.............	Weldwood Transportation Ltd. [*AAR code*]	
WTD............	Wellhead Tax [*Oil industry*]	
WT.............	Wetenschappelijke Tijdingen [*A publication*]	
WT.............	Whiffle Tree [*Structural test*] (AAG)	
WT.............	White Pennant [*Navy*] [*British*]	
WT.............	Wieczory Teatralne [*A publication*]	
WT.............	Wild Track [*Cinematography*]	
WT.............	Wild Type [*of a species*] [*Genetics*]	
WT.............	Will Talk [*Telecommunications*] (TEL)	
WTM............	William Tell Gunnery Mate	
WT.............	Wilms' Tumor [*Oncology*]	
WT.............	Wind Tunnel	
WT.............	Winterization Test (AAG)	
WT.............	[*The*] Winter's Tale [*Shakespearean work*]	
WT.............	Wire Ticket [*NASA*] (NASA)	
WT.............	Wire Transfer [*Banking*]	
WT.............	Wireless Telegraphy [*or Telephony*]	
WT.............	Wireless Transmitter	
WT.............	Wireless Truck [*British*]	
WT.............	With Tape	
WTX...........	With Title [*Bibliography*]	
WT.............	Withholding Tax [*IRS*]	
WT.............	Without	
WT.............	Wood Threshold (MSA)	
WT.............	Word Target [*Psychology*]	
WT.............	Word Terminal	
WT.............	Word Type	
W/T..........	Work Track [*Cinematography*]	
W & T	Work-and-Turn [*Printing*] (WDMC)	
WT.............	Workshop Trains [*British*]	
WT.............	World Tobacco [*A publication*]	
WT.............	Worldteam (EA)	
W & T	Wrightsville & Tennille Railroad (IIA)	
WT.............	Write Through [*Data processing*] (PCM)	
WT.............	Written Testimony (BJA)	
WT.............	Wyoming Territory	
WT's	Working Tools [*Freemasonry*]	
WTA	Tamborohano [*Madagascar*] [*Airport symbol*] (OAG)	
WTA	Washington Technological Association (MCD)	
WTA	Water Transport Association (EA)	
WTA	Welded Tube Co. of America [*AMEX symbol*] (SPSG)	
WTA	Western Timber Association (EA)	
WTA	Willingness-to-Accept [*Market research*]	
WTA	Window Test Apparatus	
WTA	Wire Traceability and Accountability [*NASA*] (NASA)	
WTA	Wissenschaftlich-Technischer Arbeitskreis fuer Denkmalpflege und Bauwerksanierung [*International Association for the Protection of Monuments and Restoration of Buildings*] (EAIO)	
WTA	Women's Tennis Association [*Later, WITA*] (EA)	
WTA	World Tax Report [*London*] [*A publication*]	
WTA	World Teleport Association [*New York, NY*] [*Telecommunications*] (TSSD)	
WTA	World Textile Abstracts [*Information service or system*] [*A publication*]	
WTA	Wyoming Trucking Association, Casper WY [*STAC*]	
WTAB	Tabor City, NC [*AM radio station call letters*]	
WTAC	Flint, MI [*AM radio station call letters*]	
WTAD	Quincy, IL [*AM radio station call letters*]	
WTAE	Pittsburgh, PA [*AM radio station call letters*]	
WTAE-TV ...	Pittsburgh, PA [*Television station call letters*]	
WTAG	Worcester, MA [*AM radio station call letters*]	
WTAI........	Melbourne, FL [*AM radio station call letters*]	
WTAJ........	Altoona, PA [*Television station call letters*]	
WTAK	Huntsville, AL [*AM radio station call letters*]	
WTAL	Tallahassee, FL [*AM radio station call letters*]	
WTAN.......	Clearwater, FL [*AM radio station call letters*]	
WTAO	Murphysboro, IL [*FM radio station call letters*]	
WTAP-TV ...	Parkersburg, WV [*Television station call letters*]	
WTAQ	La Grange, IL [*AM radio station call letters*]	
WTAR	Norfolk, VA [*AM radio station call letters*]	
WTAS........	Crete, IL [*FM radio station call letters*]	
WTAT	Charleston, SC [*Television station call letters*]	
WT Aux B ...	Water-Tube Auxiliary Boiler (DS)	
WTAW	College Station, TX [*AM radio station call letters*]	

WTAX	Springfield, IL [*AM radio station call letters*]	
W/TAX......	Withholding Tax [*IRS*] (AAG)	
WTAY	Robinson, IL [*AM radio station call letters*]	
WTAY-FM ...	Robinson, IL [*FM radio station call letters*]	
WTAZ	Morton, IL [*FM radio station call letters*]	
WTB	Wales Tourist Board (DCTA)	
WTB	War Transportation Board [*World War II*]	
WTB	Water-Tube Boiler [*Naval*]	
WTB	Welttierschutzbund [*Also known as WFPA, FMPA*] [*World Federation for the Protection of Animals*]	
WTB	Where's the Beef? [*Slogan created by the Dancer Fitzgerald Sample advertising agency for Wendy's International, Inc.*]	
WTB	Wilderness Trail Bike	
WTB	Willamette Tariff Bureau Inc., Portland OR [*STAC*]	
WTB	Woerterbuch [*Dictionary*] [*German*] (ROG)	
WTBB.......	Bonifay, FL [*FM radio station call letters*]	
WTBC.......	Williston, VT [*FM radio station call letters*]	
WTBD	Work to Be Done (ADA)	
WTBF........	Troy, AL [*AM radio station call letters*]	
WTBG	Brownsville, TN [*FM radio station call letters*]	
WTBH	Chiefland, FL [*FM radio station call letters*]	
WTBI........	Greenville, SC [*FM radio station call letters*]	
WTBI........	Pickens, SC [*AM radio station call letters*]	
WTBK.......	Manchester, KY [*FM radio station call letters*]	
WTBK.......	Westerbeke Corp. [*Avon, MA*] [*NASDAQ symbol*] (NQ)	
WTBM	Mexico, ME [*FM radio station call letters*]	
WTBN	Charlotte Amalie, VI [*FM radio station call letters*]	
WTBO	Cumberland, MD [*AM radio station call letters*]	
WTBQ	Warwick, NY [*AM radio station call letters*]	
WTBR.......	Pittsfield, MA [*FM radio station call letters*]	
WTBR.......	War Trade Board Rulings [*United States*] [*A publication*] (DLA)	
WTBS.......	Atlanta, GA [*Television station call letters*]	
WTBS.......	Water-Tube Boiler Survey (DS)	
WTB & TS ...	Watch Tower Bible and Tract Society	
WTBU	Indianapolis, IN [*Television station call letters*]	
WTBX	Hibbing, MN [*FM radio station call letters*]	
WTBY	Poughkeepsie, NY [*Television station call letters*]	
WTBZ........	Grafton, WV [*AM radio station call letters*]	
WTBZ-FM ...	Grafton, WV [*FM radio station call letters*]	
WTC	New York [*New York*] Battery Park [*Airport symbol*] (OAG)	
WTC	War Transport Council [*Later, ITWC*] [*World War II*]	
WTC	Waste Water Technology Centre [*Canada*] (ECON)	
WTC	Water Thermal and Chemical Technology Center [*University of California*] [*Research center*] (RCD)	
WTC	Waterton [*Colorado*] [*Seismograph station code, US Geological Survey*] [*Closed*] (SEIS)	
WTC	Well-Tempered Clavier [*Compositions of J. S. Bach*]	
WTC	Western Telecommunications Consulting Co. [*Los Angeles, CA*] [*Telecommunications*] (TSSD)	
WTC	Wind Temperature Correction	
WTC	Wire Test Chamber	
WTC	Women's Talent Corps [*Later, CHS*] (EA)	
WTC	Women's Theater Council	
WTC	Workload Transaction Code [*Navy*] (NG)	
WTC	World Trade Center [*New York City*]	
WTC	World Trade Center of New Orleans [*New Orleans, LA*] (EA)	
WTCA	Plymouth, IN [*AM radio station call letters*]	
WTCA	Water Terminal Clearance Authority [*Army*] (AABC)	
WTCA	Welsh Terrier Club of America (EA)	
WTCA	Wood Truss Council of America (EA)	
WTCA	World Tasar Class Association (EAIO)	
WTCA	World Trade Center Arhus [*Denmark*] (EAIO)	
WTCA	World Trade Centers Association (EA)	
WTCAJ	World Trade Center of Abidjan [*Ivory Coast*] (EAIO)	
WTCARES ...	Welsh Terrier Club of America Rescue Service (EA)	
WTCB........	Orangeburg, SC [*FM radio station call letters*]	
WTCB.......	Water Tender Construction Battalion [*Navy*]	
WTCC.......	Springfield, MA [*FM radio station call letters*]	
WTCC.......	Water Turbine Closed Coupled (MSA)	
WTCCQ	World Trade Center Club Chongqing [*China*] (EAIO)	
WTCCY	World Trade Centre - Cyprus (EAIO)	
WTCE........	Fort Pierce, FL [*Television station call letters*]	
WTCF........	Carrollton, MI [*FM radio station call letters*]	
WTCG	Andalusia, AL [*AM radio station call letters*]	
WTCGV	World Trade Center Geneva [*Switzerland*] (EAIO)	
WTCH	Shawano, WI [*AM radio station call letters*]	
WTCI........	Chattanooga, TN [*Television station call letters*]	
WTCI........	Western Telecommunications, Inc. [*Englewood, CO*] [*Telecommunications*]	
WTCIB	Women's Travelers Center and Information Bank [*Later, WIB*] (EA)	
WTCIS	World Trade Center Istanbul [*Turkey*] (EAIO)	
WTCJ	Tell City, IN [*AM radio station call letters*]	
WTCK	World Trade Center Korea	
WTCL........	Chattahoochee, FL [*AM radio station call letters*]	
WTCM	Traverse City, MI [*AM radio station call letters*]	
WTCM	Weld Timer Control Module	
WTCM-FM ...	Traverse City, MI [*FM radio station call letters*]	
WTCMM ..	World Trade Center Metro Manila [*Philippines*] (EAIO)	
WTCN	Stillwater, MN [*AM radio station call letters*]	

WTCN .... World Trade Center of Nigeria   (EAIO)
WTCNJ ..... World Trade Centre Nanjing [*China*]   (EAIO)
WTCO .... Campbellsville, KY [*AM radio station call letters*]
WTCO .... Western Transportation Co. [*AAR code*]
WTCO .... World Trade Center Oslo [*Norway*]   (EAIO)
WTCQ .... Vidalia, GA [*FM radio station call letters*]
WTCR .... Huntington, WV [*FM radio station call letters*]
WTCR .... Kenova, WV [*AM radio station call letters*]
WTCS .... Fairmont, WV [*AM radio station call letters*]
WTCS .... Windshield Temperature Control Systems
WTCSS ..... West Coast Off-Shore Tactical Control Surveillance System
          [*Navy*] (DNAB)
WTCT .... Marion, IL [*Television station call letters*]
WTCV .... Greenup, KY [*AM radio station call letters*]
WTCV .... Weapon and Tracked Combat Vehicle   (MCD)
WTCW .... Whitesburg, KY [*AM radio station call letters*]
WTCX .... Dayton, TN [*FM radio station call letters*]
WTD .... War Trade Department [*British*] [*World War II*]
WTD .... Water Turbine Direct   (MSA)
WTD .... Watertight Door
WTD .... Weapons Training Detachment [*Military*]
WTD .... Weekly Total-to-Date
WTD .... Weighted Total Demerits [*Lubricating oil test*]
WTD .... Whitland [*British depot code*]
WTD .... Wind Tunnel Data
WTD .... World Today [*London*] [*A publication*]
WTD .... World Trade Directory [*A publication*] [*Department of
          Commerce*]
wtdb .... Water-Tube Domestic Boiler   (DS)
WTDI .... WTD Industries, Inc. [*Portland, OR*] [*NASDAQ
          symbol*]   (NQ)
WTDR .... Statesville, NC [*FM radio station call letters*]
WTDR .... World Trade Directory Reports [*A publication*] [*Department of
          Commerce*]
WTDY .... Madison, WI [*AM radio station call letters*]
WTE .... International Symposium on Wave and Tidal Energy   (PDAA)
WTE .... Waste-to-Energy [*Resource recycling*]
WTE .... Wattle Tannin Equivalent [*Chemistry*]
WTE .... Westate Resources, Inc. [*Vancouver Stock Exchange symbol*]
WTE .... World Tapes for Education [*Defunct*]
WTE .... Worse than Expected [*Politics*]
WTE .... Wotje [*Marshall Islands*] [*Airport symbol*]   (OAG)
W Teach..... Western Teacher [*A publication*]
WTEB .... New Bern, NC [*FM radio station call letters*]
WTEC .... Warrantech Corp. [*New York, NY*] [*NASDAQ symbol*]   (NQ)
WTEK .... Waste Technology Corp. [*New York, NY*] [*NASDAQ
          symbol*]   (NQ)
WTEL .... Philadelphia, PA [*AM radio station call letters*]
WTEL .... Walker Telecommunications Corp. [*NASDAQ symbol*]   (NQ)
W Tel .... Warrant Telegraphist [*British military*]
WTEN .... Albany, NY [*Television station call letters*]
W Ten .... Wright's Introduction to the Law of Tenures [*A
          publication*]   (DLA)
W & T Eq Ca ... White and Tudor's Leading Cases in Equity [*9 eds.*] [*1849-
          1928*] [*A publication*]   (DLA)
W TER .... Washington Territory
WTES .... West Tennessee Experiment Station [*University of Tennessee at
          Knoxville*] [*Research center*]   (RCD)
WTF .... Waste Treatment Facility [*Nuclear energy*]   (IEEE)
WTF .... Waste Water Treatment Facility [*Nuclear energy*]   (NRCH)
WTF .... Welcome to Finland [*A publication*]
WTF .... Western Task Force [*Navy*]
WTF .... When Technology Fails [*A publication*]
WTF .... Will to Fire
WTF .... Wisconsin Test Facility [*Navy*]
WTF .... World Taekwondo Federation [*Seoul, Republic of
          Korea*]   (EAIO)
WTF .... World Timecapsule Fund   (EA)
WTFAA ..... Washington Task Force on African Affairs [*Defunct*]   (EA)
WTFDA..... Worldwide Television-FM DX Association   (EA)
WTFM........ Kingsport, TN [*FM radio station call letters*]
WTFPA ..... Wolf Trap Foundation for the Performing Arts   (EA)
WTFX........ Louisville, KY [*FM radio station call letters*]
WTG .... Waiting   (MSA)
WTG .... Weighting   (MSA)
WTG .... Williams Telecommunications Group [*Telecommunications
          service*]   (TSSD)
WTG .... Wind Tape Generation
WTG .... Wind Turbine Generator
WTG .... Worker Trait Group
WTGA .... Thomaston, GA [*AM radio station call letters*]
WTGA-FM ... Thomaston, GA [*FM radio station call letters*]
WTGC .... Lewisburg, PA [*AM radio station call letters*]
WTGE .... Baton Rouge, LA [*FM radio station call letters*]
WTGH....... Cayce, SC [*AM radio station call letters*]
WTGI .... Wilmington, DE [*Television station call letters*]
WTGL .... Cocoa, FL [*Television station call letters*]
WTGN....... Lima, OH [*FM radio station call letters*]
WTGP .... Greenville, PA [*FM radio station call letters*]
WTGP .... Union City, OH [*FM radio station call letters*]
WTGR .... Welcome to Greenland [*A publication*]

WTGS........ Hardeeville, SC [*Television station call letters*]
WTGV .... Sandusky, MI [*FM radio station call letters*]
WTGY .... Charleston, MS [*FM radio station call letters*]
WTH.......... Width   (WGA)
WTHE .... Mineola, NY [*AM radio station call letters*]
WTHE .... Workshop Test and Handling Equipment [*Military*]   (CAAL)
Wthfd .... Weatherford International, Inc. [*Associated Press
          abbreviation*]   (APAG)
WTHFRD ... Weatherford International, Inc. [*Associated Press
          abbreviation*]   (APAG)
WTHG....... Worthington Industries, Inc. [*NASDAQ symbol*]   (NQ)
WTHI .... Terre Haute, IN [*AM radio station call letters*]
WTHI-FM ... Terre Haute, IN [*FM radio station call letters*]
WTHI-TV ... Terre Haute, IN [*Television station call letters*]
W Th J .... Westminster Theological Journal [*A publication*]
WTHL .... Somerset, KY [*FM radio station call letters*]
WTHM...... Glen Arbor, MI [*FM radio station call letters*]
WTHO ...... Thomson, GA [*AM radio station call letters*]
WTHP .... Thomasville, NC [*FM radio station call letters*]
WTHPRF ... Weatherproof   (MSA)
WTHR....... Indianapolis, IN [*Television station call letters*]
WTHR....... Weather
WTHR....... Weatherford [*R. V.*] Co. [*NASDAQ symbol*]   (NQ)
WTHRA ... Weather [*London*] [*A publication*]
WTHS ...... Holland, MI [*FM radio station call letters*]
WTHT ...... Lewiston, ME [*FM radio station call letters*]
WTHU ...... Thurmont, MD [*AM radio station call letters*]
WTHWA... Weatherwise [*A publication*]
WTI .... Weapons Training Instruction   (MCD)
WTI .... Welcome to Iceland [*A publication*]
WTI .... West Texas Intermediate [*Crude oil*]   (ECON)
WTI .... Western Telematic, Inc.
WTI .... Wheelabrator Technologies, Inc. [*NYSE symbol*]   (SPSG)
WTI .... Work Training in Industry
WTI .... World Trade Institute
WTI .... World Translations Index [*International Translations Centre*]
          [*Information service or system*]
WTIC........ Hartford, CT [*AM radio station call letters*]
WTICB ...... Worldwide Travel Information Contact Book [*A publication*]
WTIC-FM ... Hartford, CT [*FM radio station call letters*]
WTIC-TV ... Hartford, CT [*Television station call letters*]
WTID .... Reform, AL [*FM radio station call letters*]
WTID .... World Travel Information Directory [*A publication*]
WTIE........ Wastewater Treatment Information Exchange [*National Small
          Flows Clearinghouse*]
WTIF .... Tifton, GA [*AM radio station call letters*]
WTIG .... Massillon, OH [*AM radio station call letters*]
WTIJ .... Roxbury, NH [*AM radio station call letters*]
WTIK........ Durham, NC [*AM radio station call letters*]
WTIL........ Mayaguez, PR [*AM radio station call letters*]
WTIM ...... Taylorville, IL [*AM radio station call letters*]
WTIN .... Ponce, PR [*Television station call letters*]
WTIQ .... Gulliver, MI [*FM radio station call letters*]
WTIQ .... Manistique, MI [*AM radio station call letters*]
WTIS........ Tampa, FL [*AM radio station call letters*]
WTIU .... Bloomington, IN [*Television station call letters*]
WTIV........ Titusville, PA [*AM radio station call letters*]
WTIX........ New Orleans, LA [*AM radio station call letters*]
WTJ .... Wedge Type Jack
WTJ .... Westminster Theological Journal [*A publication*]
WTJ .... Wrin, T. J., San Francisco CA [*STAC*]
WTJA........ Jamestown, NY [*Television station call letters*]
WTJB .... Columbus, GA [*FM radio station call letters*]
WTJC .... Springfield, OH [*Television station call letters*]
WTJH ...... East Point, GA [*AM radio station call letters*]
WTJP .... Gadsden, AL [*Television station call letters*]
WTJR .... Quincy, IL [*Television station call letters*]
WTJS .... Jackson, TN [*AM radio station call letters*]
WTJT .... Crestview, FL [*FM radio station call letters*]
WTJU....... Charlottesville, VA [*FM radio station call letters*]
WTJX........ Charlotte Amalie, VI [*Television station call letters*]
WTJY........ Taylorville, IL [*FM radio station call letters*]
WTJZ........ Newport News, VA [*AM radio station call letters*]
WTK .... Noatak [*Alaska*] [*Airport symbol*]   (OAG)
WTK .... Noatak, AK [*Location identifier*] [*FAA*]   (FAAL)
WTKB....... Huntingdon, TN [*FM radio station call letters*]
WTKC .... Kankakee, IL [*FM radio station call letters*]
WTKK .... Manassas, VA [*Television station call letters*]
WTKK .... Wen-Tzu Kai-Ko [*A publication*]
WTKL........ Baton Rouge, LA [*AM radio station call letters*]
WTKM ...... Hartford, WI [*AM radio station call letters*]
WTKM-FM ... Hartford, WI [*FM radio station call letters*]
WTKN....... Pinellas Park, FL [*AM radio station call letters*]
WTKO .... Ithaca, NY [*AM radio station call letters*]
WTKR .... Norfolk, VA [*Television station call letters*]
WTKS........ Brewer, ME [*FM radio station call letters*]
WTKT........ Georgetown, KY [*AM radio station call letters*]
WTKT-FM ... Georgetown, KY [*FM radio station call letters*]
WTKW ...... Bridgeport, NY [*FM radio station call letters*]
WTKX .... Pensacola, FL [*AM radio station call letters*]
WTKX-FM ... Pensacola, FL [*FM radio station call letters*]

WTKY .... Tompkinsville, KY [*AM radio station call letters*]
WTKY-FM ... Tompkinsville, KY [*FM radio station call letters*]
WTL .... Tuntatuliak [*Alaska*] [*Airport symbol*]   (OAG)
WTL .... Western Canadian Land [*Vancouver Stock Exchange symbol*]
WTL .... Western Trunk Line Committee, Chicago IL [*STAC*]
WTL .... Wilms' Tumor Locus [*Genetics*] [*Oncology*]
WTL .... Wyle Test Laboratories
WTLB....... Utica, NY [*AM radio station call letters*]
WTLC....... Indianapolis, IN [*FM radio station call letters*]
WTLC....... Western Tele-Communications, Inc. [*Englewood, CO*] [*NASDAQ symbol*]   (NQ)
WTLC....... Western Trunk Line Committee
W & TLC ... White and Tudor's Leading Cases in Equity [*9 eds.*] [*1849-1928*] [*A publication*]   (DLA)
WTLG .... Starke, FL [*FM radio station call letters*]
WTLH....... Bainbridge, GA [*Television station call letters*]
WTLJ .... Muskegon, MI [*Television station call letters*]
WTLK....... Taylorsville, NC [*AM radio station call letters*]
WTLK-TV ... Rome, GA [*Television station call letters*]
WTLN .... Apopka, FL [*AM radio station call letters*]
WTLN-FM ... Apopka, FL [*FM radio station call letters*]
WTLO .... Somerset, KY [*AM radio station call letters*]
WTLQ .... Pittston, PA [*FM radio station call letters*]
WTLR........ State College, PA [*FM radio station call letters*]
WTLS........ Tallassee, AL [*AM radio station call letters*]
WTLS........ West Texas Library System [*Library network*]
WTLT........ Circleville, OH [*FM radio station call letters*]
WTLV........ Jacksonville, FL [*Television station call letters*]
WTLW .... Lima, OH [*Television station call letters*]
WTLZ........ Saginaw, MI [*FM radio station call letters*]
WTM........ Western Mail [*British*] [*A publication*]
WTM........ Wind Tunnel Memorandum
WTM........ Wind Tunnel Model
WTM........ World Travel Market [*Trade show*] [*British*]   (ITD)
WTMA ...... Charleston, SC [*AM radio station call letters*]
WTMA ...... Wood Tank Manufacturers Association   (EA)
WTMB ...... Tomah, WI [*AM radio station call letters*]
WTMC ...... Ocala, FL [*AM radio station call letters*]
WTMD...... Towson, MD [*FM radio station call letters*]
WTME ...... Lewiston ME [*AM radio station call letters*]
WTMG ...... Tallahassee, FL [*FM radio station call letters*]
WTMI .... Miami, FL [*FM radio station call letters*]
WTMJ....... Milwaukee, WI [*AM radio station call letters*]
WTMJ-TV ... Milwaukee, WI [*Television station call letters*]
WTMP ...... Temple Terrace, FL [*AM radio station call letters*]
WTMR ...... Camden, NJ [*AM radio station call letters*]
WTMRF.... Westmount Resources Ltd. [*NASDAQ symbol*]   (NQ)
WTMS....... Presque Isle, ME [*AM radio station call letters*]
WTMS....... World Trade in Minerals Data Base System [*Data processing*]
WTMS-FM ... Presque Isle, ME [*FM radio station call letters*]
WTMT ...... Louisville, KY [*AM radio station call letters*]
WTMV ...... Lakeland, FL [*Television station call letters*]
WTMW ..... Arlington, VA [*Television station call letters*]
WTMX ...... Skokie, IL [*FM radio station call letters*]
WTMX ...... Wang Telephone Message Exchange [*Wang Laboratories, Inc.*] [*Telecommunications service*]   (TSSD)
WTMY ...... Sarasota, FL [*AM radio station call letters*]
WTN......... Journal of World Trade Law [*A publication*]
WTN......... Western Technical Net [*Air Force*]
WTN......... Wind Tunnel Note
WTN......... Witness
WTN......... Wroclawskie Towarzystwo Naukowe [*A publication*]
WTNC....... Thomasville, NC [*AM radio station call letters*]
WTNE .... Trenton, TN [*AM radio station call letters*]
WTNH....... New Haven, CT [*Television station call letters*]
WTNI .... Hartsville, SC [*AM radio station call letters*]
WTNJ....... Mount Hope, WV [*FM radio station call letters*]
WTNL .... Reidsville, GA [*AM radio station call letters*]
WTNN...... Farragut, TN [*AM radio station call letters*]
WTNR ...... Waynesboro, TN [*AM radio station call letters*]
WTNR-FM ... Waynesboro, TN [*FM radio station call letters*]
WTNS .... Coshocton, OH [*AM radio station call letters*]
WTNS-FM ... Coshocton, OH [*FM radio station call letters*]
WTNSTH ... Witnesseth [*Legal*] [*British*]   (ROG)
WTNT ...... Tallahassee, FL [*FM radio station call letters*]
WTNV .... Jackson, TN [*FM radio station call letters*]
WTNX ...... Lynchburg, TN [*AM radio station call letters*]
WTNY ...... Watertown, NY [*AM radio station call letters*]
WTNY-FM ... Watertown, NY [*FM radio station call letters*]
WTO......... Warsaw Treaty Organization
WTO......... Westam Oil Ltd. [*Vancouver Stock Exchange symbol*]
WTO......... WESTPAC [*Western Pacific*] Transportation Office   (CINC)
WTO......... Wireless Telegraphy Officer [*British military*]   (DMA)
WTO......... World Tourism Organization [*Madrid, Spain*]
WTO......... Wotho [*Marshall Islands*] [*Airport symbol*]   (OAG)
WTO......... Write-to-Operator [*Data processing*]   (IBMDP)
WTOB ...... Winston-Salem, NC [*AM radio station call letters*]
WTOC....... Savannah, GA [*Television station call letters*]
WTOD...... Toledo, OH [*AM radio station call letters*]
WTOE....... Spruce Pine, NC [*AM radio station call letters*]
WTOEW ... Welcome to Our Elvis World   (EA)

WTOF ...... Canton, OH [*FM radio station call letters*]
WTOG...... St. Petersburg, FL [*Television station call letters*]
WTOH...... Mobile, AL [*FM radio station call letters*]
WTOH...... Western Ohio Railroad Co. [*AAR code*]
WTOJ....... Carthage, NY [*FM radio station call letters*]
WTOK...... Meridian, MS [*Television station call letters*]
WTOL....... Toledo, OH [*Television station call letters*]
WTOM...... Cheboygan, MI [*Television station call letters*]
WTON...... Staunton, VA [*AM radio station call letters*]
WTON-FM ... Staunton, VA [*FM radio station call letters*]
WTOO...... Asheville, NC [*AM radio station call letters*]
WTOP...... Washington, DC [*AM radio station call letters*]
WTOQ...... Platteville, WI [*AM radio station call letters*]
WTOR...... Write-to-Operator with Reply [*Data processing*]   (IBMDP)
WTOS....... Skowhegan, ME [*FM radio station call letters*]
WTOS....... Western Test Range Office of Safety [*Air Force*]   (MCD)
WTOT ...... Marianna, FL [*AM radio station call letters*]
WTOV....... Steubenville, OH [*Television station call letters*]
WToVA ..... United States Veterans Administration Hospital, Tomah, WI [*Library symbol*] [*Library of Congress*]   (LCLS)
WTOW...... Washington, NC [*AM radio station call letters*]
WTOX ...... Lincoln, ME [*AM radio station call letters*]
WTOY ...... Salem, VA [*AM radio station call letters*]
WTP .... Warrant to Pollute
WTP .... Waste Water Treatment Plant [*Also, WWTP*]
WTP .... Water Treatment Plant [*Nuclear energy*]   (NRCH)
WTP .... Weapons Testing Program   (AAG)
WTP .... Wiggins Teape Paper [*Commercial firm*] [*British*]
WTP .... Willingness-to-Pay [*Market research*]
WTP .... Woitape [*Papua New Guinea*] [*Airport symbol*]   (OAG)
WTP .... World Tape Pals   (EA)
WTPA....... Mechanicsburg, PA [*FM radio station call letters*]
WTPA....... Wheelchair Tennis Players Association   (EA)
WTPBC..... Wool Textiles Production Board of Control [*British*] [*World War I*]
WTPC....... Elsah, IL [*FM radio station call letters*]
WTPI........ Indianapolis, IN [*FM radio station call letters*]
WTPM...... Aguadilla, PR [*FM radio station call letters*]
WTPR....... Paris, TN [*AM radio station call letters*]
WTPR....... Wetterau Properties, Inc. [*NASDAQ symbol*]   (NQ)
WTPS........ Water, Toxics, and Pesticides Staff [*Environmental Protection Agency*]   (GFGA)
WtPtPe ...... West Point-Pepperell, Inc. [*Associated Press abbreviation*]   (APAG)
WTQR....... Winston-Salem, NC [*FM radio station call letters*]
WTQX ...... Selma, AL [*AM radio station call letters*]
WTR .... Aquarion Co. [*NYSE symbol*]   (SPSG)
WTR .... Sierra Spring Water Co. [*AMEX symbol*]   (SPSG)
WTR .... Waiter
WTR .... War Tax Resistance [*An association*] [*Defunct*]   (EA)
WTR .... Warstar Resources, Inc. [*Vancouver Stock Exchange symbol*]
WTR .... Water
WTR .... Water Turnover Rate [*Physiology*]
WTR .... Waterford and Tranmore Railway [*British*]   (ROG)
WTR .... Waters Associates, Milford, MA [*OCLC symbol*]   (OCLC)
WTR .... Waterville [*Colby College*] [*Maine*] [*Seismograph station code, US Geological Survey*]   (SEIS)
WTR .... Weekly Transcript Reports [*New York*] [*A publication*]   (DLA)
WTR .... Well to Right [*Aviation*]   (FAAC)
WTR .... Western Test Range [*Formerly, Pacific Missile Range*] [*Air Force*]
WTR .... Westinghouse Test Reactor
WTR .... Winter
WTR .... Work Transfer Record   (KSC)
WTR .... Work Transfer Request
WTR .... World Travel [*A publication*]
WTR .... Wrightsville & Tennille R. R. [*AAR code*]
WTR .... Writer
WTRA ...... Mayaguez, PR [*Television station call letters*]
WTRB....... Ripley, TN [*AM radio station call letters*]
WTRC .... Elkhart, IN [*AM radio station call letters*]
WTRC .... Weapon Test Reports Committee [*AEC-DoD*]
WTRC .... Women's Training and Resources Corp.
WTRE....... Greensburg, IN [*AM radio station call letters*]
WTRF....... Wheeling, WV [*Television station call letters*]
WTRG ...... Rocky Mount, NC [*FM radio station call letters*]
WTRG ...... World Trade Resources Guide [*A publication*]
WTRI........ Brunswick, MD [*AM radio station call letters*]
WTRJ .... Troy, OH [*FM radio station call letters*]
WTRL........ Tomah, WI [*FM radio station call letters*]
WTRM ...... Western Test Range Manual [*Air Force*]   (MCD)
WTRM ...... Winchester, VA [*FM radio station call letters*]
WTRN ...... Tyrone, PA [*AM radio station call letters*]
WTRO....... Dyersburg, TN [*AM radio station call letters*]
WTRP....... La Grange, GA [*AM radio station call letters*]
WTRPP..... Water Pump Propeller [*on a ship*]   (DS)
WTRPRF... Waterproof   (MSA)
WTRPRFG ... Waterproofing
WTRQ....... Warsaw, NC [*AM radio station call letters*]
WTRR .... Sanford, FL [*AM radio station call letters*]
WTRS........ Dunnellon, FL [*AM radio station call letters*]

WTRS........ Waters Instruments, Inc. [*NASDAQ symbol*]   (NQ)
WTRS-FM ... Dunellon, FL [*FM radio station call letters*]
WTRSYS... Water System   (MCD)
WTRT........ Florence, AL [*Television station call letters*]
WTRTT..... Watertight   (MSA)
WTRU....... Jupiter, FL [*FM radio station call letters*]
WTRV .... Leland, MI [*FM radio station call letters*]
WTRW ...... Two Rivers, WI [*AM radio station call letters*]
WTRX .... Flint, MI [*AM radio station call letters*]
WTRY .... Rotterdam, NY [*FM radio station call letters*]
WTRY .... Troy, NY [*AM radio station call letters*]
WTRZ .... McMinnville, TN [*FM radio station call letters*]
WTRZ........ Winterize   (AAG)
WTRZN .... Winterization   (AAG)
WTS.......... Tsiroanomandidy [*Madagascar*] [*Airport symbol*]   (OAG)
WTS.......... War Training Service [*of the Civil Aeronautics Administration*] [*Formerly Civilian Pilot Training*] [*World War II*]
WTS.......... Watermen's Trade Society [*A union*] [*British*]
WTS.......... Watersport. Maandblad voor de Zeilsport. Motorbootsport [*A publication*]
WTS.......... Weapons Training Site [*Military*]
WTS.......... Western Tariff Service Inc., Oakland CA [*STAC*]
WTS.......... Westminister Theological Seminary, Philadelphia, PA [*OCLC symbol*]   (OCLC)
WTS.......... Whale Tumor Story [*Urban folklore term coined by Rodney Dale*]
WTS.......... Wind Tunnel Study
WTS.......... Wing Tank Structure
WTS.......... Winterswijk [*Netherlands*] [*Seismograph station code, US Geological Survey*]   (SEIS)
WTS.......... Women's Transport Service [*British*]
WTS.......... Women's Transportation Seminar [*Later, WTSN*]   (EA)
WTS.......... Word Terminal Synchronous
4WTS........ Four-Wire Terminating Set [*Telecommunications*]   (TEL)
WTSA........ Brattleboro, VT [*AM radio station call letters*]
WTSA....... Wood Turners and Shapers Association [*Later, WPMA*]   (EA)
WTSA-FM .. Brattleboro, VT [*FM radio station call letters*]
WTSB........ Lumberton, NC [*AM radio station call letters*]
WTSB........ Wood Turners Service Bureau [*Later, WPMA*]
WTSC........ Potsdam, NY [*FM radio station call letters*]
WTSC........ West Texas State College [*Later, WTSU*]
WTSC........ Wet Tantalum Slug Capacitor   (NASA)
WTSDET .. Wing Transportation Squadron Detachment [*Navy*]   (DNAB)
WTSF .... Ashland, KY [*Television station call letters*]
WTSFLW ... Women's Trade Society of Fancy Leather Workers [*A union*] [*British*]
WTSH .... Rockmart, GA [*FM radio station call letters*]
WTSH .... Rome, GA [*AM radio station call letters*]
WTSHRD ... Water and Toxic Substances Health Research Division [*Environmental Protection Agency*]   (GFGA)
WTSI .... Western Tar Sands, Inc. [*NASDAQ symbol*]   (NQ)
WTSJ .... Cincinnati, OH [*AM radio station call letters*]
WTSK........ Tuscaloosa, AL [*AM radio station call letters*]
WTSL........ Hanover, NH [*AM radio station call letters*]
WTSL-FM ... Hanover, NH [*FM radio station call letters*]
WTSN .... Dover, NH [*AM radio station call letters*]
WTSN .... Women's Transportation Seminar-National   (EA)
WTSNG .... Witnessing [*Legal*] [*British*]   (ROG)
WTSO .... Madison, WI [*AM radio station call letters*]
WTSP .... St. Petersburg, FL [*Television station call letters*]
WTSPT ..... Waterspout
WTSR .... Trenton, NJ [*FM radio station call letters*]
WTSS .... Scranton, PA [*AM radio station call letters*]
WTSU .... Troy, AL [*FM radio station call letters*]
WTSU .... West Texas State University [*Formerly, WTSC*]
WTSV .... Claremont, NH [*AM radio station call letters*]
WTSW ...... Wilkes-Barre, PA [*AM radio station call letters*]
WTSX .... Port Jervis, NY [*FM radio station call letters*]
WTT .... Weapon Tactics Trainer   (MCD)
WTT .... Weird Terror Tales [*A publication*]
WTT .... Western Tank Truck Carriers' Conference Inc., Denver CO [*STAC*]
WTT .... Westmount Resources Ltd. [*Toronto Stock Exchange symbol*]
WTT .... Wind Tunnel Test
WTT .... Working Timetable   (DCTA)
WTT .... World Team Tennis [*League*]
WTTA .... St. Petersburg, FL [*Television station call letters*]
WTTB .... Vero Beach, FL [*AM radio station call letters*]
WTTC .... Towanda, PA [*AM radio station call letters*]
WTTC........ Western Technical Training Command [*AAFWTTC*]
WTTC....... World Technology & Trading [*NASDAQ symbol*]   (NQ)
WTTC-FM ... Towanda, PA [*FM radio station call letters*]
WTTE........ Columbus, OH [*Television station call letters*]
WTTF........ Tiffin, OH [*AM radio station call letters*]
WTTF........ Welcome to the Faeroes [*A publication*]
WTTF-FM ... Tiffin, OH [*FM radio station call letters*]
WTTG .... Washington, DC [*Television station call letters*]
WTTI........ Dalton, GA [*AM radio station call letters*]
WTTK....... Kokomo, IN [*Television station call letters*]
WTTL........ Madisonville, KY [*AM radio station call letters*]
WTTL-FM ... Madisonville, KY [*FM radio station call letters*]

WTTM ...... Trenton, NJ [*AM radio station call letters*]
WTTN .... Watertown, WI [*AM radio station call letters*]
WTTO ...... Birmingham, AL [*Television station call letters*]
WTTR....... Westminster, MD [*AM radio station call letters*]
WTTS .... Bloomington, IN [*FM radio station call letters*]
WTTT........ Amherst, MA [*AM radio station call letters*]
WTTU .... Cookeville, TN [*FM radio station call letters*]
WTTV....... Bloomington, IN [*Television station call letters*]
WTTW ...... Chicago, IL [*Television station call letters*] [*Letters stand for "Windows to the World"*]
WTTX....... Appomattox, VA [*AM radio station call letters*]
WTTX-FM ... Appomattox, VA [*FM radio station call letters*]
WTU.......... Washington University, St. Louis, MO [*OCLC symbol*]   (OCLC)
WTU.......... Weekly TIF [*Taxpayer Information File*] Update [*IRS*]
WTU.......... Whitetails Unlimited   (EA)
WTU.......... Williams Coal Seam Gas Realty [*NYSE symbol*]   (SPSG)
WTUA .... St. Stephen, SC [*AM radio station call letters*]
WTUB .... Georgetown, SC [*FM radio station call letters*]
WTUE .... Dayton, OH [*FM radio station call letters*]
WTUF .... Boston, GA [*FM radio station call letters*]
WTUG .... Tuscaloosa, AL [*FM radio station call letters*]
WTUK .... Harlan, KY [*FM radio station call letters*]
WTUL .... New Orleans, LA [*FM radio station call letters*]
WTUN...... Pocatilico, WV [*FM radio station call letters*]
WTUP .... Tupelo, MS [*AM radio station call letters*]
WTUR .... Truro, MA [*FM radio station call letters*]
WTURB .... Water Turbine   (MSA)
WTURN.... White Turnout [*Political science*]
WTUS .... Mannington, WV [*FM radio station call letters*]
WTUX .... Indianapolis, IN [*AM radio station call letters*]
WTUZ .... Uhrichsville, OH [*FM radio station call letters*]
WTV .... Water Tank Vessel [*Navy*]
WTV .... Wound Tumor Virus [*Plant pathology*]
WTVA .... Tupelo, MS [*Television station call letters*]
WTVA .... Wider Television Access [*British*]
WTVB....... Coldwater, MI [*AM radio station call letters*]
WTVC .... Chattanooga, TN [*Television station call letters*]
WTVD ...... Durham, NC [*Television station call letters*]
WTVE .... Reading, PA [*Television station call letters*]
WTVF....... Nashville, TN [*Television station call letters*]
WTVG ...... Toledo, OH [*Television station call letters*]
WTVH....... Syracuse, NY [*Television station call letters*]
WTVI........ Charlotte, NC [*Television station call letters*]
WTVJ........ Miami, FL [*Television station call letters*]
WTVL........ Waterville, ME [*AM radio station call letters*]
WTVL-FM ... Waterville, ME [*FM radio station call letters*]
WTVM ...... Columbus, GA [*Television station call letters*]
WTVN ...... Columbus, OH [*AM radio station call letters*]
WTVO ...... Rockford, IL [*Television station call letters*]
WTVP........ Peoria, IL [*Television station call letters*]
WTVQ ...... Lexington, KY [*Television station call letters*]
WTVR ...... Richmond, VA [*AM radio station call letters*]
WTVR-FM ... Richmond, VA [*FM radio station call letters*]
WTVR-TV ... Richmond, VA [*Television station call letters*]
WTVS........ Detroit, MI [*Television station call letters*]
WTVT........ Tampa, FL [*Television station call letters*]
WTVU .... New Haven, CT [*Television station call letters*]
WTVW ...... Evansville, IN [*Television station call letters*]
WTVX .... Fort Pierce, FL [*Television station call letters*]
WTVY .... Dothan, AL [*Television station call letters*]
WTVY-FM ... Dothan, AL [*FM radio station call letters*]
WTVZ .... Norfolk, VA [*Television station call letters*]
WTw .... Joseph Mann Library, Two Rivers, WI [*Library symbol*] [*Library of Congress*]   (LCLS)
WTW .... Materials Reclamation Weekly [*A publication*]
WTW......... Wall to Wall [*Technical drawings*]
WTW .... West Thumb [*Wyoming*] [*Seismograph station code, US Geological Survey*]   (SEIS)
WTW .... Writers and Their Work [*A publication*]
WTW .... Wroclawskie Towarzystwo Naukowe [*A publication*]
WTWA ...... Thomson, GA [*AM radio station call letters*]
WTWA ...... World Trade Writers Association [*New York, NY*]   (EA)
WTWB ...... Auburndale, FL [*AM radio station call letters*]
WTWC ...... Tallahassee, FL [*Television station call letters*]
WTWF...... Woodville, FL [*AM radio station call letters*]
WTWL ...... McKinnon, TN [*FM radio station call letters*]
WTWO ...... Terre Haute, IN [*Television station call letters*]
WTWR ...... Monroe, MI [*FM radio station call letters*]
WTWS....... New London, CT [*Television station call letters*]
WTWS....... Wall to Wall Sound & Video, Inc. [*Cinnaminson, NJ*] [*NASDAQ symbol*]   (NQ)
WTWX ...... Guntersville, AL [*FM radio station call letters*]
WTWZ ...... Clinton, MS [*AM radio station call letters*]
WTX .... West Texas Utilities Co. [*AMEX symbol*]   (SPSG)
WTX .... Worldtex, Inc. [*NYSE symbol*]   (SPSG)
WTXF........ Philadelphia, PA [*Television station call letters*]
WTXI........ Ripley, MS [*FM radio station call letters*]
WTXL........ Tallahassee, FL [*Television station call letters*]
WTXT........ Fayette, AL [*FM radio station call letters*]
WTXT........ Wheatley TXT [*NASDAQ symbol*]   (SPSG)

WTXX ...... Waterbury, CT [*Television station call letters*]
WTXY ...... Whiteville, NC [*AM radio station call letters*]
WTY .... Westley Mines Ltd. [*Toronto Stock Exchange symbol*] [*Vancouver Stock Exchange symbol*]
WTYD .... New London, CT [*FM radio station call letters*]
WTYF .... World Theosophical Youth Federation [*Porto Alegre, Brazil*] (EAIO)
WTYJ .... Fayette, MS [*FM radio station call letters*]
WTYL........ Tylertown, MS [*AM radio station call letters*]
WTYL-FM ... Tylertown, MS [*FM radio station call letters*]
WTYN .... Tryon, NC [*AM radio station call letters*]
WTYR .... Soddy-Daisy, TN [*AM radio station call letters*]
W Ty R...... Washington Territory Reports [*1854-88*] [*A publication*] (DLA)
WTYS........ Marianna, FL [*AM radio station call letters*]
WTYX .... Jackson, MS [*FM radio station call letters*]
WTZ .... Weird Tales [*1973-*] [*A publication*]
WTZ .... Western Trinity Resource [*Vancouver Stock Exchange symbol*]
WTZ .... Whakatane [*New Zealand*] [*Seismograph station code, US Geological Survey*] (SEIS)
WTZA ...... Kingston, NY [*Television station call letters*]
WTZE........ Tazewell, VA [*AM radio station call letters*]
WTZE-FM ... Tazewell, VA [*FM radio station call letters*]
WTZH....... Meridian, MS [*Television station call letters*]
WTZQ .... Hendersonville, NC [*AM radio station call letters*]
WTZX........ Sparta, TN [*AM radio station call letters*]
WU .... University of Wisconsin, Madison, WI [*Library symbol*] [*Library of Congress*] (LCLS)
WU .... Weapons and Utilities Maintenance [*Military*] (GFGA)
WU .... Weather Underground (EA)
WU .... Weekly Underwriter [*A publication*]
WU .... Weight Unit [*Automobiles*]
WU .... Wesleyan University
WU .... Western European Union [*Also, WEU*] (NATG)
WU .... Western Union Telegraph Co. (TSSD)
WU .... Whitetails Unlimited (EA)
WU .... Window Unit (MSA)
WU .... Work Unit [*Air Force*] (AFM)
w/u .... Work-Up
WU .... Workshop Unit (MSA)
WU .... World Union [*Pondicherry, India*] (EA)
WU-A .... University of Wisconsin, Agricultural Library, Madison, WI [*Library symbol*] [*Library of Congress*] (LCLS)
WUA.......... Weapon Utility Analysis
WUA.......... Western Underwriters Association [*Later, ISO*]
WUA.......... Work Unit Assignment [*Navy*] (NG)
WUAA .... Wartime Unit Aircraft Activity (AFM)
WUAB....... Lorain, OH [*Television station call letters*]
WUAG....... Greensboro, NC [*FM radio station call letters*]
WUAL....... Tuscaloosa, AL [*FM radio station call letters*]
WUAR....... Women United Against Rape
WUAT....... Pikeville, TN [*AM radio station call letters*]
WUAW...... Erwin, NC [*FM radio station call letters*]
WUBE .... Cincinnati, OH [*AM radio station call letters*]
WUBE-FM ... Cincinnati, OH [*FM radio station call letters*]
WUBI .... Baxley, GA [*Television station call letters*]
WUBOA.... Wasser und Boden [*A publication*]
WUBU....... Portage, MI [*FM radio station call letters*]
WUBW...... World Union of Black Writers [*See also UEMN*] (EAIO)
WUC.......... Western Union Corp.
WUC.......... Work Unit Code
WUC.......... Writers Union of Canada
WUC.......... Wu-han [*Republic of China*] [*Seismograph station code, US Geological Survey*] (SEIS)
WU/CCM ... Washington University Center for Computational Mechanics [*St. Louis, MO*]
WU/CCR... Washington University Center for Composites Research [*St. Louis, MO*]
WUCDU.... World Union of Christian Democratic Women [*Venezuela*] [*Political party*] (EAIO)
WUCF .... Orlando, FL [*FM radio station call letters*]
WUCF .... Work Unit Code File (NASA)
WUCI .... Binghamton, NY [*FM radio station call letters*]
WUCM...... University Center, MI [*Television station call letters*]
WUCM...... Work Unit Code Manual
WUCO...... Marysville, OH [*AM radio station call letters*]
WUCOS ..... Western European Union Chiefs of Staff (NATG)
WUCPS..... World Union of Catholic Philosophical Societies (EA)
WUCT .... World Union of Catholic Teachers
WUCWO... World Union of Catholic Women's Organizations [*Rosemere, PQ*] (EAIO)
WUCX....... Bad Axe, MI [*Television station call letters*]
WUCX-FM ... Bay City, MI [*FM radio station call letters*]
WUCZ........ Carthage, TN [*FM radio station call letters*]
WuD......... Wort und Dienst. Jahrbuch der Theologischen Schule Bethel [*Bethel Bei Bielefeld*] [*A publication*]
WUDB....... Work Unit Data Bank
WU-DE...... University of Wisconsin, Center for Demography and Ecology, Madison, WI [*Library symbol*] [*Library of Congress*] (LCLS)
WUDO ...... Western European Union Defense Organization (NATG)

WUDZ....... Sweet Briar, VA [*FM radio station call letters*]
WU-E........ University of Wisconsin, Engineering Library, Madison, WI [*Library symbol*] [*Library of Congress*] (LCLS)
WUE......... Water-Use Efficiency [*Agriculture*]
WUE......... Work Unit Engineer
WUEC........ Eau Claire, WI [*FM radio station call letters*]
WUEMI .... Western Union Electronic Mail, Inc. [*McLean, VA*] [*Telecommunications*] (TSSD)
Wuerttemb Aerztebl ... Wuerttembergisches Aerzteblatt [*A publication*]
Wuerttemberg Blaetter Km ... Wuerttembergische Blaetter fuer Kirchenmusik [*A publication*]
Wuerttemb Wochenbl Landwirt ... Wuerttembergisches Wochenblatt fuer Landwirtschaft [*A publication*]
Wuerzb Jb Alt Wiss ... Wuerzburger Jahrbuecher fuer die Altertumswissenschaft [*A publication*]
Wuerzburg Geogr Arb ... Wuerzburger Geographische Arbeiten [*A publication*]
Wuerz Jb.... Wuerzburger Jahrbuecher fuer die Altertumswissenschaft [*A publication*]
WUEV....... Evansville, IN [*FM radio station call letters*]
WUEZ .... Christopher, IL [*FM radio station call letters*]
WUF .... Wattle-Urea-Formaldehyde [*Adhesive component*]
WUF .... Western United Front [*Fiji*] [*Political party*] (PPW)
WUF .... World Underwater Federation (ASF)
WUF .... World Union of Free Thinkers
WUF .... World University, Miami Learning Resource Center, Miami, FL [*OCLC symbol*] (OCLC)
WUFE .... Baxley, GA [*AM radio station call letters*]
WUFEC..... Western European Union Finance and Economic Committee (NATG)
WUFF....... Eastman, GA [*AM radio station call letters*]
WUFF-FM ... Eastman, GA [*FM radio station call letters*]
WUFI........ Rantoul, IL [*AM radio station call letters*]
WUFI........ World United Formosans for Independence [*Political party*] (EY)
WUFK ...... Fort Kent, ME [*FM radio station call letters*]
WUFL....... Sterling Heights, MI [*AM radio station call letters*]
WUFM ...... Lebanon, PA [*FM radio station call letters*]
WUFN....... Albion, MI [*FM radio station call letters*]
WUFO....... Amherst, NY [*AM radio station call letters*]
WUFR .... World Union of Free Romanians [*See also UMRL*] [*Creteil, France*] (EAIO)
WUFS....... World Union of French-Speakers [*See also UMVF*] (EAIO)
WUFT .... Gainesville, FL [*Television station call letters*]
WUFT-FM ... Gainesville, FL [*FM radio station call letters*]
WUFTU .... World Union of Free Trade Unions
WUFX ...... Buffalo, NY [*FM radio station call letters*]
WUg.......... Graham Public Library, Union Grove, WI [*Library symbol*] [*Library of Congress*] (LCLS)
WUG......... Wau [*Papua New Guinea*] [*Airport symbol*] (OAG)
WuG......... Wissenschaft und Gegenwart [*A publication*]
WUGA...... Athens, GA [*FM radio station call letters*]
WUGGAO ... Contributions to Geology. University of Wyoming [*A publication*]
WUGN ...... Midland, MI [*FM radio station call letters*]
WUGO ...... Grayson, KY [*FM radio station call letters*]
WUgSC ..... Southern Wisconsin Colony and Training School, Medical Library, Union Grove, WI [*Library symbol*] [*Library of Congress*] (LCLS)
WUH .... Wu-han [*Republic of China*] [*Seismograph station code, US Geological Survey*] (SEIS)
WUH .... Wuhan [*China*] [*Airport symbol*] (OAG)
Wuhan Univ J Nat Sci ... Wuhan University Journal. Natural Sciences [*People's Republic of China*] [*A publication*]
WUHF....... Rochester, NY [*Television station call letters*]
WUHN...... Pittsfield, MA [*AM radio station call letters*]
WUHQ...... Battle Creek, MI [*Television station call letters*]
WUHS...... Urbana, OH [*FM radio station call letters*]
WUI.......... Western Union International [*Division of WUI, Inc.*]
WUIC .... Trinity, AL [*FM radio station call letters*]
WUIS........ Water Use Information System [*Westinghouse Hanford Co.*] (IID)
WUIS........ Work Unit Information System [*Database*] [*DTIC*]
WUIV .... Icard Township, NC [*AM radio station call letters*]
WUJA ...... Caguas, PR [*Television station call letters*]
WUJC....... University Heights, OH [*FM radio station call letters*]
WUJM...... Goose Creek, SC [*AM radio station call letters*]
WUJM-FM ... Goose Creek, SC [*FM radio station call letters*]
WUJS........ World Union of Jewish Students [*Jerusalem, Israel*]
WUKEE8 .. Wuyi Science Journal [*A publication*]
WUKO....... World Union of Karatedo Organizations [*Solna, Sweden*] (EAIO)
WUKY .... Lexington, KY [*FM radio station call letters*]
WU-L......... University of Wisconsin, Law Library, Madison, WI [*Library symbol*] [*Library of Congress*] (LCLS)
WUL.......... Washington University, Law Library, St. Louis, MO [*OCLC symbol*] (OCLC)
WUL.......... Workers Unity League [*Canada*]
WULA ...... Eufaula, AL [*AM radio station call letters*]
WULA-FM ... Eufaula, AL [*FM radio station call letters*]

WULC .... West Virginia Union Catalog Interlibrary Loan Network [*Library network*]
WULDS..... Western Union Long Distance Service [*Western Union Telegraph Co.*] [*Upper Saddle River, NJ*] [*Telecommunications*] (TSSD)
WULF........ Alma, GA [*AM radio station call letters*]
WULF........ Wulf Oil Corp. [*NASDAQ symbol*] (NQ)
WU-LT...... University of Wisconsin, Land Tenure Center, Madison, WI [*Library symbol*] [*Library of Congress*] (LCLS)
WULTUO ... World Union of Liberal Trade Union Organisations [*See also WFALW*] [*Zurich, Switzerland*] (EAIO)
WU-M .... University of Wisconsin, School of Medicine, Madison, WI [*Library symbol*] [*Library of Congress*] (LCLS)
WUM........ Washington University, School of Medicine, St. Louis, MO [*OCLC symbol*] (OCLC)
WUM........ Women's Universal Movement [*Defunct*] (EA)
WUM........ Work Unit Manager
WUM........ World Union of Mapam [*See also UMM*] (EAIO)
WUMA...... Old Forge, NY [*FM radio station call letters*]
WUMB..... Boston, MA [*FM radio station call letters*]
WUMC...... Old Town, ME [*FM radio station call letters*]
WUME...... Paoli, IN [*FM radio station call letters*]
WUMF...... Farmington, ME [*FM radio station call letters*]
WUMG...... Chattahoochee, FL [*FM radio station call letters*]
WUMI....... State College, MS [*FM radio station call letters*]
WUMP...... White, Urban, Middle Class, Protestant
WUMPS.... Women Umpires [*World War II*]
WUMS....... University, MS [*FM radio station call letters*]
WUMS...... Woman's Union Missionary Society of America [*Later, UFCS*] (EA)
WUMTPT ... World Union of Martyred Towns, Peace Towns (EAIO)
WUMX...... Tallahassee, FL [*FM radio station call letters*]
WUN .... Wiluna [*Australia*] [*Airport symbol*] (OAG)
WUNC....... Chapel Hill, NC [*Television station call letters*]
WUNC-FM ... Chapel Hill, NC [*FM radio station call letters*]
WUND ...... Columbia, NC [*Television station call letters*]
W Underw ... Weekly Underwriter [*A publication*]
WUNE....... Linville, NC [*Television station call letters*]
WUNF....... Asheville, NC [*Television station call letters*]
WUNG .... Concord, NC [*Television station call letters*]
WUNH ..... Durham, NH [*FM radio station call letters*]
WUNI....... Bay City, MI [*AM radio station call letters*]
WUNJ .... Wilmington, NC [*Television station call letters*]
WUNK ...... Greenville, NC [*Television station call letters*]
Wunk .... WASP Funk [*1960's pop music*]
WUNL....... Winston-Salem, NC [*Television station call letters*]
WUNM ...... Jacksonville, NC [*Television station call letters*]
WUNN ...... Mason, MI [*AM radio station call letters*]
WUNO ...... San Juan, PR [*AM radio station call letters*]
WUNP....... Roanoke Rapids, NC [*Television station call letters*]
WUNR...... Brookline, MA [*AM radio station call letters*]
WUNS ...... Lewisburg, PA [*FM radio station call letters*]
WUNS....... World Union of National Socialists (EA)
WUNT....... Wissenschaftliche Untersuchungen zum Neuen Testament [*Tuebingen*] [*A publication*] (BJA)
WUNV....... Albany, GA [*FM radio station call letters*]
WUNY....... Utica, NY [*FM radio station call letters*]
WUOC....... Warm-Up Oxidation Catalyst [*Automotive engineering*]
WU/OEL... Washington University Optoelectronics Laboratory [*St. Louis, MO*]
WUOG ...... Athens, GA [*FM radio station call letters*]
WUOK....... West Yarmouth, MA [*AM radio station call letters*]
WUOL....... Louisville, KY [*FM radio station call letters*]
WUOM ..... Ann Arbor, MI [*FM radio station call letters*]
WUOSY .... World Union of Organizations for the Safeguard of Youth [*Later, UMOSEA*]
WUOT....... Knoxville, TN [*FM radio station call letters*]
WUOX....... Radcliff, KY [*FM radio station call letters*]
WUOY....... Wilmington, NC [*FM radio station call letters*]
WUOZ....... Belvedere, SC [*FM radio station call letters*]
WUP......... Work Unit Plan [*Navy*] (NG)
WUPA .... Wupatki National Monument
WUPE .... Pittsfield, MA [*FM radio station call letters*]
WUPI .... Presque Isle, ME [*FM radio station call letters*]
WUPJ........ World Union for Progressive Judaism (EA)
WUPL-INT ... World Union for the Protection of Life [*See also WSL-INT*] (EAIO)
WUPM...... Ironwood, MI [*FM radio station call letters*]
WUPO....... World Union of Pythagorean Organizations [*Ivybridge, Devonshire, England*] (EAIO)
WUPPE..... Wisconsin Ultraviolet Photo-Polarimeter Experiment
WUPQ....... Newberry, MI [*FM radio station call letters*]
WUPR .... Utuado-Rosa, PR [*AM radio station call letters*]
WUPS........ Houghton Lake, MI [*FM radio station call letters*]
WUPS........ World Union of Process Servers
WUPW...... Toledo, OH [*Television station call letters*]
WUPY ...... Ontonagon, MI [*FM radio station call letters*]
WUR......... World University Roundtable
WUR......... Wurltech Industries [*NYSE symbol*] (SPSG)
WURB .... Western Utilization Research Branch (MCD)
WURB .... Windsor, NC [*FM radio station call letters*]

WURC....... Holly Springs, MS [*FM radio station call letters*]
WURD....... Philadelphia, PA [*AM radio station call letters*]
WURL....... Moody, AL [*AM radio station call letters*]
Wurmser .... [*Bernhardus*] Wurmserus [*Flourished, 16th century*] [*Authority cited in pre-1607 legal work*] (DSA)
WUS .... Washington University. Studies [*A publication*]
WUS .... Wirtschaft und Statistik [*A publication*]
WUS .... Woerterbuch der Ugaritischen Sprache [*A publication*] (BJA)
WUS .... Word Underscore Character [*Data processing*]
WUS .... World University Service [*See also EUM*] [*Geneva, Switzerland*] (EAIO)
WUSA ...... Tampa, FL [*FM radio station call letters*]
WUSA ...... Washington, DC [*Television station call letters*]
WUSA ...... Waterfowl USA (EA)
WUSB ...... Stony Brook, NY [*FM radio station call letters*]
WUSC .... Columbia, SC [*FM radio station call letters*]
WUSC .... Weather of US Cities [*A publication*]
WUSC .... World University Service of Canada [*See also EUMC*]
WUSCI...... Western Union Space Communications, Inc. (MCD)
WUSF....... Tampa, FL [*FM radio station call letters*]
WUSF-TV .. Tampa, FL [*Television station call letters*]
WUSG ...... World Union Saint Gabriel [*Esher, Surrey, England*] (EAIO)
WUSI......... Olney, IL [*Television station call letters*]
WUSJ....... Elizabethton, TN [*FM radio station call letters*]
WUSL........ Philadelphia, PA [*FM radio station call letters*]
WUSL........ Washburn University School of Law (DLA)
WUSL........ Women's United Service League [*British*]
WUSM...... Hattiesburg, MS [*FM radio station call letters*]
WUSN ...... Chicago, IL [*FM radio station call letters*]
WUSO ...... Springfield, OH [*FM radio station call letters*]
WUSP....... World Union of Stockholm Pioneers (EAIO)
WUSQ....... Winchester, VA [*AM radio station call letters*]
WUSQ-FM ... Winchester, VA [*FM radio station call letters*]
WUSR ...... Scranton, PA [*FM radio station call letters*]
WU/SRL... Washington University Semiconductor Research Laboratory [*St. Louis, MO*]
WUSS....... Atlantic City, NJ [*AM radio station call letters*]
WUST ...... Washington, DC [*AM radio station call letters*]
WUS(UK) ... World University Service (United Kingdom) (DI)
WUS-US .... World University Service/USA (EA)
WUSW ..... Oshkosh, WI [*FM radio station call letters*]
WUSY ...... Cleveland, TN [*FM radio station call letters*]
WUSY ...... World Union for the Safeguard of Youth
WUT .... Warm Up Time
WUT .... Washburn University of Topeka [*Kansas*]
WUT .... Western Union Telegraph Co. [*Upper Saddle River, NJ*] [*NYSE symbol*] (SPSG)
WUTA ...... Washington University Technology Associates
WUTC .... Chattanooga, TN [*FM radio station call letters*]
WUTC .... Western Union Telegraph Co.
WUTELCO ... Western Union Telegraph Co.
WUTHH ... World Union of Tnuat Haherut Hatzorar [*Tel Aviv, Israel*] (EAIO)
WUTK .... Knoxville, TN [*AM radio station call letters*]
WUTK-FM ... Knoxville, TN [*FM radio station call letters*]
WUTM...... Martin, TN [*FM radio station call letters*]
WUTQ....... Utica, NY [*AM radio station call letters*]
WUTR....... Utica, NY [*Television station call letters*]
WUTS ...... Sewanee, TN [*FM radio station call letters*]
WUTS ...... Work Unit Time Standard [*Air Force*] (AFM)
WUTS .... Work Unit Tracking Subsystem (MCD)
WUTV .... Buffalo, NY [*Television station call letters*]
WUTWC ... Warm-Up Three-Way Catalyst [*Automotive engineering*]
WUTZ....... Summertown, TN [*FM radio station call letters*]
WUU .... Wau [*Sudan*] [*Airport symbol*] (OAG)
WUUA....... World Union for a Universal Alphabet (EA)
WUUC....... West Ulster Unionist Council [*Northern Ireland*]
WUUF .... Statesboro, GA [*FM radio station call letters*]
WUUN ...... Women United for United Nations (EA)
WUUU ...... Rome, NY [*FM radio station call letters*]
WUV......... Weighted Unit Value (MCD)
WUV......... Wuvulu Island [*Papua New Guinea*] [*Airport symbol*] (OAG)
WUVA....... Charlottesville, VA [*FM radio station call letters*]
WUVCI...... Western Union VideoConferencing, Inc. [*Defunct*] (TSSD)
WUVE....... Saginaw, MI [*FM radio station call letters*]
WUVT....... Blacksburg, VA [*FM radio station call letters*]
WUVU....... St. Augustine, FL [*FM radio station call letters*]
WUVX...... Knox, IN [*FM radio station call letters*]
WuW......... Welt und Wort [*A publication*]
WUW........ Wu-wei [*Republic of China*] [*Seismograph station code, US Geological Survey*] (SEIS)
WU-WA .... University of Wisconsin, Woodman Astronomical Library, Madison, WI [*Library symbol*] [*Library of Congress*] (LCLS)
WuWahr .... Wort und Wahrheit [*A publication*]
WuWelt .... Wissenschaft und Weltbild [*A publication*]
WUWF ...... Pensacola, FL [*FM radio station call letters*]
WUWM..... Milwaukee, WI [*FM radio station call letters*]
WUX......... Western Union Exchange [*Teleprinter*]
WUXA .... Portsmouth, OH [*Television station call letters*]
Wuyi Sci J ... Wuyi Science Journal [*A publication*]

WUZR....... Bicknell, IN [*FM radio station call letters*]
WV............ Avair Ltd. [*Ireland*] [*ICAO designator*]   (FAAC)
WV............ Diwag [*Germany*] [*Research code symbol*]
WV............ New Valley Corp. [*NYSE symbol*] [*Formerly, Western Union*]   (SPSG)
WV............ Wall Vent [*Technical drawings*]
WV............ Water Valve   (ROG)
WV............ Wave   (FAAC)
W/V.......... Weight/Volume [*Concentration*] [*Chemistry*]
WV............ West Virginia [*Postal code*]
Wv............. West Virginia Library Commission, Charleston, WV [*Library symbol*] [*Library of Congress*]   (LCLS)
WV............ West Virginia Reports [*A publication*]   (DLA)
WV............ Westminster Version of the Bible [*A publication*]   (BJA)
WV............ Whispered Voice
W/V.......... Wind Vector [*or Velocity*] [*Navigation*]
WV............ Wireless Van [*British*]
WV............ Working Voltage   (MSA)
WV............ World Vision [*An association*]   (EA)
WV............ World Vision [*A publication*]
WVA.......... Alderson-Broaddus College, Philippi, WV [*OCLC symbol*]   (OCLC)
WVA.......... War Veterans Administration [*Canada*]
WVA.......... Watervliet Arsenal [*New York*] [*Army*]
W VA........ West Virginia   (AAG)
W Va.......... West Virginia Reports [*A publication*]
W Va.......... West Virginia Supreme Court Reports [*A publication*]   (DLA)
WVA.......... West Vlaanderen Werkt [*A publication*]
WVA.......... World Veterinary Association [*See also AMV*] [*Madrid, Spain*]   (EAIO)
W Va Acad Sci Proc ... West Virginia Academy of Sciences. Proceedings [*A publication*]
W Va Acts ... Acts of the Legislature of West Virginia [*A publication*]   (DLA)
W Va Acts ... Acts of the Legislature of West Virginia [*A publication*]
W Va Ag Dept ... West Virginia. Department of Agriculture. Publications [*A publication*]
W Va Ag Exp ... West Virginia. Agricultural Experiment Station. Publications [*A publication*]
W Va Agric Exp Stn Bull ... West Virginia. Agricultural Experiment Station. Bulletin [*A publication*]
W Va Agric Exp Stn Cir ... West Virginia. Agricultural Experiment Station. Circular [*A publication*]
W Va Agric Exp Stn Circ ... West Virginia. Agricultural Experiment Station. Circular [*A publication*]
W Va Agric Exp Stn Curr Rep ... West Virginia. Agricultural Experiment Station. Current Report [*A publication*]
W Va Agric Exp Stn Misc Publ ... West Virginia. Agricultural Experiment Station. Miscellaneous Publication [*A publication*]
W Va Agric For ... West Virginia Agriculture and Forestry [*A publication*]
W Va Agric For Exp Stn Bull ... West Virginia. Agricultural and Forestry Experiment Station. Bulletin [*A publication*]
WVAB .... Virginia Beach, VA [*AM radio station call letters*]
WVAB .... War Veterans Allowance Board [*Canada*]
WVAC .... Adrian, MI [*FM radio station call letters*]
WvAC .... Concord College, Athens, WV [*Library symbol*] [*Library of Congress*]   (LCLS)
WVAC .... Norwalk, OH [*AM radio station call letters*]
WVAC .... Working Voltage, Alternating Current   (DEN)
W Va Coal Min Inst Proc ... West Virginia Coal Mining Institute. Proceedings [*A publication*]
W Va Code ... West Virginia Code [*A publication*]   (DLA)
W Va Code ... West Virginia Code [*A publication*]
W Va Const ... West Virginia Constitution [*A publication*]   (DLA)
W Va Crim Just Rev ... West Virginia Criminal Justice Review [*A publication*]   (DLA)
W Va Dent J ... West Virginia Dental Journal [*A publication*]
W Va Dep Mines Annu Rep ... West Virginia. Department of Mines. Annual Report [*A publication*]
WVAF........ Charleston, WV [*FM radio station call letters*]
W Va For Notes ... West Virginia Forestry Notes [*A publication*]
W Va Geol Econ Surv Basic Data Rep ... West Virginia. Geological and Economic Survey. Basic Data Report [*A publication*]
W Va Geol Econ Surv Bull ... West Virginia. Geological and Economic Survey. Bulletin [*A publication*]
W Va Geol Econ Surv Circ Ser ... West Virginia. Geological and Economic Survey. Circular Series [*A publication*]
W Va Geol Econ Surv Cir Ser ... West Virginia. Geological and Economic Survey. Circular Series [*A publication*]
W Va Geol Econ Surv Coal Geol Bull ... West Virginia. Geological and Economic Survey. Coal Geology Bulletin [*A publication*]
W Va Geol Econ Surv Environ Geol Bull ... West Virginia. Geological and Economic Survey. Environmental Geology Bulletin [*A publication*]
W Va Geol Econ Surv Miner Resour Ser ... West Virginia. Geological and Economic Survey. Mineral Resources Series [*A publication*]
W Va Geol Econ Surv Newsl ... West Virginia. Geological and Economic Survey. Newsletter [*A publication*]
W Va Geol Econ Surv Rep Archeol Invest ... West Virginia. Geological and Economic Survey. Report of Archeological Investigations [*A publication*]

W Va Geol Econ Surv Rep Invest ... West Virginia. Geological and Economic Survey. Report of Investigations [*A publication*]
W Va Geol Econ Surv River Basin Bull ... West Virginia. Geological and Economic Survey. River Basin Bulletin [*A publication*]
W Va Geol Surv Rep ... West Virginia. Geological Survey. Reports [*A publication*]
W Va Geol Surv Rep Invest ... West Virginia. Geological Survey. Report of Investigations [*A publication*]
W Va G S... West Virginia. Geological Survey [*A publication*]
WVAH....... Charleston, WV [*Television station call letters*]
WVaH....... West Virginia History [*A publication*]
W Va His ... West Virginia History [*A publication*]
W Va Hist ... West Virginia History. A Quarterly Magazine [*A publication*]
WVAL .... Sauk Rapids, MN [*AM radio station call letters*]
W Va Law Q ... West Virginia Law Quarterly and the Bar [*A publication*]
W Va Law R ... West Virginia Law Review [*A publication*]
W Va Law Reports ... West Virginia Reports [*A publication*]   (DLA)
W Va Lib ... West Virginia Libraries [*A publication*]
W Va Libr ... West Virginia Libraries [*A publication*]
W Va LQ.... West Virginia Law Quarterly [*A publication*]   (DLA)
W Va LR ... West Virginia Law Review [*A publication*]
W Va L Rev ... West Virginia Law Review [*A publication*]
WVALSA .. Whitewater Valley Area Library Services Authority [*Library network*]
WVAM ...... Altoona, PA [*AM radio station call letters*]
W Va Med J ... West Virginia Medical Journal [*A publication*]
WVAN .... Savannah, GA [*Television station call letters*]
W Va PSCR ... West Virginia Public Service Commission Report [*A publication*]   (DLA)
W Va PUR ... West Virginia Public Utility Commission Reports [*A publication*]   (DLA)
WVAQ ...... Morgantown, WV [*FM radio station call letters*]
WVAR ...... Richwood, WV [*AM radio station call letters*]
Wv-Ar .... West Virginia Department of Archives and History, Charleston, WV [*Library symbol*] [*Library of Congress*]   (LCLS)
WVARAY ... West Virginia University. Agricultural Experiment Station. Current Report [*A publication*]
W Va Rep... West Virginia Reports [*A publication*]   (DLA)
W Var Sports ... Women's Varsity Sports [*A publication*]
WVAS....... Montgomery, AL [*FM radio station call letters*]
WVAS........ Wake Vortex Avoidance System [*FAA*]
WVAST..... Washer Visual Acuity Screening Technique [*Visual ability test*]
W Va Univ Agric Exp Stn Curr Rep ... West Virginia University. Agricultural Experiment Station. Current Report [*A publication*]
W Va Univ Agric For Exp Stn Curr Rep ... West Virginia University. Agricultural and Forestry Experiment Station. Current Report [*A publication*]
W Va Univ Agri Exp Stn Bull ... West Virginia University. Agricultural Experiment Station. Bulletin [*A publication*]
W Va Univ Bull Proc Annu Appalachian Gas Meas Short Course ... West Virginia University. Bulletin. Proceedings. Annual Appalachian Gas Measurement Short Course [*A publication*]
W Va Univ Coal Res Bur Sch Mines Tech Rep ... West Virginia University. Coal Research Bureau. School of Mines. Technical Report [*Morgantown, West Virginia*] [*A publication*]
W Va Univ Coal Res Bur Tech Rep ... West Virginia University. Coal Research Bureau. Technical Report [*A publication*]
W Va Univ Eng Exp Sta Tech Bull ... West Virginia University. Engineering Experiment Station. Technical Bulletin [*A publication*]
W Va Univ Eng Exp Stn Bull ... West Virginia University. Engineering Experiment Station. Bulletin [*A publication*]
W Va Univ Eng Exp Stn Res Bull ... West Virginia University. Engineering Experiment Station. Research Bulletin [*A publication*]
W Va Univ Eng Exp Stn Tech Bull ... West Virginia University. Engineering Experiment Station. Technical Bulletin [*A publication*]
W Va Univ Rp Bd Reg ... West Virginia University. Report of the Board of Regents [*A publication*]
W Va U Phil ... West Virginia University. Philological Papers [*A publication*]
WVAY .... Wilmington, VT [*FM radio station call letters*]
WVAZ .... Oak Park, IL [*FM radio station call letters*]
WvB .... Beckley-Raleigh County Library, Beckley, WV [*Library symbol*] [*Library of Congress*]   (LCLS)
WVB .... Bethany College, Bethany, WV [*OCLC symbol*]   (OCLC)
WVB .... Walvis Bay [*Namibia*] [*Airport symbol*]   (OAG)
Wv-B.......... West Virginia Library Commission, Book Express Unit, Charleston, WV [*Library symbol*] [*Library of Congress*]   (LCLS)
WVBA .... Wholesale Variety Bakers Association   (EA)
WvBC .... Beckley College, Beckley, WV [*Library symbol*] [*Library of Congress*]   (LCLS)
WVBC ...... Bethany, WV [*FM radio station call letters*]
WvBeC....... Bethany College, Bethany, WV [*Library symbol*] [*Library of Congress*]   (LCLS)
WVBF........ Framingham, MA [*FM radio station call letters*]
WVBI........ Block Island, RI [*FM radio station call letters*]
WvBl .... Bluefield Public Library, Bluefield, WV [*Library symbol*] [*Library of Congress*]   (LCLS)
WvBlS........ Bluefield State College, Bluefield, WV [*Library symbol*] [*Library of Congress*]   (LCLS)
WVBR .... Ithaca, NY [*FM radio station call letters*]

WvBrA....... Appalachian Bible Institute, Bradley, WV [*Library symbol*] [*Library of Congress*] (LCLS)

WvBri......... Benedum Civic Center Public Library, Bridgeport, WV [*Library symbol*] [*Library of Congress*] (LCLS)

WVBS....... Burgaw, NC [*AM radio station call letters*]

WVBS-FM ... Burgaw, NC [*FM radio station call letters*]

WVBU....... Lewisburg, PA [*FM radio station call letters*]

WvBu....... Stonewall Jackson Regional Library, Buckhannon, WV [*Library symbol*] [*Library of Congress*] (LCLS)

WvBuW ..... West Virginia Wesleyan College, Buckhannon, WV [*Library symbol*] [*Library of Congress*] (LCLS)

WvBV .... United States Veterans Administration Hospital, Beckley, WV [*Library symbol*] [*Library of Congress*] (LCLS)

WVBX .... Georgetown, SC [*AM radio station call letters*]

WvC .... Kanawha County Public Library, Charleston, WV [*Library symbol*] [*Library of Congress*] (LCLS)

WVC .... West Virginia Code [*1899*] [*A publication*] (DLA)

WVC .... Western Veterinary Conference (EA)

WVCA .... Selma, AL [*FM radio station call letters*]

WvCA .... West Virginia Department of Agriculture, Charleston, WV [*Library symbol*] [*Library of Congress*] (LCLS)

WvCAE..... Appalachian Educational Laboratory, Inc., Charleston, WV [*Library symbol*] [*Library of Congress*] (LCLS)

WvCAP..... West Virginia Air Pollution Control Commission, Charleston, WV [*Library symbol*] [*Library of Congress*] (LCLS)

WVCB .... Shallotte, NC [*AM radio station call letters*]

WvCBHi .... West Virginia Baptist Historical Society Deposit, Department of Archives and History, Charleston, WV [*Library symbol*] [*Library of Congress*] (LCLS)

WVCC .... Linesville, PA [*FM radio station call letters*]

WvCCD ..... West Virginia Department of Civil and Defense Mobilization, Charleston, WV [*Library symbol*] [*Library of Congress*] (LCLS)

WVCF....... Ocoee, FL [*AM radio station call letters*]

WVCF....... Welsh Venture Capital Funds

WvCFM..... West Virginia State Fire Marshal's Department, Charleston, WV [*Library symbol*] [*Library of Congress*] (LCLS)

WVCG .... Coral Gables, FL [*AM radio station call letters*]

WvCGH..... Charleston General Hospital, Charleston, WV [*Library symbol*] [*Library of Congress*] (LCLS)

WVCH....... Chester, PA [*AM radio station call letters*]

WvCH........ West Virginia Department of Health, Charleston, WV [*Library symbol*] [*Library of Congress*] (LCLS)

WvCheC .... Consolidated Gas Supply Corp., Chelyan, WV [*Library symbol*] [*Library of Congress*] (LCLS)

WvCHi....... West Virginia Department of Highways, Charleston, WV [*Library symbol*] [*Library of Congress*] (LCLS)

WvCl.......... Clarksburg Public Library, Clarksburg, WV [*Library symbol*] [*Library of Congress*] (LCLS)

WvClC .... Consolidated Gas Supply Corp., Clarksburg, WV [*Library symbol*] [*Library of Congress*] (LCLS)

WvCM .... Morris Harvey College, Charleston, WV [*Library symbol*] [*Library of Congress*] (LCLS)

WVCM ...... Valdosta, GA [*FM radio station call letters*]

WvCMH.... West Virginia Department of Mental Health, Charleston, WV [*Library symbol*] [*Library of Congress*] (LCLS)

WvCMi...... West Virginia Department of Mines, Charleston, WV [*Library symbol*] [*Library of Congress*] (LCLS)

WvCNR ..... West Virginia Department of Natural Resources, Charleston, WV [*Library symbol*] [*Library of Congress*] (LCLS)

WVCO....... Loris, SC [*FM radio station call letters*]

WVCP........ Gallatin, TN [*FM radio station call letters*]

WvCPS ...... West Virginia Department of Public Safety, Charleston, WV [*Library symbol*] [*Library of Congress*] (LCLS)

WVCQ .... Brockway, PA [*AM radio station call letters*]

WVCR .... Loudonville, NY [*FM radio station call letters*]

WVCS........ California, PA [*FM radio station call letters*]

WVCT .... Keavy, KY [*FM radio station call letters*]

WvCTS ...... West Virginia State Technical Services, Charleston, WV [*Library symbol*] [*Library of Congress*] (LCLS)

WVCV .... Boalsburg, PA [*FM radio station call letters*]

WvCVR...... West Virginia Division of Vocational Rehabilitation, Charleston, WV [*Library symbol*] [*Library of Congress*] (LCLS)

WVCW ...... Barrackville, WV [*FM radio station call letters*]

WVCX .... Tomah, WI [*FM radio station call letters*]

WVCY .... Milwaukee, WI [*FM radio station call letters*]

WVCY-TV ... Milwaukee, WI [*Television station call letters*]

WVD.......... Dane County Hospital, Verona, WI [*Library symbol*] [*Library of Congress*] (LCLS)

WVD........ Davis and Elkins College, Elkins, WV [*OCLC symbol*] (OCLC)

WVD......... Waived (AABC)

WVDC....... Working Voltage, Direct Current

WVDF .... Wolverhampton Volunteer Defence Force [*British military*] (DMA)

WVE .... Water Vapor Electrolysis [*Cell*]

WVE .... Wind Velocity East (MCD)

WVEA .... Williamstown, KY [*FM radio station call letters*]

WVEC .... Hampton, VA [*Television station call letters*]

WvED .... Davis and Elkins College, Elkins, WV [*Library symbol*] [*Library of Congress*] (LCLS)

WVEE........ Atlanta, GA [*FM radio station call letters*]

WVEE........ Wheeled Vehicle Experimental Establishment [*British*]

WVEF .... Camden, SC [*AM radio station call letters*]

WVEH...... East Hampton, NY [*FM radio station call letters*]

WVEH...... Wheel Vehicle (AABC)

WVEI........ Worcester, MA [*AM radio station call letters*]

WVEL....... Pekin, IL [*AM radio station call letters*]

WVEM ...... Springfield, IL [*FM radio station call letters*]

WVEM ...... Water Vapor Electrolysis Module [*NASA*]

WVEO .... Aguadilla, PR [*Television station call letters*]

WVEP....... Martinsburg, WV [*FM radio station call letters*]

WVER .... Rutland, VT [*Television station call letters*]

WVES .... Accomac, VA [*AM radio station call letters*]

WVEU ...... Atlanta, GA [*Television station call letters*]

WVEZ ...... Louisville, KY [*FM radio station call letters*]

WVF .... Fairmont State College, Fairmont, WV [*OCLC symbol*] (OCLC)

WvF .... Marion County Public Library, Fairmont, WV [*Library symbol*] [*Library of Congress*] (LCLS)

WVF .... United States Council, World Veterans Federation (EA)

WVF .... Wave Vector Filter

WVF .... West Virginia Folklore [*A publication*]

WVF .... World Veterans Federation [*See also FMAC*] [*Paris, France*] (EAIO)

WVF .... World Veterans Fund (EA)

WvFa .... Fayette County Public Library, Fayetteville, WV [*Library symbol*] [*Library of Congress*] (LCLS)

WVFB........ Celina, TN [*FM radio station call letters*]

WVFC........ McConnellsburg, PA [*AM radio station call letters*]

WVFE........ Coral Cove, FL [*FM radio station call letters*]

WVFG .... Uniontown, AL [*FM radio station call letters*]

WVFJ .... Manchester, GA [*FM radio station call letters*]

WVFM ...... Campton, NH [*FM radio station call letters*]

WvFMHi... Marion County Historical Society, Fairmont, WV [*Library symbol*] [*Library of Congress*] (LCLS)

WvFS .... Fairmont State College, Fairmont, WV [*Library symbol*] [*Library of Congress*] (LCLS)

WVFS........ Tallahassee, FL [*FM radio station call letters*]

WVFT........ Roanoke, VA [*Television station call letters*]

WVG.......... West Virginia State College/College of Graduate Studies, Institute, WV [*OCLC symbol*] (OCLC)

WVGA ...... Valdosta, GA [*Television station call letters*]

WVGB ...... Beaufort, SC [*AM radio station call letters*]

WvGbN..... National Radio Astronomy Observatory, Green Bank, WV [*Library symbol*] [*Library of Congress*] (LCLS)

WvGlS .... Glenville State College, Glenville, WV [*Library symbol*] [*Library of Congress*] (LCLS)

WVGN....... Charlotte Amalie, VI [*FM radio station call letters*]

WVGO....... Richmond, VA [*FM radio station call letters*]

WVGR ...... Grand Rapids, MI [*FM radio station call letters*]

WVGS .... Statesboro, GA [*FM radio station call letters*]

WVH .... Marshall University, Huntington, WV [*OCLC symbol*] (OCLC)

WVH .... West Virginia History [*A publication*]

WVHA...... Wirtschaftsverwaltungshauptamt (BJA)

WvHB........ Pearl S. Buck Birthplace Museum, Hillsboro, WV [*Library symbol*] [*Library of Congress*] (LCLS)

WVHF ...... Clarksburg, WV [*FM radio station call letters*]

WvHfP....... United States Park Service, Harpers Ferry National Historical Park, Harpers Ferry, WV [*Library symbol*] [*Library of Congress*] (LCLS)

WVHI........ Evansville, IN [*AM radio station call letters*]

WVHM...... Benton, KY [*FM radio station call letters*]

WVHP....... Highland Park, NJ [*FM radio station call letters*]

WVHP....... West Virginia Association for Health, Physical Education, Recreation, and Dance. Journal [*A publication*]

WVHR...... Huntingdon, TN [*FM radio station call letters*]

WvHu .... Cabell-Huntington Public Library [*Western Counties Regional Library*], Huntington, WV [*Library symbol*] [*Library of Congress*] (LCLS)

WvHuB...... Basic Systems, Inc., Huntington, WV [*Library symbol*] [*Library of Congress*] (LCLS)

WvHuE...... United States Army, Corps of Engineers, Huntington, WV [*Library symbol*] [*Library of Congress*] (LCLS)

WvHuG...... Huntington Galleries, Huntington, WV [*Library symbol*] [*Library of Congress*] (LCLS)

WvHuH...... Holland-Suco Color Co., Huntington, WV [*Library symbol*] [*Library of Congress*] (LCLS)

WvHuM..... Marshall University, Huntington, WV [*Library symbol*] [*Library of Congress*] (LCLS)

WvHuV...... United States Veterans Administration Hospital, Huntington, WV [*Library symbol*] [*Library of Congress*] (LCLS)

WVi.......... Viroqua Public Library, Viroqua, WI [*Library symbol*] [*Library of Congress*] (LCLS)

WVI .... Watsonville, CA [*Location identifier*] [*FAA*] (FAAL)

WVI .... Work Values Inventory [*Psychometrics*]

WVI .... World Vision International

WVIA .... Scranton, PA [*Television station call letters*]

WVIA-FM ... Scranton, PA [*FM radio station call letters*]

WVIC......... East Lansing, MI [*AM radio station call letters*]

WvIC.......... West Virginia State College, Institute, WV [*Library symbol*] [*Library of Congress*] (LCLS)
WVIC-FM ... East Lansing, MI [*FM radio station call letters*]
WvICG....... West Virginia College of Graduate Studies, Institute, WV [*Library symbol*] [*Library of Congress*] (LCLS)
WVID........ Anasco, PR [*FM radio station call letters*]
WVII.......... Bangor, ME [*Television station call letters*]
WVIJ.......... Port Charlotte, FL [*FM radio station call letters*]
WVIK .... Rock Island, IL [*FM radio station call letters*]
WVIM .... Coldwater, MS [*FM radio station call letters*]
WVIN .... Bath, NY [*FM radio station call letters*]
WVIO......... Blowing Rock, NC [*AM radio station call letters*]
WVIP......... Mount Kisco, NY [*AM radio station call letters*]
WVIP-FM ... Mount Kisco, NY [*FM radio station call letters*]
WVIQ .... Christiansted, VI [*FM radio station call letters*]
WVIR .... Charlottesville, VA [*Television station call letters*]
WVIS......... Christiansted, VI [*FM radio station call letters*]
WVIT......... New Britain, CT [*Television station call letters*]
WVIT .... West Virginia Institute of Technology
WVIZ......... Cleveland, OH [*Television station call letters*]
WVJC........ Mount Carmel, IL [*FM radio station call letters*]
WVJP .... Caguas, PR [*AM radio station call letters*]
WVJP-FM ... Caguas, PR [*FM radio station call letters*]
WVJS .... Owensboro, KY [*AM radio station call letters*]
WVK .... Kanawha County Public Library, Charleston, WV [*OCLC symbol*] (OCLC)
WvK .... Keyser-Mineral County Public and Potomac Valley Regional Library, Keyser, WV [*Library symbol*] [*Library of Congress*] (LCLS)
WVK .... Manakara [*Madagascar*] [*Airport symbol*] (OAG)
WVKC .... Galesburg, IL [*FM radio station call letters*]
WvKeFW ... Bureau of Sport Fisheries and Wildlife, Eastern Fish Disease Laboratory, Kearneysville, WV [*Library symbol*] [*Library of Congress*] (LCLS)
WVKG .... Pentwater, MI [*FM radio station call letters*]
WVKM ...... Matewan, WV [*FM radio station call letters*]
WVKO .... Columbus, OH [*AM radio station call letters*]
WvKP .... Potomac State College, Keyser, WV [*Library symbol*] [*Library of Congress*] (LCLS)
WVKR .... Poughkeepsie, NY [*FM radio station call letters*]
WVKS........ Toledo, OH [*FM radio station call letters*]
WVKV .... Hurricane, WV [*AM radio station call letters*]
WVKX .... Irwinton, GA [*FM radio station call letters*]
WVKY .... Louisa, KY [*AM radio station call letters*]
WVKZ .... Clifton Park, NY [*FM radio station call letters*]
WVKZ .... Schenectady, NY [*AM radio station call letters*]
WVL .... Warfare Vision Laboratory [*Army*]
WVL .... Waterville [*Maine*] [*Airport symbol*] (OAG)
WVL .... Waterville, ME [*Location identifier*] [*FAA*] (FAAL)
WVL .... West Virginia Law Review [*A publication*]
Wv-L.......... West Virginia State Law Library, Charleston, WV [*Library symbol*] [*Library of Congress*] (LCLS)
WVLA .... Baton Rouge, LA [*Television station call letters*]
WVLB........ Wheeled Vehicle Launched Bridge (MCD)
WVLC........ Lake City, SC [*AM radio station call letters*]
WVLD .... Valdosta, GA [*AM radio station call letters*]
WvLe.......... Greenbrier County Public Library, Lewisburg, WV [*Library symbol*] [*Library of Congress*] (LCLS)
WVLE........ Scottsville, KY [*FM radio station call letters*]
WvLeG....... Greenbrier College, Lewisburg, WV [*Library symbol*] [*Library of Congress*] (LCLS)
WVLG .... Wuerttembergische Vierteljahresschrift fuer Landesgeschichte [*A publication*]
WVLK .... Lexington, KY [*AM radio station call letters*]
WVLK-FM ... Lexington, KY [*FM radio station call letters*]
WVLN .... Olney, IL [*AM radio station call letters*]
WVLQ .... West Virginia Law Quarterly [*A publication*] (DLA)
WVLR........ West Virginia Law Review [*A publication*]
Wv-LS........ West Virginia Library Commission, Library Science Department, Charleston, WV [*Library symbol*] [*Library of Congress*] (LCLS)
WVLT........ Vineland, NJ [*FM radio station call letters*]
WvM.......... Morgantown Public Library, Morgantown, WV [*Library symbol*] [*Library of Congress*] (LCLS)
WVM......... West Virginia Medical Center, Morgantown, WV [*OCLC symbol*] [*Inactive*] (OCLC)
WVM......... Wiener Voelkerkundliche Mitteilungen [*A publication*]
WvMa........ Martinsburg-Berkeley County Public Library, Martinsburg, WV [*Library symbol*] [*Library of Congress*] (LCLS)
WVMA...... Women's Veterinary Medical Association [*Later, AWV*]
WvMaV .... United States Veterans Administration Center, Martinsburg, WV [*Library symbol*] [*Library of Congress*] (LCLS)
WV-MBC .. Walking Ventilation to Maximum Breathing Capacity Ratio [*Medicine*] (MAE)
WvMBM ... United States Bureau of Mines, Morgantown, WV [*Library symbol*] [*Library of Congress*] (LCLS)
WVMC ...... Mansfield, OH [*FM radio station call letters*]
WvMc .... McMechen Public Library, McMechen, WV [*Library symbol*] [*Library of Congress*] (LCLS)
WVMG...... Cochran, GA [*AM radio station call letters*]
WVMG-FM ... Cochran, GA [*FM radio station call letters*]

WVMH...... Mars Hill, NC [*FM radio station call letters*]
WVMI ...... Biloxi, MS [*AM radio station call letters*]
WvMIL...... Institute for Labor Studies, Appalachian Center, Morgantown, WV [*Library symbol*] [*Library of Congress*] (LCLS)
WVMM..... Grantham, PA [*FM radio station call letters*]
WvMNIO .. United States Public Health Service, National Institute for Occupational Safety and Health, Appalachian Laboratory for Occupational Safety and Health Library, Morgantown, WV (LCLS)
WvMo........ City-County Public Library, Moundsville, WV [*Library symbol*] [*Library of Congress*] (LCLS)
WvMonI .... West Virginia Institute of Technology, Montgomery, WV [*Library symbol*] [*Library of Congress*] (LCLS)
WVMR...... Frost, WV [*AM radio station call letters*]
WVMT...... Burlington, VT [*AM radio station call letters*]
WVMT...... Wavemat, Inc. [*NASDAQ symbol*] (NQ)
WVMV ..... Wisteria Vein Mosaic Virus
WVMW..... Scranton, PA [*FM radio station call letters*]
WVMX ..... Stowe, VT [*FM radio station call letters*]
WVN......... Water Vapor Nitrogen [*Nuclear energy*] (NRCH)
WVN......... West Virginia Northern Railroad Co. [*AAR code*]
WVN......... Wind Velocity North (MCD)
WVN......... Woven
WVNA....... Tuscumbia, AL [*AM radio station call letters*]
WVNA-FM ... Tuscumbia, AL [*FM radio station call letters*]
WVNC...... Canton, NY [*FM radio station call letters*]
WVNE...... Leicester, MA [*AM radio station call letters*]
WVNET .... West Virginia Network for Educational Telecomputing [*Research center*] (RCD)
WVNI .... Nashville, IN [*FM radio station call letters*]
WvNiK...... West Virginia University, Kanawha Valley Graduate Center, Nitro, WV [*Library symbol*] [*Library of Congress*] (LCLS)
WVNJ .... Oakland, NJ [*AM radio station call letters*]
WVNM...... Cedar Key, FL [*FM radio station call letters*]
WvNmM.... Mobay Chemical Corp., Research Library, New Martinsville, WV [*Library symbol*] [*Library of Congress*] (LCLS)
WVNN....... Athens, AL [*AM radio station call letters*]
WVNO....... Mansfield, OH [*FM radio station call letters*]
WVNP .... Wheeling, WV [*FM radio station call letters*]
WVNR....... Poultney, VT [*AM radio station call letters*]
WVNS .... Charleston, WV [*FM radio station call letters*]
WVNU....... Greenfield, OH [*FM radio station call letters*]
WVNV....... Malone, NY [*FM radio station call letters*]
WVNW...... Burnham, PA [*FM radio station call letters*]
WVNX ...... Charlotte Amalie, VI [*FM radio station call letters*]
WVNY...... Burlington, VT [*Television station call letters*]
WVOA...... DeRuyter, NY [*FM radio station call letters*]
WVOB ...... Dothan, AL [*FM radio station call letters*]
WVOC...... Columbia, SC [*AM radio station call letters*]
WVOD...... Manteo, NC [*FM radio station call letters*]
WVOE ...... Chadbourn, NC [*AM radio station call letters*]
WVOF ...... Fairfield, CT [*FM radio station call letters*]
WVOG...... New Orleans, LA [*AM radio station call letters*]
WVOH ...... Hazlehurst, GA [*AM radio station call letters*]
WVOH-FM ... Hazlehurst, GA [*FM radio station call letters*]
WVOI ...... Toledo, OH [*AM radio station call letters*]
WVOJ ...... Jacksonville, FL [*AM radio station call letters*]
WVOK...... Birmingham, AL [*AM radio station call letters*]
WVOL ...... Berry Hill, TN [*AM radio station call letters*]
WVOM...... Iuka, MS [*AM radio station call letters*]
WVON...... Cicero, IL [*AM radio station call letters*]
WVOP...... Vidalia, GA [*AM radio station call letters*]
WVOR...... Rochester, NY [*FM radio station call letters*]
WVOS ...... Liberty, NY [*AM radio station call letters*]
WVOS-FM ... Liberty, NY [*FM radio station call letters*]
WVOT...... Wilson, NC [*AM radio station call letters*]
WVOV...... Danville, VA [*AM radio station call letters*]
WVOW...... Logan, WV [*AM radio station call letters*]
WVOW-FM ... Logan, WV [*FM radio station call letters*]
WVOX ...... New Rochelle, NY [*AM radio station call letters*]
WVOZ...... San Juan, PR [*AM radio station call letters*]
WVOZ-FM ... Carolina, PR [*FM radio station call letters*]
WvP .... Carnegie Library of Parkersburg and Wood County, Parkersburg, WV [*Library symbol*] [*Library of Congress*] (LCLS)
WVP .... Water Vapor Permeability [*Physical chemistry*]
WVP .... Women's Vote Project (EA)
WVPA .... World Veterinary Poultry Association [*See also AMVA*] [*Huntingdon, Cambridgeshire, England*] (EAIO)
WVPB....... Beckley, WV [*FM radio station call letters*]
WvPC........ Parkersburg Community College, Parkersburg, WV [*Library symbol*] [*Library of Congress*] (LCLS)
WVPE....... Elkhart, IN [*FM radio station call letters*]
WVPG ...... Parkersburg, WV [*FM radio station call letters*]
WVPH....... Piscataway, NJ [*FM radio station call letters*]
WvPhA ...... Alderson-Broaddus College, Philippi, WV [*Library symbol*] [*Library of Congress*] (LCLS)
WVPM ...... Morgantown, WV [*FM radio station call letters*]
WVPN....... Charleston, WV [*FM radio station call letters*]
WvPO .... Ohio Valley College, Parkersburg, WV [*Library symbol*] [*Library of Congress*] (LCLS)

WVPO	Stroudsburg, PA [*AM radio station call letters*]
WVPR	Windsor, VT [*FM radio station call letters*]
WVPS	Burlington, VT [*FM radio station call letters*]
WVPT	Macon, GA [*FM radio station call letters*]
WVPT	Staunton, VA [*Television station call letters*]
WVPV	Beaver Dam, KY [*AM radio station call letters*]
WVPW	Buckhannon, WV [*FM radio station call letters*]
WVR	Wakefield Volunteer Rifles [*British military*] (DMA)
WVR	Wellington Volunteer Rifles [*British military*] (DMA)
Wv-R	West Virginia Library Commission, Reference Department, WV [*Library symbol*] [*Library of Congress*] (LCLS)
WVR	West Virginia Reports [*A publication*] (DLA)
WVR	Within Visual Range [*Missile*] (MCD)
WVR	Women's Volunteer Reserve [*British*] [*World War I*]
WVRAAM ...	Within Visual Range Air-to-Air Missile
WVRC	Spencer, WV [*AM radio station call letters*]
WVRC	Wabash Valley Railroad Co. [*AAR code*]
WVRC	Wolverhampton Volunteer Rifle Corps [*British military*] (DMA)
WVRC-FM ...	Spencer, WV [*FM radio station call letters*]
WVRD	Belzoni, MS [*FM radio station call letters*]
WV Rep	West Virginia Reports [*A publication*] (DLA)
WVRK	Columbus, GA [*FM radio station call letters*]
WVRQ	Viroqua, WI [*AM radio station call letters*]
WVRQ-FM ...	Viroqua, WI [*FM radio station call letters*]
WVRRTC ...	West Virginia Rehabilitation Research and Training Center [*West Virginia University*] [*Research center*] (RCD)
WVRS	Warrenton, NC [*FM radio station call letters*]
WVRU	Radford, VA [*FM radio station call letters*]
WVRY	Waverly, TN [*FM radio station call letters*]
WVS	Water Vapor Sensor
W-V(S)	Women's Reserve, Emergency Duties [*USNR commissioned officer designation*]
WVS	Women's Voluntary Services [*Coordinated work of women for national service*] [*Later, WRVS*] [*British*] [*World War II*]
WVSA	Vernon, AL [*AM radio station call letters*]
WVSA	Weidingsvereniging van Suidelike Afrika [*Grassland Society of Southern Africa-GISSA*] (EAIO)
WvSaC	Salem College, Salem, WV [*Library symbol*] [*Library of Congress*] (LCLS)
WVSC	Somerset, PA [*AM radio station call letters*]
WVSC	West Virginia State College
W-V(S) (CEC) ...	Women's Reserve, Civil Engineering Corps Duties [*USNR commissioned officer designation*]
WVSC-FM ...	Somerset, PA [*FM radio station call letters*]
WvScU	Union Carbide Corp., South Charleston, WV [*Library symbol*] [*Library of Congress*] (LCLS)
WVSD	Itta Bena, MS [*FM radio station call letters*]
W-V(S) (DC) ...	Women's Reserve, Dental Corps Duties [*USNR commissioned officer designation*]
WVSH	Huntington, IN [*FM radio station call letters*]
WvSh	Shepherdstown Public Library, Shepherdstown, WV [*Library symbol*] [*Library of Congress*] (LCLS)
W-V(S) (H) ...	Women's Reserve, Hospital Corps Duties [*USNR commissioned officer designation*]
WvShS	Shepherd College, Shepherdstown, WV [*Library symbol*] [*Library of Congress*] (LCLS)
WVSJ	Washington Township, NJ [*AM radio station call letters*]
WVSL	Valley Station, KY [*FM radio station call letters*]
WVSM	Rainsville, AL [*AM radio station call letters*]
W-V(S) (MC) ...	Women's Reserve, Medical Corps Duties [*USNR commissioned officer designation*]
WVSR	Charleston, WV [*AM radio station call letters*]
WVSR-FM ...	Charleston, WV [*FM radio station call letters*]
WVSS	Menomonie, WI [*FM radio station call letters*]
W-V(S) (SC) ...	Women's Reserve, Supply Corps Duties [*USNR commissioned officer designation*]
WVST	Petersburg, VA [*FM radio station call letters*]
WVSU	Birmingham, AL [*FM radio station call letters*]
WVSV	Stevenson, AL [*FM radio station call letters*]
WVT	Water Vapor Transmission
WVT	Watervliet Arsenal [*New York*] [*Army*]
WVT	West Virginia Institute of Technology, Montgomery, WV [*OCLC symbol*] (OCLC)
WVTA	Windsor, VT [*Television station call letters*]
WVTB	St. Johnsbury, VT [*Television station call letters*]
WVTC	Randolph Center, VT [*FM radio station call letters*]
WVTF	Roanoke, VA [*FM radio station call letters*]
WVTF	Western Visayan Task Force [*World War II*]
WVTH	Goodman, MS [*FM radio station call letters*]
WVTK	Wavetek Corp. [*NASDAQ symbol*] (NQ)
WVTM	Birmingham, AL [*Television station call letters*]
WVTR	Marion, VA [*FM radio station call letters*]
WVTR	Water Vapor Transmission Rate
WVTU	Charlottesville, VA [*FM radio station call letters*]
WVTV	Milwaukee, WI [*Television station call letters*]
WVTY	Pittsburgh, PA [*FM radio station call letters*]
wvu	West Virginia [*MARC country of publication code*] [*Library of Congress*] (LCCP)
WVU	West Virginia University

WVU	West Virginia University Library, Morgantown, WV [*OCLC symbol*] (OCLC)
WvU	West Virginia University, Morgantown, WV [*Library symbol*] [*Library of Congress*] (LCLS)
WVUA	Tuscaloosa, AL [*FM radio station call letters*]
WvU-AE	West Virginia University, Agricultural Engineering Library, Morgantown, WV [*Library symbol*] [*Library of Congress*] (LCLS)
WVUB	Vincennes, IN [*FM radio station call letters*]
WVUBPL..	West Virginia University. Bulletin. Philological Studies [*A publication*]
WVUD	Kettering, OH [*FM radio station call letters*]
WVUE	New Orleans, LA [*Television station call letters*]
WvU-J	West Virginia University, School of Journalism, Morgantown, WV [*Library symbol*] [*Library of Congress*] (LCLS)
WvU-L	West Virginia University, College of Law, Morgantown, WV [*Library symbol*] [*Library of Congress*] (LCLS)
WVUM	Coral Gables, FL [*FM radio station call letters*]
WvU-M	West Virginia University, Medical Center, Morgantown, WV [*Library symbol*] [*Library of Congress*] (LCLS)
WvU-Mu ...	West Virginia University, Music Library, Morgantown, WV [*Library symbol*] [*Library of Congress*] (LCLS)
WV Univ Agric For Exp Stn Misc Publ ...	West Virginia University. Agriculture and Forestry Experiment Station. Miscellaneous Publication [*A publication*]
WvU-P	West Virginia University, Physical Sciences Library, Morgantown, WV [*Library symbol*] [*Library of Congress*] (LCLS)
WVUPP.....	West Virginia University. Philological Papers [*A publication*]
WVUR	Valparaiso, IN [*FM radio station call letters*]
WVUT	Vincennes, IN [*Television station call letters*]
WVUV	Leone, AS [*AM radio station call letters*]
WVUV-FM ...	Leone, AS [*FM radio station call letters*]
WVV	Whole Virus Vaccine [*Immunology*]
WVVA	Bluefield, WV [*Television station call letters*]
WVVE	Stonington, CT [*FM radio station call letters*]
WVVO	Dorchester Terrace-Brentwood, SC [*AM radio station call letters*]
WVVS	Valdosta, GA [*FM radio station call letters*]
WVVV	Blacksburg, VA [*FM radio station call letters*]
WVVW	St. Marys, WV [*AM radio station call letters*]
WVVX	Highland Park, IL [*FM radio station call letters*]
WVVY	Grifton, NC [*FM radio station call letters*]
WvW	Ohio County Public Library, Wheeling, WV [*Library symbol*] [*Library of Congress*] (LCLS)
WVW	Westview Resources [*Vancouver Stock Exchange symbol*]
WvWaB	Borg-Warner Corp., Borg-Warner Chemicals Technical Center, Washington, WV [*Library symbol*] [*Library of Congress*] (LCLS)
WVWC	Buckhannon, WV [*FM radio station call letters*]
WVWC	West Virginia Wesleyan College
WvWC	Wheeling College, Wheeling, WV [*Library symbol*] [*Library of Congress*] (LCLS)
WvWelW ...	West Liberty State College, West Liberty, WV [*Library symbol*] [*Library of Congress*] (LCLS)
WvWEPA ...	United States Environmental Protection Agency, Wheeling Field Office, Wheeling, WV [*Library symbol*] [*Library of Congress*] (LCLS)
WvWH	Wheeling Hospital, Medical Library, Wheeling, WV [*Library symbol*] [*Library of Congress*] (LCLS)
WVWI	Charlotte Amalie, VI [*AM radio station call letters*]
WvWO	Oglebay Institute, Wheeling, WV [*Library symbol*] [*Library of Congress*] (LCLS)
WVWV	Huntington, WV [*FM radio station call letters*]
WVXC	Chillicothe, OH [*FM radio station call letters*]
WVXM	West Union, OH [*FM radio station call letters*]
WVXR	Richmond, IN [*FM radio station call letters*]
WVXU	Cincinnati, OH [*FM radio station call letters*]
WVYC	York, PA [*FM radio station call letters*]
WVZA	Herrin, IL [*FM radio station call letters*]
WVZB	Erie, PA [*FM radio station call letters*]
WVZC	Montauk, NY [*FM radio station call letters*]
WVZD	Dennysville, ME [*FM radio station call letters*]
WVZE	Battle Ground, IN [*FM radio station call letters*]
WVZF	Chillocothe, OH [*FM radio station call letters*]
WVZN	Lynchburg, VA [*AM radio station call letters*]
WW	Australian Women's Weekly [*A publication*] (APTA)
W & W	De Witt and Weeresinghe's Appeal Court Reports [*Ceylon*] [*A publication*] (DLA)
WW	Israel Aircraft Industries Ltd. [*ICAO aircraft manufacturer identifier*] (ICAO)
WW	Journal of Waterway, Port, Coastal, and Ocean Engineering [*A publication*]
W & W	Wahlstrom & Widstrand [*Publisher*] [*Sweden*]
WW	Walking Wounded (ADA)
WW	Wall-to-Wall [*Carpeting*] [*Classified advertising*]
WW	Walter Winchell [*American journalist*] (IIA)
WW	Wardroom Window [*Aerospace*] (KSC)
WW	Warehouse Warrant
WW	Warrant Writer [*Navy*] [*British*]
WW	Waste Watch (EA)

WW............ Water Waste (NASA)
WW............ Water-White
WW............ Waterwall (MSA)
WW............ Waterworks
WW............ Weather Wing (MCD)
WW............ Weather Working
WW............ Weight Watchers [An association]
W/W......... Weight/Weight
WW............ Welfare Worker [British military] (DMA)
WW............ Well Water [Nuclear energy] (NRCH)
WW............ Western Waste Industries [NYSE symbol] (SPSG)
WW............ Westwater Industries Ltd. [Toronto Stock Exchange symbol]
W/W......... Wheel Well (MCD)
W & W....... White and Wilson's [or Willson's] Civil Cases, Texas Court of Appeals [A publication] (DLA)
WW............ White Wyandotte [Poultry]
WW............ Whitewall Tire [Automotive accessory]
WW............ Wholesale Wine [License]
WW............ Who's Who [A publication]
WW............ Widow [Genealogy]
W/W......... Wild Weasel [Aerospace]
WW............ Wilderness Watch (EA)
W & W....... Williams & Wilkins [Publishing company]
WW............ Winchester & Western Railroad Co. [AAR code]
W/W......... Winding to Winding (MSA)
WW............ Wines of Westhorpe [Commercial firm] [British]
WW............ Winged Warriors/National B-Body Owners Association (EA)
WW............ Wire Way [Technical drawings]
WW............ Wire Wheel [Automotive accessory]
WW............ Wire-Wound
WW............ Wire Wrap (NASA)
WW............ Wirkendes Wort [A publication]
W u W....... Wirtschaft und Wettbewerb [German] [A publication]
WW............ Wirtschaftswoche-Datenbank [Economic Week Data Bank] [Society for Public Economics] [Germany] [Information service or system] (IID)
WW............ Wishing Well [An association] (EA)
WW............ Wissenschaft und Weisheit [A publication]
WW............ With Warrants [Stock exchange term] (SPSG)
WW............ With Winch
WW............ Woman's World [A publication]
WW............ Women in the Wind [An association] (EA)
WW............ [Thomas] Woodrow Wilson [US president, 1856-1924]
WW............ Woodwind [Instrument] [Music]
WW............ Working Woman [A publication]
WW............ Working Women, National Association of Officeworkers (EA)
WW............ World War
WW............ Worldwide
WW............ Worldwide Equities Ltd. [Toronto Stock Exchange symbol]
WW............ Wound Width [Forestry]
WW............ Writers and Their Work [British Council]
Ww............ Wroclaw [A publication]
WW............ Wyatt and Webb's Reports [A publication] (DLA)
W & W....... Wyatt and Webb's Victorian Reports [A publication] (APTA)
WW............ Zas Airlines of Egypt [Egypt] [ICAO designator] (FAAC)
1WW......... Weather Wing (1st) [California] [Air Force]
2WW......... Weather Wing (2nd) [New York] [Air Force]
3WW......... Weather Wing (3rd) [Nebraska] [Air Force]
4WW......... Weather Wing (4th) [Colorado] [Air Force]
6WW......... Weather Wing (6th) [Washington, DC] [Air Force]
7WW......... Weather Wing (7th) [Illinois] [Air Force]
WWA......... Wallcovering Wholesalers Association [Later, WDA] (EA)
WWa......... Wauwatosa Public Library, Wauwatosa, WI [Library symbol] [Library of Congress] (LCLS)
WWA......... Welsh Water Authority (DCTA)
WWA......... Western Writers of America (EA)
WWA......... Who's Who in America [A publication]
WWA......... Who's Who in Art [A publication]
WWA......... Who's Who in Australia [A publication]
WWA......... With the Will Annexed
WWA......... Woolens and Worsteds of America [Defunct]
WWA......... World Warning Agency (MCD)
WWA......... World Water [A publication]
WWA......... World Waterpark Association (EA)
WWA......... World Watusi Association (EA)
WWA......... World Wide Airlines, Inc.
WWAA...... Westfalen Warmblood Association of America (EA)
WWAA...... Who's Who Among Asian Americans [A publication]
WWAB...... Lakeland, FL [AM radio station call letters]
W & W & A'B ... Wyatt, Webb, and A'Beckett's Reports [A publication] (APTA)
WW & A'B ... Wyatt, Webb, and A'Beckett's Victorian Reports [A publication] (APTA)
WWABCC ... World Wide Avon Bottle Collectors Club (EA)
WW & A'B (E) ... Wyatt, Webb, and A'Beckett's Reports (Equity) [A publication] (APTA)
W & W & A'B (Eq) ... Wyatt, Webb, and A'Beckett's Reports (Equity) [A publication] (APTA)
WW & A'B (IE & M) ... Wyatt, Webb, and A'Beckett's Reports (Insolvency, Ecclesiastical, and Matrimonial) [A publication] (APTA)

WW & A'B (M) ... Wyatt, Webb, and A'Beckett's Reports (Mining) [A publication] (APTA)
W & W & A'B (Min) ... Wyatt, Webb, and A'Beckett's Reports (Mining) [A publication] (APTA)
WWABNCP ... Worldwide Airborne Command Post [Air Force] (AFM)
WWAC...... Atlantic City, NJ [Television station call letters]
WWAC...... Western World Avon Club (EA)
WWAEA ... Water and Wastes Engineering [A publication]
WWAG...... McKee, KY [FM radio station call letters]
WWal........ Walworth Memorial Library, Walworth, WI [Library symbol] [Library of Congress] (LCLS)
WWalPS.... Walworth Public Schools, Walworth, WI [Library symbol] [Library of Congress] (LCLS)
WWalSD ... North Walworth School District Number Five, Walworth, WI [Library symbol] [Library of Congress] (LCLS)
WWaMP ... Milwaukee Psychiatric Hospital, Wauwatosa, WI [Library symbol] [Library of Congress] (LCLS)
WWAP...... Worldwide Asset Position [Military] (AABC)
WWARA ... Weltwirtschaftliches Archiv [A publication]
WWAS ...... Williamsport, PA [FM radio station call letters]
WWAS ...... World-Wide Academy of Scholars [Defunct] (EA)
WWAS ...... World Wide Air Services [Australia]
WWaSC.... Saint Camillus Hospital, Wauwatosa, WI [Library symbol] [Library of Congress] (LCLS)
WWAT ...... Chillicothe, OH [Television station call letters]
WWat .... Watertown Free Public Library, Watertown, WI [Library symbol] [Library of Congress] (LCLS)
WWATA ... Water and Waste Treatment [A publication]
WWatf ...... Waterford Public Library, Waterford, WI [Library symbol] [Library of Congress] (LCLS)
WWatfH.... Holy Redeemer College, Waterford, WI [Library symbol] [Library of Congress] (LCLS)
WWatN ..... Northwestern College, Watertown, WI [Library symbol] [Library of Congress] (LCLS)
WWau....... Waukesha Public Library, Waukesha, WI [Library symbol] [Library of Congress] (LCLS)
WWauC..... Carroll College, Waukesha, WI [Library symbol] [Library of Congress] (LCLS)
WWauH .... Waukesha Memorial Hospital, Waukesha, WI [Library symbol] [Library of Congress] (LCLS)
WWauHi ... Waukesha County Historical Society, Waukesha, WI [Library symbol] [Library of Congress] (LCLS)
WWauI ...... Waukesha County Institution, Waukesha, WI [Library symbol] [Library of Congress] (LCLS)
WWaupa.... Waupaca Free Public Library, Waupaca, WI [Library symbol] [Library of Congress] (LCLS)
WWauU..... University of Wisconsin Center-Waukesha County, Waukesha, WI [Library symbol] [Library of Congress] (LCLS)
WWAV...... Santa Rosa Beach, FL [FM radio station call letters]
WWAX...... Olyphant, PA [AM radio station call letters]
WWAY ...... Wilmington, NC [Television station call letters]
W Ways ..... Word Ways [A publication]
WWB........ Waterways Freight Bureau, Washington DC [STAC]
WWb......... West Bend Public Library, West Bend, WI [Library symbol] [Library of Congress] (LCLS)
WWB........ Women's World Banking [Financial organization]
WWB........ Writers War Board
WWBA ..... Walt Whitman Birthplace Association (EA)
WWBA ..... Western Wooden Box Association (EA)
WWBA ..... Who's Who among Black Americans [A publication]
WWBB ..... Providence, RI [FM radio station call letters]
WWBB ..... Wire-Wrapped Breadboard
WWBC ..... Cocoa, FL [AM radio station call letters]
WWBC ..... Washington Bancorporation [NASDAQ symbol] (NQ)
WWBD ..... Bamberg-Denmark, SC [AM radio station call letters]
WWBE ..... Mifflinburg, PA [FM radio station call letters]
WWBF ..... Bartow, FL [AM radio station call letters]
WWBF ..... Woodrow Wilson Birthplace Foundation (EA)
WWBH...... New Smyrna Beach, FL [AM radio station call letters]
WWBPU ... World Wide Baraca-Philathea Union (EA)
WWBR ..... Harriman, TN [AM radio station call letters]
WWBT ..... Richmond, VA [Television station call letters]
WWbU....... University of Wisconsin Center-Washington County, West Bend, WI [Library symbol] [Library of Congress] (LCLS)
WWC........ Citizen's Library, Washington, PA [OCLC symbol] (OCLC)
WWC........ Walla Walla College [Washington]
WWC........ Warren Wilson College [Swannan, NC]
WWC........ Wavy Walled Cylinder
WWC........ Who's Who in Consulting [A publication]
WWC........ William Woods College [Fulton, MO]
WWC........ World's Wristwrestling Championship (EA)
WWC........ Woven Wire Cloth
WWCA...... Gary, IN [AM radio station call letters]
WWCA...... Women's Welsh Clubs of America (EA)
WWCB ..... Corry, PA [AM radio station call letters]
WW & CB ... Weekly Weather and Crop Bulletin [A publication]
WWCC ..... Honesdale, PA [AM radio station call letters]
WWCC ..... Western Wisconsin Communications Cooperative [Independence, WI] [Telecommunications] (TSSD)
W & WCC ... White and Wilson's [or Willson's] Civil Cases, Texas Court of Appeals [A publication] (DLA)

WWCCIS .. World-Wide Command and Control Information System (MCD)
WWCD...... Grove City, OH [*FM radio station call letters*]
WWCH...... Clarion, PA [*AM radio station call letters*]
WWCICS .. Wolfe-Winrow CICS/VS Command Level Proficiency Test [*Data processing*]
W & W Civ Cases Court of Appeals ... White and Wilson's [*or Willson's*] Civil Cases, Texas Court of Appeals [*A publication*] (DLA)
WWCK...... Flint, MI [*AM radio station call letters*]
WWCK-FM ... Flint, MI [*FM radio station call letters*]
WWCL...... Lehigh Acres, FL [*AM radio station call letters*]
WWCM..... Ypsilanti, MI [*AM radio station call letters*]
WWCN...... North Fort Myers, FL [*AM radio station call letters*]
WWCO...... Waterbury, CT [*AM radio station call letters*]
W & W Con Cases ... White and Wilson's [*or Willson's*] Civil Cases, Texas Court of Appeals [*A publication*] (DLA)
W & W Con Rep ... White and Wilson's [*or Willson's*] Civil Cases, Texas Court of Appeals [*A publication*] (DLA)
WWCP ...... Johnstown, PA [*Television station call letters*]
WWCP ...... Walking Wounded Collecting Post [*Military*]
WWCS...... Canonsburg, PA [*AM radio station call letters*]
WWCT ...... Peoria, IL [*FM radio station call letters*]
WWCT Regt ... Wellington, West Coast, and Taranaki Regiment [*British military*] (DMA)
WWCTU ... World's Woman's Christian Temperance Union [*Australia*] (EAIO)
WWCU...... Cullowhee, NC [*FM radio station call letters*]
WWD......... Cape May [*New Jersey*] [*Airport symbol*] (OAG)
WWd.......... Kilbourn Public Library, Wisconsin Dells, WI [*Library symbol*] [*Library of Congress*] (LCLS)
WWD........ Weather Working Days [*Construction*]
WWD........ Weird World [*A publication*]
WWD........ Wildwood, NJ [*Location identifier*] [*FAA*] (FAAL)
WW & D .... Willmore, Wollaston, and Davison's English Queen's Bench Reports [*1837*] [*A publication*] (DLA)
WWD........ Windward (KSC)
WWD........ Women's Wear Daily [*A publication*]
WWDB...... Philadelphia, PA [*FM radio station call letters*]
WWDC...... Washington, DC [*AM radio station call letters*]
WWDCFC ... World-Wide Dave Clark Fan Club [*Defunct*] (EAIO)
WWDC-FM ... Washington, DC [*FM radio station call letters*]
WWDE...... Hampton, VA [*FM radio station call letters*]
WWdepSN ... Saint Norbert College, West De Pere, WI [*Library symbol*] [*Library of Congress*] (LCLS)
wwdFHEx ... Weather Working Days, Fridays, and Holidays Excluded [*Shipping*] (DS)
WWDJ ...... Hackensack, NJ [*AM radio station call letters*]
WWDL...... Scranton, PA [*FM radio station call letters*]
WWDM..... Sumter, SC [*FM radio station call letters*]
WWDMS .. Worldwide Data Management System
WWDMS .. Worldwide Standard Data Management System (MCD)
WWDR...... Hardeeville, SC [*FM radio station call letters*]
W Wdr .... Warrant Wardmaster [*British military*] (DMA)
WWDS ...... Muncie, IN [*FM radio station call letters*]
WWDSA ... Worldwide Digital System Architecture
WWDSHEX ... Weather Working Days, Sundays, and Holidays Excluded (DS)
WWE......... Wide World of Entertainment [*TV program*]
WWe.......... Wissenschaft und Weisheit [*A publication*]
WWE......... Worldwide Energy Corp. [*Toronto Stock Exchange symbol*] (SPSG)
W & W (E) ... Wyatt and Webb's Reports (Equity) [*A publication*] (APTA)
WWEA...... Cambridge, MA [*AM radio station call letters*]
WWea........ West Allis Public Library, West Allis, WI [*Library symbol*] [*Library of Congress*] (LCLS)
WWeaJ...... Janlen Enterprises, West Allis, WI [*Library symbol*] [*Library of Congress*] (LCLS)
WWeaM .... West Allis Memorial Hospital, West Allis, WI [*Library symbol*] [*Library of Congress*] (LCLS)
WWEB ...... Wallingford, CT [*FM radio station call letters*]
WWEC ...... Elizabethtown, PA [*FM radio station call letters*]
WWEF....... Working Women Education Fund (EA)
WWEL ...... London, KY [*AM radio station call letters*]
WWEM ..... Rochester, NH [*FM radio station call letters*]
WWEMA .. Water and Wastewater Equipment Manufacturers Association (EA)
WWENA ... Water and Water Engineering [*A publication*]
W & W (Eq) ... Wyatt and Webb's Reports (Equity) [*A publication*] (APTA)
WWER ...... Dryden, NY [*FM radio station call letters*]
WWES...... Hot Springs, VA [*AM radio station call letters*]
WWEV ...... Cumming, GA [*FM radio station call letters*]
WWEZ...... Cincinnati, OH [*FM radio station call letters*]
WWF .... War/Watch Foundation (EA)
WWF .... Washington Workshops Foundation (EA)
WWF .... Welded Wire Fabric [*Technical drawings*]
WWF .... Whole Wheat Flour (OA)
WWF .... Widowed White Female [*Classified advertising*]
WWF .... Wire Wrap Fixture
WWF .... Wonder Woman Foundation (EA)
WWF .... World Wildlife Fund (EA)
WWF .... WorldWide Fund for Nature (EA)

WWFC...... Worldwide Fair Play for Frogs Committee
WWFD...... Key West, FL [*Television station call letters*]
WWFE....... Miami, FL [*AM radio station call letters*]
WWFI........ World Wildlife Fund International [*Later, Worldwide Fund for Nature*] (EAIO)
WWFM ..... Trenton, NJ [*FM radio station call letters*]
WWFN ...... Lake City, SC [*AM radio station call letters*]
WWFO ...... Vinton, VA [*FM radio station call letters*]
WWFP...... Pearson, GA [*FM radio station call letters*]
WWFQ ..... Paw Creek, NC [*AM radio station call letters*]
WWFR ...... Okeechobee, FL [*AM radio station call letters*]
WWFS...... Kosciusko, MS [*FM radio station call letters*]
WWFS....... West Wales Field Society [*British*]
WWFT...... Key West, FL [*AM radio station call letters*]
WWF-US .. World Wildlife Fund - United States (EA)
WWFX...... Belfast, ME [*FM radio station call letters*]
WWG........ HSIA [*Halogenated Solvent Industry Alliance*] Water Work Group [*Defunct*] (EA)
WWG........ Warhead Working Group [*Military*]
WWg......... Weather Wing [*Air Force*] (AFM)
WWG........ Who's Who in Germany [*A publication*]
WWG........ Wiederwerbgesetz (BJA)
WWGC...... Carrollton, GA [*FM radio station call letters*]
WWGL...... Lexington, NC [*FM radio station call letters*]
WWGM..... Nashville, TN [*AM radio station call letters*]
WWGN...... Wildlife Working Group. Newsletter [*A publication*]
WWGP ..... Sanford, NC [*AM radio station call letters*]
WWGP ..... Ward White Group Ltd. [*NASDAQ symbol*] (NQ)
WWGS ...... Tifton, GA [*AM radio station call letters*]
WWGT ..... Portland, ME [*FM radio station call letters*]
WWGZ...... Lapeer, MI [*AM radio station call letters*]
WWGZ-FM ... Lapeer, MI [*FM radio station call letters*]
WWH .... W. W. Harrington's Reports [*31-39 Delaware*] [*A publication*] (DLA)
WW & H.... Willmore, Wollaston, and Hodges' English Queen's Bench Reports [*1838-39*] [*A publication*] (DLA)
W/WH...... With/Warhead [*Nuclear*]
WWH .... Women Working Home [*A publication*]
WWHA ..... Who's Who among Hispanic Americans [*A publication*]
W W Harr ... [*W. W.*] Harrington's Reports [*31-39 Delaware*] [*A publication*] (DLA)
W W Harr Del ... [*W. W.*] Harrington's Reports [*31-39 Delaware*] [*A publication*] (DLA)
WWHB...... Hampton Bays, NY [*FM radio station call letters*]
WWHE...... Woman Who Has Everything
WW & H (Eng) ... Willmore, Wollaston, and Hodges' English Queen's Bench Reports [*1838-39*] [*A publication*] (DLA)
WWHI....... Muncie, IN [*FM radio station call letters*]
WWhiwSD ... Whitewater Unified School District, Joint Number One, Whitewater, WI [*Library symbol*] [*Library of Congress*] (LCLS)
WWhiwU... University of Wisconsin-Whitewater, Whitewater, WI [*Library symbol*] [*Library of Congress*] (LCLS)
WWHK...... Greenville, KY [*FM radio station call letters*]
WWHL...... Cocoa, FL [*AM radio station call letters*]
WWHL...... Waterwheel
WWHN ..... Joliet, IL [*AM radio station call letters*]
WWHR...... Bowling Green, KY [*FM radio station call letters*]
WWHRAWAC ... World Wide Horse Registry for the American White and the American Creme (EA)
WWHS...... Hampden-Sydney, VA [*FM radio station call letters*]
WWHS...... Western World Haiku Society (EA)
WWHT...... Marysville, OH [*FM radio station call letters*]
WWI .... Weight Watchers International [*Commercial firm*] (EA)
WWI .... Whirlwind I
WWI .... Who's Who in Israel [*A publication*]
WWI .... Working Women's Institute (EA)
WWI .... World War I
WWIA ...... Palm Bay, FL [*FM radio station call letters*]
WWI AERO ... World War I Aeroplanes (EA)
WWIB ...... Ladysmith, WI [*FM radio station call letters*]
WW & IB... Western Weighing and Inspection Bureau
WWIC ...... Scottsboro, AL [*AM radio station call letters*]
WWiC........ Winnebago County Hospital, Winnebago, WI [*Library symbol*] [*Library of Congress*] (LCLS)
WWICS..... Woodrow Wilson International Center for Scholars (EA)
W & W (IE & M) ... Wyatt and Webb's Reports (Insolvency, Ecclesiastical, and Matrimonial) [*A publication*] (APTA)
WWIH....... High Point, NC [*FM radio station call letters*]
WWII........ Shiremanstown, PA [*AM radio station call letters*]
WWII........ Whirlwind II (SAA)
WWII........ World War II
WWIIHSLB ... World War II Honorable Service Lapel Button (AFM)
WWIII....... World War III
WWIIVM ... World War II Victory Medal [*Military decoration*]
WWil........ Barrett Memorial Library, Williams Bay, WI [*Library symbol*] [*Library of Congress*] (LCLS)
WWIL........ Wilmington, NC [*AM radio station call letters*]
WWIMS.... Worldwide Integrated Management of Subsistence [*Military*] (NVT)
WWIN....... Baltimore, MD [*AM radio station call letters*]

WWIN....... Glen Burnie, MD [*FM radio station call letters*]
WWIO....... Worldwide Inventory Objective (AABC)
WWiP........ Park View Health Center, Winnebago, WI [*Library symbol*] [*Library of Congress*] (LCLS)
WWIS........ Black River Falls, WI [*AM radio station call letters*]
WWiS........ Winnebago State Hospital, Winnebago, WI [*Library symbol*] [*Library of Congress*] (LCLS)
WWIS........ Worldwide Information Services
WWIS-FM ... Black River Falls, WI [*FM radio station call letters*]
WWIT .... Canton, NC [*AM radio station call letters*]
WWIT .... Who's Who in the Theatre [*A publication*]
WWITC..... Worldwide Improved Technical Control (MCD)
WWIVM ... World War I Victory Medal [*Military decoration*]
WWIZ .... Mercer, PA [*FM radio station call letters*]
WWJ .... Detroit, MI [*AM radio station call letters*]
WWJ .... Who's Who in Japan [*A publication*]
WWJB....... Brooksville, FL [*AM radio station call letters*]
WWJC....... Duluth, MN [*AM radio station call letters*]
WWJCC.... Worldwide Joint Coordinator Center [*NATO*] (NATG)
WWJM ..... New Lexington, OH [*FM radio station call letters*]
WWJO ...... St. Cloud, MN [*FM radio station call letters*]
WWJOA..... Water Well Journal [*A publication*]
WWJQ ...... Holland, MI [*AM radio station call letters*]
WWJR....... Sheboygan, WI [*FM radio station call letters*]
WWJY....... Crown Point, IN [*FM radio station call letters*]
WWJZ....... Mount Holly, NJ [*AM radio station call letters*]
WWK .... Continental Iron and Steel Trade Reports. Iron and Steel Trade Market Reports and Special Information [*A publication*]
WWK .... Wewak [*Papua New Guinea*] [*Airport symbol*] (OAG)
WWKA ..... Orlando, FL [*FM radio station call letters*]
WWKB ..... Buffalo, NY [*AM radio station call letters*]
WWKC...... Caldwell, OH [*FM radio station call letters*]
WWKC...... White Wolf-Kern Canyon [*Geological fault*]
WWKF ..... Fulton, KY [*FM radio station call letters*]
WWKI .... Kokomo, IN [*FM radio station call letters*]
WWKL ...... Harrisburg, PA [*FM radio station call letters*]
WWKO ...... Cocoa, FL [*AM radio station call letters*]
WWKS ...... Beaver Falls, PA [*FM radio station call letters*]
WWKT ...... Kingstree, SC [*FM radio station call letters*]
WWKX ...... Woonsocket, RI [*FM radio station call letters*]
WWKY ...... Louisville, KY [*AM radio station call letters*]
WWKZ ...... New Albany, MS [*FM radio station call letters*]
WWL .... New Orleans, LA [*AM radio station call letters*]
W & W (L) ... Wyatt and Webb's Reports (Law) [*A publication*] (APTA)
WWLA ...... Lewiston, ME [*Television station call letters*]
WWLF-TV ... Hazleton, PA [*Television station call letters*]
WWLI....... Providence, RI [*FM radio station call letters*]
WWLIS ...... Woodmen of the World Life Insurance Society (EA)
WWLK ...... Eddyville, KY [*AM radio station call letters*]
WWL2M ... Women Who Love Too Much [*Title of book by Robin Norwood*]
WWLO ...... Gainesville, FL [*AM radio station call letters*]
WWLODS ... Wire and Wire-Like Object Detection System [*Helicopter*] (MCD)
WWLP....... Springfield, MA [*Television station call letters*]
WWLR ...... Lyndonville, VT [*FM radio station call letters*]
WWLS....... Moore, OK [*AM radio station call letters*]
WWLT ...... Bamberg, SC [*FM radio station call letters*]
WWLTM... Women Who Love Too Much [*Title of book by Robin Norwood*]
WWL-TV .. New Orleans, LA [*Television station call letters*]
WWLV ...... Daytona Beach, FL [*FM radio station call letters*]
WWLX ...... Lawrenceburg, TN [*AM radio station call letters*]
WWLZ ...... Cadillac, MI [*FM radio station call letters*]
WWM........ Ons Nuis Vakblad voor de Meubelhandel, Meubelmakerij, Meubelindustrie, Interieurarchitecteur, Behangerij, Stoffeerderij, en Detailhandel in Woningtextiel [*A publication*]
WWM........ Weekly Women's Magazine [*Manila*] [*A publication*]
WWM........ Weizsaecker-Williams Method [*Physics*]
WWM........ Welded Wire Matrix
WWM........ Widowed White Male [*Classified advertising*]
WWM........ Wings West, Inc. [*Santa Monica, CA*] [*FAA designator*] (FAAC)
WWM........ Wire Wrap Machine
WWM........ Working Woman [*A publication*]
WWM........ World-Wide Missions (EA)
WWM........ Worldwide Monitor [*Vancouver Stock Exchange symbol*]
WWMCCS ... Worldwide Military Command and Communications System [*Pronounced "wimex"*]
WWMCCS ... Worldwide Military Command and Control System [*DoD*]
WWMD...... Hagerstown, MD [*FM radio station call letters*]
WWME..... Worldwide Marriage Encounter (EA)
WWMG..... Shelby, NC [*FM radio station call letters*]
WWMH .... Minocqua, WI [*FM radio station call letters*]
WWMJ ..... Ellsworth, ME [*FM radio station call letters*]
WWML..... Wood, Wire, and Metal Lathers' International Union [*Later, UBC*] (EA)
WWMMP ... Western Wood Moulding and Millwork Producers [*Later, WMMPA*] (EA)

WWMMRD ... Water and Waste Management Monitoring Research Division [*Environmental Protection Agency*] (EPA)
WWMO..... Eden, NC [*AM radio station call letters*]
WWMP..... Western Wood Moulding Producers [*Later, WMMPA*] (EA)
WWMR..... Rumford, ME [*FM radio station call letters*]
WWMS ..... Oxford, MS [*FM radio station call letters*]
WWMS ..... Water and Waste Management Staff [*Environmental Protection Agency*] (GFGA)
WWMS ..... Water and Waste Management Subsystem [*NASA*] (KSC)
WWMS ..... Who's Who in Malaysia and Singapore [*A publication*]
WWMT ..... Kalamazoo, MI [*Television station call letters*]
WWMV..... Winter Wheat (Russian) Mosaic Virus [*Plant pathology*]
WWMX..... Baltimore, MD [*FM radio station call letters*]
WWN........ Walt Whitman Newsletter [*A publication*]
WWN........ Washington Women's Network (EA)
WWN........ With Winch
WWNC...... Asheville, NC [*AM radio station call letters*]
WWNFF..... Woodrow Wilson National Fellowship Foundation (EA)
WWNH ..... Madbury, NH [*AM radio station call letters*]
WWNH ..... War Will Never Happen [*Philosophy attributed to the Defense Department by former Deputy Assistant Secretary of Defense John F. Ahearne*] [*1987*]
WWNK ...... Cincinnati, OH [*FM radio station call letters*]
WWNN ..... Pompano Beach, FL [*AM radio station call letters*]
WWNO ..... New Orleans, LA [*FM radio station call letters*]
WWNR ..... Beckley, WV [*AM radio station call letters*]
WWNS ..... Statesboro, GA [*AM radio station call letters*]
WWNS ..... World Wide News Service (BJA)
WWNSS..... Worldwide Network of Standard Seismograph [*Stations*]
WWNT ..... Dothan, AL [*AM radio station call letters*]
WWNW ..... New Wilmington, PA [*FM radio station call letters*]
WWNY ..... Carthage, NY [*Television station call letters*]
WWNZ ..... Orlando, FL [*AM radio station call letters*]
WWO .... Warrant Writer Officer [*British military*] (DMA)
WW/O....... Widow Of [*Genealogy*]
WWO .... Wing Warrant Officer [*RAF*] [*British*]
WWOC...... Avalon, NJ [*FM radio station call letters*]
WWOD ...... Lynchburg, VA [*AM radio station call letters*]
WWOF ...... Camp Lejeune, NC [*AM radio station call letters*]
WWOJ ...... Avon Park, FL [*FM radio station call letters*]
WWOK ...... Evansville, IN [*AM radio station call letters*]
WWOL ...... Forest City, NC [*AM radio station call letters*]
WWON ..... Woonsocket, RI [*AM radio station call letters*]
WWooH..... Howard Young Medical Center, Woodruff, WI [*Library symbol*] [*Library of Congress*] (LCLS)
WWOR...... Secaucus, NJ [*Television station call letters*]
W Work (Lond) ... World's Work (London) [*A publication*]
WWoVA .... United States Veterans Administration Hospital, Wood, WI [*Library symbol*] [*Library of Congress*] (LCLS)
WWOW..... Conneaut, OH [*AM radio station call letters*]
WWOZ..... New Orleans, LA [*FM radio station call letters*]
WWP .... Walden Woods Project [*An association*] (EA)
WWP .... Washington Water Power Co. [*NYSE symbol*] (SPSG)
WWP .... Water Wall (Peripheral Jet) (AAG)
WWP .... Weather Wing Pamphlet [*Air Force*] (MCD)
WWP .... Wire Wrap Panels (MCD)
WWP .... Workers World Party [*Political party*] (EA)
WWP .... Working Water Pressure
WWP .... World Weather Program [*National Science Foundation*]
WWPA ...... Western Wood Products Association (EA)
WWPA ...... Williamsport, PA [*AM radio station call letters*]
WWPA ...... Woven Wire Products Association (EA)
WWPB ...... Hagerstown, MD [*Television station call letters*]
WWPB ...... Worldwide Women Professional Bowlers (EA)
WWpC....... Central State Hospital, Waupun, WI [*Library symbol*] [*Library of Congress*] (LCLS)
WWPD ...... Marion, SC [*FM radio station call letters*]
WWPG ...... Widows' War Pensions and Gratuities [*British*]
WWPH...... Princeton Junction, NJ [*FM radio station call letters*]
WWPLS ..... World Wide Pet Lovers Society [*Defunct*] (EA)
WWPMU .. World-Wide Prayer and Missionary Union (EA)
WWPN ...... Westernport, MD [*FM radio station call letters*]
WWPR ...... Sharon, CT [*FM radio station call letters*]
W/WPR...... Windshield Wiper [*Automotive engineering*]
WWPSA..... Western World Pet Supply Association (EA)
WWPT ...... Westport, CT [*FM radio station call letters*]
WWPV ...... Colchester, VT [*FM radio station call letters*]
WWPZ ...... Petoskey, MI [*AM radio station call letters*]
WWQC...... Quincy, IL [*FM radio station call letters*]
WWQM..... Middleton, WI [*FM radio station call letters*]
WWQQ ..... Wilmington, NC [*FM radio station call letters*]
WWQR..... Morganton, NC [*Television station call letters*]
WWr.......... McMillan Memorial Library, Wisconsin Rapids, WI [*Library symbol*] [*Library of Congress*] (LCLS)
WWR........ Walt Whitman Review [*A publication*]
WWR........ Washington Weekly Report [*Independent Bankers Association of America*] [*A publication*]
WWR........ Washington Western [*AAR code*]
WWR........ Western Warner Oils [*Vancouver Stock Exchange symbol*]
WWR........ Western Weekly Reports [*Carswell Co. Ltd.*] [*Canada*] [*Information service or system*] (CRD)

WWR......... Widower [*Genealogy*]
WWR......... Wire-Wound Resistor
WWR......... Wisconsin Rapids, McMillan Library, Wisconsin Rapids, WI [*OCLC symbol*] (OCLC)
WWR......... Woodill Wildfire Registry (EA)
WWR......... Woodward, OK [*Location identifier*] [*FAA*] (FAAL)
WWRC...... Washington, DC [*AM radio station call letters*]
WWRC...... Wyoming Water Research Center [*University of Wyoming*] [*Research center*] (RCD)
WWRD...... Wilson, NC [*Television station call letters*]
WWREC.... Western Washington Research and Extension Center [*Washington State University*] [*Research center*] (RCD)
WWRF...... Who's Who Resource File [*Minority Business Development Agency*] [*Database*]
WWRI....... Worldwide Mobile Communications Routing Index (DNAB)
WWRK...... Elberton, GA [*AM radio station call letters*]
WWRK-FM ... Elberton, GA [*FM radio station call letters*]
WWRL...... New York, NY [*AM radio station call letters*]
WWRM..... St. Petersburg, FL [*FM radio station call letters*]
WWR (NS) ... Western Weekly Reports, New Series [*Canada*] [*A publication*] (DLA)
WWRS....... Wash-Water Recovery System [*in a spacecraft*] [*NASA*]
WWRT...... Scotland Neck, NC [*FM radio station call letters*]
WWRV...... New York, NY [*AM radio station call letters*]
WWRW..... Wisconsin Rapids, WI [*FM radio station call letters*]
WWRX...... Westerly, RI [*FM radio station call letters*]
WWS......... Walker Wingsail Systems [*Shipbuilding*] [*British*]
WWS......... Water Wall (Side Skegs) (AAG)
WWS......... Water and Waste Subsystem [*Aerospace*] (MCD)
WWs.......... Wausau Public Library, Wausau, WI [*Library symbol*] [*Library of Congress*] (LCLS)
WW(S)....... Well Water (System) [*Nuclear energy*] (NRCH)
WWS......... Western Writers Series [*A publication*]
WWS......... Wild Weasel Squadron [*Air Force*]
WWS......... Wind and Watermill Section [*of the Society for the Protection of Ancient Buildings*] (EA)
WWS......... Woman's Workshop (EA)
WWS......... Women's Welfare Service [*Defunct*] (EA)
WWS......... Working with Shortages (MCD)
WWS......... World Weather System
WWS......... World Wide Minerals Ltd. [*Toronto Stock Exchange symbol*] [*Vancouver Stock Exchange symbol*]
WWSA...... Walt Whitman Society of America [*Defunct*] (EA)
WWSA...... Who's Who in Saudi Arabia [*A publication*]
WWSA...... Women's War Service Auxiliary [*British military*] (DMA)
WWSB....... Sarasota, FL [*Television station call letters*]
WWSC....... Glens Falls, NY [*AM radio station call letters*]
WWSCA...... Wirtschaft und Wissenschaft [*A publication*]
WWSD...... Quincy, FL [*AM radio station call letters*]
WWSD...... Women's War Savings Division
WWSE...... Jamestown, NY [*AM radio station call letters*]
WWSF...... Andalusia, AL [*AM radio station call letters*]
WWSF....... Fort Walton Beach, FL [*FM radio station call letters*]
WWSF....... World-Wide Stroke Foundation (EA)
WWSH...... Hazleton, PA [*FM radio station call letters*]
WWSJ...... St. Johns, MI [*AM radio station call letters*]
WWSL....... Philadelphia, MS [*FM radio station call letters*]
WWsMC ... Marathon Health Care Center, Wausau, WI [*Library symbol*] [*Library of Congress*] (LCLS)
WWSN...... Dayton, OH [*FM radio station call letters*]
WWSN...... Worldwide Seismology Net [*National Bureau of Standards*]
WWSP...... Stevens Point, WI [*FM radio station call letters*]
WWSP...... Worldwide Surveillance Program [*Military*] (NG)
WWSR...... St. Albans, VT [*AM radio station call letters*]
WWSRA.... Western Winter Sports Representatives Association (EA)
WWSS....... Meredith, NH [*FM radio station call letters*]
WWSSB ..... World-Wide Software Support Branch (MCD)
WWSSN.... World-Wide Standard Seismograph Network [*Earthquake detection*]
WWSSN.... Worldwide Standardized Seismograph Network [*US Geological Survey*]
WWST....... Jeffersonville, GA [*FM radio station call letters*]
WWSU...... Dayton, OH [*FM radio station call letters*]
WWSU...... World Water Ski Union [*See also UMSN*] [*Montreux, Switzerland*] (EAIO)
WWSVA.... Worldwide Secure Voice Architecture (MCD)
WWSVCS ... World-Wide Secure Voice Communications System (MCD)
WWSVCS ... World-Wide Secure Voice Conference System (MCD)
WWSW ..... Pittsburgh, PA [*AM radio station call letters*]
WWsW...... Wausau Hospitals, Inc., Wausau, WI [*Library symbol*] [*Library of Congress*] (LCLS)
WWSW-FM ... Pittsburgh, PA [*FM radio station call letters*]
WWsWV ... Wisconsin Valley Library Service, Wausau, WI [*Library symbol*] [*Library of Congress*] (LCLS)
WWT......... Newtok [*Alaska*] [*Airport symbol*] (OAG)
WWT......... Newtok, AK [*Location identifier*] [*FAA*] (FAAL)
W & WT .... Water and Waste Treatment
WWT......... Who's Who in Technology [*A publication*]
WWTA...... Marion, MA [*FM radio station call letters*]
WWTC...... Minneapolis, MN [*AM radio station call letters*]
WWTCA ... World War Tank Corps Association (EA)

WWTCIP .. Worldwide Technical Control Improvement Program (MCD)
WWTI...... Watertown, NY [*Television station call letters*]
WWTK...... Lake Placid, FL [*AM radio station call letters*]
WWTK...... Weitek Corp. [*NASDAQ symbol*] (CTT)
WWTO...... La Salle, IL [*Television station call letters*]
WWTP...... Waste Water Treatment Plant [*Also, WTP*]
WWTR...... Bethany Beach, DE [*FM radio station call letters*]
WWTS...... Waste Water Treatment System
WWTT ...... Worldwide Tapetalk [*An association*] (EA)
WWTV...... Cadillac, MI [*Television station call letters*]
WWTV...... Western World-Samuel Communications, Inc. [*Formerly, Western-World TV*] [*NASDAQ symbol*] (NQ)
WWU......... Western Washington University
WWUF...... Waycross, GA [*FM radio station call letters*]
WWUH...... West Hartford, CT [*FM radio station call letters*]
WWUI...... Working Women's United Institute [*Later, WWI*] (EA)
WWUN...... Clarksdale, MS [*FM radio station call letters*]
WWUP...... Sault Ste. Marie, MI [*Television station call letters*]
WWUS...... Big Pine Key, FL [*FM radio station call letters*]
WWV......... Walla Walla Valley Railway Co. [*AAR code*]
WWV......... Wheeling College, Wheeling, WV [*OCLC symbol*] (OCLC)
WWV......... World Wide Time [*National Bureau of Standards call letters*] (MUGU)
WWV......... World Wide Vermiculture [*An association*] (EA)
WWVA...... Wheeling, WV [*AM radio station call letters*]
WWVH...... World Wide Time Hawaii [*National Bureau of Standards call letters*] (MUGU)
W & W Vict ... Wyatt and Webb's Victorian Reports [*1864-69*] [*Australia*] [*A publication*] (DLA)
WWVR...... West Terre Haute, IN [*FM radio station call letters*]
WWVR...... Wire-Wound Variable Resistor
WWVU...... Morgantown, WV [*FM radio station call letters*]
WWW........ Who Was Who [*A publication*]
WWW........ [*The*] Who, What, or Where Game [*Also, 3W's*] [*Television show*]
WWW........ Wide Whitewall Tire [*Automotive accessory*]
WWW........ Wolverine World Wide, Inc. [*NYSE symbol*] (SPSG)
WWW........ World Weather Watch [*World Meteorological Organization*] [*Databank*] (IID)
WWW........ World-Wide Web [*Telecommunications*] (PCM)
WWW........ Worldwide Warranty [*Canon USA, Inc.*]
WWWB..... High Point, NC [*FM radio station call letters*]
WWWC.... Wilkesboro, NC [*AM radio station call letters*]
WWWC.... World without War Council (EA)
WWWCR .. World Wide White and Creme Horse Registry (EA)
WWWE..... Cleveland, OH [*AM radio station call letters*]
WWWF..... Worldwide Wrestling Federation [*Later, WWF*]
WWWFC... [*Kitty*] Wells-[*Johnny*] Wright-[*Bobby*] Wright International Fan Club (EA)
WWWG..... Rochester, NY [*AM radio station call letters*]
WWWI...... Widows of World War I (EA)
WWWJ...... Who's Who in World Jewry [*A publication*] (BJA)
WWWK.... Ellenville, NY [*FM radio station call letters*]
WWWM... Sylvania, OH [*FM radio station call letters*]
WWWM... Toledo, OH [*AM radio station call letters*]
WWWM... [*The*] W. W. Williams Co. [*NASDAQ symbol*] (NQ)
WWWN..... Vienna, GA [*AM radio station call letters*]
WWWO.... Hartford City, IN [*FM radio station call letters*]
WWWT .... Randolph, VT [*AM radio station call letters*]
WWWTTUTWTU ... We Won't Write to Them until They Write to Us [*A servicemen's club*]
WWWV..... Charlottesville, VA [*FM radio station call letters*]
WWWV..... Women World War Veterans (EA)
WWWW.... Detroit, MI [*FM radio station call letters*]
WWWW.... Who's Who in the World of Women [*Australia*] [*A publication*]
WWWY.... Columbus, IN [*FM radio station call letters*]
WWWZ.... Summerville, SC [*FM radio station call letters*]
WWX......... World Wide Exchange [*Commercial firm*] (EA)
WWXL...... Manchester, KY [*AM radio station call letters*]
WWXL-FM ... Manchester, KY [*FM radio station call letters*]
WWY......... Warwickshire and Worcestershire Yeomanry [*British military*] (DMA)
WWY......... West Wyalong [*Australia*] [*Airport symbol*] (OAG)
WWY......... Wrigley [*Wm.*] Jr. Co. [*NYSE symbol*] (SPSG)
WWYN...... McKenzie, TN [*FM radio station call letters*]
WWYO...... Pineville, WV [*AM radio station call letters*]
WWYS...... Cadiz, OH [*FM radio station call letters*]
WWYZ...... Waterbury, CT [*FM radio station call letters*]
WWZ......... Willow Resources Ltd. [*Vancouver Stock Exchange symbol*]
WWZD...... New Albany, MS [*FM radio station call letters*]
WWZQ...... Aberdeen, MS [*AM radio station call letters*]
WWZQ-FM ... Aberdeen, MS [*FM radio station call letters*]
WWZZ...... Karns, TN [*FM radio station call letters*]
WX............ American Eagle Airlines, Inc. [*ICAO designator*] (FAAC)
WX............ Wawatay News Extra. Special Issues [*A publication*]
WX............ Wax
WX............ Weather
WX............ Westinghouse Electric Corp. [*NYSE symbol*] [*Wall Street slang name: "Wex"*] (SPSG)
WX............ Wireless [*Communications*]
WX............ Women's Extra [*Size*]

WXAC .... Reading, PA [*FM radio station call letters*]
WXAG .... Athens, GA [*AM radio station call letters*]
WXAL .... Demopolis, AL [*AM radio station call letters*]
WXAM ...... Buffalo, KY [*AM radio station call letters*]
WX-AM ..... Weather and Air Movements   (SAA)
WXAN ...... Ava, IL [*FM radio station call letters*]
WxB .... Wax Bite [*Dentistry*]
WXBA .... Brentwood, NY [*FM radio station call letters*]
WXBK .... Albertville, AL [*AM radio station call letters*]
WXBM ...... Milton, FL [*FM radio station call letters*]
WXBQ .... Bristol, TN [*FM radio station call letters*]
WXBX ...... Buffalo, NY [*AM radio station call letters*]
WXC .... Westinghouse Canada, Inc. [*Toronto Stock Exchange symbol*]
WXCC .... Williamson, WV [*FM radio station call letters*]
WXCE .... Amery, WI [*AM radio station call letters*]
WXCF .... Clifton Forge, VA [*AM radio station call letters*]
WXCF-FM ... Clifton Forge, VA [*FM radio station call letters*]
WXCI .... Danbury, CT [*FM radio station call letters*]
WXCL .... Pekin, IL [*FM radio station call letters*]
WXCL .... Peoria, IL [*AM radio station call letters*]
WXCO .... Wausau, WI [*AM radio station call letters*]
WXCON .... Pilot Reports by Qualified Weather Personnel on Weather Reconnaissance Flights [*Aviation code*]   (FAAC)
WXCT .... Hamden, CT [*AM radio station call letters*]
WXCV .... Homosassa Springs, FL [*FM radio station call letters*]
WXCY .... Havre de Grace, MD [*FM radio station call letters*]
WXD .... Meteorological RADAR Station [*ITU designation*]   (CET)
WXD .... Waxed
WXD........... Westrex Development Corp. [*Vancouver Stock Exchange symbol*]
WXDJ .... Homestead, FL [*FM radio station call letters*]
WXDR .... Newark, DE [*FM radio station call letters*]
WXDU .... Durham, NC [*FM radio station call letters*]
WXEE .... Welch, WV [*AM radio station call letters*]
WXEL .... West Palm Beach, FL [*FM radio station call letters*]
WXEL-TV ... West Palm Beach, FL [*Television station call letters*]
WXEM ...... Buford, GA [*AM radio station call letters*]
WXEW ...... Yabucoa, PR [*AM radio station call letters*]
WXFL .... Florence, AL [*FM radio station call letters*]
WXFM ...... Mt. Zion, IL [*FM radio station call letters*]
WXFX .... Prattville, AL [*FM radio station call letters*]
WXG .... Warning   (MUGU)
WXGA ...... Waycross, GA [*Television station call letters*]
WXGC .... Milledgeville, GA [*FM radio station call letters*]
WXGI .... Richmond, VA [*AM radio station call letters*]
WXGL .... Lewiston, ME [*FM radio station call letters*]
WXGM ...... Gloucester, VA [*AM radio station call letters*]
WXGM-FM ... Gloucester, VA [*FM radio station call letters*]
WXGZ .... Appleton, WI [*Television station call letters*]
WXHC....... Homer, NY [*FM radio station call letters*]
WXHD...... Mt. Hope, NY [*FM radio station call letters*]
WXHT .... Meridian, MS [*FM radio station call letters*]
WXIA .... Atlanta, GA [*Television station call letters*]
WXIC........ Waverly, OH [*AM radio station call letters*]
WXID .... Mayfield, KY [*FM radio station call letters*]
WXIE .... Oakland, MD [*FM radio station call letters*]
WXII......... Winston-Salem, NC [*Television station call letters*]
WXIL........ Parkersburg, WV [*FM radio station call letters*]
WXIN .... Indianapolis, IN [*Television station call letters*]
WXIR .... Plainfield, IN [*FM radio station call letters*]
WXIS........ Erwin, TN [*FM radio station call letters*]
WXIX....... Newport, KY [*Television station call letters*]
WXIZ....... Waverly, OH [*FM radio station call letters*]
WXJB .... Harrogate, TN [*FM radio station call letters*]
WXJD....... Oscoda, MI [*FM radio station call letters*]
WXJF .... Omega, GA [*AM radio station call letters*]
WXJI........ Grand Rapids, MI [*FM radio station call letters*]
WXJJ .... Mt. Vernon, KY [*FM radio station call letters*]
WXJM...... Washington, PA [*FM radio station call letters*]
WXJN....... Lewes, DE [*FM radio station call letters*]
WXJO ...... Bethalto, IL [*FM radio station call letters*]
WXJX....... Washington, PA [*FM radio station call letters*]
WXKC ...... Erie, PA [*FM radio station call letters*]
WXKD .... Ripley, OH [*AM radio station call letters*]
WXKE ...... Fort Wayne, IN [*FM radio station call letters*]
WXKF........ Terre Haute, IN [*FM radio station call letters*]
WXKG ...... Livingston, TN [*FM radio station call letters*]
WXKI .... Moulton, AL [*FM radio station call letters*]
WXKL........ Sanford, NC [*AM radio station call letters*]
WXKO ...... Fort Valley, GA [*AM radio station call letters*]
WXKO ...... Pana, IL [*FM radio station call letters*]
WXKQ ...... Whitesburg, KY [*FM radio station call letters*]
WXKR ...... Port Clinton, OH [*FM radio station call letters*]
WXKS....... Medford, MA [*AM radio station call letters*]
WXKS-FM ... Medford, MA [*FM radio station call letters*]
WXKW ...... Allentown, PA [*AM radio station call letters*]
WXKX ...... Parkersburg, WV [*FM radio station call letters*]
WXKZ .... Prestonsburg, KY [*FM radio station call letters*]
WXL .... Wix, Inc. [*Toronto Stock Exchange symbol*]
WXLA .... Dimondale, MI [*AM radio station call letters*]
WXLC........ Waukegan, IL [*FM radio station call letters*]

WXLE........ Johnstown, OH [*FM radio station call letters*]
WXLH .... Blue Mountain Lake, NY [*FM radio station call letters*]
WXLI........ Dublin, GA [*AM radio station call letters*]
WXLK........ Roanoke, VA [*FM radio station call letters*]
WXLL........ Decatur, GA [*AM radio station call letters*]
WXLN ...... Eminence, KY [*FM radio station call letters*]
WXLN ...... Louisville, KY [*AM radio station call letters*]
WXLO .... Fitchburg, MA [*AM radio station call letters*]
WXLO .... Fitchburg, MA [*FM radio station call letters*]
WXLP .... Moline, IL [*FM radio station call letters*]
WXLR .... Hahira, GA [*AM radio station call letters*]
WXLS........ Biloxi, MS [*AM radio station call letters*]
WXLS........ Gulfport, MS [*FM radio station call letters*]
WXLT .... McComb, MS [*FM radio station call letters*]
WXLU .... Peru, NY [*FM radio station call letters*]
WXLV ...... Schnecksville, PA [*FM radio station call letters*]
WXLW ...... Indianapolis, IN [*AM radio station call letters*]
WXLY .... North Charleston, SC [*FM radio station call letters*]
WXLZ .... Lebanon, VA [*FM radio station call letters*]
WXM .... Worcester Art Museum, Worcester, MA [*OCLC symbol*]   (OCLC)
WXMA ...... Bishopville, SC [*FM radio station call letters*]
WXMC ...... Parsippany-Troy Hills, NJ [*AM radio station call letters*]
WXMD...... White Sulphur Springs, WV [*FM radio station call letters*]
WXME ...... Avon, NY [*AM radio station call letters*]
WXMF ...... McArthur, OH [*FM radio station call letters*]
WXMG ...... Spooner, WI [*FM radio station call letters*]
WXMH ...... Mount Carmel, PA [*FM radio station call letters*]
WXMI .... Grand Rapids, MI [*Television station call letters*]
WXMJ ...... Mount Union, PA [*FM radio station call letters*]
WXMK ...... Dock Junction, GA [*FM radio station call letters*]
WXML ...... Upper Sandusky, OH [*FM radio station call letters*]
WXMT ...... Nashville, TN [*Television station call letters*]
WXMX ...... St. John's, MI [*FM radio station call letters*]
WXMY ...... Saltville, VA [*AM radio station call letters*]
WXNL ...... Baraga, MI [*FM radio station call letters*]
WXOD...... Winchester, NH [*FM radio station call letters*]
WXOK...... Baton Rouge, LA [*AM radio station call letters*]
WXON...... Detroit, MI [*Television station call letters*]
WXOQ ...... Selmer, TN [*FM radio station call letters*]
WXOW ...... La Crosse, WI [*Television station call letters*]
WXOX ...... Bay City, MI [*AM radio station call letters*]
WxP .... Wax Pattern [*Dentistry*]
WXPL........ Fitchburg, MA [*FM radio station call letters*]
WXPN ...... Philadelphia, PA [*FM radio station call letters*]
WXPQ ...... Babson Park, FL [*AM radio station call letters*]
WXPR .... Rhinelander, WI [*FM radio station call letters*]
WXPS........ Briarcliff Manor, NY [*FM radio station call letters*]
WXPT .... Kennebunkport, ME [*FM radio station call letters*]
WXPX........ West Hazleton, PA [*AM radio station call letters*]
WXPZ....... Milford, DE [*FM radio station call letters*]
WXQK ...... Spring City, TN [*AM radio station call letters*]
WXQR ...... Jacksonville, NC [*FM radio station call letters*]
WXQZ .... Canton, NY [*FM radio station call letters*]
WXR .... Radiosonde Station [*ITU designation*]   (CET)
WXR .... Weather RADAR
WXRC .... Hickory, NC [*FM radio station call letters*]
WXRCNSq ... Weather Reconnaissance Squadron [*Air Force*]
WXRECCO ... Weather Reconnaissance Flight [*Navy*]   (NVT)
WXRF........ Guayama, PR [*AM radio station call letters*]
WXRI........ Windsor, VA [*FM radio station call letters*]
WXRK ...... New York, NY [*FM radio station call letters*]
WXRL ...... Lancaster, NY [*AM radio station call letters*]
WXRO....... Beaver Dam, WI [*FM radio station call letters*]
WXRQ ...... Mount Pleasant, TN [*AM radio station call letters*]
WXRS........ Swainsboro, GA [*AM radio station call letters*]
WXRS-FM ... Swainsboro, GA [*FM radio station call letters*]
WXRT .... Chicago, IL [*FM radio station call letters*]
WXRX .... Belvidere, IL [*FM radio station call letters*]
WXRZ .... Corinth, MS [*FM radio station call letters*]
WXSB .... Benton Harbor, MI [*FM radio station call letters*]
WXSC........ Tell City, IN [*FM radio station call letters*]
WXSE .... Calhoun, TN [*FM radio station call letters*]
WXSS .... Memphis, TN [*AM radio station call letters*]
WXST .... Loudon, TN [*FM radio station call letters*]
WXTA ...... Edinboro, PA [*FM radio station call letters*]
WXTB....... Clearwater, FL [*FM radio station call letters*]
WXTC .... Charleston, SC [*AM radio station call letters*]
WXTC-FM ... Charleston, SC [*FM radio station call letters*]
WXTH ...... Alexander City, AL [*AM radio station call letters*]
WXTK ...... West Yarmouth, MA [*FM radio station call letters*]
WXTL .... Jacksonville Beach, FL [*AM radio station call letters*]
WXTN ...... Lexington, MS [*AM radio station call letters*]
WXTO ...... Winter Garden, FL [*AM radio station call letters*]
WXTQ ...... Athens, OH [*FM radio station call letters*]
WXTR ...... Waldorf, MD [*FM radio station call letters*]
WXTRN .... Weak External Reference [*Data processing*]   (BUR)
WXTS........ Toledo, OH [*FM radio station call letters*]
WXTU ...... Philadelphia, PA [*FM radio station call letters*]
WXTV ...... Paterson, NJ [*Television station call letters*]
WXTX ...... Columbus, GA [*Television station call letters*]

WXUT .... Toledo, OH [*FM radio station call letters*]
WXVA .... Charles Town, WV [*AM radio station call letters*]
WXVA-FM ... Charles Town, WV [*FM radio station call letters*]
WXVI .... Montgomery, AL [*AM radio station call letters*]
WXVK .... Coal Grove, OH [*FM radio station call letters*]
WXVL....... Crossville, TN [*FM radio station call letters*]
WXVO .... Oliver Springs, TN [*FM radio station call letters*]
WXVQ ...... De Land, FL [*AM radio station call letters*]
WXVS........ Waycross, GA [*FM radio station call letters*]
WXVT .... Greenville, MS [*Television station call letters*]
WXVU .... Villanova, PA [*FM radio station call letters*]
WXVW ...... Jeffersonville, IN [*AM radio station call letters*]
WXVX .... Monroeville, PA [*AM radio station call letters*]
WXWY ...... Robertsdale, AL [*AM radio station call letters*]
WXXA .... Albany, NY [*Television station call letters*]
WXXI........ Rochester, NY [*AM radio station call letters*]
WXXI-FM ... Rochester, NY [*FM radio station call letters*]
WXXI-TV ... Rochester, NY [*Television station call letters*]
WXXK .... Newport, NH [*FM radio station call letters*]
WXXL....... Leesburg, FL [*FM radio station call letters*]
WXXP....... Anderson, IN [*FM radio station call letters*]
WXXQ .... Freeport, IL [*FM radio station call letters*]
WXXR .... Cullman, AL [*AM radio station call letters*]
WXXU .... Cocoa Beach, FL [*AM radio station call letters*]
WXXV .... Gulfport, MS [*Television station call letters*]
WXXX .... South Burlington, VT [*FM radio station call letters*]
WXYB .... Indian Rocks Beach, FL [*AM radio station call letters*]
WXYC .... Chapel Hill, NC [*FM radio station call letters*]
WXYT .... Detroit, MI [*AM radio station call letters*]
WXYU .... Lynchburg, VA [*FM radio station call letters*]
WXYV .... Baltimore, MD [*FM radio station call letters*]
WXYX ...... Bayamon, PR [*FM radio station call letters*]
WXYZ .... Detroit, MI [*Television station call letters*]
WXZY .... Ruckersville, VA [*FM radio station call letters*]
WY............ Oman Aviation Services Co. Ltd. [*Oman*] [*ICAO designator*] (FAAC)
WY............ Warwickshire Yeomanry [*British military*] (DMA)
WY............ Washington Yards [*Navy*]
WY............ Way (ADA)
WY............ Western Yiddish (BJA)
WY............ Wey [*Unit of weight*]
WY............ Weyerhaeuser Co. [*NYSE symbol*] (SPSG)
WY............ Wherry (ROG)
WY............ Woman's Year
WY............ Wrist Yaw (MCD)
WY............ Wyeth Laboratories [*Research code symbol*]
WY............ Wyoming [*Postal code*]
WY............ Wyoming Music Educator News-Letter [*A publication*]
WY............ Wyoming Reports [*A publication*] (DLA)
Wy.............. Wyoming State Library, Cheyenne, WY [*Library symbol*] [*Library of Congress*] (LCLS)
Wy.............. Wythe's Virginia Chancery Reports [*1788-99*] [*A publication*] (DLA)
WyA........... Lincoln County Library, Afton Branch, Afton, WY [*Library symbol*] [*Library of Congress*] (LCLS)
WYA .... Whyalla [*Australia*] [*Airport symbol*] (OAG)
WYA .... Writers for Young Adults [*A publication*]
WYA .... Writers for Young Adults. Biographies Master Index [*A publication*]
WYA .... Wyangala [*Australia*] [*Seismograph station code, US Geological Survey*] [*Closed*] (SEIS)
WyAGS ..... Church of Jesus Christ of Latter-Day Saints, Genealogical Society Library, Afton Branch, Afton, WY [*Library symbol*] [*Library of Congress*] (LCLS)
WYAI .... La Grange, GA [*FM radio station call letters*]
WYAIO ..... Will You Accept, If Offered [*the position of*] (FAAC)
WYAJ .... Sudbury, MA [*FM radio station call letters*]
WYAK .... Surfside Beach-Garden City, SC [*AM radio station call letters*]
WYAK-FM ... Surfside Beach-Garden City, SC [*FM radio station call letters*]
WYAL .... Scotland Neck, NC [*AM radio station call letters*]
WYAM ...... Hartselle, AL [*FM radio station call letters*]
Wy-Ar........ Wyoming State Archives and Historical Department, Cheyenne, WY [*Library symbol*] [*Library of Congress*] (LCLS)
WYAT .... New Orleans, LA [*AM radio station call letters*]
Wyatt Prac Reg ... Wyatt's Practical Register in Chancery [*1800*] [*A publication*] (DLA)
Wyatt Pr R ... Wyatt's Practical Register in Chancery [*1800*] [*A publication*] (DLA)
Wyatt & W ... Wyatt and Webb's Reports [*A publication*] (APTA)
Wyatt W & A'B ... Wyatt, Webb, and A'Beckett's Reports [*A publication*] (DLA)
Wyatt W & A'B (Eq) ... Wyatt, Webb, and A'Beckett's Reports (Equity) [*A publication*] (APTA)
Wyatt W & A'B IE & M ... Wyatt, Webb, and A'Beckett's Reports (Insolvency, Ecclesiastical, and Matrimonial) [*A publication*] (APTA)
Wyatt W & A'B IP & M ... Wyatt, Webb, and A'Beckett's Victorian Insolvency, Probate, and Matrimonial Reports [*A publication*] (APTA)
Wyatt W & A'B Min ... Wyatt, Webb, and A'Beckett's Reports (Mining) [*A publication*] (APTA)

Wyatt & Webb ... Wyatt and Webb's Reports [*A publication*] (APTA)
Wyatt & W (Eq) ... Wyatt and Webb's Reports (Equity) [*A publication*] (APTA)
Wyatt & W (IE & M) ... Wyatt and Webb's Reports (Insolvency, Ecclesiastical, and Matrimonial) [*A publication*] (APTA)
Wyatt & W (IP & M) ... Wyatt and Webb's Reports (Insolvency, Probate, and Matrimonial) [*A publication*] (APTA)
WYAV .... Conway, SC [*FM radio station call letters*]
WYAY .... Gainesville, GA [*FM radio station call letters*]
WYAZ .... Lumpkin, GA [*FM radio station call letters*]
WYBB....... Folly Beach, SC [*FM radio station call letters*]
WYBC .... New Haven, CT [*FM radio station call letters*]
WYBE....... Philadelphia, PA [*Television station call letters*]
WYBF....... Radnor Township, PA [*FM radio station call letters*]
WYBG .... Massena, NY [*AM radio station call letters*]
WYBH....... McConnelsville, OH [*FM radio station call letters*]
WYBJ .... Greenville, MS [*FM radio station call letters*]
WYBL....... Western Young Buddhist League (EA)
WYBM ...... Minor Hill, TN [*AM radio station call letters*]
WYBT....... Blountstown, FL [*AM radio station call letters*]
WyBu......... Johnson County Library, Buffalo, WY [*Library symbol*] [*Library of Congress*] (LCLS)
WYBZ....... Crooksville, OH [*FM radio station call letters*]
WyC.......... Laramie County Library System, Cheyenne, WY [*Library symbol*] [*Library of Congress*] (LCLS)
WYC .... Warwickshire Yeomanry Cavalry [*British military*] (DMA)
WYC .... Wiley College, Marshall, TX [*OCLC symbol*] [*Inactive*] (OCLC)
WYC .... Wycombe [*England*]
WYCA ...... Hammond, IN [*FM radio station call letters*]
WyCa......... Natrona County Public Library, Casper, WY [*Library symbol*] [*Library of Congress*] (LCLS)
WyCaC .... Casper College, Casper, WY [*Library symbol*] [*Library of Congress*] (LCLS)
WyCaCH .... Wyoming State Children's Home, Casper, WY [*Library symbol*] [*Library of Congress*] (LCLS)
WyCaD ...... Wyoming School for the Deaf, Casper, WY [*Library symbol*] [*Library of Congress*] (LCLS)
WyCaGS.... Church of Jesus Christ of Latter-Day Saints, Genealogical Society Library, Casper Branch, Casper, WY [*Library symbol*] [*Library of Congress*] (LCLS)
WYCB .... Washington, DC [*AM radio station call letters*]
WYCC .... Chicago, IL [*Television station call letters*]
WyCC .... Laramie County Community College, Cheyenne, WY [*Library symbol*] [*Library of Congress*] (LCLS)
WYCC .... Write Your Congressman Club (EA)
WyCDA .... Wyoming Department of Agriculture, Cheyenne, WY [*Library symbol*] [*Library of Congress*] (LCLS)
WyCDE .... Wyoming Department of Education, Cheyenne, WY [*Library symbol*] [*Library of Congress*] (LCLS)
WYCE ...... Wyoming, MI [*FM radio station call letters*]
WYCF....... World Youth Crusade for Freedom (EA)
WYCFD..... World Youth Congress on Food and Development (EAIO)
WyCGF...... Wyoming Game and Fish Commission, Cheyenne, WY [*Library symbol*] [*Library of Congress*] (LCLS)
WyCGS...... Church of Jesus Christ of Latter-Day Saints, Genealogical Society Library, Cheyenne Branch, Cheyenne, WY [*Library symbol*] [*Library of Congress*] (LCLS)
WyCHD..... Wyoming Highway Department, Cheyenne, WY [*Library symbol*] [*Library of Congress*] (LCLS)
Wychowanie M Szkole ... Wychowanie Muzyczne w Szkole [*A publication*]
WyCHS ..... Wyoming Department of Health and Social Services, Cheyenne, WY [*Library symbol*] [*Library of Congress*] (LCLS)
WYCL........ Boyertown, PA [*FM radio station call letters*]
WYCM ...... Murfreesboro, NC [*AM radio station call letters*]
WyCMS.... Laramie County Medical Society, Cheyenne, WY [*Library symbol*] [*Library of Congress*] (LCLS)
WYCO .... Wausau, WI [*FM radio station call letters*]
WyCoB ...... Buffalo Bill Museum, Cody, WY [*Library symbol*] [*Library of Congress*] (LCLS)
WyCoGS.... Church of Jesus Christ of Latter-Day Saints, Genealogical Society Library, Cody Branch, Cody, WY [*Library symbol*] [*Library of Congress*] (LCLS)
WYCQ....... Shelbyville, TN [*FM radio station call letters*]
WYCR .... York-Hanover, PA [*FM radio station call letters*]
WYCS........ Yorktown, VA [*FM radio station call letters*]
WyCSE...... State Engineer's Office, Cheyenne, WY [*Library symbol*] [*Library of Congress*] (LCLS)
WYCV .... Granite Falls, NC [*AM radio station call letters*]
WyCV .... United States Veterans Administration Center, Cheyenne, WY [*Library symbol*] [*Library of Congress*] (LCLS)
Wy-D .... Wyoming State Documents, Cheyenne, WY [*Library symbol*] [*Library of Congress*] (LCLS)
WYDC ...... Corning, NY [*Television station call letters*]
WYDE....... Birmingham, AL [*AM radio station call letters*]
WYDH....... Atmore, AL [*FM radio station call letters*]
Wy Dic....... Wyatt's Dickens' Chancery Reports [*A publication*] (DLA)
Wy Dick.... Dickens' English Chancery Reports, by Wyatt [*A publication*] (DLA)
WYDIWYG ... What You Digitize Is What You Get
WYDM...... Batavia, NY [*Television station call letters*]

WYDN....... Worcester, MA [*Television station call letters*]
WyDo......... Converse County Library, Douglas, WY [*Library symbol*] [*Library of Congress*] (LCLS)
WYDO....... Greenville, NC [*Television station call letters*]
WYDP .... Orange Park, FL [*Television station call letters*]
WYDS .... Decatur, IL [*FM radio station call letters*]
Wydz Mat Fiz Chem Uniw Poznan Ser Fiz ... Wydzial Matematyki Fizyki i Chemii Uniwersytet Imeni Adama Mickiewicza w Poznaniu Seria Fizyka [*A publication*]
WYE .... Yengema [*Sierra Leone*] [*Airport symbol*] (OAG)
WYEA .... Sylacauga, AL [*AM radio station call letters*]
Wye Coll Dep Hop Res Annu Rep ... Wye College. Department of Hop Research. Annual Report [*A publication*]
WYED .... Goldsboro, NC [*Television station call letters*]
WY Energy Ext Serv Update ... Wyoming. Energy Extension Service. Update [*A publication*]
WYEP........ Pittsburgh, PA [*FM radio station call letters*]
WYER .... Mount Carmel, IL [*AM radio station call letters*]
WYES........ New Orleans, LA [*Television station call letters*]
WyEvGS.... Church of Jesus Christ of Latter-Day Saints, Genealogical Society Library, Evanston Branch, Evanston, WY [*Library symbol*] [*Library of Congress*] (LCLS)
WyEvSH.... Wyoming State Hospital, Evanston, WY [*Library symbol*] [*Library of Congress*] (LCLS)
WYEZ........ Elkhart, IN [*FM radio station call letters*]
WYF .... World Youth Forum [*Defunct*] (EA)
WYFA....... Waynesboro, GA [*FM radio station call letters*]
WYFB........ Gainesville, FL [*FM radio station call letters*]
WYFC....... Clinton, TN [*FM radio station call letters*]
WYFD .... Decatur, AL [*FM radio station call letters*]
WYFE........ Tarpon Springs, FL [*FM radio station call letters*]
WyFEW..... United States Air Force, Francis E. Warren Air Force Base, Cheyenne, WY [*Library symbol*] [*Library of Congress*] (LCLS)
WyFEW-I ... United States Air Force Institute of Technology, Detachment 9, Francis E. Warren Air Force Base, Cheyenne, WY [*Library symbol*] [*Library of Congress*] (LCLS)
WYFF........ Greenville, SC [*Television station call letters*]
WYFG .... Gaffney, SC [*FM radio station call letters*]
WYFH .... North Charleston, SC [*FM radio station call letters*]
WYFI........ Norfolk, VA [*FM radio station call letters*]
WYFJ .... Ashland, VA [*FM radio station call letters*]
WYFK....... Columbus, GA [*FM radio station call letters*]
WYFL .... Henderson, NC [*FM radio station call letters*]
WyFlL........ Fort Laramie Historic Site, Fort Laramie, WY [*Library symbol*] [*Library of Congress*] (LCLS)
WYFM ...... Sharon, PA [*FM radio station call letters*]
WYFN .... Nashville, TN [*AM radio station call letters*]
WYFO .... Lakeland, FL [*FM radio station call letters*]
WYFS........ Savannah, GA [*FM radio station call letters*]
WYFT........ Luray, VA [*FM radio station call letters*]
WYFV........ Cayce, SC [*FM radio station call letters*]
WYFX....... Boynton Beach, FL [*AM radio station call letters*]
WYFY........ Fisher, WV [*FM radio station call letters*]
WYFZ........ Evans, GA [*FM radio station call letters*]
WYG .... Wyoming Airlines Ltd. [*Denver, CO*] [*FAA designator*] (FAAC)
WYGC....... Gainesville, FL [*FM radio station call letters*]
WYGH....... Paris, KY [*AM radio station call letters*]
WYGINS... What You Get Is No Surprise [*Pronounced "wiggins"*] [*Coined by Dave Tarrant, president of Lotus Development Corp.'s graphics products group*]
WYGL .... Elizabethville, PA [*FM radio station call letters*]
WYGL .... Selinsgrove, PA [*AM radio station call letters*]
WYGO....... Madisonville, TN [*FM radio station call letters*]
WYGR .... Wyoming, MI [*AM radio station call letters*]
WYHS....... Hollywood, FL [*Television station call letters*]
WYHT....... Mansfield, OH [*FM radio station call letters*]
WYHY....... Lebanon, TN [*FM radio station call letters*]
WYII........ Williamsport, MD [*FM radio station call letters*]
WYIN........ Gary, IN [*Television station call letters*]
WYJCA ..... Wool Yarn Jobbers Credit Association [*Defunct*] (EA)
WYJD....... Brewton, AL [*FM radio station call letters*]
WYJZ........ Pittsburgh, PA [*AM radio station call letters*]
WYKC .... Grenada, MS [*AM radio station call letters*]
WyKc......... Johnson County Library, Kaycee Branch, Kaycee, WY [*Library symbol*] [*Library of Congress*] (LCLS)
WyKe......... Lincoln County Library, Kemmerer, WY [*Library symbol*] [*Library of Congress*] (LCLS)
Wykeham Eng Technol Ser ... Wykeham Engineering and Technology Series [*A publication*]
Wykeham Sci Ser ... Wykeham Science Series [*A publication*]
WYKK .... Quitman, MS [*FM radio station call letters*]
WYKM ...... Rupert, WV [*AM radio station call letters*]
WYKO....... Sabana Grande, PR [*AM radio station call letters*]
WYKR .... Haverhill, NH [*FM radio station call letters*]
WYKR .... Wells River, VT [*AM radio station call letters*]
WYKS........ Gainesville, FL [*FM radio station call letters*]
WYKX .... Escanaba, MI [*FM radio station call letters*]
WYKY .... Columbus, WI [*FM radio station call letters*]
WYKZ .... Beaufort, SC [*FM radio station call letters*]

WYL .... Laramie County Library System, Cheyenne, WY [*OCLC symbol*] (OCLC)
WYL .... Wyle Laboratories [*NYSE symbol*] (SPSG)
WyLan .... Fremont County Library, Lander, WY [*Library symbol*] [*Library of Congress*] (LCLS)
WyLanT .... Wyoming State Training School, Lander, WY [*Library symbol*] [*Library of Congress*] (LCLS)
WyLar........ Albany County Public Library, Laramie, WY [*Library symbol*] [*Library of Congress*] (LCLS)
WyLarBM ... United States Bureau of Mines, Laramie Petroleum Research Center, Laramie, WY [*Library symbol*] [*Library of Congress*] (LCLS)
WyLarHN ... Wyoming Health Science Network, University of Wyoming, Laramie, WY [*Library symbol*] [*Library of Congress*] (LCLS)
WyLarSh ... Sherwood Hall, Laramie, WY [*Library symbol*] [*Library of Congress*] (LCLS)
WyLarSM ... Saint Matthew's Cathedral, Laramie, WY [*Library symbol*] [*Library of Congress*] (LCLS)
WYLD .... New Orleans, LA [*AM radio station call letters*]
WYLD-FM ... New Orleans, LA [*FM radio station call letters*]
WyleLb ...... Wyle Laboratories [*Associated Press abbreviation*] (APAG)
WYLF........ Penn Yan, NY [*AM radio station call letters*]
WYLIWYS ... Where You Look Is What You Select
WY LJ .... Wyoming Law Journal [*A publication*]
WYLL........ Des Plaines, IL [*FM radio station call letters*]
WYLO .... Jackson, WI [*AM radio station call letters*]
WyLoGS.... Church of Jesus Christ of Latter-Day Saints, Genealogical Society Library, Lovell Branch, Lovell, WY [*Library symbol*] [*Library of Congress*] (LCLS)
WYLR....... Glens Falls, NY [*FM radio station call letters*]
WYLS........ York, AL [*AM radio station call letters*]
WYLT........ Raleigh, NC [*FM radio station call letters*]
WyLu .... Niobrara County Library, Lusk, WY [*Library symbol*] [*Library of Congress*] (LCLS)
WYLV....... Alcoa, TN [*FM radio station call letters*]
WYLV....... Wheat Yellow Leaf Virus [*Plant pathology*]
WYM......... Wyoming Health Science Network, Laramie, WY [*OCLC symbol*] (OCLC)
Wyman...... Wyman's Reports [*India*] [*A publication*] (DLA)
WYMB ..... Manning, SC [*AM radio station call letters*]
WYMC...... Mayfield, KY [*AM radio station call letters*]
WYMC...... Wickliffe, KY [*FM radio station call letters*]
WYMG...... Jacksonville, IL [*FM radio station call letters*]
WYMJ....... Beavercreek, OH [*FM radio station call letters*]
WYMK...... Tunkhannock, PA [*FM radio station call letters*]
WYMN...... Wyman-Gordon Co. [*NASDAQ symbol*] (NQ)
WYMS ...... Milwaukee, WI [*FM radio station call letters*]
WYMT ...... Hazard, KY [*Television station call letters*]
WYMV ...... Wheat Yellow Mosaic Virus [*Plant pathology*]
WYMX...... Greenwood, MS [*FM radio station call letters*]
WYMY ...... Bedford, VA [*FM radio station call letters*]
WYN......... Walwyn, Inc. [*Toronto Stock Exchange symbol*]
WYN......... Wyndham [*Australia*] [*Airport symbol*]
WYNA ...... Tabor City, NC [*FM radio station call letters*]
WYNB ...... Wyoming National Bancorporation [*NASDAQ symbol*] (NQ)
WYNC....... Yanceyville, NC [*AM radio station call letters*]
WYND....... De Land, FL [*AM radio station call letters*]
WYND....... Hatteras, NC [*FM radio station call letters*]
WYNE....... Kimberly, WI [*AM radio station call letters*]
WyNe......... Weston County Public Library, Newcastle, WY [*Library symbol*] [*Library of Congress*] (LCLS)
WYNF....... Tampa, FL [*FM radio station call letters*]
WYNG....... Evansville, IN [*FM radio station call letters*]
WYNI .... Monroeville, AL [*AM radio station call letters*]
WYNK....... Baton Rouge, LA [*AM radio station call letters*]
WYNK-FM ... Baton Rouge, LA [*FM radio station call letters*]
WYNN...... Florence, SC [*AM radio station call letters*]
Wynne Bov ... Wynne's Bovill's Patent Cases [*A publication*] (DLA)
Wynne Eun ... Wynne's Eunomus [*A publication*] (DLA)
WYNN-FM ... Florence, SC [*FM radio station call letters*]
Wynns........ Wynn's International, Inc. [*Associated Press abbreviation*] (APAG)
WYNO....... Nelsonville, OH [*AM radio station call letters*]
WYNS .... Lehighton, PA [*AM radio station call letters*]
WYNT .... Upper Sandusky, OH [*FM radio station call letters*]
WYNU....... Milan, TN [*FM radio station call letters*]
WYNX....... Smyrna, GA [*AM radio station call letters*]
WYNY .... Lake Success, NY [*FM radio station call letters*]
WYNZ....... Portland, ME [*AM radio station call letters*]
WYNZ....... Westbrook, ME [*FM radio station call letters*]
WYO......... US Aviation [*Riverton, WY*] [*FAA designator*] (FAAC)
WYO......... Wyoming (AAG)
WYO......... Wyoming Array [*Wyoming*] [*Seismograph station code, US Geological Survey*] (SEIS)
Wyo........... Wyoming Reports [*A publication*] (DLA)
Wyo........... Wyoming Reports [*A publication*]
Wyo Ag Exp ... Wyoming. Agricultural Experiment Station. Publications [*A publication*]
Wyo Agric Exp Stn Bull ... Wyoming. Agricultural Experiment Station. Bulletin [*A publication*]

Wyo Agric Exp Stn Cir ... Wyoming. Agricultural Experiment Station. Circular [*A publication*]

Wyo Agric Exp Stn Res J ... Wyoming. Agricultural Experiment Station. Research Journal [*A publication*]

Wyo Agric Exp Stn Sci Monogr ... Wyoming. Agricultural Experiment Station. Science Monograph [*A publication*]

Wyo Agric Ext Serv Bull ... Wyoming. Agricultural Extension Service. Bulletin [*A publication*]

WYOC....... High Springs, FL [*FM radio station call letters*]

Wyo Game Fish Comm Bull ... Wyoming. Game and Fish Commission. Bulletin [*A publication*]

Wyo Geol Assoc Earth Sci Bull ... Wyoming Geological Association. Earth Science Bulletin [*A publication*]

Wyo Geol Assoc Guideb Ann Field Conf ... Wyoming Geological Association. Guidebook. Annual Field Conference [*A publication*]

Wyo Geol Survey Bull Rept Inv ... Wyoming. Geological Survey. Bulletin. Report of Investigations [*A publication*]

Wyo Geol Surv Prelim Rep ... Wyoming. Geological Survey. Preliminary Report [*A publication*]

Wyo Geol Surv Rep Invest ... Wyoming. Geological Survey. Report of Investigations [*A publication*]

Wyo G Off B Wyo St G ... Wyoming. Geologist's Office. Bulletin. Wyoming State Geologist [*A publication*]

Wyo His Col ... Wyoming State Historical Department. Proceedings and Collections [*A publication*]

Wyo Issues ... Wyoming Issues [*A publication*]

Wyo Lib Roundup ... Wyoming Library Roundup [*A publication*]

Wyo L J ..... Wyoming Law Journal [*A publication*]

WYOM...... Wyoming (ROG)

Wyom........ Wyoming Reports [*A publication*]   (DLA)

Wyoming Geol Survey Prelim Rept ... Wyoming. Geological Survey. Preliminary Report [*A publication*]

Wyoming Hist G Soc Pr Pub ... Wyoming Historical and Geological Society. Proceedings and Collections. Publications [*A publication*]

Wyo Nurse ... Wyoming Nurse [*Formerly, Wyoming Nurses Newsletter*] [*A publication*]

Wyo Nurses News ... Wyoming Nurses Newsletter [*Later, Wyoming Nurse*] [*A publication*]

WYOO....... Springfield, FL [*FM radio station call letters*]

WYOR....... Brentwood, TN [*AM radio station call letters*]

Wyo Range Manage ... Wyoming Range Management [*A publication*]

Wyo Roundup ... Wyoming Roundup [*A publication*]

WYOS .... Nanticoke, PA [*FM radio station call letters*]

Wyo Sess Laws ... Session Laws. Wyoming [*A publication*]

Wyo Sess Laws ... Session Laws of Wyoming [*A publication*]   (DLA)

Wyo Stat .... Wyoming Statutes [*A publication*]   (ILCA)

Wyo Stat .... Wyoming Statutes [*A publication*]

Wyo St G ... Wyoming State Geologist [*A publication*]

WYOU....... Bangor, ME [*FM radio station call letters*]

WYOU....... Scranton, PA [*Television station call letters*]

Wyo Univ Dep Geol Contrib Geol ... Wyoming University. Department of Geology. Contributions to Geology [*A publication*]

Wyo Univ Nat Resour Res Inst Bull ... Wyoming University. Natural Resources Research Institute. Bulletin [*A publication*]

Wyo Univ Nat Resour Res Inst Inf Cir ... Wyoming University. Natural Resources Research Institute. Information Circular [*A publication*]

Wyo Univ Natur Resour Inst Inform Circ ... Wyoming University. Natural Resources Institute. Information Circular [*A publication*]

Wyo Univ Sch Mines B ... Wyoming University. School of Mines. Bulletin [*A publication*]

Wyo Univ Water Resour Res Inst Water Resour Ser ... Wyoming University. Water Resources Research Institute. Water Resources Series [*A publication*]

Wyo Wild Life ... Wyoming Wild Life [*A publication*]

WYOY....... Rutland, VT [*FM radio station call letters*]

WYPA .... South Boston, VA [*FM radio station call letters*]

WYPC........ Wellston, OH [*AM radio station call letters*]

WyPdS....... Sublette County Library, Pinedale, WY [*Library symbol*] [*Library of Congress*]   (LCLS)

WYPL........ Memphis, TN [*FM radio station call letters*]

WyPN........ Northwest Community College, Powell, WY [*Library symbol*] [*Library of Congress*]   (LCLS)

WYPR........ Avis, PA [*FM radio station call letters*]

Wy Pr R ..... Wyatt's Practical Register in Chancery [*England*] [*A publication*]   (DLA)

WYR .... Waybo Resources Ltd. [*Vancouver Stock Exchange symbol*]

WYR .... [*The*] West Yorkshire Regiment [*Army*] [*British*]

WYRE .... Annapolis, MD [*AM radio station call letters*]

WyRi.......... Fremont County Library, Riverton Branch, Riverton, WY [*Library symbol*] [*Library of Congress*]   (LCLS)

WyRiC .... Central Wyoming Community College, Riverton, WY [*Library symbol*] [*Library of Congress*]   (LCLS)

WYRK .... Buffalo, NY [*FM radio station call letters*]

WYRN........ Louisburg, NC [*AM radio station call letters*]

WYRQ .... Little Falls, MN [*FM radio station call letters*]

WYRS........ Rock Hill, SC [*AM radio station call letters*]

WyRsW ..... Western Wyoming College, Rock Springs, WY [*Library symbol*] [*Library of Congress*]   (LCLS)

WYRU .... Red Springs, NC [*AM radio station call letters*]

WYRV .... Cedar Bluff, VA [*AM radio station call letters*]

WYRY .... Hinsdale, NH [*FM radio station call letters*]

WYS .... West Yellowstone, MT [*Location identifier*] [*FAA*]   (FAAL)

WYS .... Wyandotte Southern Railroad Co. [*AAR code*]

WYS .... Wyse Technology [*NYSE symbol*]   (SPSG)

WYSE........ Wyse Technology [*San Jose, CA*] [*NASDAQ symbol*]   (NQ)

WYSH .... Clinton, TN [*AM radio station call letters*]

WyShCD ... Wheden Cancer Detection Foundation, Sheridan, WY [*Library symbol*] [*Library of Congress*]   (LCLS)

WyShF....... Sheridan County Fulmer Public Library, Sheridan, WY [*Library symbol*] [*Library of Congress*]   (LCLS)

WyShGS.... Wyoming Girls' School, Sheridan, WY [*Library symbol*] [*Library of Congress*]   (LCLS)

WyShMH ... Northern Wyoming Mental Health Center, Sheridan, WY [*Library symbol*] [*Library of Congress*]   (LCLS)

WyShS....... Sheridan College, Sheridan, WY [*Library symbol*] [*Library of Congress*]   (LCLS)

WyShV ...... United States Veterans Administration Hospital, Sheridan, WY [*Library symbol*] [*Library of Congress*]   (LCLS)

WYSIAYG ... What You See Is All You Get

WYSIMOLWYG ... What You See Is More or Less What You Get [*Pronounced "wizzi-mole-wig"*]

WYSIWYG ... What You See Is What You Get [*Pronounced "wizziwig"*] [*Indicates that video display on word processor bears a high-quality resemblance to printed page that will result*]

WYSL........ Avon, NY [*AM radio station call letters*]

WYSN .... Central City, PA [*FM radio station call letters*]

WYSO .... Yellow Springs, OH [*FM radio station call letters*]

WYSP........ Philadelphia, PA [*FM radio station call letters*]

WYSS .... Sault Ste. Marie, MI [*AM radio station call letters*]

WYSU .... Youngstown, OH [*FM radio station call letters*]

WYSY-FM ... Aurora, IL [*FM radio station call letters*]

WYT .... Wyandotte Terminal Railroad Co. [*AAR code*]

WYTE........ Whiting, WI [*FM radio station call letters*]

WYTH....... Madison, GA [*AM radio station call letters*]

Wythe .... Wythe's Virginia Chancery Reports [*1788-99*] [*A publication*]   (DLA)

Wythe Ch (VA) ... Wythe's Virginia Chancery Reports [*1788-99*] [*A publication*]   (DLA)

Wythe Cty Hist Rev ... Wythe County Historical Review [*A publication*]

Wythes CC ... Wythe's Virginia Chancery Reports [*1788-99*] [*A publication*]   (DLA)

Wythe's R .. Wythe's Virginia Chancery Reports [*1788-99*] [*A publication*]   (DLA)

Wythe's Rep ... Wythe's Virginia Chancery Reports [*1788-99*] [*A publication*]   (DLA)

Wythe (VA) ... Wythe's Virginia Chancery Reports [*1788-99*] [*A publication*]   (DLA)

WyThP ...... Wyoming Pioneer Home, Thermopolis, WY [*Library symbol*] [*Library of Congress*]   (LCLS)

WYTI......... Rocky Mount, VA [*AM radio station call letters*]

WyTJ......... Wesleyan Theological Journal [*A publication*]

WYTK .... Washington, PA [*FM radio station call letters*]

WYTL........ Harbor Tug, Small [*Coast Guard symbol*]   (DNAB)

WYTM ...... Buoy Tender [*Coast Guard symbol*]   (DNAB)

WYTM ...... Fayetteville, TN [*FM radio station call letters*]

WYTM ...... Floating Workship [*Coast Guard symbol*]   (DNAB)

WYTM ...... Freight Ship [*Coast Guard symbol*]   (DNAB)

WYTM ...... Harbor Craft [*Coast Guard symbol*]   (DNAB)

WYTM ...... Harbor Tug, Medium [*Coast Guard symbol*]   (DNAB)

WYTM ...... Inshore Patrol Cutter [*Coast Guard symbol*]   (DNAB)

WYTM ...... Lighthouse Tender [*Coast Guard symbol*]   (DNAB)

WYTM ...... Patrol Boat [*Coast Guard symbol*]   (DNAB)

WYTM ...... Revenue Cutter [*Coast Guard symbol*]   (DNAB)

WYTM ...... Revenue Steamer [*Coast Guard symbol*]   (DNAB)

WYTM ...... Seized Boat [*Coast Guard symbol*]   (DNAB)

WYTM ...... Station Ship [*Coast Guard symbol*]   (DNAB)

WYTM ...... Steam Derrick [*Coast Guard symbol*]   (DNAB)

WYTN ...... Youngstown, OH [*FM radio station call letters*]

WyToE ...... Eastern Wyoming College, Torrington, WY [*Library symbol*] [*Library of Congress*]   (LCLS)

WyTs .... Washakie County Library, Ten Sleep Branch, Ten Sleep, WY [*Library symbol*] [*Library of Congress*]   (LCLS)

WYTV ...... Youngstown, OH [*Television station call letters*]

WYTW ...... Cadillac, MI [*FM radio station call letters*]

WyU.......... University of Wyoming, Laramie, WY [*Library symbol*] [*Library of Congress*]   (LCLS)

WYU.......... University of Wyoming, Library, Laramie, WY [*OCLC symbol*]   (OCLC)

wyu............ Wyoming [*MARC country of publication code*] [*Library of Congress*]   (LCCP)

WyU-Ar..... University of Wyoming, Archive of Contemporary History, Laramie, WY [*Library symbol*] [*Library of Congress*]   (LCLS)

WyUp .... Weston County Public Library, Upton Branch, Upton, WY [*Library symbol*] [*Library of Congress*]   (LCLS)

WYUR .... Ripon, WI [*FM radio station call letters*]

WYUS .... Milford, DE [*AM radio station call letters*]

WYUT .... Herkimer, NY [*AM radio station call letters*]

WYUT-FM ... Herkimer, NY [*FM radio station call letters*]

WYUU....... Safety Harbor, FL [*FM radio station call letters*]

WYVC .... Camden, AL [*FM radio station call letters*]

WYVE .... Wytheville, VA [*AM radio station call letters*]
WYVN....... Martinsburg, WV [*Television station call letters*]
WYW .... Weltwirtschaft [*A publication*]
WYWCA ... World Young Women's Christian Association   (DI)
WyWo........ Washakie County Library, Worland, WY [*Library symbol*]
         [*Library of Congress*]   (LCLS)
WyWoI ...... Wyoming Industrial Institute, Worland, WY [*Library symbol*]
         [*Library of Congress*]   (LCLS)
WYWR ...... Campbell, OH [*AM radio station call letters*]
WYWY ...... Barbourville, KY [*AM radio station call letters*]
WYWY-FM ... Barbourville, KY [*FM radio station call letters*]
WYXC .... Cartersville, GA [*AM radio station call letters*]
WYXI........ Athens, TN [*AM radio station call letters*]
WYXL .... Ithaca, NY [*FM radio station call letters*]
WYXR .... Philadelphia, PA [*FM radio station call letters*]
WYXX ...... Holland, MI [*FM radio station call letters*]
WYYA .... Olive Branch, MS [*AM radio station call letters*]
WYYB ...... Dickson, TN [*FM radio station call letters*]
WYYC .... West Yorkshire Yeomanry Cavalry [*British military*]   (DMA)
WYYD ...... Amherst, VA [*FM radio station call letters*]
WYYR .... Spartanburg, SC [*AM radio station call letters*]
WYYY .... Syracuse, NY [*FM radio station call letters*]
WYYZ .... Jasper, GA [*AM radio station call letters*]
WYZ.......... Wyoming State Library, Cheyenne, WY [*OCLC symbol*]   (OCLC)
WYZB....... Mary Esther, FL [*FM radio station call letters*]
WYZD ...... Dobson, NC [*AM radio station call letters*]
WYZE....... Atlanta, GA [*AM radio station call letters*]
WYZZ ...... Bloomington, IL [*Television station call letters*]
WZ............ Royal Swazi National Airways Corp. [*Swaziland*] [*ICAO designator*]   (FAAC)
WZ............ War Zone
Wz............ Warenzeichen [*Trademark*] [*German*]
WZ............ Wiedza i Zycie [*A publication*]
WZ............ Wissenschaftliche Zeitschrift [*A publication*]
W i d Z .... Wort in der Zeit [*A publication*]
WZ............ Wort in der Zeit [*A publication*]
WZa.......... Wide Zone Alpha   (MAE)
WZAC .... Danville, WV [*FM radio station call letters*]
WZAC .... Madison, WV [*AM radio station call letters*]
WZAD .... Wurtsboro, NY [*FM radio station call letters*]
WZAK ...... Cleveland, OH [*FM radio station call letters*]
WZAL........ McDonough, GA [*AM radio station call letters*]
WZAM ...... Norfolk, VA [*AM radio station call letters*]
WZAO....... Moundsville, WV [*AM radio station call letters*]
WZAP....... Bristol, VA [*AM radio station call letters*]
WZAR .... Ponce, PR [*FM radio station call letters*]
WZAT .... Savannah, GA [*FM radio station call letters*]
WZAZ ...... Jacksonville, FL [*AM radio station call letters*]
WZBA ...... Moss Point, MS [*FM radio station call letters*]
WZBB....... Rocky Mount, VA [*FM radio station call letters*]
WZBC........ Newton, MA [*FM radio station call letters*]
WZBG ...... Litchfield, CT [*FM radio station call letters*]
WZBH ...... Georgetown, DE [*FM radio station call letters*]
WZBO ...... Edenton, NC [*AM radio station call letters*]
WZBO-FM ... Edenton, NC [*FM radio station call letters*]
WZBQ ...... Jasper, AL [*FM radio station call letters*]
WZBQ ...... Tuscaloosa, AL [*AM radio station call letters*]
WZBR ...... Ebenezer, MS [*FM radio station call letters*]
WZBS........ Ponce, PR [*AM radio station call letters*]
WZBT........ Gettysburg, PA [*FM radio station call letters*]
WZBX ...... Sylvania, GA [*FM radio station call letters*]
WZCR ...... Fort Myers Beach, FL [*FM radio station call letters*]
WZCT........ Scottsboro, AL [*AM radio station call letters*]
WzD.......... Wege zur Dichtung [*A publication*]
WZDM....... Vincennes, IN [*FM radio station call letters*]
WZDQ ...... Humboldt, TN [*FM radio station call letters*]
WZDX ...... Huntsville, AL [*Television station call letters*]
WZEA ...... Hampton, NH [*FM radio station call letters*]
WZEE........ Madison, WI [*FM radio station call letters*]
W Zegel .... Wetboek der Zegelrechten [*A publication*]
WZEL........ Young Harris, GA [*AM radio station call letters*]
WZEP........ De Funiak Springs, FL [*AM radio station call letters*]
WZEW ...... Fairhope, AL [*FM radio station call letters*]
WZEZ........ Nashville, TN [*FM radio station call letters*]
WZFL........ Centreville, MS [*AM radio station call letters*]
WZFL-FM ... Centreville, MS [*FM radio station call letters*]
WZFM...... Narrows, VA [*FM radio station call letters*]
WZFR........ Tomah, WI [*FM radio station call letters*]
WZFX....... Whiteville, NC [*FM radio station call letters*]
WZG.......... Wissenschaftliche Zeitschrift fuer Juedische Geschichte [*A publication*]   (BJA)
WZGC .... Atlanta, GA [*FM radio station call letters*]
WZGO....... Portage, PA [*AM radio station call letters*]
WZHT ...... Troy, AL [*FM radio station call letters*]
WZI .... Winzen International, Inc. [*Vancouver Stock Exchange symbol*]
WZID .... Manchester, NH [*FM radio station call letters*]
WZIP........ Akron, OH [*FM radio station call letters*]
WZJN....... Jackson, NH [*FM radio station call letters*]
WZJP .... Spencer, TN [*FM radio station call letters*]
WZJQ........ McClellanville, SC [*FM radio station call letters*]

WZJS .... Banner Elk, NC [*FM radio station call letters*]
WZJT .... Wissenschaftliche Zeitschrift fuer Juedische Theologie [*A publication*]   (BJA)
WZJTh...... Wissenschaftliche Zeitschrift fuer Juedische Theologie [*A publication*]   (BJA)
WZJY .... Mt. Pleasant, SC [*AM radio station call letters*]
WZKB ...... Wallace, NC [*FM radio station call letters*]
WZKM ...... Montgomery, WV [*FM radio station call letters*]
WZKO ...... Pineville, KY [*FM radio station call letters*]
WZKS........ Louisville, KY [*FM radio station call letters*]
WZKT .... Farmington, IL [*FM radio station call letters*]
WZKT .... Waynesboro, VA [*AM radio station call letters*]
WZKX ...... Poplarville, MS [*FM radio station call letters*]
WZKY ...... Albemarle, NC [*AM radio station call letters*]
WZKZ ...... Corning, NY [*FM radio station call letters*]
WZLA....... Abbeville, SC [*FM radio station call letters*]
WZLB....... Rome, NY [*AM radio station call letters*]
WZLE ...... Lorain, OH [*FM radio station call letters*]
WZLI .... Toccoa, GA [*FM radio station call letters*]
WZLM ...... Dadeville, AL [*FM radio station call letters*]
WZLQ ...... Tupelo, MS [*FM radio station call letters*]
WZLT .... Lexington, TN [*FM radio station call letters*]
WZLX .... Boston, MA [*FM radio station call letters*]
WZLY .... Wellesley, MA [*FM radio station call letters*]
WZLZ........ Quincy, IL [*FM radio station call letters*]
WZMB ...... Greenville, NC [*FM radio station call letters*]
WZMF ...... Danville, IL [*FM radio station call letters*]
WZMG ...... Opelika, AL [*AM radio station call letters*]
WZMP ...... Marion, MS [*FM radio station call letters*]
WZMQ ...... Key Largo, FL [*FM radio station call letters*]
WZMX ...... Hartford, CT [*FM radio station call letters*]
WZNF .... Rantoul, IL [*FM radio station call letters*]
WZNJ....... Demopolis, AL [*FM radio station call letters*]
WZNL ...... Norway, MI [*FM radio station call letters*]
WZNN ...... Rochester, NH [*AM radio station call letters*]
WZNPS...... William H. Zimmer Nuclear Power Station [*Also, ZPS*]   (NRCH)
WZNS ...... Dillon, SC [*FM radio station call letters*]
WZNT ...... San Juan, PR [*FM radio station call letters*]
WZNY ...... Augusta, GA [*FM radio station call letters*]
WZO.......... Wein Zollordnung [*Wine Duty Order*] [*German*]
WZO.......... World Zionist Organization [*Israel*]
WZOA....... Women's Zionist Organization of America
WZOB ...... Fort Payne, AL [*AM radio station call letters*]
WZOE ...... Princeton, IL [*AM radio station call letters*]
WZOE-FM ... Princeton, IL [*FM radio station call letters*]
WZOK ...... Rockford, IL [*FM radio station call letters*]
WZOL ...... Luquillo, PR [*FM radio station call letters*]
WZOM...... Defiance, OH [*FM radio station call letters*]
WZON...... Bangor, ME [*AM radio station call letters*]
WZOO....... Asheboro, NC [*AM radio station call letters*]
WZOO....... Edgewood, OH [*FM radio station call letters*]
WZOQ...... Wapakoneta, OH [*FM radio station call letters*]
WZOR ...... Immokalee, FL [*AM radio station call letters*]
WZOS ...... Oswego, NY [*FM radio station call letters*]
WZOT ...... Rockmart, GA [*AM radio station call letters*]
WZOU....... Boston, MA [*FM radio station call letters*]
WZOW ...... Goshen, IN [*FM radio station call letters*]
WZOZ ...... Oneonta, NY [*FM radio station call letters*]
WZPK....... Berlin, NH [*FM radio station call letters*]
WZPL........ Greenfield, IN [*FM radio station call letters*]
WZPQ ...... Jasper, AL [*AM radio station call letters*]
WZPR ...... Meadville, PA [*FM radio station call letters*]
WZQA ...... Flowood, MS [*AM radio station call letters*]
WZQD ...... Georgiana, AL [*FM radio station call letters*]
WZQF .... Lecanto, FL [*FM radio station call letters*]
WZQK ...... Coeburn, VA [*FM radio station call letters*]
WZQQ...... Hyden, KY [*FM radio station call letters*]
WZRC ...... New York, NY [*AM radio station call letters*]
WZRD ...... Chicago, IL [*FM radio station call letters*]
WZRH ...... Picayune, MS [*FM radio station call letters*]
WZRK ...... Hancock, MI [*FM radio station call letters*]
WZRO ...... Farmer City, IL [*FM radio station call letters*]
WZRQ ...... Ballston Spa, NY [*FM radio station call letters*]
WZRR ...... Birmingham, AL [*FM radio station call letters*]
WZRT........ Rutland, VT [*FM radio station call letters*]
WZRX ...... Jackson, MS [*AM radio station call letters*]
WZRZ ...... Hamilton, OH [*FM radio station call letters*]
WZS.......... Widespan Zoom Stereoscope   (SAA)
WZSH ...... South Bristol Township, NY [*FM radio station call letters*]
WZST .... Appomattox, VA [*FM radio station call letters*]
WZT .... Wartegg-Zeichentest [*Wartegg Symbol Test*] [*German*] [*Psychology*]
WZTA ...... Miami Beach, FL [*FM radio station call letters*]
WZTN ...... Montgomery, AL [*AM radio station call letters*]
WZTR........ Milwaukee, WI [*FM radio station call letters*]
WZTT........ Rhinelander, WI [*FM radio station call letters*]
WZTU ...... Cocoa Beach, FL [*FM radio station call letters*]
WZTV ...... Nashville, TN [*Television station call letters*]
WZTZ........ Elba, AL [*FM radio station call letters*]
WZVN....... Lowell, IN [*FM radio station call letters*]

WZVU .... Long Branch, NJ [*FM radio station call letters*]
WZW .... Worcester Public Library, Worcester, MA [*OCLC symbol*]   (OCLC)
WZWA ...... Clarksburg, WV [*FM radio station call letters*]
WZWB ...... Berwick, PA [*FM radio station call letters*]
WZWW ..... Bellefonte, PA [*FM radio station call letters*]
WZWZ ...... Kokomo, IN [*FM radio station call letters*]
WZXA .... Sturtevant, WI [*FM radio station call letters*]
WZXK .... Ashland, VA [*Television station call letters*]
WZXL .... Wildwood, NJ [*FM radio station call letters*]
WZXS .... Topsail Beach, NC [*FM radio station call letters*]
WZXV .... Palmyra, NY [*FM radio station call letters*]
WZY .... Nassau [*Bahamas*] [*Airport symbol*]   (OAG)
WZYG .... Ellettsville, IN [*FM radio station call letters*]
WZYP .... Athens, AL [*FM radio station call letters*]
WZYQ .... Braddock Heights, MD [*FM radio station call letters*]
WZYX .... Cowan, TN [*AM radio station call letters*]
WZZA .... Tuscumbia, AL [*AM radio station call letters*]
WZZB .... Seymour, IN [*AM radio station call letters*]
WZZC .... Benton, PA [*FM radio station call letters*]
WZZD .... Philadelphia, PA [*AM radio station call letters*]
WZZE .... Glen Mills, PA [*FM radio station call letters*]
WZZF .... Hopkinsville, KY [*FM radio station call letters*]
WZZI .... Manteo, NC [*FM radio station call letters*]
WZZJ .... Moss Point, MS [*AM radio station call letters*]
WZZK .... Birmingham, AL [*AM radio station call letters*]
WZZK-FM ... Birmingham, AL [*FM radio station call letters*]
WZZM ...... Corinth, NY [*FM radio station call letters*]
WZZM ...... Grand Rapids, MI [*Television station call letters*]
WZZO ...... Bethlehem, PA [*FM radio station call letters*]
WZZQ .... Terre Haute, IN [*FM radio station call letters*]
WZZR .... Stuart, FL [*FM radio station call letters*]
WZZT .... Morrison, IL [*FM radio station call letters*]
WZZU .... Burlington-Graham, NC [*FM radio station call letters*]
WZZV .... Olyphant, PA [*FM radio station call letters*]
WZZX .... Lineville, AL [*AM radio station call letters*]
WZZY .... Winchester, IN [*FM radio station call letters*]
WZZZ .... Fulton, NY [*AM radio station call letters*]

X

X .... Amino Acid, Unknown or Other [*Symbol*] [*Biochemistry*]
X .... Any Point on a Great Circle
X .... Arithmetic Mean [*Statistics*]
X .... By [*As in 9 x 12*]
X .... Central Drug Research Institute [*India*] [*Research code symbol*]
X .... Chile [*IYRU nationality code*]   (IYR)
X .... Christus [*Christ*] [*Latin*]
X .... Closed at All Times (Except When in Actual Use) [*Ship's fittings classification*]
X .... Cross [*As in X-roads*]
X .... Crystal Cut [*Symbol*]   (DEN)
X .... Drill Sergeant [*Army skill qualification identifier*]   (INF)
X .... Ethnikon Agrotikon Komma Xiton [*National Agrarian Party "X"*] [*Political party*]   (PPE)
X .... Ex-Husband [*or Ex-Wife*] [*Slang*]
X .... Ex-Interest [*Without the right to interest*] [*Finance*]
X .... Examination [*Slang*]
X .... Exchange
X .... Exclusive [*Concession in a circus or carnival*]
X .... Exercise [*British military*]   (DMA)
X .... Exhibitions [*Trade fairs, etc.*] [*Public-performance tariff class*] [*British*]
X .... Exophoria Distance [*Ophthalmology*]
X .... Experimental [*Military*]   (AABC)
X .... Explosion [*Military*]   (CAAL)
X .... Export [*Economics*]
X .... Extension   (AAG)
X .... Extra
X .... Female Chromosome
X .... Frost
X .... Horizontal Deflection [*Symbol*]   (DEN)
X .... Index [*Data processing*]
X .... Intersect   (FAAC)
X .... Kienboeck's Unit [*of x-ray dosage*]   (AAMN)
X .... Kiss [*Correspondence*]
X .... Komma Xiton Ethnikis Antistasseos [*"X" National Resistance Party*] [*Political party*]   (PPE)
X .... Lateral [*RADAR*]
X .... Midweek Travel [*Airline fare code*]
X .... Mistake [*or Error*] [*Symbol*]
X .... No Protest [*Banking*]
X .... No-Wind Distance between Pressure Pattern Observations
X .... Parallactic Angle
X .... Persons under Eighteen [*Sixteen in some localities*] Not Admitted [*Movie rating*]
X .... Psychological Problem [*Classification system used by doctors on Ellis Island to detain, re-examine, and possibly deny entry to certain immigrants*]
X .... Raw Score [*Psychology*]
X .... Reactance [*Symbol*] [*IUPAC*]   (AAG)
X .... Research [*or Experimental*] [*Designation for all US military aircraft*]
X .... St. Andrew's Cross
X .... Simes [*Italy*] [*Research code symbol*]
X .... Strike [*Bowling symbol*]
X .... Submersible Craft [*Self-propelled*] [*Navy ship symbol*]
x .... Takes [*As in K x B - King Takes Bishop*] [*Chess*]
X .... Ten [*Roman numeral*]
X .... Times [*Multiplication sign*] [*Mathematics*]
X .... Toilet [*Slang*]
X .... Transistor [*Symbol*]   (DEN)
X .... Transmit
X .... [*The First*] Unknown Quantity [*Mathematics*]   (ROG)
X .... USX Corp. [*Formerly, US Steel Corp.*] [*NYSE symbol*] [*Wall Street slang name: "Steel"*]   (SPSG)
X .... X-Axis
X .... X-Ray   (KSC)
X .... X-Ray [*Phonetic alphabet*] [*Pre-World War II*] [*World War II*] [*International*]   (DSUE)
X .... X-Ray Assistant [*British military*]
X .... X Records [*Division of RCA-Victor*] [*Record label*]

X .... Xanthosine [*One-letter symbol; see Xao*]
X .... Xerxes [*Phonetic alphabet*] [*Royal Navy*] [*World War I*]   (DSUE)
X .... Xylem [*Botany*]
x .... Xylose [*As substituent on nucleoside*] [*Biochemistry*]
x .... Xylose [*One-letter symbol; see Xyl*]
5X .... Uganda [*Aircraft nationality and registration mark*]   (FAAC)
X (Cars) ..... Designation for General Motors front-wheel-drive cars [*Citation, Omega, Phoenix, Skylark*]
X (Hour)..... Hour at which shipping evacuation is ordered from major ports [*NATO exercises*]   (NATG)
X (Mode).... Extraordinary Mode   (MCD)
XA .... Aeronautical Radio, Inc. [*ICAO designator*]   (FAAC)
XA .... Auxiliary Amplifier   (AAG)
Xa .... Chiasma [*Genetics*]   (AAMN)
xa .... Christmas Island [*Indian Ocean*] [*MARC country of publication code*] [*Library of Congress*]   (LCCP)
XA .... Experimental (Air Force)
XA .... Extended Architecture [*Data processing*]
XA .... Mexico [*Aircraft nationality and registration mark*]   (FAAC)
XA .... Transmission Adapter   (MDG)
Xa .... Xanadu [*A publication*]
Xa .... Xanthine [*Biochemistry*]
XA .... Xanthurenic Acid [*Clinical chemistry*]
XAAM ...... Experimental Air-to-Air Missile [*Air Force, NASA*]
XAARAY... US Department of Agriculture. Agricultural Research Service. ARS [*A publication*]
XACIAH ... US Department of Agriculture. Plant Inventory [*A publication*]
XACIC...... X-Ray Attenuation Coefficient Information Center [*National Institute of Standards and Technology*]
XACT........ X Automatic Code Translation   (IEEE)
XAD.......... Experimental and Development
XADMAY ... US Air Force. Technical Documentary Report. SAM-TDR [*A publication*]
XADRAF... US Army. Diamond Ordnance Fuze Laboratories. Technical Report [*A publication*]
XAFH .... X-Band Antenna Feed Horn
XAFS .... X-Ray Absorption Fine Structure [*Organic chemistry*]
XAID .... ADI Electronics [*NASDAQ symbol*]   (NQ)
XAK .... Cargo Ship, Merchant Marine Manned
XAL .... Xenon Arc Lamp
XALNA ..... Research Note FPL. Forest Products Laboratory [*United States*] [*A publication*]
XAM.......... Merchant Ship Converted to a Minesweeper [*Navy symbol*] [*Obsolete*]
Xan............ Xanthine [*Biochemistry*]
XANES...... X-Ray Absorption Near-Edge Structure [*Spectroscopy*]
XANST..... Xanthium strumarium [*Cocklebur*]
xanth......... Xanthomatosis
Xao............ Xanthosine [*Also, X*] [*A nucleoside*]
XAP .... Chapeco [*Brazil*] [*Airport symbol*]   (OAG)
XAP .... Merchant Transport [*Ship symbol*]
XAPC........ Merchant Coastal Transport, Small [*Ship symbol*]
XARM ...... Cross Arm   (AAG)
XART........ Artagraph Reproduction Technology, Inc. [*NASDAQ symbol*]   (NQ)
XAS........... Experimental Air Specification Weapons [*Navy*]   (NG)
XAS........... X-Band Antenna System
XAS........... X-Ray Absorption Spectroscopy
XASM....... Experimental Air-to-Surface Missile [*Air Force, NASA*]
XAT .... X-Ray Analysis Trial
XAV .... Auxiliary Seaplane Tender [*Ship symbol*]
XAV .... Xavier University, Cincinnati, OH [*OCLC symbol*]   (OCLC)
XAY .... Camp Atterbury, IN [*Location identifier*] [*FAA*]   (FAAL)
xb .... Cocos [*Keeling*] Islands [*MARC country of publication code*] [*Library of Congress*]   (LCCP)
XB .... Crossbar [*Bell System*]
XB .... Experimental Bomber   (MCD)
XB .... Exploding Bridge-Wire
XB .... International Air Transport Association (IATA) [*ICAO designator*]   (ICDA)

XB .... Mexico [*Aircraft nationality and registration mark*] (FAAC)
XBAR........ Crossbar
XBASIC..... Extension of BASIC [*Data processing*]
XBB .... Berne Public Library, Berne, IN [*OCLC symbol*] (OCLC)
XBC .... "B" Corp. [*Toronto Stock Exchange symbol*]
XBC .... External Block Controller
XBE .... Shasta Air, Inc. [*Yreka, CA*] [*FAA designator*] (FAAC)
XBF............ Bird Leasing, Inc. [*North Andover, MA*] [*FAA designator*] (FAAC)
XBF............ Fort Wayne, IN [*Location identifier*] [*FAA*] (FAAL)
XBG .... Bogande [*Burkina Faso*] [*Airport symbol*] (OAG)
XBG .... National Jet Corp. [*West Mifflin, PA*] [*FAA designator*] (FAAC)
XBH........... Northern Airlines [*Vineyard Haven, MA*] [*FAA designator*] (FAAC)
XBIOS....... Extended BIOS [*Basic Input/Output System*] [*Operating system*]
XBJ .... Valley Airlines [*Frenchville, ME*] [*FAA designator*] (FAAC)
XBK .... Bellair Airways [*Houston, TX*] [*FAA designator*] (FAAC)
XBK .... Xebeck [*Type of ship*] (ROG)
XBL........... Extension Bell [*Telecommunications*] (TEL)
XBL........... Northstar Aviation [*Redding, CA*] [*FAA designator*] (FAAC)
XBLD........ Extrabold [*Typography*]
XBM .... Extended BASIC Mode [*International Computers Ltd.*]
XBM .... State University of New York, College at Brockport, Brockport, NY [*OCLC symbol*] (OCLC)
XBMIA...... Report of Investigations. United States Bureau of Mines [*A publication*]
XBN .... Biniguni [*Papua New Guinea*] [*Airport symbol*] (OAG)
XBO .... Sajen Air, Inc. [*Manchester, NH*] [*FAA designator*] (FAAC)
XBP........... Bancshare Portfolio Corp. [*Toronto Stock Exchange symbol*]
XBP........... X-Ray Bright Point [*Astronomy*]
XBQ .... Denver Charters, Inc. [*Englewood, CO*] [*FAA designator*] (FAAC)
XBR .... Aero Coach Aviation International, Inc. [*Ft. Lauderdale, FL*] [*FAA designator*] (FAAC)
XBR .... Brockville [*Canada*] [*Airport symbol*] (OAG)
XBR .... Experimental Breeder Reactor
XBR .... Ozark, AL [*Location identifier*] [*FAA*] (FAAL)
XBRA........ Cross Bracing (MSA)
XBS........... Ace Air Cargo Express, Inc. [*Brook Park, OH*] [*FAA designator*] (FAAC)
XBT .... Crossbar Tandem [*Telecommunications*] (TEL)
XBT .... Desert Sun Airlines [*Long Beach, CA*] [*FAA designator*] (FAAC)
XBT .... Expendable Bathythermograph [*Oceanography*]
XBTS......... Extract Bit String [*Data processing*] (PCM)
XBU .... Arcata Flying Service [*McKinleyville, CA*] [*FAA designator*] (FAAC)
XBV .... Western Pacific Express, Inc. [*Van Nuys, CA*] [*FAA designator*] (FAAC)
XBW .... Waring Aviation, Inc. [*Charlottesville, VA*] [*FAA designator*] (FAAC)
XBX .... Air Cargo America, Inc. [*Miami, FL*] [*FAA designator*] (FAAC)
XBY .... Cosmopolitan Airlines, Inc. [*Farmingdale, NY*] [*FAA designator*] (FAAC)
XBZ .... Chesapeake Transport, Inc. [*Arlington, VA*] [*FAA designator*] (FAAC)
XC .... Air Routing International Corp. [*ICAO designator*] (FAAC)
Xc .... Capacitive Reactance
XC .... Cross-Clamp [*of carotid artery*]
XC .... Cross Country [*Also, XCY*]
X-C............. Ex-Coupon [*Without the right to coupons, as of a bond*] [*Finance*]
XC .... Excretory Cystogram [*Medicine*] (MAE)
XC .... Expandable Case
XC .... Expandable Case (MCD)
XC .... Experimental Cargo Aircraft
xc................ Maldives [*MARC country of publication code*] [*Library of Congress*] (LCCP)
XC .... Mexico [*Aircraft nationality and registration mark*] (FAAC)
XC .... X-Chromosome
XC .... Xanthomonus Campestris [*Bacteriology*]
XC .... Xerox Copy
XCA .... Air East of Delaware, Inc. [*Wilmington, DE*] [*FAA designator*] (FAAC)
XCB .... Aero Trends, Inc. [*San Jose, CA*] [*FAA designator*] (FAAC)
XCB .... Extended Core Barrel [*Drilling technology*]
XCC .... Air Vectors Airways, Inc. [*Newburg, NY*] [*FAA designator*] (FAAC)
XCD .... Air Associates Ltd. [*Kansas City, MO*] [*FAA designator*] (FAAC)
XCD .... Canadian Dollar [*Vancouver Stock Exchange symbol*]
XCE .... Aerotransit [*Danvers, MA*] [*FAA designator*] (FAAC)
XCE .... X-Band Cassegrain Experimental
XCF........... Air Niagara, Inc. [*Niagara Falls, NY*] [*FAA designator*] (FAAC)
XCG .... Atlantic Express, Inc. [*East Farmingdale, NY*] [*FAA designator*] (FAAC)
XCG .... Experimental Cargo Glider

X-CGD....... X-Linked Chronic Granulomatous Disease [*Medicine*]
XCH.......... Exchange (AAG)
XCH.......... Flight East [*North Hollywood, CA*] [*FAA designator*] (FAAC)
XCI .... X-Chromosome Inactivation [*Genetics*]
XCIT......... Excitation (AAG)
XCJ .... Eastman Airways [*Farmingdale, NJ*] [*FAA designator*] (FAAC)
XCK .... Richland Aviation [*Sidney, MT*] [*FAA designator*] (FAAC)
XCL........... Armed Merchant Cruiser [*Navy symbol*]
XCL........... Excess Current Liabilities [*Insurance*]
XCL........... Excluded from General Declassification Schedule (MCD)
XCL........... Exploration Co. of Louisiana, Inc. [*AMEX symbol*] (SPSG)
XCL........... Green Aero, Inc. [*Flint, MI*] [*FAA designator*] (FAAC)
XCL........... X-Cal Resources Ltd. [*Toronto Stock Exchange symbol*]
XCMD ...... External Command [*Data processing*]
XCN .... Northern Airways, Inc. [*Grand Forks, ND*] [*FAA designator*] (FAAC)
XCNGR .... Exchanger (AAG)
XCO.......... Cross Connection
XCOM....... Exterior Communications [*Military*] (CAAL)
XCONN..... Cross Connection
XCORA..... Xcor International, Inc. Cl A [*NASDAQ symbol*] (NQ)
XCP........... Ex-Coupon [*Without the right to coupons, as of a bond*] [*Finance*]
XCP........... Except (FAAC)
XCP........... Executive Control Program [*Data processing*] (MCD)
XCP........... Expendable Current Profiler [*Instrumentation, oceanography*]
XCPT......... Except (KSC)
XCR .... Little Falls, MN [*Location identifier*] [*FAA*] (FAAL)
XCRDA ..... Research and Development Report. United States Office of Coal Research [*A publication*]
XCS........... Cape Seppings, AK [*Location identifier*] [*FAA*] (FAAL)
XCS........... Cross-Country Skiing
XCS........... Ten Call Seconds [*Telecommunications*] (TEL)
XCS........... Xerox Computer Services [*Xerox Corp.*]
XCT .... X-Band Communications Transponder
X Ctry Skier ... X-Country Skier [*A publication*]
XCU .... Explosion Collapse, Underground Operations
XC & UC.. Exclusive of Covering and Uncovering
XCVR........ Transceiver (AAG)
XCY .... Cross Country [*Also, XC*]
XD.............. Bureau Veritas SA [*France*] [*ICAO designator*] (ICDA)
XD.............. Crossed [*Telecommunications*] (TEL)
XD.............. Ex-Directory [*Telecommunications*] (TEL)
X-D .... Ex-Dividend [*Without the right to dividend*] [*Finance*] (SPSG)
X/D .... Ex Dividendum [*Without (or Exclusive) of Dividend*] [*Finance*] (ROG)
XD.............. Examined (ROG)
XD.............. Executed (ROG)
XD.............. Executive Development [*Civil Service Commission*]
X & D........ Experiment and Development [*Flotilla*] [*Landing Craft*]
XD.............. Exploratory Development [*Military*] (MCD)
XD.............. Extra Dense
XD.............. Xylem Disease [*Plant pathology*]
XDA.......... X-Band Drive Amplifier
XDC.......... Xylene-Dioxane-Cellosolve [*Scintillation solvent*]
XD/CO ...... Ex-Directory/Calls Offered [*Telephone service*] (DI)
XDCR .... Transducer (AAG)
XDE .... Xylene-Dioxane-Ethanol [*Scintillation solvent*]
XDER .... Transducer
X & DFLOT ... Experimental and Development Flotilla [*Navy*] (DNAB)
XDH .... Xanthine Dehydrogenase [*An enzyme*]
XDI .... Xylene Diisocyanate [*Organic chemistry*]
XDIGA ...... US Geological Survey. Bulletin [*A publication*]
X-Dis......... Ex-Distribution
X-Div......... Ex-Dividend [*Without the right to dividend*] [*Finance*]
XDIVU ...... Naval Experimental Diving Unit
XDM.......... State University of New York, Agricultural and Technical College at Delhi, Delhi, NY [*OCLC symbol*] (OCLC)
XDM.......... X-Ray Density Measurement
XD/NC ...... Ex-Directory/No Connections [*Telephone service*] (DI)
XDP .... X-Ray Density Probe
XDP .... X-Ray Diffraction Powder
XDP .... Xanthosine Diphosphate [*Biochemistry*]
XDP .... Xeroderma Pigmentosum [*Inherited, disfiguring syndrome*]
XDPC........ X-Ray Diffraction Powder Camera
XDPS........ X-Band Diode Phase Shifter
XDPU .... Expanded Data Processing Unit (DNAB)
XDR .... Crusader (ROG)
XDR .... External Data Representation [*Data processing*]
XDR .... Transducer (AAG)
XDS .... Exoatmospheric Defense System [*DoD*]
XDS .... X-Ray Diffraction System
XDS .... Xerox Data Systems [*Formerly, SDS*]
XDT .... Xenon Discharge Tube
XDUCER... Transducer
XDUP .... Extended Disk Utilities Program [*Data processing*]
XDY .... Valdosta Moody Air Force Base, GA [*Location identifier*] [*FAA*] (FAAL)
XE .... Canadian Express Ltd. [*Toronto Stock Exchange symbol*] [*Vancouver Stock Exchange symbol*]
XE .... Euro Control [*Belgium*] [*ICAO designator*] (FAAC)

XE	Experimental Engine [*NASA*]
Xe	Xenon [*Chemical element*]
XEBC	Xebec [*NASDAQ symbol*] (NQ)
XEC	Execute
XECF	Experimental Engine - Cold Flow Configuration [*NERVA*]
XED	Medford, OK [*Location identifier*] [*FAA*] (FAAL)
XEDS	X-Ray Energy Dispersive System [*Microparticle analysis*]
XEF	Xenon Fluoride (MCD)
XEG	X-Ray Emission Gauge
XEG	Xerox Education Group
XEL	Excelsior Life Insurance Co. [*Toronto Stock Exchange symbol*]
XELEDOP	Transmitting Elementary Dipole with Optional Polarity (MCD)
Xen	De Xenophane [*of Aristotle*] [*Classical studies*] (OCD)
XEN	Xenia, OH [*Location identifier*] [*FAA*] (FAAL)
Xen	Xenophon [*428-354BC*] [*Classical studies*] (OCD)
XEO	Experimental Engineering Orders (DNAB)
XEOS	Xerox Electro-Optical Systems
XEPPDW	US Environmental Protection Agency. Office of Pesticide Programs. Substitute Chemical Program. EPA-540 [*A publication*]
XEQ	Execute
XER	Xerox Corp., Xerox Library Services, Webster, NY [*OCLC symbol*] (OCLC)
XER	Xerox Reproduction (AAG)
XERB	Experimental Environmental Research Buoy [*Marine science*] (MSC)
XERG	Xonics Electron Radiography [*Medical x-ray imaging equipment*]
Xerox	Xerox Corp. [*Associated Press abbreviation*] (APAG)
XES	X-Ray Emission Spectra
XES	X-Ray Energy Spectrometry
XETA	Xeta Corp. [*NASDAQ symbol*] (NQ)
XF	Experimental Fighter
XF	Extended Family [*Unitarian Universalist program*]
XF	Extra Fine
xf	Extremely Fine [*Philately*]
xf	Midway Islands [*MARC country of publication code*] [*Library of Congress*] (LCCP)
XF	Xudozestvennyj Fol'klor [*A publication*]
X15-F	Model number used by Eastman Kodak Co. [*Name is said to have been derived from symbol on magicube (X), product's place in sales line (15), and flip-flash unit that replaced magicube (F)*]
XFA	Cross-Field Acceleration
XFA	X-Ray Fluorescence Absorption
XFC	Extended Function Code
XFC	Transfer Charge [*Telecommunications*] (TEL)
XFC	X-Band Frequency Converter
XFD	Crossfeed (NASA)
XFD	X-Ray Flow Detection
XFER	Transfer (AAG)
XFES	Xerox Family Education Services
XFH	X-Band Feed Horn
XfL	Cross in Front of Left Foot [*Dance terminology*]
XFLO	Crossflow Engine [*Automotive engineering*]
XFLT	Expanded Flight Line Tester
XFM	Expeditionary Force Message [*Usually, EFM*] [*Low-rate cable or radio message selected from a list of standard wordings*]
XFM	State University of New York, College at Fredonia, Fredonia, NY [*OCLC symbol*] (OCLC)
XFM	X-Band Ferrite Modulator
XFMI	Transformer Interface
XFMR	Transformer (AAG)
XFN	Victoria, TX [*Location identifier*] [*FAA*] (FAAL)
XFQH	Xenon-Filled Quartz Helix
XFR	Transfer
XFRMR	Transformer
XFS	Fort Sill, OK [*Location identifier*] [*FAA*] (FAAL)
XFS	X-Ray Fluorescence Spectroscopy
XFS	Xenogenic Fetal Skin [*Medicine*]
XFT	Xenon Flash Tube
XFWFA7	US Fish and Wildlife Service. Fishery Bulletin [*A publication*]
XFWLAP	US Fish and Wildlife Service. Wildlife Leaflet [*A publication*]
XG	Crossing
XG	IMP Group Ltd. Aviation Services [*Canada*] [*ICAO designator*] (FAAC)
XGA	Extended Graphics Array [*IBM Corp.*]
XGAM	Experimental Guided Air Missiles
XGDS	Exempt from General Declassification Schedule (MCD)
Xge	Exchange [*Business term*]
XGG	Gorom-Gorom [*Burkina Faso*] [*Airport symbol*] (OAG)
X-Gluc.	X-Glucuronide
XGP	Experimental Geosynchronous Platform (SSD)
XGP	Xanthogranulomatous Pyelonephritis [*Medicine*]
XGP	Xerox Graphic Printer [*Xerox Corp.*]
XGPRT	Xanthine-Guanine Phosphoribosyltransferase [*An enzyme*]
XGRAPHY	Xylography [*Wood engraving*] (ROG)
XH	Experimental Helicopter
xh	Niue [*MARC country of publication code*] [*Library of Congress*] (LCCP)
XH	Sign-Filled Half-Word Designator [*Data processing*]
XH	Special Handling Service for Aircraft [*ICAO designator*] (ICDA)
XH	Xerogrammata Hochschulschriften [*A publication*]
XHAIR	Cross Hair (IEEE)
XHE	Hawaii Express [*Los Angeles, CA*] [*FAA designator*] (FAAC)
XHF	Extra-High Frequency (NVT)
XHM	X-Ray Hazard Meter
XHMO	Extended Hueckel Molecular Orbit [*Atomic physics*] (IEEE)
xho	Xhosa [*MARC language code*] [*Library of Congress*] (LCCP)
XHR	Extra-High Reliability
XHS	Indiana Historical Society, Indianapolis, IN [*OCLC symbol*] (OCLC)
XHST	Exhaust (AAG)
XHV	Extreme High Vacuum
XHVY	Extra Heavy
X-I	Ex-Interest [*Without the right to interest*] [*Finance*]
XI	International Aeradio Ltd. [*British*] [*ICAO designator*] (ICDA)
xi	St. Christopher-Nevis-Anguilla [*MARC country of publication code*] [*Library of Congress*] (LCCP)
XIA	X-Band Inteferometer Antenna
XIB	IBM Corp., Library Processing Center, White Plains, NY [*OCLC symbol*] (OCLC)
XIC	Convent of Immaculate Conception Sisters of St. Benedict, Ferdinand, IN [*OCLC symbol*] (OCLC)
XIC	Transmission Interface Converter
XIC	Xichang [*China*] [*Airport symbol*] (OAG)
XICO	Xicor, Inc. [*NASDAQ symbol*] (NQ)
XICS	Xerox Integrated Composition System [*Xerox Corp.*] [*Computer typesetting system*]
XICTMD	Xerox International Center for Training and Management Development [*Leesburg, VA*]
XID	Exchange Identification
XIDX	Xidex Corp. [*NASDAQ symbol*] (NQ)
XII	Washington, DC [*Location identifier*] [*FAA*] (FAAL)
XII P	Testaments of the Twelve Patriarchs [*Pseudepigrapha*]
XIM	Ithaca College, Ithaca, NY [*OCLC symbol*] (OCLC)
XIM	X-Ray Intensity Meter
XIMIA	Information Circular. United States Bureau of Mines [*A publication*]
XIN	Ex-Interest [*Without the right to interest*] [*Finance*]
XING	Crossing (MCD)
XINT	Ex-Interest [*Without the right to interest*] [*Finance*]
XI/O	Execute Input/Output (DEN)
XIOX	XIOX Corp. [*Burlingame, CA*] [*NASDAQ symbol*] (NQ)
XIP	Execute-in-Place [*Data processing*]
XIP	Xerox Individualized Publishing
XIPC	Extended Interprocess Communications Facilities
Xi Psi Phi Q	Xi Psi Phi Quarterly [*A publication*]
XIRS	Xenon Infrared Searchlight
XIS	Xenon Infrared Searchlight
XIS	Xerox Imaging System (PCM)
XIS	XPRESS Information Services (IID)
XIT	Extra Input Terminal
XIWSA	US Geological Survey. Water-Supply Paper [*A publication*]
XJ	Assistance Aeroportuaire de l'Aeroport de Paris [*France*] [*ICAO designator*] (ICDA)
xj	St. Helena [*MARC country of publication code*] [*Library of Congress*] (LCCP)
XJM	Schenectady County Community College, Schenectady, NY [*OCLC symbol*] (OCLC)
XJN	Milwaukee, WI [*Location identifier*] [*FAA*] (FAAL)
XJP	Jasper Public Library, Jasper, IN [*OCLC symbol*] (OCLC)
XK	Agence pour la Securite de la Navigation Aerienne en Afrique et a Madagascar (ASECNA) [*ICAO designator*] (ICDA)
xk	St. Lucia [*MARC country of publication code*] [*Library of Congress*] (LCCP)
XK	X-Band Klystron
XL	Cross-Reference List
XL	Crystal
XL	Excess Lactate
XL	Execution Language [*Data processing*]
XL	EXEL Ltd. [*NYSE symbol*] (SPSG)
XL	Extra Large [*or Long*] [*Size*]
XL	Extra Load [*Automotive engineering*]
xl	St. Pierre and Miquelon [*MARC country of publication code*] [*Library of Congress*] (LCCP)
XL	Telecomunicacoes Aeronauticas Sociedada Anonima (TASA) [*Brazil*] [*ICAO designator*] (ICDA)
XL	Unmarried Lady [*Citizens band radio slang*]
XL	X-Axis of Spacelab [*NASA*] (NASA)
XL	Xudozestvennaja Literatura [*A publication*]
XL	Xylose-Lysine [*Agar base*] [*Microbiology*]
XLA	X-Band Limiter Attenuator
XLATION	Translation
XLB	Xylem-Limited Bacteria [*Plant pathology*]
XLC	Extra Large Capacity
XLC	Extra Luxurious Chaparral
XLC	Indiana University, School of Medicine, Medical Education Resources Program, Indianapolis, IN [*OCLC symbol*] (OCLC)

XLC............ Xenon Lamp Collimator
XLD .... Experimental LASER Device (MCD)
XLD .... Xylose-Lysine-Deoxycholate [*Growth medium*]
XLDC........ XL/Datacomp, Inc. [*Hinsdale, IL*] [*NASDAQ symbol*] (NQ)
XLDT........ Xenon LASER Discharge Tube
XLE........... Columbus, GA [*Location identifier*] [*FAA*] (FAAL)
XLF........... XL Food Systems Ltd. [*Toronto Stock Exchange symbol*]
XLGX........ Xylogics, Inc. [*NASDAQ symbol*] (NQ)
xlh .... Extra Large Hinge [*Philately*]
XLI............. Extra-Low Interstitial [*Alloy*]
XLISP........ Extension of LISP [*List Processor*] 1.5 [*Programming language*] (CSR)
XLIST....... Execution List (MCD)
XLM .... St. Lawrence University, Canton, NY [*OCLC symbol*] (OCLC)
XLMR........ X-Linked Mental Retardation [*Genetics*]
XLNT .... Excellent (WGA)
XLP........... Extended-Life Protection [*Automotive engineering*]
XLP........... X-Linked Lymphoproliferative Syndrome [*Medicine*]
XLPE......... Cross-Linked Polyethylene [*Organic chemistry*] (NRCH)
XLPS .... X-Linked Lymphoproliferative Syndrome [*Medicine*]
XLPS .... Xenon Lamp Power Supply
XLR .... Experimental Liquid Rocket [*Air Force, NASA*]
XLR .... X-Linked, Lymphocyte-Regulated [*Genetics*]
XLS........... St. Louis [*Senegal*] [*Airport symbol*] (OAG)
XLS........... Xenon Light Source
XLS........... Xerox Learning Systems
XLSS .... Xenon Light Source System
XLT........... Xenon LASER Tube
XLTN .... Translation (NASA)
XLTR .... Translator (MSA)
XL & UL.... Exclusive of Loading and Unloading
XLWB....... Extra-Long Wheelbase
XM............. Christmas
XM............. Crossmatch (MAE)
XM............. Excitation Monochromator
XM............. Expanded Memory
XM............. Experimental Missile [*Air Force, NASA*]
XM............. Experimental Model
XM............. Research Missile [*NATO*]
xm .... St. Vincent [*MARC country of publication code*] [*Library of Congress*] (LCCP)
XM............. Servicios a la Navegacion en el Espacio Aereo Mexicano (SENEAM) [*Mexico*] [*ICAO designator*] (ICDA)
XMAP ...... Sweeper Device [*Navy symbol*]
XMAS....... Christmas
XMAS....... Extended Mission Apollo Simulation [*NASA*] (IEEE)
X/MBR...... Cross Member [*Automotive engineering*]
XMC .... Borough of Manhattan Community College, New York, NY [*OCLC symbol*] (OCLC)
XmC.......... Standard Microfilm Reproductions Ltd., Scarborough, ON, Canada [*Library symbol*] [*Library of Congress*] (LCLS)
XMD .... Ozark, AL [*Location identifier*] [*FAA*] (FAAL)
XME .... Medgar Evers College of the City University of New York, Brooklyn, NY [*OCLC symbol*] (OCLC)
XMED .... Xtramedics, Inc. [*NASDAQ symbol*] (NQ)
XMFR....... Transformer (AAG)
XMG......... Mahendranagar [*Nepal*] [*Airport symbol*] (OAG)
XMH .... Manihi [*French Polynesia*] [*Airport symbol*] (OAG)
XMI .... Christmas Island [*Seismograph station code, US Geological Survey*] (SEIS)
XMI .... Masasi [*Tanzania*] [*Airport symbol*] (OAG)
XMI .... Seymour-Moss International Ltd. [*Vancouver Stock Exchange symbol*]
XMIT........ Transmit [*or Transmitter*]
XML .... Miles Laboratories, Inc., Miles Pharmaceutical Division, West Haven, CT [*OCLC symbol*] (OCLC)
XML .... Minlaton [*Australia*] [*Airport symbol*] [*Obsolete*] (OAG)
XMM....... Extended Memory Manager [*Data processing*] (PCM)
XMM........ State University of New York, Agricultural and Technical College at Morrisville, Morrisville, NY [*OCLC symbol*] (OCLC)
XMOFA .... Bureau of Mines. Open File Report [*United States*] [*A publication*]
XMP .... Marion Public Library, Marion, IN [*OCLC symbol*] (OCLC)
XMP .... Xanthosine Monophosphate [*Biochemistry*]
XMR......... Cape Canaveral, FL [*Location identifier*] [*FAA*] (FAAL)
XMS .... Experimental Development Specification [*Military*] (CAAL)
XMS .... Experimental Missile Specifications
XMS .... Extended Memory Specification [*Data processing*] (PCM)
XMS .... X-Band Microwave Source
XMS .... Xavier Mission Sisters [*Catholic Mission Sisters of St. Francis Xavier*] [*Roman Catholic religious order*]
XMS .... Xerox Memory System
XMSN .... Transmission (AAG)
XMT .... Exempt (NVT)
XMT .... Transmit (MSA)
XMT .... X-Band Microwave Transmitter
XMTD .... Transmitted (MCD)
XMTG .... Transmitting
XMTL........ Transmittal (IEEE)

XMTPB..... Technical Progress Report. United States Bureau of Mines [*A publication*]
XMTR ...... Transmitter
XMT-REC ... Transmit-Receive (AAG)
XMTR-REC ... Transmitter-Receiver
XN............. Canadian National Telecommunications [*Canada*] [*ICAO designator*] (ICDA)
XN............. Christian
XN............. Ex-New [*Without the right to new stocks or shares*] [*Stock exchange term*] (SPSG)
XN............. Experimental (Navy)
XNA .... Xinhua News Agency [*China*]
XNB .... X-Band Navigation Beacon
XNBSA..... National Bureau of Standards. Special Publication [*United States*] [*A publication*]
XNC.......... Nazareth College of Rochester, Rochester, NY [*OCLC symbol*] (OCLC)
XNEW ...... Ex New Issue [*Without the right to new stocks or shares*] [*Stock exchange term*]
XNIPA...... United States. Naval Institute. Proceedings [*A publication*]
XNL .... NELINET [*New England Library Information Network*], Newton, MA [*OCLC symbol*] (OCLC)
XNN.......... Xining [*China*] [*Airport symbol*] (OAG)
XNO .... North, SC [*Location identifier*] [*FAA*] (FAAL)
XNOS .... Experimental Network Operating System
XNRX .... Xenerex Corp. [*NASDAQ symbol*] (NQ)
XNS .... Xerox Network Systems [*Telecommunications*]
XNTY .... Christianity
XNWRA ... US News and World Report [*A publication*]
XNX.......... Xenex Industries & Resources Ltd. [*Vancouver Stock Exchange symbol*]
XO............. Crystal Oscillator (IEEE)
XO............. Executive Officer [*Military*]
XO............. Expenditure Order [*Military*] (AABC)
XO............. Experimental Officer [*Also, EO, ExO*] [*Ministry of Agriculture, Fisheries, and Food*] [*British*]
XO............. Extra Old [*Designation on brandy labels*]
XO............. X-Axis of Orbiter [*NASA*] (NASA)
XO............. Xanthine Oxidase [*Also, XOD*] [*An enzyme*]
XO............. Xylenol Orange [*An indicator*] [*Chemistry*]
XOB .... Xenon Optical Beacon
XOC.......... Experimental On-Line Capabilities [*Data processing*]
XOD.......... Xanthine Oxidase [*Also, XO*] [*An enzyme*]
XOFF........ Transmitter Off (BUR)
XOID........ Xyloid [*Woody*] (ROG)
XOMA...... XOMA Corp. [*Berkeley, CA*] [*NASDAQ symbol*] (NQ)
XON .... Cross-Office Highway [*Telecommunications*] (TEL)
XON .... Exxon Corp. [*NYSE symbol*] (SPSG)
XON .... Transmitter On (BUR)
XOP .... Extended Operation
XOR.......... Exclusive Operating Room [*Medicine*] (MAE)
XOR.......... Exclusive Or [*Gates*] [*Data processing*]
XOS .... Cross-Office Slot [*Telecommunications*] (TEL)
XOS .... Extra Outsize [*Clothing*]
XOS .... Xerox Operating System
XOVR....... Exovir, Inc. [*NASDAQ symbol*] (NQ)
XOW........ Express Order Wire [*Telecommunications*] (TEL)
XOXIA ...... Xonics, Inc. Cl A [*NASDAQ symbol*] (NQ)
XP............. Expandable Processor [*IBM Corp.*] [*Data processing*]
XP............. Expansionist Party of the United States [*Political party*] (EA)
XP............. Express Paid
XP............. Express Parcel Systems [*Europe*]
XP............. Extra Person (WGA)
XP............. Fire Resistive Protected [*Insurance classification*]
XP............. Radio Aeronautica Paraguaya Sociedad Anonima (RAPSA) [*Paraguay*] [*ICAO designator*] (ICDA)
xp .... Spratly Islands [*MARC country of publication code*] [*Library of Congress*] (LCCP)
XP............. Sun Exploration & Production Co. [*NYSE symbol*] [*Later, ORX*] (CTT)
XP............. X-Axis of Payload [*NASA*] (NASA)
XP............. Xeroderma Pigmentosum [*Inherited, disfiguring syndrome*]
XPA .... Pama [*Burkina Faso*] [*Airport symbol*] (OAG)
XPA .... X-Band Parametric Amplifier
XPA .... X-Band Passive Array
XPA .... X-Band Planar Array
XPA .... X-Band Power Amplifier
XPAA........ X-Band Planar Array Antenna
XPARD6... EPA [*Environmental Protection Agency*] Environmental Protection Technology Series [*A publication*]
XPARD6... US Environmental Protection Agency. Office of Research and Development. Research Reports. Ecological Research Series [*A publication*]
XPARS ...... External Research Publication and Retrieval System [*Department of State*]
XPC........... Christus [*Christ*] [*Latin*]
XPC........... Expect (FAAC)
XPC........... Express Passenger Coach
XPD .... Cross-Polarization Discrimination [*Telecommunications*]
XPD .... Expedient Demise [*Used as title of novel by Len Deighton*]
XPD .... Expedite (MUGU)

XPDR	Transponder (MUGU)
XPG	Converted merchant ships, assigned to antisubmarine patrol or convoy escort [*Navy symbol*]
XPH	Port Heiden, AK [*Location identifier*] [*FAA*] (FAAL)
XPHS	Xylan Polyhydrogensulfate [*Antineoplastic drug*]
XPI	Cross-Polarization Interference [*in radio transmission*]
XPL	Explosive (AAG)
XPLOR	Xerox 9700 Users' Association (EA)
XPLOS	Explosive (FAAC)
XPLR	Xplor Corp. [*NASDAQ symbol*] (NQ)
XPLT	Exploit (MUGU)
XPLX	Xyplex, Inc. [*NASDAQ symbol*] (SPSG)
XPM	Expanded Metal [*Heavy gauge*]
XPM	Xerox Planning Model [*A computerized representation of the Xerox Corp.'s operations*]
XPN	Expansion (AAG)
XPNDR	Transponder (AAG)
XPONDER ...	Transponder
X-POP	X-Body Axis Perpendicular to Orbit Plane [*Aerospace*]
XPP	Express Paid Letter (ROG)
XPP	Xi Psi Phi [*Fraternity*]
XPP	Xylem Pressure Potential [*Botany*]
XPPA	X-Band Pseudopassive Array
XPPA	X-Band Pulsed Power Amplifier
XPR	Ex-Privileges [*Without the right to privileges*] [*Finance*]
x pri	Ex-Privileges [*Without the right to privileges*] [*Finance*] (DS)
XPRS	Express Cash International [*NASDAQ symbol*] (SPSG)
XPS	X-Band Phase Shifter
XPS	X-Ray Photoelectron Spectroscopy (RDA)
XPS	X-Ray Photoemission Spectroscopy
XPSW	External Processor Status Word
XPT	Crosspoint [*Switching element*] (MSA)
XPT	Export
XPT	Express Paid Telegraph
XPT	External Page Table [*Data processing*] (BUR)
X PT	Extra Point (WGA)
XPT	X-Band Pulse Transmitter
XPU	West Kuparuk, AK [*Location identifier*] [*FAA*] (FAAL)
XPW	American Ex-Prisoners of War (EA)
XQ	Cross-Question [*Transcripts*]
XQ	Experimental Target Drone [*Air Force, NASA*]
X/Q	Relative Concentration [*Symbol*] (NRCH)
XQA	Greenville, ME [*Location identifier*] [*FAA*] (FAAL)
XQH	Xenon Quartz Helix
XQM	Queens College, Flushing, NY [*OCLC symbol*] (OCLC)
XQP	Quepos [*Costa Rica*] [*Airport symbol*] (OAG)
XR	Cross Reference (MCD)
XR	Empresa de Servicios Aeronauticos [*Cuba*] [*ICAO designator*] (ICDA)
XR	Ex-Rights [*Without Rights*] [*Investment term*]
XR	Examiner (ROG)
XR	Export Reactor [*Nuclear energy*] (NRCH)
XR	Extended Range [*Film*] [*Briteline Corp.*]
XR	Extended Response (WGA)
XR	External Reset
XR	Index Register
XR	No Returns Permitted [*Business term*]
XR	RY II Financial Corp. [*Toronto Stock Exchange symbol*]
XR	X: A Quarterly Review [*A publication*]
XR	X-Ray
XRA	X-Ray Assistant [*British military*] (DMA)
XRAY	GENDEX Corp. [*NASDAQ symbol*] (NQ)
X-Ray Spect ...	X-Ray Spectrometry [*A publication*]
X-Ray Spectrum ...	X-Ray Spectrometry [*A publication*]
XRB	X-Band RADAR Beacon
XRC	Xerox Research Centre of Canada Library [*UTLAS symbol*]
XRCD	X-Ray Crystal Density
XRD	X-Ray Diffraction [*or Diffractometer*]
XRDF	X-Ray Radial Distance Function [*Surface chemistry analysis*]
XRDS	Crossroads
X-REA	X-Ray Events Analyzer (KSC)
X-REF	Cross Reference (NG)
XREP	Auxiliary Report (FAAC)
XRF	Experimental Reproduction Film (DIT)
XRF	Explosion Release Factor [*Nuclear energy*] (NRCH)
XRF	Extended Reliability Feature (HGAA)
XRF	Rockefeller Foundation, Library, New York, NY [*OCLC symbol*] (OCLC)
XRF	X-Ray Fluorescence [*Spectrometry*]
XRFS	X-Ray Fluorescence Spectrometer
XRG	X-Ray Generator [*Instrumentation*]
XRGP	Extended Range Guided Projectiles (MCD)
XRI	Xenium Resources, Inc. [*Vancouver Stock Exchange symbol*]
XRII	X-Ray Image Intensifier
XRIT	X-Rite, Inc. [*NASDAQ symbol*] (NQ)
XRL	Extended-Range Lance [*Missile*]
XRL	X-Ray LASER
XRM	External Relational Memory
XRM	Extra Range Multigrade [*Automotive engineering*]
XRM	X-Ray Microanalyzer [*or Microscopy*] (IEEE)
XRN	RY NT Financial Corp. [*Toronto Stock Exchange symbol*]
XROI	X-Ray Optical Interferometer
XRP	X-Ray and Photofluorography Technician [*Navy*]
XRP	X-Ray Polychromator
XRPM	X-Ray Projection Microscope (IEEE)
XRRAAH ..	US Forest Service. Rocky Mountain Forest and Range Experiment Station. Research Highlights. Annual Report [*A publication*]
XRS	X-Ray Spectrometry
XRT	Ex-Rights [*Without Rights*] [*Investment term*] (SPSG)
XRT	Extended-Range TOW
XRT	X-Ray Technician [*Navy*]
X-RT	X-Ray Telescope (MCD)
XRT	X-Ray Therapy [*or Treatment*]
XRTOW	Extended-Range TOW [*Tube-Launched, Optically Tracked, Wire-Guided*] [*Weapon*] (MCD)
X-RTS	Ex-Rights [*Without Rights*] [*Investment term*]
XRW	Fort Campbell, KY [*Location identifier*] [*FAA*] (FAAL)
XRX	Xerox Corp. [*NYSE symbol*] (SPSG)
XRY	Jerez De La Frontera [*Spain*] [*Airport symbol*] (OAG)
XRY	RY Financial Corp. [*Toronto Stock Exchange symbol*]
XRY	Yakima, WA [*Location identifier*] [*FAA*] (FAAL)
XS	Atmospherics (FAAC)
XS	Christus [*Christ*] [*Latin*]
XS	Cross Section
XS	Excess
XS	Expenses
XS	Extra Small
XS	Extra Strong
XS	Extremely Severe [*Rock climbing*]
XS	Societe Internationale de Telecommunications Aeronautiques, Societe Cooperative (SITA) [*ICAO designator*] (ICDA)
XS	X-Axis of Solid Rocket Booster [*NASA*] (NASA)
XS	Xerces Society (EA)
XS3	Excess Three [*Code*]
XS-11	Excess Eleven [*1967 group of scientist-astronauts selected by NASA*]
XSA	Cross-Sectional Area [*Cardiology*]
XSA	X-Band Satellite Antenna
XSAES	X-Ray Stimulated Auger Electron Spectroscopy (MCD)
XSAL	Xenon Short Arc Lamp
XSB	Xavier Society for the Blind (EA)
XSC	South Caicos [*British West Indies*] [*Airport symbol*] (OAG)
XSC	Southampton Center of Long Island University, Southampton, NY [*OCLC symbol*] (OCLC)
XSCI	Xsirius Superconductivity, Inc. [*NASDAQ symbol*] (NQ)
XSCR	Xscribe Corp. [*NASDAQ symbol*] (NQ)
XSD	Southeast Dubois County, School Corp. Library, Ferdinand, IN [*OCLC symbol*] (OCLC)
XSD	Tonopah, NV [*Location identifier*] [*FAA*] (FAAL)
XSE	Sebba [*Burkina Faso*] [*Airport symbol*] (OAG)
XSECT	Cross Section
XSF	Springfield, OH [*Location identifier*] [*FAA*] (FAAL)
XSF	X-Ray Scattering Facility
XSIR	Xsirius Scientific, Inc. [*Marina Del Ray, CA*] [*NASDAQ symbol*] (NQ)
XSL	Experimental Space Laboratory
XSM	Experimental Strategic Missile
XSM	Experimental Surface Missile
XSM	X-Ray Stress Measurement
XSMDC	Expanding Shielded Mild Detonating Cord (MCD)
XSOA	Excess Speed of Advance Authorized [*Navy*] (NVT)
X-SONAD ...	Experimental Sonic Azimuth Detector (MCD)
XSP	Singapore-Seletar [*Singapore*] [*Airport symbol*] (OAG)
XSP	Xi Sigma Pi [*Fraternity*]
XSP	Xylem Sap Potential [*Botany*]
XSPV	Experimental Solid Propellant Vehicle
XSR	X-Band Scatterometer RADAR
XSS	Experimental Space Station [*NASA*]
XSS	Xenon Solar Simulator
XST	Experimental Stealth Tactical Demonstrator [*Air Force*]
XST	Xylem Sap Tension [*Botany*]
XSTA	X-Band Satellite Tracking Antenna
XSTD	Expendable Salinity/Temperature/Depth Probe [*Oceanography*] (MSC)
XSTD	X-Band Stripline Tunnel Diode
XSTDA	X-Band Stripline Tunnel Diode Amplifier
XSTR	Extra Strong (MSA)
XSTR	Transistor (AAG)
XSTT	Excess Transit Time
XSV	Expendable Sound Velocimeter [*Oceanography*] (MSC)
XSW	X-Ray Standing Wave [*Physics*]
XT	Burkina Faso [*Aircraft nationality and registration mark*] (FAAC)
XT	Christ
XT	Cross Talk (IEEE)
XT	Exotropia Near [*Ophthalmology*]
XT	Servicos Auxiliares de Transportes Aereos (SATA) [*Brazil*] [*ICAO designator*] (ICDA)
XT	X-Axis of External Tank [*NASA*] (NASA)
XT	X-Ray Tube
XTA	X-Band Tracking Antenna

XTAL......... Crystal
XTAL......... XTAL Corp. [*Burnsville, MN*] [*NASDAQ symbol*]   (NQ)
XTALK...... Crosstalk [*Telecommunications*]   (MSA)
XTASI....... Exchange of Technical Apollo Simulation Information
            [*NASA*]   (IEEE)
XTC........... Exco Technologies Ltd. [*Toronto Stock Exchange symbol*]
XTC........... External Transmit Clock
XTE........... X-Ray Timing Explorer
XTEL........ Cross Tell   (IEEE)
XTEL......... Executive Telecommunications, Inc. [*Tulsa, OK*] [*NASDAQ
            symbol*]   (NQ)
XTEN....... Xerox Telecommunications Network [*Proposed*]   (TSSD)
XTGX........ TGX Corp. [*NASDAQ symbol*]   (NQ)
XTIAN...... Christian
XTLK........ Cross Talk [*Aviation*]   (FAAC)
XTLO........ Crystal Oscillator
XTM.......... Experimental Test Model
XTN.......... Christian   (ROG)
XTND....... Extend [*or Extended*]
XTO........... X-Band Triode Oscillator
XTON....... EXECUTONE Information Systems, Inc. [*NASDAQ
            symbol*]   (SPSG)
XTP............ Xanthosine Triphosphate [*Biochemistry*]
XTPA........ X-Band Tunable Parametric Amplifier
XTR........... X-Ray Transition Radiation
XTR........... XTRA Corp. [*NYSE symbol*]   (SPSG)
XTRA........ Extra   (ROG)
XTRA........ XTRA Corp. [*Associated Press abbreviation*]   (APAG)
XTRM....... Extreme
XTRY........ Extraordinary   (ROG)
XTS........... Cross-Tell Simulator   (IEEE)
XTV........... Xerox Team Vision [*Xerox Business Products and Systems
            Group*] [*El Segundo, CA*]   (TSSD)
XTWA...... X-Band Traveling Wave Amplifier
XTWM...... X-Band Traveling Wave MASER
XTX.......... New York Tax Exempt Income [*AMEX symbol*]   (SPSG)
XTX.......... X-Band Transmitter
XTY.......... Christianity
XU............. Aerorepresentaciones Tupac Amaru [*Peru*] [*ICAO
            designator*]   (ICDA)
XU............. Cambodia [*Aircraft nationality and registration mark*]   (FAAC)
XU............. Excretory Urogram [*Medicine*]
XU............. Fire Resistive Unprotected [*Insurance classification*]
XU............. X Unit [*A unit of wavelength*]
XU............. Xavier University [*Louisiana; Ohio*]
XUB.......... Circleville, OH [*Location identifier*] [*FAA*]   (FAAL)
XUG.......... Xyvision Users Group   (EA)
XUM......... Xenium [*Gift*]   (ROG)
XUS.......... Xavier University. Studies [*A publication*]
XUV.......... Extreme Ultraviolet
XV............. Administration de Aeropuertos y Servicios Auxiliares a la
            Nauegacion Aerea [*AASANA*] [*Bolivia*] [*ICAO
            designator*]   (FAAC)
XV............. Vietnam [*Aircraft nationality and registration mark*]   (FAAC)
XV............. X-Ray Vision
XVA.......... X-Ray Vidicon Analysis
XVERS...... Transverse   (AAG)
XVII S........ XVIIe Siecle [*A publication*]
xVit........... Xenopus Vitellogenin
XVN.......... Venice, FL [*Location identifier*] [*FAA*]   (FAAL)
XVP.......... Executive Vice President
XVR.......... Exchange Voltage Regulator [*Telecommunications*]   (TEL)
XVT.......... Extensible Virtual Toolkit [*Data processing*]
XVT.......... Rome, NY [*Location identifier*] [*FAA*]   (FAAL)
XVTR........ Transverter   (AAG)
XW............. Ex-Warrants [*Without Warrants*] [*Finance*]   (SPSG)
XW............. Experimental Warhead
XW............. Extra Wide [*Size*]
XW............. Laos [*Aircraft nationality and registration mark*]   (FAAC)
X-WARR... Ex-Warrants [*Without Warrants*] [*Finance*]
XWAVE.... Extraordinary Wave   (IEEE)
X-WAY...... Expressway
XWB.......... Ozark, Fort Rucker, AL [*Location identifier*] [*FAA*]   (FAAL)
XWC.......... Wabash-Carnegie Public Library, Wabash, IN [*OCLC
            symbol*]   (OCLC)
XWCC....... Expanded Water Column Characterization
            [*Oceanography*]   (MSC)
XWS.......... Experimental Weapon Specification
XWS.......... Experimental Weapon System
XWY......... West Union, IA [*Location identifier*] [*FAA*]   (FAAL)
XX............. Dos Equis [*Beer*] [*Standard Brands, Inc.*]
XX............. Double Excellent
XX............. Doublecross Committee [*British military*]   (DMA)
XX............. Feminine Chromosome Pair
XX............. Heavy [*Used to qualify weather phenomena such as rain, e.g.,
            heavy rain equals XXRA*] [*Aviation code*]   (FAAC)
xx.............. No Place [*or Unknown*] [*MARC country of publication code*]
            [*Library of Congress*]   (LCCP)
X-X............ Pitch Axis [*Aerospace*]   (AAG)

XX.............. Twenty Committee [*British espionage unit named after a
            "double-cross" operation it conducted during World War
            II*]
XX.............. Without Securities or Warrants [*Business term*]
XXC.......... University of South Dakota, Card Reproduction Project,
            Vermillion, SD [*OCLC symbol*]   (OCLC)
XXC.......... Xerox Canada, Inc. [*Toronto Stock Exchange symbol*]
XXL.......... Extra-Extra Large [*Size*]
XXS........... Extra-Extra Strong
XXSTR...... Double Extra Strong
XXUS........ Maxxus, Inc. [*NASDAQ symbol*]   (NQ)
XXX.......... International Urgency Signal
XXX.......... Peru, IN [*Location identifier*] [*FAA*]   (FAAL)
XXX.......... Test Flight Plan [*Aviation code*]   (FAAC)
XXX.......... Triple Excellent
XY.............. Burma [*Aircraft nationality and registration mark*]   (FAAC)
XY.............. Masculine Chromosome Pair
XY.............. Spouse [*Citizens band radio slang*]
XY.............. Xylography [*Wood engraving*]   (ROG)
XYA........... X-Y Axis
XYA........... Yandina [*Solomon Islands*] [*Airport symbol*]   (OAG)
XYAT........ X-Y Axis Table
XYC........... Irvine, KY [*Location identifier*] [*FAA*]   (FAAL)
XYD........... Daughter [*Citizens band radio slang*]
XYL........... Ex-Young-Lady [*Wife*] [*Amateur radio slang*]
XYL........... Xylocaine [*Topical anesthetic*] [*Astra trademark for lidocaine*]
XYL........... Xylophone [*Music*]
Xyl............. Xylose [*Also, x*] [*A sugar*]
XYLO........ Xylophone [*Music*]   (ADA)
XYM.......... Husband [*Citizens band radio slang*]
XYP........... X-Y Plotter
XYR........... X-Y Recorder
XYrDev...... Ten-Year Device [*Military decoration*]
XYTRON.. Xytronyx, Inc. [*Associated Press abbreviation*]   (APAG)
XYVI......... Xyvision, Inc. [*Wakefield, MA*] [*NASDAQ symbol*]   (NQ)
XYX........... Xytronyx, Inc. [*AMEX symbol*]   (SPSG)
XYXXU..... High Plains Genetics Uts [*NASDAQ symbol*]   (NQ)
XYZ........... Examine Your Zipper
XYZ........... Extra Years of Zest [*Gerontology*]
XZ............. Burma [*Aircraft nationality and registration mark*]   (FAAC)
XZY........... Philadelphia, PA [*Location identifier*] [*FAA*]   (FAAL)

Y

Y................ Admittance [*Symbol*] [*IUPAC*]
Y................ Alleghany Corp. [*NYSE symbol*] (SPSG)
Y................ Closed at Sea (for High Degree of Emergency Readiness) [*Ship's fittings classification*]
Y................ Coach [*Airline fare code*]
Y................ Doublecross [*i.e., to betray*] [*Criminal slang*]
Y................ Except Sixth Form [*For the wearing of schoolgirls' uniforms*] [*British*]
Y................ Late Operating Contact [*Symbol*] (DEN)
Y................ Luminance
Y................ Male Chromosome
Y................ Nominal Gross National Product
Y................ Pathfinder [*Army skill qualification identifier*] (INF)
Y................ Planck Function [*Symbol*] [*IUPAC*]
Y................ Prototype [*Designation for all US military aircraft*]
Y................ [*A*] Pyrimidine Nucleoside [*One-letter symbol; see Pyd*]
Y................ Symbol for Upsilon
Y................ Tanker [*Army symbol*]
Y................ Three-Phase Star Connection [*Symbol*] (DEN)
Y................ Transitional Testing [*Aircraft*]
Y................ Tyrosine [*One-letter symbol; see Tyr*]
Y................ [*The Second*] Unknown Quantity [*Mathematics*] (ROG)
Y................ Upsilon [*Symbol*] [*Quantum physics*]
Y................ Vertical Deflection [*Symbol*] (DEN)
Y................ Y-Axis
Y................ Yacht (ADA)
Y................ Yankee [*Phonetic alphabet*] [*International*] (DSUE)
Y................ Yard [*Measure*]
Y................ Yaw
Y................ Yea [*Vote*]
Y................ Year
Y................ Yeates' Pennsylvania Reports [*1791-1808*] [*A publication*] (DLA)
Y................ Yellow [*Horticulture*]
Y................ Yellow [*Phonetic alphabet*] [*Royal Navy*] [*World War II*] (DSUE)
Y................ Yen [*Monetary unit in Japan*]
Y................ Yeoman
Y................ Yersinea [*A genus of bacteria*]
Y................ Yerushalmi [*Palestinian Talmud*] (BJA)
Y................ Yield [*Stock exchange term*] [*Agriculture*]
Y................ Yoke [*Phonetic alphabet*] [*World War II*] (DSUE)
Y................ Yorker [*Phonetic alphabet*] [*Pre-World War II*] (DSUE)
Y................ Yoshitomi Pharmaceutical Ind. Co. Ltd. [*Japan*] [*Research code symbol*]
Y................ You
Y................ Young (AAMN)
Y................ Young Men's [*or Women's*] Christian Association [*Short form of reference, especially to the group's building or specific facility, as "the Y swimming pool"*]
Y................ Young Vic [*British theatrical company*]
Y................ Younger [*or Youngest*]
Y................ Young's Modulus of Elasticity [*Symbol*] [*See also E, YME*]
Y................ Your
Y................ Yttrium [*Preferred form, but see also Yt*] [*Chemical element*]
Y................ Yugoslavia [*IYRU nationality code*] (IYR)
Y................ Yukon News [*A publication*]
Y................ Yukon Standard Time [*Aviation*] (FAAC)
Y................ Yuppie [*As in Y-people*]
4Y............... Selective Service classification suggested by comedian Bob Hope for himself during World War II [*Y stood for "yellow"*]
5Y............... Kenya [*Aircraft nationality and registration mark*] (FAAC)
Y (Day) ...... June 1, 1944, the deadline for all preparations for the Normandy invasion [*World War II*]
YA.............. Afghanistan [*Aircraft nationality and registration mark*] (FAAC)
YA.............. Ash Lighter [*Navy symbol*]
YA.............. Government Civil Aviation Authority [*ICAO designator*] (ICDA)
YA.............. Yaw Axis

YA.............. Yeda-'am. Journal. Hebrew Folklore Society [*Tel-Aviv*] [*A publication*]
YA.............. YIVO Annual [*A publication*]
Y/A .... York-Antwerp Rules [*Marine insurance*]
YA.............. Yosemite Association (EA)
YA.............. Young Adult [*Refers to books published for this market*]
YA.............. Young Audiences (EA)
YAA .... Yachtsmen's Association of America (EA)
YAA .... Youth Ambassadors of America [*Later, YAI*] (EA)
YAA .... Yugoslav Survey [*A publication*]
YAAR .... Yacimientos Arqueologicos [*Database*] [*Ministerio de Cultura*] [*Spanish*] [*Information service or system*] (CRD)
YABA .... Yacht Architects and Brokers Association (EA)
YABA .... Young American Bowling Alliance (EA)
YABC .... Yesterday's Authors of Books for Children [*A publication*]
YABRI ...... Young Adult Book Review Index [*A publication*]
YAC .... Yeast Artificial Chromosome [*Genetics*] [*Biochemistry*]
YAC .... Young Adult Council of National Social Welfare Assembly (EA)
YAC .... Young Astronaut Council (EA)
YACC .... Yet Another Compiler-Complier (HGAA)
YACC .... Young Adult Conservation Corps
YACC .... Young America's Campaign Committee [*Later, FCM*] (EA)
YACE........ Yukon Alpine Centennial Expedition
Yacht........ Yachting [*A publication*]
YACN........ Yukon Anniversaries Commission Newsletter [*A publication*]
YACTOFF ... Yaw Actuator Offset (KSC)
Yad............ Yadaim (BJA)
YAD.......... Young's Nova Scotia Admiralty Decisions [*A publication*] (DLA)
Yad Energ.. Yadrena Energiya [*A publication*]
Yadernaya Fiz ... Akademiya Nauk SSSR. Yadernaya Fizika [*A publication*]
Yad Fiz...... Yadernaya Fizika [*A publication*]
Yad Geofiz ... Yadernaya Geofizika [*A publication*]
YADH........ Yeast Alcohol Dehydrogenase [*An enzyme*]
Ya Div Q .... Yale Divinity Quarterly [*New Haven, CT*] [*A publication*]
Yad Konstanty ... Yadernye Konstanty [*A publication*]
Yad Magn Rezon ... Yadernyi Magnitnyi Rezonans [*A publication*]
Yad Magn Rezon Org Khim ... Yadernyi Magnitnyi Rezonans v Organicheskoi Khimii [*A publication*]
Yad Priborostr ... Yadernoe Priborostroenie [*Former USSR*] [*A publication*]
Yad Vashem Stud Eur Jew Catastrophe Resist ... Yad Vashem Studies on the European Jewish Catastrophe and Resistance [*A publication*]
YAEC........ Yankee Atomic Electric Co.
YAF .... Asbestos Hill [*Canada*] [*Airport symbol*] [*Obsolete*] (OAG)
YAF .... Yidishe Arbeter Froyen (BJA)
YAF .... Young Americans for Freedom (EA)
YAF .... Young America's Foundation (EA)
YAF .... Yugoslavian Air Force
YAG.......... Fort Frances [*Canada*] [*Airport symbol*] (OAG)
YAG.......... Miscellaneous Auxiliary [*Self-propelled*] [*Navy ship symbol*]
YAG.......... Yagi [*Kashiwara*] [*Japan*] [*Seismograph station code, US Geological Survey*] [*Closed*] (SEIS)
YAG.......... Young Actors Guild (EA)
YAG.......... Yttrium-Aluminum Garnet [*LASER technology*]
YAGL .... Yttrium Aluminum Garnet LASER
YAGR........ Ocean RADAR Station Ship [*Navy symbol*] [*Obsolete*]
YAH.......... Alfred University, Alfred, NY [*OCLC symbol*] (OCLC)
YAH.......... Yahtse [*Alaska*] [*Seismograph station code, US Geological Survey*] (SEIS)
YAI .... Young Adult Institute and Workshop (EA)
YAI .... Youth Ambassadors International (EA)
YAIC......... Young American Indian Council
YAJ........... Yeda-'am. Journal. Hebrew Folklore Society [*Tel-Aviv*] [*A publication*]
YAJ........... Yorkshire Archaeological Journal [*A publication*]
YAK.......... Yakovlev [*Russian aircraft symbol; initialism taken from name of aircraft's designer*]
YAK.......... Yakutat [*Alaska*] [*Airport symbol*] (OAG)
YAK.......... Yakutsk [*Former USSR*] [*Geomagnetic observatory code*]

3831

YAK .... Yakutsk [*Former USSR*] [*Seismograph station code, US Geological Survey*] (SEIS)
YAKUA ..... Yakuzaigaku [*A publication*]
YAKUA2 ... Archives of Practical Pharmacy [*A publication*]
Yakugaku Zasshi J Pharmaceut Soc Jap ... Yakugaku Zasshi/Journal of the Pharmaceutical Society of Japan [*A publication*]
Yal .... Yalkut Shim'oni [*BJA*]
YAL .... Yalta [*Former USSR*] [*Seismograph station code, US Geological Survey*] [*Closed*] (SEIS)
YAL .... Yosemite Airlines [*Columbia, CA*] [*FAA designator*] (FAAC)
YAL .... Yttrium Aluminum LASER
Yale Art Gal Bul ... Yale University. Art Gallery. Bulletin [*A publication*]
Yale Associates Bul ... Yale University. Associates in Fine Arts. Bulletin [*A publication*]
Yale Bicen Pub Contr Miner ... Yale Bicentennial Publications. Contributions to Mineralogy and Petrography [*A publication*]
Yale Class Studies ... Yale Classical Studies Series [*A publication*]
Yale ClSt.... Yale Classical Studies [*A publication*]
Yale Div Q ... Yale Divinity Quarterly [*A publication*]
Yale Forestry Bull ... Yale University. School of Forestry. Bulletin [*A publication*]
Yale French Stud ... Yale French Studies [*A publication*]
Yale Fr St... Yale French Studies [*A publication*]
Yale Fr Stud ... Yale French Studies [*A publication*]
Yale Ital S ... Yale Italian Studies [*A publication*]
Yale J Biol ... Yale Journal of Biology and Medicine [*A publication*]
Yale J Biol Med ... Yale Journal of Biology and Medicine [*A publication*]
Yale J World Pub Ord ... Yale Journal of World Public Order [*A publication*]
Yale Law J ... Yale Law Journal [*A publication*]
Yale Lit Mag ... Yale Literary Magazine [*A publication*]
Yale L J ..... Yale Law Journal [*A publication*]
Yale L & Pol'y Rev ... Yale Law and Policy Review [*A publication*] (DLA)
Yale Math Monographs ... Yale Mathematical Monographs [*A publication*]
Yale R .... Yale Review [*A publication*]
Yale Rev..... Yale Review [*A publication*]
Yale Rev Law & Soc Act'n ... Yale Review of Law and Social Action [*A publication*] (DLA)
Yale Rev of L and Soc Action ... Yale Review of Law and Social Action [*A publication*] (DLA)
Yale Sci ...... Yale Scientific [*A publication*]
Yale Scient Mag ... Yale Scientific Magazine [*A publication*]
Yale Sci Mag ... Yale Scientific Magazine [*A publication*]
Yale Sc Mo ... Yale Scientific Monthly [*A publication*]
Yale Stud World PO ... Yale Studies in World Public Order [*A publication*]
Yale Stud World Pub Ord ... Yale Studies in World Public Order [*A publication*]
Yale St Wld Pub Ord ... Yale Studies in World Public Order [*A publication*]
Yale U Lib Gaz ... Yale University. Library. Gazette [*A publication*]
Yale U Libr ... Yale University. Library. Gazette [*A publication*]
Yale Univ Art Gal Bull ... Yale University. Art Gallery. Bulletin [*A publication*]
Yale Univ B ... Yale University. Art Gallery. Bulletin [*A publication*]
Yale Univ Lib Gaz ... Yale University. Library. Gazette [*A publication*]
Yale Univ Peabody Mus Nat Hist Annu Rep ... Yale University. Peabody Museum of Natural History. Annual Report [*A publication*]
Yale Univ Peabody Mus Nat Hist Bull ... Yale University. Peabody Museum of Natural History. Bulletin [*A publication*]
Yale Univ Peabody Mus Nat History Bull ... Yale University. Peabody Museum of Natural History. Bulletin [*A publication*]
Yale Univ Sch For Bull ... Yale University. School of Forestry. Bulletin [*A publication*]
Yale Univ Sch For Environ Stud Bull ... Yale University. School of Forestry and Environmental Studies. Bulletin [*A publication*]
Yalkut Le-Sivim Tekhnol U-Minhal Shel Tekst ... Yalkut Le-sivim Tekhnologyah U-Minhal Shel Tekstil [*A publication*]
Y Alm......... Yurosholayimer Almanakh [*A publication*]
YalMakh ... Yalkut Makhiri [*BJA*]
YAM .... American Museum of Natural History, New York, NY [*OCLC symbol*] (OCLC)
YAM .... Sault Ste. Marie [*Canada*] [*Airport symbol*] (OAG)
YAM .... Yamagata [*Japan*] [*Seismograph station code, US Geological Survey*] (SEIS)
YAM .... Yet Another MODEM [*Modulator-Demodulator*] [*Communications program*]
YAM .... Young Australian Male [*Lifestyle classification*]
Yamaguchi Med ... Yamaguchi Medicine [*Japan*] [*A publication*]
YAN........... Yancey Railroad Co. [*AAR code*]
YAN .... Yangoru [*Papua New Guinea*] [*Seismograph station code, US Geological Survey*] (SEIS)
YANCON ... Yankee Conference [*College sports*]
YanEnS...... Yankee Energy Systems, Inc. [*Associated Press abbreviation*] (APAG)
YANGPAT ... Yangtze Patrol, Asiatic Fleet [*Navy*]
YANK........ Yankee (ROG)
YANK .... Youth of America Needs to Know
yao.............. Yao (Bantu) [*MARC language code*] [*Library of Congress*] (LCCP)
YAO........... Yaounde [*Cameroon*] [*Airport symbol*] (OAG)
YAP .... Yap [*Caroline Islands*] [*Airport symbol*] (OAG)
YAP .... Yaw and Pitch

YAP .... Yield Analysis Pattern [*Data processing*]
Yap............. Young Aspiring Professional [*Lifestyle classification*] [*In book title "YAP; the Official Young Aspiring Professional's Fast-Track Handbook"*]
YAP .... Younger American Playwright [*Slang*]
YAPD .... Young Americans of Polish Descent (EA)
YAPLO..... Yorkshire Association of Power Loom Overlookers [*A union*] [*British*] (DCTA)
Yappie .... Young Artist Professional [*Lifestyle classification*]
YAPRA...... Yadernoe Priborostroenie [*A publication*]
YAR .... Yemen Arab Republic
YAR .... York-Antwerp Rules [*Marine insurance*]
YARA .... Young Americans for Responsible Action
Y-ARD...... Yarrow Admiralty Research Department [*Navy*] [*British*]
YARD .... Youth Associated with the Restoration of Democracy [*Kenya*] [*Political party*] (EY)
Yard R........ Yardbird Reader [*A publication*]
YARU .... Yale Arbovirus Research Unit [*Yale University*] [*Research center*] (RCD)
YAS........... Yasodhara Ashram Society (EA)
YAS........... Yaw Attitude Sensor
YASD........ Young Adult Services Division - of ALA [*American Library Association*] (EA)
YASIG .... Young Adult Special Interest Group [*Canadian Library Association*]
YASOQB... Ye Anciente and Secret Order of Quiet Birdmen (EA)
YAT .... Attawapiskat [*Canada*] [*Airport symbol*] (OAG)
YAT .... Yaldymych [*Former USSR*] [*Seismograph station code, US Geological Survey*] [*Closed*] (SEIS)
Yate-Lee..... Yates-Lee on Bankruptcy [*3rd ed.*] [*1887*] [*A publication*] (DLA)
Yates Sel Cas ... Yates' Select Cases [*1809*] [*New York*] [*A publication*] (DLA)
Yates Sel Cas (NY) ... Yates' Select Cases [*1809*] [*New York*] [*A publication*] (DLA)
YATS........ Youth Attitude Tracking Survey [*Navy*]
YAUI .... Yet Another User Interface [*Data processing*]
YAVIS .... Young, Attractive, Verbal, Intelligent, and Successful
Yawata Tech Rep ... Yawata Technical Report [*A publication*]
YAWF........ Youth Against War and Fascism (EA)
Yawnie .... Youngish Anglophone of Westmount and Notre-Dame-De-Grace [*Lifestyle classification*] [*Canadian Yuppie identified in Keith Harrison's novel "After Six Days"*]
YAWP .... Yet Another Word Processor (BYTE)
YB .... Meteorological Operational Telecommunications Network Europe [*ICAO designator*] (ICDA)
YB .... Yard Bird [*Confined to camp*] [*Military slang*]
YB .... Year Book of Reports of Cases [*A publication*]
YB .... Year Books [*Law*] [*United Kingdom*] [*A publication*]
YB .... Yearbook
Yb............... Yearbook of Comparative and General Literature [*A publication*]
YB .... Yellowknife Bear Resources, Inc. [*Toronto Stock Exchange symbol*]
YB .... Yeshiva Benarroch. Tetuan (BJA)
YB .... YIVO Bleter [*Vilna/New York*] [*A publication*]
YB .... Yorkshire Bulletin of Economic and Social Research [*A publication*]
YB .... Your Business [*A publication*] (ADA)
YB .... Ysgrifau Beirniadol [*A publication*]
Yb............... Ytterbium [*Chemical element*]
YBA .... Youth Basketball Association [*Joint program of NBA Players' Association and YMCA*]
YBAAA...... Yearbook. Association of Attenders of Alumni of the Hague Academy of International Law [*A publication*] (DLA)
Yb Agric Coop ... Yearbook of Agricultural Cooperation [*A publication*]
Yb Agric US Dep Agric ... Yearbook of Agriculture. US Department of Agriculture [*A publication*]
YB Air & Space L ... Yearbook of Air and Space Law [*A publication*] (DLA)
YB Ames.... Year Book. Ames Foundation [*A publication*] (DLA)
YBASL ...... Yearbook of Air and Space Law [*A publication*] (DLA)
YBBFC ...... Younger Brothers Band Fan Club (EA)
YBC .... Baie Comeau [*Canada*] [*Airport symbol*] (OAG)
YBC .... Yale Babylonian Collection (BJA)
YBCA........ Yearbook of Commercial Arbitration [*A publication*] (DLA)
Yb Calif Avocado Soc ... Yearbook. California Avocado Society [*A publication*]
YBCO .... Yttrium Barium Copper Oxide [*Inorganic chemistry*]
YBD .... Bowdock [*Navy symbol*]
YBD .... Yellow Band Resources [*Vancouver Stock Exchange symbol*]
YBD .... Young British Designers
YBDRE3... Year Book of Diagnostic Radiology [*A publication*]
YBDSA...... Yacht Designers and Surveyors Association (EAIO)
YBE .... Stewart Aviation Services, Inc. [*FAA designator*] (FAAC)
YBE .... Uranium City [*Canada*] [*Airport symbol*] (OAG)
YBE .... York Borough Board of Education, Professional Education Library [*UTLAS symbol*]
YB Ed I ..... Year Books of Edward I [*A publication*] (DLA)
Yb Educ...... Yearbook of Education [*A publication*]
YB Eur Conv on Human Rights ... Year Book. European Convention on Human Rights [*A publication*] (DLA)

Yb of the Eur Conv on Human Rights ... Yearbook. European Convention on Human Rights [*The Hague, Netherlands*] [*A publication*]   (DLA)
YB Europ Conv HR ... Yearbook. European Convention on Human Rights [*The Hague, Netherlands*] [*A publication*]   (DLA)
YBG .... Saguenay [*Canada*] [*Airport symbol*]   (OAG)
Yb Gen Med ... Yearbook of General Medicine [*A publication*]
Yb Gen Surg ... Yearbook of General Surgery [*A publication*]
Yb Gloucester Beekprs Ass ... Yearbook. Gloucestershire Bee-Keepers Association [*A publication*]
YBHSEQ... Year Book of Hand Surgery [*A publication*]
YB Human Rights ... Yearbook on Human Rights [*A publication*]   (DLA)
YB Hum Rts ... Yearbook on Human Rights [*A publication*]   (DLA)
YBICJ........ Yearbook. International Court of Justice [*A publication*]   (DLA)
YBICSU .... Yearbook. International Council of Scientific Unions [*A publication*]
Yb Ind Orthop Surg ... Yearbook of Industrial and Orthopedic Surgery [*A publication*]
Yb Ind Stat ... Yearbook of Industrial Statistics [*A publication*]
Yb Inter Amer M Research ... Yearbook for Inter-American Musical Research [*A publication*]
Yb Int Folk M Council ... Yearbook. International Folk Music Council [*A publication*]
YB Int L Comm ... Yearbook. International Law Community [*A publication*]   (DLA)
YB Int'l L Comm'n ... Yearbook. International Law Commission [*A publication*]   (DLA)
YB Int'l Org ... Yearbook of International Organizations [*A publication*]   (DLA)
YBJ .... Baie Johan Beetz [*Canada*] [*Airport symbol*]   (OAG)
YBK .... Baker Lake [*Canada*] [*Airport symbol*]   (OAG)
YBL........... Campbell River [*Canada*] [*Airport symbol*]   (OAG)
YB League ... Yearbook. League of Nations [*A publication*]   (DLA)
Yb of Leg Stud ... Year Book of Legal Studies [*Madras, India*] [*A publication*]   (DLA)
YbLitgSt .... Yearbook of Liturgical Studies [*Notre Dame, IN*] [*A publication*]
YBM .... State University of New York, College at Buffalo, Buffalo, NY [*OCLC symbol*]   (OCLC)
Yb Med ...... Yearbook of Medicine [*A publication*]
Yb Med Ass Great Cy NY ... Yearbook. Medical Association of the Greater City of New York [*A publication*]
Yb Neurol Psychiat Endocr ... Yearbook of Neurology, Psychiatry, Endocrinology, and Neurosurgery [*A publication*]
Y-BOCS..... Yale-Brown Obsessive-Compulsive Scale [*Psychology*]
Yb Ophthal ... Yearbook of Ophthalmology [*A publication*]
YBP............. Years before Present
YBPC......... Young Black Programmers Coalition   (EA)
Yb Pediat ... Yearbook of Pediatrics [*A publication*]
YB P1 Edw II ... Year Books, Part 1, Edward II [*A publication*]   (DLA)
Yb Phys Med Rehabil ... Yearbook of Physical Medicine and Rehabilitation [*A publication*]
Yb Phys Soc ... Yearbook. Physical Society [*A publication*]
YBPS .... Yearbook. British Pirandello Society [*A publication*]
YBR .... Brandon [*Canada*] [*Airport symbol*]   (OAG)
YBR .... Sludge Removal Barge [*Navy*]
YBR .... Yellow Brick Road [*Intelligence test*]
YBRA......... Yellowstone-Bighorn Research Association   (EA)
Yb R Hort Soc ... Yearbook. Royal Horticulture Society [*A publication*]
YB Rich II ... Bellewe's Les Ans du Roy Richard le Second [*1378-1400*] [*A publication*]   (DLA)
YBRIF .... Yellowknife Bear Resources, Inc. [*NASDAQ symbol*]   (NQ)
YB (Rolls Ser) ... Year Books, Rolls Series [*1292-1546*] [*A publication*]   (DLA)
YB (RS)..... Year Books, Rolls Series [*1292-1546*] [*A publication*]   (DLA)
YB (RS)...... Year Books, Rolls Series, Edited by Horwood [*1292-1307*] [*A publication*]   (DLA)
YB (RS)...... Year Books, Rolls Series, Edited by Horwood and Pike [*1337-46*] [*A publication*]   (DLA)
Yb R Vet Agric Coll ... Yearbook. Royal Veterinary and Agricultural College [*A publication*]
YBSC......... Year Books, Selected Cases [*A publication*]   (DLA)
YB Sch L..... Yearbook of School Law [*A publication*]   (DLA)
YB (Sel Soc) ... Year Books, Selden Society [*1307-19*] [*A publication*]   (DLA)
Yb Soc........ Yearbook. Royal Society of London [*A publication*]
Yb Soc Pol Britain ... Yearbook of Social Policy in Britain [*A publication*]
YB (SS)...... Year Books, Selden Society [*1307-19*] [*A publication*]   (DLA)
YBT .... Yale Oriental Series. Babylonian Texts [*New Haven, CT*] [*A publication*]   (BJA)
YBT .... Youssef Ben Tachfine [*Morocco*] [*Seismograph station code, US Geological Survey*]   (SEIS)
YBUN........ Yearbook of the United Nations [*A publication*]   (DLA)
Yb US Dep Agric ... Yearbook. United States Department of Agriculture [*A publication*]
YBV .... Berens River [*Canada*] [*Airport symbol*]   (OAG)
Yb Wld Aff ... Yearbook of World Affairs [*A publication*]
Yb World Aff ... Yearbook of World Affairs [*A publication*]
YB World Pol ... Yearbook of World Polity [*A publication*]   (DLA)
YBX .... Blanc Sablon [*Canada*] [*Airport symbol*]   (OAG)

Yb Yorks Beekprs Ass ... Yearbook. Yorkshire Beekeepers Association [*A publication*]
Y/C .... Luminance, Color
YC............. Open Lighter [*Non-self-propelled*] [*Navy symbol*]
YC............. Rescue Coordination Center [*ICAO designator*]   (ICDA)
YC............. Y-Chromosome
YC............. Yacht Club
YC............. Yale College   (ROG)
YC............. Yankee Conference [*College sports*]
YC............. Yard Craft [*Navy symbol*]
YC............. Yaw Channel
YC............. Yaw Coupling
YC............. Yeomanry Cavalry [*Military*] [*British*]
YC............. Yesterday's Children   (EA)
YC............. Yola Clay Loam [*A soil type*]
Y & C .... Younge and Collyer's English Chancery Reports [*1841-43*] [*A publication*]   (DLA)
Y & C .... Younge and Collyer's English Exchequer Equity Reports [*1834-42*] [*A publication*]   (DLA)
y/c .... Your Cable   (DS)
YC............. Youth Clubs [*Public-performance tariff class*] [*British*]
YC............. Youth Conservative [*Political party*] [*British*]
YCA .... Yachting Club of America   (EA)
YCA .... Yale-China Association   (EA)
YCA .... Yield Component Analysis [*Botany*]
YCA .... Young Concert Artists   (EA)
YCA .... Young Conservative Alliance of America [*Later, Campus Action Network*]   (EA)
YCAP........ Youth Committee Against Poverty
YCB .... Cambridge Bay [*Canada*] [*Airport symbol*]   (OAG)
YCB .... Yeast Carbon Base
YCB .... Yellow Creek Bluff [*Alaska*] [*Seismograph station code, US Geological Survey*]   (SEIS)
YCC .... Computer Center [*Yale University*] [*Research center*]   (RCD)
YCC .... Yearbook of Comparative Criticism [*A publication*]
YCC .... York Centre [*Vancouver Stock Exchange symbol*]
YCC .... Youth Civic Center
YCC .... Youth Conservation Corps   (EA)
YCC .... Yuma City-County Public Library, Yuma, AZ [*OCLC symbol*]   (OCLC)
YCCA .... National Youth Council on Civic Affairs [*Superseded by CCNYA*]   (EA)
YCCA .... Yorkshire Canary Club of America   (EA)
Y & CCC .... Younge and Collyer's English Chancery Cases [*62-63 English Reprint*] [*1841-43*] [*A publication*]   (DLA)
Y & C Ch ... Younge and Collyer's English Chancery Reports [*1841-43*] [*A publication*]   (DLA)
Y & C Ch Cas ... Younge and Collyer's English Chancery Cases [*62-63 English Reprint*] [*1841-43*] [*A publication*]   (DLA)
YCCIP .... Youth Community Conservation and Improvement Projects [*Department of Labor*]
YCD .... Fueling Barge [*Navy symbol*] [*Obsolete*]
YCD .... Nanaimo [*Canada*] [*Airport symbol*]   (OAG)
YCD .... Youth Correction Division [*Department of Justice*]
YCEE........ Youth Cost per Entered Employment [*Job Training and Partnership Act*]   (OICC)
Y & C Ex ... Younge and Collyer's English Exchequer Equity Reports [*1834-42*] [*A publication*]   (DLA)
Y & C Exch ... Younge and Collyer's English Exchequer Equity Reports [*1834-42*] [*A publication*]   (DLA)
YCF........... Car Float [*Non-self-propelled*] [*Navy symbol*]
YCF........... Yankee Critical Facility [*Nuclear energy*]
YCF........... Young Calvinist Federation   (EA)
YCF........... Young Conservative Foundation [*Later, CAF*]   (EA)
YCF........... Youth Citizenship Fund   (EA)
YCG .... Castlegar [*Canada*] [*Airport symbol*]   (OAG)
YCGL........ Yearbook of Comparative and General Literature [*A publication*]
YCGS........ York County Genealogical Society   (EA)
YCH .... Chatham [*Canada*] [*Airport symbol*]   (OAG)
YCHP .... Yenching Journal of Chinese Studies [*A publication*]
YCI .... Year-Class Strength Index [*Pisciculture*]
YCI .... Young Communist International [*Dissolved, 1943*]
YCJCYAQFTJB ... Your Curiosity Just Cost You a Quarter for the Jukebox [*Tavern sign*]
YCK .... Aircraft Transportation Lighter [*Navy symbol*]
YCK .... Open Cargo Lighter [*Navy ship symbol*] [*Obsolete*]
YCKKAK... Acta Gerontologica Japonica [*A publication*]
YCL........... Charlo [*Canada*] [*Airport symbol*]   (OAG)
YCL........... Yolk Cytoplasmic Layer [*Embryology*]
YCL........... Young Communist League of the United States of America   (EA)
YCL........... Youth Counseling League   (EA)
YCLA......... Young Circle League of America [*Later, Workmen's Circle*]   (EA)
YCLS......... Yale Classical Studies [*A publication*]
Y Cl St....... Yale Classical Studies Series [*A publication*]
YCM .... State University of New York, College at Cortland, Cortland, NY [*OCLC symbol*]   (OCLC)
YCM.......... Yellow, Cyan, and Magenta [*Color model*]   (WDMC)

YCM .... YMCA Camp [*Montana*] [*Seismograph station code, US Geological Survey*] [*Closed*]   (SEIS)
YCM .... Young Christian Movement [*Formerly, YCW*] [*Defunct*]
YCMD ...... Yaw Gimbal Command   (KSC)
YCN .... Cochrane [*Canada*] [*Airport symbol*]   (OAG)
YCNP .... Yellow Creek Nuclear Plant   (NRCH)
YCO .... Coppermine [*Canada*] [*Airport symbol*]   (OAG)
Y & Coll ..... Younge and Collyer's English Chancery Reports [*1841-43*] [*A publication*]   (DLA)
Y & Coll ..... Younge and Collyer's English Exchequer Equity Reports [*1834-42*] [*A publication*]   (DLA)
YCOMA .... Yearbook. Coke Oven Managers' Association [*A publication*]
YCP .... Yaw Coupling Parameter
YCp .... Yeast Centromere Plasmid [*Genetics*]
YCP .... York College of Pennsylvania, York, PA [*OCLC symbol*]   (OCLC)
YCP .... Youth Challenge Program
YCR .... Cross Lake [*Canada*] [*Airport symbol*]   (OAG)
YCS .... High School Young Christian Students   (EA)
YCS .... Yale Classical Studies [*A publication*]
YCS .... Yearbook of Construction Statistics [*A publication*]
YCS .... Yorkshire Celtic Studies [*A publication*]
YCS .... Young Christian Student   (AEBS)
YCS .... Young Collector Series [*A publication*]
YCS .... Youth Community Service [*ACTION project*]
YCSL .... Yorkridge-Calvert Savings & Loan Association [*NASDAQ symbol*]   (NQ)
YCSM .... Young Christian Student Movement
YCSN .... Yukon Conservation Society. Newsletter [*A publication*]
Y C T .... Young Cinema and Theatre [*A publication*]
YCTF .... Younger Chemists Task Force [*American Chemical Society*]
YCTSD ...... Yugoslav Center for Technical and Scientific Documentation [*Information service or system*]   (IID)
YCU .... Youth Clubs United
YCV .... Aircraft Transportation Lighter [*Non-self-propelled*] [*Navy symbol*]
YCV .... Young Citizens Volunteers [*14th (Service) Battalion, Royal Irish Rifles*] [*British military*]   (DMA)
YCW .... Young Christian Workers [*Later, YCM*]   (EA)
YCWCDP ... Acta Botanica Yunnanica [*A publication*]
YCY .... Clyde River [*Canada*] [*Airport symbol*]   (OAG)
YCZ .... Yellow Caution Zone [*Runway lighting*] [*Aviation*]
YD .... Authority Supervising the Aerodrome [*ICAO designator*]   (ICDA)
Y & D .... Bureau of Yards and Docks [*Later, NFEC*] [*Navy*]
YD .... Floating Crane [*Non-self-propelled*] [*Navy symbol*]
YD .... Floating Derrick [*Navy*]
YD .... People's Democratic Republic of Yemen [*ANSI two-letter standard code*]   (CNC)
YD .... Yard [*Navy*]
YD .... Yard [*Measure*]
YD .... Yaw Damper [*Aviation*]   (MCD)
YD .... Yaw Deviation
YD .... Yoreh De'ah. Shulhan 'Arukh   (BJA)
YD .... Yorkshire Dragoons [*British military*]   (DMA)
yd² .... Square Yard   (CDAI)
YD³ .... Cubic Yard
YDA .... Yesterday   (FAAC)
YDA .... Young Democrats of America   (EA)
YDAW .... Dawson Public Library, Yukon [*Library symbol*] [*National Library of Canada*]   (NLC)
YDAY .... Yesterday [*Business term*]
YDB .... Yield Diffusion Bonding
YDB .... Youth Development Bureau [*Department of Health and Human Services*]
YDC .... Yaw Damper Computer
YDC .... Yeast Extract - Dextrose Calcium Carbonate Agar [*Microbiology*]
YDC .... Yiddish Dictionary Committee   (EA)
YDC .... Youth for Development and Cooperation   (EAIO)
YDCA .... Young Democratic Clubs of America [*Later, YDA*]   (EA)
YDDPA ..... Youth Development and Delinquency Prevention Administration [*Later, Youth Development Bureau*] [*HEW*]
YDF .... Deer Lake [*Canada*] [*Airport symbol*]   (OAG)
YDG .... District Degaussing Vessel [*Navy symbol*]
YDG .... Yarding   (WGA)
YDI .... Youth Development, Inc.   (EA)
YDKGA ..... Yamaguchi Daigaku Kogakubu Kenkyu Hokoku [*A publication*]
YDM .... State University of New York, College of Ceramics at Alfred University, Alfred, NY [*OCLC symbol*]   (OCLC)
YDN .... Dauphin [*Canada*] [*Airport symbol*]   (OAG)
YDNGAU ... Bulletin. Faculty of Agriculture. Yamaguchi University [*A publication*]
YDP .... Yeni Dogus Partisi [*New Dawn Party*] [*Turkish Cyprus*] [*Political party*]   (EY)
YDPCK ...... Klondike National Historic Site, Parks Canada [*Lieu Historique National Klondike, Parcs Canada*] Dawson City, Yukon [*Library symbol*] [*National Library of Canada*]   (NLC)

YDPP .... Young Democratic Progressive Party [*Macedonia*] [*Political party*]   (EY)
YDQ .... Dawson Creek [*Canada*] [*Airport symbol*]   (OAG)
YDQ .... Yale Divinity Quarterly [*A publication*]
YDS .... Yards   (MCD)
YDS .... Yorkshire Dialect Society. Transactions [*A publication*]
YDSD .... Yards and Docks Supply Depot [*Obsolete*] [*Navy*]
YDSO .... Yards and Docks Supply Office [*Navy*]
YDT .... Diving Tender [*Non-self-propelled*] [*Navy symbol*]
YE .... Lighter, Ammunition [*Navy symbol*]
YE .... Year End
YE .... Yeast Enolase [*An enzyme*]
YE .... Yellow Edges
YE .... Yellow Enzyme [*Biochemistry*]
ye .... Yemen Arab Republic [*MARC country of publication code*] [*Library of Congress*]   (LCCP)
YE .... Yemen Arab Republic [*ANSI two-letter standard code*]   (CNC)
YE .... Yevreyskaya Entsiklopediya [*A publication*]   (BJA)
YE .... Youth Entry [*British military*]   (DMA)
YEA .... Yaw Error Amplifier
YEA .... Year of Energy Action
YEA .... Yeast Extract Agar [*Microbiology*]
Yea .... Yeates' Pennsylvania Reports [*1791-1808*] [*A publication*]   (DLA)
YEA .... Youth Emotions Anonymous   (EA)
YEA .... Youth Evangelism Association   (EA)
Yearb Agr Co-Op ... Yearbook of Agricultural Co-Operation [*A publication*]
Yearb Agric US Dep Agric ... Yearbook of Agriculture. US Department of Agriculture [*A publication*]
Yearb Agr USDA ... Yearbook of Agriculture. US Department of Agriculture [*A publication*]
Yearb Am Iron Steel Inst ... Yearbook. American Iron and Steel Institute [*A publication*]
Yearb Am Pulp Pap Mil Supt Assoc ... Yearbook. American Pulp and Paper Mill Superintendents Association [*A publication*]
Yearb Anesth ... Yearbook of Anesthesia [*A publication*]
Yearb Bharat Krishak Samaj ... Yearbook. Bharat Krishak Samaj [*A publication*]
Yearb Bur Miner Resour Geol Geophys ... Yearbook. Bureau of Mineral Resources. Geology and Geophysics [*A publication*]
Yearb Bur Miner Resour Geol Geo-Phys (Aus) ... Yearbook. Bureau of Mineral Resources. Geology and Geophysics (Australia) [*A publication*]
Yearb Calif Avocado Soc ... Yearbook. California Avocado Society [*A publication*]
Yearb Calif Macad Soc ... Yearbook. California Macadamia Society [*A publication*]
Yearb Carnegie Inst Wash ... Yearbook. Carnegie Institute of Washington [*A publication*]
Yearb Child Lit Assoc ... Yearbook. Children's Literature Association [*A publication*]
Yearb Coke Oven Managers' Assoc ... Yearbook. Coke Oven Managers' Association [*England*] [*A publication*]
Yearb Dermatol Syphilol ... Yearbook of Dermatology and Syphilology [*A publication*]
Yearb Drug Ther ... Yearbook of Drug Therapy [*A publication*]
Yearb Endocrinol ... Yearbook of Endocrinology [*A publication*]
Yearb Engl Stud ... Yearbook of English Studies [*A publication*]
Yearb Est Learned Soc Am ... Yearbook. Estonian Learned Society in America [*A publication*]
Yearb Fac Agr Univ Ankara ... Yearbook. Faculty of Agriculture. University of Ankara [*A publication*]
Yearb Gen Surg ... Yearbook of General Surgery [*A publication*]
Yearb Inst Geochem Sib Div Acad Sci (USSR) ... Yearbook. Institute of Geochemistry. Siberian Division. Academy of Sciences (USSR) [*A publication*]
Yearb Leo Baeck Inst ... Yearbook. Leo Baeck Institute [*A publication*]
Yearb Med ... Yearbook of Medicine [*A publication*]
Yearb Nat Farmers' Ass ... Yearbook. National Farmers' Association [*A publication*]
Yearb Natl Inst Sci India ... Yearbook. National Institute of Sciences of India [*A publication*]
Year Book Aust ... Year Book Australia [*A publication*]
Year Book Carnegie Inst Wash ... Year Book. Carnegie Institution of Washington [*A publication*]
Year Book Diagn Radiol ... Year Book of Diagnostic Radiology [*A publication*]
Yearbook East-Eur Econ ... Yearbook of East-European Economics [*A publication*]
Year Book Hand Surg ... Year Book of Hand Surgery [*A publication*]
Year Book Indian Natl Sci Acad ... Year Book. Indian National Science Academy [*A publication*]
Year Book Indian Nat Sci Acad ... Year Book. Indian National Science Academy [*A publication*]
Year Book Natl Auricula Primula Soc North Sec ... Year Book. National Auricula and Primula Society. Northern Section [*A publication*]
Year Book Nucl Med ... Year Book of Nuclear Medicine [*United States*] [*A publication*]
Year Book Obstet Gynecol ... Year Book of Obstetrics and Gynecology [*A publication*]

Yearb Pap Ind Manage Assoc ... Yearbook. Paper Industry Management Association [*A publication*]
Yearb Pathol Clin Pathol ... Yearbook of Pathology and Clinical Pathology [*A publication*]
Yearb Pediatr ... Yearbook of Pediatrics [*A publication*]
Yearb Pharm ... Yearbook of Pharmacy [*A publication*]
Yearb P7 Hen VI ... Year Books, Part 7, Henry VI [*A publication*] (DLA)
Yearb Phys Anthropol ... Yearbook of Physical Anthropology [*A publication*]
Yearb R Asiat Soc Bengal ... Yearbook. Royal Asiatic Society of Bengal [*A publication*]
Year Endocrinol ... Year in Endocrinology [*A publication*]
Year Immunol ... Year in Immunology [*A publication*]
Year Metab ... Year in Metabolism [*A publication*]
Year's Work Eng Stud ... Year's Work in English Studies [*A publication*]
Yeates .... Yeates' Pennsylvania Reports [*1791-1808*] [*A publication*] (DLA)
Yeates (PA) ... Yeates' Pennsylvania Reports [*1791-1808*] [*A publication*] (DLA)
Yeats Eliot ... Yeats Eliot Review [*A publication*]
Yeb .... Yebamoth (BJA)
YEC .... Youngest Empty Cell
YEC .... Youth Employment Competency (OICC)
YEC .... Youth Exchange Centre [*Seymour Mews House*] [*British*] (CB)
YedNum ..... Yedi'ot Numismatiyot be-Yisrael. Jerusalem (BJA)
YEDPA ...... Youth Employment and Demonstration Projects Act of 1977
YEDTA ...... Youth Employment and Demonstration Training Act [*Department of the Interior*]
YEE .... Yale Economic Essays [*A publication*]
Yeepie .... Youthful Energetic Elderly Person Involved in Everything [*Aging yuppie*] [*Lifestyle classification*]
YEER .... Youth Entered Employment Rate [*Job Training and Partnership Act*] (OICC)
Ye Et Rg Rt ... Yorkshire East Riding Regiment [*British military*] (DMA)
YEF .... Young Executives Forum [*Automotive Service Industry Association*]
YEG .... Edmonton [*Canada*] [*Airport symbol*] (OAG)
YEG .... Yeast Extract - Glucose [*Medium*]
YEH .... Yellow Enzyme, Reduced [*Biochemistry*]
YEIMEY ... Year in Immunology [*A publication*]
YEIS .... Yamaha Energy Induction System
YEK .... Eskimo Point [*Canada*] [*Airport symbol*] (OAG)
YEL .... Elliot Lake [*Canada*] [*Airport symbol*] (OAG)
YEL .... Equitable Life Assurance Society of the United States, General Library, New York, NY [*OCLC symbol*] (OCLC)
YEL .... Yellow (AAG)
Yel .... Yelverton's English King's Bench Reports [*1603-13*] [*A publication*] (DLA)
YEL .... Young England Library [*A publication*]
YEL .... Youth Employment Lobby [*Canada*]
YELD .... Yeldham [*England*]
YELL .... Yellow Freight System, Inc. of Delaware [*NASDAQ symbol*] (NQ)
YELL .... Yellowstone National Park
Yellow B R ... Yellow Brick Road [*A publication*]
Yellowstone-Bighorn Research Proj Contr ... Yellowstone-Bighorn Research Project. Contribution [*A publication*]
Yellowstone Libr and Mus Assoc Yellowstone Interpretive Ser ... Yellowstone Library and Museum Association. Yellowstone Interpretive Series [*A publication*]
yelsh .... Yellowish [*Philately*]
Yelv .... Yelverton's English King's Bench Reports [*1603-13*] [*A publication*] (DLA)
Yelv (Eng) ... Yelverton's English King's Bench Reports [*1603-13*] [*A publication*] (DLA)
YEM .... Empire State College, Saratoga Springs, NY [*OCLC symbol*] [*Inactive*] (OCLC)
YEM .... Yemen (Sanaa) [*ANSI three-letter standard code*] (CNC)
YEMI .... Youngwood Electronic Metals, Inc. [*NASDAQ symbol*] (NQ)
YEN .... Ammunition Lighter [*Navy symbol*] (DNAB)
YEO .... Yeomanry
YEO .... Yeovil [*British depot code*]
YEO .... Young Entrepreneurs Organization [*Wichita, KS*] (EA)
YEO .... Youth Employment Officer [*British*]
YEOM .... Yeomanry (WGA)
Yeomy .... Yeomanry [*British military*] (DMA)
YEp .... Yeast Episomal Plasmid [*Genetics*]
YEP .... Your Educational Plan (AEBS)
YEPD .... Yeast Extract - Peptone Dextrose [*Medium*]
YER .... Yeats Eliot Review [*A publication*]
Yer .... Yerger's Tennessee Supreme Court Reports [*A publication*] (DLA)
YER .... Yerkesik [*Turkey*] [*Seismograph station code, US Geological Survey*] (SEIS)
Yer .... Yerushalmi [*Palestinian Talmud*] (BJA)
Yerg .... Yerger's Tennessee Reports [*9-18 Tennessee*] [*A publication*] (DLA)
Yerg (Tenn) ... Yerger's Tennessee Reports [*9-18 Tennessee*] [*A publication*] (DLA)
YES .... Yankee Energy Systems, Inc. [*NYSE symbol*] (SPSG)
YES .... Yearbook of English Studies [*A publication*]
YES .... Years of Extra Savings

YES .... Yeast Extract Sucrose [*Cell growth medium*]
YES .... Yogurt Extra Smooth [*Trademark of the Dannon Co., Inc.*]
YES .... Young Entomologists' Society (EA)
YES .... Young Executive Society [*Automotive Warehouse Distributors Association*]
YES .... Youth Education Services [*Summer program*]
YES .... Youth Emergency Service
YES .... Youth Employment Service [*Department of Employment*] [*British*] (EA)
YES .... Youth Employment Support Volunteers Program [*ACTION*]
YES .... Youth Entering Service to America [*In YES Foundation, a volunteer organization proposed by the Bush administration*]
YES .... Youth for Environmental Sanity
YES .... Youth Exhibiting Stamps [*US Postal Service*]
YES .... Youths for Environment and Service [*Multinational association based in Turkey*] (EAIO)
YES/MVS ... Yorktown Expert System for Multiple Virtual Storage Environments [*Data processing*] (HGAA)
Yessis Rev ... Yessis Review of Soviet Physical Education and Sports [*A publication*]
YEST .... Yesterday (DSUE)
YESTU ...... Yellowstone Reserves Uts [*NASDAQ symbol*] (NQ)
YESTY ...... Yesterday
YET .... Youth Effectiveness Training [*A course of study*]
YETM .... Yetminster [*England*]
YETP .... Youth Employment and Training Programs [*Department of Labor*]
Yeung Nam Univ Inst Ind Technol Rep ... Yeung Nam University. Institute of Industrial Technology. Report [*A publication*]
YEV .... Inuvik [*Canada*] [*Airport symbol*] (OAG)
Yev .... Yevamot (BJA)
YF .... Aeronautical Fixed Station [*ICAO designator*] (ICDA)
YF .... Covered Lighter [*Self-propelled*] [*Navy symbol*]
YF .... Wife [*Citizens band radio slang*]
YF .... Yawmiyyaet Filastiniyya (BJA)
YF .... Yellow Fever [*Virus*] (MAE)
YF .... Yerushalmi Fragments [*A publication*] (BJA)
YF .... Young Filmakers Foundation (EA)
YFA .... Fort Albany [*Canada*] [*Airport symbol*] (OAG)
YFB .... Ferryboat or Launch [*Self-propelled*] [*Navy symbol*]
YFB .... First Boston Corp., New York, NY [*OCLC symbol*] (OCLC)
YFB .... Frobisher Bay [*Canada*] [*Airport symbol*] (OAG)
YFC .... Fredericton [*Canada*] [*Airport symbol*] (OAG)
YFC .... Yakima Firing Center (MCD)
YFC .... Young Farmers' Club [*British*]
YFCI .... Youth for Christ International [*See also JPC*] [*Singapore, Singapore*] (EAIO)
YFC/USA ... Youth for Christ/USA (EA)
YFD .... Yard Floating Dry Dock [*Non-self-propelled*] [*Navy symbol*]
YFDC .... Youth Film Distribution Center (EA)
YFE .... Forestville [*Canada*] [*Airport symbol*] (OAG)
YFEC .... Youth Forum of the European Communities [*See also FJCE*] (EAIO)
YFED .... York Financial Corp. [*York, PA*] [*NASDAQ symbol*] (NQ)
YFF .... Waltham, MA [*Location identifier*] [*FAA*] (FAAL)
YFM .... State University of New York, Agricultural and Technical College at Farmingdale, Farmingdale, NY [*OCLC symbol*] (OCLC)
YFN .... Covered Lighter [*Non-self-propelled*] [*Navy symbol*]
YFNA .... Young Friends of North America (EA)
YFNB .... Large Covered Lighter [*Non-self-propelled*] [*Navy symbol*]
YFND .... Dry Dock Companion Craft [*Non-self-propelled*] [*Navy symbol*]
YFNG .... Covered Lighter (Special Purpose) [*Later, YFNX*] [*Navy symbol*]
YFNX .... Lighter (Special Purpose) [*Non-self-propelled*] [*Navy symbol*]
YFO .... Flin Flon [*Canada*] [*Airport symbol*] (OAG)
Y-FOS .... Y-Force Operations Staff [*Army*] [*World War II*]
YFP .... Floating Power Barge [*Non-self-propelled*] [*Navy symbol*]
YFR .... Refrigerated Covered Lighter [*Self-propelled*] [*Navy symbol*]
YFRN .... Refrigerated Covered Lighter [*Non-self-propelled*] [*Navy symbol*]
YFRT .... Covered Lighter (Range Tender) [*Self-propelled*] [*Navy symbol*]
YFS .... Fort Simpson [*Canada*] [*Airport symbol*] (OAG)
YFS .... Yale French Studies [*A publication*]
YFS .... Young Flying Service [*Harlingen, TX*] [*FAA designator*] (FAAC)
YFT .... Torpedo Transportation Lighter [*Navy symbol*] [*Obsolete*]
YFTU .... Yugoslavia Federation of Trade Unions
YFU .... Harbor Utility Craft [*Self-propelled*] [*Navy symbol*]
YFU .... Why Have You Forsaken Us? Letter [*Fundraising*]
YFU .... Yard Freight Unit
YFU .... Youth for Understanding (EA)
YFV .... Yellow Fever Virus [*Virology*]
YF/VA .... Young Filmakers/Video Arts [*Also known as Young Filmakers Foundation*] (EA)
YF(XYL) .... Wife (Ex-Young-Lady) [*Amateur radio slang*]
YG .... Garbage Lighter [*Self-propelled*] [*Navy symbol*]

YG .... Yankee Group [*Boston, MA*] [*Information service or system*] [*Telecommunications*] (TSSD)
YG .... Yard Gully
YG .... Year Group
YG .... Yellow-Green
YG .... Yellow-Green Beacon [*Aviation*]
YGA .... Gagnon [*Canada*] [*Airport symbol*] (OAG)
YGB .... Gillies Bay [*Canada*] [*Airport symbol*] (OAG)
YGC .... Yahweh and the Gods of Canaan [*A publication*] (BJA)
YGF .... General Foods Technical Center, White Plains, NY [*OCLC symbol*] (OCLC)
YGJ .... Yonago [*Japan*] [*Airport symbol*] (OAG)
YGK .... Kingston [*Canada*] [*Airport symbol*] (OAG)
YGKKA ...... Yuki Gosei Kagaku Kyokaishi [*A publication*]
YGKSA ...... Yogyo Kyokai Shi [*A publication*]
YGL .... La Grande [*Canada*] [*Airport symbol*] (OAG)
YGL .... Yttrium Garnet LASER
YGM .... State University of New York, College at Geneseo, Geneseo, NY [*OCLC symbol*] (OCLC)
YGM .... Young Grandmother
YGN .... Garbage Lighter [*Non-self-propelled*] [*Navy symbol*]
YGNR .... Yukon Government News Release [*A publication*]
YGO .... Gods Narrows [*Canada*] [*Airport symbol*] (OAG)
YGP .... Gaspe [*Canada*] [*Airport symbol*] (OAG)
YGQ .... Geraldton [*Canada*] [*Airport symbol*] (OAG)
YGR .... Iles De La Madeleine [*Canada*] [*Airport symbol*] (OAG)
YGRP .... Y & A Goup, Inc. [*NASDAQ symbol*] (NQ)
YGS .... Survey Craft [*Navy symbol*]
YGS .... Yale Germanic Studies [*A publication*]
YGS .... Year of Grace Survey (DS)
YGS .... Young Guard Society [*Later, GS*] (EA)
YGT .... Target Service Task Craft [*Navy symbol*]
YGTN .... Target Barge [*Navy symbol*]
YGV .... Havre Saint Pierre [*Canada*] [*Airport symbol*] (OAG)
YGW .... Great Whale [*Canada*] [*Airport symbol*] (OAG)
YGX .... Gillam [*Canada*] [*Airport symbol*] (OAG)
YH .... Lighter, Ambulance [*Navy symbol*] [*Obsolete*]
YH .... RADAR Beacon [*Maps and charts*]
YH .... Yorkshire Hussars [*British military*] (DMA)
YH .... Youth Hostel
YHA .... Youth Hostels Association
YHB .... House Boat [*Navy symbol*]
YHD .... Dryden [*Canada*] [*Airport symbol*] (OAG)
YHHPAL .. Acta Pharmaceutica Sinica [*A publication*]
YHI .... Holman Island [*Canada*] [*Airport symbol*] (OAG)
YHIY .... Yorkshire Hussars Imperial Yeomanry [*British military*] (DMA)
YHJPCK ... Kluane National Park, Parks Canada [*Parc National Kluane, Parcs Canada*] Haines Junction, Yukon [*Library symbol*] [*National Library of Canada*] (NLC)
YHK .... Gjoa Haven [*Canada*] [*Airport symbol*] (OAG)
YHLC .... Salvage Lift Craft, Heavy [*Non-self-propelled*] [*Navy ship symbol*]
YHM .... Hamilton [*Canada*] [*Airport symbol*] (OAG)
YHM .... Hamilton College, Clinton, NY [*OCLC symbol*] (OCLC)
YHMA ...... Yukon Historical and Museums Association. Newsletter [*A publication*]
YHMAN .... Yukon Historical and Museums Association. Newsletter [*A publication*]
YHN .... Hornepayne [*Canada*] [*Airport symbol*] (OAG)
YHP .... Yokogawa Hewlett Packard Ltd. [*Japan*]
YHPA .... Your Heritage Protection Association (EA)
YHR .... Harrington Harbour [*Canada*] [*Airport symbol*] (OAG)
YHS .... Yukuharu Haiku Society [*Superseded by Yuki Teikei Haiku Society*] (EA)
YHT .... Heating Scow [*Navy symbol*]
YHT .... Young-Helmholtz Theory [*Physics*]
YHWH ...... Yahweh [*Old Testament term for God*]
YHY .... Hay River [*Canada*] [*Airport symbol*] (OAG)
YHZ .... Halifax [*Canada*] [*Airport symbol*] (OAG)
YI .... Iraq [*Aircraft nationality and registration mark*] (FAAC)
YI .... Young, Intact Animals [*Endocrinology*]
YI .... Yukon Indian News [*A publication*]
YIB .... Atikokan [*Canada*] [*Airport symbol*] (OAG)
YIBSV .... Yam Internal Brown Spot Virus [*Plant pathology*]
YICA .... Yearbook on International Communist Affairs [*A publication*]
yid .... Yiddish [*MARC language code*] [*Library of Congress*] (LCCP)
YIE .... Young Interference Experiment [*Physics*]
YIEPP .... Youth Incentive Entitlement Pilot Projects [*Department of Labor*]
YIF .... St. Augustin [*Canada*] [*Airport symbol*] (OAG)
YIFCM ...... Yaw Integrated Flight Control Module (MCD)
YIFMC ..... Yearbook. International Folk Music Council [*A publication*]
YIG .... Yttrium Iron Garnet
YIGIB .... Your Improved Group Insurance Benefits
YIH .... Yichang [*China*] [*Airport symbol*] (OAG)
YIIJS .... Young Israel Institute for Jewish Studies [*Defunct*] (EA)
YIK .... Ivugivik [*Canada*] [*Airport symbol*] (OAG)
YIL .... Yellow Indicating Light (IEEE)
YILAG .... Yidishe Landvirtshaftlekhe Gezelshaft [*A publication*] (BJA)

YIN .... Niagara County Community College, Sanborn, NY [*OCLC symbol*] (OCLC)
YIN .... Yingkow [*Republic of China*] [*Seismograph station code, US Geological Survey*] (SEIS)
YIN .... Yining [*China*] [*Airport symbol*] (OAG)
YIO .... Pond Inlet [*Canada*] [*Airport symbol*] (OAG)
YIP .... Willow Run Airport [*Michigan*] [*Airport symbol*]
YIp .... Yeast Integrating Plasmid [*Genetics*]
YIP .... Youth International Party [*Members known as "yippies"*]
YIPL .... Youth International Party Line [*Superseded by Technological American Party*]
YIPME ...... Youth Institute for Peace in the Middle East (EA)
Yippie .... Young Indicted Professional [*Lifestyle classification*]
Yiptime ...... Yipster Times [*A publication*]
YIR .... Yearly Infrastructure Report (NATG)
YIS .... Information Sheet. Yukon Territory. Bureau of Statistics [*A publication*]
YIS .... Yearbook of Italian Studies [*A publication*]
YIT............ Your Income Tax [*Computerized version of J. K. Lasser's book by the same name*]
YITB .... Yours in the Bond [*Motto of fraternity Tau Kappa Epsilon*]
Y It S .... Yale Italian Studies [*A publication*]
YIV .... Island Lake [*Canada*] [*Airport symbol*] (OAG)
YIVO .... Yidisher Visnshaftlekher Institut [*Yiddish Scientific Institute*]
YIVO .... YIVO Annual of Jewish Social Science [*A publication*]
YJ .... RADAR Homing Beacon [*Maps and charts*]
YJ .... Yellow Jacket [*Immunology*]
Y & J .... Younge and Jervis' English Exchequer Reports [*1826-30*] [*A publication*] (DLA)
YJ .... Youth Journal [*A publication*]
YJ .... Yuppie Jeep
YJCS .... Yenching Journal of Chinese Studies [*A publication*]
YJF .... Fort Liard [*Canada*] [*Airport symbol*] (OAG)
YJK .... Yellowjack Resources [*Vancouver Stock Exchange symbol*]
YJM........... Fulton-Montgomery Community College, Johnstown, NY [*OCLC symbol*] (OCLC)
YJS .... Yale Judaica Series [*A publication*] (BJA)
YJT .... Stephenville [*Canada*] [*Airport symbol*] (OAG)
YJV .... Yellow Jacket Venom [*Immunology*]
YK .... RADAR Beacon [*Maps and charts*]
YK .... Syria [*Aircraft nationality and registration mark*] (FAAC)
YK .... Yakovlev [*Former USSR*] [*ICAO aircraft manufacturer identifier*] (ICAO)
YK .... Yapi-Kredi Bank [*Turkey*] (ECON)
YK .... Yiddishe Kultur [*A publication*]
YK .... Yom Kippur (BJA)
YK .... York Antibodies [*Immunology*]
YKA .... Kamloops [*Canada*] [*Airport symbol*] (OAG)
YKA .... Yellowknife Array [*Northwest Territories*] [*Seismograph station code, US Geological Survey*] (SEIS)
YKB .... Yapi-Kredi Bank [*Turkey*]
YKB .... Yemen Kuwait Bank for Trade & Investment
YKB .... Yukon Bibliography [*Boreal Institute for Northern Studies*] [*Canada*] [*Information service or system*] [*Information service or system*] (CRD)
YKC .... Kingsborough Community College of the City University of New York, Brooklyn, NY [*OCLC symbol*] (OCLC)
YKC .... Yellowknife [*Northwest Territories*] [*Geomagnetic observatory code*]
YKC .... Yellowknife [*Northwest Territories*] [*Seismograph station code, US Geological Survey*] (SEIS)
ykc .... Yukon Territory [*MARC country of publication code*] [*Library of Congress*] (LCCP)
YKE .... Yankee Power, Inc. [*Vancouver Stock Exchange symbol*]
YKIGA .... Yokohama Igaku [*A publication*]
YKK .... Yoshido Kogyo Kabushiki-Kaishi [*Yoshida Industries Ltd.*] [*Japan*]
YKKKA ..... Yakugaku Kenkyu [*A publication*]
YKKKA8.... Japanese Journal of Pharmacy and Chemistry [*A publication*]
YKKZA...... Yakugaku Zasshi [*Journal of the Pharmaceutical Society of Japan*] [*A publication*]
YKL .... Schefferville [*Canada*] [*Airport symbol*] (OAG)
YKM .... Corning Museum of Glass, Corning, NY [*OCLC symbol*] (OCLC)
YKM .... Yaak [*Montana*] [*Seismograph station code, US Geological Survey*] (SEIS)
YKM .... Yakima [*Washington*] [*Airport symbol*] (OAG)
YKM .... Young Kibbutz Movement (EA)
YKN........... Yankton [*South Dakota*] [*Airport symbol*] (OAG)
YKN........... Yukon [*FAA*] (FAAC)
YKP .... Yeni Kibris Partisi [*New Cypus Party*] [*Turkish Cyprus*] [*Political party*] (EY)
YKQ .... Rupert House [*Canada*] [*Airport symbol*] (OAG)
YKR .... Yukon Revenue Mines [*Vancouver Stock Exchange symbol*]
YKS........... Yakushima [*Japan*] [*Seismograph station code, US Geological Survey*] [*Closed*] (SEIS)
YKS........... Yorkshire [*County in England*]
YKT .... Yakutat [*Alaska*] [*Seismograph station code, US Geological Survey*] [*Closed*] (SEIS)
YKU .... Fort George [*Canada*] [*Airport symbol*] (OAG)

YKU	Yakutat [*Alaska*] [*Seismograph station code, US Geological Survey*] (SEIS)
YKUF	Yiddisher Kultur Farband (EA)
YKW	Yom Kippur War (BJA)
YKX	Kirkland Lake [*Canada*] [*Airport symbol*] (OAG)
YKYRA	Yakubutsu Ryoho [*A publication*]
YKZ	Toronto [*Canada*] Buttonville Airport [*Airport symbol*] (OAG)
YL	Aircraft Accident Authority [*ICAO designator*] (ICDA)
YL	Approach Light Lane [*Aviation code*] (FAAC)
YL	Y-Axis of Spacelab [*NASA*] (NASA)
YL	Yad La-Kore. La-Safran ule-Pe'ile Tarbut (BJA)
YL	Yawl (ROG)
YL	Yellow [*Maps and charts*]
Y & L	York and Lancaster Regiment [*Military unit*] [*British*] (DMA)
YL	Young Lady [*Amateur radio slang*]
YL	Young Life (EA)
YL	Youth Liberation Press (EA)
YLA	Open Landing Lighter [*Navy symbol*]
YLB	Lac La Biche [*Canada*] [*Airport symbol*]
YLC	Clinton Community College, Plattsburgh, NY [*OCLC symbol*] (OCLC)
YLC	Young Life Campaign (EA)
YLD	Chapleau [*Canada*] [*Airport symbol*] (OAG)
YLD	High Income Advantage Trust [*NYSE symbol*] (SPSG)
YLD	Yield [*Investment term*]
YLDG	Yielding (ROG)
YLF	Young Leadership Forum [*Multinational association based in Israel*] (EAIO)
YLG	Yale University. Library. Gazette [*A publication*]
YLG News	Library Association. Youth Libraries Group News [*A publication*]
YLH	High-Income Advantage Trust III [*NYSE symbol*] (SPSG)
YLI	[*The*] Yorkshire Light Infantry [*Military unit*] [*British*]
YLI	Young Ladies Institute (EA)
YLJ	Meadow Lake [*Canada*] [*Airport symbol*] [*Obsolete*] (OAG)
YLJ	Yale Law Journal [*A publication*]
YLL	Lederle Laboratories, Pearl River, NY [*OCLC symbol*] (OCLC)
YLL	Lloydminster [*Canada*] [*Airport symbol*] (OAG)
YLLC	Salvage Lift Craft, Light [*Self-propelled*] [*Navy ship symbol*]
YLM	Yale Literary Magazine [*A publication*]
YLP	Mingan [*Canada*] [*Airport symbol*] [*Obsolete*] (OAG)
YLR	YAG [*Yttrium Aluminum Garnet*] LASER Range-Finder
Y & LR	York and Lancaster Regiment [*Military unit*] [*British*]
YLR	York Legal Record [*Pennsylvania*] [*A publication*] (DLA)
YLRL	Young Ladies Radio League
YLSN	Young Lawyers Section Newsletter [*Australia*] [*A publication*]
YLSTN	Yellowstone [*FAA*] (FAAC)
YLT	High Income Advantage Trust II [*NYSE symbol*] (CTT)
YLT	Yellow Light (MSA)
YLT	Yu-Yen-Hsueh Lun-Ts'ung [*Essays in Linguistics*] [*A publication*]
YLW	Kelowna [*Canada*] [*Airport symbol*] (OAG)
YLW	Yellow (ADA)
YM	Dredge [*Self-propelled*] [*Navy symbol*]
YM	Meteorological Office [*ICAO designator*] (ICDA)
YM	Prototype Missile (NATG)
YM	Yacht Measurement
YM	Yang Ming Line [*Shipping*] [*Taiwan*]
YM	Yawing Moment (KSC)
YM	Yearly Meetings [*Quakers*]
YM	Yeast Extract - Malt Extract [*Medium*]
YM	Yellow Man
YM	Yellow Metal
YM	Young Man [*A publication*]
YM	Young Men's [*Christian Association*]
YM	Young Miss Magazine [*A publication*]
YM	[*Reference*] Your Message
YMA	Mayo [*Canada*] [*Airport symbol*] (OAG)
YMA	Yarn Merchants Association [*Defunct*] (EA)
YMA	Young Menswear Association (EA)
YMB	Yeast Malt Broth
YMC	Moore-Cottrell Subscription Agencies, Inc., North Cohocton, NY [*OCLC symbol*] (OCLC)
YMC	Yeast Mold Count (OA)
YMC	Your Marketing Consultant [*An electronic publication*]
YMC	Youth and Music Canada
YMCA	Young Men's Christian Association
YMCAIPS	YMCA [*Young Men's Christian Association*] International Program Services (EA)
YMCA-USA	Young Men's Christian Associations of the United States of America (EA)
YMCU	Young Men's Christian Union
YMD	People's Democratic Republic of Yemen [*ANSI three-letter standard code*] (CNC)
YMD	[*Reference*] Your Message Date
YMDZAI	Young Men's Division - Zeirei Agudath Israel (EA)
YME	Matane [*Canada*] [*Airport symbol*] (OAG)
YME	Young's Modulus of Elasticity [*See also E, Y*]
YMF	Young Musicians Foundation (EA)
YMFS	Young Men's Friendly Society [*British*]
YMHA	Young Men's Hebrew Association [*Later, YM-YWHA*]

YMHSI	Yedi'ot ha-Makhon le-Heker ha-Shirah ha-'Ivrit. Jerusalem (BJA)
YMI	Young Men's Institute (EA)
YMISIG	Young Mensa International Special Interest Group [*Defunct*] (EA)
YMJODW	Bulletin. Yamagata University. Medical Science [*A publication*]
YML	Young Men's Lyceum
YMLC	Salvage Lift Craft, Medium [*Non-self-propelled*] [*Navy ship symbol*]
YMM	Fort McMurray [*Canada*] [*Airport symbol*] (OAG)
YMM	Yeast Minimal Medium [*Microorganism growth medium*]
YMM	Youngstown and Mahoning County Public Library, Youngstown, OH [*OCLC symbol*] (OCLC)
YMMY	Yedi'ot ha-Makhon le-Mada'ei ha-Yahadut. Jerusalem (BJA)
YMO	Moosonee [*Canada*] [*Airport symbol*] (OAG)
YMO	Yellow Magic Orchestra [*Musical group*] [*Japan*]
YMP	Motor Mine Planter [*Navy symbol*]
YMP	Yacht Materially Prejudiced [*Yacht racing*] (IYR)
YMP	Young Managing Printers [*British Printing Industries Federation*]
YMP	Youth Mobility Program (OICC)
YMPE	Year's Maximum Pensionable Earnings
YMS	Auxiliary Motor Minesweeper [*Navy symbol*]
YMS	Yaw Microwave Sensor
YMS	Yield Measurement System
YMS	Yurimaguas [*Peru*] [*Airport symbol*] (OAG)
YMT	Chibougamau [*Canada*] [*Airport symbol*] (OAG)
YMT	Motor Tug [*Navy symbol*]
YMTM	Yikal Maya Than (Mexico) [*A publication*]
Y & MV	Yazoo & Mississippi Valley Railroad Co.
YMV	Youcai Mosaic Virus [*Plant pathology*]
YMX	Montreal [*Canada*] Mirabel International Airport [*Airport symbol*] (OAG)
YM-YWHA	Young Men's and Young Women's Hebrew Association (EA)
YN	International NOTAM Office [*ICAO designator*] (ICDA)
YN	Net Tender [*Navy symbol*] [*Obsolete*]
YN	Night Coach [*Airline fare code*]
YN	Yellowknifer [*A publication*]
YN	Yeoman [*Navy rating*]
YN	Yes-No [*Response prompt*]
YN	Young Numismatist [*A publication*]
YN	[*The*] Youngstown & Northern Railroad Co. [*AAR code*]
YN1	Yeoman, First Class [*Navy rating*]
YN2	Yeoman, Second Class [*Navy rating*]
YN3	Yeoman, Third Class [*Navy rating*]
YNA	Naiashquan [*Canada*] [*Airport symbol*] (OAG)
YNB	Yanbu [*Saudi Arabia*] [*Airport symbol*] (OAG)
YNB	Yeast Nitrogen Base
YNC	Paint Hills [*Canada*] [*Airport symbol*] (OAG)
YNC	Yeoman, Chief [*Navy rating*]
YNC	Yinchuan [*Republic of China*] [*Seismograph station code, US Geological Survey*] (SEIS)
YNCM	Yeoman, Master Chief [*Navy rating*]
YNCS	Yeoman, Senior Chief [*Navy rating*]
YND	Gatineau/Hull [*Canada*] [*Airport symbol*] (OAG)
YNE	Nor East Commuter Airlines [*East Boston, MA*] [*FAA designator*] (FAAC)
YNE	Norway House [*Canada*] [*Airport symbol*] (OAG)
YNER	Yale Near Eastern Researches [*New Haven/London*] [*A publication*]
YNG	Gate Craft [*Non-self-propelled*] [*Navy symbol*]
YNG	Youngstown [*Ohio*] [*Airport symbol*] (OAG)
YNG	Youngstown State University, Youngstown, OH [*OCLC symbol*] (OCLC)
YNHA	Yosemite Natural History Association (EA)
YNHH	Yale-New Haven Hospital
YNK	Yankee Companies, Inc. [*AMEX symbol*] [*Later, NEG*] (SPSG)
YNM	Matagami [*Canada*] [*Airport symbol*] (OAG)
YNP	Young National Party [*Australia*] [*Political party*]
YNPA	Young National Party of Australia [*Political party*] (ADA)
YNPS	Yankee Nuclear Power Station (NRCH)
YNR	Yorkshire, North Riding [*County in England*] (ROG)
YNSA	Seaman Apprentice, Yeoman, Striker [*Navy rating*]
YNSN	Seaman, Yeoman, Striker [*Navy rating*]
YNT	Net Tender [*Tug Class*] [*Navy symbol*] [*Obsolete*]
YNT	Yellowstone National Travelers (EA)
YNTO	Yugoslav National Tourist Office (EA)
YNV	Yanov [*Former USSR*] [*Later, LVV*] [*Geomagnetic observatory code*]
YO	Aeronautical Information Service Unit [*ICAO designator*] (ICDA)
YO	Airline ticket that can be used on any airline
YO	Fuel Oil Barge [*Self-propelled*] [*Navy symbol*]
YO	Mayotte [*ANSI two-letter standard code*] (CNC)
YO	Y-Axis of Orbiter [*NASA*] (NASA)
YO	Yarn Over [*Knitting*]
YO	Year-Old
YO	Yes [*Citizens band radio slang*]
Yo	Yoma (BJA)

YO............. Young Officer [*British military*] (DMA)
Yo.............. Younge's English Exchequer Equity Reports [*159 English Reprint*] [*A publication*] (DLA)
YOAN........ Youth of All Nations (EA)
YOB.......... Year of Birth
YOB.......... Youth Opportunities Board
YoB .... Yushodo Booksellers Ltd., Tokyo, Japan [*Library symbol*] [*Library of Congress*] (LCLS)
YOBGAD .. Year Book of Obstetrics and Gynecology [*A publication*]
YOC.......... Old Crow [*Canada*] [*Airport symbol*] (OAG)
YOC.......... Youth Opportunity Campaign [*Civil Service Commission*]
YOC.......... Youth Opportunity Centers
YOC.......... Youth Opportunity Corps
YOCHINPROJ ... Younger Chemists International Project [*American Chemical Society*]
YOCM....... International Yogurt Co. [*NASDAQ symbol*] (NQ)
YOD.......... Cold Lake [*Canada*] [*Airport symbol*] (OAG)
YOD.......... Year of Death
YOG.......... Central Aviation, Inc. [*Chicago, IL*] [*FAA designator*] (FAAC)
YOG.......... Gasoline Barge [*Self-propelled*] [*Navy symbol*]
Yoga Jnl..... Yoga Journal [*A publication*]
YOGN....... Gasoline Barge [*Non-self-propelled*] [*Navy symbol*]
YOH .... Oxford House [*Canada*] [*Airport symbol*] (OAG)
YOINK ..... Young, One Income, No Kids [*Lifestyle classification*]
YOJ .... High Level [*Canada*] [*Airport symbol*] (OAG)
YOJ .... Yonagunijima [*Ryukyu Islands*] [*Seismograph station code, US Geological Survey*] (SEIS)
YOK.......... Yokohama [*Japan*] [*Seismograph station code, US Geological Survey*] (SEIS)
Yokogawa Tech Rep ... Yokogawa Technical Report [*Japan*] [*A publication*]
Yokohama Math J ... Yokohama Mathematical Journal [*A publication*]
Yokohama Med Bull ... Yokohama Medical Bulletin [*A publication*]
Yokohama Med J ... Yokohama Medical Journal [*Japan*] [*A publication*]
Yoko Iga..... Yokohama Igaku [*A publication*]
Yoko Med Bull ... Yokohama Medical Bulletin [*A publication*]
Yokufukai Geriatr J ... Yokufukai Geriatric Journal [*A publication*]
YOL........... Yola [*Nigeria*] [*Airport symbol*] (OAG)
YOM......... State University of New York, College at Oswego, Oswego, NY [*OCLC symbol*] (OCLC)
YOM......... Year of Marriage
Yom........... Yoma (BJA)
YON .... Fuel Oil Barge [*Non-self-propelled*] [*Navy symbol*]
YON .... Yonago [*Japan*] [*Seismograph station code, US Geological Survey*] (SEIS)
YON .... Yonkers School System, Yonkers, NY [*OCLC symbol*] (OCLC)
Yona Acta Med ... Yonago Acta Medica [*A publication*]
Yon Act Med ... Yonago Acta Medica [*A publication*]
Yonago Acta Med ... Yonago Acta Medica [*A publication*]
Yona Iga Zass ... Yonago Igaku Zasshi [*A publication*]
Yonsei Eng Rep ... Yonsei Engineering Report [*A publication*]
Yonsei Eng Rev ... Yonsei Engineering Review [*South Korea*] [*A publication*]
Yonsei J Med Sci ... Yonsei Journal of Medical Science [*A publication*]
Yonsei Med J ... Yonsei Medical Journal [*A publication*]
Yonsei Rep Trop Med ... Yonsei Reports on Tropical Medicine [*A publication*]
Yool Waste ... Yool on Waste, Nuisance, and Trespass [*1863*] [*A publication*] (DLA)
YOP .... Rainbow Lake [*Canada*] [*Airport symbol*] (OAG)
YOP .... Youth Opportunities Programme [*British*] (DCTA)
YOR.......... Bulletin of Economic Research [*A publication*]
YOR.......... Yale Oriental Research [*A publication*] (BJA)
yor .... Yoruba [*MARC language code*] [*Library of Congress*] (LCCP)
York .... York Legal Record [*Pennsylvania*] [*A publication*] (DLA)
YORK....... York Research Corp. [*NASDAQ symbol*] (NQ)
York Ass .... Clayton's English Reports, York Assizes [*A publication*] (DLA)
YorkCoHS ... York County Historical Society. Papers [*A publication*]
YorkIn........ York International Corp. [*Associated Press abbreviation*] (APAG)
York Leg Rec ... York Legal Record [*Pennsylvania*] [*A publication*] (DLA)
York Leg Record ... York Legal Record [*Pennsylvania*] [*A publication*] (DLA)
York Leg Rec (PA) ... York Legal Record [*Pennsylvania*] [*A publication*] (DLA)
York Papers Ling ... York Papers in Linguistics [*A publication*]
YORKS...... Yorkshire [*County in England*]
Yorks Beekpr ... Yorkshire Beekeeper [*A publication*]
Yorks Bull Econ Soc Res ... Yorkshire Bulletin of Economic and Social Research [*A publication*]
Yorks Geol Soc Occas Publ ... Yorkshire Geological Society. Occasional Publication [*A publication*]
Yorkshire A J ... Yorkshire Archaeological Journal [*A publication*]
Yorkshire Archaeol J ... Yorkshire Archaeological Journal [*A publication*]
Yorkshire Arch J ... Yorkshire Archaeological Journal [*A publication*]
Yorkshire Arch Journal ... Yorkshire Archaeological Journal [*A publication*]
Yorkshire Archt ... Yorkshire Architect [*A publication*]
Yorkshire Geol Soc Proc ... Yorkshire Geological Society. Proceedings [*A publication*]
Yorkshire G Polyt Soc Pr ... Yorkshire Geological and Polytechnic Society. Proceedings [*A publication*]
YOS .... Oil Storage Barge [*Non-self-propelled*] [*Navy symbol*]
YOS .... Yale Oriental Series [*A publication*]

YOS .... Years of Service [*Army*] (INF)
YOS .... Yosiwara [*Japan*] [*Seismograph station code, US Geological Survey*] [*Closed*] (SEIS)
YOSE........ Yosemite National Park
YoShiR ...... Yokohama Shiritsu Daigaku Ronso [*Bulletin. Yokohama Municipal University Society*] [*A publication*]
YOSR .... Yale Oriental Series. Researches [*A publication*]
YOT.......... Yale Oriental Texts [*A publication*] (BJA)
YOU.......... Young [*Australia*] [*Seismograph station code, US Geological Survey*] (SEIS)
YOU.......... Young Officers' Union [*Philippines*]
You............ Younge's English Exchequer Equity Reports [*159 English Reprint*] [*A publication*] (DLA)
YOU.......... Youngman Oil & Gas [*Vancouver Stock Exchange symbol*]
YOU.......... Youth Opportunities Unlimited [*Project*] (EA)
YOU.......... Youth Organizations United
You & Coll Ch ... Younge and Collyer's English Chancery Reports [*1841-43*] [*A publication*] (DLA)
You & Coll Ex ... Younge and Collyer's English Exchequer Equity Reports [*1834-42*] [*A publication*] (DLA)
You & Jerv ... Younge and Jervis' English Exchequer Reports [*A publication*] (DLA)
Young........ Young's Reports [*21-47 Minnesota*] [*A publication*] (DLA)
Young Adm ... Young's Nova Scotia Admiralty Cases [*A publication*] (DLA)
Young Adm Dec ... Young's Nova Scotia Vice-Admiralty Decisions [*A publication*] (DLA)
Young Adm Dec (Nov Sc) ... Young's Nova Scotia Vice-Admiralty Decisions [*A publication*] (DLA)
Young Athl ... Young Athlete [*A publication*]
Young Child ... Young Children [*A publication*]
Young Cinema ... Young Cinema and Theatre [*A publication*]
Younge .... Younge's English Exchequer Equity Reports [*159 English Reprint*] [*A publication*] (DLA)
Younge & C Ch ... Younge and Collyer's English Chancery Reports [*62-63 English Reprint*] [*A publication*] (DLA)
Younge & C Ch Cas (Eng) ... Younge and Collyer's English Chancery Cases [*62-63 English Reprint*] [*A publication*] (DLA)
Younge & C Exch ... Younge and Collyer's English Exchequer Equity Reports [*160 English Reprint*] [*A publication*] (DLA)
Younge & C Exch (Eng) ... Younge and Collyer's English Exchequer Equity Reports [*160 English Reprint*] [*A publication*] (DLA)
Younge & Ch Cas ... Younge and Collyer's English Chancery Cases [*62-63 English Reprint*] [*1841-43*] [*A publication*] (DLA)
Younge & Coll Ch ... Younge and Collyer's English Chancery Reports [*62-63 English Reprint*] [*A publication*] (DLA)
Younge & Coll Ex ... Younge and Collyer's English Exchequer Equity Reports [*160 English Reprint*] [*A publication*] (DLA)
Younge Exch ... Younge's English Exchequer Equity Reports [*159 English Reprint*] [*1830-32*] [*A publication*] (DLA)
Younge Exch (Eng) ... Younge's English Exchequer Equity Reports [*159 English Reprint*] [*A publication*] (DLA)
Younge & J ... Younge and Jervis' English Exchequer Reports [*148 English Reprint*] [*A publication*] (DLA)
Younge & Je ... Younge and Jervis' English Exchequer Reports [*148 English Reprint*] [*A publication*] (DLA)
Younge & J (Eng) ... Younge and Jervis' English Exchequer Reports [*148 English Reprint*] [*A publication*] (DLA)
Younge & Jerv ... Younge and Jervis' English Exchequer Reports [*148 English Reprint*] [*A publication*] (DLA)
Younge ML Cas ... Younge's English Maritime Law Cases [*A publication*] (DLA)
Young Lib .. Young Liberal [*A publication*] (APTA)
Young ML Cas ... Young's English Maritime Law Cases [*A publication*] (DLA)
Young Naut Dict ... Young's Nautical Dictionary [*A publication*] (DLA)
Young VA Dec ... Young's Nova Scotia Vice-Admiralty Decisions [*A publication*] (DLA)
YOUR........ Your Own United Resources, Inc. (OICC)
Your Comput ... Your Computer [*A publication*]
Your Mus Cue ... Your Musical Cue [*A publication*]
Your Okla Dent Assoc J ... Your Oklahoma Dental Association Journal [*A publication*]
Your Radiol ... Your Radiologist [*A publication*]
YOUSA ..... Youth Organizations USA (EA)
Youth Aid Bull ... Youth Aid Bulletin [*A publication*]
YOUTHS .. Youth Order United Toward Highway Safety (EA)
Youth Soc... Youth and Society [*A publication*]
Youth in Soc ... Youth in Society [*A publication*]
Youth and Soc ... Youth and Society [*A publication*]
Youth Train News ... Youth Training News [*A publication*]
YOW......... International Young Christian Workers [*Acronym is based on foreign phrase*] [*Belgium*]
YOW......... Ottawa [*Canada*] [*Airport symbol*] (OAG)
YOYUA .... Yoyuen [*A publication*]
YP .... Patrol Craft [*Self-propelled*] [*Navy symbol*]
YP .... Robex Collection Center [*ICAO designator*] (FAAC)
YP .... Y-Axis of Payload [*NASA*] (NASA)
YP .... Yard Patrol
YP .... Yeast Phase (AAMN)
YP .... Yellow Pine
YP .... Yield Point [*Ordinarily expressed in PSI*]

YP .... Yield Pressure (MAE)
YP .... Yorkshire Post [A publication]
YP .... Young People
YP .... Your Problem
3YP .... Three Year Plan [From George Orwell's novel, "1984"]
YPA .... Port Authority of New York and New Jersey Library, New
　　　　　　York, NY [OCLC symbol] (OCLC)
YPA .... Prince Albert [Canada] [Airport symbol] (OAG)
YPA .... Yaw Precession Amplifier
YPA .... Yearbook Printers Association (EA)
YPB........... Yeast Peptone Broth [Microbiology]
YPBF .... Yellow Sheet Price of Beef [Business term]
YPBRBML ... Yale Papyri in the Beinecke Rare Book and Manuscript Library
　　　　　　[A publication]
YPD .... Floating Pile Driver [Non-self-propelled] [Navy symbol]
YPD .... Parry Sound [Canada] [Airport symbol] (OAG)
YPD .... Yaw Phase Detector
YPD .... Yeast Extract-Peptones, Dextrose Medium [Microbiology]
YPD .... Yellow Pages Datasystem [National Planning Data Corp.]
　　　　　　[Database]
YPE........... Peace River [Canada] [Airport symbol] (OAG)
YPE........... Yoho Pitch Extractor
YPEC........ Young Printing Executives Club of New York (EA)
YPF........... Young Playwrights Festival [Foundation of the Dramatists
　　　　　　Guild]
YPG .... Yuma Proving Ground [Arizona] [Army] (AABC)
YPH.......... Port Harrison [Canada] [Airport symbol] (OAG)
YPHJA...... Yo-Up Hoeji [A publication]
YPI............ Youth Policy Institute (EA)
YPI............ Youth Pride, Inc. (EA)
YPK .... Pontoon Stowage Barge [Navy symbol] [Obsolete]
YPL........... Pickle Lake [Canada] [Airport symbol] (OAG)
YPL........... White Plains Public Library, White Plains, NY [OCLC
　　　　　　symbol] (OCLC)
YPL........... York Papers in Linguistics [A publication]
YPL........... York Public Library [UTLAS symbol]
YPL........... Young People's Literature [A publication]
YPLA .... Young People's LOGO Association (EA)
YPLA .... Your Public Lands. US Department of the Interior. Bureau of
　　　　　　Land Mangement [A publication]
YPLB .... Yellow Sheet Price of Lamb [Business term]
YPLL .... Years of Potential Life Lost [Epidemiology]
YPM .... Saint Pierre [Canada] [Airport symbol] (OAG)
YPM .... State University of New York, College at Plattsburgh,
　　　　　　Plattsburgh, NY [OCLC symbol] (OCLC)
YPM .... Yale Peabody Museum
YPM .... Yokefellowship Prison Ministry (EA)
YPN .... Port Menier [Canada] [Airport symbol] (OAG)
YPO .... Young Presidents' Organization (EA)
YPO .... Youth Programs Office [Bureau of Indian Affairs]
Y-POP ...... Y-Body Axis Perpendicular to Orbit Plane [Aerospace]
YPPK........ Yellow Sheet Price of Pork [Business term]
YPQ .... Peterborough [Canada] [Airport symbol] (OAG)
YPR .... Prince Rupert [Canada] [Airport symbol] (OAG)
YPR .... Yale Poetry Review [A publication]
YPR .... Yanks Peak Resources [Vancouver Stock Exchange symbol]
YPR .... Youth Population Ratio (OICC)
YPS........... Yards per Second
YPS........... Yellow Pages Service [Telecommunications] (TEL)
YPSCE...... Young People's Society of Christian Endeavor
YPSL .... Young Peoples Socialist League [Later, YSD] (EA)
YPSSRB .... Yukon Public Service Staff Relations Board [Canada]
YPT........... Torpedo Retriever [Navy symbol] (DNAB)
YPVS........ Yamaha Power Valve System
YPW .... Powell River [Canada] [Airport symbol] (OAG)
YPW .... Putnam-Northern Westchester BOCES [Boards of Cooperative
　　　　　　Educational Services], Yorktown Heights, NY [OCLC
　　　　　　symbol] (OCLC)
YPX .... Povungnituk [Canada] [Airport symbol] (OAG)
YPY .... Fort Chipewyan [Canada] [Airport symbol] (OAG)
YPZ........... Young Poalei Zion (BJA)
YQ .... Youth Quarterly [A publication]
YQB .... Quebec [Canada] [Airport symbol] (OAG)
YQD.......... [The] Pas [Canada] [Airport symbol] (OAG)
YQF .... Red Deer [Canada] [Airport symbol] [Obsolete] (OAG)
YQG.......... Windsor [Canada] [Airport symbol] (OAG)
YQH .... Watson Lake [Canada] [Airport symbol] (OAG)
YQI .... Yarmouth [Canada] [Airport symbol] (OAG)
YQK .... Kenora [Canada] [Airport symbol] (OAG)
YQL........... Lethbridge [Canada] [Airport symbol] (OAG)
YQM........ Moncton [Canada] [Airport symbol] (OAG)
YQQ.......... Comox [Canada] [Airport symbol] (OAG)
YQR .... Regina [Canada] [Airport symbol] (OAG)
YQR.......... Rochester Public Library, Rochester, NY [OCLC
　　　　　　symbol] (OCLC)
YQT .... Thunder Bay [Canada] [Airport symbol] (OAG)
YQU.......... Grande Prairie [Canada] [Airport symbol] (OAG)
YQV.......... Yorkton [Canada] [Airport symbol] (OAG)
YQX.......... Gander [Canada] [Airport symbol] (OAG)
YQY.......... Sydney [Canada] [Airport symbol] (OAG)
YQZ........... Quesnel [Canada] [Airport symbol] (OAG)

YR .... Airline ticket that can be used only on airline issuing it
YR .... Floating Workshop [Non-self-propelled] [Navy symbol]
YR .... Romania [Aircraft nationality and registration mark] (FAAC)
YR .... Yale Review [A publication]
YR .... Yaw Ring
Y-R............ Yaw-Roll (AAG)
YR .... Year [Online database field identifier] (EY)
Yr .... Yearbook (BJA)
YR .... Yemeni Riyal (BJA)
YR .... Young Republican
Y & R .... Young & Rubicam International [Advertising agency]
YR .... Younger
YR .... Your (AAG)
YR .... Youth Resources (EA)
YR .... Yukon Reports [Maritime Law Book Co. Ltd.] [Canada]
　　　　　　[Information service or system] (CRD)
YRA .... Yacht Racing Association [British]
YRAC .... Yacht Racing Associations Council (EA)
YRAP .... Yellow Page Rate Base Analysis Plan [Bell System]
YRB .... Resolute [Canada] [Airport symbol] (OAG)
YRB .... Submarine Repair and Berthing Barge [Non-self-propelled]
　　　　　　[Navy symbol]
YRB .... Yorbeau Resources, Inc. [Toronto Stock Exchange symbol]
YRBK........ Yearbook
Yrbk Agric ... Yearbook of Agriculture. Using Our Natural Resources [A
　　　　　　publication]
Yrbk Austl ... Yearbook Australia [A publication]
Yr Bk (Charleston SC) ... Year Book (Charleston, South Carolina) [A
　　　　　　publication]
Yrbk Compar & Gen Lit ... Yearbook of Comparative and General Literature
　　　　　　[A publication]
Yrbk Comp & Gen Lit ... Yearbook of Comparative and General Literature [A
　　　　　　publication]
Yrbk Sch Law ... Yearbook of School Law [A publication]
Yrbk Sp Educ ... Yearbook of Special Education [A publication]
Yrbk World Aff ... Yearbook of World Affairs [London] [A publication]
YRBM .... Submarine Repair, Berthing, and Messing Barge [Non-self-
　　　　　　propelled] [Navy symbol]
YRBM(L) .. Submarine Repair, Berthing, and Messing Barge (Large) [Navy
　　　　　　symbol]
YRBS .... Youth Risk Behavior Survey [Medicine]
YRC .... Submarine Rescue Chamber [Navy symbol]
YRC .... Yaw Ratio Controller (MCD)
YRDH....... Floating Dry Dock Workshop (Hull) [Non-self-propelled]
　　　　　　[Navy symbol]
YRDM .... Floating Dry Dock Workshop (Machine) [Non-self-propelled]
　　　　　　[Navy symbol]
YRDST ...... Year-Round Daylight Saving Time
YRF........... Yoga Research Foundation (EA)
YRFC........ [The] Young and the Restless Fan Club (EA)
YRFLN ..... Year Flown (MCD)
YRI .... Riviere-Du-Loup [Canada] [Airport symbol]
　　　　　　[Obsolete] (OAG)
YRI .... Yri-York Ltd. [Toronto Stock Exchange symbol]
YRINY....... Youth Research Institute of New York (EA)
YRJ .... Roberval [Canada] [Airport symbol] [Obsolete] (OAG)
YRK .... York International Corp. [NYSE symbol] (SPSG)
YRK .... York, KY [Location identifier] [FAA] (FAAL)
YRK .... York University Library [UTLAS symbol]
YRL .... Covered Lighter (Repair) [Navy symbol] [Obsolete]
YRL .... Red Lake [Canada] [Airport symbol] (OAG)
YRL .... York University Law Library [UTLAS symbol]
YRLY........ Yearly (ROG)
YRM .... Rensselaer Polytechnic Institute, Troy, NY [OCLC
　　　　　　symbol] (OCLC)
YRNF .... Young Republican National Federation (EA)
YRR .... Radiological Repair Barge [Non-self-propelled] [Navy symbol]
YRR .... Scenic Airlines [Las Vegas, NV] [FAA designator] (FAAC)
YRS........... Red Sucker Lake [Canada] [Airport symbol] (OAG)
YRS........... Yale Romanic Studies [A publication]
YRS........... Yearbook of Romanian Studies [A publication]
YRS........... Yours
YRS........... Yugoslav Relief Society
YRSI .... Yves R. Simon Institute (EA)
YRST .... Salvage Craft Tender [Non-self-propelled] [Navy ship symbol]
YRT .... Rankin Inlet [Canada] [Airport symbol] (OAG)
YRT .... Yearly Renewable Term [Insurance]
YRT .... Yellowroot Tea [Folk remedy, extract of buttercup root]
YRTMA..... Yonsei Reports on Tropical Medicine [A publication]
YS .... Aeronautical Station [ICAO designator] (ICDA)
YS .... El Salvador [Aircraft nationality and registration
　　　　　　mark] (FAAC)
YS .... Nihon Aeroplane Manufacturing Co. Ltd. [Japan] [ICAO
　　　　　　aircraft manufacturer identifier] (ICAO)
ys .... Southern Yemen (Aden) [MARC country of publication code]
　　　　　　[Library of Congress] (LCCP)
YS .... Stevedoring Barge [Navy symbol] [Obsolete]
YS .... Y-Axis of Solid Rocket Booster [NASA] (NASA)
YS .... Yacht Service [British military] (DMA)
YS .... Yard Superintendent
YS .... Yardstick

YS .... Yellow-Bellied Sapsucker [*Ornithology*]
YS .... Yellow Spot
YS .... Yidishe Shprakh [*A publication*]
YS .... Yield Spread [*Investment term*]
YS .... Yield Strength [*Ordinarily expressed in PSI*]
YS .... Yield Stress
YS .... Yolk Sac (MAE)
YS .... Yoshida Sarcoma [*Medicine*]
YS .... Young Soldier
YS .... Younger Son (ROG)
YS .... Youngstown & Southern Railway Co. [*AAR code*]
YSA........... Young Socialist Alliance (EA)
YSA........... Youth Service America (EA)
YSAF........ Young Scientists of America Foundation (EA)
YSB........... Salomon Brothers Library, New York, NY [*OCLC symbol*] (OCLC)
YSB........... Sudbury [*Canada*] [*Airport symbol*] (OAG)
YSB........... Yacht Safety Bureau (EA)
YSB........... Yield Stress Bonding
YSC........... South Central Research Library Council, Ithaca, NY [*OCLC symbol*] (OCLC)
YSC........... Yearly Spares Cost (MCD)
YSCECP Reports ... Yugoslav-Serbo-Croatian-English Contrastive Project. Reports [*A publication*]
YSCECP Studies ... Yugoslav-Serbo-Croatian-English Contrastive Project. Studies [*A publication*]
YSCO........ Yes Clothing Co. [*NASDAQ symbol*] (NQ)
YSD .... Seaplane Wrecking Derrick [*Self-propelled*] [*Navy symbol*]
YSD .... Young Social Democrats (EA)
YSDB........ Yield Stress Diffusion Bonding
YSDSA...... Youth Section of the Democratic Socialists of America (EA)
YSE........... Yale Studies in English [*A publication*]
YSE........... Yaw Steering Error
YS/E......... Yield Strength to Elastic Modulus Ratio [*Dentistry*]
YSF.......... Stoney Rapids [*Canada*] [*Airport symbol*] (OAG)
YSF.......... Yield Safety Factor (IEEE)
YSG .... Young Solicitors' Group [*British*]
YSh .... Yidishe Shprakh [*A publication*]
YSHBDP... Bulletin. Vegetable and Ornamental Crops Research Station. Series B [*Morioka*] [*A publication*]
YSI........... Sans Souci [*Canada*] [*Airport symbol*] (OAG)
YSI........... Yellow Springs Instrument Co.
YSICSA..... Yellow Springs Institute for Contemporary Studies and the Arts (EA)
YSJ .... Saint John [*Canada*] [*Airport symbol*] (OAG)
YSK........... Sanikiluaq [*Canada*] [*Airport symbol*] (OAG)
YSK........... Yokosuka [*Japan*] [*Seismograph station code, US Geological Survey*] [*Closed*] (SEIS)
YSKOD8 ... Japanese Journal of Psychopharmacology [*A publication*]
YSL........... Saint Leonard [*Canada*] [*Airport symbol*] (OAG)
YSL........... Yolk Syncytial Layer [*Embryology*]
YSL........... Young Sowers' League [*British*]
YSL........... Yves Saint Laurent [*French couturier*]
Y-SLAV ..... Yugoslavia
YSLF .... Yield Strength Load Factor (IEEE)
YSM .... Fort Smith [*Canada*] [*Airport symbol*] (OAG)
YSM .... State University of New York at Stony Brook, Stony Brook, NY [*OCLC symbol*] (OCLC)
YSM .... Yangtze Service Medal
YSM .... Young Socialist Movement
YSNC........ Youth Suicide National Center (EA)
YSO .... Young Stellar Object
YSP .... Pontoon Salvage Vessel [*Navy symbol*]
YSP........... Years Service for Severance Pay Purposes [*Military*]
YSP........... Yemen Socialist Party [*South Yemen*] [*Political party*] (PD)
YSR........... Nanisivik [*Canada*] [*Airport symbol*] (OAG)
YSR........... Sludge Removal Barge [*Non-self-propelled*] [*Navy symbol*]
YSR........... Years of Service Required
YSS........... Yuzhno-Sakhalinsk [*Former USSR*] [*Seismograph station code, US Geological Survey*] (SEIS)
YSS........... Yuzhno-Sakhalinsk [*Former USSR*] [*Geomagnetic observatory code*]
YST........... Saint Therese Point [*Canada*] [*Airport symbol*] (OAG)
YST........... Yolk Sac Tumor [*Oncology*]
YST........... Youngest
YSTC........ Yorkshire Society of Textile Craftsmen [*A union*] [*British*] (DCTA)
YSY........... Sachs Harbour [*Canada*] [*Airport symbol*] (OAG)
YSZ........... Y-Stabilized Zirconia [*Physics*]
YSZ........... Yttria-Stablized Zirconia [*Materials science*]
YT .... Harbor Tug [*Navy symbol*]
YT .... Telecommunication Authority [*ICAO designator*] (ICDA)
YT .... Y-Axis of External Tank [*NASA*] (NASA)
YT .... Yacht (ROG)
YT .... Yankee Team [*Phase of the Indochina bombing operation during US military involvement in Vietnam*]
YT .... Yaw Trim (MCD)
YT .... Yom Tov (BJA)
Yt .... Yttrium [*See also Y*] [*Chemical element*]
YT .... Yukon Territory [*Canada*] [*Postal code*]
YTA .... Pembroke [*Canada*] [*Airport symbol*] (OAG)

YTA .... Yaw Trim Angle
YTA .... Yiddish Theatrical Alliance (EA)
YTB .... Large Harbor Tug [*Self-propelled*] [*Navy symbol*]
YTB .... Yard Tug Big [*Navy*]
YTB .... Yarn to Back [*Knitting*] (ADA)
YTB .... Yield to Broker [*Investment term*]
YTB .... Yuma Test Branch [*Army*] [*Yuma, AZ*]
YTC .... Yield to Call [*Investment term*]
YTC .... Yorkshire Trust Co. [*Toronto Stock Exchange symbol*] [*Vancouver Stock Exchange symbol*]
YTCA........ Yorkshire Terrier Club of America (EA)
YTD .... Year to Date (MCD)
YTD .... Young Tree Decline [*Plant pathology*]
YTE .... Cape Dorset [*Canada*] [*Airport symbol*] (OAG)
YTEC........ Yarsley Technical Centre Ltd. [*Research center*] [*British*] (IRC)
YTELSA.... Yearbook. Estonian Learned Society in America [*A publication*]
YTEP........ Youth Training and Employment Project
YTF.......... Yad Tikvah Foundation (EA)
YTF........... Yarn to Front [*Knitting*] (ADA)
YTH.......... Thompson [*Canada*] [*Airport symbol*] (OAG)
YTHF .... Yours Till Hell Freezes [*Slang*] [*British*] (DI)
YTHJ........ Yeshivath Torah Hayim in Jerusalem
YTI........... Yeshiba Toledot Isaac. Tetuan (BJA)
YTJ .... Terrace Bay [*Canada*] [*Airport symbol*] (OAG)
YTL .... Big Trout Lake [*Canada*] [*Airport symbol*] (OAG)
YTL........... Small Harbor Tug [*Self-propelled*] [*Navy symbol*]
YTL........... Youth Tennis League (EA)
YTM .... Medium Harbor Tug [*Self-propelled*] [*Navy symbol*]
YTM .... State University of New York, College at Utica-Rome, Utica, NY [*OCLC symbol*] (OCLC)
YTM .... Yearbook for Traditional Music [*A publication*]
YTM .... Yield to Maturity [*Investment term*]
YTRC........ Yokohama Technical Research Center [*Mazda Motor Corp.*]
YTRES ...... Yankee Tractor Rocket Escape System (MCD)
YTS .... Timmins [*Canada*] [*Airport symbol*] (OAG)
YTS .... Youth Training Scheme [*British*]
YTS .... Yuma Test Station [*Missiles*]
YTT .... Torpedo Testing Barge [*Navy symbol*] [*Obsolete*]
YTTBT ..... Yield Threshold Test Ban Treaty [*1976*]
YTV .... Yaw Thrust Vector
YTV .... Yorkshire Television [*British*]
YTX .... Planned District Craft [*Navy symbol*]
YTZ .... Toronto [*Canada*] [*Airport symbol*] (OAG)
YU .... Yale Divinity School, New Haven, CT [*OCLC symbol*] [*Inactive*] (OCLC)
YU .... Yale University
YU .... Yeshiva University [*New York*]
yu............... Yugoslavia [*MARC country of publication code*] [*Library of Congress*] (LCCP)
YU .... Yugoslavia [*ANSI two-letter standard code*] (CNC)
YU .... Yugoslavia [*Aircraft nationality and registration mark*] (FAAC)
YU .... Yukon News [*A publication*]
Yu............... Yunost' [*Moscow*] [*A publication*]
Yuasa Tech Inf ... Yuasa Technical Information [*Japan*] [*A publication*]
YUB .... Tuktoyaktuk [*Canada*] [*Airport symbol*] (OAG)
YUBA .... Yuba Natural Resources, Inc. [*NASDAQ symbol*] (NQ)
Yubbie........ Young Urban Baby [*Lifestyle classification*]
Yubbie........ Young Urban Breadwinner [*Lifestyle classification*]
YuBN .... Narodna Biblioteka Socijalisticke Republike Srbije, Beograd, Yugoslavia [*Library symbol*] [*Library of Congress*] (LCLS)
YUBO........ Yucca House National Monument
YUC........ Yucana Resources, Inc. [*Vancouver Stock Exchange symbol*]
YUC.......... Yucatan
Yuca .... Young Upwardly Mobile Cuban-American [*Lifestyle classification*]
Yucca .... Young Up-and-Coming Cuban American [*Lifestyle classification*]
YUCEE...... Youth Unit of the Council for Environmental Education (EAIO)
YUCI .... Yeshiva University Cumulative Index of Films of Jewish Interest [*A publication*] (BJA)
Yuckie........ Young Ultimate Creative Kitscher [*Lifestyle classification*]
Yuckie........ Young Urban Catholic [*Lifestyle classification*]
YUEN........ Yukon Economic News [*A publication*]
YUF .... Pelly Bay [*Canada*] [*Airport symbol*] (OAG)
Yuffie........ Young Urban Failure [*Lifestyle classification*]
YUG.......... Yugawaralite [*A zeolite*]
YUG.......... Yugoslavia [*ANSI three-letter standard code*] (CNC)
Yugo Exprt ... Yugoslavia Export [*A publication*]
Yugo L. ... Yugoslav Law [*A publication*] (DLA)
Yugos .... Yugoslavia
Yugoslav L ... Yugoslav Law [*A publication*]
Yugosl Chem Pap ... Yugoslav Chemical Papers [*A publication*]
Yugosl Hop Symp Proc ... Yugoslav Hop Symposium. Proceedings [*A publication*]
Yugosl Law ... Yugoslav Law [*A publication*]
Yugosl Surv ... Yugoslav Survey [*A publication*]

Yugosl Zavod Geol Geofiz Istrazivanja Raspr ... Yugoslavia Zavod za Geoloska i Geofizicka Istrazivanja. Rasprave [*A publication*]

Yugosl Zavod Geol Geofiz Istrazivanja Vesn Geol ... Yugoslavia Zavod za Geoloska i Geofizicka Istrazivanja. Vesnik. Geologija. Serija A [*Belgrade*] [*A publication*]

Yug Soc Soil Sci Publ ... Yugoslav Society of Soil Science. Publication [*A publication*]

Yug Surv .... Yugoslav Survey [*A publication*]

YUHPAA .. Acta Horticulturalia [*Peking*] [*A publication*]

YU/IJCS ... International Journal of Comparative Sociology. York University. Department of Sociology and Anthropology [*Toronto, Canada*] [*A publication*]

YUIN .... Yukon Indian News [*A publication*]

YUK .... Youth Uncovering Krud [*Antipollution organization in Schenectady, New York*]

YUK .... Yuzhno-Kurilsk [*Former USSR*] [*Seismograph station code, US Geological Survey*] (SEIS)

YUKN .... Yukon Energy Corp. [*St. Paul, MN*] [*NASDAQ symbol*] (NQ)

Yuk Ord ..... Yukon Ordinances [*Canada*] [*A publication*] (DLA)

Yuk Rev Ord ... Yukon Revised Ordinances [*Canada*] [*A publication*] (DLA)

Yuk Stat ...... Statutes of the Yukon Territory [*A publication*]

YUL .... Montreal [*Canada*] [*Airport symbol*] (OAG)

YUL .... Yale University Library

YULG .... Yale University. Library. Gazette [*A publication*]

Yullie .... Young Urban Laborer [*Lifestyle classification*]

YUM .... Yale Medical School, New Haven, CT [*OCLC symbol*] [*Inactive*] (OCLC)

YUM .... Yuma [*Arizona*] [*Airport symbol*] (OAG)

YUM .... Yuma Gold Mines Ltd. [*Vancouver Stock Exchange symbol*]

YUM .... Yumen [*Republic of China*] [*Seismograph station code, US Geological Survey*] (SEIS)

Yummie ...... Young Upwardly Mobile Marxist [*Lifestyle classification*]

Yummie ...... Young Upwardly Mobile Mountains [*Rocky Mountains*] [*Geological take-off on the abbreviation, Yuppie*] [*Canada*]

Yummie ...... Young Urban Minister [*Lifestyle classification*]

Yummy .... Young Upwardly Mobile Mommy [*Lifestyle classification*]

Yumpie .... Young Upwardly Mobile Professional [*Lifestyle classification*]

Yumpy .... Young Upwardly Mobile Papa [*Lifestyle classification*]

YUMY .... Tofruzen, Inc. [*NASDAQ symbol*] (NQ)

YUN .... Yearbook of the United Nations [*A publication*] (DLA)

YUO .... Yuojima [*Bonin Islands*] [*Seismograph station code, US Geological Survey*] [*Closed*] (SEIS)

Yuplis .... Young Upward Professional Library Information Specialist [*Lifestyle classification*]

Yuppie .... Young Urban Professional [*Lifestyle classification*] [*In book title "The Yuppie Handbook"*]

YUR .... Yuriko Resources [*Vancouver Stock Exchange symbol*]

Yurpie .... Young, Urban Republican Professional [*Lifestyle classification*]

YUS .... Yale University, New Haven, CT [*OCLC symbol*] (OCLC)

YUS .... Yushan [*Mount Morrison*] [*Republic of China*] [*Seismograph station code, US Geological Survey*] (SEIS)

YuSaN ...... Narodne Biblioteka Bosne i Hercegovine [*National Library of Bosnia and Herzegovina*], Sarajevo, Yugoslavia [*Library symbol*] [*Library of Congress*] (LCLS)

YuSkN ...... Nacionalna Biblioteka na Makedonija "Kliment Ohridaki", Skopje, Yugoslavia [*Library symbol*] [*Library of Congress*] (LCLS)

Yussie .... Young Unescorted Single [*Lifestyle classification*]

YUTR .... Yukon Teacher [*A publication*]

YUUD .... Yukon Update [*A publication*]

YUWM ...... Yukon Water Management Bulletin. Westwater Research Centre [*A publication*]

YUX .... Hall Beach [*Canada*] [*Airport symbol*] (OAG)

YUY .... Rouyn-Noranda [*Canada*] [*Airport symbol*] (OAG)

YuZU .... Nacionalna i Sveucilisna Biblioteka [*National and University Library of Croatia*], Zagreb, Yugoslavia [*Library symbol*] [*Library of Congress*] (LCLS)

YV .... Drone Aircraft Catapult Control Craft [*Navy symbol*] [*Obsolete*]

YV .... Venezuela [*Aircraft nationality and registration mark*] (FAAC)

YV .... Yad Vashem [*An association*] [*Israel*] (EAIO)

YVA .... Moroni [*Comoro Islands*] [*Airport symbol*] (OAG)

YVA .... Yad Vashem Archives (BJA)

YVA .... Young Volunteers in ACTION

YVB .... Bonaventure [*Canada*] [*Airport symbol*] (OAG)

YVC .... Catapult Lighter [*Navy symbol*]

YVC .... Lac La Ronge [*Canada*] [*Airport symbol*] (OAG)

YVC .... Yellow Varnish Cambric

Y Viewers ... Young Viewers [*A publication*]

YVM .... Broughton [*Canada*] [*Airport symbol*] (OAG)

YVO .... Onondaga Library System, Syracuse, NY [*OCLC symbol*] (OCLC)

YVO .... Val D'Or [*Canada*] [*Airport symbol*] (OAG)

YVP .... Fort Chimo [*Canada*] [*Airport symbol*] (OAG)

YVQ .... Norman Wells [*Canada*] [*Airport symbol*] (OAG)

YVR .... Vancouver [*Canada*] [*Airport symbol*] (OAG)

YVS .... Yad Vashem Studies [*A publication*]

YVT .... Buffalo Narrows [*Canada*] [*Airport symbol*] [*Obsolete*] (OAG)

YVT .... Yakima Valley Transportation Co. [*AAR code*]

YVT .... Youth Visiting Team [*British military*] (DMA)

YW .... Military Flight Operational Control Center [*ICAO designator*] (ICDA)

YW .... Water Barge [*Self-propelled*] [*Navy symbol*]

YW .... Whitehorse Public Library, Yukon [*Library symbol*] [*National Library of Canada*] (NLC)

YW .... Year's Work in Classical Studies [*A publication*]

YW .... Year's Work in English Studies [*A publication*]

YW .... Yellow-White

YW .... Young Woman [*A publication*]

YW .... Young Women of the Church of Jesus Christ of Latter-Day Saints (EA)

YW .... Young Women's [*Christian Association*]

YW .... Yreka Western Railroad Co. [*AAR code*]

YWA .... Year's Work in Archaeology [*A publication*]

YWA .... Yukon Archives, Whitehorse, Yukon [*Library symbol*] [*National Library of Canada*] (NLC)

YWAM ...... Youth with a Mission (EA)

YWC .... Year's Work in Classical Studies [*A publication*]

YWC .... Yukon College, Whitehorse, Yukon [*Library symbol*] [*National Library of Canada*] (NLC)

YWCA .... World Young Women's Christian Association (EAIO)

YWCA .... Young Women Committed to Action [*Feminist group*]

YWCA-USA ... Young Women's Christian Association of the United States of America (EA)

YWCJCLS ... Young Women of the Church of Jesus Christ of Latter-Day Saints [*Later, YW*] (EA)

YWCS .... Year's Work in Classical Studies [*A publication*]

YWCTU ..... Young Women's Christian Temperance Union

YWDN .... Water Distilling Barge [*Non-self-propelled*] [*Navy symbol*]

YWE .... Year's Work in English Studies [*A publication*]

YWED .... Department of Economic Development: Mines and Small Business, Government of the Yukon, Whitehorse, Yukon [*Library symbol*] [*National Library of Canada*] (NLC)

YWEEP ..... Environmental Protection Service, Environment Canada [*Service de la Protection de l'Environnement, Environnement Canada*] Whitehorse, Yukon [*Library symbol*] [*National Library of Canada*] (NLC)

YWES .... Year's Work in English Studies [*A publication*]

YWF .... Young World Federalists [*Later, World Federalist Youth*]

YWFD .... Young World Food and Development [*UN Food and Agriculture Organization*]

YWG .... Winnipeg [*Canada*] [*Airport symbol*] (OAG)

YWGASOYA ... You Won't Get Ahead Sitting on Your Afterdeck [*Slang*] [*Bowdlerized version*]

YWH .... Victoria [*Canada*] [*Airport symbol*] (OAG)

YWHA .... Young Women's Hebrew Association [*Later, YM-YWHA*]

YWHHR ... Department of Health and Human Resources, Government of the Yukon, Whitehorse, Yukon [*Library symbol*] [*National Library of Canada*] (NLC)

YWHS .... Whitehorse Historical Society, Yukon [*Library symbol*] [*National Library of Canada*] (NLC)

YWHS .... Young Women's Help Society [*British*]

YWIN .... Northern Program, Indian and Northern Affairs Canada [*Programme du Nord, Affaires Indiennes et du Nord Canada*] [*Library symbol*] [*National Library of Canada*] (BIB)

YWK .... Wabush [*Canada*] [*Airport symbol*] (OAG)

YWL .... Williams Lake [*Canada*] [*Airport symbol*] (OAG)

YWL .... Yawl

YWL .... Yukon Law Library, Whitehorse, Yukon [*Library symbol*] [*National Library of Canada*] (NLC)

YWLL .... Young Workers Liberation League

YWLS .... Library Services Branch, Government of the Yukon, Whitehorse, Yukon [*Library symbol*] [*National Library of Canada*] (NLC)

YWM .... United States Military Academy, West Point, NY [*OCLC symbol*] (OCLC)

YWML ...... Year's Work in Modern Language Studies [*A publication*]

YWMLS .... Year's Work in Modern Language Studies [*A publication*]

YWN .... Ammunition Lighter [*Navy symbol*] (DNAB)

YWN .... Ammunition Pontoon [*Navy symbol*] (DNAB)

YWN .... Farm Scow [*Navy symbol*] (DNAB)

YWN .... Floating Crane [*Non-self-propelled*] [*Navy symbol*] (DNAB)

YWN .... Floating Pile Driver [*Non-self-propelled*] [*Navy symbol*] (DNAB)

YWN .... Lighterage Pontoon [*Navy symbol*] (DNAB)

YWN .... Pontoon [*Navy symbol*] (DNAB)

YWN .... Pontoon Barge [*Navy symbol*] (DNAB)

YWN .... Prison Ship [*Navy symbol*] (DNAB)

YWN .... Receiving Ship [*Navy symbol*] (DNAB)

YWN .... Sand Scow [*Navy symbol*] (DNAB)

YWN .... School Ship [*Navy symbol*] (DNAB)

YWN .... Transfer Barge [*Navy symbol*] (DNAB)

YWN .... Water Barge [*Non-self-propelled*] [*Navy symbol*]

YWN .... Winisk [*Canada*] [*Airport symbol*] (OAG)

YWN .... Yard Tug [*Navy symbol*] (DNAB)

YWOM .... [*The*] Old Log Church Museum, Whitehorse, Yukon [*Library symbol*] [*National Library of Canada*] (NLC)

YWP .... Sir Hugh Young's Working Party for Estimation of Civilian Relief Requirements [*World War II*]

YWPCN .... National Historic Sites, Parks Canada [*Lieux Historiques Nationaux, Parcs Canada*] Whitehorse, Yukon [*Library symbol*] [*National Library of Canada*]   (NLC)
YWPG .... Young World Promotion Group [*UN Food and Agriculture Organization*]
YWR .... Yorkshire, West Riding [*County in England*]   (ROG)
YWRR .... Department of Renewable Resources, Government of the Yukon, Whitehorse, Yukon [*Library symbol*] [*National Library of Canada*]   (NLC)
YWS .... Young Wales Society
YWS .... Young Workers Scheme [*British*]
YWT .... Yard-Walk-Throughs [*Navy*]   (NG)
YWTA .... Department of Territorial Affairs, Government of the Yukon, Whitehorse, Yukon [*Library symbol*] [*Obsolete*] [*National Library of Canada*]   (NLC)
YWU .... Yiddish Writers Union   (EA)
YWY .... Wrigley [*Canada*] [*Airport symbol*]   (OAG)
YX .... Military Service or Organization [*ICAO designator*]   (ICDA)
YXC .... Cranbrook [*Canada*] [*Airport symbol*]   (OAG)
YXD .... Edmonton [*Canada*] Municipal Airport [*Airport symbol*]   (OAG)
YXE .... Saskatoon [*Canada*] [*Airport symbol*]   (OAG)
YXF .... Four County Library System, Binghamton, NY [*OCLC symbol*]   (OCLC)
YXH .... Medicine Hat [*Canada*] [*Airport symbol*]   (OAG)
YXJ .... Fort St. John [*Canada*] [*Airport symbol*]   (OAG)
YXK .... Rimouski [*Canada*] [*Airport symbol*]   (OAG)
YXL .... Sioux Lookout [*Canada*] [*Airport symbol*]   (OAG)
YXO .... Houghton College, Buffalo Campus, West Seneca, NY [*OCLC symbol*]   (OCLC)
YXP .... Pangnirtung [*Canada*] [*Airport symbol*]   (OAG)
YXR .... Earlton [*Canada*] [*Airport symbol*]   (OAG)
YXS .... Prince George [*Canada*] [*Airport symbol*]   (OAG)
YXT .... Terrace [*Canada*] [*Airport symbol*]   (OAG)
YXU .... London [*Canada*] [*Airport symbol*]   (OAG)
YXX .... Abbotsford [*Canada*] [*Airport symbol*]
YXY .... Whitehorse [*Canada*] [*Airport symbol*]   (OAG)
YXZ .... Wawa [*Canada*] [*Airport symbol*]   (OAG)
YY .... Organization not allocated a 2-letter designator on an exclusive basis [*ICAO designator*]   (ICDA)
YY .... Robert Lynd [*American author, 1892-1970*] [*Pseudonym*]
Y-Y .... Yaw Axis   (AAG)
YY .... Yedi'ot Yanai   (BJA)
YYB .... North Bay [*Canada*] [*Airport symbol*]   (OAG)
YYC .... Calgary [*Canada*] [*Airport symbol*]   (OAG)
YYCI .... Youth-to-Youth Committee International   (EA)
YYD .... Smithers [*Canada*] [*Airport symbol*]   (OAG)
YYE .... Fort Nelson [*Canada*] [*Airport symbol*]   (OAG)
YYF .... Penticton [*Canada*] [*Airport symbol*]   (OAG)
YYG .... Charlottetown [*Canada*] [*Airport symbol*]   (OAG)
YYH .... Spence Bay [*Canada*] [*Airport symbol*]   (OAG)
YYJ .... Victoria [*Canada*] [*Airport symbol*]   (OAG)
YYL .... Lynn Lake [*Canada*] [*Airport symbol*] [*Obsolete*]   (OAG)
YYP .... Yarns of Yesteryear Project   (EA)
YYP .... Yeshiva University, New York, NY [*OCLC symbol*]   (OCLC)
YYQ .... Churchill [*Canada*] [*Airport symbol*]   (OAG)
YYR .... Goose Bay [*Canada*] [*Airport symbol*]   (OAG)
YYR .... Year of the Young Reader [*1989*] [*Library of Congress campaign*]
YYS .... Yo-Yo Stock [*Investment term*]
YYSCI .... Youth-to-Youth Sports Committee International   (EA)
YYT .... St. Johns [*Canada*] [*Airport symbol*]   (OAG)
YYU .... Kapuskasing [*Canada*] [*Airport symbol*]   (OAG)
YYY .... Mont-Joli [*Canada*] [*Airport symbol*]   (OAG)
YYY .... Yugntruf - Youth for Yiddish   (EA)
YYYC .... Yu-Yen Yen-Chiu [*Linguistic Researches*] [*A publication*]
YYZ .... Toronto [*Canada*] [*Airport symbol*]   (OAG)
YZ .... MET Databank [*ICAO designator*]   (ICDA)
YZA .... Albany Law School, Albany, NY [*OCLC symbol*]   (OCLC)
YZF .... Yellowknife [*Canada*] [*Airport symbol*]   (OAG)
YZG .... Sugluk [*Canada*] [*Airport symbol*]   (OAG)
YZP .... Sandspit [*Canada*] [*Airport symbol*]   (OAG)
YZR .... Sarnia [*Canada*] [*Airport symbol*]   (OAG)
YZS .... Coral Harbour [*Canada*] [*Airport symbol*]   (OAG)
YZSZ .... Yarlung Zangbo Suture Zone [*Geophysics*]
YZT .... Port Hardy [*Canada*] [*Airport symbol*]   (OAG)
YZV .... Sept-Iles [*Canada*] [*Airport symbol*]   (OAG)

Z

Z................. Administrative Aircraft [*When a suffix to Navy plane designation*]
Z................. Atomic Number [*Symbol*]
z................. Aza [*As substituent on nucleoside*] [*Biochemistry*]
Z................. Azimuth Angle
z................. Charge Number of a Cell Reaction [*Symbol*] [*Electrochemistry*]
Z................. Collision Number [*Symbol*] [*IUPAC*]
Z................. Compression Factor [*Symbol*] [*Thermodynamics*]
Z................. Contraction [*Medicine*]
Z................. Coriolis Correction
Z................. Figure of Merit [*Symbol*]   (DEN)
Z................. Glutamic Acid [*or Glutamine*] [*Also, Glx*] [*Symbol*] [*An amino acid*]
Z................. Greenwich Mean Time   (FAAC)
Z................. Impedance [*Symbol*] [*IUPAC*]
Z................. Jet Terminal Area [*Aviation symbol*]   (FAAC)
Z................. Normally Open [*Ship's fittings classification*]
z................. Partition Function, Particle [*Symbol*] [*IUPAC*]
z................. Partition Function, System [*Symbol*] [*IUPAC*]
Z................. Planning [*Aircraft classification letter*]
Z................. Stadia [*Speedways, race tracks, etc.*] [*Public-performance tariff class*] [*British*]
Z................. Standard Score [*Psychology*]
Z................. Switzerland [*IYRU nationality code*]   (IYR)
Z................. Symbol for Magnetic Reluctance   (ROG)
Z................. Tower Control [*Aviation symbol*]   (FAAC)
Z................. [*The Third*] Unknown Quantity [*Mathematics*]   (ROG)
Z................. Vertical component of the earth's magnetic field
Z................. Weekend Travel [*Also, W*] [*Airline fare code*]
Z................. Woolworth Corp. [*NYSE symbol*] [*Wall Street slang name: "Five & Dime"*] [*Toronto Stock Exchange symbol*]   (SPSG)
Z................. Z-Axis
Z................. [*Franciscus*] Zabarella [*Deceased, 1417*] [*Authority cited in pre-1607 legal work*]   (DSA)
Z................. Zagreb [*A publication*]
Z................. Zaire [*Monetary unit in Zaire*]
Z................. Zambon [*Italy*] [*Research code symbol*]
Z......... Zebra [*Phonetic alphabet*] [*Royal Navy*] [*World War I*] [*Pre-World War II*] [*World War II*]   (DSUE)
Z................. Zeitung [*Newspaper, Review*] [*German*]   (ILCA)
Z................. Zenith
Z................. Zenith Distance [*Navigation*]
Z................. Zentral-Sparkasse [*Banking*] [*Austria*]   (ECON)
Z................. Zentralblatt [*Official Gazette*] [*German*]   (ILCA)
Z................. Zentrumspartei [*Center Party*] [*German*] [*Political party*]   (PPE)
Z................. Zero
Z................. Zero Rate [*Valued added tax*]
Z................. Zerubbabel [*Freemasonry*]   (ROG)
Z................. Zinc [*Chemical symbol is Zn*]
Z................. Zionist
Z................. Zircon [*CIPW classification*] [*Geology*]
Z................. Zirconium [*Chemical element*] [*Symbol is Zr*]   (ROG)
Z................. Zivot [*A publication*]
Z................. Zloty [*Monetary unit*] [*Poland*]
Z................. Zoen Tencararius [*Flourished, 13th century*] [*Authority cited in pre-1607 legal work*]   (DSA)
Z......... Zoll [*Customs Duty*] [*German*]
Z................. Zone
Z................. Zone Marker
Z................. Zone Meridian [*Lower or upper branch*]
Z................. Zora [*A publication*]
Z................. Zuckung [*Contraction or spasm*] [*German*] [*Medicine*]
Z................. Zuender [*Fuze*] [*German military*]
Z................. Zuercher Bibel   (BJA)
Z................. Zulu [*Phonetic alphabet*] [*International*]   (DSUE)
Z................. Zulu Time [*Greenwich Mean Time*]   (AFM)
(Z).............. Zusammen [*Together*] [*Chemistry*]
Z................. Zuse [*Calculator*]   (HGAA)
Z................. Zven'ya [*A publication*]

Z................. Zwingliana [*A publication*]
Z................. Zycie [*A publication*]
Z................. Zyma AG [*Switzerland*] [*Research code symbol*]
Z8.............. Zilog Eight Bit One-Chip Microcomputer   (HGAA)
Z80............ Zilog Eight Bit Microprocessor   (HGAA)
Z8000........ Zilog Sixteen Bit Microprocessor   (HGAA)
Z (Day)....... Zero Day [*The date fixed for any important military operation*] [*British*]
ZA.............. Approach Control Office [*ICAO designator*]   (ICDA)
ZA.............. South Africa [*ANSI two-letter standard code*]   (CNC)
Za.............. Zabriskie's Reports [*21-24 New Jersey*] [*A publication*]   (DLA)
Z-A............. Zaire-Afrique [*A publication*]
za.............. Zambia [*MARC country of publication code*] [*Library of Congress*]   (LCCP)
ZA.............. Zenith Angle [*Geophysics*]
ZA.............. Zentralarchiv fuer Empirische Sozialforschung [*Central Archives for Empirical Social Research*] [*University of Cologne*] [*Information service or system*]   (IID)
ZA.............. Zero and Add
ZA.............. Zero Adjuster   (MSA)
ZA.............. Zinc-Aluminum [*An alloy*]
ZA.............. Zionist Archives [*A publication*]
ZA.............. Ziva Antika [*A publication*]
ZA.............. Zone of Action
ZA.............. Zoologischer Anzeiger [*A publication*]
ZA.............. Zunz Archive. Jewish National and University Library [*Jerusalem*] [*A publication*]
ZAA.......... Alice Arm/Kitsault [*Canada*] [*Airport symbol*]   (OAG)
ZAA.......... Zartman Association of America   (EA)
ZAA.......... Zeeman-Effect Atomic Absorption [*Spectrometry*]
ZAA.......... Zero Angle of Attack
Z Aachener Geschichtsver ... Zeitschrift. Aachener Geschichtsverein [*A publication*]
Z Aach Gesch Ver ... Zeitschrift. Aachener Geschichtsverein [*A publication*]
ZAAP........ Zero Antiaircraft Potential [*Missile*]
ZAB........... Albuquerque, NM [*Location identifier*] [*FAA*]   (FAAL)
Zab............. [*Franciscus*] Zabarella [*Deceased, 1417*] [*Authority cited in pre-1607 legal work*]   (DSA)
Zab............. Zabim   (BJA)
ZAB .... Zabrze [*Poland*] [*Seismograph station code, US Geological Survey*]   (SEIS)
ZAB .... Zinc-Air Battery
Zaba........... [*Franciscus*] Zabarella [*Deceased, 1417*] [*Authority cited in pre-1607 legal work*]   (DSA)
ZABIA .... Zastita Bilja [*A publication*]
Zab Land Laws ... Zabriskie on the Public Land Laws of the United States [*A publication*]   (DLA)
Zab (NJ) .... Zabriskie's Reports [*21-24 New Jersey*] [*A publication*]   (DLA)
ZABS......... Zab's Backyard Hots, Inc. [*Pittsford, NY*] [*NASDAQ symbol*]   (NQ)
Zaby Przyr Nieozyw ... Zabytki Przyrody Nieozywionej Ziem Rzeczpospolitej Polskiej [*A publication*]
ZACH .... Zacharias [*Old Testament book*] [*Douay version*]
ZA Ch .... Zurnal Analiticeskoj Chimii [*A publication*]
ZAD .... Zadar [*Former Yugoslavia*] [*Airport symbol*]   (OAG)
ZAD.......... Zenith Angle Distribution
ZADCC..... Zone Air Defense Control Center   (NATG)
ZADI .... Zentralstelle fuer Agrardokumentation und -Information [*Center for Agricultural Documentation and Information*] [*Databank originator*] [*Information service or system*] [*Germany*]   (IID)
Zad Rev...... Zadarska Revija [*A publication*]
ZADS........ Zeitschrift. Allgemeiner Deutsche Sprachverein [*A publication*]
ZAED .... Zentralstelle fuer Atomkernenergie-Dokumentation beim Gmelin-Institut [*Central Agency for Atomic Energy Documentation of the Gmelin Institute*] [*Germany*] [*Database originator*] [*Also, AED*]
ZAED Phys Daten ... ZAED [*Zentralstelle fuer Atomkernenergie-Dokumentation*] Physik Daten [*A publication*]
Za Ekon Mater ... Za Ekonomiyu Materialov [*A publication*]
Za Ekon Topl ... Za Ekonomiyu Topliva [*A publication*]

ZAF........... South Africa [*ANSI three-letter standard code*]   (CNC)
ZAF........... Zero Alignment Fixture
ZAG........... Zagreb [*Yugoslavia*] [*Seismograph station code, US Geological Survey*]   (SEIS)
ZAG........... Zagreb [*Former Yugoslavia*] [*Airport symbol*]   (OAG)
Zagad Ekon Roln ... Zagadnienia Ekonomiki Rolnej [*A publication*]
Zagadn Ekon Roln ... Zagadnienia Ekonomiki Rolnej [*A publication*]
Zagadn Eksploatacji Masz ... Zagadnienia Eksploatacji Maszyn [*Poland*] [*A publication*]
Zagadnienia Drgan Nieliniowych ... Zagadnienia Drgan Nieliniowych [*Nonlinear Vibration Problems*] [*A publication*]
Zagad Tech Fal Ultradziek ... Zagadnienia Techniki Fal Ultradzwiekowych [*A publication*]
Zagreber Studien ... Zagreber Germanistische Studien [*A publication*]
ZAGV .... Zeitschrift. Aachener Geschichtsverein [*A publication*]
ZAH........... Zahedan [*Iran*] [*Airport symbol*]   (OAG)
ZAHAL ..... Z'va Hagana Le'Israel [*Israel Defense Forces*] [*Hebrew*]
Zahnaerztebl (Baden-Wuerttemb) ... Zahnaerzteblatt (Baden-Wuerttemberg) [*A publication*]
Zahnaerztl Gesundheitsdienst ... Zahnaerztlicher Gesundheitsdienst [*A publication*]
Zahnaerztl Mitt ... Zahnaerztliche Mitteilungen [*A publication*]
Zahnaerztl Prax ... Zahnaerztliche Praxis [*A publication*]
Zahnaerztl Praxisfuehr ... Zahnaerztliche Praxisfuehrung [*A publication*]
Zahnaerztl Rundsch ... Zahnaerztliche Rundschau [*A publication*]
Zahnaerztl Welt ... Zahnaerztliche Welt [*A publication*]
Zahnaerztl Welt Zahnaerztl Reform ... Zahnaerztliche Welt und Zahnaerztliche Reform [*A publication*]
Zahnaerztl Welt Zahnaerztl Rundsch ... Zahnaerztliche Welt, Zahnaerztliche Rundschau [*A publication*]
Zahnerh Kd ... Zahnerhaltungskunde [*A publication*]
Zahn Inf Die ... Zahnaerztlicher Informationsdienst [*A publication*]
Zahn-Mund-Kieferheilkd ... Zahn-, Mund-, und Kieferheilkunde [*A publication*]
Zahn Prax ... Zahnaerztliche Praxis [*A publication*]
Zahn Rd ... Zahnaerztliche Rundschau [*A publication*]
Zahntechn ... Zahntechnik [*A publication*]
Zahntechn ... Zahntechniker [*A publication*]
Zahntechn Nachr ... Zahntechnische Nachrichten [*A publication*]
ZAI .... Zeirei Agudath Israel   (EA)
ZAI .... Zero Address Instruction
Zaire-Afr.... Zaire-Afrique [*A publication*]
ZAK .... Zakamensk [*Former USSR*] [*Seismograph station code, US Geological Survey*]   (SEIS)
Zakhist Rosl ... Zakhist Roslin [*A publication*]
Za Khlopk Nezavisimost ... Za Khlopkovuyu Nezavisimost [*A publication*]
Zakhyst Rosl Resp Mizhvid Temat Nauk Zb ... Zakhyst Roslyn Respublikans 'Kyi Mizhvidomchyi Tematychnyi Naukovyi Zbirnyk [*A publication*]
Zakonomern Raspred Promesnykh Tsentrov Ionnykh Krist ... Zakonomernosti Raspredeleniya Promesnykh Tsentrov v Ionnykh Kristallakh [*A publication*]
Zakonomern Razmeshcheniya Polezn Iskop ... Zakonomernosti Razmeshcheniya Poleznykh Iskopaemykh [*A publication*]
Zakupki Sel'skokhoz Prod ... Zakupki Sel'skokhozyaistvennykh Produktov [*A publication*]
ZAL .... State University of New York, Albany Library School, Albany, NY [*OCLC symbol*]   (OCLC)
ZAL .... Zionist Archives and Library   (BJA)
ZALIS....... Zinc and Lead International Service
Z Allg Oesterr Apoth Ver ... Zeitschrift. Allgemeiner Oesterreichische Apotheker-Verein [*A publication*]
ZAM .... State University of New York, Agricultural and Technical College at Alfred, Alfred, NY [*OCLC symbol*]   (OCLC)
ZAM .... Z-Axis Modulation
ZAM .... Zamboanga [*Philippines*] [*Airport symbol*]   (OAG)
Zambia Dep Game Fish Fish Res Bull ... Zambia. Department of Game and Fisheries. Fisheries Research Bulletin [*A publication*]
Zambia Dep Wildl Fish Natl Parks Annu Rep ... Zambia. Department of Wildlife, Fisheries, and National Parks. Annual Report [*A publication*]
Zambia Div For Res Annu Rep ... Zambia. Division of Forest Research. Annual Report [*A publication*]
Zambia Div For Res Res Pam ... Zambia. Division of Forest Research. Research Pamphlet [*A publication*]
Zambia For Res Bull ... Zambia Forest Research Bulletin [*A publication*]
Zambia Geogr Assoc Mag ... Zambia Geographical Association. Magazine [*A publication*]
Zambia Geol Surv Annu Rep ... Zambia. Geological Survey. Annual Report [*A publication*]
Zambia Geol Surv Dep Annu Rep ... Zambia. Geological Survey. Department Annual Report [*A publication*]
Zambia Geol Surv Dep Econ Rep ... Zambia. Ministry of Lands and Mines. Geological Survey Department. Economic Report [*A publication*]
Zambia Geol Surv Econ Rep ... Zambia. Geological Survey. Economic Report [*A publication*]
Zambia Geol Surv Rec ... Zambia. Geological Survey. Records [*A publication*]
Zambia Geol Surv Tech Rep ... Zambia. Geological Survey. Technical Report [*A publication*]

Zambia J Sci Technol ... Zambia Journal of Science and Technology [*A publication*]
Zambia LJ ... Zambia Law Journal [*A publication*]   (DLA)
Zambia Minist Lands Nat Resour For Res Bull ... Zambia. Ministry of Lands and Natural Resources. Forest Research Bulletin [*A publication*]
Zambia Minist Rural Dev For Res Bull ... Zambia. Ministry of Rural Development. Forest Research Bulletin [*A publication*]
Zambia Nurse J ... Zambia Nurse Journal [*A publication*]
Zambia Rep Geol Surv ... Zambia. Ministry of Lands and Mines. Report of the Geological Survey [*A publication*]
Zam LJ ...... Zambia Law Journal [*A publication*]   (DLA)
ZAMM ...... Zen and the Art of Motorcycle Maintenance [*A novel*]
ZAMS........ Zero-Age Main Sequence [*Astronomy*]
ZAN........... Anchorage, AK [*Location identifier*] [*FAA*]   (FAAL)
ZAN........... Zante [*Greece*] [*Seismograph station code, US Geological Survey*]   (SEIS)
ZAN........... Zantop International Airlines, Inc. [*Ypsilanti, MI*] [*FAA designator*]   (FAAC)
ZANA .... Zambia News Agency
Z Analit Chim ... Zurnal Analiticeskoj Chimii [*A publication*]
ZANC .... Zambia National Congress - Southern Rhodesia
Z An Chim ... Zurnal Analiticeskoj Chimii [*A publication*]
ZANCO Ser A ... ZANCO. Scientific Journal of Sulaimaniyah University. Series A. Pure and Applied Sciences [*A publication*]
ZANCO Ser A Pure Appl Sci ... ZANCO. Series A. Pure and Applied Sciences [*A publication*]
Zane .... Zane's Reports [*4-9 Utah*] [*A publication*]   (DLA)
ZANLA ..... Zimbabwe African National Liberation Army   (PD)
ZAnt........... Ziva Antika [*A publication*]
ZANU........ Zimbabwe African National Union [*Political party*]   (PPW)
ZANU-PF ... Zimbabwe African National Union - Patriotic Front [*Political party*]   (PD)
ZANZ .... Zanzibar
Zanzibar Protect Ann Rep Med Dept ... Zanzibar Protectorate. Annual Report on the Medical Department [*A publication*]
Zanzib Prot LR ... Zanzibar Protectorate Law Reports [*Africa*] [*A publication*]   (DLA)
Za Ovladenie Tekh Kamenougol'n Promsti ... Za Ovladenie Tekhnikoi v Kamenougol'noi Promyshlennosti [*A publication*]
ZAP .... Helionetics, Inc. [*AMEX symbol*]   (SPSG)
zap............. Zapotec [*MARC language code*] [*Library of Congress*]   (LCCP)
ZAP .... Zero Ability to Pay [*Real estate*]
ZAP .... Zero and Add Packed
ZAP .... Zero Antiaircraft Potential [*Missile*]   (MCD)
ZAP .... Znamenity Amerikansky Pisatel [*Famous American Writer*] [*Russian*]
ZAP .... Zone Axis Pattern   (MCD)
ZAP .... Zoological Action Program [*Defunct*]   (EA)
Zapadne Karpaty Ser Geol ... Zapadne Karpaty. Seria Geologia [*A publication*]
Zapadn Karpaty Ser Paleontol ... Zapadne Karpaty. Seria Paleontologia [*A publication*]
Zap Arm Otd Vses Mineral Ova ... Zapiski Armyanskogo Otdeleniya Vsesoyuznogo Mineralogicheskogo Obshchestva [*A publication*]
Zapata........ Zapata Corp. [*Associated Press abbreviation*]   (APAG)
ZAPB........ Zinc-Air Primary Battery
Zap Beloruss Gos Inst Sel'sk Lesn Khoz ... Zapiski Belorusskogo Gosudarstvennogo Instituta Sel'skogo i Lesnogo Khozyaistva [*A publication*]
Zap Cukotsk Kraeved Muz ... Zapiski Cukotskogo Kraevedceskogo Muzeja [*A publication*]
Zap GO...... Zapiski Geograficeskogo Obscestva [*A publication*]
Zap Inst Jaz Lit Ist ... Zapiski Gosudarstvennogo Instituta Jazyka, Literatury, i Istorii [*A publication*]
Zap Inst Khim Akad Nauk Ukr RSR ... Zapiski Institutu Khimii Akademiya Nauk Ukrains'koi RSR [*A publication*]
Zapisnici Srp Geol Drus ... Zapisnici Srpskog Geoloskog Drustva [*A publication*]
Zap Kalm Nauc Issl Inst Jaz Lit Ist ... Zapiski. Kalmyckij Naucno-Issledovatel'skij Institut Jazyka, Literatury, i Istorii [*A publication*]
Zap Khar'k S-Kh Inst ... Zapiski Khar'kovskogo Sel'skokhozyaistvennogo Instituta [*A publication*]
Zap Kiiv Tov Prirodozn ... Zapiski Kiivs'kogo Tovaristva Prirodoznavtsiv [*A publication*]
Zap Kirg Otd Vses Mineral Ova ... Zapiski Kirgizskogo Otdeleniya Vsesoyuznogo Mineralogicheskogo Obshchestva [*A publication*]
Zap KORGO ... Zapiski Kavkazskogo Otdela Russkogo Geograficeskogo Obscestva [*A publication*]
Zap Leningrad Sel'skokhoz Inst ... Zapiski Leningradskogo Sel'skokhozyaistvennogo Instituta [*A publication*]
Zap Leningr Gorn Inst ... Zapiski Leningradskogo Gornogo Instituta [*Former USSR*] [*A publication*]
Zap Leningr Sel'-Khoz Inst ... Zapiski Leningradskogo Sel'skokhozyaistvennogo Instituta [*A publication*]
Zap Leningr S-Kh Inst ... Zapiski Leningradskogo Sel'skokhozyaistvennogo Instituta [*A publication*]
Zap Nauchn Semin ... Zapiski Nauchnykh Seminarov [*A publication*]

Zap Nauchn Semin Leningr Otd Mat Inst Akad Nauk SSSR ... Zapiski Nauchnykh Seminarov Leningradskoe Otdelenie Matematicheskii Institut Akademia Nauk SSSR [*Former USSR*] [*A publication*]
Zap Nauchn Sem Leningrad Otdel Mat Inst Steklov (LOMI) ... Zapiski Nauchnykh Seminarov Leningradskogo Otdeleniya Matematicheskogo Instituta Imeni V. A. Steklova Akademii Nauk SSSR (LOMI) [*A publication*]
Zap Naucn Sem Leningrad Otdel Mat Inst Steklov ... Zapiski Naucnyh Seminarov Leningradskogo Otdelenija Matematiceskogo Instituta Imeni V. A. Steklova Akademii Nauk SSSR [*A publication*]
ZAPO .... Zimbabwe African People's Organization
Zap Odess Ark Obshch ... Zapiski Odesskoe Arkheologicheskoe Obshchestvo [*Odessa, USSR*] [*A publication*]
Za Prog Proizvod ... Za Progress Proizvodstva [*A publication*]
Zap Ross Mineral Ova ... Zapiski Rossiiskogo Mineralogicheskogo Obshchestva [*A publication*]
ZAPS .... Cooper Life Sciences, Inc. [*NASDAQ symbol*]   (NQ)
Zap SKK Gor NII ... Zapiski Severo-Kavkazskogo Kraevogo Gorskogo Naucno-Issledovatel'skogo Instituta [*A publication*]
Zap Sverdl Otd Vses Bot Ova ... Zapiski Sverdlovskogo Otdeleniya Vsesoyuznogo Botanicheskogo Obshchestva [*A publication*]
Zap Sverdlov Otd Vsesoyuz Bot Obshch ... Zapiski Sverdlovskogo Otdeleniya Vsesoyuznogo Botanicheskogo Obshchestva [*A publication*]
Zap Tadzh Otd Vses Mineral Ova ... Zapiski Tadzhikskogo Otdeleniya Vsesoyuznogo Mineralogicheskogo Obshchestva [*A publication*]
Zap Tsentr Kavk Otd Vses Bot Ova ... Zapiski Tsentral'no-Kavkazskogo Otdeleniya Vsesoyuznogo Botanicheskogo Obshchestva [*A publication*]
ZAPU .... Zimbabwe African People's Union
Zap Ukr Otd Vses Mineral Ova ... Zapiski Ukrainskogo Otdeleniya Vsesoyuznogo Mineralogicheskogo Obshchestva [*A publication*]
Zap Uzb Otd Vses Mineral Ova ... Zapiski Uzbekistanskogo Otdeleniya Vsesoyuznogo Mineralogicheskogo Obshchestva [*A publication*]
Zap Voronezh Sel'-Khoz Inst ... Zapiski Voronezhskogo Sel'skokhozyaistvennogo Instituta [*A publication*]
Zap Voronezh S-Kh Inst ... Zapiski Voronezhskogo Sel'skokhozyaistvennogo Instituta [*A publication*]
Zap Vost Sib Otd Vses Mineral Ova ... Zapiski Vostochno-Sibirskogo Otdeleniya Vsesoyuznogo Mineralogicheskogo Obshchestva [*A publication*]
Zap Vses Mineral Obshchest ... Zapiski Vsesoyuznogo Mineralogicheskogo Obshchestva [*A publication*]
Zap Vses Mineral O-Va ... Zapiski Vsesoyuznogo Mineralogicheskogo Obshchestva [*A publication*]
Zap Zabaik Fil Geogr Ova SSSR ... Zapiski Zabaikal'skogo Filiala Geograficheskogo Obshchestva SSSR [*A publication*]
Zap Zabaik Otd Vses Geogr O-Va ... Zapiski Zabaikal'skogo Otdela Vsesoyuznogo Geograficheskogo Obshchestva [*A publication*]
ZAR .... Zaire [*ANSI three-letter standard code*]   (CNC)
ZAR .... Zaria [*Nigeria*] [*Geomagnetic observatory code*]
ZAR .... Zero-G Antenna Range   (SSD)
ZAR .... Zeus Acquisition RADAR [*Missile defense*]
Z Arbeitsgem Oesterr Entomol ... Zeitschrift. Arbeitsgemeinschaft Oesterreichischer Entomologen [*A publication*]
Za Rekonstr Tekst Promsti ... Za Rekonstruktsiyu Tekstil'noi Promyshlennosti [*A publication*]
ZARP .... Zuid Afrikaansche Republick Politie [*South African Republic Police*]   (DSUE)
ZarSl .... Zaranie Slaskie [*A publication*]
ZAS .... Zarkani Air Services [*Egypt*]   (EY)
Zas .... [*Udalricus*] Zasius [*Deceased, 1535*] [*Authority cited in pre-1607 legal work*]   (DSA)
ZAS .... Zero Access Storage
ZAS .... Zymosan-Activated Serum [*Immunology*]
Zashch Korroz Khim Promsti ... Zashchita ot Korrozii v Khimicheskoi Promyshlennosti [*A publication*]
Zashch Met ... Zashchita Metallov [*A publication*]
Zashch Pokrytiya Met ... Zashchitnye Pokrytiya na Metallakh [*A publication*]
Zashch Rast (Kiev) ... Zashchita Rastenii (Kiev) [*A publication*]
Zashch Rast (Leningrad) ... Zashchita Rastenii (Leningrad) [*A publication*]
Zashch Rast (Mosc) ... Zashchita Rastenii (Moscow) [*A publication*]
Zashch Rast (Moscow) ... Zashchita Rastenii (Moscow) [*A publication*]
Zashch Rast Vred Bolez ... Zashchita Rastenii ot Vreditelei i Boleznei [*A publication*]
Zashch Rast Vred Bolezn ... Zashchita Rastenii ot Vreditelei i Boleznei [*A publication*]
Zashch Rast Vredit Bolez ... Zashchita Rastenii ot Vreditelei i Boleznei [*A publication*]
Zashch Truboprovodov Korroz ... Zashchita Truboprovodov ot Korrozii [*A publication*]
Zasi .... [*Udalricus*] Zasius [*Deceased, 1535*] [*Authority cited in pre-1607 legal work*]   (DSA)
Z Asiat Studien ... Zentralasiatische Studien [*Bonn*] [*A publication*]

Za Soc Zemed ... Za Socialisticke Zemedelstvi [*A publication*]
Za Sots Sel'-Khoz Nauku ... Za Sotsialisticheskuyu Sel'skokhozyaistvennuyu Nauku [*A publication*]
Za Sots Sel'skokhoz Nauku Ser A ... Za Sotsialisticheskuyu Sel'skokhozyaistvennuyu Nauku. Seriya A [*A publication*]
Zast Bilja ... Zastita Bilja [*A publication*]
ZastMat ..... Zastosowania Matematyki [*A publication*]
Zast Mater ... Zastita Materijala [*A publication*]
Zastos Mat ... Polska Akademia Nauk. Instytut Matematyczny. Zastosowania Matematyki [*A publication*]
Zastosow Mat ... Zastosowania Matematyki [*A publication*]
ZAT .... Zantop Airways, Inc.
ZAT .... Zhaotong [*China*] [*Airport symbol*]   (OAG)
ZAT .... Zinc Atmospheric Tracer
ZAT .... Zydowska Agencja Telegraficzna   (BJA)
Za Tekh Prog (Baku) ... Za Tekhnicheskii Progress (Baku) [*A publication*]
Za Tekh Prog (Gorkly) ... Za Tekhnicheskii Progress (Gorkly) [*A publication*]
ZATPA ...... Za Tekhnicheskii Progress [*A publication*]
Za Turf Ind ... Za Turfyanuyu Industriyu [*A publication*]
ZAU .... Chicago, IL [*Location identifier*] [*FAA*]   (FAAL)
ZAV .... Zavalla [*Texas*] [*Seismograph station code, US Geological Survey*] [*Closed*]   (SEIS)
Zav .... Zavim   (BJA)
Zav Lab ...... Zavodskaya Laboratoriya [*A publication*]
Zavod Lab ... Zavodskaya Laboratoriya [*A publication*]
ZAWEA ..... Zahnaerztliche Welt [*A publication*]
ZAZ .... Zaragoza [*Spain*] [*Airport symbol*]   (OAG)
ZB .... Repetitive Flight Plan Office [*ICAO designator*]   (ICDA)
ZB .... Zero Beat [*Radio*]
ZB .... Zimbabwe [*IYRU nationality code*]   (IYR)
ZB .... Zimbabwe Banking Corp. Ltd.
ZB .... Zinc Borate [*Trademark for a flame retardant compound*] [*Humphrey Chemical Co.*]
ZB .... Zoom Back [*Cinematography*]   (WDMC)
ZB .... Zuercher Bibel   (BJA)
ZB .... Zum Beispiel [*For Example*] [*German*]
ZBA .... Zero-Based Analysis   (ADA)
ZBA .... Zero Bias Anomaly
ZBA .... Zero Bracket Amount [*IRS*]
ZBA .... Zoning Board of Approval [*Generic term*]   (WGA)
ZBAA .... Beijing/Capital [*China*] [*ICAO location identifier*]   (ICLI)
Z Bayer Revisions Ver ... Zeitschrift. Bayerischer Revisions Verein [*A publication*]
ZBB .... Zero-Base Budgeting
ZBBB .... Beijing City [*China*] [*ICAO location identifier*]   (ICLI)
ZBC .... Zebec Resources [*Vancouver Stock Exchange symbol*]
ZBDC .... Zinc Dibutyldithiocarbamate [*Organic chemistry*]
ZBDLG ...... Zuercher Beitraege zur Deutschen Literatur und Geistesgeschichte [*A publication*]
ZBDSS ...... Zuercher Beitraege zur Deutschen Sprach- und Stilgeschichte [*A publication*]
ZBE .... Zinc Battery Electrode
Z Berg Gesch V ... Zeitschrift. Bergischer Geschichtsverein [*A publication*]
ZBG .... Zeitschrift. Bergischer Geschichtsverein [*A publication*]
ZBGV .... Zeitschrift. Bergischer Geschichtsverein [*A publication*]
ZBHH .... Huhhot [*China*] [*ICAO location identifier*]   (ICLI)
Zb Inst Khim Tekhnol Akad Nauk Ukr RSR ... Zbirnik Institutu Khimichnoi Tekhnologii Akademiya Nauk Ukrains'koi RSR [*A publication*]
Zbirka Izbran Poglav Fiz ... Zbirka Izbranih Poglavij iz Fizike [*A publication*]
Zbirka Izbran Poglav Mat ... Zbirka Izbranih Poglavij iz Matematike [*A publication*]
ZbirP .... Zbirnyk Prac' Naukovoji Sevcenkivs'koji Konferenciji [*A publication*]
ZBJV .... Zeitschrift. Bernischer Juristen-Verein [*A publication*]
ZBL .... Brooklyn Law School, Brooklyn, NY [*OCLC symbol*]   (OCLC)
ZBL .... Zero-Based Linearity
ZBLAN ...... Zirconium, Barium, Lanthanum, Aluminum, Sodium Fluoride [*Molar composition of glass*] [*Chemistry*]
Zbl DDR .... Zentralblatt der Deutschen Demokratischen Republik [*A publication*]   (DLA)
Zbl Soz Vers ... Zentralblatt fuer Sozialversicherung und Versorgung [*German*] [*A publication*]   (DLA)
ZBM .... State University of New York, College at Oneonta, Oneonta, NY [*OCLC symbol*]   (OCLC)
ZBMM ...... Zenana Bible and Medical Mission [*British*]   (DI)
ZBMP .... Zero-Base Media Planning
ZBN .... Brookhaven National Laboratory, Upton, NY [*OCLC symbol*]   (OCLC)
Zb Nauk Pr Aspir Kiiv Inzh Budiv Inst ... Zbirnik Naukovikh Prats Aspirantiv Kiivs'kii Inzhenerno-Budivel'nii Institut [*A publication*]
Zb Nauk Pr Aspir Kyyiv Univ Pryr Nauky ... Zbirnyk Naukovykh Prats' Aspirantiv Kyyivski Universytet Pryrodni Nauky [*A publication*]
Zb Nauk Pr Bilotserk Dos Sel Statsiya ... Zbirnyk Naukovykh Prats' Bilotserkiv'sta Doslidno-Selektvionna Statsiya [*A publication*]
Zb Nauk Pr Khim Sil'sk Hospod Ukr Sil'skohospod Akad ... Zbirnyk Naukovykh Prats' Khimicheskoho Sil'skoho Hospodarstva Ukrainskoyi Sil'skohospodarskoyi Akademiyi [*A publication*]

Zb Nauk Pr Kiiv Budiv Inst ... Zbirnik Naukovikh Prats Kiivs'kii Budivel'nii Institut [*A publication*]
Zb Nauk Pr L'viv Med Inst ... Zbirnyk Naukovykh Prats' L'viv'kyi Medychyni Instytut [*A publication*]
Zb Nauk Pr Umans'kyi Sil'skohospod Inst ... Zbirnyk Naukovykh Prats' Umans'kyi Sil'skohospodarskyi Instytut [*A publication*]
Zb Nauk Rob Khark Derzh Med Inst ... Zbirnik Naukovikh Robit Kharkivs'kogo Derzhavnogo Medichnogo Institutu [*A publication*]
ZbNPAF .... Zbirnyk Naukovych Prac' Aspirantiv z Filolohiji [*A publication*]
ZBO .... Bowen [*Australia*] [*Airport symbol*] [*Obsolete*] (OAG)
ZBO .... Zone of British Occupation [*Military*]
ZBOW .... Baotou [*China*] [*ICAO location identifier*] (ICLI)
ZBP .... Zero-Base Programming [*Military*]
ZBPE .... Beijing [*China*] [*ICAO location identifier*] (ICLI)
Zb Pr Inst Teploenerg Akad Nauk Ukr RSR ... Zbirnik Prats' Institut Teploenergetiki Akademiya Nauk Ukrains'koi RSR [*A publication*]
Zb Pr Nauk Inst Fiziol Kyyiv Univ ... Zbirnyk Prats' Naukovodoslidnyts'koho Instytuta Fiziolohiyi Kyyivs'koho Universytetu [*A publication*]
Zb Pr Naukovodosl Inst Fiziol Kyyiv Univ ... Zbirnyk Prats' Naukovodoslidnyts'koho Instytuta Fiziolohiyi Kyyivs'koho Universytetu [*A publication*]
Zb Pr Ukr Derzh Inst Nauk Prakt Vet ... Zbirnik Prats' Ukrains'kii Derzhavnii Institut Naukovoi ta Praktichnoi Veterin arii [*A publication*]
Zb Pr Ukr Inst Eksp Vet ... Zbirnik Prats' Ukrains'kogo Institutu Eksperimental'noi Veterinarii [*A publication*]
Zb Pr Zool Muz Akad Nauk Ukr RSR ... Zbirnyk Prats' Zoolohichnoho Muzeyu Akademiyi Nauk Ukrayinskoyi RSR [*A publication*]
ZBR .... Chah-Bahar [*Iran*] [*Airport symbol*] (OAG)
ZbR .... Zbirnyk Robit Aspirantiv Romano-Germans'koji i Klazycnoji Filolohiji [*A publication*]
ZBR .... Zero-Base Review
ZBR .... Zero Beat Reception [*Radio*]
ZBR .... Zero Bend Radius
ZBRA .... Zebra Technologies [*NASDAQ symbol*] (SPSG)
Zbraslav Res Inst Land Reclam Improv Sci Monogr ... Zbraslav Research Institute for Land Reclamation and Improvement. Scientific Monograph [*A publication*]
ZbRL .... Zbirnyk Robit Aspirantiv L'Vivskij Derzavnyj Universitet [*A publication*]
Zb Robit Aspir L'Viv Univ Pryr Nauk ... Zbirnyk Robit Aspirantiv L'Vivs'kyi Universytet Pryrodnykh Nauk [*A publication*]
ZBRS .... Z's Briefs. CPSU [*Cooperative Park Studies Unit, University of Alaska*] Newsletter [*A publication*]
ZBS .... Zeitschrift. Deutscher Verein fuer Buchwesen und Schrifttum [*A publication*]
ZBS .... Zivena Beneficial Society (EA)
ZBSB .... Zeitschriftenkatalog der Bayerischen Staatsbibliothek, Munchen [*Serials Catalogue of the Bavarian State Library, Munich*] [*Deutsches Bibliotheksinstitut*] [*Germany*] [*Information service or system*] (CRD)
ZBST .... ZZZZ Best Co., Inc. [*Reseda, CA*] [*NASDAQ symbol*] (NQ)
ZBT .... Zeta Beta Tau [*Fraternity*]
ZBT .... Zion Bemishpat Tipadeh (Isaiah 1:27) (BJA)
ZBTJ .... Tianjin/Zhangguizhuang [*China*] [*ICAO location identifier*] (ICLI)
ZBTQM ..... Zero-Based Tactical Quality Management [*Army*]
ZBW .... Boston, MA [*Location identifier*] [*FAA*] (FAAL)
ZBYN .... Taiyuan/Wusu [*China*] [*ICAO location identifier*] (ICLI)
Z-C .... Zapalote-Chico [*Race of maize*]
Zc .... Zechariah (BJA)
ZC .... Ziegfeld Club (EA)
ZC .... Zinfandel Club [*British*] (EAIO)
ZC .... Zone Capacity
Z of C .... Zones of Communications [*Military*]
ZCA .... Z Club of America (EA)
ZCAD .... Zycad Corp. [*NASDAQ symbol*] (NQ)
Z/CAL .... Zero Calibration (MCD)
ZCB .... Chase Manhattan Bank, New York, NY [*OCLC symbol*] (OCLC)
ZCB .... Zinc-Coated Bolt
ZCC .... Zeppelin Collectors Club (EA)
ZCC .... Zirconia-Coated Crucible
ZCCI .... Zippy Collectors Club (EA)
ZCD .... Zero Crossing Detector
ZCG .... Impedance Cardiogram (NASA)
ZChN .... Zjednoczenie Chrzescijansko-Narodowe [*Christian National Union*] [*Poland*] [*Political party*] (EY)
ZCIC .... Zirconia-Coated Iridium Crucible
ZCL .... Zacatecas [*Mexico*] [*Airport symbol*] (OAG)
ZCM .... CM Preference Corp. [*Toronto Stock Exchange symbol*]
ZCM .... State University of New York, Agricultural and Technical College at Canton, Canton, NY [*OCLC symbol*] (OCLC)
ZCMI .... Zion's Cooperative Mercantile Institution [*Department store in Salt Lake City, UT*]
ZCN .... Zinc-Coated Nut

ZCP .... Zinc Chromate Primer
ZCR .... Zero Crossing Rate
ZCR .... Zero-Temperature Coefficient Resistor
ZCS .... Zinc-Coated Screw
ZCW .... Zinc-Coated Washer
ZCZ .... Cazenovia College, Witherill Learning Center, Cazenovia, NY [*OCLC symbol*] (OCLC)
ZCzest ...... Ziemia Czestochowska [*A publication*]
ZD .... Air Traffic Flow Control Unit [*ICAO designator*] (ICDA)
ZD .... Zener Diode
ZD .... Zenith Distance [*Navigation*]
ZD .... Zero Defects
ZD .... Zielsprache Deutsch [*A publication*]
ZD .... ZIP Code Distribution
ZD .... Zone Description
ZDA .... Zinc Development Association [*British*] (EAIO)
ZDA/LDA/CA ... Zinc Development Association/Lead Development Association/Cadmium Association [*Information service or system*] (IID)
Z Dampfkesselunters Versicher Ges ... Zeitschrift. Dampfkesseluntersuchungs- und Versicherungs-Gesellschaft [*A publication*]
ZDB .... Zeitschriftendatenbank [*German Union Catalog of Serials*] [*Deutsches Bibliotheksinstitut*] [*Germany*] [*Information service or system*] (CRD)
ZDC .... Philip Crosby Association [*AMEX symbol*] (SPSG)
ZDC .... Washington, DC [*Location identifier*] [*FAA*] (FAAL)
ZDC .... Zero Defects Council
ZDC .... Zeus Defense Center [*Missile defense*]
ZDC .... Zinc Dibenzyldithiocarbamate [*Rubber accelerator*]
ZDC .... Zinc Die Casting
ZDCTBS ... Zeus Defense Center Tape and Buffer System [*Missiles*] (IEEE)
ZDD .... Zero Delay Device
ZDDB .... Zip Code Demographic Data Base [*Demographic Research Co., Inc.*] [*Information service or system*] (CRD)
ZDDL .... Zero Deletion Data Link
ZDDP .... Zinc Dialkyldithiophosphate [*Organic chemistry*]
ZDE .... Zentralstelle Dokumentation Elektrotechnik [*Electrical Engineering Documentation Center*] [*Germany*] [*Originator and database*] [*Information service or system*] (IID)
ZDEC .... Zinc Diethyldithiocarbamate [*Organic chemistry*]
Z Deut Geol Ges ... Zeitschrift. Deutsche Geologische Gesellschaft [*A publication*]
Z Deuts Morgen G ... Zeitschrift. Deutsche Morgenlaendische Gesellschaft [*Wiesbaden*] [*A publication*]
Z Deut Ver ... Zeitschrift. Deutschen Verein fuer Kunstwissenschaft [*A publication*]
ZDF .... Zucker Diabetic Fatty [*Rat strain*]
ZDF .... Zweites Deutsches Fernsehen [*Television network*] [*West Germany*]
ZDFALP .... Z Dziejow Form Artystycznych Literaturze Polskiej [*A publication*]
ZDG .... Corning Community College, Corning, NY [*OCLC symbol*] (OCLC)
ZDG .... Zinc-Doped Germanium
ZDK .... Zen-Do Kai Martial Arts Association, International (EA)
ZDKAA ..... Zdravookhranenie Kazakhstana [*A publication*]
ZDMG .... Zeitschrift. Deutsche Morgenlaendische Gesellschaft [*A publication*]
ZD Musik .. Zeitschriftendienst Musik [*A publication*]
Z DNA ...... Deoxyribonucleic Acid, Zigzag [*DNA with left-handed helix*] [*Biochemistry, genetics*]
Z Dnipr INO ... Zapiski Dnipropetrovs'kogo Institutu Narodnoi Osviti [*A publication*]
ZDP .... Zero Defects Program
ZDP .... Zero Defects Proposal
ZDP .... Zero Delivery Pressure (IEEE)
ZDP .... Zimbabwe Democratic Party [*Political party*] (PPW)
ZDPA .... Zero Defects Program Audit
ZDPG .... Zero Defects Program Guideline
ZDPO .... Zero Defects Program Objective
ZDPR .... Zero Defects Program Responsibility
ZDPV .... Zeitschrift. Deutscher Palaestinaverein [*A publication*]
ZDR .... Zentraldeutsche Rundfunk [*Central German Radio*]
ZDR .... Zeus Discrimination RADAR [*Missile defense*]
Zdrav Aktual ... Zdravotnicke Aktuality [*A publication*]
Zdrav Delo ... Zdravno Delo [*A publication*]
Zdravookhr Beloruss ... Zdravookhranenie Belorussii [*A publication*]
Zdravookhr Belorussii ... Zdravookhranenie Belorussii [*A publication*]
Zdravookhr Kaz ... Zdravookhranenie Kazakhstana [*A publication*]
Zdravookhr Kirg ... Zdravookhranenie Kirgizii [*A publication*]
Zdravookhr Ross Fed ... Zdravookhranenie Rossiiskoi Federatsii [*A publication*]
Zdravookhr Tadzh ... Zdravookhranenie Tadzhikistana [*A publication*]
Zdravookhr Turkm ... Zdravookhranenie Turkmenistana [*A publication*]
Zdrav Prac ... Zdravotnicka Pracovnice [*A publication*]
Zdrav Techn Vzduchotech ... Zdravotni Technika a Vzduchotechnika [*A publication*]
Zdrav Tech Vzduchotech ... Zdravotni Technika a Vzduchotechnika [*A publication*]

Zdrow Publiczne ... Zdrowie Publiczne [*A publication*]
ZDS .... Zenith Data Systems
ZDS .... Zinc Detection System
Zdt............. Die Zoologie des Talmuds [*L. Lewysohn*] [*A publication*] (BJA)
ZDT .... Zero-Ductility Transition (IEEE)
Z Dt Geol Ges ... Zeitschrift. Deutsche Geologische Gesellschaft [*A publication*]
Z Dtschen Morgenlaend Ges ... Zeitschrift. Deutsche Morgenlaendische Gesellschaft [*A publication*]
Z Dtsch Geol Ges ... Zeitschrift. Deutsche Geologische Gesellschaft [*A publication*]
Z Dtsch Morgenl Ges ... Zeitschrift. Deutsche Morganlaendische Gesellschaft [*A publication*]
ZDV .... Denver, CO [*Location identifier*] [*FAA*] (FAAL)
ZDV .... Zero Dead Volume [*Chromatography*]
ZDV .... Zidovudine [*Antiviral*]
ZDVGMS ... Zeitschrift. Deutscher Verein fuer die Geschichte Maehrens und Schlesiens [*A publication*]
ZDV Kw..... Zeitschrift. Deutscher Verein fuer Kunstwissenschaft [*A publication*]
ZDV f Kw... Zeitschrift. Deutscher Verein fuer Kunstwissenschaft [*A publication*]
ZDWF .... Zentrale Dokumentationsstelle der Freien Wohlfahrtspflege fuer Fluechtlinge eV [*Germany*]
ZE .... Flight Information Database [*ICAO designator*] (ICDA)
ZE .... Zenith Electronics Corp. [*NYSE symbol*] (SPSG)
ZE .... Zero Balance Entry [*Banking*]
ZE .... Zero Effusion
ZE .... Zollinger-Ellison [*Syndrome*] [*Medicine*]
ZE .... Zone Effect
ZE .... Zone Electrophoresis [*Analytical biochemistry*]
ZEA .... Zero Energy Assembly [*Nuclear energy*]
ZEA .... Zero Entropy Automorphism
Zeb............. Zebahim (BJA)
ZEB........... Zebra (ROG)
ZEBRA ...... Zebra Energy Breeder Assembly
ZEBRA ...... Zero Balance, Reimbursable Account [*Year-end reclassification of taxable income*]
ZEBRA ...... Zero Energy Breeder Reactor Assembly [*British*]
Zec .... Zechariah [*Old Testament book*]
ZEC .... Zero Energy Coefficient
ZEC .... Zinc-Electrochemical Cell
ZEC .... Zurich Energy Corp. [*Vancouver Stock Exchange symbol*]
ZECC......... Zinc-Electrochemical Cell
ZECC........ Zonal Electric Comfort Council [*Defunct*] (EA)
Zech .... Zechariah [*Old Testament book*]
ZECM........ Zonal Elementary Circulative Mechanism
ZED .... Zero Energy Deuterium [*Type of nuclear reactor*]
ZED .... Zero Express Dialing
ZED .... Zimbabwe Environment and Design [*A publication*]
ZED .... Zur Erkenntnis der Dichtung [*A publication*]
ZEDRON .. Blimp Squadron [*Later separated into BLIMPRON and Blimp-HEDRON*] [*Navy*]
ZEEP .... Zero End Expiratory Pressure [*Medicine*]
ZEEP .... Zero Energy Experimental Pile [*Nuclear reactor*] [*Canada*]
Zeews Fruittelersbl ... Zeeuws Fruittelersblad [*A publication*]
ZEF............ Elkin, NC [*Location identifier*] [*FAA*] (FAAL)
ZEG .... Senggo [*Indonesia*] [*Airport symbol*] (OAG)
ZEG .... Zero Economic Growth
ZEG .... Zero Energy Growth
ZEGL........ [*The*] Ziegler Co., Inc. [*NASDAQ symbol*] (NQ)
ZEH........... Zeit. Wochenzeitung [*A publication*]
Zei .... Das Zeichen [*A publication*]
ZEI............. Zero Environmental Impact
Zeich Zeit .. Zeichen der Zeit [*A publication*]
Zeiss Inf..... Zeiss Information [*A publication*]
Zeiss Mitt.. Zeiss Mitteilungen [*A publication*]
Zeiss-Mitt Fortschr Tech Opt ... Zeiss-Mitteilungen ueber Fortschritte der Technischen Optik [*A publication*]
Zeiss-Mitt Fortsch Tech Optik ... Zeiss-Mitteilungen ueber Fortschritte der Technischen Optik [*A publication*]
Zeitgeschic ... Zeitgeschichte [*A publication*]
Zeitw.......... Zeitwende [*A publication*]
ZEKE........ Zero Kinetic Energy [*Physics*]
Z Eks Klin Med ... Zurnal Eksperimental'noj i Kliniceskoj Mediciny [*A publication*]
Z Eksper Teoret Fiz ... Zurnal Eksperimental'noi i Teoreticeskoi Fiziki [*A publication*]
ZEL............ Bella Bella [*Canada*] [*Airport symbol*] (OAG)
ZEL............ Equitable Life Assurance Society of the United States, Medical Library, New York, NY [*OCLC symbol*] (OCLC)
ZEL............ Zelovo [*Enthusiastically*] [*Music*] (ROG)
ZEL............ Zero-Length Launch [*Missiles*]
ZELL......... Zero-Length Launch [*Missiles*] (MCD)
Zell Papier ... Zellstoff und Papier [*A publication*]
Zellstoffchem Abh ... Zellstoffchemische Abhandlungen [*A publication*]
Zellst Pap .. Zellstoff und Papier [*A publication*]
Zellst Pap (Berlin) ... Zellstoff und Papier (Berlin) [*A publication*]
Zellst Pap (Leipzig) ... Zellstoff und Papier (Leipzig) [*A publication*]

Zellwolle Dtsch Kunstseiden Ztg ... Zellwolle und Deutsche Kunstseiden-Zeitung [*A publication*]
ZELMAL .. Zero-Length Launch and Mat Landing [*Missiles*] (MCD)
ZEM .... East Main [*Canada*] [*Airport symbol*] (OAG)
ZEM .... Hobart and William Smith Colleges, Geneva, NY [*OCLC symbol*] (OCLC)
ZEM .... Zero Electrophoretic Mobility [*Analytical chemistry*]
Zem Beton ... Zement und Beton [*A publication*]
Zemed Arch ... Zemedelsky Archiv [*A publication*]
Zemed Ekon ... Zemedelska Ekonomika [*A publication*]
Zemed Tech ... Zemedelska Technika [*Czechoslovakia*] [*A publication*]
Zemed Tech Cesk Akad Zemed Ustav Vedeckotech Inf Zemed ... Zemedelska Technika. Ceskoslovenska Akademie Zemedelska Ustav Vedeckotechnickych Informaci Pro Zemedelstvi [*A publication*]
Zemed Zahr ... Zemedeistvi v Zahranici [*A publication*]
Zemex .... Zemex Corp. [*Associated Press abbreviation*] (APAG)
Zem-Kalk-Gips ... Zement-Kalk-Gips [*A publication*]
Zemled .... Zemledelie [*A publication*]
Zemled Mekh ... Zemledel'cheskaya Mekhanika [*A publication*]
Zemled Zhivotnovod Mold ... Zemledelie i Zhivotnovodstvo Moldavii [*A publication*]
Zemlerob Resp Mizhvid Temat Nauk Zb ... Zemlerobstvo Respublikans'kyi Mizhvidomchyi Tematychnyi Naukovyi Zbirnyk [*A publication*]
Zemleustroistvo Plan Sel'sk Naselennykh Punktov Geod ... Zemleustroistvo. Planirovka Sel'skikh Naselennykh Punktov i Geodeziya [*A publication*]
Zemlj Biljka ... Zemljiste i Biljka [*A publication*]
Zemlya Sib Dal'nevost ... Zemlya Sibirskaya Dal'nevostochnaya [*A publication*]
Zeml Zhivot Moldav ... Zemledelie i Zhivotnovodstvo Moldavii [*A publication*]
Zem ve Sk .. Zemepis ve Skole [*A publication*]
ZEMTR..... Zeus Early Missile Test RADAR [*Missile defense*] (AABC)
ZEN .... Zeitgeist, Enhancement, and Nonglare [*Camera lens finish developed by Sigma*]
zen .... Zenaga [*MARC language code*] [*Library of Congress*] (LCCP)
ZEN .... Zenith Laboratories, Inc. [*NYSE symbol*] (SPSG)
Zen .... Zenzelinus de Cassanis [*Deceased, 1334*] [*Authority cited in pre-1607 legal work*] (DSA)
ZENITH.... Zero Energy Nitrogen-Heated Thermal Reactor [*British*] (MCD)
ZenithE...... Zenith Electronics Corp. [*Associated Press abbreviation*] (APAG)
Zenix.......... Zenix Income Fund [*Associated Press abbreviation*] (APAG)
ZEN-NOH ... National Federation of Agricultural Cooperative Associations [*Japan*] (EAIO)
ZenNtl .... Zenith National Insurance Corp. [*Associated Press abbreviation*] (APAG)
ZENO .... Zenox, Inc. [*NASDAQ symbol*] (NQ)
ZENT .... Zentec Corp. [*NASDAQ symbol*] (NQ)
Zent Eur Giesserei Ztg ... Zentral-Europaeische Giesserei-Zeitung [*A publication*]
Zentralinst Kernforsch Rossendorf Dresden (Ber) ... Zentralinstitut fuer Kernforschung Rossendorf bei Dresden (Bericht) [*A publication*]
Zentralinst Versuchstierzucht Annu Rep ... Zentralinstitut fuer Versuchstierzucht. Annual Report [*A publication*]
Zentr Org Ges Chir ... Zentralorgan fuer die Gesamte Chirurgie und Ihre Grenzgebiete [*A publication*]
Zent Ztg Opt Mech ... Zentral-Zeitung fuer Optik und Mechanik [*A publication*]
ZENXC...... Zenex Synthetic Lubricants, Inc. [*NASDAQ symbol*] (NQ)
Zenz .... Zenzelinus de Cassanis [*Deceased, 1334*] [*Authority cited in pre-1607 legal work*] (DSA)
ZEO .... Zeolite [*Chemistry*]
ZEOS........ Zeos International Ltd. [*NASDAQ symbol*] (NQ)
Zep .... Zephaniah [*Old Testament book*]
ZEP........... Zeppelin (DSUE)
Zeph .... Zephaniah [*Old Testament book*]
ZEPHYR... Zero Energy Plutonium-Fueled Fast Reactor [*British*] (DEN)
ZEPL .... Zero Excess Propellants Line
ZEPS .... Zenith Energetic Particle Spectrometer (SSD)
ZER .... Pottsville, PA [*Location identifier*] [*FAA*] (FAAL)
Zer.............. Zera'im (BJA)
ZER .... Zero Energy Reflection
ZERA .... Zero Energy Critical Assemblies Reactor [*British*] (DEN)
ZERC........ Zero Energy Reflection Coefficient
ZERLINA ... Zero Energy Reactor for Lattice Investigation and New Assemblies [*India*]
Zernovoe Khoz ... Zernovoe Khozyaistvo [*A publication*]
Zernovye Maslichn Kul't ... Zernovye i Maslichnye Kul'tury [*A publication*]
Zero............ Zero Corp. [*Associated Press abbreviation*] (APAG)
Zero Popul Growth Natl Rep ... Zero Population Growth. National Reporter [*A publication*]
Zero Un...... Zero Un Hebdo [*A publication*]
ZERT........ Zero Reaction Tool
ZES........... Zero Energy System [*Nuclear energy*]
ZES........... Zil Elwannyen Sesel [*Formerly, Zil Eliogne Sesel, then Zil Elwagne Sesel*]

ZES............	Zollinger-Ellison Syndrome [*Medicine*]
ZES............	Zone Electrophoresis System
ZEST........	Zinc, E-Vitamin, Siberian Ginseng, Turnera [*Health product*] [*British*]
ZET...........	Zero-Gravity Expulsion Technique
ZETA........	Zero Energy Thermonuclear Apparatus [*or Assembly*] [*AEC*]
ZETF........	Zurnal Eksperimental'noi i Teoreticeskoi Fiziki [*A publication*]
ZETK........	Zetek, Inc. [*NASDAQ symbol*] (NQ)
ZETR........	Zero Energy Thermal Reactor [*British*]
Zeumer's Q St ...	Zeumer's Quellen und Studien zur Verfassungsgeschichte des Deutschen Reichs in Mittelalter und Neuzeit [*A publication*]
ZEUS........	Zero Energy Uranium System [*British*]
ZEUS........	Zeus Components, Inc. [*Port Chester, NY*] [*NASDAQ symbol*] (NQ)
ZEV	Zero Emissions Vehicle
Zev	Zevahim (BJA)
ZevE...........	Zeitschrift fuer Evangelische Ethik. Guterslosh [*A publication*] (BJA)
ZEvR.........	Zeitschrift fuer die Evangelischen Religionsunterricht [*A publication*] (BJA)
ZF	Center in charge of a Flight Information Region or an Upper Flight Information Region when the message is relevant to a VFR [*Visual Flight Rules*] Flight [*See also ZQ*] [*ICAO designator*] (ICDA)
ZF	Free Balloon [*Navy symbol*]
ZF	Zahnradfabrik Friedrichshafen AG [*West Germany*]
ZF	Zermelo-Fraenkel [*Set theory*] [*Mathematics*]
ZF	Zero Frequency
ZF	Ziegfeld Follies
ZF	Zona Fasciculata [*Of adrenal cortex*] [*Anatomy*]
ZF	Zona Franca [*A publication*]
ZF	Zone Finder [*Telecommunications*] (OA)
ZF	Zone of Fire [*Military*] (AAG)
ZF	Zweig Fund [*NYSE symbol*] (SPSG)
ZFAL.........	Zacherley Fans at Large (EA)
ZFAX........	ZFAX Image Corp. [*NASDAQ symbol*] (NQ)
ZFB...........	Signals Fading Badly
ZFC...........	Zero Failure Criteria (IEEE)
ZFC...........	Zero-Field Cooled [*Physics*]
ZFC...........	Zipp-Forming Cells [*Immunology*]
ZFC...........	Zirconia Fuel Cell
ZFDNMR ...	Zero-Field Deuterium Nuclear Magnetic Resonance
ZFE...........	Zone of Flow Establishment
ZFET	Zionist Federation Educational Trust [*British*] (DI)
ZfG...........	Zeitschrift fuer Geschichtswissenschaft [*A publication*]
ZFGBI	Zionist Federation of Great Britain and Ireland (DI)
ZFGV........	Zeitschrift. Freiburger Geschichtsvereine [*A publication*]
ZFI-Mitt....	ZFI [*Zentralinstitut fuer Isotopen- und Strahlenforschung*]-Mitteilungen [*East Germany*] [*A publication*]
ZFL...........	Zeitschrift fuer Luftrecht- und Weltraumrechtsfragen [*German*] [*A publication*] (DLA)
ZFM	Community College of the Finger Lakes, Canandaigua, NY [*OCLC symbol*] (OCLC)
ZFM	Fort McPherson [*Canada*] [*Airport symbol*] (OAG)
ZFNMR.....	Zero-Field Nuclear Magnetic Resonance
ZfP...........	Dokumentation Zerstorungsfreie Pruefung [*Nondestructive Testing Documentation*] [*Federal Institute for Materials Testing*] [*Information service or system*] (IID)
ZFP...........	Zyglo-Fluorescent Penetrant
ZFPT	Zyglo-Fluorescent Penetrant Testing
ZFS...........	Zero Field Splitting
ZFSC........	Zero-Field Splitting Constant [*Physics*]
ZFSH........	Z & Z Fashions Ltd. [*NASDAQ symbol*] (NQ)
ZFV...........	Fort Severn [*Canada*] [*Airport symbol*] (OAG)
ZfV............	Zeitschrift fuer Versicherungswesen [*German*] [*A publication*] (DLA)
ZFW	Fort Worth, TX [*Location identifier*] [*FAA*] (FAAL)
ZFW	Zero Fuel Weight [*Aviation*]
ZFYZD	Zhonghua Fangshe Yixue Yu Fanghu Zazhi [*A publication*]
ZG.............	Air Traffic Control [*ICAO designator*] (ICDA)
ZG	Zap Gun
Z-G.............	Zapalote-Grande [*Race of maize*]
ZG.............	Zero Gravity (IEEE)
ZG.............	Zerstoerergeschwader [*Twin-engine fighter wing*] [*German military - World War II*]
ZG.............	Zinc Gluconate [*Organic chemistry*]
ZG.............	Zollgesetz [*Tariff Law*] [*German*]
ZG.............	Zona Glomerulosa [*Of adrenal cortex*] [*Anatomy*]
ZG.............	Zoological Gardens
ZG.............	Zymbal Gland [*Anatomy*]
ZGA..........	Zero Grade Air
ZGCS........	Changsha/Datuopu [*China*] [*ICAO location identifier*] (ICLI)
ZGE	Zero-Gravity Effect
ZGE	Zero-Gravity Environment
ZGE	Zero-Gravity Expulsion
ZGEN	ZG Energy Corp. [*NASDAQ symbol*] (NQ)
Z Geschv (Muelheim) ...	Zeitschrift. Geschichtsverein Muelheim an der Ruhr (Muelheim, West Germany) [*A publication*]
ZGET........	Zero-Gravity Expulsion Technique
ZGF	Grand Forks [*Canada*] [*Airport symbol*] [*Obsolete*] (OAG)

ZGF	Zero Gravity Facility [*NASA*]
ZGG..........	Zero-Gravity Generator
ZGGG.......	Guangzhou/Baiyun [*China*] [*ICAO location identifier*] (ICLI)
ZGGJT	Zeitschrift. Gesellschaft fuer die Geschichte der Juden in der Tschechoslowakei [*A publication*]
ZGH..........	Zonal Gravity Harmonic
ZGHK........	Haikou [*China*] [*ICAO location identifier*] (ICLI)
ZGI	Gods River [*Canada*] [*Airport symbol*] (OAG)
ZGJT	Zeitschrift. Gesellschaft fuer die Geschichte der Juden in der Tschechoslowakei [*A publication*]
ZGKL........	Guilin [*China*] [*ICAO location identifier*] (ICLI)
ZGM.........	City University of New York, Graduate School, New York, NY [*OCLC symbol*] (OCLC)
ZGM.........	Zinc Glycinate Marker [*Immunochemistry*]
ZGMT	Zu Gott Mein Trost [*In God My Comfort*] [*German*] [*Motto of Ernst, Duke of Braunschweig-Luneburg (1564-1611)*]
ZGN..........	Zaghouan [*Tunisia*] [*Seismograph station code, US Geological Survey*] (SEIS)
ZGNN.......	Nanning/Wuxu [*China*] [*ICAO location identifier*] (ICLI)
ZGOW......	Shantou [*China*] [*ICAO location identifier*] (ICLI)
ZGR	Little Grand Rapids [*Canada*] [*Airport symbol*] (OAG)
ZGS	Gethsemani [*Canada*] [*Airport symbol*] (OAG)
ZGS	Zero Gradient Synchrotron [*AEC*]
ZGS	Zero-Gravity Shower
ZGS	Zero-Gravity Simulator
ZGS	Zirconia Grain Stabilized [*Metal alloys*]
ZGS	Zone Gradient Synchrotron [*Nickname: Ziggy*]
ZGSHG	Zeitschrift. Gesellschaft fuer Schleswig-Holsteinische Geschichte [*A publication*]
ZGT	Zero-Gravity Trainer [*NASA*] (NASA)
ZGUA........	Guangzhou City [*China*] [*ICAO location identifier*] (ICLI)
ZGWBS.....	Zero-Gravity Whole Body Shower
ZGWS........	Zane Grey's West Society (EA)
ZGZAE6....	Chinese Journal of Orthopedics [*A publication*]
ZGZJ	Zhanjiang [*China*] [*ICAO location identifier*] (ICLI)
ZGZU	Guangzhou [*China*] [*ICAO location identifier*] (ICLI)
ZH.............	Helicopter Air Traffic Control [*ICAO designator*] (ICDA)
ZH.............	Zinc Heads [*Freight*]
ZH.............	Zonal Harmonic
ZH.............	Zone Heater
zH.............	Zu Haenden [*Attention Of, Care Of, To Be Delivered To*] [*German*] (GPO)
ZHA..........	Zhangjiang [*China*] [*Airport symbol*] (OAG)
ZHCC	Zhengzhou [*China*] [*ICAO location identifier*] (ICLI)
zHd...........	Zu Haenden [*Attention Of, Care Of, To Be Delivered To*] [*German*]
Zheleznodorozhn Transp ...	Zheleznodorozhnyi Transport [*Former USSR*] [*A publication*]
Zhelezn Splavy ...	Zheleznye Splavy [*A publication*]
Zhelezobeton Konstr Chelyabinsk ...	Zhelezobetonnye Konstruktsii Chelyabinsk [*A publication*]
ZHF	Zone Heat Flux
ZHHH.......	Wuhan/Nanhu [*China*] [*ICAO location identifier*] (ICLI)
Zhidkofazn Okislenie Nepredel'nykh Org Soedin ...	Zhidkofaznoe Okislenie Nepredel'nykh Organicheskikh Soedinenii [*A publication*]
Zhilishchnoe Kommunal'n Khoz ...	Zhilishchnoe i Kommunal'noe Khozyaistvo [*A publication*]
Zhivot Nauki ...	Zhivotnovudni Nauki [*A publication*]
Zhivotnov'd Nauki ...	Zhivotnov'dni Nauki [*A publication*]
Zhivotnovod ...	Zhivotnovodstvo [*A publication*]
Zhivotnovod Vet ...	Zhivotnovodstvo i Veterinariya [*A publication*]
Zhivotnovud ...	Zhivotnovudstvo [*A publication*]
Zhivotnovud Nauki ...	Zhivotnovudni Nauki [*A publication*]
ZHJID.......	Zhongguo Jiguang [*A publication*]
ZHL..........	Hofstra University, Law School, Library, Hempstead, NY [*OCLC symbol*] (OCLC)
ZHM.........	Hunter College of the City University of New York, New York, NY [*OCLC symbol*] (OCLC)
ZHN	Honolulu, HI [*Location identifier*] [*FAA*] (FAAL)
ZHNID......	Zhongguo Niangzao [*A publication*]
ZHR..........	Zirconium Hydride Reactor
ZHSA	Zeiss Historica Society of America (EA)
ZHU	Houston, TX [*Location identifier*] [*FAA*] (FAAL)
ZHUCA.....	Zpravy Hornickeho Ustavu CSAV [*Ceskoslovenska Akademie Ved*] [*A publication*]
ZHVNAS ..	Animal Science [*Sofia*] [*A publication*]
ZHVNS	Zeitschrift. Historischer Verein fuer Niedersachsen [*A publication*]
ZHVS	Zeitschrift. Historischer Verein fuer Steiermark [*A publication*]
ZHW.........	Ziekenhuis [*A publication*]
ZHWH	Wuhan [*China*] [*ICAO location identifier*] (ICLI)
ZI	Flight Information Center [*ICAO designator*] (ICDA)
ZI	Zero Input
ZI	Zinc Institute [*Defunct*] (EA)
ZI	Zonal Index
ZI	Zone of Interior [*Military*]
Z of I	Zone of Interior [*Military*]
ZI	Zonta International (EA)
Z/I.............	Zoom In [*Cinematography and Video*]
ZIA	ZIA Airlines [*Las Cruces, NM*] [*FAA designator*] (FAAC)
ZIA	Zone of Interior Armies

ZIAD .... Ziyad, Inc. [*NASDAQ symbol*] (NQ)

ZIAX......... Zantop International Airlines, Inc. [*Air carrier designation symbol*]

ZIC............ Zirconia-Iridium Crucible

Zi de Cmo... Ziliolus de Cremona [*Authority cited in pre-1607 legal work*] (DSA)

ZICON ...... Zone of the Interior Consumers Network (MCD)

ZID .... Indianapolis, IN [*Location identifier*] [*FAA*] (FAAL)

ZID .... Zone of Initial Dilution [*Effluents*] (EG)

ZIE............ Zone Immunoelectrophoresis [*Analytical biochemistry*]

ZIEGLER ... Ziegler Co., Inc. [*Associated Press abbreviation*] (APAG)

ZIF............ Zenix Income Fund [*NYSE symbol*] (SPSG)

ZIF............ Zero Insertion Force [*Electronics*]

ZIFT .... Zygote Intrafallopian Transfer [*Obstetrics*]

ZIG .... Ziguinchor [*Senegal*] [*Airport symbol*] (OAG)

ZIG .... Zoster Immune Globulin [*Immunology*]

ZIGO .... Zygo Corp. [*NASDAQ symbol*] (NQ)

ZIH .... Hofstra University, Hempstead, NY [*OCLC symbol*] (OCLC)

ZIH .... Zihuatanejo [*Mexico*] [*Airport symbol*] (OAG)

ZIID.......... Zentralinstitut fuer Information und Dokumentation [*Central Institute for Information and Documentation*] [*Germany*] [*Information service or system*] (IID)

ZI Int......... ZI [*Ziegelindustrie*] International [*West Germany*] [*A publication*]

ZIL............ Zork Interactive Language [*Computer science*]

ZILA.......... Zila, Inc. [*NASDAQ symbol*] (NQ)

Zilla CD..... Zilla Court Decisions, Bengal, Madras, Northwest Provinces [*India*] [*A publication*] (DLA)

ZIM .... Zi Mischari [*Merchant fleet*] [*Israel*]

ZiM........... Ziemia i Morze [*A publication*]

Zim........... Zimbabwe

ZIM .... Zimchurud [*Former USSR*] [*Seismograph station code, US Geological Survey*] [*Closed*] (SEIS)

ZIM .... Zimmer Corp. [*AMEX symbol*] (SPSG)

ZIM .... Zonal Interdiction Missile (NVT)

Zimbabwe Agric J ... Zimbabwe Agricultural Journal [*A publication*]

Zimbabwe Div Livest Pastures Annu Rep ... Zimbabwe. Division of Livestock and Pastures. Annual Report [*A publication*]

Zimbabwe Eng ... Zimbabwe Engineer [*A publication*]

Zimbabwe J Agric Res ... Zimbabwe Journal of Agricultural Research [*A publication*]

Zimbabwe J Econ ... Zimbabwe Journal of Economics [*A publication*]

Zimbabwe Rhod Nurse ... Zimbabwe Rhodesia Nurse [*A publication*]

Zimbabwe Rhod Sci News ... Zimbabwe-Rhodesia Science News [*A publication*]

Zimbabwe Sci News ... Zimbabwe Science News [*A publication*]

Zimbabwe Vet J ... Zimbabwe Veterinary Journal [*A publication*]

Zimb Agric J ... Zimbabwe Agricultural Journal [*A publication*]

ZIMBANK ... Zimbabwe Banking Corp. Ltd.

Zimb Eng ... Zimbabwe Engineer [*A publication*]

Zimb J Agric Res ... Zimbabwe Journal of Agricultural Research [*A publication*]

Zimb Law J ... Zimbabwe Law Journal [*A publication*]

Zimb Libr... Zimbabwe Librarian [*A publication*]

Zimb Sci News ... Zimbabwe Science News [*A publication*]

ZIMG .... Zeitschrift. Internationale Musik Gesellschaft [*A publication*]

ZIMordASSR ... Zapiski Naucno-Issledovatel'nogo Instituta pri Sovete Ministrov Mordovskoj ASSR [*A publication*]

ZIMR........ ZIM Energy Corp. [*Houston, TX*] [*NASDAQ symbol*] (NQ)

ZIN .... Mount Zion Church [*South Carolina*] [*Seismograph station code, US Geological Survey*] [*Closed*] (SEIS)

Zinat Raksti Rigas Politeh Inst ... Zinatniskie Raksti. Rigas Politehniskais Instituts [*A publication*]

Zinc Abstr ... Zinc Abstracts [*A publication*]

Zinc/Cadmium Res Dig ... Zinc/Cadmium Research Digest [*A publication*]

Zinc Res Dig ... Zinc Research Digest [*A publication*]

ZinEB .... Zinc Ethylenebis(dithiocarbamate) [*Agricultural fungicide*]

Zink .... Zero Income, No Kids [*Lifestyle classification*]

Zinn Ca Tr ... Zinn's Select Cases in the Law of Trusts [*A publication*] (DLA)

Zinn Verwend ... Zinn und Seine Verwendung [*A publication*]

Z Int Inst Zuckerruebenforsch ... Zeitschrift. Internationales Institut fuer Zuckerruebenforschung [*A publication*]

Z Int Ver Bohring Bohrtech ... Zeitschrift. Internationaler Verein der Bohringenieure und Bohrtechniker [*A publication*]

ZIO .... Zinc Iodide-Osmium [*Biological staining procedure*]

Zion.......... Zionism (BJA)

ZION .... Zions Bancorporation [*NASDAQ symbol*] (NQ)

ZiP............ Za i Przeciw [*A publication*]

ZIP............ Zero Interest Payment [*Banking*]

ZIP............ Zigzag In-Line Package [*Wells American*] [*Data processing*]

ZIP............ Zinc Impurity Photodetector

ZIP............ ZIP Target Marketing [*A publication*]

ZIP............ Zone Improvement Plan [*Postal Service code*]

ZIP............ Zone Information Protocol (BYTE)

ZIP............ Zoster Immune Plasma [*Immunology*]

ZIPA......... Zimbabwe People's Army

ZIPE......... Zentralinstitut Physik der Erde [*Potsdam*]

ZIPP .... National Reference Publishing, Inc. [*Dallas, TX*] [*NASDAQ symbol*] (NQ)

Zipp.......... Zone of Inhibited Phage Plaques [*Immunology*]

ZIPRA .... Zimbabwe Independent People's Revolutionary Army (PD)

ZIR............ Zero Internal Resistance

Ziraat Derg ... Ziraat Dergisi [*A publication*]

Ziraat Fak Derg Ege Univ ... Ziraat Fakultesi Dergisi Ege Universitesi [*A publication*]

Zisin J Seismol Soc Jpn ... Zisin/Journal of the Seismological Society of Japan [*A publication*]

Zisin Seismol Soc Jap J ... Zisin/Seismological Society of Japan. Journal [*A publication*]

ZIS Mitt .... ZIS [*Zentralinstitut fuer Schweisstechnik*] Mitteilungen [*A publication*]

ZISS.......... Zebulun Israel Seafaring Society (EA)

ZIS (Zentralinst Schweisstech DDR) Mitt ... ZIS (Zentralinstitut fuer Schweisstechnik der Deutschen Demokratischen Republik) Mitteilungen [*A publication*]

ZIT .... Zone Information Table [*Data processing*] (PCM)

ZITI .... Sidari Corp. [*NASDAQ symbol*] (NQ)

ZITL .... Zitel Corp. [*NASDAQ symbol*] (NQ)

Ziv A .... Archiv fuer die Zivilistische Praxis [*A publication*]

Ziva .... Ziva. Casopis pro Biologickou Praci [*A publication*]

ZIVAN....... Zapiski Instituta Vostokoveden'ia Akademii Nauk SSSR [*A publication*]

Zivocisna Vyroba Cesk Akad Zemed Ustav Vedeckotech Inf Zemed ... Zivocisna Vyroba-Ceskoslovenska Akademie Zemedelska. Ustav Vedeckotechnickych Informaci pro Zemedelstvi [*A publication*]

Zivoc Vyroba ... Zivocisna Vyroba [*A publication*]

Zivotn Prostr ... Zivotne Prostredie [*A publication*]

ZIVP......... Zivotne Prostredie [*Czechoslovakia*] [*A publication*]

Ziv Pr .... Archiv fuer die Zivilistische Praxis [*A publication*]

Ziz............ Zizit (BJA)

ZJ............. Zipper Jacket

ZJ............. Zivi Jezici [*A publication*]

ZJARDK ... Zimbabwe Journal of Agricultural Research [*A publication*]

ZJC........... State University of New York, Central Administration, Albany, NY [*OCLC symbol*] (OCLC)

ZJKF .... Zpravy Jednoty Klasickych Filologu [*A publication*]

ZJSTD....... Zambia Journal of Science and Technology [*A publication*]

ZJX........... Jacksonville, FL [*Location identifier*] [*FAA*] (FAAL)

ZK............ Barrage Balloon [*Navy symbol*]

ZK............ New Zealand [*Aircraft nationality and registration mark*] (FAAC)

ZK............ Schering AG [*Germany*] [*Research code symbol*]

ZK............ Zachary Kurintner Books Ltd. [*British*]

ZK............ Zentralkommittee [*Central Committee*] [*of the Socialist Union Party of the German Democratic Republic*]

ZK............ Zera' Kodesh (BJA)

ZKA .... Zentralkatalog der Auslaendischen Literatur [*A publication*]

ZKB .... Bomber [*Russian aircraft symbol*]

ZKB .... Kasaba Bay [*Zambia*] [*Airport symbol*] (OAG)

ZKC .... Kansas City, MO [*Location identifier*] [*FAA*] (FAAL)

ZKC .... Keuka College, Lightner Library, Keuka Park, NY [*OCLC symbol*] (OCLC)

ZKE .... Kaschechewan [*Canada*] [*Airport symbol*] (OAG)

ZKG .... Kegaska [*Canada*] [*Airport symbol*] (OAG)

ZKHH .... Hamhung [*North Korea*] [*ICAO location identifier*] (ICLI)

ZKIA .... Pyongyang [*North Korea*] [*ICAO location identifier*] (ICLI)

ZKKC........ Kimchaek [*North Korea*] [*ICAO location identifier*] (ICLI)

ZKKK .... Pyongyang [*North Korea*] [*ICAO location identifier*] (ICLI)

ZKKOBW ... Cancer Research and Clinical Oncology [*A publication*]

ZKKODY .. Gerontology Extension Lectures [*A publication*]

ZKMDRVD ... Zmiesana Komisia Medzinarodnej Dohody o Rybolove vo Vodach Dunaja [*International Commission for Agreement on the Danube Fishing*] [*Former Czechoslovakia*] (EAIO)

ZKN.......... Training Balloon [*Navy symbol*]

ZKO.......... Observation Balloon [*Navy symbol*]

ZKPY........ Pyongyang/Sunan [*North Korea*] [*ICAO location identifier*] (ICLI)

ZKRVD...... Zmiesana Komisia o Rybolove vo Vodach Dunaja [*Joint Danube Fishery Commission - JDFC*] [*Zilina, Czechoslovakia*] (EAIO)

ZKSC........ Sunchon [*North Korea*] [*ICAO location identifier*] (ICLI)

ZKSR........ Sesura [*North Korea*] [*ICAO location identifier*] (ICLI)

ZKUFAK... Journal of Rural Engineering and Development [*A publication*]

ZKUJ........ Uiju [*North Korea*] [*ICAO location identifier*] (ICLI)

zkW........... Zero Kilowatt (IEEE)

ZKW.......... Zi-ka-wei [*Republic of China*] [*Seismograph station code, US Geological Survey*] (SEIS)

ZL .... Freezing Drizzle [*Meteorology*] (FAAC)

ZL .... New Zealand [*Aircraft nationality and registration mark*] (FAAC)

ZL .... Z-Axis of Spacelab [*NASA*] (NASA)

ZL .... Zavodskaja Laboratorija [*A publication*]

ZL .... Zero Lift

ZL .... Zloty [*Monetary unit*] [*Poland*] (EY)

ZL .... Zycie Literackie [*A publication*]

ZLA .... Los Angeles, CA [*Location identifier*] [*FAA*] (FAAL)

ZLAN .... Lanzhou City [*China*] [*ICAO location identifier*] (ICLI)

ZLB .... Balboa, Canal Zone [*Location identifier*] [*FAA*] (FAAL)

ZLC.......... Salt Lake City, UT [*Location identifier*] [*FAA*] (FAAL)

ZLC.......... Zero Lift Cord

ZLC............ Zinc, Lead, and Cadmium Abstracts [*Zinc Development Association/Lead Development Association/Codmium Association*] [*British*] [*Defunct*] [*Information service or system*]   (CRD)
ZLD .... Zero Level Drift
ZLD .... Zero Lift Drag
ZLD .... Zodiacal Light Device
ZLDI......... Zentralstelle fuer Luft- Raumfahrtdokumentation und Information [*Center for Documentation and Information in Aeronautics and Astronautics*] [*Information service or system*] [*West Germany*]
ZLE............ Zaba Lee Enterprises [*Vancouver Stock Exchange symbol*]
ZLG .... Zero Line Gap
ZLGIA....... Zapiski Leningradskogo Gornogo Instituta [*A publication*]
ZLH.......... Lincoln Hospital, Bronx, NY [*OCLC symbol*]   (OCLC)
ZLH.......... [*F.*] Zorell. Lexicon Hebraicum [*A publication*]   (BJA)
ZLHW....... Lanzhou [*China*] [*ICAO location identifier*]   (ICLI)
ZLIC......... Yinchuan [*China*] [*ICAO location identifier*]   (ICLI)
ZLISP....... Zilog List Processor [*Programming language*] [*1979*]   (CSR)
ZLit.......... Zycie Literackie [*Krakow*] [*A publication*]
ZLJ .... Zambia Law Journal [*A publication*]   (DLA)
ZLJM........ Zusters van Liefe Jezus en Maria [*Sisters of Charity of Jesus and Mary - SCJM*] [*Belgium*]   (EAIO)
ZLJQ......... Jiuquan [*China*] [*ICAO location identifier*]   (ICLI)
ZLK.......... Zaleski, OH [*Location identifier*] [*FAA*]   (FAAL)
ZLL........... Zero-Length Launch [*Missiles*]
ZLL........... Zero Lot Line [*Real estate*]
ZLLL .... Lanzhou/Zhongchuan [*China*] [*ICAO location identifier*]   (ICLI)
ZLM .... State University of New York, College at New Paltz, New Paltz, NY [*OCLC symbol*]   (OCLC)
ZLN .... Zwiazek Ludowo-Narodowy [*Populist-Nationalist Alliance*] [*Poland*] [*Political party*]   (PPE)
ZLO .... Manzanillo [*Mexico*] [*Airport symbol*]   (OAG)
ZLOG .... Zilog Inc. [*NASDAQ symbol*]   (SPSG)
ZLP........... Zongo [*La Paz*] [*Bolivia*] [*Seismograph station code, US Geological Survey*]   (SEIS)
ZLR.......... Zanzibar Law Reports [*1919-50*] [*A publication*]   (DLA)
ZLR.......... Zanzibar Protectorate Law Reports [*1868-1950*] [*A publication*]   (DLA)
ZLS .... Zero Level Sparing   (MCD)
ZLSIA....... Zapiski Leningradskogo Sel'skokhozyaistvennogo Instituta [*A publication*]
ZLSM .... Zeiss Light Section Microscope
ZLSN .... Xian [*China*] [*ICAO location identifier*]   (ICLI)
ZLT........... La Tabatiere [*Canada*] [*Airport symbol*]   (OAG)
ZLTO........ Zero-Length Takeoff   (MCD)
Z-LV .... Z-Axis along Local Vertical   (MCD)
ZLV.......... Zero-Length Vector
ZLXN .... Xining [*China*] [*ICAO location identifier*]   (ICLI)
ZLYA....... Yanan [*China*] [*ICAO location identifier*]   (ICLI)
ZM............ Impedance Measuring Devices [*JETDS nomenclature*] [*Military*]   (CET)
ZM............ New Zealand [*Aircraft nationality and registration mark*]   (FAAC)
ZM............ Nike-Zeus at Point Mugu [*Missile defense*]   (SAA)
ZM............ Zahnaerztliche Mitteilungen [*A publication*]
ZM............ Zambia [*ANSI two-letter standard code*]   (CNC)
ZM............ Zero Marker   (MCD)
ZM............ Zoom/MODEM [*ZOOM Telephonics, Inc.*]
Z-M........... Zuckerman-Moloff [*Sewage treatment method*]
ZM............ Zycie i Mysl [*A publication*]
ZMA .... Miami, FL [*Location identifier*] [*FAA*]   (FAAL)
ZMA .... Zinc Metaarsenite [*Insecticide, wood preservative*]
ZMag........ Z Magazine [*Zambia*] [*A publication*]
ZMAR ...... Zeus Multifunction Array RADAR [*Missile defense*]
ZMAR/MAR ... Zeus Multifunction Array RADAR / Multifunction Array RADAR [*Missile defense*]   (SAA)
ZMB .... Zambia [*ANSI three-letter standard code*]   (CNC)
ZMB .... Zero Moisture Basis [*Chemical analysis*]
ZMB .... Zinc Mercaptobenzimidazole [*Organic chemistry*]
ZMBT........ Zinc Mercaptobenzothiazole [*Organic chemistry*]
ZMBTA..... Zement und Beton [*A publication*]
ZMC .... Manhattan College, Library, Bronx, NY [*OCLC symbol*]   (OCLC)
ZMD......... Zung Measurement of Depression [*Scale*]
ZMDC....... Zinc Dimethyldithiocarbamate [*Organic chemistry*]
ZME .... Memphis, TN [*Location identifier*] [*FAA*]   (FAAL)
ZMH.......... Zeitschrift. Museum Hildesheim [*A publication*]
ZMK .... Zpravodaj Mistopisne Komise CSAV [*Ceskoslovenske Akademie Ved*] [*A publication*]
ZMKR........ Zone Marker
ZML .... Medical Library Center of New York, Standardized Cataloging Service, New York, NY [*OCLC symbol*]   (OCLC)
ZMM......... State University of New York, Maritime College, Bronx, NY [*OCLC symbol*]   (OCLC)
ZMM......... Zone Melting Model
ZMMAS.... Zodiacal Microparticle Multiparameter Analysis System [*NASA*]
ZMMD...... Zurich, Mainz, Munich, Darmstadt [*A joint European university effort on ALGOL processors*]

ZMNP .... Zurnal Ministerstva Narodnogo Prosvescenija [*A publication*]
ZMP .... Minneapolis, MN [*Location identifier*] [*FAA*]   (FAAL)
ZMP .... Zurnal Moskovskoi Patriarkhii [*Moscow*] [*A publication*]
ZMR .... Zone-Melting Recrystallization [*Crystallography*]
ZMRI........ Zinc Metals Research Institute
ZMT .... Masset [*Canada*] [*Airport symbol*]   (OAG)
ZMT .... ZIP [*Zone Improvement Plan*] Mail Translator [*Postal Service*]
ZMT .... Zoom Telephonics [*Vancouver Stock Exchange symbol*]
ZMUC........ Zoologisk Museum, University of Copenhagen [*Denmark*]
ZMX......... Zemex Corp. [*NYSE symbol*]   (SPSG)
ZN............. Airship (Nonrigid) [*Navy symbol*]
Zn.............. True Azimuth [*Symbol*]   (MUGU)
ZN............. Zenith
ZN............. Ziehl-Neelsen [*A biological stain*]
Zn.............. Zinc [*Chemical element*]
Zn.............. Znamya [*Moscow*] [*A publication*]
ZN............. Zone
ZN............. Zycie Nauki [*A publication*]
ZNA .... Nanaimo [*Canada*] Harbour Airport [*Airport symbol*]   (OAG)
ZNa.......... Zycie Nauki [*A publication*]
ZNAND.... Zootecnica e Nutrizione Animale [*A publication*]
ZNC.......... New York City Technical College, Library, Brooklyn, NY [*OCLC symbol*]   (OCLC)
ZNC.......... Nyack, AK [*Location identifier*] [*FAA*]   (FAAL)
ZNC.......... Zone of Nonproliferating Cells [*Cytology*]
ZNCAV .... Zdenku Nejedlemu Ceskoslovenska Akademie Ved [*A publication*]
ZN Ch........ Zurnal Neorganiceskoj Chimii [*A publication*]
ZND.......... Zinder [*Niger*] [*Airport symbol*]   (OAG)
ZNE.......... Newman [*Australia*] [*Airport symbol*]   (OAG)
Z Neorg Chim ... Zurnal Neorganiceskoj Chimii [*A publication*]
Zn Fl .... Zinc Flocculation [*Medical test*]   (MAE)
ZNG.......... Negginan [*Canada*] [*Airport symbol*]   (OAG)
ZnG.......... Zinc Gluconate [*Organic chemistry*]
ZNGI .... Zero Net Growth Isocline [*Ecological graph*]
ZNH .... Airship, Air-Sea Rescue [*Navy symbol*]
ZNIC .... Zonic Corp. [*NASDAQ symbol*]   (NQ)
ZNIO .... Zaklad Narodowy Imeni Ossolinskich [*A publication*]
ZNJ........... Airship, Utility [*Navy symbol*]
ZNM.......... Nioga Library System, Niagara Falls, NY [*OCLC symbol*]   (OCLC)
ZNN.......... Nonrigid Training Airship [*Navy symbol*]
ZNO.......... Nonrigid Observation Airship [*Navy symbol*]
ZNO.......... North Country Community College, Saranac Lake, NY [*OCLC symbol*]   (OCLC)
ZNO.......... Zenco Resources, Inc. [*Vancouver Stock Exchange symbol*]
ZNOE....... Zinc Oxide-Eugenol [*Dental cement*]
ZNP.......... Nonrigid Patrol Airship [*Navy symbol*]
ZNP.......... Zanzibar Nationalist Party
ZnP.......... Zinc Protoporphyrin [*Biochemistry*]
ZNP.......... Zinc Pyrithione [*Antibacterial*]
ZNP.......... Zion Nuclear Plant   (NRCH)
ZNR.......... Zinc Resistor
ZNS.......... Nonrigid Scouting Airship [*Navy symbol*]
ZnS.......... Zinc Sulfide   (BYTE)
ZNT.......... Zenith National Insurance Corp. [*NYSE symbol*]   (SPSG)
ZNTL........ Zehntel, Inc. [*Walnut Creek, CA*] [*NASDAQ symbol*]   (NQ)
ZNTS......... Zapysky Naukovoho Tovarystva Imeny Svecenka [*A publication*]
ZNTSL...... Zapysky Naukovoho Tovarystva Imeny Svecenka (Literature Series) [*A publication*]
ZNU.......... Namu [*Canada*] [*Airport symbol*] [*Obsolete*]   (OAG)
ZNXPO...... Zeus-Nike X Program Office [*Missiles*]   (MCD)
ZNY.......... New York, NY [*Location identifier*] [*FAA*]   (FAAL)
ZNZ.......... Zanzibar [*Tanzania*] [*Airport symbol*]   (OAG)
ZO............. Oceanic Air Traffic Control [*ICAO designator*]   (ICDA)
ZO............. Z-Axis of Orbiter [*NASA*]   (NASA)
ZO............. Zero Output
Zo.............. Zoen Tencararius [*Flourished, 13th century*] [*Authority cited in pre-1607 legal work*]   (DSA)
ZO............. Zoological Origin
Z/O........... Zoom Out [*Cinematography*]
ZOA.......... Oakland, CA [*Location identifier*] [*FAA*]   (FAAL)
ZOA.......... Zionist Organization of America   (EA)
Zo A .... Zoologischer Anzeiger [*A publication*]
Zoannet...... [*Franciscus*] Zoannettus [*Deceased, 1586*] [*Authority cited in pre-1607 legal work*]   (DSA)
ZOB.......... Cleveland, OH [*Location identifier*] [*FAA*]   (FAAL)
ZOBIDX.... Zoo Biology [*A publication*]
ZOBO........ Zongo [*La Paz*] [*Bolivia*] [*Seismograph station code, US Geological Survey*]   (SEIS)
Z Obsc Biol ... Zurnal Obscej Biologii [*A publication*]
Z Obsc Chim ... Zurnal Obscej Chimii [*A publication*]
ZOC.......... Zone of Convenience   (ADA)
ZOD.......... Zero Order Detector   (MCD)
ZOD.......... Zodiac   (ROG)
Zod........... Zodiac Records [*Record label*]
ZODIAC.... Zone Defense Integrated Active Capability   (IEEE)
ZOE.......... Zero Energy
ZOE.......... Zinc Oxide-Eugenol [*Dental cement*]
ZOE.......... Zone of Entry [*Military*]   (AABC)

ZOE .... Zone of Exclusion (MCD)
ZOEP .... Zoe Products, Inc. [*NASDAQ symbol*] (NQ)
Z Oesterr Entomol Ver ... Zeitschrift. Oesterreichischer Entomologe-Verein [*A publication*]
Z Oesterr Ver Gas Wasserfachmaennern ... Zeitschrift. Oesterreichischer Verein von Gas- und Wasserfachmaennern [*A publication*]
ZOF .... Ocean Falls [*Canada*] [*Airport symbol*] [*Obsolete*] (OAG)
ZOF .... Zone of Fire [*Military*]
ZOG .... Paramaribo [*Suriname*] [*Airport symbol*]
ZOG .... Zionist Occupational Government
ZOGAAV .. Zoologische Gaerten [*A publication*]
ZOH .... Zero Order Hold [*Telescope*]
ZOLD .... Zeroth Order Logarithmic Distribution
ZOLGA ..... Zoologica [*A publication*]
Zolnierz Pol ... Zolnierz Polski [*Poland*] [*A publication*]
Zolotaya Promst ... Zolotaya Promyshlennost [*A publication*]
ZOMO .... Zmotoryzowane Oddzialy Milicji Obywatelskiej [*Motorized Units of People's Militia*] [*Poland's riot police*]
ZON .... Zonda [*Argentina*] [*Seismograph station code, US Geological Survey*] (SEIS)
ZON .... Zone Petroleum Corp. [*Vancouver Stock Exchange symbol*]
Zonar .... Zonaras [*Twelfth century AD*] [*Classical studies*] (OCD)
ZOND .... [*The*] Zondervan Corp. [*NASDAQ symbol*] (NQ)
ZONEF ...... Zone Petroleum Corp. [*NASDAQ symbol*] (NQ)
Zoning and Plan L Rep ... Zoning and Planning Law Report [*A publication*]
ZOO .... Minnesota Zoological Garden, Apple Valley, MN [*OCLC symbol*] (OCLC)
ZOOACT .. Zoological Action Committee (EA)
Zoo Biol ..... Zoo Biology [*A publication*]
ZOOCHEM ... Zoochemistry (ROG)
ZOOGEOG ... Zoogeography (ROG)
ZOOL .... Zoological [*or Zoology*]
Zool Abh (Dres) ... Zoologische Abhandlungen (Dresden) [*A publication*]
Zool Afr ..... Zoologica Africana [*A publication*]
Zool Ann .... Zoologische Annalen [*A publication*]
Zool Anz .... Zoologischer Anzeiger [*A publication*]
Zool Anzeiger ... Zoologischer Anzeiger [*A publication*]
Zool Anz (Leipzig) ... Zoologischer Anzeiger (Leipzig) [*A publication*]
Zool Anz Suppl ... Zoologische Anzeiger. Supplement [*A publication*]
Zool B .... Zoological Bulletin [*A publication*]
Zool Beitr .... Zoologische Beitraege [*A publication*]
Zool Ber ..... Zoologischer Bericht [*A publication*]
Zool Bidr Upps ... Zoologiska Bidrag fran Uppsala [*A publication*]
Zool Bidr Uppsala ... Zoologiska Bidrag fran Uppsala [*A publication*]
Zool Bijdr... Zoologische Bijdragen [*A publication*]
Zool Biol Mar ... Zoologia e Biologia Marinha [*A publication*]
Zool Biol Mar (Sao Paulo) (Nova Ser) ... Zoologia e Biologia Marinha (Sao Paulo) (Nova Serie) [*A publication*]
Zool Entomol Listy ... Zoologicke a Entomologicke Listy [*A publication*]
Zool Gaert ... Zoologische Gaerten [*A publication*]
Zool Gart (Lpz) ... Zoologische Gaerten (Leipzig) [*A publication*]
Zool Inst Fac Sci Univ Tokyo Annu Rep ... Zoological Institute. Faculty of Science. University of Tokyo. Annual Report [*A publication*]
Zool Jahrb ... Zoologische Jahrbuecher-Abteilung Allgemeine Zoologie und Physiologie der Tiere [*A publication*]
Zool Jahrb Abt Allg Zool Physiol Tiere ... Zoologische Jahrbuecher. Abteilung fuer Allgemeine Zoologie und Physiologie der Tiere [*A publication*]
Zool Jahrb Abt Anat Ontog Tiere ... Zoologische Jahrbuecher. Abteilung fuer Anatomie und Ontogenie der Tiere [*A publication*]
Zool Jahrb Abt Syst (Jena) ... Zoologische Jahrbuecher. Abteilung fuer Systematik Oekologie und Geographie der Tiere (Jena) [*A publication*]
Zool Jahrb Abt Syst Oekol Geogr Tiere ... Zoologische Jahrbuecher. Abteilung fuer Systematik Oekologie und Geographie der Tiere [*A publication*]
Zool Jb .... Zoologische Jahrbuecher [*A publication*]
Zool Jb Abt Allg Zool Physiol Tiere ... Zoologische Jahrbuecher. Abteilung fuer Allgemeine Zoologie und Physiologie der Tiere [*A publication*]
Zool Jb Abt Syst Okol Geog Tiere ... Zoologische Jahrbuecher. Abteilung fuer Systematik Oekologie und Geographie der Tiere [*A publication*]
Zool Jhrb Abt Allg Zool Physiol Tiere ... Zoologische Jahrbuecher. Abteilung fuer Allgemeine Zoologie und Physiologie der Tiere [*A publication*]
Zool J Linn ... Zoological Journal. Linnean Society [*A publication*]
Zool J Linn Soc ... Zoological Journal. Linnean Society [*A publication*]
Zool Listy... Zoologicke Listy [*A publication*]
Zool Mag ... Zoological Magazine [*A publication*]
Zool Mag (Tokyo) ... Zoological Magazine (Tokyo) [*A publication*]
Zool Meded (Leiden) ... Zoologische Mededelingen (Leiden) [*A publication*]
Zool Meded Rijks Mus Nat Hist Leiden ... Zoologische Mededelingen. Rijks Museum van Natuurlijke Historie te Leiden [*A publication*]
Zool Muz Raksti Invertebrata ... Zoologijas Muzeja Raksti. Invertebrata [*A publication*]
Zoologica Pol ... Zoologica Poloniae [*A publication*]
Zoologica Scr ... Zoologica Scripta [*A publication*]
Zool Orient ... Zoologica Orientalis [*A publication*]

Zool Pol ..... Zoologica Poloniae [*A publication*]
Zool Publ Victoria Univ Wellington ... Zoology Publications. Victoria University of Wellington [*A publication*]
Zool Rec..... Zoological Record [*A publication*]
Zool Res..... Zoological Research [*A publication*]
Zool Revy... Zoologisk Revy [*A publication*]
Zool Sci..... Zoological Science [*A publication*]
Zool Sci (Tokyo) ... Zoological Science (Tokyo) [*A publication*]
Zool Scr ..... Zoologica Scripta [*A publication*]
Zool Soc Egypt Bull ... Zoological Society of Egypt. Bulletin [*A publication*]
Zool Soc London Pr ... Zoological Society of London. Proceedings [*A publication*]
Zool Soc London Proc ... Zoological Society of London. Proceedings [*A publication*]
Zool Verh... Zoologische Verhandelingen [*A publication*]
Zool Verh (Leiden) ... Zoologische Verhandelingen (Leiden) [*A publication*]
Zool Verh Rijksmus Nat Hist (Leiden) ... Zoologische Verhandelingen. Rijksmuseum van Natuurlijke Historie (Leiden) [*A publication*]
Zoonoses Res ... Zoonoses Research [*A publication*]
ZOOPH..... Zoophytology (ROG)
Zoophysiol Ecol ... Zoophysiology and Ecology [*A publication*]
Zoo Rec ..... Zoological Record [*A publication*]
ZOOREO .. Zoologica Orientalis [*A publication*]
Zootech Experiment Stn Res Bull ... Zootechnical Experiment Station. Research Bulletin [*A publication*]
Zootec Nutr Anim ... Zootecnica e Nutrizione Animale [*A publication*]
Zootec Vet ... Zootecnica e Veterinaria [*A publication*]
Zootec Vet Agric ... Zootecnica. Veterinaria e Agricoltura [*A publication*]
Zootec Vita ... Zootecnia e Vita [*A publication*]
ZOP .... Zero Order Predictor
ZOP .... Zinc Oxide Pigment
ZOPA .... Zinc Oxide Producers' Association [*European Council of Chemical Manufacturers Federations*] [*Belgium*] (EAIO)
ZOPI........ Zero Order Polynomial Interpolator
ZOPP........ Zero Order Polynomial Predictor
ZOR .... Zinc Oxide Resistor
ZOR .... Zone of Reconnaissance
ZOR .... Zorah Media Corp. [*Vancouver Stock Exchange symbol*]
ZORRO ..... Zero Offset Rapid Reaction Ordnance
ZOS .... Zapata Corp. [*NYSE symbol*] [*Toronto Stock Exchange symbol*]
ZOS .... Zoom Optical System
ZOSC........ Zoologica Scripta [*A publication*]
Z fur die Ost Gym ... Zeitschrift fuer die Oesterreichischen Gymnasien [*A publication*] (OCD)
ZOTS........ Zoom Optical Target Simulator (OA)
Zouch Adm ... Zouche's Admiralty Jurisdiction [*A publication*] (DLA)
ZOVBW .... Zeitschrift. Oesterreichischer Verein fuer Bibliothekswesen [*A publication*]
ZOW .... State University of New York, College at Old Westbury, Old Westbury, NY [*OCLC symbol*] (OCLC)
ZOX .... Ground Zero [*Nevada*] [*Seismograph station code, US Geological Survey*] [*Closed*] (SEIS)
ZP .... Air Traffic Services Reporting Office [*ICAO designator*] (ICDA)
ZP .... Paraguay [*Aircraft nationality and registration mark*] (FAAC)
ZP .... Patrol and Escort Aircraft [*Lighter-than-Air*] [*Navy symbol*] (MUGU)
ZP .... Revlon, Inc. [*Research code symbol*]
ZP .... Z-Axis of Payload [*NASA*] (NASA)
ZP .... Zadok Perspectives [*A publication*] (APTA)
ZP .... Zep Energy [*Vancouver Stock Exchange symbol*]
Zp.............. Zephaniah (BJA)
ZP .... Zona Pellucida [*Embryology*]
ZP .... Zweeppartij [*Whipping Party*] [*Political party*] [*Belgium*]
ZPA .... Zero Period Acceleration [*Nuclear energy*] (NRCH)
ZPA .... Zeus Program Analysis [*Missiles*]
ZPA .... Zone of Polarizing Activity [*Embryology, genetics*]
ZPalV .... Zeitschrift. Deutscher Palaestinaverein [*A publication*]
ZPapEpigr ... Zeitschrift fuer Papyrologie und Epigraphik [*A publication*] (BJA)
ZPAR........ Zeus Phased Array RADAR [*Missile defense*]
ZPB........... Zinc Primary Battery
ZPC........... Zero Point of Charge
ZPC........... Zinc-Phosphate Coating
ZPCA........ Zugzwang! Postal Chess Association (EA)
ZPD .... Zero Path Difference
ZPE........... Zero Point Energy
ZPE........... Zeta Phi Eta
ZPED........ Zeus Production Evaluation Program [*Missiles*] (MCD)
ZPEN........ Zeus Project Engineer Network [*Missiles*]
ZPFL .... Zanzibar and Pemba Federation of Labour
ZPG .... Airship Group [*Navy symbol*]
ZPG .... Zero Population Growth (EA)
ZPH........... Zephyrhills, FL [*Location identifier*] [*FAA*] (FAAL)
ZPI............ New York State Psychiatric Institute, Medical Library Center of New York, New York, NY [*OCLC symbol*] (OCLC)

ZPID......... Zentralstelle fuer Psychologische Information und Dokumentation [*Center for Psychological Information and Documentation*] [*Germany*] [*Database operator*] [*Information service or system*]   (IID)
ZPJIAK..... Zbirnyk Prat Jewrejskiej Istorychno-Arkheologichnoj Komisji [*Kiev*] [*A publication*]
ZPKM....... Kunming [*China*] [*ICAO location identifier*]   (ICLI)
ZPL............ Zero-Phonon Line [*Physics*]
ZPM........... State University of New York, College at Purchase, Purchase, NY [*OCLC symbol*]   (OCLC)
ZPN........... Impedance Pneumograph [*Apollo*] [*NASA*]
ZPO........... Zeus Project Office [*Missiles*]
ZPO........... Zinc Peroxide [*Pharmacology*]
ZPP........... Zimbabwe Progressive Party [*Political party*]   (PPW)
ZPP........... Zinc Protophorphyrin [*Biochemistry*]
ZPPP......... Kunming/Wujiaba [*China*] [*ICAO location identifier*]   (ICLI)
ZPPP......... Zanzibar and Pemba People's Party
ZPPR........ Zero Power Plutonium Reactor [*Nuclear energy*]
ZPR........... Zero Power Reactor [*Nuclear energy*]
Zpravy....... Zpravy pro Cestinare [*A publication*]
Zpr Cesk Keram Sklarske Spol ... Zpravy Ceskoslovenske Keramicke a Sklarske Spolecnosti [*A publication*]
ZPRF......... Zero Power Reactor Facility [*AEC*]
Z Prikl Meh i Tehn Fiz ... Zurnal Prikladnoi Mehaniki i Tehniceskoi Fiziki [*A publication*]
ZprMK...... Zpravodaj Mistopisne Komise CSAV [*Ceskoslovenske Akademie Ved*] [*A publication*]
ZPRON..... Patrol [*Lighter-than-Air*] Squadron [*Navy symbol*]
ZPRSN...... Zurich Provisional Relative Sunspot Number [*NASA*]
ZPS............ [*William H.*] Zimmer Nuclear Power Station [*Also, WZNPS*]   (NRCH)
ZPSS......... Z Polskich Studiow Slawistycznych [*A publication*]
ZPSS......... Zion Probabilistic Safety Study [*Nuclear energy*]   (NRCH)
ZPT............ Zero Power Test
ZPT............ Zoxazolamine Paralysis Time [*In experimental animals*]
ZQ.............. Center in charge of a flight information region or an upper flight information region when the message is relevant to an IFR [*Instrument Flight Rules*] flight [*See also ZF*] [*ICAO designator*]   (ICDA)
ZQC........... Queensborough Community College of the City University of New York, Library, Bayside, NY [*OCLC symbol*]   (OCLC)
ZQM......... State University of New York, College at Potsdam, Potsdam, NY [*OCLC symbol*]   (OCLC)
ZQN........... Queenstown [*New Zealand*] [*Airport symbol*]   (OAG)
ZQT........... Zero Quantum Transition [*Physics*]
ZR.............. Area Control Center [*ICAO designator*]   (ICDA)
ZR.............. Freezing Rain [*Meteorology*]   (FAAC)
ZR.............. Rigid Airship [*Navy symbol*]
ZR.............. Zadarska Revija [*A publication*]
ZR.............. Zaire [*ANSI two-letter standard code*]   (CNC)
ZR.............. Zentralrat [*Central Board*] [*German*]
ZR.............. Zero Coupon Issue (Security) [*In bond listings of newspapers*]
ZR.............. Zimmerman Registry [*An association*]   (EA)
ZR.............. Zionist Record [*A publication*]
ZR.............. Zionist Review [*A publication*]
Zr.............. Zirconium [*Chemical element*]
ZR.............. Zona Reticularis [*Of adrenal cortex*] [*Anatomy*]
ZR.............. Zone Refined
ZR.............. Zone of Responsibility
ZR.............. Zoological Record [*A publication*]
ZR.............. Zoological Record Online [*Bio Sciences Information Service*] [*Information service or system*]   (IID)
ZRA.......... Zero Range Approximation [*Nuclear science*]   (OA)
ZRA.......... Zero Resistance Ammeter [*Instrumentation*]
ZRC.......... Zenith Radio Corp.
ZRDI......... Zionic Research and Development Institute   (EA)
ZRE........... Zero Rate Error   (MCD)
ZREC........ Zoological Records [*BioSciences Information Service*]
ZRGA....... Zeitschrift. Savigny-Stiftung fuer Rechtsgeschichte. Germanistische Abteilung [*A publication*]
ZRG (GA) ... Zeitschrift. Savigny-Stiftung fuer Rechtsgeschichte. Germanistische Abteilung [*A publication*]
ZRH........... Zurich [*Switzerland*] [*Airport symbol*]   (OAG)
ZRI............ Serui [*Indonesia*] [*Airport symbol*]   (OAG)
ZRI............ Zosen [*A publication*]
ZRIO......... Zimbabwe Rhodesian Information Office [*An association*]   (EA)
ZRL........... Zagadnienia Rodzajow Literackich [*A publication*]
ZRL........... Zero Risk Level   (GFGA)
ZRM.......... Sarmi [*Indonesia*] [*Airport symbol*]   (OAG)
ZRN.......... Rigid Training Airship [*Navy symbol*]
ZRN.......... Zurn Industries, Inc. [*NYSE symbol*]   (SPSG)
ZRNI......... Zapiski Russkogo Naucnogo Instituta [*A publication*]
ZRO........... Zero Corp. [*NYSE symbol*]   (SPSG)
ZRO........... Zoological Record Online [*A publication*]
ZRO........... Zoological Record Outline
Zroshuvane Zemlerob ... Zroshuvane Zemlerobstvo [*A publication*]
Zrosh Zemlerob ... Zroshuvane Zemlerobstvo [*A publication*]
ZRP........... Rigid Patrol Airship [*Navy symbol*]
ZRP........... Zero Radial Play
ZRS........... Rigid Scouting Airship [*Navy symbol*]

ZRS........... Russell Sage College, Troy, NY [*OCLC symbol*]   (OCLC)
ZRSG......... Zoological Record Search Guide [*A publication*]
ZRSNDI... Zimbabwe Science News [*A publication*]
ZRT........... Zero Reaction Tool
ZRTLS....... Zwolse Reeks van Taal- en Letterkundige Studies [*A publication*]
ZRV........... Zero-Relative Velocity
Z/S............. Operational Display System
ZS.............. SARSAT Centre [*France*] [*ICAO designator*]   (FAAC)
ZS.............. Union of South Africa [*Aircraft nationality and registration mark*]   (FAAC)
ZS.............. Z-Axis of Solid Rocket Booster [*NASA*]   (NASA)
ZS.............. Zelena Slovenije [*Greens of Slovenia*] [*Political party*]   (EY)
ZS.............. Zellweger Syndrome [*Also, ZWS*] [*Medicine*]
ZS.............. Zero Shift
ZS.............. Zero and Subtract
ZS.............. Zero Sum [*Genetics*]
ZS.............. Zero Suppress
ZS.............. Zoological Society [*British*]
ZS.............. Zoosporangia [*Botany*]
ZSA........... San Salvador [*Bahamas*] [*Airport symbol*]   (OAG)
ZSA........... Southern Tier Library System, Corning, NY [*OCLC symbol*]   (OCLC)
ZSA........... Zero-Set Amplifier   (MSA)
ZSAM....... Xiamen [*China*] [*ICAO location identifier*]   (ICLI)
ZSAT........ Zinc Sulfide Atmospheric Tracer
ZSav.......... Zeitschrift. Savigny-Stiftung fuer Rechtsgeschichte. Romanistische Abteilung [*A publication*]
Z Savigny-Stift Rechtsgesch Kanon Abt ... Zeitschrift. Savigny-Stiftung fuer Rechtsgeschichte. Kanonistische Abteilung [*A publication*]
ZSavRG..... Zeitschrift. Savigny-Stiftung fuer Rechtsgeschichte. Romanistische Abteilung [*Weimar*] [*A publication*]
ZSB............ [*Fred*] Zeder, [*Owen*] Skelton, and [*Cart*] Breer [*Automotive engineers*]
ZSB............ Zinc Storage Battery
ZSC........... Stauffer Chemical Co., Information Services, Dobbs Ferry, NY [*OCLC symbol*]   (OCLC)
ZSC........... Zero Subcarrier Chromaticity
ZSC........... Zinc Silicate Coat
ZSC........... Zose [*Republic of China*] [*Seismograph station code, US Geological Survey*]   (SEIS)
ZSC........... Zose [*Republic of China*] [*Geomagnetic observatory code*]
ZS Ch........ Zurnal Strukturnoj Chimii [*A publication*]
Zschft f Ausl u Intl Privatr ... Zeitschrift fuer Auslaendisches und Internationales Privatrecht [*Berlin and Tubingen, Germany*] [*A publication*]   (DLA)
Zschft Luft- u Weltr-Recht ... Zeitschrift fuer Luftrecht- und Weltraumrechtsfragen [*A publication*]   (DLA)
Zschft Rechtsvergl ... Zeitschrift fuer Rechtsvergleichung [*Vienna, Austria*] [*A publication*]   (DLA)
Zschft Savigny-Germ ... Zeitschrift. Savigny-Stiftung fuer Rechtsgeschichte. Germanistische Abteilung [*A publication*]
Zschft Savigny-Kanon ... Zeitschrift. Savigny-Stiftung fuer Rechtsgeschichte. Kanonistische Abteilung [*A publication*]
Zschft Savigny-Rom ... Zeitschrift. Savigny-Stiftung fuer Rechtsgeschichte. Romanistische Abteilung
Z Schles Holst Gesch ... Zeitschrift. Gesellschaft fuer Schleswig-Holsteinische Geschichte [*Kiel, West Germany*] [*A publication*]
Z f Schweiz Recht ... Zeitschrift fuer Schweizerisches Recht/Revue de Droit Suisse/Revista di Diritto Svizzero [*Basel, Switzerland*] [*A publication*]   (DLA)
ZSCN........ Nanchang [*China*] [*ICAO location identifier*]   (ICLI)
ZSD........... Zebra Stripe Display
ZSD........... Zinc Sulfide Detector
ZSDS......... Zinc Sulfide Detection System
ZSE............ Seattle, WA [*Location identifier*] [*FAA*]   (FAAL)
ZSEV........ Z-Seven Fund, Inc. [*NASDAQ symbol*]   (NQ)
Z Sev-Dvin OIMK ... Zapiski Severo-Dvinskogo Obscestva Izucenija Mestnogo Kraja [*A publication*]
ZSFZ......... Fuzhou [*China*] [*ICAO location identifier*]   (ICLI)
ZSG........... Zero-Speed Generator
ZSGZ........ Ganzhou [*China*] [*ICAO location identifier*]   (ICLI)
ZSHA........ Shanghai [*China*] [*ICAO location identifier*]   (ICLI)
ZSHC........ Hangzhou/Jianqiao [*China*] [*ICAO location identifier*]   (ICLI)
ZSI............ Z Solar Inertial   (MCD)
ZSI............ Zero Size Image
ZSI............ Zytec Systems, Inc. [*Toronto Stock Exchange symbol*] [*Vancouver Stock Exchange symbol*]
ZSIL......... Zytec Systems, Inc. [*NASDAQ symbol*]   (NQ)
ZSJ........... St. John's University Library, Jamaica, NY [*OCLC symbol*]   (OCLC)
ZSJ........... Zangri, S. J., Chicago IL [*STAC*]
ZSJA......... Jian [*China*] [*ICAO location identifier*]   (ICLI)
ZSK........... Ze Skarbca Kultury [*A publication*]
ZSL........... Zero Sight Line   (DNAB)
ZSL........... ZEROSLOTLAN [*Avatar Technologies, Inc.*] [*In Alliance ZSL, a PC network*]
ZSL........... Zjednoczone Stronnictwo Ludowe [*United Peasants' Party*] [*Poland*] [*Political party*]   (PPW)
ZSL........... Zoological Society of London [*British*]
ZSN........... Zoological Station of Naples

ZSN .... Zurich Sunspot Number [*Astrophysics*]
ZSNED7.... Zimbabwe Science News [*A publication*]
ZSNJ .... Nanjing [*China*] [*ICAO location identifier*] (ICLI)
ZSNMAS .. Acta Rerum Naturalium. Musei Nationalis Slovaci Bratislava
.... [*A publication*]
ZSOB........ Zinc-Silver-Oxide Battery (RDA)
ZSOF .... Hefei/Luogang [*China*] [*ICAO location identifier*] (ICLI)
ZSPG .... Zero-Speed Pulse Generator
ZSQD .... Qingdao [*China*] [*ICAO location identifier*] (ICLI)
ZS-RDS..... Zung Self-Rating Depression Scale [*Psychology*]
ZSRK .... Zeitschrift. Savigny-Stiftung fuer Rechtsgeschichte.
.... Kanonistische Abteilung [*A publication*]
ZSRS .... Zung Self-Rating Scale [*For depression*]
ZSS .... Sassandra [*Ivory Coast*] [*Airport symbol*] (OAG)
ZSS .... Zen Studies Society (EA)
ZSS .... Zinc Sulfide System
ZSSA .... Shanghai City [*China*] [*ICAO location identifier*] (ICLI)
ZSSA .... Zoological Society of Southern Africa [*See also DUSA*] [*Port
.... Elizabeth, South Africa*] (EAIO)
ZSSGerm... Zeitschrift. Savigny-Stiftung fuer Rechtsgeschichte.
.... Germanistische Abteilung [*A publication*]
ZSSKanon ... Zeitschrift. Savigny-Stiftung fuer Rechtsgeschichte.
.... Kanonistische Abteilung [*Weimar*] [*A publication*]
ZSSL .... Shanghai/Longhua [*China*] [*ICAO location identifier*] (ICLI)
ZSSRGGerm ... Zeitschrift. Savigny-Stiftung fuer Rechtsgeschichte.
.... Germanistische Abteilung [*A publication*]
ZSSRGKan ... Zeitschrift. Savigny-Stiftung fuer Rechtsgeschichte.
.... Kanonistische Abteilung [*A publication*]
ZSSRGRom ... Zeitschrift. Savigny-Stiftung fuer Rechtsgeschichte.
.... Romanistische Abteilung [*A publication*]
ZSSRom .... Zeitschrift. Savigny-Stiftung fuer Rechtsgeschichte.
.... Romanistische Abteilung [*A publication*]
ZSSS.......... Shanghai/Hongqiao [*China*] [*ICAO location identifier*] (ICLI)
ZST............ Bratislava [*Czechoslovakia*] [*Seismograph station code, US
.... Geological Survey*] (SEIS)
ZST............ Stewart [*Canada*] [*Airport symbol*] (OAG)
ZST............ Zentralabteilung Strahlenschutz [*Central Department for
.... Radiation Protection*] [*Germany*]
ZST............ Zinc Sulfide Tracer
ZST............ Zone Standard Time
ZSTN........ Jinan [*China*] [*ICAO location identifier*] (ICLI)
Z Strukturn Him ... Zurnal Strukturnoi Himii. Akademija Nauk SSR.
. ... Sibirskoe Otdelenie [*A publication*]
ZSU .... San Juan, PR [*Location identifier*] [*FAA*] (FAAL)
ZSW........... Prince Rupert [*Canada*] [*Airport symbol*] [*Obsolete*] (OAG)
ZT .... Aerodrome Control Tower [*ICAO designator*] (ICDA)
ZT .... Training Aircraft [*Lighter-than-Air*] [*Navy symbol*] (MUGU)
ZT .... Union of South Africa [*Aircraft nationality and registration
.... mark*] (FAAC)
ZT .... Z-Axis of External Tank [*NASA*] (NASA)
ZT .... Zachary Taylor [*US president, 1784-1850*]
ZT .... Zipper Tubing
ZT .... Zone Time [*Navigation*]
ZT .... Zuercher Taschenbuch [*A publication*]
ZTA .... Zeta Tau Alpha [*Sorority*]
ZTAT........ Zero Turn-Around Time [*Microcomputer*] [*Hitachi Ltd.*]
ZTB........... Tete A La Baleine [*Canada*] [*Airport symbol*] (OAG)
ZTB........... Zuercher Taschenbuch [*A publication*]
Ztbl .... Zentralblatt [*Official Gazette*] [*German*]
ZTC .... Zero-Temperature Coefficient (MSA)
ZTCL......... Zytec Computers Ltd. [*Dallas, TX*] [*NASDAQ symbol*] (NQ)
Z Techn Fiz ... Zurnal Techniceskoj Fiziki [*A publication*]
Z Tech Univ (Berlin) ... Zeitschrift. Technische Universitaet (Berlin) [*A
.... publication*]
Z Tech Univ (Hannover) ... Zeitschrift. Technische Universitaet (Hannover)
.... [*German Federal Republic*] [*A publication*]
ZTG .... Zolltarifgesetz [*A publication*]
Ztg Gesunde ... Zeitung fuer Gesunde [*A publication*]
ZTH.......... Zakinthos [*Greece*] [*Airport symbol*] (OAG)
ZTJWG ..... Zeus Target Joint Working Group [*Missiles*] (AAG)
ZTL........... Atlanta, GA [*Location identifier*] [*FAA*] (FAAL)
ZTL........... Touro Law Library, New York, NY [*OCLC symbol*] (OCLC)
ZTM .... Mid-York Library System, Utica, NY [*OCLC symbol*] (OCLC)
ZTN .... Zinc Tannate of Naloxone [*Opiate antagonist*]
ZTO .... Zero Time Outage [*Nuclear energy*] (NRCH)
ZTO .... Zone Transportation Officer [*Military*]
ZTOS........ Zydowskie Towarzystwo Ochrony Sierot [*A publication*]
ZTOS........ Zydowskie Towarzystwo Opieki Spolecznej [*A publication*]
ZTP........... Zero-Temperature Plasma
ZTP........... Zydowskie Towarzystwo Przeciwgruzliczego [*A publication*]
ZTR .... Zweig Total Return Fund, Inc. [*NYSE symbol*] (CTT)
ZTRX........ Zytrex Corp. [*NASDAQ symbol*] (NQ)
ZTS .... Zoom Transfer Scope (OA)
ZTSCHR ... Zeitschrift [*Review*] [*German*]
Ztschr Tokio Med Gesellsch ... Zeitschrift. Tokio Medizinischen Gesellschaft
.... [*A publication*]
ZU.............. Union of South Africa [*Aircraft nationality and registration
.... mark*] (FAAC)
ZU.............. Upper Area Control Center [*ICAO designator*] (ICDA)
ZU.............. Utility Aircraft [*Lighter-than-Air*] [*Navy symbol*] (MUGU)

ZU.............. Zeitlich Untauglich [*Temporarily Unfit*] [*German military -
.... World War II*]
ZUA .... Agana, GU [*Location identifier*] [*FAA*] (FAAL)
ZUA .... Central New York Union List of Serials, Syracuse, NY [*OCLC
.... symbol*] (OCLC)
ZUB .... Allied Chemical Corp., Library, Solvay, NY [*OCLC
.... symbol*] (OCLC)
ZuB .... Zuercher Bibelkommentare [*A publication*]
Zubolek Pregl ... Zubolekarski Pregled [*A publication*]
ZUC .... American Foundation for Management Research, Library,
.... Hamilton, NY [*OCLC symbol*] (OCLC)
ZUCK .... Chongqing [*China*] [*ICAO location identifier*] (ICLI)
Zucker Beih ... Zucker Beihefte [*A publication*]
Zucker Frucht Gemueseverwert ... Zucker- Frucht- und Gemueseverwertung
.... [*A publication*]
Zucker Sonderbeil ... Zucker Sonderbeilage [*A publication*]
Zucker Suesswaren Wirtsch ... Zucker- und Suesswaren Wirtschaft [*A
.... publication*]
Zuck u SuesswarWirt ... Zucker- und Suesswaren Wirtschaft [*A publication*]
ZUD .... Bristol Laboratories, Library, Syracuse, NY [*OCLC
.... symbol*] (OCLC)
ZUE .... Carrier Corp., Library, Syracuse, NY [*OCLC symbol*] (OCLC)
ZUE .... Zuni Energy [*Vancouver Stock Exchange symbol*]
Zuercher Beitraege ... Zuercher Beitraege zur Geschichtswissenschaft [*A
.... publication*]
Zuercher Beitraege ... Zuercher Beitraege zur Rechtswissenschaft [*A
.... publication*]
Zuer Univ Geol Inst-Eidgenoss Tech Hochsch Geol Inst Mitt ... Zuerich
.... Universitaet. Geologisches Institut - Eidgenoessische
.... Technische Hochschule. Geologisches Institut.
.... Mitteilungen [*A publication*]
ZUG .... Community-General Hospital, Staff Library, Syracuse, NY
.... [*OCLC symbol*] (OCLC)
ZUG.......... Zugdidi [*Former USSR*] [*Seismograph station code, US
.... Geological Survey*] [*Closed*] (SEIS)
ZugerNjb ... Zuger Neujahrsblatt [*A publication*]
ZUGY .... Guiyang [*China*] [*ICAO location identifier*] (ICLI)
ZUH .... Education Opportunity Center of the State University of New
.... York, Syracuse, NY [*OCLC symbol*] (OCLC)
ZUI .... General Electric Co., Electronics Park Library, Syracuse, NY
.... [*OCLC symbol*] (OCLC)
ZUJ .... General Electric Co., Information Resources Library, Utica, NY
.... [*OCLC symbol*] (OCLC)
ZUK .... United States Veterans Administration, Hospital Library,
.... Syracuse, NY [*OCLC symbol*] (OCLC)
ZUL .... Agway, Inc., Library, Syracuse, NY [*OCLC symbol*] (OCLC)
zul............. Zulu [*MARC language code*] [*Library of Congress*] (LCCP)
ZUL .... Zurich-Lageren [*Switzerland*] [*Seismograph station code, US
.... Geological Survey*] (SEIS)
ZULS........ Lhasa [*China*] [*ICAO location identifier*] (ICLI)
ZUM......... Churchill Falls [*Canada*] [*Airport symbol*] (OAG)
ZUM......... Supreme Court, Fifth Judicial District, Law Library, Utica, NY
.... [*OCLC symbol*] (OCLC)
ZUM......... Zeitschrift fuer Urheber und Medienrecht [*Journal for
.... Copyright and Communication*] [*NOMOS Datapool*]
.... [*Database producer*]
ZUM......... Zimbabwe Unity Movement [*Political party*] (ECON)
ZUN.......... Saint Joseph's Hospital, Health Center Library, Syracuse, NY
.... [*OCLC symbol*] (OCLC)
zun............ Zuni [*MARC language code*] [*Library of Congress*] (LCCP)
ZUN.......... Zuni Pueblo, NM [*Location identifier*] [*FAA*] (FAAL)
ZUO.......... Utica Mutual Insurance Co., Library, New Hartford, NY
.... [*OCLC symbol*] (OCLC)
ZUP .... Utica/Marcy Psychiatric Center, Utica Campus Library, Utica,
.... NY [*OCLC symbol*] (OCLC)
ZuP .... Zellstoff und Papier [*A publication*]
ZUP .... Zone a Urbaniser en Priorite [*Priority Urbanization Zone*]
.... [*French*]
ZUPO .... Zimbabwe United People's Organization [*Political
.... party*] (PPW)
ZUQ.......... Saint Luke's Memorial Hospital Center, Medical Library, Utica,
.... NY [*OCLC symbol*] (OCLC)
ZUR.......... Hancock Airbase Library, Hancock Field, NY [*OCLC
.... symbol*] (OCLC)
ZUR.......... Zurfund International Ltd. [*Vancouver Stock Exchange
.... symbol*]
ZUR .... Zurich [*Switzerland*] [*Seismograph station code, US Geological
.... Survey*] (SEIS)
Zur Didak Phys Chem ... Zur Didaktik der Physik und Chemie [*A
.... publication*]
ZURF......... Zeus Up-Range Facility [*Missiles*] (AAG)
ZurnIn........ Zurn Industries, Inc. [*Associated Press abbreviation*] (APAG)
ZUS .... Utica/Marcy Psychiatric Center, Marcy Campus Library, Utica,
.... NY [*OCLC symbol*] (OCLC)
ZUS .... Zusammen [*Together*] [*Music*]
ZUT .... Maria Regina College, Library, Syracuse, NY [*OCLC
.... symbol*] (OCLC)
ZUTRON .. Airship Utility Squadron [*Navy symbol*]
ZUU.......... Masonic Medical Research Laboratory, Library, Utica, NY
.... [*OCLC symbol*] (OCLC)
ZUUU........ Chengdu [*China*] [*ICAO location identifier*] (ICLI)

ZUW .... Munson-Williams-Proctor Institute, Library, Utica, NY [*OCLC symbol*] (OCLC)
ZUX .... Mohawk Valley Learning Resource Center, Utica Library, Utica, NY [*OCLC symbol*] (OCLC)
ZUY .... Special Metals Corp., Library, New Hartford, NY [*OCLC symbol*] (OCLC)
ZUZ .... Crouse-Irving Hospital, School of Nursing, Library, Syracuse, NY [*OCLC symbol*] (OCLC)
ZUZZ .... Zug und Zerschneidezuender [*Pull-and-Cut Igniter*] [*German military - World War II*]
Z & V .... Zeiten und Voelker [*A publication*]
ZV .... Zu Verfuegung [*At Disposal*] [*Business term*] [*German*]
Zv .... Zvezda [*A publication*]
ZVA .... Jervis Public Library, Rome, NY [*OCLC symbol*] (OCLC)
ZVA .... Miandrivazo [*Madagascar*] [*Airport symbol*] (OAG)
ZVA .... Zero Order Variable Aperture Nonredundant Point Transmitted [*Compression algorithm*] (MCD)
ZVB .... Syracuse Research Corp., Library, Syracuse, NY [*OCLC symbol*] (OCLC)
ZVC .... Utica Public Library, Utica, NY [*OCLC symbol*] (OCLC)
ZVD .... Supreme Court of New York, Library, Syracuse, NY [*OCLC symbol*] (OCLC)
ZVEI .... Zentralverband der Elektrotechnischen Industrie [*Electrical Equipment Industry Association*] [*Germany*] (EY)
Z Ver Dtsch Ing ... Zeitschrift. Verein Deutscher Ingenieure [*A publication*]
Z Ver Dtsch Zucker Ind ... Zeitschrift. Verein der Deutschen Zucker-Industrie [*A publication*]
Z Ver Dtsch Zucker Ind Allg Teil ... Zeitschrift. Verein der Deutschen Zucker-Industrie. Allgemeiner Teil [*A publication*]
Z Ver Dtsch Zucker Ind Tech Teil ... Zeitschrift. Verein der Deutschen Zucker-Industrie. Technischer Teil [*A publication*]
Z Ver Hess Gesch Landesk ... Zeitschrift. Verein fuer Hessische Geschichte und Landeskunde [*A publication*]
Z Ver Hessische Gesch ... Zeitschrift. Verein fuer Hessische Geschichte und Landeskunde [*A publication*]
Zverolek Obz ... Zverolekarsky Obzor [*A publication*]
ZVF .... Zero-Velocity Fading [*Aviation*] (AIA)
ZVfD .... Zionistische Vereinigung fuer Deutschaland [*Zionist Federation of Germany*]
ZVGMS ..... Zeitschrift. Deutscher Verein fuer die Geschichte Maehrens und Schlesiens [*A publication*]
ZVHG .... Zeitschrift. Verein fuer Hamburgische Geschichte [*A publication*]
ZVHGLK .. Zeitschrift. Verein fuer Hessische Geschichte und Landeskunde [*A publication*]
ZVKPS ...... Zeitschrift. Verein fuer Kirchengeschichte in der Provinz Sachsen und Anhalt [*A publication*]
ZVM .... Mohawk Valley Community College, Utica, NY [*OCLC symbol*] (OCLC)
ZVO .... Zapiski Vostochnovo Otdeleniia [*A publication*]
ZVORAO .. Zapiski Vostochnovo Otdeleniia Imperatorskovo Ruskavo Arkheologicheskavo Obshchestva [*A publication*]
ZVR .... Zener Voltage Regulator
ZVRD .... Zener Voltage Regulator Diode
ZVS .... Zero Voltage Switch
ZVTGA...... Zeitschrift. Verein fuer Thueringische Geschichte und Altertumskunde [*A publication*]
ZVTGAK... Zeitschrift. Verein fuer Thueringische Geschichte und Altertumskunde [*A publication*]
ZVV .... Zeitschrift. Verein fuer Volkskunde [*A publication*]
ZvV .... Zvezda Vostoka [*A publication*]
ZVX .... Zygocactus Virus X [*Plant pathology*]
Z Vycisl Mat i Mat Fiz ... Zurnal Vycislitel'noi Matematiki i Matematiceskoi Fiziki [*A publication*]
ZVZ .... Zavitz Technology, Inc. [*Toronto Stock Exchange symbol*]
ZW .... Air Wisconsin [*Airline code*]
ZW .... Nike-Zeus at White Sands [*Missile defense*] (SAA)
ZW .... Zeitwende Monatsschrift [*A publication*]
ZW .... Zero Wait [*Industrial engineering*]
ZW .... Zero Wear
ZW .... Zimbabwe [*ANSI two-letter standard code*] (CNC)
Zw .... Zwischensatz [*Interpolation*] [*Music*]
ZWA .... Andapa [*Madagascar*] [*Airport symbol*] (OAG)
ZWAK ...... Aksu [*China*] [*ICAO location identifier*] (ICLI)
ZWC .... Zero Word Count
ZWC .... Zone Wind Computer
ZWE .... Zimbabwe [*ANSI three-letter standard code*] (CNC)
Zweig .... Zweig Fund [*Associated Press abbreviation*] (APAG)
ZweigTl...... Zweig Total Return Fund, Inc. [*Associated Press abbreviation*] (APAG)
ZWHM...... Hami [*China*] [*ICAO location identifier*] (ICLI)
Z Wien Ent Ges ... Zeitschrift. Wiener Entomologische Gesellschaft [*A publication*]
Z Wien Entomol Ges ... Zeitschrift. Wiener Entomologische Gesellschaft [*A publication*]
Z Wien Entomol Ver ... Zeitschrift. Wiener Entomologe-Verein [*A publication*]
Zwierzeta Lab ... Zwierzeta Laboratoryjne [*A publication*]
Z Wirtschaftsgruppe Zuckerind ... Zeitschrift. Wirtschaftsgruppe Zuckerindustrie [*A publication*]

Z Wirtschaftsgruppe Zuckerind Allg Teil ... Zeitschrift. Wirtschaftsgruppe Zuckerindustrie. Allgemeiner Teil [*A publication*]
Z Wirtschaftsgruppe Zuckerind Tech Teil ... Zeitschrift. Wirtschaftsgruppe Zuckerindustrie. Technischer Teil [*A publication*]
ZWKC .... Kuqa [*China*] [*ICAO location identifier*] (ICLI)
ZWL .... Wollaston Lake [*Canada*] [*Airport symbol*] (OAG)
ZWL .... Zero Wavelength
ZWMZDP ... Chinese Journal of Microbiology and Immunology [*Beijing*] [*A publication*]
ZWO .... Zuiver Wentenschappelijk Orderzock [*Netherlands*]
ZWOK .... Zirconium-Water Oxidation Kinetics (NRCH)
ZWP .... Zone Wind Plotter
ZWPGV ..... Zeitschrift. Westpreussischer Geschichtsverein [*A publication*]
ZWR .... ZWR. Zahnaerztliche Welt, Zahnaerztliche Rundschau, Zahnaerztliche Reform [*A publication*]
ZWS........... Zellweger Syndrome [*Medicine*]
ZWS........... Zentralwohlfahrtsstelle der Juden in Deutschland [*A publication*] (BJA)
ZWS........... Zonal Wind Stress [*Meteorology*]
ZWSH .... Kashi [*China*] [*ICAO location identifier*] (ICLI)
ZWSt .... Zentralwohlfahrtsstelle der Juden in Deutschland [*A publication*] (BJA)
ZWTN .... Hotan [*China*] [*ICAO location identifier*] (ICLI)
ZWU......... Union College, Schenectady, NY [*OCLC symbol*] (OCLC)
ZWUQ...... Urumqi [*China*] [*ICAO location identifier*] (ICLI)
ZWV .... Zero Wave Velocity
ZWW .... Zonal Westerly Wind [*Climatology*]
ZWWW .... Urumqi/Diwopu [*China*] [*ICAO location identifier*] (ICLI)
ZWYN .... Yining [*China*] [*ICAO location identifier*] (ICLI)
ZXC .... City College of New York, New York, NY [*OCLC symbol*] (OCLC)
ZXCFAR ... Zero Crossing Constant False Alarm Rate (MSA)
ZXMP....... Zero Transmission Power
ZXX .... Exxon Corp., Information Center, Technical Service Coordinator, New York, NY [*OCLC symbol*] (OCLC)
ZY .... Aerodrome Security Services [*ICAO designator*] (FAAC)
ZY .... Zayre Corp. [*NYSE symbol*] [*Later, TJX*] (SPSG)
Zy.............. Zygon [*A publication*]
ZYB .... Zionist Year Book [*A publication*] (BJA)
ZYCC........ Changchun [*China*] [*ICAO location identifier*] (ICLI)
Zycie Weteryn ... Zycie Weterynaryjne [*A publication*]
ZYDXDM ... Journal. Zhejiang Medical University [*A publication*]
ZYFV........ Zucchini Yellow Fleck Virus [*Plant pathology*]
ZYG .... Zygote Resources [*Vancouver Stock Exchange symbol*]
ZYHB .... Harbin/Yanjiagang [*China*] [*ICAO location identifier*] (ICLI)
ZYL .... Sylhet [*Bangladesh*] [*Airport symbol*] (OAG)
ZYLA........ Hailar [*China*] [*ICAO location identifier*] (ICLI)
Zymol Chem Colloidi ... Zymologica e Chemica dei Colloidi [*A publication*]
ZYMV .... Zucchini Yellow Mosaic Virus
Zy Newsl .... Zygon Newsletter [*A publication*]
ZYP........... Zefkrome Yarn Program [*Dow Chemical Co.*]
ZYQQ....... Qiqihar [*China*] [*ICAO location identifier*] (ICLI)
ZYSH .... Shenyang [*China*] [*ICAO location identifier*] (ICLI)
ZYTL........ Dalian [*China*] [*ICAO location identifier*] (ICLI)
ZYU .... New York University, New York, NY [*OCLC symbol*] (OCLC)
Zywienie Czlowieka Metab ... Zywienie Czlowieka i Metabolizm [*A publication*]
ZYYY........ Shenyang/Dongta [*China*] [*ICAO location identifier*] (ICLI)
ZZ.............. Aircraft in Flight [*ICAO designator*] (ICDA)
ZZ.............. Datum Position [*Arbitrary*] [*Navy*] [*British*]
ZZ.............. Lighter-than-Air [*Aircraft*] [*Navy symbol*] (MUGU)
Z-Z............. Roll Axis [*Aerospace*] (AAG)
Z d Z .... Zeichen der Zeit [*A publication*]
ZZ.............. Zeitschrift fuer die Wissenschaft des Judentums [*Leopold Zunz*] [*A publication*] (BJA)
ZZ.............. Zig-Zag
ZZ.............. Zinziber [*Ginger*] [*Pharmacology*] (ROG)
ZZ.............. Zu [*or Zur*] Zeit [*At This Time*] [*German*]
ZZ.............. Zugzuender [*Pull Igniter*] [*German military - World War II*]
ZZA .... Zamak Zinc Alloy
ZZB........... Zanzibar [*Tanzania*]
ZZC .... Zero-Zero Condition
ZZD .... Zig-Zag Diagram
ZZR .... Zig-Zag Rectifier
ZZR........... Zigzag Riveting (MSA)
ZZT........... Zu Zu [*Tennessee*] [*Seismograph station code, US Geological Survey*] [*Closed*] (SEIS)
ZZTFC ...... ZZ Top Fan Club (EA)
ZZV .... Zanesville, OH [*Location identifier*] [*FAA*] (FAAL)
ZZV .... Zero-Zero Visibility
ZZW .... Zero-Zero Weather
ZZZZ........ Unknown Elements in Formatted Flight Plan [*Aviation code*] (FAAC)